THE CATHOLIC STUDY BIBLE

EDITORS AND CONTRIBUTORS

Dianne Bergant

Lawrence Boadt

Richard J. Clifford

John J. Collins

Daniel J. Harrington

Leslie J. Hoppe

Luke Timothy Johnson

Kevin Madigan

Carolyn Osiek

Pheme Perkins

Eileen Schuller

Donald Senior

Ronald A. Simkins

Ronald D. Witherup

The Catholic Study Bible

Donald Senior • John J. Collins

EDITORS

The New American Bible

Including the Revised New Testament and Psalms

Translated from the Original Languages with

Critical Use of All the Ancient Sources

OXFORD

UNIVERSITY PRESS

OXFORD
UNIVERSITY PRESS

Oxford University Press, Inc., publishes works that further
Oxford University's objective of excellence
in research, scholarship, and education.

Oxford   New York
Auckland   Cape Town   Dar es Salaam   Hong Kong   Karachi
Kuala Lumpur   Madrid   Melbourne   Mexico City   Nairobi
New Delhi   Shanghai   Taipei   Toronto

With offices in
Argentina   Austria   Brazil   Chile   Czech Republic   France   Greece
Guatemala   Hungary   Italy   Japan   Poland   Portugal   Singapore
South Korea   Switzerland   Thailand   Turkey   Ukraine   Vietnam

Copyright © 1990, 2006 by Oxford University Press

Published by Oxford University Press
198 Madison Avenue, New York, New York 10016
www.oup.com

Oxford is a registered trademark of Oxford University Press

Oxford Introductions, Reading Guides, General and Reference Articles, copyright © 1990, 2006
by Oxford University Press, Inc.

Nihil Obstat	*Imprimatur*
Reverend John G. Lodge, S.S.L., S.T.D.	Reverend George J. Rassas
Reverend Robert L. Schoenstene, M.A., S.S.L.	Vicar General
Censor Deputatis	Archdiocese of Chicago
September 13, 2005	September 14, 2005

The *Nihil Obstat* and *Imprimatur* are official declarations that a book is free of doctrinal and moral error. No implication is contained therein that those who have granted the *Nihil Obstat* and *Imprimatur* agree with the content,
opinions, or statements expressed. Nor do they assume any legal responsibility associated with publication.

Scripture texts used in this work are taken from the New American Bible.
The Old Testament of the New American Bible copyright © 1970 by the Confraternity of
Christian Doctrine (CCD), Washington, D.C. (books 1 Samuel to 2 Maccabees copyright © 1969);
Revised New Testament of the New American Bible copyright © 1986 by the CCD;
Revised Psalms of the New American Bible copyright © 1991 by the CCD.

Nihil Obstat
Stephen J. Hartdegen, O.F.M., S.S.L. and Christian P. Ceroke, O. Carm., S.T.D.
Imprimatur
† Patrick Cardinal O'Boyle, D.D., Archbishop of Washington
July 27, 1970

Revised New Testament	Revised Psalms
Nihil Obstat	*Imprimatur*
Stephen J. Hartdegen, O.F.M., S.S.L., Censor Deputatis	Most Reverend Daniel E. Pilarczyk, President,
Imprimatur	National Conference of Catholic Bishops
† James A. Hickey, S.T.D., J.C.D., Archbishop of Washington	October 10, 1991
August 27, 1986	

10   9   8   7   6

Printed in Korea

CONTENTS

LIST OF SIDEBAR ESSAYS, CHARTS, AND DRAWINGS

LIST OF MAPS

New Oxford Bible Maps follow the last page of text

ABOUT THE EDITORS AND
CONTRIBUTORS

Dianne Bergant, C.S.A. Reading Guides to the Wisdom and Poetical Books: Job, Psalms, Proverbs, Ecclesiastes, Song of Songs, Wisdom, Sirach.
Dianne Bergant is Professor of Old Testament Studies at Catholic Theological Union, Chicago.

Lawrence Boadt, C.S.P., S.S.D. General Introduction to the Pentateuch. Reading Guides to Genesis, Exodus, Leviticus, Numbers, Deuteronomy.
Lawrence Boadt is Professor Emeritus of Hebrew Scriptures at Washington Theological Union.

Richard J. Clifford, S.J. Reading Guides to Isaiah, Jeremiah, Lamentations, Baruch, Ezekiel.
Richard J. Clifford is Professor of Old Testament at the Weston Jesuit School of Theology in Cambridge, Massachusetts, and is on the board of trustees and editorial board of the Catholic Biblical Association of America.

John J. Collins. Editor. Reading Guides to Daniel and the Twelve Minor Prophets: Hosea, Joel, Amos, Obadiah, Jonah, Micah, Nahum, Habakkuk, Zephaniah, Haggai, Zechariah, Malachi.
John J. Collins is Holmes Professor of Old Testament Criticism and Interpretation at Yale University. He is currently serving as president of the Society of Biblical Literature.

Daniel J. Harrington, S.J. The Bible in Catholic Life.
Daniel J. Harrington is Professor of New Testament and Chair of Biblical Studies at the Weston Jesuit School of Theology in Cambridge, Massachusetts. He is also editor of New Testament Abstracts.

Leslie J. Hoppe, O.F.M. Reading Guides to Joshua, Judges, Ruth, 1 and 2 Samuel, 1 and 2 Kings, 1 Chronicles, 2 Chronicles, Ezra, Nehemiah, Tobit, Judith, Esther, 1 Maccabees, 2 Maccabees.
Leslie J. Hoppe is Professor of Old Testament Studies at Catholic Theological Union in Chicago.

Luke Timothy Johnson. Reading Guides to Hebrews, James, 1 Peter, 2 Peter, 1 John, 2 John, 3 John, Jude, Revelation.
Luke Timothy Johnson is R.W. Woodruff Professor of New Testament and Christian Origins at Candler School of Theology at Emory University in Atlanta, Georgia. He is also a senior fellow at Emory's Center for the Study of Law and Religion.

(Editors and Contributors, continued)

Kevin Madigan. Catholic Interpretation of the Bible.
Kevin Madigan is Professor of the History of Christianity at Harvard Divinity School, Cambridge, Massachusetts.

Carolyn Osiek. Paul and His Writings. Reading Guides to Romans, 1 Corinthians, 2 Corinthians, Galatians, Ephesians, Philippians, Colossians, 1 Thessalonians, 2 Thessalonians, 1 Timothy, 2 Timothy, Titus, Philemon.
Carolyn Osiek is Charles Fischer Catholic Professor of New Testament at Brite Divinity School at Texas Christian University in Fort Worth, Texas.

Pheme Perkins. Reading Guides to Luke, John, Acts.
Pheme Perkins is Professor of Theology (New Testament) at Boston College.

Eileen Schuller. The Bible in the Lectionary.
Eileen Schuller is Professor of Religious Studies at McMaster University in Hamilton, Ontario.

Donald Senior, C.P. Editor. General Introduction. The Biblical Texts and Their Backgrounds. The Catholic Study Bible Reading Guide. Reading Guides to the Synoptic Gospels, Matthew, Mark.
Donald Senior is President and Professor of New Testament at Catholic Theological Union in Chicago.

Ronald A. Simkins. Biblical History and Archaeology.
Ronald Simkins is Director of the Center for the Study of Religion and Society at Creighton University and Associate Professor of both Theology and Classical & Near Eastern Studies at Creighton.

Ronald D. Witherup, S.S. The Challenges of Biblical Translation.
Ronald Witherup is Provincial Superior of the United States Province of Sulpicians.

ALPHABETICAL LISTING OF THE BOOKS OF THE BIBLE

Acts	1442	Job	646	Obadiah	1198
Amos	1188	Joel	1184	1 Peter	1644
Baruch	1084	John	1402	2 Peter	1651
1 Chronicles	435	1 John	1656	Philemon	1615
2 Chronicles	469	2 John	1662	Philippians	1578
Colossians	1586	3 John	1663	Proverbs	787
1 Corinthians	1516	Jonah	1200	Psalms	682
2 Corinthians	1540	Joshua	241	Revelation	1667
Daniel	1146	Jude	1665	Romans	1493
Deuteronomy	199	Judges	269	Ruth	297
Ecclesiastes	826	Judith	553	1 Samuel	303
Ephesians	1570	1 Kings	369	2 Samuel	339
Esther	569	2 Kings	403	Sirach (Ecclesiasticus)	868
Exodus	70	Lamentations	1075	Song of Songs	836
Ezekiel	1092	Leviticus	118	1 Thessalonians	1592
Ezra	509	Luke	1349	2 Thessalonians	1596
Galatians	1559	1 Maccabees	583	1 Timothy	1600
Genesis	6	2 Maccabees	619	2 Timothy	1607
Habakkuk	1213	Malachi	1233	Titus	1612
Haggai	1220	Mark	1316	Tobit	537
Hebrews	1616	Matthew	1248	Wisdom	844
Hosea	1171	Micah	1203	Zechariah	1223
Isaiah	929	Nahum	1210	Zephaniah	1217
James	1637	Nehemiah	521		
Jeremiah	1004	Numbers	151		

ABBREVIATIONS OF THE BOOKS
OF THE BIBLE

Old Testament

Gn	Genesis	Neh	Nehemiah	Lam	Lamentations
Ex	Exodus	Tb	Tobit	Bar	Baruch
Lv	Leviticus	Jdt	Judith	Ez	Ezekiel
Nm	Numbers	Est	Esther	Dn	Daniel
Dt	Deuteronomy	1 Mc	1 Maccabees	Hos	Hosea
Jos	Joshua	2 Mc	2 Maccabees	Jl	Joel
Jgs	Judges	Jb	Job	Am	Amos
Ru	Ruth	Ps(s)	Psalms	Ob	Obadiah
1 Sm	1 Samuel	Prv	Proverbs	Jon	Jonah
2 Sm	2 Samuel	Eccl	Ecclesiastes	Mi	Micah
1 Kgs	1 Kings	Song (or Sg)	Song of Songs	Na	Nahum
2 Kgs	2 Kings	Wis	Wisdom	Hb	Habakkuk
1 Chr	1 Chronicles	Sir	Sirach (Ecclesiasticus)	Zep	Zephaniah
2 Chr	2 Chronicles	Is	Isaiah	Hg	Haggai
Ezr	Ezra	Jer	Jeremiah	Zec	Zechariah
				Mal	Malachi

New Testament

Mt	Matthew	Eph	Ephesians	Heb	Hebrews
Mk	Mark	Phil	Philippians	Jas	James
Lk	Luke	Col	Colossians	1 Pt	1 Peter
Jn	John	1 Thes	1 Thessalonians	2 Pt	2 Peter
Acts	Acts of the Apostles	2 Thes	2 Thessalonians	1 Jn	1 John
Rom	Romans	1 Tm	1 Timothy	2 Jn	2 John
1 Cor	1 Corinthians	2 Tm	2 Timothy	3 Jn	3 John
2 Cor	2 Corinthians	Ti	Titus	Jude	Jude
Gal	Galatians	Phlm	Philemon	Rv	Revelation

FOOTNOTES AND REFERENCES

For greater clarity and convenience, the footnotes and cross references are printed at the bottom of each page and cross-indexed in the text itself. An *asterisk* (*) in the text indicates that there is a footnote to the text in question. Each footnote is in turn clearly marked with the number of the chapter and the verse to which it pertains. Similarly a *superior letter* (ᵃ) in the text indicates that there is a cross-reference to a particular verse. The reference itself is also clearly marked with the same letter. Hence, the reader is always aware of a footnote or a cross-reference simply by *reading the text*.

Key to Scripture References

Gn 1, 1	refers to Genesis, chapter one, verse one.
Gn 1, 1a	refers to Genesis, chapter one, first part of verse one.
Gn 1, 1f(f)	refers to Genesis, chapter one, verse one and the following verse (verses).
Gn 1, 1-10	refers to Genesis, chapter one, verses one through ten.
Gn 1, 1-10.24	refers to Genesis, chapter one, verses one through ten and verse twenty-four.
Gn 1—5	refers to Genesis, chapters one through five inclusive.
Gn 1, 1—2, 3	refers to Genesis, chapter one, verse one through chapter two, verse three inclusive.
Gn 1, 1; 2, 3	refers to Genesis, chapter one, verse one and chapter two, verse three.

READING GUIDE

GENERAL INTRODUCTION

The book you hold in your hand contains one of humanity's greatest treasures. No one can deny that the Bible has had a profound impact on world civilization. Its epic stories, its powerful language and images have left their imprint on human history, especially in cultures touched by Judaism and Christianity.

For the Christian, the Bible has an importance far more profound than its impact on culture. The Christian believes that through the turbulent and wonderful chapters of biblical history, God speaks to us. Although expressed in genuinely human terms and through very human authors, the Bible is, at the same time, the Word of God for us. Therefore, as Christians we reverence and love the Scriptures and seek to understand them as much as we can.

The purpose of this *Catholic Study Bible* is to enable the reader to read the Scriptures with new understanding and depth. The primary audience of this Study Bible is Roman Catholic. Some of the comments in the notes to the text, the Articles, and the Reading Guides deliberately reflect Catholic experience and Catholic interests. However, the editors do not wish to exclude other Christian readers from the focus of this book. In most instances, the materials included here will be useful for all Christians who want to enter deeply into the mysteries and marvels of the Bible.

In this general introduction and the two following articles, we hope to: (1) Provide a general introduction to the Bible as a whole: the nature and diversity of its contents, and how it came to be; (2) introduce the reader to the special resources for understanding the Bible provided in

this *Catholic Study Bible* edition and to suggest more profitable ways of using them.

INTRODUCING THE BIBLE

Although it is bound under one cover and bears a single title, the Bible is not a single, unified book. It is, in fact, a collection of some seventy-three different works by different authors, using very different styles and perspectives, composed over a span of several centuries, and in three different languages (Hebrew, Aramaic, Greek). Most of the Old Testament (forty-six books) was written in Hebrew, but parts of the books of Daniel (2, 4—7, 28), Ezra (4, 6—6, 18; 7, 12–26), and one verse from Jeremiah (10, 11) were originally composed in Aramaic, a Middle Eastern language related to but different from Hebrew. All twenty-seven of the New Testament books were composed in Greek.

The rich diversity of the Bible is one of its glories because it allows the story of God's people to be told from various perspectives. It also presents a challenge to the reader who should be aware of the different cultural, historical, and literary contexts of each biblical book. But there is a deeper unity to the Bible that binds together these individual pieces of literature. Through the many biblical books flows the continuing saga of God's love for Israel and for the church. Each of the biblical authors, no matter how much separated in time, culture, and literary style, shares a conviction that God's presence is felt in human history and that God invites the human family to respond with faith and integrity.

3

The Writing of the Bible

As its diverse makeup implies, the Bible was not written at a single point in history. The events covered in the Old Testament span nearly two thousand years of history, from the time of Abraham and the patriarchs (around 1800 BC) to the period of the Maccabean wars (140 BC). If one includes the epic accounts of the creation and prepatriarchal stories such as Noah and the flood, then the reach of the biblical saga goes back to the beginning of time. But the actual formulation of the biblical accounts, although making use of earlier stories and traditions, is confined to a narrower period of time, probably beginning with the monarchy (around 1000 BC) and concluding in the century before the birth of Christ.

The New Testament books were all written during the latter half of the first century AD. The letters of Paul were probably the earliest New Testament works to be put in writing, dating mainly from the decade of the fifties. The sayings of Jesus and the many stories about his ministry circulated in the Christian community all during these early decades of the church but were probably not put in writing until shortly after AD 70, with Mark the first Gospel to be written. Matthew, Luke (and his second volume, the Acts of the Apostles), and John follow, with the compositions of their Gospels taking place sometime during the last quarter of the first century. The other non-Pauline letters and writings, including the book of Revelation or the Apocalypse, also date from this period.

Forming a "Bible" from Diverse Books: The Story of the Canon

The gathering of these diverse writings into a single collection or "book" (the literal meaning of the word *Bible*) was itself a long-term and laborious process. The technical term for designating which books belong to the Bible is the *canon* (measurement). Both Judaism and Christianity had to make choices about which books to include and which books to exclude from their respective Bibles. Judaism would not make any official decision about which books belonged to its Bible until the end of the first century AD, but that does not mean it was without a Bible for so much of its history. There was little or no dispute about the major books of the Old Testament,

books which were constantly used in Jewish liturgy and teaching, but there was debate about the inclusion of later and less central works such as Tobit or the Wisdom of Solomon.

The Jewish or Hebrew canon ultimately recognizes thirty-nine books, divided into three major categories:

1. The Law (sometimes referred to as the Pentateuch, or first five books of the Bible): Genesis, Exodus, Leviticus, Numbers, Deuteronomy.

2. The Prophets: Subdivided into the "Former Prophets": Joshua, Judges, 1 and 2 Samuel, 1 and 2 Kings; and the "Latter Prophets": Isaiah, Jeremiah, Ezekiel, and the "Twelve" (=Hosea, Joel, Amos, Obadiah, Jonah, Micah, Nahum, Habakkuk, Zephaniah, Haggai, Zechariah, Malachi).

3. The Writings: Psalms, Proverbs, Job, Song of Songs, Ruth, Lamentations, Ecclesiastes, Esther, Daniel, Ezra-Nehemiah, 1 and 2 Chronicles.

As we shall explain below, not included in the official Jewish or Hebrew canon are seven other books that Roman Catholics (and Orthodox Christians) consider part of their Scriptures. Judaism reverences these books and considers them sacred, but they are not part of their canon or official list. These books are: Tobit, Judith, 1 and 2 Maccabees, Wisdom, Sirach/Ecclesiasticus, and Baruch. There are also some additional passages in the books of Daniel and Esther.

The formation of the Christian canon also took place over a considerable period of time. In fact, the official Roman Catholic decision about the canon did not come until the Council of Trent in the sixteenth century, but by that time the choice of which writings were to be included in the Bible was well established. There were many sacred writings in the early decades of the church that presumably could have been included in the Bible. We cannot always tell what criteria or decision-making processes were used to establish the canon. Some "gospels" evidently portrayed Jesus in a way unacceptable to the vast majority of Christians and so were not included. Other early writings, however, such as the *Didache* (Greek for "teaching")—a short handbook of moral behavior and church practice—seem perfectly acceptable in content and tone but were still not included. Probably the early church considered a work's content, its authorship, and the frequency of its usage in the liturgy and teaching of the churches as important criteria for judging if a sacred writing was inspired by God and worthy of inclusion in its official canon or Scriptures.

All Christians agree on the twenty-seven books to be included in the New Testament, but there is a dispute about some of the books in the Old Testament. As noted above, Roman Catholics and Orthodox Christians agree on the forty-six books that make up the Old Testament (the Orthodox include additional books in their canon: 1 and 2 Esdras; the Prayer of Manasseh; Psalm 151; 3 Maccabees). Judaism and Protestant Christians hold for the shorter list of thirty-nine books sketched above; the remaining seven are designated as the "apocryphal" books.

The reason for this divergence is that earliest Christianity used an ancient Greek translation of the Old Testament (called the Septuagint) as its Bible. This Greek version of the Bible included forty-six books. Since most of the early Christians were Greek-speaking, this is the Bible they preferred. But when Judaism officially set out to determine its canon at the end of the first century, it drew up a shorter list of thirty-nine books: those written in Hebrew. In the Reformation period, Protestants went back to this shorter, Hebrew canon, considering it more authentic.

Today, many of the doctrinal tensions that separated Catholics and Protestants have eased. Some Protestant editions of the Bible include the seven apocryphal (what Roman Catholics call *deuterocanonical*) books in an appendix of their Bibles or in a special section between the Old and New Testaments. Following usual Catholic practice, the *New American Bible* integrates the deuterocanonical books into the order of the Old Testament canon.

THE DIVERSE LITERARY FORMS AND HISTORICAL VALUE OF THE BIBLE

The broad span of biblical history and the fact that the Bible is a collection of various books signal its rich diversity. The reader of the Bible needs to be attentive not only to the historical context of a particular passage but to the varieties of literary forms and the specific style and intent of each biblical author. The prophetic oracles of Isaiah or Jeremiah are very different in literary style from the legal codes of Leviticus or the narratives of Exodus. The long lists of wise sayings in Proverbs are dramatically different in tone, style, and theology from the sweeping liturgical poetry of the Psalms. So, too, do the parables of the Gospels differ greatly from the letters of Paul or the dramatic apocalyptic scenes in the book of Revelation. The notes and Reading Guides found in this Study Bible help the reader to understand more about these various literary forms and their implications for interpreting the meaning of a particular biblical passage.

The presence of various literary forms or means of expression in the Bible also complicates the issue of the historical value of the Bible. Some Christians, particularly fundamentalist Christians, fear that admitting the Bible contains poetry, stories, and other literary forms is somehow an attack on the veracity of the Bible and dilutes its witness to history. They prefer to regard the story of creation in Genesis, or the episode of Jonah's sojourn in the belly of a great fish, as literally true.

Roman Catholic teaching—and that of many other Christian denominations—sees no incompatibility between recognizing the truth of the biblical witness and the fact that it is expressed in many forms of literary expression characteristic of human communication. Credible witness to the truth of history is not confined to an "objective" reporting of the facts in the manner of a police report or a mere "factual" description of what happened. All reporting of history involves a degree of interpretation, and such means as poetry, hymns, stories, myths, and other literary forms can also communicate historical truth about past events and the perspectives of our ancestors.

Undoubtedly, both the Old and New Testaments contain many accurate historical facts and descriptions reflecting the times and events of biblical history. But the biblical writers also wanted to interpret the *meaning* of that history and present it unabashedly from their perspectives. Previous traditions are given new interpretations and adapted to the circumstances of a different generation. In most instances their intent was not to provide a historical archive for subsequent generations but to see in the events of this history the presence of God's grace, and to communicate that conviction to their readers. The

Bible is a witness to the vitality of the people who lived its events and pondered their meaning in a spirit of faith. Each biblical passage, therefore, must be evaluated on its own terms in attempting to distinguish between factual historical data and the theological and historical interpretation provided by the biblical writer.

THE TRANSMISSION OF THE BIBLICAL TEXT AND ITS MODERN TRANSLATIONS

Each modern reader of the Bible is in debt to countless numbers of people—Jewish and Christian—who lovingly handed on to the next generations the treasures of the Bible. For much of biblical history, such transmission of the biblical tradition was done orally, not in written form. Stories, sayings of great teachers and leaders, hymns, and poetry were lovingly memorized and handed down from parents to children, teacher to disciple, from leader of prayer to congregation, and, thereby, formed the growing body of the biblical heritage.

In ancient (and some modern) cultures, oral transmission of important literature was not a casual, haphazard affair. For our modern culture, so dependent on written means of communicating information, it is hard to realize that in oral cultures subtle and often unspoken rules govern how information is shaped, retained, and transmitted from one person and one generation to another. But as styles of writing and writing materials became more sophisticated in Israel, and when it had the social organization under the monarchy to have archives and develop an educated class of scribes, then undoubtedly some parts of the Bible were preserved in written form as well.

In the New Testament, many of the Gospel materials were first preserved in oral form. Sayings of Jesus, his parables, the stories about his healings, his conflicts with opponents, and the narrative of his Passion would have been preserved and transmitted in a variety of settings such as the liturgy, instruction within the home or small Christian communities, or, perhaps even more formally, in some early centers of Christian learning. But eventually these oral materials were gathered and put in written form by the evangelists. It is likely that the oral transmission of the biblical materials, both Old and New Testaments, continued to exist and be employed even after the biblical text had been put into writing. Paul's letters and other New Testament texts such as the Catholic Epistles and the book of Revelation were composed or dictated into written form immediately.

No original manuscript of any biblical book exists. Copyists from one generation to the next transcribed the biblical materials and enabled them to be available for subsequent generations. The earliest written manuscripts we have of some Old Testament biblical materials date from the first century BC. These were part of the wealth of written materials discovered in 1948 on the northwest shore of the Dead Sea and thereafter called the "Dead Sea Scrolls." Most of the other early written materials for both the Old and the New Testaments would be papyrus fragments of biblical passages dating from the early second century AD and more complete manuscripts of the Bible on parchment from the third and fourth centuries AD.

The biblical texts of the ancient church did not have the neat format of our modern Bible. Division into the present system of chapters and verses was introduced only in the Middle Ages. Prior to that, demarcations between individual sentences and sections of a particular biblical book were much more casual and fluid. The hands of many copyists, with different personal interests and levels of skill, inevitably introduced some variations and errors into the numerous editions of the biblical text. Ancient translations or versions of manuscripts into other languages, such as Latin or Syriac or Coptic, could also introduce errors or varying interpretations not found in the original biblical language.

The science of textual criticism attempts to trace the relationships of ancient manuscripts to each other and to reestablish the most reliable form of the biblical text. The discovery of biblical texts among the Dead Sea Scrolls rolled back the age of extant biblical manuscripts several centuries. Surprisingly, although some variants exist, there is still remarkable correspondence between the state of the biblical text in the first century BC and the third or fourth century AD—testimony to the accuracy and care with which ancient peoples handed on the biblical tradition.

The *New American Bible* Translation

Most modern translations, including that found in the NAB, are based on the most reliable texts of the Bible we have and are translated from the original biblical languages rather than using any intervening translations. Many previous Catholic translations had been based on the Vulgate, or Latin version of the Bible, first prepared by Jerome in the fifth century.

As the preface to the NAB states (see pp. 3–4 of the Old Testament section), its translation was a collaborative achievement of some fifty Catholic biblical scholars, determined to use the best of modern scholarship to bring a fresh and accurate translation of the Bible to the American Catholic community.

The first full edition of the Old and New Testaments appeared in 1970. A revision of the New Testament appeared in 1986, and a revision of the Psalms in 1991. It is this fully revised edition that is used in the *Catholic Study Bible*.

Every translation, no matter how accurate and faithful, falls short in attempting to communicate the subtlety and meaning of another language. All translators have to make decisions about the purpose and audience of their translation, and the consequent principles they will use in translating the Bible from its original languages to a modern language such as American English. And, to some degree, every translation is a subtle "interpretation" of the biblical text.

The translators of the NAB wanted as much as possible to accurately reflect the nuance and form of biblical Hebrew and Greek, while recasting the language to make it compatible with the rules and style of modern English and in harmony with traditional Catholic interpretations of Scripture. The translators, however, wanted to avoid making the NAB a "paraphrase" or quasi-interpretation of the biblical text. Some modern translations attempt this. While such paraphrases perhaps make the biblical texts more palatable to a modern audience, they also risk a high degree of subjectivity in recasting the contents of the Bible. The NAB translation is faithful to the biblical text and takes its place alongside rigorously literal translations such as the Revised Standard Version. This makes it particularly suitable for deeper study of the biblical message, as well as its use in prayer and liturgy.

Accuracy of translation from one language to another also involves issues that are more than linguistic. For instance, the editors of the revised New Testament translation had to struggle with the question of inclusive language. This is a sensitive issue in modern American culture and in the Catholic Church in particular. The translators adopted a compromise stance here. Where the original biblical language clearly intended a generic reference to human beings, the translation is careful to use inclusive language. Where the original text uses a gender specific reference, however, such as many references to God through male pronouns, the translation does not attempt to use inclusive language.

Modern political issues can also cause difficulties for the translator. Such geographical terms as *Israel* or *Palestine* have highly charged meanings in the political arena of today's Middle East. But their appearance in the biblical translation of the NAB implies no endorsement of any modern political stance on these difficult issues. So, too, can modern religious sensitivities come into play. Judaism in all its modern forms, out of reverence, avoids the use of the name *Yahweh* for God. Readers in the synagogue, for example, will substitute *Adonai* (My Lord) wherever the divine name appears in the biblical text. The modern translator and commentator have to make a decision on whether to try to respect this understandable religious sensitivity.

It should be noted that the Reading Guides and major Articles included in the *Catholic Study Bible* attempt throughout to use inclusive language, and, wherever possible, to avoid offense to modern religious, cultural, or political sensitivities. The editors believed that such a spirit is in accord with both the biblical witness and sound Catholic tradition. Some use of the geographical terms *Israel* and *Palestine* was unavoidable in some of the Reading Guides, but no reference to modern geopolitical realities is intended.

READING, STUDYING, AND PRAYING THE SCRIPTURES

From the beginning of its existence, the Bible has been the object of intense study, prayerful reading, and even heated debate. The Bible is not meant to be a coffee-table book.

One could say that the Bible was formed in a

context of prayer and reflection. The various biblical authors reflected on significant events in the life of Israel, of Jesus, and of the early church. Their discovery of God's presence working within history gives the Bible its force. For all Christians the Bible has unique authority as writings inspired by God's Spirit working within the communities of Israel and the Church, and impelling the biblical writers to give expression in human words to their faith perspective. (For a Catholic view of biblical inspiration, see "The Bible in Catholic Life," RG 16–29).

Judaism has always maintained a rich tradition of reflection on its Scriptures. The rabbis lovingly studied every detail of the biblical text and saw an infinite possibility of applications to everyday life. The Scriptures were reverenced as God's Word and took a central place within the prayer life of the synagogue. Christian tradition has had the same character. Until the late Middle Ages, almost all of the Church's theology and teaching was little more than an elaboration of the biblical text.

Some of this biblical focus was lost in the Catholic Church when philosophical analysis—always important—became overdominant and theological reflection could often be far distant in focus and spirit from our biblical foundations: While biblical symbols remained dominant in Catholic liturgical life and architecture, in popular preaching and much popular piety, the Bible was a more distant echo. In the past fifty years, that trend has been radically reversed. The Second Vatican Council gave a strong impetus to a biblical renewal in every dimension of Catholicism (see "The Bible in Catholic Life," RG 16–29).

One can approach reading and study of the Bible from several vantage points.

The Historical Approach. One purpose in reading the Bible is to comb through the biblical books, seeking leads to the historical context of a given period or culture. While this is a legitimate historical enterprise, it does not correspond to the fundamentally religious character of the Bible. The Bible does have strong historical value; but its purpose is not simply to inform the reader about history but to probe the meaning of past history for the life of faith.

The Theological Approach. Another way of entering the biblical world is to seek what the Bible, or a particular biblical book, has to say on a specific doctrinal or moral issue. What, for example, does the Bible say about violence? Or what is the biblical perspective on justice? Because the Bible is such a rich and diverse body of literature, we soon discover that the Bible will yield many perspectives on such important issues. There is seldom a single biblical viewpoint on any specific theological or moral issue. Only by first understanding the context of each biblical period and biblical book, and then interrelating the Bible's varied approaches to profound questions of faith, can one weave together a biblical theology.

The Inspirational Approach. For most Christians, reading the Bible has a more modest, yet still important goal. They turn to the Scriptures for inspiration in living out their life of faith. Such inspiration can be gained in many different ways.

For some, the Scriptures are an important stimulant for prayer. The words of the Psalms, the challenge of the prophets, the compassionate mission of Jesus, the soaring words of Paul—all of these give form and expression to the longing of our own hearts as we seek the face of God. Very often the biblical words are able to express the feelings and fears and hopes we could not put into words ourselves. And in reaching out to the Bible we unite ourselves with the faith of countless generations of Christians who found the same solace and strength in the Scriptures.

For others, probing the Scriptures either in private or with a group of fellow Christians helps guide and illumine their daily life. Study of the biblical text and discussion of its meaning with other thoughtful Christians can help us understand our own experience of faith and expand our perspective on what it means to be a believer in the modern world. This approach works best when the participant is not afraid to reflect on his or her own experience, and can then relate that reflection to the ideas and images of the Bible. Very often the Bible opens its treasures when we bring to it questions and hopes that spring from our life of faith. Then, in turn, the biblical message can give new insight and nourishment to our faith experience.

A profound sense of grief or loss, for example, might lead a Christian to read with new understanding the lament psalms of the Old Testament

(RG 243–44) or the Passion of Jesus. And these biblical passages, in turn, can bring new strength to the one who suffers.

Whatever approach one takes to reading and praying the Bible, it is important from a Catholic perspective that it not be done in isolation. The Bible is the Church's book, not a private library. Only in the context of the Church's faith and tradition as a whole can the full meaning of the Bible be discovered. Some Christians who isolate themselves from common sense and from the sound wisdom of the Church community can interpret the Scriptures in a bizarre and even destructive manner. That is why the effort to understand the biblical text in its context, to sound out its possible meaning with other thoughtful

Christians, and to be open to the guidance of the Church and its teaching forms the best context for full integration of the Bible into our lives (on this see the 1993 statement of the Pontifical Biblical Commission, *The Interpretation of the Bible in the Church,* which fully endorses the use of modern biblical methods).

The *Catholic Study Bible* is designed to open the beauty and power of the Bible to the reader. The editors and the Oxford University Press hope that the guides, articles, and other resources provided in this unique volume will serve you well as you step into the marvelous world of the Bible.

Donald Senior, C.P.
General Editor

THE BIBLICAL TEXTS AND THEIR BACKGROUND

DONALD SENIOR

The biblical writings were created over a wide expanse of time. That broad historical and cultural canvas is one important cause for the Bible's rich diversity. In this Study Bible, the Reading Guides provided for each biblical book, and the introductions provided in the notes to the biblical text itself, offer specific information about the historical background of the individual books of the Bible. A clear and succinct historical summary is provided in the article "Biblical History and Archaeology" (RG 30–53). The following paragraphs sketch the relationship of the biblical books to that evolving history.

The accounts of creation and the stories about the first ancestors of the human family, such as the tragic rivalry between Cain and Abel and the story of Noah and the flood, obviously do not have the same historical grounding that later traditions could. These stories answer the question about the origin of humanity and its plight in history. Firm historical traditions begin only with the forging of Israel into an identifiable people, an event that did not begin until probably around 1250 BC. Traditions about the earlier patriarchal period starting around 1850 BC are much less certain historically, and even events from the time of Israel's sojourn in Egypt and during the period of the Exodus and early settlement in the land are sketchy since there were few means of preserving historical archives.

THE MAJOR PERIODS OF BIBLICAL HISTORY

The Time of the Patriarchs (1850–1250 BC)

The period from Abraham to Joseph is recounted in Genesis 12—50. Historically, this was a period of vast migrations in the Middle East, with clans of herders moving freely from Mesopotamia down through the Fertile Crescent into present-day Israel. Egypt had been a dominant power in the Middle East for more than two thousand years prior to that time. Egypt's might was counterbalanced by a succession of powerful dynasties at the eastern end of the Fertile Crescent, including the Persians, Assyrians, and Babylonians. Israel, located geographically between those two areas, would often be the battleground for those opposing forces. (See map #6.)

Few firm historical traditions exist from this period, but the general picture provided in the biblical traditions about the patriarchs does reflect something of the nomadic lifestyle and familial religion typical of the period.

The Exodus, Wilderness Wandering, and Settlement in the Land (1250–1130 BC)

This period is covered in Exodus, Deuteronomy, Numbers, and Joshua. The story of Israel as a unified people begins in Egypt with the stories about Moses and the miraculous exodus from Egypt. During a period of wandering in the desert, the covenant was formed with Yahweh, the LORD, the God of Israel. Under the leadership of Joshua, Israel finally breaks through into the Promised Land, driving the native Canaanites before them.

There is considerable debate about the historical background to this period. Some scholars, particularly conservative ones, are willing to accept the biblical portrayal at face value: namely that there was a mass migration of Hebrews from Egypt and that they invaded the regions of Israel

10

with military force and thereby gained possession of the land.

The lack of clear archaeological evidence supporting such a vast military conquest, and some ambiguity in the biblical traditions themselves, have led other historians to surmise that both the migration from Egypt and the possession of the land took place over a longer period of time. Some Hebrew tribes may have already settled in Israel prior to the Exodus, and joined with the incoming tribes at a later period. While some Canaanite cities may have been taken by force, some of the land was probably settled in a peaceful fashion.

In any event, the Bible sees this process as a dramatic act of deliverance by God and as the historic beginning of the story of Israel.

The Period of the Judges (1130–1020 BC)

This early period of Israelite history is narrated in the book of Judges. It is clear that the Israelites at first resisted the idea of a strong central government. They preferred a loosely organized federation of clans or tribes ruled by charismatic leaders called judges. Only the Lord could claim the right to be called King. This independent spirit and aversion to the monarchy goes deep into the consciousness of Israel.

The Monarchy (1020–587 BC)

This long, but in fact highly diverse, period of Israel's history is taken up in the books of 1 and 2 Samuel, 1 and 2 Kings, and a parallel account in 1 and 2 Chronicles.

The transition from the more informal and charismatic leadership under the judges to the more institutional form of the monarchy begins with Saul (about 1020–1000 BC) but reaches its zenith with David (1000–960 BC) and Solomon (960–930 BC). Threats from surrounding peoples and the need for more complex social organization gradually led Israel to adopt a monarchical form of government. David eventually unified diverse groups of people under a single government system, ruled from his new centrally located capital of Jerusalem. Under David and his son Solomon, Israel's territories greatly expanded.

The united kingdom forged by David did not last very long. Solomon strained it by increasing taxation and by lack of sensitivity to the old tribal loyalties. When Solomon's son Rehoboam ascended to the throne, the seams between north and south split and the separate kingdoms of Judah in the south and Israel in the north began. This divided monarchy would last until 724 BC, when the Assyrian empire would crush the Northern Kingdom. Judah would survive until the Babylonian invasion of 587 BC.

The biblical account has little respect for the northern rulers and takes a critical view of most of the kings of Judah as well, considering them unfaithful to the covenant. During this period the great prophetic movement would ignite in Israel. Elijah, Elisha, Amos, and Hosea were prophets in the northern kingdom. Isaiah served as court prophet to the kings of Judah.

Exile and Return (587–332 BC)

This crucial period of Israelite history is narrated in 2 Kings 24—25 and in the books of Ezra and Nehemiah.

The Babylonian captivity would last almost fifty years. Systematic deportation as a way of subduing conquered peoples had been used first by Assyrians and then by the Babylonians. Only a small remnant of Israelites was left behind under the firm control of Babylonian officials. When the exiled Jews eventually returned, they considered the people who had stayed behind as somehow corrupt and would not allow them to take part in the reconstruction of Israel, a source of bitterness that would lead to the sharp divisions between Jews and Samaritans so obvious in the New Testament period.

Under the leadership of Ezra and Nehemiah, Jerusalem and its Temple were rebuilt. But Israel was now only a small and fragile nation, clustered around Jerusalem and very concerned with preserving its identity.

The Greek Conquest and the Rise of the Hasmoneans (332–39 BC)

This is a turbulent part of Israelite history, reflected in 1 and 2 Maccabees and Daniel.

Alexander conquered Palestine in 332 BC, beginning a period in which Greek culture would have a strong impact on the life of Israel. After his death, the Middle Eastern portion of Alexander's empire was divided between the Seleucid dynasty, which ruled from Syria, and the Ptolemies who ruled from Egypt. The Ptolemaic dynasty controlled Israel from approximately 332 to 199 BC. Their generally benign rule gave way to the Seleucids, who attempted to impose Greek culture and taxation in a more rigorous fashion. Seleucid ruthlessness eventually triggered the Maccabean revolt, which by 160 BC had thrown off the yoke of the Seleucids against incredible odds.

The Jewish dynasty of the Hasmonean family now begins a hundred-year reign. The Hasmonean kings proved to be as corrupt and ruthless as the foreigners who had preceded them. Reactions by pious Jews to the compromises of the Hasmoneans and their Jerusalem aristocracy would give rise to protest groups such as the Essenes and Pharisees. By 60 BC, Roman influence was growing in the Middle East and brought pressure on Israel itself. The Hasmonean period came to an end with the emergence of Herod the Great, a vassal of the Romans, who would unify the country and hold it in his grip.

The Roman Period (39 BC–AD 100)

The New Testament writings emerge during this period of biblical history. With the death of

Herod in 4 BC, the Romans divided Israel among his three sons. Eventually the Romans removed the cruel and incompetent Archaelaus, taking over direct rule of Judah and Samaria. Herod Philip and Herod Antipas would continue to govern in the regions of Upper Galilee, Lower Galilee, and the Transjordan (see map #12).

Roman rule and its heavy taxation proved intolerable to the Jewish people. Tensions mounted all during the first half of the first century, exploding into revolution in AD 66. That revolt would be violently suppressed by the Romans, climaxing with the destruction of Jerusalem and its great Temple in AD 70. That event would change the complexion of Judaism forever. Another short-lived revolt would break out in AD 132. The Romans would continue to occupy Palestine until the time of the Byzantine empire. All of these events have left a profound impression on the writings of the New Testament.

THE CATHOLIC STUDY BIBLE

DONALD SENIOR

HOW TO USE THIS STUDY BIBLE

This one-volume Study Bible offers a full range of aids to help the reader discover the meaning of the Bible. The following description of its contents, and suggestions for using the book, might help you take full advantage of its unique resources.

The Resources of the Study Bible

There are seven major sections in this volume:

The *New American Bible*

Beginning on page 5 of the Old Testament section, you will find the full text and notes of the NAB. Each major section of the Bible and each biblical book has a brief introduction. Extensive notes explaining words or individual verses are found at the bottom of the page. An asterisk (*) alongside a particular word or verse signals to you that an explanatory note is provided for that biblical text. These notes are the official notes that were prepared by the editors of the NAB, and they provide a wealth of information for the studious reader.

The NAB also provides cross-references to other related biblical passages. These cross-references are signaled by a small italic letter printed within specific verses. The cross-reference is found at the bottom of the page.

Finally, along the side margins there is another set of cross-references, directing you to the Reading Guides and Articles found in other sections of the *Catholic Study Bible*. These cross-references are indicated by page numbers enclosed within a shaded box. Page numbers re-

ferring to the Reading Guides and Articles are preceded by the letters RG.

The Reading Guides

One of the special features of this Study Bible is the Reading Guides found in the front section beginning on page RG 85. There are Guides for each book of the Bible, and their purpose is precisely to lead the reader through the structure and basic message of each biblical book.

The notes found at the bottom of the page with the NAB translation provide information on specific details of a given verse. The Reading Guides add a new perspective by taking a broader look at each biblical book, tracing its major sections and themes, and making suggestions about its meaning for today. Each of them also provides references to other books and articles for readers who want to continue their study of specific issues.

The Articles

Another helpful feature of the *Catholic Study Bible* is that it provides extensive and detailed studies of key issues for understanding and using the Bible. These essays will prove especially valuable for those who want to probe deeper into a particular question. In addition to this introduction, the reader will find the following Articles:

• "The Bible in Catholic Life" explains the Roman Catholic view of Scripture and the meaning of biblical inspiration.

• "Biblical History and Archaeology" offers a succinct overview of the major periods of biblical history along with a helpful explanation of the methods and major discoveries of biblical archaeology.

• "Catholic Interpretation of the Bible" traces the history of the Church's approach to the meaning of Scripture.

• "The Challenges of Biblical Translation" shows how taking a text from one language to another is both an art and a science.

• "The Bible in the Lectionary" explains the role of the Bible in liturgy and, in particular, shows the rationale for the selection of biblical passages in the Lectionary. This will be useful for preachers or those who prepare liturgies.

Sunday and Weekday Lectionaries

The lectionaries give up-to-date cycles of readings for public services.

The Glossary

The glossary provides clear explanations of the less familiar or more technical terms used in the Bible or in the Reading Guide.

Concordance

The concordance, or word index, provides key citations for important biblical names and terms.

New Oxford Bible Maps

These extensive maps provide the reader with the entire geographical canvas on which the biblical drama is portrayed.

Suggestions for Use

The resources of the *Catholic Study Bible* enable the reader to use it in a variety of ways and settings.

For Individual Reading or Study

If your goal is to read and reflect on a single biblical book or major passage of the Bible, the two key sections of the Study Bible to use are the biblical text itself and the Reading Guides. Both should be used in tandem.

You may wish to read through the introductions to the biblical book first, both the one found in the Reading Guide and in the NAB text. In turning to the Gospel of Luke, for example, one would read the introduction in the Reading Guide on RG 397–412 and then turn to the Bible section on pp. 1349–50. After that the reader can

pick his or her way through the Gospel, noting the major characteristics of the biblical passage and its major motifs by attentive reading of the biblical text and its accompanying notes, and by referring to the information provided in the Reading Guide.

For the more ambitious reader, the "Suggested Readings" at the end of the Reading Guides and in the Articles offer leads to further study.

For Group Study

The *Catholic Study Bible* lends itself well to group use. If each member of the group has a copy, then the leader could suggest the reading of a specific biblical text and the accompanying section from the Reading Guide as a good means of preparing for the group session. Preparation always enhances group Bible study. Often the Reading Guide will provide some points of reflection that a group might find helpful as a starting point for discussion about the meaning of a passage.

Some of the articles, such as the ones on "The Bible in Catholic Life" and "The Bible in the Lectionary," could also be fruitful sources for group study and discussion. Where the group itself does not have access to individual copies, the *Catholic Study Bible* can serve as a resource for the leader or can be on hand for reference when the group discussion generates a question that needs further information.

Teaching Resource

The *Catholic Study Bible* is particularly useful for the college or religious education classroom. It provides virtually a one-volume textbook and reference library on the Bible. Experienced and imaginative teachers will find their own way to best utilize a book like this. A few suggestions might help.

The Study Bible can certainly serve as a textbook for a course on the Bible as a whole or for introductions to the Old or New Testaments. Here again interplay between pertinent sections of the Reading Guides and the biblical text and notes is very important.

Teachers in a Catholic setting may want to give special attention to the article on "The Bible in Catholic Life" as an important summary of Catholic teaching on the role of the Bible in the Church's life and thought. "The Bible in the Lectionary" will help Catholics (and Christians from other mainline denominations) understand how the liturgy is a major source of biblical inspiration for Roman Catholic tradition.

The volume will also support a course on the history and geography of the Bible. The article on the history and archaeology of the Bible provides clear and useful information. The accompanying maps enable the teacher to discuss the geography of the Bible in detail. The maps can especially be a useful illustration when studying such narratives as Exodus, the historical books, the Gospels, Acts, and Paul's letters.

Sermon and Liturgy Preparation

The thematic approach of the Reading Guides and the attempt they make to relate the biblical message to spirituality and Church teaching should prove useful for sermon and liturgy preparation.

The article on "The Bible in the Lectionary" provides important and often neglected information on the rationale for the selection and arrangement of biblical passages in the Lectionary, and offers good suggestions about relating the Bible to the liturgical year.

THE BIBLE IN CATHOLIC LIFE

DANIEL J. HARRINGTON

CHURCH LIFE TODAY

One of the great achievements of the Second Vatican Council (1962–65) has been the renewal of interest in the Bible among Catholics. How dramatic this renewal has been can be grasped by comparing Catholic practice around 1950 and the situation in the early years of the twenty-first century.

At mid-twentieth century the Scriptures were read at Mass in Latin. There were few selections from the Old Testament, and a rather small number of New Testament passages dominated the one-year cycle. In response to the mandate of the Second Vatican Council we now have a three-year cycle of Sunday readings and a two-year weekday cycle. (See "The Bible in the Lectionary," RG 76–84.) The Old Testament is very prominent, and almost the entire New Testament (Gospels and Epistles) is represented. The passages, of course, are read in the vernacular (English, Spanish, or whatever is the dominant local language).

In the 1950s study of Bible texts was not an integral part of the primary- or secondary-school curriculum in Catholic schools. At best Bible content was conveyed through summaries of the texts. Catholic college students might work through parts of the Bible with the aid of cautious and approved textbooks as guides. But now the texts of the Bible form a primary resource for Catholic religious education at all levels. And Bible courses and Bible study groups have become especially popular forums for adult education.

At mid-twentieth century Catholic seminarians took most of their Scripture courses toward the end of their theology programs. In comparison with dogma and moral theology, Scripture study was considered a minor course. Now biblical studies are a major component of the seminary curriculum at all stages. And such courses are very popular. Students in Catholic seminaries assume that much of their preaching and teaching in the future will be devoted to the Bible, and so they study it with eagerness. There is also a lively dialogue and interdisciplinary cooperation between professors of Scripture and their theological colleagues.

Since Vatican II the Bible has become prominent not only in Catholic liturgy and education but also in popular piety. The revised prayers for the sacraments and other liturgical actions use biblical language almost entirely. Charismatic groups and base communities have found biblical reflection and prayer to be the source of great spiritual energy. Even traditional Catholic observances like the Rosary are (and always have been) thoroughly biblical. The language of Catholic prayer in almost every instance derives from the Bible.

The Scriptures have also been a major element in the ecumenical movement since the Council. The serious historical and theological differences between the Christian churches remain, but the most progress has been made where the different church groups have focused on the Bible as their common heritage and have reexamined their differences in light of the Bible's language and thought patterns. When this has occurred, the usual result has been the recognition that what unites the Christian churches is more important and fundamental than what divides them. In the new and more positive relationship that has emerged between Christians and Jews in recent years, Bible study has been a vital force toward greater mutual understanding and respect.

Catholic theology since the Council gives far more attention to biblical sources and is likely to express itself more in biblical than in philosophical language. Official church documents on theological matters or current problems almost always begin from Scripture and try to ground their arguments in biblical texts. The Catholic Church today is far more biblical than it was in the mid-1950s.

BIBLE STUDY IN HISTORY

In order to understand the Bible's place in Catholic thinking today, it can be helpful to see how Christians in other times and places thought about and interpreted the Bible. The Bible has not always been studied according to the principles of modern historical criticism. Nor should scientific study of the Bible be understood as superseding, and thus making obsolete, all earlier approaches. A brief history of biblical interpretation will reveal important insights that remain valid today.

The Old Testament constituted the Bible for Jesus and the early Christians. According to the Gospels, Jesus sometimes quoted or alluded to Old Testament texts in order to establish a theological point or to suggest a way of acting. He clearly accorded these texts a certain degree of authority. Nevertheless, Jesus emerges from the New Testament as displaying flexibility toward the Old Testament and even asserting his authority over it. He distinguishes what comes from God and what comes from Moses (see Mk 10, 1–12), goes beyond certain scriptural teachings (Mt 5, 21–48), and rates love of God and neighbor (Mk 12, 28–31) over strict observance of the Sabbath.

New Testament writers such as Paul and Matthew looked upon the Old Testament Scriptures as "fulfilled" in Jesus Christ. Basing themselves on what apparently was a widespread early Christian understanding, they interpreted the Old Testament Scriptures in the light of the life, death, and resurrection of Jesus. Like other Jews

of the time, they understood the Old Testament to be a "mystery"—that is, something that could not be understood without guidance or explanation. Whereas the Qumran community (the Jewish group that gave us the Dead Sea Scrolls) found the key to the Scriptures in their own sect's history and life, the early Christians discovered Jesus to be the key that opened up the mystery of the Hebrew Bible.

By the time of the Fathers of the Church (the patristic period), the Christian Bible contained two Testaments—Old and New. These early theologians generally adopted one or the other of two basic approaches to the reading and interpretation of Scripture: the allegorical and the literal methods.

The allegorical method, favored particularly by those theologians who lived in Alexandria in Egypt, emphasized uncovering the spiritual truths beneath the surface of the biblical stories. This method had been developed by Greek thinkers who interpreted the stories in Homer's *Iliad* and *Odyssey* as symbolizing emotional or spiritual struggles within the individual. It had also been adopted by Jewish interpreters, like Philo of Alexandria, who used the method on the Hebrew Bible in order to appeal to non-Jews and especially to Jews who had come under the influence of Greek philosophy and culture. Christian theologians who used this method included Origen and Clement of Alexandria.

In contrast to this method was the more literal reading of the Bible, favored by those Christian thinkers who lived in Antioch, the capital of Syria in Roman times. The literal approach focused more on the historical realities described in Scripture, and insisted that any higher or deeper sense should be based firmly on the literal sense of the text. John Chrysostom and Theodore of Mopsuestia were among those who favored this approach.

It is important to recognize that these different emphases were not completely opposed to each other. Thus the allegorical method did not deny the historical truth of events in Scripture, nor did the literal method deny the spiritual meaning of those events. Later theologians tended to blend the two approaches, though favoring one tendency or the other. Augustine, for instance, tended toward the allegorical and Jerome toward the literal.

Medieval interpreters, building on both these approaches, distinguished four senses in a scriptural text: literal (what took place), allegorical (the hidden theological meaning), anagogical (the heavenly sense), and moral or tropological (the significance for the individual's behavior). The classic example was the word *Jerusalem* (see Gal 4, 22–31), which can refer to a city in Palestine (literal), the church (allegorical), the heavenly home of us all (anagogical), and the human soul (moral). Since this wide-ranging approach to Scripture could easily degenerate into subjectivity, careful interpreters like Thomas Aquinas insisted that "nothing necessary to faith is contained under the spiritual sense that is not elsewhere put forward by Scripture in its literal sense." Thomas Aquinas also used human reason as a tool in explaining the Scriptures and tried to bring together philosophical truth (especially as proposed by Aristotle) and biblical truth.

With the Renaissance and the rise of Humanism came a new interest in studying the Scriptures in their original languages and their historical settings. Erasmus produced a new edition of the Greek New Testament to go along with his revision of the Latin Vulgate translation. He also used the Greek and Roman classics of paganism along with the writings of the Church Fathers to interpret the biblical texts. Catholic enthusiasm for the study of the Scriptures cooled, however, in response to the claims for the Bible (*sola scriptura* or Scripture alone) made by Martin Luther and other Protestant Reformers, especially their statements about the clarity of Scripture (so that there is no need for the church as the final interpreter) and its sufficiency (so that there is no need for church tradition).

The rationalist claims of the European Enlightenment made matters even more complicated for Catholic interpreters of the Bible. For example, the philosopher Baruch Spinoza maintained that when Scripture and philosophy come into conflict (as in the case of miracles), then Scripture is to be rejected in favor of "reason." Thus the Catholic Church was backed into being the defender of biblical "truth," sometimes with unfortunate consequences.

This survey reveals some abiding principles of Catholic biblical interpretation: the central significance of Christ; the struggle to be faithful to the literal meaning while searching for spiritual meaning; the conviction that faith and reason are not opposed; the insistence that the Bible should be interpreted in the Church; and the emphasis on biblical truth against the attacks of rationalism.

MODERN DEVELOPMENTS

The gradual Catholic acceptance of scientific biblical criticism (or the historical-critical method) while remaining true to the Church's heritage can be traced with reference to a series of official Roman documents issued during the late nineteenth and the twentieth centuries. For a full collection of official Roman Catholic documents pertaining to the study of the Bible, see *The Scripture Documents: An Anthology of Official Catholic Teachings* (Dean R. Bechard, ed., Collegeville, MN: Liturgical Press, 2002).

A cautious beginning was made with the papal encyclical *Providentissimus Deus* by Pope Leo XIII in 1893, only to be blunted by fears of Modernism under Pius X and by Benedict XV's encyclical *Spiritus Paraclitus* issued in 1920. A new age dawned with the encyclical titled *Divino Afflante Spiritu* that was promulgated by Pius XII in 1943, in which the historical study of the Bible was given official approbation. The approach outlined by Pius XII was put into practice by the Pontifical Biblical Commission in its 1964 *Instruction Concerning the Historical Truth of the Gospels.*

The culmination of official Catholic pronouncements on biblical studies was the Second Vatican Council's *Dogmatic Constitution on Divine Revelation.* The nature of these documents is cumulative; that is, the latest document generally restates the teachings contained in previous documents and clarifies matters not discussed earlier in detail. However, the document of an ecumenical council has far more official weight than a papal encyclical or an instruction from the Pontifical Biblical Commission. Moreover, the Council's document on Scripture was a "dogmatic constitution," the most authoritative kind issued by Vatican II. Thus Vatican II's *Dogmatic Constitution on Divine Revelation* can be taken as the authoritative climax of a long series of developments in the Church's attitude toward the Bible.

Vatican II was a pastoral council. It sought to

address the needs of the Church and the world in the twentieth century and beyond. Its constitution on divine revelation (also known by its Latin title, *Dei verbum*)was addressed not so much to scholars or theologians as to the Church at large. In effect, the bishops were saying, "This is what the Catholic Church thinks and believes about the Bible and related matters." The document had a rocky history from its first draft in 1962 to its final form in 1965. Pope John XXIII's rejection of the initial draft, which favored a propositional understanding of revelation (revelation consists of statements of abstract truths) and a theory of two sources of revelation (Scripture and tradition), set the Second Vatican Council on its path of *aggiornamento* (Italian for "bringing up to date"). (All quotations are from the translation by Liam Walsh and Wilfrid Harrington in *Vatican Council II: The Conciliar and Post-Conciliar Documents* [Austin Flannery, ed., Northport, NY: Costello, 1975] 750–65.)

The six chapters in *Dei verbum* treat divine revelation itself, the transmission of divine revelation, Sacred Scripture—its divine inspiration and its interpretation—the Old Testament, the New Testament, and Sacred Scripture in the life of the Church. What the constitution teaches on these topics will be taken up in the remaining parts of this essay. Here, only what it teaches about scientific biblical criticism will concern us.

The conciliar statement about biblical criticism appears in paragraph 12, which is part of the chapter on the inspiration and interpretation of Scripture. It is prefaced by an acknowledgment that since God speaks in Scripture through human beings, and so in human fashion, interpreters should give careful attention to the ways in which the sacred writers thought and expressed themselves:

In determining the intention of the sacred writers, attention must be paid, *inter alia,* to literary forms for the fact is that truth is differently presented and expressed in the various types of historical writing, in prophetical and poetical texts, and in other forms of literary expression. Hence the exegete must look for that meaning which the sacred writer, in a determined situation and given the circumstances of his time and culture, intended to express and did in fact express, through the medium of a contemporary literary form. Rightly to understand what the sacred author

wanted to affirm in his work, due attention must be paid both to the customary and characteristic patterns of perception, speech and narrative which prevailed at the age of the sacred writer, and to the conventions which the people of his time followed in their dealings with one another.

The statement, which is really a condensation of Pius XII's 1943 encyclical *Divine Afflante Spiritu,* makes three points. First, it insists that we take into account the various literary forms in which the Bible is written, and it warns us against confusing historical, prophetic, and poetic texts. Next, it urges us to pay attention to the historical setting in which the sacred author wrote, suggesting that such historical awareness is necessary for grasping what the author intended. Finally, it recommends that we learn about the literary conventions and cultural assumptions that people accepted at the time when the biblical books were composed. Thus the conciliar document encourages the literary, historical, and sociological study of biblical texts.

The acceptance of biblical criticism, of course, does not reduce the Sacred Scriptures to the status of other, strictly human books. In fact, the very next sentence in the document affirms the divine authorship of the biblical texts and urges biblical interpreters to take that into consideration:

But since sacred Scripture must be read and interpreted with its divine authorship in mind, no less attention must be devoted to the content and unity of the whole of Scripture, taking into account the Tradition of the entire Church and the analogy of faith, if we are to derive their true meaning from the sacred texts.

In this way the conciliar document achieves a balance between the human and the divine contributions to Scripture. Interpreters are thereby encouraged to apply all the tools of biblical criticism, while bearing in mind the Church's longstanding conviction that the Bible contains "the Word of God in the words of men."

In 1993, to mark the one hundredth anniversary of *Providentissimus Deus* and the fiftieth anniversary of *Divino Afflante Spiritu,* the Pontifical Biblical Commission, with the full approval of Pope John Paul II, issued a document titled "The Interpretation of the Bible in the Church." Prepared by an international team of distinguished Catholic biblical scholars, this document describes various methods of and approaches to biblical interpretation, examines certain questions of a hermeneutical nature, reflects on the characteristic features of a Catholic interpretation of the Bible, and considers the place that biblical interpretation has in the life of the church. This document spells out in some detail many of the directions recommended in the papal encyclicals and in Vatican II's *Dei verbum*.

The Pontifical Biblical Commission's document describes the historical-critical method as "the indispensable method for the scientific study of the meaning of ancient texts." While giving attention to the many possible contributions from certain "new" literary and social-scientific approaches, it criticizes fundamentalism as "dangerous" and even as inviting people to "a kind of intellectual suicide." And it insists on the pastoral significance of the whole exegetical enterprise when it states: "Exegesis produces its best results when it is carried out in the context of the living faith of the Christian community, which is directed toward the salvation of the entire world."

Methods of Biblical Interpretation

The term *biblical criticism* refers to various methods of scientific biblical study that have as their goal establishing the text, understanding the content and the literary style of biblical books, and determining their origin and authenticity. This undertaking is sometimes called the "historical-critical method"—"historical" because it focuses on the original historical settings of the biblical texts and the historical processes that gave rise to them, and "critical" because it applies reason to the texts and makes judgments about them in the effort to be as objective as possible. Biblical criticism aims to understand what a text was saying to its original audience and to make clear its significance then (and now).

Textual criticism (sometimes called "lower criticism") seeks to establish the wording of the biblical text as the biblical authors wrote it. Since we no longer have direct access to the manuscripts written by the biblical authors (autographs), textual critics try to come as close as possible to the original form of the texts by gathering all the pertinent manuscript evidence (Hebrew and Aramaic for the Old Testament, Greek for the New Testament, ancient translations for

both Testaments). When the evidence has been assembled, textual critics determine where the ancient manuscripts differ and proceed to decide which reading is original and to explain how the other readings arose. The rejected readings may have been unconscious mistakes (for example, confusing similar letters of the alphabet, omitting words or phrases, inserting marginal comments into the main text) or deliberate modifications (for example, harmonizing with parallel texts, correcting grammar or style, removing "offensive" material). The accepted readings should be consistent with the content and style of the document and follow the rules of grammar and good sense.

Literary criticism attends to the words and images, the characters and their relationships, the structure and progress of thought, the literary form, and the meaning. These processes are used today in studying all kinds of literature; they are by no means confined to biblical study. Bible concordances, dictionaries, and encyclopedias make it possible to trace the development of a word (for example, *faith*) or a theme (for example, *covenant*) and to locate a particular occurrence within such a framework. Careful inspection of a text enables one to chart out the interactions among the characters or to outline the progress of the argument. The biblical writers used many different literary forms. The Old Testament consists of law codes, narratives, psalms, prophecies, proverbs, visions, and even love poetry. The New Testament contains stories of Jesus' words and deeds (Gospels), the actions of some apostles (Acts), letters (Epistles), and visions (Revelation). Rather than stating theological truths in the form of theses or propositions, the biblical authors conveyed their message in artistic and memorable ways. Literary criticism helps us to read the biblical books on their own terms and thus to appreciate their artistry and their truth.

Historical criticism concerns the world behind the biblical texts; that is, the origin and growth of the biblical documents. Scholars assume that sometimes a complicated process of composition lies behind a finished book of the Bible. Smaller literary units—for example, a saying from Jesus, or a hymn—were told and retold, or used orally in worship. Later, perhaps, a collection of sayings or hymns was generated. Still later, a writer created a longer narrative into which various sayings were fitted, or which quoted a hymn in order to make a point. At each stage, the original small unit was being used in a slightly different context, and it may have been changed in small ways in order to fit its new use better.

Scholars have various names for this sort of investigation of a biblical text, depending on what level they are examining. *Source criticism* attempts to establish where previously existing material (for example, a hymn, a saying, or a vision account) has been used by a later author in a longer work, either by accepting what is stated in the work itself or by noticing differences in content, vocabulary, and literary style. *Form criticism* seeks to classify literary genres or forms, and to isolate the historical settings in which the forms developed and functioned before they became part of the main text. A sermon, for instance, will have characteristics that are different from those of a letter or a story. *Redaction criticism* deals with the ways in which a biblical author or editor (*redactor* means editor) used sources, and sometimes changed them, to address problems and concerns facing his readers. So biblical criticism takes account of historical settings at three levels: the sources, the small units, and the finished document.

Archaeological excavations and textual discoveries such as the Ugaritic texts and the Dead Sea Scrolls can shed light on the material world and culture in which the biblical books were written. For example, ancient epics outside the Bible have helped us to appreciate the creation stories in the book of Genesis. And the Dead Sea Scrolls, besides providing the earliest extant manuscripts of the Hebrew Bible, have illumined the thought and organization of the early church.

The interpretive process can also be enriched by the application of concepts and methods used in the social sciences such as sociology, cultural anthropology, and psychology. These approaches help in exposing the cultural assumptions about the human condition and the world that people in biblical times took for granted, and in explaining the development of ancient Israel into a nation and the early Christian communities into what we call the church.

Historical criticism is sometimes defined narrowly to refer to the reality of the event behind the text, to determining what actually occurred at (for example) the first Passover or the first Easter. What really happened in detail is sometimes hard to discern, since the biblical authors were often more interested in the meaning of the events than in their precise details. Some historical critics (in the narrow sense) rule out the miraculous and divine intervention on philosophical grounds and make negative judgments about the communities that handed on the biblical texts. But this is not true of all historical critics, nor is it at all consistent with the Catholic approach to Scripture, which assumes that the biblical texts tell the "honest truth" about the events described in the texts.

While the classic historical-critical method is oriented mainly to illumining the history of the text and the world behind the text, certain new methods of literary analysis focus more on the text as it now stands (the world of the text) and on its effects on the reader today (the world before or in front of the text). *Rhetorical analysis* explores the capacity of a biblical text to persuade and convince the reader, while *narrative analysis* investigates how a text works in the sense of its success in telling a story involving plot, characters, and point of view. *Structuralist analysis* and *semiotic analysis* are modern linguistic methods that examine the various temporal and spatial relationships in a text, with an eye toward revealing the deeper patterns of meaning underlying the text.

Another set of approaches to biblical interpretation privileges the interpreter and the social location of the interpreter. *Liberation theology* takes as its starting point the lived experience of poor people today and enters into conversation with biblical texts (e.g., Israel's exodus from Egypt, or Mary's *Magnificat* in Lk 1, 46–55) as a way of illumining both the biblical text and the present situation of the poor. *Feminist interpretation* calls attention to the prominence of certain women in the Bible, exposes the patriarchal or male-centered assumptions of the cultures in which the Bible was originally produced, and challenges interpreters to recognize the liberating contributions of women to the biblical story of salvation.

Other reader-oriented resources in biblical interpretation include the *history of interpretation* (how a text has been understood by Jewish and Christian readers throughout the centuries) and the *history of effects* (the impact or influence that a text has exercised in the course of history). *Canonical criticism* focuses on the final canonical form of a biblical text, explores its place within the biblical canon as a whole, and considers its significance for the church's faith and way of life. *Hermeneutics* is concerned with discerning the present significance of a biblical text. While this is what preachers have always done, the hermeneutical phase of the interpretive task is open to and incumbent upon all Bible readers. It involves the fusion of horizons between the ancient text and the reader in the present, and envisions a process by which the reader is changed intellectually and spiritually by encounter with the biblical text.

Two terms that have recently become prominent with regard to Catholic biblical interpretation and its practical impact in church life are *actualization* and *inculturation*. The Christian Scriptures are ancient texts, and so they need to be presented in ways in which they can speak to peoples of different times (actualization) and places or cultures (inculturation). The Scriptures are made "actual" whenever their spiritual insights are presented in such a way that they can address the problems and possibilities of the present day. Likewise, the Scriptures are "inculturated" whenever they are translated, interpreted, and applied in terms that peoples from outside the ancient Mediterranean world can understand and so live out their challenges and opportunities.

One traditional way of bringing together all these different methods in a simple and coherent framework is through the traditional Catholic approach developed in monastic circles and known as *lectio divina* (divine or spiritual reading). There are four steps. The first step is *lectio* (reading); that is, a careful reading of the text from various critical perspectives (literary, historical, and theological) and the assimilation or appropriation of the text on both intellectual and emotional levels. The second step is *meditatio*, which explores what this text may be saying to me (or us) now. One can open up the text by focusing on a theme or a few phrases, by applying the senses (sight, hearing, smell, taste, touch) to the biblical scene, and by trying to make connections between the text and one's present situation. The third step is *oratio* (prayer) in which on the basis

of reading and meditating one may speak words of praise, petition, adoration, and/or thanksgiving to God. The fourth step may take the form of *contemplatio* (relishing the religious experience generated by the encounter with the text and resting in the mystery of God) and/or *actio* (coming to a decision about one's life, or finding new ways to express what one has learned— through dance, drama, artwork, group sharing, homily, etc.).

Catholic Biblical Research

Catholic institutions and scholars make important contributions to scientific biblical research. The Vatican Museum and other such institutions conserve and make available important manuscript evidence. The publishing programs of the Pontifical Biblical Institute (Rome), the Catholic Biblical Association (Washington), and the Studium Biblicum Franciscanum (Jerusalem) are among the most ambitious and respected. The research of Catholic scholars appears in prestigious journals published under Catholic auspices: *Biblica, Biblische Zeitschrift, Catholic Biblical Quarterly, Estudios Biblicos, Revue Biblique,* and *Rivista Biblica Italiana.* Of course, non-Catholic scholars are welcome to publish in these Catholic scientific journals. Catholic scholars routinely write for periodicals not under Church auspices: *Journal of Biblical Literature, New Testament Studies, Novum Testamentum, Vetus Testamentum, Zeitschrift für Neutestamentliche Wissenschaft,* and so forth. The major bibliographical services—*Old Testament Abstracts, New Testament Abstracts,* the *Elenchus of Biblica,* and the *International Review of Biblical Studies*—emanate from Catholic institutions. Articles on biblical topics frequently appear in Catholic theological journals, and popular periodicals *(The Bible Today)* and books make available to a general audience the results of scientific biblical research.

Many Catholic biblical scholars have received their professional training at the Pontifical Biblical Institute in Rome, the Ecole Biblique in Jerusalem, the Studium Biblicum Franciscanum in Jerusalem, as well as at European Catholic universities such as Louvain, the Catholic theological faculties at German universities, and the departments of theology at Catholic universities in the United States (Boston College, Catholic University in Washington, Notre Dame, Loyola of Chicago, etc.). Others have gotten philological and archaeological training at Harvard, Yale, Johns Hopkins, University of Chicago, Emory, and many other institutions. A major professional organization for biblical scholars in the United States is the Catholic Biblical Association. Catholic scholars are also heavily involved in the non-denominational Society of Biblical Literature, the American Schools of Oriental Research, and the Society of New Testament Studies.

Modern biblical scholarship is an international and interconfessional enterprise. The Catholic Church contributes to this dialogue by providing well-trained scholars and channels for publishing research. Some good examples of Catholic biblical scholarship in the United States are the *New American Bible,* the *New Jerome Biblical Commentary,* and the Sacra Pagina series of New Testament commentaries published by Liturgical Press.

Scripture as Tradition

The official Catholic emphasis on attention to the literary forms, historical settings, and cultural assumptions of the biblical writings flows from the nature of the books themselves. Far from being individual creations generated in solitude, the biblical books include many ideas, traditions, and even small pieces that already existed before being integrated into the texts in which they now stand. Biblical literature is thoroughly and deliberately traditional.

The traditional character of the Old Testament has long been acknowledged. The first five books, which are customarily called the Pentateuch or Torah, are generally recognized to incorporate material from at least four different sources (Yahwist, Elohist, Deuteronomist, Priestly; see "Introduction to the Pentateuch"). The historical books (Joshua to 2 Kings, Chronicles, Ezra, and Nehemiah) include earlier accounts, memoirs, genealogies, and the like. The prophetic books are anthologies of short pieces of poetry and prose, and the wisdom books contain ideas and sayings that circulated in the ancient Near East for centuries. The Psalms are a collection of varied kinds of songs used mainly in the Jerusalem Temple; in the Psalms there may even be remnants of non-Jewish hymns (see Psalm 29). So complicated and

so rich is the process of transmission that it is difficult in most cases to speak of *the* author of a biblical book as one may speak of an author today. The situation is further complicated by the fact that in biblical times personal creativity and originality were not important values. One displayed real creativity by using traditional ideas and expressions in new settings and in new combinations.

Given the nature of the Old Testament and the ancient concept of creativity, one would expect the New Testament to be thoroughly traditional also—and it is. The earliest complete documents in the New Testament are Paul's letters. Even these highly original and occasional pieces rely at key points on preexisting material (for example, Rom 1, 3–4; 1 Cor 13, 1–13; 15, 3–5; Phil 2, 6–11). Those epistles whose direct Pauline composition is doubtful (for example, the Pastorals, Ephesians, Colossians, 2 Thessalonians) are best understood as later attempts to bring the figure and teaching of Paul to bear on situations facing the churches in the late first century. We often regard Paul as a creative genius. However, not only did he use some traditional material, but also almost all his undisputed letters contain some indication of joint authorship (see 1 Thes 1, 1; 1 Cor 1, 1; Rom 16, 22; etc.). Moreover, throughout his letters Paul gives credit to his co-workers and encourages the collection for the Jerusalem community as a sign of solidarity with the mother church there.

The complicated process of tradition and composition also applies to the Gospels. Most scholars today place the final composition of the four canonical Gospels in the late first century: Mark around AD 70, Matthew and Luke around AD 80–90, and John around AD 90–100. Yet all scholars acknowledge that the evangelists used already existing material in their Gospels. For example, Matthew and Luke each seem to have read both Mark's Gospel and a collection of Jesus' sayings that modern scholars call *Q* (from the German word *Quelle,* meaning "source"). John utilized a collection of miracle stories (signs) and perhaps also some revelation discourses. The Markan and Johannine Passion narratives surely contain much traditional information, accounts that had been passed from one person to another.

The Gospels and the traditions incorporated in

them tell the story of Jesus of Nazareth, who was crucified around AD 30. Like other Jewish teachers of his time, Jesus taught by word (parables, proverbs, debates, other sayings) and deed (example, healings, symbolic gestures). His disciples remembered and retold his words and deeds, thus providing the basic materials for what became the Gospel tradition. Jesus did not write books. What we know of Jesus comes to us through the process of tradition from Jesus to the early church and finally to the evangelists.

The nature of the Gospels demands that interpreters attend to three stages in their development. The *Dogmatic Constitution on Divine Revelation* (*Dei verbum* 19) captures that development in this marvelously concise statement:

> The sacred authors, in writing the four Gospels, selected certain of the many elements which had been handed on, either orally or already in written form, others they synthesized or explained with an eye to the situation of the churches, the while sustaining the form of preaching, but always in such a fashion that they have told us the honest truth about Jesus.

The council's document affirms that the Gospels tell us the "honest truth" about Jesus. It recognizes that there was an intermediary stage in which traditions about Jesus circulated in oral and written forms as "preaching" about the significance of Jesus. It acknowledges that the evangelists give us only a selection (see Lk 1, 1–4; Jn 20, 30–31; 21, 25) of the traditions about Jesus. It also recognizes that the evangelists used the traditions about Jesus to address the situations of their own day. Therefore Catholics must read the Gospels as traditional documents (because they are such) and attend to three stages in their development: Jesus, the early church, and the evangelists.

Although in the past there has been some Catholic resistance to accepting the traditional character of the biblical books, this emphasis is perfectly compatible with the principles of Catholicism. There is no obligation for Catholics to be conservative historians of early Christianity (nor is there any obligation for them to be reckless or indifferent). As long as Catholic scholars make clear the link from Jesus through the early church to the evangelists, they remain faithful to their theological heritage.

In fact, an emphasis on the traditional nature

of the biblical writings is fully consistent with certain distinctively Catholic principles. The Catholic stress on the communal character of our way to God and God's way to us sensitizes Catholics to the complexity of early Christian tradition and to the role of the Church in shaping it and being formed by it. The Catholic emphasis that encounter with God is rooted in history and is a mediated experience helps us to see the continuity between Jesus and the early reflections on him, as well as the significance and correctness of those reflections. The Catholic sacramental approach, which sees God in and through all things, leads us to view the very human process of tradition as a vehicle for expressing, safeguarding, and adapting divine revelation.

Scripture and Tradition

The Catholic Church does not restrict divine revelation to the biblical text. Against the Protestant Reformation's slogan of "Scripture alone," Catholic theologians insisted on "Scripture and tradition." The term *tradition* recognizes the fact that the living reality of the Church has the task of preserving the Gospel as well as interpreting and applying it in new situations. Catholic Christianity is not simply a "religion of the Book."

While acknowledging the twofold reality of Scripture and tradition, Catholic theologians have long debated the precise relation between the two. One way of approaching the problem was to assume that Scripture and tradition constitute two separate sources of divine revelation. The Second Vatican Council rejected this view in the second chapter of its *Dogmatic Constitution on Divine Revelation* (*Dei verbum* 10): "Sacred Tradition and sacred Scripture make up a single sacred deposit of the Word of God, which is entrusted to the Church." In other words, the Word of God (or divine revelation) is the source of both tradition and Scripture.

How exactly Scripture and tradition are related remains a problem. The conciliar document uses the analogy of a wellspring or fountain to insist on their unity while preserving their diversity in *Dei verbum* 9:

> Sacred Tradition and sacred Scripture then, are bound closely together, and communicate one with the other. For both of them, flowing out from the same divine wellspring, come together in some fashion to form one thing, and move to-

wards the same goal. Sacred Scripture is the speech of God as it is put down in writing under the breath of the Holy Spirit. And Tradition transmits in its entirety the Word of God which has been entrusted to the apostles by Christ the Lord and the Holy Spirit.

The same paragraph rejects the "Scripture alone" principle of the Reformation and preserves the Catholic approach of "Scripture and tradition" by insisting that the Church does not draw certainty about all revealed truths from the holy Scriptures alone. Hence, both Scripture and tradition must be accepted and honored with equal feelings of devotion and reverence. Thus the Second Vatican Council insisted that Scripture and tradition flow from the same divine wellspring and that both must be accepted and honored. Without endorsing any one theological approach to their relation, the council rejected the opinion of those who wished to keep the two separate.

The same tension appears when the *Dogmatic Constitution* addresses the issue of authoritative interpretation of the Scriptures in *Dei verbum* 10:

... the task of giving an authentic interpretation of the Word of God, whether in its written form or in the form of Tradition, has been entrusted to the living teaching office of the Church alone. Its authority in this matter is exercised in the name of Jesus Christ. Yet this Magisterium is not superior to the Word of God, but is its servant. It teaches only what has been handed on to it. At the divine command and with the help of the Holy Spirit, it listens to this devotedly, guards it with dedication and expounds it faithfully. All that it proposes for belief as being divinely revealed is drawn from this single deposit of faith.

On the one hand, this statement entrusts authentic interpretation to the magisterium (the bishops with the pope). On the other hand, it insists that the magisterium is the servant of divine revelation and can teach only what is drawn from the single deposit of faith constituted by divine revelation.

The precise relation between Scripture and tradition also remains a problem. As a pastoral council, Vatican II avoided becoming an arbiter of theological disputes. Its insistence on the oneness of Scripture and tradition, however, did have a pastoral dimension. While not conceding to the "Scripture alone" position, it insisted that

the Bible take again its rightful place in the center of Catholic life and that appeals to tradition be judged according to their consistency with Scripture.

The Nature of the Bible

What is this book that it should be studied so intensely and guarded so carefully? The *Dogmatic Constitution on Divine Revelation* made its own a theological formula that had become prominent before Vatican II: "the words of God, expressed in the words of men" (*Dei verbum* 13). That formula derives from the classical theological definitions of the divine and human natures in the person of Jesus Christ. In speaking about the Bible in this way, the Second Vatican Council sought to hold together the transcendent nature of Scripture and its human form. Although the Bible may look like other books and may be studied profitably as other books are studied (that is, with the techniques of biblical criticism), the Bible is different with regard to its origin and its nature. The different character of the Bible is expressed by means of some rather complicated terms: revelation, inspiration, inerrancy, and canon. As with "Scripture and tradition," the Second Vatican Council used these terms without adjudicating the theological disputes surrounding them. As a pastoral council it sought to express the significance of the words for the way in which the Bible is read within the Church.

Revelation is fundamentally God's self-revelation; it is the communication of the mystery of God to the world: "It pleased God, in his goodness and wisdom, to reveal himself and to make known the mystery of his will" (*Dei verbum* 2). The Christian theological tradition affirms that God's self-revelation comes to us through creation, history, persons, society, and reason. It is also customary to refer to the Bible as a privileged revealer of God—that is, a place where the divine revelation is particularly clear. This tradition appears prominently in *Dei verbum* 6:

By divine Revelation God wished to manifest and communicate both himself and the eternal decrees of his will concerning the salvation of mankind.

The order adopted in this statement ("both himself and the eternal decrees") is significant, for it gives pride of place to the personal character of divine revelation without denying the content and the consequences. Although this point may seem obvious today, the council's emphasis on the personal dimension of revelation was correctly taken as a major step in clarifying Catholic attitudes toward Scripture. Through the Bible we encounter the mystery of God, not simply lists of commandments or interesting stories. The personal God makes those commandments and stories meaningful.

Two other theological terms for talking about the difference of the Bible from other books are *inspiration* and *inerrancy.* Again the *Dogmatic Constitution on Divine Revelation* asserts the basic point expressed by these terms without arbitrating the very complicated theological debates surrounding them. On inspiration *Dei verbum* 11 states:

> The divinely revealed realities which are contained and presented in the text of sacred Scripture have been written down under the inspiration of the Holy Spirit. For Holy Mother Church relying on the faith of the apostolic age, accepts as sacred and canonical the books of the Old and the New Testaments, whole and entire, with all their parts, on the grounds that, written under the inspiration of the Holy Spirit (cf. Jn 20, 31; 2 Tm 3, 16; 2 Pt 1, 19–21; 3, 15–16), they have God as their author, and have been handed on as such to the Church herself. To compose the sacred books, God chose certain men who, all the while he employed them in this task, made full use of their powers and faculties so that, though he acted in them and by them, it was as true authors that they consigned to writing whatever he wanted written, and no more.

The same paragraph treats inerrancy:

> Since, therefore, all that the inspired authors, or sacred writers, affirm should be regarded as affirmed by the Holy Spirit, we must acknowledge that the books of Scripture firmly, faithfully and without error teach that truth which God, for the sake of our salvation, wished to see confided to the sacred Scriptures. Thus "all Scripture is inspired by God, and profitable for teaching, for reproof, for correction and for training in righteousness, so that the man of God may be complete, equipped for every good work" (2 Tm 3, 16–17, Greek text).

The key expression in this statement is "that truth which God, for the sake of our salvation, wished to see confided to the sacred Scriptures." With-

out explicitly embracing the theory of only limited inerrancy, that statement suggests that the Bible's inerrancy consists primarily in its being a trustworthy guide on the road to salvation. Thus it expresses "inerrancy" in a positive way and avoids conceiving it as a defensive program of protecting the Bible against accusations of scientific or historical error.

The council's statement on inspiration refers to the books of the Bible as "sacred and canonical." The word *canon* (reed or measuring stick) originally meant the rule or characteristics that decided whether a particular book was judged to be part of Sacred Scripture. It now usually refers to the collection of books that are acknowledged to be authoritative in the Church and by which the Church's faith can be measured. The canon of Old Testament books traditional in Catholicism contains all the books of the Hebrew Bible (which is the same as the Protestant Old Testament canon) together with seven others that were part of the Greek and Latin Bible tradition (Judith, Tobit, Baruch, 1 and 2 Maccabees, Sirach/Ecclesiasticus, Wisdom). All Christians today share the same canon of twenty-seven New Testament books. The history of the canon's development is quite complex. The final definitive list of biblical books (including the seven additional Old Testament books) for the Catholic Church was drawn up only at the Council of Trent in 1546, though there was little disagreement about the substance of the canon from the early centuries of the Christian era.

The Bible is different. How it is different has been expressed with the help of some traditional words: revelation, inspiration, inerrancy, and canon. The Second Vatican Council in its authoritative declaration on Scripture *(Dei verbum)* took over those hallowed terms. In interpreting the Council's use of these words we must take account of the pastoral orientation of the council as a whole. Rather than working out theological subtleties or choosing among theological schools, the *Dogmatic Constitution on Divine Revelation* used those words to convey basic attitudes about how the Bible differs from other books. It affirmed that God's self-revelation comes to us through the Bible, that in some mysterious way God entered into the composition of these writings and inspired them, that the biblical books provide reliable guidance (inerrancy) for those who walk the way toward salvation with God, and that these books constitute the norm or rule (canon) by which the life of the Church is to be guided and measured in all ages. These are the basic pastoral meanings of revelation, inspiration, inerrancy, and canon.

The Authority of the Bible

The terms by which Christians express the difference of the Bible indicate that it possesses great authority for them. The Bible is the "words of God, expressed in the words of men." It is revealed, inspired, inerrant, and canonical. The *Dogmatic Constitution on Divine Revelation* goes beyond the general assertions conveyed by the traditional theological vocabulary and speaks about the authority of various parts of the Bible.

The Old Testament (see *Dei verbum* 15) prepares for and declares in prophecy the coming of Christ. It conveys our basic understanding of God and the human situation: "how a just and merciful God deals with mankind." It provides "sound wisdom" and "a wonderful treasury of prayers." The document also mentions "matters imperfect and provisional" in the Old Testament, without specifying precisely what these are (presumably legislation about sacrifices and ritual purity, "vengeful" psalms, and other such material). The unity of the two Testaments is traced back to God who "in his wisdom has so brought it about that the New should be hidden in the Old and that the Old should be made manifest in the New" (*Dei verbum* 16).

The Council accorded the Gospels a special place within the Bible "because they are our principal source for the life and teaching of the Incarnate Word, our Saviour" (*Dei verbum* 18). It insisted on the historicity and apostolicity of the Gospels, while recognizing the complex process of their composition from Jesus through the early church to the Gospel texts. Catholics find a basic continuity between Jesus and the Gospel tradition under the guidance of the Spirit working in the church. Their tendency is to insist that the tradition is basically historical. They assume that the modifications and reinterpretations made necessary by changing circumstances do not do violence to the original teaching or event. The "apostolic" character of the Gospels refers not so much to their direct composition by apostles as it does to the faithful transmission of the material

in them by those who had experienced the risen Lord and bore witness to his resurrection. The term *apostolic* describes the generation between Jesus' death (about AD 30) and the composition of the New Testament books. The claim implied by the term is that those witnesses have told us the "honest truth" about Jesus.

The New Testament also contains Paul's letters and other writings (Hebrews, the Catholic Epistles, Revelation). After affirming their composition under the inspiration of the Holy Spirit, *Dei verbum* 20 describes the contributions that these writings make in the following way:

> In accordance with the wise design of God these writings firmly establish those matters which concern Christ the Lord, formulate more and more precisely his authentic teaching, preach the saving power of Christ's divine work and foretell its glorious consummation.

It would be a mistake, however, to conclude from this description that the Epistles have a secondary status as supplements to the Gospels. In fact, Paul's authentic letters (1 Thessalonians, Galatians, 1 and 2 Corinthians, Philippians, Philemon, Romans) are the earliest complete documents in the New Testament from the standpoint of their dates of composition. Thus they give us precious information about how Paul and other early Christians in the fifties of the first century AD (some twenty-five years after the death of Jesus) understood the significance of Jesus' life, death, and resurrection. They show us how early Christians struggled to articulate their new faith in an environment that was often hostile and foreign to them. They reveal the kinds of problems that early Christians faced within their own communities (see especially 1 Cor) and so warn us against too easily viewing the apostolic period as a trouble-free and conflictless "golden age."

Enough has been said about the Bible in general (revelation, inspiration, inerrancy, and canon) and about its major parts (Old Testament, Gospels, Epistles) to indicate that it possesses great authority. But what kind of authority does the Bible have? It is surely not the coercive authority of a parent or the state or the police, which have the power to enforce a law or decision and to punish the uncooperative. It is not even the persuasive authority of the lawyer or the mathematician who convinces another by logic, arguments, proofs, and so forth. At some points in his epistles (for example, in 1 Cor 15) Paul does labor to make a convincing case on the basis of logic. But that is not his usual mode of presentation, nor is it the customary idiom of other biblical writers.

The authority that the Bible possesses can perhaps be best described as compelling. Compelling authority is the authority of the witness, the expert, the participant. Much of the Bible concerns what God's people say about God's action on their behalf. Without narrowing the testimony of the Bible to the concept of an eyewitness, it is possible to describe the Scriptures as a collection of testimonies to God. The biblical descriptions of creation, exodus, monarchy, exile, and return from exile all stress God's relatedness to Israel and Israel's responses of praise, confession, thanksgiving, and so forth. The New Testament writers portray Jesus as the revelation of God's power (and weakness). The proper response is faith, hope, and love. Thus the biblical documents contain the proclamation and articulation of people's faith about God and God's ways with creation.

God is the real basis of the Bible's authority. Insofar as the biblical books bear witness to God and thus enable us to understand better who God is and how God acts, and to grow in love for and trust in the God of the Scriptures, the Bible can be aptly called the "word of God." And so Vatican II's *Dogmatic Constitution on Divine Revelation,* which so emphasizes God's self-communication, is appropriately titled from its initial two words *Dei verbum* (Latin for "word of God").

Scripture in Church Life

This essay began with a comparison regarding the Bible's place in church life of the 1950s and today. A look at Catholic liturgy, education, piety, and theology led to the conclusion that the Catholic Church today is far more biblical than it was in the 1950s. This development mirrors some powerful statements made in the final chapter of Vatican II's *Dogmatic Constitution on Divine Revelation.*

The centrality of Scripture in Catholic liturgy involves both preaching and sacramental practice. *Dei verbum* 21 insists that "all the preaching of the Church, as indeed the entire Christian religion, should be nourished and ruled by sacred

Scripture." The same paragraph directly confronts and dissolves the opposition between word and sacrament that had been prominent since the Protestant Reformation. It does so with reference to the celebration of the Eucharist:

> The Church has always venerated the divine Scriptures as she venerated the Body of the Lord, in so far as she never ceases, particularly in the sacred liturgy, to partake of the bread of life and to offer it to the faithful from the one table of the Word of God and the Body of Christ.

The council document insists that word and sacrament belong together in the Eucharist, to the point of asserting that they form "one table."

The popularity of Scripture in Catholic education and piety responds to a very strong statement in *Dei verbum* 22: "Access to sacred Scripture ought to be wide open to the Christian faithful." The document goes on to urge the production of modern-language translations made from the ancient biblical texts. It also encourages biblical exegetes to examine and explain the sacred texts so that preachers, teachers, and catechists "may be able to distribute fruitfully the nourishment of the Scriptures to the People of God" (*Dei verbum* 23).

The importance of Scripture for Catholic theology is stated in no uncertain terms: "The 'study of the sacred page' should be the very soul of sacred theology" (*Dei verbum* 24). The document mandates that all those officially engaged in the ministry of the word should "immerse themselves in the Scriptures by constant sacred reading and diligent study" (*Dei verbum* 25). The same paragraph recommends the preparation of volumes such as the present one: "translations of the sacred texts which are equipped with necessary and really adequate explanations." There is overwhelming evidence that in response to the Second Vatican Council the Catholic Church has become much more biblical. One of its most important documents was the *Dogmatic Constitution on Divine Revelation,* which has served as our principal guide in this article. At nearly every point the post-Vatican II Church has fulfilled the mandates of that council document and thus become more biblical.

The challenge facing the Catholic Church today is to look upon *Dei verbum* not only as the end of a long development (which it was) but also as the beginning of a process that has taken us into the twenty-first century and beyond. A still more biblical church will paradoxically be better able to adjust to the rapid changes that the new millennium is already bringing upon us. A still more biblical church will be better prepared to make common cause with other Christians, with Jews and Muslims, and with all truly religious people. A still more biblical church will preserve its spiritual heritage and open its riches to others. An obvious step in the process toward a more biblical church is an increase in knowledge and love of the Scriptures.

FURTHER READING

Bechard, Dean R., ed. *The Scripture Documents: An Anthology of Official Catholic Teachings.* Collegeville, MN: Liturgical Press, 2002.

Brown, Raymond E. *Biblical Exegesis and Church Doctrine.* New York and Mahwah, NJ: Paulist Press, 1985.

——. *Responses to 101 Questions on the Bible.* New York and Mahwah, NJ: Paulist Press, 1990.

Brown, Raymond E., Joseph A. Fitzmyer, and Roland E. Murphy, eds. *The New Jerome Biblical Commentary.* Englewood Cliffs, NJ: Prentice Hall, 1990.

Fitzmyer, Joseph A. *Scripture, the Soul of Theology.* New York and Mahwah, NJ: Paulist Press, 1994.

——. *"The Interpretation of the Bible in the Church": Text and Commentary.* Rome: Editrice Pontificio Istituto Biblico, 1995.

Hagen, Kenneth and others. *The Bible in the Churches: How Various Christians Interpret the Scriptures.* 3rd ed. Milwaukee, WI: Marquette University Press, 1998.

Harrington, Daniel J. *Interpreting the Old Testament.* Collegeville, MN: Liturgical Press, 1981.

——. *Interpreting the New Testament.* Rev. ed. Collegeville, MN: Liturgical Press, 1988.

Lienhard, Joseph T. *The Bible, the Church, and Authority.* Collegeville, MN: Liturgical Press, 1995.

Schneiders, Sandra M. *The Revelatory Text. Interpreting the New Testament as Sacred Scripture.* Rev. ed. Collegeville, MN: Liturgical Press, 1999.

Williamson, Peter S. *Catholic Principles for Interpreting Scripture. A Study of the Pontifical Biblical Commission's "The Interpretation of the Bible in the Church."* Rome: Editrice Pontificio Istituto Biblico, 2001.

BIBLICAL HISTORY AND ARCHAEOLOGY

RONALD A. SIMKINS

HISTORY IN THE
BIBLICAL LITERATURE

The Bible as a Historical Source

To what extent is history—a record of actual past events—embedded in the diverse literature of the Bible? The Bible is composed of many different formal types of literature (genres), and although many of the genres present a past, no literature in the Old Testament claims or presents itself to be a work of history. History, as first practiced by the classical historians Hecataeus, Herodotus, and Thucydides, entails not only the collecting of tales and traditions about the past, but also the inquiry (which is what *historia* means) into the reliability of the traditions and plausibility of the tales. Although ancient historians used different standards to judge their source materials from those modern historians would use, the important point is that they did make *critical judgments* about their sources. In the New Testament, only the writer of Luke-Acts claims to present a work of history (Lk 1, 1–4). Whereas the writer of Luke-Acts claims to have investigated his sources in order to present a reliable account to Theophilus, the Old Testament writers made no such critical judgments. They were not historians in either the modern or classical sense.

Although the Bible is not itself a work of history, the Old Testament authors did write about Israel's past. The narrative genres present the story of the people of Israel from the creation of the world through the days of Ezra and Nehemiah. The biblical writers drew upon tales and traditions of Israel's past in order to communi-

cate an idea to their contemporaries. They were not concerned about whether the tales and traditions were reliable or plausible. Even when some attempt was made to communicate factual information, such as in the books of Kings, the writing of history was secondary to other purposes of the biblical writers. The non-narrative genres of the Bible—laws, songs, prophetic oracles, proverbs, and wisdom literature—attest to the story of Israel only indirectly. These texts too are ideological, though they also served ritual, educational, moral, and other functions in ancient Israelite society. (The various genres of biblical literature are discussed in the relevant sections of the Reading Guide.)

The extent of history embedded in the biblical texts is also questioned because of the chronological gap between the biblical writers and the events that they purport to narrate. In most cases, the biblical writers did not witness the events they describe. They often lived centuries later and were dependent upon oral traditions and perhaps some written sources (the Bible refers to a number of written sources, discussed on RG 44–46) for the composition of their narratives of the past. The reliability of these sources and their use by the biblical writers is unknown. When no source material was available—for private events, for example—the biblical writers would simply fill in the historical void in their presentation of the past one way or another, ultimately by pure invention.

Many of the biblical stories are shaped according to traditional literary or mythic patterns that make their reliability suspect. For example, the common Near Eastern myth popularly known as the conflict myth—a tale which describes a young warrior-god's rise to kingship by defeating an old god or force who poses a threat to the order and stability of the world—is transformed by the biblical writers into a literary pattern that shapes the stories of the Exodus, Joshua's conquest of Canaan, and Saul's election as king. Many other stories utilize such literary patterns. The traditional motif of the barren mother of an important person, for example, is used in the stories of Sarai and Isaac, Rachel and Joseph, and Hannah and Samuel.

The biblical writers' use of traditional literary and mythic patterns to tell their stories of Israel calls into question not only the narrative of the events but also the historical value of many details of the stories. This writing style of the biblical writers does not necessarily mean that no actual events lie beneath the narrative, but at the very least it indicates that the presentation of such events has been shaped to conform to a traditional interpretive framework. In other words, the meaning of such events as indicated by their presentation in the stories of Israel is more significant to the biblical writers than the historical reality of the events.

The Contribution of Archaeology

Archaeology is the scientific study of the material remains of past human life and activities. The material remains are discovered through excavations and surveys, and include both unwritten and written discoveries. Among the unwritten discoveries are architectural features such as temples, palaces, fortifications, public buildings, and houses; industrial features such as oil presses, wine presses, silos, ovens, and pottery kilns; and artifacts such as pottery, tools, jewelry, weapons, and statues and figurines. The written material, usually discovered during the process of excavation, is ordinarily studied by epigraphists and paleographers and includes literary documents (such as the Dead Sea Scrolls), inscriptions on stone or clay tablets, seals (bullae), and ostraca (broken pieces of pottery with words inscribed on them).

The year 1890 marks the beginning of the scientific study of Syro-Palestinian archaeology, when W. M. Flinders Petrie conducted the first systematic excavation in Palestine at Tell el-Hesi in the northern Negev. The Arabic word tell (*tel*,

in Hebrew) is used to designate the artificial mounds in the shape of truncated cones that dominate the landscape of Palestine. They are sites of ancient settlements, built up by successive levels of human occupation and destruction over the centuries. The oldest occupancy, of course, is at the bottom of the mound, and the most recent at the top. At Tell el-Hesi, Petrie laid the foundations of stratigraphy and ceramic typology, the basic interpretive principles of archaeological field method. Stratigraphy is the technique of excavating a mound (tell) layer by layer, and at the same time isolating the contents of each occupational layer (stratum). Typology is the study and classification of groups of objects (artifacts) on the basis of shared characteristics (shape, material, decoration). By correlating stratigraphy and typology archaeologists can construct a relative chronology. Using distinctive types of pottery as his dating tool, Petrie constructed a chronological framework for Palestine.

Except for a few excavations, like George Reisner's at Samaria (Sebaste) in 1909–10, archaeological excavations in Palestine before World War I resembled treasure hunts. Between World Wars I and II there was a significant advance in field techniques, largely due to William F. Albright, distinguished American archaeologist and biblical scholar. He refined pottery chronology through excavation and survey; he identified several mounds as biblical sites; he related many of the biblical episodes to archaeological contexts. Archaeological field methods advanced rapidly after World War II. Three archaeologists contributed meaningfully to this development: a Briton, Kathleen Kenyon, an Israeli, Yigael Yadin, and an American, G. Ernest Wright. At Jericho Kenyon used precise stratigraphic method to clarify the chronology of the fortification walls that had been dated incorrectly to the Late Bronze Age (1550–1200 BC). Yadin directed the first large-scale dig in modern Israel at Hazor in Upper Galilee, the largest biblical city in Palestine. In keeping with the Israeli method, Yadin concentrated on broad exposure of the monumental architecture of the site. G. Ernest Wright excavated Shechem in the central hill country, the first capital of the kingdom of Israel. Wright gave special attention to the pottery of the site as one of the most accurate indicators of ancient chronology; also, he trained a new generation of archaeologists at Shechem.

Since 1970 there has been a striking change in field method as archaeologists borrow from both the natural and the social sciences. In the first place, almost all excavation staffs are interdisciplinary: such specialists as paleobotanists, zoo-archaeologists, geologists, ecologists, and, especially, physical and cultural anthropologists collaborate with archaeologists in the field. Also, the technologies of modern science, such as carbon-14 (for dating organic substances), thermoluminescence (for dating pottery), magnetometry (for detecting the presence of metal objects), potassium argon (for dating geological samples), and neutron activation analysis (for tracing the origin of clay), are being used to analyze the data with greater precision. The purpose of this comprehensive approach, at least in theory, is to reconstruct the daily life of the people whose remains are being excavated, including their social structure and economic development, as well as their religious practices. Archaeologists' earlier interest in digging isolated tells is now also combined with regional surveys as a way of studying a tell's relationship with the surroundings. Regional study is indispensable in determining town planning, settlement patterns, and population expansion, to mention some of the concerns of modern archaeologists.

Because archaeology provides a different *kind* of evidence than that from the Bible, archaeology cannot be expected to make definitive contributions to several basic problems in the history of Israel. For example, archaeology cannot determine chronology beyond the broad limits determined by ceramic or radiocarbon dating. Archaeology addresses chronology through typologies of material remains that lack the precision of the chronological framework established by texts. The basis of typology is that human culture changes gradually and within limits. When a broad range of features and artifacts from stratified archaeological contexts are compared, a typological sequence can be established into which new features and artifacts can be placed. This typological sequence then becomes a means for dating the material uncovered in a new excavation. The major artifact used in typological dating is pottery. Pottery sherds are virtually indestructible and are found at every site in Syria-Palestine for every period since the Neolithic period. Moreover, whole pottery vessels were easily broken, leading to the production of more pottery and to rapid changes in the pottery repertoire. As a result, a large database of pottery has enabled archaeologists to establish a typological sequence by which they are able to date layers of human occupation in an excavation. Although this pottery typology is tied to an absolute chronology by occasional dated inscriptions that are found in sealed archaeological contexts, the changes within the pottery sequence provide a chronological precision of no greater than a few decades.

Other historical issues to which archaeology cannot make a definitive contribution include the problem of ethnicity. Archaeology can provide much of the material content of ethnicity, but it cannot finally define the ethnic groups because such a definition also involves shared cultural values and self-perceptions. Ethnicity involves both material and ideological components. The identification of the early Israelites in the archaeological record has been a continual problem in this regard, for the early Israelites appear to share the same material culture as the Canaanites. Some interpreters attempt to get around this problem by identifying the inhabitants of the new settlements in the central hill country at the beginning of the Iron I period as early Israelites and those inhabitants who continue to occupy the Late Bronze cities and towns as Canaanites. However, such an interpretation cannot be supported by the archaeological evidence, and in any case is only possible because of the implications of the biblical text (e.g., see Jos 17, 14–18).

The interrelation of particular human events in a political history is also beyond the scope to which archaeology can contribute. Archaeology can demonstrate that the city of Hazor in northern Israel was destroyed near the end of the Late Bronze Age, and that the city of Lachish in Judah was destroyed approximately a century later. It cannot answer the questions: Who destroyed the cities? Was the same agent responsible for the destruction of each city? Why were they destroyed? What were the causes of the cities' destruction? What happened to the inhabitants of the cities after they were destroyed? Archaeology does not deal with the evidence necessary to answer these questions. For many of the problems of political history, archaeology can only remain silent.

Finally, archaeology cannot demonstrate the truth or confirm the meaning of the biblical texts. The meaning of the biblical texts is not found in the degree to which the texts correspond to what really happened in the past. Rather, the meaning of the texts is found in the message that the biblical writers were communicating to their ancient readers, and this message is beyond the scope of archaeological research.

The focus of archaeology is on the material world, and in this regard archaeology can contribute to the historical study of ancient Israel. Archaeology provides the material context for understanding this history by presenting the material remains of a broad spectrum of Middle Eastern peoples and places. This material provides the general setting for the history of Israel, and through cross-cultural comparison is able to shed light on the Israelite material culture. For example, archaeology can provide information about the distinctive cultures of those peoples who lived near and interacted with the Israelites, such as the Philistines, Edomites, Phoenicians, Arameans, and Assyrians. Regional surveys allow us to reconstruct settlement patterns and the demographics of particular regions. The faunal and floral remains gathered from excavations enable us to reconstruct Israel's environmental setting and its changes over time.

Archaeology also provides the specific material context for many of the events narrated in the Bible, much of which the biblical narratives themselves do not address. The biblical description of King Hezekiah's rebellion against the Assyrian empire focuses primarily on the diplomatic maneuvers of the Rabshakeh of Assyria to coerce Hezekiah into submission (2 Kgs 18—19). The archaeological evidence, however, presents a picture of Hezekiah's preparations for revolt and its tragic consequences.

Ultimately, archaeological remains illuminate the daily life of the ancient Israelites, which supplements the biblical narratives. Only from archaeology can we learn about the planning and defenses of the Israelite and Judean towns and cities; the architecture of palaces, houses, temples, and public buildings; figurines, altars, and other cult objects; tombs and the Israelites' treatment of their dead; luxury items such as jewelry,

carved ivories, metal and stone vessels, and imported items; and common tools and weapons. Archaeology enables us to reconstruct aspects of the society, economy, and religion of the ancient Israelites that are neglected by the biblical tradition. Furthermore, because archaeological evidence is random—its preservation is by chance, unaffected by human selection—it provides an alternative perspective from which to view the biblical narratives. This is especially true regarding aspects of the Israelites' religious practices and beliefs. The widespread abundance of terracotta female figures, for example, attests to a dominant concern for female fertility that is given little attention in the biblical texts. Similarly, the graffiti found at Kuntillet ʿAjrud refers to "Yahweh and his asherah." The meaning of this phrase is debated, referring to a consort or a symbol of Yahweh. In either case, the phrase attests to a view of Yahweh that has been excluded from the Bible.

The Bronze Age

Chronology

Archaeologists divide the Bronze Age into three major periods, tied to the chronology of Egypt, based on changes in material culture. The Early Bronze Age (3300–2000 BC) is the first period of urbanization in Palestine. This period corresponds to the Early Dynastic period and Old Kingdom in Egypt. The Early Bronze Age is further divided into four sub-periods. Only the beginnings of urbanization are evident in Early Bronze I (3300–3000 BC). By Early Bronze II and III (3000–2200) Palestine is characterized by numerous large fortified cities. Notable excavated sites include Megiddo and Beth Yerak (Khirbet Kerak) in the north, Tell el-Farʾah (perhaps biblical Tirzah) and Ai in the central hill country, and Tel Yarmuth and Arad in the south. With the weakening of the Old Kingdom at the end of the Sixth Dynasty, Egypt entered the First Intermediate Period. Similarly, most of the urban centers in Palestine were abandoned or destroyed, with much of the population subsisting on pastoralism. This final rural period is known alternatively as Early Bronze IV, Middle Bronze I, or Intermediate Bronze (2200–2000 BC).

The Middle Bronze Age (2000–1550 BC) marks the height of prosperity and power in

Palestine with a resurgence of urbanization. The numerous large fortified cities during this period are characterized by massive fortifications consisting of ramparts, mudbrick walls, and large fortress-style gates. The large temples and palaces constructed inside the city walls attest to the prosperity of the period, and many luxury items of foreign origin give evidence of a vibrant international trade. Excavated sites of note for this period include, from north to south, Dan, Hazor, Megiddo, Aphek, Shechem, Jericho, Gezer, Ashkelon, and Tell el-ʿAjjul. The Middle Bronze Age corresponds to the Middle Kingdom and Second Intermediate Period in Egypt. In contrast to the end of the Early Bronze Age, however, the cities of Palestine continued to flourish with the collapse of the Middle Kingdom and during the rule of the foreign Hyksos kings of the Second Intermediate Period. Only when the native Egyptian kings of the Seventeenth Dynasty succeeded in driving out the Hyksos did the Middle Bronze Age come to an end, with numerous cities in Palestine being destroyed.

The Late Bronze Age (1550–1200/1150 BC) corresponds to the New Kingdom in Egypt. This largely urban period lacks the prosperity of the Middle Kingdom as the cities of Palestine became subject to the Egyptian empire. Nevertheless, the period is also characterized by internationalism, with material culture from Egypt, Greece, Cyprus, Turkey, Lebanon, and Syria found at several of the sites in Palestine. Important excavated sites for this period include, from north to south, Hazor, Megiddo, Beth Shan, Aphek, Shechem, Gezer, Lachish, Tell el-Farʾah (south), and Timna. The Late Bronze Age comes to an end with the weakening of Egypt in the Twentieth Dynasty and the withdrawal of Egypt from Palestine.

In the chronology supplied by the Bible, the Israelites' ancestors—the patriarchs Abraham, Isaac, and Jacob—are placed in the period from the end of the Early Bronze Age through the beginning of Middle Bronze Age. The exodus from Egypt is placed at the beginning of the Late Bronze Age. 1 Kings 6, 1 claims that the construction of Solomon's Temple began 480 years after the Israelites came out of Egypt in the Exodus. A conservative date for the beginning of Solomon's reign would be around 960 BC, placing the exodus event around 1440 BC. In Exodus

12, 40, the text claims that the Israelites lived in Egypt for 430 years. Thus, Joseph would have brought his father, his brothers, and their families into Egypt around 1870 BC. Further references establish a chronology for the ancestors: Abraham was 100 years old when Isaac was born (Gn 21, 5); Isaac was 60 years old when Jacob was born (Gn 25, 26); and Jacob lived 130 years before Joseph brought him to Egypt (Gn 47, 28). According to this chronology, Abraham would have been born around 2160 BC.

Although the biblical chronology is indicated fairly precisely, critical examination indicates a number of problems. First, setting aside historical problems that will be discussed below, the figure of 480 years for the period between the Exodus and the construction of the Temple is a suspiciously round number. It translates into twelve times forty, the latter being the traditional biblical length for a generation. In other words, the biblical writer is stating that the Temple was constructed twelve generations after the Exodus. The number twelve, of course, is suspicious, especially in the context of the Temple—the single most significant building in Israel—because the number often represents "all Israel." Solomon is also the twelfth generation from Judah according to some genealogies (e.g., 2 Chr 2, 1–17; 3, 1–9), and this might have served as the basis for the 480 years. The figure of 430 years for the duration of the Israelites' stay in Egypt is also problematic, but for a different reason. In Genesis 15, 13–16 the figure of 400 years is used for the same period, and this is equated with three generations. Indeed, Moses and Aaron belong to the third generation after Levi. Finally, the extremely long lives attributed to the ancestors—Abraham lived to be 175 years old, Isaac surpassed his father with 180 years, and Jacob died at the age of 147—cannot be accepted. The great ages of the ancestors reflect their proximity to the antediluvian period. Those who lived before the flood had life spans of 900 years or more, but after the flood the life spans of the people gradually diminished (indeed, Joseph only lived to be 110 years old). In the end, the biblical chronology cannot be taken simply as historical in the modern sense of the term.

The Patriarchs in History

The story of the Israelites' ancestors in Genesis is composed of numerous, originally independent, folktales. Scholars usually assume that these tales had an oral prehistory, but their written form dates from 900 BC to 400 BC (the date depends on how they understand the composition of Genesis, and there is wide disagreement on this issue). Unfortunately, there is little conclusive evidence determining the date and nature of the book's composition. Nevertheless, many anachronisms in the story indicate that it was written many centuries after the time it purports to describe. Also, as is typical of folktales, many parts of the story were written, and perhaps originally told, according to fixed patterns of storytelling in the ancient world. For example, all three of the major women in the story—Sarah, Rebekah, and Rachel—are initially barren. This is a common motif (it may reflect the social and physical reality of young girls who are married soon after their first menstruation, but unable to conceive for a few years) used in the story of the ancestors to demonstrate the providence of God. Other fixed patterns include: the rivalry between a barren, favored wife and a fertile co-wife or concubine (Sarah and Hagar, Rachel and Leah); encounter of the future betrothed at a well (Rebekah, Rachel); journey in the desert and the discovery of a well (Ishmael); revelations of a deity in a dream (Jacob); and the testament of a dying ancestor (Jacob). One fixed pattern that is found repeated in the story of the ancestors but not elsewhere is the motif of an ancestor telling a king that his wife is his sister. Abraham does this twice and Isaac once, and in each case the common motif is told in a slightly different way to fit a different context regarding whether the wife is barren, promised a child, or already has children.

Does the story of Israel's ancestors preserve any recoverable traces of actual events that took place in the Bronze Age? Some scholars have thought so. W. F. Albright placed Abraham's migration from Haran to Canaan within the context of the Amorite migrations that are attested in texts from Mesopotamia. The Amorites, known as "Amurru" in the Mesopotamian texts, were interpreted as a distinct, semi-nomadic people who migrated into southern Mesopotamia from eastern Syria and Turkey, and contributed to the collapse of the Akkad Dynasty and the rise of the First Dynasty of Babylon (whose most important king was Hammurapi). The Amorites were also given credit for the collapse of the Early Bronze

city-states in Palestine. Albright further argued that documentary evidence from texts discovered at Mari and Nuzi indicates the historicity of the patriarchal figures. Dating to the Middle Bronze Age, the Mari texts attest to many of the personal and place names mentioned in the ancestor stories; the later Nuzi texts corroborate many of the social and legal practices in the Genesis narratives. Finally, the picture in Genesis of the ancestors living a seminomadic life in the midst of fortified urban centers fits the general situation of the Middle Bronze Age.

Kathleen Kenyon, who excavated at Jericho, thought she could identify the Amorites in the archaeological record. During the Intermediate Bronze Age, Jericho was characterized by a period of occupation (perhaps in tents) prior to the construction of any permanent structures. The buildings that were built on the tell during this period were characterized by thin, rather flimsy walls. Nevertheless, the inhabitants carved hundreds of large shaft tombs out of the bedrock, in which one individual was buried in each tomb with a bronze dagger or with a few small pots. Because she also identified many foreign elements in the material culture, Kenyon argued that the evidence from Jericho attests to the arrival of nomadic invaders, whom she associated with the Amorites.

Although widely influential, Kenyon's interpretation is no longer credible. First, it is worth noting that the biblical stories do not identify the ancestors as Amorites. Abraham begins his journey not from Haran but from Ur of the Chaldeans in southern Mesopotamia; his journey goes "upstream" against the flow of Amorites into Mesopotamia. Outside Genesis, Abraham is called an Aramean (Dt 26, 5). The Amorites in the biblical tradition are presented as the native inhabitants of the land of Canaan ("Amorite" is often used synonymously with "Canaanite"), whose land would be given to Abraham's descendants. In Mesopotamian texts, the term *Amurru* simply denoted the west Semitic population of the Bronze Age. Although some groups of Amurru were nomadic, others were urbanized, occupying a wide range of socio-economic roles in the society. Second, the correspondences between the names and social and legal customs of the ancestors and those presented in the Mari and Nuzi texts are not unique to the second millennium.

Many of these names and customs can be identified in first-millennium texts during the period in which the ancestor stories themselves were written. Finally, the social situation of the ancestors as seminomads living in the midst of urban centers is also not unique to the Middle Bronze Age. In fact, this social situation is typical of virtually every period in the history of Palestine, from the Early Bronze Age through the Ottoman period. In the end, the ancestor narratives reflect the period of the Iron Age in which they were written.

The Exodus in History

The historical value of the Exodus narrative is much more difficult to assess than the story of the patriarchs. On the one hand, the Exodus narrative presents a spectacular story in which the God of Israel fights and defeats Pharaoh and his army in order to rescue his people from bondage and humiliate the Egyptians who dared to challenge the honor and kingship of God. The story is told in accordance with the widely recognized mythic pattern of the conflict myth, and many aspects of the story have a supernatural rather than a historical character. Indeed, some aspects of the story cannot be historical. The sheer magnitude of the event—that the firstborn male of every Egyptian household died (Ex 12, 29); that the entire Egyptian army pursued the Israelites to the sea and were subsequently drowned (Ex 14, 9, 28); that the number of Israelites who escaped from Egypt were 603,550 men of fighting age, not counting Levites, old men, women, and children (Nm 1, 44–47), renders it historically impossible. Other aspects of the story also exceed the bounds of a purely historical description. For example, the story does not record the name of the Egyptian king, the primary adversary of God and the Israelites. This is extremely odd since elsewhere the biblical writers mention the names of most other foreign kings—the two notable exceptions being the Egyptian king who married Sarai in Genesis 12 and the Egyptian king in the Joseph story, both of whom are known simply as Pharaoh. The depiction of the plagues is also not historically plausible. Although many of the individual plagues are natural events that can occur in Egypt, the combination of all the plagues, the scope and severity of the plagues, and the references to the plagues not affecting the Israelites or

their animals affirm a theological conviction and challenge a purely literal and historical reading of the story.

The Exodus story, on the other hand, gives evidence of the writer's familiarity with Egypt. The story is set in the context of the family of Jacob migrating into Egypt during a famine in Palestine and after Joseph had risen to the rank of vizier. Ample evidence indicates that Asiatics migrated to and lived in Egypt during all periods and especially during the Second Intermediate Period. In fact, during this period a group of Asiatics living in the eastern Delta region, known as the Hyksos, succeeded in establishing their rule over all of Lower Egypt and parts of Upper Egypt. Many scholars have noted that Joseph's ascendancy in the court of Pharaoh fits in the Hyksos period, but Asiatics also rose to prominence in later periods as well. Moreover, some parts of the Joseph story have parallels in Egyptian literature, such as the Tale of Two Brothers. Many of the names in the Exodus narrative are Egyptian. *Moses* is the Egyptian word for birth, and occurs with theophoric elements in the names of Thutmose and Ramesses. The names of Hophni, Phinehas, Shiphrah, and Puah are also Egyptian. The narrative claims that the Israelites were forced to build the store-cities Pithom and Ramesses. Ramesses can be identified with Pi-Ramesses, the capital city of Ramesses II in the eastern Delta at Tell el-Dabʿa. *Pithom* is Hebrew for Egyptian *Per-Atum,* (House of Atum,) and can be identified with either Tell el-Retabeh or nearby Tell el-Maskhuta in the eastern Delta. Evidence also indicates that foreigners living in Egypt were conscripted into the corvée labor groups used to work on the state building projects during the New Kingdom.

How do we reconcile these two opposing views of the historicity of the Exodus story? Two characteristics of biblical story telling are important in this regard. First, the biblical writers responsible for this narrative are not attempting to write a *history* of the event, in either the modern or the classical Greek sense of history. The biblical writers did not investigate or critically examine their sources, nor did they necessarily invent the story. They simply took the traditions about the past that were present in their day (probably in oral form) and constructed from them a dramatic and persuasive written narrative. The traditions might have been generated in response to actual events of the past, but, as is often the case with oral tradition, the actual events no longer resembled the traditions and cannot be reconstructed from them. Second, the biblical writers describe the significance of the event *for Israel*. The biblical writers present the Exodus as one of the most significant events in the history of Israel, yet no reference to the Israelites or the Exodus can be found in any of the Egyptian records. We would not necessarily expect the Egyptians to record what would have been a disaster for their king and army at the sea—rarely do royal scribes record the failures of their king—but we would expect to find some record of the Israelites' presence in the Delta (the "land of Goshen") or their role in state building projects. The absence of any reference to the Israelites suggests that whatever actual events might lie behind the narrative, they were insignificant from the perspective of the Egyptians. Therefore, although we might acknowledge that the Exodus narrative does preserve some traces of past events, the present form of the narrative does not provide us with any evidence from which to reconstruct those events.

Whatever events might underlie the Exodus narrative must be set in the context of what we do know about Egypt and Palestine in the Late Bronze Age. Palestine in the Late Bronze Age had a material culture that was continuous with the Middle Bronze Age, but the society itself was much poorer and less organized. This is attested in the settlement pattern. Most of the large fortified Middle Bronze cities in Palestine were destroyed at the end of the period. Many of the sites were not immediately reinhabited. Gradually, the old sites were reinhabited and new sites were settled, but the total settled area remained stable due to the abandonment of several large sites. The central hill country, which had been widely settled in the Middle Bronze Age, was now largely devoid of settlement. Most of the sites in the Late Bronze Age were small (less than twelve acres) and unfortified. The massive Middle Bronze ramparts continued to exist, but often no city wall was built on top of the ramparts. Instead, buildings were placed along the edge of the tell in a continuous line so that the outer wall of the structures offered modest protection. Few public buildings have been uncovered. The large

fortress-style temples of the Middle Bronze Age (at Shechem and Megiddo) continued to be used, but on a diminished scale. The large city of Hazor alone continued to flourish during the Late Bronze Age, perhaps due to its orientation toward the large cities in Syria rather than toward Egypt.

The Egyptian kings of Thebes, who had been ruled by the Asiatic Hyksos during the latter part of the Middle Bronze Age, now sought to extend their rule into Palestine. When Ahmose (1550–1525 BC) drove the Hyksos out of Egypt, he campaigned into Palestine to provide a buffer against further Asiatic incursions into Egypt. By the reign of Thutmose III (1492–1425 BC), all of Palestine was incorporated into the Egyptian empire. He set up an administrative system over Palestine that would endure through the remainder of the Late Bronze Age. (It is worth noting that the biblical chronology places the Exodus during the reign of Thutmose III—an impossible scenario.) Although Egypt faced opposition from the kingdoms of Mitanni (Hurrians) and Hatti (Hittites), Egypt maintained control over Palestine through the reign of Ramesses III (1184–1153 BC). Then a series of weak kings and political turmoil across the Mediterranean forced Egypt to withdraw from Palestine after approximately 350 years of control.

Evidence of the Egyptian presence and control of Palestine is found in numerous Egyptian artifacts (scarabs, jewelry, statues, stelae, anthropoid coffins) and buildings (temples and residences), especially from the end of the Late Bronze Age. Egyptian-style temples differ in distinct ways from the Syrian-style temples in Palestine that continued the Middle Bronze tradition. The Egyptian temple at Beth Shan (Strata VIII–VII), for example, consisted of a broadroom entrance hall, with benches along its walls and two pillars to support its roof. The cella in the back of the temple was raised above the floor and reached by seven steps. A platform in the cella probably held a statue of the deity. A similar temple was found at Lachish. This temple had a large central hall supported by two pillars inside an entrance chamber. From the central hall a monumental stone staircase led to a small raised chamber interpreted as the cella. Remnants of cedar beams supporting the roof and colored (Egyptian blue) plaster from the walls have survived. An Egyptian temple of a different plan was found near the copper mines at Timna in the southern Arabah. The shrine consists of a small room abutting a rock scarp. Opposite the entrance is a small niche carved into the rock face. Archaeologists have suggested that in its final phase of use the shrine was probably covered only with a cloth canopy, which is attested by the many textile fragments found on the floor. The deity worshipped at this shrine was undoubtedly Hathor, for her image has been found repeatedly carved into stones and pillars.

A number of new buildings constructed at the end of the Late Bronze Age appear to attest to the strategic concerns of the Egyptians. The buildings are similar to the private dwellings in Egypt, and thus are called "Egyptian residences." Most of these residences were built at existing sites—Beth Shan, Tell el-Far'ah (south), Megiddo, Tel Sera', Aphek, Jaffa, Tell es-Sa'idiyeh—but a few were built at uninhabited sites such as Tel Mor (near Ashdod) and Deir el-Balah (west of Gaza) and thus served as fortified outposts. The buildings are typically square with corner entrances. A square courtyard is at the center of the structure. Small chambers were built surrounding the center court, and a corner staircase would lead to a second floor. The construction of the buildings also demonstrated Egyptian techniques. The walls were thick and made of mudbrick either on a mudbrick foundation or without a foundation. The T-shaped stone doorjambs and thresholds found in the buildings are also indicative of Egyptian style.

Two episodes during the Late Bronze Age are often connected to the Bible. During the reigns of Amenhotep III (1390–1352 BC) and Akhenaten (1352–1336 BC) numerous letters sent from the local rulers of the Canaanite cities to the Egyptian court (known as the Amarna letters) refer to groups of people known as 'Apiru (or Habiru), who seem to be responsible for some of the regional turmoil. The letters imply that the 'Apiru were mercenaries or bandits, and were employed by some local rulers to promote their self-interests against other rulers. Because the term 'Apiru is etymologically similar to *Hebrew*, some scholars have suggested the Amarna letters give evidence of Hebrews—i.e., the early Israelites—in the land of Canaan. It is possible that 'Apiru is related to *Hebrew*, but at the most they probably designate

a similar social category rather than an ethnic group. In any case, if the Amarna letters refer to groups of people that can be identified as Hebrews or early Israelites, the information about them does not correspond to the biblical tradition and thus little is known about them.

The second episode occurred during the reign of Merneptah (1213–1203 BC), the son of Ramesses II. In the fifth year of his reign, he defended Egypt against a Libyan assault, and commemorated his victory on a stela where he also refers to his campaign into Palestine against Ashkelon, Gezer, Yanoam, and Israel. Whereas Ashkelon, Gezer, and Yanoam are designated in the Egyptian inscription as cities, Israel is designated as a people or tribe. This is the first reference to Israel in any Middle Eastern text, and the only reference to Israel in an Egyptian text. Unfortunately, we learn nothing about Israel, its geographic location, or its relationship to the Canaanite cities from this text. We can be certain, however, that by the reign of Merneptah a group of people known as Israel is living in the land of Canaan.

The Iron I Age

The Israelites in the Biblical Tradition

The end of the Late Bronze Age and beginning of the Iron I Age (1200/1150–1000 BC) was characterized by political turmoil. Across the Mediterranean prominent civilizations—the Mycenaeans, Minoans, Hittites—were brought to ruin, many of the Syrian and Palestinian cities were destroyed, and Egypt was forced to retreat to the Nile valley. The causes of the turmoil are many and not fully understood. One group that emerged from the turmoil was the Philistines. Originating in the Mycenaean world, they settled along the southern coast of Palestine, from Tell Qasile on the Yarkon River to Gaza, after losing a series of land and sea battles against Ramesses III in the eighth year of his reign (as recorded on the walls of his mortuary temple at Medinet Habu and in the Harris Papyrus I). They brought with them a distinct Mycenaean-style pottery that allows archaeologists to identify their settlements. The Israelites are another group that emerge during this period, but their identification in the archaeological record is not as clear as that of the Philistines.

The biblical presentation of the Israelites' conquest of Canaan and the period of the Israelite judges should presumably be set in the Iron I Age. The political vacuum that resulted from Egypt's withdrawal from Palestine would have enabled the settlement of the Israelite tribes in Canaan and the formation of new political structures, culminating in the Israelite state. The Bible's presentation of this period, however, is riddled with literary, historical, and archaeological problems.

The bulk of the stories of Israel's settlement of the land of Canaan comes from Joshua 1—12. They describe the military invasion of the land by a unified people under the leadership of Joshua. The conquest was largely successful. All the Canaanite cities were destroyed except for Gibeon, whose inhabitants deceived the Israelites into making peace with them. In its present form, the book of Joshua is part of what has come to be known as the Deuteronomistic History (along with the books of Judges, Samuel, and Kings). In the story of the conquest given in Joshua and Judges, the Deuteronomistic Historian presents an ideological tale that focuses on the Israelites' faithfulness to God as demonstrated by their fidelity to the laws of God, especially the laws of Deuteronomy. According to this ideology, the Israelites would succeed in their conquest and possession of the land of Canaan as long as they were faithful to God's covenant (Jos 1, 3–8). If they were unfaithful to the covenant—if they turned their back on Yahweh and served other gods—they would fail in taking and keeping the land. Instead, God would leave the Canaanites in the land to oppress the Israelites and to be a test of their covenant fidelity. Thus, in the story of Joshua the Israelites are faithful to the covenant and succeed in conquering the land. However, upon the death of Joshua, the people turned away from Yahweh and worshipped the Baals, and as a result God gave the Israelites over to their enemies and they were unable to stand against them (Jgs 2, 11–15). The book of Judges then describes how the people of Israel struggled in the midst of the Canaanites. The book presents the rule of each judge according to the following cycles of events: the people would suffer under the oppression of their more powerful Canaanite neighbors because they had worshipped other gods; the people would even-

tually turn to Yahweh and plead for help; God would then raise up a judge who would deliver them by defeating their enemies in battle; peace would endure throughout the life of the judge, when the people would once again reject Yahweh and the whole cycle would repeat.

From a literary perspective, numerous problems result from the Deuteronomistic Historian's presentation of the Israelite settlement. One arises from a glaring inconsistency regarding the fate of King Jabin of Hazor. In Joshua 11, the Israelites fight and defeat Jabin, put to the sword all the inhabitants of Hazor, and then burn the city. In Judges 4, however, King Jabin of Canaan who reigns in Hazor is oppressing the Israelites until they, under the leadership of Deborah and Barak, defeat his army and eventually destroy him. Although it is possible that multiple kings, especially within a dynasty, would bear the same name, it is unlikely that the king and entire population of Hazor could be killed and the city destroyed, yet emerge as a powerful force in a following generation. A more likely scenario is that the book of Judges refers to King Jabin anachronistically.

More substantial literary problems exist with the presentation of the conquest in Joshua 1—12, for the Bible preserves alternative accounts of this story. A brief tale in Joshua 17, 14–18 presents a picture in which the Israelites were militarily incapable of driving out the Canaanites because the valley-dwelling Canaanites had iron chariots. The tribes of Ephraim and Manasseh must therefore resort to clearing the forests in the inhospitable hill country in order to find enough land to subsist on. Exodus 23, 23–33 presents a situation in which the Israelites are too few in number to conquer the land of Canaan. The land can only be conquered little by little until the Israelites have sufficient population to occupy it, presumably after several generations. In Judges 1 the Israelites do not conquer the land as a unified people, but each tribe acts independently. Although the tribe of Judah has a measure of success, all of the tribes fail to drive out the Canaanite inhabitants of the land. The accounts of the allotment of the land also challenge the literary presentation of the conquest in Joshua 1—12. In Joshua 18, 2–5 Joshua divides the land among seven tribes that had failed to take possession of their land (the hill country was already occupied by the tribes of Judah and Joseph). In this account, the tribe of Benjamin had failed to take possession of its land, but the stories in Joshua 1—12 emphasize clearly that the land of Benjamin is conquered. Finally, the general picture of Israel during the lifetime of Joshua is at odds with the picture of Israel during the period of the judges. In the stories of Joshua, the Israelites are a unified people made up of twelve clearly defined tribes under the leadership of a single individual. In the stories of Judges, the Israelites are not unified. In fact, intertribal conflict is presented on more than one occasion. The judges rule over individual tribes, and the number and composition of the tribes remains fluid.

Do the books of Joshua and Judges preserve traces of events of the past? For the stories of the conquest in Joshua 1—12, the answer is probably "no," as we will explain in the following sections. The tribal allotments and boundary lists in Joshua 13—21 probably do preserve historical records of tribal boundaries, but the period to which they attest is uncertain. We should note that none of the boundary lists are given in their entirety, and the descriptions of the allotment of the land are inconsistent. The historical value of the book of Judges is a little more complicated. The overall form of the individual stories has been shaped to correspond to the ideology of the Deuteronomistic Historian, and is thus clearly secondary. Nevertheless, many biblical scholars suggest that the content of the stories preserves at least some social history and perhaps also some political history. The stories do seem to attest to early Israelite customs and social configurations, but many of these customs and social configurations may have endured well into the period of the Israelite and Judean states. Reference to conflicts with other peoples might reflect longstanding antagonism (such as with the Philistines), though some might be anachronistic for the Iron I period (such as Moab). It is possible that the text preserves the names of early tribal leaders, especially in the lists of so-called minor judges (Jgs 3, 31; 10, 1–5; 12, 7–15). The references to these judges are short, simply naming the judge, the location from where he judged, how long he judged, and often referring to his sons and where he is buried. Perhaps these lists formed part of the writer's source material. The names of the so-called major judges—Ehud,

Deborah, Gideon, Jephthah, Samson—probably also would have been included in this source material, but their stories were filled out from other, presumably oral, traditions.

Models of the Israelite Settlement

Over the last century, biblical scholars formulated three competing historical models in order to explain the settlement of the Israelites in Palestine during the Iron I Age. The Nomadic Infiltration model was first developed by Albrecht Alt and his student Martin Noth in the first half of the twentieth century. This model posits that the early Israelites were nomads or seminomads in a process of gradual sedentarization in the sparsely inhabited central hill country. The settlement was a two-stage process: The early Israelites first entered the land of Canaan in the process of changing pastures; slowly they began to settle permanently in the sparsely populated parts of the country and extended their territory as occasion offered. The whole process began by peaceful means without the use of military force. As the settlers increased in numbers, they gradually moved into the lowlands where they came into conflict with the Canaanite urban centers. This model views Joshua 1—12 as etiologically generated traditions with little historical value. Some cities such as Hazor and Bethel were destroyed by the Israelites as they moved into the lowlands, but the bulk of Joshua 1—12 is fictional. This model emphasizes the uncoordinated movements of Israelites into Canaan from different directions and at different times. If there ever was an exodus event, only a fraction of later Israel was involved.

This model is flawed in several respects. First, the model is unable to demonstrate that the Israelites originated from outside Palestine. As indicated above, all material evidence indicates that the early Israelites resembled their Canaanite neighbors. This would not be the case if the Israelites, like the Philistines, had entered Palestine from elsewhere. Second, the model presents an inadequate understanding of nomadism. Pastoral nomadism cannot be viewed as an evolutionary interval between hunting and gathering and agricultural societies. It is rather a marginal specialization of animal husbandry. The relationship between agriculturalists and pastoralists was symbiotic. Moreover, early Israelites appear to have practiced both pastoralism and agriculture.

The Military Invasion model was created in response to the Nomadic Infiltration model. The main proponents of this model—W. F. Albright, G. Ernest Wright, and John Bright—argued that archaeology has vindicated the essential historicity of the narratives in Joshua 1—12 by demonstrating that the numerous cities stated in the text to have been destroyed do in fact provide evidence of massive destruction. They acknowledge that the ancient sites of Jericho, Ai, Gibeon, and Arad pose problems to this model because they provide no evidence of occupation at the end of the Late Bronze Age. Nevertheless, they also note that the overwhelming evidence for the many other sites is decisive. Moreover, the destruction levels of most of these sites are followed by poor unfortified occupations. There is also a large number of sites with new occupation or occupation that followed centuries of abandonment. In other words, this model suggests, building on the integration of the biblical and archaeological records, that a large group of people rapidly moved into Palestine from outside the land, and their conflict with the native Canaanite inhabitants was primarily political.

The Military Invasion model has been challenged in many respects. First, the application of archaeology to Joshua 1—12 is selective. The evidence is absent for much of the text, and it is embarrassing with regard to Jericho, Ai, Gibeon, and Arad. The sites of Kadesh-Barnea, Hormah, Heshbon, Dibon, and Hebron could also be added to the list of sites in which the archaeological record does not support the biblical tradition. Second, this model has been challenged on its very assumption that archaeology could be used to verify the biblical texts in this regard, for archaeological data are inherently ambiguous. A destroyed city does not indicate the agents of destruction. Although the early Israelites could have been responsible for a site's destruction, more likely scenarios would point to the Egyptians or the Philistines (or other so-called sea peoples) as the agents of the destructions. Archaeology also raises a chronological problem for the model because not all the Late Bronze cities that give evidence of destruction were destroyed during the same time period. The destructions of Hazor and Lachish, for example, were separated by over a century. Many of the large sites that give evidence of massive destruction were in areas in which the native Canaanite inhabitants remained dominant. In other words, the material culture after the destruction of the site was similar to the material culture beforehand. Finally, the Military Invasion model also implies that the material culture of early Israel would be intrusive into the native Canaanite culture, but this is not the case.

The Peasant Revolt model was first put forward by George Mendenhall and subsequently modified by Norman Gottwald. According to this model, the Amarna letters—which refer to the internal struggles in Palestine caused by the 'Apiru—and the biblical events (especially as presented in Judges) represent the same political process: the withdrawal of large population groups from an obligation to existing political regimes, and therefore, the renunciation of any protection from these sources. There was no significant invasion of Palestine; no displacement of population; no genocide; no large scale driving out of the population, only of royal administrators. Instead, there was a peasants' revolt against the network of interlocking Canaanite city-states. The catalyst for this movement might have been the Exodus group: corvée-labor captives who escaped from Egypt and made a covenant with God at Sinai. This group espoused an ideology attractive to those oppressed in Canaan, who immediately joined them. Many of the biblical texts suggest that the people of Israel were unable to conquer the cities of the plains until David's time. Therefore, the early Israelites had geographically removed themselves from the Canaanite cities by retreating into the wooded hill country. The early Israelite settlements were in fact opening this previously uninhabited frontier; such frontiers often attract the socially disenfranchised. Credit should be given to several technological improvements—iron tools, rock terraces, lined cisterns—which made this achievement possible.

Although this model takes into account the similarities between Israelite and Canaanite material culture, it has been criticized for failing to demonstrate the existence of a true peasants' revolt in ancient Palestine and imposing modern, especially Marxist, ideologies on the early Israelites. The Peasant Revolt model overemphasizes the uniqueness of the Israelite settlement. The early highland villages of Israel are identical to other highland villages outside of Palestine; the Israelite settlement does not appear to depend on a unique religious experience or a political ideology.

The Archaeology of the Settlement

A number of new models explaining the Israelite settlement have emerged in recent years, but none has risen to the paradigmatic status of the earlier models. Rooted heavily in the new evidence gleaned from excavations and surveys, especially in the central hill country and the northern Negev, these models share numerous similarities: the Israelites emerged largely from the indigenous population of Canaan, the settlement was primarily peaceful, and the population was engaged in agricultural and pastoral activities. The models differ in their explanation of the causes of the settlement. Some models emphasize the disruption of international trade or the collapse of the Late Bronze cities; others emphasize environmental factors or long-term social processes. Undoubtedly, multiple causes are responsible for the emergence of the Israelites. The new models simply provide interpretive frameworks for the growing body of archaeological evidence of the Israelite settlement.

An explosion of new settlements in the central hill country characterizes the archaeology of the Iron I period. During the Late Bronze Age the hill country held only twenty-nine settlements (down from 220 during the preceding Middle Bronze Age). During the Iron I period, the settlements in the hill country increased to 254. The size of the settlements was quite small, averaging 4.25 acres, but most were less than 2.5 acres in size (the Late Bronze settlements on average were twice as large). Most of the settlements were founded on previously unoccupied sites, although many were founded on abandoned sites that had been occupied during the Early or Middle Bronze Ages. Except for a few major sites that show continuous settlement from the Late Bronze Age, such as Shechem and Jerusalem, most of the settlements were poor hamlets with no fortifications or public buildings.

The central hill country has gone through periods of settlement and abandonment from the Early Bronze Age through the Iron Age, and during each period the settlement pattern is fairly similar. The northern hill country (Shechem and north) is more conducive to settlement with its large valleys, moderate topography, and fertile eastern slope. The southern Judean hill country is less hospitable. As a result, more settlements are found in the north. During periods of settlement decline such as the Late Bronze Age, the percentage of settlements shifts to the north. However, during the waves of settlement such as the Iron I period, the percentage of settlements increases in the southern hill country. Similarly, an east to west settlement shift can be detected. Because the eastern side of the hill country is closer to the desert fringe, it is the location of the early wave of settlement. During settlement declines, only the eastern flank is settled. The western side of the hill country is ideal for horticulture, but it is also more mountainous and demands more permanent commitment for settlement. Thus it is not occupied until later during the waves of settlement.

This settlement pattern might be interpreted in terms of the shift from pastoral to sedentary life. The eastern and southern regions are where pastoralism is primarily practiced, and where the people would be able to make the transition from pastoral to a primarily agricultural life. The economy of these small settlements appears to be dependent primarily upon agriculture and supplemented with pastoralism. The building of many terraces throughout the hill country attests to the agricultural economy of the region. Also, pits for holding grain and cisterns for holding water are characteristic features of the Iron I sites. The domestic structures, however, attest to the importance of pastoralism, for they were adapted to serve as shelter also for the flocks. The mixed economy of farming and herding served to minimize the risks inherent in the establishment of new settlements.

Although most of the settlements simply consist of a group of houses, some of the settlements attest to planning. The common plan was the arrangement of the houses along the perimeter so that the external walls of the houses formed a defensive wall, or the ring of houses could also have created a pen for gathering the inhabitants' flocks of sheep and goats. At 'Izbet Sartah, for example, twenty-two broad-room houses formed an oval enclosure, a half-acre in area, surrounding a central open area. At Beersheba the first built-up settlement (Stratum VII, dating to the end of the Iron I period; Strata IX–VIII contained mostly pit dwellings) consisted of a ring of houses built around the perimeter of the mound, with their external walls forming a defensive barrier.

The material culture of these sites is simple and plain, and is characterized by the pillared house and the collared-rim storage jar. The pillared house is the most common architectural feature of the Iron I Age. The pillars consisted of large stone monoliths, unworked stone drums, or wooden posts placed on stone socles. Rows of pillars served to divide courtyards into roofed and unroofed areas, as well as define multiple rooms within buildings. The pillared houses followed a variety of plans, but the most common and enduring plan was the four-room house.

The basic plan of the four-room house consisted of three long rooms backed by a broad room. Pillars were usually used to separate the three long rooms; solid walls are also employed to separate the long rooms. In modified plans, the long rooms themselves (or the broad room in back) could be further subdivided. The center long room typically served as a courtyard, with ovens and food processing equipment in this room. There is debate over whether it was roofed. The side rooms separated by pillars were used to house animals, with troughs placed between the pillars. The back broad room served as the main living room. Based on the amount of charred debris in the buildings, many of these houses supported a second story. The bedrooms would have been located in the upper story over the side and back rooms. In a number of villages, the pillared houses appear in clusters or compounds in which several houses shared walls and a common courtyard. These compounds probably reflect the kinship structures of the settlers (such as the extended family). They also might attest to the economic and labor needs that the settlers faced. The shared walls of the compounds would have minimized the labor and resource needs of the settlement.

The pottery repertoire of the hill country settlements is characterized by numerous large storage jars *(pithoi),* including the collared-rim storage jar. Other utilitarian vessels are also found in lesser quantities. Painted decoration is rare, although applied or impressed decoration can be found. All of the pottery has antecedents in the pottery of the Late Bronze Age. Only a few cultic items have been found—a bronze bull at an open-air site near Mount Gilboa, a bronze figurine of a seated deity in a cult room at Hazor, pottery incense stands and small stone four-horned altars at Megiddo and Lachish—and in every case they stand firmly within the Canaanite tradition.

Who were these settlers in the central hill country? The biblical tradition, of course, would identify many of these settlers as Israelite, and indeed they became part of the states of Israel and Judah. Many of the settlers, however, might not have identified themselves as Israelites, at least not initially. In any case, the archaeological and historical evidence suggests that the settlers were a mixture of several population groups. One group undoubtedly consisted of those who left the Late Bronze urban centers in the lowlands. The settlers' knowledge of dry farming and other technological skills such as terracing, digging of cisterns, and house construction argues in favor of their origin in the Late Bronze cities. The continuities of the material culture that the settlers share with the earlier Canaanites further support this interpretation. Another group consisted of pastoralists living on the desert fringe. This group lived in a symbiotic relationship with the urban centers throughout the history of Palestine. During periods of settlement decline, the pastoral population increased and their mode of subsistence became more diverse. During periods of settlement as in the Iron I period, many in this group chose a predominantly agricultural lifestyle while others would revert to a strictly pastoral lifestyle. Finally, the settlers could have consisted of groups that are mentioned in historical texts such as the ʿApiru and the Shasu (the latter is a nomadic group mentioned in the Egyptian texts), and, perhaps, also a group of refugees who had escaped the corvée in Egypt.

Iron II Age

Historical Sources

For the Iron II Age (1000–539 BC) the historian of ancient Israel finally has at hand numerous literary and documentary sources in addition to the biblical literature. The primary and most important sources are the annals of the Assyrian kings. Beginning with Shalmaneser III (858–824 BC), the Assyrian kings began to encounter the kings of Israel in their campaigns toward the Mediterranean, and hence began to include reference to Israel in their annals and inscriptions. The annals of Shalmaneser, for example, record his battles with an Aramean coalition in which the Israelite kingdom participated. Ahab is presented as one of the stronger members, supplying the coalition with 2,000 chariots and 10,000 foot soldiers. In a later inscription on the Black Obelisk, Shalmaneser records the tribute of Jehu, the son of Omri [*sic*], and includes a relief representation of the king kneeling in submission to him. With the reign of Tiglath-pileser III (744–727 BC) the Assyrian kings also had encounters with the kings of Judah, who are now mentioned in the Assyrian annals and inscriptions. The Assyrian records are important sources for understanding Israel's relations with Damascus and other Aramean states, the events that culminated in the destruction of Samaria and the end of the Israelite kingdom, and the political events surrounding the reigns of Ahaz and Hezekiah.

The Babylonians also kept annals that shed light on the political events in the Middle East at the end of Assyrian domination. Few texts refer to Judah directly, but one chronicle does record Nebuchadnezzar's battles in Palestine, including his destruction of Jerusalem.

The Egyptian records during this period shed little light on the events involving the Israelites, for they are largely preoccupied with internal matters. During the Late Period, Egypt under the Twenty-fifth and the Twenty-sixth Dynasties is once again involved in the political affairs of Palestine, but records that attest to this involvement are few. The most notable Egyptian record of Egypt's interaction with Israel and Judah during the Iron II period is the list of conquered cities in Israel and Judah by Sheshonq I (945–924 BC; identified as the biblical Shishak), which is carved on the walls of the Karnak temple. Unfortunately, Sheshonq did not include a narrative description of his campaign, and thus his inscription offers little historical insight.

Numerous Hebrew and Aramaic inscriptions that provide important first-hand information on the events of this period have been uncovered in Palestine. The most famous of these inscriptions is the Moabite Stela, erected by King Mesha of Moab in dedication of a temple. The inscription describes how Mesha freed his land from Israelite vassalage during the reign of Omri's "son" (usually interpreted to mean Omri's grandson, Joram). The recently discovered Tel Dan inscription celebrates an unnamed king's defeat of the kings of Israel and the "house of David." The inscription was presumably erected by Hazael, king of Damascus, but the fragmentary and incomplete condition of the inscription make such an interpretation tentative. The Siloam Tunnel Inscription describes the construction of the tunnel that brought water from the Gihon spring into a pool inside the walls of Jerusalem. The inscription describes the events from the perspective of the workers, but the tunnel probably was dug at the command of Hezekiah in preparation for his rebellion against Assyria. The Lachish Letters describe diplomatic and military maneuvers during the final days of the kingdom of Judah as it was being assaulted by the Babylonians. From the same period, the Arad Letters record the provisioning of the Judean fort at Arad, but also record conflict with the Edomites who live south of Judah.

Other inscriptions attest to economic, social, and religious conditions of the Iron II period. The Gezer Calendar describes the agricultural cycle of the year. Because of the content, some scholars have interpreted this inscription to be a practice text, attesting to scribal activity. The Samaria Ostraca are a series of tax receipts that also attest to kinship structures in Israel. The Yavneh-yam Letter records the complaint of a farm worker to the commander of a fort who has deprived him of his cloak. The Kuntillet 'Ajrud Inscriptions attest to forms of Yahwism that have not been preserved in the Bible.

The primary sources in the Bible for the Iron II Age are the books of Samuel, Kings, and Chronicles (some of the prophetic books, especially Isaiah and Jeremiah, also provide historical information for this period). The stories of Samuel and Saul in 1 Samuel 1—15 are similar in kind to the stories in the book of Judges. They probably record real historical figures, and perhaps also early conflicts between the Israelites in the central hill country and the Philistines on the coastal plain. No earlier source material other than oral traditions can be recognized behind the narrative. The story of Saul and David's conflict in 1 Samuel 16—2 Samuel 1 has been shaped by an apologist on behalf of the Davidic Dynasty. Saul is presented as one driven mad by an evil spirit, whereas David is a loyal servant who refuses to raise his hand against Saul. Some of this material probably preserves traces of real historical events, such as Saul's death in battle against the Philistines, but whatever historical sources might have lain beneath the narrative are now difficult to ascertain.

The stories of 2 Samuel 2—1 Kings 11 address the period of the "United Monarchy," the reigns of David and Solomon. The historical value of these stories is currently the subject of intense debate by biblical scholars and archaeologists. This debate is compounded by the fact that this period (often labeled Iron IIA, or in some circles Iron IC) is not addressed in any nonbiblical sources, and the material remains of this period give at best an ambiguous picture. At issue is the nature and scope of the "kingdom" of David and Solomon: Was there a United Monarchy? Did David and Solomon rule over a territorial state? What was the relationship of this "kingdom" to the other "kingdoms"—Ammon, Aram, Edom, Philistia, Phoenicia—in the region? Many of the stories of David and Solomon are either legendary tales or creations of the biblical writer, perhaps based on brief historical records. Whereas the death notice of Solomon (1 Kgs 11, 41–43) refers to the "book of the chronicles of Solomon," no such source is listed in the stories of David. Texts that appear to be based on earlier sources might include the lists of David's administrators (2 Sm 8, 16–18; 20, 23–26) and his warriors (2 Sm 23, 8–39). The references to David's battles (2 Sm 8, 1–15) might also be based on an earlier source. A longer list of historical sources might be extracted from the story of Solomon: list of Solomon's officials (1 Kgs 4, 1–6); list of officials responsible for supplying food for the court (1 Kgs 4, 7–19); Solomon's use of forced labor (1 Kgs 5, 13–18); cities that Solomon built and fortified with forced labor (1 Kgs 9, 15–19); dealings with King Hiram of Tyre (1 Kgs 9, 26–28; 10, 11—12, 22); Solomon's trade in horses and chariots (1 Kgs 10, 28–29); and conflicts with Hadad of Edom, Rezon of Damascus,

and Jeroboam of Ephraim (1 Kgs 11, 14–40). Many other aspects of the stories, such as David's conquering of Jerusalem, Solomon's wisdom and wealth, and his building of the Temple, are legendary and might have been widely known oral traditions.

The stories of the separate kingdoms of Israel and Judah are found in 1 Kings 12—25. These stories are based on two groups of sources. The first source has been called the "Tales of the Prophets." This source consists of stories of prophets and especially their dealings with kings, their prophecies and their fulfillments. The source includes, for example, the story of Ahijah's prophecy that Jeroboam will become the king of the northern ten tribes of Israel (1 Kgs 11, 26–40) and his subsequent prophecy that the house of Jeroboam will be destroyed (1 Kgs 14, 1–18). Other stories are about Shemaiah (1 Kgs 12, 1–24), Jehu (1 Kgs 16, 1–4.7), Micaiah (1 Kgs 22, 1–38), Jonah (2 Kgs 14, 25–27), Isaiah (2 Kgs 18, 13–20; 19), and a number of unnamed prophets (1 Kgs 12, 25—13, 32; 1 Kgs 20; 2 Kgs 21, 10–15). The best known and largest group of stories focus on Elijah and Elisha and their interaction with the house of Ahab (1 Kgs 17—19, 21; 2 Kgs 1—10, 13). Although many of these stories are largely legendary and often reflect a later situation, they appear to have preserved some reliable historical information, particularly regarding the political situation of the period. However, it should be noted that the focus of the stories is primarily religious; the political and social context of the stories is often the backdrop for a religious message regarding the king's (and the people's) faithfulness to Yahweh.

The second major source for the book of Kings is the Israelite and Judean chronicles, which provides the framework for the story of each king. The reign of each king is introduced with a reference to his father, the age at which he began to reign and the length of his reign, and his mother's name. The reigns of the kings of Judah are synchronized with the reigns of the kings of Israel. The story of the king's reign ends with a reference to his death and the place of his burial. Mixed in with this framework are references to deeds accomplished by the king and a statement that other deeds are recorded in either the "Books of the Annals of the Kings of Israel" or the "Books of the Annals of the Kings of Judah." Although the Deuteronomistic Historian adds his own evaluation of each king's reign, the Historian does not appear to have edited or omitted information from the chronicles of the Judean kings. Less information is preserved about the Israelite kings—the king's father and mother are not listed—but this might reflect the nature of the Israelite chronicle rather than the Deuteronomistic Historian's bias. The chronicles preserve fairly reliable historical information. This information, however, is not without its problems. The chronology and synchronization of the Israelite and Judean kings, for example, does not fit within the absolute dates that can be fixed from Assyrian, Babylonian, and Egyptian records. Part of the problem might be that we are not certain how regnal years were counted in each case or whether a king's reign included a co-regency with his father. In other cases, the numbers supplied by the chronicles are incorrect. It seems impossible that Pekah could have reigned for twenty years or that Uzziah (Azariah) reigned for fifty-two years (though the latter's reign could be accounted for with a co-regency).

Other sources that could have been used by the writer of the book of Kings might be dedicatory building inscriptions (similar to the Moabite Stone) or inscriptions associated with votive dedications or biographic stelae that would have been set up in the Temple, the king's palace, or a prominent public location in Jerusalem. The existence of such inscriptions is likely and many texts in the books of Kings could be based on such inscriptions, but in the end their existence must remain speculative.

The book of Chronicles is also a source for the Iron II Age. For the stories of David and Solomon, the book of Chronicles is largely dependent upon the books of Samuel and Kings and offers little independent material. For the stories of the later kings, however, Chronicles offers some material that is not found in Kings. For example, the book of Chronicles records how the Assyrians took Manasseh as a captive to Babylon, where he repented to God who restored him to Jerusalem (2 Chr 33, 10–13). This episode is absent from the book of Kings, probably because it does not fit the ideology of the Deuteronomistic Historian, who blames the sins of Manasseh for the eventual destruction of Jerusalem by the Babylonians. In such cases, the book of

Chronicles gives us insight into sources that were not accessible to or rejected by the Deuteronomistic Historian. Moreover, this particular example should caution against placing too much confidence in the sources used by the Chronicler or other biblical writers. It is unlikely that Manasseh was ever taken to Babylon, which was a center of repeated revolt against the Assyrian empire. It is possible, however, that Manasseh was taken to Nineveh—an inscription of Esarhaddon records that Manasseh and twenty-one other kings were forced to bring building materials to Nineveh. A number of sources are named in Chronicles—History of the Prophet Nathan, Prophecy of Ahijah the Shilonite, Visions of the Seer Iddo (2 Chr 9, 29), Records of the Prophet Shemaiah and Seer Iddo (2 Chr 12, 15), Midrash of the Book of Kings (2 Chr 24, 27), Acts of Uzziah by Isaiah (2 Chr 26, 22), and Acts of Hezekiah by Isaiah (2 Chr 32, 32)—but the nature of these sources or whether they are included in the book of Kings is unknown.

The Tenth Century

The beginning of the Iron II Age is imperceptible in the archaeological record. The similarities of the tenth century with the material culture of the Iron I period have led some scholars to label the tenth century as Iron IC. The tenth century is associated with the Iron II Age primarily because the Bible claims that it is the period of statehood—the formation of the United Monarchy. Unfortunately, the United Monarchy is not clearly evident in the archaeological record. No archaeological remains can be associated with David's kingdom. There is archaeological evidence attributed to the reign of Solomon, but the significance of this evidence for understanding the history of Israel is debated.

The archaeological foundation for the United Monarchy has been the large, fortress-style, six chamber city gates and massive casemate walls at Hazor, Megiddo, and Gezer (1 Kgs 9, 15 claims that Solomon built up the walls of these cities). The gates and walls at Hazor and Gezer do appear to date to the tenth century, but the gate of Megiddo should now be dated to the ninth century (the first phase of Stratum IVA), and there is no evidence of a casemate wall surrounding the city. Instead, tenth century Megiddo (Stratum VA–IVB) consists of two large monumental palaces—palace 6000 in the north and palace 1723 in the south. No wall surrounds Megiddo at this period, though the exterior walls of the houses and two palaces built along the edge of the mound provide some protection. The palaces have foundations made of ashlars (cut stones), as does the gate of Gezer. The gate and walls of Hazor are constructed of fieldstones. The Gezer gate is also associated with guard quarters (palace 10,000) and perhaps an outer gate and solid wall. Inside the gates of Hazor and Gezer only a few buildings can be dated to the tenth century, and none is monumental or impressive. Moreover, both Hazor and Gezer are small settlements, covering only part of the tell. Elsewhere, the gradual process of urbanization is detectable in the material culture, though no monumental architecture has been found.

The significance of these archaeological remains for understanding the political structures of the tenth century is fiercely debated. For those who follow the biblical tradition and argue for a large United Monarchy, these remains provide significant, yet limited, evidence of the veracity of the tradition. For others, the material culture of the tenth century attests to some centralized building activity, but not a state, let alone a United Monarchy. A key site in this debate would presumably be Jerusalem, where the Bible claims Solomon built a Temple, a palace, and many other administrative public buildings. Unfortunately, virtually nothing from the tenth century has been uncovered in the numerous excavations of the city. Two reasons are generally given to account for this lack of evidence. First, Jerusalem was continuously occupied until Nebuchadnezzar II destroyed it in 586 BC. Evidence of tenth century Jerusalem was destroyed by later rebuilding and occupation of the city. Second, the remains of many of the Solomonic buildings would be beneath the present Temple Mount *(Haram esh-Sharif)*, which is impossible to excavate due to the religious and political situation in the city.

The Kingdom of Israel

The short-lived kingdom of Israel (931–722/1 BC) is well attested in the archaeological record. Its capital Samaria was founded in the ninth century on top of several olive-oil installations. An independently fortified royal acropolis, consisting of a large platform supported by massive retaining walls, was built on the rounded summit of a hill. The platform contained a couple of palaces and a number of administrative buildings. Most of the construction utilized finely cut ashlars. In one of the palaces a large cache of carved ivories, many imported from Phoenicia, attests to the wealth of the kingdom—the cache is usually attributed to the reign of Ahab (873–852 BC), who the Bible claims built a house of ivory (1 Kgs 22, 39). The Samaria Ostraca were found in one of the administrative buildings, and were inscribed during the reign of Jeroboam II (784–744 BC). The city was destroyed in a conflagration by Sargon II (721–705 BC), though the Assyrian assault might have begun during the reign of Shalmaneser V (726–722 BC).

Megiddo was one of the major administrative cities of the kingdom of Israel. The Israelite city (limited to Stratum IVA) was surrounded by a large wall and entered though a six-chamber gate (later rebuilt as a four-chamber gate) on its north side. A palace (380) was located on the eastern side of the city, but most of the city was dedicated to two large complexes of tripartite-pillared buildings. The southern complex consisted of five connected tripartite-pillared buildings fronted by a large walled yard. The northern complex consisted of three groups of five, two, and five connected buildings surrounding a walled yard. The interpretation of these buildings has been debated. Most commonly they are interpreted as stables for the royal chariot force. Other interpretations argue that the buildings were used for storerooms in a state-run redistribution center, or functioned as markets and fair grounds. The large water tunnel on the western side of the city, which leads to the spring outside the city wall, was constructed during this period. Tiglath-pileser III destroyed Megiddo in 732 BC and rebuilt the city (Stratum III) as an Assyrian provincial capital. The city was filled with residential buildings in an orthogonal pattern, with several Assyrian-style palaces built near the gate.

Unlike Megiddo, both Hazor and Dan in the northern Jordan Valley give evidence of several strata of occupation during this period, attesting to Israel's conflicts with Damascus and Assyria. Israelite Hazor covers the entire acropolis (the lower city was not inhabited after the Late Bronze Age). The tenth-century casemate wall is filled in to form a solid fortification wall, and another solid wall is constructed to surround the new eastern half of the city. Inside the six-chamber gate, now in the middle of the city, a single tripartite-pillared building was uncovered. Two large halls attached to the building could have functioned as a granary or storerooms to support the function of the pillared building (as a stable or market). A large citadel was built on the western end of the acropolis. Administrative buildings resembling those of Samaria were found immediately to the north and south of the citadel. The massive walls of the citadel (over six feet thick) initially served as the western fortification of the city, but at the height of the Assyrian threat at the end of the Israelite period, a new wall was added to the north, west, and south of the citadel, covering over the administrative buildings. New administrative buildings were constructed on the east side of the citadel. On the southern side of the city an enormous shaft and tunnel were dug into the aquifer beneath the city in order to supply the populace with water during a siege.

Dan was Israel's northernmost city and so often at the center of conflict with Israel's northern neighbors. The complex set of gates with multiple building phases on the southern side of the city attests to this conflict. On the north side of the tell, Avraham Biran, the excavator, uncovered a large series of structures that he identified with the high place initially built by Jeroboam I (931–911 BC; see 1 Kgs 12, 26–31). In the earliest stratum, the structure consisted of a large podium constructed of ashlars. The excavator assumed that the podium served as an open-air high place, but traces of foundations on the podium have led others to suggest that it supported a large superstructure, probably a temple. In front of the podium on the south is a large altar platform built of ashlars, with storage rooms on the west and an oil press farther south. A second phase of the temple is not well preserved. The third phase of the temple complex, dating to the eighth century, is the most developed. The podium now supported a temple. A monumental staircase made of ashlars was added to the south side of the podium. A large four-horned altar that was approached by steps and surrounded by an enclosure was constructed in front of the podium. A row of rooms on the west side of the

temple and altar functioned in support of the temple cult. Tiglath-pileser III, presumably, destroyed the temple at the end of the eighth century with the rest of the city.

The Kingdom of Judah

Judah was Israel's poorer and weaker sibling, and the material culture of Judah generally reflects this distinction. Although there were periods of friendly relations between the two kingdoms—with Judah often submitting to a more powerful Israel such as during the Omride Dynasty, and perhaps also during parts of the Jehu Dynasty—the Bible also attests to strained relations and military conflicts. The material evidence of these relations can be seen in the early fortification of some of the towns of Judah. One such site was Tell en-Nasbeh, which has been identified with biblical Mizpah and is situated at the border between Israel and Judah. At this site a massive solid inset-offset wall was built outside an earlier (tenth century) casemate wall. The wall was roughly nineteen hundred feet in length, stood forty feet above bedrock, and had an average thickness of more than twelve feet. Eleven towers fortified the wall. The wall was made from uncut fieldstones, but ashlars were used in corners and on the face of the towers. A stone glacis further protected several towers and long sections of the wall. The city was entered through a two-chamber outer gate and a four-chamber inner gate. It appears that the inner gate was the original gate, but in the ninth century the fortifications were strengthened with the construction of a new outer gate that was fortified by a massive tower. The heavy fortifications at this site attest to political tensions and perhaps military conflict between Israel and Judah.

Although the kingdom of Judah developed under relatively peaceful conditions—despite the construction of some new fortifications, few destruction levels are attested—the Assyrian threat in the eighth century led to the fortification of Judah. Unlike Israel, which had several large urban centers, the kingdom of Judah developed primarily around Jerusalem. By the end of the eighth century, Jerusalem had swelled to a large fortified city of 150 acres, larger than any city in Israel. Lachish, the second largest city in Judah, covered an area of only twenty acres. The other Judean towns averaged only five to eight acres in size. The generally peaceful conditions of Judah also enabled it to rapidly increase in population. In addition to natural population growth, the population of Judah increased due to the migration of refugees from the north, especially during the second half of the eighth century, which culminated in Israel's destruction by the Assyrians. The population increase was felt prominently in Jerusalem but also across the Judean hill country. Numerous small settlements were established during this period, many of which were unfortified and roughly two miles apart.

At the end of the eighth century, archaeology is able to provide a material context for one of the more crucial events recorded in the biblical texts: the archaeological evidence provides a picture of Hezekiah's revolt against Assyria (1 Kgs 18—19). Hezekiah fortified an enlarged Jerusalem with a massive, seven-meter thick city wall (the so-called broad wall uncovered in the Jewish Quarter). Recent excavations in the Kidron Valley have uncovered a second, outer wall around the eastern side of the city. This wall might also have been constructed by Hezekiah. In order to secure drinking water for the inhabitants of the city in case of siege, he diverted the water from the Gihon spring to a pool inside the city wall through the excavation of the Siloam tunnel. Further evidence of Hezekiah's preparation against an Assyrian assault is attested in the distribution of royal storage jars that are impressed with the inscription *lamelech* (belonging to the king). The impressions are applied to the loop handles of large ovoid jars that are 60 centimeters high, have four handles, a narrow mouth, and a short upright neck. The jars were apparently used to store liquids rather than dry goods. The seal impressions have either a winged solar disk or a four-winged scarab. The word *lamelech* is inscribed above the design. Below the design one of four towns is named: Hebron, Socoh, Ziph, and *mmsht* (the last name is unknown). These jars and seals have been securely dated to the end of the eighth century. They have been found throughout Judah, but mostly at Jerusalem and Lachish. Some scholars have argued that the jars were used to gather taxes in the form of agricultural produce such as wine and oil. Others argue that the jars represent four centers of royal wine production. Another interpretation is that the four cities inscribed on the seals represent four military divisions and

that the jars conveyed provisions to military units posted by Hezekiah throughout his kingdom. In any case, the jars attest to the king's provisioning of his cities in preparation for his revolt.

Although Jerusalem was never sacked, Hezekiah's rebellion was a complete failure. Most of the cities of Judah were destroyed, and part of Judah was placed under the domain of the Philistine king of Ekron. Hezekiah himself was forced to pay a large tribute to Sennacherib. The consequences of Hezekiah's revolt are illustrated in the Lachish reliefs found in Sennacherib's palace at Nineveh and in the excavations at Lachish. The Lachish reliefs depict in graphic detail the Assyrian assault, defeat, and plunder of Lachish. The excavations of Lachish revealed the violent destruction of Stratum III. At the southern corner of the city, the Assyrians built a massive siege ramp. Inside the city wall, the inhabitants of the city built a counterramp over their own houses in order to hold the Assyrians back. The hundreds of arrowheads and spherical slingstones attest to the intensity of the battle. The discovery of a mass grave with more than fifteen hundred bodies is grim evidence of the slaughter of the people of Lachish.

The southern border of Judah was along the Beersheba Valley and was fortified by Arad on the east and Beersheba on the west. Beersheba was a small, fortified town from the tenth century through the eighth century (Strata V–II). It provides the best example of a complete and regular city plan from the Iron II period. Although the city only occupied an area of three acres, it probably served as the major administrative center in the south. The city was fortified by a casemate wall, and entered through a four-chamber gate. Surrounding the city a stone glacis was constructed against the rampart supporting the wall. Inside the city gate was a large open square that probably served a variety of public functions. The street plan of the city was composed of concentric ovals connected by radial lanes, with the entire system converging on the plaza inside the gate. A water system was uncovered in the northeastern corner of the city. The city contained approximately seventy-five houses, most of which were designed according to a special four-room type. The back rooms of those houses that abutted the city wall along the peripheral road were incorporated into the casemates of the wall. Some of the houses have stairs preserved indicating that they had a second story. Three tripartite-pillared buildings were built east of the city gate and open onto the plaza. Together they cover an area of 600 square meters. A large building located near the city plaza at the juncture of the outer road and a radial road has been called the "governor's house." It contained three large reception halls whose entrances were built of ashlars. Beersheba was destroyed at the end of the eighth century, presumably by the Assyrians in response to Hezekiah's revolt.

The fortress of Arad was built on top of a small settlement in the ninth century (though the excavator initially dated the first fortress to the tenth century). The fortress was destroyed and rebuilt five times before finally being destroyed early in the sixth century with the destruction of the kingdom of Judah by the Babylonians. A number of letters inscribed on pottery sherds found in the fort suggest that the fort functioned primarily as a Judean bastion against the encroachment of the Edomites. The pressure of the Edomites on Judah's southern border is attested at numerous other sites in this region. At 'Ein Hatzeva in the Arabah (southeast of Arad), the large eighth century Judean fortress is replaced by a smaller Edomite fortress in the seventh century. At Horvat Qitmit in the Arad Valley (southwest of Arad) a small Edomite shrine-complex was built late in the seventh century. The fortress of Horvat 'Uza on the eastern end of the Arad Valley (southeast of Arad) was destroyed by the Edomites (as suggested by an Edomite letter found in a gate chamber) at the beginning of the sixth century. Both Aroer and Tel Malhata in the Negev (between Arad and Beersheba) present evidence of Edomite occupation by the beginning of the sixth century.

Jerusalem was destroyed in 586 BC by the Babylonian army in order to crush the rebellion by Zedekiah, Judah's last king. The archaeological remains of the City of David primarily attest to this period. Heavy ash layers in several buildings give evidence of the destruction, and numerous Babylonian iron arrowheads hint at the presumable human slaughter. One of the buildings on the eastern slope of the City of David that was destroyed in the conflagration appears to have been an archive. Dubbed the "House of the Bullae," this building contained fifty-one clay bullae that had sealed papyrus or parchment scrolls. Many of the names inscribed on the bullae are mentioned in the Bible, especially in the book of Jeremiah. The most notable bulla, found elsewhere in the city, records the name of "Baruch, son of Neriah, the scribe"—the companion of Jeremiah.

The Period of the Great Empires

The Persian Period

It is ironic that although most of the biblical books were written or compiled during the Persian period, few books actually attest to the period. The books of Ezra and Nehemiah provide the main narrative source for this period. The numerous prophetic books that attest to this period include Haggai, Zechariah, Malachi, and Isaiah 56—66, but unfortunately, these books attest to little more than the social and religious situation of the period. The books of Ezra and Nehemiah are particularly valuable for understanding this period because they seem to preserve primary sources. Each book preserves a first-hand report that has been labeled a memoir. The Nehemiah memoir is found in Nehemiah 1, 1—7, 73a; 12, 31–43; 13, 4–31; the Ezra memoir is found in Ezra 7, 27—9, 15. The book of Ezra also contains several letters from correspondence with the Persian administration. These letters also might be based on primary texts. Because many scholars have argued that Ezra is a fiction, an ideal lawgiver, his memoirs are not usually given the same status as the Nehemiah memoirs. Although Ezra has been idealized in later tradition, the presentation of him in the book of Ezra has a realistic basis and probable historical source. In any case, in their present context the memoirs and letters have been shaped by the ideological concerns of the biblical writer.

Other sources for the Persian period include the *Jewish Antiquities* of Josephus (a first-century Jewish historian). Although Josephus largely follows the biblical text, he adds information concerning the relationship between the Judeans and the Samaritans. Many Greek sources contribute to writing the history of Persia, most notably, the History of Herodotus and the works of Diodorus Siculus, but these texts give little attention to the events of Judah. The archaeological evidence for this period has not been investigated well. In terms of material culture, the spread of Phoenician and Greek influence along the coastal plain can be detected. The hill country demonstrates cultural continuities with the Iron Age. Destruction layers at numerous cities attest to military conflicts, but the dating of these destruction layers to specific events is problematic. Inscriptions and papyri, such as the Elephantine Papyri, provide evidence of the administration of the province of Judea, but they attest to little more than names of governors and high priests.

The biblical evidence refers to only two periods during the long Persian rule of Judah, and in both cases its presentation of the events is less than clear. The first period focuses on the rebuilding of the Temple by the exiles who returned to Judah from Babylon. Once Cyrus defeated Babylon (539 BC), he sought to consolidate the empire under his rule by restoring the gods and the peoples that the Babylonians had exiled. Thus Cyrus issued an edict for the Judeans to return to their homeland and rebuild the Temple of Yahweh (Ezr 6, 3–5; compare this text to an edict that has survived in the so-called Cyrus Cylinder). The book of Ezra gives a conflated presentation of who initially returned to Babylon. Sheshbazzar, who is called a prince over Judah, is credited with leading the initial return, bringing the Temple vessels from Babylon (Ezr 1, 8–11), and laying the Temple foundation (Ezr 5, 16). Yet Zerubbabel is also listed as the leader of the people, under whose direction the foundation of the Temple was laid in the second year of the return (537 BC; Ezr 3, 8–13). After a delay of several years, the rebuilding of the Temple resumed under Zerubbabel in the second year of Darius (520 BC). The Temple was completed in Darius's sixth year (515 BC).

Little is known about Sheshbazzar; no genealogy is given about him. He is often identified with Shenazzar, a son of Jehoiachin (1 Chr 3, 18), but this identification has little support. As a prince over Judah he could have been a member of the royal family, as Zerubbabel probably was, but he could simply be a leader of the people. He is called a governor just as Zerubbabel is later called. What happened to Sheshbazzar is also unknown. He probably did begin to rebuild the Temple, laying only the foundation. His leadership might have come to an end with his failure to rebuild the Temple, or in the wake of the tur-moil associated with Darius's usurpation of the Persian throne. Zerubbabel is the grandson of Jehoiachin, Judah's last king, though some scholars suggest that this is a fiction of the biblical writer. Like Sheshbazzar, he was appointed governor of Judah. When he was appointed governor is never stated in the text, although Haggai first mentions him in reference to Darius's second year (520 BC). Although he was the civil administrator of Judah, only his work in rebuilding the Temple is recorded. Once the Temple is rebuilt, no more is heard about him.

The second period that the biblical evidence addresses is the period of Ezra and Nehemiah. The relationship of these two reformers poses a significant historical problem. The stories of Ezra and Nehemiah have been artificially joined. Part of the story of Ezra has been inserted into the middle of Nehemiah's story (Neh 8—9). The biblical text places Ezra first, followed by Nehemiah, but this relationship could be artificial. The text claims that Ezra's mission began in the seventh year of Artaxerxes, whereas Nehemiah's mission began in Artaxerxes' twentieth year, but several kings by this name ruled Persia. The date of Nehemiah's mission is fairly certain. He became governor over Judah in the twentieth year of Artaxerxes I (465–424 BC), thus in 445 BC. This date is independently confirmed by a letter from the Judean community in Elephantine, Egypt, dated 25 November 407 BC, at which time a certain Bagoas was governor over Judah, referring to Delaiah and Shelemiah, the sons of Sanballat, a contemporary of Nehemiah. Nehemiah's term of office lasted until 433 BC, at which time he was recalled to the Persian court. He was appointed for a second term some time before 424 BC, the end of Artaxerxes' reign, and served as governor until some time before 411 BC, at which time Bagoas is governor.

If Ezra's mission is to be dated to the seventh year of Artaxerxes I, then his mission began in 458 BC. This relationship, however, poses several problems. The high priest Jehohanan, the grandson of Eliashib who was a contemporary of Nehemiah, is mentioned in relation to Ezra, but the Elephantine texts place him in Judah around 407 BC. The names of the high priests in the preserved lists have been corrupted because of repetition (several men named Jehohanan son of Eliashib served as high priest), thus this evidence is not conclusive. If Ezra preceded Nehemiah, then his reform does not appear to have been successful, for when Nehemiah comes on to the scene the problems addressed by Ezra continue to exist. Moreover, Nehemiah never mentions Ezra and blames his predecessors for the corrupt situation in Judah (in Neh 8, 9 the two are mentioned together, but this is clearly the result of editorial activity). Scholars have also noted that during Ezra's time Jerusalem is occupied and surrounded by a wall (Ezr 9, 9), but in Nehemiah's time Jerusalem is unoccupied and its wall has been torn down. From Nehemiah's perspective, Jerusalem could have recently been destroyed during the revolt of Megbyzus, the satrap of Abar-nahara (of which Judah was a part) in 449/8 BC, but no evidence clearly attests to this. As a result of these problems, many scholars prefer to date Ezra to the reign of Artaxerxes II (404–358 BC). Ezra's mission would then have begun in 398/7 BC, after Nehemiah. However, the biblical order of placing Ezra's mission during the reign of Artaxerxes I cannot be ruled out.

The Hellenistic and Roman Periods

The sources for understanding the history of Israel during the Hellenistic (332–63 BC) and Roman (63 BC–AD 70) periods are many, though few texts in the Bible provide much information regarding the political history of the periods. The primary biblical source for the Hellenistic period is 1 Maccabees. This book, written in the style of the book of Kings, tells of the struggle of Mattathias and his sons against the Seleucid king Antiochus IV Epiphanes and his heirs, which has come to be known as the Maccabean revolt after the name of Mattathias's eldest son, Judah Maccabee. The book is clearly biased on behalf of the Hasmoneans (as the descendants of Mattathias are known), and it seeks to legitimate the rule of John Hyrcanus and his sons, but it nevertheless preserves much historical information about the period. The other biblical books that address the period of the Maccabean revolt are Daniel and 2 Maccabees. The visions of Daniel (7—12) were composed during the revolt and thus provide the most immediate view of the events. The historical contribution of the visions, however, is in places obscured by figurative and cryptic language. 2 Maccabees, an abridgement of a five-volume history by Jason of Cyrene, covers a more limited period of time than 1 Maccabees (it ends with the death of Judas), but provides a greater depth of coverage and includes material not mentioned in 1 Maccabees. Second Maccabees is particularly valuable for its description of the Hellenistic reform, the events leading up to the revolt, especially the life and murder of Onias III, and the relations between Jerusalem and the Egyptian Diaspora.

All the books of the New Testament were written during the Roman period, but their focus is on the teaching and ministry of Jesus (Gospels) and the early church (Epistles), and they give an uneven picture of the larger Judean and Roman world in which they are set. The Gospels do not present a life of Jesus; the specific framework of the story of Jesus has been shaped by the particular focus of each evangelist. Jesus' cleansing of the Temple, for example, occurs early in his ministry in John, but during the Passion Week in Matthew, Mark, and Luke. Nevertheless, the Gospels provide information about the historical geography of Palestine, the local administration, and numerous social customs. The Epistles present an incomplete picture of the local churches to which they were written, but rarely do they address events or issues of the larger Roman world. Only the Acts of the Apostles, which presents a history of the early church, provides substantial information on the Judean and Roman world. The Acts of the Apostles also presents interesting details about a number of persons who are known from other sources: Herod Agrippa I, Herod Agrippa II, the Roman procurators Felix and Festus, and the proconsul Gallio of Achaia.

The classical authors who provide information on Judea during this period include Diodorus Siculus, Polybius, Nicholas of Damascus, Strabo, Pliny the Elder, Tacitus, Suetonius, and Dio Cassius. Two significant Jewish authors are Philo of Alexandria and Flavius Josephus. In *In Flaccum* and *Legatio ad Gaium,* Philo describes the persecutions of the Jews during the reign of Gaius Caligula, which he personally witnessed. Josephus' works, *The Jewish War* and *Jewish Antiquities*, give detailed information about the Hasmoneans, the Herodians, and the events leading up to and the consequences of the Judean revolt against Rome. Other notable sources for this period are the Zenon papyri, which attest to the administration of Judea when it was under Ptolemaic control, and the Dead Sea Scrolls, which attest to the religious diversity of the Roman period.

The archaeology of this period is dominated by the many monumental building projects sponsored by Herod the Great. In addition to the rebuilding and expansion of the Temple in Jerusalem, for which he is most known, Herod founded the port city of Caesarea Maritima on the coast south of Carmel. He rebuilt Samaria, renaming it Sebaste in honor of Augustus. He rebuilt Jericho. Both Caesarea and Sebaste included Roman-style temples dedicated to the emperor. Herod built palaces at Caesarea and at Herodian Jericho. Herod also built or rebuilt several fortresses in the Judean wilderness: Machaerus, the Herodium, and Masada. Although Herod's temple in Jerusalem was thoroughly destroyed by the Romans in AD 70 in the wake of the Judean revolt, the present Temple Mount preserves much of the platform on which Herod's temple was built. South and west of the Temple Mount, Herodian construction associated with the Temple has been uncovered: stone-paved streets with shops and piers supporting staircases to the Temple, a royal stoa, and a monumental staircase leading up to the western Double Gate and the eastern Triple Gate. West of the Temple, in the present Jewish Quarter, excavations have uncovered several large, well-decorated houses with mosaic floors and luxurious stone objects (tables, bowls, and jars). The houses were destroyed by the Romans when Titus sacked Jerusalem in AD 70. These houses attest to the affluence of Jerusalem during this period and to the violence of the Judean revolt.

Other notable archaeological sites during this period include Capernaum, Chorazin, Bethsaida, Sepphoris, and Qumran. At Capernaum and Chorazin, two towns on the northern side of the Sea of Galilee in which Jesus taught, early examples of Jewish synagogues have survived. The synagogues date to the first or second century AD, but at Capernaum traces of an earlier synagogue that dates to the period of Jesus lie beneath the later well-preserved synagogue. Also, at Capernaum the excavators have uncovered a house that Byzantine Christians identified as the house of Peter, for they built on the site a large octagon-shaped church (similar in form to the Byzantine church built at Caesarea on top of the ruins of Herod's temple to Augustus and to the Dome of the Rock on the Temple Mount). At Bethsaida, the Galilean home of several of Jesus' disciples, the excavators have uncovered several large first-century homes. In one of the homes numerous fishing implements were discovered. Sepphoris is a large Roman city with a theatre approximately four miles from Nazareth. The city was rebuilt by Antipas during Jesus' youth, and Joseph, perhaps accompanied by Jesus, would probably have been employed in its construction (the Greek term used for Joseph's occupation, *tekton,* may refer to someone who works with either wood or stone). Although it is never mentioned in the New Testament, the cultural life of Sepphoris would have been well known to Jesus. The use of the word *hypocrite* by Jesus in the Gospels, which refers to a stage actor who plays a role for an audience's approval, perhaps derives from Jesus' familiarity with the theatre of Sepphoris. The identification of the community that lived at Qumran has been debated by scholars. Although some would identify the buildings as part of a large Roman villa, the site is generally recognized as the remains of the Essene community responsible for authoring and preserving the Dead Sea Scrolls.

CATHOLIC INTERPRETATION OF THE BIBLE

KEVIN MADIGAN

The Early Church (ca. AD 100–500)

The early Catholic interpretation of the Bible, like Christianity itself, did not emerge or develop in a religious, cultural, or intellectual void. Instead, it was formed and influenced by two antecedent interpretive traditions, one Greco-Roman, the other Jewish.

The Greco-Roman tradition traces its origins back at least to the sixth century BC. This tradition originated with the followers of the brilliant Pythagoras of Samos. The Pythagoreans focused their interpretive attention upon the epic poetry of Homer, and their Platonic and Stoic successors on other classics of the Greco-Roman tradition. Confident that the poets had written under inspiration as theologians, so to speak, these interpreters concluded that great poetry was about deep cosmological and ethical realities. Accordingly, they developed a philosophy or method of interpretation called *allegoria* (allegory). Using this technique, Greek and Roman interpreters of classical literature claimed to find the deep meaning intended by the author. This meaning was usually hidden by the surface language of the poet, which could be crudely literal, enigmatic, superficially trivial, or otherwise intellectually or morally offensive. All assumed, in fact, that the literal meaning was an impediment to the "real," deep, and true (or truer) meaning of the text.

Similar assumptions and methods passed over into Diaspora Judaism no later than the turn of the first century BC and were used in the interpretation of the Septuagint, notably with the ascetic Therapeutae. Without doubt, the preemi-

nent practitioner of the allegorical method in Hellenistic Judaism was Philo of Alexandria (20 BC–AD 50). With non-Jewish Hellenistic interpreters, he shared several crucial assumptions: that the text (the Septuagint) was divinely inspired and thus permanently normative; that it contained deeper truths than those expressed superficially and contained a spiritual sense above or beyond the literal-historical; that the deeper truths were present especially where the text was, or seemed, irrational, ambiguous, absurd, sacrilegious, or otherwise difficult; and that such truths could be understood by the interpreter skilled in allegory. In addition, it was Philo's conviction that such truths were consistent with the highest insights of Stoic and Platonic thought, so that the allegorist in some sense "rewrote" the sacred text so as to harmonize it with these insights. Yet Philo insisted on literal adherence to Torah. He also observed that some texts (e.g., Nm 23, 19: "God is not like a man") were literally clear and therefore required no allegorical gloss. On several very important Christian exegetes also from Alexandria, especially Clement and Origen (who was very conscious of and explicit about his debt to Philo), Philonic hermeneutics would exercise a profound influence, which would then be felt for more than a millennium in both Eastern and Western Christianity.

With Philo and, indeed, with all contemporary Jews, the earliest Christian community agreed that "the Scriptures" referred to a collection of authoritative Jewish writings, namely that collection of writings Christians today refer to as the Old Testament. With Hellenistic Jews, early

54

Christians also shared the methodological conviction that the Scriptures could be (and sometimes should be) permitted to say things other than that which the words seemed to suggest or require.

In the application of this principle, of course, early Christians parted company with contemporary Jews. This is because the earliest Christians rapidly took those authoritative Jewish writings to attest typologically to the eschatological events that had occurred in the life, death, and resurrection of Jesus of Nazareth. That is, early Christians interpreted the events of Israelite history as *types*—intentional figural prophecies expressed in the spiritual sense of the text and recognized as prophetic only in the light of later events—of the decisive redemptive actions taken by God in the life of Jesus. Thus, typology (a form of allegory) grew up with Christianity as a hermeneutical method. (Such a hermeneutic is in evidence no later than the letters of Paul, e.g., in 1 Cor 10, 6 and Rom 5, 4). Indeed, it enabled Christians to understand the events of Christ, especially the problem of a crucified Messiah, in terms prefigured in the Hebrew Scriptures. Accordingly, it was crucial to the project of emerging Christian and ecclesiastical self-definition. That Christian typology required a thoroughgoing reinterpretation of the Scriptures the community shared with contemporary Jewish exegetes and practitioners goes without saying.

This is not to say that all early Christians, or all who so identified themselves, were comfortable with the typological method and the practical exegetical results its application effected. Some were not. Few were more uncomfortable than Marcion of Pontus, a layman of formidable wealth and missionary zeal. After having worked among the Roman Christians (ca. 144), Marcion founded a church based, exegetically, on the rejection of the typological method and of the Hebrew Scriptures and of the God revealed therein. He composed a *canon*, perhaps the first composed by any Christian, consisting solely of an expurgated version of the Gospel of Luke and a collection of ten Pauline letters. Had Marcion's position carried the day, the Old Testament would have ceased to be an arsenal of proof text to be used, in conjunction with the words of the evangelists and Paul, to establish the messiahship of Jesus. However quaint and occasion-

ally even disrespectful typological exegesis sounds to a postcritical and ecumenical age, it did preserve the Hebrew Scriptures for the use of the church.

Eventually, Marcion's views (as well as those of Gnostic Christians who also rejected the Hebrew Scriptures) were condemned by the mainstream or emerging "Catholic" Church. But Marcion's views gave considerable impetus to the formation within this Catholic Church of an authoritative list of scriptural writings. Within decades of Marcion's death—certainly no later than AD 180—the Catholic Church had composed a list, a canon, of authoritative Scriptures that resembled very closely the contents of this Study Bible. It included an "Old Testament," understood now as a collection of writings pointing typologically beyond itself to Christ, and a "New Testament." The former was the Greek Septuagint, which included the Apocrypha, books not allowed by the rabbis into the Jewish canon in the first two centuries after Jesus' birth. The contents of the latter were very much like those of our Greek New Testament, though writings later listed in the canon (e.g., James, Hebrews) were not then included.

For the remainder of the second century, the Bible was exploited above all in polemical writing against Jewish and heretical interlocutors (sometimes imaginatively configured). While these Catholic polemicists hardly ignored the New Testament, the Hebrew Bible was, as it were, the turf on which such battles were fought. Typology was the most frequently wielded arrow in the Catholic exegete's quiver. In his *Dialogue with Trypho the Jew* (ca. 160), for example, Justin Martyr attempted to demonstrate that Christ's life and especially crucifixion had been copiously, almost ubiquitously, foreshadowed in the Hebrew Scriptures. So intent was Justin on proving that the cross had been prefigured there that he found types of it in virtually any reference or allusion to wood, beginning with the Tree of Life in Genesis.

Aside from being an accomplished practitioner of the typological method, Bishop Irenaeus of Lyons (fl. 170–80) established a crucially influential principle of correct interpretation of the Bible. Dubbed by R. M. Grant "the father of authoritative exegesis in the church" and often recognized to be a father of early Catholicism,

Irenaeus argued (particularly against heretics) that only bishops in an unbroken line of succession from the apostles were to be counted as trusted interpreters. From this principle, it followed that authoritative interpretation was to be found solely within the walls of the churches and, more precisely, in those churches that could trace their origins to the apostles and whose episcopal successors had, in addition, produced short creeds to summarize the main events of salvation history contained in the Scriptures. These creeds (or rules of faith) could then be used (circularly, it might be observed) to test the orthodoxy of any scriptural interpretation.

In the Catholic interpretation of Scripture and above all in hermeneutical theory, Origen of Alexandria (ca. 185–253) towers over the third century. The fourth book of his masterwork, *On First Principles,* is dedicated solely to a theory of biblical interpretation; it is a deeply influential manifesto of Christian allegoresis. Origen's basic presumption, like that of his fellow Alexandrians, not least of all Philo, is that the Scriptures are intended to reveal not simply the historical events of salvation history but deep spiritual, theological, and cosmological truths. Such truths are revealed above all where the literal sense says things unworthy of the Deity (God planting a garden, for example), or impossible (three "days" of creation without any natural body of light), or inconsistent. (Origen was deeply impressed with the inconsistency of, among other things, the Passion and Resurrection accounts, from which he concluded they must each intend a deeper spiritual meaning.) In some cases, a biblical passage will have no literal sense. But *all* passages have a deeper spiritual sense, to which the interpreter is clued by the "stumbling blocks" of an illogical or absurd "letter." Such texts invite the skilled exegete to unearth the spiritual treasure buried below, and Origen gives quite specific rules about how to uncover this camouflaged meaning. He encourages the exegete to "search the scriptures" (Jn 5, 39) and establish the meaning of difficult passages by clear ones (a method that of course presupposed the unity of the biblical witness) and by paying attention to context and to etymology. Echoing Irenaeus, he also adds (perhaps less enthusiastically than the Bishop of Lyon) that the meaning of Scripture can be established by use of the church's Rule of

Faith. These reflections made Origen by far the most sophisticated theoretician of interpretation in ancient Christianity. He was, in addition, an enormously prolific exegete. Not to be overlooked is his *Hexapla* (sixfold), an edition of the Hebrew Scriptures which contained, in six parallel columns, one version of the Old Testament in Hebrew, one of the transliterated Hebrew, and four, including the Septuagint, in Greek. This might be called the first attempt in ecclesiastical history at textual criticism of the Hebrew Scriptures. His influence on late-antique and medieval exegetes, especially those sympathetic to allegorical interpretation (like the fourth-century Cappadocian fathers, Gregory of Nyssa and Basil), would be, if indirect, immense.

Not all were sympathetic. (We remember here Marcion.) If Alexandria nourished its scholars on allegoresis, the biblical exegetes in the important city of Antioch tended to stress the fundamental importance of the literal and historical sense of the text. According to Eusebius, the Antiochene exegetes, represented typically by John Chrysostom (407), interpreted the text "with moderation"— that is, unallegorically. This is not to say Antiochene exegetes denied that the sacred text had a higher meaning. It is to say that they were nervous about allegory. In their view, allegory simply made the text a springboard for unrestrained flights of speculation that left the natural, obvious, or contextual meaning of the text far from view. For the deeper meaning of the text, they preferred the term *theoria.* Their leader, Diodore of Tarsus (d. 390), actually composed a text titled *On the Difference between Theoria and Allegoria.* Two others, Eustathius, Bishop of Antioch, and Diodore's pupil Theodore of Mopsuestia (d. 428), wrote tracts on the same topic with the same unambiguous title—*Against Origen.*

As it turns out, the difference is largely one of emphasis, with the Antiochene school typically stressing the need to ground the higher meaning of the text in its foundational historical meaning, or at least not be opposed to it. Both men were concerned that allegoresis actually robbed the text of the meaning it purported to uncover by plunging and thus dissolving it into the murky, seemingly undisciplined universe of discourse of "spiritual understanding." (The Antiochenes would have vibrated sympathetically to von Harnack's complaint about Origen's "biblical alchemy.") Neither Antiochene was as apprehensive about, in his understandable preoccupation with the historicity of the text, what was for Origen and his Alexandrian peers the sometimes disturbingly anthropomorphic, mythical fabric of the biblical narrative. Looking ahead, one could say, somewhat simply, that in the early Latin West, the Alexandrian tradition would certainly carry the day, while in the high Middle Ages, with the reintroduction of Aristotle, the Antiochene tradition asserted its supremacy.

Even as no scholar of the fourth century did as much to explicate and make available the Bible to contemporaries, no figure exemplified ambivalence to the allegorical approach more than the great Jerome (ca. 340–420). His early commentarial efforts are highly allegorical. Later, he came under the influence of the Antiochene school through Apollinaris of Laodicea (d. ca. 390), who was later condemned for Christological heresy at the second ecumenical council of Constantinople (381). At that point, Jerome stated his desire to avoid excessive allegoresis, going so far as to claim he allegorized only when he could not determine the literal sense of a passage. However, this claim was purely theoretical, as his voluminous commentaries are replete with allegorical interpretation, about much of which, at the end of his life, he finally expressed regret.

It is difficult to imagine that such a man as Jerome could look back on his career at all ruefully. He was without doubt the greatest scholar of the fourth century. His knowledge of the history, geography, and philology of Palestine was simply unrivaled. He wrote capaciously on the Bible; indeed, he was the most prolific commentator of his day. In 382 Pope Damasus commissioned him to translate the Bible into Latin. The result was the Vulgate *(editio vulgata),* a Latin Bible translated from the original languages. To this day, it remains the edition of the Bible that has perhaps been most widely read in the West, where it had tremendous influence on language, liturgy, art, architecture, literature, politics, and theology.

One can hardly make mention of the Latin West without speaking of the importance of the North African tradition. It was there, probably by the end of the second century, that the first translation of the Bible into Latin was made, and we know there were several such translations.

Tertullian quotes from these old Latin versions as, in the mid-third century, does Bishop Cyprian of Carthage (d. 258) and as Augustine would as well. A contemporary of Jerome, Tyconius (d. ca. 400) authored the first tract on the theory of interpretation in the West worthy of comparison to Origen's. This *Liber Regularum* (Book of Rules) set out, as its title suggests, a set of principles (seven in all) for interpreting Scripture. One of the most important is that when Scripture speaks of the *head* of the church, it refers also to its *body.* In this way, statements made about Christ could be understood to refer to the church in the present age as well. Tyconius also authored a very influential commentary on the Apocalypse, which shifted the exegetical tradition away from the historic millenarian reading of the book.

Tyconius's influence was nowhere more deeply felt than in the writings of his fellow North African, Augustine of Hippo (354–430). Indeed, the influence of Tyconius on the greatest of Latin doctors has not always been recognized or conceded, because the former was a member of the schismatic Donatist church, which Augustine spent much of his life quite fiercely denouncing. But upon inspection of Augustine's own hermeneutical theory as it is expressed in his classic *On Christian Doctrine,* it will be obvious that Tyconius's influence was profound. It was felt in the wide circulation in the Middle Ages not only of Augustine's book on Christian teaching but of his own *Book of Rules,* both of which were recommended by no less a figure than Cassiodorus (d. 580).

When speaking of Augustine, it is impossible not to mention the decisive influence in his life as well as work of the allegorical method. Indeed, it might easily be said that, but for that method, Augustine might never have been baptized. It was only in the wake of hearing the Old Testament interpreted allegorically by Bishop Ambrose of Milan (ca. 339–97) that Augustine felt ready to convert. Until then, Augustine, nurtured on the classics of Roman literature, had regarded the Old Testament with a feeling bordering on contempt. Allegory enabled him to understand the Hebrew Scriptures in a new way and to harmonize them, as had Ambrose, with the Neoplatonic philosophy on which he had also been nourished. Like Origen, he offered copious guidance on how to treat difficult passages (and his advice is remarkably like Origen's). Augustine insists, as had Irenaeus, Tertullian, and Origen, on the utility of the church's Rule of Faith. But he also adds that all Scripture is to be interpreted in light of the Law of Love, so that *any* interpretation that contributed to the Reign of Charity should command assent. Augustine is also capable of sounding eerily modern, as when, in his *Harmony of the Gospels,* he is prepared to concede that the narratives in the Gospels reflect recorded community memory rather than accurate chronological narrative history. Augustine also acknowledged that Jesus' words were not always recorded verbatim; it was their sense that was communicated accurately to posterity.

The question of how many senses of Scripture there were, and what each meant, achieved authoritative definition at the end of the ancient period in Christianity in the writings of the monk John Cassian (360–435). Most ancient commentators worked with the practical distinction between literal and spiritual senses. Origen had theoretically designated three senses: literal, moral, and spiritual (*On First Principles* 4.2.4), though scrutiny of his surviving commentaries indicates he did not follow this principle slavishly. In his *Conferences,* Cassian became the first to argue that, theoretically, Scripture contained or expressed four senses: literal, allegorical, moral or tropological, and anagogical or eschatological. Eventually, this understanding was versified as follows:

Littera gesta docet, quid credas allegoria,
Moralia quid agas, quo tendas anagogia.

This little couplet basically meant that the literal sense has to do with the history of God's redemptive activity, the allegorical level with articles of belief, the moral with ethical behavior, and the anagogical with one's eternal destiny. Thus, for example, when Jerusalem is mentioned in the Bible, it would refer literally to the earthly city, allegorically to the church, morally to the soul, and anagogically to the heavenly city. Cassian's *Conferences* was one of the few texts recommended in the *Rule of Benedict.* As a consequence, his theory was absorbed in Benedictine cloisters in the early Middle Ages and passed on to interpreters for a millennium. Again, few interpreters applied this principle mechanically; many were content to distinguish in their commentaries between two or sometimes three senses.

When we survey the history of the Catholic use of Scripture in early Christianity, two important truths emerge. First, theology and scriptural interpretation were virtually one and the same activity. At the least, theology invariably began as exegesis. Second, the allegorical method, which the church did not invent, had been appropriated and baptized by it. All Christian interpreters recognized that allegory (or, with the Antiochenes, *theoria*) gave the church access to a meaning that was not frozen in time or fixed. With the allegorical method, the church had inherited, and had brilliantly exploited, a way of making the Scriptures inexhaustible. To it the ancients had bequeathed a means by which, until the modern era, it could make the Scriptures perennially relevant, above all, perhaps, in preaching.

The Medieval Era (ca. 500–1500)

One can hardly mention Benedict and early medieval monasticism without at least noting how central was the role of the Bible in the monastic life. Monastic prayer began with the *lectio divina* (divine reading) of Scripture and continued with meditation upon it. Monks were utterly immersed in the language, imagery, and thought-world of the Scriptures. So often and so carefully did they read and so assiduously ruminate upon certain parts of Scripture (the Psalter, for example) that such texts became a fundamental mark of their spiritual and mental experience. As Jean Leclercq has shown, monastic culture was a profoundly scriptural one. Monastic education was oriented almost exclusively to the ability to read and understand Scripture. In addition, early medieval scholarship on Scripture was produced almost exclusively in monastic scriptoria and by monks. One thinks of the Venerable Bede (ca. 673–735) in Northumbria, Pope Gregory the Great (590–604) in Rome, and a whole succession of eighth- and ninth-century Frankish monks, including Rabanus Maurus, Walafrid Strabo, Alcuin, Haimo, and Remigius of Auxerre, Paschasius Radbertus, to mention only a few of the most accomplished. In short, Catholic scholarship on the Bible took place almost exclusively in the setting of the monastic cloister.

It would be difficult to exaggerate the awe with which such monks beheld the patristic tradition of exegesis. Few would have dared to think of a scriptural book other than *in sensu patrum*—"in the sense of the Fathers." So understood, scholarship was prized not for novelty but for fidelity to the received tradition. Early medieval biblical scholarship was therefore traditionalist and conservative in nature. The early medieval period was, in terms of biblical scholarship, an age of compilation, not innovation. In the eighth and ninth centuries, Frankish biblical scholars produced commentaries that were, by and large, syntheses of venerable authorities. Very few dared personal commentary on the received wisdom of the Fathers. The main objective, particularly in the Carolingian era, was the transmission of patristic extracts (technically known as *florilegia*) that were authentic and otherwise reliable. Such collections are dominated by the Latin fathers, especially by Jerome, Ambrose, Augustine, and Gregory the Great. Such exposure to the Greek fathers (especially Origen) as was communicated to Western readers was achieved, largely, by presentation of the Latin fathers (like Hilary of Poitiers, Ambrose, Jerome, and Gregory) by whom they were influenced.

Most ages in church history can be identified by their interest in some discrete collection of scriptural writings, usually reflecting the theological and ecclesiological interests of the time. In the early Middle Ages, the Scriptures most used and commented were those holding a central role in monastic liturgy and thought and, to a lesser extent, doctrinal theology: the Psalter, the Song of Songs, Genesis, Paul, and Matthew (the one Gospel, curiously, that received widespread commentarial attention in the early Middle Ages). Leclercq has rightly emphasized that, for the entirety of the early Middle Ages, there is a strong and consistent link between the Bible and prayer (private and public) and, indeed, that such a link is *the* common characteristic of the use of the Bible in this period.

One of the great achievements in biblical scholarship in the early Middle Ages was the production of a standard or *Ordinary Gloss* (*Glossa Ordinaria*) of patristic commentary on the entire Bible. Nonetheless, its origins, authorship, and history of the *Gloss* have long remained obscure. Thanks to the researches of Beryl Smalley and others, we are now better in-

formed about such questions. First of all, none of the *Gloss* was produced in a Carolingian monastic setting—the so-called marginal gloss had long been attributed to the monk Walafrid of Strabo (d. ca. 850)—as had long been presupposed. Instead, it was begun in the cathedral school of Laon in the early twelfth century, at which time it, and the theological scene in Europe, was dominated by the brothers Anselm (d. 1117) and Ralph (d. ca. 1135), though the very earliest glosses on the Bible appeared in the late eighth century in England and Ireland. The former probably glossed the Psalter, Paul, and the Gospel of John; the latter the Gospel of Matthew. Others, including Gilbert the Universal, glossed much of the Hebrew Scriptures, including the Pentateuch. The entire collaborative project was completed no later than the first quarter of the thirteenth century. It usually appeared with the biblical text as a "glossed Bible," with short interlinear comments and longer marginal comments, usually of patristic origin, a form that is similar to contemporary Jewish commentary on the Talmud. Distributed in large numbers from a center in Paris, it was probably the most widely read and influential commentary on the Bible from the time of its widespread circulation ca. 1220 until the seventeenth century.

Over the course of the century that produced these two textbooks, running commentaries on the Bible came more and more to be disrupted by the introduction of theological issues or questions *(quaestiones)*. Eventually, these questions were grouped together and finally broke off from their original commentarial context altogether to form textbooks of doctrinal theology. The classic in this genre is, without doubt, Peter Lombard's *Book of Sentences*. Late in the twelfth century, scholastic masters began lecturing on the Lombard independently of the sacred page *(sacra pagina)*—the Vulgate page that had been established as a set text in the schools. This is a development of some moment. Aside from signaling the growing hegemony of the schools and the eclipse of monastic biblical scholarship and emerging universities in theological discourse, it indicates the beginning of the separation of biblical and theological studies, heretofore conceived as a single discipline.

It was, however, in the famous house of canons of St. Victor in Paris that hermeneutical and exegetical developments of great importance occurred in the twelfth century. In Hugh (d. 1141) and Andrew of St. Victor (d. 1175), the Middle Ages are sometime said to have received, respectively, their own Augustine (the former for his *Didascalicon,* often called a reworking of Augustine's *De Doctrina Christian*) and Jerome (the latter for his immense erudition, knowledge of Hebrew, and concentration on the literal-historical sense). From these men came important new reflections on the primacy and content of the primary or literal sense of Scripture, reflections that would gesture toward the ways in which biblical scholarship would change in the schools and universities and in a time during which Aristotle was being reabsorbed in Western Europe.

Like some of the Antiochenes, Hugh wrote a tract (in his case an imaginative debate) on the relationship of the literal and allegorical sense. There he described the operation of the allegorical sense with considerable precision. It was not, he argued, the language or words of Scripture that expressed the allegorical meaning, but those things to which the words pointed; the figurative meaning of the text, if such it has, belongs to the literal sense. (This was to be an issue taken up, and resolved definitively for Catholic exegesis for centuries, by St. Thomas Aquinas.) It was, he argued, on this spiritual plane or level of exegesis that the unity of Scripture was contained. It could not be on the level of the literal sense, for it was all too plain that the literal sense contradicted itself in scores of places in the Scriptures.

However, Hugh was adamant that the literal sense was of foundational importance for the allegorical sense, and he rebukes unrestrained allegorists with some sarcasm. In his book *De Scripturis,* he observes:

> I wonder how people have the face to boast themselves teachers of allegory, when they do not know the primary meaning of the letter. . . . How do you read Scripture then, if you don't read the letter? Subtract the letter and what is left?

Hugh even dares to deny Christological interpretations of texts that had long received such interpretations. Given his preoccupation with the importance of the literal sense, it is interesting to observe that Hugh was among those exegetes in twelfth-century Europe that were first to have forged ties with the Jewish exegetical community. Hugh was convinced that Jewish exegesis of the Hebrew Scriptures furnished the most literal sense of the text, and for that reason often quoted the great Jewish exegete Rabbi Solomon bar Isaac of Troyes ("Rashi," 1040–1105) as an authoritative guide to the literal sense.

If the Victorine Richard (d. 1173) undertook to refute some of Hugh's ideas, Hugh's promise was, as Beryl Smalley observed, fulfilled in the Victorine Andrew, whose obscurity she did much to overcome and on whose significance she wrote a long chapter in her groundbreaking (if not uncontroversial) book, *The Study of the Bible in the Middle Ages* (finished in 1940), which, as it were, invented the field of the study of medieval exegesis.

Andrew is without question the hero of Smalley's book, and it is because he concentrates on the historical and literal sense to the explicit exclusion of the doctrinal and moral. In this, he was quite aware that he was embarking on something new in the Middle Ages. Or, to put it another way, he saw himself continuing the work of St. Jerome. Of Andrew, Smalley observes, "No western commentator before him had set out to give a purely literal interpretation of the Old Testament." For his access to the literal truth of the Hebrew Scriptures (Andrew commented on the Pentateuch, Joshua, Judges, many of the Prophets, and some of the wisdom literature), he, too, relied on the school of Rashi. Like Hugh, he simply felt that the "Jewish explanation" of the text *was* the literal sense of the text. To the extent that he was preoccupied with establishing the literal sense of Scripture, he made extraordinary and unprecedented use of Jewish exegesis by making contact with the communities most influenced by Rashi.

One of the several other twelfth-century exegetes worthy of mention alongside Hugh of St. Victor, by whom he was influenced, is Peter Comestor or Manducator (d. ca. 1179), dean of the cathedral of Troyes and chancellor of the University of Paris. The name means "Peter the Eater," which he earned for having absorbed all of the Scriptures. His most enduring contribution to the understanding of the Scriptures was a work titled the *Historia scholastica.* This was an epitome (depending on some non-Christian authors, like Josephus) of biblical history from Creation to the events narrated in the Acts of the Apostles. As such, it fulfilled the requirements of Hugh of

St. Victor's *Didascalicon,* which called for a foundational knowledge of biblical history. It also relied heavily (though anonymously) on the commentaries of Andrew and so was in a double sense a child of the great abbey of St. Victor. Like the *Gloss,* it became a standard textbook. Judging from the number of manuscripts and early printed editions made of it, it remained very popular through the fifteenth century.

Another disciple of Andrew, perhaps the finest biblical scholar of the twelfth century, was Stephen Langton (d. 1228). Perhaps his most important contribution to biblical scholarship was the production of a new edition of the Bible. This edition was important because it divided the entire Bible into chapters (ca. 1200); Thomas Gallus (d. 1246) would later divide it into verses. This was the edition that was to become standard at Paris, and, as such, became the one used in the new university setting of the thirteenth century. The early thirteenth century was, among other things, an age in which several aids to biblical study were produced. Once Langton's Bible had been produced, with its chapter references, it was possible to produce a concordance, and indeed a concordance to the Latin of the Vulgate was produced ca. 1235 in the new Dominican priory of St. Jacques in Paris.

It was in the very different monastic setting of southern Italy that the highly innovative exegesis of Joachim of Fiore set exegesis on a radically different path—deplored once by Smalley, an enthusiast for Andrew and literal exegesis, as an attack of "senile dementia" in the spiritual sense, a prime example of the "spiritual sense in decline"—than that recommended by the great Victorines and early friars of Paris. Born in 1135 in Celico, Joachim entered the Benedictine abbey at Corazzo in 1171, of which he became prior, then abbot (ca. 1176–77). Multiple visions at the Cistercian Abbey of Casamari in 1183–84 revealed to him the fullness and harmony *(concordia)* of the Scriptures and the mystery of the Trinity. Convinced that the inner mystery of God's existence as a Trinity of Persons was linked with the structure of history, Joachim, pondering the Scriptures, saw salvation history unfolding in terms of three successive, overlapping ages *(status),* each primarily under the aegis of one of the persons of the Trinity. Thus Joachim postulates a status of the Father, of the

Son, and of the Holy Spirit, the last about to dawn.

This intricate theology of history is based on an equally complex hermeneutical theory. For Joachim, one of the major objectives of scriptural exegesis was to demonstrate the numerous literal parallels or concordances *(concordiae)* between Old Testament history and New. These *concordiae* not only shed light on the past but were also capable of revealing the future. The gifted exegete could see in both Testaments (above all in the book of Revelation) sets of concordances, which enabled him not merely to understand the first two *status* more fully but to predict the structure and meaning of the dawning third *status* of history. Joachim's exegesis was to have profound influence not only on the Franciscans of the subsequent century, who saw in Francis a herald in the new age of history just then dawning, but on many exegetes and many secular thinkers down to the twentieth century.

If Bonaventure and other Franciscan exegetes such as Peter Olivi (d. 1298) enthusiastically capitalized on Joachite hermeneutics in their own exegetical works, their Dominican confreres emphatically did not. Probably the greatest early Dominican exegete was the prolific Hugh of St. Cher (d. 1263). Intended to supplement the *Glossa Ordinaria,* his massive *Postillae in Totam Bibliam*—which relied heavily on Stephen Langton and his moralizing exegesis—was almost certainly compiled as the work of a Dominican "team" of exegetes at St. Jacques. Nonetheless, the postilla (or commentary, from the words *post illa* [*verba?*] "after those [scriptural] words"), which was a continuous gloss on every book of the Bible, bore his signature. This postilla would exercise enormous influence on contemporary exegetes (such as Bonaventure and his fellow Dominicans Albert the Great and St. Thomas Aquinas). Hugh and his collaborators also produced a *Correctorium Bibliae.* In this work, alternative readings of the Vulgate were established in an attempt to establish an authoritative text.

Hugh's fellow Dominican Thomas Aquinas is today renowned as the author of the *Summa Theologiae* and the scholastic theologian whose work was declared normative by Pope Leo XIII in 1879. Less well known is that, as part of his duties, first at Cologne, then later at Paris, he was required to lecture on the Bible. The result was a series of commentaries on Job, the Psalter, the Song of Songs, Isaiah, Jeremiah, Lamentations, Matthew, John, and the Pauline letters. Some of these exist as versions edited by Thomas, others in student lecture-notes *(reportationes)*, while others still (like the commentary on the Canticum) have been lost. Thomas also produced, at the behest of Pope Urban IV, a continuous gloss on all four Gospels. This *Catena Aurea* (Golden Chain) of mostly patristic excerpts, including an extraordinary number of Greek ones, had influence on commentaries on the Gospels down to the nineteenth century, when it was edited by Cardinal Newman, though it had its greatest impact in the Middle Ages. One of its warmest admirers would be Erasmus.

Though he commented extensively on the Bible, it was probably in the area of theory or hermeneutics that Thomas exercised the profounder influence. Thomas heightened the emphasis, begun among the twelfth-century Victorines, on the primacy of the literal sense. Indeed, he argued that upon its authority alone could a necessary theological argument be constructed *(Summa Theologiae* 1.1.10 *ad 1um)*. The literal or first sense is that intended by the author; like Augustine, Thomas agreed that this literal sense could have more than one meaning. Thomas is also clear that the literal sense could include figurative and poetic language. The spiritual sense is threefold—Thomas accepted the traditional medieval division of allegorical, moral, and anagogical spiritual senses. This threefold spiritual sense is based on the literal and presupposes it. It has to do with those spiritual realities signified by things expressed in the literal sense. Only revelation has this property, since the author of holy Scripture is God, who intends this threefold spiritual sense to be expressed by the literal sense and apprehended by the reader. In short, the literal sense for Thomas is the meaning communicated by the words; the spiritual sense is the meaning conveyed by the things *(res)* to which the literal words refer (see *Quodlibetales* 7.16.4).

In a real sense, Thomas's insistence on the primacy of the literal sense and his clear definition of it were applied to the entire Bible by a late-medieval exegete whom many have compared, for the breadth of his work, with Jerome.

Whatever the merit of that analogy, the Franciscan Nicholas of Lyra (d. 1349) is without question the dominant biblical exegete of the late Middle Ages and author, in his *Literal Postill on the Whole Bible,* of one of the most impressive works of biblical scholarship in all of ecclesiastical history.

After taking the Franciscan habit in 1300 and studying theology in Paris, Nicholas became Regent Master in Theology there in 1309. In 1322, after having been elected, three years earlier, Minister of the Province of Paris, he began his *Literal Postill,* which he finished in about a decade. From 1333 to 1339, he wrote his *Moral Commentary on the Whole Bible,* a shorter commentary that emphasized the moral and mystical meanings of the text. This was intended as a practical handbook for preachers and teachers. Unlike the postills written under the name of Hugh of St. Cher, these were all composed by Nicholas himself. The *Postilla* was the first biblical commentary to be printed (Rome, 1471–72).

Unlike most contemporary Christian exegetes, Lyra was able to read at least some Hebrew, and he knew the Talmud, the Midrash and the works of Rashi, who influenced him deeply. Lyra's great hermeneutical innovation was his teaching on the "double literal sense" *(duplex sensus literalis),* which held that citations from the Hebrew Scriptures found in the New Testament had two literal meanings. The first and more perfect meaning referred to Christ, the second and less perfect to pre-Christian history.

Lyra's influence was enormous. More than 200 manuscripts of his *Postilla Literalis* exist. Since the late fifteenth century, it has been printed 176 times. It ranks, along with the *Glossa Ordinaria,* the *Sentences* of Peter Lombard and Thomas's *Summa,* as one of the most influential theological works of the Middle Ages. Moreover, some of his commentaries are known to have influenced Luther, at least indirectly, an influence immortalized, with pardonable exaggeration, in a famous early modern couplet: *Si Lyra non lyrasset / Lutherus non saltasset* ("Had Lyra not lyred, Luther would not have danced"). Whatever the degree of his influence on Luther, Lyra did share with the reformer a revulsion for what he took to be the over-allegorization of the Bible and an emphasis on the plain, clear sense of the biblical text, an exegetical emphasis which has caused him to be known as "the clear and plain doctor."

Looking back over a millennium of the use of the Bible in medieval Catholic history, the historian is hindered by the length of the era and the complex use of the Bible from easily summarizing the main developments of the period. Nonetheless, there are certain elements of the use of the Bible, and certain trends in how and in what contexts it was interpreted, that deserve to be underscored. First of all, as we pass from the early to the high Middle Ages, we observe that biblical scholarship becomes more professionalized. Fewer and fewer Benedictine monks rank among great biblical scholars (with the exception of the great Rupert of Deutz, almost none in the twelfth century and following). Biblical scholarship moves from cloister to the schools and universities and their classrooms. It thus becomes less exclusively oriented to prayer and spiritual experience. Dominance of the field passes from the Benedictines to the new school and secular university masters, first at Laon and Paris and then to Dominicans and Franciscan friars at the University of Paris. With this development, emphasis is placed on glossing the entire Bible, often carried out in "teams." (In the late Middle Ages, we witness the reemergence of the virtuoso solo performer—Nicholas of Lyra is the primary example—who himself comments upon the entire Bible.) At the same time, a whole host of aids to Bible study are produced. These include histories of the biblical world and its geography, verbal concordances and editions of the Bible with chapters.

In terms of hermeneutics, we see an increasing emphasis, beginning in the twelfth century, on the literal and historical sense of Scripture, an emphasis reflected in many commentaries in the high and late Middle Ages. With the absorption of Aristotle in the twelfth and thirteenth centuries, the nature of each sense, and specifically how the literal is distinguished from the spiritual, received more precise definition. This hermeneutical project also boosted the ascendancy of the literal sense. Indeed, although Henri de Lubac is surely correct to insist that medieval authors never relinquished the allegorical sense to the extent argued by Smalley—it enjoyed something of a renaissance in the late Middle Ages—

it was perhaps in the high- and late-medieval emphasis on the primacy of the literal sense of Scripture that, in principle, had the most profound effect on the sixteenth-century reformers, even if, in the application of that principle, they came to radically different exegetical conclusions than their Catholic forerunners. Their efforts to translate the Bible into the vernacular made reflection on the literal sense not just desirable but imperative.

The Early Modern Period (ca. 1500–1650)

Dominating the early medieval period and contemporaneous with the reformer Martin Luther is the outstanding biblical humanist Erasmus (d. 1536). In Erasmus, we see the union of superior classical learning, the desire to reform the church by learning, and excellent biblical scholarship. His greatest contribution to the use of the Bible was his publication of the first Greek critical edition in 1516. This was a two-columned work, which contained not only the Greek New Testament but Erasmus's own Latin translation of the Greek (which corrected many perceived errors of Jerome), as well as extensive annotations at the back of the edition. For the Greek edition, Erasmus used five manuscripts he had discovered in Basel, relying especially on two of them. In later editions, his Latin translation became more and more different than Jerome's. Some of his changes, which he thought reflected the sense of the Greek more precisely, were to undermine key Catholic dogma, especially sacramental claims. For example, where Jerome translated Matthew 4, 17 *"poenitentiam agite"* (do penance), Erasmus translated it simply as "repent." This seemed to subvert the biblical foundation for the sacrament of penance. Other translations would seem to undermine other key elements of Catholic doctrine, including aspects of Mariology. Luther would make use of the 1519 edition of Erasmus's edition of the New Testament for his German translation (1522), as Tyndale would for his English version (1525). It would also serve, indirectly, as the basis for the King James version (1611) and the Textus Receptus (1633). Hundreds of commentators, well into the seventeenth century, would use his edition as well.

Erasmus also wrote a *Paraphrase on Romans*, published at virtually the same time (1517)

Luther would arrive at his own revolutionary understanding of that book. For the next seven years, he wrote paraphrases of every other book of the New Testament, save the Apocalypse. These would have special influence on the Swiss reformers. In 1547 they were placed in every parish in England and in the library of every aspiring divine. Together with the enormous influence of his edition, they easily made Erasmus the most influential Catholic biblical scholar of the early sixteenth century.

One of Luther's great theological opponents, Thomas de Vio, Cardinal Cajetan (1469–1534), certainly agreed with the Reformer and with Erasmus that reliable exegesis depended on the availability of good Hebrew and Greek texts. Although Cajetan is probably best known for his anti-Lutheran polemics and as a great admirer of Thomas (his is the commentary on the Angelic Doctor that appears in the authoritative Leonine edition of Thomas's works), he was also an accomplished exegete. Indeed, shortly after engaging in examinations of Luther's writings, he began dedicating himself to biblical translation and interpretation, producing, finally, commentaries on the Pentateuch, the historical books of the Hebrew Bible, Job, Ecclesiasticus, the Gospels, and the Epistles. Similarly, Jacopo Sadoleto, while known primarily as an opponent of Calvin, was an accomplished humanist, who also dedicated much of his life to biblical interpretation. He produced commentaries on Paul, the Gospels, and Acts. In the middle of the sixteenth century Isidorus Clarius (d. 1555) produced a revision of the Vulgate New Testament on the basis of his translation from the Greek.

The status and the authority of the Vulgate was one of the issues taken up at the Council of Trent (1545–63). At the council, it was decreed that the Vulgate was authoritative for dogma. The reason for making it so was explicitly not its proximity to the original sense of the Hebrew and Greek Scriptures but, rather, that it had been normatively so used for a millennium. Against the notion that any individual could interpret the Scripture, Trent explicitly declared:

> No one, relying on his own skill, shall, in matters of faith and of morals pertaining to the edification of the structure of Christian doctrine, wresting the sacred Scripture to his own senses, presume to interpret the said sacred Scripture

contrary to that sense which holy mother church, whose it is to judge the true sense and interpretation of the holy Scriptures, has held and does hold.

It will be perceived that, again, this is in effect a reassertion of the ancient authoritative principle found in the writings of Irenaeus. Reacting against the reformed emphasis on "scripture alone" *(sola scriptura)*, Trent defined *both* Scripture *and* tradition as sources of revelation to be received *pari affectu*—i.e., with the same reverence. This phrasing leaves it ambiguous whether the Scriptures, presumed of course to have a divine author, were a higher and more authoritative form of revelation than the writings included under the rubric "tradition."

Trent is thus largely conservative and backward-looking in its main dogmatic decrees on Scripture and interpretation. But not all Catholics in the sixteenth century were looking backward. The Catholic exegete in the sixteenth century who most anticipates modern interpretive concerns is undoubtedly Sixtus of Siena *(Senensis)* (d. 1569). A convert from Judaism, Sixtus brilliantly postulated, in a guide to the Bible entitled *Bibliotheca Sancta,* that the Psalter had multiple authors and in other ways foreshadowed the insights of modern biblical criticism.

Still, it must be conceded that Sixtus was something of an exception. Indeed, while much Catholic exegesis was absorbed in polemic with Reformed exegetes, it still shared premodern assumptions with them. Both Protestant and Catholic exegetes, however radically they differed in their dogmatic interpretation of Scriptures, shared certain crucial assumptions. Both agreed that the Scriptures were inerrant; that they were inspired; that they were heaven-sent; that revelation did not change or develop and, above all, that the Scriptures were not influenced by the cultural or historical matrices in which they were produced. At the end of the period, however, Catholic exegesis began to point to developments that would revolutionize our understanding of the original meaning of the Scriptures.

The Emergence and Development of Modern Catholic Biblical Criticism (1650–1943)

Probably no Catholic exegete so anticipated the discoveries of modern Catholic biblical criticism as Richard Simon (1638–1712). Originally a

Catholic Interpretation of the Bible

member of the French Congregation of the Oratory, Simon—like many Europeans writing under the influence of rationalistic or empirical movements and scientific discoveries, which would revolutionize Western thought in the Enlightenment—published a pathbreaking three-volume book, *Historical Criticism of the Old Testament* (1678). Simon was an immensely learned man; he knew rabbinic as well as patristic literature, and he was an accomplished patrologist. Among other things, he denied that the Pentateuch had been authored only by Moses; in fact, he maintained that Moses kept some sort of notes or annals that were later worked up by another author. Simon also argued that oral traditions usually precede their codification in written form—a crucial insight all but ignored then. Eleven years later, he followed up this daring study with a similarly bold examination of the New Testament. For these studies he paid a dear price. He felt he had to leave the Congregation on the publication of his first book. In addition, his books were condemned by the Parliament of Paris; others of his writings were later attacked by no less a figure than Louis XIV, and Jacques-Benigne Bossuet (1627–1704) was among his fiercest critics. In 1682, Simon's study of the Old Testament was placed on the Index, owing to the influence of Bossuet and his former Congregation. Nonetheless, it would be translated into English the same year and later into German. A copy of it was eventually discovered in the library of Friedrich Schleiermacher (1768–1834).

Simon's work was perfectly illustrative of the ways in which historical criticism would threaten cherished, historic dogmatic assumptions, and its condemnation a hint of how the new criticism would be received in ecclesiastical circles. For nearly two centuries after the death of Simon, Catholic biblical scholarship felt content to ignore Simon's insights. These were centuries of desiccation and dreariness in Catholic biblical scholarship practically unprecedented. Even when Julius Wellhausen (1844–1916) masterfully set out his documentary theory, many Catholic exegetes remained in a state of siege, rejecting the theory because of the rationalistic and empirical assumptions that underlay it.

In this gloomy context, the Dominican M.-J. Lagrange (1855–1938) stands out as a shining example of exegetical vigor and enlightenment.

In 1890 Lagrange founded the École Biblique in Jerusalem in order to encourage analysis of the word of God with the assistance of the historical-critical method. Two years later, he founded the first important journal in Catholic biblical studies, *Revue biblique*. At a Catholic conference in Fribourg in 1897, he urged his fellow Catholic biblical scholars to take more seriously than they heretofore had the Pentateuchal criticism. On this question, he felt, the historical evidence had to trump the literary tradition. In 1902 he started an important series of biblical commentaries titled *Etudes bibliques*. His *Historical Criticism and the Old Testament* (1905) championed the use of the historical method. In all of these endeavors, Lagrange strove to demonstrate that the historical-critical method was not necessarily destructive of immutable truth of the Catholic faith. In addition, he did pioneering work on the study of biblical genres and forms.

Not surprisingly, Lagrange failed to convince everyone that the historical-critical enterprise was compatible with the maintenance of historic dogma, and he did not emerge unscathed. After a warning from the Sacred Congregation, he turned his attention to the New Testament. Meanwhile, Pius X established the Pontifical Biblical Institute as a rival to the Ecole, and he removed Lagrange from his position there. Nonetheless, Lagrange's legacy certainly lives on, not least of all in the continuing vitality of Catholic biblical study at the École Biblique.

Shortly after Lagrange founded the École Biblique, Pope Leo XIII, who had seemed once to express the opinion that the higher criticism and Catholic dogma were compatible, issued the encyclical *Providentissimus Deus* (1893), which left a very different impression. In that encyclical, Leo demanded that the Vulgate version be used, though he allowed that other versions ought not to be neglected. He also argued that a biblical text could not contradict the sense given it by the magisterium or by the unanimous consent of the fathers, and no exegete was allowed to interpret the text so as to contradict church dogma. In a very real sense, this is again simply a modern reassertion of the ancient principle of authoritative interpretation, heard expressed in the second century by Irenaeus, that the supreme arbiter of interpretation is the church's doctrine as taught by the magisterial authority.

No Catholic interpreter of Scripture in the twentieth century ran so directly against the grain of this idea than the French biblical critic and "Modernist" Alfred Loisy (1857–1940). Loisy was a talented philologist and interpreter who taught Scripture at the Institut Catholique in Paris from 1884 to 1893. He fully accepted the methods, insights, and implications of the historical-critical method. In 1902 he wrote his classic book, *The Gospel and the Church*. In it, he concluded that many New Testament texts were ahistorical and were, in fact, produced by the early church. He dismissed the typological method and denied that the church developed in a way that Jesus could have foreseen. In later works, he sharply distinguished between the Jesus recoverable by historical method and the Christ known by faith, and argued that Jesus was unconscious of his divinity.

By the time Loisy had published these works, he had been dismissed from the Catholic Institute. More severe retribution was to follow. In 1907 his "errors" were condemned by the Holy Office in its encyclical *Lamentabili*. In the following year, Pius X issued the decree *Pascendi dominici gregis*, which condemned sixty-five "Modernist" propositions. Many of these were from Loisy's work on the New Testament (or were epitomes, more or less tendentious, of his positions). *Pascendi* denied that the authority of the church was incompetent to judge the meaning of Scripture; that the exegete could or should ignore the supernatural origin of the Bible; and that the Scriptures contained error. Classically, it denied the proposition that:

No chapter of scripture from the beginning of Genesis to the end of Revelation contains a teaching absolutely identical with that which the church sets forth on the same subject; and consequently no chapter of scripture has the same meaning for the critic as for the theologian (Proposition 61).

Not surprisingly, Loisy was excommunicated. Still, he had identified a problem that still awaits satisfactory resolution: the relationship of the truth discovered by the exegete to the dogmatic truth proclaimed magisterially by the church. Even if many Catholic exegetes have not wanted to go as far as Loisy theoretically, none of any repute has denied the reality, or the problem, of the gap he so clearly perceived. The debate has centered, rather, on the dimensions of the gap and the possibility and peril of attempting to bridge it.

The Coming of Age of Catholic Biblical Scholarship (1943–2000)

Catholic biblical scholarship, which in some sense had been plunged into a dark age with these papal pronouncements, was, in 1943 reliberated to do its work by another papal encyclical, Pope Pius XII's *Divino Afflante Spiritu*. Issued on the fiftieth anniversary of *Providentissimus Deus,* it announced its intentions to "ratify" what had been "wisely laid down" by Leo XIII. In fact, it reverses or radically recasts much of what he had to say. Where, for example, Leo had designated the Vulgate the authoritative text, Pius commanded scholars to translate and explain the original Hebrew and Greek texts. Much emphasis was laid upon determining the *literary form* the human author employed. Pius also encouraged scholars, as Leo emphatically did not, to examine the original intention and circumstances of the authors of Scripture and thus to understand the context in which they wrote. Remarkably, Pius also encouraged scholars to harmonize their conclusions with those of the profane sciences.

Even at the time, Catholic scholars recognized that *Divino Afflante Spiritu* had opened up a new epoch in the Catholic interpretation of the Bible, and its publication was hailed by the editors of *Revue biblique*. Ironically, Pius XII, who has recently been excoriated by some for his passivity in the face of the Holocaust, has been lionized by scholars as a grand patron of Catholic biblical studies. It was his pontificate that marked an about-face in Catholic attitudes toward the Bible in the twentieth century, so that so sensible an authority as Raymond Brown could once observe that *Divino Afflante* represented the Catholic Magna Charta for progress in biblical study.

Nonetheless, a renewed atmosphere of chill prevailed in Rome in the wake of Pius's death in 1958, as several professors were removed from their teaching office at the Pontifical Biblical Institute for displeasure with their historical conclusions. They were restored to their positions, however, under John XXIII and Paul VI, as the warming winds of *aggiornamento* (modernization) swept through Rome during the Second Vatican Council. The Council's dogmatic constitution on revelation (*Dei Verbum,* November 18, 1965) takes a largely positive, if cautious, attitude (reflective of the fact that it went through multiple revisions and had to reflect diplomatic compromise) toward the program laid out by Pius XII.

The efflorescence of Catholic biblical scholarship in the forty years since the Council is so great as to defeat any attempt to summarize it easily. Still, a number of crucial developments may be noted. First of all, since the Council, Protestant and Catholic interpretations of the Scriptures have been methodologically indistinguishable. Roman Catholic scholarship has accepted modern biblical criticism. Having accepted modern approaches, Roman Catholics have now produced some of the most accomplished biblical scholars in the world. As the center of gravity in biblical scholarship has shifted from the European Continent to North American, and as an increasing number of women have entered the academy since the Council, the number of outstanding Catholic women biblical scholars who have trained or who teach in the United States has soared. Adela Yarbro Collings, Margaret Mitchell, Carolyn Osiek, Pheme Perkins, and Elizabeth Schüssler-Fiorenza, to mention only a few, all have made signal contributions to the field which are recognized worldwide. Their male counterparts—among others, R. E. Brown, J. Collins, J. Donahue, J. Fitzmeyer, D. Harrington, J. Meier, D. Senior—rank at the top of their field internationally and belong to, and in many cases have led, the most important international societies of biblical studies (e.g., Society of Biblical Literature). In addition, numerous new approaches—literary-critical, liberation, feminist, structural, rhetorical, social-scientific—have given us new insight into the original meaning of the Scriptures and the communities to which they were addressed. Meanwhile, the "search for the historical Jesus" seems to have lost none of its vigor, and the renowned "Jesus seminar" includes a number of important Cath-olic participants, including John Dominic Crossan.

The overall picture, then, since Vatican II has been an overwhelmingly positive one. It will be left to twenty-first-century Catholic interpreters to address three questions, which the Catholic acceptance of modern biblical approaches has generated or made more acute. First, to what extent do new approaches involve retrojection of modern concerns and imperatives, legitimate in themselves, into the ancient biblical texts? Second, modern biblical criticism has, for those with ears to hear, only widened the gap between historical analysis of the biblical text and the historic dogmatic claims of the church. Some eminent biblical scholars, such as R. E. Brown, have heroically attempted to bridge that gap, but the results have been mixed and not inevitably convincing. How and even if the Bible and theology can be brought together is a question that, it must be admitted, has yet to receive an authentically convincing Catholic response. Finally, once the original, contextual, historical meaning of the text has been by and large established, what is left for the exegete or even the ordinary readers of Scripture? As we have seen, for the ancients and medievals, that was merely the first job of the interpreter. But we live now in an age in which the practice of allegoresis and the Platonic assumptions on which it rested have lost credibility. Few have any desire to repristinate the allegorical method. Yet the postallegorical questions linger: does the biblical text have any genuine meaning beyond or above that established by historical analysis and allied disciplines? If so how is it established and verified? Through most of the two millennia surveyed in this article, Catholic exegetes could answer those questions with confidence. Part of the pathos in the otherwise happy acceptance in Catholic biblical scholarship in the late twentieth century is that Catholic exegetes no longer know how, or even if, those questions can be answered.

THE CHALLENGES OF BIBLICAL TRANSLATION

RONALD D. WITHERUP, S.S.

For the average person in the pew, the need for new biblical translations can be bewildering. "Why do we need *new* translations?" or "What translation is the best one?" are common questions. The task of biblical translation is, however, quite complicated. There is no one biblical translation that is the best and serves all purposes equally. The translation used in this Study Bible is the *New American Bible* (revised), and special attention will be given to it. But first, one should have a general overview of the challenges posed by translating the Bible into modern English.

Presuppositions

The need for biblical translation should be self-evident. The Bible has come down to us in ancient Hebrew, Aramaic, and Greek, languages that few but scholars can use today. The Bible itself witnesses to the necessity of translation. After the Babylonian exile (sixth century BC), when the Jews dispersed throughout the ancient world and began to lose command of their native Hebrew tongue, the need arose to produce a translation of their Hebrew Bible into the vernacular of the empire, which at the time was Greek. Thus was produced one of the great translations of all time, the Septuagint (LXX), which had a major influence on the writers of the New Testament. Without translation, many of the traditions of Israel may have been lost over time, as the Jewish people struggled to retain their identity in the midst of the multiple influences of the Greco-Roman world.

No translation is perfect, however. Scholars frequently quote the adage that every translation is an interpretation. There is no such thing as a purely objective translation, yet there are some guiding presuppositions that modern translators acknowledge. The following list of five orients the discussion.

1. Language is a living reality. By nature it changes with usage and experience. No translation stands forever. The following quotation from Ronald Knox, one of the great translators of the Bible into English, affirms this reality:

> Words are living things, full of shades of meaning, full of associations; and, what is more, they are apt to change their significance from one generation to the next. The translator who understands his job feels, constantly, like Alice in Wonderland trying to play croquet with flamingoes for mallets and hedgehogs for balls; words are forever eluding his grasp. (*The Trials of a Translator* [New York: Sheed & Ward, 1949] 13)

Because living languages change, translations—even of ancient texts—must take this growth into account.

2. The task of translating from one language to another involves primarily two interrelated values: (*a*) preserving faithfully the meaning of the original text, and (*b*) enunciating the original text in clearly understood terms of the receptor language. Generally, the one cannot take absolute precedence over the other because this can lead to distorted translation. A literal translation could, for instance, lead to a total misreading of the original text because the *words* were translated but not the *meaning*. Fidelity to the original might well require a less literal translation in the receptor language. One must also consider the range of meaning of words in both the original and receptor languages.

68

A related value in the task of translation is the need to preserve in the receptor language as much as possible the form and structure of the original. Poetic and narrative forms are quite different, for example, and require separate attention. Literary form and genre is as important for translation as the actual words. Some might approach this task more loosely than others, since every language employs unique formal conventions that may or may not appear in other languages. Hebrew, for instance, has certain tendencies for repetition and simple, staccato expressions that, when translated literally into English, can seem stilted. The careful translator attempts to bridge this gap in a way that respects the linguistic uniqueness of both languages.

3. In the recent past there has been a tendency to bifurcate the task of translation into two categories: (*a*) formal equivalence (word-for-word), and (*b*) dynamic equivalence (thought-for-thought). The first is the more literal style of translation in which each word is produced as nearly as possible to preserve both the sense and the form of the original. The second approach translates more fluidly, not by replicating words and form but by conveying the *meaning* of the original in the proper form of the receptor language (that is, thought-for-thought rather than word-for-word). A third category not included in this twofold division is commonly called a *paraphrase*. This is not a translation as such but a total rephrasing of the text. It is strongly interpretive.

Recent translation theory has recognized that this duality can be misleading. Instead, translation is better viewed as a continuum ranging from a formal, one-to-one literal translation on one end to a totally free form translation or paraphrase on the other, with a range of options in between. This continuum allows for many more diverse approaches to biblical translation, which are in fact seen in the wide variety of English translations currently available. It also recognizes that the complexity of biblical translation requires more than a choice between two mutually exclusive opposites.

4. Every translation involves some interpretative moves, even if the goal is to capture as accurately as possible the original intention of the author of the text. If this principle is acknowledged, then it must be seen that not even a literal

word-for-word translation constitutes the same reality as the source text. As Eugene A. Nida, a notable Bible translator, indicates, translation always involves three realities: (*a*) loss of information; (*b*) addition of information; and (*c*) alteration of information ("Principles of Translation as Exemplified by Bible Translating," in *On Translation* [Reuben A. Brower, ed.; NY: Oxford University, 1966], 13). Words in any given language have a multiplicity of meanings and shades of nuance that do not permit one-to-one correspondence into other languages. Thus, fidelity to a biblical text does not necessarily involve an overly literal approach. This is particularly true of idioms. By their very nature idioms cannot generally be translated in literal fashion but must be compared to an appropriate, corresponding idiom in the receptor language.

The Pontifical Biblical Commission, an international body of professional consultants who provide expert advice to the Congregation for the Doctrine of the Faith in Rome, reinforces this point.

> The literal sense is not to be confused with the "literalist" sense to which fundamentalists are attached. It is not sufficient to translate a text word for word in order to obtain its literal sense. One must understand the text according to the literary conventions of the time. When a text is metaphorical, its literal sense is not that which flows immediately from a word to word translation (e.g., "Let your loins be girt": Lk 12, 35), but that which corresponds to the metaphorical use of these terms ("Be ready for action"). (*The Interpretation of the Bible in the Church* [Boston: St. Paul Books & Media, 1993], 82)

5. Translation must also take into account the influence of culture. This is a controversial point. Some believe that only a literal, word-for-word, translation is authentic to the original text. This position, however, denies that the value of all translation is to communicate faithfully the sense of the text in other cultures and contexts. If fidelity to the original text is always viewed as the ultimate value, serious mistranslation can occur. One need only ask the experience of expert Bible translators who have undertaken the task of translating biblical texts for very foreign cultures (African, Asian, indigenous peoples, etc.) to know how serious this challenge is. For example, one cannot utilize properly the biblical image of

sheep and goats and shepherds in a culture that only has experience of cattle, as in the case of some African tribes. The culture(s) represented in the biblical text are not the only ones that must be respected if the Word of God is to be communicated in modern contexts.

Again, the Pontifical Biblical Commission emphasized this point when they wrote:

> A translation, of course, is always more than a simple transcription of the original text. The passage from one language to another necessarily involves a change of cultural context: concepts are not identical and symbols have a different meaning, for they come up against other traditions of thought and other ways of life. (*The Interpretation of the Bible in the Church*, 122)

Similarly, Pope John Paul II, in an Italian address to the United Bible Societies (November 26, 2001), spoke of a threefold requirement for translators.

> A good translation is based on the three pillars that must contemporaneously support the entire work. First, there must be a deep knowledge of the language and the cultural world at the point of origin. Next, there must be a good familiarity with the language and cultural context at the point where the work will arrive. Lastly, to crown the work with success, there must be an adequate mastery of the contents and meaning of what one is translating.

Taking into account at least these five presuppositions helps to see the complexity of the trans-

lation process. It also implies that the act of translation is as much an art as it is a science. Balancing the different factors and remaining true to both the original and receptor languages and cultures is an enormous challenge.

Multiple Translations

The availability of so many modern English translations can be confusing to people. How does one choose? There are, in fact, different goals for different translations. Some are intentionally directed to a specific denominational audience, be it Catholic, mainstream Protestant, evangelical, Orthodox, or fundamentalist. Some are intended for private study, others for public reading or worship services. Many modern English translations are available in Catholic editions; they purposefully include the Old Testament apocrypha, which are often excluded from Protestant editions of the Bible.

The table below and opposite lays out some of the choices among the most well known contemporary English translations.

Now we will take a closer look at some differences of approach among these translations.

Mark 2, 1 narrates Jesus' return to his hometown. The NAB translates: "When Jesus returned to Capernaum after some days, it became known that he was *at home.*" The italicized phrase literally reads "in (the) house" (e.g., NJB), but most translations use the expression "at home" (RSV, NRSV, NIV). The NLT pro-

Translation, Date	Brief Description	Sample Text: Ps 86, 14
New American Bible (NAB) 1970 (Revised New Testament, 1986; Psalms, 1991)	The basic American Catholic translation intended for study, prayer, and use in liturgy; uses modern American English with an attempt to balance literal and thought-for-thought translation suitable for oral proclamation as well as private reading	O God, the arrogant have risen against me; a ruthless band has sought my life; to you they pay no heed.
New Revised Standard Version (NRSV) 1989	Based upon the classic Revised Standard Version (RSV), which remains a good literal translation but with sensitivity to inclusive language; uses modern idiomatic English intended for a broad appeal	O God, the insolent rise up against me; a band of ruffians seeks my life, and they do not set you before them.

The Challenges of Biblical Translation

Translation, Date	Brief Description	Sample Text: Ps 86, 14
New International Version (NIV) 1984	Intended for broad ecumenical appeal; attempts a balance between literal and thought-for-thought translation	The arrogant are attacking me, O God; a band of ruthless men seeks my life—men without regard for you.
New Jerusalem Bible (NJB) 1985, 1990	A more poetic translation from a French edition, noted for its extensive explanatory footnotes and some sensitivity to gender-inclusive language issues	Arrogant men, God, are rising up against me, a brutal gang is after my life, in their scheme of things you have no place.
Revised English Bible (REB) 1989	A modern English version utilizing spellings and idioms of English common to the United Kingdom (Great Britain, etc.)	Violent men rise to attack me, a band of ruthless men seeks my life; they give no thought to you, my God.
New Living Translation (NLT) 1996, 2004	A thorough revision of an earlier paraphrase, The Living Bible (TLB), but now based upon a translation from the original languages; leans toward explanatory translations of ambiguous passages	O God, insolent people rise up against me; a violent gang is trying to kill me. You mean nothing to them.
Contemporary English Version (CEV) 1995	Uses simple, modern, colloquial American English intended for the broadest American audience, especially young people	Proud and violent enemies, who don't care about you, have ganged up to attack and kill me.
New King James Version (NKJV) 1982	Based upon the traditional King James Version (1611) but with some refinement of the antiquated Elizabethan language; largely retains the structure and some familiar terms of seventeenth-century English	O God, the proud have risen against me, And a mob of violent *men* have sought my life, And have not set You before them.
New American Standard Bible (NASB) 1997	An updated edition of a very literal and conservative translation in contemporary English, aimed primarily at evangelical Christians	O God, arrogant men have risen up against me, And a band of violent men have sought my life, And they have not set You before them.
NET Bible (NET) 1996–2003	A totally new concept in Bible translation, making use of the Internet (www.netbible.com) and allowing for frequent changes in translation and extensive explanatory notes as new information emerges; uses contemporary American English	O God, arrogant men attack me; a gang of ruthless men, who do not respect you, seek my life.

vides a freer translation: "When Jesus returned to Capernaum several days later, the news spread quickly that he was back home."

The Greek text of Mark 2, 19 uses an expression that is an obvious Hebraism, namely, "sons of the wedding hall." Virtually all translations recognize that this is an idiom that cannot be accurately translated in literal fashion. There is a divergence in the terms that are used, however. Some use "wedding guests" (RSV, NRSV, NAB, RSV, NLT, NET), while others use "the bridegroom's attendants" (e.g., NJB).

More serious issues arise when the text is somewhat ambiguous. Hebrews 12, 2 provides an example. Many translations follow the RSV: "looking to Jesus the pioneer and perfecter of *our faith*. . . ," assuming that the text refers to the faith of believers (e.g., NRSV, NJB, NIV, NLT, NET). However, the context indicates that Jesus' faith is most likely the object of attention in the text; the modifier "our" is not found in the Greek text. Thus the NAB translation preserves the ambiguity of the text: "keeping our eyes fixed on Jesus, the leader and perfecter *of faith*." It is left to the reader to decide whether our faith or Jesus' faith is intended. An earlier version of the NLT read: "Keeping our eyes on Jesus, on whom our faith depends from start to finish." This is overly interpretive and exceeds the import of the text. The revised NLT reads: "Jesus, the champion who initiates and perfects our faith."

At times a more literal translation whose meaning is obscure is best left literally, even when it is universally recognized as a saying whose meaning is not intended to be taken literally. An example is found in Romans: "if your enemy is hungry, feed him; if he is thirsty, give him something to drink; for by so doing you will *heap burning coals upon his head*" (Rom 12, 20 NAB; cf. RSV, NRSV, NJB, NET). The saying is a proverb from the Old Testament (Prv 25, 21–22), the exact meaning of which has been debated through history. The text is not likely meant to be taken literally to pour live coals on someone's head. Rather, it appears to be an expression of bringing shame or humiliation to one's enemy by paradoxically providing a kindness.

This is the way the NLT takes the passage, which it renders: "Instead, 'If your enemies are hungry, feed them. If they are thirsty, give them something to drink. In doing this, you will heap burning coals of shame on their heads.' " While this interpretive translation may communicate the meaning of the text, this is not self-evident from the passage. Since Patristic times, various interpretations of the passage have been proposed from which one can choose an acceptable option. Thus the majority of translations simply retain the reference to burning coals. Footnotes, commentaries, or study Bibles can then offer a variety of interpretations that lie beyond the scope of the translation itself.

The Case of Inclusive Language

In the late twentieth century modern English translations have had to confront a special translating challenge that became a politically charged issue, namely, the question of "inclusive language."

Inclusive language means language that includes rather than excludes. It is usually identified with feminist concerns that traditional English translations of the Bible exhibit a vocabulary that is too patriarchally oriented and excludes the viewpoint of women. Thus, some speak of "gender-inclusive language," but the concept of inclusive language, as we will see below, actually is not restricted to feminist concerns. Yet we must acknowledge that the Bible grew out of a patriarchal culture, one in which men were dominant and women generally secondary. Thus it is not surprising to find a dominant male perspective expressed in biblical texts.

Inclusive language is divided into two categories, "horizontal inclusive language" (i.e., concerned with human beings) or "vertical inclusive language" (i.e., language about God). Bible translators have had to deal with this question directly. The NAB, for instance, has taken the stance that moderate attention to horizontal inclusive language is appropriate for a contemporary English translation. Where possible the translators avoid using the words *man* or *mankind* where the text is meant to embrace all human beings, because these terms have become increasingly more restrictive in modern English than in previous eras. Also, the literal term *sons of Israel* (an idiomatic Hebrew expression) is translated *Israelites,* since that is what the term means in most contexts. When the Pauline letters address the audience as "brothers" (Greek *adelphoi),* the NRSV utilizes the translation "brothers and sisters" (e.g., Rom 1, 13; 7, 1; 1 Cor 1, 10; etc.) because the word clearly applies to the entire community Paul is addressing. The NAB recognizes the principle (see footnote for Rom 1, 13) but has chosen to stick with the literal translation "brothers" in deference to convention. When the NAB translation was adapted for use in Roman Catholic lectionary, however, the more inclusive "brothers and sisters" has been employed where appropriate.

While the expression "inclusive language" is most frequently tied to feminist sensitivities, it has also been applied to other categories. Some translators, for instance, object to traditional expressions like "the lame" or "the blind" because they overly emphasize the handicap of an individual or class of people rather than their human dignity. They propose alternative translations like "the one who is lame" or "the one whose sight is impaired." A similar concern has arisen regarding the biblical contrasts between light and darkness (Mt 10, 27), day and night (Jn 11, 9–10; 1 Thes 5, 5), or white and black (Ps 51, 9, "whiter than snow"), because such contrasts allegedly denigrate people of color. An even more aggressive position is taken regarding a biblical title like "the Son of Man," which has Christological significance (e.g., Mk 10, 45; Jn 8, 28). They translate the phrase "child of the human one," an odd and clumsy translation that ignores the Christological implications of the title. (See *New Testament and Psalms: An Inclusive Language Version* [New York: Oxford University Press, 1989].) Most translators view such attempts as excesses that are overly intrusive in the translation process. These are examples of the imbalance of allowing modern cultural concerns to dictate absolutely how to communicate ancient texts. Such instances do not respect the integrity of the biblical text.

The principle of inclusivity has also been applied to biblical language about God (e.g., vertical inclusive language). Some object to the overabundance of masculine terminology for God in the Bible, although it is an understandable outgrowth of a patriarchal culture. They attempt to counteract this by avoiding the masculine pronouns *he* or *him* or by repeating the word *God* frequently or designing other circumlocutions for the Deity. Theologically, since God is a spirit and is neither male nor female, biblical language

about God, in fact, has its limitations. As the *Catechism of the Catholic Church* points out:

> We must therefore continually purify our language of everything in it that is limited, imagebound or imperfect, if we are not to confuse our image of God—"the inexpressible, the incomprehensible, the invisible, the ungraspable"—with our human representations. Our human words always fall short of the mystery of God. (#42)

To refer to God as "he" or to call God a rock or a fortress (2 Sm 22, 2; Ps 18, 3), a shepherd (Pss 23, 1; 80, 1), etc., is to use metaphorical and analogous language to describe how God acts toward people or how we experience God. These are not literal descriptions of God's identity. There are also feminine images for God in the Bible that should be remembered and that can provide some counterbalance to the predominance of masculine images (e.g., the image of God as a woman in labor [Is 46, 3–4] or as a tender mother [Is 49, 15; 66, 13]).

Another aspect of inclusive language is the limitation of English when utilizing singular forms of pronouns. Unlike some languages (e.g., French or Spanish), English has a limited form of third-person pronouns. For example, in French the same expression *"sa croix"* (or Spanish *"su cruz"*) can mean *his* or *her* cross, depending upon who is envisioned as the antecedent. But English requires the use of *both* modifying pronouns if one wants to apply the expression to men and women alike.

Let's take a biblical example. Jesus' saying about the necessity of taking up one's cross (Mt 10, 38) obviously applies to all Jesus' disciples, male and female. The NAB translates: *"whoever* does not take up *his cross* and follow after me is not worthy of me."* The NRSV tries to make the saying more inclusive by deleting the modifying pronoun: *"whoever* does not take up *the cross* and follow me is not worthy of me."* This solution, however, has the unfortunate side effect of making it seem that each disciple is to take up Jesus' cross rather than his or her own cross. The NLT avoids the problem by transposing the saying into second person: "If *you* refuse to take up *your cross* and follow me, *you* are not worthy of being mine."

Another example is the translation of Jesus' famous saying in Matthew 6, 24, which also applies to all followers of Jesus: *"No one* can serve two masters. *He* will either hate one and love the other, or be devoted to one and despise the other. You cannot serve God and mammon." The NRSV attempts to solve the more restrictive phrasing by inserting an implied word that is not literally present in the biblical text: *"No one* can serve two masters; for *a slave* will either hate the one and love the other, or be devoted to the one and despise the other. You cannot serve God and wealth." One also notes in this latter example the difference between the NAB's retention of the original word *mammon*—an Aramaic or Hebrew word for money or goods—and the NRSV's *wealth,* which presumably is intended to be better understood by a broad audience (cf. also NJB, NIV).

In short, English poses a peculiar problem for inclusivity that can be quite vexing for translators who wish to preserve the meaning of the original text and to remain sensitive to modern concerns. While this is not the only contemporary issue affecting biblical translation theory, it has become one of the more controversial.

Translation and Interpretation

It was noted above that all translations are essentially an interpretation. Regardless of how objective translators attempt to be, biases exist that can enter into the process. This accounts for the oft-quoted Italian saying attributed to Dante, *"Traduttore traditore"* (A translator is a traitor). Inevitably, in the history of Bible translation there have been many instances of external issues that creep into the translation process.

One example is the tendency at times for translations to make up for perceived or real mistakes in the biblical text. Matthew 1, 17 provides an example. The RSV text translates in a fairly literal fashion (see also NAB, NRSV, NIV):

> So *all the generations* from Abraham to David were *fourteen generations,* and from David to the deportation to Babylon *fourteen generations,* and from the deportation to Babylon to the Christ *fourteen generations.*

While the text is clear, anyone with a knowledge of the history of Israel recognizes that Matthew's genealogy has telescoped that history into an artificial construct and has left out of the list numerous kings and generations. This is for theological reasons. The genealogy is likely based upon a symbolic number (fourteen) that alludes

to King David and reinforces Jesus' background as the Davidic Messiah. The NLT, noting this deficiency, consequently translates the passage more loosely to rectify the apparent mistake, in a way that glosses over Matthew's theological intention:

> All *those listed above* include *fourteen generations* from Abraham to David, *fourteen* from David to the Babylonian exile, and *fourteen* from the Babylonian exile to the Messiah.

Critical questions arise also when passages of profound Christological significance are considered. A passage in the Letter to the Hebrews provides an example, especially because it quotes an Old Testament Psalm that it then applies to Jesus Christ. The NAB sticks with a fairly literal translation of Hebrews 2, 6, quoting Psalm 8, 5:

> Instead, someone has testified somewhere: "What is *man* that you are mindful of him, or *the son of man* that you care for him?"

In the context of Hebrews, the text's use of "the son of man" is meant to evoke the mysterious Christological title that the New Testament associates with Jesus (e.g., Mt 8, 20; 9, 6, etc.). At issue is not what the original meaning of Psalm 8 was, but what use was made of it by the author of the Letter to the Hebrews. The more literal translation preserves the Christological connection. The NRSV translation, however, in an effort to make the passage more inclusive, obscures the meaning of the text and glosses over its Christological significance by use of plural expressions and the substitution of "mortals" for "son of man":

> But someone has testified somewhere, "What are *human beings* that you are mindful of them, or *mortals,* that you care for *them?*"

In instances such as this, good translation requires careful attention to the context as well as the words.

Characteristics of the NAB Translation

Since the NAB is the basis for this study Bible, it is appropriate to highlight some of the characteristics of this translation.

1. The NAB falls in the middle of the continuum mentioned on RG 69 yet leans toward a more formal translation. It seeks to offer an exact rendering of the biblical text in good, modern,

American English that is not overly literal. For instance, no attempt is made to duplicate fully the Hebraisms of the Old Testament, although the parallelism of many poetic passages is retained.

2. The NAB takes into account recent finds in ancient manuscripts, such as the Dead Sea Scrolls, and more current decisions about the various families of manuscripts that are in existence. Textual critics are always attempting to ascertain the most authentic reading of ancient manuscripts based upon the latest scholarship. This is one reason why new translations are needed on a periodic basis as our knowledge of ancient texts grows.

3. Unlike its predecessor, the proposed Old Testament of the revised NAB would leave the verse order of the Masoretic text (the authoritative received text of the Hebrew Bible) intact instead of attempting a reorganization based upon scholarly theories of a more original word order.

4. A common flaw in translations can be the unevenness of translating the same word in the original text with a different English word. Unless the meaning is clearly otherwise, the NAB tries to translate the original terms with the same English equivalent consistently throughout its translation.

5. The NAB utilizes modest horizontal inclusive language wherever possible and where it would not distort the text. As much as possible, where the text necessarily requires an inclusive reading, such is rendered in the English translation. The translation does not employ vertical inclusive language.

6. The proposed NAB takes into account modern American English in its rendering of the biblical text. There is an avoidance of terms that might confuse or offend modern readers, such as *holocaust* (which can be confused with the Holocaust—the Nazi atrocity of attempting to exterminate the Jews during World War II) and *cereal offerings* (which can be confused with breakfast food rather than "grain" offerings).

7. The exegetical notes, essential for clarification and interpretation, have been thoroughly revised in the proposed NAB Old Testament to bring them more in line with the approach taken in the earlier NAB New Testament translation.

8. For Catholics, it should be noted that the NAB is published with full ecclesiastical approval and has followed the required principles for Bible translation that are standard in the Roman Catholic Church. It is thus a reliable and faithful translation that is useful for both spiritual and scholarly purposes.

The Future of Biblical Translation

In conclusion, there will always be a need for new translations. Every translation has strengths and weaknesses. In as much as translation is both a science and an art, there will always be room for improvements as time goes on. The fund of knowledge about the Bible and its world, about the ancient languages and cultures out of which it emerged, grows daily. In order for the Word of God to seep into the very lifeblood of modern English-speaking peoples, new English translations will have to take into account not only the results of scientific investigations but also the changes that continue to occur at a rapid rate within the English language. This reality ensures that Bible translation will remain an exciting field for succeeding generations who will continue to seek ways to communicate the Word of God effectively in their time and place.

FURTHER READING

Catholic International 13:4 (November 2002). Entire issue devoted to "Translation and Interpretation."

de Waard, J., and E. A. Nida. *From One Language to Another: Functional Equivalence in Bible Translating.* Nashville: Nelson, 1986.

Metzger, B. M. *The Bible in Translation: Ancient and English Versions.* Grand Rapids, MI: Baker Academic, 2001.

Nowell, Irene. "The Making of Translations: A Dilemma." *Worship* 75, 1 (2001): 58–68.

Porter, S. E., and R. E. Hess. "Translating the Bible: Problems and Prospects." *Journal of the Study of the New Testament Supplement Series,* no. 173; Sheffield: Sheffield Academic Press, 1999.

Sheeley, S. M., and R. N. Nash, Jr. *The Bible in English Translation: An Essential Guide.* Nashville: Abingdon Press, 1997.

Soukup, P. A., and R. Hodgson, eds. *Fidelity and Translation.* Franklin, WI: Sheed & Ward, 1999.

Witherup, R. D. *A Liturgist's Guide to Inclusive Language.* Collegeville, MN: Liturgical Press, 1996.

THE BIBLE IN THE LECTIONARY

EILEEN SCHULLER

One of the enduring results of the Second Vatican Council has been a renewed emphasis on the place of the Bible within Catholic life, and greater attention to its use in worship, study, and devotion. As a Church and as individuals we are discovering anew the truth of St. Jerome's insight that "ignorance of the Scriptures is ignorance of Christ." Most Catholics now own a Bible; there are Bible study groups in many parishes; children are introduced to biblical stories and actual biblical texts from the first stages of their religious education; many new hymns and much contemporary folk music are biblically based; Services of the Word (which often include a solemn enthronement of the Bible) and parish celebrations of the Liturgy of the Hours are slowly finding a place in Catholic piety.

Still, for most Catholics, their main exposure to the Bible comes at those times when the Church gathers for liturgy, to offer together praise and worship to God through Jesus. Each time the Mass is celebrated there are two or three readings from the Bible, always one from the Gospel and others from the book of Acts, the Epistles, or the Old Testament. Whenever the sacraments are celebrated (even when baptisms, marriages, and the sacrament of penance are celebrated apart from the Mass), readings from the Word of God are an integral part of the ritual. The first reading from Scripture is regularly followed by a psalm so that we might give our response in the words of Scripture. The Gospel Acclamation, the Entrance, and Communion antiphons are usually taken directly from Scripture; other prayers and texts of the Mass reflect or are based on scriptural sources (for instance, the

Glory to God in the Highest, the Lamb of God, the Lord's Prayer).

It is instructive to reflect on why the Christian tradition is so insistent that we read the Word of God whenever we gather to pray as Church. The *Constitution on the Sacred Liturgy,* one of the foundational documents of the Second Vatican Council, puts it this way: "Christ is present in His Word since it is He Himself who speaks when the holy Scriptures are read in the church" (*CSL,* 7). The *Eucharistic Instruction* of 1967 elaborates at greater length "the principal modes by which the Lord is present to his Church in liturgical celebrations. First of all, Christ is present in the assembly of the faithful gathered in his name; He is also present in his word for it is He who is speaking as the sacred Scriptures are read in the Church; in the eucharistic sacrifice, He is present both in the person of the minister . . . and above all under the eucharistic elements" (*CSL,* 9).

Roman Catholicism has traditionally placed primary emphasis (at times, almost the sole emphasis) on the eucharistic presence of Christ under the appearances of bread and wine. More recent theological reflection has emphasized that Christ is present from the moment when the people gather together in the Christian Assembly, and that He is present especially during the proclamation of the Word of God, both in the reading of Scripture and in its unfolding in the homily. The *Eucharistic Instruction* brings this all together with the beautiful imagery of food: "The Church is nourished by the bread of life, which she finds at the table both of the Word of God and the Body of Christ" (10).

The Revision of the Lectionary

Very early on in the Second Vatican Council, the Bishops of the Church, recognizing that "Sacred Scripture is of paramount importance in the celebration of the liturgy" (*Constitution on the Sacred Liturgy*, 24), called for certain reforms and changes so that this truth might become a living and pastoral reality in the Church. They said there should be "more reading from holy Scripture" and it should be "more varied and suitable" (*CSL*, 35); or, to put it in more poetic fashion, "the treasures of the Bible are to be opened up more lavishly, so that richer fare may be provided for the faithful at the table of God's Word" (*CSL*, 51). Thus, one of the first major reforms following on the Council was a revision of the Lectionary, that is, the biblical readings that are set down for each Sunday and weekday of the year, and also for use in the celebration of the sacraments, on Feast Days, at funerals, and for Votive Masses and Masses for Special Occasions.

The reforms envisaged by the Council meant not only that the readings would be in English, but that new and previously unheard sections of the Bible would need to be introduced both on Sundays and at weekday Masses. In the centuries since the Council of Trent, the *Roman Missal* of Pius V (1570) had prescribed a set series of Gospel passages on a yearly basis, and a second reading usually from the Epistles; very few passages from the Old Testament were ever heard at Sunday Mass.

To fulfill the Council's mandate, a committee was established by Rome in 1964; liturgical, scriptural, and pastoral experts, along with bishops around the world, were consulted. The work was completed in 1969 with the publication of the *Lectionary for Mass*, and introduced in all churches throughout the world on the First Sunday of Advent, 1971. In January of 1981 a second edition of the Lectionary was published with a few minor additions and changes, plus an expanded and very helpful Introduction, which explains more fully the goals and purpose of the Lectionary.

The revision of the Lectionary has been one of the most extensive and significant reforms of the Council. Unfortunately, it has not always been given the attention it deserves, nor are some of its fundamental principles always well understood,

either by the clergy who preach on these readings or by the laity who hear them. Our appreciation of the Scriptures in the liturgy can be greatly enriched by a more careful examination of the Lectionary.

Why a Lectionary at All?

Before we look at more specific questions about how the Lectionary is put together and exactly which passages are chosen, it is helpful to step back and ask the more fundamental questions: "Why a lectionary at all? What do we gain by using a lectionary?"

The decision to use a lectionary means that the readings for a given Sunday or weekday are predetermined; they are a given, and therefore they are the starting point for the planning of the liturgy as a whole and the homily. On certain other occasions (for instance, celebrations of marriages, funerals) there are more options given for Scripture readings, and a choice is to be made of what is most appropriate to the pastoral needs of a given congregation. When a special group gathers for a one-time occasion (a Retreat Day, a meeting), it is recognized that the given readings for the day may not be appropriate, and provision is made for using readings "that are more suited to the particular celebration, provided that they are chosen from the texts of an approved lectionary" (*Masses with Special Groups*, 6e). Interestingly, the greatest flexibility is allowed in choosing readings for Masses with children, although a reading from the Gospels is always to be included (*Directory for Masses with Children*, 43).

The norm in the Roman Catholic tradition is that the Scripture readings are set; they are not the choice of the priest or anyone else in the congregation. Certainly a case can be made (and has been made in the Reform and Free Church traditions) for the freedom and spontaneity to choose readings suitable to a specific community and occasion. But the Catholic tradition has opted for a structured and planned system of readings that "provides the faithful with a knowledge of the whole of God's Word, in a pattern suited to the purpose" (*CSL: Introduction*, 60).

The imposition of a lectionary seeks to lessen the temptation (although it can never remove it entirely!) to pick and choose, to listen only to those parts of the Bible that we find readily helpful and to omit those that we find difficult to understand or accept—but which may be the ones we most need to hear. For instance, if I am readily inclined to look upon God as one who is loving, merciful, kind, and forgiving, the Lectionary will certainly provide my favorite passages, but it will also force me to read those difficult passages (from both the Old and the New Testament) that speak of the wrath of God, judgment, and punishment. Or again, if I am a person with a strong social-justice orientation, firmly convinced that "actions on behalf of justice . . . are a constitutive dimension of the preaching of the gospel-message" (1971 Synod of Bishops), the Lectionary will show many of the key biblical texts both from the prophets and the Gospels; but it will also include passages that speak of the personal dimension of union with God, of a world that is passing away, even passages in praise of the monarchy and the established realm. The gift and challenge of the Lectionary is that it places before each of us passages that we might otherwise not choose to read; unrelentingly it nudges us to open ourselves to the totality of God's Word.

Foundational Principles of the Lectionary

On a first examination of the Lectionary, it is easy to get bogged down in a mass of details about different cycles and lists of what is read when, so that the whole thing can seem somewhat intimidating. Rather than trying to determine why certain texts are read on a certain day, it is more important to get an overall sense of the arrangement and rationale of the whole. The general principles and foundational decisions that have determined the basic shape and ordering of the Roman Lectionary will then be clear.

The Paschal Mystery

The focal point of the whole Lectionary is Jesus Christ, especially "the paschal mystery of his blessed passion, resurrection from the dead and glorious ascension" (*CSL*, 5). Throughout the cycle of the Church's Year, the Lectionary sets before us the totality of this central mystery of the Christian life, a mystery that was not only accomplished in Jesus, but a mystery in which we now share through Baptism and faith.

Thus, primacy is given to readings from the Gospels, which speak most directly of the person of Jesus. Furthermore, we read these texts not as individuals but as a people gathered for praise and thanksgiving. "Within the Christian assembly the proclamation of the word inevitably has a Christian aura . . . the God whom we worship in our liturgy is not, first of all, the God of the Book (which is why we freely interpret the Book by arranging it in a lectionary). Our God is the God of the Gathering" (R. Keifer, *To Hear and To Proclaim,* 115). At Mass, every passage of Scripture, whether from the Old or New Testament, is set in relationship to the Passion and Resurrection of Jesus as made present to us in the Eucharist.

The Church Year

Not everything in the Lectionary is of equal importance. The Lectionary is divided into six parts: the major section (and the one that will be the main focus of our attention) is the Temporal Cycle, that is, the readings for Sundays and weekdays throughout the Church Year; the rest of the Lectionary contains the readings for special occasions (Proper of the Saints, Commons, Ritual Masses [for examples, readings for sacraments, funerals], Masses for Various Occasions, and Votive Masses).

Within the Temporal Cycle, not all days of the year are of equal importance. Sundays have special importance, since they are the weekly celebration of the Lord's Resurrection and the occasion for the gathering of the whole community; thus, "the more important biblical passages" (*CSL: Introduction,* 65) are assigned to Sundays and the Solemnities of the Lord. The Sunday cycle is set up independent from the weekday cycle, which, in a sense, complements it.

The Church Year as a whole has its own rhythm. "The solemnity of Easter has the same kind of preeminence [in the year] . . . that Sunday has in the week" (*Norms for the Liturgical Year,* 18); there are six Sundays in Easter season, followed by Pentecost and Trinity Sundays. Then, next to Easter, the Church "holds most sacred the memorial of Christ's birth and early manifestation" (*Norms,* 32). There are two Sundays after Christmas, followed by Epiphany and the Sunday after that. These two major feasts, each with their preparatory period (Lent, with six Sundays, before Easter, and Advent, with four Sundays, before Christmas) are the primary seasons of the Church Year; the other thirty-four

Sundays, which celebrate "the mystery of Christ in all its aspects" (*Norms*, 43), form what is called simply Ordinary Time. (The Lectionary provides for more than fifty-two Sundays to allow for variations in the length of time after Easter, since Easter can fall anywhere from March 22 to April 25.)

Lectio Semicontinua and *Lectio Electa*

There are many different ways in which we could go about reading the Bible in a systematic fashion. We could start with the story of Creation and work through the events of the Old Testament chronologically, then move on to the New Testament and conclude with the book of Revelation; this would be a kind of salvation-history approach. Another option would be to organize the Scripture readings around certain great themes (grace, salvation, forgiveness, creation) or moral principles; the traditional name for this approach is *lectio electa*, "readings chosen" to suit a predetermined theme. Or, we could adopt *lectio continua*, a "continuous reading" of the Bible from beginning to end. This is the system of the Jewish synagogue in which the Torah, the first five books, are read continuously through a year; on the same day that the last chapter of Deuteronomy is finished the first chapter of Genesis is begun, so that the reading of Torah is unceasing.

The Roman Lectionary has opted for a combination of *lectio electa* (particularly in the major seasons of the Church Year) and *lectio continua* (particularly during Ordinary Time and in the weekday cycle); in fact, it is really more correct to talk of *lectio semicontinua* since no biblical book is read through in its entirety.

Although a "harmony" (to use the term from the *CSL: Introduction*, 66) exists between the different readings during Advent, Lent, and Easter, for most Masses there is no one theme in the three (Sunday) or two (weekday) readings. Thus, attempts (whether by a homilist or by musicians) to discover or impose a theme for every Mass can result in a misleading or artificial approach to the Scriptures.

Readings of Suitable Length; Omission of Difficult Sections

In the early church the custom was to read "the memoirs of the apostles or the writings of the prophets as long as there is time" (Justin Martyr, *Apol.* 67). That, however, is not the norm today; within the Mass, particularly when there are three readings, none can be too long. Narrative texts (Gospel stories, parables) are often longer (ten to fifteen verses) so that they can be complete and because they more easily hold people's attention. Other texts, particularly Sunday readings from the Epistles, are shorter (between four and eight verses) "because of the profundity of their teaching" (*CSL: Introduction*, 75). Occasionally an option is given for reading either a long or a short version of a text (for example, the story of Jesus and the Samaritan woman on the Third Sunday of Lent, A).

The Roman Lectionary also recognizes that not every passage in the Bible is either suitable or helpful for public reading in the liturgy. Decisions were made to omit entirely certain passages with "complex literary, critical, or exegetical problems" (*CSL: Introduction*, 76) that would make them difficult for most people to understand. Similarly, following the long-established practice in Roman lectionaries, at times selected verses within a reading are omitted because the passage would otherwise be too long or because a verse is "unsuitable pastorally or . . . involves truly difficult problems" (*CSL: Introduction*, 77).

Basic Arrangement of the Sunday Lectionary

After examining the possibility of spreading the readings over as little as two years or as many as four, the planners of the Sunday Lectionary decided on a three-year cycle. That is, there are different readings for each Sunday in Years A, B, and C (as they are commonly designated) and then the cycle begins over again. (Years where the sum of all the digits are divisible by three, for instance 1989, 1992, are always Year C. The year begins on the First Sunday of Advent.)

For each Sunday there are three readings: one from the Old Testament (with a few exceptions, as we will note in the Sundays after Easter), one from the Epistles or the book of Revelation, and one from the Gospels. Although provision is made for an individual Conference of Bishops to allow only two readings "for pastoral reasons" (*General Instruction*, 318), three is clearly the norm.

Since there is considerable divergence in the shape of the Lectionary during the major seasons of Advent–Christmas and Lent–Easter as compared with the Sundays of Ordinary Time, it is easier and less confusing to look at each separately, beginning with Ordinary Time.

The Gospels in Ordinary Time

One of the three Synoptic Gospels forms the central focus of each of the thirty-three (occasionally thirty-four) Sundays of each year of Ordinary Time. Year A is always the Gospel of Matthew; Year B, the Gospel of Mark; and Year C, the Gospel of Luke. The Gospel of John is not neglected, even though it does not form the core of a specific year. In accord with an ancient tradition of the Church, John has always been read during the Lent and Easter seasons "because it is the 'spiritual' Gospel in which the mystery of Christ is sounded out to greater depths" (*CSL: Introduction,* 7); in addition, because of the shortness of the Gospel of Mark, chapter 6 of John (the Bread of Life discourse) is taken up on five Sundays during Year B.

This particular arrangement of the Lectionary allows us to hear each of the Gospels in its own right; over the course of a year we come to know the distinctive picture of Jesus presented by Matthew or Mark or Luke.

The Epistles in Ordinary Time

Over the Sundays of Ordinary Time, passages are selected from the Epistles for the second reading, according to the following outline:

Year A
1 Corinthians 1—4 (Sundays 2–8)
Romans (Sundays 9–24)
Philippians (Sundays 25–28)
1 Thessalonians (Sundays 29–33)
Year B
1 Corinthians 6—11 (Sundays 2–6)
2 Corinthians (Sundays 7–14)
Ephesians (Sundays 15–21)
James (Sundays 22–26)
Hebrews 2—10 (Sundays 27–33)
Year C
1 Corinthians 12—15 (Sundays 2–8)
Galatians (Sundays 9–14)
Colossians (Sundays 15–18)
Hebrews 11—12 (Sundays 19–22)
Philemon (Sunday 23)
1 Timothy (Sundays 24–26)
2 Timothy (Sundays 27–30)
2 Thessalonians (Sundays 31–33)

Though individual passages are quite short and there is no attempt to read the Epistles in their entirety, over the three years the Lectionary gives a rich and varied exposure to the main themes and emphases of this part of Scripture. As already noted, in the Sundays in Ordinary Time there is no direct correlation between the Gospel reading and the Epistle reading; although at times they may touch on similar aspects of the Christian mystery, they have not been picked to provide a common theme.

The Old Testament Reading in Ordinary Time

In contrast to the selection of the Epistle, the first reading from the Old Testament has been carefully chosen to correlate with the Gospel text of the day. Although the intent is to highlight the unity between the Old and New Testaments, in fact there is considerable variety in how this "harmony" (*CSL: Introduction,* 67) is achieved. Sometimes it is a common theme that binds the two readings together; at other times the Old Testament will foreshadow or suggest something that is more fully developed in the Gospel (for example, on Sunday 16, Year C, the story of Martha and Mary giving hospitality to Jesus is paired with the story from Genesis of Abraham receiving his three guests). Often, if the Gospel quotes a verse from the Old Testament or refers to a specific incident, this passage will be the first reading (for example, on the Third Sunday, Year A, Matthew quotes Isaiah 8, 23—9, 1, and that Isaianic text services as the first reading). At times, the single lines given before the readings in the Lectionary are most helpful (though they are not meant to be read publicly) to indicate the point of correspondence that led to the choice of a particular reading.

While the desirability of a weekly Old Testament reading is undisputed, it is probably fair to say that the selection of Old Testament passages has been the single most controversial aspect of the Lectionary. The decision to link the first reading so closely with the Gospel imposes certain limitations. Many of the most important Old Testament passages simply do not readily lend themselves to correlation with a particular Gospel passage, and so are never heard in the Sunday assembly; often, such a brief or peripheral section of a major Old Testament story is read that it is difficult to get a sense of the whole picture. Furthermore, relatively little ever appears from the corpus of Wisdom literature (only three selections from Proverbs and two, both truncated, from the book of Job). The passages selected from the prophets are those that are readily seen to be fulfilled in Jesus, or which at least have Christological implications, but other aspects of the prophetic message are given less prominence (for example, the relatively few "social justice" passages read over the three years).

The Lent–Easter Season

As noted above, the seasons of Lent–Easter and Advent–Christmas form independent units; both cycles (the Advent even more so than the Lent) are carefully crafted so that through the Scripture readings we may be more closely initiated into the Church's understanding of these great feasts.

Easter, especially the Easter Triduum (Holy Thursday, Good Friday, and Easter Vigil on Saturday), is "the culmination of the entire liturgical year" (*Norms,* 18); Lent serves as a time of preparation, especially as a period of "closer attention to the Word of God" (*CSL,* 109). During Lent, "those important passages from the Gospels which were read to catechumens in the early centuries to prepare them for Baptism are proclaimed. These readings are directed to *all* the faithful because during Lent the whole Church, along with those about to be baptized, calls to mind the mystery of its initiation into Christ." Though it is not possible to examine closely all the readings for the Lent–Easter season, a few examples will illustrate the care and theological insight that finds expression in the arrangement of the Lectionary for this season.

The baptismal thrust is seen most clearly in Year A on the final three Sundays of Lent, where the great themes of water, light, and life are proclaimed through the reading from John's Gospel of the Samaritan woman at the well (Third Sunday), the curing of the man born blind (Fourth), and the raising of Lazarus from the dead (Fifth); so pivotal are these particular texts to the process of Christian initiation that they can be used in any of the three years, especially when there are candidates preparing for Baptism.

The readings for the first two Sundays of Lent are always the account of the Temptation and the Transfiguration respectively, read according to

the Gospel being followed in a given year. In Year B, the Gospels for the rest of Lent focus on the Crucifixion and Resurrection; in Year C, on the process of conversion.

At first glance, the choice of Old Testament readings for the Sundays of Lent might look entirely diverse and random; certainly they are not specifically linked to the Gospel. Rather, each year, they are meant to lead us through the Old Testament, presenting "the main elements of salvation history from its beginning until the promise of the New Covenant". (*CSL: Introduction,* 97):

Year A
First Sunday: Creation and fall
Second Sunday: The call of Abraham
Third Sunday: Water from the rock in the
    desert
Fourth Sunday: The anointing of David as
    king
Fifth Sunday: Promise of the restoration
Year B
First Sunday: Flood and covenant
Second Sunday: Abraham's sacrifice of his
    son
Third Sunday: The ten commandments
Fourth Sunday: Exile and destruction of the
    Temple
Fifth Sunday: Promise of the new covenant
Year C
First Sunday: Retelling the deliverance from
    Egypt
Second Sunday: The covenant with Abraham
Third Sunday: The call of Moses
Fourth Sunday: The Passover celebrated in
    the Promised Land
Fifth Sunday: Promise of a new exodus
The Epistle readings during Lent highlight themes such as faith, repentance, and baptismal motifs, and often are related to the first reading (for example, on the First Sunday of Lent, A, the passage from Romans about Christ as the Second Adam corresponds to the reading about the sin of Adam in Genesis 2).

The reading of the Gospel of John continues on most of the Sundays after Easter in all three years with texts about the Good Shepherd (Fourth Sunday) and from John's presentation of the Farewell Discourse and Prayer of Jesus (the Fifth to Seventh Sundays). This is the only time when there are no Old Testament readings; in keeping with a very ancient tradition, the Church turns to the Acts of the Apostles in all three years so that we ponder the work of the Spirit in the early Church. For the second reading, semicontinuous selections are taken from 1 Peter in Year A, 1 John in Year B (both rich in baptismal allusions), and from the book of Revelation (with its emphasis on heavenly worship) in Year C.

Advent–Christmas Season

The Lectionary for Advent is very carefully planned, with a definite movement as we progress toward the celebration of Christmas. The First Sunday emphasizes the Second Coming of Christ, picking up on a theme already sounded in the final Sunday of the Church Year (the feast of Christ the King). On the Second and Third Sundays, the Gospel is always about John the Baptist, so that the focus of attention moves more to the historical coming of a Messiah. On the Fourth Sunday, we turn to the first chapters of Matthew and Luke for events immediately prior to the birth of Jesus (the Annunciation to Mary and Joseph, and the Visitation).

In keeping with a long tradition in the Church, the Book of Isaiah with its messianic prophecies has a special place in both the Advent and Christmas readings. The Epistle readings are more general, offering exhortations and reflections; often, as the Advent focus moves to the birth of Jesus in time, the second reading serves to remind us of the Coming, which still awaits us in the future.

Throughout the Christmas season, the Lectionary preserves many of the readings that have been traditional in the Roman Church. On the Octave of Christmas, the Solemnity of Mary, Mother of God (New Year's Day), the first reading is the priestly blessing from Numbers 6, and the other two speak more specifically of Mary.

The Lectionary for Weekdays

The readings for weekdays throughout the year form a separate cycle, independent of the Sunday cycle. Even with only two readings, obviously more of the Bible can be covered on weekdays, although still only portions of many of the longer Old Testament books are included. The seasons of Advent–Christmas and Lent–Easter follow an annual cycle, that is, the readings are repeated every year; in Ordinary Time, the same Gospel passages are read every year, while the first read-

ing follows a two-year cycle (designated as Year I and Year II).

The following will give a brief outline of the weekday cycle:

Advent–Christmas Season.

During the first nine days of Advent, the Lectionary follows a very ancient custom of the Church and reads (in sequence) selected passages from the prophet Isaiah; on these days, contrary to usual practice, the Gospel is chosen to relate to this first reading. After the Thursday of the second week of Advent, the Gospel consistently speaks of John the Baptist, while the first reading is still from Isaiah or chosen to relate to the Gospel. From December 17 to 24, passages are selected from the first chapters of Matthew and Luke of events leading up to the birth of Christ; the first reading presents some of the major Old Testament messianic prophecies.

From December 27 on throughout the Epiphany season, there is a virtually continuous reading of 1 John. The Gospels relate various manifestations of Jesus; the whole of the first chapter of John's Gospel is read between December 31 and January 5.

Lent–Easter Season

Throughout Lent, the Gospel and Old Testament are rather closely related to each other and present to us different aspects of the major Lenten themes of Baptism and penance. In accord with an ancient custom in the Church, the Gospel of John is read from the fourth week on; in Holy Week the focus is more specifically on Christ's Passion.

During the Easter season, on weekdays as on Sundays, the Lectionary maintains the ancient custom of reading semicontinuously from the Acts of the Apostles. During the Octave of Easter, the Gospel selections recount the different occasions on which Christ appeared; over the next weeks there is semicontinuous reading of the teaching and prayer of Jesus at the Last Supper from John 13 through John 17.

Ordinary Time

Over the course of the year, the Gospels are read on a semicontinuous basis: Mark 1—12 in weeks 1–9, Matthew 5—25 in weeks 10–21, and Luke 4—21 in weeks 22–34. The Church Year ends with those passages from Luke that talk specifically of the Second Coming.

The first reading is completely independent from the Gospel and provides the opportunity to read selections from the majority of the Old Testament books and Epistles. Longer books are sometimes divided (for example, Genesis 1—11 is read in weeks 5–6 of Year I, Genesis 12—50 in weeks 12—14). At the very end of the Church Year, we read from Daniel in Year I and the book of Revelation in Year II with their eschatological themes.

The Responsorial Psalm

The Lectionary also introduces us to the psalms in the Bible; in fact, more than eighty psalms (or verses thereof) are used in the Sunday Lectionary and some 130 of the 150 psalms appear somewhere in the complete Lectionary. The psalm comes between the first and second reading, and is considered as "an integral part of the Liturgy of the Word" (*General Instruction*, 36).

The psalms are poetry, the majority of them certainly originally composed to be sung with musical accompaniment. The introduction to the Lectionary strongly encourages singing the psalm at Mass, preferably by a soloist (cantor) with the congregation joining in with a refrain; if the psalm is spoken, it is "to be recited in a manner conducive to meditation on the Word" (*CSL: Introduction*, 22).

Although the psalm always serves in some way as a response to the Word of God, there is considerable diversity in terms of its precise relationship to other readings. If the first reading or the Epistle or even the Gospel quotes a particular psalm verse, that psalm is usually taken up as an echo or anticipated response (for example, the use of Psalm 91 on the First Sunday of Lent, C, when a verse from this psalm, "He has put his angels in charge of you," is quoted during the temptation story in the Gospel). Often a psalm simply picks up and carries on the mood of the first reading, whether lamentation, thanksgiving, or praise. Some psalms have a long tradition of usage on particular feasts (Psalm 47, "God goes up with shouts of joy" for the Ascension; Psalm 72, "the kings of Arabia and Seba shall bring tribute. All Kings shall pay him homage, all nations shall serve him" for Epiphany). According to Lucien Deiss (a member of the committee in-

volved in the choice of psalms when the Lectionary was compiled), some psalms that would not otherwise be used were introduced primarily so that the Christian community could become more familiar with the entire Psalter (*Spirit and Song of the New Liturgy*, 110–11).

Ecumenical Import of the Lectionary

One of the unexpected and unforeseen results of the revision of the Roman Lectionary has been its adoption (with some modifications) by many Protestant churches, including Anglican/Episcopalian, Methodist, Presbyterian, Lutheran, and United Church of Canada. James White, a Methodist minister, in a much-quoted statement remarked that the Lectionary has become "Catholicism's greatest gift to Protestant preaching, just as Protestant biblical scholarship has given so much impetus to Catholic preaching" (*Christian Worship in Transition*, 139).

In recent years, many of these churches came together under the auspices of the Consultation on Common Texts and developed the *Common Lectionary*, an order of readings for use on Sundays and a few special days of the Christian year. The *Common Lectionary* basically follows the Roman Lectionary, with some significant changes in the choice of Old Testament passages in order to deal with some of the problem areas we have noted.

Although Catholics and Protestants do not share exactly the same Lectionary, tremendous progress has been made toward common reading of Scripture. The ecumenical import, even on a practical level, is significant; in many places ministers of different churches now gather together to reflect and prepare their Sunday sermons. And, although we are still not at the point of being able to be united at the table of the Lord's banquet, we can be united and nourished at the common table of his Word.

Using the Lectionary for Prayer and Study

Many people, both clergy and lay, today use the Lectionary as a basic resource for daily prayer, whether or not they are able to celebrate liturgy with the Christian community every day. Consistent use of the Lectionary over a period of years will necessarily expose us to a broad expanse of Scripture and protect us against the subjective reading of the Bible spoken about earlier. The Lectionary puts us in touch with the Church's understanding of the mysteries of our faith as presented through the Church year, helping us to recover dimensions which may have been lost in popular piety (for example, the baptismal dimension of the season of Lent as opposed to a solely ascetic focus).

Many religious educators are discovering the Lectionary as a valuable resource in catechetics; reflection on the readings as appropriate to various age groups provides a common focus when the whole community gathers in prayer. Parish study groups or Bible studies often take the Gospel of a given year as their text for study. More and more the Lectionary is being used as the core of the RCIA program to introduce the new catechumens to the life of faith and community.

Though the Lectionary contains the Word of God, the particular selection of material is a human endeavor and thus only more or less perfect. It is recognized that some choices of specific readings could have been more auspicious, and certainly revisions will probably be made in time.

In particular, two areas are surfacing that seem to call for further discussion and reflection. As we ponder the role of women today in church and society, we bring certain questions to the Lectionary; we need to ask why certain texts have been omitted (for example, the story of courageous midwives who defy Pharaoh and ensure the survival of the Hebrew people in Egypt) and whether it is either necessary or helpful pastorally to include other texts that are open to being interpreted in a way derogatory to women (for example, Eph 5, 20). The second concern is in the area of our relationship to the Jewish people; as we become more aware of "the continuity of our faith with that of the earlier covenant" (*Vatican Guidelines*, 1974), we are more sensitive to the fact that the Lectionary must "promote among the Catholic people a genuine appreciation of the special place of the Jewish people as first chosen in the history of salvation, and in no way slight the honor and dignity that is theirs" (*American Bishops' Statement on Catholic-Jewish Relations*, 1975).

The revision of the Lectionary stands as one of the most tangible and permanent implementations of the vision and challenge of the Second Vatican Council. In the Lectionary, "the treasures of the Bible are . . . opened up more lavishly so that a richer share in God's Word may be provided for the faithful" (*CSL*, 51). The Lectionary has the potential to shape the life of the Christian community, not only as the Word of God is proclaimed in the celebration of the liturgy but also as it is broken open for us in the homily, in catechetics, and in private and group study and prayer, which is rooted in Scripture. As the Lectionary is used over the cycle of years and even generations, "there is reason to hope for a new awakening of the spiritual life deriving from an increased dedication to God's word which 'abides forever' (Is 40, 8)" (*Dei Verbum*, 26).

FURTHER READING

The text of the *Constitution on the Sacred Liturgy: Introduction to the Lectionary* has been published by the United States Catholic Conference, *Lectionary for Mass: Introduction, Liturgy Documentation* Series 1, 1982.

Canadian Conference of Bishops. *National Bulletin on Liturgy,* no. 50, 1975.

Proclaim the Word: the Lectionary for Mass. Liturgy Study Text Series 8. Washington, DC: United States Catholic Conference, 1982.

Fitzsimmons, John H. *Guide to the Lectionary.* London: Mayhew-McCrimmon, 1981.

Keifer, Ralph. *To Hear and To Proclaim: Introduction, Lectionary for Mass with Commentary for Musicians and Priests.* Washington, DC: National Association of Pastoral Musicians, 1983.

Skudlarek, William. *The Word in Worship: Preaching in a Liturgical Context.* Abingdon's Preacher's Library. Nashville: Abingdon, 1981.

For discussion of some of the issues around the Bible and our relationship to the Jewish people, see Pawlikowski, John J., and James A. Wilde. *When Catholics Speak About Jews.* Chicago: Liturgy Training Program, 1987.

THE PENTATEUCH

LAWRENCE BOADT

The Nature of the Pentateuch

What Is the Pentateuch?

Beginnings are important. If we want to know what kind of a book we are reading, we skim over the first few pages to see how it starts and what point of view the author adopts. For this reason it is vital to recognize the special character of the first five books of the Old Testament. They stand apart as an introduction to the rest of the Bible and, more importantly, both the Jewish and the Christian faiths recognize them as the foundation on which the rest of the Scriptures are built. They might be called a blueprint or a constitution that becomes the standard by which all other revelation is interpreted. The name *Pentateuch* comes from the title given in the earliest Greek translation that dates to the second century BC and means a "five-part" writing. This confirms that even from biblical times the Pentateuch has always been understood as a single work. Jewish tradition calls it *Torah,* which does not so much mean "law" as "teaching." This five-book Torah contains the basic teaching of the Jewish faith.

The Pentateuch as a Part of the Canon of Scripture

A "canon" means a rule of arrangement. Biblical books are in a certain order. We do not always know clearly just when or why the Bible was ordered in exactly its present lineup, but we can be sure of one thing—it was never accidental. The order of some books changed over the centuries, but gradually each book was positioned intentionally to be read in its present order; and how we interpret the message of a book is determined at least in part by where it stands in relation to other books. So, when we begin to study the Old Testament, we must look for the clues that tell us why Genesis, Exodus, Leviticus, Numbers, and Deuteronomy are divided into five books and are lined up as they are. This must be done on two levels: (1) the religious and theological meaning of the books for our Jewish and Christian faiths today; and (2) the background of what the text and words meant to those who wrote it and put it together. This latter task also involves several other aspects: (1) the *historical* development of how the books came together and what pieces were added to them as they grew to their final size; (2) the literary shape or form of the books alone and together that give them such qualities as a plot, dramatic power, connected narrative story, and the like; and (3) whatever knowledge of Israel's *actual history* that we can discover. Thus, in all, when we set out to study the Pentateuch, we ask four questions: (1) What kind of literature is it? (2) What is it saying to us? (3) What really happened to Israel behind this account? and (4) How did this literature reach this form? It is far easier to answer the first two questions about the literary qualities and the message of the text than to rediscover after more than two thousand years how accurately all the stories from Israel's history were transmitted, or the actual way the text itself was put together by generations of biblical editors.

Reading through the Pentateuch in the *New American Bible*

The text of the NAB already provides us with several helpful tools with which we can deepen our understanding of the text of the first five books of the Old Testament. There is a brief introduction to the Pentateuch itself at the beginning, as well as specific introductions placed before the opening chapter of each individual book. These introductions sketch for the reader some of the key structures in the outline of a book and some of the major religious themes that play a crucial role in the text's message for us. They also raise a few of the major concerns of biblical scholarship for the reader to consider. In addition, there are the valuable notes at the bottom of each page of text that give us historical and scholarly information about difficult or confusing words in the text, or about the customs of ancient peoples, or about the meanings of obscure references. They sometimes also explain doctrinal beliefs of our faith that are rooted in particular biblical verses, or refer us to similar passages in other books of the Bible that throw further light on the subject under discussion.

As important as all these helps are, they are very brief. It is the purpose of this study guide to do several things to supplement them so that a serious reading of the Pentateuch will be possible without getting lost in the forest because we cannot see past all the trees. First of all, these study aids will expand the points mentioned in the introductions and notes of the NAB about the

scholarly interpretation of the text's background and development so that they can be understood as part of the larger picture that the Pentateuch paints. And second, they will explore the literary unity and artistic shaping so that the harmony of its inspired message will stand out more clearly to the modern reader. We will hopefully better appreciate how the five books all relate to one another both historically and literarily to form the foundational source of biblical faith.

The contents pages of the NAB (see p. v) include eight books in all under the title "Pentateuch." This is an unusual division, and it may be more helpful for us to look at the biblical arrangement in the threefold way that the Jewish Bible does rather than in the fourfold groupings that the NAB and other modern Christian Bibles follow. Thus, for the Jewish tradition there is the Torah (or "Law"), the Prophets, and the Writings. See diagram below.

The Catholic Bible also includes seven other books under the Writings, which are lacking in Jewish and Protestant Bibles, and are often called *deuterocanonical* because they were written in Greek and not Hebrew: Tobit, Judith, Wisdom of Solomon, Sirach/Ecclesiasticus, Baruch, and 1 and 2 Maccabees.

When ordered in columns like this, it becomes evident that prophecy includes both historical books and prophetic speakers. That is, both types are considered to call people back prophetically to the message in the Pentateuch and to show how that message was lived out or not lived out in history. The Writings, in turn, are a further

The Law (Torah)	*The Prophets*	*The Writings*
Genesis	FORMER PROPHETS	Psalms
Exodus	Joshua	Job
Leviticus	Judges	Proverbs
Numbers	1 Samuel	Ruth
Deuteronomy	2 Samuel	Song of Songs
	1 Kings	Ecclesiastes
	2 Kings	Lamentations
		Esther
	LATTER PROPHETS	Daniel
	Isaiah	Ezra–Nehemiah
	Jeremiah	1 Chronicles
	Ezekiel	2 Chronicles
	The Book of the Twelve	

grouping that should be understood primarily as books of reflection, piety, or additional explanation to help us live the message of Torah day by day. In short, all the other books of the Old Testament flow from reflection on the Torah five.

What Kind of Literature Is It?

Story and Law

Before we begin to read the text closely, several preliminary issues must be discussed more deeply in order to answer our four questions. The first is: What kind of literature is it? At first glance, the NAB reveals that it is prose rather than poetry, except in a few places (for example, Ex 15; Dt 32). But what kind of prose? A quick survey of all five books reveals a mixture of two types: *laws* and *narratives*. Generally, they are separated into large sections of each, carefully alternated, but not completely. Every narrative part contains scattered commands and laws, and every collection of laws has a healthy episode or two of story. The books break down as follows (in rough divisions):

Genesis All Narrative (Genesis 1—50);
Exodus Part Narrative (Exodus 1—19; 24; 32—34); Part Law (20—31; 35—40);
Leviticus All Law (Leviticus 1—27);
Numbers Part Narrative (Numbers 11—17; 20—26; 31—33); Part Law (Numbers 1—10; 18—19; 27—30; 34—36);
Deuteronomy Part Narrative (Deuteronomy 1—4; 31—34); Part Law (Deuteronomy 5—30).

One could illustrate this dramatically by the diagram above.

Jewish religious tradition generally identifies 613 divine commandments within the Pentateuch. The rabbis and sages have divided the breakdown of these laws as follows:

Genesis   3 laws
Exodus   111 laws
Leviticus   247 laws
Numbers   52 laws
Deuteronomy   200 laws

As shown above, the laws are contained inside a story framework that traces the "history" events from the moment of creation in Genesis 1 down to the moment when Israel stands at the edge of the Promised Land, but before it has been entered in Deuteronomy 34. But this story is really part of a much larger historical narrative that combines the Pentateuch with the so-called Deuteronomistic History (the books of Joshua, Judges, 1 and 2 Samuel, and 1 and 2 Kings) and goes from Creation to the fall of Judah, the last independent part of Israel as a nation, before the Babylonians in the sixth century BC.

What the Pentateuch proposes as a way of life through Law and Story is then narrated and judged as lived or rejected in the history of the national life on the land. 2 Kings 25 ends with a vague openness to a possible new start after the people have been defeated and exiled for their failure to obey the Word of God that was given in the Pentateuch and then proclaimed by God's prophets (see 2 Kgs 17). Because of this greater scope, we can be sure that the authors of the Pen-

Genesis	Exodus, Leviticus, & Numbers	Deuteronomy		Joshua-Judges	1 & 2 Samuel	1 & 2 Kings
From creation to the days of the patriarchs	From slavery in Egypt to the Promised Land border	Warnings on the border of the Promised Land		The people enter and settle the land	Change from tribal rule to kingship	Life under the kings up to the Exile

tateuch intended readers to see the giving of many laws as intrinsically important to their existence as a people—not just as a lesson in the past but as a continuous claim on every new generation of Israel (see diagram above).

The mixture of law and story narrative may seem boring to modern ears since we are not used to hearing long lists of regulations recited inside a good story. But to the ancient believer, knowing and accepting such laws expressed a continuity with the stories of how God dealt with their ancestors. They might say, "Our ancestors did *those* things, and we obey *these* laws, and as a result we are one and the same people of God!"

The Overall Structure

The present structure of the Pentateuch has a distinct shape to it. Not only is it story and law, it is also drama. Each book has its own subject matter that can be studied by itself, but only if the reader does not forget the larger movement of all five books. One way to look at this interlocking action among the books is to see three distinct stages:

1. The preparation period (Genesis)
2. The time of Moses in Egypt and Sinai (Exodus to Numbers)
3. The new preparation for life in the land (Deuteronomy)

This can be diagrammed as a forward movement, as shown below.

The "Plot"

This is the simplest diagram. But even more action appears when we trace the focus of God's "plan" through the developing plot. God creates the world for all peoples to praise the divine goodness, but humanity fails the divine hopes (Gn 1—11); so God chooses a single family or people that will prove faithful and teach all other nations (Gn 12—50). These in turn must learn the lesson of God's goodness through hardship and then deliverance (Ex) and become obedient and formed as truly God's holy people (Lv and Nm 1—10). Then God will lead them to a Promised Land (Nm 10—36), which they will keep only if obedient and loyal (Dt). This new articulation can be diagrammed also. See diagram at top of next page.

The Symmetrical and Artistic Unity

The Pentateuch has been divided into five books by ancient editors who found that they had so much material they needed five separate scrolls to copy it all down. They made the divisions as naturally as possible, choosing about the same lengths for each scroll and breaking between obvious changes in place or topic. But the five divisions also reveal a very carefully balanced symmetry in which the ends and middles balance

Genesis	Exodus	Leviticus	Numbers		Deuteronomy
On beginnings: God deals with the forbears in promise and person.	God rescues and covenants with the people.	Laws are given for a holy people.	Desert journey of God's guidance to the Promised Land.		A "second law" that both sums up, and looks to the land ahead.

one another in a chiastic (or ladderlike) construction that can be called an ABCBA pattern. (See diagram below.)

Many themes of call and response, promise and rescue are echoed between Genesis and Deuteronomy and between Exodus and Numbers, and key themes of obedience and faith resound in all five books.

Key Theological Themes

Certain key themes flow through the five books, sometimes limited to only one book, sometimes found in several books. The most important are:

1. The primeval history of the world before Israel's own remembered history began (Gn 1—11).

2. The promises and blessings to the great tribal ancestors, the patriarchs and matriarchs (Gn 12—50).

3. The rescue and exodus out of Egypt (Ex 1—18).

4. The giving of a covenant and laws (Ex 19, 1—Nm 10, 10).

5. Guidance in the wilderness (Ex 13—18; Nm 10, 11—36, 13).

6. The conditional warnings to guide Israel through its "salvation history" in the land (Dt).

7. The conquest of the land (Gn passim; Nm and Dt).

These all interact. Note, for example, that the promise of land is announced as God's plan of action in Exodus 3, 7–10; but it has been foreshadowed to Abraham in Genesis 12, 1–3 and then noted as fulfilled in Deuteronomy 34, 1–3, just as the conquest is to begin.

Reading the Pentateuch without Being a Fundamentalist

Each book of the Pentateuch has its own unique flavor, and each deals with a different part of the

A. Genesis	(the preface in which God calls and forms the ancestors)
B. Exodus	(the wilderness journey to the mountain of Sinai to meet God)
C. Leviticus	(the center at the top of Sinai where God gives Covenant and Law)
B. Numbers	(the wilderness journey from Sinai to the Promised Land)
A. Deuteronomy	(the epilogue in which God calls and forms Israel for the land)

story and the laws by which Israel was to live. But even if we can read each one separately, it is even more important to read them together as a single story. We have already noted how these five books tell the history (in its ancient sense) of the world and of Israel in particular from the beginnings of creation down to the hopeful moment when Israel stands on the edge of a new land and a new home in Palestine. Two things can be noted about that history mixed with laws and lessons: the first is that it is to serve as a handbook or a rule book for how Israel is to live in the land it is about to possess (see Dt 4, 1), and the second is that it certainly does not make a complete history, although it is a complete story. It picks and chooses only certain events and certain themes to treat, and these all have very significant religious lessons to teach. That is, it is a theology book as much or more than it is a real history of the people.

It is hard for us to escape a desire to see a strict modern scientific history in the stories of the Pentateuch, but let's look at one illustration to help us. In Genesis 4, Cain kills Abel when they are the only two living children of Adam and Eve according to the story. Cain is punished by God and sent far to the East. Then the text says that "Cain had relations with his wife" in Genesis 4, 17. But what wife was possible in a real history? Up to this point, the story has moved from the world's first killing to a new theme—how the world was populated—and it doesn't seem to bother the author that the second cannot fit this history just related. The only concern for the writer is to make a series of religious lessons that we can all learn from.

But the Pentateuch is not an idle story, either. It is very carefully crafted and put together to tell of the crucial things that happened in the past that we need to know in order to discover God. It tells of human weaknesses and urgings toward sin, about the failure of most of the world to know God, and the divine choice of Israel to witness the loving concern of God to others, and how God was revealed in a number of central events: (1) the choice of the patriarchs, (2) the giving of a covenant, (3) the law to be obeyed, and (4) the guidance through the wilderness to a promised land.

The Pentateuch is a great work of art. It tells a vital story of God's relationship to the world with power and beauty. It proposes history but does not allow us to question it too closely about exact descriptions. It proposes religious and theological lessons but warns us not to treat it like a textbook full of lists of truths. It proposes a story that will teach us by sharing its experience with our experience. We must read it for enjoyment and for skillful storytelling. Once we have understood the whole as literature, we can ask, "How does this literary style give us history?" and "How does it present its message?" For an overview of the history of how the Christian tradition has interpreted the Pentateuch as part of the whole Old Testament, see the article by Kevin Madigan, "Catholic Interpretation of the Bible" (RG 54–67).

Critical Interpretation of the Pentateuch

Interpretation of the Bible changed radically in the growth of modern thought after the Reformation and with the Age of Enlightenment in the seventeenth and eighteenth centuries. Much of the early efforts at a critical and historical interpretation of the Scriptures began with work on the Pentateuch. Before we look at how those scholars tried to recover the actual historical development of the Pentateuchal texts and what methods they proposed for understanding its meaning, we need to note briefly how the New Testament itself makes use of texts from the Pentateuch in order to have a point of comparison.

The New Testament

Jesus himself and the various authors of New Testament writings often cite texts from the Bible, which of course was simply the Old Testament in their day. Almost always, they cite passages from the narratives and rarely refer to the legal materials in Leviticus and Numbers, although the laws first given on Mount Sinai in Exodus 20—23 and then the speech of Moses on the law in Deuteronomy were known to them. Often the stories are cited as proofs for something that Jesus taught or that the apostles were preaching. An example is found in Jesus' teaching on divorce that is found in Matthew 19, 5 (and Mark 10, 7f). Jesus refers to Genesis 2, 24 when he says "a man shall leave his father and mother and be joined to his wife, and the two shall become one flesh."

A few stories from the Pentateuch are treated

as a *type case*. Paul in Romans 4, 9–22 cites the story of Abraham recorded in Genesis 15, 1–6 and 17, 1–5 as a forerunner of a chosen people having faith without having the law of Moses to live by. Abraham is viewed as a forerunner of the Christian believer; but in a general sense this usage may be seen as a type of prophecy—the Old Testament person foreshadows God's revelation to the Gentiles; like Abraham, they are called without living under the Law. Elsewhere, the authors of the Gospels and Acts quote Old Testament passages from the prophets and psalms as predictions of Jesus as Messiah and to help explain his death and resurrection. But occasionally, Paul uses an almost allegorical method of interpreting biblical texts. In Galatians 4, 21–31, he treats the children of Hagar and Sarah, that is, Ishmael and Isaac from Genesis 16—21, as prototypes of Jews and Christians. Hebrews 7, 1–10 does the same with the story of Melchizedek and Abraham from Genesis 14, 18–20. The author wants to show that Melchizedek represents a fore-type of Christ, who is the new and eternal high priest. To do this, however, he plays on the etymology of the name Melchizedek as "king of righteousness" and Melchizedek's position as king of Salem ("king of peace") and fancifully builds up a case that since no mention is made in the text of the king's parents, his birth, or his death after the event, he prefigures the eternal character of Jesus as divine high priest.

Overall, however, New Testament use of the Bible is nearly always focused on showing the deep connection between the meaning of earlier revelation and the person and role of Jesus. A good source for all the quotations of the Old Testament in the New is R. Bratcher, *Old Testament Quotations in the New Testament* (United Bible Societies, 1987).

The Post-Reformation Interest in Sources

The Protestant Reformation stressed the return to the study of the original texts of the Old Testament in Hebrew and other languages. This soon led to the keen observation that the vocabulary and style of passages were not consistent within the Pentateuch itself and perhaps showed signs of combining different (and older) traditions together.

The first (1678) truly modern Pentateuchal scholar was a French priest, Richard Simon. Simon noted after careful analysis that Genesis

1 and 2 seemed to differ in style, and that this was found elsewhere in Genesis and probably showed that Moses used several different sources in writing the five books of the Pentateuch. For such a modest insight, his work was condemned by church authorities and put on the index. But it opened the door. He was followed in the next century by many others who gradually explored the differences between passages that constantly called God by the proper name *Yahweh,* and those that called God by the more general term *Elohim.* The NAB always renders *Yahweh* by the English word "LORD," and *Elohim* by "God."

These could be traced as two complete parallel stories interwoven throughout the Pentateuch up to the book of Numbers. Arguments developed over whether these had been originally two separate written works that told the same history of Israel, or whether there was one original version that was supplemented or added to over many centuries to make two variants with time. In the early nineteenth century, scholars began to note that the so-called Elohist passages really represented two separate accounts themselves, one more narrative and interested in the great interventions of God, the other more concerned with priestly and ritual actions. These were named in turn the Elohist and the Priestly strands.

By the mid-nineteenth century it was commonly agreed that there had indeed been three independent versions of the Pentateuch's basic story, which could be titled by the initials J (for German *Jahwist),* E (for Elohist), and P (for Priestly). At the same time, the book of Deuteronomy was acknowledged to be a fourth and totally separate source of its own that could be labeled D naturally enough. In 1878 Julius Wellhausen published his *Prolegomena to the History of Israel,* in which he laid out the arguments for the postexilic composition of the P source. In the process he not only analyzed the arguments for the "four-source theory," as it was now called, but he supported the basic sequence of JE as monarchic, followed by D in the early exilic period, and then by P in the postexilic period, and he identified the four historical situations that led to each different telling of the history.

The Development of Form Criticism

Shortly after Wellhausen's great summary of the theory of four separate documents was published, attention turned to getting behind the four sources to the original units that comprised them. Where did all the individual incidents and poems and stories and laws come from? Thus, at the beginning of the twentieth century was born form criticism, the search for the earliest and the smallest units of the tradition. The founder of this method was Hermann Gunkel, who wrote extensively on the form-critical analysis of Genesis and the Psalms. These scholars were interested in the literary *genres* that made up the four sources. If scholars could identify the special form of a poem or a hymn or a law or a narrative, they could probably identify the situation out of which it came. Thus the victory hymn of Israel over the Egyptians in Exodus 15 can be further specified as praise of God as a divine warrior who battles alongside Israel's troops and guarantees the defeat of the enemy. This helps us realize it originates in a tribal setting before the people were settled in a kingdom, and perhaps was sung at an annual festival of God's victory.

Form criticism can even help distinguish different types of law. The Ten Commandments in Exodus 20, 1–17 are simple and direct commands to do or not to do something. They differ completely from most of the laws in the Pentateuch that specify "if you do such and such, then the penalty will be the following." Because the laws had these two differing styles, scholars assume that the first kind was more like a catechetical instruction for children to help them memorize and summarize the law; while the second type came from actual court cases in which a decision had to be made.

It can honestly be said that the work of form-critical study of the Pentateuch was the dominant task of scholarly study of the Bible in the first half of the twentieth century. As scholarship has developed in the last forty years, both source and form criticism have given way before new concerns and the new methods needed to deal with them. Before noting such shifts, what can be said of the accomplishment of these older methods?

The Fruits of Source Criticism

When scholarly criticism was born in the seventeenth and eighteenth centuries, it first noted the difficulties in the text, which suggested more than one style or author. Examples included the different names for God in the two creation stories

of Genesis 1, 1—2, 4a; and 2, 4b—3, 24. The first always calls the divine name "God," the second always uses the title "LORD God." The first is extremely formal and shows great reverence for God's transcendence, while the second makes God almost like a human being, working in clay to build a body and conferring in person with his creature. Many other places in the text show the same clear differences. Also, they noted many examples of double accounts which, except for some small differences, looked like exactly the same story being told twice. Compare Genesis 12 and 20 on Abraham passing his wife Sarah off as his sister; or the two accounts on how Hagar had to flee to the wilderness with Ishmael in Genesis 16 and 21.

After three centuries of study, scholars reached a general consensus in the late nineteenth century that there were indeed the four sources described in the section above. They can be briefly described in the following manner to reveal their individual characters and the probable date and historical situation from which they came:

The Yahwist (J)

This is the earliest and most comprehensive source of the whole story. It was written in Judah, probably Jerusalem. It was long believed to have been written under King Solomon or one of his successors in the late tenth century or early ninth century BC, but now many scholars are convinced that it was done much later in the monarchy or even in the Exile, while others believe that at least many additions can be found in the present J text that were added much later to an early version. The authors wished to show that the promises to Abraham were fulfilled in the empire founded by David. It uses the name *Yahweh* for God and has a frank and earthy language about God's closeness to those he chooses. It naturally favors strong leaders of the type of David.

The Elohist (E)

When Solomon's kingdom fell apart and the north went its own way, it needed an official account of the tradition that reflected its anti-Jerusalem view. Early source critics believed it was written shortly after the founding of the Northern Kingdom just after 900 BC, but many scholars today wonder if there ever was such an independent document; the majority perhaps believe the unique E elements are simply revisions or additions to the basic J text over the centuries. However, many of its characteristics are strong in certain sections of the Pentateuch, such as the Jacob stories or the Exodus narrative. These passages prefer the name *Elohim* for God and strongly emphasize Jacob and northern places such as Bethel, Shechem, and the like.

The Deuteronomist (D)

Deuteronomy and those books influenced by it, the so-called Deuteronomistic History (Joshua, Judges, Samuel, and Kings), are generally understood today to reflect the Exile in their final form. Many scholars trace their origins to the eighth and seventh centuries BC as a reassessment of the J and E traditions in light of pagan inroads and unfaithful kings. It has affinities to the Elohist in its stress that the covenant with Moses is more important than kingship, and on the need for total loyalty to Yahweh; and it has affinities to J with its emphasis on Jerusalem. Unlike J, the D source restricts worship of Yahweh to Jerusalem as the only legitimate center for north and south alike.

The Priestly Source (P)

Much of the P material on cult and law probably dates to the same time as Deuteronomy, but its ordering and some new materials are clearly reflective of the needs of the exilic community in the sixth century BC. It stresses obedience to the law and the permanence of God's blessing no matter how desperate the situation, and it demands personal commitment to God. Most probably the P editors arranged all four of the sources into our present Pentateuch around 500 BC. Some commentaries date it to as much as a century later. Both P and the Pentateuch as a whole reflect a definite Judean point of view in their final shapes.

J and E went along side by side as long as the two kingdoms lasted from 930 to 722 BC. When the northern kingdom fell, its E story was carried down to Judah by refugees and there combined at some point around 700 BC with J into a single account. Still later, in the time of the fall of Judah itself in 587 BC and during its exile, D and P were also combined with JE to make our final JEDP. Editors and teachers from the Priestly circles put it into final shape, and possibly it was this work that Ezra the Scribe made all the people accept as

the Book of the Law of God about 458 BC (see Neh 8—9).

Form Criticism and the Process of Tradition

Although the results of source criticism have largely stood the test of time, the interest in going back behind these written sources led to the dominant role of form criticism in this century. The heart of the form-critical method is recognition of the various literary genres and types used in biblical books. Each genre has a certain style and way of being expressed that corresponds to its purpose or function. So a letter always has a heading and salutation because a person who receives it will feel this personal touch and more likely pay attention to its message than if one just writes someone a list of facts on a page. In the opposite fashion, a telephone book always uses columns, alphabetical order, and a listlike format because a continuous letterlike paragraph would make it impossible to locate a name, which after all is the sole purpose of the directory.

Form criticism assumes that communication is socially determined by rules that reveal what kind of thing someone is trying to say. Scholars recognized that, in ancient society especially, most people depended on oral recitation and memory aids because knowledge of writing was reserved to a few, and writing materials were scarce. Thus ancient ways of speaking were stereotyped—that is, they stuck to certain well-known patterns of saying things that were used according to their intended purpose—and these genres lasted over many centuries with little variation in form. Actually, each time something was said or passed on, speakers gave it a slightly different emphasis or touch. Only when it was written down and became fixed did it stop changing altogether, yet the basic form remained constant.

To understand Pentateuch texts from a form-critical viewpoint, first see if you can find the beginning and end of a single section (what are the limits of a unit?). Then attempt to name the genre or form (is it a hymn? law? temple lament? historical narrative? fable? myth?). Next, guess at what might have been its original purpose or setting in the ancient life situation (is it part of a long epic of great heroic ancestors? Is it from the temple liturgy? Is it part of a catechism for children? Is it propaganda?). Finally, ask what purpose it plays in this narrative or section (Does it add a new episode to the plot? Does it support a line of argument? Does it explain the character of the hero?).

Our interest in the original form of a unit of biblical literature, and our investigation of where it came from in the life of ancient Israel, should draw our attention to a final critical consideration: to question the entire process of how traditions get passed on and grow or change. Both form and source criticism fall under a more general interest in the *transmission* history of the text (often called its tradition history or redaction criticism). Each original statement or story or law goes through a process of being combined with other units and then combined again in still larger works. Thus collections grow and stories are put in a new order or used in a different way for a new purpose. At the same time, each age looks at the old stories and laws and often rewrites or changes them to fit modern times.

The redaction critic tries to trace this history of transmission, editing, and adapting from the earliest stages right up to the final form as we have it in the Pentateuch today. It is a complex and difficult process that can only be done by those who know Hebrew as well as the history and literary works of the Near East. But even the new reader can get some flavor of it by carefully looking at a text, noting its structures and development, enjoying it as literature, and using the commentaries and other available tools.

Current Trends in Critical Study

Both source and form criticism work directly from what we can know of the text by comparing it with other literary styles and literary works. Much of the inspiration for form criticism, for example, came from the great work on the origins and development of fairy tales and folk stories by the brothers Grimm and Hans Christian Anderson in the early nineteenth century. But these methods have been mostly analytical; that is, they break down the narratives and laws into smaller and smaller units, and assign dates and origins to each piece. This makes it harder to read the biblical books as single works. There has been a definite movement to counterbalance this with rediscovery of methods that can be used to read the Pentateuch more fully as a whole story or literary work.

Some of these are *rhetorical criticism,* which tries to show the literary artistry in the combination of pieces into a whole and how the whole story is structured for effect; *structural analysis,* which searches for the language patterns and levels of meaning that control both the plot and the underlying message by word clues; *reader-response criticism,* which studies a text by paying attention to what the audience would hear and expect and how an author tries to reach that audience—this requires imagining ourselves in the world of the text. All of these are under the broad category of modern literary theory, and they have become very important new directions for biblical study, especially of the early books. Closely connected to these is *canonical criticism,* which tries to understand how a book like Genesis or Exodus is read as part of the larger collection of sacred books. Is there importance in Genesis being first? What happens when we read the wisdom books before the prophets in the order of our present canon?

Still another major area of new study focuses on the contributions of the social sciences. Sociology gives us models for how various types of social groupings interact together that might throw light on how ancient tribal or town or small-kingdom forms of life were lived in biblical times. Anthropology and ethnology let us study people who are still living more like the ancients did than like the way we live. Archaeology as well discovers and re-creates life as it was from stones and human remains.

Truly, Bible study today employs all the tools made available by cooperative sharing of scholarly knowledge among different sciences. At the same time, none of the gains of one movement, such as those of the early source critics, are ever thrown away as useless, but they need to be supplemented and refined by later research. And whenever one branch of study concentrates too much on just a part of the picture, we can be sure that other scholars will arise to call us back to what we have neglected.

The Historical Background of the Pentateuch

A Wide Diversity of Materials

The Pentateuch as a historical narrative begins with the creation of the earth and follows human history up to the time the Israelites enter the land of Canaan. In fact, however, few passages in the five books really reflect historical records of the past. First of all, many sections are made up of laws that have been included from collections dating to different periods in Israel's history. In a very loose way we could say they all belong under the name of Moses, the first lawgiver, because he founded the way of defining the covenant by means of religious laws.

Second, some stories are clearly not about ordinary time in history at all. All of Genesis 1—11 treats the creation of the world and the first events of human existence without any historical concreteness. As a literary genre, they do not fit the category of history telling. Instead, they are about why things are the way they are—why God made humans this way, why we sin, why we die, why it is hard to obey God, why men and women are different, why the earth is plagued with floods, how God deals with evil. Such stories about the divine purposes at the beginning of creation, and about the nature of human life as we experience it, are usually called *myths* if they are told in story form. Genesis 1—11 is almost entirely based on the myth genre. And even the stories of the patriarchs and matriarchs in Genesis 12—50 are not a modern type of recalling history but largely model hero stories built around folktale types of storytelling. Even though they are based on real history, it is often hard to pin them down to exact locations and events.

The View of the Ancient Historian

This special character of the Pentateuch as both law and story alerts us to a fundamental problem that plagues most modern believers who read the Bible. Contemporary understanding of history differs greatly from that of the ancient world. Modern people expect proof through documents, witnesses, electronic records such as audio tapes or video recordings, and careful digging to find out just what happened, without all the propaganda and personal bias of a particular interest group. This is a difficult order to fill in any case, since all of us, even trained historians, have special points of view that color what we find. It is, however, an impossible order to demand of the ancient historian. They never thought this way, and as a result did not record the events of their time

with such neutral objectivity, nor did they ever believe in telling the past as a simple and objective search for exactly what happened.

First, of course, they had no ways of getting much of the historical record. There were fewer written accounts and documents, there were no electronic or permanent ways of storing information in large and easy-to-produce books like we have, and there were no schools of science that valued exact observation as a primary end. Thus little or nothing was preserved for its own sake. Second, everything that went on told us about something important for our lives. This meant that most history was seen as a lesson for humans to learn by. History was written largely to persuade people of a certain type of behavior or a certain outlook on the world. It was viewed much as we would understand propaganda for a good cause, perhaps like newspaper editorials that take sides to explain major events or argue for their favorite causes.

The bottom line, therefore, is that ancient history was more interested in explaining *why* something happened than *what* precisely took place, and it was more interested in the message it communicated for the audience than in a record of accurate details for future study.

This insight will help us understand why the ancient historians felt no awkwardness in adding long lists of laws to a good story. The laws were vital parts of the "message" that the story was supposed to tell.

Moses as the Author of the Pentateuch

Traditionally, Moses has been considered the author of the Pentateuch. Orthodox Jews and Conservative Christians still hold this position strongly, but historical scholarship does not. Nowhere do these books actually mention an author, but frequently they state that Moses taught the people their contents, especially the laws (see Lv 23, 1–25). If Moses is the actual author, then all the laws at least would have their origin in a direct revelation from God on Mount Sinai. The book of Nehemiah relates how Ezra brought forth "the book of the law of Moses which the LORD prescribed for Israel" (Neh 8, 1), and insisted on a total commitment to its words. This passage has generally been understood to mark the beginning of a concept of canon, that is, that the book of the law of Moses was sacred and not to be revised or added to in the future. Ezra made his proclamation sometime after 458 BC, far removed from the days of Moses in the late second millennium BC. Moreover, the response of the people, and Ezra's efforts to explain it to them, suggest that they certainly did not already know this book as it was read out loud. Although they all recognized the teaching, they did not seem to be aware of this particular collection as a single work (read Neh 8—10).

For this reason, and for many others, including the fact that many of the laws belong to situations much later than the time of Moses and the people in the desert (see, for example, the laws on worshipping at the one sanctuary in Jerusalem in Deuteronomy 12), modern scholars do not try to prove that Moses was the author of the *written* books of the Pentateuch. Rather, Moses was the founder of Israelite faith as we find it in the Bible. The Pentateuch, however, contains many, many traditions, laws, stories, hymns, and reflections added by later generations from earliest times right down to the time when it was completed and Ezra declared it sacred so that further additions were no longer permitted.

Historical Dating of the Pentateuchal Traditions

Despite the difficulties in locating the exact historical events and pinning the materials to firm dates, the discoveries of other ancient tablets and chronicles, and the findings of archaeologists digging in ancient sites have given us some idea of what each different period in the second millennium BC was like. Scholars who hold a more conservative view generally situate the patriarchal narratives somewhere between 2000 and 1500 BC, the Exodus event between 1450 and 1250 BC, and the invasion of the land of Palestine around 1250 to 1200 BC. As doubts have arisen about the accuracy of the portrayal of the invasion of Canaan as recounted in the accounts of Exodus and Numbers, many scholars are expressing caution about whether the descriptions accurately reflect genuine memories of such early periods, or are rather the creations of later writers, who used some earlier materials and memories but more likely reflected the life of their own times. Many anachronisms occur in the patriarchal narratives for example, such as use of the domesticated camel, or the presence

of the Philistines, neither of which were known in the first half of the second millennium.

Arguments for some early dates are more likely than others. Thus, because Egypt had foreign rulers between 1750 BC and 1550 BC, scholars have argued that the Joseph story fits best into this time frame; because Exodus 1, 11 says the enslaved Israelites built the cities Pithom and Raamses, they would date the Exodus to the reign of Ramesses II (about 1295 to 1235 BC). On the other hand, lack of evidence for the violent destruction of Canaanite cities in the twelfth century BC can be used to argue for later tradition idealizing the past. For further discussion of dates and times, consult an introduction to the Old Testament or a short history of Israel listed in the bibliography.

A brief chart of comparative events may also be helpful (see RG 97).

Reflecting on the Message of the Pentateuch

The Theological Themes that Unite the Pentateuchal Books

In reading the Pentateuch with its vast array of materials that reflect a world of thought so different from our own, we need some guideposts. We can generally find them in those themes and topics to which the books return over and over again. The demand for obedience to the divine will would be one such example. From Adam and Eve and their failure to obey, down to Moses' own failure when striking the rock for water in Numbers 20, great stress is laid on obedience. Another way of identifying central topics is to follow the dramatic action that focuses on a certain moment or specific action. The conferring of a covenant in Exodus 19—24 is an example of this type of guidepost. The biblical tradition is so rich that there may be trouble trying to limit such important topics to ten or twenty or even thirty. Nor would it be wise to do so, since every time we read we will discover new aspects of revelation that speak to us today.

Before listing any of the major theological themes of the Pentateuch, it will help us to understand them all if we remember that the Bible is not only a book of God but about God. The central thread that weaves together all the other strands in these books tells of that God who acts in human history. More particularly, the Bible al-

	Biblical Events	Egypt	Mesopotamia	Canaan & Syria
2000			Kingdoms of Isin and Larsa in the south	
1950		Middle Kingdom Empire Dynasties 10 to 12		
1900				
1850	Patriarchs			
1800	Abraham (1900–1800) Isaac (1900–1800)			Elba Second Period
1750				
1700	Jacob (1850–1750) Joseph (1800–1700)	Semitic Conquerors From Asia (Hyksos)	Empire of Hammurapi of Babylon	
1650				
1600				
1550				
1500			Hittite Invasions	
1450	Early Exodus 1 Kgs 6,1)	New Kingdom Dynasty 18 (1550–1300)		
1400	Akhenaton Monotheism		Kingdom of the Sealand in South	
1350		Dynasty 19 (1300–1200) Pharaohs of the Exodus?		
1300	Traditional Exodus			Ugarit
1250			Assyrian Kingdom	
1200	Conquest			
1150				

most never worries about the general need for a divine principle in the world, or about the gods of other peoples, but only about this God who has been revealed as the one God and who chooses to be known to Israel in a special way. In short, the following themes all flow from the Lord's conversation with the people—and their responses!

Ten Central Themes

Creation Establishes a Good World

When Genesis 1 affirms that God created all things by speaking a word, it really means that all is ordered by the divine plan and works together in harmony. After creation was completed, God looked and "found it very good" (Gn 1, 31). Thus, no matter what evil and failure will follow in world history, we are to recall that goodness will prevail.

God Has Blessed Human Life

An important corollary of a good world is divine blessing upon it. Twice Genesis tells us that God blessed the human race (Gn 1, 28; 9, 1). Later, much is made of the blessing of Abraham (Gn 12, 2), of Sarah and Isaac (Gn 17, 16), of Jacob

(Gn 27, 27–29), of the whole people by Aaron (Nm 6, 24–26), of the nation by Balaam (Nm 23, 20), and, as the finale of the Pentateuch, of each tribe by Moses (Dt 33, 1–29).

Humanity Has a Tendency To Sin

Much of the biblical story centers on the disobedience and sinfulness of God's creatures who refuse to heed or obey the divine will. In turn, many of the laws center on atonement (in Leviticus particularly), and on the need for repentance and turning back to God (in Deuteronomy particularly).

God Delivers from All Evil

If humanity tends toward rebellion, God tends toward forgiveness and mercy. God spares Adam and Eve, Cain and Noah, and others in order to give the human race a new start each time after it sins. God is revealed above all else as a liberating God in the Exodus event. This becomes the heart of Israel's praise for God in the Passover celebration.

God Fulfills the Promises

The Pentateuch stressed again and again the fulfillment of the promise made to Noah, Abraham, Isaac, Jacob, and Moses that God will make them into a great people. The Lord was never a god patterned on the recurring cycles of nature, but always a God of the future who calls forth in Israel a trusting hope that must expect new and greater divine acts still to come.

The Covenant Binds God to Israel

Naturally all people believe their god relates to the world somehow, but only in Israel do we find a union based on love and loyalty pledged to each other in a permanent union that actually respects the role of the human partner. The covenant is the heart of biblical faith because it expresses a unique bond between God and people, built on past deeds but committed to future collaboration.

The Law Expresses Israel's Bond to God

The covenant establishes a relationship, but the laws of the Pentateuch show how that relationship can be lived out by the people—they are not restrictive rules but a dynamic way of life that expresses faithfulness to God in actions as well as words, always with a touch of joy for flavoring.

Worship Is Praise Is Thank You

This may sound like a strange heading, but the point needs emphasis: to pray is to praise, and to praise is to thank God. The Pentateuch constantly points to what God has done for Israel, and the laws point to a spirit of rejoicing and thanksgiving on Israel's part in giving back to God a part of the gift to them: namely, praising the divine goodness in everything.

Religious Life Is Life in Community

Israel is a people, not a number of all-star individuals. Discovery of the divine will and proper praise can only be given by human voices joined together. God's many faces can be seen only when memories are shared and mutual goodness is shown in action to one another.

God Directs All of History

The natural conclusion to be drawn from the preceding attributes of God is that everything falls under divine providence. The central conviction of Israel that there is one, and only one, God leads to recognition of the divine lordship over all peoples and all events. God both blesses and punishes, sets obstacles as well as shows the way to pass through them. All things are in the hands of God, and so no course of action is thinkable except to walk in the ways of the Lord.

FURTHER READING

General Introductions

Blenkinsopp, Joseph. *The Pentateuch: An Introduction to the First Five Books of the Bible.* Anchor Bible Reference Library. New York: Doubleday, 1992. An excellent scholarly analysis of modern criticism and its difficulties and achievements.

Boadt, Lawrence, C.S.P. *Reading the Old Testament: An Introduction.* Mahwah, NJ: Paulist Press, 1985. A readable overview of all the critical and theological issues of Old Testament study.

Campbell, Anthony, and Mark O'Brien. *Sources of the Pentateuch.* Minneapolis: Fortress, 1993. The authors provide texts and notes on the various documents that supposedly stand behind the Pentateuch and its growth.

Childs, Brevard. *Introduction to the Old Testament as Scripture.* Minneapolis: Fortress, 1979. A very technical but excellent introduction to each book of the Bible as it developed through the process of transmission and redaction.

General Commentaries

Barton, John, and John Muddiman. *The Oxford Bible Commentary.* Oxford and New York: Oxford University Press, 2001.

The Collegeville Old Testament Commentary. Collegeville, MN: Liturgical Press, 1985, 1987. Short, handy series written for Catholics.

The International Bible Commentary. Collegeville, MN: Liturgical Press, 1998. Scholars from every continent contribute to this work that emphasizes a literary approach to interpretation of each book, combining literary theory, historical criticism, and the history of how the book was used and interpreted throughout the centuries.

The Message of the Old Testament. Wilmington, DE: Michael Glazier, 1980, 1984. Readable middle-level commentaries on the theology of each book of the Bible.

The New Interpreter's Bible. Nashville: Abingdon Press, 1994. The combination of modern scholarship and theological reflection in a very readable format make this an excellent resource for parish libraries.

The New Jerome Biblical Commentary. Englewood Cliffs, NJ: Prentice Hall, 1990. A superb one-volume commentary on all of Scripture with fine background articles for study of the Pentateuch.

Biblical Criticism

Brueggemann, Walter, and Hans Walter Wolff. *The Vitality of Old Testament Traditions.* 2nd ed. Atlanta: John Knox, 1982. Readable essays on each of the four sources.

Friedman, Richard Elliott. *Who Wrote the Bible?* New York: Summit Books, 1987. Most readable account ever of the excitement of discovering the four sources in the Pentateuch.

Ralph, Margaret Nutting. *"And God Said What?"* Mahwah, NJ: Paulist Press, 1986. A very understandable introduction to literary forms in the Bible.

Bible Dictionaries

Achtemeier, Paul, ed. *Harper's Bible Dictionary.* New York: Harper & Row, 1985. Another excellent, up-to-date resource book.

Freedman, David Noel, ed. *Anchor Bible Dictionary.* New York: Doubleday, 1991. Comes in six large volumes and is the most complete resource tool available.

McKenzie, John L. *Dictionary of the Bible.* Milwaukee: Bruce Publishing, 1965. A superb work on almost every facet of Bible study but somewhat dated in its information on the latest trends in criticism. Its strength lies in McKenzie's incisive insights into the Catholic biblical tradition.

Metzger, Bruce M., and Michael D. Coogan. *The Oxford Companion to the Bible.* New York and Oxford: Oxford University Press, 1993.

The Individual Books of the Pentateuch

Bailey, Lloyd. *Leviticus.* Atlanta: John Knox, 1987. Simple but useful handbook to the various laws in Leviticus.

Boadt, Lawrence. *Genesis.* The International Bible Commentary. Collegeville, MN: Liturgical Press, 1998.

Childs, Brevard. *The Book of Exodus.* Old Testament Library. Philadelphia: Westminster Press, 1974. A very detailed treatment of Exodus and the origins of its traditions and its history of use in the Church.

Craighie, Peter. *The Book of Deuteronomy.* New International Commentary on the Old Testament. Grand Rapids: Eerdmans, 1976. A readable and thorough explanation of the theology of Deuteronomy.

Levine, Baruch. *Numbers 1–20.* Anchor Bible. New York: Doubleday, 1993.

Milgrom, Jacob. *Leviticus 1–16.* Anchor Bible. New York: Doubleday, 1994.

——. *Leviticus 17–22.* Anchor Bible. New York: Doubleday, 2000.

——. *Leviticus 23–27.* Anchor Bible. New York: Doubleday, 2002.

Sarna, Nahum. *Understanding Genesis: The Heritage of Biblical Israel.* New York: Schocken Books, 1966. Very fine explanation of the message and background of Genesis from a Jewish viewpoint.

——. *Exploring Exodus.* New York: Schocken Books, 1986. The follow-up to *Understanding Genesis* and just as readable, just as informative.

Weinfeld, Moshe. *Deuteronomy 1–11.* Anchor Bible. New York: Doubleday, 1991.

Westermann, Claus. *Genesis 1–11; Genesis 12–36; Genesis 37–50.* 3 vols. Minneapolis: Augsburg Press, 1984, 1987.

Other Literatures of Biblical Times

Matthews, Victor, and Don Benjamin. *Old Testament Parallels.* Rev. ed. Mahwah, NJ: Paulist Press, 1998.

Pritchard, James. *Ancient Near Eastern Texts Relating to the Old Testament.* Princeton: Princeton University Press, 1969. An excellent anthology. Referred to as ANET.

GENESIS

[see pages 6–70 of the Old Testament]

An Overview of the Book of Genesis

If we begin our study of the Bible with Genesis, it is important to remember that this is clearly *the beginning*. Whatever it contains has been chosen and put into place to provide the foundation for all that will follow in the Bible. Although it makes a great story in its own right, it also requires attention to the key themes that it develops if we are to fully understand its purpose. In order to do this effectively, first read quickly the entire fifty chapters, just glancing over them to get the drift of the "plot." After you have the basic story in mind and have gotten a small taste of its style, or better, its varied styles that change throughout the book, a second detailed study of each section will reveal much more.

The Major Divisions of Genesis

Traditionally scholars have divided Genesis into two parts: chapters 1 through 11 and 12 through 50. This is based on their subject matter and the type of literature that is found in each part. Both parts appear at first to be a single continuous story, but closer examination reveals strong differences between them. Simply put, the first eleven chapters discuss the process of creation and ideas about the earliest human ancestors as ancients understood them. The second part describes the unique traditions about the concrete clans or tribal ancestors of Israel itself. As literature, Genesis 1—11 is defined as *myth,* which is a story that attempts to explain some mystery of the relation of the gods (whom we do not know) to the world of humans (which we do know). Every myth is really also a model pattern, either bad or good, of human behavior. Although a myth in form, Genesis 1—11 is often simply called the "primeval history." In contrast, the stories of the patriarchs and matriarchs in Genesis 12—50 are more like legends, in which people recognize events from their past, although they may not have happened exactly the way they are described. They relate individual events as they have been passed down, and which have shaped the special identity of Israel.

Both types of writing give us models to follow

but, of course, not in the same way. The world of the primeval history has little in common with what we ourselves experience in the world. It is a special world when things were different and the laws of time and intimacy with the gods were different from our own time. On the other hand, Abraham, Isaac, Jacob, and the others in chapters 12 to 50 wrestle with the same world that we do, and their decisions have consequences, which are concrete and very much part of the later history of a people.

We can perhaps note some differences between them in table at top of next page.

Subdivisions of Genesis 1—50

This two-part structure can be broken down further into smaller narratives that carry the story forward and are themselves joined by a variety of means that explain how they relate to one another. See table at bottom of next page.

This is only a general sketch. Note how the four major sections of the primal history match four sections of the great founding leaders of Israel. In each the editors were skilled storytellers who wove the parts together to make one whole. But they hardly disguised their intention to show that there are stages in the history of humanity, and in the history of Israel in particular. Each period can have a major impact on the next. For world history, it was the constant spread of sin; for Israel, it was the constant development of blessing.

We could also organize the book around the stages of major figures whom God has summoned forth. Many commentators break the book down into four large blocs or stages:

• The prologue: all humankind is called to blessing; but sin prevails (Gn 1—11)

• The story of Abraham and his call, blessing, and promise (Gn 12—25)

• The stories of his son Isaac and grandson Jacob and how they carry on the blessing (Gn 26—36)

• The story of Joseph in Egypt in preparation for God's great self-revelation in the Exodus (Gn 37—50)

These four sections indicate clearly enough that the plot of Genesis focuses on major deci-

Genesis 1—11	*Genesis 12—50*
1. It is set in time that is before human history	1. It is set in historical times well known to ancient records
2. Its exact place is vague—somewhere to the the East	2. It is set in Palestine and Egypt and northern Mesopotamia exactly
3. The persons seem like symbols—nothing is known of their lives	3. The persons have names and engage in actions typical of the second millennium BC
4. Many of the stories have the form of myths like those known from Mesopotamia	4. The stories are largely sagalike or epic narratives similar to oral lore of tribal groups
5. Most of the events seem to take place in a supernatural setting unlike our own	5. The major stories keep events close to the type of experience all human eras share
6. The purpose deals only with the beginnings of humanity long before Israel's time	6. The purpose is to trace the direct tribal and clan ancestors of Israel itself

sions by key individuals. The unlikely conclusion of the story finds this people apparently in prosperity and blessing somewhere else than where they were promised. In this sense, the book of Genesis can be read as an unfinished plot of a mystery story.

Division by the Special *Toledoth* Name Lists

The NAB points out in its introduction to Genesis that the book is divided into separate sections by genealogical notices, each of which begins "These are the descendants of . . ." In the list of eleven below, it should be noted that the NAB is not always consistent in the way it translates the same Hebrew phrase, nor should this particular

method of dividing be considered necessarily the most important. It did serve one of the editor's purposes, namely to show that generations come and generations go, but God's plan moves ahead no matter what. Nevertheless, these lists are truly dividers since they often group all the members of a single family line or tribe in one place to mark a break with what has just gone before. Sometimes, however, the list is given before the events, and sometimes at the end. This can easily be discovered by looking up each example:

> **Gn 2, 4a** "The descendants of heaven and earth," that is, the second story of creation, begins after this statement. (Here the NAB refers to it as "the *story* of the heavens."

Genesis 1—3	*Genesis 12—25*
The story of God's creation and the first human sin	Abraham is chosen to receive God's blessing and give witness to others
Genesis 4—5	*Genesis 21—27*
The evil of sin grows and spreads through the world	The son, Isaac, inherits the promise and passes it on
Genesis 6—9	*Genesis 27—36; 48—50*
Evil overwhelms the world; God must begin again with a new blessing	Jacob in turn receives the promise; he is blessed with and bears the twelve sons who will become Israel
Genesis 10—11	*Genesis 37—50*
People again multiply across the earth but sin persists	Joseph brings the promise to Egypt while remaining completely faithful

Gn 5, 1 "[T]he record of the descendants of Adam," introduces the long break between the first family and the days of Noah.

Gn 6, 9 "[T]he descendants of Noah," introduces the story of the flood.

Gn 10, 1 "[T]he descendants of Noah's sons," marks the great expansion of peoples all over the world.

Gn 11, 10 "[T]he descendants of Shem," marks the addition of a new list of the nations of the world by the P source.

Gn 11, 27 "[These are] the descendants of Terah," begins the story of Abraham.

Gn 25, 12 "[T]he descendants of Abraham's son Ishmael," closes off the life of Abraham's "other" family through Hagar and Ishmael.

Gn 25, 19 "[T]he family history of Isaac," opens the story of Jacob's birth and destiny.

Gn 36, 1 "[T]he descendants of Esau," ends the role of the second brother, Esau, and directs us to Jacob's children, especially Joseph.

Gn 36, 9 This is a repetition within the Esau list, which marks its conclusion.

Gn 37, 2 "This is his [Jacob's] family history," marks the opening of the story of Joseph and his brothers, which goes to the end of Genesis.

The Primeval History in Genesis 1—11

We can now move to a more detailed analysis of the book. In studying these early chapters, several aspects should be noted: (1) They are generally described by form criticism as a combination of myths and genealogical tables. (2) They are described by source criticism as a combination of passages from the Yahwist (J) and the Priestly (P) sources. (3) Many of the individual stories have parallel narratives that are known from other ancient Near Eastern peoples, often much older than the biblical version. (4) The final masterpiece has its own purpose and beauty that makes it much more than just a collection of myths and genealogy lists.

J and P Sources

If we remember that the J stories are probably much older than the P stories, and at first stood

alone as the basic proclamation of the beginnings of the world, we can first glance at each group separately. See chart on RG 103.

It might be noted that there are several duplications in these lists: both J and P have a list of great ancestors between Adam and Noah (4, 17–26 vs. 5, 1–32); both have a flood story, which is now hopelessly intermixed as a single account; and both have a Table of Nations that spread over the earth in Genesis 10—11, which is also interwoven as a single narrative list.

The Theology of the Yahwist Source

If we look at the incidents chosen by the J source to tell its story of creation and the first humans, we find that they generally center on the tension between God's goodness given to the earth and the human response of disobedience. Each story—Adam and Eve, Cain and Abel, the angels and the women, the wicked generation of the flood, the sons of Noah, those who build the tower of Babel—all are given ample signs of God's love and bountiful providence as they fill the earth. Even so, each generation rises in disobedience according to one of the deadly vices: greed, envy, lust, pride.

The author uses a general pattern that structures the stories:

• God acts lovingly toward humanity,
• people disobey God and sin,
• God announces punishment,
• the punishment is given,
• God ends in compassion by bestowing mercy and a new blessing.

In the repetition of the pattern over and over again, J emphasizes how humanity as a whole has failed to respond to the intimate relationship of a God who once spoke to them face to face. Instead they have spread the practice of sin until it contaminated all people. Even after a new beginning following the flood, they continued to sin boldly, as is evident by the fact that God ended up confusing their languages in Gn 11, 1–9. God's hope for faithfulness and obedience from the humans in his image and likeness, and his desire to speak with them face to face, will have to take a new form; that form will be the choice of a single family or nation, through Abraham, which will respond to God's goodness and teach other people. That new promise will open chapter 12.

J (tenth century BC)	P (seventh to sixth centuries BC)
	Gn 1, 1—2, 4a The creation of the world
Gn 2, 4b—3, 24 The human condition at creation, and sin	
Gn 4, 1–26 Cain and Abel: even the children sin but God continues to care	
	Gn 5, 1–32 The list of long-lived ancestors from Adam to Noah
Gn 6, 1–4 More evil caused by the sin of angels and humans	
Gn 6, 5—9, 29 The flood story with 40 days and 7 pairs of clean animals, etc.	**Gn 6, 5—9, 29** The flood story based on 365 days and one pair of each animal only, etc.
	Gn 10, 1–7.20–24 Table of all the nations
Gn 10, 8–19.25–30 Table of Nations from a different source	
Gn 11, 1–9 The story of the tower of Babel	
	Gn 11, 10–32 The continuation of the Table of Nations down to Abraham

The Theology of the Priestly Source

We can assume that the priestly writers knew and accepted the basic J account of sin, punishment, and grace in the ages before Abraham. But they also knew that the later J promises to the ancestors Abraham, Isaac, and Jacob might be interpreted as a promise of international power and rule over other peoples, such as David and his family had exercised. Since P wrote in the sixth century BC, after Israel had known the defeat and loss of ten of the twelve tribes in 722, and the other two were in exile in Babylon from 598 to 539, they wished to refocus even the creation stories to emphasize the sovereign rule of God guiding the entire universe and constantly giving blessings much larger in scope than merely to Is-

rael. Thus in chapters 1 and 9, when God first establishes and then reestablishes the order and purpose of creation, P writes in solemn proclamations, such as the litany of the days of creation in chapter 1, the great dignity of humans created as the image of God (1, 27 and 9, 6) to populate (sharing in creation?) and govern the earth, the arbitrary and majestic creation by God's word alone, the description of the flood in terms of the solar year, and even the mighty signs in nature like the rainbow. P places the story of humankind against a vast cosmic setting as a preface to the sordid and messy succeeding history of the world and even of Israel itself.

The very neatly ordered genealogies of chapters 5 and 10—11, which record the enormous life spans of the early heroes of the earth, are also part of P's insistence that God has a plan that is not subject to human whims nor even upset by human sin. God's rule is so vast that humans must learn trust! P stresses that divine blessing can always be relied on, even as it includes the J story in which punishment follows all sin. P has enlarged the J vision from finding God anew in every crisis to reassurance that God's providence was always at work—a perfect answer to an exiled Israel, despairing that God really stood by them in their times of defeat.

The Overall Message of Genesis 1—11

The act of combining J and P, as well as all the additions and refinements made by others, including the final editors who put it all together, provided a double emphasis: (1) the eternal goodness of the creator, and (2) the moral demand on humans to obey the divine plan and come to know God. It is no accident that God begins creation by speaking the world into being and seeing that all of it is good. Nor is it accidental that God then speaks to each of the first generations—Adam and Eve, Cain and Abel, Noah, and finally Abraham—with directives. In turn, these stories and directives now stand as a prologue to the whole body of Torah teaching that fills the latter part of the Pentateuch.

The pattern of divine goodness and moral imperative established in Genesis 1—11 also demand that proper worship be given to God alone. Both J and P use familiar Near Eastern myths in order to slyly attack pagan practices (such as the way J ridicules the excessive worship of the supposed supernatural power of serpents in Gn 3). Each story intends to show that only the moral goodness of God is an adequate basis for worship, and that most Canaanite religious practices and beliefs pervert God's plan.

Some Particular Helps in Reading Individual Passages

Genesis is a literary masterpiece as well as an inspiring theological message. To appreciate it better, here are a few examples of what to note about sections as we read:

Genesis 1, 1—2, 4a

The six days of creation are divided into two panels of three days each that are matched. See chart at top of RG 105.

A comparison of the two panels reveals that in the first three days God builds a stage of heavens, water, and land; and in the corresponding second three days fills this stage with its primary actors, each in turn. The last day in each panel, days three and six, have a double task. This serves to emphasize how especially fertile the land is. Moreover, the climactic seventh day is a celebration of the goodness of this creation and becomes the model for human rest and celebration of divine goodness each week.

The pattern of creation was not invented by the P authors. The same order is followed in the ancient creation myth from Babylon called the *Enuma Elish* in which Marduk, the chief god of Babylon and young king of all the gods, fashions the world from the body of Tiamat, the mother goddess whom he had slain in battle. The *Enuma Elish* describes Marduk's creative actions in a sequence with many parallels to the account in Genesis 1. See chart at bottom of RG 105.

Genesis 2, 4b—3, 24

This is an independent account of the creation that is older than Genesis 1 and uses a number of mythic story themes known also in Mesopotamia, although the biblical version is unique as a whole and far more sophisticated in its vision than anything else we have found in the ancient world. However, similarities exist between parts of Genesis 2—3 and the following:

1. *The Myth of Etana* (ANET 114–118). A great eagle eats the young of a serpent who, in turn, catches the eagle and traps it in a pit with the help of the gods. Meanwhile, Etana, a first human being, is childless, and he prays to the gods to get to heaven to eat of the plant of birth. The sun god Shamash leads Etana to the eagle, who promises to fly him to heaven to reach the plant of birth (or new life). The story breaks off, but it seems that he gets there.

2. *The Myth of Adapa* (ANET 101–102). The gods create a first man, Adapa, who has great wisdom. He catches and breaks the wings of the south wind one day because it prevents him from fishing. When the gods begin to miss the breeze, they find out that Adapa has caused this, and so Anu, the head of the gods, summons him to heaven to account for himself. He is warned not to accept Anu's offer of the bread and water of life, because it is really the food of death. When

Prologue: Introductory Statement that God Can Control Chaos	
Day 1 Heavens and light are made	**Day 4** Specific lights fashioned in the sky
Day 2 Waters established on their own	**Day 5** Fish and sea creatures made to fill the water
Day 3 Dry land made and vegetation added	**Day 6** The animals are created for the land, and then, finally, humans
Day 7 Epilogue: God rests after completing all creation and is in total control	

Anu extends the offer, Adapa refuses what really does turn out to be the bread and water of life, and thus loses the chance for immortality for human beings.

3. *The Myth of Atrahasis* (ANET 104). This is also a story of the creation of human beings as servants to the gods to keep the world running and save the gods from laboring. In time, they also revolt against the heavy labor; when plagues fail to diminish their numbers, the gods send a flood to punish them. Only Atrahasis and his family on their ark manage to escape and restart the human race.

4. *The Myth of Baal* (ANET 129–142). Baal is the chief ruling god of the Canaanites and is known from written tablets found at Ugarit, a town in northern Syria. It tells of El, the father of the gods who lives as ruler of the heavens and the earth at the "source of the two rivers," and the struggles of Baal, one of his younger sons, the god of the Mediterranean rainstorm and the resulting fertility for the earth, to rule the earth. Baal must battle against the gods Sea and Death for the kingship. Many themes resemble those of the Enuma Elish.

4. *Ezekiel 28, 11–19*. This is an important version of creation related by Ezekiel about the king

of Tyre, which possibly reflects Canaanite beliefs that the first man was a king, paradise was a sacred mountain, that it was covered with precious stones, and that the king was known for great wisdom. Then he sinned and was driven from the mountains by means of cherubim, a kind of protective animal god.

5. *Gilgamesh* (ANET 72–99). This Babylonian myth tells the story of two great god-men heroes who challenge the gods themselves for rule of the earth. For example, the hero Gilgamesh and his friend Enkidu cut down the sacred trees in the cedar forest of the gods, which is forbidden. When the gods punish Enkidu by death, Gilgamesh searches for the key to immortality by finding the hero of the flood (which corresponds to Noah), one Utnapishtim. When Gilgamesh fails the test for immortality, he is given a second chance when given the plant of continued rejuvenation, but he loses even that to a serpent. In the end, he must return home fully mortal and learn to bear his lot.

More ancient parallels can also be found, but these should be enough to help us read the accounts of human origins and sin in the light of the pressing questions faced by all the ancient religious stories: why are the gods immortal but not

Enuma Elish		Genesis 1
1. It begins with a conquest of chaos by order	=	The opening statement of Gn 1, 1–2
2. Heavens created and separated from the water	=	Day 2, the creation of heavens and separation of the waters
3. The earth is set over the waters	=	Day 3, the land appears from the waters
4. Creation of sun and moon	=	Day 4, sun and moon are set in heaven
5. (No mention of plants or animals)	=	(Days 5–6, the creation of fish, birds, and animals)
6. Creation of human beings	=	Day 6, the creation of humans
7. The gods rest and celebrate	=	Day 7, God rests

we humans? Why do we receive punishment from the gods in life? What is our fate? The major differences between the biblical accounts and the stories of other religions center on the clear connection in the Bible between a single God's loving care for humanity, the moral refusal of people to obey God, and the justified reason that God imposed a sentence of mortality upon us together with a change in our relation to the land that now requires backbreaking labor to make it a blessing.

Genesis 4, 1–16

The story of Cain and Abel offers a moral about how when evil flourishes it leads even to fratricide. But it also builds on an age-old theme of the conflict between the farmer and the herder. The musical *Oklahoma* sings how the farmer and the cowman should be friends, but their interests conflict—the farmer wants to fence in and protect his plot of land, and the cowman requires wide-open spaces over which the cattle or sheep can move to new pastures. This was a conflict well known to the early Israelites, who as nomadic shepherds came up against the protected and settled lands of the Canaanite farmers.

Genesis 4, 17–22; 5, 1–32

The genealogies of Genesis 4—5 with the enormous ages of the patriarchs are not intended to be understood as literally exact. We can compare them to the enormous ages given to the primeval kings of Sumeria who lived before the great flood in an ancient list (ANET 265):

A-lu-lim	28,800 years
Alalgar	36,000 years
En-men-lu-anna	43,200 years
En-men-gal-anna	28,800 years
Dumuzi	36,000 years
En-sipa-zi-anna	28,800 years
En-men-dur-anna	21,000 years
Ubar-tutu	18,600 years
The flood	

Such genealogy lists are typical of many peoples who keep largely oral traditions. The parallel lists in Genesis 4 and 5 show signs of such an oral tradition. They contain some identical and many similar names, so they probably both go back to a single core list. But they differ in length, with eight generations in chapter 4 and ten in chapter 5. In oral tradition, the first and last

names in a list are carefully preserved, but the middle names tend to change from place to place, depending on where those lists are recited. Such lists are an exciting and mysterious device for imagining how far back our ancestors go and how long the world has existed. And they serve the biblical authors well as a way of linking the wondrous events of ancient days to the more historical times we all know about.

Genesis 6, 1—9, 27

Two observations should preface serious study of what the flood story means. First, this story must have been very important, because both the Yahwist and the Priestly traditions had separate versions of the flood and both were considered important enough to save. Second, it has a very strong resemblance to similar flood stories told in both Babylon and Syria, although it has some differences from both.

The more famous parallel is in the Gilgamesh myth where the hero, Utnapishtim, is warned to build an ark and take some of every kind of animal on earth aboard before the gods destroy the world with a flood. After the flood has killed all living things left on the land, the hero sends out birds (just as in Gn 8, 6–12) after the ark becomes stuck on a mountain peak. When the hero finally leaves the ark, he offers a sacrifice to the gods. They are so grateful that they bless him and make him immortal. This is quite close to the plot of Genesis except that in the pagan versions, no real cause of human evil is given for why the gods decreed a flood; in the biblical version, Noah does not receive immortality as a gift at the end. In still another ancient flood myth, Atra-Hasis, the authors retain the same basic plot, but suggest that the gods were tired of the human noise that disturbed their sleep, and so decided to do away with humans.

Again, Genesis 6—9 must be read through the eyes of the ancient Israelite who knew of the pagan versions and their account of strained relations between the divine and human worlds. The author insists that the God of Israel acted entirely out of justice and in response to moral evil in humans but still continued to love them and hold out the promise of blessing at the end. This is confirmed by restoring the earlier blessing of Genesis 1 in 9, 1–17. It is made specific to Israel as a chosen people in the final story of 9, 18–27 where the descendants of Noah's son Shem will be blessed over the peoples that stem from his other sons, Ham and Japheth.

Genesis 9, 28—10, 32

A new genealogical list is placed after the flood story to confirm that the renewed divine blessing multiplied to reconstruct an entire world of peoples and nations. This section is made up of two separate traditional lists of names for the world's peoples, one from the P school, and the other from J. The earlier list of J can be generally recognized right away in 10, 8–30 by its more narrative flavor; the P list in 9, 28—10, 7 and 10, 21–24 (and continued in 10, 31f) is much drier, simply presented as a list of names. But the editors of Genesis 1—11 have skillfully put them together to form a montage of different peoples spreading from the family home of Noah after the flood to fill the far corners of the earth.

Genesis 11, 1–9

The tower of Babel story is an excellent example of the J writer at work. It is told with humor and irony, and it makes a very pointed attack against pagan religious ideas. It is a story about words and speaking, but it is the misuse of words that is at stake. The plot pictures all people speaking the same language, which leads them to an enormous sin of pride. They seek to build a temple high enough to reach heaven so that they might have "a name for themselves," that is, to be like God. But note that as they build this tremendous monument, God looks down from heaven and can barely make it out because it is so puny by God's standards. He must come down to see it. As punishment, he halts their sinful ambition by confusing their languages. The author then ends with a bit of sharp humor. The city of such arrogance was called *Babel,* but God made it *balal,* the verb in Hebrew for "confused in language." Thus verse 9 is a pun and as such mocks the claims of Babylon and its god Marduk to rule over other peoples.

Genesis 11, 10–32

The primeval history now closes with a P list parallel to that of Genesis 5, 1–32. It links the primeval events of chapters 1 through 11 with the concrete call of Abraham in the very real towns of Ur and Harran in Mesopotamia. Like

Genesis 5, 1–32 it bridges the time between major moments or stages of divine intervention. Each patriarch is recorded with the age at which he died. The lengths are much less than those of the ten before the flood, descending from 600 years for Shem, the son of Noah, down to the four hundreds for Arpachshad, Shelah, and Eber, and rapidly down to the two hundreds for the remaining names. Of course, like the ages in chapter 5, these are not to be taken as actual ages, but as a device for showing that the "golden age" of olden times was rapidly coming to an end as the people became more and more like ourselves.

Name lists were important in the ancient world for remembering who was related to whom. And it will seem obvious, by the time we have looked at many of these lists, that the names do not really represent individuals at all, but whole tribes or peoples. This can be direct, as in 10, 22 where P writes that Shem was the father of Elam, Assyria, and the Arameans; or indirect, when a nation is identified by a famous founder or hero, such as Ishmael, the son of Abraham, who is listed as the father of the Arabs in Genesis 25, 12–18.

Structure of the Genealogies in Genesis 1—11

The name lists in Genesis 1—11 are very important parts of the overall story by highlighting the passage of time between crucial moments of sin and grace, and by serving as times of blessing between the particular stories of sin and punishment. Thus, it can be charted as shown on RG 108.

Church Use of the Genesis Story of Human Creation

It is well to note that the account of making humanity in the divine image and likeness figures significantly in a number of official Catholic church documents. For example, Pope Paul VI looked to Genesis 1, 28 as a significant reference in his development of the responsibility to subdue the earth and its resources intelligently (*Populorum Progressio* #22). And along the same vein, John Paul II went to Genesis 1, 26–30 to ground the fundamental "goodness" of creation in the Creator's eyes, which thereby also grounds the claim that redemption is possible (*Redemptor Hominis*). Likewise, the American bishops in their pastoral *Economic Justice for All* used Gen-

Key Moments of Sin, Punishment, Blessing

Genealogy Lists

Genesis 1, 1—4, 16

The story of creation and the blessings and sins of the first generations

---

Genesis 4, 17—5, 32

The long age of blessing of the ten great patriarchs before Noah's time

---

Genesis 6, 1—9, 27

Sin, flood as punishment and blessing on Noah, followed by further sin by his sons

---

Genesis 9, 28—10, 32

The list of all the nations known to ancient Israel to show the divine blessing of fertility and having dominion over the earth

---

Genesis 11, 19

Sin again rises up out of human pride after blessing

Genesis 11, 10—32

God's blessing continues, now focusing on one family, that of Terah and Abraham

---

Genesis 12, 1—?

The story of Abraham and the new direction of divine blessing

---

esis 1, 26f to show that all human relations must be based on the acknowledgment of the dignity of those created in God's image. This helps form the economic reflections of the letter.

The Great Ancestor Narratives in Genesis 12—50

As already noted above, the second major part of Genesis is arranged around the lives of four pa-

triarchal figures: Abraham, Isaac, Jacob, and Joseph. Each of these represents a forward step in the divine plan to bring about recognition of the divine blessing promised to the world—if only humanity would obey and honor God. Since humans as a whole proved very stubbornly unresponsive to God's self-revelation through long ages, God decided to turn to a new plan and work through a single chosen people who would respond and witness God's blessings to all nations.

And where is this plan laid out? Why, right at the beginning of course, in Genesis 12, 1–3. When we read this call of Abraham by God, all the subsequent themes are present:

verse 1   the promise of a land for his family

verse 2   the promise of blessing through empire and fame, and probably children ("a great nation")

verse 3   the promise to rule other nations and to mediate God's blessing to them.

These themes will echo throughout the narratives to follow, especially the combination of a son to carry on the name and a specific land. But they will not be fulfilled easily. It is very important to understand that God never promised anyone a rose garden. The narrators have constructed a story of failure and success, obedience and disobedience, a lesson of deep faith in some stories, and of a sinful lack of trust in others. Along the way, divine providence and guidance overcome all the obstacles to bringing about the promise, maintaining blessing on this small family even in the unlikely land of their enemy, Egypt.

The Literary Questions of Genesis 12—50

Scholars have identified many individual passages of both J and P throughout the patriarchal stories, and have added one more source, the Elohist (E), which is quite close to J in spirit but does not yet use the name of Yahweh to refer to God. These sources can be identified by their parallel structures, which treat the same chief events in order. If we look just at the Abraham and Sarah story of Genesis 12—25, we can get a good idea of this overlapping (table on RG 110).

Each source stresses a different aspect of the person of Abraham. J stresses his faith and trust in the promise of land and a son; E stresses his obedience even to sacrificing his heir; P stresses his fidelity in fulfilling all the divine religious prescriptions, especially circumcision.

But scholars have sought for more than these written sources alone; they wished to uncover the underlying traditions that existed before J, E, or P ever wrote a word. The form critics have noted that for the cycles of Abraham, Isaac, and Jacob, most of the incidents described are self-contained. That is, you could leave one or another of the events out, and the story could still

go on. This suggests that a long history of oral stories existed about the patriarchs and matriarchs before they were finally used in written sources. The father of form criticism was Hermann Gunkel, and he pointed to many characteristics of these particular stories that were similar to the characteristics of the Icelandic sagas of the Middle Ages. Some of these elements are:

• the stories are hero-centered around a major ancestor of a family or group;

• they don't really tell of private lives as much as of the national fortunes of their group in the past;

• they use many standard formulas, themes, and literary motifs common to folktales and hero legends;

• they are told with a highly dramatic, often poetic style of description, and not in simple narrative chronicle fashion;

• they identify major themes or beliefs of the group or tribe *today* that this ancestor initiated or began;

• they often delight in *etiological,* or causal, explanations of events or things (that is, in the why or how of the way things are). See Genesis 17, 5, where the editor explains the meaning of Abraham's name, or 21, 31, which explains how Beersheba got its name.

However, even with so many similarities between the biblical stories and medieval hero legends or family sagas, we must not forget that they only hint at the way the oldest traditions about the founding ancestors were probably originally passed down. The actual passages that we now read in the book of Genesis were carefully composed by each of the literary sources with a special religious note, and they were combined and revised numerous times to point more clearly to the lessons in the stories for the faith of later generations of Israelites. We must try to read them with an eye both to the level of their original description of the experience of God and to the complete picture painted by the finished text that sees a clear guiding hand of God through history.

The Historical Setting of the Patriarchal Stories

The general consensus of the scholarly world has been in the past that the customs and movements described in Genesis 12—50 best fit the first half

	J	E	P
Abraham receives a promise of land and/or a son	12, 1–3	15, 1–6	12, 4–9
God makes a covenant with Abraham	15, 7–12	15, 13–16	17, 1–14
A son is born and the line of the promise is secured	16, 1–16	21, 1–21	17, 15–27
	18, 1–19		
The final note of closing the life of Abraham	25, 1–6	(22, 1–13)	23, 1–20

of the second millennium BC, that is, from 1900 to 1500 BC. Some of the main reasons for this view are:

• the names of the patriarchs are not used in later periods but are known before 1500 BC;

• the wanderings from Mesopotamia to Canaan to Egypt coincide with the periods of Amorite migrations in the Near East and the time of the Middle Kingdom in Egypt (2000–1750 BC);

• customs such as the adoption of an heir (Gn 15, 1–3) and marrying a sister (12, 10–20) reflect known legal procedures from Nuzi and other towns in the second millennium;

• the story of Joseph as a prime minister in Egypt would fit well the period in Egypt when it was ruled by the Hyksos, a group of Semitic invaders from Palestine and farther East that controlled northern Egypt from about 1750 to 1500 BC;

• Abraham and Isaac and Jacob are described as seminomadic clans that settled near urban centers and dealt with the local rulers about rights for grazing, water, and travel, a way of life known from Mari documents of the eighteenth to seventeenth centuries BC.

None of these examples proves the dating of the Genesis stories, since many of these customs were also practiced at later dates. Indeed, the more archaeologists unearth artifacts and docu-

ments, the more difficult it is to date any particular custom or practice to a single period. Many particulars of the story do generally fit the conditions that prevailed in the Near East before the rise of strong Egyptian control after 1500 BC. Thus, for example, the apparent weakness of local rulers over the hill country of central Palestine in Abraham's time is supported by archaeology's failure to find any major settlement there from 2000 to 1500 BC, except possibly Shechem. On the other hand, camel caravans and mention of the Philistine states and other details support a time of writing that is much later than the period in which they have set the events.

Genesis 12—25:
The Story of Abraham and Sarah

There are several keys to getting more out of the Abraham narratives. One way is to read the story as Abraham's journey from being a landless alien in chapter 12 to its completion in chapters 23 and 25 when Sarah and then Abraham are buried in a tomb they own and in land they possess. Another way is to follow the series of promises to Abraham and Sarah as they are slowly but surely fulfilled. There are two major series in parallel: (1) the promise of land, and (2) the promise of a son to carry on the family name and to become a great people (see below).

Promise of a Son		Promise of Land	
Gn 12, 2	I make you a great nation	Gn 12, 1	"go to a land I that I will show you"
Gn 15, 5	at the night covenant	Gn 12, 7	at the terebinth of Moreh
Gn 17, 4	the P covenant	Gn 13, 14	at the departure of Lot
Gn 17, 16	the promise of Isaac	Gn 15, 18	at the night covenant
Gn 18, 10	the three angels	Gn 17, 8	the P covenant
Gn 18, 18	recap of 12, 2f	Gn 24, 7	the messenger for Isaac
Gn 21, 12	a promise to Isaac	Gn 26, 4	repeated promise to Isaac
Gn 22, 17	at the sacrifice of Isaac		
Gn 26, 4	promise repeated to Isaac		

Trusting Response		Obstacle	
Gn 12, 1–9	Abraham leaves home	Gn 12, 10–20	Abraham in Egypt
Gn 14, 1–24	War and blessing of Melchizedek	Gn 13, 1–18	Lot allowed to choose the land
Gn 15, 1–21	The covenant with God	Gn 16, 1–14	Abraham has a son by his slave wife
Gn 17, 1–27	Abraham's covenant renewed	Gn 18, 1–15	Sarah doubts the promise of a son
Gn 18, 16–33	Abraham intercedes for Sodom	Gn 20, 1–18	Abraham nearly repeats his denial of Sarah
Gn 21, 1–20	The birth of Isaac	Gn 22, 1–14	Will Abraham pass the test of sacrificing Isaac?
Gn 21, 21–33	Abraham establishes rights to water		
Gn 23, 1–20	Abraham buys land		

Genesis 12—25 can also be viewed as the story of a struggle to have trust and faith in God. Abraham and Sarah create as many obstacles to God's plan as they do helpful responses built on faith (see table above).

Still another structure can be found in the drama that leads up to the birth of the promised son, Isaac, from chapters 12 to 21. Here the series of major events are balanced in two blocs that each focus their climax on the birth of a son. See diagram on RG 112.

According to this diagram, the story moves dynamically forward through two series of parallel actions. Abraham wrestles with his call in betraying his wife and dealing with Lot but finally trusts fully in God's covenant by chapter 15, which leads to receiving a son, Ishmael. This is immediately followed by the expanded divine covenant of chapter 17, followed by further uncertain dealings with Lot and a new betrayal of his wife. But then God relents with a son Isaac, from Sarah, as fulfillment of the Promise found in chapter 12, 1–3. This entire series moves toward the great test of sacrificing his son in chapter 22. When Abraham proves himself competely obedient to God's will at that awful moment, the story comes to a rapid conclusion. Once the promise of a son is secured, purchase of a tomb in chapter 23 guarantees a claim on the land, and so Abraham's role is now ready to pass on to Isaac. And then both Sarah and Abraham pass from the scene.

Genesis 24—27:
The Story of Isaac and Rebekah

Isaac plays an important role in the life of Abraham as the promised son, but it is a passive role, even in the great scene where he is about to lose his life in chapter 22. He briefly comes to the fore in chapters 24 to 27 but they mostly duplicate scenes from the life of Abraham. The long account of arranging his marriage in chapter 24 links Isaac back to the family roots in northern Mesopotamia reported in chapter 12. His encounter with Abimelech and the surrender of his wife, as well as the concern with water rights in chapter 26, reflects two similar scenes in chapters 20 and 21; and in 26, 4 Isaac receives the renewal of the promises of land and descendants given to Abraham in chapters 12, 17, 18, 21, and 22.

Isaac's role might be best understood as permitting the transition from the role played by Abraham before him to the role played by Jacob after him, except for one thing: the remarkable person of Rebekah! The scene in chapter 24 of the messenger persuading Rebekah and her brother Laban to let her marry Isaac, and the journey home to Palestine, is a masterpiece of ancient writing art. Pay attention to how much emphasis is given to this one event—a total of sixty-seven verses. Rebekah will also become the key player in the next step of God's plan, the selection of the child Jacob over his older brother, Esau. In chapter 25, the birth of twins

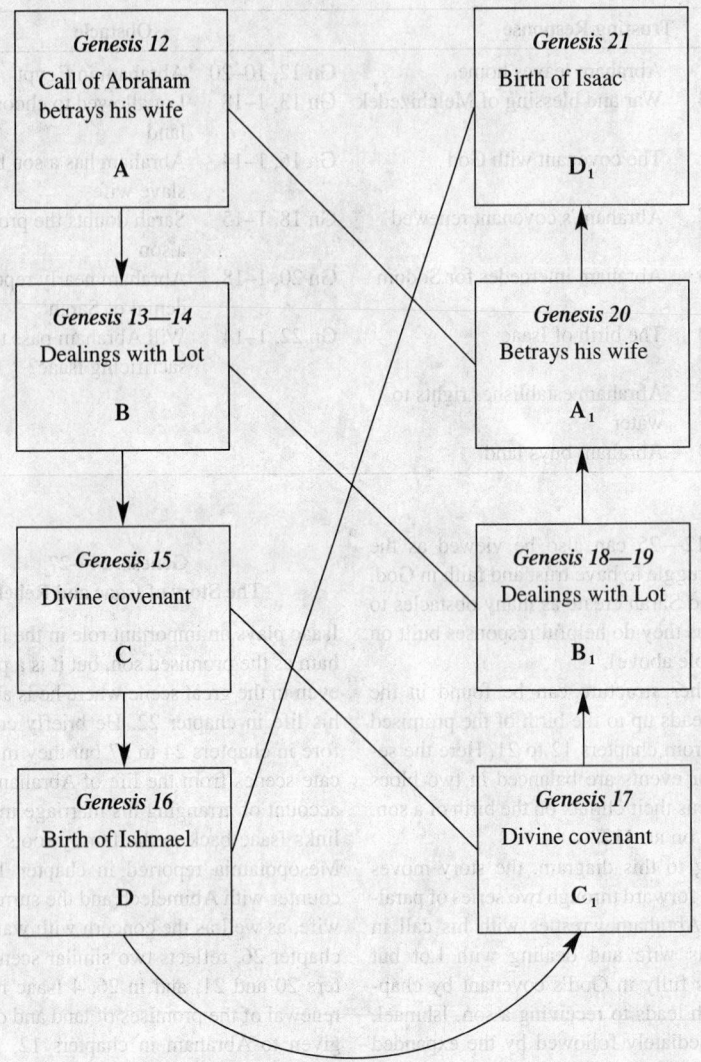

sets the stage for a great conflict that shall shadow the promise for many years ahead, the hatred of two brothers for one another, trickery on the part of Jacob, and the triumph of the younger brother over the older. And through it all, Rebekah steers a clear course that will end up winning the day.

Genesis 27—36: The Story of Jacob

In reading the story of Jacob, modern Christians are often horrified by the trickery and dishonesty involved in the way his career is presented in the text. In order to appreciate the religious message

of this part of the patriarchal history, we must be willing to read with our eyes wide open to all the possible levels that can be discovered in this very powerful piece of literature.

The following are a few initial observations and guidelines to help a better reading of these chapters: (1) Remember the overall purpose of Genesis 12—50 is to carry forward God's promise *despite all obstacles*. Thus we can expect that Jacob, like Abraham, will himself be one of those obstacles. (2) These chapters really are made up of many old sagas or folk hero stories. Although they have been gathered and polished and finally given a very religious edge, they still retain some of the early and less edifying characteristics of such traditions. (3) You as *reader* live in the twenty-first century with a modern ethical sense that is far more refined than the more basic code of conduct centered on maintaining honor, avoiding shame, demanding fair play, and upholding honesty of the ancient world. It is possible to understand the text without necessarily agreeing with everything in it. (4) This is intended as an exciting action narrative where the outcome hangs in doubt, and so we should not expect it to be a gentle, pious biography of a saint.

With these cautions in mind, we can look at all the elements that have been collected to make up the narrative as a whole:

Original Sources

The materials from which the narrative develops can be grouped into four types:

1. The conflict between the two brothers, Jacob and Esau, 25, 19–34; 27, 1–45; 32, 3–21; 33, 1–17

2. The conflict between Jacob and Laban, and the founding of a family, 27, 46—28, 9; 29, 1—32, 2

3. Divine appearance by God to Jacob to guide him, 28, 10–22; 32, 22–32; 33, 18–20; 35, 1–15

4. Special sources on the homelands of Jacob and Esau, 34, 1–31; 36, 1–43

In looking at these groupings, it immediately becomes clear that the cycles of stories about Jacob and Esau, and Jacob and Laban, are really about the struggles for identity and status of the Israelite tribes against the Edomites (Esau's people) in the first, and against the Mesopotamian peoples who are Israel's ancestors (Laban's claim over the family)in the second. These are older tales that were once recited orally to glorify Israel's past. To a modern sensitivity, Jacob may appear to be a deceiver and dishonest, but to an ancient his antics were clever, wily, and proved to be far wiser and more skillful than those of either the Edomites or Aramaeans.

Note, for example, that there are four separate conflicts between Jacob and Esau:

1. There is a struggle in the womb between them, with a prophetic word that Jacob shall triumph over Esau, his older brother (25, 21–28).

2. There is a struggle over the birthright (25, 29–34), which Jacob wins.

3. There is another struggle over the family blessing (27, 1–45) and Jacob wins again.

4. Finally, there is a great confrontation years later (32, 3—33, 17), which ends in a reconciliation between the brothers.

These incidents probably originated in bragging stories around the campfires of Israel's ancestors about how their founder Jacob outsmarted the Edomites. But they now form a series of obstacles that Jacob must overcome to carry on the divine plan, but they end in a finale of reconciliation that proves how everything works for the good in God's plan.

The same patterns can be detected in the Laban stories over the question of which wife is truly Jacob's primary spouse (and naturally therefore which sons are more important!), whose are the family gods, and whose are the possessions; in each of these conflicts, Jacob emerges the winner.

Major Themes of the Jacob Story

The Jacob stories are not intended to be a chronicle of historical events narrated in the actual order that they happened. Different factors all play a role in the development of the tradition: (1) In several cases ancient folk themes, such as the competition between the hunter and the sheepherder, or the struggle of a young shepherd against an established older one, are the source of an incident. (2) In other passages there are elements of a nationalistic boast that our clan is better than your clan. (3) Like true sagas, the personal battles stand for the tensions between actual nations. Thus, each of Jacob's twelve sons has the name of a real tribe; Esau is called "red and hairy," which in Hebrew makes a pun on the names of Edom and Seir, because he does represent Edom. (4) It is also about roots—to whom is Israel related? Certainly to the Arameans in Mesopotamia, and to the Edomites. (5) And, of course, another theme is that God writes straight with crooked lines. Examples include the choice of a younger son over the rightful older son as heir, and the triumph of the advice of a mother rather than the judgment of the father of the promise, Isaac himself.

The Appearances of God

Most importantly, the authors have added into the older folktales their strictly religious accounts of how God spoke to Jacob at various times in his life. These are also likely to be based on old stories that were cherished and retold at various shrines that grew up at the spots where God was known to have appeared, such as Bethel, Shechem, Paddan-Aram, and Penuel. But it is precisely through these scenes that the authors reveal the real purpose of the story. In the first vision at Bethel in chapter 28, Jacob receives the promise made to Abraham and Isaac; at Penuel he is designated the father of Israel as a nation, and his name is changed to match. In Shechem he acknowledges that God is the only god of Israel; and at Paddan-Aram in the final scene (chapter 35), God reconfirms that Jacob is to be the people Israel and that the promise of a great nation of descendants is on the verge of fulfillment.

The Result

When we combine all the elements that we have looked at, it presents us with a complex picture of Jacob as the model of Israel as well as its founding father. God is now about to forge these twelve sons into the future great nation, but it won't be done without problems of human blindness and often very disobedient or shortsighted or even slightly unscrupulous individuals. Jacob was all of these—but used his human talents to pursue faithfully the course that God had shown him; and lo and behold, God's plan came about! The Joseph story will illustrate the first step of building the brothers into a nation.

Genesis 37—50: The Story of Joseph

As in the preceding stories, the drama of Joseph's story can be read on two levels. The first is the search for the interesting traditions and themes that reach far back into Israel's history. The second is the overall theological purpose that the story now plays as part of the larger religious message of Genesis. On the first level, many scholars have traced the combination of the Yahwist and Elohist sources woven together to form a unified series of adventures. Perhaps even a modern reader might notice what appears to be slight differences and inconsistencies, which give away the fact that there were originally two accounts. One of the easiest places to see this is in the opening of the story in chapter 37, where J can be found in verses 3–4, 12–17,

23, 25–28, 31–34, and E in verses 1–2, 5–11, 18–22, 24, 28–30, and 36. Note, for example, such disagreements as shown in table on RG 115.

Scholars also point to two separate journeys of the brothers back and forth to Egypt: the first one, in chapter 42, is seen as E; the second, in chapter 43, is usually understood as J's parallel account.

Also still on the first level, research has pointed to the great number of parallels in the Joseph story to ancient Egyptian literary masterpieces that have been discovered. One such story tells of seven fat years followed by seven lean years of harvest (compare this to chapter 41, 1–32), while another tells the story of a young man who resists the attempts of his older brother's wife to seduce him, with the result that she screams and falsely accuses him of trying to rape her (see chapter 39, 6–20). Another famous Egyptian tale of one Sinuhe recounts how he fell out of favor with the pharaoh but was restored to favor when he proved to be a truly faithful servant of the king's interest (Joseph's imprisonment and rise to power shares some of this theme). There is yet another interesting parallel in an account found on a statue of King Idri-mi of Alalakh, a city in Syria, to be dated about the fifteenth century BC. It tells how Idri-mi's father was dethroned and the family forced to flee into exile and how Idri-mi could not get his brothers to help win back the father's kingdom; but when he managed it alone, he forgave them and took them back into his confidence.

All of these examples share some theme or another with the Joseph story, but none is more than a passing element of the whole. They do, however, confirm that the basic motifs and descriptions of chapters 37–50 are borrowed from, or echo ideas about, the world of Egypt in the second millenium BC, even if they are really the product of later imaginative creation without any basis in hard facts. Indeed, the whole way in which the Joseph story is presented connects well to the quite vague memories of the Hyksos period in Egypt (1750–1550 BC), a highly romanticized period when Semitic conquerors ruled much of the northern part of the country.

A third series of motifs on the first level of tradition is derived from the wisdom schools, perhaps as they flourished in the days of David and

J	E
The father is named Israel	The father is named Jacob
The brother Judah intercedes	The brother Reuben intercedes
The merchants are Ishmaelites	The merchants are Midianites
The long coat causes the brothers' jealousy	Joseph's dreams cause the brothers' jealousy

Solomon, but possibly, or even probably, at an even later stage of editing. Wisdom themes abound in the person of Joseph, who fits the ideal of both Egyptian wisdom sayings and those of the book of Proverbs in the Bible. He speaks only what is appropriate, keeps his own counsel, accepts misunderstanding, shows great skills as an administrator of public affairs, is adept at translating dreams, is skillful in political intrigue games, and avoids entanglement with foreign women. Above all, Joseph is attentive to God's plan, which works differently from the course of human planners (note especially the remarks of Joseph in 45, 5–8 and 50, 20, and compare these to Proverbs 16, 9 and 19, 21).

So far we have uncovered a variety of separate traditions that have gone into these chapters. What is remarkable about this particular narrative of Joseph, however, is precisely its dramatic integrity. Each step of the plot lays the groundwork for the next event. If you took away one of them, such as Joseph's imprisonment, there would be no way to get him into the king's favor in Egypt. If he didn't trick his brothers into bringing their father, Jacob, to Egypt, the master plan of God to rescue them at a later date would never have been put into place. Some scholars liken Joseph, not to the string of sagalike stories that make up the Abraham, Isaac, and Jacob cycles, but to a modern short story of fiction with a very carefully constructed plot. Some genius,

perhaps the J source itself, or one of its later editors, has taken all the old themes and separate traditions and created a literary work of art, the earliest such masterwork that we know anywhere.

Once we recognize its dramatic unity, we can begin to understand its theological message on the second level of the book of Genesis itself. Certainly, Joseph must first be understood as one of Jacob's twelve sons. Through him, one of the youngest, God will work his plan, despite the ambitions or hopes of the older and supposedly more deserving brothers. What Joseph does is entirely done through divine guidance. Joseph's vanity causes his initial problems with his brothers, and only the divine gift of dream interpretation eventually gets him out of a hopeless prison situation. By ironic twists of fate and the reversal of roles, God brings about the totally unexpected end in which a lowly Palestinian shepherd becomes the second most powerful official in Egypt. In what looks like the final triumph of the blessing of success and power and progeny promised to Abraham and Isaac, Jacob moves into Egypt. Genesis now closes with a question for all readers: what has happened to the hopes and promise to Israel that it would be a great people in possession of Canaan? Is there something yet to happen? Genesis ends with a clear message that God's work, as great as it has been, is not yet finished.

EXODUS

[see pages 70–117 of the Old Testament]

General Structure of the Book of Exodus

Exodus begins where Genesis leaves off. With Egypt now prosperous because of the efforts of Joseph, while Jacob and his sons enjoy great

blessings there themselves, one might think that all the promises to Abraham in Genesis 12, 1–3 have been fulfilled as Exodus opens. Exodus 1, 1–7 hints as much. But the drama is to continue with a cruel twist of fate in which blessing turns to desperation, and then in a surprising rebound, a new blessing unfolds that reveals Israel's destiny is not to be in the land of Egypt but in Palestine. Like Genesis, Exodus is a tension-filled dramatic play in which we discover God's mysterious purposes at work. Scholars see parallels between this book and a variety of well-known literary types, such as the classic "hero as rescuer" story, or the mythical pattern of God the mighty warrior establishing his rule over enemy powers, or the rite of passage (and purification) in which Israel goes from a slave childhood to responsible covenant adulthood. It perhaps shares elements of all of these, but stands in the end as a unique literary creation.

A Literary Overview of the Book as a Whole

We must therefore expect that this book, too, like Genesis, will be structured quite artistically and purposefully. It has two major halves: chapters 1 through 18 and 19 through 40. The first half carries the story line from success and security in the land of Egypt down through enslavement, and up again in deliverance and escape into a desolate wilderness to a meeting with God at Mount Sinai. These chapters create an exciting action story that keeps the reader wondering whether the people will really reach their goal of freedom and a new security. This is achieved by returning to each theme again and again so that they are never quite resolved; a certain tension remains whether God will be completely successful and whether the people will continue to follow where Moses is taking them—right up to the moment that they arrive at the mountain of God. Questions abound and add to the drama: Is God's promise in doubt? It seems so; yet at this same moment, God is already setting a new plan in motion with the birth of Moses. Will Moses respond to God's plan as Joseph did? Can God overcome the magic power of Pharaoh? Will the people follow Moses? When God delivers, will they believe enough to leave Egypt? In the trials of the desert, will they remain faithful? Each question receives its answer. Each stage prepares for the next. So we can diagram the book as an interlocking puzzle (see RG 117).

The second half, in chapters 19 through 40, dwells at length on two key activities that take place at the mountain. The first is the making of a covenant between God and the people, and the second is the description of two key elements of divine worship: the building of a sanctuary tent and an ark to serve as God's throne, and the establishment of priestly ministers. Dramatic tension is maintained here also, as observed in the people's idolatry in chapter 32; but much more so than in the first half, it establishes an orderly balance and state of security by the proclamation of the law by God and the people's oath to keep the covenant, followed by the orderly and well-planned description of the sanctuary and its auxiliary elements. This effect of balance is also achieved by interlocking the legal and liturgical descriptions. The descent of the glory of God into the sanctuary in chapter 40, 34–38 concludes the book, with the people united to the divine presence in harmony much as they were at the beginning of the book in chapter 1, but now with a far different destiny.

So the book is really an intricate mixture of narratives and legal regulations for the community. This did not happen by accident. The story of God's act of merciful liberation from slavery lays the foundation for his merciful guarantee to be with the people for all times that is reflected in the laws and institutions for public worship.

A Second Way of Dividing the Book

Besides the larger and more complicated plan of the book, we might better divide it for ease of study into the three geographical regions in which God meets Israel:

1. **Exodus 1—12** In the land of Egypt God works wonders to free the people from slavery;

2. **Exodus 13—18** In the wilderness God guides the people to safety and a personal encounter;

3. **Exodus 19—40** At Mount Sinai God establishes a community in covenant, law, and worship.

In each of these sections, Moses plays a leading role as God's agent, but there is never any doubt who controls the action. This is a story where God acts in each and every place with power and authority—no land or king is outside of the divine lordship. In tracing the thread of divine action through the long series of events described in the book, we need to be alert to the sudden and unexpected. What appears to be a hopeless situation where everything may be lost is suddenly changed. God turns near-defeat into victory, near-despair to triumph. In a certain way, the story is constructed like the traditional

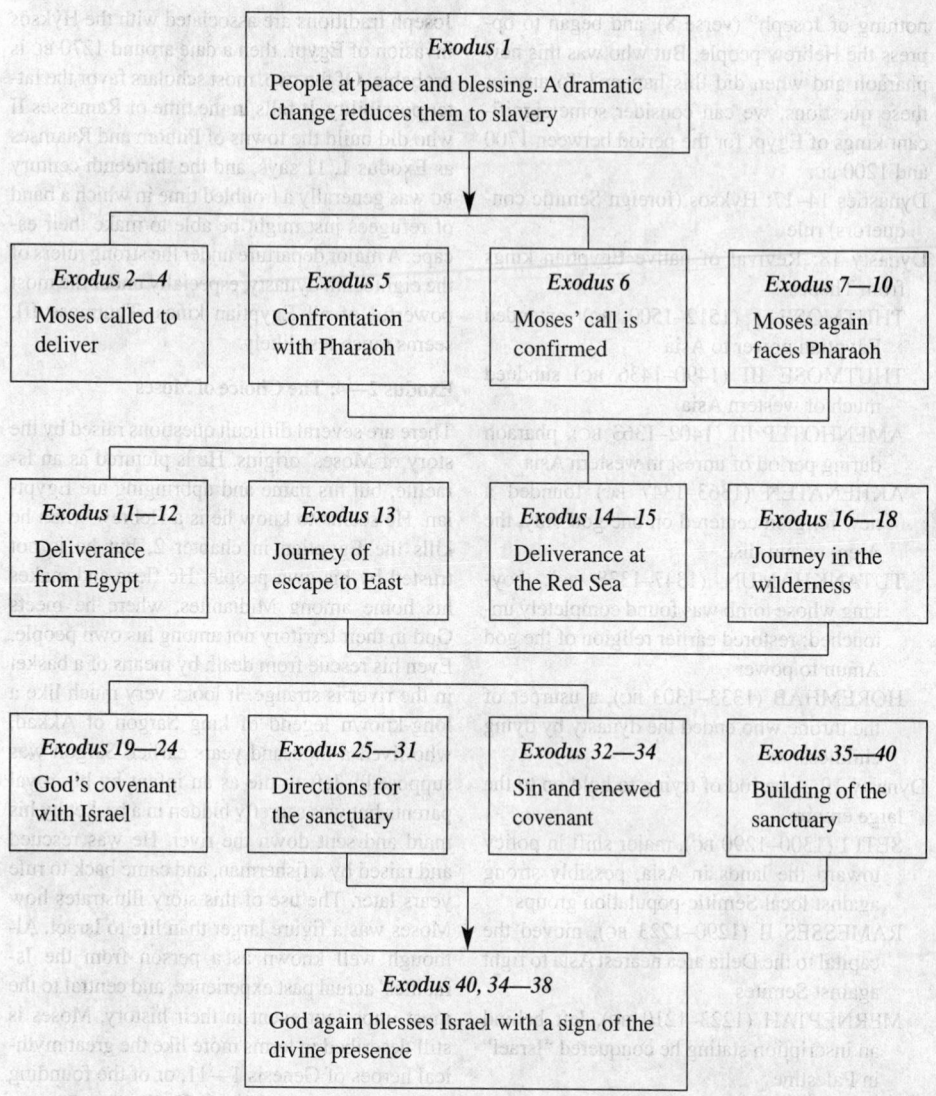

Exodus 1

People at peace and blessing. A dramatic change reduces them to slavery

Exodus 2—4

Moses called to deliver

Exodus 5

Confrontation with Pharaoh

Exodus 6

Moses' call is confirmed

Exodus 7—10

Moses again faces Pharaoh

Exodus 11—12

Deliverance from Egypt

Exodus 13

Journey of escape to East

Exodus 14—15

Deliverance at the Red Sea

Exodus 16—18

Journey in the wilderness

Exodus 19—24

God's covenant with Israel

Exodus 25—31

Directions for the sanctuary

Exodus 32—34

Sin and renewed covenant

Exodus 35—40

Building of the sanctuary

Exodus 40, 34—38

God again blesses Israel with a sign of the divine presence

psalms of lamentation that we find so often in the Psalter. A situation of desperate need calls forth a cry for help to God; God hears and answers their prayers with aid; and the people sing the divine praises (compare Psalms 7, 10, and 53).

Helps for Individual Sections of Exodus

In studying Exodus 1—18, there will be very little problem following the story line or plot of the drama. We must recall that there will be a number of inconsistencies and duplications because of the combination of the three major sources

which all reported the Exodus event. But these have been worked together smoothly for the most part, and only a careful examination will show how they are present. For many passages in these chapters, however, selected pieces of historical information or examples from other ancient peoples' literatures may help us to understand them more deeply.

Exodus 1: The Egyptian Setting

The narrative begins with a time of success in Egypt, but soon moves to a pharaoh "who knew nothing of Joseph" (verse 8), and began to oppress the Hebrew people. But who was this new pharaoh and when did this happen? To answer these questions, we can consider some significant kings of Egypt for the period between 1700 and 1200 BC.

Dynasties 14–17: Hyksos (foreign Semitic conquerors) rule

Dynasty 18: Revival of native Egyptian kings from Thebes

THUTMOSE I (1512–1500 BC) extended Egyptian power to Asia

THUTMOSE III (1490–1436 BC) subdued much of western Asia

AMENHOTEP III (1402–1363 BC), pharaoh during period of unrest in western Asia

AKHENATEN (1363–1347 BC) founded a new religion centered on one god only, the Aten, or sun-disc

TUTANKHAMUN (1347–1338 BC), boy-king whose tomb was found completely untouched; restored earlier religion of the god Amun to power

HOREMHAB (1333–1303 BC), a usurper of the throne who ended the dynasty by dying childless

Dynasty 19: A period of trying to hold on to the large empire

SETI I (1300–1290 BC), major shift in policy toward the lands in Asia, possibly strong against local Semitic-population groups

RAMESSES II (1290–1223 BC), moved the capital to the Delta area nearest Asia to fight against Semites

MERNEPTAH (1223–1210 BC), left behind an inscription stating he conquered "Israel" in Palestine

Dynasty 20: Period of loss of empire

RAMESSES III (1198–1166 BC) had to fight off the Philistines

The Bible itself gives suggested dates for the time of the Exodus. 1 Kings 6, 1 says the Temple of Solomon was built 480 years after Israel left Egypt; Exodus 12, 40 states that the Israelites had been in Egypt 430 years when they departed with Moses. If such dates are exact—and probably they are not, because they appear to be rounded out or even symbolic (12 times 40 years suggests twelve generations)—two different centuries are at stake. If the Temple was built around 960 BC, it would place the Exodus in 1440 BC; and if the

Joseph traditions are associated with the Hyksos invasion of Egypt, then a date around 1270 BC is probable. Of the two, most scholars favor the latter possibility. It falls in the time of Ramesses II who did build the towns of Pithom and Raamses as Exodus 1, 11 says, and the thirteenth century BC was generally a troubled time in which a band of refugees just might be able to make their escape. A major departure under the strong rulers of the eighteenth dynasty, especially under the most powerful of all Egyptian kings, Thutmose III, seems much less likely.

Exodus 2—4: The Choice of Moses

There are several difficult questions raised by the story of Moses' origins. He is pictured as an Israelite, but his name and upbringing are Egyptian. He seems to know he is a Hebrew when he kills the Egyptian in chapter 2, but he is not trusted by his own people. He flees and makes his home among Midianites, where he meets God in their territory not among his own people. Even his rescue from death by means of a basket in the river is strange. It looks very much like a long-known legend of king Sargon of Akkad, who lived a thousand years earlier. Sargon was supposedly left to die as an infant by his royal parents but was secretly hidden in a basket by his maid and sent down the river. He was rescued and raised by a fisherman, and came back to rule years later. The use of this story illustrates how Moses was a figure larger than life to Israel. Although well known as a person from the Israelites' actual past experience, and central to the most important event in their history, Moses is still described in terms more like the great mythical heroes of Genesis 1—11, or of the founding fathers Abraham and Jacob. He dominates every book of the Pentateuch except Genesis and, when his death is finally recorded in Deuteronomy 34, 1–8, he leaves the earth at 120 years old in the full vigor of youth and to a grave unknown. Thus, we must expect the initial encounter with such a person will be spectacular.

Note that chapters 2 through 4 form a series of scenes in a play: (1) The birth of the hero in a nearly miraculous fashion forces us to wonder what his mission in life will be; (2) The situation begins to look desperate—he is neither respected nor successful and ends up fleeing to barbarians for his safety; (3) There he is called to a nearly impossible task by God and accepts reluctantly (Ex 3, 1–12); (4) God gives him a special revelation of the divine name and an intimacy in communication not offered to others (Ex 3, 12–22); (5) God is forced to confirm the promise, reassure Moses about his mission, and give him his brother Aaron as a helper to speak on his behalf (Ex 4, 1–22); (6) Finally, the people accept him and his mission (Ex 4, 28–31).

Two notes might be added to help understand this section better:

The call of Moses has a certain pattern to it that is used throughout the Bible as the model of a call of the great prophets and leaders. Note that it is made up of the following stages:

    1. God appears or speaks to Moses (Ex 3, 1–4)

    2. He explains the reason for his coming (Ex 3, 4–9)

    3. He commissions Moses to his task (Ex 3, 10)

    4. Moses objects (Ex 3, 11)

    5. God reassures him and insists (Ex 3, 12)

    6. God follows with a sign or prediction (Ex 3, 12; 4, 1–5)

Note similar patterns for the call of the prophets and others. See table on RG 120.

The revelation of the divine name to Moses is a very special moment in the story. Note how it may be the combination of both the J and E sources because of the way it starts in Exodus 3, 1 with "the LORD" (J), and continues with "God" (E). To prepare Moses to understand the meaning of the name, God first reveals that this is the same God known to his ancestors Abraham, Isaac, and Jacob (a statement repeated three times in this chapter for emphasis!), and that God is showing love and compassion as he had done in the past when giving the promises to those earlier generations. It then comes to the moment in verse 13 when Moses asks for God's identity more clearly. The text gives several versions of the divine name: "I am who am," "I am," and "He who is" (or better, "He who causes to be"). The one certain thing is that all of these come from the same verb in Hebrew, *hayah*, the verb "to be." It is not usual to use the verb in this way. So, on the one hand, God refuses to give a regular name, but hides his real identity behind claims that He simply exists. And, on the other hand, the name suggests that God exists for something specific; in this case for the salvation

of Israel. Since the unique first person form, "I am who am," is found only here in Exodus 3, 14, the third-person form, *yhwh,* must mean either "He who makes this happen" (that is, the great act of salvation about to be performed), or, just possibly, it identifies God as the creator that causes all things to be. At least in this one event, the addition of the first person "I am" strongly suggests that God is, above all, assuring Israel that "I am always with you."

The word *Yahweh* occurs 6,823 times in the Old Testament and, following a very ancient Jewish custom, we traditionally do not use this name in prayer but replace it out of reverence for the divine greatness with the more formal "LORD." This is the practice throughout the NAB translation. Whenever the word appears in that way, printed in capitals and small capitals, it means that the underlying Hebrew word is Yahweh.

Exodus 5—12: Confrontation with the Pharaoh

The structure of these chapters also follows the pattern of a drama. There is Moses' initial attempts to show God's power to Pharaoh, and his subsequent frustration when the powers of Egyptian magicians seem as strong as God's (5, 1–13). Then the people themselves grumble that Moses is making things worse (5, 14–21). Chapter 6 opens with what seems to repeat the call of Moses from chapters 3 and 4, but scholars believe it was a separate account of the call of Moses from the P source. The editors added it to reinforce God's promise not to abandon Moses or the people, but to bring about their liberation.

The battle heats up when God begins to send plagues upon the land. There are a few inconsistencies in their presentation that suggest originally several sources were combined. Note, for example, that sometimes Moses stretches out his staff (9, 22f) and sometimes Aaron does instead (8, 1–3). The first usage is E, the second J. So, too, sometimes Pharaoh hardens his own heart, (9, 34), and sometimes God hardens his heart (10, 20). The first is J, the second is E.

The NAB notes (at 7, 14) that they are typical natural disasters that regularly trouble Egypt. The miracle is not in the actual plague, such as hail or gnats or flies, but in the timing of the contest between God and the pharaoh who has placed himself higher than the Lord. Can God

1. God appears	Jgs 6, 11f	Is 6, 1f	Jer 1, 4	Ez 1, 1–28a
2. The reason	Jgs 6, 12f	Is 6, 3–7	Jer 1, 5	Ez 1, 28b—2, 2
3. Commission	Jgs 6, 14	Is 6, 8–10	Jer 1, 5	Ez 2, 3–5
4. Objection	Jgs 6, 15	Is 6, 11	Jer 1, 6	Ez 2, 6–8
5. Reassurance	Jgs 6, 16	Is 6, 11f	Jer 1, 7f	Ez 2, 6f
6. The sign	Jgs 6, 17	-------	Jer 1, 9f	Ez 2, 8—3, 11

actually overcome the hardheartedness of the pharaoh? Each time, a plague seems to work; then it fails as the pharaoh changes his mind. The train of events struggles forward toward the climactic moment when God finally sends the tenth plague in chapter 12, 29–36. This last plague will be an act of terror and of death: by slaying Egypt's firstborn, God symbolically ends the universal leadership of Egypt and transfers divine favor to Israel's firstborn, who were spared.

It is not an accident, therefore, that this event is prefaced with an elaborate description, not of a meal as it might have been actually eaten in fear and haste, but of the full liturgical ritual of the annual feast of Passover. This feast was developed as a liturgy to recall and relive the miracle of the Exodus, the "passing over" of the angel of death and the liberation of Israel from slavery. Part of the significant theology of the book of Exodus is the unity between later rituals and the original events. What our ancestors experienced in the land of Egypt, we relive and celebrate anew in our feasts. Christianity has at least one excellent parallel to this way of thinking in that the synoptic gospel accounts of the Last Supper recount Jesus' words over the bread and wine, just as they were recited in home eucharists of the first century. To see this for yourself, compare Paul's description in 1 Corinthians 11, 23–26 with Luke 22, 14–20.

Exodus 13—15: The Escape through the Sea

These chapters can be divided into three parts. The first, in Exodus 13, 1–16, lists two further practices that the Israelites must do in order to remember how God saved them from the angel of death: (1) avoidance of leavened bread on the feast of the departure itself, and (2) the consecration of all firstborn males to God. No doubt both the avoidance of leaven and ceremonies of special dedication of a firstborn to God were practiced by Israel as well as its pagan neighbors

long before the time of the Exodus. But now they are given new meaning as a reminder that the real source of Israel's life is a God who delivered them from death. They mark the moment when God confirmed that divine favor has been transferred from Egypt's firstborn to Israel's firstborn.

The second part, in Exodus 13, 17—14, 31, gives a detailed account of how the Israelites once more escaped from the hands of the Egyptians, this time through the sea when it seemed impossible. And the third part, in Exodus 15, 1–21, recites a song of victory that celebrates the escape through the sea and may have been a hymn for a feast day. In structure this account of the great act of rescue in chapters 13 and 14 is preceded and followed by materials that come from the religious practices of later Israelite times. This is in line with the attitude expressed in chapter 12 that saw no problem relating the Passover escape side by side with a description of the much later rituals that celebrated those events.

The form of the third part, the Song of the Sea in Exodus 15, is quite old. Some scholars consider the basic text under the present enlarged form to be the oldest written text in the Bible. It uses extensive poetic parallelism for effect, and it breathes the spirit of God as a warrior chieftain in battle who comes to the rescue of his besieged people. The older part occurs in the first half, verses 1–12. It tells of the actual battle that God wages; the second part in verses 13–18 recounts how God then led victorious Israel through the desert to the Promised Land. The events that are told in verses 13–18 culminate in the establishment of a shrine (or home) of God in Palestine and could not have been written before the period of Settlement, perhaps as much as two centuries after the Exodus. Nevertheless, the hymn as a whole preserves an idea of God that belongs to the time before Israel settled in Palestine and developed a monarchy. Thus, the original poem may well have been composed sometime not long after the Exodus, during the age of the judges, with further developments added to it.

Several Egyptian documents help us to understand better the cultural background of Israel's flight from Egypt. One from shortly after the time of Moses is a report of a frontier official in the Sinai, which he sent back to headquarters in Egypt, and it reveals that Egypt regularly allowed groups of tribes to pass in and out of Egypt in times of drought or famine to save their lives:

We have finished letting the Bedouin tribes of Edom pass the fortress of Mer-ne-Ptah Hotep-hir-Maat which is in [the eastern Delta area] to go to the pools of Per–Atum . . . to keep them alive and to keep their cattle alive.

The second document is from the same period (about 1200 BC) and describes Egyptian military searches for runaway slaves:

I was sent forth from the broad halls of the palace . . . after two slaves. . . . Now when I reached the fortress, they told me that the scout had come from the desert saying that they had passed the walled place north of the fortress of Seti-Mer-ne-Ptah. . . . Which watch found their tracks? What people are after them? Write to me about all that has happened to them and how many people you sent out after them.

Two points can be made here: movement of groups was common across the Sinai borders, and the problems associated with slaves, slave escapes, and slave rebellions were of some concern to Egypt, as they were to later slave-owning societies such as Rome or the American South.

Exodus 16—18: The Hardships in the Desert of Sinai

The next stage of the journey takes the Israelites from the location of the sea to the foot of the mountain of Sinai in two months. The journey follows an itinerary which is listed for us, but unfortunately few of the places can be identified with any certainty. Even the location of Mount Sinai is open to discussion. But we can at least note some aspects with the aid of a map of the Sinai peninsula (see map 2 at the back of this book).

If we back up to the first part of the journey in chapters 13 and 14, we discover that Israel did not travel directly toward Palestine on the main highway along the coast. Egyptian forts guarded this way, and so they avoided it (13, 1–7f). Instead, they moved along the edge of the fertile Delta area just where it met the Sinai desert. The place-names in 14, 1–3 might be located either very close to the Mediterranean coast or perhaps near a swampy lake that lay along the depression line now followed by the Suez canal.

The name *Red Sea* is not certain. The Hebrew name can also mean either the "reed sea" or the "sea of chaos" or "sea of the end," which would signify doom or the final confrontation with the power of chaos in an echo of the great myths. Possibly today's Red Sea was called the "Sea of Reeds," but it is just as possible that it designated another body of water, perhaps one of several swampy lakes; on the other hand, if "sea of chaos" was intended, it could be anywhere, since the name is to be taken in a symbolic sense for the place where the Lord would finally defeat Pharaoh's army as the servants of chaotic evil.

Thus, scholars who try to identify the place-names in 15, 22 and following chapters have trouble knowing where to start. *Marah, Elim,* the desert of Sin, and *Rephidim* all remain mysteriously difficult to pinpoint. There are quite a number of oases throughout the Sinai, north and south, but none can be identified for certain with these names.

Usually three possible options for the route of the journey are given. The most northern route is the so-called Way of the Philistines and was, of necessity, avoided. The second route also went across the north somewhere and was a major caravan route to both Beersheba in Palestine and to Petra in Edom. It would also have two other strong claims: it passes very near Kadesh Barnea, Israel's main camping place where, according to Deuteronomy 2, 14, they spent thirty-eight years; and it was territory known to support nomadic groups such as the Midianites with whom Moses had spent time. It is listed on the chart as "The Way of Shur." A third possibility, and the one favored since Byzantine monks arrived at the very impressive mountain Jebel Musa in the sixth century AD, is the circular route along around the southern part of the Sinai peninsula. It has in its favor that Jebel Musa and its neighboring peaks are by far the most impressive mountains in Sinai. Moreover, there is strong evidence that Egypt itself mined the Sinai for gems and minerals in this area, using Semitic slaves. Such a mine has been found at Serabit el Khadim, and it is just possible that Moses knew the place. Finally, this longer route would permit the large number of moves that the books of Exodus and Numbers say the Israelites made. This is all we can say with our present knowledge.

Identifying the geography does not really explain the meaning of these chapters in reciting the lengthy journey of Israel away from Egypt. The events of Exodus 15, 22—18, 27 are not related to tracing the physical steps of the people as much as showing the tension between them and Moses. This is, above all, a tension between their frustrations with hardship and their duty to show gratitude to God for their freedom. At Marah, their grumbling leads to the lesson that God is a healer (15, 25f). At Sin, the dispute over food leads God to reaffirm his goodness as provider and to reinforce his demand that the Sabbath be observed (16, 16—36). At Rephidim, the people's anger over the lack of water leads to God's gift of water from the rock as a reminder of the miracle at the Red Sea (17, 1—7). The final two events, both in chapter 18, show first, a divine rejection of the Amalekites, and second, a positive relationship between Israel and the Midianites, who help organize judges and leaders to assist Moses. This is done with the assistance of Moses' father-in-law, Jethro. But it is a preparation for the greater organization around the divine commands, which are about to be given on Mount Sinai.

Exodus 19—24: The Covenant with God

These chapters describe the high point of the Pentateuch. If we wanted to draw a diagram to show this, we might draw a highway between

point A, the moment of creation, to the final point, Z, which would be the border of the promised land. This would cover the Pentateuch as a journey from Genesis 1 to Deuteronomy 34. The highway would climb steadily through Genesis and Exodus 1—15 to the top of Mount Sinai, go along its crest from Exodus 19 to the end of Numbers 10, and then descend forcefully to the shores of the Jordan River from Numbers 11 to the end of Deuteronomy. See diagram below.

On the crest of the mountain there is a long pause while God teaches Moses the laws by which Israel is to live. But these laws themselves are the fulfillment of the covenant that is established between God and the people in Exodus 19—24. So, ultimately, they are one. To understand these chapters, we should first note how they are organized into four scenes. See diagram at top of next page.

In scene one, Moses goes up and down the mountain several times, which may be a sign of more than one source combined, but it all serves to create an aura of holiness and reverence. Indeed, it so resembles the awesome experience of the Temple that many scholars have understood this to be a very late introduction built around the beautiful theological definition of Israel, found in verses 4—6: Israel is to be God's special possession.

Scene two records God's first words as a kind of summary of all that will follow. These are the key demands of any relationship with God; they cover duties toward God and toward one another and are limited to ten for easy teaching to children, who can count them on their fingers. Many of the commandments also have a special covenant motive for why they should be kept.

This is continued in scene three with an en-

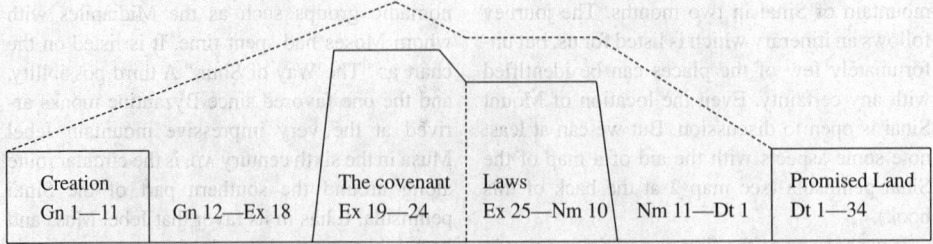

Creation	Gn 12—Ex 18	The covenant	Laws		Promised Land
Gn 1—11		Ex 19—24	Ex 25—Nm 10	Nm 11—Dt 1	Dt 1—34

19, 1–25	20, 1–21	21, 22—23, 33	24, 1–18
A	B	C	D
The purification of the people to meet God	The ten commandments as a summary of the covenant	The individual laws by which the people are to live	The solemn acceptance of the covenant

tirely different type of requirement. Unlike the Ten Commandments, which simply demand response with no answer to what will happen if you don't obey them, these requirements give a practical situation and the proper settlement of each case. The laws of chapters 21 through 23 are usually called "The Covenant Code," and are similar to civil laws throughout the ancient Near East. It is a minisample of how to act justly under the covenant.

Finally, in scene four, the people give their full assent to the divine offer of a covenant, and it is sealed by two rituals, again, perhaps, once separate from each other: a sprinkling with blood (24, 3–8), and a covenant meal in which Moses, Aaron, and the seventy elders banquet with God (24, 1.9–11).

The entire series thus combines lawgiving and ritual in an awesome setting of divine holiness and human sanctification to impress on the reader that *this* is the foundation stone of Israel's relationship to God and the source of all its religious obligations.

Exodus 25—40: Establishing God's Home in Israel

Once the Lord and Israel have been solemnly joined together, the dramatic action turns toward establishing a permanent dwelling for God in the midst of the people. Chapters 25—31 and 35—40 largely repeat each other as command and fulfillment: (1) a series of directions for building and appointing, and (2) the carrying out of those directions described in detail. The perspective on

the themes of building God's house, and establishing a special office of priests who will be consecrated and set aside for divine service, seem to stem largely from the later P source, which was concerned with showing that the Lord's Temple in Jerusalem had its original mandate at Mount Sinai. The desert tent and ark are described in terms of what a nomadic people of the wilderness might use; thus they are constructed to be portable. But all the major vessels and objects of the later Temple are already given a place during this desert period. In this manner, the text shows the unbroken continuity between God's earliest covenant bond and all later expressions of it. At the same time, these stories emphasize that the covenant cannot be observed unless worship is at its heart.

With this purpose in mind, the authors have taken the stories of Israel's first failure to keep the covenant, its idolatry with the golden calf, Moses' breaking the tablets of stone, and the regiving of the covenant words (32—34) and inserted them between the two halves of the sanctuary narratives. Worship and covenant are thus inseparably interlocked. See diagram below.

The Theology of the Covenant

Before moving on to the book of Leviticus, it will be worth a short reflection on the meaning of the term *covenant* for the faith of Israel as presented in the Pentateuch. There are several points to keep in mind:

• A covenant is a solemn agreement made with a religious ritual. In the early days it may

Exodus 19—24	*Exodus 25—31*	*Exodus 32—34*	*Exodus 35—40*
covenant given	sanctuary directions	covenant renewed	sanctuary built
A	B	A	B

have been mostly oral and put to memory, but in later biblical times it was always written in a formal document. It serves the same purpose as a contract—it is legally binding on both parties.

• Covenants can be made between individuals or between nations. Examples of individual covenants in the Pentateuch can be found in Genesis 26, 26–28; 31, 44–46. National covenants are mentioned often in the historical books: Joshua 9, 3–15; 1 Kings 5, 2–12; and 1 Kings 15, 19. It can also be made between a god and a people. For example, at the time of the flood, God promises Noah a covenant in Genesis 9, 4–12; and Abraham receives a covenant in Genesis 15, 10–21.

• These covenants between nations or with gods are modeled after typical treaties known throughout the ancient Near East. The particular type found at Mount Sinai is called a *vassal treaty* because it is made between a great king or ruler and a lesser subject state. A vassal treaty is not an equal deal. The great king promises kindness and favor; the vassal promises a long list of particular obligations that will be performed faithfully.

• These treaties were considered to be valid for all time. They could not be taken back or rejected once solemnly made.

• There are examples of covenant treaties from both seventh-century Assyria and the thirteenth-century Hittites. Biblical wording shows similarities to aspects of both forms. But the clearest model of a typical vassal treaty is known from the Hittite examples. It has six parts:

1. A preamble stating the name of the parties.
2. A historical listing of all the good things the great king has done for the vassal.
3. The laws and obligations that the vassal must perform.
4. A directive that the document be saved and read publicly.
5. A list of gods who witness the treaty.
6. Lists of curses the gods will bring on those who break the treaty, and the blessings given to the parties if they keep it.

• If we take these six steps, we can see them present in Exodus 19—24 in a general way:

1. Ex 20, 2   the preamble
2. Ex 20, 2 (19, 4)   the historical list of favors
3. Ex 20, 3–17; 20, 23—23, 17   the obligations of the vassal
4. Ex 24, 3–8; 24, 12   oath ceremony and saving the tablets
5. —   no divine witnesses
6. Ex 20, 5f; 23, 25   blessings and curses

No gods witness the treaty because in Israelite belief there are no other gods who can testify to what the Lord does. However, we must not push these similarities too far. Exodus describes, first of all, a momentous event of encountering, and then promising exclusive worship to, the Lord who has saved and shown himself a benefactor to this small refugee people.

Only later did the full legal treaty language become fixed in the tradition, such as in the covenant summary statement often found in the prophets, "You shall be my people and I will be your God" (Jer 7, 23; 11, 4; 24, 7; Ez 11, 20; 14, 11; Hos 2, 25, etc.). Perhaps closer to the original formula of the covenant relationship is the moving proclamation put first on God's own lips in Exodus 20, 5f and then again in the renewal of the covenant in 34, 6f: "The LORD, the LORD, a merciful and gracious God, slow to anger and rich in kindness and fidelity, continuing his kindness for a thousand generations, and forgiving wickedness and crime and sin; yet not declaring the guilty guiltless . . ." This same text, as indicated by John Paul II in *Dives in Misericordia,* is the basis of Israel's hope, and therefore the hope of the modern world (#4).

We can appreciate the power of the idea of a covenant because it confirms the special relationship that Israel claimed with the Lord, based on a unique and moving personal experience of the favor of that God for them. At first the covenant was mostly celebrated in worship with a national sense of destiny. Only with time do we find that later prophets like Jeremiah and Ezekiel express a growing concern to stress the legal relationship that cannot be broken even by disasters, but can require punishment and legal penalties if the covenant terms are broken.

LEVITICUS

[see pages 118–51 of the Old Testament]

Reading the Book of Leviticus Today

Jewish tradition has given a very honored place to the book of Leviticus because it contains a significant number of the laws and commandments by which Judaism defines its life and practice. Six hundred and thirteen commandments have been identified in the Pentateuch that are binding on Israel, and of these some 247 occur in Leviticus. The early rabbinic commentators of the Talmud spent many volumes examining the meaning of the statements in Leviticus and establishing practical ways in which they could still be observed many centuries after they were written down. The learned teachers of the law in the first centuries after Christ (from about AD 70 to 500) never tired of debating the myriad ways of understanding the legal materials in Leviticus and elsewhere. This may seem particularly surprising since nearly all of the laws of sacrifice that fill the first quarter of the book of Leviticus had been rendered impossible to perform by the Roman conquest of Jerusalem and after the destruction of its Temple in AD 70. It indicates, however, how richly diverse are the contents of the book, that even with the inability to perform so many of its commands, it still remains the most important statement of Torah for Judaism.

It is therefore important to recall that in Judaism *Torah* does not have the narrow and constricting meaning of "Law" so common among modern people. Torah means "teaching" or "way" and it can be best understood as a means of expressing ourselves before God as a faithful and obedient and beloved son or daughter. Jews always link Torah commands with simultaneous joy. Note the extremely upbeat and positive nature of the Bible's most famous hymn in praise of the Law, Psalm 119. The opening verses read,

> Happy those whose way is blameless,
>   who walk by the teaching of the LORD.
> Happy those who observe God's decrees,
>   who seek the LORD with all their heart,
> They do no wrong;
>   they walk in God's ways.

and it continues in this manner for another 173

verses, more than three times the length of any other psalm in the Psalter!

How opposite has been the reaction of the Christian church as it reads Leviticus. Most Christians are horrified by the idea of animal sacrifices, and they consider the questions of what should be eaten or not eaten far too restrictive; many even experience a mild case of disgust at the topics of the purity and impurity of bodily functions. Since many of the actions described in the first half of Leviticus are tied to priestly roles in the Temple, the book has become a negative symbol for Christians who emphasize the so-called freedom from the Law that Paul speaks of in his letters in the New Testament. Even the current name of the book means basically "That which pertains to the levitical priests," although in Hebrew it is called simply by its opening word, *wayyiqra'* ("And he called"). Thus it is very likely that a Christian reader will come to this book with a certain prejudice that it will be boring, irrelevant, and largely supplanted by a newer theology of the freedom of the spirit. This is not a good starting point to discover any treasure in the book, nor to realize, even in regulations that a Christian no longer observes, how profound insights into the mystery of God shine through regularly.

To gain as much appreciation for the book as we can, we need to reflect on its message on two levels. First, we can explore what religious insight and meaning the various laws and practices had for an ancient Israelite. Second, we can look at the major themes it treats in terms of how they reveal the enduring character of God's revelation and divine purpose, which gave direction and vitality to Israel's fidelity and witness through the centuries, and that have become central to Christianity's own teaching. An example of the two levels would be the understanding of sacrifice. Unless we learn the central role that sacrifice played in Leviticus as a primary means of both acknowledging God's saving blessing and also asking for forgiveness, our interpretation of Jesus' own death and the Church's explanation of the Eucharist will be seriously weakened and perhaps even incomprehensible.

The Overall Structure of the Book

Leviticus can be identified entirely with the style and theology of the Priestly source found throughout the Pentateuch. Leviticus is very interested in classifying and listing all things in their proper place, just as the P story of creation does in Genesis 1 or the list of nations does in Genesis 11, 10–32. It is also very concerned with distinguishing the realm of the sacred from that of everyday life. Most of the topics it treats deal directly with this question of what is appropriate or inappropriate in matters of approaching the divine.

The book has really two major divisions that are quite different in spirit. Chapters 1 through 16 give regulations for matters that are handled directly by the priests; chapters 17 through 27 treat the larger social areas of community behavior and public worship that express the spiritual heart of living within the covenant. In a diagram it might look like the table on RG 127.

Explanation of the Outline

Chapters 1—16. The initial collection of various regulations on sacrifice in chapters 1 through 7 is followed by a narrative explanation in chapters 8 through 10 of the proper role and status of the priestly officials, illustrated by Aaron's first major sacrifice under the covenant. Then chapters 11 through 15 contain a collection of rules and distinctions that govern the proper respect for food and bodily functions; chapter 16 follows with an elaborate description of the annual ritual that atoned for and cleansed the people of all guilt from their sins. In both parallel patterns, laws are followed by actions. Neither set is intended to comprise all the laws that must be observed, nor do the rituals described exhaust all ways of celebrating or performing sacred liturgical actions. What they do above all is establish a close connection between the ways we define our lives and the ways we celebrate in worship.

For the authors of Leviticus, this structure emphasizes that holiness is central to Israel's relationship with God, and that holiness may be defined as respect for the sacred mystery of life and for the divine presence that is found everywhere, even in ordinary day-to-day life.

Chapters 17—26. The same spirit of a holiness that sets apart areas of special divine reverence from ordinary ways of acting also governs this second part of Leviticus, which is often called simply "The Law of Holiness." It has special characteristics that mark it off as a separate set of laws from chapters 1 through 16. This set can be divided roughly into two parts: chapters 17 through 20 stress the ethical areas of life that bind us socially in communal life; chapters 21 through 25 concentrate on the sacred areas of priestly ministry and worship. They roughly correspond to the same dynamics that we find in chapters 1—16 between commands on ways of life and commands on more directly priestly ritualizing. Chapter 26 concludes this body of law, but it is so impressive in scope that it really serves as the conclusion of the whole book. It reflects much of the specific language associated with covenants. Chapter 27 was added later as an appendix.

The Literary Unity and Diversity of the Book

All scholars today recognize the basic unified viewpoint that the book takes. It is priestly. This means that it gathers together laws and directions that govern activities that should be monitored by the priests in the community. Some of these, as in the chapters on sacrifices and major feasts, have to do with public worship. Others have to do with personal behavior and conditions that affect our proper place before God. These may involve laws on food, clothing, skin diseases, sexual activity, as well as truly ethical decisions about justice, love, and right behavior between members of the covenant community.

All these laws, however, are seen to be part of what separates the sacred from the ordinary. God is holy and not to be treated in just any old way. Judaism and Christianity have always made the transcendence of God a first priority; that is, they have recognized the gulf that divides us as creatures from the one who creates. Certain moments of our lives and certain activities highlight this profound difference. Humans enter into the realm of the sacred that is set apart on a holy day or at a holy place or by the rituals performed by a consecrated (thus "holy") person. Certain features of our being, too, are holy, such as sexual-

Outline of the Book of Leviticus

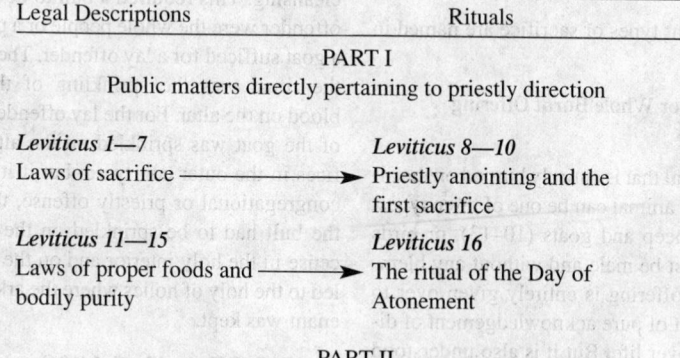

Legal Descriptions	Rituals

PART I
Public matters directly pertaining to priestly direction

Leviticus 1—7
Laws of sacrifice ——————➤

Leviticus 8—10
Priestly anointing and the first sacrifice

Leviticus 11—15
Laws of proper foods and ——➤
bodily purity

Leviticus 16
The ritual of the Day of Atonement

PART II
Daily and personal matters pertaining to the whole community

Leviticus 17—20
Moral and ethical laws on ——➤
holiness

Leviticus 21—25
Ritual requirements for holiness

PART III

Leviticus 26
Covenantal conclusion to both chapters 17—25 and to the entire book

Leviticus 27
[Appendix of laws on vows]

ity, birth, and death, because they are at the heart of the mystery of divine creation and divine control over our existence. They are to be treated with special reverence. Exodus covered the *making* of all necessary sacred objects and some ordination rites; Leviticus concentrates on *how* Israel is to act according to holy principles.

Although this theme controls every topic treated in Leviticus, the book was not written all at once. The signs of different groups of laws that at various times were joined into larger and larger collections can be seen when we look closely at the text. As an example, if we read the sacrifice rules in chapters 1—7 quickly, they may appear to be all in the same style. But we could then go back and look at particular expressions. In chapters 1—3 the sacrifices are regularly "brought *before* the Lord," so that there will be a "sweet-smelling oblation" to the Lord. These expressions are rare in chapters 4—5. Instead, these chapters deal with a special type of

offering for sin and use the label, "The Lord said to Moses . . ." more frequently. They also stress that the priest will make atonement for others. Chapters 6—7 are arranged according to a still different formula, "This is the ritual of . . ."

Probably, then, there are three slightly different sets of sacrifice laws that have been combined to make up these seven chapters. Again, the style of listing laws in chapters 1—16 is so different from the more preachy style of chapters 17—26 that all commentators have been convinced that we have separate origins for these two halves. Nevertheless, the editors have made this into one of the most unified books that we have in the Pentateuch, second only to Deuteronomy.

The Major Themes of the Individual Sections

Since much in Leviticus is foreign to modern Christian religious observances, it will be worth looking at each division with a few charts and background aids to understanding.

Leviticus 1—7: The Topic of Sacrifice

Several different types of sacrifice are named in these chapters:

The Holocaust or Whole Burnt Offering (Lv 1, 1–17)

This is an animal that is entirely burned on the altar to God. The animal can be one of three types: cattle (3–9), sheep and goats (10–13), or birds (14–17). It must be male and without any blemish. Since the offering is entirely given over to God, it is an act of pure acknowledgement of divine lordship over life. But it is also understood as an atonement for the sins of the offerer (v. 4). Yet, later in the Holiness Code, a holocaust could be offered for joyful or thankful moments (see 22, 17).

The Grain Offering (Lv 2, 1–16)

The NAB calls this the "cereal offering," but in Hebrew the word is simply "the gift offering" *(minhah)*. This may be understood in part as a substitute for expensive animals so that the poor could afford a holocaust. But more usually it was a thanksgiving to God for good crops and to celebrate joyful times. Since only the symbolic bits of grain, oil, and frankincense on the top were actually burned up, the rest went for the support of the priest.

The Peace Offering (Lv 3, 1–17)

This might better be called a "well-being sacrifice," for its main difference from the holocaust was that it was not completely burned up but largely saved and eaten by the offerers and their families. It could be taken from either cattle or sheep and goats, but not from birds. Since this offering was for a group, a bird would have been too small. Like the holocaust it had to be without blemish, but unlike the holocaust it could be either a male or a female animal. Only the fat parts (tail, inner organs and their fat, the two kidneys) were burned to God.

The Sin Offering or "Purgation Offering" (Lv 4, 1–5, 13)

This sacrifice specifically deals with those times when a sacred thing had been violated, often by accident or without knowing it. The sacrifice was necessary in order to atone for the loss of holiness and proper purity of holy things by an act of cleansing. This required a bull to be killed if the offender were the whole people or a priest; while a goat sufficed for a lay offender. The key part of the ritual was the sprinkling of the animal's blood on the altar. For the lay offender, the blood of the goat was sprinkled on the altar of sacrifices in the outer courtyard; but if it had been a congregational or priestly offense, the blood of the bull had to be sprinkled on the altar of incense in the holy interior and on the curtain that led to the holy of holies where the ark of the covenant was kept.

The Guilt Offering (Lv 5, 14–26)

This is sometimes called a "reparation offering." It differs from the sin offering just slightly in its focus (see Lv 7, 7). Where the sin offering was to cleanse the defiled sanctuary and persons, the guilt offering is strictly to give back a reparation or "payment" to God for failure in something we ought to have given or done. That is, we have cheated God or a member of the covenant community, and so not only does the wrong itself have to be fixed up, but God must be given a reparation offering over and above the actual amount that was neglected. For this offering a ram is specified, and the blood is sprinkled on the altar itself. It is clearly a ritual of atonement for sin to heal the sinner of guilt.

Instructions for the Performance of the Different Sacrifices (Lv 6,1—7, 36)

The specific actions of the priests for each of the above types of sacrifice are now spelled out in more detail in 6, 1—7, 10. Special instructions for the lay participants in the peace offerings are added on in 7, 11–36. This was necessary because, in these particular sacrifices, the offerer and his party ritually ate most of the sacrificed animal and thus needed instructions similar to those given to the priests. It did not hurt, of course, from the priestly point of view, to reemphasize to those who brought sacrifices their obligation to supply a portion to the priests for their livelihood.

Conclusion (Lv 7, 37–38)

The last two verses of chapter 7 are an especially solemn closing that underscores for the reader how seriously sacrificial regulations and the importance of this practice for the faith was to be understood.

The Anointing and Service of Aaron and His Sons (Lv 8, 1—10, 20)

Once the instructions on how sacrifice is to be done have been thoroughly learned in chapters 1—7, the action can begin. These next chapters deal with the installation of the proper priesthood, that is, Aaron and those descended from him (chapter 8); the model performance of the first sacrifices (chapter 9); and several crucial problems that need a solution (chapter 10). Thus, the section is very well organized even though there are several signs it may have originated from a variety of sources. The description of the first sacrifice in 8, 14–30 seems almost to be duplicated in the octave-day sacrifices of 9, 1–21. The story difference is that in the first, Moses actually leads Aaron; in the second, Aaron does it on his own authority.

The details of chapter 8 fulfill the requirements for proper priestly performance of the sacrifices. Verses 1–13 carry out the commands on the appointment of priests found in Exodus 29; verses 14–30 correspond to the sacrifice laws in Lv 1, 1—5, 13.

In chapter 9 three events are recorded: the first sacrifice of atonement for Aaron and the priests (9, 8–14), the first sacrifice to atone for the whole people (9, 15–21), and finally, the blessing over the people (9, 22–24). This text reinforces the lesson that sacrifices must be done correctly and with a special awareness of their sacred character. Only if they are done with such careful reverence will the glory of the Lord be present in their midst (9, 6.22–24).

In chapter 10, the lesson about God's holiness is driven home with still greater force. In the first case, verses 1–5, even the sons of Aaron will be stuck down if they fail to observe the proper awe and correct manner of approaching the divine presence. In the second case, verses 6–11, the priests must refrain from a number of behaviors that would profane the sense of holiness in the performance of their duties. These include improper dress, stepping beyond the boundary of the Tent of Meeting, and using alcoholic beverages. But they are also given the positive duty of teaching the law in its entirety to the people (v. 11). And in the third case, verses 12–20, the

correct manner of eating the sacrifices is dealt with. It is illustrated by an unusual exception that tests the rule: Eleazar and Ithamar don't eat the sacrifice as they should but give it all up as a burnt offering to God. Their excess zeal is permitted because it offered to God what they were entitled to have for themselves. If they had instead done the opposite, and taken part of God's share for themselves, one is left to imagine the death they would incur as punishment.

So then, chapters 8—10 serve two functions. They show how the laws in chapters 1—7 are performed by the true priests (see the diagram RG 127) and they fulfill the instructions given in Exodus 25—31. Those chapters gave the Lord's commands both for building a tent and ark, and for consecrating priests. But only the building program was completed by the end of Exodus. Only now does the priestly consecration finally take place. We could show the development by another diagram, on RG 130.

In this schema the Levitical editors have inserted Exodus 32—34 from the older J story of the covenant between the commands to prepare the sanctuary and priesthood and their fulfillment, both from P. This links the covenant to the regulations on worship by interlocking sections of one with the other; at the same time it integrates the two traditions of J and P. Note that it also reinforces the notion that the people easily fall into idolatry and transgress the holiness of God and so need the careful priestly performance of the cult to preserve their proper relationship to God.

The Laws of Purity (Lv 11, 1—15, 33)

These chapters take up four separate types of uncleanness associated with living beings:

1. Lv 11, 1–47   Animals
2. Lv 12, 1–8   Childbirth
3. Lv 13, 1—14, 57   Contagious diseases
4. Lv 15, 1–33   Genital discharges

The Levitical editors have made a number of important distinctions within these categories. In chapter 11, for example, some animals are considered clean, that is, fit for eating, while others are not. In general, those same animals that are unclean for eating also contaminate anyone who touches their dead bodies. In the third category, contagious diseases, special procedures are required for each different case: if it is a human

Covenant given

Exodus 19—24
The solemn conferral of
the covenant on Israel

Cult Commands

Exodus 25—27
Instructions for building
the Tent and Ark

Exodus 28—31
Instructions for
consecrating the priests

Covenant Renewal

Exodus 32—34
The covenant is broken
but God restores it

Leviticus 1—7
Instruction of the priests
on sacrifice

Cult Completion

Exodus 35—40
The construction of the
Tent and the Ark

Leviticus 8—10
Consecration of the
priests and first acts

skin disease, the person must be quarantined; if it is a fungus on a house wall, the building is quarantined; if it is a matter of sexual emissions, different rituals are prescribed for men and women.

These purity laws are based on a simple consideration, namely that many areas of human life touch the mystery of the divine, and in those areas there can be nothing that is impure or unworthy. This does not just apply to sacred spaces such as temples, or sacred moments such as birth, marriage, and high holy days; it also includes those areas of everyday experience that touch issues of life and death, including the mysterious power of sexual activity and the sometimes dangerous loss of blood and other bodily fluids.

Uncleanness refers specifically to those situations that prevent us from approaching the divine in a worthy manner. They cannot be taken lightly. The final word on the question of those who defile God's house by appearing in it in a state of uncleanness is a warning that it will cause their death (Lv 15, 31). At one point, also, the command to avoid swarming insects as unclean is identified with loyalty to God himself, and its violation defiles God's own holiness (Lv 11, 44f). Moreover, the laws can have devastating effects on the individuals involved. For example, if the skin disease does not go away, the person can be permanently exiled from the community.

Many scholars have debated the reasons why some animals are considered clean and therefore edible, while others are forbidden. Frequently they argue for a primitive science of hygiene that recognized that the unclean animals were possible carriers of disease. An example would be the pig, long known to be a possible bearer of trichinosis. Others argue that the real basis is a religious reflection on the proper order of creation as told in the Genesis creation stories. Only fish that swim, birds that fly, and animals that graze fulfill the normal pattern of God's plan; all others seem to be not quite perfect—flightless birds such as ostriches, sea creatures that walk like animals, animals that crawl close to the ground like insects, etc. A little of both views may well have influenced the theologians who made up the lists. We just do not know.

The categories covered in Leviticus 11—15 do not exhaust the realm of the clean and unclean. The Passover regulations of Exodus 12—13 deal with old leaven, which was unclean; Deuteronomy 20 demands purity conditions for waging war in God's name. But the four areas found in Leviticus usually touch those matters that come under the supervision of the priests, often require one or more sacrifices for the purification of the individuals affected, and might involve situations where the unclean person joins those who come into the Temple and would thereby consciously or unconsciously defile God's dwelling place.

The Day of Atonement (Lv 16, 1–34)

In one sense, chapter 16 takes up where the story left off in chapter 10 with the death of Aaron's sons and the need for atonement. In another sense, the ritual of a Day of Atonement described in this chapter heals all the cases of uncleanness and impurity that have defiled the land during the year. It thus sums up the proper response of the people to the dangers of impurity named in chapters 11—15. In a still larger sense, it is the climax of all the laws on sacrifice, priestly service, and purity from chapter 1 on, since they all involve the need for atonement at one level or another. The sacrifices always include some atoning function; priestly service risks constant danger of some fault in its performance that may demand atonement; and, of course, all daily cases of impurity need atoning. Going further, verse 21 tells us that the Day of Atonement ritual was to purify the people and the land of *both* unintentional *and* intentional sins and transgressions.

The actual rite is probably pre-Israelite. Similar ceremonies of transferring the sins of the people onto animals and then slaughtering them were known in many ancient cultures, including those of both Babylon and Rome. Similarly, smearing the blood of a sacrificial animal on the walls of a temple to purify it was done at Babylon. The reference to Azazel in verses 8, 10, and

26 remains uncertain. It probably refers to an ancient belief that there was a desert demon by this name that claimed the goat sent out to it. But there is no evidence for belief in any such demon here—it is a poetic way of casting out sin into the realm ruled by evil powers, the desert. It is as though the people said to the goat, "Go to hell!"

Chapter 16 carefully describes each step. It lists first the proper procedures and clothing for Aaron and any future high priest to enter the presence of God in the holy of holies; then it outlines each step of the ritual, including the prayer and hand gestures over the goat; and finally it closes with a command to do this forever. Yom Kippur, with its themes of atonement and repentance of the whole community, still occurs on the ninth day after Rosh Hashanah (the New Year) each fall. For the mixing of past and present, this passage should be compared to the parallel directions for Passover in Exodus 12.

The Holiness Code (Lv 17, 1—25, 55)

In chapters 1—16 all the topics dealt with things that needed to be observed or performed to overcome the barrier between God and human beings. Thus even the sacrifices can be included under the rubric of concern for being clean before God. Chapters 17—25 take up the opposite and just as necessary qualification of holiness: what we do *positively* to relate to God. The first sixteen chapters center on removing the blocks to our relationship; chapters 17—25 propose building new blocks in communal action in imitation of God. Actually, both areas overlap considerably with one another, and there is an excellent harmony between chapters 1 through 16 and 17 through 25.

There are nevertheless some differences. The style of 1—16 was largely listing what had to be done, but 17—25 is more like a sermon exhorting people to fidelity. Almost all of the first sixteen chapters were ritual requirements; most of 17—25 deals with ethical and social obligations. In 1—16 the accent fell on what we as mere creatures need to do to bridge the gap to the divine; in 17—25 the accent falls on how a holy people live in the image and likeness of God. In many ways the Holiness Code of 17—25 resembles the homiletic style of the book of Deuteronomy and the impassioned warnings of the prophet Ezekiel (see Ezekiel 22 for a good comparison with

Leviticus 18—20). It probably originated in the same period as Deuteronomy and Ezekiel, near the time of the Exile of 587 BC, or a little earlier. It is also a moving call to holiness and integration of all aspects of our lives around God as our central concern.

In structure, 17—25 can be divided into two parts: (a) chapters 17—20, which cover ethical demands on the whole community, and (b) chapters 21—25, which deal primarily with priestly matters of public worship. Each part has a well-ordered progression:

Part 1 (17—20)

17, 1–16 All sacrifices must be done at the central sanctuary; there must be great reverence for life by respect for the blood—it is not for human consumption but to be given back to God.

18, 1–30 Sexual behavior must be regulated by careful respect for appropriate human relationships, so that lust and orgiastic urges are controlled and that Israel does not become as carnally bankrupt as its pagan neighbors.

19, 1–37 Contains a wide variety of norms for dealing with one another as members of the covenant with God; and as verses 19–36 make clear, far differently from the way the Canaanites behave. The laws are especially concerned with protecting the rights of the weak so that there will not be a degraded serf class as was found among the Canaanite city states.

20, 1–27 Repeats many of the commands already given but adds penalties to each, often severe in respect to idolatry and incest. Once again it ends with a warning to avoid the practices of the Canaanites.

Part 2 (21—25)

21, 1–24 The role of priest demands wholeness and particular witness, so special rules governing marriage, deformities, and uncleanness are spelled out.

22, 1–33 Regulations for the wholeness and fitting perfection of the animals sacrificed are made parallel to those governing the priests.

23, 1–44 The annual feast days must be regulated with the same care as the priests and sacrifices. This section treats the weekly Sabbath as the model feast (23, 2f); and

then seven annual feast days: Passover, First Fruits, Weeks, New Year, the Day of Atonement, Booths, and the eighth day after Booths.

24, 1–23 Still further regulations of worship follow. These explain how the lamps and the showbread in the sanctuary are handled; also the death penalty for blasphemy is explained by a concrete case.

25, 1–5 A special concluding description of the *sabbatical year* every seventh year when no planting may be done; and of the *jubilee year,* every fifty years, when all property and debts return to their original owners. Both probably originated as acts of acknowledgment that God owned the land. Now they are explained as acts of social justice to restore help to the poor and landless.

These laws are an ideal code and it is not absolutely certain that some of the most idealistic among them, such as the very unlikely jubilee year, were ever put into actual practice. They stand together, however, as a vision of Israel living completely under the dominion of God and in obedience to the divine will—they are holy as God is holy, and all Israel's actions respect the integrity and purpose of God's creation. This is made clear over and over again in these nine chapters by repeating the formulas "I the Lord am your God," "I am the Lord," or "I the Lord am holy." To these is often added the reminder "I the Lord led you out of Egypt." Israel, who received such divine compassion, must always act in turn out of a like compassion for others!

The Conclusion to the Holiness Code (Lv 26, 1–46)

This is the true conclusion to the Holiness Code, but it stands apart by its form as a series of blessings on all who keep, and curses on all who violate, the covenant. In this way, it now stands as the general conclusion to chapters 1—16 and 17—25. The regulations on approaching God in worship and obeying him in society have been spelled out, and now Israel must choose. Its covenant structure resembles very closely the vassal-treaty form discussed previously in Exodus 19—24, and it has strong similarities to a closing list of blessings and curses in Deuteronomy 27.

It also reflects the thinking of the priestly editors at the end of the Exile. Not only does it foresee both blessing and eventual curse for disobedience, but it adds a short concluding word on a renewed blessing and a promise that God will not forget his covenant with Israel completely (vv. 40–46). It is imbued with the spirit of the exilic prophets Jeremiah and Ezekiel that God was about to instill a new covenant, written on the hearts of Israel, so that no longer would obedience come in response to an external law but would rise from an interior consent born of the knowledge and love of the Lord. It is at this point that the original book of Leviticus ended on a note of great hope for the future.

The Appendix on Gifts Vowed to the Sanctuary (Lv 27, 1–34)

This section was added sometime after Leviticus was completed to take care of an important problem that touched on holiness: how to handle various offerings that were vowed to the Lord but were not always appropriate for sacred use. These include such diverse subjects as persons, animals, houses, land, firstborn animals, objects vowed, and tithes. If something is not fitting to be consecrated to God, it should be sold for money for the sanctuary or be exchanged by the offerer. But once even impure offerings have touched the sanctuary, they are not to be simply returned to ordinary life again.

While these are important areas, they can be subject to rash vows by people. Note Jesus in Matthew 5, 3–9 condemns those who vow to God what belongs to the support of their parents.

NUMBERS
[see pages 151–99 of the Old Testament]

The Nature of the Book of Numbers

The name "Numbers" is taken directly from the title of the book in the Septuagint Greek translation: *Arithmoi*. It refers to the importance of taking the census of Israelites in both chapters 1 and 26. This probably reflects the early Hebrew title for the book as well, although later Jewish tradition has identified it by the name *bemidbar* ("In the desert"), the first words of the book. Generally, commentators have had trouble agreeing on the organization and purpose of the book of Numbers. They identify a rough outline of three divisions, but judge that the materials in each section are not well ordered and seem to be loose collections of topics and events that do not belong anywhere else. This approach, however, does not help us to study the book easily, and it probably reflects the difficulties that modern minds have with ancient ways of thinking, rather than being an accurate assessment of what the authors and editors of the book of Numbers thought they were doing. Several considerations might help us find more purpose and order in the book than would appear in a hasty reading.

1. Numbers Links the Mountain of Sinai and the Promised Land. It stands between the events described in Exodus and Leviticus and the situation found in Deuteronomy. It is about a journey that moves the people from Mount Sinai (Exodus and Leviticus) to the border of the Promised Land (Deuteronomy). The focus of all the stories and legal lists is either on preparations for the journey, or on problems encountered on the journey, or on attitudes that threaten the journey.

2. It Is Paired Thematically with the Book of Exodus. In the overall drama of the Pentateuch, Genesis matches Deuteronomy as first and last book because both focus on life in the land itself; Exodus matches Numbers in the second and fourth positions on both sides of Leviticus in the middle: Exodus leads up to Sinai, and Numbers away from it. Many incidents are repeated in both, such as the manna scene and Moses bringing water from a rock, but Numbers judges Israel's response differently and more judgmentally because in Numbers the Israelites have accepted the covenant and Torah and must live obediently.

3. Its Themes Build on the Laws of Leviticus. Numbers naturally flows from the materials treated in Leviticus. The central theme of Leviticus is holiness in the ordinary areas of life, such as food, clothing, sickness, moral ethics of society, and regular worship. Numbers intensifies the expectations of holiness by stressing the need for dedication and total commitment to God, in order for Israel to succeed as a nation if its goal is to live prosperously in the Holy Land. To do so, it must be obedient to divine commands and so Numbers treats rebellion and hard-heartedness as worthy of punishment.

4. Like Exodus and Leviticus, It Combines Narratives and Laws. The book contains a combination of narratives and laws just as do Exodus and Leviticus. Each collection of laws relates to the experiences and lessons learned from the past. Israel enjoyed reading these living connections that remembered the deeds of their ancestors in light of the laws they still lived by today.

5. This Is No Ordinary Journey but a Solemn March. It is a military campaign of Israel as an army advancing against the enemy. It is a journey of conquest, and it will not be completed until the end of the book of Joshua when the people have rest in the Promised Land. Most of the laws, as well as the elaborate preparations for leaving Sinai and the detailed descriptions of battles on the eastern side of the Jordan River, are framed around proper "military" behavior. This is a metaphor for obedient religious observance: a soldier in God's army must be holy and single-minded. Special aspects of this emphasized in Numbers include loyalty to Moses, rejection of paganism and pagan nations, and willingness to sacrifice for God.

6. Numbers Prepares for Deuteronomy by Centering on the Promise of the Land. The people are on the move as a great and fearsome force; they no longer need worry about the promise of a son that was the central concern in the stories of Genesis. Now the *land* dominates their thinking. It dominates as a hope for prosperity that will be in stark contrast to the deprivation and suffering of their time in the desert. And it dominates in the reflections and legal directives on how to live faithfully and loyally in the land as a people of the covenant.

The Outline of the Book of Numbers

The most common division of the book is into three large blocs that correspond to major stages of the journey narrative:

Nm 1, 1—10, 10 The proper preparation of a military expedition in a holy war.

Nm 10, 11—20, 13 The journey through the desert and the trials of the people's faith in God.

Nm 20, 14—36, 13 Final directions and campaigns to prepare for assault on the Promised Land.

This breakdown of the book's order highlights that it remains controlled by the overall sense of movement toward the divinely promised goal of the land first stated at Genesis 12, 1–3. The first bloc is a flurry of activity in getting ready to depart; the second is an actual journey from Sinai to the oasis of Kadesh Barnea; and the third division has the people move on through the Transjordan area of Edom, Moab, and the Amorites to arrive in battle array across the river from the major Canaanite stronghold of Jericho. Numbers 33 summarizes the movements of the Israelites from Egypt until they reach the edge of the Jordan by listing the stopping places where they camped. Such a record of the stages by which they traveled calls attention to the fact that, at each one, God gave special guidance and assistance, and that no movement took place without the divine initiative. But each major division of this journey contains those ritual and legal concerns that seem to fit best at that spot (see chart on RG 135).

The Development of the Major Themes in Numbers

To help us appreciate a little more the dramatic flow of the book, it might be useful to describe it narratively:

Numbers 1, 1—10, 10

The book opens with the census of all males able to go to war (1, 45). Levites, who serve in the sanctuary, are exempted. In chapter 2 these newly commissioned soldiers are then organized into a military camp prepared for defense as well as for a quick march in time of danger. The book then turns to the special role of the Levites who are to dwell around the tent and ark at the center of

The Divisions of the Book of Numbers
with a Summary of the Contents of Each Chapter

Nm 1, 1—10, 10	*Nm 10, 11—20, 13*	*Nm 20, 14—36, 13*
The camp is prepared for a holy war battle march	The journey to Kadesh with challenges to Moses' rule	Events and rules stemming from the arrival at Jordan

Chapter	Chapter	Chapter
1 Census of males for armed service	10 The battle order: the Ark is first	20 Move through Edom; death of Aaron
2 Order of the camp	11 Two occasions of rebellion	21 More victories and more murmuring
3 Special role for Levites	12 Miriam and Aaron oppose Moses	22–24 Balaam tries to stop Israel
4 Levitcal roles in bearing the Ark	13 The spies scout the Promised Land	25 The people abandon God at Baal of Peor
5 Laws of purification for battle	14 People resist taking the land	26 The census repeated and land promised
6 Vows of Nazirite dedication	15 Laws relating to possessing land	27–30 Laws on inheritance, vows, and worship
7 Sacrifices and gifts for leaving	16 Levite rebellion against Aaron	31 The Midianites are defeated
8 Levites anointed for service	17 Aaron's authority restored	32 Transjordan conquests of two and a half tribes
9 Passover celebration; camp is broken	18 Proper portions for priests and Levites	33–34 Stages of the march and boundaries
10 The trumpets sound the departure	19 Atonement for any uncleanness	35 Special Levitical cities and laws
	20 Murmuring over water	36 Inheritance laws and conclusion

camp; they represent God's ransom of all firstborn males (3, 5–12). In this way, all the fighting force becomes a consecrated army linked to holy service of the Lord through the Levitical substitutes. Then follow the duties of the Levites for moving the sanctified objects of the sanctuary when on the march (4), and a set of laws on uncleanness, theft, adultery, and other sins that would defile the army's holy status to fight for God (5). Chapter 6 completes this preparation of the camp by giving rules for those (the Nazirites) who take extra vows of rigor. Chapters 1—6 end with the blessing of Aaron over the camp (6, 22–27).

Chapters 7 through 10 then move on to the questions of proper ritual actions for the sanctuary itself, including the giving of gifts (7); the care of the lampstands, the purification of the Levites for service in the tent, and time limits for their years of duty (8); and finally the solemn celebration of the first Passover since leaving Egypt, which is to take place on the first anniversary of the miracle itself (9, 1–14). This larger division then concludes with a notice that the divine pillars of cloud and fire would move with the people, and they are to be summoned to departure by the silver trumpets (9, 15—10, 10).

Numbers 10, 11—20, 13

This traces the actual journey from Sinai toward the land of Canaan. The cloud moves, the tribes set out in marching order, all appears to be proper. But trouble immediately looms with the repetition of the grumbling of the people that had so characterized the period between their deliv-

Numbers

Numbers READING GUIDE

erance in Egypt and their arrival at Sinai in Exodus 13—18. Many of the chapters in Numbers repeat and duplicate the same grumblings recorded in the Exodus narratives. First, people complain about the lack of meat (11) and are punished by fire; but Moses intercedes and saves them. At this point, too, some of Moses' authority is shared with the elders (11, 24–30). In the next chapter, even Miriam and Aaron challenge Moses' authority and are struck with leprosy, but again Moses intercedes successfully. Next they arrive near the southern boundaries of the Promised Land and are able to advance straight into it. The scouts return with glowing reports of its bounty, but only Joshua and Caleb are fearless enough to want to attack the inhabitants. The people cringe in fear and reject Moses' leadership. God wishes to destroy them all, but Moses once again intercedes and God once again relents. But he does decree that not one shall enter the Promised Land from this generation except Caleb and Joshua, who were loyal (13—14).

Here the editors insert laws that will be required when Israel gains possession of the land (15). But again, rebellion flares up as several Levites now refuse to follow Moses. They receive death as their punishment (16), and Aaron then assumes the priestly role of reconciling and purifying the people in their relationship to God (17). This in turn is followed by a number of laws that regulate the proper payment due to priests and Levites for their services to the sanctuary, and which, to the minds of the ancient editors, fitted perfectly here after the discussion of Aaron's role.

Since uncleanness has been a major theme of these narratives, especially in the case of those who go near God's sanctuary unworthily, chapter 19 follows with a ritual that uses the ashes of a red heifer for preparing a permanent holy water to sanctify those found in an unclean state. This whole division now ends with a final case of grumbling over the lack of water in which even Moses and Aaron fail in their trust in God, and they are told that they, too, cannot enter the Promised Land.

The materials from chapters 10 to 20 have thus emphasized the fragility of the people's loyalty to the Lord, even in their state of military awareness. They also underline the need for constant purification of action and loyalty to God, if Israel is to succeed in possessing the land. Above all,

they emphasize the central role of the priests and Levites in that process of purification, and their role in developing complete fidelity through proper ritual and holiness.

Numbers 20, 14—36, 13

The action now turns to the actual conquest of the land. Their march takes them around the land of Edom and up the desert highway along the east side of the Transjordan plateau. They bypass the land of Moab and attack the Amorites farther north. This victory in chapter 21 leads the king of Moab to try to stop them. He hires a famous prophet, Balaam, to curse them. Chapters 22 through 24 consist of a very old series of stories about Balaam's efforts and his failure. They do provide a climactic statement to the patriarch's promise, as Balaam foresees the greatness of Israel in the centuries ahead.

In sharp contrast to this future greatness, however, the very next chapter records how Israel betrayed even the first commandment and fell into idolatry and the orgiastic practices of the Canaanites. All who participated are executed (25). This sets the stage for a renewed military dedication to the cause of the Lord, symbolized by taking a second census in chapter 26 to summon forth the fighting men for the war ahead.

But before any battles are fought, there is an interlude of four chapters (27—30) in which another series of regulations and laws are set forth that pertain to the organization of Israelite society when it is settled in an agricultural and urban type of life. These laws are triggered by the problem of relations between families and their obligations to one another, which the taking of the census leaves unanswered. They cover inheritance laws for the widows and daughters of men who might be slain in battle or who die prematurely. They also involve the proper rules for celebration of the feast days in a new land, and the rules governing different types of vows made by different classes of people.

Finally, fighting resumes with a major victory over Midian, which is interpreted as revenge for the Midianites' part in the idolatrous acts at Baal of Peor (31). Shortly thereafter, the tribes of Reuben, Gad, and Manasseh conquer territory on the eastern side of the Jordan River (32). This is permitted only with deep reservations since it may mean accepting less than the Promised Land itself. But those tribes promise to do their part in the conquest of Palestine when the moment comes.

The final chapters of Numbers sum up. Chapter 33 lists all the camps through which Israel had journeyed, ending with the final stopping place on the river across from Jericho. They are given a solemn command to take the land, drive out its inhabitants (33, 53–56), and divide the land among the tribes so that they fill the generous boundaries that Moses describes (34, 1–15). The book closes with a series of laws that reflect the tricky problems of legal boundaries and multiple jurisdictions. These include laws on special cities for the Levites, towns set aside as asylums for accused persons, murders in open territory between tribes, and property rights for women and the defenseless. Once again the laws illustrate the nature of the narrative that had immediately preceded them.

Conclusion

The developmental pattern of Numbers not only tells a story of adventure and difficulty, it ties this story to lessons that must be applied when the people live a totally different type of life in the Promised Land. Laws and regulations that would never apply in nomadic or seminomadic situations will become crucial when the circumstances change dramatically and the people become a settled population. The book, however, manages to unite the dramatic history of the Israelites' time in the wilderness as a people on the move—without home or power—with the later needs and practices that characterized their life in Canaan in the years following.

There are few parallels to this type of writing in modern literature, but we can learn to value and even enjoy this intense combining of (boring) laws with historical adventures, if we think of it as the answer to a profound question: How does a people preserve the lessons of the great days of salvation and guidance in the desert without losing them in later ages? They remember both the stories of the desert and the laws that came from them . . . and then observe the laws!

The Literary Unity of Numbers

Like Leviticus, Numbers reflects throughout the hand of the Priestly source guiding its order and structure. In only a few sections can we find the

J and E sources from the older tradition still present: (1) in the narrative stories of chapters 11, 13—14, 16; 21, 25, and 32; and (2) in the Balaam cycle in chapters 22—24. The major themes of J and E focus on challenges to Moses' authority and punishment for rebels who don't trust in God, as well as preparing Israel for occupation of the Promised Land. P, however, adds numerous laws that extend the reach of those already seen in Leviticus and also to make the J and E warnings even more definitive. P sections also emphasize the proper ordering of Israel's tribes, and the roles of Priests and Levites, by adding many ritual lists. Many commentators think that P is developing a response not only to J and E but also to the laws of Deuteronomy, thus placing the P sections after the Exile in the last stages of Pentateuch development. For example, the description of major feast days in Numbers 28—29 would reflect the latest development level of the many levels in the Pentateuch.

Major Priestly Religious Concerns in Numbers

These Priestly editors have emphasized certain themes above others while keeping the journey narrative moving ahead. Certainly ritual matters were important to them, for scattered references to various states of uncleanness and the rites to overcome them occur frequently in chapters 13—20. So also, numerous passages distinguish particular duties of Priests and Levites in chapters 26—36. Legal regulations for various social areas of conflict, which would arise when land is involved, are also interspersed at fitting places in the text.

And finally, the theological themes that center on God's power to bring about the promise are continued from the books of Genesis and Exodus. These include: (1) questions about the authority of leaders, namely Moses, Aaron, and the elders; (2) murmuring and lack of trust on the part of the people; (3) in the Balaam stories, the power of the prophetic word to bring about God's will; (4) the role of Joshua as sole leader to succeed Moses; and (5) the decisive victories God bestows in battle.

In order to better grasp the main religious message of these various topics scattered throughout the book, it is worth listing some of the groupings in more detail:

Numbers

Numbers   READING GUIDE

Priests and Levites. Genesis 34, 24–31 and 49, 5–7 both view Levi as a violent and renegade tribe; the book of Exodus, however, not only notes that Moses and Aaron are from the tribe of Levi but also praises the Levites in 32, 25–29 as the only tribe that remained faithful to the Lord during the golden calf incident. The tribe of Levi is therefore worthy of priestly service to the Lord. Deuteronomy 33, 8–11 adds that the Levites alone were faithful at Massah and Meribah when Moses struck water from the rock, although the two accounts (Ex 17, 1–7; Nm 20, 2–13) never mention any Levitical role. There may have been two separate traditions about the Levites, one positive and one negative. Certainly there is some reason to wonder, since in several places such as Deuteronomy, Joshua, and a few prophetic texts (Ez 43, 19—44, 15; Mal 2, 4), the Levites are referred to as priests; while in the majority of other references they are an auxiliary group to help in the Temple but are distinct from the priests, who can come only from the house of Aaron. Perhaps these conflicting reports stem from the historical reality that originally Levites were priestly in character but became subordinated to a particular branch of the family of Aaron after the Exile in 586 BC.

In Numbers, however, the Levites receive very high honor, even though the book takes the position that they are not the same as the priests and must not seek to perform priestly offices. Four sets of regulations pertain to the Levites:

• They alone have the privilege of carrying the ark of the covenant (1, 49–53), and they are also responsible for the other sacred objects in the sanctuary and for its transport during the desert years (4, 1–49).

• They are honored to be set aside as a ransom for each firstborn male among the people as a whole. Thus they are consecrated to God and may not have military roles or possess land (3, 5–20; 3, 40–51; 8, 3–24; see Dt 18, 1–5).

• In Numbers 16—17, some Levites under Korah rebel against Aaron and Moses, and demand equal priestly rights. God punishes them severely, and the story serves as a motive for why Levites are not allowed to do priestly ministry.

• Certain cities are set aside by Moses in Numbers 35, 2–8 as refuge centers for people suspected of crimes. This contradicts claims in other books that Levites had no title to land. It also provides a basis for seeing an important role for the Levites in the local administration of justice in Israel; probably they also serve as local religious leaders who functioned as priests in the small communities far from Jerusalem.

The Holy War. There is always a great amount of uneasiness when modern readers hear the stories of sacred campaigns in which the enemy—men, women, and children—are doomed and executed if Israel is victorious. Such a campaign takes place in Numbers 21, 1–3 when Israel fights Arad, and again in Numbers 31, 1–54, in the battle against the Midianites. Similar military campaigns are described in Joshua, Judges, and the books of Samuel. It is worth noting about these, however, that to the Israelite reader of the Bible who lived many years after the days of Moses, Joshua, and the judges, these accounts then belonged back in the founding days. They had a special character because it had been a life-and-death struggle between the Lord and the Canaanite gods that demanded drastic action. They knew that in their earliest traditions, God was a warrior who fought on their behalf against overwhelming odds; note in particular the description of God as a warrior in the oldest poem in the Pentateuch, Exodus 15.

Numbers gives one of the fullest explanations of Holy War theory in the passage on the Midianites in chapter 31. It is quite fierce. But in another account from about the same time as Numbers or a little earlier, Deuteronomy 20, a number of restrictions are put on such a war so that it is less than a total massacre. So, too, the first chapters of Numbers try to expand the concept of the Holy War to include the whole people as an army of the Lord on the move to Palestine. Purity and obedience are the keynotes of this army, not vengeance, and we might safely assume that already the editors of Numbers wanted to soften the stories of the old total war. They suggested, instead, that now this concept could be lived out by a total commitment of life to the way of the Lord. The battles against Arad, Midian, and finally Canaan, were still stirring episodes from the past, but they were not the way of the present! This would fit the picture painted by several prophets that war was not the way to do God's will; peace and faith were (see Is 7, 1–14; Hos 10, 13f; Jer 21, 3–10; 34, 1–5). There was a development in theology and attitude over the cen-

138

turies, and Numbers at least shows some of both viewpoints mixed together.

The Murmuring Tradition. One striking aspect of the stories in Numbers 10, 11—20, 13 is the recurrence of so many incidents of grumbling and rebellion against God by the people in the desert that resemble accounts in Exodus 14—18. Note the following:

Nm 11, 1 People grumble against Moses at Taberah; fire comes down.

Nm 11, 4f People grumble about the lack of meat at Kibroth-hattaavah; God sends a plague, but then a gift of quail for food.

Nm 12, 1–16 Miriam and Aaron rebel against the sole authority of Moses; Miriam becomes a leper, but God later heals her.

Nm 14, 1–38 The people refuse to attack Canaan; God will make them die in the desert and their children wander for forty years.

Nm 16, 1–36 Korah, Dathan, and Abiram all rebel against Aaron's authority; they are consumed by fire from heaven.

Nm 17, 6–15 The people again grumble against Moses and Aaron; the scourge of punishment is lifted by Aaron's actions.

Nm 20, 2–13 The people complain about lack of water; God has Moses strike the rock for water but keeps him from entering the Promised Land.

Nm 21, 4–9 The people again grumble about food, and God sends fiery serpents to bite them; they are saved by a bronze serpent made by Moses.

These incidents may be compared to similar examples from the book of Exodus: Exodus 14, 10; 15, 23; 16, 13; and 17, 5–7. The last case is a duplicate of Numbers 20, 1–13 in which Moses strikes the rock for water. Numbers 11, 31 seems to be the same as Exodus 16, 13, in which God sends the people quail to eat. These two cases may actually borrow material from J or E sources. The other examples in Numbers, however, all seem to have a similar interest in how God punished the people and then allowed Moses or Aaron to intercede and restore them.

Numbers, true to its priestly concern, wishes to emphasize the need of the community to atone for its sin and rebellion, and turn back to God through liturgy and purification. Even the bronze serpent in Numbers 21 implies healing through some ritual action. According to 2 Kings 18, 4 this object was receiving special veneration right up to the time that King Hezekiah reformed the religion in 715 BC and smashed the bronze serpent. Numbers tells the story—despite the obvious danger that it might be considered magically powerful—to illustrate the need to turn to God for healing.

The Roles of the Twelve Tribes in the Conquest Plan. The end of Numbers records the controversies among the tribes over whether they all must enter the land, or whether Reuben, Gad, and half of Manasseh may live on the Transjordan side of the river. A similar suggestion that harmony did not always prevail among the tribes stands out in the conflict between Joshua, Caleb, and the other scouts in Numbers 13—14. In fact, such divisions within the twelve tribes appear frequently in the books of Joshua and Judges as well. There are also numerous differences within the lists of the tribes themselves that suggest the tradition was not always uniform about which tribes made up the original people of Israel. There are seven separate listings of the tribes in the book of Numbers, and they do not always agree (see table on RG 140).

In Numbers 34, the two tribes that stayed across the Jordan, Reuben and Gad, are omitted; otherwise every list includes twelve tribes. None of these, however, mentions Levi, although he is included in all lists in Genesis and Exodus (Gn 29, 31—30, 22 plus 35, 16–20; 35, 22–26, 46, 8–25; 49, 2–27; Ex 1, 1–5). In his place, the lists in Numbers always give Joseph's two sons, Ephraim and Manasseh, as two tribes that replace those of their father, Joseph, and Levi. Several lists begin with Reuben, the firstborn son of Jacob; others begin with Judah, the chief tribe in the Priestly view. Moreover, the tribes occur in varied orders throughout the seven lists, as well as in lists in other books.

Each list came down with its own purposes in mind, of course. Numbers 2, 3–29, for example, reordered tribes to fit in a neat square around the tent and ark. We will not be too confused if we pay attention to the divergent materials and viewpoints that have been collected in Numbers and in other texts that deal with how the conquest of Palestine took place. They had no modern historians on the scene, so that much of the traditional narration of these events was in the form

The Tribal Lists in the Book of Numbers

Nm 1 5–15	Nm 1 20–43	Nm 2 3–29	Nm 7 12–83	Nm 13 4–15	Nm 26 5–50	Nm 34 19–28
Reuben	Reuben	Judah	Judah	Reuben	Reuben	Judah
Simeon	Simeon	Issachar	Issachar	Simeon	Simeon	Simeon
Judah	Gad	Zebulun	Zebulun	Judah	Gad	Benjamin
Issachar	Judah	Reuben	Reuben	Issachar	Judah	Dan
Zebulun	Issachar	Simeon	Simeon	Ephraim	Issachar	Manasseh
Ephraim	Zebulun	Gad	Gad	Benjamin	Zebulun	Ephraim
Manasseh	Ephraim	Ephraim	Ephraim	Zebulun	Manasseh	Zebulun
Benjamin	Manasseh	Manasseh	Manasseh	Manasseh	Ephraim	Issachar
Dan	Benjamin	Benjamin	Benjamin	Dan	Benjamin	Asher
Asher	Dan	Dan	Dan	Asher	Dan	Naphtali
Gad	Asher	Asher	Asher	Naphtali	Asher	
Naphtali	Naphtali	Naphtali	Naphtali	Gad	Naphtali	

of hero stories, great legendary actions of the tribes, and local memories preserved by one tribe or another. They have been organized with more neatness and more attention to continuity than may have actually been the way the events themselves happened.

No doubt some tribal groups entered Palestine separately from the main body of attackers under Joshua, while some tribes may have had large numbers of their members already in the land. Finally, the constant substitution of Ephraim and Manassah for Joseph may indicate that it was these two tribes in particular that did most of the fighting and conquering with Joshua. Indeed, to support this view, we can note that the book of Joshua indicates the action against the Canaanites largely took place in the territory of those two tribes. And the controversy with the two and a half tribes that did not want to go with the rest may only be the tip of a very large iceberg, in which the much larger hidden part is the reality of how few actually joined the invasion with Joshua.

The Balaam Oracles. The story of Balaam, the mysterious prophet summoned from the East to curse Israel, is perhaps the most fascinating part of the book of Numbers. It contains some of the older materials derived from the J and E sources that have been incorporated into the Priestly view of the conquest. In studying this part of the book, several points should be noted:

There are mixed views of Balaam in the Bible.

Numbers 22, 1—24, 25 presents Balaam as a prophet from Mesopotamia who is hired to curse Israel and then forced by God to bless them. Indeed, the folk story about Balaam and his ass in chapter 22 presents him as willing to do whatever the Lord wants. Thus one might conclude that he is presented sympathetically and perhaps even as an instrument of God. But later on in Numbers 31, 8 and 16, Balaam is slaughtered by the Israelites as a Midianite king because he led people astray at Baal of Peor. This must stem from a separate tradition than that of Numbers 22—24. This double view reappears in the book of Joshua where Balaam is the seer who curses Israel in 24, 9–10, but who was among the Midianites in 13, 22. Deuteronomy 23, 4f; Micah 6, 5, and Nehemiah 13, 2 all view Balaam as the seer. On the other side, Genesis 36, 32 describes him, under the name of Bela, as a king of Midian (also known as Edom).

Interestingly enough, the New Testament picks up a still later tradition that Balaam was greedy for money. 2 Peter 2, 16; Jude 11; Revelation 2, 14 all see him as a false teacher motivated by greed. The real Balaam may never be known, but he seems to have been famous as a prophet in other nations than Israel. A sixth-century BC Aramaic text speaks of him in this vein. So at least the basic point of Numbers 22—24 seems to be based on very old tradition.

There are four oracles in chapters 23 and 24. Most scholars hold that the two oracles in chapter 23 are from the Elohist (E) source, and the two in chapter 24 are from the Yahwist (J). Look at them closely and note the elaborate formulas of introduction in 24, 3f and 24, 15f that imply a very formal manner in which prophets in Judah may have normally spoken. These also stress the glory of the king (24, 7.17), a viewpoint typical of the Davidic monarchy. On the other hand, the oracles from the E tradition lack such elaborate formulas and stress the blessing on the whole people given by God.

Some scholars believe the words of Balaam formed the endings to both the J and the E narrative sources. In this view, the prophet looks ahead to the fulfillment of the promise in the days of the monarchy many years hence. If chapter 23 does end the E story, and chapter 24 the J story, then further stories of the conquest in Numbers 32 and in the book of Joshua that have concerns similar to those of J and E would have to be explained. We could at least say this much—that the final form of the book of Numbers sees the Balaam prophecies as important. They confirm with a divine word the coming victory of Israel's battle for the lands on both sides of the Jordan.

The Theology of the Priestly Writers

The P source probably had many earlier written pieces to draw on in putting together its descriptions in Numbers. Such might have been lists of tribal leaders (Nm 1, 5–15; 2, 3–31; 7, 12–88; 10, 14–28); the descriptions of the battle camp in chapters 2 and 10; census lists of some kind for chapters 1 and 26; Sinai place-names in Numbers 33; and, of course, J and E for such passages as Numbers 13—14, 22—24, and 32.

The P school has already stated its primary emphasis for Israel's life in Exodus 25—40: the

divine presence will be known in Israel in the sanctuary (a tent in the desert years, a temple later) and will manifest its glory there. The proper response of Israel will be observance of sacrifice and the laws of holiness. This "holy" community is given its final climactic description at the end of Leviticus in chapter 26, in the form of a warning speech.

To this, the P authors have added in Numbers some important specifications about how this holiness can be carried out through national institutions and in the relations among the tribes with respect to their possession of the land. Moreover, the cultic organization of Israel's life must be observed even in a state of exile (the idea of the battle camp in the wilderness), and even when the proper order is threatened and broken down by disobedience (the meaning of the numerous rebellions against Moses in chapters 11—21). God will certainly punish this disobedience, but the mediation of priests and leaders (Aaron and Moses) can turn away God's wrath and restore blessing. Most of all, nothing will deter the divine fulfillment; yet at the same time, God does not depend on any one leader no matter how great (even Moses can be denied entry to the Promised Land!). Although the people have no land or home now, they have all the necessary means of worship and obedience to hold on until the divine promise is fulfilled just a short time ahead.

Seen in this light, Numbers is the final statement of the Priestly theology in the Pentateuch. Now Moses can depart (note how his death should follow at the end of Numbers 36, but it is delayed until Deuteronomy 34 for editorial reasons), and the conquest begin. But first, an interlude with the book of Deuteronomy.

DEUTERONOMY

[see pages 199–241 of the Old Testament]

The *New American Bible* and the Book of Deuteronomy

The introduction to the book of Deuteronomy in the NAB points to a number of significant as-

pects for any deep study of the book. First, its style is distinctive and not like any seen up to this point in the Pentateuch. It is more like a sermon with its urgent appeals to obedience and loyalty to God, and its thundering warnings of the dire consequences that will occur if the people do not follow the deuteronomic teachings. Second, the NAB notes that scholars believe it was written near the end of Israel's time as an independent kingdom, that is to say, about the seventh century BC, and comes not at all from the time of Moses. It actually looks back on Israel's history although written as if it looked ahead to their possession of the land. Third, the NAB notes how significant Deuteronomic theology is for understanding the New Testament world of Jesus. Fourth, the NAB gives us a simple outline of how to approach Deuteronomy.

We can expand on all of these to assist us in the study of the book, as well as add some reflections on three other points: (1) The particular theological and historical perspective the book offers on Israel's earlier traditions; (2) the theology of the covenant that permeates the book; (3) its connections to the wider grouping of the historical books of Joshua, Judges, Samuel, and Kings, all of which seem to receive their inspiration from Deuteronomy. We will order these seven areas according to their logical development.

The Outline of the Book

The following detailed breakdown of the contents of Deuteronomy expands the NAB's outline and reorders it slightly to combine its parts I and II, and divide its part IV into two sections:

I. Introduction to the Deuteronomic Law Code (1, 1—11, 32)
  A. General Historical Introduction (1, 1—4, 43)
    1. Historical survey (1, 1—3, 29)
    2. Summary about the Law's goodness (4, 1–43)
  B. Particular Introduction to the Law (4, 44—11, 32)
    1. Introductory context (4, 44–49)
    2. Moses and the Ten Commandments (5, 1–33)
    3. Instruction on obeying the Law (6, 1–25)
    4. Attitudes toward foreign gods (7, 1–16)
    5. The desert lesson: depend on God! (8, 1–20)
    6. The golden calf lesson: idolatry (9, 1—10, 22)

  7. General urging to love covenant (11, 1–32)
II. The Deuteronomic Law Code (12, 1—26, 19)
  A. The Introductory Law: one sanctuary (12, 1–31)
  B. The Individual Laws (13, 1—26, 15)
    1. Laws on idolatry (13, 1–19)
    2. Ritual food laws and tithes (14, 1–29)
    3. Sabbatical release for the poor (15, 1–18)
    4. Sacrifice of the firstborn (15, 19–23)
    5. Pilgrim feast days binding on all (16, 1–17)
    6. Officials: kings, priests, prophets (16, 18—18, 22)
    7. Cities of refuge (19, 1–21)
    8. Rules for the Holy War (20, 1–20; 21, 10–14; 23, 9–14)
    9. Unknown murders (21, 1–9)
    10. Laws on social problems (21, 15—22, 12)
    11. Sexual and marriage laws (22, 13—23, 1)
    12. Divorce, marriage, and charity (23, 1—25, 19)
    13. Tithes on first fruits (26, 1–15)
  C. Conclusion: Summary of the Covenant (26, 16–19)
III. Solemn Acceptance of Covenant Law Code (27, 1—30, 20)
  A. The Covenant Ceremony (27, 1—28, 68)
    1. Curses and blessings (27, 1–26)
    2. Added curses and blessings (28, 1–46)
    3. An exilic expansion (28, 47–68)
  B. Moses' Final Exhortation on Covenant (29, 1—30, 20)
    1. Covenant warning to exiles (29, 1–27)
    2. Promise of mercy in exile (30, 1–20)
IV. The Final Conclusion of the Pentateuch as a Whole (31, 1—34, 12)
  A. The Choice of a Successor (31, 1–13.23–29)
    1. Joshua selected (31, 1–13)
    2. Law placed in the Ark (31, 23–29)

142

B. The Song of Moses (32, 1–44)

    1. Moses commanded to sing (31, 14–22)

    2. The song of Moses (31, 30—32, 44)

C. The Blessing of Moses (32, 45—33, 29)

    1. Moses' last view of the Land (32, 45–52)

    2. Moses' final blessing (33, 1–29)

D. The Death of Moses (34, 1–12)

The outline shows that the basic structure is built around a new presentation of the Law that restates many of the earlier laws of Exodus through Numbers. There is further internal evidence from the original Hebrew text of the book that it was not all written at the same time. Some of the speeches in chapters 1 through 11 and 26 through 30 are addressed to the individual Israelites, "you," while others are addressed to the plural "ye" or "you all." Certain sections, such as chapters 1 through 3 are almost entirely in this plural form, while other sections, such as chapters 4 through 11, are almost completely in the singular. This has led scholars to detect separate stages of development in the book.

It might be noted, especially, that the materials gathered in chapters 31 through 34 are not quite as tied to the laws as are those of chapters 1 through 30. These last four chapters gather together all of the diverse traditions and long-established works belonging to the memory of Moses that have not found any other place in the Pentateuch. These final chapters in some way form an appendix to the first thirty chapters.

The Covenant Structure of the Book

In looking at Exodus 1, 9–24, some general similarities stood out between the description of how Israel received its covenant and the general shape of ancient secular covenants between kings. There were six typical parts to a covenant treaty, which are reflected in a vague way in the structure of the dramatic account of those chapters. These six parts were: (1) a preamble that identified the great king giving the treaty; (2) a historical prologue listing his gracious deeds to the lesser king; (3) the legal stipulations binding on the lesser king (the vassal); (4) the provisions for public reading of the document; (5) the list of gods who witnessed the treaty; and (6) the curses

and blessings on those who break or keep the treaty.

The same pattern can be found in the book of Deuteronomy 1—30:

- the great king's self-identification (Dt 1, 1)
- the historical prologue (Dt 1, 2—4, 43)
- the laws binding on the vassal
    1. exhortatory introduction (Dt 4, 44—11, 32)
    2. the law code in detail (Dt 12, 1—26, 19)
- provisions for reading the law aloud (Dt 27, 8)
- witness of the gods — none
- curses and blessings (Dt 27, 1—28, 68)

In examining this structure, it becomes certain that the final form of Deuteronomy is made to be in the general shape of an actual treaty document. As in the Exodus narrative, there is no suggestion of divine witnesses, since there can be no other gods beside the Lord to perform that role. But, in distinction to the Exodus story, this covenant account ends with a very long series of curses and blessings that fill chapters 27 and 28. In this way it resembles the types of treaty covenants we know from the Assyrian period, especially in the seventh century BC, rather than the earlier Hittite models that perhaps influenced the Exodus accounts of the original covenant.

It is important to note at this stage, however, that the book as a whole—beginning with the first sentence and concluding with the notice of the great leader's death—combines a second format. It is framed as a farewell speech of Moses to the people. It might also be compared to an aging father's advice to his son so that the son might gain wisdom. Both forms are well known in ancient literature. Joshua 23—24 has been structured as a deathbed speech to the people, and 1 Samuel 12 serves as the prophet Samuel's farewell speech. In the New Testament, John's Gospel has gathered many of Jesus' words into a long farewell speech at the Last Supper (John 13—17). On the other hand, the form of both Proverbs 1—9 and the book of Ecclesiastes is that of a speech from an aged father who passes on the wisdom he has learned to his sons and disciples. Many Egyptian wisdom works also use this technique. Quite possibly Deuteronomy combines elements of both the deathbed legacy of the great leader and the wisdom of a father that is handed on to his sons.

The nature of the book as a covenant structure given by Moses himself, as well as its impassioned language of urgency, suggest that the authors saw it as a program for renewing the covenant by the people. Indeed, this will prove to be an important factor in trying to date the document to the seventh century BC.

The Unique Style of the Book

Deuteronomy has long been recognized as an independent source within the Pentateuch, which has no direct connection with any of the other three sources, J, E, or P. Not only is it entirely self-contained, as a speech from beginning to end, but its vocabulary and phraseology are generally unmatched anywhere among those sources. A good flavor can be found by reading chapters 4 through 11, where expressions such as the following occur repeatedly:

1. These are the ordinances, statutes, and decrees which the LORD, your God, has enjoined on you (cf. 4, 45; 5, 1; 6, 1; 6, 20; etc.).

2. Take care to observe them (4, 5; 5, 1; 6, 3; 7, 12; 8, 1; etc.).

3. You must learn them, or teach them in the land (5, 1; 5, 31; 11, 19; etc.); and teach them to your children (4, 9; 4, 10; 11, 19; etc.).

4. In the land you are about to enter to possess (5, 31; 6, 1; 6, 10; 6, 18; 9, 5; etc.).

5. So that you might live long and prosper (4, 40; 5, 33; 6, 2f; 6, 24; 11, 9; etc.).

6. You will love the LORD, your God (6, 5; 10, 12; 11, 13; etc.).

7. With all your heart and soul (4, 29; 6, 5; 10, 12; 11, 13; etc.).

8. Take to heart these words (6, 6; 11, 18).

9. Walk in his ways and fear the LORD (8, 6; 10, 20; 11, 22).

10. Do not turn aside after other gods to serve them (6, 14; 7, 4; 8, 19; 11, 16; etc.).

11. Lest God's anger flare up against you (6, 15; 7, 4; 11, 17; etc.).

12. Do not forget the LORD (8, 11; 6, 12; etc.).

13. I set before you today a blessing and a curse (11, 26; cf. 30, 19).

14. The land which the LORD swore to our fathers (6, 10; 6, 18; 6, 23; 7, 13; 10, 11; etc.); a land flowing with milk and honey (6, 3; 11, 9; etc.).

15. Do what is right and good (6, 18; cf. 12, 28; 13, 19; etc.).

Deuteronomy has a repetitive style, which serves well the preacher's need to get a message across. The type of language, with its intense use of imperatives and rhetorical piling up of several synonyms in a row for the same idea, hardly qualifies as plain narrative. It is persuasive language, calculated to move an audience to decision or change. Similarly, it uses several rhetorical devices to emphasize its major theme of obedience *in the land*. On one hand, it rarely speaks of the land simply, but names it as the land flowing with milk and honey, a good land, a land that God swore to your ancestors, and other phrases of appealing description; and on the other hand, it constantly recalls all the good deeds of the Lord toward Israel that involve divine care and help in the land, especially against foreign opposition. The authors have a perspective that seems extraordinarily concerned with warning about misuse of the land through serving other gods and at the same time disobeying all of God's commands.

The Historical Development of the Book

Arguments for dating Deuteronomy sometime in the later part of the monarchy of Judah, rather than in the time of Moses, can be given briefly. These points will focus some of the background problems and crises facing those who put it together, so that the religious message can stand out more sharply for modern readers.

Second Kings 22, 1—23, 30 narrates the events of the reign of King Josiah (640–609 BC). In the eyes of the authors of Kings, by far the most important single action of the king was his decision to reform the religious practice of the people and thus renew the covenant commitment of the nation, as a result of finding a "Book of the Law" in the Temple during its rebuilding. The king immediately consults a well-known prophetess, Huldah, who delivers a divine oracle (2 Kgs 22, 16f) that can be compared to the list of Deuteronomic phrases in the previous section. Almost all of Huldah's words are duplicated in typical Deuteronomic passages. 2 Kings 23 then records the effects of Josiah's conversion and his decision to institute a major reform. What he did conforms almost exactly to the program laid down by the law code of Deuteronomy. Note the following parallels in the table on RG 145.

2 Kings 23		Deuteronomy
23, 4.6.7.14	abolition of the asherim	7, 5; 12, 3; 16, 21
23, 4f	destroy the host of heaven	17, 3
23, 5.11	end worship of sun and moon	17, 3
23, 7	stop sacred prostitution	23, 18
23, 10	end the cult of Molech	12, 31; 18, 10
23, 13	tear down heathen high places	7, 5; 12, 2f
23, 13	remove the foreign gods	12, 1–32
23, 14	destroy the "pillars"	7, 5; 12, 3
23, 21f	Passover to be observed only in Jerusalem	16, 1–8
23, 24	forbid necromancy	18, 11

According to the text of 2 Kings, the lawbook was found in Josiah's eighteenth year (622 BC) just as he became interested in reform. In a second version, told in 2 Chronicles 34, he became interested in reform in his twelfth year (628 BC), and the book was discovered after the changes were well under way. In either case, the similarities between this lawbook, which was found in the Temple during Josiah's reign (and which led to or supported a massive reform), and the urgent preaching of Deuteronomy are too close not to refer to the same book. Scholars conclude from this that at least the core of our present book of Deuteronomy was known by 622 BC.

Close examination of the contents of Deuteronomy, however, reveals that it has strong similarities with many ideas and books, which came down from the Northern Kingdom of Israel when it was destroyed in 722 BC by the Assyrians— almost exactly one hundred years earlier. It shares a strong interest in the love of God, the covenant as relationship, and the imagery of a father leading a son, all of which made the northern prophet Hosea so unique. It has a strong polemic against Baal and the gods of Canaan, a major temptation for Israelites who lived in the northern area nearest Tyre and Sidon; it has a fierce, warlike campaign strategy against Canaanite religion typical of some of the stories told of the northern prophets Elijah and Elisha in 1 Kings 17 to 2 Kings 10. Moreover, its attitude of doubt about the king's faithfulness in chapter 17 is more typical of a northern viewpoint than of the kingdom of Judah where the house of David ruled. It also strongly supports the role of Moses as a charismatic leader, much in the style of the northern E

source in the Pentateuchal traditions of Exodus and Numbers. One could also point to the location of the covenant ceremony of curses and blessings in Deuteronomy 27—28 at Mounts Ebal and Gerizim, the traditional centers of the Northern Kingdom.

Could there be a northern origin to the earliest level of Deuteronomic traditions? The answer is a possible yes if we look to a passage in 2 Kings 18, 3–7, in which the authors state that King Hezekiah of Judah began a similar reform to that of Josiah around the time he became king, perhaps 715 BC. But did Hezekiah already know of the teachings of Deuteronomy back then? Again, it is possible that the refugees from the north brought down the fundamental Deuteronomic laws and traditions with them as they fled the Assyrians a mere seven years earlier, and it was these that Hezekiah decided to put into practice even in Judah.

What happened to the book of Deuteronomy between Hezekiah and Josiah is unknown. According to the book of Kings, King Manasseh, who ruled for most of the intervening years, violently opposed all reform (2 Kgs 21, 1–15; 23, 26f) and probably persecuted its leaders. They in turn either hid the already-written book, or kept their teachings to themselves until a more favorable king came to the throne in Judah; then they had them written down.

The Development of the Religious Perspective of the Book

With such a long and complicated history behind Deuteronomy, we must be cautious in trying to answer what particular point of view it repre-

145

sents. Possibly it developed in the following manner:

1. When the Northern Kingdom went its own way after the death of Solomon about 930 BC, this kingdom claimed that it was more faithful to the older covenant of Moses and was opposed to the claims of the house of David in Jerusalem— through which royal promise to David God redirected the covenant in 2 Samuel 7. The new northern kings, however, quickly adopted all sorts of Canaanite practices and allowed devotion to Baal, Asherah, and other deities to exist alongside the worship of the Lord. This violated the fundamental law of the covenant that there must be no god beside the Lord. The most likely source for sustained opposition to these policies came from the circles of prophets around Elijah and Elisha who violently opposed any compromise with the cult of Baal, and from among the Levitical priests charged with teaching and maintaining the covenant demands. They began to put together a new statement of the law centered on the warning that if Israel did not do better and keep its covenant, it would lose its land.

2. The defeat of the north by Assyria in 722 BC proved these reformers right, but it also left them homeless. Many fled to Judah, and there the terrible lesson that disobedience led to disaster impressed Hezekiah and his Judean priests. They tried to implement the Deuteronomic reform ideas in Judah, which did not really take hold at that time because Judah felt little need to reform after the miraculous escape from an Assyrian invasion in 701 BC, during the later years of Hezekiah. The people of Judah credited this to God's promise to David to never abandon his dynasty nor his city, Jerusalem. The Southern Kingdom became convinced God would protect them no matter what they did.

3. In the days of Josiah, Judah began to expand and retake the old Northern Kingdom of Israel because the Assyrian empire was falling apart. To win over the half-believing northerners to his side, Josiah wanted something to unite the country in faith. Once he became aware of Deuteronomy's program, from the discovery of the book in the Temple, he decided to use it. It was at this stage that the book was enlarged to its present size, except for a few chapters at the beginning and end.

4. This new setting in the kingdom of Judah led to the particular southern emphases in the book on (a) a single place of worship where God's name would dwell (12, 1–14), and (b) the frequent use throughout of the verb "choose" to describe the place God has chosen to set the divine name. The Hebrew verb is used to describe God's choosing David and is thus a kind of sacred term for the royal dynasty in Jerusalem— that God chose them—stressing God's special choice of both the house of David and the Temple of Jerusalem.

Important Themes of Deuteronomy

The development of its historical and religious perspective led Deuteronomy to give great stress to certain areas of faith over others. In reading the long introduction in chapters 1–11 and looking at the particular points that the body of laws covers in chapters 12 through 26, note these frequent themes:

The Importance of the Covenant

Deuteronomy is edited in the form of a covenant treaty between God and the people, but it is also a speech of Moses, which recalls all the covenant benefits that God has done for Israel in the desert. There is also an emphasis throughout the book on the love of father and son as a way of speaking about God and Israel. The Deuteronomic authors borrowed this from standard covenant treaties of the times, which used the motivation of love to encourage loyalty between the parties. It can be said that for Deuteronomy, covenant love and fidelity are everything!

The Law Is Not Simply Laws, but Total Commitment

Another way of approaching Deuteronomy's message is to say it demands a full commitment of heart and mind and strength to God. It is no accident that the most important statement in Deuteronomy (6, 4f) has become the daily prayer and faith confession of Jews everywhere; it was cited by Jesus himself as the greatest commandment for Christians: "Hear, O Israel! The LORD is our God, the LORD alone! Therefore, you shall love the LORD, your God, with all your heart, and with all your soul, and with all your strength."

Even the piling up of words for law, "the commandments, the statutes and decrees" (6, 1), or "ordinances, statutes and decrees" (6, 20), and similar phrases, emphasize that the great multitude of laws really points to a deeper and more permanent commitment to the Lord that lies beneath.

There Is Consistency to God's Dealings with Israel

One of the significant elements in Deuteronomy's presentation is the recital of Israel's history and the looking forward to still more problems that the people will face in the years ahead. The book sees a design in how God works in history. The pattern can be summarized briefly in this challenge: There are two choices before you—the first is to obey God, follow his ways, and be loyal with all your heart, then you shall receive the blessing of prosperity and long existence on the land. The second is to abandon God, follow the ways of the pagan gods such as Baal, and receive divine punishment and God's curse by which you will be thrown off the land and subjugated to your enemies. This pattern is given very concrete form in chapters 7 and 8, and again in 30, 15–20. A corollary of this choice is that God's wrath blazes out against any idolatry on the part of Israel.

God's Blessing Is Conditional on Israel's Response

One of the themes that sets Deuteronomy apart from earlier thinking in Israel is that God's promises either to Moses or to David are not simply guarantees that God will stand by this people with protection and help, no matter what they do. Earlier theologies of God as a divine warrior who always fights for his people is now transformed into a new view of a God who will uphold the covenant and all of its terms, including blessing and curse, according to how Israel keeps its part of the treaty. The stress falls on both faithful worship and social justice as ideals for Israel. Repentance and change of heart are often required if Israel is to return to covenant loyalty. In this way, Deuteronomy represents its call for fidelity to be a turning point that can reverse the judgment against the nation.

The Land Itself Is Conditional

Deuteronomy stresses that the covenant is tied to life in the land; misuse of the land, failure to create a just society, and dishonest policies of rulers will cost Israel its right to the land. One reason why the authors put the book into the form of a farewell speech from Moses in the desert is that it makes the warning come from a time when they had no land yet, and it hints that this may happen again if the people do not heed his words. Perhaps the book became most influential once the exile began (598–587 BC), since the readers could then recognize that they were now indeed in their sorry state because they had not obeyed the Lord as Moses had warned. It spoke to their misery and to their repentant hearts!

There Is To Be One Sanctuary

An important part of the program of Deuteronomy was to center the people's attention on Jerusalem and away from the local shrines and cultic centers, which too often had connections to pagan beliefs and practices. It was an attempt to make the people think as a single mind about unified obedience to the Lord, a unified commitment to each other as a people, and a unified source of all blessing. The kingship of the Lord over the land will then be recognized by all, so that the land, the law, and the people will finally be united as one.

Deuteronomy Updates the Covenant Law

A final point worth noting is how often the laws listed in the outline of Deuteronomy match those of the earliest law code in Israel, the "Covenant Code" found in Exodus 20, 22–23, 33. In each case, however, the older laws are stated in a way that makes them more adapted to life in the towns and cities of a kingdom in the eighth to the sixth centuries BC. They accent the obligations of citizens and members of the covenant to one another and to the weak and dispossessed so that justice can be done.

In your own study, compare the two sets of laws listed here to see if you can tell the differences:

Exodus 21—23	Deuteronomy 14—19
Ex 21, 1–11	Dt 15, 12–18
Ex 21, 12–14	Dt 19, 1–13
Ex 22, 29f	Dt 15, 19–23
Ex 22, 31	Dt 14, 3–21
Ex 23, 1	Dt 19, 16–21
Ex 23, 10f	Dt 15, 1–11
Ex 23, 14–17	Dt 16, 1–17

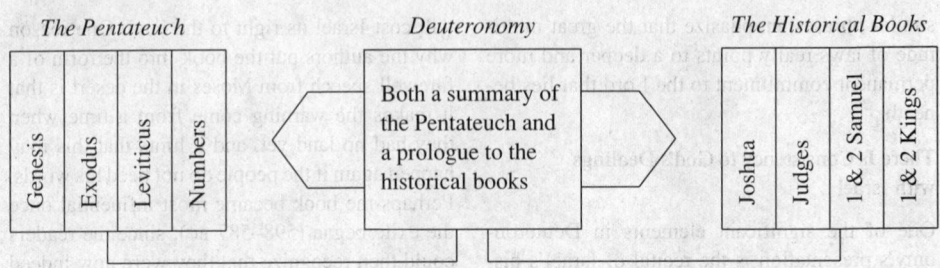

The Pentateuch   Deuteronomy   The Historical Books

Genesis | Exodus | Leviticus | Numbers — Both a summary of the Pentateuch and a prologue to the historical books — Joshua | Judges | 1 & 2 Samuel | 1 & 2 Kings

Connections of Deuteronomy and the Historical Books

Scholars in this century have stressed the strong connection between the theology of Deuteronomy listed above and the viewpoint that can be found throughout the books of Joshua, Judges, Samuel, and Kings. The same emphasis on having a choice to obey or disobey, with the resulting blessing or curse, seems to underlie how these books evaluate each major historical period and each individual leader. In comparing the book of Deuteronomy to the historical books, read together the beautiful passage in Deuteronomy 6, 3f about loving the Lord with all your heart and soul and strength, and the statement made at the end of the books of Kings about King Josiah: "Before him there had been no king who turned to the LORD as he did, with his whole heart, his whole soul, and his whole strength, in accord with the entire law of Moses" (2 Kgs 23, 25). Note also the echoes of Deuteronomy in the praise given to King Hezekiah in 2 Kings 18, 5f. These are enough to give a flavor of how Deuteronomy's thought pervades the historical accounts. For further study, look also at these key passages in the histories that reflect Deuteronomy most strongly:

Jos 1, 11–15 The promise
Jos 23—24 The covenant renewal at Shechem
Jgs 2, 11–23 The pattern of sin and curse
1 Sm 12 Samuel's final warning on fidelity
2 Sm 7 The promise to David
1 Kgs 8—9 The conditional promise to Solomon
2 Kgs 17 The reason for the fall of the North
2 Kgs 23, 25–27 The final evaluation of Judah's kings

Deuteronomy and the New Testament

The NAB lists two important citations of Deuteronomy used in Matthew's Gospel to ex-plain the temptation in the desert and to answer the question of which was the greatest commandment. We can, however, see a much greater influence of Deuteronomy than merely these two direct quotations from the book itself. It is in the overall attitude. The heart of Deuteronomy is covenant loyalty, and Deuteronomy stresses the idea of God's fatherhood and love for the people as his children. Deuteronomy also focuses on wholehearted obedience that does more than the minimum required. It sees all of life as a walking in the ways of the Lord. And finally, of course, it understands life to be full of choices made by faith; to obey or disobey. These are all the themes of Jesus' own life. Some scholars have called Luke's Gospel a new Deuteronomy, but this could be truly said of any of the Gospels. If we understand the demand of Deuteronomy for single-mindedness, together with its vast vision that all of life must be an integrated whole, we will be prepared for a deeper reading of the New Testament.

Conclusion

Deuteronomy sits last in the Pentateuch, and so sums up in a "Second Law" (from the Greek *deutero-nomos*) the essential message of the earlier Pentateuchal stories for Israel's existence as a kingdom rather than as a tribal alliance in the desert. It also looks ahead from the time of Israel's beginnings to that later life as a kingdom, which is told in the historical books. Thus, it serves as both a conclusion to the desert period and a preface to the possession of the land. It links the Pentateuch traditions with the works of the historians of its own school that put together Joshua through 2 Kings. A diagram brings this out, and so prepares us to take up the study of the historical books themselves. See diagram above.

THE DEUTERONOMISTIC HISTORY
LESLIE J. HOPPE

JOSHUA
[see pages 241–68 of the Old Testament]

Before Beginning . . .

The book of Joshua is the sixth book of the Bible and carries on the story that begins in Genesis and continues through Deuteronomy. Abraham's descendants, who had been slaves in Egypt, are ready to take possession of the land promised to their ancestors. The land was not simply a gift of God to Israel—it was the gift that made God's power and presence in Israel's life something real and tangible. It was an act of grace like no other, for the gift of the land made it possible for the people of Israel to survive. The land provided Israel with its food, clothing, and shelter. Without it, Israel could not be a people. The land as God's gift to Israel was a theme that was central to its faith. It was a motif that was at the core of ancient Israel's stories, poetry, and prophecy. The book of Joshua is one product of the storyteller's art, while the theme of the gift of the land is found in several psalms such as Psalms 105, 106, 135, and 136. The prophets based their indictment of Israel's infidelity on the gift of the land that should have led Israel to the loyal and exclusive service of its God, e.g., Jeremiah 2, 6–7; 32, 20–23.

Joshua is both the conclusion of one story and the beginning of another. It concludes the story of the liberation of the Hebrew slaves and their guidance in the wilderness to the Promised Land. It is also the first part of another story: the story of Israel in that Promised Land. The books of Judges, Samuel, and Kings are the other compo-

nents of this story. It begins with Joshua and the Israelite tribes taking control of the land, continues with stories about the judges who lead Israel in maintaining their presence in the land, and concludes with the stories of Israel's kings, who eventually lose control of that land. The story ends the same way it begins—with the Israelites outside the land. At the beginning they are ready to cross the Jordan and take control of the land; at the end they are in exile from the land, wondering about their future. It is a sad story, a tragic story. It is a story that begins with much promise and ends with great disappointment.

The ancient rabbis called the books that made up the story of Israel in its land "the Former Prophets" because they ascribed these books to prophetic authorship. Scholars have called these books "the Deuteronomistic History of Israel." But that name can be misleading since these books are not histories—at least not in the modern sense. In the form we now have, the books date to about the middle of the sixth century while Israel was in exile. The story of Israel in the Promised Land turns Israel's past into a sermon in order to provide the exiles some basis for hope by affirming that Israel can have a future, despite the terrible losses it experienced when Jerusalem fell. The book of Deuteronomy provided the theological principles that guided the telling of the story of Israel in its land. Among these principles was the importance of serving the Lord alone by shaping one's conduct according to the norms of traditional Israelite morality, as found in the Torah that God revealed to Moses. The books of Joshua to 2 Kings show what happens when Israel is obedient and what happens when it is not. The story of Israel in its land, then, asserts that Israel can have a future if it chooses—because God has set before Israel the choice of life and death (Dt 30, 15).

The book of Joshua answers two questions that were on the minds of its first readers. Is God able to restore Israel? Is God willing to do so? The answer that the book gives to the first question is a resounding yes. The book will tell the story of how Israel acquired its land ostensibly under Joshua's leadership. But as the story unfolds, it will become clear that it was God who was leading Israel all the while. The answer to the second question is a qualified yes. God has promised blessings to those who obey the Torah: if Israel chooses the path of obedience, it can expect to have a future in the land promised to its ancestors. If, however, Israel chooses the way of disobedience, there can be no hope.

Reading through the Book of Joshua

The homiletical character of the book of Joshua is evident from the very beginning. About twenty percent of the book's text describes the elaborate preparations for the entrance of the Israelite tribes into Canaan. Before the crossing of the Jordan begins, the book makes it clear the land is a gift that God is giving Israel (1, 1–5). The way to insure that Israel will be in a position to receive that gift is obedience to the Torah (1, 6–9). The rest of the book simply illustrates these two assertions. First, under Joshua's leadership, the tribes will take the land with relative ease because God is handing it to them. Second, because Israel is obedient, it takes possession of the land, which is then distributed equitably among the tribes.

Israel Enters the Promised Land
(Jos 1, 1—5, 12)

The book's first chapter consists of four speeches: the Lord to Joshua (1, 1–9); Joshua to the Israelite leadership (1, 10–11); Joshua to the tribes from east of the Jordan (1, 12–15); and the eastern tribes to Joshua (1, 16–18). These speeches are the means of conveying the central religious affirmations of the book: the presence of God with Joshua and the Israelites, the impor-

tance of obedience to the Torah, the land as a gift from God, and Joshua as the successor of Moses. These affirmations provide a framework for understanding the stories that will follow. As the stories unfold it will become clear that Israel receives the land as a gift from God given to those who obey the Torah under the guidance of Joshua. No military preparations are mentioned and none are necessary as long as Israel observes the Torah.

The episode with the two Israelite spies and Rahab, the prostitute from Jericho (2, 1–21), also betrays the book's purpose. Rahab's conversation with the two spies makes it seem as if she had been reading the book of Deuteronomy. Because she helps the Israelite spies, she is fulfilling the divine will and will escape the fate that the rest of Jericho's citizens will suffer (6, 22–25). If Israel had followed her example, the fate of Jerusalem and its exiles would have been much different. If, like Rahab, Israel now chooses the way of obedience, it will return to its land to live in peace.

The scene depicting the crossing of the Jordan (3, 1–4, 24) underscores the book's intent to present the taking of the Promised Land as a wonder performed by God to fulfill the commitment made to Israel's ancestors. The book purposely describes the crossing of the Jordan River as a miracle like the crossing of the Red Sea (4, 23), even though the Jordan is, in fact, easily fordable at several places. The miraculous crossing of the Jordan demoralizes the people of Canaan, robbing them of the will to resist (5, 1). Again, it is clear that Israel's possession of the land was God's doing.

In 5, 2–12, perspective then shifts to Israel. At God's instructions, the preparations to enter the land and face its inhabitants involve nothing of a military nature. In fact, these preparations actually render Israel's army quite vulnerable to attack because all the males had to be circumcised, making them temporarily unable to be an effective fighting force. But the mass circumcision does, however, make the community fit to celebrate the Passover (5, 2–12). Both these observances became important markers of Jewish identity during and after the exile. Certainly the book of Joshua intends to promote these practices.

The Battle for the Promised Land
(Jos 5, 13—11, 23)

Although the book of Joshua is often thought of as a chronicle of a massive invasion of Canaan by a united Israelite army under the leadership of Joshua, only one quarter of the book actually deals with the battles for the Promised Land. At the end of this section, the author comments that "Joshua captured the whole country" (11, 23). But the account of the battles fought by the Israelite tribes focuses almost entirely on the central region of Canaan (6, 1–10, 27). Battles in the south (10, 28–43) and the north (11, 1–14) are treated in summary fashion. The two places that receive the most attention are Jericho (6, 1–27) and Ai (7, 2—8, 29). But before Joshua begins the attack on Jericho, the mysterious "captain of the host of the LORD" arrives (5, 14). When this person tells Joshua that he must take off his sandals because he is standing on holy ground, the attentive reader recognizes the similarity to the story of Moses' encounter with God at the burning bush (Ex 3, 1–6) and knows that the leader of Israel as he moves out to take the land is someone other than Joshua.

Jericho was a town that had been abandoned for centuries before the time of Joshua, probably because its water source had become severely polluted, making its waters no longer drinkable. Ai was a town that flourished in the Early Bronze Age—more than a thousand years before the Israelite tribes emerged in Canaan. It too had been abandoned for centuries before the Israelite tribes made their appearance. The stories of the capture of Jericho and Ai in Joshua (6—8), then, are not historical records. But apparently, the people of Israel celebrated the gift of the land that they received from God at shrines near Jericho. Certainly, the story of Jericho's fall reads more like an account of a liturgical ceremony than that of a military adventure.

The book tells the tale of Jericho and Ai as object lessons for its readers. Neither Joshua's military leadership nor the bravery of the Israelite army was responsible for the fall of Jericho. The town was taken because Israel followed God's directions. The city's walls collapsed after an elaborate procession with the ark—not because of any military operation. This led to a complete victory, but Israel was told not to enjoy the fruits

of the victory: no one was to loot the city nor was there to be any Israelite settlement there. While Israel had no difficulty taking Jericho, Ai was another story (7, 1—8, 30). Because Joshua's spies misjudged the enemy's strength, Israel attacked Ai without sufficient force and suffered a grave defeat. The book accounts for this stunning setback by describing how Achan kept some of the booty from Jericho for himself, contrary to Joshua's instructions (6, 17–21). After Joshua prayed and Achan was punished, God provided Joshua with tactical instructions for the defeat of Ai's army.

To keep the significance of the Torah before the reader, the book tells of a detour to the north that Joshua took in order to build an altar on Mount Ebal, which flanks the valley in which Shechem is located (8, 30–35). On the stones used to make the altar, Joshua wrote the Torah. He then read the Torah—complete with the blessings and curses contained in it—to the people, reminding them that they will shape their future by the choices they make.

When the book returns to the story of the battle for Canaan, Joshua and his army are at Gilgal. Their victories led kings of the city-states in Canaan to form an alliance to stop the Israelite advance. The people of Gibeon tried a different approach. They sought an alliance with the Israelites by claiming to be, like the Israelites, newly arrived in Canaan (9, 1–27). When the Israelites discovered that they were tricked by the Gibeonites, they suggested that the Gibeonites accept a low social status in the Israelite community as laborers in the Temple.

Like Jericho and Ai, Gibeon was not inhabited in the thirteenth century BC. This story is not based on any memory of an event in Israel's past; it is another homily on obedience. Like Rahab, the Gibeonites seem to know their Bible and are familiar with the Exodus tradition and the laws of Deuteronomy regarding relations with nearby and distant towns (Dt 20). But the story also serves as a warning to consult with the Lord in difficult circumstances, which the Israelites did not do in this situation—much to their regret (Jos 9, 14). Without consulting God, Israel found itself regretting its actions. There will be several occasions in the monarchic period when Israel and Judah get into great difficulties because of the treaties they made with other nations, for example, Ahaz's alliance with Assyria (2 Kgs 16, 7–9).

One reason for Israel's regret in this case was that it had to face a coalition of Gibeon's neighbors to the south who were not happy because of its alliance with Israel. Of course, Israel was victorious, not because of its military prowess but because God enlisted the sun and moon to seal Israel's victory (10, 1–14). In the ancient Near East, the sun and the moon were gods in their own right, but here they are simply weapons in the Lord's arsenal. Verse 13 notes that the couplet celebrating this miracle came from a now lost text: the book of Jashar (see also 2 Sm 1, 18). Ancient Israel produced more literature than the Bible preserves, and occasionally the Bible will cite these texts. The book of Jashar is one example.

Following Joshua's defeat and execution of the kings allied against him, he moved against the south and brought that region under Israelite control (10, 25–43). The story of Joshua's victory over a coalition led by Jabin of Hazor (11, 1–23) is meant to account for the taking of the entire northern third of Canaan: the Jezreel Valley and the Galilee. Once the author tells of the capture of Hazor, the story of the land-taking ends. The second section of Joshua ends with summary statements (11, 15–23), the most important of which is that Joshua carried out the orders that God gave to Moses. The story of the battle for the Promised Land, then, is a story of the success that obedience brings.

The gift of the land is a motif that is woven throughout the Old Testament, but the references to how that land was acquired by Israel are not very specific. For example, though the story of Jericho's miraculous fall is an important part of Joshua, it is not mentioned elsewhere in the Old Testament. What precisely were the experiences that generated the first stories about Israel's acquisition of its land are unknown. But before they came to have their present form, they were shaped and reshaped by almost six hundred years of life in that land. Ancient Israel's storytellers witnessed the rise and fall of the two Israelite national states. These experiences certainly left their mark on the story of Joshua and the emergence of the Israelite tribes in Canaan.

The story of the battle for the Promised Land effectively turned the past into a sermon whose purpose was to stimulate the faith and hope of those who first heard or read it. They learned that there could be a future for the people of Israel if they, like Joshua's generation, were obedient to the Torah. The homiletical character of this story makes its use in reconstructing the early history of Israel problematic. Archaeological excavation supports the conclusion that the stories of conquest found in Joshua were not based on memories of actual battles that took place at Jericho, Ai, or in the environs of Gibeon. But archaeology has shown that people living in Canaan in the thirteenth century BC experienced serious disruptions. Towns and villages were destroyed and abandoned. The Israelite tribes emerged in the central highlands of Canaan precisely during this difficult period, so it is likely that Israel acquired the land that was to be the scene of its subsequent history, in part, by violence. It is difficult, from the evidence offered by the book of Joshua, to say much more. What the book does affirm unequivocally is that Israel came to possess the land because of God's power, and Israel was able to receive that land as God's gift because of its obedience. These affirmations, however, were meant to give Israel a vision of the future rather than information about the past. To those who wondered if God were capable of restoring Israel, the book of Joshua answers with a resounding yes.

Israel's Inheritance (Jos 12, 1—19, 51)

After listing the territories brought under Israelite control during the battle for the Promised Land (13, 1–7), the book of Joshua has an extensive section dealing with the distribution of the land among the Israelite tribes (13, 8—19, 51). Working through this section is difficult for modern readers since it is full of geographical detail that is meaningless to many. While the precise borders of the various tribal allotments may have been very important to the people of ancient Israel, their significance today is exclusively historical. Still, there are some details in this part of the story that even contemporary readers should attend to.

It is important to remember that ancient Israel's economy was based on agriculture. Ownership of land was crucial to survival in such an economy. Possession of a plot of land enabled the Israelite to produce enough food for his fam-

ily and livestock with a surplus to be used for re-
planting and for sacrificial offerings. Without
land, a person had no access to the means of
production. Such a person was dependent for
survival on the charity of his fellow Israelites.
Of course, there were some people who supported themselves as merchants and artisans, but
they too ultimately depended on Israel's peasant
farmers for their prosperity.

The account of the land distribution among the
tribes begins with a reminder of the areas of
Canaan that the Israelites did not control (13,
1–6). This was a necessary corrective to the ex-
aggerations in the previous section of the book,
which claimed that Joshua and the Israelite subdued "the entire land," "the whole country" (Jos
9, 24; 11, 23). Then follows a review of the territories previously allotted by Moses to those Israelites who were going to live east of the Jordan
River (13, 7–33). Israel's control over this region
was neither firm nor constant, but its inclusion
among the tribal allotments expresses Israel's
claim on that territory, even though Israel was
not always able to support that claim. When
Ezekiel described his vision of an Israel restored
after the exile, he did not have any of the tribes
living east of the Jordan (Ez 48, 1–29).

When the account of the distribution of the
land west of the Jordan begins in chapter 14, both
Eleazar the priest and Joshua preside over the
distribution (14, 1; see also Nm 34, 17). The preceding sections of the book did not emphasize
the role of the priest except for the liturgical actions (e.g., 3, 6; 6, 1–9). The priority given to
Eleazar here may reflect the more significant
role that the priests played in the leadership of
the community after the state collapsed and the
dynasty ended, as is evident from Haggai, Zechariah, and Ezra. Eleazar's presence may also be
a consequence of having the land distributed by
lot (14, 2). Although Deuteronomy explicitly
forbids attempts to determine the divine will
through the techniques of divination (Dt 18,
9–12), the casting of lots seems to have been
widely practiced and accepted as legitimate. The
lot oracle was committed to the priests (Ex 28,
30; Lv 8, 5–9). To show that the distribution of
the land was done according to God's will, it was
accomplished by the use of lots in a procedure
presided over by a priest. The New Testament
gives evidence of the continuing popularity and

acceptance of using lots to determine the divine
will (Acts 1, 26).

The report of the land's distribution among the
Israelites pays most attention to the region in
the very center of what became the territory of
the two Israelite kingdoms (14, 6—17, 17). This
is the territory that will be given to Judah,
Ephraim, and Manasseh. While the territory of
Benjamin (18, 11–20) also merits special regard
because it was coveted by both Israelite kingdoms, the allotments of the other tribes get comparatively meager attention. Judah is considered
first. Its territory comprised most of what would
be the Southern Kingdom. Since the Old Testament reflects a southern perspective, the priority
given to Judah is understandable. The territory of
Ephraim and Manasseh became the heartland of
the Northern Kingdom and could not be ignored.
The entry about the allotment of Dan is unusual
(19, 40–48). It notes that the territory given to
Dan was located along the coastal plain. This
will be the setting of the story of Samson, a Danite hero (Jgs 13—16). But the entry goes on to
note that Dan was unable to take control of that
territory from the indigenous population, and so
the tribe relocated to the far north. The story of
this relocation is told in Judges 17—18. The
story of the land's distribution concludes in 19,
49–51 with the note that Joshua received the
town in Ephraim that he requested for himself.

Special Towns (Jos 20, 1—21, 45)

Two of ancient Israel's social institutions are
the subject of the fourth section of the book
of Joshua. The first is the city of refuge. There
were six of these cities—three on each side of the
Jordan. According to Numbers 35, 9–34, it was
Moses who announced God's plan to have such
cities where a person who accidentally caused
another's death could be safe from the victim's
relatives, who might seek vengeance. Moses had
already named the three cities east of the Jordan,
and now Joshua designated three more west of
the Jordan. The books of Samuel, Kings, and
Chronicles never mention this institution since
they were not needed following the centralization of authority by the monarchy. The book of
Judges mentions two examples of private vengeance: 8, 13–21 and 20, 1–11. It is clear from
these examples that the biblical tradition does
not approve of such acts. A second set of forty-

eight towns is set aside for the Levites. The tribe of Levi received no territory of its own because the men of that tribe served as priests, who were to teach the Torah to Israel and offer sacrifice to the Lord (see Dt 33, 8–11). To fulfill these functions the priests need to be available to the people; therefore the cities where the Levites have residential and grazing rights are scattered throughout the country.

This section on special towns has been inserted in the account of the tribal allotments, as is evident from Joshua 21, 43–45. This text makes no mention of the special towns but has been detached from 19, 51 to allow for the insertion.

A Threat of Civil War (Jos 22, 1–34)

The Israelites whose territory was east of the Jordan River had joined in the battle to take control of the area west of the river. Since that battle was completed successfully, Joshua allowed them to return to their homes (vv. 1–8). This is a prelude to a conflict between the Israelites east of the river and those on the west (vv. 9–34). The tribes from the east side of the river built an altar near the Jordan, and this offended the Israelites from the west. War was averted because Phineas, Eleazar's son, succeeded in negotiating peace between the two groups. The precise nature of the offense is not obvious, though it may reflect the Deuteronomic belief that there was to be only one place where sacrifices were to be offered. Apparently, the book of Joshua assumed that this place was Shiloh. When the easterners explained that they did not intend to offer sacrifices on the altar they built (v. 26), this defused the problem. The tribes from the west of the Jordan were satisfied that those from the east side meant no offense and were not repudiating the Lord. Joshua had no role in this story; it was a priest who brought about a happy ending to what could have been a great disaster. Again, this presages the leadership role that priests assumed in Israel's life following the end of the monarchy.

An Era Ends (Jos 23, 1—24, 33)

The final testament of such an important person as Joshua was highly significant. The storyteller creates a speech for his hero that could have come right out of the book of Deuteronomy. Israel's continued presence in the land depends on its ad-

herence to "all that is written in the book of the law of Moses . . . ." (23, 6). Joshua reminds Israel to love God (23, 11), the Torah's greatest command. But then Joshua issues a warning that any failure on Israel's part to remain completely and exclusively loyal to God will have the gravest of consequences (23, 15–16). While the land is a gift from God to Israel, the gift can be revoked. Of course, this is a theological conclusion that came from Israel's experience. By the time the book of Joshua took the form that it now has, Israel did "perish from the good land" that it had received from God (23, 16). Israel's faith in God's fidelity, however, led to the hope that a new dedication to the Torah and a renewed commitment to the covenant will bring a reversal of the misfortune that Israel brought on itself. The book then describes an elaborate ceremony in which Israel of Joshua's day renews its commitment to God and the Torah (24, 1–28). Clearly this final chapter is a model for Israel of the sixth century BC, which has experienced the full consequences of its infidelity. But a renewal is possible if the people and their leaders remember how God has been faithful to fulfill the promises made to Abraham, Isaac, and Jacob. Like the ancestors in the days of Joshua, Israel must again commit itself to serve and obey God alone.

The burial notices with which the book ends (24, 29–30.32–33) are significant because of the prominence given to Eleazar, the priest. This is very likely another indication of the leadership role assumed by priests after the fall of the Israelite monarchy. Verse 31 is the verdict on the era of Joshua: it was an era marked by obedience and loyalty. That is the reason Israel came to possess the land: obedience brings God's blessing.

The Continuing Significance of the Book of Joshua

Most Christians who read the book of Joshua have a difficult time with the image of God that the book appears to have. It is a God who orders an invasion of Canaan and the annihilation of the armies sent to oppose the Israelites, and even of the civilian population of towns under attack by Israel. The conflicts depicted in the book of Joshua have been described as examples of "holy war," but this expression never appears in Joshua or anywhere else in the Bible. Still, it is true that ancient Israel did acquire control over Canaan, in some measure, by violent means. But it is difficult to be more specific than this when trying to reconstruct the process of Israel's emergence in Canaan. It is clear, however, that the image of a large Israelite armed force, organized under Joshua's leadership, invading Canaan from the east and quickly gaining control over the whole land has its roots in the religious imagination of ancient Israel rather than in the experience of the Israelite tribes.

There were serious and widespread conflicts in Canaan of the thirteenth century BC. Archaeology has shown that. But the conflicts were probably not initiated by an invading military force. They began as the centralized political and military authority over the region exercised by Egypt began to deteriorate in the fourteenth century. Canaanite city-states began fighting one another for dominance in the region. Some peasant farmers of Canaan, who bore the burden of these conflicts, withdrew their allegiance from these city-states and began to develop an alternate polity. In the central highlands, groups united by kinship and the worship of the Lord emerged as a significant force. It is possible that a group of people who worshipped the Lord, and who had escaped from slavery in Egypt, energized the people of the central highlands to resist their oppressors by telling their stories of a miraculous escape made possible by their God. In any case, the people of Israel rejected the hegemony of the city-states and ruled themselves according to traditional norms of behavior as interpreted by their elders. Over time the power of the city-states waned, and the Israelite tribes were able to strengthen their hold on the central highlands and enjoy a measure of peace and prosperity with the Lord, rather than with a human being as their sovereign. Instead of paying taxes to a human overlord, they offered tithes of their agricultural produce to the Lord at the shrines where they thanked God for the gift of the land. The Israelites believed that it was the God of their ancestors who made it possible for them to take control over their lives and destinies. This reconstruction of the emergence of the Israelite tribes in Canaan is based on the results of archaeological excavations, combined with what is known from the Bible and other ancient Near Eastern texts using models derived from anthropology and sociology.

This, however, is not the story related in the book of Joshua. That story was not written to describe the process by which the Israelite tribes came to dominate parts of Canaan. The book of Joshua was composed to encourage the exiles of Judah and Jerusalem to believe in the power of their ancestral deity to lead them from exile in Babylon back to the land promised to Abraham's descendants. The fall of Jerusalem, the destruction of its Temple, and the end of the dynasty and national state led the people of Judah to wonder about the power and the willingness of their God to save. The book of Lamentations gives voice to the questions that the exile raised in the hearts of believers. It begs God to remember what has happened to Israel and to start acting like God (Lam 5, 1.19), but Lamentations ends with what is best translated as a plaintive question: "Have you utterly rejected us?" (Lam 5, 22). The book of Joshua, then, is best understood as a response to questions such as this one—not to questions about how ancient Israel acquired its land.

The great irony of the book of Joshua was that its stories about the Israelite army conquering great cities and annihilating their populace were written at a time when ancient Israel was at its lowest ebb politically and militarily. The two Israelite national states no longer existed. Their territory was absorbed into the Babylonian provincial system. The leading citizens of Judah were taken to Babylon to prevent them from fomenting any resistance to the new order in the region. Those Judahites who remained in the land were subsistence farmers and not in a position to challenge Babylonian rule. Certainly the stories about the mighty Israelite army winning victory after victory under Joshua was a parody of the military and political impotence of Judah in the sixth century BC.

Unfortunately, the stories of the book of Joshua have served to provide support for the wars of conquest waged by Christians over the centuries. The Crusades, the wars against the Native Americans, and the Boer conquest of South Africa are just three examples of the lethal mixture of war and religion. The book of Joshua was written not to inculcate a martial spirit in its readers but instead a spirit of obedience and commitment to the Torah. The book assumes that the exile of Israel from the land that God gave it was not due to any military misadventures. Israel lost its land because of its failure to keep the Torah that God revealed to Moses. The only hope for restoration was for Judah to join their ancestors in recommitting themselves to their God: "Far be it from us to forsake the LORD for the service of other gods. For it was the LORD, our God, who brought us and our fathers up out of the land of Egypt, out of a state of slavery. He performed those great miracles before our very eyes and protected us along our entire journey and among all the peoples through whom we passed. At our approach the LORD drove out [all the peoples, including] the Amorites who dwelt in the land. Therefore we also will serve the LORD, for he is our God" (Jos 24, 16–18).

FURTHER READING

Boling, Robert G., and G. Ernest Wright. *Joshua.* Anchor Bible 6. Garden City: Doubleday, 1982.

Butler, Trent C. *Joshua.* Word Biblical Commentary 7. Waco, TX: Word, 1983.

Coote, Robert B. *Early Israel: A New Horizon.* Minneapolis: Fortress, 1990.

Gottwald, Norman K. *The Tribes of Yahweh.* Maryknoll, NY: Orbis, 1979.

Hamlin, E. John. *Inheriting the Land: A Commentary on the Book of Joshua.* International Theological Commentary. Grand Rapids, MI: Eerdmans, 1983.

Hoppe, Leslie J. *Joshua and Judges with an Excursus on Charismatic Leadership in Israel.* Old Testament Message 5. Wilmington, DE: Michael Glazier, 1982.

Lind, Millard C. *Yahweh is a Warrior.* Scottsdale, PA: Herald Press, 1980.

Mitchell, Gordon. "Together in the Land: A Reading of the Book of Joshua." *Journal for the Study of the Old Testament (JSOT),* no. 134. Sheffield: Sheffield Academic Press, 1993.

Polzin, Robert. *Moses and the Deuteronomist: A Literary Study of the Deuteronomic History, Part I, Deuteronomy, Joshua, Judges.* New York: Seabury Press, 1980.

Rowlett, Lori L. "Joshua and the Rhetoric of Violence: A New Historicist Analysis." *JSOT,* no. 226. Sheffield: Sheffield Academic Press, 1996.

JUDGES

[see pages 269–97 of the Old Testament]

Before Beginning . . .

The book of Judges is the second book in the collection the early rabbis called the "Former Prophets" and modern interpreters the "Deuteronomistic History of Israel." It is a collection of stories about several Israelite heroes set in the time between the settlement in Canaan under Joshua and the establishment of the Israelite monarchy. The title of the book comes from the designation of its principal characters. The "judges" were charismatic leaders of the Israelite community, especially in times of fierce competition over the land of Canaan. Their authority came from the Lord, and their duty was to enable Israel to live in faithful obedience. The judges had to deal with two problems: the failure of Israel to serve the Lord alone, and the competition for control of the land from other peoples. The book presents these two problems as interrelated. When Israel failed to maintain its commitment to serve the Lord exclusively, then God allowed Israel's neighbors to make its life very difficult.

The competition for control over the land of Canaan in the thirteenth century BC was very high. In the course of that competition, individuals emerged who proved very capable of managing that competition to the benefit of the Israelite tribes. Stories about these individuals and their feats circulated among the Israelites and eventually found their way into the collection we know as the book of Judges. This collection, however, served a purpose beyond simply preserving the memory of ancient heroes. Its purpose was to illustrate the consequences of Israel's failure to live in faithful obedience to the Lord. It deals with a practical and theological problem: the absence of the kind of leadership provided by Moses and Joshua. How should Israel be governed? Who would insure that Israel will live according to the Torah in the land it had received from the Lord?

The book of Judges has three parts. The first (1, 1—3, 6) provides readers with a framework for understanding the significance of the stories about these ancient heroes. The second part (3, 7—15, 20) rehearses the exploits of the judges. The book concludes with a few supplementary stories (16, 1—21, 25) that show how the Is-raelite tribes were on a path of self-destruction. Originally the stories about the individual judges served to excite a certain measure of pride in the achievements of the tribes in maintaining control over the land of Canaan. But once these stories were put into their present context in the book of Judges, the effect was to show that there was something terribly wrong about the way the Is-raelite tribes were living their lives in the land that God had given them. Readers are led to con-clude that matters could not go on like this—something had to be done, for the life of the Is-raelite tribes was degenerating into anarchy.

Reading through the Book of Judges

Understanding the Time of the Judges
(Jgs 1, 1—3, 6)

The book begins by raising the question of lead-ership: "Who shall be first among us to attack the Canaanites and to do battle with them?" (1, 1). The initial answer is Judah, the tribe that eventually became the nucleus of the Southern Kingdom. After some initial success, the tribes' progress bogged down, and the first chapter concludes with a list of areas over which the Israelites were not able to assert their control (1, 27—35). The picture here is just the opposite of that given in the book of Joshua according to which Joshua "captured the whole country, just as the LORD had foretold to Moses. Joshua gave it to Israel as their heritage, apportioning it among the tribes" (Jos 11, 23). The process by which the Israelites achieved control over Canaan was clearly long and complicated. Once the Egyptians no longer dominated the re-gion, the political and military reins they held were gone. The indigenous population of Canaan had to face raiders from the fringes of the settled areas, various kinship groups, refugees from eco-nomically and politically volatile regions, and in-vaders looking for new settlement possibilities—all of whom converged on the area between the Mediterranean Sea on the west and the desert on the east, the mountains of Lebanon on the north and the Sinai peninsula on the south. Eventually the national states of Edom, Moab, and Ammon arose east of the Jordan River. The Israelite king-doms were established west of the Jordan about two hundred years later because, apparently, the Israelite tribes seemed to prefer a more decen-tralized polity supported by a religious ideology that held that Israel's king was not a human being but the Lord. Until the rise of their national states, the Israelites had to make do with local and tem-porary leadership.

The second chapter describes the price Israel had to pay for its preferred pattern of leadership: the Israelite tribes found themselves in danger of being overcome by the other groups competing for the limited territory of Canaan. The explana-tion for this potential disaster is the failure of the Israelites to keep their covenant with the Lord. Israel will have to deal with other contenders for the land by themselves. God's help will not be forthcoming. The contrast between the period of Joshua and that of the Judges could not be more absolute. Under Joshua's leadership, "Israel served the LORD" (Jos 24, 31) and it had experi-enced victory after victory and came to possess "all the land." Without the type of leadership Joshua provided, the Israelite tribes were on the verge of annihilation because of their failure to obey the Lord. The Israelite response was lamentation at a place named *Bochim,* (weepers) (Jgs 2, 5).

The next section (2, 6—3, 6) elaborates on the religious interpretation of the problems the Is-raelite tribes had in maintaining a foothold in the land promised to their ancestors. The reason for Israel's difficulties is simple enough: "the Is-raelites offended the LORD by serving the Baals" (2, 11). The threat to Israel's continued presence in Canaan was a direct by-product of the Israelite worship of Baal, which presented a most serious threat to the exclusive service that Israel owed to its God. Baal is the title ("Lord" or "Owner") by which Hadad, the Canaanite god of the storm and fertility, was known.

One of the principal sources of anxiety in the Bronze and Iron Ages in Canaan and Israel was having enough food to eat. The problem was not the soil—it was fertile enough. The problem was water. The region was not blessed with a river system as were Egypt and Mesopotamia, whose river systems made large-scale irrigation possi-ble. In Israel, whatever moisture there was to wa-ter the land had to come as rain. The Israelites, following the lead of the Canaanites, relieved their anxiety about having enough rain to make the land provide enough food by worshipping Baal and his consort Ashtaroth (2, 13) because rain and fertility were their specialties. Israel's ancestral deity, by way of contrast, came from southern, arid regions (see Hb 3, 3). It is likely that most Israelites did not consider the worship they offered to Baal and Ashtaroth as incompatible with loyalty to the Lord, but certainly the author of Judges did. It took centuries for the people of Israel to be convinced of how critically important it was for them to serve the Lord alone. The book of Judges was an important contribution to this process.

The pattern for the way the stories of the judges will be told is set in 2, 11–23. The book introduces the narrative of each of the judges with the formula found first in 2, 11: "Israelites offended the LORD . . ." The consequence of this infidelity was domination over the Israelite tribes by their rivals for hegemony in Canaan. But the period of the judges was marked not only by divine judgment but by divine mercy. The Lord always heard the sounds of Israel's pleading and responded by raising up a leader who rescued Israel from the oppression they were experiencing. Unfortunately, at the death of the judge who rescued them, the Israelites returned to their evil ways. God determined, then, that Israel would have to continue facing the threat of extinction as long as it continued to serve the Baals (2, 16–23). The introduction to the book ends with 3, 1–6, which explains that Israel's competitors will remain in the land to test the loyalty of future generations. But one consequence of this intermingling will be that some Israelites will marry Canaanite spouses, which will often mean that the Israelite partners in such unions will abandon their ancestral religion.

Two final observations need to be made about the introduction. In the stories that follow, the threat and resistance are usually local. But Judges transforms the stories of local heroes into stories that have a significance for all Israel. Second, as readers work their way though the stories of the judges, the question arises about how long God will continue to abide Israel's infidelity. Is there some limit to God's forbearance?

The Stories of the Judges (Jgs 3, 7—15, 20)

Othniel (Jgs 3, 7–11)

The book of Judges begins with a divine oracle that names the tribe of Judah as the leader of the Israelites in the attempt to take control over Canaan (1, 1–2), and the first of the judges, Othniel, is from Judah. He has already made an appearance in the book as the conqueror of Debir, a city in the southern hill country of Judah (1, 11–13). Here Othniel's story is told with a minimum of detail, but its basic pattern will be repeated throughout this section of Judges: The Israelites served Baal instead of the Lord. God allowed an enemy to oppress them—in this case for eight years. They cried out for deliverance, and God sent a judge to rescue them. God endowed the judge with the spirit of the Lord, which empowered him to accomplish extraordinary deeds. Israel then served the Lord for the lifetime of the judge—in this case forty years.

The NAB accepts the reading of the Hebrew Bible for the name of Cushan's base: *Aram Naharaim*, a city on the Euphrates River in northern Syria. This reading cannot be correct since the judges all deal with threats from within Canaan. One suggestion is that the text should read *Armon-harim* ("fortress in the hills").

Ehud (Jgs 3, 12–30)

Ehud came from the tribe of Benjamin, whose territory is immediately north of Judah. The first detail given about Ehud is that he was left-handed. While the people of the ancient world considered left-handedness abnormal, it was a distinct advantage in hand-to-hand combat. Although the name Benjamin means "the son of my right hand," the tradition behind the book associates this tribe with a high incidence of left-handedness. Judges 20, 16 asserts that Benjamin could boast of seven hundred highly skilled left-handers.

Israel's sin was responsible for the oppression, which took the form of raids by Eglon, the king of Moab. Moab was a kingdom located in the central part of the Transjordan directly across the river from Benjaminite territory. While engaged in these raids, Eglon made "the City of Palms" (probably Jericho) his headquarters. These raids continued over an eighteen-year period. Ehud, who was supposed to bring Benjamin's tribute to Eglon, instead assassinated him. After making his escape, Ehud was able to convince men from the tribe of Ephraim to join him in expelling the Moabites from Israelite territory. So total was

Ehud's victory that Israel had peace for eighty years.

The story of Ehud's assassination of Eglon ridicules the Moabites for their carelessness, naïveté, and stupidity. Of course, the story must have been highly entertaining because it was retold countless times. Certainly one can picture the Israelite audience having a good laugh at the expense of the Moabites. The book takes this entertaining story about a Benjaminite hero and makes it part of a comprehensive theological presentation about the importance of serving the Lord alone.

Shamgar (Jgs 3, 31)

There is some doubt whether Shamgar ought to be understood as a judge like the others in the book. His name is not Semitic nor does the text claim that God raised him up in response to Israel's cries. The Song of Deborah (Jgs 5) notes that the caravan trade was interrupted "in the days of Shamgar" (v. 6). Perhaps he was responsible for this disruption. In any case, Shamgar single-handedly defeated an entire Philistine force. While his service on Israel's behalf may have been indirect, he did make life easier for some Israelites by defeating the Philistines. The book mentions him after Ehud—someone else who single-handedly delivered Israel.

Deborah and Barak (Jgs 4, 1—5, 31)

With the story of Deborah and Barak, the scene shifts northward—to the vitally important Jezreel Valley. The valley, which extended southeast from the Plain of Acco on the Mediterranean coast to the Jordan Valley, separated Galilee from the central highlands. Once under Israelite control, communication between the tribes in the Galilee and the those in the highlands to the south became possible. Also significant was the agricultural and trade potential of the Jezreel Valley. Israel had to control this important piece of real estate. But standing in its way was Jabin, the king of Hazor, who wanted to keep the Jezreel for himself. He dispatched his general Sisera with a force that included nine hundred chariots to keep Israel out of the valley. The story and poem about Deborah and Barak testify to the significance that the Jezreel Valley held. It is the celebration of a great and unexpected victory: that of an army of peasants over professional soldiers with the best of equipment.

The book of Judges presents Deborah as the hero of the conflict with Sisera's army. Barak made his contributions with great reluctance. The story labels Deborah as a prophetess and a judge (4, 4) without further explanation. Because judges and prophets were charismatic leaders, these roles were open to women. The patriarchal structures of ancient Israelite society did not obstruct the "spirit of the LORD," and clearly people understood this. Deborah shamed Barak into raising a force from Naphtali and Zebulun to oppose Sisera and his chariots. Naphtali and Zebulun were Galilean tribes, and their territory was located just to the north of the Jezreel Valley. As the reader expects, God gave victory to the Israelites. Sisera escaped the rout only to be killed by the Kenite Jael while assuming she was protecting him from the pursuing Israelites. This event fulfilled, in an unforeseen way, Deborah's prophecy, which was intended to goad Barak into action (4, 9).

The book of Judges preserves what many consider to be one of the oldest texts found in the Bible: the song of Deborah (5). This is a hymn celebrating the victory of Israel over Sisera's army. Here readers find out how the victory was achieved. A sudden rain causing a flash flood in the valley rendered the chariot force immobile and eliminated Sisera's advantage. Also, the poem asserts that the Israelite force included not only Zebulun and Naphtali but also Ephraim, Benjamin, Issachar, and Machir, which may be that portion of Manasseh west of the Jordan. Other tribes are criticized for not responding to the threat posed by Sisera: Asher, Dan, Reuben, and Gilead, which may be that portion of Manasseh east of the Jordan. The poem does not mention Judah, Gad, or Levi.

The poem contrasts two mothers: Deborah, mother of Israel, and Sisera's unnamed mother. Deborah was responsible for a great victory, while Sisera's mother came to realize that Sisera's failure to return promptly from the battle means that she would never see her son again.

Gideon (Jgs 6, 1—8, 35)

No judge receives more attention from the book of Judges than Gideon. His story begins with Israel being harassed by the Midianites, who enjoyed a great advantage over Israel. The Midianites were mounted on camels when they raided Israelite territory at harvest time. These mounted attacks made the Midianites unstoppable. They simply confiscated the harvest that the Israelites produced, making life impossible for the Israelite peasants (6, 1–6). An unnamed prophet announces the religious cause of the Midianite oppression (6, 7–10). To the angel sent to recruit Gideon to deliver Israel, the reluctant general points out his lack of suitability—a motif also found in the call of Moses (Ex 3, 10) Isaiah (Is 6, 5) and Jeremiah (Jer 1, 6).

There is a great anomaly in Gideon's story: he is frequently called *Jerubbaal,* a name that seemingly honored Baal, the Lord's rival for Israel's loyalty. The meaning of that name (let Baal sue or take action) helps explain the anomaly. Gideon's dismantling of an altar for sacrifices to Baal aroused the anger of the local populace, and they were ready to kill Gideon for his sacrilege. Gideon's father suggests that they should leave the matter up to Baal—let Baal sue—"since he destroyed his altar" (Jgs 6, 25–32).

The rest of Gideon's story describes his efforts to deal with the Midianites and others that were threatening the Israelite tribes in the central highlands. He rallied to his side not only members of his own tribe (Manasseh) but the militia of three others (Asher, Zebulun, and Naphtali). But Gideon refused to proceed without receiving another sign that his mission was from God (6, 36–40). Next came a test of Gideon's militia administered by God, who had Gideon dismiss those who lapped up drinking water and thus reduced their vigilance. Gideon received additional orders from God, requiring him to keep only three hundred fighters to insure that the militia could not ascribe the coming victory to their military skills but to God (7, 1–8). The three hundred vanquished the Midianites by a surprise nighttime attack without doing any actual fighting—again underscoring the divine origin of Israel's victory. The Ephraimite militia joined in the pursuit of the Midianites. They captured and executed two Midianite kings, Oreb and Zeeb. The story concludes with Gideon pursuing the fleeing Midianites into the Transjordan where he took two more Midianite kings, Zebah and Zalmunna. Gideon also engaged in an act of private vengeance against the town of Penuel that refused to help his men during their campaign.

Gideon's story then takes a new twist as the Israelites ask Gideon to rule as king and thus establish a dynasty to provide ongoing protection from groups like the Midianites. Gideon refused, citing the Israelite notion that the Lord is king of Israel. Gideon then uses part of the valuables confiscated from the Midianites to construct an ephod, a priestly vestment probably used for divination. The book does not consider this a positive development but notes that, nonetheless, Israel enjoyed peace for forty years (8, 22–28).

Gideon's story ends with a transition to what follows by introducing his many wives who bore him seventy children. The one child mentioned by name is Abimelech, who will be the principal character in the next story. After Gideon died, the people of Israel reverted to the worship of Baal and forgot both the Lord and Gideon's achievements (8, 29–35).

Abimelech (Jgs 9, 1–36)

Although it is in the middle of the book of Judges, the story of Abimelech is an oddity because Abimelech is not a judge. He did not free Israel from any oppression. Abimelech convinced the people of Shechem to accept him as the sole ruler of their city and its environs, replacing the more diffuse pattern of leadership as exercised by Jerubbaal's seventy sons. To solidify his one-man rule Abimelech murdered all his brothers except Jotham, who survived, cursed his brother and then fled the Shechem area— never to be heard from again.

The book places on Jotham's lips a bitter diatribe against his brother (9, 7–15). Jotham addresses Shechem's leadership in a fable about trees who were looking for a king but could persuade only a worthless thornbush to accept the position. Is this a criticism of the monarchy as an institution or merely a criticism of Abimelech? The book can barely hide its animosity toward Abimelech. It is important to remember that the book of Judges—in the form in which it now exists—was the product of someone who witnessed the fall of the Davidic dynasty and the end of the Judahite national state. Certainly the failure of the monarchy to prevent the disaster that came upon Jerusalem had to weigh heavily on the writer's mind. The role of the monarchy in Israelite life, then, was not simply a theoretical question. It is important to note that the setting of this story is Shechem, where earlier Israel had reaffirmed its covenant with the Lord (Jos 24). In

Abimelech, Shechem accepts a human being as its lord. Such a choice will be disastrous.

Abimelech's rule in Shechem was indeed a disaster for him and for the city. Although Abimelech claimed to be a Shechemite "flesh and bone" (9, 2), a revolt was fomented by Gaal, who implied that Abimelech was only a half-Shechemite. The trouble started by Gaal was serious enough that Abimelech had to be ferocious in his response (9, 42–49). Abimelech died as he was putting down the revolt. The book implies that his ignominious death was a fitting conclusion to a bad episode. In 2 Samuel, Joab and David will recall the story of Abimelech's death as they scheme to have Uriah die during the siege of Rabbath-Ammon as part of the cover-up of David's adultery with Bathsheba (2 Sm 11, 18–24). After Abimelech's death, the Israelite militia, which Abimelech also led, dispersed (Jgs 9, 22.55).

Tola and Jair (Jgs 10, 1–5)

There were several judges about whom the book provides almost no information, but they are mentioned to leave the reader with the impression that judges were part of the experience of people in every region of Israel. Tola judged in Ephraim, the western portion of the central highlands, and Jair in Gilead, the northern part of the Transjordan controlled by Israel. References to their service provide the outer frame for the much more developed story of Jephthah.

Jephthah (Jgs 10, 6—11, 40)

Because Jephthah, as the son of a prostitute, had an even lower social standing than Gideon or Deborah, he too was at first an unlikely candidate for the leadership of the Israelite militia. He did, however, possess one advantage. As the leader of a group of raiders, Jephthah had military experience and was just the kind of man that the elders of Gilead were looking for when the Ammonites were trying to push their border northward into Gilead's territory. Gilead was an Israelite territory east of the Jordan; Ammon was a kingdom to the south of Gilead.

There are several unique features to Jephthah's story. First, before resorting to armed conflict, Jephthah tried to negotiate a settlement with the Ammonites (11, 12–28). When the negotiations failed to convince the Ammonites to stop their incursions, the spirit of the Lord came upon Jephthah, empowering him for the extraordinary efforts necessary to neutralize the Ammonites. But then there is a second unusual detail in the story. Jephthah makes a hasty and carelessly worded vow before the battle. The reader wonders if this indicates that the judge was less than confident in the outcome of the approaching battle. When Jephthah handily defeated the Ammonites, it was time to act on the vow he made. The NAB translation of 11, 31 suggests that the victim was to be a human being, but that is misleading. A better translation is "the first thing to come out . . ." But Jephthah thought that he was trapped by the imprecise wording of his vow, and so he believed that he had to sacrifice the daughter who ran out to meet him on his return from the battle with the Ammonites (11, 34–35). The religious and cultural significance of the practice of lamenting for Jephthah's daughter (11, 37–40) is not clear.

The third unique episode in Jephthah's star-crossed career is a brief war between the Israelites from Gilead and those from Ephraim. The latter were jealous of Jephthah's victories and angry that they were not invited to join his expedition against the Ammonites. The conflict between Ephraim and Gilead may reflect an attempt by the former to dominate the latter. Jephthah tried negotiations a second time and failed again. In the ensuing conflict, the Ephraimites suffered severe casualties. Those who tried to escape were caught because they did not pronounce the *sh* sound in the Hebrew word *shibboleth* (current) because of their Ephraimite dialect.

Though Jephthah did neutralize the Ammonite threat and judged Israel for six years, the impression left by the book is that Jephthah's career was marked by failure and tragedy. He was not able to successfully negotiate with either the Ammonites or the Ephraimites. He lost his daughter because of a carelessly worded vow, and his victories ignited an intertribal war. The picture of Israel during the time of the judges is getting darker.

Ibzan, Elon, and Abdon (Jgs 12, 8–15)

The second part of the frame surrounding the story of Jephthah is a brief notice about three more judges, each of whom judged Israel in the region west of the Jordan River. Since Elon and Abdon were from the north, it is likely that Ibzan was too. The village of Bethlehem that was Ibzan's home was located in Zebulun (Jos 19, 15)—not in Judah. There are no warfare stories connected with any of the three.

Samson (Jgs 13, 1—15, 20)

Although Judges 15, 20 states that Samson was a judge in Israel for twenty years, his career was different from that of the judges whose stories the book has told so far. Samson never led the Israelite tribal militia. His was more of a solo act. The setting of Samson's story is the long conflict between the Israelites and the Philistines for control of Canaan. When the Egyptians and Hittites exhausted themselves vying for control of the trade routes that ran through Canaan, this left a vacuum of power waiting to be filled. The first to try to take advantage of Egypt's weakness were the Philistines. Who these people were and where they came from are not clear. Perhaps they were Mycenaeans who crossed the Mediterranean from Greece following the collapse of their empire in the thirteenth century BC. Mycenaeans served as mercenaries in the Egyptian army and knew the strengths and weaknesses of Egyptian defenses, but their invasion of Egypt still failed. The would-be conquerors of Egypt retreated to the southern part of Canaan's coastal plain, which in Hebrew was known as *peleshet*. The Bible calls these people *pelishtim* (Philistines), i.e., the people who live in the *peleshet*. The Philistines organized themselves politically into a confederation of five city-states: Gaza, Ashkelon, Ashdod, Ekron, and Gath. As the Philistines expanded to the north, they threatened the tribe of Dan, which was located on the central part of the coastal plain. Samson was a Danite.

Another unique feature of Samson's story is the narrative about the events surrounding his conception and birth that took place after Israel suffered forty years of Philistine oppression (13, 2–25). Samson's mother is told that the son she will conceive is to be a Nazirite. The word *Nazirite* comes from a Hebrew root that means "to separate, consecrate, abstain." Numbers 6 describes the lifestyle of the Nazirite. They were not to drink fermented beverages, wine, or vinegar. They were not even to drink grape juice or eat grapes or raisins. This prohibition probably was meant to insure that Nazirites would not lose the spirit of the Lord because of intoxication.

Second, Nazirites were not to cut their hair. This prohibition likely reflects a belief that a person's hair was especially significant as a place where spirits dwelt. Finally, Nazirites were not to touch any corpse because they were to remain ritually pure, and contact with a corpse rendered a person impure. A person could take the vows of a Nazirite for a set time, or a person could become a permanent Nazirite.

Samson's conflicts with the Philistines appear to be private in nature. The first comes as a result of a lost wager that Samson made with the Philistines during the celebration of his marriage to a Philistine woman (14, 1–20). The second is a reaction to his wife being given to another man (15, 1–7). The third involves an attempt by some Judahites to turn Samson over to the Philistines (15, 8–20). The story affirms three separate times that the spirit of the Lord came upon Samson. Each time the spirit gave Samson strength in situations when his life was in danger. The book implies that while Samson's struggles with the Philistines were personal, he caused the Philistines the type of setbacks that eased pressure on Dan for twenty years.

Israel's Self-Destruction (Jgs 16, 1—21, 25)

As readers make their way through the stories of the judges, the question arises, How long will God allow this pattern of apostasy and repentance to repeat itself? Will Israel ever learn to serve the Lord alone? The book of Judges answers those questions by concluding with a series of stories that show Israel clearly on the path of self-destruction. What God would not allow the Moabites, the Midianites, the Ammonites, or the Philistines to do, Israel seems bent on doing to itself. The final chapters make it appear that the Israelites become addicted to chaos—chaos that threatens their continued existence as a people.

As the previous section ends with the stories of Samson's private vendettas easing the pressure that the Philistines were bringing to bear on Israel, so this final section begins with Samson's descent into self-destruction. What is even worse is that Samson nearly took Israel with him. In Judges 16, 1–3, Samson's visit to a prostitute nearly cost him his life. Apparently, he learned nothing from that brush with death, and his affair with Delilah did end with his death. Delilah was from the Valley of Sorek, located about thirteen miles west of Jerusalem. The land there was much more agriculturally valuable than the land the Israelite tribes had in the central highlands. Its one disadvantage was that it abutted Philistine territory; there was a constant threat of harassment hanging over the Israelite farmers in the Sorek because the Philistines too had moved into that valley. The book of Judges suggests that the Philistines soon dominated the region (Jgs 13, 1). Delilah is never actually called a Philistine, but the implication is there. The cutting of a Nazirite's hair was a public statement that he was released from his vows (see Acts 18, 18). In Samson's case, it meant that he was no longer equipped to defend Israel from the Philistine threat. His hair grew back, and Samson had one more opportunity to avenge himself, but at the cost of his life (Jgs 16, 23–30). Samson's flaws proved fatal. His death presaged that of the Israelite kingdoms whose story is introduced by that of the judges.

Micah (Jgs 17, 1–13)

The scene shifts from the fate of Samson to that of Israel as a whole. The story about Micah is a symptom of the disease that afflicts Israel—the failure to serve the Lord alone. Micah built himself a shrine and, with his mother's help, outfitted it with images and an ephod, the latter probably used in divination. Micah had one of his sons serve as the priest of the shrine until a Levite happened to come by. What follows reflects the preference that Israelites had for priests from the tribe of Levi, who were likely seen as authentic representatives of the Yahwistic tradition. Indeed, Micah himself believes that as a result of his installing a Levite as a priest of his domestic shrine, he will enjoy blessings from the Lord (Jgs 17, 13). The only comment that the author of Judges makes on what he considers to be a warped notion of Israelite religious traditions is found in Judges 17, 6: "In those days there was no king in Israel; everyone did what he thought best." Without some central authority, religious anarchy reigned in Israel.

Chapter 18 describes the migration of the tribe of Dan from the central part of the coastal plain to the far north of Galilee. The story begins by repeating the refrain "At that time there was no king in Israel" (Jgs 18, 1). The story continues to describe the religious anarchy among the tribes. The Danites steal the liturgical appurtenances from Micah's shrine and abduct his priest. After they take the city of Laish, they install the Levite and the shrine in their new home, which they rename Dan. Finally, the identity of the Levite is revealed. His name is Jonathan, and he is a grandson of Moses. The book of Judges regards this shrine as illegitimate because the "house of God" was located at Shiloh (Jgs 18, 31). That Moses' grandson was associated with an illegal shrine so scandalized later scribes that they introduced another letter into the name of Moses in 18, 30, changing it to Manasseh, which was also the name of the most notorious apostate of all Judah's kings (see 2 Kgs 21).

The story of the corrupting of a young Levite from Bethlehem (Jgs 19) is followed by the story of a well-established Levite from Ephraim. This story, too, begins with the refrain: "At that time . . . there was no king in Israel" (v. 1)—a warning that what follows is another example of the religious anarchy that plagued Israel in the time of the judges. On his way home from reclaiming his secondary wife (concubine), who had returned to her father in a fit of anger, the Levite and his concubine spend the night in Gibeah, a town in the territory of Benjamin. In what has been aptly characterized as a "text of terror," the Levite's wife is gang-raped and murdered (vv. 11–30). Evidently, the hospitality and protection due a stranger in Benjamin did not extend to a secondary wife who may accompany him. Despite his own implication in facilitating this crime, the Levite summons the Israelite militia for vengeance. The tribal militia is not engaged in a defensive war against oppression but now fights in civil war. After two terrible losses, the Israelite militia finally defeats the Benjaminites, leaving only six hundred surviving males.

While the militia reassembles at Bethel, the people realize what they have done. When they seek an oracle from God to determine why one tribe has been virtually wiped out, none is forthcoming. The answer should be obvious: the Israelites try to undo what they have just done, and their solution involves them in another civil war against the people of Jabesh-gilead, who did not join in the muster against Benjamin and, thus, were likely candidates to supply wives for the six hundred remaining Benjaminites. When the war did not provide enough women, the supposedly wise elders suggested that the Benjaminites kidnap as many as they needed from Shiloh. With that, the militia disbands.

The author of Judges has painted a very bleak picture of the Israelite tribes. He leaves his readers with the by-now-familiar comment on the religious and civil anarchy that gripped the life of Israel in its land: "In those days there was no king in Israel; everyone did what he thought best" (Jgs 21, 25). What follows is the story of Israel's experience with the monarchy, which ultimately proved just as incapable of forestalling disaster for the people of Israel.

While the book of Joshua is a highly stylized portrait of Israelite beginnings, the book of Judges reflects the disordered state of life in Canaan at the end of the Late Bronze Age in Canaan. It was a very unsettled time in the region, and certainly the book of Judges gives some idea of the chaos that affected the Israelite tribes who were trying to gain a foothold in the region. This is not to suggest that the book of Judges is a historical account of events as they happened. To some extent the narratives in Judges present an idealization of the early years of Israel's existence in Canaan: the stories of local heroes are arranged in what appears to be chronological order. What these stories show is that loyalty and commitment to the Lord are what stand between Israel's well-being and its destruction.

Continuing Significance of the Book of Judges

If the modern religious reader of Judges is repulsed by its narratives, the ancient author has been successful. The picture of Israel—especially at the end of the book—is far from attractive or edifying. But it does show what happens to a nation that ignores traditional ethical and moral values. Disaster inevitably follows. If

the people of Judah would restore their community's life in the land promised to their ancestors, they need to remember the centrality of the covenant that God made with those ancestors. The stipulations of that covenant require fidelity, commitment, and absolute loyalty to the Lord. The book of Judges is an object lesson about what happens to a people when they ignore the Lord in their national life. The pattern of recurring apostasy has to be replaced by a consistent loyalty. But how does a nation evaluate its level of commitment to the moral values to which it is an heir? This will be the subject of much of the story of Israel's kings that begin in the books of Samuel and continue in the books of Kings.

FURTHER READING

Alter, Robert. *Language as Theme in the Book of Judges*. Cincinnati: University of Cincinnati Press, 1988.

Bal, M. *Death and Dissymmetry: The Politics of Coherence in the Book of Judges*. Chicago: University of Chicago Press, 1988.

Boling, Robert. *Judges*. Anchor Bible 6A. Garden City, NY: Doubleday, 1975.

Brenner, Athalya. "A Feminist Companion to Judges." *Journal for the Study of the Old Testament*. Sheffield: Sheffield Academic Press, 1993.

Finkelstein, Israel. *The Archaeology of the Israelite Settlement*. Leiden: Brill, 1988.

Hamlin, E. John. *At Risk in the Promised Land: A Commentary on the Book of Judges*. Grand Rapids, MI: Eerdmans, 1990.

Klein, Lillian R. *The Triumph of Irony in the Book of Judges*. Sheffield: Almond Press, 1988.

Mayes, A. D. H. *Israel in the Period of the Judges*. London: SMC Press, 1974.

Pannick, David. *Judges*. New York: Oxford University Press, 1987.

Soggin, J. Alberto. *Judges*. Old Testament Library. Philadelphia: Westminster, 1981.

Yee, Gale A., ed. *Judges and Method: New Approaches in Biblical Studies*. Minneapolis: Augsburg Fortress, 1995.

RUTH

[see pages 297–301 of the Old Testament]

Before Beginning . . .

The book of Ruth contains a rare and delightful story that continues to captivate its audi-

ence no matter how often it is read. Few can forget the loyalty of Ruth, the bitterness of Naomi, the forthright Boaz. The story has been of special interest to Christians since Matthew lists Ruth among the ancestors of Jesus (Mt 1, 5).

Ruth as Story

The book of Ruth is a short story, similar to the Joseph story in Gn 37—50. It is an artistically told tale with a simple plot. While the story of Joseph is set with the court of Pharaoh and deals with important personages and events, Ruth's characters are ordinary people; its events, mundane. Its closeness to life enables us to identify with its characters, to sympathize with their situation, and to rejoice when their problems are solved. The plot of the book is controlled by the problems that Ruth and Naomi have as they adjust to their new status as widows. These problems are resolved through the interaction of the book's main characters: Ruth, Naomi, and Boaz, relieving the tension created by the uncertain future that the two women faced. The principal characters are exemplary persons whose goodness is rewarded in the end, reinforcing the belief that human events are in some sense under the control of a power which insures that good triumphs. As story, its purpose is to entertain and delight, and this it does, but at the same time it also instructs. Though God never directly speaks or acts in the story, nevertheless it is clear that the story has something to teach us of the way that God is present in life.

An important element in the story is Ruth's Moabite ancestry. It is especially significant since the book presents her as the great-grandmother of David. Though Deuteronomy 22, 4 forbids a Moabite from becoming part of the Israelite community, Ruth not only does so but is a forebear of the great King David. Perhaps the author of the book made a connection between David and the Moabites because the story of David's rise to kingship has him place his parents in the safekeeping of the king of Moab, while David is trying to elude capture by Saul (1 Sm 22, 3). There is, of course, no possibility of verifying the details of Ruth's story.

Dating the Book of Ruth

It is difficult to date the book of Ruth with any certainty, for though it has been argued that it is postexilic in origin, more and more frequently arguments for a preexilic date are being advanced. Those who postulate a postexilic date

see the book of Ruth as a polemical work challenging the policies of Ezra. In his reform of the postexilic community, Ezra implemented a policy forbidding intermarriage with foreign women. The book of Ruth questions such a policy by showing that Ruth, although a foreign woman, is pious and faithful. Moreover, the kinship between Ruth and David indicates that David, the greatest of Israel's kings, was himself of mixed blood. Such a challenge to Ezra's policies would emerge close to the time of Ezra's activity, ca. 450 BC. The evidence for a preexilic date comes from an analysis of style and theology. There is nothing in the style of the book that would force one to assume a late date. Its theology is similar to that of the Joseph story (Gn 37—50) and the court history of David (2 Sm 9—20; 1 Kgs 1—2), both thought to be preexilic in origin. We cannot resolve here the complex issues surrounding the date of the book of Ruth, but the diversity of opinion cautions us against easy answers. Recent linguistic analysis of the Hebrew of Ruth suggests that a date in the early postexilic period is likely (late sixth century BC).

Ruth's Place in the Canon

While there is universal agreement about Ruth's canonical status, there is some disagreement about the book's place within the canon. Christian Bibles, including the *New American Bible*, place the book of Ruth after Judges and before 1 Samuel, following the order of books in the Septuagint, which was the version of the Old Testament read in the early church. No doubt the Septuagint placed Ruth *after* Judges because the story is set "in the time of the judges" (Ru 1, 1). It is important to note that despite its placement, the book of Ruth is not a part of the Deuteronomistic History—the story of Israel from conquest to exile found in the books of Joshua, Judges, 1 and 2 Samuel, and 1 and 2 Kings. It does not reflect the thought or style of the Deuteronomistic History; it does not have Deuteronomistic theological overtones. In Jewish Bibles, the book of Ruth is placed in the third division of the Jewish Canon—the Writings, a collection of miscellaneous works. Jewish liturgical practice includes Ruth among the five *Megilloth,* i.e., the scrolls that are read on major Jewish festivals. The book of Ruth is read on the Feast of *Shavuot* (Weeks), which Christians know as Pentecost.

Theology in the Book of Ruth

In an age when the Torah was on the way to becoming the central religious symbol of early Judaism, the book of Ruth presents three characters, Ruth, Boaz, and Naomi, whose actions go beyond what is required of them. Ruth makes a commitment to her mother-in-law, Naomi, that ignores the claims of religious traditions and national origins. Naomi shows her loving concern for Ruth by devising a scheme to induce Boaz to marry Ruth, even though that scheme could have backfired on her. Boaz ignores his self-interest to marry Ruth and thus redeem the property of Naomi's husband. The story shows how people who think of others' needs before their own find their truest happiness. God approves the conduct of these people by giving a son to Ruth and Boaz—a son who removes the emptiness and uncertainty that faced the widow Naomi. The author of Ruth is certainly saying to the book's readers: "Go you and do likewise."

How to Proceed

The book is short, and it can be read easily in one sitting. Because a story conveys its meaning in terms of what is said of its actors and their actions, it is important to pay close attention to the characterization of Ruth, Naomi, and Boaz, and what they do. Pay particular attention to the subtle presence of God in the story. Notice, too, recurring motifs and patterns that will function as clues to meaning.

The Book of Ruth in Outline

The story is worked out in scenes set between an introduction that presents the problem, and an epilogue that follows the resolution of the problem.

1, 1–5   Prologue: A Family Dies
1, 6–22   Naomi and Ruth in Bethlehem: Emptiness and Uncertainty
2, 1–23   Naomi, Ruth, and Boaz (I): A Meeting with Possibilities
3, 1–18   Naomi, Ruth, and Boaz (II): A Husband for Ruth
4, 1–12   The Climax: Boaz Acts
4, 13–17   A Son for Naomi
4, 18–22   Epilogue: A Family's Genealogy

Reading through the Book of Ruth

The Prologue: A Family Dies (Ru 1, 1–5)

A family from Bethlehem, which had been driven by hunger to Moab, is now left without any hope of progeny since the men of the family have recently died. This is a principal problem of the story: Naomi is left without husband or sons (1, 5). The author makes a special note of identifying the family's origin in Bethlehem of Judah (1, 1), noting more specifically that they were "Ephrathites from Bethlehem of Judah" (1, 2). This detail, emphasized as it was, certainly led those who first read the story of Ruth to think of the most famous of all Ephrathites: David, the son of Jesse (see 1 Sm 17, 12). Thus, the opening verses of the story hint at its eventual resolution.

The Geographical and Cultural Setting

The events recounted in these opening verses reflect conditions typical of life in Canaan. Because the region did not have a river system that made large-scale irrigation possible, agriculture was completely dependent on rain. When the rainfall was inadequate, famine was the inevitable result. One way to cope was to move to areas unaffected by the famine—usually this meant Egypt (see Gn 12, 10; 26, 1). Moab was an unusual choice. It was located east of the Dead Sea and, like the lands to the west, it too was entirely dependent on rain for agricultural productivity. Presumably a drought that affected Bethlehem would have affected Moab as well. Also unusual is that no negative comments are made regarding the marriage of Naomi's sons to Moabite women. But these details also serve to prepare the reader for an even greater anomaly coming at the end of the story.

Childless widows were particularly vulnerable in the social and economic system of the societies of the ancient Near East. A husband and sons provided a woman with security. Naomi found herself without such protection in a foreign land. She bitterly lamented her fate (Ru 1, 13), but in an unusual move one of her daughters-in-law chose to ignore her own welfare and care for Naomi. Instead of attaching herself to a man to provide for her welfare, Ruth attaches herself to Naomi, who can offer her nothing.

The Motif of Emptiness

Naomi's "emptiness" is the principal problem of the story. With great artistry the author of Ruth weaves into the story a motif of emptiness, which sets the action of the story in motion and will be reversed by the end of the story. The emptiness of the land (famine) causes Naomi's family to leave the land. The emptiness of the land gives way to the emptiness of Naomi as she loses her husband and her sons. Naomi dismisses her daughters-in-law because her "emptiness" cannot be cured. She is too old to give birth again. Naomi's emptiness is accentuated when she contrasts her previous abundance with her present destitution (1, 21). The story ends with Naomi no longer empty. She takes Ruth's child to her breast and cares for him. The women of the neighborhood congratulate her: "A son has been born to Naomi" (Ru 4, 17, literal translation).

Naomi and Ruth in Bethlehem: Emptiness and Uncertainty (Ru 1, 6–22)

The length of this scene indicates its importance for the author of Ruth. Naomi decides to return home because the famine is over in the land of Israel. Also motivating her decision must be the realization that she will have a better chance of survival among her own people than as an Israelite widow living among Moabites. Naomi's words to her daughters-in-law accentuate the tragedy of her situation. She is too old to marry and can no longer bear children. She can hope for nothing. Her daughters-in-law share Naomi's desperate situation, but she advises them to return to their people. Among their own people they may be able to find husbands and thus secure their future. With Naomi there can be no future. Ruth's loyalty is shown in her refusal to abandon her mother-in-law in spite of the hopelessness of Naomi's future; she will stay with Naomi despite the prospect of poverty.

The Character of Ruth

By drawing out the hopelessness of Naomi's situation coupled with Ruth's refusal to leave her mother-in-law, the author highlights Ruth's character: she is faithful. While there is nothing wrong with Orpah's returning home, Ruth's virtue is shown in sharp relief by the contrasting actions of these two women. Ruth is willing to share the plight of Naomi. Ruth's character is spotlighted even more in its biblical context. She is not called by God. She receives no promises. No reward awaits her. She acts solely for the good of Naomi. Her loyalty will draw the attention of Boaz, which eventually will lead to the resolution of the problem facing Ruth and Naomi, and thus everything in the story depends on this young widow.

God's Presence in the Story

It is important to note that, in the story of Ruth, most often God is referred to in the blessings and oaths that are spoken by the main characters. Naomi blesses her two daughters-in-law (1, 8f); Boaz blesses Ruth for her loyalty to Naomi (2, 12) and her good character (3, 10); Naomi blesses Boaz for his kindness to Ruth (2, 20); the blessing of fertility is bestowed upon Ruth by the citizens at the city gate (3, 10). All of these blessings are issued in God's name, but it is through the actions of the main characters that the blessings are fulfilled. God stands behind all as cause (4, 14), but God's activity is mediated by those who live faithful lives.

Other references to God in the story imply that God is the cause of all that happens. God is the one who has ended the famine in the land of Israel and filled it with food (1, 6). God is blamed for Naomi's destitution (1, 20f); God is also responsible for Naomi's abundance at the end of the story (4, 14) by enabling Ruth to conceive and bear a child (4, 13). The hand of God is to be found in all that happens in the lives of Naomi, Ruth, and Boaz. But there are no miracles, no theophanies, no signs and wonders to illuminate Ruth's way. It is through the ordinary lives of ordinary people, who demonstrate extraordinary care for each other, that the divine is manifest.

Ruth, Boaz, and Naomi (I): A Meeting with Possibilities (Ru 2, 1–23)

Ruth takes the initiative in this scene, requesting permission from her mother-in-law to glean in the fields. Picking the few stalks of grain left by the harvesters was one way that people without land were able to feed themselves. Both Leviticus and Deuteronomy require that harvesters not be so thorough as to leave nothing for the poor (Lv 19, 9f; 23, 22; Dt 24, 9). Ruth, seemingly by chance, enters the fields of Boaz, a prominent relative of Naomi. Boaz has heard of Ruth's kindness to her mother-in-law, and sees to it that she is protected and allowed to gather a considerable amount of barley.

The Character of Boaz

The story depicts Boaz as generous and noble. He insists that Ruth glean only in his fields, he extends his protection to her, he provides her with food and water, and he sees to it that she will prosper in her gleaning. The motive for his behavior toward Ruth is her kindness and loyalty to Naomi. We see in his gracious response to Ruth's faithfulness that Boaz is a person of integrity and honor.

Naomi, Ruth, and Boaz (II):
A Husband for Ruth (Ru 3, 1–18)

Naomi does not want Ruth to remain a widow, so she decides to take advantage of the positive encounter between Ruth and Boaz. She suggests a plan to Ruth that could lead to marriage with Boaz. Although the writer uses euphemisms that reflect his culture's reticence about private matters, the sexual overtones of Ruth's actions are clear. Her encounter with Boaz on the threshing floor could have turned out differently, but Boaz's integrity and generosity led in the direction Naomi hoped: Ruth will have a husband.

The Climax: Boaz Acts (Ru 4, 1–12)

The storyteller introduces a new wrinkle into his tale to complicate matters just before the denouement. For the first time in the story, Elimelech's land becomes an issue. Probably the story's first readers would have wondered when the storyteller was going to get around to dealing with this most important matter. Boaz assembles ten of the town's elders to witness how the matter of the land was going to be settled among Elimelech's relatives. The presence of the elders insured that the details of settlement became "public record." An unnamed relative who had a prior claim on the land was willing to buy it back, thus making sure that Elimelech's land would stay "in the family." Of course, doing so will benefit that man economically. But then Boaz adds that with the land came Ruth, Mahlon's widow. The land in question would pass to any child born of Ruth and the relative in ques-

tion. It is at this point that he demurs and cedes his rights to Boaz. The storyteller implies that the unnamed relative was concerned solely about his interests, unlike Naomi, Ruth, and Boaz, who, throughout the story, are concerned less about themselves and more about the welfare of others. With the tension brought on by this last complication, the storyteller can proceed to the "happy ending," which has Ruth acquire a husband, Boaz acquire both a wife and Elimelech's land, and Naomi acquire a son who will fill her emptiness.

Levirate Marriage and Land Redemption

Some interpreters suggest that the marriage of Boaz and Ruth represents a variation of the levirate marriage. A levirate marriage was the marriage of a woman with the brother of her deceased husband (*levir* is the Latin word for "brother-in-law"). Such a union was mandated if the marriage was childless (Dt 25, 5–10). The practice developed to insure that the line of the deceased man would continue, in spite of the fact that he died before his wife bore him a child. Though Boaz claims Ruth as wife to raise up a family for her late husband, he is not her brother-in-law and thus the law of levirate marriage did not apply. The storyteller presents Boaz as going beyond his obligations in order to help two widows in need.

Land redemption was a strategy that developed to make sure that circumstances that forced a man to sell his land would not lead his family into a permanent state of poverty. According to Lv 25, 23–38, it was the responsibility of a relative to buy the land before it was sold outside the family or to buy it back if it had already been sold. The land remained the property of the relative who bought it back until the Year of Jubilee, when its ownership reverted to the descendants of the man who was forced to sell it.

A Son for Naomi (Ru 4, 13–17)

Ruth's marriage to Boaz is blessed with a child. Naomi's loss is replaced by Ruth's gain; the tragedy of death, with which the story opened, is balanced by the joy of new life. Notice the women of the village congratulate Naomi as if she were the mother: "A son had been born to Naomi" (Ru 4, 17, literal translation). The storyteller thus solves the problem of Naomi's emptiness. The NAB translation obscures this point by calling the child Naomi's "grandson." While the child indeed was Naomi's grandson, the text nonetheless shows Naomi acting as if she were the mother (Ru 4, 16) and being recognized as such by the women of her village (Ru 4, 17).

The Epilogue: A Family's Genealogy (Ru 4, 18–22)

The story's epilogue takes the reader back to the prologue, which identified Naomi's family as "Ephrathites from Bethlehem" (Ru 1, 2) and thus informs the reader of the wider significance of this charming story of one family's problems. The most famous Ephrathite from Bethlehem was David, who, it turns out, was a descendant of Boaz and Ruth. Usually a genealogy serves to legitimate the status of the last person named. Here David, the last person named, serves to show the significance of what happened to three people from the village of Bethlehem for all Israel.

Continuing Significance of the Story of Ruth

While early Judaism came to regard careful observance of the Torah as the key to its future, the book of Ruth shows three people whose relationships with each other are based not on obligations but on love and concern for another in need. Such relationships have significance far beyond the lives of the three people involved directly. Jesus develops these insights in his Sermon on the Mount in which he calls his followers to go beyond the commandments—as irreplaceable as they are. The charming story of Naomi, Ruth,

and Boaz shows that an ethical system fulfills its purpose if those who accept it learn to go beyond its requirements. The Torah asserts that no Moabite is to be admitted into the Israelite community (Dt 23, 4). But the book of Ruth presents a Moabite woman whose actions on behalf of her Israelite mother-in-law proceeded from love that ignored religious and ethnic boundaries, which serve to keep people from responding to each other in love. The book of Ruth, then, presents this young Moabite woman to its readers and suggests that they follow her example. The ending of the book wishes readers to recognize that, when people give of themselves for the sake of others, they find their truest happiness. This paradox lies at the heart of the book of Ruth and makes it the charming and admirable story that it is.

FURTHER READING

Bush, Frederic W. *Ruth; Esther.* Word Biblical Commentary 9. Waco, TX: Word, 1996.

Campbell, Edward F., Jr. *Ruth.* Anchor Bible 7. Garden City, NY: Doubleday, 1975.

Fewell, Danna Nolan, and David Miller Gunn. *Compromising Redemption: Relating Characters in the Book of Ruth.* Literary Currents in Biblical Interpretation. Philadelphia: Westminster John Knox, 1990.

Hals, Ronald. *The Theology of the Book of Ruth.* Biblical Series, no. 23. Facet Books. Philadelphia: Fortress, 1969.

Larkin, Katrina J. A. *Ruth and Esther.* Old Testament Guides. Sheffield: Sheffield Academic, 1996.

Trible, P. "A Human Comedy." In *God and the Rhetoric of Sexuality.* Philadelphia: Fortress, 1978.

1 AND 2 SAMUEL

[see pages 303–368 of the Old Testament]

Before Beginning . . .

The books that we call 1 and 2 Samuel were originally one book. The division into two was the work of those responsible for the Septuagint, the third-century BC Greek translation of the Hebrew Bible. Perhaps the translators thought it was necessary to make two shorter books out of one long one. The division was introduced into the Hebrew Bible in the sixteenth century AD and has become standard ever since. Ending 1 Samuel

with the death of Saul seems to make sense until the reader realizes that this division breaks up the story of David's rise to the throne. The story of the succession to David, which begins in 2 Samuel 9 is interrupted by extraneous material in 2 Samuel 21—24 and is not completed until 1 Kings 1—2.

The books of Samuel are so named because the early rabbis believed the prophet wrote 1 Samuel 1—25. They held that the rest of 1 Samuel and the whole of 2 Samuel were the work of the prophets Nathan and Gad on the basis of 1 Chronicles 29, 29. Modern scholarship ascribes the books of Samuel in their present form to the anonymous author of the Deuteronomistic History of Israel, which begins with the book of Joshua and continues through 2 Kings. Its purpose is not historiographic but homiletical. The story of Israel in its land is told to provide the people of Judah with hope for their future and a pattern for renewing their life in the land promised to their ancestors.

Reading through the Books of Samuel

The stories in the books of Samuel revolve around three characters: Samuel (1 Sm 1—25), Saul (1 Sm 9—2 Sam 2), and David (1 Sm 10—2 Sm 24). The stories of these three figures overlap and are supplemented with stories about the ark, Jerusalem, and other members of the royal family. Through most of 1 Samuel, the story moves toward the eventual accession of David to the throne of Israel. In 2 Samuel, the story describes the clear move toward religious and political centralization in Jerusalem. The books also reveal the political and religious opposition to the attempt to center all power in the Davidic dynasty and in Jerusalem. Of course, the move to establish a dynasty and concentrate all political power in the royal house had serious economic repercussions, and these too unfold in the book. The story of Israel as it establishes a monarchy is a fascinating tale of a social, political, and economic innovation, which could advance only by overcoming the religious restraints that flowed from the belief that the only king of Israel was the Lord. Finally, though the stories seem to focus on three great figures in Samuel, Saul, and David, there is an impressive list of characters—from David's wives to Saul's crippled grandson—who have critical roles in the story of Israel as it unfolds. In fact, the apparent "little people" affect the lives of the great personages of the books of Samuel in most critical ways. But it is important to remember that for the author of the Deuteronomistic History, Israel's life in its land is shaped not by human beings nor by political or economic forces. Israel, whether it is aware of it or not, is bound to fulfill God's purposes. Israel's God is *the* principal character in the story, even though God's action is sometimes subtle and unnoticed.

Samuel (1 Sm 1, 1—8, 22)

Samuel's Birth (1 Sm 1, 1—2,10)

In one sense, the books of Samuel try to answer the question "Who is a legitimate leader in Israel?" At first, Samuel provides leadership for the tribes in an unprecedented way. He is a priest, prophet, and judge, and uniquely able to inform Israel of the Lord's will. He represents the perspective that sees God's presence in Israel as mediated by charismatic and prophetic individuals. The story of Samuel's conception and birth (1, 1–28) marks him as one whom God has chosen as an instrument. The book follows a familiar pattern to indicate Samuel's significance: he is born to a woman who had been thought of as infertile. The same motif was used to indicate the special role of Isaac (Gn 17, 15–22), Jacob (Gn 25, 19–28), Joseph (Gn 30, 22–24), and Samson (Jgs 13, 2–7). Like Samson, Samuel, it appears, was destined from birth to be a Nazirite (1 Sm 1, 11). The story of Hannah (1 Sm 1, 1—2, 11) is one of those brief episodes in which a supporting character plays a crucial role in the narrative. Samuel was born because God rewarded Hannah's persistence in praying for a child. Samuel entered God's service because of her gratitude. To conclude Hannah's story, the author of 1 Samuel inserted a poem whose theme is the reversal of fortunes brought about by the Lord in the lives of the faithful (2, 1–10). Certainly, the poem's theme reflects Hannah's experience.

Samuel and the Sons of Eli (1 Sm 2, 11–36)

The story of Samuel's career is introduced by contrasting him with the sons of Eli, the priest of Shiloh. That Samuel, rather than Eli's sons, succeeded the old priest required some explanation since the priesthood was a hereditary occupation. The answer is simple enough: Eli's sons were corrupt and abused their office to enrich themselves. The author of 1 Samuel skillfully weaves the indictment of Eli's sons (2, 12–17.22–25) with the reports about Samuel's growth to adulthood (2, 1.18–21.26). The indictment of Eli's sons prepares the reader for the judgment on the house of Eli given by the unnamed "man of God." The oracle begins with a series of questions (2, 27–29) that provide the basis for the judgment that is to follow. The man of God, then, announces God's judgment (2, 30–34). The oracle concludes with the promise that God will raise a new priestly house, and Eli's descendants will be reduced to poverty (2, 35–36). The fulfillment of this prophecy comes in two places. The immediate fulfillment comes in 1 Samuel 4, 11 with the death of Eli's sons, and its final fulfillment is noted by 1 Kings 2, 26–27 when Solomon exiles Abiathar and deprives him of the priesthood. The fulfillment of prophecy is another important motif in the story of Israel in its land.

The announcement of judgment against the house of Eli sets a pattern for understanding the story of Israel as a whole. The rehearsal of God's goodness toward Israel is followed by a listing of infidelities. The judgment makes clear the terrible consequences of infidelity—consequences that cannot be avoided. But judgment is not God's final word to Israel. Just as God raised up a new priestly dynasty to replace Eli's discredited family, so there is hope for Israel as a whole. The book offers a reason to expect God to restore Israel to the land that it lost because of its infidelity.

Samuel and Eli (1 Sm 3, 1—4, 1)

Samuel is no longer a child. It is time for him to begin his ministry on Israel's behalf. The book, however, first offers a final contrast between Samuel and the house of Eli in order to show that the role Samuel will play in the narratives to follow was sanctioned by God. Samuel's career began with an initial experience of the word of God while Samuel was in Shiloh at the shrine where the ark was kept. The book notes that such experiences were rare at the time. Though Samuel appeared unsure of himself, he did show himself to be receptive as he referred to himself as God's "servant" and asserted his willingness to obey. The message that Samuel receives is one that rehearses the condemnation of Eli's priestly dynasty in harsh and uncompromising terms. Eli accepted the verdict on his house, realizing that a new era in Israel's life was beginning. God's chosen means of communicating with Israel will be a prophet—the prophet Samuel. The book concludes the story of Samuel's call by noting that all Israel recognized Samuel's role in communicating God's word. It also affirms that God con-

tinued to speak to Samuel at Shiloh and that every word that Samuel announced came true.

In the chapters to follow, the focus will be on the fate of the ark. Samuel will not appear in the story until chapter 7. This is probably to dissociate him entirely from the reverses Israel will experience—especially the loss of the ark to the Philistines.

The Story of the Ark (1 Sm 4, 2—7, 1)

The ark was a unique element of ancient Israelite religious tradition. It served to represent the presence of God in a religion that did not allow an image of its deity to serve that purpose. But the tradition understands the immediate function of the ark differently. In some texts, it is simply a box that contained the two tablets of the Ten Commandments (Ex 25, 22; Dt 10, 3), but other traditions spoke of it as God's footstool or throne (1 Sm 4, 4; Pss 99, 5; 137, 2; 1 Chr 28, 2). In this section of 1 Samuel, however, the ark is a type of battle palladium accompanying the army of Israel as it fought against those who threatened its existence. It obviously symbolized the presence of God with the army. The first part of the ark's story describes its capture and return. The story will be taken up again when David brings the ark to Jerusalem (2 Sm 6).

The Philistines, who became the principal threat to Israel's existence, were intent on enlarging their holdings in Canaan. They controlled the area along the southern coast and were determined to expand their territory to the north and east. This move brought them into direct contact with Israel. The Philistine encampment at Aphek signaled their determination to act. After an initial defeat, the elders of Israel wondered about the cause and, thinking the ark could make a difference, they bring it to the battlefield from its shrine at Shiloh. The presence of the ark, however, did not prevent a second loss and the capture of the ark.

It is important to be aware that the numerical losses of the Israelites were not as staggering as the English text implies. In the first battle, Israel lost "four thousand men" and in the second, thirty thousand. The Hebrew word that is translated as "thousand" also represents a military unit that was relatively small—probably between five and twenty men. The book asserts that in the first battle, the Israelites lost the equivalent of four such units. In the second, they lost the equivalent of thirty such units. But, as the text makes clear, this loss was devastating nonetheless.

It is also important to note that the text does not blame the defeat of Israel on the sons of Eli, who accompanied the ark from Shiloh. The story of the ark contains no negative comments about Hophni, Phinehas, or their father, Eli, who died upon hearing the news of the disaster at Ebenezer. The first part of the ark's story ends with the naming of Phinehas's newborn child to memorialize the loss of the ark (4, 19–22).

Both the Israelites and the Philistines expected Israel to be victorious at the battle of Ebenezer (4, 4–9), but Israel suffered two crushing defeats plus the loss of the ark. To insure that readers would not draw the wrong theological conclusion from Israel's defeat, the book describes two great victories of the Lord over Dagon, the Philistine god. These two victories were mirror images of Israel's defeats, i.e., Dagon's second loss was more severe than the first. Dagon was a Mesopotamian deity imported into Canaan and honored as Baal's father. Dagon's attributes are unknown, but he is likely a fertility god since the Semitic root from which his name derives means "grain." This text asserts that there was a temple of Dagon at Ashdod, but excavations have not located one even though 1 Maccabees 10, 83–84 provides evidence that Dagon was worshipped there into the second century BC. The Lord's victory over Dagon spread panic through the Philistine cities (1 Sm 4, 3.6.11). No Philistine city wanted the ark because of all the devastation that it caused so the decision was made to return the ark to Israel.

The victory of the Lord is made all the more indisputable by the method the Philistines choose to return the ark. First, they return the ark with gifts (6, 1–5). The golden hemorrhoids and mice were given as offerings to fend off additional plagues. But to be certain about the true origin of their troubles, the Philistines set up a test (6, 7–9). Getting milk (milch) cows to overcome their maternal instincts, their lack of experience with pulling a cart, and having them arrive at a precise place would certainly indicate divine power. Of course, Israel's God passed the test, and the ark arrived back at Beth-shemesh, a town on the border of Philistine and Israelite territory. There was a siz-

able crowd to greet the ark on its return because the people were in the fields harvesting the wheat crop (6, 10–13). A large stone in the field served as a substitute altar on which the milk cows were sacrificed (6, 14) though normally only the males of the species were to be sacrificed (Lv 1, 3; 22, 19). The Philistine lords witnessed all this. The victory of Israel's God was complete.

The people of Beth-shemesh, however, did not want to keep the ark in their village, perhaps to avoid provoking the Philistines across the border. The village of Kiriath-jearim, which was a few miles farther east, accepted the ark, designating a certain Eleazar to care for it. The ark remained in that village until David brought it to Jerusalem (2 Sam 6).

Samuel and the Israelite Monarchy (1 Sm 7, 2—8, 22)

Samuel reenters the story as an adult who will have a special role in the establishment of the Israelite monarchy. While the book's attitude toward the monarchy is a bit ambiguous, it is clear from the story of Samuel's victory over the Philistines (7, 2–17) that from a military point of view, the monarchy was unnecessary. If Israel would be absolutely loyal to the Lord, no enemy could do it much harm. The story begins with Israel's return to the exclusive service of the Lord after twenty years of Philistine domination, despite the ark's presence in Israel. The book makes it clear that the ark was no guarantee that Israel would live undisturbed in its land—only the exclusive service of the Lord will bring Israel peace.

Samuel assembled the Israelite militia at Mizpah in response to the people's desire to return to the Lord. The Philistine response to this provocation was an utter failure, and Israel's victory removed the stigma of the two defeats at this very battlefield (1 Sm 4, 2–11) so Samuel renamed the place *Ebenezer*, i.e., "the stone of (God's) help." Israel remained free of Philistine domination under Samuel's leadership, making it appear unnecessary for Israel to choose a king as it would at Mizpah (1 Sm 10, 17), the scene of the great victory inspired by Samuel. The book, then, emphasizes that it was Israel's repentance—not the presence of the ark or the leadership of a king—that would secure Israel's future. Of course, when the books of Samuel were written, Israel no longer had the ark nor a king. Its only course was to return to its ancestral deity.

The effort to establish a monarchy accelerated because of the corruption of Samuel's sons (8, 1–9). The people's request, however, angered Samuel who claimed that a king would not be an instrument of justice but of oppression (8, 10–18). The people adamantly insisted on having a king "like other nations" to fight their wars, so God told Samuel to honor their request. But for Samuel, the request for a king was tantamount to apostasy. After all, God had always defended a loyal Israel. Why would Israel want a king? Samuel warned the Israelites that their rejection of God would lead to God's refusal to answer them in time of need (8, 18). They will have to depend on their king. This story, of course, reflects Israel's experience of the monarchy. It proved ineffective in preventing the disasters that eventually befell the two Israelite kingdoms. The book suggests that this outcome was, in some sense, determined by the people's sinful request for a king.

Saul (1 Sm 9, 1—15, 35)

Samuel and Saul Meet (1 Sm 9, 1—10, 16)

The story of Samuel's initial encounter with Saul, whom he eventually anointed king, knows nothing of the people's sinful request for a king. On the contrary, it presents Saul's rise to kingship very positively. Saul is a handsome man from a wealthy family, a good choice for a king. The book preserves this charming tale of a man who went looking for donkeys but found a kingdom in order to show that Saul was God's choice to be king and how he could have remained in God's good graces. But as Saul's story continues, the reader learns that the young man, endowed with so many gifts and blessed by the spirit of the Lord, squandered everything. This is the story of Israel in microcosm. Like Saul, Israel was blessed with many gifts but, in the end, it too squandered them all and found itself in exile. But will Israel's end be different from that of Saul?

The futile search for his family's donkeys led Saul to seek out a "man of God," who turned out to be Samuel. The revelation to Samuel about a "man of Benjamin" whom he would meet indicates that Saul was God's choice to be king, even though Samuel's message surprised Saul (9,

14–21). Another indication of the divine choice of Saul was the fulfillment of the signs that Samuel gave to Saul to confirm his new status. The third sign is the most significant because it promised that "the spirit of the LORD" was going to descend on Saul. This gift, of course, will enable him to do extraordinary deeds in saving Israel from its enemies (10, 1.6). Upon returning home with his family's donkeys, Saul said nothing about his peculiar encounter with Samuel. This detail is necessary to make a smooth connection with the following story that describes Saul's public acclamation as king.

A positive attitude toward Saul as king continues in the story of his public acclamation (10, 17–27). Still, there are features in the story that reflect the book's overall discomfort with the monarchy as an institution. First, Samuel assembled the people at Mizpah—the very place where he had shown that a king was unnecessary since God will always protect a repentant and loyal people (10, 17; see 1 Sm 7, 2–12). Second, Samuel, speaking in the name of God, asserted that the request for a king was another of Israel's actions rejecting their God, who had proved in the Exodus and in other situations to be a savior beyond compare (10, 18–19). Still, by using lots to select the king, Samuel demonstrates the choice of Saul was God's. The people, impressed by Saul's bearing, acclaim him as their king. Samuel then committed the laws governing the new institution to writing and dismissed the people. There were a few people, whom the text characterizes as "worthless" (10, 27), who did not support the choice of Saul. To do so, however, involved questioning the choice that God had made.

The story of Saul's public acclamation is another instance of the book's ambiguity about the establishment of the monarchy in Israel. While the story presents Saul as God's choice to be king, it also presents Israel's choice to have a king as sinful. This ambivalence is not only a theological issue; it is also a literary technique that builds up suspense in the story. Can this paradox be resolved? Can the monarchy be something that contributes positively to maintaining Israel's relationship with God? Or is it only a matter of time before the monarchy's doom becomes apparent? How can Israel reject God as its savior and still expect to survive?

The "worthless men" who did not support Saul are the only connection between the story of Saul's choice by lots (10, 17–27) and the story that follows (11, 1–15). The story of Saul's victory over the Ammonites is the high point of the Saul cycle. Here his kingship differs little from the pattern of leadership represented by the judges. He rallies all Israel to follow him in lifting the oppression brought to bear on Jabesh-gilead, a town east of the Jordan that was threatened by Ammonites, who were expanding their holdings to the north. The victory of the Israelite militia led by Saul was total. Saul proved to be magnanimous in victory as he spared the lives of the "worthless men" who opposed his accession (11, 14). Saul was then proclaimed king at the old tribal shrine at Gilgal. Saul shows what the kings of Israel should have been: the saviors of the oppressed. Unfortunately, Saul and most of his successors proved to be more obsessed with their power than with the good of the people.

The book's final reflections on the rise of the Israelite monarchy appear in chapter 12. In chapter 7 the book already showed that Israel could have gotten along very well with the Lord as its only king. Still, God acceded to the people's wishes, so having a king should have been compatible with Israel's commitment to its God. Indeed, the book does treat Saul favorably (9, 1—11, 15). That God chose Saul to be king of Israel was underscored in several ways: through the anointing, the empowerment by the spirit of the Lord, the lot oracle, the prophetic designation, the popular acclamation, the victory over the Ammonites—even by Saul's pardoning of those who opposed his accession. Samuel's presence lent credibility to the establishment of the Israelite monarchy. At the same time, the book showed less than complete support for kingship by noting that Samuel was able to keep the Philistines in check for twenty years, implying that no king was needed to defend Israel. Samuel also points out the negative social and economic impact the monarchic system will have on Israel. Finally, Samuel twice characterizes the request for a king as apostasy. But despite all this, God commanded Samuel to give in to Israel's request.

The book goes over this ground one more time in chapter 12. Samuel's address to Israel begins with a legal argument showing that both God and Samuel were blameless in the process that led up to Saul becoming king. Israel's future under its kings depends on its commitment to observe the Lord's commands (12, 14). When it rains during the dry season, the people see in this unusual occurrence additional proof that God and Samuel bear no responsibility for what will happen to Israel under its kings. The people also admit that their request for a king was sinful. But God has chosen not to abandon Israel. Samuel will be with the people to pray for them and to teach them. The implication is that as long as the people obey the prophets sent to them, God will bless them. The quality of Israel's life under its kings depends on Israel's obedience. Those who first read 1 Samuel knew that Israel and its kings failed, so the judgment that came upon the people was the fulfillment of the words spoken to Israel by Samuel as it began its life under a king.

Saul Defeats the Philistines
(1 Sm 13, 1—14, 52)

Saul's reign began well enough, at least from a military point of view. Saul maintained a small army, while allowing the bulk of the Israelite militia to return to their homes. After either Saul (13, 4) or his son Jonathan (13, 3) attacked a Philistine outpost not far from Saul's own town, both sides prepared for war. 1 Samuel 14, 1–21 describes the Israelite success in that war. That success came despite the Philistines' numerical (13, 5) and technological superiority (13, 19–22). The reason for the latter was the ability of the Philistines to forge iron. The Israelites had to make do with the less-effective bronze for their tools and weapons. The average Israelite farmer could not pay the price that the Philistine charged for iron agricultural implements—much less for iron weapons. Of the Israelite forces only Saul and Jonathan had iron swords and spears. The book, of course, implies that only a miracle could have enabled Israel to defeat the Philistines.

In the midst of the story about Saul's successful war against the Philistines, the book relates an ominous incident that took place at the tribal sanctuary at Gilgal (13, 7b–15). Because Samuel was late in arriving at Gilgal, Saul offered a sacrifice there as a prelude to the attack on the Philistines. Samuel regarded this as an offense that led God to reject Saul in favor of "a man after [God's] own heart" (13, 14), whom the reader knows to be David. The book does not specify the precise nature of Saul's offense, but Samuel regarded it as some sort of an unlawful usurpation on Saul's part. It was so serious that it ended all prospects of a Saulide dynasty.

The Philistines decided to fight the battle at Michmash, a town just nine miles northeast of Jerusalem and just over a mile east of Geba, Saul's village. Michmash was located in a canyon that was impassable on the east, so it was a good place for the Philistines to mass their troops in anticipation of an Israelite attack. That attack was led by Jonathan (14, 1–14), who did not inform Saul of his plans. When Saul heard the sound of battle, his reaction was strangely indecisive. First, he sought an oracle to determine if the Israelite army should attack, but then he stopped the process before it was completed and attacked. When the Philistines began their retreat, Saul let piety overcome his military sense. He ordered his men to fast until the victory over the Philistines was consolidated. The hungry troops not only disobeyed but ate meat that had not been properly drained of its blood (see Dt 12, 23). Jonathan, too, ate, but he ate some honey without knowing that his father had pronounced a curse on anyone who ate before the victory was complete.

When Saul heard about his soldiers' disregard of his orders, he had a ritual performed to deflect the curse on those who had eaten the meat. Then Saul sought another oracle to determine if he should continue pursuing the Philistines. When no answer was forthcoming, Saul concluded that someone had sinned, and he was determined to execute that person even if it were his son. To determine the guilty party Saul uses the lot oracle (the *urim* and *thummim;* see Dt 33, 8). Though Jonathan's guilt is discovered, the army prevented Saul from taking Jonathan's life. Saul did not continue his pursuit of the retreating Philistines. The book then appends a short notice (14, 47–52) that summarizes Saul's many battles to make it clear that God was faithful to the promise made to Samuel as reported in 1 Samuel 9, 16.

Saul and the Amalekites (1 Sm 15, 1–34)

Here is the book's final word on Saul's kingship. It simply comments that God "regretted" having made Saul king (vv. 10–35). This verdict on Saul comes after another act that Samuel regards as disobedient. Saul and his army were to take no booty from the Amalekites, whom the tradition remembered as violently opposing the entrance of the Israelite tribes into Canaan (Ex 17, 8–13; Dt 25, 17–18). When confronted by his disobedience, Saul did confess and ask for pardon, but it was too late. The prophet and the king never saw each other again alive. Samuel mourned for Saul, but God was determined to give the kingdom to another. The story of Saul describes the power of human choice. Though God selected Saul to be king, Saul was able to annul that choice by his failures. Again, this is precisely what Israel did by its disobedience.

David (1 Sm 16, 1—31, 13)

Saul and David Meet (1 Sm 16, 1–23)

The book does not hesitate to enumerate the schemes that David contrived to become king: his political moves, his marriages, and his career as a guerrilla and as a Philistine mercenary. None of this is particularly flattering to David. Despite this, the book affirms that David was God's chosen. Samuel would have anointed another of Jesse's sons, but David was God's sovereign choice, and the anointing served to commit God to David. This commitment was confirmed by the spirit of the Lord that seized David and never departed from him. But Saul, deserted by the spirit of the Lord, is a broken man, afflicted by melancholy. In a supreme irony, the old king had to look for relief from his rival for the throne. Saul's servants brought David to the court to deal with their master's moods, but the reader recognizes that their description of David makes him overqualified to be simply a musician.

David and Goliath (1 Sm 17, 1—18, 5)

The story of David and Goliath stands as a paradigm of what a person of faith can accomplish. Clearly the book wants the Jewish exiles to identify with the young David, whose words and deeds testify that it was God who brought down the Philistine giant. The story also underscores David's credentials for leadership, which even Saul recognized since he appointed David to a permanent military command, not realizing that he was paving the way for his successor. Jonathan's gift of his own clothes and weapons to David makes it appear that Saul's son is divesting himself of the right of succession in favor of his new friend, the son of Jesse. The book's rush of enthusiasm in narrating this great story led to an obvious anachronism. According to verse 35, David brought Goliath's head to Jerusalem, but that city was still in Canaanite hands and remained so until David captured it and made it his capital (see 2 Sm 5, 6–10).

Saul's Jealousy (1 Sm 18, 6–30)

Saul had good reason to be jealous of David. Not only did the people love him but so did Jonathan and Michal, Saul's children. But no matter how Saul tried to eliminate his rival, David's popularity continued to grow. Saul tried to kill David twice (v. 11), but eventually realized that David's success was divinely ordered (vv. 14–15). Saul suggested that David marry his eldest daughter. David was thrilled at the prospect of marrying into Saul's family, but Saul married her off to someone else. Recognizing David's eagerness, Saul offered David another daughter if he was willing to pay a bride-price that exposed him to great danger. But David accomplished the task, outperforming Saul's servants. When he saw how the people held David in high regard, Saul's reaction was fear and hatred.

David the Fugitive (1 Sm 19, 1—28, 2)

Saul became so obsessed with David's success that he tried to kill him. David had to flee Saul's court and take up the life of a fugitive. Coming to David's aid is an unlikely group of supporters that range from Saul's own children to the Philistines, Israel's rival for control of Canaan. In telling the story of David's life on the run, the book sees God's hand protecting David from Saul and leading the young shepherd boy inexorably to the throne of Israel.

David's successes and popular acclaim triggered Saul's first attempts on David's life, but these were unsuccessful (1 Sm 19, 1–24). First, Jonathan talked Saul out of killing David (vv. 1–7). After another one of David's military victories over the Philistines, Saul could not control his hatred and made another attempt on David's life, but the latter's dexterity saved him (vv. 8–10). Michal, Saul's daughter and David's wife, prevented a third attempt from being successful (vv. 11–17). Finally, David fled to Samuel. Saul found him but a prophetic ecstasy, which once confirmed Saul's kingship (1 Sm 10, 5–12), now

made possible David's escape (1 Sm 19, 24). The reader is meant to recognize the hand of God in David's escapes.

Though Jonathan was loyal to his father, he nonetheless recognized the injustice of Saul's intentions toward David (1 Sm 20, 1—21, 1). The story of Jonathan is a story marked by conflicting emotions as Jonathan has to stand up to Saul in order to protect David. Saul's anger led him to hurl a demeaning insult at Jonathan and his mother (v. 30). The book underscores David's innocence in all this by having different characters affirm it three times (vv. 1, 8–9, 32). The irony surrounding David's rise to kingship continues as he depends on Jonathan, the presumptive heir to Saul's throne, to insure his safety. But by saving David, Jonathan is, in effect, denying himself the throne and his father a dynasty. Although the book does not say so explicitly, the reader knows that God is guiding the events that will eventually bring David to the throne.

Jonathan, Samuel, and Michal were not the only members of Saul's entourage to help David escape from Saul. While Jonathan and Michal consciously decided to help David, Ahimelech, a priest from a sanctuary near Saul's town, was duped by David into providing him with food and a weapon (1 Sm 21, 2–10). Unfortunately for Ahimelech, Doeg, an Edomite in Saul's service, witnessed the exchange between David and Ahimelech, but the consequences of that will be clear only in 1 Samuel 22, 6–23. But the book shows the ever-widening circle of those who assisted David. In his desperation David even sought refuge in Gath, a Philistine city that was home to Goliath. But David was unable to remain incognito. He feigned lunacy, and the Philistine king fell for David's act (1 Sm 21, 11–16). David will eventually join the Philistine army (27), but the book makes it clear here that David's actions were not treasonous but were motivated by his need to escape Saul's murderous intentions.

To survive on the run David sought safety in numbers. His family joined him as he assembled a force of 400 men. Evidently, even the king of Moab was among David's supporters since the king agreed to protect members of David's family. Other help came from the prophet Gad, who advised David to seek a haven in the territory of Judah. Saul, on the other hand, massacred a group of priests that had supported his rival. Saul was now almost completely isolated. His son, daughter, the priests of Nob, and even his fellow Benjaminites were giving passive and often active support to David. In addition to all these people, Saul's atrocity at Nob drove Abiathar, the sole surviving priest, into David's camp (1 Sm 22, 1–23).

What the book implied in its accounts of David's flight from Saul, it now states explicitly in verse 14: God did not surrender David into Saul's hands. To illustrate this the book relates two of David's narrow escapes. One of these follows David's defeat of the Philistines who were raiding the Judahite town of Keilah. When Saul heard that David came to the town's defense, he saw that this afforded him the opportunity to finally capture his rival. In reversal of the usual pattern, Saul found people who were willing to betray David. But David, through divination, learned of Saul's intention and escaped. David was betrayed by the Ziphites, who also belonged to the tribe of Judah, but before Saul could act on the intelligence they provided, he had to deal with a new Philistine threat. Sandwiched between these two stories of treachery by David's fellow Judahites is another account of a Benjaminite—indeed Saul's own son and heir—declaring support for David. Jonathan had more to lose than anyone as a result of David's rise to power, but he acted in accordance with what the book presents as the will of God (1 Sm 23, 1–28).

The tables turn and David has an opportunity to kill Saul, his antagonist, but he refuses to raise his hand against the old king (1 Sm 24, 1–23). This story of David's refusal to kill Saul when he had the opportunity is a fine piece of political propaganda. The story puts David in an extremely good light and serves to legitimate his eventual ascent to Israel's throne. Indeed, even Saul recognized that David should be king. The story also serves to put a positive spin on actions that David will take to neutralize any claims to the throne that Saul's descendants might make. The implication here is clear: David was entirely blameless in the matter of the succession. The book, however, uses this story to underscore the role that God had in David's rise to kingship.

Between two accounts that make David appear reluctant to take the throne forcibly, there is one that shows him to be taking steps that make

him Saul's successor nonetheless. One of these steps involves marrying a woman from an influential Judahite family (1 Sm 25, 1–41). But before the story of David and Abigail begins, the book notes the passing of Samuel, who has had no significant role in the narratives for a while. Before the book can have Saul conjure up the spirit of Samuel (28), it is necessary that Samuel die.

One of the anomalies of the story of David's rise is the treachery of people from David's own tribe. Nabal is another Judahite who was simply not impressed with David and refused to help him. Abigail, Nabal's wife, persuaded David not to take any reprisals on her husband. When Nabal died, David immediately proposed marriage to Abigail. It will not be the first time that David will marry a woman from an influential family, who had previously been married to another. David clearly saw such marriages as helping to solve the problems he had been having with certain elements from Judah. The marriage to Abigail gave David new status in Judah.

For a second time, it was possible for David to kill Saul, and again he refused to do so (1 Sm 26, 1–25). The Lord would choose the time and circumstances of Saul's death. David upbraided Abner, Saul's general, for the lax security that gave David the opportunity to assassinate Saul. Although Saul was grateful to David, there was no reconciliation between the two, and this was the last time the two would meet. Saul's final words to David are a blessing and a prediction of David's ultimate success.

Saul's pursuit of David was relentless despite what appeared to be reconciliation between the two in chapters 24 and 26. Ironically, the only place David was safe from Saul was with Israel's implacable enemies, the Philistines (1 Sm 27, 1—28, 2). David lied his way into the trust of Achish, who once thought him mad. David claimed to have been raiding Judahite settlements while all the time raiding those of other peoples. David was put in a very awkward position when Achish announced that a raid on Israel was in the offing. He had to assure Achish of his loyalty.

Saul's Tragic Death (1 Sm 28, 3—2 Sm 1, 27)

Saul went out to meet the Philistines one last time. The place of this final confrontation was a town near Mount Gilboa, which overlooks the Jezreel Valley. The king was terrified at the prospect of having to face the Philistines again. He consulted the Lord but received no answer. He thought to consult Samuel, who had died earlier. To do so he had to engage a specialist in conjuring the spirit of the deceased—something forbidden to Israel (see Dt 18, 11). The prophet's spirit did not give the king good news: the Israelite army would be defeated. Saul's fate is sealed.

David was saved from having to fight against Saul and the Israelites because not all the Philistines trusted him. Achish allowed David to engage in raiding the Amalekites, another of Israel's traditional enemies (1 Sm 29, 1—30, 31). The story of David's conduct during these raids stands in contrast to Saul's impotence before the Philistines: David was courageous in battle; he was fair and even generous with his soldiers; he defended the Israelites who fell victim to Amalekite power; above all, he was victorious. David's victories over the Amalekites coupled with Saul's impending loss to the Philistines showed that God was behind David's rise to power.

The book relates the end of Saul with dignity and sympathy (1 Sm 31, 1–13). Saul died doing his duty as king. Though he knew that defeat was inevitable, Saul fought bravely and died by his own hand to insure that the Philistines would be deprived of making sport of him. They did, however, hang his corpse and that of Jonathan from the walls of Beth-shan, a city near Mount Gilboa. This afforded the people of Jabesh-gilead an opportunity to repay the favor that Saul did for them in better times. They took the bodies off the city wall, transported them to Jabesh, buried them, and then began a period of mourning for their one-time benefactor.

Transitions of power in the ancient Near East were rarely smooth. Palace revolts and assassinations occurred with some frequency. The book wishes to end any rumors about David's role in Saul's death, so it portrays David as deeply affected by the deaths of Saul and Jonathan (2 Sm 1, 1–27). The Amalekite confessed to Saul's murder though the reader knows that the Amalekite is lying—perhaps to ingratiate himself with David. Still, David acted on the only information he had and ordered the confessed regicide to be executed. While David came into pos-

session of the royal insignia (v. 10), he did so without any foul play on his part. The poem lamenting the tragic deaths of Saul and Jonathan, which the book places on David's lips, came from a now-lost collection called the "Book of the Just" (see also Jos 10, 13). It shows that in some quarters, the memory of Saul and Jonathan was cherished. The book has David recite these poignantly beautiful lines to demonstrate David's innocence in Saul's death.

David Becomes King (2 Sm 2, 1—5, 25)

Saul's end was sad and tragic, but the reader has a sense of relief that David has survived both Saul and the Philistines. He is now in a position to claim the kingship for which he was anointed by Samuel. Still, it will be several years before David's position over all Israel will become secure. While David had no trouble being recognized as king in Judah (2 Sm 2, 4), his position with regard to the other tribes was a different matter. Though Abner, Saul's general, placed Ishbaal, Saul's surviving son, on the throne, Ishbaal proved incompetent. This paved the way for David's rule over all the tribes. David consolidated his rule by taking Jerusalem and making it his political capital as well as Israel's religious center.

Although the book implies that a united Israel under one king was the ideal, it is clear from the story of the war between Israel and Judah in 2 Samuel 2, 12—3, 1 and subsequent stories that there were strong political differences and intense rivalry between Israel and Judah. Even a common language, religion, and culture could not overcome these differences. For most of their history, Israel and Judah were political opponents, each establishing its own national state. The story of this rivalry is told from a southern perspective. Also, the story of the civil war between the supporters of Ishbaal and David is a necessary prelude to the actions that Solomon will take in assuring his succession to David (see 1 Kgs 2, 23–33).

The list of David's children (2 Sm 3, 2–5) inserted in the account of David's struggle over the succession to Saul is important because it introduces characters who will have significant roles in the story of Solomon's succession. Amnon, Absalom, and Adonijah each had a better claim on the succession than Solomon. But it is Solomon who would follow David on the throne.

The book describes in some detail the political maneuvers that were necessary to secure the kingship for David (2 Sm 3, 6—4, 12). A rival king and his military supporters have to be eliminated, so both Abner and Ishbaal are killed. The story absolves David from any complicity in these acts, but the waters are becoming murkier. David is no longer the simple shepherd boy who saved Israel with his slingshot. The book makes it obvious that with the monarchy come intrigues, double-dealing, even murders, which are inevitable consequences of the quest for power. While the story of David's rise to kingship is not an antimonarchic tract, the book lays bare more of the consequences of Israel's decision to have a human lord in place of its Divine Lord.

Once Ishbaal was assassinated, the elders of Israel bowed to the inevitable and accepted David as king. The newly acclaimed king then moved to eliminate the one tract of land that still separated Judah from the Israelite tribes in the north. David captured Jerusalem and made it his capital. The book pauses in its story to assert that all this happened because God was with David (5, 1–12), but then it returns to the actions that David took to solidify his hold on the throne. One of these was to marry women from Jerusalem and thereby gain sympathy from its citizens (5, 13–16).

Another practical step in David's solidifying his rule over Israel is his ending the Philistine domination of Canaan (5, 17–25). David freed Israel from the Philistine threat while Saul failed to do so (see 1 Sm 9, 16; 2 Sm 3, 18). Of course, the victory over the Philistines really belonged to God who gave David the victory (2 Sm 5, 19.24)—another indication that David was God's choice to be king. The book suggests that David's victory was so overwhelming that the battlefield was named Baal-perazim, which can be translated "the Lord of the raging flood" (2 Sm 5, 20; see Is 28, 21).

The Ark in Jerusalem (2 Sm 6, 1–23)

The final step in marking the legitimacy of David's accession to kingship was the transfer of the ark. Michal's negative reaction to David's dancing before the ark suggests the displacement of Saul's family by that of David. The housing of the ark in David's city underscores the centralizing tendencies of the monarchy, which appropriates all political, military, and religious authority to itself. This attempt to make human authority absolute will ultimately lead to the undoing of the monarchy and the national state.

Temple and Dynasty (2 Sm 7, 1–29)

In the ancient Near East, the building of a temple for a nation's patron deity was a royal prerogative. Another way that David sought to legitimate his accession to Israel's throne was to build a temple for Israel's God. The book shapes its account to make two important points. The first is that a temple was not an absolute necessity in ancient Israel's religion (2 Sm 7, 5–7). The second was that God was going to establish a "house" (a dynasty) for David that would endure forever (2 Sm 7, 16). That a prophet makes this promise in God's name marks it as authoritative (vv. 4–5). It is important to note that the promise places limits on royal authority. There are obligations that the king must fulfill (v. 14; see also Ps 89, 30–32). But failure on the king's part will not nullify the promises (vv. 15–16). While a temple was built and David's dynasty did rule for four hundred years, both came to inglorious ends in the sixth century. Eventually the Temple was rebuilt but under the patronage of a foreign dynasty (see Ezr 1, 1–4.5–6). The Davidic dynasty was never restored to rule.

A member of the Davidic family ruled over the Kingdom of Judah throughout its history, except for the six years of Athaliah's reign (2 Kgs 11), and the books of Kings allude to 2 Samuel 7 and its promises several times (1 Kgs 2, 4; 8, 20.25; 9, 4–5; 11, 5.13.32.36; 15, 4; 2 Kgs 8, 19; 19, 34; 20, 6). But the storied stability of the Davidic dynasty is an illusion. Of the twenty-one kings that succeeded to David's throne, five were assassinated, three were taken into exile, three died during sieges, and one died in battle. Five kings ruled for periods of less than three years. Most ruled by the favor of imperial powers, and at least two were placed on the throne by such powers. The kings of the Davidic dynasty were unable to stave off the disaster that came to all of the small national states in the Levant once the revived Mesopotamian empires implemented their expansionist policies. The books of Kings, however, suggest that the fall of both Israelite kingdoms was due to the religious failures of the kings who ruled over them. While finding some fault with most of Judah's kings, the books of Kings lay the principal blame on Manasseh (2 Kgs 21, 8–9; 2 Kgs 23, 26–27). The collective failure of the Davidic dynasty makes the promises made to David in 2 Samuel 7 a poignant reminder of what should have been. The story of Judah's kings is the story of Israel. What began with so much promise ends tragically.

The Babylonians deposed Zedekiah, the last king of David's line, in 587 BC, and David's house was destined never to rise again. Still, there were some who believed that Israel's future was, in some way, tied to the destiny of the Davidic dynasty. The prayer of David (2 Sm 7, 18–29) and Psalms 2, 89, and 132 reflect their views. In fact, Psalm 89, 4 and 2 Samuel 23, 5 likely have 2 Samuel 7 in mind when they speak of a "covenant" that God made with David. The Davidic covenant is similar to "covenants of royal grant" in which ancient Near Eastern kings rewarded individuals who served them loyally. It is also similar to the covenant made with Abraham (Gn 15, 7–20; 17, 1–8) in which God promises Abraham a land and descendants. But the Davidic stands in some tension with the Mosaic covenant, which depends upon Israel's obedience for its durability. There are texts, however, which attempt to make the promises to David conditional, e.g., 1 Kgs 2, 4; 8, 25; 9, 4–5; Ps 132, 12. The Scriptures preserve both the Mosaic and Davidic covenants, and the two should be seen as complementary. The former emphasizes human responsibility and the latter divine constancy.

The fall of Jerusalem, the end of the Judahite state, and the deposition of the Davidic dynasty led to a reinterpretation of the promise that there would always be a descendant of David ruling from his throne (v. 16; see Is 55, 3–5), but Zerubbabel's connection with the Davidic family (1 Chr 3, 16–19) led some Jews to look for an imminent restoration of the native dynasty (see Hg 2, 2–23; Zec 3, 8; 4, 7) following the return from Babylon. The Persians did not permit this to happen, yet there remained some Jews who did expect an eventual restoration of the dynasty (see Jer 33, 14–26; Ez 37, 24–25). Such hopes could not be sustained for too long, and the restoration of the Davidic dynasty became a feature of Jew-

ish eschatological hopes. Clearly, the promises made to David were not fulfilled in a satisfactory way following the exile. Since these promises had to find fulfillment, that fulfillment would come in the future. These developed into early Jewish hopes for a "messiah." While such hopes were not prominent in early Jewish literature, renewed interest in the promises made to David did reemerge in the first century BC. The Davidic messiah is an important figure in the Dead Sea Scrolls. The New Testament exploits this expectation as it presents Jesus as the one who will inherit the throne of "David his father" (Lk 1, 32). Indeed, the Gospels refer to Jesus as "the son of David" almost twenty times.

David's Kingdom and Its Administration
(2 Sm 8, 1–18)

The book notes that David did not limit his rule to the territories given to the Israelite tribes. David mounted expeditions to extend the borders of his kingdom. Not content with limiting his role to protecting the people of Israel from external threats, David engaged in the type of expansionist militarism to which Israel and Judah would eventually fall victim. But because David was God's chosen, he was victorious (2 Sm 8, 14b). David needed people to assist him in the administration of his kingdom. The list in 2 Samuel 8, 15–18 names those who assisted David in the military and religious spheres. Though David's sons take the role of priests, eventually Levites were recognized as the sole legitimate priests; when the Chronicler gives his list of David's administrators, he calls David's sons his "chief assistants" rather than "priests" (see 1 Chr 18, 17).

David's Family and the Succession
(2 Sm 9, 1—20, 26)

The rise of David to kingship appeared to be unstoppable, but the book notes that holding on to the throne and selecting a successor were entirely different matters. Scattered throughout the story of David's rise were assurances that all happened because of God's actions. In the story of the succession to David, God is mentioned infrequently. The book shows what kind of an institution the monarchy really was, making it clear why, in the end, the monarchy failed Israel.

The story of the succession begins with David

inquiring if any of Saul's family were still alive. While David feigned concern to fulfill his commitment to Jonathan, he effectively placed a claimant to the throne and his family under house arrest (2 Sm 9, 1–13). David thus blunted any opposition that might have sought to use the disabled Meribbaal to rally against him. The war with the Ammonites and Arameans provided the framework for another of David's attempts to secure his throne more firmly. His strategy was to marry a woman who belonged to an influential family. This is the third such marriage of David (see 1 Sm 18, 20–27; 1 Sm 25). The story seemingly makes it appear as if David's encounter with Bathsheba was fortuitous, but the attentive reader recognizes a pattern in David's marriages. David married women who could help him gain and hold onto power. Bathsheba's grandfather Ahithophel was one of David's key advisers (2 Sm 16, 23), and her father, Eliam, was an important military commander (2 Sm 23, 34). The book implies that David knew exactly who Bathsheba was. He did not hesitate to use his royal power to have Bathsheba's husband eliminated so that he, David, could marry her (2 Sm 11, 2–27).

The book then transforms a tale of adultery and murder into a homily on repentance (2 Sm 12, 1–15). The prophet Nathan appeared before the king without being summoned to announce God's verdict on David's actions. The confrontation led to David's repentance so that the sentence of death was not imposed on him. The book wants to lead its readers to conclude that if they too listened to the prophets sent to them, their lives will be spared as well. David here becomes a model of repentance. Still, the power of evil that David unleashed by his sins led to the death of Bathsheba's newborn (12, 16–23). In time, Bathsheba bore David a son, who eventually would succeed his father as king. Bathsheba named her son Solomon, while Nathan named him Jedidiah (2 Sam 12, 24–25). The reason for the prophet's action is unclear since parents were responsible for naming their child. Jedidiah means "beloved of the LORD" and may signal God's choice of Solomon as David's successor. With the story of David and Bathsheba concluded for the present, the book remarks that the war against Ammon was successful (2 Sm 12, 26–31).

David's adultery with Bathsheba and his mur-

der of Uriah meant that David and his family would have the specter of sexual excess and murder hanging over their lives for a long time to come. The first to fall victim were David's eldest son, Amnon, and Tamar, his half-sister. Amnon's attraction to his sister led him to rape her (2 Sm 13, 1–21). While appalled at his son's crime, David did not punish Amnon. The disconsolate Tamar moved in with Absalom, her full-brother. Nothing more is heard of her. Absalom, however, brooded over his sister's fate for two years. When the opportunity presented itself, Absalom had Amnon murdered. Absalom then found sanctuary in Geshur, which was located in the southern part of the area now known as the Golan Heights. His maternal grandfather was king there (2 Sm 13, 23–37; see 2 Sm 3, 3).

Eventually Joab, David's nephew and general, was able to effect a reconciliation between David and Absalom, enabling Absalom to return from exile (2 Sm 14, 1–33). Absalom was impatient with the pace of his rehabilitation, and it is clear that no genuine reconciliation between father and son took place. Absalom was still harboring grudges. This led the son to take advantage of those who expressed dissatisfaction with David's rule (2 Sm 15, 1–6). Absalom's intrigues led to a full-blown revolution, which almost succeeded (2 Sm 15, 7–12). David had to flee for his life, but he had the presence of mind to instruct his priests to remain in Jerusalem to bring him news of how the rebellion was progressing and to have his friend Hushai infiltrate Absalom's retinue. Another supporter was Ziba, one of Meribbaal's servants, who provided David with supplies and informed him that Meribbaal had designs on the throne (2 Sm 16, 1–4). During this retreat from Jerusalem, David met Shimei, one of Saul's supporters, who assured him that the rebellion was just what David deserved for usurping Saul's throne (2 Sm 16, 5–14).

Upon entering Jerusalem, Absalom dramatized his break with his father in a most decisive way. He had sexual intercourse with David's concubines in full view of the people, fulfilling the curse on David pronounced by Nathan in God's name (2 Sm 12, 11–12). Ahithophel, one of David's counselors who went over to Absalom, advised quick action against the retreating David. Hushai, David's spy in Absalom's retinue, bought David time by suggesting that Absalom assemble a large force from all the tribes to deal with David. Absalom took Hushai's advice. Here is one instance where the book calls the reader's attention to the divine hand ordering events. It asserts that God prevented Absalom from taking Ahithophel's advice (2 Sm 17, 14b). David used the time bought by Hushai to prepare a successful counterattack. Absalom fled but was caught by David's troops and killed by his cousin Joab, who countermanded David's express orders that Absalom be spared. David's obvious grief over Absalom disconcerted his soldiers who risked their lives in putting down Absalom's rebellion. David regained his composure and met with his army (2 Sm 16, 20—19, 9).

The book, however, does not have David's difficulties end with the collapse of Absalom's rebellion. David had to encourage members of Judah, his own tribe, to welcome him back as king. He had to deal with Shimei who cursed him and Meribbaal who sought to take advantage of the rebellion. He spared both. David wanted to reward Barzillai's kindness, but the latter demurred. As a result of having to face an uprising led by his own son, David realized that he owed this throne to the people and their support (2 Sm 19, 23b).

Tensions among the tribes continued, presaging a split that would occur following the death of Solomon (1 Kgs 12). A more immediate consequence of this tension is a second revolt against David. Amasa, who had been a leader of the revolt that Absalom fomented, was rehabilitated by David, who charged him with putting down a second revolt led by Sheba of Benjamin, Saul's tribe. When Amasa dawdled, Joab quickly moved in, killing Amasa and leading David's forces against Sheba, who took refuge in Abel Beth-maacah, a city in the north. The revolution ended when a woman of Abel Beth-maacah persuaded the people of the town to hand over the revolutionary (2 Sm 19, 41—20, 22).

A list of David's principal officials concludes the story of David's problems in maintaining his position as king. There were two military officials: Joab, who commanded the Israelite army, and Banaiah, who led the mercenary forces. There were two civil magistrates, Shawsha and Jehoshaphat, and two priests, Zadok and Abiathar. Adoram oversaw the prisoners of war who

had to do forced labor. The duties of Ira as David's priest are unknown (2 Sm 20, 23–26).

Miscellaneous Material (2 Sm 21, 1—24, 25)

The story of David's reign is interrupted by six appendices arranged in a chiasm:

A. A famine (21, 1–14)
  B. Military Exploits (21, 15–22)
    C. David's hymn of victory (22, 1–51)
    C'. David's final hymn (23, 1–7)
  B'. Military Exploits (23, 8–39)
A'. A plague (24, 1–25)

The lack of a river system to provide for irrigation made ancient Israel particularly vulnerable to famine when rainfall was not sufficient. The book describes one such famine, which was ascribed to the failure by members of Saul's family to honor the covenant between Israel and Gibeon (see Jos 9). David allowed the Gibeonites to take their revenge on Saul's family (2 Sm 21, 1–11). The famine ended when David provided an honorable burial for Saul and Jonathan (2 Sm 21, 12–14).

The second component of the supplementary material is difficult to square with 1 Samuel 17, which describes the young David's defeat of Goliath. 2 Samuel 21, 15–19 asserts that Goliath was killed by one of David's soldiers—a certain Elhanan—while one of David's brothers is credited with killing another formidable Philistine warrior (2 Sm 21, 20–22). One attempt at harmonizing 1 Samuel 17 and 2 Samuel 21 suggests that David and Elhanan were the same person. Elhanan supposedly took the name "David" upon taking the throne of Israel. A second alternative assumes that David killed a Philistine whose name was not preserved. David's anonymous foe was then confused with Goliath whom Elhanan killed. While both solve the problem, neither has any support in the biblical text. Following the account of Israel's victories over the Philistines, the book inserts a hymn of victory that David composed. It is virtually identical to Psalm 18. Verses 21–25 assert that it was David's obedience that led to his victories—a perspective that resonated with the views of 2 Samuel.

The poetic "last words of David" (2 Sm 23, 1–7) are really a theological commentary on David and his dynasty that emphasize the importance of justice and devotion to God (v. 3). These will lead to God's blessings on the dynasty. Those who ignore the demands of justice are doomed (vv. 6–7). David's rule as king did not depend on his virtue alone but on the support of many people. Some of these are mentioned by name in 2 Samuel 23, 8–39. Ironically, the last person on the list is Uriah. His loyalty was not reciprocated by David—something that the reader knows without being told.

The last episode in 2 Samuel describes another natural disaster: a plague (2 Sm 24). David is blamed for bringing it about by taking a census of the people. The census provided the data necessary for taxation and conscription of the population. David showed that he was not content to protect the people from their enemies; he wanted to reduce them all to the status of the king's servants. The plague destroyed the value of the data. David relented, and God delivered the country from the plague.

The books of Samuel describe the transition in leadership from that of the judges to Samuel, from Samuel to Saul, and from Saul to David. The question that arises for the reader is who will succeed David as king. One son was a rapist and was murdered to avenge his crime. Another was guilty of fratricide and attempted patricide, and died in the course of a revolution against his father. The prospects for the house of David look bleak. The opening chapter of Kings will describe the solution to the problem of succession.

Continuing Significance of the Books of Samuel

As one reads the books of Samuel and its tales of jealousy, rape, murder, and revolution, one can almost hear the author of the books of Samuel saying: "If you want a monarchy, this is what you get." The contemporary reader ought to recognize the folly of making any human institution absolute. The story of David's family shows

what can happen when one is unable to keep in check the tendency to make absolute the institution of the monarchy. The ability of any society to criticize its social structure, its economic policies, its political system is necessary to keep that society from consuming itself. Second Samuel describes how Judah's royal family began to consume itself. Though monarchies are, for the most part, relics of another age, nations still succumb to the temptation of making their political, social, and economic institutions into absolutes. The story of Israel in its land shows what happens when a nation and its leader ignore the fundamental moral values.

FURTHER READING

Anderson, Arnold A. *2 Samuel*. Word Biblical Commentary 11. Waco, TX: Word, 1989.

Brueggemann, Walter. *First and Second Samuel*. Louisville: Westminister John Knox, 1990.

Halpern, Baruch. *The Constitution of the Monarchy in Israel*. Harvard Monograph Series, no. 25. Chico, CA: Scholars Press, 1981.

Frick, F. S. "The Formation of the State in Ancient Israel: A Survey of Models and Theories." *Journal for the Study of the Old Testament (JSOT)*. Sheffield:, Sheffield Academic Press 1985.

Gunn, David. "The Fate of King Saul." *JSOT*. Sheffield: Sheffield Academic Press, 1980.

———. "The Story of David." *JSOT*. Sheffield: Sheffield Academic Press, 1982.

Hertzberg, Hans W. *1 & 2 Samuel*. Old Testament Library. Philadelphia: Westminster, 1964.

Ishida, T. *Studies in the Period of David and Solomon*. Winona Lake, IN: Eisenbrauns, 1983.

Klein, Ralph W. *1 Samuel*. Word Biblical Commentary 10. Waco, TX: Word, 1983.

McCarter, P. Kyle. *1 Samuel*. Anchor Bible 8. Garden City, NY: Doubleday, 1980

———. *2 Samuel*. Anchor Bible 9. Garden City, NY: Doubleday, 1984.

Miscall, Peter D. *1 Samuel: A Literary Reading*. Bloomington, IN: Indiana University Press, 1986.

1 AND 2 KINGS

[see pages 369–435 of the Old Testament]

Before Beginning . . .

First and Second Kings continue the story of Israel in its land. They are the final two compo-

nents of the Deuteronomistic History of Israel, which turns that story into a sermon that takes its theological principles from the book of Deuteronomy. First Kings takes up where 2 Samuel 20 ended. It describes how the problem of the succession to David was resolved. The book then goes on to tell the story of the two Israelite kingdoms that arose following Solomon's death. The division between 1 and 2 Kings is artificial since it is made in the middle of telling the story of King Ahaziah of Israel. Second Kings ends rather abruptly after telling of the parole of King Jehoiachin of Judah from prison in Babylon. The book allows readers to draw their own conclusions regarding the significance of this event. There is, then, no happy ending to the story of Israel in its land. What began with so much promise ends with great tragedy.

Reading through 1 and 2 Kings

Certainly, the author of Kings used a variety of sources—from royal archives to prophetic legends—in composing his story. But in the form in which we read the book of Kings, it is probably the work of a single individual, writing during or shortly after the exile when the shape of Judah's future was unclear. The institutions that gave meaning to Israel's national and religious life were dead. The Temple of Jerusalem was in ruins and its priesthood scattered. The likelihood of a restoration of the Davidic dynasty seemed remote. The Israelite national states no longer existed. Their territory was simply incorporated into the conquering Mesopotamian empires. Imbued with the religious perspectives of the book of Deuteronomy, Kings clearly states that the downfall of Israel and Judah was a consequence of their disobedience, but it implies that Judah may still have a future if it learns obedience.

The books of Kings are anything but objective. First, they reflect a clear bias in favor of Judah and so they write off the Northern Kingdom as a complete loss. Not a single monarch from the Northern Kingdom receives a positive evaluation. Second, Kings does praise a few kings of Judah, but most are condemned. In the author's eyes, most kings promoted or at least allowed worship that did not reflect the uniqueness of Israel's God and the absolute loyalty that Israel owed to its divine patron. Third, the author is completely convinced of the centrality of the Torah in Israel's life with God. Every other religious institution is secondary to it. To make its theological points, the book uses speeches, prayers, and sometimes editorial comments. Attention to these forms will help the

reader become acquainted with the spin the book puts on the events it narrates.

Finally, the books of Kings are part of a larger work that begins with Joshua and is sometimes called the "Deuteronomistic History." It is important to remember that while the adjective Deuteronomistic is appropriate, the term history is not. The book is an exponent of Deuteronomy's theology, but the author is not a historian—at least not in the modern sense. The author is more of a preacher or moralist as he turns Israel's past into a sermon. The author of Kings directs those who want "historical" information to sources like the Chronicles of Solomon (1 Kgs 11, 41), the Chronicles of the Kings of Judah (1 Kgs 14, 29 and fourteen more times) and the Chronicles of the Kings of Israel (1 Kgs 14, 19 and sixteen more times)—sources that are, unfortunately, lost. Also, the relative chronologies of the kings of Judah and Israel do not mesh, and contemporary historians have not been able to reconcile these differences. The book passes over kings of great historical import with a few lines, while it devotes chapters to kings that the book considers models of religious commitment. One can use the books of Kings to help reconstruct the history of the Israelite kingdoms, but these books were not written for that purpose. It is important to relate the contents of the books of Kings to other ancient Near Eastern written sources and to the results of archaeological excavations. But none of this diminishes the book's theological achievements. This massive work enabled the exiles to make sense of events that challenged their most deeply held religious beliefs. The book's passion to keep Judah's faith in its ancestral deity alive despite terrible odds offers a model to all those who hand on the faith today, so reading the books of Kings can be as important today as it was millennia ago.

Solomon's Accession (1 Kgs 1, 1—2, 46)

With David a very old man, unable even to keep himself warm, the question of succession became acute. There were two competing candidates: Adonijah and Solomon. Neither was designated by a divine word given through a prophet as were Saul and David. The throne would go to the better practitioner of power politics. Adonijah was born in Hebron and was favored by David's oldest supporters: Joab and

Abiathar. Solomon was born in Jerusalem and was favored by his mother Bathsheba and those who supported David after he established himself in that city. That Adonijah was Absalom's full brother (1 Kgs 1, 6) presaged the outcome of the contest.

Adonijah and Solomon took different approaches toward the succession. Adonijah acted in his own person, claiming the throne for himself. Solomon was content to let his supporters manipulate his father into designating him as the successor to the throne. The book describes two simultaneous ceremonies—each of which was to inaugurate David's successor. The ceremonies took place near Jerusalem at two sites in shouting distance of each other. Adonijah chose En-rogel, a spring located at the juncture of the Hinnom and Kidron Valleys just south of Jerusalem; Solomon had his ceremony at the Gihon Spring, Jerusalem's main water source, at the base of the eastern slope of David's city. Solomon was able to bring more people to his ceremony; after all, he was the candidate of the Jerusalem party. When Adonijah and his supporters heard the crowd acclaim Solomon as their king, they lost heart and fled. Adonijah submitted to Solomon's authority and begged for his life, which Solomon chose to spare.

With the succession settled, the book had David make his exit. Of course, a person as important as David must have some significant last words to say. The book provides David with a schizophrenic-like testament (1 Kgs 2, 1–9). The first to speak is the "pious David" who charges his successor to be obedient to the written authoritative Torah, i.e., the book of Deuteronomy. It will be through his obedience that Solomon will secure the throne for himself and his successors (vv. 2–4). Then it is the turn of the "practical David." He knew from experience that gaining the throne and keeping the throne are two different things. The last words of David recorded in 1 Kings identify those who have shown themselves a threat to the dynasty. David was certain that Solomon would know what needed to be done (vv. 5–9).

The reader does not have to wait long to learn how Solomon dealt with potential troublemakers (1 Kgs 2, 12–46). First, he had Adonijah killed. The imprudent Adonijah gave Solomon a pretext when he asked to marry Abishag, one of David's secondary wives. Solomon chose to interpret Adonijah's foolish request as treason. The new king then dealt with Adonijah's principal supporters. He had Joab killed and sent Abiathar to internal exile. For good measure, Solomon had Shimei, David's tormentor, executed as well (see 2 Sm 16, 6–14; 19, 16–24). The book allows its readers to draw their own conclusions regarding the path Solomon took to the throne. Notably absent from these first two chapters is any statement or even a hint that God had any role in Solomon's succession.

It is important to note the role that Bathsheba, Solomon's mother, played in his rise to the throne. After he became king, she enjoyed access to him and was seated near his throne at official functions (1 Kgs 2, 19–20). The books of Kings name the mothers of seventeen other kings—all but two kings of Judah (Jehoram and Ahaz) and two kings of Israel. This had led to the conclusion that the "queen mother" has an official position and exercised political and religious power. Unfortunately, the book does not provide the type of information that would permit firm conclusions to be drawn. That the author made it a point to mention the mother of eighteen kings by name, however, makes it obvious that the "queen mother" enjoyed a specific rank and exercised some power—especially over domestic matters.

Solomon's Reign (1 Kgs 3, 1—11, 43)

The account of Solomon's reign begins with an introductory statement that encapsulates the book's ambivalence toward David's son (1 Kgs 3, 1–3). On the one hand, the reader is told that Solomon "loved the LORD" (v. 3), fulfilling the great commandment of Deuteronomy (see Dt 6, 5). But, on the other hand, he married a foreign princess and worshipped on the "high places." The Deuteronomic tradition takes a dim view of both patterns of behavior (see Dt 7, 1–4; 1 Kgs 3, 2–3 and twenty-eight more times). Like Israel's life in the land, Solomon's reign will begin well enough, but it will soon founder because of an unwillingness to be faithful to the most basic of the Torah's commands: absolute fidelity to Israel's God.

The book finally gets around to providing divine legitimation for Solomon's accession (1 Kgs 3, 4–15). It does so by having God approve of Solomon's status as king through an appearance in a dream, which the Bible considers as one way that God communicates with human beings. The story reflects an ancient Near Eastern practice (called "incubation") of seeking an oracle by sleeping in a sanctuary after offering the prescribed sacrifices. Any dream experienced during this sleep was considered a revelation from the god honored at the sanctuary. The dream concerned Solomon's request for God's help in ruling Israel wisely. The request was granted. The book follows up the account of the dream with a tale illustrating Solomon's wisdom (1 Kgs 3, 16–28). Solomon was able to settle a dispute between two women over an infant, which each claimed as her own, because he knew that the true mother would sacrifice anything to insure the welfare of her child.

The book pauses in its narrative about Solomon's reign to include information about Solomon's administration, wealth, and wisdom (1 Kgs 4, 1—5, 14). The editors of the NAB rearrange the versification of this section as follows: 4, 1–6 (Solomon's administrators); 4, 7–19; 5, 7–8 (districts for taxation); 4, 20 (the kingdom's prosperity); 5, 2–6 (Solomon's wealth); 5, 9–14 (Solomon's wisdom). First Samuel mentioned almost nothing about Saul's administration. Second Samuel named nine administrators during David's reign (see 2 Sm 8, 16–18; 20, 23–26). It is clear from the list of Solomon's administrators (1 Kgs 4, 1–19) that the centralization of all authority in the monarchy became a priority under Solomon. He developed an efficient apparatus to do what Samuel warned them that their king would do: tax them (see 1 Sm 8, 10–18). The book also makes a point of noting that Solomon set up his sons-in-law over two of the districts (1 Kgs 4, 11.15) and that Judah, Solomon's tribe, was not included among the taxation districts. The people had asked Samuel for a king to rule over them "like other nations" (1 Sm 8). The book implies that the taxation, nepotism, and cronyism assure them that they have such a king. Deuteronomy requires that the king study the Torah so that he not "become estranged from his countrymen" (Dt 17, 20). The list of the king's daily provisions (1 Kgs 5, 1–5) certainly sounded more than extravagant to Judah's subsistence farmers. The divide between the royal establishment and the general population was

becoming more pronounced. Still, 1 Kings 4, 20 (note: this verse has been moved to ch. 5) and 5, 5 describe Solomon's reign as a time of peace and prosperity.

Just as Moses was associated with Torah and David with the psalms, Solomon was remembered as a sage (see Prv 1, 1; Sir 47, 12). To conclude its initial portrait of Solomon, the book asserts that Solomon's wisdom was unsurpassed. His wisdom attracted admirers from all over the world (5, 9–14). The reader recognizes that Solomon's court is far different from that of Saul— and even David.

Next, the book describes a project with which Solomon's name is always associated: the building of the Temple (1 Kgs 5, 15–32). While the account implies that the project was ordained by God, temple building was a royal prerogative in the ancient Near East. By initiating the project of erecting a temple to Israel's patron deity in Jerusalem, his capital, Solomon was asserting, in most dramatic form, his claim to Israel's throne. The book has Solomon explain that David did not build a temple because he was almost continuously at war (1 Kgs 5, 17). Solomon also used good Deuteronomic language as he said that he was going to build a temple "for the name of God" (v. 19, literal translation). The Deuteronomic tradition usually avoided describing the Temple as God's dwelling place, preferring to speak of the Temple as the place for God's name (see Dt 12, 11). To be consistent with its portrait of Solomon as an Israelite king with an international reputation, the book has the king using his contacts to assemble the best material and artisans from surrounding countries for his project, while ordinary Israelites contributed their labor to the project.

The book goes into some detail in describing the building of the Temple. It gives the date for both the beginning and the completion of the project (1 Kgs 6, 1–37) and describes the dimensions of the building and its tripartite structure. The Temple was to have a porch, a nave, and a "holy of holies." The latter was a windowless room that was to contain the ark of the covenant, the symbol of the divine presence. In the holy of holies, there were to be two cherubim (1 Kgs 6, 23–28). A cherub was a mythical creature that had the face of a human being, the forequarters of a lion, the hindquarters of an ox, and wings of an eagle. The ark of the covenant would be placed between the two cherubim.

The book clearly wants readers to think of the Temple as a most impressive building. Solomon spared no expense in its construction and ornamentation. He overlaid the entire structure with gold (1 Kgs 6, 22). At the same time, however, the book offers an explanation for the eventual destruction of this singular structure. It presents God as warning Solomon that God will never forsake Israel, the dynasty, or the Temple if he keeps the commandments (1 Kgs 6, 12). Kings will describe how Solomon and most of Israel's kings failed, leaving God to abandon the Temple that Solomon built.

The book inserts a short description of five other structures that it credits to Solomon's building activity (1 Kgs 7, 1–12), implying that as much as the Temple was designed to show that the Lord was a great God, it and the other buildings Solomon had built were designed to show that Solomon was a great king. These five structures were the "Forest of Lebanon," which was larger than the Temple, the "Columned Hall," the "Throne Hall" (or "Hall of Justice"), and palaces for himself and for the pharaoh's daughter. Completing these projects took almost double the time it took to build the Temple (1 Kgs 6, 38; 7, 1). The text provides little information about the structures themselves, and archaeological excavation has not uncovered any such buildings.

After mentioning Solomon's other projects, the book returns to the Temple and describes some of its furnishings (1 Kgs 7, 13–51). The artisan responsible for crafting these furnishings was named Hiram though v. 40 (in the Hebrew) calls him Hirom. The Chronicler remembers him as Huram (2 Chr 4, 11) and Huram-abi (2 Chr 2, 13; 4, 16). Of particular interest are the two bronze pillars (1 Kgs 7, 15–22). Their appearance and function are difficult to reconstruct given the information in the text. They were probably symbolic because they did not support any part of the structure and because they were given names. The bronze sea (vv. 23–26), the wheeled stands (vv. 27–37), and the basins (vv. 38–39) testify to the need for large volumes of water that had to be kept in the Temple area to cleanse it from the contamination caused by the blood of the sacrifices offered there.

With the Temple and its furnishings completed, all is ready for the building's dedication. The book provides a narrative framework (1 Kgs 8, 1–9; 62–66) for a lengthy prayer that Solomon offered at the dedication. The framework describes the transfer of the ark to the newly built Temple and the sacrifices offered there for the first time. The prayer, however, seems to prepare the reader for a world without a Temple. The words of the prayer are, at times, in conflict with each other. Verses 10–13 speak about God's presence in the Temple while v. 27 asserts that God cannot be contained in the building that Solomon had just built. The prayer also appears to transform the Temple from a place of sacrificial offerings (vv. 5 and 66) into a place of prayer where Israelite and non-Israelite alike can ask for forgiveness (vv. 42–43). Indeed, one does not even need to be present in the Temple to be heard by God. All that is necessary is that one pray in the direction of Jerusalem and its Temple (vv. 38, 48; see Dn 6, 11). The author of Kings composed this prayer to help his readers cope with the loss of the Temple.

The book uses another speech to reiterate its explanation for the disastrous end of the Davidic dynasty and the destruction of the Temple (1 Kgs 9, 1–9). After all, the prayer of Solomon had just praised God for fulfilling the promise to David (1 Kgs 8, 14–29) and celebrated the dedication of the Temple. God appeared to Solomon and warned him that the future of the dynasty and the Temple depended on the fidelity of Israel's kings to the commandments and on Israel's exclusive loyalty to its ancestral deity. The conclusion is obvious: the destruction of the Temple and the end of the dynasty did not occur because of any lack of fidelity on God's part. The people of Israel and their kings bear full responsibility for the fall of the two Israelite states and the exile of their people. Of course, the book wants its readers to recognize that the converse is true as well: obedience will bring God's blessing to the people and their land.

The book brings its treatment of the temple to a close by mentioning some economic and personnel issues (1 Kgs 9, 10–25). The assistance that Hiram, the king of Tyre, gave to Solomon in completing his building projects came at a price. Solomon ceded twenty cities along the Galilean border with Tyre to Hiram. Also, the labor for the projects was supplied not by Israelites but by prisoners of war. The issue of forced labor proved to be one that undermined the relations between the king and people. Even though 1 Kings 5, 27 suggests that Solomon got skilled workers for the Temple project from Israel, 1 Kings 9, 20 asserts that the laborers came from non-Israelite prisoners of war. The Millo mentioned in 1 Kings 9, 24 was probably a structure that supported the terrace work that allowed building on the steep grades of the Ophel hill on which monarchic period Jerusalem was built.

Next, the book describes the splendor of Solomon's reign by focusing on his wealth, wisdom, and chariot forces (1 Kgs 9, 26—10, 29). Eleven times the text mentions the gold that the king amassed. It also notes that the queen of Sheba came to Jerusalem because of Solomon's renown as a sage. Sheba was located at the southwestern corner of the Arabian peninsula and was likely one of Judah's trading partners. Goods passed between these two countries through the Red Sea port at Ezion-geber. According to an Ethiopian tradition, their country was Sheba, and the results of the queen's visit to Solomon included her conversion to his religion and a son fathered by Solomon. This son visited his father and returned to Ethiopia with the ark of the covenant. While there is no biblical support for this tradition, it does explain the reason some people claim that the ark of the covenant is in Ethiopia.

From the book's perspective, the luster of all Solomon's achievements was tarnished by his failure to support the worship of the Lord alone. The reason offered for Solomon's infidelity was his marriage to non-Israelite women. Of course, the book is trying to promote marriage within the Judahite community as one way to maintain Judahite identity. To show the seriousness of Solomon's failure, the text has God speak to Solomon for a third and final time, announcing the end of the Davidic-Solomonic kingdom and the rise of another Israelite national state, which will occur after Solomon's death (1 Kgs 11, 1–13).

First Kings concludes its story of Solomon's reign by mentioning three of Solomon's rivals (1 Kgs 11, 14–40). The first is Hadad, king of Edom. Judah and Edom were perennial rivals for control of the southern part of the Levant. The second was Rezon who was "king of Damascus," the capital of Aram. Israel and Aram struggled

for many years for hegemony in the northern part of the Levant. The most serious threat, however, was an internal one. Jeroboam, one of Solomon's administrators, was supported in a bid for kingship by Egypt and with prophetic designation, threatening the rule of the Davidic dynasty. Although the rebellion was not successful at first, the book explains the origins of the two Israelite national states, Israel and Judah, as a consequence of Jeroboam's attempt to replace Solomon, who simply failed to observe the commandments and to worship the Lord alone. It is important to note that the book asserts that, despite Jeroboam, the Davidic dynasty continued in existence not only for the sake of David but also for the sake of Jerusalem. That city was destined to take on paramount importance for Judaism. The Temple, however, is not mentioned specifically. Also significant is the role played by the prophet Ahijah, who like Samuel, pronounced words of judgment on the king. The book again was suggesting that Israel listen to the prophets sent to it.

Like the reigns of his predecessors Saul and David, Solomon's began with great promise but ended with an unfavorable picture of the king, thus presaging the story of the people of Israel in their land. The book notes that Solomon was buried in the City of David after a reign of forty years and was succeeded by his son Rehoboam.

The Two Kingdoms
(1 Kgs 12, 1—2 Kgs 17, 41)

The two Israelite national states arose in the Levant sometime in the ninth century BC. Historians still have not arrived at a consensus as to the developments that led to their establishment. First Kings, however, describes the origins of the two Israelite states as the result of divine judgment on Solomon's rule, communicated by the prophet Ahijah. What Ahijah foretold was fulfilled almost immediately after Solomon's death and the accession of his son Rehoboam. But as it did with the origins of the monarchy, the book will describe the origins of the two Israelite national states in economic as well as religious terms (1 Kgs 12, 1–25). Rehoboam refused to lighten the economic burdens that Solomon imposed on his subjects, and before Rehoboam was able to consolidate his hold on his father's realm, there was a revolution that led to the establishment of the Kingdom of Israel separate from the Kingdom of Judah. When Rehoboam attempted to use military force against the rebellion, he was dissuaded by another prophetic word given through Shemaiah.

While Kings implies that the Israelites had legitimate grievances, it does not approve of religious practices, which it characterizes as obscuring the unity of Israel's ancestral deity, as violating the prohibition of images, and as ignoring the place that God chose. The book presents Jeroboam as fearing that the Jerusalem Temple will be a magnet, drawing the people to Jerusalem and to the Davidic dynasty. To counter this Jeroboam built cultic centers at Dan at the extreme north of his kingdom and at Bethel in the extreme south (1 Kgs 12, 26–33). The book makes its attitude toward these cultic centers absolutely clear when it depicts an unnamed "man of God" from Judah condemning the shrine at Bethel (1 Kgs 13, 1–10). As the story of the Northern Kingdom unfolds, every king of Israel will be condemned for maintaining these shrines and continuing "the sin of Jeroboam."

This man of God left Bethel because God had told him to eat or drink nothing there but to return to Judah. On his way home, he met an unnamed prophet, who convinced him to return to Bethel and enjoy his hospitality. Because he disobeyed God's instructions, the man of God from Judah died a violent death. But the prophet from Bethel lied to the man of God in convincing him to accept hospitality (1 Kgs 13, 11–32). Here the book exposes a practical problem connected with prophecy: how does one know whether a prophet is actually speaking in the name of God? Of course, the book wants its readers to recognize that the written authoritative Torah (the book of Deuteronomy) is the authentic, reliable, and unambiguous statement of God's will for Israel.

First Kings concludes its treatment of Jeroboam by revisiting the theme of succession (1 Kgs 14, 1–20). Abijah, Jeroboam's heir, fell ill and Jeroboam had his wife visit the prophet Ahijah in order to elicit a favorable oracle on behalf of the child. The prophet, however, predicted not only that the child was to die but also that Jeroboam's dynasty would end violently. Ahijah's speech is an intense and sometimes vulgar invective. While the prophet was not specific about Jeroboam's failures, he was quite specific about

the king's future and that of the nation. He even blamed the exile on Jeroboam (v. 16).

The book intertwines narratives about the kings of the two Israelite national states until it tells of the fall of the Northern Kingdom to the Assyrians in 2 Kings 17. The two Israelite kingdoms were rivals at first. Disputes over the border that they shared were almost continuous. The book notes that Israel and Judah fought continuously during the reigns of Jeroboam and Rehoboam (1 Kgs 14, 30). Rehoboam also had to deal with a raid by Pharaoh Shishak, who had given asylum to Jeroboam during the reign of Solomon (1 Kgs 11, 40). While the Egyptians were not in a position to reestablish the hegemony over the region, they raided 154 towns in the two kingdoms. Jerusalem was spared only because Rehoboam paid a large indemnity to Shishak (1 Kgs 14, 26). The book characterizes Rehoboam's reign as a time of apostasy (1 Kgs 14, 21–24).

The border wars between the two Israelite kingdoms continued during the reign of Abijam in Judah (1 Kgs 15, 7). The book provides no other information about Abijam's short reign except to note that he that he was nothing like David, whom the book begins to idealize even though it mentions David's lapse "in the case of Uriah" (1 Kgs 15, 5; see 2 Sm 11). The book devotes more attention to Asa, Abijam's son. He is one of the few kings of Judah whom the book commends because of his actions to rid Judah of non-Yahwistic worship. Asa also induced the Arameans to invade the Northern Kingdom. With the army of Israel occupied with the Arameans, Asa had a free hand to extend the border to Mizpeh, a town about five miles north of Jerusalem, where it remained until the fall of the Northern Kingdom in 721 BC.

The book next turns its attention to the Northern Kingdom for almost the rest of 1 Kings (15, 25—22, 40). After Jeroboam's twenty-two-year reign, the political situation in the north became very unstable. Nadab, Jeroboam's son and successor, was assassinated in the course of a war with the Philistines. The coup was led by Baasha, who purged Jeroboam's entire family in order to secure his own accession to the throne. Of course, the book sees this as a fulfillment of Ahijah's prophecy (1 Kgs 14, 10) and a consequence of Nadab's infidelity. Baasha proved to be no improvement over Nadab although he did manage to hold the throne for twenty-four years (15, 33—16, 7). Kings notes that a prophet named Jehu announced the end of Baasha's dynasty (16, 1–5.7) just as Ahijah announced the end of Jeroboam's dynasty. Jehu's words were fulfilled as Baasha's son and successor Elah was assassinated during a military coup after just two years on the throne. Zimri, the leader of the coup, purged all the descendants of Baasha to solidify his claim to the throne (16, 8–14). Omri, another Israelite general, decided to lead a coup of his own. His success led Zimri to take his life after a reign of just seven days. Of course, the book suggests Zimri's fate was the consequence of his religious infidelity. After a short civil war (1 Kgs 16, 21–22), Omri became king of Israel.

Even though Kings almost completely ignores Omri (1 Kgs 17, 23–28), he was arguably the most able ruler of the Northern Kingdom. His reign reversed Israel's fortunes. He ended the Aramean threat. He revived Israel's commercial fortunes by aligning himself with Phoenicia, sealing the alliance with the marriage of his son Ahab with Jezebel, the daughter of Ethbaal, king of Sidon. Omri ended the fifty years of fruitless conflict with Judah. He subjugated Moab and this brought the King's Highway, a major commercial highway east of the Jordan, under his control. The dynasty he established lasted four generations, providing a measure of stability to Israel. All this brought a new era of peace and prosperity to the Northern Kingdom. While Kings ignores these achievements because they do not correspond with its theological purpose, it does note that Omri established his capital at Samaria where Omri was buried.

Ahab succeeded his father Omri. It was the first successful dynastic succession in the Kingdom of Israel. From a military, economic, and political perspective, Ahab's reign was remarkably successful. His only defeat was the loss of Moab toward the end of his twenty-two-year reign. Excavations at several cities in the north show that Ahab's reign was one of economic growth and military strength. His greatest military achievement took place at the battle of Qarqar, which the book ignores. Ahab led a coalition of small states that successfully engaged the Assyrians and prevented them from taking control of the region. Ahab led the largest force in the coalition. The book chooses to focus on Ahab's serious internal

problems by introducing several stories about the prophets Elijah and Elisha. Both prophets were highly critical of the religious and social policies of Ahab and his successors.

Kings implies that Ahab's problems were caused by his Phoenician wife Jezebel, who promoted the worship of Baal. The prophet Elijah forcefully opposed her. The conflict between Elijah and Ahab over Jezebel's activity dominates the portrait of Ahab in the Bible and makes it appear as if he were a weak and ineffective ruler when the opposite was true. The worship of Baal was attractive because this god was thought to provide the rain that made Israel's survival on its land possible. To show that Baal was unable to provide rain, Elijah announced a drought (1 Kgs 17, 1). God's power to provide was obvious when a dry river bed yielded water for the prophet, and ravens brought him food. When the stream dried up again, the prophet went to beg in a Sidonian town. A poor widow from that town, who took pity on the prophet, never ran out of food despite the famine induced by the drought (1 Kgs 17, 2–16). An even more remarkable demonstration of God's power occurred when the prophet brought the widow's deceased son back to life (1 Kgs 17, 17–24).

Elijah finally met Ahab, who blamed the prophet for the drought. Of course, the reader knows that the fault lies with Ahab. While the confrontation with the prophets of Baal on Mount Carmel was another indication of the power of Israel's God (1 Kgs 18, 20–40), it was the prophet's prayer for rain that brought relief to the suffering people (1 Kgs 18, 41–46). The rain that comes on the land does not end the tension in the story because Jezebel was determined to avenge Elijah's victory at Mount Carmel. The prophet fled to the south, stopping at Beersheba, a town that abuts the Negev desert. After a brief pause, Elijah continued his journey until he reached Horeb, which is the name by which the Deuteronomic tradition knows Mount Sinai. At the place where the Israelites experienced God's presence in a most dramatic way, the prophet experienced only God's absence until he realized God was present in a "whispering sound" (1 Kgs 19, 12). God then commissioned the prophet to take specific steps to deal with the apostasy fomented by Israel's royal family. One of these steps is the anointing of a prophet to succeed him. Elijah found Elisha, whom the Lord had designated, and called him to his prophetic ministry (1 Kgs 19, 13–21).

The book sets aside its narrative about Elijah and Elisha and interjects a story about an unnamed prophet who confronts Ahab during a war between Aram and Israel (1 Kgs 20, 1–43). Aram, southern Syria with its capital Damascus, was probably the most powerful kingdom in the Levant between the eleventh and eighth centuries BC. However, historians have had problems with the stories of a war between Aram and Israel during Ahab's reign. Both Ahab and Omri were powerful kings and were not dominated by the Arameans as suggested in this story (1 Kgs 20, 1–9.34). The details of the story reflect the relations between Aram and Israel, which were characteristic of the reigns of Jehoahaz and Jehoash fifty years later when Israel was much weaker politically and militarily. Although the book may have provided this story with an incorrect setting, its theological point is clear enough as it tells a tale similar to that of Saul and the Amalekite war in 1 Samuel 15. Both Saul and Ahab fail to heed the instructions given by a prophet and stand under divine judgment. The lesson is obvious: Israel must listen to the prophets sent to it if it is to have any future.

The book returns to the conflict between king and prophet as it tells the tale of Naboth's vineyard (1 Kgs 21, 1–29). Again, it is Jezebel, Ahab's non-Israelite wife, who is responsible for the trouble. Ahab recognized that Naboth was within his rights in refusing to sell the king his vineyard. Jezebel, however, co-opted the elders of Naboth's city into convicting him on trumped-up charges of blasphemy and treason. Naboth was executed and his property forfeited to the crown, so Jezebel was able to present her husband with Naboth's vineyard. Of course, Elijah condemned this blatant injustice in God's name. Surprisingly, Ahab repented upon hearing the prophet's words of judgment, and God spared his life. Again, the book's message is obvious: if Israel listens to the prophets God sends to it, Israel's life will be spared as well.

But just as the book finished commending the prophetic word to Israel, it shows that discerning that word is not a simple matter. To do so the book describes preparations for a second war between Israel and Aram during the waning years of Ahab's reign (1 Kgs 22, 1–28). This time Ahab sought help from Jehoshaphat, the king of Judah. Relations between the two Israelite states had steadily improved since the time of Ahab's father, Omri. Indeed, Ahab offered his daughter in marriage to Jehoram, Jehoshaphat's son (2 Kgs 8, 18). The king of Judah, however, suggested seeking a word from God before embarking on any campaign against the powerful Arameans. Ahab assembled four hundred prophets to impress Jehoshaphat. After the four hundred encourage an attack, Jehoshaphat, apparently reluctant to fight the Arameans, asked if there were any more prophets who might be consulted. Ahab summoned Micaiah ben Imlah, who predicted an Aramean victory. Micaiah asserted that God put a "lying spirit" in the four hundred prophets to insure that Ahab would be defeated. How then could prophecy be a reliable guide if God can inspire prophets to lie? The book assumes that the one reliable and unimpeachable guide to Israel's life is the written, authoritative Torah, the book of Deuteronomy. The attitude of Kings toward Ahab is evident from the description of what happened when Ahab's chariot was cleansed of the fallen king's blood (1 Kgs 22, 38).

The book returns briefly to the Judahite monarchy and gives a qualified commendation to Jehoshaphat, who followed the good example of his father, Asa. The book also notes that Jehoshaphat was "at peace" with Israel, though it also claims that the king led Judah bravely in some wars but gives no details (1 Kgs 15, 45–46).

The story of Ahaziah of Israel straddles 1 and 2 Kings. Since he reigned for a little more than one year, the book gives just a brief and disapproving summary of his rule, emphasizing his promotion of Baal worship (1 Kgs 22, 52–54). The first chapter of 2 Kings offers an illustration of Ahaziah's apostasy (2 Kgs 1, 2–6). The king sought an oracle from the Baal worshipped at Ekron.

When Elijah intercepted the king's messengers and proclaimed an oracle from the God of Israel, Ahaziah sought to arrest him. But the conflict between king and prophet was no real match (2 Kgs 1, 7–16). The book is building up its case showing the failure of the monarchy. It wants to show that the political disasters that befell both Israelite kingdoms were a direct result of the apostasy of their kings (see Dt 4, 25–28).

The book presents the prophets as the foils of Israel's apostate kings, so after describing the failures of Ahab and his son Ahaziah, it turns its attention back to Elijah and Elisha and the transition from the prophetic ministry of the former to that of the latter (2 Kgs 2, 1–18). The narrative is purposely reminiscent of the traditions regarding the transition in the leadership of the Israelite community from Moses to Joshua. The book sees the succession of Elisha to the prophetic ministry as a genuine act of God. Perhaps a story with such spectacular details served to show that Elisha was a true witness to the God of Israel as was Elijah in contrast to the prophets that supported the house of Ahab (see 2 Kgs 3, 13). Fifty "guild prophets" witness the passing of the prophetic mantle to Elisha (2 Kgs 2, 15). Except for 1 Kings 20, 35, these guild prophets are always mentioned in connection with Elisha and may have been his supporters against the king and his prophets. The book concludes its introduction to the cycle of stories about Elisha with two tales that encourage Israel to obey the prophets sent to it (2 Kgs 2, 19–25).

The book shifts attention to the house of Ahab again. After the short reign of the childless Ahaziah, his brother Jehoram (Joram) became king of Israel (2 Kgs 3, 1–3). While Kings asserts that Moab's revolt took place during Jehoram's reign, it was more likely during Ahab's final years. Jehoram was simply unsuccessful in regaining control over Moab. Moab was a kingdom located east of the Dead Sea and west of the Arabian desert. It had been a vassal to Israel since the time of Omri. The Mesha stele, a monument celebrating Moab's victory over Israel, gives an account of this revolt from the Moabite perspective. Although both the biblical and Moabite accounts agree that Mesha, the king of Moab, was successful in regaining his country's independence, the book provides little historical information but a clear theological interpretation. It insists that apostasy always brings defeat. The extent of the territory under Israelite control was a tangible indication of God's blessings according to the book, and the success of Mesha's revolt and the consequent loss of Moab show that Israel was on a downward spiral because of its infidelity (2 Kgs 3, 4–27).

The book transfers the focus of its story away from kings and international political conflicts to ordinary folk in need—people whose names are never given (2 Kgs 4, 1–44). Elisha, whom this chapter refers to as a "man of God," responds to those needs with compassion. While the effect on the reader is to wonder at the miracle-working power of Elisha, the stories do not even hint that the man of God worked these miracles to establish his reputation. The book implies that Elisha did what the kings were supposed to do: respond to the needs of the lowly and poor. In fact, the reason ordinary people were in need was the economic and political policies of the monarchy. God redresses this injustice through Elisha. The prophetic task is not simply to speak words of judgment on injustice but to undo the effects of the greed that creates poverty.

With the story of Naaman, Elisha moves back into the arena of international politics (2 Kgs 5, 1–19). This is the second time the book has told a tale of someone searching for healing in a foreign country. In 2 Kings 1, it was King Ahaziah of Israel looking for healing in Ekron from Baalzebub. In 2 Kings 5, it is Naaman from Aram who looks for healing in Israel. Whereas the healings in 2 Kings 4 took place because of Elisha's compassion for those in need, here there is an overt apologetic purpose: Naaman is to learn that there was a prophet in Israel who could heal in the name of Israel's God. The Aramean general learned this lesson. There is also a homiletic character to the story. Naaman is a model for Israel. Although reluctant at first, the Aramean general obeyed the prophet and was healed. Israel surely should obey the prophets sent to it. Two more stories with a clear homiletic thrust follow (2 Kgs 5, 20—6, 7). Both stories concern the prophet's followers. In the first, Gehazi seeks to reap a monetary profit from his association with Elisha and is duly punished for his avarice. In the second, Elisha's supporters find themselves in an embarrassing situation, which the prophet resolves. The book warns against venality. Though the story of Naaman presupposes that there was peace between Aram and Israel, the book asserts that the situation changed as it describes two incidents between Israel and its neighbor to the north. The first shows that of itself Aram posed no danger to Israel (2 Kgs 6, 8–23). The prophet made the Arameans look foolish as he led them into Samaria. Fortunately for them, the prophet told the king to spare the lives of his prisoners.

The circumstances change abruptly in the story of Ben-hadad's siege of Samaria (2 Kgs 6, 24–33). A siege sought to force surrender by cutting off the supply of food. Ben-hadad's siege of the Israelite capital was working as is evident from the horrific details that the book gives (vv. 28–29). The apostasy of Omri and his successors is having its full effect as Aram jeopardized Israel's very existence. The king, of course, did not accept responsibility for Samaria's troubles; he blamed the prophet whom the book describes as cowering behind a closed door in fear of the king's anger. The Aramean threat was a harbinger of things to come. Aram here is an instrument of divine judgment on Israel's apostasy— apostasy that continued without abatement. But Israel's time had not yet come, so 2 Kings 7, 1–20 tells of the lifting of the Aramean siege of Samaria. The book makes it clear that the lifting of the siege and the relief of Samaria were not the work of Israel's military. God's power lifted the siege, and four lepers—by sheer happenstance— open the way to the city's relief from the famine. The book shows readers that Israel's God shapes human events through the prophetic word. Just as easily as God made Aram a threat to Israel, God removed that threat. This is another hint to the book's first readers that God can end their exile.

The epilogue to the story of Elisha and the woman of Shunem (2 Kgs 8, 1–6; see 2 Kgs 5, 8–37) is unusual on two counts. First, the prophet does not directly solve her problem. In fact, she is suffering economic privation precisely because she followed the prophet's instructions to relocate from Israel. Upon returning, she found her property had been confiscated. Still, just the power of the prophet's fame was enough to solve her problem. Second, it was the king who restored the woman's property. For once, an Israelite king did act for the benefit of those in need. The book illustrates the power of God to extricate people from difficult situations. That power is such that it can lead people to act contrary to their normal patterns to bring about the fulfillment of the divine will. In a sense, the woman of Shunem is Israel in microcosm. She experienced exile, loss, and eventually restoration. What happened to her, the book implies, can happen to Israel as well. It too can experience restoration after exile.

The book introduces a new character into its story of the Northern Kingdom and its kings: Hazael, who was to become king of Aram and a very serious problem for both Israel and Judah (2 Kgs 8, 7–15). Hazael was an emissary sent to seek a positive oracle for Ben-hadad, the king of Aram, who was dying. In the course of giving this oracle, the prophet became aware of the great problems Hazael would cause the Israelite kingdoms. Hazael appears to be surprised by the prophet's words. Hazael's succession was indeed irregular. He did not belong to the royal family but usurped the throne of Aram following Ben-hadad's death.

For the first time in 2 Kings, the book turns its attention to Judah as it offers judgment on the reign of Jehoram (2 Kgs 8, 16–25). The relations between Judah and Israel were peaceful, sealed by the marriage of Jehoram to Athaliah, a daughter of Ahab. Certainly in any alliance between the two kingdoms, Judah was the junior partner. The book notes that Jehoram replicated the behavior of the kings of Israel. This brought serious consequences for Judah. As Israel lost control over Moab (2 Kgs 3), so Judah's domination of Edom came to an end. The power of the Israelite kingdoms was steadily diminishing. For the book this was an obvious sign of God's displeasure with Israel, Judah, and their kings. Jehoram of Judah died after only eight years as king, leaving his twenty-one-year-old son Ahaziah to ascend David's throne. Ahaziah was a brother-in-law to Jehoram of Israel. The two kings decided to strike the Arameans under Hazael because of the threat that the Arameans posed. But Jehoram was severely wounded in battle and went to Jezreel to recover. Ahaziah went there to visit him (2 Kgs 8, 25–29). In providing these details, the book is setting the scene for the violent end that will come to the dynasty established by Omri.

To illustrate the disintegration of the Kingdom of Israel, the book describes a revolution that brought an end to the House of Omri (2 Kgs 9, 1–10, 22)—a revolution so bloody that it was still remembered with horror a century later (see Hos 1, 4–5). According to Kings, Jehu's revolution was set in motion by the apostasy and injustice practiced by Israel's kings, and the terrible end of these kings reflects the prophetic judgment on their actions (1 Kgs 14, 11; 16, 4; 21, 19–24). The book then presents Jehu's revolution not in political but theological terms; it begins with the prophet Elisha's naming of Jehu, an officer in Jehoram's army, as the one to replace the king. After Jehu assassinated Jehoram of Israel and Ahaziah of Judah, he turned to Jezebel, who taunted him as no better than Zimri, the assassin who was king of Israel for just seven days (see 1 Kgs 16, 15–19). Jezebel shared the fate of her son Jehoram at Jehu's hand (1 Kgs 9, 1–27).

As a usurper, Jehu had to eliminate claimants to the throne with better credentials. His revolutionary goals were to take Jehoram's place on the throne and end the Phoenician influence over the Kingdom of Israel. To secure his throne, Jehu purged the entire royal family (2 Kgs 10, 1–11.15–17) and to eliminate Phoenician influence, he killed the prophets of Baal and destroyed their temple (10, 18–27). Because he also killed Ahaziah of Judah, Jehu had to deal with a force from the Southern Kingdom seeking to avenge Ahaziah. But the book does not tell the story of Jehu's action to give an accurate picture of the progress of his revolution. The book wishes to describe the religious significance of that revolution. From this perspective, for all his brutal thoroughness, Jehu was a failure. He did not follow the Lord when he was king but followed instead the pattern of apostasy as set by Jeroboam. Because of this sin, Jehu did not stop Israel's slide to oblivion. Like his predecessors, Jehu witnessed Israel's power diminishing. More territory was lost—probably to Aram. Israel's doom was just a matter of time (2 Kgs 10, 28–36).

The book next shows that the baleful influence of the House of Ahab was not limited to the Northern Kingdom. The queen mother in Judah was Athaliah, a princess of the House of Ahab, who was given in marriage to Jehoram, the crown prince of Judah, thus ending the tensions between the two Israelite kingdoms. When Athaliah's son, Ahaziah, was assassinated in the course of Jehu's revolt, she decided to seize absolute power in Jerusalem. Because she, like Jehu, was a usurper, she had to eliminate all potential rivals for power so she had all the males from the House of David killed (2 Kgs 11, 1). Ahaziah's son Joash was saved by his aunt Jehosheba and escaped the massacre orchestrated by his grandmother Athaliah. During her seventh year on the throne, Athaliah was assassinated in

the course of a revolution led by Jehoiada, a priest. The temple of Baal that Athaliah built in Jerusalem was torn down, and the unprecedented rule of a woman as sovereign ended. Joash was enthroned in place of his assassinated grandmother. The book notes that support for Joash came from the people in rural areas. Jerusalem's population had evidently been co-opted by Athaliah and made no effort to support the new king (2 Kgs 11, 20).

Since Joash was placed on the throne by a priest, it is not surprising that he concerns himself with restoration of the Temple of the Lord, which probably suffered from neglect during Athaliah's reign. Still, it is important to note that the "king's secretary" oversaw the financing of the project (2 Kgs 12, 11). This is the first attempt to put more control of the Temple and its affairs in the hand of the king. Hezekiah and Josiah will continue the policy. Even though Joash developed an efficient way to finance the maintenance of the Temple, his efforts were wasted since he had to pay a heavy indemnity to Hazael, who threatened Jerusalem. Nothing else is told of this king's forty-year reign except that he was assassinated by his own courtiers. With three successive rulers assassinated, the stability of the Judahite state was seriously undermined. The book implies that the future of the Judahite state was in question.

The downward spiral of the Kingdom of Israel continued during the seventeen-year reign of Jehoahaz (2 Kgs 13, 1–9). Almost constant warfare between Israel and Aram led to the severe depletion of Israel's army (v. 7). Total disaster was averted by an unidentified "savior" (v. 5). It is likely that this savior came in the form of the Assyrian army that invaded Aram at the end of the ninth century, easing the pressure on Israel. With this account of Israel's deteriorating military power, the book begins its description of the fall of the house of Jehu. The end of Jehu's dynasty is inevitable because of the continuing apostasy of Israel's kings (v. 2).

Israel enjoyed a temporary respite from military reverses at the hand of the Arameans during the reign of Jehoash (Joash) (2 Kgs 13, 10–25). Before Elisha died, he predicted a revival of Israel's military fortunes. The short note about the revival of a corpse that touched the bones of the dead prophet illustrates how the prophetic word can bring life to the sick body of Israel, because God's saving will did not wish to bring the full force of judgment upon God's people. Tangible proofs of that were the victories of Jehoash and his recovery of Israelite territory lost to Aram.

The book's attention refocuses on Judah, which fared poorly during the reign of Amaziah (2 Kgs 14, 1–22). The king did merit qualified praise for his loyalty to God, though worship at the high places, which the book regarded as improper, continued during his rule. While the king was good, he was not good enough to insure Judah's success in the political and military sphere, which the book uses as a benchmark indicating the nation's standing before God. Amaziah was successful in bringing Edom back under Judahite domination, but when he turned his attention to the north, he was unsuccessful. He was defeated by Israel and made a prisoner of war. He witnessed the Israelite forces partially destroy Jerusalem's walls and sack the Temple. His folly in starting a war with the more powerful Northern Kingdom led finally to Amaziah's assassination. The Southern Kingdom's disintegration continues.

The book dismisses the forty-year reign of Jeroboam II in a few verses, but it cannot ignore it completely (2 Kgs 14, 23–29). Jeroboam has notable success in expanding the boundaries of his kingdom, which the book usually considers a sign of God's blessing. Here it asserts that Jeroboam's success was the fulfillment of a prophetic word given by Jonah. Although there is a book ascribed to Jonah in the collection of the prophets, the oracle given to Jeroboam is not preserved in that book or anywhere in the Bible. Kings goes on to explain the anomalous success of Jeroboam by claiming that it was the result of God's compassion on Israel (vv. 26–27). Jeroboam's reign is often described as a time of peace and prosperity; in fact it was not. The expansion of Israel's territory had to come by way of war. His building projects put a strain on the country's resources, which eventually led to the severe economic problems that Israel faced following Jeroboam's death. The chasm between rich and poor grew during Jeroboam's time.

Like Jeroboam II, Azariah of Judah enjoyed a very long reign; it was, however, marred by a skin disease that rendered him unable to perform rituals that were reserved to the king (2 Kgs 15, 1–7). His son Jotham assumed many of Azariah's duties. Even though the book praises Azariah, this praise is tempered by the comment that he did nothing about the high places that the book considered as illegitimate. Under Azariah, the Kingdom of Judah enjoyed a resurgence, which the book chooses to ignore since it does not reflect its notion of the direction Judah is heading.

Following the long reign of Jeroboam II, the Northern Kingdom began a rush to its total collapse. The text gives little more than the basic outline of a nation devolving into political chaos in the final years of its existence. Zechariah, Jeroboam's son and successor, is barely able to hold the throne for six months before he is assassinated (2 Kgs 15, 8–12). Shallum, Zechariah's assassin, managed to hold on to the throne for only one month before his assassination by Menahem, whose ruthlessness kept him on the throne for ten years (2 Kgs 15, 13–16). During Menahem's reign, Tiglath-pileser III of Assyria, which the text sometimes calls Pul, began Assyria's expansion at Israel's expense (2 Kgs 15, 17–22). Pekahiah, Menahem's son, was able to hold the throne for only two years before his assassination by Pekah (2 Kgs 15, 23–26). It was during his reign that the Assyrians began dismantling the Northern Kingdom. Pekah, too, was assassinated after a twenty-year reign by Hoshea, who was destined to be the last in the line that began with Jeroboam I. The book provides few details about the reigns of these five kings because it is more interested in the fate of Israel as a nation whose doom it is describing. The five kings each receive the usual condemnation that is given to all the kings of the north, and their individual fates presage the disaster that Northern Kingdom will experience.

The book has to break off its account of Israel's final years to tell the story of the last conflict between Israel and Judah. Pekah formed a coalition with Aram, Israel's chief rival in the Levant, to deal with a common threat: Assyria, whose expansionism and militarism imperiled them both. Pekah tried to enlist Judah in the coalition but Jotham resisted, while Kings insists that it was God who led Aram and Israel against Judah. Before the issue was decided, Jotham died (2 Kgs 15, 32–38). Jotham's son Ahaz is left to deal with the crisis.

The book has no regard for Ahaz, condemning him without reservation (2 Kgs 16, 1–20). Ahaz's desperation in the face of the invasion by the combined forces of Aram and Israel is evident from his resorting to child sacrifice as a way to gain divine favor. Ahaz's situation was grievous because he had to face hostilities on two fronts—the Edomites were moving in the south (v. 6), and Aram and Israel were coming from the north. This military pressure led Ahaz to align himself with Tiglath-pileser to whom he paid a large indemnity. The Assyrian king quickly put an end to the coalition seeking to depose Ahaz. Kings then describes in great detail changes that Ahaz made to the Temple and its altar. These are regarded as acts of apostasy (vv. 10–20).

With the account of Ahaz's reign completed, the book returns to Israel, which was on the brink of total collapse. After narrating the events that led to the end of Israel's political existence (2 Kgs 17, 1–6), the book launches into a long editorial comment to explain the fall of the Northern Kingdom as a consequence of its failure to shape its national life on the basis of the Torah (2 Kgs 17, 7–23). The Assyrians annexed the territory of the former Northern Kingdom into their provincial system. To pacify the region, they led the prominent citizens of Israel into exile and brought in people from other regions of their empire to settle in what had been the Kingdom of Israel. The author of Kings maintains that the Samaritans of his day were the descendants of these foreign settlers and describes their patterns of worship as a hybrid of Yahwism and the worship of foreign deities (2 Kgs 17, 24–41).

The Final Years of the Kingdom of Judah (2 Kgs 18, 1—25, 30)

After describing the fall of the Northern Kingdom, the book details the last years of the Southern Kingdom. Kings begins with the story of Hezekiah, a king greatly admired because of his obedience to the Torah and his destruction of the high places. Hezekiah was able to augment Judah's territories at the expense of the Philistines. In contrast to Israel, Judah and its king appeared to be prospering (2 Kgs 18, 1–12). However, the Assyrians ended Hezekiah's peace by invading Judah and besieging Jerusalem; and although Hezekiah offered an indemnity to Sen-

nacherib, the Assyrian king, the siege continued. Sennacherib demanded the surrender of Jerusalem, claiming that Judah's own patron deity had ordered him to conquer the country (2 Kgs 18, 1–37, esp. v. 25).

In his despair, Hezekiah turned to the prophet Isaiah, who assured him that Sennacherib would lift the siege and return to his country (v. 7). For reasons that are not clear to historians, the Assyrian army retreated and Sennacherib was assassinated later—just as the prophet predicted (2 Kgs 19, 1–37). Of course, Kings sees the lifting of the siege as an act of God. The final episode in Hezekiah's story puts the king's reputation under a cloud. Though God healed him and promised him a longer reign, Hezekiah wanted proof that the promises made to him by Isaiah would be fulfilled. The arrival of an ambassador from Babylon gave Isaiah the opportunity to announce Judah's approaching defeat and exile. Instead of this announcement moving Hezekiah to repentance, the king expresses relief that the disaster will come after he is gone. It is as if Hezekiah learned nothing from the near disaster brought about by the Assyrians (2 Kgs 20, 1–21).

Hezekiah was succeeded by his son Manasseh. From Kings' point of view, Judah never fell so low as it did during the fifty-five-year reign of this king. It accuses Manasseh of apostasy, idolatry, and murder, and explicitly identifies him as the Judahite Ahab, leading the Southern Kingdom to disaster as Ahab had in the Northern Kingdom. Unnamed prophets pronounced divine judgment on Manasseh's actions. There is no doubt that Manasseh kept his throne by demonstrating his loyalty to the Assyrians, in part by introducing Assyrian religious rituals to the Jerusalem Temple. He also had to be ruthless in preventing a nationalistic spirit to express itself in open revolt against the Assyrians. The book offers no reason for Manasseh's great apostasy, letting the king's actions speak for themselves. The consequences of his actions could not be set aside with an appeal to God's promises to the patriarchs or to David. Judah's fall is only a matter of time (2 Kgs 21, 1–18).

Manasseh was succeeded by his son Amon, who continued his father's policies. This led to his assassination by his own courtiers. Evidently the assassination of yet another king provoked the ordinary folk, who supported the Davidic dynasty. They likely believed that another round of assassinations would be the end of Judah, so they killed the conspirators and installed Amon's young son, Josiah, as king (2 Kgs 21, 19–26). It is during Josiah's reign that Judah made one last attempt at reform; it proved to be too late to avert divine judgment.

Josiah's reign was a short pause as Judah moved to the inevitable (2 Kgs 22, 1—23, 30). Kings describes Josiah as a monarch who "pleased the LORD" (2 Kgs 22, 2). A critical event in Josiah's reign was the discovery of a book in the course of renovations that were being made on the Temple. Kings wishes its readers to assume that the "book of the law" was what we know as the book of Deuteronomy. Josiah responded to hearing the words of the book with a gesture of repentance. He had the book authenticated by a prophet. Although Jeremiah was active at this time, the prophet consulted was an otherwise unknown woman named Huldah. She authenticated the book but announced that the curses on the unfaithful found in the book would fall on Judah and Jerusalem but not in Josiah's time.

Fortunately for Josiah, he came into power about the time Assyria's control over the Levant was waning; he moved quickly to reclaim Judah's sovereignty in matters of religion and politics. The book concentrates on Josiah's actions in the sphere of religious practice. The king took action against all types of non-Yahwistic religious activity and promoted such traditional practices as the Passover. His move into the north was likely prompted by a determination to take advantage of Assyria's weakness to extend the territory under his control. Josiah's attempts to reassert and expand Judahite sovereignty ended when he died during an ill-advised attempt to involve himself in international politics. He endeavored to stop the Egyptian army as it was advancing into Mesopotamia and was killed in battle. Josiah's "reform" died with him because Judah once again came under foreign domination. The Egyptians asserted their control over Judah by deposing Josiah's successor Jehoahaz and exiling him to Egypt. They placed another of Josiah's sons, Eliakim, on the throne, changing

his name to Jehoiakim (2 Kgs 23, 31–35). Judah had to pay an indemnity to the Egyptians. This, of course, burdened Judah's economy, which had been already made fragile by Josiah's military adventures.

With no other choice, Jehoiakim remained a loyal Egyptian vassal until Nebuchadnezzar defeated the Egyptians in two decisive battles, ending Egyptian domination of the Levant. Judah then was forced to submit to Babylon. When Babylon's fortunes changed, Jehoiakim came under Egyptian control again. But Babylon's setback was only temporary, and Judah was forced to submit to Nebuchadnezzar a second time after a siege of Jerusalem, during which Jehoiakim died. Of course, the book sees all this political and military activity as an act of divine judgment on Judah (2 Kgs 23, 36—24, 7).

Jehoiachin succeeded his father just as the Babylonian siege of Jerusalem was about to end with the city's surrender and the sacking of the Temple. While Judah was able to maintain the appearance of sovereignty, it was more firmly under Babylon's control than ever. Jehoiachin was deposed and exiled along with many of Judah's leading citizens. The Babylonians placed Mattaniah, another of Josiah's brothers on the throne, changing his name to Zedekiah. The book lets the events speak for themselves as Judah's final collapse appears to be imminent. Zedekiah was to be the last king of the Davidic line. He managed to keep his throne for eleven years. No longer able to resist calls to rebel against Babylonian domination, Zedekiah sealed the fate of the dynasty and the kingdom. The Babylonians responded to his rebellion by taking Jerusalem a second time, killing Zedekiah's sons, blinding the king, and leading him into exile. Zedekiah was never heard from again (2 Kgs 24, 18—25, 7).

Jerusalem too paid for Zedekiah's folly in revolting against Nebuchadnezzar. The city was put to the torch and its Temple was left in ruins. Many of Jerusalem's leading citizens were executed, and the rest were deported to Babylon. Nebuchadnezzar completely reorganized the government of Judah. The Babylonians appointed Gedaliah, who did not belong to the royal family, to administer what would become a new province of the Babylonian empire. They also moved Judah's administrative center from Jerusalem to Mizpah.

Assassins led by a survivor of Judah's royal family killed Gedaliah along with his Judahite and Babylonian retainers. This led many Judahites to seek refuge in Egypt, and those that remained were subject to a third deportation (see Jer 52, 30; 2 Kgs 25, 8–26). And so ends the story of Israel in its land.

As an epilogue, Kings mentions the parole of Jehoiachin from prison in Babylon (2 Kgs 25, 27–30). Unfortunately, the book does not reflect on the significance of the exiled king's new status for Judah's future. At the most critical moment in his story, the author of Kings is inexplicably reticent, leaving the reader to wonder what will become of Judah and Jerusalem. Is the divine judgment brought on by Judah's failure to be loyal to the Lord and shape its life according to Torah final? Perhaps Jehoiachin's parole is a harbinger of Judah's rehabilitation. The book does not give an explicit answer to these questions. The books of Kings end on a most ambiguous note, requiring its readers to make sense out of a tragic tale.

Continuing Significance of the Books of Kings

Like the other books that make up the Deuteronomistic History of Israel, the books of Kings put in sharp focus the consequences of failing to remain absolutely committed to the Lord and to the pattern of life given to Israel in the book of Deuteronomy. What the books illustrate is a continuing pattern of failure to live responsibly. Although Kings focuses almost exclusively on the actions of the ruling class, it certainly intended its message for a wider audience. These books remind believers today that they bear a responsibility to act on the Word. Election offers no guarantees; rather, it calls believers to greater commitment. The books of Joshua to 2 Kings tell a sad and tragic story. What began with so

much hope ends in disaster. It is not a pleasant story—especially in 2 Kings, when it becomes clear that the two Israelite kingdoms are headed toward self-destruction. But the reader today knows that Jerusalem's fall, the end of the national state, and the collapse of all Judahite religious and political institutions were not the end of the story. God's mercy triumphed over God's justice, and a renewed Judah emerged from the exile. The story of Israel in its land makes it absolutely clear that God's moral demands must be taken seriously. Failing to do so brings disaster. But despite this, believers recognize that God is still love.

FURTHER READING

Cogan, Mordechai. *1 Kings.* Anchor Bible 10. Garden City, NY: Doubleday, 2001.

Cogan, Mordechai, and Hayim Tadmor. *2 Kings.* Anchor Bible 11. Garden City, NY: Doubleday, 1988.

DeVries, Simon J. *1 Kings.* Word Biblical Commentary 12. Waco, TX: Word, 1985.

Gray, John. *1 and 2 Kings, a Commentary.* Old Testament Library. 2nd rev. ed. Philadelphia: Westminster, 1976.

Hobbs, T.R. *2 Kings.* Word Bible Commentary 13. Waco, TX: Word, 1985.

Jones, Gwilym H. *1 and 2 Kings.* 2 vols. Grand Rapids, MI: Eerdmans, 1984.

Long, Burke O. *1 Kings: With an Introduction to Old Testament Historical Literature.* Forms of Old Testament Literature 9. Grand Rapids, MI: Eerdmans, 1984.

——. *2 Kings.* Forms of Old Testament Literature 10. Grand Rapids, MI: Eerdmans, 1991.

Nelson, Richard. *First and Second Kings.* Louisville, KY: John Knox, 1987.

Rice, Gene. *Nations Under God: A Commentary on the Book of 1 Kings.* International Theological Commentary. Grand Rapids, MI: Eerdmans, 1990.

Rofé, Alexander. *The Prophetical Stories: The Narratives about the Prophets in the Hebrew Bible, Their Literary Types and History.* Jerusalem: The Magnes Press, 1988.

THE CHRONICLER'S HISTORY AND THE LATER HISTORIES

LESLIE J. HOPPE

1 CHRONICLES

[see pages 435–69 of the Old Testament]

The Chronicler's Work

As the introduction to this book notes (OT, p. 435), the first book of Chronicles is part of a larger work that includes the second book of Chronicles, Ezra, and Nehemiah. This larger work begins with Adam (1 Chr 1, 1) and concludes with the writer's own day: the fifth century following the restoration of the Jerusalem Temple after the Babylonian Exile that lasted from 587 to 539 BC. Originally 1 and 2 Chronicles formed one book. The division into two came with the printed Bible. Similarly, the books of Ezra and Nehemiah were a single work that was divided into two.

Although Chronicles begins with Adam, it repeats none of the familiar stories found in Genesis. The first nine chapters of 1 Chronicles are almost completely without narrative material. The text is little more than genealogical lists that the author gleaned from biblical texts and other sources available to him. The narrative proper begins with the story of Saul's death and burial (10, 1–14). Perhaps this is the Chronicler's way of stating that it is with David that Israel's story really begins (see note to 1, 1—9, 34, OT, p. 436).

About half of the material found in Chronicles comes from the books of Samuel and Kings. While Samuel and Kings describe and explain the rise and fall of the Israelite kingdoms, the Chronicler appears to be more interested in the future of the Israelite people. Examining how the Chronicler uses material from Samuel and Kings, and analysis of the material unique to Chronicles, reveals the Chronicler's religious message: Judah's religious institutions and their continuity with the past are critical for its future. One aim of the work is to defend the legitimacy of the Temple of Jerusalem and the significance of its worship for Israel's life. The Chronicler believed that Israel could secure its future only by worshiping its God according to the pattern set by David at God's direction. Israel's hope, then, did not reside in the restoration of its political institutions but in the renewal of legitimate worship in the Temple of Jerusalem under the direction of its priests and Levites.

Position in the Canon

The Septuagint (the ancient Greek translation of the Hebrew Bible) titled the books of Chronicles *Paraleipomena* ("things that were left out"). This was also the name for Chronicles used in the Douay-Rheims version and some other Roman Catholic versions. Evidently those responsible for the Septuagint considered Chronicles a kind of supplement to the books of Samuel and Kings. Perhaps that is why the Septuagint places Chronicles immediately following the books of Kings. Jerome followed this order in the Vulgate (his Latin translation of the Bible). English

Bibles used by both Protestant and Catholic Christians also follow this order.

The books of Chronicles are the last books in the Jewish Bible. Christian Bibles follow an arrangement that has the Old Testament end with the Prophets. The final passage is Malachi's prophecy of the return of Elijah, who will announce the "day of the Lord" (Mal 3, 23f). The Church reads a messianic meaning in this text and, following the lead of the New Testament, identifies John the Baptist, the precursor of Jesus, as the returning Elijah (Mt 11, 11–14; 17, 11–13). A prophecy regarding the precursor of the Messiah is the perfect way to lead into the story of Jesus' birth with which the New Testament begins.

In the Hebrew Bible as arranged by the rabbis, the prophetic books follow the books of Moses (the Torah or the Pentateuch), since the early rabbis viewed the prophets as expositors of the Torah. The rabbinic Bible has a third division, called the Writings, which is a miscellaneous collection of books that belong to neither the Torah nor the Prophets. The last books of this collection are 1 and 2 Chronicles. Thus the Hebrew Bible ends with the decree of Cyrus (2 Chr 36, 23) that calls for the people of Judah to return to Jerusalem and rebuild the Temple in Jerusalem. For two millennia, then, religious Jews scattered throughout the world have found that the last words of their Bible were a call to return to Jerusalem (see also the note to 2 Chr 36, 22f, OT, p. 508).

Reading the Book

The first book of Chronicles has a very simple arrangement. The first nine chapters (1, 1—9, 34) contain genealogical lists. The rest of the book narrates the story of David (9, 35—29, 30). The Chronicler's story of David idealizes the king and transforms him into the founder and sponsor of Jerusalem's Temple.

Genealogical Lists (1 Chr 1, 1—9, 34)

The genealogies of Chronicles represent an extraordinary achievement by the author. The genealogical lists extend from Adam (1, 1) to the returnees from the Babylonian Exile (9, 2–34).

The author uses the genealogies from the book of Genesis in his own tables that begin with the descent from Adam to Abraham and his sons

(1, 1–27; see Gn 5; 10; 11). From there the focus is on the twelve sons of Jacob (1, 28—2, 2). Once the genealogy reaches Judah, one of Jacob's twelve sons, the Chronicler arrives at the centerpiece of his presentation: David (see note to 2, 3—4, 23, p. 438). There is a genealogy of Judah down to David and his relatives (2, 3–17) along with lateral branches of the descendants of Judah (2, 18–55; 4, 1–23). Chapter 3 lists David's descendants, all the Davidic kings, and their descendants into the postexilic period.

The genealogies of the other tribes follow (4, 23–8, 40). These lists are not as extensive as the one for Judah except for the genealogy of the tribe of Levi (5, 27—6, 6; see note to 5, 27—6, 66, p. 442). Another interest of the Chronicler was the priestly tribe of Levi and the cult in which they ministered. Genealogies of Saul's descendants (8, 33–40; 9, 35–44) frame a list of those who returned from the Babylonian Exile (9, 1–34).

The impression left from reading these genealogies is that the true beginning of Israel was not at Sinai with the giving of the Torah, as the Priestly document would have it, but with the rise of David. The Chronicler's unique appreciation for David and his achievements becomes clear in the next section of the book.

The History of David's Reign: (1 Chr 10—29, 30)

This section begins with a report on Saul's death and burial (10, 1–12), together with a short editorial comment on the dangers Saul's reign posed for Israel because Saul was not faithful to God (see note to 10, 13f, p. 449). For the Chronicler, Saul is little more than a foil for David, whose portrait the Chronicler painted with the strokes of piety and fidelity.

The Chronicler includes nothing from the books of Samuel that compromise his idealized portrait of David. For example, he omits David's conflicts with Saul, his service with the Philistines, David's career-advancing marriages, and the political maneuvers that led to his acclamation as king of Israel. For example, 2 Samuel 2, 4 states that "the men of Judah" anointed David as the king of their tribe following Saul's death. David ruled over Judah for seven years before the elders of Israel chose him as king over the rest of the tribes (2 Sm 5, 1–5). The Chronicler, however, states that "all Israel" made David king immediately following Saul's death (1 Chr 11, 1–3). Among the notable additions to David's story as told in 2 Samuel is the story of the ark. While 2 Samuel portrays David's decision to bring the ark into Jerusalem as a decision made by David alone (2 Sm 6, 1f), the Chronicler describes the same event as an act sanctioned by all the people (1 Chr 13, 1–5). The Chronicler's account of the ark's entrance into Jerusalem highlights the role of the Levites. David appoints them to carry the ark into the city (1 Chr 15, 11–15). Since David also commissioned them to be singers in the Temple (1 Chr 15, 16–22), they sing a psalm (1 Chr 16, 7–36).

For the Chronicler, David's significance for Israel does not lie in the political sphere but in the religious. This spin on the story of David leads the Chronicler to suppress anything that sullies David's reputation. For example, the Chronicler omits the entire story of how Solomon succeeded David as king (2 Sm 9—20; 1 Kgs 1—2) from his narrative. The Chronicler says nothing about David's adultery with Bathsheba and the events that followed it, including Nathan's condemnation of David (2 Sm 12, 1–12). Similarly the Chronicler makes no mention of the two revolts against David (see 2 Sm 15—18; 20, 1–22).

The Chronicler devotes the bulk his story of David (17—29) to the plans for building the Temple, which Solomon will carry out. This, of course, makes Solomon a central figure in the Chronicler's story (see note to 22, 2ff, OT, p. 461) so the Chronicler also idealizes David's son, eliminating the stories from 1 Kings that highlight Solomon's religious and moral failings. The Chronicler's story of Solomon's succession to David appears to be a deliberate effort to imitate the account of the transition from Moses to Joshua in Deuteronomy 21 and Joshua 1. The Chronicler considered Solomon's succession to David's throne as important as Joshua's succession to the Mosaic office.

The Establishment of the Temple

The Chronicler paints the portraits of David and Solomon in order to underscore their respective roles in the establishment of the Temple and its liturgy. Worship, then, is one of the Chronicler's principal concerns. The God who is present in Judah's experience evokes a response in worship

from the people whose destiny this God guides. The Chronicler tries to show that Judah's future is dependent upon its fidelity to the proper forms of worship that God has revealed through David. There is a reciprocal relationship between God and Judah. God blesses Judah, and Judah worships God.

For the Chronicler, the Temple and its liturgy were symbols of God's continuing presence among the people of Judah. As long as the priests offered the correct sacrifices at the appropriate times in the presence of a grateful people, the Lord will dwell in Judah's midst. For the Chronicler, the history of Israel was not a series of unrelated actions by kings and prophets. Its nucleus was the worship led by the priests appointed by Moses and David. The Chronicler recognized that there were times when Judah's sin led to serious failures to offer proper worship, but Judah's sin was never fatal. Judah was always able to recover, resume proper liturgical services, and thus be certain of God's abiding presence. The fall of Jerusalem and the exile to Babylon formed an unfortunate interruption in an otherwise unbroken history of Judah as a community that offered legitimate worship to its ancestral deity. The only way to avoid a similar disaster in the future was to worship God in Jerusalem's Temple according to rituals that go back to those developed by David.

The Importance of the Temple

For proper worship of the Lord, a Temple is indispensable. Like the books of Kings, Chronicles recognizes the legitimacy of only one temple— the Temple at Jerusalem. At the time of the composition of the Chronicler's history, the worshippers of Israel's ancestral deity were not unanimous in recognizing Jerusalem's Temple as the only legitimate place of worship. There was a temple dedicated to the Lord in Samaria, and at Elephantine (a Jewish military colony located on an island near the modern city of Aswan in Egypt). In telling the story of the Northern Kingdom, the Chronicler does not even choose to mention the sanctuaries at Dan or Bethel that Jeroboam I built (see 1 Kgs 12, 26–29). For the Chronicler there could be only one Temple. David built this Temple under the same kind of divine guidance that led Moses to build the tabernacle in the wilderness. The Lord gave David the plans for the Temple in Jerusalem (1 Chr 28, 19). No other sanctuary could be a legitimate place to worship the God of Israel.

The Temple Personnel

Chapters 23 through 27 appear to be intrusive in the Chronicler's story about David and Solomon, but they are central to the Chronicler's concern to describe the contours of the proper worship of God. Chapter 23 deals with Levitical class; 24 with priestly classes; 25 with Levitical singers; 26 with the gatekeepers of the Temple, and 27 with army commanders, tribal leaders, and royal advisers. The passages that deal with the priests and Levites are important for the Chronicler's general purpose. Not only is the proper place for worshipping God crucial but so is having the proper personnel to officiate at the rites (see also 2 Chr 13, 9–11). The Chronicler provides quite a lot of detail about the people whom God chose to officiate at the liturgy in Jerusalem. At one time, any male Israelite could offer sacrificial worship. Gradually, however, members of the tribe of Levi became the preferred ministers of the ritual. Chronicles reflects a further development. Some members of the tribe of Levi were priests, who offered sacrifices, while the rest were temple singers and assistants to the priests.

The Priests

Although the Chronicler recognized the priests as the chief religious officials, there are clear indications that he did not regard them too highly (2 Chr 29, 34; 30, 3). Among the duties of the priests, there was the responsibility to blow the trumpets (1 Chr 16, 6), to minister in the inner sanctuary (2 Chr 5, 14), to offer sacrifice on the altar (2 Chr 29, 21), and to burn incense (2 Chr 26, 18). Though the Deuteronomist recognized that others besides the tribe of Levi could serve as priests, the Chronicler makes no exception other than David himself. For example, the Deuteronomist relates that David's sons were priests (2 Sm 8, 18), but in a parallel passage (1 Chr 18, 17), the Chronicler calls them "chief assistants to the king" (see the note to 18, 17, OT, p. 458). The Chronicler does depict David as exercising priestly prerogatives: he wore priestly vestments (1 Chr 15, 27), he blessed the people (16, 2), and he offered sacrifice (16, 26). David, however, was the only exception.

The Levites

The Chronicler asserts that the Levites did more than a few menial chores connected with the liturgy of the Temple. They carried the ark (1 Chr 15, 15). They were singers (15, 16–22) and gatekeepers (15, 23). The Levites fulfilled all their responsibilities under the direction of priests (1 Chr 23, 27–32). The Levites were a type of "lower clergy." They also had roles that were not directly related to worship. The Levites were judges (2 Chr 19, 8.11), prophets (2 Chr 20, 14f), and fund raisers (2 Chr 24, 5; 34, 9).

Temple Slaves

The Chronicler also describes a third group of religious personnel: the "temple slaves" (Ezr 8, 20). The Chronicler mentions them only a few times in his history. They were the lowest class of liturgical functionaries (Neh 7, 72), and their task was to help the Levites (Ezr 8, 20).

Roman Catholic Priesthood

The sacrament of Orders in the Roman Catholic Church is largely a part of our heritage from ancient Israel. The rituals of ordination recognize this heritage. The division of orders in the Roman Catholic Church into the episcopacy, presbyterate, and diaconate mirrors to some extent the Chronicler's division of temple personnel into priests, Levites, and temple slaves. Of course the status, role, and interrelationships of the orders in the Church are different from those of the Old Testament's cultic personnel, yet the concern in the Church for a hierarchy among the people directly concerned with worship is similar to that of the Chronicler.

There is not a single instance in the New Testament of anyone called a "priest" presiding at Christian worship. It is the Chronicler (and even more the Priestly strand of the Pentateuch, especially Leviticus and Numbers) who tries to make the reader sensitive to the presence of God in the act of sacrificial worship led by "official" ministers. For the Chronicler the priests and Levites were those through whom God's abiding presence among the people was evident. The rituals that they conducted were a source of blessing for the people and an act of devotion to their God. The Chronicler's God was not a hidden God. The people experienced God in worship more than anywhere else. It should be clear that the value that the Church places on the liturgy and priesthood finds a strong support in the Chronicler's history.

FURTHER READING

Ackroyd, Peter R. "The Chronicler in his Age." *Journal for the Study of the Old Testament Supplement Series,* no. 101. Sheffield: Sheffield Academic Press, 1991.

Berquist, Jon L. *Judaism in Persia's Shadow: A Social and Historical Approach.* Minneapolis: Augsburg Fortress, 1996.

Graham, M. P., ed. "The Chronicler as Historian." *JSOT Supplement Series,* no. 238. Sheffield: Sheffield Academic Press, 1997.

Mangan, Celine, O.P. *1–2 Chronicles; Ezra; Nehemiah.* Old Testament Message Series 13. Wilmington, DE: Michael Glazier.

Myers, Jacob M. *1 and 2 Chronicles.* Anchor Bible 12 and 13; Garden City, NY: Doubleday, 1965.

——. "The Kerygma of the Chronicler." In *Interpretation 20* (1966): 259–73.

Williamson, H. G. M. *1 and 2 Chronicles.* New Century Bible Commentary. Grand Rapids: Eerdmans, 1982.

2 CHRONICLES

[see pages 469–508 of the Old Testament]

Chronicles and the Israelite Kingdoms

The second book of Chronicles continues the story of Israel with the accession of Solomon to the throne of David. Comparing the way Chronicles tells this story with the narratives in the books of Kings helps to see the purpose of the Chronicler. For example, after Solomon's death and the breakup of the Davidic-Solomonic empire into the two national states of Israel and Judah, the Chronicler all but ignores the Northern Kingdom (Israel) and its kings. He focuses his attention on the Southern Kingdom (Judah). The Chronicler mentions Israel only when the story of Judah makes it necessary to do so. By contrast, throughout the books of Kings, the author synchronizes the reigns of the kings in the south with those in the north (for example, 1 Kgs 15, 1.9.25.33). In 2 Chronicles there is only one such synchronization: 2 Chronicles 13, 1. The Chronicler wishes to focus on the Davidic dynasty and what was, in his opinion, its finest achievement—the Temple in Jerusalem. Also, the Chronicler's treatment of Judah's kings focuses almost entirely on the promotion of legitimate worship and the performance of the proper ritual.

Reading the Book

Solomon

The story of Solomon (2 Chr 1—9) deals exclusively with the building of the Temple as envisioned by David. Again the Chronicler does not repeat the negative aspects of Solomon's story

that 1 Kings recounts. For example, the Chronicler omits the details about how Solomon secured his throne through the execution of potential opponents, including his half brother Adonijah (1 Kgs 2). Also unmentioned is Solomon's marriage to the daughter of Pharaoh (1 Kgs 3, 1) and other non-Israelite women (1 Kgs 11, 1–13) that the book of Kings presents as a compromise of the exclusive loyalty that Solomon owed to the God of Israel. In his description of the wealth and glory of the Temple, the Chronicler goes beyond the words of Kings (compare 2 Chr 3—4 with 1 Kgs 6—8). After Solomon's prayer of dedication, fire falls from heaven and consumes the sacrifice. God's glory fills the Temple (2 Chr 7, 1f). Here the Chronicler models the story of the Temple's dedication on that of the tabernacle in the wilderness (Ex 40, 34f). Throughout the description of Solomon's achievement in building and dedicating the Temple, the Chronicler reminds his readers of David's preparations (2, 6.13.16; 3, 1; 5, 1; 6, 3–11). In the eyes of the Chronicler, the Temple was the combined enterprise of David and Solomon, who each made his own contribution to the completion of this great work.

The Kingdom of Judah

The remaining chapters of the book (10 through 36) rehearse the history of Judah to the Babylonian Exile from the singular perspective of the Chronicler. 2 Chronicles passes over much detail important in 1 and 2 Kings without a mention because of its focus on the liturgy of the Temple. On the other hand, the Chronicler mentions various building activities, military, and administrative matters that the Deuteronomist ignores. Most of these reports occur in passages about kings that the Chronicler evaluates positively because they promoted what the Chronicler regarded as the proper worship of Israel's God.

Rehoboam, Solomon's son and successor, builds fortifications (11, 5–12) at the beginning of his career. His failure to remain completely faithful to the Law of God results in the partial conquest of his realm by the pharaoh Shishak (12, 1–5). The Chronicler is favorable to Abijah, Rehoboam's successor, in contrast to 1 Kings, which calls him Abijam (1 Kgs 15, 1–8). At the outset of a war he wages against the Northern Kingdom, Abijah addresses a long theological speech to his opponents. In it he states that the legitimate cult of Judah guarantees its victory over Israel because Israel has forsaken the true worship of the Lord (2 Chr 13, 4–12). This speech is a good indicator of the Chronicler's principal concerns. Both Asa and Jehosophat, Judah's next two kings, receive a positive evaluation from the Chronicler, who recounts their building, military, and cultic projects (14, 5—15,15; 17, 6–9; 19, 4—20, 30). Second Chronicles, then, depicts the first four kings that ruled Judah following the breakup of the Davidic-Solomonic empire as conscientious, qualified, and loyal to the Lord.

Following the lead of 2 Kings, the Chronicler rates positively several other kings from the Davidic dynasty: Uzziah (2 Chr 26, 4; see 2 Kgs 15, 3, which calls him Azariah; see also the note to 2 Kgs 14, 21, OT, p. 420), Jotham (2 Chr 27, 2; see 2 Kgs 15, 34), Hezekiah (2 Chr 29, 2; see 2 Kgs 18, 3), and Josiah (2 Chr 34, 2; see 2 Kgs 22, 2).

Chapters 29 through 31 describe a thoroughgoing reform of Judah's liturgy under Hezekiah. This reform included a confession of past neglect of proper worship (2 Chr 29, 5–11), the cleansing of the Temple (29, 16f), and the celebration of the Passover. Hezekiah invited the northerners who survived the Assyrian conquest to join the people of Judah in the renewal of the covenant (30, 1–9). The account of Hezekiah's reign in 2 Kings 18—20 says little about Hezekiah's reform because 2 Kings wished to portray Josiah as a second David who restored the covenant (2 Kgs 22—23). Another striking contrast to

2 Kings is the Chronicler's portrait of Manasseh, whom 2 Kings presents as the most evil of all Judah's kings. His sins were responsible for the fall of the Southern Kingdom (2 Kgs 21, 1–18). The Chronicler rehabilitates Manasseh by describing his conversion, which leads to a reform of Judah's worship (2 Chr 33, 11–17). It is likely that the Chronicler wanted his readers to identify with Manasseh by confessing their sins and renewing their commitment to the proper worship of Israel's God. The Chronicler's portrait of Manasseh inspired the apocryphal work known as the *Prayer of Manasseh,* a second-century BC text that is a classic of penitential devotion. (Although Jerome included a translation of this work in the Vulgate, the Council of Trent decided not to include the *Prayer of Manasseh* in the canon of the Old Testament.)

The Chronicler's version of Josiah's reform (2 Chr 34—35) distinguishes several stages. This probably reflects the actual event more accurately than the account in 2 Kings 22—23 that telescopes all the activities of the reform into a single year (see the note to 34, 3, OT, p. 504).

The Chronicler evaluates the last three kings of Judah (Jehoiachin, Jehoiakim, and Zedekiah) negatively (2 Chr 36, 5–14). After an editorial comment explaining the cause of the exile (36, 15–21), the book ends with the decree of Cyrus that calls for the restoration of Jerusalem and the rebuilding of its Temple (36, 22–23).

The Purpose of the Chronicler

Why did the Chronicler bother to retell the story of Judah's monarchy? After all, 2 Samuel through 2 Kings already told that story. Indeed, the Chronicler derived much of his story from these books. Still, when we look more closely at the Chronicler's treatment of the Judahite national state and its kings, we can see that the basic purpose of this new version of the story of David and his dynasty was to guide the Jerusalem community as it was reestablishing itself following the exile. In the eyes of the Chronicler, the one lasting contribution of the Davidic monarchy was the Temple, its rituals, and its priesthood. The Jewish community as a whole functioned as the successor of that dynasty. Once the people rebuilt the Temple and restored the proper form of its liturgy, the essential elements of Jewish life were in place. According to the Chronicler, David and Solomon combined forces to establish a divinely ordained liturgy in Jerusalem. The people, led by Ezra and Nehemiah, have resumed the service of God according to the pattern set by David. In the Chronicler's scheme, the restoration of the national state and the Davidic dynasty was not as crucial as the reestablishment of the proper worship of the Lord in Jerusalem. The people who supported the Temple and resumed the authentic worship there have fulfilled all the really important tasks of monarchy.

The Theology of the Chronicler

The Chronicler's account of the ancient Israelite monarchy differs markedly from that found in the books of Samuel and Kings. Although the Chronicler used these books as sources for his own work, he reinterpreted the material in them in order to provide his readers with a new understanding of the Davidic dynasty. While the books of Kings underscore the failure of the dynasty, the Chronicler presents the dynasty in the best possible light. The Chronicler wants to assure his readers that Judah's future depends upon the resumption of Temple service as established by David and as maintained by most of his successors. But there may have been political considerations at work in the Chronicler's telling of the story of Judah's monarchy as well. Determining this depends upon the question of dating the books of Chronicles. The introduction to 1 Chronicles dates these books to "the end of the fifth century BC" [OT, p. 436]. At this time, relations between the people of Judah and the people of the former Northern Kingdom were strained. Apparently the northerners were attempting to exert political control over Judah. This caused the animosity that grew over the years and continued into the New Testament period. The people of Judah came to regard the northerners, whom they called "Samaritans" after their ancient capital Samaria, as apostates. Both theological and political considerations combined to lead the Chronicler to reinterpret the history of Israel's monarchy in the way he did. He believed that the future of Judah depended on its absolute commitment to the authentic worship of the Lord in the Jerusalem Temple, which the Northern Kingdom rejected.

Jews and Samaritans

The books of Chronicles reflect one stage in the division that arose between the Jews and the Samaritans. Historical reconstruction has not been able to identify any sudden and dramatic act that divided the two groups irrevocably. According to Samaritan sources, the division took place at the end of the period of the judges (eleventh century BC) when Eli left Shechem and established a high-priestly line at Shiloh. According to the biblical tradition (2 Kgs 17), the separation took place in the eighth century BC, when the people of the former Northern Kingdom intermarried with foreign peoples whom the Assyrians introduced into their territory. Although it is not possible to treat either of these two accounts as straight history, they do point to important concerns. In the Chronicler's perspective, the Samaritans did not have the true priesthood (2 Chr 13, 9), and therefore their sacrificial worship was worthless.

Aside from the polemics of Jewish and Samaritan sources, the Samaritans were one example of the rich diversity in early Judaism. Their religious traditions developed independently of the leadership of the community that arose around the priests of Jerusalem. Other examples of the variety of religious perspectives in early Judaism include the Hasidim, the Essenes, and the Pharisees. An important moment in this development was the building of the Samaritan temple on Mount Gerizim (near Shechem) sometime in the early Hellenistic period (late fourth century BC). It was the building of this temple by the Samaritans and its later destruction by the Jewish king John Hyrcanus in 128 BC that led to the definitive break between the Jews and the Samaritans.

It is within this context that one should read John 4 in which Jesus meets the Samaritan woman at the well in Shechem. Her comments reflect the religious and historical conflicts between her people and the Jews. Jesus, of course, says that there will come a day when true worship of God will transcend the conflict between Jew and Samaritan (Jn 4, 21). The Chronicler's attitude toward those outside the community who worshipped the Lord centered in Jerusalem offers a striking example of an unwillingness to accept too great a diversity among those who considered themselves to be worshippers of the Lord. The reasons for the Chronicler's attitude are complex. In part they were political and economic. Apparently the province of Samaria wanted to control Jerusalem, while the leadership of the Jerusalem community wished to remain independent of such control. In part the reasons were religious and liturgical. Although the people in the north wished to help with the rebuilding of the Jerusalem Temple (Ezr 4, 2), the Judahites refused their help. Perhaps they did not believe that the northerners were sincere because of their continued use of the sanctuaries at Dan and Bethel. The Judahites considered the cult at these sanctuaries to be illegitimate. In part the reasons for the rift were historical. The Israelite tribes in the north and the south developed somewhat independently of one another, and the northerners cherished this independence fiercely. Whatever the reasons for the Chronicler's attitude toward the northerners who considered themselves to be authentic worshippers of the Lord, it was decidedly negative. It contributed to the tension between Jews and Samaritans that has lasted into the present.

The Chronicler's approach to the problem of religious diversity was understandable given the political and religious realities of the fourth century BC. The rigid application of the directives of Ezra and Nehemiah and the intensity of the Chronicler's rhetoric (see 2 Chr 13, 4–12) made it difficult for succeeding generations to overcome the division between Jew and Samaritan. Indeed, further divisions occurred within the Jewish community. The Essenes opposed the Hasmoneans. The Pharisees disputed with the Sadducees. The Herodians fought with the Zealots. In the middle of all this, Christianity emerged. Eventually, because of historical circumstances, the Pharisaic party survived the fall of Jerusalem in AD 70 and was the precursor of rabbinic Judaism. The Kairites of Babylon refused to accept the authority of the rabbis. Even within Judaism today, some Orthodox rabbis do not accept the legitimacy of Conservative and Reform Judaism. The Chronicler did not succeed in eliminating religious diversity among those who considered themselves worshippers of the Lord.

Relationships among Christian Churches

Until the Second Vatican Council, the attitude of Catholics toward other Christians was similar to the lack of tolerance that the Chronicler showed toward religious diversity. One of the principal concerns of the Council was promoting the restoration of unity among all Christians (*Decree on Ecumenism,* 1). Like the Chronicler, who is in part responsible for the rift between Jew and Samaritan, the Catholic Church, according to the Council, shares in responsibility for the divisions among Christian churches (*Decree on Ecumenism,* 3). One way to overcome these divisions is through dialogue that leads to a knowledge and appreciation of the doctrine and religious life of the many Christian churches.

Of the two main kinds of division within the Christian community, that which separates the East from the West resembles the separation between Jew and Samaritan that developed in the last four centuries before Christ. Although there were tensions between East and West for a long time, they came to a head in AD 1054 with the excommunication of the Patriarch of Constantinople by the papal legate and the patriarch's consequent excommunication of the pope's delegate. Four centuries later, other divisions arose in western Christianity as a result of the Reformation. The differences between Christian churches are not simply theological but are also historical, political, sociological, cultural, and even psychological.

To help overcome these divisions within Christianity, the Council suggested that dialogue among Christian churches focus first on those elements that the various Christian churches share: the Scriptures, belief in Christ, baptism, and the Eucharist. The diversity of customs and doctrines will not then necessarily be obstacles to unity. We will recognize them as contributing to the Church's beauty, helpful adaptations to differences of culture, necessary for the good of the faithful.

To the Christian churches that today are struggling with the project of restoring the Church's unity, the Chronicler presents an object lesson regarding what can happen when concern for the survival of one religious community leads to a type of narrow exclusivism that ignores the values of other people's approach to God. The tasks of Ezra and Nehemiah and the duty of the Chronicler were clear: to ensure the survival of the small community of the Lord surrounding Jerusalem whose continued existence was in doubt. They fulfilled their responsibilities. The responsibility of Christian churches is somewhat different today: to restore Christian unity. To make unity a possibility, Christians will need to be more willing to live with religious diversity than they have been. The Chronicler's hesitancy regarding religious diversity is understandable. Judaism was struggling for its very survival. Christianity today is not as beleaguered as was Judaism in the Chronicler's day. Achieving unity while respecting diversity should be easier for us.

FURTHER READING

Coggins, R. J. *Samaritans and Jews: The Origins of Samaritism Reconsidered.* Atlanta: John Knox, 1975.

Crown, A. D. and others, ed. *A Companion to Samaritan Studies.* Tübingen: J. C. B. Mohr, 1993.

Dexinger, F. "Limits of Tolerance in Judaism: The Samaritan Example." In *Jewish and Christian Self-Definition.* Vol. 2, *Aspects of Judaism in the Graeco-Roman Period,* edited by E. P. Sanders and others, 88–114. Philadelphia: Fortress Press, 1981.

See also 1 Chronicles.

EZRA

[See pages 509–520 of the Old Testament]

The Book of Ezra

This book and the book of Nehemiah are the only narrative accounts of the postexilic period to have survived in the Hebrew Bible. Originally the books of Ezra and Nehemiah were components of a single work. The book of Nehemiah does not even have its own title in Jewish Bibles. There is simply a marginal notation alongside Nehemiah 1, 1 that reads "The Book of Nehemiah." In most editions of the Septuagint (the second-century BC Greek version of the Hebrew Bible), the two books form a unit.

The Vulgate (St. Jerome's translation of the Bible) separated the two books, and this is how the separation came into our English Bibles. It was only during the sixteenth century AD that what was one book became two in Jewish Bibles (see the introduction to the book of Ezra, OT, p. 509).

There is some internal evidence that these books form a coherent unit. The whole period of the restoration as covered by the books of Ezra and Nehemiah is one great era of return and rebuilding framed by two celebrations of the Feast of Booths. (Booths is the fall harvest festival, also known as Tabernacles and as Sukkoth, its Hebrew name.) The first celebration takes place after the return (Ezr 3, 4) and the second after the rebuilding is complete (Neh 8, 13–18). Both celebrations are in accord with what is "written" in Torah (Ezr 3, 4; Neh 8, 14.18).

The Restoration

The books of Ezra and Nehemiah deal with the restoration of Judah following the years of exile in Babylon (587–539 BC). These books deal with two phases of the restoration. The first is the rebuilding of the Temple in Jerusalem, and the second is the reordering of Jewish life. The Temple was rebuilt in 515 BC. Determining the dates for the work of Ezra and Nehemiah, who were responsible for the reordering of Jewish life in Jerusalem, is one of the more perplexing problems for the historian of early Judaism. The problem centers on Ezra 7, 7f and Nehemiah 2, 1. The former asserts that Ezra's ministry began in the seventh year of Artaxerxes' reign, while the latter states that Nehemiah's projects began in "the twentieth year of King Artaxerxes." There were, however, three Persian monarchs who had this name and who are potential candidates for the Artaxerxes mentioned in these texts.

The biblical text appears to assume that Ezra's ministry preceded that of Nehemiah. The chronological priority is due less to historical memory than to the Bible's view that Ezra was the real restorer of Jewish life following the exile. Although there is no real consensus on this issue, it is probable that Nehemiah's ministry preceded that of Ezra. Ezra's work appears to presuppose that the reconstruction and repopulation of Jerusalem had taken place, but it was Nehemiah who was responsible for restoring the city. Then, too, the high priest during Nehemiah's time was Eliashib (Neh 3, 1.20; 13, 4) while the high priest during Ezra's time was the son of Eliashib, Johanan (Ezr 10, 6; see note on this verse, OT, p. 519). The order and names of the postexilic high priests are additional problems for historians; still it seems likely that Nehemiah preceded Ezra. It is more likely that the restoration of communal life in Jerusalem preceded the restoration of religious life. Nehemiah, then, worked during the reign of Artaxerxes I and arrived in Jerusalem in 445 BC, while Ezra worked during the reign of Artaxerxes II and arrived in Jerusalem in 398 BC.

The chronology of the Judean restoration given in the books of Ezra and Nehemiah is ambiguous. Reconstructing this chronology is not very easy. The books of Ezra and Nehemiah are more interested in presenting the religious dimension to the activities of the two men whose names they bear. Despite the many problems in reconciling the details of this narrative, the author of Ezra and Nehemiah achieved his principal goal: to describe the beginning of renewal in the life of Judah.

There are important political reasons that explain why Persian rulers expressed concern about conditions in Judah. By supporting the rebuilding of the Temple in Jerusalem, the Persian emperors were staking their claim to be the legitimate rulers of Judah. In the ancient Near East, temple building was a royal prerogative. Since the beginning of both Nehemiah's and Ezra's missions coincided with Egyptian revolts against Persian hegemony, it was important for the Persians to have a sympathetic and supportive Judah in their rear as they moved against the rebellious Egyptians.

Reading the Book of Ezra

The book of Ezra falls into two parts covering the two periods of postexilic history. Chapters 1 through 6 cover the themes of the return from exile and the rebuilding the Temple. Chapters 7 through 10 describe the mission of Ezra to reconstitute Judah as a community living in accord with the Torah.

The Return from Exile and Rebuilding of the Temple (Ezr 1, 1—6, 22)

Aramaic

The most striking feature of this section is not apparent to those who read it in translation.

While the rest of the book of Ezra is in Hebrew, 4, 7—6, 18 is in Aramaic. The author cites a few official Persian documents relating to the restoration of Judah. These documents were written in Aramaic, the common language of the diverse peoples that made up the empire and the official language of the imperial administration. The alternation between Hebrew and Aramaic shows that the people for whom the author wrote were bilingual.

Originally Aramaic was the language of the Arameans. It is a Semitic language that is akin to Hebrew. Because the Arameans were active in commercial affairs in the ancient Near East, the language became widely known. Aramaic came to be the language of diplomacy. According to 2 Kings 18, 26, both the Assyrian and Judahite officers understood the language, while the common people did not. By the sixth century BC, however, it became the most commonly used Semitic language. It was in general use in Palestine until Greek became the language of commerce, government, and literary culture after the conquests of Alexander in the fourth century BC. Aramaic, however, remained the language of the common people until the seventh century AD when Arabic replaced it. Aramaic was the language in which Jesus conversed, although he may have known Greek as well. Hebrew was not a language of everyday conversation. Rabbinic traditions, however, continued to be transmitted in Hebrew. The *Mishnah,* a collection of legal traditions, and the *Midrashim,* homiletic texts, were composed and transmitted in Hebrew. Because people did not regularly converse in Hebrew, however, it became necessary for Jews to make Aramaic versions *(Targums)* of the Old Testament. Aramaic is also the language of the Talmud (the compendium of Jewish law dating from the sixth century AD). It was not until the twentieth century that the Hebrew language was reborn and once again became a language of ordinary discourse in the modern state of Israel.

The Return of the Exiles

Chapters 1 through 3 cover the return from exile. First there is a proclamation made by Cyrus, king of Persia, that every exile from Judah who was ready to return to Jerusalem to rebuild its Temple should do so (1, 1–4). Then the following verses describe the return itself (1, 5–11). Chapter 2 gives a list of the returnees. At the top of the list is Zerubbabel, a member of the Davidic family, and Jeshua, a member of a prominent priestly family. In chapter 3, these two play important roles in the revival of worship in Jerusalem. Sacrifices begin on a provisional altar (3, 1–3). The people observe the Feast of Booths (3, 4) and they initiate the regular sacrifices (3, 5). Most important of all, they prepare for the rebuilding of the Temple (3, 6–13).

There were problems with the rebuilding. The author lists these in 4, 1—6, 13. Opposition to the project came from "the enemies of Judah and Benjamin" (4, 1) and "the people of the land" (4, 4). Both groups tried to convince the Persians that the restoration of Jerusalem was an act of political disloyalty. In 4, 7–23 there is opposition to rebuilding the walls of the city. In the end all opposition failed, and the people of Judah successfully completed their project with the full support of the Persian imperial authorities (6, 14.22).

Ezra's Mission (Ezr 7, 1—10, 44)

Ezra's Commission from the Persian Emperor

The account of Ezra's activity begins with chapter 7 and concludes with chapter 10 although Nehemiah 8 also mentions Ezra. Ezra 7—8 provide an account of Ezra's journey from Babylon to Jerusalem. The genealogy in 7, 1–5 shows that Ezra was a Zadokite priest. (The Zadokite priests were those associated with the Jerusalem Temple in the preexilic period. Zadok was the priest who served David and Solomon.) Ezra was an expert in the Torah (7, 6) which the priests who were in exile developed while in Babylon. Another Aramaic document (the credentials that Artaxerxes gave to Ezra) takes up 7, 12–26. This imperial commission includes information about contributions to the Temple in Jerusalem (vv. 13–25) and the order to reestablish Judahite society based on the "law of God" (vv. 13–15.25). It was Persian policy to restore and support the worship of national deities throughout their empire. Additionally, the Persians usually charged the priests of temple cities with codifying local customs into a legal corpus to maintain the ethnic identity and local traditions. By their acceptance or rejection of the Torah, the Judahites defined themselves as belonging to or rejecting membership in the Jewish community. The emperor granted Ezra power to establish an executive structure for the governance of the Jewish community. This means that in the view of the Persian government the priestly version of ancient Israel's ancestral faith was the "official" religion of Judah.

The account of Ezra's journey to Jerusalem begins with a list of those returning with him (8, 1–14) and Ezra's persuading of the Levites who had been unwilling to make the journey (vv. 15–20). The author seems to have modeled the rest of the chapter on the description of the Exodus from Egypt (Ex 14) and the crossing of the Jordan and the occupation of the land (Jos 3—4).

The Problem of Mixed Marriages

The remaining two chapters deal with Jews who have married outside their religious community (9, 1). Ezra finds their behavior unacceptable and recites a long penitential prayer on their behalf (9, 5–15). The people decide to set matters straight (10, 1–3), and they ask Ezra for help (10, 4–6). After a public assembly takes place, a special commission begins work (10, 7–17). It produces a list of those who married Gentiles (10, 18–44). The text of 10, 44 does not make sense in Hebrew ("and there were from them wives and they put sons"). The translators based their rendering of this text on the Septuagint, the ancient Greek version of the Old Testament. The Hebrew text is unclear about the action taken in this matter, but some Jewish men probably divorced their non-Jewish wives in response to Ezra's urging.

Exclusivism in Ezra

In denouncing mixed marriages, Ezra speaks of the Jews as a "holy race" (Ezr 9, 2). He accuses the people of Judah of desecrating themselves with "the peoples of the land." The Jewish community of the fifth century BC faced the same types of threats to its existence as did the Israelite tribes centuries before the establishment of the Israelite national state (thirteenth to the eleventh centuries BC). At that time the Israelites faced hostile neighbors. They were unable to defend themselves adequately. There was little unity or even cooperation among the tribes. In the eleventh century BC, the prophet Samuel, responding to these problems, complied with popular sentiment and established the monarchy. The king provided order and stability to the foundering Israelite tribes. The Davidic dynasty, which that lasted from the eleventh to the sixth centuries BC, furnished a sense of continuity. In the fifth century BC, Persian hegemony made the reestablishment of Judah's native dynasty impossible. Ezra provided the community with another source of stability and continuity.

Ezra offered the Jewish community the Torah, which the Jews came to see as encompassing an eternal order given by God to Israel alone. This notion of Torah had some profound effects in the social order. It made the Jewish community exclusive. It led to the idea of a "holy race" (Ezr 9, 2), which was to remain unsullied by contact with the nations. Ezra believed that the Jews were in danger of being absorbed by the non-Jewish culture that surrounded them and therefore becoming extinct. In response to this threat, he taught that there was a very specific criterion for membership in the Jewish community. A principle of heredity supplied the Jewish self-definition. It was a definition that was clear to every member of the community. Earlier traditions also attempted to deal with the loss of identity through assimilation by intermarriage with Gentiles (Ex 34, 16; Dt 7, 3; 23, 3–5). Such marriages were acceptable in some traditions (Gn 41, 45; Ru 1). Even Moses himself married a non-Israelite (Nm 12, 1). With Ezra this all changed, and mixed marriages were no longer permissible. Under Ezra, the Jewish community was not open to outsiders.

The elevation of heredity to the position of defining the people of God is understandable, yet it compromised Israel's role as a source of blessing for the nations (Gn 12, 2f) and as God's servant bringing the Torah and its peace to the nations (Is 49, 1–7). The Samaritans whom Ezra's decrees excluded from the people of God considered him their archenemy. Samaritan writings are full of derogatory comments about Ezra. In contrast, the Talmud considers Ezra to be a second Moses (Sanhedrin 2 ib) because he restored observance of the Torah when the people had forgotten about it (Sukkah 20a). Early Christianity also had to deal with Ezra's legacy as it faced the consequences of its highly successful mission to the Gentiles (Acts 10, 1—15, 35). The early Church abandoned the views of Ezra on membership in the people of God.

The Achievement of Ezra

Without the efforts of Ezra, though, the Jewish community may very well not have survived the threats to its identity that were so serious in the Persian period. It is also important to remember that, along with Ezra, the Bible has included the stories of Jonah and Ruth, both of which offer voices of dissent against the exclusivism of this book.

We need to see Ezra's notion of a holy race against the backdrop of the cultural assumptions of ancient Near Eastern people. The key word here is *holy*. The solution to Judah's problems according to Ezra was the determination of the Jews to observe the Torah. Part of this observance revolved around the notion of separation from all that was not *ritually* pure. "Holy" here is a cultic term rather than a moral one. Ezra did not imply that the Jews were morally superior to the other nations. He did believe that they were in a unique position to offer the God of their ancestors the type of worship that this God required. Unfortunately, the more the Jews associated with Gentiles the more difficult it was for them to remain ritually pure. Both Ezra and Nehemiah demanded that the Jews remove this danger to their religious observance. Books such as Jonah and Ruth reminded their readers that the Jews could not claim moral superiority. The Gentiles too could please God.

The Call to Inclusion

The book of Ezra speaks to a beleaguered religious community on the brink of extinction. It sees assimilation as one of the main threats to that existence. It fosters an attitude of separation and exclusion. Today the threat to human existence comes precisely from the ignorance, prejudice, and hatred that keep the peoples of the world apart. The Second Vatican Council recognized this when it decided to issue a separate document dealing with non-Christian religions. Originally *Nostra Aetate* (1965) was to be just a chapter in the schema on ecumenism. The bishops of the Council became aware of the importance of this topic and developed this full-scale document.

The basic assumption of *Nostra Aetate* is that

all peoples comprise a single human community. All members of this community have the same final goal: God. The religions of the world result from the universal human attempt to probe the mystery of the divine. The Council encouraged Catholics to speak and work with followers of other religions. They are to acknowledge, preserve, and promote the spiritual and moral values found in non-Christian religions.

Singled out for special attention in the Council's declaration are the two other monotheistic faiths: Judaism and Islam. In particular, the Council repudiated any form of persecution and hatred that existed between the Christians and Jews at any time and from any source (*Declaration on the Relationship of the Church to Non-Christian Religions*, 4). The Church also rejected any type of discrimination directed at people because of their religion. The bishops called upon all Catholics to maintain "good fellowship" with all peoples by living with them in peace.

The circumstances faced by the Christian communities of the Holy Land today are similar to those faced by the Jews in Ezra's day. The adverse political, social, and economic situation faced by Christians in the Holy Land makes their continued presence in the land Jesus called home very difficult. Many have chosen to leave. There is the very real danger that the Christian presence in the Holy Land will be reduced those who care

for its shrines. The very place where the Church began may be left without a living, local church. The book of Ezra stands as an object lesson in the kind of decisive action that is necessary to respond to critical circumstances. Christians cannot make use of the specific way that Ezra responded to the problems faced by the Jewish community of his day, but they can emulate his passionate commitment to the survival of his people. Christians certainly ought to commit themselves to the survival of the Christian community in the Holy Land.

FURTHER READING

Blenkinsopp, Joseph. *Ezra–Nehemiah. A Commentary.* Old Testament Library. Philadelphia: Westminster, 1988.

Fensham, F. C. *The Books of Ezra and Nehemiah.* The New International Commentary on the Old Testament. Grand Rapids, MI: Eerdmans, 1982.

Grabbe, Lester L. *Ezra–Nehemiah.* London and New York: Routledge, 1998.

Myers, Jacob M., *Ezra–Nehemiah.* Anchor Bible 14. Garden City, NY: Doubleday, 1965.

Throntveit, M. A. *Ezra–Nehemiah.* Interpretation: A Commentary for Teaching and Preaching. Louisville: John Knox, 1992.

Williamson, H. G. M. *Ezra and Nehemiah.* Old Testament Guides. Sheffield: JSOT Press, 1987.

See also 1 Chronicles.

NEHEMIAH

[see pages 521–37 of the Old Testament]

The Relation between the Books of Ezra and Nehemiah

The introduction to this book (OT, p. 521) assumes that Ezra and Nehemiah are components of what was originally a single work. The book of Nehemiah deals with the political and administrative side of the restoration, while the book of Ezra focuses on the establishment of Torah as the "constitution of the returned community."

Besides these different concerns, there is one striking difference between the two books based on literary form. According to Nehemiah 1, 1 ("The words of Nehemiah . . ."), the book is an account for which Nehemiah himself is responsible. A significant portion of the book is written

in the first person (1, 1—7, 5; 12, 31—13, 31). These are the so-called "Memoirs of Nehemiah" (see introduction, OT, p. 521).

It is important to see the work of both Nehemiah and Ezra against the deplorable conditions that the prophet Malachi depicts (see Mal 1—2). Without the type of concrete communal structures that Ezra and Nehemiah were to provide, the people found it impossible to live according to the high ideals of their ancestral religion since they lacked a healthy social and religious life.

Reading the Book

This book describes the work of Nehemiah (1, 1—7, 72) and the place of Torah in the restored community of Jerusalem (8, 1—13, 31).

The Rebuilding of Jerusalem
(Neh 1, 1—6, 19)

Because of the bad reports that came to the Persian imperial court from Jerusalem, the emperor Artaxerxes agreed to send Nehemiah, his cupbearer, to rebuild the city (1, 1—2, 8). There was opposition from both within and without the Judahite community to this project. Though Sanballat, the governor of Samaria, was Nehemiah's principal antagonist, opposition came from governors of other neighboring provinces as well (4, 1). They mocked Nehemiah's plans (2, 19f; 3, 33–37) and even proposed military action against Jerusalem (4, 1–5). When their criticism and plots failed to dissuade Nehemiah from his mission, they began plotting against his life (6, 1–14). There were also some elements within Judahite society that associated themselves with these plots against Nehemiah (6, 17–19). This internal opposition came from the upper classes who had a stake in maintaining the status quo. Their unjust behavior led to disturbances that hindered the task of rebuilding the city (5, 1–5). Nehemiah realized that rebuilding the city's walls was not enough to insure stability. He ordered the people of means to stop their economic abuse of the poor (5, 6–13). Despite all the opposition, Nehemiah completed the project of rebuilding the walls of Jerusalem in just fifty-two days (3, 1–32; 4, 9–17; 6, 15–19).

Jerusalem had been the capital of the Judahite national state. It was the location of the temple dedicated to the patron deity of that state. But the Babylonians leveled the city and its temple in 587 BC (2 Kgs 25, 10). Although the temple was rebuilt and Nehemiah refortified the city, the second temple was far less ornate than the one built by Solomon (Ezr 3, 12), and Nehemiah's walls enclosed only a fraction of the preexilic city. Jerusalem was no longer the capital of a Judahite national state. Still, it was the leading city of the Persian subprovince of Yehud. It was the center for preserving the particular worship of the Jewish community, and Persian imperial policy supported the preservation of this worship. Nehemiah's project was opposed by neighboring rulers because they saw this leading to a new economic and possibly political status for Jerusalem, which they saw as threatening their interests.

The Population of Jerusalem

Chapter 7 provides a transition from the description of Nehemiah's successful rebuilding project to the promulgation of Torah. Following the comment about the meager population of Jerusalem (7, 4), there is a repetition of the list of those who returned from Babylon (7, 6–72). This list duplicates the one found in Ezra 2, 1–67.

The Promulgation of Torah
(Neh 8, 1—13, 31)

At this point the Nehemiah memoirs break off. Chapters 8 through 10 describe a ritual that Ezra conducts. This ceremony brings to closure both the rebuilding of the city and the reconstitution of its religious life. The community of Jerusalem heard the words of Torah (8, 1–12). It responded by celebrating the Feasts of Booths according to the prescriptions of the Torah (8, 13–18). Two weeks later the community began a fast (9, 1–3), and then Ezra made a great confession of sin in the name of the people (9, 6–37).

Torah

An important theme in both Ezra and Nehemiah is the Torah as a *written* authoritative guide for the life of the Jewish community. In Nehemiah 8, Ezra reads the law. In Nehemiah 9, the people of Jerusalem confess their failure to observe the law. In Nehemiah 10, the people agree to live according to its precepts. Unfortunately for our understanding of these passages, too many Christians have a very distorted notion of the Torah. These distortions have arisen because of the polemical atmosphere in the Gospels that recount Jesus' debates with the Pharisees regarding the interpretation of Torah (Mt 5, 21–48; 23, 13–36), and the bitter exchanges between Paul and some early Christians who considered the observance of the Torah essential for all (Gal 3, 10–14).

Despite their disputes with those who opposed their teaching on the law, both Jesus and Paul could be effusive in their praise of the Torah: "Do not think that I have come to abolish the law or the prophets . . . Whoever breaks one of the least of these commandments and teaches others to do so will be called least in the kingdom of heaven" (Mt 5, 17–19) and "So then the law is holy, and the commandment is holy and righteous and good" (Rom 7, 12). Still, the word "law" has a pejorative ring to it in the ears of most Christians.

The key to understanding and appreciating the Torah is to begin with the biblical context from which it emerged. But like most theologically important words in the Hebrew Bible, the text uses the term *Torah* in several different ways within the Bible. There is even some dispute over the etymology of the word. Some hold that the word *Torah* derives from the Hebrew word *yarah,* which means to throw or to cast lots. Thus, the original meaning of Torah may have referred to the determination of the divine will with some sort of a lot-oracle. In another linguistic form, *yarah* means to point the way, to instruct. Thus Torah may have originally derived from the instructions priests gave to the people.

In the Bible, Torah usually refers to God's instructions to Moses at Sinai that he handed on to ancient Israel. Sometimes these instructions deal with specific sacrificial laws, ethical norms, regulations dealing with purity and impurity (Lv 4, 1—7, 38; 10, 10; 11, 1—13, 59; 14, 57; 23, 44). In the book of Deuteronomy, Torah takes on a more comprehensive sense and becomes that which determines Israel's cultural, religious, and national identity. Torah is the written authoritative law, which is Israel's "constitution" for life in the land that was its inheritance from God (Dt 28, 61; 29, 20; 30, 10; 31, 26).

The books of Joshua to 2 Kings follow the lead of Deuteronomy and speak of Torah in the comprehensive sense as "the book of the Torah" (Jos 1, 7f; 1 Kgs 2, 3; 2 Kgs 23, 5). The prophets use the term *Torah* in a variety of senses. Sometimes the term refers to cultic regulations (Hos 4, 6); sometimes it includes God's moral commands (Is 5, 24; 30, 9), and ethical norms (Hb 1, 4). It is also divine teaching given through the prophets (Is 1, 10; 8, 16). Sometimes the prophets use *Torah* in the comprehensive sense (Jer 6, 19; 9, 12; Is 42, 21.24; Mal 3, 22).

The Psalms praise both the Torah and those who live by it (Pss 1, 2; 19, 8; 37, 31; 40, 9; 94, 12; 112, 1; 119, 97). Psalms 19 and 119 reflect the joy of ancient Israel in the Torah. Proverbs speaks of Torah as the advice of parents or a sage (1, 8; 3, 1; 13, 14). Later Jewish sages identify wisdom and the Torah (Sir 24, 1–31; 39, 1–11).

Ezra (3, 2; 7, 6.10) and Nehemiah (8, 1; 9, 3; 10, 30; 13, 1) assume a fixed written Torah.

The early rabbis believed that they were responsible for transmitting not only the written Torah but also an oral Torah, which contained the teachings of revered sages who advanced the obligations of the law beyond the words of the written Torah, and thus made violations of the written Torah more difficult. These rabbis traced the origins of this oral Torah back to Moses *(Pirke Avot, 1,1).* Around AD 200, Rabbi Judah the Prince committed this oral law to writing in a work called the *Mishnah.* This was the beginning of the Talmud (the code of rabbinical teaching on the manner of observing the law.) Thus, in contemporary Judaism Torah refers not only to the books of Moses but to the Talmud and the entire Jewish ethical tradition.

Proverbs 1, 8 and 3, 1 may provide the key to appreciating Torah. These texts speak of Torah as parental guidance for a child. The Bible often speaks of Israel as God's children (Ex 4, 22; Dt 14, 1; 32, 10–12; Hos 11, 1; Jer 31, 9.20; Is 66, 13). Some people then understood Torah as the teaching imparted by the parent God to the child Israel. In this light, the giving of the Torah is an act of the highest love.

Another key to appreciating the Torah is the recognition that it refers not only to the vehicle of revelation but also its entire content. Torah contains both the story of Israel's election and salvation, and the stipulations of its covenantal relationship with God. Torah then includes the story of the free acts of God that presented ancient Israel with the model of righteousness. It also includes specifications of how Israel should live in obedient response to those free acts of God. The people of ancient Israel did not experience the Torah as a burden that they had to bear with patient endurance but as the way to life and a source of joy.

In the perspective of the books of Ezra and Nehemiah, obedience to the written, authoritative Torah is a condition for survival. Without careful observance Judaism is in danger of being lost in the sea of assimilation. It is assimilation that will do to the Jewish community what the exile failed to do. Thus, the Torah is Israel's life. The devotion to ethical principles, the enduring attitude of self-examination and self-correction that observance implies, the maintenance of identity by adherence to a moral code—all these are values that Christians could learn from Judaism, ancient and modern.

The word *Torah* has many meanings and reflects many different values. Perhaps only those who observe the law as an act of obedient love for God can experience its fundamental meaning. For the observant Jew it is the truth revealing God's election and salvation of Israel. It is also the way to respond to God's graciousness. It is finally the way to life. For Ezra and Nehemiah the Torah was Judah's way to the future.

The Promulgation of the Torah

The elements of the ritual found in Nehemiah 8 may have served as the model for the synagogue service that developed somewhat later in Judaism. There is the bringing of the Torah scroll (8, 2), the mounting of the platform that contains the desk for reading (8, 4), the opening of the scroll (8, 5), the blessing (v. 6a), the communal *Amen* (8, 6b). The "interpretation" that 8, 8 refers to may be an Aramaic translation of the Torah, which Ezra read in Hebrew. Some people may have needed an Aramaic translation of the Torah since they no longer understood Hebrew very well. Aramaic was the language common to all the peoples of the Persian empire and, since the sixth century BC, Aramaic was replacing Hebrew as the language of everyday speech in Judah.

The Confession

Nehemiah 9, 6–37 is one of the important creedal statements in the Old Testament. It recounts Israel's communal experience of God from the time of Abraham (9, 7) to the period of restoration (9, 33). The purpose of this confession of faith is to acknowledge Israel's failure to keep the commandments despite God's goodness and fidelity. It is also a remarkable act of faith in divine forbearance. There is a similar prayer of confession in Ezra 9, 7–15. The note to Ezra 9, 7 (OT, p. 519) suggests that these two confessions were originally parts of the same prayer.

The Agreement of the People

Chapter 10 contains a written pledge made by those listed in verses 1b–29 to observe the Torah of Moses. As the note to 10, 1–40 (OT, p. 532) suggests, this text should come after Nehemiah

13, which lists reforms of Nehemiah. The pledge made by the people could hardly be made before Nehemiah initiated the reforms. Among the specific points made in the pledge is the prohibition of marriage with Gentiles (10, 31; see 13, 20–23a) and observance of the Sabbath (10, 32; see 13, 15–22). Those who made the pledge also promise to provide firewood for the altar (10, 35; see 13, 31), first fruits for sacrifice (10, 36f; see 13, 31), and tithes for the support of the Levites (10, 38–40; see 13, 10–14).

The Resettlement of Jerusalem

Nehemiah 11 begins with a lottery used to resettle Jerusalem (11, 1–3). Then follow lists of the inhabitants of Jerusalem (11, 3–24) and of the rural areas of Judah (11, 20–30), and of the Benjaminites (11, 31–36). Nehemiah 12 begins with lists of priests and Levites (12, 1–26). Then follows a description of the dedication of the walls (12, 27–43). The book concludes with a listing of the various reform measures begun by Nehemiah (12, 44—13, 31), to the observance of which the people pledged themselves in Nehemiah 10.

Ritual Purity

Like the book of Ezra (9, 1f), Nehemiah condemns mixed marriages (Neh 13, 23–29). These books reflect the belief that if the Jews were to survive as a people, they had to keep themselves separate from other ethnic and religious groups. An important emphasis in both books, then, is the purity of the reconstituted community. On a surface level this concern appears to be a type of ethnic discrimination. There could have been some of that at work here; however, it is important to note that this emphasis on purity concerns cult and ritual. The call of Ezra and Nehemiah for purity is a call for ritual, not ethnic, purity. Ritual purity was in some sense dependent upon ancient Near Eastern ideas of order. Mixing two peoples through marriage or in worship offends this notion of order. Exclusion of Gentiles from the cult does not come from a belief in *ethnic* superiority. The call for separation from others is pervasive in Ezra and Nehemiah (Ezr 4, 1–3; 6, 21; 9—10; Neh 2, 20; 3, 3; 9, 2; 10, 29; 13, 23–29). It is a component of the directives associated with rebuilding the Temple and in the rest of the restoration program led by both Ezra and Nehemiah.

The New Testament affirms that the Christian worship transcends these patterns. According to John, Christians worship in "Spirit and truth" (Jn 4, 23). Classifications based on "flesh" are no longer relevant. Paul makes it clear that in Jesus there is "neither Jew nor Greek" (Gal 3, 28). Matthew writes that Jesus' final command was to "make disciples of all nations" (Mt 28, 19). This insight did not occur to the first Christians automatically. The Acts of the Apostles shows that the inclusion of the Gentiles into the Christian community was a matter of spirited debate among the Jewish Christians (Acts 15, 1–35).

The synagogue also struggled with the question of the exclusion/inclusion of the Gentiles. Some rabbis favored the more exclusive strain found in books such as Deuteronomy (Dt 23), Ezra, and Nehemiah. Others endorsed the more inclusive tendencies in texts such as Isaiah 56, which stated that the Temple was to be "a house of prayer for all peoples" (Is 56, 7).

The Conclusion

The last sentence of the book ("Remember this in my favor, O my God!" Neh 13, 31) may give an insight into the purpose of the book. This formula is similar to those attached to texts inscribed on walls of ancient Near Eastern temples. From the location of these texts *within* the temple, clearly those who made them were addressing the deity since only priests entered the temples themselves. This same formula, petitioning for divine remembrance, is typical of memorial inscriptions found in Jewish monumental buildings such as synagogues from a much later period. Besides being an act of piety, inclusion of this formula was probably an attempt to commend this work to its readers.

FURTHER READING

See 1 Chronicles and Ezra.

TOBIT

[see pages 537–53 of the Old Testament]

The Moral of the Story

The book of Tobit is a complex literary work with a very uncomplicated moral. The book narrates important incidents in the lives of Tobit, Sarah, and Tobiah. It tells the story of their tragedies and triumphs. The author weaves the stories of these three people together very skillfully so that the book results from the intersection of three different but related plots. This rhetorical feat of weaving the stories of these three people so tightly has a theological purpose: to show how God can manage the circumstances of people's lives in order to bring God's plans to fulfillment. Its primary religious message is simple: God rewards those who are faithful.

Approaching the Book:
The Literary Form of Tobit

The introduction to this book describes Tobit as a "religious novel" (OT, p. 537). The historical and geographical details given in the book are there simply to provide a plausible setting for the story. Tobit is not a work of history-writing. Its author confuses the kings of Assyria, shows an ignorance of the topography of Mesopotamia, and dates Tobit's exile earlier than it could have been (see notes to 1, 2.15; 5, 6; and 14, 15). Though calling Tobit a novel may not be entirely satisfactory, the book is the work of a single author and not a product of oral or literary tradition despite the author's attempt to associate his principal character with Ahiqar, a very popular figure of ancient Near Eastern wisdom tradition (see note on 1, 21; OT, p. 539). As a novel, the book of Tobit presents three characters in an intricately developed plot that the introduction summarizes on p. 537.

What is especially important to notice is how the author of Tobit tells the stories of Tobit and his relative Sarah. Both suffer undeservedly. Tobit became blind while doing an act of charity by burying the dead. In his despondency he prays for death. Sarah believes that she will remain a childless widow. A demon has killed each of her seven husbands on their respective wedding nights. Sarah too prays for death. God answers their prayers by enabling Tobiah, Tobit's son, to cure Tobit's blindness and break the power of the demon that was killing Sarah's husbands. Tobiah is able to accomplish this with the help of the angel Raphael. The action of Tobiah solves the problems of both Tobit and Sarah.

Since Tobit is such a cleverly told story, it is important that one read the story through in order to appreciate the author's message. Tobit is short enough to read in a single sitting. One key to understanding the author's purpose is the unfolding of the story and how God answers the prayers of the innocent Tobit and Sarah in a way they hardly expected.

The Religious Horizons of the Book

The basic concern of this book becomes clear as God acts through Raphael to solve the problems of Tobit, Sarah, and Tobiah. Each problem contains the germ of a solution for the others. Tobit is going to die, so he sends his son Tobiah to collect an outstanding debt. This brings Tobiah in contact with Raphael, who gives him a way to cure his father *and* to eliminate Sarah's problem. In the process of traveling to collect the debt, Tobiah meets Sarah and falls in love with her. Tobiah is able to break the power of the demon that tormented Sarah. In the end, the medicine Raphael gives Tobiah cures Tobit's blindness, Tobiah recovers the money owed to his father, Tobiah marries Sarah, and together they raise a family.

The purpose of this engaging tale is to show that God controls events and manages the circumstances in order to ensure that God's own purposes come to fruition. The story assumes God's sovereignty in people's lives and God's determination to reward the just. When the just suffer, there is a limit to that suffering. Once that limit occurs God will intervene, and sometimes that intervention is miraculous.

Tobit's reaction to his suffering and its alleviation underscores the religious views of the book. At first Tobit's response is one of despair, since he sees death as the only way of deliverance. Once he experiences God's deliverance, Tobit is eloquent in his praise of God's mercy. The book's answer to the problem of suffering is in 11, 15: ". . . it was he who scourged me, and it is he who has had mercy on me."

The Judaism of the Book

The introduction (OT, p. 537) states that the book of Tobit appeared fewer than two hundred years

before Christ. It reveals a form of Judaism that accepted magic and had a strong belief in angels and demons. Raphael, an angel of God, suggests the means for negating the power of the demon (6, 7–9), and so the magical means of dealing with demonic powers must be legitimate for any Jew. Mysterious powers in the entrails of a fish serve not only to cure illnesses but also to bind the demonic powers that harm people.

Tobit, then, represents a Judaism that sees angels and demons as having important roles to play in the drama between God and human beings. This contrasts sharply with books such as Judith and Esther where human beings are in control of their own destiny without any intervention of angelic and demonic powers. The author of Tobit considers angels to be more than simply God's messengers: they mediate prayers in God's throne room (3, 16; 12, 12–15); they oppose demons (8, 2f); they commission the writing of books (12, 11f). Belief in demons accompanies a belief in angels. While angels make their interventions for the good of people, demons are hostile powers.

The book also reflects the importance that the book of Deuteronomy came to have in early Judaism. This is especially clear in Tobit 14, 4–7, which asserts that the exile happened because of Israel's infidelity (see Dt 28, 15–68), that the exile is not God's final judgment on Israel but that there is hope for mercy (see Dt 30, 1–4), and that the Temple of Jerusalem is the only legitimate place for worship (see Dt 12, 1–14). The Judaism that Tobit depicts is a Judaism that measures fidelity to God in terms of fulfillment of the Torah, which is just what Deuteronomy preaches.

Finally Tobit seems to reflect the circumstances of Jews in the Diaspora (Jewish settlements outside of Palestine). The book portrays Gentiles as unsympathetic to Tobit's activities (2, 8) and as those responsible for persecuting him (1, 16–20). The book presents marriage within Judaism as a duty. It teaches that God is sovereign over all people and that God is present to those in exile, even in the midst of their suffering. It underscores the need to maintain Jewish identity in the Diaspora. The means to accomplish this is the family. The book's emphasis on the family is one reason that Tobit remained popular in the Church, even though the book did not become part of the Jewish canon of the Old Testament.

Reading the Book

The only way to savor the book's literary artistry and to appreciate its religious perspectives is to follow the way the author unfolds the events related to Tobit's life. Notice the suffering of Tobit, Sarah, and their families in the first part of the book. In despair they pray for death since they do not experience God's presence in this life. Notice how the stories of Tobit and Sarah parallel one another. See table below.

God hears these prayers but responds to them in a totally unexpected manner. Raphael stands as a symbol of God's presence with both Tobit and Sarah. Even though they felt abandoned by God, God was with them in the midst of their suffering. When Tobiah finishes his journey and Tobit realizes the presence of God in his own life and in the lives of his son and new daughter-in-law, he breaks into enthusiastic and joyful praise of God. The reader should notice the movement in the book from despair to thanksgiving and praise.

Angels and Demons

There are two important nonhuman characters in the book: Asmodeus, the demon who torments Sarah (3, 8) and Raphael, who reveals himself as one of the seven angels who "serve before the Glory of the Lord" (12, 15). The book of Tobit, then, reflects the belief of early Judaism in angels and demons as supernatural beings. The first form of this belief seems to be "the messenger of the Lord," which belongs to the earliest narratives in the Hebrew Bible. In some of these stories, clearly the messenger of the Lord is not different from the Lord (see Gn 16, 13; 21, 18; 31, 13). Since God confronts people directly in many of the early stories, the appearance of angels is somewhat irregular. As people begin to think of God as transcendent, far beyond the human sphere, angels become a more regular

feature of the narratives. Ideas develop about good angels and bad angels (the demons), a hierarchy of angels, and the various duties of angels. In Tobit, Raphael is one of the seven holy angels who offer up the prayers of the pious (Tb 12, 15).

Angels and demons play a prominent role in the noncanonical literature of early Judaism. For example, in the book of Enoch, Raphael is an archangel (1 Enoch 20, 3). He heals the illnesses and injuries of human beings (1 Enoch 40, 9). By the time of the New Testament, angels were thought of as spiritual beings who were God's allies in opposition to Satan and his "angels," the demons.

It is possible to see popular imagination at work in the description of angels. They wear white garments (Dn 10, 5f; 1 Enoch 87, 2). The angels have wings (Dn 9, 21 [note that the NAB follows the Septuagint and translates the Hebrew phrase "borne in winged flight" as "came in rapid flight"]; 1 Enoch 61, 1). Finally, around the turn of the era, there appears in a few Jewish texts what seems to be the belief that it was permissible to portray figures from Israel's past, especially Adam and Jacob, as angels. Evidently some Jews held that it was possible for a select few to transcend humanity and become angels.

Belief in angels was not universal in early Judaism. Acts 23, 8 asserts that the Pharisees representing more liberal and popular beliefs acknowledged the existence of angels, while the more conservative and aristocratic Sadducees rejected the existence of angels along with belief in spirits and the resurrection.

The Purpose of the Book

Why did the author tell the story of Tobit? Was it simply to entertain? Even though the book is highly entertaining as a short novel, its purpose goes far beyond the enjoyment of its readers. The author tells his story to teach while entertaining. The book calls for prayer, fasting, and especially almsgiving (4, 7–11; 12, 8). It presents the Jew-

Tobit's piety (2, 1–7)	Sarah's innocence (3, 14)
Tobit's blindness (2, 9–10)	Sarah's demon (3, 8)
Tobit's reproach (2, 14)	Sarah's reproach (3, 7–10)
Tobit's prayer (3, 1–6)	Sarah's prayer (3, 10–15)

ish family as the means of maintaining fidelity to the ancestral religion of the Jews (4, 12f). It affirms that it is possible to remain faithful to God and the Law—even in the difficult circumstances of the Diaspora. Finally, it presents repentance as the key to the future of Judaism (13, 6).

The author addresses his message to people who easily identify with the principal characters of the book. They wonder about the value of fidelity to their God since it sometimes brings them undeserved difficulties. Tobit reaffirms the value of fidelity. While there may be difficult times, God will never desert those who remain faithful, and the God who controls human events will ensure that the faithful will find their reward.

The author wishes to affirm the importance of the community. One's commitment to the community is the measure of one's commitment to God. It is important to support the poor, bury the dead, honor one's parents, marry within the community. The Jewish community will have a future as long as there are Tobits who pledge themselves to its preservation.

The purpose of the book is to move its readers from despair to prayer. The figure of Tobit is a paradigm for the pious Jews who experience not God's presence but his absence in their suffering. The central affirmation of the book is that God is

with Tobit even when Tobit does not experience the divine presence. Once Raphael makes Tobit aware that God has always been with him, Tobit launches into a song of praise (13, 1–18).

FURTHER READING

Craghan, John F. *Esther; Judith; Tobit; Jonah; Ruth.* Old Testament Message 16. Wilmington, DE: Michael Glazier, 1982.

Fitzmyer, Joseph A. *Tobit.* Berlin and New York: de Gruyter, 2003.

Levine, Amy-Jill. "Diaspora as Metaphor: Bodies and Boundaries in the Book of Tobit." In *Diaspora Jews and Judaism,* edited by J. Andrew Overman and Robert S. MacLennan. Atlanta: Scholars Press, 1992.

McCarthy, Carmel, and William Riley. "The Book of Tobit: The Pattern of Mercy." In *The Old Testament Short Story: Explorations into Narrative Spirituality,* edited by Carmel McCarthy and William Riley. Message of Biblical Spirituality 6. Wilmington, DE: Michael Glazier, 1986.

Moore, Carey A. *Tobit.* Anchor Bible 40A. NY: Doubleday, 1996.

Soll, Will. "The Book of Tobit as a Window on the Hellenistic Jewish Family." In *Passion, Vitality, and Foment: The Dynamics of Second Temple Judaism,* edited by M. Lamonette Luker. Harrisburg: Trinity, 2001.

JUDITH

[see pages 553–69 of the Old Testament]

The Book's Literary Form

There have been several attempts at classifying the book of Judith according to its literary type. The book is certainly not a historical account. The introduction points out the uselessness of trying to read this book against the "backdrop of Jewish history in relation to the empires of the ancient world" (OT, p. 554). There are just too many historical errors and anachronisms in the book. For example, the book describes Nebuchadnezzar as the king of the Assyrians (1, 1) when he was king of Babylon. His attack against Judah supposedly took place after the return from exile (4, 1–3)! The historical errors are so egregious that it is likely that the author meant

readers to recognize them as such. Is the book of Judith a historical novel, midrash (the expansion, probing, and exposition of biblical texts to find new meaning in them), or a fictional drama? None of these classifications is completely satisfactory. This book is the result of a conscious, systematic, and faith-filled meditation on God's providential care for Israel. The book attempts to show how the invisible hand of God rescues Israel through the hand of Judith.

Reading the Book

As the introduction notes (OT, p. 553), the tale of Judith is well known. Over the centuries her story has attracted a remarkable amount of attention from writers, artists, and composers.

Chiasm I			Chiasm II
1. **2, 14—3, 10**	Holofernes begins campaign; nations surrender	A. **8, 1–8**	Introduction to Judith
2. **4, 1–15**	Israel prepares for war	B. **8, 9f**	Judith plans to save Israel
3. **5, 1—6, 11**	Holofernes talks with Achior	C. **10, 9f**	Judith leaves Bethulia
3'. **6, 12–21**	Achior talks with Israel	D. **10, 11—13, 10a**	Judith overcomes Holofernes
2'. **7, 1–15**	Holofernes prepares for war	C'. **13, 10b–11**	Judith returns to Bethulia
1'. **7, 6–32**	Holofernes begins campaign; the people wish to surrender	B'. **13, 12—16, 20**	Judith plans to destroy Israel's enemies
		A'. **16, 21–25**	Conclusion about Judith

Many composers, such as Thomas Arne, Antonio Vivaldi, and Arthur Honegger, chose Judith as the subject of their oratorios and operas. Painters have represented her story on canvas, and the sculptors of the facade of the cathedral at Chartres depicted her story in stone. One reason for all this attention is that Judith's story is such a good one. It is a heroic tale in which an unlikely character overcomes the cowardice of her own people in the face of the enemy. She defeats an arrogant general who thought that he was invincible in love and war. The plot begins in part I (1, 1—7, 32) with the introduction of the antagonists: Nebuchadnezzar and his general Holofernes.

• **1, 1–16:** Nebuchadnezzar declares war on the Medes and demands that his vassals aid him in his campaign. His vassals, Judah among them, ignore his call. Despite this, Nebuchadnezzar is victorious.

• **2, 1–13:** Nebuchadnezzar commissions Holofernes to punish the disloyal vassals.

The story then focuses on the fate of Judah, whose king and people ignored Nebuchadnezzar and now await his retribution. In telling the rest of the story, the book of Judith arranges the plot in two chiasms. (A chiasm is a type of inverted parallelism.) This is a frequent rhetorical device in biblical literature. Each incident leading up to a central event is balanced in reverse order with a similar incident following the central event.

Chiasm I (2, 14—3, 10) delineates the struggle. That it is both a religious and political conflict is clear from the words of Holofernes deriding the Israelite hope for victory when be boasts: "Who are you, Achior . . . to tell us not to fight against the Israelites because their God protects them? What god is there beside Nebuchadnezzar?" (6,

2). Achior was an Ammonite whom Holofernes, Nebuchadnezzar's general, summoned to provide him with intelligence about the Israelites. Achior eventually converted to Judaism.

Chiasm II (8, 1—16, 25) introduces Judith, the heroine who relieves the tension created in Chiasm I. She defeats Holofernes and proves that the Lord alone is God. Chiasm II portrays Judith as a model of faith. She not only crushes the arrogance and pride of Nebuchadnezzar and Holofernes but overcomes the cowardice and timidity of her fellow Jews who are ready to surrender. She takes her action without any guarantee from God that she will be successful. Her only guarantee is her faith.

The Image of Judith

The heroine's name is not a proper name. It means simply "Jewish woman." Judith, then, is more than an individual; she is a composite of all the women who have saved Israel in the past by their piety, wisdom, and action. On one level, the book of Judith is a tribute to those women whose achievements and memory ancient Israel cherished. Like Miriam (Ex 15, 20f) she led Israel in a song of thanksgiving following God's deliverance of the people (Ex 15, 14–16.17). Like Deborah (Jgs 4, 4–9) she aroused the flagging faith of Israel, besieged by its enemies (Jgs 8, 9–27). Like Jael (Jgs 4, 17–21) she assassinated her people's adversary. Like the wise woman from Abel Beth-maacah (2 Sm 20, 15–22) Judith challenged the strategy of Israel's leaders and substituted her own (8, 16; 9, 2). By telling the tale of Judith, the storyteller was in effect honoring all the women whose memory ancient Israel revered. These women saved the people of ancient Israel at times when the more usual channels of leadership were not able to meet the challenges to their faith.

The first people to hear the story of Judith lived in a traditional society in which the roles assigned to men and women were distinct. The book of Judith offers a surprising dissent from the assumptions of its culture about the role and status of women. In this story, the men proved to be utter failures in the face of the threats of Nebuchadnezzar and Holofernes. As happened several times in Israel's past, God chose a woman to be the instrument of salvation. Judith, like her predecessors, is a most impressive channel of God's deliverance. The usual channels (the king, priests, and other notables) failed. The impact that this story made on a traditional society like that of early Judaism is difficult for us to appreciate because we live in a society where change occurs with greater frequency and rapidity.

Despite its countercultural veneer, the book of Judith is otherwise conservative in its outlook on the role of women in Jewish society. By rescuing her people from destruction at the hands of Gentiles, Judith is a model for the Jewish woman as the conservator of tradition. Her socially assigned role is to preserve tradition and keep her family protected from the pressures to assimilate to the dominant non-Jewish culture that threatens to envelop it. Judith is a paradigm for the Jewish woman who shields her family against incursions from the outside that threaten to dilute their loyalty to their ancestral religion. The heroine of the book carries out the role assigned to her by her culture, but she also transcends that role.

The Irony in the Book

The story of Judith is full of unexpected turns. The first and most obvious, especially to those who first heard or read Judith's story, was that a woman—not a man—saved Judah in its time of severe distress. Judith is more faithful and resourceful than any of the men of Bethulia. She is more eloquent than the king and more courageous than any of the leading citizens of the city, yet Judith is a very unlikely heroine. She is a childless widow; as such she occupied a very low place in the social hierarchy. While the king, the priests, and other leaders of Judahite society show themselves incapable of dealing with the crisis, lowly Judith stands up to the threat posed by Holofernes and takes decisive action to end it.

The means that Judith used to accomplish her end may offend some. She used her beauty to gain access to the enemy camp and to beguile Holofernes. Judith, though, was using the one weapon that she had available to her, and it happened to be a weapon that exploited the weakness of Judah's enemy. This leads to the second irony. Judith destroys Judah's enemies not with military might but with her beguiling charm and disarming beauty. The Bible sometimes portrays a woman's beauty negatively as a snare (2 Sm 11, 2–5; Prv 6, 26; Sir 9, 2f), but here it is the means of deliverance.

Finally, Judith is a childless widow, yet the book portrays her as the mother of faith. It was her faith that gave new life to Israel. That is why the high priests and elders praise her so highly (15, 9). The Latin hymn *Tota pulchra es* applies these words of praise to Mary. The liturgy finds the story of Judith as an appropriate image to speak of the Virgin Mary, who is the Mother of the Church.

The Judaism of the Book

The book of Judith asserts that the deliverance of the Jews in Bethulia depends not on power and might but on fidelity to the law. This is the point that Achior makes to Holofernes (5, 5–21) and that Judith makes to the elders of Bethulia (8, 17–21). The author portrays Judith as living according to the law as Jews interpreted it at that time. As a widow, she lived in a state of mourning marked by fasting (8, 4–6). She prayed daily at the hour of the incense offering in the Temple (9, 1). She observes the Jewish dietary laws (10, 5 and 12, 2.19). She purifies herself by bathing in running water at the appropriate time (12, 7–9). Judith criticizes the people of Bethulia for violating the law of first fruits and tithes (11, 11–14).

The book departs significantly from earlier tradition as it describes the conversion of Achior the Ammonite (14, 10). According to Deuteronomy, the Israelites were never to admit an Ammonite into their community (Dt 23, 4). Presumably the author was able to justify this by the example of Ruth, who (as a Moabite woman) belonged to the other nation that Deuteronomy excludes from ever becoming part of the Israelite community. While the book of Judith presents obedience to the Torah as the key to Israel's deliverance, it shows a type of flexibility that is able to respond to a person such as Achior, who wishes to join the Israelites in the service of God. The issue of inclusion and exclusion was a perplexing one for Judaism, as it was for the first Christians (Acts 10, 1–49; 11, 1–18; 15, 1–12).

Though the story of Judith remained a popular one among Jews for two thousand years, there is no evidence that the book was ever regarded as canonical in Palestine. It was, however, included in the Greek translation of the Old Testament made for Diaspora Jews, many of whom could no longer read Hebrew. There were continuing debates among Christians about its canonical character. The Council of Trent (1546) included Judith in its list of canonical writings, while Protestants, following Luther, did not.

The Religious Horizons of the Book

The book of Judith may date from as late as the first century (see the introduction, OT, p. 553), but in some respects it reflects the circumstances of the Maccabean revolt in the second century. For example, there are strong parallels with the defeat of Nicanor, Antiochus's general, as narrated in 1 Maccabees 7, 43–50. In some ways, Judith is the feminine counterpart of the Maccabees. The book is an eloquent statement of traditional worship of the Lord. It affirms belief in the one God (6, 2; 8, 16f; 14, 18; 16, 13). It asserts that this one God guides all human events toward their intended goal (9, 5f). Finally it describes this God as One who is present with the weak and oppressed (9, 11).

The storyteller paints a portrait of Judith much like the Israelite storytellers who told of the exploits of Ehud (Jgs 3, 12–30), Jephthah (Jgs 11, 1–40), Samson (Jgs 13—16), and David (1 Sm 16, 1—1 Kgs 2, 10). Their personal character and the means they used to save Israel did not come under careful moral scrutiny. Judith uses seduction and assassination to achieve her ends, although the text is careful to state that Judith did not have to complete her seduction of Holofernes before she could kill him (13, 16). Like these earlier stories, the book of Judith shows that God brings deliverance out of the evil

that people create for themselves. Even though the book is ostensibly about Judith, its pivotal affirmation is about the God of Israel:

> Your strength is not in numbers, nor does your power depend upon stalwart men; but you are the God of the lowly, the helper of the oppressed, the supporter of the weak, the protector of the forsaken, the savior of those without hope (9, 11).

The book of Judith then is a profession of faith in the God of Israel who saves the lowly. The story of Judith is simply an illustration of this article of ancient Israelite faith.

The book also asserts very forcefully that God's deliverance does not come except through the faithful action of people such as Judith. Unlike the king, the priests, and the elders of Bethulia who were content to pray and then surrender to Holofernes, Judith's prayer leads her to take action to save Bethulia. Though she receives no revelations or guarantees from God, her faith supplies the support she needs to begin and complete the perilous adventure that saved Israel. God saves the lowly, and prayer puts people in contact with that God, yet God's presence among the people does not absolve them from the duty to act on their beliefs. Judith is a mother of faith not only because she believed and prayed but especially because she acted on her beliefs—another perspective this book shares with 1 Maccabees.

The Image of Women in the Church

The book of Judith offers a model for the process of contemporary theological reflection on the role and status of women in the Church. It is itself one product of early Judaism's reflection on the role of women in its own social and religious system. At the very least, the book sees women as at times better fit to be instruments of salvation than men— a conclusion that was an unexpected one, given the cultural milieu in which it arose. Like Judith, Catholic women throughout the centuries have made enormous contributions to the life of the Church and are invited to see themselves as conservators of what is best in our religious heritage.

FURTHER READING

Brenner, Athalya, ed. *A Feminist Companion to Esther, Judith and Susanna.* Feminist Companion to the Bible 7. Sheffield: Sheffield Academic Press, 1995.

Craghan, John F. *Esther; Judith; Tobit; Jonah; Ruth.*
   Old Testament Message 16. Wilmington, DE:
   Michael Glazier, 1982.
Craven, Toni. *Artistry and Faith in the Book of Judith.*
   Chico, CA: Scholars Press, 1983.

Moore, Carey A. *Judith.* Anchor Bible 40B. Garden
   City, NY: Doubleday, 1985.
VanderKam, James C., ed. *No One Spoke Ill of Her:
   Essays on Judith.* Atlanta: Scholars Press, 1992.

ESTHER

[see pages 569–83 of the Old Testament]

Esther and Judith

The central character in both Esther and Judith is
a beautiful Jewish woman whose bravery and
wiles save her people from certain destruction.
The Hebrew text of Esther mentions neither God
nor any religious institutions or practices except
fasting, while the book of Judith is filled with allusions to God and numerous religious beliefs
and practices. But it was the book of Esther that
came to be included in the Jewish canon. Though
rabbis recognized Esther's canonicity after a
long debate, there is no evidence that Judith was
ever considered canonical in Palestine.

A Threat to the Jewish Community

Like the book of Judith, the central concern of
the book of Esther is the survival of the Jewish
minority in the midst of a world that is growing
more hostile to it. This book tells the story of one
threat to that survival and the removal of that
threat by relating the tale of Mordecai, a Jewish
courtier in the service of the Persian emperor.
The book of Esther makes it clear that God will
act in order to preserve the Jewish community.
God does not intervene directly to resolve the
problem but, though this divine action may be
hidden, it is nonetheless real.

The Additions to the Book

An Element of Confusion

A perplexing aspect of the shape of this book in
the *New American Bible* is the order and numbering of its chapters and verses. There are six chapters that have alphabetic identification scattered
in the midst of ten chapters that have the more familiar numerical identification. This is a result
of the way the book of Esther has come down to
us. The introduction (OT, pp. 569–70) notes that
the book of Esther has survived in two forms: a

shorter Hebrew text and a longer Greek one. The
Greek text has about 107 verses more than the Hebrew. Jerome did not believe that the additional
verses of the Greek Esther were inspired, so when
he produced his Latin translation, he took the additional verses in the Greek Esther out of their
proper context and put them in an appendix to the
book. When chapter and verse numbers were
given to biblical texts during the Middle Ages,
these additions received their numbers according
to the position they had in Jerome's Vulgate rather
than according to their proper position in the
Greek version of the book.

   The canonical status of the Greek additions
was not settled for Catholics until the Council of
Trent decided in their favor. (The Protestant
churches do not accept the additions to Esther as
canonical.) The arrangement of the text of Esther
in the NAB reflects the attempts to follow the
order of the Greek version of Esther while preserving the traditional numbering of chapters
and verses following Jerome's arrangement. This
seems to be the best solution possible in the circumstances. It allows the reader to find the additions in their proper contexts, and it preserves the
numeration of chapters and verses that is universally followed.

The Purpose of the Greek Additions

The function of the Greek additions to the Hebrew version of Esther is clear. First, the additions introduce explicit religious elements (for
example, the prayers of Mordecai and Esther in
addition C, 1–30). The Hebrew version lacks a
single reference to God except for the possible
allusion in 4, 14. Hebrew Esther is not overtly religious. It is a tale about how Jews used their wits
to outsmart their enemies. Second, by introducing "documents" (B, 1–7; E, 1–24), the additions
lend an air of authority and authenticity to the
book. The additions make the book read as if it

were a historical work. This probably was done to encourage the celebration of the Feast of Purim with which the story of Esther became associated.

The Story

At first the story sounds like a typical tale of palace intrigue. Two royal officials, Mordecai the Jew and Haman the Agagite, vie for power and position in the court of the Persian emperor. They do not hesitate to hatch plots against each other in order to secure a more important status for themselves. But in chapter 3 the story takes an ominous turn. It is no longer a tale about personal enmity between rival courtiers. Haman's plots threaten not only Mordecai but also the entire Jewish community of the Persian empire. Additions A and F (Mordecai's dream and its interpretation) with their imagery of the two dragons and the phenomena in heaven and earth (A, 4–10) transport the conflict to a cosmic level. Addition F makes it clear that it was God who saved Israel (F, 5–9).

The story that the introduction summarizes (OT, p. 569) takes place in the Diaspora (the Jewish settlements outside of the land of Israel), and it contains no references at all to the homeland of the Jews. The tension in the story revolves around the rivalry of Haman and Mordecai, but soon all the Jews find themselves swept up in the conflict because of the specifically Jewish patterns of behavior (3, 8). When Esther joins Mordecai in a plan to frustrate Haman's murderous plots, the tension is resolved. What was to be a pogrom, an officially organized massacre, against the Jews becomes a celebration of the Jews because Haman and his conspiracy fail.

The Personalities in the Story

Haman and Mordecai

The story refers to Haman as an Agagite (3, 1), i.e., a descendant of Agag, who was the king of the Amalekites whom earlier traditions remembered as the most dangerous of ancient Israel's opponents (Ex 17, 14; Dt 25, 17–19). Mordecai's genealogy (1, 1) makes him a descendant of Kish, the father of Saul (see 1 Sm 9, 1). At the conclusion of his conflict with Agag, Saul wanted to spare the life of this enemy of Israel and is criticized for it (1 Sm 15, 8f). Mordecai

makes no such mistake regarding Haman (Est 7, 9f).

Vashti and Esther

The story of Esther begins with the deposition of Vashti, the queen of Persia. Vashti lost her position as queen because she refused to obey the command of her husband, Ahasuerus, the king of Persia. During a banquet he gave, the king became drunk and ordered his wife to "display her beauty" before his male courtiers (1, 11). Because she declined to submit to this indignity, the king's officials advised the king to remove her as queen. They feared that their wives might imitate her example and refuse to be submissive and obedient (1, 16–18). The king then issued "an irrevocable royal decree" deposing Vashti and insisting that "every man should be lord in his own home" (1, 19–22). Esther, an orphaned Jewish girl who was the ward and cousin of Mordecai, won the beauty contest that determined Vashti's replacement (2, 1–10). The name Esther was a Mesopotamian name; her Jewish name was Hadassah (see note to 2, 7; OT, p. 573). Unlike Judith, Esther is hardly a model for feminists. She participates in the process to replace Vashti, who is the real heroine in this story according to a feminist reading of the text. Vashti refuses to become an "object" and insists on her dignity as a person, even though this means that she loses her position as queen. In a sense, Esther betrays Vashti by seeking to replace her.

The Historical Character of the Book

The author of Esther shows a familiarity with the royal court and administrative system of Persia. That is why interpreters favor a date toward the end of the Persian period for the bulk of the text (see the introduction, OT, p. 570). While the author describes the Persian court accurately, still the story of Esther is fictional. It is a novella on the theme of the persecuted righteous and their deliverance. The story does have a historical flavor, but it does not intend to report an actual event. (See notes to A, 1, OT, p. 570, and 1, 9, OT, p. 571, for two historical problems with the story of Esther.)

The Book of Esther and the Feast of Purim

According to F, 10, God wished the Jews to celebrate a feast on the fourteenth and fifteenth of

Adar (February/March) to celebrate their deliverance. This is the Feast of Purim. The name of the feast (Purim) means "lots" and is a reference to 3, 7 and 9, 24.26. The Bible mentions this feast nowhere else except in a possible allusion in 2 Mc 15, 36 that mentions "Mordecai's Day." The relationship between Purim and the book of Esther is not absolutely clear. Did the feast come first and the story later, or did the feast come from the book?

It may be that the Jews in the Persian diaspora adopted a local spring festival and attached a story of deliverance to it. Passover, the principal Jewish spring festival, shows a similar origin since Passover was a festival celebrated by nomads as they changed grazing areas in the spring. The Israelites attached the story of the deliverance from Egypt to this celebration. Since the Torah did not mandate the observance of Purim, the story of Esther served to promote its observance. In time, the Jews of Palestine came to observe this feast, as Josephus (a first-century AD Jewish historian and apologist) reports.

It is a mistake, however, to regard Esther 9, 20–32 as nothing more than an addition to the book that justifies the celebration of Purim. It is true that this portion of the book does make an institution of the feast and requires that future generations of Jews celebrate the festival. The text fixes the exact time and manner of its celebration. The effect of these verses is to transform the story of a frustrated pogrom and the victory of the Jews over their enemies into a religious observance.

The Jews are to observe the Feast of Purim by mourning and fasting, by the giving of gifts—especially to the poor—and by remembering the story of Esther (9, 22). These prescriptions give a religious dimension to a purely secular story. For succeeding generations the observance of Purim is to be a religious experience. The Jews are to understand their survival not just in nationalistic terms but as a religious obligation. Thus, 9, 20–32 reinterprets the book of Esther for its readers. Even though the Hebrew version of the book makes no reference to God, celebration of Mordecai's victory as a religious feast makes it clear that the victory came from God.

The Theological Horizons of the Book

Like the Joseph story (Gn 37—50) and the Succession Narrative (1 Sm 9—20; 1 Kgs 1—2),

God remains in the background in the book of Esther. The Hebrew version of the story never mentions God except for what may be an oblique reference in 4, 14 (see note to 4, 14, OT, p. 576). The rise of Esther to the position of queen of Persia allowed her to defend the Jews, just as Joseph's rise to the position as second only to the pharaoh in Egypt (Gn 41, 37–43) placed him where he could save his family (Gn 50, 20f). Similarly the succession of Solomon to David's throne was according to the divine will (2 Sm 12, 24f), but it occurred without direct divine intervention. Solomon ascended the throne of David following the successful machinations of his mother, Bathsheba, and courtiers who supported his accession (1 Kgs 1).

The story of Esther describes the Byzantine-like intrigue and plots by the antagonists and counterplots by the protagonists. The biblical text does not approve the actions of either Esther or Mordecai but only their result. What God intended was the survival of the Jewish community. God did not dictate the means to insure that survival; the human personalities involved determined these. The absence of any explicit references to God in the story may have been a deliberate attempt to emphasize the importance of the Jews taking the matter of their survival into their own hands. The additions to the Hebrew version show that some people saw this reticence as something that needed correction. These additions make the religious dimensions of the story more explicit:

Additions A and F. The story of Mordecai's dream and its interpretation make it clear that God controls the final destiny of Israel. Esther is the deliverer that God chose in answer to the prayers of the Jews.

Addition B. The decree of the Persian monarch against the Jews shows how some Gentiles regarded specifically Jewish observances as evidence of their disloyalty to the king (especially 4–7).

Addition C. This addition contains the prayers of Mordecai and Esther. The text makes it clear that the deliverance of the Jews is in response to those prayers. C, 26–29 answers any objections that readers might raise about the propriety of Esther's marriage to a non-Jew. The reference in C, 20 to the Temple is an anomaly, given the setting of the story in the Diaspora.

Addition D. Verses 2 and 8 assert that the king's change of opinion regarding the Jews resulted from God's response to the prayer of Esther.

Addition E. God condemns the enemy of Israel (vv. 2–6). The king finds the Jews innocent of all the accusations that Haman brought against them (vv. 15–16). The king acclaims the God of the Jews as sovereign over all (v. 21).

A Christian Reading of the Book

The presence of this book in the *Christian* Old Testament is a problem for some readers because of its supposed Jewish nationalism. One way to deal with this problem is to "excuse" the book's story of revenge on the enemies of the Jews by observing that the command to love one's enemies had not yet been taught by Christ (see introduction, OT, p. 570). In effect, people will dismiss the book's message because it is supposedly "sub-Christian."

The message of the book of Esther, however, has an important and positive role in the *Christian* canon. It offers an opportunity to check the tendency to spiritualize the people of ancient Israel and their contemporary descendants. The biblical text moves Christians beyond the statements made about the Jews in the Second Vatican Council's *Declaration on the Relationship of the Church to Non-Christian Religions (Nostra Aetate)*, article 4. The Council affirmed that there is a spiritual bond between Jews and Christians, that the Church received the revelation of the Old Testament from the Jews, and, above all, that the Jews are not responsible for the death of Jesus. The book of Esther asserts that the preservation of the Jewish people is a *religious obligation.* The presence of this book in the Christian canon is a statement of the religious significance of the Jewish people as an ethnic group, and it implies the abiding validity of Judaism. It makes the sin of anti-Semitism even more reprehensible than the irrational injustice that most Christians understand it to be today, and it undercuts the claim made by some Christians that God's covenant with the Jews has been replaced or superseded by Christianity.

Tales from the Diaspora and Today's Migrants

Stories about life in the Diaspora (Est, Tb, Dn 1—6) suggest that fidelity to Jewish religious traditions is not easy for Jews living outside Palestine. The special circumstances that come from living outside the Promised Land and apart from the community of faith contribute to a special feeling of vulnerability. They experience their new surroundings as hostile to the maintenance of their very identity as Jews. They see political authorities as potential or real threats to their religion and very existence. These stories show how people cut off from their roots can feel lost and menaced.

With the greater mobility that is characteristic of our age, there are more and more people who can identify with the Jewish characters in these tales from the Diaspora. Immigrants sometimes feel that they must choose between economic and political security and their own cultural and religious identities. Aware of those needs, Pope Paul VI issued his *Instruction on the Pastoral Care of People Who Migrate* (1969). Responding to the pope's initiative, the bishops of the United States issued *The Church and the Immigrant* (1976) and established the Bishops' Committee on Migration to respond to the needs of immigrants to this country. One of the main duties of this committee is to help today's immigrants adjust to their new life in a new and sometimes threatening cultural milieu. Specifically, the committee concerns itself with immigration laws, the problems of undocumented immigrants, economic and social discrimination experienced by people on the move, and pastoral initiatives to help people who feel the dislocation that comes with being an immigrant. One of the achievements of this committee was the preparation of *Together, a New People,* a pastoral statement on migrants and refugees published by the National Conference of Catholic Bishops in 1986.

FURTHER READING

Clines, David J. A. "The Esther Scroll: The Story of the Story." *Journal for the Study of the Old Testament Supplement Series,* no. 30. Sheffield: Sheffield Academic Press, 1984.

Craghan, John F. *Esther; Judith; Tobit; Jonah; Ruth.* Old Testament Message 16. Wilmington, DE: Michael Glazier, 1982.

Craig, K. *Reading Esther: A Case for the Literary Carnivalesque.* Literary Currents in Biblical Interpretation. Louisville: Westminster John Knox, 1995.

Fox, Michael. *Character and Ideology in the Book of Esther.* Columbia: University of South Carolina, 1991.

Larkin, Katrina J. A. *Ruth and Esther.* Old Testament Guides. Sheffield: Sheffield Academic Press, 1996.

Levenson, Jon D. *Esther: A Commentary.* Old Testa-

ment Library. Louisville: Westminster John Knox, 1997.

Moore, Carey A. *Esther.* Anchor Bible 7B. Garden City, NY: Doubleday, 1971.

———. *Daniel, Esther and Jeremiah: The Additions.* Anchor Bible 44. Garden City, NY: Doubleday, 1977.

1 MACCABEES

[see pages 583–619 of the Old Testament]

The Maccabees

The word *Maccabee* derives from the Hebrew word for hammer and was a nickname for Judas, a leader in the Jewish revolt against the Seleucid ruler, Antiochus Epiphanes (175–164 BC). (Seleucid is the name of the Greek dynasty that ruled in Syria following the death of Alexander the Great. It is derived from the name of Seleucus, one of Alexander's generals.) The nickname *Maccabee* later became a designation for other members of Judas's family who succeeded him as leaders in the revolt. Thus, Judas and his brothers came to be known as "the Maccabees." The term *Maccabean* came to designate the period of Jewish history that witnessed the successful revolt against the Seleucid empire.

After the revolt, the descendants of the Maccabees assumed religious and later political leadership of the Jewish community in Palestine. They ruled an independent Judah from 135 BC until Pompey conquered Palestine for Rome in 63 BC. The name given to this dynasty, the post-Maccabean generation of high priests and kings, was the "Hasmonean" dynasty. That name derives from the ancestor Asamonaeus whom Josephus (a first-century AD Jewish historian and apologist) identifies as the father of Mattathias, who was himself the father of Judas and his brothers. It was Mattathias who started the revolt against Antiochus (1 Mc 2, 15–30).

The Maccabean Literature

There are four books "of the Maccabees" that have survived from early Judaism. None of the four are in the Hebrew Bible and therefore are not in Jewish or Protestant Bibles. Jerome included the first two books of the Maccabees in the Vulgate (his translation of the Bible into

Latin), so those two books became part of the Roman Catholic canon. Third Maccabees has canonical status in Eastern Christianity. No Christian tradition accepts the fourth book of Maccabees as divinely inspired, though some Eastern churches include it as an appendix to their Bibles. Because of its focus on martyrdom, Fourth Maccabees has influenced Eastern spirituality.

The four books of the Maccabees do not form a continuous narrative like the story of Israel in its land as found in the books of Joshua to 2 Kings. First Maccabees is a historical narrative of events in the life of the Jewish community in and around Jerusalem from the reign of the Greek Seleucus IV (175–164 BC) to the accession of the Jewish ruler, John Hyrcanus (134–104 BC). Second Maccabees is an abridgement of a five-volume history of the Maccabees that no longer exists. It covers the period of Jewish history in Palestine from the time of the high priest Onias III (180 BC) to the victory of Judas Maccabee over the Greeks in 161 BC. Third Maccabees is a misnomer. It has nothing to do with the exploits of the Maccabees. The book is a first-century BC work that describes the persecution of the Jews in Egypt under Ptolemy IV (221–203 BC). Fourth Maccabees is a first-century AD discourse on religious reason as exemplified by Jewish martyrs during the Maccabean revolt.

History and Theology in 1 Maccabees

Unlike the books of Tobit, Judith, and Esther that use historical events and persons as a backdrop for what are fictional tales, 1 Maccabees is a historical narrative that is one of the main sources for reconstructing the history of the Jews in Palestine during the middle of the second century BC. This book, however, is more than a catalogue of events. Its author tries to show the significance of those events. The purpose of the work was to assert the legitimacy of the Hasmonean high-priestly dynasty. The book implies that the right of the Hasmoneans to rule is clear from the achievements of their ancestors: (1) the Maccabees saved the Jews from persecution; (2) they restored observance of the Torah; and (3) they inaugurated an era of peace and prosperity. The author of this book believed that God willed that the Hasmoneans assume the mantle of leadership over the Jews of Palestine.

Reading the Book

Setting the Scene

The story told in this book is a small part of a much larger story: *hellenization,* which was the shifting of cultural orientation from East to West, in the eastern Mediterranean region. Alexander conquered this area in the fourth century BC. It was his dream to take the culture of Greece and wed it to the cultures of the ancient Near East so that people could benefit from the best of each.

Alexander's premature death in 323 BC prevented him from fulfilling that dream. Alexander's generals divided his empire among themselves. The area of the former Israelite kingdoms came under the control of Ptolemy, who ruled from Egypt. Ptolemy permitted the Jews to practice their ancestral religion without much interference. The process of hellenization proceeded in the cultural, political, and economic spheres. The response of the Jewish community to Hellenism was equivocal: some Jews resisted hellenization; others eagerly accepted the new wave that was sweeping the world.

The region of the ancient Mesopotamian empires fell to another of Alexander's generals: Seleucus. He thought that the territory of the old Judahite and Israelite kingdoms rightfully belonged to him. The Ptolemies and Seleucids fought over this region until it passed into the hands of the Seleucids in 200 BC. At first they allowed the Jews to practice their ancestral religion without interference. But circumstances changed in 168 BC when the Seleucid king Antiochus IV Epiphanes seized upon the opportunity provided by divisions within the Jewish community. Antiochus obviously favored the hellenizers in that

community because they gave him financial support. To insure the victory of the Jewish hellenizers, Antiochus forbade the practice of the Jewish religion.

Mattathias (1 Mc 1, 1—2, 70)

The first chapter sets the scene for the bloody confrontation between the Jews and the Seleucids. It describes the hellenization of Jerusalem (1 Mc 1, 11–15), the military attacks on the city by two Seleucid armies (1 Mc 1, 16–40), and the prohibition of Jewish religious practices (1 Mc 1, 41–61). Antiochus's efforts at obliterating the Jewish religion culminated with the construction of an altar dedicated to Zeus Olympus upon the altar of holocausts, the holy place in the Temple where burnt offerings were made. This effectively transformed the Temple of Jerusalem into a shrine to Zeus (1 Mc 1, 54). Tradition remembered this act as the "horrible abomination" (Dn 11, 31; 12, 11). But the book asserts that there was opposition to the royal decrees (1 Mc 1, 62f).

The second chapter is important because it describes the specific type of opposition that the Maccabees and their followers were mounting against the hellenization of Antiochus and his Jewish collaborators. Though there were many Jews who opposed Antiochus, their responses were not always the same. For example, the book of Daniel inculcates a type of passive resistance to the Seleucid program of forced hellenization. The response of the Maccabees in the person of Mattathias is militant opposition. A key text is 2, 23–46, which describes Mattathias's fury at the prospect of Jewish apostasy. The author editorializes as he compares Mattathias's response with that of Phinehas (see Nm 25, 6–14). With this comparison, the author implies that Mattathias's action prevented God's anger from consuming the Jews because of the apostasy of some, and that this zealous action merited the high-priestly office for the Hasmoneans as the high priesthood was the reward for Phinehas's zeal against idolatry (Nm 25, 13). Besides Numbers 25, other examples of zealous action leading to priestly credentials include Exodus 32, 25–29. Mattathias became the leader of a large guerrilla force whose aim was to end Seleucid military domination of the Jews and the proscription of their religion.

1 Maccabees

The Militancy of 1 Maccabees

The response of Mattathias to the proscription of his ancestral religion was militant: he and his followers took up arms against the Seleucids and their Jewish collaborators. The United States Bishops' Pastoral, *The Challenge of Peace,* asserts the "the sacred scriptures provide the foundation for confronting war and peace today" (#27). In trying to formulate a Christian response to these issues, one has to face the militancy of 1 Maccabees. Mattathias and his sons responded to the Seleucid persecution with armed resistance. Their theological support for such a response was taken from the religious traditions of ancient Israel (see Dt 20).

It is also important to remember that the response of 1 Maccabees to the threat posed by Antiochus was not the only one among religious Jews in Palestine. Though there was agreement among religious Jews that they ought to resist Antiochus, there was a variety of viewpoints on how resistance ought to proceed. First Maccabees reflects the view of those who insisted on armed resistance. There were others who opted for martyrdom, nonviolent resistance, and even pacifism in the face of the threat posed by Antiochus's anti-Jewish laws.

While 2 Maccabees shares the militancy of 1 Maccabees, it looks at the revolution against the Seleucids from a somewhat different perspective. While it recognized the traditions associated with the wars of the Lord (see Dt 20), it also saw martyrdom as a way the faithful might contribute to the final victory over their enemies. Military prowess is not the only way. The blood of martyrs who died rather than violate the Torah cries out to God for vengeance and thereby seals the victory for the Jews.

The book of Daniel likewise describes a war between the forces of good and evil, but it believes that the real conflict takes place not on earth but in heaven, where God will be victorious over the powers of evil. Antiochus will fall, but not by human hands (Dn 8, 25). The book of Daniel holds that resistance is necessary but is nonviolent. It expresses itself in willingness to undergo suffering and even death for the sake of the Torah. Daniel can offer nonviolent resistance as an option because of its confidence in the resurrection of the faithful (Dn 12, 2f). The warfare against the forces of evil is left to God and Michael (Dn 12, 1) so the faithful do not need to fight against Antiochus since God has sealed his fate already (Dn 7, 26f). All the faithful need do is to stand up to the king by not complying with his orders to abandon their ancestral religion. The book of Daniel gives the whole credit for the inevitable victory over Antiochus to God's initiative. Daniel gives no credit to the contributions of the Maccabees at all.

Some Jews chose pacifism as a response to Antiochus's policies. This is evident from reading the *Testament of Moses,* a noncanonical work, portions of which were written about the same time as 1 Maccabees. The *Testament of Moses* has no room for the militancy of 1 Maccabees. It expected deliverance to come by direct divine intervention. The catalyst for the deliverance of the Jews is the death of those who have remained faithful to God and the Torah. The result of this deliverance will not be a Jewish state but Israel's separation from the nations and its exaltation in the heavens.

The militancy of 1 Maccabees represents just one response to the problems that the Jewish community in Palestine had because of Antiochus's persecution. The Bible and noncanonical Jewish literature offer others. In their pastoral letter, the bishops recognize that the Scriptures reflect many varied historical situations (#28). They could also have noted that the Scriptures reflect varied responses to the same historical circumstances. While we can understand the militancy of the Maccabees, such a response makes little sense in a nuclear age. There is no comparison between warfare of the second century BC and warfare today. That is precisely why the bishops of the United States spent so much time dealing with this issue and why they join recent popes in calling for nuclear disarmament.

Mattathias's Farewell

Chapter 2 concludes with Mattathias's testament (vv. 49–62) in which he consigns his military authority to his sons (vv. 65–66). Before doing that, he commends the example of Israelite heroes of the past (vv. 51–60) to his sons in order to support his militant ideology (vv. 50.66–68). He is certain that Antiochus will fall, and the suppression of Jewish religion will end with him (vv. 61–63).

Judas (1 Mc 3, 1—9, 22)

About 40 percent of the story in 1 Maccabees centers on the exploits of Judas, who succeeded his father as leader of the Jewish guerilla forces. Though the text acclaims Judas's exploits and applauds his bravery (3, 3–9; 9, 22), the author is very careful to imply that Judas's victories came about because of divine help. Judas prays before he begins any battle (3, 46; 4, 30–33; 5, 33; 7, 40–42). He boosts the morale of his army by reminding his men of how God has helped their ancestors in the face of overwhelming odds (4, 8f; 7, 41). Judas's preparations for battle (3, 47–49), his dismissal of those whom Deuteronomy exempts from war (3, 56, see Dt 20, 5–8), and the way he deals with the defeated enemy and the spoils of war (5, 28.35.51) all exemplify the beliefs of a man who is certain that he is fighting in accord with a divine command. Finally Judas praises God when he celebrates his victories (4, 24.33.55).

Hanukkah, or the Feast of the Dedication

Hanukkah is a Jewish feast celebrating the rededication of the Second Temple during the Maccabean revolt (the Hebrew word *hanukkah* means "dedication"). It was Judas Maccabee who mandated the observance of this festival (1 Mc 4, 59). Antiochus polluted the altar of the Temple (1 Mc 1, 54). This was probably the "horrible abomination" of Daniel 9, 27. When the Maccabees gained control of the area of the Temple, they purified the Temple and rebuilt the altar three years to the day of Antiochus's desecration (1 Mc 4, 36–58).

Josephus calls this festival "the feast of lights" (*Antiquities* 12:7:7) because the rededication of the Temple also involved rekindling the Temple's menorah (a lampstand with seven branches). Jews observe this festival at home by lighting one candle on a special Hanukkah menorah each night. The Talmud relates the story of how one day's supply of holy oil lasted for the full eight days of the original festival until the priests could obtain more oil for the menorah in the Temple. The significance of Hanukkah lies in its glorification of the deeds of those who refused to acquiesce in the proscription of their ancestral religion. They took up arms and won their freedom. The victory of the Maccabees over Antiochus undoubtedly enabled Judaism to survive.

Jonathan (1 Mc 9, 23—12, 54)

Judas died in battle, and his brother Jonathan succeeded him. While the text hails Jonathan's military exploits, of particular importance is his acceptance of the appointment as high priest from the Seleucid king Alexander who succeeded Antiochus (10, 20f).

Simon (1 Mc 13, 1—16, 24)

After the followers of Trypho, a pretender to the Seleucid throne, assassinated Jonathan, the leadership of the Jewish community passed to his brother Simon. Simon's stirring speech (13, 3–6) moved the people to acclaim him as their ruler (13, 8f). Later, a formal assembly composed of priests, elders, and leaders of the people ratified this popular action (1 Mc 14, 41). First Maccabees reaches its climax with the accession of Simon as leader and high priest. The purpose of the book is to present the establishment of the Hasmonean house as the legitimate political and religious dynasty for the Jews of Palestine.

The poem in 14, 4–15 is an amalgam of biblical motifs suggesting that with Simon a state of peace and prosperity has come to the Jews, the likes of which had not been seen since the days of David and Solomon. With Simon a new "golden age" has dawned. The change effected by the rule of the Hasmoneans over the thirty years since Mattathias's revolt began is dramatic. For the sake of its religion, a beleaguered minority within the Jewish community stood up to a powerful empire and prevailed. The author of 1 Maccabees considered the defeat of the Seleucids to be clear evidence that God was working through the Hasmoneans to save the Jewish community and religion.

The book, however, closes on a tragic note. After an aged Simon appointed his two eldest sons, Judas and John, as his successors, a political rival murdered Simon along with Judas and another one of his sons, Mattathias. John captured the assassin and had him executed. The succession was safe and another Hasmonean, John Hyrcanus continued the line of those "men to whom it was granted to achieve Israel's salvation" (5, 62). John ruled the Jewish community in Palestine as high priest and *ethnarch,* a title whose Greek etymology means "ruler of a people."

The Legitimacy of the Hasmoneans

The purpose of 1 Maccabees is clear: it defends the legitimacy of the Hasmonean dynasty, which ruled over the Jews in Palestine for about one hundred years until Herod the Great ended their rule. The members of this dynasty, who assumed both religious and political leadership in the Jewish community, were not without their opponents. After all, they ruled as kings when many Jews believed that the only legitimate political leaders ought to be descendants of David. As a priestly family the Hasmoneans were not members of David's tribe (Judah) let alone his family. The Hasmoneans functioned as high priests even though they were not descendants of Aaron as required by tradition. The principal opponents of the Hasmoneans were the *Hasidim* (the Pious Ones) who were the spiritual ancestors of the Essenes and the Pharisees.

The Hasidim saw themselves as careful observers of the law but held the Hasmoneans to be illegitimate interlopers as religious and political leaders. First Maccabees tried to show that the Hasmonean dynasty owed its origin to a revolutionary movement that had zeal for the Torah at its heart. According to 1 Maccabees, the Hasidim were not always very prudent in their self-styled devotion to the Torah. In their concern to have a high priest from the family of Aaron, they accepted a collaborator who betrayed them (7, 8–18). The author of 1 Maccabees considered the victories that God granted the Maccabees to be a sign from God pointing to the legitimacy of the Hasmonean dynasty. The book asserts that the most prudent approach was for the Jews to accept the dynasty until a "true prophet" will arise to say that God wishes otherwise (14, 41). This is precisely what most of the Jewish people and their leaders did (14, 28).

First Maccabees reflects a type of pragmatism that was incompatible with the religious zealotry of the Hasidim. For example, 1 Maccabees 8 is lavish in its praise of the Romans. This shows that the Hasmoneans were willing to compromise with foreigners when circumstances made it necessary. In Jesus' day, the Sadducees adopted this same position and later so did the early church (see Rm 13, 1–7 and 1 Pt 2, 13–17).

First Maccabees was not content with establishing the legitimacy of the Hasmonean dynasty on purely religious grounds. It shows that the major political powers of the day recognized the Hasmoneans as the political leaders of the Jewish people. It cites several Seleucid documents to the effect (10, 18–20; 10, 25–45; 11, 30–37; 13, 31–40; 15, 2–9). Both the Spartans (12, 5–23 and 14, 16–23) and the Romans (8, 1–32; 12, 1–4; 14, 16–19) also acknowledged the Hasmoneans as the leaders of the Jewish people.

First Maccabees in Catholic Tradition

This book is not part of the Hebrew Bible. There is no evidence that it formed part of the Qumran library, and Josephus did not include it on his list of sacred books. The book fared better among Christians. Reverence for the book by the Church's early theologians was perhaps one reason that the Councils of Florence and Trent both affirmed its canonicity. This book, however, has had no real impact on Christian theology. Its use in the liturgy is minimal. The liturgy does not make use of 1 Maccabees during the cycle of Sunday readings but reads portions of chapters 1 through 6 on four successive weekdays in Year II (nos. 497–502). Appropriately enough, the text from chapter 4 about the rededication of the altar in the Temple is a suggested reading for the Mass on the occasion of the dedication of an altar and 2, 49–52; 57–64 is the reading for the votive Mass for Persecuted Christians.

It is important to remember that 1 Maccabees was written to convince Jews that the armed revolution led by the Maccabees and their quest to expand the territory under their control to all of Palestine was ordained of God. This, of course, means that the Jewish community needed some convincing. Wars that seemingly have their basis in religion have caused so much harm that the argument of 1 Maccabees is not at all convincing to most readers today. The author of this book was able to make his argument because the Maccabean revolution succeeded. In contemporary armed conflicts, there are rarely any winners.

FURTHER READING

Bartlett, John R. *1 Maccabees*. Sheffield: Sheffield Academic Press, 1998.
Bickermann, Elias. *From Ezra to the Last of the Mac-*

cabees: The Historical Foundations of Post Biblical Judaism. New York: Schocken, 1962.

Collins, John. *Daniel, 1–2 Maccabees*. Old Testament Message 15. Wilmington, DE: Michael Glazier, 1981.

Goldstein, Jonathan A. *1 Maccabees*. Anchor Bible 41. Garden City, NY: Doubleday, 1976.

——. *2 Maccabees*. Anchor Bible 41a. New York: Doubleday, 1983.

Harrington, Daniel J. *The Maccabean Revolt: Anatomy of a Biblical Revolution*. Wilmington, DE: Michael Glazier, 1988.

Sievers, Joseph. *The Hasmoneans and Their Supporters: From Mattathias to the Death of John Hyrcanus I*. Atlanta: Scholars Press, 1990.

Williams, David S. *The Structure of 1 Maccabees*. Washington, DC: Catholic Biblical Association, 1999.

2 MACCABEES

[see pages 619–44 of the Old Testament]

The Relationship between 1 and 2 Maccabees

Second Maccabees does not continue the history of the Jewish revolt against the Seleucid empire and its aftermath, which is the subject of 1 Maccabees. The second book is an abridgment of a five-volume work on the Maccabees by one Jason of Cyrene (2, 23). This longer work has not come down to us. The unknown editor who is responsible for the present form of 2 Maccabees wished to simplify Jason's work so that readers could remember its most important features (2, 25).

Second Maccabees begins its story of the Jews in Palestine with the reign of Seleucus IV when Onias III was the high priest and ends with the defeat of the Seleucid army by Judas Maccabee. The period extends from approximately 180 to 161 BC. Thus, the story of 2 Maccabees overlaps with that in 1 Mc 1, 10—7, 5. In particular, there is quite a lot of similarity between 2 Mc 8—15 and 1 Mc 3—7.

While 2 Maccabees does not cover as much of the history of the Maccabees as does 1 Maccabees, it is a more polished literary work. Also, 2 Maccabees is less of an apology for the Hasmonean dynasty and more of an attempt to illustrate an important theological theme: God's justice in rewarding the faithful and punishing the impious. The book provides an inventory of how God dealt with both Jews and Greeks who disregarded the divine will. Its focus, however, is on those Jews who accepted death rather than be guilty of an act of disobedience. Second Maccabees highlights the death of Jewish martyrs to affect the emotions of its readers so that they may recommit themselves to faithful observance.

Reading the Book

Letters to the Jews in Egypt (2 Mc 1, 2—2, 18)

The book begins with two letters directed at the Jewish community in Egypt. Both call upon that community to celebrate a festival in honor of the rededication of the Temple following the victory of the Maccabees over the Seleucids. The feast in question is Hanukkah. Since the Torah did not mandate the celebration of this feast, the leadership of the Jewish community had to take this special step to encourage its observance.

The Jewish community in Egypt built its own temple under the direction of Onias IV, the son of the last legitimate high priest. Perhaps one purpose of these letters was to redirect these peoples' loyalty to the community in Jerusalem. Encouraging the Jews in Egypt to celebrate a festival in honor of the rededication of the Temple in Jerusalem may have been an attempt to keep them from forgetting their ties with Palestine. Also it may be that the person responsible for the present form of 2 Maccabees added these letters to the story of the triumph of the Maccabees in order to make the book into a festal scroll for Hanukkah as is the book of Esther for the Feast of Purim.

The Author's Preface (2 Mc 2, 19–32)

The person responsible for this preface is the individual who has decided to abridge the work of Jason of Cyrene. He states that he wishes to simplify Jason's work to make it helpful to more people (2, 24–26). He also advises his readers that he will add his own touches to Jason's work

(2, 29). Second Maccabees, as it stands today, is not simply a digest of a much longer work. There are portions of the book that do not come from Jason but were the product of the same person who made the abridgement.

Hellenization

Second Maccabees, like 1 Maccabees, reflects those circles in second-century BC Judaism that rejected the program of enforced hellenization imposed by Antiochus. It offers the example of martyrs who died rather than abandon their ancestral religion (see 2 Mc 6, 18—7, 42). Despite this strong objection to Hellenism, even the most pious Jews could not avoid its influence completely.

Hellenism is a term that describes the culture, ideals, and institutions that reached their apex in fifth-century BC Athens and that came to have a momentous influence throughout the eastern Mediterranean region. Until the time of Alexander the Great, this region was oriented culturally to the East. The two Israelite kingdoms were subject to the political, economic, and cultural sway of the eastern empires: Assyria, Babylon, and Persia. Alexander did more than bring Palestine into Greece's political orbit; he effected a genuine cultural reorientation. Until the Moslem conquest in the seventh century AD, the entire eastern Mediterranean region, including the territories of the former Israelite kingdoms, came under the cultural influence of the West.

The city or *polis* with its marketplace *(agora),* colonnaded streets, temples, theater, and gymnasium was the instrument of economic prosperity in the Near East and of the diffusion of Hellenism as well. Throughout Palestine the Greeks remade ancient cities. There was Ptolemais (Acco) along the Mediterranean in the north, Gaza along the Mediterranean in the south, Scythopolis (Bethshan) in the Jordan Valley, Marisa (Mareshah) in the south. Even Jerusalem was made over (1 Mc 1, 11–14).

It is not surprising that there was resistance among some Jews to hellenization. After all, the Jews had a very ancient culture and one that did not accept change very readily. There were, however, people—especially among the aristocratic stratum of Jewish society—that embraced the new cultural wave. At first, the Hellenism

that the Jews faced was mild. From the time of Alexander's death in 332 BC to about 200 BC, the Ptolemies ruled Judah from Egypt. The Ptolemies were the least culturally aggressive of all the Hellenistic dynasties. Matters changed dramatically under the Seleucid king Antiochus IV, who imposed Hellenism upon the Jews. Antiochus's policies sparked the Maccabean revolt.

Like 1 Maccabees, this work is also opposed to the forced hellenization program of Antiochus. Second Maccabees is intensely devoted to the Torah. Death, even suicide (2 Mc 14, 37–46), is preferable to violating the Torah. The reward for such loyalty for the individual is resurrection, and for the community it is the possession of Jerusalem. Despite this opposition to hellenization, it is impossible to escape the influence of Hellenistic culture. Second Maccabees itself uses rhetorical forms that come from Greek literature. For example, 2 Maccabees appeals to the emotions of its readers. The work does not hesitate to describe the death of Jewish martyrs in vivid detail. This approach is typical of Hellenistic history writing. The same is true of appeals to the supernatural (for example, 2 Mc 3, 22–30). The miraculous episodes in 2 Maccabees are comparable to episodes in Greek histories. The author does not hesitate to employ these Greek rhetorical patterns because they help the book achieve its purpose: to move its readers to renewed commitment to their ancestral religious traditions.

As opposed as 2 Maccabees is to the growing influence of Greek culture over the Jews of Palestine, the book recognizes that some Greeks are sympathetic to the Jews and their religious traditions. It even has Antiochus convert to Judaism as he is dying (9, 11–18). The book implies that the Jews do not object to the rule of the Greeks as such and that Jews can be good citizens of the empire. What they *do* object to are the excesses that came with Antiochus.

There comes a point when the pious must choose. Antiochus made the choice unavoidable. With Hellenism there came a whole bevy of gods and goddesses. There were even deified kings. More subtle were the novelties in philosophy and ethics. For the pious Jew, Hellenism represented a religious ideology and practice that was quite unfamiliar. Jewish literature of the period shows an extreme distaste for non-Israelite religion (Dn 3, 6; 1 Mc 1, 43; Wis 13, 10–19; 14, 12–21). But there was no escaping the influence of Greek culture at this time and on into the future. For example, almost seven hundred years later during the Byzantine Period (fourth to sixth centuries AD), there were a few synagogues in Palestine that had decorative motifs that included a zodiac complete with the god Helios in the center of a mosaic floor.

Second Maccabees represents the earlier view that rejected any compromise with Hellenism. There are absolute values that do not allow for any compromise. Even in the face of death, the righteous will chose fidelity to the Torah. Second Maccabees can be confident that such a choice is not in vain because of its belief in the resurrection.

The Story of the Maccabees
(2 Mc 3, 1—15, 36)

A theological purpose dominates the way 2 Maccabees tells its story: to show how the events of Jewish history—from the time of Onias the high priest to the time of Judas Maccabee—disclose a God who cares for the Jewish people by rewarding the faithful and punishing evildoers. In telling his story, the author uses a scheme first devised by the author of the story of Israel in its land as found in the books of Joshua to 2 Kings. This story, infused by Deuteronomic theology, told how Israel came to possess the land of Canaan under Joshua and then how it lost the land because of the infidelities of its kings. The story of Israel in its land (Jos through 2 Kgs) is a story of how Israel's infidelity transformed the blessing into a curse.

The story told in 2 Maccabees begins with a period of blessing (3, 1–40) during the time of Onias III when people observed the Torah (3, 1–3). During the time of the high priests Jason and Menelaus, the people and their leaders sin by violating the Torah and following the customs of the Greeks (4, 1—5, 10). This inevitably leads to punishment (5, 11—6, 17). Antiochus was the agent of God's judgment just as the Assyrians and Babylonians were agents of divine judgment in 2 Kings.

In the midst of Antiochus's persecution of the Jews, the prayers of the people, and especially the heroic death of the Jewish martyrs, led to a turning point (6, 18—8, 4). The refusal of the martyrs to sin, their obedience to the Torah, and their innocent death bring a change in circumstances. God extended mercy to the Jews and brought an end to their persecution. Although the book was aware that it was the military victories of Judas Maccabee that ended the domination of Antiochus, it assumed that it was the death of the martyrs that turned God's anger to mercy and made the Maccabean victories possible.

This section of the book has influenced the development of the Christian notion of suffering as a positive value. Suffering can be a form of divine education (6, 18—7, 42). God did not design the suffering of the Jewish people under Antiochus to destroy the people but to discipline them. God may discipline the people but does not abandon them (6, 12–16).

The suffering of the innocent led the author to affirm his belief in the resurrection of the dead (7, 9.11.14.23; 14, 46). This belief enabled the Jewish martyrs to accept their suffering because God will deliver the pious despite their death at the hands of the impious. (See the Reading Guide on Daniel, RG 337). The history of the Maccabean wars ends with a summary of Judas's victories (8, 5—15, 36) that brings salvation to the beleaguered Jewish community. The cycle is complete: blessing has returned to the Jewish people.

Parallel to this story of salvation is another story of retribution. The enemies of the Jews came to a terrible end: Antiochus died in agony (9, 8), the Greek who murdered the good high priest Onias was himself killed (4, 38), and the general who commanded the siege against Jerusalem died in battle and his head was hung from the citadel of the city (15, 35). The wicked among the Jews also suffered under divine judgment. The evil high priests Jason and Menelaus both came to miserable ends (5, 1–10 and 13, 7f).

Prayers for the Living and Dead

One of the most significant texts in this book for Roman Catholic theology is 12, 42–46. Here the author wished to show that Judas Maccabee believed in the resurrection of the dead since he ordered prayers and sacrifices for those who had fallen in battle. The author concludes that such prayers would be futile unless Judas believed that they would rise again (12, 44). Sometimes this text is used as support for the Roman Catholic belief in purgatory and the efficacy of the prayers of the living for the dead.

Another significant text for Roman Catholics is 2 Maccabees 15, 12–16. Here Judas Maccabee has a dream in which he sees the prophet Jeremiah praying for the Jews and Jerusalem. Catholic tradition accepts this text as one support for the belief in the efficacy of the intercession of the saints.

The Epilogue (2 Mc 15, 37–39)

The author ends his work rather abruptly with a hope that readers will find his work pleasant reading.

FURTHER READING

Doran, Robert. *Temple Propaganda: The Purpose and Character of 2 Maccabees.* Washington: Catholic Biblical Association, 1981.

van Henten, J. W. *The Maccabean Martyrs as Saviors of the Jewish People: A Study of 2 and 4 Maccabees.* Leiden: Brill, 1992.

See also 1 Maccabees.

THE WISDOM BOOKS

DIANNE BERGANT

Introduction

The corpus of books that we know as wisdom literature (Proverbs, Job, Ecclesiastes, Sirach or Ecclesiasticus, Wisdom of Solomon) stands apart from the other literature of the Old Testament. It asks the question, what kind of role does God play in everyday life? The answers to that question did not contribute to the national story that we have come to know as "salvation history." Instead, these books form a kind of guide for successful living. Since every person in every culture must struggle with the questions of life, there is a universal character to this literature. This might explain why, even today, people of other religious cultures often can more readily identify with the teaching of the wisdom books than with the uniquely Israelite or Christian theology found in other sections of the Bible.

The Israelites came to believe that their God was the great Creator-God, the one responsible for the world and everything in it. Observing the regularity in creation, they concluded that there was some kind of order inherent in nature itself. They believed that, if they could discern how this order operated and then harmonize their lives with it, they would be successful and at peace. The ability to perceive this order and to live in accord with it was known as wisdom.

The primary interest of the wisdom tradition is instruction in the proper ways of living. The writers made use of various teaching techniques such as storytelling, exhortation, warning, and questioning. In addition to the standard proverb, they used riddles, parables, and metaphors to instruct, advise, and persuade. There are usually very definite lessons that they wanted to teach, and so we should not be surprised when we come across what appears to be "the moral of the story."

The sages were humanists; they were concerned with the study of human beings and attentive to human welfare, values, and dignity. They taught that whatever benefited humanity was a good to be pursued, and whatever was harmful should be avoided and condemned. Training of any kind, whether within the family, the court, or in preparation for a profession, ought to impart the skills needed to succeed in the relevant setting. The criterion for judging the value of any venture was the degree of success or happiness that it brought. The sages regarded well-being and happiness as evidence that life was in accord with the order of creation. They did not advocate the pursuit of happiness for its own sake, but as a by-product of the right kind of life. Success and happiness were also considered concrete evidence of the wisdom of the successful person. The judgment of right or wrong, and the laws that supported this judgment, grew out of just such a critical reflection on the experience of life.

Although Israel's wise women and men believed that there was a right way of behaving, they did not insist on a rigid standard that would fit every circumstance. Each case was different. The wise person was the one who had a store of wisdom gained from experience and who knew which way of behaving was appropriate to each situation. There is a great deal of pragmatism in such a way of viewing life. If an approach did not accomplish the desired goal, it was discarded for one that would. This is not a case of the end justifying the means. Rather, the Israelites believed that goodness was a force that determined life. They were convinced that goodness became evident in whatever built up, sustained, or enriched life. From this point of view, the consequences of an action or the quality of the end were seen as evidence of the goodness of the means. Such an understanding of life presumed that conformity to the inherent governing principles of the world would result in a life filled with success and prosperity. On the other hand, adversity was attributed to failure to observe these authoritative directives. On occasion, this tradition does acknowledge the limitations of this point of view (Job and Ecclesiastes are prime examples). Nonetheless, the theory of retribution (the good shall be rewarded; the evil shall be punished) undergirds most of the wisdom literature.

Israel's wisdom tradition did not develop in a vacuum. It was part of a much broader movement within the ancient Near Eastern world. Reference to the sages of foreign nations can be found throughout the biblical text itself, usually within passages that depict an Israelite outstripping a non-Israelite in wisdom. For example, Joseph succeeded in interpreting Pharaoh's dream when the magicians and sages of Egypt failed (see Gn 41), and Job had a reputation that surpassed those of all the sages of the East (Jb 1, 3).

There is remarkable similarity between the biblical wisdom material and some Egyptian, Mesopotamian, and Canaanite texts. There is common subject matter, the literary forms are similar, and the worldview corresponds. Critical examination shows that the non-Israelite texts are significantly older than comparable biblical material. Israel probably borrowed from a common pool of traditions and then adapted and reinterpreted material when necessary. Despite these similarities, Israel's wisdom tradition is clearly in accord with its Yahwistic faith. It may not focus on specifics of religion, but it is highly ethical and fundamentally monotheistic, and, at times it equates wisdom with fidelity to the law of Israel.

FURTHER READING

General Introductions to Wisdom Literature:

Bergant, Dianne. *Israel's Wisdom Literature: A Liberation-Critical Reading.* Minneapolis: Fortress, 1997.

Crenshaw, James L. *Old Testament Wisdom: An Introduction.* Rev. ed. Louisville: Westminster John Knox, 1998.

Davis, Ellen E. *Proverbs, Ecclesiastes, and the Song of Songs.* Westminster Bible Companion. Louisville: Westminster John Knox, 2000.

Murphy, Roland. *The Tree of Life. An Exploration of the Biblical Wisdom Literature.* New York: Doubleday, 1990.

JOB

[see pages 646–82 of the Old Testament]

About the Book

Certain aspects of the book of Job have evoked as many interpretations as there are interpreters. Since the way we explain these points may influence our understanding of the message of the book, it might be helpful to consider some of them before proceeding. There is no agreement regarding the book's date, its place of origin, or the source of some of its parts. There is not even total agreement as to its principal theme. In fact, the richness of the book and its universal appeal prevent us from easily categorizing it. Evidence from the book itself is often given in support of a pre-exilic dating (seventh century BC). Job's complaints are reminiscent of the laments of Jeremiah, and some consider the book an outcry against the destruction of Jerusalem and deportation into exile. However, similarities with the theology and style of Deutero-Isaiah (the portion of Isaiah beginning with chapter 40) seem to carry more weight, tipping the scale in favor of a postexilic dating (sixth to fifth century BC). It is in the postexilic period (or around 400 BC) that Satan appears as the proper name of the "evil one" (1 Chr 21, 1). The book of Job must have originated sometime before Chronicles, for within its pages "the satan" is still a common term that refers to an adversary in a court of justice.

Job's struggle with suffering is a universal and perennial problem, and there is much in the book that has international flavor and appeal. There were older ancient Near Eastern accounts of innocent sufferers that may have been known to the author of Job. Several characteristics of the book, such as the names and places of origin of the three visitors, suggest foreign influence and perhaps even borrowing from other sources. Still, whatever may have originated elsewhere now clearly bears the mark of Israelite theology.

Like most pieces of ancient literature, Job is a composite rather than the work of a single author. It appears to be a prose folktale (1, 1—2, 13; 42, 7–17) within which extensive poetic speeches (3, 1—42, 6) have been inserted. In the book's present form, the two parts of the folktale serve as prologue and epilogue to the speeches. Even within these speeches, we can detect units believed to have originated from someone other than the principal author: for example, the Wisdom Poem (28), the Elihu Speeches (32—37), the second Speech of the Lord (41). Regardless of when or from whom these different sections originated, they all belong to the final form, and it is this final form that has been handed down to us as sacred Scripture. Therefore we should read the book as a unified literary work.

Finally, the universal appeal of the book stems from the nature of the questions posed by the tormented Job. Who has not struggled with the dilemma of incomprehensible suffering? Who has not cried out to God: "Why?" The principal theme of the book has been variously identified as human integrity; innocent suffering; disinterested piety; human limitations and the incomprehensibility of God; ultimate trust. Actually, these interpretations are not mutually exclusive; they are interrelated. They each express a different nuance of the all-encompassing mystery of the manner in which God is present in the world and they suggest the manner in which we should respond to that presence.

The Literary Style

Most people know the story of the innocent man who was mysteriously stricken yet remained steadfast in his loyalty and was rewarded in the end for his faithfulness. This simple understanding does not accurately represent the story; it is merely the plot of the framing folktale. The principal part of the book is the poetic dialogues. The prologue and epilogue merely set the stage and bring to conclusion the real drama. The more we understand the function of the form of the book, the better we will discover the message within it.

The dialogues consist of speeches in Hebrew poetic form. Each time Job cries out against his sorry state, Eliphaz, Bildad, or Zophar offer him counsel or attempt to convince him of his error. The orderly manner in which this exchange takes place constitutes the cycles of speeches. The third set of speeches is somewhat fragmented. Bildad's remarks are abbreviated, Zophar's are missing altogether, and Job's replies are inordinately long, often containing material that seems to contradict his basic point of view. Some scholars believe the dislocation of material that really belongs to either Bildad or Zophar explains such discrepancies, and they reconstruct the speeches in order to remedy this. Such reconstruction explains why the verses are sometimes out of numerical order in some translations.

The speeches of Elihu do not fit into any of the three cycles. While there are some differences between this Elihu section and what precedes it, the theological point of view expressed by this speaker neither fundamentally departs from nor significantly adds to that of the first three visitors. This fact has led some commentators to conclude that either the speeches are a later literary and theological addition of the original author or they are the work of another writer. This section is now part of the book, however, and cannot be discounted.

The literary form and the content of the Lord's speeches are reminiscent of an ancient Near Eastern pattern known as *onomasticon* (a Greek word meaning "list of names"). This was a constructed listing of names of things that had similar characteristics. This could include cosmological, meteorological, or other natural phenomena. These listings were probably prescientific attempts at classifying natural phenomena. They demonstrate the universal human search for understanding the universe. In the book of Job we find a creative use of this form. The author casts God in the role of wisdom teacher who poses challenging questions—a teaching technique typical of the wisdom tradition—that test Job's comprehension of the wonders of the universe. The content and the form of these questions are similar to the onomasticon. The use of nature as a means of instruction is characteristic of the wisdom tradition. While this technique occurs throughout the entire book, nowhere else does it have the effect that it does in these speeches. Because God does not directly address Job's demands, some commentators have concluded that God ignores Job's concerns. In saying this, they have not adequately considered the way the author makes use of this literary form.

The poetry found within the book is unlike most classical or contemporary poetry. There is virtually no rhyme, and the rhythm follows tonal patterns that are usually lost when the original Hebrew is translated. One characteristic that is identifiable even in translation is the correspondence of thought in successive half lines. This feature is known as parallelism. The thought in the first line can be repeated:

Does God pervert judgment,
  and does the Almighty distort justice?
    (Jb 8, 3)

or contrasted (there are no clear examples of this in Job):

Hatred stirs up disputes,
  but love covers all offenses (Prv 10, 12)

or advanced:

Pity me, pity me, O you my friends,
  for the hand of God has struck me!
    (Jb 19, 21).

Parallelism is used effectively in Job as an aid in furthering the arguments of the various speakers.

There are two other literary forms that should be mentioned. They are the lawsuit and the lament. Elements of these forms are found throughout the speeches of Job. Again and again he demands that God meet him in court where his (Job's) case will be tried and he will be found innocent (for example, 23, 2–4). Even more frequently, Job cries out to God in complaint. He laments the day of his birth (3, 1–10), and life itself (10, 1–7), and he pleads for help (13, 20–27). In all of these ways, the literary style of the author contributes to the development of the book's message.

The Drama

Each section of the book has its own dynamic and carries the story forward to its conclusion. The prose prologue plays a very important role in the unfolding of the theological message of the book. It is there that Job's innocence is estab-

lished beyond any doubt, and it is there that we see who is really responsible for Job's misfortune. It is God who permits this righteous man to suffer in order to test the quality of his integrity. Job never knows this, nor do his visitors. Only the reader is witness to what took place in heaven. It is important that we know this as we listen to the theological debate that follows. The arguments in the poetic speeches are repetitious and appear to be quite monotonous, but this is an essential part of the author's treatment of the problem. By adding layer upon layer of the same accusation and rebuttal, the author brings us into the very midst of the impasse. It does not take long for us to recognize the pointlessness of the debate. Job makes his claims, and his counselors make theirs. Neither side is convinced by the other. Only some manifestation from God can resolve the deadlock.

Job demands a hearing, and God does finally confront him—but in a manner that far surpasses Job's imagining. God breaks the cosmic silence and thunders through the heavens. Job had made his appeal to the justice of God. God answers Job from the midst of creative power. Even though his questions are not answered, the opposing tensions with which Job had struggled are clearly reconciled. But why? and how?

The epilogue and its last verses of prose complete the reworked folktale. Job is vindicated and, as was the rule in this ancient society when someone had been unjustly dispossessed, he is compensated for his losses by double payment. However, his question "Why" is never answered. As the book ends, all Job knows is that the innocent can indeed be afflicted for no apparent reason and with no guarantee that the reason will ever be disclosed.

The Message

While the book of Job is a poetic narrative, it is also a theological statement made up of several themes intricately interwoven. The way we understand this theology will influence the way we perceive the arguments in the book. The themes are treated here not in order of importance but as they appear in the book itself.

Reward and Punishment

As mentioned in the introduction, the theory of retribution undergirds most of the wisdom literature. It is, after all, the basis of any notion of justice. Goodness should be rewarded and evil should be punished. This theory probably originated from the experience of life itself. Actions frequently generate their own consequences. When it appears that this will not happen in the natural course of events, someone in authority steps in to see that justice is indeed done. We not only expect this to happen, we need it in order to live with a certain degree of security. The theory clearly plays an important role in the book of Job. Although Job endures insufferable loss and physical distress, his real agony seems to lie in the incomprehensibility of his situation. He has been a righteous man, and righteous people are not supposed to be so afflicted. Job's claim of righteousness is not an empty one. The author has taken great pains in the prologue to show us that Job is indeed a man of unsurpassed integrity. Then why should he have to bear the burden that, according to this theory, is the consequence of wickedness? Has God forgotten Job's faithfulness? Or, even worse, is God indifferent toward it? These are the kinds of questions at the heart of Job's dilemma.

It is quite clear that those who visit Job consider the theory of retribution a valid way of interpreting life. Since Job is suffering, he must be guilty of wrong. Since his suffering is so comprehensive and so intense, his sin must be serious. His visitors use every argument they can devise to convince Job of his error and persuade him to repent. They draw their conclusions about the morality of his behavior from the nature of his present situation. They do not question Job's suffering, and so they assume that he is guilty. (This same kind of thinking prompted the apostles to ask Jesus whether it was the sin of the blind man or of his parents that resulted in the man's blindness [see Jn 9, 21].) Job himself adheres to the same theory, but he makes his claims from a different point of view. He knows that he has done nothing to deserve such misfortune. Still, a strict understanding of retribution offers no other explanation for his troubles and, therefore, Job blames God. Being a man of faith, he believes that God is the architect of the order in the universe. God is the one who has made things to work as they do. Ultimately, God is the one who decides who will be rewarded and who will be punished. God usually accomplishes this through the laws that were set at creation. When they seem to fail, God can and, as the traditions of Israel claim, God does intervene to enforce justice. From Job's point of view, God has failed to do this in his case.

Since the bulk of the speeches consist of arguments in defense of or in opposition to Job's righteousness, one would think that when the Lord spoke the matter would be clarified, and we would know who was correct. When God finally does thunder from the whirlwind, the question of justice is not addressed. Instead, the focus of the divine speeches is the creative wisdom and power of God. Still, this should not be seen as avoidance of the question. Remember, in this book God is cast in the role of wisdom teacher. It is characteristic of such a teacher to ask rhetorical questions and to make reference to the natural world in order to make a point. By means of such questioning, God leads Job to see that, as there is much in nature that Job cannot understand, so there is much in human experience that is beyond him. Indirectly, God reveals the inadequacy of the theory of retribution. God shows Job that happiness and success are not demonstrable rewards for righteous living, nor are grief and failure punishment for unfaithfulness. In other words, suffering is not the sure sign of alienation from God.

The theory of retribution continues to be operative in our thinking today. When we fall upon hard times or are victims of some tragedy, we frequently ask: What have I done to deserve this? Why is God punishing me? We too have a sense of how things are supposed to work and when they don't unfold as we expect, like Job, we demand an explanation from God. Perhaps, again like Job, we will have to learn that not everything can be explained according to the theory of retribution. We will have to admit that life is too complex to be forced into one pattern.

Theodicy

Once we are convinced that certain suffering is undeserved, we are faced with a very troubling question: Why does God seem to allow injustice to occur? Theodicy (from the Greek meaning "justifying God") is the name given to our attempt to explain the problem of evil, while at the same time maintaining belief that God is a moral creator who is in control of all things and who loves those who suffer. If Job did not believe that

God is moral, the question of evil would take a totally different turn. If God is not just, then Job's suffering might be equally difficult for him to bear, but it would not be the puzzle that it is. He would know that he could not depend upon God for justice. Instead, his happiness and unhappiness would hinge on the whims of a capricious God. It is clear that such a view was foreign to Israel's faith. Job's counselors never question God's integrity, and Job does so only reluctantly and at the risk of falsely accusing God.

According to another view, God could be moral but not able to control evil completely. This is the theory advanced by several post-Holocaust Jewish thinkers who cannot explain why God allowed so many millions of innocent people to be exterminated during World War II. It is also a view expressed in the popular book by Harold S. Kushner, *When Bad Things Happen to Good People*. Although a number of recent thinkers have held this view, it is not found in the Bible. Israel believed that its God was the undisputed almighty creator (see Is 45, 7; Am 3, 6). None of the characters in the book of Job doubt God's control. In fact, if Job could believe that God was not somehow responsible, his torment might even be lessened.

A final perspective suggests that perhaps God is both moral and omnipotent, but unconcerned about simple people. Surely the almighty God has more important things to do than to worry about the fortunes or misfortunes of one man. The traditions of Israel contradict this notion as well. From the earliest stories of the ancestors (Abraham and Sarah, Isaac and Rebekah, Jacob and Rachel and Leah), we see God portrayed as attentive to the most personal needs of the individual. This is the memory of God that Job recalls as he laments his present predicament (29, 1–6). How could a gracious God who cared for him in earlier years turn against him now?

Theodicy is not an issue for the visitors, since Job's misery is not a puzzle for them. Job himself is intent on defending his own integrity rather than God's, and so theodicy is not a concern of his either. It is, however, of major importance to the author of the book, who depicts God as all-powerful and provident, and a God of unchallenged goodness. At the end of the book, the question of suffering may be left unanswered, but the integrity of God is no longer questioned.

Disinterested Piety

In a very real sense, the drama of the book stems from the satan's challenge found in 1, 9: "Is it for nothing that Job is God-fearing?" The satan insinuates that Job is righteous because of the rewards that he now enjoys and will continue to enjoy as long as he remains faithful. He claims that it is easy for Job to be loyal to God when things are going right and he is happy with life. Take away his prosperity and the good things of life, and he will not only give up his way of integrity but will actually curse God. The reader should note that God takes the dare. Twice Job is assaulted. His initial response to the tragedy that has fallen upon him proves that the satan's accusation is groundless. Job neither curses God nor veers from his attachment to God. Despite his complete reversal of fortune, Job's confidence is not shaken, and he actually praises God (see 1, 21 and 2, 10).

It is clear that Job is not God-fearing simply for the sake of blessing, for his afflictions do not diminish his devotion. Even in adversity he maintains that all things are in God's hands, and God will render whatever God deems fit. Still, Job probably did expect to be blessed for being faithful. The admonitions of his visitors as well as his own later assertions mark an expectation common to all of them (see 4, 7; 8, 20; 11, 15; 13, 16). All seem to believe that goodness will not go unrewarded nor will wickedness fail to be punished—a conviction that is fundamental to the notion of justice. Therefore, in the face of such expectation, to what extent is his piety really disinterested? The content of Job's laments and pleading show that Job does not look for recompense; he wants vindication. He is not concerned about possessions; he insists that his integrity be acknowledged. When he finally understands the lesson that God set out to teach him, he is silent and seems content with his new insights. It is apparent that the depth of Job's piety is based on his relationship with God, not on some promise of reward.

We must remember that at this time Israelites did not have a clear idea of reward or punishment in an afterlife, as Christian theology teaches. If justice was not meted out in this life, they had no hope at all for retribution. This makes Job's disinterested piety even more admirable. It also serves to challenge the quality of our own fidelity. Job's faithfulness can also be an encouragement to us. Here is a man who is not willing to accept unquestioningly what he considers a grave injustice. He rejects the instruction and counsel of those regarded as teachers of the religious tradition. Job is not blindly docile in his suffering, nor is he afraid to complain to God in his frustration. At this point we must be careful to understand Job's anger correctly. He does not argue with God because he is suffering, but because he perceives a conflict between what he considers his unwarranted suffering and his faith in the justice of God. The Job who accuses God is no less pious that the man who acknowledged, "The LORD gave and the LORD has taken away" (1, 21). Devout people certainly do have their differences with God. We are reminded of the great Teresa of Avila, who in frustration also complained to God, "No wonder you have so few friends."

Suffering

Although the customary way of understanding suffering was as punishment for sin, the book of Job does provide other explanations for it. The prologue itself tells us that God allowed Job's misfortunes to befall him so that Job's integrity might be tested (1, 11; 2, 3.5). A similar incident in the cycle of stories about Abraham comes to mind. There, "God put Abraham to the test" (Gn 22, 1) and told him to sacrifice his son Isaac. There is a significant difference here, however. In the end, Abraham was told that he had been tested (Gn 22, 16), while Job never knows about God's dealings with the satan. Job himself never regards his misfortune as a test.

Suffering is also seen as a source of moral discipline. Elihu claims that pain and sickness sometimes act as warnings against sin and as a defense against pride and complacency (33, 15–24). Other interpretations of suffering include: vicariously enduring the punishment of others (the Suffering Servant: Is 52, 13—53, 12); personal purification (Ps 66, 10); a necessary way of accomplishing the will of God (Joseph in Egypt: Gn 50, 20). Only the first two explanations are found in the book of Job.

Yet another way of understanding suffering was as the "curse of the evil deed." According to this view, those who engage in evil infect themselves in the process. This notion is behind the saying: "He who digs a pit falls into it" (Prv 26, 27). Just as the Israelites had a sense that goodness was a force that determined life, so they believed that evil carried its own consequences. This view differs from that of retribution since it does not believe that God intervenes to punish. In fact, it tends to exclude divine activity. This may explain why, in Israel, the idea of retribution seldom appeared by itself. It is always tempered by belief in God's ultimate control of good and evil.

The biblical writers seem to have been more interested in the reason and purpose of suffering than in its origin. They addressed the fact of suffering and tried to give meaning to this reality, which no one can escape. They offered provisional explanations intended to strengthen people in their struggle. These explanations were not meant to be conclusive answers, because circumstances change and they might cease to be appropriate. This is precisely the case with Job. The instruction and advice offered by his visitors may very well have been fitting in other circumstances, but in Job's situation they are empty of meaning. No one seems able to offer him an adequate explanation for his suffering. Most likely, this is precisely the reason that the book of Job has always enjoyed a place of prominence in the literature of the world and in the hearts of countless people. It demonstrates that no one is protected from undeserved personal misfortunes such as the sudden and tragic death of loved ones, human exploitation or betrayal, the unexpected collapse of a business or career, or from disasters such as flooding or fire or other ravages of nature. The horrors of war, of ethnic, racial, sexual, or other social discrimination or brutality victimize untold children, women, and men, and thus defy all standards of justice. Over the centuries this pitiable man has stood as proof that suffering is not a sure sign of infidelity. Job continues to be a source of consolation for many today who suffer innocently.

Experience and Tradition

One might conclude from this that a fundamental principle, which underlies wisdom thinking and which plays an important role in the book of Job, is the relationship between experience and tradition in the formation of new theological understanding. We have all been taught the importance of conforming our lives to the teachings of our religious tradition. A new and sometimes conflicting attitude is developing today, namely, that it is the *tradition* that must give serious consideration to contemporary life. In fact, a more complete understanding shows that there should be a dynamic correlative interaction between experience and tradition, with each influencing and refashioning the other. In the book of Job we see that neither Job nor the men who came to advise him took note of this dynamic. In the final summary of his cause, Job insists that he has always complied with the prescriptions of the law (see chapter 31). In fact, he went far beyond the demands of the law. It was precisely because of the faithfulness of his behavior that he expected a life of peace and prosperity. From where he stood, there is something seriously wrong with the order of things. Job was not willing to question his own integrity, and he was not ready to challenge the tradition. That is why, as stated earlier, he found fault with God. The others also evaluated Job's life according to the tradition. Adhering to the conventional way of interpreting suffering, they insisted that his present state of misery was the direct consequence of some sin. From where they stood, God was justified in afflicting Job, and the tradition was adequate in explaining the situation. They discounted the authenticity of Job's experience of innocent suffering.

We might miss this important theme were it not for something that God said to Eliphaz in the epilogue: ". . . you have not spoken rightly concerning me, as has my servant Job" (42, 7). Where were these men wrong and Job right? What did they say that was not part of the traditional teaching? The only issue over which there was serious disagreement was that of Job's innocence. Job insisted that God had afflicted him without cause. Upholding an inflexible interpretation of the tradition, the visitors maintained that God would never act in such a manner. We know that they are the ones who were wrong.

Job's experience of innocent suffering calls for a new and more critical look at the tradition. It is strange that neither Job nor his counselors challenged this unbending interpretation of theology, because it is precisely the ability to be faithful yet flexible in new situations that constitutes wisdom. Perhaps the author of the book wanted to demonstrate what could happen when theology is rigidly applied.

The Catholic bishops of the United States have consciously included reflection on contemporary experience in the process of writing their most recent pastoral letters. They are keenly aware of the need to be faithful to official teaching while at the same time realistic about changes in the world. They have frequently held open hearings in order to gain insights from the experience of the broader church and society before writing their documents. This practice can both endorse new wisdom and contest the old. For that reason it has been applauded by some and criticized by others.

The God of Mystery

Most of the themes considered in this reflection have focused attention on Job. Now we turn our gaze toward the depiction of God. How is God portrayed? In his complaints, Job characterizes God as powerful and oppressive when near and unconcerned when at a distance. Job's companions describe God as a prosecuting judge. However, the image revealed in the speeches of the Lord is quite different. There we see that God is indeed powerful, but it is a wondrous, awe-inspiring power (see 40, 3–5). It is also true that God is transcendent, but this does not prevent God from being solicitous for even the mountain goat about to kid (see 39, 1). Finally, God does not assume the role of judge, summoning Job before the divine tribunal, there to find him guilty and to sentence him. Instead, Job is questioned by the divine teacher and led to new horizons of insight. He is brought to understand that he has been treading on mystery—"things too wonderful for me" (42, 3). In the book of Job, God is the provident but nonetheless mysterious God of creation. It is the same God who works in the lives of each of us, yet who remains a mystery.

The Dramatic Effect of the Story

While it is true that we can dip into any section of the book of Job and draw out bits of profound teaching, the best way to read it is as a drama from beginning to end. Only in that way can we feel the frustration of the counselors mount and the desperation of Job deepen. As is the case in every good story, there is a dramatic movement here that sweeps us up into itself. We might best appreciate the richness of its message and the true-to-life description of its complexity by identifying first with Job and then with one of the visitors. Our own experience of suffering should help us to understand Job's plight. It is revealing, however, to realize how easy it is to offer empty words in our sincere attempts to console others, and to see how quickly we can become indignant when our advice is ignored.

The final effect of reading the book in this way includes an admission of the incomprehensibility of much of life. Whether we have identified with Job or with one of the others, we come to the speeches of the Lord and we realize that *no one* can answer the questions put to Job. Everyone, whether Job, Eliphaz, Bildad, Zophar, Elihu, or

the reader, when confronted with the incongruity and incomprehensibility of human life, stands silent before this transcendent God.

FURTHER READING

Habel, Norman C. *The Book of Job*. Old Testament Library. Philadelphia: Westminster, 1985.

Janzen, Gerald J. *Job*. Interpretation. Atlanta: John Knox, 1985.

Newsom, Carol A. *The Book of Job*. New Interpreter's Bible 4, 319–637. Nashville: Abingdon Press, 1996.

Perdue, Leo G. *Wisdom in Revolt: Metaphorical Theology in the Book of Job*. Sheffield: JSOT Press, 1991.

Pope, Marvin H. *Job*. Anchor Bible 15. New York: Doubleday, 1979.

Wharton, James A. *Job*. Westminster Bible Companion. Louisville: Westminster John Knox, 1999.

PSALMS

[see pages 682–787 of the Old Testament]

About the Book

The book of Psalms, also known as the Psalter, is really a collection of books each of which ends with a short doxology or hymn of praise. This is very clear to anyone who looks closely at the arrangement of the psalms. The editors of the *New American Bible* have indicated this order by adding subdivisions within the text itself. "The First Book—Psalms 1–41" ends with a doxology in 41, 14; "The Second Book—Psalms 42–72" ends with 72, 18–20; "The Third Book—Psalms 73–89" ends with 89, 53; "The Fourth Book—Psalms 90–106" ends with 106, 48; "The Fifth Book—Psalms 107–150" ends with an entire psalm of praise, Psalm 150.

There is evidence within the book of Psalms itself that our present anthology was composed of even earlier collections. Several psalms, found principally in the first book, are attributed to David. This may account for the popular, but probably not historically accurate, tradition that David himself wrote most of the psalms. Several psalms in the second and third books are ascribed to Korah and Asaph, the two great guilds of temple singers during the period of the Second Tem-

ple (confer 1 Chr 6, 33ff; 25, 1f). These groupings may have been the original collections around which other psalms clustered. Finally, the fifth book is made up of a number of Songs of Ascent and psalms of praise known as Hallel or the Hallelujah collection.

These collections have another distinguishing characteristic. They vary in the preferred name for God. *Yahweh* (translated LORD) is generally used in the first, the fourth, and the fifth collections. This has led some to refer to them together as the "Yahwist Psalter." The name *Elohim* (translated "God") is preferred in the second and third books. Together they are sometimes called the "Elohist Psalter." Many scholars believe that Elohim is a substitution made by a postexilic editor who wished to show reverence for the divine name (Yahweh) by avoiding its use.

All of these various collections overlap, and so it is difficult to identify precisely the original groupings. It is enough to know that the final compilers had an array of psalms from which to choose. The presence of psalmody in places other than the Psalter (for example, the Song of Moses in Ex 15 and the Song of Deborah in Jgs 5) indicates that there were many more psalms current in ancient Israel than have been included in the Psalter.

Types of Psalms

Commentators classify the psalms in slightly different ways. (The categories here are quite general.) There is widespread agreement, however, that the major headings are three: lament, hymn, and thanksgiving. In addition to these major groups, there are royal psalms, wisdom poems, and some psalms that might fit into more than one category. Since psalms are the prayerful responses to life experiences, a study of their forms as well as their content will throw light on the life situation of the community from which they sprang.

Laments

The type of psalm that occurs most frequently in the Psalter is the lament. Nearly a third of all the psalms belong to this category. Depending on the identity of the speaker, laments are further classified as community laments or laments of the individual. The structure of the lament is not exactly the same in every case. Not all laments appear to be complete, and even when the most common elements are present, they do not seem to have any fixed order. Still, laments are usually comprised of an invocation directed toward God; the actual lament or complaint that describes the suffering endured by the one(s) praying; a plea for deliverance from this misfortune; some kind of praise of God, often an expression of confidence that God will come to the rescue of the community or the individual; a vow to perform an act of worship in gratitude for God's intervention. Some laments also include an acknowledgment of guilt or an assertion of innocence. Finally, there is frequently a curse hurled against those believed to be responsible for the intolerable situation that precipitates the lament. This last feature has caused considerable difficulty for those who wish to use the psalms in their own prayer.

It is quite clear that the community laments (Pss 12, 14, 44, 53, 58, 60, 74, 79, 80, 83, 85, 89, 90, 94, 106, 123, 126, 137) were somehow associated with the official cultic worship of Israel. Most probably they were used when the people gathered to fast and pray on special occasions arising from national humiliation or distress. The

enemies referred to are usually national enemies who, by being opponents of Israel, were viewed as opposed to the Lord. These psalms often contain a recital of the former marvelous deeds that God had accomplished in the history of the nation. This was meant to remind God of past favors and thus encourage God to grant new ones, as well as to remind the people of God's earlier blessings in order to instill confidence in their hearts.

The laments of the individual (Pss 3—7, 13, 17, 22, 25—28, 31, 35, 36, 38—40, 42/43 [considered a single psalm, as explained in the NAB footnote], 51, 52, 54—57, 59, 61, 63, 64, 69—71, 77, 86, 88, 102, 109, 120, 130, 140–143) were most likely prayerful responses to personal misfortunes such as illness or persecution. Commentators believe that they were an integral part of personal liturgical devotion. Frequently, people who were suffering went to the Temple or to some shrine for the purpose of making a formal request to God for deliverance. Laments, with their declaration of trust in God, were simultaneously prayers to God and testimonies of hope for the benefit of the community gathered around the one suffering.

Hymns

The hymn is a song in praise of God. While many hymns appear to be the prayers of individuals, most of them seem to have been composed for use in the liturgies of Israel's major festivals. The reason for praising God, as expressed in the psalm itself, enables us to further classify certain hymns as psalms of the kingship of the Lord or as songs of Zion.

The structure of the hymn (Pss 8, 19, 29, 33, 100, 103—104, 111, 113, 114, 117, 135, 136, 145—150) is quite simple. It begins with a call to praise, which suggests that this type of psalm originated within a community setting and, at this point, some kind of liturgical leader is calling the others to prayer. This introductory exhortation is followed by an account of the wondrous acts of God, deeds that cause us to stand in awe. Depending upon the psalm, God is praised for the glories of creation (for example, Ps 8) or for the marvelous feats performed specifically for the people of Israel (among others, Ps 114). Having proclaimed God's glorious deeds, the psalm ends with a repetition of the initial call to praise, some expression of exaltation of God, and a plea for God's blessing. (This is a general description. Not all of the elements are present in every psalm.)

Hymns of the Lord's kingship (Pss 47, 93, 96—99) are a distinct group among the psalms. Their focus is the Lord, the universal king, and they have many images and motifs in common. Some scholars claim that these psalms were composed for the annual celebration of the feast of the Enthronement of the Lord. Therefore, they refer to this group as "enthronement psalms," and they place them in a category of their own. No account of such a festival can be found in the Bible itself, however. For that reason, and also because this group of psalms fits the general hymnic pattern perfectly, they are here simply classified as hymns.

The songs of Zion (Pss 46, 48, 76, 84, 87, 122) extol Mount Zion as God's holy mountain and Jerusalem as the city that God chose to inhabit. There is a variation in the structure of these psalms. Both the introductory and concluding call to praise, which are typical of hymns, are missing. Still, the body of this type of psalm celebrates the mighty God of Israel, who held back every kind of primeval attack on the city and who now dwells on its sacred mountain. As with the psalms in praise of the Lord's kingship, we are not certain about the cultic setting at which the songs of Zion were sung. We may be heirs to Israel's songs, but we do not know more than a few general facts about its cultic calendar, and we cannot reconstruct its system of worship.

Confidence and Thanksgiving

It is rather difficult to classify psalms of thanksgiving, because expressions of confidence and gratitude are often found within laments. This has led many interpreters to list these psalms with either community or individual laments. There are some psalms, however, that might be considered explicit psalms of confidence, either communal (Pss 115, 125, 129) or individual (Pss 11, 16, 23, 62, 91, 121, 131). Psalms of thanksgiving, again either communal (Pss 65—68, 75, 107, 118, 124) or individual (Pss 9/10, 30, 32, 34, 41, 92, 116, 138), also comprise a distinct category. It is the subject matter rather than the form that characterizes these psalms. Like the la-

ments, they were probably part of the communal and personal liturgical life of the people and were used in cult and devotion when the religious sentiments that they express were in order (perhaps at a time of great peril, in the case of the psalm of confidence, or during a harvest festival or after a threat had been successfully resisted, in the case of the psalm of thanksgiving.

Royal Psalms

There are several psalms that direct our attention specifically and exclusively to the king. Some scholars believe that they point to a prominent royal role in the cult. Others contend that the king did not have to be a cultic leader to enjoy a significant place in the ritual. His political and religious importance was enough to assure him of a cultic function. We must remember that Israel was a nation that perceived its king as the representative of the whole people before God and as God's special envoy for the people. This shared perception entitled the king to the prominence he enjoyed.

Various occasions in the life of the king constitute the setting of these psalms. There are coronation hymns (Pss 2, 72, 101, 110), an anniversary hymn (Ps 132), a royal wedding song (Ps 45), petitions in behalf of the warrior-king (Pss 20, 144), and prayers of thanksgiving for his successes (Pss 18, 21). These royal psalms are often referred to as "messianic psalms." "Messiah" means "anointed one," and the king is called "messiah" or "anointed" in Psalm 2. To read them as messianic psalms implies that they refer to an ideal king who is to come in the future. These psalms take on new meaning in the Christian tradition when they are applied to Jesus, the king par excellence and the one "anointed" by God.

Wisdom Poems

These poems (Pss 1, 37, 49, 73, 112, 119, 127, 128) are clearly different from those psalms that probably originated in, and were used during, liturgical celebrations. They differ in both content and style. The wisdom tradition in general is concerned with the problem of evil, the suffering of the righteous, and the justice of God. These same themes, along with language and imagery characteristic of that tradition, are found in the wisdom psalms. Finally, the manner of address here is intended to instruct rather than evoke a response. The wisdom psalms call people to listen and learn, not to pray.

Although wisdom psalms do not follow a uniform style, they do have some distinctive literary characteristics. The sages of ancient Israel made use of several techniques that were judged helpful for learning. Some of these techniques appear in the wisdom psalms. One of the most popular ones is the acrostic arrangement. This is a poetic form in which the alphabet determines the initial letter of the first word of each successive line. Several wisdom poems follow this arrangement (for example, Pss 37; 112 along with the hymns 111; 119). Because they conform to this pattern, some commentators include as wisdom poems some of the psalms listed here under other categories (hymn—Ps 145; lament—Ps 25; thanksgiving—Pss 9/10, 34).

It may be difficult to understand how and why this type of psalm originated and was included in the various collections. What may be even more puzzling is the fact that the Psalter begins with a wisdom poem (Ps 1). Most likely a postexilic compiler placed this psalm first at a time when there was neither Temple nor temple worship, and those responsible for the religious life of the community wanted to keep the psalms alive in Israelite devotion. At this particularly critical time the psalms might have been seen as a treasury for much-needed instruction as well as for prayer. The organization into five books might well have been patterned after the Torah or five books of Moses, wherein the major teachings of the faith were found.

Various Psalms

There are other psalms that quite obviously were used during a pilgrimage to or procession around Jerusalem and the Temple. The Songs of Ascent, one of the early collections alluded to above, preserves the memory of such psalms. In addition to this group, there are other psalms that were sung during processions (Pss 15, 24, 95). A few psalms appear to have been composed after the style of prophetic speech (Pss 50, 81, 82). Since people frequently came to the Temple or to a shrine in search of some word from the Lord, it is understandable that traces of this form would remain in some psalms. Finally, a small number of psalms seem to defy classification. They are

either historical recitals of the salvific feats of the Lord (Pss 78, 105), composites of other psalm forms (Pss 108, 133, 139), or general liturgical songs (Ps 134).

The Piety of the Psalmist

The psalms generally speak *to* God rather than *about* God. Although most of the important historical events of the nation, as well as the universal needs of women and men, are described or addressed somewhere in these prayers, the psalms are just that—prayers to God. If we look carefully at the sentiments expressed in these songs, we will be able to detect the major outlines of the piety of ancient Israel, a piety to which we are heirs. We have already seen that it is possible to classify the psalms according to literary form (lament, hymn, thanksgiving, etc.). A further look at these forms will show us that different types of psalms express different sentiments of devotion. Therefore it will be helpful to return to these classifications as we explore the piety of Israel contained in the psalms. (The reader is advised to consult the listings of the psalms belonging to each category. These listings are found under the heading Types of Psalms.)

Grief, Fear, Repentance, and Confidence

We all have a certain sense about how life is supposed to unfold. We learn this as we are fashioned in and by the various social groups of which we are a part. While societies may differ over values and lifestyles, all agree that basic to our nature as human beings is the desire to be happy. Our social groups train us in the acceptable ways of achieving and maintaining the happiness we seek. When we have not attained what we believe is our right, or when having once attained it, we lose it, we cry out in protest. We tend to balk at the unfairness of adversity regardless of whether we are in any way responsible for the loss. We do expect that life will be good to us. This natural human instinct, coupled with the conviction of God's special love and care, led Israel to expect security in a hostile world, success in its undertakings, and a life of serenity and prosperity for the nation as a whole and for each individual within that nation. Such a state of affairs is what the Bible refers to as *shalom* or peace. Psalms of lament grew out of the absence of just such peace.

The references in communal laments usually

apply to some national disaster that has already taken place. Depending upon the dating of the particular psalm, this calamity could have been the fall of the Northern Kingdom of Israel (about 722 BC), the Babylonian exile (about 586 BC), or the Maccabean conflict (about 167 BC). Allusions to the vulnerability of the nation would fit any one of these three emergencies. Any description of the destruction of the Temple, however, must be dated after the time of the exile and before the rebuilding of the Temple (515 BC; see Reading Guide to Ezra and to Nehemiah).

The fact that the psalmist cries out to God demonstrates Israel's belief that God has both the power and the will to intervene and deliver the nation from its present distress. Several psalms themselves indicate that this belief is based on former saving-events in the history of the people (for example, Pss 44, 2–4; 74, 2; 83, 10). Israel believed that God's might was in no way exhausted by earlier feats. On the contrary, Israel held that the all-powerful God was always ready to defend the nation whenever it was threatened with extinction. Even as the people cried out in complaint, they were proclaiming God's all-encompassing power and declaring their trust in God's continued concern for them, a concern based on divine covenantal promises. An expression of confidence, then, is an important characteristic of the lament.

As there were times when Israel felt that it was the innocent victim of the aggression of another nation, there were also instances when it admitted that the straits in which it found itself were directly related to its own sinfulness. Suffering at the hand of another was seen as punishment from God for violation of the covenant. In some of the laments, Israel admits its guilt, pleads for forgiveness and for an end to its suffering, and promises to amend its ways. One of the communal laments recounts the nation's history as if it were no more than a series of offenses against a loving God (Ps 106). Others plead that God forgive the people for their sins and restore them to divine favor (Pss 80; 5–8; 90, 7–17). In these psalms, suffering is understood as recompense from a God who is just but also forgiving.

Many of the sentiments found in the communal laments are present in individual complaints as well. The authors of these prayers claim that they are physically or spiritually afflicted or that others are wrongfully oppressing them. In their distress they turn to God for release. They do not doubt God's ultimate control over the workings of nature or the social order. Nonetheless, they might, on occasion, question why God allowed them to be besieged in the first place. Their confidence in God rests on both the recollections of past blessing and reliance on God's own faithfulness to covenant promises.

Praise

Praise is that sentiment that wells up within us as we are overwhelmed by the wonders around us or by the provident concern afforded us by the events of life and by life itself. It is not so much something that we are taught as it is something that we experience. Praise of some sort is natural to human beings. Who has not been swept away by the extravagance of a sunset, by the delicacy of spring's reawakening, by the refreshment of a gentle summer breeze, by the magnitude of the ocean's horizon or the night sky's depth? We stand in awe before the splendor of creation—and we are drawn out of ourselves. If we are attentive to the religious tendencies within ourselves, we will be moved to praise. We discover this same sentiment in the hymns. The psalmist does not seem able to find words adequate to describe the grandeur of creation (Pss 8, 29, 104, 148), and so all the forces of nature are called upon to join the psalmist in glorifying God. Underlying such sentiments of praise is the belief that God is the creator of all things and that all that God has created is beautiful, deserving of our respect, and a reminder of the majestic creator.

Other hymns applaud God for the marvelous feats performed on behalf of the Israelites (Pss 105, 114, 135). Again and again the miraculous power of God intervened for them, thus saving them from certain extinction. Since the initial and preeminent experience of deliverance was liberation from the oppression of Egypt, the Exodus became for them the symbol of all liberation. In these psalms God is perceived as tireless savior, and the psalmist's praise is an acknowledgement of the nation's total dependence on God for its continued survival.

These hymns presume that nature is benign and that God is committed to the well-being of the people. Such a view of life does not usually emerge spontaneously. It arises either from an experience of life that is basically untroubled or from a religious belief that God is indeed on our side and life should really favor us. Still, the biblical hymns are not the flights of fancy of people who have been protected from the hard realities of life or from the indifference of nature. They are also songs of praise of people who, despite misfortune, persist in their reliance on an all-powerful yet attentive God.

The Lord is further acclaimed as the sole and eternal king over all nations. The God of Israel earned this title of Champion in the primordial struggle with chaos (Pss 96, 4f; 98, 1) by undermining the influence of the other gods and ascending the heavenly throne to reign with universal and undisputed authority. The concept of God as victor in the cosmic conflict embraces the notion of creator, for the initial understanding of primordial creation is the establishment of order out of chaos (see the creation narrative in Genesis 1). Unlike the hymns discussed above, the psalms lauding the kingship of the Lord acknowledge the threatening powers present in the universe. Chaos was conquered by the Lord, but not totally destroyed. Admission of this in no way detracts from the universal reign of God proclaimed in the psalms. Instead, it was a way that Israel dealt with the fact that creation is not always friendly and life does not always appear to be favoring us. In the face of this fact, Israel believed that the Lord was truly in charge, involved in creation while ruling from the divine throne in the heavens, controlling all of the forces of the universe and, therefore, deserving of our undivided allegiance.

The songs of Zion contain some of the same imagery found in the psalms in honor of the Lord-King. Ancient Canaanite mythology, from which much of the Israelite imagery originated, recounts the cosmic battle described above. After the forces of evil were quelled, a palace was built for the victor on the summit of the highest mountain. From this vantage point the conquering hero holds sway over the entire universe. Israel revered Mount Zion as this sacred mountain and revered the Temple as the palace of the victorious creator-God. A significant shift can be detected in these psalms. Zion and the Jerusalem

Temple move the drama from the cosmic scene of primordial creation to the political and cultural world of Israel. The reality of God's divine creative power is now associated with one nation and, because of the close connection between Zion and David, specifically with the Davidic monarchy. These psalms depict God as unabashedly committed to the welfare of Israel over all other nations. The creator-God who is praised in these psalms is not distant from this people but lives in their very midst, allowing them to approach the divine presence that somehow mysteriously dwells in the Temple. (There was an attempt to balance this apparent exclusivity by inviting all other nations to worship the Lord on Zion [see Is 2, 2f; Mi 4, 1f].) Thus God is perceived as near and accessible, and Zion and the Temple command veneration.

The hymns provide us with several perceptions of God: the creator of the universe, national liberator, cosmic champion. At times these perceptions overlap, producing a collage of images intended to call forth praise. The psalmist extols God for the wonders of creation, for continued deliverance from destruction, for God's victory over the forces of evil, and for the fact of God's presence in the midst of the people. These are some of the sentiments voiced in the biblical hymns.

Gratitude

Little need be said about the expression of gratitude found in the psalms. Prayers of thanksgiving are similar to those of confidence in that the latter expect blessing and the former thank God for it. At times this gratitude flows from favors already received. At other times it anticipates the blessing that the psalmist is confident will come. The structure and content of the thanksgiving psalm resembles those of the hymn. There can be no thanksgiving until God has first been praised for the goodness that God has accomplished.

National Loyalty

The royal psalms emanated from national pride and spirit. Allegiance to the king was regarded as loyalty to the nation. Since the king was considered the representative of the whole people before God and as God's special envoy for the people, loyalty to the king and to the nation were seen as acts of devotion to God. These psalms originated out of various royal settings and they express sentiments appropriate to the respective occasion (for example, coronations, weddings, danger to the king during warfare, etc.). Despite their diversity, the sentiments of all of these songs flow from what today would be considered a type of patriotism.

An Understanding Heart

The wisdom poems generally do not address God. They are usually directed toward the community. The piety of the psalmist is not as explicit here as it is in the prayers we have already examined. Still, it can be discerned by looking carefully at the way the poet treats the themes that appear to be prominent. The problem of evil, the suffering of the righteous, and the justice of God are principal concerns of the wisdom tradition and are all facets of the same issue, namely, right order in the universe. It is clear that the wisdom psalmist presumes that there is an order to the world, and that there is a way in which we can live in this ordered world so as to be secure and prosperous. It is also evident that the psalmist sees God as the source and guarantor of this order. On the other hand, evil that clearly is not punishment can challenge the sovereignty of God. When this evil raises its head, God is expected to step in, subdue it, and restore the world to its former and appropriate state. When this does not happen, the power of God or the uprightness of God may be questioned. This might happen because either God cannot repress the evil or is unwilling to do so. While Job and Ecclesiastes live with the unanswered question of innocent suffering, and Job even demands that God take responsibility for it, the wisdom psalms do not challenge the prevailing situation. They seem to presume that the suffering of the righteous is for some legitimate purpose, which God will reveal at the appropriate time and will then correct.

The themes, language, and imagery of the wisdom poems depict God as creator of all. In this they resemble the hymns and the psalms of thanksgiving. In their insistence on justice, they are like the laments. These similarities explain why commentators classify the wisdom poems in different ways. These psalms may not be ex-

plicit expressions of Israelite piety, but they do reveal a trait that is characteristic of religious sentiment, that is, an understanding heart (see 1 Kgs 3, 9.12).

Enthusiasm, Humility, and Faithfulness

The processional psalms are charged with excitement and anticipation. They invite the observant Israelite to participate with heart and soul in various liturgical celebrations. The major festivals of ancient Israel (Passover or Unleavened Bread, Pentecost or the Feast of Weeks, Sukkoth or the Feast of Tabernacles) were all commemorated with pilgrimages to Jerusalem. Psalms were sung as the people approached the city. There were shouts of profound joy as well as humble acknowledgements of the need for pure hearts when approaching the holy city and the Temple of the Lord.

Prophetic psalms were also linked closely to the Temple. They embrace sentiments of humility and religious devotion and they summon the people to be faithful to their covenant commitment.

The wide range of religious sentiment found in the Psalter reveals the extent of Israel's piety. Every human emotion is tapped because Israel believed that God is involved in every aspect of life. It is no wonder that the psalms have touched the lives of women and men throughout the ages and that they continue to inspire the human spirit even to our own day.

The Theology in the Psalms

The expressions of piety found within the book of Psalms give us insight into the theology of ancient Israel. Although much of this theology has already been noted, it will be helpful to look at it in a more systematic fashion.

The God of Israel

The portrait of God that is sketched in the psalms draws together all of the divine faces found in the rest of the Israelite tradition. This God is the creator of the universe (Ps 8, 4) and the source of all life (Ps 36, 10), enthroned in heaven (Ps 47, 6) yet dwelling in Jerusalem (Ps 76, 3). Initially the Lord may have been perceived as Israel's exclusive liberator (Ps 66, 6), but the universal scope of God's power and protection came into view as the nation moved closer and closer to a monotheistic faith. Although uniquely committed to Israel by means of the Mosaic covenant (Ps 114, 2), and to the monarchy through the royal covenant with David (Ps 132), God is envisioned as concerned about the well-being of all people (Ps 117).

This majestic God inspires both fear (Ps 89, 8) and confidence (Ps 23), is both demanding (Ps 75, 8) and forgiving (Ps 85, 3). Above all else, the God of Israel is "merciful and gracious . . . slow to anger, abounding in kindness" (Ps 103, 8; see Ps 86, 5). The key characterization is that God is Israel's covenant partner. Everything that is important to Israel flows from this perception of God.

The Image of God

The human person is held in high regard in the psalms. (It must be noted that the psalms come from a society where the male person was the norm for what is human. The language and imagery that issued from this fact have caused great distress for many. Without perpetuating this male-preferred situation and by making appropriate substitutions while reading or meditating, we can still value the psalms for their religious insight and sentiment.) Honored as a unique manifestation of God's creative ingenuity, humanity is given responsibility for the other living creatures of the earth (Ps 8; see Gn 1). Again and again the psalmist marvels at this singular work of divine artistry. Why should God be personally committed to such an insignificant being (Pss 8, 5; 144, 3f)? As extraordinary as they are, humans live a fleeting life (Ps 39, 5f) and then perish like the flowers of the field (Ps 103, 15f). Realization of the impermanence of life becomes even starker when we remember that the psalmist did not have any clear notion of life after death. Human dignity was related to life in this world.

There is no doubt in the mind of the psalmist that human beings are thoroughly understood by and totally dependent upon God (Ps 139). God provides for their basic physical needs (Ps 65, 10–14) and protects them from harm (Ps 121). In a special way, God is the guardian of the poor and afflicted (Ps 40, 18), the defenseless widows and orphans (Ps 68, 6), and the *anawim* or lowly ones (Ps 147, 6). The psalmist goes to great lengths to show that what appears to be

the insignificance of the human creature is, in fact, the occasion for the solicitude and tender care of God.

Natural Creation

The psalms reveal a special regard for natural creation as the handiwork of God (Ps 104). This may well have originated from a polytheistic belief that the mysterious powers in nature are really manifestations of various deities. As Israel's understanding of God developed, expanded, and incorporated within itself reverence for these extraordinary manifestations, these powers came to be seen as expressions of the Lord. God is revealed in the thunderstorm (Ps 29) and in the design of the natural world (Ps 65, 7). Creation was thus no longer seen as a rival for the homage of the people. Instead, it became a partner in the praise of God (Ps 148).

The Future

Ancient Israel was interested in both the future of the nation and the fate of the individual. The positive view that it takes on this issue, which is called eschatology, stems from its faith in the goodness of God toward all creation. Despite the struggles that the nation faced in its attempts to survive and to flourish in a contentious world, Israel believed that the final victory would be the Lord's and that through God's triumph it too would prosper. Individuals also looked to God to remedy the injustices of a burdensome life. They clung to the conviction that God would eventually right all wrongs, and they would then enjoy the happiness that was their due.

The psalms that praise the kingship of the Lord and describe God's defeat of the forces of evil, also promise the restoration of the nation (Ps 14, 7). When this happens, the gods of the other nations will be recognized as the empty idols they are (Ps 96, 5), and all the peoples will join in praising the Lord (96, 7–10). According to some of the royal psalms, this decisive turning point in history will be brought about through the agency of a "messiah" (Ps 2, 7–9).

Great attention is paid in the psalms to the fate of the individual. Although earlier theology taught that reward and punishment would be worked out within the community or down through the generations (see Ex 20, 5), the post-exilic prophets maintained that retribution would be meted out according to one's own deeds (see Ez 18). In the face of this new perspective, the prosperity of the wicked challenged the theory of retribution. In response, the psalmist claimed that such prosperity would not last and so the upright should not envy sinners (Ps 37, 1). Still, the apparently peaceful death of those who were wicked and prosperous, and the unmerited suffering or adversity of the righteous, remained an unresolved problem.

The psalms say very little about life beyond the grave, but they frequently mention the shadowy existence known as *Sheol* (Ps 49, 15). This was not a place of retribution; it included neither reward nor punishment. It was simply a place of darkness and dust. It probably referred to nothing more than the grave, the abode of the dead. Still, it suggests that while Israel did not have a clear idea of life after death, it entertained the possibility that the dead did not cease to exist.

The Psalms and the New Testament

We may not always appreciate the specific theological importance of the psalms because today we tend to distinguish between explicit theological statements on the one hand and prayer on the other. In many ways, this is a false distinction. Statements of faith may well be the reflection on or development of theological thought, but prayer is theology as it is experienced. It is quite clear that the early Christians seldom made such distinctions. For them, the psalms were not only vehicles of prayer but they also contained important statements of faith, statements that found their fulfillment in the person and mission of Jesus (see Lk 24, 44).

The New Testament both alludes to and specifically cites various psalms. Five of them seem to be referred to more than the rest. They are the messianic psalms 2 and 110; the individual laments 22 and 69; and the communal psalm of thanksgiving 118. The first two are cited in discussions of Jesus' messianic preeminence (see Acts 13, 33; Heb 1, 5). Motifs from the two laments are used in accounts of his passion and death, interpreted by some as evidence that the psalmist was really foretelling Jesus' suffering. Psalm 118 speaks of the rejected stone that becomes the cornerstone (v. 22; see Mt 21, 42) and the blessedness of the one who comes in the name of the Lord (v. 26; see Mk 11, 9), themes that the

New Testament writers see fulfilled in Jesus. Thus the early Christian theologians developed the theology of the psalms in ways that would enhance their own understanding of Jesus the Christ.

The Psalms Today

Most people are acquainted with the psalms because they are incorporated into the regular prayer of the church. Others may be more familiar with some of them through their own personal use in private devotion. Everyone interested in the psalms will also want to know more about how they function as means of prayer. Moreover, a study of the psalms would be incomplete if we did not address the role that they have played and continue to play in shaping the minds and hearts of believers. We cannot arrive at this insight by limiting our examination exclusively to historical or literary analyses. While the psalms are certainly religious literature they are at the same time means to spiritual transformation.

Poetic Imagery

The psalms are poetry. They are, in fact, some of the most beautiful poetry that the human spirit has created. The imagery is vivid, the verbs are energetic, and all can share the sentiments expressed. One need not be familiar with the historical situations from which the psalms sprang in order to appreciate their enduring worth. Like all classic literature, they express fundamental human values that speak to every culture and every age. By merely reading the psalms thoughtfully and respecting their integrity, we can be touched by their lyrical artistry and drawn into the dynamic world that they envision.

This reflective, even contemplative, reading can plunge us into the religious dispositions of the psalmist, for the words and the images that grew from these dispositions can now readily serve as vehicles carrying us back into them. We may not come to the psalms with hearts filled with praise or thanksgiving or grief, but the world mirrored there, a world that is real though perhaps not identical with ours, often resonates deep within us. It is as if we know that world, or at least we sense that we should know it and, recognizing it, we cry out in praise or thanksgiving or grief. In this way the poetic imagery can be the starting point of our meditation on the psalms.

Genuine Prayer

For Jews and Christians, the psalms are much more than profoundly moving poetry. They are the voice of our respective religious faiths. First heard centuries ago in a land far removed from ours, they have been on the lips of believers in every historical period since that time. It is not merely that we use the psalms to express our devotion; they in fact profoundly shape our religious consciousness. The psalms have served as a prism that spreads before us the many facets of our relationship with God. Gilead, Manasseh, and Ephraim (see Ps 60, 9) may be unfamiliar names to many, but they were beneficiaries of God's promise of protection of which we are heirs, and so we identify with them. We "join in procession with leafy branches up to the horns of the altar" (Ps 118, 27), convinced that our prayers too will be answered.

Liturgy is not merely a celebration of some past event. It is an enactment in which and through which promises and claims that were made in the past become present realities. The Exodus was certainly a concrete historical event. Whenever Israel reenacted this event, however (see Jos 24), the reality of the Exodus became present with all of its power and possibility. The participants of the liturgical celebration were not participants of the original escape. "When the Egyptians maltreated and oppressed us, imposing hard labor upon us, we cried to the LORD, the God of our fathers, and he heard our cry and saw our affliction, our toil and our oppression. He brought us out of Egypt" (Dt 26, 6–8a). The psalms have a role to play in this creative reenactment. Not only do they address God in sentiments appropriate to what has been described, but they also fashion a world wherein *we* interact with God by means of these very sentiments. When we really enter the world sketched in the laments, *we* are plunged into fear and distress and *we* cry out to the Lord. Now this is *our* world; these are *our* sentiments; this is *our* prayer.

When we pray the psalms in this way, we are not simply using their religious imagery to express our own personal devotion. Nor are we merely calling to memory events of the past in order to be inspired by the saving acts of God in our history. We are entering into and carrying forward our creative, dynamic religious heritage. In this way the heritage becomes the inspiration of our personal devotion, and our devotion is shaped by this biblical heritage.

The World beyond the Psalms

The psalms not only invite us into the world created by their imagery and sentiments, they also prompt us to move beyond this world, back into our own world and circumstances, there to reengage in the transformation we ourselves have already undergone. The implications of this transformation of our world and the forms it may take will vary according to the sentiments found within the psalm. (Once again it will be helpful to return to the classification of psalms outlined above under the heading Types of Psalms.)

Laments

The laments, the largest category of psalms found in the Bible, continues to cause considerable difficulty for many contemporary believers. Some people think that prayer should be primarily praise, petition, or thanksgiving. The fact that many of the sections of the laments, which contain accusations against God or the cursing of antagonists, have been deleted from liturgical texts seems to support this misconception. We have become so accustomed to seeing ourselves as "Alleluia People" that we relegate any mention of suffering and pain to the prayers of petition. This is unfortunate because it prevents us from dealing honestly and straightforwardly in worship with the grief and frustration we experience in the face of national crisis or personal misfortune. It is natural to complain, even to complain to God. Laments are often admissions of guilt, pleas for forgiveness, and promises of amendment. When we pray the laments in this spirit we confess that God is a just yet forgiving judge, and we pledge ourselves to lives of faithfulness to our own covenant responsibilities.

The laments are not only protests of our grief or fear or anger, but they are also testimonies of our trust in God's faithfulness to covenant promises. They do not originate in the hearts of nonbelievers. Rather, they spring from the conviction that God is on our side, willing and able to provide for us in our distress. Remembrance of past protection is at the heart of this conviction. If God was compassionate in the past, surely

God will show us the same compassion in the future.

Finally, there is another way to enter the world of the laments. It is through solidarity with those who suffer and are oppressed. While laments may not come easily to the lips of the comfortable, they are integral to the prayer of those who are in distress. As we share or stand by them in their suffering, their prayer becomes our own; as we enter into the sentiments of the laments, we begin to understand and identify with their suffering. Laments can strengthen us in our commitment to justice and peace.

Hymns

As we praise God for the splendor of creation and acknowledge that the universe belongs to this divine architect and not to us, we should also be moved to profound respect for the world of which we are a part. We may exercise a kind of dominion over the animals with whom we share the earth, but we exercise this rule in God's stead. Hymns of praise can instill in us the dispositions necessary to become responsible stewards of the treasures of creation.

The hymns extolling the Lord for having delivered Israel from the threats of extinction depict God as an ever-present savior. This nation has been rescued from oppressive policies that threaten its well-being and prevent its self-determination. In praising God as a faithful liberator, Israel is also acknowledging God's enduring commitment to justice. God's people—and that includes all people—must be free to follow the inspiration of God as they receive it. As we pray these hymns, we too should find ourselves committed to justice toward and respect for the autonomy of all nations.

The Lord is also acclaimed as champion in the cosmic struggle with the threatening forces of chaos. Acknowledging that these forces were never completely destroyed, psalms that acclaim the kingship of the Lord declare that God is still in charge and, thus, deserving of our undivided devotion. If we praise the Lord in this fashion, we can hardly allow anything—whether wealth, power, or national loyalty—to rival the allegiance we have pledged to God.

The final division of hymns consists of the songs of Zion, which honor the mountain on which the Lord dwells, from which the Lord reigns, and to which all the nations are invited. We have seen that in these psalms the drama has moved from the cosmic plane to the world of history. The Lord is not in some distant remote place, inaccessible to the people. On the contrary, God is in the midst of the people, approachable, even inviting. We may have no allegiance to Zion itself, but with these psalms we are really acknowledging God's commitment to our well-being and God's faithful presence in our midst. A word of caution is in order here lest we fall into the trap of national chauvinism. Zion has significance because the Lord chose it, not because it chose the Lord. Whenever Israel confused being *elect* with being *elite,* it faced prophetic condemnation (see the prophet's reprimand of Jerusalem and the Temple in Jer 7; 26). We today are not preserved from this same temptation. The songs honoring Zion must be understood for what they are—hymns in praise of God, not simply songs of national pride. In fact, long-standing Christian tradition saw in the imagery of Zion, with its connection to Jerusalem and the Temple, a foretaste of the Church itself where God would dwell in the midst of his people.

Psalms of Thanksgiving

It is very difficult to be sincerely grateful when we think we deserve the good fortune that is ours. Psalms of thanksgiving help us to remember that whatever we enjoy has come to us from the hand of a gracious God. When these psalms are associated with laments, they serve as expressions of gratitude for deliverance. This suggests that Israel recognized that its own security and prosperity were blessings from God. Psalms of thanksgiving will be genuine prayer only when they spring from the conviction that our blessings also are gratuitous gifts from God. We cannot claim them by right, and so we would do well to be as generous with them with others as God has been with them with us.

Other Psalms

As with the songs of Zion, we must be on guard against national chauvinism when praying the royal psalms. Israel may have believed that loyalty to the king was an act of devotion to God, but the king was accountable to the same covenantal responsibilities as were the rest of the people. The law of the nation was an early attempt to guarantee protection and prosperity to each member of the community. (Since this was a patriarchal society, full membership was restricted to adult men.) Rather than exempting the monarchy from covenantal obligations, the royal psalms proclaim that the king was an agent through whom the blessings of fidelity were bestowed upon the people. These psalms provide us with language and imagery to celebrate the benefits we receive from God as citizens of our own country.

One of the characteristics of the wisdom poetry is its lavish use of nature imagery. The balance and regularity of the natural world are held up as examples after which society and human relationships should be patterned. This may help us understand why several "New Age" or "Creation-Centered Spirituality" movements turn to the wisdom tradition of the Bible for inspiration. We can all benefit from the insights of these groups, for this dimension of our tradition has for too long been overlooked and reclaiming it can only enrich us. Still, we cannot allow reflection on the harmony in nature to hinder us from addressing the more challenging social issues of the wisdom psalms. These poems confront us with their interest in the problem of evil, the suffering of the righteous, and the justice of God. As these hymns become our own, their interests will become our commitments.

The excitement and enthusiasm that permeate the processional psalms reveal a nation that takes its liturgical celebrations seriously. There is unfeigned joy at the thought of approaching the throne of God, but there is also humble realization that only the pure of heart will be granted access. In many ways, our own access to the divine enjoys a kind of familiarity. In a society such as ours, which is so focused on human progress and accomplishment together with technological advances and secularization, many people have lost an appreciation of the transcendent. Processional psalms remind us that, while God is indeed in our midst and accessible to us, God is still God, holy and transcendent.

It should be clear from this consideration of the psalms that their real importance is not primarily in their literary meaning but in their religious nature. As believers, we cannot be uninterested in our study of the primary prayers of our tradition, for we come to the psalms not only with open minds but also with open hearts.

FURTHER READING

Brueggemann, W. *The Psalms and the Life of Faith.* Minneapolis: Fortress, 1995.

Limburg, James. *Psalms.* Westminster Bible Commentary. Louisville: Westminster John Knox, 2000.

Mays, James L. *Psalms.* Interpretation. Louisville: John Knox, 1994.

McCann, J. C. *A Theological Introduction to the Psalms: The Psalms as Torah.* Nashville: Abingdon, 1993.

———. *The Book of Psalms.* New Interpreter's Bible 4, 641–1280. Nashville: Abingdon Press, 1996.

Miller, P. D. *Interpreting the Psalms.* Philadelphia: Fortress, 1986.

———. *They Cried to the Lord. The Form and Theology of Israelite Prayer.* Minneapolis: Fortress, 1994.

PROVERBS

[see pages 787–826 of the Old Testament]

About the Book

Proverbs is probably the biblical book that best characterizes the wisdom tradition. It appears to be the "guide for successful living" referred to in the introduction. Its primary purpose is to teach wisdom. It makes its appeal to various groups of people in different walks of life. It exhorts children (not necessarily or only young children) to heed the teaching of their parents (1, 8), and it directs citizens to act with respect toward the king (16, 10–15). It warns young men of the dangers of undisciplined living (5, 1–14; 23, 29–35), and it offers a portrait of the model wife for women to emulate (31, 10–31).

The book is composed of eight discernible collections of didactic teaching. These are quite distinct sections. Several of them are identified within the biblical text itself. Others can be distinguishable by means of their particular literary forms.

The first section consists of a general introduction to the entire book (1, 1–7) and a collection of instructions (1, 8f.18). It is in this section that we find the student addressed again and again as "my son" and exhorted to listen to the teaching that is advanced. Fifteen of the twenty-three instances of this address appear in the first seven chapters of the book. The form clearly marks this section as instruction. The second section (10, 1—22, 16) is explicitly identified as "The Proverbs of Solomon" (10, 1). Each verse in this section is a saying in its own right whose meaning does not depend on what precedes it or on what follows it. Some scholars classify this as sentence literature. A second characteristic of this section is the antithetical nature of each proverb. (This poetic feature will be discussed below.) These characteristics clearly delineate the section as a distinctive collection.

It is possible that the third section of the book (22, 17—24, 22), instructions titled "The sayings of the wise" (22, 17), is patterned after a collection of an Egyptian scribe, Amen-em-Ope (22, 19). If this is the case, it is probably the most obvious example in the wisdom tradition of Israel's literary borrowing (see RG 236). The fourth section (24, 23–34), a group of sentences designated "also . . . sayings of the wise" (24, 23), is quite short. It is followed by a much longer collection of sentence literature (25, 1—29, 27) titled "the proverbs of Solomon" (25, 1). This collection is further linked with the sages of the court of Hezekiah, the Judean king who ruled around the turn of the seventh century BC. It seems that he inaugurated a period of religious reform and literary activity. The mention of his name in a collection of proverbs may be evidence of this movement.

The sixth section, called "The words of Agur" (30, 1), is the shortest (30, 1–6). It is followed by a collection of proverbs that are distinguished by their literary form (30, 7–33). These numerical proverbs, so named because of their use of numbers (x, x + 1), have much in common with the riddle. The latter is a form mentioned in one of the introductory verses (1, 6) and in other places of the Bible (see the riddle of Samson, Jgs 14, 12, and the test of the queen of Sheba, 1 Kgs 10, 1), but are found nowhere in the book of Proverbs itself. The eighth and last section can be divided into two parts: instruction (31, 1–9), titled "The words of Lemuel" (31, 1); and a poem describing the ideal wife (31, 10–31).

The first verse of the book states that Solomon is the author of the proverbs. There was a tradition that this king was not only versed in human wisdom (see 1 Kgs 3, 16–18) but had encyclopedic knowledge as well (see 1 Kgs 3, 4–14). Ancient people believed that wisdom belonged by right to the god and, since the king was the human representative of the god, it was the special possession of the king. Since Solomon ruled during a time of splendor and enlightenment, he became known in popular devotion as the wise man par excellence. His reputation gave credibility to wisdom writing and, as more wisdom writing was attributed to him, his reputation grew. Ascribing Solomonic authorship to Proverbs gives the book the status of official teaching and credits the king with comprehensive wisdom. There is a possibility that the real royal authority behind the Proverbs is Hezekiah. Collections of proverbs could well have been compiled during the time of his religious reform, and he himself could have ascribed them to Solomon. We do not have enough information to reconstruct accurately this historical period. The book of Proverbs itself, however, attests to both Hezekiah's influence (25, 1) and Solomon's reputation (1, 1; 10, 1; 25, 1).

The Proverb

There is no English word that adequately translates the Hebrew *mashal* (translated "proverb"). It embraces a broad category of literary forms: oracle (Nm 23, 7); discourse (Jb 29, 1); parable (Ps 78, 2); taunt-song (Is 14, 4). In each case there is a lesson to be learned, and for this reason the *mashal* might best be understood as "an example from life" intended to instruct. (Although some scholars understand *mashal* in the limited sense of a specific form, it will be used here as a general category unless otherwise indicated.) This is the word that identifies two major collections as "The Proverbs of Solomon" (10, 1; 25, 1) and from which the book itself receives its name. The root meaning of *mashal* is "likeness" or "comparison" as in "Like mother like daughter," or in the contrast "Better safe than sorry." As a comparison, it usually consists of two parts in some kind of poetic construction. The *sentence* (10, 2ff), the purest form of the proverb, is distinct from the *instruction* (22, 17ff), which is a much longer unit, sometimes almost a short essay. Sentence and instruction alike, however, are expressed in poetic form, the two parts being either compared or contrasted in parallel balance of "thought rhyme." This *parallelism* is an easily recognizable feature of Hebrew poetry (see RG 238).

While there are various types of parallelism, it is usually some form of balanced equivalence or opposition. An example of the first is:

> On the way of wisdom I direct you,
> I lead you on straightforward paths (4, 11).

An example of the latter is:

> The memory of the just will be blessed,
> but the name of the wicked will rot (10, 7).

It is clear that the first type does not demand exact equivalence, nor does the second require precise contrast. Thus the second part of each of these poetic lines can be drawn from a wide variety of possibilities. The result is a collection of sayings, which are remarkable for their accuracy of insight and fluidity of expression. It is precisely this openness to interpretation and application that distinguishes a proverb in the strictest sense from a simple simile or metaphor whose interpretation is indicated and whose use is thereby limited.

It is important to appreciate the prominence of poetry in the Bible. Israel did not casually choose to express itself in poetic form. Its very perception of reality was poetic. The modern world of science and technology does not always grasp, much less appreciate, the aesthetic perspective of the ancient world. It insists on the language of exact sciences because it tends to perceive reality scientifically. Ancient Israel did not. Its encounter with reality was aesthetic and, therefore, it expressed itself in artistic thought patterns and literary forms. This does not minimize the validity of its perception and the truthfulness of its expression, or ours for that matter. They are two very different ways of looking at reality and talking about it.

The proverb itself serves two important functions. It depicts a situation from the past, and from this depiction it suggests a way of acting in the future. Understanding how this literary form works should help us to grasp the dynamics of the wisdom tradition. Wisdom is not a collection of quaint catchy phrases, which in some simplistic fashion suggest that life will unfold according to plan if we just follow the directions. Proverbs are artistically honed images of specific facets of life, and from these we can learn something about our own living. They direct our attention to the commonplace and there, usually by some type of comparison or contrast, provide us with an opportunity to gain insight into the complexities of life. Different proverbs do this in different ways. The wise person is the one who understands life from more than one proverbial point of view and can discern the appropriate way of responding to it.

Our comprehension of proverbs depends upon our ability to recognize what very different things might have in common:

> The way of an eagle in the air,
> the way of a serpent upon a rock,
> the way of a ship on the high seas,
> and the way of a man with a maiden (30, 19).

What do these dissimilar realities have in common? It is apparent that none of these "ways" is a distinctly defined route. The kind of analogy present in a proverb operates according to the same principles, as do the riddles, which people might use to challenge each other's wit. Different realities have something in common; what is it?

Proverbs do not command, they persuade. They do not dictate what must be done. Rather, they describe how things work. Their purpose is not to indoctrinate, but to educate. They are not precepts that call for obedience, but adages that invite prudent response. The book of Proverbs clearly insists on the importance of living an ethical life. The ethics it promotes, however, issued from reflection on life rather than from conformity to law.

The Teacher and the Student

Scholars hold various opinions regarding the identity of the wisdom teachers and the settings within which they taught. Some believe that there was a professional class of teachers attached to the court and appointed to train young men in the arts of diplomacy. They claim that much of the wisdom that we find in Proverbs is specialized knowledge imparted in well-defined schools. Others maintain that the elders of the family were the recognized teachers of wisdom who handed down the tradition to the next generation. These others believe that wisdom was part of the common cultural heritage of the people, and all members of the society were fashioned in its teaching.

All scholars agree that the primary education of ancient Israelite youth took place in the home and was the responsibility of the father and, as Proverbs 1, 8 tells us, the mother. (Some commentators do not believe that women played a role in the education of sons. They contend that the inclusion of "mother" is merely for the sake of poetic balance of thought [see *parallelism* above]. While that may be the case in this instance, such a poetic construction probably would not have been envisioned without some grounding in experience.) The pertinent information and operating principles of hereditary occupations were also handed down within the confines of the family, perhaps within an extended family. Such hereditary professions included the monarchy, the priesthood, and the scribal class. Education in these professions might well have been an extension of family training.

The biblical texts show that Israelite kings modeled their courts after the pattern of other ancient Near Eastern nations. They appointed men to advise them, to administer royal policies, and to keep official records. It is obvious that these men had to be trained. We should not, however, automatically conclude that such centers were the exclusive or even the principal settings for the teaching of wisdom. Some insist that since the relationship between teacher and student was analogous to that between father and son, (in patriarchal societies women seldom benefit from the educational system) the address "My son," should not be viewed exclusively as familial. While this may be true, the inclusion of "your mother's teaching" (1, 8) argues for a family setting.

If wisdom is basically the way a culture addresses the fundamental questions of life, then all members of the society are trained in it and all possess this wisdom in varying degrees and live it out in their lives in diverse ways. The "way of wisdom" may have been very general and indistinguishable, or specialized and distinctive. Intelligence may be an innate quality, but wisdom is acquired by learning from others and

from life experience. Such wisdom is neither static nor the exclusive domain of an official class. It grew up within the people, and it was their public property.

The Way of Wisdom

Wisdom came to be understood in several ways. Consequently, "the way of wisdom," a phrase that scholars use, refers to the proper way of doing things, whether in human society, in the world of nature, or on the cosmic plane. The first of these is the kind of wisdom that has been described thus far. Often called practical or folk wisdom, it is primarily concerned with the consequences of social interaction. Since peace and harmony can exist only where some kind of social order is maintained, whatever guaranteed such order was pursued, and whatever threatened it was avoided. This, in fact, is the dimension of wisdom thinking that gave rise to the theory of retribution—the wise will enjoy peace and security; the fool will suffer the consequences of foolishness:

> The virtue of the upright saves them,
> > but the faithless are caught in their own
> > > intrigue (11, 6).

Proverbs declare that there are only two ways open to women and men: the way of the wise (those who learn from experience), and the way of the foolish (those who do not learn). Since successful living demands an ongoing search for meaning, one can never settle for the solutions of the past. New situations constantly present themselves; new choices must be made. The ever-developing tradition of wisdom provides various examples of behavior that resulted in success as well as behavior that ended in disaster. The wise, enriched by this store of practical knowledge, will take to heart these lessons. They are the ones who have developed a certain facility in drawing from the accumulated wisdom of the past and, in an imaginative way, successfully bring it to bear on new situations. Thus they follow "the way of wisdom."

A second kind of wisdom deals with our need to survive and prosper in the natural world. Reflective observation of nature and the movements within it led people to recognize a certain amount of regularity in its operations and similarity in its various manifestations. This regularity was charted, the similarities noted, and a kind of nature wisdom developed that was a precursor of the physical sciences. People learned how to live in harmony with nature and, through comparison and contrast, they drew lessons from nature for their daily lives:

Like snow in summer, or rain in harvest,
    honor for a fool is out of place (26, 1).

This too was "the way of wisdom."

Some have questioned the religious value of folk wisdom, because there is no mention of God. The proverbs appear to be anthropocentric (human-centered) rather than theocentric (God-centered). We must be careful not to compare an ancient Near Eastern humanistic point of view with a kind of modern humanism that is faithless. Biblical Israel was not a secular society. It never questioned the divine power working to hold the world in proper balance. It might not understand God's actions, but it did not doubt God's power. The wisdom tradition was built on the conviction that God expected people to use their human abilities to the fullest. Whether or not there is explicit mention of God, Israelite wisdom was religious teaching, and the ethical orientation of the proverbs should be seen as evidence of their religious character.

Finally, people in the ancient Near East believed that there was a kind of wisdom that was beyond their grasp and their comprehension. Their belief rested on the conviction that there was some kind of cosmic order within which they lived, an order that was reliable though mysterious, an order that revealed the wisdom of the creator-god. They maintained that this cosmic order not only predated the natural world but also was actually somehow responsible for its existence. The primordial wisdom associated with this cosmic order fashioned the world and keeps it functioning properly. Of all the kinds of wisdom, it alone contains the secrets of the universe and the complete answers to all questions. The sages knew that this was the only wisdom that would satisfy the human search for meaning. Since it was clearly beyond human reach, it was considered a cosmic reality and it was described as such:

From of old I was poured forth,
    at the first, before the earth (8, 23).

Creation is "the way of wisdom" on this cosmic plane. Israel believed that God was creator of all things, and thus it spoke of a theological dimension to each of these three manifestations of wisdom. Although theological expression is more explicit in later writings, it was never absent from Israel's worldview. The optimistic view of life that permeates the book of Proverbs flows from the conviction that there is an order to the universe and, with God's help, we can discover it, live in harmony with it, and thus enjoy peace and prosperity. This, above all, is "the way of wisdom."

The Teachings of the Wise

Before we look at some of the specifics of the wisdom teaching, it is important for us to remember a few fundamentals of the movement. Here, emphasis is on the human person in general rather than on the nation as a collective group. Its scope is universal, not exclusively Israelite. The counsel offered addresses issues from everyday life rather than cultic experience. It is concerned with pragmatic ends, not transcendent values. If we expect this teaching to address questions not found within its range, not only will we find it wanting but also we might even fail to appreciate the riches that are to be found there.

Fear of the Lord

"The fear of the LORD is the beginning of wisdom." Several variations of this familiar saying appear in the book of Proverbs (1, 7; 9, 10; 15, 33). This notion of fear is based on the recognition of the holiness of God. There may very well be a certain dimension of terror in those who behold the awesomeness of God and realize their own deficiency in the face of it, but this is not the primary meaning that "fear of the LORD" intends to convey. This fear is better characterized as awe and reverence than as terror and dread. Awe, not dread, is awakened when one realizes the transcendence of a God who is protective, not threatening.

Israel did not view this reverential fear as merely an attitude of mind. It was the foundation of its moral conduct. It included respect, loyalty, obedience, and covenant love. Owing to the special character of Yahweh, "fear of the LORD" (the Hebrew word that we translate as LORD is *Yahweh,* the name of Israel's God) becomes a uniquely Israelite expression. Eventually, this phrase became the summation of Israelite religion and piety. In Proverbs this "fear of the LORD" is linked with wisdom, which is practical knowledge that comes from reflection on experience. These are two quite distinct ideas that, when brought together, significantly reinterpret the meaning of wisdom. Comparing two proverbs can see this:

The beginning of wisdom is: get wisdom . . . (4, 7)
The beginning of wisdom is the fear of the LORD . . . (9, 10).

In the first proverb, ordinary life is the source of wisdom. In the second, wisdom flows from religious faith. This change in perspective may be the result of sages trying to bridge the gap between the wisdom teaching that they held in common with other Near Eastern nations and that which was distinctively Israelite.

"Fear of the LORD" might be understood in another way. The Israelites believed that behind the breathtaking order of the universe was an all-wise and all-powerful God. They believed that the more they knew about their world, the more they would discover about God. The reverse was also held. Knowledge about God was the beginning of true knowledge about the world. The more one was committed to God, the more one was in harmony with the order placed in the world by this same God. Thus, the proper religious attitude toward God was the source of wisdom.

Training in Virtue

As stated above, the emphasis in the wisdom tradition is on the individual person rather than on the nation. This should not be understood as a kind of privatized individualism as we know today. It was precisely as a member of the covenant community that an Israelite searched for meaning in the events of life. The social ramifications of one's personal life were seldom far from the minds of the people. (It is merely for the sake of this investigation that we separate personal virtues from social virtues. The former characterize behavior in every kind of situation. The latter suggest specific social settings implied in the proverbs themselves.)

The connection between wisdom and personal virtue is clear and frequently stated. The way of wisdom is the way of virtue. It is also the only way to happiness (see Prv 10—13). Many proverbs praise self-control, especially restraint in speech (21, 23). They direct one to speak with words that are pleasing (16, 24), not foolish (14, 23). They admonish discipline in other areas of life as well. For instance, the student is counseled: "With closest custody, guard your heart" (4, 23). Honesty (13, 5), diligence (6, 6–11), docility (13, 10), and humility (22, 4) are but a few of the virtues that are recommended to the young who, if they live their lives according to this counsel, are promised a good reputation (22, 1) and long life (10, 27). Once again we see that the people are advised to put their trust in the Lord and not be overconfident of their own ability (3, 5).

There are numerous warnings against the seduction of adulterous women. In a strict patriarchal society, the virtue of men is of primary concern; women are frequently regarded as property and are confined in restrictive seclusion in order to guarantee their fidelity and thus assure the legitimacy of the male's offspring. Only women of questionable virtue move freely in such societies, and these are precisely the women against whom the young men are cautioned (see 2, 16–19; 6, 20–35).

A significant amount of instruction is unmistakably social in its focus. It is bent on developing relationships necessary for societal tranquility. The proverbs themselves provide glimpses into the social settings within which they might be effective. It is obvious that the family plays a prominent role as the initial setting for education. Several proverbs admonish young people to heed the teaching of their parents (1, 8; 6, 20). The sages realized that the family is the foundation of society, and social virtues are cultivated there. They understood that the lessons of respect and obedience learned within the family go a long way in other less personal social situations. A fair amount of counsel about training and chastisement can also be found (22, 6; 13, 1; 24; 19, 18). This advice might be directed either to training within the family or to occupational education (see The Teacher and the Student).

The distinct influence of Yahwism may not be easily detected in some proverbial instruction, but the call to justice in Proverbs is similar to what we find in the covenant. It manifests itself in concern for the relationship between the rich and the poor. Despite the fact that riches were viewed as fitting reward for righteous living, the inherent dangers of possessing wealth were still acknowledged (28, 3.8; 11, 28; 21, 13). The poor were to be respected, for they too came from the hand of God (14, 31; 22, 2) and were sometimes more virtuous than the rich (28, 6).

Advice is given to both the ruled and the ruler. Subjects are told to esteem the king, because he exercises considerable power over them (16, 14f). Kings, on the other hand, are bound to be fair and upright (16, 10–12). The demand that kings observe justice is part of the ideology of kingship throughout the ancient Near East.

Moral teaching such as this might presuppose an almost mechanical view of retribution. It suggests that the universal order upon which the world depends is neat and reliable. The rewards and punishments, considered the consequences of particular styles of living, seem almost to issue from impersonal laws inherent in the actions themselves, or they are deemed the direct intervention of a God who is executing justice. The book of Proverbs may appear to oversimplify the complexities of human life. It does not question the status quo. One will have to look elsewhere for a critique of social structures or of the prevailing philosophy of life. The applicability of the theory of retribution is not challenged in this book as it is in Job and in Ecclesiastes.

The Figure of Wisdom

An interesting feature of this book is the figure of Wisdom personified. In the very first chapter (1, 20–33), wisdom is depicted as a woman who goes through the city looking for disciples. Many of the traits that characterize her are found throughout the book in proverbs that describe either the wise teacher or the wisdom teaching itself. This woman is frequently contrasted with a second woman, Folly (9, 13), who attempts to seduce the simple into her ways. It is not unusual to find personification itself in Hebrew poetry. The prophets used it:

> Break out together in song,
>   O ruins of Jerusalem! (Is 52, 9)

as did the psalmists:

> Let the rivers clap their hands,
>   the mountains shout with them for joy
>   (Ps 98, 8).

What is unusual here is that wisdom is characterized as a woman. Several explanations for this have been advanced. Some believe that this is a remnant of ancient Near Eastern (even Israelite) worship of a goddess of wisdom. Others see it as merely a development from the feminine form of the word *hokmah,* "wisdom." A widely accepted explanation for this might be found in the nature of the society itself. Wisdom was regarded as the most desirable possession. In this patriarchal male-preferred society, it is understandable that what is desired would be personified as a woman. The same is true for folly. Women are no more inherently seductive than are men. However, they are a better representation of what men find enticing.

This might explain certain features of the figure of the woman in the market place (8, 1–21), but the real mystery lies in the identity of the figure that was present at creation (8, 22–31). Over the centuries this figure has been interpreted in various ways.

The Bible quite explicitly states again and again that God alone is the creator. However, there we also find Wisdom claiming to have exercised some role in creation (8, 30). This claim must be reconciled with the traditional Israelite faith. One way to do this has been to understand the figure of Wisdom as the personification of a divine attribute. According to this view, the personification is merely a stylistic feature of the author. Such an imaginative technique is not foreign to the Bible. The kindness, truth, and justice of God have also been personified (see Ps 85, 10–14).

As helpful as this explanation may be, it does not take into account the fact that Wisdom is identified as an entity separate from the creator (8, 22). Such a characterization is more than personification. It is closer to *hypostasization* (taking what is normally a personal trait and transforming it into a person with its own existence). It is apparent that once Wisdom is created, she has a life of her own. It is also clear that she is a creature with cosmic dimensions. She existed before the rest of creation, and she appears to be active beyond the confines of space and time. According to some commentators, this suggests a mythological origin. Such an interpretation would not be against biblical religion, for there are several other sections of the Bible that con-

Proverbs

tain mythological elements (for example, the garden with the talking serpent [Gn 2—3]; the sea dragon [Is 27, 1]).

A third interpretation of this mysterious figure is gaining more prominence today. It claims that Wisdom was originally a goddess. Some say that she was a Canaanite deity; others argue that she was actually early Israelite. Scholars have long maintained that Israel moved from believing in many gods (polytheism), to acknowledging that other nations might have their gods but Israel would worship only one (monolatry), to insisting that there is only one God (monotheism). It is possible that the ancestors of Israel once believed in a goddess of wisdom from whom Woman Wisdom originated.

Whatever the origin of this enigmatic figure, she is no longer perceived as a goddess. She probably represents that inaccessible dimension of wisdom that all people desire but which resides with God alone, the kind of wisdom that is within creation but beyond us. This is the wisdom that explains the universe but which we cannot attain. The mysterious figure, whatever her origin, reminds us that the fullness of wisdom cannot be gained through human experience. It belongs to God.

The Role of Wisdom Today

There are several reasons why Proverbs may not be popular reading. It seems to describe a world that does not exist, a world where life has a proper order and events follow a cause-and-effect sequence. We know to the contrary that life is very unpredictable. We may be able to discern some of the order in nature, but the events of life itself cannot be charted or foreseen. Consequently, Proverbs appears to be very naive and somewhat static.

Furthermore, the world of Proverbs seems to be the world of the comfortable, not the world of those who struggle. Even directions about justice are given from the point of view of those who are in charge, and the advice does not question the way things are. Since people supported by the status quo seldom challenge it, Proverbs might well be perceived as a guide to "Win Friends, Influence People, and Get Ahead in the World as It Is." Advocates of justice and peace usually turn to the prophets for inspiration, not to the proverbs.

Such an evaluation of the wisdom tradition misses a few very important points. First, proverbs do not claim to describe everything, but they do depict a bit of the world. Each proverb reflects a snippet of life. Together they offer a collage, not a blueprint. Second, the process that produces proverbs may be more significant than the content of the proverbs themselves. It teaches us the importance of serious reflection on experience and the need to adjust both our understanding and our behavior as circumstances change. The wise person is the one who can adequately assess the demands of a situation and who is experienced and flexible enough to behave in a way that is appropriate to that particular situation. If we read proverbs as directions that we must follow rather than as examples from which we can learn, we will misunderstand the force of their teaching. However, if we read them rightly, we will discover that the way of wisdom is neither naive nor static.

Although people do not turn to the proverbs for prophetic inspiration, the wisdom method of reflection on life experience found there has gained prominence in recent years. Frequently, experience is the starting point from which contemporary theologians develop their insights. This approach has spread from the base Christian communities to Bible discussion groups around the world. People are beginning again to realize that they encounter God *through* human experience, not *despite* it.

The charge that Proverbs is a book of upper-class ethics can be debated. It is true that several proverbs seem suited to the court or to some other diplomatic setting. However, most of them could easily have been used in the normal everyday training of youth. They do presume an underlying order that is stable and reliable, but that is common in most initial training programs. Proverbs is the kind of teaching that socializes members into the group. It does not question the credibility of the group and so it lacks a prophetic edge. However, Proverbs does offer an appreciation of life and an encouragement to live it to the fullest.

FURTHER READING

Clifford, R. J. *Proverbs*. Old Testament Library. Louisville: Westminster, 1999.

Fox, M. V. *Proverbs 1–9.* Anchor Bible 18A. New York: Doubleday, 2000.

Perdue, Leo G. *Proverbs.* Interpretation. Louisville: John Knox, 2000.

Murphy, Roland E. *Proverbs.* Word Bible Commentary. Waco, TX: Word, 1998.

ECCLESIASTES

[see pages 826–36 of the Old Testament]

Ecclesiastes does not enjoy the renown that belongs to other writings of the wisdom tradition, specifically Job or Psalms. However, even people who are unfamiliar with the book often use expressions that arise from its provocative view of life. Sayings such as "You can't take it with you!" or "There's nothing new under the sun!" show that the thinking of Ecclesiastes is not foreign to our own contemporary worldview.

About the Book

Ecclesiastes manifests some of the literary characteristics of a *Royal Testament,* a common type of literature of the ancient Near East intended for the instruction of the king's successor. The Royal Testament was written in the first person and claimed to be advice gleaned from the experience of life. Although the book begins with a kind of third-person descriptive prologue (1, 1–11) and ends with an epilogue also in the third person (12, 9–14), everything else within it suggests but one speaker and, despite some conflicting statements, one point of view. There are also several unresolved literary questions regarding the book's authorship, dating, place of origin, composition, and structure.

The very first verse of the book describes rather than identifies the speaker as "David's son, Qoheleth, king in Jerusalem." (See the Solomonic attribution of the book of Proverbs, early in the Reading Guide to that book.) Since there is no biblical mention of a Davidic son by the name of Qoheleth, some other connotation must be intended. The exact meaning of the name Qoheleth is debated. It probably comes from the Hebrew word *qahal,* meaning assembly. The form of the word suggests that it is not a name but a participle that designates someone who does something. This explains why most commentators maintain that the word refers to someone who calls forth or presides over a meeting, perhaps for the purpose of teaching. The

Greek word used to translate *qahal* is *ekklesia,* meaning a citizens' assembly in Greece. In this biblical book, the one who presides over the assembly is called Ecclesiastes or Preacher.

The man is further designated as the son of David, king of Israel. The reference is obviously to Solomon, the one revered in popular devotion as the wise king par excellence. The author seems to be claiming that Solomon is the speaker, and therefore the teaching in the book has the authority of Solomon's wisdom. Although this claim appears only in the first two chapters, it sets the tone for the rest of the instruction. From the outset the teaching has authority even though it may prove to be unorthodox.

The language of the book resembles the kind of Hebrew that appeared during a very late biblical period and was used almost exclusively for literary purposes. The inclusion of several Aramaic words has led scholars to date the book around the third century BC. The place of origin is more difficult to determine. Some say it was Phoenicia, others suggest Egypt. The international character of the wisdom tradition adds to the complexity of precise identification (see introduction to the Wisdom Books, RG 236).

There are also different opinions regarding the structure of the book. Some believe that it is simply a collection of wisdom pieces lacking organization. Others divide the book into two major parts: Qoheleth's observations of life, and the conclusions that he draws. (The *New American Bible* belongs to this latter group.) Since there is only one speaker, a structure based on alternate speeches is ruled out.

Besides instruction, the author makes use of several other teaching techniques. These include proverbial quotations, contrasting proverbs, and rhetorical questions. Several of these forms are mentioned in the prologue to Proverbs, ". . . proverb and parable, the words of the wise and their riddles" (Prv 1, 6). All of this fosters the characterization of Qoheleth as a respected teacher of wisdom.

Ecclesiastes is one of the five books that make up the *Megilloth,* or "Scrolls," a special collection that includes Song of Songs, Ruth, Lamentations, and Esther. These books were read during various liturgical festivals and were gathered together for the sake of convenience. Ecclesiastes was read during the harvest celebration of Sukkoth, also known as Tabernacles or Booths. This major pilgrim feast was so called because the harvesters lived in booths as they gathered in their crops. It is not clear how this practice of reading began or why Ecclesiastes was chosen for this festival. Perhaps the somber tone of the book, the seasoned reflections of an aging sage, fit the maturity of harvest. Although reading the book was not always a consistent synagogue practice, Ecclesiastes continues to be considered part of the Megilloth.

The book clearly begins with the distinctive "Vanity of vanities, says Qoheleth, vanity of vanities! All things are vanity!" (1, 2) and ends on the same tone "Vanity of vanities, says Qoheleth, all things are vanity!" (12, 8). What some consider a kind of prologue (1, 1–11) might well come from the original author. The epilogue (12, 9–14) is different: at least one, possibly two people besides the primary have added something. Verses 9–11 praise Qoheleth as a wise teacher and compiler of wisdom sayings. Whoever added these verses plainly agreed with Qoheleth's conclusions despite their critical and sometimes unconventional viewpoint. The tone changes, though, with verse 12, which begins with the same Hebrew word as does verse 9. Some hold that this is textual evidence of a second epilogue. This is the only place in the book where the student is identified in a manner found frequently in Proverbs. However, the student is warned against too much speculation and is advised to trust in the retributive justice of God, a theme that Qoheleth consistently challenges.

It would appear from all this, that the author created a literary character, Qoheleth, and ascribed Solomonic authority to him in order to give his own instruction credibility. A later editor further authenticated this teaching by explicitly assuring the reader of Qoheleth's wisdom. However, with two short verses a second editor tried to temper some of Qoheleth's statements.

There are two possible explanations for this inconsistent ending: (1) The book was already well enough accepted so that its critics could not dismiss it. Still, someone was in a position to append a caution to what might be considered questionable teaching. (2) If there was only one editor who agreed with Qoheleth's teaching, that person realized that without some kind of tempering it would not be preserved. In order to assure acceptance, the last verses restate the traditional view of retribution and seem to return the entire teaching to the circle of orthodoxy.

A Critical Point of View

There is a wide range of scholarly opinion regarding the meaning of the book. Qoheleth has been described as a skeptic, a cynic, or, more positively, a pragmatist. His view of life has been called everything from pessimistic and fatalistic to realistic. Some judge his religious outlook hedonistic or pleasure-seeking, while others think it is faithful to Israelite values. It is clear that he is disillusioned with certain facets of his society, yet he lacks the enthusiasm of a reformer and the vision of a mystic. This has led some critics to label him a frustrated man who is resigned to the injustice and meaninglessness of life and who is intent on making the most of any fleeting pleasures, in the spirit of Epicureanism. It is difficult to make a distinction between a challenge to the way life is understood and dissatisfaction with life itself. Perhaps in the actual living of life, it is impossible to separate the two. A careful reading of Qoheleth, however, will show that he does not really despair of life but only of unrealistic expectations regarding it. Qoheleth's real struggle is with the meaning of life, especially life viewed from the perspective of the theory of retribution (see introduction).

A Chase after Wind

Qoheleth sets out to discover everything of value within human experience (1, 13). Since he is identified as a king, he has both the wealth and the leisure to embark on this quest. As possessor of extraordinary wisdom (1, 16), he of all people is equipped to experience life to the full. The text states that he has acquired wisdom, but satisfaction in what he sought was always beyond his grasp, "a chase after wind" (1, 17). It is clear that in his search for wisdom, he was looking for something else as well. Qoheleth next turned to the pursuit of self-gratification, and in many different ways he was successful in this pursuit, but still he was not satisfied (2, 1–11). It seems that he accomplished everything to which he had set his mind in his search to answer the fundamental question: "What profit has man from all the labor which he toils at under the sun?" (1, 3). He consistently arrived at the same conclusion, however. There is no lasting gain, no tangible dividend, "with nothing gained under the sun" (2, 11).

The theory of retribution claims that there is a direct relation between the uprightness of one's behavior and the good or ill fortune that one enjoys or endures. According to this theory, Qoheleth's wisdom and wealth would be perceived as concrete proof of his goodness and a guarantee of future prosperity. But Qoheleth does not really enjoy his good fortune, and so he questions its value. Since death comes to all, he wonders, "why then should I be wise? Where is the profit for me?" (2, 15). It is not life as such, nor the search for fulfillment in life, that frustrates him. What he loathes (2, 17) is the profitlessness of human striving. It is not fulfilling. Since Qoheleth did attain the wisdom and wealth and pleasure that he sought, his frustration must stem from his failure to attain something in addition to these goals. Qoheleth is asking more of life than merely success and prosperity.

He is also troubled about the inevitability of death and the sense of futility it often imparts. Regardless of how one lives, death is the ultimate fate of all. Any advantage that one might have because of righteousness, wisdom, or wealth is only temporary and, therefore, questionable. In fact, the fool who disregards societal rules may actually have an edge over the one who conforms to them at the cost of enjoyment. Death and the total relinquishment that it demands force Qoheleth to question the value of any human accomplishment and to wonder if perhaps life itself is "a chase after wind."

Nothing Is New under the Sun

We have already seen how the wisdom teachers appealed to the obvious order within the natural world as they urged people to live in compliance with acceptable social custom (see Proverbs: The Way of Wisdom, RG 257f). The author of Job

used the same technique with a slightly different twist. There we see that Job was overwhelmed by the wonders of nature and led to acknowledge the incomprehensible dimension of life (see Job: Reward and Punishment, RG 238f). The author of Ecclesiastes also directs our attention to the regularity in nature (1, 2–11), but he does so in order to highlight its monotony. The activity of the earth does not change; it seems constant. The sun rises and sets and rises again and sets again in the same mode day after day. Although the wind appears at times to be irregular, it follows certain paths that, upon observation, can be predicted. Even the sea, though constantly fed, is never full. The regularity detected in nature appears to be devoid of any progress. There is nothing new under the sun.

What advantage does the earth have in being constant? What does the sun accomplish by rising and setting if it must repeat the cycle again and again with no variation and no advance? What profit comes from the wind's endless movement if it never arrives at any destination? To what avail do the streams nourish an insatiable sea? Qoheleth urges us to learn yet another lesson from nature. Human striving for gain is nothing but wearisome labor that must be repeated and repeated with no promise of conclusion and no assurance of gratification. Human life is basically the same regardless of the society or the generation into which one is born. Life itself follows the same cycles, and experiences are quite similar. Momentous events do occur, but they seldom interfere with the fundamental rhythms of existence. Nature repeats itself and so does human history. Nothing seems to have lasting significance.

In what may be the most familiar section of the entire book (3, 1–9), Qoheleth declares that each event of human life has its own appointed time. Here, each event is linked in poetic construction with its opposite. There are two ways of understanding this pattern. First, juxtaposing opposites is a poetic way of expressing totality. It creates an inclusion that encompasses both poles and everything in between. Examples of this include: "knowledge of good and bad" (see Gn 2, 9.17) meaning comprehensive knowledge; "bone and flesh" (see Gn 2, 23) referring to the entire body. The contemporary phrase "flesh and blood" has the same meaning.

The second way of understanding this poetic form is as an expression of relativity. There is an inevitability to human events that is nonetheless relative. The circumstances of life determine what is fitting and what is not. What is appropriate at one time or in one situation can be out of place when the circumstances change. This may be the author's way of insisting that there are no absolutes; that is, everything is always relative to all else. There is a time to die as well as a time to be born. Neither seems to have an advantage over the other. However, we do not know the rules that govern these appointed times, and so we are helpless to control them and may feel that we are at their mercy.

The task of living is not easy. Qoheleth explains why in 3, 11. This verse may be the most difficult one of the book because of the questions surrounding the translation and interpretation of the Hebrew *olam*. Although some versions translate this word as "world," or "future," or even "ignorance," the NAB renders it as "the timeless." God has put *olam* in the human heart, and we want to know, to understand, and even to control everything in the world. It seems that while human beings are finite, their desires transcend the limits of time. Qoheleth has described the world as fixed and closed. There is, nonetheless, urgency within the human heart that seeks to burst the confines of restrictive determinism in order to delight in the wonders of freedom and mystery. We are reminded of St. Augustine's famous saying: "You have made us for yourself, O Lord, and our hearts are restless until they rest in you."

All Is Vanity!

"All is vanity" is the expression that has come to characterize the entire book. The Hebrew word *hebel*, which is here translated as "vanity," can also be rendered as "vapor" or "thin air." It means pointlessness or futility, and it refers to something that may be real but that has little or no lasting substance. We have seen that Qoheleth has accomplished everything he set out to do. He has acquired wisdom and wealth; he has enjoyed pleasure and prosperity; he has achieved all of his goals. And yet he declares "All is vanity!" All of the energy he put into his projects was pointless; all of his toil was futile. One might expect him to advise against ever trying to be happy, but

he does not. Quite the contrary! We will see that he urges people to enjoy what they have. Then what about life does he regard as vanity?

Qoheleth observed in the lives of others what Job experienced in his own life: The righteous do not always enjoy the good things of life, nor are the wicked always deprived of them (4, 1; 8, 10f). Life itself has shown both Job and Qoheleth the inadequacy of the theory of retribution. This theory may be helpful in explaining some things and in encouraging a certain kind of behavior, but it falls short in many areas. While both men seem to have arrived at this insight, Qoheleth's dissatisfaction in the face of his own prosperity and success has led him a step further in challenging the theory. It is not only that a righteous person sometimes does not prosper; it is also that, even when one does realize some desired goal, there is no guarantee of fulfillment. To suppose that the attainment of goals, even noble goals, can fulfill human longings is, according to Qoheleth, vanity!

The Wisdom of the Sage

The wisdom of Qoheleth consists not only in a critical examination of everything that is supposed to bring happiness but also in providing positive counsel. Although he finds fault with some aspects of human striving, he advises something that is often overlooked in times of feverish activity, something that is always within reach and may well be the key to true happiness and contentment. He exhorts his hearers to relish the simple pleasures that are at hand (2, 24; 3, 13.22; 5, 19; 8, 15; 9, 9). These pleasures can be experienced in the very act of living: in eating, in drinking, in labor itself rather than in the wealth that one may hope to produce by it. According to Qoheleth, this pleasure, like everything else in life, has come from the hand of God and should be enjoyed.

One cannot calculate this enjoyment or manipulate it as might be possible in a purely business transaction. Life is not a business transaction and to expect a strict quid pro quo (this for that) return, as one might expect in a rigid interpretation of retribution, will only end in disappointment. Qoheleth believes the enjoyment should be sought in the doing rather than in the outcome. To wait in anticipation of something more than the natural satisfaction that accompanies human activity is foolish, because the future is uncertain.

Qoheleth does not spurn the search for wisdom or the normal human striving for success and prosperity. He objects to making human accomplishment the primary or exclusive goal in life. He calls upon all to find pleasure in what they are doing and, if they are fortunate enough to become successful in the process, to see this as a gift from God as well.

A Challenge for Today

Ecclesiastes is not an account of Qoheleth's journey in faith. It is more like jottings or a report of his experiments in living. He did not share Job's struggle with theodicy (a defense of God against the accusation of injustice). Rather, Qoheleth addressed human misconceptions about divine activity, not the incomprehensible itself. He seems to have gone right to the core of things. He scrutinized some of the primary undertakings and fundamental goals of people.

Qoheleth would probably be unrelenting in his criticism of many of the attitudes found within our contemporary society. He knew that prosperity is often fleeting and cannot ensure happiness, even when it is at one's disposal. The complexity of modern society and the instability of the world's economy make it more difficult to amass wealth today than may have been the case in the past. For this reason, the strain and conflict that often accompany the struggle for "upward mobility" have been heightened. This is true for nations as well as for individuals. Much of the injustice in present society stems from greed and an avaricious devouring of the wealth of the world. Too many people believe that having more will make them happy.

Qoheleth never disparaged ingenuity or hard work. Rather, he criticized those who judged the worth of human endeavor by the amount of output rather than the quality of input. There is a very thin line between directing all of one's energies toward accomplishing a noble goal and sacrificing everything for the sake of success. Qoheleth wholeheartedly endorsed the former while he condemned the latter. He would most likely criticize any attitude or system that places more value on the product than on the person producing it. Today's business practices, whether local, na-

tional, or international, would come under his scrutiny in this regard.

The struggle for upward mobility is not the only dimension of contemporary society that Qoheleth would most likely challenge. Many people spend a lifetime climbing the ladder of prominence and power. Others will do almost anything to gain acceptability in prestigious social, professional, or political circles. And who does not aspire to a reputation for wisdom or exceptional intelligence? Qoheleth would challenge us to put all such ambition in the right perspective.

This sage teacher was not blind to the many disappointments and tragedies of life, but neither was he an advocate of radical social change. He cautions against wishing for what cannot be, and he urges his hearers to make the most of what they have. This may not be an encouraging message for those who are deprived of the necessities of life, but most likely it was not intended for them. He is not contesting the justice of the social order. He is questioning the value of the motivation behind obsessive striving for success.

Finally, Qoheleth was convinced that the future is not totally under our control. It cannot be manipulated by human decision nor determined by human behavior. A strict interpretation of retribution frequently includes the notion that God is bound to respond to our actions with appropriate reward or punishment, whichever the case may be. This normally unconscious attitude surfaces when we are faced with unexplained reverses of fortune. We wonder what we have done to bring adversity upon ourselves, or we accuse God of behaving unfairly toward us. Qoheleth would remind us that God is not bound by our interpretive theories. We can accurately predict neither success nor failure.

Qoheleth would insist that the primary goal of life is living. All work, all progress has one principal purpose and that is the enhancement and promotion of life. Every other end is at best secondary or otherwise "a chase after the wind." This is a profoundly religious teaching, for Qoheleth believed that it was the creator who placed the desire for happiness within each human heart, made living an exciting adventure, and willed that every person be given the chance to find pleasure in life. He would strongly object to any materialistic point of view that might minimize or deny this basic conviction. Qoheleth was a champion of the greatest of God's gifts—life itself.

FURTHER READING

Brown, William P. *Ecclesiastes*. Interpretation. Louisville: Westminster John Knox, 2000.

Crenshaw, James L. *Ecclesiastes*. Old Testament Library. Philadelphia: Westminster, 1987.

Murphy, Roland E. *Ecclesiastes*. Word Bible Commentary 23A. Waco, TX: Word, 1992.

Seow, C. L. *Ecclesiastes*. Anchor Bible 18C. New York: Doubleday, 1997.

Towner, W. Sibley. *The Book of Ecclesiastes*. New Interpreter's Bible 5. Nashville, TN: Abingdon Press, 1997.

THE SONG OF SONGS

[see pages 836–43 of the Old Testament]

No book of the Old Testament is more difficult to interpret than the Song of Songs. It is clearly a collection of love poems full of sensuous imagery. It promotes no apparent theological or moral values, and it never even mentions God. It is no wonder that its acceptance into the canon of inspired writings was seriously questioned. The very character of the book has led to many quite distinct interpretations.

About the Book

Scholars vary in their explanation of the book, but they agree that it did not originate as a single composition. They concur that it is a collection of poems of various lengths, but they propose different ways of grouping these poems. Some have suggested a movement from longing to union and then to separation. This pattern is repeated through the eight short chapters. Others maintain that, while the lyrics do express such sentiments, the arrangement of the poems lacks any definite pattern. The book may have no clearly defined structure, but it is marked by frequent repetitions (for example, 2, 7; 3, 5; 8, 4). Since there is no narrative plot and the speakers are neither identified nor introduced, one can only speculate about the compiler's original intention.

This relatively short book has an unusually large number of uncommon words. Its 117 verses contain forty-nine words that appear nowhere else in the Old Testament. This adds to the difficulty of comprehension, for we are prevented from comparing the meaning of the word found in one context with its meaning in another. This obscure vocabulary also opens the poem to a multiplicity of interpretations, thus making it somewhat cryptic but also allowing for a rich diversity of meanings.

Like Proverbs and Ecclesiastes, the Song is associated with Solomon. This ascription to the famous king is found only in the editorial introduction (1, 1) and is preceded by a preposition that can be translated in various ways: "by" Solomon; "to" Solomon; "for" Solomon; "of" Solomon; "concerning" Solomon. The attribution need not imply authorship. Still, ascribing the book to Solomon probably gave it credibility, linked it with the other wisdom traditions, and contributed to one of its best-known allegorical interpretations. The book does include other references to Solomon (3, 7.9.11; 8, 11f), and this has convinced some interpreters of the Solomonic identity of the amorous shepherd. However, in none of these passages does Solomon speak, and the references could actually be merely figurative allusions to fabulous wealth.

The geographic references within the Song are quite wide reaching. Northern locations are mentioned (2, 1; 3, 9; 4, 8; 6, 4; 7, 5–6), as are places in Transjordan (4, 1) and Judah (1, 14; 3, 5). This variety may reflect the early northern Israelite source of some of the original poems and a later southern, perhaps Jerusalem, setting for the final edition. The appearance of the Persian word for orchard or park (4, 13) suggests a postexilic date (after 539 BC).

The Song of Songs is also found in the *Megilloth* scroll (see Reading Guide to Ecclesiastes, RG 262). It is read on the last day of the celebration of Passover. Perhaps the announcement of the end of winter (2, 11) made the poem suitable for use during a spring festival. Many consider the reference to the horses and chariots of Pharaoh (1, 9) a clear allusion to the Exodus, the event commemorated at Passover.

Voices in the Song

There are letters in the left-hand margins of the NAB that identify the speaker of the verses. These letters are in fact an interpretation. The references to the "Daughters of Jerusalem" (see 1, 5; 2, 7; 3, 5; 5, 8.16) do not present any problem, but the meaning of "bride" (see 4, 8–12; 5, 1) is not clear. The Hebrew text clearly refers to the young woman in this way, but the word itself designates a woman who is betrothed but not yet married to a man. While the text does allude to the sexual union of the lovers, it never describes a marriage and so the male partner is not necessarily a "groom." (The reference in 3, 11 is to the splendor of Solomon, not to the marriage of the lovers in the Song.) Furthermore, there seem to be two distinct portraits of this elusive lover. One of them is a royal figure from Jerusalem (see 1, 12–17; 3, 6–11), and the other is a rustic youth from the north (see 1, 7f; 2, 8–17). Nowhere in the book do we find an explicit combination of the two.

Who are these mysterious lovers? The way one understands the meaning and function of the book will influence the way one identifies the characters within it. If these are ancient wedding songs, then, of course, the lovers are a bride and a groom. If this is love poetry of the type we know existed in ancient Egypt, then "bride" can be understood in the figurative sense of a lover, and her partner is the man with whom she is intimately involved. He is called "lover" or "beloved" (see 1, 13; 2, 16; 5, 8; etc.), not husband. It is only as the result of some interpretive approach that one might identify the young man as Solomon and thus understand the Song as a poem composed on the occasion of one of his marriages to some foreign princess.

Form and Meaning

For more than two thousand years, the Song of Songs has been not only a fascination but also something of a riddle. It is its very uniqueness that has made it a challenge to understand. There are basically four ways of interpreting it: allegorical, cultic, dramatic, and literal. Each of these interpretive approaches reveals different facets of the literary quality of the book and opens up possibilities for our religious enrichment. All of them have gained acceptance within Roman Catholic tradition. The book itself contains characteristics that support each of these methods, thus lending it to any one of the approaches. It is interesting to note that while currently the first and preferred method of interpretation of most of the Bible has been the literal approach, the opposite has been true with this book. Perhaps much of the sexual imagery has been so explicit or suggestive as to offend the sensitivities of many of the faithful. Thus, commentators have presumed that the poems were not meant to be understood literally, and therefore they must have some concealed religious meaning.

When we talk about interpretation, it is important to distinguish between what the book *meant* in the past and what it might *mean* for the present. Those interpreters who employ a strict historical-critical approach (cf. Harrington) insist that the original sense must be the focus of our explanation. For them, discovering the earliest form and meaning of the book is crucial. They believe that it is this original meaning that continues to be revelatory for us today. Other commentators believe that the book can be interpreted in various ways. These latter interpreters do not categorize approaches as right or wrong but as helpful or not helpful. They would be more open than the former group to various interpretations of the Song of Songs.

Allegorical Interpretation

An allegory is an analogy or a comparison of two areas of human experience, usually a more concrete or everyday area and one that is more abstract or farther removed from ordinary experience. Our understanding of the more abstract area is helped by the analogy with our everyday experience. For example, in our courts Justice is often represented as a beautiful woman wearing a blindfold and holding balancing scales. The woman's beauty symbolizes the attractions of Justice: as we are drawn to beauty, so should we be drawn to Justice. Her blindfold symbolizes the impartiality of Justice: no matter how important or unimportant the person who appears before her, she is concerned only with the merits of the case presented. The balancing scales symbolize the objective nature of Justice: decisions are made according to public standards, and anyone can observe how they are made. Thus by using concrete images, the allegorical figure helps us understand our ideals of Justice.

An allegorical method of interpretation presumes that the real significance of the material under consideration is more than just its factual or historical content. In this view, the surface meaning is a figure of speech that signifies some deeper spiritual truth. This interpretive approach was quite prevalent in ancient Jewish circles (Philo, 20 BC–AD 54) as well as among early Christian writers (Origen, AD 185–254). Jewish commentators who allegorized the Song interpreted it as symbolizing God's dealings with Israel. They claimed that the book narrates this relationship, tracing it from the time of the Exodus to the coming of the messiah. They believed that it extols the steadfast love that God bestowed on Israel and describes the fickleness that characterized Israel's attitude toward its divine lover.

As the Christians began to read the Hebrew traditions in light of their faith in Christ, this allegorical method produced new meanings. One of their interpretations identified the lovers in the Song as Christ and the Church. Another read it as a description of the mystical union of God and the individual soul. Some of the most profound theology in the Christian mystical tradition is grounded in this kind of allegorical interpretation of the Song. The works of saints Bernard of Clairvaux and John of the Cross are the chief examples of this kind of writing. The bride has even been identified as the Virgin Mary. Although this interpretation is not easily accommodated to the poems, it has become quite prominent within Roman Catholic tradition. One reason for this is the belief that Mary is the exemplar of the individual soul in union with God. A second and probably stronger reason for the acceptance of this representation is the fact that sections from the Song are read during the liturgy on several Marian feasts. Thus by association this particular allegorical interpretation has been introduced into popular devotion.

Cultic Interpretation

A second way of understanding the Song of Songs assumes that it was originally a liturgical reenactment of a drama that takes place in nature

each spring. This drama is reflected in a well-known fertility myth of the ancient Near Eastern world. The great god (the Canaanite Baal or the Babylonian Tammuz) dies after the harvest and is mourned by the fertility goddess (Anath or Ishtar respectively). She frantically searches for him during the barren winter. Her efforts are finally successful, and they are eventually united. Nature is revived with the coming of spring, and the cycle of life is repeated. The fact that this book was read during the spring festival of Passover seems to support the theory that Israel was indeed influenced by the agricultural celebrations of the time.

There is ample evidence in the Bible of Israel's appropriation and subsequent reinterpretation of Canaanite cultic practices. Passover itself is probably a combination of two festivals: an early nomadic celebration meant to ensure the fertility of the flock, and an agricultural one, the Feast of Unleavened Bread, meant to ensure the growth of the crop. The nomadic festival took on historical significance as it was used to commemorate God's deliverance of the people from Egyptian bondage, and it was associated with the Feast of Unleavened Bread after the people had settled in Canaan and had moved from a nomadic to an agricultural form of life. These two very different festivals merged into one celebration, and elements of both became details of the standard story of the first Passover celebration (see Ex 12).

The Song itself includes several features that are characteristic of fertility liturgies. Women always play a prominent role in these cultic reenactments. There is frequently a chorus of women, and the chief character is a goddess who is separated from her lover. The speakers are seldom named, and their speeches are more monologues than dialogues. The goddess is sometimes a bride, sometimes a sister, sometimes a mother; the beloved is depicted as a king, but more frequently as a shepherd. It is quite possible that, while this ritual drama was never incorporated into the official liturgy of Israel, it enjoyed widespread acceptance in the isolated rural communities (see Ez 8, 14). Those who endorse this theory of interpretation contend that the book was included in the canon precisely because of this popular use. Commentators who reject the cultic theory do so because there is no explicit evidence that Israel included the rite of the dying/rising god in its own ritual. They do not deny the possibility of popular acceptance, but they insist that any association with fertility religion would work against the book's inclusion in the canon. They regard the cultic interpretation as merely a sophisticated form of the allegorical approach.

Dramatic Interpretation

The third approach has a long history in the church's tradition. As early as the second century of the Christian era, Origen claimed that the Song was a wedding poem written in dramatic form by Solomon himself. Some interpreters today divide the book into a drama of five movements: the anticipation and tryst (1, 1—2, 17); the separation (3, 1–11); reunion (4, 1—5, 1) a second separation (5, 2—6, 3); and final union (6, 4—8, 14). Such a division attempts to show how the Song includes the dramatic elements of conflict and resolution. The fact that there are only speeches and no narrative sections lends support to this theory of interpretation. However, it is the commentators not the author(s) who assign the speeches to the characters, as is done in the left-hand margins of the NAB, and who identify the various scenes by means of subtitles within the text.

The two major characters of the drama are the royal shepherd and the Shulammite maiden. A two-character interpretation has serious deficiencies, however. There is no dramatic development, and the book lacks ethical purpose. A three-character approach was developed to address these weaknesses. It distinguishes two male individuals, the king and the shepherd. The former tries to win the love of the beautiful maiden, but she remains faithful to her shepherd lover. The difference between these two interpretations is obvious. In the first one, the royal shepherd is noble and worthy of the faithful love of the Shulammite. This royal personage might well represent Solomon. In the second interpretation, the king is a villain who tries to seduce the maiden with the promise of luxury and comfort. One wonders how such a disapproving portrait of Solomon could survive as part of the wisdom tradition, a tradition ascribed to the wisdom of the very king who is maligned by this depiction. The weaknesses of this approach are obvious. Since the biblical text does not supply speech

designations, the decisions about their identification are influenced by the biases of the interpreter. Stage directions are also imposed from without rather than discovered within the poems themselves. Finally, there is neither story line nor character development, essential traits of good drama.

Literal Interpretation

It may be that the original meaning of the Song is found in its literal interpretation. Most likely, the Song of Songs is simply a collection of love poems that neither symbolized divine love nor developed from fertility rites. The poems teach no lessons, tell no story. They simply celebrate the passion of human love. Some believe that these are secular poems. Others doubt that purely secular love songs would ever have been admitted into the canon. These latter commentators believe that the poems are examples of Judean wedding songs. They also discover in them traces of a poetic form called the *wasf,* an Arabic word meaning description. These are poems that use images from nature to describe parts of the male or female body. This literary form might explain some of the strange imagery found in the Song (see 4, 1–5; 7, 2–6).

If this literary reading is really the meaning of the Song of Songs, a fundamental question surfaces: Why was the book considered inspired and thus included in the Bible? One can only offer a hypothetical answer. Israel may have followed the same wedding customs, as did its Syrian neighbor, celebrating the event for seven days. During the festivities the bride was characterized as "maiden" and the groom as "king." On the eve of the wedding itself the girl would dance for her lover and recite *wasf* for his enjoyment. The representation of the man as "king" and the extravagance of the celebration could blend quite easily with the tradition about Solomon's erotic exploits (see 1 Kgs 11, 1). Some believe that one of the poems was actually composed on the occasion of one of his marriages (3, 6–11). Thus, what was initially a collection of wedding songs was now regarded as a description of the king's sexual adventures and was joined with two other writings that claim divine inspiration and Solomonic authorship, namely, Proverbs and Ecclesiastes. Each of these three books explicitly attributed to Solomon addresses some of the central issues of life, issues that are basic to the wisdom thinking of the ancient Near East, Israel included. Proverbs provides directions on how to achieve peace and prosperity. Qoheleth addresses the search for meaning in life. The Song of Songs celebrates a fundamental human emotion, namely, erotic love. None of these books fits into the category of salvation history, but each one is an example of the way of wisdom.

Once writings were associated with Solomon and the wisdom attributed to him, it was not long before they possessed their own authoritative significance. This seems to have been enough to ensure inclusion in the canon. These three books may be quite distinct from each other, but they have come to represent different moments in the life of the same man. The Song of Songs reveals a young, passionate, unguarded Solomon; Proverbs shows a moderate but optimistic man who has learned from his experience of life; the musings of Qoheleth come from someone who approaches the end of life challenging the enduring value of human accomplishment. The quality of these anthropological, but nonetheless theological, concerns is evidence of their religious value. Solomonic ascription provided the books with canonical status.

Wisdom Teaching

Each of the interpretive approaches described above leads us to the central question: What is the book's theological value? Since it belongs to the wisdom tradition, we might also ask: What does it teach us? We have considered four different methods of interpretation, and we should not be surprised if we discover four quite distinct answers to these questions.

The allegorical approach provides us with a figurative way of understanding the nature of our relationship with God. It portrays the relationship as dynamic, energizing, mutually loving, and intensely intimate. This depiction of God runs counter to the images of an impassive creator or an avenging judge, characterizations that may be the prominent images of God held by many people. We may be familiar with the notion of God as a loving parent or of Jesus as a faithful friend, but the Song of Songs offers us a portrait of a passionate lover, one who desires union with us. Some might find this notion scandalous, but the wisdom tradition (specifically Job and Eccle-

siastes) repeatedly teaches something about God or human nature that is unconventional.

At the heart of the dying/rising ritual is the conviction that death does not have the final victory. The love of the grieving goddess is strong enough to bring her lover back to her and to revitalize the lifeless earth. To the proverb: "For love is strong as death" (8, 6; *Revised Standard Version* translation), one might add: "In Spring a young woman's fancy turns to thoughts of love."

The dramatic interpretation depicts an example of faithful love. Whether one favors the two- or the three-character account, the fidelity of the bride is held up for all to admire and imitate. She is unrelenting in her search and steadfast in her commitment. This image of a faithful woman conforms to the one found in other places of the wisdom tradition (see Prv 31, 10–31).

The literal understanding of the Song skirts all symbolic interpretation and makes no apology for its erotic imagery. It affirms that sexuality is one of the gifts that God gave for our enjoyment (see Prv 5, 15–21; Eccl 9, 9). Still, sexual pleasure is not sought promiscuously. It is pursued only within the context of faithful and exclusive commitment.

Finally, the portrait of the maiden in the Song of Songs is exceptional for literature that originated in a patriarchal culture. The woman is not portrayed as naïve or passive, solely dependent upon a man for protection and sustenance. She takes the initiative in the romantic exchange of the poem, uttering twice as much of the erotic poetry as does the man. The maiden is portrayed as an independent and mature person in her own right. She has her own vineyard (1, 6) and is encouraged to pasture her flocks (1, 8), occupations normally assigned to men. Through its use of the metaphor of human love, the Song of Songs proclaims a biblical conviction that will also be amplified in sound Christian tradition: human sexuality—male and female—is a creation of God and, expressed in accord with God's law, is both noble and enobling.

FURTHER READING

Fox, Michael V. *The Song of Songs and the Ancient Egyptian Love Songs.* Madison, WI: University of Wisconsin, 1985.

Murphy, Roland E. *The Song of Songs.* Hermeneia. Minneapolis: Fortress, 1990.

WISDOM

[see pages 844–68 of the Old Testament]

The Hellenization of the World

The last half of the fourth century BC saw rapid and sweeping changes in the ancient world. The conquests of Alexander the Great had brought the entire eastern world under the influence of Greek culture. This served to unify an otherwise diverse and disorganized world. It also threatened the integrity of other cultures and religious perspectives. With Alexander's death in 323 BC, the empire was divided among his followers, and three independent and mutually hostile kingdoms were formed. Two of these kingdoms played significant roles in the affairs of the Jewish nation. Ptolemy gained control of Egypt and established himself in Alexandria; Seleucus triumphed over Babylon and made Antioch his center. In its own way, each kingdom contributed to the shaping of biblical tradition.

The hellenization that was forced upon the Jewish community by the Seleucid ruler Antiochus Epiphanes was the background for the Jewish war of independence known as the Maccabean revolt (167–142 BC). This struggle is narrated in 1 and 2 Maccabees (see Reading Guides on Maccabees) and is the real context for the story found in the book of Daniel. The military and religious victory the Jewish people gained at this time is celebrated each year at the feast of Hanukkah.

The influence of the Ptolemies is more relevant to an understanding of the wisdom literature. It occurred earlier than that of the Seleucids and appears to have been quite well received. A large colony of Jews lived in Alexandria and accommodated itself to Greek language and culture. This was the group that translated its religious traditions from Hebrew into Greek, thus producing the basis of what has come to be known as the Septuagint (Latin for seventy, frequently designated LXX). A tradition grew up claiming that seventy scribes, working independent of each other, labored over the translation for seventy days in seventy different locations and produced identical versions. This marvel was seen as evidence of the inspired nature of the translation. Most likely the task took decades, but this fact did not detract from the reverence accorded the Septuagint over the years.

The Alexandrian or Greek version of the Scriptures was probably the one in popular use during the first century of the Christian era. During this same period, however, the Jewish community adopted the older Palestinian or Hebrew version as its official text. The Christian practice of adding its own writings to the collection may have contributed to this decision.

Christians continued to revere the Alexandrian tradition. In fact, by comparing the Old Testament citations used by New Testament writers, scholars conclude that a good number, if not most of them, come from the Alexandrian rather than from the earlier Palestinian version. At the time of the Reformation, the official version of the Old Testament became a point of disagreement among Christian denominations. Protestant churches retained the shorter Hebrew canon and thus preserve the more ancient Jewish version of the tradition. The Roman church accepted the wider Greek canon and thereby preserves an authentic early church tradition. The collection of those books not found within the Hebrew canon are called *deuterocanonical* (second-listing) by Roman Catholics and *apocryphal* (originally meaning "hidden," now understood as inspirational but not canonical) by Protestants. This explains why some Bibles include such books as Wisdom and Sirach, while others do not.

About the Book

Over the centuries this book has been called "The Book of Wisdom" (from the Latin translations), "The Wisdom of Solomon" (from the Septuagint), or variations of either title. Although the author does not explicitly identify himself as Solomon, the identification is implied in several first person references (7, 5; 8, 21; 9, 7f; see 1 Kgs 3, 5–15). This might be due to the author's presumption that the somewhat unconventional character of the book's ideas might require Solomonic authority to be accepted as orthodox teaching. (For an explanation of Solomonic authorship see Proverbs, RG 254; Ecclesiastes, RG 262; Song, RG 267, 270.)

The book itself suggests an origin from within the Jewish community of Alexandria. It is clear that the author was steeped in the history of the Exodus (11, 2–16; 12, 23–27; 16, 2–19.22), was acquainted with the religious practices of Egypt (15, 14—16,1), and was well versed in Hellenistic philosophy and science (6, 22—11, 1). The author reinterpreted his own religious heritage and critiqued the traditions, practices, and insights of the other two cultures. He did this in an attempt to support those Jews who were questioning the relevance of their ancient faith in the face of the radical cultural changes they were undergoing.

Most scholars date this book somewhere around the turn of the era, during the first century BC. At this period of history, the primary threat did not arise from the hellenizing Greeks but from the hellenized Jews themselves. The oppression from outside the community that had led to the Maccabean revolt had given way to a subtle undermining of traditional teaching and values. Even the religious leaders were not immune to this kind of worldliness. The author appears to have been concerned that the pious not be led astray, that those enthralled by Greek culture be convinced of the excellence of the biblical heritage, and that those already carried away by the currents of change be rescued.

Literary features of the book confirm that it originated in Greek. The form of the language is natural and free-flowing, not awkward, as might be the case if this were a translation from Hebrew. The extensive scientific vocabulary reveals an author who possessed an exceptional comprehension of Hellenistic learning. References to earlier religious tradition correspond to the style of the Alexandrian rather than to that of the Palestinian version. The thought is similar to what is found in Jewish-Alexandrian works of this period. The author frequently employed a form of expression that resembles the diatribe, a method of argument developed by the Cynic and Stoic philosophers of Greece that creates imaginary opponents who raise questions that the philosopher refutes.

Despite these Greek characteristics, this is basically a Jewish work. It is not difficult to detect the influence of Hebrew parallelism in the poetry. (For an explanation of parallelism see Job, RG 238.) The description of God's care during the Exodus is a kind of homiletic *midrash* (a method of interpretation that the Jewish community devised in order to apply the Bible to new situations). Thus a law was restated as *halakah*, and a narrative is retold as *haggadah* in such a way as to give direction to a new generation. On the other hand, the Greeks, particularly Philo, developed allegory as a principal method of interpreting traditions. It is significant that the author of Wisdom employed midrash rather than allegory. This characteristic of the book further substantiates its Jewish, rather than Greek, origin.

The structure of Wisdom is a matter of dispute. There are not obvious divisions as can be found in some books of the wisdom tradition. The editors of the NAB have adopted a fairly general thematic division: (1) The Reward of Justice; (2) Praise of Wisdom by Solomon; (3) Special Providence of God during the Exodus.

Wisdom Teaching

The unifying theme of this biblical book is "the praise of wisdom." Each of the three major sections addresses this theme from its own distinctive point of view. A cursory examination of each section will highlight significant theological elements found there.

The Reward of Justice (1, 1—6, 21)

The first section is often called "The Book of Eschatology." (Traditionally, eschatology refers to the last or final things: the end of the age, death, judgment, reward, and punishment.) In it we find the destinies of the righteous and of the wicked described in vivid contrast. The former, regardless of their obvious suffering, "are in the hand of God" (3, 1), while the latter "shall receive a punishment to match their thoughts" (3, 10). This entire section serves as a summons to fidelity to the religious traditions of Israel, a fidelity that will guarantee the rewards of wisdom.

At first glance this teaching might seem to be merely a restatement of the doctrine of retribution. A closer look will show that it is instead a radical departure from the traditional understanding. The author not only challenged some traditional views but also introduced several radically new ideas. First, he insisted that childlessness, a condition that by itself brought reproach in ancient society (see Gn 16, 4; 1 Sm 1, 7) is not a mark of divine displeasure (3, 13f; 4, 1). Regardless of the importance of offspring for the survival of the race, moral not physical fruitfulness is emphasized here.

The author further denied that suffering itself presupposes sin. In fact, an untimely death may be a righteous person's rescue from the wickedness of life (4, 14). We are reminded of the adage: The good die young. This author agreed with both Job and Qoheleth that virtue is not always rewarded in this life, nor is evil always punished. He went on to suggest, however, that whoever thinks that the death of the righteous is affliction or destruction is foolish (3, 2f). Such death is, rather, a trial that they must endure in order to be with God (3, 5f).

It is in this book that the reader of the Old Testament is first introduced to the Greek concept *psyche* (soul, 1, 11; 3, 1). Although in some passages the word is used with the same meaning as the Hebrew *nephesh* (being or life, 12, 6; 14, 5; 16, 9), in other places it clearly marks the adoption of the body-soul dualism, which was part of the Greek understanding of human nature. The Greeks held that human nature was a combination of an impermanent material body and an eternal spiritual soul. This combination was dissolved at death. Caution is in order here. We must be careful not to take accommodation to Greek thought farther than the author did. Nowhere does this book speak of an immortal soul.

A second and related idea is that of life after death. This notion is quite different from the earlier perceptions of Sheol, the abode of the dead (see Psalms, RG 250). There is just enough ambiguity in the use of the words "immortality" (3, 4; 4, 1; 8, 13.17; 15, 3) and "incorruptibility" (2, 23; 6, 18f) to prevent us from making too many definite statements about the author's view. One thing does seem clear, however. Immortality is not an inherent quality of human nature; it is the fruit of union with wisdom (8, 13.17; 15, 3). Although 2, 23 claims that God made humans to be incorruptible (imperishable), 6, 18 suggests that incorruptibility is contingent upon fidelity to wisdom. We are not sure whether the author was speaking merely of physical death, or of physical death followed by spiritual death, or of spiritual death alone. The thought does seem to pass over physical death, and attention is directed toward spiritual death. Later in history, Saint Paul will have to face this same question when dealing with the unexpected deaths of Christians (1 Thes 4, 13–18). Unlike the author of Wisdom, his answer will be quite specific.

Finally, the author of the book of Wisdom brought the two earlier creation narratives together and reinterpreted them. The statement about being made in God's image (2, 23), an allusion to Genesis 1, 16.28, is followed by the claim that the devil's envy brought death into the world (2, 24), a reinterpretation of Genesis 3. (A few commentators believe that the latter reference is to the envy of Cain, which resulted in the death of Abel [Gn 4, 1–8]. However, in a nonbiblical Jewish text, another writer of this time stated that Gadreel, a fallen angel, led Eve astray [1 Enoch 69, 6]. This latter citation supports the interpretation offered here.) The author of Wisdom was the first biblical writer to identify the serpent of the Genesis account with the devil.

Praise of Wisdom by Solomon (6, 22—11, 1)

The second major section of the book is an address acclaiming the glories of wisdom. It is from this section that the book receives its name, and it is here that we find a representation of personified Wisdom (see Proverbs, RG 260). This characterization of Wisdom is quite different from that found in the earlier tradition. The author may have realized the unconventional nature of his depiction and felt that claiming Solomonic authority would be necessary in order to gain acceptance for this reinterpretation. At any rate, this section begins with an account of his own humble origin, his prayer for wisdom, and God's bestowal of this immeasurable gift in answer to his pleading (7, 1–7; also see 9, 1–18). This is unquestionably an allusion to the prayer of Solomon (1 Kgs 3, 5–15), and it characterizes the author as the wise king.

The actual description of Wisdom is composed of elements from various sources: Israelite tradition (7, 22a; see Prv 8, 30); from the cult of the Egyptian deity Isis, goddess of wisdom and patron of culture, whose praises were extolled in the form of listings similar to that found in 7, 22—8, 1; and from Hellenistic philosophy and science (see 8, 7 for mention of the cardinal virtues of Plato). This section may well be the heart of the author's argument in favor of the superiority of the religion of Israel.

Earlier traditions spoke of "a spirit of wisdom" (Is 11, 2), but here Wisdom itself is called a spirit (1, 6; 7, 22). The author has brought two quite distinct and dissimilar concepts together by merging the notion of intelligence, the basic meaning of wisdom, with that of energy or power, the central idea in spirit. Having done this, he could then speak of the wisdom-spirit as "an aura of the might of God" (Wis 7, 25). It is in this book that Wisdom is referred to as "the spirit of the LORD" (1, 7). (The theology in this verse functions significantly in the liturgy of Pentecost.) Although spirit played a major role in Stoic philosophy, it was clearly a prominent theme in Jewish tradition as well. In his description of the nature and dignity of Wisdom (7, 22–24), the author may well have employed the attributes of the world spirit, a concept found in Stoic philosophy. However, when he recounted the early history of Israel he equated Wisdom with the spirit of the Lord. He did this by ascribing to Wisdom what earlier Israelite writers attributed to the spirit of the Lord: the creative power in the world (7, 22a; see Jdt 16, 14); the source of Joseph's honor in Egypt (10, 13; see Gn 41, 38); the inspiration that prepared Moses for the Exodus and led the people through the wilderness (10, 16f; see Is 63, 11.14).

There has been a significant amount of discussion regarding the influence of this figure of Wisdom on New Testament writings. Some scholars believe that the influence was direct. Others hold that the obvious similarities suggest that there was a general treasury of thought, imagery, and language that served as a common source. Whichever position is more accurate, early Christian theologians reinterpreted the figure of personified Wisdom as they struggled to understand Jesus the Christ. Paul explicitly referred to Christ as the wisdom of God (1 Cor 1, 24.30). The most obvious example of this reinterpretation, however, is found in the Gospel according to John. There we find Jesus described in ways that Wisdom had been depicted earlier: as being with God in the beginning before the world existed (Jn 1, 1; 17, 5; see Wis 2, 22); as sent from heaven to accomplish the will of God (Jn 6, 38; see Wis 9, 10). Current scholarship is only beginning to pursue the implications of Wisdom imagery for Christology.

This section of the book ends with a summary of the way that Wisdom guided the ancestors of Israel, brought them out of Egypt, and, through the agency of Moses (see Hos 12,14), enabled them to prosper (10, 1—11, 1). It is clear that this Wisdom, once thought to be the possession of the king, was now considered the constant companion of true Israelites, those faithful ones of the past as well as the committed Jews of the present.

Special Providence of God during the Exodus (11, 2—19, 22)

Here the book shows an observable shift in focus. The poem in praise of Wisdom gives way to midrash that extols the ancestral God of Israel. This version of the experience of the Exodus and the time in the wilderness illustrates two points: (1) the sufferings that befell the Egyptians were the direct result of their sinfulness (11, 16); and (2) the very elements that afflicted the Egyptians benefited the Israelites (11, 5). This rereading of the past is done through a creative selection of biblical data as well as the addition of material not found elsewhere. The author did not set out to recount historical facts or to repeat traditional testimonies. He seemed intent on addressing the challenge raised by Hellenism. His goal was to remind Alexandrian Jews that once before they had suffered at the hands of the Egyptians and, in the face of impossible odds, had been rescued. This midrash provides "historical" basis for continued trust in the God of Israel.

There are two digressions within this third division of the book. Both of them are found in the second example of God's providence. The first is a testimony to God's mercy (11, 17—12, 22). Although it breaks the midrashic line of thought, it may have been prompted by the mention of punishment in the preceding line (11, 16). The second digression is a condemnation of idolatry (13, 1—15, 17). It follows the claim that the Egyptians "saw and recognized the true God whom before they had refused to know" (12, 27), yet they continued in their idolatry. It should be noted that the language used in the condemnation of nature worship (13, 1–9) might be the best example of the author's broad grasp of scientific knowledge.

Theology in a New Context

The author of Wisdom did not set out in search of new theological insights. Since he was committed to prove the enduring value of the religion of

Israel, he explained traditions and themes that were familiar to the Jews of his day. What made his contribution unique was the method that he employed as he went about his task. He incorporated elements of other cultures into this theological thinking.

Throughout its history, Israel had been forced by circumstances to deal with the religious and cultural traditions of other societies. The Bible itself shows that these encounters were sometimes peaceful and beneficial, and at other times violent and destructive. Whatever the situation may have been, elements from those cultures found their way into the traditions of Israel. The religion of Israel reinterpreted features of the other cultures and then assimilated these new ideas into its own perspective. Israel seldom assumed the fundamental religious worldview of the other culture. This changed with the hellenization of the world. It was precisely the attraction of Greek civilization that threatened Jewish faith. Now the community wrestled with an agonizing dilemma: Could one accept the prevailing culture and remain faithful to the traditions of the ancestors? The author of Wisdom undertook the task of answering this question in the affirmative. In doing so, he did not try to reconcile Judaism with Hellenism. Instead, he used the ideas, the language, and the literary style of Greek culture to demonstrate the excellence of the Jewish faith.

In taking Greek culture seriously, this theologian did what theologians after him would have to do whenever cultural lines were crossed. The challenge of interpretation facing him was not so different from the one facing us today; that is, to render a religious heritage that originated in one cultural context into another very different one. The purpose of the author of the book of Wisdom was apologetic. He sought to defend his ancestral faith. Our purpose in reinterpretation is usually evangelical. We seek to proclaim the word of God in a variety of contexts. In this we have much to learn from both the message of this wisdom teacher and from his method of theological reinterpretation.

FURTHER READING

Collins, John J. *Jewish Wisdom in the Hellenistic Age.* Louisville: Westminster John Knox, 1997.

Kolarcik, Michael. *The Book of Wisdom.* New Interpreter's Bible 5, 435–600. Nashville: Abingdon Press, 1997. Fine literary and theological commentary.

Winston, David. *The Wisdom of Solomon.* Anchor Bible 43. New York: Doubleday, 1979.

SIRACH (ECCLESIASTICUS)

[see pages 868–927 of the Old Testament]

About the Book

Over the years the book of Sirach has been known by different names: "The Wisdom of Jesus Ben Sira"; "The Book of Sirach" (Sirach is a shortened form of the Greek *Sirachides,* grandson of Sira); "Ecclesiasticus" (from the Latin for book of the church, a designation that probably stems from its frequent use as a catechetical aid in the early centuries of the Western Church).

Sirach is the only biblical book that identifies its author (50, 27), refers to its translator (a grandson of the Ben Sira), and dates its translation ("the thirty-eighth year of the reign of King Euergetes," sometime after 132 BC—information found in the foreword). Although the prophetic books claim not only to have originated from specific prophets

and to locate the ministry of those prophets during the reigns of specific kings (for example, Hos 1, 1; Is 1, 1; Jer 1, 2f; etc.), the references there are to prophetic activity and not to the books that bear the names of the prophets. Here we have a clear reference to literary activity.

The foreword also provides us with some interesting information about the composition of the biblical canon (the official list of inspired books). Three times the grandson of Ben Sira speaks of "the law, the prophets, and the later authors" (or "the rest of the books"). This reference tells us that by the second century BC the Jewish community already had what has come to be known as a tripartite (three-part) Bible. Scholars believe that the first two parts (the Law and the Prophets) most likely included the books as we have them today. The third part (the Writings) was probably quite fluid until well into the Christian era.

Like the book of Wisdom, Sirach belongs to the collection called *deuterocanonical* by Roman Catholics or *apocryphal* by Protestants (see Wisdom, RG 272). The foreword, which is considered historical introduction and not inspired instruction, recounts the translator's arrival in Egypt, where he discovered that the Jews' "valuable teaching" had been translated from Hebrew into Greek, the language of the day. This inspired him to undertake the translation of his own grandfather's teachings. The Hebrew version from which he worked seems to have dropped out of sight until copies of it were found in 1896.

It is not clear why the Jews did not accept Sirach as canonical. Some commentators offer a twofold reason: (1) Ben Sira was interested in the Temple and the cult (concerns of a first-century AD group called Sadducees); and (2) he did not seem to believe in the resurrection of the body (a position held by a rival religious group of the first century called the Pharisees). Therefore the Pharisaic rabbis who decided on the canon rejected Sirach. Whatever the case may have been, its absence from the Jewish list explains its exclusion from the Protestant canon.

The manner in which the high priest Simon is described (50, 1–21) leads one to conclude that he had only recently died. This would locate the writing of the original Hebrew version of Sirach sometime during the first quarter of the second century (200–175 BC). The description of Simon's priestly performance suggests that the author was quite familiar with the Jerusalem ritual. Perhaps he was even a resident of the city. Many commentators believe that Jerusalem was in fact the place of the book's composition.

The book appears to be a collection of proverbs organized in such a way as to resemble short essays. While there is no explicit arrangement in the book itself, one can divide the material both thematically and according to literary form. Chapters 1 through 43 principally deal with moral instruction, a characteristic that Sirach has in common with the rest of the wisdom literature. This first section can be further subdivided into two parts, each of which is introduced by a poem praising wisdom (see 1, 1–29 and 24, 1–31). The entire

first section ends with a poem extolling God's activity in nature (42, 15—43, 35). The poems that acclaim time-honored heroes of Israel (44, 1—49, 16) and the high priest Simon (50, 1–24) are followed by a kind of epilogue, which contains a denunciation of some of the traditional enemies of Israel and a subscription identifying the author (50, 25–29). The book closes with two appendices: a psalm of thanksgiving for deliverance from danger (51, 1–12); and a personal testimony in the form of an acrostic poem (51, 13–30; see Psalms, RG 245).

The Reason for Writing

The hellenization of the Near East had already taken hold among the educated upper classes by the time Ben Sira put his teachings into writing (see Wisdom, RG 272). Many Jews must have wondered whether their ancient traditions could match the comprehension and depth of Greek thought. Being a well-traveled man (34, 11), Ben Sira would have witnessed the decline in fervor that overtook his coreligionists. Being an observant Jew, he would have been greatly troubled by this. It seems clear that his object in writing was to show the Jews of his day that real wisdom was to be found in the traditions of Israel and not in the godless Greek philosophy of the day. He intended his work to be a comprehensive authoritative reference wherein could be found guidance and instruction for every circumstance of life.

Ben Sira exhorted his readers to study the ancient traditions to find there the kind of direction needed to cope with their new and challenging situation (2, 10). He warned against trying to live according to the standards of both Judaism and Hellenism (2, 12), and he condemned those who chose the latter over the former (2, 13f). Using a traditional wisdom figure of speech (those who fear the Lord), he identified the wise as those who were faithful to the religion of Israel (2, 15–17). While the content of most of his wisdom teaching is quite conventional, the way Ben Sira blended it with Israel's history, and its legal and cultic traditions is distinctive. Earlier wisdom writing showed little interest in specifically Israelite matters. Ben Sira claimed that true wisdom resides in Israel (24, 1–21), and later he used history to support this claim (44, 1—49, 16). He identified Wisdom with the Law of

Moses (24, 22), and in that way he accorded the Law of Moses a place of honor above the traditions of other cultures. Unlike other wisdom teachers, he demonstrated a profound concern for the cult and the role of the priesthood (46, 6–20; 47, 12f; 50, 1–21). All of this was, no doubt, Ben Sira's way of arguing in favor of fidelity to Judaism.

If we are correct in determining the date of the translation, the final form of this book probably appeared after the Maccabean revolt but before the writing of the Wisdom of Solomon. Such historical reconstruction will help us to see how Israel's response to Hellenism varied with time. Ben Sira did not make accommodations to the process of hellenization to the extent that the author of Wisdom did. If "traditionalist" means maintaining unchanged the answers of the past because they alone are adequate to meet the problems of the present, then Ben Sira can be called "traditionalist" in his response to Hellenism.

Wisdom Teaching

In many ways the teaching of Ben Sira resembles that of the book of Proverbs. Its primary focus is moral guidance. The book lends itself to being an instructional manual containing maxims, many of which are grouped according to topic. The result is a series of short essays addressing topics such as duties toward God, toward one's parents, and toward rulers. There are instructions on how to train children, how to choose friends, and how to guard one's speech. There are warnings against excess, sloth, and foolishness. Whatever one needs to succeed in life, while at the same time remaining faithful to the traditions of the elders, is addressed in the instructional section of this book.

Sirach is also like Proverbs in its celebration of the glories of personified Wisdom (chapters 1 and 24). It is distinctive, however, in the way it takes this characterization a step further than did the earlier work. Here we see Wisdom searching for a place to dwell and finally pitching her tent in Jerusalem. Allusions to this poetic characterization can be found in the prologue to the Gospel of John where the Word, present with God from the beginning and involved in the creation of all things, "pitched his tent among us" (Jn 1, 1–14). Ben Sira's poems describing the role of divine

wisdom in creation (16, 22—17, 18; 39, 12–35; 42, 15—43, 35) are really commentaries on the opening chapters of Genesis. The rather technical way he developed his thought shows us the extent to which Ben Sira was influenced by the scientific knowledge of his day.

This book contains some of the harshest statements about women found anywhere in the Bible. Proverbs may have warned the naive youth to beware of wily and seductive women, but this author seems to speak disparagingly against women in general. Ben Sira is the one who blames woman for sin and death (25, 23). It is further apparent that he expected wives to be subservient to their husbands, for he seems to advocate punishment, even including divorce, if they refuse to obey (25, 24f). Perhaps the worst example of this misogyny is found in the description of the unwed daughter (42, 9–14). The author clearly considers her a liability, and his concern is exclusively with the reputation of the father.

The author holds a thoroughly traditional view of retribution (4, 11–19; 7, 1–3; 16, 1–21; 21, 1–10). The possibility of rewards or punishments after death does not seem to have been considered by this wisdom teacher (14, 15–19). He counsels mourning at the death of another, but he admonishes his reader to moderation even in the acceptable expression of grief. The reason why the display should be temperate is that the dead are dead, and nothing can be changed by uncontrolled sorrow (38, 1–23).

While this view of life and death may have been in agreement with earlier notions of retribution, it was clearly not universally held in Israel at this time. Hope of reward after death for fidelity during persecution is found in other writings of this period (for example, Dn 12, 1–3; 2 Mc 7, 9.23.29). Although Ben Sira probably lived before the Maccabean revolt (events surrounding this period are recorded in the other books mentioned above), his grandson-translator certainly lived after the rebellion, and he upheld Ben Sira's traditional view.

Ben Sira's adherence to the traditional notion of retribution and its consequent rejection of any notion of life after death, coupled with his support of the priesthood and interest in the cult, have prompted many interpreters to regard him as a Proto-Sadducee. Although Sadducees as a group probably did not yet exist until after the Maccabean revolt, many of the theological views found in this book were eventually adopted by this aristocratic priestly party.

The Influence of Sirach

Since the New Testament writers seem to have preferred the Alexandrian Bible, it is not surprising that the influence of Sirach can be detected in some of their writings. The Letter of James is a clear example of this. Both books address questions of pride (Sir 10, 7; Jas 4, 6) and humility (Sir 3, 18; Jas 1, 9), of rich and poor (Sir 10, 19–24; Jas 2, 1–6), and of true wisdom (Sir 19, 17–21; Jas 3, 13–17), to name but a few examples. There are also obvious parallels between directives found in Sirach and those found in the Gospels. This includes teaching on magnanimity (Sir 29, 12; Mt 6, 19) and forgiveness (Sir 28, 2; Mk 11, 25) and against placing false hopes in possessions (Sir 11, 18f; Lk 12, 16–21).

While the canonical status of Sirach was and remains a question for debate, from the time of its appearance it has exerted significant influence in both the Jewish and the Christian communities. Over the years it has served as a kind of handbook of practical ethics, and its teachings can be found in the liturgical texts of both religious groups. The discovery at Qumran of a scroll of Ben Sira is evidence that the book was widely known before the turn of the era. It also appears in copies of liturgical scrolls that were read in synagogues around the tenth century AD. Finally, the book is also quoted at least once in the Talmud. The early church theologians Cyprian (third century AD) and Jerome (fourth century AD) attest to Christian use of the book. Clement of Alexandria (second century AD) quotes it so often that his citations have come to be considered an authoritative version of the text. This controversial book continues to exercise its influence even today. Passages from Sirach are used as lectionary readings. For many, perhaps most, Catholics, the liturgical celebration is their primary exposure to the Bible. Within this context the teachings of Ben Sira continue to exhort hearers to fidelity to the tradition and to upright moral living.

It is interesting to note that in response to the Vatican document *Decree on the Training of Priests* (16), moral theologians are reexamining the moral instructions found in Scripture. They do not turn there in search of ageless answers to contemporary questions but in an attempt to discover how moral decisions were made in the past. Biblical specialists provide them with insights into the manner in which writers, especially the teachers of wisdom, brought the time-honored religious tradition to bear on new situations. The book of Sirach, with its essaylike instruction, remains a source of information in this area. It opens a window into a community struggling with its identity as it finds itself at the crossroads of traditional religion and contemporary culture. Sirach and Wisdom provide us with two ways of responding to this challenge. While we may not be able to follow their specific advice, we can learn from their example ways of reinterpreting the tradition creatively, while at the same time remaining loyal to its revelatory message.

FURTHER READING

Collins, John J. *Jewish Wisdom in the Hellenistic Age*, 21–111. Louisville: Westminster, 1997.

———. *The Wisdom of Jesus Son of Sirach*. The Oxford Bible Commentary, 667–98. Edited by J. Barton and J. Muddiman. Oxford: Oxford University Press, 2001.

Crenshaw, James L. *The Book of Sirach*. New Interpreter's Bible 5, 603–867. Nashville: Abingdon Press, 1997. Excellent theological commentary.

Skehan, P. W., and A. A. DiLella. *The Wisdom of Ben Sira*. Anchor Bible 39. New York: Doubleday, 1987.

THE MAJOR PROPHETS, BARUCH, AND LAMENTATIONS

RICHARD J. CLIFFORD

ISAIAH

[see pages 929–1003 of the Old Testament]

In the Jewish Bible (Tanakh), Isaiah, Jeremiah, Ezekiel, and "the Twelve" (the Minor Prophets) are in the second section, which is called "The Latter Prophets." Together with "The Former Prophets" (Joshua to Kings), they come after the Pentateuch (Torah), and before the Writings. Jews regard the Latter Prophets primarily as expositors of the instructions and laws contained in the Torah. The Christian Bible, in contrast, places the Prophets in the third and concluding section of the Old Testament (after the historical and wisdom books), a position that links the prophetic books directly to the New Testament and emphasizes the prophets as heralds of the last days, the time of Jesus Christ. Both Jewish and Christian understandings of prophecy prize the book of Isaiah, for it insists equally on exclusive faith in God (e.g., 7, 1–9; 28, 14–22) and social justice (e.g., 5, 1–24), and it instills hope for a renewed Zion and Davidic king (8, 23—9, 6; 11, 1–9).

The book of Isaiah contains a wide variety of styles and material. Chapters 1 through 39 blend denunciations of Zion and Judah, promises of blessings, announcements of interventions ("judgments") of God, oracles about foreign nations, and narratives about the prophet. The dominant foreign nation threatening Israel is Assyria. Chapters 40 through 55 are quite different. They contain no narratives, denunciations, or prophetic biography, but they have carefully crafted speeches announcing forgiveness of sins to the exiles in Babylonia and inviting them to return to Zion. The dominant foreign nations in these chapters are Babylon and Persia (Cyrus in 44, 28; 45, 1.13 is the king of Persia). Chapters 56 through 66 are also distinctive. They presume an audience that is back in Zion and intent on rebuilding itself; criticisms and promises center on Zion, and some sections (e.g., 56, 1–6; 60—62; 65—66) deliberately refer back to chapters 1 through 39. This section contains no prophetic biography nor does it mention any dominant foreign power. Like chapters 40 through 55, no author is mentioned. From these and other data, biblical scholarship from the late eighteenth century forward has come to agree there are "three Isaiahs" in the sense of three distinct sections: Chapters 1 through 39 preserve the preaching and deeds of Isaiah of Jerusalem of the late eighth century (though the editing of these chapters is later); chapters 40 through 55 interpret the Isaian legacy for exiles in the mid-sixth century; and chapters 56 through 66 interpret the same legacy for the rebuilding of Zion. Scholars conventionally refer to the three sections as First, Second, and Third Isaiah, though it is possible there were actually only two prophets. It is possible that "Second Isaiah" was the author of chapters 56 through 66 as well as of chapters 40 through 55. Over the last four decades, study of the book of Isaiah has taken a new turn. Without abandoning the views sketched above, scholars have turned their interest to the book of Isaiah as a unified literary work and are concerned with the way that its three sections relate to each other.

The following pages will discuss the historical background, literary structure, and message of the three sections, and then will give an overall view of the book.

Isaiah of Jerusalem (First Isaiah)

Historical Background of First Isaiah

Why did the writing prophets, Hosea, Amos, and Isaiah, appear in the mid-eighth century? Although a complete explanation is not possible, two significant ones are the emergence of Assyria as a superpower, and gross inequalities in the society of the time, especially concerning land tenure. Israel's enemies in the previous century, the ninth-century Aramean city-states to the north such as Damascus and Hamath, were more or less on a par with Israel; it was possible to mount a defense against them and go to war with some hope of victory. In the first half of the eighth century, the Arameans were in decline, which enabled the two halves of the divided kingdom, Israel in the north and Judah in the south, to flourish. The Neo-Assyrian Empire revived in the mid-eighth century, however, and turned its gaze to the eastern coastlands of the Mediterranean (the Levant). For the next two hundred years Assyria dominated the Levant, though the quality of its presence varied according to the strength of individual kings. Assyrian pressure destabilized the Northern Kingdom of Israel (a process recorded by Hosea). In 722 Shalmaneser V (728–722) conquered Samaria, the capital of the Northern Kingdom (Israel), though Sargon falsely claimed credit; and the Northern Kingdom was divided into Assyrian provinces (2 Kgs 17; 18, 1–12). Judah had to play thereafter the role of loyal vassal, although it did on occasion join with neighboring states and with Egypt against Assyria, most notably against Sennacherib in 701. Despite these occasional forays, the Southern Kingdom managed to retain its vassal status, chiefly by paying large tribute to the Assyrians.

For the prophet Isaiah, the Assyrian presence in the holy land of Israel provoked a major crisis. Unlike Egyptian and Aramean forays in Palestine in previous centuries, Assyria was a super-power against which no state in the Levant could possibly defend itself. So invincible was Assyria that its presence in the holy land called into question the sacred story that Israel lived by. In one version of that story, Israel had been rescued from Pharaoh's dominion in Egypt and led through the wilderness to the Lord's own land there to enjoy his protection and nurture (e.g., Pss 44, 78, 105, 136). Another version, used by Isaiah, focused on Zion (another name for Jerusalem), which was regarded as unconquerable as befitted the dwelling of the Lord. In Zion reigned the Lord's lieutenant on earth, the Davidic king, dispensing divine blessings and protection upon the land. Mighty Assyria bestriding the land seemed to invalidate the symbols of Zion and the king and the story told about them. In response to this crisis of meaning, Isaiah offered an interpretation of the tradition: far from being a violator of a holy place, he asserted, the Assyrian king had been invited by the Lord to punish Israel for its unjust behavior (10, 5–19). In due course, Assyria would be punished for its excesses, but now Judah must regard the Assyrian king as carrying out the judgment of the Lord. In putting forth this viewpoint to his contemporaries, Isaiah met strong resistance. To publicize his view and make it available to the next generation, Isaiah wrote his message down: "The record is to be folded and the sealed instruction kept among my disciples. For I will trust in the LORD, who is hiding his face from the house of Jacob; yes, I will wait for him. . . . And when they say to you, 'Inquire of mediums and fortune-tellers (who chirp and mutter!); should not a people inquire of their gods, apply to the dead on behalf of the living?'—then this document will furnish its instruction" (Is 8, 16–20).

The second historical factor in the rise of writing prophets was the increase of cruel and violent behavior among the people, which was especially directed against the poor. Though direct evidence of the condition of Israelite society is scarce, the prophets speak with such a unified voice about the inequality and social abuses that one must conclude such behavior was rampant. Isaiah goes so far as to speak in God's name to reject sacrifice until justice is done for the poor (1, 12–16). He is scathing against those who form estates from land seized from the poor (5, 8–10) and against those whose wealth made them arrogant (5, 11–12). The people's unequal access to the land provoked a crisis in the ancient traditions no less troubling to faithful Israelites than that caused by the Assyrian threat. In both cases, the people were unable to enjoy the fruits of the land that, according to their sacred traditions, the Lord owned and had given them for their use. Leviticus 25, 23 stated the ideal with unmistakable clarity: "The land shall not be sold in perpetuity; for the land is mine, and you are but aliens who have become my tenants." Isaiah's interpretation is that Zion (which in his thinking seems to stand for the holy land) would have to be purged to restore its original purity (e.g., 1, 21–28; 28, 1–8) and that Assyria was to be the instrument of purgation.

Several major interactions between Israel/ Judah and the Assyrian Empire are reflected in the book of Isaiah. In his first western campaign, 743–738, the Assyrian king Tiglath-pileser III (745–728) crushed a coalition of Hamath and northern coastal cities led by King Uzziah of Judah. Subsequently, there were three important periods of conflict between the two states, the first being the Syro-Ephraimite War (735–732) in which Damascus ("Syro-") and Israel ("Ephraimite") attempted to force King Ahaz of Judah to join their coalition against Assyria. Ahaz refused (chapter 7), called in Assyria to defend Judah, being happy, it seems, to enjoy some of the privileges of being a vassal of a great empire. Damascus and Israel failed in their war against Assyria, and the Northern Kingdom regions of Megiddo, Dor, and Gilead became Assyrian provinces (8, 23—9, 6).

A second period of conflict between Assyria and Judah came in 715–705 when King Hezekiah of Judah made several attempts to join anti-Assyrian alliances, notably a rebellion in the Philistine city of Ashdod in 713–711 (Is 20, 1–6; 18, 1—19, 15; 14, 28–32). The third period was in 701 when Hezekiah revolted against Sennacherib, assuming leadership of an alliance consisting of Phoenicia, Philistia, and Egypt. Sennacherib of Assyria marched west, pacified Phoenicia and Philistia without difficulty, and defeated Egyptian troops of Shabaka at Elteqeh. Hezekiah sued for peace (22, 9–11). Isaiah 36 through 38 refers to the same events, although it contains a legendary section that complicates interpretation. Most probably 2 Kings 18, 13–16 is a factual chronicle, to which a legendary account (2 Kgs 18, 17—19, 37) was appended.

Literary Structure

Most scholars regard chapter 1 as an introduction of the main themes of the whole book: imminent divine judgment, the necessity of social justice, and the painful process that transforms Zion into a holy and righteous city. Chapter 39, at the other end, seems to be an editorial transition to chapters 40 through 55, hinting at Judean arrogance that will eventually lead to the Babylonian captivity. Chapters 2 through 12, mainly concerned with the Syro-Ephraimite War (735–732), clearly form a unit. Built around a core, chapters 6 through 9 narrate the commission of Isaiah, King Ahaz's refusal to believe, and further threats and promises. This unit ends with a thanksgiving (chapter 12) that anticipates the salvation of Zion. Chapters 13 through 23, containing oracles concerning foreign nations, conclude with the upholding of Zion and punishing of the city that is counter to Zion (24—27). Chapters 28 through 33 blend denunciations and promises concerning Zion; chapters 34—35 describe the Day of the Lord and healing of nature in the style of Second Isaiah; and chapters 36—38 are a third-person narrative about the prophet and King Hezekiah in the Assyrian crisis of 701.

Lawrence Boadt has suggested that the editors arranged the three blocks, 2 to 12, 13 to 33, and 34 to 38, into three stages in order to make Isaiah's preaching applicable to later audiences. Each of the three stages displays a tripartite or ABC pattern: the Day of the Lord (appearance of the Lord as a warrior), human response, and divine act. The appearance of the Lord (A) invites a response by the people or the king (B), which is followed by (C) a divine intervention implementing justice. The pattern makes it possible for any reader of the Isaiah scroll to experience the powerful coming of the Lord and to respond accordingly. Thanks to the ABC structure, later readers of Isaiah are at no disadvantage compared to the original listeners or readers. The following four paragraphs suggest how the ABC pattern operates in chapters 2 through 38.

The pattern is clearest in Stage 1 (2—12). It should be noted that the opening scene (2, 1–5)— Jerusalem as the preeminent place of instruction and the goal of the nations' pilgrimage—falls outside the pattern. Its function in the book is to introduce the pilgrimage to Zion that is such an important motif in the book. The procession to Zion comes to a preliminary conclusion in chapter 12 and to a final conclusion in chapters 60 to 62 and 56 to 66.

The tripartite pattern of 2, 6–22 actually begins with the Day of the Lord "against all that is proud and arrogant, all that is high" in v. 12. The Day of the Lord section ends positively with a promise of glory for Zion (4, 2–6). The B section of the pattern (5, 1—9, 6) can be subtitled "rebelliousness and its royal example." It indicts the people for unjust conduct, shows the commissioning of Isaiah and his condemnation of King Ahaz for refusing to trust in God's promises to defend Zion and thus protect the king. The chapters go on to promise a better king (8, 23—9, 6). Salvation is impeded, but not ended, by the king's disbelief. The C section (9, 7—12, 6) can be titled "sin, judgment, and restoration of Zion." It begins with a condemnation of the people (9, 7—10, 4), tells of the choosing of Assyria as the punisher who will be punished later on (10, 5–34), gives a promise of a better king (11), and concludes with an anticipatory thanksgiving (12).

Stage 2 (13 through 33) also displays the tripartite pattern. It begins with the dramatic depiction of the Day of the Lord (against Babylon) in chapter 13. Denunciations of other foreign nations follow; Assyria, Egypt, Moab, Damascus (and Jerusalem) are severely chastised for not accepting the sovereign design of the Lord. The mention of "Babylon" in chapter 13 raises difficulties to First Isaian authorship, for Babylon was Israel's enemy in the late seventh and sixth centuries, not the eighth century. The occurrences of "Babylon" elsewhere in the section (14, 2 and 22, and 21, 9) are not problematic, for 14, 2 and 22 are in the frame of the poem (where they could have been added later), not in the body of the poem; Isaiah 21, 9 ("fallen is Babylon, and all the images of her gods") can refer to Assyria's documented destruction of Babylonian images in 689. To explain the occurrence of "Babylon" in chapter 13, several solutions have been proposed: (1) Chapter 13 was written in the seventh or sixth century when Babylon was the world power and inserted when the entire scroll was edited in the sixth or fifth century (the ma-

jority view); (2) Babylon referred to in chapter 13 is turn-of-the-eighth-century Babylon under Merodach-baladan, which rebelled against Assyria, and had to be recaptured at least four times (in 708, 703, 700, and 689); and (3) Isaiah 13, 1—14, 27 was originally written against Assyria by First Isaiah and later editors inserted Babylon in the sixth century. The last solution is the most probable since Assyria and Babylon, both great empires, became symbols of organized hostility to God; their names became virtually interchangeable as proverbial enemies of God.

Chapters 24 through 27 seem to stand apart from the rest of First Isaiah. Scholars sometimes entitle them "The Isaiah Apocalypse," but the name is unsatisfactory. The chapters speak of universal destruction and then speak of two cities: one the city of God, and the other a city opposed to God. Lack of specific references make interpretation of these chapters tentative. The chapters are perhaps best understood as the conclusion to chapters 13 through 23, generalizing the particular descriptions in the earlier chapters. Evidently, chapters 24 through 27 conclude the oracles against the foreign nations by showing the universal and timeless outreach of the Lord. The sovereignty of God encompasses the nations of the world. At any rate, in the tripartite editing, the chapters vividly portray the Day of the Lord.

The B section in Stage 2 appears in chapters 28 through 31, which contain examples of sinful alliances (especially on the part of the Northern Kingdom, called Ephraim). Judah is no better than her northern sister, the text asserts, yet the promises concerning Zion invite the people to repent. Section C (32—33) gives assurances that Assyria will be destroyed in the end and that an obedient king will be part of the new order for Israel.

Stage 3 (34 through 38), like the other two stages, begins with the Day of the Lord that punishes the wicked (in this case Edom as the representative of Israel's enemies) and upholds the faithful who return to Zion (34 through 35). The latter chapters employ components familiar from the pattern: the inevitable defeat of Assyrian arrogance, the king who responds for the people (unlike Ahaz, Hezekiah trusts), and Zion's salvation. This time, however, salvation is immediate and not postponed to the future. Hezekiah turns to the Lord fully, and his trust makes him a model for all the people.

The Theology of First Isaiah: the Plan of the Lord

Of the many possible ways of approaching the theology of Isaiah of Jerusalem, one of the most fruitful is to examine his understanding of the Lord's "plan" or "work." There are many synonyms for the divine plan or work in Isaiah and in Second Isaiah: "work, deeds" (5, 12; 41, 4; 45, 11) "thoughts (plans)" (55, 8–9), the phrase "the Lord was pleased to . . ." (42, 21; 53, 10), "deed" (5, 19; 28, 21), "word" (e.g., 2, 3; 5, 24; 30, 12; 44, 26). The most illuminating Isaian word, however, is "plan," which the prophet uses both as a noun and a verb. The best illustration of "plan" is 5, 19, which attacks those who deny the Lord is acting in the present crisis, "those who say, 'Let [the Lord] make haste and speed his *work*, that we may see it; on with the *plan* of the Holy One of Israel! let it come to pass, that we may know it!' " In Isaiah, words for "plan" or "work" are used in two different contexts: (1) for God's plan that will inevitably be realized and (2) for human plans or works that will inevitably fail. An example of the second usage is 8, 10, addressed to the hostile nations: "Form a plan, and it shall be thwarted; make a resolve, and it shall not be carried out, for 'With us is God!' " (cf. 19, 3.11). The passage shows that the prophet believes, contrary to the people, that the Lord has a plan for Israel and the nations, and he, Isaiah, is to announce it and help the people respond positively to it. The divine plan is clear in Isaiah: Israel's social injustice has necessitated divine judgment with the goal of renewal, and it will be carried out by Assyria. Later, Assyria will be punished for its excesses and arrogance. Judah and Zion must respond with openness and trust in the Lord's promises concerning Zion and the Davidic king. The plan concerns divine judgment. "Judgment" is not a negative concept in the Bible; it is an intervention by which justice is brought about by punishing evildoers and upholding the righteous. In First Isaiah, the attack of Assyria is part of a process of restorative justice that will end with the renewal of Israel. Though "plan" in First Isaiah describes the punishment of Jerusalem and eventual destruction of

Assyria (e.g., 14, 26), in Second Isaiah "plan" always has a positive sense, as in 44, 26, where "I carry out the *plan* announced by my messengers; I say to Jerusalem: Be inhabited; to the cities of Judah: Be rebuilt; I will raise up their ruins" (cf. 46, 10–11). First Isaiah establishes clearly that God has a plan, a judgment that involves the Assyrians as a temporary agent. The plan requires a response from the people, and it will ultimately lead to the renewal of Israel. It will fall to Second Isaiah to elaborate the plan of Isaiah of Jerusalem.

The Traditions Isaiah Used

One cannot appreciate the First Isaian "plan of the Lord," or indeed his entire message, without some idea of his use of traditions. Of the traditions he used, the most important were those celebrating the Lord as the king of heaven and earth (e.g., 6, 5; 33, 22) who chose Mount Zion as his dwelling (e.g., 1, 21–28; 2, 1–4; 4, 2–6; 28, 14–22; 31, 4–9; 33; 37, 22–29) and David as his client king (e.g., 7, 1–17; 32, 1–8; 17—24; 36—38). His favored title "Lord of Hosts" (sixty-two times) implies kingship over heavenly beings, typically won by a victory that no other heavenly being could achieve. Behind the title and these traditions lies a worldview that generated the stories through which people explained reality, making it possible for them to answer basic questions concerning human existence. The stories and the answers found expression in cultural symbols, and they also inculcated a way of living. Zion and the Davidic king were cultural symbols in this profound sense.

From what story do the Isaian symbols of Zion (the divine dwelling) and Davidic kingship derive their meaning? The story is called the combat myth by modern scholars. Of the versions of the myth in the ancient Near East, the following version was the most widely known: a monstrous force (often Sea) threatens cosmic order, and the gods are at a loss how to respond. The gods finally commission a young god who defeats the monstrous threat and restores (or creates) order and fertility. The gods acclaim him king, and he constructs a palace to symbolize his kingship. The myth is also attested in the Bible. A good example of the Israelite adaptation of the myth is Ps 93.

The LORD is king, robed with majesty;
  the LORD is robed, girded with might.
The world will surely stand in place,
  never to be moved.
Your throne stands firm from of old;
  you are from everlasting, LORD.
The flood has raised up, LORD;
  the flood has raised up its roar;
  the flood has raised its pounding waves.
More powerful than the roar of many waters,
  more powerful than the breakers of the sea,
  powerful in the heavens is the LORD.
Your decrees are firmly established;
  holiness belongs to your house, LORD,
  for all the length of days. (Ps 93, 1–5)

The psalm acclaims the Lord as king, robed with the glorious garments of a victorious warrior (v. 1a), ruling over a world that is now stable and safe from the cosmic threat personified by Sea (vv. 1b–2). Verses 3 and 4 tell of the great battle and the Lord's victory, and verse 5 describes the decrees the Lord speaks and the palace the Lord builds.

Such is the mythological background of Mount Zion, where the Lord rules as the incomparable Holy One and king of the universe. No wonder that the poets call Zion the highest mountain in the world (Ps 2, 2) and the dwelling of the Holy One (e.g., Pss 4, 3–5; 8, 18; 12, 6). The Davidic king was part of the same story. In some psalms, his commission as king was linked to the creation of the world. In Psalm 89, David is appointed as the "Most High over the kings of the earth" (89, 28), just as the Lord is superior to all the gods (89, 6–15).

Isaiah employed the traditions of the Lord as the king of the universe, Mount Zion as the dwelling of the incomparable Holy One, and the Davidic king as the delegate of the Lord. Jeremiah preferred to work with the Exodus, and Ezekiel worked with the full range of traditions, those of the holy Temple and land, Exodus, and divine king. Though it is probable that these prophets were aware of the full range of Israel's traditions, they selected those traditions that best suited their own temperament and pastoral aims.

Messianic Passages in Isaiah

The English word *messiah* comes from a Hebrew word meaning "anointed one." The Greek translation, *christos* (English "Christ"), appears in the New Testament. The Old Testament uses messiah of certain officials who were anointed with oil for their office—priests (e.g., Ex 40, 15) and especially the Davidic kings (e.g., 1 Sm 9, 10). Although the Davidic dynasty was regarded as everlasting in the sense that there would always be a son of David on the throne, the Old Testament never uses messiah of future kings. Only in the first century BC is a future son of David called a messiah, in the Dead Sea Scrolls and in the noncanonical Psalms of Solomon. The earliest New Testament books use "Christ" (Messiah) as the second name of Jesus (e.g., 1 Thes 1, 11). Paul inverts the order of words to "Christ Jesus" and announces that Jesus has fulfilled the expectations of the messiah, which are rooted in the Old Testament.

Popular usage is less exact, however. It often uses the term *messianic* of any Old Testament passage that speaks of a future son of David as in the above title, "Messianic Passages in Isaiah." In this broad sense, there are several messianic passages in Isaiah, notably in chapters 7 through 9, and 11, which have played an enormously important role in Christian reflection on Jesus. Isaiah 7, 1–17 is the most famous messianic passage in the entire Old Testament. The historical context is the attempt by the Northern Kingdom (Israel) and Damascus to force Ahab, king of Judah, to fight with them against Assyria. Isaiah, who opposed this alliance, challenges Ahab to place his trust in the promise of divine protection made to his ancestor David and not to fear "these two stumps of smoldering brands." When Ahab refuses to ask for a sign confirming the promise, Isaiah gives him one: "Therefore the Lord himself will give you this sign: the virgin shall be with child, and bear a son, and shall name him Immanuel" (Is 7, 14). Most probably, Isaiah says to the king that the sign is the pregnancy of your wife whose son (and not you) will one day bear the happy name Immanuel ("God is with us") and embody the divine protection of Jerusalem. A sign is a hint or foretaste of the divine power that will later appear in full. Such protection of Jerusalem is mentioned in such psalms as 46, 48, and 76. The son mentioned in the Isaian oracle was evidently Hezekiah (king from 715–687/6 BC), who in fact turned out to be a faithful son of David. How can a word uttered in the eighth century have significance for later generations? The answer is that Isaiah's sign, being a word of God, was not fully realized in eighth-century events to which it was originally addressed. Rather, the word retained its power so that, Christians believe, it was fulfilled completely only in the birth of Jesus. In Mt 1, 23, Joseph is told that Mary's child is from the Holy Spirit. The assurance is explained by quoting Is 7, 14, "Look, the *virgin* shall conceive and bear a son." Expansions to the promise in Is 7, 18–25 show that even in the very earliest times interpreters regarded the promise to the son of David as enormously significant.

Another important messianic oracle is Isaiah 8, 23—9, 6 (9, 1–7 in some versions): "First he degraded the land of Zebulun and the land of Naphtali; but in the end he has glorified the seaward road, the land west of the Jordan, the District of the Gentiles. Anguish has taken wing, dispelled is darkness: for there is no gloom where until now there was distress. The people who walked in darkness have seen a great light; upon those who dwelt in the land of gloom a light has shone. . . . For a child is born to us, a son is given us; upon his shoulder dominion rests. They name him Wonder-Counselor, God-Hero, Father-Forever, Prince of Peace. His dominion is vast and forever peaceful, from David's throne, and over his kingdom, which he confirms and sustains by judgment and justice, both now and forever. The zeal of the LORD of hosts will do this!" Like Isaiah 7, 14, this oracle arose in a specific historical circumstance—the coronation of a Davidic king of Judah, possibly Hezekiah. Whenever a new Davidic king was installed, people remembered the ancient Davidic promises (cf. 2 Sm 7) and hoped the promises of prosperity and protection would be realized under the new king. The old tribal areas (Zebulun and Naphtali) had become, in the Assyrian conquest of 722 BC, three Assyrian provinces: Galilee, Dor, and Gilead. For the unfortunate Israelites living in the conquered territories, light has dawned because the newly installed Davidic king will, the prophet hopes, replace Assyrian rule with the Lord's. Like Isaiah 7, 14, an oracle uttered at a particular time and place (late eighth century, Jerusalem) retained its force after the eighth century to take further effect at a later day. In Luke 1, 32, the angel alludes to the passage when he tells Mary that her son "will be great and will be called Son of the Most High,

and the Lord God will give him the throne of David his father, and he will rule over the house of Jacob forever, and of his kingdom there will be no end."

The last of the famous Isaian messianic prophecies is 11, 1–9, "But a shoot shall sprout from the stump of Jesse, and from his roots a bud shall blossom. The spirit of the LORD shall rest upon him: a spirit of wisdom and of understanding, a spirit of counsel and of strength, a spirit of knowledge and of fear of the LORD, and his delight shall be the fear of the LORD. Not by appearance shall he judge, nor by hearsay shall he decide, but he shall judge the poor with justice, and decide aright for the land's afflicted. He shall strike the ruthless with the rod of his mouth, and with the breath of his lips he shall slay the wicked. Justice shall be the band around his waist, and faithfulness a belt upon his hips. Then the wolf shall be a guest of the lamb, and the leopard shall lie down with the kid; the calf and the young lion shall browse together, with a little child to guide them. The cow and the bear shall be neighbors, together their young shall rest; the lion shall eat hay like the ox. The baby shall play by the cobra's den, and the child lay his hand on the adder's lair. There shall be no harm or ruin on all my holy mountain; for the earth shall be filled with knowledge of the LORD, as water covers the sea."

Like the previous oracles, Isaiah 11, 1–9 has a very specific origin. It seems to have been the installation or the anniversary of the installation of the king. The "shoot" that shall sprout (verse 1) is a reference to the Davidic dynasty, which had seemed a mere stump to its enemies (Is 10, 33–34). As the agent of the Lord's justice, the king would surely be endowed with power and wisdom (verses 2–3a). Divine justice is not necessarily the same as human justice, so that the king will not judge by human standards (verses 3b–5). The result of the king's rule will usher in an idyllic age, free of violence, when all will be taught by God. The language of the oracle is influenced by "court style"—poems about the king used embellished and exaggerated speech. The king is the agent through whom the Lord will bring about the peaceable kingdom. The Septuagint translation adds another gift to the six mentioned in the Hebrew text—"piety"—providing the biblical basis for the traditional Christian seven gifts of the Holy Spirit. For Christians, this passage predicts the outpouring of the Spirit in the New Testament.

The Message of Isaiah of Jerusalem

Only when one knows Isaiah's traditions can one appreciate the originality of his interpretation and the pastoral program that he proposed. The traditions of Zion and David were pure reassurance. Knowing that the time of judgment had come, Isaiah had to alter the triumphant ideology of king and temple. He believed that the coming judgment would not end in destruction but in salvation if the people trusted the Lord's plan. Astonishingly, he teaches that the historical means of judgment is Assyria ("Woe to Assyria! My rod in anger, my staff in wrath" (10, 5). The people must allow the Assyrian king free reign as the agent of judgment. If Judah rebels by entering into alliances with Egypt and neighboring city-states, Zion will be destroyed and the king cast aside, and salvation, if it comes at all, will be deferred to the far future. In Isaiah's radical thinking, Israel's refusal to believe in the Lord's "plan" is tantamount to political rebellion and idolatry (28, 14–22). With a kind of "political trust," the people must believe in the Lord's plan and cooperate with it.

Isaiah interprets the sacred (and reassuring) traditions for a new historical context: social injustice had become rampant, and an unstoppable superpower (Assyria) loomed over the defenseless nation. For Isaiah, the triumphal traditions of Zion's inviolability and the Davidic king's universal rule can have no validity as long as injustice and idolatry are triumphant (chapters 2, 5, and 28) and the leaders refuse to accept Assyria as the divine instrument. Isaiah's pastoral strategy flows directly from his analysis of the situation. He exhorts the people to rely solely on the Lord, to accept his plan that Assyria will be his instrument of justice, and to give up trying to stop Assyria. He urges them to favor the poor and the dispossessed (the king has a special role here). Only then will their Temple offerings be accepted and God bless them. In Isaiah, interpretation and ethics are intrinsically linked: his theology is preaching and his preaching is theology.

In summary, Isaiah recognized that the relationship of the Lord and Israel had reached a critical point in the late eighth century. With a prophet's radical eye, he saw on the one hand the people's failure to live in accord with the dictates of the Holy One in their midst and, on the other, the presence of a new kind of enemy on their borders, the superpower Assyria. He recognized a connection between the two facts: Assyria was God's instrument to "judge" Israel, that is, to force Israel to go through a process of purgation. If they accepted in faith God's ruling in this difficult time, the people would emerge purified and pleasing to the Lord. There was no easy path to renewal; it involved judgment. Isaiah reminded the people that the institutions through which the Lord had met and governed them, the temple and the king, did not operate automatically but only if the people approached them in faith and trust. The king played an important role as the one chosen by the Lord and in some sense as a representative of the people. But the king had to trust in the Lord and would be reckoned as good or bad to the extent that he trusted in the promises about Zion and his kingship.

Isaiah's message remains powerful today, largely because his message has been written down in the threefold pattern described above under "Literary Structure": (A) the appearance of the Lord in power (B) requiring a response by the people or their representative (C) followed by a divine intervention that implements justice. When one reads Isaiah today, one confronts the Lord who demands justice of human hearers and yet will inevitably bring about a just world. Isaiah never doubts that the Lord will remain faithful to the people and eventually bring about a renewed Israel ("I will restore your judges as at first, and your counselors as in the beginning; after that you shall be called city of justice, faithful city" 1, 26). Christians will revere Isaiah for his teaching about the Davidic king's major role in a renewed Israel, his insistence on embracing divine judgment for a renewed Israel, and his portrayal of all holy God who delights in living in the midst of Israel.

Second Isaiah

Scholarly analysis of Second Isaiah has been hindered because of a lack of consensus on the length of the poems. Scholars have given an exceptionally wide range of answers to the question of how many poems should be distinguished. They range from fifteen to seventy distinct poems. Judgment of poetic length is crucial for the interpretation of the prophet's message. If one assumes chapters 40 through 55 to be a collection of very short pieces, one will be inclined to view the prophet as a lyric poet given to short outbursts. But if one judges these same chapters to consist of lengthy poems, then one will be inclined to regard the author as a thinker who develops ideas in a complex way.

Why has there been such a wide range of assessments? In the early decades of the twentieth century, many scholars were influenced by the assumption of form criticism that the prophets borrowed literary forms from daily life, such as accusations from the law court, hymns and laments from temple worship, and love songs. That assumption is in fact largely correct, for the prophets communicated in language and genres that were familiar to their audience. Yet the prophets, especially Second Isaiah, were also theologians who developed their ideas in new ways in order to persuade people to certain modes of action. Thus they went far beyond popular speech and the familiar genres of everyday life. This essay takes the view that Second Isaiah was a thinker and theologian who composed lengthy poems to develop his ideas. The list below proposes the following poems in Second Isaiah and for each gives a title expressing in very brief form the content and point of the poems.

1. The Lord speaks good news to Israel (40, 1–11)

2. Strength for an exhausted people (40, 12–31)

3. Judgment in favor of Israel (41, 1—42, 9)

4. The divine warrior removes the obstacles to his people's return (42, 10—43, 8)

5. Israel raised to be a witness to the Lord (43, 9—44, 5)

6. Witness to their Maker (44, 6–23)

7. The Lord appoints Cyrus king (44, 24—45, 13)

8. The Lord will not leave the holy city in ruins (45, 14–25)

9. The Lord carries his people to his city (46)

10. The destruction of Dame Babylon (47)

11. Openness to the interpreting word (48)

12. The servant performs his task in the sight of the nations (49)

13. The light that follows punishing darkness (50, 1—51, 8)

14. A prayer that the Lord destroy the foe and bring his people to Zion (51, 9—52, 12)

15. The many confess that the Lord upholds his servant (52, 13—53, 12)

16. Zion, the secure city of the Lord (54)

17. Come into the life-giving presence of the Lord! (55)

Second Isaiah wrote in the mid-sixth century, about a century and a half after First Isaiah (in modern terms the span of time between the American Civil War and the present). The prophet's audience was in Babylon, not Palestine as in chapters 2 through 38 and 56 through 66. The traditions he employed differed strikingly from First Isaiah's. Instead of traditions concerning Mount Zion and the Davidic king, Second Isaiah preferred to work with those concerning the Creation and the Exodus. He employed different genres: chiefly, trial scenes and oracles of salvation rather than the biographical narratives and warnings about social justice favored by First Isaiah. His message, too, was distinctive: not warnings to prepare for the judgment, but calls to return to Zion. How then can Second Isaiah be said to continue the preaching of First Isaiah?

The reason that Second Isaiah can be called his legitimate successor, despite his differences from First Isaiah, is that he had the same view of the judgment process as First Isaiah and regarded his commission as continuing the commission given earlier to First Isaiah. The judgment was an ongoing process, in his view, continuing into his own day. Second Isaiah, too, felt called to monitor its progress and to invite the people to play their part as it unfolded. The difference in Second Isaiah was that a new stage had been reached: the earlier phase of punishment and destruction was over and a new phase was about to begin—rebuilding. Second Isaiah received the commission to preach consolation (40, 1–11) in the very same divine assembly where First Isaiah earlier had received the commission to announce devastation (6, 1–11). These passages calls are portrayed as parallel commissions. As Isaiah of Jerusalem had lamented his people's suffering, "Woe is me, I am doomed! For I am a man of unclean lips, living among a people of unclean lips" (6, 5), so Second Isaiah likewise felt obliged to express the vast suffering the people have already undergone, "The grass withers, the flower wilts, when the breath of the LORD blows upon it.

[So then, the people is the grass]" (40, 7). At first sight, Second Isaiah's commission seems to be the opposite of the first: "Comfort, give comfort to my people, says your God" (40, 1) versus First Isaiah's commission, "You are to make the heart of this people sluggish, to dull their ears and close their eyes; else their eyes will see, their ears hear, their heart understand, and they will turn and be healed" (6, 10). In fact, the commissions are complementary, for the second reveals the next stage in a seamless plan of destruction and rebuilding. The pastoral task now consists in summoning the people back to Zion rather than in calling them to social justice.

There is a second striking progression in the judgment process. The pagan royal instrument of God is Cyrus of Persia rather than the king of Assyria. Instead of "Woe to Assyria! My rod in anger . . . Against an impious nation I send him!" (10, 5–6), Second Isaiah announces "Thus says the LORD to his anointed, Cyrus, whose right hand I grasp, subduing nations before him, and making kings run in his service, opening doors before him and leaving the gates unbarred" (45, 1). Both kings are unaware of the divine choice (10, 7; 45, 4).

The commission to announce the divine plan provides the basis for the continuity between First and Second Isaiah. The divine plan in chapters 40 through 55 is a mirror image of the plan in chapters 1 through 39, which accounts for the correspondences between the two prophets. It is the mirror imaging of the main points of the message of one prophet in the other that one most readily senses the continuity between them.

As with First Isaiah, the revelation to Second Isaiah demanded a response on the part of the people. Theory and practice were not sharply distinct in the prophets. Second Isaiah heard a member of the heavenly council give the orders, "In the desert prepare the way of the LORD! Make straight in the wasteland a highway for our God!" (40, 3), that is, build a road through the desert from Babylon to Zion so the exiles can return home. Convinced that his task was to persuade people to embark on the journey, he announced: "Go forth from Babylon, flee from Chaldea!" (48, 20). The exiles were to return to their native city and begin anew. It would, however, be a mistake to view Second Isaiah solely as a pragmatist whose only task was to make cer-

tain that the people returned home as quickly as possible. In the prophet's dramatic view of national vocation, the people had ceased to be Israel when they were removed from the land that gave them their identity. To become Israel fully, they must do what Israel had originally done to become a people—participate in an exodus from the land of bondage to the land of promise. Israel was far from their homeland like the Hebrews in Egypt; the wilderness was like the Red Sea, and the servant who will lead them was like Moses (49, 1–6). The new exodus advertised to the nations that the Lord, the God of Israel, still acted in the world.

As was common in Hebrew rhetoric, the new exodus was depicted with mythic as well as historical qualities. The mythic dimension gives the event a universal scope. A good example of the mixing of historical and mythic levels is 51, 9–11, where the prophet prays that the Lord act, invoking his powerful arm:

Awake, awake, put on strength,
    O arm of the LORD!
Awake as in the days of old,
    in ages long ago!
Was it not you who crushed Rahab,
    you who pierced the dragon?
Was it not you who dried up the sea,
    the waters of the great deep,
Who made the depths of the sea into a way
    for the redeemed to pass over?" (Is 51,
    10–11).

Blending even more obviously mythic and historical elements is 43, 16–21:

Thus says the LORD,
    who opens a way in the sea
    and a path in the mighty waters,
Who leads out chariots and horsemen,
    a powerful army,
Till they lie prostrate together, never to rise,
    snuffed out and quenched like a wick.
Remember not the events of the past,
    the things of long ago consider not;
See, I am doing something new!
    Now it springs forth, do you not perceive it?
In the desert I make a way,
    in the wasteland, rivers.
Wild beasts honor me,
    jackals and ostriches,
For I put water in the desert
    and rivers in the wasteland
    for my chosen people to drink,

The people whom I formed for myself,
   that they might announce my praise.

The old exodus is depicted both as the conquest of Sea and the military defeat of Pharaoh, and the new exodus is depicted both as the conquest of desert and a journey through the wilderness to Palestine.

Though the above paragraphs have stressed continuity between the programs of First and Second Isaiah, there were discontinuities as well. One of the most striking was the role of the Davidic king who was the delegate of the divine king (6, 5). In the time of Second Isaiah, there was no reigning Davidic king. What did Second Isaiah do with this central tradition that no longer had meaning? He mentioned the Davidic king in only one verse, and that verse transferred the representative role of the king to the people.

Come to me heedfully,
   listen, that you may have life.
I will renew with you (plural) the everlasting
   covenant,
   the benefits assured to David.
As I made him a witness to the peoples,
   a leader and commander of nations,
So shall you summon a nation you knew not,
   and nations that knew you not shall run to
   you,
Because of the LORD, your God,
   the Holy One of Israel, who has glorified
   you" (Is 55, 3–5).

The verses have sometimes been interpreted as a wholesale democratizing of kingship, a transfer from individual kingship to a kind of corporate kingship; they are, however, much more limited in scope. They transfer only the Davidic king's witnessing of his patron deity's glory to the nations as in Ps 18, 44–45, "You rescued me from the strife of peoples; you made me head over nations. A people I had not known became my slaves; as soon as they heard of me they obeyed. Foreigners cringed before me." The people's embarking on a new exodus made them witnesses of their patron deity's power to determine the course of world history.

In summary, Second Isaiah freely selected omitted, or developed earlier, Isaian traditions because he saw himself as an inspired proclaimer continuing the divine plan first discerned by his predecessor. The plan has its times and seasons, and God propels it through different situations as a farmer nurtures and processes different crops with different means (cf. 28, 23–29). Second Isaiah focused on the Exodus traditions, rather than on the Zion and David traditions, because this tradition best served his strategy of moving the people from Babylon to Zion in a new exodus—land taking. Using historical and mythical language, he showed the urgency and significance of the great project. Engaging in the new exodus will bring Israel back into existence and show the nations that the Lord is supreme by reason of this act.

The Servant of the Lord in Second Isaiah

Among the most important and much discussed features of Second Isaiah is the servant of the Lord. The word *servant* occurs twenty-one times in chapters 40 through 55. In all but eight instances, *servant* refers to the people Israel. At the end of the eighteenth century, with the advent of modern biblical scholarship, many scholars singled out four passages about the servant (42, 1–9; 49, 1–7; 50, 4–11; 52, 13—53, 12) and claimed that these passages refer, not to the nation, but to an individual. (Many scholars still identify the servant as Israel in ideal form.) They differ on the identity of this individual; among the proposals are Moses as an ideal figure, Cyrus the Persian king (cf. 44, 28; 45, 1.13), and the prophet himself. The first two suggestions are unlikely. It is hard to imagine what meaning an abstract figure would have for an exiled population undergoing suffering and deprivation. Cyrus is virtually excluded because his role in the book is as antitype to the Assyrian king, not as servant, as explained in the section above. A substantial minority of scholars have always believed that the servant in these passages is the people Israel, but personified with traits of Moses and the prophets. A mediating position is suggested here: the servant is the prophet in a dialectic relationship to the people, like that of Moses or the prophets to Israel. Moses and the prophets stood between the Lord and the people. They were "out front," often undergoing in advance those events that would later happen to the people. In Exodus, Moses fled Egypt pursued by Pharaoh and met the Lord at Sinai; later, the people fled Egypt and met the Lord at Sinai. Moses' example showed them how to do it. Isaiah and Jeremiah also offered examples of obedience and patient suffering to the people, for they too underwent in advance what the people would later undergo. One can interpret the four servant songs in a similar fashion. The prophet is fulfilling the vocation of the people Israel, offering them an example and a warning. His songs evoke the great servant of the Lord, Moses, as well as Jeremiah and, of course, his great predecessor, Isaiah of Jerusalem.

Though scholars continue to discuss the identity of the servant, there is no doubt about the purpose of the servant songs. They proclaim to the nations that Israel's exile and great sufferings do not mean that the Lord is ineffectual, but that he is just and compassionate in a new way. He continues to reign. Israel's sufferings show God's justice and compassion.

The servant songs were influential on later biblical literature. Several verses from the fourth servant song were particularly influential: "See, my servant shall prosper (Hebrew *yaskil*), he shall be raised high and greatly exalted" (52, 13); "If he gives his life as an offering for sin, he shall see his descendants in a long life, and the will of the LORD shall be accomplished through him"; "Because of his affliction he shall see the light in fullness of days; through his suffering, my servant shall justify many, and their guilt he shall bear"(53, 10–11). The influence of these verses can be seen in Dn 11, 33–35 (italics show the borrowing from Is 52—53: "The nation's *wise men (maskilim) shall instruct the many;* though for a time they will become victims of the sword, of flames, exile, and plunder. . . . *Of the wise men,* some shall fall, so that the rest may be tested, refined, and purified, until the end time which is still appointed to come." The group who sponsored the book of Daniel saw themselves as "the wise" who instructed "the many" in Israel, even to the point of dying for them.

The fourth servant song influenced the portrayal of Jesus in the New Testament. When Jesus rebukes the apostles' unseemly striving for honor in Mark 10, 35-45, he concludes his criticism with a borrowing from Isaiah 52, 13—53, 12: "For the Son of Man did not come to be served but to serve and to give his life as a ransom for many." The most explicit New Testament text on the suffering servant is Acts 8, 26–40, the encounter of Philip, the deacon, with the Ethiopian eunuch. The eunuch, an official in the kingdom of Meroe, was reading Isaiah 53,

7–8. He asked Philip, " 'I beg you, about whom is the prophet saying this? About himself, or about someone else?' Then Philip opened his mouth and, beginning with this scripture passage, he proclaimed Jesus to him." Philip's response is not preserved, but one can infer from the eunuch's request for baptism that the text was very important in early Christian instruction, providing a way of understanding the death and resurrection of Jesus.

An important question is whether Jesus historically saw himself as the servant whose sufferings redeemed Israel. Scholars are divided on the issue. Some believe that the early church interpreted Jesus as the suffering servant subsequently, in the light of further reflection on the Scriptures. Even though the question cannot be definitively answered, it would be exceedingly strange if Jesus, so in tune with the Hebrew Scriptures, had not profoundly reflected on such a key Old Testament text and applied it to himself as he faced his death.

Third Isaiah

Chapters 56 through 66 were written several decades later in Palestine rather than in Babylon. It is possible that the author, now older and facing different issues, was also the author of chapters 40 through 55. It is equally possible that he was another person who felt authorized to continue and complete Second Isaiah's work. It is impossible to decide. Chapters 56 through 66 presume that many exiles have returned to Zion, and that they, along with those who remained in Palestine, are busy rebuilding the community. Second Isaiah's task had been to announce to the people that a new stage in the unfolding of the divine plan had been decreed—restoration rather than destruction—and to persuade them to respond by returning to Zion. Yet how were the people to rebuild once they were in Zion? What must they do to become a new people? It is precisely these questions that Third Isaiah addresses. His theme is rebuilding the community in its twofold sense of building a city and forming a people (60—62; 66).

The various speeches of Third Isaiah have been edited into a coherent whole. Chapters 60 through 62, concerning the glorification of Zion, is the centerpiece, for five poems precede (56, 1–8; 56, 9—57, 13; 57, 14–21; 58; 59) and five follow (63, 1–6; 63, 7—64, 12; 65; 66, 1–16.17–24). The centerpiece is framed on one side by a lament plus a brief description of the coming of the Lord to Zion (59, 1–20.21) and, on the other, by a brief description of the coming of the Lord to Zion plus a lament (63, 1–6; 63, 7—64, 1). It is helpful to give a schematic presentation of chapters 56 through 66, and to give to each poem a title that summarizes its essence.

1. The Lord will gather yet more worshippers (56, 1–8)

2. Punishment for the idolatrous oppressors of the faithful (56, 9—57, 13)

3. God will lead the humble faithful (57, 14–21)

4. The fast that the Lord wants (58)

5. Those who repent in Zion will be saved (59)

6. Zion's glory (60)

7. The prophet is sent to the poor (61)

8. Prayer for the city's restoration (62)

9. Day of punishment for the nations (63, 1–6)

10. Communal lament (63, 7—64, 12)

11. The righteous are upheld in judgment: they shall inherit the land (65)

12. Judgment in Jerusalem in favor of the righteous (66, 1–16)

13. Jerusalem as the goal of the nations' pilgrimage (66, 17–24)

With regard to inherited traditions, Third Isaiah shows the same freedom as does Second Isaiah. Third Isaiah does not use, for example, the royal traditions so dear to First Isaiah, and the Exodus traditions dear to Second Isaiah appear only once or twice. Third Isaiah's favored traditions are the mountain of the Holy One, and Zion as the goal of pilgrimage (chapters 60, 62) and place of divine judgment (65, 1–6; 65; 66, 17–24). How then can Third Isaiah be said to continue the preaching of the two previous prophets? How is this section linked to the preceding two? The answer is the same as for Second Isaiah—the prophet is concerned with the same divine plan as his predecessors. Third Isaiah believes the divine plan continues to operate, and that he has been authorized by God to monitor the judgment-process as it appears in his own day, helping the audience respond to its ethical demands.

Here, then, is the program of Third Isaiah. To the returnees, uncertain about their claim on the land and their identity as Israel in a still devastated city, the prophet announces that the Lord will rebuild the community in Zion so as to reveal the divine glory. To be Israel in an authentic and meaningful way means to adhere to God's commandments, especially those concerning right worship and social justice (57—58), and to await in faith the visitation of God that will transform the city (e.g., 59, 15–21; 65; 66). The visitation will separate *true* Israel from the *counterfeit* Israel that oppresses its neighbors and closes itself off from the coming renewal. Third Isaiah declares that living in the city of Zion is not enough; one must live in accord with the commands of the Holy God dwelling there, and one must await in lively faith the Lord's initiatives. This point is made at the very beginning of the prophet's message. To emphasize the holiness expected of inhabitants in Zion, Third Isaiah invites to "my holy mountain" two hitherto excluded categories, eunuchs and foreigners, solely on the basis of their sincere commitment to the covenant (56, 1–8). The nations and Israel are given one and the same criterion for admission to Mount Zion: "Observe what is right, do what is just; for my salvation is about to come, my justice, about to be revealed" (56, 1).

The Unity of the Book of Isaiah

One might not expect a book recording the prophetic deeds and utterances of three prophets and editors over two and half centuries to have much unity. The book begins when Israel and Judah were independent kingdoms; it records Assyria's destruction or partition of Israel and subjugation of Judah in the late eighth century, the effects of the destruction of Jerusalem and exile of Judahites a century later, and finally the return and initial efforts at rebuilding Zion in the sixth century. As has been shown above, despite the upheavals and discontinuities of the history, all the Isaian writers discerned a single ongoing judgment-process aimed at renewing Zion. Zion was a symbol of the people and their sacred land. All the prophets in this tradition announced the progress of divine action and invited the people to suitable response, whether repentance, hope, return, or rebuilding.

Editorially, the unity of the book is reinforced and signaled by a number of literary devices. It is not certain who the final editors were. Were they scribes who edited and published the literary legacy of preexilic Israel for the postexilic generations? Or did the author of Second and Third Isaiah gather and edit the whole? A few scholars have suggested that Second Isaiah wrote chapters 40 through 55 and 56 through 66, and then arranged 1 through 39 so the entire scroll would form a coherent message. At any rate, it is clear that the last half of Third Isaiah (60—62; 63, 7—66, 24) is particularly important in the structure of the book. A good example of editing is the placement of the scenes of the pilgrimage of the nations to Zion. First Isaiah begins with a preface (1, 2–4) depicting a pilgrimage of the nations to Zion to listen to the instruction of the Lord. Chapters 60 through 66 is the other end of the great arc begun in chapter 2. In chapter 60, the nations stream toward a brilliantly lit Zion, and in 66, 15–24 the nations come to Zion with gifts, bringing the book to a conclusion.

Another indication of unity is the theme of the judgment and rebuilding of Zion. Chapter 1 indicted an obtuse people for not realizing that their present misery was the result of their infidelity and injustice (1, 2–20). The important poem in 1, 21–30 describes an attack on the city of Zion by the Lord himself in order to purify it from the injustice that has taken over the city. The divine attack is an act of judgment that puts down wickedness and upholds justice. The promise of such a judgment is repeated in Isaiah 4, 2–6; 28, 14–22; 33, 17–24. The elaborate community lament in 63, 7—64, 11 is a long and urgent appeal for a transformative visitation: "Zion is a desert, Jerusalem a waste. Our holy and glorious temple in which our fathers praised you has been burned with fire; all that was dear to us is laid waste. Can you hold back, O LORD, after all this? Can you remain silent, and afflict us so severely?" Responding to that lament, Isaiah 65 describes the longed-for judgment that transforms Jerusalem into the righteous city promised by First Isaiah. Isaiah 65, 17–19 declares, "Lo, I am about to create new heavens and a new earth. . . . Instead, there shall always be rejoicing and happiness in what I create; for I create Jerusalem to be a joy and its people to be a delight; I will rejoice in Jerusalem and exult in my people." Chapter 65 seems to reverse the threat of 1, 24–27, "Now, therefore, says the Lord, the LORD of hosts, the Mighty One of Israel: Ah! I will take vengeance on my foes and fully re-

pay my enemies! . . . I will restore your judges as at first, and your counselors as in the beginning; after that you shall be called city of justice, faithful city. Zion shall be redeemed by judgment, and her repentant ones by justice."

Two word pairs occur throughout the scroll and play an important role in elucidating its message. The first word pair is *mishpat* and *sedaqah* in Hebrew, which are usually translated as "justice and righteousness" or, as in the NAB, "judgment and justice." The two words convey one idea, the social and personal justice that should inform human actions. The word pair occurs only in First and Third Isaiah. Using the word pair, First Isaiah indicts Israel for its lack of judgment and justice, as in 5, 7: "The vineyard of the LORD of hosts is the house of Israel, and the men of Judah are his cherished plant; he looked for judgment, but see, bloodshed! for justice, but hark, the outcry!" Even the holy city Zion lacks these qualities, requiring God to restore them in the future, "Zion shall be redeemed by judgment, and her repentant ones by justice" (1, 27). The rebuilding of Zion (in the sense of city and people) must include judgment and justice, for it was the lack of these qualities that led to the destruction of Zion. It is no surprise, therefore, that when Third Isaiah speaks about the rebuilding of Zion, he insists on precisely these two qualities, for without them all rebuilding is in vain (56, 1; 58, 2bc; 59, 4; 59, 9.14).

The second important word pair in Isaiah is "salvation and justice" (*yeshuaʿ* and *sedaqah*, with variation in the order of words). This pair occurs only in Second and Third Isaiah, as in 45, 8: "Let the earth open and salvation bud forth; let justice also spring up! I, the LORD, have created this," and in 56,1, "my salvation is about to come, my justice, about to be revealed." As the first pair expresses *human* response to God's initiatives, so the second word pair expresses *divine* action that is saving and righteous. Only the two latter prophets had the good fortune to see God's restoration and rebuilding, which they describe as "salvation." Significantly, Third Isaiah's opening line (56, 1) brings both word pairs together in a synthesis, implying that the long-sought justice of Isaiah of Jerusalem can at last be realized because of the turning point in history signaled by the return from exile: "Thus says the LORD: Observe judgment, do justice, for my salvation is about to come, my justice, about to be revealed" (Author's translation). The first colon expresses a moral demand of humans, and the second line, the coming divine order. Now is the time for both to be realized! Renewed Zion demands conduct befitting its holiness. The use of the word pairs suggests a careful editor, who attempted to show that the indictment of First Isaiah can be overcome in the renewal of Zion, and the promises of return and renewal in Second Isaiah can be realized in Third Isaiah's day.

Zion is made holy by divine judgment (65). Being righteous, it becomes a magnet to the nations (66, 15–24), a role that fulfills the promise of 2, 1–5. Third Isaiah redefines Zion: it is no longer simply a place of assured blessings and safety, but the goal of pilgrimage for the nations and site of a teaching that is authoritative for the nations.

Conclusions

The unity of Isaiah does not come from the traditions used by the three prophets, for each used different ones. Still less does its unity come from an ongoing "school of Isaiah" postulated by an earlier generation of scholars; there is no evidence for such a school. Isaian unity comes from the unified plan or work of the Lord, which all three sections of the book announce and promote. It had been revealed to Isaiah of Jerusalem that the Lord had begun a process (judgment) to rectify the pervasive injustice marring Zion, and that the process would ultimately bring about a renewed people and land. Second and Third Isaiah were convinced that God had revealed to them a new stage in the divinely led process or judgment initially revealed to First Isaiah. The progress of the judgment was not determined in advance, but, like other important divine responses, changed according to the behavior of Israel and circumstances of history. Second Isaiah discerned a turn in world history that permitted the exiles to return to Zion and gave them the opportunity to be witnesses to the nations that the Lord is supreme. Following in his footsteps, Third Isaiah discerned a further stage, the rebuilding of Zion in accord with divine righteousness. All three prophets entrusted the completion of the plan to God and thus left the future open.

A special contribution of First Isaiah is his view that divine judgment is realized in human history. God uses human agencies, even the enemies of Israel, and guides them to bring about a righteous world. The judgment can involve destruction as well as salvation. What is rebellious will be destroyed; what is righteous will be upheld. In every one of its phases, the Lord's plan calls for human response and participation. Isaiah's view of history proved to be invaluable for Israelite thinkers of the exilic period trying to make sense of Israel when the monarchy collapsed and the Temple and the city were destroyed. The old traditions celebrating the Lord in the midst of a people living happily and safely in the land had lost all credibility. One cannot help wondering what exilic thinkers would have done if Isaiah had not earlier taught that the most sacred institutions do not offer protection on their own, but only because the Holy One is graciously present in them. Times change, and God is present to his people in new ways.

The Influence of Isaiah on Biblical Books

Isaiah's view of history—that the great empire was the Lord's means of "judging" or making Zion just—deeply influenced the prophet Jeremiah a century and a half later. Though for Jeremiah the great empire was not Assyria but Babylon, he taught that it was the Lord who brought "the enemy from the north" (i.e., Babylon; Jer 4—10) as an instrument of judgment. Judeans should submit to this chosen instrument with the hope that the Lord would renew them and ultimately bring them home (e.g., Jer 20, 4–6; 25, 9–12; 29, 1–24). Isaiah's view of history also influenced the author of Daniel in the second century. According to chapters 2 and 7, the Lord controlled the succession of four world empires, the last of which would be punished as Israel rose to supremacy.

In the second and first centuries BC, Jewish sectarians at Qumran on the Dead Sea believed that Isaiah 40, 1–11 was about to come true: "In the desert prepare the way of the LORD! Make straight in the wasteland a highway for our God! . . . Then the glory of the LORD shall be revealed, and all mankind shall see it together; for the mouth of the LORD has spoken" (Is 40, 3.5). Therefore, they waited on the edge of the desert for the Lord to enter the land and inaugurate a new age. Jesus shared some of this lively expectation of the return of the Lord to Zion and an outpouring of the holy Spirit, as is evidenced by the preachment "Repent, for the Kingdom (rule) of God is at hand!" and the outpouring of the Spirit (Mk 1, 12–13; Lk 4, 16–30; Rom 8). The Gospel of Mark interprets Isaiah 40, 1–5: "Behold, I am sending my messenger ahead of you; he will prepare your way. A voice of one crying out in the desert: 'Prepare the way of the Lord, make straight his paths.' John (the) Baptist appeared in the desert proclaiming a baptism of repentance for the forgiveness of sins." The exegesis of the time referred these verses to the return of the exiles at the end of days, accompanied by spiritual renewal and indeed renewal of the cosmos itself. Isaiah's proclamation of the birth of a son of David in Isaiah 7, 14 ("Therefore the Lord himself will give you this sign: the virgin shall be with child, and bear a son, and shall name him Immanuel") was of enormous significance in the gospels (Mt 1, 22–23; Lk 1, 31). Matthew 1, 22–23 is explicit: "All this took place to fulfill what the Lord had said through the prophet: 'Behold, the virgin shall be with child and bear a son, and they shall name him Emmanuel,' which means 'God is with us.' " The spiritual endowments of the king in Isaiah 11, 1–9 provided images for Christian writers in Matthew 2, 23; 1 Peter 4, 14; Revelation 1, 4; and Ephesians 6, 14. Isaian words and images were taken up by Christian writers. The Christian liturgical season of Advent draws heavily on the texts of Isaiah. The intellectual and spiritual achievement of Isaiah of Jerusalem turned out to be exceptionally long-lived and productive.

FURTHER READING

First Isaiah

Barton, John. *Isaiah 1–39*. Old Testament Reading Guide. Sheffield: Sheffield Academic Press, 1995. Well balanced, clearly written introduction; it is not a commentary.

Blenkinsopp, Joseph. *Isaiah 1–39; Isaiah 40–55; Isaiah 56–66*. Anchor Bible 19; 19A; 19B. New York: Doubleday, 2000, 2001, 2002. It is an advantage to have a major commentary on all sixty-six chapters from one scholar. The book is up to date and very well done. For advanced students.

Boadt, Lawrence. "Re-examining a Pre-exilic Redaction of Isaiah." In *Imagery and Imagination in Biblical Literature: Essays in Honor of Aloysius Fitzgerald*. Catholic Biblical Quarterly Monograph Series 32: 169–70. Washington, DC: Catholic Biblical Association, 2001. Argues for editorial unity in chapters 1 through 39.

Brueggemann, Walter. *Isaiah 1–39*. Westminster Bible Companion. Louisville: Westminster John Knox, 1998. Canonical approach, written with lay Christians in mind.

Childs, Brevard S. *Isaiah*. Old Testament Library. Louisville: Westminster John Knox, 2001. Written from a canonical perspective that stresses the book as Scripture.

Clements, R. E. *Isaiah 1–39*. New Century Bible Commentary. Grand Rapids: Eerdmans, 1980. Clear and balanced commentary.

Collins, John J. *Isaiah*. Collegeville Bible Commentary 13. Collegeville, MN: Liturgical Press, 1986. Succinct, competent, a popular explanation.

Goldingay, John. *Isaiah*. New International Biblical Commentary. Peabody, MA: Hendrickson, 2001. Concerned with showing the coherence of Isaiah for a wide readership. Suitable for pastors and students.

Jensen, Joseph, O.S.B. *Isaiah 1–39*. Old Testament Message 9. Wilmington, DE: Michael Glazier, 1984. Excellent commentary, combining exact scholarship and theological analysis.

Schmitt, John J. *Isaiah and His Interpreters*. New York: Paulist Press, 1986. A helpful and readable survey of the scholarship on Isaiah.

Seitz, Christopher R. *Isaiah 1–39*. Interpretation. Louisville: John Knox, 1993. Largely concerned with the coherence and structure of the book.

———. *The Book of Isaiah 40–66*. The New Interpreter's Bible 1, 307–552. Nashville: Abingdon Press, 2001. Concerned with theological themes and biblical theology.

Tucker, Gene M. *The Book of Isaiah 1–39*. New Interpreter's Bible 1, 25–305. Nashville: Abingdon Press, 2001. Thorough and well balanced, with a strong interest in pastoral application.

Wildberger, Hans. *Isaiah 1–12; Isaiah 13–27; Isaiah 28–39*. Continental Commentary. Minneapolis: Fortress, 1991, 1997, 2002. The most detailed commentary on First Isaiah. Recommended for advanced students and scholars.

Second and Third Isaiah

Baltzer, Klaus. *Deutero-Isaiah*. Hermeneia. Minneapolis: Fortress, 2001. Baltzer assumes throughout that the book reflects a drama, an assumption that limits the usefulness of the volume.

Blenkinsopp, Joseph. *Isaiah 40–55; Isaiah 56–66*. Anchor Bible 19A; 19B. See comments above.

Clifford, Richard J. *Fair Spoken and Persuading*. New York: Paulist Press, 1984. Studies the literary and theological side of the chapters.

Scullion, John. *Isaiah 40–66*. Old Testament Message 12. Wilmington, DE: Michael Glazier, 1982.

JEREMIAH

[see pages 1004–1075 of the Old Testament]

Jeremiah began his prophetic ministry in 627 BC, during the reform initiated by King Josiah (640–609) and is last heard from as an unwilling exile in Egypt in the period between 582 and 570. Though his ministry began in a period of bright promise and reform, his recorded preaching focused on the disintegration of Judah from 609 forward, after King Josiah was killed and Babylon's assaults began. Especially noteworthy is his preaching during the grim period leading up to the destruction of Jerusalem and the Temple in 586 and its aftermath. The Hebrew version of Jeremiah falls into three main parts: (1) chapters 1 through 25, poetic oracles of judgment against Judah and Jerusalem, including sermons, reports of prophetic actions, and laments; (2) chapters 26 through 45, chiefly narratives about the prophet with some sermons; (3) chapters 46 through 51, oracles concerning foreign nations. Chapter 52, a historical appendix, provides further information about Zedekiah, the fall of Jerusalem and the exile.

Historical Background

To understand Jeremiah's ministry, one must have some grasp of events in Israel and Judah (the southern and northern kingdoms) from the time of Isaiah in the late eighth century to the Babylonian Exile (conventionally 586 to 539). Isaiah of Jerusalem, whose words and deeds are recorded in Isaiah 1—39, exercised his prophetic ministry from ca. 738 to the rebellion of 701 and possibly to the death of King Hezekiah in 687. His successor, Manasseh (687–642), was weak, choosing submission rather than resistance to Assyrian rule. He is remembered in the Bible as a faithless and false leader (2 Kgs 21, 9–17; Jer 15, 4). During the first three quarters of the seventh century, the Assyrian Empire flourished in the eastern Mediterranean. It even conquered Egypt and, for a time, occupied it. Assurbanipal (669–ca. 627) was the last great Assyrian king. After him, the empire, already overextended, collapsed with exceptional speed. In 612 a coalition of King Cyaxares of Media and King Nabopolassar of Babylon brought it down, and the entire Near East celebrated.

The long dominance and sudden collapse of the Assyrian empire are sensitively reflected in Judean politics. In 640, at the age of eight, Josiah came to the throne aided by people eager for reform, but Assyrian power kept him quiet in his early years. Beginning in 627, the year of the death of Assurbanipal that precipitated the rapid slide of Assyria, Josiah led a resurgence of national and religious rebuilding. He restored the old boundaries of the kingdom of David, annexing the former Assyrian provinces of Samaria, Gilead, and Galilee (2 Kgs 23, 19). Further impetus was given to his reform when, in 622, workers restoring the Temple found an ancient law book. The book was the nucleus of Deuteronomy and became the basis of religious reform (2 Kgs 22, 1—23, 27). Unfortunately, the promising reform was cut short by Josiah's unexpected death at the hands of the pharaoh Neco in 609 (2 Kgs 23, 28–30; 2 Chr 35, 20–24). At about the same time, Babylon began its rise to power in the west. First Egypt and then (after 605) Babylon became the dominant power in Palestine.

Where was Jeremiah during these extraordinary events? Even though he was commissioned a prophet in 627 and thus lived through Josiah's reform (Jer 1, 2; cf. also 3, 6; 36, 2), he is, surprisingly, not recorded as supporting it with his preaching. Some scholars suggest he rejected Josiah's reform efforts as too little too late, although it is more likely that his oracles in support of it have been reused and applied to the new situation following Josiah's death. A good example is the famous "Book of Consolation" in chapters 30 and 31, which seems to have been addressed originally to "Israel," that is, the Northern Kingdom, the inhabitants of Samaria, Gilead, and Galilee, whom King Josiah invited into his Davidic empire. In several passages (e.g., Jer 30, 3.4), the phrase "and Judah" seems tacked on to "Israel" (Northern Kingdom), the group originally addressed.

After the tragedy of 609, Josiah's son Jehoahaz (also called Shallum) succeeded him as king, but within three months the Egyptians replaced him with Jehoiakim, another son of Josiah. Judah paid tribute to Egypt. Jehoiakim was denounced by Jeremiah for using forced labor to build himself a fine palace (22, 13–19). When the Babylonians defeated the Egyptians at the decisive battle of Carchemish (605), Babylon became the major political power in the Levant (the eastern Mediterranean coast), and Jehoiakim duly transferred his loyalties to the victorious power. In the same year occurred the famous incident of Jehoiakim burning column by column the scroll containing Jeremiah's preaching (36, 1.23). He was offended by Jeremiah's prediction that Babylon would destroy Israel. Harboring hopes of independence, Jehoiakim revolted after three years. Nebuchadnezzar responded with troops from Moab, Ammon, and Aram, though Judah limped on for a few more years (2 Kgs 24, 2; Jer 25, 11). Jehoiakim died in 598, either by natural causes (implied by 2 Kgs 24, 6) or after being captured by Nebuchadnezzar and taken to Babylon (2 Chr 36, 5–8). His son Jehoiachin succeeded him, reigning only three months before he too was taken to Babylon in 597 with other leaders. The prophet Ezekiel was in this deportation. Nebuchadnezzar installed yet another son of Josiah, Zedekiah, as vassal king. Jeremiah wrote down his vision of the good and bad figs (24, 1–10) to tell the exiles that God would make them the basis of a remnant in preference to those who stayed behind in Jerusalem. Rumors of revolt were rife in Jerusalem. Such rumors provoked Jeremiah's symbolic action of carrying the ox-yoke (27, 1–22), his confrontation with the prophet Hananiah (28, 1–17), and his letter to the exiles (29, 1–32).

Finally, in July 586, the unthinkable happened: the walls of Jerusalem were breached, the city was set afire, and the Temple was looted and destroyed. The rebellious King Zedekiah was captured and forced to look on as his two sons were murdered; then his own eyes were put out, and he was taken in chains to Babylon (2 Kgs 25; Jer 39, 7). After Jerusalem fell, the Babylonians, grateful for Jeremiah's exhortations to his countrymen to submit to them, freed him from the prison where he had been consigned (Jer 39, 11–14; 40, 1–6).

Nebuchadnezzar established his seat of government at Mizpeh and appointed Gedaliah, a member of an important Judean family, as governor (2 Kgs 25, 22–26). Gedaliah, however, was assassinated by Ishmael and other fanatical nationalists ca. 582 (Jer 40, 7—43, 7). Fearful of another Babylonian deportation, a group of prominent Judeans fled to Egypt and took a reluctant Jeremiah with them (Jer 43, 8—44, 30). Active for a while in Egypt, he finally disappears from the historical record.

Dateable Utterances and Events in the Book of Jeremiah

The previous section sketched the history and politics of the period from Isaiah of Jerusalem to Jeremiah, and made a few passing references to passages in Jeremiah. This section focuses on the passages in the book that carry a date or can be dated from the context. Although the book was not edited according to a strict chronology, dateable passages provide a good way to understand the prophet's response to the events of his time. For many of the oracles and sermons, an editor took great care to provide information on their time and place. The dates provide valuable clues to understanding a complex and dense book. Although the events described in the passages below are dated to chronological periods, one must always recognize that the passages themselves may in some cases have been edited at a later time in view of the whole message of Jeremiah.

The first passage is 1, 4–19, the prophet's call, which dates to the thirteenth year of Josiah's reign (1, 2) in 627. A few scholars believe 627 was the year of Jeremiah's birth and the call came much later, but few scholars have been persuaded by the arguments in support of it. The year is important, for it shows Jeremiah began his ministry during the early years of the Josianic reform, which was inspired in part by the "book of the law [or instruction]" found in the Temple (2 Kgs 22), the nucleus of the present book of Deuteronomy. In Deuteronomy, Moses proclaims the law to the people about to cross over into the promised land so that they will know how to live in the land so as to enjoy God's blessing. Significantly, Jeremiah's call is modeled on that of Moses (Ex 3—4); like Moses, he first resists until the divine word is placed in his mouth. Deuteronomic themes are important in the book: avoidance of idols, insistence on wholehearted observance of Moses' words, association of heart and covenant, inevitability of divine punishment for breach of covenant yet possibility of renewal and return. Another passage that seems to reflect the early ministry of Jeremiah in the time of Josiah is Jer 16, 1–13, where the Lord commands the prophet not to take a wife. Such a command, contrary to the culture of the time, must have been given when Jeremiah was at an age to choose a wife, that is, when he was a young man. Many scholars believe that chapters 30 and 31 were originally addressed to Israel, the Northern Kingdom. Evidently, Jeremiah supported Josiah's invitation to the former Assyrian provinces in the north to join their kinfolk in the south and become again one people as in the great days of the united monarchy under David and Solomon. Chapters 30 and 31 were later reinterpreted as applying not to the exiles of the former Assyrian provinces but to the sixth-century exiles scattered in Babylon and Egypt. There is no reason why Jeremiah himself could not have redirected his own oracles.

With Josiah's death in 609, his reform collapsed. Any lingering hopes attaching to Josiah's son Jehoahaz were shattered when the Egyptians replaced him with another son of Josiah, Jehoiakim. Among the passages interpreting this frustrating turn of events is 22, 10–19, which evaluates the three kings of the period, Josiah, Jehoahaz, and Jehoiakim. Jeremiah's bold sermon attacking mindless confidence in the Temple (7, 1–15; abbreviated in 26, 1–24) was given in 609 according to 26, 1. It would have been natural for Jeremiah to support Josiah's son as he supported his father, but by this time the prophet appears to have reached the conclusion that Josiah's reform was dead and that the Babylonians were the instrument of divine judgment. Isaiah's earlier interpretation of Assyria as the instrument of Israel's punishment provided a precedent for a similar interpretation of Babylon. The lackluster performance of the sons of Josiah only reinforced his gloomy conclusion.

In the fourth year of Jehoiakim (605), Jeremiah dictated to his secretary Baruch his oracles up to the present (Jer 36). When the scroll was read to the king, he was outraged and personally burned the scroll, making it necessary for Jeremiah to dictate the scroll again. The scroll that Jeremiah dictated to replace the burned scroll is presumably the basis of the present text of Jeremiah, and scholars have speculated endlessly

about its contents. From Jehoiakim's reaction, one can assume that the scroll contained predominantly prophecies of woe and vigorous criticism of the king and the establishment. These are the chief themes of chapters 1 through 25. After the stressful conflict with the king, Jeremiah spoke reassuring words to his secretary Baruch, who was caught in a situation that was not of his own making. Those words were reinterpreted as applying to the greater distress of the exile (Jer 45). Jeremiah's praise of the austere lifestyle of the Rechabites is editorially linked to chapter 36, so is likely to have taken place at the same time as the encounter with Jehoiakim. In the same year, Jeremiah predicted the Babylonian captivity and specifically identified "the enemy from the north" as Babylon (25, 1–14). Perhaps three or four years later, Jeremiah smashed the clay jug, a prophetic gesture symbolizing the Lord's smashing of the people (19, 1–15). The gesture provoked the priest Pashhur's punishment (20, 1–6).

Two passages are concerned with Jehoiachin's three-month reign in 597: Jeremiah 22, 24–30 regards the king as having no hope of success; 24, 1–10 with its vision of the basket of good figs and the basket of bad figs, teaches that the deportees, not those left behind, will form the basis of a new community.

Another important date is 594, when emissaries from Edom, Moab, Ammon, Tyre, and Sidon came to Jerusalem to persuade King Zedekiah (597–587) to rebel against the Babylonians. Egypt would also join them, some hoped. Jeremiah vigorously opposed the plan with the shocking assertion that the Lord intends that all those nations submit to Babylon (27, 1–22). Such assertions did not go unchallenged. The prophet Hananiah vehemently opposed Jeremiah (though ultimately to his own cost, 28, 1–17) in that same year. It was then that Jeremiah wrote a letter to the exiles telling them to resist such prophets of weal and prepare for an exile of seventy years (29, 1–32; 51, 59–64). The above chronology is based on the Septuagint (Greek) rendering of Jeremiah 28, 1.

The largest number of dated passages occur in the period leading up to the destruction of Jerusalem and the Temple in 589–587. Zedekiah asked Jeremiah to inquire of the Lord as Babylon closed in (21, 1–10), but, according to 34, 1–7, the prophet predicted that Babylon would burn down Jerusalem and capture the king. When King Zedekiah freed Hebrew slaves in an attempt to gain divine favor in the crisis and then reneged, Jeremiah excoriated him: "But then you changed your mind and profaned my name by taking back your male and female slaves to whom you had given their freedom; you forced them once more into slavery. Therefore, thus says the LORD: You did not obey me by proclaiming your neighbors and kinsmen free. I now proclaim you free, says the LORD, for the sword, famine, and pestilence. I will make you an object of horror to all the kingdoms of the earth" (34, 16–17). In contrast to such waffling, Jeremiah during the crisis redeemed a relative's field to demonstrate his trust that the exiles would eventually come back to Judah. Chapters 37 and 38 narrate how during that tumultuous time Jeremiah was imprisoned.

In 586 Jerusalem was destroyed (Jer 39). Jeremiah was freed from prison and given the opportunity of going to Babylon (40, 1–6), but he declined. The final dated passages narrate events of 586–582, when civil order was collapsing and groups were making plans to leave the ruined city (40, 7—43, 7). After receiving the word of the Lord, Jeremiah counseled people to remain in Jerusalem (42, 7–17). The prophet, however, ended up in Egypt, having been forced to accompany a group trying to escape further Babylonian violence (43, 8–13).

The Biography of Jeremiah

More than any other prophet, Jeremiah made himself the message. His own life, especially his anguish over the ruin of Israel, was the palette supplying the colors of his preaching. His inner life is revealed in the very first chapter, where he wrestles with his call to be a prophet. His laments in chapters 11 to 20 are the most famous examples of his highly personal understanding of the prophetic task of proclaiming the divine word as it guides history. One can say that the events that would later happen to the people first played themselves out in Jeremiah's life, so that he could reflect on them and prepare the people for what was coming.

Jeremiah's ancestry can be traced back to Eli, the priest in charge of the sanctuary at Shiloh (1 Sm 1–4; 14, 3). King Solomon exiled Eli's

great-great-grandson, Abiathar, to Anathoth, a town three and a half miles northeast of Jerusalem (1 Kgs 2, 26). Jeremiah hailed from this town (1, 1). Jeremiah's name, like most names of the time, is a sentence name, derived from the Hebrew verbal root *rûm,* "be high, exalted, rise." It means "May Yahweh (-*iah*) exalt/raise him up" (*Jerem-*), expressing the hope that the Lord would give him honor during his life.

Politics helped forge the message of Jeremiah. As Assurbanipal, the last great Assyrian king, grew old, the empire began to disintegrate. In Jerusalem, King Josiah repudiated the Assyrian gods. To have done so earlier would have been considered treason by Assyria and would have cost him his throne. In the year that Assurbanipal died (627), civil war wracked the empire and Babylon, Assyria's ancient rival to the south, secured its independence. That same year Jeremiah received a call to prophesy (Jer 1, 1–14), and in 621 King Josiah inaugurated his great "Deuteronomic reform" (2 Kgs 22—23). The collapse of the Assyrian empire enabled him to invite the northern tribes, formed into Assyrian provinces a hundred years earlier (2 Kgs 17), to join to the kingdom of Judah. Jeremiah 30 and 31 preserve some of his preaching of this time. Jeremiah also condemned idolatry at Jerusalem (Jer 2—6). Tragically, Josiah was killed by the Egyptians in 609 (2 Kgs 23, 29f) and was eventually succeeded by his son Jehoiakim whom Jeremiah severely criticized (Jer 22, 13–19). Babylon, under Nebuchadnezzar, had become the world power in place of Assyria. When Jehoiakim revolted, the Babylonians recaptured the city, plundered it, and took many prominent Israelites into exile. Jeremiah urged the next king, Zedekiah, to refrain from joining the Egyptian party in another revolt. Weak and easily swayed, Zedekiah secretly consulted Jeremiah but took public positions against him (Jer 38). In July 586 the Babylonians stormed the city and a month later burned Jerusalem and its Temple to the ground. After the king witnessed the slaughter of his sons, the Babylonians blinded him and carted him off into oblivion (2 Kgs 25; Jer 52).

Jeremiah was treated well by the Babylonians, probably because he persistently urged Judah to submit to them. The Babylonians gave him the choice of either enjoying a palace in Babylon or remaining behind in the land. He chose the latter

(40, 1–6). When the remnant in Jerusalem rejected his advice and fled into Egypt, they dragged the prophet with them (Jer 42, 1—43, 7). There Jeremiah died, to become a tradition and a book.

The character of Jeremiah shines from every page of this extraordinary book: joyful optimism (31); honest, painful struggling with God (12, 1–5; 15, 10–21; 20, 7–18); courage in confronting kings (37); anguish over the tragic fate of Jerusalem (8, 18—9, 10); perseverance amid continuous rejection (20, 9). At times he is petulant and revengeful as his confessions show (12, 1–5; 15, 10–21; 17, 12–18; 18, 18–23; 20, 7–18).

Jeremiah responded sensitively to life and beauty, to the growth and blossoming of nature: the almond tree's first flowering in spring (1, 11); the silence of the air when the last bird has flown away (4, 25); the gurgling freshness of spring water (2, 13). Celibacy was not an easy decision, and he felt its loneliness severely (16, 1–4). Paradoxically, it bonded Jeremiah with the people in their most difficult moments of loss and so led the way to peace with God.

Stylistically, Jeremiah extended the vocabulary of prayer in Israel, contributing especially to the individual lament (more precisely, petition with extended complaint) and the argumentative questioning of God. Moses argued with God (Ex 32, 11–14). So did Jeremiah's contemporary, Habakkuk, who devoted two chapters of his prophecy to such challenges. Jeremiah's confessions, however, pushed this moment of defiance to its extreme. Job further developed the genre, demanding an audience with God to press his case (Job 13, 14; 19, 26; 31, 35–37).

Jeremiah's life spanned a tumultuous age in religion, politics, and war. It began with national independence and religious revival, and it saw the downfall of the Assyrian empire and its replacement by the Babylonian empire. The period witnessed the defeat and violent death of Josiah, the collapse of his reform, ineffective Judean kings, and the Temple's disintegration in fire and smoke. From this vantage point, one can understand Jeremiah's emotional highs and lows, admire his passion and courage, and appreciate his ability to find grounds of hope.

The Traditions That Jeremiah Used

Rather than writing a theological treatise as a modern preacher might, the prophets of Israel interpreted the traditions of their people. The people evidently knew their traditions well and could appreciate the variations and the new slants the prophets introduced. The national traditions were usually in the form of *narratives* that dealt with serious issues of national identity, found expression in *symbols* (institutions like the Temple or events like the Exodus), and included a way of living, *action*. Each prophet focused on different aspects of the national traditions. Isaiah of Jerusalem, for example, employed the traditions about Mount Zion (the site of the Temple) and about the Davidic king as the legate of the Holy One whose task was helping the people serve their Lord. In contrast, Jeremiah concentrated on the Exodus, which for him was the Lord's great act of love for Israel, which demanded a sincere response of exclusive fidelity. The Exodus was the time when Israel was faithful to the relationship (e.g., Jer 2, 1–13; cf. 31, 2–6). The Exodus also included symbols, such as the law given on Mount Sinai (9, 12; 16, 11; 31, 33) and the teaching office of Moses. The Exodus entailed action, for the people were expected to respond in faithful love to the Lord who had loved and chosen them, and they were expected as well to obey the commandments given on Sinai. A sign of how powerful the Exodus was for Jeremiah is his call, for 1, 4–10 is modeled on the call of Moses (Ex 4, 10–12). Like Moses, he resists the call of God and must have his resistance overcome by divine reassurances. There are differences, however. One is that, unlike Moses (15, 1), Jeremiah is expressly forbidden to exercise the traditional prophetic role of interceding for the people (Jer 7, 16; 11, 14) in contrast to Moses' magnificent intercession in Ex 32—34; Dt 9, 20. Another tradition important for the prophet is that of the Davidic king, which is most clearly set out in 2 Samuel 7, and widely celebrated thereafter, especially in the psalms (e.g., 2, 72, 89, etc.). As noted, Jeremiah once promoted King Josiah's reform. Even when he excoriated Josiah's royal successors, he did so with a keen sense of their dignity and responsibility as legates of the Lord. Jerusalem was rich with traditions about the grandeur of Zion as the city of the Lord and the site of the divine dwelling (e.g., Pss 46, 48, 76, 87; Is 2, 1–4; 60—62). Although Jeremiah did not employ the exalted language about Zion and the Temple that was in the tradition, he regarded Zion with awe, for it was the Lord's beloved city. But he expressly rejected blind trust in the Temple (Jer 7, 1–15; 8, 19). Though Zion was devastated and forlorn (4, 31; 26, 18; 30, 17), he promised that the people would one day return there in peace (3, 14; 31, 2–6). Such were the major traditions and symbols that Jeremiah interprets. It is obvious that in the book they were not mere items in a list of national lore, but powerful stories and symbols feeding people's imagination and stirring them to action.

How did Jeremiah interpret these venerable traditions and symbols for the sake of the people in their hour of crisis? As regards the Exodus, his early preaching gives the clearest indication: it was a time when Israel's identity was formed and they were faithful to the Lord.

> I remember the devotion of your youth,
>   how you loved me as a bride,
> Following me in the desert,
>   in a land unsown.
> Sacred to the LORD was Israel,
>   the first fruits of his harvest (2, 2–3)

Jeremiah believed that the people became corrupted when they entered the land and worshipped the local deities: "When I brought you into the garden land to eat its goodly fruits, you entered and defiled my land, you made my heritage loathsome. The priests asked not, 'Where is the LORD?' Those who dealt with the law knew me not: the shepherds rebelled against me. The prophets prophesied by Baal, and went after useless idols" (2, 7–8). Amos might indict the people for not observing specific precepts of the Mosaic law (Am 2, 4—3, 2), but Jeremiah was concerned with the quality of the relationship itself. The people's fault, he never tired of repeating, was that they corrupted the relationship and pursued other gods (2—6). His concern with the sincerity of the people's commitment to the Sinai covenant prompted him to mention again and again the inclination of the human heart to rebel against the commands of the Lord (e.g., 5, 23; 7, 24; 9, 13; 11, 8). He used the striking metaphor of the uncircumcised heart (4, 4; 9, 25). In short, Jeremiah proclaimed that the people violated the Sinai covenant. His task was not completed with this announcement, however. A pastor as well as theologian, he had the task of moving them to respond with appropriate *action,* in this case to ac-

cept the divine punishment—the Babylonian invasion—and to wait in hope for restoration in the form of a new exodus (16, 14–15; 23, 7–8; 31, 8).

He also interpreted the traditions about the Davidic king. Though critical of the kings of his time (with the exception of Josiah in 22, 15–16), Jeremiah and the Jeremiah tradition envisioned a blessed future with the Davidic king playing a positive role: "Behold, the days are coming, says the LORD, when I will raise up a righteous shoot to David; as king he shall reign and govern wisely, he shall do what is just and right in the land" (23, 5; cf. 33, 14–26). The most explicit vision of the future is the Book of Consolation in chapters 30 and 31. These chapters (apart from 30, 9) do not, however, assign a major role to the king.

Some of the traditions Jeremiah used are associated with those that had evolved in the Northern Kingdom. Among these traditions are the sermons collected in the book of Deuteronomy and the stories in the Deuteronomistic books of Joshua, Judges, 1 and 2 Samuel, and 1 and 2 Kings. By contrast, Isaiah of Jerusalem was a "southerner," attached to Jerusalem and its Temple, to the covenant with the Davidic dynasty, and to the promises granted to each of these institutions.

The Contents of the Book

On a first reading, the arrangement of material in the book of Jeremiah is like that of Isaiah and Ezekiel: oracles of doom against Israel, oracles concerning foreign nations, oracles of salvation, and historical narratives. Although the Hebrew text of Jeremiah (the basis of all modern translations) breaks this pattern by placing the oracles concerning foreign nations at the end (46—51), the more original Greek version placed the oracles concerning foreign nations after the oracles of doom against Israel (beginning in 25, 13), so that the original book followed the traditional order.

The oracles of doom against Israel are concentrated in chapters 1 through 25, though the chapters do not form a coherent whole. There is a common viewpoint in the chapters, but the individual units are quite diverse in content and style. Prose alternates with poetry. Such variety suggests that multiple authors contributed to the section, though one should not conclude simplistically that the poetry comes from Jeremiah and the prose comes from disciples or editors. For one thing, Hebrew poetry is not always sharply distinguishable from rhythmic prose, and, for another, modern translations sometimes do not print poetry in sense lines.

Chapters 26 through 34 are concerned with future salvation: 26 through 29 deal with true and false prophets, and 30 through 34 with future salvation. Chapters 35 through 45, all in prose, narrate the sufferings of Jeremiah in the final period of his ministry. The oracles concerning the foreign nations, 46 through 51, are mostly in poetic form. Chapter 52, drawn from 2 Kings 24, 18–25, concludes the book. The following paragraphs examine the sections in more detail.

The commission narrative in 1, 4–10, is supplemented by two visions followed by a summary of Jeremiah's main themes (1, 14–19). Chapters 2 through 6 contain separate oracles largely concerned with the Northern Kingdom and the threat of "the enemy from the north" (1, 13–15; 4, 6; 6, 1.22), the prophet's designation for an invader that was later identified explicitly with Babylon. Chapter 2 is a covenant lawsuit indicting Israel for its lack of love and loyalty to its Lord, and chapter 3 follows with insistent demands for conversion (Hebrew *shub,* literally "turn," occurs ten times). Chapters 4 through 6 are a good sample of Jeremiah's preaching. Though some destruction has already taken place, the prophet does not dwell on it as if there is no future. The invasion of Babylon is regarded both as an inevitable historical event *and* a divine judgment on sin. Chapters 2 and 3 specify Israel's sin as apostasy and idolatry, whereas chapters 4 through 6 specify the sin as social injustice and the corruption of leadership.

These threats and anticipatory laments are interrupted by 7, 1—8, 3, the Temple sermon and related oracles, but reappear in 8, 4—10, 25 with an even greater emphasis on lament. Though several voices interact in the chapters—God, the prophet, the people mourning or praising—a recurring process is discernible, which proceeds from sin to judgment to lament. The people's sin is uncovered; divine judgment will punish it; lament (prayer emphasizing distress) attempts to assuage God's anger, and bring respite and salvation. Chapter 10 attacks other gods and their

images. Though using new images and different perspectives, these chapters continue the themes of chapters 2 through 6: the enemy from the north, the insistence on repentance ("turning"), the people's malicious hearts, the failure of the leaders, and the prophets who speak falsely in God's name.

The long section, Jer 11, 1—20, 18 is a collection of diverse material: laments, oracles, and prophetic actions. Dominating the section are Jeremiah's seven "confessions" (actually petitions making special use of complaints and laments): 11, 18–23; 12, 1–6; 15, 10–21; 17, 14–18; 18, 18–23; and 20, 7–13; 20, 14–18. The usual structure has two parts, the prophet's complaint and the Lord's response. How these laments are to be understood is debated. They are certainly related to the public presentation of the prophet, elaborating the original commission (1) and vindicating the divine judgments in 2 through 10 by portraying Jeremiah as an example of one who has suffered *and* been upheld by God's mercy. Judgment in the Bible, it must be noted, is a process involving punishment of the wicked and upholding of the righteous. It is a synonym for punishment. Also found within the section are divine oracles (including divine lament, 12, 7–13), prophetic speeches, and prophetic actions. These prophetic actions (13, 1–14; 16, 1–13; 17, 19–27; 18, 1–12; 19, 1—20, 6) are interspersed like the "confessions" throughout the section. In this section the earlier emphasis on repentance lessens, and more attention is paid to the negative side of judgment. The section ends with the most despairing of Jeremiah's laments (20, 14–18), which demonstrates the prophet's sincerity and also provides a model of the national suffering and vindication awaiting the whole nation.

The next section, Jeremiah 21, 1—25, 38 is concerned with the leadership of Judah at the time of the fall of the Kingdom of Judah. The prophet inveighs against King Jehoiakim for extravagant building projects at the expense of the poor (22, 13–19) and later dashes royal hopes by declaring that King Zedekiah will fall into the hands of the Babylonians (21, 1–10). False prophets, a particular problem for Jeremiah, come in for severe attack (23, 9–40). Chapter 25 has a dual role in the book, concluding the first part of the book by the summary in 25, 1–14, and pointing forward in verse 13 to the scroll Jeremiah dictated to Baruch in chapter 36, "Against that land I will fulfill all the words I have spoken against it (all that is written in this scroll [NAB "book"], which Jeremiah prophesied against all the nations" (25, 13).

Jeremiah 26, 1—36, 32 consist of blocks of material (all are in prose except 30 and 31) describing scenes of conflict or comfort. Chapter 26 is a version of the Temple sermon in chapter 7, reiterating the Jeremianic theme that the only way forward is to allow full freedom to the Lord's work of judgment. It serves as prologue both to Jeremiah's attacks on the foolish utopian schemes detailed in 27 through 29 and to his invitation to genuine hope beyond judgment in 30 through 33. Like chapter 36, chapter 26 is set in the opening years of Jehoiakim's reign (609); it is probable that these two chapters form a frame around the section in between. Chapter 34, on the conditional freeing of slaves, provides a negative contrast to the full hearted following of the Lord by the austere Rechabites in chapter 35. Chapter 36 brings the section to a close, for King Jehoiakim, attempting to destroy the scroll of Jeremiah (probably much of chapters 2 through 25), unwittingly insures that the words of the scroll will continue to guide the people even after Jeremiah himself leaves the scene.

A good title for chapters 37 through 45 is "The last days of Judah and the last days of the prophet." The chaos just before and during the final catastrophe is narrated in 37 through 39. The desperation of the people and King Zedekiah is reflected in his alternately consulting and imprisoning Jeremiah, who nonetheless insists on only one counsel: do not resist, for it is by divine will that the Babylonians will triumph. Chapters 40 and 41 tell of the political changes as Babylon takes over the governance of the land. Jeremiah's counsel to people fearful of further Babylonian assaults that they should remain in the land is ignored. A frightened group of Judeans takes him to Egypt, where his words fall on deaf ears (42—43). The final chapter (45) in the section promises that Baruch will survive, a pointer to the preservation of Jeremiah's words for future generations.

Oracles concerning the nations close the book in the Hebrew version (46—51). Such words are expected, for Jeremiah had been appointed as a prophet to the nations (1, 5). Various countries are named and come under critique: Egypt, Philistia, Moab, Ammon, Edom, Damascus, Arabian tribes, Elam, and, most extensively, Babylon. Some are long, others are short; some are bitter, others are not; and a few even promise restoration after the judgment. Reasons for the punishment are given for some but not for all. One can surmise that at least some of these nations violated treaties with Israel and Judah, or inflicted grave injuries upon them. Or perhaps Jeremiah simply assumed that the great judgment operative in Judah and Jerusalem must inevitably affect its near neighbors as well.

Chapter 52, a slightly adapted version of 2 Kings 24, 18—25, 30, summarizes the Babylonian destruction of the Temple and of Jerusalem, concluding importantly with the release from prison of King Jehoiachin, the Davidic scion. Jeremiah 23, 5–8, had spoken about raising up a righteous branch for the house of David, and the editor wants the book to end on a hopeful note.

The Composition of the Book

The book of Jeremiah poses severe difficulties for modern readers. A brief, passionate poetic oracle may be followed by a prose sermon in the style of Deuteronomy, and then by a biographical account in the style of the book of Kings. Some passages are pure doom, whereas others speak confidently of restoration and rebuilding. What kind of editorial process produced a book of such diversity? Scholars have given much thought to the question, and their answers show a considerable range. For example, William L. Holladay's detailed two-volume commentary (1986, 1989) believes that much of the material can be dated to specific moments in Jeremiah's life, whereas Robert P. Carroll (1986) regards the book not as a collection of Jeremiah's words and deeds but as a stream of tradition to which a variety of authors contributed, including postexilic authors wishing to legitimate the rebuilding of Jerusalem and Judah. Because the evidence is sparse, scholarly unanimity on the composition of the book is unlikely. Nonetheless, it is possible to give some account of the problem of the sources and their use in the book.

Scholars generally single out three categories of material in the book. The first category is the "authentic words" *by* Jeremiah, which are found largely in the poetic traditions preserved in chapters 1 through 25. The second is the historical narratives *about* Jeremiah, for example, 19, 1—20, 6; 26; 28; 36; 37—38; 40, 7—43, 12. These sections are usually attributed to Jeremiah's secretary, Baruch, who, according to chapter 36, wrote down the preaching of the prophet. The third category is the "Deuteronomic" sections, sections that resemble the sermons found in the book of Deuteronomy, for example, 7, 1—8, 3; 11, 1–14; 18, 1–12; and most of chapters 32 through 35. Scholars disagree whether the sermons and other prose pieces are based directly on Jeremiah's oral preaching (perhaps even written down by the prophet) or whether they are free compositions written long afterwards by others.

The first and the third category deserve comment. Regarding the first category, Jeremiah's alleged authentic words, it is very difficult, if not impossible, to get at the very words of *any* ancient teacher, especially in the ancient Near East. Teachers stood within a circle of disciples who carefully pondered and then repeated, sometimes with variants and illustrations, their master's teachings. "Authentic" and "inauthentic" mean something entirely different in that world than in ours. Poetic form as such is no guarantee that Jeremiah is the author, nor does prose form prove he is not. It is likely that most of the poetic oracles in chapters 1 through 25 are from Jeremiah; their reiterated themes and consistent viewpoint expressed in ever fresh images and new angles suggest as much. It must be admitted, however, that followers of Jeremiah might have learned the style, and that some of their work, "elaborations of the work of the master" they would have called it, made it into the final collection. The third category, the "Deuteronomic sermon," requires more precision. "Deuteronomic" is used of both the book of Deuteronomy (especially of its law-based sermons in 5—26) and also of the Deuteronomic History (Deuteronomy–Kings). Both works contain preaching typical of the period prior to and during the exile (late seventh to sixth centuries BC). It is not surprising that the sermons in Jeremiah resemble other sermons written at the same period. The inconsistencies in the oracles and the sermons can be explained by the different demands of the genre and the different periods in which they were written. That some sections offer hope and others speak unrelievedly of doom is not necessarily a sign of mul-

tiple authorship. Jeremiah, like other prophets, regarded divine judgment as a *process* that established justice on earth. Destruction was not its goal but the means to a just and peaceful world. For Jeremiah, doom was not the last word of God. Though he saw the Babylonian invasion with all of its horrors as inevitable, it was not for him ultimate. For this reason, oracles of salvation in the book should not too quickly be judged "late" or "secondary."

There are three sources that do not fit into the categories mentioned above and deserve special treatment: the laments in chapters 11 through 20, the Book of Consolation in 30 and 31, and the oracles concerning foreign nations in 46 through 51.

1. The personal laments (confessions) of Jeremiah with their divine responses are found in 11, 18–23; 12, 1–6; 15, 10–21; 17, 14–18; 18, 18–23; 20, 7–13; and 20, 14–18. Some scholars have regarded them primarily as autobiographical, that is, the record of the inner anguish of a gifted and sensitive soul. Such a judgment does not explain, however, why the record of purely private grief would end up in a book dealing with national issues. The confessions are rather petitions of a beleaguered prophet employing the lament style of the Psalter and Job. Suffering under the burden of a prophetic commission he cannot renounce, Jeremiah confronts evil embodied in enemies who seek to silence, imprison, and even kill him. He struggles to understand how God could have left him alone to face enemies of the prophetic word. What is especially striking is not that Jeremiah composed and used these laments (every human being at some point probably uses such prayers), but that he made them public. They are part of his preaching and have a dual purpose. First, Jeremiah wants to differentiate himself from false prophets by showing that his word does not come from himself but from God. Why would he ever put himself in such danger and anguish by speaking an unpopular message? Second, he himself is an example of one who is suffering divine judgment. His anguish will later be every Israelite's, and he wants to show the people how to suffer faithfully and not lose hope that the destruction is only the first stage in the process of divine judgment that will end in redemption. His laments are interspersed throughout the section chapters 11 through 20

and are perhaps meant to complement the similarly interspersed prophetic actions described in 13, 1–14; 16, 1–13; 17, 19–27; 18, 1–12; 19, 1—20, 6. Both lament and prophetic gesture illustrate the process of divine judgment.

2. Chapters 30 and 31 are known as the Book of Consolation, and the same theme of restoration is continued in chapter 32 (Jeremiah's purchase of a field in view of eventual return) and chapter 33 (promises of restoration). As already suggested, 30 and 31 were originally addressed to the Northern Kingdom of Israel during the reign of Josiah, which in 722 had come under Assyrian rule, to assure her that she still had a future as part of the chosen people. References assuring Judah that she too could look forward to a similar bright future have been added (e.g., "Israel *and Judah*" in 30, 1.4). Though some scholars deny chapters to Jeremiah because of their alleged Deuteronomic phraseology and theology, it is hard to understand it as a purely sixth-century exilic piece. Why, for example, would an exilic author use chiefly Ephraimite (northern) traditions and appeal to the old Northern Kingdom rather than to *all* Israel, north and south? The adjective "Deuteronomic" does not necessarily imply a sixth century date. The most satisfying explanation is that the core (31, 2–22.31–34) was written by the young Jeremiah to support Josiah's restoration of the old Davidic empire by inviting people of the former Assyrian provinces in the north (2 Kgs 23, 19; 2 Chr 35, 17). Jeremiah 31, 31–33 is the famous reference to the new covenant: "I will make a new covenant with the house of Israel and the house of Judah . . . not be like the covenant I made with their fathers the day I took them by the hand to lead them forth from the land of Egypt. . . . I will place my law within them, and write it upon their hearts; I will be their God, and they shall be my people." It appears to be related to the discovery of the ancient law book in the Temple in 622. With the death of Josiah and collapse of his reform, Jeremiah applied the promises to the far greater dispersion of the sixth-century exile in the belief that God's words must ultimately prove true.

3. Oracles concerning or "against" (the Hebrew preposition has both meanings) foreign nations occur also in Isaiah, Ezekiel, and Amos. In the Greek version of Jeremiah, these oracles appear in the middle of the book (as they do in Isaiah and Ezekiel), following immediately after 25, 13. Some scholars believe collections of oracles against foreign nations were in general circulation, and that editors of Jeremiah simply selected preexisting material to insert into the book. The oracles in chapters 46 through 51, however, are compatible with Jeremiah's views, for example, the oracles concerning Egypt in chapter 46. Although the hostile pronouncements against Babylon in chapters 50 and 51 differ sharply from the more positive view of Babylon elsewhere in the book, it is possible that Jeremiah regarded Babylon in the same way as Isaiah regarded Assyria: as the Lord's instrument of judgment that would itself fall under judgment because of its excesses. There is, however, material found also in other prophets, for example, passages about Moab in 48, 1–47 has strong similarities to Isaiah 15—16, and the passage about Edom in Jeremiah 49, 7–22 is similar to Obadiah 1—10. Collections of poems against Israel's enemies might have been drawn upon to complete the book.

The Message of Jeremiah

Jeremiah's outlook is far reaching, extending even to the nations as one might expect from his commission, "before you were born I dedicated you, a prophet to the nations I appointed you" (1, 5). He is concerned with a world view that finds expression in story, symbol, and action. The worldview is not static or fixed, however, for it is profoundly shaped by events, the movement of history, which the prophets believe is directed by the Lord. To the prophets is revealed the significance of that history for Israel. To Jeremiah in particular was revealed the significance for Israel of the decline of the Assyrian Empire and the rise of the Babylonian, as well as the significance of the inability of the people and their leaders to reform their lives and respond to the Lord. Many prophets, like Hananiah (28), assured the people that the hostile empires were a passing phase, and that God would rescue them or bring them back from Babylon after a very short stay. No change in the attitude of the people was called for. Jeremiah knew better. Rejecting such false comfort, he was convinced that the people had to go through a terrible process of judgment before there could be any restoration. He believed the false prophets had dreamed up their soothing message. He asked them the crucial question:

"Who has stood in the council of the LORD, to see him and to hear his word? Who has heeded his word, so as to announce it?" (23, 18). The answer: only Jeremiah. Why would he invent a message that cost him such suffering?

Jeremiah's message cannot be separated from the traditions that he chooses to retell and interpret. The Exodus in all its breadth was the tradition that most captivated the prophet's imagination and shaped his message. He viewed it not as a wonder of the past but as a divine deed that was still powerful. He had a tremendous trust in the Exodus as the founding event of Israel. In the Exodus, God established the community by freeing them from Egyptian tyranny and forming them into a new people. This dual action, liberation and formation, showed the Lord's love and invited in turn an affectionate and exclusive response from the people. Once upon a time, in the early days of Josiah, Jeremiah expected the king's reform to purify hearts and engender the love and devotion of the original Exodus. Events taught Jeremiah something else: first there must be divine judgment, a process that will punish and, he hoped, purify the people so that God and people could enter into that relationship afresh. Judgment would be accomplished within history, by Babylon (here he was taught by Isaiah's view of Assyria), and only after purgation could restoration take place. Meanwhile, the prophet must make the people understand that the enemy from the north is inevitable; it is the Lord's instrument. The people must accept the Babylonian incursion from the Lord's hand, and not deceive themselves by entering into anti-Babylonian alliances or by credulous acceptance of prophets who proclaimed "Peace! Peace!" Jeremiah's own struggle with this hard divine decision could serve as a model for the people as they face this bitter process.

Characteristic of Jeremiah is his fidelity to the Exodus of which the covenant is an essential component. Despite the bitterness of his message about the immediate prospects of the people, his view of the future is positive because it is based upon the Exodus as an enduring event done by the Lord.

The New Covenant

Though a few modern scholars separate the Exodus from Egypt from the giving of the law at Sinai, Jeremiah regarded them as constituting one great event. When he spoke about the covenant, he implied that God had first initiated the relationship in the liberation from Egyptian bondage. The new covenant spoken of in the Book of Consolation (chapters 30 and 31) is shorthand for the entire Exodus. As already suggested, the chapters seem to have been originally addressed to people of the former Northern Kingdom of Israel and was adapted to the inhabitants of Jerusalem within the Southern Kingdom of Judah. The covenant had been annulled by the people's apostasy (11, 1–17; cf. 2 Kgs 17, 1–24; 22, 10–15). Jeremiah knew, however, that the Mosaic covenant, immediately after being mediated by Moses at Mount Sinai, had been broken when the people worshipped the golden calf (Ex 32). Yet God forgave even that apostasy after Moses' strenuous intercession: "If I find favor with you, O LORD, do come along in our company. . . . 'Here, then,' said the LORD 'is the covenant I will make. Before the eyes of all your people I will work such marvels as have never been wrought in any nation anywhere on earth, so that this people among whom you live may see how awe-inspiring are the deeds which I, the LORD, will do at your side' " (Ex 34, 9–10).

This forgiveness of the people in the Sinai wilderness can be considered a renewed or "new" covenant, and it served as a precedent for Jeremiah's new covenant. Aware that in his own day the people had again rejected the covenant, Jeremiah proclaimed that the people could keep it only if God changed their hearts. In the Bible, the heart is the organ of memory and decision rather than the organ of affections. The new heart is a metaphor for a fresh initiative by God to strengthen the will of the people. In mentioning the heart, Jeremiah was not eliminating teachers and preachers; otherwise, he himself would have no right to preach! But he was emphasizing God's role in helping human beings to respond to the divine word.

It is important to remember two things about the new covenant. First, the new covenant does not replace the old. Old does not mean worn out and ready to be discarded; it means venerable yet capable of being renewed, like the Sinai covenant after the apostasy of the golden calf (Ex 32—34). Second, the exiled people of Judah were included in Jeremiah's new covenant, for they returned to the land and observed once again their ancient covenant with the Lord. One need not hold that the new covenant of the New Testament invalidates the old covenant in the Old Testament. In his first epistle John paradoxically plays with the idea of the old and the new:

> Beloved, I am writing no new commandment to you but an old commandment that you had from the beginning. The old commandment is the word that you have heard. And yet I do write a new commandment to you, which holds true in him and among you, for the darkness is passing away, and the true light is already shining. (1 Jn 2, 7–8)

The old became new in a distinctive way within the "coming days" through the death and resurrection of Jesus (Rom 1, 1–4; 1 Cor 15, 12–28). This new covenant is commemorated in each Eucharist (Lk 22, 20; 1 Cor 11, 25). The "newness" of the new covenant appears ever more clearly in one of the final New Testament compositions, Hebrews 11, 7–13. Finally, Vatican II's document on the Church turned to this passage as a biblical foundation for rediscovering a communitarian model of the Church as the "people of God" (*Lumen Gentium*, n. 9).

Sin and Atonement

The prophet declares realistically that sin inevitably brings its own punishment. If the people "went after empty idols, [then they] became empty themselves" (Jer 2, 5), and again in the same chapter: "Your own wickedness chastises you" (2, 19). One is transformed for good or bad into that which one desires.

Another aspect of Jeremiah's theology of sin and atonement becomes clear through the Hebrew verb for "chastise": *yasar*. It stresses the purifying and strengthening results of punishment as well as God's compassion:

> I hear, I hear Ephraim pleading:
> You chastised me, and I am chastened; . . .
> If you allow me, I will return,
> . . .
> Is Ephraim not . . .
> the child in whom I delight? . . . .
> My heart stirs for him,
> I must show him mercy, says the LORD (31, 18.20).

This sequence of sin-suffering-repentance-forgiveness-new life is also found in the Deu-

teronomistic History (Deuteronomy to 2 Kings); Judges 2, 10—23 is a particularly good example. Jeremiah develops the tradition. In the movement from sin to suffering, Jeremiah was never far removed from the agony of the people Israel (3, 19–25). In this way he understood his call to celibacy (16, 1–4). Yet, as another passage points out, hope is always stirring within the barren earth (17, 5–8).

Faith and Prayer

Jeremiah is continually laying bare the anguish of his heart. Nowhere, however, does he wrestle with God so fiercely as in his confessions: 12, 1–5; 15, 10–21; 17, 12–18; 18, 18–23; 20, 7–18. Here Jeremiah confronts God with defiant questions, yet stands on the solid rock of faith in God's fidelity and concern. In 12, 1 Jeremiah begins with faith but immediately proceeds to question that faith. Translated literally, verse 1 sternly speaks its message:

> You [are] just, LORD! Yet I must argue my case publicly against you. Why does the way of the godless prosper?

God never answers Jeremiah's question but rather expects his faith to become even sturdier. A literal translation of 12, 5 reads:

> If running against human beings wearies you,
>   how will you race against horses?
> If you are secure only in a land of peace,
>   what will you do in the thickets of the Jordan?

Symbolically Jeremiah is admitting that things must get worse before they can get better. He will in any case plunge ahead.

True and False Prophecy

Jeremiah defies the conventional expectations of an authentic prophet. First of all, he seldom if ever claims this title; editors or biographers bestow it upon him. Another proof for an authentic prophet's mission from the Lord was to be found in the fulfillment of prophecy (Dt 18, 21–22; Jer 28). Jeremiah's prediction about the return of the northern tribes in 31, 1–20 seems never to have come true in the literal sense initially intended by the prophet, but only in its extended form as applied to all the Babylonian exiles. Another kind of fulfillment of the same passage was Matthew 2, 16–23, which applies Jeremiah's words to the return of Jesus to Palestine after the tyrant no longer threatens the child.

In chapter 23, Jeremiah stressed moral integrity as a sign of true prophecy. He lashed out angrily:

> Concerning the prophets:
> My heart within me is broken,
> my bones all tremble . . .
> Because of the LORD,
> because of his holy words.
> With adulterers the land is filled . . .
> Both prophet and priest are godless!
> In my very house I find their wickedness,
> says the LORD. (23, 9–11)

In calling the priests and temple prophets adulterers, Jeremiah is speaking metaphorically; in their ministry they have betrayed the supreme and intimate love of God. To justify their own halfhearted and wicked ways, they failed to warn the people, who were guilty of injustices and sensuality.

Yet personal faultlessness is a difficult criterion of true prophecy. Few if any prophets were without faults. For instance, someone might use against Jeremiah and Amos their own bitter, revengeful language (Am 4, 1; Jer 18, 19–23; 22, 18f).

Some may think that prophets are genuine if they carry within themselves a strong conviction of their divine call. Against this credential is Jeremiah's own indecisiveness, waiting "some time" (28, 12) or "ten days" (42, 7) before replying. His confessions reveal still more trepidation and uncertainty. Still another credential, advanced for true prophecy, comes from community acceptance. Against this condition we think at once of Jesus' remark: "no prophet is accepted in his own native place" (Lk 4, 24). Jeremiah is the classic example of the rejected prophet.

Judgment and Restoration

One of the enduring contributions of Jeremiah is his conviction that Israel must undergo a kind of death before it can be given new life by God. Evidently he once thought that royal reforms could remake the people, but after viewing the warlike Babylonians, the cowardly kings after Josiah, and the moral failings of his people, he came to the conclusion that destruction was inevitable. Believing in the Lord's control of God of history,

his justice, and his love for Israel, Jeremiah concluded that the divine judgment about to fall, however horrible, would in fact bring about divine justice. The people Israel had nothing ultimately to fear from their Lord who even in judgment was liberating and forming them, as in the Exodus of old. Their "death," accepted with trust, would lead to their "resurrection." Just as Jeremiah continued to believe in the Lord who plunged him into a furnace of suffering in the hope he would rescue him from it, so the people must trust in their just and loving Lord. Judgment was a process that involved more than punishment; it brought restoration of a purified people and made possible a new covenant.

The Text of Jeremiah and Its Transmission

There are two versions of the book of Jeremiah. The Masoretic Text (in Hebrew), used by Jews and Christians today and the basis of all modern translations, is one-eighth longer and has a different organization (after Jer 25, 13a) than the Greek (Septuagint) version. The oracles concerning the nations appear at the end of the Hebrew text in chapters 46 through 51, and in the Greek in the middle in chapters 26 through 31. Prior to the discovery of the Dead Sea Scrolls, it was generally thought that the Hebrew text was original and that the Greek text was an abbreviation. Study of the Dead Sea Scrolls caused a change in that judgment, for among the many biblical manuscripts (dating from the third century BC to the first century AD) were four Hebrew fragments of Jeremiah matching the Greek textual tradition rather than the Hebrew. As a result, scholars now regard the Greek text as a translation of a Hebrew text current in Egypt; the translation was made sometime between 250 and 150 BC. The Greek version seems to preserve the first edition of the book, whereas the Masoretic Text preserves the second edition. Changes in the second edition include duplications (e.g., 8, 10b–13 duplicates 6, 13–15), additions (e.g., 33, 14–26 and 51, 44b–49a), and expansions of proper names and formulas. These facts suggest many stages in the composition of the book. Evidently not only Jeremiah the man but also Jeremiah the book underwent a long and difficult journey before arriving at the present authoritative Scripture.

The Influence of Jeremiah on Other Biblical Literature and the New Testament

In the second century BC, Daniel 9, 22–27 reinterpreted Jeremiah's famous prediction that the exile would last seventy years (Jer 25, 11–12; 29, 10); it would last seventy weeks of years, that is, seven times seventy. The apocryphal Letter of Jeremiah of the second century BC ridicules divine images, developing biblical attacks (cf. Dt 4, 27–28; Is 40, 18–20, and Jer 10, 2–16). Rabbinic literature remembers Jeremiah as the great prophet of doom. The Talmud evidently places Jeremiah at the beginning of the Latter Prophets.

Christian tradition regards Jeremiah as a type and model of Jesus Christ. Isaiah announces the promised Messiah by words, so to speak, and Jeremiah by his life. So many details parallel the life and ministry of Jesus that one is not surprised to hear the answer to Jesus' question, "Who do people say that the Son of Man is?" as, "Some say John the Baptist, others Elijah, still others Jeremiah or one of the prophets" (Mt 16, 14). With Jeremiah it was more a matter of works than words. God was offering in Jeremiah a model for imitation rather than a message for study. The same event in Jeremiah's career—for instance, called from the mother's womb—applies to others besides Jesus, in this case the suffering servant of Isaiah (Is 49, 1) and John the Baptist (Lk 1, 39–45). Rather, both Jesus and especially the evangelists turned continually to Jeremiah to contemplate and illuminate the mystery of where God was directing their life and ministry. Jeremiah's prophecy is a rich source for appreciating Jesus' words and actions.

The following points of resemblance, by no means exhaustive, show up between Jesus and Jeremiah: (a) confirmed in grace from the mother's womb (Jer 1, 5; Lk 1, 26–38); (b) unmarried (Jer 16, l–3); (c) hounded by hometown citizens and family (Jer 12, 6; Lk 4, 24.29); (d) weeping over Jerusalem (Jer 8, 23; Lk 19, 41); (e) speaking of the Temple as "a den of thieves" (Jer 7, 11; Mt 21, 13); (f) consulted secretly and fearfully by those who believe (Jer 37, 17; Jn 3, 1–21); (g) foreseeing a new covenant (Jer 31, 31–34; Lk 22, 20).

FURTHER READING

Basic Commentaries

Achtemeier, Elizabeth. *Jeremiah*. Knox Preaching Guides. Atlanta: John Knox Press, 1987. Background and summaries lead up to solid application.

Boadt, Lawrence, C.S.P. *Jeremiah 1–25; Jeremiah 26–52; Habakkuk; Zephaniah; Nahum*. Old Testament Message. 2 vols. Wilmington, DE: Michael Glazier Inc., 1982. Well-balanced treatment and does not neglect the religious value of Jeremiah.

Brueggemann, Walter. *A Commentary on Jeremiah: Exile and Homecoming*. 2 vols. Grand Rapids: Eerdmans, 1998. A fine commentary, accessible, with theological reflection and preaching application.

Clements, Ronald. *Jeremiah*. Interpretation. Atlanta: John Knox, 1988. Emphasis on the theological and homiletic use of Jeremiah.

Couturier, Guy, C.S.C. *Jeremiah*. New Jerome Biblical Commentary, 265–304. Englewood Cliffs, NJ: Prentice Hall, 1990. Well-balanced treatment.

Miller, Patrick D. *The Book of Jeremiah*. New Interpreter's Bible 1, 555–926. Nashville: Abingdon Press, 2001. Up to date. A fine blend of historical, literary, and theological approaches.

Nicholson, E. W. *Jeremiah 1–25; Jeremiah 26–52*. 2 vols. Cambridge Bible Commentary on the New English Bible. New York: Cambridge University Press, 1973, 1975. Clear, short explanations, especially of historical, geographical details.

O'Connor, Kathleen. *Jeremiah*. Oxford Bible Dictionary, 487–528. New York: Oxford University Press, 2001. Detailed, yet accessible.

Overholt, Thomas. *Jeremiah*. HarperCollins Bible Commentary, 538–76. San Francisco: Harper, 2000. Brief, scholarly, yet accessible.

Advanced commentaries

Carroll, Robert P. *Jeremiah*. Old Testament Library. Philadelphia: Westminster, 1986. Skeptical that this book contains the words and deeds of Jeremiah; rather it was an ever-growing "stream of tradition."

Holladay, William L. *Jeremiah 1; Jeremiah 2*. Hermeneia. Philadelphia: Fortress, 1989. Detailed and technical, interested in locating the prophecy in the life of the prophet.

Keown, Gerald L., Pamela J. Scalise, and Thomas J. Smothers. *Jeremiah 26–52*. Word Bible Commentary 27. Dallas: Word, 1995. Judicious and thorough.

Lundbom, Jack R. *Jeremiah 1–20*. Anchor Bible 21A. New York: Doubleday, 1999. Technical treatment, with a special interest in literary and rhetoric matters.

McKane, William L. *A Critical and Exegetical Commentary on Jeremiah*. 2 vols. International Critical Commentary. Edinburgh: T & T Clark, 1986. Technical, strong on textual and philological matters.

LAMENTATIONS

[see pages 1075–83 of the Old Testament]

The book of Lamentations consists of five prayers of complaint, mourning before God the destruction of Jerusalem and the Temple. Since Jerusalem and the Temple were destroyed by the Babylonians in 586 and a new one constructed in 520, the prayers must have been composed in the sixty-six-year period when the Temple lay in ruins. The confusion and anguish of the prayers suggest they were composed shortly after the destruction in 586. In form, the poems are acrostic, that is, the initial word of each verse or each stanza begins with a successive letter of the twenty-two-letter Hebrew alphabet. Each poem, therefore, has either twenty-two stanzas or twenty-two verses. Although the fifth poem does not use initial letters of the alphabet, it also has twenty-two verses and so, in a broad sense, is acrostic. In the Hebrew Bible, the poems are called by the opening word of the first line of the first poem, *'ekah*, "*How* lonely she is now, the once crowded city!*" In antiquity, literary works were often known by their opening words. Jewish tradition follows this ancient usage. In the Christian Bible, "Lamentations" is the title of the work; it is the English translation of the Septuagint (Greek) title *threnoi*, "lamentations."

First-time readers may find the five poems dreary, repetitive, and far too comfortable with the role of victim. Closer study reveals subtle dramatic movement within each poem and between the poems; a range of emotions is skillfully explored and expressed—grief, anger, something near despair, acceptance, glimmers of hope and joy, and an indomitable will to carry on. Though many people today tend to exclude such "negative" feelings from their prayers and thoughts, Lamentations considers such feelings an inescapable part of life and makes them the stuff of prayer.

Historical Background

In the two centuries before the Lamentations were composed, Israel was in political decline, and its religious and national traditions in crisis. For those two centuries (from ca. 738 to 539 BC), with the exception of a brief resurgence under King Josiah during 627–609, the people lived under the control of two great empires, Assyria and then Babylon. The early sixth century, when Lamentations was written, was particularly difficult. That period witnessed Babylonian pressure, uncertain Judean leadership, and ultimately the destruction of Jerusalem and the Temple and large deportations to Babylonia. The countryside was devastated, and the economy destroyed. Such dismal conditions called into question the national traditions that had provided earlier generations with meaning and helped them make sense of everyday life. The traditions proclaimed that Israel's God was supreme over all gods and nations and had liberated Israel from the Egyptians and given them the land of Canaan; the Lord made the land fertile and protected the people from their enemies. For most of the two centuries prior to Lamentations, the nation's experience had been otherwise. The nation's brilliant traditions seemed to mock the nation's bitter experience. The people were not liberated; their land belonged to others; many of them had been shipped off to servitude in Babylon. Where was the Lord in all this? What could the people hope for? Though the immediate cause of the composition of Lamentations was the destruction of the city and Temple in 586, the poems actually mourn a much longer period of divine absence and national humiliation.

Destruction of the Temple dealt a terrible blow to the ordinary way in which public prayer was carried out. Public prayer texts such as the psalms presupposed that the Lord chose to dwell on Zion (Jerusalem) and there receive the praise and petitions of Israel. Zion was the privileged place of encounter between Yahweh and the holy people. Through its elaborate ceremonies the Lord received the honor due the sovereign of the entire universe. The reform measures of King Josiah (622–609; see 2 Kgs 22—23 and 2 Chr 34—35) served to reinforce the position of Jerusalem as the center of Israelite worship. Among the hopes connected to Zion was that the nations would make pilgrimages to Zion to hear the Lord's word and offer their gifts to the supreme God (Is 2, 1–4; 60—61; 66, 18–21). The Temple deeply influenced the prayer of Israelites no matter where they lived. Even exiles customarily prayed in the direction of the Temple (1 Kgs 8, 35; Dn 6, 10; 1 Esd 4, 58) in order to enter into its prayer rhythms. Texts such as the psalms allowed individual Israelites to align their own prayer to the worship conducted in the Temple.

Moderns might assume that the Lord can appear equally at any time and any place, but ancients thought otherwise. Though Yahweh, the God of Israel, might appear and act in other places, Zion was his preeminent place of disclosure and encounter with Israel; only here was Israel fully "before the Lord." Here the Lord was enthroned upon the cherubim (Pss 80, 1; 99, 1) and "judged," that is, governed Israel and the nations. Zion was the goal of the three annual feasts of pilgrimage. Though the universe might totter, Zion, it was believed, would remain unshaken and secure (Pss 46, 2–3; 48, 4–8; 76, 3). The "Songs of Zion" (Pss 46, 48, 76, 84, 87, 121, 122) celebrated the city as the site of the victory over primordial enemies and the residence of Yahweh, patron of the Davidic dynasty. But with the Temple lying in ruins, Israelite worship changed profoundly. Lamentations attempted to find new modes of prayer—prayer in time of destruction.

Genre of the Book

Two traditional genres (or types) of prayer influenced the book of Lamentations. One was the communal lament found in the Psalter, and the other was the city lament, common in Mesopotamian religious literature and found here and there in the Bible. It is instructive to compare Lamentations to the community laments that also mourn a national loss. For example, Psalm 89 laments the defeat of the Davidic king, Psalms 44, 77, and 80 the loss of sacred territory, and Psalm 74 the destruction of the Temple. A major difference between the Psalms and Lamentations is that the lament psalms *remember,* that is, narrate in words (and perhaps in ritual actions) the divine act that installed the king, gave the land, or built the Temple in order that the Lord will renew the original act. With confidence in God's great acts of the past, they pray for God to renew those powerful acts now. Lamentations, on the other hand, does not *remember* in that sense; the poems do not work from the same confidence in the national traditions. Lamentations rather chooses the lyrical option; the poems explore the human emotions

evoked by the catastrophe—the sorrow, guilt, anger, and hope—and bring them before the Lord. Just as the Psalms made it possible for every Israelite, even those far from Jerusalem, to participate in the worship carried out in the Temple, so Lamentations made it possible for all Israelites during the exile to explore and express their grief, anger, and hope concerning the Temple and the God who once dwelt there. Today, the book makes it possible for all Christians and Jews to explore and express their own sorrows and forms of exile.

It is important to underline that Lamentations are prayers asking God to do something for Israel. They are not merely expressions of personal and communal misery. Even though their tone is disappointed and often bitter, they believe that the Lord is behind the present distress of the community and has the power to turn and bring healing and prosperity. The strategy of the prayers is to remind God of his failure to carry out his promises to protect the people and make them prosperous. The people's wretched state advertises the ineffectiveness and callousness of their deity. Thus, they proclaim that they are miserable and abandoned in the hope (however dim) that God will finally "get it" and come to their rescue. The prayers equivalently ask the Lord to turn from his callous ways.

Though it shares features with the communal lament found in the Psalter, Lamentations has the strongest affinity with the city lament, a literary genre found in ancient Mesopotamia (modern Iraq). Temples were composed of mudbrick and other nondurable materials and had frequently to be restored and rebuilt. In order to placate the gods of the city temples for the destruction that preceded the rebuilding, city laments were recited. They described the destruction of the city and its chief shrines, acknowledged the god's "abandonment" of his or her sanctuary, and prayed for the eventual return of the god to the temple. They described the enemies' attack and the laments of the city's chief goddess. Obviously, these city laments did not envision an unhappy future. The temple would be rebuilt and the god would return. Lamentations seems to draw on this genre. The biblical book is not, however, slavishly dependent on Mesopotamian models. It appears that the city lament was at home in Israel long before Lamentations. Isaiah 1, 21–28 is an example: "How has she turned adulteress, the faithful city, so upright! Justice used to lodge within her, but now, murderers. Your silver is turned to dross, your wine is mixed with water" (Is 1, 21–22). The major difference between the Mesopotamian and biblical city laments is that the biblical laments cannot count on the return of the deity to the temple. They are not "playacting." Lamentations ends bitterly, without any assurances that the Lord will return to the Temple.

Poetic Analysis of the Book

The literary structure of Lamentations blends the fixed forms of Hebrew poetry with exceptionally free movement. The first four poems follow the alphabetic or acrostic arrangement: the first letters of the stanzas in Hebrew are the letters of the alphabet, in order. In the third Lamentation all three lines of a stanza start with the same letter. The first four songs follow the *qinah* meter of lament, one of the clearest metric styles in Hebrew poetry. The common Hebrew poetic line has two parts with equal number of accents in each part. The *qinah* meter has five beats, 3 + 2, so that a beat is missing in the second part. The final moment remains suspended and unfinished. It is associated with the topics of lament and loss.

An exceptional variety of attitudes follow one another: national and individual laments of misery (1, 12–16; 3, 43–45); prayer for help (1, 9c); confidence (3, 22–25); faith in the wisdom of God to assure that all receive what they deserve (3, 26–42); hymn of praise (5, 19). Jerusalem is addressed by the congregation (1, 1) and also speaks in her own name (1, 12–16).

While lamenting how chaos erupts everywhere (even cannibalism in 2, 20 and 4, 10), the author surrounds the entire exposition with the strict rules of alphabetic poetry and *qinah* meter. The poetry implies that God is still in control; all is not lost. Good order must return, and Israel's theology must absorb and teach the lessons of Jerusalem's destruction and exile. Lamentations asks that this process not be hurried. Israel needs space for mourning, time for disorder. Theology too cannot be hurried in unraveling an explanation of redemptive suffering.

Authorship and Place in the Bible

The irregularity of the book shows up in still other ways. Despite later tradition, quite a few signs point to someone other than Jeremiah as the author. Lamentations speaks favorably of the Davidic kings (4, 20, "The anointed one of the LORD, our breath of life, was caught in their snares, he in whose shadow we thought we could live on among the nations"), whereas Jeremiah suffered severely from them (Jer 22, 13–19; 37) and did not center his hopes for the future on them. The vocabulary and religious perspective of the two books are quite different. The most ancient manuscripts of Lamentations do not mention Jeremiah as the author. Moreover, the two books are found in different parts of the Hebrew Bible, Jeremiah among the Prophets, and Lamentations among the Writings. The ascription of the book to Jeremiah came much later, an instance of the ancient practice of ascribing originally anonymous works to a famous hero. The statement in 2 Chronicles 35, 25 that Jeremiah composed a lamentation over King Josiah, "which can be found written in the Lamentations," does not refer to the present book of Lamentations. In the Septuagint, the second-century BC Greek translation, this book and that of Baruch (see Jer 36) are found immediately after the prophecy of Jeremiah. A Christian tradition points to a hillside cave north of the walled city of Jerusalem as the place where Jeremiah wept over the city and composed these laments. So common was the ascription to Jeremiah that the Council of Trent's enumeration of the inspired books of the Old Testament does not name Lamentations, but only "Jeremiah with Baruch" (Session IV, April 8, 1546). Lamentations became a part of the tradition of Jeremiah in reflecting upon suffering as a way of expiating sin.

Lamentations has a special affinity with the prophecies in the second and third parts of Isaiah (Is 40—55 and 56—66). Each deals with the horrendous problem of the destruction of Jerusalem, the Babylonian exile, and the return to a miserable postexilic Jerusalem. Both books have common images: the tongue parched with thirst (Lam 4, 4; Is 41, 17); the pouring out of wrath (Lam 2, 4; 4, 11; Is 42, 25); the call to the mind or heart (Lam 3, 21; Is 44, 19). The almost hopeless agony and strong pleading of Lamentations still resound for us today:

> Our holy and glorious temple
>   in which our fathers praised you
> Has been burned with fire;
>   all that was dear to us is laid waste.

Can you hold back, O LORD, after all this?
    Can you remain silent, and afflict us so
        severely? (Is 64, 10f)

Prayer linked the disciples of Isaiah in exile with those of Jeremiah among the ruins of Jerusalem. In addition to these shared traditions, Lamentations seems to receive and develop traditions found in Deuteronomy and Hosea. These books, with their stress on sensitivity, compassion, and fidelity, nourished the authors of Lamentations as they lamented their national catastrophe before God.

Was there a single author of Lamentations? Even though the five poems of Lamentations have much in common, it is difficult to decide upon a single author. They are better explained by traditions of prayer amid Israelites struggling to survive in the rubble of Jerusalem.

Praying with the Book

The five chapters are not intended to solve the problem of suffering; rather, they let us remain, sorrowing in God's presence. Prayer, like friendship, is not meant to accomplish something, only to be aware of the one we love. Nonetheless, we may find help in a few markers along the way.

The first lamentation begins with the sorrow of the author at the sight of the ruined city (vv. 1–11). Then Jerusalem herself confesses her sins, her hopes and her anger against the enemy (vv. 12–22).

The second lamentation lays the devastated city before God (vv. 1–10). Technically this is the style of a lament: simply to present the situation as it is in its pain and horror. After revealing personal sorrow (vv. 11f), the poet addresses the city from the depths of compassion (vv. 13–22), beginning: "To what can I liken or compare you, O daughter Jerusalem?"

The third lamentation turns into an *individual* cry of sorrow. It begins with an assertiveness that startles us at a time when people's spirits, like their homes, are broken apart:

I am a man who knows affliction
    from the rod of his [God's] anger.
One whom he has led and forced to walk
    in darkness, not in the light.

While the poet speaks in his or her own name during most of the poem, in verses 25–47 other voices speak from a group of sages or wise persons and

other friends, baffled by the tragedy (vv. 40–47). This poem is the most complex of all.

The fourth lamentation returns to the style and mood of the first two. The opening verses tell the end of nobles and children (vv. 1–10), followed by a meditation on Jerusalem (vv. 11f). After the responsibility is placed upon the religious leaders (vv. 13–20), the poem ends with a curse upon the enemy (vv. 21f).

The fifth and last lamentation was titled by the Latin Vulgate "The Prayer of Jeremiah." This liturgical prayer sustains its beauty and serenity despite its topic of rejection and tragedy. It asks very little, only that the Lord remember.

Prayer beyond Theology

Lamentations allows us to remain with grief and tragedy long enough to mourn beauty and goodness as they deserve. If we do not mourn adequately, we may assume that nothing too precious was lost. We remain with God, even if events seemingly destroyed God's promises and, in the case of Lamentations, God's presence with us in the Temple. If our sorrow extends beyond the limits of our reasoning, then we plunge into a moment of time not for arguing theology but for allowing emotions to rush forward. Lamentations gushes from the dark, subterranean wellsprings of faith and sears the highest heavens in an outcry of anguish.

Without ever giving a reason, the book of Lamentations allows us to absorb a good purpose even in meaningless suffering. God, compassionate enough to bear our human outrage, walks us through dark gullies to a plateau of peace. This book is a triumph of faith over theology, at least theology in the days of the prophet Jeremiah. Because the Davidic dynasty and the holy city of Jerusalem received promises of God's eternal protection (Pss 46; 89; 132), priests and other prophets wanted Jeremiah killed for threatening the city with destruction (Jer 26). National laments, other than Lamentations, had already plunged beyond the limits of theology. In its second part of lament and reflection (vv. 10–23), Psalm 44 reverses the theological statements of the introduction (vv. 2–9) and introduces its final section almost blasphemously: "Awake! Why do you sleep, O Lord?" Blasphemous, because Psalm 121 declares: "The LORD, the maker of heaven and earth . . . never slumbers nor sleeps."

The LORD is your guardian" (vv. 2 and 4). It is not that theology is false, only that it has its limits. At such times contemplative prayer does what nothing else can do for us; it sustains us in God's presence with our agony and outrage.

Israelites prayed to God in the place which God had abandoned (Ez 10, 18–23). They gathered in the Temple ruins (Jer 41, 4–7), a dead place that paradoxically comes alive to address the assembly:

> Come, all you who pass by the way,
>   look and see
> Whether there is any suffering like my
>   suffering . . .
> When the LORD afflicted me
>   on the day of his blazing wrath (Lam 1, 12).

Other prayers besides Lamentations were being composed: for instance, Isaiah 63, 7—64, 11; Pss 79 and 80. Israel seemed to survive less by theological tradition, more within a community at prayer before a compassionate God. This same God admits publicly in Second Isaiah that Israel has received double for all her sins (Is 40, 2), that is, too much. There are instances, again beyond the limits of theology, where God regrets divine anger and punishment (Ex 32, 14; 2 Sm 24, 16; Jer 42, 10).

Influence of Lamentations in Judaism and Christianity

Later Jewish tradition counted Lamentations as one of the five festival scrolls (the Megilloth), with Song of Songs, Ruth, Ecclesiastes, and Esther. Lamentations was read in the liturgy on the "ninth of Ab," sorrowfully remembering the two destructions of Jerusalem, by the Babylonians in 587 BC and by the Romans in AD 70.

The Christian church has used Lamentations in reference to Christ's Passion. In the Latin church, Lamentations played an important and memorable role in the Holy Week services prior the reforms of Vatican II. They were sung during the ceremony of Tenebrae ("darkness"), probably named from the custom of extinguishing one candle after each psalm until the church was

left in darkness. Several of the Tenebrae texts (though not Lamentations) have survived in the revised morning offices for Good Friday and Holy Saturday. In general, the Lamentations are used sparingly in the Roman Catholic lectionary; there are only three selections among the many Old Testament selections for masses for the dead and only one in the readings for masses "for any need." It remains a challenge for the church to learn how to incorporate laments into its public prayer so that the pains and difficulties of Christian discipleship are represented as fully as the peace and joy of faith.

FURTHER READING

Basic Commentaries

Dobbs-Allsopp, F. W. *Lamentations*. Interpretation. Louisville: John Knox Press, 2000. Excellent; scholarly, yet accessible to first-time readers.

Fischer, James A., G.M. *Song of Songs; Ruth; Lamentations; Ecclesiastes; Esther.* Collegeville Bible Commentary 24. Collegeville, MN: Liturgical Press, 1986. Very brief and good treatment.

Gottwald, Norman K. *Lamentations*. HarperCollins Bible Commentary, 577–82. San Francisco: Harper, 2000. Gottwald has long worked on Lamentations; this short commentary is the fruit of his labors.

Guinan, Michael D. *Lamentations*. New Jerome Biblical Commentary, 558–62. Englewood Cliffs, NJ: Prentice Hall, 1990. Balanced and concise.

Kodell, Jerome. O.S.B., *Lamentations . . . Baruch*. Old Testament Message. Wilmington, DE: Michael Glazier Inc., 1982. A good, though brief, exposition.

O'Connor, Kathleen M. *Lamentations*. New Interpreter's Bible 6. 1011–73. Nashville, TN: Abingdon Press, 2001. A fine analysis.

——. *Lamentations and the Tears of the World*. Maryknoll, NY: Orbis Books, 2002. A perceptive commentary with reflections on the meaning of the book for today.

Advanced Commentary

Hillers, Delbert R. *Lamentations*. Anchor Bible 7A. Garden City, NY: Doubleday, 1992. Interested in the linguistic questions and in comparable laments in the ancient world.

BARUCH

[see pages 1084–92 of the Old Testament]

Baruch, son of Neriah, was the secretary of the great prophet Jeremiah. He wrote down the prophet's preaching to preserve it for later generations, and on occasion he read that preaching to audiences when Jeremiah was not able to do so (Jer 32; 36; 45). Much more than a simple record keeper, he was from an important Jerusalem family and scribe in the employ of the palace. Sharing Jeremiah's fate as an exile in Egypt, he is last heard from in that country around 582 BC (Jer 43, 5–7). The book bearing his name is a collection of four sections, probably of separate origin, which were written long after Baruch, probably in the second or early first centuries. In the Second Temple period (520 BC to AD 70), it was not unusual to use the name of a well-known ancient personage as the title of a contemporary work in order to link the work to earlier traditions and enhance its authority.

The book of Baruch has four sections: an introduction (1, 1–14), a long confession of sin (1, 15—3, 8), a poem on wisdom (3, 9—4, 4), and a consoling poem (4, 5—5, 9). In Roman Catholic Bibles, the so-called Letter of Jeremiah is often printed as the sixth chapter of Baruch. When included in the book of Baruch, as it sometimes is, it makes a fifth section. Though the sections may have had separate origins, they are linked to one another, giving the book a clear unity. It is generally agreed that Baruch was written in Hebrew. No Hebrew manuscript survives, however. The Greek version serves as the basis of modern translations. Other ancient versions are in Syriac, Latin, Coptic, Ethiopic, Arabic, and Armenian.

Baruch is in the Orthodox and Roman Catholic canon of sacred Scripture. In the Protestant canon it is classed among the Apocrypha. Catholic Bibles such as the *New American Bible* add the Epistle of Jeremiah to Baruch as its sixth chapter.

The Historical Background of the Book

When was the book of Baruch written? Evidence must be indirect, for there are no references to contemporary events in the book. Historical inconsistencies and inaccuracies in the introduction (e.g., that Baruch lived in Babylon rather than Egypt, contrary to Jer 43, 6, and the strange "fifth year" in 1, 2) indicate the book was written long after the early sixth century when the historical Baruch lived. Since the prayer in chapters 1 and 2 (especially 1, 15—2, 5) depends on Daniel 9 (ca. 164) and the wisdom poem (3, 9—4, 4) depends on Sirach 24 (ca. 180), Baruch must have been written after the completion of these works, unless the two sources were in existence before the composition of the books in which they now appear. Many scholars therefore suggest that the date of composition was sometime in the late second or early first centuries.

What had happened in the history of Israel from the sixth to the second centuries to make the book of Baruch possible? The Babylonian exile is conventionally dated 586 to 539. Babylonian deportations in the early sixth century impoverished Jerusalem and Judah. The Temple ceased operation, and the economy was devastated. In 539 the Persians entered Babylon and effectively ended the empire. The period from 539 to 333 is known as the Persian period and the period from 333 to 63 as the Hellenistic (Greek) period. The defeat of Babylon by Cyrus the Persian greatly benefited people in Judah and in the exiled community. Cyrus authorized the rebuilding of the Temple and the return of the sacred vessels, and permitted the return of the exiles (Ezr 1, 1–4; 6, 1–5). Most exiles stayed where they were, however, and the Diaspora (dispersion) communities in Babylon and elsewhere grew and flourished in the centuries that followed. Only in 520 was the Temple rebuilt (on a very modest scale), a sign of the practical difficulties in returning to normal and a sign too of the animosity of neighboring peoples. The rebuilt Temple became the center of the restored community, even though, as Isaiah 56 through 66 clearly shows, the people struggled with different visions of restoration.

The postexilic period was a time of literary creativity. Most Old Testament books underwent final editing at this time, including the Pentateuch, the Deuteronomistic History, and the pro-

315

phetic books. Other books were composed later in this period, among them Chronicles and Ezra-Nehemiah. Some of the late books looked back at the preexilic period with awe and reverence, regarding its literature as timeless standards. Their authors paid homage to the golden-age works by allusions and borrowings. The attribution of the book of Baruch to the sixth-century secretary of Jeremiah is an example of such reverence. Another indication is Baruch's multiple allusions to Deuteronomy (especially Dt 28 and 30), Jeremiah (e.g., Jer 8, 1; 11, 17; 24, 7.9; 31, 33), Deutero-Isaiah (Is 40—55), and Daniel (especially Dn 9). Among the abiding concerns of exilic literature were the Jerusalem Temple, the meaning of exile, and the problem of authority in a changed society. With the disappearance of the old institutions of religion and government in Judea, where was the divine presence to be found and who had religious authority? Related questions were where wisdom was to be found and the location of authoritative teaching or *torah*. These concerns are addressed in the book of Baruch.

In the course of time, the Persian Empire expanded westward and came into conflict with Greece, which eventually led to the defeat of the Persians. In 333 Alexander the Great swept down the coast of the western Mediterranean and conquered the Phoenician coast. Jerusalem surrendered and became a province in yet another empire, the Ptolemaic empire (capital in Egypt) and then the Seleucid (capital in Antioch). More important, it came under the influence of Greek culture. The new culture raised several points relevant to the book of Baruch. One was the question of Jewish identity. New centers of Judaism rivaled Jerusalem: Alexandria in Egypt and Babylon in Mesopotamia. As most Jews now lived outside the boundaries of Palestine and did not speak Hebrew, the question of what made a Jew became pressing. What was the relation of the diaspora communities to the Jerusalem and the Judean community? When would the exile completely end so that Judah might be independent and have its own king? Was the period of divine wrath ongoing? These questions concerning the identity of Judah among the nations appear in the book of Baruch.

Analysis of the Book

1. **Introduction (1, 1–14).** According to the opening lines of Baruch, on the fifth anniversary of the destruction of the Temple in Jerusalem, Baruch read the book to Jehoiachin (Jeconiah) and to all who could come—nobles, princes, elders, everyone high and low. Jehoiachin was the Davidic king who had been exiled to Babylon in 598/597 and represented hopes for a restored monarchy (2 Kgs 25, 27–30; Jer 52, 31–34). When they heard it, they wept, fasted, and prayed, and then took up a collection for the high priest and the people in Jerusalem. Baruch arranged for the return of the silver vessels that Nebuchadnezzar robbed from the Temple. The verses evoke golden-age scenes of leaders gathering the people and speaking authoritative words to them, for example, Moses in Deuteronomy, King Josiah in 2 Kings 22—23, and (in a reverse of the present scene) Baruch reading the book to the unreceptive King Jehoiakim in Jeremiah 36. Baruch here speaks with scriptural authoritativeness; such is the sense of verse 3, literally "Baruch read the words . . . in the ears of all the people who came to hear the book." Not only do Baruch and the people send vessels to Jerusalem; they also send money for offerings, suggest what the Jerusalemites should pray for (the welfare of the king and the forgiveness of the sins of the exiles), and even write a prayer for Temple worship (1, 10–14). The latter is not a private prayer; it is to be read on feast days in the Temple. The text of the prayer follows in 1, 15—3, 8, which links the first and second parts of the book.

The key to the opening scene is that Baruch, the secretary of the great Jeremiah and his sometime spokesman, is the speaker. Baruch's interpretation of the prophet's famous letter to the exiles in Babylon in Jeremiah 29 is accepted as authoritative by the leaders in Babylon: "Promote the welfare of the city to which I have exiled you; pray for it to the LORD, for upon its welfare depends your own. Thus says the LORD: Only after seventy years have elapsed for Babylon will I visit you and fulfill for you my promise to bring you back to this place. . . . Yes, when you seek me with all your heart, you will find me with you, says the LORD, and I will change your lot; I will gather you together from all the nations and all the places to which I have banished you, says the LORD, and bring you back to the place from which I have exiled you" (Jer 29, 7–15). Baruch apparently reinterprets "seventy years" to mean an indefinite period of time. Daniel 9, 20–27 had famously reinterpreted the seventy years to seventy weeks of years, that is, seven times seventy (= 490 years), but Baruch's interpretation is even more open-ended. According to him, the exiles must serve the king of Babylon for "many days" (Bar 1, 12). The wrath of God has not yet turned away from the exiles (1, 13). In the meantime, Baruch advises fervent prayer (1, 15—3, 8) and, in the following passages, teaches the exiles how to seek life-giving wisdom in this less than perfect situation.

2. **A prayer that the Lord might relent and once again be gracious (1, 15—3, 8).** It is assumed that prayer offered in the Jerusalem Temple is more efficacious than private prayer. The confession acknowledges that the people have sinned and that the covenant curses listed in Deuteronomy 28 have been unleashed. All the ills that have come upon the people are deserved; no excuses are offered. The first part of the poem (1, 15—2, 5) is to be said by the people of Jerusalem, and the second part by the exiles (2, 6–16). 1, 15 ("Justice is with the LORD, our God; and we today are flushed with shame, we men of Judah and citizens of Jerusalem") matches 2, 6 ("Justice is with the LORD, our God; and we, like our fathers, are flushed with shame even today"), suggesting that both verses begin parallel sections. Furthermore, 2, 13–14 indicates that the exiles are speaking, so it is natural to regard 2, 6 as the point where the exiles' prayer begins. The prayer draws heavily on Daniel 9, 7–8.10–14; almost every word in Daniel finds an echo in Baruch. Jeremiah and Deuteronomy are also quarried. In the prayer, the people give up all claims of righteousness and place all hopes of rescue in the character of God, the Lord's care for his good name.

3. **Wisdom is to be found in Israel's law (3, 9—4, 5).** Where can wisdom be found? Always elusive (Job 28), life-giving wisdom is especially hard to find in the exilic crisis. After the prayer, which gives up all human sources of salvation (1, 15—3, 8), the book begins a new section with the authoritative command, "Hear, O Israel, the commandments of life" (3, 9). It is an apt sum-

mons, for the people live in a foreign land, virtually among the dead (3, 11). The charge that they "have forsaken the fountain of wisdom" (3, 12) is probably an allusion to Jeremiah 2, 13, "Two evils have my people done: they have forsaken me, the source of living waters; they have dug themselves cisterns, broken cisterns, that hold no water." Borrowing from the wisdom poem in Job 28 (among other biblical texts), the poem insists that human beings cannot lay hold of wisdom by their own efforts; it must be given by God. God has in fact given wisdom to Israel—in the form of their *torah* or law: "[Wisdom] is the book of the precepts of God, the law that endures forever; all who cling to her will live, but those will die who forsake her. Turn, O Jacob, and receive her: walk by her light toward splendor" (4, 1–2). Baruch here draws on Sirach 24 (ca. 180), which also teaches that divine wisdom is to be found in the law given to Israel, "All this [wisdom] is true of the book of the Most High's covenant, the law which Moses commanded us as an inheritance for the community of Jacob" (Sir 24, 22).

Three points about this wisdom poem should be noted. First, it comes immediately after the community confession of helplessness and blindedness, suggesting that wisdom is God's answer to the people's quandary. The hymn sings of the inaccessibility of wisdom and nonetheless asserts it can be found. This is just what the community, adrift, needed to hear. Second, the focus on *torah* was an important religious development in early Judaism. The old markers of community identity no longer played the role that they once did—the Temple, a common land, a king and independent government. New boundary markers were necessary so that the community might define itself among the nations. Among the new markers were the law or *torah* and the Scriptures. What was written could be read by people of different lands, cultures, and languages. Eventually, the word *torah* came to be applied to the Pentateuch, the great authoritative narrative. Third, the wisdom hymn associates wisdom preeminently with one nation, Israel. Previously, wisdom was more "international"; to pursue it was the duty of every human being. The "nationalizing" of wisdom can be seen as early as Deuteronomy 4, 6, probably from the sixth century: "Observe [the statutes] carefully, for thus will you give evidence of your wisdom and intelligence to the nations, who will hear of all these statutes and say, 'This great nation is truly a wise and intelligent people.' " In a memorable phrase, Baruch says that to live according to the wisdom of the *torah* is to "walk by her light toward splendor" (4, 2). Israel has the great privilege of knowing what is pleasing to God (4, 3).

4. **A poem of encouragement (4, 5—5, 9).** Like the two preceding sections, this section alludes to the writings of the golden age, especially Isaiah 40 through 55. Isaiah personified Babylon (Is 37) and Zion (Is 49, 14–26; 54) as queens, imagining them as wives of the national god and mothers of their citizens (cf. Ps 87). With the destruction of the city and the exile of its citizens, each personified city lost her husband and her children. In Isaiah 40 through 55, Woman Zion is assured by her Lord that her children will return. Isaiah 60 and 62 envision the return of Zion's exiled children and her husband: "Raise your eyes and look about; they all gather and come to you: Your sons come from afar, and your daughters in the arms of their nurses" (Is 60, 4), and "No more shall men call you 'Forsaken,' or your land 'Desolate,' but you shall be called 'My Delight,' and your land 'Espoused.' For the LORD delights in you, and makes your land his spouse" (Is 62, 4). In Baruch, personified Zion is not yet fully restored. Despite her great suffering, however, she thinks only of the suffering of her children. With great compassion, she explains their real situation to them: their sins angered the just God who punished them by bringing a distant nation against them (4, 15). Zion intercedes with God on their behalf (4, 17–20), setting an example of hope (4, 21–26) and faithfulness (4, 27–29). Though bereft of her children, Zion continues to act as a true mother of her children.

The second section of the poem of consolation (4, 30—5, 9) is addressed to Zion. Reprising a key verb from Zion's speech, "*Fear not, my children; call out to God! He who brought this upon you will remember you*" (4, 27), the new poem begins by responding to her, "*Fear not, Jerusalem! He who gave you your name is your encouragement.*" The second part of the poem is the divine answer to the words of Woman Zion in 4, 5–29. She had told her children she was interceding for them with sackcloth and prayer (4, 20) and expressed her steadfast hope they would return to her. The second section (4, 30—5, 9) as-

sures Zion that her hope will come true. Three verbs in the imperative mood introduce the three sections of the speech: (1) "Fear not, Jerusalem" in 4, 30; (2) "Look to the east, Jerusalem! behold the joy that comes to you from God" in 4, 36; and (3) "Up, Jerusalem! stand upon the heights; look to the east and see your children" in 5, 5. Section 1 asserts that Zion's enemies will be punished; section 2 that her children will return and that she can take off her widow's garments; and section 3 that the hills and valleys have been leveled to make a beautiful highway for the exiles to walk as they return home to Zion. Baruch here draws on Isaiah 40 through 55.

5. **The Letter of Jeremiah.** In Roman Catholic Bibles, the Letter of Jeremiah is often printed as chapter 6 of Baruch. Protestant editions of the Bible place both Baruch and the Letter of Jeremiah among the Apocrypha, and print the Letter of Jeremiah as a separate work immediately after Baruch. Addressed to the exiles in Babylon like Baruch, the Letter of Jeremiah develops themes of Jeremiah's famous letter to the exiles (Jer 29). The Letter of Jeremiah interprets Jeremiah's "seventy years" (Jer 25, 11–12; 29, 10) as seven generations (Bar 6, 3). Its chief concern, however, is in launching a satiric attack on idols (Jer 10, 2—16): avoid divine images and worship Israel's God exclusively. In the exilic and post-exilic periods Israelite thinkers became more reflective about their monotheistic faith. Part of that reflection was expressed in satirical attacks on divine images, which were, in the ancient Near East, the normal means of encountering the deity. Jeremiah 10 and Baruch 6 are not the only satires on divine images in the Bible. Others are found in Deuteronomy 4, 27–28; Psalms 115, 4–8; 135, 15–18; Isaiah 40, 18–20; 44, 9–10; 46, 1–7. The Letter of Jeremiah consists of ten warnings, all but the last ending in a refrain that the statues are not divine and that people should not "fear" them, that is, accord them divine honor.

The work is attributed to Jeremiah because it furthers his work of preaching to the exiles. It was known to the author of 2 Maccabees 2, 1–3, and must therefore have been written toward the end of the second century. The original language seems to have Hebrew or Aramaic, for the extant Greek occasionally reflects Semitic syntax.

The Message of the Book of Baruch

Baruch, the secretary of Jeremiah, preserved and interpreted the words of his master for a new time and situation. By the time Baruch was written (probably the late second or early first century BC), the exile had gone on far longer than what Jeremiah predicted. Jeremiah's "seventy years" had come and gone and the exile continued. "Exile" had come to mean something more complex than absence from one's homeland. It meant also subjugation to a foreign government, high rates of taxation, harassment, and arbitrary treatment by an occupying power. The author of the book believes in the authority of the Jeremiah tradition but realizes it has to be interpreted for a new situation. Jeremiah's seventy years of exile (Jer 25, 1–12; 29, 10) become in Baruch "many days" (Bar 1, 12; 4, 35, literal translation; NAB "long" and "long time"). In the Letter of Jeremiah, it becomes "many years, a period seven generations long" (Bar 6, 2). Jeremiah advised the exiles to settle down and pray for the welfare of Babylon (Jer 29, 5–7) and promised that the Lord had a plan to bring the exiles back provided they were constant in prayer (Jer 29, 10–14), "When you call me, when you go to pray to me, I will listen to you" (Jer 29, 12). Baruch provides a model of such prayer (Bar 1, 15—3, 8): the nation abases itself and places all its hopes in the Lord. Baruch also shows the people that there are other ways to gain life during exile, especially the pursuit of wisdom, which is to be found in the law of the Lord (3, 9—4, 5). Mother Zion instructs the people how they are to live so that the Lord will bring them back: maintain a lively hope that the Lord will bring them back to Zion (4, 5—5, 9).

Baruch shows that many Jews, at least in Judea, considered the exile to be still continuing. It had not ended when the first exiles returned in the latter part of the sixth century. Rather, it continues as long as Israel is not free and another empire rules their land, as long as their Temple is subject to foreign supervision, and their rulers govern under the direction of others. Such subordination is an insult to the Lord of heaven and earth who is Israel's God.

For modern readers, Baruch shows how ancient Scripture can be interpreted to give life and meaning to people in new situations. The book's insistence that one must place all one's hope in the Lord, that one can find the Lord in the inspired Scriptures, and that one must hear words of hope make it perennially valuable for all ages.

Influence in Judaism and Christianity

The Hebrew text was not preserved in Judaism. According to Jerome, in the late fourth century AD, the Jews did not even possess a Hebrew text. In early Christianity, however, Baruch was widely quoted and cited as sacred Scripture. Baruch 3, 36–37, concerning the appearance on earth of the wisdom of God, was a particular favorite because it was given a Christological reference. Fathers of the Church often quoted it, though they sometimes cite it as "Jeremiah," because in the Septuagint (Greek) translation Baruch was an appendix to Jeremiah. The work appears in several canonical lists of Greek fathers but never in lists compiled by Latin fathers. The book was included in the canonical list of the Council of Trent in 1546 and was ratified by Vatican I in 1870. Luther and other reformers followed Jerome's example and excluded Baruch from the canon. Protestants place it among the Apocrypha.

FURTHER READING

Fitzgerald, Aloysius, F.S.C. *Baruch*. The New Jerome Biblical Commentary, 563–67. Englewood Cliffs, NJ: Prentice Hall, 1990. Fine short commentary.

Harrington, Daniel J., S.J. *Baruch. Letter of Jeremiah*. HarperCollins Bible Commentary, 781–88. San Francisco: Harper, 2000. Concise, competent, the best short commentary.

Kodell, Jerome, O.S.B. *Lamentations; Baruch*. Old Testament Message 14. Wilmington, DE: Michael Glazier, 1982. Good basic commentary.

Nickelsburg, George D. "Baruch and the Epistle of Jeremiah." In *Jewish Writings in the Second Temple Period*, edited by M. E. Stone, 140–48. Assen: Van Gorcum, 1984. Authoritative essay.

Saldarini, Anthony J. *The Book of Baruch. The Letter of Jeremiah*. New Interpreter's Bible 6. 927–1010. Nashville, TN: Abingdon Press, 2001. The most recent, thorough, and judicious commentary.

EZEKIEL

[see pages 1092–1146 of the Old Testament]

The book of Ezekiel is a unique blend of divine utterance (rather than prophetic utterance), strange imagery, and careful arrangement. It is the only prophetic book displaying a chronological order. There are four major blocks of material, which are in the same sequence as in the books of Isaiah and Jeremiah. Chapters 1 through 24 are oracles concerning Judah and Jerusalem; chapters 25 through 32 are oracles concerning the nations; chapters 33 through 37 announce restoration; and chapters 38 through 48 describe the final battle and the vision of the new Temple and city. This essay discusses the historical background, the dated oracles and life of the prophet, the traditions Ezekiel used, the literary structure of the book, some key passages, the theology of the book, the Hebrew and Greek text, and the influence of Ezekiel on early Judaism and on the New Testament.

Historical Background

To understand Ezekiel's message, one must go back a century and a half before Ezekiel, to the earliest writing prophets—Amos, Hosea, Micah, and Isaiah of Jerusalem. What provoked these individuals to initiate a new religious movement and write down their prophecies and publicize them for the widest possible audience? Though we will probably never understand the reasons fully, two factors played a major role: (1) the prophets' conviction that the Lord's relationship to Israel had reached a crisis point; and (2) the fact that Israel faced a new kind of enemy, a superpower (Assyria) against which it could not defend itself. The earliest prophet, Amos, it is true, did not mention Assyria, but stated decisively that Israel's special relationship to the Lord had ended (8, 1–3) and that Judah and Israel, like the nations, now stood under the severe judgment of God (2, 4—3, 2). Before the rise of the writing prophets, prophets fought for the Lord and the cause of righteousness in Israel, but never called into question the relationship itself. Reform measures would bring the people back into right relationship with the Lord, they thought. Indeed, it was possible to mount de-

fenses against the modestly scaled armies that attacked Israel in those days. In the last third of the eighth century BC, however, Assyria moved into the area. Massive, relentless, and superior in war, it could not be defeated in any meaningful sense. The best one could do was to pay tribute.

How did these two new factors—the military situation and the prophets' conviction that the relationship had ended—affect Israel's traditions? These two factors severely damaged the credibility of the traditions, for the usual version of the national story, preserved in such psalms as 105, 114, and 136, proclaimed that the Lord set Israel apart for himself, freed them from Egyptian bondage, and gave them the Promised Land. The political changes of the mid-eighth century made the people's possession of their land precarious and uncertain. Israel's identity as a special people was called into question when the Lord remained silent before this new threat. Prophets were needed to reinterpret the ancient traditions for a radically new turn of events and to make it possible for the people to respond in a new situation. Each prophet emphasized in his own way the centrality of the relationship to the Lord and guided the people to appropriate actions. Hosea, for example, used the metaphor of marriage and the prospect of a new exodus to exhort Israel to remain faithful to the relationship. Amos mercilessly exposed the social injustice of the people and revised the traditional notion of the Day of the Lord to mean that the Lord might attack *Israel* rather than its enemies. Isaiah uncovered forgotten aspects of the Zion and David traditions to show that the promises were demands for fidelity as well as assurances of divine help. Jeremiah used the Exodus tradition and attempted to show that the divine judgment the people were experiencing could have a positive outcome if the people were obedient. Ezekiel, it will be shown below, interpreted the same historical events as Jeremiah, but saw them from a quite different perspective—that of a priest. The writing prophets, therefore, had a twofold task: to interpret the national traditions in the light of the ever-changing course of history, and to persuade peo-

320

ple to act in accord with the required changes. Theory and practice, interpretation and praxis, were inseparable for the prophets.

Shortly before Ezekiel appears on the scene, in the last quarter of the seventh century, the hitherto dominant Assyrian empire collapsed with astonishing speed, enabling small states in the Levant such as Judah to regain their freedom and rebuild. (The Levant is the land area bordering the eastern Mediterranean.) Under Assyrian rule, the Northern Kingdom of Israel had become an Assyrian province, and Judah, with territory reduced, was a vassal state. These were the times of the prophets Hosea, Micah, and Isaiah, who had the task of explaining to the people that what was happening, however horrific, was the work of the Lord, that the events did not necessarily mean the end of Israel, and that the divine work demanded a faithful response.

In 640 BC, Josiah came to the throne in Judah. A child just eight years old, Josiah was assisted by a group of people loyal to the Lord and the authentic traditions of Israel. The death of the Assyrian king Assurbanipal, in 627 BC, freed him to launch a reform and reclaim the people's national and religious identity. Josiah sought to restore the old boundaries of the kingdom of David, annexing the former Assyrian provinces of Samaria, Gilead, and Galilee (2 Kgs 23, 19). In 622 BC, an ancient law book, the nucleus of the present book of Deuteronomy, was found in the Temple in the course of restoration work. It became the basis of a wide-ranging religious reform (2 Kgs 22, 1—23, 27). Unfortunately, the promising reform collapsed with Josiah's unexpected death in 609 BC (2 Kgs 23, 28–30). Judah was again reduced to a vassal state, first under Egypt and then, after Nebuchadnezzar defeated Egypt at the battle of Carchemish (in northern Syria) in 605 BC, under Babylon. Descendants of Josiah came to the throne in succession, all at the command of foreign powers: Jehoahaz (609, three months), Jehoiakim (609–598) and his son, Jehoiachin (598/7, three months), and Jehoiachin's uncle, Zedekiah (597–587/6). Though it had to yield control of Palestine to Babylon, Egypt remained a formidable state, never letting an opportunity pass to encourage Judah to rebel against Babylon. Jehoiakim and Zedekiah, for their part, played one great power against the other, but found, to their cost, that Egypt was weak and unreliable. Jeremiah vigorously opposed such attempts to fend off Babylon, which he regarded as God's instrument to punish and purge Judah. Jeremiah was right. Judean political juggling roused the Babylonians, and in 598 its army sacked the city and deported many of its leaders to Babylonia (2 Kgs 24, 8–17). Jehoiakim died during the siege, and the Babylonians took his eighteen-year-old son Jehoiachin to Babylon as a hostage to prevent further rebellion. Many people placed their hopes for eventual restoration in Jehoiachin, a king in the line of David; to them, his release from prison was a good omen (2 Kgs 25, 19; Jer 52, 31–33). Jehoiachin's uncle Zedekiah was named regent (2 Kgs 24, 18–20), and he continued his predecessors' rebellious policies. Nebuchadnezzar responded with force. After a campaign lasting three years (588–586 BC), he destroyed the cities of Judah and looted and burned Jerusalem and its Temple (2 Kgs 25; Jer 52). Babylon had done what Assyria had not done—destroy Jerusalem and the Temple.

King Zedekiah had to face the awful consequences. Captured, he was forced to look on as his two sons were murdered, then his own eyes were put out (2 Kgs 25). Among the eight or ten thousand deportees of 597 (2 Kgs 24, 14–16 give both figures) was Ezekiel (Ez 1, 1), evidently a Zadokite priest. With other exiles, he settled in Nippur and seems to have occupied a prominent place in the transplanted community and was often consulted by them (Ez 8, 1; 14, 1; 20, 1). To judge by his commission to stand in opposition to the community and by his vigorous criticism of their opinions, he had a very different understanding of the exile than they did. He saw the exile as a long process of judgment that required faith. The people, on the other hand, saw themselves as helpless victims and hoped for a speedy and trouble-free return. No wonder that the Lord said to the prophet: "Hard of face and obstinate of heart are they to whom I am sending you. But you shall say to them: Thus says the Lord GOD!" (2, 4).

Dated Oracles in the Book of Ezekiel

The book contains two series of seven dates that introduce selected oracles throughout the book.

(The first date [1, 1] is outside of the sequence.) One series of seven dates introduces foreign oracles in chapters 25 through 32 (26, 1; 29, 1.17; 30, 20; 31, 1; 32, 1.17), and range from 587/586 to 571; all but one, 29, 1.17, are in chronological order. The sections describe specific actions of enemy nations. The other series of seven dates (1, 2; 3, 16; 8, 1; 20, 1; 24, 1; 33, 21; 40, 1) introduces important moments in the prophet's ministry. Ezekiel 1, 2 and 3, 16 mark his call and commission. The crucial vision of the departure of the divine glory from the Temple in chapters 8 through 11 is signaled by the date heading in 8, 1. The fourth date, 20, 1, is less certain; it may allude to the beginning of Zedekiah's rebellion, which was so fraught with consequences for the nation. The fifth date, 24, 1, marks the beginning of the siege of Jerusalem in January 588. The last two dates are concerned with restoration: 33, 21 is the date of the arrival of the news that Jerusalem has fallen, indicating that the prophet can now devote his attention to the revival of the nation; 40, 1 begins the final vision of the new city and its Temple in 573. Carefully arranged in chronological order, these dates show how Ezekiel's preaching corresponded with God's judgment that unfolded over time. The number seven, which often expresses fullness and completion in the Bible, underlines the comprehensive nature of the divine plan. The dates suggest that the plan will come to completion even if human beings resist it.

Two dates require special comment. Ezekiel 1, 1 gives the date of his call, "In the thirtieth year, on the fifth day of the fourth month, while I was among the exiles by the river Chebar, the heavens opened, and I saw divine visions," whereas the immediately following date (1, 2) gives the date as July 593, "On the fifth day of the month, the fifth year, that is, of King Jehoiachin's exile, the word of the LORD came to the priest Ezekiel." To what does "the thirtieth year" refer? It could mean several things: Ezekiel's age at the time of his call (a priest could begin work in the Temple at thirty, according to Nm 4, 3); the year when the book was finally edited; or thirty years after an event known to Ezekiel's original readers but not to us. The first suggestion makes the most sense: though Ezekiel was at the proper age for ordination, he could not be ordained in Babylonia because he could not go to the Temple; he

would therefore serve at the Temple through visions (see 8—11 and 40—48). The other date, March/April 571 (19, 17) is not in the proper chronological sequence; it may update an oracle originally given earlier.

The dates link Ezekiel's preaching to specific events in human history. Since Ezekiel employed divine speech and visionary experiences more than any other prophet, the date formulas remind readers that he was interpreting real events and urging hearers to practical action.

The Biography of Ezekiel

According to the date formula in 1, 2, Ezekiel's prophetic ministry began with his call in July 593 near a canal ("River Chebar" in NAB) near Nippur, a few miles south of the city of Babylon. He was among the eight or ten thousand able men exiled to Babylonia after the siege of Jerusalem in 597 BC (2 Kgs 24, 14.16). (Evidently other family members were not counted in the census.) The last dated formula in the book is March/April 571 (29, 17), which introduces a promise that Babylonia will plunder Egypt. The time span between the first and the last oracle is twenty-two years. To judge from the contents of the oracles, most of his ministry took place from 593 to 585. Ezekiel, however, may well have continued teaching and writing after 571 about matters that did not require a date, for example, the future events depicted in chapters 33 through 48. His public career was spent completely in dismal circumstances. The period from 593 to 571 was one of unrelieved doom—unhindered Babylonian domination, inept and cowardly Judean leadership, the fiery destruction of Jerusalem and the Temple, and exile in humiliation and poverty. These were the events that required Ezekiel's attention and comment. No wonder that the scroll in his inaugural vision "was covered with writing front and back, and written on it was: Lamentation and wailing and woe!" (2, 10). It is a tribute to his faith and imagination that the prophet's message is ultimately about the bright future God has in store for his people.

The fact that Ezekiel is called a priest is of enormous significance: "The word of the LORD came to the priest Ezekiel, the son of Buzi, in the land of the Chaldeans by the river Chebar. There the hand of the LORD came upon me" (1, 3). It has already been noted that his call "in the thirtieth year" most probably refers to the age of ordination. Priestly ordination was complex, however, requiring animal sacrifice (Ex 29 and Lv 8), which could only be carried out in Temple precincts. Ezekiel seems to be saying that normal ordination and priestly service was impossible for him, for he had no access to the Temple. He would be present in Jerusalem and exercise his priestly service in a new way, through *visionary experience*. Like that of Isaiah (Is 6), Ezekiel's inaugural vision is one of the throne of the Lord (1, 26). In chapters 8 through 11, he will tour the Temple in a vision and will show how profoundly it has been corrupted by unholy conduct. In chapters 40 through 48, he will go on a visionary tour of the new city and the new Temple. As a priest, his categories are purity and impurity, and the boundaries between profane and sacred. As a prophet his purview included social justice and the fidelity required by the covenant. Holiness implied social justice (cf. Lv 19) and social justice implied right worship (cf. Is 1, 2–20). Ezekiel demands both exactness in rituals and compassion toward one's neighbor. An example is 18, 5, "If a man is virtuous—if he does what is right and just, if he does not eat on the mountains, nor raise his eyes to the idols of the house of Israel; if he does not defile his neighbor's wife, nor have relations with a woman in her menstrual period . . . ," (18, 5–6). The fact that he is a priest, even if not actually ordained in the Temple, does not take away in the least from his calling as a prophet. He often prophesies about Israel's problems and possibilities in priestly terms: how God will dwell in the midst of a sinful people, rebuild the Temple to protect its holiness, and arrange the people in the zones of holiness around the Temple. (See "The Traditions That Ezekiel Used.")

Ezekiel does not tell us very much about his personal life, for evidently he did not consider it significant for his public task. We know that his wife died in 588 only because it was important to his preaching (24, 15–27). To dramatize how devastating would be the loss of "the delight of your eyes" (referring to the Temple), Ezekiel was forbidden by God to perform the customary mourning rites for his wife ("the delight of your eyes") when she died. The examples show that the book is not a biography but a record of preaching.

Several verses show Ezekiel's style of communicating to the elders of the people (8, 1; 14, 1; 20, 1). The elders gathered around him to consult the Lord. The verb "to consult the Lord" was a technical term for seeking an oracle from the Lord. That the elders would come to Ezekiel shows that they recognized him as an authentic prophet. Like a true prophet, he had no hesitation in criticizing them vigorously (14, 1). Though his frequent use of divine speech might suggest that he did not converse with his hearers, several oracles directly respond to sayings current among the people. An example: "What is the meaning of this proverb that you recite in the land of Israel: 'Fathers have eaten green grapes, thus their children's teeth are on edge'?" (18, 2). Ezekiel proceeded to a detailed refutation of this popular saying. Other popular sayings provoked a similar critique (12, 22.23.27; 22, 28; 37, 11). Some exiles dismissed him as no more than an entertaining figure, as the Lord informed the prophet: "Your countrymen are talking about you along the walls and in the doorways of houses. They say to one another, 'Come and hear the latest word that comes from the LORD.' My people come to you as people always do; they sit down before you and hear your words, but they will not obey them, for lies are on their lips and their desires are fixed on dishonest gain. For them you are only a ballad singer, with a pleasant voice and a clever touch. They listen to your words, but they will not obey them" (33, 30–32).

Ezekiel's style has caused some modern commentators to question his balance and even his sanity. Chapters 1, 8, 10, 37, and 40 describe ecstatic visions seizing the prophet's whole person. Among his prophetic gestures are clapping his hands and stamping his feet (6, 11), digging through the wall of his house at night with a pack on his back to illustrate the exile (12, 5), lying on his side for 390 days, and arranging his cut hair in three piles (5, 1–17). Though some scholars of the previous generation argued that such behavior indicated mental instability, most today recognize that the actions are prophetic gestures, like Isaiah walking naked in Jerusalem for three years to dramatize the Assyrian conquest of Egypt (Is 20). They are a kind of living parable, designed to shock and provoke reflection. They do not provide a glimpse of "the real Ezekiel," whose personality (in the modern sense of personality) is largely hidden from our eyes.

The Traditions That Ezekiel Used

Every prophet favors certain traditions out of the many in Israel's lore. Isaiah made great use of the traditions about Zion and the Davidic king. Though Jeremiah cited the royal traditions, they were less important to him than the Exodus, which was the event that established the relationship between the Lord and the people. The traditions, it should be noted, do not exist as separate entities; they are related to one another as parts of a whole.

Ezekiel employed several traditions: the Exodus (especially the building of the tabernacle with its *kabod,* "glory") and the wilderness journey; Israelite and ancient Near Eastern traditions about the Temple and temple-city; and mythological traditions about the creation and maintenance of the world. The Exodus figures especially in one passage, chapter 20, where it is given an extraordinary reinterpretation. Unlike Amos and Jeremiah who regarded the Exodus as the golden moment of Israel's fidelity before the corrupting influence of the land, Ezekiel saw Israel's infidelity as beginning in the founding moment itself. Even before they left Egypt, the people had compromised themselves. To the elders consulting him, Ezekiel received the oracle: "Make known to them the abominations of their ancestors in these words . . . ; in the land of Egypt I revealed myself to them and swore: I am the LORD, your God. That day I swore to bring them out of the land of Egypt to the land I had scouted for them, a land flowing with milk and honey, a jewel among all lands. Then I said to them: Throw away, each of you, the detestable things that have held your eyes; do not defile yourselves with the idols of Egypt: I am the LORD, your God. But they rebelled against me and refused to listen to me; none of them threw away the detestable things that had held their eyes, they did not abandon the idols of Egypt" (20, 4–8). Only zeal for the divine name held back the Lord from pouring out his anger against them then and again during rebellions at the giving of the law and at the rise of the next generation.

Why did Ezekiel radically devalue the revered traditions of the Exodus? The elders consulted him in 591 (20, 1); in four years the siege would begin that will bring down Jerusalem and the Temple. Ezekiel had to prepare the people to believe that the destruction would be the Lord's doing. The prophet must unmask the false hopes that have deluded the people up to this point. He could not allow even the Exodus, the sacred moment of foundation, to be a source of pride. Israel was unfaithful even then. The people's only hope was the Lord, and in the last part of chapter 20 (vv. 33–44) Ezekiel outlined in glowing terms how the Lord, with a dazzling display of power, would enter into judgment with the people and lead them in a new exodus.

Another instance of the centrality of the Exodus is found in the account of the new temple-city and worship in chapters 40 through 48. Ezekiel 45, 7–17.21–25 and 46, 1–18 speak of the prince (Hebrew *nasi*) instead of the king. Why? Because, it seems, the prophet wants to return to the ideals of the Exodus period, before there was a king. In ancient tradition, the *nasi* was the leader of each tribe in the march in the desert (Nm 2 and 7). Another indication of the importance of the Exodus is Ezekiel's demotion of the Levitical priests and promotion of the Zadokites (44, 6–16; 48, 11). The warrant for demoting one group and promoting another was apparently inspired by the people's apostasy and punishment in Numbers 25. Phineas, of the line of Aaron, killed the apostates and it was reckoned "for him and for his descendants after him the pledge of an everlasting priesthood, because he was zealous on behalf of his God and thus made amends for the Israelites" (Nm 25, 13). A true priest rejects all foreigners in worship. The Levitical priests had been lax in excluding them from preexilic worship (Ez 8—11; 44, 10–14). In contrast, the ancestor of Zadok, Phineas, had shown himself a zealous defender of orthodox worship, and so it is only fitting that his descendants, the Zadokites, are made priests in the renewed liturgy. One may also note that the mountain in chapters 40 through 48 is associated with Mount Sinai; chapters 40 through 48 is the only body of law not uttered by Moses; and Ezekiel plays the role of Moses providing the plans for a Temple and arranging for the encampment of the tribes. To Ezekiel is revealed the blueprint of the divine dwelling, as it was to Moses in Exodus 25, 9. The purpose of the revelation on the mountain in Ezekiel is right worship and the proper ordering of the community, the same purpose as the legal material in Exodus, Leviticus, and Numbers.

The most important traditions for Ezekiel are

priestly, although it is difficult to trace exactly all the antecedents of his vision in the existing priestly traditions in Exodus 25—31 and 35—40 (the tabernacle with its equipment and rituals), Leviticus, and Numbers 1 through 10. There are similarities in Ezekiel to the so-called Holiness Code (Lv 17—26), a collection of laws concerned with the holiness of the people and the land they are entering. Examples of such similarities are the phrase, "for I, the LORD, am your God" (Lv 26, 2; in Ezekiel, "I am the Lord") as a motive to act rightly, and the mixing of "ritual" and "moral" laws (e.g., Lv 19). Some scholars distinguish two traditions in Leviticus, a "priestly code" in chapters 1 through 16 (abbreviated P) and a "holiness code" in chapters 17 through 26 (abbreviated H). Each tradition has distinctive ideas about sin and holiness. In P, the Temple is the primary locale of holiness, and in H, it is the land. Ezekiel seems to straddle the two viewpoints: Chapters 8 through 11 focus on the holiness in the Temple, and chapters 40 through 48 focus on the holiness in the land in its concern to arrange the tribal allotments around the Temple in the center. His priestly outlook is consistent. For him, Israel's sin consisted in defiling the sanctuary (5, 11), in committing "abominations" (a term used in worship, e.g., 5, 9; 7, 4; chapters 8 and 11), and in worshipping images (14, 3–5). An important metaphor for him is the priestly one of uncleanness (e.g., 20, 30–31; 22, 26; 36, 18). Uncleanness plays an important role in the long allegory of the two sisters in chapters 16 and 23, and in his attack on against the mountains, corrupted by the people's abominations. In chapter 18, Ezekiel gives a priestly torah, or teaching, on the question whether the guilt of one generation is passed on to the next.

Ezekiel also draws on mythological traditions. According to one definition, a myth is a traditional story set in the primordial past and involving supernatural elements. Myth and history are not necessarily opposed; mythological concepts and language were employed by biblical authors to show the transcendent significance of the historical laws and events they interpreted. Ezekiel, for example, used mythological language to describe his vision at the Chebar canal: the Lord appears to him in a storm cloud, luminous yet dark with water, borne by four composite figures having traits of animals and humans. The Lord is here portrayed as the divine warrior, a familiar portrayal in ancient Near Eastern religion and art (and in the Bible as well, for example, in Ex 15; 1 Kgs 18, 41–46; 19, 1–18). How much more effective and "true" is Ezekiel's mythic-historical report of his experience in 1, 3—3, 15 than a bare and unadorned statement that the Lord had appeared to him! Ezekiel's language conveys a sense of the transcendent. The mythic motifs are not mere decoration, however. They occur within a story, called by modern scholars "the combat myth," which was widely known in the ancient Near East from the third millennium BC to well into the common era. Ezekiel assumes that his hearers and readers know the story.

Though every version of the combat myth was unique, there was a basic plot: a power (often depicted as a monster) threatens the cosmic and political order of the universe. The assembly of the gods cannot find a senior god to repel the monster; the assembly appoints a young god, promising him kingship if he succeeds. Defeating the monster, the god restores the prethreat order (in some versions creates the world), builds a palace, and is acclaimed king by the gods. In biblical adaptations of the combat myth, the victory of the warrior God is normally the creation of the world or the creation of Israel. Ezekiel's adaptation of the combat myth is clearest in chapters 38 through 48. Before the Lord can build his palace and city, an enemy, greater and more resistant than the historical nations mentioned in chapters 25 through 32, must be faced and defeated. That enemy is Gog of the land of Magog. Only when he and his armies are defeated (38—39) can the Temple be built. With Gog of the land of Magog eliminated, the Lord can build his city and decree new ordinances. When one appreciates the mythic nature of these chapters, one realizes that Ezekiel is speaking of the *far future* in these chapters. Before the new world can come in definitively, evil itself, which is more than the evil of any one nation, has to be defeated. One can see how a mythological perspective enables the prophet to speak of matters that transcend history as such, yet without cutting loose from history, for he is speaking of history's goal.

The Literary Structure of the Book

Of all the prophetic books, Ezekiel is arranged with the most skill and purpose. To some extent, the structure is the message. Chapters 1 through

24 are oracles against Judah; 25 through 32 are oracles against foreign nations; and 33 through 48 are oracles of restoration for Judah and Jerusalem. Since the oracles *against* the foreign nations are by that fact *for* Judah, they can be viewed under restoration. The whole book falls into two equal parts, doom (1—24) and restoration (25—48). Like a good sentinel (3, 16–21; 33, 1–6), Ezekiel preached doom and warning right up to the fall of Jerusalem in 586 BC. After that great event, his task was to preach restoration. The two halves of the book are closely connected. The first part announced the fall of the city and urged Israel to give up its delusions and false hopes of speedy relief. Divine judgment had to come, for only a divine action makes possible the reign of God. The reign of God means, first, the overturning of the false rule of the pagan nations (25—32) and, second, the implementation of the justice of God in the land (33—48). The implementation has three aspects: (1) a new exodus and conquest of the land (33—37); (2) the vanquishing of primordial evil greater than that in any one nation (38—39); and (3) the new temple-city, the return of the Lord who departed in chapter 11, the regulations of the new worship, the river coming from the Temple, and the new encampment of the tribes around the temple-city (40—48). A detailed outline illuminates the significance of the structure. See outline, RG 327.

Three visions provide a complementary structure: chapters 1 to 3, 8 to 11, and 40 to 48. The first depicts the prophet's call, the second is the judgment against Jerusalem and the Temple, and the third is the restoration of the Temple and the arrangement of the holy land. Ezekiel 43, 3 expressly relates the three visions: "The vision was like that which I had seen when he came to destroy the city, and like that which I had seen by the river Chebar." Although there are visions in other prophetic books (Zec 1—6), only in Ezekiel are they woven into the architecture of the book. In the first vision, Ezekiel sees the glory (Hebrew *kabod*) of God that dwelt in the tabernacle in the wilderness and in the Temple in Jerusalem. Phrasing carefully in order to safeguard the sacrality and otherness of the glory, the prophet describes only the wheels of the divine throne. The throne is mobile; it is in Babylon rather than Jerusalem. This opening scene foreshadows the departure of the glory from Jerusalem in 10, 1—11, 25 and the return in 43, 1–12. A deity able to move, unlike the traditional picture of the deity dwelling in the Temple in Jerusalem, is an ominous beginning to the book. Ezekiel's unpopular message has evidently isolated him from the other exiles as he sits alone at the banks of the canal. God finds him by a canal outside the city. The next vision (8—11) is pivotal in the book: an angelic figure transports Ezekiel from Babylon to Jerusalem, gives him a tour of the Temple, and points out men committing cultic abominations and injustice against others. Angelic servants kill all those within who have not been marked as contrite, a harbinger of the slaughter that will take place when the Temple is destroyed. In the ancient Near East no temple is destroyed unless its god has already abandoned it. The glory abandons the city, lifted up by the wings of the cherubim. Ezekiel describes the vision to his fellow exiles and attempts to show them its significance. In the last vision (40—48) the Lord returns to the temple-city, rebuilt on a heavenly model and protected from all corrupting foreign influence. A new torah or authoritative teaching is given and all is made ready for a new people.

Within the structure, there are some correspondences between chapters 1 through 24 and 25 through 48. The news of the destruction of Jerusalem plays a key role in the book. Shortly before the city fell in July 586, Ezekiel's wife died, and the prophet was forbidden to perform the mourning rites for her as a symbol of the loss of the city (24, 15–27). He was also struck dumb (3, 26–27; 24, 27). When the news comes, he was able to speak (34, 21–22) and proclaimed the Lord's restoration. In 3, 16–21, Ezekiel was made a sentinel charged with telling his people of their impending destruction. When the destruction took place, his sentinel task was reaffirmed (33, 1–9) for the new phase in God's plan for the people. In 36, 1–5, the prophet blessed the mountains of Israel, reversing his earlier denunciations in 6, 1–10; the mountains evidently stand for the entire land.

Some Key Chapters in the Book

In the vision of the throne chariot and the commission (1, 2—3, 15), the prophet stood alone beside the Chebar canal and saw a large lumi-

Outline of the Book of Ezekiel

I. Impending Doom (1—24)
  A. Title and introduction (1, 1–3)
  B. Vision of the Enthroned One and Commission of Ezekiel
    1. Vision of the divine throne (1, 1–28)
    2. Commissioning of the prophet (2, 1—3, 27)
  C. Symbolic Acts and Oracles
    1. Three symbolic actions (4, 1—5, 4)
    2. Three matching oracles (5, 5—7, 27)
  D. Vision of Divine Judgment on the Temple
    1. The abominations committed in the Temple (8, 1—9, 11)
    2. God departs from the city (10, 1—11, 25)
  E. Condemnation of Leaders and People
    1. Symbolic gesture foreshadowing the exile (12, 1–28)
    2. Condemnation of false prophets (13, 1–23)
    3. Idolatry *versus* right behavior (14, 1–23)
  F. Allegories and Metaphors of Judgment
    1. Allegory of the vine wood (15, 1–8)
    2. Allegory of Jerusalem as God's faithless wife (16, 1–63)
    3. Allegory of the two eagles (17, 1–24)
    4. Priestly decisions on intergenerational responsibility (18, 1–32)
    5. Two allegories on the king (19, 1–14)
  G. Final Indictment and Condemnation
    1. Review of the Exodus (20, 1–44)
    2. The sword oracles (20, 1—21, 32)
    3. The guilt of Jerusalem (22, 1–31)
    4. The allegory of the two sisters (23, 1–49)
    5. Two signs of the end (24, 1–27)
II. Restoration (33—48)
  A. Oracles against Foreign Nations
    1. Against neighboring states (25, 1–17)
    2. Against Tyre (26, 1—28, 19)
    3. Against Sidon (28, 20–26)
    4. Against Egypt (29, 1—32, 32)
  B. Justice in the Land
    1. The second commission of the prophet (33, 1–33)
    2. The good Shepherd replaces false shepherds (34, 1–31)
    3. Oracles against the mountains of Edom (35, 1–15)
    4. Blessings on the mountains of Israel (36, 1–15)
    5. Renewal of Israel (36, 16–38)
    6. The people are brought back to life
      a. Vision of dry bones (37, 1–14)
      b. The two sticks rejoined (37, 15–28)
  C. The conquest of Gog of Magog
    1. Gog's attack on the people of God (38, 1–23)
    2. God's victory (39, 1–29)
  D. The New Temple and the New Worship
    1. Description of the new Temple
      a. The Temple court (40, 1–47)
      b. Inside of the Temple (40, 48—42, 20)

nous cloud moving in his direction. It was radiant (1, 4), like the luminous clouds that accompanied appearances of the Lord in such ancient traditions as Exodus 19, 9; 24, 16; 33, 9; and 34, 5. As it came near, he discerned four creatures, all radiant, in its lower part; they had human feet and hands but with four wings and four faces. They moved as one; below and alongside each there was a wheel rimmed with eyes, and above them was a shining expanse. As the creatures' wings slackened and the apparition came to a halt, the prophet looked up and saw a sapphire throne upon which a human figure sat, glowing, ringed by a rainbow. It was the throne of God. The order of the narrative is the order of the prophet's perception: sights, then sounds; the lower part of the vision, then the upper; the movement of the apparition, then the halting. (These remarks do not apply to 1, 8b–12, which are dislocated.) Though unparalleled in its bold portrayal of divinity, the vision is also traditional; Psalms 18, 8–14 (parallel in 2 Sm 22) is a similar storm appearance; the composite creatures are found in Isaiah 6 and attested in Mesopotamian and Syrian religious symbolism. To perceive the full significance of the divine manifestation, one must take into consideration the commission in 1, 28—3, 15. As Moshe Greenberg points out, one can assume from the commission to preach to a hardhearted people that Ezekiel was already an outcast from his community. Instead of facing the impending disaster, the people put their faith in prophets who said the whole thing would soon be over. The majestic vision vindicated the prophet's minority view; the Lord told him his community would not believe his message and yet he must speak, saying, "Thus says the LORD God." Further, in 3, 1–3 the

Lord commanded him to eat the scroll like Jeremiah, "When I found your words, I devoured them; they became my joy and the happiness of my heart" (Jer 15, 16; cf. Pss 119, 103). Though the gesture of eating the scroll seems bizarre, it was typical of Ezekiel to use traditional material with unusual concretization and dramatization. In any event, Ezekiel's *writings* seem to have been arranged with exceptional artistry and confidence in the power of the written word to instruct and teach. One last point: the mobile throne shows the Lord able to leave the Jerusalem Temple and meet the exiles in their new residence; such mobility will be demonstrated negatively by the departure in chapter 11 and positively by the return in chapter 43.

More than any other prophet, Ezekiel uses gestures to provoke his audience to question him (e.g., 4, 1–3.4–8.9–17; 5, 1–4; 12, 1–11; 37, 15–24). The gestures are a kind of street theater to capture the attention of an unreceptive audience. On one occasion, Ezekiel was told to take a brick, sketch a city on it, build miniature siege works against it, and put a metal plate between himself and the city; he then was told to lie on his left side for 390 days, then on his right side for forty days. He had also to eat bread made of different grains (as one might in a siege) and ration his water. This action was an anticipation of the disasters lying ahead for the people when Jerusalem would be destroyed (chapter 4). The prophet was evidently acting out the disaster that the people were refusing to face as they clung to hopes of a speedy return to their normal lives in Judah. The people will lie helpless as they "bear their punishment." The prophet's sign of not mourning one's wife in 24, 15–27 is an example of a sign provoking a reaction: "Then the people asked me, 'Will you not tell us what all these things that you are doing mean for us?' " (24, 19).

The vision of the corruption of the Temple and the departure of the glory (8, 1—11, 25) can be confusing. Chapters 8 through 11 are linked to the opening vision in chapters 1 through 3 in reverse order: the luminous figure in 8, 2 is linked to 1, 27; the throne in 10, 1, to the throne in 1, 26; the sounds of wings in 10, 5, to the sounds of wings in 1, 24; the wheels in 10, 9–13, to the wheels in 1, 15–18, and the faces in 10, 14, to the faces in 1, 10. The "cherubim" in chapter 10 are the same as the "living creatures" in chapter 1. According to Greenberg, a chiasm, or sandwich structure, shapes chapters 8 through 11:

A. Ezekiel converses with the elders (8, 1a)
  B. The hand of the Lord fell upon him (8, 1b)
    C. A luminous figure (8, 2–3)
    C'. The glory of the Lord (11, 22–23)
  B'. The spirit lifted him up (11, 24b)
A'. Ezekiel tells the exiles what the Lord has revealed to him (11, 25)

In the section framed by this chiasm (8, 4—11, 21), the angelic guide gives Ezekiel a tour of the corrupt practices that have polluted the Temple and the social wrongs that have ruined the people (8, 5–18). Punishment is imposed (9, 10–11). Meanwhile, the glory of the Lord begins to move, on its way to leave the Temple (10, 4–5); the cherubim stop at the entrance of the east gate (10, 8–22). Next, in a passage that balances the description of the first group of men in Chapter 8, the spirit brings Ezekiel to the east gate to view more evidence of wicked behavior (11, 1–13). In 11, 14–21, a reassuring word comes to Ezekiel that the exiles will not lose their property back in Judah. Though the Lord removed them far away among the nations, yet he has been a sanctuary to them for a little while in the countries where they have gone (11, 16, different translation from NAB). The Lord abandons his Temple. At the time of this vision, perhaps not too long after the prophet's commission in 593, the exiles were unprepared for the possibility that the Temple might be destroyed.

Chapter 18, one of the most famous chapters in Ezekiel, gives priestly decisions (torah) on questions that had become especially pressing because of the people's situation. Though sometimes misinterpreted as a charter of religious in-

dividualism, chapter 18 makes two distinct points: (1) 18, 1–20 teaches that one generation will not have to suffer for the sins of a previous generation, contrary to an older view preserved in Exodus 20, 5, "For I, the LORD, your God, am a jealous God, inflicting punishment for their fathers' wickedness on the children of those who hate me, down to the third and fourth generation"; (2) 18, 21–28 teaches that past sins do not encumber a person currently leading a good life. These teachings were provoked by a fashionable proverb of the time, "Fathers have eaten green grapes, thus their children's teeth are on edge." The proverb implicitly accused God of punishing the innocent descendants of wicked forbears. The prophet denies any "vertical" guilt (between generations) but insists on "horizontal" guilt, that is, the present generation must bear its own guilt. The people are not simply victims of someone else's sin.

Other chapters of the book are long essays detailing the history of the Lord's relationship with the people—chapters 16 (the Lord's relationship with personified Jerusalem), 20 (the retelling of the Exodus), and 23 (the story of the two sisters, Oholah and Oholibah, respectively Samaria and Jerusalem). In the two allegories (16 and 23), the Lord came upon helpless women and made them noble, yet they fought him every step of the way. What is the purpose of these exceedingly negative retellings of Israel's history? One must be aware that Israel found its identity by telling its national story. A comparison may be helpful. A modern person's identity arises largely from his or her own story: who one's parents were and of what social class; where one grew up, went to school, where one worked, and whom one married. If one becomes unhappy or dysfunctional, one examines one's story and seeks to find a new and more productive way of telling that story. Similarly, Ezekiel felt the people misunderstood their national story; they had to be shown that their version no longer made sense; it was not uniformly glorious as the people commonly believed. So Ezekiel retold the story in new and perverse ways. He said that the people were unfaithful from the beginning; their history gave them no reason for pride.

Ezekiel's retellings of the story in chapters 16 and 23 can offend modern readers. Two things must be noted. First, Ezekiel has a peculiar strategy of dramatizing a reality and, to modern tastes, exaggerating it. His use of the marital metaphor for the relationship of the Lord and Israel is an example. The metaphor was at least as old as Hosea 1—3; Ezekiel makes it concrete far beyond any usage in Hosea, drawing out the personification and dwelling on its sexual aspects. Second, Ezekiel describes the infidelity of Israel as flagrant sexual misconduct: she is a prostitute and deserves to be humiliated and punished. The prophet is a child of his time, portraying the broken relationship as a woman's betrayal of a man, and the deity's act of justice as satisfying his male rage and jealousy (e.g., 16, 23–24). Furthermore, either Ezekiel or an editor in 23, 46–49 goes on to make the story a warning against all women's lewd behavior. The warning, of course, makes a legitimate point: lewd conduct is wrong in women (as well as in men). One must be careful, however, not to imply that women are usually unfaithful. In speaking about such biblical passages, it is pastorally advisable to speak of the marriage metaphor as a favored metaphor for the relationship of the Lord and Israel. The metaphor expresses a relationship that is mutual, passionate, self-giving, nurturing, and faithful.

Unlike chapters 16 and 23, chapter 20 speaks without allegory about the people's past and future. The occasion for this essay is an inquiry to Ezekiel by some of the elders for an oracular response. Instead, the Lord tells the prophet to indict them, to make known to them the abominations of their ancestors (v. 5). To indict them, he tells the history of the people in four stages: Egypt (vv. 5–10), the first wilderness generation (vv. 11–17), the second wilderness generation (vv. 18–26), and in the land (vv. 27–29). Verses 30–44 are the application and consequences: God refuses again to respond to an inquiry (vv. 30–31) and then reveals a new exodus (vv. 32–44): "I will lead you to the desert of the peoples, where I will enter into judgment with you face to face" (v. 35), and the people will finally come into the land and serve the Lord on the holy mountain (v. 40). The prophet retells the history in such a way as to take away all cause for pride. The people's task is to allow the Lord in the future to redo the Exodus so that the result will be a faithful people.

The oracles against the foreign nations are in chapters 25 through 32, the center of the book, the same placement as Isaiah (chapters 13—27) and the Greek text of Jeremiah (25, 13; 31). Ezekiel's arrangement is careful: chapters 25—28 are oracles against six nations (Ammon, Moab, Edom, Philistia, Tyre, and Sidon), beginning with the nation directly east (Ammon) and then proceeding clockwise ending in the direction of northwest (Sidon). Geographically, one would expect the list to end with the north, the direction from which the enemy of Israel at this time, Babylon, would invade. Jeremiah 25, 9 even calls Babylon the "the enemy from the north." For Ezekiel, however, Babylon is not the enemy but the instrument of the Lord's judgment, even exercising judgment against the seven nations (e.g., Ez 26, 7; 19, 18; 30, 10). Instead, the book places Egypt in the seventh and climactic arrangement. Moreover, there are seven oracles against Egypt (29—32). One is prepared for the concentration on Egypt by the lengthy oracles against Tyre (26—28). The placement of the oracles in this part of the book contributes to the meaning of the prophet's message in at least three ways: (1) since the Lord of all the world has judged Judah and Jerusalem, surrounding nations are affected by that judgment; (2) the punishment of the nations that persecuted Judah is the first step in the restoration of Judah, which will be announced in more positive form in chapters 33—37; (3) chapters 25 through 32 prepare for chapters 38 and 39: just as the defeat of the nations makes possible the restoration of Judah upon its land, so the defeat of all human and cosmic evil in chapters 38 and 39 makes possible the definitive kingdom in chapters 40 through 48.

Chapters 33 through 37 contain a message of restoration. The opening chapter recalls earlier passages and moves one into a new age for Israel. The prophet as watchman (33, 1–9) harks back to 3, 16–21 and Ezekiel's initial call; the passage on individual retribution (33, 10–20) has relevance for chapter 18, which treats sin, guilt, and punishment; the arrival of the fugitive from Jerusalem and the end of Ezekiel's muteness (32, 22) alludes to 3, 22–27 and 24, 25–27. Ezekiel 33, 23–33 insist that salvation is reserved for those in exile who have been transformed. It anticipates 36, 16–38. Chapter 34, the divine king as shepherd, stands in the tradition of referring to kings as shepherds: 2 Sm 5, 2; Mi 5, 4; Jer 2, 8;

3, 15; 23, 1–6. Ezekiel's passage in turn influenced Zec 11, 4–17, and together they helped to form New Testament passages on the divine shepherd like Mark 6, 34 and John 10.

Ezekiel 36, 16–38 makes points similar to those in Jeremiah 31, 31–37. Both passages speak of an interior renewal. As a priest, Ezekiel introduces a number of ritual details to accompany the interior transformation: cease to profane my holy name; witness to my holiness; sprinkle with clean (or holy) water; be cleansed of idols; observe my decrees. Chapter 37 uses two different images to recount Israel's revival: dry bones scattered across a field are fitted together, covered with sinews and flesh, and brought to life by the breathing of the spirit and the two sticks brought together.

The final part of the book begins with chapter 38, not chapter 40, for the battle of Gog of the land of Magog against the Lord is the necessary prelude to the construction of a new temple-city, its regulations, and the positioning of the holy people around it. Chapters 38 and 39 presume that Israel has returned from exile and dwells peacefully on its own land (38, 12). In a grand finale, God, the divine warrior, musters the armies of the world and lures them into a massive battle that results in their annihilation and his glory. Such a divine initiative was, according to 38, 17, predicted in such earlier prophetic passages as Isaiah 29, 7; Micah 8, 11–13; Jeremiah 1, 14. Isaiah 14, 24–27 predicted that the great empire Assyria would be destroyed in the midst of the holy land. Furthermore, Exodus texts said that the Lord was glorified by the defeat of the Egyptians: "Thus will I make Pharaoh so obstinate that he will pursue them. Then I will receive glory through Pharaoh and all his army, and the Egyptians will know that I am the LORD" (Ex 14, 4). Such a statement sounds very much like Ezekiel 39, 13, which describes the victory as the day the Lord reveals his glory. To a first-time reader, the text of chapters 38 and 39 seems confused, and indeed there may have been revisions or additions to underline the meaning. Its structure, however, seems clear: 38, 1–16, Gog's attack on Israel; 38, 17–23, God's war against Gog; 39, 1–16, God's victory (39, 1–3 is parallel to 38, 1–6); 39, 17–29, God's glory is revealed to all. Although based vaguely on historical characters (Gog seems based on the Lydian ruler Gyges; Magog, his homeland, was probably created to rhyme with Gog; Gomer is from the Cimmerians), the scene is *transhistorical;* it is an event that will happen at an unspecified future time. Divine initiative is stressed repeatedly, just as it is in the Exodus accounts. Gog does not attack on his own initiative; the Lord brings the army into the holy land so that he can destroy it on the mountains of Israel. The text seems to presume that there is some primordial evil, greater than any one empire that must be identified and destroyed before Israel can live in complete peace. In a sense, the composite battle and victory is a theological reflection on evil and a statement of the hope that God will someday eradicate every vestige of that evil.

According to the combat myth, after winning the cosmic battle, the victorious deity is recognized as the supreme god and builds his palace (temple), announcing his decrees for the ruling of the world. In chapter 40, 1–4, the hand of the Lord brought Ezekiel in a vision to the land of Israel and set him down on a very high mountain on which there was a city and a temple. An angelic figure shows him the ground plan (there are no elevations in the plan) of the Temple area; the tour is a counterpart to the tour of chapters 8—11. The order of topics in 40 through 48 follows generally those of the priestly writings of the Pentateuch (Ex 25—31; 33—40; Lv; Nm 1—10; 32; 34—35). The temple plan follows generally the latest form of the Solomonic Temple but with an emphasis on safeguarding the sanctity of the temple from profane contact. For example, the eastern gate ("the gate which faced the east," 40, 5) is a military gate, like gates found in Gezer, Hazor, and Megiddo, which contain four successive recesses so that guards can interrupt chariots rushing the gate. The nearness of the king's palace to the temple in the old system is vigorously criticized (43, 6–12). The Lord returns to the temple (43, 1–5), and Ezekiel sees "that the temple was filled with the glory of the LORD" (v. 5).

The next section of the vision (43, 13—46, 24) is concerned with the altar, the reorganization of the clergy making the Zadokites alone full priests (45, 15–31), the territory set apart for them (45, 1–9), and the prince's responsibilities for supporting the temple (46) and overseeing justice (45, 9). "Prince" is an ancient premonarchic title that Ezekiel revives in place of "king," which for him had become a symbol of failed leadership. The third section is introduced by 47, 1–11, the water flowing from the temple throughout the land, which serves as a transition from temple to land. Water in Ezekiel is associated with the deity (1, 24 and 43, 2). The sacred mountain is the garden of God, the source of all fertilizing waters (Gn 2, 10–14; cf. Ez 28, 13; 31, 8–9; 36, 35). Mount Zion is also associated with that tradition (e.g., Ps 46, 4 and Is 12, 3; 33, 20–24). One of the four great rivers arising in the garden of Eden was the Gihon, which is, according to 1 Kings 1, 33, the river of Jerusalem. The remaining chapters speak of the boundaries of the future land of Israel (essentially the same as Nm 34, 1–12), the redistricting of the tribes in equal east-west strips, each with coastal land, uplands, and territory in the Jordan-Dead Sea depression. The new name given to Jerusalem, "The Lord is there," is the last verse in the book.

The Theology of the Book

Ezekiel's theology originated in his prophetic interpretation of the situation of his community—the Judeans living as exiles in Babylonia—and his counsels on how they should live in their new circumstances. His theology includes praxis, or observance. Although Ezekiel is concerned with the actions of the Lord and the course of Israelite history, he must also deal with the people's immediate anxieties and concerns, among which are concerns about whether they have title to their land and whether they have a future as a people. In other words, should they give up their dreams of being the Lord's special people and, instead, acculturate themselves into the Babylonian empire? As many exiles saw things, their ancestors' sins definitively severed the relationship of the Lord to Israel. This bitter truth was especially visible among the landless and unhappy exiles. Ezekiel thus had to explain concrete issues without losing sight of the overall purposes of the Lord whose spokesman he was.

At the basis of his theology was the great founding moment of Israel—the Exodus from Egypt and entry into Canaan *as seen through priestly eyes*. It has already been pointed out that the Priestly source deeply influenced the prophet. An example of its influence is the dominant structuring device of the glorious Lord on the throne of wheels: the glory appeared to the exiled prophet

(1, 28; 3, 23), departed from the Jerusalem Temple (10, 18; 11, 23), and will return to the temple-city (43, 2–5), to fill the Temple (44, 4) as the glory once filled the tabernacle in the wilderness in Exodus 40, 34. The mobility expressed by the throne with wheels is very important: the Lord is not tied down to one place or to a particular way. Like Micah's prediction, affirmed by Jeremiah, that the Temple was not sacrosanct and could be destroyed (Mi 3, 12; Jer 7, 4), and like Isaiah's prediction that the Lord was doing a new thing (Is 43, 19; 48, 6), Ezekiel strikes a blow for the freedom of God. It is important to note, however, that the Lord does not leave the Jerusalem Temple to become a spiritual presence available in every time and place. Rather, the Lord will come back to a specific place, there to meet the people in a purified and sacred place. The great empires, Assyria and then Babylonia, and the writing prophets' assessment that Israel had failed to live up to its covenantal responsibilities, changed forever the situation of Israel, in a sense "requiring" the Lord to do a new thing. What is the "new thing"? Those empires will be the instruments of Israel's purification ("judgment") and eventual return to the Lord. Hence, exile and destruction are not the end of the relationship; rather they constitute the judgment process that will establish justice, that is, uphold the righteous and put down the wicked. God is not absent from the process. Ezekiel does not hesitate to affirm that the Lord is present among the exiled population and that if people give up their delusions and their sinful ways, the Lord will raise them from the death of exile and give them a new city and temple. In the general picture of exile and restoration just presented, Ezekiel did not differ significantly from his prophetic predecessors. What then was his peculiar contribution to the Bible and to the contemporary church?

Though not cited as often by Christians as other prophetic books, Ezekiel says much to modern Christians. It insists on the Lord's transcendence and freedom; one can be overwhelmed and transformed by the presence of the Lord whom one cannot see. The Lord moves easily from the Temple to the exile and back to a restored Temple. Yet this utterly free and sovereign Lord has fallen in love with Israel and cannot leave or abandon her. Ezekiel insists more than any other prophet that the Lord acts because of the Lord's own reasons, not because of Israel's virtues or miseries. In fact, the prophet insists on this point with such vehemence that some modern readers are offended. The text locates the authority of the prophetic oracle in the Lord: the prophet is constantly referred to as "son of man," that is, mere human in comparison with God. The phrase "oracle of the Lord" occurs eighty-five times; the so-called recognition formula "that they may know that I am the Lord" occurs fifty-four times; and the assertion that the Lord acts so his name will not be profaned among the nations is constant. Although at first reading they might suggest a self-centered deity, they actually make a positive statement, for they locate the reason for God acting *in God's very self* in the divine character. How dangerous it would be if God acted because of human righteousness! God acts because of who he is, not because of who Israel is. That is the basis of true hope, and it is why Ezekiel is so intent on destroying all human grounds for hope. True hope is based in God, not in human beings.

Another important contribution of the book is its careful literary structure. Ezekiel is a writer as well as a speaker. The structure in a sense frees Ezekiel from his immediate context to address a wider audience. In the book, one sees the glorious Lord, obligated to no human institution, choosing an individual to announce a painful judgment on beloved Israel that will eventuate in the renewal of that people. The metaphors for this process are dominantly those of love (marriage and betrothal) and personal presence (departing and returning), even though Ezekiel employs the metaphors in his peculiarly concrete and dramatic way. The judgment process extends to other nations as well and has as its ultimate aim restoration rather than destruction. When the final blow comes (the destruction of the Temple), the judgment process enters a new phase, that of restoration. Again, this phase uses relational metaphors—a loving shepherd, the mountain lands of Israel, dry bones, and a stick rejoined. The restoration phase addresses the problem of permanent and residual evil in the universe in the great victory over Gog of Magog. Only after that evil is destroyed (in some future time) is it possible for the Lord's own palace and city to be constructed. Chapters 33 through 37 speak of the *immediate* future and chapters 38 through 48 of the *indefinite* future. It is his vision of the process of

judgment that Ezekiel makes his greatest contribution to the Christian Bible.

In the confusing and destructive events of the early sixth century, Ezekiel recognized the judgment of the Lord. He allowed the Lord to act in justice and compassion and do a new thing—bring about a restored people living peacefully and happily with God at the center. Without panic, steadily and insistently, he instructed the people how to live in the judgment process. He showed them its immediate goal (33—37) and its ultimate goal (40—48). They thus could endure, trust in God alone, and hope in the world that God would bring in. Ezekiel illuminates the New Testament, in which judgment leading to life plays a significant role. The book illuminates as well the life of Jesus, who underwent his own process of judgment: a righteous poor person, killed by sinners, but raised up to life.

Another important contribution of the book is its insistence that the Lord has a dwelling among human beings and among the people of Israel. God is not abstract and universal. Rather, God provides a place where people can hear and encounter him, and where fertilizing waters can flow over the earth from that precious center.

The Text of Ezekiel

The Hebrew text at times seems repetitive and overloaded. In the view of many scholars, it contains doublets (repeated verses) and expansions by disciples or scribes. The problem is particularly acute in the vision of the divine chariot in chapters 1 and 10. The Septuagint, the Greek translation made in the second century BC, is about 4 or 5 percent shorter than the Hebrew text and seems to be an earlier edition of the book. The Hebrew text is a later form of that text, which has been supplemented by systematic additions, some of which resemble language and concepts in Deuteronomy. The additions are mostly minor: additions of parallel words or phrases, explanations, filling out of the context, harmonizing additions, and Deuteronomistic formulations. The textual situation is much like that in Jeremiah, where the Greek text is 15 percent shorter than the Hebrew, and is an earlier version of the text. Scholars are divided on how to explain the longer Hebrew text and the apparent doublets, repetitions, and expansions, many of which are in the Greek text as well as the Hebrew. A few scholars defend the position that Ezekiel is the author of virtually the entire book and so attribute the repetitions and expansions to the prophet's rhetorical style. The older position, which is still the majority position today, believes that that additions and expansions were added to the text in course of copying it. Many expansions could have been made by Ezekiel himself, who apparently realized early on that the prophetic book itself could carry on his God-given task of instructing Israel. Walther Zimmerli, a respected recent interpreter, suggests, for example, that 16, 1–43 is the original core of this long chapter, and that verses 44–58 and 59–63 are expansions.

Oral proclamation can change greatly when written down, because the writer or disciple now has a new and quite different audience in mind. The arrangement of the entire book can take on a entirely new significance, for it helps *readers* to interpret the prophet's proclamation for a different situation. The editing and arranging of Ezekiel was done with such care and intelligence that it is a further step in the prophetic task of interpretation and exhortation. Thus, the additions to the book of Ezekiel do not obscure his purpose but make it available to readers. Israel never regarded the prophetic books primarily as biographies or histories. Rather, the books were and are still regarded as preaching the divine word to every generation.

Ezekiel in Jewish and Christian Tradition

In rabbinic literature, Ezekiel became a favorite of unorthodox forms of Judaism and thus was regarded with some caution by the rabbis. Four aspects of Ezekiel's prophecy were singled out. First, the divine chariot revelation in chapter 1 became the basis of Jewish mysticism and also of heretical speculation of various kinds. The mysticism is sometimes referred to as "merkabah (chariot) mysticism." Second, the rabbis feared that Ezekiel's severe denunciations of Israel in the first part of the book could be used by Christians in an anti-Jewish way and so were unacceptable. Third, the resurrection of the dry bones in 37, 1–14 was a favorite of sectarian groups and hence was played down by the rabbis. Fourth, Ezekiel's vision of the future temple and

his laws seemed to contradict the Pentateuchal instructions and nearly led to the exclusion of the book from the canon.

In the New Testament, the Gospels do not quote any text from Ezekiel. Matthew 13, 32 refers to Ezekiel 17, 23; Matthew 25, 35 to Ezekiel 18, 17, and there are a few more allusions. The most obvious debt is the portrayal of Jesus as the Good Shepherd (Mt 18, 12–14; Jn 10, 1–18), which comes from Ezekiel 34. First Peter 3, 9 harks back to Ezekiel 18, 23 and 33, 11. The New Testament book that makes constant reference to Ezekiel is Revelation (Apocalypse), usually in brief snatches and allusions. A few examples: Revelation 4, 1–8 develops the throne vision of Ezekiel 1; and Revelation 5, 1; 10, 1–4.8–11 pick up the image of the eating of the scroll from Ezekiel 2, 8–9; Revelation 17, 1–6.15–18 use the figure of the prostitute (Ez 16 and 23) to condemn Babylon; Revelation 19 and 20 derive the image of God from Ezekiel 38, 19; and Revelation 11, 21–22 are built on the vision of the new temple-city in Ezekiel 40—48. Revelation 7, 1–4 is linked to Ezekiel 7, 2 and 9, 4–6; Revelation 21, 15–16 uses Ezekiel 40, 3–5. Among the Apostolic Fathers, Ezekiel is the least cited of the prophets; in one count he is cited nine times in contrast to Isaiah, who is cited fifty-four times.

FURTHER READING

Basic Commentaries

Blenkinsopp, Joseph. *Ezekiel*. Interpretation. Louisville: Westminster John Knox, 1990. Readable, geared to pastors.

Boadt, L. *Ezekiel*. New Jerome Commentary, 305–28. Englewood Cliffs, NJ: Prentice Hall, 1990. Though relatively brief, extremely fine commentary.

Cody, Aelred. O.S.B. *Ezekiel*. Old Testament Message. Wilmington, DE: Michael Glazier, 1984. Theological focus with a particular interest in priestly matters, yet popular in style.

Craven, Toni. *Ezekiel. Daniel*. Collegeville Bible Commentary. Collegeville, MN: Liturgical Press, 1986. Good basic commentary.

Darr, Katheryn Pfisterer. *The Book of Ezekiel*. New Interpreter's Bible 6, 1075–1607. Nashville: Abingdon Press, 2001. Detailed, yet accessible. Reader-oriented method.

Galambush, Julie. *Ezekiel*. The Oxford Bible Commentary, 533–62. Oxford: Oxford University Press, 2001. Up to date, well informed.

Gowan, Donald E. *Ezekiel.* Knox Preaching Guides. Atlanta: John Knox Press, 1985. Pastoral application.

Wilson, Robert R. *Ezekiel.* HarperCollins Bible Commentary, 583–622. San Francisco: HarperCollins, 2000. Critical and concise.

Advanced Commentaries

Block, Daniel I. *The Book of Ezekiel: Chapters 1–24; The Book of Ezekiel: Chapters 25–48.* New International Commentary on the Old Testament. Grand Rapids, MI: Eerdmans, 1997, 1998. Massive, detailed, judicious, with large bibliography on each section, written from an evangelical viewpoint.

Eichrodt, Walther. *Ezekiel.* Old Testament Library. Translated by C. Quin. Philadelphia: Westminster, 1970. Classic commentary in the German Protestant tradition, focus on theological interpretation.

Greenberg, Moshe. *Ezekiel 1–20.* Anchor Bible. Garden City, NY: 1983. Helpful for the religious challenges in Ezekiel's world and for postbiblical Jewish writers.

Levenson, Jon D. *Theology of the Program of Restoration of Ezekiel 40–48.* Harvard Semitic Monographs 10. Cambridge, MA: Scholars Press, 1976. Important study that shows chapters 40 through 48 are a carefully articulated program of restoration.

Zimmerli, Walther. *Ezekiel 1; Ezekiel 2.* Hermeneia. Philadelphia: Fortress Press, 1979, 1983. A much admired and influential commentary, successfully demonstrating Ezekiel was a serious and consistent theologian.

DANIEL AND THE MINOR PROPHETS

JOHN J. COLLINS

DANIEL

[see pages 1146–70 of the Old Testament]

The book of Daniel falls into three sections. The first (chapters 1—6) consists of stories in which Daniel and his three companions are the heroes. The second (7—12) is made up of revelations told by Daniel in the first person. The third (13—14) contains short stories that are not found in the Hebrew/Aramaic text of Daniel but only in the Greek and Latin versions. Jews and Protestant Christians do not accept these stories as canonical, but Protestants include them in the Apocrypha, a collection of ancient Jewish writings, which they consider edifying even if not inspired. The different kinds of material in the three divisions of Daniel reflect the gradual growth of the book. The stories in chapters 1 through 6 are the oldest part and may originally have been independent stories. We know that the revelations were composed during the persecution of the Jews by Antiochus IV Epiphanes of Syria in 168–164 BC. The "Additions" were added some time later, probably before the beginning of the Christian era.

The Tales

The stories in the first six chapters are similar in kind to historical novels—they mention historical names and places but are, nevertheless, fictional. At several points they contradict what we know from other sources about the history of the times. For instance, Belshazzar is presented as a king of Babylon and son of Nebuchadnezzar. Ancient Babylonian inscriptions show that he was son of Nabonidus (a slightly later king), and

that he served as deputy ruler in Babylon but was never king. Darius the Mede is not attested independently of the book of Daniel, but Darius was the name of an early Persian king.

In each of these cases the book of Daniel has a smattering of history, but it is not ultimately concerned with historical accuracy. The stories are means of conveying a religious message, like the parables of Jesus, and so the occasional historical characters and places are not the main point. Daniel, like Noah and Job (with whom he is mentioned in Ez 14, 14), may never have existed, but the religious value of the stories is none the less for that.

The stories paint a picture of the life of Jewish exiles in Babylon. It is an ideal rather than a realistic picture, but it expresses hopes and defines acceptable behavior. There is a certain analogy between the situation of the Jews in a pagan world and the modern situation of Christians in a secular world, which makes the message of the tales still relevant today. This message has two facets: it affirms the possibility of life in a Gentile environment, and insists on the importance of fidelity to the essentials of the Jewish tradition.

Affirmation of the Gentile Environment

Daniel and his companions are taken into the service of the Babylonian king and are trained in "the language and literature of the Chaldeans." They express no reservations about this training. Indeed they outshine the Babylonians at their own skills (1, 20). The point of chapter 2 is that Daniel can interpret the king's dream when the Babylonian wise men fail, because of the assistance of his God. His superior ability to interpret mysteries is again in evidence in chapters 4 and 5.

King Nebuchadnezzar's dream in chapter 2 provides an interesting case study in Daniel's attitude to Gentile kingship. The dream concerns the famous statue of four metals symbolizing four kingdoms, which will all be destroyed by a stone and which symbolizes the kingdom of God. This dream foretells that ultimately *all* Gentile kingdoms will be destroyed. There is no urgency about this prophecy, however. God has allotted a lengthy period of time for Gentile rule, and during that period Jews can find fulfillment in the service of a pagan king. The spirit of the passage is similar to that of Jeremiah 27, 6–8, which affirms that all nations must serve Babylon until its time too shall come.

Chapters 4 and 5 present two case studies of pagan rule in action. In chapter 4, Nebuchadnezzar becomes proud because of his great kingdom. For this he is punished by being reduced to the condition of a beast. After a time his reason is restored, and he gives praise to God. He is then restored to his kingdom. In chapter 5, Belshazzar behaves arrogantly at a feast and profanes the sacred vessels of the Jews. Mysterious writing appears on the wall, which only Daniel can read. It pronounces judgment on the king. Because Belshazzar did not learn from the experience of Nebuchadnezzar, he is weighed in the balance and found wanting, and his kingdom is given to the Medes and the Persians. In short, Gentile kings must be subject to God in the fundamental sense that they must temper their arrogance and behave with restraint. If they do this, Daniel has no objection to their rule, and indeed he shows sympathetic concern for Nebuchadnezzar. Only when the kings exceed their limits do they incur the judgment of God.

The Importance of Fidelity

Despite their success at the pagan court, Daniel and his companions remain faithful to their Jewish religion. In chapter 1, they refuse to eat the king's food, because it is not *kosher.* (See the laws concerning clean and unclean food in chapter 11 of the book of Leviticus.) In chapter 3 the

three youths refuse to worship the king's statue at the risk of death, and in chapter 6 Daniel likewise refuses to depart from his custom of daily prayer even at the cost of being thrown into the lions' den. In each case the Jews ultimately win the respect of their rulers and emerge more successful than before. The stories of the fiery furnace and the lions' den, like all miracle stories, are meant to arouse a sense of wonder. They are not realistic stories. The long history of Christian martyrdoms and of the persecution of Jews (down to the lethal furnaces of Auschwitz) shows that God does not usually intervene to rescue the innocent. Christian tradition appropriately understood the stories of the furnace and lions' den as representing resurrection from the dead. The essential point in Daniel's stories, however, is that God has the power to save, or to do whatever is for the best. Daniel and his companions have trust in God, and this liberates them to do whatever they ought to do regardless of the immediate consequences. The attitude of the tales is well expressed in the words of the three youths (3, 17f): "If our God, whom we serve, can save us from the white-hot furnace and from your hands, O king, may he save us! But even if he will not, know, O king, that we will not serve your god or worship the golden statue which you set up." Their fidelity is not conditional. It is a matter of integrity, and this integrity is the key to their success.

The tales in Daniel 1 through 6 have a very optimistic view of the Gentile world. The Jews have enemies at the royal court, largely for reasons of envy, but the kings are well disposed and repeatedly praise and acknowledge the God of Daniel. In chapter 6, King Darius is dismayed when he is tricked into throwing Daniel to the lions. He is delighted when Daniel survives and readily confesses "the living God, enduring forever." The stories stop short of having the king convert to Judaism. In a sense it is even more gratifying to have a pagan king acknowledge the power of the God of the Jews. These tales express confidence that the truth of Jewish religion is powerful enough to impress any person of goodwill. Judaism has nothing to fear from the Gentile or secular world.

Daniel 1 through 6 conveys a sense that God is in control and that all will work out for the best. The kingdom of God can be exercised through

Daniel

the rule of pagan kings. True religion does not require any particular political system. This optimistic view of the world arose from the experience of Jews in foreign lands in much of the ancient world. It is similar to the liberal theology that has flourished in modern times wherever Christians or Jews have lived under tolerant political regimes. It is an attractive view of the world, which emphasizes the good in human nature, and is a viable theology in normal times. Unfortunately, times are not always normal, and there are occasions when we have to give more recognition to the forces of evil in the world. One such occasion in antiquity was the persecution of the Jews in the Maccabean period (see "Bible History and Archaeology," RG 52), and it was in this situation that the apocalyptic visions of Daniel (7—12) were written.

The Revelations

The Apocalyptic Genre

Daniel's visions belong to the genre of apocalyptic literature, which takes its name from the book of Revelation in the New Testament. "Apocalypse" *(apokalypsis)* is simply the Greek word for revelation, but the word has come to be associated with a particular kind of revelation, with certain recurring characteristics.

One trademark of the Jewish apocalypses (though not of the book of Revelation) is pseudonymity—that is, the real authors (whose names are not known) wrote under the names of famous people who had lived long before. Enoch, the most popular visionary, was supposed to have lived before Noah and the flood. (Enoch appears in Gn 5, 18–24.) Surprisingly, the people of the second century BC do not appear to have been skeptical about his authorship. Rather, his great antiquity added to the prestige of his writings.

Another trademark of an apocalypse is the presence of a mediating angel. An angel explains the visions to Daniel. In other apocalypses, which are not included in the canon, a visionary such as Enoch is taken on a tour of the heavens, accompanied by an angel as tour guide. The presence of the angel emphasizes the supernatural character of the experience and adds to the sense of mystery. (The interpreting angel first appears in biblical literature in the book of Zechariah.)

Apocalypses also have a typical subject matter. This deals on the one hand with the heavenly world of the angels, and on the other with predictions of the future, especially of a final judgment. This kind of writing was developed in Judaism from the third century BC on and was very popular in early Christianity. The most important Jewish apocalypses are 1 Enoch, 2 Enoch, 2 Esdras, 2 Baruch, 3 Baruch.

No genre of biblical literature is more difficult for the modern reader than the apocalypses. This literature is exceptional even within the Bible. In the modern world liberal Christians tend to avoid it, while fundamentalists too easily adapt it to their own ends. Several factors contribute to the difficulty.

The Heavy Use of Symbolism

Apocalypses do not speak directly but veil their meaning in symbolic language, which is closely related to the language of dreams. All scholars agree that King Antiochus Epiphanes is a major figure in Daniel 7—12 (see note on 7, 7). Yet the king is never mentioned by name. Instead we read of a beast with ten horns, which sprouts an eleventh, and we can infer from other historical information that the eleventh is Antiochus. The text gives us a clue. It tells us that the four beasts, of which the horned beast is the last, are four kingdoms, but it never identifies them explicitly. The lack of specificity is typical of oracles in the ancient world. It adds a sense of mystery, and strengthens the impression that the prophecy is of supernatural origin. It also has an effect on the long-term interpretation of the apocalypse. Two hundred years after Daniel was written, people could interpret the fourth kingdom as Rome, and the eleventh horn as a Roman emperor. Down through the centuries the beast could be interpreted as the villain of the day. This kind of reinterpretation is helpful if it is done with proper understanding. The apocalyptic vision describes types of characters who reappear in history. Antiochus Epiphanes was not the only tyrant worthy of being described as a beast. One of the uses of an apocalyptic vision is that it gives us language to describe new situations: the scene of beasts rising from the sea could be applied appropriately to the outbreak of World War II. It is important to realize, however, that Daniel was not predicting this war. He was speaking of a persecution in the second century BC, and his vision can be applied to other situations only by analogy. Fundamentalists often read Daniel or the New Testament Apocalypse as if they were written to predict our modern situation. In fact, they were written for their own time and place, but they can help us understand our modern situation because they describe patterns that recur throughout history.

Angels and Demons

Some modern Christians find the prominence of angels and demons in apocalyptic literature to be a problem. For Daniel, the battles between Jews and Greeks are only a reflection of a battle in heaven. Moreover, it is not God who fights for the Jews but the archangel Michael, who is mentioned here by name for the first time. Most people in the ancient world believed that the heavens were peopled with supernatural beings. Usually these were called "gods," but Jewish and Christian tradition makes a sharp distinction between the supreme deity and the lesser heavenly beings, called angels. The modern secular world, with its scientific approach to the heavens, has little room for such beings. An apocalypse, however, is not a scientific treatise but a work of imagination. To say that there is a battle in heaven between the patron angels of Greece and Judah is to say that earthly war is not entirely subject to human control. Angels provide a vivid way of dramatizing providence or divine control. To understand an apocalypse, we should not ask, "Do these angels exist?" but "What do they stand for?" and especially, "If we imagine a world with angels, what effect does this have on the way we view human life?"

Pseudonymity

We have noted above that all Jewish apocalypses are pseudonymous. This device added to the authority of a book. In an apocalypse it had another advantage: it enabled Daniel to "predict" four hundred years of history, which were already past when the book was written. Since the prediction was demonstrably accurate over these four hundred years, people were more likely to believe the real prediction of what was still to come. From a modern viewpoint this practice seems deceptive and therefore unethical. We consider pseudonymous writing a forgery. The

practice was widely accepted, however, in the Greek and Roman world as well as in Judaism. While the common people presumably believed that the revelations were genuinely old, the real authors must have been known to an inner circle. It is difficult for us to reconstruct the mindset of people who wrote pseudonymous books, but it is certain that they did not regard their work as deceptive. It is possible that the authors put themselves in the place of Enoch and Daniel, and imagined that they were actually describing the visions of these ancient worthies. In any case, the enduring value of the apocalypses does not lie in the accuracy of their predictions but in the kind of conduct they inspired and supported. In the case of Daniel, the question is not whether Daniel really predicted all these things in advance, but whether his stance in the face of religious persecution is a good one.

Determinism

Apocalyptic literature typically assumes that history has a fixed duration and can be divided into a set number of periods (for example, four kingdoms or seventy weeks of years). The course of events can be predicted centuries in advance. Consequently, history appears to be predetermined. It is important to realize that this does not mean that human decisions are predetermined. On the contrary, the book of Daniel is basically a call for decision in a time of crisis. The course of history is set, and the fate of the righteous and the wicked is predetermined. The fate of any individuals, however, remains to be decided and will be determined by the kinds of decisions they make.

Predictions of the End

Perhaps the aspect of apocalyptic literature that most offends modern sensibilities is the attempt to predict exactly the time of the end. (In Daniel, the end in question is the end of the persecution. In later apocalypticism it is often the end of the world.) Down through the centuries, apocalyptic groups have often set a date for the end of the world, only to see it come and go. Naturally such predictions have been discredited by their frequent failure. The book of Daniel actually gives three very precise dates for the end of the persecution. In 8, 14, an angel says that the Temple will be desolate for 2,300 evenings and mornings, or 1,150 days. At the end of chapter 12, however, we are given two different figures: 1,290 days and 1,335 days.

Presumably the number was increased when the end was delayed. We can understand the function of these numbers in the time of persecution: it was easier to keep going if one believed that relief would come on a specific day. Remarkably enough, however, the failure of these exact predictions did not discredit the book of Daniel. Later interpreters assumed that the figures must have some symbolic meaning and were not to be taken literally. In fact, the attempt to predict the end is only a very minor element in apocalyptic literature, and its importance should not be blown out of proportion. It served a limited purpose in its historical setting, but it must be admitted that such attempts were ultimately counterproductive. This is not an aspect of apocalyptic literature that anyone should try to imitate in a modern setting.

Information or Exhortation?

The problems of interpreting apocalyptic literature in the modern world can be summarized by asking whether we should read these books for information or for exhortation. It is a fact that any apocalypse combines the two aspects. It tries to teach us a view of the world, and if we accept that view we will be disposed to act in a certain way. The problem is that the apocalyptic view of the world is no longer acceptable. Angels and demons are not part of our universe, and we can no longer believe that the duration of history is coming to an end. Much of the "information" provided by an apocalypse is now incredible if taken literally. It still has value, however, if we regard it as symbolism and focus on the attitudes and actions it was designed to support. Such an ethical focus is fundamentally important for understanding the book of Daniel and its relevance to modern times.

A Symbolic Vision

Chapter 7 is one of the most famous and influential of all apocalyptic visions. In part it resembles Nebuchadnezzar's dream in chapter 2: it describes four human kingdoms, which will be followed by a kingdom set up by God. The imagery, however, is very different. Instead of four metals, Daniel 7 describes four beasts that rise out of the sea. In biblical poetry the sea is often a symbol of chaos, of all that is opposed to God, and it is sometimes said to be inhabited by monsters (for instance, Is 27, 1: God "will slay the dragon that is in the sea"; compare Is 51, 9f). When chapter 7 in Daniel represents the pagan kingdoms as beasts from the sea, then the point is that they are rebellious and opposed to God. This represents a view of the pagan kingdoms, which is much more negative than anything in Daniel 1—6.

After the vision of the four beasts, Daniel sees a judgment scene in which an "Ancient One" sits on a throne, surrounded by thousands of angels, and the fourth beast is condemned to the fire. Then "one like a son of man" appears on the clouds of heaven. Christian tradition, beginning with the Gospels, identified this figure as Jesus Christ, but the passage could not have been understood in that way by Jews in the second century BC. Jewish tradition identified the "son of man" as the messiah. Modern scholarship is divided between two interpretations: some see the figure as a collective symbol for Israel, others as the archangel Michael. It is quite clear that he represents the triumph of the Jewish people over their persecutors. The issue in dispute is how that triumph was understood. The view that the son of man figure is Michael relies on the analogy with Daniel 10—12, where Michael represents Israel in a heavenly battle with the angelic prince of Greece. The triumph of the Jews, then, is imagined in the apocalypse as a victory by their heavenly patron. The son of man is always understood as a heavenly individual in other Jewish apocalypses (1 Enoch, 2 Esdras).

Daniel 7 was written during the persecution of the Jews by Antiochus Epiphanes of Syria, which is described in 1 and 2 Maccabees. The experience of persecution colored the author's perception of all Gentile kingdoms. The message of the vision is that pagan rulers are evil and in rebellion against God, but that they will be defeated by the power of God. The symbolism of the vision, however, with its beasts and fire and figure riding on the clouds, expresses this idea with exceptional power and vividness. Consequently, the imagery has been used over and over again in new situations. It provides language that can express the evil, which erupts from time to time in human affairs (think of the Holocaust as a modern example) and which can also express a hope that does not depend on human power. The message of the vision is one of hope. Although the forces against us may be demonic, the power of God and the angels will ultimately prevail. The imagery of this vision is used repeatedly in the Gospels and most elaborately in the book of Revelation.

Daniel 8 is a symbolic vision very similar to chapter 7. Even some of its imagery (the little horn) is taken from the earlier chapter. In this case the central episode of the imagery concerns the revolt of the little horn against the host of heaven. There is a reminiscence here of the morning star, son of the dawn in Isaiah 14, which rises above the stars of God but is then cast down to the depths. Antiochus Epiphanes is identified as an example of the general pattern represented by the Isaianic passage. Again, the prophecy is one of hope since the pattern guaranteed the fall of the rebel.

A Prophecy Reinterpreted

A different kind of revelation is found in chapter 9. In this case, a biblical prophecy provides the point of departure. Jeremiah had prophesied that the land would be subject to Babylon for seventy years. According to 2 Chronicles 36, 20f, this prophecy was fulfilled by the restoration under Cyrus of Persia (although only fifty years had elapsed). Zechariah 1, 12 related it to the rebuilding of the Temple (about sixty-six years after its destruction). The author of Daniel evidently did not think that the restoration of the Persian period satisfied the prophecy. Rather than discard the prophecy as a failure, however, he reinterpreted it. Seventy years really means seventy weeks of years, or 490 years. The way of interpreting Scripture here is basically the same as the way of interpreting dreams and visions in the previous chapters. (It is also typical of the Pesharim, or biblical commentaries, found among the Dead Sea Scrolls.) The numbers in Jeremiah's prophecy are taken as symbolic. The implications of this procedure are far-reaching. When the visionary says that only three and a half years are left before the end, we cannot be sure that this will not turn out to mean three and a half weeks of years. In short, the impression of precise prediction, which we get from the use of numbers, is misleading. What Daniel ultimately affirms is not the particular timetable but the re-

liability of the promises of God, however mysterious their timing may be.

Chapter 9 also includes a remarkable prayer on the lips of Daniel. The prayer is of a type common in the postexilic period. (See for example Neh 9.) Its theology is typical of the tradition influenced by the book of Deuteronomy. Israel is punished for its own sin and can only appeal for the mercy of God. This theology is rather different from the usual theology of Daniel. The primary cause of Israel's suffering in apocalyptic theology lies in the wickedness of the nations that rebel against God, and indeed in the predetermined plan of history. In response to the prayer, Daniel receives a revelation, but there is no question of forgiveness, or of shortening the time of trial because of repentance. From the viewpoint of the book of Daniel, it is appropriate to express repentance, as Daniel does, but we should not expect our prayers to alter the course of events.

Another Dimension of History

Daniel's apocalyptic view of history is most fully laid out in chapters 10 through 12, which make up one long vision. There, an angel explains to Daniel that there is an ongoing battle in heaven between the archangels Michael and Gabriel on the one hand and the angelic "princes" of Persia and Greece on the other (10, 13.20f). This battle is reflected on earth in the wars of the Hellenistic age, which are described at length in chapter 11, and especially in the career of Antiochus Epiphanes who takes up approximately half the chapter (11, 21–45). At the end Michael will arise in victory (12, 1), and the resurrection will follow.

This long passage makes several claims about history, which would not be apparent to the typical observer:

First, what is involved is not just warfare between human kingdoms, but a battle between angelic powers, and the outcome of this cannot be decided by human power.

Second, the course of history is fixed in advance. The battles of the Hellenistic age can be revealed to Daniel in the Babylonian exile. In fact, the passage was written during the persecution under Antiochus Epiphanes. It gives an accurate account of history down to that time (11, 39). Such "prophecy after the fact" implies that the course of history is predetermined, and it inspires confidence in the actual prediction with which the passage concludes (in this case, the imminent death of the king 11, 40–45, and the resurrection, 12, 1–3).

Third, history culminates with the resurrection of the dead. Daniel is the only book in the Hebrew Bible that clearly affirms the resurrection of individuals. Earlier prophecy sometimes uses the language of resurrection for the restoration of the Jewish nation, as in Isaiah 26, 19 and Ezekiel 37. The book of Wisdom, which was composed in Greek about the time of Christ, also has a clear doctrine of immortality. The idea of resurrection had probably been introduced into Judaism before the time of the Maccabees. The noncanonical 1 Enoch, chapter 22, which describes the abodes of the dead as they wait for resurrection, is probably older than Daniel. There is no doubt, however, that the experience of martyrdom in the time of persecution made the Jews more receptive to belief in resurrection than they had been before. The importance of resurrection in that setting can be seen from the story of the seven brothers in 2 Maccabees 7.

Belief in resurrection made an enormous difference to Judaism, and was essential to the origin of Christianity. Traditional Jewish religion had taught that the reward for a just life was to see one's children's children, to the fourth generation, and the welfare of the nation as a whole. In the time of the Maccabees, however, pious Jews were put to death precisely for obeying the Law and so were cut off from the traditional reward for a just life. Belief in life beyond the grave, in the company of the angels, provided an entirely new perspective. Martyrdom was no longer an absurdity, but the means to a greater end. So Daniel announced that the wise would take their stand in the time of persecution, even though some of them would fall (11, 33–35). These "wise" do not, apparently, join the Maccabees to fight for national independence. Rather, they put their trust in Michael and the heavenly world and choose the way of passive resistance. The stand of these wise teachers exemplifies the ethical stance of the book of Daniel, which is the most enduring message of the book.

There is clear continuity between the apocalyptic message of Daniel 10—12 and the older stories of the fiery furnace and the lions' den. On the one hand there is the belief that God rules all kingdoms and has the power to save. On the other is the conviction that one must act with integrity even at the cost of life itself. The belief in resurrection makes this conviction easier to maintain.

The apocalyptic visions offer a much less optimistic view of the Gentile world than the tales of chapters 1 through 6. This again is not a view for all seasons but for situations of crisis, which we should hope are exceptional. Pagan powers are not always "beasts from the sea," although they may be so on occasion. The ethical stance advocated by the "wise" in Daniel 11, that of passive resistance, is not necessarily normative for all situations either. The militant revolution of the Maccabees is also canonized in the Old Testament. The book of Daniel exemplifies one possible way in which a faithful Jew or Christian may respond to a situation of oppression and persecution. Whether it is the right way can only be decided in light of the specific circumstances of each situation, but it always demands serious consideration.

The Additions

Daniel 13 and 14 are rightly labeled as an Appendix in the *New American Bible,* as they are independent stories in which Daniel happens to play a part. Susanna is placed before Daniel 1 in one Greek translation (that attributed to Theodotion), since Daniel appears there as a young boy, but there is no doubt that the story was originally independent.

Susanna

In the story of Susanna, Daniel appears as the wise judge. This role is suggested by his name (*Dan* comes from the Hebrew verb, to judge) but not by anything in Daniel 1—12. His judgment recalls that of Solomon in 1 Kings 3. The story as a whole may be described as a parable, insofar as it is a short story that reverses our expectations in some important respect. (Compare Nathan's parable in 2 Sm 11 and several of Jesus' parables.) Normally elders who have been appointed judges are the righteous ones, and the word of a young woman would carry little weight against theirs. Yet it is characteristic of biblical narrative that the underdog prevails or is justified. (A comparable story involving a woman, Tamar, can be found in Gn 38.) The story of Susanna loses some of its dramatic effect by telling us at the outset that the judges are wicked. Nonetheless the story provides a nice illustration of the unreliability of conventional expectations.

In one respect, at least, the story of Susanna has the same viewpoint as the rest of the book of Daniel. In verse 23, when Susanna is trapped, she declares: "Yet it is better for me to fall into your power without guilt than to sin before the Lord" (Dn 13, 23). This is the same lesson that we learned from the three young men, from Daniel in the lions' den, and again from the martyrs of the Maccabean period. The story is closer to Daniel 1—6 than to 10—12, since it envisages salvation in this life, and, appropriately, the execution of Susanna's accusers.

Bel and the Dragon

Daniel 14 contains two stories that make fun of pagan idolatry. These stories are caricatures. They should not be taken as accurate descriptions of Babylonian religion, any more than anti-Catholic caricatures should be taken as fair representations of the Catholic veneration of statues.

The Babylonians in the stories are excessively stupid, and their devices are too easily exposed. The story of the dragon shares with Daniel 6 the motif of the lions' den but does not necessarily depend on the earlier chapter. All we can say is that Daniel was associated with the lions' den in oral tradition, and that both these stories made use of the motif. Bel and the Dragon is more fantastic than Daniel 6: he remains in the den for six days and the prophet Habakkuk is transported from Judea by an angel to feed him. These fantastic elements give the tale a lighthearted quality, but the background here is more tense than in Daniel 1—6. Daniel confronts the Babylonian religion in a way that he never does in the earlier chapters. The Babylonians threaten him because of his religious zeal, not because of professional envy as in chapter 6.

There is a sense here that Judaism and paganism are fundamentally incompatible. The king is still benevolent, but the Babylonians suspect that he has become a Jew. There is, of course, ample precedent for demanding a clear-cut choice between the Lord and other deities (compare Elijah

in 1 Kgs 18). Daniel 1 through 6 also presupposed such a choice, but did not present it as starkly as chapter 14. There are times when confrontation can be avoided and fruitful interaction is possible. Bel and the Dragon, on the other hand, does not allow for any ecumenical relations with pagan religion. Presumably this attitude reflects the situation in which the story was written. Here again we see that the biblical stories are not timeless in character but are shaped by historical circumstances. Their modern relevance, likewise, depends on the circumstances in which we read them.

FURTHER READING

Collins, John J. *Daniel; 1–2 Maccabees.* Old Testament Message, 15. Wilmington, DE: Glazier, 1981. Introductory commentary, along the lines of this Reading Guide.

Seow, C. L.. *Daniel.* Westminster Bible Companion; Louisville: Westminster John Knox, 2003. Clear, introductory commentary intended for lay readers.

Smith-Christopher, D. L. *The Book of Daniel.* New Interpreter's Bible 7, 19–152. Nashville: Abingdon, 1996. Commentary designed for preachers. Liberationist, postcolonial perspective.

For more detailed, scholarly commentary see:

Collins, John J. *Daniel. A Commentary on the Book of Daniel, with an essay, "The Influence of Daniel on the New Testament," by Adela Yarbro Collins.* Hermeneia. Minneapolis: Fortress, 1993. Detailed commentary on the full book, including the additions.

Montgomery, James A. *The Book of Daniel.* International Critical Commentary. Edinburgh: Clark, 1927. Reprint, 1979. Classic scholarly commentary, although out of date in some respects.

For the Additions to Daniel see:

Moore, C. A. *Daniel, Esther and Jeremiah: The Additions.* Anchor Bible 44. Garden City, NY: Doubleday, 1977.

The noncanonical apocalyptic literature can be found in:

Charlesworth, J. H., ed. *The Old Testament Pseudepigrapha.* Vol. 1. Garden City, NY: Doubleday, 1983.

Sparks, H. F. D., ed. *The Apocryphal Old Testament.* Oxford: Oxford University Press, 1984.

For a study of this material see:

Collins, J. J. *The Apocalyptic Imagination.* 2nd ed. Grand Rapids, MI: Eerdmans, 1998.

THE TWELVE MINOR PROPHETS

The Book of the Twelve is a collection of prophetic oracles that were composed over a period of about 300 years. The number *twelve* is probably chosen because of the twelve tribes of Israel. At least in some cases the books are artificial—for example, it is quite clear that Zechariah 9—14 do not come from the same prophet as Zechariah 1—8. While we will review the books in their canonical order, it may be helpful at the outset to group them according to their origin.

1. Three prophets, Amos, Hosea, and Micah, were active in the eighth century BC, and were contemporary with the earlier part of Isaiah's career. Hosea was a northern prophet and Micah a southern, while Amos was a native of the Southern Kingdom who prophesied in the north. (On the two kingdoms, see the historical sketch, RG 45–50.)

2. Another cluster of three prophets can be dated in the Babylonian period, toward the end of the seventh century BC. Zephaniah is dated to the time of King Josiah (640–609 BC), Nahum proclaimed the fall of Nineveh in 612 BC, and Habakkuk prophesied when the Babylonians were already advancing westward (605–597 BC).

3. Two prophets, Haggai and Zechariah are known to have been active in the rebuilding of the Jerusalem Temple in 520–518 BC. Again, only chapters 1 through 8 of the book of Zechariah can be attributed to this prophet.

4. The remaining four books, Joel, Jonah, Obadiah, and Malachi, and the latter part of Zechariah, come from the postexilic period, but their dates cannot be determined precisely. Malachi may be roughly contemporary with Ezra in the fifth century BC. The book of Jonah and the second part of Zechariah could be as early as the fifth century or as late as the Hellenistic period (after 330 BC).

Most of these books are made up of short poetic oracles. (The book of Jonah, which is a short story, is an exception.) The nature of prophecy is that it addresses specific situations, and so it is important to know something of the time and place of the different prophets, when this is possible. At the same time, these oracles were preserved because they had enduring relevance and could be applied to new situations by analogy. All of this material was handed down orally for some time before it was put in written form. Consequently, there is often reason to doubt whether a particular prophecy was actually uttered by the prophet to whom it is ascribed. So, for example, Micah 4, 1–3 contains a passage that is also found in Isaiah 2, 1–4. We cannot now be sure which, if either, of these prophets originally spoke these lines. Moreover, these books were edited in the postexilic period, and the editors also added some passages. While it is always helpful to know the situation in which an oracle was originally given, it is not possible to be sure of the original setting of each passage.

As we might expect, there is considerable diversity in this collection, but there are also some dominant themes:

1. Most of these prophets focus their attention on the sins of their own people. There are exceptions. The oracles of Obadiah and Nahum consist entirely of condemnations of foreign nations. Haggai and Zechariah, in the period immediately after the Babylonian exile, are exceptionally supportive of their leaders and institutions. Nonetheless, most of these prophets were characterized by their critical spirit.

2. The sins they denounced were both social and cultic. The social agenda of prophecy was set by the great eighth-century BC prophets, especially Amos and Micah, but concern for the weak and unprotected persists throughout the corpus, down to the oracles of Malachi. Hosea engages in extensive polemic against the worship of gods other than the Lord, and this concern reappears from time to time in the other prophets. The prophets were even more concerned, however, with abuses in the worship of the Lord, even when there were no pagan elements involved. Amos and Micah denounced the cult of their day because it made the people complacent and distracted them from the injustice of their society. At the end of the collection, we still find Malachi criticizing the priests for failing to live up to the ideals of their office. People who performed the prescribed rituals were not necessarily pleasing to God for that reason. The prophetic critiques do not mean that ritual is not

important. On the contrary, it is precisely because it is vitally important to the religious life of
a community that they devote so much attention
to it.

3. It is common in biblical theology to say that
God acts in history. The prophets say more than
this: they teach that whatever actually happens is
the work of God. So they understood the great
calamities, which befell the Northern Kingdom
of Israel in 721 BC and the Southern Kingdom of
Judah in 587/6 BC, as acts of divine judgment. Indeed these catastrophes added to the authority of
the prophets, since they were seen as the fulfillment of their oracles. The constant reference to
historical events ensures an element of realism in
the preaching of the prophets. They are not only
concerned with moral ideals, but also with what
works in practice.

4. The theme of judgment undergoes some development in the later prophets. This can be seen
by following the motif of the Day of the Lord.
This motif first appears in Amos. In the context
it seems clear that the Israelites expected the Day
of the Lord to vindicate them against their immediate enemies. For Amos, however, the Day
of the Lord would be the occasion of judgment
on Israel. In the postexilic period, Joel anticipates a day of judgment for all nations in the valley of Jehoshaphat. In Zechariah 14 it is the day
when all the nations assemble for battle against
Jerusalem, to be defeated by the Lord. The Book
of the Twelve ends with a forward look to "the
day of the Lord, the great and terrible day." Increasingly, it is a day of definitive universal
judgment.

5. The theme of the salvation of Israel is also
more prominent in the postexilic period. Already
in the eighth century BC, Hosea looked beyond
the impending destruction by the Assyrians and
spoke of a new beginning like the Exodus of old.
After the exile it made little sense to speak of further destruction of Israel. Very often the prophets
imagine a situation that is different from the
present. When Jerusalem was in ruins, or restored in only modest circumstances, they revived the dream of Zion, the holy mountain, and
divine abode (so Joel, Zephaniah, and a postexilic passage in Micah 4). Similarly, the hope for
a restored Davidic monarchy is at home in the
period after the exile (Mi 5; Zec 9). The phrase
"on that day" frequently introduces prophecies
of the great transformation that is to come (for
example, Zec 14, 6.8.13.20). It is likely that at
least some of these oracles were inserted by
those who put this collection together, gathering
and arranging the scattered materials. These editors wanted to insure that the recollection of the
past did not outweigh the hope for the future. The
tendency of the editors to put the words of judgment in perspective is most strikingly evident at
the end of the book of Amos. After the prophet's
threat that God would wipe Israel off the face of
the earth, the editor adds, "but I will not destroy
the house of Jacob completely" (9, 8) and goes
on to prophesy the restoration of the Davidic dynasty.

Taken as a whole, the Book of the Twelve is
both a reflection on the past and a lesson for the
future. The order of the oracles is not easily apparent, and this makes reading through the collection difficult. They are certainly not arranged
in chronological order, and even the thematic order is only occasional. We can, however, find a
pattern, in which sin is followed by judgment and
judgment by salvation. Not all the individual
prophets saw this full pattern. Some, like Amos,
simply announced the imminent judgment. Others, like Haggai and Zechariah, focused on the
moment of restoration. The editors of the
prophetic books were heavily influenced by the
theology of Deuteronomy. According to that
theology, sin does not go unpunished, but God
is ultimately merciful and wants only the repentance and restoration of Israel. The collected
prophets, then, can be read as a call for repentance,
to be sustained until the final Day of the Lord. The
first book in the collection, Hosea, ends with the
invitation, "Return, O Israel, to the LORD, your
God" (Hos 14, 2). The final book, Malachi, ends
with a reminder to keep the law of Moses, and a
promise that Elijah will come to reconcile parents
and children. In this way, the lesson of the
prophets is tied in nicely with that of the Pentateuch.

FURTHER READING

Blenkinsopp, J. *A History of Prophecy in Israel.* 2nd
　　ed. Louisville: Westminster John Knox, 1996.
　　Comprehensive, reliable introduction to the
　　prophetic books.
Petersen, D. L. *The Prophetic Literature. An Introduc-*

tion, 169–214. Louisville: Westminster John Knox, 2002. Focuses on the literary character of the collection.

Sweeney, M. *The Twelve Prophets.* Collegeville: Liturgical Press, 2000. A commentary on the twelve minor prophets.

von Rad, G. *Old Testament Theology.* Vol. 2. Louisville: Westminster John Knox, 2001. Reprint of 1965 edition. Still very useful theological introduction.

HOSEA

[see pages 1171–83 of the Old Testament]

Hosea is not the first of the prophets chronologically, but he provides a good introduction to the prophetic corpus, as he is unrivaled for the beauty of his poetry and the emotional power of his oracles. He lived at a time of great crisis for the Northern Kingdom of Israel. He began his career in the middle of the eighth century (about 750 BC). Little more than a decade later Israel came under threat from the mighty Assyrian empire, which was expanding westward. The king of Israel became a vassal, or subject, of Assyria in 732 BC, the kingdom was brought to an end, and its capital Samaria destroyed, in 722 BC. In the period between the death of King Jeroboam II (who is mentioned in Hos 1,1) in 746 BC and the first submission of Israel in 732 BC, no fewer than five kings sat on the throne (and a sixth succeeded in 732 BC). It was, then, a period of great instability. While we cannot specify the occasions of Hosea's individual prophecies, it is important to be aware of this general background.

As noted in the *New American Bible,* the first three chapters stand apart from the rest of the book because of the theme of the prophet's marriage. It is difficult to discern any pattern in chapters 4 through 14. Most of the oracles proclaim the destruction of Israel, but the book ends with an invitation to repentance (14, 2–9). There is also an important prophecy of restoration at 11, 8–11.

The Metaphor of Marriage

The attractiveness of Hosea's prophecy springs from his use of metaphor and symbol, especially imagery drawn from human relationships. His most fundamental metaphor is that of marriage. The book opens with one of the most bizarre commands in all the Bible, "Go, take a harlot wife. . . ." It may be that the woman, Gomer, was not a harlot when she married, and that the command anticipates her later behavior. There is an alternative view, however, held by many scholars, which sees the choice of a harlot wife as a deliberate symbolic act on the part of the prophet (compare the bizarre symbolic acts in Isaiah 20 and Ezekiel 4). Some scholars think that Gomer was not only a prostitute but a cult prostitute, devoted to the worship of the pagan god Baal. By marrying such a person, Hosea would have attracted considerable attention, and dramatized his message that "the land gives itself to harlotry" (1, 2). In any case, the prophet uses the experience of infidelity in marriage, all too familiar to his audience, to convey an understanding of Israel's behavior toward the Lord, the God of Israel. The metaphor was appropriate for several reasons:

1. It is a fundamental presupposition of Hosea that Israel is bound to God by the covenant given to Moses. A covenant is a contractual arrangement, like a marriage. The relationship can be expressed in the declarations "You are my people" and "My God" (2, 25) on the analogy of the standard marriage formula "she is my wife, he is my husband."

2. One of the major problems addressed by Hosea was idolatry, specifically the cult of the Canaanite god Baal. The word *baal* was used in Hebrew as the common word for husband. Moreover, Baal was attractive to the people because he was a fertility god who was supposed to guarantee the productivity of land, animals, and people. Some scholars have supposed that the worship of Baal involved sexual acts with sacred prostitutes. This is now viewed as unlikely, but the imagery of prostitution and fornication is often used to symbolize idolatry. Hosea was contrasting the covenant with the Lord, understood

as a marriage, with the cult of Baal, understood as prostitution. The prophet's wife exemplified the behavior of Israel, by straying from the marital relationship.

3. Hosea's whole understanding of God is based on the assumption that God is like the best in human nature, only more so. Since marriage is the culmination of love between man and woman, it is appropriate that it should also provide the analogy for understanding the love between the Lord and Israel.

The fact that the prophet uses the most intimate aspect of his own life to convey his message is indicative of his total involvement in his prophecy. The involvement extends to his children, who are given such symbolic names as "not pitied" (Lo-ruhama, 1, 6) and "not my people" (Lo-ammi, 1, 8). There is no concern for private, personal life. The prophet and his family are at the disposal of God for the welfare of the people.

The Lord and Baal

In the great poem in chapter 2, Hosea argues that the people are mistaken when they credit Baal with providing the grain, the wine, and the oil. It is the Lord who really controls fertility. What is involved here is not simply a matter of knowing the most appropriate name for the God of nature. To acknowledge the Lord as lord is to accept the Sinai covenant, with its code of ethics for society. Israel's infidelity in worshipping Baal is the symptom of a pervasive disease. Hosea's grievance against the people is summed up in 4, 1–3:

There is no fidelity, no mercy,
no knowledge of God in the land.
False swearing, lying, murder, stealing and
adultery!
in their lawlessness, bloodshed follows
bloodshed.
Therefore the land mourns. . . .

The list of offenses closely follows the Ten Commandments, but the point is not just that specific laws are broken. It is a question of fundamental attitude. Infidelity manifests itself in sexual behavior, in idolatry, in the repeated assassination of rulers, in wavering political alliances. This lack of constancy certainly had an effect on the political fortunes of the nation. Hosea believed that it also had an effect on the land itself. He

may have been right insofar as the rulers neglected the proper care of the land because of intrigue and opportunism.

Land and Desert

In the poem in Hosea 2, the prophet plays on the rich associations of the promised land. The foundation of Israel's identity was the story of the Exodus. The escape from Egypt had been followed by forty years of wandering in the desert. After that experience, Israel had indeed looked like "a land flowing with milk and honey." Now the prophet threatened to take all that away: "I will make her like the desert, reduce her to an arid land." To appreciate the full force of this threat we must remember that for ancient Israel the gift of the land was the primary expression of salvation. There was no belief among Israelites of that time in a blessed hereafter. To reduce the land to a desert would be, in effect, to undo the Exodus. In fact, the devastation of the Assyrian invasion might well be said to do that, some years after Hosea spoke.

The desert, however, was not only a place of death. It was also a place of hope. Israel wandered in the desert in "the days of her youth." Hosea changes his metaphor in 2, 16 and plays on the positive connotations of the desert, as a place where a man might take a young woman in privacy, away from the town, to court her. What he is suggesting is that the destruction at the hands of Assyria is not the end. It is rather a transitional stage, necessary to clear away the cult of Baal and the other abuses in Israel. When Israel has been stripped down, so to speak, by the Assyrians, a new beginning will be possible, in effect a new Exodus.

The motif of a new Exodus, introduced here for the first time, would later be important for Second Isaiah (Is 40—55) after the Babylonian exile. It would be taken up again by the people who wrote the Dead Sea Scrolls, shortly before the time of Christ, and it is implied in the career of John the Baptist (Mk 1, 2f).

Criticism of the Cult

The cult of Baal was attractive in part because it was a matter of ritual rather than of ethical conduct. The Israelites were also willing to perform rituals for the Lord. Hosea complains at the facile way in which they professed repentance, only to have the sentiment vanish as soon as they left the Temple (6, 1–4). In the course of this passage the Israelites say: "He will revive us after two days; on the third day he will raise us up." This reference to raising up on the third day has often been related to the resurrection of Christ. In its context, however, it simply expresses the hope that God would restore the fortunes of the people after a short time.

Hosea goes on to enunciate one of the classic formulations of biblical religion in 6, 6: "It is love that I desire, not sacrifice, and knowledge of God rather than holocausts." Sacrifice was not bad in itself, but it was only as good as the attitude it represented. Without the love that expressed itself in ethical conduct, sacrifice was meaningless, no matter what it cost. The inadequacy of sacrifice without the practice of justice is one of the major themes that runs through the prophetic corpus.

The Importance of Metaphors

The power of Hosea's prophecy comes in large part from his stock of striking metaphors. Israel is compared to a "cake unturned" (7, 8), a "wild ass" (8, 9), or a "luxuriant vine" (10, 1). These metaphors have an emotional effect because of the associations they carry with them, and this enhances their power of communication. Nowhere is this more evident than in chapter 11, which begins "When Israel was a child I loved him." The reference is to the Exodus, but the effect is very different from the rather violent accounts in the Pentateuch. By comparing Israel to a child, Hosea paints a vivid picture of God as the loving parent, teaching the infant to walk and lifting it up. By implication, Israel should have the same kind of elemental bond with the Lord that a toddler has with its parents.

Development of this metaphor leads Hosea to one of the most remarkable passages in the Old Testament. The thought of destroying his or her own child is repugnant to any normal parent. The Lord, too, asks "how could I give you up, O Ephraim?" (11, 8). Following the thrust of the metaphor the answer is inevitable: "I will not give vent to my blazing anger, I will not destroy Ephraim again." The rationale may surprise us, however—"for I am God and not man." Human parents are fallible and may be overcome by

anger; God is not subject to weakness. The difference between God and humanity is that we fall short of what we know to be best, while God has no such limitation.

Hosea, like all the great prophets, was a realist. He recognized that Israel would be destroyed, and whatever actually happened was the work of God (a point which will be made again by Amos). The same God whose heart is stirred to pity in chapter 11 declares that "My eyes are closed to compassion" in 13, 14. There is an apparent contradiction here. The mood of the prophet might naturally swing with changing circumstances, but if the Lord is "God and not man," we expect consistency. Hosea was not a systematic theologian, however, and all his insights do not fit neatly together. He was a shrewd enough observer to realize what would befall Samaria at the hands of the Assyrians—little ones dashed to pieces, expectant mothers ripped open (14, 1). Yet he affirmed that God still loved Israel like a child, or, in the imagery of chapter 2, that after God had divorced Israel he would start over again with a new courtship. In this his faith is like that of a modern Jew who still believes in the love of God after the Holocaust. The conviction that God is love, despite all the evidence for random brutality and hatred in the world, is also an integral part of Christian faith.

One of Hosea's harshest words of judgment is given an ironic twist in the New Testament. In 13, 14 the Lord asks, through the prophet, "Where are your plagues, O death! where is your sting, O nether world!" The point of the passage is that God is about to use the sting of death against Israel. In 1 Corinthians 15, 54f, Saint Paul quotes this passage. In this case, however, the question is a mocking one—the sting of death has been broken by the resurrection of Christ. While Paul changes the meaning of the passage he quotes, the new meaning is not altogether alien to Hosea, since he too looked beyond the death of the nation Israel and hoped for its "resurrection."

The Relevance of Hosea

Hosea's message of divine love and the need for fidelity has lost none of its relevance in the modern world. The most important lesson to be learned from Hosea, however, may well be a matter of theological method. The way to the knowledge of God is through the observation of human experience. We know that it is better to pity than to destroy because of our experience in raising children. We know that infidelity is destructive because of the experience of our relationships, or because we have seen it in the relationships of others. Our knowledge of God is inferred from those basic human values which we know intuitively. Essentially the same theological method can be found in the parables of Jesus (for example, the Prodigal Son and the Good Samaritan) which are based to a great degree on the observation of human relationships.

FURTHER READING

King, P. J. *Amos, Hosea, Micah—An Archaeological Commentary.* Philadelphia: Westminster, 1988. Good use of archaeology to illustrate the prophetic texts.

Mays, J. L. *Hosea, A Commentary.* Philadelphia: Westminster, 1969. Balanced exegetical commentary.

Wolff, H. W. *Hosea.* Hermeneia. Philadelphia: Fortress, 1974. The best detailed commentary.

Yee, G. A. *The Book of Hosea.* New Interpreter's Bible 7, 197–297. Nashville: Abingdon Press, 1996. Homiletical commentary with feminist sensitivity.

JOEL

[see pages 1184–88 of the Old Testament]

In sharp contrast to Hosea, the book of Joel makes no reference to known historical events, which would enable us to establish when it was written. It is safe to say, however, that it is one of the later prophetic books, and the date 400 BC (OT, p. 1184) is a reasonable guess. Two considerations favor a relatively late date. First, according to 4, 6 some people of Judah were sold as slaves to the Greeks. This reference suggests a date after the Babylonian exile, when Judah was weak and contacts between the Greeks and the Near East were increasing. Second, the imagery of the Day of the Lord and the judgment of the nations has a strongly apocalyptic character. Such imagery is characteristic of the postexilic period.

The reference to Jews sold into slavery is indicative of the circumstances in which the book was written. It was a time of deprivation and exploitation. The first two chapters refer to a plague of locusts that had ravaged the harvests of Judah, thereby aggravating the problems of the poor. These circumstances are significant for understanding why the prophet predicts cosmic upheaval and radical change.

The book is characterized by movement from specific concern with the plague of locusts to a more general prophecy of universal judgment. Joel 1, 1—2, 17 combines description of the plague with exhortations and prayers for deliverance. Chapter 2, verses 18 to 27 give a reply and reassurance from God. All of this may reflect an actual Temple liturgy for relief from the disaster.

Chapter 3 is concerned with a future time, when God will intervene to pour out the spirit and save a remnant of the people. Chapter 4 proclaims the final judgment of the nations and salvation of God's elect.

The Day of the Lord

The theme of the Day of the Lord runs through the book as a unifying thread. The earliest mention of the Day of the Lord is in Amos 5, 18. It is apparent from that passage that this was originally a festive day, to which people looked forward in joyful anticipation. Amos, however, declared that it would be a day of darkness and not light. By the time the book of Joel was written, any great disaster could be dubbed a "Day of the Lord." In Joel 1—2 the reference is quite specifically to a plague of locusts, which transforms the land from being like "the garden of Eden" to a "desert waste" (2, 3). Joel speaks of the locusts as an invading army, with the Lord at their head (2, 11)—whatever actually happens is the work of God. The people respond to the emergency in ways typical of the ancient world, by bringing offerings and libations. It is characteristic of the Hebrew prophets, however, that a crisis such as this is made into an occasion for reform and repentance. The exhortation in 2, 13 is a classic expression of the prophetic view of proper ritual: "Rend your hearts, not your garments."

In the modern secular world we do not usually regard natural disasters such as locusts or tornadoes as visitations from God, nor do we rely on rituals for relief. It would indeed be unfortunate if recourse to ritual kept people from taking whatever practical measures were possible to resolve their problems. The situation in Joel, however, was beyond human control, at least in that time and place. The ritual, then, was all that people could do. It was their way of expressing their desperate concern and their hope that God would give them relief. In urging them to use the crisis as an occasion for reform, the prophet is bringing some good out of a bad situation. He is also recognizing that all of life has religious significance. The prophetic idea of salvation is primarily concerned with the welfare of the people on earth. Anything that threatens that welfare is worthy of the prophet's attention, even if it is not the result of human activity in any evident sense.

The plague of locusts was undoubtedly traumatic for those who experienced it, but it was not an event of great historical moment. We do not even know when it took place. In the context of the book of Joel it takes on a broader significance. It is a prefiguration of a greater Day of the Lord, when God will come to judge the nations. The destruction of the land by the locusts is a small-scale rehearsal for the final judgment. In chapter 3, then, the Day of the Lord takes on a different meaning from what it had in the first two chapters. It now refers to the Day of Judgment. The description in 3, 1–5 has become a classic passage because it is quoted in Acts 2, 17–21. The imagery suggests the end of the world—the sun will be turned to darkness and the moon to blood. Such imagery is increasingly common in prophecy of the postexilic period (compare Is 13, 9–11; 34, 1–4).

Despite the vividness of the imagery, Joel does not envisage the end of the world, in the sense familiar from the book of Revelation. The language here is metaphorical. The darkening of sun and moon is a way of expressing that there will be a time of great tumult and confusion. The world order as we know it will be turned upside down and, most importantly, the foreign nations who have oppressed the Jews will be overthrown. The magnitude of this upheaval is expressed through the imagery of the physical universe. This kind of imagery is very common in the apocalyptic literature from the second century BC on, (see the Reading Guide to Daniel).

The later apocalyptic writers, however, took the imagery more literally and came to believe in an actual end of the world. This is not yet the case in Daniel, but it is commonplace by New Testament times. In 2 Esdras 7, 30 (a Jewish writing from the end of the first century AD), the earth is turned back to primeval silence for seven days before the resurrection, so that the new creation is clearly separated from the old. Joel, in contrast, has no resurrection, and looks for a transformation of this world rather than a new creation.

A Vision of Plenty

There are two aspects of Joel's hope for the transformation of the earth. First is the universal human hope for freedom from hunger. This is a natural reaction to the locust plague. In a time of scarcity Joel comforts his people with the promise that they will eat and be filled (2, 26) and even rhapsodizes that "the mountains shall drip new wine, and the hills shall flow with milk" (4, 18). This kind of prediction is very common in the Prophets (see, for example, Is 11). It evidently involves a strong element of wish fulfillment. More than two thousand years later, the world is still a long way from being rid of hunger. The optimistic prophecy has two functions. It gives hope to the poor, not certainty indeed but a hope that is within the bounds of possibility, and it reminds us all of a goal toward which we should work. The role of the prophecy is to sustain energy and morale in depressing times. In itself, the prophecy did not feed the hungry, but then humanity does not live by bread alone, and the prophet supplied strength in other ways.

Vengeance on the Nations

The second aspect of the Day of the Lord is one that Christians sometimes find distasteful, although Christians have certainly indulged it in the course of history. This is the desire for vengeance. It is not enough that Judah flow with wine and milk, the hated neighbor Edom must be a desert waste (4, 19). If the Philistines have sold Jews as slaves, their own children must be sold in turn (4, 4–8). Where other prophets called on people to beat their swords into plowshares (Is 2, 4; Mi 4, 3), Joel reverses the call and looks forward to a showdown in the valley of Jehoshaphat. Vengeance is not one of the nobler human emotions, but it is certainly understandable and sometimes irresistible. Distaste for vengeance should not distract us from the more fundamental problems that give rise to it. The prophets' call for vengeance is usually a call for justice. In the case of Joel it is a protest of the powerless who had seen their children sold into slavery. Slavery was a far more fundamental sin against humanity than vengeance, real or imagined.

In the modern world, the vengefulness of the prophet often finds its counterpart in the feelings of Third World countries toward the more developed West. Vengeance is all the more distasteful when it is directed against ourselves, for reasons we seldom understand. Since the Hebrew prophets are part of our own tradition, they may help us reach some understanding of the mentality of those who see themselves as oppressed and want to see the tables turned on their more powerful neighbors. This is not to approve of vengefulness, but to affirm that we can learn something even from a somewhat distasteful text.

FURTHER READING

Achtemeier, E. *The Book of Joel.* New Interpreter's Bible 7, 301–36. Nashville: Abingdon Press, 1996. Brief homiletical commentary.

Crenshaw, J. L. *Joel.* Anchor Bible 24C. New York: Doubleday, 1995. Excellent, up-to-date commentary.

Wolff, H. W. *Joel and Amos.* Hermeneia. Philadelphia: Fortress, 1977. Classic detailed commentary.

AMOS

[see pages 1188–98 of the Old Testament]

Amos is the earliest of the prophets who have books in their names. In fact, his oracles were transmitted orally and were only collected in book form much later. The opening verse mentions the kings Uzziah of Judah and Jeroboam II of Israel, who are the earliest kings mentioned in Hosea 1, 1. The later kings listed in connection with Hosea are not mentioned in Amos. The historical background of the two prophets is very much the same. The dominant factor is the threat of destruction by Assyria. Nonetheless, the problems on which the two prophets focus are quite different. Hosea paid great attention to idolatry and cultic behavior, which symbolized the deeper problems of the society. Amos also comments on the cult but scarcely hints that idolatry is a problem. Instead he speaks directly to the issue of social justice, with a vigor unparalleled anywhere in the Bible.

The Career of Amos

We know very little about the career of Amos. He came from the village of Tekoa in the Southern Kingdom of Judah, but he delivered his oracles in the Northern Kingdom, especially around the temple of Bethel, just north of the border. He did not, in any case, attach great importance to political boundaries. It is a theme of his prophecy that all peoples are equal in the sight of God.

Only one episode from his career is recounted in the book. In 7, 10–17 we hear of an encounter between Amos and the priest of Bethel. The priest was worried because Amos was prophesying against the king in the Temple precincts. The priest could not afford to offend the king, and so he told Amos to go back to Judah. Amos's reply has given rise to much debate. Literally the Hebrew says "No prophet I, nor the son of a prophet." The NAB opts for one possible interpretation of this utterance: "I was no prophet" (until the Lord called me). An alternative view is that he rejected the very name "prophet." In either case, the point at issue is that Amos is not a member of a guild of professional prophets, such as we see in action in 1 Kings 22, the story of Micaiah, son of Imlah. He was an independent agent. He was a shepherd and a dresser of sycamores (the fruit, resembling a fig, had to be tended in order to prevent insects from destroying it), and so had his own means. He did not depend on king or priest for support and was not beholden to them, and thus did not require their permission to prophesy. This independence left him free to speak the truth as he saw it, without political constraint.

The style of Amos is blunt, even offensive. He calls the women of Samaria "cows of Bashan" (4, 1) and tells the priest Amaziah that his wife

Amos

will be a harlot in the city (7, 17). This is not the way to make friends and influence people, and it is not a style recommended by professors of homiletics. Amos makes no attempt to win the sympathy of his audience, as Nathan did with David (2 Sm 12) or as Jesus does in the parables. He is a prophet in the mold of Elijah, whose denunciations come close to cursing. This crude style of preaching must be seen in its social context. Nathan was a trusted adviser to David and could expect to have an effect on him. Amos, like Elijah, was an outsider. He did not have the ear of the king and saw no likelihood that the upper classes would change their ways. Consequently, he does not appeal for repentance. He simply proclaims the doom that is coming. He testifies to the conditions of his time and puts them on record, but he does not suggest that the catastrophe could be avoided.

The oracles of Amos are grouped in distinct blocks. The first two chapters contain a series of oracles against various nations, culminating in a denunciation of Israel. Amos 3, 1—5, 9 contains three long oracles (or strings of short utterances), which are introduced as "words." These are followed in 5, 7—6, 14 by three "woes" against Israel and Judah. (The verses in 5, 7–9 are out of order and must be rearranged. See OT, p. 1193.) Chapters 7, 1 through 9, 8b contain a series of visions of destruction. Chapter 9, 8c–15 is an epilogue, probably added by a later editor.

The Oracles against the Nations

The book begins with oracles of judgment against Israel's immediate neighbors, in the area now occupied by Lebanon, Syria, Jordan, and part of the occupied territory of Palestine. The oracle against Judah may have been added by the editor of the book to bring it up to date, after Israel had been destroyed. It was not unusual in the ancient world for a prophet from one country to denounce or curse other nations: see Numbers 22—24, where Balaam is called to curse Israel. What is unusual here is that Amos doesn't stop after he has denounced the other nations, but goes on to pronounce a similar judgment on Israel. His listeners would surely have expected to hear that Israel would be glorified when Edom was humiliated (as we saw in Joel 4). Amos, however, insists that Israel is no different from other nations in the eyes of God. Any nation that sins deserves punishment. The sins of the other nations are not all offenses against Israel. Moab is condemned for burning to lime the bones of the king of Edom (2, 1), which is an outrage against humanity as such, or against natural law. The sins of Israel, too, are sins against humanity: they sell the just man for silver and the poor man for a pair of sandals (2, 6).

The oracle against Israel in Amos 2, 6–16 can be read as a "covenant lawsuit," that is, a speech in which the prophet indicts Israel for failing to keep the Sinai covenant. The covenant had three essential elements: (1) the recollection of salvation history, culminating in the Exodus; (2) the commandments, and (3) blessings for keeping the commandments and curses for breaking them. The history as well as the curses and blessings both provided motivation to keep the commandments. The typical argument of a "covenant lawsuit" is that (1) God earned the loyalty of Israel by bringing it out of Egypt but, (2) Israel proved disloyal by breaking the commandments. In Amos 2, the sins of Israel are listed first (vv. 6–8). Then the prophet recalls the Exodus and the obligation it entailed. He concludes with a threat, which is in effect a curse: "Beware, I will crush you into the ground" (2, 13). Many scholars think, however, that the recollection of the Exodus here was added by an editor, who wanted to put the prophetic preaching in the context of the theology of Deuteronomy (which is also exemplified in the books of Joshua, Judges, Samuel, and Kings). Amos himself had a wider frame of reference. The practices he condemns are, to be sure, forbidden by the law of Moses, but that is not the point in Amos. People of any nation should recognize that it is criminal to sell a just man for silver. So it makes no difference to Amos whether or not a particular nation knows the law of Moses. The basic requirements of justice should be obvious to all. In short, Amos appeals to natural law, as it was understood in the ancient Near East. The law of Moses coincided with that law to a great extent, but the essentials of ethical behavior should be known even to pagans. In the New Testament, Saint Paul makes the same point in Romans 1, where he says that pagan idolaters have no excuse, "for what can be known about God is evident to them."

Amos and the Covenant

The equivalence of Israel and other nations in the sight of God is a theme that runs through the book of Amos. It raises a question as to whether the prophet regarded Israel as a chosen nation in any sense. He was certainly familiar with the story of the Exodus and the recitation of salvation history. For Amos, however, the Exodus guarantees Israel no privilege, but only adds to its responsibility. Two other passages in the book address this question very directly.

1. In 3, 2 we read "You alone have I favored, more than all the families of the earth." We expect this statement to be followed by a reassurance, such as "therefore I will protect you like the apple of my eye" or the like. Instead we read "Therefore I will punish you for all your crimes." Here, as in the oracles against the nations, Amos deliberately shocks his audience by telling them what they neither expect nor want to hear. (Jesus uses a similar technique in the parable of the good Samaritan.) In a sense he is only spelling out the implications of the covenant, which always carried the threat of the curses for breaking the laws as well as the promise of the blessings for obedience. This is not how most people in Israel understood the covenant, however. They thought, naturally enough, that the Exodus guaranteed them divine protection, that they were already "saved." According to Amos, the only way Israel differs from the other nations is that it should know better and therefore is all the more blameworthy for its crimes.

2. Amos puts the Exodus in perspective even more bluntly in 9, 7: "Are you not like the Ethiopians to me? . . . Did I not bring the Israelites from the land of Egypt as I brought the Philistines from Caphtor and the Arameans from Kir?" Israel is special in the eyes of God . . . but so is every other people. The Philistines and Syrians had their salvation history too. None of this means that the Exodus was not important. It was absolutely fundamental to the identity of Israel. It did not, however, mean that Israel would be favored in any way, except that it should know more clearly than others what was demanded of it.

Amos's sustained denial that Israel was any different from other peoples has its best parallel in the Wisdom literature (especially Proverbs), which ignores the special revelation to Israel and focuses on the universal moral law. Amos seems to have been an educated man. He displays an impressive knowledge of international affairs, and he was certainly no ignorant peasant. We do not know how he acquired his learning. He was probably well versed in traditional wisdom, whether he was formally educated in a school setting or not.

The Words and Woes

The three "words" of Amos are really a string of shorter oracles, mainly concerned with the sins of the Israelites. In 3, 3–8, however, he lays out some of his theological presuppositions. He assumes that there is an order in nature and things do not happen by chance ("Does a lion roar . . . when it has no prey?"). This order is the work of God. Amos is a radical monotheist, not only in the sense that he ignores other gods but that he regards everything that happens as the work of the Lord. Religious people always credit God with the good things that happen. Amos goes further: "If evil befalls a city, has not the Lord caused it?" God is responsible for the bad as well as the good. (Remember the Israelite religion at this time had no devil on whom evil could be blamed.) The acts of God in history, then, are not confined to special events like the Exodus, but embrace everything that actually happens. This conviction lays the foundation for a thoroughgoing realism in his view of international politics. If Assyria is more powerful than Israel, this is not by chance but is the will of God. Jeremiah took a similar view of the power of Babylon when it destroyed Jerusalem.

Amos directs many of his oracles against the cult at Bethel. When people go to make offerings to atone for sin at Bethel, Amos says that they "come to Bethel and sin" (4, 4). There is a pun in the Hebrew because of the similarity of the terms for "sin-offering" and "sin," and Amos uses the word play to equate the two. His sharpest critique of the cult, however, is delivered in the famous "Woe" against those who yearn for the Day of the Lord (5, 18–25). The Day of the Lord was a major festival day, most probably the Feast of Tabernacles or Sukkoth, a harvest festival in the fall. It was an occasion for celebrating the victory of the God of Israel and the defeat of his enemies. Amos, characteristically, tells the people that it will be the opposite of what they expect. The real Day of the Lord, when God appears before the people, will be a day of judgment. Amos was the first prophet to speak of the Day of the Lord as a day of judgment on Israel, and thereby he introduced one of the major themes of the prophetic literature.

Amos goes on to issue a broadside against all the festivals of Israel. He implies that Israel survived for the forty years in the desert without offering sacrifices (5, 25). His point is not that all ritual is necessarily bad, but that it is not of the essence of religion. For Amos, the essence of religion is social justice. If ritual furthers justice, well and good, but too often it does not. In the prophet's view, the Israelite cult only made the upper classes complacent. They identified themselves as "Israel" and felt that they were God's chosen people. Their cultic celebrations reminded them of the Exodus and the great things God had done for them, and reassured them that God would deliver them from danger again. They need not, then, be too concerned about the plight of the poor. When the festival was over, they could go back to cheating in the marketplace (8, 5). Amos insisted that all this was self-delusion. God would not overlook the injustice of the society because of the sound of the harps, and the Assyrians would rudely shatter the naive belief that God would protect Israel no matter what.

The final "Woe" in chapter 6 paints a vivid picture of "the complacent in Zion [and] the overconfident on the mount of Samaria," the upper classes of both kingdoms of Israel. These were the people who sold the poor into slavery while they lived in luxury themselves. Amos announces with evident anticipation that these would be the first to go into exile. This was not mere wish fulfillment on the prophet's part. He knew the practice of the Assyrians, which was to take the upper classes into exile so that there would be no one left to lead a revolt. In his view, it was a fate that they richly deserved.

The Visions

Chapters 7 through 9 are primarily visions of the destruction of Israel. At first the prophet is moved by the enormity of the destruction and intercedes with God on behalf of Israel. After the vision of the locusts and of the fire, God relents, but the time for forgiveness runs out. The message is summed up in the vision of a basket of ripe fruit. The Hebrew here involves another pun. The word for "ripe fruit" is very similar to the word for "end." Amos 8, 2 "the time is ripe" can also be translated "the end has come." This was the first time the idea of an "end" was proclaimed in ancient Israel. The end in question was the end of Israel as an independent nation. Later biblical writers would extend the idea and envisage an end of history or of the world. (The technical theological term "eschatology," which refers to the doctrine of the last things, is derived from the Greek word for "end.") Amos, however, was not speaking of the end of the world. The end of Israel in the eighth century BC, which he predicted, was final, in the sense that the political entity that had existed for two hundred years was wiped off the map and never restored. The influence of Amos on later tradition was undoubtedly increased by the fact that his prophecy was so completely fulfilled.

The Israel whose end Amos announced was primarily the Israel of the upper classes, who held political power. They were the ones who identified themselves as Israel in the cult and in international political relations. The peasants would undoubtedly suffer during the Assyrian invasion, but ultimately it may not have made much difference whether one paid taxes to a foreign power or to predatory Israelite landlords. From the viewpoint of the peasants, and of Amos, the survival of Israel as a nation was not of great importance. What mattered was not political identity but the living conditions of the poor within the society.

The Epilogue

Much of the force of Amos's prophecy derived from its finality. When he said that God would destroy the kingdom of Israel off the face of the earth (9, 8), that was his last word. A later editor felt that this stark conclusion did not do justice to history. Israel in the broader sense of the people of the Lord, north and south, was not terminated. The message of the prophetic corpus as a whole is ultimately not one of destruction but of hope. What the epilogue does, then, is put the prophecy of Amos in a broader perspective. Death and destruction have their time and place, but there remains the hope for an ideal future, as we have seen in the prophecy of Joel. This ultimate optimism is an essential ingredient of biblical faith.

Three points in the epilogue deserve special attention.

1. Amos 9, 9f suggests that God's judgment on Israel will be selective, so that only the sinners will die. Obviously the Assyrians were not so selective, nor were the Babylonians after them. The preexilic prophets spoke of the fate of the whole nation, not of individuals, and this was realistic if divine judgment was executed through warfare. In the postexilic period, however, there is increasing sensitivity to individual responsibility. (See the great reflection on this subject in Ez 18.) In the apocalyptic literature (for example, Daniel) the problem is resolved by the belief that just and wicked receive their appropriate retribution after death.

2. The hope for the future is focused on "the fallen hut of David." This oracle probably comes from the period after the exile when there was no longer a Davidic king on the throne in Jerusalem. The hope expressed here is messianic, but should not be confused with the later Christian understanding of the Messiah. The hope here is that the native Jewish kingship will be restored.

3. Finally, the ideal state of the end-time is decidedly earthly in character. The hope is for peace and prosperity, with an abundance of wine and fruit. One of the major points that the Hebrew Bible can contribute to Christian spirituality is a healthy appreciation of the good things of this world.

The Relevance of Amos

No prophet is more easily related to the modern world than Amos, for the social inequities that he denounced in eighth-century BC Israel are still very much with us. The American bishops adopt a much milder tone than Amos in their pastoral letter on the economy, but their concerns are very much in line with his. The bishops insist that "government has a moral function: protecting human rights and securing justice for all members of the commonwealth" (*Economic Justice for All,* p. 35), and that "the fulfillment of the basic needs of the poor is of the highest priority" (p. 27). In the ancient world it was the role of the prophet to be the conscience of the nation and

speak up for the powerless. In the modern world, that role falls to religious leaders, who are not themselves involved in the business of government and so can view it with some perspective.

The first lesson to be learned from Amos is that social justice is the business of religion. The test of piety is what happens in the marketplace rather than what happens in the church or temple.

A second lesson is less obvious at first, but bears some thought. Amos was convinced that there is an intrinsic connection between the justice of a society and its long-term prosperity. This conviction arose from his radical monotheism. The God who gives prosperity is also the God of justice. In the modern world we are hesitant to see such an immediate connection between morality and success. Nonetheless it is probably true that the greed of the Israelite upper classes contributed to their own downfall. On the one hand their aspiration to power and independence brought them into conflict with Assyria. On the other hand the exploitation of the poor, and the individualism of the rich, weakened the society internally. The Assyrians might have rolled over Israel whether it was a just society or not, but the blow might not have been so severe if its leaders had been less concerned with political power and more concerned with equality and justice.

FURTHER READING

Coote, R. B. *Amos Among the Prophets: Composition and Theology.* Philadelphia: Fortress, 1981. Lively presentation of the message of Amos.

Gowan, D. E. *The Book of Amos.* New Interpreter's Bible 7, 339–431. Nashville: Abingdon Press, 1996. Homiletical commentary.

Jeremias, J. *The Book of Amos.* Louisville: Westminster John Knox, 1998. Exegetical commentary with emphasis on the composition of the book.

King, P. J. *Amos, Hosea, Micah—An Archaeological Commentary.* Philadelphia: Westminster, 1988. Uses archaeology to illustrate the teaching of the prophet.

Mays, J. L. *Amos, A Commentary.* Philadelphia: Westminster, 1969. Balanced exegetical commentary.

Wolff, H. W. *Amos the Prophet, The Man and His Background.* Philadelphia: Fortress, 1973. Summary of the findings of the author's commentary.

The best detailed scholarly commentary is that of H. W. Wolff, *Joel and Amos* (Hermeneia. Philadelphia: Fortress, 1977).

OBADIAH

[see pages 1198–1200 of the Old Testament]

With only twenty-one verses, the book of Oba-diah is the shortest of the prophetic books. It con-sists of a series of short oracles against Edom (vv. 1–14), then an oracle against all the nations (15f), followed by a prediction of the restoration of Judah. Edom was a small state to the south of Judah. (It was later called Idumaea.) The Edomites incurred the lasting hatred of the Jews in the sixth century BC by exploiting the weak-nesses of Judah and pillaging its territory after the Babylonian invasion. Relations remained very bitter when the Jews returned from the exile and restored the city of Jerusalem. The prophecy of Obadiah belongs to this general period (sixth or early fifth century BC) but contains no indica-tion of its specific date. The hatred between Ju-dah and Edom was intense and lasting. Long af-ter Edom had ceased to be a threat to the Jews, the name Edom was used in rabbinic literature as a code name for Rome, the hated enemy of the day.

Oracles against Edom

Oracles of vengeance against Edom were com-mon in the postexilic period. Compare the re-lated utterances in Jeremiah 49, 7–22. For the modern reader, these oracles pose the usual prob-lem of how to deal with vengeance. In fairness, it should be noted that the logic of Obadiah is quite similar to that of Amos. There is a natural moral law that applies to the actions of all peoples. That law forbids violence against one's neighbors and then gloating over their distress. One who vio-lates that law, however, loses its protection. The underlying principle is succinctly stated in verse 15: "As you have done, so shall it be done to you." The natural law requires that the punish-ment fit the crime. Obadiah indicts Edom for be-havior similar to that for which Amos indicted Is-rael. While it may seem more noble to direct criticism against one's own people, the moral principle is the same. Edom deserved the pro-phetic denunciation.

Judgment upon the Nations

In broadening his attack to all the foreign na-tions, Obadiah uses the now familiar motif of the Day of the Lord (see the guide to Amos). Here the judgment is directed only against the foreign nations. Israel did not need a word of judgment at this time. The Day of the Lord here is simply the day of judgment. It implies a decisive change in the course of events, but nothing like the end of history or of the world. The judgment will be governed by the law of retribution: as you have done to others, so shall it be done to you. Oba-diah applies this principle to whole nations rather than to individuals.

The Restoration of Judah

The idea that a remnant will be saved on Mount Zion was developed especially by Isaiah. In the present context one is struck by the modesty of the hope. The kingship of God does not imply that Judah will rule all the nations, only its im-mediate neighbors who have most recently af-flicted it. While a note of vengeance is present it should not be exaggerated. The oracle is really a testimony to the indomitable hope of a people who had been reduced to poverty and insignifi-cance, and were at the mercy of their neighbors. Belief in the kingship of God on Mount Zion was a deep-rooted part of the Jerusalem cult under the monarchy (see for example, Pss 93; 97—99). In the aftermath of the exile it became a source of hope for deliverance.

FURTHER READING

Pagán, S. *The Book of Obadiah.* New Interpreter's Bible 7, 435–59. Nashville: Abingdon Press, 1996. Brief homiletical commentary.

Raabe, P. R. *Obadiah.* Anchor Bible 24D. New York: Doubleday, 1996. Thorough philological commen-tary.

Wolff, H. W. *Obadiah and Jonah: A Commentary.* Minneapolis: Augsburg, 1986. Classic scholarly commentary.

JONAH

[see pages 1200–1202 of the Old Testament]

The book of Jonah is unique among the Prophets for two reasons. First, it is not a collection of oracles but a narrative, and second, Jonah is in many ways an antiprophet, whose behavior is approximately the opposite of what we expect from a prophet. The story may be termed a fable, because of the role of the fish (compare the role of animals in Aesop's fables). It can also be considered as a parable, in the sense that it is a short story that goes against our expectations, like many of the parables of Jesus. The story is set in the Assyrian period (like the prophecies of Hosea and Amos), but there is general agreement that it comes from a much later time. While we cannot pinpoint the time of composition, it was certainly sometime in the postexilic period. The actual setting, then, was close to the time of Joel and Obadiah, but Jonah has a very different perspective on the problems of the period.

The division of the book is adequately represented by the chapters. The long psalm in chapter 2 stands out from its context. It may have been added by a later editor who was more interested in the miracle of Jonah's survival than was the original author.

Three considerations are especially important for appreciating the book of Jonah:

1. The story is quite deliberately humorous,

2. Its primary subject matter is the proper attitude to foreign nations, not Jonah's miraculous escape from drowning,

3. The story gives a mildly critical perspective on the religious zeal that is a trademark of prophecy.

The Humor of the Story

The humorous quality should be apparent from the opening verses. Where else do we ever hear of a prophet who so flagrantly disobeys a divine command? The idea that one could get away from the Lord by sailing to a remote place is not only naive but deliberately ridiculous. The pagan sailors exhibit more "fear of the Lord" than does Jonah. When he finally goes to Nineveh, the Assyrians respond with a fervor unparalleled in Israel. Even the animals join in the repentance. The author of this passage is not concerned with his-

torical plausibility—everyone knew that Assyria had never turned from its "evil way." The fantastic repentance of the Assyrians simply adds to the enjoyment of the tale.

The centerpiece of the humor of the story is even more fantastic than the repentance of the Assyrians. A great fish arrives just in time to catch Jonah when he is thrown overboard and vomits him up on the shore. Nothing could be more remote from the spirit of this story than to believe that this actually happened. The episode of Jonah and the fish has rich theological implications, especially for Christians, but there is no theological virtue in mistaking a fantastic joke for literal fact.

The humor of the story has an ironic quality. It refuses to give the prophet the dignity associated with the office, or to take his convictions seriously. It invites us to reconsider our stereotypes of both pagans and prophets. Unlike the oracles of Amos, it assumes the goodwill of its readers and tries to lead them to new insight.

The Attitude to Foreign Nations

The primary subject matter of the book is indicated at the outset when the prophet is sent to preach to the Assyrians rather than to his own people. The wickedness of Assyria is not in doubt; it is the premise of the story. Jonah, naturally enough, wants to see justice done and is upset at God's excessive mercy. The incredible repentance of the Assyrians forces the issue: does Assyria, the most destructive tyrant of its day, deserve divine forgiveness? It is as if the Nazi leaders made a show of repentance after World War II and were pardoned. Jonah is not exceptionally narrow-minded here. His demand for justice is just as reasonable as that at the Nuremberg trials. It is not accepted, however. God speaks here as creator, to whom the Assyrians are as important as the Israelites (or, in modern terms, Nazis are as important as Jews or Christians). The concluding verse of the book recognizes that "the Assyrian in the street" is no more guilty of the crimes of his nation than are the cattle, but guilt or innocence is not the point. The book of Jonah sees God in the same terms as the much later book of Wisdom 11, 24: "For you love all things that are and loathe nothing that you have made; for what you hated, you would not have fashioned." The magnanimity of this sentiment is astonishing, especially when we consider the situation of the Jews in the postexilic period, when they had every reason to resent foreign powers. We may compare this story to Jesus' parable of the good Samaritan. The parable presupposes that most Jews would have regarded "good Samaritan" as a contradiction in terms. The penitent Assyrian is at least as great a contradiction, and as hard to accept. Admittedly, when the book of Jonah was written the Assyrian invasion was already ancient history, and it did not arouse emotions to the same degree as the Holocaust in our time. Nevertheless, it is not that Jonah was exceptionally narrow-minded here, but rather that God is exceptionally tolerant.

The Perspective on Prophetic Zeal

Jonah reacts to God's mercy by sulking and praying for death (4, 8). He is not the first prophet to do so. The great Elijah also sat under a tree and asked God to take his life (1 Kgs 19, 4f). Elijah, more than any prophet, was known for his zeal in destroying sinners (witness his treatment of the prophets of Baal in 1 Kgs 18, 40). Jonah is a prophet in the same mold. In this case, however, the zeal of the prophet does not meet with approval. The book of Jonah sees the limitations of prophetic zeal. God's rebuke is mild. Jonah is well intentioned and is acting in accordance with a long tradition. Conformity with tradition is not enough, however. Hosea had marked a breakthrough in the Israelite tradition by the recognition that it is more fitting for God to have mercy than to punish. The book of Jonah extends that insight to the treatment of foreign nations. Even the prophet must learn that reconciliation holds a higher value than strict retribution. Not all the prophetic books reflect this insight, but it is certainly the view affirmed for Christianity in the Gospels.

The Sign of Jonah

The episode in the belly of the fish is a minor humorous motif in the original story, but it acquires greater significance in later tradition. In Matthew 12, 39f, Jonah's stay in the belly of the fish is taken to prefigure Jesus' time in the tomb,

and Jonah is often used as a symbol of resurrection in early Christian art. The symbolic significance of this episode appears already in the psalm in chapter 2. There the belly of the fish is equated with the netherworld, and Jonah's rescue is equivalent to resurrection from the dead. In the context of the Old Testament, the resurrection is metaphorical and means simply that the psalmist is delivered from desperate circumstances. It is a confession of the power of God to give life and take it away. We should note that what Jonah regrets about the netherworld is that he is separated from the presence of God. What he asks is not just continued survival but restoration to that presence. Fullness of life, for most Old Testament writers, is not life without end but the experience of God's grace, which is so satisfying that it is better to have "one day in your courts than a thousand elsewhere" (Ps 84, 11).

The Relevance of Jonah

Jonah's message of tolerance and forgiveness is as urgent in the modern world as it was in the fifth century BC. It is a hard word and should not be sentimentalized. It demands not only tolerance and understanding for those who are different from us, but forgiveness for those who have truly behaved wickedly, if they are willing to accept it. It is not yet a demand for unconditional forgiveness, since it has the precondition of repentance, but it is not an easy demand for all that.

The sign of Jonah caught the imagination of later generations as a sign of hope. That hope nicely undergirds the message of tolerance and forgiveness, since the wicked deeds of the oppressor are not as final as they seem. Those who hope for deliverance from the belly of death can afford to forgive the injustices of life. Belief in resurrection is often associated with the hope that the wicked will be damned. The book of Jonah, read in the light of the New Testament and Christian tradition, suggests that resurrection can also give a larger perspective on life, which has room for tolerance and forgiveness.

FURTHER READING

Limburg, J. *Jonah*. Louisville: Westminster John Knox, 1993. Commentary, with interest in later interpretations of Jonah in literature and art.

Sasson, J. *Jonah*. Anchor Bible 24B. New York: Doubleday, 1990. Full commentary, with interest in folkloric motifs.

Trible, P. *Jonah*. New Interpreter's Bible 7, 463–529. Nashville: Abingdon Press, 1996. Excellent literary commentary.

Wolff, H. W. *Obadiah and Jonah: A Commentary.* Minneapolis: Augsburg, 1986. Classic scholarly commentary.

MICAH

[see pages 1203–10 of the Old Testament]

Micah was a prophet of the eighth century BC, contemporary with Amos, Hosea, and Isaiah. As a prophet of the Southern Kingdom of Judah, he most closely resembles Isaiah. The book that bears his name does not all come from his hand. There is general agreement that his words are preserved in chapters 1 through 3, probably also in chapter 6, and in parts of chapter 7. Chapters 4 and 5, however, were probably added after the Babylonian exile. The original words of Micah, like those of Amos, are largely preoccupied with issues of social justice and the coming Assyrian invasion.

The Impending Judgment

The first oracle begins with a classic description of a *theophany,* or apparition of God. Traditionally such a theophany was associated with divine deliverance, as in Deuteronomy 33 and Judges 5 (compare also the theophany on Sinai). Micah's theophany, however, is like Amos's Day of the Lord. God is not coming to save but to judge. The immediate presence of God is destructive for a sinful people. In eighth-century BC Israel, the presence of God was not experienced as fire and earthquake but as the invasion of the Assyrian army. The destruction would fall most heavily on Samaria and Jerusalem, the major cities, homes of the royal houses and ruling classes.

The reasons for the coming destruction are spelled out most clearly in chapter 2. The problem is that the rich devise ways to force the smaller landowners into debt and then seize their property. Isaiah 5, 8 complains about the same problem ("Woe to you who join house to house, who connect field with field, till no room remains, and you are left to dwell alone in the midst of the land"). From the prophet's viewpoint, it was only fitting that this land would be seized again by the Assyrians, so that the greed of the big landowners would be in vain.

Micah also discusses another fact of life in ancient Israel, which was only hinted at by Amos but was later a major theme in the prophecy of Jeremiah. The professional prophets were leading the people astray (3, 5). This is why Amos made his protest "No prophet I." The phenomenon is natural enough. Prophets found that people liked to be reassured and told that all was well, and they tailored their message to their market. They were concerned with their own well-being more than that of the nation. A classic illustration of the professional prophets in action can be found in 1 Kings 22. In contrast, Micah saw the task of the true prophet as "to declare to Jacob his crimes and to Israel his sins" (3, 8). Compare the assertion of Jeremiah that "From of old, the prophets who were before you and me prophesied war, woe, and pestilence" (Jer 28, 8). Such a prophet would never be popular, but at least there could be no doubt about his sincerity.

The true prophet here, as so often in the history of Israel, finds himself in opposition to the religious leaders, the priests, and the official prophets (3, 11). On the surface of things, the priests appear to have great faith: no evil can come upon Israel because the Lord is in its midst. Such faith is no virtue for Micah. Rather virtue lies in the practice of justice and in facing reality honestly. He regarded the Temple on Mount Zion, often the focal point of Jewish religion in antiquity, as a negative force. According to the psalmist, Mount Zion was "the holy dwelling of the Most High. God is in its midst; it shall not be shaken" (Ps 46, 6). If kings came to attack it, they would be seized with terror and put to flight (Ps 48, 5f). Micah realized that the Assyrians would not panic at the sight of Jerusalem. The belief that Zion could not be destroyed was a source of complacency and illusion. So Micah uttered his radical prophecy that Zion would be plowed like a field. This prophecy is quoted in Jeremiah 26, 18 as a precedent for the equally radical prophecy of Jeremiah. It was not fulfilled in Micah's time, but it was not forgotten either, and it was justified in time. Faith cannot be based on any religious institution, no matter how sacred. No temple is permanent, and no one is guaranteed the unconditional protection of God.

The Indictment of Israel

Chapter 6 presents an example of the "covenant lawsuit," which we have discussed above in connection with Amos. According to the logic of the Sinai covenant, Israel was bound to keep the commandments because God had brought it out of the land of Egypt. If the people kept the commandments they would be blessed, if not they would be cursed. In Micah 6, 1–5 God indicts Israel by recalling that the divine part of the obligation had been satisfied in the Exodus. It is not necessary to spell out how Israel has failed to keep its part, or what the consequences will be.

Micah does not suggest that the Israelites were indifferent to religion. On the contrary, they were willing to perform any ritual that might further their interests, even human sacrifice (6, 7). According to 2 Kings 21, 6, a king of Judah, Manasseh, immolated his son by fire in the seventh century BC. The prophet cuts through the pretenses of such superstition with a succinct formulation of the essence of religion: "to do the right and to love goodness, and to walk humbly with your God" (6, 8). No special beliefs or cultic observances are required. There was general agreement on what it meant to do the right. The anguished quest for the right sacrifice, then, is shown to be mere hypocrisy. The business of religion is quite straightforward. It only requires the will to do what we know we ought. It is significant that the American bishops used Micah 6, 8 as a summary of the heritage of the biblical prophets in setting the tone for the entire letter *Economic Justice for All* (n. 4). We might compare this passage with the Judgment scene in Matthew 25, 31–46. There the Son of Man does not ask about beliefs or ritual practices, but whether one fed the hungry and clothed the naked.

The Faith of the Prophet

The prophets only rarely provide glimpses of their personal faith, such as we find in the "confessions" of Jeremiah. One such glimpse is provided in Micah 7, 7–10. Micah appears as a lonely figure, as we might expect in view of his relationship to the other prophets. His attempt to reach his public appears to have failed, but he is sustained by the conviction that God will vindicate him. In all of this he resembles Jeremiah, whose trials are described at greater length. The experience of prophets such as these contributed to the ideal of the Suffering Servant (Is 53), which has played such an important part in Christian theology.

The Prophecies of Restoration

The oracles inserted in Micah 4—5 in the postexilic period include two that are especially memorable. The prophecy of the restoration of the house of the Lord in Micah 4, 1–3 is also found in Isaiah 2, 2–4. The author of this oracle is unknown. The idea that all nations would find a spiritual center in Jerusalem may be quite old, but it flourished especially in the postexilic period when Jews who lived in other lands went to Jerusalem on pilgrimage. The prophecy is artfully placed here, immediately after the prediction that Zion would become a plowed field. The editors of the prophetic books typically placed an oracle of hope after one of judgment. In Micah's day the influence of the Temple was such that he needed to remind people that it would not last forever. By the time the book was edited the need for judgment had passed, and it was appropriate to remember the potential of the Temple for good.

Micah 5, 1–4 speaks of a ruler who will come from Bethlehem. This prophecy has been treasured by Christians for obvious reasons. In the Jewish context, the significance of Bethlehem lies in the fact that it was the birthplace of David. The prophecy, then, is that the Davidic line will be restored. In mentioning Bethlehem rather than Jerusalem, however, the prophet is making a further point. He is recalling the humble origins of the monarchy, when it was associated with a village rather than with a city, and was not yet tainted with the corruption of Solomon's empire. The hope for restoration of the native kingship, which would bring peace to the land, is similar to what is described in more rhapsodic language in Isaiah 11.

FURTHER READING

Hillers, D. R. *Micah*. Hermeneia. Philadelphia: Fortress, 1984. Interprets Micah as a prophet of a revitalization movement.

King, P. J. *Amos, Hosea, Micah—An Archaeological Commentary*. Philadelphia: Westminster, 1988. Uses archaeology to illustrate the prophetic book.

Mays, J. L. *Micah, A Commentary*. Philadelphia: Westminster, 1976. Balanced exegetical commentary.

Simundson, D. J. *The Book of Micah*. New Interpreter's Bible 7, 531–89. Nashville: Abingdon Press, 1996. Helpful homiletical commentary.

Wolff, H. W. *Micah, A Commentary*. Minneapolis: Augsburg, 1990. Classic scholarly commentary.

——. *Micah the Prophet*. Philadelphia: Fortress, 1981. Summarizes findings of the author's commentary.

NAHUM

[see pages 1210–13 of the Old Testament]

The oracles of Nahum are concerned with a single event, the fall of Nineveh in 612 BC. The euphoria of the prophet is understandable. Never again would Judah be invaded by Assyria. Some centuries later the author of Jonah might pity Nineveh, but that was more than could be expected at the time of its downfall. It is characteristic of biblical prophecy that the fall of one Gentile nation at the hands of another is assumed to be the work of the Lord.

A Jealous God

The opening verse of Nahum's prophecy is somewhat shocking to modern ears: "A jealous and avenging God is the LORD." Such a characterization of God was not new. One of the oldest descriptions of the biblical God is found in Exodus 15, 3: "The LORD is a warrior" and on Sinai the Lord declares that he is a jealous God (Ex 20, 5). This aspect of the divinity was never thought to be incompatible with mercy and love. It is simply the expression of justice: "the LORD never leaves the guilty unpunished." The wrath of God is only the manifestation of the moral order in the universe. Events like the fall of Nineveh were precious, because they showed that justice eventually prevailed. Nahum also says that the Lord is slow to anger (1, 3) and emphasizes his goodness to the righteous (1, 7). The immediate demonstration of that goodness was that God gave the smaller peoples of the Near East the satisfaction of seeing the fall of Assyria.

A Shortsighted Prophecy

The most striking thing about Nahum's prophecy, however, is how shortsighted it was. While Judah was freed from one oppressor it would soon be subjected to another, no less destructive. A mere fifteen years after Nahum proclaimed security, Jerusalem would again be under siege.

The lesson to be learned from Nahum is a two-edged one. The fall of Assyria is a reminder that all tyrants fall sooner or later and therefore is a cause of hope. The hope is tempered by the realization that the fall of a particular tyrant is not the end of all tyranny. History is full of surprises, not all of them pleasant. Nahum's exultation over the fall of Nineveh is echoed in the New Testament in John of Patmos's anticipation of the fall of Rome (Revelation 17—18). John uses the image of the harlot, which is found in Nahum 3, 4. Rome, too, fell eventually, but other tyrants took its place. Yet there is consolation in the knowledge that no power lasts forever.

FURTHER READING

Boadt, L. *Jeremiah 26–52; Habakkuk; Zephaniah; Nahum*. Old Testament Message 10. Wilmington, DE: Glazier, 1981. Helpful brief commentary.

Roberts, J. J. M. *Nahum, Habakkuk and Zephaniah*. Louisville: Westminster, 1991. Concise scholarly commentary.

HABAKKUK

[see pages 1213–16 of the Old Testament]

The prophecy of Habakkuk is considerably more reflective than that of Nahum. He prophesied a few years later, when the Babylonian threat had become obvious. Habakkuk, however, not only reacts to the immediate danger but ponders the underlying problem. Why do the wicked circumvent the just? Why do the wicked devour those more righteous than themselves? Granted that the blame falls on humanity, why does God allow such a situation to prevail? The question, in short, is one of *theodicy,* or the justice of God and is more typical of wisdom literature than of prophecy. The classic treatment is found in the book of Job. The question of theodicy arises later in the apocalyptic literature especially in the great apocalypse of 2 Esdras, which is printed with the Apocrypha in Protestant editions of the Bible.

Habakkuk was concerned first of all with the injustice within Jewish society. It is illuminating to compare the "woes" in chapter 2 with Jeremiah's critique of King Jehoiakim (609–598 BC), which accuses the king of oppression and exploitation, especially in building a cedar palace by forced labor (Jer 22, 13–19). Jehoiakim might well be accused of storing up what is not his (Hb 2, 6) and of setting his nest on high (2, 9), and even the violence done to Lebanon (2, 17) may refer to his use of cedar. The critique, however, is couched in general terms and can apply to any wealthy and arrogant man.

Habakkuk's answer to the question of theodicy anticipates the kind of response that the apocalyptic writers would later offer. He does not provide an explanation but a promise that the situation will be rectified in time. At first the solution seems worse than the problem: God will raise up the Babylonians (1, 6–11). Isaiah (chapter 10) had spoken of Assyria as the rod of the Lord's anger. Babylon apparently fills this role in Habakkuk, by bringing about the downfall of King Jehoiakim. In Isaiah the rod itself would eventually be broken. The eventual destruction of Babylon is implied in Habakkuk too. The prophet cannot have been unaware that Babylon was a prime example of the wicked who devours one more just than

himself and whose throat was insatiable as death (2, 5). Because of the similarity between the behavior of Babylon and that of the wicked in Judah, it is sometimes unclear to which Habakkuk is referring. The lesson, however, is clear. Even though justice is not apparent in the world, one should trust in the Lord and be patient.

Righteousness and Faith

The most famous utterance of Habakkuk is undoubtedly 2, 4, "the just man, because of his faith, shall live," which acquired pivotal importance in the theology of Paul (Rom 1, 17; Gal 3, 11). In its original context, "faith" does not have the pregnant sense that it has in Paul. It is simply the trust in God that enables one to wait for the future, closer perhaps to hope than to faith in the traditional Christian sense. The contrast here is between the rash man (the fool, in the terminology of Proverbs) and the one who is able to take a longer view. The person who judges only in light of the immediate present sees no justice in the world and may be tempted to conclude that there is no divine control. The righteous, or wise, person, in contrast, trusts that justice will prevail and is content to wait for it.

The faith of Habakkuk finds its most poetic expression in chapter 3. The description of the theophany, which has God come in triumph as a warrior, stands in a long tradition of such hymns (compare Dt 33; Jgs 5; Mi 1). The early hymns of this kind referred to God's past activity on behalf of Israel. Habakkuk expects such a manifestation in the future. It will be directed against "the people who attack us" (3, 16), presumably the Babylonians, although Jewish oppressors may also be included. What the prophet envisages is a decisive intervention of God, to wipe out all wickedness and oppression. In this he is close to the kind of future hope that we find later in the apocalyptic literature, except that he does not envisage any judgment of the dead. It is not surprising then that Habakkuk was popular in apocalyptic circles. The Dead Sea Scrolls include a commentary (called a *pesher*) on Habakkuk, which interpreted the prophecy with reference to the history of the Qumran sect (taking the Chaldeans as the Romans). The notion that "the vision still has its time" (Hb 2, 3) is echoed in Daniel 8, 17, in a context where people were again asking "how long, O LORD?"

The faith of Habakkuk is a faith against appearances: "Though the fig tree blossom not nor fruit be on the vines . . . Yet will I rejoice in the LORD" (3, 17f). It is based on the conviction that God is just, and so justice must ultimately prevail. The only question is "how long?" It is a question that has been repeated in every generation and has yet to receive a final answer. In the meantime, those who share the faith of Habakkuk find strength to go on. The value of such faith does not depend on the fulfillment of its expectations but on its power to transform the lives of the faithful.

FURTHER READING

Boadt, L. *Jeremiah 26–52; Habakkuk; Zephaniah; Nahum.* Old Testament Message 10. Wilmington, DE: Glazier, 1981.

Gowan, D. E. *The Triumph of Faith in Habakkuk.* Atlanta: John Knox, 1976.

Hiebert, T. *The Book of Habakkuk.* New Interpreter's Bible 7, 623–55. Nashville: Abingdon Press, 1996. Brief homiletical commentary.

Roberts, J. J. M. *Nahum, Habakkuk and Zephaniah.* Louisville: Westminster, 1991. Concise scholarly commentary.

ZEPHANIAH

[see pages 1217–20 of the Old Testament]

Zephaniah prophesied a little earlier than Nahum and Habakkuk in the reign of Josiah, the king who instituted the Deuteronomic reform (2 Kgs 22—23). One of his themes concerns idolatry (1, 4–6). He may have been active before the reform, but Josiah was not very successful in his attempt to stamp out foreign cults in any case. Indeed, the prophet inveighs against the king's sons for adopting foreign customs (1, 8). Zephaniah was contemporary with the early career of Jeremiah. The surviving oracles are almost entirely taken up with the proclamation of the Day of the Lord.

A Day of Judgment for Judah

The first oracle on the Day of the Lord is directed against Judah. The main offenses, which he denounces, are idolatry and lack of faith in the Lord (1, 12). In the context of Josiah's time, rejection of the Lord was rejection of the Deuteronomic law. The emphasis of Zephaniah is not on the sins of Judah but on the destructiveness of the Day of the Lord. It is portrayed in cosmic terms: God will make an end of all who live on earth. The day of judgment is seen as the vindication of the majesty of God against the unworthiness of the people. Compare the destructive effect of the holiness of God in Isaiah 6.

A Day of Judgment on the Nations

The wrath of the Lord is not only directed against Judah. Chapter 2 catalogues the surrounding peoples, most of whom have been guilty of offending Judah in some way. The list extends to Assyria, the most arrogant of all. The boast of Nineveh ("There is no other than I") is the same as that of Babylon in Isaiah 47, 10. The most fundamental human sin is self-divinization. This was already the temptation of Adam and Eve, and it is a charge often made by the prophets (see, for example, Is 14 and Dn 4). Zephaniah's prophecies of the Day of the Lord dramatize the gulf between God and humanity and are basically a put-down of all human pride.

Reproach and Promise for Jerusalem

The final chapter does not use the catchword "Day of the Lord" but deals with related themes. The phrase "on that day" (3, 11) refers to the Day of the Lord and is often used to introduce additions to the prophetic books in the postexilic period.

In the opening oracle of the chapter (3, 1–8), Jerusalem is denounced as the tyrannical city that accepts no correction. The reference may be to the failure of the Deuteronomic reform or simply to the rejection of the prophet himself. The concluding oracle, however (3, 11–20), prophesies restoration for Jerusalem, when God "will leave as a remnant in your midst a people humble and lowly." The motif of the remnant is familiar from the preaching of Isaiah, a century before Zephaniah, and there is no doubt that Isaiah had considerable influence on the later prophet. It is possible, then, that Zephaniah uttered this oracle, but it is more likely that here we have another example of an optimistic oracle added on to the end of a prophetic book by an editor.

While the concluding oracle may not have come from Zephaniah, it has its own validity. The judgments of the Assyrian and Babylonian

eras were not God's last word to Israel. Even after the destructive Day of the Lord, hope was still possible.

FURTHER READING

Berlin, A. *Zephaniah*. Anchor Bible 25A. New York: Doubleday, 1994. Careful technical commentary.
Boadt, L. *Jeremiah 26–52; Habakkuk; Zephaniah; Nahum*. Old Testament Message 10. Wilmington, DE: Glazier, 1981. Helpful brief commentary.
Roberts, J. J. M. *Nahum, Habakkuk and Zephaniah*. Louisville: Westminster, 1991. Brief scholarly commentary.

HAGGAI

[see pages 1220–23 of the Old Testament]

The activity of Haggai can be dated quite precisely to the year 520 BC, almost two decades after the return of the Jews from the Babylonian exile. During that time various problems had beset the returned exiles, and they had not succeeded in rebuilding the Temple. We know from Ezra 5, 1f that it was at the urging of Haggai and Zechariah that the task was finally brought to completion. The book of Haggai preserves both the words Haggai used to exhort the Jews to finish the building and his attempt to cope with their disappointment after it was finished.

The Exhortation to Rebuild

The first chapter of Haggai paints a vivid picture of the impoverished state of the Jewish community after the return. The difficulty of their situation was compounded by drought and crop failure. Haggai offered a daring interpretation of this situation: their difficulties were due to the fact that they had not rebuilt the Temple but had concentrated instead on rebuilding their own houses. We find here a classical case study in religious priorities. Socially minded critics tend to see Haggai as merely superstitious. The people needed the shelter of their own houses. God did not need a temple. This criticism is congenial to modern thought, but we also find it in antiquity. The anonymous prophet in Isaiah 66, 1–2 asks: "The heavens are my throne, the earth is my footstool. What kind of house can you build for me?" That

passage very probably comes from Haggai's time and suggests that there were other prophets who opposed the rebuilding. Yet there was social wisdom in Haggai's position. The morale of the community was at a low ebb. One way of raising that morale was to engage in a community project, which would encourage people to think of the good of the community as a whole rather than dwell on their own misfortune. This is not to suggest that Haggai thought consciously in such sociological terms but, in fact, by urging the people to think of God rather than of themselves he was directing their attention to the greater good of the community. A comparable situation occurred in the United States in the late nineteenth and early twentieth centuries. The immigrant communities from Europe were made up of poor working-class people. Nonetheless they took pride in erecting great churches and schools in cities like New York and Boston. These edifices were put up at no small sacrifice, but their value to the communities was enormous. While success was difficult for individuals, it was possible for communities that banded together. The buildings were simultaneously an offering to their God and an expression of their own self-worth.

The Reaction to the Finished Temple

We are told in the book of Ezra that when the foundation of the new Temple was laid, the old men who remembered Solomon's Temple cried out in sorrow, and their laments could not be distinguished from the shouts of joy. This was because the new Temple was puny in comparison with the old (Ezr 3, 12f). Haggai 2, 3 records this reaction. Besides, the completion of the Temple did not bring about the dramatic reversal of fortunes that Haggai had predicted. Haggai's reaction to this situation is typical of prophets through the ages whose predictions have not come to pass. First, he tells the people to wait "a little while." The prediction is not wrong, only the time is delayed. Second, he diagnoses a reason for the delay. The people are not observing purity laws and their offerings are unclean. He ends by reaffirming that God will shake the heavens and the earth when conditions are right.

It must be admitted that this reaction shows some embarrassment on the part of the prophet, which can only have increased with the passage of time when his predictions remained unfulfilled. The case of Haggai points out the Achilles heel of predictive prophecy. The hopes raised by the prophet were good for the morale of the community, but only for a time. When they were not fulfilled, they led to disillusionment. The same problem would beset the apocalyptic and messianic expectations of later generations, and eventually tend to discredit them.

The Lesson of Haggai

There are, then, two lessons to be learned from Haggai. One is that hope should not be focused on specific predictions. The faith of Habakkuk was secure because it was a faith in ultimate justice and did not depend on specific events coming to pass within a short space of time. Haggai's more specific prediction gives rise to problems. The other is that he has a positive lesson to offer on the value of religious symbols and ritual as a means of bringing the community together. It was largely through his efforts that the Temple was rebuilt. While the Temple may not have satisfied immediate expectations, its contribution to Jewish life over the next five hundred years was enormous, and would far outweigh the initial disappointment which many felt when it was completed.

FURTHER READING

Hanson, P. D. *The Dawn of Apocalyptic,* 240–62. Philadelphia: Fortress, 1975. Groundbreaking study of postexilic Judah.

March, W. E. *The Book of Haggai.* New Interpreter's Bible 7, 707–32. Nashville: Abingdon Press, 1996. Brief homiletical commentary.

Meyers, C. L., and E. M. Meyers. *Haggai, Zechariah 1–8.* Anchor Bible 25B. Garden City, NY: Doubleday, 1987. Thorough scholarly commentary.

Petersen, D. L. *Haggai and Zechariah 1–8,* 17–106. Philadelphia: Westminster, 1984. Concise but excellent scholarly commentary.

Wolff, H. W. *Haggai.* Minneapolis: Augsburg, 1988. Classic scholarly commentary.

ZECHARIAH

[see pages 1223–33 of the Old Testament]

The book of Zechariah contains the work of more than one prophet. It takes its name from the contemporary of Haggai who was also instrumental in the completion of the Temple. "Deutero-Zechariah" (Zec 9—14) comes from a much later time. Some scholars even distinguish a "Trito-Zechariah" in chapters 12 through 14.

The Original Zechariah

The original oracles of Zechariah are characterized by a series of visions that are explained to the prophet by an angel. The interpreting angel appears here for the first time in biblical literature. It becomes a standard feature of apocalyptic literature, beginning with Daniel 7—12. These symbolic visions disclose the prophet's view of what is really going on in the postexilic period by revealing a dimension of these events, which is hidden from the ordinary observer. So the first vision shows four (presumably angelic) horsemen whom the Lord had sent to patrol the earth. The implication is that God is indeed in control, although the divine activity may not be obvious. The visions in chapter 2 show four heavenly blacksmiths coming to beat down the horns of the nations and an angelic "man" making preparations for the restoration of Jerusalem. In all of these visions the hidden, heavenly activity is reassuring and a source of confidence for the fledgling Jewish community.

High Priest and King

Down to the time of the Babylonian exile, the prophets had been sharply critical of the monarchy and usually also of the priesthood. When Zechariah prophesied, the monarchy was no more, but Zerubbabel, a descendant of the Davidic line, held the position of governor under the rule of the Persians. In the absence of a king, the high priest enjoyed new power and authority. Both Zerubbabel and the high priest of the day, Joshua, had their critics. Zechariah, in sharp contrast to earlier prophets, came to the defense of the community's leaders. The vision in chapter 3 is a remarkable defense of Joshua. In the vision, Joshua stands before the angel of the Lord and is accused by Satan. This is one of the earliest appearances of Satan in the Old Testament. (He also appears in Job 1—2 and 1 Chr 21, 1.) He has not yet taken on the character of the Devil of later mythology. Rather he is an angel in the service of God, whose mission is to detect and prosecute wrongdoers in the manner of a federal attorney. The fact that Satan is said to bring accusations against Joshua is the prophet's way of dramatizing the opposition to the high priest in the Jewish community. Satan symbolizes Joshua's critics. He receives a stinging rebuke from the angel of the Lord. The point is not that Joshua is faultless, but that criticism is not appropriate when the community is struggling. Joshua is "a brand snatched from the fire" (Zec 3, 2)—that is, most of the leadership and institutions of Judaism had been destroyed, and what was left should be supported not criticized. So Joshua's faults are cast aside like dirty clothes, and he is affirmed in the sight of the Lord. Zechariah does not give Joshua a blank check. He is charged to walk in the ways of the Lord (3, 7). Nonetheless, the contrast with earlier prophetic attitudes to the priesthood is striking. In earlier times, religious institutions were often problematic insofar as they bred complacency in the people, and so a prophet like Amos spoke as if the sacrificial cult could be abolished. After the experience of the exile, however, Zechariah recognized the importance of institutions. While they are not an end in themselves, no society can live without them.

The prophet is equally positive about Zerub-babel, who is extolled for laying the foundation of the Temple. The two leaders are pictured as olive trees in chapter 4, because both priest and king were anointed with oil—hence the title "messiah" or "anointed one." The people of the Dead Sea Scrolls followed the lead of Zechariah and expected two messiahs, a priestly messiah of Aaron and a royal messiah of Israel. In chapter 6, the prophet is told to make a crown and to put it on the head of the high priest Joshua. Most scholars have recognized that the text has been altered here. (See the note on p. 1227, OT.) Originally, it would have provided crowns for *both* Joshua and Zerubbabel. The coronation of a Davidic prince would have been a highly dangerous undertaking, because the Persian overlords would surely have taken it as a gesture of rebellion. We do not know whether Zechariah ever carried it out. At some point the text was changed to eliminate the crown for Zerubbabel and thus avoid the suggestion of rebellion.

The understanding of the monarchy became increasingly idealized in the period after the exile, when the shortcomings of the actual kings were forgotten. The future king would be the messiah, the anointed one who would make Jerusalem again a holy city (8, 3). Zerubbabel could hardly have lived up to those expectations if he had been crowned, but his career, and that of Zechariah, helped keep alive the dream of independence for Judah.

The Appreciation of Ritual

Just as Zechariah shows a renewed appreciation for the institutions of priesthood and monarchy, he also has a more positive view of ritual than some earlier prophets. In 5, 5–11 he sees wickedness in the form of a woman, who is put in a bushel container and carried off to Babylon. The vision suggests that wickedness can be gotten rid of by a symbolic physical action. This idea is very similar to the scapegoat ritual in Leviticus 16 and shows that the prophet appreciated the power of ritual. While wickedness cannot be put in a container and disposed of, the ritual action expresses the human desire—and strengthens the resolve—to rid the society of evil. It has its effect on the emotions and motivations of the people who perform it.

Zechariah also appreciated the limits of ritual. In chapter 7 he is asked about the proper number of fast days. He answers that motivation is more important than keeping the exact number. What is most important is to "render true judgment, and show kindness and compassion toward each other" (7, 9). Here Zechariah echoes the sentiment of Hosea 6, 6: "it is love that I desire, not sacrifice." After the experience of the exile and the destruction of the Temple, Zechariah knew that sacrifice was important too, but his priorities are still the same as those of Hosea.

Zechariah 9—11

Two passages in chapters 9 through 11 merit special attention: the messianic oracle in chapter 9, and the allegory of the shepherds in chapter 11.

The Messianic Oracle

The messianic oracle in 9, 9f is famous because of its association with Palm Sunday in Matthew 21, 5 and John 12, 15. The ass was not as humble an animal in the ancient world as in modern times and was the vehicle of nobility in Genesis and Judges, but in the postexilic context it was a throwback to an earlier, simpler time. The hope is for a ruler who will restore Solomon's empire ("from the river to the ends of the earth") but will avoid the arrogance of the monarchy (symbolized by horses and chariots) and will be closer in style to the Judges.

As in Micah 4 and Isaiah 2, the messianic age will be a time of universal disarmament. One could scarcely describe Zechariah 9 as pacifistic, however. The logic of the passage is that the Lord will fight for Judah so that "they shall drink blood like wine" (9, 15). The mentality of this passage is close to what we find later in the apocalyptic books. In Daniel, it is Michael the archangel who fights the battles of Israel. The human role is to maintain purity and be obedient to the law. For Deutero-Zechariah, the Lord assumes the role of warrior directly, in accordance with much of Israelite tradition (for example, Ex 15, 3). The Jewish people will not need the warrior's bow because God will kill their enemies for them.

This oracle could have been written at almost any time in the postexilic period when the monarchy was no more, and the Jewish people, in any case, were not equipped with horses and chariots. If the reference to Yavan (Greece) in verse 13 is original, the setting may be about the

time of Alexander's conquests. The modest messiah, riding on an ass, provides an attractive contrast to the mighty Macedonian conqueror.

The Allegory of the Shepherds

The allegory of sheep and shepherds is very widespread in the ancient Near East, with the shepherds representing kings and rulers. The allegory of Zechariah 11 must be understood against the background of two passages in Ezekiel. Ezekiel 34 has an extended prophecy against the shepherds of Israel who exploited their flock. The movement of the prophecy, however, is from judgment to salvation, as the Lord takes over the job of shepherd. In Ezekiel 37, 15–22, the prophet takes two sticks, representing Israel and Judah, and joins them together, signifying that they would henceforth be one nation under David their king. In Zechariah 11 we also find exploitative shepherds (compare Zec 10, 2f), but there is no movement to salvation. The flock is designated for slaughter from the outset. The prophet is assigned to shepherd it for a while, but even he gives up on it and in the end they are given over to a foolish shepherd who takes no care of them. The wage of the prophet is the price of a slave, which is the value that the sheep merchants (foreign powers) attach to the God of Israel. It is also the wage of Judas in Matthew 26, 15. The two staffs of Zechariah 11 symbolize two covenants, one with the nations, and the other between Judah and Israel. Both are broken in the course of the prophecy. In all, then, Deutero-Zechariah reverses Ezekiel's predictions of salvation.

There is no agreement among scholars as to just when this prophecy was written or what context it addressed. All we can say is that it is an expression of extreme dissatisfaction and disillusionment from the postexilic period. The author of this passage is very far from the trust in the institutional leaders that characterized the original Zechariah in chapters 1 through 8. There is no confidence here either in the Jewish leaders or in their foreign masters. All the prophet can do is protest, in the traditional language of prophecy: "woe to my foolish shepherd . . ." Like every great prophet from the time of Elijah, the anonymous speaker of these lines uses the power of the word to proclaim judgment and even to curse. Even if there is little hope of changing the situation, it is the duty of the prophet to testify and to ensure that people see reality for what it is.

Zechariah 12—14

The last three chapters of Zechariah are even more confusing than the previous three. There is persistent criticism of the rulers. Chapter 13 includes a "song of the sword" (compare Ez 21) against the "shepherd" and predicts that only one-third of the people will be spared. More surprising than this is the prediction of the end of prophecy (13, 1–6).

The Decline of Prophecy

Prophecy had been discredited for various reasons. One was the failure of predictions, especially the prophecies of glorious restoration after the exile. Another was the conflict between prophets themselves and the willingness of some to mislead the people for their personal gain. This had been a problem already in the time of Micaiah, son of Imlah (1 Kgs 22) and was severe in the time of Jeremiah. It was only natural then that prophets would come to be viewed with suspicion. In Zechariah 13, 3 even a prophet's parents assume that an oracle spoken in the name of the Lord is a lie.

After Haggai and Zechariah, prophets seem to have lost status. We do not even know the real names of the prophets whom we call Third Isaiah, Deutero-Zechariah, and Malachi. The visionaries of the Maccabean period attributed their visions to ancient heroes such as Daniel and Enoch. Undoubtedly there were prophets in Judaism in the Hellenistic period (John the Baptist is a late example), but they did not command the same respect as those of the Assyrian and Babylonian eras.

The Final Battle

The motif that runs through these chapters is that of a final battle in Jerusalem. The traditional motif was that in the last days all the nations would assemble to fight against Mount Zion (for example Ps 2; Ez 38—39). This motif is elaborated here in chapters 12 and 14. Chapter 12 suggests that there has been some tension between Judah and Jerusalem. Judah must be saved first so that

Jerusalem will not gloat over it. Rivalry between city and countryside is natural enough and does not help us identify the situation in which the oracle was composed. In Zechariah 12 the emphasis falls on reconciliation. Jerusalem and the Davidic house will be compassionate and will "look on him whom they have thrust through" (12, 10). This enigmatic allusion has given rise to endless speculation. Some scholars have thought that the reference was to King Josiah, who was killed in battle at Megiddo in 609 BC, but this oracle is certainly from a much later time. Others have thought the figure is deliberately mysterious like the Suffering Servant in Isaiah. John 19, 37 saw the fulfillment of this prophecy in the piercing of the side of Christ on the cross. We cannot now be sure whether the passage referred to a specific individual in its Jewish context. What is clear is that the prophet looked for a time when the leaders in Jerusalem would show compassion for the people they had oppressed and be reconciled with them.

The final oracle, in chapter 14, also envisages reconciliation between Judah and the nations, so that even the Egyptians will celebrate the Feast of Tabernacles. There is a threat of coercion, which betrays the prophet's awareness that such a conversion of the Gentiles was implausible. Nonetheless, the future hope of Zechariah 14 is remarkable for its broadminded universalism, insofar as it wants to include the Egyptians in the worship of the true God.

FURTHER READING

Hanson, P. D. *The Dawn of Apocalyptic*, 280–380. Philadelphia: Fortress, 1975.

Meyers, C. L., and E. M. Meyers. *Haggai; Zechariah 1—8*. Anchor Bible 25B. Garden City, NY: Doubleday, 1987.

——. *Zechariah 9—14*. Anchor Bible 25C. New York: Doubleday, 1993.

Ollenburger, B. C. *The Book of Zechariah*. New Interpreter's Bible 7, 735–840. Nashville: Abingdon Press, 1996. Useful commentary with homiletical reflections.

Petersen, D. L. *Haggai and Zechariah 1—8*, 109–320. Philadelphia: Westminster, 1984.

MALACHI

[see pages 1233–38 of the Old Testament]

The three chapters that make up the last book of the prophetic corpus are, like Deutero-Zechariah, anonymous—we do not know who wrote them. Malachi is not a proper name but means "my messenger." The word is taken from 3, 1 ("Lo, I am sending my messenger") to designate the one through whom this word of the Lord was given. The book is made up of 6 oracles: 1, 2–5; 1, 6—2, 9; 2, 10–16; 2, 17—3, 5; 3, 6–12; and 3, 13–21. There are two short appendixes in 3, 22–24.

The first oracle, 1, 2–5, is a standard polemical oracle against Edom, Judah's neighbor and bitter enemy in the postexilic period. This oracle is rather atypical of Malachi, however, as the others are all critical of Judah itself. He is especially critical of the priesthood and of breaches of faith by the people.

The Priesthood (1, 6—2, 9)

Malachi stands in a long line of prophets, beginning with Amos, who were critical of the priesthood. In this case, the charge is that the priests have been offering cheap sacrifices, disposing of sick and lame animals instead of offering the best ones. The logic of Malachi's argument deserves notice. No one would offer a sick animal to the governor, yet the priests make such offerings to God. An offering has symbolic significance and reflects the attitude of the one who brings it. Malachi is not opposed to the priesthood as such. Far from it. He speaks of a covenant with Levi (2, 4), which is never mentioned in the Pentateuch or historical books. (Levi is, however, set apart for a special role in Dt 10, 8f and 33, 9f.) He has the greatest respect for the ideal of the priesthood. Because so much is expected of the priests they are all the more guilty.

The most striking statement in this passage, however, is the declaration that "from the rising of the sun, even to its setting, my name is great among the nations" (1, 11). The Gentile nations certainly did not worship the Lord explicitly, so it is not certain what the prophet had in mind. One theory holds that the reference is to the Jewish Diaspora, the scattering of Jewish exiles among the nations, but Jews were not supposed to offer sacrifices outside of Jerusalem, although

they sometimes did. Two considerations may throw light on this problem. First, the Persian kings were generous in providing funds for the support of the Jewish Temple, and Malachi may have recognized this support as an offering to the Lord. Second, in the official correspondence in the books of Ezra and Nehemiah, the Lord is called the God of heaven (for example, Ezr 6, 10). The high god of the Persians, and other sovereign deities could also be acknowledged as "the God of Heaven," and so the Gentiles could be understood to worship the same God as the Jews. This view of pagan religion would be decidedly broad-minded and liberal.

Breaches of Faith

The most controversial passage in the book of Malachi is found in the third oracle, 2, 10–16. The prophet begins with the rhetorical question: "Have we not all the one Father?" He goes on to denounce two breaches of faith. First, Judah "has married an idolatrous woman" (literally, "the daughter of a foreign god," 2, 11). The second problem is the divorce of "the wife of your youth," (2, 14).

It is reasonable to assume that the background of this oracle is related to the situation described in Ezra 9, where the leaders of the people inform Ezra that "neither the Israelite laymen nor the priests nor the Levites have kept themselves aloof from the peoples of the land . . . . for they have taken some of their daughters as wives . . ." The usual explanation of the passage in Malachi is that Jewish men were divorcing the Jewish wives of their youth and marrying Gentile women, possibly for social reasons. Inevitably, they then became implicated in the cult of pagan deities. On this interpretation, the question, "have we not all one Father?" is addressed *only* to Jews and is not as universalistic as it initially seems.

This interpretation is certainly possible. There is no doubt that Malachi disapproved of mixed marriages. There is no other evidence, however, that Jews in the postexilic period divorced their Jewish wives. In fact, the only instance of divorce for which we have evidence is found in

Ezra 10, where the Jewish men who had taken foreign wives send them away at Ezra's command. Malachi's categorical statement, "for I hate divorce, says the LORD" (2, 16), is hard to reconcile with Ezra's policy. It is possible, then, that Malachi is quite universalistic, despite his disapproval of mixed marriages. Once a marriage had been entered into, it was sacred. The Jewish men should have taken care that their offspring were "godly" (2, 15) rather than try to undo the marriage. Conversion of the spouses, rather than divorce, was the solution. On this interpretation, the "one Father" is the creator of all, Jews and Gentiles. Ethnic distinctions do not matter if one is willing to recognize the one God. The "daughter of a foreign god" only becomes so by her choice of which God to worship. If this interpretation is correct, Malachi exhibits some of the spirit of Saint Paul in his openness to the Gentiles. He would have been in direct conflict with Ezra, had they been contemporaries. We know that there was some diversity of opinion in Judaism at this period. Ezekiel 44, 7 insisted that no "foreigners, uncircumcised both in heart and flesh" be admitted to the Temple. In contrast, an oracle preserved in Isaiah 56 shows a very open attitude to "the foreigners who join themselves to the LORD," and assures them of a place on the holy mountain. Malachi may be seen as part of this "liberal" tradition, which welcomed foreigners if they were willing to convert to Judaism.

The Day of the Lord

The final chapter of the book is dominated by the expectation that God will come in judgment. The image of the refiner's fire is embedded in our memory by Handel's *Messiah*. The idea of a day

of destructive judgment is, of course, an adaptation of the traditional Day of the Lord. The most distinctive aspect of Malachi's use of the theme is the motif of the messenger who prepares the way. In the final appendix, this messenger is identified as Elijah the prophet. Since Elijah had not died but was taken up alive to heaven (2 Kgs 2, 11), there was speculation that he would return to complete his earthly course. In the New Testament, John the Baptist is cast in this role (Mt 11, 14; 17, 12f). Elijah's task is to warn the people and give them a last chance at repentance. It is likely that the prophet we call Malachi saw himself as performing this task.

The final oracle of Malachi is also the conclusion of the prophetic corpus. The editors of the prophetic books specifically wanted the collection to reinforce the laws of the Pentateuch: "Remember the law of Moses. . ." (3, 22). They also underlined the theme of the coming judgment, which runs throughout the collection. The purpose of the collected prophetic books is not only to remind us of the past but especially to motivate us in the present by making us look to the future.

FURTHER READING

Hill, A. D. *Malachi*. Anchor Bible 25D. New York: Doubleday, 1998. Thorough scholarly commentary.

Petersen, D. L. *Zechariah 9–14 and Malachi*. Louisville: Westminster John Knox, 1995. Concise but excellent commentary.

Schuller, E. M. *The Book of Malachi*. New Interpreter's Bible 7, 843–77. Nashville: Abingdon Press, 1996. Helpful commentary with homiletical reflections.

THE GOSPELS AND ACTS

DONALD SENIOR AND PHEME PERKINS

INTRODUCTION TO THE SYNOPTIC GOSPELS

The Similarities and Differences among the Synoptic Gospels

Because of their striking similarities, the three Gospels of Matthew, Mark, and Luke have traditionally been called *synoptic,* from the Greek meaning to "view together." The observer of these three Gospels would, in fact, notice many parallels among these stories of Jesus if they were laid side by side.

At the same time, the general structure and style of the Synoptic Gospels are distinctively different from John's Gospel. For example, in each of the Synoptic Gospels, Jesus begins his public ministry of teaching and healing in Galilee, travels with his disciples on a single purposeful journey to Jerusalem, and there experiences final rejection, death and, ultimately, resurrection. Jesus' sayings in these Gospels are generally either succinct and pointed or in the story form of the parable; his actions are characterized by marvelous healings and exorcisms; a major theme of his preaching is the advent of the "Rule of God." In John, on the other hand, Jesus moves back and forth between Galilee and Judea, and his teaching is often expressed in long, meditative discourses. There are no parables in John, no exorcisms, and fewer healing stories; the Rule of God motif plays a very minor role.

But it would be a mistake to consider Matthew, Mark, and Luke as carbon copies of each other. As the Reading Guides and *New American Bible* introductions make clear, modern biblical

scholarship has emphasized the unique style and theological perspective of each of the Gospels. While obviously related to each other in form and content, the three Synoptic Gospels develop their own distinct view of Jesus and his mission. Mark, for instance, begins his story of Jesus with his baptism at the Jordan, whereas Matthew, by means of the infancy narrative at the beginning of the Gospel, traces Jesus' origin back into the history of Israel. Luke, too, begins with an infancy narrative but gives much more positive emphasis to Jerusalem than either Mark or Matthew. In Luke's Gospel the young Jesus goes to Jerusalem to listen to the teachers in the Temple courtyard, and the disciples of Jesus will gather to pray in the Jerusalem Temple after his resurrection. Luke also adds a second volume to his Gospel; the Acts of the Apostles picks up the story of Jesus and his apostles where the Gospel left off, and shows its continuing force as the community of the Risen Christ moves out into the world.

The "Synoptic Problem"

Both the similarities and the distinctive differences among the Synoptic Gospels have led to ongoing debate about their interrelationship, or the "synoptic problem" as it is called. The canonical order of the Gospels—Matthew, Mark, Luke—influenced scholars in the early church, such as Augustine, to assume that Matthew was the first Gospel written, with Mark and Luke dependent on it.

In the late nineteenth and early twentieth centuries, however, this general consensus was challenged. Analyses of the style and content of Mark led scholars to conclude that Mark was the first Gospel written, with Matthew and Luke directly dependent on Mark. The presence of other material in Matthew and Luke that was not found in Mark, such as the sayings of Jesus in the Sermon on the Mount, led to the hypothesis of an additional source for Matthew and Luke. This hypothetical source of material—which scholars call "Q" (from the German word *Quelle* or "source")—was probably a collection of sayings and parables of Jesus that circulated in the earliest Christian community. Independently of each other, if this hypothesis is correct, Matthew and Luke blended this source with their new renditions of Mark and perhaps with some other materials or traditions specific to their own communities.

This hypothesis about the interrelationship of the Synoptic Gospels is called the "two-source hypothesis" because it postulates two literary sources for the Gospels of Matthew and Luke, namely the Gospel of Mark and Q. It presumes that Mark was the first Gospel to be written and that Mark, in fact, set the basic format for the story of Jesus, a format that both Matthew and Luke used as the starting point for their own narratives. This relationship would account for the similarities among the Gospels. Each Gospel writer's particular interpretation of Mark, the use of other sources, and the unique pastoral and theological perspectives of the writers and their local churches, would lead to the distinctiveness of each of the Synoptics.

Most New Testament scholars today, including Roman Catholics, accept the two-source hypothesis as the most plausible explanation of the interrelationship among the Synoptics. But even though a majority of scholars accept it, it is still a theory and therefore vigorous debate continues about other solutions to the synoptic problem. There are those who are convinced that Matthew or even Luke should be considered the first Gospel to be written, or others who are not persuaded that there was any literary contact among the Synoptic Gospels, but rather that each developed independently from a common gospel tradition.

The issue of the relationship of John's Gospel to the Synoptics is even more problematic. Until the midpoint of this century, most modern biblical scholars assumed that John knew of the Synoptic Gospels and that his own Gospel was a very distinctive variation on the synoptic tradition. But more recently, a significant number of scholars speculate that John may represent an independent stream of tradition that had little, if any, contact with the Synoptic Gospels.

The Synoptic Gospels and Their Portrayal of Jesus

Whatever may be the ultimate solution to the synoptic problem, it is clear that the Gospels of Matthew, Mark, and Luke have made an essential contribution to our understanding of Jesus and his ministry. The strongly transcendent Jesus of John's Gospel, with its emphasis on the preexistent Word and the incarnation of that Word in human flesh, has had a profound influence on Catholic Christology. But in the twenty-first century, Catholic theology has turned with renewed energy to the portrayals of Jesus in the Synoptic Gospels. The overarching symbol of the Rule of God proclaimed by Jesus in the Synoptics has provided an important framework for understanding the social and liberating implications of Jesus' message. Modern Christology's deep interest in the humanity of Jesus also turns to the portrayals found in Mark, Matthew, and Luke. The trauma of the Holocaust and the Christian-Jewish dialogue have led to a new appreciation of the Jewishness of Jesus, and here, too, the Synoptics' portrayal of Jesus and his milieu has provided an important backdrop. Interest in the literary quality of the Gospels has also focused attention on the Synoptic Gospels with their rich variety of sayings, parables, healing stories, conflicts, and other types of literary forms.

In short, the Synoptic Gospels are a major and essential source for a genuine understanding of Jesus and his message. That richness is described in detail in the Reading Guides that follow.

D.S.

MATTHEW

[see pages 1248–1315 of the New Testament]

Before Beginning . . .

As pointed out in the introduction (NT pp. 1248–52), Matthew's Gospel has long held a special place in the life and teaching of the church. The special character of this Gospel alerts us to some things to keep in mind as we set out to study it more closely.

A Story

Like each of the Gospels, Matthew's work is a story or a narrative. It begins with the roots of Jesus' family tree, describes the circumstances of his birth, and then turns to the events of his ministry, culminating in his death, resurrection, and final appearances to his disciples.

Even though Matthew's way of telling a story is influenced by his time and culture, his narrative has many of the same characteristics as storytelling today. There is an unfolding plot that carries the story from the beginning of Jesus' life, with its mixture of success and opposition, through to the death and triumph of its conclusion. There are characters (Jesus, the disciples, the opponents, etc.): some of them are quite developed (for example, Jesus and Peter), some seem one-dimensional (for example, the Pharisee opponents), others have only minor roles (the mother of James and John). All of these elements play a part as one reads or studies the Gospel of Matthew.

In describing Matthew's Gospel as a story we are not implying that it has no historical basis. There is no doubt that Matthew uses materials rooted in history (most of which he draws from the Gospel of Mark, one of his principal sources). But the evangelist, or Gospel writer, casts these traditions about Jesus into the form of a running story. A story or narrative helps catch up the reader into the dynamism and feeling of the events being recounted. This feature of the Gospel can engage us when we come to study or read it in more depth.

A Fund of Teaching

While Matthew's Gospel remains a dynamic story, it is also enriched—more than any of the other Gospels—with the sayings of Jesus. This feature has led commentators over the centuries to consider Matthew a kind of "catechism" or teacher's manual. In addition to the basic story of Jesus' life and ministry, which Matthew drew mainly from the Gospel of Mark, he also had a fund of the important sayings of Jesus (many of which he shares in common with the Gospel of Luke). The evangelist has organized many of these sayings into discourses or speeches of Jesus (see introduction pp. 1249–51). These are not transcripts of actual talks given by Jesus because there is little logical progression found in the discourses as a whole. Rather, the evangelist has clustered the sayings of Jesus around basic motifs. Explanations of many of the sayings are found in the notes to the biblical text; later in the study guide we will discuss some of the major themes of the discourses. These discourses bring the reader of Matthew's Gospel into vital contact with the power of Jesus' teaching.

The Jewish Heritage of Jesus and the Early Church

While all of the New Testament writings illustrate the essential dependence of Jesus and the early church on Judaism, none does it more forcefully than Matthew's Gospel. In fact, one of the primary purposes of this Gospel may have been the attempt to link the story of Jesus with the history of Israel. Any reader of Matthew who wants to go deeply into this Gospel must be alert to its Jewish background.

This feature of Matthew springs to our attention from the opening lines of the Gospel, which begin with a genealogy or family tree, tying Jesus into the history of Israel. The frequent use of Old Testament quotations, the concern with the Jewish law and customs of purity and prayer, the sharp critique of the Jewish leaders for their rejection of Jesus and for their failure to lead a life of holiness—all of these show that Matthew was absorbed with Jesus' Jewish heritage.

But it is also apparent that Matthew is concerned with how this Jewish Jesus is Messiah for the whole world. As we will indicate below, the universal mission of the church is also a prime motif of this Gospel. In fact, Matthew seems to be telling the story of Jesus so that it can help both the Jewish Christians and the Gentile converts of his community. After reading the Gospel they would be able to understand that Jesus fulfills the hopes and dreams God planted in the people of Israel, and now extends the offer of God's salvation to all the world.

Strange as it may seem, Matthew's Jewish roots may also explain another difficult feature of his Gospel: his strong critique of the Jewish leaders. The Jesus of Matthew's Gospel blisters his opponents for their hypocrisy and lack of faith. They are held up to the reader of the Gospel as negative examples of what an authentic disciple should avoid becoming. The sharp edge to Matthew's critique may stem from the tragic division and hostility that grew between Judaism and Jewish Christianity in the early decades of the church. For Matthew, the fact that most of Israel did not accept Jesus or the Gospel—while many Gentiles did accept it—was a baffling and unexpected turn in salvation history, and his telling of the story of Jesus reflects this. Unfortunately, Matthew's characterization of the Jewish leaders also provided an opportunity for later anti-Semitism to develop (itself a violation of the Gospel's teaching).

How to Proceed

Since Matthew's Gospel is a story, it would be best to begin at the beginning! Although one could approach the Gospel thematically, that is, taking a certain topic (for instance, discipleship) and tracking passages throughout the Gospel that relate to this theme or motif, the best method might be to let the story line of the Gospel be your guide. Begin where Matthew begins (chapter one, verse one) and let overarching ideas or themes emerge as the story of Jesus unfolds. This will be the method of the study guide: for each major section of the Gospel, we will discuss some key themes. You will find more detailed commentary on each section in the ample notes that accompany the Gospel text itself.

Working through Matthew's Gospel

The outline or major segments of Matthew's Gospel can be determined only by paying attention to the contours of his story. In harmony with the discussion found in the introduction (see NT, pp. 1248–52), we propose the following division:

• *The Origin of Jesus* (1, 1—2, 23). Here Matthew presents the events surrounding Jesus' birth and infancy.

• *Preparation for the Ministry of Jesus* (3, 1—4, 7). The test in the desert and the ministry of John the Baptist help prepare for the formal beginning of Jesus' mission.

• *The Galilean Ministry of Jesus* (4, 7—16, 12). This major section spans the ministry of Jesus from his entrance into Galilee until his announcement of the Passion and his intent to go to Jerusalem. It can be subdivided into other important segments:

1. The Sermon on the Mount (4, 17—7, 29)
2. Jesus the Healer (8, 1—9, 35)
3. The Mission Discourse (9, 36—11, 1)
4. Mounting Hostility to Jesus (11, 2—12, 50)
5. The Parable Discourse (13, 1—53)
6. The Kingdom and the Disciples (13, 54—16, 12). This section includes the ongoing activity of Jesus and reactions to it, but with special emphasis on Jesus' relationship with Peter and the rest of the disciples.

• *The Way to Jerusalem* (16, 13—20, 34). Jesus' fateful journey to Jerusalem with his disciples dominates this section. Three times during this journey Jesus predicts his Passion and Resurrection (16, 21; 17, 22f; 20, 17–19) and instructs his disciples on the cost of following him. There is also the important discourse on community life (18, 1–35).

• *Final Teaching in Jerusalem* (21, 1—25, 46). This section of the Gospel takes place in Jerusalem. It concentrates on Jesus' final exchanges with his opponents (esp. 21, 12—22, 46), his condemnation of the scribes and Pharisees (23, 1–39), and the long discourse on the final age and judgment (24, 1—25, 46).

• *Death and Resurrection* (26, 1—28, 20). The concluding segment of the narrative contains the Passion narrative and the account of Jesus' burial (26, 1—27, 66), the events surrounding the discovery of the empty tomb (28, 1–15), and Jesus' final appearance to the eleven disciples on a Galilean mountaintop (28, 16–20).

Reading through Matthew's Gospel

This section traces major themes and characteristics in each segment of Matthew's Gospel. It supplements the introduction and notes that accompany the Gospel text itself.

The Origin of Jesus (Mt 1, 1—2, 23)

The first two chapters of Matthew's Gospel are like a prologue to a great drama, sounding major themes that will be played out in the rest of the story. In this way the evangelist or Gospel writer alerts the reader to the particular tones he will give his portrayal of Jesus.

A Messiah Rooted in the Hopes of Israel

The Jewish heritage of Jesus is stressed in the very first lines of this Gospel. He is the "son of David, the son of Abraham" (1, 1) and his messianic lineage is traced through Jewish history from Abraham to Joseph, the husband of Mary (1, 2–18). Explicit quotations from the Old Testament (for example, 1, 23; 2, 6; 2, 15; 2, 18; 2, 23) are augmented by numerous allusions to Old Testament figures and events (for instance, the hostility of Herod recalls the rage of Pharaoh against the Israelites; the reference to a star recalls the prophecy of Balaam about a future deliverer for Israel in Nm 24, 17; Joseph, who is guided to protect the holy family through dreams and goes into Egypt, is reminiscent of another Joseph who was also a dreamer and one who rescued Israel in Egypt during a time of famine and distress). In all these ways Matthew proclaims something that echoes throughout the Gospel: Jesus is the promised *Messiah,* the one through whom God's longed-for salvation would be achieved. Thus continuity with the Old Testament is stressed (compare Mt 5, 17).

A Messiah Close to His People

The experiences of Jesus and his family evoke another theme important to this Gospel, namely Jesus' identification with the "least." The Matthean Christmas story has a sober mood to it. Right from the beginning, Jesus and his family are threatened with death by a tyrant. Innocent people are killed because they are identified with Jesus. The holy family is forced into exile (just as Israel had been in its tortured history). Even when they return from Egypt (a new exodus?) they are unable to go home to Bethlehem but must become displaced persons, living in Nazareth (2, 22f).

This identification with the great events of Israel's struggle to be free may help explain one of the names given Jesus in Matthew's story. He is to be called *Emmanuel,* that is, "God is with us" (1, 23). As subsequent events of the Gospel will show, the Matthean Jesus has extraordinary compassion for the suffering (see, for example, the healings in chapters 8 and 9), explicitly identifies himself with the "least" (see Mt 25, 31–46; 10, 42), and promises to remain with his church as it continues its mission in the world (28, 20; 18, 20).

Jesus as Messiah of Israel and Savior of the World

While Matthew stresses the Jewish roots of Jesus and his messianic mission, he also signals the ultimate worldwide scope of that mission. As Herod and the leaders of Jerusalem plot to destroy Jesus, the magi, Gentile wise men, come seeking to pay homage to him (2, 1–12). Even in the family tree of Jesus, Matthew may be hinting at the wider horizons of Jesus' mission. While most of the genealogy traces the male line of Jesus' ancestry, there are several women mentioned—Tamar, Rahab, Ruth, Bathsheba—all of whom were foreigners whose entry into Jewish history was under unusual, sometimes even scandalous, circumstances. Even Mary, the mother of Jesus, seems to be put in this category since her association with the royal Davidic line is not by natural means but only through the initiative of the Spirit—something that causes consternation to Joseph (1, 18–19).

Thus from the beginning outsiders had been part of Jesus' history. This is a major theme of Matthew's Gospel. He will emphasize the rejection Jesus experiences from the Jewish leaders and at the same time provide scattered examples of Gentiles groping toward faith (for example, the centurion in 8, 5–13; the Gadarene demoniacs in 8, 28–34; the Canaanite woman in 15, 21–28). Matthew carefully notes that Jesus' historical ministry focused on Israel (10, 5) but with the new age of resurrection, that mission of salvation would now extend to all nations (28, 19).

The infancy narrative also hints at the kind of salvation Jesus will bring. Of all the Gospels, Matthew alone stresses the significance of the name *Jesus.* The angel gives the divine instruction that the child is to be named Jesus "because he will save his people from their sins" (see the explanatory note at 1, 21). Jesus is depicted as *savior* throughout the Gospel as he delivers people from their burdens of sickness, oppression, and sin. This is a Jesus who thirsts for justice or righteousness (3, 15) and blesses those who, like the prophets before them, suffer in the pursuit of justice (5, 10). Jesus exercises divine power in forgiving sins (see 9, 1–8) and urges his disciples to reflect this same sense of reconciliation in dealing with each other (see especially 5, 43–48; 18, 21–35).

The overall mood of Matthew's Christmas story is quite different from that of Luke's. There are no triumphant angels, no picturesque gathering of shepherds, little focus on a tender vision of mother and child. Instead there are ominous plots against the child, outbreaks of violence, displacement, and exile. But throughout there is also the promise of God's abiding presence, bringing salvation in spite of sin and rejection. Perhaps we can think of Matthew's infancy Gospel as an "adult" Christmas story, one that has a special truth for the many people experiencing violence and persecution today. It tells a story that begins in the strength and beauty of a particular history and culture but will ultimately reach across boundaries to touch all peoples. In any case, these two chapters prepare us for the story that will follow, a story that will trace Jesus' mission of salvation through bitter rejection to ultimate triumph.

Preparation for the Ministry of Jesus (3, 1—4, 17)

This transition section brings the reader from the infancy narrative into the beginning of Jesus' ministry in Galilee. It opens with the preaching of John in the desert and closes with the first footstep of Jesus into Galilee, the northern region of Israel where he proclaims the advent of the Kingdom.

Two characteristic Matthean themes dominate this segment of Matthew's narrative.

The Dawn of a New Age

Throughout his Gospel, Matthew is conscious that the coming of Jesus was the decisive turning point in the history of salvation. In Jesus, God was offering the world salvation; the final age longed for by Israel was now beginning. This conviction is expressed through the figure of John the Baptist, whose appearance is reminis-

cent of Elijah, the great prophet expected to return at the end of the world (see note to 3, 4) and whose message heralds the imminent approach of God's Kingdom (3, 2). That message will be driven home by Jesus himself. He, too, preaches the nearness of the Kingdom (4, 17). Whereas John is clearly a prophet preparing the way, Jesus is the one who brings the Kingdom to reality. Jesus is clearly superior to John: the Spirit of God descends on Jesus (3, 16) and a "voice from heaven" (a Jewish way of speaking obliquely about God) declares that Jesus "is my beloved Son" (3, 17). Jesus' entry into the region of Galilee and the start of his mission there will be light and hope to people who languish in darkness and the fear of death, (see 4, 13–16). Even at this early stage of his Gospel, the evangelist hints at the universal scope of Jesus' message (see note to 4, 12–17).

Repentance and Good Deeds

Both John and Jesus call people to repentance. The reality of God's kingdom and the consciousness of living in a new and decisive age of salvation should move Israel to change its way of thinking and its way of acting. Throughout his Gospel, Matthew will insist that the touchstone of authentic repentance is good deeds. So here John the Baptist challenges the Jewish leaders: "Produce good fruit as evidence of your repentance" (3, 8). It is not sufficient for them to claim to be children of Abraham (3, 9); status within God's reign is not dependent on blood lines or rank but on one's response to God's love embodied in Jesus.

The testing of Jesus in the desert also illustrates this point (see notes to 4, 1–11). As was the case in the infancy narrative, Jesus recapitulates the experience of Israel. In their wandering through the desert, Israel and its leaders had often failed God's covenant, but Jesus, faithful Jew and faithful Son of God, will not fail, despite the efforts of Satan to draw him away from his messianic mission. The Jesus of Matthew's Gospel shows a fierce and loving loyalty to God. As he tells John, he must "fulfill all righteousness" (3, 15). Jesus is not content merely to preach fidelity to God; he demonstrates it here in the mysterious realm of the desert test and in his commitment to his mission even to the point of death on the cross.

The Galilean Ministry of Jesus (4, 17—16, 12)

A major section of the Gospel begins with Jesus' entry into Galilee and the inauguration of his ministry of teaching and healing. We will consider the material in six segments, following the flow of Matthew's narrative.

The Sermon on the Mount (4, 17—7, 29)

The Sermon on the Mount, the first of Jesus' five great discourses in this Gospel, is perhaps the best-known passage of Matthew's Gospel.

The Sermon itself spans chapters 5 through 7, but preparation for this great discourse begins in chapter 4. After sounding the theme of the Kingdom of God (4, 17), Jesus calls his first disciples to follow him and to share in his mission (4, 18–22). Jesus is committed to teaching, proclaiming the Kingdom of God, and healing (4, 23). That liberating mission draws a response from every point of the compass as throngs of broken and needy people surge toward Jesus and his message of God's mercy (4, 24f). Jesus' teaching, Matthew implies, is not mere abstract truth. Jesus' words and his healing touch have the power to transform lives.

The Sermon on the Mount does not have a neat progressive structure; rather, sayings of Jesus are clustered around basic motifs. We will note some of them here:

A New Teaching for a New Age. Matthew's conviction that Jesus is the Messiah, and therefore the authoritative teacher of God's will, runs throughout the Sermon. With Jesus the final age of salvation dawns and, with it, new insight into God's will. Matthew's Jesus sees that will of God as being in continuity with the revelation that came through the Law of Moses in the Old Testament, but now bringing that law to its fullest and most compelling expression. In the opening verses of the Sermon Jesus states: "Do not think that I have come to abolish the law or the prophets. I have come not to abolish but to fulfill" (5, 17; see the comments in the notes to this text).

The conviction that the end of the world will be a triumph of God's grace—a conviction based on belief in the life, death, and resurrection of Jesus—runs throughout the Sermon and gives it special force. The false values assumed by the world are crumbling. This is the message of the

beatitudes (5, 3–12): those who are "poor in spirit" or who "hunger and thirst for righteousness" or are "peacemakers" are blessed because God will vindicate their hopes. Similarly, because it is a new age with new possibilities, the old wisdom is no longer adequate. A series of six antitheses or contrast statements mark off the difference between former interpretation of the Jewish law and Jesus' own radical teaching (see 5, 21–48).

The Supreme Law of Love Expressed in Committed Action. Matthew's emphasis on good deeds, cited above (see comments on Preparation for the Ministry of Jesus [3, 1—4, 17]), is clearly in evidence here. The words of Jesus at the conclusion of the Sermon are unequivocal: "Not everyone who says to me, 'Lord, Lord,' will enter the kingdom of heaven, but only the one who does the will of my Father in heaven" (7, 21). But the Sermon demonstrates that Matthew's Jesus is not simply talking about frenetic action. The heart and soul of Jesus' teaching is the command to love. That comes to its fullest expression in the last of the contrast statements where Jesus tells his disciples they are to love even the enemy (5, 44) because God's own love is lavish and indiscriminate, bathing both just and unjust in its light and refreshment (5, 45). Matthew is consistent on this point throughout the Gospel (see 7, 12; 22, 34–40). Asking his disciples to strive for love of enemies—the most challenging demand that can be made on the human heart—expresses the ultimate spirit of all of Jesus' teaching on human relationships. For this reason, the disciple is to strive for complete honesty (5, 33–37), avoid retaliation for injury (5, 38–39), and is not to violate another through lust or manipulation (5, 27–30).

Jesus' teaching roots all of this in God's relationship to us. The teaching on love of enemy and nonretaliation is, therefore, not a peripheral part of the Gospel nor is it an abstract ideal. This fundamental teaching of Jesus remains a challenge for Christians who wrestle with what this Gospel teaching demands of us who live in a violent world where the use of force is commonplace.

Revelation of a Close and Compassionate God. Jesus' teaching in this part of the Gospel also gives a profound insight into the Gospel's image of God. God's boundary-breaking love is not based on merit but reaches out even to the unjust and the "enemy" (5, 45–48). God cares for us more than for birds of the air or the wild flowers, whose freedom and beauty are signs of God's provident love (6, 25–32). Therefore, the disciple is to have complete trust in God and to pray with confidence and without pretense (7, 7–11). Jesus' model prayer (6, 9–15) catches up much of the spirit of the entire Sermon. There is a wonderful simplicity and honesty about the instructions on piety in the Sermon (6, 1–18); God's relationship to us is direct and close. There is no place for posturing before such a loving God.

The Authority of the Sermon. How to live with the Sermon on the Mount has been a constant point of discussion in the church. Are these demanding words to be taken as impossible ideals, meant only for a perfect world or for perfect people? Or do they make sense only in the setting of Jesus' own times, when people thought the end of the world was near and so might be capable of responding heroically in such an emergency situation?

None of these solutions are adequate. The instructions of Jesus are not a system of clear-cut laws spelling out exactly how we are to act in every circumstance, nor are they abstract or impossible ideals. These teachings give us practical guidance as we seek to live a life faithful to the Gospel. They illustrate the core spirit of Jesus' teaching, a spirit we must embody in our own circumstances. The possibility of living in accord with the teaching of Jesus is based on God's grace; the Sermon illustrates the difference grace can make in a person's life and relationships. Within the array of moral choices that confront us, the examples Jesus gives in the Sermon such as the call for integrity in our relationships, for nonretaliation, and for a commitment to reconciliation help direct us in the right way.

Jesus the Healer (8, 1—9, 34)

Introduction: This is a powerful section of the Gospel in which Matthew displays another dimension of Jesus: he teaches, he also heals. As the notes to the text state (see comments under 8, 1), Matthew draws most of these stories from his source, Mark's Gospel, but the evangelist significantly reedits this material. He abbreviates many of Mark's stories, omitting some of the colorful details in order to concentrate on Jesus'

essential actions and accompanying words. Matthew also clusters the nine major stories of these chapters into three segments (a tenth miracle is reported but barely narrated in 9, 32; it serves to contrast the reactions of the Pharisees with that of the crowds): 8, 1–17; 8, 18—9, 17; 9, 18–34.

Each of these clusters of stories seems to have a dominant motif. In 8, 1–17 the emphasis falls on Jesus' power to heal. The second section, 8, 18—9, 17, concentrates on the demands of discipleship. And the final section, 9, 18–34, illustrates the essential role of faith in the healing narratives. These motifs are by no means exclusive, however; the richness of the healing stories allows the Gospel to proclaim many levels of meaning at the same time. We will examine more closely each of these dominant themes.

Christology. By narrowing the spotlight on Jesus in the first three stories, Matthew emphasizes the divine power that works through the Messiah. Jesus cleanses the leper, heals the servant of a Gentile soldier, and dispels the fever of Simon's mother-in-law. Except in the case of the centurion, there is little attention to the plight or disposition of the sick person in these stories. The concluding verse of the section (8, 17) makes Matthew's intended point; by his healing touch Jesus fulfills the prophetic promise of Isaiah 53, 4: "He took away our infirmities and bore our diseases."

By their very nature the healing stories serve Matthew's purpose. All of us experience sickness or disability at one time or another in our life. We all experience our limitations and realize too well that death looms before us. Jesus is moved with compassion (9, 3.36) and does not hesitate to stand in solidarity with those whose condition makes them "outsiders" (see his association with the leper, the Gentile, the tax collectors).

The Conditions of Discipleship. In the second set of stories Matthew illustrates some of the demands of discipleship. Only those fully committed to proclaiming the Kingdom of God and following Jesus are able to go with him across the sea (see 8, 18–23). But even for those who remain, following Jesus can mean the threatening experience of the storm at sea (8, 24–27) and strange encounters with the power of evil (8, 28–34). The true disciple is one who learns that mercy and compassion drive Jesus, a lesson the

Pharisees (whom Matthew consistently portrays in negative tones) seem unable to grasp (9, 9–13).

Faith. The healing stories often serve to illustrate the meaning of faith. Faith is, first of all, trust in Jesus' power to heal and transform us. That faith is evident in the leper who approaches Jesus (even though the law forbade him to do so), in the centurion who pleads on behalf of his servant (see 8, 10), in the friends who bring the paralytic to Jesus (9, 2), in the woman with the hemorrhage who touches the tassel of his cloak (9, 22), and in the two blind men who trust that Jesus can do what no one else can (9, 28f).

Note, too, the faith illustrated in these stories often takes a very active form. The leper boldly comes up to Jesus; the woman dares to touch him; the Gentile swallows his pride and pleads with a Jewish healer; the friends of the paralytic gain him access to Jesus. The sick and disabled can teach us this lesson: trusting in God does not mean mere passivity, waiting for a bolt from heaven. Transformation comes when we exercise our trust in God, and commit our own resources to seeking a new life.

The Mission Discourse (9, 35—11, 1)

Now that Matthew has completed his portrait of Jesus as teacher and healer, he moves to a new segment of the Gospel. Using his own mission as a model, Jesus gathers his twelve apostles and commissions them to proclaim the Kingdom of God, and to heal. The motivation for their mission is the same that animated Jesus' own energetic healing in the previous two chapters: the crowds are "troubled and abandoned, like sheep without a shepherd" (see Mt 9, 36–38).

This forms the second of the five great discourses of Matthew's Gospel. The evangelist draws some of the material in this discourse from chapter 13 of Mark's Gospel (see especially the material in Mt 10, 16–23); the rest comes from Q, the sayings source he holds in common with Luke (see introduction), or from Matthew's own sources.

Note that the discourse can be read from two different perspectives: (1) as part of the unfolding story of Jesus' ministry and his relationship with his disciples; (2) and an instruction for the post-Easter church. In the former time frame, Jesus tells his apostles to restrict their mission to Israel, the chosen people of God (10, 5f); but in the new age, when the gospel must be proclaimed to all the world (see 28, 16–20), Jesus' words apply to the universal mission of the church.

Typical Matthean themes run through the discourse. The Twelve (including Matthew the tax collector, 10, 3) share in Jesus' own mission of proclaiming the Kingdom and healing those in need (10, 7f). Note that the apostles are not yet commissioned to "teach"—that comes only after the Resurrection (see 28, 20) when they have a deeper grasp of Jesus' mission. Any disciple who follows Jesus can expect to meet indifference, hostility, or rejection (see, for example, 10, 16–25.34–39). The discourse is not naive but clearly warns the apostles about the cost of proclaiming the gospel in an authentic way.

But there is also strong affirmation of the power of the gospel and of the sense of confidence that should go with those on mission. They are not to be afraid of those who threaten their lives (10, 26–28) or flinch before the divisions that may come. The loving God who has an eye for the sparrows and counts the hairs on our heads will not abandon those who follow the way of Jesus. Christians who live in circumstances of persecution and violence understand well these words of Jesus. Those who live in more comfortable circumstances need to ask themselves if the gospel values they reverence are not sometimes co-opted by the seductions of the dominant culture.

Matthew's concern with the mission of the church will reemerge in the final scene of the Gospel when the mission of Jesus, confined to Israel during his lifetime, bursts out into the world through the mission of the church (28, 16–20).

Mounting Hostility to Jesus and His Mission (11, 2—12, 50)

In the mission discourse Jesus warned his disciples to expect opposition when they preached the gospel. Now Jesus himself becomes embroiled in conflict because of his mission. For the next two chapters Matthew traces the opposition that swirls around John the Baptist and Jesus.

The motif of conflict is apparent from the first words of chapter 11—John the Baptist is in prison and soon to die. He sends his disciples to Jesus with the key question: "Are you the one who is to come, or should we look for another?" (11, 3). That question leads to a summary of Jesus' great deeds, and to Jesus' reflection on John's ministry and his own.

The opposition to Jesus is crystallized in "this generation" (11, 16), which understood neither the ascetical John nor the gentle and compassionate Jesus (11, 18f). "Wisdom," that is, God's message to Israel embodied in Jesus himself, will be proven present in the liberating works that Jesus performs in his ministry (11, 19).

Matthew weaves together in this section profound insight into the bond between Jesus and his Father (11, 25–27)—one of the most beautiful passages of the Gospel—with tumultuous scenes of conflict, as the enemies of Jesus fail to perceive that he is the Messiah and attack him for healing on the Sabbath (see the series of stories in chapter 12). Judgment, another typical Matthean motif emerges from all this. The Jewish towns that refuse to transform their lives in the light of the gospel bear the responsibility for their failure. Matthew's emphasis on judgment goes hand in hand with his emphasis on the necessity of good deeds. Living out the gospel should not be confused with mere noble aspirations and religious rhetoric. A tree is known by the fruit it produces (12, 33).

The section closes with this insistence: the true family of Jesus are not those who merely claim kinship with him but those who do the will of God (12, 50).

The Parable Discourse (13, 1–50)

Parables were the trademarks of Jesus' teaching style. As the notes to the text explain (see 13, 11), these pointed stories both reveal and veil the mystery of the Kingdom. Unless the listeners are willing to probe beneath the surface of the parables, the true meaning of Jesus' words will escape them (13, 14f).

Typical themes of Matthew's Gospel emerge again in this discourse. The certain triumph of the Kingdom, which was a strong theme of the Sermon on the Mount, dominates the parable of the sower (13, 1–9) as well as the parables of the mustard seed (13, 31f) and the yeast (13, 33f). Discipleship motifs stand out in the parables of the treasure and the pearl (13, 44–46): true followers of Jesus are to put aside everything and be

fully committed to the compelling beauty of God's reign.

Many of the parables in Matthew's Gospel have obvious moral messages (see also the stories in chapters 24 and 25). The parable of the weeds sown among wheat (13, 24–30; explanation, 13, 36–43) makes the point that the church, like the world itself, is a mix of good and evil. The disciples should not be discouraged by this but be confident that God's grace will triumph at the end of time, and evil will be punished. The theme of judgment present in the previous section of the Gospel reemerges here.

The conclusion of the parable discourse seems almost to be a signature of the Gospel writer (13, 52). The scribe who is instructed (literally: "discipled") in the kingdom of heaven is like the householder who can bring from the storehouse "both the new and the old." Preserving the best of the past and yet making it come alive for a new generation seems to be one of the main purposes of Matthew's Gospel (see introduction p. 1249). Matthew was convinced that Jesus did not destroy the beautiful traditions of Judaism but gave them new meaning. Bridging past and present in an open and respectful manner is one of the greatest challenges of religious leadership in any age.

The Kingdom and the Disciples (13, 51—16, 12)

It is difficult to characterize this long section of Matthew's story under any single heading. Jesus' ministry of teaching and healing continues but now begins to burst beyond the confines of Galilee into Gentile territory. Clashes with his opponents, mainly the Pharisees, also continue to erupt. But the haunting story of Jesus' walking on the water and Peter's awkward attempts to trust his master (14, 22–33) may give us a clue to the special character of this section. With new intensity Jesus begins to instruct his disciples on the mystery of the Kingdom, and they begin to realize the awesome identity of the Messiah. Several motifs run through these chapters:

The Inclusive Mission of Jesus. Following the lead of Mark's Gospel, Matthew begins to trace the boundary-breaking nature of Jesus' ministry (see Reading Guide to Mark's Gospel, RG 391–92). After another conflict with the Pharisees (15, 1–20), Jesus ventures near the Gentile region of Tyre and Sidon and there encounters a "Canaanite" woman (15, 21–28). This is one of the most intriguing stories in the Gospel. At first Jesus resists the woman's entreaties on behalf of her daughter. The Matthean Jesus remains committed *only* to the people of Israel (see 10, 5f). But the woman's insistence, an expression of her active faith, breaks down Jesus' resistance and seems to open the horizons of his own vision. Matthew uses this story to instruct his own church: they, too, may have had too narrow a concept of their mission, thinking that only Jews could become Christians. But the needs and genuine faith of the Gentiles showed the early church that God intended to extend the boundaries of the Kingdom to include all people.

The two stories of the miraculous feedings (14, 13–21; 15, 32–39) give a similar impression of expansiveness. Jesus will not let the vast crowds go hungry and uses the occasion to instruct his disciples. Another epic scene takes place on the mountaintop, a favorite place of revelation in Matthew's Gospel (15, 29–31). Similar to the vista at the beginning of the Sermon on the Mount (see 4, 23–25), vast crowds of the sick and disabled surge toward Jesus and he cures them. Once again the disciples can observe the boundless compassion that drives Jesus.

Opposition and Rejection. Despite the mercy of Jesus, his opponents continue to resist and misunderstand his message. The parable discourse had warned that some would prefer not to "see" and not to "hear" what Jesus preached. That prediction comes true in Nazareth (13, 54–58) where Jesus' own people rebuff him and take offense at his "wisdom and mighty deeds." The story of Herod and the death of John the Baptist (14, 1–12) are early warning signs about Jesus' own fate. His enemies were so immersed in their opposition that they would carry it to the point of trying to destroy Jesus.

In this conflict about the tradition of washing hands before eating (15, 1–20), the Gospel offers one explanation of the intransigence of Jesus' opponents. They have allowed their own traditions to "nullify the word of God" (15, 6). In other words, they had lost a sense of priority, placing good but not essential values ahead of those that were most fundamental. Matthew continues to stress that Jesus was not opposed or indifferent to the Law, but he wanted to inject new life into its observance by insisting that the love command was the basis of all fidelity (see discussion at 5, 17).

The Disciples. The story of Peter walking on the water contains material unique to Matthew's Gospel and illustrates both the importance of Petrine traditions in this Gospel and the evangelist's view of discipleship. Peter begins to sink in the waves because he "doubted" or "hesitated" and because he has "little faith" (14, 31). The latter phrase is particularly characteristic of Matthew's Gospel (see p. 1250). Matthew's portrayal is sympathetic and realistic: the disciples believe but their faith is weak. Deeper trust in Jesus is needed.

At the same time, the disciples are quite different from the opponents of Jesus. While the opponents reject Jesus and align him with Satan (12, 24), the disciples acclaim Jesus as "the Son of God" (14, 33). The enemies of Jesus cannot understand his teaching, but the disciples, albeit hesitantly, do "understand" (16, 12; see also 13, 16.51).

The Way to Jerusalem (16, 13—20, 34)

A dramatic shift in the setting of the Gospel story is about to take place. Jesus goes with his disciples to the northernmost reaches of Israel, Caesarea Philippi (16, 13). There he will ask the fundamental question of the Gospel: "Who do you say that I am?" (16, 15). Jesus' question and Peter's response represent a turning point in the narrative. "From that time" (16, 21) Jesus will begin to speak openly about his approaching death, and the action of the Gospel will point toward Jerusalem and the events of the Passion and Resurrection.

The announcement of Jesus' journey to Jerusalem (16, 21) thus introduces the motif of a "journey," a theme already present in Mark's Gospel (see comments on Mark 8—10) and one greatly expanded in the Gospel of Luke (see comments on journey narrative in Luke RG 406–8). The threefold prediction of the Passion (in Matthew, see 16, 21; 17, 22f; 20, 17–19) punctuates the journey and keeps the reader's attention directed to Jerusalem and Jesus' death and resurrection. That great climax to the Gospel, already alluded to as early as the infancy gospel (see comments in RG 375), dominates the entire narrative and gives urgency to Jesus' teaching. The transfiguration reflects this: immediately after Jesus predicts his death for the first time, the light of resurrection glory seems to emanate from his person in a mountaintop scene reminiscent of the revelation given to Moses on Sinai (see the notes to 17, 1).

During the journey narrative, the spotlight seems to fall with new intensity on Jesus' relationship with his disciples. Although some conflicts with the Pharisees take place (see, for example, the dispute about divorce, 19, 1–12), most of Jesus' words are directed to his disciples, revealing to them what it means to follow a Crucified Messiah. Special Petrine traditions are present in this section, too, including Peter's confession at Caesarea Philippi and Jesus' blessing upon him, his mediating role in paying the Temple tax on behalf of Jesus and himself (17, 24–27), and his lead question about forgiveness in the discourse on community life (18, 21).

The Ministry of Leadership

Matthew gives special attention to Peter in his Gospel (see comments on 14, 22–33).

Although the disciples had already confessed Jesus as "the Son of God" (14, 33), Peter himself has an opportunity to confess his own belief that Jesus is "the Messiah, the Son of the Living God" (16, 16). Thus the focus in the Caesarea Philippi scene is not on the disciples in general but on Peter and his faith in Jesus. Peter's firm belief in Jesus is rewarded by a special blessing. He receives a new name, "Peter" or "Rock" (see comments in notes to 16, 18, p. 1282) because he will be the foundation upon which Jesus' church will be built. Peter is given the "keys of the kingdom of heaven" and empowered to "bind" and "loose." Both of these images, as the notes to the text indicate, refer to the responsibilities of leadership entrusted to Peter. He becomes, in effect, the prime minister of the community.

Matthew will balance out this focus on Peter by also asserting the authority of the community in chapter 18, but at this point in the Gospel he is showing the important role entrusted to the leader of the community. Undoubtedly this reflects a ministry of leadership already present in

Matthew's church. The Gospel uses Peter as a model for leadership. Historically, Peter had been an important leader in the church. In Acts we are told that he helped mediate between the Jewish Christian church of Jerusalem and the emerging Gentile churches (see Acts 10—15). Paul, too, acknowledges the importance of "Cephas" (see, for example Gal 1, 18; 2, 11–14). And the Letters of Peter, even if not written directly by the Apostle, testify to the importance of his memory in the early church (see Reading Guides to 1 and 2 Peter).

While it would be going too far to impose on this Gospel scene the full-blown institution of the papal office, Roman Catholic tradition can legitimately see in the figure of Peter the founding model for the later emergence of this office in the church. Peter is blessed because of his strong faith in Jesus and because he served a key role in maintaining the unity of the church. Equally important to remember, however, is that the gospel refuses to idealize Peter or to place him above the demands of the gospel. The same Peter that Jesus blesses lavishly here is also called "Satan" and "obstacle" (16, 23), will underestimate the need for reconciliation (18, 21), and will deny his discipleship in the face of the Passion (26, 69–75). Leaders within the community must remain disciples (see 23, 10).

Life in the Community

The fourth discourse of Matthew's Gospel, the discourse on community, occurs in this section of the Gospel (18, 1–35). The notes supply detailed commentary on this powerful example of Jesus' teaching. Matthew gathers here two parables of Jesus (the lost sheep, and the unforgiving servant) and several sayings, and he molds them into a discourse.

Two key sayings divide the chapter and strike its major themes. At the end of the first major section, Jesus tells the disciples: "In just the same way, it is not the will of your heavenly Father that one of these little ones be lost" (18, 14). The call to urgently seek out and care for the "little ones," that is, the weak or alienated members of the community, dominates the first half of the discourse. The members of the community are not to seek their own aggrandizement (18, 1–5) and are never to "scandalize" or despise those on the margins of the church (18, 6–10). Matthew's version of the lost sheep parable drives that lesson home: the leaders of the community are to seek out the stray, not to condemn them.

The second half of the discourse concludes with another key saying: "So will my heavenly Father do to you, unless each of you forgives his brother (or sister) from the heart" (18, 35). The need for reconciliation dominates the latter half of the discourse. Disputes are to be settled in a fair and practical manner (18, 15–17), and even if strong discipline must be taken toward a recalcitrant member, he or she is to be treated "like a Gentile or a tax collector"—a poignant note in a Gospel where Jesus seeks out just such people (see, for example, 9, 9–13)! Those who have experienced limitless forgiveness from God should not put limits on reconciliation within the community. That is the radical message of Jesus' reply to Peter, and the concluding parable of the story. Its message is similar in content to Jesus' teaching on love of enemies in the Sermon on the Mount (see 5, 43–48). We are to strive to love even the enemy because God's own love is lavish and indiscriminate.

This entire chapter offers a remarkable model for the church. There is little concern here for structures and budgets (important as they are for us and may have been for Matthew's community, too); emphasis falls rather on the care we need to have for each other if we are to be followers of Jesus.

Final Teaching in Jerusalem (21, 1—25, 46)

The Gospel drama now enters Jerusalem, the capital city, where Jesus will experience death and resurrection. The great temple of Herod dominated this city in the time of Jesus, and its shadow falls across the scenes Matthew narrates in these chapters.

Jesus the Messiah enters his city in triumph, but he is seated on a donkey's colt, which Matthew interprets as a sign of Jesus' humility (see comment on 21, 5). As a fearless prophet, Jesus cleanses the house of God, another sign of his God-given mission to call Israel to repentance. The next day Jesus returns to the Temple compound and begins to teach the crowds (21, 13). There follows a number of key texts that reveal the heart of Jesus' message. But the Jewish authorities (the Pharisees now joined by the "chief priests and elders of the people," all members of the Sanhedrin, an informal ruling body whose base would, in fact, have been Jerusalem) remain hostile to Jesus and his message. This section of the Gospel is filled with sharp clashes between Jesus and his opponents.

Two important clusters of sayings and parables are found here. In the first, 23, 1–39, Jesus excoriates the scribes and the Pharisees, portraying them in purely negative tones for their hypocrisy and lack of fidelity. As we will discuss below, this is Matthew's most intense assault on the Jewish leaders. The second collection of sayings and parables forms the fifth and final discourse of the Gospel, the so-called eschatological discourse or discourse on the end of the world (see the note to 24, 1). While gazing at the stunning Temple from the Mount of Olives, Jesus reflects on the fate of the Temple and the end of human history. This leads to a series of parables, some of them unique to Matthew, urging the disciples to remain faithful and to exemplify that fidelity through good deeds (see 24, 36—25, 46).

The Authority of Jesus

Matthew portrays Jesus in strong, authoritative tones in this section. The Messiah enters the royal city in triumph with the acclamations of the crowds filling the air (21, 1–11). "The Lord of the sabbath" (12, 8) asserts his authority over the Temple by driving out the merchants and money changers, reclaiming God's house (21, 12–17). He meets head-on the challenges of each of the major religious authorities of Israel: the scribes, the Pharisees, the chief priests, the elders of the people, the Sadducees. Even though Jesus will soon be a prisoner, Matthew wants to leave no doubt in the mind of the reader: Jesus is the Messiah, the true Teacher of Israel.

The foundation of that authority is Jesus' identity as God's Son. The parable of the tenants reaffirms that (21, 33–46); Jesus describes himself in this allegory (see note in text, p. 1295) as the son of the vineyard owner, the "heir," whose maltreatment will bring judgment on the tenants. He is more than David's Son—even David the King had to call the future Messiah "Lord" (22, 41–46).

Matthew also presents Jesus dealing with questions of the law in characteristic fashion. The law is not rejected out of hand but reinterpreted. The dispute about the greatest commandment of the law (22, 34–40) is most revealing: "the whole law and the prophets" depend on the love command. The core of Jesus' teaching and the basis for all interpretation of tradition are the values of love and compassion (see 5, 43–48, and comments on chapter 18).

Jesus and His Opponents

In chapter 23 Matthew presents Jesus as launching into a fierce assault on the hypocrisy and infidelity of the scribes and Pharisees. As the notes observe (see comments on 23, 1–39), they become, in effect, negative examples—the reverse side of the portrayal of the faithful disciple found in the Sermon on the Mount. Reading this discourse tells us what values Matthew's Jesus holds most dear: practicing what one preaches (23, 3), being compassionate rather than laying heavy burdens on others (23, 4), not using religion as a means of self-aggrandizement (23, 5f), having a proper sense of values and therefore understanding that mercy and justice are always the highest priority in interpreting the law (23, 23–28). Jesus urges his disciples to be leaders who have a sense of solidarity with the community rather than viewing others as inferior and subordinate (23, 8–12).

This strong indictment of the failings of the leaders is not intended solely to pummel the opponents of Jesus. Rather it is meant as a sober instruction for the Christian readers of the Gospel. Nevertheless, the negative stereotyping of the Jewish leaders, especially when it is read apart from its historical context in the Gospel, can have destructive effects. We who live in the horrible shadow of the Holocaust must be responsible readers of this Gospel and, while taking to heart the important lessons of this discourse, must not allow its negative image of the Jewish leaders to influence our attitude to Jews today. Every modern pope and the teaching of the Second Vatican Council has attacked anti-Semitism and reminded Catholics of their spiritual and historical roots in the living faith of Judaism (see particularly, the 2002 statement of the Pontifical Biblical Commission, *The Jewish People and Their Sacred Scriptures in the Christian Bible*).

Judgment

The parables that make up the eschatological discourse have a familiar Matthean ring to them

(see 24, 36—25, 46). Once again the evangelist dwells on the importance of doing good deeds as the authenticating expression of one's discipleship. The "faithful and prudent servant" is the one who is found taking care of the household and distributing food to those in need (24, 45f); the wise virgins have their lamps filled with oil and are ready to respond at the proper moment (25, 1–13); the servant who employs his or her talents is the one blessed on the master's return from a long journey (25, 14–30); those who will be invited to inherit the Kingdom are those who carried out the love command—feeding the hungry, clothing the naked, visiting the prisoner, and welcoming the stranger (25, 31–46).

The climactic parable of the sheep and the goats illustrates how far Matthew is prepared to press his insistence on good deeds. The "sheep" had not even recognized the Risen Lord present in the needy but yet acted out of compassion. They are blessed by the Son of Man in his glory because they have proven to be faithful servants. More than once in his Gospel Matthew has stated that doing the good deeds of compassion and justice weigh far more than knowing the right words and wearing the right vestments (see a similar message in the parable of the two sons, 21, 28–32). There is little tolerance for religious hypocrisy in this Gospel.

The Death and Resurrection of God's Son (26, 1—28, 20)

The Passion (26, 1—27, 66)

The Passion story moves quickly from Jesus' prediction of the plot against him (26, 1–5), through the last supper with his disciples (26, 20–30), his anguished prayer and arrest in Gethsemane (26, 36–56), the interrogation and trial before the Sanhedrin or Jewish Council (26, 57–75), the Roman trial before Pilate (27, 1–31), and the final scene of crucifixion, mockery, and death (27, 32–56). The burial in Joseph of Arimathea's tomb and the Pharisees' demand that Pilate post a guard (27, 57–66) prepare the reader for the explosive events of the Resurrection.

The peculiar emphases Matthew gives the Passion story can be summarized under three major themes:

The Majesty of Jesus. Even in the Passion story, Jesus remains the majestic Messiah of Israel. This is already true in Mark's account but it is given particular emphasis by Matthew. Jesus is imbued with prophetic knowledge of the events about to take place: he predicts the plot of the leaders (26, 1f), is fully aware of his impending death (26, 12.18), knows the identity of his betrayer (26, 25), and the certainty of Peter's denials (26, 34). His captors cannot seize him until Jesus confronts Judas with his treachery (26, 50). And when the high priest commands with an oath that Jesus reveal his identity, Jesus predicts with calm majesty his eventual triumph as the Son of Man who will be exalted at the right hand of God (26, 64). Death cannot destroy or defeat God's Son—that is the heart of Matthew's message in the Passion story. The parade of mockers who file past the cross jeer Jesus and ridicule his claim to be God's Son (27, 39–44). But as death comes, Jesus is acclaimed as the true Son of God, and nature itself erupts in testimony to Jesus' victory (see comments on 27, 51–54).

The Dawn of the New Age. The death of Jesus is the center point of sacred history in Matthew's perspective. As discussed above (see comments on RG 381), Matthew, along with all of the New Testament, considered Jesus as the advent of the final and decisive age of salvation promised by God to Israel. The death of Jesus was the climactic act of his entire mission: here all of his love and commitment were compressed into one intense act of fidelity to the will of his Father. Thus the death of Jesus becomes in a special way the turning point between the old and the new age. With the death (and resurrection) of Jesus the final age of human history had begun and, therefore, humanity must respond to God's grace in a new way.

Several features of Matthew's Passion story proclaim this theology of history. At the moment of death (27, 51–57) signs of the new age break out: nature convulses, the tombs are split open, and the dead are liberated—just as the dream of the prophet Ezekiel had envisioned, with the dead bones of Israel's hopes taking flesh and escaping the tomb (see Ez 37). The age of death is over; the age of resurrection begins.

The attention Matthew gives to the response of the leaders and people of Israel to Jesus is another part of his theology of history (see, for example, 27, 24f). Paradoxically, because Israel rejects Jesus, the way will now be open for the gospel to be proclaimed to the Gentiles. This does not mean that Matthew despairs of having the Jews accept the message of Jesus (he seems to offer some hope of this in 23, 39), but he does believe that the mission to the Gentiles is now possible in the new and final age of salvation, and one of the catalysts for that mission was the fact that the mission to Israel had failed. Paul, too, has a similar theology in Romans 9—11, where he reminds his readers that in the mystery of God's providence the failure of Israel becomes a moment of grace for the Gentiles. For Paul, Israel remains special because God is faithful and will never forget the promises made to the chosen people. This biblical teaching is reaffirmed in the theology of the Second Vatican Council where in the document on relationships with non-Christian religions *(Nostra Aetate)* the Council explicitly refers to Romans 9—11 to state that the Jewish people have a special and enduring place in the history of salvation. Pope John Paul II in his historic visit to the synagogue of Rome affirmed that Catholicism has a relationship with Judaism "which we do not have with any other religion." For these reasons the Pontifical Biblical Commission declared that "an attitude of respect, esteem and love for the Jewish people is the only truly Christian attitude in a situation which is mysteriously part of the beneficent and positive plan of God" *(The Jewish People and Their Sacred Scriptures in the Christian Bible,* par. 87).

Examples and Counterexamples. The Passion story also serves Matthew's teaching about discipleship. In the crucible of suffering and death, one's true character is revealed. The Passion is filled with examples, both positive and negative, of how people respond to the gospel in crisis. The leaders remain implacably hostile to Jesus and demand his death. Peter and the rest of the disciples prove their "little faith," with Peter denying he knows Jesus and the others fleeing in panic. Judas betrays his master and gives in to despair rather than seeking repentance (27, 3f).

There are also bright moments: the woman of Bethany who performs a last kindness for Jesus, anointing him for burial despite the protests of the disciples (26, 6–13); Pilate's wife who pleads on behalf of "that righteous man" (27, 19); the centurion and his companions who acclaim the crucified Jesus as the "Son of God" (27, 54);

the women who stand by Jesus at the cross and see to his burial (27, 56); Joseph of Arimathea, the rich disciple who risks his reputation by burying a publicly executed man in his own new tomb (27, 57–61). And, of course, Jesus himself is the prime exemplar of fidelity—seeking God's will despite the threat of death, refusing violence at the moment of his arrest, and trusting in God even as his life's breath is taken from him.

There is no doubt that Matthew intended the readers of the Passion to place themselves in the story and to ask the troubled question posed by the disciples: "Is it I, Lord?" (26, 22).

The Resurrection (28, 1–20)

The Gospel concludes with the events surrounding the empty tomb and Jesus' appearances to his disciples. None of the Gospels attempts to narrate the resurrection itself, but Matthew comes closest to that in mentioning an "earthquake" and an "angel of the Lord" who comes from heaven to roll back the stone from the tomb (28, 2). Marvelous events such as these and the opening of the tombs at the moment of Jesus' death (see 27, 51–53) continue to signal the final and glorious age when God's presence would be felt in a vivid way.

Mark's original ending does not include the report of any appearances of the Risen Christ; the discovery of the empty tomb, and the words of the heavenly messenger about Jesus' triumph over death are enough to proclaim the message (see Mk 16, 1–8). But in Matthew's Gospel, Jesus appears first to the women as they leave the empty tomb (28, 9f), and then to the eleven disciples (here Matthew does not forget Judas's tragic fate) in Galilee (28, 16–20). Matthew's denunciation of the Jewish leaders continues right to the end of the Gospel: when the chief priests and elders learn from the soldiers about the astounding events at the tomb, instead of believing in Christ's triumph, they concoct a false story about the disciples stealing the body of Jesus (28, 11–15).

The final scene of the Gospel (28, 16–20) is on a mountaintop, the favored site of special revela-

tion throughout the Gospel (see, for example, the temptation, the Sermon on the Mount, the transfiguration, the healing of the crowds, 15, 29–31). The Risen Christ comes in triumph, as he had predicted during his Passion, and commissions his disciples to go to "all nations," making disciples, baptizing them into the community, and teaching them to observe all that Jesus had commanded.

Major themes of the Gospel are compressed into this scene: Matthew's concern with the universal mission of the church; his emphasis on Jesus as teacher; his realistic portrayal of the disciples (who even now "hesitate" as they encounter the Risen Christ, see 28, 17!); his interest in the church. This scene has inspired countless Christian missionaries throughout the centuries to leave their homeland to bring the gospel to others. Above all, the Gospel's majestic portrayal of Jesus as the church's firm foundation and abiding hope is reaffirmed. No matter how turbulent will be the church's future, the Risen Jesus will not abandon it. Matthew concludes his Gospel with the final promise of one who was named *Emmanuel*, "God is with us" (see 1, 23): "I am with you always, until the end of the age" (28, 20).

D.S.

FURTHER READING

Carter, Warren. *Matthew: Storyteller, Interpreter, Evangelist.* Peabody, MA: Hendrickson, 1996.

Davies, W. D., and Dale C. Allison. *Matthew.* International Critical Commentary. Vols. 1–3. Edinburgh: T & T Clark, 1988, 1997.

Harrington, Daniel J., S.J. *The Gospel of Matthew.* Sacra Pagina. Collegeville, MN: Liturgical Press, 1991.

Senior, Donald. *The Death of Jesus in the Gospel of Matthew.* Passion Series 1. Wilmington, DE: Michael Glazier, 1985.

——. *What Are They Saying About Matthew?* Rev. ed. Mahweh, NJ: Paulist Press, 1996.

——. *Matthew.* Abingdon New Testament Commentaries; Nashville: Abingdon Press, 1998.

MARK

[see pages 1316–48 of the New Testament]

Before Beginning . . .

As the introduction in the text suggests (see p. 1317), Mark's Gospel was probably the first Gospel to be written. Mark can take credit for shaping the Christian message into its most effective and moving form, that of a story about Jesus. The evangelist knitted together sayings of Jesus and stories about his ministry into a single dynamic narrative, tracing the life of Jesus from his first encounter with John the Baptist at the Jordan to his dynamic mission in Galilee, and on to his death and resurrection in Jerusalem. Mark's purpose was not simply to preserve the church's memory about Jesus but to make that memory take on new force in the lives of his readers.

Although we cannot be sure of the date, Mark probably wrote for Roman Christians, shortly after the persecutions of Nero (AD 64), when the community was still reeling from that tyrant's cruelty. Some Christians had reacted to Nero's attacks with heroic martyrdom, but others had betrayed the community or slipped away in fear. Mark's story of the crucified Jesus and his disciples who struggled to remain faithful would have been a powerful lesson for this early Christian church.

Characteristics of Mark's Gospel

There are some typical features and motifs, or themes, of Mark's Gospel that the reader should be alert to.

A Theology in Narrative

One of the most obvious features of Mark's Gospel, but one that should not be overlooked, is the fact that it is a narrative, a "story," about Jesus. Mark proclaims to his readers the good news of salvation (the literal meaning of the term *gospel*), but he does it not by a series of abstract statements or propositions but through a dynamic story that grips the reader with its force and emotion.

Some of the characteristics of Mark's narrative style reveal his theological message. The pace of the story is urgent. Jesus moves rapidly from place to place; there is little wasted motion and a minimum of verbiage. The dynamism and urgency of the Gospel coincide with Mark's conviction that the mission of Jesus is compelling and one must respond to it without hesitation. The Gospel is also filled with conflicts between Jesus and his opponents and between Jesus and the demons; the climactic passion story dominates the whole Gospel. Here, too, Mark's theological perspective is at work: because the message of Jesus calls for radical change and challenges the powers of this world, it is not surprising that conflict and suffering have such a major role to play in Mark's story.

Christology

The central and guiding question of Mark's Gospel is posed in 8, 29: "Who do you say that I am?" Understanding the mystery of Jesus' identity and responding to it with faith are the major concerns of the Gospel. Mark proclaims that Jesus is the Son of God and the Messiah, typical convictions of the entire New Testament, but the evangelist proclaims this fundamental faith by means of his story. Jesus' healings, his parables, his instruction of the disciples, his encounters with demons, his conflicts with opponents, and, above all, his death and resurrection reveal the profound mystery of Christ. Jesus' dynamic ministry of healing and exorcisms demonstrates that, through him, God's liberating rule was now breaking into history and freeing people from the grip of death.

For Mark, however, the most important means of revealing Jesus' identity was the cross. The cross becomes the touchstone of all authentic faith in Jesus; in his death for others Jesus reveals the heart of his mission. All of the other titles and images applied to Jesus such as "Messiah" *(Christ),* or "Son of Man," or healer, take on their true meaning when seen in the context of Jesus' redemptive death. Throughout Mark's narrative we will see this focus on Jesus at work.

Discipleship

Mark's Gospel is also concerned with what it means to follow Jesus; the disciples of Jesus play an important role in Mark's story. Jesus commis-

on the struggles of the community as it awaits the consummation of human history.

• 14, 1—15, 47. The climactic Passion account.

• 16, 1–8. The Gospel closes with the discovery of the empty tomb and the heavenly messenger's announcement of Jesus' victory over death.

As the notes explain (see comments on 16, 9–20) there are additional endings appended to Mark's Gospel, but these were added later by someone other than the evangelist. In our comments on the Gospel we will assume that the original ending to Mark's Gospel was 16, 1–8.

Reading through Mark's Gospel

The goal of this section is to trace major themes and characteristics of each segment of Mark's Gospel. What is said here complements the more detailed commentary found in the introduction and in the notes to the biblical text.

Overture (Mk 1, 1–13)

Like an overture to a musical piece, these verses sound major themes that will echo throughout Mark's Gospel. The setting for these opening scenes is the Judean desert, that haunting place so full of symbolism in the Bible. It was in the desert that Israel was first forged into a people, as God led them from slavery to freedom and sealed a covenant with them at Sinai. The desert was a place of new beginnings, and Jesus, like John, comes here to start his mission. But the desert is also a place of testing, the parched arena where the children of Israel rebelled against God and where the forbidding terrain revealed the true character of those who dared its stretches. Here, too, Jesus would be tested by Satan before the beginning of his mission in Galilee.

Mark signals several major themes in these brief opening scenes:

• John comes dressed like Elijah (see note to 1, 6, p. 1318), the great prophet who was expected to return at the end of the world. By presenting John in this fashion, Mark indicates that the old age is coming to an end and a new age is beginning. That is the reason for the urgent message of repentance John preaches. This sense of a new age dawning with Jesus moves throughout the Gospel.

• Mark also clearly identifies Jesus as the Son of God. The divine voice from heaven leaves no doubt about Jesus' awesome identity (1, 11). The Spirit of God descends on Jesus and imbues him with the power to carry out his mission as the Messiah, God's anointed one who would liberate the world from death (1, 10). As we noted in the introduction, Christology is a major concern of the Gospel.

• The desert test (1, 12f) where Jesus wrestles with the demon is also a preview of the ministry of Jesus. In his mission of healing, Jesus casts out demons and liberates the sick and disabled from the shackles of pain. To carry out his mission, Jesus must often struggle with opponents; from the opening scene of the Gospel, Mark tells us that the process of saving human life can be filled with conflict. Experience bears this out: very often true liberation from sin and false values comes only through great struggle.

The Galilean Ministry of Jesus (1, 14—8, 21)

This major section spans almost one half of the Gospel, and covers Jesus' ministry of teaching and healing in the northern region of Galilee. We can divide it into five segments, each with distinctive tones.

The Keynote of Jesus' Mission (1, 14f)

These two verses condense much of the Gospel message. As he enters into his home region of Galilee, Jesus sounds the major theme of his ministry: "the kingdom of God is at hand" (1, 15). Each phrase evokes a major Markan theme:

"This is the time of fulfillment" (1, 15). The new and final age of salvation—longed for by Israel over centuries—now dawns with the advent of Jesus. That new age will call for new responses by those graced to experience it (see Jesus' teaching on catching the mood of the times and the need to pour new wine into new wineskins, 2, 18–22).

"The kingdom of God is at hand" (1, 15). This biblical symbol expresses Israel's hope for salvation, for the time when God would come once and for all to rule Israel with justice and peace, not in the manner of the Jewish kings who so many times had failed the people and been themselves agents of oppression. The Gospel portrays Jesus not only as the messenger of that coming Kingdom but as actually inaugurating God's rule through his healing touch, his commitment to

justice, and the liberating act of giving his life for others.

"Repent, and believe in the gospel" (l, lf). God's offer of salvation through Jesus calls for a response. Those who hear the good news should "repent." The literal meaning of the Greek word *metanoiein* means to change one's mind or perspective. Throughout his Gospel Mark uses images of perception—hearing, seeing, understanding—to describe faith. The disciples of Jesus are asked to see reality—God's reality—with the new eyes of faith and to transform their lives accordingly.

The Call of the Disciples and Jesus' First Day of Ministry (1, 16–45)

The remaining verses of chapter 1 present the first day of Jesus' dynamic mission. This section is most characteristic of Mark's portrayal of Jesus: After choosing his first disciples, Jesus plunges into the sickness and pain of his world, healing and casting out demons. The action takes place around Capernaum, the small fishing village on the northwest corner of the Sea of Galilee, the arena for most of Jesus' ministry in Mark's account.

The Call of the Disciples (1, 16–20). The meaning of discipleship is a major theme of the Gospel. Right at the beginning of his mission, therefore, Jesus calls disciples to follow him and to share in his own ministry of fishing for people. This rapid-fire story condenses the early church's theology of discipleship: (a) discipleship is a gift; all of the initiative comes from Jesus, not from the disciples themselves; (b) the essence of discipleship is following Jesus, an allegiance that takes precedence over every other value; (c) the disciple is privileged to share in the mission of Jesus, here expressed in terms of "fishing" for people. In the Bible (see, for example, Jer 16, 16; Hb 1, 14f), that image of fishing is used to describe the gathering of people for the final day of judgment. Jesus' own ministry has similar strong tones.

Exorcism and Healing (1, 20–45). This whole section is filled with reports of exorcisms and healings. The first action of Jesus is typical of his entire ministry. He enters the synagogue at Capernaum on a Sabbath and liberates a man whose life was tormented by an "unclean spirit" (1, 23).

Exorcism, or the expulsion of evil spirits who hold human beings in their tormenting grip, is frequently mentioned in Mark's Gospel. Here the demons recognize that they are struggling with "the Holy One of God" and know that Jesus has come to destroy them. The people who witness the liberation of the man respond: "A new teaching with authority!" For Mark, such liberating acts are precisely the "new teaching" of Jesus, and that is why the evangelist highlights the exorcisms. They present in dramatic form the ultimate meaning of Jesus' ministry: he has come to destroy the power of death in all its forms and to free humanity from its grip.

The ancient world attributed many psychic and physical ailments to the power of evil spirits, a recognition that their lives were ruled by powers they could not control. While our own modern world view may be less inclined to attribute illness to evil powers, the message of the Gospel is still relevant. We can still learn from Jesus' fierce commitment to alleviating pain and to freeing people from situations and powers that oppress them. And there are many situations where human beings are caught in the grip of overpowering evil, whether it be economic oppression, systemic violence, obsessive or addictive behaviors, or racism—situations often beyond the control of any individual. The Gospel tells us that God's will and the goal of all authentic Christian mission is to liberate humans from such tyrannies of evil.

Conflict (2, 1–3, 6)

The reader will notice a significant change of tone in this section of the Gospel. As Jesus continues his ministry of healing, he meets with strong oppression from the Jewish leaders. The five conflict stories in this section reach their climax in 3, 6 where the leaders begin to plot Jesus' death. Right from the beginning of his story Mark draws our attention to the Passion. Like some distant tolling of a bell, warnings had already been given in 1, 14 where Mark, almost offhandedly, mentions that Jesus begins his ministry in Galilee "after John had been arrested." And the fierce struggle with the demon in the synagogue of Capernaum (1, 21–28) was a preview of more deadly conflicts to come.

An important point to notice in these stories

is that the conflicts revolve around the central values of Jesus' ministry. The scribes object because Jesus claims the power to forgive sins and to heal (2, 1–12). Pharisees take offense at his association with sinners and outcasts (2, 16f) and at his compassionate interpretation of the law (2, 23–28). His healing of a man's withered arm on a Sabbath is the final affront (3, 1–6). Thus Mark implies that fidelity to the good news of mercy and compassion can, paradoxically, lead to conflict with those who have other values and other priorities.

The discussion about fasting that stands in the middle of this section (2, 18–22) gives the reader another clue about Mark's message. A series of sayings emphasize that, with Jesus, a new age has dawned. It is the time of the "bridegroom"; a time for replacing the whole cloth, not just a patch; a time for new wine and new wineskins. Each of these images stresses that the new age of salvation is present in Jesus and, therefore, new things are possible. The Pharisees and scribes miss this reality and blindly oppose Jesus. As we mentioned above, Mark employs perception metaphors—seeing, hearing, understanding—to describe the experience of faith (see comments, RG 389).

Finally, in this section, we should not overlook Mark's continuing concern about discipleship. Another call story similar to that in 1, 16–20 takes place when Jesus encounters the toll collector Levi, sitting at his customs or toll post (Capernaum was a border town between the territories ruled by the vassal kings Herod Agrippa and Phillip). Once again, the call story emphasizes that faith and discipleship are a gift to which we must respond. This story also reminds us that the community is open to everyone: the just and the sinner. The opponents of Jesus are blind to this fact, too, and take offense at his sharing a meal with "tax collectors and sinners" (2, 16). But Jesus responds that being a "physician" to the sinners was precisely his mission (2, 17).

This entire section has strong lessons for Christian life. It reminds us that true fidelity to the gospel has a price and that we should not be surprised to encounter opposition and conflict, even deadly hostility, from those whose values are challenged by the justice and compassion of the gospel. Jesus' compassion and his strong commitment to include the disabled, the sick, and other social outcasts in the community can also instruct us on the nature of the church and its mission.

The Mystery of the Kingdom (3, 7—4, 34)

By means of a summary, Mark continues his reporting of Jesus' dynamic ministry of healing and exorcisms (3, 7–12). The disciples' stake in all this is made clear in 3, 13–19: Jesus climbs to the top of a mountain (a typical place of revelation in the Bible) and solemnly commissions the Twelve "to be with him," "to preach," and "to have authority to drive out demons." The disciples share fully in the ministry of Jesus.

But the note of conflict and misunderstanding sounded in the previous section continues to dominate here. All of the people close to Jesus seem to be out of sympathy with him. His own relatives want to take him back home because they think "he is out of his mind" (3, 21). Mark follows through with this incident in a later scene where Jesus' "mother and his brothers" arrive to take him back home (3, 31–35). But Jesus puts distance between himself and his uncomprehending family when he looks at the circle of disciples who are inside the house with him and says: "Here are my mother and my brothers . . . whoever does the will of God is my brother and sister and mother" (3, 35).

The parable discourse (4, 1–34) attempts to give a reason for all this misunderstanding. The parables, like Jesus himself, are a mysterious revelation of the Kingdom of God. Those not in sympathy with Jesus cannot understand his words. But those called to be disciples are "granted the mystery of the Kingdom of God" (see note to 4, 11–12, p. 1323). While honoring human freedom, Mark wants to affirm that God's providence guides all of human life, even in the darkest moments such as the rejection of Jesus.

Mark's reflection on the parables also reaffirms that faith in Jesus is a gift; it is not something we control or achieve solely through our own efforts. The disciples are "given" the mystery of the Kingdom of God.

Other important themes of Mark's Gospel are communicated in the parables. The stories of the sower casting small, vulnerable seeds on rough ground (4, 3–9), the tiny mustard seed (4,

30–32), and that of the seed growing without the farmer's knowledge (4, 26–29) affirm, on the one hand, that the reality of God's Kingdom seeps into our lives in a hidden and often unnoticed fashion. Such is often the case in Mark's Gospel when people fail to recognize *who* Jesus is because they are looking for another type of Messiah. On the other hand the parables proclaim that God's kingdom will be wonderfully triumphant despite opposition: the harvest of new life and peace will be abundant, "thirty, sixty, and a hundredfold" (4, 8).

Throughout this section Mark's portrayal of the disciples remains constant. Even though they are privileged to be chosen as followers of Jesus, they still have a hard time understanding his message (4, 13).

The Universal Mission of Jesus (4, 35—8, 21)

This concluding section of Jesus' Galilean ministry embraces a large amount of material that can be loosely gathered under the theme of the universal scope of Jesus' mission. The Sea of Galilee begins to be an important factor, not simply as a geographical phenomenon in the center of Galilee, but as an important symbolic boundary between Jew and Gentile (consult the map of Galilee, map #13; the region to the west of the Sea was mainly Jewish in population, while on the eastern shore the population was mainly Gentile).

Jesus and his disciples cross the sea several times in this section, occasionally having to endure its turbulent storms. The first time is in 4, 35 when they cross through the storm and arrive in the Gentile territory of the Gerasenes (5, 1). There Jesus will liberate a Gentile man from a terrible demon. Another missionary journey begins in 7, 24, after Jesus' dispute with the Pharisees. This begins to the northwest where Jesus encounters the Syrophoenician woman (7, 24–30) and extends around once more to the Decapolis on the eastern side of the lake (7, 31). The entire section ends with Jesus and his disciples again in the boat together heading for the Gentile shore (8, 13).

Other important blocks of material give a mission flavor to this section, such as the commissioning of the Twelve and sending them out (6, 7—13, 30f). The flashback to the death of John the Baptist at the hands of Herod is a reminder about the true cost of discipleship (6, 14–29). So, too, are Jesus' continuing disputes with his opponents (see, for example, 7, 1–23 and 8, 11–13). Two of Jesus' greatest signs also tell us something about the nature of Jesus' mission; once on the Jewish side and once on the Gentile side of the lake, Jesus miraculously feeds massive crowds of hungry people (6, 34–44; 8, 1–10).

The following are some of the major themes of this section:

The Universality of the Gospel. Even though Jesus' ministry was confined mainly to Israel, Mark's Gospel shows the universal character of Jesus' words and actions. God's saving love was not meant exclusively for one group or one region. The stories of Jesus' healing Gentiles such as the Gerasene man (5, 1–20), the Greek woman's daughter (7, 24–30), and the deaf-mute from the Decapolis (7, 31–37) illustrate this. So, too, does the fact that Jesus feeds Gentiles as well as Jews.

But crossing religious and cultural boundaries, and being open to people who are different from us, does not come easily for the human spirit, as history has repeatedly demonstrated. The early church, too, struggled with the need to reach out beyond its own boundaries (see, for example, the story of Cornelius's conversion in Acts 10—11). Mark hints at this in his Gospel, too. To cross to the Gentile side of the lake, Jesus and the disciples must brave the terror of the storm (4, 35–41). Jesus himself seems hesitant before the request of the Syrophoenician woman (7, 27), and the disciples want the crowds to be sent home rather than take the responsibility to feed them (8, 4).

The universal character of the church has become more apparent to Christianity in modern times as the church has become less dominated by its European and Western traditions, but we still struggle to be a truly global church and thus open to people of different races, nationalities, and economic status. There are deep tensions between peoples of different religious traditions, and racism is still strong. This section of Mark's Gospel reminds us that the message of Jesus was inclusive from the beginning.

Nourishing God's People. The two feeding stories are eloquent statements of Jesus' mission. As God did during the Exodus from Egypt with manna, so Jesus, too, feeds God's hungry people. These feeding stories illustrate the justice dimension of the Gospel; the hungry are not to be sent away on their own thin resources (as the disciples suggest to Jesus!). Jesus came to feed them—a clear instruction for the mission of the church. At the same time, the feeding stories also evoke the Eucharist (Jesus' gestures of blessing and distributing the bread are identical to the Last Supper, 14, 22); Jesus' mission was to reach across boundaries and to gather God's people into one body.

The Struggle of the Disciples. As the Galilean ministry of Jesus comes to a close, the disciples' difficulty in understanding Jesus seems only to increase. They are completely baffled at his mysterious power in calming the storm (4, 38–41), and walking on the sea (6, 45–51)—two haunting stories that reveal the divine power of Jesus. They are out of sympathy with Jesus' compassion for the crowds (6, 35f; 8, 4). And the section ends with their complete confusion about the meaning of Jesus' words and deeds (8, 14–21). Jesus had come to break one loaf for the many, but there was still a long journey ahead before the disciples would grasp the meaning of that mission.

The Journey from Galilee to Jerusalem (8, 22—10, 52)

Mark's story now comes to a major turning point. Jesus and his disciples travel to the northern boundary of Israel, to the town of Caesarea Philippi. Along the way, Jesus poses the key question of the Gospel: "Who do you say that I am?" (8, 29).

The Gospel has been answering that question for the reader all throughout the preceding chapters as it revealed—through Jesus' eloquent words and powerful ministry of healing and exorcism—his identity as God's Messiah and savior. But Jesus' opponents proved blind to that revelation, and even the disciples have been unable to grasp it. In this section Jesus provides more urgent instruction on his mission and the demands of discipleship. For the first time in the Gospel he begins to speak openly of his death and resurrection. Three Passion predictions punctuate these chapters (8, 31; 9, 31; 10, 33–34). The cross, as a sign of Jesus' total commitment to his Father's will and his compassionate and selfless love for others, becomes the touchstone for understanding who Jesus is and what discipleship means.

Geography and the symbol of a journey also give a special character to these key chapters of the Gospel. Jesus and his disciples will travel from Caesarea Philippi in the north to Judea and its capital city of Jerusalem in the south (see map 13). But this is no routine journey in Mark's perspective. This purposeful journey toward Jerusalem is also Jesus' journey toward the cross where he will experience death and victory. The disciples must follow this same path if they are to be faithful to Jesus and his message. Thus this journey evokes other biblical journeys, especially the journey of the Israelites from Egypt to the promised land; that, too, was a journey from death to life. As we will see in the next section of the Gospel (11, 1—13, 37), Jerusalem, with its great Temple and the priests who attend it, becomes a negative symbol in Mark's theology. There Jesus will suffer his final rejection. Because of that, the Jerusalem Temple will give way to a new temple, Jesus himself.

The disciples are also an important focal point in this section. While disputes with opponents and other incidents take place, most of the action revolves around Jesus and his followers. After each of the Passion predictions, the disciples display their extraordinary lack of understanding of Jesus and his message. Peter attempts to silence Jesus (8, 32); all of the disciples argue about which of them is the greatest (9, 33f); the sons of Zebedee ask for special places of influence and power with Jesus, triggering the jealousy of the rest of the disciples (10, 35–37.41). The disciples also try to discourage the children from coming to Jesus (10, 13); they are unable to perform an exorcism on a sick boy (9, 18) despite being given the power to do so (see 6, 7), and they continue to be baffled by Jesus' teaching (see, for example, 10, 24–26).

In response to their lack of understanding Jesus gives even more intense instruction on the meaning of discipleship after each of the Passion predictions. The disciples must be willing to "take up the cross" and follow Jesus; to "lose" their lives for the sake of Jesus and the gospel (8, 34–38). Instead of being absorbed with self-aggrandizement, the disciples should imitate the child and seek to be the "servant of all" (10, 35f). To follow Jesus means putting aside whatever holds us back from being free to serve others, such as excessive possessions (10, 17–31). True greatness is not defined by "lording it over" others but by giving our lives for them (10, 42–45).

In all of these instructions, the image of the cross is key. Jesus, the Son of Man (see the note to 8, 31 for this important title in Mark), came not to be served but to serve, "to give his life as a ransom for many" (10, 45). The death of Jesus on the cross is seen not as a tragic failure but as the ultimate expression of Jesus' entire mission. His death—like his life—was an act of love for others. Therefore the disciple, too, must "take up the cross" and make giving of life for others the animating principle of every action.

Because the disciples were absorbed in their own interests and fears, they understood Jesus' message dimly at best. Mark frames this entire section of the Gospel with two stories about Jesus' healing blind men. In 8, 22–26 it is a case of deep-seated blindness. Jesus must lay hands on the man's eyes twice before he can see clearly. In the beautiful story of Bartimaeus (10, 46–52), the focus shifts to the blind person's own determination to reach Jesus. Even though the bystanders attempt to stifle his cries for mercy, Bartimaeus's pleas reach Jesus' ears. Jesus poses a profound question: "What do you want me to do for you?" Bartimaeus replies: "Master, I want to see." That humble trust and honest expression of need save Bartimaeus. He receives his sight and begins to follow Jesus on the journey of discipleship (10, 52). Mark has clearly interpreted this healing story as a discipleship story.

These two stories are penetrating commentary on the plight of the disciples. The disciples are blind in a sense far more disabling than that of physical blindness; they have a deep-seated block to understanding Jesus and his message. Bartimaeus, by contrast, reaches out to Jesus in his need and asks for the light of faith; that is the solution the disciples have yet to discover.

Death and Resurrection in Jerusalem (11, 1—16, 8)

Beginning with chapter 11, Mark's story enters its final phase. Jesus and his disciples have completed their journey from Galilee to Jerusalem. As the triumphant Messiah, Jesus enters the city of David where he will face determined opposition, death itself, and then final victory.

The material in these chapters can be subdivided into four major sections: the first two focusing on the Temple; the latter two comprising the Passion narrative and the discovery of the empty tomb.

Jesus and the Temple (11, 1—12, 44)

Jesus enters Jerusalem in seeming triumph; there are admiring crowds and acclamations of hosanna. For this brief moment, at least, the true identity of Jesus—so prone to be misunderstood by the characters in the Gospel—shines out clearly. But the mood of this section soon turns somber. Mark surrounds the story of Jesus' cleansing of the Temple (11, 15–19) with the curious incident about the fig tree (11, 12—14, 20f). The fig tree is cursed and withers because its fruits are not ready at the proper time for Jesus to harvest them. The fruitless tree becomes a sign of the Temple's own failure. Jesus' stern prophetic actions in the Temple area take on added meaning in Mark's text—the Temple is not only cleansed of abuses, it is declared no longer valid. Mark's Gospel foresees a new temple and a new worshipping community emerging in Jesus and his future community of disciples. This will be reaffirmed in the Passion story when Jesus is accused of predicting a temple "not made by hands" (14, 58) and when the Temple veil is torn asunder at the moment of Jesus' death (15, 38). This same motif is alluded to at the end of the parable of the tenants: the rejected Son who is killed by the tenants will become the "cornerstone" of a new edifice.

Thus Mark takes a dim view of the Jerusalem Temple because he sees it as symbolic of religious practice that has become hollow. This also emerges in the conflict stories that abound in this section. Like a great champion, Jesus seems to wrestle with each faction of the leaders: the chief priests, the elders, the scribes, the Herodians, the Pharisees, the Sadducees. They challenge the authority of Jesus but are reduced to silence by his penetrating answers.

These scenes underscore the power and majesty of Jesus, even as death approaches. He is indeed one greater than David (see 12, 35–37), one who is Lord of the Temple. But the encounters with the Jewish leaders also help reaffirm important facets of Jesus' teaching. A scribe (who, in fact, seems in sympathy with Jesus and is representative of all those who seek God with a sincere heart) is led to an insight that goes to the heart of Jesus' message: "to love God with all your heart, with all your understanding, with all your strength, and to love your neighbor as yourself is worth more than all burnt offerings and sacrifice" (12, 33).

The entire section ends with sharply contrasting images that also ram home the message Mark emphasizes in this section of the Gospel: Jesus excoriates the leaders who love the trappings of religion while "devouring the houses of widows," but he blesses the poor widow who gives everything she has to God (12, 38–44).

Toward the End-Time (13, 1–37)

This final discourse of Jesus to his disciples is one of the most enigmatic yet important passages in Mark's Gospel. It provides us with a powerful reflection on the ultimate meaning of history. The setting for the discourse is Jesus' prediction that the majestic Temple of Herod would one day be destroyed (as it was in AD 70), thus continuing the negative view of the Temple from the previous section.

The real focus of the chapter is on the future of the Christian community as it will carry out its mission in history, after the death and resurrection of Jesus. This discourse is not a transcript of a single speech by Jesus. The evangelist weaves together in this chapter sayings of Jesus with numerous quotations from the Old Testament, especially the apocalyptic literature that dwells on crisis. The chapter's main themes represent a profound reflection on the community's future:

Warnings about Persecutions and Divisions as the Community Carries Out Its Mission. Mark clearly asserts that before the end of the world can come, the church must complete its mission of proclaiming the gospel to all the world (13, 10). In the course of that mission, however, will come persecution from both Jews and Gentiles (13, 9–11) and internal divisions (13, 12f). Mark's story has already illustrated how Jesus himself experienced opposition from his opponents and misunderstanding by his family and disciples.

The Christian Is to "Stay Awake." As the community moves out into history, it must be alert and sober, ready to catch glimpses of God's presence breaking into history (13, 33–37). Mark makes it clear that this does not mean that the

community is to be anxiously scanning the calendar and speculating about the end of the world. In fact, such doomsday predictions are branded as the words of "false Christs" and "false prophets" (13, 5f.21f). Rather, the Christian is to be committed to proclaiming the gospel and to living with the realization of God's imminent presence in history.

God's Triumph in History. The most important message of the chapter is to affirm that the final moment of human history will not be chaos or the defeat of goodness but the triumph of grace. Jesus, the Son of Man, will return to gather his disciples from the four corners of the earth and lead them to God (13, 24–27). While acknowledging the reality of human suffering and the crises that the Christian community will have to face, Mark's view of history is ultimately full of hope.

The Passion (14, 1—15, 47)

These two chapters form the longest single narrative in the whole Gospel, reaffirming the importance the Passion holds for Mark's perspective. Jesus' death for others sums up his entire mission and is the ultimate revelation of his identity as the Son of God.

The Passion story moves rapidly to its climax at the cross. The opening scenes (14, 1–11) set the mood as the leaders and Judas plot Jesus' death, while a faithful woman anoints his body for death. The Last Supper with the disciples dominates the next section (14, 12–31); the breaking of the bread and the sharing of the cup are living signs of Jesus' impending death for others. The mood darkens when Jesus and his disciples go to Gethsemane (14, 32–52). While Jesus earnestly prays for the strength to follow God's will, the disciples sleep. Then Judas leads an armed band into the garden to arrest Jesus. In the face of that threat, the disciples all flee in panic. The trials before the Sanhedrin (14, 53–72) and before Pilate (15, 1–20) dominate the rest of the Passion narrative. The crucifixion, death, and burial of Jesus bring the great drama to its conclusion (15, 21–47).

Two major motifs move throughout the Passion story:

The Crisis of Discipleship. The disciples' inability to understand Jesus, so apparent throughout the Gospel, leads ultimately to their failure in the crisis of the Passion. Despite their bravado at the Last Supper (14, 31), all of the disciples abandon Jesus at the moment of his arrest (14, 50–52), and Peter publicly denies he even knows Jesus (14, 66–72). Mark gives his reader a sober lesson: suffering and persecution can prompt heroism, but it can also expose weak faith and superficial commitment (see 4, 17).

The disciples' failure is in sharp contrast to the courageous loyalty and faith of other characters in the drama, such as the anonymous woman who anoints Jesus (over the protests of some of his followers, 14, 3–9), the Roman centurion who acclaims Jesus at the moment of his death (15, 39), the faithful women who stand by the cross (15, 40f), and Joseph of Arimathea, a member of the Sanhedrin, who takes courage and asks to bury the crucified Jesus (15, 42–47). These "unexpected" people—women, a Gentile soldier, a member of the opposition—illustrate the true meaning of faithful discipleship, an obvious lesson for the church.

The Revelation of Jesus as the Christ, the Son of God. The Passion story provides the final answer to the question that underlies all of Mark's Gospel: Who is Jesus? As Jesus courageously proclaims to the Sanhedrin: he is the Christ, the Son of God (14, 61ff). But coming in the midst of the Passion narrative, with Jesus standing as a prisoner about to be condemned and executed, the use of these titles takes on new meaning. Jesus is the Christ or Messiah, God's royal son who comes to liberate Israel; but he is not a liberator or monarch in the usual triumphant mode one might expect. Jesus liberates not through dominating power but by giving his life for others (see the key text of 10, 45, p. 1337). Jesus truly is the Son of God, but the God he reveals is not an exalted potentate but a God revealed in the apparent "weakness" of a life totally committed to others.

In the perspective of Mark's Gospel, the Passion provides the right context for understanding who Jesus is. (See a similar conviction in Paul's 1 Cor 1, 18–31.)

The Empty Tomb (16, 1–8)

Although brief, this concluding scene of the Gospel proclaims a substantial message. An author later than Mark added a longer ending, but this story of the empty tomb was probably the original conclusion to Mark's story (see the discussion in the notes to 16, 1–8).

Jesus' Victory over Death. The fundamental message of the passage is that the crucified Jesus is triumphant over death. That is the powerful symbolism of an empty tomb and the explicit message of the mysterious "young man" the women discover there: "You seek Jesus of Nazareth, the crucified. He has been raised; he is not here" (16, 6). Without this assurance Mark's story would not be "gospel"—good news.

Reconciliation with the Disciples. This scene also picks up the story of the absent disciples. The women are instructed: "But go and tell his disciples and Peter, 'He is going before you to Galilee; there you will see him, as he told you' "(16, 7). Even though the disciples had deserted and denied Jesus, the Risen Christ does not abandon them. He had promised that at the Last Supper: "after I am raised up I shall go before you to Galilee" (14, 28). Now, that promised reconciliation is about to take place. In a very true sense, the disciples had "died" during the Passion; they, too, would experience resurrection to a new life of discipleship.

Back to Galilee: The Mission Begins. The disciples will "see" Jesus in Galilee, the place where Jesus had carried out his universal mission of healing and teaching, and the place where he had first called his followers to be with him and to share in his ministry. What precise meeting with Jesus does Mark have in mind—resurrection appearances? Or the final meeting with the Risen Christ at the end of the world? Or does he mean that the Risen Jesus would be with his disciples as they take up their mission? Mark leaves the question unanswered and perhaps has all of these encounters in mind.

The Gospel ends on a note of awe; the women leave the tomb, trembling and bewildered, struck silent by the awesome message entrusted to them (16, 8). Some interpreters understand their silence as another instance of discipleship failure; the message given them is never delivered because of paralyzing fear. But it is unlikely Mark wants to suggest that the women never told the disciples about the empty tomb. The notes of awe and silence and fear are Mark's way of expressing profound reverence for the events he narrates. In Jesus' victory over death, God's power has transformed the world forever.

D.S.

FURTHER READING

Donahue, John, S.J., and Daniel J. Harrington, S.J. *The Gospel of Mark*. Sacra Pagina. Collegeville, MN: Liturgical Press, 2002.

Moloney, Francis J. *The Gospel of Mark: A Commentary*. Peabody: Hendrickson, 2002.

Reiser, William. *Jesus in Solidarity With His People: A Theologian Looks at Mark*. Collegeville, MN: Liturgical Press, 2000.

Senior, Donald. *The Death of Jesus in the Gospel of Mark*. Passion Series 2. Wilmington, DE: Michael Glazier, 1984.

LUKE

[see pages 1349–1401 of the New Testament]

Before Beginning . . .

Luke tells us that he was not an eyewitness to the events of Jesus' ministry. He is dependent upon others who have already put the testimony of such witnesses in narrative form (1, 2). Scholars have identified three of the sources that Luke used: Mark's Gospel; a collection of Jesus' sayings that was also used by Matthew, called *Q;* and a source for additional material about Jesus, which scholars designate *L* (see *New American Bible*, introduction, p. 1350). Luke seems to preserve the order of sayings in his written source rather than shifting them to new discourse units as in Matthew. The introduction suggests that Luke is a second- or third-generation Christian looking back on the founding years of the movement. Luke's ability to write in different styles—including that of the Septuagint, the Greek translation of the Hebrew Scriptures, which was the Bible for most of the early Christian communities—and to use conventions of Hellenistic literature, such as the opening dedication to a prominent patron, suggest a well-educated author. To have received a literary education of this sort, Luke probably came from a prosperous urban family. Unlike the other Gospel writers, Luke's account did not end with the Gospel. He wrote a second volume, Acts, which showed that God's salvation, begun in Jesus, moved beyond Jerusalem and the pious of Israel into the whole world.

Luke's Gospel provides an account of Jesus' life and teaching for that universal mission. Today, people sometimes think that Christianity and its Gospels belong to North American and European culture. They wonder whether Christians can spread the message to people in other cultures without destroying those cultures. We need to remember that the story of Jesus originated in a Semitic culture. Luke and other early Christians were already engaged in intercultural dialogue when they retold the story of Jesus for the Greek-speaking, non-Jewish converts who inhabited cities in the eastern part of the Roman empire. Their example shows that the gospel message is not limited to any one culture. The story of Jesus belongs to all peoples.

An Assured Teaching

Luke's desire to establish Christianity within the larger world of the Roman empire is evident in references to Roman emperors and events. For example, he links the birth of Jesus to Caesar Augustus (2, 1). People have sometimes thought that Luke was attempting to write what we would call a history of Jesus and the earliest disciples. Most of the "historical" references, however, are not accurate even by ancient standards. Luke calls his work a *diegesis,* meaning a "narrative account," not a history. He claims that it is thorough, accurate, and orderly. He has traced the events that have occurred among "us" (that is, the Christian community) from the beginning (1, 1–4). The purpose of his writing is to provide *asphaleia,* "assurance" for the instruction that Christians give. In other words, Luke's book will show that what the church preaches is rooted in the ministry of Jesus and the preaching of the first apostles.

Luke takes patterns for his story from biblical history. This literary device is especially evident in the infancy narratives, which show God's promises of salvation being fulfilled in Jesus. When Luke claims that his narrative is "orderly," he refers to the literary order, which sets out the periods of salvation. Luke also provides assurance for the Christian preaching by showing that the Spirit of God has guided the whole process from the earliest days of Israel through the ministry of Jesus. In the second volume, Acts, he shows the same Spirit at work in the developments in the early community. Civic authorities were suspicious of new religious movements. Luke's work addresses those fears by highlighting the high moral standards and social value of Christianity.

An Ordered Narrative

Luke has told us that he is dependent upon earlier accounts but that he has reworked his material to provide a more accurate and orderly account. We have seen that accuracy and order do not refer to historical inquiry but to Luke's desire to set forth the way in which God's plan of salvation is fulfilled in the Christian movement. Scholars have made detailed studies of additions, deletions, and changes that Luke has made in the order of material taken over from Mark. There are three major additions that even the beginning Gospel reader can spot. Mark begins abruptly with the appearance of John the Baptist. Luke (as does Matthew) begins with an account of Jesus' birth (1, 5—2, 40). He adds a tale about the child Jesus (2, 41–52). Then, between the baptism and temptation stories, Luke reintroduces Jesus by giving his genealogy (3, 23–38). A long section in which Jesus is journeying toward Jerusalem with the disciples (9, 51—19, 27) contains much of the teaching of Jesus. It includes parables that Luke has taken from Q (and from his special tradition) and retold in a way that serves as instruction for the church. By contrast, Mark's Gospel has only a short section of instruction to the disciples on the trip to Jerusalem.

Finally, you will notice several differences in the Passion and the Resurrection materials. Mark ends with the women running from the empty tomb. Luke 24, on the other hand, has accounts of appearances by the Risen Lord as well as instructions to the disciples. Luke's Passion narrative differs from Mark (and Matthew) as well. Jesus is never formally tried by the Jewish court. There is an unusual episode in which Pilate sends Jesus to be investigated by Herod (23, 6–12). Pilate persists in declaring that Jesus is innocent of the charges against him (23, 4.14f.22). The dying Jesus prays for forgiveness for his enemies (23, 34) and enacts the message of the gospel by

promising salvation to a repentant criminal who dies with him (23, 39–43).

Each of these sections contributes to our sense that God's plan of salvation is being carried out. The infancy narratives recapitulate the hopes of the faithful people of Israel. As Jesus begins the journey to Jerusalem, he knows that he is to be taken up from there in death (9, 51). This journey is a time to prepare the disciples both for the events in Jerusalem and for their future role as witnesses to Jesus' teaching. In the narrative of Jesus' death and resurrection, Luke emphasizes the fact that it "was necessary"—that is, part of God's plan already set out in the Prophets—for the Messiah to suffer and die in Jerusalem (see 22, 22; 24, 26f). The episode with the repentant criminal shows that the death of Jesus extends salvation and forgiveness to others.

The Tragedy of Israel

Luke's strong narrative sense of a divine plan moving toward its fulfillment often dominates our imagination as we read Luke-Acts. If we allow this sense of divine purpose to lull us into accepting as good or necessary all the events through which God's plan is achieved, then we will miss another component in Luke's story—the tragedy of Israel. The infancy stories awaken the joyful expectation that Israel's messianic king has arrived to bring salvation. Through him, God's peace and blessings will come to both Jews and Gentiles (2, 29–32). Yet, as the story unfolds, this promise will not be fulfilled.

Persistent rejection, first of Jesus and then of the disciples' mission, leaves Israel excluded. Luke points out the tragedy of this situation in a series of prophetic laments that Jesus utters over Jerusalem and her inhabitants. The first is a Q tradition (13, 34f; Mt 23, 37–39), which Luke has attached to an episode from his special tradition (13, 31–33). The episode contained a warning that Herod was seeking Jesus' life. Jesus connects the divine necessity that he die in Jerusalem (13, 33) with a lament for the city. The second, from Luke's special tradition, occurs as Jesus is looking out over the city where he is to die (19, 41–44). Jesus weeps at the thought of the peace that will elude the city and the terrible devastations of war that she is to suffer. The final lament, also from L, occurs as Jesus is on the way to his death. He looks out at the weeping women of Jerusalem and warns them to weep for themselves instead (23, 27–31).

The church has constantly reminded Catholics that, even though the ancestors of today's Jews chose not to accept Jesus as Messiah, Christians cannot reject or persecute Jews. She has also insisted that Christians share a common heritage with the Jewish people that is rooted in the Hebrew Scriptures. Luke's narrative insists that the heritage of the Christian movement lies in the faithful and just persons of Israel. Jesus' own family are among the righteous ones who trust in God for salvation. Though Luke's Passion narrative holds certain Jewish leaders responsible for some of the events, Jesus does not condemn them but asks God's forgiveness. Luke also presents us with a Jesus who is able to weep as he foresees the terrible fate of Jerusalem. The prosperous and beautiful city of his day will be reduced to the rubble of war. She will not enjoy the peace that God so longs to give the people.

Reading through Luke

Before you sit down to study Luke, read through the whole Gospel. Many of the stories will be familiar to you, since Luke contains some of the best-loved stories in the Gospels. You will notice that Luke is a gifted storyteller. Even in the parables of Jesus, he creates short episodes and switches from the third-person report into dialogue between the characters. Young children often enjoy the stories in Luke more than those in the other Gospels. As you are reading, you might note passages that particularly appeal to you. Do you find any common themes in those stories? Here are some of the themes that you will find running through the Gospel.

Salvation Is a Joyous Surprise

You will soon notice that Luke has many images of celebration and rejoicing. From the very beginning of the story to the very last verse, people are praising and thanking God for the salvation that they experience in Jesus. Salvation is a "surprise" or gift because those who receive it could never have anticipated that it would come. Mary's *Magnificat* (1, 46–55) sets the tone. God has come and rescued the humble, poor, oppressed, and lowly people of the land. Jesus begins his ministry

(4, 18) by quoting a promise from Isaiah: a threefold release from poverty, from sickness, and from sin. Luke drives home this point about salvation by showing that Jesus has the power to forgive sins and to heal people (see 5, 17–26). Even the rich tax collector Zacchaeus hears the message, demonstrates his repentance by making restitution to those he had cheated, and expresses his joy by throwing a banquet (19, 1–10).

God's mercy is the source of this salvation. Christians are to show mercy in the same way that God is merciful (6, 36). When Jesus gives examples of what God's mercy and forgiveness are like, he uses very active images. God is not waiting for people to come crawling back, begging forgiveness. God is out looking for people to help like the shepherd and the lost sheep, the woman and the lost coin, or the wayward son's father, who goes running out of the house and immediately orders a large celebration (see 15, 3–32). The elder brother in the story of the Prodigal Son shows us the other side of the coin. Jesus recognizes that some people find it difficult to accept this open-handed offer of forgiveness to sinners, when they themselves have struggled all their lives to do everything that they are required to do and have never even had a banquet to celebrate.

Salvation Includes Everyone

In Acts, Luke will show us that God directed the disciples to take the gospel to all the peoples of the earth. The Gospel demonstrates the universality of God's love and salvation in a different way. It stresses the fact that Jesus reached out to all sorts of people, even to those who seemed to have no chance at salvation. Zacchaeus, the tax collector, was a sinner who had defrauded people to enrich himself (19, 1–10). The Samaritans, traditional enemies of the Jews, turn out to be examples of Jesus' teaching. The mercy shown by the Good Samaritan (10, 37) is so well known that we can speak of anyone who shows mercy or unmerited assistance to another as a "Samaritan." Less well known is the Samaritan leper (17, 12–19) who is the only one of the group healed by Jesus to return and give him thanks. Women—often excluded from higher education, public leadership, and cultural events in antiquity—are constantly included in Jesus' ministry. A sinful woman provides a better demonstration of love and hospitality than the Pharisee. Her sins are forgiven (7, 31–50). Mary is permitted to sit and listen to Jesus as a disciple. She does not have to busy herself with the traditional woman's business of serving the male guests that has her sister so distracted (10, 38–42).

Today, many women experience the tension between Martha and Mary in their own lives. On the one hand, they are anxious to participate in opportunities for education, careers, and involvement with the community outside the home. On the other hand, they are still responsible for most of the work and caregiving that goes on within the home. Some women who are financially able to devote themselves to homemaking and volunteer community activities on a full-time basis report that they feel "looked down on" because they do not have a paying job. When Jesus defended Mary's place as listening to his teaching, he was not condemning Martha's devotion to serving her guests or the traditional tasks of women in the home. Jesus was really issuing an invitation to her to join her sister. Martha was so busy that she was missing the one necessary thing, to hear Jesus' message about the Kingdom (10, 41f). As our lives continue to fill up with activities at home, work, and in the community, we need to ask whether we are shoving out the time we need for the one necessary thing, hearing the word of the Lord.

Special Concern for Those in Need

We have already seen that salvation has very concrete aspects in Luke. Those who are poor, helpless, in prison, sick, and the like are promised release. Jesus and the apostles are able to relieve the suffering of the sick by healing. Acts contains many stories in which God intervenes to free the apostles from prison. To achieve this goal, however, miraculous events are not required. The story of the Good Samaritan (10, 25–37) shows how this salvation can come about through concrete actions. The Samaritan uses his own resources to see that the man beaten up by robbers is restored to health, even though, as a Jew, the victim is his enemy. The parable of the Great Supper, in which the host replaces with the poor the friends who refused to come, and the sayings about showing aid to those who cannot repay (14, 12–24) are other examples of how salvation can come to those in need.

You may have noticed in reading through Luke how often it returns to the theme of rich and poor. The rich often fail to receive salvation because they are trapped by their own desires for money or pleasure (see 12, 13–21; 16, 19–30). Even those who are good people like the Rich Ruler (18, 18–24) are so locked in by possessions that they cannot achieve the eternal life they desire. That does not mean that Luke thinks all rich people are excluded from the Kingdom. The Samaritan, Zacchaeus, and anyone else who is willing to share his or her wealth generously with those who are in need can become a disciple of Jesus. Acts will return to this theme in its picture of sharing possessions in the early community. Luke also retains the sayings of Jesus that call upon followers to renounce material goods in order to become disciples (6, 35; 9, 3; 10, 4; 12, 33; 14, 33; 16, 13). By doing so, Jesus, and later the apostles, demonstrate that they are completely dedicated to God. But Luke knows that such discipleship is possible only if the basic needs of the group are met through the generosity of others. He reports that a group of women followers provided the necessary support (8, 1–3). In Acts, he reports that Paul achieved the same end by laboring at his trade (Acts 20, 33–35).

Mary Is the First Disciple

Catholic Christians have always paid special honor to Mary, the mother of Jesus. Since much of the elaborate Marian piety of the church did not develop until medieval times, people sometimes feel that Mary has been left out in the biblical renewal. Luke's Gospel provides the basis for the devotion that we show to Mary. Her assent to God's work of salvation initiates the whole story. Her *Magnificat* is a strong affirmation of God's faithfulness and mercy. Sometimes people think that we honor Mary simply because she experienced a miracle in Jesus' birth. That is not Luke's picture. For Luke she is both the epitome of the faithful people of Israel who wait confidently for God's salvation, and the beginning of the new life of those who will be disciples of Jesus. Jesus defines her role in 8, 21. She is one who hears and does the word of God. He repeats this affirmation in 11, 27f. The crowd praises Jesus' biological mother. Jesus corrects them by insisting that hearing and keeping the word of God constitutes the true source of blessing.

The infancy narrative demonstrates that Mary has this quality of true discipleship. She has accepted God's will in the Annunciation scene. Later she keeps in her heart words spoken to her about Jesus, as well as the extraordinary events that she witnesses (2, 19.51). Simeon includes her in his oracle about the impact of Jesus' ministry in Israel (2, 34f). She too will be caught in the divisions to come. But Mary remains among the faithful disciples of Jesus. She was present among those disciples gathered in Jerusalem after the Resurrection (Acts 1, 14).

An Outline of Luke

Luke's Gospel falls into a neat pattern that moves from the infancy narrative, in which we are among the righteous of Israel in Jerusalem, through the ministry in Galilee, back to the Jerusalem Temple, and finally to Jesus' death and resurrection. The Gospel leaves us with the disciples in Jerusalem awaiting the coming of the Spirit. Acts will take the Gospel from Jerusalem out into the world. Jerusalem forms a symbolic center to the Gospel, as much of the narrative takes place either in or on the way to the holy city. The major divisions in the story are clearly marked transitions in the unfolding of the plot:

Prologue (1, 1–4)
Infancy Narrative (1, 5—2, 52)
Preparation for the Public Ministry
(3, 1—4, 13)
The Ministry in Galilee (4, 14—9, 50)
The Journey to Jerusalem (9, 51—19, 27)
Teaching Ministry in Jerusalem
(19, 28—21, 38)
The Passion Narrative (22, 1—23, 56)
The Resurrection Narrative (24, 1–53)

Now it is time to read through Luke in detail. We will be looking to see how Luke develops a picture of Jesus, salvation, and Christian discipleship. Since Luke preserves important blocks of the teaching of Jesus, we will also be interested in how Luke presents the teaching of Jesus for Christians in his time. Discipleship requires doing the word as well as hearing it.

Prologue (1, 1–4)

Luke introduces his Gospel with a prologue, because he considers that his work belongs alongside other Hellenistic literature. The prologue consists of a single complex Greek sentence that ends with the word *asphaleia,* "assurance." Luke intends the orderly account of the events that constitute the Christian story of salvation to demonstrate the integrity of the Christian message that the church in his day proclaims. (A close parallel for this use of *kathexes,* "orderly," appears in Acts 11, 4. Peter is going to narrate the events that led him to baptize the Gentile Cornelius and his household and to share table fellowship with them. This account will persuade the leaders of the church in Jerusalem that God was operating behind those events.)

The Infancy Narrative (1, 5—2, 52)

Structure of the Lucan Infancy Narrative

This section is built on an elaborate parallelism between Jesus and John the Baptist. In each case, Jesus is greater than the Baptist, who is only the forerunner of the Messiah. The most detailed parallels occur between the two angelic birth announcements (John, 1, 5–25; Jesus, 1, 26–38): (a) neither parent is expecting a child; (b) an angel appears, the parent is troubled and told not to fear; (c) the child is announced, his name given, and a statement is made about his future greatness; (d) the parent raises a question about how this can happen; (e) the angel gives an assertion that it will happen, and a sign; (f) Zechariah is forced to be silent; Mary's spontaneous answer affirms God's will. The birth announcements are followed by an episode that brings the two together and confirms the angel's statement to Mary, the Visitation (1, 39–56). In this episode the Baptist testifies to the presence of Jesus as savior by moving in the womb.

The next cycle recounts the births (John, 1, 57f; Jesus, 2, 1–20) and circumcision/naming of the two children (John, 1, 57–80; Jesus, 2, 21–40). Each birth section includes an affirmation of the joy attending the birth. Each naming section concludes with an affirmation that the child grew. This cycle is followed by an episode that prefigures Jesus' last days, the Finding in the Temple (2, 41–52). Jesus will return to the Temple to teach before his death (see the outline of the Gospel). The narratives make it clear that God is responsible for the origins of both children. For the Baptist, God has overcome the barrenness of his parents, just as other barren women in the Hebrew Bible, like Sarah and Hannah, had been given children. For Jesus, God has done something even greater by bringing the child into existence in the womb of his virgin mother.

Songs of Salvation: The Canticles

These episodes contain several canticles, which have become a treasured part of Christian worship: Mary's *Magnificat* (1, 46–55); Zechariah's *Benedictus* (1, 68–79); the canticle of the angels (2, 13f); Simeon's *Nunc Dimittis* (2, 29–32). Many scholars think that Luke has taken the *Magnificat,* the *Benedictus,* and perhaps the *Nunc Dimittis* from a Jewish Christian source. They employ a mosaic of expressions taken from the Hebrew Bible and other Jewish psalms and hymns from the time of Jesus. Mary's *Magnificat* is an individual song of praise, which seems to be modeled on the Song of Hannah (1 Sm 2, 1–10). After celebrating God's greatness toward the lowly handmaid, the second strophe (vv. 51–53), in a series of strong, active verbs, alludes to God's past deeds of salvation. The final verses (54f) relate the career of Jesus to the covenant God had made with Abraham. Scholars think that this hymn originated among Jewish Christians who identified themselves with the "poor ones," the *anawim,* of Israel. The term designated those who were unfortunate, lowly, sick, downtrodden. The rich and powerful, those who feel no need of God, are opposed to the *anawim* (see Ps 149,4; Is 49, 13; 66, 2). The poor ones are the righteous remnant in Israel who know that they must look to God for salvation.

The *Benedictus* begins as a song of thanksgiving (vv. 71–75) recalling the dynastic oracle concerning the house of David (see 2 Sm 7, 12f). The hymn affirms that Jesus will fulfill this messianic role. It then shifts to the form of an oracle concerning the destiny of the newborn child (vv. 76–79). The Baptist will prepare God's people for the coming Messiah. We are reminded that God comes to save the people out of merciful compassion. Luke will make the theme of mercy a central motif in the ministry of Jesus.

The *Nunc Dimittis* draws upon two passages of Isaiah (Is 40, 5; 49, 6). Simeon has now seen the salvation which they promised. The image of an aged patriarch blessed with a glimpse of God's promise is rooted in the Hebrew Bible (see Joseph, Gn 46, 30; Moses, Dt 32, 49–50; 34, 1–5; Anna and Tobit, Tb 11, 9.14). Verses 31–32 point to another important theme in Luke: God's salvation is given for all peoples. Endowed with the prophetic spirit, the aged Simeon not only recognizes the dawning of salvation, he also warns that Jesus' coming will bring about divisions. God's plan includes the rejection of the Messiah by his own people (see 4, 29; 13, 33–35; 19, 44.47f; 20, 14.17).

Virgin Birth and Christology in the Infancy Narrative

We have already seen that the canticles celebrate Jesus' coming as the fulfillment of all God's promises to the faithful people of Israel. The *Benedictus* pointed to Jesus as the anticipated Messiah of the Davidic house. The most striking Christological statements in the infancy narrative occur in the angelic birth announcement (1, 28–37). The announcement proceeds in two stages. Verses 32f parallel 2 Sm 7, 9.13.14.16. Jesus will inherit the Davidic throne and rule over Jacob's house forever as "son" of God. The second stage in the announcement moves beyond these messianic promises to the special sense in which Jesus is Son of God: Jesus is begotten through God's intervention. Some scholars suggest that Luke has created this two-step process from older Christological affirmations like Romans 1, 3f. There, Jesus is "Son of David" during his earthly life and is designated "Son of God" through the power of the Holy Spirit when he is exalted to God's right hand at the Resurrection. The announcement to Mary speaks of God's Spirit overshadowing her and bringing into being a child who is Son of God from the time he is conceived. For Luke, Jesus is fully human but is never just another ordinary human being.

Mary's virginity serves to sharpen the Christological focus: the child to be born is God's Son. The step-parallelism between the Baptist and Jesus provides additional literary evidence that Luke considers the birth of Jesus to be an even greater example of divine power than that of the

Baptist. Mary is not like the barren woman, someone whose womb could unexpectedly open and produce a child. As a virgin, there is no human way for her to have a child without God's unique presence in that process. Ancient Greek biology taught that the spirit in a father's sperm gave shape to the material in a mother's womb. The more active the spirit, the more closely a child resembled its father. Thus Mary's virginity indicates a relationship between Jesus and God unlike that of any other human being. The honor that Mary enjoys is not due to the fact of her virginity but to her willingness to accept a role in God's plan for the salvation of humanity.

A second angelic announcement, that of the angels to the shepherds, accompanies the story of Jesus' birth (2, 1–20). Luke introduces this section with a reference to Caesar Augustus and the expansion of Roman rule indicated by the census. Historically, there was no worldwide census under Quirinius. When the Romans took over administration of Judea in AD 6, they took a census of that province. Residents of Galilee, which was still ruled by one of Herod's sons, would not have been obligated to return to an ancestral village in Judea. Matthean tradition claims that Jesus was born toward the end of the rule of Herod, the Great, who died in 4 BC. Though Luke lacks precise historical information in this scene, its Roman associations permit a symbolic contrast. Augustus emphasized the fact that his rule had brought peace in the world. The doors to the temple of war, pictured on coins, were shown closed. Luke uses the angelic announcement (2, 10–14) to show that the true source of peace lies elsewhere: in the Savior, Messiah, the Lord who has been born in the Davidic town, Bethlehem.

Preparation for the Public Ministry (3, 1—4, 13)

Many of the themes in the ministry of Jesus have been anticipated in the infancy narratives. We have seen that Jesus fulfills God's promises of salvation, and we have heard some of the major Christological titles: Son of David, Messiah, Savior, Lord, and Son of God. The Spirit, which overshadowed Mary at his conception, will remain with Jesus throughout the ministry. Mary's *Magnificat* introduced the images for salvation as "reversal," a lifting up of the poor ones, those who have no one but God to turn to in their need.

We have seen the importance of thanksgiving, rejoicing, and prayer as well as the posture of the faithful disciple who hears the word of God. But we have also heard the warning that all of Israel will not rush to greet its Messiah with the same joy found in these stories. Before Luke begins to recount the public ministry, he introduces three additional blocks of material: (a) the Baptist's mission in preparing the way for Jesus and Jesus' baptism; (b) a genealogy, and (c) the temptation of Jesus.

The Baptist's Ministry (3, 1–22)

Luke has gathered together traditions about John the Baptist from different sources. John is fulfilling the mission given him to serve as forerunner for God's Messiah. Luke has arranged his account so that the fiery preacher of repentance also serves as precursor to Jesus in the content of his message: (a) repentance and forgiveness, two of the effects of salvation in Luke, and (b) the requirements for dealing with material possessions: share with those who have nothing, avoid greed and injury to others, act fairly. The ethical section of John's preaching (vv. 10–14) illustrates the "good fruit," which must come from repentance (v. 9). When we bear in mind the whole sweep of salvation history in Luke, the warning that God can raise up children of Abraham from the stones takes on a more ominous note. As the episode comes to a conclusion, the Baptist responds to speculation about his own status by separating himself clearly from the Messiah who is about to come with the Spirit and fire. John belongs to the age of prophetic figures. Jesus will inaugurate the messianic age. Luke then completes the story of the Baptist by reporting the fact that John was imprisoned by Herod Antipas before Jesus appears on the scene. This order creates some chaos in the account of Jesus' baptism, which follows it (vv. 21f). For Luke, the baptism of Jesus can never suggest that Jesus was dependent upon the Baptist. Rather, the episode permits a divine affirmation that Jesus is son of God and provides the occasion for the Spirit to descend on Jesus and inaugurate his ministry.

Genealogy of Jesus (3, 23–38)

This unusual genealogy corrects a misapprehension about Jesus. People may think he is the son of Joseph. The Christian community knows better. It traces Jesus' ancestry back to the first "son of God," Adam, and thus links Jesus to the entire human race, not just to the house of David.

Temptation of Jesus (4, 1–13)

Jesus goes to the desert under the impulse of the Spirit. The temptations Satan poses are challenges to Jesus' identity as "Son of God," which has been the central title in Luke's narrative to this point. Temptation, in this sense, is not an impulse toward some sinful act. Rather, as in the testing of Abraham by the demand that he sacrifice Isaac, temptation puts the person before a crisis that will demonstrate whether the individual's faith in God can be destroyed. Jesus refuses to use his status as Son for personal gain. Though Satan is silenced, the story ends on an ominous note; though Jesus' ministry will undermine demonic power (10, 18; 13, 16), Satan may yet return. In Luke 22, 31f Jesus speaks of a confrontation with Satan on behalf of his disciples; though they will be seriously tested by the events of the Passion, Jesus has prayed that their faith will not fail. When the temptations are finished, Jesus has demonstrated that he is the obedient Son of God who will carry out God's plan of salvation—whatever the cost.

The Ministry in Galilee (4, 14—9, 50)

The introduction to this section (4, 14f) highlights the power of the Spirit active in the ministry of Jesus (1, 35; 3, 22; 4, 1.14.18).

In Nazareth and Capernaum (4, 16–44)

Luke's sources had Jesus' ministry begin in Capernaum (see Mk 1, 21–35). Luke has reordered events (v. 23 refers to the Capernaum tradition) to open with a sermon in Nazareth that depicts Jesus as the one who fulfills what the Hebrew prophets foretold (vv. 17–21). Throughout Luke-Acts, programmatic announcements occur in synagogues and at the Temple. Jesus announces the joyous freedom of the Year of Jubilee (combining Is 61, 1–11 and Is 58, 6). Luke's genealogy has prepared readers for the skepticism attributed to those who think that Jesus cannot possibly be the messiah, since he was considered to be Joseph's son (3, 23; 4, 22). Once again, Luke previews the story yet to come. Jesus points to Hebrew prophets Elijah and Elisha,

who were directed to assist persons who were not Israelites. These words provoke a deadly hostility in the hearers (vv. 25–30).

The rest of the chapter consists of healing stories that illustrate the liberation Jesus has just announced. The demons acknowledge that Jesus is "from God." However, the popular acclaim, which results from the miracles, makes it so difficult for Jesus even to move about that he leaves for synagogues in Judea (vv. 42–44).

Jesus Gathers Disciples (5, 1–39)

Jesus' activities in Nazareth and Capernaum come before he has any disciples. This arrangement provides those who are called with some reason for following Jesus. By the time he gathers his first disciples, Jesus already has a reputation as healer and teacher. Simon Peter's call to follow Jesus is linked with a tale of a miraculous catch of fish. Peter's acknowledgment that he is a "sinner" would make the ancient reader think of stories like those in Homer that he or she heard at school. Mortals cannot see the gods, but certain events make their presence evident. So Peter, viewing the catch, announces that he is unworthy to be in the presence of the divine (v. 8). Peter's reaction to the catch is also similar to the "fear" exhibited at the appearance of the angels in the birth announcement stories. Like the angel, Jesus first tells Peter not to be afraid. Then he states what Peter's future destiny is to be: "from now on you will be catching men" (v. 10). The Christian reader knows of Peter's role as missionary apostle in Acts. Peter and the sons of Zebedee, James and John, respond as exemplary disciples. They will leave everything to follow Jesus.

Jesus continues to establish his authority through healings, first of a leper (vv. 12–16), then of a paralyzed man (vv. 17–26). When Luke took over the account of the healing of the paralyzed man, it was already a controversy story over Jesus' authority to forgive sins (see Mk 2, 1–12). The reader already knows that Jesus has the power to heal anyone he wishes. In this case, the miracle becomes both an occasion to free the man from sin through forgiveness *and* a demonstration of the authority by which Jesus can claim that the man's sins have been forgiven. Its introduction (v. 17) recalls the boy Jesus in the Temple (2, 46–47): there are Pharisees and scribes gathered from the villages of Galilee and Judea as well as Jerusalem. The crowd goes home praising God, but the Pharisees and scribes have become suspicious of Jesus. His offer of forgiveness appears to be a blasphemous attempt by a human being to seize a power that belongs to God (v. 21). Luke's reader knows that Jesus is not just any human being but the obedient Son of God. Jesus would never seize any power that rightly belongs to God (see 4, 5–8).

As Jesus calls his next disciple, the toll collector Levi, he incurs further complaints from the Pharisees and scribes. They go to Jesus' disciples to ask why he eats with persons who are considered sinners. Jesus first cites a proverb in defense of his actions and then insists that the goal of his mission is to call sinners. He is not out to preach to the righteous.

Jesus is accused of not instructing his disciples in piety as a true teacher would do. The disciples of both the Baptist and the Pharisees fast. Jesus' disciples do not. Jesus' defense consists of a brief parable and a string of proverbs (5, 33–39). The first employs a human analogy: it is impossible to fast at a wedding. The abundance of the wedding feast was also a common metaphor for the time of salvation. When Jesus is no longer present, Christians will fast (v. 35). The proverbs demonstrate the absurdity of trying to mix the old ways of life with the new time of salvation. Persons accustomed to the old may find it difficult to accept the new (v. 39).

Jesus then defends his disciples against charges of breaking the Sabbath (6, 1–5), first by appeal to Scripture (1 Sm 21, 1–6), then by insistence upon his authority as Son of Man (compare 5, 24), and finally on humanitarian grounds: it is always right to preserve rather than destroy life (vv. 6–11). The section concludes with the choice of the Twelve from the larger group of disciples who will share Jesus' mission and serve as witnesses to what Jesus has done and said.

Sermon on the Plain (6, 17–49)

Jesus' first major sermon sounds familiar notes of reversal from the *Magnificat* as well as the opening of his ministry (4, 18). The Kingdom is good news for the poor and oppressed, and divine judgment against the wealthy and prosperous. As the stories of Christian missionaries in Acts will demonstrate, Christians must expect rejection and

persecution for preaching about Jesus (see Acts 7, 52). Juxtaposing the command to love enemies with sayings on persecution provides a concrete context in which that love is to be practiced (vv. 27–30). The love command covers all forms of mercy since it is to be modeled on the mercy of God. Examples point to general ethical precepts: give to one who asks; lend to those who cannot repay; treat others as you would be treated. Judgment sayings strengthen this ethical teaching. We are judged by the judgments we make about others (vv. 37–42).

Jesus Is the Promised Savior (7, 1—9,18)

Jesus' ministry in Galilee continues with a series of traditional miracle stories told so that they testify to Jesus' identity: (a) cure of the centurion's slave indicates that there is greater faith among the Gentiles than in Israel (7, 9); (b) the widow's son evokes the allusions to Elijah and Elisha in the opening sermon (4, 25f); awestruck, the people acknowledge that a great prophet has arisen (7, 16). Further miracles demonstrate the truth of Jesus' reply to the Baptist's disciples, that he is indeed the one to come (vv. 18–23). Luke edits his sources to draw a distinction between those who received John's baptism and also receive Jesus with praise, and those who reject the plan of God—the lawyers and Pharisees (vv. 28–30). The call of Levi (5, 27–32) illustrated the conversion of tax collectors. This contrast prepares the reader for the sharp contrast between the Pharisee Simon, who failed to show Jesus the hospitality due an honored guest, and the sinful woman, who anoints Jesus and whose sins are forgiven (7, 36–50). The parable of the Pharisee and the tax collector makes a similar point (18, 9–14).

Examples of women who followed Jesus (8, 1–3) and Jesus' mother as model disciple, one who hears and keeps the word of God (8, 19–21), frame the instruction about discipleship provided by the parable of the sower (8, 4–15), the lamp (8, 16–17), and a general warning to be careful how one hears the word (v. 18). The interpretation of the sower parable indicates the threats to discipleship: (a) some will not believe the initial preaching; (b) some will be turned from discipleship by temptation, cares, riches, and pleasure; and (c) still others will lack the patient endurance necessary to bring forth the harvest.

Another series of miracles emphasizes Jesus' power to save. The disciples are rescued from the storm (8, 22–25); the Gerasene saved from the multitude of demons that made it impossible for any human bonds to restrain him (vv. 26–37). The concluding instructions are pointed toward Christians as well: go and declare what God has done for you (vv. 38f). The healing of Jairus's daughter and the woman with the hemorrhage focus on the faith of the recipients (vv. 40–56). Jesus expands his mission of preaching and healing by sending out the Twelve (9, 1–6). The brief notice about Herod's perplexity raises expectations about Jesus' true identity. If he is not the Baptist returned, then he must be like one of the great prophets of old such as Elijah (9, 7–9). This section concludes with the feeding of the five thousand (9, 13–17). As Luke shapes the story, this miracle represents food for the hungry (6, 21) as well as a response to Satan's challenge to turn stones into bread (4, 3f). Jesus does live by the word of God alone.

The Messiah Who Must Suffer (9, 18–50)

None of the external opinions about Jesus' identity capture the truth that Jesus is the Messiah who must suffer. Luke applies this insight to the followers of Jesus by insisting that the disciple must be ready to take up the cross "daily" (9, 23). Not only does God affirm Jesus' sonship at the Transfiguration (as in Mark 9, 7), but Moses and Elijah also converse with Jesus about his coming departure from the world at Jerusalem (9, 30f). Luke has omitted Markan material critical of the disciples from the Passion prediction (Mk 8, 33), the Transfiguration (Mk 9, 6), and the healing of an epileptic boy (Mk 9, 28–29). In doing so, Luke brings the dramatic theophany of the Transfiguration into closer proximity with the predictions of the Passion. God prevents the disciples from understanding what Jesus has said to them. Their arguments over greatness and jealousy of a outsider who uses Jesus' name (9, 46–50) show that they are not yet ready to follow Jesus in suffering.

The Journey to Jerusalem (9, 51—19, 27)

The journey to Jerusalem is the time of preparation for the disciples. Teachings of Jesus, especially extended narrative parables, dominate this section of the Gospel. Miracles underline Jesus' conflict with the Pharisee teachers over the mer-

ciful application of the Law (13, 10–17; 14, 1–6); they point to the virtues of faith and gratitude (shown by a Samaritan, 17, 11–19), and they anticipate Jesus' triumphal entry into Jerusalem (18, 35–43). We will pick out some of the key themes in this section.

Criticism of the Pharisee Opponents of Jesus

The shape of this criticism was anticipated by the story of the sinful woman in the house of a Pharisee (7, 36–50). Luke sharpens the charges and also generalizes them to apply to Christians as well: (a) it is hypocritical to use the Law to condemn in one case what one's actions in another approve; applications of purity regulations demonstrate this principle (11, 37–44); (b) lack of love of God leads to self-aggrandizement and even persecution of those sent by God (11, 45–52). The Pharisees are persistently pictured as driven by love of money, desire for honor among others, and self-justification that stems from their application of the Law. The first two characteristics (16, 14f) reappear in Acts as typical of magicians and false prophets in paganism (see Acts 8, 9–25).

Luke is using the Pharisees as characters to warn Christians about dangers that they face. We should not take a superior attitude as though such failings only happen to persons who reject Jesus' teaching. Legalistic condemnation of one group for actions that our own practices tolerate in another context, such as racism or other forms of discrimination, cannot be acceptable Christian behavior. Nor can we claim to be Christians and yet spend our lives pursuing money, social status, and other forms of power over others.

Warnings about Judgment

Luke does not anticipate the return of Jesus in judgment in the immediate future. Consequently, warnings to be watchful apply to both Jesus' opponents and Luke's Christian readers. Jesus speaks prophetic woes against unrepentant cities (10, 13–15). Demands for a sign only prove that there was more wisdom among Gentiles in the past than among God's people in the present (11, 29–32). Hypocrisy can never be hidden from God's judgment (12, 1–3). The stories of faithful and unfaithful servants warn against presuming that the delay in Jesus' return means that all restraints are removed (12, 35–48). Although they can read the signs of the weather, Jesus' contemporaries are unable to see what is before them in Jesus (12, 54–56). People must not fall into the false confidence born of the tragedies that happen to others. The fact that we have not suffered the disasters that happen to others does not mean that those who suffer are worse that we are, or that God is more pleased with us (13, 1–5). The parable of the barren fig tree provides an alternate reading of the situation. It could be that we are like the tree being given its one last chance (13, 6–9). The narrow door and shut door warn that Jesus' audience could be excluded and replaced with foreigners in the Kingdom (13, 22–30). Framing the parable of the servants entrusted with the master's wealth with the parable of the ruler who had gone into a distant country emphasizes the problem of discipleship in a time of delay (19, 11–27). Delay need not mean the absence of the Kingdom. Luke preserves sayings that point out the presence of the Kingdom for Jesus' disciples as well as its sudden arrival (17, 20–37). Luke expands the traditional saying about the coming of the Son of Man in judgment with another affirmation that the Son of Man must first suffer and be rejected by his own generation (17, 25).

Discipleship: Renunciation, Devotion, and Suffering

The journey opens with sayings that warn would-be disciples that they must be completely devoted to the Kingdom (9, 57–62). Such disciples renounce normal human ties to family. They are the ones sent to heal and to preach the approach of the Kingdom (10, 9). Their words are equivalent to the words of Jesus (10, 16). Luke 10, 17–20 acknowledges the potential dangers that the disciples face. However, Satan's fall from heaven indicates that the mission is weakening evil's power over humanity. Stories of the apostles in Acts will illustrate the certainty of divine protection. Sayings against anxiety require the disciple to have confidence in the generosity of others (12, 22–34). Luke's addition to the traditional saying—sell possessions, give alms, and so provide yourself with heavenly treasure (v. 22)—points to one way in which the material needs were met.

The church's economic teaching reminds Catholics that they have a moral obligation to

work for a society that provides for the needs of its weakest members. The good news for the poor depends upon consistent efforts by all Christians to help those who are disadvantaged. Our social programs should not make such people feel despised or rejected. Jesus and the early church welcomed such people into the community in addition to providing food and clothing for them.

The Martha and Mary story (10, 38–42) also illustrates a discipleship that abandons the cares of this world, even the obligations of hospitality, for the one thing necessary to salvation—hearing and keeping the word of Jesus (also see 11, 27–38).

Disciples must also expect division. Jesus' ministry brings division even within families (12, 49–53; see also 2, 34f). Jesus challenges disciples to recognize the full cost of being a disciple: both suffering and patient endurance to follow Jesus to the end are required (14, 25–33). The slave can never tell the master, "I quit" (17, 7–10).

Discipleship and Material Possessions

Riches can be a major hurdle to becoming or remaining a disciple of Jesus (8, 14; 18, 18–25). Disciples have left everything to follow Jesus (18, 26–30). Lucan parables demonstrate the folly of being possessed by wealth: the rich farmer dies before he can build his barns (12, 13–21), and the rich man who cannot see the poor Lazarus at his door is so blind to his sinful behavior that he thinks he can bargain even with Abraham from hell (16, 19–31). Alongside the call for renouncing everything, Luke presents another way in which Christians can use material possessions: they can share them with the unfortunate as the Good Samaritan does (10, 30–36). Instead of feasting with friends, they can provide for the poor, lame, homeless persons who have no resources (14, 12–24). Luke presents the parable of the dishonest steward as a warning to Christians that they cannot mix service to God with the pursuit of wealth (16, 1–13). The final episode in the travel narrative, the parable of the pounds (19, 11–27) draws on a common experience in a world without instant communications, uncertainty about the fate or return of those on a journey. Luke recognizes that Jesus may not return in judgment for a long time. Disciples must remain faithful stewards of what God has given them.

Prayer in the Life of Disciples

The infancy narrative showed the exemplary piety of those righteous persons for whom the Messiah came. Jesus frequently turns to prayer (3, 21; 6, 12; 9, 18.28; 11, 2; 22, 32.41; 23, 46), and he instructs the disciples about prayer as a response to their request to be taught as the Baptist had taught his disciples (11, 1; see also 5, 33). Luke follows the Lord's Prayer (11, 2–4) with the parable of the persistent friend (vv. 5–8) and instruction on the efficacy of prayer (vv. 9–13). The issue of efficacy returns in the parable of the importunate widow (18, 1–6). If an unjust judge with no moral conscience can be badgered into hearing the widow, how much the more quickly will God respond to the pleas of the suffering lowly ones? After all, God is not withdrawn, waiting for humans to come begging, but is actively seeking those who are lost (see chapter 15).

Jesus' Teaching Ministry in Jerusalem (19, 28—21, 38)

Jesus' arrival in Jerusalem brings the narrative back to its beginning.

The Messiah Comes to City and Temple (19, 28–48)

The Messiah who should have brought peace to Jerusalem will not be able to do so (19, 41–44). Luke has revised the story of Jesus' entry (Mk 11, 1–10) so that the crowd consists of followers testifying to the works Jesus has done in Galilee (v. 37). Jesus proceeds directly to the Temple so that the entry reflects the Greek version of Mal 3, 1, "the Lord whom you seek shall suddenly come to his own temple." But Jesus has not come to set up the kingdom of David (19, 11; Acts 1, 4). The conclusion of the acclamation resembles the angelic announcement that peace is coming to God's faithful (2, 14). Here, the city is the object of a prophetic lament—peace comes in the heavens, not on earth (v. 38). Allusion to Hb 2, 11, the stones crying out from the walls against a nation that plunders the people (19, 39f), heightens the narrative sense of a city about to meet its divine destiny. Jesus purges the Temple so that it can be a place of prayer as well as the location for Jesus' teaching in Jerusalem (19, 45–48).

Jesus Teaches Daily in the Temple (20, 1—21,4)

A traditional series of pronouncement stories (Mk 11, 27—12, 44) provides the content of Jesus' teaching now that he has returned to "his Father's house" (2, 49).

The Authority For Jesus' Actions. Jesus responds with a counterquestion hinting that those who reject him do not believe the Baptist either. Compare Jesus' answer (20, 8) with his response to the Council when they demand to know whether Jesus is Messiah (22, 67). If Jesus speaks they do not believe; if Jesus asks a question they do not answer.

Wicked Tenants. Christians have traditionally read this parable as an allegory for the replacement of Israel as God's covenant people. Today we recognize that neither Jesus nor Luke think that a faithful God would give up on the Jewish people. Jesus directs this tale at his opponents. Luke has expanded the narrative with the owner's soliloquy and increasing violence against servants. Luke also adds an image of persons being crushed by the rejected stone (compare 2, 34), which intensifies the judgmental overtones of the saying.

Tribute Due God and Caesar. Luke's addition of verse 20 intensifies the hostility implied in the question. Jesus' opponents are seeking evidence for charges of stirring up political rebellion to bring against Jesus at trial (see 23, 2–5). The spies pose their malicious question under the guise of pious flattery. Jesus, they say, teaches the truth and exhibits a godlike impartiality toward persons. Again, Jesus responds with a counterquestion. He forces the opponents to acknowledge that they are carrying coins with Caesar's image and they utter Caesar's name. Jesus' reply serves as a judgment against their failure to pay God the honor due God. Readers know that Jesus' disciples have left coins and human positions of honor behind. They recognize that only God claims our loyalty. Thus, this passage does not teach the doctrine of separate powers of church and state that has traditionally been attached to it.

Resurrection of the Dead. The final challenge receives a double answer. The absurd case based on a hypothetical reading of levirate marriage (that is, that a man must marry his dead brother's wife if she had not yet borne children [see Dt 25, 5; Gn 38, 8]) probably came from the debates between Sadducees and Pharisees over resurrection. Jesus' first answer affirms that the "children of God" (note the contrast with the woman who dies childless) are resurrected to an angelic existence. His second answer (20, 37f) points to the revelation of God to Moses. If God is God of the patriarchs, they must be living.

Jesus Challenges the Opposition. Having silenced those who came to question him, Jesus poses challenges of his own. The question about how David's Son can be greater than his ancestor draws upon Psalm 110, 1, a text frequently used in early Christianity to speak of Jesus' exaltation. The warning about the scribes (20, 45–47) invokes the Lucan contrast between the wealthy and the oppressed poor. Jesus emerges as advocate for the poor. Finally, the comment on the widow's offering (21, 1–4) repeats the contrast between a poor person and the wealthy. The radical gift of the widow condemns the abundance that stands behind the gifts of the rich. Jesus is not approving the poverty in which the widow lives, but he is asserting that her acts demonstrate a piety greater than that of the rich.

Fate of the Temple and the Coming End-Time (21, 5–38)

The Jerusalem teaching ends with Luke's version of the apocalyptic sayings in Mark 13. He has recast the traditional material to support the view that the end-time is not about to come by separating the destruction of the Temple (21, 5–7) from events which signal the end-time.

Even traditional signs of the end, false messiahs and rebellions, do not point to an immediate second coming (vv. 8–11). They are part of a time of persecution. God protects the Christian who must face hostility or even death from Jews, Gentiles, and even family (21, 12–19). The fall of Jerusalem does not lead to the end-time. Instead, it inaugurates a new stage in salvation history. Jerusalem will be overrun until the age of the pagans reaches its conclusion (21, 20–24). After all these events the Son of Man will return in glory (21, 25–28). The Christian who lives in the world between Jesus' ascent to heaven and the second coming can remain confident that Jesus' words will never pass away (21, 29–33). Christians remain watchful and pray for strength

to endure and appear before the Son of Man (21, 24–36).

The Passion Narrative (22, 1—23, 56a)

The Passion narrative is not a court record of what happened but a narrative shaped by the conviction that Jesus is the suffering Messiah, the obedient Son who has been raised by God. Apologetic motifs dominate Luke's version of the Passion. Political charges (23, 2.5.18f) are false and recognized as such by Pilate, who declares Jesus innocent three times (vv. 4, 14f. 22). Pilate yields to pressure from Jewish leaders, to whom he hands over Jesus for crucifixion (23, 23–26).

Conspiracy to Kill Jesus (22, 1–6)

Luke blames only certain Jewish leaders for the plot that costs Jesus his life (22, 1–2). Acts 1, 16–20 reports a legend that divine retribution took the life of Jesus' betrayer, Judas.

The Last Supper (22, 7–38)

Jesus is aware of the suffering he is about to undergo. It provides a symbolic interpretation of the cups of wine and bread at the Passover meal. A new covenant will be made in the death of Jesus. As the Jews had been told to remember the Exodus during Passover, Jesus tells his disciples to remember his death as the new focal point of salvation history.

The second element in the Last Supper scene is the farewell speech. Such speeches were delivered by dying patriarchs to their children, encouraging them to remember the ancestor's example by remaining faithful to the Law and then predicting their failures to do so. Luke creates Jesus' speech out of four independent sayings: (a) oracle against the betrayer (22, 21–23); (b) the disciples' place in the Kingdom (vv. 24–30); (c) prophecy of Peter's denial and eventual restoration (vv. 31–34), and (d) a saying about two swords (vv. 35–38). Jesus sets the disciples an example in his death. The worst sin committed by a disciple is Judas's betrayal, which is rendered even more heinous by the echoes of covenant sacrifice associated with the meal.

Division and backsliding are set themes in betrayal stories. Luke relocates the dispute about greatness (see Mk 10, 42–45) to the Supper, where it forms a contrast with Jesus' example as "one who serves" (22, 27). The sayings critique cultural patterns of benefactor and client obligations that dominated social relationships in ancient society (vv. 22–25). Jesus' earlier instructions to invite persons to your banquet who cannot repay you rather than invite those, like you, who can afford to give banquets, and Jesus' own appearance as slave rather than master, provide additional illustrations of the Lucan theme of reversal in the Kingdom.

Beyond the ominous events of Jesus' death, Judas's betrayal, and Peter's denial, the discourse presents images of fulfillment. The Twelve who stand by Jesus will occupy the twelve thrones of the tribes of Israel. (Judas will be replaced; see Acts 1, 15–26). The meal anticipates a future celebration with Jesus in glory—a communal celebration with Jesus, not the ranked banquets of those whose idea of greatness Jesus rejects. Before this banquet can occur, Jesus must suffer to enter glory. Satan makes the threatened return (4, 13) in Judas (22, 3) and in testing Peter. Jesus' prayer prevents the sifting of the disciples from being more severe (22, 31f; for sifting as an act of judgment see Amos 9, 9). This perception that the future will be more difficult than during Jesus' life appears in the saying about the swords. Jesus cancels the earlier rules against taking provisions (22, 35–36; see also 10, 1–12), meaning that missionaries may now provide themselves with purse, knapsack, and sandals.

Arrest of Jesus (22, 39–53)

Jesus demonstrates his fidelity to God as obedient Son in prayer before his Passion. Luke deflects criticism of the disciples for failing to stay awake by alluding to their grief. They are warned that they must pray to avoid being tested. Jesus exhibits his freedom from fear over his fate in his words to those who come to seize him. He is no robber in hiding. They could have taken him publicly in the Temple, but the present hour of darkness is permitted by God's plan (v. 53).

Trial of Jesus (22, 54—23,25)

Fulfillment of Jesus' predictions provides further evidence that God's will, not the plan of his enemies, controls the events around Jesus' death. Luke puts the story of Peter's denial before the trial of Jesus begins. Jesus reminds Peter of the earlier prediction by looking at him; Peter breaks

down in tears. When Jesus' captors challenge him to prophesy as a form of mockery (22, 64), readers have evidence from the Peter episode to show that Jesus is a true prophet. Luke does not report a legal trial by Jewish authorities. The false accusations and the verdict have been fixed before the Passion even begins. Jesus responds to the question about his messiahship with a judgment saying about the Son of Man. The Sanhedrin concludes that Jesus claims to be "Son of God" (22, 66–71). Readers know (22, 42) that Jesus will suffer death as the obedient Son of the Father.

Luke's version of the trial before Pilate insists that Jesus was innocent of the charges of stirring up political rebellion used to secure his death. Luke adds the geographical note, "from Galilee where he began even to here" (23, 5), and then clears Jesus from guilt in Galilee by having him appear before Herod (vv. 6–12). That scene represents the climax of the earlier accounts of Herod's reaction to Jesus, which shifted from fascination to opposition (9, 9; 13, 31–33). Herod desires a miracle, but all he sees is the silent prisoner who is the object of violent accusations and mockery. Ironically, the incident creates peace between the old enemies, Herod and Pilate (v. 12). Even though Pilate persists in affirming Jesus' innocence, he is manipulated by the angry crowd into handing Jesus over for crucifixion. The leaders who orchestrated Jesus' death are really the ones fostering rebellion. They ask for the release of a known murderer and rebel (23, 25).

Crucifixion and Burial of Jesus (23, 26–56a)

As he is led to his death, Jesus prophesies the terrible fate awaiting Jerusalem once more (23, 26–32; 19, 41–44). Scorned and considered a criminal, Jesus is able to offer salvation to the repentant sinner (23, 39–43). The crowd challenges Jesus to save himself from his fate, which, as it turns out, is the entry into paradise for both himself and those who repent and are forgiven (see 22, 28–30; the disciples who feast with Jesus in the Kingdom are those who have endured with him in his trials). This episode shows the reader that God's mercy can be experienced even in the midst of brutal hostility. Apocalyptic signs accompany Jesus' death, which is witnessed by the women and other followers from

Galilee. The centurion proclaims Jesus' innocence while the crowd laments (23, 44–48).

Joseph, a member of the Council, buries Jesus as an act of piety. He represents the righteous of Israel who sought the Kingdom of God (v. 51). The women prepare to anoint the body, but they are interrupted by the Sabbath. The burial scene shows that Jesus was buried with honor, not like a criminal, and that the place was known to his followers. Luke is telling us that when the women return to complete the anointing, there can be no possibility that they have mistaken the place of burial.

Resurrection of Jesus (23, 56b—24, 53)

Jesus' departure takes place in Jerusalem on the third day (24, 21.51). Luke has rewritten traditional stories about the empty tomb and about mealtime appearances of the Risen Lord in order to create a sequence of three scenes. Luke arranges these scenes so that the Resurrection faith is more and more explicitly spelled out. The Gospel concludes with the disciples offering prayer and praise in Jerusalem while waiting for the Holy Spirit to initiate the next stage in the drama of salvation, the spread of the gospel from Jerusalem to the whole world.

The Women at the Tomb (23, 56b—24, 12)

The first of the three scenes opens when the women return to the tomb. Angels chide them for seeking the living among the dead (compare 20, 38). Instead of a simple proclamation of the Easter faith as one finds in Mark 16, 6b, Luke's angels remind the women of Jesus' predictions of the Passion and Resurrection. The women report that the angels said Jesus was alive (24, 22f). When Luke repeats variants of a scene, we can expect the subsequent accounts to expand on hints in the first version.

Jesus Appears on the Road to Emmaus (24, 13–35)

Confirmation of the women's report about the tomb had not yet led to disciples seeing the Risen Lord. In the second scene, Luke uses a folktale motif: the appearance of a divine being disguised as a stranger who must be shown hospitality. Jesus expands on what the angels at the tomb said, and he interprets Moses and the Prophets in order to demonstrate that the suffering of the Messiah was

God's plan. Then a new theme comes in: the manifestation of Jesus in the breaking of bread. (John 21, 1–14 contains a variant of the manifestation of Jesus in the guise of a stranger at a meal.) The Messiah has suffered, entered into glory, and now renews his presence to the disciples in the meal.

Jesus Appears to the Disciples in Jerusalem (24, 36–43)

Luke knows the tradition that Jesus had appeared to Peter (24, 34; see 1 Cor 15, 5) but recounts only the appearance to the disciples at a meal. The third appearance confirms the fact that the Jesus who appears is the crucified one, raised up by God, not some ghost or other psychic phenomenon. The body that was missing from the tomb has been taken up by the risen Jesus.

That bodily transformation distinguishes Christian belief in resurrection from theories about the immortality of the soul or reincarnation. Neither near-death experiences nor so-called psychic phenomena provide support for our Christian faith in resurrection.

Jesus Commissions the Disciples (24, 44–49)

In the third scene, as in the previous two episodes, Luke reminds us that the Messiah had to suffer and die in order to fulfill Scripture (vv. 44–46). The story then takes up the central element in all resurrection appearance stories: commissioning the recipients. These stories all point to the future mission of the disciples and founding of Christian communities in which Jesus continues to be present. The commission in verses 47–49 is a prelude to the story of the first apostles, which Luke will tell in Acts. The disciples' mission to preach repentance and baptism to all nations in Jesus' name, beginning from Jerusalem, continues the preaching that occurred during Jesus' ministry and reflects a new stage in salvation history. (Matthew 28, 19f reports a variant tradition in which the disciples are to make disciples of the nations, baptizing them, and teaching them to observe Jesus' teaching.)

Jesus Departs (24, 50–53)

The ending of the Gospel reflects the departure that Jesus discussed with Moses and Elijah (9, 31), as well as showing the Son of Man in glory at the right hand of God (22, 69). Jesus' resurrection appearances are understood to be from his place of glory with God (24, 26). The stories have introduced ways in which Jesus will now be present to the church, through the Spirit promised by the Father (verse 49), and in the breaking of the bread (verse 35). The church's mission will be to take Jesus' teaching throughout the world.

Things We Have Learned from Luke

Jesus Is Savior for All Peoples

From the very beginning, Luke shows that the hopes that poor, weak, suffering, righteous persons have are fulfilled in the coming of Jesus. The Gospel shows that women as well as men; foreigners and Gentiles as well as Israelites; sick, weak, sinful, and despised persons as well as the well-off and respected people can come to Jesus. God seeks to reverse the situation of the poor and suffering. Consequently, Jesus comes as a suffering, servant Messiah, not as a liberator or king, who will take his place with the powerful of this world. Jesus' parables reveal that the love and mercy of God prompts this gift of salvation.

Disciples Participate in the Mission of Jesus

The disciples do not simply preach about Jesus or the Kingdom of God, they also participate in the reversal of roles, status, and concerns that the coming of salvation brings. Some disciples renounce everything that ties them to the social structures of the world. Others use their material resources in ways quite different from those around them. They do not seek exchanges between friends, which would create obligations to reciprocate. They do not try to pile up wealth or to indulge themselves and their friends in consuming luxurious goods. Their lives are not dom-

inated by concern for acquiring and preserving material things. Instead, they aid people who will never be able to repay them. They give away wealth to meet the needs of other people.

Their only "anxiety" is acquiring heavenly treasure. All disciples are willing to follow Jesus' example of suffering service rather than demanding that others honor and serve them.

Prayer and Worship Are the Center of Christian Life

Even acts of mercy and compassion would not establish a relationship with God if people did not praise God in worship and ask God's assistance in meeting the challenges that the life of discipleship poses. Throughout the Gospel, Jesus sets the example. He worships with others in the synagogue and withdraws for prayer at critical moments. The disciples turn to prayer and praise after the Resurrection. Luke also contains examples of prayer in the Lord's Prayer and the canticles of the infancy narrative. Jesus warned disciples in the garden that they would have to pray to be spared testing, a reminder of the last petition of the Lord's Prayer. In Acts, the early community will continue to follow the example set by Jesus.

P.P.

FURTHER READING

Bovon, F. *Luke 1: A Commentary on the Gospel of Luke 1:1—9:50*. Hermeneia. Minneapolis: Fortress Press, 2002.

Fitzmyer, J. A. *The Gospel According to Luke 1–9 and 10–24*. Anchor Bible 28; 28A. Garden City, NY: Doubleday, 1981, 1985.

Johnson, L. T. *The Gospel of Luke*. Sacra Pagina 3. Collegeville, MN: Liturgical Press/Michael Glazier, 1991.

JOHN

[see pages 1402–41 of the New Testament]

Before Beginning . . .

The Fourth Gospel has a double conclusion. After the Resurrection stories in Jerusalem, we are told that Jesus did many other signs but that those in the book seek to lead to belief in Jesus as Son of God (20, 30f). After the Resurrection stories in

Galilee, we learn that the Beloved Disciple was the source of the Johannine tradition and that all the things Jesus did could not be written down (21, 24f). Expanded or revised editions of a book were not uncommon in antiquity. Both conclusions remind readers that the Gospel has been written to inspire and confirm their faith in Jesus.

Composition of the Fourth Gospel

The double ending indicates that John's Gospel has revised an earlier version. Other additions to the narrative and awkward transitions between sections also lead to this conclusion (see introduction to John, *New American Bible*). For example, John 14, 31 brings the discourse to an end. Yet the Gospel as we have it contains three more chapters of discourse material. John 12, 44–50 appears to be tacked on at the end of chapter 12. Some of the additional material may have been added to the Gospel by later disciples of the author. As you read the Gospel, you will also see that Jesus often identifies with great religious symbols like light, life, water, bread, shepherd, and vine. The author of the Gospel assumes that its readers will recognize that these symbols have roots in the Hebrew Scriptures. This symbolic way of speaking about Jesus was probably developed within a community of Christians, which included the Beloved Disciple, followers who compiled the final edition of the Gospel, and another teacher who wrote the Johannine letters.

The Fourth Gospel and the Other Gospels

John is very different from the other Gospels. You will immediately notice that Jesus speaks in long symbolic discourses, not in short sayings and episodes that end in sayings. The only piece of ethical teaching in the Fourth Gospel is the love command. There are also major differences in the order of events. John pictures Jesus' ministry extending over three Passovers. The cleansing of the Temple comes at the beginning (2, 13–22), not at the end of Jesus' ministry. Jesus' death is attributed to the following that he gained when he restored Lazarus to life. John attaches symbolic discourses to many of the miracles so that the miracle becomes a claim about Jesus' relationship to God. Most scholars think that John draws on traditions about Jesus that were independent of those preserved in the Synoptic (Matthew, Mark, Luke) Gospels.

Symbols, Irony, and Misunderstanding

The Fourth Gospel uses symbols to present its message that Jesus is the unique Son of God. No one who persists in taking Jesus' words literally can understand the truth that Jesus reveals (see the rejection of literal understandings of Jesus' words and deeds in 3, 4–10; 4, 10–15; 6, 26–33). The reader knows the true meaning of Jesus' words when the characters in the story do not.

The Fourth Gospel and the Jews

Though some Jews, like Nicodemus, are sympathetic to Jesus (3, 1–11; 7, 50–52; 12, 42), the Gospel often uses the expression "the Jews" as a symbol for all those who oppose Jesus. They display a murderous desire to kill God's envoy and will be condemned by the founders of their own tradition, who testify to Jesus (Moses, 5, 41–47; Abraham, 8, 48–59). The hostility in the Johannine account may have had its roots in the expulsion of Christian Jews from the synagogues, referred to in John 9, 27 and 16, 1–4a (see introduction).

If you read carefully, you will notice that John often does not bother to distinguish the various groups within Judaism of Jesus' day, such as Sadducees, Herodians, scribes, lawyers, and Pharisees. He often speaks of "the Jews" as though summarizing a story in which Jesus is facing "the bad guys." This habit creates a tension between the fact that Jesus and his followers were also Jews and the way in which the Gospel is using "Jews" as a term for a role in the story. John 18, 35f illustrates this tension. Pilate treats Jesus with scorn because Jesus is a Jew, handed over by fellow Jews. Jesus' answer distinguishes himself and his followers from "the Jews," that is, the group opposed to him. John is not making a statement about the Jewish people when he uses "the Jews" to fill the role of "bad guys." The Vatican has reminded Catholics that anti-Semitism is one of the worst forms of racism. We must acknowledge that in the past people have not distinguished between John's use of "the Jews" as characters and the Jewish people. Today, we must be very careful not to continue that misreading. In some contexts, it might be appropriate to substitute another phrase like "Jesus' enemies" or a more literal rendering of the term used for "the Jews," "the Judeans," when retelling the Johannine story in order to avoid confusion. Such substitutions are particularly important when working with young children who cannot make the distinction easily between "the Jews" as characters in a story and their Jewish classmates and neighbors.

Reading through John

In reading John, we must be sensitive to the use of symbols, irony, and misunderstanding. The characters who interact with Jesus in the story are at different levels of understanding as to who Jesus is. The disciples begin with faith that Jesus fulfills the messianic promises to Israel, but this faith is not yet knowledge of Jesus as the revelation of God. Their faith must be completed by the post-Resurrection process of coming to understand Jesus, the perspective which the evangelist shares with the readers (16, 25). Jewish sympathizers and the crowds have a vague idea that Jesus might be "from God" or even be the Messiah. John often divides the opinions of the crowd in two. One opinion is wrong or literal-minded; the other is partially correct (12, 27–29). Unlike the Jewish crowds, who sometimes accept Jesus, John also uses the expression "the Jews" to represent religious authorities hostile to Jesus. They reject all testimony to the truth that Jesus comes from God, and they are the ones responsible for his death.

Signs and Faith in the Fourth Gospel

The symbolic perspective influences John's account of miracles (see introduction). Taken literally, they cannot lead a person to faith (2, 23–25), but seen as "signs" pointing to Jesus' identity with God, his "glory" (2, 11), they may serve as the beginning point for faith. John embeds four of the miracles in discourses, which interpret their symbolic meaning. The symbols of life, light, and bread point to Jesus as the source of eternal life for all who believe.

Today, people continue to wonder whether they should "believe in miracles." There is no doubt that Jesus was well known for his ability to heal. The Gospels insist that Jesus used his healing power to bring people closer to God. He never used miracles to enrich himself or to gain popularity. Even though miracles can be a sign that God is working through Jesus, they can also be a trap. Sometimes people think they can bargain with God. If God will just heal them of disease or help them out of a jam, then they will become faithful Christians. John reminds us that our faith is not based on miracles. Our relationship with God is based on what Jesus has shown us about God's love for the world. It is not wrong

to seek healing through prayer. Sometimes God will express love by a miraculous healing, but we should not think that miracles are anything more than a small sign of God's greatness.

Dualism in the Fourth Gospel

The Gospel uses a number of dualistic expressions, such as light/dark, life/death, from above (heavenly)/from below (earthly), not judged/condemned. They illuminate a process of division that occurs within the story. Persons confronted with Jesus' word either believe and become children of God who will inherit eternal life, or they reject Jesus and are condemned by God. This dualism gives John a certain harshness. There is no middle ground between belief and unbelief (12, 44–50). Believers are united with Jesus and the Father. They may even experience the larger world as hostile (15, 1–27). Dualistic imagery and a negative picture of the nonbelieving world often appears in sectarian groups. The notes in the NAB point out significant parallels between Johannine symbols and those used by the sectarian Jewish community at Qumran.

Belief and Eternal Life

Christians usually think of salvation or eternal life as a reward that comes in the future when they join Jesus in heaven (14, 2f; 17, 24) or when Jesus returns to judge the world (5, 27–29). John retains this traditional language but introduces a new perspective on salvation. Belief brings persons into unity with Jesus. Therefore, they can be spoken of as already having passed through death to life (5, 24–26; 3, 16–21). Those who reject Jesus are already condemned. Judgment really occurs when Jesus, who has come into the world as light, is accepted or rejected. Though various witnesses provide testimony—the Baptist, Scripture, and the deeds which Jesus does—the believer must accept Jesus' word about God. Only Jesus comes from heaven to reveal God (3, 31–36).

Jesus as God in the Fourth Gospel

The Gospel presents Jesus "from above" by identifying him with the Word, which is always present to God and through which God created the world (1, 1–5). John defends the claim that Jesus is equal to God in functional terms: (1) Jesus makes God known; (2) Jesus exercises functions attributed to God, giving life and judging; (3) humans ought to respond to Jesus with the honor appropriate to God. John also emphasizes the special Father/Son relationship between Jesus and God. Jesus is obedient to the mission the Father has given him. Jesus' death will be a sign of God's love for humanity. The disputes between Jesus and "the Jews" (chapters 5—12) turn on the issue of Jesus' relationship to God. This section ends with the ironic fact that Jesus' opponents seek to kill the source of life.

An Outline of John

The plot of the Fourth Gospel follows a pattern of descent and ascent. Jesus comes into the world from the Father seeking "his own," those who will believe. Then, Jesus confronts the world. His ministry divides believers from unbelievers. The hostility of unbelief leads to the "hour" of his crucifixion, which John treats as an exaltation. Jesus returns to the glory that he had enjoyed with the Father from the beginning. The Gospel is clearly divided into two parts: first, the account of Jesus' confrontation with the world, which many scholars refer to as the "book of signs" (chapters 1 through 12); and second, the account of Jesus' return to the Father when the destined hour arrives, referred to as the "book of glory" (chapters 13 through 20).

• *Prologue* (1, 1–18). A hymnic section introduces us to Jesus as God's Word, which has come into the world.

• *The Book of Signs* (1, 19—12, 50). Jesus' confrontation with the world represents God's judgment against unbelief. This section falls into two parts:

Gathering Witnesses to Jesus (1, 19—4, 54). Jesus demonstrates his glory to disciples and others who will believe in him before the confrontation with unbelief begins.

Confrontation with the World (5, 1—12, 50). The light has come into the world for judgment. Jesus confronts those who refuse to believe with testimony to his divine origin.

• *The Book of Glory* (13, 1—20, 31). Jesus' whole life has been moving toward the hour of his glorification and return to the Father. This section falls into two parts:

Preparing the Disciples for the Hour (13, 1—17, 26). At the Last Supper, Jesus delivers lengthy discourses about his return to the Father and its meaning for the disciples.

Jesus' Arrest, Crucifixion, and Resurrection (18, 1—20, 31). John understands the crucifixion as the moment of Jesus' life-giving exaltation and return to the Father.

• *Epilogue: Resurrection Appearance in Galilee* (21, 1–25). Second conclusion reports further appearances of Jesus and points toward the destiny of two leading disciples, Peter and the Beloved Disciple.

Now it is time to read through the Gospel. You will find it easy to pick out the symbols and the sharp divisions between characters in the story. Remember that John wrote to encourage faith in Jesus as Son of God, because that faith is the source of eternal life. What happens to faith in each episode? Why do some characters move toward a more complete faith in Jesus while others pull away and become hostile?

The Prologue (1, 1–18)

A Hymn to the Divine Word

The introduction to John is different from all of the other Gospels. It begins even before creation. John might even be following the opening words of Genesis 1 in which God creates the world out of formless chaos by speaking. Because of Jesus, John has a new insight about the divine Word. The Word is not simply speech or some abstract power that God can use to create. The Word actually became known to us in a person, Jesus. We speak of the Incarnation, of God becoming human. This idea of God is the special revelation of Christianity. It differs from the monotheism of Judaism and Islam, which insists that the unity of God cannot be shared. The Christian claim that Jesus can be spoken of as God is at the core of the controversies in the Fourth Gospel. John makes it clear right at the beginning that we can speak about God under two distinct aspects, God as the ultimate source of all things (that is, the Father) and the Word, through whom God creates and sustains the world and guides humans (that is, the Son). Later in the Gospel we will also learn that the Spirit comes from God to those who believe. Christians believe that the Father, Son, and Spirit are three distinct persons that make up the one God.

You will notice that many of the verses in this

section have a poetic quality made up of short parallel lines that employ the symbols of life, light, darkness, and glory. You will also notice that other verses speak of the role of John the Baptist as witness to the light (1, 6–8.15). Still other verses speak in the first person plural of what "we" have received from the coming of the light (vv. 12.14b.16). "We" clearly means the Christian community that believes in Jesus. They have received the power to become children of God thanks to Jesus (v. 12). Many scholars think that the poetic verses belonged to an early hymn, which John has used for the introduction. The NAB prints these verses in a poetic form so that you can distinguish them from the prose comments that the author inserted to create the introduction.

Salvation, a Gift from the Word

This section makes it clear that only those people who receive Jesus as the incarnate Word can attain salvation. The Word actually existed before anything was created, but people may still fail to receive the Word when it comes to them. The Prologue contains several hints about the fate of the light when it comes into our world. People who should have received Jesus, do not. But those who do, receive the grace of becoming children of God and coming to know God as revealed by Jesus. The contrast between the Law that came through Moses and the "grace and truth," probably a rendering of the Hebrew expression for God's love and fidelity to the covenant (see note to 1, 14), anticipates the conflict between Jesus and the Jewish leaders. Jesus will establish a new covenant between God and those people who come to believe in him.

The Book of Signs (1, 19—12, 50)

John uses the word "signs" to emphasize the symbolic role of Jesus' miracles in pointing to Jesus' true, divine origin. In order to understand the truth revealed by the signs, a person must think of their symbolic reality, not of the literal words or events. The "Jews" will be portrayed as persons who are unable to see the symbolic truth of Jesus' words.

Gathering Witnesses to Jesus (1, 19—4, 54)

The Prologue told us that the Baptist was sent to testify to Jesus. He opens this section with that

testimony (1, 19–34). Although there are hints of hostility to come, the first four chapters are generally positive. Jesus gathers followers who believe in his divine mission.

John Testifies to Jesus (1, 19–34)

The Baptist testifies on different occasions to two different groups of officials that he is not the Messiah. He is simply preparing the way for the one who is coming (1, 19–28). The Synoptic Gospels contain a scene in which Jesus is baptized and hears God announce that he is God's beloved Son (see Mk 1, 9–11). Jesus has no need of such a revelation in the Fourth Gospel. The evangelist transforms the traditional scene into another example of testimony about Jesus. The Baptist sees the Spirit descend from heaven like a dove and remain on Jesus. God has given him that sign to identify the Messiah, who will baptize with the Spirit and will take away the sin of the world (1, 29–34).

Jesus Gathers Disciples (1, 35–51)

A series of brief scenes shows us how Jesus gathered the rest of his disciples. They follow a set pattern. Persons who come to Jesus through the testimony of others have their own experience with Jesus, which makes them true disciples. The Baptist sends Jesus the first disciples (vv. 35–37). Notice that this chapter is collecting all of the titles that early Christians used to speak of Jesus: Lamb of God (v. 36); Messiah (v. 41); the one predicted by Moses and the prophets (v. 45); Son of God (v. 49); King of Israel (v. 49); and Son of Man (v. 51). The final verse is very enigmatic. It hints at the story of the ladder, which Jacob saw in a dream vision (Gn 28, 12). But Jesus as the heavenly figure, the Son of Man, has replaced the ladder. According to John, no one sees God except through Jesus (see 1, 18).

Cana Miracle Manifests His Glory (2, 1–12)

Now that he has gathered the disciples, Jesus' first miracle reveals his divine glory to them. The real revelation of Jesus' glory, however, cannot come until the Crucifixion. Therefore, Jesus first appears to reject his mother's request (vv. 4f). A wedding feast was often used as a symbol for the time of rejoicing that would follow God's judgment. Jesus has provided the wine for such a feast. We will see that Jesus replaces some of the most important Jewish feasts and customs. Christians no longer follow traditional patterns of worship. Here, Jesus replaces the water, which was to be used for ritual purification.

Cleansing of the Temple (2, 13–25)

Unlike the Synoptic Gospels, which include only one visit to Jerusalem in Jesus' ministry, John has three different Passover visits as well as episodes during other feasts. The other Gospels link the cleansing of the Temple with the Passover of Jesus' death. John puts that episode much earlier. It enables him to tell the Christian reader that Jesus will also replace the Temple. The evangelist reminds readers that Jesus' disciples could not have understood the saying until after the Resurrection (2, 22). The end of the chapter warns against faith that is based simply on miracles (vv. 23–25). Many attracted by Jesus' miracles will not remain faithful.

Dialogue with Nicodemus (3, 1–21)

The next two dialogues, with Nicodemus and with the Samaritan woman, employ the technique of misunderstanding in which the person to whom Jesus speaks takes Jesus' words literally and thus provokes further comment. You will notice that Jesus always responds with an even more difficult statement than the one that provoked the original misunderstanding. In this case, Jesus' words appear to leave Nicodemus behind, but he will reappear as someone sympathetic to Jesus (7, 50–52). Since Jewish writings of the period also speak of a cleansing of the righteous by the Holy Spirit, Nicodemus might have been expected to understand that Jesus was speaking about a rebirth "from above," that is, through the Spirit rather than "again" (see note to 3, 3). John's Christian readers probably saw an allusion to baptism in the insistence that people had to be reborn to enter the Kingdom. The episode marks a clear distinction between the teacher of Israel who cannot even understand the idea of spiritual rebirth, and Jesus who is, in fact, the very source of life.

A sudden shift to the plural "we" and "you people" echoes the confrontation between Christians and their synagogue opponents in the evangelist's time (v. 11). Verses 12–15 follow a pattern similar to 1, 50f. Belief on the grounds of some "earthly" sign is challenged by the heavenly reality, which is to be revealed in Jesus. In both cases a saying about the Son of Man represents the higher truth. Drawing upon the story of Moses lifting up a bronze serpent in the wilderness (Nm 21, 9), the evangelist asserts that Jesus will have to be lifted up (on the cross) to become a source of eternal life for all believers. Verses 16–21 speak to the Christian reader about the coming of Jesus. Elsewhere in the Gospel "world" is a negative symbol for those who are hostile to the Word. Here the world refers to all humans as the object of God's love. Though darkness did not overcome the light (1, 5), humanity can still reject the light. The passage offers one explanation for the tragic fact that people will prefer darkness to light; they would rather hide their evil ways than "live the truth," a Semitic expression for following the will of God revealed in the Law.

We should remember this human tendency to "prefer darkness to light" when we confront issues of moral or personal reform today. When we are faced with situations in which people are addicted to drugs or alcohol, we find that the most difficult step is overcoming the denial of the problem. We may become frustrated in our efforts to help such people because it seems that they would rather destroy their lives and those of others than accept available help. Certainly, we should not write off people who need our help, but this passage shows us that we cannot always expect easy results.

Jesus and John the Baptist (3, 22—4,3)

John once again testifies to Jesus as the one to come. The saying about the Bridegroom appears in the Synoptic Gospels as part of an exchange over fasting. John's disciples fast while Jesus' do not (see Mk 2, 18–19). In John's Gospel the emphasis lies on the identity of the two men. The Baptist's role ends once he has given witness to Jesus. Verse 27 points to the importance of grace in the Gospel: no one can have anything that God has not given to that person. Verses 3, 31–36 seem to be the evangelist's summary of the entire chapter. The Son is the one who has been given "everything" by the Father (v. 35). His mission is to give the Spirit—or eternal life—to those who believe (vv. 33f.36). The contrast between the "one from heaven," who testifies to the truth and speaks the words of God, and those who belong to earth, who reject the Son, once again demonstrates that the coming of the Son also brings judgment (v. 36b).

The Samaritan Woman (4, 4–42)

John has divided this story into a series of scenes that progressively reveal the truth about Jesus and his mission. Jesus comes to be known as greater than the patriarch Jacob, who met his future wife at a well. Legend had it that in the new age, the water would bubble to the top of Jacob's well so that people did not have to labor at drawing water. Jesus is more than a messiah figure who would vindicate the Jews by exalting Jerusalem. Jesus is more than the prophet like Moses whom the Samaritans expected to establish their version of the Law and place of worship against the claims of their Judean neighbors. Readers know that when Jesus speaks of a gift of living (that is, flowing) water, he speaks symbolically of the gift of the Spirit (3, 8). The woman persists in treating Jesus' words literally until the enigmatic reference to her marital status persuades her that Jesus is a prophet. When Jesus responds to her challenge to settle the old dispute between Jews and Samaritans over *where* to worship God by speaking of worship in "Spirit and truth," Jesus is alluding to himself as the replacement of the Temple (see 2, 13–22). The woman finally accepts Jesus as Messiah. Like the disciples in chapter 1, she puts that insight into action by bringing others to Jesus (v. 29).

Jesus' dialogue with his disciples about mission and harvest (4, 31–38) indicates that, like the woman, they too are sent to preach to others. Along with the previous episode, in which Jesus was said to be baptizing more people than the Baptist, this story makes it clear that Jesus was able to convert people with his preaching. The hostile controversies of the next section might otherwise give the impression that Jesus' mission was largely a failure. The large numbers of Samaritans who come to Jesus indicate the truth of Jesus' words to the disciples about the rich harvest. The story concludes with the ringing affirmation that Jesus is "Savior of the world."

Healing the Royal Official's Son (4, 43–54)

The section on gathering followers concludes with a second miracle in Cana. Jesus' word spoken at a distance is enough to heal the official's son (4, 53). Now that Jesus' identity as the Son

sent from God to save the world has been established, we are ready for the confrontation between Jesus and those who do not believe.

Confrontation with the World (5, 1—12, 50)

The sharp confrontation with unbelief that makes up this section of the Gospel does not represent failure, since it leads to the hour of Jesus' exaltation and return to the Father. Jesus succeeds in gathering as children of God those persons who believe his words despite all the obstacles that others put in their way.

Healing on the Sabbath:
Jesus Gives Life and Judges (5, 1–47)

The tradition that Jesus provoked hostility among religious leaders by healing a paralyzed man on the Sabbath and associating that healing with the forgiveness of sins is well established in the tradition (see Mk 2, 1–12). John uses the discourse that follows the miracle story to draw out what the real issue is: Jesus' claim to equality with God (5, 16–18). Opposing teachers could appeal to the Law of Moses to argue that no human being can claim to do things which are God's alone, to give life to the dead and to judge (see notes to 5, 21.22). We have already seen that in John's view the decisive encounter with Jesus is the moment of judgment (see vv. 24–26). Jesus defends his claim to give life and judge by appealing to the special relationship he enjoys with God. As "Son," Jesus does what the Father has given him to do. He does not act on his own authority (v. 30). Furthermore, those who question his behavior should look to the witnesses he can bring forward: the Baptist (vv. 31–35), the deeds which God has enabled him to do (v. 36), and the witness that God has given through Scripture (vv. 37–39). Jesus accuses his opponents of failing to recognize that he is from God because they are not really concerned with the glory that belongs to God. They are only interested in the human glory they receive from other people. He warns them that their confidence in Moses is misplaced. Moses witnesses to Jesus and will condemn anyone who rejects that testimony (vv. 40–47).

Jesus Is the Bread from Heaven (6, 1–71)

Chapter 6 is based upon a traditional cycle of material that included the feeding of the multitude, calming the storm at sea, a demand that

Jesus give people a sign, a challenge to Jesus based on his human origins, and Peter's confession of faith in Jesus as Messiah. John reshapes this material by including a lengthy discourse on Jesus as the bread of life, which has come down from heaven (vv. 22–59). Those who fail to see the symbolism of the feeding miracle or who focus on earthly facts about Jesus will not receive Jesus as the bread of life. Just as Jesus had promised the Samaritan woman a gift of water that would lead to eternal life, he promises bread that will give life to the believer. But the "Jews" are going to copy the behavior of their ancestors, who murmured against Moses. John explains that those who do come to believe in Jesus have been brought to him by God (vv. 37–39.44f). The comment that Jesus will not cast out those who come to him (v. 37) probably refers to the members of John's church who had been expelled from the Jewish community by officials. That experience is prefigured in the story of the blind man (9, 22).

Jesus' words are the source of eternal life in the first part of the discourse. Christian tradition associates the manna and the "bread of life" with the Eucharist. This tradition appears in 6, 51–59. It is necessary to eat the life-giving bread and wine, the flesh and blood of Jesus. This meal establishes a special relationship between Jesus and the believer: they "abide in" one another. Just as the Father is the source of Jesus' life, so Jesus becomes the source of life for the Christian. In this episode we learn that receiving eternal life is not the result simply of *thinking* that Jesus is God's Son. It really involves an entirely new relationship with God that is possible in Jesus. John 6, 51–58 places the Eucharist at the center of that relationship. If Jesus' words about eating his flesh and blood were taken literally, they would be a blasphemous participation in a human sacrifice. Even if Jesus' audience understood that Jesus was speaking symbolically, they might be horrified at the idea that Jesus could identify himself with God so closely.

The chapter concludes with a reaction among Jesus' followers, which shows that these words were too difficult for many to accept. Faced with the possibility of abandoning Jesus, Peter confesses that there is no one else to whom they could turn. Only Jesus has the words of eternal life.

Conflict and Division at the Feast of Tabernacles (7, 1—8, 59)

The episodes in this section occur at the Feast of Tabernacles and at an unnamed feast that follows it. The symbolism of light and water were part of the Tabernacles ritual, and Jesus uses them to express his identity (7, 37–39; 8, 12). Throughout the section we are reminded that officials are seeking Jesus' death even when they deny that fact (7, 1.19f.25; 8, 39f). Jesus is accused of "leading the people astray." He is also accused of being possessed by a demon. Since it is not yet Jesus' hour, however, attempts to arrest (7, 32.44), legally condemn (7, 45–52), and stone (8, 59) Jesus fail. Several scenes picture the divided opinion among the crowd. These scenes may also provide answers to Jewish objections against Jesus: (a) Jesus did not keep the Law in healing on the Sabbath, but the Law permits activities like circumcision on the Sabbath (7, 19–24); (b) Jesus' origins make it impossible for him to be the Messiah, yet Jesus' real origins are "from heaven," and the signs he has done testify to that fact (7, 25–31.40–44); (c) Jesus is not an established teacher of the Law, yet Jesus has received his words and teaching from God so that he does not seek personal glory as human teachers do (7, 15–18).

Jesus begins to prepare the reader for his departure. He speaks of it in a symbolic way, which the crowd cannot fully understand. Jesus will go to a place where they cannot follow him (7, 32–36). The crowd thinks that Jesus will go to the Jewish communities outside Palestine. There is a symbolic truth in that statement: Christianity will spread in those communities. Or, perhaps, Jesus intends to commit the blasphemous act of killing himself (8, 21f). The ironic truth of that statement is that Jesus will give up his life on behalf of others. He predicts that when his enemies have executed him, they will find that Jesus is the one who comes from the Father. Jesus even bears the divine name "I AM" (8, 28). The bitter conflict between Jesus and the Jewish leaders in chapter 8 repeats this identification of Jesus with God's I AM in a dispute over descent from Abraham. Those who seek to kill Jesus cannot be descendants of Abraham, since what Abraham saw and rejoiced in was Jesus. Therefore, they are branded children of Satan (8, 39–59). The story acknowledges the difficulty of Jesus' words. He is asking us to identify a human being with the God revealed to Abraham and to Moses.

The Blind Man Believes in Jesus (9, 1–41)

This story shows that it was possible for the blind man to move *from* the miracle by which Jesus restored his sight *to* true faith in Jesus. He does so as the religious authorities pressure him to condemn Jesus. He comes to recognize more and more clearly that Jesus cannot be a sinner, and therefore Jesus must have come from God. The fear that "Jews" (= authorities) will drive them out of the synagogue keeps the man's parents from testifying (9, 22f). This story may represent the experience of members of the Johannine community. Jesus returns at the end of the story to show the man his identity and condemn the blindness of the Jewish leaders (vv. 39–41).

True Shepherd Gives His Life (10, 1–42)

We already know that Jesus' death is an expression of God's love for the world (3, 16). Religious authorities have said that Jesus deserves death for leading people astray (7, 45–52). Here, parables of the shepherd and his sheep demonstrate that Jesus is the true leader of the people—at least for those whom God has enabled to respond to his call (10, 1–30). Jesus will even give his life for the sheep, something that none of the hired hands who claim to lead the people will do. Offended by his claim to identity with the Father (vv. 30–39), the crowd again tries to stone Jesus. We are reminded that Jesus' death is a free offering on his part, not a victory for those allied against him (vv. 17f).

Raising Lazarus: Gift of Life Means Death (11, 1–57)

John has used the raising of Lazarus to bring out the irony of what the religious leaders are seeking to do. Jesus is the source of life (vv. 24–26), yet they think that they can silence Jesus by killing him. The Lazarus episode also serves to remind Christians that if they truly believe that Jesus is resurrection and life, then they should not mourn physical death as others do. Jesus often seems remote from others, but here Jesus displays his love for Lazarus and his sisters. Ironically, the following that Jesus gained from his greatest sign led to the formal decision of the Jewish Council to arrange his death (11, 45–57).

Although the high priest does not know the truth of his words, it will turn out to be a good thing that one person dies for the people, and, as the evangelist points out, for all the peoples of the world (vv. 50–52).

The Light Is Departing (12, 1–50)

John locates the traditional story of Jesus' anointing at Bethany (Mk 14, 3–9) in the home of Lazarus and identifies the anonymous woman as his sister Mary. She recognizes the approach of Jesus' death. Ironically, the traitor, Judas, is the one who protests (vv. 1–8). Hints of the future Christian mission are evident in the Pharisees' response to the entry, "the whole world has gone after him," (v. 19) and the coming of some Greeks to seek Jesus. Their arrival marks the hour of Jesus' death. He prophesies that when he is lifted up on the cross, he will draw all people to himself (vv. 20–32). The "Book of Signs" concludes with reflections on the tragedy of disbelief (vv. 39–43 and 44–50).

The Book of Glory (13, 1—20, 31)

We already know that Jesus offers his life out of love; that Jesus' crucifixion is the moment of his exaltation and return to the Father; that this death is the source of eternal life for all who believe and the manifestation of a new relationship between believers and God. The truth about Jesus' death lies in the revelation that occurs on the cross, not in the plots of Jesus' enemies.

The Supper Discourses (13, 1—17, 26)

Jesus prepares the disciples for the events to come, as well as their future life as a community of believers. The foot-washing not only reflects the service Jesus is about to perform in his death, it also sets a pattern for relationships among disciples. They are going to be the ones sent to represent Jesus and must follow the model given by their teacher (13, 1–20). John has never let us forget that one of Jesus' disciples, Judas, does not really belong to Jesus. He is the agent of God's purpose even though he is in the grip of Satan (6, 70f; 12, 4–6; 13, 2.11.21–30; 17, 12). Throughout this section, the evangelist reminds us that the disciples understood the significance of what Jesus said and did only after he had been glorified (13, 7; 14, 29; 16, 4.25). As Judas is about to depart, a new character, the Beloved

Disciple, appears in the narrative. He is closer to Jesus than any other disciple (13, 23) and will show special insight into events of the Passion and Resurrection. The Johannine community revered the Beloved Disciple as the source of its tradition.

The discourses in 13, 31—17, 26 may have been composed as independent units. John 13, 36—14, 31 treats the disciples' grief, Jesus' departure and return, and the coming of the Advocate. Jesus also returns to the disciples as an indwelling presence along with the Father. John 16, 4b–33 also deals with the disciples' grief, Jesus' departure and return, and the coming of the Advocate. It lacks the development of the return theme, however, as the mutual indwelling of Father and Son. John 15, 1—16, 4a encourages the disciples to remain united with Jesus the true vine and to love one another. This unity may be severely tested, since the disciples must also expect hatred, persecution, and even death from the world (15, 18—16, 4a). Finally, John 17, 1–26 contains a prayer in which Jesus speaks to the Father about the disciples he is leaving behind. They are the evidence that Jesus has completed the task he was sent into the world to accomplish (17, 6–11a). Left in the world, the disciples are no more "of the world" than Jesus, but without Jesus they require God's protection (17, 13–19). As the Father sent him, so Jesus is sending the disciples into the world. The prayer looks beyond the immediate community of disciples to the community that will be the result of their preaching. Jesus expresses a vision of Christian community that runs throughout these discourses. The community is to express the love and unity, which has its source in the love and unity that exists between the Father and the Son (17, 20–26).

Mutual love and unity grounded in their vision of God are the focal points of the discourses. You may have noticed that the only explicit commandment given in the Fourth Gospel is the command to love one another (13, 34f). This love expresses the love of God (14, 21.23f; 17, 23) and of Jesus for "his own," which is about to be demonstrated on the cross (13, 1; 14, 21b; 15, 11–15). These discourses also suggest that mutual love and unity will be severely tested. The disciples do not yet fully understand what Jesus has revealed to them. The Advocate, who comes from God, must continue the process of bringing understanding to the community (14, 25f; 16, 13–15). Hatred and persecution from outsiders may also take their toll, as the synagogue exclusion apparently did. The Advocate will help the disciples who have to stand trial (15, 26f) and convict the world of its unrighteousness and sin (16, 8–11). The community may not remain in the "name of God," which Jesus has revealed (17, 11). If you read 1 John, you will see that the Johannine churches suffered serious internal divisions. These discourses remind us that Jesus' revelation of God's love is the foundation of Christian unity. Christians who follow this ideal face a hostile world in which their faithfulness to it survives only if they remember its source and persist in praying for the guidance of the Spirit necessary to achieve mutual love and unity.

Jesus' Arrest, Crucifixion, and Resurrection (18, 1—20, 31)

Throughout his Passion, Jesus remains in complete control of his destiny. Jesus lays down his life; others do not take it from him. When Jesus identifies himself with the name I AM, used of God in the Old Testament, all those who came to seize him fall to the ground (18, 1–14). Jesus confronts his accusers with the evidence of his public teaching. He demands that they bring evidence against him, which they are unable to do (18, 19–24). Jewish officials try to hand Jesus over to Pilate without a formal charge (18, 28–32). Consequently, the inquiry that Pilate conducts picks up the theme of kingship. John's use of double meanings throughout the Gospel has prepared us for the dialogue that follows. Jesus both denies any earthly kingship and assents to the title "King of the Jews" (18, 33–38). Nor are we surprised to find the soldiers' mockery turn Jesus into a king symbolically and then to see Pilate present the "king" to the Jewish people (19, 1–5).

When Jesus is presented as "king," the trial scene breaks out into vicious hostility. Pilate knows Jesus is innocent but can only speak to the Jewish officials and to Jesus with bitterness and sarcasm. He knows nothing about truth (18, 38). Jesus does not accept Pilate's claim to authority (19, 10f). Pilate is the one who fears the political power of others. He will give in to threats of being denounced to Caesar and execute an innocent man. At the same time, he retaliates against those responsible by insisting that the charge read "King of the Jews." The chief priests demonstrate how far away from God they are by proclaiming that they have no king but Caesar (19, 12–22). The violent cruelty and bitterness of this scene show us what brute force and political power are like when those in power have no awareness of their responsibilities toward God. Pilate is interested only in asserting Roman control over the conquered Jews. The death of an obscure Galilean is of no concern to him. When we meditate on this passage, we should recognize that we have a responsibility to protest such abuses of power in our own world. We cannot stand by and permit innocent people to be brutalized and even killed to support tyrannical power.

Details in the crucifixion scene, which fulfill passages of Scripture, demonstrate that everything is happening according to God's plan (19, 23f.28.33–37). Jesus provides for those faithful to him by entrusting his mother to the Beloved Disciple as "son" (19, 25–27). Unlike the others crucified, whose legs were broken to hasten their death (19, 31–33), Jesus departs to the Father as soon as his mission is accomplished (19, 30).

Jesus' crucifixion and death are witnessed by friends and enemies alike. When Pilate releases the body to Joseph of Arimathea and Nicodemus for burial, we know that Jesus has really died and been buried according to accepted customs (19, 38–42). Consequently, Mary's reaction to discovering the tomb open is to conclude that "they" (possibly hostile authorities) have taken the body (20, 1f). Though the Beloved Disciple arrives at the tomb first and is said to believe, all he and Peter discover is the grave wrappings in one pile and the face cloth rolled up in another place. The evangelist comments that they could not understand what had happened because they did not know the Scripture about Jesus' Resurrection (20, 9).

Mary of Magdala's encounter with the Risen Lord combines the old tradition of an angelic appearance to the women at the tomb, announcing the Resurrection, with the tradition that Jesus himself appeared to the women in the vicinity of the tomb (20, 11–18; see Mt 28, 1–10). As in the other tomb stories, Mary receives a message for the disciples. She is not to cling to the Lord but to announce Jesus' return to God. John's

account puts the occurrence of all the events—Resurrection, ascent to the Father, and bestowing the Spirit on the disciples—on Easter. When Jesus appears among the disciples, the marks on his body prove that the Risen Lord is the one who had been crucified. The disciples are now officially sent to the world as Jesus had been, and they receive the promised gift of the Spirit, a sign that Jesus' mission has been completed (7, 39; 3, 34). Forgiveness of sins as an activity of the Spirit within the Christian community (21, 23) appears only here in John's Gospel, but it is familiar from the Synoptics (see Lk 24, 47; Mt 18, 18). First John presupposes some form of "forgiveness" available within the community (see 1 Jn 1, 8—2, 2; 5, 16f).

John creates a second episode from the tradition of Thomas's doubt. The demand for physical evidence is a sign of unbelief. Christians who have not seen and yet believed are the ones who are really blessed (20, 28f).

Epilogue (21, 1–25)

This chapter seems to have been added to the Gospel by another hand sometime after its completion (see introduction, p. 1402). It elaborates on a tradition of Resurrection appearances in Galilee. The miraculous catch of fish has a parallel in the miracle associated with the calling of Peter in Luke 5, 1–11. This chapter focuses upon the two heroes from the apostolic age: Peter, who inherited Jesus' role as shepherd, and the Beloved Disciple, who established the Johannine tradition. Peter had died a martyr's death. The Beloved Disciple lived a long time but has also died. Johannine Christians can look back upon that generation of disciples as faithful witnesses to Jesus.

Things We Have Learned from John

John has presented us with a unique story of Jesus. Instead of collecting sayings and parables in which Jesus spoke about the Kingdom of God, the evangelist focuses our attention on the special relationship between Jesus and God. We need to remember this special relationship between Jesus and God, because we often slip into thinking of Jesus as though he were just another human religious leader. If we think that way, then Jesus becomes something of a hero, someone who could just as easily be replaced by another person whose life and message seemed more inspiring at another time in our lives. We need to remember that Jesus is more than a great human being. Jesus is our revelation of God.

Jesus Is the Unique Son of God

No one can come away from the Fourth Gospel without recognizing that Jesus is identified with God. The Prologue described that relationship as the Word, which is always with God and through which God acts in the world. In the narrative, Jesus appears as the unique Son of the Father. The Son is the only one who can reveal the Father. Father and Son are united by a common love and the Son's obedience to everything the Father requires.

Salvation Comes through Belief in the Son

Salvation, which John usually describes as eternal life, requires belief in Jesus as God's Son. It cannot be delivered by human institutions such as those the Jewish leaders think will provide security. Salvation consists in a new relationship to God through Jesus. This relationship is open to anyone to whom God has given the grace to believe in Jesus. Sometimes we meet evangelical Christians who tell us that unless we accept Jesus Christ as our personal Lord and savior, we cannot be saved. They try to suggest that there is something wrong with the belief in Jesus that we have unless we go through the type of conversion experience typical of members of that church. Reading the Gospel of John makes it clear that anyone who believes that his or her salvation has come through the revelation that Jesus brought has already accepted Jesus as Lord and Savior. That special relationship is what we mean when we talk about faith.

Jesus' Death Expresses God's Love for Humanity

Jesus is not the victim of human injustice even though those who killed him were evil people. Jesus chose to offer his life for others so that they could see God's love revealed on the cross. When we see God's love on the cross, we are reminded that God identifies with the lowly, suffering people of the world by joining with them. God does not approve of the injustice that creates such suffering. Jesus reminded Pilate that his own death was an "offering," not the triumph of Pilate's power. Christians must look for ways of identifying with and helping the suffering, rather than expecting God to act through the powers of the world.

Mutual Love and Unity in the Church Express the Love of God

The love shown by Christians is not simply an expression of a moral virtue. Christians always have the example of Jesus' love to follow. They also have the experience of the Father and Son dwelling in the community to inspire their efforts to achieve unity.

P.P.

FURTHER READING

Brown, R. E. *The Gospel According to John 1–12 and 13–21*. Anchor Bible 29; 29A. Garden City, NY: Doubleday, 1966, 1971.

Moloney, F. J. *The Gospel of John*. Sacra Pagina 4. Collegeville, MN: Liturgical Press/Michael Glazier, 1998.

Smith, D. Moody, Jr. *John*. Abingdon New Testament Commentaries. Nashville: Abingdon Press, 1999.

ACTS

[see pages 1442–91 of the New Testament]

Before Beginning . . .

Acts continues the story that began with Luke's Gospel. What began with Jesus' life did not end on Easter. God's plan requires another act: the gospel must spread beyond Jerusalem to all the peoples of the earth (Lk 24, 47; Acts 1, 8). Luke recounts the deeds of the first generation of apostles by which God took the movement out of the Galilean and Judean environment of its birth. He has not provided a detailed chronicle of everything that occurred during the period between the resurrection of Jesus and Paul's arrival in Rome (ca. AD 30–62). Peter disappears from the story once Paul's mission to the Gentiles is established as God's plan. Acts ends with Paul under benign house arrest in Rome, able to preach to visitors (28, 17–31). We hear nothing of the martyrdom of Peter and Paul there under Nero, although allusions show that Luke's readers are expected to know of Paul's death (20, 25; 21, 13).

A Story of God's Salvation

Acts has an unusual ending. One of its heroes is under arrest in Rome, and we never find out what happens to him. As soon as you read Paul's letter to the Romans, you find out that he was not the first missionary to reach Rome. There was an established Christian community before he arrived (1, 8–15). Paul mentions a number of people associated with that church at the end of the letter (16, 1–16).

Luke did know about these people. He mentions the fact that two famous missionaries, Aquila and Priscilla (Acts 18, 2; see Rom 16, 3f), had had to leave Italy when the Emperor Claudius expelled Jews from Rome. Roman sources tell us that riots over the name of "Chrestus" was the cause (Suetonius, *Life of Claudius* 25). This event may have taken place as early as AD 40 (see note to Acts 18, 2). While Luke has not included all of the events in early Christian history that were known to his readers, he has adopted a literary genre close to what the ancients would consider an "historical monograph." Unlike secular histories of great wars, lives of emperors, the founding of states, and the like, Luke has models for history writing in the Jewish Scriptures. Biblical history wants to show how God's plan of salvation worked out through special people and events. We use the expression "salvation history" for this type of writing.

Understanding Salvation History

How do we even know what God's plan is? You will see as you read the stories in Acts that even the disciples did not know what God intended. They had certain guideposts. The most important was what they knew about Jesus. Jesus had also told them in very general terms that a new stage in God's plan was about to unfold and that they would be an essential part of carrying it out. They also knew passages from the Old Testament that had helped them understand how Jesus' life and death fitted into God's plan. Luke makes it very clear, however, that even with these resources the disciples would not have

been able to figure out God's plan in advance. God intervenes through the Holy Spirit at the critical turning points in the story.

Though God's intervention is crucial to salvation history, human beings are not manipulated like puppets. You will notice that the disciples in the story have to figure out the significance of the unusual experiences that happen to them during their mission. They ask for further assistance from God in prayer. They also discuss the events that have occurred as they prepare to take new steps in preaching the gospel. Their ability to look back on past examples of God's action helps them understand what God is doing in the present. Sometimes they might even have taken the wrong step if God had not intervened. Acts 16, 6–10 reports that the Spirit of Jesus actually caused Paul to change his travel plans in Asia Minor and then to go over to Greece. It was time for Paul to spread the word farther to the west.

The Plan of Salvation History in Acts

Perhaps you have figured out a way of understanding the end of Acts from this passage. The book employs a geographical plan for the spread of the gospel. We begin where the ministry of Jesus had ended, in Jerusalem. We move west until we come to the center of the empire that embraced the whole circle of the Mediterranean: Rome. By the end of the book, you will see that Christianity is no longer confined to the band of followers in Jerusalem. Christian churches dot the empire. Take a look at the map of Paul's missionary journeys in Acts. (See map #14.) You will notice that Paul touches the major cities along the roads and sea routes of his time.

As you read through Acts, you will also notice another feature of the early mission. The disciples preach first to Jews and then to Gentiles. Apollos is active in the synagogues (Acts 18, 26–28). Some of Luke's summaries refer to converts from both Jews and "Greeks," an expression used for non-Jews, or Gentiles, rather than for persons of Greek descent (see Acts 18, 10). But often the mission to non-Jews begins only when influential people in the synagogue turn the audience against the missionaries (see Acts 13, 44–52). Israel has first place in the plan of salvation. She receives another chance after the rejection of Jesus when the disciples begin to preach the gospel (see 3, 11–26). The pattern of rejection by Jews followed by enthusiastic reception on the part of Gentiles, makes us aware of a turning point in the story of salvation. The Hebrew Scriptures and the public ministry of Jesus told of God's dealings with Israel. From now on, the story of salvation would involve all the peoples of the world. Luke's pattern of Jews first, then Gentiles, also reminds us that Christianity is indebted to Judaism. That link is not a trivial cultural accident but part of the divine plan of salvation. The Catholic church has called upon Christians to acknowledge this common heritage by rejecting all forms of anti-Semitism. Through interreligious discussions with Jewish believers, Catholics can come to appreciate the contribution that Jewish traditions have made to their own faith in God.

Reading through Acts

Before you sit down to study Acts, read through the whole book. You will notice that there are some types of stories that occur again and again. The apostles are put in jail. They must make speeches before various courts and officials. Sometimes God rescues them from jail or some other hostile action. Besides the legal speeches, Luke adds the drama of speeches that announce the gospel. The apostles frequently gain attention through miracles, which they are able to work in Jesus' name. In other stories, the apostles challenge the religious beliefs, superstitions, and magical practices of the Gentiles. As the gospel moves out from Jerusalem, these dramatic episodes are fitted into a pattern of journeys.

Acts as Entertainment

We have already seen that Acts has been structured to make a religious point about God's plan of salvation. As Luke tells the story, he provides the reader with a number of entertaining incidents (confusing Paul and Barnabas with pagan gods in Acts 14, 8–18, for example). Persecutions, trials, imprisonments, journeys, and dramatic shipwrecks all had their counterparts in novels that were popular during this period. The novels usually had a romantic theme rather than a religious one, but the use of comparable tales reminds us that Acts provided readers with pleasure as well as instruction.

Acts and the Early Community

You will also notice as you read through Acts that there appears to be great harmony among Christians in the early communities. We know from Paul's letters that the early churches were sometimes torn by dissent and often had to be encouraged by the apostle to demonstrate in their actions the love that Christians were to show one another.

Luke knows that the early communities were not always perfect. Acts shows us how the churches ought to live together. It even shows us how Christians should work out difficulties that they face. They are never to forget that their purpose is to thank God for the salvation they have received and to preach the same message to others. There is no place for the love of money, for the jealousy, maliciousness, and deceitful behavior that those who persecute the apostles demonstrate.

An Outline of Acts

• *Preparation for the Christian Mission* (1, 1—2, 13). This section includes all of the events between Easter and the first missionary sermon that Peter preaches on Pentecost.

    Waiting in Jerusalem (1, 1–14)

    Replacing Judas (1, 15–26)

    Pentecost, the Coming of the Spirit (2, 1–13)

• *The Mission in Jerusalem* (2, 14—8, 3)

    Two Sermons by Peter (2, 14—3, 26)

    Peter and John before the Sanhedrin (4, 1–31)

    Sharing Possessions in the Community (4, 31—5, 16)

    Trial before the Sanhedrin (5, 17–42)

    Deacons for the Hellenists (6, 1–7)

    Trial and Death of Stephen (6, 8—8, 3)

• *Mission in Judea and Samaria* (8, 4—9, 43). The gospel begins to spread into areas around Jerusalem.

    Philip Preaches Outside Jerusalem (8, 4–40)

    Conversion of Paul (9, 1–30)

    The Church Continues to Grow (9, 31–43)

• *Inauguration of the Gentile Mission* (10, 1—15, 35). These chapters set the stage for the mission of Paul by showing that the Gentile mission began from Jerusalem itself.

Conversion of Cornelius (10, 1—11, 26)

Paul's First Missionary Journey (11, 27—14, 28)

Gentile Mission Confirmed in Jerusalem (15, 1–35)

• *Paul's Mission to the Ends of the Earth* (15, 36—28, 31). Paul now fulfills the mission that God gave him by carrying the gospel throughout the Roman empire from Jerusalem to Rome itself.

Second Missionary Journey (15, 36—18, 23)

Third Missionary Journey (18, 24—21, 14)

Paul's Arrest and Imprisonment at Jerusalem (21, 17—26, 32)

Paul's Journey to Rome (27, 1—28, 31)

Now it is time to read through each section of Acts in detail. We will be looking to see how Luke describes the development of the early church. Even though the apostles do not always know where God is leading, they remain open to the Spirit. Even though the apostles experience hostility and some deaths, they never cease to tell people about Jesus. God has shown them that Jesus came to be the savior for all the nations of the world.

The Preparation for the Christian Mission (1, 1—2, 13)

Waiting in Jerusalem (1, 1–14)

Acts continues the story that Luke's Gospel had ended with Easter (Lk 24, 50–53). The New Testament refers to a number of different appearances by the Risen Lord (see 1 Cor 15, 3–7).

Jesus did not continue to appear to his disciples indefinitely. Nor did he remain with them continuously as he had during his lifetime (see Jn 20, 19–29). Luke has used the biblical number of forty to set a time frame for the appearance of the Lord (see note to Acts 1, 3). He insists that the risen Jesus is identical with the person who had died on the cross (v. 3a). Jesus' teaching during this interim period repeats the Kingdom theme of the Gospel. The disciples must wait in Jerusalem until the Holy Spirit comes on them as it had come on Jesus at the beginning of his mission (see Lk 3, 22). This event will mark the transition to a new phase of the salvation story—

the age of the church. The Ascension (vv. 6–12) also marks a change in the idea of how God will bring salvation. Jesus has not gone to heaven so that he can return with divine power and set up God's kingdom in Jerusalem as some people thought (1, 6–7). After receiving the Holy Spirit, Jesus' disciples will become witnesses to Jesus throughout the world.

The apostles and other followers of Jesus, including his mother, Mary, and some other women, form the first community. Luke emphasizes the importance of prayer in the life of the church. Gathering for prayer and celebration of the meal together is one pillar of the church. We will see that the other is charity toward the poor.

Replacing Judas (1, 15–26)

The number of apostles has to be restored to Twelve. The Twelve represented the twelve tribes of Israel (see Lk 22, 30). This group, however, did not become a permanent office or council in the early church. The church was to become the new Israel (see note to 1, 26). By using lots to determine which of two candidates would take Judas's place, the early Christians are permitting God to have the final say in this decision. The qualifications for the candidates—that they followed Jesus from the beginning to the end of his ministry—reflect Luke's understanding of the apostles as the "witnesses" who guarantee the validity of the gospel that is being preached in the churches (see Lk 24, 48; Acts 1, 8). Luke also takes this occasion to repeat a legend about the death of Judas (vv. 17–20). Peter uses Scripture to show that Judas's betrayal did not destroy God's plan. Judas's death reflects divine punishment for a person who has committed a blasphemous act against God. (A different legend about Judas's death appears in Mt 27, 3–10.)

Pentecost, the Coming of the Spirit (2, 1–13)

Fire and strong winds are typical elements in appearances of God (see notes to 2, 2f). The Greek translation of Isaiah 66, 15.18 says of God's coming: "For behold the Lord will come as a fire, with a flame of fire . . . I am coming to gather all the nations and tongues." The new turn in salvation history, represented by Acts, shows us that God is gathering the "nations and tongues" into one church through the Christian mission. Luke makes Pentecost a double miracle. Not only does the Spirit inspire the disciples' speech, but persons from different nations are able to understand their message. Pentecost anticipates the goal of the missionary effort which the Spirit will inspire in the Church.

The Mission in Jerusalem (2, 14—8, 3)

Two Sermons by Peter (2, 14—3, 26)

Luke follows a similar pattern in all of Peter's sermons. His Pentecost sermon is the most famous (2, 14–36). It begins with the theme of prophetic fulfillment. The prophets anticipated a powerful outpouring of God's Spirit in the last days. Though the world is *not* ending, God has given that Spirit to the disciples. Peter uses several Old Testament quotations to demonstrate that the risen Jesus is the Messiah whom God had promised. God has established the crucified Jesus as Lord and Christ in heaven (v. 36).

Peter's speech has a profound impact on the crowd. The universality of the Christian mission is represented by these converts from the distant corners of the earth. Baptism is the rite though which the new converts receive forgiveness of sins and the gift of the Holy Spirit (2, 37–41). Acts 2, 42–47 describe the unity of the growing community. The fundamental elements of Christian community are presented: teaching, fellowship, breaking bread, and prayer.

Christians demonstrate their care for one another by giving to the poor. The early church did not force members to renounce everything, as Peter and the others had done. Many would continue to own property and practice their trade. In this the church was different from groups like the Jewish sect called the Essenes. It expected members to turn over property to the sect as a condition of joining monastic-like groups. Essenes who lived in villages were required to turn over a set number of days wages to the group's overseer. Ancient philosophers described the ideal relationship between friends as sharing all things in common. Acts depicts a Christian community that spontaneously fulfills such ideals.

Luke frequently uses miracles to provide evidence for the faith that people should have in Jesus. The healing of a crippled man (3, 1–10) provides the occasion for Peter's second speech

(3, 11–26). Once again the speech is a brief recitation of the salvation history, which has been fulfilled in Jesus. God's promise to Abraham has been realized in Jesus (3, 25f).

Peter and John before the Sanhedrin (4, 1–31)

This scene is the first of a number of trial scenes in Acts. A pattern is developed: (a) the miracle attracts attention; (b) the apostles teach those who have been attracted by the miracle; (c) arrest of the missionary by jealous (Jewish) officials; (d) trial of the missionary; (e) miraculous escape or vindication of the mission. At first, the trials are orderly. The judges take a moderate approach and only warn the disciples, but opposition to the Christian mission will increase until Stephen is murdered by an enraged mob. You will notice that the apostles never claim any miraculous powers for themselves. Miracles are done in the name of Jesus (v. 10). All of the miracles have some connection with the mission to spread the gospel. Acts 4, 12 expresses the belief that motivates preaching the gospel throughout the world: "There is no salvation through anyone else, nor is there any other name under heaven given to the human race by which we are to be saved."

The communal prayer that follows the apostles' release (4, 23–31) shows that Christians never lost their confidence in God's power to rescue them from danger. What happened to Jesus, and will shortly happen to martyrs like Stephen, is not a defeat for Christians. God's plan for salvation can make use of such events. God responds to this prayer with a second Pentecost: the Holy Spirit comes to all who are present.

Sharing Possessions in the Community (4, 32—5, 16)

Luke elaborates on the theme of shared property. He first presents striking examples of generosity by persons who were willing to follow the sayings of Jesus that encouraged people to sell all and become disciples (see Lk 12, 33; 16, 9.11.13). The story of Ananias and Sapphira provides a somewhat comic illustration of what might happen to persons who attempt to pretend that they have the generosity of disciples while secreting money for their own use (compare the Rich Fool, Lk 12, 16–21). Once again, death is viewed as God's judgment against persons who have done something blasphemous. They were not required to sell the property in order to be part of the community. Their sin was in the attempt to deceive the Holy Spirit. Human beings can be taken in by fraud, but God will always know what is in a person's heart. No one can cheat God. We may refuse to follow these examples of Christians helping those in need. We may even devise a scheme to appear to help the poor while keeping more for ourselves, but if we do, we will have to answer to God.

Trial before the Sanhedrin (5, 17–42)

The miracles of the previous passage lead to jealousy and another imprisonment. This time we learn that no one could keep the apostles in jail if God wished them to continue preaching elsewhere. An angel takes them from prison to preach in the Temple area. This miraculous sign further enrages the opposition. The apostles are released thanks to the judicial prudence of Gamaliel, a Pharisee who demonstrates respect for God's plan (v. 39), but some people are now angry enough to kill the apostles (v. 33).

Deacons for the Hellenists (6, 1–7)

This passage presents several difficulties, since it does not fit with what follows. The distinction between Hebrews and Hellenists seems to be based on an individual's mother tongue. The Hellenists would be Jewish converts to Christianity who spoke Greek. The description of the Seven as persons who would take care of the distribution of food, so that the apostles could devote themselves to prayer and preaching, suggests that the Seven were to be like deacons in the church at a later date. They must oversee the material arrangements and aid to the poor. Verse 6 describes the process, prayer, and laying on of hands by which persons were installed in offices in the church during Luke's time. In the next episode (v. 8) we learn that the most famous of the persons chosen engages in ministry of preaching like Peter and the other apostles.

Trial and Death of Stephen (6, 8—8, 3)

This trial scene is the longest in Acts. Stephen emphasizes Israel's past failures. His speech prepares for the mission to the Gentiles as it develops in the plot of Acts. Luke creates a link between Stephen and the hero of that mission, Paul, by picturing Paul—who tells us that he had persecuted the church out of zeal for ancestral tradition (see Gal 1, 13; 1 Cor 15, 9b; Phil 3, 6)—as a witness to Stephen's death (8, 1). Luke's Paul later refers to this event as evidence of his initial hostility to Christianity (22, 20). Luke also uses the Stephen episode to tie the emergence of a non-Jewish Christianity to the ministry of Jesus. The charges against Stephen (6, 13f) are similar to those brought against Jesus. False witnesses testify that Stephen attacks the Temple and the Law, and they predict that Jesus will destroy the Temple. The tradition that Jesus' predictions about the destruction of the Temple were brought into his Jewish trial is well established in the Synoptic Gospels (see Mk 14, 58; Mt 26, 61; Mk 15, 29; Mt 27, 40). Luke omits this detail from the appearance of Jesus before the Council in his Gospel and places it here.

Predictions that God will destroy a corrupt Temple to establish one that is a holy place appear in the Prophets (see Jer 7, 11; Zec 14, 21; Mal 3, 1; Is 56, 7). The Jewish sect (known as the Essenes) was severely critical of the corrupt priesthood and calendar used in the Temple. Their criticism stems from a concern for more exact observance of the Law. By contrast, the Stephen episode ties criticism of the Temple to an attack on the Law.

Later in Acts, similar suspicions will be voiced against Paul (see 22, 20f). Like Stephen, he will be seized on the grounds that he is attacking the Temple (= "this place") and the Law. Two further charges are made against Paul. He speaks against the Jewish people, and he has committed a sacrilegious act by bringing a Gentile into the area reserved for Jews (22, 28). Luke's narrative shows that Stephen and Paul were not attacking the Law. Luke has shown that the Jerusalem Christians were constantly in the Temple praying. There is no basis for the accusations brought against either Stephen or Paul, just as there had been no basis for the charges against Jesus (see Lk 23, 4f.13–15.22).

Many interpreters have suggested that Luke is using the trial scenes in Acts to defend Christianity against the suspicions of outsiders (see introduction to Acts, p. 1443). Political insurrection, disregard for ancestral traditions, and acts of impiety like defiling a temple were terrible deeds, all of which could stir local as well as Roman officials to punish the perpetrators. The Roman authorities were particularly suspicious of groups that they thought might lead to rebellion among the peoples of the empire. At the same time, the Romans protected sacred places and traditional religious practices. Special edicts from the emperor prohibited local officials from taking advantage of their Jewish populace by seizing money collected for the Temple in Jerusalem, forcing Jews to appear in court on the Sabbath, and the like. Christians were particularly suspect, since their religious practices were not the traditions of an ancient people. Luke may be attempting to answer this objection by demonstrating that Christianity is the true heir of the Jewish tradition.

Stephen's speech (7, 2–53) recites salvation history to indict Israel for failure to obey God's commands. Such a speech would not be out of place in a Jewish context. One of the rule books of the Essene sect, *The Damascus Document*, begins in a similar way. It concludes that because Israel had been unfaithful, even though she had suffered punishment for various misdeeds, God had taken the promises away from the nation as a whole. Only the small remnant of righteous Jews who made up the Essene sect will experience the blessings of salvation when the Messiah comes.

By implying that the audience shares an ancestral hostility to God's prophets (vv. 51–53), Stephen fuels a rage that not only kills him but also spawns persecution against other Christians. Since it scatters Christians outside Jerusalem (8, 1), this hostility indirectly furthers God's plan. Stephen's vision of the risen Lord exalted in heaven recalls a saying that Mark reports Jesus using before the high priest (Mk 14, 62). Visions of the heavenly Son of Man usually carry overtones of divine judgment in the New Testament (compare Rv 1, 7–18). As readers, we know that God will vindicate the faithful witness. You may have picked up another similarity between the death of Stephen and that of Jesus. Stephen dies peacefully with words of forgiveness on his lips (compare Lk 23, 34.46). There is one important difference. Jesus had prayed to God, the Father; Stephen addresses his prayer to Jesus whom he has seen standing at God's right hand.

Mission in Judea and Samaria (8, 4—9, 43)

Philip Preaches outside Jerusalem (8, 4–40)

The gospel begins to be spread outside Jerusalem to those who have some contact with Judaism: the Samaritans, who had their own version of the Law of Moses, and an Ethiopian, who was already interested in the traditions of the Jewish people. Several Lucan themes appear in this section. Philip's instruction about Isaiah (8, 30–35) shows that Jesus is the fulfillment of what is written in the Prophets. Unlike the Jerusalem crowd who had turned a deaf ear to such arguments, the Ethiopian demonstrates the proper response: he becomes a disciple of Jesus by being baptized. This story also introduces a minor theme, which some scholars consider part of Luke's apologetic task. Prominent people either become Christians, listen to the apostles' preaching with sympathy and often ask them to return, or provide some other form of assistance.

The conversion of the Samaritans and the conflict with Simon the magician introduce two more themes: the continuity of the new Christian mission with the Jerusalem apostolate and the superiority of Christianity to all forms of pagan superstition and religion. We have already seen that the gift of the Holy Spirit defines Christian baptism for Luke (Acts 2, 38; 10, 48), who contrasts it with the water baptism of John the Baptist (Lk 3, 16; Acts 1, 5; 11, 16; 18, 25; 19, 3f). Christians are baptized in the name of Jesus. Baptism involves forgiveness of the past sins of a life without God, as well as receiving the Spirit. Acts 8, 16 departs from the normal pattern, since Philip has baptized in the name of the Lord, but his converts did not receive the Spirit until Peter and John came from Jerusalem to lay hands on them (8, 14–17).

In Catholic tradition this text has been cited as one of the biblical foundations for the sacrament of confirmation in which the Spirit is conferred subsequent to baptism (see, for example, *The Catholic Catechism*, No. 1288). Pentecostal Christians affirm that persons who have not experienced the Spirit coming over them are not yet fully Christian. As presented in the Acts of the Apostles, episodes in which the Spirit is separated from water baptism reflect exceptional oc-currences. In the conversion of Cornelius, for example, the Spirit will indicate that God has ac-cepted the new converts even before water bap-tism. Here, the separation between water bap-tism and receiving the Spirit allows Luke to show that the new mission takes place under the sponsorship of Jerusalem. Luke indicates that the Spirit always operates in and through the church.

The encounter with Simon the magician al-lows Luke to address another possible objection to Christianity. We have seen that Luke fre-quently uses miracle stories or references to mir-acle working to initiate interest in the Christian preaching. In antiquity, healings and other ex-traordinary events that occurred through assis-tance from a god or goddess might be called mir-acles, but a hostile bystander might accuse the miracle worker of being nothing more than a magician. The contest between Moses and the magicians at Pharaoh's court (Ex 7, 8f.12) pro-vides a biblical pattern for evaluating magic. Even though they may duplicate some of Moses' miracles, no magician can duplicate or withstand the power that comes from the Lord. The Si-mon incident demonstrates the power of Chris-tianity to destroy such superstitions. Luke men-tions another common charge against religious charlatans: greed. The Christian mission is not driven by desire for money (3, 1–10). Christians sell property and share their possessions.

Conversion of Paul (9, 1–30)

Paul's conversion demonstrates God's power to use everything, even the hostile persecutor, to achieve the divine purpose. Paul himself tells us little about the call from God that transformed him from being an enemy of the Jesus movement to being its advocate (see Gal 1, 11–24). Luke then presents three versions of Paul's conversion (Acts 9, 1–19; 22, 4–16.17–21; 26, 12–18), which differ from each other. Each of the four ac-counts serves an apologetic purpose. Paul's own account in Galatians 1 belongs to an impassioned defense of his preaching to the Gentiles. He must show that, in telling them they could be saved through belief in Jesus without also taking on ob-ligations of the Jewish Law, he is not distorting the gospel or breaking agreements made with Je-rusalem. Acts 9 must vindicate Paul as the repre-sentative of God's offer of salvation to the Gen-

tiles. The next two accounts (Acts 22 and 26) of Paul's conversion occur in speeches that Paul gives while imprisoned in Jerusalem.

Luke's accounts share a core of details: (a) let-ters from the high priest; (b) Paul is approaching Damascus; (c) light from heaven shines around Paul [and in #3, Acts 26, around those with him]; (d) he [#3: we] falls to the ground; (e) hears a voice speaking to him (#3: in Hebrew); (f) "Saul, Saul, why are you persecuting me?" [#3: "hard for you to kick against the goad"); (f) asks iden-tity of speaker; and (g) "Jesus, whom you are persecuting." This core suggests a common story about Paul's conversion. After this point the three accounts diverge. Acts 9, 12–16 expands on the theme of Paul's blindness. Ananias comes to Paul as "healer" (note the emphasis on the cure in v. 18). Acts 22, 11a.12f gives a more ab-breviated account, and Acts 26 omits these de-tails altogether as it does the details about the ac-tions of Paul's companions after the appearance, the visit of Ananias, and Paul's baptism. In Acts 9, 16, the Lord tells Ananias of Paul's commis-sion. In Acts 22, 14f, Ananias gives the commis-sion to Paul, but in 26, 16b–18, Paul receives the commission directly from the Lord.

The blinding/healing sequence in Acts 9, 12–19 suggests that the blinding of Paul is an act of God's displeasure similar to the temporary blindness God inflicts on the magician Elymas (Acts 13, 9–11; see also the threat of divine pun-ishment in Acts 8, 22–24). Paul's own version and the later stories in Acts emphasize Paul's commission, but this plays no role in the narra-tive about Paul. God uses it as an argument to persuade Ananias to go to Paul. Acts 9, 15 has been phrased so that it reflects the commission given the disciples in 1, 8. The ensuing versions of the story will relate the commission to Paul's vision of Christ and to the details of his specific role in the Gentile mission as it has unfolded in Acts. Here, Luke uses the story of the miraculous conversion of the persecutor of Christianity to initiate the preparation for that global mission, which is the subject of this section of the book.

The Church Continues to Grow (9, 32–43)

Luke concludes the section with two stories from Peter's mission. The healing of Tabitha follows the same pattern as Jesus' own healing of Talitha (see Mk 5, 41; Lk 7, 15). Tabitha indicates the important roles that women believers play in the growth of Christianity. Not only is she an example of piety and charity, but she also has a group of poor widows who assemble in her home. This period of peace and growth shows that the community has successfully weathered the storm of persecution that began with Stephen's martyrdom.

Inauguration of the Gentile Mission (10, 1—15, 35)

Conversion of Cornelius (10, 1—11, 26)

Before Paul can fulfill his role as one who carries the gospel from Jerusalem to Rome, the leaders of the church must formally accept Gentiles into the Christian fellowship. The common meal was the basic expression of Christian unity. Paul reports an episode in which Jewish Christians from Jerusalem were unwilling to eat with the Gentile members of the Antioch church, presumably because they felt that such behavior would have violated the food laws that set Jews apart from other peoples. Paul says that before these people came, Peter himself was willing to share the meal with Gentile Christians, but that when the stricter Jewish Christians arrived, Peter, Barnabas, and other Jewish Christians began to celebrate a separate meal (see Gal 2, 11–14). Peter may have been attempting to preserve harmony in the church by not offending Jewish Christians who could not bring themselves to change a whole lifetime of kosher food laws. The story of how Peter came to accept Gentile converts, which Luke repeats here, bears traces of that old dispute. God must direct Peter, in a vision, to renounce his former understanding of what represented clean and unclean food.

Peter takes others with him to Cornelius's house so that he has witnesses to what has happened. His sermon acknowledges the fact that God is impartial. Anyone can receive salvation through Jesus if that person honors God and acts justly. The Spirit even demonstrates to Peter and the others that Gentiles are to be accepted into the church by granting Cornelius and his household a mini-Pentecost before they are baptized (10, 44–48). Upon his return to Jerusalem, Peter gains official approval for his actions from the other leaders there. He reports everything that

had happened in connection with the Cornelius episode so that those in Jerusalem agree that "God has then granted life-giving repentance to the Gentiles too" (11, 18).

The first church to include Jews and Gentiles in a single fellowship is founded by anonymous Christians in Antioch. Quickly, however, they obtain the services of two famous apostles, Barnabas and Paul. Barnabas is sent by the authorities in Jerusalem. He provides the link between Antioch and the church in Jerusalem (11, 19–26). Acts 11, 26 notes that the name "Christians" originated in Antioch. It appears that this name was first given to followers of Jesus by outsiders. It may have implied some scorn for the leader whom Christians worshipped, as appears to be the case when Agrippa uses it in Acts 26, 28.

Paul's First Missionary Journey (11, 27—14, 28)

The missionary efforts of Barnabas and Paul illustrate one of the principles of Luke's account of salvation history. Jewish rejection of the gospel leads the apostles to turn to the Gentiles, who receive God's salvation with joy. Paul's letters contain a number of references to an offering from his Gentile churches, which he took to Christians in Jerusalem (see Gal 2, 10; 1 Cor 16, 1–4; 2 Cor 8f). He does not deliver that collection until the final visit to Jerusalem (Rom 15, 30–32). Many scholars think that Luke has confused that episode with another tradition about some form of famine relief that had been associated with the predictions of a Christian prophet (Acts 11, 27–30).

The Jerusalem church suffers yet another round of persecution. We are told that James, the son of Zebedee, was martyred by the Jewish king and that Peter was imprisoned. He would have been executed if God had not intervened to rescue him from jail (Acts 12, 1–19). Herod Agrippa suffers a tortured death as divine punishment for his impiety (12, 20–24). In ancient stories, being eaten by worms was a typical punishment for tyrants who scorned the gods. A Jewish account of Herod's death has been preserved by the historian Josephus. His version agrees with Luke that Herod had accepted divine honors from his subjects and so been struck down. Josephus says, however, that the occasion was the celebration of athletic games at Caesarea.

Paul's first missionary journey establishes the pattern of first preaching in Jewish synagogues and then turning to the Gentiles. Paul makes this principle explicit in his sermon at Pisidian Antioch (13, 44–47). We have already seen that Luke wishes to show that Christianity is superior to pagan superstition. Paul overcomes a Jewish magician who had had influence with the Roman proconsul on Cyprus (13, 4–12), and in keeping with Luke's interest in the conversion of prominent persons, the proconsul becomes a believer. At Lystra, Paul and Barnabas must actually prevent the people from offering sacrifices to them as if they were pagan gods in human form (14, 8–18). Throughout this journey the apostles are plagued by hostility from Jews at the same time that they receive warm receptions from the Gentiles.

Gentile Mission Confirmed in Jerusalem (15, 1–35)

All of these events prove to the leaders of the church that God does want them to accept Gentiles into the church. They must face the objections of Jewish Christians, however, who feel that to admit Gentiles without requiring them to observe the Law contradicts the whole story of God's covenant with Israel. They insisted that Jesus was the Messiah for those who sought to be faithful children of Abraham and followers of Moses. In addition to Acts, we have Paul's report of the council in Jerusalem (Gal 2, 1–10). The two versions of the meeting in Jerusalem do not agree in many of their details. Some scholars think that Paul is referring to an earlier meeting. When the agreement to divide missionary efforts, with Peter going to Jews and Paul to Gentiles, failed to resolve the difficulties that arose in mixed churches like Antioch, another meeting was held. At that meeting some restrictions were laid on the Gentiles. They had to avoid idolatry, avoid meat that Jewish law would have considered impure, and not enter into marriages that Jewish law considered incestuous. The decree is mentioned again in Acts 21, 25. The list of prohibitions is based on rules in Leviticus 17—18 that regulate the behavior of non-Jews who live among Jews. Adopting these rules would make it possible for Jewish and Gentile Christians to enjoy table fellowship.

Luke knew of a letter sent by James to Antioch that stated these rules. He presumed that they came from the same meeting at which Paul and Barnabas received authorization for a mission to the Gentiles that would not require the Gentiles to observe Jewish practices. Paul insists that there were no rules imposed on the Gentiles (Gal 2, 6). By Luke's time, the problem of table fellowship had disappeared, as most churches were predominantly Gentile. The significance of the Jerusalem Council lies in the way in which church leaders were able to recognize and officially affirm the new direction in salvation history that would permit expansion of the gospel beyond the nation and culture in which it was born to all peoples of the earth.

The Mission of Paul to the Ends of the Earth (15, 36—28, 31)

Second Missionary Journey (15, 36—18, 23)

Paul now begins the journeys that will take the gospel throughout the rest of the empire. On this journey, he will take the decisive step of crossing from Asia Minor into Greece, where some of the most important Pauline churches would be founded. The New Testament contains Paul's own letters to churches in Thessalonica, Philippi, and Corinth. When Paul arrives in Europe, the narrative style suddenly changes from the third person to the first person "we." Sections of journey narrative in the "we" style appear throughout the rest of Acts (16, 6–12 [beginning of the European mission]; 20, 1–7.13–16; 21, 1–9.15–17 [last journey to Jerusalem]; 27, 1—28, 16 [voyage to Rome]). Some scholars attribute the "we" sections to a travel diary kept by a companion of Paul. The content of these sections matches that of the journeys that Luke has already used to describe the Pauline mission. A shift into the first-person plural was often used by ancient authors for its literary effect. The change in style may represent Luke's way of telling us that *we* have now arrived at the mission for which the rest of the narrative has prepared us. The gospel is to be taken completely beyond Judaism. In time these Gentile Christians will be the sole custodians of a tradition, which God has been preparing since Abraham. It will be their responsibility to see to it that the gospel continues to be preached in all the nations of the earth.

A dream vision takes Paul into Macedonia (16, 6–16). Dream visions were frequently cited as the source of divine guidance in the ancient world. Paul's first major foundation is at Philippi, a Roman colony that enjoyed the rights of an Italian city. Paul's letter to the Philippians indicates that he enjoyed close relationships with this church. They sent assistance to Paul when he was imprisoned or working in other areas, and both men and women from the Philippian church worked as missionaries preaching the gospel to others (see Phil 1, 14; 4, 2f). Acts does not contain much information about the extensive periods of time that Paul lived in communities like Philippi, Thessalonica, and Corinth, nor does Luke refer to persons and issues mentioned in Paul's letters to those churches. There is no evidence in Acts that Luke was familiar with any of Paul's letters. If he had accompanied Paul on some part of his missionary work (see Phlm 24; Col 4, 14), Luke cannot have been involved in the major events of Paul's mission in the way that Timothy, Titus, and Silvanus were.

Luke appears to have drawn upon anecdotal material for the major events in each of the cities. He then shapes that material to illustrate his understanding of the growth of the early church. The Philippi episode repeats themes that we have already encountered. Christian preaching is well received by wealthy, respectable citizens, in this case Lydia, a woman who trades in purple cloth (16, 12–15). Christianity triumphs over pagan superstition and exploitation of the supernatural for personal gain when Paul exorcises the demon from a slave girl (16, 16–18). Like the demons in the Gospel stories (see Lk 4, 31–37), this demon recognizes the purpose for which the apostles have come.

Jealousy and lost profits once again fuel false charges against the apostles as persons who incite disorder and destroy ancestral customs. The real opponents of Roman order are the accusers, who stir up the mob with the charges, and the magistrates, who violate Roman law by flogging a Roman citizen. In this case, another miraculous deliverance from prison permits a dramatic conclusion in which the apostle confronts the magistrates with the illegality of their own behavior

(16, 19–39). It also provides an opportunity for the gospel to be heard by the jailer and his household. We have evidence from Paul's own letters that his preaching in prison resulted in converts (see Philemon).

The episodes at Thessalonica (17, 1–9) and Beroea (17, 10–15) repeat the patterns of the Philippi episode. Initial success, including prominent converts, leads to jealousy and charges that the apostles are destroying public order and encouraging revolt against Rome. Luke's readers already know that such accusations are false and that hostility will not impede the apostles' mission.

Paul tells us nothing of his stay in Athens except that he remained there alone after sending Timothy to strengthen the faith of the recent converts in Thessalonica (1 Thes 3, 1f). Paul may not have succeeded in establishing a church there. Luke, however, uses the occasion to advance his case for the religious superiority of Christianity by showing it to be equal to the philosophical understanding of the divine principle governing the universe, and not simply another form of religious cult, magic, or superstition that sought to sway the masses for the financial gain of its preachers. Its reputation was built on its philosophic schools. Luke refers to the two most popular types of philosophy among the Romans, Epicurean and Stoic (17, 18–21). The speech which Paul delivers at their request (17, 22–34) touches on common themes in the philosophical account of religion, which was opposed to the superstitious beliefs about the gods found among the masses. God, the invisible, omnipresent creator and sustainer of the universe, is not swayed by rituals nor partial to one group of people over another. Hellenistic Jews had also taken over the language of philosophical monotheism to advocate the superiority of their religious tradition.

Athenians were well known for their piety and their curiosity. Following the practice of ancient rhetoric, the speech opens by seeking to render the audience friendly to the speaker. Paul praises them for these traits. In composing the speech, Luke has apparently modified a common type of altar inscription, ". . . altars of the gods, named unknown, and heroes. . ." to the singular (v. 23). Paul then develops three claims about God that were philosophic commonplaces among both pagan and Jewish authors: (a) God is the creator of the entire universe and consequently has no need of human service or temples (vv. 24f); (b) God has allotted certain zones of the earth for the nations of human beings, who should be grateful for God's ordering of the universe and seek to serve God, who sustains and is present to all created things (vv. 26–28); (c) true worship of God will reject all superstitious practices, such as identifying the creator with the products of human artistry and imagination (v. 29).

The conclusion shifts from the common ground between the Christian preacher and philosophical enlightenment to an appeal for conversion (vv. 30f). It recalls the "unknown" taken from the altar inscriptions, which had served as an example of Athenian piety in verse 24. Inscriptions to unknown deities are a feature of polytheism, since they point to an anxiety to honor deities who might influence events but who are not "named" in the local traditions. Now is the time for a true monotheism. God is not an abstract, creative, sustaining principle, called by many names in the different nations. God is the one who calls on Paul's listeners to repent (= abandon even their philosophical paganism) and accept the message about Jesus as the one in whom all the nations of the earth are to receive salvation. As was the case in earlier missionary speeches, the Resurrection appears as God's evidence for the status of Jesus as judge of all. This departure from the common ground with philosophical theism, however, only draws skepticism or, at best, a puzzled willingness to hear more. The church-founding conversions of other missionary episodes do not occur.

Luke's account of Paul's extensive work in Corinth (18, 1–17) refers to the fact that Paul worked at his trade while preaching there, as he did in all of his churches (see 1 Thes 2, 9; 1 Cor 4, 12; 9). Luke supplies the additional information that Paul's trade was that of tentmaker, probably someone making tents of leather and rough cloth, as well as other items, such as harnesses. He mentions two of Paul's close associates from that mission, Priscilla and Aquila (1 Cor 16, 19; Rom 16, 3). Luke also tells the story of their instruction of Apollos (18, 24–28), whose apostolic work in Corinth Paul mentions in 1 Corinthians 1—4. Luke's brief account of the founding follows the line he has already established: after success in at-

tracting influential persons, hostility from the Jews forces the apostle to turn to the Gentiles. They bring Paul before the Roman proconsul Gallio, who refuses to hear a charge involving Jewish religious law. Gallio's response (v. 14f) reflects what Luke considers to be the ideal response when Christians accused of disturbances, which are internal Jewish affairs, are brought before officials. His reference to Priscilla and Aquila's suffering exile from Rome (18, 2) indicates that he knows that Romans often responded differently to disputes that Christian preaching generated within the Jewish community. Gallio's indifference is demonstrated in "burlesque" fashion— that is, by exaggerated and stereotyped actions— in verse 17. He remains indifferent when they beat Sosthenes, the ruler of the synagogue, before his tribunal.

Third Missionary Journey (18, 24—21, 14)

This section of Acts builds on episodes about the mission in Ephesus, which was the residence of the governor of the province of Asia and the fourth largest city in the empire. Ephesus was also the location of a famous temple of the goddess Artemis, which was one of the wonders of the Hellenistic world. Silver coins from the city depict the temple with the statue of the goddess inside. Paul's confrontation with that cult occupies most of the account of his mission there (19, 8–41). Later Paul delivers his farewell speech to leaders of the church in Ephesus (20, 17–38). Luke's emphasis on Ephesus may have led him to locate two episodes there that seem to come from separate traditions: (a) the instruction of Apollos, who had received only the baptism of John (18, 24–28) and (b) the conferring of the Spirit on persons who had received only the baptism of John (19, 1–7). Luke's account assumes that Priscilla and Aquila have moved to Ephesus from Corinth and that Ephesian Christians urged Apollos to go to Corinth. Luke seems to assume that Apollos and Paul had not met (19, 1), although Paul writes 1 Corinthians from Ephesus or its environs and says that Apollos was unwilling to return to Corinth (1 Cor 16, 8.12). And although Apollos had only received John's baptism, he is not rebaptized. Priscilla and Aquila are able to bring persons into full Christian discipleship. Yet, the disciples of 19, 1–7 have not even heard of the Holy Spirit! Scholars have suggested that this episode would be more appropriate in the area of Syro-Palestine where Jewish baptismal sects would continue to exist well into the third century.

The episode is similar to one in which Peter and John confer the Spirit on Samaritan converts (8, 14–25). It serves two functions in Luke's schema for the expanding mission: (a) it shows that Paul is able to win over Jewish sectarians, and (b) it demonstrates the continuity between the Pauline mission and the activity of the Jerusalem church. He brings persons into the community that the Holy Spirit has been creating through the apostles since Pentecost.

Paul's mission in Ephesus is the last story of Paul's activity that is not shadowed by his impending arrest at Jerusalem. Luke's summary continues the pattern of synagogue preaching followed by withdrawal to a Gentile environment. Miracles draw attention to the new movement. They also demonstrate the power of Christianity to destroy superstition and magical practices among the people (19, 8–20). The success of Christian preaching, however, awakens hostility from persons who exploit the presence of the temple of Artemis. Demetrius's speech (see v. 26) to his fellow silversmiths alludes to the speech of Acts 17, 24f. Christian preaching teaches people that human temples and artifacts do not represent God. As had been the case in earlier conflicts with magicians, fears for the economic loss that would result from accepting the Christian gospel spark the hostility. As in the Gallio case, the local town clerk refuses to become involved. The Christians have not committed any impious acts such as robbing the temple or dishonoring the goddess. Demetrius is the one who is endangering public order by inciting the crowds.

This conclusion seems to represent an ideal rather than reality. As Luke fills out the rest of the journey with brief notices of stops and miracles performed by the apostle (20, 1–16), he makes it appear that Paul left Ephesus of his own volition and that he avoided returning there in order to save time needed to reach Jerusalem by Pentecost (20, 16). Yet the summons to the officials of the church in Ephesus for a farewell meeting at Miletus (20, 17f) suggests that in fact Paul may have been banished from Ephesus. Paul's obscure reference to conflict in Ephesus (see 1 Cor 15, 32a) implies that at one time he suffered imprisonment or punishment there.

Paul's farewell to the Ephesians (20, 17–35) provides the occasion for Luke to reflect on the transition from the generation of the apostles to the church of his own day. The farewell speech of the dying patriarch was an established genre in Hellenistic Jewish writing. The Old Testament contains a farewell speech from Moses to Israel (Dt 29—32). In such speeches, the dying patriarch exhorts his offspring to follow the Law, anticipates their future disobedience (in most cases), and sets before them the example of his own life. Moses also provides for the future leadership of the people by appointing Joshua as his successor. You can see that Luke has incorporated many of these elements in this speech. The Spirit has been warning Paul that he faces imprisonment and hardship in Jerusalem. He holds up his own life as an exemplary model of complete devotion to bearing witness to the gospel no matter what the circumstances. Unlike the pagans, who sought to enrich themselves from the superstitions of the people, Paul has never sought money from his converts. He commends his own example of working at a trade, not only because it frees the apostle and his associates from suspicion of greed but also provides the opportunity to give aid to the weak (v. 35). Thus we find Paul's final word of admonition returning to the example that the earliest Jerusalem community had set. Christians donate their property for support of the poor.

The farewell speech is also the time to look from the ideal of the past into the dangers of the future. Paul warns of divisions even within the ranks of the community's leaders. He admonishes the presbyters and "overseers" (v. 28; see Phil 1, 1), who have charge of the community left behind by the apostles, to watch over themselves as well as the church. They must continue proclaiming the gospel and exhorting others to faith and repentance. In Luke's narrative we have now seen the completion of the apostolic period. Officials from local churches, who are called "elders" or "overseers," must take over the community. These persons have been appointed by apostles and commissioned by imposition of hands (14, 23). In that sense, they appear as successors to the apostles. But just as Joshua could not be another Moses, so they are not replacement apostles. The Spirit that has guided the church throughout the developments of the apostolic period must continue to direct her course.

Paul's dedication to his mission, even in the face of sure suffering, leads him to continue the journey (21, 4). Even the Christian prophet Agabus, whom we know to be reliable because he predicted the famine under Claudius (see 11, 28), warns Paul that in Jerusalem the Jews will bind him and hand him over to the Romans. See what Paul himself wrote to the Romans just before he left for Jerusalem (Rom 15, 31). He was concerned about what he might suffer from unbelievers as well as the fact that the Jewish Christian church might reject the offering that he brings.

Paul's Arrest and Imprisonment at Jerusalem (21, 15—26, 32)

As soon as Paul arrives in Jerusalem, James warns him that devout Jewish Christians suspect Paul of leading Christians who are Jewish away from their ancestral traditions. James proposes that Paul demonstrate his own piety by paying the expenses for some persons who had taken a private vow. Ironically, Paul's participation in these rites leads to his arrest. We have already seen that the charges against him for turning people against the Law and the Temple were anticipated in the story of Stephen's martyrdom. Luke uses the situation of Paul's imprisonment in Jerusalem to provide speeches in which Paul defends and explains his mission. His first speech to the Jerusalem crowd (22, 1–21) points to the extreme piety of his early life. Only the direct intervention of God could change Paul's behavior. Paul refers to his conversion as evidence for God's direction of his life and ministry. This theme is underlined by a second vision of Christ as Paul is praying in the Temple (22, 17–21).

During his imprisonment at Philippi, Paul said nothing about his Roman citizenship until after he had been flogged (16, 37). Here he stops the Roman commander as he is about to interrogate Paul under torture (22, 25–29). Though Paul is able to stall the Sanhedrin by pitting the Pharisees against the Sadducees, the Romans must intervene by moving Paul to Caesarea under heavy guard (Acts 23). With the transfer to Caesarea, Paul is now in Roman hands. However

sympathetically they listen to Paul's preaching, the Roman authorities take no steps to gain his release. Paul's first speech before Felix, the Roman procurator of Judea, defends the Jewish character of his own personal conduct (24, 10–21). He remains in prison through a change in the Roman administration of the province. The Jews hope that the new procurator will turn Paul over to them. Faced with the possibility that he might be tried in Jerusalem, Paul invokes the ultimate privilege of a Roman citizen, the right to be heard by a court in Rome itself (25, 1–12). The Roman procurator repeats the details of Paul's situation to the visiting Jewish king, Herod Agrippa II. Festus, Felix's successor as procurator, clearly understands that Paul has not been charged with any crime under Roman law. At best, the squabble concerns points of Jewish law. Since Agrippa is curious about Paul, Felix arranges for a final speech by the apostle (26, 1–23). Paul defends himself by repeating the circumstances of his life as a devout Jew who was converted by a divine vision which no one could ignore. In this account of Paul's conversion, Luke focuses upon the divine commission to be a missionary to the Gentiles (26,16–18). After the hearing, both Festus and Agrippa agree that Paul is innocent. Luke may be following the pattern set out in Jesus' trial. Pilate and Herod both agree that Jesus is innocent. But Paul cannot be released, since he has demanded a hearing in the imperial court (26, 30–32).

Paul's Journey to Rome (27, 1—28, 31)

We have already seen that the conclusion of Acts, in which Paul is preaching the gospel at Rome, though under house arrest (28, 17–31), brings Luke's plot to a climax. The gospel has reached the capital of the civilized world. Luke's account of how Paul came to Rome makes use of another type of ancient adventure story, the sea voyage. Such voyages frequently included descriptions of how the hero escaped from shipwreck, pirates, and other such dangers. The story of Paul's journey is told with all the high drama of such tales. During the vicious storm that destroys the ship and has the survivors washed up on the beach at Malta, Paul demonstrates his own confidence in God and superiority to the fears of the ship's crew. Paul is even able to celebrate a meal of bread, which he has blessed (27, 35f). The wording reminds Christians of the Eucharist (note to 27, 35). It is impossible to sail across the Mediterranean in winter, so the group is forced to stay on Malta. The episode associated with that stay includes the drama of native peoples watching the shipwrecked party. When Paul is unharmed by a poisonous snake, they conclude that he must be a god (28, 3–6). Paul wins more friends on the island by healing the sick, and they are provided with everything needed to continue the journey (vv. 7–10). Although clearly narrated with an eye toward entertaining the reader, the Malta story also points out that God will provide whatever is necessary for the apostle to fulfill his mission. The superstitious pagans had ignored Paul's prophetic warning that attempting to sail so close to winter would destroy both ship and cargo. The island natives thought that the snake was divine punishment for some evil Paul had committed until they saw that he escaped unharmed. In each case, the apostle comes through the threat to his life because he places all of his trust in the Lord.

Things We Have Learned from Acts

Now that we have finished reading through Acts, we should take some time to reflect on the impact of the narrative as a whole. Luke has made striking use of traditions he inherited about the apostles—a plan of salvation history and the art of storytelling to instruct us about the development of God's plan of salvation in the apostolic age.

Judaism Is the Inherited Tradition of the Church

The church developed according to a divine plan of salvation, which remains rooted in the experiences of Israel. When God led the church to turn toward the Gentiles, this heritage was not forgotten although it was no longer necessary for a person to be culturally and legally a Jew in order to experience salvation.

God Seeks the Salvation of All the Peoples on Earth

Acts shows us that the apostles had to venture beyond their own Jewish culture in order to take the gospel to the ends of the earth. Though they found this task difficult, since it often resulted in hostility from fellow Jews, all the apostles accepted this growth toward becoming a truly universal church as an expression of God's will. The task is not over. The church still must venture into other lands and cultures to fulfill the mission that is hers until the end of time: to bear witness to the gospel everywhere.

The Church Is a Spirit-Guided Institution

You will notice that in Acts the Spirit works in and through the official leaders and structures of the community. Developments like the admission of Gentiles were clearly difficult adjustments, but we see that the leaders of the community in Jerusalem eventually come to express what is the will of God. Furthermore, as the apostle Paul leaves the scene, he has established "elders" or "overseers" in his churches. It is necessary that persons be designated as leaders now that the apostolic age has passed. Although many people think that an institution can never be the vehicle for the Spirit, Acts insists that the church is such a vehicle.

Christians Must Be Willing to Suffer for the Gospel

Since the apostles overcome the sufferings and imprisonments they face, we may forget how relentless the onset of hostility is. No form of suffering causes any of the apostles to stray from the mission given by God and cease to proclaim the gospel. There is no instance in which preaching the gospel does not awaken some form of resistance.

The Christian Fellowship Has Special Marks of Its Identity

Luke has presented us with ideal pictures of what the church should be. We see the harmonious gathering of diverse peoples for prayer, preaching by the apostles, and community meals. We also see a community in which concern for the weak and needy is one of the most important parts of its communal life.

The Church Calls People to Religious Conversion

Because the church preaches religious conversion, it comes into conflict with all forms of pseudo-religion and superstition. Magical practices have no place in Christian life, nor do movements that use the religious sentiments of the masses to collect money from those who are taken in by the propaganda of such false cults. Christians give their resources to help those in need. They speak out against any false idea of God that would require buildings and other material goods for God or God's servants. Christians remain loyal to the basic institutions of their society, even when those institutions seem to be used against them by persons who do not like the criticism of false beliefs and behavior that comes from the gospel.

P.P.

FURTHER READING

Barrett, C. K. *The Acts of the Apostles.* Vol. 1: *Preliminary Introduction and Commentary on Acts 1–14;* Vol. 2: *Introduction and Commentary on Acts 15–28.* International Critical Commentary. Edinburgh: T. & T. Clark, 1994, 1998.

Fitzmyer, J. A. *The Acts of the Apostles.* Anchor Bible 31. New York: Doubleday, 1998.

Johnson, L. T. *The Acts of the Apostles.* Sacra Pagina 5. Collegeville, MN: Liturgical Press/Michael Glazier, 1992.

Klauck, Hans-Josef. *Magic and Paganism in Early Christianity: The World of the Acts of the Apostles.* Minneapolis: Fortress, 2003.

PAUL AND HIS WRITINGS

CAROLYN OSIEK

According to Acts, Paul was born in Tarsus, a city on the eastern end of the Mediterranean Sea, in what is now Turkey, around AD 10. He was a Roman citizen from birth, a status that carried certain privileges. He was also, according to Acts, a student of Gamaliel, a renowned rabbi, and a Pharisee, that is, a member of a strictly observant Jewish party. His own writings indicate that he was well educated in the Greek language and in Pharisaic methods of biblical interpretation. Both Paul and Acts say that he was so zealous for the Jewish Law before his conversion that he persecuted those who, he believed, had strayed from the Law by believing that Jesus was the Christ. During this earlier part of the sketch of Paul's life in Acts, he is called by his Jewish name, Saul. When in the narrative he begins to encounter the Roman world (13, 9), Luke calls him by his Roman name, Paul.

After experiencing a revelation of the Risen Christ from God, however, Paul himself joined these followers of "the Way" as a young adult, about AD 34. He firmly believed that his conversion included a call to preach the Christian message of salvation to all people, including Gentiles. Paul spent the rest of his life, about thirty years, in pursuit of this mission. After three years in Arabia and a brief visit to Jerusalem, he embarked on his missionary career. After some years working in the Eastern Mediterranean area as far west as Greece, he visited Jerusalem to deliver relief funds collected in Asia Minor and Greece. He then intended to visit Rome and Spain, but in Jerusalem he met with increasing opposition from some Jewish leaders and was arrested and brought to Rome around AD 60. Between AD 48 and his death around AD 62, Paul wrote letters to communities with which he had worked, answering their questions and preaching the gospel as he understood it to have been revealed to him.

Sources

We learn about Paul's life from his own letters and from Luke's account in the Acts of the Apostles (cf. Acts 9, 1–30; 11, 1—28, 31). There are some discrepancies between what Paul says and what Luke records about certain incidents of Paul's career: for example, Luke and Paul do not agree about whether the Council of Jerusalem, around AD 50, stipulated that the Gentiles should keep some aspects of the Jewish Law (see Acts 15 and Galatians 2, 1–10). We must remember that when Luke writes about Paul's life, his account is a secondary source: it was written more than a generation after Paul (about AD 85), at a time when the major issue of non-Jewish converts was no longer as pressing. Luke minimizes the tensions involved in integrating the Gentiles into the church.

The Epistles of Paul

There are thirteen letters or epistles ascribed to Paul, but most commentators recognize only seven of these as definitely written by the apostle; the others are attributed to disciples of Paul. The seven letters certainly written by Paul himself are Romans, 1 and 2 Corinthians, Galatians, Philippians, 1 Thessalonians, and Philemon. The remaining six letters (that is, Ephesians, Colossians, 2 Thessalonians, 1 and 2 Timothy, and Titus) are often called "Deutero-Pauline." Among the latter group, the Pauline authorship of 2 Thessalonians and Colossians is most disputed. For various reasons commentators believe that these six letters were not actually written by Paul but instead were written by later Christians familiar with his teachings. Disciples could have claimed to be writing in Paul's name in order to gain authority for their own adaptations of his teaching, an accepted practice among the ancients. In the New Testament, the Pauline writings are arranged in two groups: first, letters to communities; second, letters to individuals. Within each group they run roughly from the longest to the shortest. The letters are not arranged in the order in which they were written.

Letters and Epistles

Paul's letters follow the fairly simple structure of a letter in Greek or Roman culture. Such letters were not placed in envelopes, so the address is given right at the start. Then follows the body of the letter; finally, the conclusion contains personal greetings and instructions. Some scholars have suggested a distinction between more formal, systematic "epistles" and informal "letters." In this way of thinking, Romans would be an example of a formal epistle, whereas Philemon or Titus would be examples of an informal letter. Even some of those letters supposedly written to individuals may really be formal "epistles" intended for wider circulation. Many interpreters have also noted a fundamental structure discernible in many of Paul's writings, but most clearly in Romans. Paul first outlines his most basic teachings in a section sometimes called the doctrinal or "indicative" part. This is followed by an application of these teachings in Paul's exhortations to the community, a section called the "imperative" or "parenetical" (that is, exhortatory) part of the body of the letter.

The Apostle and His Gospel

Much of the Christian vocabulary we have become so familiar with and associate with the ministry of Jesus actually originated with Paul. For example, Paul was, as far as we know, the first to coin a Christian meaning for the words *apostle, gospel, charism, ministry,* and many doctrinal phrases such as "justification by faith." As the first Christian writer, Paul began to develop specifically Christian terminology, even though many of the terms he uses will have roots in Judaism, or other meanings in secular Greek.

Paul's writings predate any of our written Gospels. Paul is the first to speak about preaching the gospel, although he does not conceive this as a story about the life and ministry of Jesus. The idea of the gospel, which appears even in the Old Testament (see, for example, Is 61, 1–2, "glad tidings") means the "good news." For Paul this is the message of salvation now accessible to all through faith in Jesus Christ. In Romans, Paul describes the gospel as the "power of God" to save all who believe (Rom 1, 16). Thus, Paul does not think of the gospel as a story of the events in Jesus' life, nor even as a set of beliefs about Jesus. Rather, the gospel is the "good news" that all who believe in Jesus are already saved.

Paul rarely speaks of any actions or words of Jesus during his lifetime. Rather, he focuses on God's power, working through the death and resurrection of Jesus, to save Jews and Greeks (that is, all people) alike. While reading Paul it is well to remember that, for him, the term *gospel* means the proclamation of faith in God's forgiveness or the realization in human life of the "good news" that Jesus Christ has come to bring salvation to all people.

In his writings, Paul usually identifies himself as an apostle (Rom 1, 1; 11, 13; 1 Cor 1, 1; 4, 9; 9, 1f.5; 15, 9; 2 Cor 1, 1; 11, 5.13; 12, 11.12; and so on). The term *apostle* literally means "one sent," who represents the sender and is entrusted with the sender's authority and message. God is the source of Paul's apostleship.

The Letters in Circulation

The apostle's authority was in his words and example. It became real when the community as a whole discerned Paul's meaning and decided on the actions, which they as believers should derive from Paul's words. In his letters, Paul teaches, exhorts, encourages, and corrects. The communities reverenced his instructions, reading and preserving them. They circulated these letters, sharing them with other communities. In this way the letters eventually gained the authority of Christian Scriptures as the communities were increasingly strengthened, formed, and informed by a common tradition. Most people in Pauline communities probably could not read, so a reader would read Paul's letter aloud to the assembly of believers. There they reflected together on its contents. From Paul's writings we can get a picture of how the early church operated, how it worshipped and governed itself, and how it grew.

ROMANS

[see pages 1493–1515 of the New Testament]

Before Beginning . . .

The placement of Romans at the beginning of the New Testament letters is appropriate not only because it is the longest of Paul's letters but also because it may very well be his most important work. Romans has always held a special place among Paul's writings. Especially since the time of the Protestant Reformation in the sixteenth century, the importance of the doctrine of "justification by faith," which Paul develops in Romans (and, in a more succinct version, in Galatians) has been recognized by Catholics and Protestants alike as one of the most significant teachings of Paul and, in fact, of Christianity.

Paul and the Roman Christians

The Roman Christian community must have been fairly large by the time of Paul's arrival there. It is estimated that the Jewish community of Rome in the early first century numbered 50,000. Among Christians, it seems from Paul's letter that there were both Jews and Gentiles. Some of the information given in chapter 16 indicates quite a few house churches. Of course, Paul did not intend to arrive in Rome as a prisoner but as a free missionary. Yet according to the account in Acts, he arrived not the way he intended, but rather under arrest.

Several unique characteristics of Romans distinguish this letter from the other writings of Paul. In this letter, Paul addresses a church he has not founded. He writes to introduce himself and his gospel and to seek the Roman community's acceptance and help. Before fulfilling his desire to come to Rome on the way to Spain (cf. Rom 15, 22–33), Paul must first deliver the collection of money from the Gentile churches for the "poor among the holy ones in Jerusalem" (15, 26), who have been suffering from a famine. When these funds are delivered, his sights will be set for Rome.

So it is that both the Jewish mission field represented by the church in Jerusalem and the open-ended Gentile mission represented by Rome and Spain are on Paul's mind as he writes this letter. Paul is concerned about unity among Christians. Although he has not founded the Roman church, he refers to the common faith he shares with believers there. He stresses the common fund of teaching from which both he and they draw. The issues of community in faith and of reconciliation permeate all of Romans and contribute to its perennial appeal to believers of every age.

Except for chapter 16, which may have been added later (cf. below, our commentary on this chapter, and the notes of the NAB), Romans lacks the personal tone characteristic of most of Paul's letters. Some manuscripts omit the words "in Rome" in 1, 7 and 15. Without this designation and the greetings of chapter 16, Romans might be considered as a circular letter, a general development of Paul's most basic theological ideas. In Romans, Paul expounds upon universal salvation, upon the notion of justification by faith, and on the relationship between Israel and the church as transformed by Christ. These are some of the most important and generally applicable aspects of all of Paul's theology. The general nature and universal applicability of Romans contribute to its wide appeal as an introduction to Paul.

Romans as "Diatribe"

More than any other Pauline writing, Romans is like a formal treatise, a summary of Paul's theology that serves both as a self-introduction to a community not yet personally acquainted with Paul and as a summary for the message Paul preaches. Even though Romans has the formal features of an epistle, it can also be understood as a philosophical diatribe, a written exposé that tries to anticipate real or supposed objections or rebuttal. The diatribe, used by some ancient philosophers in teaching and writing, often interjected traces of dialogue in order to answer questions expected of opponents. For example, Paul brings his arguments forward by interspersing throughout Romans such rhetorical questions as "What advantage is there then in being a Jew?" (3, 1) or "Well, then, are we better off?" (3, 9) or "What then can we say that Abraham found, our ancestor according to the flesh?" (4, 1). Thus, in comparison to Paul's other works, Romans is structured more as a philosophical treatise. Most of the other letters reflect more the give and take of real dialogue among people actually working and interacting together.

Working through Romans

The typical Greco-Roman letter form applied to Romans yields the following divisions: the *address,* consisting of a greeting and a thanksgiving, is contained in Rom 1, 1–15; the *body* of the letter comprises 1, 16—15, 13. It contains the essential message of Paul, basically following what has helpfully been called the "indicative-imperative" structure (see "Letters and Epistles," RG 440). The *conclusion* in 15, 14—16, 27 contains Paul's travelogue, his personal greetings, and a final doxology.

A working outline of Romans follows:

  I. The Address (Rom 1, 1–15)
 II. The Body of the Letter (1, 16–15, 13)
    A. The Theme; the "Indicative" (1, 16–17)
    B. The Common Predicament of Gentiles and Jews (1, 18—3, 20)
    C. Central Declaration of Justification by Faith (3, 21–31)
    D. Abraham, Model of Faith (4, 1–25)
    E. The Two Adams (5, 1–21)
    F. A Preliminary "Imperative" (6, 1–23)
    G. Life without the Spirit (7, 1–25)
    H. Life in the Spirit (8, 1–39)
    I. But What of Israel? (9, 1—11, 36)
    J. The Final "Imperative" (12, 1—15, 13)
III. Conclusion (15, 14—16, 27)

Reading through Romans

The Address (1, 1–15)

The address typically includes greetings and a thanksgiving. The greeting of Romans, identifying the sender, Paul, and his addressees, is an elaboration of the standard form of Greco-Roman letters (see note 1, 1–7, p. 1494, and "Letters and Epistles," RG 440). Here and in

some other letters, notably Philippians, Paul has woven this brief feature into an extended prayer. In no other authentic Pauline letter besides Romans does Paul write in his name alone. He usually has with him some co-worker known to the recipients. In chapter 16, this is certainly the case. But even in Romans, Paul is not entirely independent. He needs the Romans' acceptance. He is grateful for their perseverance, and he looks forward to being strengthened by them through their common faith (1, 11). Paul says that although he is personally unknown to the Romans, the gospel or Christian message he preaches is the same as that which they have received from other Christian missionaries.

Although Paul usually refers to his addressees as "the church in _____," he does not use the term "church" in the address of Romans. But he does remind the Roman Christians of their vocation to holiness. In developing a Christian terminology in the Greek language, Paul will consistently draw upon images and phrases that appear in the Hebrew Scriptures. An example is Paul's description of the believing community as holy, as saints, called and sanctified by God (for instance, 1 Cor 1, 2). Israel is a "kingdom of priests, a holy nation," according to Exodus 19, 6. The Law sets Israel apart, making it distinct from its neighbors because it has a covenant relationship with God. This holiness has nothing to do with the virtue of the members but arises from the fact of God's call. Their personal holiness is then a response to that call.

The Body of the Letter (1, 16—15, 13)

The Theme (1, 16–17)

Romans 1, 16–17 states the theme. In the chapters that follow, the gospel is described as the power of God for universal salvation. This theme is developed in both its positive and negative implications. Positively, Paul insists that faith is accessible to all through Christ. But Paul also realizes some negative implications, even of his belief that all are saved in Christ. For example, it is clear that all have sinned and are in need of salvation. The emphasis on universal sinfulness deserving of God's wrath is the negative pole of the theme of Romans. There is no human means of achieving salvation for ourselves; it must be given.

Note that for Paul the starting point is not that all have sinned but rather that all have been saved. This is the conviction of faith. Paul considers sin to be an illustration of the universal need for salvation. This explains why Paul's hope, eloquently expressed especially in chapters 5, 8, and 15, is so deep and certain. No human sin is sufficient to separate us from the love of God that saves us.

Paul's Fundamental Conviction

The Greek words that we translate "just," "justice," "justify," and "righteousness" are all derived from the same root word, *dikaios* (just), *dikaiosyn* (justice, righteousness, or justification). Even more important, for Paul the concepts are closely linked. He connects the justice of God with God's power and will to "justify" all people, that is, to regard them as just.

The Scriptures show that God's justice is revealed, that is, it cannot be completely attained through human effort or study. Isaiah reminds us that God's thoughts are not human thoughts, and God's ways not our ways (see Is 55, 7–8). Yet the Scriptures also tell us that we are to be just, that we must act in imitation of God, that we are to walk blamelessly before God and be perfect (see Gn 17, 1; Hos 6, 6). Thus, justice is not completely foreign to us. The God-fearing Israelite seeks to act justly, that is, in ways that are acceptable to God and in accord with God's covenant. These ways are also revealed through the Jewish Torah ("instruction") or Law. The Torah was handed down from Moses and interpreted throughout the history of the Jewish people, who reverenced it as the revealed will of God. So, for example, Abraham in Genesis (Gn 15, 6) and Joseph in the infancy narrative (Mt 1, 19) are described as "righteous" *(dikaios)* men.

It is not that acting justly or keeping the Law earns salvation or God's approval, but rather the opposite. The covenant is God's gift to Israel. Israel's response is to keep the Law. The Jewish person seeking justice is enjoined to study and to follow the Torah or the instruction of God. In the covenant is the hope of being justified, that is, "made just" in God's sight. Thus, for the Old Testament as for Paul, the related terms "justice," "just," and "justified" all originate in God, who reveals how we are to act and judges us accordingly. Although all people are sinners, Jew-

ish theology teaches that we may expect to learn the way of justice through a faithful following of the Law in all things. This is the background for Paul's understanding of justification through Jesus Christ.

There are two main ideas that we must understand if we are to grasp the argument about justification that Paul puts forth in Romans and in some of his other writings. The first is the meaning for him of trying to attain justification or salvation by obeying the Law. (This is dealt with particularly in chapter 3 of his Letter to the Galatians; see the Reading Guide to Galatians.) The second main idea pertains to Paul's explanation of how the Gentiles, or those who do not have the Law, are justified.

First, for Paul, justification through the works of the Law is a false hope for several reasons. The idea that the Law held the key to justification was the position of the Jews who did not become Christians as well as of the Christian-Jewish group, led by Peter and James, who constituted the majority of the church when Paul began his mission. The theological challenge Paul faces is that his experience of the Risen Christ and his mission to preach that justification is available to all, both Jews who have the Law and the Gentiles who do not, convinced Paul that justification is an act of God, given freely to all who believe. Like his Jewish contemporaries, Paul himself was zealous for the Law (cf. Rom 10, 1–3; Phil 3, 3–7; Gal 1, 11–14), but now his experience has taught him that this is not the way to go. Now in his zeal to win people over to the way he is convinced is right, Paul argues that the Law is impossible to keep and can only lead to frustration and self-righteousness. This caricature of the Law must be understood as rhetorical attempts to persuade Gentiles attracted by Law observance to his point of view.

Second, justification through the Law is insufficient because it excludes the Gentiles, who, as Paul has described the situation in Romans 1, 18—3, 31, are in the same sinful predicament as the Jews. But both Abraham and Christ show that the Gentiles, no less than the Jews, are now justified through faith. According to the Law, Jesus was condemned to death. But God overturned the Law's verdict in raising Jesus to life (see Gal 3, 10–14). Thus, for Paul, the Law has been superseded by the death and resurrection of Jesus.

As a consequence of this, the Gentiles are now included among the justified. By accepting Jesus' gift of justification, and consequently living in accord with God's will, Jews and Gentiles both are saved. Following the just requirements of the Law or the precepts of the church is not a *prerequisite* for but a *result of being justified.*

Paul understands justification as already having taken place through the death and resurrection of Christ. Salvation is in the future, promised to those who believe in Christ and live according to this belief. As Paul himself says it, "Indeed, if, while we were enemies, we were reconciled to God through the death of his Son, how much more, once reconciled, will we be saved by his life" (Rom 5, 10).

We must also comprehend Paul's idea of faith in order to understand the argument of Romans. It may seem that he is simply replacing one human action, obedience to the Law, with another human action, faith in Jesus Christ. But for Paul faith is trust: the belief that it is God's power, not our own, and our reliance on God, not on our own abilities, that saves us. Paul saw the obvious danger for sinful people: the danger that they would continue in their wrong behavior and so close themselves off from God forever. But Paul also saw the danger for those people who seemed moral and upright: the danger that they would believe God was forced to save them because they had earned their way into God's love.

For Paul, this thinking is a fatal mistake. It assumes that we can manipulate God by our actions. Paul breaks through this misunderstanding by his assertion of the necessity of faith. Faith is our acknowledgment that it is God's power that saves us, not our own efforts; that we are helpless, in that we are all sinners; and that we can trust in God.

We should note that Paul begins with the affirmation of faith in God's work of salvation to which all have access in Christ. He does not start with the premise of defeat nor emphasize that each person must individually become convicted of sin. Rather, Paul stresses first the goodness and power of God to save, and then tries to demonstrate the universal need for salvation to be given.

Paul uses terms such as "redeem" and "justify" and "reconcile" in relationship to one another and sometimes almost interchangeably

(see Rom 5, 9–11 and discussion on that passage below). These terms originally belonged to the world of finance; for Paul they appropriately illustrate the economy of salvation. The "debit" columns of sin and guilt and punishment are converted by God into the "credit" columns of forgiveness, redemption, and reconciliation. Through faith we are reconciled to God and to one another. We are redeemed by the blood of Christ, and our sins are forgiven.

Paul came to believe that the revelation of the Law was fulfilled and superseded by the death-resurrection of Christ. In Romans, Paul will develop a dichotomy between what was "formerly" and what is "now." For Paul, God's justice is only fully revealed in Jesus. The emphasis on "now" also implies an emphasis on the accessibility of God's justice to all through faith. The Law (or Torah) formerly divided humanity into "Jews and Gentiles," the latter not sharing in the promise represented by the Law. This division is overcome, and all now have equal access to God's revelation of justice expressed in Christ.

The Common Predicament of Gentiles and Jews (1, 18—3, 20)

Having stated his conviction that the gospel is God's power to save all people through faith (1, 1–16f), Paul proceeds to demonstrate the need of all for salvation. Universal sin illustrates this need. Paul shows that "all," both Gentiles and Jews, have sinned and incurred the wrath of God. The "wrath of God" is being revealed in that the Gentiles are experiencing disastrous consequences of their own behavior (Rom 1, 18–32). The wrath of God is an image borrowed from the Old Testament prophets (see Is 9, 8–12; 10, 5; Jer 50, 11–17; Ez 5, 13; 36, 5–6). It depicts God's rejection or "abandonment" (Rom 1, 24.26.28) of people to their own sin. The story of Saul's disobedience to God in 1 Samuel 15 dramatizes this dynamic: from the moment when God no longer accepts Saul's kingship, Saul's downfall is certain.

Although the Gentiles *could* know God through creation, the evidence of their godless lives means that they have rejected knowledge of God. Belief in God is no mere intellectual affair but involves a conversion to "the living and true God" (see 1 Thes 1, 9) expressed in a virtuous life. Paul adopts the Old Testament notion of the

relationship between idolatry and immorality evident among the pagans. (But see the NAB note
on 1, 18–32 that cautions that the lives of many
in the Greco-Roman culture could serve as models for Christians today.) Paul speaks in general-
ities here, trying first to indict the Gentiles (1,
18–31) and later (in 2, 1—3, 9) the Jews, in an effort to show the effects of universal sin and the
need of all humanity for God's salvation.

Central Declaration of Justification by Faith (3, 21–31)

Paul summarizes his previous demonstration of
universal sinfulness (3, 23) but prefaces it with
the way out, accomplished by God through
Christ, then makes the central assertion: we are
justified by faith apart from the works of the Law
(3, 28). He emphasizes that God's just judgment
comes upon all people, for God shows no partiality (2, 11; see also Dt 10, 17; 2 Chr 19, 7; Sir
35, 12f; Acts 10, 34; Gal 2, 6; Eph 6, 9; Col 3,
2.5; 1 Pt 1, 17). Having indicated that the Gentiles are sinners, Paul turns to concentrate
throughout Rom 2, 1—3, 20 on the Jews. Here
Paul adopts the language of the prophets, who
not only charged sinfulness to the pagans but
also accused the Jews of having "a stubborn and
impenitent heart."

Abraham, Model of Faith (4, 1–25)

For Paul, Abraham is a type of Christ; that is,
Abraham follows the pattern of Christ. Adam
and Moses, on the other hand, are antitypes—
reverse patterns. For Jews, circumcision, the ritual removal of the foreskin of the penis of infant
boys, symbolizes the individual's membership
in the people of God, and therefore the individual's acceptance of God's law and teaching.
Since Abraham was justified before his circumcision, he was justified independently of the
Law. Therefore Abraham is the ancestor of both
Jews and Gentiles. Abraham's example illustrates the theme of Romans: all have access now
to salvation through faith. (For further discussion
of the image of Abraham for Paul, see the Reading Guide to Galatians.)

The Two Adams (5, 1–21)

In chapter 5 Paul contrasts Christ's saving actions (that is, his death and resurrection) with the
devastating consequences of the sin of the first

Adam. By the time of Paul, it was generally understood that the first human beings were created
immortal (Wis 2, 23f) but that their sin brought
death into the world. Subsequent generations
continue the sentence of death by continuing to
sin (Rom 5, 12). Adam represents all people under sin with its curse of death. But Adam is also
a figure drawing out God's promise of redemption. The writer of Genesis portrays the situation
of Adam as obviously in need of some divine action: even before the curse for sin is pronounced
in Genesis 3, 16–19, God promises to save the
human family in the end (Gn 3, 15). The early
church Fathers, above all Augustine, used these
passages, especially Romans 5, 12, as a basis for
description of the devastating effects of original
sin, although Paul does not use this terminology.
Rather, he argues that if the first sin had such
widespread effects that since Adam all people
have been under its influence, how much more
effective and powerful is the gift of salvation
won through Jesus Christ. That gift is called
grace, which brings eternal life (5, 21). The
mode of argument here is a familiar rhetorical
construction: from lesser to greater. If so much
damage was caused by the first human being,
Adam, how much greater is the grace and redemption won by the ultimate human being,
Christ.

Paul insists that Christ's death and resurrection have affected all of human history. His argument is basically this: if the sin of Adam was so
far reaching, how much more encompassing is
the gift of God in Christ for all. Paul's thinking is
at the basis of the church's ecstatic thanksgiving,
"O happy fault that has merited so great a redeemer!" The Roman liturgy recalls this prayer
during the Easter Vigil each year in the recitation
of the *Exsultet*.

Salvation is a reality that Paul describes here
and elsewhere (see 1 Cor 6, 11; 2 Cor 5, 10–15;
10, 5–10), using multiple terms like reconciliation, redemption, justification, and sanctification. The verb "to save" refers to God's intervening action when human beings are in need. It
connotes actual, sometimes physical, rescue as
well as deliverance in spiritual distress. The Old
Testament often refers to God as "Savior." Reference to God's saving action is one of the
Bible's most frequent ways of referring to God,
appearing literally hundreds of times. In the New

Testament this term is often used in connection with Jesus. The disciples, for example, prayed "Lord, save us" (for example, Mt 8, 25). Paul assumes we are familiar with the long Old Testament tradition of God's saving actions on behalf of people. But Paul, in relating God's action to the death and resurrection of Christ, gives a new emphasis in the theology of salvation or "soteriology." Many scholars point out that all of Paul's Christology or thinking about Christ is really a soteriology or doctrine of how God saves through Christ.

A Preliminary "Imperative" (6, 1–23)

Paul's view of humankind, that is, his theological anthropology, is evident in this chapter. He considers all people to be under some dominant influence, living either for God under grace or living for sin. This is a different perspective from our contemporary one that considers human freedom as an autonomous, absolute ideal. For Paul, freedom is related to life for God (6, 10) in contrast with slavery to sin (6, 6). By means of the opposites of death and life, Paul contrasts the former condition of sin and death to the new life of freedom won by Christ and obtained by the believer through baptism.

The term *baptism* means "immersion," and Paul plays on this original sense even as he has the initiatory rite in view. He coins several expressions in chapter 6, compounding verbs with the prefix *syn*—(meaning "with") that signify believers' solidarity with Christ. We have "died with" him and are "buried with" him; therefore we will be "raised with" him and now "live with" him. This incorporation into the death-resurrection of Christ by means of baptism necessarily has implications for the moral life. As a result of this incorporation, we "walk" (a term designating moral living) in the newness of life (6, 4). Paul will postpone a fuller discussion of the implications of this "newness of life" until chapters 12 through 15.

Life without the Spirit (7, 1–25)

The major part of chapter 7 follows the style of a diatribe (see the NAB notes on chapter 7 and RG 441). Paul anticipates the objections of real or imaginary opponents in a kind of dialogue designed to present his own ideas in an orderly fashion. The most important aspects of Paul's argument are three. First, the Christian views the Law

differently now, having been freed from its service (Paul says "bondage") by participation in the death of Christ. Second, the function of the Law is to specify what is sinful. Thus the Law did not encourage grace or freedom but only identified sin. Third, anticipating an objection that the Law is therefore sin, Paul responds emphatically, "No!" Yet knowledge of what is good does not enable us to do what is good. The Law is one more factor, then, in the judgment against humanity, convicting all of sin. The Law concurs with human conscience, judging us as sinners. This is the meaning of the expression, "the good that I want to do I avoid and the evil I wish to avoid I do" (see 7, 19–21). But it is important to realize that his statements about this unhappy predicament are rhetorical, not autobiographical. They are not expressions of his personal conscience but of the situation of humanity without God.

Life in the Spirit (8, 1–39)

Chapter 8 celebrates the message of salvation. "There is no condemnation for those who are in Christ Jesus" (8, 1). "[Nothing can] separate us from the love of God in Christ Jesus our Lord" (8, 38f). Nowhere is Paul's understanding of the role of the Spirit more eloquently expressed than here. Paul begins chapter 8 with a consideration of the opposition between the flesh and the spirit. He often tries to illustrate his meaning by opposing two poles of thought. This is a way of showing the mutually exclusive categories of sin and death versus grace and life. Paul adapts the Greek notion of the *flesh* in order to express the sinful condition of humanity before grace. In the Greek philosophical tradition, flesh, like spirit, had several connotations. The flesh means, of course, that which pertains to the body. But it can also mean the inferior aspect of human existence, whatever in human life is weak or limited. For the Greeks, the flesh referred to what they regarded as baser desires, which for them included sensual and sexual instincts. The flesh is mortal and must be controlled by the spirit (that is, the mind and will), which in Greek thought is immortal. Paul adapts this notion to sometimes speak of the flesh as the moral equivalent of sin. For Paul, however, sins of the flesh include not just bodily sins, such as gluttony, but also spiritual sins, such as pride. Drawing on the same tradition, Paul uses the term *spirit* to refer to the new life accessible to all through Christ. In stressing the life of the spirit, Paul contrasts the present salvation with the past that was characterized by sin, death, and slavery to the dictates of the flesh.

The Holy Spirit is an advocate, coming to our aid and strengthening us. Like the Israelites in Egypt, we formerly could only groan in the suffering and weakness caused by sin. The Spirit converts our incoherent cries into a prayer that recognizes God as Father and ourselves as children of God. Thus through the Spirit we are liberated from slavery to sin and enabled to pray as the children of God, saying *Abba* (8, 15). From Paul's use of this prayer, we can assume that he is indirectly referring to the Gospel tradition that tells us that Jesus himself addressed God as "*Abba*, Father" (Mk 14, 36). We are confident, too, that the suffering we experience and witness is as nothing compared to the glory that is to come. All creation shared in the sin of Adam and groans with humanity in its suffering. Now all creation awaits the revelation of the children of God (8, 20–25).

At the end of chapter 8, Paul exclaims that nothing can separate us from the love of God. But he goes on to acknowledge in chapters 9 through 11 that the Jewish rejection of the Christian message is a challenge to this belief. Some may say that now God has run out of patience with Israel. But if Israel's rejection of Christ limits God's fidelity to the covenant and God's justice, what does that mean not only for Israel but for the Christian church, which is adopting the prerogatives of Israel? Has God had a change of mind? These are some of the questions Paul puzzles out in these chapters in a remarkable review of the history of salvation.

But What of Israel? (9, 1—11, 36)

The form of this three-chapter unit is a philosophical diatribe. Paul responds to anticipated questions or challenges in the form of an artificial dialogue. In the course of developing his views, he makes abundant use of the Old Testament. Before dealing with some ethical conclusions to the doctrines in chapters 12 through 15, Paul senses the necessity of taking up this personally painful question about God's fidelity to the Jews. Israel's rejection of Christ was clearly a problem not only for Paul but also for the early church. Paul's consideration of this question

properly belongs with the doctrinal development of Romans.

Paul's summary of the privileges of Israel in Romans 9, 1–5 prompts him to redefine the term *Israel* in chapters 9 through 11. Israel is not a mere ethnic or historical reality, but one that always had theological connotations. The Jewish Scriptures show, Paul argued, that "not all who are of Israel are Israel" (9, 6). The element of divine choice was operating throughout Jewish history, illustrating that God is free to show mercy as God wishes. Not all are children of Abraham simply because they descended from him, as the preference for Isaac over Ishmael shows (see 9, 7–9; Gal 4, 22–31). God chose Jacob over Esau (Rom 9, 10–13). God hardens some, as in the case of Pharaoh; but divine mercy is shown to Moses and the Hebrews in Egypt (9, 15–17). Paul also cites examples from the prophets, especially Jeremiah, Hosea, and Isaiah to support God's freedom to choose. For Paul, God's mercy is God's justice. Paul carefully builds his arguments to show how God is now including the Gentiles among the new "Israel of God" (Gal 6, 16).

Paul begins chapter 10, as he had chapter 9, with a defense of his kinspeople. He testifies to Jewish zeal in pursuit of the Law as he himself was zealous for the Law prior to his faith in Christ (see Gal 1, 14). But as "end of the law" (Rom 10, 4), Christ brings justification for all who believe. Thus Christ renders the Law useless and eliminates the differences between Jew and Gentile. To support his assertion that Christ is the end of the Law, Paul develops an explanation of Scripture in the style of a Jewish *midrash* or "running commentary." Paul applies the Old Testament to Christ and so gives an example of how the "law and the prophets testify" to the righteousness given by God in Christ (cf. Rom 3, 2ff). Paul argued that there is only one God of Jews and Gentiles in Romans 3, 21–31. Similarly, here in chapter 10, Paul says that there is only one Lord over all and accessible to all who call upon him. That Lord is Christ. Near the end of the chapter, in 10, 14–21, Paul echoes the traditional prophetic denunciation of Israel who alone is responsible for her infidelity. But God continues to reach out to a "disobedient people" (10, 21).

God's fidelity, proven in the past and present

(chapters 9 and 10) will ultimately be for the salvation of "all Israel" in the future (Rom 11). God has not finally abandoned Israel since a remnant remains faithful to God as a sign of the ultimate salvation of "all Israel" (Rom 11, 26). Paul cautions the Gentiles, included by the action of Christ into "all Israel," to remember that it is only by grace that they are saved. This is a mystery revealing God's infinite mercy. The power of God is the divine compassion by which all are enfolded into the salvation of "all Israel."

The Final "Imperative" (12, 1—15, 13)

Paul's ethical conclusions apply his teaching, and form the "imperative" or "parenetic," exhortatory part of the letter. This can be subdivided into consideration of the church and the world (12, 1—13, 14) and a call for reconciliation and unity (14, 1—15, 13). Romans 12, 1–2 has been called the heart of Pauline ethics. Here Christians, who do not yet have a sacrificial ritual like most of their neighbors in their temples and like the Jews in Jerusalem, learn that their lives are their living sacrifice, purifying them to be able to live not in conformity to the world (seen as being in opposition to God), but with transformed understanding. In describing the Christian community, Paul adapts the image of the "body" (12, 4–8), a popular image used by Stoic philosophers to illustrate the interdependence of members in a state. Older Catholics may be familiar with this image for the church and probably relate it to ideas developed by Pope Pius XII in an encyclical titled "The Mystical Body" *(Mystici Corporis)*. This encyclical stressed the various ways members of the Christian community, both now and in past ages, are related to one another. We can also note that Paul develops the image to stress the very real mutual dependency of Christians who should not think of themselves "more highly than one ought to think" (12, 3) but as "one body" (12, 4) having many parts. The image of the body provides the transition between the liturgical language that describes Christians' behavior as "spiritual worship" (12, 1), and the obligations of the mutual love that is to be characteristic of Christians.

Romans 13, 1–7 takes up the question of the Christian community's relation to civil government. We must remember that Paul is speaking to a minority community within an alien state. At first glance his advice appears simplistic. Paul says that all authority is ordained by God and has its origin in God. Christians in Paul's time were trying simply to survive. Society expected citizens to follow the religion of the state. Paul instructs Christians to be good citizens while not being conformed to the standards of the world around them. Then, having spoken about giving society its due, Paul considers the question of the debt believers owe one another: love is the fulfillment of the law. Apparently Paul is acquainted with the love command of Jesus (see Rom 13, 8–10). He reviews the commandments from adultery to covetousness, repeating finally in verse 10 what he stated in verse 8: "Love is the fulfillment of the law."

Divisions over Observances and the Call to Unity (14, 1—15, 13)

Paul frequently enjoins his addressees to be of one and the same mind (for example, Phil 2, 1–4). Yet disputes over ethical issues threaten the unity that should characterize the Christian church. The Roman Christians disagree over dietary matters and the observance of certain feast days. In a mixed community of Jewish and Gentile Christians, such questions could not help but arise.

Referring to the different sides of this debate, Paul speaks of those with "weak" and those with "strong" faith. His emphasis is not so much on the opinions or positions of individual believers but on the common attitudes to be cultivated among believers. He refers to the faith of the community and of members' responsibility to be united with the faith of the whole body.

Paul exhorts the Christians to a fundamental harmony that is expressed in mutual respect and concern for one another. Paul reminds the Roman Christians, many of whom are Jewish, that the Scriptures are written for our instruction and encouragement. The term *encouragement* is linked to the hope that abounds in the community "by the power of the holy Spirit" (15, 13). Hope, joy, and peace are linked to belief. Faith is a confession about the meaning of Jesus' death and resurrection (see Rom 10, 9). But it is also, according to 15, 7–13, acceptance of other members of the Christian community.

Conclusion (15, 14—16, 27)

Paul reminds the Romans again, as he did at the beginning of his letter, about their common faith and his confidence in them. In 15, 14–33 the apostle speaks of his need for their hospitality soon; he requests prayers as he embarks on his mission to Jerusalem to take the collection there. Although Paul is personally unacquainted with the Romans, he has written "boldly" because he is a "minister" of Jesus Christ. He describes his ministry in liturgical language, as a "priestly" *(leitourgos)* duty (15, 16). Paul is of course not referring to a sacramental priesthood, since Christians have not yet developed a theology of sacrificial cult, but to his mission to preach the Christian message to the Gentiles. He uses language common to the Jerusalem Temple priesthood and to other religious worship of the day.

Paul reports that his immediate plans include a visit to Rome in passing on the way to Spain, after taking the collection to Jerusalem. He understands the collection as a symbol linking Jews and Gentiles, the fulfillment of a responsibility he accepted at the Jerusalem council (Gal 2, 10). There is yet only the unfinished matter of taking the offering from the Gentiles to Jerusalem. This material gift represents a debt owed the Jews whose spiritual heritage is now shared by the Gentiles. The term *debt* occurred in Romans 13, 8–10 where Paul described love as the only legitimate debt a believer can incur. Since spiritual blessings are much greater than material things, the Gentiles owe these lesser goods to the Jews as a consequence of their inheriting Israel's spiritual blessings now through Jesus Christ. Common faith makes kin of Jews and Gentiles and links both in mutual responsibility. Paul's strategy, then, is twofold: to ensure that the offering is sizable and that it is accepted as symbolic of the true faith and equal status of the Gentile Christians. If the Jewish Christians accept the gift, they are thereby accepting the mission to the Gentiles.

Chapter 16 consists mostly of greetings to and from various people known to Paul. It is possible that it was originally part of a letter intended for Ephesus, and was for some reason later added to the preceding fifteen chapters of Romans. This chapter seems almost like an af-terthought, and further examination suggests it even contains some discrepancies to material stated or implied in the first fifteen chapters. Paul commends Phoebe, bearer of the letter to the Romans, speaking of her as *diakonos* (the only named person in the New Testament who is a "deacon" of a particular church) and *prostatis,* that is, his patron and benefactor. Then he greets numerous people as if he is well known to them and as if he and the Romans have a number of mutual acquaintances. Until now the apostle has maintained a certain distance from the Roman Christians, insinuating that his introduction to himself and to his gospel could serve in lieu of the personal contact he usually has with communities he has founded. But if Paul knows as many Romans as this chapter indicates, the uncharacteristically general and impersonal tone of chapters 1 through 15 of the letter is strange. The note on 16, 1–23 draws attention to the mixture of Jewish and Gentile names, representative of the mixed background of the Roman community. Much valuable social information about acquaintances and collaborators of Paul, both male and female, whether in Ephesus or Rome, is contained in these verses.

The placement and originality of the final doxology or blessing is debated (see note). But its appropriateness at the end of this epistle is undisputed. The doxology echoes several themes developed in the course of the letter. Paul speaks of "my gospel" (see 1, 16–17), the mystery kept secret for long ages (11, 25–32), manifested through prophetic writings (numerous allusions to the Old Testament throughout this epistle), and to the obedience of faith (see 1, 5; 15, 28). Paul has pronounced a blessing at various points throughout his development (7, 24; 8, 35–39; 11, 33–36), as if carried away by the abundance of God's wisdom and mercy. This reflects the Jewish custom of celebrating the wonders of God with praise. Nowhere is the doxology more fitting than after Paul has reviewed the fundamentals of his gospel, with emphasis on the universality of redemption and the imminence of God's victory over all evil in the triumph of Jesus Christ.

Concluding Remarks

Throughout our commentary on Romans we have tried to show the relevance of the major themes developed here: justification by faith, the emphasis on the present reality of justification contrasted with the former life of sin, and most importantly, the inclusion of all—Jews and Gentiles—in a new Israel of God, the church.

The ethical section of Romans may be seen as a description of the church living in but not of the world. It would be hard to overestimate the influence of Romans in the development of Christian doctrine and morality throughout history.

THE LETTERS TO THE CORINTHIANS

Introduction

The letters to the Corinthians reveal Paul the pastoral theologian in ways that his other surviving letters do not. The sheer number of pastoral problems posed and answered, especially in 1 Corinthians, leads us to think that here Paul was most challenged to apply the principles he knew to real, new circumstances in the lives of his community. The Corinthians could never be accused of lack of initiative. Rather, they seem to have taken seriously (perhaps more so than Paul would have liked) his encouragement to find new freedom in Christ, so that his relationship with them was complex and tumultuous.

Corinth was the capital and central city of the Roman province of Achaia, which comprised southern Greece. Its location near the isthmus dividing the Peloponnesus from mainland Greece made it a major seaport and trading center. It was also a Roman freedmen's colony and therefore its population was made up of various peoples, but with a heavy concentration of Roman citizens and Roman interests. With its mixture of national and religious groups, rich and poor, Jews, pagans, and Christians, and moral and immoral people, it was an exciting but difficult environment for the small Christian community, which

was predominantly Gentile but probably had a small Jewish minority.

The letters we call 1 and 2 Corinthians formed part of a larger collection that originally consisted of several letters Paul wrote to the community. He speaks in 1 Corinthians 5, 9 of a previous letter written to the Corinthians instructing them to avoid immoral people. Such a letter no longer exists and nowhere do we have this instruction from Paul, unless, as has been suggested, a piece of it survives as 2 Corinthians 6, 14—7, 1. Similarly, the reference to a letter written in "much affliction and anguish of heart" (2 Cor 2, 4) hardly fits the tone of 1 Corinthians. Furthermore, 2 Corinthians is characterized by discontinuity, suggesting that it is actually a composite of several letters (see *New American Bible,* introduction to 2 Corinthians).

We learn that the Corinthians also wrote to Paul (see 1 Cor 7, 1), and that the Corinthian church, difficult as it was for Paul, preserved and honored his advice, undoubtedly reading his letters at liturgical gatherings as Paul had instructed them to do. We are left with the impression that the extant letters reflect an editing and combining of writings, compiled as the community processed and integrated the words of the apostle.

1 CORINTHIANS

[see pages 1516–40 of the New Testament]

Before Beginning . . .

In writing 1 Corinthians around AD 56, Paul was responding to some disquieting reports he had received about the community. First Corinthians addresses real, not theoretical, situations. Paul's knowledge of what was going on was based

on verbal accounts from reliable sources, letters from members of the community, and Paul's own eighteen-month experience of living amidst this community (Acts 18, 11).

First Corinthians is a particularly fruitful source of reflection for our contemporary church because it raises so many issues that are still relevant: divisions based on ideologies or different world views, incest, lawsuits among Christians, scandal, marriage and celibacy, theology of woman and the participation of women in the church, the proper way to celebrate Eucharist, charismatic gifts, and belief in the Resurrection. We, like the Corinthians, are challenged to find the right role and qualifications of leadership in a pluralistic society. Like the Corinthians we need to recognize that behavior is an indicator of what we believe.

In a sense, the singular "community" might misrepresent the Corinthians. We may tend to think of the community as a specific group that met at the house of a particular individual in a city. But the Corinthians were not a single large community. It is probable that in that particular city there were several Christian communities that congregated at different houses. Apparently these communities represented different competitive factions. Each community was developing divergent expressions of Christian life and worship. Some groups were homogeneous, preferring to worship with like-minded people from similar social and religious backgrounds, who followed certain diets and enjoyed certain prestigious spiritual gifts.

A variety of liturgical celebrations developed. The Corinthians disagreed about whether Christians ought to marry or, if married, should remain married after baptism. Paul responds to these issues among the Christians at Corinth. Although our problems and divisions may be expressed somewhat differently, Paul's admonitions to the Corinthians on the importance of unity, charity, and mutual respect based on a common faith provide us with a model for approaching our own problems. First Corinthians discloses to us the pastor Paul, who encourages the Corinthians to imitate him as he imitates Christ (11, 1).

Working through 1 Corinthians

Our comments on the major themes and relevance of this epistle will follow the structure suggested in the NAB introduction (p. 1517), with some rather minor adjustments. First Corinthians contains the usual letter format: an *address* in 1, 1–9, the *body of the letter* in 1, 10—15, 58, and a *conclusion* in 16, 1–24.

Since this letter is a response to the concerns of the Corinthians, there is not the same kind of objective, formal structure we saw in Romans. Yet we can detect in 1 Corinthians a structural pattern that helps shed some light on the emphasis and meaning of Paul's message. Paul's general approach to issues follows an A-B-A' pattern by which Paul introduces and begins to develop a topic (A), disrupts his reflections by bringing up a second issue (B), and then returns to the original topic (A'). Often he uses this pattern to emphasize the middle, or B, statement. One illustration is Paul's discussion of abuses in the celebration of the Eucharist. He describes the abuses in 1 Corinthians 11, 17–22 (A) and in verses 26–34 (A'). Paul interjects into the middle of this description his account of Jesus' Last Supper the night before he died (see 11, 23–25, [B]). In this way Paul tries to remedy the abuses at Corinth by recalling what Jesus did and reminding the Corinthians that they are to act "in memory of" Jesus. Further examples of Paul's use of the A-B-A' pattern will be discussed as they appear in this letter. For the moment simply note that the pattern has the effect of emphasizing the B section as a corrective for the situations described in A and A'.

A working outline of 1 Corinthians is the following:

I. Address (1, 1–9)

II. The Body of the Letter (1, 10—15, 58)
   A. Reported Divisions and Abuses (1, 10—6, 20)
     1. Factions (1, 10—4, 21)
     2. Immoral Behavior (5, 1—6, 20)
   B. Answers to the Corinthians' Questions (7, 1—11, 1)
     1. Marriage and Virginity (7, 1–40)
     2. Food Offered to Idols (8, 1—11, 1)
       a. Exercising knowledge and love (8, 1–13; 10, 1—11, 1)
       b. The example of Paul (9, 1–27)
   C. Problems in Liturgical Assemblies (11, 2—14, 40)
     1. Dress and Decorum in the Assembly (11, 2–16)
     2. Celebration of the Eucharist (11, 17–34)
     3. The Spiritual Gifts (12, 1—14, 40)
   D. The Resurrection (15, 1–58)

III. Conclusion (16, 1–24)

Reading through 1 Corinthians

The Address (1, 1–9)

The address contains a greeting (1, 1–3) and thanksgiving (1, 4–9). In the greeting, Paul refers to himself as an "apostle of Jesus Christ" and identifies a "brother," Sosthenes, as co-author who, however, does not reappear in the letter. He is perhaps to be identified with the synagogue official of the same name in Acts 18, 17. Paul addresses the community as a "church" *(ekklesia),* which has been "sanctified in Christ Jesus" and "called to be holy." Paul thus reminds the Corinthians that they have a common vocation *(ekklesia* literally means "called out of"). This is Paul's usual word for the assembly of believers, taken from the civic word for the assembly of citizens in a free city-state. It may also be a conscious translation of the Hebrew *qahal,* the biblical assembly of Israel. The Corinthians have a new identity, rooted in God, that distinguishes them from the world around them.

Paul's adaptation of the thanksgiving usually found in Hellenistic letters focuses on the blessings received by his addressees. Moreover, the thanksgiving announces themes Paul will develop in the letter. The Corinthians lack no spiritual gift whatsoever (1, 7). The factions among them that so concerned Paul are rooted precisely in their envy of and competition for extraordinary gifts.

The Body of the Letter (1, 10—15, 58)

The whole of 1 Corinthians addresses specific issues that caused dissension and strained the fabric of the Corinthian community. In the first section of the body or main part of the letter, Paul discusses the divisions he has heard about among the Corinthians (1, 10—6, 20). He then turns to address matters that the Corinthians had themselves directed to him (see 7, 1—11, 1). Finally, Paul will consider other issues relevant to the Corinthian community; namely appropriate ways of celebrating the Eucharist (11, 2—14, 40), and the meaning of the Resurrection (15, 1–58). Following this general outline, we can now comment on the main message of 1 Corinthians.

Reported Divisions and Abuses (1, 10—6, 20)

Reports from Chloe's people (see 1, 11) identified some problems at Corinth stemming from two matters: (1) factions (1, 10—4, 21) and (2) immoral behavior (5, 1—6, 20).

Factions in Corinth (1, 10—4, 21). The variety of backgrounds of its members caused many problems in the community of Corinth. Various members of the community turned to different leaders, and groups began to vie with one another for superiority and recognition. Paul first takes up the slogans adopted by groups who profess allegiance to the various leaders. He names group leaders, specifically Cephas (that is, Peter), Apollos, and himself. He shows the absurdity of divisions based on leadership, which is superficial compared to the common baptism by which all Christians are sanctified and saved.

The Corinthians disagreed among themselves about which leaders were the most important and which group of Christians was the most prestigious. They may have taken their lead from disagreements among the great figures themselves. James disagreed with Paul, for example, about whether any aspects of the Jewish Law were required of Gentile Christians (Gal 2). Peter favored at least minimal requirements, while Paul advocated complete freedom from the Jewish Law for Gentile converts. First Corinthians suggests that the leaders' disagreement affected the Corinthians and caused many to side with one leader against another. But the Corinthians also had their own divisions.

Another leader was Apollos who, for very different reasons, had a following that competed for the Corinthians' loyalty. Apollos attracted many Corinthians because of his eloquence in speaking (see Acts 18, 24–28). Meanwhile, some of the Corinthians cited Paul's unimpressive physical presence and speaking abilities as reason to reject him (1 Cor 2, 1–5; 2 Cor 1, 10). Paul chided the Corinthians for judging by human standards, not by God's as revealed in the cross of Christ. Paul reminded them that neither he nor Peter nor Apollos were crucified for them. The Corinthians were baptized in Christ's name and belonged to Christ. The formation of competitive groups within the Christian community is absurd. Paul admonishes the Corinthians to remember who they are—that by worldly standards few among them have any reason to boast (1, 26–31)—but that "in the Lord" they can boast that they are saved and form a "new creation" (2 Cor 5, 17). They do not have wealth or nobility or education, but they are rich in the blessings of the Spirit of God. The "not many of you" in verse 26 has been read both ways: Paul is stressing the humble origins and status of most, but in saying this he suggests that some really were of higher social status and wealth.

The first part of this letter (1, 10—4, 21) may be summarized as the gospel paradox, the teaching that God's wisdom is greater than human wisdom, that the power of the cross outweighs all human power. The Corinthians portrayed themselves as sophisticated, mature, and truly wise. Paul describes them as rather immature, of the "flesh" rather than spiritual (3, 1), deceiving themselves and therefore lacking in the most fundamental knowledge. They erroneously judged according to standards that are transitory rather than eternal. The riches and wisdom of God surpass all understanding and may be perceived only through wisdom that is revealed by the Spirit (2, 10).

Immoral Behavior (5, 1—6, 20). In chapters 5 and 6, Paul gives instances when judgments on the appropriate behavior for believers would be necessary. The Christian message of salvation has many implications—doctrinal, liturgical, ethical. Certain behavior is inconsistent with belonging to the Christian community. Chapters 5 and 6 specifically mention incest, bringing lawsuits against other members of the community, and sexual promiscuity, as liable to the community's judgment.

The Corinthians were complacent about keeping in their community someone who violated Jewish incest laws by living with his stepmother. Paul uses a traditional image of "yeast" to help describe the impact of the presence of such a one in their midst. The proverb "a little yeast leavens all the dough" illustrates the extent to which the sinner's action corrupts the whole community. Jesus uses this same image to warn about the influence of the Pharisees on the disciples (Mt 16, 6; Mk 8, 15; Lk 12, 1). Paul was concerned about the impact of the sinner on the community and the "contagion" of sinful actions. Throughout this letter, a fundamental point of Christian the-

ology is emphasized: namely, as Christians we cannot act alone without regard for one another. Our actions affect others, for good or evil. Paul sees conversion as turning "from idols to serve the living and true God" (1 Thes 1, 9). This conversion requires a readiness to change not only our hearts but also our actions so that we may live in accordance with our baptism. Continuing the yeast image, Paul cites the formula of the paschal lamb and unleavened bread, pure and free from yeast. Yeast, as it is here, is usually a negative symbol. The connection is especially relevant at the time of the year in which Paul writes, the season of Passover (16, 8).

It troubles Paul to hear that some in the community are bringing lawsuits against one another, when what they should be doing is suffering wrongs in imitation of Christ. At best, they should settle such disputes among themselves. He reminds them of the eschatological scenario in which God's holy ones will judge the earth. They therefore have no business submitting their grievances to unbelieving judges now. Nor do they know what they are doing by participation in prostitution. "Everything is lawful" to the one who is free in Christ, but this does not mean everything is acceptable. The body of every believer is a temple of the Holy Spirit that cannot be profaned.

Answers to the Corinthians' Questions (7, 1—11, 1)

Paul then takes up the Corinthians' own questions about how daily life is an expression of their faith. The Corinthians themselves identified certain issues within their community that were disturbing their unity. They wrote to Paul about these two types of questions: those about marriage and virginity (see 7, 1–40), and those pertaining to the eating of idol meats and participation at pagan meals (8, 1—11, 1).

Marriage and Virginity (7, 1–40). In chapter 7 Paul specifically discusses three life choices that many Christians believed were affected by baptism with an advantage on one side: marriage or virginity (7, 1–7.16), fidelity to Judaism signified by circumcision versus uncircumcision (vv. 18–20), and slavery versus manumission or freedom (vv. 21–24). According to 1 Corinthians 7, a specific question arose concerning whether married Christians ought to remain married. An un-

1 Corinthians

derstanding of baptism as initiation into the eschatological community seemed to imply that the baptized should renounce the constraints and responsibilities of marriage. Jesus' opposition to divorce is first attested here (7, 10.11). Some asked whether a Christian married to an unbeliever could or should remain in the marriage. Some men wondered if there was an advantage to circumcision. Some slaves thought, and perhaps expected, that they would be better off freed.

Paul's general advice is to "remain in the state in which you were called" (see 7, 17.20.24). His reasoning is that the time is short (7, 29.31), too short for unnecessary social entanglements. It is debatable whether Paul believed literally that the eschatological end was imminent or whether this was his way to see all of life as contingent on the absolute power and will of God. Although Christians are "in" the world, they are not "of" it as John says (Jn 17, 14–16). The particular circumstances of believers do not interfere with or lessen the effect of the new status of their identity in Christ. Christians have always sensed the need to express the implications of their new identity as baptized persons with an appropriate way of life.

Paul agreed with a position held by some in Corinth, that "it is a good thing . . . not to touch a woman" (1 Cor 7, 1). Paul acknowledged his own preference for celibacy that leaves one "free of anxieties" (7, 32). The Gospels record Jesus' saying that "in heaven there is neither giving nor taking in marriage" (see Mk 12, 25 and parallel passages). Sexuality, circumcision, even slavery do not have significance in the new age. Indeed, the hope for a new society of equals was one of the reasons Christianity was so appealing to many "minority" groups, including women, slaves, and others who lacked status in the Greco-Roman world.

Paul's response is to advocate no change in social status since it is unimportant in the Christian context. Responding to those who challenge the right of Christians to marry, Paul drew on the word of Jesus regarding the indissolubility of marriage (7, 10–11). Yet Paul added an exception that considerably weakens the effect of Jesus' statement. In the case of unwillingness of the unbelieving spouse to remain married to a baptized person, they may separate. Furthermore, Paul applied the exception to both men and women, giving women the same rights as men.

We should note Paul's remarkable freedom in relating Jesus' words to the pastoral situation of Corinth. In all of the questions with which he has to deal, Paul demonstrates a surprising creativity and flexibility.

Food Offered to Idols (8, 1—11, 1). Here Paul responds to three very practical situations about which the Corinthians must make everyday decisions: whether they should (1) eat meat bought in the marketplace that was probably originally offered in sacrifice at a pagan temple; (2) accept dinner invitations in rented banquet rooms in pagan temples, during which there was a sacrificial libation to the god in whose temple they were; (3) accept dinner invitations to the homes of unbelievers. He asserts a basic theological position that these gods are not really gods at all, supporting it with reference to Israel's history as recorded in the Scriptures (10, 1–13) and with the example of his own experience. But the bottom line is the unity of the community. If anyone of weaker conscience will be scandalized, then it is not to be done.

Exercising Knowledge and Love (8, 1–7 and 10, 23—11, 1). Paul quotes a Corinthian slogan, acknowledging the truth that "all of us have knowledge" (8, 1). The Corinthians apparently assumed that such knowledge made some of them superior to others. So, for example, it was their "knowledge" that allowed them to overlook incest in one of their members (see chapter 5). It was the competition for the gifts considered superior that was disrupting their assemblies (14, 20–33) and even the Lord's Supper (11, 17–18). Paul proposes charity as a remedy for the rivalry of the various kinds of "knowledge" that inflate the ego and that were causing factions in the Corinthian church. Whereas knowledge divides, love unites, enabling the Corinthians' many gifts to supply various needs in the community, helping them to "build up" (see the description of the role of prophecy in 1 Cor 14, 3), rather than destroy (1 Cor 11, 17–34).

In discussing the factions between the "weak and the strong," Paul speaks of "conscience," a term that appears almost exclusively in Pauline writings with little impact on other New Testament authors (for instance, Rom 2, 15; 9, 1; 13, 5; 1 Cor 8, 7.10.12; 10, 25.27.28.29; 2 Cor 1, 12;

1 Tm 1, 5; 2 Tm 1, 3; Ti 1, 15; see also Acts 23, 1; Heb 9, 9.14; 1 Pt 2, 19; 3, 16.21). In biblical thinking, conscience is never an individualist function. It always has to do with how one sees oneself in relation to one's community. Paul gives a communal meaning to conscience and places it in a new Christian context. In this context, the personal consciences of both the "weak" and the "strong" are subordinate to the obligations of mutual charity. The weak must not judge the strong and the strong not scandalize the weak. For Paul, conscience is not autonomous. It cannot be the last court of appeal among Christians. It is subject to charity and concern for one "for whom Christ has died" (8, 11).

In 1 Corinthians 10, 23—11, 1, Paul summarizes his discussion of knowledge of the specific issues regarding pagan meals and customs, and of imitation of his own example. Quoting another Corinthian slogan (as he did in 8, 1 where he said "all of us have knowledge"), Paul agrees "Everything is lawful" (10, 23). Yet, he continues, not everything is beneficial. The merit of an action is related to its effects on the community. Concrete questions about whether to eat or not should be resolved in view of their effect on the other members of the community. For Paul, the morality of a decision depends upon its impact on the conscience of other brothers and sisters. Paul's attempt to win others over rather than to alienate them keeps their salvation in view. Thus he concludes that Corinthian Christians ought to imitate him as he does Christ (11, 1).

The Example of Paul (9, 1–27). To support his argument about mutual love and avoidance of scandal, Paul inserts between the two parts of the argument the example of his own conduct. (Chapter 9 represents B in the A-B-A' pattern discussed in the introduction.) Though he could demand material support, though he could exercise a great deal more freedom and authority, he instead tries to become all things to everyone by being as much like them as possible. The hint is clear: you too do not need to exercise all the freedom to which you have a right, but you can subordinate some of it sometimes for the good of the whole. The Corinthians' problems reflect their mixed makeup of predominantly Gentile but also partly Jewish members, as well as a certain level of education and intellectual refinement. Greek intellectual life valued gifts of mind and spirit,

such as knowledge and eloquent reasoning. Such gifts contributed to the status of the individuals who possessed them, sometimes to the detriment of charity.

In many of his letters Paul refers to the fact that he works with his hands and thus gives an example for his addressees to follow (1 Thes 2, 9; 2 Thes 3, 7–10). Paul freely forfeited the apostolic privilege of support in order "not to place an obstacle to the gospel of Christ" (1 Cor 9, 12). He served all—Jews, Gentiles, the "strong and the weak"—so that through this service the gospel message would be available to them. No one should be denied the gospel because of inability to pay. This forfeiting of privilege makes Paul freer to serve. Yet, as he will argue in 2 Corinthians 8, 1—9, 15, after receiving the gospel message Christians have a responsibility to contribute to the support of other Christians in need. Here he ends this digression about his own example with an athletic image. Just like a professional athlete, he disciplines himself, training not for a perishable crown of laurel or celery, as did the athletes of the day, but for an imperishable one.

Asceticism has played an important role in Christian spirituality throughout the history of the church. Paul legitimizes asceticism or self-denial for apostolic reasons. Today we live in a world that encourages individual freedom without constraints and the pursuit of happiness almost to any length. Such a mentality is not so distant from the sophisticated world of the Corinthians. Paul's corrective view suggests another approach altogether. The community's pursuit of charity should be the focus of the individual's energies and form the individual's conscience. Freedom is for the service of the gospel message. A person's rights are subject to God's call to preach the gospel. The charity of God compels us, training us in the school of self-denial and the pursuit of God's will in our lives.

Problems in Liturgical Assemblies (11, 2—14, 40)

Paul now turns to issues affecting the ways that the Corinthians are worshipping together. They fall into three categories: decorum at assemblies (11, 2–16), celebration of the Lord's Supper (11, 17–34), and the unity and variety of spiritual gifts (12, 1—14, 40).

Dress and Decorum in the Assembly (11, 2–16). This is a problematic passage that has received much attention. Throughout the ancient Mediterranean world, among Jews, Greeks, and Romans alike, the subordination of women to men was a common part of the thinking, even though by this time women of sufficient wealth and status exercised a great deal of social and economic autonomy. It was common custom that respectable adult women veiled themselves in public, even though that custom was changing in social circles that were more sensitive to Roman customs. In more traditional circles, as is still the case in some cultures, the unveiled female head was a sign of sexual availability. It appears that some female members of the Corinthian church, however, were combining their knowledge of newer social customs with Paul's own preaching about freedom in the Spirit, and concluded that the veil was no longer necessary in some circumstances, particularly the church assembly, where others, including Paul, judged that it was. While never questioning women's right to pray and prophesy publicly (11, 5), he simply judged that it must be done with traditional dress. In his attempt to provide a theological explanation, Paul draws on traditional images of headship and subordination, using as illustration three parallel examples: Christ and man, man and woman, God and Christ. He then goes on to appeal to "nature," which really means "common sense," that is, what people were used to. Finally, he realizes that he has not proved his case and simply withdraws to the position of authority: we just don't do it that way (11, 16)! While affirming women's full position in the church, he capitulates on the question of dress in favor of something that will not cause scandal among conservative outsiders (and perhaps some insiders, too) who are undoubtedly watching this new movement.

Celebration of the Eucharist (11, 17–34). There were divisions among the Corinthians on social and economic grounds. Wealthy Christians apparently boasted great meals at which the poor were either not welcomed or treated badly. Some became drunk while others went away hungry (11, 20–22.33–34). Paul says that this is not the Lord's Supper and that the Corinthians are eating and drinking their own condemnation (see 11, 27–29). Within the context of the discussion of abuses in the community's liturgical celebrations, Paul inserts his account of the institution of the Last Supper in order to put the troubles in the proper context. This is the earliest written account of the institution of the Lord's Supper in the New Testament (see the note on 11, 23–25). Paul's version, also reflected in Luke 22, 14–20, contains at least three significant differences from the version given in Mk 14, 22–25; Mt 26, 26–29. These variants are in the additions of the words "for you," the command "Do this in remembrance of me" (v. 24), and the qualifier "new" before "covenant" in 11, 25. These variants witness to several early versions of the eucharistic sayings.

By emphasizing that Jesus' body was given "for you," Paul reminds the Corinthians of Jesus' self-giving act in which they participate by receiving the bread and the cup. They are then warned that an "unworthy" reception would not bring salvation but rather condemnation. The command to do this in memory of Jesus calls the Christians to offer a fitting memorial, including calling to mind Jesus' self-offering and imitating him in this. The insertion of "new" before "covenant" reminds the Corinthians that Jeremiah's prophecy of a "new covenant" is fulfilled in Christ (see Jer 31, 31; 2 Cor 3, 3.6). This is an inclusive covenant, one that is already proclaimed in ancient Israel and that will be extended to all, one that provides the basis for a new society and a new relationship with God. It is important to realize that Paul's critique of the Corinthian Eucharist is not proper reverence toward the sacrament, but proper reverence toward the poor and all members who participate in it.

The Spiritual Gifts (12, 1—14, 40). The divisions among the Corinthians based on competition for the higher gifts continues to occupy Paul. He reminds the Corinthians that when they were pagans they were "attracted and led away" by idols (12, 2). Idolatry attributes the honor and devotion that belongs to God to false gods. Paul advises the Corinthians that in true conversion to Jesus Christ there is unity with others who also worship the same God.

The hymn of love in 1 Corinthians 13, inserted within the context of chapters 12 and 14 on the variety of gifts, may not be a Pauline composition but something borrowed from Stoic sources, which he found helpful to illustrate the unity that should characterize the Corinthians (see note on 13, 1–13). In chapter 11, Paul alluded to the divisions between the wealthy and the poor at the common table. In chapters 12 and 14, it is not so much the social distinctions as striving for spiritual gifts that threatens the Corinthians' unity. As remedy, Paul offers reflections on the community as the body of Christ (12, 12–27), a new adaptation of an old image of social unity. A very high estimation is placed on prophecy, the action of the Spirit through members of the community. But the new context Paul provides emphasizes that love is the highest spiritual gift, one to which all believers must aspire to achieve (13, 13). Love remains the most important of all the spiritual gifts in the church. This is not to diminish faith and hope and the other spiritual gifts such as teaching and administration. Love is an expression of God's own love, enabling us to act mercifully and kindly toward one another. Love in action, at the service of others, is the essential message of the gospel.

The Resurrection (15, 1–58)

For Paul, the death, burial, and resurrection of Christ are the central mystery of the Christian life—but not in isolation. If we are to experience death and burial, we are also to experience resurrection. Paul claims to have met the Risen Christ directly, and we can assume that some of his assertions about the Resurrection are derived from that experience (Gal 1, 12.15–16). Others perhaps came from his meeting with Cephas (Gal 1, 18), who had participated in the post-Easter appearances, and from his own apocalyptic theology in Pharisaic context. Paul implies that if the Corinthians really grasped and accepted the Resurrection and its implications, many of the problems he has addressed throughout the letter would have been resolved. In the first part of this chapter (15, 1–11), he states the fundamental teaching on the resurrection of Christ and recites the earliest surviving creed and list of appearances. He stresses the appearances of the Risen Christ that were the foundational experiences, beginning with Peter's and ending with his own.

A second section (15, 12–28) states emphatically, "If Christ has not been raised, your faith is in vain" (15, 14.17). The resurrection of Christ

forms the basis of faith and causes believers to reassess all of life and death. By his resurrection, Christ is revealed as the "firstfruits of those who have fallen asleep" (15, 20). Christ is our hope, our assurance that we too will have the same experience. Without it, perseverance in faith, including the sacrifices involved in suffering persecution, is pointless.

In a third section (15, 29–34), Paul is trying to shame the Corinthians by showing them the absurdities of some Christian practices and beliefs without faith in the Resurrection as the fate of all the faithful. The slogan quoted by Paul, "Let us eat and drink, for tomorrow we die" (15, 32) is the wisdom of those without hope in the life to come.

In the next section (15, 35–50), he takes up those who speculate on the nature of resurrection and the risen body. He uses the example of dissimilar creatures such as birds and fish, the sun and the moon, to show the qualitative difference between bodies, as a way of stressing, without going into detail, the differences in our bodies before and after the resurrection. The seed sown in the ground is not the same as the green shoot that springs from it, yet the shoot is continuous with the life of the seed that must die in order to produce it. Paul draws a contrast between the first Adam, the earthly, corruptible one whose image we now bear, and the last Adam, Christ, the incorruptible and eternal one, whose image we will bear in the resurrection.

The last section of 1 Corinthians 15 (vv. 51–58) incorporates a hymnic celebration of God's victory through Christ over sin and death, compiled from verses of Isaiah and Hosea. Conquered by Christ, sin and death have lost their sting. By the resurrection of Christ, God has shown us that sin and death are not the last word, but only lead to life. Therefore Paul sings God's praises for the hope that the Resurrection gives. He reminds the Corinthians that their "labor is not in vain in the Lord" (1 Cor 15, 58). The rousing message of the chapter is: hang on! The best is yet to come!

Conclusion (16, 1–24)

Finally, Paul speaks of the collection and how it is to be taken to alleviate the suffering of the saints (16, 1–4). Paul then reports his travel plans, sends greetings to his friends, and concludes with a blessing. Comparison of the persons named with those mentioned in 1 Corinthians 1 and Acts 18 renders an interesting profile of the Corinthian community with its mixture of notable men and women, rich and poor, powerful and ordinary citizens. Paul greets representatives of all categories, personally demonstrating the acceptance and unity he has been advocating.

Concluding Remarks

Some readers may find it surprising to realize that Paul deals in 1 Corinthians with some of the same questions that continue to challenge the church today. Christians still struggle with whether there are more limits on the freedom allowed to women than to men. The rights and responsibilities of ministers in the church are at the heart of the renewal of the priesthood initiated by Vatican II and continued in various important pastoral and ecclesial efforts locally and in the universal church. Issues such as the requirements for a sacramental marriage and qualifications for the ordained ministry, the possibilities for lay ministries, or the role of the sacraments (especially baptism and the Eucharist) in Christian life were not answered by Paul, or even by Vatican II, once and for all. But the church continues to use

Paul's pastoral approach to guide and to respond to the needs of its members.

The Corinthians were a church like ours—real people with real problems. They struggled for charity in the midst of disagreements, for respect for leaders without exaggerating these leaders' roles. Paul stressed the role of ministers as servants of God and Jesus Christ. Paul recognizes the authority of the church to discipline its members, including the immoral, those in dispute, the strong as well as the weak. Paul tried to help remedy their problems by advising them to seek spiritual gifts, especially charity. Paul advocated a healthy respect for the body without failing to see the value of asceticism. Paul recognized roles for both women and men in the liturgy. He gave some concrete examples of practical implications of living the gospel message as a community of equals. He protests discrimination against the poor or those considered inferior because they possess lesser gifts. Further, Paul stresses already in 1 Corinthians, and more so in 2 Corinthians, the necessity of aiding the less fortunate. The first epistle to the Corinthians is truly an interpretation of the gospel message that continues to challenge us with its many implications.

2 CORINTHIANS

[see pages 1540–59 of the New Testament]

Before Beginning . . .

Second Corinthians features some of the most profound moments of Paul's theology, but in a puzzling arrangement. If 1 Corinthians has a structure that is clear and easy to follow, his second letter to the same church is characterized by disorderly sequence, to such a degree that many scholars think it is actually a composite of several letters Paul sent to the same church. The tone tends to be more defensive than most of his letters, and the flow of thought choppy. Some fragments (for example, 6, 14—7, 1) appear completely out of context. The transition from 2, 13 to 2, 14 is very rough, while 7, 5 seems to pick up exactly where 2, 13 left off. Further, chapters 8 and 9 seem to have been originally two separate

letters, each dealing with the collection, but neither assuming the other nor conditioned by the whole context of chapters 1 through 7 and 10 through 13. Finally, chapters 10 through 13 could stand alone as an "apologia," an explanation in defense of Paul's own spiritual experience, his vocation, and apostolic credentials. Certainly 2 Corinthians exhibits traces of an ongoing conversation.

Yet the lack of cohesion in Paul's thought may be only apparent. It is also possible that there is an order to the letter that demonstrates Paul's typical A-B-A' pattern, which also influenced 1 Corinthians. So, for example, Paul begins and ends 2 Corinthians with personal testimony about the painful difficulties both he and the Corinthians have experienced in the course of their relationship (see 1, 12—7, 16 as A, and 10, 1—13, 10 as A'). Within this frame, the two middle chapters, 8 and 9, dealing with the collection for the poor in Jerusalem (B section) illustrate that for Paul, the generosity of the Corinthians symbolizes the success of the Gentile mission. The older scholarship, with its emphasis on literary sources and redactions, is more prone to see the letter as composed of several fragments. In this case, a later editor combined the pieces into the whole that we now have, but the parts sometimes do not fit together well. If this is the case, an explanation is needed as to why the editor did such a poor job. Newer scholarship, with its emphasis on literary analysis, tends to try to look at the letter as a unified whole. In this case, the disruptions in the flow of the text are due to Paul's deliberate digressions for rhetorical effect.

Whichever may be the true situation, we need to work through 2 Corinthians in its final, canonical form, even if it also represents originally separate letters or letter fragments. We approach 2 Corinthians as part of the New Testament canon, a letter preserved by the early church and read at liturgical gatherings in spite of its criticisms of the Corinthians and the many challenges it raised for the church there. Despite the many troubles and misunderstandings between them, the Corinthians seem to have respected Paul's authority enough to preserve his words, reflect on them, and circulate them to other churches. Lest we think that ours is the only age in which deep divisions appear in the church, this letter reveals that Christian community in the first years was no idyllic experience. The Corinthian letters will serve as a corrective to such mistaken idealism.

Working through 2 Corinthians

Some initial observations about the connection of parts of the text will help us read 2 Corinthians with better understanding. As already indicated, 2 Corinthians follows a rather disrupted and choppy sequence. Following the usual Greco-Roman letter structure, 2 Corinthians has the three main parts of the *address* in 1, 1–7, the *body* of the letter in 1, 8—13, 10, and the *conclusion* in 13, 11–13. Our comments will consider each of these parts. A working outline of 2 Corinthians is as follows:

I. The Address (1, 1–7)
II. The Body of the Letter (1, 8—13, 10)
  A. Crisis Between Paul and the Corinthians (1, 8—7, 16)
    1. Past Difficulties and Relationships (1, 9—2, 13)
    2. Paul's Ministry (2, 14—7, 4)
    3. Resolution of the Crisis (7, 5–16)
  B. The Collection for Jerusalem (8, 1—9, 15)
  C. Paul's Defense of His Ministry (10, 1—13, 10)
III. Conclusion (13, 11–13)

Reading through 2 Corinthians

The Address (1, 1–7)

In the *address* Paul names Timothy as co-author. Timothy and Titus (2, 13; 7, 6; 8, 16.23; see also Gal 2, 1) were apparently more trusted by the Corinthians than Paul himself. Timothy is not named again in 2 Corinthians although some suppose he is the unnamed "brother" who accompanies Titus with the collection. Luke tells us that Timothy was a faithful companion of Paul, especially on the second and third missionary journeys (see "The Pastoral Letters," RG 486–7).

The greeting includes a doxology or prayer glorifying and praising God whose "encouragement" is strength in affliction (see 2 Cor 1, 3–4). This encouragement *(paraklesis)* in noun or verbal form occurs ten times in five verses, 3 through 7. This addition gives us a hint as to the overriding mood of 2 Corinthians. Paul and the Corinthians have experienced much misunderstanding, but Paul wants to move on to great consolation. Transcending all the pain is the certainty of God's presence with them and Paul's confidence that God is at work in their lives.

The Body of the Letter (1, 8—13, 10)

The message of 2 Corinthians is developed in three main parts: (A) In the first part (1, 8—7, 16), Paul reviews his past relationship with the Corinthians; (B) Chapters 8 and 9 form a second part in which Paul develops a theology of giving, speaking of the collection among the Gentiles and specifically of the generosity of the Corinthians as a symbol of the fruitfulness of the Gentile mission; (A') In the third part, 10, 1—13, 10, Paul revisits topics he raised in the first part and returns to the theme of his credentials as an apostle, accenting his own weakness and the call of God. It is here that Paul develops a theology of suffering, speaking candidly and with great feeling about his own experience of the grace of God. Many in the history of Christianity have seen in these chapters a spiritual reality by which they are helped to interpret their own personal experience of God: "My grace is sufficient for you, for power is made perfect in weakness" (12, 9). We can read through these three parts of the body of 2 Corinthians, reflecting on the relevance of this composite letter for our own experience as Christians.

The Crisis between Paul and the Corinthians (1, 8—7, 16)

The relationship between Paul and the Corinthians seems to have been marked by crisis. This is evident in both 1 and 2 Corinthians. We shall focus now on the problems Paul mentions in the first part of 2 Corinthians. The apostle first reviews his past relationship with the Corinthians and then his ministry with them. Paul mentions several instances of mistrust and tension between himself and the Corinthians in his review of their past relationship.

Past Difficulties and Relationships (1, 8—2, 13)

First, Paul reviews the difficulties he had in "Asia," meaning the Roman province that covered the western part of Asia Minor. He probably alludes to Ephesus, where because of this and 1 Corinthians 15, 32 many scholars think he endured an imprisonment not recorded in Acts. Paul then focuses on several areas—a change of plans and the Corinthians' subsequent accusation of inconstancy and lack of sincerity; his confrontation with an offending member of the community and his plea for leniency in the punishment of this person whom he has forgiven; and Paul's anxiety about the lack of information about the Corinthians from Titus. Paul appears frustrated at the apparent lack of communication, sympathy, and confidence. The factions that were mentioned in 1 Corinthians could have made a simple change of mind such as this a

source of strife. Paul's detractors accused him of being unreliable.

Paul appeals to God's own fidelity as part of his response (1, 18), showing that his word is sincere and his care constant. Yet he decided to change his plans in view of the recent painful letter (2, 4) that he had found it necessary to write to the Corinthians. He postponed a promised visit only to give time for healing (2, 1–4). With sufficient reflection Paul is confident that the Corinthians would realize the abundant love he has for them (2, 4).

Apparently someone in the community publicly offended Paul (2, 5–11), though the nature of the offense remains obscure. As in 1 Corinthians 5, Paul advocates a judgment not by outsiders but within the church. The action by the majority was acceptable and judged sufficient by Paul. In the case of the incestuous man of 1 Corinthians, he recommended expulsion from the church (see 1 Cor 5, 2.4–5). But in 2 Corinthians 2, 5–11 Paul says that the time has come for forgiveness and reintegration lest Satan be granted a victory in the offender. Like many other biblical writers Paul sees the world as an arena where the conflict between good and evil forces is ongoing, each vying for human allegiance. The church is entrusted with the "ministry of reconciliation" as Paul describes it in 2 Corinthians 5, 11–16. The forgiveness of the one who offended Paul is a specific example of that ministry in practice.

In 2, 12–13 Paul mentions the anguish he felt at his inability to find Titus and receive news about the Corinthians. This anxiety is a further indication of Paul's sincere affection for the Corinthians. In 1, 12–24 he defends his change of plans and insists on his anxious concern for the Corinthians. It would seem that this was written before Paul received the happy news from Titus described in 7, 5–16.

Paul's Ministry (2, 14—7, 4)

Paul interrupts his review of the events that troubled his relationship to the Corinthians in order to describe in more general theological terms his apostolic ministry. Within the overall A-B-A' structure of 2 Corinthians we see subsections like 1, 12—7, 16 also exhibiting this same pattern. In this instance, 2, 14—7, 4 (B), describing

Paul's ministry, is framed by, and grounds theologically, the practical and painful experience of Paul's relationship with the community described in 1, 12—2, 13 (A) and 7, 5–16 (A'). Paul's description of his ministry develops several important themes:

the new covenant enacted by Christ
(3, 1–18);

the paradox of the ministry: strength in weakness (4, 1–18);

the ministry of reconciliation entrusted to them (5, 1–21).

This description begins (2, 14–17) and ends (7, 2–4) with expressions of confidence in God and in the Corinthians. We will briefly discuss each of the three Pauline themes.

The New Covenant Enacted by Christ (3, 1–18). Here, Paul's reasoning is based on the Old Testament passages and on one of his favorite contrasts, between spirit and flesh (see Rom 8, 1–10; Gal 2, 3; 5, 17–23). It exemplifies the method taught him in his biblical training, taking several passages from different sources and combining them to produce a new conclusion. Jeremiah's promise of a "new covenant" (31, 31–34) is combined with Ezekiel's prophecy of God's promise to replace human hearts of stone with hearts of flesh and to give a covenant in the spirit (Ez 36, 26–36). Exodus 34 described the relationship between God and Moses as so glorious that Moses had to come down from Mount Sinai with a veil covering his head lest the Israelites die at the sight of his glowing face (Ex 34, 33–35). These passages from the Prophets and the Law provide the scriptural basis for Paul's argument that the ministry *(diakonia)* of the new covenant, to which Paul is devoted, is superior to that of Moses. Using the familiar rhetorical method from lesser to greater, Paul argues that if Moses' covenant was so spectacular yet was still written on stone and in hearts of flesh, how much greater is Christ's covenant, which is the fulfillment of the prophetic promise of the Spirit!

Paul contrasts the Mosaic covenant written "in ink" or "on stone" with the "new covenant" written by the "Spirit" on "hearts of flesh." In the process he uses the phrase "old covenant" (2 Cor 3, 14), the only instance of this expression in the Scriptures. This "old" covenant was that enacted by God with Moses. Jeremiah and Ezekiel had

spoken of a new enactment of the covenant reality, in which intimate access to God would be realized. Paul picks up this theme to write that this promise of a "new covenant" is realized in the work of Jesus. The difference between the covenants illustrates the contrast between Moses and Christ, and indicates the superiority of the covenant in Christ. Paul and the Corinthians are ministers or agents *(diakonoi)* of the new covenant that brings life and the Spirit. In the last part of the passage, he switches the image of the veil to apply it not as a protection on Moses' face to prevent injury to the people but as an obstacle to clear vision, now upon the faces of those who are unable to see the glory of the new covenant in Jesus (3, 14–18). Christian readers today should remember that Paul was working within the Jewish context of biblical interpretation to work in a new way with familiar texts and images. While his message was definitely that a new thing had been done in Christ that would fully include the Gentiles, he was not drawing a contrast between an old Jewish covenant, now obsolete, and a new Christian covenant that would replace it. Rather, he wanted new Gentile members of the church to realize their debt to our Jewish brothers and sisters for the spiritual heritage they preserved and which we share with them. The Old Testament Scriptures continue to provide a fertile field for mutual reflection and understanding among Christians and Jews.

The Paradox of the Ministry: Strength in Weakness (4, 1–18). Even though Paul is a minister of this great new covenant, he knows that the glory is God's, not his, and that the mystery of reception in faith is not within his control. He expresses the weakness and fragility of this ministry by the familiar image: "We hold this treasure in earthen vessels" (4, 7), a poetic translation of meaning that could be said more prosaically: "We hold these treasures in clay pots," as a reminder that the power is from God, not from human agents. Paul recalls the price to be paid: "We are afflicted in every way . . . perplexed . . . persecuted . . . constantly being given up to death for the sake of Jesus" (4, 8–11). But Paul continuously alludes to God as the source of his own hope, confidence, and power.

Grace is given in greater and greater abundance through the mystery of Christ for the glory of God. Even while they experience diminishment of their "outer self," the "inner self" grows stronger. The afflictions they experience are passing, but the invisible power of God is what lasts forever.

The Ministry of Reconciliation (5, 1–21). Throughout 2 Corinthians 2, 14—7, 4 Paul wrestles with the redemptive aspects of suffering for the sake of the Christian message. This aspect has several implications: first, the negative is not overwhelming; rather, there is always some experience of rescue or salvation. Second, the experience of suffering ends not with the apostle but redounds to the good of the community and, beyond the community, relates to the will of God. Third, for Paul, redemption effects a radical change in believers, taking them out of a particular sinful mode of existence and introducing them into another mode of reality that is in Christ. Fourth and finally, Paul and the Corinthians, like all ministers of the gospel, are involved in the ministry of reconciliation of the whole world to God.

Earthly existence is fraught with difficulties. In Paul's words, we "groan and are weighed down" (5, 4) by the difficulties of human existence and of fidelity to the work entrusted to us. We are longing to be covered not with a "tent" but with a heavenly dwelling not made with human hands. We walk by faith (5, 7), trying to please the Lord by whom, in the end, we will be judged (5, 10) not only on our own deeds but also on the effect of those deeds on others' actions. Catholic interpretation has always emphasized the communal responsibility or the obligations believers have toward others. Paul goes on to explain in the remainder of chapter 5 (vv. 11–21) that Christ's work is a ministry of reconciling the world to God. But that work is not finished once and for all. Through Christ we have been given the astounding mission and responsibility of carrying on that work of reconciliation (5, 17–20). In this context, Paul pleads with the Corinthians to be reconciled with God and thus, implicitly, with him.

Resolution of the Crisis (7, 5–16)

Paul returns to the concrete situation in Corinth, alluding to his anguished wait until he encountered Titus. Paul's representative, Titus, had now furnished good news about the Corinthians' reception of Paul's difficult letter (2, 4 and 7, 8), which some argue is actually chapters 10 through 12 of the present letter. Now the conflict between Paul and the Corinthians was apparently resolved. Paul's exuberant gratitude overshadows all of the former sadness and anxiety. It appears as though all is completely restored, and there is no more reason for concern.

If we have been reading along with Paul, we have noted that some of the problems that afflict our church were present in the experience of the earliest Christians. Paul was an itinerant preacher who normally traveled from community to community preaching the gospel. But Paul lived among the Corinthians longer than with any other community (eighteen months [Acts 18, 11]). He invested enormous energy in this community and could not be indifferent to their problems and questions and mistakes. No one can doubt that this is a problematic relationship, yet it was not severed. The deliberate rhetorical contrast in this letter is between the apparently conflicting data of 2 Corinthians 1, 12—7, 16: the lofty statements about the ministry of the new covenant as well as the insinuations of distrust, discouragement, and anxiety between apostle and community. Paul describes the Christian ministry as a ministry of reconciliation, but he also reminds us of the fragility of the human agents, as earthen vessels holding the treasure. All the hardships are apparently forgotten in Paul's exuberant conclusion: "I rejoice, because I have confidence in you in every respect" (7, 16).

The Collection for Jerusalem (8, 1—9, 15)

Chapters 8 and 9 appear originally to have been two independent "fund-raising letters" on the importance of a generous and substantial offering to the Jerusalem church. This collection for Jerusalem presumably was the condition for acceptance there of Paul's mission to the Gentiles in Gal 2, 10. Jerusalem may have been a collection center for distribution of relief to other churches of Palestine and Syria. This collection is important because it represents the full participation of the Gentile Christians in the community of the new Israel, the Church. On the one hand Paul encourages the Corinthians to give generously, seeing this request as a "test [of] the genuineness of your love by your concern for others" (8, 8). On the other hand Paul will see the acceptance of the Gentiles' offering as evidence of the Jewish Christians', and specifically of the Jerusalem church's, willingness to accept the Gentile mission (Rom 15, 22–33).

Paul uses the tactic of creating competition among the Gentile churches. He encourages the Corinthians to give as generously as the Macedonians (Philippi and Thessalonica), who were generous even when they themselves were "tested by affliction" (8, 2). But in 9, 2 Paul claims that he has boasted of the Corinthians' generosity to the Macedonians. In Romans he says that both the Achaians (the Corinthians) and the Macedonians were only too happy to contribute because they understood it as their obligation (Rom 15, 27). The Gentiles were "indebted" to the mother church in Jerusalem and to the other Jewish Christian churches whose spiritual heritage they shared. The language of wealth and poverty in these passages is rhetorical and should not be taken as economic indicators. At the end of the chapter Paul speaks of envoys or messengers from and to the churches, among whom is Titus. The others are unnamed but probably known to the recipients of the letter. They are in fact called "apostles" of the churches (8, 23). Along with this title applied to Epaphroditus in Philippians 2, 25 and to Andronicus and Junia in Romans 16, 7, it indicates that the title of apostle was held by many in the Pauline churches.

Paul begins chapter 9 as if he has not written chapter 8. Although he has just encouraged generosity in the collection, he says in 9, 1, "It is superfluous for me to write to you" about the collection. There are many other ideas repeated in chapter 9 that were raised in chapter 8. It would be very strange for Paul to say the difficult things he says to the Corinthians before and after these chapters and even deal with their accusations against him (chapter 10), while here in the middle asking them for money! These arguments, and the apparent independence of these chapters not only from each other but also from the context of the rest of the letter, prompt many interpreters to consider them as originally separate letters or letter fragments. For us, however, they represent a crucial example of the importance of Paul's role as apostle to the Corinthians. This is the role he reviewed in chapters 1 through 7 and ardently defends in chapters 10 through 13, to which we now turn.

Paul's Defense of His Ministry (10, 1—13, 10)

In the course of defending his ministry again, Paul can be seen following the A-B-A' pattern, by which he introduced arguments in 10, 1–18 (A), which he will continue in a concluding section in 12, 19—13, 10 (A'). Between these he interjects 11, 1—12, 18 (B), his own experience with the Corinthians and his sufferings as an apostle. Thus Paul's development includes responses to accusations that continue among the Corinthians: he is weak (10, 1–2), not an eloquent speaker (10, 10), not supported by the community (11, 7–10). Paul reminds the Corinthians at the beginning (10, 2.11) and end (12, 20—13, 2.10) that he intends to visit them soon and deal with such issues in person. In the midst of his responses to charges, Paul develops in a famous and memorable passage (11, 1—12, 18) his own lived theology of the cross.

Paul's Response (10, 1–18; 12, 19—13, 10)

Paul's impatient tone in chapters 10 through 13 suggests that he has already dealt with their accusations against him, and they ought to have been laid to rest. The Corinthians appear to be elitists, perceiving themselves to be superior in knowledge and gravitating toward those they suppose possess superior gifts. These include eloquence and an impressive appearance. Some of the Corinthians apparently favored Apollos' eloquence over the "contemptible speech" of Paul (see 1 Cor 3, 4–5; 4, 6–7). They noted Peter's freedom, his authority, the fact that he accepts support from the community (see 1 Cor 9, 6), and challenged Paul's reasons for refusing community support. Apparently the Corinthians are affronted by Paul's refusal to accept their patronage and continue to see Paul's forfeiture of this "apostolic right" to support as an admission that Paul is not of the same stature as Peter.

The Corinthians' complaint that Paul is an impressive writer but that his presence is disappointing (10, 1.10) is arrogant but perhaps speaks a truth that led him to rely so strongly on the written word. Oratory was highly prized; perhaps Paul did not measure up to expectations in that regard. In response, Paul warned that he was empowered by Christ to "act boldly." He would use spiritual weapons to subdue in the end every enemy and disobedient thought in all to make all things subject to Christ (10, 2–6). Paul warned the Corinthians against false pride and conceits and jealousies. He had earlier told the Corinthians to decide whether he came peacefully or "with a rod" (1 Cor 4, 21). Now he promises to visit again soon and warns that he shall not be lenient with them (13, 1–10). The Corinthians should examine themselves and see whether Christ is in them. For his part Paul is confident that Christ is with him. This warning tone is difficult to imagine in the same letter with and following the reconciling tone of 7, 5–10.

Paul Boasts of His Labors and His Weakness (11, 1–12, 18)

Since the Corinthians are attracted by knowledge, Paul proposes to speak of "foolishness," and asks their indulgence. Remember that in 1 Corinthians 1—3 Paul described the wisdom of God as folly for humans and added that God confounds the wise with the wisdom of the cross. In this section of 2 Corinthians, Paul talks about the role of the cross in his own life.

Again, it is Paul's opponents who draw out this vehement testimony about the source of his authority. There are those Paul sarcastically calls the "superapostles" (11, 5), with the same tone with which one might say "supermouse" or "superrabbit"; a few verses later, they are labeled for what Paul really thinks of them, as "false apostles" (11, 13; see the "false brothers" of Gal 2, 4). In any case, others are leading the Corinthians astray; Paul fears that the Corinthians are like Eve (11, 3), deceived by the serpent's cunning. This little aside indicated Paul's acceptance of the prevailing male wisdom of his time, since Sirach 25, 23, that Eve represented the more easily seduced segment of humankind. The comparison with Eve, so regarded, would be insulting to

the lofty Corinthians, a strategy Paul uses to bring them back to humility.

Continuing his paradoxical development of knowledge and foolishness, Paul describes the wisdom he has learned through suffering. His beautiful testimony can hardly be adequately paraphrased. It must be read and reflected upon. The experiences which the Corinthians construe as "failures"—the beatings, humiliations, imprisonments, dangers—are Paul's apostolic credentials. He has experienced visions and revelations and ecstasies. He might have been tempted to pride in these (as he suggests the Corinthians would be). But Paul also experienced a "thorn in the flesh . . . an angel of Satan, to beat me" (2 Cor 12, 7). The wisdom Paul learned from this suffering, so beautifully expressed, is that God's power is made perfect in his human weakness. In the end we can understand why Paul says, "I boast most gladly of my weaknesses, in order that the power of Christ may dwell with me" (12, 9).

Conclusion (13, 11–13)

The conclusion is brief and encouraging, and could be the conclusion to any Pauline letter. It does not reveal the depth of pain involved in some of its earlier content. By following Paul's apparently circuitous arguments, we are enriched far beyond the effort of understanding the specific situation Paul addressed in Corinth centuries ago. An outcome of studying 2 Corinthians is the realization that all the suffering involved in creating the church among limited human beings bears fruit in fidelity and hope. From 2 Corinthians we are brought to a whole new appreciation of the role of the cross in the Christian vocation to holiness.

GALATIANS
[see pages 1559–70 of the New Testament]

Before Beginning . . .

Galatians is the only Pauline letter written as a circular letter to various churches of a geographical region rather than an urban center. The old territory of Galatia comprised a large central and northern area of Asia Minor. The Roman prov-

ince of Galatia, to which Paul probably refers, included some of the cities, such as Iconium, Lystra, and Derbe, in which Paul worked, according to Acts.

Paul's tone in the opening lines of Galatians is defensive and emotional, shown by the absence of the usual prayer of thanksgiving following the address, which is a common characteristic of Paul's letters. Paul sees the problem in the Galatian communities as a great threat not only to his own reputation and mission but to the gospel itself. Other missionaries, whom scholars commonly call "Judaizers," came into Galatia after Paul and claimed that Gentiles must follow some aspects of the Jewish law, including circumcision, in order to be fully Christian. Perhaps they said that Paul taught the fundamentals, and they would now give the Galatians the full Christian message. They were undermining Paul's authority and the sufficiency of faith in Christ that Paul preached. Consequently, he writes heatedly to convince the recipients that he has the full truth. From the emotional tone of chapters 1 and 2, he passes to the complex biblical demonstrations of chapters 3 and 4, finally into the ethical teaching of chapters 5 and 6.

The issues of freedom and faith, diversity of teaching and different understandings of the gospel message, and the relationship of Christianity to Judaism are as important to us as they were to Paul's addressees in Galatia. Yet today's reader of Galatians must see past the combative tone of this letter, the circumstances of its writing, and the historical context in which Paul first developed his dichotomy between faith and works. These tasks are well worth the effort if we are to understand this important epistle of Paul. It is also essential to realize that this letter in which Paul talks the most about freedom is also the letter in which he most identifies with the cross of Christ. Freedom is for the sake of service.

Jews and Gentiles in the Pauline Churches

We cannot adequately comprehend Galatians without recognition of an important historical issue that was at the basis of Paul's missionary perspective. That issue involves the relationship between Judaism and the infant church that struggled to integrate the non-Jews or Gentiles into a new "Israel of God" (Gal 6, 16), and between Jews and Gentiles in that church. Although this may seem like a remote issue unrelated to the problems the church faces today, it is actually quite relevant for us with our increasing ethnic diversity and ecumenical concerns. The question of "Who shall belong?" had to be resolved differently than it was in Judaism, where

circumcision was the sign of initiation, and obedience to the Mosaic Law signified membership.

Those Christians who were already ethnically and religiously Jewish saw the message of Jesus largely within the context of Judaism. Indeed, Christianity might have remained as a sect within Judaism had it revolved only around belief that Jesus was the Messiah. Early Christianity, however, was almost immediately open to the conversion of the Gentiles (sometimes called the "nations" or the "pagans" in translations). We must also remember that before his conversion to Christ, Paul the Pharisee was so zealous for the observance of the Law that he persecuted the church (Gal 1, 13). According to Acts, Paul obtained authorization to hunt down and bring to trial in Jerusalem those fellow Jews who had become convinced that Jesus was the Messiah (Acts 9, 1–2). As a strict Jew, Paul had perceived along with many others that the message of Christ was a threat to Jewish claims to a unique access to the one true God through the covenant. The Pharisaism to which Paul belonged already was open to Gentile membership, based on the universal vision of the later prophets, especially Second and Third Isaiah, but with the requirement that they convert to Judaism. After Paul had accepted the messianic identity of Jesus through revelation and had begun to proclaim it as a missionary (1, 15–16), he held the conviction that this new movement must be able to absorb both Jews and Gentiles, but in a new way. His own special attraction, based on a personal revelation, was to preach the gospel to Gentiles, an attraction that he says the leaders in Jerusalem accepted (2, 7–9). Through his pastoral experience, he had come to the conclusion that the only way to integrate Jews and Gentiles fully into the churches was to eliminate the need for conversion to Judaism on the part of the Gentiles.

In other words, Paul reassessed, as a result of his vocation, the role of the Jewish Law to which he had always been devoted. In light of his God-given vocation to preach the message of Christ to non-Jews, Paul began to see the Law as superseded. According to the Law as it was then understood, the Gentiles had been excluded from salvation. Through Christ, Paul taught, they are included—and on their own terms, not as converts to Judaism. As a result of a revelation from

God, Paul identified himself as an apostle to the Gentiles. Consequently Paul felt as committed to the Gentile mission as he ever had felt formerly with regard to the Jewish Law.

The Gentile mission, however, did not begin with Paul. Stephen (see Acts 6) and others, including Peter (Acts 10), had preached to Gentiles and baptized them before Paul. Nevertheless, not all of the early Christian leaders felt the same degree of freedom from the Jewish Law as Paul did. Nor did everyone agree that Gentiles who were becoming part of the church should neglect the prescriptions of the Jewish Law. Peter and James, for example, who were recognized Christian leaders, both felt that some observance of Jewish Law should be required of the Gentiles. James was a very significant figure in the Jerusalem mother church. Peter, of course, was one of the Twelve and a leader of the Jerusalem community as well as a known authority in the predominantly Jewish Christian community at Antioch. Representatives from James apparently were preaching at least a minimal observance of Jewish Law and gaining a significant hearing among the Gentile converts (see Acts 11, 1–26; Gal 2, 1–10).

The matter was confusing for several reasons. Christianity incorporated the monotheism and the high ethical principles of Judaism, which were very attractive to many Gentiles. The appeal of these basics of Judaism made more reasonable the position of those who "Judaized" (a verb Paul uses only in Gal 2, 14, where it is translated "live like Jews"). The "Judaizers" claimed that Gentiles should fulfill some basic requirements of the Jewish Law, particularly circumcision and some dietary restrictions, in order to demonstrate that they had actually converted from pagan ways. But from the beginning of the Christian preaching, faith in Jesus crucified and raised from death by God had been the only requirement for baptism. Even Peter testified that the Gentiles, like the Jews, were saved through faith and that "God shows no partiality" (Acts 15, 9; Gal 2, 6). Paul vehemently opposed any additional requirements for the Gentiles. He believed that these additions would, in fact, constitute deviation from the firm conviction that salvation is a work of God accomplished through grace that is accepted by faith in Jesus as the Christ.

Working through Galatians

Galatians represents Paul's effort to defend his preaching against alternative interpretations and to correct some misrepresentations about the message he preaches. Galatians exhibits the three main parts of a letter: the *address* (1, 1–5), the *body* (1, 6—6, 10), which contains teaching (1, 6—4, 31) and ethical applications (5, 1—6, 10), and a *conclusion* (6, 11–18). We will comment on these main divisions of Galatians; a more detailed outline is given in the NAB:

I. Address (1, 1–5)
II. The Body of the Letter (1, 6—6, 10)
   A. Defense of Paul's Gospel and Authority (1, 6—2, 21)
     1. Paul's Vocation (1, 6–24)
     2. Paul and the Jerusalem Authorities (2, 1–21)
   B. Faith, Freedom, and the Scriptures (3, 1—4, 31)
     1. Abraham, Father of Faith (3, 6–16)
     2. Example of the Human Will (3, 17–23)
     3. Example of the Child-Minder (3, 24—4, 11)
     4. Assurance of Paul's Affection (4, 12–20)
     5. Allegory of the Two Wives of Abraham (4, 21–31)
   C. Exhortations for Christian Life (5, 1—6, 10)
III. Conclusion (6, 11–18)

Reading through Galatians

The Address (1, 1–5)

This address, in which Paul greets the recipients, is abbreviated and assertive. It lacks the usual thanksgiving characteristic of the opening of a Pauline letter. Perhaps Paul's eagerness to get to the heart of his message explains this omission. Perhaps, too, he is so distressed at what he has heard about the events in Galatia that he cannot feel thankful. He asserts from the beginning that his credentials are not from any human source, but from God and Jesus Christ.

The Body of the Letter (1, 6—6, 10)

In Galatians we see Paul on the defensive, strongly insisting on his loyalty to the gospel.

This defense is occasioned by accusations that he seeks only to please other human beings. He develops several themes as part of his defense of the message he preached and that his authority came from God. Key themes in this defense are Paul's vocation, the coherence of his message with that of Jerusalem, and the biblical proofs of the truth of his preaching.

Defense of Paul's Preaching and Authority (1, 6—2, 21)

Paul expresses amazement that the Galatians have so quickly deserted the one who called them and who remains faithfully rooted in Christ, while they have deserted to "a different gospel" (1, 6). He is about to prove to them that they and those who have taught them this way are wrong.

Paul's Vocation (1, 6–24). Apparently there were those who accused Paul of lying. They claimed that Paul neglected to inform the Gentiles that their baptism involved following prescriptions of the Jewish Law. According to these opponents, Paul did not fully explain the gospel to his converts. But Paul countered that it was the opponents, rather than he, who were perverting the message of Christ. There cannot be two versions of the true gospel message. Paul understood the challenge to his authority as also a threat to the message he preached. His appeal to the divine origin of his call serves to emphasize that there can only be one true gospel. Even if he himself or any other church leader or an "angel from heaven" (1, 8) would teach otherwise, the one true gospel is the one the Galatians heard from Paul. It does not need to be augmented with certain prescriptions from the Jewish Law.

Although we often speak about his conversion, Paul himself describes what happened as a "vocation." This was not merely a personal call as we might think of vocation today. Paul's call from God involves also a mission specifically to the Gentiles. Paul insists that this call came from God and underlines its divine origin by contrasting it with the role played by human beings, including his own initial unwillingness to accept Christ. It is precisely because he was in conflict with many others, including leaders of the church, that Paul begins Galatians by emphasizing that his call is from God. Paul has received an "apocalypse" or "revelation." He did not even go

to Jerusalem nor meet any other apostle until three years after his call (which most scholars date around AD 34–35).

Paul uses language from the great prophets to describe his call, suggesting that he stands in their line. He claims that he was called from his "mother's womb," echoing the description of Jeremiah's call (Jer 1, 4; see also Is 49, 1). Paul reviews his own efforts to destroy the church, insisting that it was zeal for the Jewish Law that caused him to seek the authority to bring to trial in Jerusalem his fellow Jews who believed in Christ. Paul insists that he did not consult nor compromise with "flesh and blood," referring to the church authorities such as Peter, whom he did not even meet until later.

Paul and the Jerusalem Authorities (2, 1–21). According to the authentic gospel preaching, faith in Jesus as the Christ is sufficient for salvation, without any other obligations to the Jewish Law. The single gospel message, Paul argues in Galatians 2, 1–10, was confirmed by a meeting in Jerusalem with all the leaders of the church. Scholars place this meeting around AD 50 (see Acts 11 and 15). The only stipulation the leaders expressed was that Paul and the Gentiles be mindful of the poor, which probably refers to the collection of money from the Gentile churches for a common fund in Jerusalem (see comment on 2 Cor 8 and 9). Paul insists that he was eager to do this. Nevertheless, the Gentiles probably needed to learn that concern for the poor was a priority of Christian life (see 2 Cor 8, 1—9, 15). The Gentiles would not have benefited from the long Jewish ethical tradition that mandated taking care of the poor. Although this just concern was part of Jewish Law, the Law is not the reason Paul gives for accepting this stipulation. Rather, he insists that there was neither discussion nor agreement about the Gentiles following any prescriptions of the Law. This account from Paul is quite at odds with the account of presumably the same Jerusalem meeting in Acts 15, 20.29, where observance of Jewish marital and sexual customs and basic dietary laws are enjoined on the Gentiles. Scholars have always had difficulty with the two versions, some assuming that Luke invented the cultic observances that the Gentiles were expected to observe, others assuming that Paul ignored them. Here Paul insists that no restrictions were part of the accord but were only added *after* the Jerusalem meeting and only because of pressure from the Jerusalem church headed by James. In Galatians 5, 3 Paul will remind the Galatians that those who are circumcised must observe the whole Law, not just selected precepts.

The issue of imposing at least a minimal observance of the Jewish Law, including circumcision, on the Gentiles was introduced, Paul asserts, by "representatives from James," only after the Jerusalem Conference. Paul accuses them of bad faith, saying that they had come to "spy on our freedom . . . in Christ Jesus" (2, 4). The notion of Christian freedom will be more developed in Galatians 5. Here it is introduced as characteristic of Christians in the Pauline churches. Paul confronted Peter later in Antioch because Peter caved in to the pressure of the "Judaizing" delegation from James in Jerusalem. The picture Paul paints is of a change of mind on the part of James and Peter after the Jerusalem agreement, which had the impact of undermining Paul's authority in Galatia and elsewhere. The "Judaizers" of Galatia may have been witnesses to this discrepancy and thus felt authorized to challenge Paul's authority there. Paul had accused Peter of influencing the Gentiles to "live like Jews" in the observance of some basics of the Law, including circumcision. Peter, who had also baptized Gentiles (Acts 10), was beginning to compromise the Gentiles' freedom after the Jerusalem meeting.

This historical conflict provides the context for Paul's important concept of "justification by faith." Within the framework of his conflict with Peter and James, Paul reminds Peter as a fellow Jew that "we who are Jews . . . know that a person is not justified by works of the [Jewish] law but through faith in Jesus Christ" (2, 15–16). Paul appeals to the faith he has in common with Peter and with other Jewish Christians. All Christians of Jewish descent share the belief that Jesus is the Christ. It is Jesus rather than the Jewish Law that justifies all. Generations later in the church, when the preponderance of believers were of Gentile rather than Jewish origin, the historical context of this dispute was forgotten. Since then, Christians have sometimes mistakenly interpreted Paul's message as somehow considering faith as opposed to works. Furthermore, the word "alone" was added to the formula

"justification by faith," and the phrase was understood in an absolute sense. So, for example, Luther portrayed the gospel as "law-free" in his famous objection to indulgences, which were undoubtedly carried to extremes in his day. The Reformers used Paul's doctrine of justification by faith to oppose any notion of salvation as dependent on good works, such as they alleged the Catholic doctrine of salvation taught. They distorted the Catholic teaching of works as a response to faith. For their part, Catholics have sometimes exaggerated the role of meritorious deeds to gain grace. Both Protestants and Catholics have based their arguments on Paul, especially on Galatians and Romans, and both have distorted the Jewish understanding of Law observance as the response of the faithful to the gift of the covenant. As a result, some Christians erroneously read into Paul's message a dichotomy between faith and works that does not accurately interpret Paul's original meaning, and a theological anti-Judaism that characterizes the Jewish way of life as oppressively bound in Law as contrasted to liberating Christian freedom.

We see in all of Paul's letters that his doctrine is consistently followed by ethical applications. Thus Paul teaches that faith is expressed in the moral life. Good works are a response to faith. Even in passages where Paul speaks of freedom (for example, in Galatians 5) he advocates at the same time the practice of good works. Paul's understanding of Christianity includes a highly developed ethic or lifestyle. He would see no opposition between faith and freedom on one side and good works and obedience on the other, as he will show in the next major section of Galatians.

Faith, Freedom, and the Scriptures (Gal 3, 1—4, 31)

Here Paul begins his theological and biblical explanation of his gospel. He appeals first to the experience of the Galatians, then to the biblical exposition of several texts, then to several human examples.

Paul insists that his converts in Galatia have heard the true and complete gospel message from him and that, as a result of their conversion to Christ, they have received the Spirit of God. He asks them a question to which they all know the answer, in order to shame them into attention: did you receive the Spirit through Law or through faith (3, 2)? They know it was through his preaching of faith without Law. In order to emphasize the importance of continuing to live the life of faith, Paul employs a contrast between the "flesh" and the "spirit" designed to show that these are mutually exclusive. Today's reader will find such a contrast problematic unless we understand the Greek philosophical mindset of Paul's audience and the special meanings he attaches to the words.

Today we tend to equate "flesh" with body or material existence, and to affirm the body as a positive and even essential expression of self-fulfillment and human happiness. But the Greeks stressed the tension between the flesh and the spirit, which presupposed the superiority of the spirit and the inferiority of the flesh. For them, the spirit represented the immortal, life-giving aspect of human experience, whereas the body or flesh signified the weaker, sensual, mortal aspect that had to be subordinated to the spirit in order to find happiness. Though the Hebrews did not generally share this mindset, still earlier biblical language will sometimes use "flesh" or "flesh and blood" to mean the weakness and vulnerability of human existence without the assistance of God (see even 1 Cor 15, 50). This is usually Paul's meaning for "flesh": human arrogance that tries to live independently of God's grace. To further complicate our task of interpreting Paul's meaning, we note that Paul sometimes refers to the Spirit of God or Holy Spirit (at times simply called the "Spirit"), and at other times he designates the human spirit. Often it is hard for the reader to distinguish the two. In English translations God's Spirit is usually capitalized, but that is at the call of the translator, and sometimes the difference is not clear. Paul asserts that the Spirit of God was conferred upon the Galatians by faith, not by "works of the flesh" such as circumcision. Paul therefore concludes that it would be an absurd regression to "end in the flesh" what had begun in the spirit. Faith transferred the Galatians and all believers from the domain of the flesh to that of the spirit. The Spirit of God enables us to share fully in the inheritance of the promise made to Abraham and fulfilled now in Christ. Thus Paul moves from a review of the Galatian experience of the gospel to an illustration of the validity of that experience taken from the Scriptures.

Abraham, Father of Faith (3, 6–16). Paul reinforces his teaching on justification by faith by giving examples from the Scriptures showing that faith in Christ is sufficient for salvation. Using the exegetical methods in which he was trained, he draws out several biblical passages from different places and puts them together into a new argument to show that Abraham received the promise and was considered to have been justified in God's sight *before* he was given the precept of circumcision (Gen 12, 3; 15, 6). Then the crucified Christ took upon himself the curse of the Law by hanging on a tree (Dt 27, 26; Hb 2, 4; Lv 18, 5; Dt 21, 23). Paul relates the experience of Abraham and his sons to the experience of the Galatians. Through faith the Galatians (a predominantly Gentile community) became the "children of Abraham" (3, 7). "Abraham believed God, and it was credited to him as righteousness" (3, 6). God gave a promise to Abraham because of his faith. This promise included the "nations" or Gentiles who are blessed through Abraham. Now, Paul says, the Gentiles have received the blessing of Abraham. The promise has been fulfilled in Christ.

Example of the Human Will (3, 17–23). Paul then uses the example of a last will or testament (in Greek, the words, will, testament, and covenant are all the same, *diatheke,* which helps make the analogy in a way that is lost in English). Once made and ratified, it cannot be changed by something that comes along later. In like manner, the covenant with Abraham could not be altered by the Mosaic Law that came later. The original covenant through faith is the prior one that cannot be annulled, and this is the one in which all persons of faith belong.

Example of the Child-Minder (3, 24—4, 11). The next human analogy that Paul uses would have been perfectly comprehensible to his contemporaries, but it needs some explanation today. The "custodian" was a slave in a wealthy family who had authority over the minor son and was responsible for his discipline and education. Once the son came of age and became the heir, the roles were reversed. Paul uses this example to argue that the Law was a temporary custodian until Christ came, which is the time set by the father for our spiritual coming of age. At that point, the Law has no more power over us.

As illustration for this maturity in Christ that

we now have, Paul uses one of his most famous sayings, probably a baptismal formula that he quotes for effect. All who have been baptized in Christ have a new identity, so that there is no longer Jew or Greek, slave or free, male and female, but all are one in Christ Jesus (3, 27–28). We would like to know how seriously this proclamation was taken in Paul's day. The tension between Jew and Greek (that is, Gentile) continued, but it was precisely to this that Paul was devoting much of his effort. Nevertheless, Christian persecution of Jews increased rather than decreased in following centuries. Slavery certainly continued for centuries in Christian households and states. Problems between men and women in the church have not yet subsided. Disparities in treatment based on ethnicity, social status, and gender are perennial. This prophetic text remains a challenge for the church in every age.

Assurance of Paul's Affection (4, 12–20). In spite of the harsh things Paul had to say to the Galatians in the beginning of the letter, he now softens a bit to express his continued affection for them and his remembrance of how well they treated him when he was there. Verse 15 leads some commentators to suppose that Paul had some kind of eye disease that made him less impressive in person (see 2 Cor 10, 10), but this is speculation. He hopes to come again to be with them and to be able to speak more affectionately than he has had to do in this letter.

Allegory of the Two Wives of Abraham (4, 21–31). Paul goes on to illustrate his teaching with yet another scriptural example, namely that of Abraham's two sons by two women. The first, Ishmael, is the son of a slave woman, Hagar, whose name never actually occurs here (but see Gn 21). Isaac is Sarah's son, born free. Ishmael and his mother were expelled from Abraham's sight and did not inherit the promise. Paul develops his commentary as an allegory, understanding Ishmael and Hagar to represent slavery to the covenant on Mount Sinai. Isaac represents the promise fulfilled in the freedom of faith without the restrictions of the Law. The words originally spoken to Sarah, who had been barren, are fulfilled in the believers who inherit the promise (4, 27). Paul says of the Galatians that they, like Isaac, are children of the promise, that is, the promise of grace and with it, freedom from the

Law. Thus Paul's reading of the Scriptures reinforces his insistence that the Galatians are justified without the Law and freed from the Law. Therefore, to return to the Law's restrictions would be a great foolishness (see 3, 1).

Exhortations for Christian Living (Gal 5, 1—6, 10)

Paul draws implications for Christian living from his teaching. While insisting on freedom, he shows how faith has its consequences in Christian life. Chapters 5 and 6 exhort believers to exercise their faith in their relationships with one another. These exhortations focus on the responsibilities Christians share for developing the community. We are struck by Paul's emphasis on social responsibility. Note that Paul does not dwell on a believer's personal, interior life so much as on the relationships that should characterize the Christian community, which is living the blessings of the Spirit of God (see 5, 21–23). The term "freedom" recurs here (5, 1.13). For Paul freedom is not lawlessness but the liberty to live for God (see Rom 6, 4) and to serve one another through love (Gal 5, 13). The choice between slavery and freedom is the choice between the works of the Law and the works of the Spirit. For Paul, all humans are under some power— either of "sin" and the "flesh," or of the Spirit of God and faith.

In 5, 2–12 Paul refers again to the specific problem that occasioned this urgent letter. The Judaizers are agitating the Galatians, trying to convince them to be circumcised and follow some of the elements of the Jewish Law. Paul reminds the Galatians of a principle certainly upheld by Jews, that circumcision of itself is nothing if not a sign of commitment to follow the whole Law (5, 3). The problem Paul confronts is the imposition of circumcision on the Gentiles. Galatians 5, 11 implies that Paul, even as a Christian, did "preach circumcision" for Jews; perhaps he did at one time earlier in his career, and the Galatians have heard of it. Paul does not dispute the role of the Law in Jewish life. Although some accused Paul of undermining the Law for Jews, he considers himself innocent of that charge (see Rom 9, 1–5; 1 Cor 9, 20; Acts 21, 20–26). The list of "works of the flesh" in 5, 20–21 show that Paul does not equate flesh with the body; many of them are perversions of mind.

In Galatians 6, 1–10 Paul continues to reflect on community life, advocating the virtues of charity, service, and humility. Christians are obliged to "bear one another's burdens." Although they are also called to "do good to all," even those outside the church, special priority is given to those in the family of faith (6, 10).

Conclusion (6, 11–18)

Paul adds a final note for emphasis and concludes with a short prayer. He probably dictated this letter to a scribe. He adds his own closing remarks, beginning at verse 11. Here he adds a new dimension to the arguments against the agitators: they are insincere, since they themselves do not follow the Law. They are only trying to escape persecution by other Jews, or possibly the Romans (see note on 6, 12–15). Paul contrasts their cowardice and insincerity with his own boldness and consistency, referring to the "marks of Jesus" on his body. All that matters, Paul says, is that we are created anew (6, 15). He concludes with a prayer for peace and mercy, calling down a blessing on his brothers and sisters in Christ.

Concluding Remarks

The letter to the Galatians may be one of the most difficult for us to approach without prior knowledge of the historical circumstances in which it was written, yet no one knows very much about those circumstances. Paul's message here is nevertheless especially appropriate today. Despite painful differences with other leaders, Paul focuses on a single gospel message that all authentic Christian missionaries preach. This message emphasizes the role of faith and the significance of community. Paul's use of Scripture illustrates that this is the same message that has been repeated and refined throughout the Old Testament. Faith is the expression of the bond between God and us, a bond lived out in relationships with others. Paul's exhortation to Christians is to "be free" and therefore responsible for one another. There is no conflict between faith and works, according to Paul. Faith is necessarily expressed in the everyday life of believers. Paul does, however, stress that the works of faith are a result of the gift of the Spirit and a response to it, not a requirement for receiving the Spirit or for meriting salvation.

EPHESIANS

[see pages 1570–78 of the New Testament]

Before Beginning . . .

Ephesians displays a well-developed theology of the church. The four major epistles of Paul (Romans, 1 and 2 Corinthians, and Galatians) are all addressed to specific congregations in various important locations in the Greco-Roman world. Ephesians envisions not a single congregation but the universal church seen as a spiritual reality entrusted with the worldwide mission of Christ. Here the word "church" *(ekklesia)* acquires that new meaning of universal reality.

There are significant parallels between Ephesians and Colossians. The advanced Christology and ecclesiology, the apparent absence of Jewish-Gentile tensions, and, finally, the unusual vocabulary unique to these two epistles among the Pauline letters prompt many interpreters to assert that Ephesians and Colossians were written in an era after the death of Paul. If that is the case, the disciple who wrote these letters was familiar with Pauline theology and style and adapted Paul's message to new times and circumstances. In our comments we will follow the usual practice of referring to the author of Ephesians and the other "Deutero-Pauline" writings (see "Paul and His Writings," RG 439–40) as "Paul," all the while keeping in mind that nearly all Pauline scholars think of Ephesians as not from Paul himself, and a majority think the same of Colossians.

Working through Ephesians

Ephesians follows the pattern of a Greco-Roman letter, beginning with an *address* (1, 1–14) and ending with a *conclusion* (6, 21–24). Moreover, it follows the pattern of a Pauline letter, with initial blessing or prayer in the address and conclusion adapted to a liturgical assembly. These stylized elements enclose the *body* of the letter (1, 15—6, 20), which presents a teaching or doctrine on the church and then applies this teaching to the daily life of believers. We will follow the NAB outline (p. 1571) emphasizing the major themes developed in Ephesians. This outline is as follows:

I. The Address (1, 1–14)
II. The Body of the Letter (1, 15—6, 20)
   A. The Teaching on the Church (1, 15—4, 24)
     1. Unity of the Church (1, 15—2, 22)
     2. World Mission of the Church (3, 1—4, 24)
   B. Ethical Applications (4, 25—6, 20)
III. Conclusion (6, 21–24)

Reading through Ephesians

The Address (1, 1–14)

Ephesians identifies the sender as "Paul, an apostle of Christ Jesus by the will of God." The absence from some manuscripts of the designation "in Ephesus" (1, 1) is one reason why Ephesians is considered by some to be a circular letter—intended for a wider audience rather than for the specific community at Ephesus alone. No particularities regarding the Ephesian community are mentioned as is customary when Paul writes to a community he knows as well as he should have known the Ephesians (see Acts 19, 10). The lack of a personalized greeting further supports the view that this is a letter to all the churches written by a Pauline disciple.

A doxology or blessing of God replaces the personal thanksgiving characteristic of Paul's letters (Eph 1, 3–6). As if conscious of the great mystery of the church he is about to describe, the author begins by proclaiming the blessedness of God. The recurrence of the term "blessed" and the many liturgical references suggest that this prayer of praise is inspired by the Jewish liturgies in which believers, mindful of the wondrous works of God, cannot but bless the Creator. The focus is on God's blessing in Christ in whom the divine plan for the salvation of all people is achieved. The Holy Spirit is described as the "first installment" (1, 14) of our inheritance toward redemption.

The Body of the Letter (1, 15—6, 20)

The message of Ephesians has two parts. The first or doctrinal section (1, 15—4, 24) unfolds the church as the fulfillment of God's plan for salva-

tion, inaugurated in Christ. A second section (4, 25—6, 20) contains ethical "imperatives" concerning the daily conduct of believers, providing practical applications of Paul's teaching.

The Teaching on the Church (1, 15—4, 24)

Ephesians develops the New Testament teaching about the unity of the church and the church's worldwide mission. Integral to this mission is the significant role of the apostle in its promotion. We shall briefly consider each of these teachings.

Unity of the Church (1, 15—2, 22). The ecclesiology, or theology of the church, in Ephesians is integrally linked to its Christology. That is to say that its view of the church follows from its view of Christ and Christ's saving work. Therefore, to understand the emphasis on the unity of the church that occurs in Ephesians, we must see the perspective on Christ developed there. The Christology and ecclesiology in Ephesians and Colossians is developed beyond that in Paul's major letters to the Corinthians and the Romans. Yet this development has its roots in Paul, for whom the image of the church as the body of Christ helps to express the unity of Christians and the salvific work of Christ's death and resurrection.

The description of the church as the Body of Christ appears first in 1 Corinthians 12, 12–27 and Romans 12, 4–8. Paul urged the Christians in Corinth and Rome to express their unity in mutual love as members of the same body, Christ. But in Ephesians and Colossians there is a major change in the image. Here Christ is referred to as the "head of the body, the church" (Eph 1, 22–23; Col 1, 18). This shift in the image leads away from the mutual participation and responsibility of all the members to centralized authority in the person of Christ, who is portrayed as above every principality, authority, and dominion (cf. Eph 1, 21–22). Nevertheless, the recipients are still reminded that in the body of Christ, we are members of one another (4, 15) and of Christ (5, 30).

By his resurrection, Paul asserts, Jesus became Lord of all, Jews and Gentiles and every creature (see 1 Cor 12, 3). This is so because in Christ's resurrection God has conquered sin and death; it is the beginning of a new era. Paul's writings speak of the humiliation (death) and exaltation (resurrection) of Christ by which God vindicated Jesus because of his obedience. Jesus now sits at God's right hand. At Jesus' name, every knee bends and every tongue proclaims that Jesus is Lord (Phil 2, 6–11). This is one of the oldest Christological proclamations (Rom 10, 9). Jesus' lordship is an expression of his sovereignty over all created things and his word reconciling the whole of creation to God. Yet even now the universal recognition of Jesus' lordship has not been completed. The mission of preaching Christ's lordship and bringing all creation under God's reign is entrusted to the church.

Some time after AD 50, when Paul was writing Galatians and Romans, it is clear that one of the major problems facing the church was the reconciliation of Jews and Gentiles under one God and one Lord. Distinctions between Jews and Gentiles were symbolized by such practices as circumcision, dietary laws, and restrictions regarding table fellowship, intermarriage, and other forms of social interaction. These, Paul insisted, were obliterated by Christ's death. Yet the apostle himself had to struggle to resolve the tensions between Israel and the Gentiles (see, for example, Romans 9—11). The teaching about the church in Ephesians seems to reflect a time or place in which these tensions are resolved. The Gentiles are portrayed as those who were once "far off . . . strangers to the covenants of promise." Now they have "become near by the blood of Christ" (2, 13). The images of the church as the body of Christ and Christ as the head of the church serve to illustrate the intrinsic unity of the church of Jews and Gentiles, that is, of all people in Christ.

World Mission of the Church (3, 1—4, 24). The author of Ephesians identifies himself as "Paul, a prisoner of Christ [Jesus] for you Gentiles" (3, 1). He then abruptly interrupts this self-introduction to elaborate on his role in the mystery of God's plan for the salvation of the world. Now imprisoned, Paul continues the work of intercession. Through prayer Paul brings the Gentiles to God. The church—the body of Christ and the family of God—is entrusted with the work of salvation that is to fill all things "with the fullness of God" (3, 19). Paul understands his work to be essential in God's plan, and yet he is unperturbed either by his own imprisonment or by the failure of some to accept the message of Christ. Salvation as well as creation is in God's hands, and God's plan is being fulfilled in inscrutable mystery.

Again the language reflects that introduced by Paul in his earlier writings. But the conception of the divine plan of salvation is more developed. The church, under the impetus of the Spirit, is bringing all to the "one God and Father of all, who is over all and through all and in all" (4, 6). Paul's prayer is that "you may be filled with all the fullness of God" (3, 19). The mystery of God who ordained that "all Israel will be saved" (Rom 11, 26) now prescribes that we "no longer live as the Gentiles do" (Eph 4, 17), but "put on the new self, created in God's way in righteousness and holiness of truth" (4, 24). Having described this mystery, Paul goes on to exhort the Ephesians to express their common call to holiness and unity in their daily life.

Ethical Applications (4, 25—6, 20)

Ephesians 5 illustrates how its teaching on the church has practical consequences in the daily lives of believers. Ephesians 5, 1 says, "So be imitators of God, as beloved children, and live in love." This could be the summary of the whole of Christian life. The author of Ephesians draws out some implications of imitating God by living in love. Much of this section consists of general moral exhortation, description of what the ideal Christian life with one another should look like.

Christians relate to one another in ways already established and governed, at least to some extent, by outward society. So, for example, wives and husbands, children and parents, slaves and masters all follow Greco-Roman social norms, which give some direction about the rights and duties of people who are in these kinds of relationships. The author adopts and adapts the traditional philosophical approach to household life that is at least as old as Aristotle and that we call "household rules." In ordinary Greco-Roman society the lines of authority and of subservience were clearly drawn. Husbands, parents, and masters all have great power over wives, children, and slaves in a rigid social hierarchy.

For Paul these rules or principles become practical applications of faith for members of the "household of God" (2, 19), giving directives for various segments of society in their relationships to one another. Paul does not offer a radical critique of certain social contracts, such as slavery or male dominance. Yet for him, relationships among Christians must reflect a new perspective. Christians are motivated to a new way of thinking, determined by their common baptism. Christians share the conviction that all are one in Christ and saved by Christ. This leads to innovations in the usual treatment of household rules: here both parties in a relationship are addressed, whereas in the traditional form, only the male authority would be addressed, and here the inferior party is even addressed first. The Ephesians are urged to "live in a manner worthy of the call you have received . . . bearing with one another through love" (Eph 4, 1f). They are exhorted to "be subordinate to one another" (5, 21), to "nourish and cherish" one another, because they are members of one body (5, 29–30). The extra verses spent on the analogy of husband to Christ and wife to the church are the springboard for much later mysticism, even as they also have been justification for continued subordinate positions for women. Such a passage as this, along with the exhortations to slave obedience, are paradoxical combinations of beauty, grace, and what today can only be seen as social oppression in the name of faith. They require careful interpretation both in the context of the author's world and of ours.

If we do not let these thorny problems be major obstacles, reading Ephesians today can inspire us to a powerful vision of the church. It leads us to reassess the ordinary way of approaching one another as colleagues, family, clients, and the like. We, like the Ephesians, are urged to remember our real identity and to respect others by relating to everyone in a way worthy of members of the "household of God." The ordinary hierarchical system that prevails in the world is superseded by a new way of relating to one another in Christ.

Paul finally urges the Ephesians to "pray at every opportunity in the Spirit" (6, 18). He again asks for prayers for himself, that he may speak "the mystery of the gospel" with boldness and courage even though he is in chains (6, 19–20).

Conclusion (6, 21–24)

Ephesians does not exhibit the usual personal tone and greetings of Paul's authentic letters. In the conclusion, however, the author indicates that he sends the letter with Tychicus (6, 21), the name of Paul's messenger of Colossians as well

(Col 4, 7). The final prayers are for peace and love and grace.

Concluding Remarks

Ephesians strikes a balance between reflection on the church as a universal, spiritual reality and application in the daily lives of Christians of their new identity as members of this spiritual creation. The letter also emphasizes the congruence between Christians' personal spirituality and their responsibilities in relationships with one another. Through baptism we are renewed. We have put off the "old humanity," symbolized by Adam; we have been transformed into a "new humanity," in Christ. We are called to be imitators of God and to reflect God's love and compassion in our daily lives.

As part of our Christian Scriptures, Ephesians stands as a continual challenge calling us beyond the present to a deeper reality where all things are in the care of God. The present with its trials, temptations, failures, and limitations can indeed discourage us. The problems of resolving tensions and enduring suffering are temporary. Ephesians is a letter from prison, addressing a church afflicted with oppression from the outside, confusion and dissension from within. Ephesians testifies to the author's faith and by the hope of God's plan for the salvation of the entire world—a plan that will be fulfilled despite, and even by means of, apparent obstacles. When we are confronted by the limitations of our present circumstances or hampered by fear, Ephesians provides encouragement. For us as Christians, the liturgy celebrates a communion with God. Faith is conviction of things unseen, especially about the triumph of God in Christ.

Ephesians is one of the most hope-filled and confident of all the Pauline letters. It may lack the usual personal tone expected of communities Paul knew well. But Ephesians expresses fundamental Christian beliefs that continue to characterize the church today. For example, despite suffering and failures, the church celebrates the reality of salvation already experienced in the daily life of Christians. In our world, where many families are in crisis, we read Paul's advice about mutual relationships with members of God's household and take courage in the admonition to serve one another in love. Like the writer of Ephesians, the modern church at Vatican II complemented reflection on the nature of the church with the role of the church in the modern world. The church as Christ's body, no matter what its limitations, is called and empowered to reconcile the whole world to God. Each of us, as members of the church, has a role in this mission.

PHILIPPIANS

[see pages 1578–85 of the New Testament]

Before Beginning . . .

Philippians is one of the most appealing of Paul's letters. Along with Ephesians, Colossians, and Philemon, Philippians is traditionally called a "captivity letter" because in all four the author refers to his imprisonment. The authentic Pauline authorship of Philippians and Philemon is never doubted, although there is disagreement regarding the authorship of Ephesians and Colossians.

There are several theories about the location and occasion of the imprisonment from which Paul writes. The oldest and traditional view is that he writes from Rome in his final imprisonment there; this would date the letter to the late fifties or early sixties of the first century. Some have questioned the feasibility of this location, given the apparent frequent exchanges implied in the letter and the great distance from Rome to Philippi. So a second location has been suggested, Caesarea Maritima on the Palestinian coast, during the two years of confinement recorded in Acts 24—26. Still, that is a great distance, requiring a month or more of travel. A third suggestion is that Paul was imprisoned earlier in his life in Ephesus, and that Philippians and Philemon date from that time, perhaps in the middle years of the fifties. The mysterious references to trouble in Asia (Ephesus was the principal city of the Roman province of Asia) in 1 Corinthians 15, 32 and 2 Corinthians 1, 8–10 support this idea, as does Paul's avoidance of Ephesus on his journey to Jerusalem (Acts 20, 16). In that case, travel back and forth from Paul's prison to Philippi would have been much easier and faster.

If the Pauline authorship of Philippians is unquestioned, the unity of the letter poses some challenges. The choppy nature of this letter has led many interpreters to suggest that Philippians was originally at least three letters. A later editor (according to this theory), adapting the initial and final greeting, combined the originally separate messages into one edited "letter" for the purpose of later circulation. On the other hand, many more recent interpreters, using methods derived from the principles of ancient rhetoric, argue for the unity of the letter in spite of the rough edges here and there. Whichever is the case, the end result, the "canonical letter," provides the rich spiritual legacy called Philippians, so beloved in the Christian tradition.

Important Pauline themes are developed in Philippians, particularly that of unity. We see in the letter the deep love Paul feels for this community. Disregarding the dangers facing him, Paul focuses on the sufferings of the community caused by external persecution and internal divisions. We hear of Paul's gratitude for the material support he has received from the community. We witness his fears about the problems within the community and the pressure from outside, but he subordinates those concerns to expressions of joy for the strength of the Philippians' church. In a surprisingly vehement outburst against those who advocate a return to the Jewish Law, he reminds us that this issue, so central to Galatians and Romans, is not forgotten elsewhere.

Working through Philippians

We can discuss the main themes of Philippians according to the following outline. The basic letter contains the usual *address* (1, 1–11), *body* (1, 12—3,1), and *conclusion* (4, 21 –23).

   I. Address and Thanksgiving (1, 1–11)
  II. The Body of the Letter (1, 12—4, 20)
     A. Paul's Situation and the Progress of the Gospel (1, 12–26)
     B. Exhortations for Community Unity; Example of Jesus (1, 27—2, 18)
     C. Travel of Paul and Assistants (2, 19—3, 1)
     D. Digression and Warning (3, 1–4a)
     E. Example of Paul (3, 4b–21)
     F. Specific Appeal to Unity (4, 1–9)
     G. A Thank-you Note (4, 10–20)
  III. Conclusion (4, 21–23)

Reading through Philippians

The Address (1, 1–11)

The opening line names Paul and Timothy as senders of the letter, but the speaker quickly changes to "I" in verse 3, for Paul is really the author. Timothy will be mentioned as an ideal companion in 2, 19–24. The address is unique among Pauline letters in its acknowledgment of local leaders by title, "overseers and ministers," which by using later meanings of the words could also mean "bishops and deacons," but there is no evidence that the connotations later brought to those words are active here. Nevertheless, the address shows the beginnings of official titles and functions in the church.

A thanksgiving (1, 3–8) and a prayer (1, 9–11) complete the address. This is one of the longest and most beautifully developed of the Pauline thanksgivings. It introduces the themes of joy and community, themes that recur throughout Philippians. The paradox expressed in this letter is that the intense suffering experienced by Paul and the Philippians pales in comparison to the confident joy they share. Although separated because of Paul's imprisonment, and threatened on all sides, Paul and the Philippians are "partners," participating together in the spread of the gospel message. Paul draws strength from the Philippians' affection and display of concern for him. He prays (1, 9–11) that they will be strengthened and that their love will grow even amid hardships. Together they all await the "day of Christ," which Paul longs for and strains forward to obtain.

The Body of the Letter (1, 12—4, 20)

Paul's Situation and the Progress of the Gospel (1, 12–26)

Paul links faith in suffering and the spread of the gospel. Nowhere is this link more eloquently expressed than in Philippians 1, 12–26 where he refers to the effect his own imprisonment has had on the progress of the gospel message. Paul rejoices that even his enemies are using the opportunity represented by his present circumstances to energetically pursue the spread of the Christian message. For him, the priority is that "in every way . . . Christ is being proclaimed" (1,

18). This position stands in some contrast to his insistence elsewhere, even in 3, 2–3 of this letter, that only he has the right gospel. Paul speaks of joy even though he is in prison and the outcome is uncertain. He could be facing death. As a committed and passionate apostle, Paul worked tirelessly to promote acceptance of the gospel message by Gentiles everywhere. Now, in prison, Paul is equally peaceful, knowing that even should he die the preaching will be continued.

If 1 Corinthians, especially chapters 1 and 2, represents a theoretical development of Paul's theology of the cross, Philippians represents Paul's own faith as he lives this theology. The wisdom of the cross is that God's power is made perfect in weakness. By this transforming power of the cross, Paul's brothers and sisters take encouragement from his imprisonment and preach the gospel all the more fearlessly. By the wisdom of the cross Paul considers death to be "gain," and what he formerly considered "gain" to be "rubbish" (see 3, 7–8). Imprisoned, Paul draws strength from the community. He speaks with confidence and joy, expressing hope that is firmly rooted in God.

Exhortations for Community Unity and the Example of Jesus (1, 27—2, 18)

As he does in several other letters, Paul expresses concern that the opposition the Philippians experience will threaten their faith. He knows of internal divisions among these Christians. By appealing to them to have a common mind and heart, Paul alludes first to his own suffering and imprisonment and then to the example of Christ.

The beautiful hymn about the abasement of Christ of 2, 6–11 is probably taken from an already existing piece of early Christian poetry with which the Philippians are familiar. It recalls their source of encouragement, and is a cherished expression of faith in the redemptive aspects of Christ's suffering and death. The example of Christ's death must, above all else, influence the believing community in its own practical acceptance of and obedience to God's will. Thus, Christ who "emptied himself" is the example of behavior for the Philippians who are having trouble preserving unity in the congregation. Further, Christ by his death became "Lord" so that all who profess his Lordship are subject to him. In homage they recognize that they are brothers and sisters, members with one another of one believing community. So Christ is the example and the empowerment of selfless, mutual service in the church. Following the hymn, Paul draws out some implications: the Philippians are to remain blameless and innocent in the midst of adversity and wickedness, waiting for the day of Christ (2, 16). Conceiving of the Christian life as a liturgical sacrifice, Paul says that even though he is "poured out as a libation," (wine that is offered in sacrifice) he rejoices. He asks only that the Philippians share his joy.

Travel of Paul and Assistants (2, 19—3, 1)

The travel account given here and other indications suggest relatively free and frequent exchanges between the prisoner, Paul, and the Philippians. This would be more easily understood with an imprisonment closer to Philippi than to Rome, hence the Ephesian theory. The news about Epaphroditus's illness and recovery seem to indicate different visits. He probably came from Philippi and was not able to continue his apostolic work because of illness. Timothy is extolled as an ideal assistant, a second example of unity after Jesus. The trust among Paul, Timothy, and Epaphroditus stands in contrast to the squabbling between Euodia and Syntyche and other members of the Philippian community (4, 2–3).

Digression and Warning (3, 2–4a)

The abrupt change of tone and content between the first two chapters of Philippians and the strong warning in 3, 2–4 is one of the strongest arguments that these were originally separate communications. Even so, a skilled rhetorician could also just as abruptly switch topic and tone in order to get his audience's attention. This sudden theme of resistance to those who agitate for the Gentiles to be circumcised, presented in an insulting tone, is brief and does not reappear in this letter.

Example of Paul (3, 4b–21)

After presenting the example of Jesus and then in a lesser way of Timothy, Paul now proposes himself as example of one who knows how to give up privilege and status for the good of others. He gives us some of our best biographical information about himself, then reflects on the conse-quences of his encounter with Christ. Using athletic imagery, Paul encourages the Philippians to strain toward the goal of a "perfect maturity." He urges them not to regress into the past, seeking glory in shame (possible allusions to circumcision) or in other practices of the "flesh" such as observances of certain dietary rules. These, Paul says, are earthly things. Paul himself used to glory in his religious accomplishments, but since his conversion he no longer regards these as significant. Indeed, his former system of valuing is "rubbish" compared with his new way of seeing things in Christ. This is the wisdom of the cross. Those who do not accept this wisdom are "enemies of the cross" (3, 18).

Specific Appeal to Unity (4, 1–9)

Paul turns to an internal crisis that is just as destructive and threatening to the community. He begins chapter 4 by urging the Philippians to live in harmony, a theme he had already developed in chapters 1 and 2. But now he is specific in his appeal to unity, and all the previous rhetoric on the subject may be leading to this climax. There is a conflict between some leading women of the community, Euodia and Syntyche, and Paul solemnly begs them to stop. What position these women occupy we do not know, but their division is obviously central to the community's problems, so they may be significant leaders. Paul addresses a comrade and enlists the help of an otherwise unknown man named Clement to aid in the reconciliation of these women, for the betterment of the whole community.

A Thank-you Note (4, 10–20)

Paul expresses thanks for the help received from the Philippians and sent with Epaphroditus. He adds, however, that his gratitude is not so much that he was personally aided as that the Philippians' generosity is "profit that accrues to your account" (4, 17). Paul testifies to his own indifference and ability to do without. Yet he humbly accepted aid not only to alleviate his own need but as a symbol of the affection that linked him to the Philippians. Paul speaks of this aid in liturgical terms, referring to it as "a fragrant aroma . . . a sacrifice, pleasing to God" (4, 18–19; see also 2 Cor 2, 14–16). This is the ancient language of liturgical offering and sacrifice. The idea of an offering of mutual love and aid by Christians to one another as a "liturgy" appears also in Romans 12, 1–2, and 15, 17–20.

Conclusion (4, 21–23)

The conclusion of the letter sends greetings to everyone there from everyone here. The reference to "Caesar's household" is to the vast imperial network of civil servants that were present in every major city. We know from this reference that there were Christians among them.

Concluding Remarks

Since the writing of Philippians, the Christian community has been inspired not only by the words of the apostle but by the example of the imprisoned leader who speaks with such affection, hope, and faith. One of the most beautiful and well known of Paul's letters, Philippians represents a reflection on the meaning of fidelity in the midst of trial. Paul's confidence that in all things "Christ is . . . proclaimed" (1, 18) transcends the threat of others' jealousy and rivalry. The Christological hymn of Philippians 2 not only inspired the Philippians to greater unity but also continues to invite believers of every age to imitate Christ. Paul's prayer for his fellow Christians is that they always be happy (Phil 4, 4–9). This serves as a model for our prayers for one another. Paul puts his own life before the Philippians, encouraging them to follow him in everything that he does and says. Paul then promises that the "God of peace will be with you" (4, 9). Such should be our prayer in attracting others to live the Christian life.

COLOSSIANS

[see pages 1586–92 of the New Testament]

Before Beginning . . .

It is customary to refer to the author of Colossians as Paul, even though many interpreters question whether Paul himself wrote this brief letter. Many characteristics of the letter seem to suggest Paul's presence behind it. The lively style and personal greetings are typical of Paul. Most of the personal names mentioned here also appear in Philemon, a letter that has always been attributed to Paul himself. Yet there are strange speculative expressions, new terminology, and a new understanding of the church that many scholars think indicates a different author here, writing in Paul's name with the hope of using Paul's authority. A compromise position is that Paul entrusted the message to a secretary who composed it in his own terms and with his own style.

Paul himself did not establish the church at Colossae. Possibly Epaphras, a disciple of Paul, was the founding missionary there. The context is that erroneous teachers implied that Christ's work of redemption was incomplete—that certain other religious practices were required to supplement Christ's saving death and resurrection. These suggested practices were drawn from Jewish as well as non-Jewish or pagan religions. They amounted to ascetical and superstitious additions to the message Paul and Epaphras had taught. As in Galatians, but less emotionally, Paul adamantly insists in Colossians that adding to the gospel message is really subtracting from grace. Only as a member of Christ's body and under his headship can we fill up "what is lacking in the afflictions of Christ" (1, 24), that is, continuing Christ's redemptive suffering in the world.

At issue in the discussion at Colossae is the primary role of Christ in the salvation of the world. The power and authority of Christ and his relation to the rest of creation are challenged. False teachings at Colossae suggested that other spiritual beings were rivals to Christ's role, and that certain ascetical practices were a means of becoming more spiritual, while also helping to appease these spiritual beings. Using categories and labels present in these false teachings, Paul insists on the primacy of Christ and the sufficiency of his saving action on our behalf. Ethical imperatives follow from this fundamental faith rather than from the necessity of placating angelic spirits or following some ascetical ideals.

Working through Colossians

The *address and thanksgiving* (1, 1–14) and *conclusion* (4, 7–18) enclose the *body* of this letter in 1, 15—4, 6. The body of Colossians follows the basic indicative-imperative pattern characteristic of Paul. The structure of Colossians then is the following:

I. Address and Thanksgiving (1, 1–14)
II. The Body of the Letter (1, 15—4, 6)
   A. Instruction about Christ and False Teaching (1, 15—2, 23)
   B. Ethics Characterizing the True Christian (3, 1—4, 6)
III. Conclusion (4, 7–18)

Reading through Colossians

The Address (1, 1–14)

The *address* includes not only the usual greeting (1, 1–2) and thanksgiving (1, 3–8) but also a prayer for the continued progress of the Colossians (1, 9–14). Both the *address* and *conclusion* (4, 7–18) contain greetings and personal references that are typical of Paul.

The Body of the Letter (1, 15—4, 6)

Colossians' main message is correct teaching and warnings against false teachings (1, 15—2, 23). This is followed by exhortations to exercise fundamental beliefs in daily Christian living (3, 1—4, 6).

Instruction about Christ and False Teaching (1, 15—2, 23)

Paul is confident that Epaphras has given the community a solid foundation. He reminds the Colossians that by Christ's saving death, "[God] delivered us from the power of darkness and transferred us to the kingdom of his beloved Son" (1, 13). This transference from the realm of sin and error into that of grace and truth is effected in baptism and must be lived out in the daily lives of Christians. The doctrinal presentation of the first major part of Colossians falls into three sections: the Christological hymn and its implications (1, 15–23), Paul's own ministry and example (1, 24—2, 3), and warnings against false teachers and their teaching (2, 4–23).

The Christological Hymn (1, 15–23). In order to teach a correct Christology and clarify errors, Paul quotes a liturgical hymn apparently familiar to the Colossians (1, 15–20; see also Phil 2, 6–11). Many interpreters believe that this hymn predates Paul and was already in use by the early Christian communities. The poetic rhythm and language suggest that it was a hymn and that it was at home in the liturgy. Since Paul generally writes in prose, the insertion of a hymn here is easily discerned in the Greek. In this hymn Christians profess and celebrate the authority of Christ in whom all "the fullness was pleased to dwell, and through him to reconcile all things for him." Paul stresses the redemption and peace won for us through Christ. He does not badger or scold the Colossians for their errors, but presents Christ's role of reconciling the world to God as the basis of common faith among all believers. The text adapts a variety of traditions about the figure of Wisdom and a cosmic savior to the person of Christ, who begins, as in the prologue of John's Gospel, in the heavenly realm. But he is also the head of the church and firstborn from the dead, so that his saving action works in our history.

Paul's Ministry and Example (1, 24—2, 3). Emphasis on his own example is a remarkable trait of Paul's letters, one expected of a great teacher in his day (see further 1 Thes 1, 6; 2 Cor 11–12). It is also significant that upon reviewing Christ's work of redemption, Paul immediately attaches his own example as a model for the Colossians to emulate. At first this advice may strike us as surprising and almost shocking. How can Paul claim to be a model for all to imitate (see 1 Cor 11, 1; Phil 4, 8)? It springs from the apostle's humility and transparent confidence. Paul is so firmly rooted in God that he dares to advise his addressees to follow his example. By studying Paul's life, others may know the power of God and be converted. Paul always reveals the source of his confidence, which is not self-reliance but hope in God. This hope is best expressed in Christ's gift of salvation evidenced in the life of the apostle. The apostle glories in his vocation and fidelity while also accentuating his sufferings in the service of the gospel.

In describing his own ministry, Paul adapts categories important to the Colossians and to the false teachers who are disturbing them. They are emphasizing "wisdom" and "perfection," so Paul speaks about the "knowledge of the mystery of God, Christ, in whom are hidden all the treasures of wisdom and knowledge" (2, 2–3). Paul identifies the goal of his mission to "present everyone perfect in Christ" (1, 28). For this he labors and struggles in accord with God's power "working within me" (1, 29).

Warnings against False Teachings (2, 4–23). Paul encourages the Colossians in their faith, reminding them of their identity in Christ. He observes the "good order and the firmness of your faith in Christ." He celebrates this fidelity and encourages the Colossians to be grateful, with a thanksgiving rooted in faith. Finally, he warns against the seduction of false teaching that is according to mere human tradition and not grounded in Christ. The false teaching was probably a combination of Jewish and pagan philosophies and pagan ideals. Paul denounces the "circumcision administered by human hands" and the ascetical practices regarding "food and drink" alleged to be required at certain times and days (2, 16). Some teachers flaunted their visions and self-abasement, and were involved in complicated devotions to angelic beings. Paul labeled all these as transitory fads, "shadows of things to come" and "things destined to perish." By contrast, in Christ dwells the fullness of God. All are members of Christ, who is the head of the body, the church. Here and in Ephesians, this specific role of Christ within the church is introduced. Christians are united in one church under one Lord who is Christ. Their common task is the reconciliation of the world to God under Christ.

Ethics Characterizing the True Christian (3, 1—4, 6)

Paul does not really present a new, uniquely Christian ethical system but draws from several existing systems. Often Paul lists vices or virtues similar to lists found in Stoic or other Greek philosophers. The "household rules" found in Colossians (see Eph 5, 21—6, 9; Ti 2, 1—3, 8; 1 Pt 2, 11—3, 7) have parallels in contemporary Greco-Roman literature where elements of household management are discussed. The submission of wives, children, and slaves to the male household head was an expected part of the social order. A fundamental difference for Paul is the motivation and the empowerment to fulfill these ethical principles. The church as the body of Christ distinguishes itself from the outside world in that the love command operates to create a new way for Christians to relate to one an-

other. Paul says that the Colossians once conducted themselves as pagans who practiced immorality, greed, and passion (see 3, 5–7). Now they have "put on the new self, which is being renewed . . . in the image of its creator" (3, 10). In Christ the usual sexual, social, and ethnic distinctions do not exist, "but Christ is all and in all" (3, 11).

Conclusion (4, 7–18)

Tychicus is the messenger entrusted with the letter to the Colossians. Many think that the Onesimus mentioned as his companion (4, 9) is the former slave who returned to Colossae with the letter from Paul to Philemon (see Reading Guide to Philemon). The other companions mentioned at the end of Colossians are well-known Christians named in other Pauline letters except for Nympha (4, 15), a woman who hosts a house church. This list of personal references reminds us about the common Christian teaching upon which Paul depends and to which he urges the Colossians to hold firm.

Concluding Remarks

Today no less than in the times of the Colossians, Christians are pulled in various directions and people are still searching for spiritual guides and nourishment. The exotic, speculative language in Colossians does not seem so strange to us when we consider the attraction of certain superstitions, the popularity of astrology, the following of television evangelists who promise reprieves from effort in the spiritual life and shortcuts to wholeness and holiness. The epistle to the Colossians stresses the reconciliation of all things in Christ as the fundamental faith assertion with enormous ethical repercussions. As the firstborn of all creation, Christ is a symbol of the value of all creation and a promise of the ultimate salvation of all. That truth translates into the church's responsibility for stewardship in the world, assuming that in preaching reconciliation the rights of all are respected. In carrying out its mission, the church must be a symbol of peace, since Christ is the head of the church and Christ made peace by the blood of the cross.

THE LETTERS TO THE THESSALONIANS

Introduction

As far as we know, the Christian community at Thessalonica was among the earlier ones that Paul established and, although Paul's tone is affectionate in these letters, the apostle experienced a great deal of persecution from both Jews and Gentiles as a result of his preaching there. In his letters to the Thessalonians, Paul addresses real problems that arose in the community, such as mutual charity, the need to be responsible about work, and the issue of the death of Christians. The specific nature of these problems does not in any way detract from the enduring value of these letters as models for the Christian pastor and community. Before turning to the letters themselves, let us briefly describe some of the main elements of Paul's apocalyptic perspective that is so important in the Thessalonian correspondence as well as in Paul's other writings. (For more about apocalyptic literature, see the Reading Guides to Daniel and Revelation.)

Paul's Apocalyptic Perspective

Apocalyptic literature was born of the syncretistic blending of Wisdom and Prophetic traditions from the Bible with some elements of cosmic philosophy and mysticism from the Greco-Roman world. It spoke powerfully to those who were oppressed and suffering, encouraging them in the midst of their suffering. The apocalyptic writer was concerned with why the world was not as it ought to be. Jewish and Christian apocalypticism looked to God to bring about a radical transformation of the present world into something more like what God intended. We can only outline here some of the ways that the apocalyptic perspective influenced Paul.

First, *God's reign is universal.* The Jewish apocalyptic writers interpreted all of history, the good and the bad, as evolving according to a divine plan for the ultimate salvation of Israel, though some also foresaw a definite place for the Gentiles as well. Paul's call taught him to affirm and expand that insight. Throughout his writings Paul emphasizes that salvation is accessible to all now that Christ has come. God shows no partiality (see Rom 1, 16; 3, 22.29; 10, 12; Eph 2, 14;

Acts 10, 34; 15, 9–11). Paul says, "There is neither Jew nor Greek . . . neither slave nor free person . . . not male and female; for you are all one in Christ Jesus" (Gal 3, 28). The Gentiles have turned "from idols to serve the living and true God" (1 Thes 1, 9).

Second, Paul's thinking, like that of other apocalyptic writers, was characterized by a *dualism* that envisioned the ultimate salvation of the faithful and punishment of the wicked. Paul speaks of those who are "saved" and those who are "perishing" (see 1 Cor 1, 18; 2 Thes 2, 10). He pictures the judgment seat of Christ before whom we all must appear, "so that each one may receive recompense" (2 Cor 5, 10). The faithful are delivered from the wrath of God (1 Thes 1, 10), but it will not be withheld forever from the "enemies of the cross" (Phil 3, 18; see 1 Thes 2, 16). The basis for judgment is acceptance or rejection of the gospel. This dualism also gives rise to tensions and even hostility between the present and the age to come. The Lordship of Christ is a cosmic domain; Christ is in the process of returning all things to God (1 Cor 15, 28). The role of believers is to continue in faith and faithful life.

Third, there is language of expectation that the *time of transformation is imminent,* another characteristic of apocalyptic literature, which Paul borrows. For instance, this influences his views on the insignificance of one's marital or social status (for example, 1 Cor 7), his warnings to prayerful vigilance (1 Thes 5, 1–11), and his encouragement to endure suffering or oppression while striving to build up the community (Phil 2, 12–18). The just vigilantly await the savior (see Phil 3, 20), believing that he is coming to transform their mortal bodies into incorruptibility (Phil 3, 21). But we must be careful not to take this kind of language literally. It functioned as a reminder of the radical contingency of time and all things, and the possibility of God's powerful intervention at any time.

Paul adapts these elements, avoiding the extremes of some apocalyptic thinkers. He introduces significant modifications based on his own experience as apostle of the Gentiles, and his conviction that the end-times have already begun in Christ.

1 THESSALONIANS

[see pages 1592–96 of the New Testament]

Before Beginning . . .

Thessalonica was the capital and major city of the Roman province of Macedonia, about one hundred miles southwest of Philippi along a major Roman road. The communities at Thessalonica and Philippi were among Paul's first converts in Greece. This letter indicates that he encountered many troubles there from both Jews and Greeks. The beginning of Paul's ministry in Thessalonica was characterized by suffering and humiliation. He was "insolently treated at Philippi," an incident to which he does not allude in his letter there (see 2, 2; see also Acts 20, 34; 1 Cor 4, 12; 9, 3–18; 2 Thes 3, 7–9). The Thessalonians, too, shared in some of that persecution (2, 14–16). Persecution, illness, misunderstanding, and other forms of suffering plague Paul's ministry. Yet he constantly has hope of being found worthy by God to be entrusted with the preaching of the gospel (2, 4).

Working through 1 Thessalonians

Following the usual letter format, 1 Thessalonians has an *address and thanksgiving* (1, 1–10) and *conclusion* (5, 26–28), which envelop the *body* of Paul's message (2, 1—5, 25). This message falls into two parts: the indicative (2, 1—3, 13) followed by the ethical exhortations (4, 1—5, 25).

The structure of 1 Thessalonians can be outlined as follows:
 I. The Address (1, 1–10)
 II. The Body of the Letter (2, 1—5, 25)
  A. Paul's Account and Defense of His Ministry (2, 1—3, 13)
  B. Specific Exhortations and Instructions (4, 1—5, 22)
 III. Conclusion (5, 23–28)

Reading through 1 Thessalonians

The Address and Thanksgiving (1, 1–10)

The address contains a short greeting (1, 1) and an extended thanksgiving (1, 2–10). A distinctive feature of Paul's letters is that the thanksgiving focuses on what God has done for Paul's addressees. In other correspondence of the time, the thanksgiving normally centers on the health and benefits enjoyed by the sender and a wish for the prosperity of the recipient. Paul's co-authors are Silvanus and Timothy. Following his custom, Paul writes not only in his own name but as a member of a team of Christian missionaries. Unlike many others of his letters that begin with several names, here the second person plural is maintained throughout the letter, Paul's "I" breaking through only at 2, 18 and 5, 27. In what we believe is the first extant letter from Paul, there is a greeting that will become Paul's trademark: "To the church of _____, grace and peace to you in (or from) God the Father and the Lord Jesus." This greeting is seen in its simplest form here; in later letters Paul will elaborate on this basic form.

A function of the thanksgiving in the address is often to anticipate the themes of a letter. In the case of 1 Thessalonians, thanksgiving itself is a major theme. Paul is grateful for the reception of the word of God by the Thessalonians and for the impact that their faith has had on other communities. Paul claims that he himself does not even have to testify to the fruitfulness of the Thessalonian mission—word of it has spread throughout the Greek world (Macedonia and Achaia include the whole of Greece, 1, 8). Besides the initial thanksgiving of 1, 2–10 that properly belongs to the address, two other thanksgivings appear in 2, 13–16; 3, 9–13. In all three places, Paul speaks of the relationship between faith and charity and of the expectation of the *Parousia* or second coming of Jesus Christ. These are the major themes of 1 Thessalonians.

The Body of the Letter (2, 1—5, 25)

The body contains Paul's main message in two parts; Paul's account and defense (2, 1—3, 13) followed by teachings and exhortation (4, 1—5, 25).

Paul's Account and Defense of his Ministry (2, 1—3, 13)

Paul states clearly that his motives are without guile in his work with them. If we can read between the lines, we can surmise the accusations of unworthy motives on his part against which he defends himself. He stresses his gratitude to God for the success of this community and presents a defense of his ministry among them.

Thanksgiving is a persistent thread that runs throughout 1 Thessalonians. Yet Paul is not a naive optimist. He is aware that this community is experiencing several problems. Although he will return to the theme of gratitude, he launches into a defense of his own ministry with the Thessalonians, thereby implying that some have questioned his authority or actions. Throughout Paul's ministry career, he insists that he is an apostle, called by God to preach the gospel message. Paul's defense of himself and his authority are linked to the call he has from God. He is under a divine compulsion to preach the gospel, and his confidence derives from this vocation. His defense of his ministry is also prompted by some of the dangers represented by false teachers agitating the Thessalonians in Paul's absence. Although this is a painful and threatening problem, Paul interrupts this defense with thanksgivings, as if to say that he is confident in the Thessalonians' perseverance despite the interference of the agitators.

One of the most difficult yet persistent problems that faced the early church was that of false prophets or false teachers. In the ancient world, where travel was difficult and communications took time, often philosophers or religious teachers joined others who traveled for business or personal reasons. News was gathered and disseminated by such traveling groups; new converts were often made along the way. First Thessalonians reflects this kind of mobility where Paul speaks about his own past visits with the Thessalonians as well as his thwarted plans to return. He promises to visit again soon. He warns the Thessalonians about other types of ministers—those who are greedy or who flatter (2, 5) or who rely on the community for support (2, 9). Paul's own example stands out in contrast to these, for he has been "gentle as a nursing mother" among them (2, 7).

Despite his grateful recognition of the sturdy faith of the Thessalonians, Paul found it necessary to remind them of the sacrifices and dedication they saw in him and his companions. Among his characteristic practices, Paul repeatedly notes

that he is self-supporting. He "toiled day and night" among them and in so doing, he gave them an example that they ought to imitate. This practice of working with his hands and supporting himself was unusual. The Corinthians misinterpreted it, and he did accept gifts of support from the Philippians (Phil 4, 10–20).

Specific Exhortations and Instructions (4, 1—5, 22)

Concrete ethical applications or "imperatives" follow from Paul's grateful description of the Christian community at Thessalonica. This parenetic or exhortatory section may be considered a specific example of Paul's concern that faith be exercised in practical living, particularly as expressed in charity.

Sexual Conduct (4, 3–8). These verses refer to sexual morality, but it is not clear how. The text may refer to a man being faithful to his wife (the usual translation), or to the need for his own sexual control, with no wife mentioned, and verse 6 may refer again to marital fidelity against adultery, or to cheating in business matters. In any case, the text raises a variety of ethical concerns including sexual conduct and business ethics.

For their part, the Jews considered the obligations of marriage and the family to be linked to the covenant relationship with God. This link was an important one Paul wished to adopt for the Gentile Christians. Paul therefore stresses the obligation of believers to develop relationships worthy of them, reflecting respect for one another and for their call to holiness. Charity among believers, in turn, has an effect even on those outside the community who will be impressed with the example of high moral conduct of the Christians.

Death and the Need for Vigilance (4, 13—5, 11). Paul and other early Christians seem to have believed that the Parousia or return of Jesus was very near. Now members of the Thessalonian community are dying before this event, which was a problem for their faith that Jesus would truly return. They wondered how the dead would participate in the triumphant day of Christ's return. Paul encourages the Thessalonians to persevere in faith and joins to this a warning about continued vigilance. Enthusiastic faith can often wane at the onslaught of opposition, suffering, and frustrated expectations. Paul fears that the

say that these are signs of Paul's true authorship, but perhaps the insistence on Paul's authority seems more than a little defensive. Writing in Paul's name assured that a letter would be taken seriously. This practice of Paul's disciples was also an attempt to give continuity to the apostle's message, explicitly interpreting the Pauline traditions in a new context. Despite the reservations of interpreters about Pauline authorship, it is customary to refer to the writer of 2 Thessalonians as "Paul."

There is good reason to believe that 2 Thessalonians was written a decade or more after Paul's death. It is addressed to the same community as 1 Thessalonians but a community that is troubled by the mistaken preaching that the Day of the Lord had now arrived. The preoccupation of early Christians with the times and circumstances accompanying the return of Christ is a problem addressed by many of the New Testament writers, including the Gospels of Matthew, Mark, and Luke, and the book of Revelation. The "apocalyptic" message of 2 Thessalonians is not a frightening one that heightens with fear the anticipation of Christ's return, but is instead a message of consolation and hope for the Christians suffering persecution and confusion. The term "apocalyptic" has come into vogue again in our own times as we, like the early Christians, face an uncertain future. We need to understand biblical apocalyptic as emphasizing hope for all those who persevere.

Working through 2 Thessalonians

Second Thessalonians exhibits the usual letter characteristics of an *address and thanksgiving* (1, 1–12) and *conclusion* (3, 15–18) enclosing the message or *body* of the letter in 2, 1—3, 16.
  I. The Address (1, 1–12)
  II. The Body of the Letter (2, 1—3, 15)
  III. Conclusion (3, 16–18)

Reading through 2 Thessalonians

The Address and Thanksgiving (1, 1–12)

The address includes a greeting (1, 1–2), a thanksgiving (1, 3–10), and a prayer (1, 11–12). The greeting is an almost slavish imitation of the greeting of 1 Thessalonians. Paul joins himself with Silvanus and Timothy, fellow missionaries to the Thessalonians (see 1 Thes 1, 1). Also sim-

ilar to 1 Thessalonians is the fact that thanksgiving is not only a part of the initial address as a formal characteristic of a letter; gratitude is also a central theme in the development of Paul's teaching (see 2, 13–17).

The Body of the Letter (2, 1—3, 15)

Paul's message to the Thessalonians can be subdivided into instruction on right thinking (2, 1–17) and right conduct in the daily life of the Christians at Thessalonica (3, 1–16).

Paul's Teaching on Right Thinking (2, 1–17)

The early Christians' expectation of an imminent return of Christ needed to be adjusted and corrected as the community developed. Unforeseen crises arose, and answers had to be sought in the basics of the Christian preaching. Time passed and the danger was that Christians would become disenchanted and would lose faith, especially in the midst of adversity. First Thessalonians had warned the community about maintaining faith, hope, and love even amid trials such as the death of fellow Christians. There Paul focused on the Day of the Lord, which, he assured them, was coming soon. This reminder served as a warning that behavior would be judged, and the faithful would be rewarded, whereas the unfaithful would be punished.

By the time of the writing of 2 Thessalonians, it seems the eschatological expectation was being taken too seriously, and this caused new problems. As time passed, the early Christians were wondering about the accuracy of their hope that Christ would return soon. They became alarmed by prophecies and by a letter that they thought came from Paul; it seems to have said that the expected "day of the Lord" had arrived (2, 2). The author denies this and lists a number of events that must come first. This change in 2 Thessalonians 2, 1–10 from the expectation of the near return of Christ seen in 1 Thessalonians is one of the main reasons interpreters suspect that 2 Thessalonians is from a later, second generation Pauline Christian. The early Christians had experienced persecution. History had already shown that any expectation that Christ would speedily return with power, to punish the oppressors of the Christians, was wrong.

The message underlying the apocalyptic references in 2 Thessalonians is "do not be alarmed."

The writer avoids any kind of futile speculation concerning times and circumstances of the Parousia. He uses standard apocalyptic images portraying the conflict between good and evil, and the ultimate victory of God over evil. Yet he studiously avoids any specific description. It is sufficient that his readers focus on the hope of God's victory and that they remain vigilant against deception or alarm.

Paul's Teaching on Right Conduct (3, 1–15)

The admonition in 3, 10 not to feed anyone who will not work, and the general exhortation against idleness is probably connected to the apocalyptic expectation discussed earlier. Some thought that there was no further point to building the human community. But Paul warns that idlers only disrupt the peace of the community. Thus he connects idleness and a lack of charity. The apostle presents himself as a model to the contrary to be imitated. His work with his hands is apparently a topic of discussion among his converts. Perhaps, like the Corinthians, the Thessalonians despise labor and prefer the leisure that is considered more conducive to the development of the mind and spirit. Paul gives both social and theological reasons showing that he was not constrained to work but does so freely. Part of the legacy he left with the community was his example of working. This

may have been a form of self-abasement Paul practiced in order to "be all things to all people" (see 1 Cor 9, 21–22). Paul stresses that his aim is to make the gospel accessible to all.

Conclusion (3, 16–18)

The author adds a greeting "in his own hand," apparently to insure authenticity. Yet it is such characteristics that make Pauline authorship of 2 Thessalonians suspect. There are no personal greetings and no originality to the abrupt closing of this letter. The author seems to be copying Paul's style rather than adding a more personalized signature as Paul would have done.

Concluding Remarks

Christians today can understand the need for restraint on the belief that the return of Christ was imminent. Perhaps more than ever before, we can appreciate the important balance introduced by 2 Thessalonians between faith that indeed the return of Christ would come, and emphasis on the need to work diligently to create a better society. Second Thessalonians offers us a message of hope and encouragement. The events that must come to pass before the end of the world are opportunities inviting us to a change of heart, expressed in careful stewardship of our lives, of the church, and of the world.

THE PASTORAL LETTERS

Introduction

The two letters to Timothy and the single letter to Titus have been called the "Pastoral Letters" since they deal largely with issues regarding pastoral care in Pauline communities. Most scholars consider them not to have been written by Paul but by a later writer, since they reflect a degree of church organization not present in Paul's day. We are indebted to these communities for preserving this distinctive correspondence that describes the initial development of church offices and organization. The Pastorals might be read as reflections on Christian ministry. In keeping with the tradition of authorship by Paul we will refer to the writer as "Paul," although most interpreters would agree that these letters are written at least a generation after Paul's death. In form they are

personal letters written to one disciple, but in reality, they are open letters to communities on church policy in various issues.

Paul himself traveled far and wide preaching the message of Christ, founding churches, and writing letters back to communities he had established. Throughout his missionary career, Paul was joined by others and worked with others. He depended upon others. He kept in touch with local leadership. His letters request prayers and sometimes aid for himself and for his mission. In writing letters, Paul often names co-workers as co-authors. He sends emissaries to communities, sometimes for diplomatic reasons and sometimes because he is prohibited from coming at the time and needs to send a messenger. Among his most trusted and reliable partners in the spread of Christianity were Timothy and Titus.

We have references to the work and reputation of these companions of Paul in the authentic Pauline letters. Galatians 2, 2–3 says that Titus accompanied Paul and Barnabas to Jerusalem and that, although he was a Gentile, the Jerusalem authorities did not insist that Titus be circumcised. Luke mentions Timothy as a companion of Paul on the second (Acts 16, 1–4) and third (Acts 19, 22) missionary journeys. Luke does not mention Titus, but he was a trusted messenger of Paul who eased the apostle's difficult communications, especially with the Corinthians (see 2 Cor 2, 12–13; 7, 7; 8, 16–24).

Timothy and Titus served Christian congregations in ancient Greece. The traditional understanding, reflected in these letters, is that Timothy later became a church leader in Ephesus (1 Tm 1, 3) and Titus in Crete (Tit 1, 5). Both were struggling with the challenge of those who offered alternatives to the teachings of Paul. Paul writes to reinforce the faith of these pastors and to encourage them, reminding them of their own Christian vocation.

1 TIMOTHY

[see pages 1600–1607 of the New Testament]

Before Beginning . . .

Both of the two letters addressed to Timothy struggle with the nagging threat of false teaching. This is a problem that afflicted the church from the beginning.

Working through 1 Timothy

The content matter of this letter is diverse, and any particular outline seems arbitrary and artificial. Our discussion of 1 Timothy is based on the following structure:

I. The Address and Thanksgiving (1, 1–2.12–17)
II. The Body of the Letter (1, 3–11; 1, 18—6, 19)
    A. Paul's Message to Timothy (1, 3–11; 1, 18—4, 16)
    B. Duties Toward Others (5, 1—6, 19)
III. Conclusion (6, 20–21)

Reading through 1 Timothy

The Address and Thanksgiving (1, 1–2.12–17)

The address consists of a brief greeting in Pauline form (1, 1–2) with the thanksgiving delayed until 1, 12–17. A warning against false doctrines (1, 3–11) appears between these two parts of the address. This intrusion breaks the usual structure of a letter but manifests the gravity of the author's concern. The thanksgiving (1, 12–17) recalls Paul's former blasphemy and persecution of the church, evidence that his call was

unmerited and unsolicited (1, 12–17). Paul's example is a primary instance of the transforming power of grace. Because he sinned grievously (though in ignorance), the grace bestowed upon Paul had to be abundant. Notice that the author does not dwell on guilt or remorse. His allusion to Paul's sinful past only serves to illustrate the gratuity of God's mercy. These reflections prompt him to praise God in a short doxology or blessing (1, 17).

The Body of the Letter (1, 3–11; 1, 18—6, 19)

The message of 1 Timothy is primarily a warning against the dangers of false teaching. The writer reminds Timothy about the qualities he should look for in assistants who are true ministers of the gospel, and he discusses Christians' duties toward others.

Paul's Message to Timothy (1, 3–11; 1, 18—4, 16)

The Warning Against False Teaching (1, 3–11.18–20). The teaching attacked in 1 Timothy is a form of *gnosis* (knowledge) that involved "myths and . . . genealogies [and] . . . speculations" (1, 4). All three Pastorals, but especially 1 Timothy, are aimed at secure knowledge of the truth and secure ways of acting it out. These are reflections on the genuine applications of a teaching or knowledge that Timothy knows well.

The threat Paul combats in 1 Timothy is the pursuit of gnosis without any ethical or practical applications for living (1 Tm 1, 4; see 2 Tm 2, 14;

3, 7; Ti 3, 9). Thus the practicalities of Christian living and church life together are emphasized, along with a pastorally oriented theology. This letter attacks those who would reduce Christianity to a mere doctrine or intellectual exercise, to the neglect of the ethical implications. The letter presumes a common fund of knowledge and emphasizes that authentic Christianity should work itself out in everyday life.

Life and Leadership in the Community (2, 1—4, 16). The primary example of authentic Christian living is the minister of the gospel message. Timothy has a great responsibility entrusted to him by God and verified in the church (1, 3.18–20; 4, 6–16; 6, 11–16.20–21). The writer impresses on Timothy the importance of his role as example for the church.

The advice to Timothy in this letter proceeds from the admonition to draw strength from the "prophetic words once spoken about you" (1, 18) and the suggestion to "attend to yourself and to your teaching" (4, 16). Timothy should concentrate on "righteousness, devotion, faith, love, patience, and gentleness" (6, 11). He should ignore the seduction of "profane babbling and the absurdities of so-called knowledge" (6, 20). Constancy and perseverance in the faith are required in order to attract and encourage other believers. Timothy is urged to demonstrate to all his reliance on God.

The discussion of how each group of persons should act toward others is an adaptation of the "household codes" used in Eph 5, 21—6, 9 and Col 3, 18—4, 1. Here men and women, young and old, male and female should treat each other with the respect due them in traditional society (also 5, 1–2; 6, 1–2). The duties of bishop and deacons (3, 1–13) are drawn from typical descriptions of virtue. The text speaks of a single bishop and a number of deacons, both male and female (or, possibly, of male deacons and their wives, 3, 11). We know from Phil 1, 1 that these titles were used very early on. Presbyters are not mentioned in this passage (3, 1–7), but only in 5, 17–19. It does not seem, therefore, that there is as yet a triple-tiered ministry of bishop, presbyters, and deacons, which will come in the next years.

In one way, 1 Timothy may be read as a list of rules for people in various offices and positions within the community. There is, however, a common theme in all of Paul's advice. Members of the Christian community should distinguish themselves by their love for and service to one another. Even the dress and decorum of men and women at the liturgy, for example, should contribute to the building up of the community (2, 8–10).

The particular advice to women, which has been controversial throughout Christian history, should be understood in the context of charity and the importance of good example. False teachers advocating asceticism, especially in the form of renunciation of marriage or restrictions on certain foods (4, 1–3), were particularly successful with women whom the author of 1 Timothy perceives as especially susceptible. The prevailing male wisdom taught that women were gullible and subject to error, as symbolized in the story of Eve who was seduced by the serpent. Contrary to the false teachers, Paul supports marriage and sees the family as conducive to holiness. He therefore advocates the "submission" of women, which was part of traditional views about the well-run family. This, he insists, is not a lifestyle unworthy of Christian women but a way in which women may, like Timothy, "persevere in faith and love and holiness" (2, 15). The same thinking drives the advice to slaves in a later passage to honor and respect their owners (6, 1–2), with the warning that believing slaves are not to think of themselves as equal to their owners but to be even more respectful. This kind of thinking, as can be imagined, has caused mayhem in later centuries when those who appeal to the authority of the Bible resist social change. In his own context, however, Paul is simply trying to uphold human dignity within a social structure that he cannot change.

Duties toward Others (5,1 —6, 19)

This is really a rather artificial division, since the whole letter is preoccupied with community relationships. There is ambiguity in the discussion about widows (5, 3–16), perhaps indication of uneven editing. First, widows who have no other means of support are to be supported by the church (5, 3–8.16). Then, there is some kind of enrollment of widows who are at least sixty years old, distinguished for practicing virtue, and resolved to remain unmarried—hardly issues to consider if a widow is starving. Some kind of service organization is envisioned in 5, 9–15, returning again in verse 16 to the assistance of needy widows. Given lower life expectancy, few women would live beyond sixty, and younger widows are to remarry, so they could not hope to qualify later to be enrolled as those married only once (5, 9).

The concrete advice regarding bishops and deacons and other ministers to the community stresses the power of example. This is especially important in those offices that have visibility in the community and represent a community trust. Many interpreters assume that the degree of development of the offices mentioned suggests a late composition of 1 Timothy. It would seem to have taken some years for the church to develop such a variety of roles and recognized ministries. On the other hand, we know that these ministries were beginning to develop already in Paul's day. They pertain to basic needs that arose as the church struggled to respond to its mission in the world. The office of bishop or overseer developed out of the custom of holding all things in common so that the surplus of the rich would supply the needs of the poor in the Christian community (see 2 Cor 8 and 9). The ministry of deacons reflected the priority of preaching the word, while not neglecting the physical and material needs of the church's members (Rom 16, 2; Acts 6, 1–6). The earliest writings of Paul, and in fact all of the New Testament, stress the social dimension of the Christian message. Therefore, the stewardships that would assure this dimension were created as soon as the priority was recognized.

Conclusion (6, 20–21)

The conclusion (6, 20–21) is in the form of a final recommendation and warning. First Timothy ends by restating the main message of the letter: "Guard the trust" (see 1, 3–10; 4, 7; 6, 3–5). Authority is stewardship. Many have been deceived by gnosis or false knowledge. Timothy is urged to hold firm to what he knows and to live it quietly.

Concluding Remarks

First Timothy represents several challenges for the modern interpreter. The author's view that women are more susceptible to error than men, for example, betrays the bias of a male-dominated culture. Changing attitudes throughout history facilitated the education of women, and consequently the underlying premise of their greater gullibility has been proven false. First Timothy stresses the responsibility of leaders to interpret the essentials of the Christian message and to insure charity as distinctive of the Christian community. Interpreters today distinguish between the culturally based bias against women and the essential message that included all in the life of charity to be lived by the community. This is a life in which all may grow and mature, women as well as men. Later generations were able to change oppressive structures of slavery. The responsibility of leaders and pastors is to nurture that life, providing in their own lives a model of charity for other Christians to emulate.

2 TIMOTHY

[see pages 1607–12 of the New Testament]

Before Beginning . . .

The same preoccupations appear here as we saw in 1 Timothy: warnings about false teachings, and Paul's exhortation to Timothy as a minister of the gospel like himself. Second Timothy is written in a warmer, more personal tone than 1 Timothy, and therefore its lack of formal structure is understandable. It is really a testament in the form of a letter. Like Moses in Deuteronomy 29—30 or Jesus in John 14—16, the elder Paul, imprisoned in Rome (1, 16–17), looks back on his life with the knowledge of his imminent

death (4, 6–8) and gives the younger man the benefit of his experience. He begins and ends the letter with references to his own experiences and the vocation of Timothy, thus linking the two. Their ties of affection and of common vocation are deep and very significant for Paul. The elder apostle speaks of his own life, his loneliness, his lack of confidence in other human beings. Yet he is not discouraged. God is the source of strength for both Paul and Timothy. The deeply personal tone of this letter has led some recent commentators to reevaluate the question of Pauline authorship, and to suggest that while

1 Timothy and Titus are of a later era, perhaps 2 Timothy is not.

Working through 2 Timothy

The *address and thanksgiving* (1, 1–5) and *conclusion* (4, 9–22) envelop the *body* of the letter in 1, 6—4, 8. The main themes of 2 Timothy are the minister's experience of God and warnings against false teaching.

    I. The Address and Thanksgiving (1, 1–5)
    II. The Body of the Letter (1, 6—4, 8)
        A. Instructions to Timothy (1, 6—2, 13)
        B. Warnings about False Teaching
           (2, 14—3, 9)
        C. Final advice (3, 10—4, 8)
    III. Conclusion (4, 9–22)

Reading through 2 Timothy

The Address and Thanksgiving (1, 1–5)

The address (1, 1–5) consists of a greeting (1, 1–2) and a thanksgiving (1, 3–5), following the authentic Pauline style.

The Body of the Letter (1, 6—4, 8)

We have noted previously that Paul generally follows a basic pattern of first presenting his fundamental teaching on various issues and then drawing ethical conclusions from this teaching, though these two parts do not always follow one another in neat order. First Timothy does not follow this pattern very well, and 2 Timothy even less so, primarily because it is more of a personal communication that combines reminders about teaching with advice in an informal way. The informal structure of this letter focuses on two main themes that are developed here: the minister's experience of God and warnings against false teaching.

Instructions to Timothy (1, 6—2, 13)

Timothy is not to be ashamed of the gospel or his commission to testify to the truth at all times. He also has the responsibility to keep that truth intact as he has received it. The apostle often uses himself as an example, as a source of inspiration and motivation. Paul lives with such integrity that he urges Christians to imitate him in everything (see Phil 4, 8–10). Timothy is reminded that those who follow Christ will suffer persecution. This echoes Jesus' warning to his disciples

(Mt 24, 9–14; Mk 13, 9–13; Lk 21, 12–19; Jn 15, 11–27). In the face of such pressure, Timothy is to remain constant.

Warnings about False Teaching (2, 14—3, 9)

Like the other Pastorals, 2 Timothy is aimed at false teachings that promote a certain gnosis or knowledge and a consequent asceticism or strict discipline. The false teachings Paul attacks attach superior value to those who are "enlightened" with such knowledge and practice stringent customs regarding sexuality and diet. These practices set them apart from others, contributing to their sense of superiority. In all three letters, Paul was assuming that his addressees held the right beliefs, so that it was not necessary to review the correct teaching or doctrine that the writer and recipient hold in common. Therefore Paul spoke in vague and abstract terms about the false teaching, concentrating instead on the appropriate ethical applications that follow from true gospel preaching. Paul urges Timothy not to become embroiled in debates: "Charge [people] . . . to stop disputing about words . . . avoid profane [and] idle talk" (2, 14.16). One of the false teachings actually identified is that baptized Christians are already risen with Christ and that there is no future bodily resurrection (see note on 2, 14–19). Paul understands Christians as living in the last days when there are many dangers and threats to faith.

While warnings about false teaching are given throughout this section, in verses 1–9 they are concentrated and seem aimed at a specific group of people, although they could also be intended more generally. The disparagement of women's intellectual ability that we have seen surface in 1 Timothy is again present (3, 6–7), with perhaps the opposite effect: in fact, the author is telling us that missions among women were very successful, which means that the women were intellectually alert and responsive.

Final Advice (3, 10—4, 8)

Paul describes his life and impending death as a liturgical sacrifice; he is being poured out like a libation, an offering of wine (4, 6). He has run and finished the course (4, 7). He awaits with longing the reward of God (4, 6–8). Such confidence is based in God and meant to serve as encouragement to Timothy who still runs the course. Like other biblical heroes (including Moses and Jesus), Paul is represented in 2 Timothy as giving a kind of farewell address near the end of his life (4, 6–8). In this speech the hero warns his followers about impending dangers and threats to fidelity. They are commissioned with authority and reminded about the source of their confidence. They are promised that God will remain with them and that they will endure. Paul reminds Timothy to hold to the essentials of sound doctrine: Scripture, and the example of Christ and of other Christians. He reminds Timothy that those who live the gospel message will be persecuted. Paul urges Timothy to be faithful in waiting for the appearance of Jesus Christ.

Conclusion (4, 9–22)

The personal tone and greetings of 2 Timothy mark this as the closest Pastoral Letter to Paul's own style. Paul often experienced failure in his relationships with others. The author of 2 Timothy experiences similar problems. Like Paul, he says that such difficulties are the occasion for more converts to the gospel message. The letter

ends with a prayer for God's spirit to be with Timothy ("your" is singular). The plural in the last line may indicate the letter's being read and reflected upon in the assembly.

Concluding Remarks

The church is not a perfect society nor are its ministers without human faults and failings. Conflicts over a variety of issues have plagued believers from the beginning, making it sometimes difficult to discern right from false teaching and practice. The church has experienced crises of leadership and problems with authority and obedience. Relationships among Christians have often been strained. Paul and other New Testament authors are not strangers to such tensions and problems. The author of 2 Timothy manifests a remarkable vulnerability to the strains in his own relationships with others, but this does not in any way detract from his visions or hopes for the church. In fact, with amazing confidence and humility, the author of 2 Timothy shows that even his failures are opportunities for the spread of the Christian message.

TITUS

[see pages 1612–15 of the New Testament]

Before Beginning . . .

The third Pastoral Letter is addressed to Titus, who is charged with the administration of the church in the large area of Crete (1, 5). The letter to Titus has many parallels with 1 Timothy and manifests the same concerns for the maintenance duties of those entrusted with the care of the local communities. They are to give particular care to the appointment of reliable assistants and to the presentation of sound church teaching, protecting it from the many threats and dangers of false teaching.

Working through Titus

The *address* in 1, 1–4 is not followed by the usual thanksgiving, but the text goes directly into the *body* of the letter in 1, 5—3, 11. This message presents the pastoral charge or responsibilities, especially that of working with others in the preaching of the Christian message. The entire

letter may be seen as an exhortation of encouragement from one pastor to another. A short *conclusion* (3, 12–15), giving personal information, brings the letter to a close. The simple structure is as follows:

    I. Address (1, 1–4)
   II. The Body of the Letter (1, 5—3, 11)
      A. Pastoral Charge (1, 5–16)
      B. Teaching the Christian Life
        (2, 1—3, 11)
  III. Conclusion (3, 12–15)

Reading through Titus

The Address (1, 1–4)

The address follows the usual Pauline pattern, but here it consists of a greeting only. It is slightly more elaborate than Paul's usual greetings but exhibits many of the features of Paul's thinking. As in the other Pastorals, the author emphasizes the apostle's role in the spread of the worldwide mission of Christ. This mission is now entrusted to Paul's "child," Titus, a fellow worker encouraged through this letter to insure the continuing line of good pastors and to preserve the faithful teaching of Christian life. The great dangers that face Titus and the church of Crete are the false teachers and those who would corrupt the Christian message.

The Body of the Letter (1, 5—3, 11)

Pastoral Charge (1, 5–16)

Verses 5 through 9 are parallel to the instruction of 1 Timothy 3, 1–7. Paul is an itinerant preacher who, nevertheless, is keenly aware of the need for stabilized leadership, especially to protect the church against heretical or false teaching. Therefore, the instructions given to Titus concerning the administration of the church at Crete are related first to the appointment of trustworthy and reliable pastors for the various duties required for the growth and development of the church there.

One of the important offices was that of *presbyter* (elder, v. 5), a term that in meaning is quite close in this letter to *episkopos* (overseer or bishop, v. 7). The two statements seem to be about the same people, as they could also be in 1 Timothy 3, 1–7; 5, 17–20. The main function of the bishop was apparently the overseeing of the financial or material matters in the church. Again, as in Philippians 1, 1, it is difficult to translate *episkopos* accurately, since the title "bishop" has such different connotations today. This bishop is God's "steward," entrusted with the distribution of goods and accountable to the members of the community. Therefore his own life ought to be exemplary. He must not only avoid excesses but also represent a model Christian life in his own family. As in 1 Timothy 3, 2–13, the description of the virtues of office-holders is taken from typical descriptions in literature on virtue.

Leaders of the church are to offer an alternative example to that of the false teachers who preach for personal gain, living off the community and seeking personal recognition and recompense. These kinds of accusations against one's opponents are also part of traditional rhetoric and should not be taken at face value. The conduct of the presbyters or bishops should,

however, be above reproach. Primary among the false teachers are the Judaizers who continue to advocate observance of some aspects of the Jewish Law, a custom that was attractive to some Christians for many centuries. The writer stoops to an ethnic slur by quoting an earlier author to the effect that Cretans are by their very nature prone to deceit, dishonesty, and laziness, thus making them all the more susceptible to falsehoods (1, 12).

Teaching the Christian Life (2, 1—3, 11)

Titus is encouraged to hold on to sound faith in teaching, while resisting pressures from all sides. Since the imagery of moral preaching often depicted the church as the new family, its members are here taught to relate to one another as older and younger people would in a well-ordered family in which respect dominates. Groups singled out include older men and younger men, older and younger women, slaves, and those in authority. Christians must not act in accordance with the world around them. Yet they must survive in an alien world. Paul's instructions focus on how to survive in this world while offering an alternative lifestyle and developing integrity as Christians. The domestic role for women is reinforced. The author reminds them of their duties to be examples within the marital context. Likewise slaves are directed not to rebel against the control of their masters (2, 9–10). The author urges them to fidelity and kindness within the context of slavery. Citizens were also inclined to see Christianity as an alternative to obedience to a corrupt state. The author of Titus advocates exemplary citizenship based on the status of Christians as already justified and relying on the mercy of God. Paul summarizes his advice to Titus, reminding him to avoid controversies and to maintain his integrity in the true faith. The false teachers disturb the community and its ministers. Paul exhorts to vigilance and constancy.

Conclusion (3, 12–15)

The final lines include very specific travel directives and recommendations for travelers passing through Crete. Titus is told to come with an assistant whom he will send, to join Paul at Nicopolis, a common city name; probably the one in western Greece is intended. Mediterranean Sea travel shut down from November 10 to March 10, and a traveler thus had to "winter" somewhere waiting out the passage of those months. Paul closes with personal greetings. The final greeting "grace be with you all" is the simplest of closing forms. Some manuscripts add "of the Lord" or "of God" and "Amen," which are closer to the usual elaborations of Paul himself.

Concluding Remarks

Christians continue to wrestle with questions relating practice or behavior to belief. Christianity, like Judaism, has always emphasized the importance of deeds rather than mere knowledge or doctrine alone. Ministers of the gospel are entrusted with the responsibility to preserve teach-

ing while also presenting exemplary lives. The letter to Titus reminds us of the difficulties, yet the importance, of working with others for the advance of the gospel message.

The challenge of the Pastoral Letters for today's church can hardly be overestimated. The Catholic view of Paul has long been unduly influenced by his portrait in these letters. Catholic Christians in particular have inherited a long tradition stressing the communal dimensions of Christian teaching. We do not receive the Christian message individually nor can we live it in isolation from each other. This emphasis on communal responsibility is part of the legacy of the Pastoral Letters.

PHILEMON

[see pages 1615–16 of the New Testament]

Before Beginning . . .

Paul's letter to Philemon is a gem of early Christian exchange, and the only true personal letter that we have from Paul. No one seriously challenges Philemon as an authentic Pauline letter and an integral part of the New Testament. As contrasted with an "epistle" that embodies more stereotypic, stylized forms and features (for instance, Romans), Philemon appears to be a letter between individuals, dealing with a very concrete matter rather than with generalized, abstract theological principles. Neither Paul nor the early Christian community intended to attack slavery directly, so we may well wonder why this letter was preserved at all and why it might be significant for us.

Despite its brevity and apparent succinctness, Paul's letter to Philemon is full of interpretive problems and has been intensively studied in recent years. The traditional story line behind it since the fourth century has been that Onesimus, a slave, had run away from his master, Philemon, and had come to Paul for protection. Paul had converted Onesimus to Christianity, and now sent him back to Philemon, carrying this letter. But more recently, this interpretation has been questioned and several other possible scenarios proposed. One is that, according to Roman law, a slave who goes to a third party to mediate a dispute with his or her owner is not to be considered

a fugitive. If one reads the letter from this perspective, it also fits. A third argument is that Onesimus is not a slave at all, but Philemon's brother, whom Philemon is treating like a slave (Phlm 16). Paul asks him to reconcile and treat him as he deserves. The interpretation that Onesimus is indeed a slave is the majority one, but why he went to Paul remains an open question, as does what Paul really wants Philemon to do. But it is clear that the relationship between Philemon and Onesimus is not good, and Paul is trying to patch it up.

The informal conversational tone does not detract from the letter's impressive significance within the Christian context. Each part of this letter underscores its ecclesial or community context and gives us a glimpse into the structure of relationship and exchange in the early Christian church. Because nearly all the names mentioned in the letter also occur in Colossians, the usual supposition is that Philemon's house church is located in Colossae.

Working through Philemon

The letter to Philemon has the usual features of a Pauline letter: an *address and thanksgiving* (1–6), the *body* (7–22) and *conclusion* (23–25). Philemon follows a simple outline:

I. Address and Thanksgiving (1–6)

II. The Body of the Letter (7–22)

III. Conclusion (23–25)

Reading through Philemon

The Address and Thanksgiving (1–6)

It is not Philemon alone who is addressed, but Apphia, perhaps Philemon's wife, Archippus, another member of the household, and the whole "church [that meets] at your house" (1–2). The thanksgiving (4–6) notes the renowned love and faith Philemon has always shown the "holy ones," a reference to his fellow Christians. Paul also names Philemon a "partner" in faith, emphasizing the common life in Christ that they share, which is the basis for the new society that Paul envisions.

The Body of the Letter (7–22)

The varied expressions of Paul's complex relationship with Philemon serve as a model for the new relationships Philemon now has with Onesimus. Their common baptism provides a basis for Philemon and Onesimus (as well as for the whole church) to create an entirely new way of relating to one another and to resolve the tensions between them. In no other Pauline letter is the relationship between the "indicative" or statement of Christian reality (signified by a common baptism) so integrally bound up with the "imperative" implications or exhortations that flow from this reality. From a structural viewpoint, it is impossible to separate the "indicative" from the "imperative" in this letter as we have done in others.

In 1 Corinthians 7, 21–23, Paul says that slavery or freedom is indifferent in the Christian life. It is not clear in this letter whether Paul appeals to Philemon to manumit Onesimus, that is, free him from slavery. He may expect that the two of them now continue in a good relationship of master and slave. But if Onesimus is a runaway, normal punitive measures against an errant slave (who perhaps also stole from his master, 18–19) are prohibited by Paul. Master and slave are fellow Christians. The community context should help them work out a new way of relating to one another as "brothers." Because of whatever way Onesimus has wronged Philemon, Philemon is in a delicate position. If he does not punish Onesimus, he is lacking in necessary discipline, and his social peers will think him weak. If he does

insist on punishment, he will violate his Christian obligation to forgiveness and Paul's express desires. The whole house church is watching to see what he will do! Unfortunately, we do not know the answer.

Paul describes himself as a prisoner (9), as Philemon's brother (7.20), and as father of Onesimus (10). Paul says he is an old man (9), an anticipated guest of Philemon (22), and one to whom Philemon is indebted (19). These descriptions illustrate the various ways in which the patronage system of the culture interacted with Christian expressions of interdependence and ultimately equality in Christ. They are a way of redefining Paul's relationship to Philemon and to the church in Colossae. They also serve as a model for Philemon to develop a new relationship between himself and Onesimus. The letter is a masterpiece of rhetorical strategy. Paul does not mandate any specific set of actions, but rather appeals to Philemon and to the whole community to read and reflect on this letter in light of their common baptism, and to discern a course of action toward Onesimus that will reflect the Christian faith they share.

Conclusion (23–25)

The final greetings mention names of Paul's co-workers also found in Colossians (1, 7; 2, 1; 4, 12–13) and 2 Timothy (4, 9–13). Together with the liturgical blessing (Phlm 25), these greetings underscore once again the communal context in which this letter was written and in which it ought to be reflected upon and acted upon. Philemon draws out some implications of the baptismal formula quoted in Galatians 3, 28: "There is neither Jew nor Greek, there is neither slave nor free person, there is not male and female; for you are all one in Christ Jesus" (see also Col 3, 11).

Concluding Remarks

The letter to Philemon raises interesting challenges for its original recipients and for us. Apparently Onesimus himself is bearer of this letter from Paul to his master. The letter is to be read at the liturgy when the Christian community will help Philemon reintegrate Onesimus back into his household as a fellow Christian. The very fact that the community preserved this letter—

and that it comes down to us included in the canon of the New Testament—testifies to the spirit of openness, humility, and generosity of Philemon and his congregation that must have successfully resolved this matter. Today the church as a whole and local churches are faced with perplexing social problems, especially with regard to social expectations and their clash with faith values. We can take hope that what was written long ago was written for our instruction. We can well afford to contemplate the role of such a pastoral letter and of the community's reflection on its contents.

FURTHER READING

Dunn, James D. G. *The Theology of Paul the Apostle.* Grand Rapids, MI: Eerdmans, 1998.

Fitzmyer, Joseph A. *According to Paul: Studies in the Theology of the Apostle.* Mahwah, NJ: Paulist, 1993.

Murphy-O'Connor, Jerome. *Paul: A Critical Life.* Oxford: Clarendon, 1996.

Roetzel, Calvin J. *The Letters of Paul: Conversations in Context.* 4th ed. Louisville, KY: Westminster John Knox, 1998.

——. *Paul: The Man and the Myth.* Minneapolis, MN: Fortress, 1999.

Stendahl, Krister. *Paul among Jews and Gentiles.* Philadelphia: Fortress, 1976.

THE GENERAL LETTERS AND REVELATION

LUKE TIMOTHY JOHNSON

HEBREWS

[see pages 1616–36 of the New Testament]

Before Beginning . . .

Hebrews is not a real letter but a sermon (see introduction, NT, 1616–18) The best way to experience Hebrews is by reading it out loud from beginning to end. Subtle points of Greek rhetoric—such as the alliteration in the opening verses—will still escape the contemporary reader. But oral recitation helps to catch the sermonic rhythms of Hebrews, its use of "we" and "you" (so natural to the sermon), and its alternating pattern of exposition and exhortation. Note, for example, how the opening argument of 1, 5–14 leads naturally to the "therefore, we must attend all the more" in 2, 1–5. Reading straight through also enables the reader to grasp the powerful argument that is the outstanding characteristic of this early Christian writing.

Toward Understanding Hebrews

Hebrews has significantly shaped the liturgy, doctrine, and spirituality of the church. Although other New Testament writings speak of Jesus' death as a sacrifice, Hebrews' unique reflection on Melchizedek (chapter 7) and on Jesus as the Great High Priest influenced the development of Catholic liturgy. Hebrews' insistence on Jesus' full divinity and equally full participation in human nature contributed to the understanding of Jesus' identity as God's Son (1—2). And Hebrews' vision of faith as a pilgrimage toward God (11—12) created a symbolic framework for the Christian understanding of discipleship as a "journey." For all its riches, Hebrews resists easy assimilation for two reasons: the first is that it presents a sustained argument from beginning to end; the second is that its symbols are hard to understand. Dealing with these difficulties clears the way to more intelligent and satisfactory reading.

The Argument

Some parts of the New Testament, like the Gospel parables, can be read out of their original context and still make sense. But each part of Hebrews plays a role in a complicated interplay of argument and explanation concerning Jesus and Christian life. Hebrews resists being excerpted. It uses a form of argument, found both in Greek philosophy and rabbinic Judaism, called "from the lesser to the greater." The argument goes, "If something is true in a smaller matter, it is even more true in an analogous greater matter." In Hebrews, the contrast is between the partial revelation of God in the past through angels, law, and priesthood, and the perfect revelation "in the last of these days" through God's Son, Jesus, between that former "lesser" salvation and the present "greater" salvation.

The argument in Hebrews is not theoretical but practical. The real point is the contrast between the response to God's word by the people of the past, and the response demanded of the people today. A greater blessing and hope require a greater degree of obedience and loyalty, just as disobedience carries a greater penalty. The stakes are higher all around.

Hebrews

The Symbols

The symbols of Hebrews are sufficiently strange
to shake any assumption that the New Testament
world was "just like ours." Hebrews demands of
its readers, for example, a far more sophisticated
grasp of Scripture than that possessed by most
Christians today. Much of its argument, in fact, is
based on complex modes of scriptural interpretation that, while strange to us, were common in
the first century. The version of Scripture used by
Hebrews (as by other New Testament writings)
was not Hebrew but Greek. Its citations and allusions are from the Septuagint. This study edition
gives some assistance by providing complete
Scripture references. Citations in the text are
flagged with small letters; passages are identified at the bottom of each page. To fully appreciate Hebrews' virtuosity, study the citations in
their original context as well as how Hebrews
can turn them to fit its argument (as in 10, 5–7).

Hebrews' view of the world is strikingly different from that of present-day Christians in an
even more fundamental sense. Hebrews works
within a philosophical tradition called Platonism,
which saw a great gulf between the spiritual realm
and the material world. Spiritual things are eternal, unchanging; material things are transitory. As
a result, spiritual things are both more real and better than the material. For Platonic Jews and Christians, the "spiritual" and "material" realms were
understood in terms of "heaven" and "earth."

This is the framework for grasping Hebrews'
point about the superiority of Jesus' priesthood.
By his resurrection, Jesus entered heaven, where
he is a "priest forever" (5, 6), in contrast to the
Jewish priesthood, which could only be temporary. Likewise the "heavenly sanctuary" is superior to the physical tent of worship described in
Scripture (8—9). The symbolism at times becomes dense and requires patience to disentan-
gle, but the basic point is clear. The human Messiah Jesus now shares God's life in heaven. His
priesthood is therefore both the ultimate and
eternal "source of salvation" to others (5, 9).

The Readers

The original hearers of this sermon had experienced the loss of property and friends (10,
32–34). They were tempted to lose hope and
seek a more stable framework than that offered

by a crucified messiah. Hebrews addresses their
longing for stability by offering the hope for "a
better homeland, a heavenly one" (11, 16). The
first readers' experience can be translated into
that of every age: all of us in various ways experience loss, desperation, alienation, despair. Hebrews' message to us is as sharp as it was to
them: "Oh, that today you would hear his voice:
Harden not your hearts" (4, 7). We also are called
to go on pilgrimage through our troubled circumstances, looking to Jesus, who is still and always the "leader and perfecter of faith" (12, 2).

The Prologue (1, 1–4)

The opening sentence is elegantly constructed
and introduces Hebrews' central themes. First is
the contrast between God's partial revelation in
the past ("to our ancestors") and the perfect revelation now ("to us") made through God's Son,
which establishes the basic thesis: Jesus is superior to the old dispensation, or covenant (see 8,
13). Second, Jesus' divine status is clearly if metaphorically expressed by calling him the "imprint" of God. The exalted identity attributed to
the Son is similar to that in John and Paul (see,
for example, Jn 1, 1–4 and 1 Cor 8, 6). Third, the
prologue states that the way God "spoke" in
Jesus was through his death for others (the purification from sins), and his resurrection.

Note the image of enthronement: Jesus "took
his seat at the right hand." This alludes to Psalm
110, 1, the favorite resurrection psalm of early
Christians: "The LORD said to my lord: 'Take
your throne at my right hand, while I make your
enemies your footstool' " (see also 1, 13). Hebrews will also exploit the fourth verse of this
psalm when he develops the comparison between Jesus and Melchizedek in chapter 7. The
image of enthronement runs throughout the sermon. Jesus is both priest and king. Finally, we
notice that Jesus "inherits" a name better than
that of the angels. Jesus is here portrayed as a
forerunner. If they follow him, Christians also
will enter into an inheritance (1, 14; 6, 12). The
mention of angels, in turn, provides a transition
to Hebrews' argument.

**The Son Is Higher than the Angels
(1, 5—2, 18)**

A series of Scripture citations proves that the Son
is superior to angels. The notes in the New Testa-

ment pp. 1618–20 discuss details of the citations. The pertinent question for us is, why do angels require putting in place, anyway? Our contemporary view of the world has small room for angels! But in the world of the New Testament, especially in the writings of Judaism, angels were regarded as the most powerful intermediaries between God and humans. The tendency to exalt their role is attested in Galatians 4, 9 and Colossians 2, 18. What concern does the author address? Jesus in his humanity did not appear so impressive as these "spiritual" beings. He was not only human; he suffered and died. Hebrews must overcome the scandal of a "lowly" Messiah.

Citations from Scripture do not by themselves demonstrate the point. As in other New Testament writings (for example, Gal 3, 1–5), Hebrews argues "the greater" from the fact of the readers' own *experience*. The work of God's Spirit among them is itself powerful "witness" to the salvation accomplished through Jesus (2, 3f). And never content with the speculative, Hebrews drives home the exhortation. This "greater salvation" demands of the readers a greater response of alertness (2, 1f).

From the perspective of the power of the Risen Lord, Hebrews takes up the issue of Jesus' "lowliness." On the basis of Psalm 8, the author asserts that Jesus was "lower than the angels" only temporarily. And the reason was so that he could "taste death for everyone," that is, act as priest. On the basis of a messianic reading of Isaiah 8, 18f, Hebrews next affirms God's (and the Messiah's) solidarity with humanity. Then, Hebrews turns the tables, and makes Jesus' humanity a positive criterion for authentic priesthood. Because Jesus is one with those he represents before God—he shares the way they are "tested," and the way they "fear death"—he can be a compassionate and merciful priest. It is significant that Hebrews defines priesthood in terms of his personal identity and experience rather than in terms of religious ceremony. Hebrews thereby anticipates an important principle of later doctrine: "what is not assumed [by God] cannot be saved." Precisely *because* he is human, Jesus can save humanity.

Jesus, Faithful and Compassionate High Priest (3, 1—5, 10)

Moses was so central a figure for Jews that he became a natural point of contrast for Christian

claims about Jesus (see, for example, Jn 1, 17). Hebrews now contrasts Moses as "the servant of [God's] house," and Jesus as "son over the house" (3, 4f). The real contrast in this section, however, is between the people that Moses led and the Christians the author of Hebrews addresses in terms of disobedience and obedient faith (3, 7–13). Hebrews agrees with Paul's argument in 1 Corinthians 10, 1–13 that what happened to Israel in the desert is a warning for the present.

The argument here uses complex ancient rules for interpreting Scripture. Much is made, for example, of the occurrence of specific words, such as "rest" and "today," without regard for their original contexts. The premise for such a procedure is that Scripture speaks to every age in each of its words, and that every part of Scripture interprets every other part. On that premise, Hebrews asserts that the "rest" to which Moses led the people (the land) was not the "rest of God," namely, God's own life. For that matter, neither did people of old even succeed in entering *that* earthly rest because of their disobedience. Christians in contrast have hope for the real rest—of God's own life—won by Jesus' resurrection. The point? They are to obey the call of God and not fall away (4, 6). The message of Hebrews is not a trivial one. The readers are not engaged in a trivial conquest of territory; they are called to a share in God's life, a far more awesome prospect (4, 12f).

Hebrews has identified obedient faith as the fundamental response demanded by God. The comparison to the wandering Israelites also establishes Hebrews' basic image of the church as the people of God on *pilgrimage*. The image suggests that the church is not simply an institution like other institutions. It is never fully "at home" in the world. The church exists with reference to a higher goal—the "heavenly city"—toward which it must steadily move like a pilgrim, although this side of death the goal is never reached. Pilgrims need the sort of attentiveness, patience, obedience, and endurance demanded by Hebrews. Above all, they need *hope* (see 6, 18). They can move lightly through this worldly existence only if convinced that their destination is truly "greater" than their present abode.

Hebrews points the reader again to the leader of the pilgrimage, the "apostle and high priest of our confession" (3, 1). In the description of Jesus as priest (4, 14—5, 9), Hebrews combines what has come to be called both "high" and "low" Christologies (understandings of Jesus). Jesus is definitely "from above"; he is God's Son in the fullest sense, but he is also fully human, "from below." It is his *human* existence that defines the path "all the children" are to follow. As priest, he is exemplar. Jesus is not only "faithful" (3, 1f) as all are called to be; he "learned obedience from what he suffered" (5, 8). The full implications of this statement will become clear only later (see 12, 1–11), but we already understand that Jesus' suffering deepened his faith, and his obedience was itself a form of suffering. Jesus progressively *became,* in his humanity, perfect Son of God, and therefore the "leader" of all who follow him.

Jesus' Eternal Priesthood and Sacrifice (5, 11—10, 39)

The long middle section of the sermon argues for the superiority of Jesus' priesthood. It begins with an extended exhortation (5, 11—6, 20), and then focuses on Jesus' priestly identity and activity (7—10).

Hebrews presupposes the readers' grasp of the "basic teaching about Christ" (6, 1), but, in a rebuke as much as an exhortation, he urges them beyond the milk fit for babes to the meat meant for the mature (compare Paul's use of this imagery in 1 Cor 3, 1–3). This "mature teaching" is by no means a matter of moving beyond Jesus or abandoning Jesus. Such apostasy from Christ Hebrews calls "recrucifying the Son of God" (6, 6). Indeed, God's promise based on Jesus' resurrection is utterly reliable; Jesus is the "anchor of the soul" (6, 19), to whose priesthood God has bound himself by oath (6, 13). The nature and implications of Jesus' priesthood, however, are precisely what require explication. By it the Christian hope is made secure. By it Christians are able to become "imitators of those who, through faith and patience, are inheriting the promises" (6, 12).

The consideration of Jesus as priest is the climax of the "lesser to the greater" argument. But because the procedures and symbols of Jewish cult are foreign to us today, this section makes for some of the hardest reading in the New Testament. It is important to remember from the start that Hebrews' argument is based on the Christian experience of the Spirit and conviction that Jesus is Risen Lord, and he has entered into the life of God (2, 3–4). Only this premise makes Hebrews' reinterpretation of Scripture reasonable. Once that premise is granted, then the major turning points of the exposition make sense.

Jesus and Melchizedek (7, 1–28)

Why does Hebrews devote so much attention to a figure who appears only twice in Scripture? Because both appearances are understood as pointing forward to Christ. In Genesis 14, 17–20, Melchizedek is named a priest of God (although he was a Gentile), whom even Abraham acknowledged by giving him tithes. Logically, then, a priest descended from Melchizedek would be superior to one descended from Abraham! Melchizedek's second scriptural appearance is in verse 4 of the very Psalm 110 that Christians regard as a prophecy of Jesus' resurrection. Melchizedek's being "without beginning or end" (because Scripture records neither his birth nor his death) is therefore an anticipation of the Son of God whose priesthood is eternally valid. Jesus is a priest forever, "like Melchizedek" (Ps 110, 4) because through his resurrection, Jesus became priest "by the power of a life that cannot be destroyed" (7, 16). He "remains forever" (7, 24). His sacrifice is "once for all" (7, 27). He "lives forever to make intercession" (7, 25). The Jewish priesthood descended from Abraham cannot compete.

The Old and New Covenant (8, 1–13)

God's revelation in Jesus does more than continue the story of God's people; it raises it to a new plane. Jesus' death and resurrection mark an absolute beginning. Here, Hebrews' Platonic worldview and its convictions concerning the resurrected Lord converge. In 8, 1–6, we see the use of Platonic language, when Moses' desert sanctuary is called "the copy and shadow of the heavenly sanctuary" (8, 5). Heaven is greater than earth. More dramatically, Hebrews turns this Platonism into an interpretation of history: the old covenant is likewise a "shadow" of the new, pointing to but replaced by the work of God in Jesus. Hebrews exploits Jeremiah's promise of a new covenant "in the heart" to affirm that the old order is in fact obsolescent.

The Priestly Act of Jesus (9, 1—10, 18)

The comparison of covenants now becomes a specific contrast between ancient cult and Jesus' death and resurrection. The complexity of the imagery here is daunting. The reader is offered some help by the notes in New Testament pp. 1627–30. Even more helpful would be a careful reading of Exodus 25—27 (which describes the Tent of the Wilderness) and Leviticus 16 (which describes the ritual for the Day of Atonement). Hebrews hammers at two basic points. First, because Jewish sacrifices had to be repeated, it is obvious they were not effective—they could not truly purify the human conscience (9, 6.25; 10, 1–3.11). In contrast, Jesus entered "real" life, so his sacrifice is eternally valid (9, 12.24–28; 10, 10–12). Second, the old cult sacrificed animals, whereas Jesus gave his own life for others in obedience to God (8, 12–14; 10, 5–10.19). As both priest and victim, furthermore, he showed himself to be a personal example that others could follow. All believers have "confidence of entrance into the sanctuary by the new and living way he opened for us" (10, 19f).

Exhortation to Fidelity (10, 19–39)

In the light of this "greater salvation," Hebrews warns again of the consequences of apostasy (10, 26–31). Despite their losses and trials, Christians are called to a still deeper loyalty (10, 32–39). By mentioning endurance and faith as requisites for receiving the promises (10, 36–38), Hebrews prepares for its final stirring exhortation.

Examples, Discipline, Disobedience (11, 1—12, 29)

The sermon's long argument reaches its climax in this exhortation to faith, understood as loyalty, endurance, and hope. The recital of heroes and heroines of the past serves to provide *examples* for the readers to imitate. Why? Just as the readers had lost property and had been persecuted, so also had the believers who preceded them. Yet the ancestors persevered in the search for a better homeland (11, 14). The repetition of the phrase "by faith" summons the readers to join ranks with those on pilgrimage to God's presence. Unlike the desert generation that fell by the way because of disobedience, these exemplars continued faithful, even though they themselves

did not receive the full promise (11, 39)! It was left to Jesus, the "leader and perfecter of faith" (12, 2) to provide complete access to God through his death and resurrection. Because Christians can now look to him (12, 2), there is solid reason to hope while still on the journey.

By summoning such a "cloud of witnesses" (12, 1) to support the commitment of the readers, Hebrews states a conviction that eventually became an article of the Christian creed, "the communion of saints." Those struggling for God on earth are not alone. They are joined in a larger fellowship of faith with those who have died and who now support them with their prayers. The people of faith have solidarity in hope.

This is not blind optimism: the alienation, suffering, and persecution experienced by the ancients is not trivialized. And Jesus, before he could sit on the throne, had to "endure the cross, despising its shame" (12, 2). Jesus' human response to God is the perfect example for the faith of Christians. Faith is always "evidence of things not seen" (11, 1), which means that it is always a risk taken in the face of a pain more palpably present than the promise. Thus, also, the Christian experience of prayer has as an essential component the "dark night" of the soul when God seems more absent than present.

The connection between Sonship and suffering continues in 12, 5–13. The remarks about fathers disciplining their children at first seem banal if not regressive. But when we remember that Jesus, "Son though he was, . . . learned obedience from what he suffered" (5, 8), we come to appreciate the profound correspondence between Christology and Christian existence. What we suffer in our lives, if we can perceive and accept such suffering in faith, enables God to shape Jesus' own "sonship" in us. Ancient Greeks had the maxim *mathein pathein,* "to learn it is necessary to suffer." Being educated as children of God requires a painful transformation, for the goal is the holy God (12, 10).

Hebrews reminds its readers that they have undertaken not a pleasant stroll but a terrible path toward "the city of the living God" (12, 22), a pilgrimage whose completion means life eternal but whose abandonment means not seeing the Lord (12, 14). Nowhere else does the New Testament give a sterner reminder of life's tragic depths and terrifying heights than in this simple conclusion, "for our God is a consuming fire" (12, 29).

Final Exhortation, Blessing, Greetings (13, 1–25)

Although the final chapter is mainly practical, it is intimately joined to the theological argument of chapters 1 through 12. Notice, for example, the plea to "imitate the faith" of leaders, and the motivation of that faith being the eternal priesthood of Jesus who is "the same yesterday, today, and forever" (13, 7f). The mix of advice about hospitality, marriage, and possessions (13, 1–4) with the command to "go to Jesus outside the camp . . . for here we have no lasting city, but we seek the one that is to come" (13, 13) is altogether typical of this sermon (see also 10, 25) and of the early Christian understanding of existence. Christians live in the world like other people and participate in its structures. But they are not defined by this world or its values, even its

religious values (13, 9–11). No institutional cult or sacrificial priesthood is legitimated by this severe writing; everything necessary has been accomplished already by Jesus. Christians are defined not by their liturgy but by their following the one who suffered "outside the gate, to consecrate the people by his own blood" (13, 12). Christians are never entirely at ease in the world or even in the church. They are pilgrims, struggling toward the "God of peace" into whose care the final blessing (13, 20f) entrusts the readers of this profound and powerful sermon.

FURTHER READING

Attridge, H. W. *Epistle to the Hebrews*. Hermeneia. Philadelphia: Fortress Press, 1989.
Koester, C. R. *Hebrews, A New Translation with Introduction and Commentary*. Anchor Bible 36. New York: Doubleday, 2001.
Lane, W. L. *Hebrews*. 2 vols. Word Biblical Commentary. Waco: Word, 1991.

JAMES

[see pages 1637–44 of the New Testament]

Before Beginning . . .

James as Moral Exhortation

Letter writing was so popular in antiquity that the epistolary form became a package capable of holding many materials. In the case of James (as noted in the introduction, NT, pp. 1637–38), the letter format is the frame for a moral exhortation intended for a general readership.

Before turning to an analysis of the text, it is helpful to consider some of its literary features and major themes. James is not terribly difficult to understand; its style is lucid, its message is straightforward. The reader's task is putting into practice what James teaches. Our task here is simply the deeper appreciation of a clear witness.

The Writing

The form of Greco-Roman moral exhortation called *parenesis* was concerned with reminding readers of traditional values rather than with constructing theory. Such reminders often took the form of short maxims. James's first chapter in

particular has such maxims, which are less connected to each other than to other sections of the composition. Chapters 2 through 5 take the form of short essays. The maxims in chapter 1 set themes that are developed in the essays of chapters 2 through 5. Note how the control of the tongue in 1, 26 is elaborated by 3, 1–12. Moral exhortation also presented models of virtue for readers to imitate. In James, the figures of Abraham, Rahab, Job, and Elijah provide examples from Scripture of the practical virtue James encourages.

James, however, is more than a moral treatise. It is a religious writing that uses the symbols of Scripture. James resembles the *Wisdom* tradition in its use of maxims, and in advocating a "wisdom from above" as the measure of life (3, 13–18). James uses the language and perspective of the *Prophets* in its attack on rich oppressors (5, 1–6). James also uses the *Law*. For James, both the Decalogue and the Law of Love are binding for Christians. They are to be understood, however, in light of the teachings of Jesus. James has many allusions to the words of Jesus (see, for example, 1, 12; 2, 5; 3, 12; 5, 12).

The Message

James advocates living faith and practical love. His concern is behavior. Like other moralists of his age, he is impatient with fine words that go nowhere (see, for example, 1, 22–25). Above all, faith that is not expressed in love is a charade.

James's target is the Christian who is "of two minds" (1, 8; 4, 8). This person wants to live by two standards at once: that of God, and that of the world. James demands a choice. Not only speech but also the use of possessions and the practice of fairness within the community lie within the range of his concern. He especially attacks envy, which perfectly illustrates the morals of "the world" opposed to God (see, for example, 3, 13—4, 10).

Readers may be surprised to find that Jesus is mentioned only twice (1, 1; 2, 1), with no reference at all to the messianic message of salvation through Jesus' death and resurrection. But James does not lack theology. He bases his exhortations on the one God who creates and judges all humanity. James centers attention on God rather than on Christ.

This study guide divides the text differently than the *New American Bible*. No major issue is involved, only a judgment concerning what goes better with what. The paragraph headings in the NAB are helpful, as also are the notes.

The Two Measures (1, 1–27)

Although chapter 1 is made up of separate aphorisms with only loose internal connections, the chapter does more than simply provide a table of contents for the essays to follow. The opening statements also make clear that humans must live by either one sort of measure or another.

The first verses have some word-linkages, but they don't form an easily followed argument. Like the book of Proverbs, they offer a set of maxims that invite testing against the reader's own experience of life. Although the same Greek word *(peirasmos)* is used in both verses, for example, the meaning of "trial" in 1, 2 is not the same as "temptation" in 1, 13.

The aphorisms are not, however, simply a random collection of wise sayings. The maxims in chapter 1 provide something of an index to the contents of chapters 2 through 5. The theme of enduring trials (1, 2–4.12–15) is developed in 5,

7–11; the opposition between rich and poor (1, 9–11) recurs in 4, 13—5, 6. Control of the tongue (1, 19–21) is expanded in 3, 1–12. Carrying out words in speech (1, 22–26) is enlarged by 2, 14–26. The theme of true wisdom (1, 5–8.16–18) is argued by 3, 13—4, 10. The prayer of faith (1, 6f) is amplified by 5, 12–18.

The aphorisms also introduce the basic pattern that structures the whole of James: the contrast between the measure of the world and the measure of God. The measure of the world is expressed by envy: "desire conceives and brings forth sin, and when sin reaches maturity it gives birth to death" (1, 15). The values of the world are self-deceptive (1, 16.27), are expressed in wrathful behavior (1, 19), and in every sort of excess (1, 21) especially the pursuit of illusory wealth (1, 11). These values are based on the perception of life as a closed system; God has no part. Therefore all humans are in competition: one person's gain is another's loss.

The measure of faith is the opposite. All creation—life itself—is a gift: "all good giving and every perfect gift is from above, coming down from the Father of lights" (1, 17). Because God has created humans by "the word of truth" (1, 18), humans are able to receive the implanted word from him (1, 21) and live in the way God does, giving "generously and ungrudgingly" (1, 5). In the Greek, these words suggest the opposite of envy, which always grasps for more. Life by God's measure is expressed by "care for orphans and widows in their affliction" (1, 27). One is thereby "unstained by the world" by living according to a different value system (1, 27).

The greeting in verse 1, "to the twelve tribes in the dispersion," can therefore be understood as referring to the condition of Christians "in the world but not of the world." As in Hebrews and 1 Peter, Christians are regarded as pilgrims and sojourners. They are not hostile to the world but neither are they defined by it. James's whole effort is to persuade those "of two minds" (1, 8) to live by God's measure which is the perfect "wisdom from above" (see 3, 15).

Discrimination and the Law of Love (2, 1–13)

The first essay reveals a voice that resembles Paul in Galatians. James uses the same oral, dialogical style known as the diatribe. Vivid and lively, it is filled with rhetorical questions, exclamations, and abrupt transitions. The effect is a direct challenge to every reader—then and now. The challenge is even more clearly heard when the text is read aloud.

Christians, James says, must live consistently with their convictions. "Faith in our . . . Lord Jesus Christ" (2, 1) is incompatible with any form of discrimination within the community. James sketches a lively scene that probably reflects a general situation rather than a local incident. The context is judgment within the community, like that carried out in the diaspora synagogue to settle disputes. In the background is the injunction of Leviticus 19, 15 that forbids partiality in judgment. How plausible and true to life is his portrayal of a community pandering to rich members and slighting their poor!

That James intends us to see discrimination as an offense against love as well as faith in his allusion to Leviticus 19, 15 is shown immediately by his explicit citation of Leviticus 19, 18 in 2, 8. The "law of love" is also identified by Jesus as the summation of Scripture. James calls it the "royal" law, and he means the standard regulating relations in the community. It is the "law of the kingdom." James spells out this commandment by alluding to the Ten Commandments (2, 11), and also to the specific commandments found in the original context of Leviticus 19 that accompany the original exhortation, "love your neighbor as yourself" (see Jas 4, 11; 5, 4.9.12.20). James says that breaking any commandment means breaking the whole law, because sin is not against a law but against a lawgiver. Faith in the one God excludes picking and choosing between commandments, just as it excludes picking and choosing between fellow Christians!

Active Faith (2, 14–26)

The following section is often misunderstood. Because James speaks of "faith" and "works" (terms often used by Paul), people think James is responding to Paul's teaching. In fact, his perspective is entirely different. James speaks not of the commandments of the law but of active faith. He is a moralist and is concerned with the way speech gets converted to action. Like all moralists, his concern is efficacy: "of what use is it?" The examples of Abraham and Rahab illustrate James's point. Their faith expressed itself in effective action. Abraham was willing to sacrifice

his son; Rahab showed hospitality to God's scouts. James is not debating with Paul over the question of how people are saved. His exhortation is intensely practical and arises from the situation pictured in 2, 14–16: pious talk does not feed or clothe the needy. Such faith is as "dead" as a corpse; such religion is fraudulent (see 1, 26f).

We discover here two distinctive aspects of James. His teaching is not based on what is specifically *Christian*, but on faith in the one God shared by other monotheistic traditions. For James, the "faith of Christ" and teachings of Jesus do not oppose but refine Torah. James therefore also contains the opening to genuine *social ethics*. His moral teaching is not confined to the Christian community; it can be extended to the world. If there is no partiality in the community, based in the law of God, then forms of discrimination in the wider world can be combated on the same basis. If sister and brother in the community are to be fed, then the community as such should also feed the needy of the world in every changing circumstance.

James also warns us that this can cut both ways. If the Christian community does not live up to its own calling, and is unjust, then it bears no witness to the world and is itself subject to condemnation (2, 5–7).

The Power of the Tongue (3, 1–12)

James's concern for the proper use of speech (see 1, 19.26) now becomes thematic. Preoccupation with speech is typical of ancient moralists. Taciturnity as a sign of wisdom was proverbial (see, for example, Prv 10, 19; 11, 12). That such "control of the tongue" was almost insurmountably difficult to achieve was also well known. James therefore considers control of speech to be a mark of perfection (3, 2).

James makes two related points using conventional imagery from Greek philosophy. The first compares the tongue to a horse's bit or a ship's rudder, showing not only how a small organ can direct a large body but also how much that organ itself, with its disproportionate power, needs to be controlled by someone with a sense of direction! James's second point concerns the potential for *harm* in uncontrolled speech. It is like a flame "setting the entire course of our lives on fire" (3, 6).

The capacity of speech to do evil is more impressive than its power for good: "no human being can tame the tongue. It is a restless evil, full of deadly poison" (3, 8). Sadly, the story of human discourse from the Garden of Eden to the latest garden party only confirms James's harsh judgment. No wonder the ancients valued taciturnity: better no speech than destructive speech. The dangers inherent in speech also undergird the value of silence in the monastic/contemplative tradition of both the East and the West. Silence is the necessary precondition to "welcome the word that . . . is able to save your souls" (1, 21).

The theological implications of speech are central to James's exhortation. In 3, 9–12, he contrasts the speech that "blesses God" with that which "curses human beings" who are made in God's image! Once again James combats the "two-minded" person, who thinks that it is possible to have a relationship with God that disregards human obligations. As in 2, 14–17, James insists that religious language and practical human care must go together. The same source cannot yield two kinds of water, and a Christian should not speak with two tongues. Action should follow conviction; speech should conform to faith.

The warning is directed most of all at those who desire to be teachers in the faith community (3, 1). If care is required for all speech, it is even more necessary for those who shape the minds of others according to the measure of God and not of the world.

Friendship with God or the World
(3, 13—4, 10)

Although the paragraph division of modern translations hides what is clearer in Greek, 3, 13—4, 10 is a self-contained essay stating the central theological framework for understanding James as a whole.

Formally, it is a call of conversion. In 3, 13—4, 6, James presents an indictment. In 4, 7–10, he exhorts his readers to repentance. A powerful spatial metaphor governs both parts, a contrast between what comes "from above" (true wisdom, God's gift), and that which originates "from below" (false wisdom, human arrogance).

Correspondingly, the readers are told to "humble" themselves, so that God can "exalt" them (4, 10). The spatial metaphor points to differing measures of reality. That "from below" James calls "the world." It treats life as though God had no claim; human success is measured by human accomplishment and acquisition. But God's measure says that everything comes as a gift from "the Father of lights" (1, 17), and that arrogance is empty pretence. James, as always, has as his main target the "two-minded" person (4, 8) who wants to live by both measures at once.

Within this call to conversion, James develops the theme of envy as exemplifying the measure of the world. Notice the occurrence of "jealousy" in 3, 14.16; 4, 2 and climactically in 4, 5. This last verse is notoriously difficult to translate, not least because we have no verse of Scripture saying what James suggests. The best solution is to render 4, 5 as two rhetorical questions (a technique common in this essay): "Do you think the scripture speaks in vain? Is the spirit God has made to dwell in us for envy?" The word for "envy" here is never used of God (whereas "jealous" sometimes is), and never occurs in Greek with a positive connotation. The point clearly is that God's spirit has nothing to do with envy. Envy comes from the "wisdom from below." James associates with envy all the vices commonly attributed to it in Greek moral discourse, especially social unrest, murder, and war.

Why is envy so singled out? Because its underlying assumption is that your gain is my loss. This is the opposite of the Spirit of community, where all gain by anyone's growth and all rejoice in anyone's good fortune. Envy causes me to sorrow when another has something that I lack. And when life is measured simply in terms of what I possess—"I am what I have"—then for another to have and me to lack is intolerable. Envy drives the acquisitive instinct: "you covet" (4, 2). It is a short step to conflict, war, and murder, between individuals and among nations. Like other Greek moralists, James assigns the cause of war to envy (4, 1–3). It is remarkable that this passage, which alone in the New Testament analyzes the causes of human conflict, should play so little role in moral discussions of war and peace.

At the climax of the indictment (4, 4), James accuses his readers of being "adulterers" because they have broken covenant both with God and with their fellow humans. The covenant is about loyalty and love. There is no connection between those attitudes and the self-seeking of envy. James also uses the language of Greek philosophy concerning "friendship." He contrasts "friendship with the world" and "friendship with God" as opposing ways of life. James is not condemning the world understood as the place of human activity or God's creation. Rather, it is a system of values that excludes consideration of God. To be "friends with the world" therefore means to live by a measure that leaves God's claim aside.

To this closed system James opposes the measure of faith: God is the source of "all good giving and every perfect gift" (1, 17). God gives more grace to the humble even while resisting the arrogant (4, 6). God is not envious of humans but gives to all generously and without grudging (see 1, 5). Those who submit to God are therefore also lifted up by God (4, 10). Their tears of repentance will rapidly turn to joy, because—a remarkable statement—when humans draw near to God, God also draws near to them (4, 8).

Against Arrogance (4, 11—5, 6)

James now turns to three forms of arrogance, which exemplify life according to the measure of the world. The first is the practice of slandering a neighbor (4, 11f). Such critical speech naturally involves both a condemnation of the other and an implied assertion of one's own superiority: "I am in a position to judge." James insists that such judgment breaks the law of love (see Lv 19, 16) and reminds his readers that the lawgiver is also the judge. God alone can both save and destroy life (see 1, 21).

A second form of arrogance is demonstrated by those who make great business plans without ever considering the fragile nature of their own existence (4, 13–17). Once more, their speech gives them away; they assume control over the present and the future. James comments: "You are boasting in your arrogance. All such boasting is evil" (4, 16). The speech of one living by God's measure is also revealing: "If the Lord wills . . ." This is more than pious talk; it refers all of life and all of life's projects to the one who gives and can alone sustain life.

Finally, with a prophetic rage like that of Amos, James attacks the insolence of the rich who withhold wages from their laborers. The security gained by such fraud is illusory; the rich fatten themselves for the day of judgment (5, 5). They sin because they "know the right thing to do but do not do it" (4, 17). How do they know? Because the scriptural context for the law of love in Leviticus 19, 18 states plainly, "you shall not withhold overnight the wages of your day laborer" (Lv 19, 13).

Patience, Plain Speech, Prayer (5, 7–20)

Having called the double-minded to conversion and excoriated the arrogant, James turns to the community's inner life. Speech is again the underlying theme, this time with reference to the proper uses of speech in the church.

The attack on oppressors (5, 1–6) leads naturally to the condition of those who suffer persecution from without. James recommends patience and extends the example of Job (5, 11). Patience is possible for them as it is for a farmer, because the fruitful outcome of their loyalty is certain: "the coming of the Lord is at hand." In the meantime, nothing would be more natural than for the afflicted to turn on each other in resentment and hurt. James again uses Leviticus 19 when he tells them, "Do not complain about one another that you may not be judged" (see Lv 19, 17f).

Christians should speak plainly. In 5, 12 James repeats the commandment of Jesus (Mt 5, 33–37) that speech should be unadorned and straightforward, without oaths. And in his last exhortation, James encourages the sort of mutual correction that can build up the identity of the church (5, 20).

Because the church is constituted by the word of truth (1, 18), it should above all express that truth in its communal life of prayer. James enumerates the sorts of prayer that are appropriate to the community's diverse circumstances (5, 13f) and then elaborates the prayer with anointing for a sick member. This ritual is the basis for the sacrament of anointing for the sick and has roots in the healing ministry of Jesus (see 5, 15). James's last example from Torah is the prophet Elijah, whose prayer demonstrates the power of faith for those who live by God's measure (5, 17f; cf. 1, 6–8). These final exhortations, down to earth and humane, summarize beautifully the character of James, who from beginning to end finds wisdom in practical faith and active love.

FURTHER READING

Adamson, J. B. *James: The Man and His Message.* Grand Rapids: Eerdmans, 1989.

Harris, Patrick J. *James.* Sacra Pagina. Collegeville, MD: Liturgical Press, 2003.
Johnson, L. T. *The Letter of James.* Anchor Bible 37A. New York: Doubleday, 1995.
Wall, R. W. *Community of the Wise: The Letter of James.* Valley Forge, PA: Trinity Press International, 1997.

1 PETER

[see pages 1644–51 of the New Testament]

Before Beginning . . .

First Peter bears all the marks of a real letter. It was written to Christians scattered throughout the provinces of Asia Minor. Although written in clear and even elegant Greek, and although containing an exhortation and witness (5, 12) at once simple and profound, 1 Peter is given far less attention than it deserves. Partly this is because many contemporary scholars think that the letter is pseudonymous and a product of second generation rather than primitive Christianity (see, for example, introduction, NT, pp. 1644–45). There are, however, excellent reasons for considering Peter the disciple to have been the author of 1 Peter. In any case, the authority of New Testament writings does not derive from the identity of the author. Whether it was the apostle or someone writing in his name, this letter speaks powerfully to a situation of early believers and retains enduring value for readers in every age.

A Letter to the Gentile Christians

The Situation of the Readers

Since the letter is addressed to Christians spread over a large geographical area (1, 1), we do not expect the detailed treatment of local problems. By reading between the lines, however, we are able to learn something about their shared characteristics. They seem to have been recently converted. Peter reminds them repeatedly of their former life of vice (1, 18–20; 4, 3–4), as well as their initiation into the messianic community through baptism (1, 3; 1, 22—2, 3). They seem, furthermore, to be direct converts from paganism rather than from Judaism. They were themselves Gentiles and continued to live among the symbols and social structures of the Empire. They in-

evitably felt pulled between an allegiance to their new calling and an attraction to the values of the world they had left. They were, finally, converts who were experiencing suffering. On the basis of 4, 12, some have considered this to be a state-sponsored persecution such as was later the lot of Christians. But Peter's positive view of the state (2, 12–17) does not fit that reconstruction. It is more likely that Peter's readers were experiencing the sort of verbal abuse and social ostracism that Christians experienced from the beginning. The suffering was no less serious. Martyrdom is painful but swift. The corrosion of confidence is slower but terribly effective.

Christian Apologetic

First Peter can best be understood as a form of apologetic literature. This form of writing originated among Diaspora Jews and was taken over by Christians. Ostensibly it explains one's distinctive beliefs to the wider world in terms outsiders can understand. Indirectly, it supports community identity. First Peter has many of the characteristics of this genre. It is positive and open to the dominant culture. Christians are not to flee the world or its structures. They are to be good citizens within those social structures. And they are to be ready to demonstrate by their behavior and their speech that they pose no threat to others (3, 15–16).

At the same time, Peter works to build up the identity of the community. He reminds his readers that they are called to holiness and a standard of behavior higher than that of their neighbors (2, 11–12; 4, 1–2). He reminds them of the fundamental transformation they had undergone in their baptism. He assures them that although they are "sojourners" in the world (2, 11), they are part of the "household of God" (2, 4–5; 4, 17). In so doing, Peter appropriates for these new Gentile believers all the scriptural titles and symbols used of Israel, to give them a sense of continuity with God's people, even though once they were "no people." In 1 Peter we observe a thoroughly Gentile Christianity regarding itself as the "New Israel," taking up a place in the Diaspora not against the world but as a witness to the world.

The Greeting (1, 1–2)

The greeting of this circular letter establishes more than the simple identification of author and addressees. No need to elaborate the simple designation, "Peter, apostle of Jesus Christ," for Peter's authority is unquestioned (see, in contrast, 2 Peter). But the "diaspora" of Asia Minor has religious as well as geographical connotations. We see here a theme found also in James and Hebrews and in the Christian literature of the second century: Christians are in exile from their true homeland in heaven so long as they are on earth. They are, in fact, "sojourners" precisely because they have been "chosen" by God and have an identity distinct from that of their neighbors. They should therefore cultivate attitudes appropriate to exiles and pilgrims (see, for example, 2, 11). The greeting also reminds the readers of the rich complexity of their experience of God: The Father has chosen them; the Son saved them, by his obedient sacrifice; and the Spirit has sanctified them.

The Gift and Call of God (1, 3–21)

The opening prayer (1, 3–9) is based on the blessing formula of Jewish worship: God is blessed for his gifts to humans. In this case, Peter gives thanks for the new life his readers have been granted through the resurrection of Jesus. Their new life is real, yet not complete. Their inheritance is one that is kept for them in heaven (1, 4f). They, of course, still remain on earth. This tension establishes them as pilgrims and sojourners. As their salvation "waits for them," so also must they "wait for it." In the meantime, they must experience the trials and sufferings inherent to the life of faith (1, 6f). Peter places his readers between the "already" of God's grace and the "not yet" of salvation fully achieved (1, 9), in a manner typical of New Testament writings. But what they hope for is secure, a "living hope" (1, 3) because it is based not simply in hu-

man longing but in the "power of God" at work among them (1, 5).

Despite the fact that his readers have converted from paganism, Peter inserts them into the story of Israel. In speaking of an "inheritance in heaven," Peter implies a contrast to the "inheritance of the land," which was the hope of Israel. Likewise, 1, 10–12 develops a contrast between stages in the story. Peter asserts that the prophets of old did not speak of their own times (1, 12) but spoke of the "sufferings destined for Christ and the glories to follow them" (1, 11). Three aspects of this striking statement deserve notice. First, the superiority of the Christians' present experience is clearly asserted; as in Hebrews the claims of the earlier covenant are made secondary. What the Christians have received in the gospel transcends even what angels can know (1, 12)! Second, Scripture is taken over completely as messianic prophecy. Everything in Scripture points to Jesus. Third, as in Luke-Acts, the pattern of the Messiah is spelled out in terms of "suffering, then glory." That his readers must follow after this same pattern becomes explicit later in the letter.

Having asserted the reality of God's gift, Peter now sketches the demands it places on those who receive it (1, 13–21). They are to direct their lives by the new form of existence given to them. This means a radical obedience to the giver of the gift, an obedience spelled out in terms of holiness (1, 15f). As their lives have changed, so must their behavior. They must not act as they formerly did but are to become "different." They are to shape themselves in a manner consonant with the one who called them with the gift of the "precious blood of Christ" (1, 19). Peter again calls his readers "sojourners" (1, 17). Jews of the Diaspora were to be different from pagans; Christians are to be "different" (holy) in the world as they wait for the fulfillment of their salvation (see 1, 9). They are not defined by the norms of others (1, 14.18) but by their allegiance to God, so that "your faith and hope are in God" (1, 21).

A Gospel People (1, 22—2, 10)

To strengthen their grasp on their special identity Peter reminds his readers of the basis of their new life in "the living and abiding word of God" (1, 23). By this, Peter explicitly means the good news (1, 25). This is the message of a crucified

Messiah who was raised to new life. By the obedient acceptance of that strange proclamation, they were given "new birth" (1, 23). Immediately, however, Peter asserts the need for them to grow. The "spiritual milk" they now imbibe is appropriate to new converts who have just "tasted and seen that the Lord is good" (see also 1 Cor 3, 1–3; Heb 6, 13), but they are to mature "in Christ" by patterning their life according to a new standard of moral behavior. They must leave aside deceit in favor of truth, envy for love.

Peter is not only concerned with the transformation of individuals, but, as much as Paul, with the identity of the community also. In 2, 4–10, therefore, he reminds them of their communal identity as God's house and people. This section interweaves scriptural passages and allusions. The references at the bottom of New Testament pages 1646–47 provide valuable assistance. The choice of passages is strikingly similar to that in Romans 9, 25–33. It is less likely that Peter used Romans than that both Paul and Peter used community traditions of scriptural interpretation developed from the first days of the church.

The first set of passages (2, 6–8) portrays the paradox of Christian faith. The stone that God intended to be the basis for his people Israel was rejected by them; yet the rejected one became the basis of a new people, a "spiritual house" made up of living persons (2, 4). The reference here is clearly to the crucified Jesus who was a scandal (a stone of stumbling) to his fellow Jews who expected a messiah with more obvious and impressive credentials than suffering for others (see 1 Cor 1, 18–23).

For the Christian community, however, the *rejected* Messiah is the basis for a new life and shared identity. In the second set of texts, Peter strings together the most precious epithets applied to Israel as God's people in Torah. Now, they apply to these Gentiles, "once no people, but now God's people." In the messianic community, these aliens have a home (see also Eph 2, 19–22).

Where is the place of the historical Jewish people? It must be confessed that 1 Peter simply does not take them into account. He appropriates the symbols of Torah for the exclusive use of Gentile believers. Readers today cannot expect to find in this text an answer to the many questions concerning the relations of Christians to Jews, for 1 Peter does not address them.

Life within the World's Structures
(2, 11—3, 7)

Christians are to maintain distance from the values of this world as "aliens and sojourners" (2, 11). At the same time, they must live within the social structures of the world. Peter is convinced that if they are good citizens, they will turn away from slander and persecution. The practice of "good works" is the community's basic witness (2, 12).

Peter uses the traditional form of "household ethics" to sketch the Christians' social obligations. Greek philosophy had elaborated the mutual duties of people who lived in a stratified social order. Over the empire as a whole, the emperor was considered head of the household. In individual families, husbands ruled wives, parents ruled children, and masters ruled slaves. This was simply the conventional arrangement of that time. Neither Paul (see Col 3, 18—4, 1) nor Peter thought that the Christian message demanded the dismantling of society's structures.

In 2, 13–17, Peter portrays the empire and its agents in positive terms. Submission to legitimate authority is both right and expedient, since the state punishes only the wicked: such an outlook is inconceivable if Christians were in fact being harassed by the state as such. Yet, even here, the relationship with God is primary. Social obligations, if they conflict with that relationship, must give way to it: "Be free, yet without using freedom as a pretext for evil, but as slaves of God" (2, 16). Obedience to God comes before all; and before God, all are slaves.

We might expect in the next section exhortations to both masters and slaves (compare Col 3, 22—4, 1). Perhaps the absence of masters says something about the Christians' social status. But since Peter thinks of all Christians as slaves (2, 16), this exhortation to servants becomes a general teaching to the community at large. The most striking aspect of this teaching is the invocation of Jesus as an explicit example to be imitated, for all who suffer unjustly (2, 21–23). Jesus not only won salvation for others by his death on the cross. In his very manner of suffering, he provided the model for how Christians were to act.

Not only what Jesus did but also how he did it becomes a source of life to the community.

The exhortation to wives (3, 1–6) is much more extensive than that to husbands (3, 7). Traditional Jewish and Greek motifs, which stress the value of internal virtue over external adornment, are used to support the command to be submissive. Women are to be subordinate, we notice, not to all men, but to their husbands (3, 1.5). In return, men are to regard women as fully equal in their relationship before the Lord. Women are "joint heirs of the gift of life" (3, 7).

In these instructions, we do not find a divinely inspired blueprint for the ideal social order or Christian family structure. What we find is the best available moral teaching applied to the real world of that age. Just as the social structures of the past cannot be transferred directly to the present, neither can the relationships appropriate to those structures be directly imitated. Yet for families both ancient and modern, for societies then and now, good order, mutual respect, obedience, and authority are very much required. The style of those structures, happily, is left to human creativity.

Witness in a Hostile World (3, 8—4, 6)

The Christians of Asia Minor were not suffering persecution, torture, and death. Their suffering was nevertheless real and painful. Social ostracism works a slow and insidious poison into a community's sense of identity. They were being "insulted" (3, 9), maligned and defamed (3, 16), and "vilified" (4, 4). Why? Probably they were abused because they no longer followed the ways of their neighbors (4, 3f). They have become different (holy), and people who insist on being different generate resentment.

Peter's response to the community's experience of suffering is remarkable. He does not advocate withdrawal from society or hostility toward outsiders. Instead, Christians are to remain in the world (see 2, 13—3, 7) and are to engage outsiders in dialogue. They are to be ready to "give an explanation to anyone who asks you for a reason for your hope" (3, 15). The expectation that such explanation would be helpful pays a high compliment to the basic reasonableness and goodwill of outsiders. Christians are also to follow the exhortation of Jesus to return a blessing

for a curse (see Mt 5, 44). In order to act in this way toward outsiders, they must cultivate the same qualities of sympathy and love toward each other in the community (3, 8). Within their own hearts, furthermore, they are to "sanctify Christ as Lord" (3, 15), which, Peter asserts, will free them from fear of outsiders (3, 14). How will this happen?

They are to remember how Jesus not only "suffered for sins once" (3, 18) but also how he was raised from the dead in power. Using traditions found in apocalyptic literature (such as 1 Enoch), Peter symbolically expresses the conviction that the resurrection was not simply an event concerning the person Jesus but had cosmic extension. "In the spirit" Jesus went to the spirits in prison to preach the good news (3, 19–22). This dramatic announcement is the basis for the statement in the Apostles' Creed that says Jesus "descended into hell." It means that God's power to save reaches everywhere, even to the farthest reaches of human sin and alienation.

Peter's immediate point, however, is that by baptism (3, 21), the Christians of Asia Minor have been given the same power. They need not fear human slander, for the power of God is at work among them. They are like those to whom Jesus preached after his resurrection, "though condemned in the flesh in human estimation . . . alive in the spirit in the estimation of God" (4, 6).

Community Attitudes (4, 7—5, 14)

First Peter does not portray the Christians' moral situation in stark black-and-white tones, but like most New Testament writings it has a keen sense that the time for decision is now. The final exhortations are colored by the conviction that "the end of all things is at hand" (4, 7). The time of judgment is soon (4, 17). Therefore, Christian life means "resisting the devil" who through affliction such as they are experiencing "seeks to devour them" (5, 8f). Such circumstances call for a "serious, sober" attitude and one that is "vigilant" (4, 7; 5, 8). Those who experience affliction are to regard their sufferings as a share in Christ's own (5, 13f), knowing that they will share in his glory (4, 13; 5, 10). Within the community, attitudes of mutual service are to prevail (4, 9–11), demonstrated by good order and humility (5, 1–16).

When exhorting the community's leaders, Peter forbids lording it over the flock. Leaders are rather to provide a positive example (5, 3). The image of the shepherd recalls the portrayal of Jesus as the "shepherd and guardian of your souls" (in 2, 25). The connection is made explicit in 5, 4: with characteristic optimism, Peter promises such good leaders that, "when the chief Shepherd is revealed, you will receive the unfading crown of glory."

The New Testament contains no writing more positive in its evaluation of the world yet more compelling in its call to holiness than 1 Peter. As Martin Luther correctly noted, it is one of the New Testament compositions that truly "show thee Christ."

FURTHER READING

Achtemeier, P. J. *1 Peter: A Commentary on First Peter.* Edited by E. J. Epp. Hermeneia. Minneapolis: Fortress Press, 1996.

Elliot, John H. *1 Peter.* The Anchor Bible 37B. New York: Doubleday, 2000.

Kelly, J. N. D. *A Commentary on the Epistles of Peter and Jude.* Harper New Testament Commentary. New York: Harper & Row, 1969.

Senior, Donald. *1 Peter.* Sacra Pagina. Collegeville, MD: Liturgical Press, 2003.

2 PETER

[see pages 1651–56 of the New Testament]

Before Beginning . . .

An appreciative understanding of 2 Peter demands more than the normal effort. Hard work is necessary to uncover the situation addressed by the letter. Perhaps even more difficult is the hurdle presented by the letter's sustained argumentative tone. Such effort finds its rewards, however, in the surprising discovery that a writing which at first appears as the New Testament's most irrelevant can emerge as having perennial pertinence.

A Defense of God's Judgment

The circumstances of 2 Peter's composition are obscure (see introduction, NT, pp. 1651–52). The same author did not write both 1 and 2 Peter. The style, outlook, and concerns of the two letters are too disparate for a common authorship. The main thing they have in common is the mention of Noah and the flood. Second Peter has far more in common with Jude (with which it shares the polemical material of chapter 2) than with 1 Peter. In all likelihood, 2 Peter is a pseudonymous composition. Despite the self-presentation of chapter 1, it is not "Symeon Peter" who writes, but someone who invokes his authority as a support for shared traditions being threatened by deviance. This sermon in the form of a letter may have been addressed to a single church, but it may also have been intended for a larger audience, all "those who have received a faith of equal value to ours" (1, 1). It is thus considered a "general" epistle. The title "Catholic Epistles" was applied to 1 and 2 Peter, James, 1, 2, 3 John, and Jude because they were written for a broader audience than a local church (in Greek, "catholic" = "pertaining to the whole"). Some readers also consider 2 Peter "catholic" in another sense: its concern for tradition anticipates the emergence of the Catholic Church in the second century.

At first reading, 2 Peter seems to be a loose collection of observations within which talk about Jesus' second coming plays a particularly significant part. Some scholars have therefore thought that the "delay of the *Parousia*" was the crisis that stimulated composition. Closer analysis, however, shows that "Peter" and his opponents are debating a deeper and more perennial problem: does God judge the world? Underlying that issue, in turn, is a still more fundamental one concerning the reality of God and God's relationship to the world. The debate, in short, is between living faith and practical atheism. It is a debate still in progress. The contribution of 2 Peter is worth hearing.

Far from a random collection of statements, the letter as a whole presents a coherent argument. Chapter 1 establishes the authority of the writer and of the Scripture that will be used as the source of proof. Chapter 2 attacks the opponents' "destructive teachings" on the basis of Scripture. Chapter 3 presents the proper understanding of the tradition concerning God's judgment.

The Common Tradition (1, 1–21)

The first section of the letter establishes the authority of the writer and of the shared tradition (1, 1) that the author represents. Extraordinary emphasis is put on the person of Peter and on the fact that he will soon die (1, 13f). These touches recall the literary genre popular in early Christianity called the "Farewell Discourse." In this sort of composition, a figure from the past, speaking shortly before his death, predicts catastrophes to come and enjoins fidelity on his followers. We notice in this case, however, an equally strong emphasis on *memory* (1, 9.12.13.15). The opponents "forget" the proper knowledge, and Peter seeks to "remind" his readers of it. The emphasis on memory makes the letter resemble as well the form of moral exhortation called *parenesis*. The connection to parenesis is most obvious in 2 Peter 1, 5–8. Parenesis spelled out moral obligations in terms of maxims. Here, Peter lists the sort of qualities that should follow upon the readers' faith. More important even than the specific items is the overall point made by the list: more than knowledge or faith is involved in being Christian. A whole way of life is demanded. Those who have "forgotten" this lead lives that are "idle and unfruitful" (1, 8f). There is a sharp polemical edge to this comment. In chapter 2, Peter will show that the opponents' "destructive heresies" bring about destructive behavior, which in turn brings down God's judgment.

A complex statement provides the basis for Peter's overall argument and a transition to his attack on opponents (1, 16–21). In a passage that clearly corresponds to the Synoptic Gospels' story of Jesus' transfiguration (see Mt 17, 1–8), he asserts the reality of the Christian experience of God. The tradition out of which Peter writes is not speculation ("cleverly devised myths," 1, 16), but is a power he and others experience personally; "we" saw and heard on the mountain (1, 16–18)! The community's tradition is based not in fancy but in fact. The experience, moreover, was of "the power and coming" of the Lord Jesus Christ. As we will learn, the promise concerning Jesus' return is the bone of contention in chapter 3. Peter claims that the expectation of his return is based on the reality of his already having come.

The disciples' experience of Jesus also grounds the "prophetic message" about Jesus' return for judgment. Peter places this prophecy of Jesus (see Mt 24, 29–31) among the prophecies of Scripture. As with scriptural prophecies, interpretation is not to be personal or idiosyncratic but a decision of the community that is guided by the same Spirit that gave utterance in the first place. With this alignment, Peter has provided the basis for arguing the whole issue of God's judgment (and therefore of Jesus' return) on the truthfulness of Scripture as properly interpreted by the tradition.

Condemnation of False Teachers (2, 1–22)

The claim to a true "prophetic message" in 1, 19 provides a transition to the attack on "false teachers" (2, 1) who are placed in the line of "false prophets." As we will learn more fully in chapter 3, the opponents are denying the power of God to judge, that is, to intervene in the affairs of the world (3, 4). By denying God's ability to judge, they bring judgment on themselves! Their "destructive heresies" bring on them "destruction" (2, 1). But their teaching has proven successful, convincing many (2, 2); Peter's response must therefore be vigorous and pointed.

We saw in 1, 5–8 that Peter was concerned with the moral consequences of faith. The ancient world knew what our world sometimes ignores, that people act on their ideas, and that bad ideas can lead to bad behavior. A real misconception of what life is about leads to a distorted existence. Showing how certain teachings lead to immoral behavior is a way of proving that the ideas are false. Peter therefore pays particular attention to the *way of life* generated by these doctrines. He attacks the "licentious ways" of the opponents (2, 2), their "greed" and "lies" (2, 3). They are people of "depraved desires" (2, 10), are "irrational" (2, 12) and "adulterous" (2, 14). The catalogue of vices reaches a rhetorical climax in 2, 17f, then takes a sharp turn: "They promise them freedom, though they themselves are slaves of corruption, for a person is a slave of whatever overcomes him" (2, 19).

What sort of "freedom" did the opponents promise? Apparently, it was freedom from the fear of punishment. If God does not intervene in human affairs to punish the wicked and reward the good, then (they said) one can live immorally, looking out only for oneself, indulging in antisocial behavior.

Peter's first rebuttal is based on the nature of vice. They are slaves of their dominating appetite, which controls their behavior. They are not sophisticated or liberated. They are as compulsive as dogs returning to their vomit, these Christians who once knew righteousness but have now turned back to a novel version of an old atheism: "Fools say in their hearts, 'There is no God' " (Ps 14, 1).

The second part of Peter's rebuttal is based on the conviction that the Bible stories relate the facts of history. When Scripture says therefore that God *did* punish and reward, that is proof of God's ability still to do so. Peter relates the cases of the wicked angels (2, 4), of Noah (2, 5), of Sodom and Gomorrah (2, 6–10) and of Balaam (2, 15f) as evidence of God's intervention. In contrast to the letter of Jude (with which much of this material is shared), Peter not only emphasizes punishment; God also rewards those who are faithful. Here, the issue is whether God acts in human history at all. Peter's recitation from Scripture asserts that in fact God does.

The Coming of the Lord (3, 1–18)

The specific nature of the debate emerges for the first time in this final section. Here, not simply a question of fact but a matter of principle is at stake.

The question of fact is not really in dispute. Jesus clearly had not yet returned to judge the world as all Christians had been expecting. But quite different conclusions were being drawn from that undisputed fact. The "scoffers" challenge the very *promise* of his coming (3, 4).

They base their denial on the immutability of the world "from the beginning." They hold the position of ancient skeptics such as the Epicureans and (among the Jews) Sadducees, who denied divine providence. If there was a god, he did not meddle with the world, which was, therefore, a closed system of natural forces and human desires. God was not a factor to be considered, never had been, never would be. The failure of Jesus to return, therefore, was only one more piece of evidence proving that all such prophecies were empty.

Theirs is a real threat to the whole structure of faith. They challenge not only the reality of the Parousia but the very reality of a living God! Is God, then, merely a figment of the imagination, a projection of human longing, a societal superego? The whole concept of revelation is obviously challenged as well. There can be no real "promise" if there is no living God to speak, or to act.

In this argument, both sides base their position on a claim of *experience,* which then interprets reality as a whole. The skeptics say that experience shows no evidence for God's activity: "nothing has changed." Peter argues that Scripture (which is after all the record of human history) proves that God *does* intervene (see all of chapter 2). God created by a word and can destroy by a word (3, 5f). Furthermore—and this is the significance of 1, 16–19—Peter and his companions themselves *experienced* such an intervention in the transfiguration of Jesus! Thus, their tradition is based on the prophets, on the Lord Jesus, and on the apostles (3, 2).

If God does intervene, how is his apparent absence to be interpreted? Peter invokes the arguments used by other defenders of divine providence. God's time cannot be measured by human time: there is an infinite distance between God and humans (3, 7). God's apparent delay is to bring people to repentance (3, 8f).

Ultimately, those whose experience is different are not likely to be convinced. Peter appeals not to the opponents but to those attracted to their position. He reasserts the conviction that Jesus will come "like a thief in the night" (see Mt 24, 43; 1 Thes 5, 2; Rv 3, 3), and that his coming will inaugurate "new heavens and a new earth in which righteousness dwells" (3, 13; see Rv 21, 1). His concern throughout this letter, however, has been most of all with the behavior of his readers, and he reasserts "what sort of persons they are to be" during this time of waiting (3, 11). After all debate is over, only the truth of human existence validates doctrine.

The letter concludes with a reference to Paul's letters that the opponents are distorting (3, 15f). The fact that the author refers to "all" of Paul's letters, that he makes them equivalent to "Scripture," and that there is already a history of interpreting (or misinterpreting) them, are strong indications that this "Peter" is a writer of the second generation who defends a tradition common to the historical Peter and Paul against the threat of doctrinal and behavioral deviance.

FURTHER READING

Bauckham, R. J. *Jude; 2 Peter.* Word Biblical Commentary. Waco, TX: Word, 1983.

Harrington, Daniel, S.J. *Jude and 2 Peter.* Sacra Pagina. Collegeville: Liturgical Press, 2003.

Neyrey, J. H. *2 Peter; Jude* Anchor Bible 37C. New York: Doubleday, 1993.

1 JOHN

[see pages 1656–62 of the New Testament]

Before Beginning . . .

Exhortation to a Divided Church

The New Testament contains three letters attributed to John. How these letters connect to the Gospel according to John and the book of Revelation is not easy to determine. Scholars agree that all came from a community of "Johannine Christianity" in the late first century, but neither their precise authorship nor sequence has been established. We are not even sure of the location of this "Johannine Christianity," although Asia Minor seems most likely. In such a state of ignorance, hypotheses abound. The introductions to each of these letters in the NAB give some sense of the options (cf. New Testament pp. 1656–57, 1662, 1663–64).

What we can learn of "Johannine Christianity" derives from the writings themselves. Apart from the connection to John, what common characteristics marked this version of messianism? First, the figure of Jesus played a central role in the identity of the community. Second, these churches had experienced tragic division. In the Gospel and Revelation, there is conflict between these messianists and the Jews. In the letters and Revelation, there is also evidence of divisions within the churches. Third, this experience of division sharpened the community's symbols into a stark dualism: light and darkness, life and death, truth and falsehood, flesh and spirit.

The Three Letters

In the three letters, we see conflict happening within the churches. Disputes involve the proper understanding of Jesus. The letters provide a window on this early Christian conflict, revealing at once its multiple dimensions and its seriousness. It is impossible to say at this distance exactly how the letters relate to each other or to the situation. Second and 3 John are real letters

and claim to come from "the Elder." First John is anonymous and not really a letter so much as a sermonic exhortation.

Some think that the three letters show three stages of the community's conflict. This hypothesis is possible, but a better one is that the three documents were written at the same time by the same author and sent to a single church aligned with "The Elder." Each letter fulfills a specific function: 3 John recommends the mailman, Demetrius, to the church leader, Gaius. Second John is a cover letter to be read publicly to the church. First John is the centerpiece, an exhortation to a community divided by conflict. The Study Guides for 2 and 3 John will describe how they fulfill their functions. Let us concentrate first on 1 John.

The Character of 1 John

Because it is not so closely tied to the particulars of a specific community's life, 1 John lends itself more readily to every time and place. For a document generated by bitter conflict, it is amazingly positive and loving in tone. Christians through the ages have rightly considered it one of the great spiritual witnesses of the New Testament.

The structure of this writing is not obvious. Certainly it is not a genuine letter. Even as a sermon, it tends to wander a bit, repeating the same points. First John at times has the appearance of an argument but none of the substance. Readers are sometimes shocked at the lack of consistency. What is stated positively is sometimes denied only a short time later. The reason for this alternation of ideal and real lies in the circumstances being addressed.

The Johannine Christians saw their lives defined by a choice. Their first and basic choice was to follow Jesus. They considered that truth, life, and light characterized them; while falsehood, darkness, and death characterized those who did not follow Jesus. The Christians were the community of true prophecy. But now, the community finds itself divided into two hostile camps, and the cause of division is precisely what should have been the centerpiece of this unity: the proper understanding of the nature and role of Jesus.

First John's apparent indecisiveness reflects the chastened perspective caused by the trauma of division. The symbols of unity and perfection need reshaping. The author urges his readers away from a smug sense of their own perfection, to an awareness of their need to repent. Not only "those who went out from us" have sinned; all have sinned and need the expiation offered by Jesus.

Opening Exhortation (1, 1—2, 17)

First John opens with a poetic prologue (1, 1–4) that resembles the prologue to the Fourth Gospel (Jn 1, 1–8) in its deliberate allusion to Genesis 1, 1 ("in the beginning"), and its emphasis on the "word of life." In the epistle's prologue, however, the stress is placed on the community's *experience* of the Word in Jesus. The writer testifies to what he has "seen and heard and touched" (compare Jn 19, 35). The experience, furthermore, is one shared by the readers. The language of fellowship dominates 1, 3f. The believers have fellowship with God the Father through Jesus. They are also, by that same agency, to have fellowship among themselves. The textual variant in 1, 4 illustrates the dense interweaving. Manuscripts differ on reading "your" joy, or "our" joy. For this writer, both meanings coincide.

The section closes with another deliberately rhetorical statement of purpose: "I am writing to you because" (2, 12–14). Different groups in the community are addressed, but the message is basically one message and is more clearly spelled out by 2, 15–17: the church is to live by the "will of God" and not by the standards of the "world." John's talk about "love of the world" here is very close to that in the letter of James about the "lover of the world" (Jas 4, 4) and means much the same thing. The writer does not forbid love for humanity; he denounces the "worldliness" that denies God's claim on his creation and bases existence on "sensual lust, enticement for the eyes, and a pretentious life" (2, 16).

Within the framework provided by the pro-logue and the statement of purpose, the rest of the opening section of this sermon serves to remind the readers of the need to live by the "message we have heard from him and proclaim to you" (1, 5).

The community has, to be sure, already heard that "God is light, and in him there is no darkness at all" (1, 5). But now, because of the division in this community, a new sense of reality is required. Behavior must match their ideals. They can no longer simply assume that "we are the light" without hesitation. In fact, sin does occur among them, and they need to repent of it. They cannot claim to be "in the light" while their behavior shows that they "walk in darkness" (1, 6). That is a lie. Likewise, they cannot claim to "know God" while not keeping God's commandments (2, 4).

With a different vocabulary than James, but with a quite similar concern, John seeks to make his readers' actions conform to their convictions. And the great commandment of God that is to govern the life of the community is also—as in James—the law of love for neighbor, the test whether one is "in the light" or "in the darkness." For 1 John, it is not simply doctrinal correctness that spells true fellowship in the community, but ethical consistency.

First John places special emphasis on the role of Jesus as expiation for sin (1, 7; 2, 2) and advocate for believers (2, 1). The community's failure, demonstrated in its division into hostile parties, makes the need for intercession clear. They cannot do it alone. It also makes clear that "love" is not simply a state of mind, but something to be performed. In an atmosphere of hurt and separation, such performance is difficult.

The Divided Community (2, 18—3, 24)

The severity of the community's crisis is indicated by the fact that the writer thinks the end of all things is at hand. The author calls those who have left the community "antichrists." In apocalyptic literature, the presence of antichrist is a sign of the final tribulation (see Mt 24, 24). The theme of Jesus' return occurs again in 2, 28 and 3, 2. Typical of apocalyptic also is the exhortation to stand fast ("remain in him," 2, 24.27.28; 3, 6) and to avoid being deceived (2, 26).

The threat to the community is the greater because former members make it: "they went out

from us." It is impossible for this writer to acknowledge fully that they had ever been of one
spirit with the community: "they were not really
of our number." What proof does he have? "If
they had been, they would have remained" (2,
19). This is desperate logic. It indicates the shock
given to a church devoted to unity and opposition
to a world "out there" when it experiences conflict and division from within. The very identity
of the community is called into question.

We cannot be sure exactly what the bone of
contention was between those who left and those
who stayed, only that it involved the proper understanding of Jesus. The author uses the language of "denial" and "confession" (2, 22f), and
it seems clear that a formal *doctrinal* issue is at
stake (see also 2 Jn 7). The briefest description of
the deviance is that they deny "Jesus is the
Christ." This obviously qualifies them to be
"anti-Christs" in the narrow sense, but it is hard
to imagine how such people could ever have
been part of the messianic community. Such a
denial is more appropriate to nonbelieving Jews.
To complicate matters, the author adds other features in 3, 23; 4, 2f; 5, 1.10. These make it appear
that outsiders deny either the full divine origin of
Jesus (that he is "God's son") or his full humanity (that he "came in the flesh"). In short, John is
convinced his party has the full understanding of
Jesus and his opponents do not; beyond that general statement we cannot advance.

Characteristic of this writing, however, is its
ability to combine a claim to possession of "the
truth" (2, 21), with a demand at the same time for
transformation. The community is not yet perfect. They are indeed, to use one of their favorite
expressions, "children of God" (see Jn 1, 12), but
they still need to mature. Only when he appears
will they become "like him, for we shall see him
as he is" (3, 2). Having the truth means living the
truth, which demands strict ethical norms. In 3,
4–18, John develops the strongest possible contrast between the way of the world governed by
the devil (4, 8; 5, 19) and the way revealed by
God through the Messiah Jesus. The way of the
world is driven by the envy that leads to murder
(the example of Cain, 3, 12; compare Jas 4, 1–5).
The way Jesus reveals is exactly the opposite. It
does not take away life but gives it, and in the
giving of life reveals love: "the way we came to
know love was that he laid down his life for us."

The moral correlative follows at once: "so we
ought to lay down our lives for our brothers" (3,
16). The New Testament contains no more direct
connection between the work of the Messiah and
the pattern of Christian existence. And lest anyone think the giving of life can be accomplished
in attitude only or once for all, John spells it out
in terms of the sharing of material possessions
with the needy, and concludes in a manner familiar to us from Paul and James, "let us love not
in word or speech but in deed and truth."

Finally, the claim to be in possession of the
truth must be qualified by the deeper statement
of humility in 3, 19–21. It is because they are in
the hands of the one who is "greater than our
hearts and knows everything" that they know
they belong to the truth. It is not their accomplishment but his gift; their adequate response is
to act as he did, in love (3, 23f).

The Remnant Community (4, 1—5, 21)

Because the community is divided, shared symbols are now being interpreted by opposing parties to the dispute. More careful judgment is
therefore required. John reminds his readers of
the need to "test the spirits to see whether they
belong to God" (4, 1). As earlier he had spoken
of the opponents as "antichrists," now he applies
to them the epithet "false prophets," another favorite designation in apocalyptic (see Mt 24, 11).
In this case, the proper confession of Jesus is the
criterion for true and false prophecy, certifying
whether the speaker belongs to God or to "the
world" (4, 2–4; 13–16).

Within the remnant community itself, discernment is also required. How can the church be
sure that it lives by the Spirit of God? That it has
the right confession of Jesus is taken for granted.
But John adds the ethical dimension; keeping the
commandment of God shows their love for God
(5, 2f). What is that commandment? It is that
they are to love each other. John indissolubly
joins love of God and neighbor; doing one is doing the other: "If anyone says 'I love God' but
hates his brother, he is a liar" (4, 20). As earlier
in 3, 15f, John grounds such love in the way God
has revealed himself to be for humans in the
sending of his son and Jesus' expiatory death: "In
this is love: not that we have loved God, but that
he loved us and sent his Son as expiation for our
sins" (4, 10). Since humans do not have direct

access to God (4, 12; see Jn 1, 18), their relationship to God is mediated by their relationships with each other (4, 12.20f).

The last section of this sermon is filled with a mixture of confidence and caution. The community living by God's love and faith is sure of victory "over the world" (5, 4f), even though "the whole world is under the power of the evil one" (5, 19). This is because the community's testimony is not isolated. It is supported by the testimony of Father, Son, and Spirit, each working in and through the church (5, 6–9). The community is confident of its gift of "eternal life" (2, 25; 5, 11.13). But the victory over sin and death (see 3, 7–14) is not yet complete. Idolatry is a temptation that needs to be avoided (5, 21); perfect love has not yet driven out fear (4, 18); mutual correction is required (5, 16f). For this divided community, nothing can any longer be taken for granted; division has given new urgency to discernment (5, 20).

FURTHER READING

Brown, R. E. *The Epistles of John*. Anchor Bible 30. Garden City, NY: Doubleday, 1982.

Painter, John. *1, 2, and 3 John*. Sacra Pagina. Collegeville: Liturgical Press, 2002.

Rensberger, David. *1 John; 2 John; 3 John*. Abingdon New Testament Commentaries; Nashville: Abingdon, 1997.

Sloyan, G. S. *Walking in the Truth: Preservers and Deserters—The First, Second, and Third Letters of John*. Valley Forge, PA: Trinity Press International, 1995.

2 JOHN

[see pages 1662–63 of the New Testament]

Before Beginning . . .

A Cover Letter to the Church

Unless 2 and 3 John are connected to the same moment of crisis that generated 1 John, it is hard to explain their preservation by a local church, their exchange between churches, and their eventual inclusion in the New Testament canon. In the Reading Guide to 1 John (RG 513), the suggestion is made that all three letters were sent in a single packet by the emissary Demetrius to the local leader Gaius (see 3 Jn) who was still loyal to "the Elder" in the dispute dividing Johannine Christianity into hostile factions.

Whereas 1 John lacks all epistolary character and appears as a sermon to be delivered aloud to an assembly (or even a number of assemblies), 2 John bears the marks of a genuine letter. It has the formal elements of greeting (1–3), body (4–12) and farewell (13). It mentions the desire of the writer to visit the addressees (12). Unlike 3 John, however, which is addressed to an individual, 2 John is written to the "chosen Lady" and her children (1). The designation is almost certainly an honorary title for the church itself. The argument that it refers to a specific woman leader is doubtful, if the rest of the reconstruction here being suggested makes sense. The "children," of course, are the ones really being addressed; the second-person verbs are predominantly in the plural.

The symbols of Johannine Christianity are very much in evidence. Notice the emphasis on "truth" (1–3) and on "walking in the truth" (4); on "keeping the commandment," which is not new but from the beginning (5); on love for one another as the fulfillment of that commandment (6); on the creation of mutual joy as the mark of fellowship (12). Surely, such a cluster of distinctive themes makes best sense when read together with 1 John.

What distinguishes 2 John is its function. In 3 John 9, the Elder says that he "is writing" (or "wrote") something to the church. In all likelihood, this refers to 1 John, the exhortation to a remnant community. Second John, then, is undoubtedly a letter of introduction to the community as such, to be read before the sermon is delivered, to identify its author, to emphasize its main teaching, and to suggest some practical actions to be taken by the community. These may or may not be fully in accord with the spirit of 1 John, but they are certainly recognizable as a response to the crisis signaled by 3 John.

Strategies for Survival

Again we meet the split between those who "walk in truth" and the "many deceivers who have gone out into the world" (7). As in 1 John, these are designated antichrists because they "do not acknowledge Jesus Christ as coming in the flesh." In the Reading Guide to 1 John, we suggest how difficult it is to determine precisely what this denial implies. For the Elder, however, the opponents appear as "progressives" who have gone too far in their interpretation and no longer "remain in the teaching of the Christ" (or "about" the Christ). The Elder's community is therefore portrayed as defending the traditional understanding of Jesus. The importance of right doctrine is underscored by the equation: having Christ is having God (see 1 Jn 4, 3). For Johannine Christianity, the unique mediation of salvation by Jesus is axiomatic. He alone is the "way and the truth and the life" (Jn 14, 6). The lesson is clear: misconstruing the mediator means missing the good news entirely. If the Elder's readers do not hold to the proper understanding, they will "lose what they worked for."

The community crisis is so severe that the Elder calls for the extraordinary practice of excommunication. They are neither to offer heretics hospitality nor even to greet them as brothers (10). Notice the connection, everywhere assumed in the New Testament, between message and messenger. Physical fellowship implies spiritual unanimity. Thus, "whoever greets him shares in his evil works" (11). Only those who deliver the proper doctrine (10) are to be welcomed. Here the Elder advocates the same practice of shunning and exclusion of which he accuses Diotrephes in 3 John. The battle is a bitter one.

It is difficult to know what positive instruction one should draw from these ancient fragments of hostile conflicts. Perhaps it is important for the church to remember in every age that it has never been easy to establish or to secure its identity; deviance and dispute are part of community life. Perhaps also, however, it is important for the church in every age to reflect whether proper doctrine is more important than the fellowship of love. Even in an age of ecumenism that issue remains unresolved.

FURTHER READING

See the bibliography for 1 John, and:

Brown, R. E. *The Community of the Beloved Disciple.* New York: Paulist Press, 1979.

Rensberger, D. *1 John; 2 John; 3 John.* Nashville: Abingdon, 1997.

3 JOHN

[see pages 1663–65 of the New Testament]

Before Beginning . . .

A Letter of Recommendation

The New Testament contains two letters written explicitly to individuals—Paul's letter to Philemon, and the Elder's letter to Gaius, which we know as 3 John. Both Paul and John take up matters of community concern, while having the same specific function, that of recommending the bearer of the letter to the addressee. In the case of Philemon, Paul seeks to return a slave who had run away and to assure his welcome. In the case of 3 John, the Elder recommends to the local church leader his emissary Demetrius. He has a good reputation from all, and "we give our testimonial as well, and you know our testimony is true" (12).

The ancient world had conventions for these letters. They were widely used in early Christianity, as we learn elsewhere in Paul's correspondence (see 2 Cor 3, 1; Rom 16). It was natural for a missionary movement to certify its agents (apostles) with such letters, in order to ensure them a safe reception and the hospitality due such "co-workers in the truth" (8). Receiving such messengers, as we see also in 2 John, meant accepting their message as well, an understanding widespread in Judaism and reflected as well in the sayings of Jesus: "Whoever listens to you listens to me. Whoever rejects you rejects me. And whoever rejects me rejects the one who sent me" (Lk 10, 16). This principle became problematic when the movement itself divided into hostile parties. Paul complained of the Corinthians' preference for apostles other than himself (2 Cor 10, 12; 11, 4). 3 John points us directly to such a situation.

Third John is so tied to particular practical problems and so devoid of any real theology that it is doubtful that either it or 2 John would have been preserved or made part of the canon were it not associated with a writing that did transcend those circumstances by its religious message. This Reading Guide has proposed that the three letters of John were all part of the same packet delivered to Gaius from the Elder through Demetrius, and that the two smaller letters owe their preservation to the theological weightiness of 1 John.

But if its survival was accidental and its theology minimal, 3 John is all the more precious to readers today. It provides the key to the historical circumstances presupposed by 2 and 1 John. Without it, their religious emphasis would be less intelligible. And without 3 John, an appreciation for the travails of early Christianity would be appreciably diminished.

The Politics of Ecclesial Power

Third John reveals clearly that the struggle for the soul of Johannine Christianity involved structure as much as symbol, power as much as piety. Indeed, the two levels of conflict were intimately connected. On one side we see the Elder writing to his loyal colleague Gaius. On the other side is Diotrephes, who "loves to dominate." Diotrephes not only asserts authority over Gaius at the local level, but he also refuses to acknowledge the authority of the Elder over the regional church. The author says that when he comes, he will "draw attention to what he is doing" (10), but this is a small threat to a rebellious local chieftain. The position of the Elder is threatened. He needs the personal loyalty of Gaius, and his financial assistance as well.

We are thereby brought to the political maneuvering at the heart of this battle. Diotrephes is not content to "spread evil nonsense" about the Elder. He takes positive action to suppress the

Elder's authority. He refuses himself to receive the Elder's delegates, and, even more, Diotrephes expels from the church those who want to receive them (10). We can understand why the Elder appreciates Gaius's reception of Demetrius, and we can grasp the significance of verses 5–8. The Elder needs to provide an alternative source of hospitality and missionary outfitting, since Diotrephes has taken up a position among those who "went out from us" (1 Jn 2, 19) and no longer supports the Elder's teaching.

Gaius is being asked to receive Demetrius (and his companions) as well as equip them for their next stage of travel. Perhaps by implication the Elder's future emissaries are also included in the request. Since the Johannine missionaries accept nothing from the "pagans" ("the world"), the need for a network of hospitality and financial support is obvious (7). As in 2 John, financial sharing is tantamount to spiritual fellowship. Helping such missionaries is being "co-workers in the truth" (8). It is clear as well that both parties to the dispute are using the same tactics. Here, Diotrephes is the one shunning and excommunicating. But in 2 John we find the Elder advocating the same actions among his followers.

The internecine struggles of early Christianity are not terribly edifying, but they are instructive. Christians who long for a golden age of harmony should be reminded that there never was one. Among history's benefits is liberation from myth. And edifying or not, these letters testify to another truth. The struggle for identity is never simply a matter of ideas or even symbols. It involves inevitably the messy realities of money and political power.

FURTHER READING

See the bibliographies for 1 and 2 John, and:
Malherbe, A. J. "Hospitality and Inhospitality in the Church." *Social Aspects of Early Christianity*. 2nd ed., 92–112. Philadelphia: Fortress Press, 1983.
Smalley, S. S. *1, 2, 3 John*. Word Biblical Commentary; Waco: Word, 1984.

JUDE

[see pages 1665–67 of the New Testament]

Before Beginning . . .

The Obscurity of Jude

Although Jude is among the shortest writings in the New Testament, it bristles with difficulties. Some of these have to do with placing the composition in the historical development of early Christianity. Others involve grasping its language, which has a number of obscure allusions. The two sorts of problems are related. Our ignorance of the author and his circumstances prevents us from having a secure context for reading the letter. But because Jude so obviously was responding to some kind of specific crisis, every attempt must be made to construct such a context if the letter is to yield any sense at all.

The introduction in the NAB (New Testament, p. 1665) states the majority scholarly opinion on most of the questions concerning authorship and occasion. Jude is considered a general epistle of relatively late date. It is an attack on false teachers, probably representing some form of Gnosticism (an early deviant form of Christianity stressing "self-fulfillment"). Another reading of the evidence suggests that Jude could have been written at virtually any period and was concerned less with false teaching than with bad behavior. This minority view will be developed in the paragraphs to follow. The main point, of course, is to make as good sense as possible out of the letter.

Literary Connections

Far more puzzling than the identity of Jude is the placement of his letter among other early Christian literature. The author mentions an earlier draft he had begun, when the crisis among his readers demanded his turning attention to the polemic now being read by them (3). What was that earlier version? A not entirely unrelated issue is the relation of Jude to 2 Peter. Everyone recognizes that the material in 2 Peter 2 is similar to that in Jude 5–13. Less clear is whether one author depended on the other, or both relied on a shared earlier tradition. Neither should the resemblance be overstated. Jude is not simply a source for 2 Peter. Each sharpens the material to a different polemical point.

Further literary puzzles are provided by Jude's literary allusions. He cites examples of sinners being punished. Some are readily apparent from the Bible, although a few (like Balaam) may derive as well from Jewish biblical interpretation. Jude also cites the apocryphal writing known as 1 Enoch as though it were Scripture (14). And his version of the dispute between Michael and Satan over the body of Moses appears to derive from another apocryphal writing, The Assumption of Moses (9). His reference to the "words spoken by the apostles" (17) is no clearer, since it is more an amalgam of early Christian statements on the end-time (cf., for example, Mk 13, 22; 1 Tim 4, 1–3) than a specific citation.

That an author could assume familiarity with such sources among his readers seems to presuppose either a Jewish-Christian readership, or a Gentile one familiar with Jewish apocrypha. What the ancient readers presumably understood, we do not, and the lack of literary context continues to make this letter obscure to present-day readers.

Historical Setting

Writings like 2 Peter and Jude remind us how little we know about early Christianity apart from the chronology provided by Acts and Paul's letters. We cannot fit them into any development we know about and must rely on guesswork. Every hypothesis, furthermore, is based solely on the text itself. Precision concerning what the text does and does not say is obviously critical to the value of any reconstruction.

Jude clearly takes a polemical stand against opponents and exhorts its readers to remain steadfast. Contrary to the usual opinion, however, the text contains no clear indication that Jude was opposing "false teachers" or that they were purveying any "heresy." Their "scorning of Lordship" (4.8) seems to have been practical rather than theoretical. Jude attacks immoral behavior rather than false teaching. So thorough is his disparagement, indeed, that it is hard to know even what they were doing. He specifically accuses them of disrupting the community love feasts. The term is usually taken to mean eucharistic meals. They are also accused of carousing and of looking after only themselves (literally: "shepherding themselves," 12). He also calls their behavior "divisive" (19). Otherwise, Jude uses all the standardized charges common to the polemic of the ancient world: they are sexually immoral (7), greedy (11.16), slanderous (15), and living for their own desires (16). In short, they "live on the natural plane, devoid of the Spirit" (19). They "pervert the grace of our God into licentiousness" (4).

Living by God's Grace

Letters of Paul such as 1 Corinthians attest how difficult it was for the early Christians to translate the gift of God (grace) into consistent patterns of moral behavior. Legitimate disagreement could exist on matters of diet, work, use of possessions, and the like. It was not immediately obvious in all cases what "life in the Spirit" meant behaviorally. In the case of Jude, however, it appears that disagreement has overstepped the boundary into true moral deviance; hence the outrage of the author. The opponents are "perverting the gift."

Jude's first line of defense is an attack on the immoral people. He tries to demonstrate from Scripture how there have always been such troublemakers, and they have always been punished. These will be punished as well. In contrast to 2 Peter 2, in which the emphasis is on the power of God to judge the righteous and unrighteous, in Jude the stress is entirely on the punishment of the rebellious.

The polemic is not random but carefully argued, with some rhetorical polish. Notice the repetition of "these people" in verses 8, 10, 12, 16, and 19, which brings the examples of old to

bear on the present circumstances. Jude also plays on the Greek words for "keep" in verses 1, 6, 13, 21, and 24. His opponents fail to "keep their place," but Jude's readers are to "keep themselves in the love of God" who is, in turn, able to "keep them from stumbling."

Jude's second line of defense is to edify ("build up") his readers in their "most holy faith" (20). He reminds them that God dealt with troubles like these from of old, and in fact the apostles of Jesus had foretold the emergence of such rebellious "scoffers" (17f). He reassures them that they are being "kept safe for Jesus Christ" despite this turmoil (1). Jude does not suggest that it is the believers' role to punish the reprobate. He exhorts them to avoid such immoral behavior (23) and to build up their own faith. If the opponents are "devoid of spirit," the believers are to "pray in the holy Spirit" (20). But their love for God is to be demonstrated in an attitude of mercy and care for those who waver and even for those who appear to be lost (22f).

Jude's witness is a limited one. But the use of moral outrage is not entirely exhausted by the circumstances of the first century. The tendency to turn grace into libertinism is a perennial one. Combining justifiable outrage at license with mercy for the licentious is a delicate and difficult art. Few writings have carried it off as well as Jude.

FURTHER READING

Harrington, Daniel, S.J. *Jude and 2 Peter.* Sacra Pagina. Collegeville: Liturgical Press, 2003.

Kelly, J. N. D. *The Epistles of Peter and Jude.* Harper New Testament Commentary. New York: Harper & Row, 1969.

Kraftchick, S. J. *Jude; 2 Peter.* Abingdon New Testament Commentaries. Nashville: Abingdon, 2002.

REVELATION

[see pages 1667–94 of the New Testament]

Before Beginning . . .

A Book of Christian Prophecy

The book of Revelation makes for difficult reading. Many interpretations of it over the centuries

have led to disastrous consequences both for individuals and communities. The fundamental error is to take Revelation as a literal set of predictions from the past about current events. Reading Revelation that way has been popular for a long time, but it has become an obsession for many contemporaries. Such readings have successively been disconfirmed by facts; the "end-time" has been awaited many times without occurring. Such readings have caused the distortion of lives. Many have abandoned livelihood and loved ones to meet the New Jerusalem, only to have their dreams destroyed. Such readings also miss the real religious message of Revelation. They reduce its value to that of an astrological chart.

Although the text itself virtually calls out for such an interpretation, with its promise to reveal "what must happen soon" (22, 6), it is critical to recognize that just such statements are standard features of a specific literary genre of the ancient world, called apocalyptic. Two convictions should guide faithful study of Revelation. First, as with all the biblical writings, the Word of God was addressed first to the original audience; a text's "fuller" meaning for successive ages is secondary and never to be divorced from that first, historical, meaning. Second, as in all literature, religious or otherwise, literary genre dictates meaning. Newspapers and poetry do not communicate their respective "truths" in identical ways. Knowing the conventions of a literary form is necessary to intelligent reading.

Revelation as Apocalyptic

Beginning at least with the book of Daniel in the Old Testament, the apocalyptic style was widely used in Judaism during the New Testament period. Generated by persecution from without and the threat of apostasy from within, this "literature of the oppressed" quickly gained certain standard features: revelations about the future are experienced in dreams or visions, and the insights are communicated through a complex symbolism involving numbers, animals, and cosmic phenomena. The element of prediction is actually a fiction. The seer interprets events of his own age, using a figure of the past (such as Enoch) or an angelic being as a spokesperson.

These literary features serve to express an interpretation of history. Apocalyptic defends God's justice. Events appear to be under the control of evil people or even satanic powers, since those devoted to God are being persecuted. Such is the "present age." But apocalyptic places God's blessing in a future time, "the age to come." Just when things become humanly im-

possible on earth, God will intervene (as through a Messiah) to save his own, and thus inaugurate the "kingdom of God." Apocalyptic reconciles the conviction that God controls history with the experience that suggests God does not. The religious message of apocalyptic is simple. To the faithful, it says, "hold on"; to the wavering, "stand fast." It offers the hope of eventual vindication to those now oppressed but remaining loyal to the one God.

Revelation as Prophecy

Revelation fits the apocalyptic genre well. It has visions, animals, numbers, and cosmic catastrophes. It has a two-age interpretation of history. And its basic religious message is a call for the "endurance of the holy ones" (13, 10; 14, 12). In other ways, however, Revelation transcends apocalyptic. The author is not a fictional sage from the past but a leader well known to his readers. The voice of prophecy is directed explicitly (and not in coded fashion) to the seven churches of Asia Minor in chapters 2 and 3. Most importantly, the turn of the ages has already begun. The victory of God over evil has in principle been accomplished through the death and resurrection of Jesus; even more impressively, the faithful who have been killed already share in that victory in heaven.

The self-understanding of the church in this writing is thoroughly prophetic. Those who follow Jesus are "servants and prophets and holy ones" (11, 18). Their witness is the "spirit of prophecy" (19, 10). Jesus is the first and "faithful witness" (1, 5) whose mission they continue. The nature of their prophecy is to bear witness to the reality of God in the world. In the letters of chapters 2 and 3, this is expressed as fidelity in face of corruption or apostasy. In the visions of chapters 4 through 21, it is expressed as loyalty in face of the idolatrous claims of the state and even of possible death.

The Opening Vision (1, 1–20)

The prologue (1, 1–3) and the epilogue (22, 6–21) provide an explicit prophetic framework for the entire work and reveal a self-conscious literary awareness as well (cf. 1, 3; 22, 18). The understanding of prophecy as *witness,* which becomes the major theme of the book, is sounded at once (1, 2).

The popularity of letter writing in early Christianity is shown by the fact that this apocalyptic writing contains letters to the seven churches of Asia Minor (Rv 2—3), and even has an epistolary greeting to introduce the work (1, 4–8). The author identifies himself as one known to his readers and recounts the vision that provides the basis for the rest of the book. The phrasing of 1, 9 suggests that John is on the Greek island of Patmos as a punishment for his witness to Jesus. The vision that now comforts him becomes an exhortation to all who are likewise oppressed.

The Risen Jesus is encountered as the Son of Man (the central figure in much apocalyptic), described in the most transcendent terms available. The reader is now in the realm of visions, which means the realm of symbols. The terms are obviously not meant literally, any more than the later fantastic descriptions of heaven. The terms used here and elsewhere are not fresh-minted but are the coinage of biblical symbolism. Of all apocalyptic writings, Revelation most artfully weaves together the themes of classical prophecy, especially of the prophet Ezekiel. The footnotes and cross-references in the NAB will repay the effort required. One should quickly realize that Revelation is a self-conscious and complex literary construction.

The Son of Man appears with the stars in his hands, standing amid seven lampstands. Revelation makes clear from the start that it is the risen and powerful Lord (in cosmic control) who is revealed, and that he is present to the churches (1, 20), the concerns of which are taken up in the letters that follow.

Letters to the Seven Churches (2, 1—3, 22)

In what are literally "spirit letters" (see 2, 7) from the Risen Jesus, seven churches of well-known cities in Asia Minor receive individualized prophecies. Revelation understands "prophecy" as exhortations to remain faithful to the integrity of their calling. The trials and lapses of the Christians in these communities are here put on remarkable display. We also hear fragments of sayings (such as in 2, 3) that occur elsewhere in the New Testament literature (see 1 Thes 5, 2 and Mk 13, 33).

The letters all follow the same format. There is a greeting, followed by an elaborate designation of Jesus. The Risen Lord analyzes each commu-

nity's spiritual condition and concludes with words of warning or of promise. The description of the church's struggles show how they faced opposition from without (as from the Jews), but even more, division within (as with the Nicolaitans). Corruption, too, appears as a vivid possibility. Typical for Johannine literature, the opposition is pictured in terms of false prophecy (2, 20). The focus of praise and of persuasion in these letters is endurance.

The imagery of the letters is lush. Who can resist the almost fairy-tale quality of this statement: "I shall also give a white amulet upon which is inscribed a new name, which no one knows except the one who receives it" (2, 17)? Beneath the poetry, however, lies grim reality. The difficulty in these letters of maintaining loyalty in the face of social exclusion and human laxity is raised, in the visions that follow, to the level of a cosmic conflict between the Lord and the forces of evil.

God and the Lamb in Heaven (4, 1—5, 14)

John is "caught up in spirit" (4, 2), and the rest of Revelation consists in the visions he experienced in his ecstatic state. The vision is a staple of apocalyptic. It is found with equal frequency in early Jewish mysticism, called *Merkabah,* or "throne-chariot" mysticism. In prayer, the adept ascended through the heavens to the throne of God's presence. Much of the celestial furniture here resembles that of the *Merkabah:* the jewel-encrusted throne room (4, 3f); the sea of glass (4, 6); the angelic creatures (4, 6–9), and the numinous hymns sung in praise of God (5, 9–13).

A dramatic departure from standard symbolism is the appearance of "the Lamb that seemed to have been slain" (5, 6). Jesus is also called "Lamb of God" in John's Gospel (1, 29; see also Jn 19, 36, a reference to the Passover lamb). It is a bold stroke to picture Jesus in such paradoxical animal terms. The salient aspect of the lamb is its sacrificial function: Jesus was slain. But this lamb is also "the lion of the tribe of Judah," who has triumphed over death (5, 5). In a powerful assertion of Jesus' status after his resurrection, the lamb is at "the right hand of the one who sat on the throne" (5, 7; see Ps 110, 1). Both figures receive the praise of the heavenly creatures (5, 9–11) and indeed of all creation (5, 13f).

The special character of the visions of Revelation is shown by the problem of the "scroll" (5, 1). It contains the secrets to be revealed, and because of its use in Ezekiel it is immediately recognizable as a symbol for prophecy (10, 8–11 and Ez 2, 9—3, 4). Because of his resurrection, Jesus is empowered to open the scroll (5, 5). What follows, therefore, is both a revelation of and from Jesus Christ (see 1, 1). The visions will show "what must happen afterwards" (4, 1), but the reader is not frightened, knowing from this first vision that the fundamental victory has already been accomplished.

Visions of Cosmic Conflict (6, 1—16, 21)

The next section of Revelation is the most difficult to make sense of, and, not surprisingly, the most worked over for signs of the end. The candidates selected to fit the profile of the "Beast" with the number 666 (13, 18) have ranged from Nero to Hitler.

The visions are so structured as to give the illusion of temporal sequence, linked together as they are by the phrase "and then I saw. . ." It is indeed tempting to translate a series of visions into a sequence of historical events, so readers have tried to compute the overlapping series of sevens: seals (6, 1–17; 8, 1), trumpets (8, 1—9, 21; 11, 15), plagues (15, 1–8), and bowls (16, 1–20). But neither the events reported by headlines nor elaborate literary analyses have ever satisfactorily unlocked this dense poetry. It is in fact more likely that all the visions repeat the same basic message. The saints on earth, locked in conflict with hostile forces, find a cosmic counterpart in the struggle between God and Satan.

Thus, on one side we see all the "beasts" who oppose the faithful: the dragon (12, 1–8), the first beast (13, 1–10), and the second beast (13, 11–17). These are not separate enemies but successive masks of the one force of evil. As in modern horror films, the destruction of one gives rise to another more horrifying still. Beneath the different manifestations, one visible enemy is most prevalent: the idolatrous state that persecutes the saints, enslaves them, and seeks to kill them (13, 7–18).

On the other side are those loyal to God, the "servants, prophets, and holy ones" (11, 18; 19, 9f). They continue Jesus' own faithful witness to God by witnessing to Jesus. By so doing, they re-

ject the idolatrous claims of the state on their obeisance. They suffer the consequences, some of them by shedding blood. Revelation establishes the connection between "witness" and "martyr" by the disciples' imitation of Jesus' death. The prophetic self-consciousness of this church is most clearly stated in the account of the two witnesses (11, 1–13). This earthly interlude shows two people, who both "witness" and "testify" (the terms are interchangeable). They are killed in imitation of Jesus (11, 7). They are also called into heaven (11, 12). The vignette describes the conviction of Revelation that those who share Jesus' death also share his triumph in heaven. Thus, alternating with scenes of suffering on earth below are serene descriptions of the saints in heaven celebrating the anticipated and certain victory of the Lamb (5, 9f; 6, 9–11; 7, 4–7; 14, 1–5; 15, 2–4). In standard apocalyptic, history moves downward to ever more dismal circumstances, until God finally intervenes. In Revelation, however, the final outcome is not in doubt. Not only Jesus but also those "defeated" with him by evil already share in the resurrection triumph. The earthly conquest is just a matter of tidying up.

It is useless to tease such poetry into a train schedule. The vision here is not one of history unfolding like clockwork; it is a religious vision of God's ultimate conquest despite current appearances. Once the reader lets go of the obsessive "need to know" that twists beauty into charts and tables, it is possible to wonder at the powerful poetic and religious imagination at work in these glorious images. On the side of evil, what genius to make the second beast, who is a "false prophet," mimic the features but betray the nature of the true prophet: "it had two horns like a lamb's but spoke like a dragon" (13, 11). On the side of good, what beauty in the prayer that speaks to the suffering of all humankind, that hopes "the Lamb who is in the center of the throne will shepherd them and lead them to springs of life-giving water, and God will wipe away every tear from their eyes" (7, 17).

Punishment of Babylon (17, 1—20, 15)

The masks fall away, revealing as the real enemy of God's people the Roman empire, "the great harlot who lives near the many waters" (17, 1). Rome is called Babylon (17, 5) because in the biblical tradition it was Babylon above all that symbolized the desecration of the Temple and the exile of the people. In typical apocalyptic fashion, the sequence of events is laid out: God has given temporary rule to this evil empire to accomplish his ends. It does battle against the Lamb and the people.

The persecution and suffering were undoubtedly real. These Christians were faced with the choices of all who suffer oppression. Were they to resist violently and seek the overthrow of Rome? That was futile as well as contrary to their ethos. Were they simply to cooperate? That would be to lose their identity. They chose the path of passive resistance. They did not fight the beast, but neither would they do its bidding. The path of martyrdom, however slow or fast, is not easy. For those who survive, the psychic toll is considerable. Anger at the enemy can easily turn inward; patient endurance is hard. They were convinced that "the Lamb will conquer" (17, 14), but in their earthly condition they had not yet seen it happen. Rome's fall is therefore described in delicious detail. The pent-up fury of the oppressed is released in glee over the degradation of the oppressor. Much of this is obviously and literally wish fulfillment, the stuff of fantasy. The anger of a downtrodden people is deflected to a punishing God.

The end-time reveals how "the words of God are accomplished" (17, 17). The "Word of God" himself (19, 13) leads the climactic battle and inaugurates the messianic age, when the saints "will reign with Christ for a thousand years" (20, 4–6). But this is not yet the end. There is another outbreak of demonic destruction (20, 7–10) and the tossing of the Devil into the fire, then the resurrection of the dead for final judgment (20, 11–15). These stages lack poetry, but the final vision overcomes this deficiency.

The New Creation (21, 1—22, 21)

The conclusion to Revelation is a fitting conclusion to the Bible as a whole. The vision of a new creation (21, 1) is central to the New Testament (see, for example, 2 Cor 5, 17). The Christian experience of Christ was an absolute beginning, rooted in the ever-new life of God himself. God can say, "Behold, I make all things new" (21, 5) because God is "the Alpha and the Omega, the beginning and the end" of all things (21, 6; 22,

13). As Genesis began with the creation by a word, so the vision of the end-time recapitulates that beginning: creation is renewed.

The hope expressed by Revelation is not simply that souls be saved after death, or that evil be conquered, or even that saints reign for a thousand years over a burnt-out terrain. The hope is that creation itself be transformed. So the sight of a "New Jerusalem coming down out of heaven from God" is the vision of a civilized order, one that is intrinsically holy in the proper sense. Human society is based on the recognition of God's power and presence. No place for those, now, who refuse the "dwelling place of God with the human race" (21, 3.7f).

In this city, there is not even need for "religion" as a separate compartment of life. The temple of the city is "the Lord God almighty and the Lamb" (21, 22). And all the city's people will be priests of [the Lord] God (20, 6), showing at last that the fundamental human vocation is praise of God (22, 9). There need be no division between peoples. Nothing is here accursed (22, 3). The nations will walk by the light of the Lamb (21, 24), and the trees of the city "serve as medicine for the nations" (22, 2). And what medicine! There will be "no more death or mourning, wailing or pain, [for] the old order has passed away" (21, 4).

Great harm has come to those millenarians who have tried by force to make this vision a reality, and establish a thousand-year reign of the saints on earth. Great despair has come to the utopians who have tried on the basis of goodwill to construct a society like the New Jerusalem.

The vision has its value precisely as challenge, as ever-receding prophecy to all human effort for renewal. This does not come about by human cunning but by God's gift. The transformation is not technical but organic. But so compelling is the vision that no one who hears it can help joining in the plaintive cry of the epilogue, "Amen! Come, Lord Jesus!" The epilogue also reminds us that we are still in the in-between time when the world is not re-created. There is still need for the witness of prophecy and for endurance of the saints, for "the wicked still act wickedly, and the filthy still be filthy. The righteous must still do right, and the holy still be holy" (22, 11). Here is a call to the saints.

FURTHER READING

Aune, D. E. *Revelation*. 3 vols. Word Biblical Commentary; Waco: Word, 1997–98.

Boring, M. Eugene. *Revelation*. Interpretation Commentaries. Louisville: John Knox, 1989.

Caird, G. B. *A Commentary of the Revelation of St. John the Divine*. Harper New Testament Commentary. New York: Harper & Row, 1966.

Harrington, Wilfrid J., O.P. *Revelation*. Abington New Testament Commentaries; Nashville: Abingdon, 1998.

Minear, P. *I Saw a New Earth: An Introduction to the Vision of The Apocalypse*. Washington, DC: Corpus Publications, 1968.

Thompson, Leonard L. *Revelation*. Sacra Pagina. Collegeville, MD: Liturgical Press, 1993.

THE OLD TESTAMENT

NEW AMERICAN BIBLE

PREFACE TO THE *NEW AMERICAN BIBLE*

Old Testament

On September 30, 1943, His Holiness Pope Pius XII issued his now famous encyclical on scripture studies, *Divino Afflante Spiritu*. He wrote: "We ought to explain the original text which was written by the inspired author himself and has more authority and greater weight than any, even the very best, translation whether ancient or modern. This can be done all the more easily and fruitfully if to the knowledge of languages be joined a real skill in literary criticism of the same text."

Early in 1944, in conformity with the spirit of the encyclical, and with the encouragement of Archbishop Cicognani, Apostolic Delegate to the United States, the Bishops' Committee of the Confraternity of Christian Doctrine requested members of The Catholic Biblical Association of America to translate the sacred scriptures from the original languages or from the oldest extant form of the text, and to present the sense of the biblical text in as correct a form as possible.

The first English Catholic version of the Bible, the Douay-Rheims (1582–1609/10), and its revision by Bishop Challoner (1750) were based on the Latin Vulgate. In view of the relative certainties more recently attained by textual and higher criticism, it has become increasingly desirable that contemporary translations of the sacred books into English be prepared in which due reverence for the text and strict observance of the rules of criticism would be combined.

The New American Bible has accomplished this in response to the need of the church in America today. It is the achievement of some fifty biblical scholars, the greater number of whom, though not all, are Catholics. In particular, the editors-in-chief have devoted twenty-five years to this work. The collaboration of scholars who are not Catholic fulfills the directive of the Second Vatican Council, not only that "correct translations be made into different languages especially from the original texts of the sacred books," but that, "with the approval of the church authority, these translations be produced in cooperation with separated brothers" so that "all Christians may be able to use them."

The text of the books contained in *The New American Bible* is a completely new translation throughout. From the original and the oldest available texts of the sacred books, it aims to convey as directly as possible the thought and individual style of the inspired writers. The better understanding of Hebrew and Greek, and the steady development of the science of textual criticism, the fruit of patient study since the time of St. Jerome, have allowed the translators and editors in their use of all available materials to approach more closely than ever before the sense of what the sacred authors actually wrote.

Where the translation supposes the received text—Hebrew, Aramaic, or Greek, as the case may be—ordinarily contained in the best-known editions, as the original or the oldest extant form, no additional remarks are necessary. But for those who are happily able to study the original text of the scriptures at firsthand, a supplementary series of textual notes pertaining to the Old Testament was added originally in an appendix to the typical edition. (It is now obtainable in a separate booklet from The Catholic Biblical Association of America, The Catholic University of America, Washington, DC 20064.) These notes furnish a guide in those cases in which the editorial board judges that the manuscripts in the original languages, or the evidence of the ancient versions, or some similar source, furnish the correct reading of a passage, or at least a reading more true to the original than that customarily printed in the available editions.

The Massoretic text of 1 and 2 Samuel has in numerous instances been corrected by the more ancient manuscripts Samuel a, b, and c from Cave 4 of Qumran, with the aid of important evidence from the Septuagint in both its oldest form and its Lucianic recension. Fragments of the lost Book of Tobit in Aramaic and in Hebrew, recovered from Cave 4 of Qumran, are in substantial agreement with the Sinaiticus Greek recension used for the translation of this book. The lost original Hebrew text of 1 Maccabees is replaced by its oldest extant form in Greek. Judith, 2 Maccabees, and parts of Esther are also translated from the Greek.

The basic text for the Psalms is not the Massoretic but one which the editors considered closer to the original inspired form, namely the Hebrew text underlying the new Latin Psalter of the Church, the *Liber Psalmorum* (1944[1], 1945[2]). Nevertheless they retained full liberty to establish the reading of the original text on sound critical principles.

The translation of Sirach, based on the original Hebrew as far as it is preserved and corrected from the ancient versions, is often interpreted in the light of the traditional Greek text. In the Book of Baruch the basic text is the Greek of the Septuagint, with some readings derived from an underlying Hebrew form no longer extant. In the deuterocanonical sections of Daniel (3, 24—90; 13, 1—14, 42), the basic text is the Greek text of Theodotion, occasionally revised according to the Greek text of the Septuagint.

In some instances in the Book of Job, in Proverbs, Sirach, Isaiah, Jeremiah, Ezekiel, Hosea, Amos, Micah, Nahum, Habakkuk, and Zechariah there is good reason to believe that the original order of lines was accidentally disturbed in the transmission of the text. The verse numbers given in such cases are always those of the current Hebrew text, though the arrangement differs. In these instances the textual notes advise the reader of the difficulty. Cases of exceptional dislocation are called to the reader's attention by footnotes.

The Books of *Genesis to Ruth* were first published in 1952; the Wisdom Books, *Job to Sirach,* in 1955; the Prophetic Books, *Isaiah to Malachi,* in 1961; and the Historical Books, *Samuel to Maccabees,* in 1969. In the present edition of *Genesis to Ruth* there are certain new features: a general introduction to the Pentateuch, a retranslation of the text of Genesis with an introduction, cross-references, and revised textual notes, besides new and expanded exegetical notes which take into consideration the various sources or literary traditions.

The revision of *Job to Sirach* includes changes in strophe division in Job and Proverbs and in titles of principal parts and sections of Wisdom and Ecclesiastes. Corrections in the text of Sirach are made in 39, 27—44, 17 on the basis of the Masada text, and in 51, 13–30 on the basis of the occurrence of this canticle in the Psalms scroll from Qumran Cave 11. In this typical edition, new corrections are reflected in the textual notes of Job, Proverbs, Wisdom, and Sirach. In the Psalms, the enumeration found in the Hebrew text is followed instead of the double enumeration, according to both the Hebrew and the Latin Vulgate texts, contained in the previous edition of this book.

In the Prophetic Books *Isaiah to Malachi,* only minor revisions have been made in the structure and wording of the texts, and in the textual notes.

The spelling of proper names in *The New American Bible* follows the customary forms found in most English Bibles since the Authorized Version.

The work of translating the Bible has been characterized as "the sacred and apostolic work of interpreting the word of God and of presenting it to the laity in translations as clear as the difficulty of the matter and the limitations of human knowledge permit" (A. G. Cicognani, Apostolic Delegate, in *The Catholic Biblical Quarterly,* 6, [1944], 389–90). In the appraisal of the present work, it is hoped that the words of the encyclical *Divino afflante Spiritu* will serve as a guide: "Let all the sons of the church bear in mind that the efforts of these resolute laborers in the vineyard of the Lord should be judged not only with equity and justice but also with the greatest charity; all moreover should abhor that intemperate zeal which imagines that whatever is new should for that very reason be opposed or suspected."

Conscious of their personal limitations for the task thus defined, those who have prepared this text cannot expect that it will be considered perfect; but they can hope that it may deepen in its readers "the right understanding of the divinely given Scriptures," and awaken in them "that piety by which it behooves us to be grateful to the God of all providence, who from the throne of his majesty has sent these books as so many personal letters to his own children" *(Divino afflante Spiritu).*

THE PENTATEUCH

See RG
85-99

The Pentateuch, which consists of the first five books of the Bible (Genesis, Exodus, Leviticus, Numbers, Deuteronomy), enjoys particular prestige among the Jews as the "Law," or "Torah," the concrete expression of God's will in their regard. It is more than a body of legal doctrine, even though such material occupies many chapters, for it contains the story of the formation of the People of God: Abraham and the patriarchs, Moses and the oppressed Hebrews in Egypt, the birth of Israel in the Sinai covenant, the journey to the threshold of the Promised Land, and the "discourses" of Moses.

The grandeur of this historic sweep is the result of a careful and complex joining of several historic traditions, or sources. These are primarily four: the so-called Yahwist, Elohist, Priestly and Deuteronomic strands that run through the Pentateuch. (They are conveniently abbreviated as J, E, P and D.) Each brings to the Torah its own characteristics, its own theological viewpoint—a rich variety of interpretation that the sensitive reader will take pains to appreciate. A superficial difference between two of these sources is responsible for their names: the Yahwist prefers the name *Yahweh* (represented in translation as LORD) by which God revealed himself to Israel; the Elohist prefers the generic name for God, *Elohim*. The Yahwist is concrete, imaginative, using many anthropomorphisms in its theological approach, as seen, e.g., in the narrative of creation in Gn 2, compared with the Priestly version in Gn 1. The Elohist is more sober, moralistic. The Priestly strand, which emphasizes genealogies, is more severely theological in tone. The Deuteronomic approach is characterized by the intense hortatory style of Dt 5—11, and by certain principles from which it works, such as the centralization of worship in the Jerusalem temple.

However, even this analysis of the Pentateuch is an over-simplification, for it is not always possible to distinguish with certainty among the various sources. The fact is that each of these individual traditions incorporates much older material. The Yahwist was himself a collector and adapter. His narrative is made up of many disparate stories that have been reoriented, and given a meaning within the context in which they now stand; e.g., the story of Abraham and Isaac in Gn 22. Within the J and P traditions one has to reckon with many individual units; these had their own history and life-setting before they were brought together into the present more or less connected narrative.

This is not to deny the role of Moses in the development of the Pentateuch. It is true we do not conceive of him as the author of the books in the modern sense. But there is no reason to doubt that, in the events described in these traditions, he had a uniquely important role, especially as lawgiver. Even the later laws which have been added in P and D are presented as a Mosaic heritage. Moses is the lawgiver *par excellence,* and all later legislation is conceived in his spirit, and therefore attributed to him. Hence, the reader is not held to undeviating literalness in interpreting the words, "the LORD said to Moses." One must keep in mind that the Pentateuch is the crystallization of Israel's age-old relationship with God.

In presenting the story of the birth of the People of God, the Pentateuch looks back to the promises made to the patriarchs, and forward to the continuing fulfillment of these promises in later books of the Bible. The promises find their classic expression in Gn 12, 1ff. The "God of the Fathers" challenges Abraham to believe: the patriarch is to receive a people, a land, and through him the nations will somehow be blessed.

The mysterious and tortuous way in which this people is brought into being is described: Despite Sarah's sterility, Isaac is finally born—to be offered in sacrifice! The promises are renewed to him eventually, and also to the devious Jacob, as if to show that the divine design will be effected, with or without human cunning. The magnificent story of Joseph is highlighted by the theme of Providence; the promise of a people is taking shape.

Israel is not formed in a vacuum, but amid the age-old civilization of Mesopotamia and the Nile. Oppression in Egypt provokes a striking intervention of God.

Yahweh reveals himself to Moses as a savior, and the epic story of deliverance is told in Exodus. This book also tells of the Sinai covenant, which is rightfully regarded as the key to the Old Testament. Through the covenant Israel becomes Yahweh's people, and Yahweh becomes Israel's God. This act of grace marks the fulfillment of the first promise; that Abraham will be the father of a great nation, God's special possession. The laws in Exodus and Leviticus (P tradition) are both early and late. They spell out the proper relationship of the federation of the Twelve tribes with the LORD. He is a jealous God, demanding exclusive allegiance; he cannot be imaged; he takes vengeance upon the wicked, and shows mercy to the good. Slowly the LORD reveals himself to his people; with remarkable honesty, Israel records the unsteady response—the murmurings and rebellions and infidelities through the desert wanderings up to the plain of Moab.

This sacred history was formed within the bosom of early Israel, guided by the spirit of God. It was sung beside the desert campfires; it was commemorated in the liturgical feasts, such as Passover; it was transmitted by word of mouth from generation to generation—until all was brought together in writing, about the sixth century B.C., when the literary formation of the Pentateuch came to an end.

The Book of Deuteronomy has a history quite peculiar to itself. Its old traditions and law code (12—26) are put forth in the form of "discourses" of Moses before his death. The extraordinarily intense and hortatory tone fits the mood of a discourse. The book contains possibly the preaching of the Levites in the northern kingdom of Israel before its fall in 721 B.C. If this book is situated in its proper historical perspective, its true impact is more vividly appreciated. It is the blueprint of the great "Deuteronomic" reform under King Josiah (640–609 B.C.). This was an attempt to galvanize the people into a wholehearted commitment to the covenant ideals, into an obedience motivated by the great commandment of love (Dt 6, 4ff). Israel has yet another chance, if it obeys. The people are poised between life and death; and they are exhorted to choose life—today (Dt 26, 16-19; 30, 15-20).

See RG
100–115

The Book of Genesis

Genesis, the first book of the Bible, opens with the Hebrew word bereshit, which means "in the beginning." The title "Genesis" was given to the Septuagint (Greek) translation of the book because of its concern with the origin of the world (Gn 1, 1; 2, 4), of the human race, and, in particular, of the Hebrew people.

Eleven structural units (toledoth), of unequal length and importance, present the unity and purpose of the book in terms of God's universal sovereignty, his dealings with men, and his choice and formation of a special people to be the instrument of his plan of salvation.

The tracing of the direct descendance from Adam to Jacob constitutes the major part of the book, while the genealogical tables of lateral branches are not so developed nor of such interest as those that pertain to the story of the Israelite people. In fact, these lateral branches gradually disappear from the narrative. And with the introduction of Abraham and his covenant with God, the history of humanity as such becomes contracted to the story of the descendants of Abraham through Isaac and Jacob—the chosen people.

Despite its unity of plan and purpose, the book is a complex work, not to be attributed to a sin-

6

gle original author. Several sources, or literary traditions, that the final redactor used in his composition are discernable. These are the Yahwist (J), Elohist (E) and Priestly (P) sources, which in turn reflect older oral traditions (see Introduction to the Pentateuch).

In Genesis, the Yahwist source is the most important by reason of its teaching, its antiquity, and the continuity it gives the book. It constitutes a sacred history, continually drawing attention to the working out of God's design through his interventions in the affairs of men. The Elohist source, less well preserved, is found in fragmentary form only, depicting God's manifestations through visions and dreams rather than theophanies. Angels are God's intermediaries with men. Moreover, there is a solicitude for the divine transcendence and greater sensitivity toward the moral order. The Priestly source contains those elements—chronological data, lists, genealogies—that construct the framework of Genesis and bind its contents together. To the J and E sources it adds such legal institutions as the sabbath rest, circumcision and the alliances between God and Noah and God and Abraham.

The interpreter of Genesis will recognize at once the distinct object that sets chapters 1—11 apart: the recounting of the origin of the world and of man (primeval history). To make the truths contained in these chapters intelligible to the Israelite people destined to preserve them, they needed to be expressed through elements prevailing among that people at that time. For this reason, the truths themselves must therefore be clearly distinguished from their literary garb.

With the story of the patriarchs Abraham, Isaac and Jacob (Gn 11, 27—50, 26), the character of the narrative changes. While we do not view the account of the patriarchs as history in the strict sense, nevertheless certain of the matters recounted from the time of Abraham onward can be placed in the actual historical and social framework of the Near East in the early part of the second millennium B.C. (2000–1500), and documented by non-biblical sources.

Genesis contains many religious teachings of basic importance: the preexistence and transcendence of God, his wisdom and goodness, his power through which all things are made and on which they all depend; the special creation of man in God's image and likeness, and of woman from the substance of man; the institution of marriage as the union of one man with one woman; man's original state of innocence; man's sin of pride and disobedience, its consequences for the protoparents and their posterity. Despite the severity of their punishment, hope of reconciliation is offered by God through the first as well as the subsequent promises of salvation and blessing. Abraham is blessed for his faith and obedience, and he is to be a blessing for all nations through his offspring, Isaac, Jacob, and Jacob's sons (Gn 12, 3; 18, 18; 22, 18), of whom the Messiah, mankind's greatest blessing, will eventually be born (Gal 3, 8).

Frequent references to Genesis are found in the New Testament. Christ becomes the antithesis of Adam: sin and death come to mankind through Adam, justification and life through Jesus Christ (Rom 5, 12. 17ff). Noah's ark becomes the symbol of the church, by which men are saved from destruction through the waters of baptism (1 Pt 3, 20ff); Abraham's faith is the model for all believers; the sacrifice of his son Isaac typifies the sacrifice of Christ, Son of the Father. The liturgy, too, relates the persons of Abel, Abraham and Melchizedek to Christ in his act of sacrifice.

The Book of Genesis is divided as follows:

I: The Primeval History (1, 1—11, 26).

II: The Patriarch Abraham (11, 27—25, 18).

III: The Patriarchs Isaac and Jacob (25, 19—36, 43).

IV: Joseph and His Brothers (37, 1—50, 26).

I: The Primeval History

CHAPTER 1

See RG
104

First Story of Creation. [*] [1] In the beginning, when God created the heavens and the earth,[a] [2] the earth was a formless wasteland, and darkness covered the abyss,[*] while a mighty wind swept over the waters.[b]

1, 1—2, 4a: This section introduces the whole Pentateuch. It shows how God brought an orderly universe out of primordial chaos.

1, 2: The abyss: the primordial ocean according to the an-

a: Gn 2, 1.4; Pss 8, 4; 38—39; 90, 2; Wis 11, 17; Sir 16, 24; Jer 10, 12; 2 Mc 7, 28; Acts 14, 15; Col 1, 16f; Heb 1, 2f; 3, 4; 11, 3; Rv 4, 11. *b:* Jer 4, 23.

[3]Then God said, "Let there be light," and there was light.[c] [4]God saw how good the light was. God then separated the light from the darkness. [5]God called the light "day," and the darkness he called "night." Thus evening came, and morning followed—the first day.[*]

[6]Then God said, "Let there be a dome in the middle of the waters, to separate one body of water from the other." And so it happened: [7]God made the dome, and it separated the water above the dome from the water below it.[d] [8]God called the dome "the sky." Evening came, and morning followed—the second day.

[9]Then God said, "Let the water under the sky be gathered into a single basin, so that the dry land may appear." And so it happened: the water under the sky was gathered into its basin, and the dry land appeared.[e] [10]God called the dry land "the earth," and the basin of the water he called "the sea." God saw how good it was. [11f]Then God said, "Let the earth bring forth vegetation: every kind of plant that bears seed and every kind of fruit tree on earth that bears fruit with its seed in it." And so it happened: [12]the earth brought forth every kind of plant that bears seed and every kind of fruit tree on earth that bears fruit with its seed in it. God saw how good it was. [13]Evening came, and morning followed—the third day.

[14]Then God said: "Let there be lights in the dome of the sky, to separate day from night. Let them mark the fixed times, the days and the years,[g] [15]and serve as luminaries in the dome of the sky, to shed light upon the earth." And so it happened: [16]God made the two great lights, the greater one to govern the day, and the lesser one to govern the night; and he made the stars.[h] [17]God set them in the dome of the sky, to shed light upon earth, [18]to govern the day and the night, and to separate the light from the darkness. God saw how good it was. [19]Evening came, and morning followed—the fourth day.

[20i]Then God said, "Let the water teem with an abundance of living creatures, and on the earth let birds fly beneath the dome of the sky." And so it happened: [21]God created the great sea monsters and all kinds of swimming creatures with which the water teems, and all kinds of winged birds. God saw how good it was, [22]and God blessed them, saying, "Be fertile, multiply, and fill the water of the seas; and let the birds multiply on the earth."[j] [23]Evening came, and morning followed—the fifth day.

[24k]Then God said, "Let the earth bring forth all kinds of living creatures: cattle, creeping things, and wild animals of all kinds." And so it happened: [25]God made all kinds of wild animals, all kinds of cattle, and all kinds of creeping things of the earth. God saw how good it was. [26l]Then God said: "Let us make man in our image, after our likeness. Let them have dominion over the fish of the sea, the birds of the air, and the cattle, and over all the wild animals and all the creatures that crawl on the ground."[*]

[27] God created man in his image;
in the divine image he created him;
male and female he created them.

[28]God blessed them, saying to them: "Be fertile and multiply; fill the earth and subdue it. Have dominion over the fish of the sea, the birds of the air, and all the living things that move on the earth."[m] [29n]God also said: "See,

---

cient Semitic cosmogony. After God's creative activity, part of this vast body forms the salt-water seas (vv 9f); part of it is the fresh water under the earth (Ps 33, 7; Ez 31, 4), which wells forth on the earth as springs and fountains (Gn 7, 11; 8, 2; Prv 3, 20). Part of it, "the upper water" (Ps 148, 4; Dn 3, 60), is held up by the dome of the sky (Gn 1, 6f) from which rain descends on the earth (Gn 7, 11; 2 Kgs 7, 2. 19; Ps 104, 13). A mighty wind: literally, "a wind of God," or "a spirit of God"; cf Gn 8, 1.

1, 5: In ancient Israel a day was considered to begin at sunset. According to the highly artificial literary structure of Gn 1, 1—2, 4a, God's creative activity is divided into six days to teach the sacredness of the sabbath rest on the seventh day in the Israelite religion (Gn 2, 2f).

1, 26: Man is here presented as the climax of God's creative activity; he resembles God primarily because of the dominion God gives him over the rest of creation.

c: 2 Cor 4, 6.   *d:* Prv 8, 27f; 2 Pt 3, 5.   *e:* Jb 38, 8; Ps 33, 7; Jer 5, 22.   *f:* Ps 104, 14.   *g:* Jb 26, 10; Ps 19, 1f; Bar 3, 33.   *h:* Dt 4, 19; Ps 136, 7ff; Wis 13, 2ff; Jer 31, 35.   *i:* Jb 12, 7-10.   *j:* Gn 8, 17.   *k:* Sir 16, 27f; Bar 3, 32.   *l:* 26f: Gn 5, 1. 3; 9, 6; Ps 8, 5f; Wis 2, 23; 10, 2; Sir 17, 1. 3f; Jas 3, 7; 1 Cor 11, 7; Eph 4, 24; Col 3, 10; Mt 19, 4; Mk 10, 6.   *m:* Gn 8, 17; 9, 1; Pss 8, 6-9; 115, 16; Wis 9, 2.   *n:* 29f: Gn 9, 3; Ps 104, 14f.

The Major Divisions of Genesis

First section: 1, 1 to 11, 9	Primeval history, the origins of humankind, and failure through sin.
Second section: 11, 10 to 25, 34	Abraham, his call and response, his blessing and promise, his son Isaac and Isaac's sons Jacob (Israel) and Esau
Third section: 26, 1 to 36, 43	Isaac, Jacob, and the sons of Jacob (Israel)
Fourth section: 37, 1 to 50, 26	The sons of Israel, and Jacob and the Israelites in Egypt

I give you every seed-bearing plant all over the earth and every tree that has seed-bearing fruit on it to be your food; *30*and to all the animals of the land, all the birds of the air, and all the living creatures that crawl on the ground, I give all the green plants for food." And so it happened. *31*God looked at everything he had made, and he found it very good. Evening came, and morning followed—the sixth day.*o*

See RG 104

CHAPTER 2

*1*Thus the heavens and the earth and all their array were completed.*p* *2*Since on the seventh day God was finished with the work he had been doing, he rested on the seventh day from all the work he had undertaken.*q* *3*So God blessed the seventh day and made it holy, because on it he rested from all the work he had done in creation.*r*

*4*Such is the story of the heavens and the earth at their creation.

*Second Story of Creation.** At the time when the LORD God made the earth and the heavens— *5*while as yet there was no field shrub on earth and no grass of the field had sprouted, for the LORD God had sent no rain upon the earth and there was no man to till

the soil, *6*but a stream was welling up out of the earth and was watering all the surface of the ground— *7*the LORD God formed man out of the clay of the ground* and blew into his nostrils the breath of life, and so man became a living being.*s*

*8*Then the LORD God planted a garden in Eden,* in the east, and he placed there the man whom he had formed.*t* *9*Out of the ground the LORD God made various trees grow that were delightful to look at and good for food, with the tree of life in the middle of the garden and the tree of knowledge of good and bad.*u*

*10*A river rises* in Eden to water the garden; beyond there it divides and becomes four branches. *11*The name of the first is the Pishon; it is the one that winds through the whole land of Havilah, where there is gold. *12*The gold of that land is excellent; bdellium and lapis lazuli are also there. *13*The name of the second river is the Gihon; it is the one that winds all through the land of Cush.*v* *14*The name of the third river is the Tigris; it is the one that flows east of Asshur. The fourth river is the Euphrates.

*15*The LORD God then took the man and settled him in the garden of Eden, to culti-

---

2, 4b-25: This section is chiefly concerned with the creation of man. It is much older than the narrative of Gn 1, 1—2, 4a. Here God is depicted as creating man before the rest of his creatures, which are made for man's sake.

2, 7: God is portrayed as a potter molding man's body out of clay. There is a play on words in Hebrew between adam ("man") and adama ("ground"). Being: literally, "soul."

2, 8: Eden: used here as the name of a region in southern Mesopotamia; the term is derived from the Sumerian word eden, "fertile plain." A similar-sounding Hebrew word means "delight"; the garden in Eden could therefore be understood as the "garden of delight," so that, through the Greek version, it is now known also as "paradise," literally, a "pleasure park."

2, 10-14: Rises: in flood to overflow its banks. Beyond there: as one travels upstream. Branches: literally, "heads," i.e., upper courses. Eden is near the head of the Persian Gulf, where the Tigris and the Euphrates join with two other streams to form a single river. The land of Cush here and in Gn 10, 8, is not Ethiopia (Nubia) as elsewhere, but the region of the Kassites east of Mesopotamia.

---

o: 1 Tm 4, 4. *p:* Is 45, 12; Jn 1, 3. *q:* Ex 20, 9ff; 31, 17; Heb 4, 4. 10. *r:* Ex 20, 11; Dt 5, 14; Neh 9, 14. *s:* Gn 3, 19; 18, 27; Tb 8, 6; Jb 34, 15; Pss 103, 14; 104, 29; Eccl 3, 20; 12, 7; Wis 7, 1; Sir 33, 10; 1 Cor 15, 45. *t:* Is 51, 3; Ez 31, 9. *u:* Gn 3, 22; Prv 3, 18; Rv 2, 7; 22, 2. 14. *v:* Sir 24, 25.

vate and care for it.[w] [16]The LORD God gave man this order: "You are free to eat from any of the trees of the garden[x] [17]except the tree of knowledge of good and bad. From that tree you shall not eat; the moment you eat from it you are surely doomed to die."[y]

[18]The LORD God said: "It is not good for the man to be alone. I will make a suitable partner for him."[z] [19]So the LORD God formed out of the ground various wild animals and various birds of the air, and he brought them to the man to see what he would call them; whatever the man called each of them would be its name. [20]The man gave names to all the cattle, all the birds of the air, and all the wild animals; but none proved to be the suitable partner for the man.

[21]So the LORD God cast a deep sleep on the man, and while he was asleep, he took out one of his ribs and closed up its place with flesh.[a] [22]The LORD God then built up into a woman the rib that he had taken from the man. When he brought her to the man, [23]the man said:

"This one, at last, is bone of my bones
    and flesh of my flesh;
This one shall be called 'woman,'
    for out of 'her man' this one has been
        taken."[*]

[24b]That is why a man leaves his father and mother and clings to his wife, and the two of them become one body.[*]

[25]The man and his wife were both naked, yet they felt no shame.

CHAPTER 3

See RG 104-6

The Fall of Man. [1]Now the serpent was the most cunning of all the animals that the LORD God had made. The serpent asked the woman, "Did God really tell you not to eat from any of the trees in the garden?" [2]The woman answered the serpent: "We may eat of the fruit of the trees in the garden;

[3c]it is only about the fruit of the tree in the middle of the garden that God said, 'You shall not eat it or even touch it, lest you die.' " [4]But the serpent said to the woman: "You certainly will not die![d] [5]No, God knows well that the moment you eat of it your eyes will be opened and you will be like gods who know[*] what is good and what is bad." [6]The woman saw that the tree was good for food, pleasing to the eyes, and desirable for gaining wisdom. So she took some of its fruit and ate it; and she also gave some to her husband, who was with her, and he ate it.[e] [7]Then the eyes of both of them were opened, and they realized that they were naked; so they sewed fig leaves together and made loincloths for themselves.

[8]When they heard the sound of the LORD God moving about in the garden at the breezy time of the day,[*] the man and his wife hid themselves from the LORD God among the trees of the garden.[f] [9]The LORD God then called to the man and asked him, "Where are you?" [10]He answered, "I heard you in the garden; but I was afraid, because I was naked, so I hid myself." [11]Then he asked, "Who told you that you were naked? You have eaten, then, from the tree of which I had forbidden you to eat!" [12]The man replied, "The woman whom you put here with me—she gave me fruit from the tree, so I ate it." [13]The LORD God then asked the woman, "Why did you do such a thing?" The woman answered, "The serpent tricked me into it, and so I ate it."[g]

[14]Then the LORD God said to the serpent:

"Because you have done this, you shall
        be banned
    from all the animals
    and from all the wild creatures;
On your belly shall you crawl,
    and dirt shall you eat
    all the days of your life.[h]

2, 23: There is a play on the similar-sounding Hebrew words ishsha ("woman") and ishah ("her man, her husband").

2, 24: One body: literally "one flesh"; classical Hebrew has no specific word for "body." The sacred writer stresses the fact that conjugal union is willed by God.

3, 5: Like gods who know: or "like God who knows."

3, 8: The breezy time of the day: literally "the wind of the day." On most days in Palestine a cooling breeze

blows from the sea shortly before sunset.

---

w: Sir 7, 15.   *x:* Ps 104, 14.   *y:* Gn 3, 2f; Rom 6, 23.   *z:* Tb 8, 6; Sir 36, 24; 1 Cor 11, 9; 1 Tm 2, 13.   *a:* Sir 17, 1; 1 Cor 11, 8f; 1 Tm 2, 13.   *b:* Mt 19, 5; Mk 10, 7; 1 Cor 7, 10f; Eph 5, 31.   *c:* Gn 2, 17; Rom 6, 23.   *d:* 4f: Wis 2, 24; Sir 25, 14; Is 14, 14; Jn 8, 44; 2 Cor 11, 3.   *e:* Gn 3, 22; 1 Tm 2, 14.   *f:* Jer 23, 24.   *g:* 2 Cor 11, 3.   *h:* Is 65, 25; Mi 7, 17; Rv 12, 9.

15 I will put enmity between you and the woman,
and between your offspring and hers;
He will strike at your head,
while you strike at his heel."*i

16To the woman he said:

"I will intensify the pangs of your childbearing;
in pain shall you bring forth children.
Yet your urge shall be for your husband,
and he shall be your master."j

17To the man he said: "Because you listened to your wife and ate from the tree of which I had forbidden you to eat,

"Cursed be the ground because of you!
In toil shall you eat its yield
all the days of your life.k
18 Thorns and thistles shall it bring forth to you,
as you eat of the plants of the field.
19 By the sweat of your face
shall you get bread to eat,
Until you return to the ground,
from which you were taken;
For you are dirt,
and to dirt you shall return."l

20The man called his wife Eve, because she became the mother of all the living.* 21For the man and his wife the LORD God made leather garments, with which he clothed them. 22Then the LORD God said: "See! The man has become like one of us, knowing what is good and what is bad! Therefore, he must not be allowed to put out

his hand to take fruit from the tree of life also, and thus eat of it and live forever."m 23The LORD God therefore banished him from the garden of Eden, to till the ground from which he had been taken. 24When he expelled the man, he settled him east of the garden of Eden; and he stationed the cherubim and the fiery revolving sword, to guard the way to the tree of life.*

CHAPTER 4

See RG
106

Cain and Abel. 1The man had relations with his wife Eve, and she conceived and bore Cain, saying, "I have produced a man with the help of the LORD."* 2Next she bore his brother Abel. Abel became a keeper of flocks, and Cain a tiller of the soil. 3In the course of time Cain brought an offering to the LORD from the fruit of the soil, 4while Abel, for his part, brought one of the best firstlings of his flock.n The LORD looked with favor on Abel and his offering, 5but on Cain and his offering he did not. Cain greatly resented this and was crestfallen. 6So the LORD said to Cain: "Why are you so resentful and crestfallen? 7If you do well, you can hold up your head; but if not, sin is a demon lurking* at the door: his urge is toward you, yet you can be his master."o

8Cain said to his brother Abel, "Let us go out in the field." When they were in the field, Cain attacked his brother Abel and killed him.p 9Then the LORD asked Cain, "Where is your brother Abel?" He answered, "I do not know. Am I my brother's keeper?" 10The LORD then said: "What have you done! Listen: Your brother's blood cries out

---

3, 15: He will strike . . . at his heel: since the antecedent for he and his is the collective noun offspring, i.e., all the descendants of the woman, a more exact rendering of the sacred writer's words would be, "They will strike . . . at their heels." However, later theology saw in this passage more than unending hostility between snakes and men. The serpent was regarded as the devil (Wis 2, 24; Jn 8, 44; Rv 12, 9; 20, 2), whose eventual defeat seems implied in the contrast between head and heel. Because "the Son of God appeared that he might destroy the works of the devil" (1 Jn 3, 8), the passage can be understood as the first promise of a Redeemer for fallen mankind. The woman's offspring then is primarily Jesus Christ.
3, 20: This verse seems to be out of place; it would fit better after v 24. The Hebrew name hawwa ("Eve") is related to the Hebrew word hay ("living").

3, 24: The above rendering is based on the ancient Greek version; that of the current Hebrew is, When he expelled the man, he settled east of the garden of Eden, the cherubim.
4, 1: The Hebrew name qayin ("Cain") and the term qaniti ("I have produced") present another play on words.
4, 7: Demon lurking: in Hebrew, robes, literally "croucher," is used here, like the similar Akkadian term rabisu, to designate a certain kind of evil spirit.

i: Is 7, 14; 9, 5; Rom 16, 20; 1 Jn 3, 8; Rv 12, 17.   j: 1 Cor 11, 3; Eph 5, 22f; 1 Tm 2, 12.   k: Gn 5, 29; Rom 5, 12; 8, 20; Heb 6, 8.   l: Gn 2, 7; Jb 10, 9; 34, 15; Pss 90, 3; 103, 14; Eccl 3, 20; 12, 7; Wis 15, 8; Sir 10, 9; 17, 2; Rom 5, 12; 1 Cor 15, 21; Heb 9, 27.   m: Gn 2, 9; Rv 22, 2. 14.   n: Ex 34, 19; Heb 11, 4.   o: Sir 7, 1; Jude 11.   p: Wis 10, 3; Mt 23, 35; Lk 11, 51; 1 Jn 3, 12; Jude 11.

to me from the soil! *11*Therefore you shall be banned from the soil that opened its mouth to receive your brother's blood from your hand.*q* *12*If you till the soil, it shall no longer give you its produce. You shall become a restless wanderer on the earth." *13*Cain said to the LORD: "My punishment is too great to bear. *14*Since you have now banished me from the soil, and I must avoid your presence and become a restless wanderer on the earth, anyone may kill me at sight." *15*"Not so!" the LORD said to him. "If anyone kills Cain, Cain shall be avenged sevenfold." So the LORD put a mark* on Cain, lest anyone should kill him at sight. *16*Cain then left the LORD's presence and settled in the land of Nod,* east of Eden.

Descendants of Cain and Seth. *17**Cain had relations with his wife, and she conceived and bore Enoch. Cain also became the founder of a city, which he named after his son Enoch. *18*To Enoch was born Irad, and Irad became the father of Mehujael; Mehujael became the father of Methusael, and Methusael became the father of Lamech. *19*Lamech took two wives; the name of the first was Adah, and the name of the second Zillah. *20*Adah gave birth to Jabal, the ancestor of all who dwell in tents and keep cattle. *21*His brother's name was Jubal; he was the ancestor of all who play the lyre and the pipe. *22*Zillah, on her part, gave birth to Tubalcain, the ancestor of all who forge instruments of bronze and iron. The sister of Tubalcain was Naamah. *23*Lamech said to his wives:

"Adah and Zillah, hear my voice;
  wives of Lamech, listen to my
    utterance:
I have killed a man for wounding me,
  a boy for bruising me.
24 If Cain is avenged sevenfold,
  then Lamech seventy-sevenfold."

*25*Adam again had relations with his wife, and she gave birth to a son whom she called Seth. "God has granted* me more offspring in place of Abel," she said, "because Cain slew him." *26*To Seth, in turn, a son was born, and he named him Enosh.

At that time men began to invoke the LORD by name.*r*

CHAPTER 5

See RG 106

Generations: Adam to Noah.* *1s*This is the record of the descendants of Adam. When God created man, he made him in the likeness of God; *2*he created them male and female. When they were created, he blessed them and named them "man."

*3t*Adam was one hundred and thirty years old when he begot a son in his likeness, after his image; and he named him Seth.*u* *4*Adam lived eight hundred years after the birth of Seth, and he had other sons and daughters. *5*The whole lifetime of Adam was nine hundred and thirty years; then he died.

*6*When Seth was one hundred and five years old, he became the father of Enosh. *7*Seth lived eight hundred and seven years after the birth of Enosh, and he had other

4, 15: A mark: probably a tattoo. The use of tattooing for tribal marks has always been common among the nomads of the Near Eastern deserts.

4, 16: The land of Nod: not a definite geographic region. The term merely means "the land of nomads."

4, 17-22: In vv 12-16 Cain was presented as the archetype of nomadic peoples. The sacred author in this section follows another ancient tradition that makes Cain the prototype of sedentary peoples with higher material culture.

4, 25f: Has granted: Hebrew shat, a wordplay on the name shet ("Seth"). Enosh: in Hebrew, a synonym of adam ("man"). At the time . . . name: men began to call God by his personal name, Yahweh, rendered as "the Lord" in this version of the Bible. The ancient, so-called Yahwist source used here employs the name Yahweh long before the time of Moses. Another ancient source, the Elohist (from its use of the term Elohim, "God," instead of Yahweh, "Lord," for the pre-Mosaic period), makes Moses the first to use Yahweh as the

proper name of Israel's God, previously known by other names as well; cf Ex 3, 13ff.

5, 1-32: Although this chapter, with its highly schematic form, belongs to the relatively late "Priestly document," it is based on very ancient traditions. Together with Gn 11, 10-26, its primary purpose is to bridge the genealogical gap between Adam and Abraham. Adam's line is traced through Seth, but several names in the series are the same as, or similar to, certain names in Cain's line (Gn 4, 17ff). The long lifespans attributed to these ten antediluvian patriarchs have a symbolic rather than a historical value. Babylonian tradition also recorded ten kings with fantastically high ages who reigned successively before the flood.

q: Dt 27, 24. *r:* 1 Chr 1, 1; Lk 3, 38. *s:* Gn 1, 27; Wis 2, 23; Sir 17, 1; 1 Cor 11, 7; Jas 3, 9. *t:* Gn 4, 25. *u:* 3-32: 1 Chr 1, 1-4; Lk 3, 36ff.

The *Toledoth* ("Generations") Lists

I N THE TEXT of Genesis, the Hebrew word ***toledoth*** (pronounced "tole-uh-DOTE" and meaning "generations" or "descendants") serves as a marker for the end of one section of the narrative and the beginning of the next. Here are the places where the word occurs:

2, 4a	The second creation story
5, 1	Introduces the section between the first human family and the days of Noah
6, 9	Introduces the story of the flood
10, 1	The expansion of people over the earth
11, 10	A new list of the nations of the earth
11, 27	The beginning of Abraham's story
25, 12	The end of the story of Hagar and Ishmael, Abraham's other family
25, 19	Introduces Jacob's story
36, 1	The end of Esau's story and the beginning of the story of Jacob's children
36, 9	The conclusion of the list
37, 2	The beginning of the story of Joseph and his brothers

sons and daughters. [8]The whole lifetime of Seth was nine hundred and twelve years; then he died.

[9]When Enosh was ninety years old, he became the father of Kenan. [10]Enosh lived eight hundred and fifteen years after the birth of Kenan, and he had other sons and daughters. [11]The whole lifetime of Enosh was nine hundred and five years; then he died.

[12]When Kenan was seventy years old, he became the father of Mahalalel. [13]Kenan lived eight hundred and forty years after the birth of Mahalalel, and he had other sons and daughters. [14]The whole lifetime of Kenan was nine hundred and ten years; then he died.

[15]When Mahalalel was sixty-five years old, he became the father of Jared. [16]Mahalalel lived eight hundred and thirty years after the birth of Jared, and he had other sons and daughters. [17]The whole lifetime of Mahalalel was eight hundred and ninety-five years; then he died.

[18]When Jared was one hundred and sixty-two years old, he became the father of Enoch. [19]Jared lived eight hundred years af-ter the birth of Enoch, and he had other sons and daughters. [20]The whole lifetime of Jared was nine hundred and sixty-two years; then he died.

[21]When Enoch was sixty-five years old, he became the father of Methuselah. [22]Enoch lived three hundred years after the birth of Methuselah, and he had other sons and daughters. [23]The whole lifetime of Enoch was three hundred and sixty-five years. [24]Then Enoch walked with God,* and he was no longer here, for God took him.[v]

[25]When Methuselah was one hundred and eighty-seven years old, he became the father of Lamech. [26]Methuselah lived seven hundred and eighty-two years after the birth of Lamech, and he had other sons and daughters. [27]The whole lifetime of Methuselah was nine hundred and sixty-nine years; then he died.

[28]When Lamech was one hundred and eighty-two years old, he begot a son [29w]and named him Noah, saying, "Out of the very ground that the LORD has put under a curse, this one shall bring us relief from our work and the toil of our hands."* [30]Lamech lived

---

5, 24: In place of the usual formula, Then he died, the change to Enoch walked with God clearly implies that he did not die, but like Elijah (2 Kgs 2, 11f) was taken alive to God's abode.

5, 29: There is a similarity in sound between the Hebrew word noah, "Noah," and the verbal phrase yenahamenu, "he

will bring us relief"; this latter refers both to the curse put on the soil because of the fall of man (Gn 3, 17ff) and to Noah's success in agriculture, especially in raising grapes for wine (Gn 9, 20f).

---

v: Wis 4, 10f; Sir 44, 16; 49, 14; Heb 11, 5.   *w:* Gn 3, 17ff.

five hundred and ninety-five years after the birth of Noah, and he had other sons and daughters. *31*The whole lifetime of Lamech was seven hundred and seventy-seven years; then he died.

*32*When Noah was five hundred years old, he became the father of Shem, Ham and Japheth.*x*

CHAPTER 6

See RG
106–7

*Origin of the Nephilim.** *1*When men began to multiply on earth and daughters were born to them, *2*the sons of heaven* saw how beautiful the daughters of man were, and so they took for their wives as many of them as they chose.*y* *3*Then the LORD said: "My spirit* shall not remain in man forever, since he is but flesh. His days shall comprise one hundred and twenty years."

*4*At that time the Nephilim appeared on earth (as well as later*), after the sons of heaven had intercourse with the daughters of man, who bore them sons. They were the heroes of old, the men of renown.*z*

Warning of the Flood. *5**When the LORD saw how great was man's wickedness on earth, and how no desire that his heart conceived was ever anything but evil,*a* *6*he re-

gretted that he had made man on the earth, and his heart was grieved.

*7*So the LORD said: "I will wipe out from the earth the men whom I have created, and not only the men, but also the beasts and the creeping things and the birds of the air, for I am sorry that I made them." *8*But Noah found favor with the LORD.

*9*These are the descendants of Noah. Noah, a good man and blameless in that age,*b* *10*for he walked with God, begot three sons: Shem, Ham and Japheth.

*11*In the eyes of God the earth was corrupt and full of lawlessness.*c* *12*When God saw how corrupt the earth had become, since all mortals led depraved lives on earth,*d* *13*he said to Noah: "I have decided to put an end to all mortals on earth; the earth is full of lawlessness because of them. So I will destroy them and all life on earth.*e*

Preparation for the Flood. *14*"Make yourself an ark of gopherwood,* put various compartments in it, and cover it inside and out with pitch. *15*This is how you shall build it: the length of the ark shall be three hundred cubits, its width fifty cubits, and its height thirty cubits.* *16*Make an opening for daylight* in the ark, and finish the ark a cu-

---

6, 1-4: This is apparently a fragment of an old legend that had borrowed much from ancient mythology. The sacred author incorporates it here, not only in order to account for the prehistoric giants of Palestine, whom the Israelites called the Nephilim, but also to introduce the story of the flood with a moral orientation—the constantly increasing wickedness of mankind.

6, 2: The sons of heaven: literally "the sons of the gods" or "the sons of God," i.e., the celestial beings of mythology.

6, 3: My spirit: the breath of life referred to in Gn 2, 7. His days . . . years: probably the time God would still let men live on earth before destroying them with the flood, rather than the maximum span of life God would allot to individual men in the future.

6, 4: As well as later: According to Nm 13, 33, when the Israelites invaded Palestine and found there the tall aboriginal Anakim, they likened them to the Nephilim; cf Dt 2, 10f. Perhaps the huge megalithic structures in Palestine were thought to have been built by a race of giants, whose superhuman strength was attributed to semi-divine origin. The heroes of old: the legendary worthies of ancient mythology.

6, 5—8, 22: The story of the great flood here recorded is a composite narrative based on two separate sources interwoven into an intricate patchwork. To the Yahwist source, with some later editorial additions, are usually assigned 6, 5-8; 7, 1-5. 7-10. 12. 16b. 17b. 22-23; 8, 2b-3a. 6-12. 13b. 20-22. The other sections come from the "Priestly document."

The combination of the two sources produced certain duplications (e.g., 6, 13-22 of the Yahwist source, beside 7, 1-5 of the Priestly source); also certain inconsistencies, such as the number of the various animals taken into the ark (6, 19f; 7, 14f of the Priestly source, beside 7, 2f of the Yahwist source), and the timetable of the flood (8, 3-5. 13f of the Priestly source, beside 7, 4. 10. 12. 17b; 8, 6. 10. 12 of the Yahwist source). Both biblical sources go back ultimately to an ancient Mesopotamian story of a great flood, preserved in the eleventh tablet of the Gilgamesh Epic. The latter account, in some respects remarkably similar to the biblical account, is in others very different from it.

6, 14: Gopherwood: an unidentified wood not mentioned elsewhere; gopher is merely the Hebrew word for it.

6, 15: The dimensions of Noah's ark were approximately 440 × 73 × 44 feet, a foot and a half to the cubit. The ark of the Babylonian flood story was an exact cube, 120 cubits in length, width, and height.

6, 16: Opening for daylight: a conjectural rendering of the Hebrew word sohar, occurring only here. The reference is probably to an open space on all sides near the top of the ark to admit light and air. The ark also had a window or hatch, which could be opened and closed (Gn 8, 6).

x: Gn 6, 10; 10, 1.   *y:* Mt 24, 38; Lk 17, 26f.   *z:* Wis 14, 6; Bar 3, 26.   *a:* Ps 14, 2f.   *b:* Wis 10, 4; Sir 44, 17.   *c:* Jb 22, 15ff. *d:* Ps 14, 2.   *e:* Sir 40, 9f; 44, 17; Mt 24, 37ff.

bit above it. Put an entrance in the side of the ark, which you shall make with bottom, second and third decks. [17]I, on my part, am about to bring the flood [waters] on the earth, to destroy everywhere all creatures in which there is the breath of life; everything on earth shall perish.[f] [18]But with you I will establish my covenant; you and your sons, your wife and your sons' wives, shall go into the ark.[g] [19]Of all other living creatures you shall bring two into the ark, one male and one female, that you may keep them alive with you. [20]Of all kinds of birds, of all kinds of beasts, and of all kinds of creeping things, two of each shall come into the ark with you, to stay alive. [21]Moreover, you are to provide yourself with all the food that is to be eaten, and store it away, that it may serve as provisions for you and for them." [22]This Noah did; he carried out all the commands that God gave him.

CHAPTER 7

See RG
106-7 [1]Then the LORD said to Noah: "Go into the ark, you and all your household, for you alone in this age have I found to be truly just.[h] [2]Of every clean animal, take with you seven pairs, a male and its mate; and of the unclean animals, one pair, a male and its mate; [3]likewise, of every clean bird of the air, seven pairs, a male and a female, and of all the unclean birds, one pair, a male and a female. Thus you will keep their issue alive over all the earth. [4]Seven days from now I will bring rain down on the earth for forty days and forty nights, and so I will wipe out from the surface of the earth every moving creature that I have made."[i] [5]Noah did just as the LORD had commanded him.

The Great Flood. [6]Noah was six hundred years old when the flood waters came upon the earth. [7]Together with his sons, his wife, and his sons' wives, Noah went into the ark because of the waters of the flood.[j] [8]Of the clean animals and the unclean, of the birds, and of everything that creeps on the ground,

[9][two by two] male and female entered the ark with Noah, just as the LORD had commanded him.[k] [10]As soon as the seven days were over, the waters of the flood came upon the earth.

[11]In the six hundredth year of Noah's life, in the second month, on the seventeenth day of the month: it was on that day that

All the fountains of the great abyss* burst forth,
  and the floodgates of the sky were opened.

[12]For forty days and forty nights heavy rain poured down on the earth.

[13]On the precise day named, Noah and his sons Shem, Ham and Japheth, and Noah's wife, and the three wives of Noah's sons had entered the ark, [14]together with every kind of wild beast, every kind of domestic animal, every kind of creeping thing of the earth, and every kind of bird. [15]Pairs of all creatures in which there was the breath of life entered the ark with Noah. [16]Those that entered were male and female, and of all species they came, as God had commanded Noah. Then the LORD shut him in.

[17]The flood continued upon the earth for forty days. As the waters increased, they lifted the ark, so that it rose above the earth. [18]The swelling waters increased greatly, but the ark floated on the surface of the waters. [19]Higher and higher above the earth rose the waters, until all the highest mountains everywhere were submerged, [20]the crest rising fifteen cubits higher than the submerged mountains. [21]All creatures that stirred on earth perished: birds, cattle, wild animals, and all that swarmed on the earth, as well as all mankind.[l] [22]Everything on dry land with the faintest breath of life in its nostrils died out. [23]The LORD wiped out every living thing on earth: man and cattle, the creeping things and the birds of the air; all were wiped out from the earth. Only Noah and those with him in the ark were left.

7, 11: Abyss: the subterranean ocean; see note on Gn 1, 2.

f: Gn 7, 4. 21; 2 Pt 2, 5.   g: Gn 9, 9; Wis 14, 6; Heb 11, 7; 1 Pt 3, 20.   h: Wis 10, 4; Sir 44, 17; 2 Pt 2, 5.   i: Gn 6, 17; 2 Pt 2, 5.
j: Wis 14, 6; 1 Pt 3, 20; 2 Pt 2, 5.   k: Gn 6, 19.   l: 21ff; Jb 22, 16; Mt 24, 39; Lk 17, 27; 2 Pt 3, 6.

See RG
106-7

CHAPTER 8

7, 24*The waters maintained their crest over the earth for one hundred and fifty days, *1*and then God remembered Noah and all the animals, wild and tame, that were with him in the ark. So God made a wind sweep over the earth, and the waters began to subside. *2*The fountains of the abyss and the floodgates of the sky were closed, and the downpour from the sky was held back. *3*Gradually the waters receded from the earth. At the end of one hundred and fifty days, the waters had so diminished *4*that, in the seventh month, on the seventeenth day of the month, the ark came to rest on the mountains of Ararat.* *5*The waters continued to diminish until the tenth month, and on the first day of the tenth month the tops of the mountains appeared.

*6*At the end of forty days Noah opened the hatch he had made in the ark,* *7*and he sent out a raven, to see if the waters had lessened on the earth. It flew back and forth until the waters dried off from the earth. *8*Then he sent out a dove, to see if the waters had lessened on the earth. *9*But the dove could find no place to alight and perch, and it returned to him in the ark, for there was water all over the earth. Putting out his hand, he caught the dove and drew it back to him inside the ark. *10*He waited seven days more and again sent the dove out from the ark. *11*In the evening the dove came back to him, and there in its bill was a plucked-off olive leaf! So Noah knew that the waters had lessened on the earth. *12*He waited still another seven days and then released the dove once more; and this time it did not come back.

*13*In the six hundred and first year of Noah's life, in the first month, on the first day of the month, the water began to dry up on the earth. Noah then removed the covering of the ark and saw that the surface of the ground was drying up. *14*In the second month, on the twenty-seventh day of the month, the earth was dry.

*15*Then God said to Noah: *16*"Go out of the ark, together with your wife and your sons and your sons' wives. *17*Bring out with you every living thing that is with you—all bodily creatures, be they birds or animals or creeping things of the earth—and let them abound on the earth, breeding and multiplying on it."*m* *18*So Noah came out, together with his wife and his sons and his sons' wives; *19*and all the animals, wild and tame, all the birds, and all the creeping creatures of the earth left the ark, one kind after another.

*20*Then Noah built an altar to the LORD, and choosing from every clean animal and every clean bird, he offered holocausts on the altar. *21*When the LORD smelled the sweet odor, he said to himself: "Never again will I doom the earth because of man, since the desires of man's heart are evil from the start;* nor will I ever again strike down all living beings, as I have done.*n*

22 As long as the earth lasts,
seedtime and harvest,
cold and heat,
Summer and winter,
and day and night
shall not cease."*o*

CHAPTER 9

See RG
106-7

Covenant with Noah. *1*God blessed Noah and his sons and said to them: "Be fertile and multiply and fill the earth.*p* *2*Dread fear of you shall come upon all the animals of the earth and all the birds of the air, upon all the creatures that move about on the ground and all the fishes of the sea; into your power they are delivered. *3q*Every creature that is alive shall be yours to eat; I give them all to you as I did the green plants.* *4r*Only flesh

---

7, 24: This verse belongs to chapter 7 but its contents properly introduce chapter 8.

8, 4: Ararat: ancient Urartu, north of the Mesopotamian plain, part of modern Armenia.

8, 6: In the original Yahwist source, from which this verse is taken, the forty days refer to the full period of the flood itself (cf Gn 7, 4. 17); in the present context, however, they seem to refer to a period following the date just given in v 5 from the Priestly source.

8, 21: From the start: literally "from his youth." It is uncertain whether this means from the beginning of the human race or from the early years of the individual.

9, 3: Antediluvian creatures, including man, are depicted

---

m: Gn 1, 22. 28.   *n:* Sir 44, 18; Is 54, 9; Rom 7, 18.   *o:* Jer 33, 20. 25.   *p:* Gn 1, 22, 28; 8, 17; Jas 3, 7.   *q:* Gn 1, 29f; Dt 12, 15.   *r:* Lv 7, 26f; 17, 4; Dt 12, 16. 23; 1 Sm 14, 33; Acts 15, 20.

with its lifeblood still in it you shall not eat.* [5]For your own lifeblood, too, I will demand an accounting: from every animal I will demand it, and from man in regard to his fellow man I will demand an accounting for human life.[s]

[6] If anyone sheds the blood of man,
    by man shall his blood be shed;
For in the image of God
    has man been made.[t]

[7]Be fertile, then, and multiply; abound on earth and subdue it."[u]

[8]God said to Noah and to his sons with him: [9]"See, I am now establishing my covenant with you and your descendants after you[v] [10]and with every living creature that was with you: all the birds, and the various tame and wild animals that were with you and came out of the ark. [11]I will establish my covenant with you, that never again shall all bodily creatures be destroyed by the waters of a flood; there shall not be another flood to devastate the earth."[w] [12]God added: "This is the sign that I am giving for all ages to come, of the covenant between me and you and every living creature with you: [13x]I set my bow in the clouds to serve as a sign of the covenant between me and the earth. [14]When I bring clouds over the earth, and the bow appears in the clouds, [15]I will recall the covenant I have made between me and you and all living beings, so that the waters shall never again become a flood to destroy all mortal beings.[y] [16]As the bow appears in the clouds, I will see it and recall the everlasting covenant that I have established between God and all living beings—all mortal creatures that are on earth." [17]God told Noah:

"This is the sign of the covenant I have established between me and all mortal creatures that are on earth."

Noah and His Sons. [18*]The sons of Noah who came out of the ark were Shem, Ham and Japheth. (Ham was the father of Canaan.)[z] [19]These three were the sons of Noah, and from them the whole earth was peopled.

[20]Now Noah, a man of the soil, was the first to plant a vineyard. [21]When he drank some of the wine, he became drunk and lay naked inside his tent.[a] [22]Ham, the father of Canaan, saw his father's nakedness, and he told his two brothers outside about it. [23]Shem and Japheth, however, took a robe, and holding it on their backs, they walked backward and covered their father's nakedness; since their faces were turned the other way, they did not see their father's nakedness. [24]When Noah woke up from his drunkenness and learned what his youngest son had done to him, [25]he said:

"Cursed be Canaan!
    The lowest of slaves
    shall he be to his brothers."[b]

[26]He also said:

"Blessed be the LORD, the God of Shem!*
    Let Canaan be his slave.
[27] May God expand Japheth,*
    so that he dwells among the tents of
        Shem;
    and let Canaan be his slave."

[28]Noah lived three hundred and fifty years after the flood. [29]The whole lifetime of Noah was nine hundred and fifty years; then he died.

---

as vegetarians (Gn 1, 29f), becoming carnivorous only after the flood.

9, 4: Because a living being dies when it loses most of its blood, the ancients regarded blood as the seat of life, and therefore as sacred. Although in itself the prohibition against eating meat with blood in it is comparable to the ritual laws of the Mosaic code, the Jews considered it binding on all men, because it was given by God to Noah, the new ancestor of all mankind; therefore the early Christian Church retained it for a time (Acts 15, 20. 29).

9, 18-27: This story seems to be a composite of two earlier accounts; in the one, Ham was guilty, whereas in the other, it was Canaan. One purpose of the story is to justify the Israelites' enslavement of the Canaanites because of certain indecent sexual practices in the Canaanite religion. Obvi-

ously the story offers no justification for enslaving African Negroes, even though Canaan is presented as a "son" of Ham because the land of Canaan belonged to Hamitic Egypt at the time of the Israelite invasion.

9, 26: Blessed . . . Shem: perhaps the text read originally, "Blessed of the Lord be Shem," which would be expected in the context.

9, 27: In the Hebrew text there is a play on the words yapt ("expand") and yepet ("Japheth").

s: Gn 4, 10f; Ex 21, 12. *t:* Gn 1, 26f; Lv 24, 17; Nm 35, 33; Jas 3, 9. *u:* Gn 1, 28; 8, 17; 9, 2. *v:* Gn 6, 18. *w:* Sir 44, 18; Is 54, 9. *x:* Sir 43, 12. *y:* Is 54, 9. *z:* Gn 5, 32; 10, 1. *a:* Lam 4, 21; Heb 2, 15. *b:* Dt 27, 16; Wis 12, 11.

See RG
107

CHAPTER 10

*Table of the Nations.** *1*These are the descendants of Noah's sons, Shem, Ham and Japheth, to whom sons were born after the flood.

2 *c*The descendants of Japheth:
Gomer,* Magog, Madai, Javan, Tubal, Meshech and Tiras.*d*
3 The descendants of Gomer:
Ashkenaz,* Riphath and Togarmah.
4 The descendants of Javan:
Elishah,* Tarshish, the Kittim and the Rodanim.

*5*These are the descendants of Japheth, and from them sprang the maritime nations, in their respective lands—each with its own language—by their clans within their nations.

6 The descendants of Ham:
Cush,* Mizraim, Put and Canaan.
7 The descendants of Cush:
Seba, Havilah, Sabtah, Raamah and Sabteca.
The descendants of Raamah:
Sheba and Dedan.

*8*Cush* became the father of Nimrod, who was the first potentate on earth. *9*He was a mighty hunter by the grace of the LORD; hence the saying, "Like Nimrod, a mighty hunter by the grace of the LORD." *10*The chief cities of his kingdom were Babylon, Erech and Accad, all of them in the land of Shinar.* *11*From that land he went forth to Asshur,* where he built Nineveh, Rehoboth-Ir and Calah, *12*as well as Resen, between Nineveh and Calah,* the latter being the principal city.

*13e*Mizraim became the father of the Ludim, the Anamim, the Lehabim, the Naphtuhim, *14*the Pathrusim,* the Casluhim, and the Caphtorim from whom the Philistines sprang.

*15*Canaan became the father of Sidon, his first-born, and of Heth;* *16*also of the Jebusites, the Amorites, the Girgashites, *17*the Hivites, the Arkites, the Sinites, *18*the Arvadites, the Zemarites and the Hamathites. Afterward, the clans of the Canaanites spread out, *19*so that the Canaanite borders extended from Sidon all the way to Gerar, near Gaza, and all the way to Sodom, Gomorrah, Admah and Zeboiim, near Lasha.*

*20*These are the descendants of Ham, according to their clans and languages, by their lands and nations.

*21*To Shem also, Japheth's oldest brother and the ancestor of all the children of Eber, sons were born.

10, 1-32: This chapter presents a remarkably good classification of the various peoples known to the ancient Israelites; it is theologically important as stressing the basic family unity of all men on earth. The relationship between the various peoples is based partly on linguistic, partly on geographic, and partly on political grounds according to their . . . languages, . . . lands and nations: (v 31). In general, the descendants of Japheth (vv 2-5) are the peoples of the Indo-European languages to the north and west of Mesopotamia and Syria; the descendants of Ham (vv 6-20) are the Hamitic-speaking peoples of northern Africa; and the descendants of Shem (vv 21-31) are the Semitic-speaking peoples of Mesopotamia, Syria and Arabia. But there are many exceptions to this rule; the Semitic-speaking peoples of Canaan, for instance, are considered descendants of Ham, because at the time they were subject to Hamitic Egypt (vv 6. 15-19). This chapter is a composite from the Yahwist source (vv 8-19. 21. 24-30) of about the ninth century B.C., and the Priestly source (vv 1-7. 20. 22f. 31f) of a few centuries later. That is why certain tribes of Arabia are listed under both Ham (v 7) and Shem (vv 26ff).

10, 2: Gomer: the Cimmerians; Madai: the Medes; Javan: the Greeks.

10, 3: Ashkenaz: the Scythians.

10, 4: Elishah: Cyprus; the Kittim: certain inhabitants of Cyprus; the Rodanim: the inhabitants of Rhodes.

10, 6: Cush: Biblical Ethiopia, modern Nubia. Mizraim: Egypt; Put: either Punt in East Africa or Libya.

10, 8: Cush: here, the Kassites; see note on Gn 2, 10-14. Nimrod: probably Tukulti-Ninurta I (thirteenth century B.C.), the first Assyrian conqueror of Babylonia and a famous city-builder at home.

10, 10: Shinar: ancient Sumer in southern Mesopotamia, mentioned also in Gn 11, 2; 14, 1.

10, 11: Asshur: Assyria. Rehoboth-Ir: literally "wide-streets city," was probably not the name of another city, but an epithet of Nineveh; cf Jon 3, 3.

10, 12: Calah: Assyrian Kalhu, the capital of Assyria in the ninth century B.C.

10, 14: The Pathrusim: the people of upper (southern) Egypt; cf Is 11, 11; Jer 44, 1; Ez 29, 14; 30, 14. Caphtorim: Crete; for Caphtor as the place of origin of the Philistines, cf Dt 2, 23; Am 9, 7; Jer 47, 4.

10, 15: Heth: the biblical Hittites; see note on Gn 23, 3.

10, 19: Lasha: the reading of this name is uncertain; perhaps it should be "Bela"; cf Gn 14, 2.

c: 2-8: 1 Chr 1, 5-10. *d:* Ez 38, 2. *e:* 13-18: 1 Chr 1, 11-16.

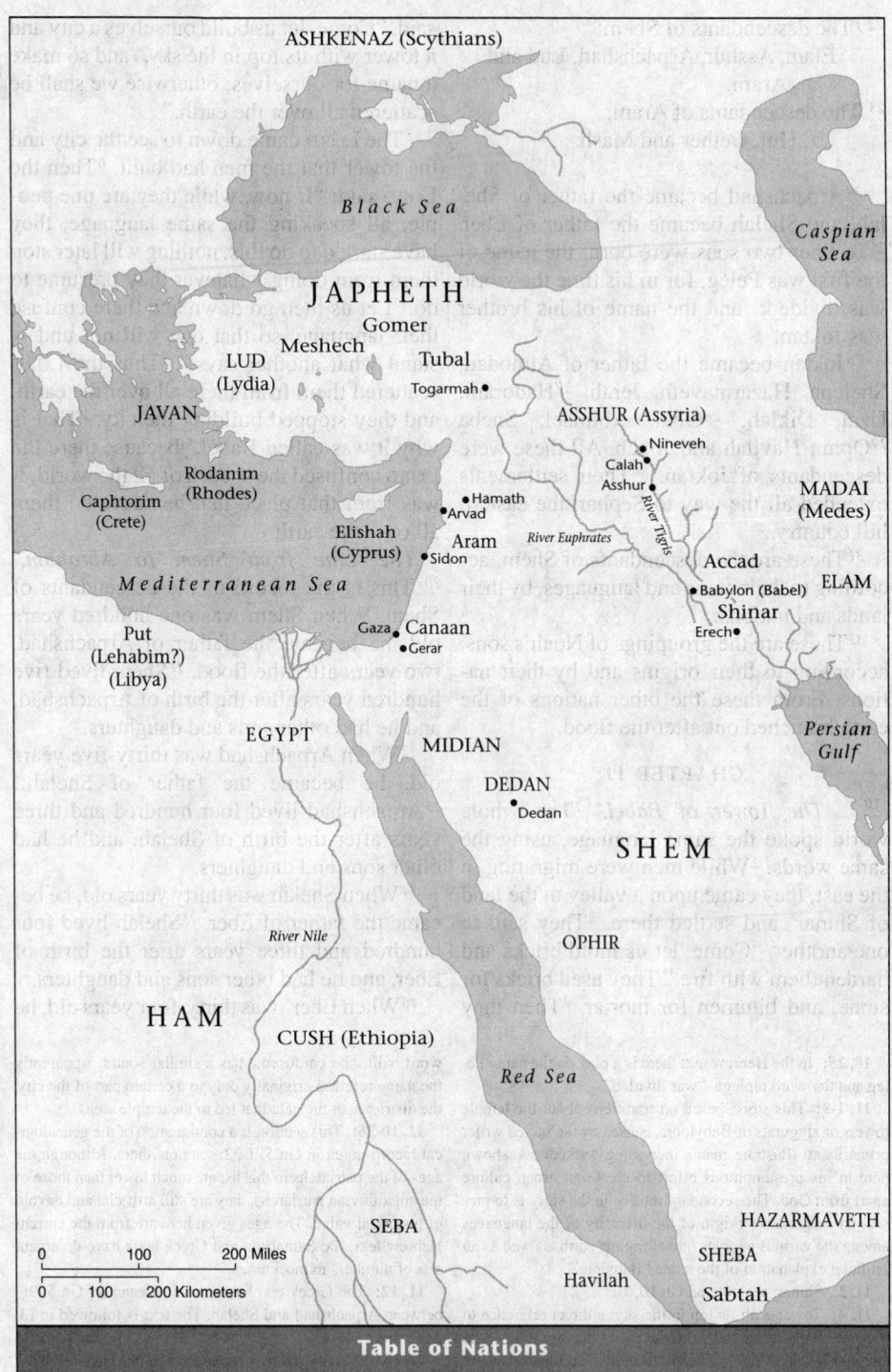

ASHKENAZ (Scythians)

Black Sea

Caspian Sea

JAPHETH

Gomer
Meshech
LUD   Tubal
(Lydia)   Togarmah •

JAVAN

Rodanim
(Rhodes)

Caphtorim
(Crete)   Elishah   Hamath
(Cyprus)   • Arvad
Aram
• Sidon

Mediterranean Sea

Gaza • Canaan
• Gerar

Put
(Lehabim?)
(Libya)

ASSHUR (Assyria)
• Nineveh
Calah •
Asshur •
MADAI
(Medes)

River Euphrates   *River Tigris*

Accad
• Babylon (Babel)   ELAM
Shinar
Erech •

Persian Gulf

EGYPT   MIDIAN
• DEDAN
• Dedan

River Nile   SHEM

OPHIR

HAM   CUSH (Ethiopia)

Red Sea

SEBA   HAZARMAVETH
SHEBA
Havilah   Sabtah

0   100   200 Miles
0   100   200 Kilometers

Table of Nations

19

22 ᶠThe descendants of Shem:
Elam, Asshur, Arpachshad, Lud and
Aram.
23 The descendants of Aram:
Uz, Hul, Gether and Mash.

24 Arpachshad became the father of Shelah, and Shelah became the father of Eber.
25 To Eber two sons were born: the name of
the first was Peleg, for in his time the world
was divided;* and the name of his brother
was Joktan.
26 Joktan became the father of Almodad,
Sheleph, Hazarmaveth, Jerah, 27Hadoram,
Uzal, Diklah, 28Obal, Abimael, Sheba
29Ophir, Havilah and Jobab. All these were
descendants of Joktan. 30Their settlements
extended all the way to Sephar, the eastern
hill country.
31 These are the descendants of Shem, according to their clans and languages, by their
lands and nations.
32 These are the groupings of Noah's sons,
according to their origins and by their nations. From these the other nations of the
earth branched out after the flood.

See RG
107

CHAPTER 11

The Tower of Babel.* 1The whole
world spoke the same language, using the
same words. 2While men were migrating in
the east, they came upon a valley in the land
of Shinar* and settled there. 3They said to
one another, "Come, let us mold bricks and
harden them with fire." They used bricks for
stone, and bitumen for mortar. 4Then they
said, "Come, let us build ourselves a city and
a tower with its top in the sky,* and so make
a name for ourselves; otherwise we shall be
scattered all over the earth."
5 The LORD came down to see the city and
the tower that the men had built. 6Then the
LORD said: "If now, while they are one people, all speaking the same language, they
have started to do this, nothing will later stop
them from doing whatever they presume to
do. 7Let us then go down and there confuse
their language, so that one will not understand what another says." 8Thus the LORD
scattered them from there all over the earth,
and they stopped building the city. 9That is
why it was called Babel,* because there the
LORD confused the speech of all the world. It
was from that place that he scattered them
all over the earth.

The Line from Shem to Abraham.*
10 gThis is the record of the descendants of
Shem. When Shem was one hundred years
old, he became the father of Arpachshad,
two years after the flood. 11Shem lived five
hundred years after the birth of Arpachshad,
and he had other sons and daughters.
12 When Arpachshad was thirty-five years
old, he became the father of Shelah.*
13 Arpachshad lived four hundred and three
years after the birth of Shelah, and he had
other sons and daughters.
14 When Shelah was thirty years old, he became the father of Eber. 15Shelah lived four
hundred and three years after the birth of
Eber, and he had other sons and daughters.
16 When Eber* was thirty-four years old, he

10, 25: In the Hebrew text there is a play on the name Peleg and the word niplega, "was divided."

11, 1-9: This story, based on traditions about the temple
towers or ziggurats of Babylonia, is used by the sacred writer
primarily to illustrate man's increasing wickedness, shown
here in his presumptuous effort to create an urban culture
apart from God. The secondary motive in the story is to present an imaginative origin of the diversity of the languages
among the various peoples inhabiting the earth, as well as an
artificial explanation of the name "Babylon."

11, 2: Shinar: see note on Gn 10, 10.

11, 4: Tower with its top in the sky: a direct reference to
the chief ziggurat of Babylon, the E-sag-ila, signifying "the
house that raises high its head." Babylonian ziggurats were
the earliest skyscrapers.

11, 9: Babel: the Hebrew form of the name "Babylon"; the
native name, Bab-ili, means "gate of the gods." The Hebrew

word balil, "he confused," has a similar sound. Apparently
the name referred originally only to a certain part of the city,
the district near the gate that led to the temple area.

11, 10-26: This section is a continuation of the genealogical record given in Gn 5, 1-32; see note there. Although the
ages of the patriarchs in this list are much lower than those of
the antediluvian patriarchs, they are still artificial and devoid
of historical value. The ages given here are from the current
Hebrew text; the Samaritan and Greek texts have divergent
sets of numbers in most cases.

11, 12: The Greek text has a certain Kenan (cf Gn 5, 9f)
between Arpachshad and Shelah. The text is followed in Lk
3, 36.

11, 16: Eber: the eponymous ancestor of the Hebrews, "descendants of Eber" (Gn 10, 21. 24-30); see note on Gn 14, 13.

f: 22-29: 1 Chr 1, 17-23. g: 10-26: 1 Chr 1, 24-27; Lk 3, 34ff.

became the father of Peleg. [17]Eber lived four hundred and thirty years after the birth of Peleg, and he had other sons and daughters.

[18]When Peleg was thirty years old, he became the father of Reu. [19]Peleg lived two hundred and nine years after the birth of Reu, and he had other sons and daughters.

[20]When Reu was thirty-two years old, he became the father of Serug. [21]Reu lived two hundred and seven years after the birth of Serug, and he had other sons and daughters.

[22]When Serug was thirty years old, he became the father of Nahor. [23]Serug lived two hundred years after the birth of Nahor, and he had other sons and daughters.

[24]When Nahor was twenty-nine years old, he became the father of Terah. [25]Nahor lived one hundred and nineteen years after the birth of Terah, and he had other sons and daughters.

[26]When Terah was seventy years old, he became the father of Abram, Nahor and Haran.[h]

II: The Patriarch Abraham

Terah. [27]This is the record of the descendants of Terah. Terah became the father of Abram, Nahor and Haran, and Haran became the father of Lot. [28]Haran died before his father Terah, in his native land, in Ur of the Chaldeans.[*] [29]Abram and Nahor took wives; the name of Abram's wife was Sarai, and the name of Nahor's wife was Milcah, daughter of Haran, the father of Milcah and Iscah.[i] [30]Sarai was barren; she had no child. [31]Terah took his son Abram, his grandson Lot, son of Haran, and his daughter-in-law Sarai, the wife of his son Abram, and brought them out of Ur of the Chaldeans, to go to the land of Canaan.[*] But when they reached Haran, they settled there.[j] [32]The lifetime of Terah was two hundred and five years; then Terah died in Haran.[*]

CHAPTER 12

See RG 110-11

Abram's Call and Migration. [1]The LORD said to Abram: "Go forth from the land of your kinsfolk and from your father's house to a land that I will show you.[k]

[2] "I will make of you a great nation,
    and I will bless you;
I will make your name great,
    so that you will be a blessing.[l]
[3] [m]I will bless those who bless you
    and curse those who curse you.
All the communities of the earth
    shall find blessing in you."[*]

[4][n]Abram went as the LORD directed him, and Lot went with him. Abram was seventy-five years old when he left Haran. [5]Abram took his wife Sarai, his brother's son Lot, all the possessions that they had accumulated, and the persons[*] they had acquired in Haran, and they set out for the land of Canaan. When they came to the land of Canaan, [6]Abram passed through the land as far as the sacred place at Shechem, by the terebinth of Moreh. (The Canaanites were then in the land.)

[7]The LORD appeared to Abram and said, "To your descendants I will give this land." So Abram built an altar there to the LORD

11, 28: Ur of the Chaldeans: Ur was an extremely ancient city of the Sumerians (later, of the Babylonians) in southern Mesopotamia. The Greek text has "the land of the Chaldeans." In either case, the term Chaldeans is an anachronism, because the Chaldeans were not known to history until approximately a thousand years after Abraham's time.

11, 31: The Samaritan and Greek texts include Nahor and his wife in Terah's migration to Haran. Although this is probably due to scribal harmonization, Nahor's family actually did migrate to Haran; cf Gn 24, 10; 27, 43.

11, 32: Since Terah was seventy years old when his son Abraham was born (v 26), and Abraham was seventy-five when he left Haran (Gn 12, 4), Terah lived in Haran for sixty years after Abraham's departure. According to the tradition in the Samaritan text, Terah died when he was one hundred and forty-five years old, therefore, in the same year in which Abraham left Haran. This is the tradition followed in St. Stephen's speech: Abraham left Haran "after his father's death" (Acts 7, 4).

12, 3: Shall find blessing in you: the sense of the Hebrew expression is probably reflexive, "shall bless themselves through you" (i.e., in giving a blessing they shall say, "May you be as blessed as Abraham"), rather than passive, "shall be blessed in you." Since the term is understood in a passive sense in the New Testament (Acts 3, 25; Gal 3, 8), it is rendered here by a neutral expression that admits of both meanings. So also in the blessings given by God to Isaac (Gn 26, 4) and Jacob (Gn 28, 14).

12, 5: Persons: slaves and retainers that formed the social aggregate under the leadership of Abraham; cf Gn 14, 14.

---

h: Jos 24, 2; 1 Chr 1, 27. i: Gn 17, 15; 20, 12. j: Jos 24, 3; Neh 9, 7; Jdt 5, 6-9; Acts 7, 4. k: Acts 7, 3; Heb 11, 8. l: Gn 17, 6; Sir 44, 20; Rom 4, 17-22. m: Gn 18, 18; 22, 18; Acts 3, 25; Gal 3, 8. n: 4f: Gn 11, 31; Jos 24, 3; Acts 7, 4.

who had appeared to him.*o* *8*From there he moved on to the hill country east of Bethel, pitching his tent with Bethel to the west and Ai to the east. He built an altar there to the LORD and invoked the LORD by name. *9*Then Abram journeyed on by stages to the Negeb.*

Abram and Sarai in Egypt. *10*There was famine in the land; so Abram went down to Egypt to sojourn there, since the famine in the land was severe.*p* *11*When he was about to enter Egypt, he said to his wife Sarai: "I know well how beautiful a woman you are. *12*When the Egyptians see you, they will say, 'She is his wife'; then they will kill me, but let you live. *13*Please say, therefore, that you are my sister,* so that it may go well with me on your account and my life may be spared for your sake."*q* *14*When Abram came to Egypt, the Egyptians saw how beautiful the woman was; *15*and when Pharaoh's courtiers saw her, they praised her to Pharaoh. So she was taken into Pharaoh's palace. *16*On her account it went very well with Abram, and he received flocks and herds, male and female slaves, male and female asses, and camels.*

*17*But the LORD struck Pharaoh and his household with severe plagues because of Abram's wife Sarai.*r* *18*Then Pharaoh summoned Abram and said to him: "How could you do this to me! Why didn't you tell me she was your wife? *19*Why did you say, 'She is my sister,' so that I took her for my wife? Here, then, is your wife. Take her and be gone!"

*20*Then Pharaoh gave men orders concerning him, and they sent him on his way, with his wife and all that belonged to him.

CHAPTER 13

See RG 110–11

Abram and Lot Part. *1*From Egypt Abram went up to the Negeb with his wife and all that belonged to him, and Lot accompanied him.*s* *2*Now Abram was very rich

in livestock, silver and gold.*t* *3*From the Negeb he traveled by stages toward Bethel, to the place between Bethel and Ai where his tent had formerly stood, *4*the site where he had first built the altar; and there he invoked the LORD by name.*u*

*5*Lot, who went with Abram, also had flocks and herds and tents, *6*so that the land could not support them if they stayed together; their possessions were so great that they could not dwell together. *7*There were quarrels between the herdsmen of Abram's livestock and those of Lot's. (At this time the Canaanites and the Perizzites were occupying the land.)

*8*So Abram said to Lot: "Let there be no strife between you and me, or between your herdsmen and mine, for we are kinsmen. *9*Is not the whole land at your disposal? Please separate from me. If you prefer the left, I will go to the right; if you prefer the right, I will go to the left." *10*Lot looked about and saw how well watered the whole Jordan Plain was as far as Zoar, like the LORD's own garden, or like Egypt. (This was before the LORD had destroyed Sodom and Gomorrah.) *11*Lot, therefore, chose for himself the whole Jordan Plain and set out eastward. Thus they separated from each other; *12*Abram stayed in the land of Canaan, while Lot settled among the cities of the Plain, pitching his tents near Sodom. *13*Now the inhabitants of Sodom were very wicked in the sins they committed against the LORD.*v*

*14*After Lot had left, the LORD said to Abram: "Look about you, and from where you are, gaze to the north and south, east and west;*w* *15*all the land that you see I will give to you and your descendants forever.*x* *16*I will make your descendants like the dust of the earth; if anyone could count the dust of the earth, your descendants too might be

---

12, 9: The Negeb: the semidesert land of southern Palestine.

12, 13: You are my sister: although Abraham's deceit may not be fully defensible, his statement was at least a half-truth; Sarah was indeed his relative, called "a sister" in Hebrew; cf Gn 20, 12. Moreover, the ancient traditions on which this story and the parallel ones in Gn 20, 1-18 and 26, 6-11 are based, probably come from the Hurrian custom of wife-sister marriage. Among the Hurrians, with whom Abraham's clan lived in close contact at Haran, a man could adopt his wife as his sister and thus give her higher status.

12, 16: Camels: domesticated camels probably did not come into common use in the ancient Near East until the end of the 2nd millennium B.C. Thus the mention of camels at the time of the patriarchs (Gn 24, 11-64; 30, 43; 31, 17. 34; 32, 8. 16; 37, 25) is seemingly an anachronism.

o: Ex 33, 1; Dt 34, 4; Acts 7, 5. p: Gn 26, 1. q: Gn 20, 12f; 26, 7. r: Ps 105, 14. s: Gn 12, 9. t: Ps 112, 1ff; Prv 10, 22. u: Gn 12, 8. v: Gn 18, 20; Ez 16, 49; 2 Pt 2, 6ff; Jude 1, 7. w: Gn 28, 14. x: Gn 12, 7; Mt 5, 4; Lk 1, 55; Acts 7, 5; Gal 3, 16.

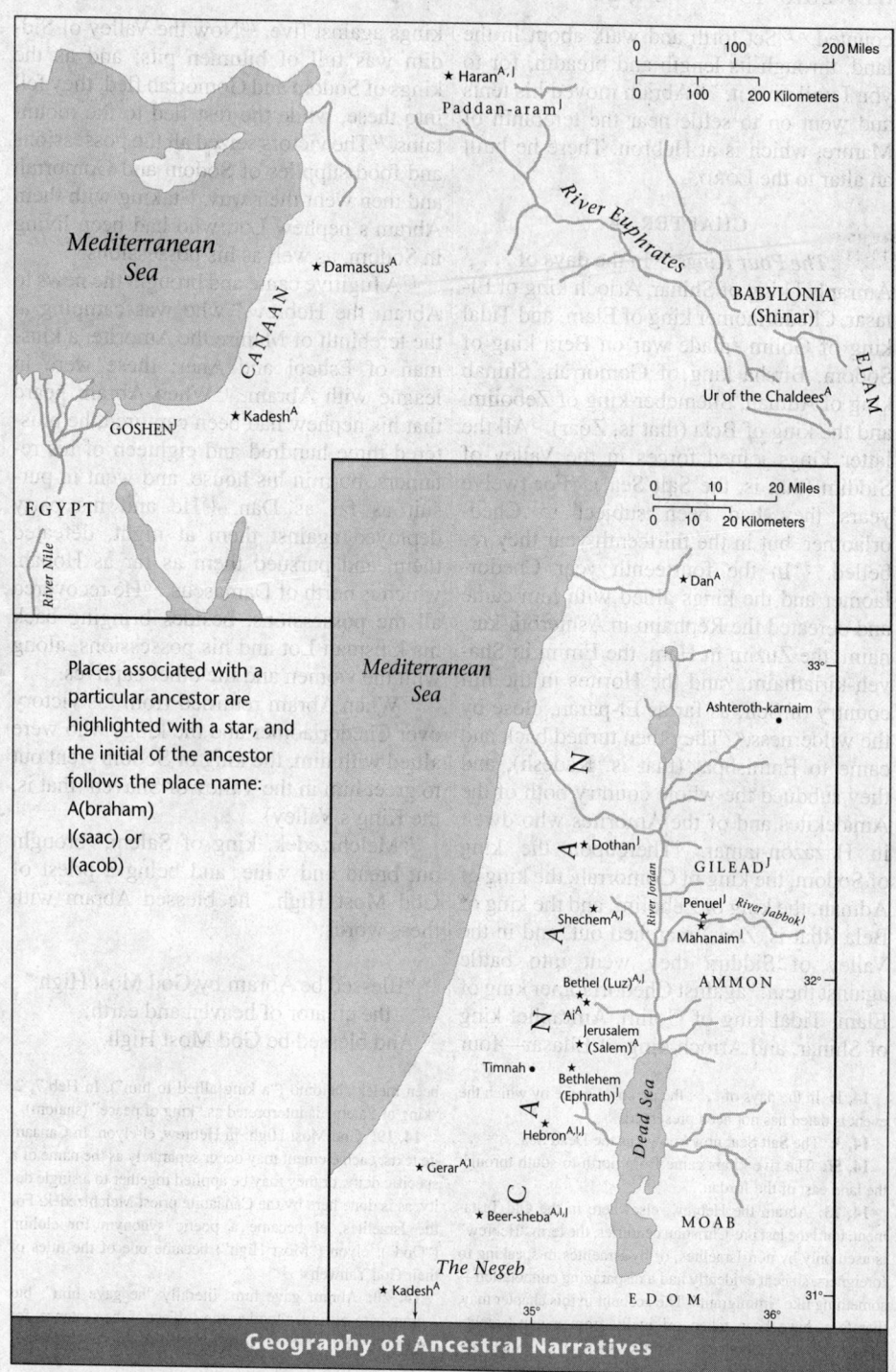

Places associated with a particular ancestor are highlighted with a star, and the initial of the ancestor follows the place name:
A(braham)
I(saac) or
J(acob)

Mediterranean Sea

CANAAN

EGYPT

GOSHEN[J]

★ Kadesh[A]

River Nile

★ Haran[A,I]

Paddan-aram[I]

River Euphrates

BABYLONIA
(Shinar)

ELAM

★ Damascus[A]

Ur of the Chaldees[A]

0   100   200 Miles
0   100   200 Kilometers

Mediterranean Sea

★ Dan[A]

Ashteroth-karnaim

★ Dothan[J]

GILEAD[J]

Shechem[A,J]

Penuel[I] River Jabbok[I]

Mahanaim[I]

Bethel (Luz)[A,J]

Ai[A]

AMMON

Jerusalem
(Salem)[A]

Timnah ●

Bethlehem
(Ephrath)[I]

Hebron[A,I,J]

★ Gerar[A,I]

C A N A A N

River Jordan

Dead Sea

AMMON

★ Beer-sheba[A,I,J]

MOAB

The Negeb

★ Kadesh[A]

EDOM

0   10   20 Miles
0   10   20 Kilometers

33°

32°

35°

36°

31°

Geography of Ancestral Narratives

23

counted.^{y} ^{17}Set forth and walk about in the land, through its length and breadth, for to you I will give it." ^{18}Abram moved his tents and went on to settle near the terebinth of Mamre, which is at Hebron. There he built an altar to the LORD.^{z}

See RG 110-11

CHAPTER 14

The Four Kings. ^{1}In the days of . . . ,* Amraphel king of Shinar, Arioch king of Ellasar, Chedorlaomer king of Elam, and Tidal king of Goiim ^{2}made war on Bera king of Sodom, Birsha king of Gomorrah, Shinab king of Admah, Shemeber king of Zeboiim, and the king of Bela (that is, Zoar). ^{3}All the latter kings joined forces in the Valley of Siddim (that is, the Salt Sea*). ^{4}For twelve years they had been subject to Chedorlaomer, but in the thirteenth year they rebelled. ^{5*}In the fourteenth year Chedorlaomer and the kings allied with him came and defeated the Rephaim in Ashteroth-karnaim, the Zuzim in Ham, the Emim in Shaveh-kiriathaim, ^{6}and the Horites in the hill country of Seir, as far as El-paran, close by the wilderness.^{a} ^{7}They then turned back and came to Enmishpat (that is, Kadesh), and they subdued the whole country both of the Amalekites and of the Amorites who dwelt in Hazazon-tamar. ^{8}Thereupon the king of Sodom, the king of Gomorrah, the king of Admah, the king of Zeboiim, and the king of Bela (that is, Zoar) marched out, and in the Valley of Siddim they went into battle against them: ^{9}against Chedorlaomer king of Elam, Tidal king of Goiim, Amraphel king of Shinar, and Arioch king of Ellasar—four

kings against five. ^{10}Now the Valley of Siddim was full of bitumen pits; and as the kings of Sodom and Gomorrah fled, they fell into these, while the rest fled to the mountains. ^{11}The victors seized all the possessions and food supplies of Sodom and Gomorrah and then went their way, ^{12}taking with them Abram's nephew Lot, who had been living in Sodom, as well as his possessions.^{b}

^{13}A fugitive came and brought the news to Abram the Hebrew,* who was camping at the terebinth of Mamre the Amorite, a kinsman of Eshcol and Aner; these were in league with Abram. ^{14}When Abram heard that his nephew had been captured, he mustered three hundred and eighteen of his retainers, born in his house, and went in pursuit as far as Dan. ^{15}He and his party deployed against them at night, defeated them, and pursued them as far as Hobah, which is north of Damascus. ^{16}He recovered all the possessions, besides bringing back his kinsman Lot and his possessions, along with the women and the other captives.

^{17}When Abram returned from his victory over Chedorlaomer and the kings who were allied with him, the king of Sodom went out to greet him in the Valley of Shaveh (that is, the King's Valley).

^{18}Melchizedek, king of Salem,* brought out bread and wine, and being a priest of God Most High,* he blessed Abram with these words:^{c}

^{19} "Blessed be Abram by God Most High,*
　　the creator of heaven and earth;
^{20} And blessed be God Most High,

14, 1: In the days of . . . : the personal name by which the event is dated has not been preserved.

14, 3: The Salt Sea: now known as the Dead Sea.

14, 5f: The five kings came from north to south through the land east of the Jordan.

14, 13: Abram the Hebrew: elsewhere in the Old Testament, until the last pre-Christian centuries, the term "Hebrew" is used only by non-Israelites, or by Israelites in speaking to foreigners, since it evidently had a disparaging connotation— something like "immigrant." The account in this chapter may, therefore, have been taken originally from a non-Israelite source, in which Abraham, a warlike sheik of Palestine, appears as a truly historical figure of profane history.

14, 18: Salem: traditionally identified with Jerusalem (Ps 76, 3), but the Hebrew text is not certain; instead of the present *melek shalem* ("king of Salem") the original may have

been *melek shelomo* ("a king allied to him"). In Heb 7, 2, "king of Salem" is interpreted as "king of peace" (shalom).

14, 19: God Most High: in Hebrew, el-elyon. In Canaanite texts, each element may occur separately as the name of a specific deity, or they may be applied together to a single deity, as is done here by the Canaanite priest Melchizedek. For the Israelites, el became a poetic synonym for elohim ("God"); elyon ("Most High") became one of the titles of their God Yahweh.

14, 20: Abram gave him: literally "he gave him"; but Abram is to be understood as the subject of the sentence, for the tithes were the tenth part assigned to priests; cf Heb 7, 4-10.

---

y: Gn 22, 17; Nm 23, 10.   *z:* Gn 14, 13.   *a:* Dt 2, 12.   *b:* Gn 13, 10ff.   *c:* Ps 110, 4; Heb 5, 6. 10; 7, 1.

24

who delivered your foes into your hand."

Then Abram gave him* a tenth of everything. *21*The king of Sodom said to Abram, "Give me the people; the goods you may keep." *22*But Abram replied to the king of Sodom: "I have sworn to the LORD, God Most High,* the creator of heaven and earth, *23*that I would not take so much as a thread or a sandal strap from anything that is yours, lest you should say, 'I made Abram rich.' *24*Nothing for me except what my servants have used up and the share that is due to the men who joined me—Aner, Eshcol and Mamre; let them take their share."

See RG 110–11

CHAPTER 15

The Covenant with Abram. *1*Some time after these events, this word of the LORD came to Abram in a vision:

"Fear not, Abram!
I am your shield;
I will make your reward very great."

*2*But Abram said, "O Lord GOD, what good will your gifts be, if I keep on being childless and have as my heir the steward of my house, Eliezer?" *3*Abram continued, "See, you have given me no offspring, and so one of my servants will be my heir." *4*Then the word of the LORD came to him: "No, that one shall not be your heir; your own issue shall be your heir."*d* *5*He took him outside and said, "Look up at the sky and count the stars, if you can. Just so," he added, "shall your descendants be."*e* *6f*Abram put his faith in the LORD, who credited it to him as an act of righteousness.*

*7*He then said to him, "I am the LORD who brought you from Ur of the Chaldeans to give you this land as a possession."*g* *8*"O Lord GOD," he asked, "how am I to know that I shall possess it?" *9*He answered him, "Bring me a three-year-old heifer, a three-year-old she-goat, a three-year-old* ram, a turtledove, and a young pigeon."*h* *10*He brought him all these, split them in two, and placed each half opposite the other; but the birds he did not cut up. *11*Birds of prey swooped down on the carcasses, but Abram stayed with them. *12*As the sun was about to set, a trance fell upon Abram, and a deep, terrifying darkness enveloped him.

*13*Then the LORD said to Abram: "Know for certain that your descendants shall be aliens in a land not their own, where they shall be enslaved and oppressed for four hundred years.*i* *14*But I will bring judgment on the nation they must serve, and in the end they will depart with great wealth.*j* *15*You, however, shall join your forefathers in peace; you shall be buried at a contented old age. *16*In the fourth time-span* the others shall come back here; the wickedness of the Amorites will not have reached its full measure until then."*k*

*17*When the sun had set and it was dark, there appeared a smoking brazier* and a flaming torch, which passed between those pieces. *18*It was on that occasion that the LORD made a covenant* with Abram, saying: "To your descendants I give this land, from the Wadi of Egypt to the Great River [the Euphrates],*l* *19m*the land of the Kenites, the Kenizzites, the Kadmonites, *20*the Hittites, the Perizzites, the Rephaim, *21*the Amorites, the Canaanites, the Girgashites, and the Jebusites."

14, 22: Abraham uses the name of the Canaanite god el-elyon ("God, the Most High") in apposition to the name of his God, Yahweh ("the LORD").

15, 6: Abraham's faith in God's promises was regarded as an act of righteousness, i.e., as expressing the "right" attitude of man toward God. In turn, God credited this to Abraham, i.e., gave him title to the fulfillment of God's promises. St. Paul (Rom 4, 1-25; Gal 3, 6-9) makes Abraham's faith a model for that of Christians.

15, 9: Three-year-old: ritually mature.

15, 16: Time-span: the Hebrew term dor is commonly rendered as "generation," but it may signify a period of varying length. Neither this passage nor the statement about the four hundred years has any value for determining how long the Israelites were in Egypt.

15, 17: Brazier: literally "oven"; a portable one is meant here. The smoke and fire represent God's presence. Although the text does not mention it, Abraham no doubt also walked between the split carcasses. For the meaning of this strange ceremony, see note on Jer 34, 18ff.

15, 18: Made a covenant: literally "cut a covenant"; the expression derives from the ceremony of cutting the animals in two.

d: Gn 17, 16. *e:* Gn 22, 17; 28, 14; Ex 32, 13; Dt 1, 10; Sir 44, 21; Rom 4, 18; Heb 11, 12. *f:* 1 Mc 2, 52; Rom 4, 3. 9. 22; Gal 3, 6f; Jas 2, 23. *g:* Gn 11, 31; 12, 1; Ex 32, 13; Neh 9, 7f; Acts 7, 2f. *h:* Lv 1, 14. *i:* Ex 12, 40; Nm 20, 15; Jdt 5, 9f; Is 52, 4; Acts 13, 20; Gal 3, 17. *j:* Ex 3, 8. 21f. *k:* 1 Kgs 21, 26. *l:* Ex 32, 13; Neh 9, 8; Ps 105, 11; Sir 44, 21. *m:* 19f: Dt 7, 1.

CHAPTER 16

See RG
110–11

Birth of Ishmael. [1]*Abram's wife Sarai had borne him no children. She had, however, an Egyptian maidservant named Hagar.[n] [2]Sarai said to Abram: "The LORD has kept me from bearing children. Have intercourse, then, with my maid; perhaps I shall have sons through her." Abram heeded Sarai's request.[o] [3]Thus, after Abram had lived ten years in the land of Canaan, his wife Sarai took her maid, Hagar the Egyptian, and gave her to her husband Abram to be his concubine. [4]He had intercourse with her, and she became pregnant. When she became aware of her pregnancy, she looked on her mistress with disdain.[p] [5q]So Sarai said to Abram: "You are responsible for this outrage against me. I myself gave my maid to your embrace; but ever since she became aware of her pregnancy, she has been looking on me with disdain. May the LORD decide between you and me!" [6]Abram told Sarai: "Your maid is in your power. Do to her whatever you please." Sarai then abused her so much that Hagar ran away from her.

[7]The LORD's messenger* found her by a spring in the wilderness, the spring on the road to Shur,[r] [8]and he asked, "Hagar, maid of Sarai, where have you come from and where are you going?" She answered, "I am running away from my mistress, Sarai." [9]But the LORD's messenger told her: "Go back to your mistress and submit to her abusive treatment. [10]I will make your descendants so numerous," added the LORD's messenger, "that they will be too many to count.[s] [11]Besides," the LORD's messenger said to her:

"You are now pregnant and shall bear a
    son;
    you shall name him Ishmael,*
    for the LORD has heard you,
        God has answered you.

[12] He shall be a wild ass of a man,
    his hand against everyone,
        and everyone's hand against him;
    in opposition to all his kin
        shall he encamp."[t]

[13]To the LORD who spoke to her she gave a name, saying, "You are the God of Vision";* she meant, "Have I really seen God and remained alive after my vision?"[u] [14]That is why the well is called Beer-lahai-roi.* It is between Kadesh and Bered.

[15]Hagar bore Abram a son, and Abram named the son whom Hagar bore him Ishmael.[v] [16]Abram was eighty-six years old when Hagar bore him Ishmael.

CHAPTER 17

See RG
110–11

Covenant of Circumcision. [1]When Abram was ninety-nine years old, the LORD appeared to him and said: "I am God the Almighty.* Walk in my presence and be blameless.[w] [2]Between you and me I will establish my covenant, and I will multiply you exceedingly."[x]

[3]When Abram prostrated himself, God continued to speak to him: [4]"My covenant with you is this: you are to become the father of a host of nations.[y] [5]No longer shall you be called Abram; your name shall be Abraham,* for I am making you the father of a host of nations.[z] [6]I will render you exceedingly fertile; I will make nations of you; kings shall stem from you. [7]I will maintain my covenant

---

16, 1-6: Sarah's actions are all in keeping with the laws of the time, as known from ancient extra-biblical sources.

16, 7: The LORD's messenger: a manifestation of God in human form; therefore in v 13 the messenger is identified with the Lord himself.

16, 11: Ishmael: in Hebrew the name means "God has heard."

16, 13: The God of Vision: in Hebrew, el-roi; hence the name of the spring. Remained alive: for the ancient notion that a person died on seeing God, cf Gn 32, 31; Ex 20, 19; Dt 4, 33; Jgs 13, 22.

16, 14: Beer-lahai-roi: probably "the well of living sight," i.e., the well where one can see (God) and yet live.

17, 1: The Almighty: traditional but incorrect rendering of the divine title shaddai, of uncertain meaning.

17, 5: Abram and Abraham are merely two forms of the same name, both meaning, "the father is exalted"; another variant form is Abiram (Nm 16, 1; 1 Kgs 16, 34). The additional -ha- in the form Abraham is explained by folk etymology as coming from ab-hamon goyim, "father of a host of nations."

n: Gn 11, 30. o: Gn 21, 8f; Gal 4, 22. p: 1 Sm 1, 6; Prv 30, 23. q: 5-16: Gn 21, 10-19. r: Ex 15, 22. s: Gn 17, 20; 21, 13. 18; 25, 12-18. t: Gn 21, 20; 25, 18. u: Gn 24, 62. v: Gn 16, 2; Gal 4, 22. w: Gn 35, 11; Ex 6, 3. x: Gn 12, 2; 13, 16; Ex 32, 13. y: Sir 44, 21; Rom 4, 17. z: Neh 9, 7.

with you and your descendants after you throughout the ages as an everlasting pact, to be your God and the God of your descendants after you.*a* *8*I will give to you and to your descendants after you the land in which you are now staying, the whole land of Canaan, as a permanent possession; and I will be their God."*b*

*9*God also said to Abraham: "On your part, you and your descendants after you must keep my covenant throughout the ages. *10*This is my covenant with you and your descendants after you that you must keep: every male among you shall be circumcised.*c* *11*Circumcise the flesh of your foreskin, and that shall be the mark of the covenant between you and me.*d* *12*Throughout the ages, every male among you, when he is eight days old, shall be circumcised, including houseborn slaves and those acquired with money from any foreigner who is not of your blood.*e* *13*Yes, both the houseborn slaves and those acquired with money must be circumcised. Thus my covenant shall be in your flesh as an everlasting pact. *14*If a male is uncircumcised, that is, if the flesh of his foreskin has not been cut away, such a one shall be cut off from his people; he has broken my covenant."

*15*God further said to Abraham: "As for your wife Sarai, do not call her Sarai; her name shall be Sarah.* *16*I will bless her, and I will give you a son by her. Him also will I bless; he shall give rise to nations, and rulers of peoples shall issue from him."*f* *17*Abraham prostrated himself and laughed* as he said to himself, "Can a child be born to a man who is a hundred years old? Or can Sarah give birth at ninety?"*g* *18*Then Abraham said to God, "Let but Ishmael live on by your favor!" *19*God replied: "Nevertheless, your wife Sarah is to bear you a son, and you shall call him Isaac. I will maintain my covenant with him as an everlasting pact, to be

his God and the God of his descendants after him.*h* *20*As for Ishmael, I am heeding you: I hereby bless him. I will make him fertile and will multiply him exceedingly. He shall become the father of twelve chieftains, and I will make of him a great nation.*i* *21*But my covenant I will maintain with Isaac, whom Sarah shall bear to you by this time next year."*j* *22*When he had finished speaking with him, God departed from Abraham.

*23*Then Abraham took his son Ishmael and all his slaves, whether born in his house or acquired with his money—every male among the members of Abraham's household—and he circumcised the flesh of their foreskins on that same day, as God had told him to do. *24*Abraham was ninety-nine years old when the flesh of his foreskin was circumcised,*k* *25*and his son Ishmael was thirteen years old when the flesh of his foreskin was circumcised. *26*Thus, on that same day Abraham and his son Ishmael were circumcised; *27*and all the male members of his household, including the slaves born in his house or acquired with his money from foreigners, were circumcised with him.

CHAPTER 18

See RG 110–11

Abraham's Visitors. *1*The LORD appeared to Abraham by the terebinth of Mamre, as he sat in the entrance of his tent, while the day was growing hot. *2*Looking up, he saw three men standing nearby. When he saw them, he ran from the entrance of the tent to greet them; and bowing to the ground,*l* *3*he said: "Sir,* if I may ask you this favor, please do not go on past your servant. *4*Let some water be brought, that you may bathe your feet, and then rest yourselves under the tree. *5*Now that you have come this close to your servant, let me bring you a little food, that you may refresh yourselves; and afterward you may go on your way." "Very well," they replied, "do as you have said."

17, 15: Sarai and Sarah are variant forms of the same name, both meaning "princess."

17, 17: Laughed: yishaq, which is the Hebrew form of the name "Isaac"; other similar explanations of the name are given in Gn 18, 12 and 21, 6.

18, 3: Abraham addresses the leader of the group, whom he does not yet recognize as Yahweh; in the next two verses he speaks to all three men. The other two are later

(Gn 19, 1) identified as messengers.

a: Ps 105, 42; Lk 1, 72f; Gal 3, 16. *b:* Ex 32, 13; Dt 1, 8; 14, 2; Lk 1, 55; Acts 7, 5. *c:* Jn 7, 22; Acts 7, 8; Rom 4, 11. *d:* Sir 44, 21. *e:* Lv 12, 3; Lk 1, 59; 2, 21. *f:* Gn 18, 10; Gal 4, 23. *g:* Rom 4, 19; Heb 11, 11f. *h:* Gn 11, 30; 21, 2; Ex 32, 13; Sir 44, 22. *i:* Gn 16, 10; 21, 13. 18; 25, 12-16. *j:* Gn 18, 14; 21, 2; 26, 2-5; Rom 9, 7. *k:* Gn 17, 10; Rom 4, 11. *l:* Heb 13, 1f.

6 Abraham hastened into the tent and told Sarah, "Quick, three seahs* of fine flour! Knead it and make rolls." 7 He ran to the herd, picked out a tender, choice steer, and gave it to a servant, who quickly prepared it. 8 Then he got some curds* and milk, as well as the steer that had been prepared, and set these before them; and he waited on them under the tree while they ate.

9 "Where is your wife Sarah?" they asked him. "There in the tent," he replied. 10 One of them* said, "I will surely return to you about this time next year, and Sarah will then have a son." Sarah was listening at the entrance of the tent, just behind him.m 11 Now Abraham and Sarah were old, advanced in years, and Sarah had stopped having her womanly periods.n 12 So Sarah laughed* to herself and said, "Now that I am so withered and my husband is so old, am I still to have sexual pleasure?" 13 But the LORD said to Abraham: "Why did Sarah laugh and say, 'Shall I really bear a child, old as I am?' 14 Is anything too marvelous for the LORD to do? At the appointed time, about this time next year, I will return to you, and Sarah will have a son."o 15 Because she was afraid, Sarah dissembled, saying, "I didn't laugh." But he said, "Yes you did."

Abraham Intercedes for Sodom. 16 The men set out from there and looked down toward Sodom; Abraham was walking with them, to see them on their way. 17 The LORD reflected: "Shall I hide from Abraham what I am about to do, 18 now that he is to become a great and populous nation, and all the nations of the earth are to find blessing in him?p 19 Indeed, I have singled him out that he may direct his sons and his posterity to keep the way of the LORD by doing what is right and just, so that the LORD may carry into effect for Abraham the promises he made about him." 20q Then the LORD said: "The outcry against Sodom and Gomorrah is so great, and their sin so grave,* 21 that I must go down and see whether or not their actions fully correspond to the cry against them that comes to me. I mean to find out."

22 While the two men walked on farther toward Sodom, the LORD remained standing before Abraham. 23 Then Abraham drew nearer to him and said: "Will you sweep away the innocent with the guilty? 24 Suppose there were fifty innocent people in the city; would you wipe out the place, rather than spare it for the sake of the fifty innocent people within it? 25 Far be it from you to do such a thing, to make the innocent die with the guilty, so that the innocent and the guilty would be treated alike! Should not the judge of all the world act with justice?"r 26 The LORD replied, "If I find fifty innocent people in the city of Sodom, I will spare the whole place for their sake." 27 Abraham spoke up again: "See how I am presuming to speak to my Lord, though I am but dust and ashes!s 28 What if there are five less than fifty innocent people? Will you destroy the whole city because of those five?" "I will not destroy it," he answered, "if I find forty-five there." 29 But Abraham persisted, saying, "What if only forty are found there?" He replied, "I will forbear doing it for the sake of the forty." 30 Then he said, "Let not my Lord grow impatient if I go on. What if only thirty are found there?" He replied, "I will forbear doing it if I can find but thirty there." 31 Still he went on, "Since I have thus dared to speak to my Lord, what if there are no more than twenty?" "I will not destroy it," he answered, "for the sake of the twenty." 32 But he still

18, 6: Three seahs: one ephah, about half a bushel.

18, 8: Curds: a type of soft cheese or yoghurt.

18, 10: One of them: i.e., the Lord. Abraham now realizes this for the first time when he hears the prediction of a miraculous birth. About this time next year: literally "when the time becomes alive," i.e., at the time when birth is due after the period of gestation; the conception is understood as taking place soon after the prediction.

18, 12: Sarah laughed: see note on Gn 17, 17.

18, 20: Israelite tradition was unanimous in ascribing the destruction of Sodom and Gomorrah to the wickedness of these cities, but tradition varied in regard to the nature of this wickedness. According to the present account of the Yahwist, the sin of Sodom was homosexuality (Gn 19, 4f), which is therefore also known as sodomy; but according to Isaiah (1, 9f; 3, 9), it was a lack of social justice; Ezekiel (16, 46-51) described it as a disregard for the poor, whereas Jeremiah (23, 14) saw it as general immorality.

m: Gn 17, 19; 21, 1; 2 Kgs 4, 16; Rom 9, 9. n: Gn 17, 17; Rom 4, 19; Heb 11, 11f. o: Mt 19, 26; Mk 10, 27; Lk 1, 37; 18, 27; Rom 4, 21. p: Lk 1, 55. q: Gn 19, 13; Is 3, 9; Lk 17, 28; Jude 1, 7. r: Dt 32, 4; Jb 8, 3. 20; Wis 12, 15. s: Sir 10, 9; 17, 27.

persisted, "Please, let not my Lord grow angry if I speak up this last time. What if there are at least ten there?" "For the sake of those ten," he replied, "I will not destroy it."[t]

[33]The LORD departed as soon as he had finished speaking with Abraham, and Abraham returned home.

CHAPTER 19

See RG 110–11

Destruction of Sodom and Gomorrah. [1]The two angels reached Sodom in the evening, as Lot was sitting at the gate of Sodom. When Lot saw them, he got up to greet them; and bowing down with his face to the ground, [2]he said, "Please, gentlemen,* come aside into your servant's house for the night, and bathe your feet; you can get up early to continue your journey." But they replied, "No, we shall pass the night in the town square."[u] [3]He urged them so strongly, however, that they turned aside to his place and entered his house. He prepared a meal for them, baking cakes without leaven, and they dined.

[4v]Before they went to bed, all the townsmen of Sodom, both young and old—all the people to the last man—closed in on the house. [5]They called to Lot and said to him, "Where are the men who came to your house tonight? Bring them out to us that we may have intimacies with them." [6]Lot went out to meet them at the entrance. When he had shut the door behind him, [7]he said, "I beg you, my brothers, not to do this wicked thing. [8]I have two daughters who have never had intercourse with men. Let me bring them out to you, and you may do to them as you please. But don't do anything to these men, for you know they have come under the shelter of my roof." [9]They replied, "Stand back! This fellow," they sneered, "came here as an immigrant, and now he dares to give

orders! We'll treat you worse than them!" With that, they pressed hard against Lot, moving in closer to break down the door.[w] [10]But his guests put out their hands, pulled Lot inside with them, and closed the door; [11]at the same time they struck the men at the entrance of the house, one and all, with such a blinding light* that they were utterly unable to reach the doorway.

[12]Then the angels said to Lot: "Who else belongs to you here? Your sons [sons-in-law]* and your daughters and all who belong to you in the city—take them away from it![x] [13]We are about to destroy this place, for the outcry reaching the LORD against those in the city is so great that he has sent us to destroy it."[y] [14]So Lot went out and spoke to his sons-in-law, who had contracted marriage with his daughters.* "Get up and leave this place," he told them; "the LORD is about to destroy the city." But his sons-in-law thought he was joking.

[15]As dawn was breaking, the angels urged Lot on, saying, "On your way! Take with you your wife and your two daughters who are here, or you will be swept away in the punishment of the city." [16]When he hesitated, the men, by the LORD's mercy, seized his hand and the hands of his wife and his two daughters and led them to safety outside the city. [17]As soon as they had been brought outside, he was told: "Flee for your life! Don't look back or stop anywhere on the Plain. Get off to the hills at once, or you will be swept away."[z] [18]"Oh, no, my lord!" replied Lot. [19]"You have already thought enough of your servant to do me the great kindness of intervening to save my life. But I cannot flee to the hills to keep the disaster from overtaking me, and so I shall die. [20]Look, this town ahead is near enough to escape to. It's only a small place.* Let me

---

19, 2: Gentlemen: Lot does not yet know that the distinguished-looking men are God's messengers; cf Gn 18, 3.

19, 11: Blinding light: a preternatural flash that temporarily dazed the wicked men and revealed to Lot the true nature of his guests.

19, 12: Since Lot apparently had no sons, a glossator interpreted the term to mean sons-in-law.

19, 14: It is uncertain whether Lot's sons-in-law were fully married to his daughters or only "engaged" to them (Israelite "engagement" was the first part of the marriage cere-

mony), or even whether the daughters involved were the same as, or different from, the two daughters who were still in their father's house.

19, 20: A small place: the Hebrew word misar, literally "a little thing," has the same root consonants as the name of the town Zoar in v 22.

t: Jer 5, 1; Ez 22, 30. *u:* Wis 10, 6; Sir 16, 8; Ez 16, 50; Heb 13, 1f. *v:* 4-9; Jgs 19, 22-25; Jude 1, 7. *w:* Gn 13, 12; 2 Pt 2, 7f. *x:* 2 Pt 7, 9. *y:* Is 1, 7. 9; Zep 2, 9; Lk 17, 29. *z:* Wis 10, 6.

flee there—it's a small place, isn't it?—that my life may be saved." *21*"Well, then," he replied, "I will also grant you the favor you now ask. I will not overthrow the town you speak of. *22*Hurry, escape there! I cannot do anything until you arrive there." That is why the town is called Zoar.*a*

*23*The sun was just rising over the earth as Lot arrived in Zoar;*b* *24*at the same time the LORD rained down sulphurous fire upon Sodom and Gomorrah [from the LORD out of heaven].*c* *25*He overthrew* those cities and the whole Plain, together with the inhabitants of the cities and the produce of the soil.*d* *26*But Lot's wife looked back, and she was turned into a pillar of salt.*e*

*27*Early the next morning Abraham went to the place where he had stood in the LORD's presence. *28*As he looked down toward Sodom and Gomorrah and the whole region of the Plain,* he saw dense smoke over the land rising like fumes from a furnace.*f*

*29*Thus it came to pass: when God destroyed the Cities of the Plain, he was mindful of Abraham by sending Lot away from the upheaval by which God overthrew the cities where Lot had been living.

Moabites and Ammonites.* *30*Since Lot was afraid to stay in Zoar, he and his two daughters went up from Zoar and settled in the hill country, where he lived with his two daughters in a cave. *31*The older one said to the younger: "Our father is getting old, and there is not a man on earth to unite with us as was the custom everywhere. *32*Come, let us ply our father with wine and then lie with him, that we may have offspring by our father." *33*So that night they plied their father with wine, and the older one went in and lay

with her father; but he was not aware of her lying down or her getting up. *34*Next day the older one said to the younger: "Last night it was I who lay with my father. Let us ply him with wine again tonight, and then you go in and lie with him, that we may both have offspring by our father." *35*So that night, too, they plied their father with wine, and then the younger one went in and lay with him; but again he was not aware of her lying down or her getting up.

*36*Thus both of Lot's daughters became pregnant by their father. *37*The older one gave birth to a son whom she named Moab, saying, "From my father."* He is the ancestor of the Moabites of today.*g* *38*The younger one, too, gave birth to a son, and she named him Ammon, saying, "The son of my kin."* He is the ancestor of the Ammonites of today.*h*

CHAPTER 20

See RG 110-11

Abraham at Gerar.* *1*Abraham journeyed on to the region of the Negeb, where he settled between Kadesh and Shur. While he stayed in Gerar, *2*he said of his wife Sarah, "She is my sister." So Abimelech, king of Gerar, sent and took Sarah. *3*But God came to Abimelech in a dream one night and said to him, "You are about to die because of the woman you have taken, for she has a husband." *4*Abimelech, who had not approached her, said: "O Lord, would you slay a man even though he is innocent? *5*He himself told me, 'She is my sister,' and she herself also stated, 'He is my brother.' I did it in good faith and with clean hands." *6*God answered him in the dream: "Yes, I know you did it in good faith. In fact, it was I who kept you from sinning against me; that is why I

19, 25: Overthrew: the consistent use of this term, literally "turned upside down," to describe the destruction of the Cities of the Plain seems to imply that their upheaval (v 29) was caused primarily by an earthquake; this would naturally be accompanied by a disastrous fire, especially in a region containing bitumen (Gn 14, 10) and its accompanying gases.

19, 28f: From the height east of Hebron, Abraham could easily see the region at the southern end of the Dead Sea, where the Cities of the Plain were probably located.

19, 30-38: This Israelite tale about the origin of Israel's neighbors east of the Jordan and the Dead Sea was told partly to ridicule these racially related but rival nations and partly to give folk etymologies for their names.

19, 37: From my father: in Hebrew, meabi, similar in sound to the name "Moab."

19, 38: The son of my kin: in Hebrew, ben-ammi, similar in sound to the name "Ammonites."

20, 1-18: This story from the Elohist source (see note on Gn 4, 25) combines elements found in the two very similar but distinct stories of the Yahwist source in Gn 12, 10-20 and 26, 6-11.

a: Wis 10, 6.   *b:* Pss 9, 6; 11, 6; 107, 34.   *c:* Wis 10, 7; Is 1, 9; 13, 19; Lam 4, 6; 17, 29; 2 Pt 2, 6.   *d:* Dt 29, 22; Jer 50, 40; Am 4, 11.   *e:* Wis 10, 7; Lk 17, 32.   *f:* Rv 9, 2; 14, 10f.   *g:* Dt 2, 9.   *h:* Dt 2, 19.

did not let you touch her. [7]Therefore, return the man's wife—as a spokesman* he will intercede for you—that your life may be saved. If you do not return her, you can be sure that you and all who are yours will certainly die."

[8]Early the next morning Abimelech called all his court officials and informed them of everything that had happened, and the men were horrified. [9]Then Abimelech summoned Abraham and said to him: "How could you do this to us! What wrong did I do to you that you should have brought such monstrous guilt on me and my kingdom? You have treated me in an intolerable way. [10]What were you afraid of," he asked him, "that you should have done such a thing?" [11]"I was afraid," answered Abraham, "because I thought there would surely be no fear of God in this place, and so they would kill me on account of my wife. [12]Besides, she is in truth my sister, but only my father's daughter, not my mother's; and so she became my wife.[i] [13]When God sent me wandering from my father's house, I asked her: 'Would you do me this favor? In whatever place we come to, say that I am your brother.' "

[14]Then Abimelech took flocks and herds and male and female slaves and gave them to Abraham; and after he restored his wife Sarah to him, [15]he said, "Here, my land lies at your disposal; settle wherever you please." [16]To Sarah he said: "See, I have given your brother a thousand shekels of silver.* Let that serve you as a vindication before all who are with you; your honor has been preserved with everyone." [17]Abraham then interceded with God, and God restored health to Abimelech, that is, to his wife and his maidservants, so that they could bear children; [18]for God had tightly closed every womb in Abimelech's household on account of Abraham's wife Sarah.

CHAPTER 21

See RG 110-11

Birth of Isaac. [1]The LORD took note of Sarah as he had said he would; he did for her as he had promised.[j] [2]Sarah became pregnant and bore Abraham a son in his old age, at the set time that God had stated.[k] [3]Abraham gave the name Isaac to this son of his whom Sarah bore him.[l] [4]When his son Isaac was eight days old, Abraham circumcised him, as God had commanded.[m] [5]Abraham was a hundred years old when his son Isaac was born to him. [6]Sarah then said, "God has given me cause to laugh, and all who hear of it will laugh with me.[n] [7]Who would have told Abraham," she added, "that Sarah would nurse children! Yet I have borne him a son in his old age." [8]Isaac grew, and on the day of the child's weaning Abraham held a great feast.

[9]*Sarah noticed the son whom Hagar the Egyptian had borne to Abraham playing with her son Isaac; [10]so she demanded of Abraham: "Drive out that slave and her son! No son of that slave is going to share the inheritance with my son Isaac!"[o] [11]Abraham was greatly distressed, especially on account of his son Ishmael. [12]But God said to Abraham: "Do not be distressed about the boy or about your slave woman. Heed the demands of Sarah, no matter what she is asking of you; for it is through Isaac that descendants shall bear your name.[p] [13]As for the son of the slave woman, I will make a great nation of him also, since he too is your offspring."

[14]Early the next morning Abraham got some bread and a skin of water and gave them to Hagar. Then, placing the child on her back,* he sent her away. As she roamed

---

20, 7: Spokesman: the Hebrew term nabi used here is regularly translated as "prophet," but it simply means "one who speaks on behalf of another," whether the latter is God, as in almost all cases, or another man, as in Ex 4, 16.

20, 16: A thousand shekels of silver: not a gift distinct from that of the animals and the slaves (v 14), but the monetary value of these.

21, 9-19: This story of Hagar's expulsion, in the Elohist source, is in general a duplicate of the one from the Yahwist source in Gn 16, 5-14; but the two stories differ greatly in detail.

21, 14: Placing the child on her back: the phrase is translated from an emended form of the Hebrew text. In the current faulty Hebrew text, Abraham put the bread and the waterskin on Hagar's back, while her son apparently walked beside her. This reading seems to be a scribal attempt at harmonizing the present passage with the data of the Priestly source, in which Ishmael would have been at least fourteen

i: Gn 12, 13.   *j:* Gn 17, 19; 18, 10.   *k:* Gal 4, 23; Heb 11, 11.
l: Mt 1, 2; Lk 3, 34.   *m:* Gn 17, 10ff; Acts 7, 8.   *n:* Gn 17, 17.
o: Jgs 11, 2; Gal 4, 30.   *p:* Rom 9, 7; Heb 11, 18.

aimlessly in the wilderness of Beer-sheba, [15]the water in the skin was used up. So she put the child down under a shrub, [16]and then went and sat down opposite him, about a bowshot away; for she said to herself, "Let me not watch to see the child die." As she sat opposite him, he began to cry. [17]God heard the boy's cry, and God's messenger called to Hagar from heaven: "What is the matter, Hagar? Don't be afraid; God has heard the boy's cry in this plight of his.[q] [18]Arise, lift up the boy and hold him by the hand; for I will make of him a great nation." [19]Then God opened her eyes, and she saw a well of water. She went and filled the skin with water, and then let the boy drink.

[20]God was with the boy as he grew up. He lived in the wilderness and became an expert bowman, [21]with his home in the wilderness of Paran. His mother got a wife for him from the land of Egypt.

The Pact at Beer-sheba. [22]About that time Abimelech, accompanied by Phicol, the commander of his army,* said to Abraham: "God is with you in everything you do. [23]Therefore, swear to me by God at this place* that you will not deal falsely with me or with my progeny and posterity, but will act as loyally toward me and the land in which you stay as I have acted toward you." [24]To this Abraham replied, "I so swear."

[25]Abraham, however, reproached Abimelech about a well that Abimelech's men had seized by force. [26]"I have no idea who did that," Abimelech replied. "In fact, you never told me about it, nor did I ever hear of it until now."

[27]Then Abraham took sheep and cattle and gave them to Abimelech and the two made a pact. [28]Abraham also set apart seven ewe lambs of the flock, [29]and Abimelech asked him, "What is the purpose of these seven ewe lambs that you have set apart?" [30]Abraham answered, "The seven ewe lambs you shall accept from me that thus I may have your acknowledgment that the well was dug by me." [31]This is why the place is called Beer-sheba;* the two of them took an oath there. [32]When they had thus made the pact in Beer-sheba, Abimelech, along with Phicol, the commander of his army, left and returned to the land of the Philistines.

[33]Abraham planted a tamarisk at Beer-sheba, and there he invoked by name the LORD, God the Eternal.* [34]Abraham resided in the land of the Philistines for many years.

CHAPTER 22

See RG 110–11

The Testing of Abraham. [1]Some time after these events, God put Abraham to the test.* He called to him, "Abraham!" "Ready!" he replied.[r] [2]Then God said: "Take your son Isaac, your only one,† whom you love, and go to the land of Moriah. There you shall offer him up as a holocaust on a height that I will point out to you."[s] [3]Early the next morning Abraham saddled his donkey, took with him his son Isaac, and two of his servants as well, and with the wood that he had cut for the holocaust, set out for the place of which God had told him.

[4]On the third day Abraham got sight of the place from afar. [5]Then he said to his servants: "Both of you stay here with the donkey, while the boy and I go on over yonder. We will worship and then come back to you." [6]Thereupon Abraham took the wood for the holocaust and laid it on his son Isaac's shoul-

---

years old when Isaac was born; compare Gn 16, 16 with 21, 5; cf 17, 25. But in the present Elohist story Ishmael is obviously a little boy, not much older than Isaac; cf vv 15, 18.

21, 22: Here and in v 32 the Greek text has ". . . Abimelech, accompanied by Ahuzzath, his councilor, and Phicol . . ."; but this is probably a secondary harmonization with Gn 26, 26. Abimelech took Phicol with him in order to intimidate Abraham by a show of strength.

21, 23: This place: Beer-sheba (v 31). Abimelech had come from Gerar (Gn 20, 2), about thirty miles west of Beer-sheba.

21, 31: Beer-sheba: the Hebrew name really means "the well of the seven," i.e., the place where there are seven wells,

alluded to in the episode of the seven ewe lambs, vv 28ff; but it can also be interpreted to mean "the well of the oath."

21, 33: God the Eternal: in Hebrew, el olam, perhaps the name of the deity of the pre-Israelite sanctuary at Beer-sheba, but used by Abraham merely as a title of Yahweh; cf Is 40, 28.

22, 1: God put Abraham to the test: to prove the firmness of Abraham's faith in God's promise that through Isaac all the nations of the earth would find blessing; cf Gn 18, 10. 18; 21, 12.

22, 2: Only one: uniquely precious, especially loved; therefore the same term is rendered in vv 12. 16 as "beloved."

q: Gn 16, 7.   *r:* Sir 44, 20.   *s:* 2 Chr 3, 1; 1 Mc 2, 52; Heb 11, 17.

ders, while he himself carried the fire and the knife. [7]As the two walked on together, Isaac spoke to his father Abraham: "Father!" he said. "Yes, son," he replied. Isaac continued, "Here are the fire and the wood, but where is the sheep for the holocaust?" [8]"Son," Abraham answered, "God himself will provide the sheep for the holocaust." Then the two continued going forward.

[9]When they came to the place of which God had told him, Abraham built an altar there and arranged the wood on it. Next he tied up his son Isaac, and put him on top of the wood on the altar.[t] [10]Then he reached out and took the knife to slaughter his son.[u] [11]But the LORD's messenger called to him from heaven, "Abraham, Abraham!" "Yes, Lord," he answered. [12]"Do not lay your hand on the boy," said the messenger. "Do not do the least thing to him. I know now how devoted you are to God, since you did not withhold from me your own beloved son."[v] [13]As Abraham looked about, he spied a ram caught by its horns in the thicket. So he went and took the ram and offered it up as a holocaust in place of his son. [14]Abraham named the site Yahweh-yireh;* hence people now say, "On the mountain the LORD will see."

[15]Again the LORD's messenger called to Abraham from heaven [16w]and said: "I swear by myself, declares the LORD, that because you acted as you did in not withholding from me your beloved son, [17]I will bless you abundantly and make your descendants as countless as the stars of the sky and the sands of the seashore; your descendants shall take possession of the gates of their enemies,[x] [18]and in your descendants all the nations of the earth shall find blessing—all this because you obeyed my command."[y]

[19]Abraham then returned to his servants, and they set out together for Beer-sheba, where Abraham made his home.

*Nahor's Descendants.** [20]Some time afterward, the news came to Abraham: "Milcah too has borne sons, to your brother Nahor: [21]Uz, his first-born, his brother Buz, Kemuel (the father of Aram), [22]Chesed, Hazo, Pildash, Jidlaph and Bethuel." [23]Bethuel became the father of Rebekah. These eight Milcah bore to Abraham's brother Nahor. [24]His concubine, whose name was Reumah, also bore children: Tebah, Gaham, Tahash and Maacah.

CHAPTER 23

See RG 110-11

Purchase of a Burial Place. [1]The span of Sarah's life was one hundred and twenty-seven years. [2]She died in Kiriath-arba (that is, Hebron) in the land of Canaan, and Abraham performed the customary mourning rites for her. [3]Then he left the side of his dead one and addressed the Hittites:* [4]"Although I am a resident alien* among you, sell me from your holdings a piece of property for a burial ground, that I may bury my dead wife."[z] [5]The Hittites answered Abraham: "Please, sir, [6]listen to us! You are an elect of God among us. Bury your dead in the choicest of our burial sites. None of us would deny you his burial ground for the burial of your dead." [7]Abraham, however, began to bow low before the local citizens, the Hittites, [8]while he appealed to them: "If you will allow me room for burial of my dead, listen to me! Intercede for me with Ephron, son of Zohar, asking him [9]to sell me the cave of Machpelah that he owns; it is at the edge of his field. Let him sell it to me in your presence, at its full price, for a burial place."

22, 14: Yahweh-yireh: a Hebrew expression meaning "the Lord will see"; the reference is to the words in v 8, "God himself will see to it."

22, 20-24: A list of Aramean tribes who lived to the east and northeast of Israel, twelve in number, like the twelve tribes of Israel (Gn 35, 23) and the twelve tribes of Ishmael (Gn 25, 12-16).

23, 3: The Hittites: a non-Semitic people in Canaan; their relationship to the well-known Hittites of Asia Minor is uncertain.

23, 4: A resident alien: literally "a sojourner and a settler," i.e., a long-term resident alien. Such a one would normally

not have the right to own property. The importance of Abraham's purchase of the field in Machpelah, which is worded in technical legal terms, lies in the fact that it gave his descendants their first, though small, land rights in the country that God had promised the patriarch they would one day inherit as their own. Abraham therefore insists on purchasing the field and not receiving it as a gift.

t: Jas 2, 21. *u:* Wis 10, 5. *v:* Rom 8, 32; 1 Jn 4, 9. *w:* 16f: Gn 15, 5; Ex 32, 13; Lk 1, 73; Rom 4, 13; Heb 6, 13f; 11, 12. *x:* Gn 24, 60. *y:* Gn 12, 3; 18, 18; 26, 4; Sir 44, 21; Acts 3, 25; Gal 3, 16. *z:* Gn 33, 19; Acts 7, 16; Heb 11, 9.

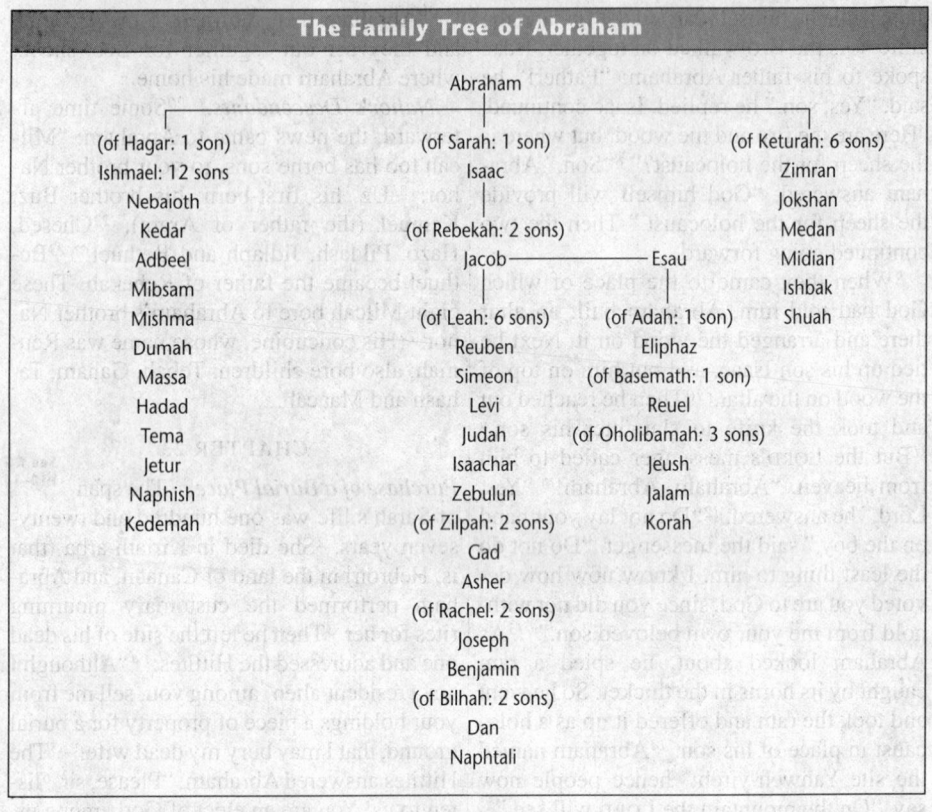

The Family Tree of Abraham

Abraham

(of Hagar: 1 son)	(of Sarah: 1 son)	(of Keturah: 6 sons)
Ishmael: 12 sons	Isaac	Zimran
Nebaioth		Jokshan
Kedar	(of Rebekah: 2 sons)	Medan
Adbeel	Jacob ——————— Esau	Midian
Mibsam		Ishbak
Mishma	(of Leah: 6 sons)	(of Adah: 1 son)	Shuah
Dumah	Reuben	Eliphaz
Massa	Simeon	(of Basemath: 1 son)
Hadad	Levi	Reuel
Tema	Judah	(of Oholibamah: 3 sons)
Jetur	Isaachar	Jeush
Naphish	Zebulun	Jalam
Kedemah	(of Zilpah: 2 sons)	Korah
	Gad	
	Asher	
	(of Rachel: 2 sons)	
	Joseph	
	Benjamin	
	(of Bilhah: 2 sons)	
	Dan	
	Naphtali	

[10]Now Ephron was present with the Hittites. So Ephron the Hittite replied to Abraham in the hearing of the Hittites who sat on his town council:* [11]"Please, sir, listen to me! I give you both the field and the cave in it; in the presence of my kinsmen I make this gift. Bury your dead!" [12]But Abraham, after bowing low before the local citizens, addressed Ephron in the hearing of these men: [13]"Ah, if only you would please listen to me! I will pay you the price of the field. Accept it from me, that I may bury my dead there." [14]Ephron replied to Abraham, "Please, [15]sir, listen to me! A piece of land worth four hundred shekels* of silver—what is that between you and me, as long as you can bury your dead?" [16a]Abraham accepted Ephron's terms; he weighed out to him the silver that Ephron had stipulated in the hearing of the Hittites, four hundred shekels of silver at the current market value.*

[17b]Thus Ephron's field in Machpelah, facing Mamre, together with its cave and all the trees anywhere within its limits, was conveyed [18]to Abraham by purchase in the presence of all the Hittites who sat on Ephron's town council. [19]After this transaction, Abraham buried his wife Sarah in the cave of the field of Machpelah, facing Mamre (that is, Hebron) in the land of Canaan. [20]Thus the field with its cave was transferred from the Hittites to Abraham as a burial place.

23, 10: Who sat on his town council: probable meaning of the literal translation, "who came in at the gate of his city"; so also in v 18.

23, 15: Four hundred shekels: probably an exorbitant sum; Jeremiah (32, 9) paid only seventeen shekels for his field in Anathoth, though the Babylonian invasion no doubt helped to reduce the price.

23, 16: The current market value: the standard weight called a shekel varied according to time and place.

a: Acts 7, 16.   b: 17f: Gn 49, 29f.

CHAPTER 24

See RG 111–12

Isaac and Rebekah. [1]Abraham had now reached a ripe old age, and the LORD had blessed him in every way. [2c]Abraham said to the senior servant of his household, who had charge of all his possessions: "Put your hand under my thigh,* [3]and I will make you swear by the LORD, the God of heaven and the God of earth, that you will not procure a wife for my son from the daughters of the Canaanites among whom I live,[d] [4]but that you will go to my own land and to my kindred to get a wife for my son Isaac." [5]The servant asked him: "What if the woman is unwilling to follow me to this land? Should I then take your son back to the land from which you migrated?" [6]"Never take my son back there for any reason," Abraham told him. [7]"The LORD, the God of heaven, who took me from my father's house and the land of my kin, and who confirmed by oath the promise he then made to me, 'I will give this land to your descendants'—he will send his messenger before you, and you will obtain a wife for my son there.[e] [8]If the woman is unwilling to follow you, you will be released from this oath. But never take my son back there!" [9]So the servant put his hand under the thigh of his master Abraham and swore to him in this undertaking.

[10]The servant then took ten of his master's camels, and bearing all kinds of gifts from his master, he made his way to the city of Nahor* in Aram Naharaim. [11]Near evening, at the time when women go out to draw water, he made the camels kneel by the well outside the city. [12]Then he prayed: "LORD, God of my master Abraham, let it turn out favorably for me* today and thus deal graciously with my master Abraham. [13]While I stand here at the spring and the daughters of the townsmen are coming out to draw water, [14]if I say to a girl, 'Please lower your jug, that I may drink,' and she answers, 'Take a drink, and let me give water to your camels, too,' let her be the one whom you have decided upon for your servant Isaac. In this way I shall know that you have dealt graciously with my master."

[15]He had scarcely finished these words when Rebekah (who was born to Bethuel, son of Milcah, the wife of Abraham's brother Nahor) came out with a jug on her shoulder. [16]The girl was very beautiful, a virgin, untouched by man. She went down to the spring and filled her jug. As she came up, [17]the servant ran toward her and said, "Please give me a sip of water from your jug." [18]"Take a drink, sir," she replied, and quickly lowering the jug onto her hand, she gave him a drink. [19]When she had let him drink his fill, she said, "I will draw water for your camels, too, until they have drunk their fill." [20]With that, she quickly emptied her jug into the drinking trough and ran back to the well to draw more water, until she had drawn enough for all the camels. [21]The man watched her the whole time, silently waiting to learn whether or not the LORD had made his errand successful. [22]When the camels had finished drinking, the man took out a gold ring weighing half a shekel, which he fastened on her nose, and two gold bracelets weighing ten shekels, which he put on her wrists. [23]Then he asked her: "Whose daughter are you? Tell me, please. And is there room in your father's house for us to spend the night?" [24]She answered: "I am the daughter of Bethuel the son of Milcah, whom she bore to Nahor. [25]There is plenty of straw and fodder at our place," she added, "and room to spend the night." [26]The man then bowed down in worship to the LORD, [27]saying: "Blessed be the LORD, the God of my master Abraham, who has not let his

---

24, 2: Put your hand under my thigh: the symbolism of this act was apparently connected with the Hebrew concept of children issuing from their father's "thigh" (Gn 46, 26; Ex 1, 5). Perhaps the man who took such an oath was thought to bring the curse of sterility on himself if he did not fulfill his sworn promise. Jacob made Joseph swear in the same way (Gn 47, 29). In both these instances, the oath was taken to carry out the last request of a man upon his death.

24, 10: Nahor: it is uncertain whether this is to be under-

stood as the name of Abraham's brother (Gn 11, 27), Rebekah's grandfather (Gn 24, 15), or the city of the same name (as known from the Mari documents); Aram Naharaim, situated near Haran (Gn 11, 31) in northern Mesopotamia.

24, 12: Let it turn out favorably for me: let me have a favorable omen; cf end of v 14.

c: 2f: Gn 47, 29. d: Gn 24, 37; 28, 1f; Jgs 14, 3; Tb 4, 12. e: Gn 12, 7; Ex 6, 8; Tb 5, 17; Gal 3, 16. f: Gn 22, 23.

constant kindness toward my master fail. As for myself also, the LORD has led me straight to the house of my master's brother."

²⁸Then the girl ran off and told her mother's household about it. ²⁹ᵍNow Rebekah had a brother named Laban. ³⁰As soon as he saw the ring and the bracelets on his sister Rebekah and heard her words about what the man had said to her, Laban rushed outside to the man at the spring. When he reached him, he was still standing by the camels at the spring. ³¹So he said to him: "Come, blessed of the LORD! Why are you staying outside when I have made the house ready for you, as well as a place for the camels?" ³²The man then went inside; and while the camels were being unloaded and provided with straw and fodder, water was brought to bathe his feet and the feet of the men who were with him. ³³But when the table was set for him, he said, "I will not eat until I have told my tale." "Do so," they replied.

³⁴"I am Abraham's servant," he began. ³⁵"The LORD has blessed my master so abundantly that he has become a wealthy man; he has given him flocks and herds, silver and gold, male and female slaves, and camels and asses. ³⁶My master's wife Sarah bore a son to my master in her old age, and he has given him everything he owns. ³⁷My master put me under oath, saying: 'You shall not procure a wife for my son among the daughters of the Canaanites in whose land I live; ³⁸instead, you shall go to my father's house, to my own relatives, to get a wife for my son.' ³⁹When I asked my master, 'What if the woman will not follow me?' ⁴⁰he replied: 'The LORD, in whose presence I have always walked, will send his messenger with you and make your errand successful, and so you will get a wife for my son from my own kindred of my father's house.ʰ ⁴¹Then you shall be released from my ban. If you visit my kindred and they refuse you, then, too, you shall be released from my ban.'

⁴²"When I came to the spring today, I prayed: 'LORD, God of my master Abraham, may it be your will to make successful the errand I am engaged on! ⁴³While I stand here at the spring, if I say to a young woman who comes out to draw water, Please give me a little water from your jug, ⁴⁴and she answers, Not only may you have a drink, but I will give water to your camels, too—let her be the woman whom the LORD has decided upon for my master's son.'

⁴⁵"I had scarcely finished saying this prayer to myself when Rebekah came out with a jug on her shoulder. After she went down to the spring and drew water, I said to her, 'Please let me have a drink.' ⁴⁶She quickly lowered the jug she was carrying and said, 'Take a drink, and let me bring water for your camels, too.' So I drank, and she watered the camels also. ⁴⁷When I asked her, 'Whose daughter are you?' she answered, 'The daughter of Bethuel, son of Nahor, born to Nahor by Milcah.' So I put the ring on her nose and the bracelets on her wrists. ⁴⁸Then I bowed down in worship to the LORD, blessing the LORD, the God of my master Abraham, who had led me on the right road to obtain the daughter of my master's kinsman for his son. ⁴⁹If, therefore, you have in mind to show true loyalty to my master, let me know; but if not, let me know that, too. I can then proceed accordingly."

⁵⁰ⁱLaban and his household said in reply: "This thing comes from the LORD; we can say nothing to you either for or against it. ⁵¹Here is Rebekah, ready for you; take her with you, that she may become the wife of your master's son, as the LORD has said." ⁵²When Abraham's servant heard their answer, he bowed to the ground before the LORD. ⁵³Then he brought out objects of silver and gold and articles of clothing and presented them to Rebekah; he also gave costly presents to her brother and mother. ⁵⁴After he and the men with him had eaten and drunk, they spent the night there.

When they were up the next morning, he said, "Give me leave to return to my master."ʲ ⁵⁵Her brother and mother replied, "Let the girl stay with us a short while, say ten days; after that she may go." ⁵⁶But he said to them, "Do not detain me, now that the LORD has made my errand successful; let me go

g: Gn 27, 43.   h: Tb 5, 17; 10, 13.   i: 50f; Tb 7, 12.   j: Tb 7, 14; 8, 20.

back to my master." [57]They answered, "Let us call the girl and see what she herself has to say about it." [58]So they called Rebekah and asked her, "Do you wish to go with this man?" She answered, "I do." [59]At this they allowed their sister Rebekah and her nurse to take leave, along with Abraham's servant and his men. [60]Invoking a blessing on Rebekah, they said:

"Sister, may you grow
    into thousands of myriads;
And may your descendants gain
        possession
    of the gates of their enemies!"[k]

[61]Then Rebekah and her maids started out; they mounted their camels and followed the man. So the servant took Rebekah and went on his way.

[62]Meanwhile Isaac had gone from Beer-lahai-roi and was living in the region of the Negeb.[l] [63]One day toward evening he went out . . .* in the field, and as he looked around, he noticed that camels were approaching. [64]Rebekah, too, was looking about, and when she saw him, she alighted from her camel [65]and asked the servant, "Who is the man out there, walking through the fields toward us?" "That is my master," replied the servant. Then she covered herself with her veil.

[66]The servant recounted to Isaac all the things he had done. [67]Then Isaac took Rebekah into his tent; he married her, and thus she became his wife. In his love for her Isaac found solace after the death of his mother Sarah.

See RG 110–12

CHAPTER 25

Abraham's Sons by Keturah. [1m]*Abraham married another wife, whose name was Keturah. [2]She bore him Zimran, Jokshan, Medan, Midian, Ishbak and Shuah. [3]Jokshan became the father of Sheba and Dedan. The descendants of Dedan were the Asshurim, the Letushim, and the Leummim.[n] [4]The descendants of Midian were Ephah, Epher, Hanoch, Abida and Eldaah. All of these were descendants of Keturah.

[5]Abraham deeded everything that he owned to his son Isaac. [6]To his sons by concubinage, however, he made grants while he was still living, as he sent them away eastward, to the land of Kedem,* away from his son Isaac.

Death of Abraham. [7]The whole span of Abraham's life was one hundred and seventy-five years. [8]Then he breathed his last, dying at a ripe old age, grown old after a full life; and he was taken to his kinsmen. [9o]His sons Isaac and Ishmael buried him in the cave of Machpelah, in the field of Ephron, son of Zohar the Hittite, which faces Mamre, [10]the field that Abraham had bought from the Hittites; there he was buried next to his wife Sarah. [11]After the death of Abraham, God blessed his son Isaac, who made his home near Beer-lahai-roi.

Descendants of Ishmael. [12]These are the descendants of Abraham's son Ishmael, whom Hagar the Egyptian, Sarah's slave, bore to Abraham. [13p]These are the names of Ismael's sons, listed in the order of their birth: Nebaioth (Ishmael's first-born), Kedar, Adbeel, Mibsam,[q] [14]Mishma, Dumah, Massa, [15]Hadad, Tema, Jetur, Naphish and Kedemah. [16]These are the sons of Ishmael, their names by their villages and encampments; twelve chieftains of as many tribal groups.[r]

[17]The span of Ishmael's life was one hundred and thirty-seven years. After he had breathed his last and died, he was taken to his kinsmen. [18]The Ishmaelites ranged from Havilah-by-Shur, which is on the border of Egypt, all the way to Asshur; and each of them pitched camp* in opposition to his various kinsmen.[s]

24, 63: He went out: the meaning of the Hebrew term that follows this is obscure.

25, 1-11: Though mentioned here, Abraham's marriage to a "concubine," or wife of secondary rank, and his death are not to be understood as happening chronologically after the events narrated in the preceding chapter.

25, 6: The land of Kedem: or "the country of the East," the region inhabited by the Kedemites or Easterners (Gn 29, 1; Jgs 6, 3. 33; Jb 1, 3; Is 11, 14). The names mentioned in vv

2ff, as far as they can be identified, are those of tribes in the Arabian desert.

25, 18: Pitched camp: literally "fell"; the same Hebrew verb is used in Jgs 7, 12 in regard to the hostile encampment

k: Gn 22, 17.   *l:* Gn 16, 13f; 25, 11.   *m:* 1-4; 1 Chr 1, 32f.
n: Is 21, 13.   *o:* 9f: Gn 23, 3-20.   *p:* 13-16: 1 Chr 1, 29ff.
q: Is 60, 7.   *r:* Gn 17, 20.   *s:* Gn 16, 12.

III: The Patriarchs Isaac and Jacob

Birth of Esau and Jacob. [19]This is the family history of Isaac, son of Abraham; Abraham had begotten Isaac. [20]Isaac was forty years old when he married Rebekah, the daughter of Bethuel the Aramean of Paddan-aram and the sister of Laban the Aramean.[t] [21]Isaac entreated the LORD on behalf of his wife, since she was sterile. The LORD heard his entreaty, and Rebekah became pregnant. [22]But the children in her womb jostled each other so much that she exclaimed, "If this is to be so, what good will it do me!" She went to consult the LORD, [23]and he answered her:

"Two nations are in your womb,
   two peoples are quarreling while still
      within you;
But one shall surpass the other,
   and the older shall serve the younger."[u]

[24]When the time of her delivery came, there were twins in her womb.[v] [25]The first to emerge was reddish,[*] and his whole body was like a hairy mantle; so they named him Esau. [26]His brother came out next, gripping Esau's heel;[*] so they named him Jacob. Isaac was sixty years old when they were born.[w]

[27]As the boys grew up, Esau became a skillful hunter, a man who lived in the open; whereas Jacob was a simple man, who kept to his tents.[x] [28]Isaac preferred Esau, because he was fond of game; but Rebekah preferred Jacob. [29]Once, when Jacob was cooking a stew, Esau came in from the open, famished. [30]He said to Jacob, "Let me gulp down some of that red stuff;[*] I'm starving." (That is why he was called Edom.) [31]But Jacob replied, "First give me your birthright[*] in exchange for it."[y] [32]"Look," said Esau, "I'm on the point of dying. What good will any birthright do me?" [33]But Jacob insisted, "Swear to me first!" So he sold Jacob his birthright under oath.[z] [34]Jacob then gave him some bread and the lentil stew; and Esau ate, drank, got up, and went his way. Esau cared little for his birthright.

CHAPTER 26

See RG 111–12

Isaac and Abimelech. [1a]There was a famine in the land (distinct from the earlier one that had occurred in the days of Abraham), and Isaac went down to Abimelech, king of the Philistines in Gerar.[b] [2]The LORD appeared to him and said: "Do not go down to Egypt, but continue to camp wherever in this land I tell you. [3]Stay in this land, and I will be with you and bless you; for to you and your descendants I will give all these lands, in fulfillment of the oath that I swore to your father Abraham.[c] [4]I will make your descendants as numerous as the stars in the sky and give them all these lands, and in your descendants all the nations of the earth shall find blessing—[d] [5]this because Abraham obeyed me, keeping my mandate (my commandments, my ordinances and my instructions)."

[6][*]So Isaac settled in Gerar. [7]When the men of the place asked questions about his wife, he answered, "She is my sister." He was afraid, if he called her his wife, the men of the place would kill him on account of Rebekah, since she was very beautiful. [8]But when he had been there for a long time,

---

of Bedouin tribes. The present passage shows the fulfillment of the prediction contained in Gn 16, 12.

25, 25: Reddish: in Hebrew, admoni, a reference to Edom, another name for Esau (v 30; 36, 1). Edom, however, was really the name of the country south of Moab where the descendants of Esau lived. It was called the "red" country because of its reddish sandstone. Hairy: in Hebrew, sear, a reference to Seir, another name for Edom (Gn 36, 8). One might expect the text to say, "So they named him Seir"; but Esau (esaw) also means "hairy."

25, 26: Esau's heel: the Hebrew is baaqeb esaw, a reference to the name Jacob; cf Gn 27, 36. Probably, however, the name Jacob has no true etymological connection with the Hebrew word for "heel" (aqeb), but is instead a shortened form of some such name as yaaqob-el ("may God protect").

25, 30: Red stuff: in Hebrew, adom; another play on the word Edom, the "red" land.

25, 31: Birthright: the privilege that entitled the first-born son to a position of honor in the family and to a double share in the possessions inherited from the father.

26, 6-11: The Yahwist's version of the wife-sister episode at Gerar; the Elohist's version (Gn 20, 1-18) is connected with Abraham and Sarah.

---

t: Gn 24, 66.   *u:* Gn 27, 29; Nm 24, 18; Mal 1, 2-5; Rom 9, 11f.   *v:* Hos 12, 3.   *w:* Mt 1, 2   *x:* Gn 27, 6f.   *y:* Dt 21, 17.   *z:* Heb 12, 16.   *a:* 1-14; Gn 12, 10-20.   *b:* Gn 12, 1.   *c:* Gn 12, 7; 15, 18; Ex 32, 13; Ps 105, 9; Sir 44, 22; Heb 11, 9.   *d:* Gn 12, 3; 22, 17f; 28, 14; Ex 32, 13.

Abimelech, king of the Philistines, happened to look out of a window and was surprised to see Isaac fondling his wife Rebekah. ⁹He called for Isaac and said: "She must certainly be your wife! How could you have said, 'She is my sister'?" Isaac replied, "I thought I might lose my life on her account." ¹⁰"How could you do this to us!" exclaimed Abimelech. "It would have taken very little for one of the men to lie with your wife, and you would have thus brought guilt upon us!" ¹¹Abimelech therefore gave this warning to all his men: "Anyone who molests this man or his wife shall forthwith be put to death."

¹²*Isaac sowed a crop in that region and reaped a hundredfold the same year. Since the LORD blessed him, ¹³ᵉhe became richer and richer all the time, until he was very wealthy indeed. ¹⁴He acquired such flocks and herds, and so many work animals, that the Philistines became envious of him. (¹⁵ᶠThe Philistines had stopped up and filled with dirt all the wells that his father's servants had dug back in the days of his father Abraham.) ¹⁶So Abimelech said to Isaac, "Go away from us; you have become far too numerous for us." ¹⁷Isaac left there and made the Wadi Gerar his regular campsite. (¹⁸Isaac reopened the wells which his father's servants had dug back in the days of his father Abraham and which the Philistines had stopped up after Abraham's death; he gave them the same names that his father had given them.) ¹⁹But when Isaac's servants dug in the wadi and reached spring water in their well, ²⁰the shepherds of Gerar quarreled with Isaac's servants, saying, "The water belongs to us!" So the well was called Esek,* because they had challenged him there. ²¹Then they dug another well, and they quarreled over that one too; so it was called Sitnah.* ²²When he had moved on from there, he dug still another well; but over this one they did not quarrel. It was called Rehoboth, because he said, "The LORD has now given us ample room, and we shall flourish in the land."

²³From there Isaac went up to Beer-sheba. ²⁴The same night the LORD appeared to him and said: "I am the God of your father Abraham. You have no need to fear, since I am with you. I will bless you and multiply your descendants for the sake of my servant Abraham."ᵍ ²⁵So he built an altar there and invoked the LORD by name. After he had pitched his tent there, his servants began to dig a well nearby.

²⁶ʰAbimelech had meanwhile come to him from Gerar, accompanied by Ahuzzath, his councilor, and Phicol, the general of his army. ²⁷Isaac asked them, "Why have you come to me, seeing that you hate me and have driven me away from you?" ²⁸They answered: "We are convinced that the LORD is with you, so we propose that there be a sworn agreement between our two sides—between you and us. Let us make a pact with you: ²⁹you shall not act unkindly toward us, just as we have not molested you, but have always acted kindly toward you and have let you depart in peace. Henceforth, 'The LORD's blessing be upon you!' " ³⁰Isaac then made a feast for them, and they ate and drank. ³¹Early the next morning they exchanged oaths. Then Isaac bade them farewell, and they departed from him in peace.

³²That same day Isaac's servants came and brought him news about the well they had been digging; they told him, "We have reached water!" ³³He called it Shibah;* hence the name of the city, Beer-sheba, to this day.

³⁴*When Esau was forty years old, he

26, 12-33: The Yahwist's version of the story about the wells at Beer-sheba; again, the Elohist's version (Gn 21, 22f) is connected with Abraham. A redactor joined the two accounts by means of the parenthetical verses 15 and 18.
26, 20: Esek: "challenge."
26, 21: Sitnah: "opposition"; one might expect the text to be continued by some such words as "because they were in opposition there."
26, 33: Shibah: "seven," for the sake of a closer assonance with Beer-sheba; but the present version of the story says nothing about there being seven wells there as implied in Gn

21, 28-31. The Greek version understood the Hebrew text more logically as shebua, "oath," in keeping with the present story.
26, 34f: These verses from the Priestly source, which have no logical connection with the preceding stories, serve as an introduction to the following section on Esau's loss of his birthright by suggesting a motivation for this in Isaac's and Rebekah's dislike for Esau's Canaanite wives.

e: 13f: Jb 1, 3. f: 15-24: Gn 21, 25-31. g: Gn 46, 3. h: 26-33: Gn 21, 22-31; Prv 16, 7.

married Judith, daughter of Beeri the Hittite, and Basemath, daughter of Elon the Hivite.[i] [35]But they became a source of embitterment to Isaac and Rebekah.

CHAPTER 27

See RG 112–14

Jacob's Deception.[*] [1]When Isaac was so old that his eyesight had failed him, he called his older son Esau and said to him, "Son!" "Yes, father!" he replied. [2]Isaac then said, "As you can see, I am so old that I may now die at any time. [3]Take your gear, therefore—your quiver and bow—and go out into the country to hunt some game for me. [4]With your catch prepare an appetizing dish for me, such as I like, and bring it to me to eat, so that I may give you my special blessing[*] before I die."

[5]Rebekah had been listening while Isaac was speaking to his son Esau. So when Esau went out into the country to hunt some game for his father,[j] [6]Rebekah said to her son Jacob, "Listen! I overheard your father tell your brother Esau, [7]'Bring me some game and with it prepare an appetizing dish for me to eat, that I may give you my blessing with the LORD's approval before I die.' [8]Now, son, listen carefully to what I tell you. [9]Go to the flock and get me two choice kids. With these I will prepare an appetizing dish for your father, such as he likes. [10]Then bring it to your father to eat, that he may bless you before he dies." [11]"But my brother Esau is a hairy man," said Jacob to his mother Rebekah, "and I am smooth-skinned![k] [12]Suppose my father feels me? He will think I am making sport of him, and I shall bring on myself a curse instead of a blessing." [13]His mother, however, replied: "Let any curse against you, son, fall on me! Just do as I say. Go and get me the kids."

[14]So Jacob went and got them and brought them to his mother; and with them she pre-pared an appetizing dish, such as his father liked. [15]Rebekah then took the best clothes of her older son Esau that she had in the house, and gave them to her younger son Jacob to wear; [16]and with the skins of the kids she covered up his hands and the hairless parts of his neck. [17]Then she handed her son Jacob the appetizing dish and the bread she had prepared.

[18]Bringing them to his father, Jacob said, "Father!" "Yes?" replied Isaac. "Which of my sons are you?" [19]Jacob answered his father: "I am Esau, your first-born. I did as you told me. Please sit up and eat some of my game, so that you may give me your special blessing." [20]But Isaac asked, "How did you succeed so quickly, son?" He answered, "The LORD, your God, let things turn out well with me." [21]Isaac then said to Jacob, "Come closer, son, that I may feel you, to learn whether you really are my son Esau or not." [22]So Jacob moved up closer to his father. When Isaac felt him, he said, "Although the voice is Jacob's, the hands are Esau's." [23](He failed to identify him because his hands were hairy, like those of his brother Esau; so in the end he gave him his blessing.) [24]Again he asked him, "Are you really my son Esau?" "Certainly," he replied. [25]Then Isaac said, "Serve me your game, son, that I may eat of it and then give you my blessing." Jacob served it to him, and Isaac ate; he brought him wine, and he drank. [26]Finally his father Isaac said to him, "Come closer, son, and kiss me." [27]As Jacob went up and kissed him, Isaac smelled the fragrance of his clothes. With that, he blessed him, saying,

"Ah, the fragrance of my son
  is like the fragrance of a field
    that the LORD has blessed![l]

[28] "May God give to you
  of the dew of the heavens

27, 1-45: What Jacob did in deceiving his father and thereby cheating Esau out of Isaac's deathbed blessing is condemned as blameworthy, not only by Hosea (12, 4) and Jeremiah (9, 3), but also, indirectly, by the Yahwist narrator of the present story, who makes the reader sympathize with Esau as the innocent victim of a cruel plot, and shows that Jacob and his mother, the instigator of the plot, paid for it by a lifelong separation from each other. The story was told because it was part of the mystery of God's ways in salvation history—his use of weak, sinful men to achieve his own ultimate purpose.

27, 4: My special blessing: "the blessing of my soul." The same expression is used also in vv 19. 25. 31. In the context it must mean something like a solemn deathbed blessing, believed to be especially efficacious.

i: 34f: Gn 27, 46.　*j:* Gn 25, 28.　*k:* Gn 25, 25.　*l:* Gn 22, 17f; Heb 11, 20.

And of the fertility of the earth
abundance of grain and wine.

29 *m*"Let peoples serve you,
and nations pay you homage;
Be master of your brothers,
and may your mother's sons bow
down to you.

"Cursed be those who curse you,
and blessed be those who bless you."

30 Jacob had scarcely left his father, just after Isaac had finished blessing him, when his brother Esau came back from his hunt. 31 Then he too prepared an appetizing dish with his game, and bringing it to his father, he said, "Please, father, eat some of your son's game, that you may then give me your special blessing." 32 "Who are you?" his father Isaac asked him. "I am Esau," he replied, "your first-born son." 33 With that, Isaac was seized with a fit of uncontrollable trembling. "Who was it, then," he asked, "that hunted game and brought it to me? I finished eating it just before you came, and I blessed him. Now he must remain blessed!" 34 On hearing his father's words, Esau burst into loud, bitter sobbing. "Father, bless me too!" he begged. 35 When Isaac explained, "Your brother came here by a ruse and carried off your blessing," 36 Esau exclaimed, "He has been well named Jacob! He has now supplanted me* twice! First he took away my birthright, and now he has taken away my blessing." Then he pleaded, "Haven't you saved a blessing for me?"*n* 37 Isaac replied: "I have already appointed him your master, and I have assigned to him all his kinsmen as his slaves; besides, I have enriched him with grain and wine. What then can I do for you, son?" 38 But Esau urged his father, "Have you only that one blessing, father? Bless me too!" Isaac, however, made

no reply; and Esau wept aloud.*o* 39 Finally Isaac spoke again and said to him:

"Ah, far from the fertile earth
shall be your dwelling;
far from the dew of the heavens
above!*p*

40 "By your sword you shall live,
and your brother you shall serve;
But when you become restive,
you shall throw off his yoke from your
neck."*q*

41 Esau bore Jacob a grudge because of the blessing his father had given him. He said to himself, "When the time of mourning for my father comes, I will kill my brother Jacob."*r* 42 When Rebekah got news of what her older son Esau had in mind, she called her younger son Jacob and said to him: "Listen! Your brother Esau intends to settle accounts with you by killing you. 43 Therefore, son, do what I tell you: flee at once to my brother Laban in Haran, 44 and stay with him a while until your brother's fury subsides 45 [until your brother's anger against you subsides] and he forgets what you did to him. Then I will send for you and bring you back. Must I lose both of you in a single day?"

Jacob Sent to Laban. 46 *Rebekah said to Isaac: "I am disgusted with life because of the Hittite women. If Jacob also should marry a Hittite woman, a native of the land, like these women, what good would life be to me?"*s*

CHAPTER 28

See RG 112-14

1 Isaac therefore called Jacob, greeted him with a blessing, and charged him: "You shall not marry a Canaanite woman!*t* 2 Go now to Paddan-aram, to the home of your mother's father Bethuel, and there choose a wife for yourself from among the daughters

---

27, 36: He has now supplanted me: in Hebrew, wayya-qebeni, a wordplay on the name Jacob, yaaqob; see Jer 9, 3 and note, as well as Gn 25, 26. There is also a play between the Hebrew words bekora ("birthright") and beraka ("blessing").

27, 46—28, 9: This section, which is from the Priestly source and a direct sequel of Gn 26, 34f, presents a different, though not contradictory, reason for Jacob's going to Paddan-aram: namely, to preserve racial purity among the chosen people. The account of Esau's marriages is given for the pur-

pose of explaining the racial mixture of the Edomites, who were descended in part from tribes related to Israel, in part from older peoples in Edom called Hittites, Horites or Hivites, and in part from the Ishmaelite (Arabian) tribes who later invaded the region.

m: Gn 25, 23; 49, 8; Nm 24, 9.   *n:* Gn 25, 26. 29-34; Hos 12, 4.   *o:* Heb 12, 17.   *p:* Heb 11, 20.   *q:* 2 Kgs 8, 20. 22; 2 Chr 21, 8.   *r:* Wis 10, 10; Ob 1, 10.   *s:* Gn 26, 34f.   *t:* Gn 24, 3f; 26, 35.

of your uncle Laban.*u* *3*May God Almighty bless you and make you fertile, multiply you that you may become an assembly of peoples. *4*May he extend to you and your descendants the blessing he gave to Abraham, so that you may gain possession of the land where you are staying, which he assigned to Abraham."*v* *5*Then Isaac sent Jacob on his way; he went to Paddan-aram, to Laban, son of Bethuel, the Aramean, and brother of Rebekah, the mother of Jacob and Esau.*w*

*6*Esau noted that Isaac had blessed Jacob when he sent him to Paddan-aram to get himself a wife there, charging him, as he gave him his blessing, not to marry a Canaanite woman, *7*and that Jacob had obeyed his father and mother and gone to Paddan-aram. *8*Esau realized how displeasing the Canaanite women were to his father Isaac, *9*so he went to Ishmael, and in addition to the wives he had, married Mahalath, the daughter of Abraham's son Ishmael and sister of Nebaioth.*x*

Jacob's Dream at Bethel. *10*Jacob departed from Beer-sheba and proceeded toward Haran. *11*When he came upon a certain shrine,* as the sun had already set, he stopped there for the night. Taking one of the stones at the shrine, he put it under his head and lay down to sleep at that spot. *12*Then he had a dream: a stairway* rested on the ground, with its top reaching to the heavens; and God's messengers were going up and down on it.*y* *13*And there was the LORD standing beside him and saying: "I, the LORD, am the God of your forefather Abraham and the God of Isaac; the land on which

you are lying I will give to you and your descendants.*z* *14*These shall be as plentiful as the dust of the earth, and through them you shall spread out east and west, north and south. In you and your descendants all the nations of the earth shall find blessing.*a* *15*Know that I am with you; I will protect you wherever you go, and bring you back to this land. I will never leave you until I have done what I promised you."*b*

*16*When Jacob awoke from his sleep, he exclaimed, "Truly, the LORD is in this spot, although I did not know it!" *17*In solemn wonder he cried out: "How awesome is this shrine! This* is nothing else but an abode of God, and that is the gateway to heaven!" *18*Early the next morning Jacob took the stone that he had put under his head, set it up as a memorial stone,* and poured oil on top if it.*c* *19*He called that site Bethel,* whereas the former name of the town had been Luz.*d*

*20*Jacob then made this vow: "If God remains with me, to protect me on this journey I am making and to give me enough bread to eat and clothing to wear, *21*and I come back safe to my father's house, the LORD shall be my God. *22*This stone that I have set up as a memorial stone shall be God's abode. Of everything you give me, I will faithfully return a tenth part to you."

CHAPTER 29

See RG 112-14

Arrival in Haran. *1e*After Jacob resumed his journey, he came to the land of the Easterners.* *2*Looking about, he saw a well in the open country, with three droves of sheep huddled near it, for droves were watered from that well. A large stone covered

---

28, 11: Shrine: literally "place," often used specifically of a sacred site. Here the place was Bethel (v 19), a sacred site as early as the time of Abraham (Gn 12, 8).

28, 12: Stairway: in Hebrew, sullam, traditionally but inaccurately, translated as "ladder." The corresponding verb, salal, means "to heap up" something, such as dirt for a highway or ramp. The imagery in Jacob's dream is derived from the Babylonian ziggurat or temple tower, "with its top in the sky" (Gn 11, 4), and with brick steps leading up to a small temple at the top.

28, 17: This: the stone Jacob used as a headrest; cf v 22. That: the stairway Jacob saw in his dream.

28, 18: Memorial stone: in Hebrew, masseba, a stone which might vary in shape and size, set upright and usually intended for some religious purpose. Since the custom of

erecting such "sacred pillars" in Palestine went back to its pre-Israelite period, their pagan associations were often retained; therefore, later Israelite religion forbade their erection (Lv 26, 1; Dt 16, 22) and ordered the destruction of those that were associated with paganism (Ex 34, 31; Dt 12, 3).

28, 19: Bethel: i.e., "house of God"; the reference is to the abode of God in v 17.

29, 1: Easterners: see note on Gn 25, 6.

---

u: Gn 22, 22; 17, 1f. 4f. *v:* Ex 32, 13. *w:* Jdt 8, 26. *x:* Gn 36, 2f. *y:* Jn 1, 51. *z:* Dt 1, 8; Mi 7, 28. *a:* Gn 12, 3; 13, 14f; 15, 5f; 18, 18; 22, 17f; 26, 4; Dt 19, 8; Sir 44, 21. *b:* Gn 31, 3. *c:* Gn 31, 13; 35, 14f. *d:* Gn 35, 6; 48, 3; Jos 18, 13; Jgs 1, 23; Hos 12, 4. *e:* Wis 10, 10.

the mouth of the well.^{f} ^{3}Only when all the shepherds were assembled there could they roll the stone away from the mouth of the well and water the flocks. Then they would put the stone back again over the mouth of the well.

^{4}Jacob said to them, "Friends, where are you from?" "We are from Haran," they replied. ^{5}Then he asked them, "Do you know Laban, son of Nahor?" "We do," they answered.^{g} ^{6}He inquired further, "Is he well?" "He is," they answered; "and here comes his daughter Rachel with his flock." ^{7}Then he said: "There is still much daylight left; it is hardly the time to bring the animals home. Why don't you water the flocks now, and then continue pasturing them?" ^{8}"We cannot," they replied, "until all the shepherds are here to roll the stone away from the mouth of the well; only then can we water the flocks."

^{9}While he was still talking with them, Rachel arrived with her father's sheep; she was the one who tended them. ^{10}As soon as Jacob saw Rachel, the daughter of his uncle Laban, with the sheep of his uncle Laban, he went up, rolled the stone away from the mouth of the well, and watered his uncle's sheep. ^{11}Then Jacob kissed Rachel and burst into tears.* ^{12}He told her that he was her father's relative, Rebekah's son, and she ran to tell her father. ^{13}When Laban heard the news about his sister's son Jacob, he hurried out to meet him. After embracing and kissing him, he brought him to his house. Jacob then recounted to Laban all that had happened, ^{14}and Laban said to him, "You are indeed my flesh and blood."*

Marriage to Leah and Rachel. After Jacob had stayed with him a full month, ^{15}Laban said to him: "Should you serve me for nothing just because you are a relative of mine? Tell me what your wages should be." ^{16}Now Laban had two daughters; the older

was called Leah, the younger Rachel. ^{17}Leah had lovely eyes,* but Rachel was well formed and beautiful. ^{18}Since Jacob had fallen in love with Rachel, he answered Laban, "I will serve you seven years for your younger daughter Rachel."* ^{19}Laban replied, "I prefer to give her to you rather than to an outsider. Stay with me." ^{20}So Jacob served seven years for Rachel, yet they seemed to him but a few days because of his love for her.^{h}

^{21}Then Jacob said to Laban, "Give me my wife, that I may consummate my marriage with her, for my term is now completed." ^{22}So Laban invited all the local inhabitants and gave a feast. ^{23}At the nightfall he took his daughter Leah and brought her to Jacob, and Jacob consummated the marriage with her. ^{24}(Laban assigned his slave girl Zilpah to his daughter Leah as her maidservant.) ^{25}In the morning Jacob was amazed:* it was Leah! So he cried out to Laban: "How could you do this to me! Was it not for Rachel that I served you? Why did you dupe me?" ^{26}"It is not the custom in our country," Laban replied, "to marry off a younger daughter before an older one. ^{27}Finish the bridal week* for this one, and then I will give you the other too, in return for another seven years of service with me."^{i}

^{28}Jacob agreed. He finished the bridal week for Leah, and then Laban gave him his daughter Rachel in marriage. ^{29}(Laban assigned his slave girl Bilhah to his daughter Rachel as her maidservant.) ^{30}Jacob then consummated his marriage with Rachel also, and he loved her more than Leah. Thus he remained in Laban's service another seven years.^{j}

Jacob's Children. ^{31}When the LORD saw that Leah was unloved, he made her fruitful, while Rachel remained barren. ^{32}Leah conceived and bore a son, and she named him

---

29, 11: Burst into tears: literally "raised his voice and wept," i.e., for joy.

29, 14: Flesh and blood: literally "bone and flesh," i.e., a close relative; on the Hebrew idiom, see Gn 2, 23.

29, 17: Lovely eyes: The adjective modifying eyes is often translated as "weak," but "lovely" is the more probable word.

29, 18: Jacob offers to render service (Jos 15, 16f; 1 Sm 17, 25; 18, 17) in lieu of the customary bridal price (Ex

22, 16f; Dt 22, 29).

29, 25: Jacob was amazed: he had not recognized Leah because a bride was veiled when she was brought to her bridegroom; cf Gn 24, 65.

29, 27: The bridal week: an ancient wedding lasted for seven days of festivities; cf Jgs 14, 12.

---

f: Gn 24, 11f. *g:* Tb 7, 4. *h:* Hos 12, 13. *i:* Hos 12, 13. *j:* Dt 21, 15ff.

Reuben;* for she said, "It means, 'The LORD saw my misery; now my husband will love me.' "*k 33She conceived again and bore a son, and said, "It means, 'The LORD heard that I was unloved,' and therefore he has given me this one also"; so she named him Simeon.* 34Again she conceived and bore a son, and she said, "Now at last my husband will become attached to me, since I have now borne him three sons"; that is why she named him Levi.* 35Once more she conceived and bore a son, and she said, "This time I will give grateful praise to the LORD"; therefore she named him Judah.* Then she stopped bearing children.*l

See RG
112-14

CHAPTER 30

1When Rachel saw that she failed to bear children to Jacob, she became envious of her sister. She said to Jacob, "Give me children or I shall die!"*m 2In anger Jacob retorted, "Can I take the place of God, who has denied you the fruit of the womb?"*n 3She replied, "Here is my maidservant Bilhah. Have intercourse with her, and let her give birth on my knees,* so that I too may have offspring, at least through her."*o 4So she gave him her maidservant Bilhah as a consort,* and Jacob had intercourse with her. 5When Bilhah conceived and bore a son, 6Rachel said, "God has vindicated me; indeed he has heeded my plea and given me a son." Therefore she named him Dan.* 7Ra-

chel's maidservant Bilhah conceived again and bore a second son, 8and Rachel said, "I engaged in a fateful struggle with my sister, and I prevailed." So she named him Naphtali.*

9When Leah saw that she had ceased to bear children, she gave her maidservant Zilpah to Jacob as a consort. 10So Jacob had intercourse with Zilpah, and she conceived and bore a son. 11Leah then said, "What good luck!" So she named him Gad.* 12Then Leah's maidservant Zilpah bore a second son to Jacob; 13and Leah said, "What good fortune!"—meaning, "Women call me fortunate." So she named him Asher.*

14One day, during the wheat harvest, when Reuben was out in the field, he came upon some mandrakes* which he brought home to his mother Leah. Rachel asked Leah, "Please let me have some of your son's mandrakes." 15Leah replied, "Was it not enough for you to take away my husband, that you must now take my son's mandrakes too?" "Very well, then!" Rachel answered. "In exchange for your son's mandrakes, Jacob may lie with you tonight." 16That evening, when Jacob came home from the fields, Leah went out to meet him. "You are now to come in with me," she told him, "because I have paid for you with my son's mandrakes." So that night he slept with her, 17and God heard her prayer; she conceived and bore a fifth son to Jacob.

29, 32: Reuben: The literal meaning of the Hebrew name is "look, a son!" But in this case, as also with the names of all the other sons of Jacob, a symbolic rather than an etymological interpretation of the name is given, because the name and the persons were regarded as closely interrelated. The symbolic interpretation of Reuben's name, according to the Yahwist source, is based on the similar-sounding, raa beonyi, "he saw my misery." In the Elohist source, the name is explained by the similar-sounding yeehabani, "he will love me."

29, 33: Simeon: in popular etymology, related to shama, "he heard."

29, 34: Levi: related to yillaweh, "he will become attached."

29, 35: Judah: related to odeh, "I will give grateful praise."

30, 3: On my knees: in the ancient Near East, a father would take a newborn child in his lap to signify that he acknowledged it as his own; Rachel uses the ceremony in order to adopt the child and establish her legal rights to it.

30, 4: Consort: the Hebrew word normally means "wife," but here it refers to a wife of secondary rank, who did not

have the full legal rights of an ordinary wife.

30, 6: Dan: explained by the term dannanni, "he has vindicated me."

30, 8: Naphtali: explained by the phrase naptule elohim niptalti, literally, "in a divine wrestling match I have wrestled," perhaps implying the concept of an ordeal; hence the above rendering, I engaged in a fateful struggle.

30, 11: Gad: explained by the Hebrew term begad, literally "in luck," i.e., what good luck!

30, 13: Asher: explained by the term beoshri, literally "in my good fortune," i.e., what good fortune, and by the term ishsheruni, "they call me fortunate."

30, 14: Mandrakes: an herb whose root was anciently thought to promote conception. The Hebrew word for mandrakes, dudaim, has erotic connotations, since it sounds like the words daddayim ("breasts") and dodim ("sexual pleasure").

---

k: Gn 49, 3. *l:* Mt 1, 2; Lk 3, 33. *m:* Prv 30, 16. *n:* 2 Kgs 5, 7. *o:* Gn 16, 2ff.

[18]Leah then said, "God has given me my reward for having let my husband have my maidservant"; so she named him Issachar.* [19]Leah conceived again and bore a sixth son to Jacob; [20]and she said, "God has brought me a precious gift. This time my husband will offer me presents, now that I have borne him six sons"; so she named him Zebulun.* [21]Finally, she gave birth to a daughter, and she named her Dinah.

[22]Then God remembered Rachel; he heard her prayer and made her fruitful. [23]She conceived and bore a son, and she said, "God has removed my disgrace."*p* [24]So she named him Joseph,* meaning, "May the LORD add another son to this one for me!"

Jacob Outwits Laban. [25]After Rachel gave birth to Joseph, Jacob said to Laban: "Give me leave to go to my homeland. [26]Let me have my wives, for whom I served you, and my children, too, that I may depart. You know very well the service that I have rendered you." [27]Laban answered him: "If you will please. . . .

"I have learned through divination that it is because of you that God has blessed me. [28]So," he continued, "state what wages you want from me, and I will pay them." [29]Jacob replied: "You know what work I did for you and how well your livestock fared under my care; [30]the little you had before I came has grown into very much, since the LORD's blessings came upon you in my company. Therefore I should now do something for my own household as well." [31]"What should I pay you?" Laban asked. Jacob answered: "You do not have to pay me anything outright. I will again pasture and tend your flock, if you do this one thing for me: [32]go through your whole flock today and remove from it every dark animal among the sheep and every spotted or speckled one among the goats.* Only such animals shall be my wages. [33]In the future, whenever you check on these wages of mine, let my honesty testify against me: any animal in my possession that is not a speckled or spotted goat, or a dark sheep, got there by theft!" [34]"Very well," agreed Laban. "Let it be as you say."

[35]That same day Laban removed the streaked and spotted he-goats and all the speckled and spotted she-goats, all those with some white on them, as well as the fully dark-colored sheep; these he left . . . in charge of his sons.* [36]Then he put a three days' journey between himself and Jacob, while Jacob continued to pasture the rest of Laban's flock.

[37]Jacob, however, got some fresh shoots of poplar, almond and plane trees, and he made white stripes in them by peeling off the bark down to the white core of the shoots. [38]The rods that he had thus peeled he then set upright in the watering troughs, so that they would be in front of the animals that drank from the troughs. When the animals were in heat as they came to drink, [39]*the goats mated by the rods, and so they brought forth streaked, speckled and spotted kids. [40]The sheep, on the other hand, Jacob kept apart, and he set these animals to face the streaked or fully dark-colored animals of Laban. Thus he produced special flocks of his own, which he did not put with Laban's flock. [41]Moreover, whenever the hardier animals were in heat, Jacob would set the rods in the troughs in full view of these animals, so that they mated by the rods; [42]but with the

---

30, 18: Issachar: explained by the terms, sekari, "my reward," and in v 16, sakor sekartika, literally "I have hired you," i.e., I have paid for you.

30, 20: Zebulun: related to the Akkadian word zubullum, "bridegroom's gift," is explained by the terms, zebadani . . . zebed tob, "he has brought me a precious gift," and yizbeleni, "he will offer me presents."

30, 24: Joseph: explained by the words yosep, "may he add," and in v 23, asap, "he has removed."

30, 32: Dark . . . sheep . . . spotted or speckled . . . goats: In the Near East the normal color of sheep is light gray, whereas that of goats is uniform dark brown or black. Ordinarily, therefore, Jacob would have received but few animals.

30, 35: By giving the abnormally colored animals to his

sons, Laban not only deprived Jacob of his first small wages, but he also designed to prevent in this way the future breeding of such animals in the part of his flock entrusted to Jacob.

30, 39-42: Jacob's stratagem was based on the widespread notion among simple people that visual stimuli can have prenatal effects on the offspring of breeding animals. Thus, the rods on which Jacob had whittled stripes or bands or chevron marks were thought to cause the female goats that looked at them to bear kids with lighter-colored marks on their dark hair, while the gray ewes were thought to bear lambs with dark marks on them simply by visual cross-breeding with the dark goats.

---

p: Lk 1, 25.

45

weaker animals he would not put the rods there. So the feeble animals would go to Laban, but the sturdy ones to Jacob. [43]Thus the man grew increasingly prosperous, and he came to own not only large flocks but also male and female servants and camels and asses.

See RG 112-14

CHAPTER 31

Flight from Laban. [1]Jacob learned that Laban's sons were saying, "Jacob has taken everything that belonged to our father, and he has accumulated all this wealth of his by using our father's property." [2]Jacob perceived, too, that Laban's attitude toward him was not what it had previously been. [3]Then the LORD said to Jacob, "Return to the land of your fathers, where you were born, and I will be with you."[q]

[4]So Jacob sent for Rachel and Leah to meet him where he was in the field with his flock. [5]There he said to them: "I have noticed that your father's attitude toward me is not as it was in the past; but the God of my father has been with me. [6]You well know what effort I put into serving your father; [7]yet your father cheated me and changed my wages time after time. God, however, did not let him do me any harm.[r] [8]*Whenever your father said, 'The speckled animals shall be your wages,' the entire flock would bear speckled young; whenever he said, 'The streaked animals shall be your wages,' the entire flock would bear streaked young. [9]Thus God reclaimed your father's livestock and gave it to me. [10]Once, in the breeding season, I had a dream in which I saw mating he-goats that were streaked, speckled and mottled. [11]In the dream God's messenger called to me, 'Jacob!' 'Here!' I replied.

[12]Then he said, 'Note well. All the he-goats in the flock, as they mate, are streaked, speckled and mottled, for I have seen all the things that Laban has been doing to you. [13]I am the God who appeared to you in Bethel, where you anointed a memorial stone and made a vow to me. Up, then! Leave this land and return to the land of your birth.' "[s]

[14]Rachel and Leah answered him: "Have we still an heir's portion in our father's house? [15]Are we not regarded by him as outsiders?* He not only sold us; he has even used up the money that he got for us! [16]All the wealth that God reclaimed from our father really belongs to us and our children. Therefore, do just as God has told you."[t]

[17]Jacob proceeded to put his children and wives on camels, [18]and he drove off with all his livestock and all the property he had acquired in Paddan-aram, to go to his father Isaac in the land of Canaan.

[19]Now Laban had gone away to shear his sheep, and Rachel had meanwhile appropriated her father's household idols.[u] * [20]Jacob had hoodwinked* Laban the Aramean by not telling him of his intended flight. [21]Thus he made his escape with all that he had. Once he was across the Euphrates, he headed for the highlands of Gilead.

[22]On the third day, word came to Laban that Jacob had fled. [23]Taking his kinsmen with him, he pursued him for seven days* until he caught up with him in the hill country of Gilead. [24]But that night God appeared to Laban the Aramean in a dream and warned him, "Take care not to threaten Jacob with any harm."[v]

Jacob and Laban in Gilead. [25]When Laban overtook Jacob, Jacob's tents were pitched in the highlands; Laban also pitched

---

31, 8-12: This Elohist account of the miraculous increase in Jacob's flock differs somewhat from the Yahwist account given in Gn 30, 32-42.

31, 15: Outsiders: literally "foreign women"; they lacked the favored legal status of native women. Used up: literally "eaten, consumed"; the bridal price that a man received for giving his daughter in marriage was legally reserved as her inalienable dowry.

31, 19: Household idols: in Hebrew, teraphim, figurines used in divination (Ez 21, 26; Zec 10, 2). Laban calls them his "gods" (v 30).

31, 20: Hoodwinked: literally "stolen the heart of," i.e.,

lulled the mind of. Aramean: The earliest extra-biblical references to the Arameans date from several centuries after the time of Jacob; to call Laban an Aramean and to have him speak Aramaic (v 47) would seem to be an anachronism.

31, 23: For seven days: literally "a way of seven days," a general term to designate a long distance; it would have taken a camel caravan many more days to travel from Haran to Gilead, the region east of the northern half of the Jordan.

q: Gn 26, 3; 28, 15; 32, 10.   *r:* Jdt 8, 26.   *s:* Gn 28, 18.   *t:* Wis 10, 10f.   *u:* Gn 19, 34; 1 Sm 19, 13.   *v:* Wis 10, 12.

his tents there, on Mount Gilead. ²⁶"What do you mean," Laban demanded of Jacob, "by hoodwinking me and carrying off my daughters like war captives?* ²⁷Why did you dupe me by stealing away secretly? You should have told me, and I would have sent you off with merry singing to the sound of tambourines and harps. ²⁸You did not even allow me a parting kiss to my daughters and grandchildren! What you have now done is a senseless thing. ²⁹I have it in my power to harm all of you; but last night the God of your father said to me, 'Take care not to threaten Jacob with any harm!' ³⁰Granted that you had to leave because you were desperately homesick for your father's house, why did you steal my gods?" ³¹"I was frightened," Jacob replied to Laban, "at the thought that you might take your daughters away from me by force. ³²But as for your gods, the one you find them with shall not remain alive! If, with my kinsmen looking on, you identify anything here as belonging to you, take it." Jacob, of course, had no idea that Rachel had stolen the idols.

³³Laban then went in and searched Jacob's tent and Leah's tent, as well as the tents of the two maidservants; but he did not find the idols. Leaving Leah's tent, he went into Rachel's. ³⁴Now Rachel had taken the idols, put them inside a camel cushion, and seated herself upon them. When Laban had rummaged through the rest of her tent without finding them,ʷ ³⁵Rachel said to her father, "Let not my lord feel offended that I cannot rise in your presence; a woman's period is upon me." So, despite his search, he did not find his idols.

³⁶Jacob, now enraged, upbraided Laban. "What crime or offense have I committed," he demanded, "that you should hound me so fiercely? ³⁷Now that you have ransacked all my things, have you found a single object taken from your belongings? If so, produce it here before your kinsmen and mine, and let them decide between us two.

³⁸"In the twenty years that I was under you, no ewe or she-goat of yours ever miscarried, and I have never feasted on a ram of your flock. ³⁹ˣI never brought you an animal torn by wild beasts; I made good the loss myself. You held me responsible for anything stolen by day or night.* ⁴⁰How often the scorching heat ravaged me by day, and the frost by night, while sleep fled from my eyes! ⁴¹Of the twenty years that I have now spent in your household, I slaved fourteen years for your two daughters and six years for your flock, while you changed my wages time after time. ⁴²If my ancestral God, the God of Abraham and the Awesome One of Isaac, had not been on my side, you would now have sent me away empty-handed. But God saw my plight and the fruits of my toil, and last night he gave judgment."ʸ

⁴³*Laban replied to Jacob: "The women are mine, their children are mine, and the flocks are mine; everything you see belongs to me. But since these women are my daughters, I will now do something for them and for the children they have borne. ⁴⁴Come, then, we will make a pact, you and I; the LORD shall be a witness between us."

⁴⁵Then Jacob took a stone and set it up as a memorial stone.ᶻ ⁴⁶Jacob said to his kinsmen, "Gather some stones." So they got some stones and made a mound; and they had a meal there at the mound. ⁴⁷Laban called it Jegar-sahadutha,* but Jacob named it Galeed. ⁴⁸"This mound," said Laban, "shall be a witness from now on between you and me." That is why it was named Galeed— ⁴⁹and also Mizpah,* for he said: "May the LORD keep watch between you and me

---

31, 26: War captives: literally "women captured by the sword"; the women of a conquered people were treated as part of the victor's booty; cf 1 Sm 30, 2; 2 Kgs 5, 2.

31, 39: Laban's actions were contrary to the customs of the ancient Near East, as recorded in the Code of Hammurabi: "If in a sheepfold an act of god has occurred, or a lion has made a kill, the shepherd shall clear himself before the deity, and the owner of the fold must accept the loss" (par. 266); cf Ex 22, 12.

31, 43-54: In this account of the treaty between Laban and Jacob, the Yahwist and Elohist sources are closely interwoven.

The mound or cairn of stones comes from the Yahwist source, the memorial stone or stele comes from the Elohist one.

31, 47: Jegar-sahadutha: an Aramaic term meaning "mound of witness." Galeed: in Hebrew, galed, with the same meaning; also offers an explanation of the regional name Gilead.

31, 49: Mizpah: a town in Gilead; cf Jgs 10, 17; 11, 11. 34; Hos 5, 1. The Hebrew name mispa ("lookout") is allied to

---

w: Gn 31, 19.　x: Ex 22, 12.　y: Gn 19, 24. 29.　z: Gn 28, 18; 35, 14.

when we are out of each other's sight. [50]If you mistreat my daughters, or take other wives besides my daughters, remember that even though no one else is about, God will be witness between you and me."

[51]Laban said further to Jacob: "Here is this mound, and here is the memorial stone that I have set up between you and me. [52]This mound shall be witness, and this memorial stone shall be witness, that, with hostile intent, neither may I pass beyond this mound into your territory nor may you pass beyond it into mine. [53]May the God of Abraham and the god of Nahor [their ancestral deities] maintain justice between us!" Jacob took the oath by the Awesome One of Issac. [54]He then offered a sacrifice on the mountain and invited his kinsmen to share in the meal. When they had eaten, they passed the night on the mountain.

CHAPTER 32

See RG 112-14 [1]Early the next morning, Laban kissed his grandchildren and his daughters goodbye; then he set out on his journey back home, [2]while Jacob continued on his own way. Then God's messengers encountered Jacob. [3]When he saw them he said, "This is God's encampment." So he named that place Mahanaim.*

Embassy to Esau. [4]Jacob sent messengers ahead to his brother Esau in the land of Seir, the country of Edom,[a] [5]with this message: "Thus shall you say to my lord Esau: 'Your servant Jacob speaks as follows: I have been staying with Laban and have been detained there until now. [6]I own cattle, asses and sheep, as well as male and female servants. I am sending my lord this information in the hope of gaining your favor.' " [7]When the messengers returned to Jacob, they said,

"We reached your brother Esau. He is now coming to meet you, accompanied by four hundred men."

[8]Jacob was very much frightened. In his anxiety, he divided the people who were with him, as well as his flocks, herds, and camels, into two camps. [9]"If Esau should attack and overwhelm one camp," he reasoned, "the remaining camp may still survive." [10]Then he prayed, "O God of my father Abraham and God of my father Isaac! You told me, O LORD, 'Go back to the land of your birth, and I will be good to you.'[b] [11]I am unworthy of all the acts of kindness that you have loyally performed for your servant: although I crossed the Jordan here with nothing but my staff, I have now grown into two companies. [12]Save me, I pray, from the hand of my brother Esau! Otherwise I fear that when he comes he will strike me down and slay the mothers and children.[c] [13]You yourself said, 'I will be very good to you, and I will make your descendants like the sands of the sea, which are too numerous to count.' "

[14]After passing the night there, Jacob selected from what he had with him the following presents for his brother Esau: [15]two hundred she-goats and twenty he-goats; two hundred ewes and twenty rams; [16]thirty milch camels and their young; forty cows and ten bulls; twenty she-asses and ten he-asses. [17]He put these animals in charge of his servants, in separate droves, and he told the servants, "Go on ahead of me, but keep a space between one drove and the next." [18]To the servant in the lead he gave this instruction: "When my brother Esau meets you, he may ask you, 'Whose man are you? Where are you going? To whom do these animals ahead of you belong?' [19]Then you shall answer, 'They belong to your brother Jacob,

---

yisep yhwh ("may the Lord keep watch"), and also echoes the word masseba ("memorial pillar").

32, 3: Mahanaim: a town in Gilead (Jos 13, 26. 30; 21, 38; 2 Sm 2, 8; etc.). The Hebrew name means "two camps." There are other allusions to the name in vv 8. 11.

32, 25: Some man: a messenger of the Lord in human form, as is clear from vv 29ff.

32, 29: Israel: the first part of the Hebrew name Yisrael is given a popular explanation in the word sarita, "you contended"; the second part is the first syllable of elohim, "divine beings." The present incident, with a similar allusion to the

name Israel, is referred to in Hos 12, 5, where the mysterious wrestler is explicitly called an angel.

32, 31: Peniel: a variant of the word Penuel (v 32), the name of a town on the north bank of the Jabbok in Gilead (Jgs 8, 8f. 17; 1 Kgs 12, 25). The name is explained as meaning "the face of God," peni-el. Yet my life has been spared: see note on Gn 16, 13.

a: Gn 36, 6.   b: Gn 31, 3.   c: Gn 28, 14; 48, 16; Ex 32, 13; Heb 11, 12.

but they have been sent as a gift to my lord Esau; and Jacob himself is right behind us.' " [20]He gave similar instructions to the second servant and the third and to all the others who followed behind the droves, namely: "Thus and thus shall you say to Esau, when you reach him; [21]and be sure to add, 'Your servant Jacob is right behind us.' " For Jacob reasoned, "If I first appease him with gifts that precede me, then later, when I face him, perhaps he will forgive me." [22]So the gifts went on ahead of him, while he stayed that night in the camp.

Struggle with the Angel. [23]In the course of that night, however, Jacob arose, took his two wives, with the two maidservants and his eleven children, and crossed the ford of the Jabbok. [24]After he had taken them across the stream and had brought over all his possessions, [25]Jacob was left there alone. Then some man* wrestled with him until the break of dawn. [26]When the man saw that he could not prevail over him, he struck Jacob's hip at its socket, so that the hip socket was wrenched as they wrestled.[d] [27]The man then said, "Let me go, for it is daybreak." But Jacob said, "I will not let you go until you bless me." [28]"What is your name?" the man asked. He answered, "Jacob."[e] [29]Then the man said, "You shall no longer be spoken of as Jacob, but as Israel,* because you have contended with divine and human beings and have prevailed." [30]Jacob then asked him, "Do tell me your name, please." He answered, "Why should you want to know my name?" With that, he bade him farewell. [31]Jacob named the place Peniel,* "Because I have seen God face to face," he said, "yet my life has been spared."[f]

[32]At sunrise, as he left Penuel, Jacob limped along because of his hip. [33]That is why, to this day, the Israelites do not eat the sciatic muscle that is on the hip socket, inasmuch as Jacob's hip socket was struck at the sciatic muscle.

See RG 112–14

CHAPTER 33

Jacob and Esau Meet. [1]Jacob looked up and saw Esau coming, accompanied by four hundred men. So he divided his children among Leah, Rachel and the two maidservants, [2]putting the maids and their children first, Leah and her children next, and Rachel and Joseph last. [3]He himself went on ahead of them, bowing to the ground seven times, until he reached his brother. [4]Esau ran to meet him, embraced him, and flinging himself on his neck, kissed him as he wept.

[5]When Esau looked about, he saw the women and children. "Who are these with you?" he asked. Jacob answered, "They are the children whom God has graciously bestowed on your servant." [6]Then the maidservants and their children came forward and bowed low; [7]next, Leah and her children came forward and bowed low; lastly, Rachel and her children came forward and bowed low. [8]Then Esau asked, "What did you intend with all those droves that I encountered?" Jacob answered, "It was to gain my lord's favor." [9]"I have plenty," replied Esau; "you should keep what is yours, brother." [10]"No, I beg you!" said Jacob. "If you will do me the favor, please accept this gift from me, since to come into your presence is for me like coming into the presence of God, now that you have received me so kindly. [11]Do accept the present I have brought you; God has been generous toward me, and I have an abundance." Since he so urged him, Esau accepted.

[12]Then Esau said, "Let us break camp and be on our way; I will travel alongside you." [13]But Jacob replied: "As my lord can see, the children are frail. Besides, I am encumbered with the flocks and herds, which now have sucklings; if overdriven for a single day, the whole flock will die. [14]Let my lord, then, go on ahead of me, while I proceed more slowly at the pace of the livestock before me and at the pace of my children, until I join my lord in Seir." [15]Esau replied, "Let me at least put at your disposal some of the men who are with me." But Jacob said, "For what reason? Please indulge me in this, my lord." [16]So on the same day that Esau began his journey back to Seir, [17]Jacob journeyed to Succoth. There he built a home for himself and made

d: Hos 12, 4.   e: Gn 35, 10; 1 Kgs 18, 31; 2 Kgs 17, 34.   f: Jgs 13, 22.

booths for his livestock. That is why the place was called Succoth.*

[18]Having thus come from Paddan-aram, Jacob arrived safely at the city of Shechem, which is in the land of Canaan, and he encamped in sight of the city.[g] [19]The plot of ground on which he had pitched his tent he bought for a hundred pieces of bullion* from the descendants of Hamor, the founder of Shechem.[h] [20]He set up a memorial stone there and invoked "El, the God of Israel."[i]

See RG
112–14

CHAPTER 34

The Rape of Dinah. [1]*Dinah, the daughter whom Leah had borne to Jacob, went out to visit some of the women of the land. [2]When Shechem, son of Hamor the Hivite,* who was chief of the region, saw her, he seized her and lay with her by force. [3]Since he was strongly attracted to Dinah, daughter of Jacob, indeed was really in love with the girl, he endeavored to win her affection. [4]Shechem also asked his father Hamor, "Get me this girl for a wife."

[5]Meanwhile, Jacob heard that Shechem had defiled his daughter Dinah; but since his sons were out in the fields with his livestock, he held his peace until they came home. [6]Now Hamor, the father of Shechem, went out to discuss the matter with Jacob, [7]just as Jacob's sons were coming in from the fields. When they heard the news, the men were shocked and seethed with indignation. What Shechem had done was an outrage in Israel; such a thing could not be tolerated.[j]

[8]Hamor appealed to them, saying, "My son Shechem has his heart set on your daughter. Please give her to him in marriage. [9]Intermarry with us; give your daughters to us, and take our daughters for yourselves. [10]Thus you can live among us. The land is open before you; you can settle and move about freely in it, and acquire landed property here." [11]Then Shechem, too, appealed to Dinah's father and brothers: "Do me this fa-

vor, and I will pay whatever you demand of me. [12]No matter how high you set the bridal price, I will pay you whatever you ask; only give me the maiden in marriage."

Revenge of Jacob's Sons. [13]Jacob's sons replied to Shechem and his father Hamor with guile, speaking as they did because their sister Dinah had been defiled. [14]"We could not do such a thing," they said, "as to give our sister to an uncircumcised man; that would be a disgrace for us. [15]We will agree with you only on this condition, that you become like us by having every male among you circumcised. [16]Then we will give you our daughters and take yours in marriage; we will settle among you and become one kindred people with you. [17]But if you do not comply with our terms regarding circumcision, we will take our daughter and go away."

[18]Their proposal seemed fair to Hamor and his son Shechem. [19]The young man lost no time in acting in the matter, since he was deeply in love with Jacob's daughter. Moreover, he was more highly respected than anyone else in his clan. [20]So Hamor and his son Shechem went to their town council and thus presented the matter to their fellow townsmen: [21]"These men are friendly toward us. Let them settle in the land and move about in it freely; there is ample room in the country for them. We can marry their daughters and give our daughters to them in marriage. [22]But the men will agree to live with us and form one kindred people with us only on this condition, that every male among us be circumcised as they themselves are. [23]Would not the livestock they have acquired—all their animals—then be ours? Let us, therefore, give in to them, so that they may settle among us."

[24]All the able-bodied men of the town agreed with Hamor and his son Shechem, and all the males, including every able-bodied man in the community,* were circumcised. [25]On the third day, while they were

---

33, 17: Succoth: an important town near the confluence of the Jabbok and the Jordan (Jos 13, 27; Jgs 8, 5-16; 1 Kgs 7, 46). Booths: in Hebrew, sukkot, of the same sound as the name of the town.

33, 19: Pieces of bullion: in Hebrew, kesita, a monetary unit of which the value is now unknown. Descendants of Ha-

mor: Hamorites, "the men of Hamor"; cf Jgs 9, 28. Hamor was regarded as the eponymous ancestor of the pre-Israelite inhabitants of Shechem.

g: Gn 12, 6; Jn 4, 6. h: Jos 24, 32; Jn 4. 5; Acts 7, 16. i: Jgs 6, 24. j: 2 Sm 13, 12.

still in pain, Dinah's full brothers Simeon and Levi, two of Jacob's sons, took their swords, advanced against the city without any trouble, and massacred all the males.*k* *26*After they had put Hamor and his son Shechem to the sword, they took Dinah from Shechem's house and left.*l* *27*Then the other sons of Jacob followed up the slaughter and sacked the city in reprisal for their sister Dinah's defilement. *28*They seized their flocks, herds and asses, whatever was in the city and in the country around. *29*They carried off all their wealth, their women, and their children, and took for loot whatever was in the houses.*m*

*30*Jacob said to Simeon and Levi: "You have brought trouble upon me by making me loathsome to the inhabitants of the land, the Canaanites and the Perizzites. I have so few men that, if these people unite against me and attack me, I and my family will be wiped out." *31*But they retorted, "Should our sister have been treated like a harlot?"

CHAPTER 35

See RG
112–14

Bethel Revisited. *1*God said to Jacob: "Go up now to Bethel. Settle there and build an altar there to the God who appeared to you while you were fleeing from your brother Esau."*n* *2*So Jacob told his family and all the others who were with him: "Get rid of the foreign gods* that you have among you; then purify yourselves and put on fresh clothes. *3*We are now to go up to Bethel, and I will build an altar there to the God who answered me in my hour of distress and who has been with me wherever I have gone." *4*They therefore handed over to Jacob all the foreign gods in their possession and also the

rings* they had in their ears. *5*Then, as they set out, a terror from God fell upon the towns round about, so that no one pursued the sons of Jacob.

*6*Thus Jacob and all the people who were with him arrived in Luz [that is, Bethel] in the land of Canaan.*o* *7*There he built an altar and named the place Bethel, for it was there that God had revealed himself to him when he was fleeing from his brother.*p*

*8*Death came to Rebekah's nurse Deborah; she was buried under the oak below Bethel, and so it was called Allon-bacuth.*

*9*On Jacob's arrival from Paddan-aram, God appeared to him again and blessed him. *10*God said to him:

"You whose name is Jacob
    shall no longer be called Jacob,
    but Israel shall be your name."*q*

Thus he was named Israel. *11*God also said to him:

"I am God Almighty;
    be fruitful and multiply.
A nation, indeed an assembly of nations,
    shall stem from you,
    and kings shall issue from your loins.
12 The land I once gave
    to Abraham and Isaac
    I now give to you;
And to your descendants after you
    will I give this land."*r*

*13*Then God departed from him. *14*On the site where God had spoken with him, Jacob set up a memorial stone, and upon it he made a libation and poured out oil.*s* *15*Jacob named the site Bethel, because God had spoken with him there.

34, 1-31: Behind the story of the rape of Dinah and the revenge of Jacob's sons on the men of the city of Shechem there probably lies a dimly recollected historical event connected with an armed conflict between the earliest Israelite tribes invading central Canaan and the Hurrian inhabitants of the Shechem region.

34, 2: Hivite: The Greek text has "Horite"; the terms were apparently used indiscriminately to designate the Hurrian or other non-Semitic elements in Palestine.

34, 24: Every able-bodied man in the community: literally "all those who go out at the gate of the city," apparently meaning the men who go out to war. By temporarily crippling them through circumcision, Jacob's sons deprived the city of its defenders.

35, 2: Foreign gods: pagan images, including household idols (see note on Gn 31, 19), that Jacob's people brought with them from Paddan-aram.

35, 4: Rings: Earrings were often worn as amulets connected with pagan magic.

35, 8: This verse may have stood originally in some other context. Rebekah's nurse is spoken of without a name, in Gn 24, 59. Allon-bacuth: the Hebrew name means "oak of weeping."

---

k: Gn 49, 6.   *l:* Jdt 9, 2.   *m:* Jdt 9, 3f.   *n:* Gn 28, 12f.   *o:* Gn 28, 19; Jos 18, 13; Jgs 1, 22f.   *p:* Gn 28, 12f.   *q:* 1 Kgs 18, 31; 2 Kgs 17, 34.   *r:* Ex 32, 13; Heb 11, 9.   *s:* Gn 28, 18; 31, 45.

Jacob's Family. [16]Then they departed from Bethel: but while they still had some distance to go on the way to Ephrath, Rachel began to be in labor and to suffer great distress. [17]When her pangs were most severe, her midwife said to her, "Have no fear! This time, too, you have a son." [18]With her last breath—for she was at the point of death—she called him Ben-oni;* his father, however, named him Benjamin. [19]*t*Thus Rachel died; and she was buried on the road to Ephrath [that is, Bethlehem].* [20]Jacob set up a memorial stone on her grave, and the same monument marks Rachel's grave to this day.

[21]Israel moved on and pitched his tent beyond Migdal-eder. [22]While Israel was encamped in that region, Reuben went and lay with Bilhah, his father's concubine. When Israel heard of it, he was greatly offended.*u*

The sons of Jacob were now twelve. [23]The sons of Leah: Reuben, Jacob's first-born, Simeon, Levi, Judah, Issachar, and Zebulun; [24]*the sons of Rachel: Joseph and Benjamin; [25]the sons of Rachel's maid Bilhah: Dan and Naphtali; [26]the sons of Leah's maid Zilpah: Gad and Asher. These are the sons of Jacob who were born to him in Paddan-aram.

[27]Jacob went home to his father Isaac at Mamre, in Kiriath-arba [that is, Hebron], where Abraham and Isaac had stayed. [28]The lifetime of Isaac was one hundred and eighty years; [29]then he breathed his last. After a full life, he died as an old man and was taken to his kinsmen. His sons Esau and Jacob buried him.

See RG 112–14

CHAPTER 36

Edomite Lists. [1]These are the descendants of Esau [that is, Edom]. [2]*Esau took his wives from among the Canaanite women: Adah, daughter of Elon the Hittite; Oholibamah, granddaughter through Anah of Zibeon the Hivite;*v* [3]and Basemath, daughter of Ishmael and sister of Nebaioth. [4]Adah bore Eliphaz to Esau; Basemath bore Reuel;*w* [5]and Oholibamah bore Jeush, Jalam and Korah. These are the sons of Esau who were born to him in the land of Canaan.*x*

[6]Esau took his wives, his sons, his daughters, and all the members of his household, as well as his livestock comprising various animals and all the property he had acquired in the land of Canaan, and went to the land of Seir, out of the way of his brother Jacob.*y* [7]Their possessions had become too great for them to dwell together, and the land in which they were staying could not support them because of their livestock. [8]So Esau settled in the highlands of Seir. [Esau is Edom.]*z* [9]These are the descendants of Esau, ancestor of the Edomites, in the highlands of Seir.

[10]These are the names of Esau's sons: Eliphaz, son of Esau's wife Adah; and Reuel, son of Esau's wife Basemath. [11]*a*The sons of Eliphaz were Teman, Omar, Zepho, Gatam and Kenaz. [12](Esau's son Eliphaz had a concubine Timna, and she bore Amalek to Eliphaz.) These are the descendants of Esau's wife Adah. [13]The sons of Reuel were Nahath, Zerah, Shammah and Mizzah. These are the descendants of Esau's wife Basemath.*b* [14]The descendants of Esau's wife Oholibamah—granddaughter through Anah of Zibeon—whom she bore to Esau were Jeush, Jalam and Korah.*c*

[15]The following are the clans of Esau's descendants. The descendants of Eliphaz, Esau's first-born: the clans of Teman, Omar,

---

35, 18: Ben-oni: means either "son of my vigor" or, more likely in the context, "son of affliction." Benjamin: "son of the right hand." This may be interpreted to signify a son who is his father's help and support, but more likely its original meaning was "southerner." In the Hebrew idiom, the south lies to one's right hand, and Benjamin was the southernmost of the Rachel tribes.

35, 19: Bethlehem: the gloss comes from a later tradition that identified the site with Bethlehem, also called Ephrath or Ephratha (Jos 15, 59; Ru 4, 11; Mi 5, 1). But Rachel's grave was actually near Ramah (Jer 31, 15), a few miles north of Jerusalem, in the territory of Benjamin (1 Sm 20, 2).

35, 24ff: Benjamin is here said to have been born in Pad-

dan-aram, either because all twelve sons of Jacob are considered as a unit, or because the Priestly source, from which vv 23-29 are taken, follows a tradition different from that of the Elohistic source found in vv 16-20.

36, 2-14: The names of Esau's wives and of their fathers given here differ considerably from their names cited from other old sources in Gn 26, 34 and 28, 9. Zibeon the Hivite: In v 20 he is called a "Horite"; see note on Gn 34, 2.

t: Gn 48, 7; 1 Sm 10, 2; Mi 5, 2.   *u:* Gn 49, 4; 1 Chr 5, 1.   *v:* Gn 26, 34.   *w:* 1 Chr 1, 35.   *x:* 1 Chr 1, 35.   *y:* Gn 32, 4.   *z:* Dt 2, 4f; Jos 24, 4.   *a:* 11f: 1 Chr 1, 36.   *b:* 1 Chr 1, 37.   *c:* 1 Chr 1, 35.

Zepho, Kenaz, [16]Korah, Gatam and Amalek. These are the clans of Eliphaz in the land of Edom; they are descended from Adah. [17]The descendants of Esau's son Reuel: the clans of Nahath, Zerah, Shammah and Mizzah. These are the clans of Reuel in the land of Edom; they are descended from Esau's wife Basemath. [18]The descendants of Esau's wife Oholibamah: the clans of Jeush, Jalam and Korah. These are the clans of Esau's wife Oholibamah, daughter of Anah. [19]Such are the descendants of Esau [that is, Edom] according to their clans.

[20]The following are the descendants of Seir the Horite,* the original settlers in the land: Lotan, Shobal, Zibeon, Anah,[d] [21]Dishon, Ezer and Dishan; they are the Horite clans descended from Seir, in the land of Edom. [22e]Lotan's descendants were Hori and Hemam, and Lotan's sister was Timna. [23]Shobal's descendants were Alvan, Mahanath, Ebal, Shepho and Onam. [24]Zibeon's descendants were Aiah and Anah. (He is the Anah who found water in the desert while he was pasturing the asses of his father Zibeon.) [25]The descendants of Anah were Dishon and Oholibamah, daughter of Anah. [26]The descendants of Dishon were Hemdan, Eshban, Ithran and Cheran. [27]The descendants of Ezer were Bilhan, Zaavan and Akan. [28]The descendants of Dishan were Uz and Aran. [29]These are the Horite clans: the clans of Lotan, Shobal, Zibeon, Anah, [30]Dishon, Ezer and Dishan; they were the clans of the Horites, clan by clan, in the land of Seir.

[31f]The following are the kings who reigned in the land of Edom before any king reigned over the Israelites.* [32]Bela, son of Beor, became king in Edom; the name of his city was Dinhabah. [33]When Bela died, Jobab, son of Zerah, from Bozrah, succeeded him as king. [34]When Jobab died, Husham, from the land of the Temanites, succeeded him as king. He defeated the Midianites in the country of Moab; the name of his city was Avith.

[35]When Husham died, Hadad, son of Bedad, succeeded him as king. [36]When Hadad died, Samlah, from Masrekah, succeeded him as king. [37]When Samlah died, Shaul, from Rehoboth-on-the-River, succeeded him as king. [38]When Shaul died, Baal-hanan, son of Achbor, succeeded him as king. [39]When Baal-hanan died, Hadar succeeded him as king; the name of his city was Pau. (His wife's name was Mehetabel; she was the daughter of Matred, son of Mezahab.)

[40]The following are the names of the clans of Esau individually according to their subdivisions and localities: the clans of Timna, Alvah, Jetheth, [41]Oholibamah, Elah, Pinon, [42]Kenaz, Teman, Mibzar, [43]Magdiel and Iram. These are the clans of the Edomites, according to their settlements in their territorial holdings. [Esau was the father of the Edomites.]

IV: Joseph and His Brothers

CHAPTER 37

See RG 114-15

Joseph Sold into Egypt. [1]Jacob settled in the land where his father had stayed, the land of Canaan. [2]This is his family history. When Joseph was seventeen years old, he was tending the flocks with his brothers; he was an assistant to the sons of his father's wives Bilhah and Zilpah, and he brought his father bad reports about them.

[3]Israel loved Joseph best of all his sons, for he was the child of his old age; and he had made him a long tunic. [4]When his brothers saw that their father loved him best of all his sons, they hated him so much that they would not even greet him.

[5]Once Joseph had a dream, which he told to his brothers:[g] [6]"Listen to this dream I had. [7]There we were, binding sheaves in the field, when suddenly my sheaf rose to an upright position, and your sheaves formed a ring around my sheaf and bowed down to it." [8]"Are you really going to make yourself

---

36, 20: Seir the Horite: According to Dt 2, 12, the highlands of Seir were inhabited by Horites before they were occupied by the Edomites.

36, 31: Before any king reigned over the Israelites: obviously this statement was written after the time of Saul, Israel's first king.

---

d: 20f: 1 Chr 1, 38. e: 22-28: 1 Chr 1, 39-42. f: 31-43: 1 Chr 1, 45-54. g: Gn 42, 9.

king over us?" his brothers asked him. "Or impose your rule on us?" So they hated him all the more because of his talk about his dreams.[h]

[9]Then he had another dream, and this one, too, he told to his brothers. "I had another dream," he said; "this time, the sun and the moon and eleven stars were bowing down to me." [10]When he also told it to his father, his father reproved him. "What is the meaning of this dream of yours?" he asked. "Can it be that I and your mother and your brothers are to come and bow to the ground before you?" [11]So his brothers were wrought up against him but his father pondered the matter.

[12]One day, when his brothers had gone to pasture their father's flocks at Shechem, [13]Israel said to Joseph, "Your brothers, you know, are tending our flocks at Shechem. Get ready; I will send you to them." "I am ready," Joseph answered. [14]"Go then," he replied; "see if all is well with your brothers and the flocks, and bring back word." So he sent him off from the valley of Hebron. When Joseph reached Shechem, [15]a man met him as he was wandering about in the fields. "What are you looking for?" the man asked him. [16]"I am looking for my brothers," he answered. "Could you please tell me where they are tending the flocks?" [17]The man told him, "They have moved on from here; in fact, I heard them say, 'Let us go on to Dothan.'" So Joseph went after his brothers and caught up with them in Dothan. [18]They noticed him from a distance, and before he came up to them, they plotted to kill him. [19]They said to one another: "Here comes that master dreamer! [20]Come on, let us kill him and throw him into one of the cisterns here; we could say that a wild beast devoured him. We shall then see what comes of his dreams."[i]

[21]*When Reuben heard this, he tried to save him from their hands, saying, "We must not take his life. [22]Instead of shedding blood," he continued, "just throw him into that cistern there in the desert; but don't kill him outright." His purpose was to rescue him from their hands and restore him to his father.[j] [23]So when Joseph came up to them, they stripped him of the long tunic he had on; [24]then they took him and threw him into the cistern, which was empty and dry.

[25]They then sat down to their meal. Looking up, they saw a caravan of Ishmaelites coming from Gilead, their camels laden with gum, balm and resin to be taken down to Egypt.[k] [26]Judah said to his brothers: "What is to be gained by killing our brother and concealing his blood?[l] [27]Rather, let us sell him to these Ishmaelites, instead of doing away with him ourselves. After all, he is our brother, our own flesh." His brothers agreed. [28]They sold Joseph to the Ishmaelites for twenty pieces of silver.*

Some Midianite traders passed by, and they pulled Joseph up out of the cistern and took him to Egypt.[m] [29]When Reuben went back to the cistern and saw that Joseph was not in it, he tore his clothes, [30]and returning to his brothers, he exclaimed: "The boy is gone! And I—where can I turn?" [31]They took Joseph's tunic, and after slaughtering a goat, dipped the tunic in its blood. [32]They then sent someone to bring the long tunic to their father, with the message: "We found this. See whether it is your son's tunic or not." [33]He recognized it and exclaimed: "My son's tunic! A wild beast has devoured him! Joseph has been torn to pieces!"[n] [34]Then Jacob rent his clothes, put sackcloth on his loins, and mourned his son many days. [35]Though his sons and daughters tried to console him, he refused all consolation, saying, "No, I will go down mourning to my son in the nether world." Thus did his father lament him.[o]

[36]The Midianites, meanwhile, sold Joseph

37, 21-36: The chapter thus far is from the Yahwist source, as are also vv 25-28a. But vv 21-24 and 28b-36 are from the Elohist source. In the latter, Reuben tries to rescue Joseph, who is taken in Reuben's absence by certain Midianites; in the Yahwist source, it is Judah who saves Joseph's life by having him sold to certain Ishmaelites. Although the two variant forms in which the story was handed down in early oral tradition differ in these minor points, they agree on the essential fact that Joseph was brought as a slave into

Egypt because of the jealousy of his brothers.

37, 28: They sold Joseph . . . silver: in the Hebrew text, these words occur between out of the cistern and (they) took him to Egypt at the end of the verse.

---

h: Gn 50, 17. i: Gn 44, 28. j: Gn 42, 22. k: Gn 43, 11. l: Jb 16, 18. m: Ps 105, 17; Wis 10, 13; Acts 7, 9. n: Gn 44, 28. o: Gn 42, 38.

in Egypt to Potiphar, a courtier of Pharaoh and his chief steward.^p

in Egypt to Potiphar, a courtier of Pharaoh and his chief steward.*p*

See RG
114–15

CHAPTER 38*

Judah and Tamar. ¹About that time Judah parted from his brothers and pitched his tent near a certain Adullamite named Hirah. ²There he met the daughter of a Canaanite named Shua, married her, and had relations with her.*q* ³She conceived and bore a son, whom she named Er. ⁴Again she conceived and bore a son, whom she named Onan. ⁵Then she bore still another son, whom she named Shelah. They were in Chezib* when he was born.*r*

⁶Judah got a wife named Tamar for his first-born, Er. ⁷But Er, Judah's first-born, greatly offended the LORD; so the LORD took his life.*s* ⁸*t*Then Judah said to Onan, "Unite with your brother's widow, in fulfillment of your duty as brother-in-law, and thus preserve your brother's line."* ⁹Onan, however, knew that the descendants would not be counted as his; so whenever he had relations with his brother's widow, he wasted his seed on the ground, to avoid contributing offspring for his brother. ¹⁰What he did greatly offended the LORD, and the LORD took his life too. ¹¹Thereupon Judah said to his daughter-in-law Tamar, "Stay as a widow in your father's house until my son Shelah grows up"—for he feared that Shelah also might die like his brothers. So Tamar went to live in her father's house.

¹²Years passed, and Judah's wife, the daughter of Shua, died. After Judah completed the period of mourning, he went up to Timnah for the shearing of his sheep, in company with his friend Hirah the Adullamite. ¹³When Tamar was told that her father-in-law was on his way up to Timnah to shear his sheep, ¹⁴she took off her widow's garb, veiled her face by covering herself with a shawl, and sat down at the entrance to Enaim, which is on the way to Timnah; for she was aware that, although Shelah was now grown up, she had not been given to him in marriage.*u* ¹⁵When Judah saw her, he mistook her for a harlot, since she had covered her face. ¹⁶So he went over to her at the roadside, and not realizing that she was his daughter-in-law, he said, "Come, let me have intercourse with you." She replied, "What will you pay me for letting you have intercourse with me?" ¹⁷He answered, "I will send you a kid from the flock." "Very well," she said, "provided you leave a pledge until you send it." ¹⁸Judah asked, "What pledge am I to give you?" She answered, "Your seal and cord,* and the staff you carry." So he gave them to her and had intercourse with her, and she conceived by him. ¹⁹When she went away, she took off her shawl and put on her widow's garb again.

²⁰Judah sent the kid by his friend the Adullamite to recover the pledge from the woman; but he could not find her. ²¹So he asked the men of the place, "Where is the temple prostitute,* the one by the roadside in Enaim?" But they answered, "There has never been a temple prostitute here." ²²He went back to Judah and told him, "I could not find her; and besides, the men of the place said there was no temple prostitute there."

38, 1-30: This chapter, from the Yahwist source, has nothing to do with the Joseph story in which Judah is still living with his father and brothers. The sacred author inserted this independent account from the life of Judah at this place to mark the long lapse of time during which Joseph's family knew nothing of his life in Egypt. This is apparently a personalized history of the early days of the tribe of Judah, which interbred with several Canaanite clans, though some of these soon became extinct.

38, 5: Chezib: a variant form of Achzib (Jos 15, 44; Mi 1, 14), a town in the Judean Shephelah.

38, 8: Preserve your brother's line: literally, "raise up seed for your brother." The ancient Israelites regarded as very important their law of levirate, or "brother-in-law" marriage; see notes on Dt 25, 5; Ru 2, 20. In the present story, it is primarily Onan's violation of this law, rather than the means he used to

circumvent it, that brought on him God's displeasure (vv 9f).

38, 18: Seal and cord: the cylinder seal, through which a hole was bored lengthwise so that it could be worn from the neck by a cord, was a distinctive means of identification. Apparently a man's staff was also marked with his name (Nm 17, 16f) or other sign of identification.

38, 21: Temple prostitute: the Hebrew term qedesha, literally "consecrated woman," designates a woman who had ritual intercourse with men in pagan fertility rites; cf Dt 23, 18; Hos 4, 14, where the same Hebrew word is used. Hirah the Adullamite uses a word that refers to a higher social class than that designated by the term zona, common "harlot," used in vv 15. 24.

---

p: Ps 105, 17.　*q:* 1 Chr 2, 3.　*r:* 1 Chr 4, 21.　*s:* 1 Chr 2, 3.
t: Dt 25, 5; Mt 22, 24; Mk 12, 19; Lk 20, 28.　*u:* Prv 7, 10.

[23]"Let her keep the things," Judah replied; "otherwise we shall become a laughingstock. After all, I did send her the kid, even though you were unable to find her."

[24]About three months later, Judah was told that his daughter-in-law Tamar had played the harlot and was then with child from her harlotry. "Bring her out," cried Judah; "she shall be burned." [25]But as they were bringing her out, she sent word to her father-in-law, "It is by the man to whom these things belong that I am with child. Please verify," she added, "whose seal and cord and whose staff these are." [26]Judah recognized them and said, "She is more in the right than I am, since I did not give her to my son Shelah." But he had no further relations with her.

[27]When the time of her delivery came, she was found to have twins in her womb.[v] [28]While she was giving birth, one infant put out his hand; and the midwife, taking a crimson thread, tied it on his hand, to note that this one came out first. [29][w]But as he withdrew his hand, his brother came out; and she said, "What a breach you have made for yourself!" So he was called Perez.[*] [30]Afterward his brother came out; he was called Zerah.[x] [*]

See RG 114–15

CHAPTER 39

Joseph's Temptation. [1]When Joseph was taken down to Egypt, a certain Egyptian (Potiphar, a courtier of Pharoah and his chief steward[*]) bought him from the Ishmaelites who had brought him there. [2][y]But since the LORD was with him, Joseph got on very well and was assigned to the household of his Egyptian master. [3]When his master saw that the LORD was with him and brought him success in whatever he did, [4]he took a liking to Joseph and made him his personal attendant; he put him in charge of his household and entrusted to him all his possessions.[z] [5]From the moment that he put him in charge of his household and all his possessions, the LORD blessed the Egyptian's house for Joseph's sake; in fact, the LORD's blessing was on everything he owned, both inside the house and out. [6]Having left everything he owned in Joseph's charge, he gave no thought, with Joseph there, to anything but the food he ate.

Now Joseph was strikingly handsome in countenance and body. [7]After a time, his master's wife began to look fondly at him and said, "Lie with me." [8]But he refused. "As long as I am here," he told her, "my master does not concern himself with anything in the house, but has entrusted to me all he owns. [9]He wields no more authority in this house than I do, and he has withheld from me nothing but yourself, since you are his wife. How, then, could I commit so great a wrong and thus stand condemned before God?" [10]Although she tried to entice him day after day, he would not agree to lie beside her, or even stay near her.[a]

[11]One such day, when Joseph came into the house to do his work, and none of the household servants were then in the house, [12]she laid hold of him by his cloak, saying, "Lie with me!" But leaving the cloak in her hand, he got away from her and ran outside. [13]When she saw that he had left his cloak in her hand as he fled outside, [14]she screamed for her household servants and told them, "Look! My husband has brought in a Hebrew slave to make sport of us! He came in here to lie with me, but I cried out as loud as I could. [15]When he heard me scream for help, he left his cloak beside me and ran away outside."

[16]She kept the cloak with her until his master came home. [17]Then she told him the same story: "The Hebrew slave whom you brought here broke in on me, to make sport of me. [18]But when I screamed for help, he

---

38, 29: He was called Perez: the Hebrew word means "breach."

38, 30: He was called Zerah: a name connected here by popular etymology with a Hebrew verb for the red light of dawn, alluding apparently to the crimson thread.

39, 1: (Potiphar . . . chief steward): These words in the text serve to harmonize ch 39 from the Yahwist source, with Gn 37, 36, and 40, 1-23, from the Elohist. In the former, the Ishmaelites who bought Joseph from his brothers (Gn 37, 28)

sold him to the unnamed "Egyptian master" of ch 39. In the latter, the Midianites who kidnaped Joseph (Gn 37, 28; 40, 15) sold him to Potiphar, Pharaoh's chief steward (Gn 37, 36), whose house was used as a royal prison (Gn 40, 2f).

v: 1 Chr 2, 4. w: Rv 4, 12; Mt 1, 3; Lk 3, 33. x: Nm 26, 20; 1 Chr 2, 4; Mt 1, 3. y: 1 Sm 3, 19; 10, 7; 18, 14; 2 Sm 5, 10; 2 Kgs 18, 7; Acts 7, 9. z: Dn 1, 9. a: 1 Mc 2, 53.

left his cloak beside me and fled outside." [19]As soon as the master heard his wife's story about how his slave had treated her, he became enraged. [20]He seized Joseph and threw him into the jail where the royal prisoners were confined.[b]

But even while he was in prison, [21]the LORD remained with Joseph; he showed him kindness by making the chief jailer well-disposed toward him.[c] [22]The chief jailer put Joseph in charge of all the prisoners in the jail, and everything that had to be done there was done under his management. [23]The chief jailer did not concern himself with anything at all that was in Joseph's charge, since the LORD was with him and brought success to all he did.

CHAPTER 40

See RG 114–15

The Dreams Interpreted. [1]Some time afterward, the royal cupbearer and baker gave offense to their lord, the king of Egypt. [2]Pharaoh was angry with his two courtiers, the chief cupbearer and the chief baker, [3]and he put them in custody in the house of the chief steward (the same jail where Joseph was confined). [4]The chief steward assigned Joseph to them, and he became their attendant.

After they had been in custody for some time, [5]the cupbearer and the baker of the king of Egypt who were confined in the jail both had dreams on the same night, each dream with its own meaning. [6]When Joseph came to them in the morning, he noticed that they looked disturbed. [7]So he asked Pharaoh's courtiers who were with him in custody in his master's house, "Why do you look so sad today?" [8]They answered him, "We have had dreams, but there is no one to interpret them for us." Joseph said to them, "Surely, interpretations come from God. Please tell the dreams to me."[d]

[9]Then the chief cupbearer told Joseph his dream. "In my dream," he said, "I saw a vine in front of me, [10]and on the vine were three branches. It had barely budded when its blossoms came out, and its clusters ripened into grapes. [11]Pharaoh's cup was in my hand; so I took the grapes, pressed them out into his cup, and put it in Pharaoh's hand." [12]Joseph said to him: "This is what it means. The three branches are three days; [13]within three days Pharaoh will lift up your head* and restore you to your post. You will be handing Pharaoh his cup as you formerly used to do when you were his cupbearer. [14]So if you will still remember, when all is well with you, that I was here with you, please do me the favor of mentioning me to Pharaoh, to get me out of this place. [15]The truth is that I was kidnaped from the land of the Hebrews, and here I have not done anything for which I should have been put into a dungeon."

[16]When the chief baker saw that Joseph had given this favorable interpretation, he said to him: "I too had a dream. In it I had three wicker baskets on my head; [17]in the top one were all kinds of bakery products for Pharaoh, but the birds were pecking at them out of the basket on my head." [18]Joseph said to him in reply: "This is what it means. The three baskets are three days; [19]within three days Pharaoh will lift up your head and have you impaled on a stake, and the birds will be pecking the flesh from your body."

[20]And in fact, on the third day, which was Pharaoh's birthday, when he gave a banquet to all his staff, with his courtiers around him, he lifted up the heads of the chief cupbearer and chief baker. [21]He restored the chief cupbearer to his office, so that he again handed the cup to Pharaoh; [22]but the chief baker he impaled—just as Joseph had told them in his interpretation. [23]Yet the chief cupbearer gave no thought to Joseph; he had forgotten him.

CHAPTER 41

See RG 114–15

Pharaoh's Dream. [1]After a lapse of two years, Pharaoh had a dream. He saw himself standing by the Nile, [2]when up out of the Nile came seven cows, handsome and fat; they grazed in the reed grass. [3]Behind them seven other cows, ugly and gaunt, came up out of the Nile; and standing on the

---

40, 13: Lift up your head: signifying "pardon you." In v 19 "to lift up the head" means "to behead"; and finally, in v 20, the same expression means "to review the case (of someone)." Joseph couches his interpretation of the dreams in equivocal terms.

---

b: Ps 105, 18.   *c:* Acts 7, 9f.   *d:* Gn 41, 16.

bank of the Nile beside the others, [4]the ugly, gaunt cows ate up the seven handsome, fat cows. Then Pharaoh woke up.

[5]He fell asleep again and had another dream. He saw seven ears of grain, fat and healthy, growing on a single stalk. [6]Behind them sprouted seven ears of grain, thin and blasted by the east wind; [7]and the seven thin ears swallowed up the seven fat, healthy ears. Then Pharaoh woke up, to find it was only a dream.

[8]Next morning his spirit was agitated. So he summoned all the magicians and sages of Egypt and recounted his dreams to them; but no one could interpret his dreams for him. [9]Then the chief cupbearer spoke up and said to Pharaoh: "On this occasion I am reminded of my negligence. [10]Once, when Pharaoh was angry, he put me and the chief baker in custody in the house of the chief steward. [11]Later, we both had dreams on the same night, and each of our dreams had its own meaning. [12]There with us was a Hebrew youth, a slave of the chief steward; and when we told him our dreams, he interpreted them for us and explained for each of us the meaning of his dream.[e] [13]And it turned out just as he had told us: I was restored to my post, but the other man was impaled."

[14]Pharaoh therefore had Joseph summoned, and they hurriedly brought him from the dungeon. After he shaved and changed his clothes, he came into Pharaoh's presence.[f] [15]Pharaoh then said to him: "I had certain dreams that no one can interpret. But I hear it said of you that the moment you are told a dream you can interpret it." [16]"It is not I," Joseph replied to Pharaoh, "but God who will give Pharaoh the right answer."[g]

[17]Then Pharaoh said to Joseph: "In my dream, I was standing on the bank of the Nile, [18]when up from the Nile came seven cows, fat and well-formed; they grazed in the reed grass. [19]Behind them came seven other cows, scrawny, most ill-formed and gaunt. Never have I seen such ugly specimens as these in all the land of Egypt! [20]The gaunt, ugly cows ate up the first seven fat cows. [21]But when they had consumed them, no one could tell that they had done so, because they looked as ugly as before. Then I woke up. [22]In another dream, I saw seven ears of grain, fat and healthy, growing on a single stalk. [23]Behind them sprouted seven ears of grain, shriveled and thin and blasted by the east wind; [24]and the seven thin ears swallowed up the seven healthy ears. I have spoken to the magicians, but none of them can give me an explanation."

[25]Joseph said to Pharaoh: "Both of Pharaoh's dreams have the same meaning. God has thus foretold to Pharaoh what he is about to do. [26]The seven healthy cows are seven years, and the seven healthy ears are seven years—the same in each dream. [27]So also, the seven thin, ugly cows that came up after them are seven years, as are the seven thin, wind-blasted ears; they are seven years of famine. [28]It is just as I told Pharaoh: God has revealed to Pharaoh what he is about to do. [29]Seven years of great abundance are now coming throughout the land of Egypt; [30]but these will be followed by seven years of famine, when all the abundance in the land of Egypt will be forgotten. When the famine has ravaged the land, [31]no trace of the abundance will be found in the land because of the famine that follows it—so utterly severe will that famine be. [32]That Pharaoh had the same dream twice means that the matter has been reaffirmed by God and that God will soon bring it about.

[33]"Therefore, let Pharaoh seek out a wise and discerning man and put him in charge of the land of Egypt. [34]Pharaoh should also take action to appoint overseers, so as to regiment the land during the seven years of abundance. [35]They should husband all the food of the coming good years, collecting the grain under Pharaoh's authority, to be stored in the towns for food. [36]This food will serve as a reserve for the country against the seven years of famine that are to follow in the land of Egypt, so that the land may not perish in the famine."

[37]This advice pleased Pharaoh and all his officials.[h] [38]"Could we find another like him," Pharaoh asked his officials, "a man so

e: Dn 1, 17.   f: Ps 105, 20.   g: Gn 40, 8.   h: Acts 7, 10.

endowed with the spirit of God?" [39] So Pharaoh said to Joseph: "Since God has made all this known to you, no one can be as wise and discerning as you are. [40] You shall be in charge of my palace, and all my people shall dart at your command. Only in respect to the throne shall I outrank you.[i] [41] Herewith," Pharaoh told Joseph, "I place you in charge of the whole land of Egypt." [42] With that, Pharaoh took off his signet ring* and put it on Joseph's finger. He had him dressed in robes of fine linen and put a gold chain about his neck. [43] He then had him ride in the chariot of his vizier, and they shouted "Abrek!"* before him.

Thus was Joseph installed over the whole land of Egypt. [44] "I, Pharaoh, proclaim," he told Joseph, "that without your approval no one shall move hand or foot in all the land of Egypt." [45] Pharaoh also bestowed the name of Zaphenath-paneah* on Joseph, and he gave him in marriage Asenath, the daughter of Potiphera, priest of Heliopolis. [46] Joseph was thirty years old when he entered the service of Pharaoh, king of Egypt.

After Joseph left Pharaoh's presence, he traveled throughout the land of Egypt. [47] During the seven years of plenty, when the land produced abundant crops, [48] he husbanded all the food of these years of plenty that the land of Egypt was enjoying and stored it in the towns, placing in each town the crops of the fields around it. [49] Joseph garnered grain in quantities like the sands of the sea, so vast that at last he stopped measuring it, for it was beyond measure.

[50] Before the famine years set in, Joseph became the father of two sons, born to him by Asenath, daughter of Potiphera, priest of Heliopolis.[j] [51] He named his first-born Manasseh,* meaning, "God has made me forget entirely the sufferings I endured at the hands of my family"; [52] and the second he named Ephraim,* meaning, "God has made me fruitful in the land of my affliction."

[53] When the seven years of abundance enjoyed by the land of Egypt came to an end, [54] the seven years of famine set in, just as Joseph had predicted. Although there was famine in all the other countries, food was available throughout the land of Egypt.[k] [55] When hunger came to be felt throughout the land of Egypt and the people cried to Pharaoh for bread, Pharaoh directed all the Egyptians to go to Joseph and do whatever he told them. [56] When the famine had spread throughout the land, Joseph opened all the cities that had grain and rationed it to the Egyptians, since the famine had gripped the land of Egypt. [57] In fact, all the world came to Joseph to obtain rations of grain, for famine had gripped the whole world.

CHAPTER 42

The Brothers' First Journey to Egypt.

See RG 114–15

[1] When Jacob learned that grain rations were available in Egypt, he said to his sons: "Why do you keep gaping at one another? [2] I hear," he went on, "that rations of grain are available in Egypt. Go down there and buy some for us, that we may stay alive rather than die of hunger."[l] [3] So ten of Joseph's brothers went down to buy an emergency supply of grain from Egypt. [4] It was only Joseph's full brother Benjamin that Jacob did not send with the rest, for he thought some disaster might befall him. [5] Thus, since there was famine in the land of Canaan also, the sons

---

41, 42: Signet ring: a finger ring in which was set a stamp seal, different from the cylinder seal such as Judah wore; see note on Gn 38, 18. This is an authentic detail. By receiving Pharaoh's signet ring, Joseph was made vizier of Egypt (v 43); the vizier was known as "seal-bearer of the king of Lower Egypt." Another authentic detail is the gold chain, a symbol of high office in ancient Egypt.

41, 43: Abrek: apparently a cry of homage, though the word's derivation and actual meaning are uncertain.

41, 45: Zaphenath-paneah: a Hebrew transcription of an Egyptian name meaning "the god speaks and he (the newborn child) lives." Asenath: means "belonging to (the Egyptian goddess) Neith." Potiphera: means "he whom Ra (the

Egyptian god) gave"; a shorter form of the same name was borne by Joseph's master (Gn 37, 36). Heliopolis: in Hebrew, On, a city seven miles northeast of modern Cairo, site of the chief temple of the sun god; it is mentioned also in v 50; Gn 46, 20; Ez 30, 17.

41, 51: Manasseh: allusion to this name is in the Hebrew expression, nishshani, "he made me forget."

41, 52: Ephraim: related to the Hebrew expression hiphrani, "(God) has made me fruitful."

---

i: Ps 105, 21; Wis 10, 14; 1 Mc 2, 53; Acts 7, 10. *j:* Gn 46, 20; 48, 5. *k:* Ps 105, 16; Acts 7, 11. *l:* Acts 7, 12.

of Israel were among those who came to procure rations.[m]

[6]It was Joseph, as governor of the country, who dispensed the rations to all the people. When Joseph's brothers came and knelt down before him with their faces to the ground,[n] [7]he recognized them as soon as he saw them. But he concealed his own identity from them and spoke sternly to them. "Where do you come from?" he asked them. They answered, "From the land of Canaan, to procure food."

[8]When Joseph recognized his brothers, although they did not recognize him, [9]he was reminded of the dreams he had about them. He said to them: "You are spies.[o] You have come to see the nakedness of the land."* [10]"No, my lord," they replied. "On the contrary, your servants have come to procure food. [11]All of us are sons of the same man. We are honest men; your servants have never been spies." [12]But he answered them: "Not so! You have come to see the nakedness of the land." [13]"We your servants," they said, "were twelve brothers, sons of a certain man in Canaan; but the youngest one is at present with our father, and the other one is gone."[p] [14]"It is just as I said," Joseph persisted; "you are spies. [15]This is how you shall be tested: unless your youngest brother comes here, I swear by the life of Pharaoh that you shall not leave here. [16]So send one of your number to get your brother, while the rest of you stay here under arrest. Thus shall your words be tested for their truth; if they are untrue, as Pharaoh lives, you are spies!" [17]With that, he locked them up in the guardhouse for three days.

[18]On the third day Joseph said to them: "Do this, and you shall live; for I am a God-fearing man. [19]If you have been honest, only one of your brothers need be confined in this prison, while the rest of you may go and take home provisions for your starving families. [20]But you must come back to me with your youngest brother. Your words will thus be verified, and you will not die." To this they agreed.[q] [21]To one another, however, they said: "Alas, we are being punished because of our brother. We saw the anguish of his heart when he pleaded with us, yet we paid no heed; that is why this anguish has now come upon us."[r] [22]"Didn't I tell you," broke in Reuben, "not to do wrong to the boy? But you wouldn't listen! Now comes the reckoning for his blood."[s] [23]They did not know, of course, that Joseph understood what they said, since he spoke with them through an interpreter. [24]But turning away from them, he wept. When he was able to speak to them again, he had Simeon taken from them and bound before their eyes. [25]Then Joseph gave orders to have their containers filled with grain, their money replaced in each one's sack, and provisions given them for their journey. After this had been done for them, [26]they loaded their donkeys with the rations and departed.

[27]*At the night encampment, when one of them opened his bag to give his donkey some fodder, he was surprised to see his money in the mouth of his bag. [28]"My money has been returned!" he cried out to his brothers. "Here it is in my bag!" At that their hearts sank. Trembling, they asked one another, "What is this that God has done to us?"

[29]When they got back to their father Jacob in the land of Canaan, they told him all that had happened to them. [30]"The man who is lord of the country," they said, "spoke to us sternly and put us in custody as if we were spying on the land. [31]But we said to him: 'We are honest men; we have never been spies. [32]There were twelve of us brothers, sons of the same father; but one is gone, and the youngest one is at present with our father in the land of Canaan.' [33]Then the man who is lord of the country said to us: 'This is how I shall know if you are honest men: leave one of your brothers with me, while the rest

42, 9. 12: The nakedness of the land: the military weakness of the land, like human nakedness, should not be seen by strangers.

42, 27-28: These two verses are from the Yahwist source, whereas the rest of the chapter is from the Elohist source, in which the men find the money in their sacks (not "bags"—a different Hebrew word) only when they arrive home (v 35); cf Gn 43, 21.

m: Jdt 5, 10; Acts 7, 11. n: Ps 105, 21. o: Gn 37, 5. p: Gn 44, 20. q: Gn 43, 5. r: Gn 37, 18-27. s: Gn 37, 22.

of you go home with rations for your starving families. [34]When you come back to me with your youngest brother, and I know that you are honest men and not spies, I will restore your brother to you, and you may move about freely in the land.' "

[35]When they were emptying their sacks, there in each one's sack was his moneybag! At the sight of their moneybags, they and their father were dismayed. [36]Their father Jacob said to them: "Must you make me childless? Joseph is gone, and Simeon is gone, and now you would take away Benjamin! Why must such things always happen to me!" [37]Then Reuben told his father: "Put him in my care, and I will bring him back to you. You may kill my own two sons if I do not return him to you." [38]But Jacob replied: "My son shall not go down with you. Now that his full brother is dead, he is the only one left. If some disaster should befall him on the journey you must make, you would send my white head down to the nether world in grief."

CHAPTER 43[*]

See RG 114-15

The Second Journey to Egypt. [1]Now the famine in the land grew more severe. [2]So when they had used up all the rations they had brought from Egypt, their father said to them, "Go back and procure us a little more food." [3]But Judah replied: "The man strictly warned us, 'You shall not appear in my presence unless your brother is with you.'[u] [4]If you are willing to let our brother go with us, we will go down to procure food for you. [5]But if you are not willing, we will not go down, because the man told us, 'You shall not appear in my presence unless your brother is with you.' "[v] [6]Israel demanded, "Why did you bring this trouble on me by telling the man that you had another brother?" [7]They answered: "The man kept asking about ourselves and our family: 'Is your father still living? Do you have another brother?' We had to answer his questions. How could we know that he would say, 'Bring your brother down here'?"

[8]Then Judah urged his father Israel: "Let the boy go with me, that we may be off and on our way if you and we and our children are to keep from starving to death.[w] [9]I myself will stand surety for him. You can hold me responsible for him. If I fail to bring him back, to set him in your presence, you can hold it against me forever.[x] [10]Had we not dilly-dallied, we could have been there and back twice by now!"

[11]Their father Israel then told them: "If it must be so, then do this: Put some of the land's best products in your baggage and take them down to the man as gifts: some balm and honey, gum and resin, and pistachios and almonds.[y] [12]Also take extra money along, for you must return the amount that was put back in the mouths of your bags; it may have been a mistake. [13]Take your brother, too, and be off on your way back to the man. [14]May God Almighty dispose the man to be merciful toward you, so that he may let your other brother go, as well as Benjamin. As for me, if I am to suffer bereavement, I shall suffer it."

[15]So the men got the gifts, took double the amount of money with them, and, accompanied by Benjamin, were off on their way down to Egypt to present themselves to Joseph. [16]When Joseph saw Benjamin with them, he told his head steward, "Take these men into the house, and have an animal slaughtered and prepared, for they are to dine with me at noon." [17]Doing as Joseph had ordered, the steward conducted the men to Joseph's house. [18]But on being led to his house, they became apprehensive. "It must be," they thought, "on account of the money put back in our bags the first time, that we are taken inside; they want to use it as a pretext to attack us and take our donkeys and seize us as slaves." [19]So they went up to Joseph's head steward and talked to him at the entrance of the house. [20]"If you please, sir," they said, "we came down here once before to procure food.[z] [21]But when we arrived at a night's encampment and opened our bags, there was each man's money in the mouth of his bag—

43, 1-34: This chapter and the following one are from the Yahwist source, in which Judah, not Reuben as in the Elohist source, volunteers to go surety for Benjamin.

t: Gn 37, 35.   *u:* Gn 44, 23.   *v:* Gn 42, 20.   *w:* Gn 42, 37.   *x:* Gn 44, 32.   *y:* Gn 45, 23.   *z:* Gn 42, 3.

our money in the full amount! We have now brought it back.*a* *22*We have brought other money to procure food with. We do not know who put the first money in our bags." *23*"Be at ease," he replied; "you have no need to fear. Your God and the God of your father must have put treasures in your bags for you. As for your money, I received it." With that, he led Simeon out to them.

*24*The steward then brought the men inside Joseph's house. He gave them water to bathe their feet, and got fodder for their donkeys. *25*Then they set out their gifts to await Joseph's arrival at noon, for they had heard that they were to dine there. *26*When Joseph came home, they presented him with the gifts they had brought inside, while they bowed down before him to the ground. *27*After inquiring how they were, he asked them, "And how is your aged father, of whom you spoke? Is he still in good health?"*b* *28*"Your servant our father is thriving and still in good health," they said, as they bowed respectfully. *29*When Joseph's eye fell on his full brother Benjamin, he asked, "Is this your youngest brother, of whom you told me?" Then he said to him, "May God be gracious to you, my boy!"*c* *30*With that, Joseph had to hurry out, for he was so overcome with affection for his brother that he was on the verge of tears. He went into a private room and wept there.

*31*After washing his face, he reappeared and, now in control of himself, gave the order, "Serve the meal." *32*It was served separately to him,* to the brothers, and to the Egyptians who partook of his board. (Egyptians may not eat with Hebrews; that is abhorrent to them.) *33*When they were seated by his directions according to their age, from the oldest to the youngest, they looked at one another in amazement; *34*and as portions were brought to them from Joseph's table,

Benjamin's portion was five times as large as* anyone else's. So they drank freely and made merry with him.

CHAPTER 44

See RG 114–15

Final Test. *1**Then Joseph gave his head steward these instructions: "Fill the men's bags with as much food as they can carry, and put each man's money in the mouth of his bag. *2*In the mouth of the youngest one's bag put also my silver goblet, together with the money for his rations." The steward carried out Joseph's instructions. *3*At daybreak the men and their donkeys were sent off. *4*They had not gone far out of the city when Joseph said to his head steward: "Go at once after the men! When you overtake them, say to them, 'Why did you repay good with evil? Why did you steal the silver goblet from me? *5*It is the very one from which my master drinks and which he uses for divination.* What you have done is wrong.' "

*6*When the steward overtook them and repeated these words to them, *7*they remonstrated with him: "How can my lord say such things? Far be it from your servants to do such a thing! *8*We even brought back to you from the land of Canaan the money that we found in the mouths of our bags. Why, then, would we steal silver or gold from your master's house? *9*If any of your servants is found to have the goblet, he shall die, and as for the rest of us, we shall become my lord's slaves." *10*But he replied, "Even though it ought to be as you propose, only the one who is found to have it shall become my slave, and the rest of you shall be exonerated." *11*Then each of them eagerly lowered his bag to the ground and opened it; *12*and when a search was made, starting with the oldest and ending with the youngest, the goblet turned up in Benjamin's bag. *13*At this, they tore their clothes. Then, when each

43, 32: Separately to him: that Joseph did not eat with the other Egyptians was apparently a matter of rank.

43, 34: Five times as large as: probably an idiomatic expression for "much larger than."

44, 1f: Replacement of the money in the men's bags is probably a redactional addition here, taken from the Yahwist account of the first visit. It is only the goblet in Benjamin's bag, not any replaced money, that plays a part in the rest of the chapter.

44, 5: Divination: seeking omens through liquids poured into a cup or bowl was a common practice in the ancient Near East; cf v 15. Even though divination was frowned on in later Israel (Lv 19, 31), it is in this place an authentic touch which the sacred author does not hesitate to ascribe to Joseph, the wisest man in Egypt.

a: Gn 42, 27f.   *b:* Tb 7, 4.   *c:* Gn 42, 13.

man had reloaded his donkey, they returned to the city.

[14] As Judah and his brothers reentered Joseph's house, he was still there; so they flung themselves on the ground before him. [15] "How could you do such a thing?" Joseph asked them. "You should have known that such a man as I could discover by divination what happened." [16] Judah replied: "What can we say to my lord? How can we plead or how try to prove our innocence? God has uncovered your servants' guilt.* Here we are, then, the slaves of my lord—the rest of us no less than the one in whose possession the goblet was found." [17] "Far be it from me to act thus!" said Joseph. "Only the one in whose possession the goblet was found shall become my slave; the rest of you may go back safe and sound to your father."

[18] Judah then stepped up to him and said: "I beg you, my lord, let your servant speak earnestly to my lord, and do not become angry with your servant, for you are the equal of Pharaoh. [19]* My lord asked your servants, 'Have you a father, or another brother?' [20] So we said to my lord, 'We have an aged father, and a young brother, the child of his old age. This one's full brother is dead, and since he is the only one by that mother who is left, his father dotes on him.'[d] [21] Then you told your servants, 'Bring him down to me that my eyes may look on him.' [22] We replied to my lord, 'The boy cannot leave his father; his father would die if he were to leave him.' [23] But you told your servants, 'Unless your youngest brother comes back with you, you shall not come into my presence again.'[e] [24] When we returned to your servant our father, we reported to him the words of my lord.

[25] "Later, our father told us to come back and buy some food for the family. [26] So we reminded him, 'We cannot go down there; only if our youngest brother is with us can we go, for we may not see the man if our youngest brother is not with us.' [27] Then your servant our father said to us, 'As you know, my wife bore me two sons. [28] One of them, however, disappeared, and I had to conclude that he must have been torn to pieces by wild beasts; I have not seen him since.'[f] [29] If you now take this one away from me, too, and some disaster befalls him, you will send my white head down to the nether world in grief.'

[30] "If then the boy is not with us when I go back to your servant my father, whose very life is bound up with his, he will die as soon as he sees that the boy is missing; [31] and your servants will thus send the white head of our father down to the nether world in grief. [32] Besides, I, your servant, got the boy from his father by going surety for him, saying, 'If I fail to bring him back to you, father, you can hold it against me forever.'[g] [33] Let me, your servant, therefore, remain in place of the boy as the slave of my lord, and let the boy go back with his brothers. [34] How could I go back to my father if the boy were not with me? I could not bear to see the anguish that would overcome my father."

CHAPTER 45

See RG 114–15

The Truth Revealed. [1] Joseph could no longer control himself in the presence of all his attendants, so he cried out, "Have everyone withdraw from me!" Thus no one else was about when he made himself known to his brothers. [2] But his sobs were so loud that the Egyptians heard him, and so the news reached Pharaoh's palace. [3][h] "I am Joseph," he said to his brothers. "Is my father still in good health?" But his brothers could give him no answer, so dumbfounded were they at him.

[4] "Come closer to me," he told his brothers. When they had done so, he said: "I am your brother Joseph, whom you once sold into Egypt. [5] But now do not be distressed, and do not reproach yourselves for having sold me here. It was really for the sake of saving lives that God sent me here ahead of you.[i] [6] For two years now the famine has been in the land, and for five more years tillage will yield no harvest. [7] God, therefore, sent me on ahead of you to ensure for you a

---

44, 16: Guilt: in trying to do away with Joseph when he was young.

44, 19: My lord . . . your servants: such frequently repeated expressions in Judah's speech show the formal court style used by a subject in speaking to a high official.

d: Gn 42, 13.   e: Gn 43, 3.   f: Gn 37, 20. 33.   g: Gn 43, 9.   h: 3f: Acts 7, 13.   i: Gn 50, 20; Sir 49, 15.

remnant on earth and to save your lives in an extraordinary deliverance. [8]So it was not really you but God who had me come here; and he has made of me a father to Pharaoh,* lord of all his household, and ruler over the whole land of Egypt.

[9]*"Hurry back, then, to my father and tell him: 'Thus says your son Joseph: God has made me lord of all Egypt; come to me without delay.'[j] [10]You will settle in the region of Goshen,* where you will be near me—you and your children and grandchildren, your flocks and herds, and everything that you own. [11]Since five years of famine still lie ahead, I will provide for you there, so that you and your family and all that are yours may not suffer want.' [12]Surely, you can see for yourselves, and Benjamin can see for himself, that it is I, Joseph, who am speaking to you. [13]Tell my father all about my high position in Egypt and what you have seen. But hurry and bring my father down here." [14]Thereupon he flung himself on the neck of his brother Benjamin and wept, and Benjamin wept in his arms. [15]Joseph then kissed all his brothers, crying over each of them; and only then were his brothers able to talk with him.

[16]When the news reached Pharaoh's palace that Joseph's brothers had come, Pharaoh and his courtiers were pleased. [17]So Pharaoh told Joseph: "Say to your brothers: 'This is what you shall do: Load up your animals and go without delay to the land of Canaan. [18]There get your father and your families, and then come back here to me; I will assign you the best land in Egypt, where you will live off the fat of the land.'[k] [19]Instruct them further: 'Do this. Take wagons from the land of Egypt for your children and your wives and to transport your father on your way back here. [20]Do not be concerned about your belongings, for the best in the whole land of Egypt shall be yours.'"

[21]The sons of Israel acted accordingly. Joseph gave them the wagons, as Pharaoh had ordered, and he supplied them with provisions for the journey. [22]He also gave to each of them fresh clothing, but to Benjamin he gave three hundred shekels of silver and five sets of garments. [23]Moreover, what he sent to his father was ten jackasses loaded with the finest products of Egypt and ten jennies loaded with grain and bread and other provisions for his journey. [24]As he sent his brothers on their way, he told them, "Let there be no recriminations on the way."

[25]So they left Egypt and made their way to their father Jacob in the land of Canaan. [26]When they told him, "Joseph is still alive—in fact, it is he who is ruler of all the land of Egypt," he was dumbfounded; he could not believe them. [27]But when they recounted to him all that Joseph had told them, and when he saw the wagons that Joseph had sent for his transport, the spirit of their father Jacob revived. [28]"It is enough," said Israel. "My son Joseph is still alive! I must go and see him before I die."

CHAPTER 46

Migration to Egypt. [1]Israel set out with all that was his. When he arrived at Beer-sheba, he offered sacrifices to the God of his father Isaac. [2]There God, speaking to Israel in a vision by night, called, "Jacob! Jacob!" "Here I am," he answered. [3]Then he said: "I am God,* the God of your father. Do not be afraid to go down to Egypt, for there I will make you a great nation. [4]Not only will I go down to Egypt with you; I will also bring you back here, after Joseph has closed your eyes."

[5]So Jacob departed from Beer-sheba, and the sons of Israel put their father and their wives and children on the wagons that Pharaoh had sent for his transport. [6]They took with them their livestock and the possessions they had acquired in the land of Canaan. Thus Jacob and all his descendants mi-

See RG 114-15

45, 8: Father to Pharaoh: a term applied to a vizier in ancient Egypt.

45, 9-15: In these verses, as in Gn 46, 31—47, 5a, all from the Yahwist source, Joseph in his own name invites his father and brothers to come to Egypt. Only after their arrival is Pharaoh informed of the fact. On the other hand, in 45, 16-20 from the Elohist source, it is Pharaoh himself who invites Joseph's kinsmen to migrate to his domain.

45, 10: The region of Goshen: modern Wadi Tumilat in the eastern part of the Nile Delta.

46, 3: I am God: more precisely according to the Hebrew text, "I am El." "El" is here a divine name, not the common noun "god."

j: Acts 7, 14. k: Acts 7, 14.

grated to Egypt.^{l} ^{7}His sons and his grandsons, his daughters and his granddaughters—all his descendants—he took with him to Egypt.

^{8}These are the names of the Israelites, Jacob and his descendants, who migrated to Egypt.

*Reuben, Jacob's first-born,^{m} ^{9}and the sons of Reuben: Hanoch, Pallu, Hezron and Carmi.^{n} ^{10}The sons of Simeon: Nemuel, Jamin, Ohad, Jachin, Zohar, and Shaul, son of a Canaanite woman.^{o} ^{11}The sons of Levi: Gershon, Kohath and Merari.^{p} ^{12}The sons of Judah: Er, Onan, Shelah, Perez and Zerah—but Er and Onan had died in the land of Canaan; and the sons of Perez were Hezron and Hamul.^{q} ^{13}The sons of Issachar: Tola, Puah, Jashub and Shimron.^{r} ^{14}The sons of Zebulun: Sered, Elon and Jahleel.^{s} ^{15}These were the sons whom Leah bore to Jacob in Paddan-aram, along with his daughter Dinah—thirty-three persons in all, male and female. ^{16}The sons of Gad: Zephon, Haggi, Shuni, Ezbon, Eri, Arod and Areli.^{t} ^{17}The sons of Asher: Imnah, Ishvah, Ishvi and Beriah, with their sister Serah; and the sons of Beriah: Heber and Malchiel.^{u} ^{18}These were the descendants of Zilpah, whom Laban had given to his daughter Leah; these she bore to Jacob—sixteen persons in all.

^{19}The sons of Jacob's wife Rachel: Joseph and Benjamin. ^{20}In the land of Egypt Joseph became the father of Manasseh and Ephraim, whom Asenath, daughter of Potiphera, priest of Heliopolis, bore to him.^{v} ^{21}The sons of Benjamin: Bela, Becher, Ashbel, Gera, Naaman, Ahiram, Shupham, Hupham and Ard.^{w} ^{22}These were the sons whom Rachel bore to Jacob—fourteen persons in all.

^{23}The sons of Dan: Hushim.^{x} ^{24}The sons of Naphtali: Jahzeel, Guni, Jezer and Shillem.^{y} ^{25}These were the sons of Bilhah, whom La-

ban had given to his daughter Rachel; these she bore to Jacob—seven persons in all.

^{26}Jacob's people who migrated to Egypt—his direct descendants, not counting the wives of Jacob's sons—numbered sixty-six persons in all.^{z} ^{27}Together with Joseph's sons who were born to him in Egypt—two persons—all the people comprising Jacob's family who had come to Egypt amounted to seventy persons* in all.^{a}

^{28}Israel had sent Judah ahead to Joseph, so that he might meet him in Goshen. On his arrival in the region of Goshen, ^{29}Joseph hitched the horses to his chariot and rode to meet his father Israel in Goshen. As soon as he saw him, he flung himself on his neck and wept a long time in his arms. ^{30}And Israel said to Joseph, "At last I can die, now that I have seen for myself that Joseph is still alive."

^{31}Joseph then said to his brothers and his father's household: "I will go and inform Pharaoh, telling him: 'My brothers and my father's household, whose home is in the land of Canaan, have come to me. ^{32}The men are shepherds, having long been keepers of livestock; and they have brought with them their flocks and herds, as well as everything else they own.' ^{33}So when Pharaoh summons you and asks what your occupation is, ^{34}you must answer, 'We your servants, like our ancestors, have been keepers of livestock from the beginning until now,' in order that you may stay in the region of Goshen, since all shepherds are abhorrent to the Egyptians."

CHAPTER 47

Settlement in Goshen. ^{1}Joseph went and told Pharaoh, "My father and my brothers have come from the land of Canaan, with their flocks and herds and everything else they own; and they are now in the region of Goshen." ^{2}He then presented to Pharaoh five of his brothers whom he had selected from

See RG 114-15

46, 8-27: This genealogical list has here been inserted by a redactor who based it on the clan lists (Nm 26, 5-50) at the time of Moses. Therefore it includes some of Jacob's grandchildren, who would hardly have been born when Joseph was still a relatively young man. The number fourteen (v 22) is based on a garbled version of the genealogical list.

46, 27: Seventy persons: either to be understood as a round number, or arrived at by including Jacob and Joseph with the preceding persons, who add up to sixty-eight.

l: Ex 1, 1; Jos 24, 4; Jdt 5, 10; Acts 7, 15.   *m:* Ex 1, 2.   *n:* Ex 6, 14; Nm 26, 5; 1 Chr 5, 3.   *o:* Ex 6, 15; Nm 26, 12; 1 Chr 4, 24.   *p:* Ex 6, 16; Nm 3, 17; 26, 57; 1 Chr 6, 1.   *q:* Gn 38, 3-10. 29f; Nm 26, 19; Rv 4, 18-22; 1 Chr 2, 5.   *r:* Nm 26, 23f; 1 Chr 7, 1.   *s:* Nm 26, 26.   *t:* Nm 26, 15f.   *u:* Nm 26, 44; 1 Chr 7, 30f.   *v:* Gn 41, 50; Nm 26, 28. 35.   *w:* Nm 26, 38; 1 Chr 7, 6; 8, 1-4.   *x:* Nm 26, 42.   *y:* Nm 26, 48f; 1 Chr 7, 13.   *z:* Ex 1, 5.   *a:* Ex 1, 5; Dt 10, 22; Acts 7, 14.

their full number. *3*When Pharaoh asked them what their occupation was, they answered, "We, your servants, like our ancestors, are shepherds. *4*We have come," they continued, "in order to stay in this country, for there is no pasture for your servants' flocks in the land of Canaan, so severe has the famine been there. Please, therefore, let your servants settle in the region of Goshen."*b* *5*Pharaoh said to Joseph, "They may settle in the region of Goshen; and if you know any of them to be qualified, you may put them in charge of my own livestock."

Thus, when Jacob and his sons came to Joseph in Egypt, and Pharaoh, king of Egypt, heard about it, Pharaoh said to Joseph, "Now that your father and brothers have come to you, *6*the land of Egypt is at your disposal; settle your father and brothers in the pick of the land." *7*Then Joseph brought his father Jacob and presented him to Pharaoh. After Jacob had paid his respects to Pharaoh, *8*Pharaoh asked him, "How many years have you lived?" *9*Jacob replied: "The years I have lived as a wayfarer amount to a hundred and thirty. Few and hard have been these years of my life, and they do not compare with the years that my ancestors lived as wayfarers."* *10*Then Jacob bade Pharaoh farewell and withdrew from his presence.

*11*As Pharaoh had ordered, Joseph settled his father and brothers and gave them holdings in Egypt on the pick of the land, in the region of Rameses.* *12*And Joseph sustained his father and brothers and his father's whole household, down to the youngest, with food.

Joseph's Land Policy. *13*Since there was no food in any country because of the extreme severity of the famine, and the lands of Egypt and Canaan were languishing from hunger, *14*Joseph gathered in, as payment for the rations that were being dispensed, all the money that was to be found in Egypt and Canaan, and he put it in Pharaoh's palace.

*15*When all the money in Egypt and Canaan was spent, all the Egyptians came to Joseph, pleading, "Give us food or we shall perish under your eyes; for our money is gone." *16*"Since your money is gone," replied Joseph, "give me your livestock, and I will sell you bread in return for your livestock." *17*So they brought their livestock to Joseph, and he sold them food in return for their horses, their flocks of sheep and herds of cattle, and their donkeys. Thus he got them through that year with bread in exchange for all their livestock. *18*When that year ended, they came to him in the following one and said: "We cannot hide from my lord that, with our money spent and our livestock made over to my lord, there is nothing left to put at my lord's disposal except our bodies and our farm land. *19*Why should we and our land perish before your very eyes? Take us and our land in exchange for food, and we will become Pharaoh's slaves and our land his property; only give us seed, that we may survive and not perish, and that our land may not turn into a waste."

*20*Thus Joseph acquired all the farm land of Egypt for Pharaoh, since with the famine too much for them to bear, every Egyptian sold his field; so the land passed over to Pharaoh, *21*and the people were reduced to slavery, from one end of Egypt's territory to the other. *22*Only the priests' lands Joseph did not take over. Since the priests had a fixed allowance from Pharaoh and lived off the allowance Pharaoh had granted them, they did not have to sell their land.

*23*Joseph told the people: "Now that I have acquired you and your land for Pharaoh, here is your seed for sowing the land. *24*But when the harvest is in, you must give a fifth of it to Pharaoh, while you keep four-fifths as seed for your fields, and as food for yourselves and your families [and as food for your children]." *25*"You have saved our lives!" they answered. "We are grateful to my lord that we can be Pharaoh's slaves." *26*Thus Joseph

---

47, 9: Wayfarer . . . wayfarers: man is merely a sojourner on earth; cf Ps 39, 13.

47, 11: The region of Rameses: same as the region of Goshen; see note on Gn 45, 10. The name Rameses, however, is an anachronism, since this royal name did not come into use before the end of the fourteenth century B.C., long after the time of Joseph.

---

b: Ex 23, 9; Dt 23, 8.

made it a law for the land in Egypt, which is still in force, that a fifth of its produce should go to Pharaoh. Only the land of the priests did not pass over to Pharaoh.

Jacob Blesses Ephraim and Manasseh. [27]Thus Israel settled in the land of Egypt, in the region of Goshen. There they acquired property, were fertile, and increased greatly.[c] [28]Jacob lived in the land of Egypt for seventeen years; the span of his life came to a hundred and forty-seven years. [29]When the time approached for Israel to die, he called his son Joseph and said to him: "If you really wish to please me, put your hand under my thigh as a sign of your constant loyalty to me; do not let me be buried in Egypt. [30]When I lie down with my ancestors, have me taken out of Egypt and buried in their burial place."[d] [31]"I will do as you say," he replied. But his father demanded, "Swear it to me!" So Joseph swore to him. Then Israel bowed at the head of the bed.*

See RG
114–15

CHAPTER 48

[1]Some time afterward, Joseph was informed, "Your father is failing." So he took along with him his two sons, Manasseh and Ephraim. [2]When Jacob was told, "Your son Joseph has come to you," he rallied his strength and sat up in bed.

[3e]Jacob then said to Joseph: "God Almighty appeared to me at Luz* in the land of Canaan, and blessing me, [4]he said, 'I will make you fertile and numerous and raise you into an assembly of tribes, and I will give this land to your descendants after you as a permanent possession.' [5]Your two sons, therefore, who were born to you in the land of Egypt before I joined you here, shall be mine; Ephraim and Manasseh shall be mine as much as Reuben and Simeon are mine. [6]Progeny born to you after them shall remain yours; but their heritage shall be recorded in the names of their two brothers.

[7f]I do this because, when I was returning from Paddan, your mother Rachel died, to my sorrow, during the journey in Canaan, while we were still a short distance from Ephrath; and I buried her there on the way to Ephrath [that is, Bethlehem].'"

[8]When Israel saw Joseph's sons, he asked, "Who are these?" [9]"They are my sons," Joseph answered his father, "whom God has given me here." "Bring them to me," said his father, "that I may bless them." [10](Now Israel's eyes were dim from age, and he could not see well.) When Joseph brought his sons close to him, he kissed and embraced them. [11]Then Israel said to Joseph, "I never expected to see your face again, and now God has allowed me to see your descendants as well!"

[12]Joseph removed them from his father's knees and bowed down before him with his face to the ground. [13]Then Joseph took the two, Ephraim with his right hand, to Israel's left, and Manasseh with his left hand, to Israel's right, and led them to him. [14]But Israel, crossing his hands, put out his right hand and laid it on the head of Ephraim, although he was the younger, and his left hand on the head of Manasseh, although he was the first-born. [15]Then he blessed them with these words:

"May the God in whose ways
    my fathers Abraham and Isaac walked,
The God who has been my shepherd
    from my birth to this day,[g]
[16] The Angel who has delivered me from all harm,
    bless these boys
That in them my name be recalled,
    and the names of my fathers, Abraham and Isaac,
And they may become teeming multitudes
    upon the earth!"

47, 31: Israel bowed at the head of the bed: meaning perhaps that he gave a nod of assent and appreciation as he lay on his bed. By reading with different vowels the Hebrew word for "bed," the Greek version translated it as "staff," and understood the phrase to mean that he bowed in worship, leaning on the top of his staff; it is thus quoted in Heb 11, 21.

48, 3: Luz: an older name of Bethel (Gn 28, 19).

48, 7: Since her early death prevented Rachel from bearing more than two sons, Jacob feels justified in treating her two grandsons as if they were her own offspring.

---

c: Ex 1, 7. d: Gn 50, 5. e: 3f: Gn 28, 12-15; 35, 6. f: Gn 35, 19. g: Heb 11, 21.

[17]When Joseph saw that his father had laid his right hand on Ephraim's head, this seemed wrong to him; so he took hold of his father's hand, to remove it from Ephraim's head to Manasseh's, [18]saying, "That is not right, father; the other one is the first-born; lay your right hand on his head!" [19]But his father resisted. "I know it, son," he said, "I know. That one too shall become a tribe, and he too shall be great. Nevertheless, his younger brother shall surpass him, and his descendants shall become a multitude of nations." [20]So when he blessed them that day and said, "By you shall the people of Israel pronounce blessings; may they say, 'God make you like Ephraim and Manasseh,' " he placed Ephraim before Manasseh.[h]

[21]Then Israel said to Joseph: "I am about to die. But God will be with you and will restore you to the land of your fathers. [22i]As for me, I give to you, as to the one above his brothers, Shechem, which I captured from the Amorites with my sword and bow.'"*

CHAPTER 49

See RG
114–15   *Jacob's Testament.* [1]Jacob called his sons and said: "Gather around, that I may tell you what is to happen to you in days to come.

[2] "Assemble and listen, sons of Jacob,
   listen to Israel, your father.

[3] "You, Reuben, my first-born,
   my strength and the first fruit of my
      manhood,
   excelling in rank and excelling in
      power!
[4] Unruly as water, you shall no longer excel,
   for you climbed into your father's bed
   and defiled my couch to my sorrow.[j]

[5] "Simeon and Levi, brothers indeed,
   weapons of violence are their knives.*
[6] Let not my soul enter their council,
   or my spirit be joined with their
      company;
   For in their fury they slew men,
      in their willfulness they maimed oxen.[k]
[7] Cursed be their fury so fierce,
   and their rage so cruel!
   I will scatter them in Jacob,
   disperse them throughout Israel.

[8] "You, Judah, shall your brothers praise
   —your hand on the neck of your
      enemies;
   the sons of your father shall bow down
      to you.
[9] Judah, like a lion's whelp,
   you have grown up on prey, my son.
   He crouches like a lion recumbent,
      the king of beasts—who would dare
         rouse him?[l]
[10] The scepter shall never depart from Judah,
   or the mace from between his legs,
   While tribute is brought to him,*
      and he receives the people's homage.
[11] He tethers his donkey to the vine,
      his purebred ass to the choicest stem.
   In wine he washes his garments,
      his robe in the blood of grapes.*
[12] His eyes are darker than wine,
   and his teeth are whiter than milk.

[13] "Zebulun shall dwell by the seashore
   [This means a shore for ships],
   and his flank shall be based on Sidon.

[14] "Issachar is a rawboned ass,
   crouching between the saddlebags.
[15] When he saw how good a settled life was,
   and how pleasant the country,

48, 22: Both the meaning of the Hebrew and the historical reference in this verse are obscure. By taking the Hebrew word for Shechem as a common noun meaning shoulder or mountain slope, some translators render the verse, "I give you one portion more than your brothers, which I captured . . ." The reference may be to the capture of Shechem by the sons of Jacob (Gn 34, 24-29). Shechem lay near the border separating the tribal territory of Manasseh from that of Ephraim (Jos 16, 4-9; 17, 1f. 7).

49, 5: Knives: if this is the meaning of the obscure Hebrew word here, the reference may be to the knives used in circumcising the men of Shechem (Gn 34, 24; cf Jos 5, 2).

49, 10: While tribute is brought to him: this translation is based on a slight change in the Hebrew text, which, as it stands would seem to mean, "until he comes to Shiloh." A somewhat different reading of the Hebrew text would be, "until he comes to whom it belongs." This last has been traditionally understood in a Messianic sense. In any case, the passage foretells the supremacy of the tribe of Judah, which found its fulfillment in the Davidic dynasty and ultimately in the Messianic Son of David, Jesus Christ.

49, 11: In wine . . . the blood of grapes: Judah's clothes are poetically pictured as soaked with grape juice from trampling in the wine press, the rich vintage of his land; cf Is 63, 2.

h: Heb 11, 21.   i: Jos 17, 14. 17f; Jn 4. 5.   j: Gn 35, 22; 1 Chr 5, 1f.   k: Gn 34, 25.   l: 1 Chr 5, 2.

He bent his shoulder to the burden
and became a toiling serf.

16 "Dan shall achieve justice* for his
    kindred
    like any other tribe of Israel.
17 Let Dan be a serpent by the roadside,
    a horned viper by the path,
That bites the horse's heel,
    so that the rider tumbles backward.

18 "[I long for your deliverance, O LORD!]

19 "Gad shall be raided by raiders,
    but he shall raid at their heels.*

20 "Asher's produce is rich,
    and he shall furnish dainties for kings.

21 "Naphtali is a hind let loose,
    which brings forth lovely fawns.

22 "Joseph is a wild colt,
    a wild colt by a spring,
    a wild ass on a hillside.
23 Harrying and attacking,
    the archers opposed him;
24 But each one's bow remained stiff,
    as their arms were unsteady,
By the power of the Mighty One of Jacob,
    because of the Shepherd, the Rock of
        Israel,
25 The God of your father, who helps you,*
    God Almighty, who blesses you,
With the blessings of the heavens above,
    the blessings of the abyss that
        crouches below,
The blessings of breasts and womb,
26   the blessings of fresh grain and
        blossoms,
The blessings of the everlasting
        mountains,
    the delights of the eternal hills.
May they rest on the head of Joseph,
    on the brow of the prince among his
        brothers.

27 "Benjamin is a ravenous wolf;
    mornings he devours the prey,
    and evenings he distributes the spoils."

Farewell and Death. 28 All these are the
twelve tribes of Israel, and this is what their
father said about them, as he bade them
farewell and gave to each of them an appropriate message. 29 Then he gave them this
charge: "Since I am about to be taken to my
kindred, bury me with my fathers in the cave
that lies in the field of Ephron the Hittite,
30 the cave in the field of Machpelah, facing
on Mamre, in the land of Canaan, the field
that Abraham bought from Ephron the Hittite for a burial ground.m 31 There Abraham
and his wife Sarah are buried, and so are
Isaac and his wife Rebekah, and there, too, I
buried Leah— 32 the field and the cave in it
that had been purchased from the Hittites."
33 When Jacob had finished giving these
instructions to his sons, he drew his feet into
the bed, breathed his last, and was taken to
his kindred.

CHAPTER 50

See RG
114–15

Jacob's Funeral. 1 Joseph threw himself on his father's face and wept over him as
he kissed him. 2 Then he ordered the physicians in his service to embalm his father.
When they embalmed Israel, 3 they spent
forty days at it, for that is the full period of
embalming; and the Egyptians mourned him
for seventy days. 4 When that period of
mourning was over, Joseph spoke to Pharaoh's courtiers. "Please do me this favor," he
said, "and convey to Pharaoh this request of
mine. 5 Since my father, at the point of death,
made me promise on oath to bury him in the
tomb that he had prepared for himself in the
land of Canaan, may I go up there to bury
my father and then come back?"n 6 Pharaoh
replied, "Go and bury your father, as he
made you promise on oath."
7 So Joseph left to bury his father; and
with him went all of Pharaoh's officials who
were senior members of his court and all the
other dignitaries of Egypt, 8 as well as Joseph's whole household, his brothers, and
his father's household; only their children
and their flocks and herds were left in the

49, 16: In Hebrew the verb for achieve justice is from the
same root as the name Dan.
49, 19: In Hebrew there is a certain assonance between the
name Gad and the words for "raided," "raiders" and "raid."

49, 25f: A very similar description of the agricultural
riches of the tribal land of Joseph is given in Dt 33, 13-16.

m: Gn 23, 17.   n: Gn 47, 30.

region of Goshen. ⁹Chariots, too, and charioteers went up with him; it was a very large
retinue.

¹⁰When they arrived at Goren-ha-atad,* which is beyond the Jordan, they held there a very great and solemn memorial service; and Joseph observed seven days of mourning for his father. ¹¹When the Canaanites who inhabited the land saw the mourning at Goren-ha-atad, they said, "This is a solemn funeral the Egyptians are having." That is why the place was named Abel-mizraim. It is beyond the Jordan.

¹²Thus Jacob's sons did for him as he had instructed them. ¹³They carried him to the land of Canaan and buried him in the cave in the field of Machpelah, facing on Mamre, the field that Abraham had bought for a burial ground from Ephron the Hittite.ᵒ

¹⁴After Joseph had buried his father he returned to Egypt, together with his brothers and all who had gone up with him for the burial of his father.

Plea for Forgiveness. ¹⁵Now that their father was dead, Joseph's brothers became fearful and thought, "Suppose Joseph has been nursing a grudge against us and now plans to pay us back in full for all the wrong we did him!" ¹⁶So they approached Joseph and said: "Before your father died, he gave us these instructions: ¹⁷'You shall say to Joseph, Jacob begs you to forgive the criminal

wrongdoing of your brothers, who treated you so cruelly.' Please, therefore, forgive the crime that we, the servants of your father's God, committed." When they spoke these words to him, Joseph broke into tears. ¹⁸Then his brothers proceeded to fling themselves down before him and said, "Let us be your slaves!" ¹⁹But Joseph replied to them: "Have no fear. Can I take the place of God? ²⁰Even though you meant harm to me, God meant it for good, to achieve his present end, the survival of many people.ᵖ ²¹Therefore have no fear. I will provide for you and for your children." By thus speaking kindly to them, he reassured them.�q

²²Joseph remained in Egypt, together with his father's family. He lived a hundred and ten years. ²³He saw Ephraim's children to the third generation, and the children of Manasseh's son Machir were also born on Joseph's knees.ʳ

Death of Joseph. ²⁴Joseph said to his brothers: "I am about to die. God will surely take care of you and lead you out of this land to the land that he promised on oath to Abraham, Isaac and Jacob."ˢ ²⁵Then, putting the sons of Israel under oath, he continued, "When God thus takes care of you, you must bring my bones up with you from this place."ᵗ ²⁶Joseph died at the age of a hundred and ten. He was embalmed and laid to rest in a coffin in Egypt.ᵘ

50, 10f: Goren-ha-atad: "Threshing Floor of the Brambles." Abel-mizraim: although the name really means "watercourse of the Egyptians," it is understood here, by a play on the first part of the term, to mean "mourning of the Egyptians." The site has not been identified through either reading of the name. But it is difficult to see why the mourning rites should have been held in the land beyond the Jordan when the burial was at He-

bron. Perhaps an earlier form of the story placed the mourning rites beyond the Wadi of Egypt, the traditional boundary between Canaan and Egypt (Nm 34, 5; Jos 15, 4. 47).

o: Gn 23, 16; Acts 7, 16.   p: Gn 45, 5; Sir 49, 15.   q: Gn 47, 12.   r: Nm 32, 39; Jos 17, 1.   s: Ex 3, 8; Jos 24, 32; Heb 11, 22.   t: Ex 13, 19; Heb 11, 22.   u: Sir 49, 15.

See RG
115–24

The Book of Exodus

The second book of the Pentateuch is called Exodus from the Greek word for "departure," because the central event narrated in it is the departure of the Israelites from Egypt. It continues the history of the chosen people from the point where the Book of Genesis leaves off. It recounts the oppression by the Egyptians of the ever-increasing descendants of Jacob and their miraculous deliv-

erance by God through Moses, who led them across the Red Sea to Mount Sinai where they entered into a special covenant with the Lord.

These events were of prime importance to the chosen people, for they became thereby an independent nation and enjoyed a unique relationship with God. Through Moses God gave to the Israelites at Mount Sinai the "law": the moral, civil and ritual legislation by which they were to become a holy people, in whom the promise of a Savior for all mankind would be fulfilled.

The principal divisions of Exodus are:

I: The Israelites in Egypt (1, 1—12, 36).

II: The Exodus from Egypt and the Journey to Sinai (12, 37—18, 27).

III: The Covenant at Mount Sinai (19, 1—24, 18).

IV: The Dwelling and Its Furnishings (25, 1—40, 38).

I: The Israelites In Egypt

CHAPTER 1

See RG 117-18

Jacob's Descendants in Egypt. [1]These are the names of the sons of Israel[*] who, accompanied by their households, migrated with Jacob into Egypt: [2*]Reuben, Simeon, Levi and Judah; [3]Issachar, Zebulun and Benjamin; [4]Dan and Naphtali; Gad and Asher. [5]The total number of the direct descendants[*] of Jacob was seventy.[a] Joseph was already in Egypt.

[6]Now Joseph and all his brothers and that whole generation died.[b] [7]But the Israelites were fruitful and prolific. They became so numerous and strong that the land was filled with them.

The Oppression. [8]Then a new king, who knew nothing of Joseph,[*] came to power in Egypt.[c] [9]He said to his subjects, "Look how numerous and powerful the Israelite people are growing, more so than we ourselves! [10]Come, let us deal shrewdly with them to stop their increase; otherwise, in time of war they too may join our enemies to fight against us, and so leave our country."

[11]Accordingly, taskmasters were set over the Israelites to oppress them with forced labor.[d] Thus they had to build for Pharaoh[*] the supply cities of Pithom and Raamses. [12]Yet the more they were oppressed, the more they multiplied and spread. The Egyptians, then, dreaded the Israelites [13]and reduced them to cruel slavery, [14]making life bitter for them with hard work in mortar[*] and brick and all kinds of field work—the whole cruel fate of slaves.

Command to the Midwives. [15]The king of Egypt told the Hebrew midwives, one of whom was called Shiphrah and the other Puah, [16]"When you act as midwives for the Hebrew women and see them giving birth,[*] if it is a boy, kill him; but if it is a girl, she may live." [17]The midwives, however, feared God; they did not do as the king of Egypt had ordered them, but let the boys live. [18]So the king summoned the midwives and asked them, "Why have you acted thus, allowing the boys to live?" [19]The midwives answered Pharaoh, "The Hebrew women are not like the Egyptian women. They are robust and give birth before the midwife arrives." [20]Therefore God dealt well with the midwives. The people, too, increased and grew strong. [21]And because the midwives feared God, he built up families for them. [22]Pharaoh then commanded all his subjects, "Throw into the river[*] every boy that is born to the Hebrews,[e] but you may let all the girls live."

CHAPTER 2

See RG 118-19

Birth and Adoption of Moses. [1]Now a certain man of the house of Levi married a Levite woman,[f] [2]who conceived and bore a son. Seeing that he was a goodly child, she

---

1, 1: Sons of Israel: here literally the first-generation sons of Jacob. Cf v 5. However, beginning with Ex 1, 7 the same Hebrew phrase refers to the more remote descendants of Jacob; hence, from there on, it is ordinarily rendered as "the Israelites." Households: the family in its fullest sense, including wives, children and servants.

1, 2: The sons of Jacob are listed here according to the respective mothers. Cf Gn 29, 31; 30, 30; 35, 16-26.

1, 5: Direct descendants: literally, persons coming from the loins of Jacob; hence, wives and servants are here excluded. Cf Gn 46, 26.

1, 8: Who knew nothing of Joseph: this king ignored the services that Joseph had rendered to Egypt.

1, 11: Pharaoh: not a personal name, but a title common to all the kings of Egypt.

1, 14: Mortar: either the wet clay with which the bricks were made, as in Na 3, 14, or the cement used between the bricks in building, as in Gn 11, 3.

1, 16: And see them giving birth: the Hebrew text is uncertain.

1, 22: The river: the Nile, which was "the" river for the Egyptians.

a: Gn 46, 27; Dt 10, 22; Acts 7, 14.   b: Gn 50, 26.   c: 8ff: Acts 7, 18.   d: Dt 26, 6.   e: Acts 7, 19.   f: Ex 6, 20; Nm 26, 59.

hid him for three months.[g] [3]When she could hide him no longer, she took a papyrus basket,* daubed it with bitumen and pitch, and putting the child in it, placed it among the reeds on the river bank. [4]His sister stationed herself at a distance to find out what would happen to him.

[5]Pharaoh's daughter came down to the river to bathe, while her maids walked along the river bank. Noticing the basket among the reeds, she sent her handmaid to fetch it. [6]On opening it, she looked, and lo, there was a baby boy, crying! She was moved with pity for him and said, "It is one of the Hebrews' children." [7]Then his sister asked Pharaoh's daughter, "Shall I go and call one of the Hebrew women to nurse the child for you?" [8]"Yes, do so," she answered. So the maiden went and called the child's own mother. [9]Pharaoh's daughter said to her, "Take this child and nurse it for me, and I will repay you." The woman therefore took the child and nursed it. [10]When the child grew,* she brought him to Pharaoh's daughter, who adopted him as her son[h] and called him Moses; for she said, "I drew him out of the water."

Moses' Flight to Midian. [11]On one occasion, after Moses had grown up,* when he visited his kinsmen[i] and witnessed their forced labor, he saw an Egyptian striking a Hebrew, one of his own kinsmen. [12]Looking about and seeing no one, he slew the Egyptian and hid him in the sand. [13]The next day he went out again, and now two Hebrews were fighting! So he asked the culprit, "Why are you striking your fellow Hebrew?" [14]But he replied, "Who has appointed you ruler and judge over us? Are you thinking of

killing me as you killed the Egyptian?" Then Moses became afraid and thought, "The affair must certainly be known."

[15]Pharaoh, too, heard of the affair and sought to put him to death. But Moses fled from him and stayed in the land of Midian.[j] As he was seated there by a well, [16]seven daughters of a priest of Midian came to draw water and fill the troughs to water their father's flock. [17]But some shepherds came and drove them away. Then Moses got up and defended them and watered their flock. [18]When they returned to their father Reuel,* he said to them, "How is it you have returned so soon today?" [19]They answered, "An Egyptian* saved us from the interference of the shepherds. He even drew water for us and watered the flock!" [20]"Where is the man?" he asked his daughters. "Why did you leave him there? Invite him to have something to eat." [21]Moses agreed to live with him, and the man gave him his daughter Zipporah in marriage. [22]She bore him a son, whom he named Gershom;* for he said, "I am a stranger in a foreign land."[k]

The Burning Bush. [23]A long time passed, during which the king of Egypt died. Still the Israelites groaned and cried out because of their slavery. As their cry for release went up to God,[l] [24]he heard their groaning and was mindful of his covenant[m] with Abraham, Isaac and Jacob. [25]He saw the Israelites and knew. . . .

CHAPTER 3

See RG 118-19

[1]Meanwhile Moses was tending the flock of his father-in-law Jethro, the priest of Midian. Leading the flock across the desert, he came to Horeb, the mountain

---

2, 3: Basket: literally, "chest" or "ark"; the same Hebrew word is used in Gn 6, 14 for Noah's ark. Here, however, the chest was made of papyrus stalks.

2, 10: When the child grew: probably when he was weaned or a little later. Moses: in Hebrew, Mosheh; the Hebrew word for "draw out" is mashah. The explanation of the name is not intended as a scientific etymology but as a play on words. The name is probably derived from an Egyptian word for "has been born," referring the birth to a god thought to be its sponsor.

2, 11: After Moses had grown up: Acts 7, 23 indicates that this was after an interval of nearly forty years. Cf Ex 7, 7. Striking: probably in the sense of "flogging"; according to some, "slaying."

2, 18: Reuel: he was also called Jethro. Cf Ex 3, 1; 4, 18; 18, 1.

2, 19: An Egyptian: Moses was probably wearing Egyptian dress, or spoke Egyptian to Reuel's daughters.

2, 22: Gershom: the name is explained as if it came from the Hebrew word ger, "stranger," joined to the Hebrew word sham, "there." Some Greek and Latin manuscripts add here a passage taken from Ex 18, 4.

---

g: Acts 7, 20; Heb 11, 23.   h: Acts 7, 21; Heb 11, 24.   i: 11-14: Acts 7, 23-28.   j: Acts 7, 29; Heb 11, 27.   k: Ex 18, 3.   l: Ex 3, 7. 9; Dt 26. 7.   m: Ex 6, 5; Pss 105, 8f; 106, 44f.

of God.* *2*There an angel of the LORD* appeared to him in fire flaming out of a bush.*n* As he looked on, he was surprised to see that the bush, though on fire, was not consumed. *3*So Moses decided, "I must go over to look at this remarkable sight, and see why the bush is not burned."

The Call of Moses. *4*When the LORD saw him coming over to look at it more closely, God called out to him from the bush, "Moses! Moses!" He answered, "Here I am." *5*God said, "Come no nearer!*o* Remove the sandals from your feet, for the place where you stand is holy ground. *6p*I am the God of your father," he continued, "the God of Abraham, the God of Isaac, the God of Jacob."* Moses hid his face, for he was afraid to look at God. *7*But the LORD said, "I have witnessed the affliction of my people in Egypt and have heard their cry of complaint against their slave drivers, so I know well what they are suffering. *8*Therefore I have come down* to rescue them from the hands of the Egyptians and lead them out of that land into a good and spacious land, a land flowing with milk and honey, the country of the Canaanites, Hittites, Amorites, Perizzites, Hivites and Jebusites.*q* *9*So indeed the cry of the Israelites has reached me, and I have truly noted that the Egyptians are oppressing them. *10*Come, now! I will send you to Pharaoh to lead my people, the Israelites, out of Egypt."

*11*But Moses said to God, "Who am I* that I should go to Pharaoh and lead the Israelites out of Egypt?" *12*He answered, "I will be with you; and this shall be your proof that it is I who have sent you: when you bring my people out of Egypt, you will worship God on this very mountain." *13*But," said Moses to God, "when I go to the Israelites and say to them, 'The God of your fathers has sent me to you,' if they ask me, 'What is his name?' what am I to tell them?" *14*God replied, "I am who am."* Then he added, "This is what you shall tell the Israelites: I AM sent me to you."

*15*God spoke further to Moses, "Thus shall you say to the Israelites: The LORD, the God of your fathers, the God of Abraham, the God of Isaac, the God of Jacob, has sent me to you.

"This is my name forever;*r*
    this is my title for all generations.

16"Go and assemble the elders* of the Israelites, and tell them: The LORD, the God of your fathers, the God of Abraham, Isaac and Jacob, has appeared to me and said: I am concerned about you and about the way you are being treated in Egypt; *17*so I have decided to lead you up out of the misery of Egypt into the land of the Canaanites, Hittites, Amorites, Perizzites, Hivites and Jebusites, a land flowing with milk and honey.

18"Thus they will heed your message. Then you and the elders of Israel shall go to the king of Egypt and say to him:*s* The LORD,

3, 1: The mountain of God: probably given this designation because of the divine apparitions which took place there, such as on this occasion and when the Israelites were there after the departure from Egypt.

3, 2: An angel of the LORD: the visual form under which God appeared and spoke to men is referred to indifferently in some Old Testament texts either as God's angel or as God himself. Cf Gn 16, 7. 13; Ex 14, 19. 24f; Nm 22, 22-35; Jgs 6, 11-18.

3, 6: The God of Abraham . . . Jacob: cited by Christ in proof of the resurrection since the patriarchs, long dead, live on in God who is the God of the living. Cf Mt 22, 32; Mk 12, 26; Lk 20, 37. Afraid: The appearance of God caused fear of death, since it was believed that no one could see God and live; cf Gn 32, 30.

3, 8: I have come down: a figure of speech signifying an extraordinary divine intervention in human affairs. Cf Gn 11, 5. 7. Flowing with milk and honey: an expression denoting agricultural prosperity, which seems to have been proverbial in its application to Palestine. Cf Ex 13, 5; Nm 13,

27; Jos 5, 6; Jer 11, 5; 32, 22; Ez 20, 6. 15.

3, 11: Who am I: besides naturally shrinking from such a tremendous undertaking, Moses realized that, as a fugitive from Pharaoh, he could hardly hope to carry out a mission to him. Perhaps he also recalled that on one occasion even his own kinsmen questioned his authority. Cf Ex 2, 14.

3, 14: I am who am: apparently this utterance is the source of the word Yahweh, the proper personal name of the God of Israel. It is commonly explained in reference to God as the absolute and necessary Being. It may be understood of God as the Source of all created beings. Out of reverence for this name, the term Adonai, "my Lord," was later used as a substitute. The word Lord in the present version represents this traditional usage. The word "Jehovah" arose from a false reading of this name as it is written in the current Hebrew text.

3, 16: Elders: the Israelite leaders, who were usually older men. They were representatives of the people.

n: 2-10; Acts 7, 30-35.   *o:* Jos 5, 15.   *p:* Ex 4, 5; Mt 22, 32; Mk 12, 36; Lk 20, 37.   *q:* 8f: Gn 15, 19ff.   *r:* Ps 135, 13.   *s:* Ex 5, 3.

the God of the Hebrews, has sent us word. Permit us, then, to go a three-days' journey in the desert, that we may offer sacrifice to the LORD, our God.

¹⁹"Yet I know that the king of Egypt will not allow you to go unless he is forced. ²⁰I will stretch out my hand, therefore, and smite Egypt by doing all kinds of wondrous deeds there. After that he will send you away. ²¹I will even make the Egyptians so well-disposed toward this people that, when you leave, you will not go empty-handed. ²²'Every woman shall ask her neighbor and her house guest for silver and gold articles* and for clothing to put on your sons and daughters. Thus you will despoil the Egyptians."

See RG 118–19

CHAPTER 4

Confirmation of Moses' Mission. ¹"But," objected Moses, "suppose they will not believe me, nor listen to my plea? For they may say, 'The LORD did not appear to you.'" ²The LORD therefore asked him, "What is that in your hand?" "A staff," he answered. ³The LORD then said, "Throw it on the ground." When he threw it on the ground it was changed into a serpent,ᵘ and Moses shied away from it. ⁴"Now, put out your hand," the LORD said to him, "and take hold of its tail." So he put out his hand and laid hold of it, and it became a staff in his hand. ⁵"This will take place so that they may believe," he continued, "that the LORD, the God of their fathers, the God of Abraham, the God of Isaac, the God of Jacob, did appear to you."

⁶Again the LORD said to him, "Put your hand in your bosom." He put it in his bosom, and when he withdrew it, to his surprise his hand was leprous, like snow. ⁷The LORD then said, "Now, put your hand back in your bosom." Moses put his hand back in his bosom, and when he withdrew it, to his surprise it was again like the rest of his body. ⁸"If they will not believe you, nor heed the message of the first sign, they should believe the message of the second. ⁹And if they will not believe even these two signs, nor heed your plea, take some water from the river and pour it on the dry land. The water you take from the river will become blood on the dry land."ᵛ

Aaron's Office as Assistant. ¹⁰Moses, however, said to the LORD, "If you please, Lord, I have never been eloquent, neither in the past, nor recently, nor now that you have spoken to your servant; but I am slow of speech and tongue."ʷ ¹¹The LORD said to him, "Who gives one man speech and makes another deaf and dumb? Or who gives sight to one and makes another blind? Is it not I, the LORD? ¹²Go, then! It is I who will assist you in speaking and will teach you what you are to say." ¹³Yet he insisted, "If you please, Lord, send someone else!"* ¹⁴Then the LORD became angry with Moses and said, "Have you not your brother, Aaron the Levite? I know that he is an eloquent speaker. Besides, he is now on his way to meet you. ¹⁵When he sees you, his heart will be glad. You are to speak to him, then, and put the words in his mouth. I will assist both you and him in speaking and will teach the two of you what you are to do. ¹⁶He shall speak to the people for you: he shall be your spokesman,* and you shall be as God to him.ˣ ¹⁷Take this staff* in your hand; with it you are to perform the signs."

Moses' Return to Egypt. ¹⁸After this Moses returned to his father-in-law Jethro and said to him, "Let me go back, please, to my kinsmen in Egypt, to see whether they are still living." Jethro replied, "Go in peace."*

3, 22: Articles: probably jewelry. Despoil: this was permissible, that the Israelites might compensate themselves for their many years of servitude; besides, the Egyptians would give these things willingly. Cf Ex 12, 33-36.

4, 13: Send someone else: literally, "Send by means of him whom you will send," that is, "Send whom you will."

4, 16: Spokesman: literally, "mouth"; Aaron was to serve as a mouthpiece for Moses, as a prophet does for God; hence the relation between Moses and Aaron is compared to that between God and his prophet. Cf Ex 7, 1.

4, 17: This staff: probably the same as that of vv 2ff; but some understand it here of a new staff now given by God to Moses.

4, 18: Moses did not tell his father-in-law his main reason for returning to Egypt, but this secondary motive which he offered was also true.

---

t: 21f: Ex 11, 2f; 12, 35f.   *u:* Ex 7, 10.   *v:* Ex 7, 17. 19f.
w: Ex 6, 12.   *x:* 15f: Ex 7, 1.

[19]In Midian[y] the LORD said to Moses, "Go back to Egypt, for all the men who sought your life are dead." [20]So Moses took his wife and his sons, and started back to the land of Egypt, with them riding the ass. The staff of God he carried with him. [21]The LORD said to him, "On your return to Egypt, see that you perform before Pharaoh all the wonders I have put in your power. I will make him obstinate,* however, so that he will not let the people go. [22z]So you shall say to Pharaoh: Thus says the LORD: Israel is my son, my first-born. [23]Hence I tell you: Let my son go, that he may serve me. If you refuse to let him go, I warn you, I will kill your son, your first-born."[a]

[24]*On the journey, at a place where they spent the night, the Lord came upon Moses and would have killed him. [25b]But Zipporah took a piece of flint and cut off her son's foreskin and, touching his person, she said, "You are a spouse of blood to me." [26]Then God let Moses go. At that time she said, "A spouse of blood," in regard to the circumcision.

[27]The LORD said to Aaron, "Go into the desert to meet Moses." So he went, and when they met at the mountain of God, Aaron kissed him. [28]Moses informed him of all the LORD had said in sending him, and of the various signs he had enjoined upon him. [29]Then Moses and Aaron went and assembled all the elders of the Israelites. [30]Aaron told them everything the LORD had said to Moses, and he performed the signs before the people. [31]The people believed, and when they heard that the LORD was concerned about them and had seen their affliction, they bowed down in worship.

CHAPTER 5

See RG 119–20

Pharaoh's Obduracy. [1]After that, Moses and Aaron went to Pharaoh and said, "Thus says the LORD, the God of Israel: Let my people go, that they may celebrate a feast to me in the desert." [2]Pharaoh answered, "Who is the LORD, that I should heed his plea to let Israel go? I do not know the LORD; even if I did, I would not let Israel go." [3]They replied, "The God of the Hebrews has sent us word. Let us go a three days' journey in the desert, that we may offer sacrifice to the LORD, our God;[c] otherwise he will punish us with pestilence or the sword."

[4]The king of Egypt answered them, "What do you mean, Moses and Aaron, by taking the people away from their work? Off to your labor! [5]Look how numerous the people of the land are already," continued Pharaoh, "and yet you would give them rest from their labor!"

[6]That very day Pharaoh gave the taskmasters and foremen* of the people this order: [7]"You shall no longer supply the people with straw for their brickmaking* as you have previously done. Let them go and gather straw themselves! [8]Yet you shall levy upon them the same quota of bricks as they have previously made. Do not reduce it. They are lazy; that is why they are crying, 'Let us go to offer sacrifice to our God.' [9]Increase the work for the men, so that they keep their mind on it and pay no attention to lying words."

[10]So the taskmasters and foremen of the people went out and told them, "Thus says Pharaoh: I will not provide you with straw. [11]Go and gather the straw yourselves, wherever you can find it. Yet there must not be the slightest reduction in your work." [12]The people, then, scattered throughout the land of Egypt to gather stubble for straw, [13]while the taskmasters kept driving them on, saying, "Finish your work, the same daily amount as when your straw was supplied."

Complaint of the Foremen. [14]The foremen of the Israelites, whom the taskmasters of Pharaoh had placed over them, were beaten, and were asked, "Why have you not

---

4, 21: Make him obstinate: literally, "harden his heart." God permitted Pharaoh to be stubborn in his opposition to the departure of the Israelites. Cf Rom 9, 17f.
4, 24ff: Apparently God was angry with Moses for having failed to keep the divine command given to Abraham in Gn 17, 10ff. Moses' life is spared when his wife circumcises their son.
5, 6: The taskmasters and foremen: the former were higher officials and probably Egyptians; the latter were lower officials, chosen from the Israelites themselves. Cf v 14.
5, 7: Straw was mixed with the clay to give the sun-dried bricks greater consistency.

y: Ex 2, 15, 23.   z: Sir 36, 11.   a: Ex 11, 5; 12, 29.   b: Is 6, 2; 7, 20.   c: Ex 3, 18.

completed your prescribed amount of bricks yesterday and today, as before?" ¹⁵Then the Israelite foremen came and made this appeal to Pharaoh: "Why do you treat your servants in this manner? ¹⁶No straw is supplied to your servants, and still we are told to make bricks. Look how your servants are beaten! It is you who are at fault." ¹⁷Pharaoh answered, "It is just because you are lazy that you keep saying, 'Let us go and offer sacrifice to the LORD.' ¹⁸Off to work, then! Straw shall not be provided for you, but you must still deliver your quota of bricks."

¹⁹The Israelite foremen knew they were in a sorry plight, having been told not to reduce the daily amount of bricks. ²⁰When, therefore, they left Pharaoh and came upon Moses and Aaron, who were waiting to meet them, ²¹they said to them, "The LORD look upon you and judge! You have brought us into bad odor with Pharaoh and his servants and have put a sword in their hands to slay us."

Renewal of God's Promise. ²²Moses again had recourse to the LORD and said, "Lord, why do you treat this people so badly? And why did you send me on such a mission? ²³Ever since I went to Pharaoh to speak in your name, he has maltreated this people of yours, and you have done nothing to rescue them."

CHAPTER 6

See RG
119–20

¹Then the LORD answered Moses, "Now you shall see what I will do to Pharaoh. Forced by my mighty hand, he will send them away; compelled by my outstretched arm, he will drive them from his land."

²God also said to Moses, "I am the LORD. ³As God the Almighty I appeared[d] to Abraham, Isaac and Jacob, but my name, LORD, I did not make known to them. ⁴I also established my covenant with them, to give them the land of Canaan, the land in which they were living as aliens.[e] ⁵And now that I have heard the groaning of the Israelites, whom the Egyptians are treating as slaves, I am mindful of my covenant.[f] ⁶Therefore, say to the Israelites: I am the LORD. I will free you from the forced labor of the Egyptians and will deliver you from their slavery. I will rescue you by my outstretched arm and with mighty acts of judgment. ⁷I will take you as my own people, and you shall have me as your God.[g] You will know that I, the LORD, am your God when I free you from the labor of the Egyptians ⁸and bring you into the land which I swore to give to Abraham, Isaac and Jacob. I will give it to you as your own possession—I, the LORD!" ⁹But when Moses told this to the Israelites, they would not listen to him because of their dejection and hard slavery.

¹⁰Then the LORD said to Moses, ¹¹"Go and tell Pharaoh, king of Egypt, to let the Israelites leave his land." ¹²But Moses protested to the LORD, "If the Israelites would not listen to me, how can it be that Pharaoh will listen to me, poor speaker[h] that I am!" ¹³Still, the LORD, to bring the Israelites out of Egypt, spoke to Moses and Aaron and gave them his orders regarding both the Israelites and Pharaoh, king of Egypt.

Genealogy of Moses and Aaron. ¹⁴These are the heads of the ancestral houses.* The sons of Reuben,[i] the first-born of Israel, were Hanoch, Pallu, Hezron and Carmi; these are the clans of Reuben. ¹⁵The sons of Simeon[j] were Jemuel, Jamin, Ohad, Jachin, Zohar and Shaul, who was the son of a Canaanite woman; these are the clans of Simeon. ¹⁶The names of the sons of Levi,[k] in their genealogical order, are Gershon, Kohath and Merari. Levi lived one hundred and thirty-seven years.

¹⁷The sons of Gershon,[l] as heads of clans, were Libni and Shimei. ¹⁸The sons of Kohath[m] were Amram, Izhar, Hebron and Uzziel. Kohath lived one hundred and thirty-three years. ¹⁹The sons of Merari[n] were Mahli and Mushi. These are the clans of Levi in their genealogical order.

6, 14: The purpose of the genealogy here is to give the line from which Moses and Aaron sprang. Reuben and Simeon are first mentioned because, as older brothers of Levi, their names occur before his in the genealogy.

d: Gn 17, 1; 35, 11.   e: Gn 15, 18; 17, 4-8.   f: Ex 2, 24.   g: Lv 26, 12.   h: Ex 6, 30.   i: Nm 26. 5f; 1 Chr 5, 3   j: Nm 26, 12; 1 Chr 4, 24.   k: Nm 3, 17; 1 Chr 6, 1. 16; 23, 6.   l: Nm 3, 21; 1 Chr 6, 17; 23, 7.   m: Nm 3, 27; 1 Chr 6, 2. 18.   n: Nm 3, 20; 1 Chr 6, 19; 23, 21.

²⁰Amram married his aunt* Jochebed,ᵒ who bore him Aaron, Moses and Miriam. Amram lived one hundred and thirty-seven years. ²¹The sons of Izhar were Korah, Nepheg and Zichri. ²²The sons of Uzziel were Mishael, Elzaphan and Sithri. ²³Aaron married Amminadab'sᵖ daughter, Elisheba, the sister of Nahshon; she bore him Nadab, Abihu, Eleazar and Ithamar. ²⁴The sons of Korah were Assir, Elkanah and Abiasaph. These are the clans of the Korahites. ²⁵Aaron's son, Eleazar, married one of Putiel's daughters, who bore him Phinehas. These are the heads of the ancestral clans of the Levites. ²⁶This is the Aaron and this the Moses to whom the LORD said, "Lead the Israelites from the land of Egypt, company by company." ²⁷These are the ones who spoke to Pharaoh, king of Egypt, to bring the Israelites out of Egypt—the same Moses and Aaron.

Moses and Aaron before Pharaoh. ²⁸On the day the LORD spoke to Moses in Egypt ²⁹he said, "I am the LORD. Repeat to Pharaoh, king of Egypt, all that I tell you." ³⁰But Moses protested to the LORD, "Since I am a poor speaker,�q how can it be that Pharaoh will listen to me?"

See RG 119–20

CHAPTER 7

¹The LORD answered him, "See! I have made you as God to Pharaoh,ʳ and Aaron your brother shall act as your prophet.* ²You shall tell him all that I command you. In turn, your brother Aaron shall tell Pharaoh to let the Israelites leave his land. ³Yet I will make Pharaoh so obstinate that, despite the many signs and wonders that I will work in the land of Egypt, ⁴he will not listen to you. Therefore I will lay my hand on Egypt and by great acts of judgment I will bring the hosts of my people, the Israelites, out of the land of Egypt, ⁵so that the Egyptians may learn that I am the LORD, as I stretch out my hand against Egypt and lead the Israelites out of their midst."

⁶Moses and Aaron did as the LORD had commanded them. ⁷Moses was eighty years old and Aaron eighty-three when they spoke to Pharaoh.

The Staff Turned into a Snake. ⁸The LORD told Moses and Aaron, ⁹"If Pharaoh demands that you work a sign or wonder, you shall say to Aaron: Take your staff and throw it down before Pharaoh, and it will be changed into a snake."ˢ ¹⁰Then Moses and Aaron went to Pharaoh and did as the LORD had commanded. Aaron threw his staff down before Pharaoh and his servants, and it was changed into a snake. ¹¹Pharaoh, in turn, summoned wise men and sorcerers, and they also, the magiciansᵗ of Egypt, did likewise by their magic arts. ¹²Each one threw down his staff, and it was changed into a snake. But Aaron's staff swallowed their staffs. ¹³Pharaoh, however, was obstinate and would not listen to them, just as the LORD had foretold.

First Plague: Water Turned into Blood. ¹⁴*Then the LORD said to Moses, "Pharaoh is obdurate in refusing to let the people go. ¹⁵Tomorrow morning, when he sets out for the water, go and present yourself by the river bank, holding in your hand the staff that turned into a serpent. ¹⁶Say to him: The LORD, the God of the Hebrews, sent me to you with the message: Let my people go to worship me in the desert. But as yet you have not listened. ¹⁷The LORD now says: This is how you shall know that I am the LORD. I will strike the water of the river with the staff I hold, and it shall be changed into blood.ᵘ ¹⁸The fish in the river shall die, and the river itself shall become so polluted that the Egyptians will be unable to drink its water."

¹⁹The LORD then said to Moses, "Say to Aaron: Take your staff and stretch out your

---

6, 20: His aunt: more exactly, "his father's sister." Later on such a marriage was forbidden. Cf Lv 18, 12. Hence, the Greek and Latin versions render here, "his cousin."

7, 1: Just as God had his prophets to speak to men in his name, so Moses had Aaron as his "prophet" to speak to Pharaoh. Cf Ex 4, 16.

7, 14: Most of the ten plagues of Egypt seem to be similar to certain natural phenomena of that country; but they are represented as supernatural at least in their greater intensity and in their occurring exactly to Moses' commands.

o: Nm 26, 59. p: Ru 4, 19f; 1 Chr 2, 10. q: Ex 6, 12. r: Ex 4, 15f. s: Ex 4, 3. t: 2 Tm 3, 8. u: 17-21: Ex 4, 9; Pss 78, 44; 105, 29; Wis 11, 5-7.

hand over the waters of Egypt—their streams and canals and pools, all their supplies of water—that they may become blood. Throughout the land of Egypt there shall be blood, even in the wooden pails and stone jars."

²⁰Moses and Aaron did as the LORD had commanded. Aaron raised his staff and struck the waters of the river in full view of Pharaoh and his servants, and all the water of the river was changed into blood. ²¹The fish in the river died, and the river itself became so polluted that the Egyptians could not drink its water. There was blood throughout the land of Egypt. ²²But the Egyptian magicians did the same by their magic arts. So Pharaoh remained obstinate and would not listen to Moses and Aaron, just as the LORD had foretold. ²³He turned away and went into his house, with no concern even for this. ²⁴All the Egyptians had to dig in the neighborhood of the river for drinking water, since they could not drink the river water.

Second Plague: the Frogs. ²⁵Seven days passed after the LORD had struck the river. ²⁶*Then the LORD said to Moses, "Go to Pharaoh and tell him:ᵛ Thus says the LORD: Let my people go to worship me. ²⁷If you refuse to let them go, I warn you, I will send a plague of frogs over all your territory. ²⁸The river will teem with frogs. They will come up into your palace and into your bedroom and onto your bed, into the houses of your servants, too, and your subjects, even into your ovens and your kneading bowls. ²⁹The frogs will swarm all over you and your subjects and your servants."

See RG 119-20

CHAPTER 8

¹The LORD then told Moses, "Say to Aaron: Stretch out your hand and your staff over the streams and canals and pools, to make frogs overrun the land of Egypt." ²Aaron stretched out his hand over the waters of Egypt, and the frogs came up and

covered the land of Egypt. ³But the magicians did the same by their magic arts. They, too, made frogs overrun the land of Egypt.

⁴Then Pharaoh summoned Moses and Aaron and said, "Pray the LORD to remove the frogs from me and my subjects, and I will let the people go to offer sacrifice to the LORD." ⁵Moses answered Pharaoh, "Do me the favor of appointing the time when I am to pray for you and your servants and your subjects, that the frogs may be taken away from you and your houses and be left only in the river." ⁶"Tomorrow," said Pharaoh. Then Moses replied, "It shall be as you have said, so that you may learn that there is none like the LORD, our God. ⁷The frogs shall leave you and your houses, your servants and your subjects; only in the river shall they be left."

⁸After Moses and Aaron left Pharaoh's presence, Moses implored the LORD to fulfill the promise he had made to Pharaoh about the frogs; ⁹and the LORD did as Moses had asked. The frogs in the houses and court-yards* and fields died off. ¹⁰Heaps and heaps of them were gathered up, and there was a stench in the land. ¹¹But when Pharaoh saw that there was a respite, he became obdurate and would not listen to them, just as the LORD had foretold.

Third Plague: the Gnats. ¹²Thereupon the LORD said to Moses, "Tell Aaron to stretch out his staff and strike the dust of the earth, that it may be turned into gnatsʷ throughout the land of Egypt."* ¹³They did so. Aaron stretched out his hand, and with his staff he struck the dust of the earth, and gnats came upon man and beast. The dust of the earth was turned into gnats throughout the land of Egypt. ¹⁴Though the magicians tried to bring forth gnats by their magic arts, they could not do so.ˣ As the gnats infested man and beast, ¹⁵the magicians said to Pharaoh, "This is the finger of God."* Yet Pharaoh remained obstinate and would not listen to them, just as the LORD had foretold.

Fourth Plague: the Flies. ¹⁶Again the

7, 26—8, 28: This is Ex 8, 1-32 in the verse enumeration of the Vulgate.

8, 9: Courtyards: some render "farmhouses."

8, 12. 17: Gnats, flies: it is uncertain what species of troublesome insects are here meant.

8, 15: The finger of God: understood by the magicians as the staff mentioned in Ex 8, 13. Cf Lk 11, 20.

v: 26-29: Pss 78, 45; 105, 30.   w: 12f: Ps 105, 31.   x: Wis 17, 7.

LORD told Moses, "Early tomorrow morning present yourself to Pharaoh when he goes forth to the water, and say to him: Thus says the LORD: Let my people go to worship me. [17]If you will not let my people go, I warn you, I will loose swarms of flies upon you and your servants and your subjects and your houses. The houses of the Egyptians and the very ground on which they stand shall be filled with swarms of flies. [18]But on that day I will make an exception of the land of Goshen: there shall be no flies where my people dwell, that you may know that I am the LORD in the midst of the earth. [19]I will make this distinction between my people and your people. This sign shall take place tomorrow." [20]This the LORD did. Thick swarms of flies entered the house of Pharaoh and houses of his servants; throughout Egypt the land was infested with flies.[y]

[21]Then Pharaoh summoned Moses and Aaron and said to them, "Go and offer sacrifice to your God in this land." [22]But Moses replied, "It is not right to do so, for the sacrifices we offer to the LORD, our God, are an abomination to the Egyptians.[*] If before their very eyes we offer sacrifices which are an abomination to them, will not the Egyptians stone us? [23]We must go a three days' journey in the desert to offer sacrifice to the LORD, our God, as he commands us." [24]"Well, then," said Pharaoh, "I will let you go to offer sacrifice to the LORD, your God, in the desert, provided that you do not go too far away and that you pray for me." [25]Moses answered, "As soon as I leave your presence I will pray to the LORD that the flies may depart tomorrow from Pharaoh and his servants and his subjects. Pharaoh, however, must not play false again by refusing to let the people go to offer sacrifice to the LORD." [26]When Moses left Pharaoh's presence, he prayed to the LORD; [27]and the LORD did as Moses had asked. He removed the flies from Pharaoh and his servants and subjects. Not one remained. [28]But once more Pharaoh became obdurate and would not let the people go.

CHAPTER 9

See RG 119-20

Fifth Plague: the Pestilence. [1]Then the LORD said to Moses, "Go to Pharaoh and tell him: Thus says the LORD, the God of the Hebrews: Let my people go to worship me. [2]If you refuse to let them go and persist in holding them, [3]I warn you, the LORD will afflict all your livestock in the field—your horses, asses, camels, herds and flocks—with a very severe pestilence. [4]But the LORD will distinguish between the livestock of Israel and that of Egypt, so that none belonging to the Israelites will die." [5]And setting a definite time, the LORD added, "Tomorrow the LORD shall do this in the land." [6]And on the next day the LORD did so. All the livestock of the Egyptians died,[z] but not one beast belonging to the Israelites. [7]But though Pharaoh's messengers informed him that not even one beast belonging to the Israelites had died, he still remained obdurate and would not let the people go.

Sixth Plague: the Boils. [8]Then the LORD said to Moses and Aaron, "Take a double handful of soot from a furnace, and in the presence of Pharaoh let Moses scatter it toward the sky. [9]It will then turn into fine dust over the whole land of Egypt and cause festering boils on man and beast throughout the land."

[10]So they took soot from a furnace and stood in the presence of Pharaoh. Moses scattered it toward the sky, and it caused festering boils on man and beast. [11]The magicians could not stand in Moses' presence, for there were boils on the magicians no less than on the rest of the Egyptians. [12]But the LORD made Pharaoh obstinate, and he would not listen to them, just as the LORD had foretold to Moses.

Seventh Plague: the Hail. [13]Then the LORD told Moses, "Early tomorrow morning present yourself to Pharaoh and say to him: Thus says the LORD, the God of the He-

---

8, 22: The Egyptians would fiercely resent the sacrifice of any animal they considered sacred. Certain animals were worshiped in Egypt, at least as the symbols of various deities.

---

y: Pss 78, 45; 105, 31; Wis 16, 9.   *z:* Ps 78, 48.

brews: Let my people go to worship me, [14]or this time I will hurl all my blows upon you and your servants and your subjects, that you may know that there is none like me anywhere on earth. [15]For by now I would have stretched out my hand and struck you and your subjects with such pestilence as would wipe you from the earth. [16]But this is why I have spared you: to show you* my power and to make my name resound throughout the earth![a] [17]Will you still block the way for my people by refusing to let them go? [18]I warn you, then, tomorrow at this hour I will rain down such fierce hail as there has never been in Egypt from the day the nation was founded up to the present. [19]Therefore, order all your livestock and whatever else you have in the open fields to be brought to a place of safety. Whatever man or beast remains in the fields and is not brought to shelter shall die when the hail comes upon them." [20]Some of Pharaoh's servants feared the warning of the LORD and hurried their servants and livestock off to shelter. [21]Others, however, did not take the warning of the LORD to heart and left their servants and livestock in the fields.

[22]The LORD then said to Moses, "Stretch out your hand toward the sky, that hail may fall upon the entire land of Egypt, on man and beast and every growing thing in the land of Egypt." [23]When Moses stretched out his staff toward the sky, the LORD sent forth hail[b] and peals of thunder. Lightning flashed toward the earth, and the LORD rained down hail upon the land of Egypt; [24]and lightning constantly flashed through the hail, such fierce hail as had never been seen in the land since Egypt became a nation. [25]It struck down every man and beast that was in the open throughout the land of Egypt; it beat down every growing thing and splintered every tree in the fields. [26]Only in the land of Goshen, where the Israelites dwelt, was there no hail.

[27]Then Pharaoh summoned Moses and Aaron and said to them, "I have sinned again! The LORD is just; it is I and my sub-jects who are at fault. [28]Pray to the LORD, for we have had enough of God's thunder and hail. Then I will let you go; you need stay no longer." [29]Moses replied, "As soon as I leave the city I will extend my hands to the LORD; the thunder will cease, and there will be no more hail. Thus you shall learn that the earth is the LORD's. [30]But you and your servants, I know, do not yet fear the LORD God."

[31]Now the flax and the barley were ruined, because the barley was in ear and the flax in bud. [32]But the wheat and the spelt were not ruined, for they grow later.

[33]When Moses had left Pharaoh's presence and had gone out of the city, he extended his hands to the LORD. Then the thunder and the hail ceased, and the rain no longer poured down upon the earth. [34]But Pharaoh, seeing that the rain and hail and thunder had ceased, sinned again: he with his servants became obdurate, [35]and in his obstinacy he would not let the Israelites go, as the LORD had foretold through Moses.

CHAPTER 10

See RG 119-20

Eighth Plague: the Locusts. [1]Then the LORD said to Moses, "Go to Pharaoh, for I have made him and his servants obdurate in order that I may perform these signs of mine among them [2]and that you may recount to your son and grandson how ruthlessly I dealt with the Egyptians and what signs I wrought among them, so that you may know that I am the LORD."[c]

[3]So Moses and Aaron went to Pharaoh and told him, "Thus says the LORD, the God of the Hebrews: How long will you refuse to submit to me? Let my people go to worship me. [4]If you refuse to let my people go, I warn you, tomorrow I will bring locusts into your country. [5]They shall cover the ground, so that the ground itself will not be visible. They shall eat up the remnant you saved unhurt from the hail, as well as all the foliage that has since sprouted in your fields. [6]They shall fill your houses and the houses of your servants and of all the Egyptians; such a sight your fathers or grandfathers have not

---

9, 16: To show you: some ancient versions read, "to show through you." Cf Rom 9, 17.

a: Rom 9, 17.   *b:* 23f; Pss 78, 47; 105, 32f.   *c:* Dt 6, 20ff.

seen from the day they first settled on this soil up to the present day." With that he turned and left Pharaoh.

⁷But Pharaoh's servants said to him, "How long must he be a menace to us? Let the men go to worship the LORD, their God. Do you not yet realize that Egypt is being destroyed?" ⁸So Moses and Aaron were brought back to Pharaoh, who said to them, "You may go and worship the LORD, your God. But how many of you will go?" ⁹"Young and old must go with us," Moses answered, "our sons and daughters as well as our flocks and herds must accompany us. That is what a feast of the LORD means to us." ¹⁰"The LORD help you,"* Pharaoh replied, "if I ever let your little ones go with you! Clearly, you have some evil in mind. ¹¹No, no! Just you men can go and worship the LORD.* After all, that is what you want." With that they were driven from Pharaoh's presence.

¹²The LORD then said to Moses, "Stretch out your hand over the land of Egypt, that locusts*d* may swarm over it and eat up all the vegetation and whatever the hail has left." ¹³So Moses stretched out his staff over the land of Egypt, and the LORD sent an east wind* blowing over the land all that day and all that night. At dawn the east wind brought the locusts. ¹⁴They swarmed over the whole land of Egypt and settled down on every part of it. Never before had there been such a fierce swarm of locusts, nor will there ever be. ¹⁵They covered the surface of the whole land, till it was black with them. They ate up all the vegetation in the land and the fruit of whatever trees the hail had spared. Nothing green was left on any tree or plant throughout the land of Egypt.

¹⁶Hastily Pharaoh summoned Moses and Aaron and said, "I have sinned against the LORD, your God, and against you. ¹⁷But now, do forgive me my sin once more, and pray the LORD, your God, to take at least this deadly pest from me." ¹⁸When Moses left the presence of Pharaoh, he prayed to the LORD, ¹⁹and the LORD changed the wind to a very strong west wind, which took up the locusts and hurled them into the Red Sea.* But though not a single locust remained within the confines of Egypt, ²⁰the LORD made Pharaoh obstinate, and he would not let the Israelites go.

Ninth Plague: the Darkness. ²¹Then the LORD said to Moses, "Stretch out your hand toward the sky, that over the land of Egypt there may be such intense darkness* that one can feel it." ²²So Moses stretched out his hand toward the sky, and there was dense darkness*e* throughout the land of Egypt for three days. ²³Men could not see one another, nor could they move from where they were, for three days. But all the Israelites had light where they dwelt.

²⁴Pharaoh then summoned Moses and Aaron and said, "Go and worship the LORD. Your little ones, too, may go with you. But your flocks and herds must remain." ²⁵Moses replied, "You must also grant us sacrifices and holocausts to offer up to the LORD, our God. ²⁶Hence, our livestock also must go with us. Not an animal must be left behind. Some of them we must sacrifice to the LORD, our God, but we ourselves shall not know which ones we must sacrifice to him until we arrive at the place itself." ²⁷But the LORD made Pharaoh obstinate, and he would not let them go. ²⁸"Leave my presence," Pharaoh said to him, "and see to it that you do not appear before me again! The day you appear before me you shall die!" ²⁹Moses replied, "Well said! I will never appear before you again."

10, 10: The LORD help you . . . : literally, "May the LORD be with you in the same way as I let you . . ."; a sarcastic blessing intended as a curse.

10, 11: Pharaoh realized that if the men alone went they would have to return to their families. He suspected that the Hebrews had no intention of returning.

10, 13: East wind: coming across the desert from Arabia, the strong east wind brings Egypt the burning sirocco and, at times, locusts. Cf Ex 14, 21.

10, 19: The Red Sea: according to the traditional transla-tion, but the Hebrew is literally, "the Reed Sea"; hence the Red Sea of Exodus was probably a body of shallow water somewhat to the north of the present deep Red Sea.

10, 21: Darkness: at times a storm from the south, called the khamsin, blackens the sky of Egypt with sand from the Sahara; the dust in the air is then so thick that the darkness can, in a sense, "be felt."

d: 12ff: Pss 78, 46; 105, 34f.   *e:* Ps 105, 28.

See RG
119-20

CHAPTER 11

Tenth Plague: the Death of the First-born. ¹Then the LORD told Moses, "One more plague will I bring upon Pharaoh and upon Egypt. After that he will let you depart. In fact, he will not merely let you go; he will drive you away. ²Instruct your people that every man is to ask his neighbor, and every woman her neighbor, for silver and gold articles and for clothing."*f* ³The LORD indeed made the Egyptians well-disposed toward the people; Moses himself was very highly regarded by Pharaoh's servants and the people in the land of Egypt.

⁴Moses then said, "Thus says the LORD: At midnight I will go forth through Egypt.*g* ⁵Every first-born in this land shall die,*h* from the first-born of Pharaoh on the throne to the first-born of the slave-girl at the handmill, as well as all the first-born of the animals. ⁶Then there shall be loud wailing throughout the land of Egypt, such as has never been, nor will ever be again. ⁷But among the Israelites and their animals not even a dog shall growl, so that you may know how the LORD distinguishes between the Egyptians and the Israelites. ⁸*i*All these servants of yours shall then come down to me, and prostrate before me, they shall beg me, 'Leave us, you and all your followers!' Only then will I depart." With that he left Pharaoh's presence in hot anger.

⁹The LORD said to Moses, "Pharaoh refuses to listen to you that my wonders may be multiplied in the land of Egypt." ¹⁰Thus, although Moses and Aaron performed these various wonders in Pharaoh's presence, the LORD made Pharaoh obstinate, and he would not let the Israelites leave his land.

See RG
119-20

CHAPTER 12

The Passover Ritual Prescribed. ¹The LORD said to Moses and Aaron in the land of Egypt, ²"This month* shall stand at the head of your calendar; you shall reckon it the first month of the year.*j* ³Tell the whole community of Israel: On the tenth of this month every one of your families must procure for itself a lamb, one apiece for each household. ⁴If a family is too small for a whole lamb, it shall join the nearest household in procuring one and shall share in the lamb* in proportion to the number of persons who partake of it. ⁵The lamb must be a year-old male and without blemish. You may take it from either the sheep or the goats. ⁶You shall keep it until the fourteenth day of this month, and then, with the whole assembly of Israel present, it shall be slaughtered during the evening twilight. ⁷They shall take some of its blood and apply it to the two doorposts and the lintel of every house in which they partake of the lamb. ⁸That same night they shall eat its roasted flesh with unleavened bread and bitter herbs. ⁹It shall not be eaten raw or boiled, but roasted whole, with its head and shanks and inner organs. ¹⁰None of it must be kept beyond the next morning; whatever is left over in the morning shall be burned up.

¹¹"This is how you are to eat it: with your loins girt, sandals on your feet and your staff in hand, you shall eat like those who are in flight. It is the Passover* of the LORD. ¹²For on this same night I will go through Egypt, striking down every first-born of the land, both man and beast, and executing judgment on all the gods of Egypt—I, the LORD! ¹³But the blood will mark the houses where you are. Seeing the blood, I will pass over you; thus, when I strike the land of Egypt, no destructive blow will come upon you.*k*

¹⁴"This day shall be a memorial feast for you, which all your generations shall celebrate with pilgrimage to the LORD, as a perpetual institution. ¹⁵For seven days you must eat unleavened bread. From the very first day you shall have your houses clear of all leaven. Whoever eats leavened bread from

---

12, 2: This month: Abib, the month of "ripe grain." Cf Ex 13, 4; 23, 15; 34, 18; Dt 16, 1. It occurred near the vernal equinox, March-April. Later it was known by the Babylonian name of Nisan. Cf Neh 2, 1; Est 3, 7.

12, 4: Share in the lamb: probably, in the expenses of its purchase. Some explain, "reckon for the lamb the number of persons required to eat it." Cf Ex 12, 10.

12, 11: Passover: in Hebrew, pesach, in Aramaic, pascha.

In the following verses the same root is used in the verb "to pass over." The word may be originally Egyptian, pesach, "the blow," i.e., the final plague which destroyed the Egyptian first-born.

f: 2f: Ex 3, 21f; 12, 35f. *g:* Ex 12, 12. *h:* 5f: Ex 12, 29f. *i:* Ex 12, 31ff. *j:* 2-20: Lv 23, 5-8; Nm 9, 2-5; 28, 16ff; Dt 16, 1-8. *k:* Heb 11, 28.

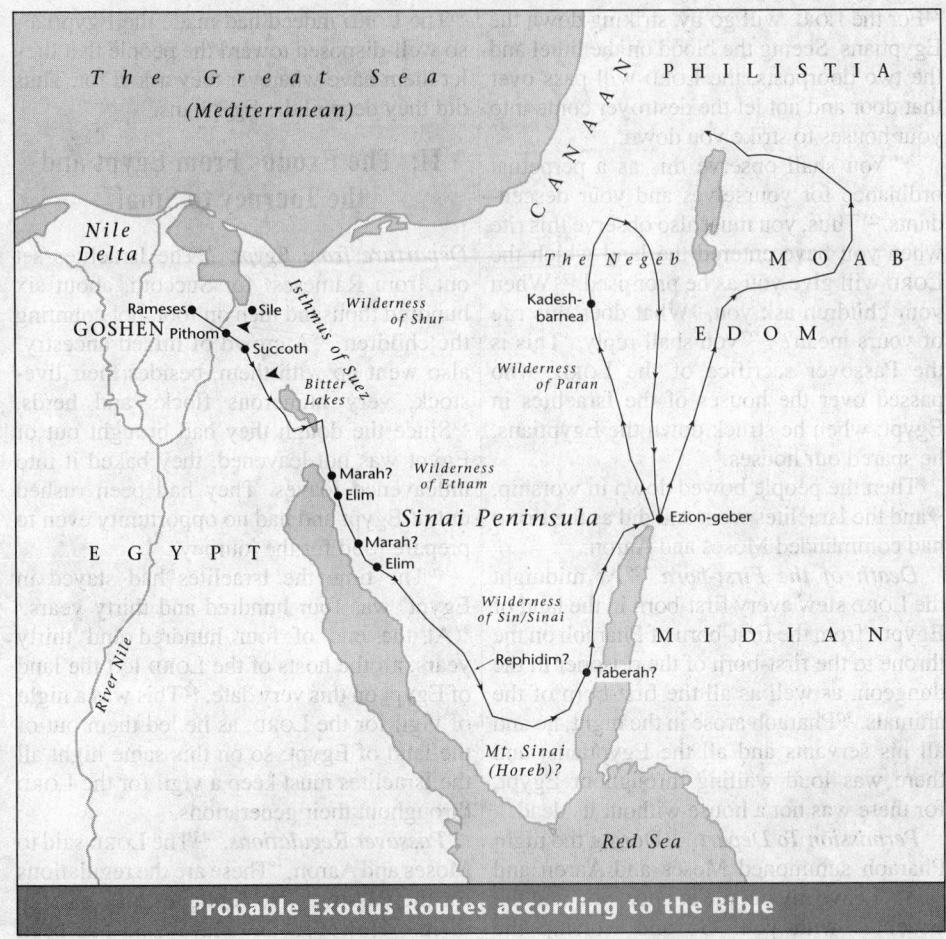

The Great Sea
(Mediterranean)

CANAAN   PHILISTIA

Nile
Delta

The Negeb   M O A B

Rameses   Sile   *Wilderness*   Kadesh-
GOSHEN Pithom   *of Shur*   barnea   E D O M

Succoth   *Wilderness*
of Paran

Bitter
Lakes

Marah?   *Wilderness*
Elim   *of Etham*

Sinai Peninsula   Ezion-geber

E G Y P T   Marah?
Elim

Wilderness   M I D I A N
of Sin/Sinai

Rephidim?   Taberah?

Mt. Sinai
(Horeb)?

Red Sea

Probable Exodus Routes according to the Bible

the first day to the seventh shall be cut off from Israel. [16]On the first day you shall hold a sacred assembly, and likewise on the seventh. On these days you shall not do any sort of work, except to prepare the food that everyone needs.

[17]"Keep, then, this custom of the unleavened bread.[l] Since it was on this very day that I brought your ranks out of the land of Egypt, you must celebrate this day throughout your generations as a perpetual institution. [18]From the evening of the fourteenth day of the first month until the evening of the twenty-first day of this month you shall eat unleavened bread.

[19]For seven days no leaven may be found in your houses. Anyone, be he a resident alien or a native, who eats leavened food shall be cut off from the community of Israel. [20]Nothing leavened may you eat; wherever you dwell you may eat only unleavened bread."

Promulgation of the Passover. [21]Moses called all the elders of Israel and said to them, "Go and procure lambs for your families, and slaughter them as Passover victims. [22]Then take a bunch of hyssop,[*] and dipping it in the blood that is in the basin, sprinkle the lintel and the two doorposts with this blood.[m] But none of you shall go outdoors until morning.

12, 22: Hyssop: a plant with many woody branchlets that make a convenient sprinkler.

l: Ex 13, 3.   *m:* 22f: Ex 12, 7. 13.

[23] For the LORD will go by, striking down the Egyptians. Seeing the blood on the lintel and the two doorposts, the LORD will pass over that door and not let the destroyer come into your houses to strike you down. [24] "You shall observe this as a perpetual ordinance for yourselves and your descendants. [25] Thus, you must also observe this rite when you have entered the land which the LORD will give you as he promised. [26] When your children ask you, 'What does this rite of yours mean?'[n] [27] you shall reply, 'This is the Passover sacrifice of the LORD, who passed over the houses of the Israelites in Egypt; when he struck down the Egyptians, he spared our houses.' "

Then the people bowed down in worship, [28] and the Israelites went and did as the LORD had commanded Moses and Aaron.

Death of the First-born. [29] At midnight the LORD slew every first-born in the land of Egypt,[o] from the first-born of Pharaoh on the throne to the first-born of the prisoner in the dungeon, as well as all the first-born of the animals. [30] Pharaoh arose in the night, he and all his servants and all the Egyptians; and there was loud wailing throughout Egypt, for there was not a house without its dead.

Permission To Depart. [31] During the night Pharaoh summoned Moses and Aaron and said, "Leave my people at once, you and the Israelites with you! Go and worship the LORD as you said. [32] Take your flocks, too, and your herds, as you demanded, and be-gone; and you will be doing me a favor."

[33] The Egyptians likewise urged the people on, to hasten their departure from the land; they thought that otherwise they would all die. [34] The people, therefore, took their dough before it was leavened, in their kneading bowls wrapped in their cloaks on their shoulders. [35] The Israelites did as Moses had commanded: they asked the Egyptians for articles of silver and gold and for clothing.[p]

[36] The LORD indeed had made the Egyptians so well-disposed toward the people that they let them have whatever they asked for. Thus did they despoil the Egyptians.

II: The Exodus From Egypt and the Journey to Sinai

Departure from Egypt. [37] The Israelites set out from Rameses[q] for Succoth, about six hundred thousand men on foot, not counting the children. [38] A crowd of mixed ancestry* also went up with them, besides their live-stock, very numerous flocks and herds. [39] Since the dough they had brought out of Egypt was not leavened, they baked it into unleavened loaves. They had been rushed out of Egypt and had no opportunity even to prepare food for the journey.

[40] The time the Israelites had stayed in Egypt* was four hundred and thirty years.[r] [41] At the end of four hundred and thirty years, all the hosts of the LORD left the land of Egypt on this very date. [42] This was a night of vigil for the LORD, as he led them out of the land of Egypt; so on this same night all the Israelites must keep a vigil for the LORD throughout their generations.

Passover Regulations. [43] The LORD said to Moses and Aaron, "These are the regulations for the Passover. No foreigner may partake of it. [44] However, any slave who has been bought for money may partake of it, pro-vided you have first circumcised him. [45] But no transient alien or hired servant may par-take of it. [46] It must be eaten in one and the same house; you may not take any of its flesh outside the house.[s] You shall not break any of its bones.* [47] The whole community of Israel must keep this feast. [48] If any aliens[t] living among you wish to celebrate the Passover of the LORD, all the males among them must first be circumcised, and then they may join in its observance just like the

---

12, 38: Mixed ancestry: half-Hebrew and half-Egyptian. Cf Nm 11, 4; Lv 24, 10f.

12, 40: In Egypt: according to some ancient sources, "in Canaan and Egypt," thus reckoning from the time of Abra-ham. Cf Gal 3, 17.

12, 46: You shall not break any of its bones: the application of these words to our Lord on the cross shows that the Paschal lamb was a prophetic type of Christ, immolated to free men from the bondage of sin. Cf also 1 Cor 5, 7; 1 Pt 1, 19.

n: 26f: Ex 13, 8. 14; Dt 6, 20f.   o: 29f: Ex 11, 4ff; Pss 78, 51; 105, 36; 136, 10; Wis 18, 10-16.   p: 35f: Ex 3, 21f; 11, 2f; Ps 105, 37f.   q: Nm 33, 3ff.   r: Gn 15, 13; Acts 7, 6; Gal 3, 17.   s: Nm 9, 12; Jn 19, 36.   t: 47f: Nm 9, 14.

natives. But no man who is uncircumcised may partake of it. [49]The law shall be the same for the resident alien as for the native."

[50]All the Israelites did just as the LORD had commanded Moses and Aaron. [51]On that same day the LORD brought the Israelites out of Egypt company by company.

CHAPTER 13

See RG 120–21

Consecration of First-born. [1]The LORD spoke to Moses and said, [2]"Consecrate to me every first-born that opens the womb among the Israelites,[u] both of man and beast, for it belongs to me."

[3]Moses said to the people, "Remember this day on which you came out of Egypt, that place of slavery.[v] It was with a strong hand that the LORD brought you away. Nothing made with leaven must be eaten. [4]This day of your departure is in the month of Abib. [5]Therefore, it is in this month that you must celebrate this rite, after the LORD, your God, has brought you into the land of the Canaanites, Hittites, Amorites, Hivites and Jebusites, which he swore to your fathers he would give you, a land flowing with milk and honey. [6]For seven days you shall eat unleavened bread, and the seventh day shall also be a festival to the LORD. [7]Only unleavened bread may be eaten during the seven days; no leaven and nothing leavened may be found in all your territory. [8]On this day you shall explain to your son, 'This is because of what the LORD did for me when I came out of Egypt.' [9]It shall be as a sign on your hand and as a reminder on your forehead;[w] thus the law of the LORD will ever be on your lips, because with a strong hand the LORD brought you out of Egypt. [10]Therefore, you shall keep this prescribed rite at its appointed time from year to year.

[11]"When the LORD, your God, has brought you into the land of the Canaanites, which he swore to you and your fathers he would give you, [12]you shall dedicate to the LORD every son that opens the womb;[x] and all the male firstlings of your animals shall belong to the LORD. [13]Every first-born of an ass you shall redeem with a sheep. If you do not redeem it, you shall break its neck. Every first-born son you must redeem. [14]If your son should ask you later on, 'What does this mean?' you shall tell him, 'With a strong hand the LORD brought us out of Egypt, that place of slavery. [15]When Pharaoh stubbornly refused to let us go, the LORD killed every first-born in the land of Egypt, every first-born of man and of beast. That is why I sacrifice to the LORD everything of the male sex that opens the womb, and why I redeem every first-born of my sons.' [16]Let this, then, be as a sign on your hand and as a pendant on your forehead: with a strong hand the LORD brought us out of Egypt."[y]

Toward the Red Sea. [17]Now, when Pharaoh let the people go, God did not lead them by way of the Philistines' land,[*] though this was the nearest; for he thought, should the people see that they would have to fight, they might change their minds and return to Egypt. [18]Instead, he rerouted them toward the Red Sea by way of the desert road. In battle array the Israelites marched out of Egypt. [19]Moses also took Joseph's bones[z] along, for Joseph had made the Israelites swear solemnly that, when God should come to them, they would carry his bones away with them.

[20]Setting out from Succoth, they camped at Etham[a] near the edge of the desert.

[21]The LORD preceded them, in the daytime by means of a column of cloud to show them the way, and at night by means of a column of fire[*] to give them light.[b] Thus they could travel both day and night. [22]Neither the column of cloud by day nor the column of fire by night ever left its place in front of the people.

13, 17: By way of the Philistines' land: the most direct route from Egypt to Palestine, along the shore of the Mediterranean.

13, 21: A column of cloud . . . a column of fire: probably one and the same preternatural phenomenon, a central nucleus of fire surrounded by smoke; only at night was its luminous nature visible. Cf Ex 40, 38.

---

u: Ex 13, 12-15. *v:* 3-10: Ex 12, 2-20. *w:* Ex 13, 16; Dt 6, 8; 11, 18. *x:* 12-15; Ex 13, 2; 22, 29f; 34, 19f: Nm 3, 12f; 8, 16; 18, 15; Dt 15, 19. *y:* Ex 13, 9. *z:* Gn 50, 25; Jos 24, 32. *a:* Nm 33, 6. *b:* 21f: Ex 40, 38; Nm 9, 15-22; Dt 1, 33; Neh 9, 19; Pss 78, 14; 105, 39; Wis 10, 17.

See RG
120–21

CHAPTER 14

[1] Then the LORD said to Moses, [2]*"Tell the Israelites to turn about and camp before Pi-hahiroth, between Migdol and the sea.[c] You shall camp in front of Baal-zephon, just opposite, by the sea. [3]Pharaoh will then say, 'The Israelites are wandering about aimlessly in the land. The desert has closed in on them.' [4]Thus will I make Pharaoh so obstinate that he will pursue them. Then I will receive glory through Pharaoh and all his army, and the Egyptians will know that I am the LORD."

This the Israelites did. [5]When it was reported to the king of Egypt that the people had fled, Pharaoh and his servants changed their minds about them. "What have we done!" they exclaimed. "Why, we have released Israel from our service!" [6]So Pharaoh made his chariots ready and mustered his soldiers— [7]six hundred first-class chariots and all the other chariots of Egypt, with warriors on them all. [8]So obstinate had the LORD made Pharaoh that he pursued[d] the Israelites even while they were marching away in triumph. [9]The Egyptians, then, pursued them; Pharaoh's whole army, his horses, chariots and charioteers, caught up with them as they lay encamped by the sea, at Pi-hahiroth, in front of Baal-zephon.

Crossing of the Red Sea. [10]Pharaoh was already near when the Israelites looked up and saw that the Egyptians were on the march in pursuit of them. In great fright they cried out to the LORD. [11]And they complained to Moses, "Were there no burial places in Egypt that you had to bring us out here to die in the desert? Why did you do this to us? Why did you bring us out of Egypt? [12]Did we not tell you this in Egypt, when we said, 'Leave us alone. Let us serve the Egyptians'? Far better for us to be the slaves of the Egyptians than to die in the desert." [13]But Moses answered the people, "Fear not! Stand your ground, and you will see the victory the LORD will win for you today. These Egyptians whom you see today you will never see again. [14]The LORD himself will fight for you; you have only to keep still."

[15]Then the LORD said to Moses, "Why are you crying out to me? Tell the Israelites to go forward. [16]And you, lift up your staff and, with hand outstretched over the sea, split the sea in two, that the Israelites may pass through it on dry land. [17]But I will make the Egyptians so obstinate that they will go in after them. Then I will receive glory through Pharaoh and all his army, his chariots and charioteers. [18]The Egyptians shall know that I am the LORD, when I receive glory through Pharaoh and his chariots and charioteers."

[19]The angel of God, who had been leading Israel's camp, now moved and went around behind them. The column of cloud also, leaving the front, took up its place behind them, [20]so that it came between the camp of the Egyptians and that of Israel. But the cloud now became dark,* and thus the night passed without the rival camps coming any closer together all night long. [21]Then Moses stretched out his hand over the sea, and the LORD swept the sea with a strong east wind throughout the night and so turned it into dry land.[e] When the water was thus divided, [22]the Israelites marched into the midst of the sea on dry land, with the water like a wall to their right and to their left.

Destruction of the Egyptians. [23]The Egyptians followed in pursuit; all Pharaoh's horses and chariots and charioteers went after them right into the midst of the sea. [24]In the night watch just before dawn the LORD cast through the column of the fiery cloud upon the Egyptian force a glance that threw it into a panic; [25]and he so clogged their chariot wheels that they could hardly drive. With that the Egyptians sounded the retreat

---

14, 2: These places have not been definitively identified. Even the relative position of Pi-hahiroth and Baal-zephon is not clear; perhaps the former was on the west shore of the sea, where the Israelites were, and the latter on the opposite shore.

14, 20: The cloud now became dark: the light which it ordinarily cast at night would now have been a help to the Egyptians; its present obscurity serves as a shield for the Israelites. However, the reading of the original text here is not quite certain.

---

c: Nm 33, 7f.   d: 5-8: Wis 19, 3; 1 Mc 4, 9.   e: 21f: Ex 15, 19; Pss 66, 6; 78, 13; 136, 13f; Wis 10, 18; 19, 7f; Is 63, 12f; Heb 11, 29.

before Israel, because the Lord was fighting for them against the Egyptians.

²⁶Then the Lord told Moses, "Stretch out your hand over the sea, that the water may flow back upon the Egyptians, upon their chariots and their charioteers." ²⁷So Moses stretched out his hand over the sea, and at dawn the sea flowed back to its normal depth. The Egyptians were fleeing head on toward the sea, when the Lord hurled them into its midst. ²⁸As the water flowed back, it covered the chariots and the charioteers of Pharaoh's whole army*f* which had followed the Israelites into the sea. Not a single one of them escaped. ²⁹But the Israelites had marched on dry land through the midst of the sea, with the water like a wall to their right and to their left. ³⁰Thus the Lord saved Israel on that day from the power of the Egyptians. When Israel saw the Egyptians lying dead on the seashore ³¹and beheld the great power that the Lord had shown against the Egyptians, they feared the Lord and believed in him*g* and in his servant Moses.

CHAPTER 15

See RG
120–21

¹Then Moses and the Israelites sang*h* this song to the Lord:*

I will sing to the Lord, for he is
    gloriously triumphant;
    horse and chariot he has cast into the sea.
² My strength and my courage is the Lord,
    and he has been my savior.
He is my God, I praise him;
    the God of my father, I extol him.*i*
³ The Lord is a warrior,
    Lord is his name!
⁴ Pharaoh's chariots and army he hurled
    into the sea;
    the elite of his officers were
      submerged in the Red Sea.

⁵ The flood waters covered them,
    they sank into the depths like a stone.*j*
⁶ Your right hand, O Lord, magnificent in
    power,

your right hand, O Lord, has shattered
    the enemy.
⁷ In your great majesty you overthrew your
    adversaries;
you loosed your wrath to consume
    them like stubble.
⁸ At a breath of your anger the waters piled
    up,
the flowing waters stood like a mound,
the flood waters congealed in the
    midst of the sea.
⁹ The enemy boasted, "I will pursue and
    overtake them;
I will divide the spoils and have my
    fill of them;
I will draw my sword; my hand shall
    despoil them!"
¹⁰ When your wind blew, the sea covered
    them;
like lead they sank in the mighty
    waters.
¹¹ Who is like to you among the gods,
    O Lord?
Who is like to you, magnificent in
    holiness?
O terrible in renown, worker of wonders,
¹²   when you stretched out your right
    hand, the earth swallowed them!
¹³ In your mercy you led the people you
    redeemed;
in your strength you guided them to
    your holy dwelling.
¹⁴ The nations heard and quaked:
    anguish gripped the dwellers in
    Philistia.
¹⁵ Then were the princes of Edom
    dismayed;
    trembling seized the chieftains of Moab;
All the dwellers in Canaan melted away;
¹⁶   terror and dread fell upon them.*k*
By the might of your arm they were
    frozen like stone,
while your people, O Lord, passed
    over,
while the people you had made your
    own passed over.

15, 1-21: This canticle (used in Christian liturgy) celebrates God's saving power, miraculously delivering his people from their enemies, and leading them to the victorious conquest of the Promised Land.

f: 28f: Dt 11, 4; Ps 106, 11.   *g:* 31f: Ps 106, 12; Wis 10, 20.   *h:* Ex 15, 21.   *i:* Ps 118, 14; Is 12, 2.   *j:* Neh 9, 11.   *k:* 16f: Ps 78, 53ff.

17 And you brought them in and planted
them on the mountain of your
inheritance—
the place where you made your seat,
O LORD,
the sanctuary, O LORD, which your
hands established.

*18*The LORD shall reign forever and ever.

*19*They sang thus because Pharaoh's
horses and chariots and charioteers had gone
into the sea, and the LORD made the waters
of the sea flow back upon them, though the
Israelites had marched on dry land through
the midst of the sea.*l* *20*The prophetess Miriam, Aaron's sister, took a tambourine in her
hand, while all the women went out after her
with tambourines, dancing; *21*and she led
them* in the refrain:

Sing to the LORD, for he is gloriously
triumphant;
horse and chariot he has cast into the
sea.*m*

At Marah and Elim. *22nThen Moses led
Israel forward from the Red Sea, and they
marched out to the desert of Shur. After traveling for three days through the desert without finding water, *23*they arrived at Marah,
where they could not drink the water, because it was too bitter. Hence this place was
called Marah. *24*As the people grumbled
against Moses, saying, "What are we to
drink?" *25*he appealed to the LORD, who
pointed out to him a certain piece of wood.
When he threw this into the water, the water
became fresh.*o*

It was here that the LORD, in making rules
and regulations for them, put them to the
test. *26*"If you really listen to the voice of the
LORD, your God," he told them, "and do

what is right in his eyes: if you heed his
commandments and keep all his precepts, I
will not afflict you with any of the diseases
with which I afflicted the Egyptians;*p* for I,
the LORD, am your healer."

*27*Then they came to Elim, where there
were twelve springs of water and seventy
palm trees, and they camped there near the
water.*q*

CHAPTER 16

See RG 121-22

The Desert of Sin. *1*Having set out
from Elim, the whole Israelite community
came into the desert of Sin, which is between Elim and Sinai, on the fifteenth day of
the second month* after their departure from
the land of Egypt. *2*Here in the desert the
whole Israelite community grumbled
against Moses and Aaron. *3*The Israelites
said to them, "Would that we had died at the
LORD's hand in the land of Egypt, as we sat
by our fleshpots and ate our fill of bread! But
you had to lead us into this desert to make
the whole community die of famine!"

The Quail and Manna. *4*Then the LORD
said to Moses,*r* "I will now rain down bread
from heaven* for you. Each day the people
are to go out and gather their daily portion;
thus will I test them, to see whether they follow my instructions or not. *5*On the sixth
day, however, when they prepare what they
bring in, let it be twice as much as they
gather on the other days." *6*So Moses and
Aaron told all the Israelites, "At evening you
will know that it was the LORD who brought
you out of the land of Egypt; *7*and in the
morning you will see the glory of the LORD,
as he heeds your grumbling against him.*s*
But what are we that you should grumble
against us? *8*When the LORD gives you flesh
to eat in the evening," continued Moses,
"and in the morning your fill of bread, as he

15, 21: She led them: Miriam's refrain re-echoes the
first verse of this song and was probably sung as an
antiphon after each verse.

16, 1: On the fifteenth day of the second month: just one
full month after their departure from Egypt. Cf Ex 12, 2. 51;
Nm 33, 3f. They encamped in the desert of Sin on a Friday;
the murmuring (vv 2f) occurred on the sabbath, the arrival of
the quail (v 13) the evening before Sunday, followed by six
mornings (vv 14-27) of collecting manna before the next
sabbath.

16, 4: Bread from heaven: as a gift from God, the manna
is said to come down from the sky. Cf Ps 78, 25; Wis 16, 20.
Perhaps it was similar to a natural substance that is still found
in small quantities on the Sinai peninsula, but here it is, at
least in part, clearly miraculous. Our Lord referred to the
manna as a type of the Blessed Eucharist. Cf Jn 6, 32. 49-52.

l: Ex 14, 21-29.   *m:* Ex 15, 1.   *n:* 22f: Nm 33, 8.   *o:* Sir 38, 5.
p: Dt 7, 15.   *q:* Nm 33, 9.   *r:* Pss 78, 24f; 105, 40; Jn 6, 31f;
1 Cor 10, 3.   *s:* 6f: Ex 16, 12.

heeds the grumbling you utter against him, what then are we? Your grumbling is not against us, but against the LORD."

⁹Then Moses said to Aaron, "Tell the whole Israelite community: Present yourselves before the LORD, for he has heard your grumbling." ¹⁰When Aaron announced this to the whole Israelite community, they turned toward the desert, and lo, the glory of the LORD appeared in the cloud! ¹¹The LORD spoke to Moses and said, ¹²"I have heard the grumbling of the Israelites. Tell them: In the evening twilight you shall eat flesh, and in the morning you shall have your fill of bread, so that you may know that I, the LORD, am your God."

¹³In the evening quail*ᵗ* came up and covered the camp. In the morning a dew lay all about the camp, ¹⁴and when the dew evaporated, there on the surface of the desert were fine flakes like hoarfrost on the ground. ¹⁵On seeing it, the Israelites asked one another, "What is this?"* for they did not know what it was. But Moses told them, "This is the bread which the LORD has given you to eat.*ᵘ*

Regulations Regarding the Manna. ¹⁶"Now, this is what the LORD has commanded. So gather it that everyone has enough to eat, an omer for each person, as many of you as there are, each man providing for those of his own tent." ¹⁷The Israelites did so. Some gathered a large and some a small amount. ¹⁸*But when they measured it out by the omer, he who had gathered a large amount did not have too much, and he who had gathered a small amount did not have too little.*ᵛ* They so gathered that everyone had enough to eat. ¹⁹Moses also told them, "Let no one keep any of it over until tomorrow morning." ²⁰But they would not listen to him. When some kept a part of it over until the following morning, it became wormy and rotten. Therefore Moses was displeased with them.

²¹Morning after morning they gathered it, till each had enough to eat; but when the sun grew hot, the manna melted away. ²²On the sixth day they gathered twice as much food, two omers for each person. When all the leaders of the community came and reported this to Moses, ²³he told them, "That is what the LORD prescribed. Tomorrow is a day of complete rest, the sabbath, sacred to the LORD. You may either bake or boil the manna, as you please; but whatever is left put away and keep for the morrow." ²⁴When they put it away for the morrow, as Moses commanded, it did not become rotten or wormy. ²⁵Moses then said, "Eat it today, for today is the sabbath of the LORD. On this day you will not find any of it on the ground. ²⁶On the other six days you can gather it, but on the seventh day, the sabbath, none of it will be there." ²⁷Still, on the seventh day some of the people went out to gather it, although they did not find any. ²⁸Then the LORD said to Moses, "How long will you refuse to keep my commandments and laws? ²⁹Take note! The LORD has given you the sabbath. That is why on the sixth day he gives you food for two days. On the seventh day everyone is to stay home and no one is to go out." ³⁰After that the people rested on the seventh day.

³¹The Israelites called this food manna.*ʷ* It was like coriander seed,* but white, and it tasted like wafers made with honey.

³²Moses said, "This is what the LORD has commanded. Keep an omerful of manna for your descendants, that they may see what food I gave you to eat in the desert when I brought you out of the land of Egypt." ³³Moses then told Aaron, "Take an urn* and put an omer of manna in it. Then place it before the LORD in safekeeping for your descendants."*ˣ* ³⁴So Aaron placed it in front of the commandments* for safekeeping, as the LORD had commanded Moses.

16, 15: What is this: the original man hu is thus rendered by the ancient versions, which understood the phrase as a popular etymology of the Hebrew word man, "manna"; some render, "This is manna."

16, 18: St. Paul cites this passage as an example of equitable sharing. Cf 2 Cor 8, 15.

16, 31: Coriander seed: small, round, aromatic seeds of bright brown color; the comparison, therefore, refers merely

to the size and shape, not to the taste or color of the manna.

16, 33: Urn: according to the Greek translation, which is followed in Heb 9, 4, this was a golden vessel.

16, 34: The commandments: the two tablets of the ten commandments, which were kept in the ark. Cf Ex 25, 16. 21f.

t: Nm 11, 31; Ps 78, 27f.   *u:* Dt 8, 3.   *v:* 2 Cor 8, 15.   *w:* Nm 11, 7.   *x:* Heb 9, 4.

35The Israelites ate this manna for forty years, until they came to settled land;*y* they ate manna until they reached the borders of Canaan. 36[An omer is one tenth of an ephah.]

See RG
121–22

CHAPTER 17

Water from the Rock. 1From the desert of Sin the whole Israelite community journeyed by stages, as the LORD directed, and encamped at Rephidim.*z*

Here there was no water for the people to drink. 2They quarreled, therefore, with Moses and said, "Give us water to drink."*a* Moses replied, "Why do you quarrel with me? Why do you put the LORD to a test?" 3Here, then, in their thirst for water, the people grumbled against Moses, saying, "Why did you ever make us leave Egypt? Was it just to have us die here of thirst with our children and our livestock?" 4So Moses cried out to the LORD, "What shall I do with this people? A little more and they will stone me!" 5The LORD answered Moses, "Go over there in front of the people, along with some of the elders of Israel, holding in your hand, as you go, the staff with which you struck the river. 6I will be standing there in front of you on the rock in Horeb. Strike the rock, and the water will flow from it for the people to drink."*b* This Moses did, in the presence of the elders of Israel. 7The place was called Massah and Meribah,* because the Israelites quarreled there and tested the LORD, saying, "Is the LORD in our midst or not?"*c*

Battle with Amalek. 8At Rephidim, Amalek* came and waged war against Israel.*d* 9Moses, therefore, said to Joshua, "Pick out certain men, and tomorrow go out and engage Amalek in battle. I will be standing on top of the hill with the staff of God in my hand." 10So Joshua did as Moses told him: he engaged Amalek in battle after Moses had climbed to the top of the hill with Aaron and Hur. 11As long as Moses kept his hands raised up, Israel had the better of the fight, but when he let his hands rest, Amalek had the better of the fight. 12Moses' hands, however, grew tired; so they put a rock in place for him to sit on. Meanwhile Aaron and Hur supported his hands, one on one side and one on the other, so that his hands remained steady till sunset. 13And Joshua mowed down Amalek and his people with the edge of the sword.

14Then the LORD said to Moses, "Write this down in a document as something to be remembered, and recite it in the ears of Joshua.*e* I will completely blot out the memory of Amalek from under the heavens." 15Moses also built an altar there, which he called Yahweh-nissi;* 16for he said, "The LORD takes in hand his banner; the LORD will war against Amalek through the centuries."

CHAPTER 18

See RG
121–22

Meeting with Jethro. 1Now Moses' father-in-law Jethro, the priest of Midian, heard of all that God had done for Moses and for his people Israel: how the LORD had brought Israel out of Egypt. 2So his father-in-law Jethro took along Zipporah, Moses' wife, whom Moses had sent back to him, 3and her two sons. One of these was called Gershom;*f* for he said, "I am a stranger in a foreign land." 4The other was called Eliezer; for he said, "My father's God is my helper; he has rescued me from Pharaoh's sword." 5Together with Moses' wife and sons, then, his father-in-law Jethro came to him in the desert where he was encamped near the mountain of God, 6and he sent word to Moses, "I, Jethro, your father-in-law, am coming to you, along with your wife and her two sons."

7Moses went out to meet his father-in-law, bowed down before him, and kissed him. Having greeted each other, they went into the tent. 8Moses then told his father-in-law of all that the LORD had done to Pharaoh and the Egyptians for the sake of Israel, and of all the hardships they had had to endure

17, 7: Massah . . . Meribah: Hebrew words meaning respectively, "the (place of the) test," and "the (place of the) quarreling."
17, 8: Amalek: the Amalekites were an aboriginal people of southern Palestine and the Sinai peninsula. Cf Nm 24, 20.
17, 15: Yahweh-nissi: meaning, "the LORD is my banner."

y: Jos 5, 12.   *z*: Nm 33, 12ff.   *a*: 2-7: Nm 20, 2-13.   *b*: 5f: Dt 8, 15; Pss 78, 15f; 105, 41; Wis 11, 4; Is 43, 20; 48, 21.   *c*: Ps 95, 8f.
d: Dt 25, 17; 1 Sm 15, 2.   *e*: Nm 24, 20; 1 Sm 15, 3. 20.   *f*: Ex 2, 22.

on their journey, and how the LORD had come to their rescue. [9]Jethro rejoiced over all the goodness that the LORD had shown Israel in rescuing them from the hands of the Egyptians. [10]"Blessed be the LORD," he said, "who has rescued his people from the hands of Pharaoh and the Egyptians. [11]Now I know that the LORD is a deity great beyond any other; for he took occasion of their being dealt with insolently to deliver the people from the power of the Egyptians." [12]Then Jethro, the father-in-law of Moses, brought a holocaust and other sacrifices to God, and Aaron came with all the elders of Israel to participate with Moses' father-in-law in the meal before God.

Appointment of Minor Judges. [13]The next day Moses sat in judgment for the people, who waited about him from morning until evening. [14]When his father-in-law saw all that he was doing for the people, he inquired, "What sort of thing is this that you are doing for the people? Why do you sit alone while all the people have to stand about you from morning till evening?" [15]Moses answered his father-in-law, "The people come to me to consult God. [16]Whenever they have a disagreement, they come to me to have me settle the matter between them and make known to them God's decisions and regulations."

[17]"You are not acting wisely," his father-in-law replied. [18]"You will surely wear yourself out, and not only yourself but also these people with you. The task is too heavy for you;[g] you cannot do it alone. [19]Now, listen to me, and I will give you some advice, that God may be with you. Act as the people's representative before God, bringing to him whatever they have to say. [20]Enlighten them in regard to the decisions and regulations, showing them how they are to live and what they are to do. [21]But you should also look among all the people for able and God-fearing men, trustworthy men who hate dishonest gain, and set them as officers over groups of thousands, of hundreds, of fifties, and of tens.[h] [22]Let these men render decisions for the people in all ordinary cases. More important cases they should refer to you, but all the lesser cases they can settle themselves. Thus, your burden will be lightened, since they will bear it with you. [23]If you do this, when God gives you orders you will be able to stand the strain, and all these people will go home satisfied."

[24]Moses followed the advice of his father-in-law and did all that he had suggested. [25]He picked out able men from all Israel and put them in charge of the people as officers over groups of thousands, of hundreds, of fifties, and of tens. [26]They rendered decisions for the people in all ordinary cases. The more difficult cases they referred to Moses, but all the lesser cases they settled themselves. [27]Then Moses bade farewell to his father-in-law, who went off to his own country.

III: The Covenant at Mount Sinai

CHAPTER 19

See RG 122

Arrival at Sinai. [1i]In the third month after their departure from the land of Egypt, on its first day, the Israelites came to the desert of Sinai. [2]After the journey from Rephidim to the desert of Sinai, they pitched camp.

While Israel was encamped here in front of the mountain, [3]Moses went up the mountain to God. Then the LORD called to him and said, "Thus shall you say to the house of Jacob; [4]tell the Israelites: You have seen for yourselves how I treated the Egyptians and how I bore you up on eagle wings and brought you here to myself.[j] [5]Therefore, if you hearken to my voice and keep my covenant, you shall be my special possession, dearer to me than all other people,[k] though all the earth is mine. [6]You shall be to me a kingdom of priests,* a holy nation.[l] That is

---

19, 6: Kingdom of priests: inasmuch as the whole Israelite nation was consecrated to God in a special way, it formed a race of royal priests who participated in the liturgical sacrifices, even though the actual offering of the sacrifices was the exclusive prerogative of the Aaronic priesthood. The same condition exists in the New Dispensation as regards the whole Christian people and the Christian priesthood in the strict sense. Cf Is 61, 6; 1 Pt 2, 5. 9.

g: Nm 11, 14. h: 21. 25: Dt 1, 15; 16, 18. i: 1f: Nm 33, 15. j: Dt 32, 11. k: Dt 7, 6; 14, 2; 26, 18f; 32, 8f. l: 1 Pt 2, 9.

what you must tell the Israelites." [7]So Moses went and summoned the elders of the people. When he set before them all that the LORD had ordered him to tell them, [8]the people all answered together, "Everything the LORD has said, we will do." Then Moses brought back to the LORD the response of the people.

[9]The LORD also told him, "I am coming to you in a dense cloud,[m] so that when the people hear me speaking with you, they may always have faith in you also." When Moses, then, had reported to the LORD the response of the people, [10]the LORD added, "Go to the people and have them sanctify themselves today and tomorrow. Make them wash their garments [11]and be ready for the third day; for on the third day the LORD will come down on Mount Sinai before the eyes of all the people. [12]Set limits for the people all around the mountain,[n] and tell them: Take care not to go up the mountain, or even to touch its base. If anyone touches the mountain he must be put to death. [13]No hand shall touch him; he must be stoned to death or killed with arrows. Such a one, man or beast, must not be allowed to live. Only when the ram's horn resounds may they go up to the mountain." [14]Then Moses came down from the mountain to the people and had them sanctify themselves and wash their garments. [15]He warned them, "Be ready for the third day. Have no intercourse with any woman."

The Great Theophany. [16]On the morning of the third day there were peals of thunder and lightning, and a heavy cloud over the mountain, and a very loud trumpet blast, so that all the people in the camp trembled. [17]But Moses led the people out of the camp to meet God, and they stationed themselves at the foot of the mountain.[o] [18]Mount Sinai was all wrapped in smoke, for the LORD came down upon it in fire. The smoke rose from it as though from a furnace, and the whole mountain trembled violently. [19]The trumpet blast grew louder and louder, while Moses was speaking and God answering him with thunder.

[20]When the LORD came down to the top of Mount Sinai, he summoned Moses to the top of the mountain, and Moses went up to him. [21]Then the LORD told Moses, "Go down and warn the people not to break through toward the LORD in order to see him; otherwise many of them will be struck down. [22]The priests, too, who approach the LORD must sanctify themselves; else he will vent his anger upon them." [23]Moses said to the LORD, "The people cannot go up to Mount Sinai, for you yourself warned us to set limits around the mountain to make it sacred." [24]The LORD repeated, "Go down now! Then come up again along with Aaron. But the priests and the people must not break through to come up to the LORD; else he will vent his anger upon them." [25]So Moses went down to the people and told them this.

CHAPTER 20

See RG 122

The Ten Commandments. [1]Then God delivered all these commandments:*

[2p]"I, the LORD, am your God, who brought you out of the land of Egypt,[q] that place of slavery. [3]You shall not have other gods besides me. [4]You shall not carve idols[r] for yourselves in the shape of anything in the sky above or on the earth below or in the waters beneath the earth; [5]you shall not bow down before them or worship them.[s] For I, the LORD, your God, am a jealous* God, inflicting punishment for their fathers' wickedness on the children of those who hate me, down to the third and fourth generation; [6]but bestowing mercy down to the thousandth generation, on the children of those who love me and keep my commandments.

[7]"You shall not take the name of the LORD, your God, in vain.[t] For the LORD will not leave unpunished him who takes his name in vain.

20, 1-17: The precise division of these precepts into "ten commandments" is somewhat uncertain. Traditionally among Catholics vv 1-6 are considered as only one commandment, and v 17 as two. Cf Dt 5, 6-21.

20, 5: Jealous: demanding exclusive allegiance, such as a wife must have for her husband.

m: Ex 20, 21; 24, 15-18.   *n:* 12f: Ex 34, 3; Heb 12, 18f.   *o:* 16ff: Dt 4, 10ff.   *p:* 2-17; Dt 5, 6-21.   *q:* Lv 26, 13; Ps 81, 10; Hos 13, 4.   *r:* Ex 34, 17; Lv 26, 1; Dt 4, 15-19; 27, 15.   *s:* Ex 34, 7. 14; Nm 14, 18; Dt 4, 24; 6, 15.   *t:* Lv 19, 12; 24, 16.

8"Remember to keep holy the sabbath day. *9*Six days you may labor and do all your work, *10*but the seventh day is the sabbath of the LORD, your God.*u* No work may be done then either by you, or your son or daughter, or your male or female slave, or your beast, or by the alien who lives with you. *11*In six days the LORD made the heavens and the earth, the sea and all that is in them; but on the seventh day he rested.*v* That is why the LORD has blessed the sabbath day and made it holy.

12w"Honor your father and your mother, that you may have a long life in the land which the Lord, your God, is giving you.*x*

13"You shall not kill.*y*

14"You shall not commit adultery.*z*

15"You shall not steal.*a*

16"You shall not bear false witness against your neighbor.*b*

17"You shall not covet your neighbor's house. You shall not covet your neighbor's wife, nor his male or female slave, nor his ox or ass, nor anything else that belongs to him."*c*

The Fear of God. *18*When the people witnessed the thunder and lightning, the trumpet blast and the mountain smoking, they all feared and trembled.*d* So they took up a position much farther away *19*and said to Moses, "You speak to us, and we will listen; but let not God speak to us, or we shall die." *20*Moses answered the people, "Do not be afraid, for God has come to you only to test you and put his fear upon you, lest you should sin." *21*Still the people remained at a distance, while Moses approached the cloud where God was.

*22*The LORD told Moses, "Thus shall you speak to the Israelites: You have seen for yourselves that I have spoken to you from heaven. *23*Do not make anything to rank with me; neither gods of silver nor gods of gold shall you make for yourselves.*e*

24"An altar of earth you shall make for me, and upon it you shall sacrifice your holocausts and peace offerings, your sheep and your oxen.*f* In whatever place I choose for the remembrance of my name* I will come to you and bless you. *25*If you make an altar of stone for me,*g* do not build it of cut stone, for by putting a tool to it you desecrate it. *26*You shall not go up by steps to my altar, on which you must not be indecently uncovered.

CHAPTER 21

See RG 122

Laws Regarding Slaves. *1*"These are the rules* you shall lay before them. *2h*When you purchase a Hebrew slave, he is to serve you for six years, but in the seventh year he shall be given his freedom without cost. *3*If he comes into service alone, he shall leave alone; if he comes with a wife, his wife shall leave with him. *4*But if his master gives him a wife and she bears him sons or daughters, the woman and her children shall remain the master's property and the man shall leave alone. *5*If, however, the slave declares, 'I am devoted to my master and my wife and children; I will not go free,' *6*his master shall bring him to God* and there, at the door or doorpost, he shall pierce his ear with an awl, thus keeping him as his slave forever.

7"When a man sells his daughter as a slave, she shall not go free as male slaves do. *8*But if her master, who had destined her* for himself, dislikes her, he shall let her be redeemed. He has no right to sell her to a foreigner, since he has broken faith with her. *9*If he destines her for his son, he shall treat her like a daughter. *10*If he takes another wife, he

---

20, 24: I choose for the remembrance of my name: literally, "where I make my name to be remembered": at the sacred site where God wishes to be worshiped and his name revered.

21, 1: Rules: judicial precedents to be used in settling questions of law and custom. This introductory phrase serves as the title of the following collection of civil and religious laws (chapters 21–23) which is called in Ex 24, 7, the book of the covenant.

21, 6: To God: to the sanctuary; or perhaps the phrase is to be rendered, "to the gods," in the sense of "to the judges." Cf Ps 82, 1. Since the expression "to have an open ear" meant to

"obey," a pierced ear lobe was an ancient symbol of obedience. Cf Ps 40, 7.

21, 8: Destined her: intended her as a wife of second rank.

u: 8ff; Ex 23, 12; 31, 13-16; 34, 21; 35, 2; Lv 23, 3. *v*: Ex 31, 17; Gn 2, 2f. *w*: 12-16: Mt 19, 18f; Mk 10, 19; Lk 18, 20; Rom 13, 9. *x*: Mt 15, 4; Mk 7, 10; Eph 6, 2f. *y*: Mt 5, 21. *z*: Lv 18, 20; 20, 10; Dt 22, 22; Mt 5, 27. *a*: Lv 19, 11. *b*: Ex 23, 1; Dt 19, 16ff; Prv 19, 5. 9; 24, 28. *c*: Rom 7, 7. *d*: 18-21: Dt 4, 11; 5, 22-27; 18, 16; Heb 12, 18f. *e*: Ex 20, 3f. *f*: Dt 12, 5. 11; 14, 23; 16, 6. *g*: Dt 27, 5; Jos 8, 31. *h*: 2-6: Lv 25, 39ff; Dt 15, 12-18; Jer 34, 14.

shall not withhold her food, her clothing, or her conjugal rights. [11]If he does not grant her these three things, she shall be given her freedom absolutely, without cost to her.

Personal Injury. [12]"Whoever strikes a man a mortal blow must be put to death.[i] [13]He, however, who did not hunt a man down, but caused his death by an act of God, may flee to a place which I will set apart for this purpose. [14]But when a man kills another after maliciously scheming to do so, you must take him even from my altar and put him to death. [15]Whoever strikes his father or mother shall be put to death.

[16]"A kidnaper, whether he sells his victim or still has him when caught, shall be put to death.[j]

[17]"Whoever curses his father or mother shall be put to death.[k]

[18]"When men quarrel and one strikes the other with a stone or with his fist, not mortally, but enough to put him in bed, [19]the one who struck the blow shall be acquitted, provided the other can get up and walk around with the help of his staff. Still, he must compensate him for his enforced idleness and provide for his complete cure.

[20]"When a man strikes his male or female slave with a rod so hard that the slave dies under his hand, he shall be punished. [21]If, however, the slave survives for a day or two, he is not to be punished, since the slave is his own property.

[22]"When men have a fight and hurt a pregnant woman, so that she suffers a miscarriage, but no further injury, the guilty one shall be fined as much as the woman's husband demands of him, and he shall pay in the presence of the judges.[l] [23]*But if injury ensues, you shall give life for life, [24]eye for eye, tooth for tooth, hand for hand, foot for foot, [25]burn for burn, wound for wound, stripe for stripe.

[26]"When a man strikes his male or female slave in the eye and destroys the use of the eye, he shall let the slave go free in compensation for the eye. [27]If he knocks out a tooth of his male or female slave, he shall let the slave go free in compensation for the tooth.

[28]"When an ox gores a man or a woman to death, the ox must be stoned; its flesh may not be eaten. The owner of the ox, however, shall go unpunished. [29]But if an ox was previously in the habit of goring people and its owner, though warned, would not keep it in; should it then kill a man or a woman, not only must the ox be stoned, but its owner also must be put to death. [30]If, however, a fine is imposed on him, he must pay in ransom for his life whatever amount is imposed on him. [31]This law applies if it is a boy or a girl that the ox gores. [32]But if it is a male or a female slave that it gores, he must pay the owner of the slave thirty shekels of silver, and the ox must be stoned.

Property Damage. [33]"When a man uncovers or digs a cistern and does not cover it over again, should an ox or an ass fall into it, [34]the owner of the cistern must make good by restoring the value of the animal to its owner; the dead animal, however, he may keep.

[35]"When one man's ox hurts another's ox so badly that it dies, they shall sell the live ox and divide this money as well as the dead animal equally between them. [36]But if it was known that the ox was previously in the habit of goring and its owner would not keep it in, he must make full restitution, an ox for an ox; but the dead animal he may keep.

[37]*"When a man steals an ox or a sheep and slaughters or sells it, he shall restore five oxen for the one ox, and four sheep for the one sheep.[m]

CHAPTER 22

See RG 122

[1]"[If a thief is caught* in the act of housebreaking and beaten to death, there is

---

21, 23ff: This section is known as the lex talionis, the law of tit for tat. The purpose of this law was not merely the enforcement of rigorous justice, but also the prevention of greater penalties than would be just. Christ refers to this passage when he exhorts Christians to cede their lawful rights for the sake of charity. Cf Mt 5, 38ff.

21, 37—22, 30: In the Vulgate, 22, 1-31.

22, 1f: If a thief is caught: this seems to be a fragment of what was once a longer law on housebreaking, which has

been inserted here into the middle of a law on stealing animals. At night the householder would be justified in killing a burglar outright, but not so in the daytime, when the burglar could more easily be caught alive. He must make full restitution: this stood originally immediately after 21, 37.

---

i: 12ff: Lv 24, 17; Nm 35, 15-29; Dt 4, 41f; 19, 2-5.   *j:* Dt 24, 7.
k: Lv 20, 9; Prv 20, 20; Mt 15, 4; Mk 7, 10.   *l:* 22-25: Lv 24, 18-21; Dt 19, 21; Mt 5, 38.   *m:* 2 Sm 12, 6.

no bloodguilt involved. ²But if after sunrise he is thus beaten, there is bloodguilt.] He must make full restitution. If he has nothing, he shall be sold to pay for his theft. ³If what he stole is found alive in his possession, be it an ox, an ass or a sheep, he shall restore two animals for each one stolen.

⁴*"When a man is burning over a field or a vineyard, if he lets the fires spread so that it burns in another's field, he must make restitution with the best produce of his own field or vineyard. ⁵If the fire spreads further, and catches on to thorn bushes, so that shocked grain or standing grain or the field itself is burned up, the one who started the fire must make full restitution.

Trusts and Loans. ⁶"When a man gives money or any article to another for safekeeping and it is stolen from the latter's house, the thief, if caught, must make twofold restitution. ⁷If the thief is not caught, the owner of the house shall be brought to God,* to swear that he himself did not lay hands on his neighbor's property. ⁸In every question of dishonest appropriation, whether it be about an ox, or an ass, or a sheep, or a garment, or anything else that has disappeared, where another claims that the thing is his, both parties shall present their case before God; the one whom God convicts must make two-fold restitution to the other.

⁹"When a man gives an ass, or an ox, or a sheep, or any other animal to another for safekeeping, if it dies, or is maimed or snatched away, without anyone witnessing the fact, ¹⁰the custodian shall swear by the LORD that he did not lay hands on his neighbor's property; the owner must accept the oath, and no restitution is to be made. ¹¹But if the custodian is really guilty of theft, he must make restitution to the owner. ¹²If it has been killed by a wild beast, let him bring it as evidence, and he need not make restitution for the mangled animal.ⁿ

¹³"When a man borrows an animal from his neighbor, if it is maimed or dies while the owner is not present, the man must make restitution. ¹⁴But if the owner is present, he need not make restitution. If it was hired, this was covered by the price of its hire.

Social Laws. ¹⁵"When a man seduces a virgin who is not betrothed, and lies with her, he shall pay her marriage price and marry her.º ¹⁶If her father refuses to give her to him, he must still pay him the customary marriage price for virgins.*

¹⁷"You shall not let a sorceress live.ᵖ

¹⁸"Anyone who lies with an animal shall be put to death.�q

¹⁹"Whoever sacrifices to any god, except to the LORD alone, shall be doomed.ʳ

²⁰"You shall not molest or oppress an alien, for you were once aliens yourselves in the land of Egypt.ˢ ²¹You shall not wrong any widow or orphan. ²²If ever you wrong them and they cry out to me, I will surely hear their cry. ²³My wrath will flare up, and I will kill you with the sword; then your own wives will be widows, and your children orphans.

²⁴"If you lend money to one of your poor neighbors among my people, you shall not act like an extortioner toward him by demanding interest from him. ²⁵If you take your neighbor's cloak as a pledge, you shall return it to him before sunset; ²⁶for this cloak of his is the only covering he has for his body. What else has he to sleep in? If he cries out to me, I will hear him; for I am compassionate.

²⁷"You shall not revile God,* nor curse a prince of your people.ᵘ

²⁸"You shall not delay the offering of your harvest and your press. You shall give me the first-born of your sons. ²⁹You must do the same with your oxen and your sheep; for seven days the firstling may stay with its

22, 4: The Greek and Latin versions understood this verse as a prohibition against allowing one's cattle to graze in the field of another.

22, 7: Brought to God: see note on Ex 21, 6. Cf also Ex 22, 10.

22, 16: The customary marriage price for virgins: fifty shekels according to Dt 22, 29.

22, 27: God: or perhaps "the gods," in the sense of "the

judges," as the parallel with a prince of your people suggests.

n: Gn 31, 39. o: 15f: Dt 22, 28f. p: Lv 19, 26. 31; 20. 6. 27; Dt 18, 10f. q: Lv 18, 23; Dt 27, 21. r: Dt 13; 17, 2-7. s: 20-23: Ex 23, 9; Lv 19, 33f; Dt 10, 18f; 24, 17f; 27, 19; Zec 7, 10. t: 24-26: Lv 25, 35-38; Dt 23, 19f; 24, 10-13; Ez 18, 7f. 17f. u: Acts 23, 5.

mother, but on the eighth day you must give it to me.^y

³⁰"You shall be men sacred to me. Flesh torn to pieces in the field you shall not eat; throw it to the dogs.^w

CHAPTER 23

See RG 122

¹"You shall not repeat a false report. Do not join the wicked in putting your hand, as an unjust witness, upon anyone.^{x 2}Neither shall you allege the example of the many as an excuse for doing wrong, nor shall you, when testifying in a lawsuit, side with the many in perverting justice. ³You shall not favor a poor man in his lawsuit.^y

⁴"When you come upon your enemy's ox or ass going astray, see to it that it is returned to him.^{z 5}When you notice the ass of one who hates you lying prostrate under its burden, by no means desert him; help him, rather, to raise it up.

⁶"You shall not deny one of your needy fellow men his rights in his lawsuit. ⁷You shall keep away from anything dishonest. The innocent and the just you shall not put to death, nor shall you acquit the guilty. ⁸Never take a bribe, for a bribe blinds even the most clear-sighted and twists the words even of the just.^{a 9}You shall not oppress an alien; you well know how it feels to be an alien, since you were once aliens yourselves in the land of Egypt.^b

Religious Laws. ^{10c}"For six years you may sow your land and gather in its produce. ¹¹But the seventh year you shall let the land lie untilled and unharvested, that the poor among you may eat of it and the beasts of the field may eat what the poor leave. So also shall you do in regard to your vineyard and your olive grove.

¹²"For six days you may do your work, but on the seventh day you must rest,^d that your ox and your ass may also have rest, and

that the son of your maidservant and the alien may be refreshed. ¹³Give heed to all that I have told you.

"Never mention the name of any other god; it shall not be heard from your lips.

^{14e}"Three times a year you shall celebrate a pilgrim feast to me.* ¹⁵You shall keep the feast of Unleavened Bread. As I have commanded you, you must eat unleavened bread for seven days at the prescribed time in the month of Abib, for it was then that you came out of Egypt. No one shall appear before me* empty-handed. ¹⁶You shall also keep the feast of the grain harvest with the first of the crop that you have sown in the field; and finally, the feast at the fruit harvest at the end of the year, when you gather in the produce from the fields. ¹⁷Thrice a year shall all your men appear before the LORD God.

¹⁸"You shall not offer the blood of my sacrifice with leavened bread;^f nor shall the fat of my feast be kept overnight till the next day. ¹⁹The choicest first fruits of your soil you shall bring to the house of the LORD, your God.

"You shall not boil a kid in its mother's milk.*

Reward of Fidelity. ²⁰"See, I am sending an angel^g before you, to guard you on the way and bring you to the place I have prepared. ²¹Be attentive to him and heed his voice. Do not rebel against him, for he will not forgive your sin. My authority resides in him.* ²²If you heed his voice and carry out all I tell you, I will be an enemy to your enemies and a foe to your foes.

²³"My angel will go before you and bring you to the Amorites, Hittites, Perizzites, Canaanites, Hivites and Jebusites; and I will wipe them out. ²⁴Therefore, you shall not bow down in worship before their gods, nor shall you make anything like them;* rather, you must demolish them and smash their sa-

---

23, 14: These three feasts are elsewhere called the Passover, Pentecost and Booths. Cf Ex 34, 18-26; Lv 23; Dt 16.

23, 15: Appear before me: the original expression was "see my face"; so also in several other places, as Ex 23, 17; 34, 23f; Dt 16, 16; 31, 11.

23, 19: Boil a kid in its mother's milk: this was part of a Canaanite ritual; hence it is forbidden here as a pagan ceremony.

23, 21: My authority resides in him: literally, "My name is within him."

23, 24: Make anything like them: some render, "act according to their conduct." Sacred pillars: objects of religious veneration at Canaanite sanctuaries.

---

v: Ex 13, 2; 34, 19; Lv 22, 27; Dt 15, 19.   *w:* Lv 7, 24; 17, 15; 22, 8.   *x:* 1f; Dt 19, 16ff.   *y:* Lv 19, 15.   *z:* Dt 22, 1ff.   *a:* Dt 16, 19; 27, 25; Sir 20, 28.   *b:* Ex 22, 21.   *c:* 10f; Lv 25, 3-7.   *d:* Ex 20, 8.   *e:* 14-17; Ex 34, 18. 22ff; Lv 23; Dt 16, 1-17.   *f:* 18f; Ex 34, 25f.   *g:* Ex 14, 19; 32, 34; 33, 2.

Calendar

THE YEAR WAS COMPOSED of twelve lunar months (beginning on the day of the new moon), with an intercalary month added periodically (see perhaps 1 Kgs 12, 33). In some traditions, and perhaps originally, the year began in the fall, at the autumnal equinox (see Ex 23, 16; 34, 22). In others, following Babylonian practice, the new year was celebrated in the spring. The fall new year became standard in postbiblical Judaism.

Months in the Bible are usually identified by ordinal numbers, beginning with the spring new year. Some months (in boldface in the following list) are also designated with names derived either from a Canaanite calendar or, in postexilic texts, from a Babylonian one; the names of months not found in the Bible are known from other ancient sources.

	Canaanite Name	Babylonian/Aramaic Name	Modern Equivalent
First	**Abib**	**Nisan**	March–April
Second	**Ziv**	Iyar	April–May
Third		**Sivan**	May–June
Fourth		Tammuz	June–July
Fifth		Av	July–August
Sixth		**Elul**	August–September
Seventh	**Ethanim**	Tishri	September–October
Eighth	**Bul**	Marheshvan	October–November
Ninth		Chislev	November–December
Tenth		**Tebeth**	December–January
Eleventh		**Shebat**	January–February
Twelfth		**Adar**	February–March

The Jewish calendar is based on the lunar month, which is a bit longer than 29½ days, so Jewish lunar months are 29 or 30 days long. Twelve lunar months usually amount to 354 days, 11 days short of a solar year. In order for the festivals to stay in the correct season in relation to the solar year, an extra month is added every few years. Following ancient Babylonian models, the calendar runs on a 19-year cycle: years 3, 6, 8, 11, 14, 17, and 19 of the cycle are intercalated or "leap" years, containing an extra month of Adar, sometimes called *Adar Sheni* (second Adar). Adar was chosen for intercalation because it is the last month of the Babylonian year and of the biblical year beginning in Nisan (an alternate calendar, the one now in use, begins the year in Tishri with Rosh Ha-Shanah). The next 19-year intercalation cycle will begin in 5768 (2007–2008 A.D.).

Observances fall within the calendar as follows:

Rosh Ha-Shanah (the New Year)	1–2 Tishri
Yom Kippur (the Day of Atonement)	10 Tishri
Succoth (Booths) begins	15 Tishri
Hanukkah begins	25 Chislev
Purim	14 Adar (15 Adar in Jerusalem and other ancient walled cites)
Passover begins	15 Nisan
Shavuot (Weeks) begins	6 Sivan
Tish'ah be'av	9 Ab

cred pillars.*h* 25The LORD, your God, you shall worship; then I will bless your food and drink, and I will remove all sickness from your midst; 26no woman in your land will be barren or miscarry; and I will give you a full span of life.

27"I will have the fear of me precede you, so that I will throw into panic every nation you reach.*i* I will make all your enemies turn from you in flight, 28and ahead of you I will send hornets* to drive the Hivites, Canaanites and Hittites out of your way. 29But not in one year will I drive them all out before you; else the land will become so desolate that the wild beasts will multiply against you. 30Instead, I will drive them out little by little before you, until you have grown numerous enough to take possession of the land. 31jI will set your boundaries from the Red Sea to the sea of the Philistines,* and from the desert to the River; all who dwell in this land I will hand over to you to be driven out of your way. 32You shall not make a covenant with them or their gods. 33They must not abide in your land, lest they make you sin against me by ensnaring you into worshiping their gods."*k*

CHAPTER 24

See RG 122

Ratification of the Covenant. 1Moses himself was told, "Come up to the LORD, you and Aaron, with Nadab, Abihu, and seventy of the elders of Israel. You shall all worship at some distance, 2but Moses alone is to come close to the LORD; the others shall not come too near, and the people shall not come up at all with Moses."

3When Moses came to the people and related all the words and ordinances of the LORD, they all answered with one voice, "We will do everything that the LORD has told us."*l* 4Moses then wrote down all the words of the LORD and, rising early the next day, he erected at the foot of the mountain an altar and twelve pillars* for the twelve tribes of Israel. 5Then, having sent certain young men of the Israelites to offer holocausts and sacrifice young bulls as peace offerings to the LORD, 6Moses took half of the blood and put it in large bowls; the other half he splashed on the altar. 7Taking the book of the covenant, he read it aloud to the people, who answered, "All that the LORD has said, we will heed and do." 8Then he took the blood and sprinkled it on the people, saying, "This is the blood of the covenant which the LORD has made with you in accordance with all these words of his."*m*

9Moses then went up with Aaron, Nadab, Abihu, and seventy elders of Israel, 10and they beheld the God of Israel. Under his feet there appeared to be sapphire tilework, as clear as the sky itself. 11Yet he did not smite these chosen Israelites. After gazing on God,* they could still eat and drink.

Moses on the Mountain. 12The LORD said to Moses, "Come up to me on the mountain and, while you are there, I will give you the stone tablets*n* on which I have written the commandments intended for their instruction." 13So Moses set out with Joshua, his aide, and went up to the mountain of God. 14The elders, however, had been told by him, "Wait here for us until we return to you. Aaron and Hur are staying with you. If anyone has a complaint, let him refer the matter to them." 15After Moses had gone up, a cloud covered the mountain. 16The glory of the LORD settled upon Mount Sinai. The cloud covered it for six days, and on the seventh day he called to Moses from the midst of the cloud.*o* 17To the Israelites the glory of the LORD was seen as a consuming fire on the mountaintop.*p* 18But Moses passed into

---

23, 28: Hornets: some understand this figuratively of various troublesome afflictions; others translate the Hebrew word as "leprosy." Cf Dt 7, 20; Jos 24, 12; Wis 12, 8.

23, 31: The sea of the Philistines: the Mediterranean. The River: the Euphrates. Only in the time of David and Solomon did the territory of Israel come near to reaching such distant borders.

24, 4: Pillars: stone shafts or slabs, erected as symbols of the fact that each of the twelve tribes had entered into this covenant with God; not idolatrous as in Ex 23, 24, although the same He-

brew word is used in both passages. See note on Gn 28, 18.

24, 11: After gazing on God: the ancients thought that the sight of God would bring instantaneous death. Cf Ex 33, 20; Gn 16, 13; 32, 31; Jgs 6, 22f; 13, 22. Eat and drink: partake of the sacrificial meal.

---

h: 23f: Ex 34, 10-16; Nm 33, 51f; Dt 7, 24ff.   *i:* 27ff: Dt 2, 25; 7, 20ff.   *j:* Gn 15, 18; Dt 11, 24; Jos 1, 4.   *k:* 32f: Ex 34, 12-16; Dt 7, 2ff.   *l:* Ex 19, 8.   *m:* 5-8: Heb 9, 18ff.   *n:* Ex 31, 18; 32, 15f; Dt 5, 22.   *o:* Sir 45, 4.   *p:* Ex 19, 18; Heb 12, 18.

the midst of the cloud as he went up on the mountain; and there he stayed for forty days and forty nights.*q*

IV: The Dwelling and Its Furnishings

CHAPTER 25

See RG 123

Collection of Materials. [1]This is what the LORD then said to Moses:*r* [2]"Tell the Israelites to take up a collection for me. From every man you shall accept the contribution that his heart prompts him to give me. [3]These are the contributions you shall accept from them: gold, silver and bronze;*s* [4]violet, purple and scarlet yarn; fine linen and goat hair; [5]rams' skins dyed red, and tahash* skins; acacia wood; [6]oil for the light; spices for the anointing oil and for the fragrant incense; [7]onyx stones and other gems for mounting on the ephod and the breastpiece.

[8]"They shall make a sanctuary for me, that I may dwell in their midst.*t* [9]This Dwelling and all its furnishings you shall make exactly according to the pattern that I will now show you.*u*

Plan of the Ark. [10]"You shall make an ark of acacia wood,*v* two and a half cubits long, one and a half cubits wide, and one and a half cubits high. [11]Plate it inside and outside with pure gold, and put a molding of gold around the top of it. [12]Cast four gold rings and fasten them on the four supports of the ark, two rings on one side and two on the opposite side. [13]Then make poles of acacia wood and plate them with gold. [14]These poles you are to put through the rings on the sides of the ark, for carrying it; [15]they must remain in the rings of the ark and never be withdrawn. [16]In the ark you are to put the commandments which I will give you.

[17]"You shall then make a propitiatory* of pure gold, two cubits and a half long, and one and a half cubits wide. [18]Make two cherubim* of beaten gold for the two ends of the propitiatory, [19]fastening them so that one cherub springs direct from each end. [20]The cherubim shall have their wings spread out above, covering the propitiatory with them; they shall be turned toward each other, but with their faces looking toward the propitiatory. [21]This propitiatory you shall then place on top of the ark. In the ark itself you are to put the commandments which I will give you. [22]There I will meet you and there, from above the propitiatory, between the two cherubim on the ark of the commandments, I will tell you all the commands that I wish you to give the Israelites.

The Table. [23]"You shall also make a table of acacia*w* wood, two cubits long, a cubit wide, and a cubit and a half high. [24]Plate it with pure gold and make a molding of gold around it. [25]Surround it with a frame,* a handbreadth high, with a molding of gold around the frame. [26]You shall also make four rings of gold for it and fasten them at the four corners, one at each leg, [27]on two opposite sides of the frame as holders for the poles to carry the table. [28]These poles for carrying the table you shall make of acacia wood and plate with gold. [29]Of pure gold you shall make its plates* and cups, as well as its pitchers and bowls for pouring libations. [30]On the table you shall always keep showbread set before me.*x*

The Lampstand. [31]"You shall make a lampstand of pure beaten gold*y*—its shaft

---

25, 5: Tahash: perhaps the name of a marine animal, such as the dugong or the porpoise. The Greek and Latin versions took it for the color hyacinth.

25, 17: Propitiatory: this traditional rendering of the Hebrew term, which may mean merely "cover," is derived from its connection with the ceremony of the Day of Atonement whereby God was rendered "propitious." Cf Lv 16, 14ff.

25, 18ff: Cherubim: probably in the form of human-headed winged lions. The cherubim over the ark formed the throne for the invisible Lord. Cf Ps 80, 2. For a more detailed description of the somewhat different cherubim in the temple of Solomon, see 1 Kgs 6, 23-28; 2 Chr 3, 10-13.

25, 25: A frame: probably placed near the bottom of the

legs to keep them steady. The golden table of Herod's temple is pictured thus on the Arch of Titus.

25, 29f: The plates held the showbread, that is, the holy bread which was placed upon the table every sabbath as an offering to God, and was later eaten by the priests. The cups held the incense which was strewn upon the bread. Cf Lv 24, 5-9. The libation wine was poured from the pitchers into the bowls. All these vessels were kept on the golden table.

---

q: Ex 34, 28; Dt 9, 9. *r*: 1-7: Ex 35, 4-9. 20-29. *s*: Ex 35, 4-9. *t*: 8f: Ex 26, 1-30; 36, 8-38. *u*: Acts 7, 44. *v*: 10-22: Ex 37, 1-9; Heb 9, 1-5. *w*: 23-30: Ex 37, 10-16. *x*: Lv 24, 5ff. *y*: 31-40: Ex 37, 17-24.

Structure of the Tabernacle

and branches—with its cups and knobs and petals springing directly from it. *32*Six branches are to extend from the sides of the lampstand, three branches on one side, and three on the other. *33**On one branch there are to be three cups, shaped like almond blossoms, each with its knob and petals; on the opposite branch there are to be three cups, shaped like almond blossoms, each with its knob and petals; and so for the six branches that extend from the lampstand. *34*On the shaft there are to be four cups,* shaped like almond blossoms, with their knobs and petals, *35*including a knob below each of the three pairs of branches that extend from the lampstand. *36*Their knobs and branches shall so spring from it that the whole will form but a single piece of pure beaten gold. *37**You shall then make seven lamps*z* for it and so set up the lamps that they shed their light on the space in front of the lampstand. *38*These, as well as the trimming shears and trays,* must be of pure gold. *39*Use a talent of pure gold for the lampstand and all its appurtenances. *40*See that you make them according to the pattern shown you on the mountain.*a*

CHAPTER 26

The Tent Cloth. *1*"The Dwelling itself you shall make out of sheets* woven of fine linen twined and of violet, purple and scarlet yarn, with cherubim embroidered on them.*b* *2*The length of each shall be twenty-eight cubits, and the width four cubits; all the sheets shall be of the same size. *3*Five of the sheets are to be sewed together, edge to edge; and the same for the other five. *4*Make

See RG
123

25, 33: In keeping with the arrangement of the ornaments on the shaft, the three sets of ornaments on each branch were probably so placed that one was at the top and the other two equally spaced along the length of the branch. Knob: the cup-shaped seed capsule at the base of a flower.

25, 34f: Of the four ornaments on the shaft, one was at the top and one was below each of the three sets of side branches.

25, 37: The lamps were probably shaped like small boats, with the wick at one end; the end with the wick was turned

toward the front of the lampstand.

25, 38: Trays: small receptacles for the burnt-out wicks.

26, 1: Sheets: strips of tapestry, woven of white linen, the colored threads being used for the cherubim which were embroidered on them. These sheets were stretched across the top of the Dwelling to form a roof, their free ends hanging down inside the boards which formed walls.

z: Lv 24, 2ff; Nm 8, 2.   *a:* Heb 8, 5.   *b:* 1-14: Ex 36, 8-19.

loops of violet yarn along the edge of the end sheet in one set, and the same along the edge of the end sheet in the other set. [5]There are to be fifty loops along the edge of the end sheet in the first set, and fifty loops along the edge of the corresponding sheet in the second set, and so placed that the loops are directly opposite each other. [6]Then make fifty clasps of gold, with which to join the two sets of sheets, so that the Dwelling forms one whole.

[7]"Also make sheets woven of goat hair, to be used as a tent covering* over the Dwelling. [8]Eleven such sheets are to be made; the length of each shall be thirty cubits, and the width four cubits: all eleven sheets shall be of the same size. [9]Sew five of the sheets, edge to edge, into one set, and the other six sheets into another set. Use the sixth sheet double at the front of the tent.* [10]Make fifty loops along the edge of the end sheet in one set, and fifty loops along the edge of the end sheet in the second set. [11]Also make fifty bronze clasps and put them into the loops, to join the tent into one whole. [12]There will be an extra half sheet of tent covering, which shall be allowed to hang down over the rear of the Dwelling. [13]Likewise, the sheets of the tent will have an extra cubit's length to be left hanging down on either side of the Dwelling to protect it. [14]Over the tent itself you shall make a covering of rams' skins dyed red, and above that, a covering of tahash skins.

The Wooden Walls. [15c]"You shall make boards of acacia wood as walls for the Dwelling. [16]The length of each board is to be ten cubits, and its width one and a half cubits. [17]Each board shall have two arms* that shall serve to fasten the boards in line. In this way all the boards of the Dwelling are to be made. [18]Set up the boards of the Dwelling as follows: twenty boards on the south side, [19]with forty silver pedestals under the twenty boards, so that there are two pedestals under each board, at its two arms; [20]twenty boards on the other side of the Dwelling, the north side, [21]with their forty silver pedestals, two under each board; [22]six boards for the rear of the Dwelling, to the west; [23]and two boards for the corners at the rear of the Dwelling. [24]These two shall be double at the bottom, and likewise double at the top, to the first ring. That is how both boards in the corners are to be made. [25]Thus, there shall be in the rear eight boards, with their sixteen silver pedestals, two pedestals under each board. [26]Also make bars of acacia wood: five for the boards on one side of the Dwelling, [27]five for those on the other side, and five for those at the rear, toward the west. [28]The center bar, at the middle of the boards, shall reach across from end to end. [29]Plate the boards with gold, and make gold rings on them as holders for the bars, which are also to be plated with gold. [30]You shall erect the Dwelling according to the pattern shown you on the mountain.

The Veils. [31]"You shall have a veil woven of violet, purple and scarlet yarn,[d] and of fine linen twined, with cherubim embroidered on it.[e] [32]It is to be hung on four gold-plated columns of acacia wood, which shall have hooks* of gold and shall rest on four silver pedestals. [33]Hang the veil from clasps. The ark of the commandments you shall bring inside, behind this veil which divides the holy place from the holy of holies. [34]Set the propitiatory on the ark of the commandments in the holy of holies.

[35]"Outside the veil you shall place the table and the lampstand, the latter on the south side of the Dwelling, opposite the table, which is to be put on the north side. [36]For the entrance of the tent make a variegated* curtain of violet, purple and scarlet yarn and of fine linen twined. [37]Make five columns of acacia wood for this curtain;

26, 7: Tent covering: the cloth made of sheets of goat hair to cover the Dwelling.

26, 9: Half the width of the end strip was folded back at the front of the Dwelling, thus leaving another half-strip to hang down at the rear. Cf v 12.

26, 17: Arms: literally, "hands." According to some, they served as "tongue and groove" to mortise the boards together; according to others, they were pegs at the bottom of the boards and fitted into sockets in the pedestals.

26, 32: Hooks: probably placed near the tops of the columns, to hold the rope from which the veils and curtains hung.

26, 36: Variegated: without definite designs such as the cherubim on the inner veil.

c: 15-30: Ex 36, 20-34.   d: 2 Chr 3, 14.   e: 31-37: Ex 36, 35-38.

have them plated with gold, with their hooks of gold; and cast five bronze pedestals for them.

CHAPTER 27

See RG
123

The Altar of Holocausts. *1*"You shall make an altar*f* of acacia wood, on a square, five cubits long and five cubits wide; it shall be three cubits high. *2*At the four corners there are to be horns, so made that they spring directly from the altar. You shall then plate it with bronze. *3*Make pots for removing the ashes, as well as shovels, basins, forks and fire pans, all of which shall be of bronze. *4*Make a grating* of bronze network for it; this to have four bronze rings, one at each of its four corners. *5*Put it down around the altar, on the ground. This network is to be half as high as the altar. *6*You shall also make poles of acacia wood for the altar, and plate them with bronze. *7*These poles are to be put through the rings, so that they are on either side of the altar when it is carried. *8*Make the altar itself in the form of a hollow* box, just as it was shown you on the mountain.

Court of the Dwelling. *9g*"You shall also make a court for the Dwelling. On the south side the court shall have hangings a hundred cubits long, woven of fine linen twined, *10*with twenty columns and twenty pedestals of bronze; the hooks and bands on the columns shall be of silver. *11*On the north side there shall be similar hangings, a hundred cubits long, with twenty columns and twenty pedestals of bronze; the hooks and bands on the columns shall be of silver. *12*On the west side, across the width of the court, there shall be hangings, fifty cubits long, with ten columns and ten pedestals. *13*The width of the court on the east side shall be fifty cubits. *14*On one side there shall be hangings to the extent of fifteen cubits, with three columns and three pedestals; *15*on the other side there shall be hangings to the extent of fifteen cubits, with three columns and three pedestals.

16"At the entrance of the court there shall be a variegated curtain, twenty cubits long, woven of violet, purple and scarlet yarn and of fine linen twined. It shall have four columns and four pedestals. *17*All the columns around the court shall have bands and hooks of silver, and pedestals of bronze. *18*The enclosure of the court is to be one hundred cubits long, fifty cubits wide, and five cubits high. Fine linen twined must be used, and the pedestals must be of bronze. *19*All the fittings of the Dwelling, whatever be their use, as well as all its tent pegs and all the tent pegs of the court, must be of bronze.

Oil for the Lamps. *20*"You shall order the Israelites to bring you clear oil of crushed olives, to be used for the light, so that you may keep lamps burning regularly.*h* *21*From evening to morning Aaron and his sons shall maintain them before the LORD in the meeting tent, outside the veil which hangs in front of the commandments. This shall be a perpetual ordinance for the Israelites throughout their generations.

CHAPTER 28

See RG
123

The Priestly Vestments. *1i*"From among the Israelites have your brother Aaron, together with his sons Nadab, Abihu, Eleazar and Ithamar, brought to you, that they may be my priests. *2*For the glorious adornment of your brother Aaron you shall have sacred vestments made. *3*Therefore, to the various expert workmen whom I have endowed with skill, you shall give instructions to make such vestments for Aaron as will set him apart for his sacred service as my priest. *4*These are the vestments they shall make: a breastpiece, an ephod, a robe, a brocaded tunic, a miter and a sash. In making these sacred vestments which your brother Aaron and his sons are to wear in serving as my priests, *5*they shall use gold, violet, purple and scarlet yarn and fine linen.

27, 4: Grating: it is not clear whether this was flush with the altar or at some small distance from it; in the latter case the space between the altar and the grating would be filled with stones and serve as a platform around the altar, which would otherwise be too high for the priest to reach conveniently.

27, 8: Hollow: probably filled with earth or stones when in use. Cf Ex 20, 24f.

f: 1-8: Ex 38, 1-7. *g:* 9-19: Ex 38, 9-20. *h:* 20f: Lv 24, 1-4. *i:* 1-5: Ex 39, 1; Sir 45, 7.

The Ephod and Breastpiece. [6]"The ephod* they shall make of gold thread and of violet, purple and scarlet yarn, embroidered on cloth of fine linen twined.[j] [7]It shall have a pair of shoulder straps joined to its two upper ends. [8]The embroidered belt on the ephod shall extend out from it and, like it, be made of gold thread, of violet, purple and scarlet yarn, and of fine linen twined.

[9]"Get two onyx stones and engrave on them the names of the sons of Israel: [10]six of their names on one stone, and the other six on the other stone, in the order of their birth. [11]As a gem-cutter engraves a seal, so shall you have the two stones engraved with the names of the sons of Israel and then mounted in gold filigree work. [12]Set these two stones on the shoulder straps of the ephod as memorial stones of the sons of Israel. Thus Aaron shall bear their names on his shoulders as a reminder before the LORD. [13]Make filigree rosettes of gold,[k] [14]as well as two chains of pure gold, twisted like cords, and fasten the cordlike chains to the filigree rosettes.

[15]"The breastpiece* of decision you shall also have made, embroidered like the ephod with gold thread and violet, purple and scarlet yarn on cloth of fine linen twined.[l] [16]It is to be square when folded double, a span high and a span wide. [17]On it you shall mount four rows of precious stones: in the first row, a carnelian, a topaz and an emerald; [18]in the second row, a garnet, a sapphire and a beryl; [19]in the third row, a jacinth, an agate and an amethyst; [20]in the fourth row, a chrysolite, an onyx and a jasper. These stones are to be mounted in gold filigree work, [21]twelve of them to match the names of the sons of Israel, each stone engraved like a seal with the name of one of the twelve tribes.

[22]"When the chains of pure gold, twisted like cords, have been made for the breastpiece, [23]you shall then make two rings of gold for it and fasten them to the two upper ends of the breastpiece. [24]The gold cords are then to be fastened to the two rings at the upper ends of the breastpiece, [25]the other two ends of the cords being fastened in front to the two filigree rosettes which are attached to the shoulder straps of the ephod. [26]Make two other rings of gold and put them on the two lower ends of the breastpiece, on its edge that faces the ephod. [27]Then make two more rings of gold and fasten them to the bottom of the shoulder straps next to where they join the ephod in front, just above its embroidered belt. [28]Violet ribbons shall bind the rings of the breastpiece to the rings of the ephod, so that the breastpiece will stay right above the embroidered belt of the ephod and not swing loose from it.

[29]"Whenever Aaron enters the sanctuary, he will thus bear the names of the sons of Israel on the breastpiece of decision over his heart as a constant reminder before the LORD. [30]In this breastpiece of decision[m] you shall put the Urim and Thummim,* that they may be over Aaron's heart whenever he enters the presence of the LORD. Thus he shall always bear the decisions for the Israelites over his heart in the LORD's presence.

Other Vestments. [31]"The robe of the ephod[n] you shall make entirely of violet material. [32]It shall have an opening for the head in the center, and around this opening there shall be a selvage, woven as at the opening of a shirt, to keep it from being torn. [33]All around the hem at the bottom you shall make pomegranates, woven of violet, purple and scarlet yarn and fine linen twined, with gold

---

28, 6: Ephod: this Hebrew word is retained in the translation because it is the technical term for a peculiar piece of the priestly vestments, the exact nature of which is uncertain. It seems to have been a sort of apron that hung from the shoulders of the priest by shoulder straps (v 7) and was tied around his waist by the loose ends of the attached belt (v 8).

28, 15-30: Breastpiece: in shape like a modern altar burse, it was a pocketlike receptacle for holding the Urim and Thummim (v 30), and formed an integral part of the ephod, to which it was attached by an elaborate system of rings and chains. Both the ephod and its breastpiece were made of brocaded linen.

28, 17-20: The translation of the Hebrew names of some of these gems is quite conjectural.

28, 30: Urim and Thummim: both the meaning of these Hebrew words and the exact nature of the objects so designated are uncertain. They were apparently lots of some kind which were drawn or cast by the priest to ascertain God's decision in doubtful matters. Hence, the burse in which they were kept was called "the breastpiece of decision."

j: 6-12: Ex 39, 2-7; Sir 45, 8-14.   *k:* 13f: Ex 28, 22. 25; 39, 15. 18.   *l:* 15-21: Ex 39, 15-21.   *m:* Lv 8, 8; Sir 45, 11.   *n:* 31-35: Ex 39, 20ff; Lv 8, 9; Sir 45, 10.

bells between them; [34]first a gold bell, then a pomegranate, and thus alternating all around the hem of the robe. [35]Aaron shall wear it when ministering, that its tinkling may be heard as he enters and leaves the LORD's presence in the sanctuary; else he will die.

[36]"You shall also make a plate of pure gold and engrave on it, as on a seal engraving, "Sacred to the LORD." [37]This plate is to be tied over the miter with a violet ribbon in such a way that it rests on the front of the miter,[o] [38]over Aaron's forehead. Since Aaron bears whatever guilt the Israelites may incur in consecrating any of their sacred gifts, this plate must always be over his forehead, so that they may find favor with the LORD.

[39p]"The tunic of fine linen shall be brocaded. The miter shall be made of fine linen. The sash shall be of variegated work.

[40]"Likewise, for the glorious adornment of Aaron's sons you shall have tunics and sashes and turbans made. [41]With these you shall clothe your brother Aaron and his sons. Anoint and ordain them,[*] consecrating them as my priests. [42]You must also make linen drawers for them, to cover their naked flesh from their loins to their thighs.[q] [43]Aaron and his sons shall wear them whenever they go into the meeting tent or approach the altar to minister in the sanctuary, lest they incur guilt and die. This shall be a perpetual ordinance for him and for his descendants.

See RG 123

CHAPTER 29

Consecration of the Priests. [1]"This is the rite you shall perform in consecrating them as my priests.[r] Procure a young bull and two unblemished rams. [2]With fine wheat flour make unleavened cakes mixed with oil, and unleavened wafers spread with oil, [3]and put them in a basket. Take the basket of them along with the bullock and the two rams. [4]Aaron and his sons you shall also bring to the entrance of the meeting tent, and there wash them with water. [5]Take the vestments and clothe Aaron with the tunic, the robe of the ephod, the ephod itself, and the breastpiece, fastening the embroidered belt of the ephod around him. [6]Put the miter on his head, the sacred diadem on the miter. [7]Then take the anointing oil and anoint him with it, pouring it on his head. [8]Bring forward his sons also and clothe them with the tunics, [9]gird them with the sashes, and tie the turbans on them.[s] Thus shall the priesthood be theirs by perpetual law, and thus shall you ordain Aaron and his sons.

Ordination Sacrifices. [10t]"Now bring forward the bullock in front of the meeting tent. There Aaron and his sons shall lay their hands on its head. [11]Then slaughter the bullock before the LORD, at the entrance of the meeting tent. [12]Take some of its blood and with your finger put it on the horns of the altar. All the rest of the blood you shall pour out at the base of the altar. [13]All the fat that covers its inner organs, as well as the lobe of its liver and its two kidneys, together with the fat that is on them, you shall take and burn on the altar. [14]But the flesh and hide and offal of the bullock you must burn up outside the camp, since this is a sin offering.[u]

[15]"Then take one of the rams, and after Aaron and his sons have laid their hands on its head, [16]slaughter it. The blood you shall take and splash on all the sides of the altar. [17]Cut the ram into pieces; its inner organs and shanks you shall first wash, and then put them with the pieces and with the head. [18]The entire ram shall then be burned on the altar, since it is a holocaust, a sweet-smelling oblation to the LORD.

[19]"After this take the other ram, and when Aaron and his sons have laid their hands on its head, [20]slaughter it. Some of its blood you shall take and put on the tip of Aaron's right ear and on the tips of his sons' right ears and on the thumbs of their right hands and the great toes of their right feet. Splash the rest of the blood on all the sides of the altar. [21]Then take some of the blood that is on the altar, together with some of the anointing oil, and sprinkle this on Aaron and his vestments, as well as on his sons and their vest-

---

28, 41: Ordain them: literally, "fill their hands," a technical expression used solely for the installation of priests. The phrase probably originated in the custom of placing in the priests' hands the instruments or other symbols of the sacerdotal office.

o: Ex 39, 31; Lv 8, 9.   *p:* 39-43: Ex 39, 27ff.   *q:* Ez 44, 18.   *r:* 1-8: Lv 8, 1-9.   *s:* Lv 8, 13.   *t:* 10-26: Lv 8, 14-30.   *u:* Heb 13, 11.

ments, that his sons and their vestments may be sacred.

22"Now, from this ram you shall take its fat: its fatty tail,* the fat that covers its inner organs, the lobe of its liver, its two kidneys with the fat that is on them, and its right thigh, since this is the ordination ram; 23then, out of the basket of unleavened food that you have set before the LORD, you shall take one of the loaves of bread, one of the cakes made with oil, and one of the wafers. 24All these things you shall put into the hands of Aaron and his sons, so that they may wave them as a wave offering* before the LORD. 25After you have received them back from their hands, you shall burn them on top of the holocaust on the altar as a sweet-smelling oblation to the LORD. 26Finally, take the breast of Aaron's ordination ram and wave it as a wave offering before the LORD; this is to be your own portion.

27*"Thus shall you set aside the breast of whatever wave offering is waved,v as well as the thigh of whatever raised offering is raised up, whether this be the ordination ram or anything else belonging to Aaron or to his sons. 28Such things are due to Aaron and his sons from the Israelites by a perpetual ordinance as a contribution. From their peace offerings, too, the Israelites shall make a contribution, their contribution to the LORD.

29"The sacred vestmentsw of Aaron shall be passed down to his descendants, that in them they may be anointed and ordained. 30The descendant who succeeds him as priest and who is to enter the meeting tent to minister in the sanctuary shall be clothed with them for seven days.

31x"You shall take the flesh of the ordination ram and boil it in a holy place. 32At the entrance of the meeting tent Aaron and his sons shall eat the flesh of the ram and the bread that is in the basket. 33They themselves are to eat of these things by which atonement was made at their ordination and consecration; but no layman may eat of them, since they are sacred. 34If some of the flesh of the ordination sacrifice or some of the bread remains over on the next day, this remnant must be burned up; it is not to be eaten, since it is sacred. 35Carry out all these orders in regard to Aaron and his sons just as I have given them to you.y

"Seven days you shall spend in ordaining them, 36zsacrificing a bullock each day as a sin offering, to make atonement. Thus also shall you purge the altar* in making atonement for it; you shall anoint it in order to consecrate it. 37Seven days you shall spend in making atonement for the altar and in consecrating it. Then the altar will be most sacred, and whatever touches it will become sacred.

38*"Now, this is what you shall offer on the altar: two yearling lambsa as the sacrifice established for each day; 39one lamb in the morning and the other lamb at the evening twilight. 40With the first lamb there shall be a tenth of an ephah of fine flour mixed with a fourth of a hin of oil of crushed olives and, as its libation, a fourth of a hin of wine. 41The other lamb you shall offer at the evening twilight, with the same cereal offering and libation as in the morning. You shall offer this as a sweet-smelling oblation to the LORD. 42Throughout your generations this established holocaust shall be offered before the LORD at the entrance of the meeting tent, where I will meet you and speak to you.

43"There, at the altar, I will meet the Israelites; hence, it will be made sacred by my glory.b 44Thus I will consecrate the meeting tent and the altar, just as I also consecrate Aaron and his sons to be my priests. 45I will dwell in the midst of the Israelites and will

29, 22: Fatty tail: the thick layer of fat surrounding the tails of sheep and rams bred in Palestine even today. It is regarded as a choice food. Cf Lv 3, 9.

29, 24-26: Wave offering: the portions of a peace offering, breast and right thigh, which the officiating priest moved to and fro (waved) in the presence of the LORD. They were reserved for Aaron and his sons.

29, 27-30: These verses are a parenthetical interruption of the ordination ritual; v 31 belongs logically immediately after v 26.

29, 36f: Purge the altar: the construction of an altar by profane hands rendered it impure. The anointing and consecration of the altar purified it and made it sacred.

29, 38-42: A parenthesis inserted into the rubrics for consecrating the altar; v 43 belongs directly after v 37.

v: 27f: Lv 7, 31-34; 10, 14f; Nm 18, 18f; Dt 18, 3.   w: Nm 20, 26. 28.   x: 31-34: Lv 8, 31f.   y: Lv 8, 36.   z: 36f: Lv 8, 33ff.   a: 38-42: Nm 28, 3-8.   b: Ex 25, 22.

be their God. [46]They shall know that I, the LORD, am their God who brought them out of the land of Egypt, so that I, the LORD, their God, might dwell among them.

See RG 123

CHAPTER 30

Altar of Incense. [1]"For burning incense you shall make an altar of acacia wood,[c] [2]with a square surface, a cubit long, a cubit wide, and two cubits high, with horns that spring directly from it. [3]Its grate on top, its walls on all four sides, and its horns you shall plate with pure gold. Put a gold molding around it. [4]Underneath the molding you shall put gold rings, two on one side and two on the opposite side, as holders for the poles used in carrying it. [5]Make the poles, too, of acacia wood and plate them with gold. [6]This altar you are to place in front of the veil that hangs before the ark of the commandments where I will meet you.[d]

[7]"On it Aaron shall burn fragrant incense. Morning after morning, when he prepares the lamps, [8]and again in the evening twilight, when he lights the lamps, he shall burn incense. Throughout your generations this shall be the established incense offering before the LORD. [9]On this altar you shall not offer up any profane incense, or any holocaust or cereal offering; nor shall you pour out a libation upon it. [10]Once a year Aaron shall perform the atonement rite on its horns.[e] Throughout your generations this atonement is to be made once a year with the blood of the atoning sin offering. This altar is most sacred to the LORD."

Census Tax. [11]The LORD also said to Moses, [12]"When you take a census[f] of the Israelites who are to be registered, each one, as he is enrolled, shall give the LORD a forfeit for his life, so that no plague may come upon them for being registered. [13]Everyone who enters the registered group must pay a half-shekel, according to the standard of the sanctuary shekel, twenty gerahs to the shekel. This payment of a half-shekel is a contribution to the LORD.[g] [14]Everyone of twenty years or more who enters the registered group must give this contribution to the LORD. [15]The rich

need not give more, nor shall the poor give less, than a half-shekel in this contribution to the LORD to pay the forfeit for their lives. [16h]When you receive this forfeit money from the Israelites, you shall donate it to the service of the meeting tent, that there it may be the Israelites' reminder, before the LORD, of the forfeit paid for their lives."

The Laver. [17]The LORD said to Moses, [18]"For ablutions you shall make a bronze laver with a bronze base. Place it between the meeting tent and the altar, and put water in it.[i] [19]Aaron and his sons shall use it in washing their hands and feet.[j] [20]When they are about to enter the meeting tent, they must wash with water, lest they die. Likewise when they approach the altar in their ministry, to offer an oblation to the LORD, [21]they must wash their hands and feet, lest they die. This shall be a perpetual ordinance for him and his descendants throughout their generations."

The Anointing Oil. [22]The LORD said to Moses, [23]"Take the finest spices: five hundred shekels of free-flowing myrrh; half that amount, that is, two hundred and fifty shekels, of fragrant cinnamon; two hundred and fifty shekels of fragrant cane; [24]five hundred shekels of cassia—all according to the standard of the sanctuary shekel; together with a hin of olive oil; [25]and blend them into sacred anointing oil,[k] perfumed ointment expertly prepared. [26l]With this sacred anointing oil you shall anoint the meeting tent and the ark of the commandments, [27]the table and all its appurtenances, the lampstand and its appurtenances, the altar of incense [28]and the altar of holocausts with all its appurtenances, and the laver with its base. [29]When you have consecrated them, they shall be most sacred; whatever touches them shall be sacred. [30]Aaron and his sons you shall also anoint and consecrate as my priests.[m] [31]To the Israelites you shall say: As sacred anointing oil this shall belong to me throughout your generations. [32]It may not be used in any ordinary anointing of the body, nor may you make any other oil of a like mixture. It is sacred, and shall be treated as

---

c: 1-5; Ex 37, 25-28.   d: Ex 40, 26.   e: Lv 16, 18.   f: Nm 1, 2f; 26, 2.   g: Mt 17, 24-27.   h: Ex 38, 25.   i: Ex 38, 8; 40, 7. 30.   j: 19ff; Ex 40, 31f.   k: Ex 37, 29.   l: 26-29; Ex 40, 9ff; Lv 8, 10; Nm 7, 1.   m: Ex 29, 7; Lv 8, 12.

sacred by you. ³³Whoever prepares a perfume like this, or whoever puts any of this on a layman, shall be cut off from his kinsmen."

The Incense. ³⁴ⁿThe LORD told Moses, "Take these aromatic substances: storax and onycha and galbanum, these and pure frankincense in equal parts; ³⁵and blend them into incense. This fragrant powder, expertly prepared, is to be salted and so kept pure and sacred. ³⁶Grind some of it into fine dust and put this before the commandments in the meeting tent where I will meet you. This incense shall be treated as most sacred by you. ³⁷You may not make incense of a like mixture for yourselves; you must treat it as sacred to the LORD. ³⁸Whoever makes an incense like this for his own enjoyment of its fragrance, shall be cut off from his kinsmen."

CHAPTER 31

See RG 123

Choice of Artisans. ^{1o}The LORD said to Moses, ²"See, I have chosen Bezalel, son of Uri, son of Hur, of the tribe of Judah, ³and I have filled him with a divine spirit of skill and understanding and knowledge in every craft: ⁴in the production of embroidery, in making things of gold, silver or bronze, ⁵in cutting and mounting precious stones, in carving wood, and in every other craft. ⁶As his assistant I have appointed Oholiab, son of Ahisamach, of the tribe of Dan. I have also endowed all the experts with the necessary skill to make all the things I have ordered you to make: ^{7p}the meeting tent, the ark of the commandments with the propitiatory on top of it, all the furnishings of the tent, ⁸the table with its appurtenances, the pure gold lampstand with all its appurtenances, the altar of incense, ⁹the altar of holocausts with all its appurtenances, the laver with its base, ¹⁰the service cloths,* the sacred vestments for Aaron the priest, the vestments for his sons in their ministry, ¹¹the anointing oil, and the fragrant incense for the sanctuary. All these things they shall make just as I have commanded you."

Sabbath Laws. ^{12q}The LORD said to Moses, ¹³"You must also tell the Israelites: Take care to keep my sabbaths, for that is to be the token between you and me throughout the generations, to show that it is I, the LORD, who make you holy. ¹⁴Therefore, you must keep the sabbath as something sacred. Whoever desecrates it shall be put to death. If anyone does work on that day, he must be rooted out of his people. ¹⁵Six days there are for doing work, but the seventh day is the sabbath of complete rest, sacred to the LORD. Anyone who does work on the sabbath day shall be put to death. ¹⁶So shall the Israelites observe the sabbath, keeping it throughout their generations as a perpetual covenant. ¹⁷Between me and the Israelites it is to be an everlasting token; for in six days the LORD made the heavens and the earth, but on the seventh day he rested at his ease."

¹⁸When the LORD had finished speaking to Moses on Mount Sinai, he gave him the two tablets of the commandments, the stone tablets inscribed by God's own finger.^r

CHAPTER 32

See RG 123

The Golden Calf. ¹When the people became aware of Moses' delay in coming down from the mountain, they gathered around Aaron and said to him, "Come, make us a god who will be our leader; as for the man Moses who brought us out of the land of Egypt, we do not know what has happened to him."^s ²Aaron replied, "Have your wives and sons and daughters take off the golden earrings they are wearing, and bring them to me." ³So all the people took off their earrings and brought them to Aaron, ⁴who accepted their offering, and fashioning this gold with a graving tool, made a molten calf. Then they cried out, "This is your God, O Israel, who brought you out of the land of Egypt."^t ⁵On seeing this, Aaron built an altar before the calf and proclaimed, "Tomorrow is a feast of the LORD."* ⁶Early the next day

---

31, 10: The service cloths: so the Greek. They were perhaps the colored cloths mentioned in Nm 4, 4-15.

32, 5: The calf . . . a feast of the LORD: from this it is clear that the golden calf was intended as an image, not of a false god, but of the Lord himself, his strength being symbolized by the strength of a young bull. The Israelites, however, had been forbidden to represent the Lord under any visible form. Cf Ex 20, 4.

n: 34ff: Ex 25, 6; 37, 29.   o: 1-6: Ex 35, 30-35.   p: 7-11: Ex 35, 10-19.   q: 12-17: Ex 20, 8-11; 35, 1-3.   r: Ex 24, 12; 32, 15f; Dt 5, 22.   s: Ex 32, 23; Acts 7, 40.   t: Ex 32, 8; 1 Kgs 12, 28.

the people offered holocausts and brought peace offerings. Then they sat down to eat and drink, and rose up to revel.*u*

[7] With that, the LORD said to Moses, "Go down at once to your people, whom you brought out of the land of Egypt, for they have become depraved. [8]*v* They have soon turned aside from the way I pointed out to them, making for themselves a molten calf and worshiping it, sacrificing to it and crying out, 'This is your God, O Israel, who brought you out of the land of Egypt!' [9] I see how stiff-necked this people is,"*w* continued the LORD to Moses. [10] "Let me alone, then, that my wrath may blaze up against them to consume them. Then I will make of you a great nation."

[11] But Moses implored the LORD, his God, saying,*x* "Why, O LORD, should your wrath blaze up against your own people, whom you brought out of the land of Egypt with such great power and with so strong a hand? [12] Why should the Egyptians say, 'With evil intent he brought them out, that he might kill them in the mountains and exterminate them from the face of the earth'? Let your blazing wrath die down; relent in punishing your people. [13] Remember your servants Abraham, Isaac and Israel, and how you swore to them by your own self, saying,*y* 'I will make your descendants as numerous as the stars in the sky; and all this land that I promised, I will give your descendants as their perpetual heritage.' " [14] So the LORD relented in the punishment he had threatened to inflict on his people.

[15] Moses then turned and came down the mountain with the two tablets of the commandments in his hands,*z* tablets that were written on both sides, front and back; [16] tablets that were made by God, having inscriptions on them that were engraved by God himself.*a* [17] Now, when Joshua heard the noise of the people shouting, he said to Moses, "That sounds like a battle in the camp." [18] But Moses answered, "It does not sound like cries of victory, nor does it sound like cries of defeat; the sounds that I hear are cries of revelry." [19] As he drew near the camp, he saw the calf and the dancing. With that, Moses' wrath flared up, so that he threw the tablets down and broke them on the base of the mountain.*b* [20] Taking the calf they had made, he fused it in the fire and then ground it down to powder, which he scattered on the water* and made the Israelites drink.*c*

[21] Moses asked Aaron, "What did this people ever do to you that you should lead them into so grave a sin?" Aaron replied, "Let not my lord be angry. [22] You know well enough how prone the people are to evil. [23] They said to me, 'Make us a god to be our leader; as for the man Moses who brought us out of the land of Egypt, we do not know what has happened to him.' [24] So I told them, 'Let anyone who has gold jewelry take it off.' They gave it to me, and I threw it into the fire, and this calf came out."

[25] When Moses realized that, to the scornful joy of their foes, Aaron had let the people run wild, [26] he stood at the gate of the camp and cried, "Whoever is for the LORD, let him come to me!" All the Levites*d* then rallied to him, [27] and he told them, "Thus says the LORD, the God of Israel: Put your sword on your hip, every one of you! Now go up and down the camp, from gate to gate, and slay your own kinsmen,* your friends and neighbors!" [28] The Levites carried out the command of Moses, and that day there fell about three thousand of the people. [29] Then Moses said, "Today you have been dedicated to the LORD,* for you were against your own sons and kinsmen, to bring a blessing upon yourselves this day."

The Atonement. [30] On the next day Moses said to the people,*e* "You have committed a grave sin. I will go up to the LORD, then; per-

32, 20: The water: the stream that flowed down Mount Sinai. Cf Dt 9, 21.

32, 27: Slay your own kinsmen: those who were especially guilty of the idolatry.

32, 29: Dedicated to the LORD: because of their zeal for the true worship of the Lord, the Levites were chosen to be special ministers of the ritual service. However, the meaning of the Hebrew here is somewhat disputed.

u: 1 Cor 10, 7. *v:* 7f: Dt 9, 12. 16. *w:* 9f: Dt 9, 13; Ps 106, 23. *x:* 11f: Nm 14, 13ff; Dt 9, 28. *y:* Gn 22, 16f. *z:* Dt 9, 15. *a:* Ex 31, 18. *b:* Dt 9, 16f. *c:* Dt 9, 21. *d:* 26-29: Dt 33, 8f. *e:* 30-34: Dt 9, 18ff.

haps I may be able to make atonement for your sin." [31]So Moses went back to the LORD and said, "Ah, this people has indeed committed a grave sin in making a god of gold for themselves! [32]If you would only forgive their sin! If you will not, then strike me out of the book that you have written."* [33]The LORD answered, "Him only who has sinned against me will I strike out of my book. [34]Now, go and lead the people whither I have told you. My angel will go before you. When it is time for me to punish, I will punish them for their sin."

[35]Thus the LORD smote the people for having had Aaron make the calf for them.

CHAPTER 33

See RG 123

[1]The LORD told Moses, "You and the people whom you have brought up from the land of Egypt, are to go up from here to the land which I swore to Abraham, Isaac and Jacob I would give to their descendants.*f* [2]Driving out the Canaanites, Amorites, Hittites, Perizzites, Hivites and Jebusites, I will send an angel before you*g* [3]to the land flowing with milk and honey. But I myself will not go up in your company, because you are a stiff-necked people; otherwise I might exterminate you on the way." [4]When the people heard this bad news, they went into mourning, and no one wore his ornaments.

[5]The LORD said to Moses, "Tell the Israelites: You are a stiff-necked people. Were I to go up in your company even for a moment, I would exterminate you. Take off your ornaments, therefore; I will then see what I am to do with you." [6]So, from Mount Horeb onward, the Israelites laid aside their ornaments.

Moses' Intimacy with God. [7]The tent,*h* which was called the meeting tent,* Moses used to pitch at some distance away, outside the camp. Anyone who wished to consult the LORD would go to this meeting tent outside the camp. [8]Whenever Moses went out to the tent, the people would all rise and stand at the entrance of their own tents, watching Moses until he entered the tent. [9]As Moses entered the tent, the column of cloud would come down and stand at its entrance while the LORD spoke with Moses. [10]On seeing the column of cloud stand at the entrance of the tent, all the people would rise and worship at the entrance of their own tents. [11]The LORD used to speak to Moses face to face,*i* as one man speaks to another. Moses would then return to the camp, but his young assistant, Joshua, son of Nun, would not move out of the tent.

[12]Moses said to the LORD, "You, indeed, are telling me to lead this people on;*j* but you have not let me know whom you will send with me. Yet you have said, 'You are my intimate friend,' and also, 'You have found favor with me.' [13]Now, if I have found favor with you, do let me know your ways so that, in knowing you, I may continue to find favor with you. Then, too, this nation is, after all, your own people." [14]"I myself,"* the LORD answered, "will go along, to give you rest." [15]Moses replied, "If you are not going yourself, do not make us go up from here. [16]For how can it be known that we, your people and I, have found favor with you, except by your going with us? Then we, your people and I, will be singled out from every other people on the earth." [17]The LORD said to Moses, "This request, too, which you have just made, I will carry out, because you have found favor with me and you are my intimate friend."

[18]Then Moses said, "Do let me see your glory!" [19]He answered, "I will make all my beauty pass before you, and in your presence I will pronounce my name, 'LORD'; I who show favors to whom I will, I who grant mercy to whom I will.*k* [20]But my face you cannot see,*l* for no man sees me and still

---

32, 32: The book that you have written: the list of God's intimate friends. In a similar sense St. Paul wished to be anathema from Christ for the sake of his brethren. Cf Rom 9, 3.

33, 7-11: The meeting tent is mentioned here by anticipation; its actual construction is described in the following chapters.

33, 14: I myself: literally, "my face," that is, "my presence." To give you rest: in the Promised Land; some understand, "to put your mind at rest"; others, by a slight emendation in the text, render, "to lead you."

f: Gn 12, 7. *g:* Ex 23, 23. *h:* Ex 29, 42f. *i:* Nm 12, 8; Dt 34, 10; Sir 45, 4-6. *j:* Ex 32, 34. *k:* Rom 9, 15. *l:* Jn 1, 18; 1 Tm 6, 16.

lives. [21]Here," continued the LORD, "is a place near me where you shall station yourself on the rock. [22]When my glory passes I will set you in the hollow of the rock and will cover you with my hand until I have passed by. [23]Then I will remove my hand, so that you may see my back;* but my face is not to be seen."

See RG 123

CHAPTER 34

Renewal of the Tablets. [1]The LORD said to Moses, "Cut two stone tablets like the former,[m] that I may write on them the commandments which were on the former tablets that you broke. [2]Get ready for tomorrow morning, when you are to go up Mount Sinai and there present yourself to me on the top of the mountain. [3]No one shall come up with you, and no one is even to be seen on any part of the mountain;[n] even the flocks and the herds are not to go grazing toward this mountain." [4]Moses then cut two stone tablets like the former, and early the next morning he went up Mount Sinai as the LORD had commanded him, taking along the two stone tablets.

[5]Having come down in a cloud, the LORD stood with him there and proclaimed his name, "LORD." [6]Thus the LORD passed before him and cried out, "The LORD, the LORD, a merciful and gracious God, slow to anger and rich in kindness and fidelity, [7]continuing his kindness for a thousand generations, and forgiving wickedness and crime and sin; yet not declaring the guilty guiltless, but punishing children and grandchildren to the third and fourth generation for their fathers' wickedness!"[o] [8]Moses at once bowed down to the ground in worship. [9]Then he said, "If I find favor with you, O LORD, do come along in our company. This is indeed a stiff-necked people; yet pardon our wickedness and sins, and receive us as your own."

Religious Laws. [10]"Here, then," said the LORD, "is the covenant I will make. Before the eyes of all your people I will work such marvels as have never been wrought in any nation anywhere on earth, so that this people among whom you live may see how awe-inspiring are the deeds which I, the LORD, will do at your side. [11]But you, on your part, must keep the commandments I am giving you today.[p]

"I will drive out before you the Amorites, Canaanites, Hittites, Perizzites, Hivites, and Jebusites. [12q]Take care, therefore, not to make a covenant with these inhabitants of the land that you are to enter; else they will become a snare among you. [13]Tear down their altars; smash their sacred pillars, and cut down their sacred poles.* [14]You shall not worship any other god, for the LORD is 'the Jealous One';* a jealous God is he. [15]Do not make a covenant with the inhabitants of that land; else, when they render their wanton worship to their gods and sacrifice to them, one of them may invite you and you may partake of his sacrifice. [16]Neither shall you take their daughters as wives for your sons; otherwise, when their daughters render their wanton worship to their gods, they will make your sons do the same.

[17]"You shall not make for yourselves molten gods.[r]

[18]"You shall keep the feast of Unleavened Bread.[s] For seven days at the prescribed time in the month of Abib you are to eat unleavened bread, as I commanded you; for in the month of Abib you came out of Egypt. [19]"To me belongs every first-born male that opens the womb among all your livestock, whether in the herd or in the flock.[t] [20]The firstling of an ass you shall redeem with one of the flock; if you do not redeem it, you must break its neck. The first-born among your sons you shall redeem.

"No one shall appear before me empty-handed.

33, 23: You may see my back: man can see God's glory as reflected in creation, but his "face," that is, God as he is in himself, mortal man cannot behold. Cf 1 Cor 13, 12.

34, 13: Sacred poles: "Ashera" was the name of a Canaanite goddess. In her honor wooden poles (asherot) were erected, just as stone pillars (massebot) were erected in honor of the god Baal. Both were placed near the altar in a Canaanite shrine.

34, 14: The LORD is 'the Jealous One': see note on Ex 20, 5. Some, by a slight emendation, render, "The LORD is jealous for his name." Cf Ez 39, 25.

---

m: Dt 10, 1f. n: Ex 19, 12f. 21. o: 6f: Ex 20, 5f; Nm 14, 18; Dt 5, 9f; Jer 32, 18. p: Ex 13, 5; 33, 2. q: 12-16: Ex 23, 32f; Dt 7, 1-5; 12, 2f. r: Lv 19, 4; 5, 8f. s: Ex 12, 15ff; 13, 3f. t: 19f: Ex 13, 2. 12f; 23, 15.

[21]"For six days you may work,[u] but on the seventh day you shall rest; on that day you must rest even during the seasons of plowing and harvesting.

[22v]"You shall keep the feast of Weeks* with the first of the wheat harvest; likewise, the feast at the fruit harvest at the close of the year. [23]Three times a year all your men shall appear before the Lord, the LORD God of Israel. [24]Since I will drive out the nations before you to give you a large territory, there will be no one to covet your land when you go up three times a year to appear before the LORD, your God.

[25]"You shall not offer me the blood of sacrifice with leavened bread, nor shall the sacrifice of the Passover feast be kept overnight for the next day.

[26]"The choicest first fruits of your soil you shall bring to the house of the LORD, your God.

"You shall not boil a kid in its mother's milk."[w]

Radiance of Moses' Face. [27]Then the LORD said to Moses, "Write down these words, for in accordance with them I have made a covenant with you and with Israel." [28]So Moses stayed there with the LORD for forty days and forty nights,[x] without eating any food or drinking any water, and he wrote on the tablets the words of the covenant, the ten commandments.

[29]As Moses came down from Mount Sinai with the two tablets of the commandments in his hands, he did not know that the skin of his face had become radiant while he conversed with the LORD. [30]When Aaron, then, and the other Israelites saw Moses and noticed how radiant the skin of his face had become, they were afraid to come near him. [31]Only after Moses called to them did Aaron and all the rulers of the community come back to him. Moses then spoke to them. [32]Later on, all the Israelites came up to him,

and he enjoined on them all that the LORD had told him on Mount Sinai. [33]When he finished speaking with them, he put a veil over his face.* [34]Whenever Moses entered the presence of the LORD to converse with him, he removed the veil until he came out again.[y] On coming out, he would tell the Israelites all that had been commanded. [35]Then the Israelites would see that the skin of Moses' face was radiant; so he would again put the veil over his face until he went in to converse with the LORD.

CHAPTER 35

See RG 123

Sabbath Regulations. [1]Moses assembled the whole Israelite community and said to them,[z] "This is what the LORD has commanded to be done. [2]On six days work may be done, but the seventh day shall be sacred to you as the sabbath of complete rest to the LORD. Anyone who does work on that day shall be put to death. [3]You shall not even light a fire in any of your dwellings on the sabbath day."

Collection of Materials. [4]Moses told the whole Israelite community, "This is what the LORD has commanded: [5a]Take up among you a collection for the LORD. Everyone, as his heart prompts him, shall bring, as a contribution to the LORD, gold, silver and bronze; [6]violet, purple and scarlet yarn; fine linen and goat hair; [7]rams' skins dyed red, and tahash skins; acacia wood; [8]oil for the light; spices for the anointing oil and for the fragrant incense; [9]onyx stones and other gems for mounting on the ephod and on the breastpiece.

Call for Artisans. [10b]"Let every expert among you come and make all that the LORD has commanded: [11]the Dwelling, with its tent, its covering, its clasps, its boards, its bars, its columns and its pedestals; [12]the ark, with its poles, the propitiatory, and the curtain veil; [13]the table, with its poles and all its

---

34, 22: Feast of Weeks: the festival of thanksgiving for the harvest, celebrated seven weeks or fifty days after the beginning of the harvest. It was also called Pentecost (fiftieth) and coincided with the giving of the law on Mount Sinai, fifty days after the offering of the first fruits; cf Lv 23, 10f; Dt 16, 9.

34, 33: He put a veil over his face: St. Paul sees in this a symbol of the failure of the Jews to recognize Jesus as the

promised Messiah. The true spiritual meaning of the writings of Moses and the prophets is still veiled from the unbelieving Jews. Cf 2 Cor 3, 7-18.

---

u: Ex 20, 9f.   v: 22f: Ex 23, 16f; Dt 16, 10. 13. 16.   w: 25f: Ex 23, 18f.   x: Ex 24, 18; Dt 9, 9. 18; 10, 2. 4.   y: 33f: 2 Cor 3, 13. 16.   z: 1-3: Ex 31, 13-17.   a: 5-9: Ex 25, 2-7.   b: 10-19: Ex 31, 6-11.

appurtenances, and the showbread; *14*the lampstand, with its appurtenances, the lamps, and the oil for the light; *15*the altar of incense, with its poles; the anointing oil, and the fragrant incense; the entrance curtain for the entrance of the Dwelling; *16*the altar of holocausts, with its bronze grating, its poles, and all its appurtenances; the laver, with its base; *17*the hangings of the court, with their columns and pedestals; the curtain for the entrance of the court; *18*the tent pegs for the Dwelling and for the court, with their ropes; *19*the service cloths for use in the sanctuary; the sacred vestments for Aaron, the priest, and the vestments worn by his sons in their ministry."

The Contribution. *20*When the whole Israelite community left Moses' presence, *21*everyone, as his heart suggested and his spirit prompted, brought a contribution to the LORD for the construction of the meeting tent, for all its services, and for the sacred vestments. *22*Both the men and the women, all as their hearts prompted them, brought brooches, earrings, rings, necklaces and various other gold articles.*c* Everyone who could presented an offering of gold to the LORD. *23*Everyone who happened to have violet, purple or scarlet yarn, fine linen or goat hair, rams' skins dyed red or tahash skins, brought them. *24*Whoever could make a contribution of silver or bronze offered it to the LORD; and everyone who happened to have acacia wood for any part of the work, brought it. *25*All the women who were expert spinners brought hand-spun violet, purple and scarlet yarn and fine linen thread. *26*All the women who possessed the skill, spun goat hair. *27*The princes brought onyx stones and other gems for mounting on the ephod and on the breastpiece; *28*as well as spices, and oil for the light, anointing oil, and fragrant incense. *29*Every Israelite man and woman brought to the LORD such voluntary offerings as they thought best, for the various kinds of work which the LORD had commanded Moses to have done.

The Artisans. *30*Moses said to the Israelites,*d* "See, the LORD has chosen Bezalel,

son of Uri, son of Hur, of the tribe of Judah, *31*and has filled him with a divine spirit of skill and understanding and knowledge in every craft: *32*in the production of embroidery, in making things of gold, silver or bronze, *33*in cutting and mounting precious stones, in carving wood, and in every other craft. *34*He has also given both him and Oholiab, son of Ahisamach, of the tribe of Dan, the ability to teach others. *35*He has endowed them with skill to execute all types of work: engraving, embroidering, the making of variegated cloth of violet, purple and scarlet yarn and fine linen thread, weaving, and all other arts and crafts.

CHAPTER 36

See RG 123

1"Bezalel, therefore, will set to work with Oholiab and with all the experts whom the LORD has endowed with skill and understanding in knowing how to execute all the work for the service of the sanctuary, just as the LORD has commanded."*e*

*2*Moses then called Bezalel and Oholiab and all the other experts whom the LORD had endowed with skill, men whose hearts moved them to come and take part in the work. *3*They received from Moses all the contributions which the Israelites had brought for establishing the service of the sanctuary. Still, morning after morning the people continued to bring their voluntary offerings to Moses. *4*Thereupon the experts who were executing the various kinds of work for the sanctuary, all left the work they were doing, *5*and told Moses, "The people are bringing much more than is needed to carry out the work which the LORD has commanded us to do." *6*Moses, therefore, ordered a proclamation to be made throughout the camp: "Let neither man nor woman make any more contributions for the sanctuary." So the people stopped bringing their offerings; *7*there was already enough at hand, in fact, more than enough, to complete the work to be done.

The Tent Cloth and Coverings. *8f*The various experts who were executing the

c: 22-28: Ex 25, 3-7.   d: 30-35: Ex 31, 1-6.   e: 1f: Ex 31, 1. 6.   f: 8-19: Ex 26, 1-14.

work, made the Dwelling with its ten sheets woven of fine linen twined, having cherubim embroidered on them with violet, purple and scarlet yarn. ⁹The length of each sheet was twenty-eight cubits, and the width four cubits; all the sheets were of the same size. ¹⁰Five of the sheets were sewed together, edge to edge; and the same for the other five. ¹¹Loops of violet yarn were made along the edge of the end sheet in the first set, and the same along the edge of the end sheet in the second set. ¹²Fifty loops were thus put on one inner sheet, and fifty loops on the inner sheet in the other set, with the loops directly opposite each other. ¹³Then fifty clasps of gold were made, with which the sheets were joined so that the Dwelling formed one whole.

¹⁴Sheets of goat hair were also woven as a tent over the Dwelling. Eleven such sheets were made. ¹⁵The length of each sheet was thirty cubits and the width four cubits; all eleven sheets were of the same size. ¹⁶Five of these sheets were sewed edge to edge into one set; and the other six sheets into another set. ¹⁷Fifty loops were made along the edge of the end sheet in one set, and fifty loops along the edge of the corresponding sheet in the other set. ¹⁸Fifty bronze clasps were made with which the tent was joined so that it formed one whole. ¹⁹A covering for the tent was made of rams' skins dyed red, and above that, a covering of tahash skins.

The Boards. ²⁰ᵍBoards of acacia wood were made as walls for the Dwelling. ²¹The length of each board was ten cubits, and the width one and a half cubits. ²²Each board had two arms, fastening them in line. In this way all the boards of the Dwelling were made. ²³They were set up as follows: twenty boards on the south side, ²⁴with forty silver pedestals under the twenty boards, so that there were two pedestals under each board, at its two arms; ²⁵twenty boards on the other side of the Dwelling, the north side, ²⁶with their forty silver pedestals, two under each board; ²⁷six boards at the rear of the Dwelling, to the west; ²⁸and two boards at the corners in the rear of the Dwelling.

²⁹These were double at the bottom, and likewise double at the top, to the first ring. That is how both boards in the corners were made. ³⁰Thus, there were in the rear eight boards, with their sixteen silver pedestals, two pedestals under each board. ³¹Bars of acacia wood were also made, five for the boards on one side of the Dwelling, ³²five for those on the other side, and five for those at the rear, to the west. ³³The center bar, at the middle of the boards, was made to reach across from end to end. ³⁴The boards were plated with gold, and gold rings were made on them as holders for the bars, which were also plated with gold.

The Veil. ³⁵ʰThe veil was woven of violet, purple and scarlet yarn, and of fine linen twined, with cherubim embroidered on it. ³⁶Four gold-plated columns of acacia wood, with gold hooks, were made for it, and four silver pedestals were cast for them.

³⁷The curtain for the entrance of the tent was made of violet, purple and scarlet yarn, and of fine linen twined, woven in a variegated manner. ³⁸Its five columns, with their hooks as well as their capitals and bands, were plated with gold; their five pedestals were of bronze.

CHAPTER 37

See RG 123

The Ark. ¹Bezalel made the ark of acacia wood, two and a half cubits long, one and a half cubits wide, and one and a half cubits high. ²The inside and outside were plated with gold, and a molding of gold was put around it. ³Four gold rings were cast and put on its four supports, two rings for one side and two for the opposite side. ⁴Poles of acacia wood were made and plated with gold; ⁵these were put through the rings on the sides of the ark, for carrying it.

⁶The propitiatory was made of pure gold, two and a half cubits long and one and a half cubits wide. ⁷Two cherubim of beaten gold were made for the two ends of the propitiatory, ⁸one cherub fastened at one end, the other at the other end, springing directly from the propitiatory at its two ends. ⁹The cherubim had their wings spread out above,

g: 20-34: Ex 26, 15-29.   h: 35-38: Ex 26, 31-37.

covering the propitiatory with them. They were turned toward each other, but with their faces looking toward the propitiatory.[i]

The Table. [10j]The table was made of acacia wood, two cubits long, one cubit wide, and one and a half cubits high. [11]It was plated with pure gold, and a molding of gold was put around it. [12]A frame a handbreadth high was also put around it, with a molding of gold around the frame. [13]Four rings of gold were cast for it and fastened, one at each of the four corners. [14]The rings were alongside the frame as holders for the poles to carry the table. [15]These poles were made of acacia wood and plated with gold. [16]The vessels that were set on the table, its plates and cups, as well as its pitchers and bowls for pouring libations, were of pure gold.

The Lampstand. [17k]The lampstand was made of pure beaten gold—its shaft and branches as well as its cups and knobs and petals springing directly from it. [18]Six branches extended from its sides, three branches on one side and three on the other. [19]On one branch there were three cups, shaped like almond blossoms, each with its knob and petals; on the opposite branch there were three cups, shaped like almond blossoms, each with its knob and petals; and so for the six branches that extended from the lampstand. [20]On the shaft there were four cups, shaped like almond blossoms, with their knobs and petals, [21]including a knob below each of the three pairs of branches that extended from the lampstand. [22]The knobs and branches sprang so directly from it that the whole formed but a single piece of pure beaten gold. [23]Its seven lamps, as well as its trimming shears and trays, were made of pure gold. [24]A talent of pure gold was used for the lampstand and its various appurtenances.

The Altar of Incense. [25l]The altar of incense was made of acacia wood, on a square, a cubit long, a cubit wide, and two cubits high, having horns that sprang directly from it. [26]Its grate on top, its walls on all four sides, and its horns were plated with pure gold; and a molding of gold was put around it. [27]Underneath the molding gold rings were placed, two on one side and two on the opposite side, as holders for the poles to carry it. [28]The poles, too, were made of acacia wood and plated with gold.

[29]The sacred anointing oil and the fragrant incense were prepared in their pure form by a perfumer.[m]

CHAPTER 38

See RG 123

The Altar of Holocausts. [1]The altar of holocausts[n] was made of acacia wood, on a square, five cubits long and five cubits wide; its height was three cubits. [2]At the four corners horns were made that sprang directly from the altar. The whole was plated with bronze. [3]All the utensils of the altar, the pots, shovels, basins, forks and fire pans, were likewise made of bronze. [4]A grating of bronze network was made for the altar and placed round it, on the ground, half as high as the altar itself. [5]Four rings were cast for the four corners of the bronze grating, as holders for the poles, [6]which were made of acacia wood and plated with bronze. [7]The poles were put through the rings on the sides of the altar for carrying it. The altar was made in the form of a hollow box.

[8]The bronze laver,[o] with its bronze base, was made from the mirrors of the women who served[*] at the entrance of the meeting tent.

The Court. [9p]The court was made as follows. On the south side of the court there were hangings, woven of fine linen twined, a hundred cubits long, [10]with twenty columns and twenty pedestals of bronze, the hooks and bands of the columns being of silver. [11]On the north side there were similar hangings, one hundred cubits long, with twenty columns and twenty pedestals of bronze, the hooks and bands of the columns being of silver. [12]On the west side there were hangings, fifty cubits long, with ten

---

38, 8: The reflecting surface of ancient mirrors was usually of polished bronze. The women who served: cf 1 Sm 2, 22.

i: 1-9: Ex 25, 10-22.   j: 10-16: Ex 25, 23-30.   k: 17-24: Ex 25, 31-39.   l: 25-28: Ex 30, 1-5.   m: Ex 30, 23ff. 34ff.   n: 1-7: Ex 27, 1-8; 2 Chr 1, 5.   o: Ex 30, 18-21.   p: 9-20: Ex 27, 9-19.

columns and ten pedestals, the hooks and bands of the columns being of silver. [13]On the east side the court was fifty cubits long. [14]Toward one side there were hangings to the extent of fifteen cubits, with three columns and three pedestals; [15]toward the other side, beyond the entrance of the court, there were likewise hangings to the extent of fifteen cubits, with three columns and three pedestals. [16]The hangings on all sides of the court were woven of fine linen twined. [17]The pedestals of the columns were of bronze, while the hooks and bands of the columns were of silver; the capitals were silver-plated, and all the columns of the court were banded with silver.

[18]At the entrance of the court there was a variegated curtain, woven of violet, purple and scarlet yarn and of fine linen twined, twenty cubits long and five cubits wide, in keeping with the hangings of the court. [19]There were four columns and four pedestals of bronze for it, while their hooks were of silver. [20]All the tent pegs for the Dwelling and for the court around it were of bronze.

Amount of Metal Used. [21]The following is an account of the various amounts used on the Dwelling, the Dwelling of the commandments, drawn up at the command of Moses by the Levites under the direction of Ithamar, son of Aaron the priest. [22]However, it was Bezalel, son of Uri,[q] son of Hur, of the tribe of Judah, who made all that the Lord commanded Moses, [23]and he was assisted by Oholiab, son of Ahisamach, of the tribe of Dan, who was an engraver, an embroiderer, and a weaver of variegated cloth of violet, purple and scarlet yarn and of fine linen.

[24]All the gold used in the entire construction of the sanctuary, having previously been given as an offering, amounted to twenty-nine talents and seven hundred and thirty shekels, according to the standard of the sanctuary shekel. [25]The amount of the silver received from the community was one hundred talents and one thousand seven hundred and seventy-five shekels, according to the standard of the sanctuary shekel; [26]one bekah apiece, that is, a half-shekel apiece, according to the standard of the sanctuary shekel, was received from every man of twenty years or more who entered the registered group; the number of these was six hundred and three thousand five hundred and fifty men.[r] [27]One hundred talents of silver were used for casting the pedestals of the sanctuary and the pedestals of the veil, one talent for each pedestal, or one hundred talents for the one hundred pedestals. [28]The remaining one thousand seven hundred and seventy-five shekels were used for making the hooks on the columns, for plating the capitals, and for banding them with silver. [29]The bronze, given as an offering, amounted to seventy talents and two thousand four hundred shekels. [30]With this were made the pedestals at the entrance of the meeting tent, the bronze altar with its bronze gratings and all the appurtenances of the altar, [31]the pedestals around the court, the pedestals at the entrance of the court, and all the tent pegs for the Dwelling and for the court around it.

CHAPTER 39

See RG 123

The Vestments. [1]With violet, purple and scarlet yarn were woven the service cloths for use in the sanctuary, as well as the sacred vestments[s] for Aaron, as the LORD had commanded Moses.

[2]The ephod was woven of gold thread and of violet, purple and scarlet yarn and of fine linen twined. [3]Gold was first hammered into gold leaf and then cut up into threads, which were woven with the violet, purple and scarlet yarn into an embroidered pattern on the fine linen. [4]Shoulder straps were made for it and joined to its two upper ends. [5]The embroidered belt on the ephod extended out from it, and like it, was made of gold thread, of violet, purple and scarlet yarn, and of fine linen twined, as the LORD had commanded Moses. [6]The onyx stones were prepared and mounted in gold filigree work; they were engraved like seal engravings with the names of the sons of Israel.

q: 22f: Ex 31, 2. 6; 35, 30. 34; 36, 1.   *r:* Nm 1, 46.   *s:* Ex 31, 10.   *t:* 2-10: Ex 28, 6-12.

[7]These stones were set on the shoulder straps of the ephod as memorial stones of the sons of Israel, just as the LORD had commanded Moses.

[8u]The breastpiece was embroidered like the ephod, with gold thread and violet, purple and scarlet yarn on cloth of fine linen twined. [9]It was square and folded double, a span high and a span wide in its folded form. [10]Four rows of precious stones were mounted on it: in the first row a carnelian, a topaz and an emerald; [11]in the second row, a garnet, a sapphire and a beryl; [12]in the third row a jacinth, an agate and an amethyst; [13]in the fourth row a chrysolite, an onyx and a jasper. They were mounted in gold filigree work. [14]These stones were twelve, to match the names of the sons of Israel, and each stone was engraved like a seal with the name of one of the twelve tribes.

[15v]Chains of pure gold, twisted like cords, were made for the breastpiece, [16]together with two gold filigree rosettes and two gold rings. The two rings were fastened to the two upper ends of the breastpiece. [17]The two gold chains were then fastened to the two rings at the ends of the breastpiece. [18]The other two ends of the two chains were fastened in front to the two filigree rosettes, which were attached to the shoulder straps of the ephod. [19]Two other gold rings were made and put on the two lower ends of the breastpiece, on the edge facing the ephod. [20]Two more gold rings were made and fastened to the bottom of the two shoulder straps next to where they joined the ephod in front, just above its embroidered belt. [21]Violet ribbons bound the rings of the breastpiece to the rings of the ephod, so that the breastpiece stayed right above the embroidered belt of the ephod and did not swing loose from it. All this was just as the LORD had commanded Moses.

The Other Vestments. [22]The robe of the ephod was woven entirely of violet yarn, [23]with an opening in its center like the opening of a shirt, with selvage around the opening to keep it from being torn. [24]At the hem of the robe pomegranates were made of vio-let, purple and scarlet yarn and of fine linen twined; [25]bells of pure gold were also made and put between the pomegranates all around the hem of the robe: [26]first a bell, then a pomegranate, and thus alternating all around the hem of the robe which was to be worn in performing the ministry—all this, just as the LORD had commanded Moses.

[27]For Aaron and his sons there were also woven tunics of fine linen;[w] [28]the miter of fine linen; the ornate turbans of fine linen; drawers of linen [of fine linen twined]; [29]and sashes of variegated work made of fine linen twined and of violet, purple and scarlet yarn, as the LORD had commanded Moses. [30]The plate of the sacred diadem was made of pure gold[x] and inscribed, as on a seal engraving: "Sacred to the LORD." [31]It was tied over the miter with a violet ribbon, as the LORD had commanded Moses.

Presentation of the Work to Moses. [32]Thus the entire work of the Dwelling of the meeting tent was completed. The Israelites did the work just as the LORD had commanded Moses. [33]They then brought to Moses the Dwelling, the tent with all its appurtenances, the clasps, the boards, the bars, the columns, the pedestals, [34]the covering of rams' skins dyed red, the covering of tahash skins, the curtain veil; [35]the ark of the commandments with its poles, the propitiatory, [36]the table with all its appurtenances and the showbread, [37]the pure gold lampstand with its lamps set up on it and with all its appurtenances, the oil for the light, [38]the golden altar, the anointing oil, the fragrant incense; the curtain for the entrance of the tent, [39]the altar of bronze with its bronze grating, its poles and all its appurtenances, the laver with its base, [40]the hangings of the court with their columns and pedestals, the curtain for the entrance of the court with its ropes and tent pegs, all the equipment for the service of the Dwelling of the meeting tent; [41]the service cloths for use in the sanctuary, the sacred vestments for Aaron the priest, and the vestments to be worn by his sons in their ministry. [42]The Israelites had carried out all the work just as the LORD had com-

u: 8-14: Ex 28, 15-21.   *v:* 15-21: Ex 28, 31-35.   *w:* 27ff: Ex 28, 39-42.   *x:* 30f: Ex 28, 36f.

manded Moses. [43]So when Moses saw that all the work was done just as the LORD had commanded, he blessed them.

CHAPTER 40

See RG 123

Erection of the Dwelling. [1]Then the LORD said to Moses, [2]y"On the first day of the first month* you shall erect the Dwelling of the meeting tent.[z] [3]Put the ark of the commandments in it, and screen off the ark with the veil.[a] [4]Bring in the table and set it. Then bring in the lampstand and set up the lamps on it. [5]Put the golden altar of incense in front of the ark of the commandments, and hang the curtain at the entrance of the Dwelling. [6]Put the altar of holocausts in front of the entrance of the Dwelling of the meeting tent. [7]Place the laver between the meeting tent and the altar, and put water in it. [8]Set up the court round about, and put the curtain at the entrance of the court.

[9b]"Take the anointing oil and anoint the Dwelling and everything in it, consecrating it and all its furnishings, so that it will be sacred. [10]Anoint the altar of holocausts and all its appurtenances, consecrating it, so that it will be most sacred. [11]Likewise, anoint the laver with its base, and thus consecrate it.

[12c]"Then bring Aaron and his sons to the entrance of the meeting tent, and there wash them with water. [13]Clothe Aaron with the sacred vestments and anoint him, thus consecrating him as my priest. [14]Bring forward his sons also, and clothe them with the tunics. [15]As you have anointed their father, anoint them also as my priests. Thus, by being anointed, they shall receive a perpetual priesthood throughout all future generations."

[16]Moses did exactly as the LORD had commanded him. [17]On the first day of the first month of the second year the Dwelling was erected. [18]It was Moses who erected the Dwelling. He placed its pedestals, set up its boards, put in its bars, and set up its columns. [19]He spread the tent over the Dwelling and put the covering on top of the tent, as the LORD had commanded him. [20d]He took the

commandments and put them in the ark; he placed poles alongside the ark and set the propitiatory upon it. [21]He brought the ark into the Dwelling and hung the curtain veil, thus screening off the ark of the commandments, as the LORD had commanded him. [22]He put the table in the meeting tent, on the north side of the Dwelling, outside the veil, [23]and arranged the bread on it before the LORD, as the LORD had commanded him.[e] [24]He placed the lampstand in the meeting tent, opposite the table, on the south side of the Dwelling, [25]and he set up the lamps before the LORD, as the LORD had commanded him. [26]He placed the golden altar in the meeting tent, in front of the veil, [27]and on it he burned fragrant incense, as the LORD had commanded him. [28]He hung the curtain at the entrance of the Dwelling. [29]He put the altar of holocausts in front of the entrance of the Dwelling of the meeting tent, and offered holocausts and cereal offerings on it, as the LORD had commanded him. [30f]He placed the laver between the meeting tent and the altar, and put water in it for washing. [31]Moses and Aaron and his sons used to wash their hands and feet there, [32]for they washed themselves whenever they went into the meeting tent or approached the altar, as the LORD commanded Moses. [33]Finally, he set up the court around the Dwelling and the altar and hung the curtain at the entrance of the court. Thus Moses finished all the work.

God's Presence in the Dwelling. [34g]Then the cloud covered the meeting tent, and the glory of the LORD filled the Dwelling. [35]Moses could not enter the meeting tent, because the cloud settled down upon it and the glory of the LORD filled the Dwelling. [36]Whenever the cloud rose from the Dwelling, the Israelites would set out on their journey. [37]But if the cloud did not lift, they would not go forward; only when it lifted did they go forward. [38]In the daytime the cloud of the LORD was seen over the Dwelling; whereas at night, fire was seen in the cloud by the whole house of Israel in all the stages of their journey.

40, 2: On the first day of the first month: almost a year after the departure of the Israelites from Egypt. Cf v 17.

y: 2-8: Ex 40, 16-33.   z: Ex 26, 30.   a: 3ff: Ex 26, 33ff.   b: 9ff: Ex 30, 26-29.   c: 12-15: Ex 28, 41; 29, 4-9; Lv 8, 1-13.   d: 20ff: Ex 25, 16, 21; 26, 33ff.   e: Ex 25, 30.   f: 30ff: Ex 30, 18ff.   g: 34-38; Nm 9, 15-22.

See RG
125–33

The Book of Leviticus

The name "Leviticus" was bestowed on the third book of the Pentateuch by the ancient Greek translators because a good part of this book consists of sacrificial and other ritual laws prescribed for the priests of the tribe of Levi.

Continuing the legislation given by God to Moses at Mount Sinai, Leviticus is almost entirely legislative in character; the rare narrative portions are subordinate to the main legislative theme. Generally speaking, the laws contained in this book serve to teach the Israelites that they should always keep themselves in a state of legal purity, or external sanctity, as a sign of their intimate union with the Lord. Accordingly, the central idea of Leviticus is contained in its oft-repeated injunction: "You shall be holy, because I, the LORD, am holy."

The main divisions of Leviticus are:

I: Ritual of Sacrifices (1—7).

II: Ceremony of Ordination (8—10).

III: Laws regarding Legal Purity (11—16).

IV: Code of Legal Holiness (17—26).

V: Redemption of Offerings (27).

I: Ritual of Sacrifices

See RG
128

CHAPTER 1

Holocausts. ¹The LORD called Moses, and from the meeting tent gave him this message: ²ᵃ"Speak to the Israelites and tell them: When any one of you wishes to bring an animal offering to the LORD, such an offering must be from the herd or from the flock.*

³"If his holocaust* offering is from the herd, it must be a male without blemish.ᵇ To find favor with the LORD, he shall bring it to the entrance of the meeting tent ⁴and there lay his hand on the head of the holocaust, so that it may be acceptable to make atonement for him.ᶜ ⁵He shall then slaughter the bull before the LORD, but Aaron's sons, the priests, shall offer up its blood by splashing it on the sides of the altar which is at the entrance of the meeting tent.ᵈ ⁶Then he shall skin the holocaust and cut it up into pieces. ⁷After Aaron's sons, the priests, have put some burning embers on the altar and laid some wood on them, ⁸they shall lay the pieces of meat, together with the head and the suet, on top of the wood and embers on the altar. ⁹The inner organs and the shanks, however, the offerer shall first wash with water. The priest shall then burn the whole offering on the altar as a holocaust, a sweet-smelling oblation to the LORD.ᵉ

¹⁰"If his holocaust offering is from the flock, that is, a sheep or a goat, he must bring a male without blemish. ¹¹This he shall slaughter before the LORD at the north side of the altar. Then Aaron's sons, the priests, shall splash its blood on the sides of the altar. ¹²When the offerer has cut it up into pieces, the priest shall lay these, together with the head and suet, on top of the wood and the fire on the altar. ¹³The inner organs and the shanks, however, the offerer shall first wash with water. The priest shall offer them up and then burn the whole offering on the altar as a holocaust, a sweet-smelling oblation to the LORD.

¹⁴"If he offers a bird as a holocaust to the LORD, he shall choose a turtledove or a pigeon as his offering.ᶠ ¹⁵Having brought it to the altar where it is to be burned, the priest shall snap its head loose and squeeze out its blood against the side of the altar.ᵍ ¹⁶Its crop and feathers shall be removed and thrown on the ash heap at the east side of the altar.

1, 2: From the herd or from the flock: the only animals which could be used as sacrificial victims were either of the bovine class (bulls, cows and calves) or the ovine class (sheep and lambs, goats and kids). Excluded, therefore, were not only all wild animals, but also such "unclean" domestic animals as the camel and the ass. See note on Lv 11, 1ff.

1, 3: Holocaust: from the Greek word meaning "wholly burned," this is the technical term for the special type of sacrifice in which an entire animal except its hide was consumed in the fire on the altar. The primary purpose of this complete gift was to render glory and praise to God.

---

a: Lv 22, 18. 19. *b:* Ex 12, 5. *c:* Lv 3, 2. 8. 13; 4, 15; 8, 14. 22; 16, 21; Ex 29, 10. 15. *d:* Lv 3, 8. *e:* Lv 3, 5. 16; Ex 29, 18. *f:* Lv 5, 7; 12, 8; Lk 2, 24. *g:* Lv 5, 8.

[17]Then, having split the bird down the middle without separating the halves, the priest shall burn it on the altar, over the wood on the fire, as a holocaust, a sweet-smelling oblation to the LORD.

CHAPTER 2

See RG 128

Cereal Offerings. [1]"When anyone wishes to bring a cereal offering to the LORD, his offering must consist of fine flour. He shall pour oil on it and put frankincense over it.[h] [2]When he has brought it to Aaron's sons, the priests, one of them shall take a handful of this fine flour and oil, together with all the frankincense, and this he shall burn on the altar as a token offering,* a sweet-smelling oblation to the LORD.[i] [3]The rest of the cereal offering belongs to Aaron and his sons. It is a most sacred oblation to the LORD.[j]

[4]"When the cereal offering you present is baked in an oven, it must be in the form of unleavened cakes made of fine flour mixed with oil, or of unleavened wafers spread with oil. [5]If you present a cereal offering that is fried on a griddle, it must be of fine flour mixed with oil and unleavened.[k] [6]Such a cereal offering must be broken into pieces, and oil must be poured over it. [7]If you present a cereal offering that is prepared in a pot, it must be of fine flour, deep-fried in oil. [8]A cereal offering that is made in any of these ways you shall bring to the LORD, offering it to the priest, who shall take it to the altar. [9]Its token offering the priest shall then lift from the cereal offering and burn on the altar as a sweet-smelling oblation to the LORD. [10]The rest of the cereal offering belongs to Aaron and his sons. It is a most sacred oblation to the LORD.

[11]"Every cereal offering that you present to the LORD shall be unleavened, for you shall not burn any leaven or honey as an oblation to the LORD.[l] [12]Such you may indeed present to the LORD in the offering of first fruits, but they are not to be placed on the altar for a pleasing odor. [13]However, every cereal offering that you present to the LORD shall be seasoned with salt.[m] Do not let the salt of the covenant of your God* be lacking from your cereal offering. On every offering you shall offer salt.

[14]"If you present a cereal offering of first fruits to the LORD, you shall offer it in the form of fresh grits of new ears of grain, roasted by fire. [15]On this cereal offering you shall put oil and frankincense. [16]For its token offering the priest shall then burn some of the grits and oil, together with all the frankincense, as an oblation to the LORD.

CHAPTER 3

See RG 128

Peace Offerings. [1]"If someone in presenting a peace offering* makes his offering from the herd, he may offer before the LORD either a male or a female animal, but it must be without blemish.[n] [2]He shall lay his hand on the head of his offering,[o] and then slaughter it at the entrance of the meeting tent; but Aaron's sons, the priests, shall splash its blood on the sides of the altar. [3]From the peace offering he shall offer as an oblation to the LORD the fatty membrane over the inner organs, and all the fat that adheres to them,[p] [4]as well as the two kidneys, with the fat on them near the loins, and the lobe of the liver,* which he shall sever above the kidneys. [5]All this Aaron's sons shall then burn on the altar with the holocaust,[q] on the wood over the fire, as a sweet-smelling oblation to the LORD.

[6]"If the peace offering he presents to the

2, 2: Token offering: literally, "reminder." Instead of burning the whole cereal offering, they burned only this part of it on the altar; it thus corresponded to the fat of the peace offering. See note on Lv 3, 1.

2, 13: The salt of the covenant of your God: the partaking in common of salt by those seated together at table was an ancient symbol of friendship and alliance. Cf Mk 9, 49 and Col 4, 6; and see note on Nm 18, 19.

3, 1: Peace offering: thus the ancient versions have rendered the Hebrew word, which perhaps means more exactly, "fulfillment sacrifice," offered up in fulfillment of a vow. Cf

Prv 7, 14. Its characteristic feature was the sacred banquet at which the offerer and his guests partook of the meat of the sacrificed animal. Cf Lv 7, 11-21.

3, 4: The lobe of the liver: some render, "the fatty covering of the liver."

h: Nm 15, 4. *i:* Lv 6, 15. *j:* Lv 7, 9f; Sir 7, 31; 1 Cor 9, 13. *k:* 1 Chr 23, 29. *l:* Lv 6, 16f; Mt 16, 12; Mk 8, 15; Lk 12, 1; 1 Cor 5, 7; Gal 5, 9. *m:* Ez 43, 24. *n:* Lv 22, 21. *o:* Lv 1, 4. *p:* Ex 29, 13. 22. *q:* Lv 6, 12.

LORD is from the flock, he may offer either a male or a female animal, but it must be without blemish. [7]If he presents a lamb as his offering, he shall bring it before the LORD, [8]and after laying his hand on the head of his offering, he shall slaughter it before the meeting tent; but Aaron's sons shall splash its blood on the sides of the altar. [9]As an oblation to the LORD he shall present the fat of the peace offering: the whole fatty tail,* which he must sever close to the spine, the fatty membrane over the inner organs, and all the fat that adheres to them,[r] [10]as well as the two kidneys, with the fat on them near the loins, and the lobe of the liver, which he must sever above the kidneys. [11]All this the priest shall burn on the altar as the food of the LORD's oblation.

[12]"If he presents a goat, he shall bring it before the LORD, [13]and after laying his hand on its head, he shall slaughter it before the meeting tent; but Aaron's sons shall splash its blood on the sides of the altar. [14]From it he shall offer as an oblation to the LORD the fatty membrane over the inner organs, and all the fat that adheres to them, [15]as well as the two kidneys, with the fat on them near the loins, and the lobe of the liver, which he must sever above the kidneys. [16]All this the priest shall burn on the altar as the food of the sweet-smelling oblation. All the fat belongs to the LORD. [17]This shall be a perpetual ordinance for your descendants wherever they may dwell. You shall not partake of any fat* or any blood."[s]

CHAPTER 4

Sin Offerings: For Priests. [1]The LORD said to Moses, [2]"Tell the Israelites: When a person inadvertently commits a sin* against some command of the LORD by doing one of the forbidden things,[t] [3]if it is the anointed priest* who thus sins and thereby makes the people also become guilty, he shall present to the LORD a young, unblemished bull as a sin offering for the sin he committed.[u] [4]Bringing the bullock to the entrance of the meeting tent, before the LORD, he shall lay his hand on its head and slaughter it before the LORD.[v] [5]The anointed priest shall then take some of the bullock's blood and bring it into the meeting tent, [6]where, dipping his finger in the blood, he shall sprinkle it seven times before the LORD, toward the veil of the sanctuary.[w] [7]The priest shall also put some of the blood on the horns of the altar[x] of fragrant incense which is before the LORD in the meeting tent. The rest of the bullock's blood he shall pour out at the base of the altar of holocausts which is at the entrance of the meeting tent. [8]From the sin-offering bullock he shall remove all the fat: the fatty membrane over the inner organs, and all the fat that adheres to them, [9]as well as the two kidneys, with the fat on them near the loins, and the lobe of the liver, which he must sever above the kidneys. [10]This is the same as is removed from the ox of the peace offering; and the priest shall burn it on the altar of holocausts. [11]The hide of the bullock and all its flesh, with its head, legs, inner organs and offal,[y] [12]in short, the whole bullock, shall be brought outside the camp to a clean place where the ashes are deposited and there be burned up in a wood fire. At the place of the ash heap, there it must be burned.

For the Community. [13]"If the whole community of Israel inadvertently and without even being aware of it does something that the LORD has forbidden and thus makes itself guilty,[z] [14]should it later on become known that the sin was committed, the community shall present a young bull as a sin offering. They shall bring it before the meeting tent, [15]and here, before the LORD, the elders of the community shall lay their hands on the bullock's head.[a] When the bullock has

---

3, 9: The whole fatty tail: see note on Ex 29, 22.

3, 17: Any fat: only the fat mentioned in vv 9f. 14f is meant; other fat could be eaten by the Israelites.

4, 2: A sin: not necessarily a moral fault; included are all the cases of ritual uncleanness which people necessarily incurred in certain unavoidable circumstances.

4, 3: The anointed priest: his violation of the ceremonial law brought a sort of collective guilt on all the people whom

he represented before God. Sin offering: more exactly, "sacrifice for remitting sin"; sin is here understood as explained above.

r: Lv 9, 19. *s:* Lv 17, 10-14; Gn 9, 4; Dt 12, 16. 23; 15, 23. *t:* Lv 5, 15. 17; Nm 15, 22-29. *u:* Heb 7, 27. *v:* Lv 1, 3f. *w:* Lv 8, 11. *x:* Lv 8, 15; 9, 9; 16, 18; Ex 29, 12. *y:* Lv 8, 17; 9, 11; Ex 29, 14; Nm 19, 5. *z:* Lv 5, 2-4; Nm 15, 24-26. *a:* Lv 1, 4.

been slaughtered before the LORD, *16*the anointed priest shall bring some of its blood into the meeting tent, *17*and dipping his finger in the blood, he shall sprinkle it seven times before the LORD, toward the veil. *18*He shall also put some of the blood on the horns of the altar of fragrant incense which is before the LORD in the meeting tent. The rest of the blood he shall pour out at the base of the altar of holocausts which is at the entrance of the meeting tent. *19*All of its fat he shall take from it and burn on the altar, *20*doing with this bullock just as he did with the other sin-offering bullock. Thus the priest shall make atonement for them, and they will be forgiven. *21*This bullock must also be brought outside the camp and burned, just as has been prescribed for the other one. This is the sin offering for the community.

For the Princes. *22*"Should a prince commit a sin inadvertently by doing one of the things which are forbidden by some commandment of the LORD, his God, and thus become guilty, *23*if later on he learns of the sin he committed, he shall bring as his offering an unblemished male goat. *24*Having laid his hands on its head, he shall slaughter the goat as a sin offering before the LORD, in the place where the holocausts are slaughtered. *25*The priest shall then take some of the blood of the sin offering on his finger and put it on the horns of the altar of holocausts. The rest of the blood he shall pour out at the base of this altar. *26*All of the fat he shall burn on the altar like the fat of the peace offering.*b* Thus the priest shall make atonement for the prince's sin, and it will be forgiven.

For Private Persons. *27*"If a private person commits a sin inadvertently*c* by doing one of the things which are forbidden by the commandments of the LORD, and thus becomes guilty, *28*should he later on learn of the sin he committed, he shall bring an unblemished she-goat as the offering for his sin. *29*Having laid his hand on the head of the sin offering,*d* he shall slaughter it at the place of the holocausts. *30*The priest shall then take

some of its blood on his finger and put it on the horns of the altar of holocausts. The rest of the blood he shall pour out at the base of the altar. *31*All the fat shall be removed, just as the fat is removed from the peace offering, and the priest shall burn it on the altar for an odor pleasing to the LORD.*e* Thus the priest shall make atonement for him, and he will be forgiven.

32"If, however, for his sin offering he presents a lamb, he shall bring an unblemished female. *33*Having laid his hand on its head, he shall slaughter this sin offering in the place where the holocausts are slaughtered. *34*The priest shall then take some of the blood of the sin offering on his finger and put it on the horns of the altar of holocausts. The rest of the blood he shall pour out at the base of the altar. *35*All the fat shall be removed, just as the fat is removed from the peace-offering lamb,*f* and the priest shall burn it on the altar with the other oblations of the LORD. Thus the priest shall make atonement for the man's sin, and it will be forgiven.

CHAPTER 5

For Special Cases. *1*"If any person refuses to give the information which, as a witness of something he has seen or learned, he has been adjured to give, and thus commits a sin and has guilt to bear;*g* *2*or if someone, without being aware of it, touches any unclean thing, as the carcass of an unclean wild animal,*h* or that of an unclean domestic animal, or that of an unclean swarming creature, and thus becomes unclean and guilty; *3*or if someone, without being aware of it, touches some human uncleanness, whatever kind of uncleanness this may be, and then recognizes his guilt; *4*or if someone, without being aware of it, rashly utters an oath*i* to do good or evil, such as men are accustomed to utter rashly, and then recognizes that he is guilty of such an oath; *5*then whoever is guilty in any of these cases shall confess the sin he has incurred,*j* *6*and as his sin offering for the sin

See RG 128

---

b: Lv 3, 3-5.   *c:* Nm 15, 27.   *d:* Lv 1, 4.   *e:* Lv 1, 9; 3, 3-5.   *f:* Lv 3, 9.   *g:* Prv 29, 24.   *h:* Lv 11, 24. 31. 39; 12; 13; 15.   *i:* Jgs 11, 30f; 1 Sm 14, 24; Mk 6, 23; Acts 23, 12.   *j:* Lv 26, 40; Nm 5, 7.

he has committed he shall bring to the L ORD a female animal from the flock, a ewe lamb or a she-goat. The priest shall then make atonement for his sin.

[7] "If, however, he cannot afford an animal of the flock, he shall bring to the L ORD as the sin offering for his sin two turtledoves or two pigeons, one for a sin offering and the other for a holocaust.[k] [8] He shall bring them to the priest, who shall offer the one for the sin offering first. Snapping its head loose at the neck, yet without breaking it off completely,[l] [9] he shall sprinkle some of the blood of the sin offering against the side of the altar.[m] The rest of the blood shall be squeezed out against the base of the altar. Such is the offering for sin. [10] The other bird shall be offered as a holocaust in the usual way. Thus the priest shall make atonement for the sin the man committed, and it will be forgiven. [11] "If he is unable to afford even two turtledoves or two pigeons, he shall present as a sin offering for his sin one tenth of an ephah of fine flour. He shall not put oil or frankincense on it, because it is a sin offering. [12] When he has brought it to the priest, the latter shall take a handful of this flour as a token offering, and this he shall burn as a sin offering on the altar with the other oblations of the L ORD. [13] Thus the priest shall make atonement for the sin that the man committed in any of the above cases, and it will be forgiven.[n] The rest of the flour, like the cereal offerings, shall belong to the priest."

Guilt Offerings. [14] The L ORD said to Moses, [15] "If someone commits a sin by inadvertently cheating* in the L ORD's sacred dues, he shall bring to the L ORD as his guilt offering an unblemished ram from the flock, valued at two silver shekels according to the standard of the sanctuary shekel. [16] He shall also restore what he has sinfully withheld from the sanctuary, adding to it a fifth of its

value.[o] This is to be given to the priest, who shall then make atonement for him with the guilt-offering ram, and he will be forgiven.

[17] [p] "If someone, without being aware of it,* commits such a sin by doing one of the things which are forbidden by some commandment of the L ORD, that he incurs guilt for which he must answer, [18] he shall bring as a guilt offering to the priest an unblemished ram of the flock of the established value. The priest shall then make atonement for the fault which was unwittingly committed, and it will be forgiven. [19] Such is the offering for guilt; the penalty of the guilt must be paid to the L ORD."

[20] The L ORD said to Moses, [21] "If someone commits a sin of dishonesty against the L ORD by denying his neighbor a deposit or a pledge for a stolen article, or by otherwise retaining his neighbor's goods unjustly, [22] or if, having found a lost article, he denies the fact and swears falsely about it with any of the sinful oaths that men make in such cases, [23] he shall therefore, since he has incurred guilt by his sin, restore the thing that was stolen or unjustly retained by him or the deposit left with him or the lost article he found [24] or whatever else he swore falsely about; on the day of his guilt offering he shall make full restitution of the thing itself, and in addition, give the owner one fifth of its value. [25] As his guilt offering he shall bring to the L ORD an unblemished ram of the flock of the established value. When he has presented this as his guilt offering to the priest, [26] the latter shall make atonement for him before the L ORD, and he will be forgiven whatever guilt he may have incurred."

CHAPTER 6

See RG
128

The Daily Holocaust. [1] The L ORD said to Moses, [2] "Give Aaron and his sons the following command: This is the ritual* for holocausts. The holocaust is to remain on the

---

5, 15: Cheating: not offering the full amount in tithes, first fruits, etc. Guilt offering: its characteristic was a certain additional penalty imposed as reparation for the injustice involved in the fault which was atoned for by this sacrifice. However, in certain passages, e.g., Lv 14, 12f; Nm 6, 12; Ezr 10, 19, the term "guilt offering" is used for more important cases of "sin offerings" where no apparent injustice is involved.

5, 17: Without being aware of it: the case naturally pre-

supposes that later on the offender learns of his mistake. Cf Lv 4, 13f.

6, 2: Ritual: literally, "law, instruction." Here, and in the following paragraphs, are given additional prescriptions for various kinds of sacrifices which were, in part, treated of in the preceding chapters.

k: Lv 12, 8; Lk 2, 24. l: Lv 1, 15. 17. m: Lv 1, 15. n: Lv 4, 26. 35. o: Lv 22, 14. p: Lv 4, 2.

hearth of the altar all night until the next morning, and the fire is to be kept burning on the altar. [3]The priest, clothed in his linen robe and wearing linen drawers on his body, shall take away the ashes to which the fire has reduced the holocaust on the altar, and lay them at the side of the altar. [4]Then, having taken off these garments and put on other garments, he shall carry the ashes to a clean place outside the camp. [5]The fire on the altar is to be kept burning; it must not go out. Every morning the priest shall put firewood on it. On this he shall lay out the holocaust and burn the fat of the peace offerings. [6]The fire is to be kept burning continuously on the altar; it must not go out.

Daily Cereal Offering. [7]"This is the ritual of the cereal offering. One of Aaron's sons shall first present it before the LORD, in front of the altar. [8]Then he shall take from it a handful of its fine flour and oil, together with all the frankincense that is on it, and this he shall burn on the altar as its token offering, a sweet-smelling oblation to the LORD. [9]The rest of it Aaron and his sons may eat; but it must be eaten in the form of unleavened cakes and in a sacred place: in the court of the meeting tent they shall eat it. [10]It shall not be baked with leaven. I have given it to them as their portion from the oblations of the LORD; it is most sacred, like the sin offering and the guilt offering. [11]All the male descendants of Aaron may partake of it as their rightful share in the oblations of the LORD perpetually throughout your generations. Whatever touches the oblations becomes sacred."

[12]*The LORD said to Moses, [13]"This is the offering that Aaron and his sons shall present to the LORD [on the day he is anointed]: one tenth of an ephah of fine flour for the established cereal offering, half in the morning and half in the evening. [14]It shall be well kneaded and fried in oil on a griddle when you bring it in. Having broken the offering into pieces, you shall present it as a sweet-smelling oblation to the LORD. [15]Aaron's descendant who succeeds him as the anointed priest shall do likewise. This is a perpetual ordinance: for the Lord the whole offering shall be burned. [16]Every cereal offering of a priest shall be a whole burnt offering; it may not be eaten."

Sin Offerings. [17]The LORD said to Moses, [18]"Tell Aaron and his sons: This is the ritual for sin offerings. At the place where holocausts are slaughtered, there also, before the LORD, shall the sin offering be slaughtered.[q] It is most sacred. [19]The priest who presents the sin offering may partake of it; but it must be eaten in a sacred place,[r] in the court of the meeting tent. [20]Whatever touches its flesh shall become sacred. If any of its blood is spilled on a garment, the stained part must be washed in a sacred place. [21]A clay vessel in which it has been cooked shall thereafter be broken;[s] if it is cooked in a bronze vessel, this shall be scoured afterward and rinsed with water. [22]All the males of the priestly line may partake of the sin offering, since it is most sacred.[t] [23]But no one may partake of any sin offering of which some blood has been brought into the meeting tent[u] to make atonement in the sanctuary; such an offering must be burned up in the fire.

CHAPTER 7

See RG 128–29

Guilt Offerings. [1]"This is the ritual for guilt offerings, which are most sacred. [2]At the place where the holocausts are slaughtered, there also shall the guilt offering be slaughtered.[v] Its blood shall be splashed on the sides of the altar. [3]wAll of its fat shall be taken from it and offered up: the fatty tail, the fatty membrane over the inner organs, [4]as well as the two kidneys with the fat on them near the loins, and the lobe of the liver, which must be severed above the kidneys. [5]All this the priest shall burn on the altar as an oblation to the LORD. This is the

---

6, 12-16: This is another law about the daily or "established" cereal offering. It differs in some respects from the preceding law (vv 7-11) and also from the law in Ex 29, 38-42. Hence, the words *on the day he is anointed* were probably added by some later scribe in order to avoid the difficulty of harmonizing this law with the other two laws on the same matter.

q: Lv 7, 2.   *r:* Lv 10, 17.   *s:* Lv 11, 33; 15, 12.   *t:* Lv 7, 6; Nm 18, 10.   *u:* Lv 4, 5; Heb 13, 11.   *v:* Lv 6, 18.   *w:* 3-5: Lv 3, 4. 9f. 14-16; 4, 8f.

guilt offering. [6]All the males of the priestly line may partake of it; but it must be eaten in a sacred place, since it is most sacred.[x]

[7]"Because the sin offering and the guilt offering are alike, both having the same ritual, the guilt offering likewise belongs to the priest who makes atonement with it. [8]Similarly, the priest who offers a holocaust for someone may keep for himself the hide of the holocaust that he has offered. [9y]Also, every cereal offering that is baked in an oven or deep-fried in a pot or fried on a griddle shall belong to the priest who offers it, [10]whereas all cereal offerings[z] that are offered up dry or mixed with oil shall belong to all of Aaron's sons without distinction.

Peace Offerings. [11]"This is the ritual for the peace offerings that are presented to the LORD. [12]When anyone makes a peace offering in thanksgiving, together with his thanksgiving sacrifice he shall offer unleavened cakes mixed with oil, unleavened wafers spread with oil, and cakes made of fine flour mixed with oil and well kneaded. [13]His offering shall also include loaves of leavened bread* along with the victim of his peace offering for thanksgiving. [14]From each of his offerings he shall present one portion as a contribution to the LORD; this shall belong to the priest who splashes the blood of the peace offering.

[15a]"The flesh of the thanksgiving sacrifice shall be eaten on the day it is offered; none of it may be kept till the next day. [16]However, if the sacrifice is a votive or a free-will offering, it should indeed be eaten on the day the sacrifice is offered, but what is left over may be eaten on the next day. [17]Should any flesh from the sacrifice be left over on the third day, it must be burned up in the fire. [18]If, therefore, any of the flesh of the peace offering is eaten on the third day, it shall not win favor for him nor shall it be reckoned as to his credit; rather, it shall be considered as refuse, and anyone who eats of it shall have his guilt to bear. [19]Should the flesh touch anything unclean, it may not be eaten, but shall be burned up in the fire.

"All who are clean may partake of this flesh. [20]If, however, someone while in a state of uncleanness eats any of the flesh of a peace offering belonging to the LORD, that person shall be cut off from his people. [21]Likewise, if someone touches anything unclean, whether the uncleanness be of human or of animal origin or from some loathsome crawling creature, and then eats of a peace offering belonging to the LORD, that person, too, shall be cut off from his people."

Prohibition against Blood and Fat. [22]The LORD said to Moses, [23]"Tell the Israelites: You shall not eat the fat* of any ox or sheep or goat.[b] [24]Although the fat of an animal that has died a natural death or has been killed by wild beasts may be put to any other use, you may not eat it.[c] [25]If anyone eats the fat of an animal from which an oblation is made to the LORD, such a one shall be cut off from his people. [26]Wherever you dwell, you shall not partake of any blood, be it of bird or of animal. [27]Every person who partakes of any blood shall be cut off from his people."[d]

The Portions for Priests. [28]The LORD said to Moses, [29]"Tell the Israelites: He who presents a peace offering to the LORD shall bring a part of it as his special offering to him, [30]carrying in with his own hands the oblations to the LORD. The fat is to be brought in, together with the breast, which is to be waved as a wave offering* before the LORD. [31]The priest shall burn the fat on the altar,[e] but the breast belongs to Aaron and his sons. [32]Moreover, from your peace offering you shall give to the priest the right leg as a raised offering. [33]The descendant of Aaron who offers up the blood and fat of the

---

7, 13: Leavened bread: these loaves were not burned on the altar (cf Lv 2, 11), but were eaten at the "communion" meal which followed the sacrifice. See note on Lv 3, 1.

7, 23: The fat: only the particular portions specified in Lv 3, 9f. 14f are meant. Ox or sheep or goat: such animals as could be sacrificed; the fat of other clean animals could be eaten.

7, 30-34: A wave offering . . . a raised offering: these ceremonies are described in Ex 29, 24-28. The Hebrew word for "raised offering" is also rendered, in certain contexts, as "contribution."

x: Lv 6, 22.   y: Lv 2, 3-10; Nm 18, 9; Ez 44, 29.   z: Lv 2, 14f.   a: 15-18: Lv 19, 6f.   b: Lv 3, 17.   c: Lv 22, 8.   d: Lv 17, 10.   e: Lv 3, 11, 16.

peace offering shall have the right leg as his portion, [34]for from the peace offerings of the Israelites I have taken the breast that is waved and the leg that is raised up, and I have given them to Aaron, the priest, and to his sons by a perpetual ordinance as a contribution from the Israelites."[f]

[35]This is the priestly share* from the oblations of the LORD, allotted to Aaron and his sons on the day he called them to be the priests of the LORD; [36]on the day he anointed them the LORD ordered the Israelites to give them this share by a perpetual ordinance throughout their generations.

[37]This is the ritual for holocausts, cereal offerings, sin offerings, guilt offerings, [ordination offerings] and peace offerings, [38]which the LORD enjoined on Moses at Mount Sinai at the time when he commanded the Israelites in the wilderness of Sinai to bring their offerings to the LORD.

II: Ceremony of Ordination

CHAPTER 8

See RG 129

Ordination of Aaron and His Sons. [1]The LORD [g] said to Moses,* [2]"Take Aaron and his sons, together with the vestments,* the anointing oil, the bullock for a sin offering, the two rams, and the basket of unleavened food. [3]Then assemble the whole community at the entrance of the meeting tent." [4]And Moses did as the LORD had commanded. When the community had assembled at the entrance of the meeting tent, [5]Moses told them what the LORD had ordered to be done. [6]Bringing forward Aaron and his sons, he first washed them with water.[h] [7]Then he put the tunic on Aaron,[i] girded him with the sash, clothed him with the robe, placed the ephod on him, and girded him with the embroidered belt of the ephod, fastening it around him. [8][j]He then set the breastpiece on him, with the Urim and Thummim* in it, [9][k]and put the miter on his head, attaching the gold plate, the sacred diadem, over the front of the miter, at his forehead, as the LORD had commanded him to do.

[10]Taking the anointing oil, Moses anointed and consecrated the Dwelling, with all that was in it.[l] [11]Then he sprinkled some of this oil seven times on the altar, and anointed the altar, with all its appurtenances, and the laver, with its base, thus consecrating them. [12]He also poured some of the anointing oil on Aaron's head, thus consecrating him.[m] [13]Moses likewise brought forward Aaron's sons, clothed them with tunics, girded them with sashes, and put turbans on them, as the LORD had commanded him to do.

Ordination Sacrifices. [14]When he had brought forward the bullock for a sin offering, Aaron and his sons laid their hands on its head. [15]Then Moses slaughtered it, and taking some of its blood, with his finger he put it on the horns around the altar, thus purifying the altar. He also made atonement for the altar by pouring out the blood at its base when he consecrated it.[n] [16]Taking all the fat that was over the inner organs, as well as the lobe of the liver and the two kidneys with their fat,[o] Moses burned them on the altar. [17]The bullock, however, with its hide and flesh and offal he burned in the fire outside the camp, as the LORD had commanded him to do.

[18]He next brought forward the holocaust ram, and Aaron and his sons laid their hands on its head. [19]When he had slaughtered it, Moses splashed its blood on all sides of the altar. [20]After cutting up the ram into pieces, he burned the head, the cut-up pieces and the suet; [21]then, having washed the inner organs and the shanks with water, he also burned these remaining parts of the ram on the altar as a holocaust, a sweet-smelling oblation to the LORD, as the LORD had commanded him to do.

[22]Then he brought forward the second ram, the ordination ram, and Aaron and his sons laid their hands on its head. [23]When he

---

7, 35: The priestly share: literally, "the anointed part."

8, 1—9, 21: Though presented in the form of a narrative, this description of Aaron's ordination was intended to serve as a guide for all future ordinations.

8, 2: The vestments, etc.: already described in Ex 28– 29.

8, 8: The Urim and Thummim: see note on Ex 28, 30.

f: Ex 29, 27f. g: 1-36: cf Ex 29. h: 6f: Ex 40, 12f. i: 7ff: Sir 45, 8-13. j: Ex 28, 30. k: Ex 28, 36. l: Ex 30, 26. m: Sir 45, 15. n: Lv 4, 7; Heb 9, 22. o: 16f: Lv 3, 4; 4, 8-11.

had slaughtered it, Moses took some of its blood and put it on the tip of Aaron's right ear, on the thumb of his right hand, and on the big toe of his right foot.*p* 24Moses had the sons of Aaron also come forward, and he put some of the blood on the tips of their right ears, on the thumbs of their right hands, and on the big toes of their right feet. The rest of the blood he splashed on the sides of the altar. 25He then took the fat: the fatty tail and all the fat over the inner organs, the lobe of the liver and the two kidneys with their fat, and likewise the right leg; 26from the basket of unleavened food that was set before the LORD he took one unleavened cake, one loaf of bread made with oil, and one wafer; these he placed on top of the portions of fat and the right leg. 27He then put all these things into the hands of Aaron and his sons, whom he had wave them as a wave offering before the LORD. 28When he had received them back, Moses burned them with the holocaust on the altar as the ordination offering, a sweet-smelling oblation to the LORD. 29He then took the breast and waved it as a wave offering before the LORD; this was Moses' own portion of the ordination ram. All this was in keeping with the LORD's command to Moses. 30Taking some of the anointing oil and some of the blood that was on the altar, Moses sprinkled with it Aaron and his vestments, as well as his sons and their vestments, thus consecrating both Aaron and his vestments and his sons and their vestments.

31Finally, Moses said to Aaron and his sons, "Boil the flesh at the entrance of the meeting tent, and there eat it with the bread that is in the basket of the ordination offering, in keeping with the command I have received: 'Aaron and his sons shall eat of it.' 32What is left over of the flesh and the bread you shall burn up in the fire. 33Moreover, you are not to depart from the entrance of the meeting tent for seven days, until the days of your ordination are completed; for your ordination is to last for seven days. 34*The LORD has commanded that what has been done today be done to make atonement for you. 35Hence you must remain at the entrance of the meeting tent day and night for seven days, carrying out the prescriptions of the LORD; otherwise you shall die; for this is the command I have received." 36So Aaron and his sons did all that the LORD had commanded through Moses.

CHAPTER 9

See RG
129

Octave of the Ordination. 1On the eighth day Moses summoned Aaron and his sons, together with the elders of Israel, 2and said to Aaron, "Take a calf for a sin offering and a ram for a holocaust, both without blemish, and offer them before the LORD. 3Tell the elders of Israel, too: Take a he-goat for a sin offering, a calf and a lamb, both unblemished yearlings, for a holocaust, 4and an ox and a ram for a peace offering, to sacrifice them before the LORD, along with a cereal offering mixed with oil; for today the LORD will reveal himself to you." 5So they brought what Moses had ordered. When the whole community had come forward and stood before the LORD, 6Moses said, "This is what the LORD orders you to do, that the glory of the LORD may be revealed to you. 7Come up to the altar," Moses then told Aaron, "and offer your sin offering and your holocaust in atonement for yourself and for your family; then present the offering of the people in atonement for them, as the LORD has commanded."

8Going up to the altar, Aaron first slaughtered the calf that was his own sin offering. 9When his sons presented the blood to him, he dipped his finger in the blood and put it on the horns of the altar. The rest of the blood he poured out at the base of the altar. 10He then burned on the altar the fat, the kidneys and the lobe of the liver that were taken from the sin offering, as the LORD had commanded Moses; 11but the flesh and the hide he burned up in the fire outside the camp. 12Then Aaron slaughtered his holocaust. When his sons brought him the blood, he splashed it on all sides of the altar. 13They

---

8, 34: The sense is not quite clear. Either the verse gives merely the reason why God ordered this ceremony, or it contains God's command that the same ceremony be used in all future ordinations, or it decrees a repetition of the entire ceremony on each of the seven days. At least a sin offering for atonement was made on each of these days. Cf Ex 29, 29-36.

p: Lv 14, 14.

then brought him the pieces and the head of the holocaust, and he burned them on the altar. [14]Having washed the inner organs and the shanks, he burned these also with the holocaust on the altar.

[15]Thereupon he had the people's offering brought up. Taking the goat that was for the people's sin offering, he slaughtered it and offered it up for sin as before. [16]Then he brought forward the holocaust, other than the morning holocaust, and offered it in the usual manner. [17]He then presented the cereal offering; taking a handful of it, he burned it on the altar. [18]Finally he slaughtered the ox and the ram, the peace offering of the people. When his sons brought him the blood, Aaron splashed it on all sides of the altar. [19]The portions of fat from the ox and from the ram, the fatty tail, the fatty membrane over the inner organs, the two kidneys, with the fat that is on them, and the lobe of the liver,[q] [20]he placed on top of the breasts and burned them on the altar, [21r]having first waved the breasts and the right legs as a wave offering before the LORD, in keeping with the LORD's command to Moses.

Revelation of the Lord's Glory. [22]Aaron then raised his hands over the people and blessed them. When he came down from offering the sin offering and holocaust and peace offering, [23]Moses and Aaron went into the meeting tent.[s] On coming out they again blessed the people. Then the glory of the LORD was revealed to all the people. [24]Fire came forth from the LORD's presence[t] and consumed the holocaust and the remnants of the fat on the altar. Seeing this, all the people cried out and fell prostrate.

CHAPTER 10

Nadab and Abihu. [1]During this time Aaron's sons Nadab and Abihu* took their censers and, strewing incense on the fire they had put in them,[u] they offered up before the LORD profane fire, such as he had not authorized. [2]Fire* therefore came forth from the LORD's presence and consumed them,[v] so that they died in his presence. [3]Moses then said to Aaron, "This is as the LORD said:

Through those who approach me I will
  manifest my sacredness;*
In the sight of all the people I will
  reveal my glory."[w]

But Aaron said nothing. [4]Then Moses summoned Mishael and Elzaphan, the sons of Aaron's uncle Uzziel, with the order, "Come, remove your kinsmen from the sanctuary and carry them to a place outside the camp." [5]So they went in and took them, in their tunics,* outside the camp, as Moses had commanded.

Conduct of the Priests. [6]Moses said to Aaron and his sons Eleazar and Ithamar, "Do not bare your heads* or tear your garments,[x] lest you bring not only death on yourselves but God's wrath also on the whole community. Your kinsmen, the rest of the house of Israel, shall mourn for those whom the LORD's fire has smitten; [7]but do not you go beyond the entry of the meeting tent, else you shall die; for the anointing oil of the LORD is upon you." So they did as Moses told them.

[8]The LORD said to Aaron, [9]"When you are to go to the meeting tent, you and your sons are forbidden under pain of death, by a perpetual ordinance throughout your generations, to drink any wine or strong drink.[y] [10]You must be able to distinguish between what is sacred and what is profane, between what is clean and what is unclean;[z] [11]you must teach the Israelites all the laws that the LORD has given them through Moses."[a]

The Eating of the Priestly Portions. [12]Moses said to Aaron and his surviving

10, 1: Nadab and Abihu: the older sons of Aaron. Cf Ex 6, 23f.

10, 2: Fire: perhaps after the manner of lightning.

10, 3: I will manifest my sacredness: the presence of God is so sacred that it strikes dead those who approach him without the proper holiness. Cf Nm 20, 13; Ez 28, 22.

10, 5: In their tunics: they were buried just as they were, with no shroud or funeral solemnities.

10, 6: Bare your heads: go without the customary head covering, as a sign of mourning. Some interpreters, however,

understand it as the cutting off of one's hair, which ordinarily all the Israelites, men as well as women, let grow long. Cf Is 15, 2; Jer 7, 29. Still others understand the verb to mean "to let one's hair hang loose and wild." Cf Lv 13, 45; 21, 10, where the same phrase is used.

q: 19f: Lv 3, 3ff.   r: Lv 7, 31f.   s: Nm 6, 23-26.   t: 1 Kgs 18, 38; 2 Chr 7, 1.   u: Lv 16, 1; Nm 3, 4; 26, 61; 1 Chr 24, 2.   v: Nm 16, 35.   w: Lv 21, 17. 21.   x: Lv 21, 10.   y: Ez 44, 21.   z: Lv 11, 47; 20, 25; Ez 22, 26; 44, 23.   a: Sir 45, 16.

sons, Eleazar and Ithamar, "Take the cereal offering left over from the oblations of the LORD, and eat it beside the altar in the form of unleavened cakes.*b* Since it is most sacred, *13*you must eat it in a sacred place. This is your due from the oblations of the LORD, and that of your sons; such is the command I have received. *14c*With your sons and daughters you shall also eat the breast of the wave offering and the leg of the raised offering, in a clean place; for these have been assigned to you and your children as your due from the peace offerings of the Israelites. *15*The leg of the raised offering and the breast of the wave offering shall first be brought in with the oblations, the fatty portions, that are to be waved as a wave offering before the LORD. Then they shall belong to you and your children by a perpetual ordinance, as the LORD has commanded."

16*When Moses inquired about the goat of the sin offering, he discovered that it had all been burned. So he was angry with the surviving sons of Aaron, Eleazar and Ithamar, and said, *17d*"Why did you not eat the sin offering in the sacred place, since it is most sacred? It has been given to you that you might bear the guilt of the community and make atonement for them before the LORD. *18*If its blood was not brought into the inmost part of the sanctuary, you should certainly have eaten the offering in the sanctuary, in keeping with the command I had received." *19*Aaron answered Moses, "Even though they presented their sin offering and holocaust before the LORD today, yet this misfortune has befallen me. Had I then eaten of the sin offering today, would it have been pleasing to the LORD?" *20*On hearing this, Moses was satisfied.

III: Laws Regarding Legal Purity

CHAPTER 11

See RG
129-31

Clean and Unclean Food. *1*The LORD said to Moses and Aaron,* *2*"Speak to the Israelites and tell them: Of all land animals these are the ones you may eat: *3*any animal that has hoofs you may eat, provided it is cloven-footed and chews the cud. *4*But you shall not eat any of the following that only chew the cud or only have hoofs: the camel, which indeed chews the cud, but does not have hoofs and is therefore unclean for you; *5*the rock badger,* which indeed chews the cud, but does not have hoofs and is therefore unclean for you; *6*the hare, which indeed chews the cud, but does not have hoofs and is therefore unclean for you; and the pig, *7*which does indeed have hoofs and is cloven-footed, but does not chew the cud and is therefore unclean for you. *8*Their flesh you shall not eat, and their dead bodies you shall not touch; they are unclean for you.

9"Of the various creatures that live in the water, you may eat the following: whatever in the seas or in river waters has both fins and scales you may eat. *10*But of the various creatures that crawl or swim in the water, whether in the sea or in the rivers, all those that lack either fins or scales are loathsome for you, *11*and you shall treat them as loathsome. Their flesh you shall not eat, and their dead bodies you shall loathe. *12*Every water creature that lacks fins or scales is loathsome for you.

13"Of the birds, these you shall loathe and, as loathsome, they shall not be eaten:* the eagle, the vulture, the osprey, *14*the kite, the various species of falcons, *15*the various species of crows, *16*the ostrich, the nightjar,

---

10, 16-19: Eleazar and Ithamar burned the entire goat of the sin offering (Lv 9, 15) instead of eating it in a sacred place (Lv 6, 19) to bear the guilt of the community. Aaron defends this action of his sons against Moses' displeasure by implying that they did not have sufficient sanctity to eat the flesh of the victim and thus perform the expiation of the people. They themselves still labored under the blow of the divine anger which struck their brothers Nadab and Abihu.

11, 1ff: These distinctions between edible and inedible meats were probably based on traditional ideas of hygiene, but they are here given a moral, religious basis: the inedible varieties are classified as "unclean" to remind the Israelites

that they are to be a pure and holy people, dedicated to the Lord.

11, 5f: According to modern zoology, the rock badger (hyrax Syriacus) is classified as an ungulate, and the hare as a rodent; neither is a ruminant. They appear to chew their food as the true ruminants do, and it is upon this appearance that the classification in the text is based.

11, 13-19. 30: The identification of the various Hebrew names for these birds and reptiles is in many cases uncertain.

b: Lv 6, 16.   *c:* 14f; Lv 7, 34.   *d:* Lv 6, 18f.

Purity, Cleanliness, and Ritual

In the thinking of the ancient Israelites, there were certain boundaries within nature that should not be crossed or confused. These boundaries separated things of one kind from things of another kind, and things that went together were seen to have certain characteristics in common. Take, for instance, the category of "creatures that live in the water" (11, 9): along with living in the water, these creatures were supposed to have fins and scales. If a creature—such as an oyster or a lobster—lived in the waters but did not have fins and scales, it did not fulfill all of the characteristics of its kind, and it therefore confused the boundaries of "creatures that live in the water" and was unclean. In the same way, the Israelites believed that animals that chewed the cud—ruminants, such as the cow—should have cloven, or divided, hoofs. The cow has divided hoofs, so it is clean. But the pig, which has divided hoofs, does not chew the cud, so it is unclean. It has confused a natural category, and is therefore to be avoided. See also Deuteronomy 14, 3-21.

The clearest and strongest boundary was the one between life and death, and one had to be very careful when dealing with anything that was dead.

the gull, the various species of hawks, *17*the owl, the cormorant, the screech owl, *18*the barn owl, the desert owl, the buzzard, *19*the stork, the various species of herons, the hoopoe, and the bat.*

20"The various winged insects that walk on all fours are loathsome for you. *21*But of the various winged insects that walk on all fours you may eat those that have jointed legs for leaping on the ground; *22*hence of these you may eat the following: the various kinds of locusts,* the various kinds of grasshoppers, the various kinds of katydids, and the various kinds of crickets. *23*All other winged insects that have four legs are loathsome for you.

24"Such is the uncleanness that you contract, that everyone who touches their dead bodies shall be unclean until evening, *25*and everyone who picks up any part of their dead bodies shall wash his garments and be unclean until evening. *26*All hoofed animals that are not cloven-footed* or do not chew the cud are unclean for you; everyone who touches them becomes unclean. *27*Of the various quadrupeds, all those that walk on paws* are unclean for you; everyone who touches their dead bodies shall be unclean

until evening, *28*and everyone who picks up their dead bodies shall wash his garments and be unclean until evening. Such is their uncleanness for you.

29"Of the creatures that swarm on the ground, the following are unclean for you: the rat, the mouse, the various kinds of lizards, *30*the gecko, the chameleon, the agama, the skink, and the mole. *31*Among the various swarming creatures, these are unclean for you. Everyone who touches them when they are dead shall be unclean until evening. *32*Everything on which one of them falls when dead becomes unclean. Any such article that men use, whether it be an article of wood, cloth, leather or goat hair, must be put in water and remain unclean until evening, when it again becomes clean. *33*Should any of these creatures fall into a clay vessel, everything in it becomes unclean, and the vessel itself you must break. *34*Any solid food that was in contact with water, and any liquid that men drink, in any such vessel become unclean. *35*Any object on which one of their dead bodies falls, becomes unclean; if it is an oven or a jar-stand, this must be broken to pieces; they are unclean

---

11, 19: The bat: actually a mammal, but listed here with the birds because of its wings.

11, 22: The Hebrew distinguishes four classes of edible locust-like insects, but the difference between them is quite uncertain. Cf Mt 3, 4.

11, 24-28: This paragraph sharpens the prohibition against

unclean animals: not only is their meat unfit for food, but contact with their dead bodies makes a person ritually unclean.

11, 26: All hoofed animals that are not cloven-footed: such as the horse and the ass.

11, 27: All those that walk on paws: such as dogs and cats.

and shall be treated as unclean by you. [36]However, a spring or a cistern for collecting water remains clean; but whoever touches the dead body* becomes unclean. [37]Any sort of cultivated grain remains clean even though one of their dead bodies falls on it; [38]but if the grain has become moistened, it becomes unclean when one of these falls on it.

[39]"When one of the animals that you could otherwise eat, dies of itself, anyone who touches its dead body shall be unclean until evening; [40]and anyone who eats of its dead body shall wash his garments and be unclean until evening;[e] so also, anyone who removes its dead body shall wash his garments and be unclean until evening.

[41]"All the creatures that swarm on the ground are loathsome and shall not be eaten. [42]Whether it crawls on its belly, goes on all fours, or has many legs, you shall eat no swarming creature: they are loathsome. [43]Do not make yourselves loathsome or unclean with any swarming creature through being contaminated by them.[f] [44]For I, the LORD, am your God; and you shall make and keep yourselves holy, because I am holy.[g] You shall not make yourselves unclean, then, by any swarming creature that crawls on the ground. [45]Since I, the LORD, brought you up from the land of Egypt that I might be your God, you shall be holy, because I am holy.

[46]"This is the law for animals and birds and for all the creatures that move about in the water or swarm on the ground, [47]that you may distinguish between the clean and the unclean, between creatures that may be eaten and those that may not be eaten."[h]

See RG 129-31

CHAPTER 12

Uncleanness of Childbirth. [1]The LORD said to Moses, [2]"Tell the Israelites: When a woman has conceived and gives birth to a boy, she shall be unclean* for seven days, with the same uncleanness as at her menstrual period.[i] [3]On the eighth day, the flesh of the boy's foreskin shall be circumcised,[j] [4]and then she shall spend thirty-three days more in becoming purified of her blood; she shall not touch anything sacred nor enter the sanctuary till the days of her purification are fulfilled. [5]If she gives birth to a girl, for fourteen days she shall be as unclean as at her menstruation, after which she shall spend sixty-six days in becoming purified of her blood.

[6]"When the days of her purification for a son or for a daughter are fulfilled,[k] she shall bring to the priest at the entrance of the meeting tent a yearling lamb for a holocaust and a pigeon or a turtledove for a sin offering. [7]The priest shall offer them up before the LORD to make atonement for her, and thus she will be clean again after her flow of blood. Such is the law for the woman who gives birth to a boy or a girl child. [8]*If, however, she cannot afford a lamb, she may take two turtledoves or two pigeons,[l] the one for a holocaust and the other for a sin offering. The priest shall make atonement for her, and thus she will again be clean."

CHAPTER 13

See RG 129-31

Leprosy. [1]The LORD said to Moses and Aaron, [2m]"If someone has on his skin* a scab or pustule or blotch which appears to be the sore of leprosy, he shall be brought to Aaron, the priest, or to one of the priests among his descendants, [3]who shall examine the sore on his skin. If the hair on the sore has turned white and the sore itself shows that it has penetrated below the skin, it is indeed the sore of leprosy; the priest, on see-

---

11, 36: Whoever touches the dead body: to remove the dead insect from the water supply.

12, 2f: The uncleanness of the woman was more serious during the first period, the seven days after the birth of a boy or the fourteen days after the birth of a girl; only during this period would the rules given in Lv 15, 19-24 apply.

12, 8: Forty days after the birth of Jesus, his Virgin Mother made this offering of the poor (Lk 2, 22. 24); since the holocaust was offered in thanksgiving for the birth of the child, this was most fittingly offered by Mary. However, because of her miraculous delivery, she was not really obliged to make the sin offering of purification.

13, 2ff: Various kinds of skin blemishes are treated here which were not contagious but simply disqualified their subjects from association with others, especially in public worship, until they were declared ritually clean. The Hebrew term used does not refer to Hansen's disease, currently called leprosy.

e: Lv 17, 15; 22, 8. f: 43f: Lv 20, 25f. g: Lv 19, 2; 20, 7. 26; Mt 5, 48; 1 Pt 1, 16. h: Lv 10, 10. i: Lv 15, 19. j: Gn 17, 12; Jn 7, 22. k: Lk 2, 22. l: Lv 1, 14; Lk 2, 24. m: Dt 24, 8.

ing this, shall declare the man unclean. [4]If, however, the blotch on the skin is white, but does not seem to have penetrated below the skin, nor has the hair turned white, the priest shall quarantine the stricken man for seven days. [5]On the seventh day the priest shall again examine him. If he judges that the sore has remained unchanged and has not spread on the skin, the priest shall quarantine him for another seven days, [6]and once more examine him on the seventh day. If the sore is now dying out and has not spread on the skin, the priest shall declare the man clean; it was merely eczema. The man shall wash his garments and so become clean. [7]But if, after he has shown himself to the priest to be declared clean, the eczema spreads at all on his skin, he shall once more show himself to the priest. [8]Should the priest, on examining it, find that the eczema has indeed spread on the skin, he shall declare the man unclean; it is leprosy.

[9]"When someone is stricken with leprosy, he shall be brought to the priest. [10]Should the priest, on examining him, find that there is a white scab on the skin which has turned the hair white and that there is raw flesh in it, [11]it is skin leprosy that has long developed. The priest shall declare the man unclean without first quarantining him, since he is certainly unclean. [12]If leprosy breaks out on the skin* and, as far as the priest can see, covers all the skin of the stricken man from head to foot, [13]should the priest then, on examining him, find that the leprosy does cover his whole body, he shall declare the stricken man clean; since it has all turned white, the man is clean. [14]But as soon as raw flesh appears on him, he is unclean; [15]on observing the raw flesh, the priest shall declare him unclean, because raw flesh is unclean; it is leprosy. [16]If, however, the raw flesh again turns white, he shall return to the priest; [17]should the latter, on examining him, find that the sore has indeed turned white, he shall declare the stricken man clean, and thus he will be clean.

[18]"If a man who had a boil on his skin which later healed, [19]should now in the place of the boil have a white scab or a pink blotch, he shall show himself to the priest. [20]If the latter, on examination, sees that it is deeper than the skin and that the hair has turned white, he shall declare the man unclean: it is the sore of leprosy that has broken out in the boil. [21]But if the priest, on examining him, finds that there is no white hair in it and that it is not deeper than the skin and is already dying out, the priest shall quarantine him for seven days. [22]If it has then spread on the skin, the priest shall declare him unclean; the man is stricken. [23]But if the blotch remains in its place without spreading, it is merely the scar of the boil; the priest shall therefore declare him clean.

[24]"If a man had a burn on his skin, and the proud flesh of the burn now becomes a pink or a white blotch, [25]the priest shall examine it. If the hair has turned white on the blotch and this seems to have penetrated below the skin, it is leprosy that has broken out in the burn; the priest shall therefore declare him unclean and stricken with leprosy. [26]But if the priest, on examining it, finds that there is no white hair on the blotch and that this is not deeper than the skin and is already dying out, the priest shall quarantine him for seven days. [27]Should the priest, when examining it on the seventh day, find that it has spread at all on the skin, he shall declare the man unclean and stricken with leprosy. [28]But if the blotch remains in its place without spreading on the skin and is already dying out, it is merely the scab of the burn; the priest shall therefore declare the man clean, since it is only the scar of the burn.

[29]"When a man or a woman has a sore on the head or cheek, [30]should the priest, on examining it, find that the sore has penetrated below the skin and that there is fine yellow hair on it, the priest shall declare the person unclean, for this is scall,* a leprous disease of the head or cheek. [31]But if the priest, on examining the scall sore, finds that it has not penetrated below the skin, though the hair on it may not be black, the priest shall quar-

---

13, 12ff: If leprosy breaks out on the skin: the symptoms described here point to a form of skin disease which is merely on the surface and therefore easily cured.

13, 30: Scall: a scabby or scaly eruption of the scalp. According to some, "ringworm."

antine the person with scall sore for seven days, [32] and on the seventh day again examine the sore. If the scall has not spread and has no yellow hair on it and does not seem to have penetrated below the skin, [33] the man shall shave himself, but not on the diseased spot. Then the priest shall quarantine him for another seven days. [34] If the priest, when examining the scall on the seventh day, finds that it has not spread on the skin and that it has not penetrated below the skin, he shall declare the man clean; the latter shall wash his garments, and thus he will be clean. [35] But if the scall spreads at all on his skin after he has been declared clean, [36] the priest shall again examine it. If the scall has indeed spread on the skin, he need not look for yellow hair; the man is surely unclean. [37] If, however, he judges that the scall has remained in its place and that black hair has grown on it, the disease has been healed; the man is clean, and the priest shall declare him clean.

[38] "When the skin of a man or a woman is spotted with white blotches, [39] the priest shall make an examination. If the blotches on the skin are white and already dying out, it is only tetter* that has broken out on the skin, and the person therefore is clean.

[40] "When a man loses the hair of his head, he is not unclean merely because of his bald crown. [41] So too, if he loses the hair on the front of his head, he is not unclean merely because of his bald forehead. [42] But when there is a pink sore on his bald crown or bald forehead, it is leprosy that is breaking out there. [43] The priest shall examine him; and if the scab on the sore of the bald spot has the same pink appearance as that of skin leprosy of the fleshy part of the body, [44] the man is leprous and unclean, and the priest shall declare him unclean by reason of the sore on his head.

[45] "The one who bears the sore of leprosy shall keep his garments rent and his head bare, and shall muffle his beard; he shall cry out, 'Unclean, unclean!' [46] As long as the sore is on him he shall declare himself unclean, since he is in fact unclean.[n] He shall dwell apart, making his abode outside the camp.

Leprosy of Clothes. [47] "When a leprous infection* is on a garment of wool or of linen, [48] or on woven or knitted material of linen or wool, or on a hide or anything made of leather, [49] if the infection on the garment or hide, or on the woven or knitted material, or on any leather article is greenish or reddish, the thing is indeed infected with leprosy and must be shown to the priest. [50] Having examined the infection, the priest shall quarantine the infected article for seven days.

[51] "On the seventh day the priest shall again examine the infection. If it has spread on the garment, or on the woven or knitted material, or on the leather, whatever be its use, the infection is malignant leprosy, and the article is unclean. [52] He shall therefore burn up the garment, or the woven or knitted material of wool or linen, or the leather article, whatever it may be, which is infected; since it has malignant leprosy, it must be destroyed by fire. [53] But if the priest, on examining the infection, finds that it has not spread on the garment, or on the woven or knitted material, or on the leather article, [54] he shall give orders to have the infected article washed and then quarantined for another seven days.

[55] "Then the priest shall again examine the infected article after it has been washed. If the infection has not changed its appearance, even though it may not have spread, the article is unclean and shall be destroyed by fire. [56] But if the priest, on examining the infection, finds that it is dying out after the washing, he shall tear the infected part out of the garment, or the leather, or the woven or knitted material. [57] If, however, the infection again appears on the garment, or on the woven or knitted material, or on the leather article, it is still virulent and the thing infected shall be destroyed by fire. [58] But if, after the

---

13, 39: Tetter: vitiligo, a harmless form of skin disease.

13, 47: A leprous infection: some mold or fungus growth resembling human leprosy.

---

n: Nm 5, 2; 12, 14f; 2 Kgs 15, 5; Lk 17, 12.

washing, the infection has left the garment, or the woven or knitted material, or the leather article, the thing shall be washed a second time, and thus it will be clean. [59]This is the law for leprous infection[o] on a garment of wool or linen, or on woven or knitted material, or on any leather article, to determine whether it is clean or unclean."

CHAPTER 14

See RG
129-31

Purification after Leprosy. [1]The LORD said to Moses, [2p]"This is the law for the victim of leprosy at the time of his purification. He shall be brought to the priest, [3]who is to go outside the camp to examine him. If the priest finds that the sore of leprosy has healed in the leper, [4]he shall order the man who is to be purified, to get two live, clean birds, as well as some cedar wood, scarlet yarn,[*] and hyssop. [5]The priest shall then order him to slay one of the birds over an earthen vessel with spring water[*] in it. [6]Taking the living bird with the cedar wood, the scarlet yarn and the hyssop, the priest shall dip them all in the blood of the bird that was slain over the spring water, [7]and then sprinkle seven times the man to be purified from his leprosy. When he has thus purified him, he shall let the living bird fly away over the countryside. [8]The man being purified shall then wash his garments and shave off all his hair and bathe in water; only when he is thus made clean may he come inside the camp; but he shall still remain outside his tent for seven days. [9]On the seventh day he shall again shave off all the hair of his head, his beard, his eyebrows, and any other hair he may have, and also wash his garments and bathe his body in water; and so he will be clean.

Purification Sacrifices. [10]"On the eighth day he shall take two unblemished male lambs, one unblemished yearling ewe lamb, three tenths of an ephah of fine flour mixed with oil for a cereal offering, and one log of oil. [11]The priest who performs the purification ceremony shall place the man who is being purified, as well as all these offerings, before the LORD at the entrance of the meeting tent. [12]Taking one of the male lambs, the priest shall present it as a guilt offering, along with the log of oil, waving them as a wave offering before the LORD. [13](This lamb he shall slaughter in the sacred place where the sin offering and the holocaust are slaughtered; because, like the sin offering, the guilt offering belongs to the priest and is most sacred.) [14]Then the priest shall take some of the blood of the guilt offering and put it on the tip of the man's right ear, the thumb of his right hand, and the big toe of his right foot.[q] [15]The priest shall also take the log of oil and pour some of it into the palm of his own left hand; [16]then, dipping his right forefinger in it, he shall sprinkle it seven times before the LORD. [17]Of the oil left in his hand the priest shall put some on the tip of the man's right ear, the thumb of his right hand, and the big toe of his right foot, over the blood of the guilt offering. [18]The rest of the oil in his hand the priest shall put on the head of the man being purified. Thus shall the priest make atonement for him before the LORD. [19]Only after he has offered the sin offering in atonement for the man's uncleanness shall the priest slaughter the holocaust [20]and offer it, together with the cereal offering, on the altar before the LORD. When the priest has thus made atonement for him, the man will be clean.

Poor Leper's Sacrifice. [21]"If a man is poor and cannot afford so much, he shall take one male lamb for a guilt offering, to be used as a wave offering in atonement for himself, one tenth of an ephah of fine flour mixed with oil for a cereal offering, a log of oil, [22]and two turtledoves[*] or pigeons, which he can more easily afford, the one as a sin offering and the other as a holocaust. [23]On the eighth day of his purification he shall bring them to the priest, at the entrance of the meeting tent before the LORD. [24]Taking the guilt-offering lamb, along with the log of oil,

---

14, 4: Scarlet yarn: probably used for tying the hyssop sprig to the cedar branchlet.

14, 5: Spring water: literally, "living water," taken from some source of running water, not from a cistern.

14, 22: Two turtledoves: substitutes for the two additional lambs, similar to the offering of a poor woman after childbirth. Cf Lv 12, 8.

o: Lv 14, 54.   p: Mt 8, 4; Mk 1, 44; Lk 5, 14.   q: Lv 8, 23f.

the priest shall wave them as a wave offering before the LORD. [25]When he has slaughtered the guilt-offering lamb, he shall take some of its blood, and put it on the tip of the right ear of the man being purified, on the thumb of his right hand, and on the big toe of his right foot. [26]The priest shall then pour some of the oil into the palm of his own left hand [27]and with his right forefinger sprinkle it seven times before the LORD. [28]Some of the oil in his hand the priest shall also put on the tip of the man's right ear, the thumb of his right hand, and the big toe of his right foot, over the blood of the guilt offering. [29]The rest of the oil in his hand the priest shall put on the man's head. Thus shall he make atonement for him before the LORD. [30]Then, of the turtledoves or pigeons, such as the man can afford, [31]the priest shall offer up one as a sin offering and the other as a holocaust, along with the cereal offering. Thus shall the priest make atonement before the LORD for the man who is to be purified. [32]This is the law for one afflicted with leprosy who has insufficient means for his purification."

Leprosy of Houses. [33]The LORD said to Moses and Aaron, [34]"When you come into the land of Canaan, which I am giving you to possess, if I put a leprous infection on any house of the land you occupy, [35]the owner of the house shall come and report to the priest, 'It looks to me as if my house were infected.' [36]The priest shall then order the house to be cleared out before he goes in to examine the infection, lest everything in the house become unclean. Only after this is he to go in to examine the house. [37]If the priest, on examining it, finds that the infection on the walls of the house consists of greenish or reddish depressions which seem to go deeper than the surface of the wall, [38]he shall close the door of the house behind him and quarantine the house for seven days. [39]On the seventh day the priest shall return to examine the house again. If he finds that the infection has spread on the walls, [40]he shall order the infected stones to be pulled out and cast in an unclean place outside the city. [41]The whole inside of the house shall then be scraped, and the mortar that has been scraped off shall be dumped in an unclean place outside the city. [42]Then new stones shall be brought and put in the place of the old stones, and new mortar shall be made and plastered on the house.

[43]"If the infection breaks out once more after the stones have been pulled out and the house has been scraped and replastered, [44]the priest shall come again; and if he finds that the infection has spread in the house, it is corrosive leprosy, and the house is unclean. [45]It shall be pulled down, and all its stones, beams and mortar shall be hauled away to an unclean place outside the city. [46]Whoever enters a house while it is quarantined shall be unclean until evening. [47]Whoever sleeps or eats in such a house shall also wash his garments. [48]If the priest finds, when he comes to examine the house, that the infection has in fact not spread after the plastering, he shall declare the house clean, since the infection has been healed. [49]To purify the house, he shall take two birds, as well as cedar wood, scarlet yarn, and hyssop. [50]One of the birds he shall slay over an earthen vessel with spring water in it. [51]Then, taking the cedar wood, the hyssop and the scarlet yarn, together with the living bird, he shall dip them all in the blood of the slain bird and the spring water, and sprinkle the house seven times. [52]Thus shall he purify the house with the bird's blood and the spring water, along with the living bird, the cedar wood, the hyssop, and the scarlet yarn. [53]He shall then let the living bird fly away over the countryside outside the city. When he has thus made atonement for it, the house will be clean.

[54]"This is the law for every kind of human leprosy and scall, [55r]for leprosy of garments and houses, [56]as well as for scabs, pustules and blotches, [57]so that it may be manifest when there is a state of uncleanness and when a state of cleanness. This is the law for leprosy."

CHAPTER 15

Personal Uncleanness. [1]The LORD said to Moses and Aaron, [2]"Speak to the Is-

See RG
129-31

r: Lv 13, 47-58.

raelites and tell them: Every man who is afflicted with a chronic flow from his private parts is thereby unclean.*s* *3*Such is his uncleanness from this flow that it makes no difference whether the flow drains off or is blocked up; his uncleanness remains. *4*Any bed on which the man afflicted with the flow lies, is unclean, and any piece of furniture on which he sits, is unclean. *5*Anyone who touches his bed shall wash his garments, bathe in water, and be unclean until evening. *6*Whoever sits on a piece of furniture on which the afflicted man was sitting, shall wash his garments, bathe in water, and be unclean until evening. *7*Whoever touches the body of the afflicted man shall wash his garments, bathe in water, and be unclean until evening. *8*If the afflicted man spits on a clean man, the latter shall wash his garments, bathe in water, and be unclean until evening. *9*Any saddle on which the afflicted man rides, is unclean. *10*Whoever touches anything that was under him shall be unclean until evening; whoever lifts up any such thing shall wash his garments, bathe in water, and be unclean until evening. *11*Anyone whom the afflicted man touches with unrinsed hands shall wash his garments, bathe in water, and be unclean until evening. *12*Earthenware touched by the afflicted man shall be broken; and every wooden article shall be rinsed with water.

13"When a man who has been afflicted with a flow becomes free of his affliction, he shall wait seven days for his purification. Then he shall wash his garments and bathe his body in fresh water, and so he will be clean. *14*On the eighth day he shall take two turtledoves or two pigeons, and going before the LORD, to the entrance of the meeting tent, he shall give them to the priest, *15*who shall offer them up, the one as a sin offering and the other as a holocaust. Thus shall the priest make atonement before the LORD for the man's flow.

16"When a man has an emission of seed, he shall bathe his whole body in water and be unclean until evening. *17*Any piece of cloth or leather with seed on it shall be washed with water and be unclean until evening.

18"If a man lies carnally with a woman, they shall both bathe in water and be unclean until evening.

19"When a woman has her menstrual flow, she shall be in a state of impurity for seven days.*t* Anyone who touches her shall be unclean until evening. *20*Anything on which she lies or sits during her impurity shall be unclean. *21*Anyone who touches her bed shall wash his garments, bathe in water, and be unclean until evening. *22*Whoever touches any article of furniture on which she was sitting, shall wash his garments, bathe in water, and be unclean until evening. *23**But if she is on the bed or on the seat when he touches it, he shall be unclean until evening. *24*If a man dares to lie with her, he contracts her impurity and shall be unclean for seven days;*u* every bed on which he then lies also becomes unclean.

25"When a woman is afflicted with a flow of blood for several days outside her menstrual period, or when her flow continues beyond the ordinary period,*v* as long as she suffers this unclean flow she shall be unclean, just as during her menstrual period. *26*Any bed on which she lies during such a flow becomes unclean, as it would during her menstruation, and any article of furniture on which she sits becomes unclean just as during her menstruation. *27*Anyone who touches them becomes unclean; he shall wash his garments, bathe in water, and be unclean until evening.

28"If she becomes freed from her affliction, she shall wait seven days, and only then is she to be purified. *29*On the eighth day she shall take two turtledoves or two pigeons and bring them to the priest at the entrance of the meeting tent. *30*The priest shall offer up one of them as a sin offering and the other as a holocaust. Thus shall the priest make atonement before the LORD for her unclean flow.

31"You shall warn the Israelites of their

15, 23: What is added to the legislation by this verse is uncertain in both the Hebrew and the Greek.

s: Nm 5, 2.   t: Lv 12, 2. 5.   u: Lv 18, 19.   v: Mt 9, 20; Mk 5, 25; Lk 8, 43.

uncleanness, lest by defiling my Dwelling, which is in their midst, their uncleanness be the cause of their death.

[32]"This is the law for the man who is afflicted with a chronic flow, or who has an emission of seed, and thereby becomes unclean; [33]as well as for the woman who has her menstrual period, or who is afflicted with a chronic flow; the law for male and female; and also for the man who lies with an unclean woman."

See RG 131

CHAPTER 16

The Day of Atonement. [1]After the death of Aaron's two sons, who died when they approached the LORD's presence, the LORD spoke to Moses [2]and said to him,[w] "Tell your brother Aaron that he is not to come whenever he pleases into the sanctuary, inside the veil,* in front of the propitiatory on the ark; otherwise, when I reveal myself in a cloud above the propitiatory, he will die. [3]Only in this way may Aaron enter the sanctuary. He shall bring a young bullock for a sin offering and a ram for a holocaust. [4]He shall wear the sacred linen tunic, with the linen drawers next his flesh, gird himself with the linen sash and put on the linen miter. But since these vestments are sacred, he shall not put them on until he has first bathed his body in water. [5]From the Israelite community he shall receive two male goats for a sin offering and one ram for a holocaust.[x]

[6]"Aaron shall bring in the bullock, his sin offering to atone for himself and for his household. [7]Taking the two male goats, and setting them before the LORD at the entrance of the meeting tent, [8]he shall cast lots to determine which one is for the LORD and which for Azazel.* [9]The goat that is determined by lot for the LORD, Aaron shall bring in and offer up as a sin offering. [10]But the goat determined by lot for Azazel he shall set alive before the LORD, so that with it he may make atonement by sending it off to Azazel in the desert.

[11]"Thus shall Aaron offer up the bullock, his sin offering, to atone for himself and for his family. When he has slaughtered it, [12]he shall take a censer full of glowing embers from the altar before the LORD, as well as a double handful of finely ground fragrant incense, and bringing them inside the veil, [13]there before the LORD he shall put incense on the fire, so that a cloud of incense may cover the propitiatory over the commandments; else he will die.* [14]Taking some of the bullock's blood, he shall sprinkle it with his finger on the fore part of the propitiatory and likewise sprinkle some of the blood with his finger seven times in front of the propitiatory.[y]

[15]"Then he shall slaughter the people's sin-offering goat, and bringing its blood inside the veil, he shall do with it as he did with the bullock's blood, sprinkling it on the propitiatory and before it.[z] [16]Thus he shall make atonement for the sanctuary because of all the sinful defilements and faults of the Israelites. He shall do the same for the meeting tent, which is set up among them in the midst of their uncleanness. [17]No one else may be in the meeting tent from the time he enters the sanctuary to make atonement until he departs. When he has made atonement for himself and his household, as well as for the whole Israelite community, [18]he shall come out to the altar before the LORD and make atonement for it also. Taking some of the bullock's and the goat's blood, he shall put it on the horns around the altar,[a] [19]and with his finger sprinkle some of the blood on it seven times. Thus he shall render it clean and holy, purged of the defilements of the Israelites.

The Scapegoat. [20]"When he has completed the atonement rite for the sanctuary, the meeting tent and the altar, Aaron shall bring forward the live goat. [21]Laying both

---

16, 2: The sanctuary, inside the veil: the innermost part of the sanctuary, known also as "the holy of holies." Cf Ex 26, 33f. Here the high priest was allowed to enter only once a year, on Yom Kippur, the Day of Atonement. In Heb 9, 3-12 this ceremony is applied to Christ's single act of Redemption, whereby he won for us an everlasting atonement. Propitiatory: see note on Ex 25, 17.

16, 8: Azazel: perhaps a name of Satan, used only in this chapter. The ancient versions translated this word as "the escaping goat," whence the English word "scapegoat."

16, 13: Else he will die: the smoke is to conceal the resplendent majesty of God, the sight of which would strike any man dead.

w: Heb 9, 6-12.   *x*: Nm 29, 11.   *y*: Heb 9, 13. 25.   *z*: Heb 5, 1; 6, 19.

hands on its head, he shall confess over it all the sinful faults and transgressions of the Israelites, and so put them on the goat's head.[b] He shall then have it led into the desert by an attendant. [22] Since the goat is to carry off their iniquities to an isolated region, it must be sent away into the desert.[c]

[23]*"After Aaron has again gone into the meeting tent, he shall strip off and leave in the sanctuary the linen vestments he had put on when he entered there. [24] After bathing his body with water in a sacred place, he shall put on his vestments, and then come out and offer his own and the people's holocaust, in atonement for himself and for the people, [25] and also burn the fat of the sin offering on the altar.

[26]"The man who has led away the goat for Azazel shall wash his garments and bathe his body in water; only then may he enter the camp. [27] The sin-offering bullock and goat whose blood was brought into the sanctuary to make atonement, shall be taken outside the camp,[d] where their hides and flesh and offal shall be burned up in the fire. [28] The one who burns them shall wash his garments and bathe his body in water; only then may he enter the camp.

The Fast. [29e]"This shall be an everlasting ordinance for you: on the tenth day of the seventh month every one of you, whether a native or a resident alien, shall mortify himself* and shall do no work. [30] Since on this day atonement is made for you to make you clean, so that you may be cleansed of all your sins before the LORD, [31] by everlasting ordinance it shall be a most solemn sabbath for you, on which you must mortify yourselves.

[32]"This atonement is to be made by the priest who has been anointed and ordained to the priesthood in succession to his father.

He shall wear the linen garments, the sacred vestments, [33] and make atonement for the sacred sanctuary, the meeting tent and the altar, as well as for the priests and all the people of the community. [34] This, then, shall be an everlasting ordinance for you: once a year atonement shall be made for all the sins of the Israelites."[f]

Thus was it done, as the LORD had commanded Moses.

IV: Code of Legal Holiness

CHAPTER 17

See RG 131-32

Sacredness of Blood. [1] The LORD said to Moses, [2] "Speak to Aaron and his sons, as well as to all the Israelites, and tell them: This is what the LORD has commanded. [3]*Any Israelite who slaughters an ox or a sheep or a goat, whether in the camp or outside of it, [4] without first bringing it to the entrance of the meeting tent to present it as an offering to the LORD in front of his Dwelling, shall be judged guilty of bloodshed; and for this, such a man shall be cut off from among his people. [5] Therefore, such sacrifices as they used to offer up in the open field the Israelites shall henceforth offer to the LORD, bringing them to the priest at the entrance of the meeting tent and sacrificing them there as peace offerings to the LORD. [6] The priest shall splash the blood on the altar of the LORD at the entrance of the meeting tent and there burn the fat for an odor pleasing to the LORD. [7] No longer shall they offer their sacrifices to the satyrs to whom they used to render their wanton worship.[g] This shall be an everlasting ordinance for them and their descendants.

[8]"Tell them, therefore: Anyone, whether of the house of Israel or of the aliens residing among them, who offers a holocaust or

---

16, 23: This verse is best read after v 25. According to later Jewish practice the high priest again went into the holy of holies to remove the censer.

16, 29: Mortify himself: literally, "afflict his soul"; traditionally understood by the Jews as signifying abstinence from all food. This is the only fast day prescribed in the Mosaic law.

17, 3ff: The ancients considered blood the seat and sign of life, and therefore something sacred, even in animals. Cf Gn 9, 4f. Hence, even the ordinary butchering of an animal for

meat was looked upon as having a sacrificial character, so that it should be performed at the sanctuary. This law, however, could not be carried out without great difficulty when the Israelites were scattered throughout Palestine, and so was modified in Dt 12, 20ff.

a: Ex 30, 12. *b:* Is 53, 6; 2 Cor 5, 21. *c:* Is 53, 11. 12; Jn 1, 29; 1 Pt 2, 24. *d:* Heb 13, 11. *e:* Lv 23, 27. 32; Nm 29, 7. *f:* Heb 9, 7. 25. *g:* Ex 34, 15; Dt 32, 17; 2 Chr 11, 15; 1 Cor 10, 20.

sacrifice [9] without bringing it to the entrance of the meeting tent to offer it to the LORD, shall be cut off from his kinsmen. [10] And if anyone, whether of the house of Israel or of the aliens residing among them, partakes of any blood, I will set myself against that one who partakes of blood and will cut him off from among his people.[h] [11][i] Since the life of a living body is in its blood, I have made you put it on the altar, so that atonement may thereby be made for your own lives,* because it is the blood, as the seat of life, that makes atonement. [12] That is why I have told the Israelites: No one among you, not even a resident alien, may partake of blood.

[13] "Anyone hunting, whether of the Israelites or of the aliens residing among them, who catches an animal or a bird that may be eaten, shall pour out its blood and cover it with earth. [14] Since the life of every living body is its blood, I have told the Israelites: You shall not partake of the blood of any meat.[j] Since the life of every living body is its blood, anyone who partakes of it shall be cut off.

[15][k] Everyone, whether a native or an alien, who eats of an animal that died of itself or was killed by a wild beast, shall wash his garments, bathe in water, and be unclean until evening, and then he will be clean. [16] If he does not wash or does not bathe his body, he shall have the guilt to bear."

See RG
131-32

CHAPTER 18

The Sanctity of Sex. [1] The LORD said to Moses, [2] "Speak to the Israelites and tell them: I, the LORD, am your God. [3] You shall not do as they do in the land of Egypt, where you once lived, nor shall you do as they do in the land of Canaan, where I am bringing you; do not conform to their customs. [4] My decrees you shall carry out, and my statutes you shall take care to follow. I, the LORD, am your God. [5] Keep, then, my statutes and decrees, for the man who carries them out will find life through them. I am the LORD.[l]

[6] *"None of you shall approach a close relative to have sexual intercourse with her. I am the LORD. [7][m] You shall not disgrace your father by having intercourse with your mother. Besides, since she is your own mother, you shall not have intercourse with her. [8] You shall not have intercourse with your father's wife,[n] for that would be a disgrace to your father. [9] You shall not have intercourse with your sister, your father's daughter or your mother's daughter, whether she was born in your own household or born elsewhere. [10] You shall not have intercourse with your son's daughter or with your daughter's daughter, for that would be a disgrace to your own family. [11] You shall not have intercourse with the daughter whom your father's wife bore to him, since she, too, is your sister. [12][o] You shall not have intercourse with your father's sister, since she is your father's relative. [13] You shall not have intercourse with your mother's sister, since she is your mother's relative. [14] You shall not disgrace your father's brother by being intimate with his wife,[p] since she, too, is your aunt. [15] You shall not have intercourse with your daughter-in-law; she is your son's wife, and therefore you shall not disgrace her. [16] You shall not have intercourse with your brother's wife,* for that would be a disgrace to your brother.[q] [17] You shall not have intercourse with a woman and also with her daughter, nor shall you marry and have intercourse with her son's daughter or her daughter's daughter; this would be shameful, because they are related to her. [18] While

17, 11: That atonement may thereby be made for your own lives: hence, the sacrifice of an animal was a symbolic act which substituted the victim's life for the life of the offerer, who thus acknowledged that he deserved God's punishments for his sins. This idea of sacrifice is applied in Heb 9–10 to the death of Christ, inasmuch as "without the shedding of blood there is no forgiveness" (Heb 9, 22).

18, 6-18: These laws are formulated as directed to the male Israelites only, but naturally the same norms of consanguinity and affinity would apply to the women as well. Marriage, as well as casual intercourse, is here forbidden between men and women of the specified degrees of relationship.

18, 16: With your brother's wife: it was the violation of this law which aroused the wrath of John the Baptist against Herod Antipas. Cf Mk 6, 18. An exception to this law is made in Dt 25, 5.

h: Lv 3, 17. *i:* Gn 9, 4. *j:* Lv 7, 26f. *k:* Lv 11, 39f; 22, 8. *l:* Gal 3, 12. *m:* 7-16: Lv 20, 11-21. *n:* Dt 23, 1; 27, 20; 1 Cor 5, 1. *o:* 12f: Lv 20, 19. *p:* Lv 20, 20. *q:* Lv 20, 21; Mt 14, 3f; Mk 6, 18.

your wife is still living you shall not marry her sister as her rival; for thus you would disgrace your first wife.

19"You shall not approach a woman to have intercourse with her while she is unclean from menstruation. *20*You shall not have carnal relations with your neighbor's wife, defiling yourself with her. *21r*You shall not offer any of your offspring to be immolated to Molech,* thus profaning the name of your God. I am the LORD. *22*You shall not lie with a male as with a woman; such a thing is an abomination.*s 23*You shall not have carnal relations with an animal, defiling yourself with it; nor shall a woman set herself in front of an animal to mate with it; such things are abhorrent.*t*

24"Do not defile yourselves by any of these things by which the nations whom I am driving out of your way have defiled themselves. *25*Because their land has become defiled, I am punishing it for its wickedness, by making it vomit out its inhabitants. *26*You, however, whether natives or resident aliens, must keep my statutes and decrees forbidding all such abominations *27*by which the previous inhabitants defiled the land; *28*otherwise the land will vomit you out also for having defiled it, just as it vomited out the nations before you. *29*Everyone who does any of these abominations shall be cut off from among his people. *30*Heed my charge, then, not to defile yourselves by observing the abominable customs that have been observed before you.*u* I, the LORD, am your God."

CHAPTER 19

See RG 131–32 *Various Rules of Conduct.* *1*The LORD said to Moses, *2*"Speak to the whole Israelite community and tell them: Be holy, for I, the LORD, your God, am holy.*v 3*Revere your mother and father,*w* and keep my sabbaths. I, the LORD, am your God.

4"Do not turn aside to idols, nor make molten gods for yourselves.*x* I, the LORD, am your God.

5"When you sacrifice your peace offering to the LORD, if you wish it to be acceptable, *6*it must be eaten on the very day of your sacrifice or on the following day. Whatever is left over until the third day shall be burned up in the fire. *7*If any of it is eaten on the third day, the sacrifice will be unacceptable as refuse;*y 8*whoever eats of it then shall pay the penalty for having profaned what is sacred to the LORD. Such a one shall be cut off from his people.

9"When you reap the harvest of your land, you shall not be so thorough that you reap the field to its very edge, nor shall you glean the stray ears of grain.*z 10*Likewise, you shall not pick your vineyard bare, nor gather up the grapes that have fallen. These things you shall leave for the poor and the alien. I, the LORD, am your God.

11"You shall not steal. You shall not lie or speak falsely to one another.*a 12*You shall not swear falsely by my name, thus profaning the name of your God.*b* I am the LORD.

13"You shall not defraud or rob your neighbor. You shall not withhold overnight the wages of your day laborer.*c 14*You shall not curse the deaf, or put a stumbling block in front of the blind, but you shall fear your God. I am the LORD.

15"You shall not act dishonestly in rendering judgment. Show neither partiality to the weak nor deference to the mighty, but judge your fellow men justly.*d 16*You shall not go about spreading slander among your kinsmen; nor shall you stand by idly when your neighbor's life is at stake. I am the LORD.

17"You shall not bear hatred for your brother in your heart.*e* Though you may have to reprove your fellow man, do not incur sin because of him. *18*Take no revenge and cherish no grudge against your fellow country-

---

18, 21: Immolated to Molech: the reference is to the Canaanite custom of sacrificing children to the god Molech. The little victims were first slain and then cremated. Cf Ez 16, 20ff; 20, 26. 31; 23, 37.

r: Lv 20, 2-5; Dt 18, 10; 2 Kgs 16, 3; 21, 6.   *s:* Lv 20, 13; Rom 1, 27; 1 Cor 6, 9f.   *t:* Lv 20, 15f; Ex 22, 18.   *u:* Lv 20, 23; Dt 18, 9. *v:* Lv 11, 44; Mt 5, 48; 1 Pt 1, 16.   *w:* Ex 20, 12.   *x:* Lv 26, 1; Ex 20, 3-5; 34, 17; Dt 27, 15.   *y:* Lv 7, 18.   *z:* Lv 23, 22; Dt 24, 19ff. *a:* Ex 20, 15f.   *b:* Ex 20, 7; Mt 5, 33.   *c:* Dt 24, 14f.   *d:* Ex 23, 2f; Dt 1, 17; 16, 19; Ps 82, 2; Prv 24, 23.   *e:* Mt 18, 15; Lk 17, 3; Gal 6, 1; 1 Jn 3, 14.

men. You shall love your neighbor as your-self.* I am the LORD.ᶠ

¹⁹"Keep my statutes: do not breed any of your domestic animals with others of a different species; do not sow a field of yours with two different kinds of seed; and do not put on a garment woven with two different kinds of thread.

²⁰*"If a man has carnal relations with a female slave who has already been living with another man but has not yet been redeemed or given her freedom, they shall be punished but not put to death, because she is not free. ²¹The man, moreover, shall bring to the entrance of the meeting tent a ram as his guilt offering to the LORD. ²²With this ram the priest shall make atonement before the LORD for the sin he has committed, and it will be forgiven him.

²³"When you come into the land and plant any fruit tree there, first look upon its fruit as if it were uncircumcised.* For three years, while its fruit remains uncircumcised, it may not be eaten. ²⁴In the fourth year, however, all of its fruit shall be sacred to the LORD as a thanksgiving feast to him. ²⁵Not until the fifth year may you eat its fruit. Thus it will continue its yield for you. I, the LORD, am your God.

²⁶"Do not eat meat with the blood still in it.ᵍ Do not practice divination or soothsaying. ²⁷*Do not clip your hair at the temples, nor trim the edges of your beard.ʰ ²⁸Do not lacerate your bodies for the dead, and do not tattoo yourselves. I am the LORD.

²⁹"You shall not degrade your daughter by making a prostitute of her; else the land will become corrupt and full of lewdness. ³⁰Keep my sabbaths, and reverence my sanctuary.ⁱ I am the LORD.

³¹"Do not go to mediums or consult for-tune-tellers, for you will be defiled by them.ʲ I, the LORD, am your God.

³²"Stand up in the presence of the aged, and show respect for the old; thus shall you fear your God. I am the LORD.

³³"When an alien resides with you in your land, do not molest him.ᵏ ³⁴You shall treat the alien who resides with you no differently than the natives born among you; have the same love for him as for yourself; for you too were once aliens in the land of Egypt.ˡ I, the LORD, am your God.

³⁵"Do not act dishonestly in using measures of length or weight or capacity. ³⁶You shall have a true scale and true weights, an honest ephah and an honest hin.ᵐ I, the LORD, am your God, who brought you out of the land of Egypt. ³⁷Be careful, then, to observe all my statutes and decrees. I am the LORD."

CHAPTER 20

See RG 131-32

Penalties for Various Sins. ¹The LORD said to Moses, ²"Tell the Israelites: Anyone, whether an Israelite or an alien residing in Israel, who gives any of his offspring to Molech shall be put to death.ⁿ Let his fellow citizens stone him. ³I myself will turn against such a man and cut him off from the body of his people; for in giving his offspring to Molech, he has defiled my sanctuary and profaned my holy name. ⁴Even if his fellow citizens connive at such a man's crime of giving his offspring to Molech, and fail to put him to death, ⁵I myself will set my face against that man and his family and will cut off from their people both him and all who join him in his wanton worship of Molech. ⁶Should anyone turn to mediums and fortune-tellers and follow their wanton ways,ᵖ I will turn against such a one and cut him off from his people. ⁷Sanctify your-

19, 18: You shall love your neighbor as yourself: cited by our Lord as the second of the two most important commandments of God. Cf Mt 22, 39; Mk 12, 31. Although in the present context the word "neighbor" is restricted to "fellow countrymen," in Lk 10, 29-37 Christ extends its meaning to embrace all men, even enemies. Cf also Mt 5, 43ff.

19, 20ff: This law seems out of its proper context here; perhaps it stood originally after Lv 20, 12. Female slave . . . given her freedom: reference is to the case treated of in Ex 21, 7-11.

19, 23ff: Uncircumcised: by analogy with a newborn boy,

the newly planted tree was considered impure until "circumcised" by offering to the Lord all the fruit it bore in the fourth year.

19, 27: See note on Lv 21, 5.

 f: Mt 5, 43; 19, 19; 22, 39; Mk 12, 31; Rom 13, 9; Gal 5, 14; Jas 2, 8. g: Lv 3, 17; Dt 18, 10; 2 Kgs 17, 17; 21, 6; 2 Chr 33, 6. h: Lv 21, 5. i: Lv 26, 2; Ex 20, 8. j: Lv 20, 6. 27; Dt 18, 11; Is 8, 19. k: Ex 22, 20; 23, 9; Jer 22, 3; Mal 3, 5. l: Dt 10, 19. m: Dt 25, 13. 15; Prv 11, 1; 16, 11; 20, 10; Ez 45, 10. n: Lv 18, 21. o: Ez 23, 39. p: Lv 19, 31.

selves, then, and be holy; for I, the LORD, your God, am holy.*q* *8*Be careful, therefore, to observe what I, the LORD, who make you holy, have prescribed.

9"Anyone who curses his father or mother shall be put to death;*r* since he has cursed his father or mother, he has forfeited his life. *10*If a man commits adultery with his neighbor's wife, both the adulterer and the adulteress shall be put to death.*s* *11*If a man disgraces his father*t* by lying with his father's wife, both the man and his stepmother shall be put to death; they have forfeited their lives. *12*If a man lies with his daughter-in-law,*u* both of them shall be put to death; since they have committed an abhorrent deed, they have forfeited their lives. *13*If a man lies with a male as with a woman,*v* both of them shall be put to death for their abominable deed; they have forfeited their lives. *14*If a man marries a woman and her mother also,*w* the man and the two women as well shall be burned to death for their shameful conduct, so that such shamefulness may not be found among you. *15*If a man has carnal relations with an animal, the man shall be put to death,*x* and the animal shall be slain. *16*If a woman goes up to any animal to mate with it,*y* the woman and the animal shall be slain; let them both be put to death; their lives are forfeit. *17*If a man consummates marriage with his sister or his half-sister,*z* they shall be publicly cut off from their people for this shameful deed; the man shall pay the penalty of having had intercourse with his own sister. *18*If a man lies in sexual intercourse with a woman during her menstrual period,*a* both of them shall be cut off from their people, because they have laid bare the flowing fountain of her blood. *19*You shall not have intercourse with your mother's sister or your father's sister;*b* whoever does so shall pay the penalty of incest. *20*If a man disgraces his uncle by having intercourse with his uncle's wife, the man and his aunt shall pay the penalty by dying childless. *21*If a man marries his brother's wife and thus disgraces his brother, they shall be childless because of this incest.

22"Be careful to observe all my statutes and all my decrees; otherwise the land where I am bringing you to dwell will vomit you out. *23*Do not conform, therefore, to the customs of the nations*c* whom I am driving out of your way, because all these things that they have done have filled me with disgust for them. *24*But to you I have said:*d* Their land shall be your possession, a land flowing with milk and honey. I am giving it to you as your own, I, the LORD, your God, who have set you apart from the other nations. *25e*You, too, must set apart, then, the clean animals from the unclean, and the clean birds from the unclean, so that you may not be contaminated with the uncleanness of any beast or bird or of any swarming creature in the land that I have set apart for you. *26*To me, therefore, you shall be sacred; for I, the LORD, am sacred,*f* I, who have set you apart from the other nations to be my own.

27*"A man or a woman who acts as a medium or fortune-teller*g* shall be put to death by stoning; they have no one but themselves to blame for their death."

CHAPTER 21

See RG
131–32

Sanctity of the Priesthood. *1*The LORD said to Moses, "Speak to Aaron's sons, the priests, and tell them: None of you shall make himself unclean for any dead person* among his people,*h* *2*except for his nearest relatives, his mother or father, his son or daughter, his brother *3*or his maiden sister, who is of his own family while she remains unmarried; for these he may make himself unclean. *4*But for a sister who has married out of his family he shall not make himself unclean; this would be a profanation. *5**"The priests shall not make bare the

20, 27: This verse is best read immediately after v 6.

21, 1: Unclean for any dead person: by preparing the corpse for burial. Cf Nm 6, 6; 19, 11-19.

21, 5: Such mourning customs of the Canaanites were forbidden to all the Israelites, but especially to the priests. Cf Lv 19, 27f.

q: Lv 11, 44; 19, 2; 1 Pt 1, 16.   *r:* Ex 21, 17; Prv 20, 20; Mt 15, 4; Mk 7, 10.   *s:* Lv 18, 20; Dt 22, 22; Jn 8, 5.   *t:* Lv 18, 7f.   *u:* Lv 18, 15.   *v:* Lv 18, 22.   *w:* Lv 18, 17; Dt 27, 23.   *x:* Ex 22, 18; Dt 27, 21.   *y:* Lv 18, 23.   *z:* Lv 18, 9; Dt 27, 22.   *a:* Lv 18, 19.   *b:* Lv 18, 12f.   *c:* Lv 18, 30.   *d:* Ex 3, 8. 17; 6, 8.   *e:* Lv 11, 2-47; Dt 14, 4-20.   *f:* Lv 11, 44; Ex 19, 6; 1 Pt 1, 16.   *g:* Lv 19, 31; Ex 22, 17; Dt 18, 11.   *h:* Ez 44, 25.

crown of the head, nor shave the edges of the beard,[i] nor lacerate the body. [6]To their God they shall be sacred,* and not profane his name; since they offer up the oblations of the LORD, the food of their God, they must be holy.

[7]"A priest shall not marry a woman who has been a prostitute or has lost her honor, nor a woman who has been divorced by her husband; for the priest is sacred to his God.[j] [8]Honor him as sacred who offers up the food of your God; treat him as sacred, because I, the LORD, who have consecrated him, am sacred.

[9]"A priest's daughter who loses her honor by committing fornication and thereby dishonors her father also, shall be burned to death.

[10]"The most exalted of the priests, upon whose head the anointing oil has been poured and who has been ordained to wear the special vestments, shall not bare his head* or rend his garments, [11]nor shall he go near any dead person. Not even for his father or mother may he thus become unclean [12]or leave the sanctuary;[k] otherwise he will profane the sanctuary of his God, for with the anointing oil upon him, he is dedicated to his God, to me, the LORD.

[13]"The priest shall marry a virgin. [14]Not a widow or a woman who has been divorced or a woman who has lost her honor as a prostitute, but a virgin, taken from his own people, shall he marry;[l] [15]otherwise he will have base offspring among his people. I, the LORD, have made him sacred."

Irregularities. [16]The LORD said to Moses, [17]"Speak to Aaron and tell him: None of your descendants, of whatever generation, who has any defect shall come forward to offer up the food of his God. [18]Therefore, he who has any of the following defects may not come forward: he who is blind, or lame, or who has any disfigurement or malformation, [19]or a crippled foot or hand, [20]or who is humpbacked or weakly or walleyed, or who

is afflicted with eczema, ringworm or hernia. [21]No descendant of Aaron the priest who has any such defect may draw near to offer up the oblations of the LORD; on account of his defect he may not draw near to offer up the food of his God. [22]He may, however, partake of the food of his God: of what is most sacred as well as of what is sacred. [23]Only, he may not approach the veil nor go up to the altar on account of his defect; he shall not profane these things that are sacred to me, for it is I, the LORD, who make them sacred."

[24]Moses, therefore, told this to Aaron and his sons and to all the Israelites.

CHAPTER 22

See RG 131-32

Sacrificial Banquets. [1]The LORD said to Moses, [2]"Tell Aaron and his sons to respect the sacred offerings which the Israelites consecrate to me; else they will profane my holy name. I am the LORD.

[3]"Tell them: If any one of you, or of your descendants in any future generation, dares, while he is in a state of uncleanness, to draw near the sacred offerings which the Israelites consecrate to the LORD, such a one shall be cut off from my presence. I am the LORD.

[4]"No descendant of Aaron who is stricken with leprosy, or who suffers from a flow, may eat of these sacred offerings, unless he again becomes clean.[m] Moreover, if anyone touches a person who has become unclean by contact with a corpse, or if anyone has had an emission of seed, [5]or if anyone touches[n] any swarming creature or any man whose uncleanness, of whatever kind it may be, is contagious, [6]the one who touches such as these shall be unclean until evening and may not eat of the sacred portions until he has first bathed his body in water;[o] [7]then, when the sun sets, he again becomes clean. Only then may he eat of the sacred offerings, which are his food. [8]He shall not make himself unclean by eating of any animal that has died of itself or has been killed by wild beasts.[p] I am the LORD.

21, 6: Sacred: the same Hebrew word has both the active meaning of "holy," that is, keeping oneself free from profane impurities, and the passive meaning of "sacred," that is, set apart from what is profane and therefore treated with religious reverence.

21, 10: Bare his head: see note on Lv 10, 6.

i: Ez 44, 20. *j:* Ez 44, 22. *k:* Lv 10, 7. *l:* Ez 44, 22. *m:* Lv 7, 20; 15, 16. *n:* Lv 11, 24. 43. *o:* Heb 10, 22. *p:* Lv 17, 15; Dt 14, 21; Ez 44, 31.

9"They shall keep my charge and not do wrong in this matter; else they will die for their profanation. I am the LORD who have consecrated them.

10"Neither a lay person nor a priest's tenant or hired servant may eat of any sacred offering.*q* *11*But a slave whom a priest acquires by purchase or who is born in his house may eat of his food. *12*A priest's daughter who is married to a layman may not eat of the sacred contributions. *13*But if a priest's daughter is widowed or divorced and, having no children, returns to her father's house, she may then eat of her father's food as in her youth. No layman, however, may eat of it. *14r*If such a one eats of a sacred offering through inadvertence, he shall make restitution to the priest for the sacred offering, with an increment of one fifth of the amount. *15*The sacred offerings which the Israelites contribute to the LORD the priests shall not allow to be profaned*s* *16*nor in the eating of the sacred offering shall they bring down guilt that must be punished; it is I, the LORD, who make them sacred."

Unacceptable Victims. *17*The LORD said to Moses, *18*"Speak to Aaron and his sons and to all the Israelites, and tell them: When anyone of the house of Israel, or any alien residing in Israel, who wishes to offer a sacrifice, brings a holocaust as a votive offering or as a free-will offering to the LORD, *19*if it is to be acceptable, the ox or sheep or goat that he offers must be an unblemished male.*t* *20*You shall not offer one that has any defect, for such a one would not be acceptable for you.*u* *21*When anyone presents a peace offering*v* to the LORD from the herd or the flock in fulfillment of a vow, or as a free-will offering, if it is to find acceptance, it must be unblemished; it shall not have any defect. *22*One that is blind or crippled or maimed, or one that has a running sore or mange or ringworm, you shall not offer to the LORD; do not put such an animal on the altar as an oblation to the LORD. *23*An ox or a sheep that is in any way ill-proportioned or stunted you

may indeed present as a free-will offering, but it will not be acceptable as a votive offering. *24*One that has its testicles bruised or crushed or torn out or cut off you shall not offer to the LORD. You shall neither do this in your own land *25*nor receive from a foreigner any such animals to offer up as the food of your God; since they are deformed or defective,*w* they will not be acceptable for you."

*26*The LORD said to Moses, *27*"When an ox or a lamb or a goat is born, it shall remain with its mother for seven days; only from the eighth day onward will it be acceptable, to be offered as an oblation to the LORD.*x* *28*You shall not slaughter an ox or a sheep on one and the same day with its young. *29*Whenever you offer a thanksgiving sacrifice to the LORD, so offer it that it may be acceptable for you; *30*it must, therefore, be eaten on the same day; none of it shall be left over until the next day.*y* I am the LORD.

31"Be careful to observe the commandments which I, the LORD, give you, *32*and do not profane my holy name; in the midst of the Israelites I, the LORD, must be held as sacred. It is I who made you sacred *33*and led you out of the land of Egypt, that I, the LORD, might be your God."

CHAPTER 23

See RG 131-32

Holy Days. *1*The LORD said to Moses, *2*"Speak to the Israelites and tell them: The following are the festivals of the LORD, my feast days, which you shall celebrate with a sacred assembly.

3"For six days work may be done; but the seventh day is the sabbath rest, a day for sacred assembly, on which you shall do no work. The sabbath shall belong to the LORD wherever you dwell.*z*

Passover. *4*"These, then, are the festivals of the LORD which you shall celebrate at their proper time with a sacred assembly.*a* *5*The Passover of the LORD falls on the fourteenth day of the first month, at the evening twilight.*b* *6*The fifteenth day of this month is the LORD's feast of Unleavened Bread. For

q: 1 Sm 21, 6; Mt 12, 4. *r:* Lv 5, 16; 27, 13. 15. 19. *s:* Lv 19, 8; Nm 18, 32. *t:* Lv 1, 3. 10. *u:* Dt 15, 21; 17, 1; Mal 1, 8. 14. *v:* Lv 3, 1. 6. *w:* Mal 1, 14. *x:* Ex 22, 29. *y:* Lv 7, 15. *z:* Ex 20, 8-11; 23, 12; 31, 14f; 34, 21; Dt 5, 12-15; Lk 13, 14. *a:* Ex 23, 14-19. *b:* Nm 9, 2f; 28, 16.

seven days you shall eat unleavened bread.*c* ⁷On the first of these days you shall hold a sacred assembly and do no sort of work.*d* ⁸On each of the seven days you shall offer an oblation to the LORD. Then on the seventh day you shall again hold a sacred assembly and do no sort of work."

⁹The LORD said to Moses, ¹⁰"Speak to the Israelites and tell them: When you come into the land which I am giving you, and reap your harvest, you shall bring a sheaf of the first fruits of your harvest to the priest, ¹¹who shall wave the sheaf before the LORD that it may be acceptable for you. On the day after the sabbath* the priest shall do this. ¹²On this day, when your sheaf is waved, you shall offer to the LORD for a holocaust an unblemished yearling lamb. ¹³Its cereal offering shall be two tenths of an ephah of fine flour mixed with oil, as a sweet-smelling oblation to the LORD; and its libation shall be a fourth of a hin of wine. ¹⁴Until this day, when you bring your God this offering, you shall not eat any bread* or roasted grain or fresh kernels. This shall be a perpetual statute for you and your descendants wherever you dwell.

Pentecost. ¹⁵"Beginning with the day after the sabbath, the day on which you bring the wave-offering sheaf, you shall count seven full weeks,*e* ¹⁶and then on the day after the seventh week, the fiftieth* day,*f* you shall present the new cereal offering to the LORD. ¹⁷For the wave offering of your first fruits to the LORD, you shall bring with you from wherever you live two loaves of bread made of two tenths of an ephah of fine flour and baked with leaven. ¹⁸Besides the bread, you shall offer to the LORD a holocaust of seven unblemished yearling lambs, one young bull, and two rams, along with their cereal offering and libations, as a sweet-smelling oblation to the LORD. ¹⁹One male goat shall be sacrificed as a sin of-

fering, and two yearling lambs as a peace offering.*g* ²⁰The priest shall wave the bread of the first fruits and the two lambs as a wave offering before the LORD; these shall be sacred to the LORD and belong to the priest. ²¹On this same day you shall by proclamation have a sacred assembly, and no sort of work may be done. This shall be a perpetual statute for you and your descendants wherever you dwell.

²²"When you reap the harvest of your land, you shall not be so thorough that you reap the field to its very edge, nor shall you glean the stray ears of your grain. These things you shall leave for the poor and the alien. I, the LORD, am your God."

New Year's Day. ²³The LORD said to Moses, ²⁴"Tell the Israelites: On the first day of the seventh month you shall keep a sabbath rest, with a sacred assembly and with the trumpet blasts as a reminder; ²⁵you shall then do no sort of work, and you shall offer an oblation to the LORD."

The Day of Atonement. ²⁶*h*The LORD said to Moses, ²⁷"The tenth of this seventh month is the Day of Atonement,*i* when you shall hold a sacred assembly and mortify yourselves and offer an oblation to the LORD. ²⁸On this day you shall not do any work, because it is the Day of Atonement, when atonement is made for you before the LORD, your God. ²⁹Anyone who does not mortify himself on this day shall be cut off from his people; ³⁰and if anyone does any work on this day, I will remove him from the midst of his people. ³¹This is a perpetual statute for you and your descendants wherever you dwell: you shall do no work, ³²but shall keep a sabbath of complete rest and mortify yourselves. Beginning on the evening of the ninth of the month, you shall keep this sabbath of yours from evening to evening."

The Feast of Booths. ³³The LORD said to

23, 11: The sabbath: according to the Jewish tradition this was the feast day itself, the fifteenth of Nisan, which was a special day of rest. Cf v 7. However, some understand here the Saturday of the Passover week, or even the Saturday following it; cf Jn 19, 31.

23, 14: Any bread: made from the new grain. The harvest had first to be sanctified for man's use by this offering to God.

23, 16: The fiftieth: from the Greek word for this we have the name "Pentecost." Cf 2 Mc 12, 31; Acts 2, 1. It was also

called "the feast of the Seven Weeks," or simply "the feast of Weeks" (Nm 28, 26; Dt 16, 10; Tb 2, 1). The new cereal offering: of flour made from the new grain. Pentecost was the thanksgiving feast at the end of the grain harvest, which began after Passover. Later tradition made it a commemoration of the giving of the law at Sinai.

c: Ex 12, 18; 13, 3. 10; 23, 15; 34, 18.   *d:* Ex 12, 15; Nm 28, 18. 25.   *e:* Ex 34, 22; Nm 28, 26; Dt 16, 9.   *f:* Acts 2, 1.   *g:* Nm 28, 30.   *h:* Lv 25, 9.   *i:* Lv 16, 29f; Nm 29, 7.

Moses, [34]"Tell the Israelites: The fifteenth day of this seventh month[j] is the LORD's feast of Booths,* which shall continue for seven days. [35]On the first day there shall be a sacred assembly, and you shall do no sort of work. [36]For seven days you shall offer an oblation to the LORD, and on the eighth day you shall again hold a sacred assembly and offer an oblation to the LORD. On that solemn closing you shall do no sort of work.

[37]"These, therefore, are the festivals of the LORD on which you shall proclaim a sacred assembly, and offer as an oblation to the LORD holocausts and cereal offerings, sacrifices and libations, as prescribed for each day, [38]in addition to those of the LORD's sabbaths, your donations, your various votive offerings and the free-will offerings that you present to the LORD.

[39]"On the fifteenth day, then, of the seventh month, when you have gathered in the produce of the land,[k] you shall celebrate a pilgrim feast of the LORD for a whole week. The first and the eighth day shall be days of complete rest. [40]On the first day you shall gather foliage* from majestic trees, branches of palms and boughs of myrtles and of valley poplars, and then for a week you shall make merry before the LORD, your God. [41]By perpetual statute for you and your descendants you shall keep this pilgrim feast of the LORD for one whole week[l] in the seventh month of the year. [42]During this week every native Israelite among you shall dwell in booths, [43]that your descendants[m] may realize that, when I led the Israelites out of the land of Egypt, I made them dwell in booths. I, the LORD, am your God."

[44]Thus did Moses announce to the Israelites the festivals of the LORD.

CHAPTER 24

See RG 131–32

The Sanctuary Light. [1]The LORD said to Moses, [2]"Order the Israelites to bring you clear oil of crushed olives for the light, so that you may keep lamps burning regularly.[n] [3]In the meeting tent, outside the veil that hangs in front of the commandments, Aaron shall set up the lamps to burn before the LORD regularly, from evening till morning. Thus, by a perpetual statute for you and your descendants, [4]the lamps shall be set up on the pure gold lampstand,[o] to burn regularly before the LORD.

The Showbread. [5]"You shall take fine flour and bake it[p] into twelve cakes, using two tenths of an ephah of flour for each cake. [6]These you shall place in two piles, six in each pile, on the pure gold table before the LORD. [7]On each pile put some pure frankincense, which shall serve as an oblation to the LORD, a token offering for the bread. [8]Regularly on each sabbath day this bread shall be set out afresh[q] before the LORD, offered on the part of the Israelites by an everlasting agreement. [9]It shall belong to Aaron and his sons, who must eat it in a sacred place, since, as something most sacred among the various oblations to the LORD, it is his by perpetual right."

Punishment of Blasphemy. [10]Among the Israelites there was a man born of an Israelite mother (Shelomith, daughter of Dibri, of the tribe of Dan) and an Egyptian father. [11]This man quarreled publicly with another Israelite and cursed and blasphemed the LORD's name. So the people brought him to Moses, [12]who kept him in custody till a decision from the LORD should settle the case for them. [13]The LORD then said to Moses, [14]"Take the blasphemer outside the camp, and when all who heard him have laid their hands on his head, let the whole community stone him. [15]Tell the Israelites: Anyone who curses his God shall bear the penalty of his sin; [16]whoever blasphemes the name of the LORD shall be put to death.[r] The whole com-

---

23, 34: Feast of Booths: the joyful observance of the vintage and fruit harvest. Cf Dt 16, 13. During the seven days of the feast the Israelites camped in booths of branches erected on the roofs of their houses or in the streets in commemoration of their wanderings in the desert, where they dwelt in booths.

23, 40: Foliage: literally, "fruit," but here probably used in the general sense of "produce, growth." These branches were used for constructing the "booths" or huts in which the peo-

ple lived during the feast. Cf Neh 8, 15. However, from about the time of Christ on, the Jews have understood this of "fruit" in the strict sense; hence, branches of lemons and oranges were carried with the other branches in joyous procession.

---

j: Nm 29, 12; Dt 16, 13; 2 Mc 1, 9. 18; Jn 7, 2.   *k:* Ex 23, 16; Dt 16, 13.   *l:* Nm 29, 12-38.   *m:* Dt 31, 10-13.   *n:* Ex 27, 20f.   *o:* Ex 25, 31.   *p:* Ex 25, 30; 1 Kgs 7, 48; 2 Chr 4, 19; 13, 11; Heb 9, 2.   *q:* 1 Chr 9, 32.   *r:* 1 Kgs 21, 10. 13; Mt 26, 65f; Jn 10, 33.

munity shall stone him; alien and native alike must be put to death for blaspheming the LORD's name.

[17]"Whoever takes the life of any human being shall be put to death;[s] [18]whoever takes the life of an animal shall make restitution of another animal. A life for a life![t] [19]Anyone who inflicts an injury on his neighbor shall receive the same in return. [20]Limb for limb, eye for eye, tooth for tooth! The same injury that a man gives another shall be inflicted on him in return.[u] [21]Whoever slays an animal shall make restitution, but whoever slays a man shall be put to death. [22]You shall have but one rule, for alien and native alike.[v] I, the LORD, am your God."

[23]When Moses told this to the Israelites, they took the blasphemer outside the camp and stoned him;[w] they carried out the command that the LORD had given Moses.

See RG 131-32

CHAPTER 25

The Sabbatical Year. [1]The LORD said to Moses on Mount Sinai, [2]"Speak to the Israelites and tell them: When you enter the land that I am giving you, let the land, too, keep a sabbath for the LORD. [3]For six years you may sow your field, and for six years prune your vineyard, gathering in their produce.[x] [4]But during the seventh year the land shall have a complete rest, a sabbath for the LORD,[y] when you may neither sow your field nor prune your vineyard. [5]*The aftergrowth of your harvest you shall not reap, nor shall you pick the grapes of your untrimmed vines in this year of sabbath rest for the land. [6]While the land has its sabbath, all its produce will be food equally for you yourself and for your male and female slaves, for your hired help and the tenants who live with you, [7]and likewise for your livestock and for the wild animals on your land.

The Jubilee Year. [8]"Seven weeks of years shall you count—seven times seven years— so that the seven cycles amount to forty-nine years. [9]Then, on the tenth day of the seventh month let the trumpet resound; on this, the Day of Atonement, the trumpet blast shall re-echo throughout your land. [10]This fiftieth year* you shall make sacred by proclaiming liberty in the land for all its inhabitants.[z] It shall be a jubilee for you, when every one of you shall return to his own property, every one to his own family estate. [11]In this fiftieth year, your year of jubilee, you shall not sow, nor shall you reap the aftergrowth or pick the grapes from the untrimmed vines. [12]Since this is the jubilee, which shall be sacred for you, you may not eat of its produce, except as taken directly from the field.

[13]"In this year of jubilee, then, every one of you shall return to his own property. [14]Therefore, when you sell any land to your neighbor or buy any from him, do not deal unfairly. [15]On the basis of the number of years since the last jubilee shall you purchase the land from him;[a] and so also, on the basis of the number of years for crops, shall he sell it to you. [16]When the years are many, the price shall be so much the more; when the years are few, the price shall be so much the less. For it is really the number of crops that he sells you. [17]Do not deal unfairly, then; but stand in fear of your god. I, the LORD, am your God.

[18]"Observe my precepts and be careful to keep my regulations, for then you will dwell securely in the land. [19]The land will yield its fruit and you will have food in abundance, so that you may live there without worry.[b] [20]Therefore, do not say, 'What shall we eat in the seventh year, if we do not then sow or reap our crop?'[c] [21]I will bestow such blessings on you in the sixth year that there will then be crop enough for three years. [22]When you sow in the eighth year, you will continue

25, 5ff: As long as the produce of the sabbatical year remains on the field, it remains available to everyone; cf v 12. In Ex 23, 10f the poor and the wild beasts that have no other source of nourishment are alone mentioned.

25, 10: Fiftieth year: to arrive at this number, the preceding year of jubilee is included in the count, and therefore this is more exactly the forty-ninth year, the seventh sabbatical year. Liberty: Israelite slaves were set free (v 50) and landed property was returned to its original owner (v 13): two im-

portant laws for preserving the social and economic equilibrium. Jubilee: derived from the Hebrew word yobel, "ram's horn," which was blown on this occasion.

s: Gn 9, 5f; Ex 21, 12; Nm 35, 31; Dt 19, 11f.   *t:* Ex 21, 33f.   *u:* Dt 19, 21; Mt 5, 38.   *v:* Lv 19, 34; Ex 12, 49; Nm 15, 16.   *w:* Acts 7, 57f.   *x:* Ex 23, 10f.   *y:* 1 Mc 6, 49. 53.   *z:* Nm 36, 4; Is 61, 2; Ez 46, 17; Lk 4, 19.   *a:* Lv 27, 18. 23.   *b:* Lv 26, 5.   *c:* Mt 6, 25. 31; Lk 12, 22. 29.

to eat from the old crop; and even into the ninth year, when the crop comes in, you will still have the old to eat from.*d*

Redemption of Property. *23e*"The land shall not be sold in perpetuity; for the land is mine, and you are but aliens who have become my tenants. *24*Therefore, in every part of the country that you occupy, you must permit the land to be redeemed. *25*When one of your countrymen is reduced to poverty and has to sell some of his property, his closest relative, who has the right to redeem it, may go and buy back what his kinsman has sold.*f* *26*If, however, the man has no relative to redeem his land, but later on acquires sufficient means to buy it back in his own name, *27*he shall make a deduction from the price in proportion to the number of years since the sale, and then pay back the balance to the one to whom he sold it, so that he may thus regain his own property. *28*But if he does not acquire sufficient means to buy back his land, what he has sold shall remain in the possession of the purchaser until the jubilee, when it must be released and returned to its original owner.*g*

29"When someone sells a dwelling in a walled town, he has the right to buy it back during the time of one full year from its sale. *30*But if such a house in a walled town has not been redeemed at the end of a full year, it shall belong in perpetuity to the purchaser and his descendants; nor shall it be released in the jubilee. *31*However, houses in villages that are not encircled by walls shall be considered as belonging to the surrounding farm land; they may be redeemed at any time, and in the jubilee they must be released.

32"In levitical cities the Levites shall always have the right to redeem the town houses that are their property. *33*Any town house of the Levites in their cities that had been sold and not redeemed, shall be released in the jubilee; for the town houses of the Levites are their hereditary property in the midst of the Israelites. *34*Moreover, the pasture land belonging to their cities shall not be sold at all;*h* it must always remain their hereditary property.

35"When one of your fellow countrymen is reduced to poverty and is unable to hold out beside you, extend to him the privileges of an alien or a tenant, so that he may continue to live with you.*i* *36*Do not exact interest from your countryman either in money or in kind, but out of fear of God let him live with you. *37j*You are to lend him neither money at interest nor food at a profit. *38*I, the LORD, am your God, who brought you out of the land of Egypt to give you the land of Canaan and to be your God.

39"When, then, your countryman becomes so impoverished beside you that he sells you his services, do not make him work as a slave.*k* *40*Rather, let him be like a hired servant or like your tenant, working with you until the jubilee year, *41*when he, together with his children, shall be released from your service and return to his kindred and to the property of his ancestors. *42*Since those whom I brought out of the land of Egypt are servants of mine, they shall not be sold as slaves to any man. *43*Do not lord it over them harshly, but stand in fear of your God.

44"Slaves, male and female, you may indeed possess, provided you buy them from among the neighboring nations. *45*You may also buy them from among the aliens who reside with you and from their children who are born and reared in your land. Such slaves you may own as chattels, *46*and leave to your sons as their hereditary property, making them perpetual slaves. But you shall not lord it harshly over any of the Israelites, your kinsmen.*l*

47"When one of your countrymen is reduced to such poverty that he sells himself to a wealthy alien who has a permanent or a temporary residence among you, or to one of the descendants of an immigrant family, *48*even after he has thus sold his services he still has the right of redemption; he may be redeemed by one of his own brothers, *49*or by his uncle or cousin, or by some other relative or fellow clansman; or, if he acquires the means, he may redeem himself. *50*With

d: Lv 26, 10. *e:* 1 Pt 2, 11. *f:* Ru 2, 20; 4, 4. 6; Jer 32, 7f. *g:* Lv 27, 24. *h:* Nm 35, 3. *i:* Dt 15, 7. 8. *j:* Dt 23, 19. *k:* 1 Kgs 9, 22. *l:* Is 14, 1f.

his purchaser he shall compute the years from the sale to the jubilee, distributing the sale price over these years as though he had been hired as a day laborer. [51]The more such years there are, the more of the sale price he shall pay back as ransom; [52]the fewer years there are left before the jubilee year, the more he has to his credit; in proportion to his years of service shall he pay his ransom. [53]The alien shall treat him as a servant hired on an annual basis, and he shall not lord it over him harshly under your very eyes. [54]If he is not thus redeemed, he shall nevertheless be released, together with his children, in the jubilee year.[m] [55]For to me the Israelites belong as servants; they are servants of mine, because I brought them out of the land of Egypt, I, the LORD, your God.

See RG 132-33

CHAPTER 26

The Reward of Obedience. [1]"Do not make false gods for yourselves. You shall not erect an idol or a sacred pillar for yourselves, nor shall you set up a stone figure for worship in your land;[n] for I, the LORD, am your God. [2]Keep my sabbaths,[o] and reverence my sanctuary. I am the LORD.

[3]*"If you live in accordance with my precepts and are careful to observe my commandments, [4]I will give you rain in due season, so that the land will bear its crops, and the trees their fruit;[p] [5]your threshing will last till vintage time, and your vintage till the time for sowing, and you will have food to eat in abundance, so that you may dwell securely in your land. [6]I will establish peace in the land, that you may lie down to rest without anxiety. I will rid the country of ravenous beasts, and keep the sword of war from sweeping across your land. [7]You will rout your enemies and lay them low with your sword. [8]Five of you will put a hundred of your foes to flight, and a hundred of you will chase ten thousand of them, till they are cut down by your sword. [9]I will look with favor

upon you, and make you fruitful and numerous, as I carry out my covenant with you. [10]So much of the old crops will you have stored up for food that you will have to discard them to make room for the new.[q] [11r]I will set my Dwelling among you, and will not disdain you. [12]Ever present in your midst, I will be your God, and you will be my people; [13]for it is I, the LORD, your God, who brought you out of the land of the Egyptians and freed you from their slavery, breaking the yoke they had laid upon you and letting you walk erect.

Punishment of Disobedience. [14]"But if you do not heed me and do not keep all these commandments, [15]if you reject my precepts and spurn my decrees, refusing to obey all my commandments and breaking my covenant, [16]then I, in turn, will give you your deserts. I will punish you with terrible woes—with wasting and fever to dim the eyes and sap the life. You will sow your seed in vain, for your enemies will consume the crop. [17]I will turn against you, till you are beaten down before your enemies and lorded over by your foes. You will take to flight though no one pursues you.[s]

[18]"If even after this you do not obey me, I will increase the chastisement for your sins sevenfold, [19]to break your haughty confidence. I will make the sky above you as hard as iron, and your soil as hard as bronze, [20]so that your strength will be spent in vain; your land will bear no crops, and its trees no fruit.

[21]"If then you become defiant in your unwillingness to obey me, I will multiply my blows another sevenfold, as your sins deserve. [22]I will unleash the wild beasts against you, to rob you of your children and wipe out your livestock, till your population dwindles away and your roads become deserted.

[23]"If, with all this, you still refuse to be chastened by me and continue to defy me, [24]I, too, will defy you and will smite you for your sins seven times harder than before.[t] [25]I

26, 3-45: Since God's covenant was with the Israelite nation as a whole, these promises and threats are made primarily to the entire community. The rewards and punishments are of a temporal nature because the community as such exists only here on earth, not in the hereafter.

m: Ex 21, 2f.   *n:* Lv 19, 4; Ex 20, 4; Nm 33, 52; Dt 5, 8.   *o:* Ex 20, 8.   *p:* Ps 85, 13.   *q:* Lv 25, 22.   *r:* 11f: Ex 29, 45; Ez 39, 26ff; 2 Cor 6, 16.   *s:* Dt 28, 25.   *t:* 24f: Jer 2, 30; Ez 5, 17; 14, 17.

will make the sword, the avenger of my covenant, sweep over you. Though you then huddle together in your walled cities, I will send in pestilence among you, till you are forced to surrender to the enemy. [26]And as I cut off your supply of bread, ten women will need but one oven for baking all the bread they dole out to you in rations[u]—not enough food to still your hunger.

[27]"If, despite all this, you still persist in disobeying and defying me, [28]I, also, will meet you with fiery defiance and will chastise you with sevenfold fiercer punishment for your sins, [29v]till you begin to eat the flesh of your own sons and daughters.* [30]I will demolish your high places,[w] overthrow your incense stands, and cast your corpses on those of your idols. In my abhorrence of you, [31]I will lay waste your cities and devastate your sanctuaries, refusing to accept your sweet-smelling offerings. [32]So devastated will I leave the land that your very enemies who come to live there will stand aghast at the sight of it.[x] [33]You yourselves I will scatter among the nations[y] at the point of my drawn sword, leaving your countryside desolate and your cities deserted. [34]Then shall the land retrieve its lost sabbaths during all the time it lies waste, while you are in the land of your enemies; then shall the land have rest and make up for its sabbaths[z] [35]during all the time that it lies desolate, enjoying the rest that you would not let it have on the sabbaths when you lived there.

[36]"Those of you who survive in the lands of their enemies I will make so fainthearted that, if leaves rustle behind them, they will flee headlong, as if from the sword, though no one pursues them; [37]stumbling over one another as if to escape a weapon, while no one is after them—so helpless will you be to take a stand against your foes! [38]You will be lost among the Gentiles, swallowed up in your enemies' country. [39]Those of you who

survive in the lands of their enemies will waste away for their own and their fathers' guilt.[a]

[40]"Thus they will have to confess that they and their fathers were guilty of having rebelled against me and of having defied me, [41]so that I, too, had to defy them and bring them into their enemies' land. Then, when their uncircumcised hearts are humbled and they make amends for their guilt, [42]I will remember my covenant with Jacob, my covenant with Isaac, and my covenant with Abraham;[b] and of the land, too, I will be mindful. [43]But the land must first be rid of them, that in its desolation it may make up its lost sabbaths, and that they, too, may make good the debt of their guilt for having spurned my precepts and abhorred my statutes. [44]Yet even so, even while they are in their enemies' land, I will not reject or spurn them, lest, by wiping them out, I make void my covenant with them; for I, the LORD, am their God. [45]I will remember them because of the covenant I made with their forefathers, whom I brought out of the land of Egypt under the very eyes of the Gentiles,[c] that I, the LORD, might be their God."

[46]*These are the precepts, decrees and laws which the LORD had Moses promulgate on Mount Sinai in the pact between himself and the Israelites.

V: Redemption of Offerings

CHAPTER 27

See RG 133

Redemption of Votive Offerings. [1]The LORD said to Moses, [2]"Speak to the Israelites and tell them: When anyone fulfills a vow of offering one or more persons to the LORD, who are to be ransomed at a fixed sum of money, [3]for persons between the ages of twenty and sixty, the fixed sum, in sanctuary shekels, shall be fifty silver shekels for a man, [4]and thirty shekels for a woman; [5]for

---

26, 29: Eat the flesh of your own sons and daughters: extreme famine in cities under siege often forced their inhabitants to such dire means of subsistence. Cf Dt 28, 53; Jer 19, 9; Ez 5, 10; 2 Kgs 6, 28f.

26, 46: The Book of Leviticus seems originally to have ended here; the following chapter is an appendix.

---

u: Is 9, 19; Ez 4, 16; 5, 16; 14, 13; Mi 6, 14.   *v:* Is 9, 18.   *w:* 2 Chr 14, 5; 34, 3. 4. 7; Ez 6, 3-6.   *x:* 1 Kgs 9, 8; Jer 9, 11; 18, 16; 19, 8; 25, 18; Ez 5, 15.   *y:* Jer 9, 16; Zec 7, 14.   *z:* Lv 25, 2; 2 Chr 36, 21.   *a:* Ez 4, 17; 24, 23; 33, 10.   *b:* Ex 6, 5; 2 Kgs 13, 23; Ps 106, 45; Ez 16, 60.   *c:* Ex 12, 51.

persons between the ages of five and twenty, the fixed sum shall be twenty shekels for a youth, and ten for a maiden; [6]for persons between the ages of one month and five years, the fixed sum shall be five silver shekels for a boy, and three for a girl; [7]for persons of sixty or more, the fixed sum shall be fifteen shekels for a man, and ten for a woman. [8]However, if the one who took the vow is too poor to meet the fixed sum, the person must be set before the priest, who shall determine the sum for his ransom in keeping with the means of the one who made the vow.

[9]"If the offering vowed to the LORD is an animal that may be sacrificed, every such animal, when vowed to the LORD, becomes sacred. [10]The offerer shall not present a substitute for it by exchanging either a better for a worse one or a worse for a better one. If he attempts to offer one animal in place of another, both the original and its substitute shall be treated as sacred. [11]If the animal vowed to the LORD is unclean and therefore unfit for sacrifice, it must be set before the priest, [12]who shall determine its value* in keeping with its good or bad qualities, and the value set by the priest shall stand. [13]If the offerer wishes to redeem the animal, he shall pay one fifth more than this valuation.[d]

[14]"When someone dedicates his house as sacred to the LORD, the priest shall determine its value in keeping with its good or bad points, and the value set by the priest shall stand. [15]If the one who dedicated his house wishes to redeem it, he shall pay one fifth more than the price thus established, and then it will again be his.

[16]"If the object which someone dedicates to the LORD is a piece of his hereditary land, its valuation shall be made according to the amount of seed required to sow it, the acreage sown with a homer of barley seed being valued at fifty silver shekels. [17]If the dedication of a field is made at the beginning of a jubilee period, the full valuation shall hold; [18]but if it is some time after this, the priest shall estimate its money value according to the number of years left until the next jubilee year, with a corresponding rebate on the valuation.[e] [19]If the one who dedicated his field wishes to redeem it, he shall pay one fifth more than the price thus established, and so reclaim it. [20]If, instead of redeeming such a field, he sells it to someone else, it may no longer be redeemed; [21]but at the jubilee it shall be released as sacred to the LORD; like a field that is doomed, it shall become priestly property.

[22]"If the field that some man dedicates to the LORD is one he had purchased and not a part of his hereditary property, [23]the priest shall compute its value in proportion to the number of years until the next jubilee, and on the same day the price thus established shall be given as sacred to the LORD; [24]at the jubilee,[f] however, the field shall revert to the hereditary owner of this land from whom it had been purchased.

[25]"Every valuation shall be made according to the standard of the sanctuary shekel. There are twenty gerahs to the shekel.

Offerings Not To Be Redeemed. [26]"Note that a first-born animal,[g] which as such already belongs to the LORD, may not be dedicated by vow to him. If it is an ox or a sheep, it shall be ceded to the LORD; [27]but if it is an unclean animal,* it may be redeemed by paying one fifth more than its fixed value. If it is not redeemed, it shall be sold at its fixed value.

[28]"Note, also, that any one of his possessions which a man vows as doomed to the LORD, whether it is a human being or an animal or a hereditary field, shall be neither sold nor ransomed; everything that is thus doomed becomes most sacred to the LORD.[h] [29]All human beings that are doomed* lose the right to be redeemed; they must be put to death.

27, 12: Determine its value: fix the price at which the animal may be sold to someone else. Only the original owner must pay the twenty percent tax, as a penalty for buying back what he had vowed to God. So also for houses and fields that are vowed to the Lord, as treated of in the following verses. The money from the sale or from the redemption of such vowed property naturally goes to the sanctuary.

27, 27: An unclean animal: such as the first-born of an ass,

which was unfit for sacrifice. According to Ex 13, 13; 34, 20, a first-born ass was to be redeemed by offering a sheep in its stead, or was to have its neck broken. The present law is probably a later modification of the earlier one.

d: Lv 22, 14.   e: Lv 25, 15f.   f: Lv 25, 10. 28. 41.   g: Ex 13, 2.
h: 1 Sm 15, 21.

30"All tithes of the land, whether in grain from the fields or in fruit from the trees, belong to the LORD, as sacred to him.*i* *31*If someone wishes to buy back any of his tithes, he shall pay one fifth more than their value. *32*The tithes of the herd and the flock shall be determined by ceding to the LORD as sacred every tenth animal as they are counted by the herdsman's rod. *33*It shall not

matter whether good ones or bad ones are thus chosen, and no exchange may be made. If any exchange is attempted, both the original animal and its substitute shall be treated as sacred, without the right of being bought back."

*34*These are the commandments which the LORD gave Moses on Mount Sinai for the Israelites.

27, 29: All human beings that are doomed: according to some interpreters, this signifies the idolatrous Canaanites, who were doomed to destruction by divine authority; according to others, this drastic law was enacted for the purpose of discour-

aging private persons from rashly vowing their slaves or other dependents as offerings to God. Cf Ex 22, 19; Dt 13, 13-19.

i: Nm 18, 21. 24; 2 Chr 31, 5f. 12; Mal 3, 8. 10.

The Book of Numbers

See RG 133–41

The Book of Numbers derives its name from the account of the two censuses of the Hebrew people taken, one near the beginning and the other toward the end of the journey in the desert (chapters 1 and 26). It continues the story of that journey, begun in Exodus, and describes briefly the experiences of the Israelites for a period of thirty-eight years, from the end of their encampment at Sinai to their arrival at the border of the Promised Land. Numerous legal ordinances are interspersed in the account, making the book a combination of law and history.

The various events described clearly indicate the action of God, who punishes the murmuring of the people by prolonging their stay in the desert, at the same time preparing them by this discipline to be his witnesses among the nations.

In the New Testament Christ and the Apostles derive useful lessons from such events in the Book of Numbers as the brazen serpent (Jn 3, 14f), the sedition of Korah and its consequences (1 Cor 10, 10), the prophecies of Balaam (2 Pt 2, 15f), and the water gushing from the rock (1 Cor 10, 4).

The chief divisions of the Book of Numbers are as follows:

I: Preparation for the Departure from Sinai

CHAPTER 1

See RG 134–35

The Census. *1*In the year following that of the Israelites' departure from the land of Egypt, on the first day of the second month, the LORD said to Moses in the meeting tent in the desert of Sinai: *2**"Take a census of the whole community of the Israelites,*a* by clans and ancestral houses, registering each male individually. *3*You and Aaron shall enroll in companies all the men in Israel of twenty years or more who are fit for military service.

Moses' Assistants. *4*"To assist you there shall be a man from each tribe, the head of his ancestral house. *5b*These are the names of those who are to assist you:

from Reuben: Elizur, son of Shedeur;
6 from Simeon: Shelumiel, son of
    Zurishaddai;
7 from Judah: Nahshon, son of Amminadab;
8 from Issachar: Nethanel, son of Zuar;
9 from Zebulun: Eliab, son of Helon;
10 from Ephraim: Elishama, son of Ammihud,
    and from Manasseh: Gamaliel, son of
    Pedahzur, for the descendants of
    Joseph;

1, 2: All Israel was divided into tribes, each tribe into clans, and each clan into ancestral houses.

a: 2f: Nm 14, 29; 26, 2-51. *b:* 5-15: Nm 10, 14-27.

11 from Benjamin: Abidan, son of Gideoni;
12 from Dan: Ahiezer, son of Ammishaddai;
13 from Asher: Pagiel, son of Ochran;
14 from Gad: Eliasaph, son of Reuel;
15 from Naphtali: Ahira, son of Enan."

16c These were councilors of the community, princes of their ancestral tribes, chiefs of the troops* of Israel. *17* So Moses and Aaron took these men who had been designated, *18* and assembled the whole community on the first day of the second month. Every man of twenty years or more then declared his name and lineage according to clan and ancestral house, *19* as the LORD had commanded Moses.

Count of the Twelve Tribes. This is their census as taken in the desert of Sinai. *20* Of the descendants of Reuben, the first-born of Israel, registered by lineage in clans and ancestral houses: when all the males of twenty years or more who were fit for military service were polled, *21* forty-six thousand five hundred were enrolled in the tribe of Reuben.

22 Of the descendants of Simeon, registered by lineage in clans and ancestral houses: when all the males of twenty years or more who were fit for military service were polled, *23* fifty-nine thousand three hundred were enrolled in the tribe of Simeon.

24 Of the descendants of Gad, registered by lineage in clans and ancestral houses: when all the males of twenty years or more who were fit for military service were polled, *25* forty-five thousand six hundred and fifty were enrolled in the tribe of Gad.

26 Of the descendants of Judah, registered by lineage in clans and ancestral houses: when all the males of twenty years or more who were fit for military service were polled, *27* seventy-four thousand six hundred were enrolled in the tribe of Judah.

28 Of the descendants of Issachar, registered by lineage in clans and ancestral houses: when all the males of twenty years or more who were fit for military service were polled, *29* fifty-four thousand four hundred were enrolled in the tribe of Issachar.

30 Of the descendants of Zebulun, registered by lineage in clans and ancestral houses: when all the males of twenty years or more who were fit for military service were polled, *31* fifty-seven thousand four hundred were enrolled in the tribe of Zebulun.

32 Of the descendants of Joseph—

Of the descendants of Ephraim, registered by lineage in clans and ancestral houses: when all the males of twenty years or more who were fit for military service were polled, *33* forty thousand five hundred were enrolled in the tribe of Ephraim.

34 Of the descendants of Manasseh, registered by lineage in clans and ancestral houses: when all the males of twenty years or more who were fit for military service were polled, *35* thirty-two thousand two hundred were enrolled in the tribe of Manasseh.

36 Of the descendants of Benjamin, registered by lineage in clans and ancestral houses: when all the males of twenty years or more who were fit for military service were polled, *37* thirty-five thousand four hundred were enrolled in the tribe of Benjamin.

38 Of the descendants of Dan, registered by lineage in clans and ancestral houses: when all the males of twenty years or more who were fit for military service were polled, *39* sixty-two thousand seven hundred were enrolled in the tribe of Dan.

40 Of the descendants of Asher, registered by lineage in clans and ancestral houses: when all the males of twenty years or more who were fit for military service were polled, *41* forty-one thousand five hundred were enrolled in the tribe of Asher.

42 Of the descendants of Naphtali, registered by lineage in clans and ancestral houses: when all the males of twenty years or more who were fit for military service were polled, *43* fifty-three thousand four hundred were enrolled in the tribe of Naphtali.

44 It was these who were registered, each according to his ancestral house, in the census taken by Moses and Aaron and the

---

1, 16: Troops: literally "thousands"; this division of the Israelites, with its subdivisions of "hundreds, fifties and tens," was primarily for military and judicial purposes. Cf Ex 18, 21: 2 Sm 18, 1.

---

c: Ex 18, 21. 25.

Tribal Lists in Genesis, Numbers, and Deuteronomy

The lists of the names of the tribes that made up the people of Israel are not always identical. This indicates that there were slight variations in the traditions that stand behind these lists. The list in Numbers 34 omits the tribes of Reuben and Gad, who did not cross the Jordan. The lists in Numbers also do not include the names of Joseph or Levi, but instead substitute the names of Joseph's sons, Ephraim and Manasseh. (For purposes of comparison, the order of the names is the same in each of these lists, but the numbers beneath each name show its position in the list given in the biblical text.)

Genesis 49, 1–22	Numbers 1, 5–15	Numbers 1, 20–43	Numbers 2, 3–29 7,12-83	Numbers 13, 4–15	Numbers 26, 5–50	Numbers 34, 19–28	Deuteronomy 33, 1–29
Reuben 1	Reuben 1	Reuben 1	Reuben 4	Reuben 1	Reuben 1	——	Reuben 1
Simeon 2	Simeon 2	Simeon 2	Simeon 5	Simeon 2	Simeon 2	Simeon 2	Levi 3
Judah 4	Judah 3	Judah 4	Judah 1	Judah 3	Judah 4	Judah 1	Judah 2
Issachar 6	Issachar 4	Issachar 5	Issachar 2	Issachar 4	Issachar 5	Issachar 8	Issachar 8
Zebulun 5	Zebulun 5	Zebulun 6	Zebulun 3	Zebulun 7	Zebulun 6	Zebulun 7	Zebulun 7
Joseph 11	Ephraim 6	Ephraim 7	Ephraim 7	Ephraim 5	Ephraim 8	Ephraim 6	Ephraim 5
Levi 3	Manasseh 7	Manasseh 8	Manasseh 8	Manasseh 8	Manasseh 7	Manasseh 5	Manasseh 6
Benjamin 12	Benjamin 8	Benjamin 9	Benjamin 9	Benjamin 6	Benjamin 9	Benjamin 3	Benjamin 4
Dan 7	Dan 9	Dan 10	Dan 10	Dan 9	Dan 10	Dan 4	Dan 10
Asher 9	Asher 10	Asher 11	Asher 11	Asher 10	Asher 11	Asher 9	Asher 12
Gad 8	Gad 11	Gad 3	Gad 6	Gad 12	Gad 3	——	Gad 9
Naphtali 10	Naphtali 12	Naphtali 12	Naphtali 12	Naphtali 11	Naphtali 12	Naphtali 10	Naphtali 11

twelve princes of Israel. [45]The total number of the Israelites of twenty years or more who were fit for military service, registered by ancestral houses, [46]was six hundred and three thousand five hundred and fifty.

Levites Omitted in the Census. [47]The Levites, however, were not registered[d] by ancestral tribe with the others.* [48]For the LORD had told Moses, [49]"The tribe of Levi alone you shall not enroll nor include in the census along with the other Israelites. [50]You are to give the Levites charge of the Dwelling of the commandments with all its equipment and all that belongs to it. It is they who shall carry the Dwelling with all its equipment and who shall be its ministers.[e] They shall there-

1, 47: The Levites were not enrolled in this census, which was principally for military purposes, but a separate census was made of them. Cf Nm 3, 15f. 39.

d: Nm 2, 33; 3, 14-39; 26, 57-62.   e: Nm 3, 7f; 4, 2-49; 1 Chr 6, 48.

fore camp around the Dwelling. *51*When the Dwelling is to move on, the Levites shall take it down; when the Dwelling is to be pitched, it is the Levites who shall set it up.*f* Any layman who comes near it shall be put to death. *52*While the other Israelites shall camp by companies, each in his own division of the camp,*g* *53*the Levites shall camp around the Dwelling of the commandments.*h* Otherwise God's wrath will strike the Israelite community. The Levites, then, shall have charge of the Dwelling of the commandments." *54*All this the Israelites fulfilled as the LORD had commanded Moses.

See RG 134-35

CHAPTER 2

Arrangement of the Tribes. *1*The LORD said to Moses and Aaron: *2*"The Israelites shall camp, each in his own division, under the ensigns of their ancestral houses.*i* They shall camp around the meeting tent, but at some distance from it.

3*"Encamped on the east side, toward the sunrise, shall be the divisional camp of Judah, arranged in companies. [The prince of the Judahites was Nahshon, son of Amminadab, *4*and his soldiers amounted in the census to seventy-four thousand six hundred.] *5*With Judah shall camp the tribe of Issachar [their prince was Nethanel, son of Zuar, *6*and his soldiers amounted in the census to fifty-four thousand four hundred] *7*and the tribe of Zebulun. [Their prince was Eliab, son of Helon, *8*and his soldiers amounted in the census to fifty-seven thousand four hundred. *9*The total number of those registered by companies in the camp of Judah was one hundred and eighty-six thousand four hundred.] These shall be first on the march.

10"On the south side shall be the divisional camp of Reuben, arranged in companies. [Their prince was Elizur, son of Shedeur, *11*and his soldiers amounted in the census to forty-six thousand five hundred.] *12*Beside them shall camp the tribe of Simeon [their prince was Shelumiel, son of Zurishaddai, *13*and his soldiers amounted in the

census to fifty-nine thousand three hundred] *14*and next the tribe of Gad. [Their prince was Eliasaph, son of Reuel, *15*and his soldiers amounted in the census to forty-five thousand six hundred and fifty. *16*The total number of those registered by companies in the camp of Reuben was one hundred and fifty-one thousand four hundred and fifty.] These shall be second on the march.

17"Then the meeting tent and the camp of the Levites shall set out in the middle of the line. As in camp, so also on the march, every man shall be in his proper place, with his own division.

18"On the west side shall be the divisional camp of Ephraim, arranged in companies. [Their prince was Elishama, son of Ammihud, *19*and his soldiers amounted in the census to forty thousand five hundred.] *20*Beside them shall camp the tribe of Manasseh [their prince was Gamaliel, son of Pedahzur, *21*and his soldiers amounted in the census to thirty-two thousand two hundred] *22*and the tribe of Benjamin. [Their prince was Abidan, son of Gideoni, *23*and his soldiers amounted in the census to thirty-five thousand four hundred. *24*The total number of those registered by companies in the camp of Ephraim was one hundred and eight thousand one hundred.] These shall be third on the march.

25"On the north side shall be the divisional camp of Dan, arranged in companies. [Their prince was Ahiezer, son of Ammishaddai, *26*and his soldiers amounted in the census to sixty-two thousand seven hundred.] *27*Beside them shall camp the tribe of Asher [their prince was Pagiel, son of Ochran, *28*and his soldiers amounted in the census to forty-one thousand five hundred] *29*and next the tribe of Naphtali. [Their prince was Ahira, son of Enan, *30*and his soldiers amounted in the census to fifty-three thousand four hundred. *31*The total number of those registered by companies in the camp of Dan was one hundred and fifty-seven thousand six hundred.] These shall be the last of the divisions on the march."

*32 j*This was the census of the Israelites

2, 3-31: A similar arrangement of the tribes around the central sanctuary in the ideal Israelite state is given in Ez 48.

f: Nm 3, 10. 38; 18, 7; 2 Sm 6, 6f; 1 Chr 13, 10.   *g:* Nm 2, 2. 34.   *h:* Nm 3, 7f. 38; 8, 19; 18, 4f.   *i:* Nm 1, 52.   *j:* 32-33: Nm 1, 46-49.

taken by ancestral houses. The total number of those registered by companies in the camps was six hundred and three thousand five hundred and fifty. [33] The Levites, however, were not registered with the other Israelites, for so the LORD had commanded Moses. [34] The Israelites did just as the LORD had commanded Moses; both in camp and on the march they were in their own divisions, every man according to his clan and his ancestral house.

See RG
134-35

CHAPTER 3

The Sons of Aaron. [1] The following were the descendants of Aaron and Moses at the time that the LORD spoke to Moses on Mount Sinai. [2] The sons of Aaron were Nadab his first-born, Abihu, Eleazar, and Ithamar.[k] [3] These are the names of the sons of Aaron, the anointed priests who were ordained to exercise the priesthood. [4] But when Nadab and Abihu offered profane fire before the LORD in the desert of Sinai, they met death[l] in the presence of the LORD, and left no sons. Thereafter only Eleazar and Ithamar performed the priestly functions under the direction of their father Aaron.

Levites in Place of the First-born. [5] Now the LORD said to Moses: [6] "Summon the tribe of Levi and present them to Aaron the priest, as his assistants.[m] [7] They shall discharge his obligations and those of the whole community before the meeting tent[n] by serving at the Dwelling. [8] They shall have custody of all the furnishings of the meeting tent and discharge the duties of the Israelites in the service of the Dwelling. [9] You shall give the Levites to Aaron and his sons;[o] they have been set aside from among the Israelites as dedicated to me. [10] But only Aaron and his descendants shall you appoint to have charge of the priestly functions.[p] Any layman who comes near shall be put to death."

[11] The LORD said to Moses, [12] "It is I who have chosen the Levites from the Israelites in place of every first-born that opens the womb among the Israelites.[q] The Levites, therefore, are mine, [13] because every first-born is mine. When I slew all the first-born in the land of Egypt, I made all the first-born in Israel sacred to me, both of man and of beast. They belong to me; I am the LORD."

Census of the Levites. [14] The LORD said to Moses in the desert of Sinai, [15] "Take a census of the Levites by ancestral houses and clans, registering every male of a month or more."[r] [16] Moses, therefore, took their census in accordance with the command the LORD had given him.

[17s] The sons of Levi were named Gershon, Kohath and Merari. [18] The descendants of Gershon, by clans, were named Libni and Shimei. [19] The descendants of Kohath, by clans, were Amram, Izhar, Hebron and Uzziel. [20] The descendants of Merari, by clans, were Mahli and Mushi. These were the clans of the Levites by ancestral houses.

Duties of the Levitical Clans. [21] To Gershon belonged the clan of the Libnites and the clan of the Shimeites; these were the clans of the Gershonites. [22] When all their males of a month or more were registered, they numbered seven thousand five hundred. [23] The clans of the Gershonites camped behind the Dwelling, to the west. [24] The prince of their ancestral house was Eliasaph, son of Lael. [25t] At the meeting tent they had charge of whatever pertained to the Dwelling,* the tent and its covering, the curtain at the entrance of the meeting tent, [26] the hangings of the court, the curtain at the entrance of the court enclosing both the Dwelling and the altar, and the ropes.

[27] To Kohath belonged the clans of the Amramites, the Izharites, the Hebronites, and the Uzzielites; these were the clans of the Kohathites. [28] When all their males of a month or more were registered, they num-

---

3, 25f: The Gershonites had two wagons for transporting these things; cf Nm 7, 7. For a description of the Dwelling, see Ex 26, 1-6; the tent, Ex 26, 7-13; its covering, Ex 26, 14; the curtain at the entrance, Ex 26, 36; the hangings of the court, Ex 27, 9-15; the curtain at the entrance of the court, Ex 27, 16; the ropes of the Dwelling, Ex 35, 18.

k: Ex 6, 23. *l:* Nm 26, 61; Lv 10, 1f; 1 Chr 24, 2. *m:* Nm 18, 2. *n:* Nm 8, 24. *o:* Nm 8, 19. *p:* Nm 1, 51; 18, 7. *q:* 12f: Nm 3, 41; 8, 16f; Ex 13, 2. 12. 15. *r:* Nm 3, 39; 26, 62. *s:* 17-20: Nm 26, 57; Gn 46, 11; Ex 6, 16-19; 1 Chr 6, 1f. 16-19. *t:* 25-26: Ex 26, 7. 14. 36; 36, 14.

bered eight thousand three hundred. They had charge of the sanctuary. [29]The clans of the Kohathites camped at the south side of the Dwelling. [30]The prince of their ancestral house was Elizaphan, son of Uzziel. [31]They had charge of whatever pertained to the ark, the table, the lampstand, the altars, the utensils with which the ministry of the sanctuary was exercised, and the veil.* [32]The chief prince of the Levites, however, was Eleazar, son of Aaron the priest; he was supervisor over those who had charge of the sanctuary.

[33]To Merari belonged the clans of the Mahlites and the Mushites; these were the clans of Merari. [34]When all their males of a month or more were registered, they numbered six thousand two hundred. [35]The prince of the ancestral house of the clans of Merari was Zuriel, son of Abihail. They camped at the north side of the Dwelling. [36]*The Merarites were charged with the care of whatever pertained to the boards of the Dwelling, its bars, columns, pedestals, and all its fittings, [37]as well as the columns of the surrounding court with their pedestals, pegs and ropes.

[38]East of the Dwelling, that is, in front of the meeting tent, toward the sunrise, were camped Moses and Aaron and the latter's sons. They discharged the obligations of the sanctuary for the Israelites. Any layman who came near was to be put to death. [39]The total number of male Levites a month old or more whom Moses had registered by clans in keeping with the LORD's command, was twenty-two thousand.

Census and Ransom of First-born. [40]The LORD then said to Moses, "Take a census of all the first-born males of the Israelites a month old or more, and compute their total number. [41]Then assign the Levites to me, the LORD, in place of all the first-born of the Israelites, as well as their cattle in place of all the first-born among the cattle of the Israel-

ites." [42]So Moses took a census of all the first-born of the Israelites, as the LORD had commanded him. [43]When all the first-born males of a month or more were registered, they numbered twenty-two thousand two hundred and seventy-three.

[44]The LORD said to Moses: [45]"Take the Levites in place of all the first-born of the Israelites, and the Levites' cattle in place of their cattle, that the Levites may belong to me. I am the LORD. [46]As ransom for the two hundred and seventy-three first-born of the Israelites who outnumber the Levites, [47]you shall take five shekels for each individual, according to the standard of the sanctuary shekel, twenty gerahs to the shekel.[u] [48]Give this silver to Aaron and his sons as ransom for the extra number." [49]So Moses took the silver as ransom from those who were left when the rest had been redeemed by the Levites. [50]From the first-born of the Israelites he received in silver one thousand three hundred and sixty-five shekels according to the sanctuary standard. [51]He then gave this ransom silver to Aaron and his sons, as the LORD had commanded him.

CHAPTER 4

See RG 134-35

Duties Further Defined. [1]The LORD said to Moses and Aaron: [2]"Among the Levites take a total of the Kohathites, by clans and ancestral houses, all the men of the Kohathites [3]between thirty* and fifty years of age; these are to undertake obligatory tasks in the meeting tent.[v]

[4]"The service of the Kohathites in the meeting tent concerns the most sacred objects. [5]In breaking camp, Aaron and his sons shall go in and take down the screening curtain* and cover the ark of the commandments with it. [6]Over these they shall put a cover of tahash skin, and on top of this spread an all-violet cloth. They shall then put the poles in place. [7]On the table of the

---

3, 31: The Kohathites had to carry these sacred objects on their shoulders; cf Nm 7, 9. For a description of the ark, see Ex 25, 10-22; the table, Ex 25, 23-30; the lampstand, Ex 25, 31-40; the altars, Ex 27, 1-8; 30, 1-10.

3, 36f: The Merarites had four wagons for transporting this heavy material; cf Nm 7, 8. For a description of the boards, bars, etc., of the Dwelling, see Ex 26, 15-30; the columns, pedestals, etc., of the court, Ex 27, 9-19.

4, 3: Thirty: at a later period the Levites began to serve when they were twenty-five (Nm 8, 24) or even only twenty years old (1 Chr 23, 24. 27; 2 Chr 31, 17; Ezr 3, 8; but cf 1 Chr 23, 3).

4, 5: The screening curtain: the veil between the inner and the outer rooms of the sanctuary. Cf Ex 26, 31-33.

---

u: Nm 18, 16; Ex 30, 13; Lv 27, 25; Ez 45, 12.   *v:* Nm 8, 24; 1 Chr 23, 24-27.

Presence they shall spread a violet cloth and put on it the plates and cups, as well as the bowls and pitchers for libations; the established bread offering shall remain on the table. *8*Over these they shall spread a scarlet cloth and cover all this with tahash skin. They shall then put the poles in place. *9*They shall use a violet cloth to cover the lampstand with its lamps, trimming shears, and trays, as well as the various containers of oil from which it is supplied. *10*The lampstand with all its utensils they shall then enclose in a covering of tahash skin, and place on a litter. *11*Over the golden altar* they shall spread a violet cloth, and cover this also with a covering of tahash skin. They shall then put the poles in place. *12*Taking the utensils of the sanctuary service, they shall wrap them all in violet cloth and cover them with tahash skin. They shall then place them on a litter. *13*After cleansing the altar* of its ashes, they shall spread a purple cloth over it. *14*On this they shall put all the utensils with which it is served: the fire pans, forks,* shovels, basins, and all the utensils of the altar. They shall then spread a covering of tahash skin over this, and put the poles in place.

15"Only after Aaron and his sons have finished covering the sacred objects and all their utensils on breaking camp, shall the Kohathites enter to carry them. But they shall not touch the sacred objects; if they do they will die.*w* These, then, are the objects in the meeting tent that the Kohathites shall carry.

16"Eleazar, son of Aaron the priest, shall be in charge of the oil for the light, the fragrant incense, the established cereal offering, and the anointing oil. He shall be in charge of the whole Dwelling with all the sacred objects and utensils that are in it."

*17*The LORD said to Moses and Aaron: *18*"Do not let the group of Kohathite clans perish from the body of the Levites. *19*That they may live and not die when they approach the most sacred objects, this is what you shall do for them: Aaron and his sons shall go in and assign to each of them his task and what he must carry; *20*but the Kohathites shall not go in to look upon the sacred objects, even for an instant; if they do, they will die."*x*

*21*The LORD said to Moses, *22*"Take a total among the Gershonites also, by ancestral houses and clans, *23*of all the men between thirty and fifty years of age; these are to undertake obligatory tasks in the meeting tent. *24*This is the task of the clans of the Gershonites, what they must do and what they must carry: *25*they shall carry the sheets of the Dwelling, the meeting tent with its covering and the outer wrapping of tahash skin, the curtain at the entrance of the meeting tent, *26*the hangings of the court, the curtain at the entrance of the court that encloses both the Dwelling and the altar, together with their ropes and all other objects necessary in their use. Whatever is to be done with these things shall be their task. *27*The service of the Gershonites shall be entirely under the direction of Aaron and his sons, with regard to what they must do and what they must carry; you shall make each man of them responsible for what he is to carry. *28*This, then, is the task of the Gershonites in the meeting tent; and they shall be under the supervision of Ithamar, son of Aaron the priest.

29"Among the Merarites, too, you shall enroll by clans and ancestral houses *30*all their men between thirty and fifty years of age; these are to undertake obligatory tasks in the meeting tent. *31y*This is what they shall be responsible for carrying, all the years of their service in the meeting tent: the boards of the Dwelling with its bars, columns and pedestals, *32*and the columns of the surrounding court with their pedestals, pegs and ropes. You shall designate for each man of them all the objects connected with his service, which he shall be responsible for carrying. *33*This, then, is the task of the clans of the Merarites during all their service in the meeting tent under the supervision of Ithamar, son of Aaron the priest."

4, 11: The golden altar: the altar of incense. Cf Ex 30, 1-6.
4, 13: The altar: the bronze altar of holocausts. Cf Ex 27, 1-8.
4, 14: Forks: used in turning over the sacrificed animal on the fire of the altar. Basins: to receive the sacrificial blood; cf Zec 9, 15.

w: 2 Sm 6, 6f; 1 Chr 13, 9f.   *x:* 1 Sm 6, 19.   *y:* Nm 3, 36f.

Number of Adult Levites. [34]So Moses and Aaron and the princes of the community made a registration among the Kohathites, by clans and ancestral houses, [35]of all the men between thirty and fifty years of age. These were to undertake obligatory tasks in the meeting tent; [36]as registered by clans, they numbered two thousand seven hundred and fifty. [37]Such was the census of all the men of the Kohathite clans who were to serve in the meeting tent, which Moses took, together with Aaron, as the LORD bade him.

[38]The registration was then made among the Gershonites, by clans and ancestral houses, [39]of all the men between thirty and fifty years of age. These were to undertake obligatory tasks in the meeting tent; [40]as registered by clans and ancestral houses, they numbered two thousand six hundred and thirty. [41]Such was the census of all the men of the Gershonite clans who were to serve in the meeting tent, which Moses took, together with Aaron, at the LORD's bidding.

[42]Then the registration was made among the Merarites, by clans and ancestral houses, [43]of all the men from thirty up to fifty years of age. These were to undertake obligatory tasks in the meeting tent; [44]as registered by clans, they numbered three thousand two hundred. [45]Such was the census of the men of the Merarite clans which Moses took, together with Aaron, as the LORD bade him.

[46]Therefore, when Moses and Aaron and the Israelite princes had completed the registration among the Levites, by clans and ancestral houses, [47]of all the men between thirty and fifty years of age who were to undertake tasks of service or transport of the meeting tent, [48]the total number registered was eight thousand five hundred and eighty. [49]According to the LORD's bidding to Moses, they gave them their individual assignments for service and for transport; so the LORD had commanded Moses.

CHAPTER 5

See RG 134-35

The Unclean Expelled. [1]The LORD said to Moses: [2]"Order the Israelites to expel from camp every leper, and everyone suffering from a discharge, and everyone who has become unclean by contact with a corpse.*[z] [3]Male and female alike, you shall compel them to go out of the camp; they are not to defile the camp in which I dwell."[a] [4]The Israelites obeyed the command that the LORD had given Moses; they expelled them from the camp.

Unjust Possession. [5]*The LORD said to Moses, [6]b"Tell the Israelites: If a man (or woman) commits a fault against his fellow man and wrongs him, thus breaking faith with the LORD, [7]he shall confess the wrong he has done, restore his ill-gotten goods in full, and in addition give one fifth of their value to the one he has wronged. [8]However, if the latter has no next of kin* to whom restoration of the ill-gotten goods can be made, the goods to be restored shall be the LORD's and shall fall to the priest; this is apart from the atonement ram with which the priest makes amends for the guilty man. [9]Likewise, every sacred contribution that the Israelites are bound to make shall fall to the priest.[c] [10]Each Israelite man may dispose of his own sacred contributions; they become the property of the priest to whom he gives them."[d]

Ordeal for a Suspected Adulteress. [11]The LORD said to Moses, [12]"Speak to the Israelites and tell them: If a man's wife goes astray and becomes unfaithful to him [13]by having intercourse with another man,[e] though her husband has not sufficient evidence of the fact, so that her impurity remains unproved for lack of a witness who might have caught her in the act; [14]or if a man is overcome by a feeling of jealousy that makes him suspect his wife, whether she was actually impure or

---

5, 2: For the laws regarding victims of leprosy, see Lv 13–14; those suffering from a discharge, Lv 15; the unclean by contact with a corpse, Nm 19, 11-22; Lv 21, 1-4.

5, 5-10: The basic law on unjust possession is given in Lv 5, 14-26. The new item here concerns the case where the injured party has died and left no heirs, in which case the restitution must be made to the priest.

5, 8: Next of kin: literally, "redeemer," a technical term

denoting the nearest relative, upon whom devolved the obligation of "redeeming" the family property, in order to keep it within the family. Cf Lv 25, 25; Ru 4, 1-6.

---

z: Nm 19, 11. 13; Lv 13, 46; 21, 1; 22, 4.   *a:* Nm 35, 34.   *b:* 6ff: Lv 5, 21-25.   *c:* Dt 18, 3f; Ex 44, 29f.   *d:* Lv 10, 12-15.   *e:* Lv 18, 20; Jn 8, 4.

not: [15]he shall bring his wife to the priest and shall take along as an offering for her a tenth of an ephah of barley meal. However, he shall not pour oil on it nor put frankincense over it, since it is a cereal offering of jealousy, a cereal offering for an appeal in a question of guilt.

[16]"The priest shall first have the woman come forward and stand before the LORD. [17]In an earthen vessel he shall meanwhile put some holy water,* as well as some dust that he has taken from the floor of the Dwelling.[f] [18]Then, as the woman stands before the LORD, the priest shall uncover her head and place in her hands the cereal offering of her appeal,* that is, the cereal offering of jealousy, while he himself shall hold the bitter water that brings a curse. [19]Then he shall adjure the woman, saying to her, 'If no other man has had intercourse with you, and you have not gone astray by impurity while under the authority of your husband, be immune to the curse brought by this bitter water. [20]But if you have gone astray while under the authority of your husband and have acted impurely by letting a man other than your husband have intercourse with you'— [21]so shall the priest adjure the woman with this oath of imprecation—'may the LORD make you an example of malediction and imprecation* among your people by causing your thighs to waste away and your belly to swell! [22]May this water, then, that brings a curse, enter your body to make your belly swell and your thighs waste away!'[g] And the woman shall say, 'Amen, amen!'* [23]The priest shall put these imprecations in writing and shall then wash them off into the bitter water, [24]which he is to have the woman

drink, so that it may go into her with all its bitter curse. [25]But first he shall take the cereal offering of jealousy from the woman's hand, and having waved this offering before the LORD, shall put it near the altar, [26]where he shall take a handful of the cereal offering as its token offering and burn it on the altar.[h] Only then shall he have the woman drink the water. [27]Once she has done so, if she has been impure and unfaithful to her husband, this bitter water that brings a curse will go into her, and her belly will swell and her thighs will waste away, so that she will become an example of imprecation among her people. [28]If, however, the woman has not defiled herself, but is still pure, she will be immune and will still be able to bear children.

[29]"This, then, is the law for jealousy: When a woman goes astray while under the authority of her husband and acts impurely, [30]or when such a feeling of jealousy comes over a man that he becomes suspicious of his wife, he shall have her stand before the LORD, and the priest shall apply this law in full to her. [31]The man shall be free from guilt,* but the woman shall bear such guilt as she may have."

CHAPTER 6

Laws Concerning Nazirites. [1]The LORD said to Moses: [2]"Speak to the Israelites and tell them: When a man (or a woman) solemnly takes the nazirite* vow to dedicate himself to the LORD, [3]he shall abstain from wine and strong drink;[i] he may neither drink wine vinegar, other vinegar, or any kind of grape juice, nor eat either fresh or dried grapes. [4]As long as he is a nazirite he shall not eat anything of the produce of the vine;

See RG 134-35

5, 17: Holy water: water from the laver that stood in the court of the Dwelling.

5, 18: Appeal: by which she invokes the Lord and refers her case to his decision.

5, 21: An example of malediction and imprecation: the woman's name would be used in curses and oaths to invoke a similar misfortune on another person or on oneself. Cf Is 65, 15; Jer 29, 22.

5, 22: Amen: a Hebrew word meaning, "certainly, truly," used to give assent to a statement, a curse, a blessing, a prayer, or the like; in this sense of "so be it," the Christian liturgy also uses it after prayers and blessings.

5, 31: Free from guilt: by fulfilling his obligation of obtaining a decision in the matter.

6, 1ff: Nazirite: from the Hebrew word nazir, meaning "set apart as sacred, dedicated, vowed." The nazirite vow could be either for a limited period or for life. Those bound by this vow had to abstain from all the products of the grapevine, from cutting or shaving their hair, and from contact with a corpse. They were regarded as men of God like the prophets; cf Am 2, 11f. Examples of lifelong nazirites were Samson (Jgs 13, 4f. 7; 16, 17), Samuel (1 Sm 1, 11), and John the Baptizer (Lk 1, 15). At the time of Christ the practice of taking the nazirite vow for a limited period seems to have been quite common, even among the early Christians; cf Acts 18, 18; 21, 23f. 26.

f: Nm 19, 17.   *g:* Ps 109, 18.   *h:* Lv 5, 12.   *i:* 3f: Jgs 13, 7. 14.

not even unripe grapes or grapeskins. [5]While he is under the nazirite vow, no razor shall touch his hair.[j] Until the period of his dedication to the LORD is over, he shall be sacred, and shall let the hair of his head grow freely. [6]As long as he is dedicated to the LORD, he shall not enter where a dead person is.[k] [7]Not even for his father or mother, his sister or brother, should they die, may he become unclean, since his head bears his dedication to God. [8]As long as he is a nazirite he is sacred to the LORD.

[9]"If someone dies very suddenly in his presence, so that his dedicated head becomes unclean, he shall shave his head on the day of his purification, that is, on the seventh day. [10]On the eighth day he shall bring two turtledoves or two pigeons to the priest at the entrance of the meeting tent. [11]The priest shall offer up the one as a sin offering and the other as a holocaust, thus making atonement for him for the sin he has committed by reason of the dead person. On the same day he shall reconsecrate his head [12]and begin anew the period of his dedication to the LORD as a nazirite, bringing a yearling lamb as a guilt offering. The previous period is not valid, because his dedicated head became unclean.

[13]"This is the ritual for the nazirite:[l] On the day he completes the period of his dedication he shall go to the entrance of the meeting tent, [14]bringing as his offering to the LORD one unblemished yearling lamb for a holocaust, one unblemished yearling ewe lamb for a sin offering, one unblemished ram as a peace offering, along with their cereal offerings and libations, [15]and a basket of unleavened cakes of fine flour mixed with oil and of unleavened wafers spread with oil. [16]The priest shall present them before the LORD, and shall offer up the sin offering and the holocaust for him. [17]He shall then offer up the ram as a peace offering to the LORD, with its cereal offering and libation, and the basket of unleavened cakes. [18]Then at the entrance of the meeting tent the nazirite shall shave his dedicated head,[m] collect the hair, and put it in the fire that is under the peace offering. [19]After the nazirite has shaved off his dedicated hair, the priest shall take a boiled shoulder of the ram, as well as one unleavened cake and one unleavened wafer from the basket, and shall place them in the hands of the nazirite. [20]The priest shall then wave them as a wave offering before the LORD. They become sacred and shall belong to the priest, along with the breast of the wave offering and the leg of the raised offering. Only after this may the nazirite drink wine.

[21]"This, then, is the law for the nazirite; this is the offering to the LORD which is included in his vow of dedication apart from anything else which his means may allow. Thus shall he carry out the law of his dedication in keeping with the vow he has taken."

The Priestly Blessing. [22]The LORD said to Moses: [23]"Speak to Aaron and his sons and tell them: This is how you shall bless the Israelites. Say to them:

[24] The LORD bless you and keep you!
[25] The LORD let his face shine* upon you,
and be gracious to you!
[26] The LORD look upon you kindly and give
you peace!*

[27]So shall they invoke my name upon the Israelites, and I will bless them."

CHAPTER 7

See RG
134-35

Offerings of Princes. [1]Now, when Moses had completed the erection of the Dwelling and had anointed and consecrated it with all its equipment[n] (as well as the altar with all its equipment), [2]an offering was made by the princes of Israel, who were heads of ancestral houses; the same princes of the tribes who supervised the census. [3]The offering they brought before the LORD consisted of six baggage wagons and twelve oxen, that is, a wagon for every two princes, and an ox for every prince. These they presented as their offering before the Dwelling.

6, 25: Let his face shine: a Hebrew idiom for "smile."
6, 26: Peace: the Hebrew word includes the idea of "prosperity, happiness."

j: Jgs 13, 5; 16, 17; 1 Sm 1, 11.   *k:* Nm 19, 11. 16; Lv 21, 11.   *l:* Acts 21, 24. 26.   *m:* Acts 18, 18; 21, 24.   *n:* Ex 40, 17.

⁴The LORD then said to Moses, ⁵"Accept their offering, that these things may be put to use in the service of the meeting tent. Assign them to the Levites, to each group in proportion to its duties." ⁶So Moses accepted the wagons and oxen, and assigned them to the Levites. ⁷He gave two wagons and four oxen to the Gershonites° in proportion to their duties, ⁸and four wagons and eight oxen to the Merarites in proportion to their duties, under the supervision of Ithamar, son of Aaron the priest. ⁹He gave none to the Kohathites, because they had to carry on their shoulders the sacred objects which were their charge.ᵖ

¹⁰For the dedication of the altar also, the princes brought offerings before the altar on the day it was anointed.�q ¹¹But the LORD said to Moses, "Let one prince a day present his offering for the dedication of the altar."

¹²*The one who presented his offering on the first day was Nahshon, son of Amminadab, prince of the tribe of Judah. ¹³His offering consisted of one silver plate weighing a hundred and thirty shekels according to the sanctuary standard and one silver basin weighing seventy shekels, both filled with fine flour mixed with oil for a cereal offering; ¹⁴one gold cup of ten shekels' weight filled with incense; ¹⁵one young bull, one ram, and one yearling lamb for a holocaust; ¹⁶one goat for a sin offering; ¹⁷and two oxen, five rams, five goats, and five yearling lambs for a peace offering. This was the offering of Nahshon, son of Amminadab.

¹⁸On the second day Nethanel, son of Zuar, prince of Issachar, made his offering. ¹⁹He presented as his offering one silver plate weighing a hundred and thirty shekels according to the sanctuary standard and one silver basin weighing seventy shekels, both filled with fine flour mixed with oil for a cereal offering; ²⁰one gold cup of ten shekels' weight filled with incense; ²¹one young bull, one ram, and one yearling lamb for a holocaust; ²²one goat for a sin offering; ²³and two oxen, five rams, five goats, and five yearling lambs for a peace offering. This was the offering of Nethanel, son of Zuar.

²⁴On the third day it was the turn of Eliab, son of Helon, prince of the Zebulunites. ²⁵His offering consisted of one silver plate weighing a hundred and thirty shekels according to the sanctuary standard and one silver basin weighing seventy shekels, both filled with fine flour mixed with oil for a cereal offering; ²⁶one gold cup of ten shekels' weight filled with incense; ²⁷one young bull, one ram, and one yearling lamb for a holocaust; ²⁸one goat for a sin offering; ²⁹and two oxen, five rams, five goats, and five yearling lambs for a peace offering. This was the offering of Eliab, son of Helon.

³⁰On the fourth day it was the turn of Elizur, son of Shedeur, prince of the Reubenites. ³¹His offering consisted of one silver plate weighing a hundred and thirty shekels according to the sanctuary standard and one silver basin weighing seventy shekels, both filled with fine flour mixed with oil for a cereal offering; ³²one gold cup of ten shekels' weight filled with incense; ³³one young bull, one ram, and one yearling lamb for a holocaust; ³⁴one goat for a sin offering; ³⁵and two oxen, five rams, five goats, and five yearling lambs for a peace offering. This was the offering of Elizur, son of Shedeur.

³⁶On the fifth day it was the turn of Shelumiel, son of Zurishaddai, prince of the Simeonites. ³⁷His offering consisted of one silver plate weighing a hundred and thirty shekels according to the sanctuary standard and one silver basin weighing seventy shekels, both filled with fine flour mixed with oil for a cereal offering; ³⁸one gold cup of ten shekels' weight filled with incense; ³⁹one young bull, one ram, and one yearling lamb for a holocaust; ⁴⁰one goat for a sin offering; ⁴¹and two oxen, five rams, five goats, and five yearling lambs for a peace offering. This was the offering of Shelumiel, son of Zurishaddai.

⁴²On the sixth day it was the turn of Eliasaph, son of Reuel, prince of the Gadites.

7, 12-88: The repetitious account of the same offerings brought by each of the twelve tribal princes and the summary of them are characteristic of an official registration.

o: 7f: Nm 4, 24-33.   *p:* Nm 3, 31; 4, 4-15.   *q:* Nm 7, 84.

⁴³His offering consisted of one silver plate weighing a hundred and thirty shekels according to the sanctuary standard and one silver basin weighing seventy shekels, both filled with fine flour mixed with oil for a cereal offering; ⁴⁴one gold cup of ten shekels' weight filled with incense; ⁴⁵one young bull, one ram, and one yearling lamb for a holocaust; ⁴⁶one goat for a sin offering; ⁴⁷and two oxen, five rams, five goats, and five yearling lambs for a peace offering. This was the offering of Eliasaph, son of Reuel.

⁴⁸On the seventh day it was the turn of Elishama, son of Ammihud, prince of the Ephraimites. ⁴⁹His offering consisted of one silver plate weighing a hundred and thirty shekels according to the sanctuary standard and one silver basin weighing seventy shekels, both filled with fine flour mixed with oil for a cereal offering; ⁵⁰one gold cup of ten shekels' weight filled with incense; ⁵¹one young bull, one ram, and one yearling lamb for a holocaust; ⁵²one goat for a sin offering; ⁵³and two oxen, five rams, five goats, and five yearling lambs for a peace offering. This was the offering of Elishama, son of Ammihud.

⁵⁴On the eighth day it was the turn of Gamaliel, son of Pedahzur, prince of the Manassehites. ⁵⁵His offering consisted of one silver plate weighing a hundred and thirty shekels according to the sanctuary standard and one silver basin weighing seventy shekels, both filled with fine flour mixed with oil for a cereal offering; ⁵⁶one gold cup of ten shekels' weight filled with incense; ⁵⁷one young bull, one ram, and one yearling lamb for a holocaust; ⁵⁸one goat for a sin offering; ⁵⁹and two oxen, five rams, five goats, and five yearling lambs for a peace offering. This was the offering of Gamaliel, son of Pedahzur.

⁶⁰On the ninth day it was the turn of Abidan, son of Gideoni, prince of the Benjaminites. ⁶¹His offering consisted of one silver plate weighing a hundred and thirty shekels according to the sanctuary standard and one silver basin weighing seventy shekels, both filled with fine flour mixed with oil for a cereal offering; ⁶²one gold cup of ten shekels' weight filled with incense;

⁶³one young bull, one ram, and one yearling lamb for a holocaust; ⁶⁴one goat for a sin offering; ⁶⁵and two oxen, five rams, five goats, and five yearling lambs for a peace offering. This was the offering of Abidan, son of Gideoni.

⁶⁶On the tenth day it was the turn of Ahiezer, son of Ammishaddai, prince of the Danites. ⁶⁷His offering consisted of one silver plate weighing a hundred and thirty shekels according to the sanctuary standard and one silver basin weighing seventy shekels, both filled with fine flour mixed with oil for a cereal offering; ⁶⁸one gold cup of ten shekels' weight filled with incense; ⁶⁹one young bull, one ram, and one yearling lamb for a holocaust; ⁷⁰one goat for a sin offering; ⁷¹and two oxen, five rams, five goats, and five yearling lambs for a peace offering. This was the offering of Ahiezer, son of Ammishaddai.

⁷²On the eleventh day it was the turn of Pagiel, son of Ochran, prince of the Asherites. ⁷³His offering consisted of one silver plate weighing a hundred and thirty shekels according to the sanctuary standard and one silver basin weighing seventy shekels, both filled with fine flour mixed with oil for a cereal offering; ⁷⁴one gold cup of ten shekels' weight filled with incense; ⁷⁵one young bull, one ram, and one yearling lamb for a holocaust; ⁷⁶one goat for a sin offering; ⁷⁷and two oxen, five rams, five goats, and five yearling lambs for a peace offering. This was the offering of Pagiel, son of Ochran.

⁷⁸On the twelfth day it was the turn of Ahira, son of Enan, prince of the Naphtalites. ⁷⁹His offering consisted of one silver plate weighing a hundred and thirty shekels according to the sanctuary standard and one silver basin weighing seventy shekels, both filled with fine flour mixed with oil for a cereal offering; ⁸⁰one gold cup of ten shekels' weight filled with incense; ⁸¹one young bull, one ram, and one yearling lamb for a holocaust; ⁸²one goat for a sin offering; ⁸³and two oxen, five rams, five goats, and five yearling lambs for a peace offering. This was the offering of Ahira, son of Enan.

⁸⁴These were the offerings for the dedica-

tion of the altar, given by the princes of Israel on the occasion of its anointing: twelve silver plates, twelve silver basins, and twelve gold cups. [85]Each silver plate weighed a hundred and thirty shekels, and each silver basin seventy, so that all the silver of these vessels amounted to two thousand four hundred shekels, according to the sanctuary standard. [86]The twelve gold cups that were filled with incense weighed ten shekels apiece, according to the sanctuary standard, so that all the gold of the cups amounted to one hundred and twenty shekels. [87]The animals for the holocausts were, in all, twelve young bulls, twelve rams, and twelve yearling lambs, with their cereal offerings; those for the sin offerings were twelve goats. [88]The animals for the peace offerings were, in all, twenty-four oxen, sixty rams, sixty goats, and sixty yearling lambs. These, then, were the offerings for the dedication of the altar after it was anointed.

The Voice. [89]When Moses entered the meeting tent to speak with him, he heard the voice addressing him from above the propitiatory[r] on the ark of the commandments, from between the two cherubim; and it spoke to him. . . .

See RG
134-35 **CHAPTER 8**

The Lamps Set Up. [1]The LORD spoke to Moses, and said, [2]"Give Aaron this command: When you set up the seven lamps,[s] have them throw their light toward the front of the lampstand." [3]Aaron did so, setting up the lamps to face toward the front of the lampstand, just as the LORD had commanded Moses. [4]The lampstand was made of beaten gold[t] in both its shaft and its branches, according to the pattern which the LORD had shown Moses.

Purification of the Levites. [5]The LORD said to Moses: [6]"Take the Levites from among the Israelites and purify them.* [7]This is what you shall do to them to purify them.

Sprinkle them with the water of remission;* then have them shave their whole bodies and wash their clothes, and so purify themselves. [8]They shall take a young bull, along with its cereal offering of fine flour mixed with oil; you shall take another young bull for a sin offering. [9]Then have the Levites come forward in front of the meeting tent, where you shall assemble also the whole community of the Israelites. [10]While the Levites are present before the LORD, the Israelites shall lay their hands upon them. [11]Let Aaron then offer the Levites before the LORD as a wave offering from the Israelites, thus devoting them to the service of the LORD. [12]The Levites in turn shall lay their hands on the heads of the bullocks, which shall then be immolated, the one as a sin offering and the other as a holocaust to the LORD, in atonement for the Levites. [13]Thus, then, shall you have the Levites stand before Aaron and his sons, to be offered as a wave offering to the LORD; [14]and thus shall you set aside the Levites from the rest of the Israelites, that they may be mine.[u]

[15]"Only then shall the Levites enter upon their service in the meeting tent. You shall purify them and offer them as a wave offering; [16]because they, among the Israelites, are strictly dedicated to me; I have taken them for myself in place of every first-born that opens the womb among the Israelites.[v] [17]Indeed, all the first-born among the Israelites, both of man and of beast, belong to me; I consecrated them to myself on the day I slew all the first-born in the land of Egypt.[w] [18]But in place of all the first-born Israelites I have taken the Levites; [19]and I have given these dedicated Israelites to Aaron and his sons[x] to discharge the duties of the Israelites in the meeting tent and to make atonement for them, so that no plague may strike among the Israelites should they come near the sanctuary."

[20]Thus, then, did Moses and Aaron and the whole community of the Israelites deal

---

8, 6: Purify them: in the language of the Pentateuch only the priests were "consecrated," that is, made sacred or set aside for the Lord, in an elaborate ceremony described in Ex 29; Lv 8. The Levites were merely "purified," that is, made ritually clean for their special work.

8, 7: Water of remission: literally, "water of sin," that is, for the remission of sin.

r: Ex 25, 22.   *s:* Ex 25, 37.   *t:* Ex 25, 31. 40.   *u:* Nm 3, 45.
v: Nm 3, 12. 45.   *w:* Nm 3, 13; 13, 2; Lk 2, 23.   *x:* Nm 3, 9f.

with the Levites, carrying out exactly the command which the LORD had given Moses concerning them. [21] When the Levites had cleansed themselves of sin* and washed their clothes, Aaron offered them as a wave offering before the LORD, and made atonement for them to purify them. [22] Only then did they enter upon their service in the meeting tent under the supervision of Aaron and his sons. The command which the LORD had given Moses concerning the Levites was carried out.

Age Limits for Levitical Service. [23] The LORD said to Moses: [24] "This is the rule for the Levites. Each from his twenty-fifth year onward shall perform the required service in the meeting tent.[y] [25] When he is fifty years old, he shall retire from the required service and work no longer. [26] His service with his fellow Levites shall consist in sharing their responsibilities in the meeting tent, but he shall not do the work. This, then, is how you are to regulate the duties of the Levites."

See RG 134-35

CHAPTER 9

Second Passover. [1] In the first month of the year following their departure from the land of Egypt, the LORD said to Moses in the desert of Sinai, [2] "Tell the Israelites to celebrate the Passover at the prescribed time. [3] The evening twilight of the fourteenth day of this month[z] is the prescribed time when you shall celebrate it, observing all its rules and regulations." [4] Moses, therefore, told the Israelites to celebrate the Passover. [5] And they did so, celebrating the Passover in the desert of Sinai during the evening twilight of the fourteenth day of the first month, just as the LORD had commanded Moses.

[6] There were some, however, who were unclean because of a human corpse and so could not keep the Passover that day. These men came up to Moses and Aaron that same day [7] and said, "Although we are unclean because of a corpse, why should we be de-prived of presenting the LORD's offering at its proper time along with the other Israelites?" [8] Moses answered them, "Wait until I learn what the LORD will command in your regard."

[9] The LORD then said to Moses: [10] "Speak to the Israelites and say: If any one of you or of your descendants is unclean because of a corpse, or if he is absent on a journey, he may still keep the LORD's Passover. [11] But he shall keep it in the second month,[a] during the evening twilight of the fourteenth day of that month, eating it with unleavened bread and bitter herbs, [12] and not leaving any of it over till morning, nor breaking any of its bones,[b] but observing all the rules of the Passover. [13] However, anyone who is clean and not away on a journey, who yet fails to keep the Passover, shall be cut off from his people, because he did not present the LORD's offering at the prescribed time. That man shall bear the consequences of his sin.

[14] "If an alien* who lives among you wishes to keep the LORD's Passover, he too shall observe the rules and regulations for the Passover. You shall have the same law for the resident alien as for the native of the land."[c]

The Fiery Cloud. [15] On the day when the Dwelling was erected, the cloud* covered the Dwelling, the tent of the commandments; but from evening until morning it took on the appearance of fire over the Dwelling.[d] [16] It was always so: during the day the Dwelling was covered by the cloud, which at night had the appearance of fire. [17] Whenever the cloud rose from the tent, the Israelites would break camp; wherever the cloud came to rest, they would pitch camp.[e] [18] At the bidding of the LORD the Israelites moved on, and at his bidding they encamped.[f] As long as the cloud stayed over the Dwelling, they remained in camp. [19] Even when the cloud tarried many days over the Dwelling, the Israelites obeyed the

8, 21: Cleansed themselves of sin: by having the "water of remission" sprinkled on them as prescribed in v 7.

9, 14: An alien: this passage presupposes that he is already circumcised as prescribed in Ex 12, 48.

9, 15: The cloud: already mentioned at the departure from Egypt; cf Ex 13, 21f.

y: Nm 4, 3. 23.   z: Ex 12, 6; Lv 23, 5.   a: 2 Chr 30, 2-15.   b: Ex 12, 46; Jn 19, 36.   c: Ex 12, 48f.   d: Ex 13, 21.   e: Wis 18, 3.
f: 1 Cor 10, 1.

LORD and would not move on; [20]yet sometimes the cloud was over the Dwelling only for a few days. It was at the bidding of the LORD that they stayed in camp, and it was at his bidding that they departed. [21]Sometimes the cloud remained there only from evening until morning; and when it rose in the morning, they would depart. Or if the cloud lifted during the day, or even at night, they would then set out. [22]Whether the cloud tarried over the Dwelling for two days or for a month or longer, the Israelites remained in camp and did not depart; but when it lifted, they moved on. [23]Thus, it was always at the bidding of the LORD that they encamped, and at his bidding that they set out; ever heeding the charge of the LORD, as he had bidden them through Moses.

CHAPTER 10

See RG 134-35

The Silver Trumpets. [1]The LORD said to Moses: [2]"Make two trumpets of beaten silver, which you shall use in assembling the community and in breaking camp. [3]When both are blown, the whole community shall gather round you at the entrance of the meeting tent; [4]but when one of them is blown, only the princes, the chiefs of the troops of Israel, shall gather round you. [5]When you sound the first alarm, those encamped on the east side shall set out; [6]when you sound the second alarm, those encamped on the south side shall set out; when you sound the third alarm, those encamped on the west side shall set out; when you sound the fourth alarm, those encamped on the north side shall set out. Thus shall the alarm be sounded for them to depart. [7]But in calling forth an assembly you are to blow an ordinary blast, without sounding the alarm.

[8]"It is the sons of Aaron, the priests, who shall blow the trumpets; and the use of them is prescribed by perpetual statute for you and your descendants. [9]g When in your own land you go to war against an enemy that is attacking you, you shall sound the alarm on the trumpets, and the LORD, your God, will re-

member you and save you from your foes. [10]On your days of celebration,* your festivals, and your new-moon feasts, you shall blow the trumpets over your holocausts and your peace offerings;h this will serve as a reminder of you before your God. I, the LORD, am your God."

II: From Sinai to the Plains of Moab

Departure from Sinai. [11]In the second year, on the twentieth day of the second month, the cloud rose from the Dwelling of the commandments. [12]The Israelites moved on from the desert of Sinai by stages, until the cloud came to rest in the desert of Paran.

[13]The first time that they broke camp at the bidding of the LORD through Moses, [14]ithe camp of the Judahites, under its own standard and arranged in companies, was the first to set out. Nahshon, son of Amminadab, was over their host, [15]and Nethanel, son of Zuar, over the host of the tribe of Issachar, [16]and Eliab, son of Helon, over the host of the tribe of Zebulun. [17]Then, after the Dwelling was dismantled, the clans of Gershon and Merari set out, carrying the Dwelling. [18]The camp of the Reubenites, under its own standard and arranged in companies, was the next to set out, with Elizur, son of Shedeur, over their host, [19]and Shelumiel, son of Zurishaddai, over the host of the tribe of Simeon, [20]and Eliasaph, son of Reuel, over the host of the tribe of Gad. [21]The clan of Kohath then set out, carrying the sacred objects for the Dwelling, which was to be erected before their arrival. [22]The camp of the Ephraimites next set out, under its own standard and arranged in companies, with Elishama, son of Ammihud, over their host, [23]and Gamaliel, son of Pedahzur, over the host of the tribe of Manasseh, [24]and Abidan, son of Gideoni, over the host of the tribe of Benjamin. [25]Finally, as rear guard for all the camps, the camp of the Danites set out, under its own standard and arranged in companies, with Ahiezer, son of Amishaddai, over their host,

---

10, 10: Days of celebration: special holidays, such as the occasion of a victory. Festivals: the great annual feasts of the Passover, Pentecost and Booths described in Lv 23; Nm 28–29.

g: 2 Chr 13, 14.   *h:* Nm 29, 1; 2 Chr 29, 26ff.   *i:* 14ff: Nm 2, 3. 5. 7.

²⁶and Pagiel, son of Ochran, over the host of the tribe of Asher, ²⁷and Ahira, son of Enan, over the host of the tribe of Naphtali. ²⁸This was the order of departure for the Israelites, company by company.

Hobab as Guide. As they were setting out, ²⁹Moses said to his brother-in-law Hobab, son of Reuel the Midianite, "We are setting out for the place which the LORD has promised to give us. Come with us, and we will be generous toward you, for the LORD has promised prosperity to Israel." ³⁰*But he answered, "No, I will not come. I am going instead to my own country and to my own kindred." ³¹Moses said, "Please, do not leave us; you know where we can camp in the desert, and you will serve as eyes for us. ³²If you come with us, we will share with you the prosperity the LORD will bestow on us."

Into the Desert. ³³*j*They moved on from the mountain of the LORD,* a three days' journey, and the ark of the covenant of the LORD which was to seek out their resting place went the three days' journey with them. ³⁴And when they set out from camp, the cloud of the LORD was over them by day.

³⁵Whenever the ark set out, Moses would say,

"Arise, O LORD, that your enemies may
          be scattered,
and those who hate you may flee
          before you."

³⁶And when it came to rest, he would say,

"Return, O LORD, you who ride upon the
          clouds,
to the troops of Israel."

**See RG
135-36**

CHAPTER 11

Discontent of the People. ¹Now the people complained in the hearing of the LORD;*k* and when he heard it his wrath flared up so that the fire of the LORD burned among

them and consumed the outskirts of the camp. ²But when the people cried out to Moses, he prayed to the LORD and the fire died out. ³Hence that place was called Taberah,* because there the fire of the LORD burned among them.

⁴The foreign elements among them were so greedy for meat that even the Israelites lamented again,*l* "Would that we had meat for food! ⁵We remember the fish we used to eat without cost in Egypt, and the cucumbers, the melons, the leeks, the onions, and the garlic. ⁶But now we are famished; we see nothing before us but this manna."*m*

⁷*n*Manna was like coriander seed* and had the appearance of bdellium. ⁸When they had gone about and gathered it up, the people would grind it between millstones or pound it in a mortar, then cook it in a pot and make it into loaves, which tasted like cakes made with oil. ⁹At night, when the dew fell upon the camp, the manna also fell.*o*

¹⁰When Moses heard the people, family after family, crying at the entrance of their tents, so that the LORD became very angry, he was grieved. ¹¹"Why do you treat your servant so badly?" Moses asked the LORD. "Why are you so displeased with me that you burden me with all this people? ¹²Was it I who conceived all this people? or was it I who gave them birth, that you tell me to carry them at my bosom, like a foster father carrying an infant, to the land you have promised under oath to their fathers? ¹³Where can I get meat to give to all this people? For they are crying to me, 'Give us meat for our food.' ¹⁴I cannot carry all this people by myself, for they are too heavy for me. ¹⁵If this is the way you will deal with me, then please do me the favor of killing me at once, so that I need no longer face this distress."

The Seventy Elders. ¹⁶Then the LORD said to Moses, "Assemble for me seventy of the elders of Israel, men you know for true el-

---

10, 30ff: Hobab wished to be coaxed before granting the favor. From Jgs 1, 16 it seems probable that he did accede to Moses' request.

10, 33: The mountain of the Lord: Sinai (Horeb), elsewhere always called "the mountain of God."

11, 3: Taberah: means "the burning."

11, 7: Coriander seed: see note on Ex 16, 31. Bdellium: a

transparent, amber-colored gum resin, which is also mentioned in Gn 2, 12.

j: Dt 1, 33.   *k:* Dt 9, 22.   *l:* Ps 78, 18.   *m:* 5f: Nm 21, 5; Ex 16, 3; Acts 7, 39.   *n:* 7f: Ex 16, 14f. 31; Ps 78, 24; Wis 16, 20; Jn 6, 31.   *o:* Ex 16, 14f.

ders and authorities among the people, and bring them to the meeting tent. When they are in place beside you, [17]I will come down and speak with you there. I will also take some of the spirit that is on you and will bestow it on them, that they may share the burden of the people with you. You will then not have to bear it by yourself.

[18]"To the people, however, you shall say: Sanctify yourselves for tomorrow, when you shall have meat to eat. For in the hearing of the LORD you have cried, 'Would that we had meat for food! Oh, how well off we were in Egypt!' Therefore the LORD will give you meat for food, [19]and you will eat it, not for one day, or two days, or five, or ten, or twenty days, [20]but for a whole month—until it comes out of your very nostrils and becomes loathsome to you. For you have spurned the LORD who is in your midst, and in his presence you have wailed, 'Why did we ever leave Egypt?' "

[21]But Moses said, "The people around me include six hundred thousand soldiers; yet you say, 'I will give them meat to eat for a whole month.' [22]Can enough sheep and cattle be slaughtered for them? If all the fish of the sea were caught for them, would they have enough?" [23]The LORD answered Moses, "Is this beyond the LORD's reach? You shall see now whether or not what I have promised you takes place."

The Spirit on the Elders. [24]So Moses went out and told the people what the LORD had said. Gathering seventy elders of the people, he had them stand around the tent. [25]The LORD then came down in the cloud and spoke to him. Taking some of the spirit that was on Moses, he bestowed it on the seventy elders; and as the spirit came to rest on them, they prophesied.*

[26]Now two men, one named Eldad and the other Medad, were not in the gathering but had been left in the camp. They too had been on the list, but had not gone out to the tent; yet the spirit came to rest on them also, and they prophesied in the camp. [27]So, when a young man quickly told Moses, "Eldad and Medad are prophesying in the camp," [28]Joshua, son of Nun, who from his youth had been Moses' aide, said, "Moses, my lord, stop them." [29]But Moses answered him, "Are you jealous for my sake? Would that all the people of the LORD were prophets! Would that the LORD might bestow his spirit on them all!" [30]Then Moses retired to the camp, along with the elders of Israel.

The Quail. [31]There arose a wind[p] sent by the LORD, that drove in quail from the sea and brought them down over the camp site at a height of two cubits from the ground* for the distance of a day's journey all around the camp. [32][q]All that day, all night, and all the next day the people gathered in the quail. Even the one who got the least gathered ten homers of them. Then they spread them out* all around the camp. [33]But while the meat was still between their teeth, before it could be consumed, the LORD's wrath flared up against the people, and he struck them with a very great plague. [34]So that place was named Kibroth-hattaavah,* because it was there that the greedy people were buried.

[35]From Kibroth-hattaavah the people set out for Hazeroth.

CHAPTER 12

Jealousy of Aaron and Miriam. While they were in Hazeroth, [1]Miriam and Aaron spoke against Moses on the pretext of the marriage he had contracted with a Cushite woman.* [2]They complained,* "Is it

See RG 135-36

11, 25: They prophesied: in the sense, not of foretelling the future, but of speaking in enraptured enthusiasm. Such manifestations of mystic exaltation occurred in the early days of Hebrew prophecy (1 Sm 10, 10ff; 19, 20ff) and in the first years of the Church (Acts 2, 6-11. 17; 19, 6; 1 Cor 12–14).

11, 31: At a height of two cubits from the ground: exhausted by the storm, the quail could take but short, low flights, so that they were easily captured. To give food to the hungry people, God may have used the natural phenomenon of the annual migration of quail across the Sinai Peninsula. In the spring large flocks of these birds cross the Gulf of Aqabah

flying toward the west; in the fall they fly back eastward from the Mediterranean. The sea mentioned here probably refers to the former body of water.

11, 32: They spread them out: to cure by drying.

11, 34: Kibroth-hattaavah: means "graves of greed."

12, 1: Cushite woman: apparently Zipporah, the Midianitess, is meant; cf Ex 2, 21. Perhaps the term is used here merely in the sense of "despised foreigner."

12, 2: The real reason for Miriam's quarrel with her

p: Ps 78, 26ff.   q: 32f: 78, 26-31; 1 Cor 10, 6-7.

through Moses alone that the LORD speaks? Does he not speak through us also?" And the LORD heard this. *3r*Now, Moses himself was by far the meekest man on the face of the earth. *4*So at once the LORD said to Moses and Aaron and Miriam, "Come out, you three, to the meeting tent." And the three of them went. *5*Then the LORD came down in the column of cloud, and standing at the entrance of the tent, called Aaron and Miriam. When both came forward, *6*he said, "Now listen to the words of the LORD:

> Should there be a prophet among you,
>   in visions will I reveal myself to him,
>   in dreams will I speak to him;
> *7* Not so with my servant Moses!
> Throughout my house he bears my trust:*s*
> *8*   face to face I speak to him,*t*
>   plainly and not in riddles.
> The presence of the LORD he beholds.

Why, then, did you not fear to speak against my servant Moses?"

Miriam's Leprosy. *9*So angry was the LORD against them that when he departed, *10*and the cloud withdrew from the tent, there was Miriam,*u* a snow-white leper!* When Aaron turned and saw her a leper, *11*"Ah, my lord!" he said to Moses, "please do not charge us with the sin that we have foolishly committed! *12*Let her not thus be like the stillborn babe that comes forth from its mother's womb with its flesh half consumed." *13*Then Moses cried to the LORD, "Please, not this! Pray, heal her!" *14*But the LORD answered Moses, "Suppose her father had spit in her face, would she not hide in shame for seven days? Let her be confined outside the camp for seven days; only then may she be brought back." *15*So Miriam was confined outside the camp for seven days, and the people did not start out again until she was brought back.

*16*After that the people set out from Hazeroth and encamped in the desert of Paran.

CHAPTER 13

See RG 135-36

The Twelve Scouts. *1*The LORD said to Moses, *2*"Send men to reconnoiter the land of Canaan, which I am giving the Israelites. You shall send one man from each ancestral tribe, all of them princes." *3v*So Moses dispatched them from the desert of Paran, as the LORD had ordered. All of them were leaders among the Israelites; *4*by name they were:

> Shammua, son of Zaccur, of the tribe of Reuben;
> *5* Shaphat, son of Hori, of the tribe of Simeon;
> *6* Caleb, son of Jephunneh, of the tribe of Judah;
> *7* Igal [son of Joseph] of the tribe of Issachar;
> *10* Gaddiel, son of Sodi, of the tribe of Zebulun;
> *11* Gaddi, son of Susi, of the tribe of Manasseh, for the Josephites, with
> *8* Hoshea, son of Nun, of the tribe of Ephraim;
> *9* Palti, son of Raphu, of the tribe of Benjamin;
> *12* Ammiel, son of Gemalli, of the tribe of Dan;
> *13* Sethur, son of Michael, of the tribe of Asher;
> *14* Nahbi, son of Vophsi, of the tribe of Naphtali;
> *15* Geuel, son of Machi, of the tribe of Gad.

*16*These are the names of the men whom Moses sent out to reconnoiter the land. But Hoshea, son of Nun, Moses called Joshua.*

*17*In sending them to reconnoiter the land of Canaan, Moses said to them, "Go up here in the Negeb, up into the highlands, *18*and see what kind of land it is. Are the people living there strong or weak, few or many?

---

brother Moses was her jealousy of his superior position; his Cushite wife served only as an occasion for the dispute. Aaron merely followed his sister in her rebellion; hence she alone was punished.

12, 10: A snow-white leper: afflicted with "white leprosy," a skin disease that generally is not serious or of long duration. Cf Lv 13, 3-6.

13, 16: Joshua: in Hebrew, "Jehoshua," which was later modified to "Jeshua," the Hebrew pronunciation of the name "Jesus." Hoshea and Joshua are variants of one original name meaning "the LORD saves." Cf Mt 1, 21.

r: Sir 45, 1f. *s:* Sir 45, 3; Heb 3, 2. 5. *t:* Ex 33, 11; Dt 34, 10. *u:* Dt 24, 9. *v:* 3-33: Dt 1, 22-28.

[19] Is the country in which they live good or bad? Are the towns in which they dwell open or fortified? [20] Is the soil fertile or barren, wooded or clear? And do your best to get some of the fruit of the land." It was then the season for early grapes.

[21] So they went up and reconnoitered the land from the desert of Zin* as far as where Rehob adjoins Labo of Hamath. [22w] Going up by way of the Negeb, they reached Hebron, where Ahiman, Sheshai and Talmai, descendants of the Anakim,* were living. [Hebron had been built seven years before Zoan in Egypt.] [23] They also reached the Wadi Eshcol,* where they cut down a branch with a single cluster of grapes on it, which two of them carried on a pole, as well as some pomegranates and figs. [24] It was because of the cluster the Israelites cut there that they called the place Wadi Eshcol.[x]

Their Return. [25] After reconnoitering the land for forty days they returned, [26y] met Moses and Aaron and the whole community of the Israelites in the desert of Paran at Kadesh, made a report to them all, and showed them the fruit of the country. [27] They told Moses: "We went into the land to which you sent us. It does indeed flow with milk and honey, and here is its fruit. [28] However, the people who are living in the land are fierce, and the towns are fortified and very strong.[z] Besides, we saw descendants of the Anakim there. [29] Amalekites live in the region of the Negeb; Hittites, Jebusites and Amorites dwell in the highlands, and Canaanites along the seacoast and the banks of the Jordan."

[30] Caleb, however, to quiet the people toward Moses, said, "We ought to go up and seize the land, for we can certainly do so." [31] But the men who had gone up with him

said, "We cannot attack these people; they are too strong for us." [32] So they spread discouraging reports[a] among the Israelites about the land they had scouted, saying, "The land that we explored is a country that consumes its inhabitants. And all the people we saw there are huge men, [33b] veritable giants* [the Anakim were a race of giants]; we felt like mere grasshoppers, and so we must have seemed to them."

CHAPTER 14

See RG 135-36

Threats of Revolt. [1] At this, the whole community broke out with loud cries, and even in the night the people wailed. [2c] All the Israelites grumbled against Moses and Aaron, the whole community saying to them, "Would that we had died in the land of Egypt, or that here in the desert we were dead! [3] Why is the LORD bringing us into this land only to have us fall by the sword? Our wives and little ones will be taken as booty. Would it not be better for us to return to Egypt?" [4] So they said to one another, "Let us appoint a leader and go back to Egypt."

[5] But Moses and Aaron fell prostrate before the whole assembled community of the Israelites; [6] while Joshua, son of Nun, and Caleb, son of Jephunneh, who had been in the party that scouted the land, tore their garments [7] and said to the whole community of the Israelites,[d] "The country which we went through and explored is a fine, rich land. [8] If the LORD is pleased with us, he will bring us in and give us that land, a land flowing with milk and honey. [9e] But do not rebel against the LORD! You need not be afraid of the people of that land; they are but food for us!* Their defense has left them, but the LORD is with us. Therefore, do not be afraid

---

13, 21: The desert of Zin: north of Paran and southwest of the Dead Sea. It is quite distinct from "the desert of Sin" near the border of Egypt (Ex 16, 1; 17, 1; Nm 33, 11). Labo of Hamath: a town near Riblah (Jer 39, 5f) at the southern border of Hamath, an independent kingdom in southern Syria. David's conquests extended as far as Hamath (2 Sm 8, 9ff), and Labo thus formed the northern border of the ideal extent of Israel's possessions (Nm 34, 7ff; Ez 47, 15; 48, 1). Some commentators think that this verse is a later addition to the text; cf Dt 1, 24.

13, 22. 28: Anakim: an aboriginal race in southern Palestine, largely absorbed by the Canaanites before the Israelite

invasion. Either because of their tall stature or because of the massive stone structures left by them the Israelites regarded them as giants.

13, 23: Eshcol: means "cluster."

13, 33: Giants: in Hebrew, "nephilim." Cf Gn 6, 4.

14, 9: They are but food for us: that is, "we can easily consume and destroy them." This is the answer to the pessimistic report that this land "consumes its inhabitants" (Nm 13, 32).

w: Jos 11, 21f. x: Nm 32, 9; Dt 1, 24f. y: 26f: Ex 3, 8. 17.
z: 28f: Dt 9, 1f. a: Nm 32, 9; Jos 14, 8. b: Dt 2, 10. c: Ex 16, 3; Ps 106, 25. d: 7f: Dt 1, 25. e: Dt 7, 18.

of them." [10]In answer, the whole community threatened to stone them.

The Lord's Sentence. But then the glory of the LORD appeared at the meeting tent to all the Israelites. [11]And the LORD said to Moses, "How long will this people spurn me? How long will they refuse to believe in me, despite all the signs I have performed among them?[f] [12]I will strike them with pestilence and wipe them out. Then I will make of you a nation greater and mightier than they."[g]

[13h]But Moses said to the LORD: "Are the Egyptians to hear of this? For by your power you brought out this people from among them. [14]And are they to tell of it to the inhabitants of this land? It has been heard that you, O LORD, are in the midst of this people; you, LORD, who plainly reveal yourself! Your cloud stands over them, and you go before them by day in a column of cloud and by night in a column of fire.[i] [15]If now you slay this whole people, the nations who have heard such reports of you will say, [16]'The LORD was not able to bring this people into the land he swore to give them; that is why he slaughtered them in the desert.'[j] [17]Now then, let the power of my Lord be displayed in its greatness, even as you have said, [18k]'The LORD is slow to anger and rich in kindness, forgiving wickedness and crime; yet not declaring the guilty guiltless, but punishing children to the third and fourth generation for their fathers' wickedness.' [19]Pardon, then, the wickedness of this people in keeping with your great kindness, even as you have forgiven them from Egypt until now."[l]

[20]The LORD answered: "I pardon them as you have asked. [21]Yet, by my life and the LORD's glory that fills the whole earth, [22]of all the men who have seen my glory and the signs I worked in Egypt and in the desert,[m] and who nevertheless have put me to the test ten times already and have failed to heed my voice, [23]not one shall see the land which I promised on oath to their fathers. None of these who have spurned me shall see it. [24]But because my servant Caleb has a different spirit and follows me unreservedly,[n] I will bring him into the land where he has just been, and his descendants shall possess it. [25]But now, since the Amalekites and Canaanites are living in the valleys,* turn away tomorrow and set out in the desert on the Red Sea road."

[26]The LORD also said to Moses and Aaron: [27]"How long will this wicked community grumble against me?[o] I have heard the grumblings of the Israelites against me. [28]Tell them:* By my life, says the LORD, I will do to you just what I have heard you say. [29]Here in the desert[p] shall your dead bodies fall. Of all your men of twenty years or more, registered in the census, who grumbled against me, [30]not one shall enter the land where I solemnly swore to settle you, except Caleb, son of Jephunneh, and Joshua, son of Nun. [31]Your little ones, however, who you said would be taken as booty, I will bring in, and they shall appreciate the land you spurned.[q] [32]But as for you, your bodies shall fall here in the desert, [33]here where your children must wander for forty years, suffering for your faithlessness, till the last of you lies dead in the desert.[r] [34]Forty days you spent in scouting the land; forty years shall you suffer for your crimes: one year for each day. Thus you will realize what it means to oppose me. [35]I, the LORD, have sworn to do this to all this wicked community that conspired against me: here in the desert they shall die to the last man."

[36]And so it happened to the men whom Moses had sent to reconnoiter the land[s] and who on returning had set the whole community grumbling against him by spreading discouraging reports about the land; [37]these men who had given out the bad report about

14, 25: The valleys: the low-lying plains in the Negeb and along the seacoast and in the Jordan depression as well as the higher valleys in the mountains farther north; cf Nm 14, 45.

14, 28f: God punished the malcontents by giving them their wish; cf v 2. Their lack of faith and of confidence in God is cited in 1 Cor 10, 10, and Heb 3, 12-18, as a warning for Christians.

f: Ps 78, 22. 32.   g: Ex 32, 10.   h: 13-16: Ex 32, 12; Dt 9, 26ff; Ps 106, 23.   i: Ex 13, 21; Jos 2, 9f.   j: Ex 32, 12; Dt 9, 28.   k: Ex 20, 5; 34, 6f; Pss 103, 8; 145, 8.   l: Ps 78, 38.   m: 22f: Dt 1, 35.   n: Jos 14, 8f.   o: Ex 16, 7. 12.   p: Dt 1, 35; Heb 3, 17.   q: Dt 1, 39.   r: 33f: Nm 13, 26; 32, 13; Ps 95, 10; Ez 4, 6.   s: 36f: Nm 13, 17. 32f; 1 Cor 10, 10.

the land were struck down by the LORD and died. [38]Of all the men who had gone to reconnoiter the land, only Joshua, son of Nun, and Caleb, son of Jephunneh, survived.[t]

Unsuccessful Invasion. [39]When Moses repeated these words to all the Israelites, the people felt great remorse. [40]Early the next morning they started up into the foothills, saying, "Here we are, ready to go up to the place that the LORD spoke of:[u] for we were indeed doing wrong." [41]But Moses said, "Why are you again disobeying the LORD's orders? This cannot succeed. [42]Do not go up, because the LORD is not in your midst; if you go, you will be beaten down before your enemies.[v] [43]For there the Amalekites and Canaanites face you, and you will fall by the sword. You have turned back from following the LORD; therefore the LORD will not be with you."

[44]Yet they dared to go up into the foothills,[w] even though neither the ark of the covenant of the LORD nor Moses left the camp. [45]And the Amalekites and Canaanites who dwelt in that hill country came down and defeated them, beating them back as far as Hormah.*

See RG
135-36

CHAPTER 15

Secondary Offerings. [1]The LORD said to Moses, [2]*"Give the Israelites these instructions: When you have entered the land that I will give you for your homesteads, [3]if you make to the LORD a sweet-smelling oblation from the herd or from the flock, in holocaust, in fulfillment of a vow, or as a freewill offering, or for one of your festivals, [4]whoever does so shall also present to the LORD a cereal offering consisting of a tenth of an ephah of fine flour mixed with a fourth of a hin of oil, [5]as well as a libation of a fourth of a hin of wine, with each lamb sacrificed in holocaust or otherwise. [6]With each

sacrifice of a ram you shall present a cereal offering of two tenths of an ephah of fine flour mixed with a third of a hin of oil, [7]and a libation of a third of a hin of wine, thus making a sweet-smelling offering to the LORD. [8]When you sacrifice an ox as a holocaust, or in fulfillment of a vow, or as a peace offering to the LORD, [9]with it you shall present a cereal offering of three tenths of an ephah of fine flour mixed with half a hin of oil, [10]and a libation of half a hin of wine, as a sweet-smelling oblation to the LORD. [11]The same is to be done for each ox, ram, lamb or goat. [12]Whatever the number you offer, do the same for each of them.

[13]"All the native-born shall make these offerings in the same way, whenever they present a sweet-smelling oblation to the LORD. [14]Likewise, in any future generation, any alien residing with you permanently or for a time, who presents a sweet-smelling oblation to the LORD, shall do as you do. [15]There is but one rule for you and for the resident alien, a perpetual rule for all your descendants. Before the LORD you and the alien are alike, [16]with the same law and the same application of it for the alien residing among you as for yourselves."

[17]The LORD said to Moses, [18]"Speak to the Israelites and tell them: When you enter the land into which I will bring you [19]and begin to eat of the food of that land, you shall offer the LORD a contribution [20]consisting of a cake of your first batch of dough.* You shall offer it just as you offer a contribution from the threshing floor.[x] [21]Throughout your generations you shall give a contribution to the LORD from your first batch of dough.

Sin Offerings. [22]*"When through inadvertence you fail to carry out any of these commandments which the LORD gives to Moses,[y] [23]and through Moses to you, from the time the LORD first issues the command-

---

14, 45: Hormah: one of the Canaanite royal cities in southern Judea (Jos 12, 14), known at this time as "Zephath"; the origin of the later name is told in Nm 21, 3; Jgs 1, 17.

15, 2-16: These laws on sacrifice are complementary to those of Lv 1–3. Since the food of the Israelites consisted not only of meat but also of bread, oil and wine, so, besides the animal oblations, they offered flour, wine and oil in sacrifice to the Lord.

15, 20: Dough: some render, "barley grits." This word is

used elsewhere only in Ez 44, 30 and Neh 10, 33; a related Hebrew word is used in Lv 2, 14.

15, 22ff: Although no moral guilt is incurred by an inadvertent violation of God's commandments, the sanctity of the law can require some reparation even for such violations.

t: Nm 26, 65.   *u:* Nm 13, 18; Dt 1, 42.   *v:* Dt 1, 42.   *w:* Dt 1, 43.   *x:* 19-20: Ez 44, 30.   *y:* 22f; Lv 4, 13f.

ment down through your generations: [24]if the community itself unwittingly becomes guilty of the fault of inadvertence, the whole community shall offer the holocaust of one young bull as a sweet-smelling oblation pleasing to the LORD, along with its prescribed cereal offering and libation, as well as one he-goat as a sin offering. [25z]Then the priest shall make atonement for the whole Israelite community; thus they will be forgiven the inadvertence for which they have brought their holocaust as an oblation to the LORD. [26]Not only the whole Israelite community, but also the aliens residing among you, shall be forgiven, since the fault of inadvertence affects all the people.

[27]"However, if it is an individual who sins inadvertently,[a] he shall bring a yearling she-goat as a sin offering, [28]and the priest shall make atonement before the LORD for him who sinned inadvertently; when atonement has been made for him, he will be forgiven. [29]You shall have but one law for him who sins inadvertently, whether he be a native Israelite or an alien residing with you.

[30]"But anyone who sins defiantly,[b] whether he be a native or an alien, insults the LORD, and shall be cut off from among his people. [31c]Since he has despised the word of the LORD and has broken his commandment, he must be cut off. He has only himself to blame."

The Sabbath-breaker. [32]While the Israelites were in the desert, a man was discovered gathering wood on the sabbath day. [33]Those who caught him at it brought him to Moses and Aaron and the whole assembly. [34]But they kept him in custody, for there was no clear decision* as to what should be done

with him.[d] [35]Then the LORD said to Moses, "This man shall be put to death; let the whole community stone him outside the camp." [36]So the whole community led him outside the camp and stoned him to death, as the LORD had commanded Moses.

Tassels on the Cloak. [37]The LORD said to Moses, [38]"Speak to the Israelites and tell them that they and their descendants must put tassels* on the corners of their garments, fastening each corner tassel with a violet cord.[e] [39]When you use these tassels, let the sight of them remind you to keep all the commandments of the LORD, without going wantonly astray after the desires of your hearts and eyes. [40]Thus you will remember to keep all my commandments and be holy to your God. [41]I, the LORD, am your God who, as God, brought you out of Egypt that I, the LORD, may be your God."[f]

CHAPTER 16

See RG 135-36

Rebellion of Korah. [1]Korah, son of Izhar, son of Kohath, son of Levi,* [and Dathan and Abiram, sons of Eliab, son of Pallu, son of Reuben] took [2]two hundred and fifty Israelites who were leaders in the community, members of the council and men of note. They stood before Moses, [3]and held an assembly against Moses and Aaron, to whom they said,[g] "Enough from you! The whole community, all of them, are holy; the LORD is in their midst. Why then should you set yourselves over the LORD's congregation?"

[4]When Moses heard this, he fell prostrate. [5]Then he said to Korah and to all his band, "May the LORD make known tomorrow morning who belongs to him and who is the holy one and whom he will have draw near to

15, 34: No clear decision: they already knew that a willful violation of the sabbath was a capital offense, but they did not yet know how the death penalty was to be inflicted.

15, 38: Tassels: at the time of Christ these tassels were worn by all pious Jews, including our Lord (Mt 9, 20f; Mk 6, 56); the Pharisees wore very large ones in ostentation of their zeal for the law (Mt 23, 5).

16, 1ff: The evidence seems to show that there were two distinct rebellions: one of Korah and his band (Nm 27, 3) and the other of Dathan and Abiram (Dt 11, 6); cf Ps 106. The present account combines both events into one narrative; but even here it is rather easy to separate the two, once certain proper names (vv 1. 6. 24. 32. 35) have been identified as glosses. The rebellion of the Reubenites, Dathan and

Abiram, was of a political nature, against Moses alone as the civil leader; these rebels were punished by being swallowed alive in an earthquake. The rebellion of Korah was of a religious nature, against the religious leadership of both Moses and Aaron; about two hundred and fifty malcontents joined Korah's band; they were punished by fire. The parts of the present section which refer to the rebellion of Dathan and Abiram are vv 12-15 and vv 25-34 of chapter 16; rest of chapter 16 and all of chapter 17 concern the rebellion of Korah.

z: Lv 4, 20. *a:* 27f: Lv 4, 27f. *b:* Dt 17, 12. *c:* Prv 13, 13.
d: Lv 24, 12. *e:* Dt 22, 12. *f:* Lv 22, 32f. *g:* Ps 106, 16ff; Sir 45, 19; 1 Cor 10, 10.

him! Whom he chooses, he will have draw near him. *6*Do this: take your censers [Korah and all his band] *7*and put fire in them and place incense in them before the LORD tomorrow. He whom the LORD then chooses is the holy one. Enough from you Levites!"

*8*Moses also said to Korah, "Listen to me, you Levites! *9h*Is it too little for you that the God of Israel has singled you out from the community of Israel, to have you draw near him for the service of the LORD's Dwelling and to stand before the community to minister for them? *10*He has allowed you and your kinsmen, the descendants of Levi, to approach him, and yet you now seek the priesthood too. *11*It is therefore against the LORD that you and all your band are conspiring. For what has Aaron done that you should grumble against him?"

Rebellion of Dathan and Abiram. *12*Moses summoned Dathan and Abiram, sons of Eliab, but they answered, "We will not go.* *13*Are you not satisfied with having led us here away from a land flowing with milk and honey, to make us perish in the desert, that you must now lord it over us? *14*Far from bringing us to a land flowing with milk and honey, or giving us fields and vineyards for our inheritance, will you also gouge out our eyes?* No, we will not go."

*15*Then Moses became very angry and said to the LORD, "Pay no heed to their offering. I have never taken a single ass from them, nor have I wronged any one of them."*i*

Korah. *16*Moses said to Korah, "You and all your band shall appear before the LORD tomorrow—you and they and Aaron too. *17*Then each of your two hundred and fifty followers shall take his own censer, put incense in it, and offer it to the LORD; and you and Aaron, each with his own censer, shall do the same." *18*So they all took their censers, and laying incense on the fire they had put in them, they took their stand by the entrance of the meeting tent along with Moses and Aaron. *19*Then, when Korah had assembled all his band against them at the entrance of the meeting tent, the glory of the LORD appeared to the entire community, *20*and the LORD said to Moses and Aaron, *21*"Stand apart from this band, that I may consume them at once." *22*But they fell prostrate and cried out, "O God, God of the spirits of all mankind, will one man's sin make you angry with the whole community?" *23*The LORD answered Moses, *24*"Speak to the community and tell them: Withdraw from the space around the Dwelling" [of Korah, Dathan and Abiram].

Punishment of Dathan and Abiram. *25*Moses, followed by the elders of Israel, arose and went to Dathan and Abiram.* *26*Then he warned the community, "Keep away from the tents of these wicked men and do not touch anything that is theirs: otherwise you too will be swept away because of all their sins." *27*When Dathan and Abiram had come out and were standing at the entrances of their tents with their wives and sons and little ones, *28*Moses said, "This is how you shall know that it was the LORD who sent me to do all I have done, and that it was not I who planned it: *29*if these men die an ordinary death, merely suffering the fate common to all mankind, then it was not the LORD who sent me. *30*But if the LORD does something entirely new, and the ground opens its mouth and swallows them alive down into the nether world, with all belonging to them, then you will know that these men have defied the LORD." *31j*No sooner had he finished saying all this than the ground beneath them split open, *32*and the earth opened its mouth and swallowed them and their families [and all of Korah's men] and all their possessions. *33*They went down alive to the nether world with all belonging to them; the earth closed over them, and they perished from the community. *34*But all the Israelites near them fled at their shrieks, saying, "The earth might swallow us too!"

Punishment of Korah. *35*So they withdrew from the space around the Dwelling [of Korah,* Dathan and Abiram]. And fire from

16, 12: We will not go: to appear before Moses' tribunal.
16, 14: Gouge out our eyes: blind us to the real state of affairs.
16, 25: Since Dathan and Abiram had refused to go to Moses (vv 12ff), he, with the elders as witnesses, was obliged to go to their tent.

16, 35: This verse continues v 24; the first sentence is transposed from v 27.

h: Dt 10, 8. *i:* 1 Sm 12, 3. *j:* 31ff: Nm 26, 10; Lv 10, 2; Dt 11, 6; Ps 106, 7f.

the LORD came forth which consumed the two hundred and fifty men who were offering the incense.

CHAPTER 17

See RG
135–36

[1]The LORD said to Moses, [2]"Tell Eleazar, son of Aaron the priest, to remove the censers from the embers; and scatter the fire some distance away, [3]*for these sinners have consecrated the censers at the cost of their lives. Have them hammered into plates to cover the altar, because in being presented before the LORD they have become sacred. In this way they shall serve as a sign to the Israelites." [4]So Eleazar the priest had the bronze censers of those burned during the offering hammered into a covering for the altar, [5]in keeping with the orders which the LORD had given him through Moses. This cover was to be a reminder to the Israelites that no layman, no one who was not a descendant of Aaron, should approach the altar to offer incense before the LORD, lest he meet the fate of Korah and his band.

[6]The next day the whole Israelite community grumbled against Moses and Aaron, saying, "It is you who have slain the LORD's people." [7]But while the community was deliberating against them, Moses and Aaron turned toward the meeting tent, and the cloud now covered it and the glory of the LORD appeared. [8]Then Moses and Aaron came to the front of the meeting tent, [9]and the LORD said to Moses and Aaron, [10]"Depart from this community, that I may consume them at once." But they fell prostrate.

[11]Then Moses said to Aaron, "Take your censer, put fire from the altar in it, lay incense on it, and bring it quickly to the community to make atonement for them; for wrath has come forth from the LORD and the

blow is falling."[k] [12]Obeying the orders of Moses, Aaron took his censer and ran in among the community, where the blow was already falling on the people. Then, as he offered the incense and made atonement for the people, [13]standing there between the living and the dead, the scourge was checked. [14]Yet fourteen thousand seven hundred died from the scourge, in addition to those who died because of Korah. [15]When the scourge had been checked, Aaron returned to Moses at the entrance of the meeting tent.

Aaron's Staff. [16]The LORD now said to Moses, [17]"Speak to the Israelites and get one staff* from them for each ancestral house, twelve staffs in all, one from each of their tribal princes. Mark each man's name on his staff; [18]and mark Aaron's name on Levi's staff,* for the head of Levi's ancestral house shall also have a staff. [19]Then lay them down in the meeting tent, in front of the commandments, where I meet you. [20]There the staff of the man of my choice shall sprout. Thus will I suppress from my presence the Israelites' grumbling against you."

[21]So Moses spoke to the Israelites, and their princes gave him staffs, twelve in all, one from each tribal prince; and Aaron's staff was with them. [22]Then Moses laid the staffs down before the LORD in the tent of the commandments. [23]The next day, when Moses entered the tent, Aaron's staff, representing the house of Levi, had sprouted and put forth not only shoots, but blossoms as well, and even bore ripe almonds! [24]Moses thereupon brought out all the staffs from the LORD's presence to the Israelites. After each prince identified his own staff and took it, [25]the LORD said to Moses, "Put back Aaron's staff in front of the commandments, to be kept there as a warning to the rebellious, so

17, 3: Whatever was brought into intimate contact with something sacred shared in its sacredness. See note on Nm 19, 20.

17, 17: The staff was not merely an article of practical use, but also a symbol of authority; cf Gn 49, 10; Nm 24, 17; Jer 48, 17. Hence, the staff of a leader of a tribe was considered the emblem of his tribe; in fact, certain Hebrew words for "staff" also means "tribe." Perhaps for this reason, to avoid confusion, the author here uses the term "ancestral house" instead of the ordinary word for "tribe."

17, 18: Levi's staff: it is not clear whether this is consid-

ered as one of the twelve mentioned in the preceding verse, or as a thirteenth staff. Sometimes Levi is reckoned as one of the twelve tribes (e.g., Dt 27, 12f), but more often the number twelve is arrived at by counting the two sub-tribes of Joseph, i.e., Ephraim and Manasseh, as distinct tribes. In this passage also it seems probable that the tribe of Levi is considered apart from the other twelve.

17, 27f: Logically these two verses belong immediately after Nm 16, 35.

k: Wis 18, 20f.

that their grumbling may cease before me; if it does not, they will die." *26*And Moses did as the LORD had commanded him.

Charge of the Sacred Things. *27**Then the Israelites cried out to Moses, "We are perishing; we are lost, we are all lost! *28*Every time anyone approaches the Dwelling of the LORD, he dies! Are we to perish to the last man?"

See RG 135–36

CHAPTER 18

*1*The LORD said to Aaron,* "You and your sons as well as the other members of your ancestral house shall be responsible for the sanctuary; but the responsibility of the priesthood shall rest on you and your sons alone. *2*Bring with you also your other kinsmen of the tribe of Levi, your ancestral tribe, as your associates* and assistants, while you and your sons are in front of the tent of the commandments. *3*They shall look after your persons and the whole tent; however, they shall not come near the sacred vessels or the altar, lest both they and you die. *4*As your associates they shall have charge of all the work connected with the meeting tent. But no layman* shall come near you. *5*You shall have charge of the sanctuary and of the altar, that wrath may not fall again upon the Israelites.

6"Remember, it is I who have taken your kinsmen, the Levites, from the body of the Israelites; they are a gift to you,*l* dedicated to the LORD for the service of the meeting tent. *7m*But only you and your sons are to have charge of performing the priestly functions in whatever concerns the altar and the room within the veil.* I give you the priesthood as a gift. Any layman who draws near shall be put to death."

The Priests' Share of the Sacrifices. *8*The LORD said to Aaron,* "I myself have given you charge of the contributions made to me in the various sacred offerings of the Israelites;*n* by perpetual ordinance I have assigned them to you and to your sons as your priestly share. *9*You shall have the right to share in the oblations that are most sacred, in whatever they offer me as cereal offerings or sin offerings or guilt offerings; these shares shall accrue to you and to your sons. *10*In eating them you shall treat them as most sacred; every male among you may partake of them. As sacred, they belong to you.

11"You shall also have what is removed from the gift in every wave offering* of the Israelites; by perpetual ordinance I have assigned it to you and to your sons and daughters.*o* All in your family who are clean may partake of it. *12*I have also assigned to you all the best*p* of the new oil and of the new wine and grain that they give to the LORD as their first fruits; *13*and likewise, of whatever grows on their land, the first products that they bring in to the LORD shall be yours; all of your family who are clean may partake of them. *14*Whatever is doomed* in Israel shall be yours. *15*Every living thing that opens the womb, whether of man or of beast, such as are to be offered to the LORD, shall be yours;*q* but you must let the first-born of man, as well as of unclean animals, be redeemed. *16*The ransom for a boy is to be paid when he is a month old; it is fixed at five silver shekels according to the sanctuary standard, twenty gerahs to the shekel. *17*But the first-born of cattle, sheep or goats shall not be redeemed; they are sacred. Their blood you must splash on the altar and their fat you must burn as a sweet-smelling oblation to

---

18, 1ff: This law, which kept unqualified persons from contact with sacred things, is the answer to the Israelites' cry in Nm 17, 28. It is followed by other laws concerning priests and Levites.

18, 2: Associates: in Hebrew this word alludes to the popular etymology of the name "Levi." Cf Gn 29, 34.

18, 4: Layman: here, "one who is not a Levite"; in v 7, "one who is not a priest."

18, 7: Veil: the outer veil, or "curtain," is probably meant.

18, 8ff: Two classes of offerings are here distinguished: the most sacred offering, which only the male members of the priestly families could eat (vv 8ff), and the other offerings,

which even the women of the priestly families could eat (vv 11-19).

18, 11: Wave offering: this included the breast and right leg (v 18), the shoulder of the peace offering (Lv 7, 30-34), and portions of the nazirite sacrifice (Nm 6, 19f).

18, 14: Doomed: in Hebrew, *herem*, which means here "set aside from profane use and made sacred to the Lord." Cf Lv 27, 21. 28.

l: Nm 3, 9; 8, 19. *m:* Nm 3, 10. *n:* Nm 5, 9. *o:* Ex 29, 27f; Lv 7, 34; 10, 14. *p:* 12f: Dt 18, 4; 26, 2. *q:* Ex 13, 2.

the LORD. [18r]Their meat, however, shall be yours, just as the breast and the right leg of the wave offering belong to you. [19]By perpetual ordinance I have assigned to you and to your sons and daughters all the contributions from the sacred gifts which the Israelites make to the LORD; this is an inviolable covenant* to last forever before the LORD, for you and for your descendants." [20s]Then the LORD said to Aaron,* "You shall not have any heritage in the land of the Israelites nor hold any portion among them; I will be your portion and your heritage among them.

Tithes Due the Levites. [21]"To the Levites, however, I hereby assign all tithes in Israel as their heritage in recompense for the service they perform in the meeting tent.[t] [22]The Israelites may no longer approach the meeting tent; else they will incur guilt deserving death. [23]Only the Levites are to perform the service of the meeting tent, and they alone shall be held responsible; this is a perpetual ordinance for all your generations. The Levites, therefore, shall not have any heritage among the Israelites, [24]for I have assigned to them as their heritage the tithes which the Israelites give as a contribution to the LORD. That is why I have ordered that they are not to have any heritage among the Israelites."

Tithes Paid by the Levites. [25]The LORD said to Moses, [26]"Give the Levites these instructions: When you receive from the Israelites the tithes I have assigned you from them as your heritage, you are to make a contribution from them to the LORD, a tithe of the tithes; [27]and your contribution will be credited to you as if it were grain from the threshing floor or new wine from the press. [28]Thus you too shall make a contribution from all the tithes you receive from the Israelites, handing over to Aaron the priest the part to be contributed to the LORD. [29]From all the gifts that you receive, and from the best parts, you are to consecrate to the LORD your own full contribution.

[30]"Tell them also: Once you have made your contribution from the best part, the rest of the tithes will be credited to you Levites as if it were produce of the threshing floor or of the wine press. [31]Your families, as well as you, may eat them anywhere, since they are your recompense for service at the meeting tent. [32]You will incur no guilt so long as you make a contribution of the best part. Do not profane the sacred gifts of the Israelites and so bring death on yourselves."

CHAPTER 19

See RG 135-36

Ashes of the Red Heifer. [1]The LORD said to Moses and Aaron: [2]"This is the regulation which the law of the LORD prescribes. Tell the Israelites to procure for you a red heifer that is free from every blemish and defect and on which no yoke has ever been laid. [3]This is to be given to Eleazar the priest, to be led outside the camp* and slaughtered in his presence. [4]Eleazar the priest shall take some of its blood on his finger and sprinkle it seven times toward the front of the meeting tent.* [5]Then the heifer shall be burned in his sight, with its hide and flesh, its blood and offal; [6]and the priest shall take some cedar wood, hyssop and scarlet yarn and throw them into the fire in which the heifer is being burned. [7]The priest shall then wash his garments and bathe his body in water. He remains unclean until the evening, and only afterward may he return to the camp. [8]Likewise, he who burned the heifer shall wash his garments, bathe his body in water, and be unclean until evening. [9]Finally, a man who is clean shall gather up

---

18, 19: An inviolable covenant: literally, "a covenant of salt." Cf 2 Chr 13, 5. The reference may perhaps be to the preservative power of salt (cf Mt 5, 13); but more likely the phrase refers to the custom of partaking of the same salt in common to render a contract unbreakable. See note on Lv 2, 13.

18, 20: The priests and Levites were forbidden to own hereditary land such as the other Israelites possessed; therefore in the allotment of the land they were not to receive any portion of it. Certain cities, however, were assigned to them for their residence; cf Nm 35, 1-8.

19, 3: Outside the camp: several Fathers of the Church saw in this a prefiguring of the sacrificial death of Christ outside the walls of Jerusalem; cf Jn 19, 20; Heb 13, 12; in the purifying water, into which the ashes of the red heifer were put, they saw a type of the water of Baptism.

19, 4: Toward the front of the meeting tent: since the tabernacle faced the east (Ex 26, 15-30), the killing of the heifer took place east of the camp; in later times it was done on the Mount of Olives, east of the Temple.

r: Lv 7, 31-34.   s: Dt 10, 9; 18, 1f; Jos 13, 33; Ez 44, 28.   t: Heb 7, 5.

the ashes of the heifer and deposit them in a clean place outside the camp. There they are to be kept for preparing lustral water for the Israelite community. The heifer is a sin offering. ¹⁰He who has gathered up the ashes of the heifer shall also wash his garments and be unclean until evening. This is a perpetual ordinance, both for the Israelites and for the aliens residing among them.

Use of the Ashes. ¹¹"Whoever touches the dead body of any human being shall be unclean for seven days; ¹²he shall purify himself with the water on the third and on the seventh day, and then he will be clean again. But if he fails to purify himself on the third and on the seventh day, he will not become clean. ^{13u}Everyone who fails to purify himself after touching the body of any deceased person, defiles the Dwelling of the LORD and shall be cut off from Israel. Since the lustral water has not been splashed over him, he remains unclean: his uncleanness still clings to him.

¹⁴"This is the law: When a man dies in a tent, everyone who enters the tent, as well as everyone already in it, shall be unclean for seven days; ¹⁵likewise, every vessel that is open, or with its lid unfastened, shall be unclean. ¹⁶Moreover, everyone who in the open country touches a dead person, whether he was slain by the sword or died naturally, or who touches a human bone or a grave, shall be unclean for seven days. ¹⁷*For anyone who is thus unclean, ashes from the sin offering shall be put in a vessel, and spring water shall be poured on them. ¹⁸Then a man who is clean shall take some hyssop, dip it in this water, and sprinkle it on the tent and on all the vessels and persons that were in it, or on him who touched a bone, a slain person or other dead body, or a grave. ¹⁹The clean man shall sprinkle the unclean on the third and on the seventh day; thus purified on the seventh day, he shall

wash his garments and bathe his body in water, and in the evening he will be clean again. ²⁰*Any unclean man who fails to have himself purified shall be cut off from the community, because he defiles the sanctuary of the LORD. As long as the lustral water has not been splashed over him, he remains unclean. ²¹This shall be a perpetual ordinance for you.

"One who sprinkles the lustral water shall wash his garments, and anyone who comes in contact with this water shall be unclean until evening. ²²Moreover, whatever the unclean person touches becomes unclean itself, and anyone who touches it becomes unclean until evening."

CHAPTER 20

See RG
135-36

Death of Miriam. ¹The whole Israelite community arrived in the desert of Zin in the first month,* and the people settled at Kadesh. It was here that Miriam died, and here that she was buried.

Water Famine at Kadesh. ²As the community had no water, they held a council against Moses and Aaron. ³The people contended with Moses, exclaiming, "Would that we too had perished with our kinsmen in the LORD's presence! ⁴Why have you brought the LORD's community into this desert where we and our livestock are dying? ⁵Why did you lead us out of Egypt, only to bring us to this wretched place which has neither grain nor figs nor vines nor pomegranates? Here there is not even water to drink!" ⁶But Moses and Aaron went away from the assembly to the entrance of the meeting tent, where they fell prostrate.

Sin of Moses and Aaron. Then the glory of the LORD appeared to them, ⁷and the LORD said to Moses, ⁸"Take the staff and assemble the community, you and your brother Aaron, and in their presence order the rock to yield its waters. From the rock you shall

---

19, 17ff: "If . . . the sprinkled ashes of a heifer sanctify the unclean unto the cleansing of the flesh, how much more will the blood of Christ . . . cleanse your conscience from dead works?" (Heb 9, 13f).

19, 20: Ritual uncleanness is, as it were, contagious; so also sacredness; see note on Nm 17, 3.

20, 1: The desert of Zin: a barren region with a few good oases, southwest of the Dead Sea. See note on Nm 13, 21.

The first month: we would expect the mention also of the day and of the year (after the exodus) when this took place; cf similar dates in Nm 1, 1; 10, 11; 33, 38; Dt 1, 3. Here the full date seems to have been lost. Probably the Israelites arrived in Kadesh in the third year after the exodus. Cf Dt 1, 46.

u: Lv 15, 31.

bring forth water for the community and their livestock to drink." [9]So Moses took the staff from its place before the LORD, as he was ordered. [10]He and Aaron assembled the community in front of the rock, where he said to them,[v] "Listen to me, you rebels! Are we to bring water for you out of this rock?" [11][w]Then, raising his hand, Moses struck the rock twice* with his staff, and water gushed out in abundance for the community and their livestock to drink. [12]*But the LORD said to Moses and Aaron, "Because you were not faithful to me in showing forth my sanctity before the Israelites, you shall not lead this community into the land I will give them."

[13]These are the waters of Meribah,[x] where the Israelites contended against the LORD, and where he revealed his sanctity among them.

Edom's Refusal. [14]From Kadesh Moses sent men to the king of Edom with the message: "Your brother Israel* has this to say: You know of all the hardships that have befallen us, [15]how our fathers went down to Egypt, where we stayed a long time, how the Egyptians maltreated us and our fathers, [16]and how, when we cried to the LORD,[y] he heard our cry and sent an angel who led us out of Egypt. Now here we are at the town of Kadesh at the edge of your territory. [17]Kindly let us pass through your country. We will not cross any fields or vineyards, nor drink any well water, but we will go straight along the royal road* without turning to the right or to the left, until we have passed through your territory."

[18]But Edom answered him, "You shall not pass through here; if you do, I will advance against you with the sword." [19]The Israelites insisted, "We want only to go up along the highway. If we or our livestock drink any of your water, we will pay for it. Surely there is no harm in merely letting us march through." [20]But Edom still said, "No, you shall not pass through,"[z] and advanced against them with a large and heavily armed force. [21]Therefore, since Edom refused to let them pass through their territory, Israel detoured around them.

Death of Aaron. [22][a]Setting out from Kadesh, the whole Israelite community came to Mount Hor.* [23]There at Mount Hor, on the border of the land of Edom, the LORD said to Moses and Aaron, [24]"Aaron is about to be taken to his people; he shall not enter the land I am giving to the Israelites, because you both rebelled against my commandment at the waters of Meribah. [25]Take Aaron and his son Eleazar and bring them up on Mount Hor.[b] [26]Then strip Aaron of his garments and put them on his son Eleazar; for there Aaron shall be taken in death."

[27]Moses did as the LORD commanded. When they had climbed Mount Hor in view of the whole community, [28]Moses stripped Aaron of his garments and put them on his son Eleazar. Then Aaron died there on top of the mountain.[c] When Moses and Eleazar came down from the mountain, [29]all the community understood that Aaron had passed away; and for thirty days the whole house of Israel mourned him.

CHAPTER 21

Victory over Arad. [1]When the Canaanite king of Arad,* who lived in the Negeb,[d] heard that the Israelites were com-

See RG 136-37

20, 11: Twice: perhaps because he had not sufficient faith to work the miracle with the first blow. Cf v 12.

20, 12f: The sin of Moses and Aaron consisted in doubting God's mercy toward the ever-rebellious people. In showing forth my sanctity: God's sacred power and glory: an allusion to the name of the place, Kadesh, which means "sanctified, sacred." Meribah means "contention." Cf Ex 17, 7.

20, 14: Your brother Israel: the Edomites were descended from Esau, the brother of Jacob. Their country, to the southeast of the Dead Sea, was also known as Seir; cf Gn 25, 24ff; 36, 1. 8f.

20, 17: The royal road: an important highway, running north and south along the plateau east of the Dead Sea. In ancient times it was much used by caravans and armies; later it

was improved by the Romans, and large stretches of it are still clearly recognizable.

20, 22: Mount Hor: not definitively identified, but probably to be sought in the vicinity of Kadesh. According to Dt 10, 6, Aaron died at Moserah (cf "Moseroth" in Nm 33, 30f), which is apparently the name of the region in which Mount Hor is situated.

21, 1-3: The account of this episode seems to be a later insertion here, for Nm 21, 4, belongs logically immediately after Nm 20, 29. Perhaps this is the same event as that mentioned in Jgs 1, 16f.

v: Ex 17, 5f.   w: Ps 78, 15f; Wis 11, 4; 1 Cor 10, 4.   x: Nm 27, 14: Ex 17, 7.   y: Ex 2, 23.   z: Jgs 11, 17.   a: 21f: Nm 33, 37. b: 25f: Dt 32, 50.   c: Nm 33, 38.   d: Nm 33, 40.

ing along the way of Atharim, he engaged them in battle and took some of them captive. ²Israel then made this vow to the LORD: "If you deliver this people into my hand, I will doom their cities."^e ³Later, when the LORD heeded Israel's prayer and delivered up the Canaanites,^f they doomed them and their cities. Hence that place was named Hormah.*

The Bronze Serpent. ⁴From Mount Hor they set out on the Red Sea road, to bypass the land of Edom. But with their patience worn out by the journey, ⁵the people complained^g against God and Moses, "Why have you brought us up from Egypt to die in this desert, where there is no food or water? We are disgusted with this wretched food!"*

⁶In punishment the LORD sent among the people saraph* serpents, which bit^h the people so that many of them died. ⁷Then the people came to Moses and said, "We have sinned in complaining against the LORD and you. Pray the LORD to take the serpents from us." So Moses prayed for the people, ⁸and the LORD said to Moses, "Make a saraph and mount it on a pole, and if anyone who has been bitten looks at it, he will recover."* ⁹Moses accordingly made a bronze serpent* and mounted it on a pole, and whenever anyone who had been bitten by a serpent looked at the bronze serpent, he recovered.ⁱ

Journey around Moab. ¹⁰The Israelites moved on and encamped in Oboth.^j ¹¹Setting out from Oboth, they encamped in Iyeabarim* in the desert fronting Moab on the east. ¹²Setting out from there, they encamped in the Wadi Zered. ¹³Setting out

from there, they encamped on the other side of the Arnon, in the desert that extends from the territory of the Amorites; for the Arnon forms Moab's boundary with the Amorites. ¹⁴Hence it is said in the "Book of the Wars of the LORD"*:

> "Waheb in Suphah and the wadies,
> ¹⁵ Arnon and the wadi gorges
> That reach back toward the site of Ar
>   and slant to the border of Moab."

¹⁶From there they went to Beer,* where there was the well of which the LORD said to Moses, "Bring the people together, and I will give them water." ¹⁷Then it was that Israel sang this song:

> "Spring up, O well!—so sing to it—
> ¹⁸ The well that the princes sank,
>   that the nobles of the people dug,
>   with their scepters and their staffs."

From Beer they went to Mattanah, ¹⁹from Mattanah to Nahaliel, from Nahaliel to Bamoth, ²⁰from Bamoth to the cleft in the plateau of Moab at the headland of Pisgah that overlooks Jeshimon.*

Victory over Sihon. ²¹Now Israel sent men to Sihon, king of the Amorites, with the message, ²²"Let us pass through your country. We will not turn aside into any field or vineyard, nor will we drink any well water, but we will go straight along the royal road until we have passed through your territory." ²³Sihon,^k however, would not let Israel pass through his territory, but mustered all his forces and advanced into the desert against Israel. When he reached Jahaz, he engaged

---

21, 3: Hormah: related to the Hebrew word herem, meaning "doomed." See notes on Nm 14, 45; 18, 14.

21, 5: This wretched food: apparently the manna is meant.

21, 6: Saraph: the Hebrew name for a certain species of venomous snakes; the word probably signifies "the fiery one," these snakes being so called from the burning effect of their poisonous bite.

21, 8: If anyone who has been bitten looks at it, he will recover: "and as Moses lifted up the serpent in the desert, even so must the Son of Man be lifted up, that those who believe in him may not perish, but may have life everlasting" (Jn 3, 14f).

21, 9: King Hezekiah, in his efforts to abolish idolatry, "smashed the bronze serpent which Moses had made" (2 Kgs 18, 4).

21, 11: Iye-abarim: probably means "the ruins in the Abarim (Mountains)." See note on Nm 27, 12.

21, 14: The "Book of the Wars of the Lord": an ancient collection of Israelite songs, now lost. Waheb in Suphah: since neither place is mentioned elsewhere, it is quite uncertain whether these dubious Hebrew words are even to be considered as place names; some Hebrew words apparently lost must have preceded this phrase.

21, 16: Beer: means a well.

21, 20: Jeshimon: "the wasteland"; in 1 Sm 23, 19. 24, and 26, 1. 3, this is the desert of Judah, on the western side of the Dead Sea, but here and in Nm 23, 28, it seems to refer to the southern end of the Jordan valley where Beth-jeshimoth was situated.

---

e: Jos 6, 17; Jgs 1, 17. *f:* Nm 14, 45. *g:* Nm 11, 6; Ex 16, 3. *h:* Dt 8, 15; Wis 16, 5; 1 Cor 10, 9. *i:* Wis 16, 6f. 10; Jn 3, 14f. *j:* Nm 33, 43f. *k:* Dt 2, 32; Jgs 11, 20.

Israel in battle. [24]But Israel defeated him at the point of the sword, and took possession of his land from the Arnon to the Jabbok and as far as the country of the Ammonites, whose boundary was at Jazer. [25l]Israel seized all the towns here and settled in these towns of the Amorites, in Heshbon and all its dependencies. [26]Now Heshbon was the capital of Sihon, king of the Amorites, who had fought against the former king of Moab and had seized all his land from Jazer to the Arnon. [27]That is why the poets say:

"Come to Heshbon, let it be rebuilt,
     let Sihon's capital be firmly
          constructed.
[28] For fire went forth from Heshbon
     and a blaze from the city of Sihon;
It consumed the cities of Moab
     and swallowed up the high places of
          the Arnon.
[29] Woe to you, O Moab!
     You are ruined, O people of
          Chemosh!*
He let his sons become fugitives
     and his daughters be taken captive
          by the Amorite king Sihon.
[30] Their plowland is ruined from Heshbon
          to Dibon;
     Ar is laid waste; fires blaze as far as
          Medeba."

[31]When Israel had settled in the land of the Amorites, [32]Moses sent spies to Jazer; Israel then captured it with its dependencies and dispossessed the Amorites who were there.

Victory over Og. [33m]Then they turned and went up along the road to Bashan. But Og, king of Bashan, advanced against them with all his people to give battle at Edrei. [34]The LORD, however, said to Moses, "Do not be afraid of him; for into your hand I will deliver him with all his people and his land. Do to him as you did to Sihon, king of the Am-

orites, who lived in Heshbon."[n] [35]So they struck him down with his sons and all his people, until not a survivor was left to him, and they took possession of his land.

See RG 136–37

CHAPTER 22

[1]Then the Israelites moved on and encamped in the plains of Moab* on the other side of the Jericho stretch of the Jordan.

III: On the Plains of Moab

Balaam Summoned. [2]Now Balak, son of Zippor, saw all that Israel did to the Amorites. [3]Indeed, Moab feared the Israelites greatly because of their numbers, and detested them. [4]So Moab said to the elders of Midian, "Soon this horde will devour all the country around us as an ox devours the grass of the field." And Balak, Zippor's son, who was king of Moab at that time, [5]sent messengers to Balaam, son of Beor, at Pethor on the Euphrates, in the land of the Amawites, summoning him with these words, "A people has come here from Egypt who now cover the face of the earth and are settling down opposite us! [6]Please come and curse this people for us;* they are stronger than we are. We may then be able to defeat them and drive them out of the country. For I know that whoever you bless is blessed and whoever you curse is cursed." [7]Then the elders of Moab and of Midian left with the divination fee in hand and went to Balaam. When they had given him Balak's message, [8]he said to them in reply, "Stay here overnight, and I will give you whatever answer the LORD gives me." So the princes of Moab lodged with Balaam.

[9]Then God came to Balaam and said, "Who are these men visiting you?" [10]Balaam answered God, "Balak, son of Zippor, king of Moab, sent me the message: [11]'This people that came here from Egypt now cover the face of the earth. Please come and lay a

---

21, 29: Chemosh: the chief god of the Moabites, and mentioned as such in the famous inscription of Mesha, king of Moab, who was the contemporary of the dynasty of Omri in Israel. Cf 1 Kgs 11, 7. 33; 2 Kgs 23, 13; Jer 48, 7. 13.

22, 1: The plains of Moab: the lowlands to the northeast of the Dead Sea, between the Jordan and the foothills below Mount Nebo. Here the Israelites remained until they crossed the

Jordan, as told in Jos 1–4. Jericho lay to the west of the Jordan.

22, 6: Curse this people for us: Balak believed that if Balaam forecast an evil omen for Israel, this evil would come to pass, as if by magic. Balaam was a soothsayer or foreteller; cf Jos 13, 22.

l: 25f: Jos 21, 39; Jgs 11, 26. *m:* Dt 3, 1ff. *n:* Ps 136, 17ff.

curse on them for us; we may then be able to give them battle and drive them out.' " [12]But God said to Balaam, "Do not go with them and do not curse this people, for they are blessed." [13]The next morning Balaam arose and told the princes of Balak, "Go back to your own country, for the LORD has refused to let me go with you." [14]So the princes of Moab went back to Balak with the report, "Balaam refused to come with us."

Second Appeal to Balaam. [15]Balak again sent princes, who were more numerous and more distinguished than the others. [16]On coming to Balaam they told him, "This is what Balak, son of Zippor, has to say: Please do not refuse to come to me. [17]I will reward you very handsomely and will do anything you ask of me. Please come and lay a curse on this people for me." [18o]But Balaam replied to Balak's officials, "Even if Balak gave me his house full of silver and gold, I could not do anything, small or great, contrary to the command of the LORD, my God. [19]But, you too shall stay here overnight, till I learn what else the LORD may tell me."

[20]That night God came to Balaam and said to him, "If these men have come to summon you, you may go with them; yet only on the condition that you do exactly as I tell you." [21]So the next morning when Balaam arose, he saddled his ass, and went off with the princes of Moab.

The Talking Ass. [22]But now the anger of God flared up* at him for going, and the angel of the LORD stationed himself on the road to hinder him as he was riding along on his ass, accompanied by two of his servants. [23]When the ass saw the angel of the LORD standing on the road with sword drawn, she turned off the road and went into the field, and Balaam had to beat her to bring her back on the road. [24]Then the angel of the LORD took his stand in a narrow lane between vineyards with a stone wall on each side. [25]When the ass saw the angel of the LORD there, she shrank against the wall; and since she squeezed Balaam's leg against it, he beat her again. [26]The angel of the LORD then went ahead, and stopped next in a passage so narrow that there was no room to move either to the right or to the left. [27]When the ass saw the angel of the LORD there, she cowered under Balaam. So, in anger, he again beat the ass with his stick.

[28p]But now the LORD opened the mouth of the ass, and she asked Balaam, "What have I done to you that you should beat me these three times?" [29]"You have acted so willfully against me," said Balaam to the ass, "that if I but had a sword at hand, I would kill you here and now." [30]But the ass said to Balaam, "Am I not your own beast, and have you not always ridden upon me until now? Have I been in the habit of treating you this way before?" "No," replied Balaam.

[31]Then the LORD removed the veil from Balaam's eyes, so that he too saw the angel of the LORD standing on the road with sword drawn; and he fell on his knees and bowed to the ground. [32]But the angel of the LORD said to him, "Why have you beaten your ass these three times? It is I who have come armed to hinder you because this rash journey of yours is directly opposed to me. [33]When the ass saw me, she turned away from me these three times. If she had not turned away from me, I would have killed you; her I would have spared." [34]Then Balaam said to the angel of the LORD, "I have sinned. Yet I did not know that you stood against me to oppose my journey. Since it has displeased you, I will go back home." [35]But the angel of the LORD said to Balaam, "Go with the men; but you may say only what I tell you." So Balaam went on with the princes of Balak.

[36]When Balak heard that Balaam was coming, he went out to meet him at the boundary city Ir-Moab on the Arnon at the end of the Moabite territory. [37]And he said to Balaam, "I sent an urgent summons to you! Why did you not come to me? Did you think I could not reward you?" [38]Balaam an-

---

22, 22: The anger of God flared up: not merely because Balaam was going to Balak, for he had God's permission for the journey (v 20), but perhaps because he was tempted by avarice to curse Israel against God's command. "They have followed the way of Balaam, son of Bosor, who loved the wages of wrongdoing" (2 Pt 2, 15); "and have rushed on thoughtlessly into the error of Balaam for the sake of gain" (Jude 11). Cf v 32 and compare Ex 4, 18-26.

o: Nm 24, 13.   p: 2 Pt 2, 16.

swered him, "Well, I have come to you after all. But what power have I to say anything? I can speak only what God puts in my mouth." [39]Then Balaam went with Balak, and they came to Kiriath-huzoth. [40]Here Balak slaughtered oxen and sheep, and sent portions to Balaam and to the princes who were with him.

The First Oracle. [41]The next morning Balak took Balaam up on Bamoth-baal, and from there he saw some of the clans.

CHAPTER 23

See RG 136–37

[1]Then Balaam said to Balak, "Build me seven altars, and prepare seven bullocks and seven rams for me here." [2]So he did as Balaam had ordered, offering a bullock and a ram on each altar. And Balak said to him, "I have erected the seven altars, and have offered a bullock and a ram on each." [3]Balaam then said to him, "Stand here by your holocaust while I go over there. Perhaps the LORD will meet me, and then I will tell you whatever he lets me see." He went out on the barren height, [4]and God met him. [5]When he had put an utterance in Balaam's mouth, the LORD said to him, "Go back to Balak, and speak accordingly." [6]So he went back to Balak, who was still standing by his holocaust together with all the princes of Moab. [7]Then Balaam gave voice to his oracle:

From Aram* has Balak brought me here,
  Moab's king, from the Eastern
    Mountains:[q]
"Come and lay a curse for me on Jacob,
  come and denounce Israel."
[8] How can I curse whom God has not
    cursed?
  How denounce whom the LORD has
    not denounced?
[9] For from the top of the crags I see him,
  from the heights I behold him.

Here is a people that lives apart*
  and does not reckon itself among the
    nations.
[10] Who has ever counted the dust of Jacob,
  or numbered Israel's wind-borne
    particles?*
May I die the death of the just,
  may my descendants be as many as
    theirs!

[11]"What have you done to me?" cried Balak to Balaam. "It was to curse my foes that I brought you here; instead, you have even blessed them." [12]Balaam replied, "Is it not what the LORD puts in my mouth that I must repeat with care?"

The Second Oracle. [13]Then Balak said to him, "Please come with me to another place* from which you can see only some and not all of them, and from there curse them for me." [14]So he brought him to the lookout field on the top of Pisgah, where he built seven altars and offered a bullock and a ram on each of them. [15]Balaam then said to Balak, "Stand here by your holocaust, while I seek a meeting over there." [16]Then the LORD met Balaam, and having put an utterance in his mouth, he said to him, "Go back to Balak, and speak accordingly." [17]So he went back to Balak, who was still standing by his holocaust together with the princes of Moab. When Balak asked him, "What did the LORD say?" [18]Balaam gave voice to his oracle:

Be aroused, O Balak, and hearken;
  give ear to my testimony, O son of
    Zippor!
[19] God is not man that he should speak
    falsely,
  nor human, that he should change his
    mind.
Is he one to speak and not act,
  to decree and not fulfill?

23, 7: Aram: the ancient name of the region later known as Syria. The Eastern Mountains: the low ranges in the Syrian desert near the Euphrates and Balaam's town of Pethor; cf Nm 22, 5.

23, 9: A people that lives apart: Israel, as the chosen people of God, occupied a unique place among the nations, from which they kept themselves aloof.

23, 10: The dust of Jacob . . . Israel's wind-borne particles: the Israelites will be as numerous as dust in a desert

sandstorm. May I . . . as many as theirs: a formula by which Balaam swears he is speaking the truth; he sees the reward of virtue in having numerous descendants.

23, 13: To another place: Balak thought that if Balaam would view Israel from a different site, he could forecast a different kind of omen.

q: Nm 22, 6.

²⁰ It is a blessing I have been given to
  pronounce;
 a blessing which I cannot restrain.
²¹ Misfortune is not observed in Jacob,
  nor misery* seen in Israel.
 The LORD, his God, is with him;
  with him is the triumph of his King.
²² It is God who brought him out of
  Egypt,^r
 a wild bull of towering might.*
²³ No, there is no sorcery against Jacob,
  nor omen against Israel.
 It shall yet be said of Jacob,
  and of Israel, "Behold what God has
  wrought!"
²⁴ Here is a people that springs up like a
  lioness,
 and stalks forth like a lion;
 It rests not till it has devoured its prey
 and has drunk the blood of the slain.^s

²⁵"Even though you cannot curse them," said Balak to Balaam, "at least do not bless them." ²⁶But Balaam answered Balak, "Did I not warn you that I must do all that the LORD tells me?"

The Third Oracle. ²⁷Then Balak said to Balaam, "Come, let me bring you to another place; perhaps God will approve of your cursing them for me from there." ²⁸So he took Balaam to the top of Peor, that overlooks Jeshimon. ²⁹Balaam then said to him, "Here build me seven altars; and here prepare for me seven bullocks and seven rams." ³⁰And Balak did as Balaam had ordered, offering a bullock and a ram on each altar.

See RG
136-37
CHAPTER 24

¹Balaam, however, perceiving that the LORD was pleased to bless Israel, did not go aside as before to seek omens, but turned his gaze toward the desert. ²When he raised his eyes and saw Israel encamped, tribe by tribe, the spirit of God came upon him, ³and he gave voice to his oracle:

The utterance of Balaam, son of Beor,
 the utterance of the man whose eye is
  true,
⁴ The utterance of one who hears what
  God says,
 and knows what the Most High
  knows,
Of one who sees what the Almighty sees,
 enraptured, and with eyes unveiled:
⁵ How goodly are your tents, O Jacob;
 your encampments, O Israel!
⁶ They are like gardens beside a stream,
 like the cedars planted by the LORD.
⁷ His wells shall yield free-flowing waters,
 he shall have the sea within reach;
 His king shall rise higher than. . . .
 and his royalty shall be exalted.
⁸ It is God who brought him out of Egypt,
 a wild bull of towering might.
 He shall devour the nations like grass,
 their bones he shall strip bare.^t
⁹ He lies crouching like a lion,
 or like a lioness; who shall arouse
  him?
 Blessed is he who blesses you,
 and cursed is he who curses you!^u

¹⁰Balak beat his palms* together in a blaze of anger at Balaam and said to him, "It was to curse my foes that I summoned you here; yet three times now you have even blessed them instead!^{v 11}Be off at once, then, to your home. I promised to reward you richly, but the LORD has withheld the reward from you!" ¹²Balaam replied to Balak, "Did I not warn the very messengers whom you sent to me, ¹³'Even if Balak gave me his house full of silver and gold, I could not of my own accord do anything, good or evil, contrary to the command of the LORD'? Whatever the LORD says I must repeat.^w

The Fourth Oracle. ¹⁴"But now that I am about to go to my own people, let me first warn you what this people will do to your people in the days to come." ¹⁵Then Balaam gave voice to his oracle:

23, 21: Misfortune . . . misery: Balaam admits that he is unable to predict any evils for Israel.
23, 22: A wild bull of towering might: the reference is to Israel, rather than to God.
24, 10: Balak beat his palms: a sign of disclaiming any responsibility for paying the promised reward.

r: Nm 24, 8. s: Nm 24, 9; Gn 49, 9. t: Nm 23, 22. u: Nm 23, 24; Gn 12, 3; 27, 29; 49, 9. v: Nm 23, 11. w: Nm 22, 18.

The utterance of Balaam, son of Beor,
the utterance of the man whose eye is
true,
[16] The utterance of one who hears what
God says,
and knows what the Most High
knows,
Of one who sees what the Almighty sees,
enraptured and with eyes unveiled.
[17] I see him, though not now;
I behold him, though not near:
A star shall advance from Jacob,
and a staff* shall rise from Israel,
That shall smite the brows of Moab,[x]
and the skulls of all the Shuthites,
[18] Till Edom is dispossessed,
and no fugitive is left in Seir.
Israel shall do valiantly,
[19] and Jacob shall overcome his foes.

[20]Upon seeing Amalek, Balaam gave voice
to his oracle:

First* of the peoples was Amalek,
but his end is to perish forever.[y]

[21]Upon seeing the Kenites,* he gave voice to
his oracle:

Your abode is enduring, O smith,
and your nest is set on a cliff;
[22] Yet destined for burning—
even as I watch—are your inhabitants.

[23]Upon seeing . . . he gave voice to his oracle:

*Alas, who shall survive of Ishmael,
[24] to deliver his people from the hands of
the Kittim?
When they have conquered Asshur and
conquered Eber,
He too shall perish forever.

[25]Then Balaam set out on his journey
home; and Balak also went his way.

CHAPTER 25

See RG 136–37

Worship of Baal of Peor. [1]While Israel was living at Shittim,* the people degraded themselves by having illicit relations
with the Moabite women.[z] [2]These then invited the people to the sacrifices of their god,
and the people ate of the sacrifices[a] and worshiped their god. [3]When Israel thus submitted to the rites of Baal of Peor,[b] the LORD's
anger flared up against Israel, [4c]and he said
to Moses, "Gather all the leaders of the people, and hold a public execution* of the
guilty ones before the LORD, that his blazing
wrath may be turned away from Israel." [5]So
Moses told the Israelite judges, "Each of you
shall kill those of his men who have submitted to the rites of Baal of Peor."

Zeal of Phinehas. [6]Yet a certain Israelite
came and brought in a Midianite woman* to
his clansmen in the view of Moses and of the
whole Israelite community, while they were
weeping at the entrance of the meeting tent.
[7d]When Phinehas, son of Eleazar, son of
Aaron the priest, saw this, he left the assem-

24, 17: A star . . . a staff: many of the Fathers have understood this as a Messianic prophecy, although it is not referred to
anywhere in the New Testament; in this sense the star is Christ
himself, just as he is the staff from Israel; cf Is 11, 1. But it is
doubtful whether this passage is to be connected with the "star
of the Magi" in Mt 2, 1-12. The Shuthites: mentioned in other
documents of this period as nomads on the border of Palestine.

24, 20: First: literally "the beginning." Amalek was an
aboriginal people in Palestine and therefore considered as of
great antiquity. There is a deliberate contrast here between the
words first and end.

24, 21: The Kenites lived in high strongholds in the mountains of southern Palestine and the Sinai Peninsula, and were
skilled in working the various metals found in their territory.
Their name is connected, at least by popular etymology, with
the Hebrew word for "smith"; of similar sound is the Hebrew
word for "nest"—hence the play on words in the present passage.

24, 23f: The translation of this short oracle is based on a
reconstructed text and is rather uncertain. Ishmael: the sur-

vival of Ishmael is indicated in Gn 17, 20; 21, 13. 18.

25, 1: Shittim: the full name was Abel-shittim, a locality
at the foot of the mountains in the northeastern corner of the
plains of Moab (Nm 33, 49). Illicit relations: perhaps as part
of the licentious worship of Baal of Peor.

25, 4: Hold a public execution: the same phrase occurs in
2 Sm 21, 6-14, where the context shows that at least a part of
the penalty consisted in being denied honorable burial. In
both passages, dismemberment as a punishment for the
breaking of covenant pledges is a current understanding of
the phrase.

25, 6: Midianite woman: at this time the Midianites were
leagued with the Moabites in opposing Israel; cf Nm 22, 4. 7.
Balaam had induced both the Midianites (Nm 31, 16) and the
Moabites (Rv 2, 14) to lure the Israelites to the obscene rites
of Baal of Peor. They were weeping: on account of the plague
that had struck them; cf v 8.

---

x: 2 Sm 8, 2.   y: Ex 17, 14; 1 Sm 15, 3.   z: Nm 31, 16.   a: Ex
34, 15f.   b: Ps 106, 28; Hos 9, 10.   c: Dt 4, 3.   d: Ps 106, 30.

bly, and taking a lance in hand, [8]followed the Israelite into his retreat where he pierced the pair of them, the Israelite and the woman. Thus the slaughter of Israelites was checked; [9]but only after twenty-four thousand had died.

[10]Then the LORD said to Moses, [11]"Phinehas, son of Eleazar, son of Aaron the priest, has turned my anger from the Israelites by his zeal for my honor* among them; that is why I did not put an end to the Israelites for the offense to my honor. [12e]Announce, therefore, that I hereby give him my pledge of friendship, [13]which shall be for him and for his descendants after him the pledge of an everlasting priesthood, because he was zealous on behalf of his God and thus made amends for the Israelites."

[14*]The Israelite slain with the Midianite woman was Zimri, son of Salu, prince of an ancestral house of the Simeonites. [15]The slain Midianite woman was Cozbi, daughter of Zur, who was head of a clan, an ancestral house, in Midian.

Vengeance on the Midianites. [16*]The LORD then said to Moses, [17f]"Treat the Midianites as enemies and crush them, [18]for they have been your enemies by their wily dealings with you as regards Peor and as regards their kinswoman Cozbi, the daughter of the Midianite prince, who was killed at the time of the slaughter because of Peor."

CHAPTER 26

See RG
136-37

The Second Census. [19]After the slaughter* [1]the LORD said to Moses and Eleazar, son of Aaron the priest, [2]"Take a census, by ancestral houses, throughout the community of the Israelites of all those of twenty years or more who are fit for military service in Israel."[g] [3]So on the plains of Moab along the Jericho stretch of the Jordan, Moses and the priest Eleazar registered [4]those of twenty years or more, as the LORD had commanded Moses.

The Israelites who came out of the land of Egypt were as follows:

[5h]Of Reuben, the first-born of Israel, the Reubenites by clans were: through Hanoch the clan of the Hanochites, through Pallu the clan of the Palluites, [6]through Hezron the clan of the Hezronites, through Carmi the clan of the Carmites. [7]These were the clans of the Reubenites, of whom forty-three thousand seven hundred and thirty men were registered.

[8]From Pallu descended Eliab, [9]and the descendants of Eliab were Dathan and Abiram[i]—the same Dathan and Abiram, councilors of the community, who revolted against Moses and Aaron [like Korah's band when it rebelled against the LORD]. [10]The earth opened its mouth and swallowed them as a warning [Korah too and the band that died when the fire consumed two hundred and fifty men. [11]The descendants of Korah, however, did not die out].

[12]The Simeonites by clans were: through Nemuel* the clan of the Nemuelites, through Jamin the clan of the Jaminites, through Jachin the clan of the Jachinites, [13]through Sohar the clan of the Soharites, through Shaul the clan of the Shaulites. [14]These were the clans of the Simeonites, of whom twenty-two thousand two hundred men were registered.

[15]The Gadites by clans were: through Zephon the clan of the Zephonites, through Haggi the clan of the Haggites, through Shuni the clan of the Shunites, [16]through Ozni the clan of the Oznites, through Eri the clan of the Erites, [17]through Arod the clan of the Arodites, through Areli the clan of the Arelites. [18]These were the clans of the Gadites, of whom forty thousand five hundred men were registered.

[19]The sons of Judah who died in the land of Canaan were Er and Onan.[j] [20]The Judahites by clans were: through Shelah the clan of the

25, 11: For my honor: by taking vengeance on those who had made Baal of Peor a rival of the Lord.

25, 14f: The nobility of the slain couple is mentioned in order to stress the courage of Phinehas in punishing them. The zeal of Phinehas became proverbial; cf Ps 106, 30; Sir 45, 23; 1 Mc 2, 26. 54.

25, 16ff: The account of the execution of this command is given in Nm 31, 1-18.

26, 19: This is the last verse of Ch 25.

26, 12: Nemuel: so also in Gn 46, 10; 1 Chr 4, 24. In Ex 6, 15, the same man is called "Jemuel"; it is uncertain which form is correct.

e: 12f: Sir 45, 23f; Ps 106, 31; 1 Mc 2, 26. 54. *f:* 17f: Nm 31, 2-12. *g:* Nm 1, 2f. *h:* 5f: 1 Chr 5, 3. *i:* 9f: Nm 16, 1. 32. *j:* Gn 38, 7. 10; 46, 12; 1 Chr 2, 3.

Shelahites, through Perez the clan of the Perezites, through Zerah the clan of the Zerahites. ²¹The Perezites were: through Hezron the clan of the Hezronites, through Hamul the clan of the Hamulites. ²²These were the clans of Judah, of whom seventy-six thousand five hundred men were registered.

²³The Issacharites by clans were: through Tola the clan of the Tolaites, through Puvah the clan of the Puvahites, ²⁴through Jashub the clan of the Jashubites, through Shimron the clan of the Shimronites. ²⁵These were the clans of Issachar, of whom sixty-four thousand three hundred men were registered.

²⁶The Zebulunites by clans were: through Sered the clan of the Seredites, through Elon the clan of the Elonites, through Jahleel the clan of the Jahleelites. ²⁷These were the clans of the Zebulunites, of whom sixty thousand five hundred men were registered.

²⁸The sons of Joseph were Manasseh, and Ephraim. ²⁹The Manassehites by clans were: through Machir the clan of the Machirites, through Gilead, a descendant of Machir, the clan of the Gileadites. ³⁰The Gileadites were: through Abiezer the clan of the Abiezrites, through Helek the clan of the Helekites, ³¹through Asriel the clan of the Asrielites, through Shechem the clan of the Shechemites, ³²through Shemida the clan of the Shemidaites, through Hepher the clan of the Hepherites. ³³ᵏZelophehad, son of Hepher, had no sons, but only daughters, whose names were Mahlah, Noah, Hoglah, Milcah and Tirzah. ³⁴These were the clans of Manasseh, of whom fifty-two thousand seven hundred men were registered.

³⁵The Ephraimites by clans were: through Shuthelah the clan of the Shuthelahites, through Becher the clan of the Bechrites, through Tahan the clan of the Tahanites. ³⁶The Shuthelahites were: through Eran the clan of the Eranites. ³⁷These were the clans of the Ephraimites, of whom thirty-two thousand five hundred men were registered.

These were the descendants of Joseph by clans.

³⁸The Benjaminites by clans were: through Bela the clan of the Belaites, through Ashbel the clan of the Ashbelites, through Ahiram the clan of the Ahiramites, ³⁹through Shupham the clan of the Shuphamites, through Hupham the clan of the Huphamites. ⁴⁰The descendants of Bela were Arad and Naaman: through Arad the clan of the Aradites, through Naaman the clan of the Naamanites. ⁴¹These were the Benjaminites by clans, of whom forty-five thousand six hundred men were registered.

⁴²The Danites by clans were: through Shuham the clan of the Shuhamites. These were the clans of Dan, ⁴³of whom sixty-four thousand four hundred men were registered.

⁴⁴The Asherites by clans were: through Imnah the clan of the Imnites, through Ishvi the clan of the Ishvites, through Beriah the clan of the Beriites, ⁴⁵through Heber the clan of the Heberites, through Malchiel the clan of the Malchielites. ⁴⁶The name of Asher's daughter was Serah. ⁴⁷These were the clans of Asher, of whom fifty-three thousand four hundred men were registered.

⁴⁸The Naphtalites by clans were: through Jahzeel the clan of the Jahzeelites, through Guni the clan of the Gunites, ⁴⁹through Jezer the clan of the Jezerites, through Shillem the clan of the Shillemites. ⁵⁰These were the clans of Naphtali, of whom forty-five thousand four hundred men were registered.

⁵¹These six hundred and one thousand seven hundred and thirty were the Israelites who were registered.

Allotment of the Land. ⁵²*The LORD said to Moses, ⁵³ˡ"Among these groups the land shall be divided as their heritage in keeping with the number of individuals in each group. ⁵⁴ᵐTo a large group you shall assign a large heritage, to a small group a small heritage, each group receiving its heritage in proportion to the number of men registered

26, 52-56: The division of Canaan among the various tribes and clans and families was determined partly by the size of each group and partly by lot. Perhaps the lots determined the respective locality of each tribal land and the section reserved for each clan, while the relative size of the allotted locality and section depended on the numerical strength of each group. The Hebrews considered the outcome of the drawing of lots as an expression of God's will; cf Acts 1, 23-26.

k: Nm 27, 1; 36, 11; Jos 17, 3. l: Jos 11, 23. m: Nm 33, 54; 35, 8.

in it. ⁵⁵But the land shall be divided by lot, as the heritage of the various ancestral tribes. ⁵⁶As the lot falls shall each group, large or small, be assigned its heritage."

Census of the Levites. ⁵⁷The Levites registered by clans were: through Gershon the clan of the Gershonites, through Kohath the clan of the Kohathites, through Merari the clan of the Merarites. ⁵⁸These also were clans of Levi: the clan of the Libnites, the clan of the Hebronites, the clan of the Mahlites, the clan of the Mushites, the clan of the Korahites.

Among the descendants of Kohath was Amram, ⁵⁹whose wife was named Jochebed. She also was of the tribe of Levi, born to the tribe in Egypt. To Amram she bore Aaron and Moses and their sister Miriam. ⁶⁰To Aaron were born Nadab and Abihu, Eleazar and Ithamar. ⁶¹But Nadab and Abihu died when they offered profane fire before the LORD.

⁶²The total number of male Levites one month or more of age, who were registered, was twenty-three thousand.ⁿ They were not registered with the other Israelites, however, for no heritage was given them among the Israelites.

⁶³These, then, were the men registered by Moses and the priest Eleazar in the census of the Israelites taken on the plains of Moab along the Jericho stretch of the Jordan. ⁶⁴Among them there was not a man of those who had been registered by Moses and the priest Aaron in the census of the Israelites taken in the desert of Sinai. ⁶⁵ᵒFor the LORD had told them that they would surely die in the desert, and not one of them was left except Caleb, son of Jephunneh, and Joshua, son of Nun.

CHAPTER 27

Zelophehad's Daughters. ¹Zelophehad, son of Hepher, son of Gilead, son of

Machir, son of Manasseh, son of Joseph, had daughters named Mahlah, Noah, Hoglah, Milcah and Tirzah.^p They came forward, ²and standing in the presence of Moses, the priest Eleazar, the princes, and the whole community at the entrance of the meeting tent, said: ³"Our father died in the desert. Although he did not join those who banded together against the LORD* [in Korah's band], he died for his own sin without leaving any sons. ⁴But why should our father's name be withdrawn from his clan merely because he had no son? Let us, therefore, have property among our father's kinsmen."

Laws Concerning Heiresses. ⁵*When Moses laid their case before the LORD, ⁶the LORD said to him, ⁷"The plea of Zelophehad's daughters is just; you shall give them hereditary property among their father's kinsmen, letting their father's heritage pass on to them. ⁸Therefore, tell the Israelites: If a man dies without leaving a son, you shall let his heritage pass on to his daughter; ⁹if he has no daughter, you shall give his heritage to his brothers; ¹⁰if he has no brothers, you shall give his heritage to his father's brothers; ¹¹if his father had no brothers, you shall give his heritage to his nearest relative in his clan, who shall then take possession of it." This is the legal norm for the Israelites, as the LORD commanded Moses.^q

Joshua To Succeed Moses. ¹²The LORD said to Moses, "Go up here into the Abarim Mountains* and view the land that I am giving to the Israelites.^r ¹³When you have viewed it, you too shall be taken to your people, as was your brother Aaron,^s ¹⁴because in the rebellion of the community in the desert of Zin you both rebelled against my order to manifest my sanctity to them by means of the water."^t [This is the water of Meribah of Kadesh in the desert of Zin.]

¹⁵Then Moses said to the LORD, ¹⁶"May the LORD, the God of the spirits of all

27, 3: He did not join . . . against the Lord: had he done so, he and his heirs could have rightly been deprived of the privilege of receiving a portion in the Promised Land.

27, 5-11: The purpose of this law, as also that of the related laws in Nm 36, 2-10 (heiresses to marry within the same tribe), Dt 25, 5-10 (levirate marriage), and Lv 25, 10 (return of property in the jubilee year), was to keep the landed property within the proper domain of each tribe.

27, 12: The Abarim Mountains: the range on the eastern side of the Dead Sea.

n: Nm 3, 39. o: Nm 14, 22ff. 29. p: Nm 26, 33; Jos 17, 3. q: Jer 32, 6-9. r: Dt 3, 27; 32, 49; 34, 1. s: 13f: Nm 20, 12. 24. t: Dt 32, 51.

mankind,* set over the community a man [17]who shall act as their leader in all things, to guide them in all their actions; that the LORD's community may not be like sheep without a shepherd." [18]And the LORD replied to Moses, "Take Joshua, son of Nun,[u] a man of spirit,* and lay your hand upon him. [19]Have him stand in the presence of the priest Eleazar and of the whole community, and commission him before their eyes. [20]Invest him with some of your own dignity, that the whole Israelite community may obey him. [21]He shall present himself to the priest Eleazar, to have him seek out for him the decisions of the Urim* in the LORD's presence; and as he directs, Joshua, all the Israelites with him, and the community as a whole shall perform all their actions."

[22]Moses did as the LORD had commanded him. Taking Joshua and having him stand in the presence of the priest Eleazar and of the whole community, [23]he laid his hands on him and gave him his commission, as the LORD had directed through Moses.

CHAPTER 28

See RG
136-37

General Sacrifices. [1]The LORD said to Moses, [2]"Give the Israelites this commandment: At the times I have appointed, you shall be careful to present to me the food offerings that are offered to me as sweet-smelling oblations.

Each Morning and Evening. [3v]"You shall tell them therefore: This is the oblation which you shall offer to the LORD: two unblemished yearling lambs each day as the established holocaust,* [4]offering one lamb in the morning and the other during the evening twilight, [5]each with a cereal offer-

ing of one tenth of an ephah of fine flour mixed with a fourth of a hin of oil of crushed olives.* [6]This is the established holocaust that was offered at Mount Sinai as a sweet-smelling oblation to the LORD. [7]And as the libation for the first lamb, you shall pour out to the LORD in the sanctuary* a fourth of a hin of wine. [8]The other lamb, to be offered during the evening twilight, you shall offer with the same cereal offering and the same libation as in the morning, as a sweet-smelling oblation to the LORD.

On the Sabbath. [9]"On the sabbath day you shall offer two unblemished yearling lambs, with their cereal offering, two tenths of an ephah of fine flour mixed with oil, and with their libations. [10]Each sabbath there shall be the sabbath holocaust in addition to the established holocaust and its libation.

At the New Moon Feast. [11]"On the first of each month* you shall offer as a holocaust to the LORD two bullocks, one ram, and seven unblemished yearling lambs, [12]with three tenths of an ephah of fine flour mixed with oil as the cereal offering for each bullock, two tenths of an ephah of fine flour mixed with oil as the cereal offering for the ram, [13]and one tenth of an ephah of fine flour mixed with oil as the cereal offering for each lamb, that the holocaust may be a sweet-smelling oblation to the LORD. [14]Their libations shall be half a hin of wine for each bullock, a third of a hin for the ram, and a fourth of a hin for each lamb. This is the new moon holocaust for every new moon of the year. [15]Moreover, one goat shall be sacrificed as a sin offering to the LORD. These are to be offered in addition to the established holocaust and its libation.

27, 16: The God of the spirits of all mankind: the sense is either that God knows the character and abilities of all men and therefore knows best whom to appoint (cf Acts 1, 24), or, more probably, that God is Master of life and death and therefore can call Moses from this world whenever he wishes; cf the same phrase in Nm 16, 22, where "spirit" evidently means "the life principle."

27, 18: A man of spirit: literally, "a man in whom there is spirit": one who has the qualities of a good leader—courage, prudence, and strength of will. Cf Gn 41, 38; Dt 34, 9.

27, 21: The Urim: certain sacred objects which the Hebrew priests employed to ascertain the divine will, probably by obtaining a positive or negative answer to a given question. The full expression was "the Urim and Thummim"; cf

Ex 28, 30; Lv 8, 8; Dt 33, 8; Ezr 2, 63; Neh 7, 65. Joshua was ordinarily not to receive direct revelations from God as Moses had received them.

28, 3: The established holocaust: "the tamid holocaust," the technical term for the daily sacrifice.

28, 5: Oil of crushed olives: this oil, made in a mortar, was purer and more expensive than oil extracted in the olive press.

28, 7: In the sanctuary: according to Sir 50, 15, it was at the base of the altar.

28, 11: On the first of each month: literally, "at the new moons"; beginning on the evening when the crescent of the new moon first appeared.

---

u: Dt 34, 9.   *v:* 3-8: Ex 29, 38-42.

At the Passover. [16]"On the fourteenth day* of the first month falls the Passover of the LORD,[w] [17]and the fifteenth day of this month is the pilgrimage feast. For seven days unleavened bread is to be eaten. [18]On the first of these days you shall hold a sacred assembly, and do no sort of work.[x] [19]As an oblation you shall offer a holocaust to the LORD, which shall consist of two bullocks, one ram, and seven yearling lambs that you are sure are unblemished, [20]with their cereal offerings of fine flour mixed with oil, offering three tenths of an ephah for each bullock, two tenths for the ram, [21]and one tenth for each of the seven lambs; [22]and offer one goat as a sin offering in atonement for yourselves. [23]These offerings you shall make in addition to the established morning holocaust: [24]you shall make exactly the same offerings each day for seven days as food offerings, in addition to the established holocaust with its libation, for a sweet-smelling oblation to the LORD. [25]On the seventh day you shall hold a sacred assembly, and do no sort of work.[y]

At Pentecost. [26]"On the day of first fruits,* on your feast of Weeks,[z] when you present to the LORD the new cereal offering, you shall hold a sacred assembly, and do no sort of work. [27]You shall offer as a sweet-smelling holocaust to the LORD two bullocks, one ram, and seven yearling lambs that you are sure are unblemished, [28]with their cereal offerings of fine flour mixed with oil; offering three tenths of an ephah for each bullock, two tenths for the ram, [29]and one tenth for each of the seven lambs. [30]Moreover, one goat shall be offered as a sin offering in atonement for yourselves. [31]You shall make these offerings, together with their libations, in addition to the established holocaust with its cereal offering.

CHAPTER 29

See RG 136-37

On New Year's Day. [1]"On the first day of the seventh month* you shall hold a sacred assembly, and do no sort of work; it shall be a day on which you sound the trumpet.[a] [2]You shall offer as a sweet-smelling holocaust to the LORD one bullock, one ram, and seven unblemished yearling lambs, [3]with their cereal offerings of fine flour mixed with oil; offering three tenths of an ephah for the bullock, two tenths for the ram, [4]and one tenth for each of the seven lambs. [5]Moreover, one goat shall be offered as a sin offering in atonement for yourselves. [6]These are to be offered in addition to the ordinary new moon holocaust with its cereal offering, and in addition to the established holocaust with its cereal offering, together with the libations prescribed for them, as a sweet-smelling oblation to the LORD.

On the Day of Atonement. [7]"On the tenth day of this seventh month* you shall hold a sacred assembly, and mortify yourselves, and do no sort of work.[b] [8]You shall offer as a sweet-smelling holocaust to the LORD one bullock, one ram, and seven yearling lambs that you are sure are unblemished, [9]with their cereal offerings of fine flour mixed with oil; offering three tenths of an ephah for the bullock, two tenths for the ram, [10]and one tenth for each of the seven lambs. [11]Moreover, one goat shall be sacrificed as a sin offering. These are to be offered in addition to the atonement sin offering,* the established holocaust with its cereal offering, and their libations.

*On the Feast of Booths.** [12]"On the fifteenth day of the seventh month you shall hold a sacred assembly,[c] and do no sort of

---

28, 16: On the fourteenth day: toward evening at the end of this day; cf Ex 12, 6. 18.

28, 26: The day of first fruits: a unique term for this feast, which is usually called "the feast of Weeks"; it was celebrated as a thanksgiving for the wheat harvest seven weeks after the barley harvest (Passover). In the time of Christ it was commonly known by the Greek word "Pentecost," that is, "fiftieth" (day after the Passover); see note on Lv 23, 16.

29, 1: The first day of the seventh month: (about September-October) is now the Jewish New Year's Day. In the older calendar the year began with the first of Nisan (March-April); cf Ex 12, 2.

29, 7: The tenth day of this seventh month: the Day of Atonement. Mortify yourselves: literally, "afflict your souls," that is, with fasting.

29, 11: The atonement sin offering: the bullock prescribed in Lv 16, 11f.

29, 12: This feast of Booths celebrating the vintage harvest was the most popular of all and therefore had the most elaborate ritual. See note on Lv 23, 34.

w: Ex 12, 18; Lv 23, 5; Dt 16, 1. *x:* Ex 12, 16; Lv 23, 7. *y:* Ex 12, 16; 13, 6; Lv 23, 8. *z:* Ex 34, 22. *a:* Nm 10, 10; Lv 23, 24. *b:* Lv 16, 29; 23, 27f. 32. *c:* Lv 23, 34f.

work; then, for seven days following, you shall celebrate a pilgrimage feast to the LORD. [13]You shall offer as a sweet-smelling holocaust to the LORD thirteen bullocks,* two rams, and fourteen yearling lambs that are unblemished, [14]with their cereal offerings of fine flour mixed with oil; offering three tenths of an ephah for each of the thirteen bullocks, two tenths for each of the two rams, [15]and one tenth for each of the fourteen lambs. [16]Moreover, one goat shall be sacrificed as a sin offering. These are to be offered in addition to the established holocaust with its cereal offering and libation.

[17]"On the second day you shall offer twelve bullocks, two rams, and fourteen unblemished yearling lambs, [18]with their cereal offerings and libations as prescribed for the bullocks, rams and lambs in proportion to their number, [19]as well as one goat for a sin offering, besides the established holocaust with its cereal offering and libation.

[20]"On the third day you shall offer eleven bullocks, two rams, and fourteen unblemished yearling lambs, [21]with their cereal offerings and libations as prescribed for the bullocks, rams and lambs in proportion to their number, [22]as well as one goat for a sin offering, besides the established holocaust with its cereal offering and libation.

[23]"On the fourth day you shall offer ten bullocks, two rams, and fourteen unblemished yearling lambs, [24]with their cereal offerings and libations as prescribed for the bullocks, rams and lambs in proportion to their number, [25]as well as one goat for a sin offering, besides the established holocaust with its cereal offering and libation.

[26]"On the fifth day you shall offer nine bullocks, two rams, and fourteen unblemished yearling lambs, [27]d with their cereal offerings and libations as prescribed for the bullocks, rams and lambs in proportion to their number, [28]as well as one goat for a sin

offering, besides the established holocaust with its cereal offering and libation.

[29]"On the sixth day you shall offer eight bullocks, two rams, and fourteen unblemished yearling lambs, [30]with their cereal offerings and libations as prescribed for the bullocks, rams and lambs in proportion to their number, [31]as well as one goat for a sin offering, besides the established holocaust with its cereal offering and libation.

[32]"On the seventh day you shall offer seven bullocks, two rams, and fourteen unblemished yearling lambs, [33]with their cereal offerings and libations as prescribed for the bullocks, rams and lambs in proportion to their number, [34]as well as one goat for a sin offering, besides the established holocaust with its cereal offering and libation.

[35]"On the eighth day[e] you shall hold a solemn meeting,* and do no sort of work. [36]You shall offer up in holocaust as a sweet-smelling oblation to the LORD one bullock, one ram, and seven unblemished yearling lambs, [37]with their cereal offerings and libations as prescribed for the bullocks, rams and lambs in proportion to their number, [38]as well as one goat for a sin offering, besides the established holocaust with its cereal offering and libation.

[39]"These are the offerings you shall make to the LORD on your festivals, besides whatever holocausts, cereal offerings, libations, and peace offerings you present as your votive or free-will offerings."

CHAPTER 30

See RG 136-37

[1]Moses then gave the Israelites these instructions, just as the LORD had ordered him.

Validity and Annulment of Vows. [2]Moses said to the heads of the Israelite tribes, "This is what the LORD has commanded: [3]When a man makes a vow to the LORD or binds himself under oath to a pledge* of abstinence, he shall not violate his word, but must fulfill exactly the promise he has uttered.[f]

29, 13: Thirteen bullocks: the number of bullocks sacrificed before the octave day was seventy, arranged on a descending scale so that the number on the seventh day was the sacred number seven.

29, 35: A solemn meeting: the Hebrew word is the technical term for the closing celebration of the three major feasts of the Passover, Pentecost and Booths, or of other special feasts that

lasted for a week. Cf Lv 23, 36; Dt 16, 8; 2 Chr 7, 9; Neh 8, 18.

30, 3: A vow . . . a pledge: here the former signifies the doing of some positive good deed, in particular the offering of some sacrifice; the latter signifies the abstaining from some otherwise licit action or pleasure; cf v 14.

---

d: Nm 29, 30. 37. *e:* Lv 23, 36; Jn 7, 37. *f:* Dt 23, 22; Eccl 5, 3f.

[4]"When a woman, while still a maiden in her father's house, makes a vow to the LORD, or binds herself to a pledge, [5]if her father learns of her vow or the pledge to which she bound herself and says nothing to her about it, then any vow or any pledge she has made remains valid. [6]But if on the day he learns of it her father expresses to her his disapproval, then any vow or any pledge she has made becomes null and void; and the LORD releases her from it, since her father has expressed to her his disapproval.

[7]"If she marries while under a vow or under a rash pledge to which she bound herself, [8]and her husband learns of it, yet says nothing to her that day about it, then the vow or pledge she had made remains valid. [9]But if on the day he learns of it her husband expresses to her his disapproval, he thereby annuls the vow she had made or the rash pledge to which she had bound herself, and the LORD releases her from it. [10]The vow of a widow or of a divorced woman, or any pledge to which such a woman binds herself, is valid.

[11]"If it is in her husband's house* that she makes a vow or binds herself under oath to a pledge, [12]and her husband learns of it yet says nothing to express to her his disapproval, then any vow or any pledge she has made remains valid. [13]But if on the day he learns of them her husband annuls them, then whatever she has expressly promised in her vow or in her pledge becomes null and void; since her husband has annulled them, the LORD releases her from them.

[14]"Any vow or any pledge that she makes under oath to mortify herself, her husband can either allow to remain valid or render null and void. [15]But if her husband, day after day, says nothing at all to her about them, he thereby allows as valid any vow or any pledge she has made; he has allowed them to remain valid, because on the day he learned of them he said nothing to her about them. [16]If, however, he countermands them* some

time after he first learned of them, he is responsible for her guilt."

[17]These are the statutes which the LORD prescribed through Moses concerning the relationship between a husband and his wife, as well as between a father and his daughter while she is still a maiden in her father's house.

CHAPTER 31

See RG 136-37

Extermination of the Midianites. [1]The LORD said to Moses,* [2]"Avenge the Israelites on the Midianites, and then you shall be taken to your people." [3]So Moses told the people, "Select men from your midst and arm them for war, to attack the Midianites and execute the LORD's vengeance on them. [4]From each of the tribes of Israel you shall send a band of one thousand men to war." [5]From the clans of Israel, therefore, a thousand men of each tribe were levied, so that there were twelve thousand men armed for war. [6]Moses sent them out on the campaign, a thousand from each tribe, with Phinehas, son of Eleazar, the priest for the campaign, who had with him the sacred vessels and the trumpets for sounding the alarm. [7]They waged war against the Midianites, as the LORD had commanded Moses, and killed every male among them. [8]Besides those slain in battle, they killed the five Midianite kings:* Evi, Rekem, Zur, Hur and Reba; and they also executed Balaam, son of Beor, with the sword. [9]But the Israelites kept the women of the Midianites with their little ones as captives, and all their herds and flocks and wealth as spoil, [10]while they set on fire all the towns where they had settled and all their encampments. [11]Then they took all the booty, with the people and beasts they had captured, and brought the captives, together with the spoils and booty, [12]to Moses and the priest Eleazar and to the Israelite community at their camp on the plains of Moab, along the Jericho stretch of the Jordan.

30, 11: In her husband's house: after her marriage. This contrasts with the case given in vv 7ff.

30, 16: He countermands them: he prevents their fulfillment. Since he has first allowed the vows to remain valid, he can no longer annul them.

31, 1ff: The narrative of Israel's relations with Midian, which was interrupted after Nm 25, 18, is now resumed.

31, 8: The five Midianite kings: they are called "Midianite princes, Sihon's vassals" in Jos 13, 21.

Treatment of the Captives. [13]When Moses and the priest Eleazar, with all the princes of the community, went outside the camp to meet them, [14]Moses became angry with the officers of the army, the clan and company commanders, who were returning from combat. [15]"So you have spared all the women!" he exclaimed. [16]"Why, they are the very ones who on Balaam's advice prompted the unfaithfulness of the Israelites toward the LORD in the Peor affair,[g] which began the slaughter of the LORD's community. [17]*Slay, therefore, every male child and every woman who has had intercourse with a man. [18]But you may spare and keep for yourselves all girls who had no intercourse with a man.

Purification after Combat. [19]"Moreover, you shall stay outside the camp for seven days, and those of you who have slain anyone or touched anyone slain in battle shall purify yourselves on the third and on the seventh day. This applies both to you and to your captives. [20]You shall also purify every article of cloth, leather, goats' hair, or wood."

[21]Eleazar the priest told the soldiers who had returned from combat: "This is what the law, as prescribed by the LORD to Moses, ordains: [22]Whatever can stand fire, such as gold, silver, bronze, iron, tin and lead, [23]you shall put into the fire, that it may become clean; however, it must also be purified with lustral water.* But whatever cannot stand fire you shall put into the water. [24]On the seventh day you shall wash your clothes, and then you will again be clean. After that you may enter the camp."

Division of the Booty. [25]The LORD said to Moses: [26]"With the help of the priest Eleazar and of the heads of the ancestral houses, count up all the human captives and the beasts that have been taken; [27]then divide them evenly,* giving half to those who took

active part in the war by going out to combat, and half to the rest of the community. [28]You shall levy a tax for the LORD on the warriors who went out to combat: one out of every five hundred persons, oxen, asses and sheep [29]in their half of the spoil you shall turn over to the priest Eleazar as a contribution to the LORD. [30]From the Israelites' half you shall take one out of every fifty persons, and the same from the different beasts, oxen, asses and sheep, and give them to the Levites, who have charge of the LORD's Dwelling." [31]So Moses and the priest Eleazar did this, as the LORD had commanded Moses.

Amount of Booty. [32]This booty, what was left of the loot which the soldiers had taken, amounted to six hundred and seventy-five thousand sheep, [33]seventy-two thousand oxen, [34]sixty-one thousand asses, [35]and thirty-two thousand girls who were still virgins.

[36]The half that fell to those who had gone out to combat was: three hundred and thirty-seven thousand five hundred sheep, [37]of which six hundred and seventy-five fell as tax to the LORD; [38]thirty-six thousand oxen, of which seventy-two fell as tax to the LORD; [39]thirty thousand five hundred asses, of which sixty-one fell as tax to the LORD; [40]and sixteen thousand persons, of whom thirty-two fell as tax to the LORD. [41]The taxes contributed to the LORD, Moses gave to the priest Eleazar, as the LORD had commanded him.

[42]The half for the other Israelites, which fell to the community when Moses had taken it from the soldiers, was: [43]three hundred and thirty-seven thousand five hundred sheep, [44]thirty-six thousand oxen, [45]thirty thousand five hundred asses, [46]and sixteen thousand persons. [47]From this, the Israelites' share, Moses, as the LORD had ordered, took one out of every fifty, both of persons and of

---

31, 17: There are later references to Midian in Jgs 6–8; 1 Kgs 11, 18; Is 60, 6. The present raid was only against those Midianites who were dwelling at this time near the encampment of the Israelites.

31, 23: Lustral water: water mixed with the ashes of the red heifer as prescribed in Nm 19, 9.

31, 27: Divide them evenly: for a similar division of the

booty into two equal parts, between those who engaged in the fray and those who stayed with the baggage, cf 1 Sm 30, 24. But note that here the tax on the booty of the non-combatants is ten times as much as that on the soldier's booty.

g: 2 Pt 2, 15; Rv 2, 14.

beasts, and gave them to the Levites, who had charge of the LORD's Dwelling.

Gifts of the Officers. [48]Then the officers who had been clan and company commanders of the army came up to Moses [49]and said to him, "Your servants have counted up the soldiers under our command, and not one is missing. [50]*So, to make atonement for ourselves before the LORD, each of us will bring as an offering to the LORD some gold article he has picked up, such as an anklet, a bracelet, a ring, an earring, or a necklace." [51]Moses and the priest Eleazar accepted this gold from them, all of it in well-wrought articles. [52]The gold that they gave as a contribution to the LORD amounted in all to sixteen thousand seven hundred and fifty shekels. This was from the clan and company commanders; [53]what the common soldiers had looted each one kept for himself. [54]Moses, then, and the priest Eleazar accepted the gold from the clan and company commanders, and put it in the meeting tent as a memorial for the Israelites before the LORD.

See RG 136-37

CHAPTER 32

Request of Gad and Reuben. [1]Now the Reubenites and Gadites had a very large number of livestock. Noticing that the land of Jazer and of Gilead* was grazing country, [2]they came to Moses and the priest Eleazar and to the princes of the community and said, [3]*"The region of Ataroth, Dibon, Jazer, Nimrah, Heshbon, Elealeh, Sebam, Nebo and Baal-meon, [4]which the LORD has laid low before the community of Israel, is grazing country. Now, since your servants have livestock," [5]they continued, "if we find favor with you, let this land be given to your servants as their property. Do not make us cross the Jordan."

Moses' Rebuke. [6]But Moses answered the Gadites and Reubenites: "Are your kinsmen, then, to engage in war, while you remain here? [7]Why do you wish to discourage the Israelites from crossing to the land the LORD has given them? [8]That is just what your fathers did when I sent them from Kadesh-barnea to reconnoiter the land.[h] [9]They went up to the Wadi Eshcol and reconnoitered the land, then so discouraged the Israelites that they would not enter the land the LORD had given them. [10i]At that time the wrath of the LORD flared up, and he swore, [11]'Because they have not followed me unreservedly, none of these men of twenty years or more who have come up from Egypt shall ever see this country I promised under oath to Abraham and Isaac and Jacob, [12j]except the Kenizzite* Caleb, son of Jephunneh, and Joshua, son of Nun, who have followed the LORD unreservedly.' [13]So in his anger with the Israelites the LORD made them wander in the desert forty years, until the whole generation that had done evil in the sight of the LORD had died out. [14]And now here you are, a brood of sinners, rising up in your fathers' place to add still more to the LORD's blazing wrath against the Israelites. [15]If you turn away from following him, he will make them stay still longer in the desert, and so you will bring about the ruin of this whole nation."

Counter Proposal. [16]But they were insistent with him: "We wish only to build sheepfolds here for our flocks, and towns for our families; [17]but we ourselves will march as troops in the van of the Israelites,[k] until we have led them to their destination. Meanwhile our families can remain here in the fortified towns, safe from attack by the natives. [18]We will not return to our homes until every one of the Israelites has taken possession of his heritage, [19l]and will not claim any heritage with them once we cross the

---

31, 50: The precise nature and use of some of these articles of gold is not certain.

32, 1: Gilead: the name of the western part of the plateau east of the Jordan, sometimes signifying the whole region from the Yarmuk to the Jordan, sometimes only the northern part of this region, and sometimes, as here, only its southern part. Jazer lay to the east of southern Gilead.

32, 3: The places named in this verse, as well as the additional ones given in vv 34-38, were all in the former kingdom of Sihon, that is, in the region between the Jabbok and the Arnon. Cf Nm 21, 23f; Jos 13, 19-21. 24-27.

32, 12: Kenizzite: a member of the clan of Kenaz, which, according to Gn 36, 11. 15. 42, was Edomitic; hence, although Caleb belonged to the tribe of Judah (Nm 13, 6; 34, 19), he must have had Edomite blood in his veins; cf also Jos 14, 6. 14.

h: 8f: Nm 13, 31ff; Dt 1, 22. i: 10f: Dt 1, 34f. j: Nm 14, 24; Dt 1, 36. k: Jos 4, 12f. l: Jos 13, 8.

Jordan, so long as we receive a heritage for ourselves on this eastern side of the Jordan."

Agreement Reached. [20]*Moses said to them in reply: "If you keep your word to march as troops in the LORD's vanguard [21]and to cross the Jordan in full force before the LORD until he has driven his enemies out of his way [22]and the land is subdued before him, then you may return here, quit of every obligation to the LORD and to Israel, and this region shall be your possession before the LORD.[m] [23]But if you do not do this, you will sin against the LORD, and you can be sure that you will not escape the consequences of your sin. [24]Build the towns, then, for your families, and the folds for your flocks, but also fulfill your express promise."

[25]The Gadites and Reubenites answered Moses, "Your servants will do as you command, my lord. [26n]While our wives and children, our herds and other livestock remain in the towns of Gilead, [27]all your servants will go across as armed troops to battle before the LORD, just as your lordship says."

[28]Moses, therefore, gave this order in their regard to the priest Eleazar, to Joshua, son of Nun, and to the heads of the ancestral tribes of the Israelites: [29]"If all the Gadites and Reubenites cross the Jordan with you as combat troops before the LORD, you shall give them Gilead as their property when the land has been subdued before you. [30]But if they will not go across with you as combat troops before the LORD, you shall bring their wives and children and livestock across before you into Canaan, and they shall have their property with you in the land of Canaan."

[31]To this the Gadites and Reubenites replied, "We will do what the LORD has commanded us, your servants. [32]We ourselves will go across into the land of Canaan as troops before the LORD, but we will retain our hereditary property on this side of the Jordan." [33]So Moses gave them [*the Gadites and Reubenites, as well as half the tribe of Manasseh, son of Joseph, the kingdom of Sihon, king of the Amorites, and the kingdom of Og, king of Bashan,] the land with its towns and the districts that surrounded them.[o]

[34]The Gadites rebuilt the fortified towns of Dibon, Ataroth, Aroer, [35]Atroth-shophan, Jazer, Jogbehah, [36]Beth-nimrah and Beth-haran, and they built sheepfolds. [37]The Reubenites rebuilt Heshbon, Elealeh, Kiriathaim, [38]Nebo, Baal-meon [names to be changed!],* and Sibmah. These towns, which they rebuilt, they called by their old names.

Other Conquests. [39]The descendants of Machir, son of Manasseh, invaded Gilead and captured it, driving out the Amorites who were there. [40][Moses gave Gilead to Machir,[p] son of Manasseh, and he settled there.] [41]Jair,[q] a Manassehite clan, campaigned against the tent villages, captured them and called them Havvoth-jair. [42]Nobah also campaigned against Kenath, captured it with its dependencies and called it Nobah after his own name.

CHAPTER 33

See RG 136-37

Stages on the Journey. [1]The following are the stages by which the Israelites journeyed up by companies from the land of Egypt under the guidance of Moses and Aaron.* [2]By the LORD's command Moses

---

32, 20ff: Since the ark of the Lord was borne into battle with the Israelite army, the vanguard was said to march before the Lord.

32, 33: The preceding is concerned solely with the two tribes of Gad and Reuben and with the land of the former kingdom of Sihon; hence it seems probable that the sudden reference here to the half-tribe of Manasseh and to their territory in Bashan, the former kingdom of Og, is a later addition to the text.

32, 38: The phrase in brackets is a gloss, warning the reader either to change the order of the preceding names, or, more probably, to read some other word, such as bosheth, "shame," for Baal. They called by their old names: literally, "they called by their names" (see Textual Notes); however, some understand the current Hebrew text to mean, "they called by new names."

33, 1ff: This list of camping sites was drawn up by Moses, as v 2 expressly states. However, in its present form it probably includes some glosses. Moreover, a comparison with the more detailed accounts of the journey as given elsewhere shows that this is not complete. It records just forty camping sites, not counting the starting place, Rameses, and the terminus, the plains of Moab. This number, which corresponds exactly to the forty years of wandering in the desert, is probably a schematic device. Besides, it seems that in its present form the order of some of these names has been disturbed. Several names listed here are not recorded elsewhere.

---

m: Jos 1, 15. n: Jos 1, 14. o: Dt 3, 12; 29, 7; Jos 12, 6; 13, 8.
p: Dt 3, 15. q: Dt 3, 14.

Journey from the Wilderness to Canaan

recorded the starting places of the various stages. The starting places of the successive stages were:

3 *They set out from Rameses in the first month,
  on the fifteenth day of the first month.
On the Passover morrow the Israelites went forth
  in triumph, in view of all Egypt,
4 While the Egyptians buried their first-born
  all of whom the LORD had struck down;
  on their gods, too, the LORD executed judgments.*

From Egypt to Sinai. 5Setting out from Rameses, the Israelites camped at Succoth. 6Setting out from Succoth, they camped at Etham near the edge of the desert. 7Setting out from Etham, they turned back to Pi-hahiroth, which is opposite Baal-zephon, and they camped opposite Migdol.* 8Setting out from Pi-hahiroth, they crossed over through the sea into the desert,* and after a three days' journey in the desert of Etham, they camped at Marah. 9Setting out from Marah, they came to Elim, where there were twelve springs of water and seventy palm trees, and they camped there.* 10Setting out from Elim, they camped beside the Red Sea. 11Setting out from the Red Sea, they camped in the desert of Sin. 12Setting out from the desert of Sin, they camped at Dophkah. 13Setting out from Dophkah, they camped at Alush. 14Setting out from Alush, they camped at Rephidim, where there was no water for the people to drink.* 15Setting out from Rephidim, they camped in the desert of Sinai.*

From Sinai to Kadesh. 16Setting out from the desert of Sinai, they camped at Kibroth-hattaavah. 17Setting out from Kibroth-hattaavah, they camped at Hazeroth.* 18Setting out from Hazeroth, they camped at Rithmah.

33, 3f: These two verses were probably borrowed from some ancient song celebrating the exodus from Egypt.

r: 4f: Ex 12, 12. 29. 37.   s: Ex 14, 2.   t: Ex 15, 22.   u: Ex 15, 27.   v: Ex 17, 1.   w: Ex 19, 2.   x: 17f: Nm 11, 34f.

[19]Setting out from Rithmah, they camped at Rimmon-perez. [20]Setting out from Rimmon-perez, they camped at Libnah. [21]Setting out from Libnah, they camped at Rissah. [22]Setting out from Rissah, they camped at Kehelathah. [23]Setting out from Kehelathah, they camped at Mount Shepher. [24]Setting out from Mount Shepher, they camped at Haradah. [25]Setting out from Haradah, they camped at Makheloth. [26]Setting out from Makheloth, they camped at Tahath. [27]Setting out from Tahath, they camped at Terah. [28]Setting out from Terah, they camped at Mithkah. [29]Setting out from Mithkah, they camped at Hashmonah. [30]*Setting out from Hashmonah,—

From Mount Hor to Ezion-geber. They camped at Moseroth. [31]Setting out from Moseroth, they camped at Bene-jaakan. [32]Setting out from Bene-jaakan, they camped at Mount Gidgad. [33]Setting out from Mount Gidgad, they camped at Jotbathah. [34]Setting out from Jotbathah, they camped at Abronah. [35]Setting out from Abronah, they camped at Ezion-geber. [36]Setting out from Ezion-geber,—

From Kadesh to Mount Hor. They camped in the desert of Zin, at Kadesh.[y] [37]Setting out from Kadesh, they camped at Mount Hor on the border of the land of Edom. [38][Aaron the priest ascended Mount Hor.[z] at the LORD's command, and there he died in the fortieth year from the departure of the Israelites from the land of Egypt, on the first day of the fifth month. [39]Aaron was a hundred and twenty-three years old when he died on Mount Hor. [40]*Now, when the Canaanite king of Arad, who lived in the Negeb in the land of Canaan, heard that the Israelites were coming. . . .] [41]Setting out from Mount Hor,—

*From Ezion-geber to the Plains of Moab.** They camped at Zalmonah. [42]Setting out from Zalmonah, they camped at Punon.

[43]Setting out from Punon, they camped at Oboth. [44]Setting out from Oboth, they camped at Iye-abarim on the border of Moab. [45]Setting out from Iye-abarim, they camped at Dibon-gad. [46]Setting out from Dibon-gad, they camped at Almon-diblathaim. [47]Setting out from Almon-diblathaim, they camped in the Abarim Mountains opposite Nebo. [48]Setting out from the Abarim Mountains, they camped on the plains of Moab along the Jericho stretch of the Jordan. [49]Their camp along the Jordan on the plains of Moab extended from Beth-jeshimoth to Abel-shittim.

Conquest and Division of Canaan. [50]The LORD spoke to Moses on the plains of Moab beside the Jericho stretch of the Jordan and said to him: [51]"Tell the Israelites: When you go across the Jordan into the land of Canaan, [52]drive out all the inhabitants of the land before you; destroy all their stone figures and molten images, and demolish all their high places.[a]

[53]"You shall take possession of the land and settle in it, for I have given you the land as your property. [54]You shall apportion the land among yourselves by lot, clan by clan, assigning a large heritage to a large group and a small heritage to a small group.[b] Wherever anyone's lot falls, there shall his property be within the heritage of his ancestral tribe.

[55]"But if you do not drive out the inhabitants of the land before you, those whom you allow to remain will become as barbs in your eyes and thorns in your sides, and they will harass you in the country where you live,[c] [56]and I will treat you as I had intended to treat them."

CHAPTER 34

See RG 136–37

The Boundaries. [1]The LORD said to Moses, [2]"Give the Israelites this order: When you enter the land of Canaan, this is the terri-

---

33, 30-36: Moseroth is mentioned in Dt 10, 6 (in the form of "Moserah"), as the place where Aaron died. It must therefore have been close to Mount Hor; cf Nm 20, 22ff. It seems very probable that the section vv 36b–41a stood originally immediately after v 30a.

33, 40: The verse begins the same account of the victory over Arad as is given in Nm 21, 1ff, where it also follows the

account of Aaron's death.

33, 41b-49: It seems that this section stood originally immediately after v 36a.

---

y: 36f: Nm 20, 1. 22.   *z:* Nm 20, 25; Dt 32, 50.   *a:* Ex 23, 31; 34, 13; Dt 7, 5; 12, 3.   *b:* Nm 26, 53ff.   *c:* Jos 23, 13; Jgs 2, 3.

tory that shall fall to you as your heritage—the land of Canaan with its boundaries:

[3]"Your southern boundary shall be at the desert of Zin along the border of Edom;[d] on the east it shall begin at the end of the Salt Sea, [4]and turning south of the Akrabbim Pass, it shall cross Zin, and extend south of Kadesh-barnea to Hazar-addar; thence it shall cross to Azmon,[e] [5]and turning from Azmon to the Wadi of Egypt, shall terminate at the Sea.[f]

[6]"For your western boundary you shall have the Great Sea* with its coast; this shall be your western boundary.

[7]"The following shall be your boundary on the north: from the Great Sea you shall draw a line to Mount Hor,* [8]and shall continue it from Mount Hor to Labo in the land of Hamath, with the boundary extending through Zedad. [9]Thence the boundary shall reach to Ziphron and terminate at Hazarenan. This shall be your northern boundary.

[10]"For your eastern boundary you shall draw a line from Hazar-enan to Shepham. [11]From Shepham the boundary shall go down to Ar-Baal, east of Ain, and descending further, shall strike the ridge on the east side of the Sea of Chinnereth; [12]thence the boundary shall continue along the Jordan and terminate with the Salt Sea.

"This is the land that shall be yours, with the boundaries that surround it."

[13]Moses also gave this order to the Israelites: "This is the land, to be apportioned among you by lot, which the LORD has commanded to be given to the nine and one half tribes. [14]For all the ancestral houses of the tribe of Reuben, and the ancestral houses of the tribe of Gad, as well as half of the tribe of Manasseh, have already received their heritage; [15]these two and one half tribes have received their heritage on the eastern side of the Jericho stretch of the Jordan, toward the sunrise."

Supervisors of the Allotment. [16]The LORD said to Moses, [17]"These are the names of the men who shall apportion the land among you: Eleazar the priest, and Joshua, son of Nun, [18][g]and one prince from each of the tribes whom you shall designate for this task. [19]These shall be as follows:

from the tribe of Judah: Caleb, son of Jephunneh;

[20] from the tribe of Simeon: Samuel, son of Ammihud;

[21] from the tribe of Benjamin: Elidad, son of Chislon;

[22] from the tribe of Dan: Bukki, son of Jogli;

[23] from the tribe of Manasseh: Hanniel, son of Ephod; and

[24] from the tribe of Ephraim: Kemuel, son of Shiphtan, for the descendants of Joseph;

[25] from the tribe of Zebulun: Elizaphan, son of Parnach;

[26] from the tribe of Issachar: Paltiel, son of Azzan;

[27] from the tribe of Asher: Ahihud, son of Shelomi;

[28] from the tribe of Naphtali: Pedahel, son of Ammihud."

[29]These are they whom the LORD commanded to assign the Israelites their heritage in the land of Canaan.

CHAPTER 35

See RG 136-37

Cities for the Levites. [1]The LORD gave these instructions to Moses on the plains of Moab beside the Jericho stretch of the Jordan: [2][h]"Tell the Israelites that out of their hereditary property they shall give the Levites cities for homes, as well as pasture lands around the cities. [3]The cities shall serve them to dwell in, and the pasture lands shall serve their herds and flocks and other animals. [4]The pasture lands of the cities to be assigned the Levites shall extend a thousand cubits from the city walls in each direction. [5]Thus you shall measure out two thousand cubits outside the city along each side—east, south, west and north—with the city lying in the center. This shall serve them as the pasture lands of their cities.

34, 6: The Great Sea: the Mediterranean.
34, 7f: Mount Hor: different from the one where Aaron died; cf Nm 20, 22; 33, 37f.

---

d: Jos 15, 1f.   *e:* Jos 15, 3.   *f:* Jos 15, 4.   *g:* Nm 1, 4.   *h:* Jos 14, 3f; 21, 2.

6i"Now these are the cities you shall give to the Levites: the six cities of asylum which you must establish as places where a homicide can take refuge, and in addition forty-two other cities— *7*a total of forty-eight cities with their pasture lands to be assigned the Levites. *8**In assigning the cities from the property of the Israelites, take more from a larger group and fewer from a smaller one, so that each group will cede cities to the Levites in proportion to its own heritage."

Cities of Asylum. *9*The LORD said to Moses, *10*"Tell the Israelites: When you go across the Jordan into the land of Canaan, *11*select for yourselves cities*j* to serve as cities of asylum, where a homicide who has killed someone unintentionally may take refuge. *12*These cities shall serve you as places of asylum from the avenger of blood,* so that a homicide shall not be put to death unless he is first tried before the community. *13*Six cities of asylum shall you assign: *14*three beyond the Jordan, and three in the land of Canaan. *15*These six cities of asylum shall serve not only the Israelites but all the resident or transient aliens among them, so that anyone who has killed another unintentionally may take refuge there.

Murder and Manslaughter. *16**"If a man strikes another with an iron instrument and causes his death, he is a murderer and shall be put to death.*k* *17*If a man strikes another with a death-dealing stone in his hand and causes his death, he is a murderer and shall be put to death. *18*If a man strikes another with a death-dealing club in his hand and causes his death, he is a murderer and shall be put to death. *19*The avenger of blood may execute the murderer, putting him to death on sight.

20"If a man pushes another out of hatred, or after lying in wait for him throws something at him, and causes his death,*l* *21*or if he strikes another out of enmity and causes his death, he shall be put to death as a murderer. The avenger of blood may execute the murderer on sight.

22m"However, if a man pushes another accidentally and not out of enmity, or if without lying in wait for him he throws some object at him, *23*or without seeing him throws a death-dealing stone which strikes him and causes his death, although he was not his enemy nor seeking to harm him: *24*then the community, deciding the case between the slayer and the avenger of blood in accordance with these norms, *25*shall free the homicide from the avenger of blood and shall remand him to the city of asylum where he took refuge;*n* and he shall stay there until the death of the high priest who has been anointed with sacred oil. *26*If the homicide of his own accord leaves the bounds of the city of asylum where he has taken refuge, *27*and the avenger of blood finds him beyond these bounds and kills him, the avenger incurs no blood-guilt; *28*the homicide was bound to stay in his city of asylum until the death of the high priest. Only after the death of the high priest may the homicide return to his own district.

29"These shall be norms for you and all your descendants, wherever you live, for rendering judgment.

Witnesses. *30*"Whenever someone kills another, the evidence of witnesses is required for the execution of the murderer.*o* The evidence of a single witness is not sufficient for putting a person to death.

No Indemnity. *31*"You shall not accept indemnity in place of the life of a murderer who deserves the death penalty; he must be put to death. *32*Nor shall you accept indemnity to allow a refugee to leave his city of asylum and again dwell elsewhere in the land before the death of the high priest. *33*You shall not desecrate the land where you live. Since bloodshed desecrates the land,

---

35, 8: This provision was hardly observed in the actual assignment of the levitical cities as narrated in Jos 21.

35, 12: The avenger of blood: one of the close relatives of the slain (2 Sm 14, 7) who, as executor of public justice, had the right and duty to take the life of the murderer; cf Dt 19, 6. 12; Jos 20, 3. 5. 9.

35, 16-25: Here, as also in Dt 19, 1-13, there is a casuistic development of the original law as stated in Ex 21, 12ff.

---

i: Dt 4, 41f; Jos 20, 2.   *j:* 10ff; Dt 19, 2; Jos 20, 2ff.   *k:* Ex 21, 12; Lv 24, 17.   *l:* Ex 21, 14; Dt 19, 11.   *m:* Jos 20, 3.   *n:* Jos 20, 6.
o: Dt 17, 6; 19, 15; Jn 8, 17; 2 Cor 13, 1; 1 Tm 5, 19.

the land can have no atonement for the blood shed on it except through the blood of him who shed it. ³⁴Do not defile the land in which you live and in the midst of which I dwell;ᵖ for I am the LORD who dwells in the midst of the Israelites."

See RG 136-37

CHAPTER 36

Property of Heiresses. ¹The heads of the ancestral houses in the clan of descendants of Gilead, son of Machir, son of Manasseh—one of the Josephite clans—came up and laid this plea before Moses and the priest Eleazar and before the princes who were the heads of the ancestral houses of the other Israelites. ²They said: "The LORD commanded you, my lord, to apportion the land by lot among the Israelites;�q and you, my lord, were also commanded by the LORD to give the heritage of our kinsman Zelophehad to his daughters. ³But if they marry into one of the other Israelite tribes, their heritage will be withdrawn from our ancestral heritage and will be added to that of the tribe into which they marry; thus the heritage that fell to us by lot will be diminished. ⁴When the Israelites celebrate the jubilee year,* the heritage of these women will be permanently added to that of the tribe into which they marry and will be withdrawn from that of our ancestral tribe."

⁵*So Moses gave this regulation to the Israelites according to the instructions of the LORD: "The tribe of the Josephites are right in what they say. ⁶This is what the LORD commands with regard to the daughters of Zelophehad: They may marry anyone they please, provided they marry into a clan of their ancestral tribe, ⁷so that no heritage of the Israelites will pass from one tribe to another, but all the Israelites will retain their own ancestral heritage. ⁸Therefore, every daughter who inherits property in any of the Israelite tribes shall marry someone belonging to a clan of her own ancestral tribe, in order that all the Israelites may remain in possession of their own ancestral heritage. ⁹Thus, no heritage can pass from one tribe to another, but all the Israelite tribes will retain their own ancestral heritage."

¹⁰The daughters of Zelophehad obeyed the command which the LORD had given to Moses. ¹¹Mahlah, Tirzah, Hoglah, Milcah and Noah, Zelophehad's daughters, married relatives on their father's side ¹²within the clans of the descendants of Manasseh, son of Joseph; hence their heritage remained in the tribe of their father's clan.

Conclusion. ¹³These are the commandments and decisions which the LORD prescribed for the Israelites through Moses, on the plains of Moab beside the Jericho stretch of the Jordan.

36, 4: Before the jubilee year various circumstances, such as divorce, could make such property revert to its original tribal owners; but in the jubilee year it became irrevocably attached to its new owners.

36, 5-9: This is a supplement to the law given in Nm 27, 5-11.

p: Ex 29, 45.   q: Nm 26, 55; 27, 6; Jos 17, 3f.

See RG 141-48

The Book of Deuteronomy

The fifth and last book of the Pentateuch is called Deuteronomy, meaning "second law." In reality, what it contains is not a new law but a partial repetition, completion and explanation of the law proclaimed on Mount Sinai. The historical portions of the book are also a résumé of what is related elsewhere in the Pentateuch. The chief characteristic of this book is its vigorous oratorical style. In a series of eloquent discourses Moses presents the theme of covenant renewal in a vital religious framework. He exhorts, corrects and threatens his people, appealing to their past glory, their historic mission, and the promise of future triumph. His aim is to enforce among the Israelites the Lord's claim to their obedience, loyalty and love. The events contained in the Book of Deuteronomy took place in the plains of Moab (1, 5) between the end of the wanderings in the desert (1, 3) and the crossing of the Jordan River (Jos 4, 19), a period of no more than forty days.

The Book of Deuteronomy, written after the Israelites had for centuries been resident in the Land of Promise, takes the form of a testament of Moses, the great leader and legislator, to his people on the eve of his death. At the time of our Lord's coming, it shared with the Psalms a preeminent religious influence among the Old Testament books. The Savior quoted passages of Deuteronomy in overcoming the threefold temptation of Satan in the desert (Mt 4; Dt 6, 13. 16; 8, 3; 10, 20), and in explaining to the lawyer the first and greatest commandment (Mt 22, 35-39; Dt 6, 4).

The book is divided as follows:

I: Historical Review and Exhortation (1, 1— 4, 43).

II: God and His Covenant (4, 44—11, 32).

III: Exposition of the Law (12, 1—26, 19).

IV: Final Words of Moses (27, 1—34, 12).

I: Historical Review and Exhortation

CHAPTER 1

See RG 141-48

Introduction. [1]These are the words which Moses spoke to all Israel beyond the Jordan [* in the desert, in the Arabah, opposite Suph, between Paran and Tophel, Laban, Hazeroth and Dizahab; [2]it is a journey of eleven days from Horeb to Kadeshbarnea by way of the highlands of Seir].

[3]In the fortieth year, on the first day of the eleventh month, Moses spoke to the Israelites all the commands that the LORD had given him in their regard. [4]After he had defeated Sihon, king of the Amorites, who lived in Heshbon,[a] and Og, king of Bashan, who lived in Ashtaroth and in Edrei, [5]Moses began to explain the law in the land of Moab beyond the Jordan, as follows:

Departure from Horeb. [6]"The LORD, our God, said to us at Horeb, 'You have stayed long enough at this mountain. [7]*Leave here and go to the hill country of the Amorites and to all the surrounding regions,[b] the land of the Canaanites in the Arabah, the mountains, the foothills, the Negeb and the seacoast; to Lebanon, and as far as the Great River [the Euphrates]. [8]I have given that land over to you.[c] Go now and occupy the land I swore to your fathers, Abraham, Isaac and Jacob, I would give to them and to their descendants.'

Appointment of Elders. [9]"At that time I said to you, 'Alone, I am unable to carry you.* [10]The LORD, your God, has so multiplied you that you are now as numerous as the stars in the sky.[d] [11]May the LORD, the God of your fathers, increase you a thousand times over, and bless you as he promised! [12]But how can I alone bear the crushing burden that you are, along with your bickering? [13e]Choose wise, intelligent and experienced men from each of your tribes, that I may appoint them as your leaders.' [14]You answered me, 'We agree to do as you have proposed.' [15]So I took outstanding men of your tribes, wise and experienced, and made them your leaders as officials over thousands, over hundreds, over fifties and over tens, and other tribal officers. [16]I charged your judges at that time, 'Listen to complaints among your kinsmen, and administer true justice to both parties even if one of them is an alien.[f] [17]In rendering judgment, do not consider who a person is; give ear to the lowly and to the great alike, fearing no man, for judgment is God's. Refer to me any case that is too hard for you and I will hear it.' [18]Thereupon I gave you all the commands you were to fulfill.

The Twelve Scouts. [19]"Then, in obedience to the command of the LORD, our God, we set out from Horeb and journeyed through the whole desert, vast and fearful as you have seen,[g] in the direction of the hill country of the Amorites. We had reached Kadesh-

---

1, 1: The local setting of all these discourses is in the land of Moab beyond the Jordan (cf v 5), also known as the plains of Moab (Nm 36, 13).

1, 7: The Amorites and the Canaanites formed the principal part of the pre-Israelite population of Palestine. The foothills: the hills on the western slope of the Judean mountain range. The Arabah: the valley of the Jordan and the depression south of the Dead Sea. The Negeb: the arid land in southern Palestine.

1, 9: Carry you: cf v 31.

---

a: Dt 3, 2; Nm 21, 21-35.   *b:* Nm 13, 29.   *c:* Gn 12, 7; 15, 18; 17, 7f; 28, 13f.   *d:* Dt 10, 22; Gn 15, 5.   *e:* 13ff: Ex 18, 21-25.   *f:* 16f: Ex 18, 26; 2 Chr 19, 6f; Prv 24, 23; Jn 7, 24; Jas 2, 9.   *g:* Dt 8, 15; 32, 10.

barnea [20] when I said to you, 'You have come to the hill country of the Amorites, which the LORD, our God, is giving us. [21] The LORD, your God, has given this land over to you. Go up and occupy it, as the LORD, the God of your fathers, commands you. Do not fear or lose heart.' [22h] Then all of you came up to me and said, 'Let us send men ahead to reconnoiter the land for us and report to us on the road we must follow and the cities we must take.' [23] Agreeing with the proposal, I chose twelve men from your number, one from each tribe. [24] They set out into the hill country as far as the Wadi Eshcol, and explored it. [25] Then, taking along some of the fruit of the land, they brought it down to us and reported, 'The land which the LORD, our God, gives us is good.'

Threats of Revolt. [26] "But you refused to go up,[i] and after defying the command of the LORD, your God, [27] you set to murmuring in your tents,* 'Out of hatred for us the LORD has brought us up out of the land of Egypt,[j] to deliver us into the hands of the Amorites and destroy us. [28] What shall we meet with up there? Our kinsmen have made us fainthearted by reporting that the people are stronger and taller than we, and their cities are large and fortified to the sky; besides, they saw the Anakim there.'[k]

[29] "But I said to you, 'Have no dread or fear of them. [30] The LORD, your God, who goes before you, will himself fight for you, just as he took your part before your very eyes in Egypt, [31] as well as in the desert, where you saw how the LORD, your God, carried you, as a man carries his child, all along your journey until you arrived at this place.' [32] Despite this, you would not trust the LORD, your God, [33] who journeys before you to find you a resting place—by day in the cloud, and by night in the fire, to show the way you must go.[l] [34] When the LORD heard your words, he was angry; [35] and he swore, 'Not one man of this evil generation shall look upon the good land I swore to give to your fathers,[m] [36] except Caleb,* son of Jephunneh; he shall see it. For to him and to his sons I will give the land he trod upon, because he has followed the LORD unreservedly.'

[37] "The LORD was angered against me also on your account, and said, 'Not even you shall enter there,[n] [38] but your aide Joshua,[o] son of Nun, shall enter. Encourage him, for he is to give Israel its heritage. [39] Your little ones, who you said would become booty, and your children, who as yet do not know good from bad—they shall enter; to them I will give it, and they shall occupy it.[p] [40] But as for yourselves: turn about and proceed into the desert on the Red Sea road.'

Unsuccessful Invasion. [41q] "In reply you said to me, 'We have sinned against the LORD. We will go up ourselves and fight, just as the LORD, our God, commanded us.' And each of you girded on his weapons, making light of going up into the hill country. [42] But the LORD said to me, 'Warn them: Do not go up and fight, lest you be beaten down before your enemies, for I will not be in your midst.' [43] I gave you this warning but you would not listen. In defiance of the LORD's command you arrogantly marched off into the hill country. [44] Then the Amorites living there came out against you and, like bees, chased you, cutting you down in Seir as far as Hormah. [45] On your return you wept before the LORD, but he did not listen to your cry or give ear to you. [46] That is why you had to stay as long as you did at Kadesh.

CHAPTER 2

See RG 141-48

Northward along Edom. [1] "When we did turn and proceed into the desert on the Red Sea road,[r] as the LORD had commanded me, we circled around the highlands of Seir for a long time. [2] Finally the LORD said to me, [3] 'You have wandered round these highlands long enough; turn and go north. [4] Give

1, 27: In your tents: among yourselves.

1, 36: Except Caleb: Joshua also was allowed to enter, but he is not referred to here because special mention is made of him in v 38 as the successor of Moses.

h: 22-28: Nm 13, 2-34. i: Dt 9, 23. j: Dt 9, 28; Nm 14, 1-4; Ps 106, 25. k: Dt 9, 1f. l: Ex 13, 21; Nm 10, 33f; 14, 14. m: 34ff: Nm 14, 22f. 28-38; Jos 14, 9. n: Dt 4, 21; 34, 4; Nm 20, 12. o: Dt 31, 3. 7; Nm 27, 18ff; 34, 17. p: 39f: Nm 14, 31. q: 41-45: Nm 14, 40. 42-45. r: Dt 1, 40; Nm 14, 25; 21, 4.

this order to the people: You are now about to pass through the territory of your kinsmen, the descendants of Esau, who live in Seir. Though they are afraid of you, be very careful [5]not to come in conflict with them, for I will not give you so much as a foot of their land, since I have already given Esau possession of the highlands of Seir. [6]You shall purchase from them with silver the food you eat and the well water you drink. [7]The LORD, your God, has blessed you in all your undertakings; he has been concerned about your journey through this vast desert. It is now forty years that he has been with you, and you have never been in want.'[s]

Along Moab. [8]"Then we left behind us the Arabah route, Elath, Ezion-geber, and Seir, where our kinsmen, the descendants of Esau, live; and we went on toward the desert of Moab.[t] [9]And the LORD said to me, 'Do not show hostility to the Moabites or engage them in battle, for I will not give you possession of any of their land, since I have given Ar to the descendants of Lot as their own.[u] [10][Formerly the Emim lived there, a people strong and numerous and tall like the Anakim;[v] [11]like them they were considered Rephaim. It was the Moabites who called them Emim. [12]In Seir, however, the former inhabitants were the Horites;[w] the descendants of Esau dispossessed them, clearing them out of the way and taking their place, just as the Israelites have done in the land of their heritage which the LORD has given them.] [13]Get ready, then, to cross the Wadi Zered.'[x] So we crossed it. [14]Thirty-eight years had elapsed between our departure from Kadesh-barnea and that crossing; in the meantime the whole generation of soldiers had perished from the camp, as the LORD had sworn they should.[y] [15]For it was the LORD's hand that was against them, till he wiped them out of the camp completely.

Along Ammon. [16]"When at length death had put an end to all the soldiers among the people, [17]the LORD said to me, [18]'You are now about to leave Ar and the territory of Moab behind. [19]As you come opposite the Ammonites,[z] do not show hostility or come in conflict with them, for I will not give you possession of any land of the Ammonites, since I have given it to the descendants of Lot as their own. [20][This also was considered a country of the Rephaim from its former inhabitants, whom the Ammonites called Zamzummim, [21]a people strong and numerous and tall like the Anakim. But these, too, the LORD cleared out of the way for the Ammonites, who ousted them and took their place. [22]He had done the same for the descendants of Esau, who dwell in Seir, by clearing the Horites out of their way, so that the descendants of Esau have taken their place down to the present. [23]So also the Caphtorim,[*] migrating from Caphtor, cleared away the Avvim, who once dwelt in villages as far as Gaza, and took their place.]

Defeat of Sihon. [24]" 'Advance now across the Wadi Arnon.[a] I now deliver into your hands Sihon, the Amorite king of Heshbon, and his land. Begin the occupation; engage him in battle. [25]This day I will begin to put a fear and dread of you into every nation under the heavens, so that at the mention of your name they will quake and tremble before you.'

[26]"So I sent messengers from the desert of Kedemoth to Sihon, king of Heshbon, with this offer of peace: [27]'Let me pass through your country by the highway; I will go along it without turning aside to the right or to the left. [28]For the food I eat which you will supply, and for the water you give me to drink, you shall be paid in silver. Only let me march through, [29]as the descendants of Esau who dwell in Seir[b] and the Moabites who dwell in Ar have done, until I cross the Jordan into the land which the LORD, our God, is about to give us.' [30]But Sihon, king of Heshbon, refused to let us pass through his land, because the LORD, your God, made him stubborn in mind and obstinate in heart

2, 23: The Caphtorim: members of one of the groups of sea peoples who invaded the coast of Egypt and the southern part of Palestine about 1200 B.C. Caphtor: the ancient name of the island of Crete. Cf Am 9, 7.

s: Dt 8, 2ff.   *t:* Jgs 11, 18.   *u:* Gn 19, 36f.   *v:* Dt 1, 28.   *w:* Gn 36, 20f.   *x:* Nm 21, 12.   *y:* Nm 14, 29. 33. 35.   *z:* Gn 19, 38.
a: Nm 21, 13; Jgs 11, 19-22.   *b:* Dt 2, 5. 8f; Jgs 11, 17.

that he might deliver him up to you, as indeed he has now done.

31"Then the LORD said to me, 'Now that I have already begun to hand over to you Sihon and his land, begin the actual occupation.' *32*So Sihon and all his people advanced against us to join battle at Jahaz; *33*but since the LORD, our God, had delivered him to us, we defeated him and his sons and all his people.*c 34*At that time we seized all his cities and doomed* them all, with their men, women and children; we left no survivor.*d 35*Our only booty was the livestock and the loot of the captured cities. *36*From Aroer on the edge of the Wadi Arnon and from the city in the wadi itself, as far as Gilead,*e* no city was too well fortified for us to whom the LORD had delivered them up. *37*However, in obedience to the command of the LORD, our God, you did not encroach upon any of the Ammonite land, neither the region bordering on the Wadi Jabbok, nor the cities of the highlands.*f*

See RG 141-48

CHAPTER 3

Defeat of Og. *1*"Then we turned and proceeded toward Bashan. But Og, king of Bashan,*g* advanced against us with all his people to give battle at Edrei. *2*The LORD, however, said to me,*h* 'Do not be afraid of him, for I have delivered him into your hand with all his people and his land. Do to him as you did to Sihon, king of the Amorites, who lived in Heshbon.' *3*And thus the LORD, our God, delivered into our hands Og, king of Bashan, with all his people. We defeated him so completely that we left him no survivor. *4*At that time we captured all his cities, none of them eluding our grasp, the whole region of Argob, the kingdom of Og in Bashan: sixty cities in all, *5*to say nothing of the great number of unwalled towns. All the cities were fortified with high walls and gates and bars. *6i*As we had done to Sihon, king of Heshbon, so also here we doomed all the cities, with their men, women and children;

*7*but all the livestock and the loot of each city we took as booty for ourselves.

8"And so at that time we took from the two kings of the Amorites beyond the Jordan the territory from the Wadi Arnon to Mount Hermon *9*[which is called Sirion by the Sidonians and Senir by the Amorites], *10*comprising all the cities of the plateau and all Gilead and all the cities of the kingdom of Og in Bashan including Salecah and Edrei. *11*[Og, king of Bashan, was the last remaining survivor of the Rephaim. He had a bed of iron,* nine regular cubits long and four wide, which is still preserved in Rabbah of the Ammonites.]

Allotment of the Conquered Lands. *12j*"When we occupied the land at that time, I gave Reuben and Gad the territory from Aroer, on the edge of the Wadi Arnon, halfway up into the highlands of Gilead, with the cities therein. *13*The rest of Gilead and all of Bashan, the kingdom of Og, the whole Argob region, I gave to the half-tribe of Manasseh. [All this region of Bashan was once called a land of the Rephaim. *14*Jair, a Manassehite clan,*k* took all the region of Argob as far as the border of the Geshurites and Maacathites, and called it after his own name Bashan Havvoth-jair, the name it bears today.] *15*To Machir I gave Gilead, *16*and to Reuben and Gad the territory from Gilead to the Wadi Arnon—including the wadi bed and its banks—and to the Wadi Jabbok, which is the border of the Ammonites, *17*as well as the Arabah with the Jordan and its eastern banks from Chinnereth to the Salt Sea of the Arabah, under the slopes of Pisgah.*l*

18"At that time I charged them* as follows: 'The LORD, your God, has given you this land as your own. But all you troops equipped for battle must cross over in the vanguard of your brother Israelites.*m 19*Only your wives and children, as well as your livestock, of which I know you have a large

---

2, 34: Doomed: see notes on Nm 18, 14; 21, 3.

3, 11: Bed of iron: some translate, "a sarcophagus of basalt."

3, 18: I charged them: the words which follow were spoken to the men of Reuben and Gad (cf Nm 32).

---

c: Dt 29, 7; Nm 21, 23-32.   *d:* Dt 3, 6; 29, 7f.   *e:* Dt 3, 12; Jos 13, 9. 16; Jgs 11, 26.   *f:* Nm 21, 24; Jos 12, 2.   *g:* Dt 29, 6; Nm 21, 33.   *h:* 2f: Nm 21, 34f.   *i:* Ps 135, 10ff.   *j:* 12f: Nm 32, 29. 32f; Jos 13, 8. 29.   *k:* Nm 32, 41; Jos 13, 11. 13.   *l:* Dt 4, 49; Jos 12, 3.   *m:* Jos 1, 14; 4, 12.

number, shall remain behind in the towns I have given you,[n] [20]until the LORD has settled your kinsmen as well, and they too possess the land which the LORD, your God, will give them on the other side of the Jordan.[o] Then you may all return to the possessions I have given you.'

[21]"It was then that I instructed Joshua, 'Your eyes have seen all that the LORD, your God, has done to both these kings; so, too, will the LORD do to all the kingdoms which you will encounter over there. [22]Fear them not, for the LORD, your God, will fight for you.'

Refusal to Moses. [23]"And it was then that I besought the LORD, [24]'O Lord GOD, you have begun to show to your servant your greatness and might. For what god in heaven or on earth can perform deeds as mighty as yours? [25]Ah, let me cross over and see this good land beyond the Jordan, this fine hill country, and the Lebanon!' [26]But the LORD was angry with me on your account and would not hear me.[p] 'Enough!' the LORD said to me. 'Speak to me no more of this. [27]Go up to the top of Pisgah and look out to the west, and to the north, and to the south, and to the east. Look well, for you shall not cross this Jordan.[q] [28]Commission Joshua,[r] and encourage and strengthen him, for he shall cross at the head of this people and shall put them in possession of the land you are to see.' [29]This was while we were in the ravine opposite Beth-peor.

CHAPTER 4

See RG 141–48

Advantages of Fidelity. [1]"Now, Israel, hear the statutes and decrees which I am teaching you to observe, that you may live, and may enter in and take possession of the land which the LORD, the God of your fathers, is giving you. [2]In your observance of the commandments of the LORD, your God,[s] which I enjoin upon you, you shall not add to what I command you nor subtract from it. [3]You have seen with your own eyes what the

LORD did at Baal-peor:[t] the LORD, your God, destroyed from your midst everyone that followed the Baal of Peor; [4]but you, who clung to the LORD, your God, are all alive today. [5]Therefore, I teach you the statutes and decrees as the LORD, my God, has commanded me, that you may observe them in the land you are entering to occupy. [6]Observe them carefully, for thus will you give evidence of your wisdom and intelligence to the nations, who will hear of all these statutes and say, 'This great nation is truly a wise and intelligent people.' [7]"For what great nation is there that has gods so close to it as the LORD, our God, is to us whenever we call upon him? [8]Or what great nation has statutes and decrees that are as just as this whole law which I am setting before you today?

Revelation at Horeb. [9]"However, take care and be earnestly on your guard not to forget the things which your own eyes have seen, nor let them slip from your memory as long as you live, but teach them to your children[v] and to your children's children: [10]*There was the day on which you stood before the LORD, your God, at Horeb, and he said to me,[w] 'Assemble the people for me; I will have them hear my words, that they may learn to fear me as long as they live in the land and may so teach their children.' [11]You came near and stood at the foot of the mountain,[x] which blazed to the very sky with fire and was enveloped in a dense black cloud. [12]Then the LORD spoke to you from the midst of the fire.[y] You heard the sound of the words, but saw no form; there was only a voice. [13]He proclaimed to you his covenant, which he commanded you to keep: the ten commandments, which he wrote on two tablets of stone. [14]The LORD charged me at that time to teach you the statutes and decrees which you are to observe over in the land you will occupy.

Danger of Idolatry. [15]"You saw no form at all on the day the LORD spoke to you at Horeb from the midst of the fire.[z] Be strictly

---

4, 10: Beginning here and continuing on for several verses (at least to the end of v 14) is the "reminiscence," the account of the things that the Israelites should recall and teach their children.

---

n: Nm 32, 1. 4; Jos 1, 14. o: Jos 22, 4. p: Dt 4, 21. q: Dt 34, 4; Nm 27, 12f. r: Dt 1, 38; 31, 7; Nm 27, 22f. s: Dt 13, 1. t: Nm 25, 3-9. u: 2 Sm 7, 23. v: Dt 11, 19; Ps 78, 3-6. w: Heb 12, 18f. x: Ex 19, 17f. y: Dt 4, 33. 36; 5, 4. z: Ex 24, 12; 31, 18; 34, 28.

on your guard, therefore, [16]not to degrade yourselves by fashioning an idol to represent any figure, whether it be the form of a man or of a woman,[a] [17]of any animal on the earth or of any bird that flies in the sky, [18]of anything that crawls on the ground or of any fish in the waters under the earth. [19]And when you look up to the heavens and behold the sun or the moon or any star among the heavenly hosts, do not be led astray into adoring them and serving them.[b] These the LORD, your God, has let fall to the lot of all other nations under the heavens; [20]but you he has taken and led out of that iron foundry,* Egypt, that you might be his very own people, as you are today.[c] [21]Since the LORD was angered against me on your account[d] and swore that I should not cross the Jordan nor enter the good land which he is giving you as a heritage, [22]I myself shall die in this country without crossing the Jordan; but you will cross over and take possession of that good land.[e] [23]Take heed, therefore, lest, forgetting the covenant which the LORD, your God, has made with you, you fashion for yourselves against his command an idol in any form whatsoever.[f] [24]For the LORD, your God, is a consuming fire, a jealous God.

God's Fidelity. [25]"When you have children and grandchildren, and have grown old* in the land, should you then degrade yourselves by fashioning an idol in any form and by this evil done in his sight provoke the LORD, your God, [26]I call heaven and earth this day to witness against you, that you shall all quickly perish from the land which you will occupy when you cross the Jordan. You shall not live in it for any length of time but shall be promptly wiped out. [27]The LORD will scatter you among the nations, and there shall remain but a handful of you among the nations to which the LORD will lead you.[g] [28]There you shall serve gods fashioned by the hands of man out of wood and stone, gods which can neither see nor hear, neither eat nor smell.[h] [29]Yet there too you shall seek the LORD, your God; and you shall indeed find him when you search after him with your whole heart and your whole soul.[i] [30]In your distress, when all these things shall have come upon you, you shall finally return to the LORD, your God, and heed his voice. [31]Since the LORD, your God, is a merciful God, he will not abandon and destroy you, nor forget the covenant which under oath he made with your fathers.[j]

Proofs of God's Love. [32]"Ask now of the days of old, before your time, ever since God created man upon the earth; ask from one end of the sky to the other: Did anything so great ever happen before? Was it ever heard of? [33]Did a people ever hear the voice of God speaking from the midst of fire, as you did, and live?[k] [34]Or did any god venture to go and take a nation for himself from the midst of another nation, by testings,* by signs and wonders,[l] by war, with his strong hand and outstretched arm, and by great terrors, all of which the LORD, your God, did for you in Egypt before your very eyes? [35]All this you were allowed to see that you might know the LORD is God and there is no other. [36]Out of the heavens he let you hear his voice to discipline you; on earth he let you see his great fire, and you heard him speaking out of the fire. [37]For love of your fathers he chose their descendants and personally led you out of Egypt by his great power, [38]driving out of your way nations greater and mightier than you, so as to bring you in and to make their land your heritage, as it is today. [39]This is why you must now know, and fix in your heart, that the LORD is God in the heavens above and on earth below, and that there is no other.[m] [40]You must keep his statutes and commandments which

4, 20: Egypt is called an iron foundry, or furnace for smelting iron, because God allowed the Israelites to be afflicted there for the sake of their spiritual purification; the same expression for Egypt occurs also in 1 Kgs 8, 51; Jer 11, 4; compare the expression, "the furnace of affliction," in Is 48, 10.

4, 25: Grown old: Israel will lose the freshness of its youthful fervor.

4, 34: Testings: the demonstrations of God's power as in the ten great plagues of Egypt; cf Dt 7, 19; 29, 2.

a: Dt 5, 8; Ex 20, 4. *b:* Dt 17, 3; Jb 31, 26ff. *c:* 1 Kgs 8, 51; Jer 11, 4. *d:* Dt 1, 37; 3, 26. *e:* Dt 3, 27. *f:* Dt 4, 16. *g:* 27f: Dt 28, 36. 62. 64. *h:* Ps 135, 15ff; Is 44, 9. *i:* Jer 29, 13. *j:* Dt 31, 8. *k:* Dt 4, 36; 5, 24. 26; Ex 20, 19. *l:* Dt 7, 19; 26, 8; 29, 2; Ex 7, 3; 15, 3-10; Jer 32, 21. *m:* Dt 4, 35.

I enjoin on you today, that you and your children after you may prosper, and that you may have long life on the land which the LORD, your God, is giving you forever."[n]

Cities of Refuge. [41o] Then Moses set apart three cities in the region east of the Jordan, [42] that a homicide might take refuge there if he unwittingly killed his neighbor to whom he had previously borne no malice, and that he might save his life by fleeing to one of these cities: [43] Bezer in the desert, in the region of the plateau, for the Reubenites; Ramoth in Gilead for the Gadites; and Golan in Bashan for the Manassehites.

II: God and His Covenant

Introduction. [44] This is the law which Moses set before the Israelites. [45] These are the ordinances, statutes and decrees which he proclaimed to them when they had come out of Egypt [46] and were beyond the Jordan in the ravine opposite Beth-peor, in the land of Sihon, king of the Amorites, who dwelt in Heshbon and whom Moses and the Israelites defeated after coming out of Egypt. [47] They occupied his land and the land of Og, king of Bashan, as well—the land of these two kings of the Amorites in the region east of the Jordan: [48] from Aroer on the edge of the Wadi Arnon to Mount Sion* (that is, Hermon) [49] and all the Arabah east of the Jordan, as far as the Arabah Sea under the slopes of Pisgah.[p]

See RG 141-48

CHAPTER 5

The Covenant at Horeb. [1] Moses summoned all Israel and said to them, "Hear, O Israel, the statutes and decrees which I proclaim in your hearing this day, that you may learn them and take care to observe them. [2] The LORD, our God, made a covenant with us at Horeb;[q] [3] not with our fathers did he make this covenant, but with us, all of us who are alive here this day. [4] The LORD spoke with you face to face on the mountain from the midst of the fire. [5r] Since you were afraid of the fire and would not go up the mountain, I stood between the LORD and you at that time, to announce to you these words of the LORD:

The Decalogue. [6s] 'I, the LORD, am your God, who brought you out of the land of Egypt,[t] that place of slavery. [7u] You shall not have other gods besides me. [8] You shall not carve idols for yourselves[v] in the shape of anything in the sky above or on the earth below or in the waters beneath the earth; [9*] you shall not bow down before them or worship them. For I, the LORD, your God, am a jealous God,[w] inflicting punishments for their fathers' wickedness on the children of those who hate me, down to the third and fourth generation [10] but bestowing mercy, down to the thousandth generation,[x] on the children of those who love me and keep my commandments.

[11] 'You shall not take the name of the LORD, your God, in vain.[y] For the LORD will not leave unpunished him who takes his name in vain.

[12] 'Take care to keep holy the sabbath day as the LORD, your God, commanded you. [13] Six days you may labor and do all your work; [14] but the seventh day is the sabbath of the LORD, your God.[z] No work may be done then, whether by you, or your son or daughter, or your male or female slave, or your ox or ass or any of your beasts, or the alien who lives with you. Your male and female slave should rest as you do. [15] For remember that you too were once slaves in Egypt,[a] and the LORD, your God, brought you from there with his strong hand and outstretched arm. That is why the LORD, your God, has commanded you to observe the sabbath day.

[16b] 'Honor your father and your mother, as the LORD, your God, has commanded you,

---

4, 48: Sion: another name for Mount Hermon, besides those mentioned in Dt 3, 9.

5, 9f: God does not punish us for another's sins, but because of the solidarity of human society, the good or evil deeds of one generation may make their effects felt even in later generations. Yet note how God's mercy allows the good effects of virtue to last much longer than the bad effects of vice: a thousand generations compared to three or four.

---

n: Dt 6, 2f; 12, 28.   *o:* 41ff: Dt 19, 2-13; Nm 35, 6-29; Jos 20, 8; 21, 27. 36f; 1 Chr 6, 71. 80.   *p:* Dt 3, 17.   *q:* Dt 28, 69.   *r:* Ex 24, 2.
s: 6-21: Ex 20, 2-17.   *t:* Ps 81, 11.   *u:* Ps 81, 10.   *v:* Dt 27, 15; Lv 26, 1; Ps 97, 7.   *w:* Ex 34, 14.   *x:* Dt 7, 9; Ex 20, 6.   *y:* Mt 5, 33.
z: Gn 2, 2; Ex 20, 8; 23, 12; Heb 4, 4.   *a:* Dt 15, 15; 16, 12; 24, 18. 22.   *b:* Sir 3, 2-16; Mt 15, 4; Mk 7, 10; Lk 18, 20; Eph 6, 2.

"Hear, O Israel"

This statement of belief (6, 4–9) is the most important one for Israel, and is also partly quoted in the New Testament by Jesus (Mark 12, 29-30). It is known as the *Shema*, from its first word in Hebrew, the command "Hear!"

that you may have a long life and prosperity in the land which the LORD, your God, is giving you.

17c 'You shall not kill.

18 'You shall not commit adultery.

19 'You shall not steal.

20 'You shall not bear dishonest witness against your neighbor.

21 'You shall not covet your neighbor's wife.

'You shall not desire your neighbor's house or field, nor his male or female slave, nor his ox or ass, nor anything that belongs to him.'

Moses as Mediator. *22* "These words, and nothing more, the LORD spoke with a loud voice to your entire assembly on the mountain from the midst of the fire and the dense cloud. He wrote them upon two tablets of stone and gave them to me. *23* But when you heard the voice from the midst of the darkness, while the mountain was ablaze with fire, you came to me in the person of all your tribal heads and elders, *24* and said, 'The LORD, our God, has indeed let us see his glory and his majesty! We have heard his voice from the midst of the fire*d* and have found out today that a man can still live after God has spoken with him. *25* But why should we die now? Surely this great fire will consume us. If we hear the voice of the LORD, our God, any more, we shall die.*e* *26* For what mortal has heard, as we have, the voice of the living God speaking from the midst of fire, and survived? *27* Go closer, you, and hear all that the LORD, our God, will say, and then tell us what the LORD, our God, tells you; we will listen and obey.' *f*

28 "The LORD heard your words as you were speaking to me and said to me, 'I have heard the words these people have spoken to you, which are all well said.*g* *29* Would that they might always be of such a mind, to fear me and to keep all my commandments! Then they and their descendants would prosper forever. *30* Go, tell them to return to their tents. *31* Then you wait here near me and I will give you all the commandments, the statutes and decrees you must teach them, that they may observe them in the land which I am giving them to possess.'

32 "Be careful, therefore, to do as the LORD, your God, has commanded you, not turning aside to the right or to the left, *33* but following exactly the way prescribed for you by the LORD, your God, that you may live and prosper, and may have long life in the land which you are to occupy.*h*

CHAPTER 6

See RG
141-48

1 "These then are the commandments, the statutes and decrees*i* which the LORD, your God, has ordered that you be taught to observe in the land into which you are crossing for conquest, *2* so that you and your son and your grandson may fear the LORD, your God, and keep, throughout the days of your lives, all his statutes and commandments*j* which I enjoin on you, and thus have long life. *3* Hear then, Israel, and be careful to observe them, that you may grow and prosper the more, in keeping with the promise of the LORD, the God of your fathers, to give you a land flowing with milk and honey.

The Great Commandment. *4* * "Hear, O Israel! The LORD is our God, the LORD alone!*k*

6, 4f: This passage contains the basic principle of the whole Mosaic law, the keynote of the Book of Deuteronomy: since the Lord alone is God, we must love him with an undivided heart. Christ cited these words as "the greatest and the first commandment," embracing in itself the whole law of God (Mt 22, 37f and parallels).

c: 17-20: Mt 5, 21. 27; Lk 18, 20; Jas 2, 11.   *d:* Dt 4, 33.   *e:* Dt 18, 16.   *f:* Ex 20, 19.   *g:* Dt 18, 17.   *h:* Dt 4, 40.   *i:* Dt 4, 1; 5, 31; 12, 1.   *j:* Dt 4, 40; 5, 29; 10, 12f.   *k:* Mk 12, 29.

[5]Therefore, you shall love the LORD, your God, with all your heart, and with all your soul, and with all your strength.[l] [6]Take to heart these words which I enjoin on you today. [7]Drill them into your children.[m] Speak of them at home and abroad, whether you are busy or at rest. [8]Bind them at your wrist as a sign[*] and let them be as a pendant on your forehead.[n] [9]Write them on the doorposts of your houses and on your gates.[o]

Fidelity in Prosperity. [10]"When the LORD, your God, brings you into the land which he swore to your fathers, Abraham, Isaac and Jacob, that he would give you, a land with fine, large cities that you did not build,[p] [11]with houses full of goods of all sorts that you did not garner, with cisterns that you did not dig, with vineyards and olive groves that you did not plant; and when, therefore, you eat your fill, [12q]take care not to forget the LORD, who brought you out of the land of Egypt, that place of slavery. [13r]The LORD, your God, shall you fear; him shall you serve,[*] and by his name shall you swear. [14]You shall not follow other gods, such as those of the surrounding nations, [15]lest the wrath of the LORD, your God, flare up against you and he destroy you from the face of the land;[s] for the LORD, your God, who is in your midst, is a jealous God.

[16t]"You shall not put the LORD, your God, to the test, as you did at Massah. [17]But keep the commandments of the LORD, your God, and the ordinances and statutes he has enjoined on you. [18]Do what is right and good in the sight of the LORD, that you may, according to his word, prosper, and may enter in and possess the good land which the LORD promised on oath to your fathers, [19]thrusting all your enemies out of your way.[u]

Instruction to Children. [20]"Later on, when your son asks you what these ordinances, statutes and decrees mean[v] which the LORD, our God, has enjoined on you, [21]you shall say to your son, 'We were once slaves of Pharaoh in Egypt, but the LORD brought us out of Egypt with his strong hand[w] [22]and wrought before our eyes signs and wonders, great and dire, against Egypt and against Pharaoh and his whole house. [23]He brought us from there to lead us into the land he promised on oath to our fathers, and to give it to us. [24]Therefore, the LORD commanded us to observe all these statutes in fear of the LORD, our God, that we may always have as prosperous and happy a life as we have today; [25]and our justice before the LORD, our God, is to consist in carefully observing all these commandments he has enjoined on us.'

CHAPTER 7

See RG 141–48

Destruction of Pagans. [1]"When the LORD, your God, brings you into the land which you are to enter and occupy, and dislodges great nations before you—the Hittites, Girgashites, Amorites, Canaanites, Perizzites, Hivites and Jebusites:[x] seven nations more numerous and powerful than you— [2]and when the LORD, your God, delivers them up to you and you defeat them, you shall doom them. Make no covenant with them[y] and show them no mercy. [3]You shall not intermarry with them, neither giving your daughters to their sons nor taking their daughters for your sons.[z] [4]For they would turn your sons from following me to serving other gods, and then the wrath of the LORD would flare up against you and quickly destroy you.

[5]"But this is how you must deal with them:[a] Tear down their altars, smash their sacred pillars, chop down their sacred poles,[*] and destroy their idols by fire. [6]For

---

6, 8: Bind them . . . as a sign: these injunctions were probably meant merely in a figurative sense; cf Ex 13, 9. 16. However, the later Jews understood them literally, and tied on their wrists and foreheads "phylacteries," boxes containing strips of parchment on which the words were inscribed; cf Mt 23, 5.

6, 13: Him shall you serve: here, to "serve" God means especially to "worship" him; in this sense it is quoted by our Lord (Mt 4, 10) as an argument against worshiping the devil.

7, 5: Sacred pillars . . . poles: see note on Ex 34, 13.

l: Dt 10, 12; 11, 13; Mt 22, 37; Mk 12, 30; Lk 10, 27.   *m:* 6f: Dt 4, 9; 11, 18; 32, 46.   *n:* Dt 11, 18; Ex 13, 9. 16; Mt 23, 5.   *o:* Dt 11, 20.   *p:* 10f: Jos 24, 13.   *q:* Dt 5, 6.   *r:* Dt 10, 20; Mt 4, 10; Lk 4, 8.   *s:* 14f: Dt 8, 19; 11, 16. 28.   *t:* Nm 20, 1-13.   *u:* Ex 23, 27; 34, 11.   *v:* Ex 12, 26; 13, 14.   *w:* Ex 20, 2.   *x:* Ex 23, 23; 33, 2.   *y:* Ex 34, 12.   *z:* 3f: Ex 34, 16; 1 Kgs 11, 1f.   *a:* Dt 12, 3; Ex 13, 14.

you are a people sacred to the LORD, your God; he has chosen you from all the nations on the face of the earth to be a people peculiarly his own.[b] [7]It was not because you are the largest of all nations that the LORD set his heart on you and chose you, for you are really the smallest of all nations. [8]It was because the LORD loved you and because of his fidelity to the oath he had sworn to your fathers, that he brought you out with his strong hand from the place of slavery, and ransomed you from the hand of Pharaoh, king of Egypt. [9c]Understand, then, that the LORD, your God, is God indeed, the faithful God who keeps his merciful covenant down to the thousandth generation toward those who love him and keep his commandments, [10]but who repays with destruction the person who hates him; he does not dally with such a one, but makes him personally pay for it. [11]You shall therefore carefully observe the commandments, the statutes and the decrees which I enjoin on you today.

Blessings of Obedience. [12d]"As your reward for heeding these decrees and observing them carefully, the LORD, your God, will keep with you the merciful covenant which he promised on oath to your fathers. [13]He will love and bless and multiply you; he will bless the fruit of your womb and the produce of your soil, your grain and wine and oil, the issue of your herds and the young of your flocks, in the land which he swore to your fathers he would give you.[e] [14]You will be blessed above all peoples; no man or woman among you shall be childless nor shall your livestock be barren. [15]The LORD will remove all sickness from you; he will not afflict you with any of the malignant diseases that you know from Egypt, but will leave them with all your enemies.

[16]"You shall consume all the nations which the LORD, your God, will deliver up to you. You are not to look on them with pity, lest you be ensnared into serving their gods. [17]Perhaps you will say to yourselves,[f] 'These nations are greater than we. How can we dispossess them?' [18]But do not be afraid of them. Rather, call to mind what the LORD, your God, did to Pharaoh and to all Egypt: [19]the great testings which your own eyes have seen, the signs and wonders, his strong hand and outstretched arm with which the LORD, your God, brought you out.[g] The same also will he do to all the nations of whom you are now afraid. [20]Moreover, the LORD, your God, will send hornets among them, until the survivors who have hidden from you are destroyed.[h] [21]Therefore, do not be terrified by them, for the LORD, your God, who is in your midst, is a great and awesome God. [22]He will dislodge these nations before you little by little. You cannot exterminate them all at once, lest the wild beasts become too numerous for you.[i] [23]The LORD, your God, will deliver them up to you and will rout them utterly until they are annihilated.[j] [24]He will deliver their kings into your hand, that you may make their names perish from under the heavens. No man will be able to stand up against you,[k] till you have put an end to them. [25]The images of their gods you shall destroy by fire. Do not covet the silver or gold on them, nor take it for yourselves, lest you be ensnared by it; for it is an abomination to the LORD, your God. [26]You shall not bring any abominable thing into your house, lest you be doomed with it; loathe and abhor it utterly as a thing that is doomed.

CHAPTER 8

See RG 141-48

God's Care. [1]"Be careful to observe all the commandments[l] I enjoin on you today, that you may live and increase, and may enter in and possess the land which the LORD promised on oath to your fathers. [2]Remember how for forty years now the LORD, your God, has directed all your journeying in the desert,[m] so as to test you by affliction and find out whether or not it was your intention to keep his commandments. [3]He therefore let you be afflicted with hunger, and then fed you with manna,[n] a food unknown to you and your fathers, in order to show you that

b: Dt 14, 2; 26, 18; Ex 19, 6.   c: 9f: Dt 5, 9f.   d: 12-16: Dt 28, 1-14; Ex 23, 22-26; Lv 26, 3-13.   e: Dt 30, 9.   f: 17f: Dt 1, 28ff.   g: Dt 4, 34.   h: Ex 23, 28ff.   i: Ex 23, 29f.   j: Dt 7, 2.   k: Dt 11, 25.   l: Dt 4, 1; 6, 1.   m: Dt 2, 7; 29, 4; Am 2, 10.   n: Ex 16, 12-15. 35; Nm 11, 6-9; Mt 4, 4; Lk 4, 4.

not by bread alone* does man live, but by every word that comes forth from the mouth of the LORD. [4]The clothing did not fall from you in tatters, nor did your feet swell these forty years.[o] [5]So you must realize that the LORD, your God, disciplines you even as a man disciplines his son.

Danger of Prosperity. [6]"Therefore, keep the commandments of the LORD, your God, by walking in his ways and fearing him. [7]For the LORD, your God, is bringing you into a good country,[p] a land with streams of water, with springs and fountains welling up in the hills and valleys, [8]a land of wheat and barley, of vines and fig trees and pomegranates, of olive trees and of honey, [9]a land where you can eat bread without stint and where you will lack nothing, a land whose stones contain iron and in whose hills you can mine copper. [10]But when you have eaten your fill, you must bless the LORD, your God, for the good country he has given you. [11]Be careful not to forget the LORD, your God, by neglecting his commandments and decrees and statutes which I enjoin on you today: [12]lest, when you have eaten your fill, and have built fine houses and lived in them, [13]and have increased your herds and flocks, your silver and gold, and all your property, [14]you then become haughty of heart and unmindful of the LORD, your God, who brought you out of the land of Egypt, that place of slavery; [15]who guided you through the vast and terrible desert with its saraph serpents and scorpions, its parched and waterless ground; who brought forth water for you from the flinty rock[q] [16]and fed you in the desert with manna, a food unknown to your fathers, that he might afflict you and test you, but also make you prosperous in the end. [17]Otherwise, you might say to yourselves,[r] 'It is my own power and the strength of my own hand that has obtained for me this wealth.' [18]Remember then, it is the LORD, your God, who gives you the power to acquire wealth, by fulfilling, as he has now done, the covenant which

he swore to your fathers. [19]But if you forget the LORD, your God, and follow other gods, serving and worshiping them,[s] I forewarn you this day that you will perish utterly. [20]Like the nations which the LORD destroys before you, so shall you too perish for not heeding the voice of the LORD, your God.

CHAPTER 9

See RG 141–48

Unmerited Success. [1]"Hear, O Israel! You are now about to cross the Jordan to enter in and dispossess nations greater and stronger than yourselves, having large cities fortified to the sky,[t] [2]the Anakim, a people great and tall.[u] You know of them and have heard it said of them, 'Who can stand up against the Anakim?' [3]Understand, then, today that it is the LORD, your God, who will cross over before you as a consuming fire; he it is who will reduce them to nothing and subdue them before you, so that you can drive them out and destroy them quickly, as the LORD promised you.[v] [4]After the LORD, your God, has thrust them out of your way, do not say to yourselves, 'It is because of my merits that the LORD has brought me in to possess this land';[w] for it is really because of the wickedness of these nations that the LORD is driving them out before you. [5]No, it is not because of your merits or the integrity of your heart that you are going in to take possession of their land; but the LORD, your God, is driving these nations out before you on account of their wickedness and in order to keep the promise which he made on oath to your fathers, Abraham, Isaac and Jacob. [6]Understand this, therefore: it is not because of your merits that the LORD, your God, is giving you this good land to possess, for you are a stiff-necked people.

The Golden Calf. [7]"Bear in mind and do not forget how you angered the LORD, your God, in the desert. From the day you left the land of Egypt until you arrived in this place, you have been rebellious toward the LORD.[x] [8]At Horeb you so provoked the LORD that he was angry enough to destroy you,[y] [9]when I

8, 3: Not by bread alone, etc.: quoted by our Lord in Mt 4, 4. The sense is: God takes care of those who love him even when natural means seem to fail them.

---

o: Dt 29, 4; Neh 9, 21.   *p:* Dt 11, 10ff.   *q:* Wis 11, 4.   *r:* Dt 9, 4.   *s:* Dt 4, 25f; 30, 18.   *t:* Dt 1, 28; 4, 38.   *u:* Nm 13, 33.   *v:* Dt 31, 3; Ex 23, 27.   *w:* Dt 8, 17.   *x:* Dt 31, 27; Ex 14, 11; Nm 14, 11.   *y:* Ex 32, 4; Ps 106, 19.

had gone up the mountain to receive the stone tablets of the covenant which the LORD made with you.^z Meanwhile I stayed on the mountain forty days and forty nights without eating or drinking, ¹⁰till the LORD gave me the two tablets of stone inscribed, by God's own finger,^a with a copy of all the words that the LORD spoke to you on the mountain from the midst of the fire on the day of the assembly. ¹¹Then, at the end of the forty days and forty nights, when the LORD had given me the two stone tablets of the covenant, ¹²he said to me,^b 'Go down from here now, quickly, for your people whom you have brought out of Egypt have become depraved; they have already turned aside from the way I pointed out to them and have made for themselves a molten idol. ¹³I have seen now how stiff-necked this people is,' the LORD said to me. ¹⁴'Let me be, that I may destroy them and blot out their name from under the heavens. I will then make of you a nation mightier and greater than they.'

¹⁵"When I had come down again from the blazing, fiery mountain, with the two tablets of the covenant in both my hands,^c ¹⁶I saw how you had sinned against the LORD, your God: you had already turned aside from the way which the LORD had pointed out to you by making for yourselves a molten calf! ¹⁷Raising the two tablets with both hands I threw them from me and broke them before your eyes.^d ¹⁸Then, as before, I lay prostrate before the LORD for forty days and forty nights without eating or drinking, because of all the sin you had committed in the sight of the LORD and the evil you had done to provoke him.^e ¹⁹For I dreaded the fierce anger of the LORD against you: his wrath would destroy you.^f Yet once again the LORD listened to me. ²⁰With Aaron, too, the LORD was deeply angry, and would have killed him had I not prayed for him also at that time. ²¹Then, taking the calf, the sinful object you had made, and fusing it with fire, I ground it down to powder as fine as dust, which I threw into the wadi that went down the mountainside.^g

²²"At Taberah, at Massah, and at Kibroth-hattaavah likewise, you provoked the LORD to anger.^h ²³And when he sent you up from Kadesh-barnea to take possession of the land he was giving you, you rebelled against this command of the LORD, your God, and would not trust or obey him.ⁱ ²⁴Ever since I have known you, you have been rebels against the LORD.

²⁵"Those forty days, then, and forty nights, I lay prostrate before the LORD, because he had threatened to destroy you. ²⁶This was my prayer to him: O Lord GOD, destroy not your people, the heritage which your majesty has ransomed and brought out of Egypt with your strong hand. ²⁷Remember your servants, Abraham, Isaac and Jacob. Look not upon the stubbornness of this people nor upon their wickedness and sin, ²⁸lest the people from whose land you have brought us say, 'The LORD was not able to bring them into the land he promised them'; or 'Out of hatred for them he brought them out to slay them in the desert.'^j ²⁹They are, after all, your people and your heritage, whom you have brought out by your great power and with your outstretched arm.^k

CHAPTER 10

See RG 141–48

¹"At that time the LORD said to me, 'Cut two tablets of stone like the former;^l then come up the mountain to me. Also make an ark of wood. ²I will write upon the tablets the commandments that were on the former tablets that you broke, and you shall place them in the ark.' ³So I made an ark of acacia wood, and cut two tablets of stone like the former, and went up the mountain carrying the two tablets.^m ⁴The LORD then wrote on them, as he had written before, the ten commandments which he spoke to you on the mountain from the midst of the fire on the day of the assembly. After the LORD had given them to me, ⁵I turned and came down the mountain, and placed the tablets in the ark I had made.^o There they have remained, in keeping with the command the LORD gave me.

---

z: Ex 24, 12. 18; 34, 28.   a: Ex 31, 18.   b: 12ff: Ex 32, 7-10.   c: Ex 32, 15.   d: 16f: Ex 32, 19.   e: Ex 32, 31; 34, 28.   f: Dt 10, 10; Ex 32, 10.   g: Ex 32, 20.   h: Ex 17, 7; Nm 11, 1ff. 34.   i: Nm 14, 1-4; Ps 106, 24f.   j: Nm 14, 14ff.   k: Dt 4, 20; Ex 6, 6f.   l: Ex 34, 1.   m: Ex 34, 4.   n: Ex 20, 1-17; 34, 28.   o: Ex 40, 20; 1 Kgs 8, 9.

⁶[The Israelites set out from Beeroth Bene-jaakan*p* for Moserah, where Aaron died and was buried, his son Eleazar succeeding him in the priestly office. ⁷From there they set out for Gudgodah, and from Gudgodah for Jotbathah,*q* a region where there is water in the wadies.]

⁸"At that time the LORD set apart the tribe of Levi to carry the ark of the covenant of the LORD,*r* to be in attendance before the LORD and minister to him, and to give blessings in his name, as they have done to this day. ⁹For this reason, Levi has no share in the heritage with his brothers;*s* the LORD himself is his heritage, as the LORD, your God, has told him.

¹⁰After I had spent these other forty days and forty nights on the mountain, and the LORD had once again heard me and decided not to destroy you, ¹¹he said to me, 'Go now and set out at the head of your people,*t* that they may enter in and occupy the land which I swore to their fathers I would give them.'

The Lord's Majesty. ¹²"And now, Israel, what does the LORD, your God, ask of you but to fear the LORD, your God, and follow his ways exactly, to love and serve the LORD, your God, with all your heart and all your soul,*u* ¹³to keep the commandments and statutes of the LORD which I enjoin on you today for your own good? ¹⁴Think! The heavens, even the highest heavens,* belong to the LORD, your God, as well as the earth and everything on it.*v* ¹⁵Yet in his love for your fathers the LORD was so attached to them as to choose you, their descendants, in preference to all other peoples, as indeed he has now done.*w* ¹⁶Circumcise your hearts,* therefore, and be no longer stiff-necked. ¹⁷For the LORD, your God, is the God of gods, the LORD of lords, the great God, mighty and awesome, who has no favorites, accepts no bribes;*x* ¹⁸who executes justice for the orphan and the widow, and befriends the alien, feeding and clothing him. ¹⁹So you too must befriend the alien, for you were once aliens yourselves in the land of Egypt.*y* ²⁰The LORD, your God, shall you fear, and him shall you serve; hold fast to him and swear by his name.*z* ²¹He is your glory, he, your God, who has done for you those great and terrible things which your own eyes have seen. ²²Your ancestors went down to Egypt seventy strong,*a* and now the LORD, your God, has made you as numerous as the stars of the sky.

CHAPTER 11 See RG 141–48

The Wonders of the Lord. ¹"Love the LORD, your God, therefore, and always heed his charge: his statutes, decrees and commandments. ²It is not your children, who have not known it from experience, but you yourselves who must now understand the discipline of the LORD, your God; his majesty, his strong hand and outstretched arm; ³the signs and deeds he wrought among the Egyptians, on Pharaoh, king of Egypt, and on all his land;*b* ⁴what he did to the Egyptian army and to their horses and chariots, engulfing them in the water of the Red Sea as they pursued you,*c* and bringing ruin upon them even to this day; ⁵what he did for you in the desert until you arrived in this place; ⁶and what he did to the Reubenites Dathan and Abiram, sons of Eliab, when the ground opened its mouth and swallowed them up out of the midst of Israel, with their families and tents and every living thing that belonged to them.*d* ⁷With your own eyes you have seen all these great deeds that the LORD has done. ⁸Keep all the commandments, then, which I enjoin on you today, that you may be strong enough to enter in and take possession of the land into which you are crossing, ⁹and that you may have long life on the land which the

---

10, 14: Even the highest heavens: literally, "and the heavens of the heavens"; compare the phrase, "the third heaven," in 2 Cor 12, 2.

10, 16: Circumcise your hearts: cf Dt 30, 6; Jer 4, 4; Rom 2, 29. The "uncircumcised heart" (Lv 26, 41; Jer 9, 25; Ez 44, 7. 9) is closed and unreceptive to divine grace and guidance, just as "uncircumcised ears" (Jer 6, 10) are closed to sound, and "uncircumcised lips" (Ex 6, 12. 30) do not open well in speech.

---

p: Nm 33, 31.   *q:* Nm 33, 32f.   *r:* Nm 3, 6; 6, 23-27; 16, 9.   *s:* Nm 18, 20.   *t:* Ex 32, 34; 33, 1.   *u:* Dt 6, 2. 5.   *v:* Neh 9, 6.   *w:* Dt 7, 6ff.   *x:* 2 Chr 19, 7; Jb 34, 19; Wis 6, 7; Acts 10, 34; Rom 2, 11; Gal 2, 6.   *y:* Ex 22, 21; 23, 9; Lv 19, 33f.   *z:* Dt 6, 13; Mt 4, 10; Lk 4, 8.   *a:* Gn 46, 27; Ex 1, 5; Acts 7, 14.   *b:* Dt 6, 22; Ps 78, 42-51.   *c:* Ex 14, 26ff; 15, 9; Pss 78, 53; 106, 11.   *d:* Nm 16, 31ff.

LORD swore to your fathers he would give to them and their descendants, a land flowing with milk and honey. *The Gift of Rain.* *10*"For the land which you are to enter and occupy is not like the land of Egypt from which you have come, where you would sow your seed and then water it by hand, as in a vegetable garden. *11e*No, the land into which you are crossing for conquest is a land of hills and valleys that drinks in rain from the heavens, *12*a land which the LORD, your God, looks after; his eyes are upon it continually from the beginning of the year to the end. *13**If, then, you truly heed my commandments which I enjoin on you today, loving and serving the LORD, your God, with all your heart and all your soul,*f 14*I will give the seasonal rain to your land, the early rain* and the late rain, that you may have your grain, wine and oil to gather in; *15*and I will bring forth grass in your fields for your animals.*g* Thus you may eat your fill. *16*But be careful lest your heart be so lured away that you serve other gods and worship them.*h 17*For then the wrath of the LORD will flare up against you and he will close up the heavens, so that no rain will fall, and the soil will not yield its crops, and you will soon perish from the good land he is giving you. *Reward of Fidelity.* *18i*"Therefore, take these words of mine into your heart and soul. Bind them at your wrist as a sign, and let them be a pendant on your forehead. *19*Teach them to your children, speaking of them at home and abroad, whether you are busy or at rest. *20*And write them on the doorposts of your houses and on your gates, *21*so that, as long as the heavens are above the earth, you and your children may live on in the land which the LORD swore to your fathers he would give them.

22"For if you are careful to observe all these commandments I enjoin on you, loving the LORD, your God, and following his ways exactly, and holding fast to him, *23*the LORD will drive all these nations out of your way,*j* and you will dispossess nations greater and mightier than yourselves. *24k*Every place where you set foot shall be yours: from the desert and from Lebanon, from the Euphrates River to the Western Sea,* shall be your territory. *25*None shall stand up against you; the LORD, your God, will spread the fear and dread of you through any land where you set foot, as he promised you.*l*

A Blessing and a Curse. *26m*"I set before you here, this day, a blessing and a curse: *27*a blessing for obeying the commandments of the LORD, your God, which I enjoin on you today; *28*a curse if you do not obey the commandments of the LORD, your God, but turn aside from the way I ordain for you today, to follow other gods, whom you have not known. *29*When the LORD, your God, brings you into the land which you are to enter and occupy, then you shall pronounce the blessing on Mount Gerizim,*n* the curse* on Mount Ebal. *30*[Are they not beyond the Jordan, on the other side of the western road in the country of the Canaanites who live in the Arabah, opposite the Gilgal beside the terebinth of Moreh?] *31*For you are about to cross the Jordan to enter and occupy the land which the LORD, your God, is giving you. When therefore, you take possession of it and settle there, *32*be careful to observe all the statutes and decrees that I set before you today.

III: Exposition of the Law
CHAPTER 12

See RG 141-48

One Sanctuary. *1*"These are the statutes and decrees which you must be careful to observe in the land which the LORD, the

---

11, 13ff: As often in the Prophets, the discourse passes into the words of God himself. Cf Dt 7, 4; 17, 3; 28, 20; 29, 4f.

11, 14: The early rain: the rains which begin in October or November and continue intermittently throughout the winter. The late rain: the heavy showers of March and April. In Palestine the crops are sown in the autumn and reaped in the spring.

11, 24: The Western Sea: the Mediterranean.

11, 29: You shall pronounce the blessing . . . the curse: for

the full ceremony, see chapters 27 and 28. Gerizim . . . Ebal: adjacent mountains in Samaria with a deep ravine between them. Their summits command an excellent view of the entire country.

---

e: 11f: Dt 8, 7. *f:* 13f: Dt 10, 12; Lv 26, 4. *g:* Ps 104, 14. *h:* 16f: Dt 4, 25f; 6, 14. *i:* 18-21: Dt 6, 6-9. *j:* Dt 7, 1; 9, 1. *k:* Ex 23, 31. *l:* Dt 2, 25; 7, 24; Ex 23, 27. *m:* 26ff: Dt 28, 2-45; 30, 1. 15. 19. *n:* Dt 27, 12f.

God of your fathers, has given you to occupy, as long as you live on its soil. [2]Destroy without fail every place on the high mountains, on the hills, and under every leafy tree where the nations you are to dispossess worship their gods.[o] [3]Tear down their altars, smash their sacred pillars, destroy by fire their sacred poles, and shatter the idols of their gods, that you may stamp out the remembrance of them in any such place.

[4]"That is not how you are to worship the LORD, your God. [5]Instead,[p] you shall resort to the place which the LORD, your God, chooses out of all your tribes and designates as his dwelling [6]and there you shall bring your holocausts and sacrifices, your tithes and personal contributions, your votive and freewill offerings, and the firstlings of your herds and flocks. [7]There, too, before the LORD, your God, you and your families shall eat and make merry over all your undertakings, because the LORD, your God, has blessed you. [8]You shall not do as we are now doing; here, everyone does what seems right to himself, [9]since you have not yet reached your resting place, the heritage which the LORD, your God, will give you. [10]But after you have crossed the Jordan and dwell in the land which the LORD, your God, is giving you as a heritage, when he has given you rest from all your enemies round about and you live there in security, [11]then to the place which the LORD, your God, chooses as the dwelling place for his name you shall bring all the offerings I command you: your holocausts and sacrifices, your tithes and personal contributions, and every special offering you have vowed to the LORD. [12]You shall make merry before the LORD, your God, with your sons and daughters, your male and female slaves, as well as with the Levite who belongs to your community but has no share of his own in your heritage. [13]Take care not to offer up your holocausts in any place you fancy, [14]but offer them up in the place which the LORD chooses from among your tribes; there you shall make whatever offerings I enjoin upon you.

Profane and Sacred Meals. [15]"However, in any of your communities you may slaughter and eat to your heart's desire as much meat as the LORD, your God, has blessed you with; and the unclean as well as the clean may eat it, as they do the gazelle or the deer. [16]Only, you shall not partake of the blood, but must pour it out on the ground like water.[q] [17]Moreover, you shall not, in your own communities, partake of your tithe of grain or wine or oil, of the first-born of your herd or flock, of any offering you have vowed, of your freewill offerings, or of your personal contributions. [18]These you must eat before the LORD, your God, in the place he chooses, along with your son and daughter, your male and female slave, and the Levite who belongs to your community; and there, before the LORD, you shall make merry over all your undertakings. [19]Take care, also, that you do not neglect the Levite as long as you live in the land.[r]

[20]"After the LORD, your God, has enlarged your territory, as he promised you,[s] when you wish meat for food,* you may eat it at will, to your heart's desire; [21]and if the place which the LORD, your God, chooses for the abode of his name is too far, you may slaughter in the manner I have told you any of your herd or flock that the LORD has given you, and eat it to your heart's desire in your own community. [22]You may eat it as you would the gazelle or the deer: the unclean and the clean eating it alike. [23]But make sure that you do not partake of the blood; for blood is life, and you shall not consume this seat of life with the flesh. [24]Do not partake of the blood, therefore, but pour it out on the ground like water. [25]Abstain from it, that you and your children after you may prosper for doing what is right in the sight of the LORD. [26]However, any sacred gifts or votive offerings that you may have, you shall bring with you to the place which the LORD chooses, [27]and there you must offer both the flesh and the blood of your holocausts on the altar of the LORD, your God; of your other

---

12, 20: Meat for food: as on special feasts. Meat was not eaten every day in Israel, even by the wealthy.

o: 2f: Dt 7, 5; Ex 23, 24; 34, 13.   p: 5-7. 11f: Dt 14, 22-26; 15, 19f; 16, 2. 10f. 14f; 26, 2.   q: Dt 15, 23; Gn 9, 4; Lv 3, 17.   r: Dt 14, 27.   s: Dt 19, 8; Gn 28, 14; Ex 34, 24.

sacrifices the blood indeed must be poured out against the altar of the LORD, your God,[t] but their flesh may be eaten. [28]Be careful to heed all these commandments I enjoin on you, that you and your descendants may always prosper for doing what is good and right in the sight of the LORD, your God.

Pagan Rites. [29]"When the LORD, your God, removes the nations from your way as you advance to dispossess them, be on your guard! Otherwise, once they have been wiped out before you and you have replaced them and are settled in their land, [30]you will be lured into following them. Do not inquire regarding their gods, 'How did these nations worship their gods? I, too, would do the same.' [31]You shall not thus worship the LORD, your God, because they offered to their gods every abomination that the LORD detests, even burning their sons and daughters to their gods.[u]

See RG
141-48

CHAPTER 13

Penalties for Idolatry. [1]"Every command that I enjoin on you, you shall be careful to observe, neither adding to it nor subtracting from it.

[2]"If there arises among you a prophet or a dreamer* who promises you a sign or wonder, [3]urging you to follow other gods, whom you have not known, and to serve them: even though the sign or wonder he has foretold you comes to pass, [4]pay no attention to the words of that prophet or that dreamer; for the LORD, your God, is testing you to learn whether you really love him with all your heart and with all your soul. [5]The LORD, your God, shall you follow, and him shall you fear; his commandment shall you observe, and his voice shall you heed, serving him and holding fast to him alone. [6][v]But that prophet or that dreamer shall be put to death, because, in order to lead you astray from the way which the LORD, your God, has directed you to take, he has preached apostasy from the LORD, your God, who brought you out of the land of Egypt and

ransomed you from that place of slavery. Thus shall you purge the evil from your midst.

[7]"If your own full brother, or your son or daughter, or your beloved wife, or your intimate friend, entices you secretly to serve other gods, whom you and your fathers have not known, [8]gods of any other nation, near at hand or far away, from one end of the earth to the other: [9]do not yield to him or listen to him, nor look with pity upon him, to spare or shield him, [10]but kill him. Your hand shall be the first raised to slay him; the rest of the people shall join in with you. [11]You shall stone him to death, because he sought to lead you astray from the LORD, your God, who brought you out of the land of Egypt, that place of slavery. [12]And all Israel, hearing of it, shall fear and never again do such evil as this in your midst.

[13]"If, in any of the cities which the LORD, your God, gives you to dwell in, you hear it said [14]that certain scoundrels have sprung up among you and have led astray the inhabitants of their city to serve other gods whom you have not known, [15]you must inquire carefully into the matter and investigate it thoroughly. If you find that it is true and an established fact that this abomination has been committed in your midst, [16][w]you shall put the inhabitants of that city to the sword, dooming the city and all life that is in it, even its cattle, to the sword. [17]Having heaped up all its spoils in the middle of its square, you shall burn the city with all its spoils as a whole burnt offering to the LORD, your God. Let it be a heap of ruins forever, never to be rebuilt. [18]You shall not retain anything that is doomed, that the blazing wrath of the LORD may die down and he may show you mercy and in his mercy for you may multiply you as he promised your fathers on oath; [19]because you have heeded the voice of the LORD, your God, keeping all his commandments which I enjoin on you today, doing what is right in his sight.

13, 2. 4. 6: Dreamer: a false prophet who pretended to have received revelations from God in his dreams; cf Jer 23, 25-32; Zec 10, 2. But dreams could also be a channel of true prophecy (Nm 12, 6; Jl 3, 1) and of genuine revelations (Gn 20, 3. 6; 31, 10. 24; 37, 5. 9; Mt 1, 20; 2, 12f. 19; etc.).

t: Lv 17, 11.   *u:* Lv 18, 21; Jer 7, 31.   *v:* 6-10. 14: Dt 6, 14; 17, 2-7.   *w:* 16f: Jos 6, 18. 24; 7, 26; 8, 28.

See RG
141–48

CHAPTER 14

Pagan Mourning Rites. [1]"You are children of the LORD, your God. You shall not gash yourselves nor shave the hair above your foreheads for the dead.[x] [2]For you are a people sacred to the LORD, your God, who has chosen you from all the nations on the face of the earth to be a people peculiarly his own.[y]

Clean and Unclean Animals. [3]"You shall not eat any abominable thing.[z] [4a]These are the animals you may eat: the ox, the sheep, the goat, [5]the red deer, the gazelle, the roe deer, the ibex, the addax, the oryx,* and the mountain sheep. [6]Any animal that has hoofs you may eat, provided it is cloven-footed and chews the cud. [7]But you shall not eat any of the following that only chew the cud or only have cloven hoofs: the camel, the hare and the rock badger, which indeed chew the cud, but do not have hoofs and are therefore unclean for you; [8]and the pig, which indeed has hoofs and is cloven-footed, but does not chew the cud and is therefore unclean for you. Their flesh you shall not eat, and their dead bodies you shall not touch.[b]

[9]"Of the various creatures that live in the water, whatever has both fins and scales you may eat, [10]but all those that lack either fins or scales you shall not eat; they are unclean for you.

[11]"You may eat all clean birds. [12]But you shall not eat any of the following: the eagle, the vulture, the osprey, [13]the various kites and falcons, [14]all the various species of crows, [15]the ostrich, the nightjar, the gull, the various species of hawks, [16]the owl, the screech owl, the ibis, [17]the desert owl, the buzzard, the cormorant, [18]the stork, the various species of herons, the hoopoe, and the bat. [19]*All winged insects, too, are unclean

for you and shall not be eaten. [20]But you may eat any clean winged creatures.

[21]"You must not eat any animal that has died of itself, for you are a people sacred to the LORD, your God.[c] But you may give it to an alien who belongs to your community, and he may eat it, or you may sell it to a foreigner.

"You shall not boil a kid in its mother's milk.*

Tithes. [22]"Each year you shall tithe all the produce that grows in the field you have sown;[d] [23]then in the place which the LORD, your God, chooses as the dwelling place of his name[e] you shall eat in his presence your tithe of the grain, wine and oil, as well as the firstlings of your herd and flock, that you may learn always to fear the LORD, your God. [24]If, however, the journey is too much for you and you are not able to bring your tithe, because the place which the LORD, your God, chooses for the abode of his name is too far for you, considering how the LORD has blessed you,* [25]you may exchange the tithe for money and, with the purse of money in hand, go to the place which the LORD, your God, chooses. [26]You may then exchange the money for whatever you desire, oxen or sheep, wine or strong drink, or anything else you would enjoy, and there before the LORD, your God, you shall partake of it and make merry with your family. [27]But do not neglect the Levite who belongs to your community, for he has no share in the heritage with you.[f]

[28]"At the end of every third year you shall bring out all the tithes of your produce for that year and deposit them in community stores, [29]that the Levite who has no share in the heritage with you, and also the alien, the orphan and the widow who belong to your community, may come and eat their fill;[g] so that the LORD, your God, may bless you in all that you undertake.

14, 5: The gazelle, the addax, the oryx: species of antelopes. The ibex: a species of wild goat.

14, 19f: The apparent contradiction is to be resolved in the light of Lv 11, 20-23; the unclean winged insects are those that walk on the ground; the clean winged creatures are those that leap on the ground, such as certain species of locusts.

14, 21: Boil a kid in its mother's milk: see note on Ex 23, 19.

14, 24: Considering how the Lord has blessed you: should the Israelite farmer be blessed with an abundant harvest, a tenth of this would be too much to transport for a great distance.

x: Lv 19, 28.   y: Dt 7, 6.   z: Ez 4, 14; Acts 10, 14.   a: 4-20; Lv 11, 2-23.   b: Lv 11, 26.   c: Ex 22, 30; 23, 19; 34, 26.   d: Lv 27, 30.   e: 23f: Dt 12, 5ff.   f: Dt 12, 12. 19.   g: 28f: Dt 26, 12.

See RG
141–48

CHAPTER 15

Debts and the Poor. [1]"At the end of every seven-year period* you shall have a relaxation of debts,[h] [2]which shall be observed as follows. Every creditor shall relax his claim on what he has loaned his neighbor; he must not press his neighbor, his kinsman, because a relaxation in honor of the LORD has been proclaimed. [3]You may press a foreigner, but you shall relax the claim on your kinsman for what is yours.[i] [4]Nay, more! since the LORD, your God, will bless you abundantly in the land he will give you to occupy as your heritage, there should be no one of you in need. [5]If you but heed the voice of the LORD, your God, and carefully observe all these commandments which I enjoin on you today, [6]you will lend to many nations, and borrow from none;[j] you will rule over many nations, and none will rule over you, since the LORD, your God, will bless you as he promised. [7]If one of your kinsmen in any community is in need in the land which the LORD, your God, is giving you, you shall not harden your heart nor close your hand to him in his need. [8]Instead, you shall open your hand to him and freely lend him enough to meet his need.[k] [9]Be on your guard lest, entertaining the mean thought that the seventh year, the year of relaxation, is near, you grudge help to your needy kinsman and give him nothing; else he will cry to the LORD against you and you will be held guilty. [10]When you give to him, give freely and not with ill will; for the LORD, your God, will bless you for this in all your works and undertakings. [11]The needy will never be lacking* in the land; that is why I command you to open your hand to your poor and needy kinsman in your country.[l]

Hebrew Slaves. [12]"If your kinsman, a Hebrew man or woman, sells himself to you, he is to serve you for six years, but in the seventh year you shall dismiss him from your service, a free man.[m] [13]When you do so, you shall not send him away empty-handed, [14]but shall weight him down with gifts from your flock and threshing floor and wine press, in proportion to the blessing the LORD, your God, has bestowed on you. [15]For remember that you too were once slaves in the land of Egypt, and the LORD, your God, ransomed you. That is why I am giving you this command today.[n] [16]If, however, he tells you that he does not wish to leave you, because he is devoted to you and your household, since he fares well with you, [17]you shall take an awl and thrust it through his ear* into the door, and he shall then be your slave forever.[o] Your female slave, also, you shall treat in the same way. [18]You must not be reluctant to let your slave go free, since the service he has given you for six years was worth twice a hired man's salary; then also the LORD, your God, will bless you in everything you do.

Firstlings. [19][p]"You shall consecrate to the LORD, your God, all the male firstlings of your herd and of your flock. You shall not work the firstlings of your cattle, nor shear the firstlings of your flock. [20]Year after year you and your family shall eat them before the LORD, your God, in the place he chooses.[q] [21]If, however, a firstling is lame or blind or has any other serious defect, you shall not sacrifice it to the LORD, your God, [22]but in your own communities you may eat it, the unclean and the clean eating it alike, as you would a gazelle or a deer. [23]Only, you shall not partake of its blood, which must be poured out on the ground like water.[r]

CHAPTER 16

See RG
141–48

Feast of the Passover. [1]"Observe the month of Abib* by keeping the Passover of the

---

15, 1: At the end of every seven-year period: in every seventh, or sabbatical, year. Cf Dt 15, 9; 31, 10; and compare Jer 34, 14 with Dt 15, 12. A relaxation of debts: it is uncertain whether a full cancellation of debts is meant, or merely a suspension of payment on them or on their interest among the Israelites. Cf Ex 23, 11 where the same Hebrew root is used of a field that is "let lie fallow" in the sabbatical year.

15, 11: The needy will never be lacking: compare the words of Christ, "The poor you have always with you" (Mt 26, 11).

15, 17: His ear: cf Ex 21, 6 and the note there.

16, 1: Abib: "ear of grain, ripe grain," the name of the month in which the barley harvest fell, corresponding to our March and April; at a later period this month received the Babylonian name of "Nisan."

h: Neh 10, 31.   i: Dt 23, 20.   j: Dt 28, 12f.   k: Lv 25, 35; Sir 29, 1f; Mt 5, 42.   l: Dt 15, 8; Sir 29, 12.   m: Ex 21, 2; Jer 34, 14.   n: Dt 5, 15.   o: 16f: Ex 21, 5f.   p: Ex 13, 11.   q: Dt 14, 23.   r: 21ff: Dt 12, 15f; Lv 22, 20.

LORD, your God,[s] since it was in the month of Abib that he brought you by night out of Egypt. [2] You shall offer the Passover sacrifice from your flock or your herd to the LORD, your God, in the place which he chooses as the dwelling place of his name. [3t] You shall not eat leavened bread with it. For seven days you shall eat with it only unleavened bread, the bread of affliction, that you may remember as long as you live the day of your departure from the land of Egypt; for in frightened haste you left the land of Egypt. [4] Nothing leavened may be found in all your territory for seven days, and none of the meat which you sacrificed on the evening of the first day shall be kept overnight for the next day.

[5] "You may not sacrifice the Passover in any of the communities which the LORD, your God, gives you; [6] only at the place which he chooses as the dwelling place of his name, and in the evening at sunset, on the anniversary of your departure from Egypt, shall you sacrifice the Passover. [7] You shall cook and eat it at the place the LORD, your God, chooses; then in the morning you may return to your tents. [8] For six days you shall eat unleavened bread, and on the seventh there shall be a solemn meeting in honor of the LORD, your God; on that day you shall not do any sort of work.

Feast of Weeks. [9u] "You shall count off seven weeks, computing them from the day when the sickle is first put to the standing grain. [10] You shall then keep the feast of Weeks* in honor of the LORD, your God, and the measure of your own freewill offering shall be in proportion to the blessing the LORD, your God, has bestowed on you. [11] In the place which the LORD, your God, chooses as the dwelling place of his name,[v] you shall make merry in his presence together with your son and daughter, your male and female slave, and the Levite who belongs to your community, as well as the alien, the orphan and the widow among you. [12] Remember that you too were once slaves in Egypt, and carry out these statutes carefully.

Feast of Booths. [13w] "You shall celebrate the feast of Booths for seven days, when you have gathered in the produce from your threshing floor and wine press.* [14] You shall make merry at your feast,[x] together with your son and daughter, your male and female slave, and also the Levite, the alien, the orphan and the widow who belong to your community. [15] For seven days you shall celebrate this pilgrim feast in honor of the LORD, your God, in the place which he chooses; since the LORD, your God, has blessed you in all your crops and in all your undertakings, you shall do naught but make merry.

[16] "Three times a year,[y] then, every male among you shall appear before the LORD, your God, in the place which he chooses: at the feast of Unleavened Bread, at the feast of Weeks, and at the feast of Booths. No one shall appear before the LORD empty-handed, [17] but each of you with as much as he can give, in proportion to the blessings which the LORD, your God, has bestowed on you.

Judges. [18] "You shall appoint judges and officials throughout your tribes to administer true justice for the people in all the communities which the LORD, your God, is giving you. [19] You shall not distort justice; you must be impartial.[z] You shall not take a bribe; for a bribe blinds the eyes even of the wise and twists the words even of the just. [20] Justice and justice alone shall be your aim, that you may have life and may possess the land which the LORD, your God, is giving you.

Pagan Worship. [21]* "You shall not plant a sacred pole of any kind of wood beside the altar of the LORD, your God, which you will build;[a] [22] nor shall you erect a sacred pillar,* such as the LORD, your God, detests.

16, 10: Feast of Weeks: later known more commonly as "Pentecost."

16, 13: See note on Lv 23, 34.

16, 21—17, 7: This section seems to be out of its proper place, since it interrupts the natural sequence of the laws for the judges (Dt 16, 18-20 and 17, 8-13). It probably belongs to the similar section, Dt 12, 29—14, 2.

16, 21f: Sacred pole . . . sacred pillar: see note on Ex 34, 13.

---

s: 1-8: Ex 12, 2-20; 23, 15; Nm 28, 16ff. 24f.   t: 3f: Ex 13, 6f; 34, 18.   u: 9-12: Lv 23, 15-21.   v: Dt 12, 5. 7. 12. 18.   w: 13-15: Ex 23, 16; Lv 23, 34-43; Nm 29, 12-38.   x: Dt 16, 11.   y: Ex 23, 14f. 17; 34, 23; 2 Chr 8, 13.   z: Dt 1, 17; Ex 23, 8.   a: 1 Kgs 14, 15; 2 Chr 33, 3.

CHAPTER 17

See RG
141–48

1"You shall not sacrifice to the LORD, your God, from the herd or from the flock an animal with any serious defect;*b* that would be an abomination to the LORD, your God.

2c"If there is found among you, in any one of the communities which the LORD, your God, gives you, a man or a woman who does evil in the sight of the LORD, your God, and transgresses his covenant, *3*by serving other gods, or by worshiping the sun or the moon or any of the host of the sky, against my command;*d* *4*and if, on being informed of it, you find by careful investigation that it is true and an established fact that this abomination has been committed in Israel: *5*you shall bring the man (or woman) who has done the evil deed out to your city gates* and stone him to death. *6*The testimony of two or three witnesses is required for putting a person to death;*e* no one shall be put to death on the testimony of only one witness. *7*At the execution, the witnesses are to be the first to raise their hands against him; afterward all the people are to join in.*f* Thus shall you purge the evil from your midst.

Judges. *8*"If in your own community there is a case at issue which proves too complicated for you to decide, in a matter of bloodshed or of civil rights or of personal injury, you shall then go up to the place which the LORD, your God, chooses, *9*to the levitical priests or to the judge who is in office at that time. They shall study the case and then hand down to you their decision.*g* *10*According to this decision that they give you in the place which the LORD chooses, you shall act, being careful to do exactly as they direct. *11*You shall carry out the directions they give you and the verdict they pronounce for you, without turning aside to the right or to the left from the decision they hand down to you. *12*Any man who has the insolence to refuse to listen to the priest* who officiates there in the ministry of the LORD, your God, or to the judge, shall die. Thus shall you purge the evil from your midst. *13*And all the people, on hearing of it, shall fear, and never again be so insolent.

The King. *14*"When you have come into the land which the LORD, your God, is giving you, and have occupied it and settled in it, should you then decide to have a king over you like all the surrounding nations,*h* *15*you shall set that man over you as your king whom the LORD, your God, chooses.*i* He whom you set over you as king must be your kinsman; a foreigner, who is no kin of yours, you may not set over you. *16*But he shall not have a great number of horses;* nor shall he make his people go back again to Egypt to acquire them, against the LORD's warning that you must never go back that way again.*j* *17*Neither shall he have a great number of wives, lest his heart be estranged;*k* nor shall he accumulate a vast amount of silver and gold. *18*When he is enthroned in his kingdom, he shall have a copy of this law made from the scroll that is in the custody of the levitical priests.*l* *19*He shall keep it with him and read it all the days of his life that he may learn to fear the LORD, his God, and to heed and fulfill all the words of this law and these statutes. *20*Let him not become estranged from his countrymen through pride, nor turn aside to the right or to the left from these commandments. Then he and his descendants will enjoy a long reign in Israel.

CHAPTER 18

See RG
141–48

Priests. *1*"The whole priestly tribe of Levi shall have no share in the heritage with Israel; they shall live on the oblations of the LORD and the portions due to him.*m* *2*Levi

---

17, 5: Out to your city gates: outside the gates in an unclean place; cf Lv 24, 14; Nm 15, 36; Acts 7, 58; Heb 13, 12.

17, 12: The priest: the high priest; the judge: a layman. The former presided over the court in cases which directly concerned religion, the latter in cases of a more secular nature; cf 2 Chr 19, 8-11.

17, 16: Horses: chariotry for war. The Lord's warning: the same warning is also referred to in Dt 28, 68, although it is not mentioned explicitly elsewhere in the Pentateuch. We know from other sources that Egypt used to export war horses to Palestine. The danger envisioned here is that some king might make Israel a vassal of Egypt for the sake of such military aid.

---

b: Lv 22, 20. *c:* 2-7: Dt 13, 6-15. *d:* Dt 4, 19. *e:* Dt 19, 15; Nm 35, 30; Mt 18, 16; Jn 8, 17; 2 Cor 13, 1. *f:* Dt 13, 10. *g:* Dt 21, 5; 2 Chr 19, 8. *h:* 1 Sm 8, 5. 19f. *i:* 1 Sm 9, 16; 10, 24; 16, 12. *j:* Dt 28, 68; 1 Kgs 4, 26; 10, 26. *k:* 1 Kgs 11; 3f; Neh 13, 26. *l:* Dt 31, 9. 26. *m:* Nm 18, 8f. 20-24; 1 Cor 9, 13.

shall have no heritage among his brothers; the LORD himself is his heritage, as he has told him. *3*The priests shall have a right to the following things from the people: from those who are offering a sacrifice, whether the victim is from the herd or from the flock, the priest shall receive the shoulder, the jowls and the stomach. *4*You shall also give him the first fruits of your grain and wine and oil,*n* as well as the first fruits of the shearing of your flock; *5*for the LORD, your God, has chosen him and his sons out of all your tribes to be always in attendance to minister in the name of the LORD.

6"When a Levite goes from one of your communities anywhere in Israel in which he ordinarily resides, to visit, as his heart may desire, the place which the LORD chooses, *7*he may minister there in the name of the LORD, his God, like all his fellow Levites who are in attendance there before the LORD. *8*He shall then receive the same portions to eat as the rest, along with his monetary offerings and heirlooms.

Prophets. *9*"When you come into the land which the LORD, your God, is giving you, you shall not learn to imitate the abominations of the peoples there.*o* *10*Let there not be found among you anyone who immolates his son or daughter*p* in the fire,* nor a fortune-teller, soothsayer, charmer, diviner, *11*or caster of spells, nor one who consults ghosts and spirits or seeks oracles from the dead. *12*Anyone who does such things is an abomination to the LORD, and because of such abominations the LORD, your God, is driving these nations out of your way.*q* *13*You, however, must be altogether sincere toward the LORD, your God. *14*Though these nations

whom you are to dispossess listen to their soothsayers and fortune-tellers, the LORD, your God, will not permit you to do so.

15"A prophet like me* will the LORD, your God, raise up for you from among your own kinsmen; to him you shall listen.*r* *16*This is exactly what you requested of the LORD, your God, at Horeb on the day of the assembly, when you said, 'Let us not again hear the voice of the LORD, our God, nor see this great fire any more, lest we die.'*s* *17*And the LORD said to me, 'This was well said. *18*I will raise up for them a prophet like you from among their kinsmen, and will put my words into his mouth; he shall tell them all that I command him. *19*If any man will not listen to my words which he speaks in my name, I myself will make him answer for it.*t* *20*But if a prophet presumes to speak in my name*u* an oracle that I have not commanded him to speak, or speaks in the name of other gods, he shall die.'

21"If you say to yourselves, 'How can we recognize an oracle which the LORD has spoken?', *22*know that, even though a prophet speaks in the name of the LORD, if his oracle is not fulfilled or verified, it is an oracle which the LORD did not speak. The prophet has spoken it presumptuously, and you shall have no fear of him.

CHAPTER 19

See RG 141-48

Cities of Refuge. *1*"When the LORD, your God, removes the nations whose land he is giving you, and you have taken their place and are settled in their cities and houses, *2v*you shall set apart three cities* in the land which the LORD, your God, is giving you to occupy. *3*You shall thereby divide

---

18, 10f: Immolates his son or daughter in the fire: to Molech. See note on Lv 18, 21. Such human sacrifices are classed here with other pagan superstitions because they were believed to possess magical powers for averting a calamity; cf 2 Kgs 3, 27. Three other forms of superstition are listed here: augury (by a fortune-teller, a soothsayer or a diviner); black magic (by a charmer . . . or caster of spells); and necromancy (by one who consults ghosts and spirits or seeks oracles from the dead).

18, 15: A prophet like me: from the context (opposition to the pagan soothsayers) it seems that Moses is referring in general to all the true prophets who were to succeed him. But since Christ is the Great Prophet in whom the prophetic office finds its fulfillment and completion, this passage was understood in a special Messianic sense both by the Jews (Jn 6, 14;

7, 40) and by the Apostles (Acts 3, 22; 7, 37).

19, 2: Set apart three cities: the Israelites were to have at least six cities of refuge, three in the land east of the Jordan and three in the land of Canaan west of the Jordan (Nm 35, 9-34); but since the three cities east of the Jordan had now been appointed (Dt 4, 41-43), reference is made here only to the three west of the Jordan. The execution of this command is narrated in Jos 20.

n: Nm 18, 12; 2 Chr 31, 5. *o:* Dt 12, 29ff; Lv 18, 26-30. *p:* 10f: Lv 18, 21; 19, 31; 20, 27; 1 Sm 28, 7; 2 Kgs 17, 17; 21, 6. *q:* Dt 9, 4. *r:* Jn 1, 45; 6, 14; Acts 3, 22; 7, 37. *s:* Ex 20, 19. *t:* Acts 3, 23. *u:* 20. 22: Dt 13, 2ff. *v:* Dt 4, 41ff; Ex 21, 13; Nm 35, 10-15; Jos 20, 2. 8.

into three regions the land which the LORD, your God, will give you as a heritage, and so arrange the routes that every homicide will be able to find a refuge.

⁴"It is in the following case that a homicide may take refuge in such a place to save his life: when someone unwittingly kills his neighbor to whom he had previously borne no malice.ʷ ⁵For example, if he goes with his neighbor to a forest to cut wood, and as he swings his ax to fell a tree, its head flies off the handle and hits his neighbor a mortal blow, he may take refuge in one of these cities to save his life. ⁶Should the distance be too great, the avenger of blood* may in the heat of his anger pursue the homicide and overtake him and strike him dead, even though he does not merit death since he had previously borne the slain man no malice. ⁷That is why I order you to set apart three cities.

⁸ˣ"But if the LORD, your God, enlarges your territory, as he swore to your fathers, and gives you all the land he promised your fathers he would give ⁹in the event that you carefully observe all these commandments which I enjoin on you today, loving the LORD, your God, and ever walking in his ways: then add three cities to these three. ¹⁰Thus, in the land which the LORD, your God, is giving you as a heritage, innocent blood will not be shed and you will not become guilty of bloodshed.

¹¹ʸ"However, if someone lies in wait for his neighbor out of hatred for him, and rising up against him, strikes him mortally, and then takes refuge in one of these cities, ¹²the elders of his own city shall send for him and have him taken from there, and shall hand him over to be slain by the avenger of blood. ¹³Do not look on him with pity, but purge from Israel the stain of shedding innocent blood, that you may prosper.

Removal of Landmarks. ¹⁴"You shall not move your neighbor's landmarks erected by your forefathers in the heritage you receive in the land which the LORD, your God, is giving you to occupy.ᶻ

False Witnesses. ¹⁵"One witness alone shall not take the stand against a man in regard to any crime or any offense of which he may be guilty; a judicial fact shall be established only on the testimony of two or three witnesses.ᵃ

¹⁶"If an unjust witness takes the stand against a man to accuse him of a defection from the law, ¹⁷the two parties in the dispute shall appear before the LORD in the presence of the priests or judges in office at that time;ᵇ ¹⁸and if after a thorough investigation the judges find that the witness is a false witness and has accused his kinsman falsely, ¹⁹you shall do to him as he planned to do to his kinsman.ᶜ Thus shall you purge the evil from your midst. ²⁰The rest, on hearing of it, shall fear, and never again do a thing so evil among you. ²¹Do not look on such a man with pity. Life for life, eye for eye, tooth for tooth, hand for hand, and foot for foot!ᵈ

CHAPTER 20

See RG 141–48

Courage in War. ¹"When you go out to war against your enemies and you see horses and chariots and an army greater than your own, do not be afraid of them, for the LORD, your God, who brought you up from the land of Egypt, will be with you.

²"When you are about to go into battle, the priest shall come forward and say to the soldiers: ³'Hear, O Israel! Today you are going into battle against your enemies. Be not weakhearted or afraid; be neither alarmed nor frightened by them. ⁴For it is the LORD, your God, who goes with you to fight for you against your enemies and give you victory.'ᵉ

⁵"Then the officials shall say to the soldiers,ᶠ 'Is there anyone who has built a new house and not yet had the housewarming? Let him return home, lest he die in battle and another dedicate it. ⁶Is there anyone who has planted a vineyard and never yet enjoyed its

---

19, 6: The avenger of blood: see note on Nm 35, 12.

---

w: Dt 4, 42; Nm 35, 15; Jos 20, 3. 5. *x:* Gn 15, 18-21; 28, 14; Ex 23, 31; 34, 24. *y:* 11ff: Ex 21, 12. 14; Nm 35, 20f. *z:* Dt 27, 17; Prv 23, 10; Hos 5, 10. *a:* Dt 17, 6; Nm 35, 30; Mt 18, 16; Jn 8, 17; 2 Cor 13, 1. *b:* Dt 17, 8f. *c:* 18f: Dn 13, 61f. *d:* Ex 21, 23f; Lv 24, 20; Mt 5, 38. *e:* Dt 1, 30; 3, 22; Jos 23, 10. *f:* 5ff: 1 Mc 3, 56.

fruits? Let him return home, lest he die in battle and another enjoy its fruits in his stead. [7]Is there anyone who has betrothed a woman and not yet taken her as his wife? Let him return home, lest he die in battle and another take her to wife.'[g] [8]In fine, the officials shall say to the soldiers, 'Is there anyone who is afraid and weakhearted?[h] Let him return home, lest he make his fellows as faint-hearted as himself.'

[9]"When the officials have finished speaking to the soldiers, military officers shall be appointed over the army.

Cities of the Enemy. [10]"When you march up to attack a city, first offer it terms of peace. [11]If it agrees to your terms of peace and opens its gates to you, all the people to be found in it shall serve you in forced labor. [12]But if it refuses to make peace with you and instead offers you battle, lay siege to it, [13]and when the LORD, your God, delivers it into your hand, put every male in it to the sword; [14]but the women and children and livestock and all else in it that is worth plundering you may take as your booty, and you may use this plunder of your enemies which the LORD, your God, has given you.[i]

[15]"That is how you shall deal with any city at a considerable distance from you, which does not belong to the peoples of this land. [16]But in the cities of those nations which the LORD, your God, is giving you as your heritage, you shall not leave a single soul alive. [17]You must doom them all—the Hittites, Amorites, Canaanites, Perizzites, Hivites and Jebusites[j]—as the LORD, your God, has commanded you, [18]lest they teach you to make any such abominable offerings as they make to their gods, and you thus sin against the LORD, your God.

Trees of a Besieged City. [19]"When you are at war with a city and have to lay siege to it for a long time before you capture it, you shall not destroy its trees by putting an ax to them. You may eat their fruit, but you must not cut down the trees. After all, are the trees of the field men, that they should be included in your siege? [20]However, those trees which you know are not fruit trees you may destroy, cutting them down to build siege-works with which to reduce the city that is resisting you.

CHAPTER 21

See RG 141–48

Expiation of Untraced Murder. [1]"If the corpse of a slain man* is found lying in the open on the land which the LORD, your God, is giving you to occupy, and it is not known who killed him, [2]your elders and judges shall go out and measure the distances to the cities that are in the neighborhood of the corpse. [3]When it is established which city is nearest the corpse, the elders of that city shall take a heifer that has never been put to work as a draft animal under a yoke, [4]and bringing it down to a wadi with an ever-flowing stream at a place that has not been plowed or sown, they shall cut the heifer's throat there in the wadi.* [5]The priests, the descendants of Levi, shall also be present, for the LORD, your God, has chosen them to minister to him and to give blessings in his name, and every case of dispute or violence must be settled by their decision.[k] [6]Then all the elders of that city nearest the corpse shall wash their hands* over the heifer whose throat was cut in the wadi, [7]and shall declare, 'Our hands did not shed this blood,* and our eyes did not see the deed. [8]Absolve, O LORD, your people Israel, whom you have ransomed, and let not the guilt of shedding innocent blood remain in the midst of your people Israel.' Thus they shall be absolved from the guilt of blood-

21, 1-9: This paragraph is best read immediately after Dt 19, 21. The slain man may not necessarily have been murdered; he may have been killed by a wild beast. But the blood of the slain cries out to God from the soil where it was shed; cf Gn 4, 10. Therefore a religious ceremony of propitiation is here prescribed in order to avert God's anger on the community.

21, 4: They shall cut the heifer's throat there in the wadi: its blood is to be carried away by the stream, signifying thereby the removal of the human blood from the soil. This is

not a sacrifice but a symbolic action; the priests are present merely as official witnesses.

21, 6: Wash their hands: a symbolic gesture in protestation of one's own innocence when human blood is unjustly shed; cf Mt 27, 24.

21, 7: This blood: the blood of the slain man as symbolized by the heifer's blood.

g: Dt 24, 5.   h: Jgs 7, 3.   i: 13f: Nm 31, 7. 9. 11; Jos 22, 8.   j: 16f: Dt 7, 1f; Jos 10, 40; 11, 14.   k: Dt 19, 17.

shed, [9]and you shall purge from your midst the guilt of innocent blood, that you may prosper for doing what is right in the sight of the LORD.

Marriage with a Female Captive. [10]"When you go out to war against your enemies and the LORD, your God, delivers them into your hand, so that you take captives, [11]if you see a comely woman among the captives and become so enamored of her that you wish to have her as wife, [12]you may take her home to your house. But before she may live there, she must shave her head* and pare her nails [13]and lay aside her captive's garb. After she has mourned her father and mother for a full month, you may have relations with her, and you shall be her husband and she shall be your wife. [14]However, if later on you lose your liking for her, you shall give her her freedom, if she wishes it; but you shall not sell her or enslave her, since she was married to you under compulsion.

Rights of the First-born. [15]"If a man with two wives loves one and dislikes the other; and if both bear him sons, but the first-born is of her whom he dislikes: [16]when he comes to bequeath his property to his sons he may not consider as his first-born the son of the wife he loves, in preference to his true first-born, the son of the wife whom he dislikes. [17]On the contrary, he shall recognize as his first-born the son of her whom he dislikes, giving him a double share of whatever he happens to own, since he is the first fruits of his manhood, and to him belong the rights of the first-born.

The Incorrigible Son. [18]"If a man has a stubborn and unruly son who will not listen to his father or mother, and will not obey them even though they chastise him, [19]his father and mother shall have him appre-hended and brought out to the elders at the gate* of his home city, [20]where they shall say to those city elders, 'This son of ours is a stubborn and unruly fellow who will not listen to us; he is a glutton and a drunkard.' [21]Then all his fellow citizens shall stone him to death. Thus shall you purge the evil from your midst, and all Israel, on hearing of it, shall fear.

Corpse of a Criminal. [22]"If a man guilty of a capital offense is put to death and his corpse hung on a tree,* [23]it shall not remain on the tree overnight.[l] You shall bury it the same day; otherwise, since God's curse rests on him who hangs on a tree,* you will defile the land which the LORD, your God, is giving you as an inheritance.

CHAPTER 22

See RG
141–48

Care for Lost Animals. [1]"You shall not see your kinsman's ox or sheep driven astray without showing concern about it; see to it that it is returned to your kinsman.[m] [2]If this kinsman does not live near you, or you do not know who he may be, take it to your own place and keep it with you until he claims it; then give it back to him. [3]You shall do the same with his ass, or his garment, or anything else which your kinsman loses and you happen to find; you may not be unconcerned about them. [4]You shall not see your kinsman's ass or ox foundering on the road without showing concern about it; see to it that you help him lift it up.

Various Precepts. [5]"A woman shall not wear an article proper to a man, nor shall a man put on a woman's dress; for anyone who does such things is an abomination to the LORD, your God.

[6]"If, while walking along, you chance upon a bird's nest with young birds or eggs in it, in any tree or on the ground, and the

---

21, 12f: Shave her head . . . : these symbolic actions are meant to signify the purification of the woman from her pagan defilement or perhaps the end of her period of mourning for her previous husband.

21, 19: The gate: in the city walls. This open space served as the forum for the administration of justice. Cf Dt 22, 15; 25, 7; Ru 4, 1f. 11; Is 29, 21; Am 5, 10. 12. 15.

21, 22: Hung on a tree: some understand, "impaled on a stake." In any case the hanging or impaling was not the means used to execute the criminal; he was first put to death by the ordinary means, stoning, and his corpse was then exposed on high as a salutary warning for others. Cf Jos 8, 29; 10, 26; 1 Sm 31, 10; 2 Sm 21, 9.

21, 23: God's curse rests on him who hangs on a tree: St. Paul quotes these words in Gal 3, 13, where he applies them to the crucified Savior, who "redeemed us from the curse of the law, becoming a curse for us."

l: Gal 3, 13.   m: 1-4: Ex 23, 4f.

mother bird is sitting on them, you shall not take away the mother bird along with her brood; [7]you shall let her go, although you may take her brood away. It is thus that you shall have prosperity and a long life.

[8]"When you build a new house, put a parapet around the roof; otherwise, if someone falls off, you will bring blood-guilt upon your house.

[9]n"You shall not sow your vineyard with two different kinds of seed; if you do, its produce shall become forfeit,* both the crop you have sown and the yield of the vineyard. [10]You shall not plow with an ox and an ass harnessed together. [11]You shall not wear cloth of two different kinds of thread, wool and linen, woven together.

[12]"You shall put twisted cords* on the four corners of the cloak that you wrap around you.o

Crimes against Marriage. [13]"If a man, after marrying a woman and having relations with her, comes to dislike her, [14]and makes monstrous charges against her and defames her by saying, 'I married this woman, but when I first had relations with her I did not find her a virgin,' [15]the father and mother of the girl shall take the evidence of her virginity* and bring it to the elders at the city gate. [16]There the father of the girl shall say to the elders, 'I gave my daughter to this man in marriage, but he has come to dislike her, [17]and now brings monstrous charges against her, saying: I did not find your daughter a virgin. But here is the evidence of my daughter's virginity!' And they shall spread out the cloth before the elders of the city. [18]Then these city elders shall take the man and chastise him,* [19]besides fining him one hundred silver shekels, which they shall give to the girl's father, because the man defamed a virgin in Israel. Moreover, she shall remain his wife, and he may not divorce her as long as he lives.

[20]"But if this charge is true, and evidence of the girl's virginity is not found, [21]they shall bring the girl to the entrance of her father's house and there her townsmen shall stone her to death, because she committed a crime against Israel by her unchasteness in her father's house. Thus shall you purge the evil from your midst.

[22]"If a man is discovered having relations with a woman who is married to another, both the man and the woman with whom he has had relations shall die.p Thus shall you purge the evil from your midst.

[23]"If within the city a man comes upon a maiden who is betrothed,* and has relations with her, [24]you shall bring them both out to the gate of the city and there stone them to death: the girl because she did not cry out for help though she was in the city, and the man because he violated his neighbor's wife. Thus shall you purge the evil from your midst.

[25]"If, however, it is in the open fields that a man comes upon such a betrothed maiden, seizes her and has relations with her, the man alone shall die. [26]You shall do nothing to the maiden, since she is not guilty of a capital offense. This case is like that of a man who rises up against his neighbor and murders him: [27]it was in the open fields that he came upon her, and though the betrothed maiden may have cried out for help, there was no one to come to her aid.

[28]q"If a man comes upon a maiden that is not betrothed, takes her and has relations with her, and their deed is discovered, [29]the man who had relations with her shall pay the girl's father fifty silver shekels and take her as his wife, because he has deflowered her. Moreover, he may not divorce her as long as he lives.

CHAPTER 23

See RG 141–48

[1]"A man shall not marry his father's wife,* nor shall he dishonor his father's bed.

22, 9: Become forfeit: to the sanctuary; cf Lv 19, 19; Jos 6, 19.

22, 12: Twisted cords: referred to as "tassels" on "violet cords" in Nm 15, 38. See note there.

22, 15: The evidence of her virginity: the bridal garment or sheet stained with a little blood from the first nuptial relations.

22, 18: Chastise him: flog him, as prescribed in Dt 25, 1-3.

22, 23: A maiden who is betrothed: a girl who is married but not yet brought to her husband's home and whose marriage is therefore still unconsummated.

23, 1: Father's wife: stepmother. Dishonor: cf Dt 27, 20.

n: 9. 11: Lv 19, 19.   o: Nm 15, 38; Mt 23, 5.   p: Lv 20, 10; Jn 8, 4f.   q: 28f: Ex 22, 16.

Membership in the Community. ²"No one whose testicles have been crushed or whose penis has been cut off, may be admitted into the community of the LORD. ³No child of an incestuous union may be admitted into the community of the LORD, nor any descendant of his even to the tenth generation. ⁴*ʳ*No Ammonite or Moabite may ever be admitted into the community of the LORD, nor any descendants of theirs even to the tenth generation, ⁵*ˢ*because they would not succor you with food and water on your journey after you left Egypt, and because Moab hired Balaam, son of Beor, from Pethor in Aram Naharaim, to curse you; ⁶though the LORD, your God, would not listen to Balaam and turned his curse into a blessing for you, because he loves you. ⁷Never promote their peace and prosperity as long as you live. ⁸*ᵗ*But do not abhor the Edomite, since he is your brother, nor the Egyptian, since you were an alien in his country. ⁹Children born to them may in the third generation be admitted into the community of the LORD.

Cleanliness in Camp. ¹⁰"When you are in camp during an expedition against your enemies, you shall keep yourselves from everything offensive. ¹¹If one of you becomes unclean because of a nocturnal emission, he shall go outside the camp, and not return until, ¹²toward evening, he has bathed in water; then, when the sun has set, he may come back into the camp. ¹³Outside the camp you shall have a place set aside to be used as a latrine. ¹⁴You shall also keep a trowel in your equipment and with it, when you go outside to ease nature, you shall first dig a hole and afterward cover up your excrement. ¹⁵Since the LORD, your God, journeys along within your camp to defend you and to put your enemies at your mercy, your camp must be holy; otherwise, if he sees anything indecent in your midst, he will leave your company.

Various Precepts. ¹⁶"You shall not hand over to his master a slave who has taken refuge from him with you. ¹⁷Let him live with you wherever he chooses, in any one of your communities* that pleases him. Do not molest him. ¹⁸*"There shall be no temple harlot among the Israelite women, nor a temple prostitute among the Israelite men.*ᵘ* ¹⁹You shall not offer a harlot's fee or a dog's price as any kind of votive offering in the house of the LORD, your God; both these things are an abomination to the LORD, your God.

²⁰"You shall not demand interest from your countrymen on a loan of money or of food or of anything else on which interest is usually demanded.*ᵛ* ²¹You may demand interest from a foreigner, but not from your countryman, so that the LORD, your God, may bless you in all your undertakings on the land you are to enter and occupy.

²²"When you make a vow to the LORD, your God, you shall not delay in fulfilling it; otherwise you will be held guilty, for the LORD, your God, is strict in requiring it of you. ²³Should you refrain from making a vow, you will not be held guilty. ²⁴But you must keep your solemn word and fulfill the votive offering you have freely promised to the LORD.

²⁵"When you go through your neighbor's vineyard, you may eat as many of his grapes as you wish, but do not put them in your basket. ²⁶When you go through your neighbor's grainfield, you may pluck some of the ears with your hand, but do not put a sickle to your neighbor's grain.

CHAPTER 24

See RG 141-48

Marriage Laws. ¹"When a man,* after marrying a woman and having relations with

---

23, 17: In any one of your communities: from this it would seem that the slave in question is a fugitive from a foreign country.

23, 18f: The pagans believed that they could enter into special relationship with their gods and goddesses by having sexual relations with the pagan priests and priestesses who prostituted themselves for this purpose. The money paid for this was considered a sort of votive offering made to the pagan sanctuary. Such abominations were naturally forbidden in Israel. A dog's price: the money paid the pagan priest for his indecent service.

24, 1-4: This law is directly concerned only with forbid-ding divorced couples to remarry each other, and indirectly with checking hasty divorces, by demanding sufficient cause and certain legal formalities. Divorce itself is taken for granted and tolerated as an existing custom whose evils this law seeks to lessen. Cf Dt 22, 19. 29; Mal 2, 14ff. Christ gave the authentic interpretation of this law: "Moses, by reason of the hardness of your heart, permitted you to put away your wives; but it was not so from the beginning" (Mt 19, 8f).

---

r: Neh 13, 1f. *s:* Nm 24, 10. *t:* Gn 25, 24ff. *u:* 1 Kgs 14, 24; 22, 46; 2 Kgs 23, 7. *v:* Ex 22, 25; Lv 25, 37; Lk 6, 34f.

her, is later displeased with her because he finds in her something indecent,* and therefore he writes out a bill of divorce and hands it to her, thus dismissing her from his house: [2]if on leaving his house she goes and becomes the wife of another man, [3]and the second husband, too, comes to dislike her and dismisses her from his house by handing her a written bill of divorce; [4]or if this second man who has married her, dies; then her former husband, who dismissed her, may not again take her as his wife after she has become defiled. That would be an abomination before the LORD, and you shall not bring such guilt upon the land which the LORD, your God, is giving you as a heritage.

[5w]"When a man is newly wed, he need not go out on a military expedition, nor shall any public duty be imposed on him. He shall be exempt for one year for the sake of his family, to bring joy to the wife he has married.

Justice, Equity and Charity. [6]*"No one shall take a hand mill or even its upper stone as a pledge for debt, for he would be taking the debtor's sustenance as a pledge.

[7]"If any man is caught kidnaping a fellow Israelite in order to enslave him and sell him, the kidnaper shall be put to death.[x] Thus shall you purge the evil from your midst.

[8y]"In an attack of leprosy you shall be careful to observe exactly and to carry out all the directions of the levitical priests. Take care to act in accordance with the instructions I have given them. [9z]Remember what the LORD, your God, did to Miriam on the journey after you left Egypt.

[10]*"When you make a loan of any kind to your neighbor, you shall not enter his house to receive a pledge from him, [11]but shall wait outside until the man to whom you are making the loan brings his pledge outside to you. [12]If he is a poor man, you shall not sleep in the mantle he gives as a pledge, [13]but shall return it to him at sunset that he himself may

sleep in it.[a] Then he will bless you, and it will be a good deed of yours before the LORD, your God.

[14]"You shall not defraud a poor and needy hired servant, whether he be one of your own countrymen or one of the aliens who live in your communities. [15]You shall pay him each day's wages before sundown on the day itself, since he is poor and looks forward to them.[b] Otherwise he will cry to the LORD against you, and you will be held guilty.

[16]"Fathers shall not be put to death for their children, nor children for their fathers; only for his own guilt shall a man be put to death.[c]

[17]"You shall not violate the rights of the alien or of the orphan, nor take the clothing of a widow as a pledge.[d] [18]For, remember, you were once slaves in Egypt, and the LORD, your God, ransomed you from there; that is why I command you to observe this rule.

[19e]"When you reap the harvest in your field and overlook a sheaf there, you shall not go back to get it; let it be for the alien, the orphan or the widow, that the LORD, your God, may bless you in all your undertakings. [20]When you knock down the fruit of your olive trees, you shall not go over the branches a second time; let what remains be for the alien, the orphan and the widow. [21]When you pick your grapes, you shall not go over the vineyard a second time; let what remains be for the alien, the orphan, and the widow. [22]For remember that you were once slaves in Egypt; that is why I command you to observe this rule.

CHAPTER 25

See RG 141-48

[1]"When men have a dispute and bring it to court, and a decision is handed down to them acquitting the innocent party and condemning the guilty party, [2]if the latter

---

24, 1: Something indecent: a rather indefinite phrase, meaning perhaps "immodest conduct." At the time of Christ the rabbis differed in opinion concerning the sufficient grounds for divorce; cf Mt 19, 3.

24, 6: Since the Israelites ground their grain into flour only in sufficient quantity for their current need, to deprive a debtor of his hand mill was virtually equivalent to condemning him to starve to death.

24, 10f: The debtor had the right to select the pledge that the creditor demanded as a guarantee for his loan.

w: Dt 20, 7.   x: Ex 21, 16.   y: Lv 13, 1-14.   z: Nm 12, 10-15. a: Ex 22, 26.   b: 14f: Lv 19, 13; Tb 4, 15; Sir 34, 25f; Jer 22, 13. c: 2 Kgs 14, 6; 2 Chr 25, 4; Ez 18, 20.   d: Ex 22, 22; 23, 9. e: 19ff: Lv 19. 9f; 23, 22.

deserves stripes, the judge shall have him lie down and in his presence receive the number of stripes his guilt deserves. *3*Forty stripes* may be given him, but no more;*f* lest, if he were beaten with more stripes than these, your kinsman should be looked upon as disgraced because of the severity of the beating.

4*"You shall not muzzle an ox when it is treading out grain.*g*

Levirate Marriage. *5*"When brothers live together* and one of them dies without a son, the widow of the deceased shall not marry anyone outside the family; but her husband's brother shall go to her and perform the duty of a brother-in-law by marrying her.*h 6i*The first-born son she bears shall continue the line of the deceased brother, that his name may not be blotted out from Israel. *7*If, however, a man does not care to marry his brother's wife, she shall go up to the elders at the gate and declare, 'My brother-in-law does not intend to perform his duty toward me and refuses to perpetuate his brother's name in Israel.' *8*Thereupon the elders of his city shall summon him and admonish him. If he persists in saying, 'I am not willing to marry her,' *9**his sister-in-law, in the presence of the elders, shall go up to him and strip his sandal from his foot and spit in his face, saying publicly, 'This is how one should be treated who will not build up his brother's family!' *10*And his lineage shall be spoken of in Israel as 'the family of the man stripped of his sandal.'

Various Precepts. *11*"When two men are fighting and the wife of one intervenes to save her husband from the blows of his opponent, if she stretches out her hand and

seizes the latter by his private parts, *12*you shall chop off her hand without pity.

13"You shall not keep two differing weights in your bag, one large and the other small;*j 14*nor shall you keep two different measures in your house, one large and the other small. *15*But use a true and just weight, and a true and just measure, that you may have a long life on the land which the LORD, your God, is giving you. *16*Everyone who is dishonest in any of these matters is an abomination to the LORD, your God.

17"*Bear in mind what Amalek did to you on the journey after you left Egypt,*k 18*how without fear of any god he harassed you along the way, weak and weary as you were, and cut off at the rear all those who lagged behind. *19*Therefore, when the LORD, your God, gives you rest from all your enemies round about in the land which he is giving you to occupy as your heritage, you shall blot out the memory of Amalek from under the heavens.*l* Do not forget!

CHAPTER 26

See RG 141-48

Thanksgiving for the Harvest. *1*"When you have come into the land which the LORD, your God, is giving you as a heritage, and have occupied it and settled in it, *2*you shall take some first fruits*m* of the various products of the soil which you harvest from the land which the LORD, your God, gives you, and putting them in a basket, you shall go to the place which the LORD, your God, chooses for the dwelling place of his name. *3*There you shall go to the priest in office at that time and say to him, 'Today I acknowledge to the LORD, my God, that I have indeed come into the land which he swore to

---

25, 3: Forty stripes: a relatively mild punishment in ancient times. Later Jewish practice limited the number to thirty-nine; cf 2 Cor 11, 24.

25, 4: St Paul argues from this verse that a laborer has the right to live on the fruits of his labor; cf 1 Cor 9, 9; 1 Tm 5, 18.

25, 5: When brothers live together: when relatives of the same clan, though married, hold their property in common. It was only in this case that the present law was to be observed, since one of its purposes was to keep the property of the deceased within the same clan. Such a marriage of a widow with her brother-in-law is known as a "levirate" marriage from the Latin word levir, meaning "a husband's brother."

25, 9f: The penalty decreed for a man who refuses to comply with this law of family loyalty is public disgrace (the

widow is to spit in his face) and the curse of poverty; sandals were proverbially a man's cheapest possession (cf Am 2, 6; 8, 6), and therefore "a man without sandals" was the poorest of the poor. Some commentators, however, connect this symbolic act with the ceremony mentioned in Ru 4, 7f.

25, 17-19: This attack on Israel by Amalek is not mentioned elsewhere in the Old Testament, although it probably was connected with the battle mentioned in Ex 17, 8. A campaign against Amalek was carried out by Saul; cf 1 Sm 15.

f: 2 Cor 11, 24.   *g:* 1 Cor 9, 9; 1 Tm 5, 18.   *h:* Mt 22, 24; Mk 12, 19; Lk 20, 28.   *i:* 6-9; Ru 4, 5-10.   *j:* 13ff: Lv 19, 35f; Prv 16, 11; Ez 45, 10; Ml 6, 11.   *k:* Ex 17, 8.   *l:* Ex 17, 14; 1 Sm 15, 2f.   *m:* Ex 23, 19; 34, 26.

our fathers he would give us.' [4]The priest shall then receive the basket from you and shall set it in front of the altar of the LORD, your God. [5]Then you shall declare before the LORD, your God, 'My father was a wandering Aramean* who went down to Egypt with a small household and lived there as an alien.[n] But there he became a nation great, strong and numerous. [6o]When the Egyptians maltreated and oppressed us, imposing hard labor upon us, [7]we cried to the LORD, the God of our fathers, and he heard our cry and saw our affliction, our toil and our oppression. [8]He brought us out of Egypt with his strong hand and outstretched arm, with terrifying power, with signs and wonders;[p] [9]and bringing us into this country, he gave us this land flowing with milk and honey.[q] [10]Therefore, I have now brought you the first fruits of the products of the soil which you, O LORD, have given me.' And having set them before the LORD, your God, you shall bow down in his presence. [11]Then you and your family, together with the Levite and the aliens who live among you, shall make merry over all these good things which the LORD, your God, has given you.[r]

Prayer with the Tithes. [12]"When you have finished setting aside all the tithes of your produce in the third year,[s] the year of the tithes, and you have given them to the Levite,* the alien, the orphan and the widow, that they may eat their fill in your own community, [13]you shall declare before the LORD, your God, 'I have purged my house of the sacred portion and I have given it to the Levite, the alien, the orphan and the widow, just as you have commanded me. In this I have not broken or forgotten any of your commandments: [14]*I have not eaten any of the tithe as a mourner; I have not brought any of it out as one unclean; I have not offered any of it to the dead. I have thus hearkened to the voice of the LORD, my God, doing just as you have commanded me. [15]Look

down, then, from heaven, your holy abode, and bless your people Israel and the soil you have given us in the land flowing with milk and honey which you promised on oath to our fathers.'

The Covenant. [16]"This day the LORD, your god, commands you to observe these statutes and decrees. Be careful, then, to observe them with all your heart and with all your soul. [17]Today you are making this agreement with the LORD: he is to be your God and you are to walk in his ways and observe his statutes, commandments and decrees, and to hearken to his voice.[t] [18]And today the LORD is making this agreement with you: you are to be a people peculiarly his own,[u] as he promised you; and provided you keep all his commandments, [19]he will then raise you high in praise and renown and glory above all other nations he has made, and you will be a people sacred to the LORD, your God, as he promised."

IV: Final Words of Moses
CHAPTER 27

See RG 141-48

Ceremonies. [1]Then Moses, with the elders of Israel, gave the people this order: "Keep all these commandments which I enjoin on you today. [2]On the day you cross the Jordan into the land which the LORD, your God, is giving you, set up some large stones and coat them with plaster. [3]Also write on them,[v] at the time you cross, all the words of this law, that you may thus enter into the land flowing with milk and honey, which the LORD, your God, and the God of your fathers, is giving you as he promised you. [4]When, moreover, you have crossed the Jordan, besides setting up on Mount Ebal these stones concerning which I command you today, and coating them with plaster, [5]you shall also build to the LORD, your God, an altar made of stones that no iron tool has touched.[w] [6]You shall make this altar of the

---

26, 5: Aramean: either in reference to the origin of the patriarchs from Aram Naharaim (cf Gn 24, 10; 25, 20; 28, 5; 31, 20. 24), or merely in the sense of "nomad," in the same way as "Arab" was later used; cf Jer 3, 2.

26, 12: And you have given them to the Levite . . . : as prescribed in Dt 14, 28f.

26, 14: These are allusions to pagan religious practices.

n: Gn 46, 6f; Acts 7, 14f.   o: 6f: Ex 1, 8-22; 2, 23ff; 3, 9; Nm 20, 15f.   p: Ex 12, 51.   q: Ex 3, 8.   r: Dt 12, 7. 12.   s: Dt 14, 28f.   t: Ex 24, 7.   u: 18f: Dt 7, 6; 14, 2; 28, 1; Ex 19, 5.   v: Jos 8, 32.   w: Ex 20, 25; Jos 8, 31.

LORD, your God, with undressed stones, and shall offer on it holocausts to the LORD, your God. ⁷You shall also sacrifice peace offerings and eat them there, making merry before the LORD, your God. ⁸On the stones* you shall inscribe all the words of this law very clearly."

⁹Moses, with the levitical priests, then said to all Israel: "Be silent, O Israel, and listen! This day you have become the people of the LORD, your God.ˣ ¹⁰You shall therefore hearken to the voice of the LORD, your God, and keep his commandments and statutes which I enjoin on you today."

¹¹That same day Moses gave the people this order: ¹²"When you cross the Jordan, Simeon, Levi, Judah, Issachar, Joseph and Benjamin shall stand on Mount Gerizimʸ to pronounce blessings over the people, ¹³while Reuben, Gad, Asher, Zebulun, Dan and Naphtali shall stand on Mount Ebal to pronounce curses.

The Twelve Curses. ¹⁴"The Levites shall proclaim aloud to all the men of Israel: ¹⁵'Cursed be the man who makes a carved or molten idolᶻ—an abomination to the LORD, the product of a craftsman's hands—and sets it up in secret!' And all the people shall answer, 'Amen!'*

¹⁶'Cursed be he who dishonors his father or his mother!'ᵃ And all the people shall answer, 'Amen!'

¹⁷'Cursed be he who moves his neighbor's landmarks!'ᵇ And all the people shall answer, 'Amen!'

¹⁸'Cursed be he who misleads a blind man on his way!'ᶜ And all the people shall answer, 'Amen!'

¹⁹'Cursed be he who violates the rights of the alien, the orphan or the widow!'ᵈ And all the people shall answer, 'Amen!'

²⁰'Cursed be he who has relations with his father's wife, for he dishonors his father's bed!'ᵉ And all the people shall answer, 'Amen!'

²¹'Cursed be he who has relations with any animal!'ᶠ And all the people shall answer, 'Amen!'

²²'Cursed be he who has relations with his sister or his half-sister!'ᵍ And all the people shall answer, 'Amen!'

²³'Cursed be he who has relations with his mother-in-law!'ʰ And all the people shall answer, 'Amen!'

²⁴'Cursed be he who slays his neighbor in secret!'ⁱ And all the people shall answer, 'Amen!'

²⁵'Cursed be he who accepts payment for slaying an innocent man!' And all the people shall answer, 'Amen!'

²⁶'Cursed be he who fails to fulfill any of the provisions of this law!'ʲ And all the people shall answer, 'Amen!'

CHAPTER 28*

See RG
141-48

Blessings for Obedience. ¹"Thus, then,ᵏ shall it be:ˡ if you continue to heed the voice of the LORD, your God, and are careful to observe all his commandments which I enjoin on you today, the LORD, your God, will raise you high above all the nations of the earth.ᵐ ²When you hearken to the voice of the LORD, your God, all these blessings will come upon you and overwhelm you:

³ "May you be blessed in the city,
  and blessed in the country!

⁴ "Blessed be the fruit of your womb,
  the produce of your soil and the
    offspring of your livestock,
  the issue of your herds and the young
    of your flocks!ⁿ

⁵ "Blessed be your grain bin and your
    kneading bowl!

⁶ "May you be blessed in your coming in,
  and blessed in your going out!*

27, 8: On the stones: cf vv 3f; not the stones of the altar.

27, 15-26: Amen: see note on Nm 5, 22.

28, 1-69: This chapter would read better immediately after chapter 26.

28, 6: In your coming in . . . in your going out: at the beginning and end of every action, or in all actions in general.

x: Dt 26, 17ff. y: 12f: Dt 11, 29; Jos 8, 33f. z: Ex 20, 4. 23; Lv 19, 4; Wis 14, 8. a: Dt 21, 18-21; Ex 21, 17; Lv 20, 9. b: Dt 19, 14. c: Lv 19, 14. d: Dt 24, 17; Ex 22, 21f. e: Dt 22; 23, 1; Lv 18, 8; 20, 11. f: Ex 22, 18; Lv 18, 23; 20, 15. g: Lv 18, 9; 20, 17. h: Lv 18, 17; 20, 14. i: Ex 20, 13; 21, 12; Nm 35, 20f. j: Gal 3, 10. k: 1-68: Lv 26, 1-45. l: 1-14: Dt 7, 12-16. m: Dt 26, 19. n: Dt 7, 13; 30. 9.

Victory and Prosperity. [7]"The LORD will beat down before you the enemies that rise up against you; though they come out against you from but one direction, they will flee before you in seven.* [8]The LORD will affirm his blessing upon you, on your barns and on all your undertakings, blessing you in the land that the LORD, your God, gives you. [9]Provided that you keep the commandments of the LORD, your God, and walk in his ways, he will establish you as a people sacred to himself, as he swore to you;*o* [10]so that, when all the nations of the earth see you bearing the name of the LORD,* they will stand in awe of you.*p* [11]The LORD will increase in more than goodly measure the fruit of your womb, the offspring of your livestock, and the produce of your soil, in the land which he swore to your fathers he would give you. [12]The LORD will open up for you his rich treasure house of the heavens, to give your land rain in due season, blessing all your undertakings, so that you will lend to many nations and borrow from none.*q* [13]The LORD will make you the head, not the tail,* and you will always mount higher and not decline, as long as you obey the commandments of the LORD, your God, which I order you today to observe carefully; [14]not turning aside to the right or to the left from any of the commandments which I now give you, in order to follow other gods and serve them.

Curses for Disobedience. [15]"But if you do not hearken to the voice of the LORD, your God,*r* and are not careful to observe all his commandments which I enjoin on you today, all these curses shall come upon you and overwhelm you:

[16] "May you be cursed in the city,
  and cursed in the country!

[17] "Cursed be your grain bin and your
  kneading bowl!

[18] "Cursed be the fruit of your womb,
  the produce of your soil and the
   offspring of your livestock,
  the issue of your herds and the young
   of your flocks!

[19] "May you be cursed in your coming in,
  and cursed in your going out!

Sickness and Defeat. [20]"The LORD will put a curse on you, defeat and frustration in every enterprise you undertake, until your are speedily destroyed and perish for the evil you have done in forsaking me. [21]The LORD will bring a pestilence upon you that will persist until he has exterminated you from the land you are entering to occupy. [22]The LORD will strike you with wasting and fever, with scorching, fiery drought, with blight and searing wind, that will plague you until you perish. [23]The sky over your heads will be like bronze and the earth under your feet like iron.*s* [24]For rain the LORD will give your land powdery dust, which will come down upon you from the sky until you are destroyed. [25]The LORD will let you be beaten down before your enemies; though you advance against them from one direction, you will flee before them in seven, so that you will become a terrifying example to all the kingdoms of the earth.*t* [26]Your carcasses will become food for all the birds of the air and for the beasts of the field, with no one to frighten them off. [27]The LORD will strike you with Egyptian boils*u* and with tumors, eczema and the itch, until you cannot be cured. [28]And the LORD will strike you with madness, blindness and panic, [29]so that even at midday you will grope like a blind man in the dark, unable to find your way.

Despoilment. "You will be oppressed and robbed continually, with no one to come to your aid. [30]Though you betroth a wife, another man will have her. Though you build a house, you will not live in it. Though you plant a vineyard, you will not enjoy its fruits.

28, 7. 25: From but one direction . . . in seven: in one compact mass, contrasted with many scattered groups.

28, 10: You bearing the name of the Lord: literally, "The LORD's name is called over you," an expression signifying ownership and protection. Cf 2 Sm 12, 28; 1 Kgs 8, 43; Is 4, 1; 63, 19; Jer 7, 10f; 14, 9; 15, 16; 25, 29; Am 9, 12.

28, 13: The head, not the tail: in the honorable position as leader. Cf Is 9, 14; 19, 15.

o: Dt 26, 18; Ex 19, 5f. *p:* Dt 2, 25; 11, 25. *q:* Dt 15, 6. *r:* Bar 1, 20; Dn 9, 11; Mal 2, 2. *s:* 22f: Lv 26, 19. *t:* Lv 26, 17. 37. *u:* Ex 9, 9ff.

³¹Your ox will be slaughtered before your eyes, and you will not eat of its flesh. Your ass will be stolen in your presence, but you will not recover it. Your flocks will be given to your enemies, with no one to come to your aid. ³²Your sons and daughters will be given to a foreign nation while you look on and grieve for them in constant helplessness. ³³A people whom you do not know will consume the fruit of your soil and of all your labor, and you will be oppressed and crushed at all times without surcease, ³⁴until you are driven mad by what your eyes must look upon. ³⁵*The LORD will strike you with malignant boils of which you cannot be cured, on your knees and legs, and from the soles of your feet to the crown of your head.

Exile. ³⁶ᵛ"The LORD will bring you, and your king whom you have set over you, to a nation which you and your fathers have not known, and there you will serve strange gods of wood and stone, ³⁷and will call forth amazement, reproach and barbed scorn from all the nations to which the LORD will lead you.

Fruitless Labors. ³⁸"Though you spend much seed on your field, you will harvest but little, for the locusts will devour the crop.ʷ ³⁹Though you plant and cultivate vineyards, you will not drink or store up the wine, for the grubs will eat the vines clean.ˣ ⁴⁰Though you have olive trees throughout your country, you will have no oil for ointment, for your olives will drop off unripe.ʸ ⁴¹Though you beget sons and daughters, they will not remain with you, but will go into captivity.ᶻ ⁴²Buzzing insects will infest all your trees and the crops of your soil. ⁴³The alien residing among you will rise higher and higher above you, while you sink lower and lower. ⁴⁴He will lend to you, not you to him. He will become the head, you the tail.

⁴⁵"All these curses will come upon you, pursuing you and overwhelming you, until you are destroyed, because you would not hearken to the voice of the LORD, your God, nor keep the commandments and statutes he gave you. ⁴⁶They will light on you and your descendants as a sign and a wonder* for all time. ⁴⁷Since you would not serve the LORD, your God, with joy and gratitude for abundance of every kind, ⁴⁸therefore in hunger and thirst, in nakedness and utter poverty, you will serve the enemies whom the LORD will send against you. He will put an iron yoke on your neck, until he destroys you.

Invasion and Siege. ⁴⁹ᵃ"The LORD will raise up against you a nation from afar, from the end of the earth, that swoops down like an eagle, a nation whose tongue you do not understand, ⁵⁰a nation of stern visage, that shows neither respect for the aged nor pity for the young. ⁵¹They will consume the offspring of your livestock and the produce of your soil, until you are destroyed; they will leave you no grain or wine or oil, no issue of your herds or young of your flocks, until they have brought about your ruin. ⁵²They will besiege you in each of your communities, until the great, unscalable walls you trust in come tumbling down all over your land. They will so besiege you in every community throughout the land which the LORD, your God, has given you, ⁵³that in the distress of the siege to which your enemy subjects you, you will eat the fruit of your womb, the flesh of your own sons and daughtersᵇ whom the LORD, your God, has given you. ⁵⁴The most refined and fastidious man among you will begrudge his brother and his beloved wife and his surviving children ⁵⁵any share in the flesh of his children that he himself is using for food when nothing else is left him in the straits of the siege to which your enemy will subject you in all your communities. ⁵⁶The most refined and delicate woman among you, so delicate and refined that she would not venture to set the sole of her foot on the ground, will begrudge her beloved husband and her son and daughter ⁵⁷the afterbirth that issues from her womb and the infant she brings forth

---

28, 35: This verse is best read with v 27.

28, 46: A sign and a wonder: an ominous example, attracting attention; cf Dt 29, 21-28.

---

v: 1 Kgs 9, 7ff; 2 Chr 7, 20ff; 33, 11; 36, 6. 20.   w: Ml 6, 15; Hg 1, 6.   x: Zep 1, 13.   y: Mi 6, 15.   z: Lam 1, 5.   a: 49-52: Jer 5, 15ff; Bar 4, 15f.   b: Lv 26, 29; 2 Kgs 6, 28f; Jer 19, 9; Lam 4, 10; Bar 2. 3.

when she secretly uses them for food for want of anything else, in the straits of the siege to which your enemy will subject you in your communities.

Plagues. [58]"If you are not careful to observe every word of the law which is written in this book, and to revere the glorious and awesome name of the LORD, your God, [59]he will smite you and your descendants with severe and constant blows, malignant and lasting maladies. [60]He will again afflict you with all the diseases of Egypt* which you dread, and they will persist among you.[c] [61]Should there be any kind of sickness or calamity not mentioned in this book of the law, that too the LORD will bring upon you until you are destroyed. [62]Of you who were numerous as the stars in the sky,[d] only a few will be left, because you would not hearken to the voice of the LORD, your God.

Exile. [63]"Just as the LORD once took delight in making you grow and prosper,[e] so will he now take delight in ruining and destroying you, and you will be plucked out of the land you are now entering to occupy. [64]The LORD will scatter you among all the nations from one end of the earth to the other,[f] and there you will serve strange gods of wood and stone, such as you and your fathers have not known. [65]Among these nations you will find no repose, not a foot of ground to stand upon, for there the LORD will give you an anguished heart and wasted eyes* and a dismayed spirit. [66]You will live in constant suspense and stand in dread both day and night, never sure of your existence. [67]In the morning you will say, 'Would that it were evening!' and in the evening you will say, 'Would that it were morning!' for the dread that your heart must feel and the sight that your eyes must see. [68]The LORD will send you back in galleys* to Egypt, to the region I told you that you were never to see again;[g] and there you will offer yourselves for sale to your enemies as male and female slaves, but there will be no buyer."

[69]These are the words of the covenant which the LORD ordered Moses to make with the Israelites in the land of Moab, in addition to the covenant which he made with them at Horeb.

CHAPTER 29

See RG 141–48

Past Favors Recalled. [1]Moses summoned all Israel and said to them, "You have seen all that the LORD did in the land of Egypt before your very eyes to Pharaoh and all his servants and to all his land; [2]the great testings your own eyes have seen, and those great signs and wonders.[h] [3]But not even at the present day has the LORD yet given you a mind to understand, or eyes to see, or ears to hear.* [4]'I led you for forty years in the desert.[i] Your clothes did not fall from you in tatters nor your sandals from your feet; [5]bread was not your food, nor wine or beer your drink. Thus you should know that I, the LORD, am your God.' [6j]When we came to this place, Sihon, king of Heshbon, and Og, king of Bashan, came out to engage us in battle, but we defeated them [7]and took over their land, which we then gave as a heritage to the Reubenites, Gadites, and half the tribe of Manasseh.[k] [8]Keep the terms of this covenant, therefore, and fulfill them, that you may succeed in whatever you do.

All Israel Bound to the Covenant. [9]"You are all now standing before the LORD, your God—your chiefs and judges, your elders and officials, and all of the men of Israel, [10]together with your wives and children and the aliens who live in your camp, down to those who hew wood and draw water for you— [11]that you may enter into the covenant of the LORD, your God, which he concluded with you today under this sanction of a curse;* [12]so

---

28, 60: He will again afflict you with all the diseases of Egypt: such as the Lord had promised to remove from his people; cf Dt 7, 15.

28, 65: Wasted eyes: worn out and disappointed in their longing gaze.

28, 68: In galleys: in the ships of the Phoenician slave traders (Ez 27, 13; Jl 4, 6; Am 1, 9), who also dealt with Egypt (Is 23, 3).

29, 3: Eyes to see . . . ears to hear: with inner, spiritual discernment. Cf Mt 13, 43.

29, 11: Sanction of a curse: the present pact binds under penalty of the curses mentioned in this book. Cf v 20.

c: Dt 28, 27. *d:* Dt 1, 10; Jer 42, 2. *e:* Dt 30, 9. *f:* Lv 26, 33. *g:* Hos 8, 13; 9, 3. *h:* Dt 4, 34; Ex 19, 4. *i:* Dt 8, 2. 4. *j:* Dt 2, 24. 32; 3, 1; Nm 21, 33ff. *k:* Dt 3, 16; Nm 32, 33.

that he may now establish you as his people and he may be your God, as he promised you and as he swore to your fathers Abraham, Isaac and Jacob. *13* But it is not with you alone that I am making this covenant, under this sanction of a curse; *14* it is just as much with those who are not here among us* today as it is with those of us who are now here present before the LORD, our God.

Warning against Idolatry. *15* "You know in what surroundings we lived in the land of Egypt and what we passed by in the nations we traversed, *16* and you saw the loathsome idols of wood and stone, of gold and silver, that they possess. *17* Let there be, then, no man or woman, no clan or tribe among you, who would now turn away their hearts from the LORD, our God, to go and serve these pagan gods! Let there be no root that would bear such poison and wormwood among you! *18* If any such person, upon hearing the words of this curse, should beguile himself into thinking that he can safely persist in his stubbornness of heart, as though to sweep away both the watered soil and the parched ground,* *19* the LORD will never consent to pardon him. Instead, the LORD's wrath and jealousy will flare up against that man, and every curse mentioned in this book will alight on him. The LORD will blot out his name from under the heavens *20* and will single him out from all the tribes of Israel for doom, in keeping with all the curses of the covenant inscribed in this book of the law.

Punishment for Infidelity. *21* "Future generations, your own descendants who will rise up after you, as well as the foreigners who will come here from far-off lands, when they see the calamities of this land and the ills with which the LORD has smitten it— *22* all its soil being nothing but sulphur and salt, a burnt-out waste, unsown and unfruitful, without a blade of grass, destroyed like Sodom and Gomorrah,*l* Admah and Zeboiim, which the

LORD overthrew in his furious wrath— *23* they and all the nations will ask, 'Why has the LORD dealt thus with this land? Why this fierce outburst of wrath?'*m* *24* And the answer will be, 'Because they forsook the covenant which the LORD, the God of their fathers, had made with them when he brought them out of the land of Egypt, *25* and they went and served other gods and adored them, gods whom they did not know and whom he had not let fall to their lot: *26* that is why the LORD was angry with this land and brought on it all the imprecations listed in this book; *27* in his furious wrath and tremendous anger the LORD uprooted them from their soil and cast them out into a strange land,*n* where they are today.' *28* [Both what is still hidden* and what has already been revealed concern us and our descendants forever, that we may carry out all the words of this law.]

CHAPTER 30

See RG 141–48

Mercy for the Repentant. *1* "When all these things which I have set before you, the blessings and the curses, are fulfilled in you,*o* and from among whatever nations the LORD, your God, may have dispersed you, you ponder them in your heart: *2* then, provided that you and your children return to the LORD, your God, and heed his voice with all your heart and all your soul,*p* just as I now command you, *3* the LORD, your God, will change your lot; and taking pity on you, he will again gather you from all the nations wherein he has scattered you. *4* Though you may have been driven to the farthest corner of the world, even from there will the LORD, your God, gather you; even from there will he bring you back. *5* The LORD, your God, will then bring you into the land which your fathers once occupied, that you too may occupy it, and he will make you more prosperous and numerous than your fathers. *6* The LORD, your God, will circumcise your hearts* and the hearts of

---

29, 14: Not here among us: this includes their descendants.

29, 18: To sweep away both the watered soil and the parched ground: apparently a proverb signifying that such an unfaithful Israelite will cause God to punish the good with the wicked, to root out the good plants growing in irrigated soil, together with the worthless plants growing in the dry ground.

29, 28: What is still hidden: the events of the future. What

has already been revealed: God's law and the punishments in store for those who break it. Leave the future to God; our business is to keep his law.

30, 6: Circumcise your hearts: see note on Dt 10, 16.

---

l: Gn 14, 10f; 19, 24f.   *m:* 23f: 1 Kgs 9, 8f; Jer 22, 8f.   *n:* Dn 9, 11-14.   *o:* Dt 11, 26ff.   *p:* 2f: Neh 1, 9.

your descendants,[q] that you may love the LORD, your God, with all your heart and all your soul, and so may live. [7]But all those curses the LORD, your God, will assign to your enemies and the foes who persecuted you. [8]You, however, must again heed the LORD's voice and carry out all his commandments which I now enjoin on you. [9]Then the LORD, your God, will increase in more than goodly measure the returns from all your labors, the fruit of your womb, the offspring of your livestock, and the produce of your soil;[r] for the LORD, your God, will again take delight in your prosperity, even as he took delight in your fathers', [10]if only you heed the voice of the LORD, your God, and keep his commandments and statutes that are written in this book of the law, when you return to the LORD, your God, with all your heart and all your soul.

God's Command Clear. [11]*"For this command which I enjoin on you today is not too mysterious and remote for you. [12]It is not up in the sky, that you should say, 'Who will go up in the sky to get it for us and tell us of it, that we may carry it out?' [13]Nor is it across the sea, that you should say, 'Who will cross the sea to get it for us and tell us of it, that we may carry it out?' [14]No, it is something very near to you, already in your mouths* and in your hearts; you have only to carry it out.

The Choice before Israel. [15]"Here, then, I have today set before you life and prosperity, death and doom. [16]If you obey the commandments of the LORD, your God, which I enjoin on you today, loving him, and walking in his ways, and keeping his commandments, statutes and decrees, you will live and grow numerous, and the LORD, your God, will bless you in the land you are entering to occupy. [17]If, however, you turn away your hearts and will not listen, but are led astray and adore and serve other gods, [18]I tell you now that you will certainly perish;

you will not have a long life on the land which you are crossing the Jordan to enter and occupy. [19]I call heaven and earth today to witness against you:[s] I have set before you life and death, the blessing and the curse.[t] Choose life, then, that you and your descendants may live, [20]by loving the LORD, your God, heeding his voice, and holding fast to him. For that will mean life for you, a long life for you to live on the land which the LORD swore he would give to your fathers Abraham, Isaac and Jacob."

CHAPTER 31

See RG 141–48

The Lord's Leadership. [1]When Moses had finished speaking these words to all Israel, [2]he said to them, "I am now one hundred and twenty years old[u] and am no longer able to move about freely; besides, the LORD has told me that I shall not cross this Jordan. [3]It is the LORD your God, who will cross before you; he will destroy these nations before you, that you may supplant them.[v] [It is Joshua who will cross before you, as the LORD promised.] [4w]The LORD will deal with them just as he dealt with Sihon and Og, the kings of the Amorites whom he destroyed, and with their country. [5]When, therefore, the LORD delivers them up to you, you must deal with them exactly as I have ordered you.[x] [6]Be brave and steadfast; have no fear or dread of them, for it is the LORD, your God, who marches with you; he will never fail you or forsake you."[y]

Call of Joshua. [7]Then Moses summoned Joshua and in the presence of all Israel said to him,[z] "Be brave and steadfast, for you must bring this people into the land which the LORD swore to their fathers he would give them; you must put them in possession of their heritage. [8]It is the LORD who marches before you; he will be with you and will never fail you or forsake you. So do not fear or be dismayed."

30, 11-14: God has revealed his will so clearly that ignorance of his law can be no excuse. St. Paul in Rom 10, 6-10, applies these words to the ease with which we can come to faith and salvation in Christ.

30, 14: In your mouths: that you may readily talk about it; cf Dt 6, 7; 11, 19. And in your hearts: that you may easily remember it; cf Dt 6, 6; 11, 18.

---

q: Dt 6, 5.   r: Dt 28, 11.   s: Dt 4, 26.   t: Dt 11, 26ff; 28, 2. 15.   u: Dt 34, 7; Nm 20, 12.   v: Dt 9, 3.   w: Nm 21, 21-35.   x: Dt 7, 2.   y: Dt 20, 3f.   z: 7f: Jos 1, 6f. 9.

The Reading of the Law. [9]When Moses had written down this law, he entrusted it to the levitical priests who carry the ark of the covenant of the LORD, and to all the elders of Israel, [10]giving them this order: "On the feast of Booths,[a] at the prescribed time in the year of relaxation* which comes at the end of every seven-year period, [11]when all Israel goes to appear before the LORD, your God, in the place which he chooses, you shall read this law* aloud in the presence of all Israel. [12]Assemble the people—men, women and children, as well as the aliens who live in your communities—that they may hear it and learn it, and so fear the LORD, your God, and carefully observe all the words of this law. [13]Their children also, who do not know it yet, must hear it and learn it, that they too may fear the LORD, your God, as long as you live on the land which you will cross the Jordan to occupy."

Commission of Joshua. [14]The LORD said to Moses, "The time is now approaching for you to die. Summon Joshua, and present yourselves at the meeting tent that I may give him his commission." So Moses and Joshua went and presented themselves at the meeting tent.* [15]And the LORD appeared at the tent in a column of cloud, which stood still at the entrance of the tent.

A Command to Moses. [16]The LORD said to Moses, "Soon you will be at rest with your fathers, and then this people will take to rendering wanton worship to the strange gods among whom they will live in the land they are about to enter.[b] They will forsake me and break the covenant which I have made with them. [17]At that time my anger will flare up against them; I will forsake them and hide my face from them, so that they will become a prey to be devoured, and many evils and troubles will befall them. At that time they will indeed say, 'Is it not because our God is not among us that these evils have befallen us?' [18]Yet I will be hiding my face from them at that time only because

of all the evil they have done in turning to other gods. [19]Write out this song,[c] then, for yourselves. Teach it to the Israelites and have them recite it, so that this song may be a witness for me against the Israelites. [20]For when I have brought them into the land flowing with milk and honey which I promised on oath to their fathers, and they have eaten their fill and grown fat, if they turn to other gods and serve them, despising me and breaking my covenant; [21]then, when many evils and troubles befall them, this song, which their descendants will not have forgotten to recite, will bear witness against them. For I know what they are inclined to do even at the present time, before I have brought them into the land which I promised on oath to their fathers." [22]So Moses wrote this song that same day, and he taught it to the Israelites.

Commission of Joshua. [23]Then the LORD commissioned Joshua, son of Nun, and said to him, "Be brave and steadfast, for it is you who must bring the Israelites into the land which I promised them on oath.[d] I myself will be with you."

The Law Placed in the Ark. [24]When Moses had finished writing out on a scroll the words of the law in their entirety, [25]he gave the Levites[e] who carry the ark of the covenant of the LORD this order: [26]"Take this scroll of the law and put it beside the ark of the covenant of the LORD, your God, that there it may be a witness against you. [27]For I already know how rebellious and stiff-necked you will be. Why, even now, while I am alive among you, you have been rebels against the LORD! How much more, then, after I am dead! [28f]Therefore, assemble all your tribal elders and your officials before me, that I may speak these words for them to hear, and so may call heaven and earth to witness against them. [29g]For I know that after my death you are sure to become corrupt and to turn aside from the way along which I directed you, so that evil will befall you in

---

31, 10: The year of relaxation: cf Dt 15, 1ff and the note there.

31, 11ff: Reading the law not only instructed the people but also consoled them by the assurance of the divine goodness.

31, 14f. 23: V 23 is best read immediately after v 15; perhaps the original order was vv 7-8. 14-15. 23.

a: 10f: Dt 16, 13ff. b: Jgs 2, 12. 17. c: Dt 31, 21; 32, 1-43. d: Dt 31, 7f; Jos 1, 5ff. e: 24f: Dt 31, 9. f: Dt 32, 1-43. g: Jgs 2, 19.

some future age because you have done evil in the LORD's sight, and provoked him by your deeds."

The Song of Moses. [30]Then Moses recited the words of this song from beginning to end, for the whole assembly of Israel to hear:

See RG
141-48

CHAPTER 32

A

[1] Give ear, O heavens, while I speak;*
    let the earth hearken to the words of
       my mouth!
[2] May my instruction soak in like the rain,
    and my discourse permeate like the
       dew,
    Like a downpour upon the grass,
    like a shower upon the crops:
[3] For I will sing the LORD's renown.
    Oh, proclaim the greatness of our God!
[4] The Rock—how faultless are his deeds,
    how right all his ways!
    A faithful God, without deceit,
    how just and upright he is![h]

[5] Yet basely has he been treated by his
       degenerate children,
    a perverse and crooked race![i]
[6] Is the LORD to be thus repaid by you,
    O stupid and foolish people?
    Is he not your father who created you?
    Has he not made you and established
       you?[j]

[7] Think back on the days of old,
    reflect on the years of age upon age.
    Ask your father and he will inform you,
    ask your elders and they will tell you:[k]
[8] When the Most High assigned the
       nations their heritage,
    when he parceled out the descendants
       of Adam,[l]

He set up the boundaries of the peoples
    after the number of the sons of God;*
[9] While the LORD's own portion was
       Jacob,
    his hereditary share was Israel.[m]

[10] He found them in a wilderness,
    a wasteland of howling desert.
    He shielded them and cared for them,
    guarding them as the apple of his eye.[n]

[11] As an eagle incites its nestlings forth
    by hovering over its brood,
    So he spread his wings to receive them
    and bore them up on his pinions.[o]
[12] The LORD alone was their leader,
    no strange god was with him.
[13] He had them ride triumphant over the
       summits of the land*
    and live off the products of its fields,
    Giving them honey to suck from its rocks
    and olive oil from its hard, stony
       ground;

[14] Butter from its cows and milk from its
       sheep,
    with the fat of its lambs and rams;
    Its Bashan* bulls and its goats,
    with the cream of its finest wheat;
    and the foaming blood of its grapes
       you drank.

B

[15] [So Jacob ate his fill,]
    the darling* grew fat and frisky;
    you became fat and gross and gorged.
    They spurned the God who made them
    and scorned their saving Rock.[p]
[16] They provoked him with strange gods
    and angered him with abominable
       idols.[q]

32, 1-43: In the style of the great prophets, the speaker is often God himself. The whole song is a poetic sermon, having for its theme God's benefits to Israel (vv 1-14) and Israel's ingratitude and idolatry in turning to the gods of the pagans, which sins will be punished by the pagans themselves (vv 15-29); in turn, the foolish pride of the pagans will be punished, and the Lord's honor will be vindicated (vv 30-43).

32, 8: The sons of God: the angels; cf Jb 1, 6; 2, 1; 38, 7; Ps 89, 7f. Here the various nations are portrayed as having their respective guardian angels. Cf Dn 10, 20f; 12, 1.

32, 13: The land: Canaan.

32, 14: Bashan: a fertile grazing land east of the Jordan, famous for its strong cattle. Cf Ps 22, 13; Ez 39, 18; Am 4, 1.

32, 15: The darling: a probable meaning of the Hebrew word yeshurun, a term of endearment for "Israel." Cf Dt 33, 5. 26; Is 44, 2.

h: Ps 92, 15; Rv 15, 3. *i:* Dt 31, 29; Ps 78, 8; Lk 9, 41. *j:* Ex 4, 22; Is 63, 16; 64, 8; Jer 31, 9. *k:* Dt 4, 32; Ps 44, 2. *l:* Gn 10, 1-32; Acts 17, 26. *m:* Ex 19, 5; Ps 33, 12. *n:* Dt 8, 15; Jer 2, 6; Zec 2, 8. *o:* Ex 19, 4. *p:* Dt 31, 20. *q:* Nm 25, 2f; Ps 78, 58.

¹⁷ They offered sacrifice to demons, to
  "no-gods,"
    to gods whom they had not known
      before,
  To newcomers just arrived,
    of whom their fathers had never stood
      in awe.
¹⁸ You were unmindful of the Rock that
      begot you,
    You forgot the God who gave you
      birth.ʳ
¹⁹ When the LORD saw this, he was filled
      with loathing
    and anger toward his sons and
      daughters.
²⁰ "I will hide my face from them," he said,
    "and see what will then become of
      them.
  What a fickle race they are,
    sons with no loyalty in them!ˢ
²¹ "Since they have provoked me with their
      'no god'
    and angered me with their vain idols,
  I will provoke them with a 'no-people';
    with a foolish nation I will anger
      them.ᵗ

²² "For by my wrath a fire is enkindled
    that shall rage to the depths of the
      netherworld,
  Consuming the earth with its yield,
    and licking with flames the roots of
      the mountains.ᵘ
²³ I will spend on them woe upon woe
    and exhaust all my arrows against
      them:

²⁴ "Emaciating hunger and consuming fever
      and bitter pestilence,
  And the teeth of wild beasts I will send
      among them,
    with the venom of reptiles gliding in
      the dust.

²⁵ "Snatched away by the sword in the
      street
    and by sheer terror at home

Shall be the youth and the maiden alike,
    the nursing babe as well as the hoary
      old man.ᵛ

²⁶ "I would have said, 'I will make an end
      of them
    and blot out their name from men's
      memories,'
²⁷ Had I not feared the insolence of their
      enemies,
    feared that these foes would
      mistakenly boast,
  'Our own hand won the victory;
    the LORD had nothing to do with it.' "

²⁸ For they are a people devoid of reason,*
    having no understanding.
²⁹ If they had insight they would realize
      what happened,
    they would understand their future and
      say,

C
³⁰ "How could one man rout a thousand,
    or two men put ten thousand to flight,
  Unless it was because their Rock sold
      them
    and the LORD delivered them up?"
³¹ Indeed, their "rock" is not like our Rock,
    and our foes are under condemnation.

³² They are a branch of Sodom's
      vine-stock,
    from the vineyards of Gomorrah.
  Poisonous are their grapes
    and bitter their clusters.
³³ Their wine is the venom of dragons
    and the cruel poison of cobras.

³⁴ "Is not this preserved in my treasury,
    sealed up in my storehouse,
³⁵ Against the day of vengeance and
      requital,
    against the time they lose their
      footing?"
  Close at hand is the day of their disaster,
    and their doom is rushing upon them!

32, 28-35: The reference is to the pagan nations, not to Israel.

r: Jer 2, 32.   *s:* Dt 31, 17.   *t:* Rom 10, 19.   *u:* Lam 4, 11.   *v:* Lv 26, 25.

³⁶ Surely, the LORD shall do justice for his
  people;
  on his servants he shall have pity.
  When he sees their strength failing,
  and their protected and unprotected*
  alike disappearing,ʷ

³⁷ He will say, "Where are their godsˣ
  whom they relied on as their 'rock'?
³⁸ Let those who ate the fat of your sacrifices
  and drank the wine of your libations
  Rise up now and help you!
  Let them be your protection!

³⁹ "Learn then that I, I alone, am God,
  and there is no god besides me.
  It is I who bring both death and life,
  I who inflict wounds and heal them,
  and from my hand there is no rescue.ʸ

⁴⁰ "To the heavens I raise my hand and swear:
  As surely as I live forever,

⁴¹ I will sharpen my flashing sword,
  and my hand shall lay hold of my quiver.

"With vengeance I will repay my foes
  and requite those who hate me.
⁴² I will make my arrows drunk with blood,
  and my sword shall gorge itself with
  flesh—
With the blood of the slain and the
  captured,
  Flesh from the heads of the enemy
  leaders."

⁴³ Exult with him, you heavens,
  glorify him, all you angels of God;
For he avenges the blood of his servants
  and purges his people's land.

⁴⁴So Moses, together with Joshua, son of
Nun, went and recited all the words of this
song for the people to hear.

Final Appeal. ⁴⁵When Moses had finished
speaking all these words to all Israel, ⁴⁶he
said,ᶻ "Take to heart all the warning which I
have now given you and which you must impress on your children, that you may carry
out carefully every word of this law. ⁴⁷For
this is no trivial matter for you; rather, it
means your very life, since it is by this means
that you are to enjoy a long life on the land
which you will cross the Jordan to occupy."

Moses to View Canaan. ⁴⁸On that very
day the LORD said to Moses, ⁴⁹"Go up on
Mount Nebo, here in the Abarim Mountains
[it is in the land of Moab facing Jericho], and
view the land of Canaan, which I am giving
to the Israelites as their possession.ᵃ ⁵⁰Then
you shall die on the mountain you have
climbed, and shall be taken to your people,
just as your brother Aaron died on Mount
Hor and there was taken to his people;ᵇ ⁵¹be-
cause both of you broke faith with me
among the Israelites at the waters of Meribath-kadesh in the desert of Zin by failing to
manifest my sanctity among the Israelites.ᶜ
⁵²You may indeed view the land at a distance, but you shall not enter that land which
I am giving to the Israelites."ᵈ

CHAPTER 33

See RG
141–48

Blessing upon the Tribes. ¹This is the
blessing which Moses, the man of God, pronounced upon the Israelites before he died.
²He said:

"The LORD came from Sinai*
  and dawned on his people from Seir;
He shone forth from Mount Paran
  and advanced from Meribath-kadesh,
While at his right hand a fire blazed forth
  and his wrath devastated the nations.ᵉ
³ But all his holy ones were in his hand;*
  they followed at his feet
  and he bore them up on his pinions.
⁴ A law he gave to us;

32, 36: Their protected and unprotected: the meaning of
the Hebrew is uncertain; according to some, the idea is
"slaves and freemen."

33, 2-5. 26-29: These verses seem to form an independent
hymn describing, in the form of a theophany, the conquest of
Canaan. The first section of this hymn (vv 2-5) serves here as
an introduction to the various "blessings"; the second section
(vv 26-29), as their conclusion.

33, 3: His holy ones were in his hand: the Israelites were
protected by the Lord.

---

w: 2 Mc 7, 6. *x:* 37f: Jgs 10, 14; Jer 2, 28. *y:* Dt 4, 35; Tb 13,
2; Wis 16, 13. *z:* Dt 4, 9. *a:* Nm 27, 12; 33, 47f. *b:* Nm 20,
24ff. 28; 27, 13; 33, 38. *c:* Nm 20, 12; 27, 14. *d:* Dt 3, 27; 34,
4. *e:* Ex 19, 18. 20; Jgs 5, 4f.

he made the community of Jacob his
domain,*f*
5 and he became king of his darling,*
When the chiefs of the people assembled
and the tribes of Israel came together.
6 "May Reuben live and not die out,*g*
but let his men be few."*

7 The following is for Judah. He said:
"The LORD hears the cry of Judah;
you will bring him to his people.*
His own hands defend his cause
and you will be his help against his
foes."*h*

8 Of Levi he said:
"To Levi belong your Thummim,
to the man of your favor your Urim;*
For you put him to the test at Massah
and you contended with him at the
waters of Meribah.*i*
9 He said of his father, 'I regard him not';
his brothers he would not
acknowledge,
and his own children he refused to
recognize.
Thus the Levites keep your words,
and your covenant they uphold.*
10 They promulgate your decisions to Jacob
and your law to Israel.
They bring the smoke of sacrifice to your
nostrils,
and burnt offerings to your altar.*j*
11 Bless, O LORD, his possessions
and accept the ministry of his hands.
Break the backs of his adversaries
and of his foes, that they may not rise."

12 Of Benjamin he said:
"Benjamin is the beloved of the LORD,

who shelters him all the day,
while he abides securely at his
breast."*k*

13 Of Joseph he said:*l*
"Blessed by the LORD is his land
with the best of the skies above
and of the abyss crouching beneath;
14 With the best of the produce of the year,
and the choicest sheaves of the
months;
15 With the finest gifts of the age-old
mountains
and the best from the timeless hills;
16 With the best of the earth and its fullness,
and the favor of him who dwells in the
bush.*
These shall come upon the head of
Joseph
and upon the brow of the prince
among his brothers,
17 The majestic bull, his father's first-born,
whose horns are those of the wild ox
With which to gore the nations,
even those at the ends of the earth."
[These are the myriads of Ephraim,
and these the thousands of Manasseh.]

18 Of Zebulun he said:*m*
"Rejoice, O Zebulun, in your pursuits,
and you, Issachar, in your tents!
19 You who invite the tribes to the
mountains
where feasts are duly held,
Because you suck up the abundance of
the seas*
and the hidden treasures of the sand."

20 Of Gad he said:*n*
"Blessed be he who has made Gad so vast!

33, 5. 26: The darling: see note on Dt 32, 15.

33, 6: In keeping with the other blessings, probably this verse was once introduced by the phrase, "Of Reuben he said." It is to be noted that there is no blessing here for Simeon.

33, 7: Bring him to his people: this probably refers to the isolated position of the tribe of Judah during the conquest of the Promised Land (cf Jgs 1, 17-19); according to some commentators the reference is to the divided kingdom.

33, 8: Thummim . . . Urim: see note on Ex 28, 30.

33, 9: The reference is probably to the Levites' slaughter of their brethren after the affair of the golden calf in the desert; cf Ex 32, 27-29.

33, 16: Him who dwells in the bush: a title given to the Lord because of his appearance to Moses in the burning bush; cf Ex 3.

33, 19: The abundance of the seas: perhaps the wealth that comes from sea-borne trade or from fishing. The hidden treasures of the sand: possibly an allusion to the valuable purple dye extracted from certain marine shells found on the coast of northern Palestine.

---

f: Jn 1, 17; 7, 19.   *g:* Gn 49, 3f.   *h:* Gn 49, 8-12.   *i:* Gn 49, 5; Ex 17, 7; 28, 30; Nm 20, 13.   *j:* Ex 30, 7f.   *k:* Gn 49, 27.   *l:* 13-17: Gn 49, 22-26.   *m:* 18f: Gn 49, 13ff.   *n:* 20f: Gn 49, 19.

He lies there like a lion
that has seized the arm and head of the
prey.

21 He saw that the best should be his
when the princely portion* was
assigned,
while the heads of the people were
gathered.
He carried out the justice of the
LORD
and his decrees respecting Israel."o

22 Of Dan he said:
"Dan is a lion's whelp,p
that springs forth from Bashan!"*

23 Of Naphtali he said:
"Naphtali is enriched with favors
and filled with the blessings of the
LORD;
The lake* and south of it are his
possession!"q

24 Of Asher he said:r
"More blessed than the other sons be
Asher!
May he be the favorite among his
brothers,
as the oil of his olive trees runs over
his feet!*

25 May your bolts be of iron and bronze;
may your strength endure through all
your days!"

26 "There is no god like the God of the
darling,
who rides the heavens in his power,
and rides the skies in his majesty;

27 He spread out the primeval tent;
he extended the ancient canopy.
He drove the enemy out of your way
and the Amorite he destroyed.

28 Israel has dwelt securely,

and the fountain of Jacob has been
undisturbed.
In a land of grain and wine,
where the heavens drip with dew.s

29 How fortunate you are, O Israel!
Where else is a nation victorious in the
LORD?
The LORD is your saving shield,
and his sword is your glory.
Your enemies fawn upon you,
as you stride upon their heights."t

CHAPTER 34

See RG
141-48

Death and Burial of Moses. 1Then
Moses went up from the plains of Moab to
Mount Nebo,u the headland of Pisgah which
faces Jericho, and the LORD showed him all
the land—Gilead, and as far as Dan, 2all
Naphtali, the land of Ephraim and Manasseh, all the land of Judah as far as the Western Sea, 3the Negeb, the circuit of the Jordan
with the lowlands at Jericho, city of palms,
and as far as Zoar. 4The LORD then said to
him, "This is the landv which I swore to
Abraham, Isaac and Jacob that I would give
to their descendants. I have let you feast
your eyes upon it, but you shall not cross
over." 5So there, in the land of Moab, Moses,
the servant of the LORD, diedw as the LORD
had said; 6and he was buried in the ravine
opposite Beth-peor in the land of Moab, but
to this day no one knows the place of his burial. 7Moses was one hundred and twenty
years oldx when he died, yet his eyes were
undimmed and his vigor unabated. 8For
thirty days the Israelites wept for Moses in
the plains of Moab, till they had completed
the period of grief and mourning for Moses.

9Now Joshua, son of Nun,y was filled with
the spirit of wisdom, since Moses had laid
his hands upon him; and so the Israelites
gave him their obedience, thus carrying out
the LORD's command to Moses.

33, 21: The princely portion: Moses gave the tribe of Gad their land on the east of the Jordan only on condition that they
would help the other tribes conquer the land west of the river; cf Nm 32; Jos 22.

33, 22: The sense is, "May he leap up like a lion of Bashan"; the heavily wooded hills of Bashan were notorious for their
lions, but the tribe of Dan was not settled in this region.

33, 23: The lake: the Lake of Gennesaret on which the land of this tribe bordered.

33, 24: The land of the tribe of Asher was covered with olive groves.

o: Nm 32, 1. 5. 16-19. 31f; Jos 1, 12-15; 1 Chr 5, 18-22.   p: Gn 49, 16f.   q: Gn 49, 21; Jos 19, 32-39.   r: 24f: Gn 49, 20.   s: Gn 27,
28.   t: Dt 4, 7f.   u: Dt 3, 27.   v: Dt 3, 27; 32, 52; Gn 12, 7; 15, 18.   w: Dt 32, 50.   x: Dt 31, 2.   y: Nm 27, 18. 23; Jos 1, 17.

[10z]Since then no prophet has arisen in Israel like Moses, whom the LORD knew face to face. [11a]He had no equal in all the signs and wonders the LORD sent him to perform in the land of Egypt against Pharaoh and all his servants and against all his land, [12]and for the might and the terrifying power that Moses exhibited in the sight of all Israel.

z: Ex 33, 11.   a: Dt 4, 34.

The Book of Joshua

See RG 149–56

The Book of Joshua derives its name from the successor of Moses, with whose deeds it is principally concerned. The purpose of the book is to demonstrate God's fidelity in giving to the Israelites the land he had promised them for an inheritance (Gn 15, 18ff; Jos 1, 2ff; 21, 41ff; 23, 14ff).

Their occupation of the country is begun with the crossing of the Jordan and the conquest of Jericho (ch 1–6), in both of which the Lord intervenes on their behalf. This is followed by a first foothold on the Palestinian mountain range, at Ai, Bethel and Gibeon (ch 7–9), and two sweeping campaigns against the city-states in the south of the country (ch 10) and in the north (ch 11), with a summary in Jos 12. The broad claim to total sovereignty thus established is spelled out by a combined list of tribal boundaries and of the towns contained within each area or administrative district (ch 13–19), including cities of asylum and cities for the Levites (ch 20, 21). The book closes with a narrative about the tribes east of the Jordan (ch 22), a warning speech by Joshua (ch 23), and a renewal at Shechem (ch 24) of the covenant with the Lord, already affirmed there near the beginning (8, 30-35) of the conquest.

Like the books which precede it, the Book of Joshua was built up by a long and complex process of editing traditional materials. Both Jewish and Christian believers have always regarded it as inspired.

The entire history of the conquest of the Promised Land is a prophecy of the spiritual conquest of the world through the Church under the leadership of Jesus the Messiah.

The Book of Joshua may be divided as follows:

I: Conquest of Canaan (1, 1—12, 24).
II: Division of the Land (13, 1—21, 45).

III: Return of the Transjordan Tribes and Joshua's Farewell (22, 1—24, 33).

I: Conquest of Canaan

CHAPTER 1

See RG 150

Divine Promise of Assistance. [1]After Moses, the servant of the LORD, had died, the LORD said to Moses' aid Joshua, son of Nun: [2]"My servant Moses is dead. So prepare to cross the Jordan here, with all the people, into the land I will give the Israelites. [3]As I promised Moses, I will deliver to you every place where you set foot. [4]*Your domain is to be all the land of the Hittites, from the desert and from Lebanon east to the great river Euphrates and west to the Great Sea.[a] [5]No one can withstand you while you live. I will be with you as I was with Moses:[b] I will not leave you nor forsake you. [6]Be firm and steadfast, so that you may give this people possession of the land which I swore to their fathers I would give them. [7]Above all, be firm and steadfast, taking care to observe the entire law which my servant Moses enjoined on you. Do not swerve from it either to the right or to the left, that you may succeed wherever you go. [8]Keep this book of the law on your lips. Recite it by day and by night, that you may observe carefully all that is written in it; then you will successfully attain your goal. [9]I command you: be firm and steadfast! Do not fear nor be dismayed, for the LORD, your God, is with you wherever you go."[c]

1, 4: The ideal frontiers are given: in the south the desert of Sinai, in the north the Lebanon range, in the east the Euphrates, and in the west the Great Sea, the Mediterranean.

a: 3f: Jos 14, 9; Gn 15, 18; Dt 11, 24.   b: Dt 31, 8; Heb 13, 5.   c: 7. 9: Dt 31, 7f.

[10]So Joshua commanded the officers of the people: [11]"Go through the camp and instruct the people, 'Prepare your provisions, for three days from now you shall cross the Jordan here, to march in and take possession of the land which the LORD, your God, is giving you.' "[d]

The Transjordan Tribes. [12]Joshua reminded the Reubenites, the Gadites, and the half-tribe of Manasseh: [13]"Remember what Moses, the servant of the LORD, commanded you when he said, 'The LORD, your God, will permit you to settle in this land.' [14]Your wives, your children, and your livestock shall remain in the land Moses gave you here beyond the Jordan.[e] But all the warriors among you must cross over armed ahead of your kinsmen and you must help them [15]until the LORD has settled your kinsmen, and they like you possess the land which the LORD, your God, is giving them. Afterward you may return and occupy your own land, which Moses, the servant of the LORD, has given you east of the Jordan."[f] [16]"We will do all you have commanded us," they answered Joshua, "and we will go wherever you send us. We will obey you as completely as we obeyed Moses. [17]But may the LORD, your God, be with you as he was with Moses. [18]If anyone rebels against your orders and does not obey every command you give him, he shall be put to death. But be firm and steadfast."

See RG 150

CHAPTER 2

Spies Saved by Rahab. [1]Then Joshua, son of Nun, secretly sent out two spies from Shittim, saying, "Go, reconnoiter the land and Jericho." When the two reached Jericho, they went into the house of a harlot* named Rahab,[g] where they lodged. [2]But a report was brought to the king of Jericho that some Israelites had come there that night to spy out the land. [3]So the king of Jericho sent Rahab the order, "Put out the visitors who have entered your house, for they have come to spy out the entire land." [4]The woman[h] had taken the two men and hidden them, so she said, "True, the men you speak of came to me, but I did not know where they came from. [5]At dark, when it was time for the gate to be shut, they left, and I do not know where they went. You will have to pursue them immediately to overtake them." [6]Now, she had led them to the roof, and hidden them among her stalks of flax spread out* there. [7]But the pursuers set out along the way to the fords of the Jordan, and once they had left, the gate was shut.

[8]Before the spies fell asleep, Rahab* came to them on the roof [9]and said: "I know that the LORD has given you the land, that a dread of you has come upon us, and that all the inhabitants of the land are overcome with fear of you.[i] [10]For we have heard how the LORD dried up the waters of the Red Sea before you when you came out of Egypt,[j] and how you dealt with Sihon and Og, the two kings of the Amorites beyond the Jordan, whom you doomed to destruction. [11]At these reports, we are disheartened; everyone is discouraged because of you, since the LORD, your God, is God in heaven above and on earth below.[k] [12]Now then, swear to me by the LORD that, since I am showing kindness to you, you in turn will show kindness to my family;[l] and give me an unmistakable token [13]that you are to spare my father and mother, brothers and sisters, and all their kin, and save us from death." [14]"We pledge our lives for yours," the men answered her. "If you do not betray this errand of ours, we will be faithful in showing kindness to you when the LORD gives us the land."

[15]Then she let them down through the window with a rope; for she lived in a house built into the city wall.* [16]"Go up into the hill country," she suggested to them, "that your

---

2, 1: Harlot: this is the regular equivalent of the Hebrew word, but perhaps it is used here of Rahab in the broader sense of a woman who kept a public house. Joshua's spies hoped to remain undetected at such an inn.

2, 6: Stalks of flax spread out: to dry in the sun, after they had been soaked in water, according to the ancient process of preparing flax for linen-making. In the Near East the flax harvest occurs near the time of the feast of the Passover (Jos 4, 19; 5, 10); cf Ex 9, 31.

2, 8-11: Rahab's faith and good works are praised in the New Testament; cf Heb 11, 31; Jas 2, 25.

2, 15: A house built into the city wall: such houses, which used the city wall for their own inner walls, have been found at ancient sites. The upper story of Rahab's house was evi-

d: Dt 11, 31. *e:* Nm 32, 26. *f:* Jos 22, 4; Dt 3, 20. *g:* Mt 1, 5; Jas 2, 25. *h:* Jos 6, 17. *i:* Ex 15, 15f; 23, 27. *j:* Jos 4, 23; Ex 14, 21; Nm 21, 23-26. 33ff. *k:* Dt 4, 39. *l:* Jos 2, 18; 6, 23. 25.

pursuers may not find you. Hide there for three days, until they return; then you may proceed on your way." [17]The men answered her, "This is how we will fulfill the oath you made us take: [18]When we come into the land, tie this scarlet cord in the window through which you are letting us down; and gather your father and mother, your brothers and all your family into your house. [19]Should any of them pass outside the doors of your house, he will be responsible for his own death, and we shall be guiltless. But we shall be responsible if anyone in the house with you is harmed. [20]If, however, you betray this errand of ours, we shall be quit of the oath you have made us take." [21]"Let it be as you say," she replied, and bade them farewell. When they were gone, she tied the scarlet cord in the window.

[22]They went up into the hills, where they stayed three days until their pursuers, who had sought them all along the road without finding them, returned. [23]Then the two came back down from the hills, crossed the Jordan to Joshua, son of Nun, and reported all that had befallen them. [24]They assured Joshua, "The LORD has delivered all this land into our power; indeed, all the inhabitants of the land are overcome with fear of us."

<table>
<tr><td>See RG
150</td></tr>
</table>

CHAPTER 3

Preparations for Crossing the Jordan. [1]Early the next morning, Joshua[m] moved with all the Israelites from Shittim to the Jordan, where they lodged before crossing over. [2]Three days later the officers went through the camp [3]and issued these instructions to the people: "When you see the ark of the covenant of the LORD, your God, which the levitical priests will carry, you must also break camp and follow it, [4]that you may know the way to take, for you have not gone over this road before. But let there be a space of two thousand cubits be-

tween you and the ark. Do not come nearer to it." [5]Joshua also said to the people, "Sanctify yourselves, for tomorrow the LORD will perform wonders among you." [6]And he directed the priests to take up the ark of the covenant and go on ahead of the people; and they did so.

[7]Then the LORD said to Joshua, "Today I will begin to exalt you in the sight of all Israel, that they may know I am with you, as I was with Moses.[n] [8]Now command the priests carrying the ark of the covenant to come to a halt in the Jordan when they reach the edge of the waters."

[9]So Joshua said to the Israelites, "Come here and listen to the words of the LORD, your God." [10]He continued: "This is how you will know that there is a living God in your midst, who at your approach will dispossess the Canaanites, Hittites, Hivites, Perizzites, Girgashites, Amorites and Jebusites.[o] [11]The ark of the covenant of the LORD of the whole earth will precede you into the Jordan. [12][Now choose twelve men,[p] one from each of the tribes of Israel.] [13]When the soles of the feet of the priests carrying the ark of the LORD, the Lord of the whole earth, touch the water of the Jordan, it will cease to flow; for the water flowing down from upstream will halt in a solid bank."

The Crossing Begun. [14]The people struck their tents to cross the Jordan, with the priests carrying the ark of the covenant ahead of them. [15]No sooner had these priestly bearers of the ark waded into the waters at the edge of the Jordan, which overflows all its banks during the entire season of the harvest,* [16]than the waters flowing from upstream halted, backing up in a solid mass[q] for a very great distance indeed, from Adam, a city in the direction of Zarethan; while those flowing downstream toward the Salt Sea of the Arabah disappeared entirely.*

dently higher than the city wall. It was through the window of such a house that St. Paul escaped from Damascus; cf Acts 9, 25; 2 Cor 11, 33.

3, 15: Season of the harvest: toward the end of March and the beginning of April, when the grain and other crops that grew during the rainy season of winter were reaped. The crossing took place "on the tenth day of the first month" of the Hebrew year, which began with the first new moon after the spring equinox; cf Jos 4, 19. At this time of the year the Jordan would be swollen as a result of the winter

rains and the melting snow of Mount Hermon.

3, 16: The sudden damming of the river could have been caused by a landslide, as has happened on other occasions. The miraculous character of this event would not thereby be removed because God, who foretold it (Jos 3, 13), also caused it to take place at precisely the right moment (Jos 3, 15), whether or not he used natural forces to accomplish his will.

m: Jos 2, 1.   *n:* Jos 1, 5; 4, 14.   *o:* Ex 33, 2; Dt 7, 1.   *p:* Jos 4, 2. 4.   *q:* Ps 114, 3.

Thus the people crossed over opposite Jericho. [17]While all Israel crossed over on dry ground, the priests carrying the ark of the covenant of the LORD remained motionless on dry ground in the bed of the Jordan[r] until the whole nation had completed the passage.

CHAPTER 4

See RG 150

Memorial Stones. [1]After the entire nation had crossed the Jordan, the LORD said to Joshua, [2]"Choose twelve men[s] from the people, one from each tribe, [3]and instruct them to take up twelve stones from this spot in the bed of the Jordan where the priests have been standing motionless.[t] Carry them over with you, and place them where you are to stay tonight."

[4]Summoning the twelve men whom he had selected from among the Israelites, one from each tribe, [5]Joshua said to them: "Go to the bed of the Jordan in front of the ark of the LORD, your God; lift to your shoulders one stone apiece, so that they will equal in number the tribes of the Israelites. [6]In the future, these are to be a sign among you. When your children ask you what these stones mean to you, [7]you shall answer them, 'The waters of the Jordan ceased to flow before the ark of the covenant of the LORD when it crossed the Jordan.'[u] Thus these stones are to serve as a perpetual memorial to the Israelites." [8]The twelve Israelites did as Joshua had commanded: they took up as many stones from the bed of the Jordan as there were tribes of the Israelites, and carried them along to the camp site, where they placed them, according to the LORD's direction. [9]Joshua also had twelve stones set up in the bed of the Jordan on the spot where the priests stood who were carrying the ark of the covenant. They are there to this day.

[10]*The priests carrying the ark remained in the bed of the Jordan until everything had been done that the LORD had commanded Joshua to tell the people. The people crossed over quickly, [11]and when all had reached the other side, the ark of the LORD, borne by the priests, also crossed to its place in front of them. [12]The Reubenites, Gadites, and half-tribe of Manasseh, armed, marched in the vanguard of the Israelites, as Moses had ordered.[v] [13]About forty thousand troops equipped for battle passed over before the LORD to the plains of Jericho.

[14]That day the LORD exalted Joshua in the sight of all Israel,[w] and thenceforth during his whole life they respected him as they had respected Moses.

[15]Then the LORD said to Joshua, [16]"Command the priests carrying the ark of the commandments to come up from the Jordan."[x] [17]Joshua did so, [18]and when the priests carrying the ark of the covenant of the LORD had come up from the bed of the Jordan, as the soles of their feet regained the dry ground, the waters of the Jordan resumed their course and as before overflowed all its banks.

[19]The people came up from the Jordan on the tenth day of the first month, and camped in Gilgal on the eastern limits of Jericho. [20]At Gilgal Joshua set up the twelve stones which had been taken from the Jordan, [21]saying to the Israelites, "In the future, when the children among you ask their fathers what these stones mean, [22]you shall inform them, 'Israel crossed the Jordan here on dry ground.' [23]For the LORD, your God, dried up the waters of the Jordan in front of you until you crossed over, just as the LORD, your God, had done at the Red Sea, which he dried up in front of us until we crossed over;[y] [24]in order that all the peoples of the earth may learn that the hand of the LORD is mighty, and that you may fear the LORD, your God, forever."

CHAPTER 5

See RG 150-51

Rites at Gilgal. [1]When all the kings of the Amorites to the west of the Jordan and all the kings of the Canaanites by the sea heard that the LORD had dried up the waters of the Jordan before the Israelites until they crossed over, they were disheartened and lost courage at their approach.

4, 10-18: After the digression about the two sets of memorial stones, the author resumes the narrative by briefly repeating the story of the crossing, which he had already told in Jos 3, 14-17.

---

r: Jos 4, 7. 22. *s:* Jos 3, 12. *t:* Jos 3, 13; 4, 8f; Dt 27, 2. *u:* Jos 3, 13. 16. *v:* Dt 3, 18. *w:* Jos 3, 7. *x:* Jos 3, 6. *y:* Ex 14, 21.

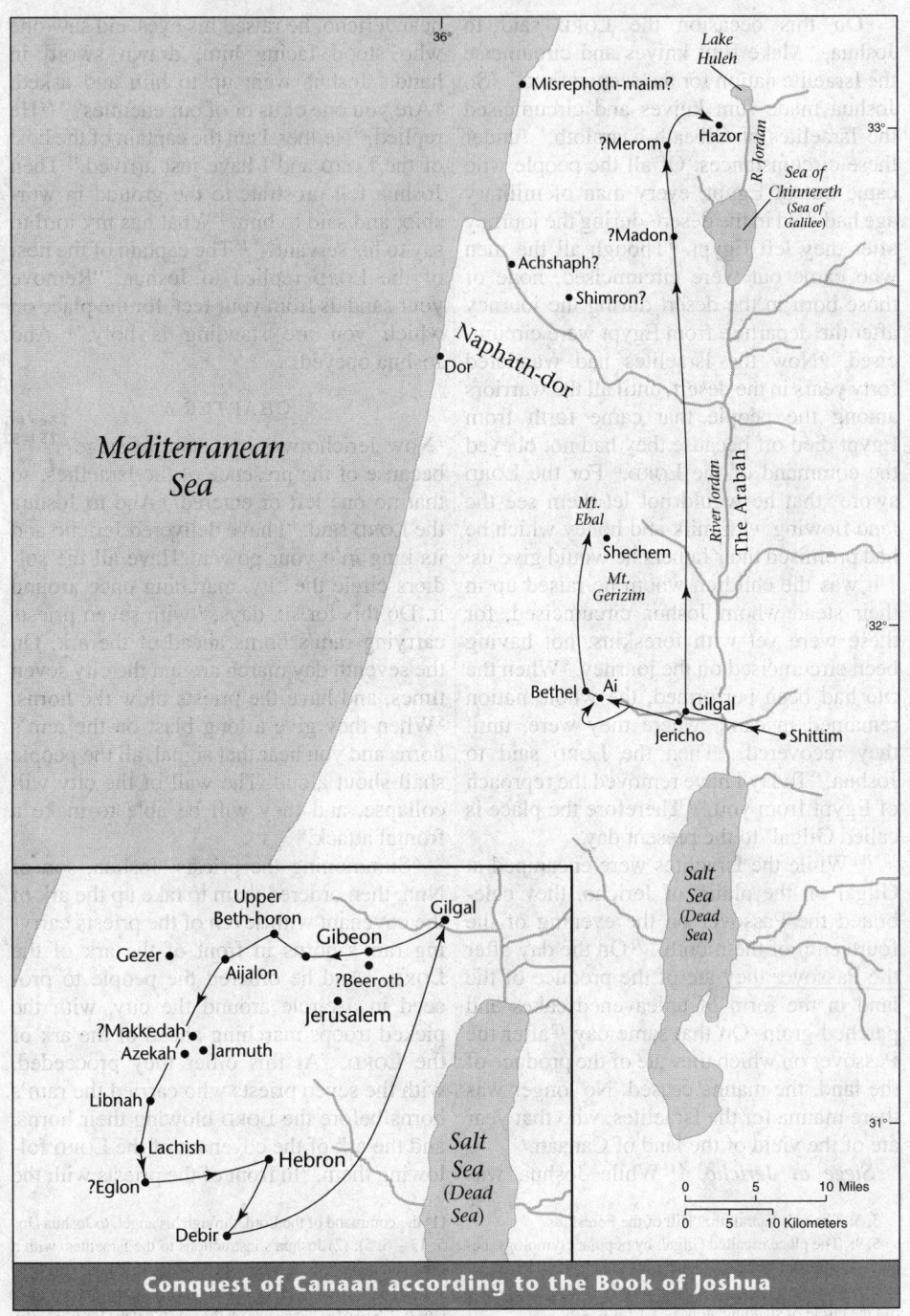

Conquest of Canaan according to the Book of Joshua

**Labels on main map:**

Lake Huleh

Misrephoth-maim?

?Merom

Hazor

R. Jordan

Sea of Chinnereth (Sea of Galilee)

?Madon

Achshaph?

Shimron?

Naphath-dor

Dor

Mediterranean Sea

Mt. Ebal

Shechem

Mt. Gerizim

River Jordan

The Arabah

Bethel

Ai

Gilgal

Jericho

Shittim

Salt Sea (Dead Sea)

**Labels on inset map:**

Upper Beth-horon

Gilgal

Gibeon

Gezer

Aijalon

?Beeroth

?Makkedah

Jerusalem

Azekah

Jarmuth

Libnah

Lachish

Hebron

Salt Sea (Dead Sea)

?Eglon

Debir

0   5   10 Miles

0   5   10 Kilometers

[2]On this occasion the LORD said to Joshua, "Make flint knives and circumcise the Israelite nation for the second time." [3]So Joshua made flint knives and circumcised the Israelites at Gibeath-haaraloth,[*] [4]under these circumstances: Of all the people who came out of Egypt, every man of military age had died in the desert[z] during the journey after they left Egypt. [5]Though all the men who came out were circumcised, none of those born in the desert during the journey after the departure from Egypt were circumcised. [6]Now the Israelites had wandered forty years in the desert, until all the warriors among the people that came forth from Egypt died off because they had not obeyed the command of the LORD.[a] For the LORD swore[b] that he would not let them see the land flowing with milk and honey which he had promised their fathers he would give us. [7c]It was the children whom he raised up in their stead whom Joshua circumcised, for these were yet with foreskins, not having been circumcised on the journey. [8]When the rite had been performed, the whole nation remained in camp where they were, until they recovered. [9]Then the LORD said to Joshua, "Today I have removed the reproach of Egypt from you."[d] Therefore the place is called Gilgal[*] to the present day.

[10e]While the Israelites were encamped at Gilgal on the plains of Jericho, they celebrated the Passover on the evening of the fourteenth of the month.[*] [11]On the day after the Passover they ate of the produce of the land in the form of unleavened cakes and parched grain. On that same day [12]after the Passover on which they ate of the produce of the land, the manna ceased. No longer was there manna for the Israelites, who that year ate of the yield of the land of Canaan.[f]

Siege at Jericho. [13*]While Joshua was near Jericho, he raised his eyes and saw one who stood facing him, drawn sword in hand.[g] Joshua went up to him and asked, "Are you one of us or of our enemies?" [14]He replied, "Neither. I am the captain of the host of the LORD and I have just arrived." Then Joshua fell prostrate to the ground in worship, and said to him, "What has my lord to say to his servant?" [15]The captain of the host of the LORD replied to Joshua, "Remove your sandals from your feet, for the place on which you are standing is holy."[h] And Joshua obeyed.

CHAPTER 6

See RG 151–52

[1]Now Jericho was in a state of siege because of the presence of the Israelites, so that no one left or entered. [2]And to Joshua the LORD said, "I have delivered Jericho and its king into your power. [3]Have all the soldiers circle the city, marching once around it. Do this for six days, [4i]with seven priests carrying ram's horns ahead of the ark. On the seventh day march around the city seven times, and have the priests blow the horns. [5]When they give a long blast on the ram's horns and you hear that signal, all the people shall shout aloud. The wall of the city will collapse, and they will be able to make a frontal attack."

[6]Summoning the priests, Joshua, son of Nun, then ordered them to take up the ark of the covenant with seven of the priests carrying ram's horns in front of the ark of the LORD. [7]And he ordered the people to proceed in a circle around the city, with the picked troops marching ahead of the ark of the LORD. [8]At this order they proceeded, with the seven priests who carried the ram's horns before the LORD blowing their horns, and the ark of the covenant of the LORD following them. [9]In front of the priests with the

---

5, 3: Gibeath-haaraloth: "Hill of the Foreskins."

5, 9: The place is called Gilgal: by popular etymology, because of the similarity of sound with the Hebrew word gallothi, "I have removed." Gilgal probably means "(the place of) the circle of standing stones." Cf Jos 4, 4-8.

5, 10: The month: the first month of the year, later called Nisan; see note on Jos 3, 15. The crossing of the Jordan occurred, therefore, about the same time of the year as did the equally miraculous crossing of the Red Sea; cf Ex 12–14.

5, 13—6, 26: The account of the siege of Jericho embraces:

(1) the command of the Lord, through his angel, to Joshua (Jos 5, 13—6, 5); (2) Joshua's instructions to the Israelites, with a brief summary of how these orders were carried out (Jos 6, 6-11); (3) a description of the action on each of the first six days (Jos 6, 12-14); (4) the events on the seventh day (Jos 6, 15-26).

---

z: Nm 14, 29; 26, 64f; Dt 2, 16; Ps 106, 26; 1 Cor 10, 5. *a:* Nm 14, 29. *b:* Heb 3, 11. 17. *c:* Dt 1, 39. *d:* Jos 4, 19. *e:* Ex 12, 6; Lv 23, 5; Nm 9, 3-5. *f:* Ex 16, 35. *g:* Ex 23, 20. *h:* Ex 3, 5; Acts 7, 33. *i:* Nm 10, 8f.

horns marched the picked troops; the rear guard followed the ark, and the blowing of horns was kept up continually as they marched. [10]But the people had been commanded by Joshua not to shout or make any noise or outcry until he gave the word: only then were they to shout. [11]So he had the ark of the LORD circle the city, going once around it, after which they returned to camp for the night.

[12]Early the next morning, Joshua had the priests take up the ark of the LORD. [13]The seven priests bearing the ram's horns marched in front of the ark of the LORD, blowing their horns. Ahead of these marched the picked troops, while the rear guard followed the ark of the LORD, and the blowing of horns was kept up continually. [14]On this second day they again marched around the city once before returning to camp; and for six days in all they did the same.

[15]On the seventh day, beginning at daybreak, they marched around the city seven times in the same manner; on that day only did they march around the city seven times. [16]The seventh time around, the priests blew the horns and Joshua said to the people, "Now shout, for the LORD has given you the city [17]and everything in it.[j] It is under the LORD's ban. Only the harlot Rahab and all who are in the house with her are to be spared, because she hid the messengers we sent. [18k]But be careful not to take, in your greed, anything that is under the ban;[*] else you will bring upon the camp of Israel this ban and the misery of it. [19]All silver and gold, and the articles of bronze or iron, are sacred to the LORD. They shall be put in the treasury of the LORD."

The Fall of Jericho. [20]As the horns blew, the people began to shout. When they heard the signal horn, they raised a tremendous shout. The wall collapsed,[*] and the people stormed the city in a frontal attack and took it.[l] [21]They observed the ban by putting to the sword all living creatures[m] in the city: men and women, young and old, as well as oxen, sheep and asses.

[22]Joshua directed the two men who had spied out the land, "Go into the harlot's house and bring out the woman with all her kin, as you swore to her you would do."[n] [23]The spies entered and brought out Rahab, with her father, mother, brothers, and all her kin.[o] Her entire family they led forth and placed them outside the camp of Israel. [24]The city itself they burned with all that was in it,[p] except the silver, gold, and articles of bronze and iron, which were placed in the treasury of the house of the LORD. [25*]Because Rahab the harlot had hidden the messengers whom Joshua had sent to reconnoiter Jericho, Joshua spared her with her family and all her kin, who continue in the midst of Israel to this day.

[26q]On that occasion Joshua imposed the oath: Cursed before the LORD be the man who attempts to rebuild this city, Jericho. He shall lose his first-born when he lays its foundation, and he shall lose his youngest son when he sets up its gates.[*]

[27]Thus the LORD was with Joshua so that his fame spread throughout the land.[r]

CHAPTER 7

See RG 151–52

Defeat at Ai. [1]But the Israelites violated the ban; Achan, son of Carmi, son of Zerah, son of Zara of the tribe of Judah, took goods that were under the ban,[s] and the anger of the LORD flared up against the Israelites.

[2]Joshua next sent men from Jericho to Ai, which is near Bethel on its eastern side, with instructions to go up and reconnoiter the land. When they had explored Ai, [3]they re-

---

6, 18: That is under the ban: that is doomed to destruction; see notes on Lv 27, 29; Nm 18, 14; 21, 3.

6, 20: The wall collapsed: by the miraculous intervention of God. The blowing of the horns and the shouting of the people were a customary feature of ancient warfare, here intended by God as a test of the people's obedience and of their faith in his promise; cf Heb 11, 30.

6, 25: From Mt 1, 5, we learn that Rahab married Salmon of the tribe of Judah and thus became the great-great-grandmother of David, Christ's ancestor; cf Ru 4, 18-22.

6, 26: He shall lose his first-born . . . its gates: this curse was fulfilled when Hiel rebuilt Jericho as a fortified city during the reign of Ahab, king of Israel; cf 1 Kgs 16, 34. Till then Jericho was merely an unwalled village; cf Jos 18, 12. 21; Jgs 3, 13; 2 Sm 10, 5.

j: Jos 2, 4; Dt 20, 17; Heb 11, 31.   k: Jos 7, 12. 25; Dt 13, 18.   l: 2 Mc 12, 15; Heb 11, 30.   m: Dt 7, 2.   n: Jos 2, 14.   o: Jos 2, 13; Heb 11, 31.   p: Jos 8, 2.   q: 1 Kgs 16, 34.   r: Jos 1, 5.   s: Jos 6, 18; 22, 20; 1 Chr 2, 7.

turned to Joshua and advised, "Do not send all the people up; if only about two or three thousand go up, they can overcome Ai. The enemy there are few; you need not call for an effort from all the people." ⁴About three thousand of the people made the attack, but they were defeated by those at Ai, ⁵who killed some thirty-six of them. They pressed them back across the clearing in front of the city gate till they broke ranks, and defeated them finally on the descent, so that the confidence of the people melted away like water.

⁶Joshua, together with the elders of Israel, rent his garments and lay prostrate before the ark of the LORD until evening; and they threw dust on their heads. ⁷"Alas, O Lord GOD," Joshua prayed, "why did you ever allow this people to pass over the Jordan, delivering us into the power of the Amorites, that they might destroy us? Would that we had been content to dwell on the other side of the Jordan. ⁸Pray, Lord, what can I say, now that Israel has turned its back to its enemies? ⁹When the Canaanites and the other inhabitants of the land hear of it, they will close in around us and efface our name from the earth. What will you do for your great name?"

¹⁰The LORD replied to Joshua: "Stand up. Why are you lying prostrate? ¹¹Israel has sinned: they have violated the covenant which I enjoined on them. They have stealthily taken goods subject to the ban, and have deceitfully put them in their baggage. ¹²If the Israelites cannot stand up to their enemies, but must turn their back to them, it is because they are under the ban.ᵘ I will not remain with you unless you remove from among you whoever has incurred the ban. ¹³Rise, sanctify the people.ᵛ Tell them to sanctify themselves before tomorrow, for the LORD, the God of Israel, says: You are under the ban, O Israel. You cannot stand up to your enemies until you remove from among you whoever has incurred the ban. ¹⁴In the morning you must present yourselves by tribes. The tribe which the LORD

designates shall come forward by clans; the clan which the LORD designates shall come forward by families; the family which the LORD designates shall come forward one by one. ¹⁵He who is designated as having incurred the ban shall be destroyed by fire, with all that is his, because he has violated the covenant of the LORD and has committed a shameful crime in Israel."

Achan's Guilt and Punishment. ¹⁶Early the next morning Joshua had Israel come forward by tribes, and the tribe of Judah was designated.* ¹⁷Then he had the clans of Judah come forward, and the clan of Zerah was designated. He had the clan of Zerahʷ come forward by families, and Zabdi was designated. ¹⁸Finally he had that family come forward one by one, and Achan, son of Carmi, son of Zabdi, son of Zerah of the tribe of Judah, was designated. ¹⁹Joshua said to Achan, "My son, give to the LORD, the God of Israel, glory and honor by telling me what you have done; do not hide it from me." ²⁰Achan answered Joshua, "I have indeed sinned against the LORD, the God of Israel. This is what I have done: ²¹Among the spoils, I saw a beautiful Babylonian mantle, two hundred shekels of silver, and a bar of gold fifty shekels in weight; in my greed I took them. They are now hidden in the ground inside my tent, with the silver underneath." ²²The messengers whom Joshua sent hastened to the tent and found them hidden there, with the silver underneath. ²³They took them from the tent, brought them to Joshua and all the Israelites, and spread them out before the LORD.

²⁴Then Joshua and all Israel took Achan, son of Zerah, with the silver, the mantle, and the bar of gold, and with his sons and daughters, his ox, his ass and his sheep, his tent, and all his possessions, and led them off to the Valley of Achor. ²⁵Joshua said, "The LORD bring upon you today the misery with which you have afflicted us!"ˣ And all Israel stoned him to death ²⁶and piled a great heap of stones over him, which remains to the present day.ʸ Then the anger of the LORD re-

---

7, 16ff: Was designated: probably by means of the Urim and Thummim; cf 1 Sm 14, 38-42. See note on Ex 28, 30.

t: Jos 6, 17-19.   *u:* Jos 6, 18.   *v:* Jos 3, 5; Lv 20, 7; 1 Sm 16, 5.   *w:* Nm 26, 20.   *x:* Jos 6, 18; 22, 20; 1 Chr 2, 7.   *y:* Jos 8, 29.

lented. That is why the place is called the Valley of Achor* to this day.

CHAPTER 8

See RG 151–52

Capture of Ai. ¹The LORD then said to Joshua, "Do not be afraid or dismayed. Take all the army with you and prepare to attack Ai.ᶻ I have delivered the king of Ai into your power, with his people, city, and land. ²Do to Ai and its king what you did to Jericho and its king; except that you may take its spoil and livestock as booty.ᵃ Set an ambush behind the city." ³So Joshua and all the soldiers prepared to attack Ai. Picking out thirty thousand warriors,* Joshua sent them off by night ⁴with these orders: "See that you ambush the city from the rear, at no great distance; then all of you be on the watch. ⁵The rest of the people and I will come up to the city, and when they make a sortie against us as they did the last time, we will flee from them. ⁶They will keep coming out after us until we have drawn them away from the city, for they will think we are fleeing from them as we did the last time. When this occurs, ⁷rise from ambush and take possession of the city, which the LORD, your God, will deliver into your power. ⁸When you have taken the city, set it afire in obedience to the LORD's command. These are my orders to you." ⁹Then Joshua sent them away. They went to the place of ambush, taking up their position to the west of Ai, toward Bethel. Joshua, however, spent that night in the plain.

¹⁰Early the next morning Joshua mustered the army and went up to Ai at its head, with the elders of Israel. ¹¹When all the troops he led were drawn up in position before the city, they pitched camp north of Ai, on the other side of the ravine. ¹²[He took about five thousand men and set them in ambush between Bethel and Ai, west of the city.] ¹³Thus the people took up their stations, with the main body north of the city and the ambush west of it, and Joshua waited overnight among his troops. ¹⁴The king of Ai saw this, and he and all his army came out very early in the morning to engage Israel in battle at the descent toward the Arabah, not knowing that there was an ambush behind the city. ¹⁵Joshua and the main body of the Israelites fled in seeming defeat toward the desert, ¹⁶till the last of the soldiers in the city had been called out to pursue them. ¹⁷Since they were drawn away from the city, with every man engaged in this pursuit of Joshua and the Israelites, not a soldier remained in Ai [or Bethel], and the city was open and unprotected.

¹⁸Then the LORD directed Joshua, "Stretch out the javelin in your hand toward Ai, for I will deliver it into your power." Joshua stretched out the javelin in his hand toward the city, ¹⁹and as soon as he did so, the men in ambush rose from their post, rushed in, captured the city, and immediately set it on fire. ²⁰By the time the men of Ai looked back, the smoke from the city was already sky-high. Escape in any direction was impossible, because the Israelites retreating toward the desert now turned on their pursuers; ²¹for when Joshua and the main body of Israelites saw that the city had been taken from ambush and was going up in smoke, they struck back at the men of Ai. ²²Since those in the city came out to intercept them, the men of Ai were hemmed in by Israelites on either side, who cut them down without any fugitives or survivorsᵇ ²³except the king, whom they took alive and brought to Joshua.

²⁴All the inhabitants of Ai who had pursued the Israelites into the desert were slain by the sword there in the open, down to the last man. Then all Israel returned and put to the sword those inside the city. ²⁵There fell that day a total of twelve thousand men and

---

7, 26: Achor: "misery, affliction." The reference is to the saying of Joshua in v 25, with an allusion also to the similar-sounding name of Achan.

8, 3: Thirty thousand warriors: this figure of the Hebrew text, which seems extremely high, may be due to a copyist's error; some manuscripts of the Septuagint have "three thousand," which is the number of the whole army in the first, unsuccessful attack (Jos 7, 4); the variant reading in v 12 mentions "five thousand."

z: Jos 2, 24.   *a:* Jos 6, 21. 24; Dt 20, 14.   *b:* Dt 7, 2.

women, the entire population of Ai.
[26c]Joshua kept the javelin in his hand
stretched out until he had fulfilled the doom
on all the inhabitants of Ai. [27]However, the
Israelites took for themselves as booty the
livestock and the spoil of that city, according
to the command of the LORD issued to
Joshua. [28]Then Joshua destroyed the place
by fire, reducing it to an everlasting mound
of ruins, as it remains today.[d] [29]He had the
king of Ai hanged on a tree until evening;[e]
then at sunset Joshua ordered the body removed from the tree and cast at the entrance
of the city gate, where a great heap of stones
was piled up over it, which remains to the
present day.

Altar on Mount Ebal. [30]*Later Joshua
built an altar to the LORD, the God of Israel,
on Mount Ebal, [31]of unhewn stones on
which no iron tool had been used,[f] in keeping with the command to the Israelites of
Moses, the servant of the LORD, as recorded
in the book of the law. On this altar they offered holocausts and peace offerings to the
LORD. [32]There, in the presence of the Israelites, Joshua inscribed upon the stones a
copy of the law written by Moses.[g] [33]And
all Israel, stranger and native alike, with
their elders, officers and judges, stood on
either side of the ark facing the levitical
priests who were carrying the ark of the
covenant of the LORD.[h] Half of them were
facing Mount Gerizim and half Mount
Ebal, thus carrying out the instructions of
Moses, the servant of the LORD, for the
blessing of the people of Israel on this first
occasion. [34i]Then were read aloud all the
words of the law, the blessings and the
curses, exactly as written in the book of the
law. [35j]Every single word that Moses had
commanded, Joshua read aloud to the entire community, including the women and
children, and the strangers who had accompanied Israel.

CHAPTER 9

See RG 151-52

Confederacy against Israel. [1]When
the news reached the kings west of the Jordan, in the mountain regions and in the
foothills, and all along the coast of the Great
Sea as far as Lebanon: Hittites, Amorites,
Canaanites, Perizzites, Hivites and Jebusites,[k]
[2]they all formed an alliance to launch a common attack against Joshua and Israel.

The Gibeonite Deception. [3]On learning
what Joshua had done to Jericho and Ai, the
inhabitants of Gibeon[l] [4]put into effect a device of their own. They chose provisions for
a journey, making use of old sacks for their
asses, and old wineskins, torn and mended.
[5]They wore old, patched sandals and shabby
garments; and all the bread they took was
dry and crumbly. [6]Thus they journeyed to
Joshua in the camp at Gilgal, where they
said to him and to the men of Israel, "We
have come from a distant land to propose
that you make an alliance with us."[m] [7]But the
men of Israel replied to the Hivites,* "You
may be living in land that is ours. How, then,
can we make an alliance with you?" [8]But
they answered Joshua, "We are your servants." Then Joshua asked them, "Who are
you? Where do you come from?" [9]They answered him, "Your servants have come from
a far-off land, because of the fame of the
LORD, your God. For we have heard reports
of all that he did in Egypt[n] [10]and all that he
did to the two kings of the Amorites beyond
the Jordan,[o] Sihon, king of Heshbon, and
Og, king of Bashan, who lived in Ashtaroth.
[11]So our elders and all the inhabitants of our
country said to us, 'Take along provisions
for the journey and go to meet them. Say to
them: We are your servants; we propose that
you make an alliance with us.' [12]This bread
of ours was still warm when we brought it
from home as provisions the day we left to
come to you, but now it is dry and crumbled.

8, 30-35: These ceremonies were prescribed in Dt 11, 29, and Dt 27, 2-26. See notes on those passages.

9, 7: The Hivites: apparently the Gibeonites belonged to this larger ethnic group (cf also Jos 11, 19), although in 2 Sm 21, 2 they are classed as Amorites; both groups are listed among the seven nations in Canaan whom the Israelites were to exter-minate; cf Dt 7, 1f.

---

c: Ex 17, 11ff. d: Dt 13, 16. e: Jos 10, 26f; Dt 21, 22f; Jn 19, 31. f: Ex 20, 24f; Dt 27, 5f. g: Dt 27, 2. 8. h: Jos 3, 3; Dt 11, 27; 27, 12; 31, 9. 12. i: Dt 28, 2-68; 30, 19; 31, 11; Neh 8, 2f. j: Dt 31, 12. k: Jos 3, 10; Ex 3, 8. 17; 23, 23; Dt 1, 7. l: Jos 6, 21. 24; 11, 19. m: Ex 23, 32; Dt 7, 2. n: Jos 2, 10. o: Nm 21, 25. 33.

[13]Here are our wineskins, which were new when we filled them, but now they are torn. Look at our garments and sandals, which are worn out from the very long journey." [14]Then the Israelite princes partook of their provisions, without seeking the advice of the LORD.[p] [15]So Joshua made an alliance with them and entered into an agreement to spare them,[q] which the princes of the community sealed with an oath.

Gibeonites Made Vassals. [16]Three days after the agreement was entered into, the Israelites learned that these people were from nearby, and would be living in Israel. [17]The third day on the road, the Israelites came to their cities of Gibeon, Chephirah, Beeroth and Kiriath-jearim, [18]but did not attack them, because the princes of the community had sworn to them by the LORD, the God of Israel. When the entire community grumbled against the princes, [19]these all remonstrated with the people, "We have sworn to them by the LORD, the God of Israel, and so we cannot harm them. [20]Let us therefore spare their lives and so deal with them that we shall not be punished for the oath we have sworn to them." [21]Thus the princes recommended that they be let live, as hewers of wood and drawers of water* for the entire community; and the community did as the princes advised them.

[22]Joshua summoned the Gibeonites and said to them, "Why did you lie to us and say that you lived at a great distance from us, when you will be living in our very midst? [23]For this are you accursed: every one of you shall always be a slave [hewers of wood and drawers of water] for the house of my God." [24]They answered Joshua, "Your servants were fully informed of how the LORD, your God, commanded his servant Moses that you be given the entire land and that all its inhabitants be destroyed before you. Since, therefore, at your advance, we were in great

fear for our lives, we acted as we did.[r] [25]And now that we are in your power, do with us what you think fit and right." [26]*Joshua did what he had decided: while he saved them from being killed by the Israelites, [27]at the same time he made them, as they still are, hewers of wood and drawers of water for the community and for the altar of the LORD, in the place of the LORD's choice.[s]

CHAPTER 10

See RG 151–52

The Siege of Gibeon. [1]Now Adonizedek, king of Jerusalem, heard that, in the capture and destruction of Ai, Joshua had done to that city and its king as he had done to Jericho and its king.[t] He heard also that the inhabitants of Gibeon had made their peace with Israel, remaining among them, [2]and that there was great fear abroad, because Gibeon was large enough for a royal city, larger even than the city of Ai, and all its men were brave. [3]So Adonizedek, king of Jerusalem, sent for Hoham, king of Hebron, Piram, king of Jarmuth, Japhia, king of Lachish, and Debir, king of Eglon, [4]to come to his aid for an attack on Gibeon, since it had concluded peace with Joshua and the Israelites.[u] [5]The five Amorite kings, of Jerusalem, Hebron, Jarmuth, Lachish and Eglon,* united all their forces and marched against Gibeon, where they took up siege positions. [6]Thereupon, the men of Gibeon sent an appeal to Joshua in his camp at Gilgal: "Do not abandon your servants. Come up here quickly and save us. Help us, because all the Amorite kings of the mountain country have joined forces against us."[v]

Joshua's Victory. [7]So Joshua marched up from Gilgal with his picked troops and the rest of his soldiers. [8]Meanwhile the LORD said to Joshua, "Do not fear them, for I have delivered them into your power. Not one of them will be able to withstand you." [9]And when Joshua made his surprise attack upon

---

9, 21: Hewers of wood and drawers of water: proverbial terms for the lowest social class in the Israelite community; cf Dt 29, 10f.

9, 26f: Later on, Saul violated the immunity of the Gibeonites, but David vindicated it; cf 2 Sm 21, 1-9.

10, 5: Hebron . . . Eglon: these four cities were to the south and southwest of Jerusalem.

---

p: Nm 27, 21.   *q:* Jos 11, 19; 2 Sm 21, 2.   *r:* Ex 23, 27f; Dt 7, 1f.   *s:* Dt 12, 5.   *t:* Jos 9, 15; 6, 21. 24; 8, 26-29.   *u:* Jos 9, 15.   *v:* Jos 9, 6.

them after an all-night march from Gilgal, [10]the LORD threw them into disorder before him. The Israelites inflicted a great slaughter on them at Gibeon and pursued them down the Beth-horon slope, harassing them as far as Azekah and Makkedah.

[11]While they fled before Israel along the descent from Beth-horon, the LORD hurled great stones from the sky* above them all the way to Azekah, killing many.[w] More died from these hailstones than the Israelites slew with the sword. [12]On this day, when the LORD delivered up the Amorites to the Israelites,

Joshua prayed to the LORD,
and said in the presence of Israel:
Stand still, O sun, at Gibeon,
O moon, in the valley of Aijalon!
[13] And the sun stood still,
and the moon stayed,
while the nation took vengeance on its
foes.[x]

Is this not recorded* in the Book of Jashar? The sun halted in the middle of the sky; not for a whole day did it resume its swift course. [14]Never before or since was there a day like this, when the LORD obeyed the voice of a man; for the LORD fought for Israel. [15][Then Joshua and all Israel returned to the camp at Gilgal.]

Execution of Amorite Kings. [16]Meanwhile the five kings who had fled, hid in a cave at Makkedah. [17]When Joshua was told that the five kings had been discovered hiding in a cave at Makkedah, [18]he said, "Roll large stones to the mouth of the cave and post men over it to guard them. [19]But do not remain there yourselves. Pursue your enemies, and harry them in the rear. Do not allow them to escape to their cities, for the LORD, your God, has delivered them into your power."

[20]Once Joshua and the Israelites had finally inflicted the last blows in this very great slaughter, and the survivors had escaped from them into the fortified cities, [21]all the army returned safely to Joshua and the camp at Makkedah, no man uttering a sound against the Israelites. [22]Then Joshua said, "Open the mouth of the cave and bring out those five kings to me." [23]Obediently, they brought out to him from the cave five kings, of Jerusalem, Hebron, Jarmuth, Lachish and Eglon. [24]When they had done so, Joshua summoned all the men of Israel and said to the commanders of the soldiers who had marched with him, "Come forward and put your feet on the necks of these kings." They came forward and put their feet upon their necks. [25]Then Joshua said to them, "Do not be afraid or dismayed, be firm and steadfast. This is what the LORD will do to all the enemies against whom you fight." [26y]Thereupon Joshua struck and killed them, and hanged them on five trees, where they remained hanging until evening. [27]At sunset they were removed from the trees at the command of Joshua and cast into the cave where they had hidden; over the mouth of the cave large stones were placed, which remain until this very day.

Conquest of Southern Canaan. [28z]Makkedah, too, Joshua captured and put to the sword at that time. He fulfilled the doom on the city, on its king, and on every person in it, leaving no survivors. Thus he did to the king of Makkedah what he had done to the king of Jericho. [29]Joshua then passed on with all Israel from Makkedah to Libnah, which he attacked. [30]Libnah also, with its king, the LORD delivered into the power of Israel. He put it to the sword with every person there, leaving no survivors. Thus he did to its king what he had done to the king of Jericho. [31]Joshua next passed on with all Is-

---

10, 11: Great stones from the sky: the hailstones mentioned in the next sentence.

10, 13: Is this not recorded: the reference is to the preceding, poetic passage. Evidently the Book of Jashar, like the Book of the Wars of the Lord (Nm 21, 14), recounted in epic style the exploits of Israel's early heroes. The sun halted: though it is widely supposed that this passage describes in popular language and according to external appearances a miraculous lengthening of the day, it is equally probable that

Joshua's prayer was rather for an abrupt obscuration of the sun, which would impede his enemies in their flight homeward and also prevent them from rallying their forces; this request would have been answered by the hailstorm (cf Sir 46, 5) and by a darkness relieved only twenty-four hours later, well into the next day.

---

w: Jb 38, 22. x: Sir 46, 4; Is 28, 21; Heb 3, 11. y: 26f: Jos 8, 29; Dt 21, 22f. z: Jos 6, 21.

rael from Libnah to Lachish, where they set up a camp during the attack. [32]The LORD delivered Lachish into the power of Israel, so that on the second day Joshua captured it and put it to the sword with every person in it, just as he had done to Libnah. [33]At that time Horam, king of Gezer, came up to help Lachish, but Joshua defeated him and his people, leaving him no survivors. [34]From Lachish, Joshua passed on with all Israel to Eglon; encamping near it, they attacked it [35]and captured it the same day, putting it to the sword. He fulfilled the doom that day on every person in it, just as he had done at Lachish. [36]From Eglon, Joshua went up with all Israel to Hebron, which they attacked [37]and captured. They put it to the sword with its king, all its towns, and every person there, leaving no survivors, just as Joshua had done to Eglon. He fulfilled the doom on it and on every person there. [38]Then Joshua and all Israel turned back to Debir and attacked it, [39]capturing it with its king and all its towns. They put them to the sword and fulfilled the doom on every person there, leaving no survivors. Thus was done to Debir and its king what had been done to Hebron, as well as to Libnah and its king.

[40a]Joshua conquered the entire country; the mountain regions, the Negeb, the foothills, and the mountain slopes, with all their kings. He left no survivors, but fulfilled the doom on all who lived there, just as the LORD, the God of Israel, had commanded. [41]Joshua conquered from Kadesh-barnea to Gaza, and all the land of Goshen* to Gibeon. [42]All these kings and their lands Joshua captured in a single campaign, for the LORD, the God of Israel, fought for Israel. [43]Thereupon Joshua with all Israel returned to the camp at Gilgal.

CHAPTER 11

See RG 151-52

Northern Confederacy. [1]When Jabin, king of Hazor,* learned of this, he sent a message to Jobab, king of Madon, to the king of Shimron, to the king of Achshaph, [2]and to the northern kings in the mountain regions and in the Arabah near Chinneroth, in the foothills, and in Naphath-dor to the west.[b] [3]These were Canaanites to the east and west, Amorites, Hittites, Perizzites and Jebusites in the mountain regions, and Hivites at the foot of Hermon in the land of Mizpah. [4]They came out with all their troops, an army numerous as the sands on the seashore, and with a multitude of horses and chariots. [5]All these kings joined forces and marched to the waters of Merom,* where they encamped together to fight against Israel.

[6]The LORD said to Joshua, "Do not fear them, for by this time tomorrow I will stretch them slain before Israel. You must hamstring their horses and burn their chariots." [7]Joshua with his whole army came upon them at the waters of Merom in a surprise attack. [8]The LORD delivered them into the power of the Israelites, who defeated them and pursued them to Greater Sidon, to Misrephoth-maim,[c] and eastward to the valley of Mizpeh. They struck them all down, leaving no survivors. [9]Joshua did to them as the LORD had commanded: he hamstrung their horses and burned their chariots.

Conquest of Northern Canaan. [10]At that time Joshua, turning back, captured Hazor and slew its king with the sword; for Hazor formerly was the chief of all those kingdoms. [11]He also fulfilled the doom by putting every person there to the sword, till none was left alive. Hazor itself he burned. [12]Joshua thus captured all those kings with their cities and put them to the sword, fulfilling the doom on them, as Moses, the servant of the LORD, had commanded.[d] [13]However, Israel did not destroy by fire any of the cities built on raised sites, except Hazor,

---

10, 41: Goshen: a town and its surrounding district at the southern end of the Judean mountains (cf Jos 11, 16; 15, 51); not to be confused with the land of Goshen in northeastern Egypt (Gen 45, 10), although in the current Hebrew Bible both names are spelled the same.

11, 1ff: Hazor, Madon, Shimron, and Chinneroth: cities and their surrounding districts in eastern Galilee. Achshaph and Naphath-dor: southwest of Galilee. The mountain regions: in central and northern Galilee.

11, 5: The waters of Merom: a stream in central Galilee that flows southeast to water the fertile Arabah, or plain of Chinneroth on the western shore of the lake of Gennesaret.

a: Dt 20, 16f. *b:* Jos 12, 3; Jgs 1, 27. *c:* Jos 13, 6. *d:* Dt 7, 2; 20, 16f.

which Joshua burned. *14*The Israelites took all the spoil and livestock of these cities as their booty; but the people they put to the sword, until they had exterminated the last of them, leaving none alive. *15*As the LORD had commanded his servant Moses, so Moses commanded Joshua, and Joshua acted accordingly.*e* He left nothing undone that the LORD had commanded Moses should be done.

Survey of the Conquest. *16*So Joshua captured all this land: the mountain regions, the entire Negeb, all the land of Goshen, the foothills, the Arabah, as well as the mountain regions and foothills of Israel,*f* *17*from Mount Halak that rises toward Seir*g* as far as Baal-gad in the Lebanon valley at the foot of Mount Hermon. All their kings he captured and put to death. *18*Joshua waged war against all these kings for a long time. *19*With the exception of the Hivites who lived in Gibeon, no city made peace with the Israelites; all were taken in battle.*h* *20*For it was the design of the LORD to encourage them to wage war against Israel, that they might be doomed to destruction and thus receive no mercy, but be exterminated, as the LORD had commanded Moses.*i*

21*At that time Joshua penetrated the mountain regions and exterminated the Anakim in Hebron,*j* Debir, Anab, the entire mountain region of Judah, and the entire mountain region of Israel. Joshua fulfilled the doom on them and on their cities, *22*so that no Anakim were left in the land of the Israelites. However, some survived in Gaza, in Gath, and in Ashdod. *23k*Thus Joshua captured the whole country, just as the LORD had foretold to Moses. Joshua gave it to Israel as their heritage, apportioning it among the tribes. And the land enjoyed peace.*

CHAPTER 12*

See RG 152-53

Lists of Conquered Kings. *1*The kings of the land east of the Jordan, from the River Arnon to Mount Hermon, including all the eastern section of the Arabah, whom the Israelites conquered and whose lands they occupied, were: *2*First, Sihon, king of the Amorites, who lived in Heshbon. His domain extended from Aroer, which is on the bank of the Wadi Arnon, to include the wadi itself, and the land northward through half of Gilead to the Wadi Jabbok, *3*as well as the Arabah from the eastern side of the Sea of Chinnereth, as far south as the eastern side of the Salt Sea of the Arabah in the direction of Beth-jeshimoth,*m* to a point under the slopes of Pisgah. *4*Secondly, Og, king of Bashan, a survivor of the Rephaim, who lived at Ashtaroth and Edrei.*n* *5*He ruled over Mount Hermon, Salecah, and all Bashan as far as the boundary of the Geshurites and Maacathites, and over half of Gilead as far as the territory of Sihon, king of Heshbon. *6*After Moses, the servant of the LORD, and the Israelites conquered them, he assigned their land to the Reubenites, the Gadites, and the half-tribe of Manasseh, as their property.*o*

*7*This is a list of the kings whom Joshua and the Israelites conquered west of the Jordan and whose land, from Baal-gad in the Lebanon valley to Mount Halak which rises toward Seir, Joshua apportioned to the tribes of Israel. *8*It included the mountain regions and foothills, the Arabah, the slopes, the desert, and the Negeb, belonging to the Hittites, Amorites, Canaanites, Perizzites, Hivites and Jebusites. *9*They were the kings of Jericho,*p* Ai (which is near Bethel), *10*Jerusalem, Hebron, *11*Jarmuth, Lachish,*q* *12*Eglon, Gezer,*r* *13*Debir, Geder,*s* *14*Hormah, Arad, *15*Libnah, Adullam,*t* *16*Makkedah,

---

11, 21ff: Most of the land assigned to the tribe of Judah was not conquered by it till the early period of the Judges. See note on Jgs 1, 1-36.

11, 23: The land enjoyed peace: of a limited and temporary nature. Many of the individual tribes had still to fight against the remaining Canaanites; cf Jos 15, 13-17; 17, 12f. This verse forms the conclusion to the first part of the book. Cf note on Jos 12, 1-24.

12, 1-24: This chapter, inserted between the two principal parts of the book (chapters 1-11 and 13-21), resembles the

lists of conquered cities which are inscribed on monuments of the Egyptian and Assyrian monarchs. Perhaps it was copied here from some such public Israelite record.

e: Dt 7, 2. *f:* Jos 10, 41; 12, 8. *g:* Jos 12, 7; Dt 7, 24. *h:* Jos 9, 3. 7. 15. *i:* Dt 2, 30; 20, 16f. *j:* Jos 15, 13f; Nm 13, 22; Dt 1, 28. *k:* Jos 14, 1-19, 51; Nm 34, 2-12. *l:* 2-5: Nm 21, 21-26. 33ff. *m:* Jos 13, 20. *n:* Jos 13, 11f. *o:* Nm 32, 33; Dt 3, 12f. *p:* Jos 6, 2; 8, 23. *q:* 10f: Jos 10, 23. *r:* Jos 10, 23. 33. *s:* Jos 10, 38f; 15, 36. *t:* Jos 10, 29f; 15, 35.

Bethel,*u* *17*Tappuah, Hepher,*v* *18*Aphek, La-
sharon,*w* *19*Madon, Hazor,*x* *20*Shimron,
Achshaph,*y* *21*Taanach, Megiddo,*z* *22*Kedesh,
Jokneam (at Carmel),*a* *23*and Dor (in
Naphath-dor), the foreign king at Gilgal,*b*
*24*and the king of Tirzah, thirty-one kings in
all.

II: Division of the Land

CHAPTER 13

See RG
152-53 *Division of Land Commanded.*
*1*When Joshua was old and advanced in
years, the LORD said to him:*c* "Though now
you are old and advanced in years, a very
large part of the land still remains to be conquered. *2*This additional land includes all
Geshur* and all the districts of the Philistines
3(from the stream adjoining Egypt to the
boundary of Ekron in the north is reckoned
Canaanite territory, though held by the five
lords of the Philistines in Gaza, Ashdod,
Ashkelon, Gath and Ekron); also where the
Avvim are in the south;*d* *4*all the land of the
Canaanites from Mearah of the Sidonians to
Aphek, and the boundaries of the Amorites;
*5*and the Gebalite territory; and all the Lebanon on the east, from Baal-gad at the foot of
Mount Hermon to Labo in the land of Hamath. *6*At the advance of the Israelites I will
drive out all the Sidonian inhabitants of the
mountain regions between Lebanon and
Misrephoth-maim;*e* at least include these areas in the division of the Israelite heritage,
just as I have commanded you. *7*Now, therefore, apportion among the nine tribes and the
half-tribe of Manasseh the land which is to
be their heritage."

The Eastern Tribes. *8f* Now the other half
of the tribe of Manasseh, as well as the Reubenites and Gadites, had received their heritage which Moses, the servant of the LORD,
had given them east of the Jordan: *9*from
Aroer on the bank of the Wadi Arnon and the

city in the wadi itself, through the tableland
of Medeba and Dibon, *10*with the rest of the
cities of Sihon, king of the Amorites, who
reigned in Heshbon, to the boundary of the
Ammonites; *11*also Gilead and the territory
of the Geshurites and Maacathites, all
Mount Hermon, and all Bashan as far as Salecah, *12*the entire kingdom in Bashan of Og,
a survivor of the Rephaim, who reigned at
Ashtaroth and Edrei. Though Moses conquered and occupied these territories, *13*the
Israelites did not dislodge the Geshurites
and Maacathites, so that Geshur and Maa-
cath survive in the midst of Israel to this day.
*14g*However, to the tribe of Levi Moses assigned no heritage since, as the LORD had
promised them, the LORD, the God of Israel,
is their heritage.

Reuben. *15h*What Moses gave to the Reubenite clans:*i* *16*Their territory reached from
Aroer, on the bank of the Wadi Arnon, and
the city in the wadi itself, through the tableland about Medeba, *17*to include Heshbon
and all its towns which are on the tableland,
Dibon, Bamoth-baal, Beth-baal-meon, *18*Jahaz, Kedemoth, Mephaath, *19*Kiriathaim,
Sibmah, Zereth-shahar on the knoll within
the valley, *20*Beth-peor, the slopes of Pisgah,
Beth-jeshimoth, *21*and the other cities of the
tableland and, generally, of the kingdom of
Sihon. This Amorite king, who reigned in
Heshbon, Moses had killed, with his vassals, the princes of Midian, who were settled in the land: Evi, Rekem, Zur, Hur and
Reba;*j* *22*and among their slain followers the
Israelites put to the sword also the soothsayer Balaam, son of Beor.*k* *23*The boundary
of the Reubenites was the bank of the Jordan. These cities and their villages were the
heritage of the clans of the Reubenites.

Gad. *24*What Moses gave to the Gadite
clans: *25*Their territory included Jazer, all the
cities of Gilead, and half the land of the Ammonites as far as Aroer, toward Rabbah

---

13, 2: Geshur: not to be confused with the large Aramaean district of the same name in Bashan (vv 11-13; Dt 3, 14); here
it is a region to the south of the Philistine country, since vv 2-5 list the unconquered lands along the coast from south to north;
cf also 1 Sm 27, 8.

u: Jos 8, 17; 10, 28. *v:* Jos 15, 34. *w:* Jos 15, 53. *x:* Jos 11, 1. 10. *y:* Jos 11, 1. *z:* Jos 17, 11. *a:* Jos 19, 37. *b:* Jos 11, 2.
c: Jos 23, 1. *d:* Jgs 3, 3. *e:* Jos 11, 8. *f:* Jos 12, 6; Nm 32, 33. *g:* Jos 14, 3f; Nm 18, 20-24. *h:* 15-31; Dt 3, 12-17. *i:* 15-23;
Nm 21, 25-31; 32, 37f. *j:* Nm 21, 24; 31, 8; Dt 3, 10. *k:* Nm 31, 8. *l:* 24-28; Nm 32, 34ff.

26(that is, from Heshbon to Ramath-mizpeh and Betonim, and from Mahanaim to the boundary of Lodebar); 27and in the Jordan valley: Beth-haram, Beth-nimrah, Succoth, Zaphon, the other part of the kingdom of Sihon, king of Heshbon, with the bank of the Jordan to the southeastern tip of the Sea of Chinnereth. 28These cities and their villages were the heritage of the clans of the Gadites.

Manasseh. 29mWhat Moses gave to the clans of the half-tribe of Manasseh: 30Their territory included Mahanaim, all of Bashan, the entire kingdom of Og, king of Bashan, and all the villages of Jair, which are sixty cities in Bashan.n 31Half of Gilead, with Ashtaroth and Edrei, once the royal cities of Og in Bashan, fell to the descendants of Machir, son of Manasseh, for half the clans descended from Machir.

32These are the portions which Moses gave when he was in the plains of Moab, beyond the Jordan east of Jericho. 33However, Moses gave no heritage to the tribe of Levi, since the LORD himself, the God of Israel, is their heritage, as he promised.o

CHAPTER 14

See RG 152–53

The Western Tribes. 1Here follow the portions which the Israelites received in the land of Canaan.p Eleazar the priest, Joshua, son of Nun, and the heads of families in the tribes of the Israelites determined 2their heritage by lot, in accordance with the instructions the LORD had given through Moses concerning the remaining nine and a half tribes.q 3For to two and a half tribes Moses had already given a heritage beyond the Jordan; and though the Levites were given no heritage among the tribes,r 4the descendants of Joseph formed two tribes, Manasseh and Ephraim. The Levites themselves received no share of the land except cities to live in, with their pasture lands for the cattle and flocks.s

5Thus, in apportioning the land, did the Israelites carry out the instructions of the LORD to Moses.

Caleb's Portion. 6tWhen the Judahites came up to Joshua in Gilgal, the Kenizzite Caleb, son of Jephunneh, said to him: "You know what the LORD said to the man of God, Moses, about you and me in Kadesh-barnea. 7uI was forty years old when the servant of the LORD, Moses, sent me from Kadesh-barnea to reconnoiter the land; and I brought back to him a conscientious report. 8vMy fellow scouts who went up with me discouraged the people, but I was completely loyal to the LORD, my God. 9On that occasion Moses swore this oath, 'The land where you have set foot shall become your heritage and that of your descendants forever, because you have been completely loyal to the LORD, my God.' 10Now, as he promised, the LORD has preserved me while Israel was journeying through the desert, for the forty-five years since the LORD spoke thus to Moses; and although I am now eighty-five years old,w 11I am still as strong today as I was the day Moses sent me forth, with no less vigor whether for war or for ordinary tasks.x 12Give me, therefore, this mountain region which the LORD promised me that day, as you yourself heard. True, the Anakim are there, with large fortified cities, but if the LORD is with me I shall be able to drive them out, as the LORD promised."y 13Joshua blessed Caleb, son of Jephunneh, and gave him Hebron as his heritage.z 14Therefore Hebron remains the heritage of the Kenizzite Caleb, son of Jephunneh, to the present day, because he was completely loyal to the LORD, the God of Israel. 15Hebron was formerly called Kiriath-arba, for Arba, the greatest among the Anakim.a And the land enjoyed peace.

CHAPTER 15

See RG 152–53

Boundaries of Judah. 1The lot for the clans of the Judahite tribe fell in the extreme south toward the boundary of Edom, the desert of Zin in the Negeb.b 2cThe boundary there ran from the bay that forms the southern end of the Salt Sea, 3southward below

m: 29-31: Nm 32, 39ff.   n: Nm 32, 41.   o: Jos 18, 7; Nm 18, 20.   p: Jos 17, 4; 21, 1; Nm 34, 17f.   q: Nm 26, 55; 33, 54; 34, 13. r: Jos 13, 8. 14. 33.   s: Jos 21, 3-40; Gn 48, 5.   t: Nm 14, 24. 30; 32, 12; Dt 1, 36. 38.   u: Nm 14, 6-9.   v: Nm 13, 31ff; 14, 24; 32, 12; Dt 1, 36.   w: Nm 14, 30.   x: Sir 46, 1ff.   y: Jos 11, 21.   z: Jos 10, 36f; 15, 13-19; 21, 11f.   a: Jgs 1, 10.   b: Nm 34, 3.   c: 2-4: Nm 34, 3ff.

the pass of Akrabbim, across through Zin, up to a point south of Kadesh-barnea, across to Hezron, and up to Addar; from there, looping around Karka, [4]it crossed to Azmon and then joined the Wadi of Egypt before coming out at the sea. [This is your southern boundary.] [5]The eastern boundary was the Salt Sea as far as the mouth of the Jordan.

[6d]The northern boundary climbed from the bay where the Jordan meets the sea, up to Beth-hoglah, and ran north of Beth-arabah, up to Eben-Bohan-ben-Reuben. [7]Thence it climbed to Debir, north of the vale of Achor,[e] in the direction of the Gilgal that faces the pass of Adummim, on the south side of the wadi; from there it crossed to the waters of En-shemesh and emerged at En-rogel. [8]Climbing again to the Valley of Ben-Hinnom* on the southern flank of the Jebusites [that is, Jerusalem], the boundary rose to the top of the mountain at the northern end of the Valley of Rephaim,[f] which bounds the Valley of Hinnom on the west. [9]From the top of the mountain it ran to the fountain of waters of Nephtoah,[g] extended to the cities of Mount Ephron, and continued to Baalah, or Kiriath-jearim. [10]From Baalah the boundary curved westward to Mount Seir and passed north of the ridge of Mount Jearim (that is, Chesalon); thence it descended to Beth-shemesh, and ran across to Timnah. [11]It then extended along the northern flank of Ekron, continued through Shikkeron, and across to Mount Baalah, thence to include Jabneel, before it came out at the sea. [12]The western boundary was the Great Sea and its coast. This was the complete boundary of the clans of the Judahites.

Conquest by Caleb. [13h]As the LORD had commanded, Joshua gave Caleb, son of Jephunneh,[i] a portion among the Judahites, namely, Kiriath-arba (Arba was the father of Anak), that is, Hebron. [14j]And Caleb drove out from there the three Anakim, the descendants of Anak: Sheshai, Ahiman and Talmai. [15]From there he marched up against the inhabitants of Debir,[k] which was formerly called Kiriath-sepher. [16]Caleb said, "I will give my daughter Achsah in marriage to the one who attacks Kiriath-sepher and captures it." [17*]Othniel, son of Caleb's brother Kenaz, captured it, and so Caleb gave him his daughter Achsah in marriage. [18]On the day of her marriage to Othniel, she induced him to ask her father for some land. Then, as she alighted from the ass, Caleb asked her, "What is troubling you?" [19]She answered, "Give me an additional gift! Since you have assigned to me land in the Negeb, give me also pools of water." So he gave her the upper and the lower pools.

Cities of Judah. [20*]This is the heritage of the clans of the tribe of Judahites: [21]The cities of the tribe of the Judahites in the extreme southern district toward Edom were: Kabzeel, Eder, Jagur, [22]Kinah, Dimonah, Adadah, [23]Kedesh, Hazor and Ithnan; [24]Ziph, Telem, Bealoth, [25]Hazor-hadattah, and Kerioth-hezron (that is, Hazor); [26]Amam, Shema, Moladah, [27]Hazar-gaddah, Heshmon, Beth-pelet, [28]Hazar-shual, Beersheba, and Biziothiah, [29]Baalah, Iim, Ezem, [30]Eltolad, Chesil, Hormah, [31]Ziklag,[l] Madmannah, Sansannah, [32]Lebaoth, Shilhim and En-rimmon; a total of twenty-nine cities with their villages.

[33]In the foothills:* Eshtaol, Zorah, Ashnah, [34]Zanoah, Engannim, Tappuah, Enam, [35]Jarmuth, Adullam, Socoh, Azekah, [36]Shaaraim, Adithaim, Gederah, and Gederothaim; fourteen cities and their villages. [37]Zenan, Hadashah, Migdal-gad, [38]Dilean, Mizpeh, Joktheel, [39]Lachish, Bozkath, Eglon, [40]Cabbon, Lahmam, Chitlish, [41]Gede-

15, 8: The Valley of Ben-hinnom: the southern limit of Jerusalem. Ben-hinnom means "son of Hinnom." The place was also called Valley of Hinnom, in Hebrew ge-hinnom, whence the word "Gehenna" is derived.

15, 17-19: The story of Othniel is told again in Jgs 1, 13-15; cf also Jgs 3, 9-11.

15, 20-62: This elaborate list of the cities of Judah was probably taken from a document made originally for administrative purposes; the cities are divided into four provincial districts, some of which have further subdivisions. For simi-

lar lists of the cities of Judah, cf Jos 19, 2-7; 1 Chr 4, 28-32; Neh 11, 25-30. This list has suffered in transmission, so that the totals given in vv 32 and 36 are not exact, and some of the names are probably misspelled; many of the cities cannot be identified.

15, 33: In the foothills: see note on Dt 1, 7.

d: Jos 18, 18f. 22.   e: Jos 7, 26; 18, 16ff: 2 Sm 17, 17.   f: Jos 18, 16.   g: Jos 18, 15.   h: 13-19: Jgs 1, 10-15.   i: Jos 14, 13ff.   j: Nm 13, 22; Jgs 1, 20.   k: Jos 10, 38.   l: 1 Sm 27, 6.

roth, Beth-dagon, Naamah and Makkedah; sixteen cities and their villages. ⁴²Libnah, Ether, Ashan, ⁴³Iphtah, Ashnah, Nezib, ⁴⁴Keilah, Achzib and Mareshah; nine cities and their villages. ⁴⁵Ekron and its towns and villages; ⁴⁶from Ekron to the sea, all the towns that lie alongside Ashdod and their villages; ⁴⁷Ashdod and its towns and villages; Gaza and its towns and villages, as far as the Wadi of Egypt and the coast of the Great Sea.

⁴⁸In the mountain regions: Shamir, Jattir, Socoh, ⁴⁹Dannah, Kiriath-sannah (that is, Debir), ⁵⁰Anab, Eshtemoh, Anim, ⁵¹Goshen, Holon and Giloh; eleven cities and their villages. ⁵²Arab, Dumah, Eshan, ⁵³Janim, Beth-tappuah, Aphekah, ⁵⁴Humtah, Kiriath-arba (that is, Hebron), and Zior; nine cities and their villages. ⁵⁵Maon, Carmel, Ziph, Juttah, ⁵⁶Jezreel, Jokdeam, Zanoah, ⁵⁷Kain, Gibbeah and Timnah; ten cities and their villages. ⁵⁸Halhul, Beth-zur, Gedor, ⁵⁹Maarath, Beth-anoth and Eltekon; six cities and their villages. Tekoa, Ephrathah (that is, Bethlehem), Peor, Etam, Kulom, Tatam, Zores, Karim, Gallim, Bether and Manoko; eleven cities and their villages. ⁶⁰Kiriath-baal (that is, Kiriath-jearim) and Rabbah: two cities and their villages.^m

⁶¹In the desert:* Beth-arabah, Middin, Secacah, ⁶²Nibshan, Ir-hamelah and En-gedi; six cities and their villages. ⁶³[But the Jebusites who lived in Jerusalem the Judahites could not drive out; so the Jebusites dwell in Jerusalem beside the Judahites to the present day.ⁿ]

See RG 152-53

CHAPTER 16

The Joseph Tribes. ¹The lot that fell to the Josephites* extended from the Jordan at Jericho to the waters of Jericho east of the desert; then the boundary went up from Jericho to the heights at Bethel.* ²Leaving

Bethel for Luz, it crossed the ridge to the border of the Archites at Ataroth, ³and descended westward to the border of the Japhletites, to that of Lower Beth-horon, and to Gezer, ending thence at the sea.^o

Ephraim. ⁴Within the heritage of Manasseh and Ephraim, sons of Joseph, ⁵the dividing line* for the heritage of the clans of the Ephraimites ran from east of Ataroth-addar to Upper Beth-horon^p ⁶and thence to the sea. From Michmethath^q on the north, their boundary curved eastward around Taanath-shiloh, and continued east of it to Janoah; ⁷from there it descended to Ataroth and Naarah, and skirting Jericho, it ended at the Jordan. ⁸From Tappuah^r the boundary ran westward to the Wadi Kanah and ended at the sea. This was the heritage of the clans of the Ephraimites, ⁹including the villages that belonged to each city set aside for the Ephraimites within the territory of the Manassehites.^s ¹⁰But they did not drive out the Canaanites living in Gezer,^t who live on within Ephraim to the present day, though they have been impressed as laborers.

CHAPTER 17

See RG 152-53

Manasseh. ¹Now as for the lot that fell to the tribe of Manasseh^u as the firstborn of Joseph: since his eldest son, Machir, the father of Gilead, was a warrior, who had already obtained Gilead and Bashan, ^{2v}the allotment was now made to the other descendants of Manasseh, the clans of Abiezer, Helek, Asriel, Shechem, Hepher and Shemida, the other male children of Manasseh, son of Joseph.

³Furthermore, Zelophehad, son of Hepher,^w son of Gilead, son of Machir, son of Manasseh, had had no sons, but only daughters, whose names were Mahlah, Noah, Hoglah, Milcah, and Tirzah. ⁴These presented themselves to Eleazar the priest, to

---

15, 61: In the desert: in the Jordan rift near the Dead Sea.

16, 1—17, 18: The boundaries and cities of Judah, the most important tribe, having been given, the land of the next most important group, the two Josephite tribes of Ephraim and Manasseh, is now described, though it was separated from Judah by the territories of Benjamin (Jos 18, 11-20) and Dan (Jos 19, 40-48).

16, 1-3: This line formed the southern boundary of Ephraim and the northern boundaries of Benjamin and of Dan.

16, 5: The dividing line: separating Ephraim from Manasseh. Ephraim's northern border (v 5) is given in an east-to-west direction; its eastern border (v 6f) in a north-to-south direction.

---

m: Jos 18, 14. *n:* Jgs 1, 21; 2 Sm 5, 6. *o:* Jos 10, 10. 33. *p:* Jos 18, 13. *q:* Jos 17, 7. *r:* Jos 17, 7. *s:* Jos 17, 9. *t:* Jgs 1, 29. *u:* Gn 41, 51; 46, 20; 48, 18; 50, 23; Nm 26, 29; Dt 3, 13. 15. *v:* Nm 26, 29-32. *w:* Nm 26, 33; 27, 1; 36, 2.

Joshua, son of Nun, and to the princes, saying, "The LORD commanded Moses to give us a heritage among our kinsmen." So in obedience to the command of the LORD a heritage was given to each of them among their father's kinsmen.[x] [5]Thus ten shares fell to Manasseh apart from the land of Gilead and Bashan beyond the Jordan,[y] [6]since these female descendants of Manasseh received each a portion among his sons. The land of Gilead fell to the rest of the Manassehites.

[7]Manasseh bordered on Asher.[*] From Michmethath, near Shechem, another boundary ran southward to include the natives of En-Tappuah, [8]because the district of Tappuah belonged to Manasseh, although Tappuah itself was an Ephraimite city on the border of Manasseh. [9]This same boundary continued down to the Wadi Kanah.[z] The cities that belonged to Ephraim from among the cities of Manasseh were those to the south of the wadi; thus the territory of Manasseh ran north of the wadi and ended at the sea. [10]The land on the south belonged to Ephraim and that on the north to Manasseh; with the sea as their common boundary, they reached Asher on the north and Issachar on the east.

[11][a]Moreover, in Issachar and in Asher Manasseh was awarded Beth-shean[b] and its towns, Ibleam and its towns, Dor and its towns and the natives there, Endor and its towns and natives, Taanach and its towns and natives, and Megiddo and its towns and natives [the third is Naphath-dor]. [12]Since the Manassehites could not conquer these cities, the Canaanites persisted in this region. [13]When the Israelites grew stronger they impressed the Canaanites as laborers, but they did not drive them out.

Protest of Joseph Tribes. [14]The descendants of Joseph said to Joshua, "Why have you given us only one lot and one share as our heritage?[c] Our people are too many, because of the extent to which the LORD has blessed us." [15]Joshua answered them, "If you are too many, go up to the forest and clear out a place for yourselves there in the land of the Perizzites and Rephaim, since the mountain regions of Ephraim are so narrow." [16]For the Josephites said, "Our mountain regions are not enough for us; on the other hand, the Canaanites living in the valley region all have iron chariots, in particular those in Beth-shean and its towns, and those in the valley of Jezreel."[d] [17]Joshua therefore said to Ephraim and Manasseh, the house of Joseph, "You are a numerous people and very strong. You shall have not merely one share, [18]for the mountain region which is now forest shall be yours when you clear it. Its adjacent land shall also be yours if, despite their strength and iron chariots, you drive out the Canaanites."

CHAPTER 18

See RG
152-53

[1]After they had subdued the land, the whole community of the Israelites assembled at Shiloh, where they set up the meeting tent.[e]

The Seven Remaining Portions. [2]Seven tribes among the Israelites had not yet received their heritage. [3]Joshua therefore said to the Israelites, "How much longer will you put off taking steps to possess the land which the LORD, the God of your fathers, has given you? [4]Choose three men from each of your tribes; I will commission them to begin a survey of the land, which they shall describe for purposes of inheritance. When they return to me, [5]you shall divide it into seven parts. Judah is to retain its territory in the south,[f] and the house of Joseph its territory in the north. [6]You shall bring here to me the description of the land in seven sections. I will then cast lots for you here before the LORD, our God. [7]For the Levites have no share among you,[g] because the priesthood of the LORD is their heritage; while Gad, Reuben, and the half-tribe of Manasseh have al-

---

17, 7: Manasseh bordered on Asher: only at the extreme northwestern section of Manasseh's territory. The boundary given in the following sentences (vv 7-10) is a more detailed description of the one already mentioned in Jos 16, 5ff, as separating Manasseh from Ephraim.

x: Nm 27, 6f; 36, 2.   y: Jos 13, 30f.   z: Jos 16, 8f.   a: 1 Chr 7, 29.   b: 11ff; Jgs 1, 27f.   c: Jos 16, 4; Gn 48, 19f. 22.   d: Jgs 6, 33.
e: Jos 19, 51.   f: Jos 15, 1—17, 18.   g: Jos 13, 8. 33.

ready received the heritage east of the Jordan which Moses, the servant of the LORD, gave them."

[8]When those who were to map out the land were ready for the journey, Joshua instructed them to survey the land, prepare a description of it, and return to him; then he would cast lots for them there before the LORD in Shiloh. [9]So they went through the land, listed its cities in writing in seven sections, and returned to Joshua in the camp at Shiloh. [10]Joshua then divided up the land for the Israelites into their separate shares, casting lots for them before the LORD in Shiloh.

Benjamin. [11]One lot fell to the clans of the tribe of Benjaminites. The territory allotted them lay between the descendants of Judah and those of Joseph. [12][h]Their northern boundary* began at the Jordan and went over the northern flank of Jericho, up westward into the mountains, till it reached the desert of Beth-aven. [13]From there it crossed over to the southern flank of Luz (that is, Bethel). Then it ran down to Ataroth-addar, on the mountaintop south of Lower Beth-horon.[i] [14]For the western border, the boundary line swung south from the mountaintop opposite Beth-horon till it reached Kiriath-baal (that is, Kiriath-jearim), which city belonged to the Judahites. This was the western boundary. [15]The southern boundary began at the limits of Kiriath-jearim and projected to the spring at Nephtoah. [16]It went down to the edge of the mountain on the north of the Valley of Rephaim, where it faces the Valley of Ben-hinnom; and continuing down the Valley of Hinnom along the southern flank of the Jebusites, reached En-rogel.[j] [17]Inclining to the north, it extended to En-shemesh, and thence to Geliloth, opposite the pass of Adummim. Then it dropped to Eben-Bohan-ben-Reuben, [18]across the northern flank of the Arabah overlook, down into the Arabah.[k]

[19]From there the boundary continued across the northern flank of Beth-hoglah and extended to the northern tip of the Salt Sea, at the southern end of the Jordan. This was the southern boundary. [20]The Jordan bounded it on the east. This was how the heritage of the clans of the Benjaminites was bounded on all sides.

[21]Now the cities belonging to the clans of the tribe of the Benjaminites were: Jericho, Beth-hoglah, Emek-keziz, [22]Beth-arabah, Zemaraim, Bethel, [23]Avvim, Parah, Ophra, [24]Chephar-ammoni, Ophni and Geba; twelve cities and their villages. [25]Also Gibeon, Ramah, Beeroth, [26]Mizpeh, Chephirah, Mozah, [27]Rekem, Irpeel, Taralah, [28]Zela, Haeleph, the Jebusite city (that is, Jerusalem), Gibeah and Kiriath; fourteen cities and their villages. This was the heritage of the clans of Benjaminites.

CHAPTER 19

See RG 152-53

Simeon. [1]The second lot fell to Simeon. The heritage of the clans of the tribe of Simeonites lay within that of the Judahites. [2][l]For their heritage they received Beer-sheba, Shema, Moladah, [3]Hazar-shual, Balah, Ezem, [4]Eltolad, Bethul, Hormah, [5]Ziklag, Beth-marcaboth, Hazar-susah, [6]Beth-lebaoth and Sharuhen; thirteen cities and their villages. [7]Also En-rimmon, Ether and Ashan; four cities and their villages, [8]besides all the villages around these cities as far as Baalath-beer (that is, Ramoth-negeb). This was the heritage of the clans of the tribe of the Simeonites. [9]This heritage of the Simeonites was within the confines of the Judahites; for since the portion of the latter was too large for them, the Simeonites obtained their heritage within it.

Zebulun. [10]*The third lot fell to the clans of the Zebulunites. The limit of their heritage was at Sarid. [11]Their boundary went up west

---

18, 12-20: Benjamin's northern boundary (vv 12f) corresponded to part of the southern boundary of Ephraim (Jos 16, 1f). Their western border (v 14) was the eastern border of Dan (cf Jos 19, 40-47). Their southern boundary (vv 15-19) corresponded to part of the northern boundary of Judah (Jos 15, 6-9).

19, 10-16: Zebulun's territory was in the central section of the Plain of Esdraelon and of southern Galilee; it was bounded on the south by Manasseh, on the southeast by Issachar, on the

northeast and north by Naphtali, and on the west by Asher. The site of the later city city of Nazareth was within its borders. Bethlehem of Zebulun was, of course, distinct from the city of same name in Judah. Twelve cities: apparently seven of the names are missing from v 15, unless some of the places mentioned in vv 12-14 are to be included in the number.

---

h: Jos 16, 1.   *i:* Jos 16, 2f. 5; Gn 28, 19.   *j:* Jos 15, 7f.   *k:* Jos 15, 6.   *l:* 2-8: 1 Chr 4, 28-33.

... and through Mareal, reaching Dabbesheth and the wadi that is near Jokneam. *12*From Sarid eastward it ran to the district of Chisloth-tabor, on to Daberath, and up to Japhia. *13*From there it continued eastward to Gath-hepher and to Eth-kazin, extended to Rimmon, and turned to Neah. *14*Skirting north of Hannathon, the boundary ended at the valley of Iphtahel. *15*Thus, with Kattath, Nahalal, Shimron, Idalah and Bethlehem, there were twelve cities and their villages *16*to comprise the heritage of the clans of the Zebulunites.

Issachar. *17**The fourth lot fell to Issachar. The territory of the clans of the Issacharites *18*included Jezreel, Chesulloth, Shunem, *19*Hapharaim, Shion, Anaharath, *20*Rabbith, Kishion, Ebez, *21*Remeth, En-gannim, En-haddah and Beth-pazzez. *22*The boundary reached Tabor, Shahazumah and Beth-shemesh, ending at the Jordan. These sixteen cities and their villages *23*were the heritage of the clans of the Issacharites.

Asher. *24**The fifth lot fell to the clans of the tribe of the Asherites. *25*Their territory included Helkath, Hali, Beten, Achshaph, *26*Allammelech, Amad and Mishal, and reached Carmel on the west, and Shihor-libnath. *27*In the other direction, it ran eastward of Beth-dagon, reached Zebulun and the valley of Iphtahel; then north of Beth-emek and Neiel, it extended to Cabul, *28*Mishal, Abdon, Rehob,*m* Hammon and Kanah, near Greater Sidon. *29*Then the boundary turned back to Ramah and to the fortress city of Tyre; thence it cut back to Hosah and ended at the sea. Thus, with Mahalab, Achzib, *30*Ummah, Acco, Aphek and Rehob, there were twenty-two cities and their villages *31*to comprise the heritage of the clans of the tribe of the Asherites.

Naphtali. *32**The sixth lot fell to the Naphtalites. The boundary of the clans of the Naphtalites *33*extended from Heleph, from the oak at Zaanannim to Lakkum, including Adami-nekeb and Jabneel, and ended at the Jordan. *34*In the opposite direction, westerly, it ran through Aznoth-tabor and from there extended to Hukkok; it touched Zebulun on the south, Asher on the west, and the Jordan on the east. *35*The fortified cities were Ziddim, Zer, Hammath, Rakkath, Chinnereth, *36*Adamah, Ramah, Hazor, *37*Kedesh, Edrei, En-hazor, *38*Yiron, Migdal-el, Horem, Beth-anath and Beth-shemesh;*n* nineteen cities and their villages, *39*to comprise the heritage of the clans of the tribe of the Naphtalites.

Dan. *40**The seventh lot fell to the clans of the tribe of Danites. *41*Their heritage was the territory of Zorah, Eshtaol, Ir-shemesh, *42*Shaalabbin, Aijalon, Ithlah,*o* *43*Elon, Timnah, Ekron, *44*Eltekoh, Gibbethon, Baalath, *45*Jehud, Bene-berak, Gath-rimmon, *46*Mejarkon and Rakkon, with the coast at Joppa. *47p*But the territory of the Danites was too small for them; so the Danites marched up and attacked Leshem,* which they captured and put to the sword. Once they had taken possession of Leshem, they renamed the settlement after their ancestor Dan. *48*These cities and their villages were the heritage of the clans of the tribe of the Danites.

Joshua's City. *49*When the last of them had received the portions of the land they were to inherit, the Israelites assigned a heritage in their midst to Joshua, son of Nun. *50*In obedience to the command of the LORD, they gave him the city which he requested, Timnah-serah*q* in the mountain region of Ephraim. He rebuilt the city and made it his home.

*51*These are the final portions into which Eleazar the priest, Joshua, son of Nun, and the heads of families in the tribes of the Isra-

---

19, 17-23: Issachar's land was on the eastern watershed of the Plain of Esdraelon, but also included the southeastern end of the Galilean mountains. It was surrounded by Manasseh on the south and east, by Naphtali on the north, and by Zebulun on the west. Jezreel (v 18) dominated the plain to which it gave its name, the later form of which was Esdraelon.

19, 24-31: Asher inherited the western slope of the Galilean hills as far as the sea, with Manasseh to the south, Zebulun and Naphtali to the east, and Phoenicia to the north.

19, 32-39: Naphtali received eastern Galilee; Asher was to the west and Zebulun and Issachar were to the south, while the upper Jordan and Mount Hermon formed the eastern border. Part of the tribe of Dan later on occupied the northern extremity of Naphtali's lands, at the sources of the Jordan (v 47).

19, 40-46: The original territory of Dan was a small enclave between Judah, Benjamin, Ephraim and the Philistines.

19, 47: Leshem: called Laish in Jgs 18, where the story of the migration of the Danites is told at greater length.

m: 28f: Jgs 1, 31.   *n:* Jgs 1, 33.   *o:* Jgs 1, 35.   *p:* Jgs 18, 27-29.
q: Jos 24, 30; Jgs 2, 9.

elites divided the land by lot in the presence of the LORD, at the door of the meeting tent in Shiloh.

CHAPTER 20

See RG 153-54

Cities of Asylum. ¹The LORD said to Joshua:* ²"Tell the Israelites to designate the cities of which I spoke to them through Moses,ʳ ³to which one guilty of accidental and unintended homicide may flee for asylum from the avenger of blood. ⁴To one of these cities the killer shall flee, and standing at the entrance of the city gate, he shall plead his case before the elders, who must receive him and assign him a place in which to live among them. ⁵Though the avenger of blood pursues him, they are not to deliver up the homicide who slew his fellow man unintentionally and not out of previous hatred. ⁶Once he has stood judgment before the community, he shall live on in that city till the death of the high priest who is in office at the time. Then the killer may go back home to his own city from which he fled."ˢ

List of Cities. ⁷So they set apart Kedesh in Galilee in the mountain region of Naphtali, Shechem in the mountain region of Ephraim, and Kiriath-arba (that is, Hebron) in the mountain region of Judah.ᵗ ⁸And beyond the Jordan east of Jericho they designated Bezer on the open tableland in the tribe of Reuben, Ramoth in Gilead in the tribe of Gad, and Golan in Bashan in the tribe of Manasseh.ᵘ ⁹These were the designated citiesᵛ to which any Israelite or stranger living among them who had killed a person accidentally might flee to escape death at the hand of the avenger of blood, until he could appear before the community.

CHAPTER 21

See RG 153-54

Levitical Cities. ¹The heads of the Levite families* came up to Eleazar the priest, to Joshua, son of Nun, and to the heads of families of the other tribes of the Israelitesʷ ²at Shiloh in the land of Canaan, and said to them, "The LORD commanded, through Moses, that cities be given us to dwell in, with pasture lands for our livestock."ˣ ³Out of their own heritage, in obedience to this command of the LORD, the Israelites gave the Levites the following cities with their pasture lands.

⁴When the first lot among the Levites fell to the clans of the Kohathites, the descendants of Aaron the priest obtained thirteen cities by lot from the tribes of Judah, Simeon and Benjamin. ⁵The rest of the Kohathites obtained ten cities by lot from the clans of the tribe of Ephraim, from the tribe of Dan, and from the half-tribe of Manasseh. ⁶The Gershonites obtained thirteen cities by lot from the clans of the tribe of Issachar, from the tribe of Asher, from the tribe of Naphtali, and from the half-tribe of Manasseh. ⁷The clans of the Merarites obtained twelve cities from the tribes of Reuben, Gad and Zebulun. ⁸These cities with their pasture lands the Israelites allotted to the Levites in obedience to the LORD's command through Moses.ʸ

Cities of the Priests. ⁹ᶻFrom the tribes of the Judahites and Simeonites they designated the following cities, ¹⁰and assigned them to the descendants of Aaron in the Kohathite clan of the Levites, since the first lot fell to them: ¹¹first, Kiriath-arba (Arba was the father of Anak), that is, Hebron, in the mountain region of Judah, with the adjacent pasture lands, ¹²although the open country and villages belonging to the city had been given to Caleb, son of Jephunneh, as his property.ᵃ ¹³Thus to the descendants of Aaron the priest were given the city of asylum for homicides at Hebron, with its pasture lands; also, Libnah with its pasture lands, ¹⁴Jattir with its pasture lands, Eshtemoa with its pasture lands, ¹⁵Holon with its pasture lands, Debir with its pasture lands,

---

20, 1-9: The laws concerning the cities of refuge are given in Nm 35, 9-28; Dt 19, 1-13; see notes on Nm 35, 16-25; Dt 19, 2.

21, 1: The order to establish special cities for the Levites is given in Nm 35, 1-8. The forty-eight cities listed here were hardly the exclusive possession of the Levites; at least the more important of them, such as Hebron, Shechem and Ramoth in Gilead, were certainly peopled for the most part by the tribe in whose territory they were situated. But in all these cities the Levites had special property rights which they did not possess in other cities; cf Lv 25, 32ff.

r: Ex 21, 13; Nm 35, 10-14; Dt 4, 41-43; 19, 2-9. s: Nm 35, 12. 24f. t: Jos 15, 13; 19, 37; 21, 21. u: Jos 21, 27. 36f. v: Nm 35, 15. w: Ex 6, 16-19; Nm 3, 17-20. x: Nm 35, 2. y: Nm 35, 2. z: 9-19: 1 Chr 6, 54-60. a: Jos 14, 14; 15, 13.

JOSHUA 21:16—22:1

(faded underlying text visible through map on right margin)

Mediterranean
Sea

★ Kedesh

33°

ASHER

NAPHTALI

Abdon

MANASSEH

Rehob

Rimmon
(Dimnah)

★ Golan

ZEBULUN
Daberath
Hammath-dor

BASHAN

Helkath ● Jokneam

● Kishion

ISSACHAR

Jarmuth

★ Ramoth-gilead?

● Taanach

MANASSEH

GILEAD

GAD

Shechem

32°

● Mahanaim

Gath-rimmon

● Shiloh

DAN

EPHRAIM

● Jazer

● Elteke?

Beth-horon
Gibeon

Gibbethon
Gezer ● Aijalon

● Geba
BENJAMIN
● Almon

Anathoth

Beth-shemesh

Heshbon

★ Bezer?

● Holon?

REUBEN

Libnah

Hebron
(Kiriath-arba)
★

Dead
Sea

● Kedemoth?

JUDAH

● Juttah
Debir ●
● Eshtemoa
● Jattir

31°

SIMEON

0   10   20 Miles

0   10   20 Kilometers

35°

36°

Levitical Cities

263

16 Ashan with its pasture lands, Juttah with its pasture lands, and Beth-shemesh with its pasture lands: nine cities from the two tribes mentioned. 17 From the tribe of Benjamin they obtained the four cities of Gibeon with its pasture lands, Geba with its pasture lands, 18 Anathoth[b] with its pasture lands, and Almon with its pasture lands. 19 These cities which with their pasture lands belonged to the priestly descendants of Aaron, were thirteen in all.

Cities of the Other Kohathites. 20c The rest of the Kohathite clans among the Levites obtained by lot, from the tribe of Ephraim, four cities. 21 They were assigned, with its pasture lands, the city of asylum for homicides at Shechem in the mountain region of Ephraim; also Gezer with its pasture lands, 22 Kibzaim with its pasture lands, and Beth-horon with its pasture lands. 23 From the tribe of Dan they obtained the four cities of Elteke with its pasture lands, Gibbethon with its pasture lands, 24 Aijalon with its pasture lands, and Gath-rimmon with its pasture lands; 25 and from the half-tribe of Manasseh the two cities of Taanach with its pasture lands and Ibleam with its pasture lands. 26 These cities which with their pasture lands belonged to the rest of the Kohathite clans were ten in all.

Cities of the Gershonites. 27d The Gershonite clan of the Levites received from the half-tribe of Manasseh two cities: the city of asylum for homicides at Golan with its pasture lands; and also Beth-Astharoth with its pasture lands. 28 From the tribe of Issachar they obtained the four cities of Kishion with its pasture lands, Daberath with its pasture lands, 29 Jarmuth with its pasture lands, and En-gannim with its pasture lands; 30 from the tribe of Asher, the four cities of Mishal with its pasture lands, Abdon with its pasture lands, 31 Helkath with its pasture lands, and Rehob with its pasture lands; 32 and from the tribe of Naphtali, three cities: the city of asylum for homicides at Kedesh in Galilee, with its pasture lands; also Hammath with its pasture lands, and Rakkath with its pasture lands. 33 These cities which with their pasture lands belonged to the Gershonite clans were thirteen in all.

Cities of the Merarites. 34e The Merarite clans, the last of the Levites, received from the tribe of Zebulun the four cities of Jokneam with its pasture lands, Kartah with its pasture lands, 35 Rimmon with its pasture lands, and Nahalal with its pasture lands; 36 also, across the Jordan, from the tribe of Reuben, four cities: the city of asylum for homicides at Bezer with its pasture lands, Jahaz with its pasture lands, 37 Kedemoth with its pasture lands, and Mephaath with its pasture lands; 38 and from the tribe of Gad a total of four cities: the city of asylum for homicides at Ramoth in Gilead with its pasture lands, also Mahanaim with its pasture lands, 39 Heshbon with its pasture lands, and Jazer with its pasture lands. 40 The cities which were allotted to the Merarite clans, the last of the Levites, were therefore twelve in all.

41 Thus the total number of cities[f] within the territory of the Israelites which, with their pasture lands, belonged to the Levites, was forty-eight. 42 With each and every one of these cities went the pasture lands round about it.

43 And so the LORD gave Israel all the land he had sworn to their fathers he would give them.[g] Once they had conquered and occupied it, 44 the LORD gave them peace on every side, just as he had promised their fathers. Not one of their enemies could withstand them; the LORD brought all their enemies under their power. 45 Not a single promise[h] that the LORD made to the house of Israel was broken; every one was fulfilled.

III: Return of the Transjordan Tribes and Joshua's Farewell

CHAPTER 22

See RG 154

The Eastern Tribes Dismissed. 1 At that time Joshua summoned the Reubenites, the Gadites, and the half-tribe of Manasseh

---

b: Jer 1, 1.   c: 20-26: 1 Chr 6, 66-70.   d: 27-33: 1 Chr 6, 71-76.   e: 34-38: 1 Chr 6. 77-81.   f: Nm 35, 7.   g: Gn 12, 7; 13, 15; 15, 18; 26, 3; 28, 4. 13.   h: Jos 23, 14f.

²and said to them:ⁱ "You have done all that Moses, the servant of the LORD, commanded you, and have obeyed every command I gave you. ³For many years now you have not once abandoned your kinsmen, but have faithfully carried out the commands of the LORD, your God. ⁴Since, therefore, the LORD, your God, has settled your kinsmen as he promised them, you may now return to your tents beyond the Jordan; to your own land, which Moses, the servant of the LORD, gave you.ʲ ⁵But be very careful to observe the precept and law which Moses, the servant of the LORD, enjoined upon you: love the LORD, your God;ᵏ follow him faithfully; keep his commandments; remain loyal to him; and serve him with your whole heart and soul." ⁶Joshua then blessed them and sent them away to their own tents.

⁷(For, to half the tribe of Manasseh Moses had assigned land in Bashan;ˡ and to the other half Joshua had given a portion along with their kinsmen west of the Jordan.) What Joshua said to them when he sent them off to their tents with his blessing was, ⁸"Now that you are returning to your own tents with great wealth, with very numerous livestock, with silver, gold, bronze and iron, and with a very large supply of clothing, divide these spoils of your enemies with your kinsmen there."ᵐ ⁹So the Reubenites, the Gadites, and the half-tribe of Manasseh left the other Israelites at Shiloh in the land of Canaan and returned to the land of Gilead, their own property, which they had received according to the LORD's command through Moses.ⁿ

The Altar beside the Jordan. ¹⁰When the Reubenites, the Gadites, and the half-tribe of Manasseh came to the region of the Jordan in the land of Canaan, they built there at the Jordan a conspicuously large altar. ¹¹The other Israelites heard the reportᵒ that the Reubenites, the Gadites, and the half-tribe of Manasseh had built an altar in the region of the Jordan facing the land of Canaan,* across from them, ¹²and therefore they assembled their whole community at Shiloh to declare war on them.*

Accusation of the Western Tribes. ¹³First, however, they sent to the Reubenites, the Gadites, and the half-tribe of Manasseh in the land of Gilead an embassy consisting of Phinehas, son of Eleazar the priest,ᵖ ¹⁴and ten princes, one from every tribe of Israel, each one being both prince and military leader of his ancestral house. ¹⁵When these came to the Reubenites, the Gadites, and the half-tribe of Manasseh in the land of Gilead, they said to them: ¹⁶q"The whole community of the LORD sends this message: What act of treachery is this you have committed against the God of Israel? You have seceded from the LORD this day, and rebelled against him by building an altar of your own! ¹⁷For the sin of Peor, a plague came upon the community of the LORD.ʳ ¹⁸We are still not free of that; must you now add to it? You are rebelling against the LORD today and by tomorrow he will be angry with the whole community of Israel! ¹⁹If you consider the land you now possess unclean,* cross over to the land the LORD possesses, where the Dwelling of the LORD stands,ˢ and share that with us. But do not rebel against the LORD, nor involve us in rebellion, by building an altar of your own in addition to the altar of the LORD, our God. ²⁰When Achan, son of Zerah,ᵗ violated the ban, did not wrath fall upon the entire community of Israel? Though he was but a single man, he did not perish alone* for his guilt!"

22, 11: In the region of the Jordan facing the land of Canaan: on the eastern side of the Jordan valley. The river itself formed the boundary between these eastern tribes and the rest of the tribes who lived in what was formerly Canaan—though the term Canaan could also be used of both sides of the Jordan valley (cf v 10). The Transjordan tribes naturally built their altar in their own territory.

22, 12: To declare war on them: the western Israelites considered this altar, which seemed to violate the customary unity of the sanctuary (cf Lv 17, 1-9; Dt 12, 4-14), as a sign of secession and dangerous to national unity. The motives for the war were political as well as religious.

22, 19: Unclean: not sanctified by the Dwelling of the Lord.

22, 20: Achan . . . did not perish alone: his guilt caused the failure of the first attack on Ai (Jos 7, 4-23); this fact is adduced as an argument for the solidarity and mutual responsibility of all the Israelites.

i: Jos 1, 16f; Nm 32, 20ff; Dt 3, 18ff.   *j:* Jos 1, 13; 13, 8; Nm 32, 33.   *k:* Dt 6, 5f. 17; 10, 12; 11, 1. 13. 22.   *l:* Jos 17, 5.   *m:* Nm 31, 27.   *n:* Jos 18, 1; Nm 32, 1. 26. 29.   *o:* Dt 13, 13ff.   *p:* Ex 6, 25; Sir 45, 28.   *q:* Lv 17, 8f.   *r:* Nm 25, 3f; Dt 4, 3.   *s:* Jos 18, 1.   *t:* Jos 7, 1. 5.

Reply of the Eastern Tribes. [21]The Reubenites, the Gadites, and the half-tribe of Manasseh replied to the military leaders of the Israelites: "The LORD is the God of gods. [22]The LORD, the God of gods,* knows and Israel shall know. If now we have acted out of rebellion or treachery against the LORD, our God, [23]and if we have built an altar of our own to secede from the LORD, or to offer holocausts, grain offerings or peace offerings upon it, the LORD himself will exact the penalty. [24]We did it rather out of our anxious concern lest in the future your children should say to our children: 'What have you to do with the LORD, the God of Israel? [25]For the LORD has placed the Jordan as a boundary between you and us. You descendants of Reuben and Gad have no share in the LORD.' Thus your children would prevent ours from revering the LORD. [26]So we decided to guard our interests by building this altar of our own: not for holocausts or for sacrifices, [27u]but as evidence for you on behalf of ourselves and our descendants, that we have the right to worship the LORD in his presence with our holocausts, sacrifices, and peace offerings. Now in the future your children cannot say to our children, 'You have no share in the LORD.' [28]Our thought was, that if in the future they should speak thus to us or to our descendants, we could answer: 'Look at the model of the altar of the LORD which our fathers made, not for holocausts or for sacrifices, but to witness* between you and us.' [29]Far be it from us to rebel against the LORD or to secede now from the LORD by building an altar for holocaust, grain offering, or sacrifice in addition to the altar of the LORD, our God, which stands before his Dwelling."

[30]When Phinehas the priest and the princes of the community, the military leaders of the Israelites, heard what the Reubenites, the Gadites and the Manassehites had to say, they were satisfied. [31]Phinehas, son of Eleazar the priest, said to the Reubenites, the Gadites and the Manassehites, "Now we know that the LORD is with us. Since you have not committed this act of treachery against the LORD, you have kept the Israelites free from punishment by the LORD."

[32]Phinehas, son of Eleazar the priest, and the princes returned from the Reubenites and the Gadites in the land of Gilead to the Israelites in the land of Canaan, and reported the matter to them. [33]The report satisfied the Israelites, who blessed God and decided against declaring war on the Reubenites and Gadites or ravaging the land they occupied.

[34]The Reubenites and the Gadites gave the altar its name* as a witness among them that the LORD is God.

CHAPTER 23

See RG 154

Joshua's Final Plea. [1]Many years later, after the LORD had given the Israelites rest from all their enemies round about them, and when Joshua was old and advanced in years,[v] [2]he summoned all Israel (including their elders, leaders, judges and officers) and said to them: "I am old and advanced in years. [3]You have seen all that the LORD, your God, has done for you against all these nations; for it has been the LORD, your God, himself who fought for you. [4w]Bear in mind that I have apportioned among your tribes as their heritage the nations that survive [as well as those I destroyed] between the Jordan and the Great Sea in the west. [5]The LORD, your God, will drive them out and dislodge them at your approach, so that you will take possession of their land as the LORD, your God, promised you. [6]Therefore strive hard to observe and carry out all that is written in the book of the law of Moses, not straying from it in any way,[x] [7]or mingling with these nations while they survive among you. You must not invoke their gods, or

---

22, 22: The LORD, the God of gods: the Hebrew, which cannot be adequately rendered in English here, adds to the divine name Yahweh ("the LORD") two synonymous words for "God," el and elohim. The repetition of these three sacred words adds force to the protestations of fidelity and innocence.

22, 28: To witness: far from being destined to form a rival sanctuary, the model of the altar was intended by the eastern tribes solely as a means of teaching their children to be faithful to the one true sanctuary beyond the Jordan.

22, 34: The name of this altar was the Hebrew word for "witness," [c] ed.

u: Dt 12, 5f. 17f.   v: Jos 13, 1.   w: Jos 13, 2-7; 14, 2; 18, 10; Ps 78, 55.   x: Jos 1, 7.

swear by them, or serve them, or worship them,[y] [8]but you must remain loyal to the LORD, your God, as you have been to this day. [9]At your approach the LORD has driven out large and strong nations, and to this day no one has withstood you. [10]One of you puts to flight a thousand, because it is the LORD, your God, himself who fights for you,[z] as he promised you. [11]Take great care, however, to love the LORD, your God. [12]For if you ever abandon him and ally yourselves with the remnant of these nations while they survive among you, by intermarrying and intermingling with them,[a] [13]know for certain that the LORD, your God, will no longer drive these nations out of your way. Instead they will be a snare and a trap for you, a scourge for your sides and thorns for your eyes, until you perish from this good land which the LORD, your God, has given you.

[14]"Today, as you see, I am going the way of all men.* So now acknowledge with your whole heart and soul that not one of all the promises the LORD, your God, made to you has remained unfulfilled. Every promise has been fulfilled for you, with not one single exception. [15]But just as every promise the LORD, your God, made to you has been fulfilled for you, so will he fulfill every threat,* even so far as to exterminate you from this good land which the LORD, your God, has given you. [16]If you transgress the covenant of the LORD, your God, which he enjoined on you, serve other gods and worship them, the anger of the LORD will flare up against you and you will quickly perish from the good land which he has given you."

See RG 154

CHAPTER 24

Reminder of the Divine Goodness. [1]Joshua gathered together all the tribes of Israel at Shechem, summoning their elders, their leaders, their judges and their officers. When they stood in ranks before God,

[2]Joshua addressed all the people: "Thus says the LORD, the God of Israel: In times past your fathers, down to Terah,[c] father of Abraham and Nahor, dwelt beyond the River* and served other gods. [3]But I brought your father Abraham from the region beyond the River and led him through the entire land of Canaan.[d] I made his descendants numerous, and gave him Isaac. [4]To Isaac I gave Jacob and Esau.[e] To Esau I assigned the mountain region of Seir in which to settle, while Jacob and his children went down to Egypt.

[5]"Then I sent Moses and Aaron, and smote Egypt with the prodigies which I wrought in her midst.[f] [6]Afterward I led you out of Egypt, and when you reached the sea, the Egyptians pursued your fathers to the Red Sea with chariots and horsemen.[g] [7]Because they cried out to the LORD,[h] he put darkness between your people and the Egyptians, upon whom he brought the sea so that it engulfed them. After you witnessed what I did to Egypt, and dwelt a long time in the desert, [8]I brought you into the land of the Amorites who lived east of the Jordan. They fought against you, but I delivered them into your power. You took possesion of their land, and I destroyed them [the two kings of the Amorites] before you. [9]Then Balak, son of Zippor, king of Moab, prepared to war against Israel. He summoned Balaam, son of Beor, to curse you; [10]but I would not listen to Balaam. On the contrary, he had to bless you, and I saved you from him. [11]Once you crossed the Jordan[l] and came to Jericho, the men of Jericho fought against you, but I delivered them also into your power. [12]And I sent the hornets* ahead of you which drove them [the Amorites, Perizzites, Canaanites, Hittites, Girgashites, Hivites and Jebusites] out of your way; it was not your sword or your bow.[m] [13]"I gave you a land which you had not tilled and cities which you had not built, to

---

23, 14: Going the way of all men: drawing near to death, the inevitable goal of all; cf 1 Kgs 2, 1f.

23, 15: Every threat: mentioned especially in Dt 28, 15-68.

24, 2: Beyond the River: east of the Euphrates; cf Gn 11, 28-31.

24, 12: The hornets: see note on Ex 23, 28.

---

y: Dt 7, 2ff.   z: Ex 14, 14; Lv 26, 8; Dt 3, 22.   a: Ex 34, 16; Dt 7, 3.   b: Lv 26, 14-39; Dt 28, 15-68.   c: Gn 11, 26. 31; 31, 53.
d: Gn 12, 1; Acts 7, 2-4.   e: Gn 25, 24ff; 36, 8; 46, 1. 6; Acts 7, 15.   f: Ex 3, 10; 7, 14-12, 30.   g: Ex 12, 37. 51; 14, 9.   h: Ex 14,
10. 20. 27f.   i: Nm 21, 21-35.   j: Nm 22, 2-5.   k: Nm 23, 1-24, 25.   l: Jos 3, 14; 6, 1.   m: Jos 11, 20; Ex 23, 28; Dt 7, 20.

dwell in; you have eaten of vineyards and olive groves which you did not plant.[n]

[14o]"Now, therefore, fear the LORD and serve him completely and sincerely. Cast out the gods your fathers served beyond the River and in Egypt, and serve the LORD. [15p]If it does not please you to serve the LORD, decide today whom you will serve, the gods your fathers served* beyond the River or the gods of the Amorites in whose country you are dwelling. As for me and my household, we will serve the LORD."

Renewal of the Covenant. [16]But the people answered, "Far be it from us to forsake the LORD for the service of other gods. [17]For it was the LORD, our God, who brought us and our fathers up out of the land of Egypt, out of a state of slavery. He performed those great miracles before our very eyes and protected us along our entire journey and among all the peoples through whom we passed. [18]At our approach the LORD drove out [all the peoples, including] the Amorites who dwelt in the land. Therefore we also will serve the LORD, for he is our God."

[19]Joshua in turn said to the people, "You may not be able* to serve the LORD, for he is a holy God; he is a jealous God[q] who will not forgive your transgressions or your sins. [20]If, after the good he has done for you, you forsake the LORD and serve strange gods, he will do evil to you and destroy you."

[21]But the people answered Joshua, "We will still serve the LORD." [22]Joshua therefore said to the people, "You are your own witnesses that you have chosen to serve the LORD." They replied, "We are, indeed!"

[23]"Now, therefore, put away the strange gods that are among you and turn your hearts to the LORD, the God of Israel." [24]Then the people promised Joshua, "We will serve the LORD, our God, and obey his voice."

[25]So Joshua made a covenant with the people that day and made statutes and ordinances for them at Shechem, [26]which he recorded in the book of the law of God. Then he took a large stone and set it up there under the oak that was in the sanctuary of the LORD.[r] [27]And Joshua said to all the people, "This stone shall be our witness,[s] for it has heard all the words which the LORD spoke to us. It shall be a witness against you, should you wish to deny your God." [28]Then Joshua dismissed the people, each to his own heritage.[t]

Death of Joshua. [29u]After these events, Joshua, son of Nun, servant of the LORD, died at the age of a hundred and ten. [30]He was buried within the limits of his heritage at Timnath-serah[v] in the mountain region of Ephraim north of Mount Gaash. [31]Israel served the LORD during the entire lifetime of Joshua and that of the elders who outlived Joshua and knew all that the LORD had done for Israel. [32w]The bones of Joseph,* which the Israelites had brought up from Egypt, were buried in Shechem in the plot of ground Jacob had bought from the sons of Hamor, father of Shechem, for a hundred pieces of money. This was a heritage of the descendants of Joseph. [33]When Eleazar, son of Aaron, also died, he was buried on the hill which had been given to his son Phinehas[x] in the mountain region of Ephraim.

24, 15: The gods your fathers served: Abraham's ancestors were polytheists.

24, 19: You may not be able: fidelity to God's service is not easy, and therefore those who take such solemn obligations on themselves must be ever vigilant against human weakness.

24, 32: The bones of Joseph: the mummified body of Joseph (Gn 50, 25f), which the Israelites took with them as they left Egypt (Ex 13, 19), was fittingly buried at the ancient city of Shechem, near the border between the two Josephite tribes of Ephraim and Manasseh.

---

n: Dt 6, 10f. o: Dt 10, 12; 1 Sm 7, 3; 12, 24; Tb 14, 9. p: Dt 30, 15-19. q: Ex 20, 5; 23, 21; 34, 14; Lv 19, 2. r: Gn 28, 18; 31, 45; Jgs 9, 6. s: Gn 31, 48. 52; Dt 31, 19. 21. 26. t: Jgs 2, 6. u: 29ff; Jgs 2, 7ff. v: Jos 19, 50; Jgs 2, 9. w: Gn 33, 19; 50, 24; Ex 13, 19. x: Jos 22, 13.

See RG
156-64

The Book of Judges

The Book of Judges derives its title from the twelve heroes of Israel whose deeds it records. They were not magistrates, but military leaders sent by God to aid and to relieve his people in time of external danger. They exercised their activities in the interval of time between the death of Joshua and the institution of the monarchy in Israel. Six of them—Othniel, Ehud, Barak, Gideon, Jephthah and Samson—are treated in some detail and have accordingly been styled the Major Judges. The other six, of whose activities this book preserves but a summary record, are called the Minor Judges. There were two other judges, whose judgeships are described in 1 Samuel— Eli and Samuel, who seem to have ruled the entire nation of Israel just before the institution of the monarchy. The twelve judges of the present book, however, very probably exercised their authority, sometimes simultaneously, over one or another tribe of Israel, never over the entire nation.

The purpose of the book is to show that the fortunes of Israel depended upon the obedience or disobedience of the people to God's law. Whenever they rebelled against him, they were oppressed by pagan nations; when they repented, he raised up judges to deliver them (cf Jgs 2, 10-23).

The accounts of various events, whether written shortly after their occurrence or orally transmitted, were later skillfully unified according to the moral purpose of the redactor sometime during the Israelite monarchy.

The book is divided as follows:

I: Palestine after the Death of Joshua (1, 1—3, 6).

II: Stories of the Judges (3, 7—16, 31).

III: The Tribes of Dan and Benjamin in the Days of the Judges (17, 1—21, 25).

I: Palestine After the Death of Joshua

CHAPTER 1

See RG
157-58

Pagan Survivors in Palestine. [1]After the death of Joshua* the Israelites consulted the LORD, asking, "Who shall be first among us to attack the Canaanites and to do battle with them?"[a] [2]The LORD answered, "Judah shall attack: I have delivered the land into his power." [3]Judah then said to his brother Simeon, "Come up with me into the territory allotted to me, and let us engage the Canaanites in battle. I will likewise accompany you into the territory allotted to you." So Simeon went with him.

[4]When the forces of Judah attacked, the LORD delivered the Canaanites and Perizzites into their power, and they slew ten thousand of them in Bezek. [5]It was in Bezek that they came upon Adonibezek and fought against him. When they defeated the Canaanites and Perizzites, [6]Adonibezek fled. They set out in pursuit, and when they caught him, cut off his thumbs and his big toes. [7]At this Adonibezek said, "Seventy kings, with their thumbs and big toes cut off, used to pick up scraps under my table. As I have done, so has God repaid me." He was brought to Jerusalem, and there he died. [8][The Judahites fought against Jerusalem and captured it, putting it to the sword; then they destroyed the city by fire.]

[9b]Afterward the Judahites went down to fight against the Canaanites who lived in the mountain region, in the Negeb, and in the foothills, [10c]Judah also marched against the Canaanites who dwelt in Hebron, which was formerly called Kiriath-arba, and defeated Sheshai, Ahiman and Talmai.[d] [11]From there they marched against the inhabitants of Debir, which was formerly called Kiriath-se-

---

1, 1-36: This chapter summarizes events most of which occurred shortly after the death of Joshua. Perhaps because they were planned and inaugurated by him, they are also attributed to him in the last half of the preceding book (Jos 14—22).

a: Jgs 20, 18: Nm 27, 21.   b: Jos 10, 40; 11, 16; 12, 8.   c: Jos 15, 13-19.   d: Nm 13, 22; Jos 14, 15.

pher. [12]And Caleb said, "I will give my daughter Achsah in marriage to the one who attacks Kiriath-sepher and captures it." [13e]Othniel, son of Caleb's younger brother Kenaz, captured it; so Caleb gave him his daughter Achsah in marriage. [14]On the day of her marriage to Othniel she induced him to ask her father for some land. Then, as she alighted from the ass, Caleb asked her, "What is troubling you?" [15]"Give me an additional gift," she answered. "Since you have assigned land in the Negeb to me, give me also pools of water." So Caleb gave her the upper and the lower pool. [16]The descendants of the Kenite, Moses' father-in-law,* came up with the Judahites from the city of palms to the desert at Arad [which is in the Negeb]. But they later left and settled among the Amalekites.[f]

[17g]Judah then went with his brother Simeon, and they defeated the Canaanites who dwelt in Zephath. After having doomed the city to destruction, they renamed it Hormah. [18h]Judah, however, did not occupy Gaza with its territory, Ashkelon with its territory, or Ekron with its territory. [19i]Since the LORD was with Judah, he gained possession of the mountain region. Yet he could not dislodge those who lived on the plain, because they had iron chariots. [20]As Moses had commanded, Hebron was given to Caleb, who then drove from it the three sons of Anak.[j]

[21]*The Benjaminites did not dislodge the Jebusites who dwelt in Jerusalem, with the result that the Jebusites live in Jerusalem beside the Benjaminites to the present day.[k] [22]The house of Joseph, too, marched up against Bethel, and the LORD was with them. [23]The house of Joseph had a reconnaissance made of Bethel, which formerly was called Luz.[l] [24]The scouts saw a man coming out of the city and said to him, "Show us a way into the city, and we will spare you." [25]He showed them a way into the city, which they then put to the sword; but they let the man and his whole clan go free. [26]He then went to the land of the Hittites, where he built a city and called it Luz, as it is still called.

[27]Manasseh did not take possession of Beth-shean with its towns or of Taanach with its towns. Neither did he dislodge the inhabitants of Dor and its towns, those of Ibleam and its towns, or those of Megiddo and its towns.[m] The Canaanites kept their hold in this district. [28]When the Israelites grew stronger, they impressed the Canaanites as laborers, but did not drive them out. [29]Similarly, the Ephraimites did not drive out the Canaanites living in Gezer, and so the Canaanites live in Gezer in their midst.[n]

[30]Zebulun did not dislodge the inhabitants of Kitron or those of Nahalol; the Canaanites live among them, but have become forced laborers.

[31o]Nor did Asher drive out the inhabitants of Acco or those of Sidon, or take possession of Mahaleb, Achzib, Helbah, Aphik or Rehob. [32]The Asherites live among the Canaanite natives of the land, whom they have not dislodged.

[33p]Naphtali did not drive out the inhabitants of Beth-shemesh or those of Beth-anath, and so they live among the Canaanite natives of the land. However, the inhabitants of Beth-shemesh and Beth-anath have become forced laborers for them.

[34]The Amorites hemmed in the Danites in the mountain region, not permitting them to go down into the plain.[q] [35]The Amorites had a firm hold in Harheres, Aijalon and Shaalbim, but as the house of Joseph gained the upper hand, they were impressed as laborers.

[36]The territory of the Amorites extended from the Akrabbim pass to Sela and beyond.

CHAPTER 2

See RG 157-58

Infidelities of the Israelites. [1r]An angel of the LORD went up from Gilgal to

---

1, 16: Moses' father-in-law: Reuel; cf Nm 10, 29-32 and note. City of palms: Jericho (cf Dt 34, 3), or a town in the Negeb.

1, 21: According to Jos 18, 16, Jerusalem was assigned to the tribe of Benjamin. But it was not actually taken from the Jebusites until David captured it (2 Sm 5, 6-9) and made it his capital, outside the tribal organization.

e: Jgs 3, 9. f: Jgs 4, 11; Nm 10, 29-32. g: Nm 21, 3. h: Jos 11, 22. i: Jos 17, 16ff. j: Jos 14, 9. 13; 15, 14. k: Jos 15, 63. l: Gn 28, 19; 35, 6; 48, 3; Jos 18, 13. m: 27f; Jos 17, 11ff. n: Jos 16, 10. o: 31f; Jos 19, 24-31. p: Jos 19, 32-39. q: Jos 19, 47f. r: 1ff; Jgs 6, 8ff.

Bochim and said, "It was I who brought you up from Egypt and led you into the land which I promised on oath to your fathers. I said that I would never break my covenant with you, [2]but that you were not to make a pact with the inhabitants of this land, and you were to pull down their altars. Yet you have not obeyed me.[s] What did you mean by this? [3]For now I tell you, I will not clear them out of your way; they shall oppose you and their gods shall become a snare for you."[t]

[4]When the angel of the LORD had made these threats to all the Israelites, the people wept aloud; [5]and so that place came to be called Bochim.[*] They offered sacrifice there to the LORD.

[6u]When Joshua dismissed the people, each Israelite went to take possession of his own hereditary land. [7]The people served the LORD during the entire lifetime of Joshua, and of those elders who outlived Joshua and who had seen all the great work which the LORD had done for Israel. [8]Joshua, son of Nun, the servant of the LORD, was a hundred and ten years old when he died; [9]and they buried him within the borders of his heritage at Timnath-heres in the mountain region of Ephraim north of Mount Gaash.[v]

[10]But once the rest of that generation were gathered to their fathers, and a later generation arose that did not know the LORD, or what he had done for Israel, [11]the Israelites offended the LORD by serving the Baals.[*w] [12]Abandoning the LORD, the God of their fathers, who had led them out of the land of Egypt, they followed the other gods of the various nations around them, and by their worship of these gods provoked the LORD.

[13]Because they had thus abandoned him and served Baal and the Ashtaroth,[*] [14]the anger of the LORD flared up against Israel, and he delivered them over to plunderers who despoiled them. He allowed them to fall into the power of their enemies round about whom they were no longer able to withstand. [15]Whatever they undertook, the LORD turned into disaster for them, as in his warning he had sworn he would do, till they were in great distress.[x] [16]Even when the LORD raised up judges to deliver them from the power of their despoilers, [17]they did not listen to their judges, but abandoned themselves to the worship of other gods. They were quick to stray from the way their fathers had taken, and did not follow their example of obedience to the commandments of the LORD. [18]Whenever the LORD raised up judges for them, he would be with the judge and save them from the power of their enemies as long as the judge lived; it was thus the LORD took pity on their distressful cries of affliction under their oppressors. [19]But when the judge died, they would relapse and do worse than their fathers, following other gods in service and worship, relinquishing none of their evil practices or stubborn conduct.[y]

[20]In his anger toward Israel the LORD said, "Inasmuch as this nation has violated my covenant which I enjoined on their fathers, and has disobeyed me, [21]I for my part will not clear away for them any more of the nations which Joshua left when he died." [22]Through these nations the Israelites were to be made to prove whether or not they would keep to the way of the LORD and continue in it as their fathers had done; [23]therefore the LORD allowed them to remain instead of expelling them immediately, or delivering them into the power of Israel.

CHAPTER 3

See RG 157-59

[1]The following are the nations which the LORD allowed to remain, so that through them he might try all those Israelites who had no experience of the battles with Canaan [2][just to instruct, by training them in battle,

---

2, 5: Bochim: the Hebrew word for "weepers."

2, 11: Baals: the chief god of the Canaanites and the Phoenicians was called "Baal," a word meaning "lord." He was honored by various titles, hence the plural form here, equivalent to "the pagan gods."

2, 13: Ashtaroth: the Canaanite Phoenician goddess of love and fertility was Astarte. The plural form used here refers to her various titles and images and is equivalent to "goddesses."

s: Ex 34, 12f. 15; Dt 7, 2. 5; 21, 2f.   t: Nm 33, 55; Jos 23, 13.   u: 6-9: Jos 24, 28-31.   v: Jos 19, 50.   w: 11. 14; Jgs 3, 7f; 4, 1f; 6, 1; 10, 6f; 13, 1.   x: Dt 28, 15-68.   y: Jgs 3, 12; 4, 1; 6, 1; 8, 33.   z: 20f; Jos 23, 16.

those generations only of the Israelites who would not have had that previous experience]: *3a*the five lords of the Philistines;* and all the Canaanites, the Sidonians, and the Hivites who dwell in the mountain region of Lebanon between Baal-hermon and the entrance to Hamath. *4*These served to put Israel to the test, to determine whether they would obey the commandments the LORD had enjoined on their fathers through Moses. *5*Besides, the Israelites were living among the Canaanites, Hittites, Amorites, Perizzites, Hivites and Jebusites. *6*In fact, they took their daughters in marriage, and gave their own daughters to their sons in marriage, and served their gods.

II: Stories of the Judges

Othniel. *7b*Because the Israelites had offended the LORD by forgetting the LORD, their God, and serving the Baals and the Asherahs,* *8*the anger of the LORD flared up against them, and he allowed them to fall into the power of Cushan-rishathaim, king of Aram Naharaim, whom they served for eight years. *9*But when the Israelites cried out to the LORD, he raised up for them a savior, Othniel, son of Caleb's younger brother Kenaz, who rescued them. *10*The spirit of the LORD came upon him, and he judged Israel.*c* When he went out to war, the LORD delivered Cushan-rishathaim, king of Aram, into his power, so that he made him subject. *11*The land then was at rest for forty years,*d* until Othniel, son of Kenaz, died.

Ehud. *12*Again the Israelites offended the LORD, who because of this offense strengthened Eglon, king of Moab, against Israel. *13*In alliance with the Ammonites and Amalekites, he attacked and defeated Israel, taking possession of the city of palms. *14*The Israelites then served Eglon, king of Moab, for eighteen years.

*15*But when the Israelites cried out to the LORD, he raised up for them a savior, the Benjaminite Ehud, son of Gera, who was left-handed. It was by him that the Israelites sent their tribute to Eglon, king of Moab. *16*Ehud made himself a two-edged dagger a foot long, and wore it under his clothes over his right thigh. *17*He presented the tribute to Eglon, king of Moab, who was very fat, *18*and after the presentation went off with the tribute bearers. *19*He returned, however, from where the idols are, near Gilgal, and said, "I have a private message for you, O king." And the king said, "Silence!" Then when all his attendants had left his presence, *20*and Ehud went in to him where he sat alone in his cool upper room, Ehud said, "I have a message from God for you." So the king rose from his chair, *21*and then Ehud with his left hand drew the dagger from his right thigh, and thrust it into Eglon's belly. *22*The hilt also went in after the blade, and the fat closed over the blade because he did not withdraw the dagger from his body.

*23*Then Ehud went out into the hall, shutting the doors of the upper room on him and locking them. *24*When Ehud had left and the servants came, they saw that the doors of the upper room were locked, and thought, "He must be easing himself in the cool chamber." *25*They waited until they finally grew suspicious. Since he did not open the doors of the upper room, they took the key and opened them. There on the floor, dead, lay their lord!

*26*During their delay Ehud made good his escape and, passing the idols, took refuge in Seirah. *27*On his arrival he sounded the horn in the mountain region of Ephraim, and the Israelites went down from the mountains with him as their leader. *28*"Follow me," he said to them, "for the LORD has delivered your enemies the Moabites into your power." So they followed him down and seized the fords of the Jordan leading to Moab, permitting no one to cross.*e* *29*On that occasion they slew about ten thousand Moabites, all of them strong and valiant men. Not a man escaped. *30*Thus was Moab

---

3, 3: The Philistines: non-Semitic invaders, who gave their name to all Palestine, although they occupied only its southwestern plains. Their confederation embraced the five leading cities of Gaza, Ashkelon, Ashdod, Gath and Ekron.

3, 7: Asherahs: elsewhere rendered "sacred poles." See

note on Ex 34, 13 and on Dt 7, 5. Here the word seems to mean "goddesses."

---

a: Jos 13, 2-6. *b:* Jgs 2, 11ff. *c:* Jgs 6, 34; 11, 29; 13, 25; 14, 6. 19; 15, 14. *d:* Jgs 5, 31; 8, 28. *e:* Jgs 4, 7. 14; 7, 9. 15.

brought under the power of Israel at that time; and the land had rest for eighty years.

Shamgar. [31]After him there was Shamgar, son of Anath, who slew six hundred Philistines with an oxgoad. He, too, rescued Israel.

CHAPTER 4

See RG 159

Deborah and Barak. [1]After Ehud's death, however, the Israelites again offended the LORD. [2]So the LORD allowed them to fall into the power of the Canaanite king, Jabin, who reigned in Hazor.[f] The general of his army was Sisera, who dwelt in Harosheth-ha-goiim. [3]But the Israelites cried out to the LORD; for with his nine hundred iron chariots he sorely oppressed the Israelites for twenty years.

[4]At this time the prophetess Deborah, wife of Lappidoth, was judging Israel. [5]She used to sit under Deborah's palm tree, situated between Ramah and Bethel in the mountain region of Ephraim, and there the Israelites came up to her for judgment. [6]She sent and summoned Barak, son of Abinoam,[g] from Kedesh of Naphtali. "This is what the LORD, the God of Israel, commands," she said to him; "go, march on Mount Tabor, and take with you ten thousand Naphtalites and Zebulunites. [7]I will lead Sisera, the general of Jabin's army, out to you at the Wadi Kishon,[h] together with his chariots and troops, and will deliver them into your power." [8]But Barak answered her, "If you come with me, I will go; if you do not come with me, I will not go." [9]"I will certainly go with you," she replied, "but you shall not gain the glory in the expedition on which you are setting out, for the LORD will have Sisera fall into the power of a woman." So Deborah joined Barak and journeyed with him to Kedesh.

[10]Barak summoned Zebulun and Naphtali to Kedesh, and ten thousand men followed him. Deborah also went up with him.[i]

[11]*Now the Kenite Heber had detached himself from his own people, the descendants of Hobab, Moses' brother-in-law,[j] and had pitched his tent by the tere-binth of Zaanannim, which was near Kedesh.

[12]It was reported to Sisera that Barak, son of Abinoam, had gone up to Mount Tabor. [13]So Sisera assembled from Harosheth-ha-goiim at the Wadi Kishon all nine hundred of his iron chariots and all his forces. [14]Deborah then said to Barak, "Be off, for this is the day on which the LORD has delivered Sisera into your power. The LORD marches before you." So Barak went down Mount Tabor, followed by his ten thousand men. [15]And the LORD put Sisera[k] and all his chariots and all his forces to rout before Barak. Sisera himself dismounted from his chariot and fled on foot. [16]Barak, however, pursued the chariots and the army as far as Harosheth-ha-goiim. The entire army of Sisera fell beneath the sword, not even one man surviving.

[17]*Sisera, in the meantime, had fled on foot to the tent of Jael, wife of the Kenite Heber, since Jabin, king of Hazor, and the family of the Kenite Heber were at peace with one another. [18]Jael went out to meet Sisera and said to him, "Come in, my lord, come in with me; do not be afraid." So he went into her tent, and she covered him with a rug. [19]He said to her, "Please give me a little water to drink. I am thirsty." But she opened a jug of milk for him to drink, and then covered him over.[l] [20]"Stand at the entrance of the tent," he said to her. "If anyone comes and asks, 'Is there someone here?' say, 'No!' " [21]Instead Jael, wife of Heber, got a tent peg and took a mallet in her hand. While Sisera was sound asleep, she stealthily approached him and drove the peg through his temple down into the ground, so that he perished in death.[m] [22]Then when Barak came in pursuit of Sisera, Jael went out to meet him and said to him, "Come, I

4, 11: Most of the Kenites occupied a district in the southern part of Judah (Jgs 1, 16). A group of them, however, had detached themselves and settled in lower Galilee.

4, 17-22: It is to be noted that the sacred author merely records the fact of the murder of Sisera. We must not construe this as approval of Jael's action.

f: Jos 11, 1. 10; Ps 83, 10; 1 Sm 12, 9.   *g:* Heb 11, 32.   *h:* Jgs 5, 21; Ps 83, 10.   *i:* Jgs 5, 18.   *j:* Nm 10, 29.   *k:* Ps 83, 10.   *l:* Jgs 5, 25.   *m:* Jgs 5, 26.

Mediterranean
Sea

ARAM (SYRIA)

Sidon

Kedesh

Hazor

NAPHTALI

Bethlehem

ZEBULUN

ISSACHAR

MANASSEH

MANASSEH

Shechem
Mt. Gerizim
Arumah

Zaphon?
Penuel
Succoth
River Jabbok

GILEAD

EPHRAIM

Ramah

Bethel
Ophrah

Jogbehah

DAN

Aijalon
Mizpah

AMMON

Ekron
Timnah
Zorah

Heshbon

Ashdod

Lehi?

Gath?

Ashkelon

PHILISTIA

Gaza

Dead
Sea

R. Arnon

Karkor

MOAB

AMALEK

0   10   20 Miles
0   10   20 Kilometers

MIDIAN

35°   36°

Important Cities Mentioned in Judges

Harosheth-
ha-goiim?

Mt. Tabor

Hill of
Moreh

Wadi Kishon

V. of Jezreel

Hill Country
of Ephraim

Thebez?

32°

31°

274

will show you the man you seek." So he went in with her, and there lay Sisera dead, with the tent peg through his temple.

²³Thus on that day God humbled the Canaanite king, Jabin, before the Israelites; ²⁴their power weighed ever heavier upon him, till at length they destroyed the Canaanite king, Jabin.

See RG 159

CHAPTER 5

Canticle of Deborah. ¹On that day Deborah [and Barak, son of Abinoam] sang this song:

² Of chiefs who took the lead in Israel,*
  of noble deeds by the people who
    bless the LORD,
³ Hear, O kings! Give ear, O princes!
  I to the LORD will sing my song,
  my hymn to the LORD, the God of
    Israel.

⁴ O LORD, when you went out from Seir,
  when you marched from the land of
    Edom,
The earth quaked and the heavens were
    shaken,
  while the clouds sent down showers.
⁵ Mountains trembled
  in the presence of the LORD, the One
    of Sinai,ⁿ
  in the presence of the LORD, the God
    of Israel.ᵒ

⁶ In the days of Shamgar, son of Anath,ᵖ
  in the days of slavery caravans ceased;
Those who traveled the roads
  went by roundabout paths.
⁷ Gone was freedom beyond the walls
  gone indeed from Israel.

When I, Deborah, rose,
  when I rose, a mother in Israel,
⁸ New gods* were their choice;
  then the war was at their gates.

Not a shield could be seen, nor a lance,
  among forty thousand in Israel!

⁹ My heart is with the leaders of Israel,
  nobles of the people who bless the
    LORD;
¹⁰ They who ride on white asses,
  seated on saddlecloths as they go their
    way;
¹¹ Sing of them to the strains of the harpers
    at the wells,
  where men recount the just deeds of
    the LORD,
  his just deeds that brought freedom to
    Israel.

¹² Awake, awake, Deborah!
  awake, awake, strike up a song.
Strength! arise, Barak,
  make despoilers your spoil, son of
    Abinoam.
¹³ Then down came the fugitives with the
    mighty,
  the people of the LORD came down for
    me as warriors.

¹⁴ From Ephraim, princes were in the valley;*
  behind you was Benjamin, among
    your troops.
From Machir came down commanders,
  from Zebulun wielders of the
    marshal's staff.

¹⁵ With Deborah were the princes of
    Issachar;
  Barak, too, was in the valley, his
    course unchecked.

Among the clans of Reuben
  great were the searchings of heart.�q
¹⁶ Why do you stay beside your hearths
  listening to the lowing of the herds?
Among the clans of Reuben
  great were the searchings of heart!

5, 2-31: This canticle is an excellent example of early Hebrew poetry, even though some of its verses are now obscure.

5, 8: New gods: pagan deities; cf Dt 32, 16-18. God punished the idolatry of the Israelites by leaving them relatively unarmed before the attacks of their enemies, who had better weapons, made of iron; cf 1 Sm 13, 19-22.

5, 14-22: Praise for the tribes which formed the Israelite league against Sisera: Ephraim, Benjamin, Manasseh (represented by Machir), Zebulun, Issachar, and Naphtali (led by Barak). The tribes of Reuben, Gad (Gilead), Dan, and Asher are chided for their lack of co-operation. The more distant tribes of Judah and Simeon are not mentioned.

n: Dt 33, 2; 2 Sm 22, 8; Pss 18, 8; 68, 9.   *o:* Ex 19, 16; Dt 4, 11; Ps 97, 5.   *p:* Jgs 3, 31.   *q:* Jgs 4, 14.

¹⁷ Gilead, beyond the Jordan, rests;
    why does Dan spend his time in ships?
Asher, who dwells along the shore,
    is resting in his coves.
¹⁸ Zebulun is the people defying death;
    Naphtali, too, on the open heights!^r

¹⁹ The kings came and fought;
    then they fought, those kings of
        Canaan,
At Taanach by the waters of Megiddo;
    no silver booty did they take.^s
²⁰ From the heavens the stars, too, fought;[*]
    from their courses they fought against
        Sisera.^t

²¹ The Wadi Kishon swept them away;
    a wadi . . . , the Kishon.^u
²² Then the hoofs of the horses pounded,
    with the dashing, dashing of his
        steeds.

²³ "Curse Meroz,"[*] says the LORD,
    "hurl a curse at its inhabitants!
For they came not to my help,
    as warriors to the help of the LORD."

²⁴ Blessed among women be Jael,
    blessed among tent-dwelling women.^v
²⁵ He asked for water, she gave him milk;^w
    in a princely bowl she offered curds.
²⁶ With her left hand she reached for the
        peg,
    with her right, for the workman's
        mallet.
She hammered Sisera, crushed his head;
    she smashed, stove in his temple.
²⁷ At her feet he sank down, fell, lay still;
    down at her feet he sank and fell;
    where he sank down, there he fell,
        slain.

²⁸ From the window peered down and
        wailed
    the mother of Sisera, from the lattice:
"Why is his chariot so long in coming?

why are the hoofbeats of his chariots
    delayed?"
²⁹ The wisest of her princesses answers her,
    and she, too, keeps answering herself:
³⁰ "They must be dividing the spoil they
        took:
    there must be a damsel or two for each
        man,
Spoils of dyed cloth as Sisera's spoil,
    an ornate shawl or two for me in the
        spoil."
³¹ May all your enemies perish thus,
    O LORD!^x
    but your friends be as the sun rising in
        its might!

And the land was at rest for forty years.

CHAPTER 6

See RG 159-60

The Call of Gideon. ¹The Israelites offended the LORD, who therefore delivered them into the power of Midian for seven years, ²so that Midian held Israel subject. For fear of Midian the Israelites established the fire signals on the mountains, the caves for refuge, and the strongholds. ³And it used to be that when the Israelites had completed their sowing, Midian, Amalek and the Kedemites would come up,^y ⁴encamp opposite them, and destroy the produce of the land as far as the outskirts of Gaza, leaving no sustenance in Israel, nor sheep, oxen or asses. ⁵For they would come up with their livestock, and their tents would become as numerous as locusts; and neither they nor their camels could be numbered, when they came into the land to lay it waste. ⁶Thus was Israel reduced to misery by Midian, and so the Israelites cried out to the LORD.

⁷When Israel cried out to the LORD because of Midian, ^{8z}he sent a prophet to the Israelites who said to them, "The LORD, the God of Israel, says: I led you up from Egypt; I brought you out of the place of slavery. ⁹I rescued you from the power of Egypt and of

---

5, 20f: It would seem that nature aided the Hebrews in some way. Perhaps the torrential rains swelled the waters of Kishon, which then overwhelmed the Canaanites.

5, 23: Meroz: an unknown locality in which Hebrews probably resided, since its inhabitants are cursed for their failure to proffer aid.

---

r: Jgs 4, 10. *s:* Jgs 1, 27; Jos 17, 11. *t:* Jgs 4, 15; Jos 10, 14. *u:* Jgs 4, 7. 13. *v:* Jgs 4, 17; Jdt 13, 17; Lk 1, 28. 42. *w:* 25f: Jgs 4, 19. 21. *x:* Ps 83, 10-19. *y:* 3f: Jgs 7, 12; Dt 28, 30ff. *z:* 8ff: Jgs 2, 1f; 10, 11-14.

all your other oppressors. I drove them out before you and gave you their land. [10]And I said to you: I, the LORD, am your God; you shall not venerate the gods of the Amorites in whose land you are dwelling. But you did not obey me."

[11]Then the angel of the LORD came and sat under the terebinth in Ophrah that belonged to Joash the Abiezrite. While his son Gideon was beating out wheat in the wine press to save it from the Midianites, [12]the angel of the LORD appeared to him and said, "The LORD is with you, O champion!" [13]"My Lord," Gideon said to him, "if the LORD is with us, why has all this happened to us? Where are his wondrous deeds of which our fathers told us when they said, 'Did not the LORD bring us up from Egypt?' For now the LORD has abandoned us and has delivered us into the power of Midian." [14]The LORD turned to him and said, "Go with the strength you have and save Israel from the power of Midian. It is I who send you." [15]But he answered him, "Please, my lord, how can I save Israel? My family is the meanest in Manasseh, and I am the most insignificant in my father's house." [16]"I shall be with you," the LORD said to him, "and you will cut down Midian to the last man." [17]He answered him, "If I find favor with you, give me a sign that you are speaking with me. [18]Do not depart from here, I pray you, until I come back to you and bring out my offering and set it before you." He answered, "I will await your return."

[19]So Gideon went off and prepared a kid and an ephah of flour in the form of unleavened cakes. Putting the meat in a basket and the broth in a pot, he brought them out to him under the terebinth and presented them. [20]The angel of God said to him, "Take the meat and unleavened cakes and lay them on this rock; then pour out the broth."[a] When he had done so, [21]the angel of the LORD stretched out the tip of the staff he held, and touched the meat and unleavened cakes. Thereupon a fire came up from the rock which consumed the meat and unleavened cakes, and the angel of the LORD disappeared from sight. [22b]Gideon, now aware that it had been the angel of the LORD, said, "Alas, Lord GOD, that I have seen the angel of the LORD face to face!" [23]The LORD answered him, "Be calm, do not fear. You shall not die." [24]So Gideon built there an altar to the LORD and called it Yahweh-shalom.* To this day it is still in Ophrah of the Abiezrites.

[25]That same night the LORD said to him, "Take the seven-year-old spare bullock and destroy your father's altar to Baal and cut down the sacred pole* that is by it. [26]You shall build, instead, the proper kind of altar to the LORD, your God, on top of this stronghold. Then take the spare bullock and offer it as a holocaust on the wood from the sacred pole you have cut down." [27]So Gideon took ten of his servants and did as the LORD had commanded him. But through fear of his family and of the townspeople, he would not do it by day, but did it at night. [28]Early the next morning the townspeople found that the altar of Baal had been destroyed, the sacred pole near it cut down, and the spare bullock offered on the altar that was built. [29]They asked one another, "Who did this?" Their inquiry led them to the conclusion that Gideon, son of Joash, had done it. [30]So the townspeople said to Joash, "Bring out your son that he may die, for he has destroyed the altar of Baal and has cut down the sacred pole that was near it." [31]But Joash replied to all who were standing around him, "Do you intend to act in Baal's stead, or be his champion? If anyone acts for him, he shall be put to death by morning. If he whose altar has been destroyed is a god, let him act for himself!" [32]So on that day Gideon was called Jerubbaal,* because of the words, "Let Baal take action against him, since he destroyed his altar."[c]

[33]Then all Midian and Amalek and the Kedemites mustered and crossed over into the valley of Jezreel, where they encamped. [34]The spirit of the LORD enveloped Gideon;

6, 24: Yahweh-shalom: Hebrew for "the LORD is peace," a reference to the Lord's words, "Be calm," literally, "Peace be to you!"

6, 25: The sacred pole: see note on Ex 34, 13.

6, 32: Jerubbaal: similar in sound to the Hebrew words meaning, "Let Baal take action."

a: Jgs 13, 19.   *b:* 22f: Gn 32, 31; Dt 5, 24ff.   *c:* 1 Sm 12, 11.

he blew the horn that summoned Abiezer to follow him. [35]He sent messengers, too, throughout Manasseh, which also obeyed his summons; through Asher, Zebulun and Naphtali, likewise, he sent messengers and these tribes advanced to meet the others. [36]Gideon said to God, "If indeed you are going to save Israel through me, as you promised, [37]I am putting this woolen fleece on the threshing floor. If dew comes on the fleece alone, while all the ground is dry, I shall know that you will save Israel through me, as you promised." [38]That is what took place. Early the next morning he wrung the dew from the fleece, squeezing out of it a bowlful of water. [39]Gideon then said to God, "Do not be angry with me if I speak once more. Let me make just one more test with the fleece. Let the fleece alone be dry, but let there be dew on all the ground." [40]That night God did so; the fleece alone was dry, but there was dew on all the ground.

Battles of Gideon

See RG 159-60

CHAPTER 7

Defeat of Midian. [1]Early the next morning Jerubbaal[d] (that is, Gideon) encamped by Enharod with all his soldiers. The camp of Midian was in the valley north of Gibeath-hammoreh. [2]The LORD said to Gideon, "You have too many soldiers with you for me to deliver Midian into their power, lest Israel vaunt itself against me and say, 'My own power brought me the victory.' [3]Now proclaim to all the soldiers, 'If anyone is afraid or fearful, let him leave.' "[e] When Gideon put them to this test on the mountain, twenty-two thousand of the soldiers left, but ten thousand remained. [4]The LORD said to Gideon, "There are still too many soldiers. Lead them down to the water and I will test them for you there. If I tell you that a certain man is to go with you, he must go with you. But no one is to go if I tell you he must not." [5*]When Gideon led the soldiers down to the water, the LORD said to him, "You shall set to one side everyone

who laps up the water as a dog does with its tongue; to the other, everyone who kneels down to drink." [6]Those who lapped up the water raised to their mouths by hand numbered three hundred, but all the rest of the soldiers knelt down to drink the water. [7]The LORD said to Gideon, "By means of the three hundred who lapped up the water I will save you and will deliver Midian into your power. So let all the other soldiers go home." [8]Their horns, and such supplies as the soldiers had with them, were taken up, and Gideon ordered the rest of the Israelites to their tents, but kept the three hundred men. Now the camp of Midian was beneath him in the valley.

[9]That night the LORD said to Gideon, "Go, descend on the camp, for I have delivered it up to you. [10]If you are afraid to attack, go down to the camp with your aide Purah. [11]When you hear what they are saying, you

---

7, 5: The Lord desired not numerous but reliable soldiers. Those who drank from their hands were alert, standing ready to resist attack, whereas the others were careless and undependable. The cowardly soldiers had already been dismissed (v 3); cf Dt 20, 8.

---

d: Jgs 6, 32.   *e:* Dt 20, 8.

will have the courage to descend on the camp." So he went down with his aide Purah to the outposts of the camp. *12*The Midianites, Amalekites, and all the Kedemites lay in the valley, as numerous as locusts. Nor could their camels be counted, for these were as many as the sands on the seashore. *13**When Gideon arrived, one man was telling another about a dream. "I had a dream," he said, "that a round loaf of barley bread was rolling into the camp of Midian. It came to our tent and struck it, and as it fell it turned the tent upside down." *14*"This can only be the sword of the Israelite Gideon, son of Joash," the other replied. "God has delivered Midian and all the camp into his power." *15*When Gideon heard the description and explanation of the dream, he prostrated himself. Then returning to the camp of Israel, he said, "Arise, for the LORD has delivered the camp of Midian into your power."

*16*He divided the three hundred men into three companies, and provided them all with horns and with empty jars and torches inside the jars. *17*"Watch me and follow my lead," he told them. "I shall go to the edge of the camp, and as I do, you must do also. *18*When I and those with me blow horns, you too must blow horns all around the camp and cry out, 'For the LORD and for Gideon!' " *19*So Gideon and the hundred men who were with him came to the edge of the camp at the beginning of the middle watch,* just after the posting of the guards. They blew the horns and broke the jars they were holding. *20*All three companies blew horns and broke their jars. They held the torches in their left hands, and in their right the horns they were blowing, and cried out, "A sword for the LORD and Gideon!" *21*They all remained standing in place around the camp, while the whole camp fell to running and shouting and fleeing. *22*But the three hundred men kept blowing the horns, and throughout the camp the

LORD set the sword of one against another.*f* The army fled as far as Beth-shittah in the direction of Zarethan, near the border of Abel-meholah at Tabbath.

*23*The Israelites were called to arms from Naphtali, from Asher, and from all Manasseh, and they pursued Midian. *24*Gideon also sent messengers throughout the mountain region of Ephraim to say, "Go down to confront Midian, and seize the water courses against them as far as Beth-barah, as well as the Jordan." So all the Ephraimites were called to arms, and they seized the water courses as far as Beth-barah, and the Jordan as well. *25g*They captured the two princes of Midian, Oreb and Zeeb, killing Oreb at the rock of Oreb and Zeeb at the wine press of Zeeb. Then they pursued Midian and carried the heads of Oreb and Zeeb to Gideon beyond the Jordan.

CHAPTER 8

See RG
159–60

*1*But the Ephraimites said to him, "What have you done to us, not calling us when you went to fight against Midian?" And they quarrelled bitterly with him. *2*"What have I accomplished now in comparison with you?" he answered them. "Is not the gleaning of Ephraim better than the vintage of Abiezer?*h* *3*Into your power God delivered the princes of Midian, Oreb and Zeeb. What have I been able to do in comparison with you?" When he said this, their anger against him subsided.

*4*When Gideon reached the Jordan and crossed it with his three hundred men, they were exhausted and famished. *5*So he said to the men of Succoth, "Will you give my followers some loaves of bread? They are exhausted, and I am pursuing Zebah and Zalmunna, kings of Midian." *6*But the princes of Succoth replied, "Are the hands of Zebah and Zalmunna already in your possession, that we should give food to your army?"*

7, 13: The barley loaf represents the agricultural Hebrews while the tent refers to the nomadic Midianites. The overthrow of the tent indicates the victory of the Hebrews over their Midianite oppressors.

7, 19: At the beginning of the middle watch: about two hours before midnight. The ancient Hebrews divided the night into three watches of about four hours each. At the beginning of a watch the sentinels were changed.

8, 6: Are the hands . . . in your possession . . . ?: i.e., can you already boast of victory? The hands as well as the heads of slain enemies were cut off and counted as trophies; cf 2 Sm 4, 8; 2 Kgs 10, 7f; and the Ugaritic Anath Epic, V AB, II 10ff.

f: 22f: Ps 83, 10; Is 9, 4.   *g:* Jgs 8, 3; Ps 83, 12; Is 10, 26.   *h:* Jg 6, 34.

[7]Gideon said, "Very well; when the LORD has delivered Zebah and Zalmunna into my power, I will grind your flesh in with the thorns and briers of the desert." [8]He went up from there to Penuel and made the same request of them, but the men of Penuel answered him as had the men of Succoth. [9]So to the men of Penuel, too, he said, "When I return in triumph, I will demolish this tower."

[10]Now Zebah and Zalmunna were in Karkor with their force of about fifteen thousand men; these were all who were left of the whole Kedemite army, a hundred and twenty thousand swordsmen having fallen. [11]Gideon went up by the route of the nomads east of Nobah and Jogbehah, and attacked the camp when it felt secure. [12]Zebah and Zalmunna fled. He pursued them and took the two kings of Midian, Zebah and Zalmunna, captive, throwing the entire army into panic. [13]Then Gideon, son of Joash, returned from battle by the pass of Heres. [14]He captured a young man of Succoth, who upon being questioned listed for him the seventy-seven princes and elders of Succoth. [15]So he went to the men of Succoth and said, "Here are Zebah and Zalmunna, with whom you taunted me, 'Are the hands of Zebah and Zalmunna already in your possession, that we should give food to your weary followers?' " [16]He took the elders of the city, and thorns and briers of the desert, and ground these men of Succoth into them. [17]He also demolished the tower of Penuel and slew the men of the city.

[18]Then he said to Zebah and Zalmunna, "Where now are the men you killed at Tabor?" "They all resembled you," they replied. "They appeared to be princes." [19]"They were my brothers, my mother's sons," he said. "As the LORD lives, if you had spared their lives, I should not kill you." [20]Then he said to his first-born, Jether, "Go, kill them." Since Jether was still a boy, he was afraid and did not draw his sword. [21]Zebah and Zalmunna said, "Come, kill us yourself, for a man's strength is like the man." So Gideon stepped forward and killed Zebah and Zalmunna. He also took the crescents that were on the necks of their camels.

[22]The Israelites then said to Gideon, "Rule over us—you, your son, and your son's son—for you rescued us from the power of Midian." [23]But Gideon answered them, "I will not rule over you, nor shall my son rule over you. The LORD must rule over you."

[24]Gideon went on to say, "I should like to make a request of you. Will each of you give me a ring from his booty?" (For being Ishmaelites,* the enemy had gold rings.) [25]"We will gladly give them," they replied, and spread out a cloak into which everyone threw a ring from his booty. [26]The gold rings that he requested weighed seventeen hundred gold shekels, in addition to the crescents and pendants, the purple garments worn by the kings of Midian, and the trappings that were on the necks of their camels. [27]Gideon made an ephod out of the gold and placed it in his city Ophrah. However, all Israel paid idolatrous homage to it there, and caused the ruin of Gideon and his family.

[28]Thus was Midian brought into subjection by the Israelites; no longer did they hold their heads high. And the land had rest for forty years, during the lifetime of Gideon.

Gideon's Son Abimelech. [29]Then Jerubbaal, son of Joash, went back home to stay. [30i]Now Gideon had seventy sons, his direct descendants, for he had many wives. [31]His concubine* who lived in Shechem also bore him a son, whom he named Abimelech. [32]At a good old age Gideon, son of Joash, died and was buried in the tomb of his father Joash in Ophrah of the Abiezrites. [33]But after Gideon was dead, the Israelites again abandoned themselves to the Baals, making Baal of Berith* their god [34]and forgetting the LORD, their God, who had delivered them from the power of their enemies all around them. [35]Nor were they grateful to the family of Jerubbaal [Gideon] for all the good he had done for Israel.

8, 24: Ishmaelites: here as in Gn 37, 25-28, the designation is not ethnic; it refers rather to their status as nomads.

8, 31: Concubine: a wife of secondary rank.

8, 33: Baal of Berith: one of the titles of Baal as worshiped by the Canaanites of Shechem, meaning "the lord of the covenant."

i: Jgs 9, 2. 5.

CHAPTER 9

See RG
160–61

¹Abimelech, son of Jerubbaal, went to his mother's kinsmen in Shechem,ʲ and said to them and to the whole clan to which his mother's family belonged, ²"Put this question to all the citizens of Shechem: 'Which is better for you: that seventy men, or all Jerubbaal's sons, rule over you, or that one man rule over you?' You must remember that I am your own flesh and bone." ³When his mother's kin repeated these words to them on his behalf, all the citizens of Shechem sympathized with Abimelech, thinking, "He is our kinsman." ⁴They also gave him seventy silver shekels from the temple of Baal of Berith, with which Abimelech hired shiftless men and ruffians as his followers. ⁵He then went to his ancestral house in Ophrah, and slew his brothers, the seventy sons of Jerubbaal, on one stone. Only the youngest son of Jerubbaal, Jotham, escaped, for he was hidden. ⁶Then all the citizens of Shechem and all Beth-millo came together and proceeded to make Abimelech king by the terebinth at the memorial pillar in Shechem.

⁷When this was reported to him, Jotham went to the top of Mount Gerizim, and standing there, cried out to them in a loud voice: "Hear me, citizens of Shechem, that God may then hear you! ⁸Once the trees went to anoint a king over themselves. So they said to the olive tree, 'Reign over us.'ᵏ ⁹But the olive tree answered them, 'Must I give up my rich oil, whereby men and gods are honored,* and go to wave over the trees?' ¹⁰Then the trees said to the fig tree, 'Come; you reign over us!' ¹¹But the fig tree answered them, 'Must I give up my sweetness and my good fruit, and go to wave over the trees?' ¹²Then the trees said to the vine, 'Come you, and reign over us.' ¹³But the vine answered them, 'Must I give up my wine that cheers gods* and men, and go to wave over the trees?' ¹⁴Then all the trees said to the buckthorn, 'Come; you reign over us!' ¹⁵But the buckthorn replied to the trees, 'If you wish to anoint me king over you in good faith, come and take refuge in my shadow. Otherwise, let fire come from the buckthorn and devour the cedars of Lebanon.'

¹⁶*"Now then, if you have acted in good faith and honorably in appointing Abimelech your king, if you have dealt well with Jerubbaal and with his family, and if you have treated him as he deserved— ¹⁷for my father fought for you at the risk of his life when he saved you from the power of Midian; ¹⁸but you have risen against his family this day and have killed his seventy sons upon one stone, and have made Abimelech, the son of his handmaid,ˡ king over the citizens of Shechem, because he is your kinsman— ¹⁹if, then, you have acted in good faith and with honor toward Jerubbaal and his family this day, rejoice in Abimelech and may he in turn rejoice in you. ²⁰But if not, let fire come forth from Abimelech to devour the citizens of Shechem and Beth-millo, and let fire come forth from the citizens and from Beth-millo to devour Abimelech." ²¹Then Jotham went in flight to Beer, where he remained for fear of his brother Abimelech.

²²When Abimelech had ruled Israel for three years, ²³God put bad feelings between Abimelech and the citizens of Shechem, who rebelled against Abimelech. ²⁴This was to repay the violence done to the seventy sons of Jerubbaal and to avenge their blood upon their brother Abimelech, who killed them, and upon the citizens of Shechem, who encouraged him to kill his brothers. ²⁵The citizens of Shechem then set men in ambush for him on the mountaintops, and these robbed all who passed them on the road. But it was reported to Abimelech.

9, 9: Whereby men and gods are honored: oil was used in the worship both of the true God and of false gods; it was prescribed in the worship of Yahweh (Lv 2, 1. 6. 15; 24, 2). It was also used to consecrate prophets, priests and kings (Ex 30, 25. 30; 1 Sm 10, 1; 16, 13).

9, 13: Cheers gods: wine was used in the libations both of the Temple of Jerusalem and of pagan temples.

9, 16: Just as the noble trees refused the honor of royalty and were made subject to a mean plant, so did Abimelech of less noble birth than the seventy sons of Gideon now tyrannize over the people.

---

j: Jgs 8, 31.   *k:* Jgs 8, 22f.   *l:* Jgs 8, 31.

²⁶Now Gaal, son of Ebed, came over to Shechem with his kinsmen. The citizens of Shechem put their trust in him, ²⁷and went out into the fields, harvested their grapes and trod them out. Then they held a festival and went to the temple of their god, where they ate and drank and cursed Abimelech. ²⁸Gaal, son of Ebed, said, "Who is Abimelech? And why should we of Shechem serve him? Were not the son of Jerubbaal and his lieutenant Zebul once subject to the men of Hamor, father of Shechem?ᵐ Why should we serve him? ²⁹Would that this people were entrusted to my command! I would depose Abimelech. I would say to Abimelech, 'Get a larger army and come out!' "

³⁰At the news of what Gaal, son of Ebed, had said, Zebul, the ruler of the city, was angry ³¹and sent messengers to Abimelech in Arumah with the information: "Gaal, son of Ebed, and his kinsmen have come to Shechem and are stirring up the city against you. ³²Now rouse yourself; set an ambush tonight in the fields, you and the men who are with you. ³³Promptly at sunrise tomorrow morning, make a raid on the city. When he and his followers come out against you, deal with him as best you can."

³⁴During the night Abimelech advanced with all his soldiers and set up an ambush for Shechem in four companies. ³⁵Gaal, son of Ebed, went out and stood at the entrance of the city gate. When Abimelech and his soldiers rose from their place of ambush, ³⁶Gaal saw them and said to Zebul, "There are men coming down from the hilltops!" But Zebul answered him, "You see the shadow of the hills as men." ³⁷But Gaal went on to say, "Men are coming down from the region of Tabbur-Haares, and one company is coming by way of Elon-Meonenim." ³⁸Zebul said to him, "Where now is the boast you uttered, 'Who is Abimelech that we should serve him?' Are these not the men for whom you expressed contempt? Go out now and fight with them." ³⁹So Gaal went out at the head of the citizens of Shechem and fought against Abimelech. ⁴⁰But Abimelech routed him, and he fled before him; and many fell slain right up to the entrance of the gate. ⁴¹Abimelech returned to Arumah, but Zebul drove Gaal and his kinsmen from Shechem, which they had occupied.

⁴²The next day, when the people were taking the field, it was reported to Abimelech, ⁴³who divided the men he had into three companies, and set up an ambush in the fields. He watched till he saw the people leave the city, and then rose against them for the attack. ⁴⁴Abimelech and the company with him dashed in and stood by the entrance of the city gate, while the other two companies rushed upon all who were in the field and attacked them. ⁴⁵That entire day Abimelech fought against the city, and captured it. He then killed its inhabitants and demolished the city, sowing the site with salt.*

⁴⁶When they heard of this, all the citizens of Migdal-shechem went into the crypt of the temple of El-berith. ⁴⁷It was reported to Abimelech that all the citizens of Migdal-shechem were gathered together. ⁴⁸So he went up Mount Zalmon with all his soldiers, took his ax in his hand, and cut down some brushwood. This he lifted to his shoulder, then said to the men with him, "Hurry! Do just as you have seen me do." ⁴⁹So all the men likewise cut down brushwood, and following Abimelech, placed it against the crypt. Then they set the crypt on fire over their heads, so that every one of the citizens of Migdal-shechem, about a thousand men and women, perished.

⁵⁰Abimelech proceeded to Thebez, which he invested and captured. ⁵¹Now there was a strong tower in the middle of the city, and all the men and women, in a word all the citizens of the city, fled there, shutting themselves in and going up to the roof of the tower. ⁵²Abimelech came up to the tower and fought against it, advancing to the very entrance of the tower to set it on fire. ⁵³But a certain woman cast the upper part of a millstone down on Abimelech's head, and it

9, 45: Sowing the site with salt: a severe measure, which was a symbol of desolation, and even more, since it actually rendered the ground barren and useless.

m: Gn 34, 2. 6.

fractured his skull.[n] [54]He immediately called his armor-bearer and said to him, "Draw your sword and dispatch me, lest they say of me that a woman killed me."[o] So his attendant ran him through and he died. [55]When the Israelites saw that Abimelech was dead, they all left for their homes.

[56]Thus did God requite the evil Abimelech had done to his father in killing his seventy brothers. [57]God also brought all their wickedness home to the Shechemites, for the curse of Jotham, son of Jerubbaal, overtook them.

CHAPTER 10

See RG
161

Tola. [1]After Abimelech there rose to save Israel the Issacharite Tola, son of Puah, son of Dodo, a resident of Shamir in the mountain region of Ephraim. [2]When he had judged Israel twenty-three years, he died and was buried in Shamir.

Jair. [3]Jair the Gileadite came after him and judged Israel twenty-two years. [4]He had thirty sons who rode on thirty saddle-asses* and possessed thirty cities in the land of Gilead; these are called Havvoth-jair to the present day.[p] [5]Jair died and was buried in Kamon.

Oppression by the Ammonites. [6]The Israelites again offended the LORD, serving the Baals and Ashtaroths, the gods of Aram, the gods of Sidon, the gods of Moab, the gods of the Ammonites, and the gods of the Philistines. Since they had abandoned the LORD and would not serve him, [7]the LORD became angry with Israel and allowed them to fall into the power of [the Philistines and] the Ammonites. [8]For eighteen years they afflicted and oppressed the Israelites in Bashan, and all the Israelites in the Amorite land beyond the Jordan in Gilead. [9]The Ammonites also crossed the Jordan to fight against Judah, Benjamin, and the house of Ephraim, so that Israel was in great distress.

[10]Then the Israelites cried out to the LORD, "We have sinned against you; we have forsaken our God and have served the Baals." [11][q]The LORD answered the Israelites: "Did

The Twelve Judges

not the Egyptians, the Amorites,[r] the Ammonites, the Philistines, [12]the Sidonians, the Amalekites, and the Midianites oppress you?[s] Yet when you cried out to me, and I saved you from their grasp, [13]you still forsook me and worshiped other gods. Therefore I will save you no more. [14]Go and cry out to the gods you have chosen; let them save you now that you are in distress." [15]But the Israelites said to the LORD, "We have sinned. Do to us whatever you please. Only save us this day." [16]And they cast out the foreign gods from their midst and served the LORD, so that he grieved over the misery of Israel.

[17]The Ammonites had gathered for war and encamped in Gilead, while the Israelites assembled and encamped in Mizpah.[t] [18]And among the people the princes of Gilead said to one another, "The one who begins the war against the Ammonites shall be leader of all the inhabitants of Gilead."[u]

10, 4: Saddle-asses: a sign of rank and wealth; cf Jgs 5, 10; 12, 14.

n: 2 Sm 11, 21.   o: 1 Sm 31, 4; 1 Chr 10, 4.   p: Dt 3, 14.   q: 11-14: Jgs 2, 1ff; 6, 8ff.   r: Nm 21, 21-32.   s: Jgs 6, 3.   t: Jgs 11, 29.
u: Jgs 11, 5-11.

CHAPTER 11

See RG
161

Jephthah. *1*There was a chieftain, the Gileadite Jephthah, born to Gilead of a harlot. *2*Gilead's wife had also borne him sons, and on growing up the sons of the wife had driven Jephthah away, saying to him, "You shall inherit nothing in our family, for you are the son of another woman." *3*So Jephthah had fled from his brothers and had taken up residence in the land of Tob. A rabble had joined company with him, and went out with him on raids.

*4*Some time later, the Ammonites warred on Israel. *5*When this occurred the elders of Gilead went to bring Jephthah from the land of Tob. *6*"Come," they said to Jephthah, "be our commander that we may be able to fight the Ammonites." *7*"Are you not the ones who hated me and drove me from my father's house?" Jephthah replied to the elders of Gilead. "Why do you come to me now, when you are in distress?" *8*The elders of Gilead said to Jephthah, "In any case, we have now come back to you; if you go with us to fight against the Ammonites, you shall be the leader of all of us who dwell in Gilead." *9*Jephthah answered the elders of Gilead, "If you bring me back to fight against the Ammonites and the LORD delivers them up to me, I shall be your leader." *10*The elders of Gilead said to Jephthah, "The LORD is witness between us that we will do as you say."

*11*So Jephthah went with the elders of Gilead, and the people made him their leader and commander.*v* In Mizpah, Jephthah settled all his affairs before the LORD. *12*Then he sent messengers to the king of the Ammonites to say, "What have you against me that you come to fight with me in my land?" *13*He answered the messengers of Jephthah, "Israel took away my land from the Arnon to the Jabbok and the Jordan when they came up from Egypt.*w* Now restore the same peaceably."

*14*Again Jephthah sent messengers to the king of the Ammonites, *15*saying to him, "This is what Jephthah says: Israel did not take the land of Moab or the land of the Ammonites.*x* *16*For when they came up from Egypt, Israel went through the desert to the Red Sea and came to Kadesh. *17*Israel then sent messengers to the king of Edom saying, 'Let me pass through your land.' But the king of Edom did not give consent. They also sent to the king of Moab, but he too was unwilling. So Israel remained in Kadesh.*y* *18*Then they went through the desert, and bypassing the land of Edom and the land of Moab, went east of the land of Moab and encamped across the Arnon.*z* Thus they did not go through the territory of Moab, for the Arnon is the boundary of Moab. *19a*Then Israel sent messengers to Sihon, king of the Amorites, king of Heshbon. Israel said to him, 'Let me pass through your land to my own place.' *20*But Sihon refused to let Israel pass through his territory. On the contrary, he gathered all his soldiers, who encamped at Jahaz and fought Israel. *21*But the LORD, the God of Israel, delivered Sihon and all his men into the power of Israel, who defeated them and occupied all the land of the Amorites dwelling in that region, *22*the whole territory from the Arnon to the Jabbok, from the desert to the Jordan. *23*If now the LORD, the God of Israel, has cleared the Amorites out of the way of his people, are you to dislodge Israel? *24*Should you not possess that which your god Chemosh* gave you to possess, and should we not possess all that the LORD, our God, has cleared out for us?*b* *25*Again, are you any better than Balak, son of Zippor, king of Moab? Did he ever quarrel with Israel, or did he war against them*c* *26*when Israel occupied Heshbon and its villages, Aroer and its villages, and all the cit-

11, 24: Chemosh: the chief god of the Moabites—not of the Ammonites, whose leading deity was called Molech or Milcom; cf Nm 21, 29; 1 Kgs 11, 7; 2 Kgs 23, 13. The error is probably due to an ancient copyist. Jephthah argues from the viewpoint of his adversaries, the Ammonites, that they were entitled to all the land they had conquered with the aid of their god. It does not necessarily follow that Jephthah himself believed in the actual existence of this pagan god.

v: Jgs 10, 18.   *w:* Nm 21, 13. 24ff.   *x:* Dt 2, 9. 19.   *y:* Nm 20, 1. 14. 18-21; Dt 1, 46.   *z:* Nm 21, 4. 11. 13; 22, 36; Dt 2, 8.
a: 19-22: Nm 21, 21-26; Dt 2, 26-36.   *b:* Nm 21, 29; 1 Kgs 11, 7.   *c:* Nm 22, 2; Jos 24, 9; Mi 6, 5.

ies on the banks of the Arnon?^{d} Three hundred years have passed; why did you not recover them during that time? ^{27}I have not sinned against you, but you wrong me by warring against me. Let the LORD, who is judge, decide this day between the Israelites and the Ammonites!" ^{28}But the king of the Ammonites paid no heed to the message Jephthah sent him.

Jephthah's Vow. ^{29}The spirit of the LORD came upon Jephthah. He passed through Gilead and Manasseh, and through Mizpah-Gilead as well, and from there he went on to the Ammonites. ^{30}*Jephthah made a vow to the LORD. "If you deliver the Ammonites into my power," he said, ^{31}"whoever comes out of the doors of my house to meet me when I return in triumph from the Ammonites shall belong to the LORD. I shall offer him up as a holocaust."

^{32}Jephthah then went on to the Ammonites to fight against them, and the LORD delivered them into his power, ^{33}so that he inflicted a severe defeat on them, from Aroer to the approach of Minnith (twenty cities in all) and as far as Abel-keramim. Thus were the Ammonites brought into subjection by the Israelites. ^{34}When Jephthah returned to his house in Mizpah, it was his daughter who came forth, playing the tambourines and dancing. She was an only child: he had neither son nor daughter besides her. ^{35}When he saw her, he rent his garments and said, "Alas, daughter, you have struck me down and brought calamity upon me. For I have made a vow to the LORD and I cannot retract."^{e} ^{36}"Father," she replied, "you have made a vow to the LORD. Do with me as you have vowed, because the LORD has wrought vengeance for you on your enemies the Ammonites." ^{37}Then she said to her father, "Let me have this favor. Spare me for two months, that I may go off down the mountains to mourn my virginity* with my com-

panions." ^{38}"Go," he replied, and sent her away for two months. So she departed with her companions and mourned her virginity on the mountains. ^{39}At the end of the two months she returned to her father, who did to her as he had vowed. She had not been intimate with man. It then became a custom in Israel ^{40}for Israelite women to go yearly to mourn the daughter of Jephthah the Gileadite for four days of the year.

CHAPTER 12

The Shibboleth Incident. ^{1}The men of Ephraim gathered together and crossed over to Zaphon. They said to Jephthah, "Why do you go on to fight with the Ammonites without calling us to go with you? We will burn your house over you."^{f} ^{2}Jephthah answered them, "My soldiers and I were engaged in a critical contest with the Ammonites. I summoned you, but you did not rescue me from their power. ^{3}When I saw that you would not effect a rescue, I took my life in my own hand and went on to the Ammonites, and the LORD delivered them into my power. Why, then, do you come up against me this day to fight with me?"

^{4}Then Jephthah called together all the men of Gilead and fought against Ephraim, whom they defeated; for the Ephraimites had said, "You of Gilead are Ephraimite fugitives in territory belonging to Ephraim and Manasseh." ^{5}The Gileadites took the fords of the Jordan toward Ephraim. When any of the fleeing Ephraimites said, "Let me pass," the men of Gilead would say to him, "Are you an Ephraimite?" If he answered, "No!" ^{6}they would ask him to say "Shibboleth."* If he said "Sibboleth," not being able to give the proper pronunciation, they would seize him and kill him at the fords of the Jordan. Thus forty-two thousand Ephraimites fell at that time.

See RG 161-62

11, 30-40: The text clearly implies that Jephthah vowed a human sacrifice, according to the custom of his pagan neighbors; cf 2 Kgs 3, 27. The inspired author merely records the fact; he does not approve of the action.

11, 37: Mourn my virginity: to bear children was woman's greatest pride; to be childless was regarded as a great misfortune. Hence Jephthah's daughter asks permission to mourn the fact that she will be put to death before she can bear children.

12, 6: Shibboleth: "an ear of grain." But this Hebrew word can also mean "flood water" as in Ps 69, 3. 16. Apparently the Gileadites engaged the Ephraimites in conversation about the "flood water" of the Jordan. Differences in enunciating the initial sibilant of the Hebrew word betrayed different tribal affinities.

d: Nm 21, 25; Dt 2, 36.   *e:* Nm 30, 3.   *f:* Jgs 8, 1.

[7]After having judged Israel for six years, Jephthah the Gileadite died and was buried in his city in Gilead.

Ibzan. [8]After him Ibzan of Bethlehem judged Israel. [9]He had thirty sons. He also had thirty daughters married outside the family, and he brought in as wives for his sons thirty young women from outside the family. After having judged Israel for seven years, [10]Ibzan died and was buried in Bethlehem.

Elon. [11]After him the Zebulunite Elon judged Israel. When he had judged Israel for ten years, [12]the Zebulunite Elon died and was buried in Elon in the land of Zebulun.

Abdon. [13]After him the Pirathonite Abdon, son of Hillel, judged Israel. [14]He had forty sons and thirty grandsons who rode on seventy saddle-asses. After having judged Israel for eight years, [15]the Pirathonite Abdon, son of Hillel, died and was buried in Pirathon in the land of Ephraim on the mountain of the Amalekites.

CHAPTER 13

See RG
162

The Birth of Samson. [1]The Israelites again offended the LORD, who therefore delivered them into the power of the Philistines for forty years.[g]

[2]There was a certain man from Zorah, of the clan of the Danites, whose name was Manoah. His wife was barren and had borne no children. [3]An angel of the LORD appeared to the woman and said to her, "Though you are barren and have had no children, yet you will conceive and bear a son.[h] [4]Now, then, be careful to take no wine or strong drink and to eat nothing unclean. [5]As for the son you will conceive and bear, no razor shall touch his head,[i] for this boy is to be consecrated* to God from the womb. It is he who will begin the deliverance of Israel from the power of the Philistines."

[6]The woman went and told her husband, "A man of God came to me; he had the appearance of an angel of God, terrible indeed.

I did not ask him where he came from, nor did he tell me his name. [7]But he said to me, 'You will be with child and will bear a son. So take neither wine nor strong drink, and eat nothing unclean. For the boy shall be consecrated to God from the womb, until the day of his death.' " [8]Manoah then prayed to the LORD. "O LORD, I beseech you," he said, "may the man of God whom you sent, return to us to teach us what to do for the boy who will be born."

[9]God heard the prayer of Manoah, and the angel of God came again to the woman as she was sitting in the field. Since her husband Manoah was not with her, [10]the woman ran in haste and told her husband. "The man who came to me the other day has appeared to me," she said to him; [11]so Manoah got up and followed his wife. When he reached the man, he said to him, "Are you the one who spoke to my wife?" "Yes," he answered. [12]Then Manoah asked, "Now, when that which you say comes true, what are we expected to do for the boy?" [13]The angel of the LORD answered Manoah, "Your wife is to abstain from all the things of which I spoke to her. [14]She must not eat anything that comes from the vine, nor take wine or strong drink, nor eat anything unclean. Let her observe all that I have commanded her." [15]Then Manoah said to the angel of the LORD, "Can we persuade you to stay, while we prepare a kid for you?" [16]But the angel of the LORD answered Manoah, "Although you press me, I will not partake of your food. But if you will, you may offer a holocaust to the LORD." Not knowing that it was the angel of the LORD, [17]Manoah said to him, "What is your name, that we may honor you when your words come true?" [18]The angel of the LORD answered him,[j] "Why do you ask my name, which is mysterious?"* [19][k]Then Manoah took the kid with a cereal offering and offered it on the rock to the LORD, whose works are mysteries. While Manoah and his wife were looking on, [20]as the flame rose to

---

13, 5: Consecrated: In Hebrew, nazir. Samson therefore was for life to be under the nazirite vow, which obliged him to abstain from drinking wine or having his hair cut; cf Nm 6, 2-8.

13, 18: Mysterious: incomprehensible, above human understanding. Hence, the angel speaks in the name of the Lord himself, to whom Manoah at once offers a sacrifice.

g: Jgs 10, 6.   *h:* 3f: 1 Sm 1, 20; Lk 1, 31.   *i:* Nm 6, 5.   *j:* Gn 32, 29.   *k:* 19f: Jgs 6, 19ff.

the sky from the altar, the angel of the LORD ascended in the flame of the altar. When Manoah and his wife saw this, they fell prostrate to the ground; *21*but the angel of the LORD was seen no more by Manoah and his wife. Then Manoah, realizing that it was the angel of the LORD, *22*said to his wife, "We will certainly die, for we have seen God."*l* *23*But his wife pointed out to him, "If the LORD had meant to kill us, he would not have accepted a holocaust and cereal offering from our hands! Nor would he have let us see all this just now, or hear what we have heard."

*24*The woman bore a son and named him Samson.*m* The boy grew up and the LORD blessed him; *25*the spirit of the LORD first stirred him in Mahaneh-dan, which is between Zorah and Eshtaol.

CHAPTER 14

See RG
162

Marriage of Samson. *1*Samson went down to Timnah and saw there one of the Philistine women.* *2*On his return he told his father and mother, "There is a Philistine woman I saw in Timnah whom I wish you to get as a wife for me." *3*His father and mother said to him, "Can you find no wife among your kinsfolk or among all our people, that you must go and take a wife from the uncircumcised Philistines?" But Samson answered his father, "Get her for me, for she pleases me." *4nNow his father and mother did not know that this had been brought about by the LORD, who was providing an opportunity against the Philistines; for at that time they had dominion over Israel.

*5*So Samson went down to Timnah with his father and mother. When they had come to the vineyards of Timnah, a young lion came roaring to meet him. *6*But the spirit of the LORD came upon Samson, and although he had no weapons, he tore the lion in pieces as one tears a kid. *7*However, on the journey

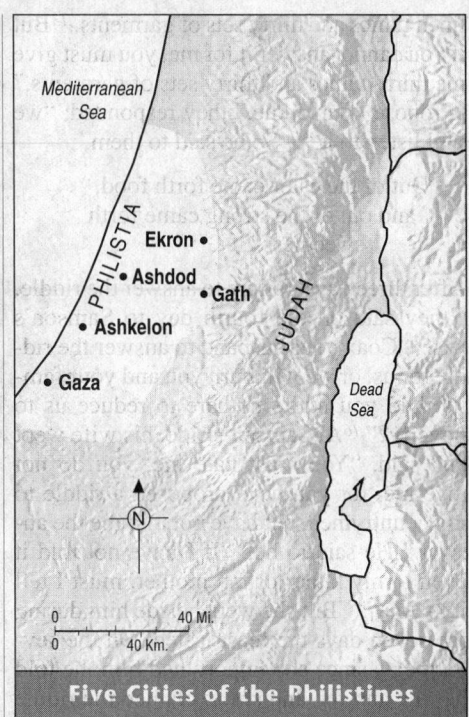

Mediterranean Sea

PHILISTIA

Ekron •

• Ashdod
• Gath

• Ashkelon

JUDAH

• Gaza

Dead Sea

N

0   40 Mi.
0   40 Km.

Five Cities of the Philistines

to speak for the woman, he did not mention to his father or mother what he had done. *8*Later, when he returned to marry the woman who pleased him, he stepped aside to look at the remains of the lion and found a swarm of bees and honey in the lion's carcass. *9*So he scooped the honey out into his palms and ate it as he went along. When he came to his father and mother, he gave them some to eat, without telling them that he had scooped the honey from the lion's carcass.

*10*His father also went down to the woman, and Samson gave a banquet there, since it was customary for the young men to do this. *11*When they met him, they brought thirty men to be his companions.* *12*Samson said to them, "Let me propose a riddle to you. If within the seven days of the feast you solve it for me successfully, I will give you thirty

---

14, 1-3: Marriages were arranged by the parents of the bridegroom as well as of the bride; cf Gn 24, 2-8; 34, 3-6. The Mosaic law specified only seven pagan nations, not including the Philistines, in the prohibition against mixed marriages; cf Dt 7, 1-4. But national and religious sentiment was against any marriage with a non-Israelite; cf Gn 28, 1f; 1 Kgs 11, 1-10.

14, 5ff: Although Samson was accompanied by his parents on the journey to Timnah, v 7 implies that he

was not near them when he tore the lion in pieces.

14, 11: Companions: known at a later period as "the friends of the bridegroom" (1 Mc 9, 39; Mk 2, 19), the best man and his fellows. Here they are Philistines (v 16), appointed by the family of the bride, who would also have several bridesmaids; cf Mt 25, 1-13.

---

l: 21f: Jgs 6, 22f.   *m:* Heb 11, 32.   *n:* Jgs 15, 11.

linen tunics and thirty sets of garments. [13]But if you cannot answer it for me, you must give me thirty tunics and thirty sets of garments." "Propose your riddle," they responded; "we will listen to it." [14]So he said to them,

"Out of the eater came forth food,
 and out of the strong came forth
   sweetness."

After three days' failure to answer the riddle, [15]they said on the fourth day to Samson's wife, "Coax your husband to answer the riddle for us, or we will burn you and your family. Did you invite us here to reduce us to poverty?" [16]At Samson's side, his wife wept and said, "You must hate me; you do not love me, for you have proposed a riddle to my countrymen, but have not told me the answer." He said to her, "If I have not told it even to my father or my mother, must I tell it to you?" [17]But she wept beside him during the seven days the feast lasted. On the seventh day, since she importuned him, he told her the answer, and she explained the riddle to her countrymen.

[18]On the seventh day, before the sun set, the men of the city said to him,

"What is sweeter than honey,
 and what is stronger than a lion?"

He replied to them,

"If you had not plowed with my heifer,
 you would not have solved my riddle."

[19]The spirit of the LORD came upon him, and he went down to Ashkelon, where he killed thirty of their men and despoiled them; he gave their garments to those who had answered the riddle. Then he went off to his own family in anger, [20]and Samson's wife was married to the one who had been best man at his wedding.o

See RG 162

CHAPTER 15

Samson Defeats the Philistines. [1]After some time, in the season of the wheat harvest, Samson visited his wife, bringing a kid. But when he said, "Let me be with my wife in private," her father would not let him en-ter, [2]saying, "I thought it certain you wished to repudiate her; so I gave her to your best man. Her younger sister is more beautiful than she; you may have her instead." [3]Samson said to them, "This time the Philistines cannot blame me if I harm them." [4]So Samson left and caught three hundred foxes. Turning them tail to tail, he tied between each pair of tails one of the torches he had at hand. [5]He then kindled the torches and set the foxes loose in the standing grain of the Philistines, thus burning both the shocks and the standing grain, and the vineyards and olive orchards as well.

[6]pWhen the Philistines asked who had done this, they were told, "Samson, the son-in-law of the Timnite, because his wife was taken and given to his best man." So the Philistines went up and destroyed her and her family by fire. [7]Samson said to them, "If this is how you act, I will not stop until I have taken revenge on you." [8]And with repeated blows, he inflicted a great slaughter on them. Then he went down and remained in a cavern of the cliff of Etam.

[9]The Philistines went up and, from a camp in Judah, deployed against Lehi. [10]When the men of Judah asked, "Why have you come up against us?" they answered, "To take Samson prisoner; to do to him as he has done to us." [11]Three thousand men of Judah went down to the cavern in the cliff of Etam and said to Samson, "Do you not know that the Philistines are our rulers? Why, then, have you done this to us?" He answered them, "As they have done to me, so have I done to them." [12]They said to him, "We have come to take you prisoner, to deliver you over to the Philistines." Samson said to them, "Swear to me that you will not kill me yourselves." [13]"No," they replied, "we will certainly not kill you but will only bind you and deliver you over to them."q So they bound him with two new ropes and brought him up from the cliff. [14]When he reached Lehi, and the Philistines came shouting to meet him, the spirit of the LORD came upon him: the ropes around his arms became as flax that is consumed by fire and his bonds melted away

o: Jgs 15, 2. 6.   p: Jgs 14, 20.   q: Jgs 16, 11f.

from his hands. ¹⁵Near him was the fresh jawbone of an ass; he reached out, grasped it, and with it killed a thousand men. ¹⁶Then Samson said,

"With the jawbone of an ass
    I have piled them in a heap;
With the jawbone of an ass
    I have slain a thousand men."

¹⁷As he finished speaking he threw the jawbone from him; and so that place was named Ramath-lehi.* ¹⁸Being very thirsty, he cried to the LORD and said, "You have granted this great victory by the hand of your servant. Must I now die of thirst or fall into the hands of the uncircumcised?" ¹⁹Then God split the cavity in Lehi, and water issued from it, which Samson drank till his spirit returned and he revived. Hence that spring in Lehi is called En-hakkore* to this day.

²⁰Samson judged Israel for twenty years in the days of the Philistines.ʳ

CHAPTER 16

See RG
162-64

¹Once Samson went to Gaza, where he saw a harlot and visited her. ²Informed that Samson had come there, the men of Gaza surrounded him with an ambush at the city gate all night long. And all the night they waited, saying, "Tomorrow morning we will kill him." ³Samson rested there until midnight. Then he rose, seized the doors of the city gate and the two gateposts, and tore them loose, bar and all. He hoisted them on his shoulders and carried them to the top of the ridge opposite Hebron.

Samson and Delilah. ⁴After that he fell in love with a woman in the Wadi Sorek whose name was Delilah. ⁵The lords of the Philistines came to her and said, "Beguile him and find out the secret of his great strength, and how we may overcome and bind him so as to keep him helpless. We will each give you eleven hundred shekels of silver."

⁶So Delilah said to Samson, "Tell me the secret of your great strength and how you may be bound so as to be kept helpless." ⁷"If they bind me with seven fresh bowstrings which have not dried," Samson answered her, "I shall be as weak as any other man." ⁸So the lords of the Philistines brought her seven fresh bowstrings which had not dried, and she bound him with them. ⁹She had men lying in wait in the chamber and so she said to him, "The Philistines are upon you, Samson!" But he snapped the strings as a thread of tow is severed by a whiff of flame;ˢ and the secret of his strength remained unknown.

¹⁰Delilah said to Samson, "You have mocked me and told me lies. Now tell me how you may be bound." ¹¹"If they bind me tight with new ropes, with which no work has been done," he answered her, "I shall be as weak as any other man."ᵗ ¹²So Delilah took new ropes and bound him with them. Then she said to him, "The Philistines are upon you, Samson!" For there were men lying in wait in the chamber. But he snapped them off his arms like thread.

¹³Delilah said to Samson again, "Up to now you have mocked me and told me lies. Tell me how you may be bound." He said to her, "If you weave my seven locks of hair into the web and fasten them with the pin, I shall be as weak as any other man." ¹⁴So while he slept, Delilah wove his seven locks of hair into the web, and fastened them in with the pin. Then she said, "The Philistines are upon you, Samson!" Awakening from his sleep, he pulled out both the weaver's pin and the web.

¹⁵Then she said to him, "How can you say that you love me when you do not confide in me? Three times already you have mocked me, and not told me the secret of your great strength!" ¹⁶She importuned him continually and vexed him with her complaints till he was deathly weary of them. ¹⁷So he took her completely into his confidence and told her, "No razor has touched my head,ᵘ for I have been consecrated to God from my mother's womb. If I am shaved, my strength will leave me, and I shall be as weak as any other man!"

15, 17: Ramath-lehi: "heights of the jawbone."
15, 19: En-hakkore: "the spring of him who cries out," an allusion to Samson's cry in v 18.

r: Jgs 16, 31.   s: Jgs 15, 14.   t: Jgs 15, 13.   u: Jgs 13, 5.

[18]When Delilah saw that he had taken her completely into his confidence, she summoned the lords of the Philistines, saying, "Come up this time, for he has opened his heart to me." So the lords of the Philistines came and brought up the money with them. [19]She had him sleep on her lap, and called for a man who shaved off his seven locks of hair. Then she began to mistreat him, for his strength had left him. [20]When she said, "The Philistines are upon you, Samson!", and he woke from his sleep, he thought he could make good his escape as he had done time and again, for he did not realize that the LORD had left him. [21]But the Philistines seized him and gouged out his eyes. Then they brought him down to Gaza and bound him with bronze fetters, and he was put to grinding in the prison. [22]But the hair of his head began to grow as soon as it was shaved off.

The Death of Samson. [23v]The lords of the Philistines assembled to offer a great sacrifice to their god Dagon* and to make merry. They said,

"Our god has delivered into our power
    Samson our enemy."

[25]When their spirits were high, they said, "Call Samson that he may amuse us." So they called Samson from the prison, and he played the buffoon before them. [24]When the people saw him, they praised their god. For they said,

"Our god has delivered into our power
    our enemy, the ravager of our land,
    the one who has multiplied our slain."

Then they stationed him between the columns. [26]Samson said to the attendant who was holding his hand, "Put me where I may touch the columns that support the temple and may rest against them." [27]The temple was full of men and women: all the lords of the Philistines were there, and from the roof about three thousand men and women looked on as Samson provided amusement.

[28]Samson cried out to the LORD and said, "O Lord GOD, remember me! Strengthen me, O God, this last time that for my two eyes I may avenge myself once and for all on the Philistines." [29]Samson grasped the two middle columns on which the temple rested and braced himself against them, one at his right hand, the other at his left. [30]And Samson said, "Let me die with the Philistines!" He pushed hard, and the temple fell upon the lords and all the people who were in it. Those he killed at his death were more than those he had killed during his lifetime.

[31]All his family and kinsmen went down and bore him up for burial in the grave of his father Manoah between Zorah and Eshtaol. He had judged Israel for twenty years.[w]

III: The Tribes of Dan and Benjamin in the Days of the Judges

CHAPTER 17

See RG 163–64

Micah and the Levite. [1]There was a man in the mountain region of Ephraim whose name was Micah. [2]He said to his mother, "The eleven hundred shekels of silver over which you pronounced a curse in my hearing when they were taken from you, are in my possession. It was I who took them; so now I will restore them to you." [3]When he restored the eleven hundred shekels of silver to his mother, she took two hundred of them and gave them to the silversmith, who made of them a carved idol* overlaid with silver.[x] [4]Then his mother said, "May the LORD bless my son! I have consecrated the silver to the LORD as my gift in favor of my son, by making a carved idol overlaid with silver." It remained in the house of Micah. [5]Thus the layman Micah had a sanctuary. He also made an ephod and household idols,[y] and consecrated one of his sons, who became his priest. [6]In those days there was no king in Israel; everyone did what he thought best.[z]

16, 23: Dagon was originally a Mesopotamian deity, whom the Philistines came to worship as their own god of grain.

17, 3: Idol: an image, not of a pagan god, but of the Lord. The Mosaic law forbade the making of an image even of the true God.

---

v: 1 Sm 5, 2-5.   *w:* Jgs 15, 20.   *x:* Ex 20, 4; Lv 19, 4.   *y:* Jgs 18, 14. 17.   *z:* Jgs 18, 1; 21, 25.

[7]There was a young Levite who had resided within the tribe of Judah at Bethlehem of Judah. [8]From that city he set out to find another place of residence. On his journey he came to the house of Micah in the mountain region of Ephraim. [9]Micah said to him, "Where do you come from?" He answered him, "I am a Levite from Bethlehem in Judah, and am on my way to find some other place of residence." [10]"Stay with me," Micah said to him. "Be father and priest to me,[a] and I will give you ten silver shekels a year, a set of garments, and your food." [11]So the young Levite decided to stay with the man, to whom he became as one of his own sons. [12]*Micah consecrated the young Levite, who became his priest, remaining in his house. [13]Therefore Micah said, "Now I know that the LORD will prosper me, since the Levite has become my priest."

See RG 162-64

CHAPTER 18

Migration of the Danites. [1]At that time there was no king in Israel.[b] Moreover the tribe of Danites were in search of a district to dwell in, for up to that time they had received no heritage among the tribes of Israel.*

[2]So the Danites sent from their clan a detail of five valiant men of Zorah and Eshtaol, to reconnoiter the land and scout it. With their instructions to go and scout the land, they traveled as far as the house of Micah in the mountain region of Ephraim, where they passed the night. [3]Near the house of Micah, they recognized the voice* of the young Levite[c] and turned in that direction. "Who brought you here and what are you doing here?" they asked him. "What is your interest here?" [4]"This is how Micah treats me," he replied to them. "He pays me a salary and I am his priest."[d] [5]They said to him, "Consult God, that we may know whether the undertaking we are engaged in will succeed." [6]The priest said to them, "Go and prosper:

the LORD is favorable to the undertaking you are engaged in."

[7]So the five men went on and came to Laish. They saw that the people dwelling there lived securely after the manner of the Sidonians, quiet and trusting, with no lack of any natural resources. They were distant from the Sidonians and had no contact with other people. [8]When the five returned to their kinsmen in Zorah and Eshtaol and were asked for a report, [9]they replied, "Come, let us attack them, for we have seen the land and it is very good. Are you going to hesitate? Do not be slothful about beginning your expedition to possess the land. [10]Those against whom you go are a trusting people, and the land is ample. God has indeed given it into your power: a place where no natural resource is lacking."

[11]So six hundred men of the clan of the Danites, fully armed with weapons of war, set out from where they were in Zorah and Eshtaol, [12]and camped in Judah, up near Kiriath-jearim; hence to this day the place, which lies west of Kiriath-jearim, is called Mahaneh-dan.[e]

[13]From there they went on to the mountain region of Ephraim and came to the house of Micah. [14]The five men who had gone to reconnoiter the land of Laish said to their kinsmen, "Do you know that in these houses there are an ephod, household idols, and a carved idol overlaid with silver?[f] Now decide what you must do!" [15]So turning in that direction, they went to the house of the young Levite at the home of Micah and greeted him. [16]The six hundred men girt with weapons of war, who were Danites, stood by the entrance of the gate, and the priest stood there also. [17]Meanwhile the five men who had gone to reconnoiter the land went up and entered the house of Micah. [18]When they had gone in and taken the ephod, the household idols, and the carved idol overlaid with silver, the

---

17, 12f: According to Nm 18, 1-7 only those Levites who were descended from Aaron could be consecrated as priests.

18, 1: The tribe of Dan had been assigned a territory with definite limits in central Palestine. However they were unable to gain possession of the better portion of their land (Jgs 1, 34). So they now seek territory elsewhere in Palestine.

18, 3: Recognized the voice: perhaps they noticed the peculiar pronunciation of his south Hebrew dialect.

a: Jgs 18, 19.   b: Jos 19, 40-48.   c: Jgs 17, 7.   d: Jgs 17, 10.
e: Jgs 13, 25.   f: Jgs 17, 4f.

priest said to them, "What are you doing?" [19]They said to him, "Be still: put your hand over your mouth. Come with us and be our father and priest.[g] Is it better for you to be priest for the family of one man or to be priest for a tribe and a clan in Israel?" [20]The priest, agreeing, took the ephod, household idols, and carved idol and went off in the midst of the band. [21]As they turned to depart, they placed their little ones, their livestock, and their goods at the head of the column.

[22]The Danites had already gone some distance, when those in the houses near that of Micah took up arms and overtook them. [23]They called to the Danites, who turned about and said to Micah, "What do you want, that you have taken up arms?" [24]"You have taken my god, which I made, and have gone off with my priest as well," he answered. "What is left for me? How, then, can you ask me what I want?" [25]The Danites said to him, "Let us hear no further sound from you, lest fierce men fall upon you and you and your family lose your lives." [26]The Danites then went on their way, and Micah, seeing that they were stronger than he, returned home.

[27]Having taken what Micah had made, and the priest he had had, they attacked Laish, a quiet and trusting people; they put them to the sword and destroyed their city by fire. [28]No one came to their aid, since the city was far from Sidon and they had no contact with other people. The Danites then rebuilt the city, which was in the valley that belongs to Beth-rehob, and lived there. [29]They named it Dan after their ancestor Dan, son of Israel. However, the name of the city was formerly Laish. [30]The Danites set up the carved idol for themselves, and Jonathan, son of Gershom, son of Moses, and his descendants were priests for the tribe of the Danites until the time of the captivity of the land.[*] [31]They maintained the carved idol Micah had made as long as the house of God was in Shiloh.

CHAPTER 19

See RG 162-64

The Levite from Ephraim. [1]At that time, when there was no king in Israel,[h] there was a Levite residing in remote parts of the mountain region of Ephraim who had taken for himself a concubine from Bethlehem of Judah. [2]His concubine was unfaithful to him and left him for her father's house in Bethlehem of Judah, where she stayed for some four months. [3]Her husband then set out with his servant and a pair of asses, and went after her to forgive her and take her back. She brought him into her father's house, and on seeing him, the girl's father joyfully made him welcome. [4]He was detained by the girl's father, and so he spent three days with this father-in-law of his, eating and drinking and passing the night there. [5]*On the fourth day they rose early in the morning and he prepared to go. But the girl's father said to his son-in-law, "Fortify yourself with a little food; you can go later on." [6]So they stayed and the two men ate and drank together. Then the girl's father said to the husband, "Why not decide to spend the night here and enjoy yourself?" [7]The man still made a move to go, but when his father-in-law pressed him he went back and spent the night there.

[8]On the fifth morning he rose early to depart, but the girl's father said, "Fortify yourself and tarry until the afternoon." When he and his father-in-law had eaten, [9]and the husband was ready to go with his concubine and servant, the girl's father said to him, "It is already growing dusk. Stay for the night. See, the day is coming to an end. Spend the night here and enjoy yourself. Early tomorrow you can start your journey home." [10]The man, however, refused to stay another night; he and his concubine set out with a pair of saddled asses, and traveled till they came opposite Jebus, which is Jerusalem. [11]Since they were near Jebus with the day far gone, the servant said to his master, "Come, let us turn off to this city of the Jebusites and

---

18, 30: Until . . . land: about the year 734 B.C., when the Assyrian emperor Tiglath-pileser III subjected northern Palestine.

19, 5-9: Such importuning of guests to prolong their stay

at the home of their host is characteristic of Oriental hospitality.

g: Jgs 17, 10. h: Jgs 17, 6.

spend the night in it." [12]But his master said to him, "We will not turn off to a city of foreigners, who are not Israelites, but will go on to Gibeah.[i] [13]Come," he said to his servant, "let us make for some other place, either Gibeah or Ramah, to spend the night."[j] [14]So they continued on their way till the sun set on them when they were abreast of Gibeah of Benjamin.

[15]*There they turned off to enter Gibeah for the night.[k] The man waited in the public square of the city he had entered, but no one offered them the shelter of his home for the night. [16]In the evening, however, an old man came from his work in the field; he was from the mountain region of Ephraim, though he lived among the Benjaminite townspeople of Gibeah. [17]When he noticed the traveler in the public square of the city, the old man asked where he was going, and whence he had come. [18]He said to him, "We are traveling from Bethlehem of Judah far up into the mountain region of Ephraim, where I belong. I have been to Bethlehem of Judah and am now going back home; but no one has offered us the shelter of his house. [19]We have straw and fodder for our asses, and bread and wine for the woman and myself and for our servant; there is nothing else we need." [20]"You are welcome," the old man said to him, "but let me provide for all your needs, and do not spend the night in the public square." [21]So he led them to his house and provided fodder for the asses. Then they washed their feet, and ate and drank.[l]

The Outrage at Gibeah. [22m]While they were enjoying themselves, the men of the city, who were corrupt,* surrounded the house and beat on the door. They said to the old man whose house it was, "Bring out your guest, that we may abuse him." [23]The owner of the house went out to them and said, "No, my brothers; do not be so wicked. Since this man is my guest, do not commit this crime.

[24]Rather let me bring out my maiden daughter or his concubine. Ravish them, or do whatever you want with them; but against the man you must not commit this wanton crime." [25]When the men would not listen to his host, the husband seized his concubine and thrust her outside to them. They had relations with her and abused her all night until the following dawn, when they let her go. [26]Then at daybreak the woman came and collapsed at the entrance of the house in which her husband was a guest, where she lay until the morning. [27]When her husband rose that day and opened the door of the house to start out again on his journey, there lay the woman, his concubine, at the entrance of the house with her hands on the threshold. [28]He said to her, "Come, let us go"; but there was no answer. So the man placed her on an ass and started out again for home.

[29]*On reaching home, he took a knife to the body of his concubine, cut her into twelve pieces, and sent them throughout the territory of Israel. [30n]Everyone who saw this said, "Nothing like this has been done or seen from the day the Israelites came up from the land of Egypt to this day. Take note of it, and state what you propose to do."

CHAPTER 20

See RG 162–64

Assembly of Israelites. [1]So all the Israelites came out as one man: from Dan to Beer-sheba,* and from the land of Gilead, the community was gathered to the LORD at Mizpah. [2]The leaders of all the people and all the tribesmen of Israel, four hundred thousand foot soldiers who were swordsmen, presented themselves in the assembly of the people of God. [3]Meanwhile, the Benjaminites heard that the Israelites had gone up to Mizpah. The Israelites asked to be told how the crime had taken place, [4]and the Levite, the husband of the murdered woman, testified: "My concubine and I went into

---

19, 15: Private hospitality was the customary means of providing comfort to travelers where public facilities were so rare.

19, 22: Who were corrupt: literally "sons of Belial," indicating extreme perversion; cf Gn 19, 4-8. This crime and its punishment made the name Gibeah proverbial as a place of shameful wickedness; cf Hos 9, 9; 10, 9.

19, 29: A drastic means for arousing the tribes to avenge the unheard of crime of the Benjaminites.

20, 1: From Dan to Beer-sheba: from north to south. The land of Gilead: all the territory east of the Jordan.

i: Jgs 1, 21.   j: Jos 18, 25.   k: Jgs 20, 4.   l: Gn 18, 4; 24, 32; 43, 24.   m: 22-25: Gn 19, 4-9.   n: Hos 9, 9; 10, 9.

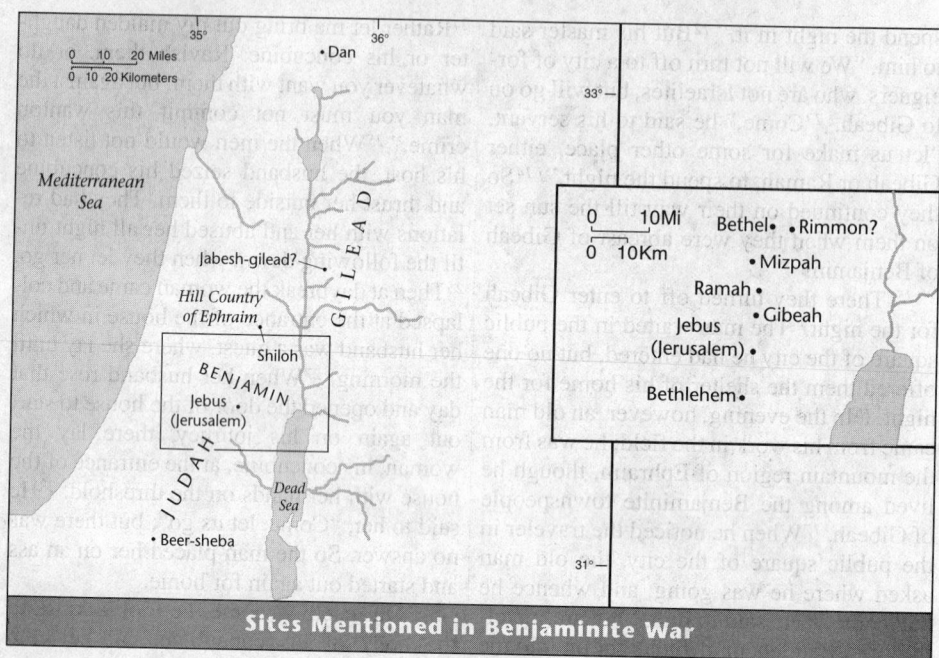

Sites Mentioned in Benjaminite War

Gibeah of Benjamin*ᵒ* for the night. ⁵*ᵖ*But the citizens of Gibeah rose up against me by night and surrounded the house in which I was. Me they attempted to kill, and my concubine they abused so that she died. ⁶*�q*So I took my concubine and cut her up and sent her through every part of the territory of Israel, because of the monstrous crime they had committed in Israel. ⁷*Now that you are all here, O Israelites, state what you propose to do."*ʳ* ⁸All the people rose as one man to say, "None of us is to leave for his tent or return to his home. ⁹Now as for Gibeah, this is what we will do: We will proceed against it by lot, ¹⁰taking from all the tribes of Israel ten men for every hundred, a hundred for every thousand, a thousand for every ten thousand, and procuring supplies for the soldiers who will go to deal fully and suitably with Gibeah of Benjamin for the crime it committed in Israel."

¹¹When, therefore, all the men of Israel without exception were leagued together against the city, ¹²*the tribes of Israel sent men throughout the tribe of Benjamin to say, "What is this evil which has occurred among you? ¹³Now give up these corrupt men of Gibeah, that we may put them to death and thus purge the evil from Israel." But the Benjaminites refused to accede to the demand of their brothers, the Israelites. ¹⁴Instead, the Benjaminites assembled from their other cities to Gibeah, to do battle with the Israelites. ¹⁵The number of the Benjaminite swordsmen from the other cities on that occasion was twenty-six thousand, in addition to the inhabitants of Gibeah. ¹⁶Included in this total were seven hundred picked men who were left-handed, every one of them able to sling a stone at a hair without missing. ¹⁷Meanwhile the other Israelites who, without Benjamin, mustered four hundred thousand swordsmen ready for battle, ¹⁸moved on to Bethel and consulted God.

20, 7: The Israelites were asked to decide at once what action to take concerning this crime; cf 2 Sm 16, 20. The Levite undoubtedly addressed the tribal heads who would speak in behalf of the multitude.

20, 12: Before the crime at Gibeah was punished, the Benjaminites were invited to join their brethren, the Israelites, in punishing the crime. Since they failed to respond, special messengers were sent asking them to deliver up the guilty ones. They replied by gathering their forces for combat.

o: Jgs 19, 14f. *p:* Jgs 19, 22-27. *q:* Jgs 19, 29. *r:* Jgs 19, 30.

When the Israelites asked who should go first in the attack on the Benjaminites,ˢ the LORD said, "Judah shall go first."* ¹⁹The next day the Israelites advanced on Gibeah with their forces.

War with Benjamin. ²⁰On the day the Israelites drew up in battle array at Gibeah for the combat with Benjamin, ²¹the Benjaminites came out of the city and felled twenty-two thousand men of Israel. ²³Then the Israelites went up and wept before the LORD until evening. "Shall I again engage my brother Benjamin in battle?" they asked the LORD; and the LORD answered that they should. ²²But though the Israelite soldiers took courage and again drew up for combat in the same place as on the previous day, ²⁴when they met the Benjaminites for the second time, ²⁵once again the Benjaminites who came out of Gibeah against them felled eighteen thousand Israelites, all of them swordsmen. ²⁶So the entire Israelite army went up to Bethel, where they wept and remained fasting before the LORD until evening of that day, besides offering holocausts and peace offerings before the LORD. ²⁷ᵗWhen the Israelites consulted the LORD (for the ark of the covenant of God was there in those days, ²⁸and Phinehas, son of Eleazar, son of Aaron, was ministering to him in those days), and asked, "Shall I go out again to battle with Benjamin, my brother, or shall I desist?" the LORD said, "Attack! for tomorrow I will deliver him into your power." ²⁹ᵘSo Israel set men in ambush around Gibeah.*

³⁰The Israelites went up against the Benjaminites for the third time and formed their line of battle at Gibeah as on other occasions. ³¹The Benjaminites went out to meet them, and in the beginning they killed off about thirty of the Israelite soldiers in the open field, just as on the other occasions. ³²Therefore the Benjaminites thought, "We are defeating them as before"; not realizing that disaster was about to overtake them. The Israelites, however, had planned the flight so as to draw them away from the city onto the highways. They were drawn away from the city onto the highways, of which the one led to Bethel, the other to Gibeon. ³³And then all the men of Israel rose from their places. They re-formed their ranks at Baal-tamar, and the Israelites in ambush rushed from their place west of Gibeah, ³⁴ten thousand picked men from all Israel, and advanced against the city itself. In a fierce battle, ³⁵the LORD defeated Benjamin before Israel; and on that day the Israelites killed twenty-five thousand one hundred men of Benjamin, all of them swordsmen.

³⁶To the Benjaminites it had looked as though the enemy were defeated, for the men of Israel gave ground to Benjamin, trusting in the ambush they had set at Gibeah. ³⁷But then the men in ambush made a sudden dash into Gibeah, overran it, and put the whole city to the sword. ³⁸Now, the other Israelites had agreed with the men in ambush on a smoke signal they were to send up from the city. ³⁹And though the men of Benjamin had begun by killing off some thirty of the men of Israel, under the impression that they were defeating them as surely as in the earlier fighting, the Israelites wheeled about to resist ⁴⁰as the smoke of the signal column began to rise up from the city. It was when Benjamin looked back and saw the whole city in flames against the sky ⁴¹that the men of Israel wheeled about. Therefore the men of Benjamin were thrown into confusion, for they realized the disaster that had overtaken them. ⁴²They retreated before the men of Israel in the direction of the desert, with the fight being pressed against them. In their very midst, meanwhile, those who had been in the city were spreading destruction. ⁴³The men of Benjamin had been surrounded, and were now pursued to a point east of Gibeah, ⁴⁴while eighteen thousand of them fell, warriors to a man. ⁴⁵The rest turned and fled through the desert to the rock Rimmon.ᵛ But on the highways the Israelites picked off five

20, 18: Judah shall go first: the same response as in Jgs 1, 1f, but without the assurance of immediate success. Only after the Israelites were punished at the hands of the Benjaminites for their own grossness, and had performed penance, did they succeed in punishing the latter for their part in the crime of rape and murder, by gaining the victory over them.

20, 29-46: This stratagem proved more useful to the Israelites than force, as in the siege of Ai (Jos 8, 3-21). In the par-

s: Jgs 1, 1f.   t: 1 Sm 4, 3f.   u: 29-46: Jos 8, 4-24.   v: Jgs 21, 13.

thousand men among them, and chasing them up to Gidom, killed another two thousand of them there. [46]Those of Benjamin who fell on that day were in all twenty-five thousand swordsmen, warriors to a man. [47]But six hundred others who turned and fled through the desert reached the rock Rimmon, where they remained for four months.

[48]The men of Israel withdrew through the territory of the Benjaminites, putting to the sword the inhabitants of the cities, the livestock, and all they chanced upon. Moreover they destroyed by fire all the cities they came upon.

CHAPTER 21

See RG 162-64

Wives for the Survivors. [1]Now the men of Israel[*] had sworn at Mizpah that none of them would give his daughter in marriage to anyone from Benjamin. [2]So the people went to Bethel and remained there before God until evening, raising their voices in bitter lament.[w] [3]They said, "LORD, God of Israel, why has it come to pass in Israel that today one tribe of Israel should be lacking?" [4]Early the next day the people built an altar there and offered holocausts and peace offerings. [5]Then the Israelites asked, "Are there any among all the tribes of Israel who did not come up to the LORD for the assembly?" For they had taken a solemn oath that anyone who did not go up to the LORD at Mizpah should be put to death without fail.[x]

[6*]The Israelites were disconsolate over their brother Benjamin and said, "Today one of the tribes of Israel has been cut off. [7]What can we do about wives for the survivors, since we have sworn by the LORD not to give them any of our daughters in marriage?" [8]And when they asked whether anyone among the tribes of Israel had not come up to the LORD in Mizpah, they found that none of the men of Jabesh-gilead had come to the encampment for the assembly. [9]A roll call of the army established that none of the inhabitants of that city were present. [10]The community, therefore, sent twelve thousand warriors with orders to go to Jabesh-gilead and put those who lived there to the sword, including the women and children. [11]They were told to include under the ban[*] all males and every woman who was not still a virgin.[y] [12]Finding among the inhabitants of Jabesh-gilead four hundred young virgins, who had had no relations with men, they brought them to the camp at Shiloh in the land of Canaan. [13z]Then the whole community sent a message to the Benjaminites at the rock Rimmon, offering them peace. [14]When Benjamin returned at that time, they gave them as wives the women of Jabesh-gilead whom they had spared; but these proved to be not enough for them.

[15]The people were still disconsolate over Benjamin because the LORD had made a breach[*] among the tribes of Israel. [16]And the elders of the community said, "What shall we do for wives for the survivors? For every woman in Benjamin has been put to death." [17]They said, "Those of Benjamin who survive must have heirs, else one of the Israelite tribes will be wiped out. [18*]Yet we cannot give them any of our daughters in marriage, because the Israelites have sworn, 'Cursed be he who gives a woman to Benjamin!'" [19]Then they thought of the yearly feast of the LORD at Shiloh, north of Bethel, east of the highway that goes up from Bethel to Shechem, and south of Lebonah. [20]And they instructed the Benjaminites, "Go and lie in wait in the vineyards. [21]When you see the girls of Shiloh come out to do their dancing, leave the vineyards and each of you seize one of the

---

allel accounts the first (vv 29-35) is a summary of the second (vv 36-46).

21, 1-3: The anger of the Israelites led them to destroy their brethren, the Benjaminites. Having realized their goal, however, they were soon filled with dismay, and sought to restore the tribe they had all but exterminated.

21, 6-9: This account is summarized in the parallel passage in vv 2-5.

21, 11: Under the ban: see note on Nm 21, 3.

21, 15: Had made a breach: what is here attributed to God was in reality the free and deliberate act of the Israelites and happened only by the permissive will of God. The ancients attributed to the first primary cause what is more directly due to secondary causes.

21, 18: Regardless of the serious consequences of their vow, the Israelites considered themselves obliged to fulfill it; cf Jgs 11, 31. 35f. 39.

---

w: Jgs 20, 26.   x: Jgs 20, 8ff.   y: Nm 31, 17.   z: Jgs 20, 47.

girls of Shiloh for a wife, and go to the land of Benjamin. [22]When their fathers or their brothers come to complain to us, we shall say to them, 'Release them to us as a kindness, since we did not take a woman apiece in the war. Had you yourselves given them these wives, you would now be guilty.' "

[23]The Benjaminites did this; they carried off a wife for each of them from their raid on the dancers, and went back to their own territory, where they rebuilt and occupied the cities. [24]Also at that time the Israelites dispersed; each of them left for his own heritage in his own clan and tribe.

[25]*In those days there was no king in Israel; everyone did what he thought best.[a]

21, 25: Cf Jgs 17, 6; 18, 1; 19, 1. The verse gives the reason why the lawlessness of the period of judges, and the events described herein, were possible.

a: Jgs 17, 6; 18, 1; 19, 1,

See RG
164–69

The Book of Ruth

The Book of Ruth is named after the Moabite woman who was joined to the Israelite people by her marriage with the influential Boaz of Bethlehem.

The book contains a beautiful example of filial piety, pleasing to the Hebrews especially because of its connection with King David, and useful both to Hebrews and to Gentiles. Its aim is to demonstrate the divine reward for such piety even when practiced by a stranger. Ruth's piety (2, 11), her spirit of self-sacrifice, and her moral integrity were favored by God with the gift of faith and an illustrious marriage whereby she became the ancestress of David and of Christ. In this, the universality of the messianic salvation is foreshadowed.

In the Greek and Latin canons the Book of Ruth is placed just after Judges, to which it is closely related because of the time of its action, and just before Samuel, for which it is an excellent introduction, since it traces the ancestry of the Davidic dynasty. One might characterize the literary form of this book as dramatic, since about two-thirds of it is in dialogue. Yet there is every indication that, as tradition has always held, it contains true history.

There is no certainty about the author of the book. It was written long after the events had passed (4, 7), which took place "in the time of the judges" (1, 1).

CHAPTER 1

See RG
166–67

Naomi in Moab. [1]Once in the time of the judges* there was a famine in the land; so a man from Bethlehem of Judah departed with his wife and two sons to reside on the plateau of Moab. [2]The man was named Elimelech, his wife Naomi, and his sons Mahlon and Chilion; they were Ephrathites from Bethlehem of Judah. Some time after their arrival on the Moabite plateau, [3]Elimelech, the husband of Naomi, died, and she was left with her two sons, [4]who married Moabite women, one named Orpah, the other Ruth. When they had lived there about ten years, [5]both Mahlon and Chilion died also, and the woman was left with neither her two sons nor her husband. [6]She then made ready to go back from the plateau of Moab because word reached her there that the LORD had visited his people and given them food.

[7]She and her two daughters-in-law left the place where they had been living. Then as they were on the road back to the land of Judah, [8]Naomi said to her two daughters-in-law, "Go back, each of you, to your mother's house!* May the LORD be kind to you as you were to the departed and to me! [9]May the LORD grant each of you a husband and a home in which you will find rest." She kissed them good-by, but they wept with

1, 1f: In the time of the judges: three generations before the end of the period of Judges; cf Ru 4, 21f. Bethlehem of Judah: to distinguish it from the town of the same name in the tribe of Zebulun (Jos 19, 15). Ephrathites from Bethlehem: belonging to a Judean clan which settled in Bethlehem; cf 1 Sm 17, 12; 1 Chr 2, 50f; 4, 4.

1, 8: Mother's house: the women's part of the dwelling; cf Jgs 4, 17; Song 3, 4.

Places in Ruth

[15]"See now!" she said, "your sister-in-law has gone back to her people and her god. Go back after your sister-in-law!" [16]*But Ruth said, "Do not ask me to abandon or forsake you! for wherever you go I will go, wherever you lodge I will lodge, your people shall be my people, and your God my God. [17]Wherever you die I will die, and there be buried. May the LORD do so and so to me, and more besides, if aught but death separates me from you!" [18]Naomi then ceased to urge her, for she saw she was determined to go with her.

The Return to Bethlehem. [19]So they went on together till they reached Bethlehem. On their arrival there, the whole city was astir over them, and the women asked, "Can this be Naomi?" [20a]But she said to them, "Do not call me Naomi.* Call me Mara, for the Almighty has made it very bitter for me. [21]I went away with an abundance, but the LORD has brought me back destitute. Why should you call me Naomi, since the LORD has pronounced against me and the Almighty has brought evil upon me?" [22]Thus it was that Naomi returned with the Moabite daughter-in-law, Ruth, who accompanied her back from the plateau of Moab. They arrived in Bethlehem at the beginning of the barley harvest.*

CHAPTER 2

The Meeting. [1]Naomi had a prominent kinsman named Boaz,[b] of the clan of her husband Elimelech. [2]Ruth the Moabite said to Naomi, "Let me go and glean ears of grain* in the field of anyone who will allow me that favor."[c] Naomi said to her, "Go, my daughter," [3]and she went. The field she entered to glean after the harvesters happened to be the section belonging to Boaz of the clan of Elimelech. [4]Boaz himself came from Bethlehem and said to the harvesters, "The

See RG 167-68

loud sobs, [10]and told her they would return with her to her people. [11]"Go back, my daughters!" said Naomi. "Why should you come with me? Have I other sons in my womb who may become your husbands?* [12]Go back, my daughters! Go, for I am too old to marry again. And even if I could offer any hopes, or if tonight I had a husband or had borne sons, [13]would you then wait and deprive yourselves of husbands until those sons grew up? No, my daughters! my lot is too bitter for you, because the LORD has extended his hand against me." [14]Again they sobbed aloud and wept; and Orpah kissed her mother-in-law good-by, but Ruth stayed with her.

1, 11: Have I other sons . . . husbands?: Naomi insisted that her daughters-in-law remain in their own country only for the sake of posterity. If she had had other sons, the levirate law would have obliged them to marry the widows of her deceased sons to perpetuate the names of the deceased; cf Gn 38, 8; Dt 25, 5f.

1, 16f: An example of heroic fidelity and piety. Ruth's decision, confirmed with an oath, to adhere to her mother-in-law impelled her to abandon her country and its pagan worship.

1, 20f: Naomi: means "amiable" or "pleasant," suggesting

God's favor toward her. The Almighty has brought evil upon me: the ancients regarded adversity as a punishment from God for personal sin, as if good and evil were always repaid in a temporal and material manner.

1, 22: Barley harvest: early April. This circumstance favored the events of the narrative that follow.

2, 2: Let me go and glean . . . grain: even the poor, the widow, the stranger, and the orphan had a right to glean at harvest time; cf Lv 19, 9f; 23, 22; Dt 24, 19-22.

---

a: Ex 15, 23.   *b:* Ru 3, 2. 12; 4, 21; Mt 1, 5.   *c:* Dt 24, 19.

LORD be with you!'"* and they replied, "The LORD bless you!" *5*Boaz asked the overseer of his harvesters, "Whose girl is this?" *6*The overseer of the harvesters answered, "She is the Moabite girl who returned from the plateau of Moab with Naomi.*d 7*She asked leave to gather the gleanings into sheaves after the harvesters; and ever since she came this morning she has remained here until now, with scarcely a moment's rest."

*8*Boaz said to Ruth, "Listen, my daughter! Do not go to glean in anyone else's field; you are not to leave here. Stay here with my women servants. *9*Watch to see which field is to be harvested, and follow them; I have commanded the young men to do you no harm. When you are thirsty, you may go and drink from the vessels the young men have filled." *10*Casting herself prostrate upon the ground, she said to him, "Why should I, a foreigner, be favored with your notice?" *11e*Boaz answered her: "I have had a complete account of what you have done for your mother-in-law after your husband's death; you have left your father and your mother and the land of your birth, and have come to a people whom you did not know previously. *12*May the LORD reward what you have done! May you receive a full reward from the LORD, the God of Israel, under whose wings you have come for refuge." *13*She said, "May I prove worthy of your kindness, my lord: you have comforted me, your servant, with your consoling words; would indeed that I were a servant of yours!" *14*At mealtime Boaz said to her, "Come here and have some food; dip your bread in the sauce." Then as she sat near the reapers, he handed her some roasted grain and she ate her fill and had some left over. *15*She rose to glean, and Boaz instructed his servants to let her glean among the sheaves themselves without scolding her, *16*and even to let drop some handfuls and leave them for her to glean without being rebuked.

*17*She gleaned in the field until evening, and when she beat out what she had gleaned it came to about an ephah of barley, *18*which she took into the city and showed to her mother-in-law. Next she brought out and gave her what she had left over from lunch. *19*So her mother-in-law said to her, "Where did you glean today? Where did you go to work? May he who took notice of you be blessed!" Then she told her mother-in-law with whom she had worked. "The man at whose place I worked today is named Boaz," she said. *20f*"May he be blessed by the LORD, who is ever merciful to the living and to the dead," Naomi exclaimed to her daughter-in-law; and she continued, "He is a relative of ours, one of our next of kin."* *21*"He even told me," added Ruth the Moabite, "that I should stay with his servants until they complete his entire harvest." *22*"You would do well, my dear," Naomi rejoined, "to go out with his servants; for in someone else's field you might be insulted." *23*So she stayed gleaning with the servants of Boaz until the end of the barley and wheat harvests.

CHAPTER 3

See RG 168

Ruth Again Presents Herself. When she was back with her mother-in-law, *1*Naomi said to her, "My daughter, I must seek a home for you that will please you. *2g*Now is not Boaz, with whose servants you were, a relative of ours? This evening he will be winnowing barley at the threshing floor. *3*So bathe and anoint yourself; then put on your best attire and go down to the threshing floor. Do not make yourself known to the man before he has finished eating and drinking. *4*But when he lies down, take note of the place where he does so. Then go, uncover a place at his feet,* and lie down. He will tell you what to do." *5*"I will do whatever you advise," Ruth replied. *6*So she went down to

---

2, 4: The Lord be with you: courtesy and religious feeling characterize the salutations of the Hebrews. This greeting is used in the Christian liturgy.

2, 20: One of our next of kin: literally "our redeemer," a near relative of the same clan who had the right and duty to restore the land which an impoverished kinsman had alienated (Lv 25, 25-28), and to marry the widow of a relative who

had died without male offspring so as to raise up posterity to his name (Dt 25, 5-10).

3, 4: Uncover a place at his feet . . . : confident of the virtue of Ruth and Boaz, Naomi advises this unusual expedient to her daughter-in-law for the purpose of introducing her claim.

d: Ru 1, 22.   *e:* Ru 1, 14-17.   *f:* Ru 3, 9.   *g:* Ru 1.

the threshing floor and did just as her mother-in-law had instructed her.

⁷Boaz ate and drank to his heart's content. Then when he went and lay down at the edge of the sheaves, she stole up, uncovered a place at his feet, and lay down. ⁸In the middle of the night, however, the man gave a start and turned around to find a woman lying at his feet. ⁹He asked, "Who are you?" And she replied, "I am your servant Ruth. Spread the corner of your cloak over me,* for you are my next of kin." ¹⁰He said, "May the LORD bless you, my daughter! You have been even more loyal now than before in not going after the young men, whether poor or rich.ʰ ¹¹So be assured, daughter, I will do for you whatever you say; all my townspeople know you for a worthy woman. ¹²ⁱNow, though indeed I am closely related to you, you have another relative still closer.* ¹³Stay as you are for tonight, and tomorrow, if he wishes to claim you, good! let him do so. But if he does not wish to claim you, as the LORD lives, I will claim you myself. Lie there until morning."ʲ ¹⁴So she lay at his feet until morning, but rose before men could recognize one another. Boaz said, "Let it not be known that this woman came to the threshing floor." ¹⁵Then he said to her, "Take off your cloak and hold it out." When she did so, he poured out six measures of barley, helped her lift the bundle,ᵏ and left for the city.

¹⁶Ruth went home to her mother-in-law, who asked, "How have you fared, my daughter?" So she told her all the man had done for her, ¹⁷and concluded, "He gave me these six measures of barley because he did not wish me to come back to my mother-in-law empty-handed!" ¹⁸Naomi then said,

"Wait here, my daughter, until you learn what happens, for the man will not rest, but will settle the matter today."

CHAPTER 4

See RG
168–69

Boaz Marries Ruth. ¹Boaz went and took a seat at the gate;* and when he saw the closer relativeˡ of whom he had spoken come along, he called to him by name, "Come and sit beside me!" And he did so. ²Then Boaz picked out ten of the elders* of the city and asked them to sit nearby. When they had done this, ³he said to the near relative: "Naomi, who has come back from the Moabite plateau, is putting up for sale the piece of land that belonged to our kinsman Elimelech. ⁴*So I thought I would inform you, bidding you before those here present, including the elders of my people, to put in your claim for it if you wish to acquire it as next of kin.ᵐ But if you do not wish to claim it, tell me so, that I may be guided accordingly, for no one has a prior claim to yours, and mine is next." He answered, "I will put in my claim."

⁵*Boaz continued, "Once you acquire the field from Naomi, you must take also Ruth the Moabite,ⁿ the widow of the late heir, and raise up a family for the departed on his estate." ⁶The near relative replied, "I cannot exercise my claim lest I depreciate my own estate. Put in a claim yourself in my stead, for I cannot exercise my claim." ⁷Now it used to be the custom in Israel that, to make binding a contract of redemption or exchange, one party would take off his sandal* and give it to the other. This was the form of attestation in Israel. ⁸So the near relative, in saying to Boaz, "Acquire it for yourself,"

3, 9: Spread the corner of your cloak over me: be my protector by marrying me according to the duty of a near kinsman; cf Dt 25, 5; Ez 16, 8.

3, 12: Relative still closer: who had a prior right and duty to marry Ruth.

4, 1: Took a seat at the gate: i.e., of the city, where business affairs were settled.

4, 2: Ten of the elders: to serve as judges in legal matters as well as witnesses of the settlement of business affairs; cf Dt 25, 7-9.

4, 4: Poverty had obliged Naomi to sell the land of her deceased husband. The law permitted the nearest kinsman to redeem the land and thus preserve the family patrimony; cf Lv 25, 25.

4, 5f: The heir of Elimelech's field had died without children (Ru 1, 5). The nearest of kin could now redeem the land but he must also take Ruth, the widow of the late heir, to wife to perpetuate the family of the deceased; cf Dt 25, 5f. The first male child of such a marriage would be the legal son of Mahlon and grandson of Elimelech.

4, 7: Take off his sandal . . . : by this act the near relative renounced his legal right, both to the field of Elimelech and to the marriage with Ruth. The custom mentioned in Dt 25, 6 is somewhat different.

---

h: Dt 25, 5.   i: Ru 4, 1.   j: Ru 4, 5; Dt 25, 5.   k: Ru 2, 17.   l: Ru 3, 12.   m: Lv 25, 25.   n: Ru 3, 13; Dt 25, 5.

drew off his sandal. ⁹Boaz then said to the elders and to all the people, "You are witnesses today that I have acquired from Naomi all the holdings of Elimelech, Chilion and Mahlon. ¹⁰I also take Ruth the Moabite, the widow of Mahlon, as my wife, in order to raise up a family for her late husband on his estate, so that the name of the departed may not perish among his kinsmen and fellow citizens. Do you witness this today?" ¹¹ₒAll those at the gate, including the elders, said, "We do so. May the LORD make this wife come into your house like Rachel and Leah, who between them built up the house of Israel. May you do well in Ephrathah and win fame in Bethlehem. ¹²ₚWith the offspring the LORD will give you from this girl, may your house become like the house of Perez, whom Tamar bore to Judah."*

¹³Boaz took Ruth. When they came together as man and wife, the LORD enabled her to conceive and she bore a son. ¹⁴Then the women said to Naomi, "Blessed is the LORD who has not failed to provide you today with an heir! May he become famous in Israel! ¹⁵He will be your comfort and the support of your old age, for his mother is the daughter-in-law who loves you. She is worth more to you than seven sons!" ¹⁶Naomi took the child, placed him on her lap,* and became his nurse. ¹⁷And the neighbor women gave him his name,�q at the news that a grandson had been born to Naomi. They called him Obed. He was the father of Jesse, the father of David.*

¹⁸ᵣThese are the descendants of Perez: Perez was the father of Hezron,ˢ ¹⁹Hezron was the father of Ram, Ram was the father of Amminadab, ²⁰ᵗAmminadab was the father of Nahshon, Nahshon was the father of Salmon, ²¹Salmon was the father of Boaz, Boaz was the father of Obed, ²²ᵘObed was the father of Jesse, and Jesse became the father of David.

4, 12: Perez, whom Tamar bore to Judah: the right which Judah unwittingly satisfied for his daughter-in-law Tamar (Gn 38), Boaz willingly rendered to Ruth.

4, 16: Placed him on her lap: took him as her own; cf Gn 30, 3; 48, 12; Nm 11, 12.

4, 17: The father of Jesse, the father of David: indicating the place of Obed, Jesse and David in the line of Judah and the ancestry of Christ, the Messiah; cf Mt 1, 5f.

o: Gn 29, 31-30, 24; 35, 19.   p: Gn 38, 29.   q: Lk 1, 58.   r: 18-22: 1 Chr 2, 4-15; Mt 1, 3-6.   s: Gn 46, 12; 1 Chr 4, 1.   t: Ex 6, 23; Nm 1, 7.   u: 1 Sm 16, 10-13.

THE HISTORICAL BOOKS

The historical books include 1 and 2 Samuel, 1 and 2 Kings, 1 and 2 Chronicles, Ezra, Nehemiah, 1 and 2 Maccabees. To these are added the special literary group of Tobit, Judith, and Esther.

The Books of Tobit, Judith, and 1 and 2 Maccabees, as well as parts of Esther, are called deuterocanonical: they are not contained in the Hebrew canon but have been accepted by the Catholic Church as canonical and inspired.

By means of a series of episodes involving the persons of Samuel, Saul, and David, a century of history unfolds in 1 and 2 Samuel from the close of the period of Judges to the rise and establishment of the monarchy in Israel. Most important is God's promise to David of a lasting dynasty (2 Sm 7), from which royal messianism in the Bible developed.

In 1 and 2 Kings the religious history of Israel extends another four centuries, from the last days of David to the Babylonian captivity and the destruction of Jerusalem (587 B.C.). The various sources for these books are woven into a uniform pattern based on the principle of fidelity to Yahweh for rulers and people alike. The sequence of regnal chronicles in both books is interrupted by a cycle of traditions surrounding the prophets Elijah (1 Kgs) and Elisha (2 Kgs).

Chronicles, Ezra, and Nehemiah form a historical work, uniform in style and basic ideas. Chronicles records the long period from the reign of Saul to the return from exile, not so much with exactitude of detail as with concern for the meaning of the facts which demonstrate God's intervention in history. The Ezra-Nehemiah chronicle constitutes the most important source for the formation of the Jewish religious

community after the Babylonian exile; the two persons most responsible for the reorganization of Jewish life were Ezra and Nehemiah.

1 and 2 Maccabees contain independent accounts of partially identical events which accompanied the attempted suppression of Judaism in Palestine in the second century B.C. Vigorous reaction to this attempt established for a time the religious and political independence of the Jews. 1 Maccabees portrays God as the eternal benefactor of the Jews and their unfailing source of help. The people are required to be devoted to his exclusive worship and to observe exactly the law he has given them. 2 Maccabees, besides supplementing the former volume, gives a theological interpretation of the history of the period and contains teaching on the resurrection from the dead, intercession of the saints, and suffrages for the dead.

Tobit, Judith, and Esther are examples of free composition—the religious novel used for purposes of edification and instruction. Interest in whatever historical data these books may contain is merely intensified by the addition of vivid details. Judith is a lesson in Providence: a pious reflection on the annual Passover observance to convey the reassurance that God is still the master of history who saves Israel from her enemies. Esther's purpose is the glorification of the Jewish people and the explanation of the origin, significance, and date of the feast of Purim. It is a literary development of the principle of reversal of fortune through punishment of the prosperous rich and reward for the virtuous who are oppressed.

Samuel to Maccabees demonstrates that before as well as during the millennium of history with which it is concerned, Israel was a covenanted people, bound to Yahweh, Lord of the universe, by the ties of faith and obedience. This required observance of the law and worship in his temple, the consequent rewards of which were divine favor and protection. In this way these books anticipate and prepare for the coming of him who would bring type and prophecy to fulfillment, history to term, and holiness to perfection: Christ, the Son of David and the promised Messiah.

The Books of Samuel

See RG
169–83

Originally but one book, the scroll of Samuel was early divided into two. The Greek translators called these the first and second Books of Kingdoms, a title St. Jerome later modified to "Kings." The Hebrew title, "Samuel," alludes to the leading figure in the first book, who was responsible for the enthronement of David. It is David's history that the second book recounts.

This sacred work thus comprises the history of about a century, describing the close of the age of the Judges and the beginnings of monarchy in Israel under Saul and David. It is not a complete and continuous history, nor a systematic account of the period, but rather a series of episodes centered around the persons of Samuel, Saul and David, the principal figures leading up to the establishment of the royal dynasty of David.

The final editor is unknown, nor are we certain of the time at which the various strands of the narrative were put together, though one may think of the period, perhaps late in the seventh century B.C., when the other volumes of the "Former Prophets," from Joshua through Kings, were built into a more or less continuous historical corpus.

The Samuel-Saul-David narratives clearly depend on several written sources: a Samuel cycle, two sets of stories about Saul and David, and a family history of David. This last (2 Sm 9—20; 1 Kgs 1—2), one of the most vivid historical narratives surviving from ancient times, probably originated early in the reign of Solomon.

One of the most significant theological contributions of the Old Testament is found in 2 Samuel 7, the oracle of Nathan. David is here promised an eternal dynasty, and this becomes the basis for the development of royal messianism throughout the Bible. With this promise to David one should compare 2 Chr 17; Pss 89, 20-38; 132, 11ff; Acts 2, 30; and Heb 1, 5.

The contents of this work may be divided as follows:

I: History of the Last Judges, Eli and Samuel (1 Sm 1, 1—7, 17).
II: Establishment of the Monarchy in Israel (1 Sm 8, 1—12, 25).
III: Saul and David (1 Sm 13, 1—2 Sm 2, 7).
IV: The Reign of David (2 Sm 2, 8—20, 26).
V: Appendixes (2 Sm 21, 1—24, 25).

The First Book of Samuel

I: History of the Last Judges, Eli and Samuel

See RG
170

CHAPTER 1

Elkanah and His Family at Shiloh. ¹There was a certain man from Ramathaim, Elkanah by name, a Zuphite from the hill country of Ephraim. He was the son of Jeroham, son of Elihu, son of Tohu, son of Zuph, an Ephraimite.ᵃ ²He had two wives, one named Hannah, the other Peninnah; Peninnah had children, but Hannah was childless. ³This man regularly went on pilgrimage from his city to worship the LORD of hosts and to sacrifice to him at Shiloh, where the two sons of Eli, Hophni and Phinehas, were ministering as priests of the LORD.ᵇ ⁴When the day came for Elkanah to offer sacrifice, he used to give a portion each to his wife Peninnah and to all her sons and daughters, ⁵but a double portion to Hannah because he loved

a: 1 Chr 6, 19f.   b: Ex 23, 14-17; 34, 23; Dt 16, 16; Jgs 21, 19.

303

her, though the LORD had made her barren.[c] [6]Her rival, to upset her, turned it into a constant reproach to her that the LORD had left her barren.[d] [7]This went on year after year; each time they made their pilgrimage to the sanctuary of the LORD, Peninnah would approach her, and Hannah would weep and refuse to eat. [8]Her husband Elkanah used to ask her: "Hannah, why do you weep, and why do you refuse to eat? Why do you grieve? Am I not more to you than ten sons?"[e]

Hannah's Prayer. [9]Hannah rose after one such meal at Shiloh, and presented herself before the LORD; at the time, Eli the priest was sitting on a chair near the doorpost of the LORD's temple. [10]In her bitterness she prayed to the LORD, weeping copiously, [11]and she made a vow, promising: "O LORD of hosts, if you look with pity on the misery of your handmaid, if you remember me and do not forget me, if you give your handmaid a male child, I will give him to the LORD* for as long as he lives; neither wine nor liquor shall he drink, and no razor shall ever touch his head."[f] [12]As she remained long at prayer before the LORD, Eli watched her mouth, [13]for Hannah was praying silently; though her lips were moving, her voice could not be heard. Eli, thinking her drunk, [14]said to her, "How long will you make a drunken show of yourself? Sober up from your wine!" [15]"It isn't that, my lord," Hannah answered. "I am an unhappy woman. I have had neither wine nor liquor; I was only pouring out my troubles to the LORD. [16]Do not think your handmaid a ne'er-do-well; my prayer has been prompted by my deep sorrow and misery." [17]Eli said, "Go in peace, and may the God of Israel grant you what you have asked of him." [18]She replied, "Think kindly of your maidservant," and left. She went to her quarters, ate and drank with her husband, and no longer appeared downcast. [19]Early the next morning they worshiped before the LORD, and then returned to their home in Ramah.

Hannah Bears a Son. When Elkanah had relations with his wife Hannah, the LORD remembered her. [20]She conceived, and at the end of her term bore a son whom she called Samuel, since she had asked* the LORD for him. [21]The next time her husband Elkanah was going up with the rest of his household to offer the customary sacrifice to the LORD and to fulfill his vows, [22]Hannah did not go, explaining to her husband, "Once the child is weaned, I will take him to appear before the LORD and to remain there forever; I will offer him as a perpetual nazirite." [23]Her husband Elkanah answered her: "Do what you think best; wait until you have weaned him. Only, may the LORD bring your resolve to fulfillment!" And so she remained at home and nursed her son until she had weaned him.

Samuel Is Offered to God. [24]Once he was weaned, she brought him up with her, along with a three-year-old bull, an ephah* of flour, and a skin of wine, and presented him at the temple of the LORD in Shiloh. [25]After the boy's father had sacrificed the young bull, Hannah, his mother, approached Eli [26]and said: "Pardon, my lord! As you live, my lord, I am the woman who stood near you here, praying to the LORD. [27]I prayed for this child, and the LORD granted my request. [28]Now I, in turn, give him to the LORD; as long as he lives, he shall be dedicated to the LORD." She left him there; *[1]and as she worshiped the LORD, she said:

CHAPTER 2

See RG 170–71

"My heart exults in the LORD,*
 my horn* is exalted in my God.
I have swallowed up my enemies;
 I rejoice in my victory.[g]

1, 11: Give him to the Lord: some ancient texts call Samuel a nazir in this context; see note on Nm 6, 1ff.

1, 20: Since she had asked: this explanation would be more directly appropriate for the name Saul, which means "asked"; Samuel means "name of God."

1, 24: An ephah: a little more than a bushel.

1, 1: And . . . said: this belongs to ch 2.

2, 1-10: A hymn attributed to Hannah, the mother of Samuel, as her thanksgiving to God because she has borne a son despite her previous sterility. She praises God as the helper of the weak (1ff), who casts down the mighty and raises up the lowly (3ff), and who alone is the source of true strength (8ff); the hymn ends with a prayer for the king (v 10). This canticle has several points of resemblance with our Lady's Magnificat.

2, 1: Horn: the symbol of strength; cf Pss 18, 3; 75, 5; 89, 18; 112, 9.

---

c: Dt 21, 15ff. *d:* Gn 16, 4f. *e:* Ru 4, 15. *f:* Nm 6, 1-5; Jgs 13, 2-5; 16, 17; Lk 1, 15. *g:* Dt 33, 17; 2 Sm 22, 3; Ps 18, 2; Is 61, 10; Lk 1, 47. 69

2 There is no Holy One like the LORD;
 there is no Rock like our God.*h*

3 "Speak boastfully no longer,
 nor let arrogance issue from your
  mouths.*
For an all-knowing God is the LORD,
 a God who judges deeds.*i*
4 The bows of the mighty are broken,
 while the tottering gird on strength.*j*
5 The well-fed hire themselves out for
  bread,
 while the hungry batten on spoil.
The barren wife bears seven sons,
 while the mother of many languishes.
6 "The LORD puts to death and gives life;
 he casts down to the nether world;
 he raises up again.*k*
7 The LORD makes poor and makes rich,
 he humbles, he also exalts.
8 He raises the needy from the dust;
 from the ash heap he lifts up the poor,
To seat them with nobles
 and make a glorious throne their
  heritage.*l*
He gives to the vower his vow,
 and blesses the sleep of the just.

"For the pillars of the earth are the LORD's,
 and he has set the world upon them.
9 He will guard the footsteps of his faithful
  ones,
 but the wicked shall perish in the
  darkness.
For not by strength does man prevail;
10 the LORD's foes shall be shattered.
The Most High in heaven thunders;
 the LORD judges the ends of the earth.
Now may he give strength to his king
 and exalt the horn of his anointed!"*m*

11 When Elkanah returned home to Ramah, the child remained in the service of the LORD under the priest Eli.

Wickedness of Eli's Sons. 12 Now the sons of Eli were wicked; they had respect neither for the LORD 13 nor for the priests' duties toward the people. When someone offered a sacrifice, the priest's servant would come with a three-pronged fork, while the meat was still boiling,*n* 14 and would thrust it into the basin, kettle, caldron, or pot. Whatever the fork brought up, the priest would keep. That is how all the Israelites were treated who came to the sanctuary at Shiloh. 15 In fact, even before the fat was burned, the priest's servant would come and say to the man offering the sacrifice, "Give me some meat to roast for the priest. He will not accept boiled meat from you, only raw meat." 16 And if the man protested to him, "Let the fat be burned first as is the custom, then take whatever you wish," he would reply, "No, give it to me now, or else I will take it by force."*o* 17 Thus the young men sinned grievously in the presence of the LORD; they treated the offerings to the LORD with disdain.

The Lord Rewards Hannah. 18 Meanwhile the boy Samuel, girt with a linen apron,* was serving in the presence of the LORD. 19 His mother used to make a little garment for him, which she would bring him each time she went up with her husband to offer the customary sacrifice. 20 And Eli would bless Elkanah and his wife, as they were leaving for home. He would say, "May the LORD repay you with children from this woman for the gift she has made to the LORD!" 21 The LORD favored Hannah so that she conceived and gave birth to three more sons and two daughters, while young Samuel grew up in the service of the LORD.*p*

Eli's Futile Rebuke. 22 When Eli was very old, he heard repeatedly how his sons were treating all Israel [and that they were having relations with the women serving at the entry of the meeting tent.]* 23 So he said to them: "Why are you doing such things?

2, 3: Speak . . . mouths: addressed to the enemies mentioned in v 1.
2, 18: Linen apron: called in Hebrew "ephod," but not the same as the high priest's ephod (Ex 28, 6-14) or the ephod used in divination (v 28). Samuel wore a simple apron such as was worn by the priests (1 Sm 22, 18), and on one occasion also by David (2 Sm 6, 14).
2, 22: The bracketed words, which recall Ex 38, 8, are a gloss in the received text; they are lacking in the oldest Greek translation, and in a Hebrew manuscript from Qumran.

h: 2 Sm 22, 3; Ps 18, 2.   *i:* Ps 75, 4.   *j:* Is 40, 29.   *k:* Dt 32, 39; Tb 4, 19; Jb 5, 11; Ps 30, 4; Wis 16, 13; Lk 1, 52.   *l:* Jb 9, 6; 38, 6; Ps 104, 32; 121, 3.   *m:* Ps 98, 9.   *n:* 13-15: Ex 29, 27f; Lv 7, 29-36; Dt 18, 3.   *o:* Lv 3, 3ff.   *p:* 1 Sm 3, 19.

²⁴No, my sons, you must not do these things! It is not a good report that I hear the people of the LORD spreading about you. ²⁵If a man sins against another man, one can intercede for him with the LORD; but if a man sins against the LORD, who can intercede for him?" But they disregarded their father's warning, since the LORD had decided on their death. ²⁶Meanwhile, young Samuel was growing in stature and in worth in the estimation of the LORD and of men.�q

Doom of Eli's House. * ²⁷A man of God came to Eli and said to him: "This is what the LORD says: 'I went so far as to reveal myself to your father's family when they were in Egypt as slaves to the house of Pharaoh. ²⁸I chose them out of all the tribes of Israel to be my priests, to go up to my altar, to burn incense, and to wear the ephod* before me; and I assigned all the oblations of the Israelites to your father's family.ʳ ²⁹Why do you keep a greedy eye on my sacrifices and on the offerings which I have prescribed? And why do you honor your sons in preference to me, fattening yourselves with the choicest part of every offering of my people Israel?' ³⁰ˢThis, therefore, is the oracle of the LORD, the God of Israel: 'I said in the past that your family and your father's family should minister in my presence forever. But now,' the LORD declares, 'away with this! for I will honor those who honor me, but those who spurn me shall be accursed. ³¹Yes, the time is coming when I will break your strength and the strength of your father's family, so that no man in your family shall reach old age. ³²You shall witness as a disappointed rival all the benefits enjoyed by Israel, but there shall never be an old man in your family. ³³I will permit some of your family to remain at my altar, to wear out their eyes in consuming greed; but the rest of the men of your family shall die by the sword. ³⁴You shall have a sign in what will

happen to your two sons, Hophni and Phinehas: both shall die on the same day.ᵗ ³⁵I will choose a faithful priest who shall do what I have in heart and mind. I will establish a lasting house for him which shall function in the presence of my anointed forever. ³⁶Then whoever is left of your family will come to grovel before him for a piece of silver or a loaf of bread, and will say: Appoint me, I beg you, to a priestly function, that I may have a morsel of bread to eat.' "ᵘ

CHAPTER 3

See RG 171

Revelation to Samuel. ¹During the time young Samuel was minister to the LORD under Eli, a revelation of the LORD was uncommon* and vision infrequent. ²One day Eli was asleep in his usual place. His eyes had lately grown so weak that he could not see. ³The lamp of God was not yet extinguished, and Samuel was sleeping in the temple of the LORD where the ark of God was.ᵛ ⁴The LORD called to Samuel, who answered, "Here I am." ⁵He ran to Eli and said, "Here I am. You called me." "I did not call you," Eli said. "Go back to sleep." So he went back to sleep. ⁶Again the LORD called Samuel, who rose and went to Eli. "Here I am," he said. "You called me." But he answered, "I did not call you, my son. Go back to sleep." ⁷At that time Samuel was not familiar with the LORD, because the LORD had not revealed anything to him as yet. ⁸The LORD called Samuel again, for the third time. Getting up and going to Eli, he said, "Here I am. You called me." Then Eli understood that the LORD was calling the youth. ⁹So he said to Samuel, "Go to sleep, and if you are called, reply, 'Speak, LORD, for your servant is listening.' " When Samuel went to sleep in his place, ¹⁰the LORD came and revealed his presence, calling out as before, "Samuel, Samuel!" Samuel answered, "Speak, for

---

2, 27-36: These verses propose the punishment of Eli from a point of view contemporary with the reform of Josiah (2 Kgs 23, 9; cf v 36); they hint at the events recorded in 1 Sm 22, 18-23 and 1 Kgs 2, 27. The older story of this divine warning is that in 1 Sm 3, 11-14.

2, 28: Ephod: a portable container, presumably of cloth, for the lots used in ritual consultation of God during the days of the Judges (Jgs 17, 5; 18, 14-15) and down into the time of David (1 Sm 14, 3ff; 23, 6ff; 30, 7f). The ephod of the high priest de-

scribed in Ex 28, 6ff becomes a garment upon which a breastpiece of decision symbolizes, but no longer serves for, such consultation. The Exodus text codifies a later form of the tradition.

3, 1: Uncommon: prophetic communications from God were almost unknown.

---

q: Lk 2, 52.   r: 1 Sm 23, 9; 30, 7f; Jgs 17, 5.   s: 30f: 2 Sm 22, 26; 1 Kgs 2, 27; Ps 18, 25.   t: 1 Sm 4, 11.   u: 2 Kgs 23, 9.   v: Ex 25, 22; 27, 20f; Lv 24, 2. 4; 2 Chr 13, 11.

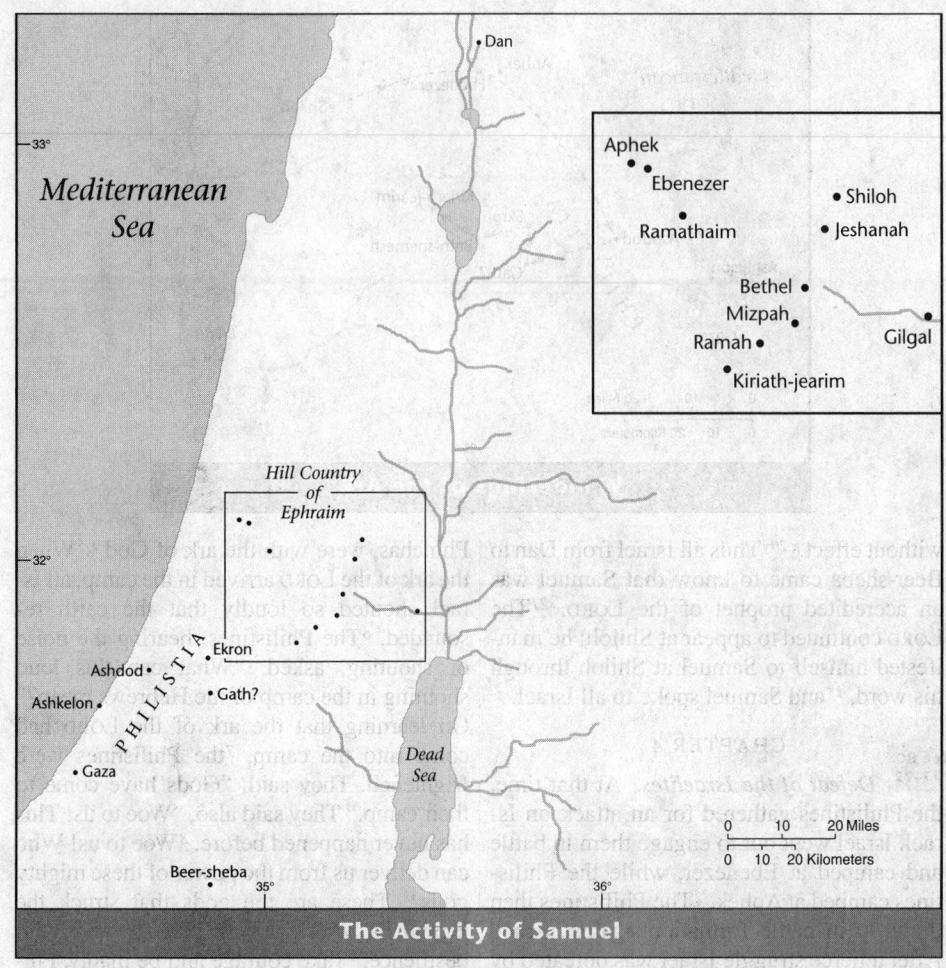

Mediterranean
Sea

Aphek
Ebenezer
Shiloh
Ramathaim
Jeshanah
Bethel
Mizpah
Ramah
Gilgal
Kiriath-jearim

Dan

33°

Hill Country
of
Ephraim

32°

Ekron
Ashdod
Gath?
Ashkelon

PHILISTIA

Gaza

Dead
Sea

Beer-sheba
35°
36°

0   10   20 Miles
0   10   20 Kilometers

The Activity of Samuel

your servant is listening." *11*The LORD said to Samuel: "I am about to do something in Israel that will cause the ears of everyone who hears it to ring. *12*On that day I will carry out in full against Eli everything I threatened against his family. *13*I announce to him that I am condemning his family once and for all, because of this crime: though he knew his sons were blaspheming God, he did not reprove them.*w* *14*Therefore, I swear to the family of Eli that no sacrifice or offering will ever expiate its crime." *15*Samuel then slept until morning, when he got up early and opened the doors of the temple of the LORD. He feared to tell Eli the vision, *16*but Eli called to him, "Samuel, my son!" He replied, "Here I am." *17*Then Eli asked, "What did he say to you? Hide nothing from me! May God do thus and so to you* if you hide a single thing he told you." *18*So Samuel told him everything, and held nothing back. Eli answered, "He is the LORD. He will do what he judges best."

Samuel Acknowledged as Prophet. *19*Samuel grew up, and the LORD was with him, not permitting any word of his to be

3, 17: May God do thus and so to you: the Biblical writers avoid repeating for us the specific terms of a curse as the speaker would have uttered it.

w: 1 Sm 2, 27-36.

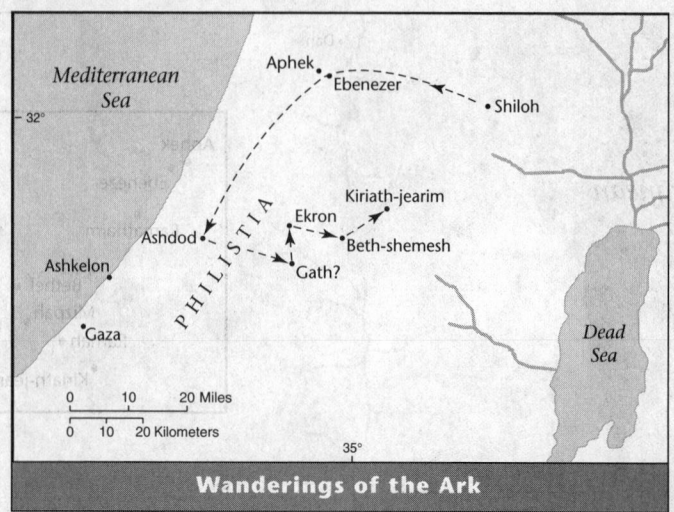

Wanderings of the Ark

without effect.[x] [20y]Thus all Israel from Dan to Beer-sheba came to know that Samuel was an accredited prophet of the LORD. [21]The LORD continued to appear at Shiloh; he manifested himself to Samuel at Shiloh through his word, [1*]and Samuel spoke to all Israel.

See RG 171–72

CHAPTER 4

Defeat of the Israelites. At that time, the Philistines gathered for an attack on Israel. Israel went out to engage them in battle and camped at Ebenezer, while the Philistines camped at Aphek. [2]The Philistines then drew up in battle formation against Israel. After a fierce struggle Israel was defeated by the Philistines, who slew about four thousand men on the battlefield. [3]When the troops retired to the camp, the elders of Israel said, "Why has the LORD permitted us to be defeated today by the Philistines? Let us fetch the ark of the LORD from Shiloh that it may go into battle among us and save us from the grasp of our enemies."

Loss of the Ark. [4]So the people sent to Shiloh and brought from there the ark of the LORD of hosts, who is enthroned upon the cherubim.* The two sons of Eli, Hophni and Phinehas, were with the ark of God.[z] [5]When the ark of the LORD arrived in the camp, all Israel shouted so loudly that the earth resounded. [6]The Philistines, hearing the noise of shouting, asked, "What can this loud shouting in the camp of the Hebrews mean?" On learning that the ark of the LORD had come into the camp, [7]the Philistines were frightened. They said, "Gods have come to their camp." They said also, "Woe to us! This has never happened before. [8]Woe to us! Who can deliver us from the power of these mighty gods?* These are the gods that struck the Egyptians with various plagues and with pestilence. [9]Take courage and be manly, Philistines; otherwise you will become slaves to the Hebrews, as they were your slaves. So fight manfully!" [10]The Philistines fought and Israel was defeated; every man fled to his own tent. It was a disastrous defeat, in which Israel lost thirty thousand foot soldiers.[a] [11]The ark of God was captured, and Eli's two sons, Hophni and Phinehas, were among the dead.[b]

Death of Eli. [12]A Benjaminite fled from the battlefield and reached Shiloh that same day, with his clothes torn and his head covered with dirt.[c] [13]When he arrived, Eli was

3, 1: And . . . Israel: this belongs to ch 4.

4, 4: Enthroned upon the cherubim: this title of the Lord seems to have originated in the sanctuary at Shiloh; it represents the divine Majesty as seated upon a throne on which he can be borne through the heavens by winged creatures somewhat as in the visions of Ez 1 and 10.

4, 8: These mighty gods: the Philistines, who were polytheists, are represented as supposing the Israelites honored several gods.

x: 1 Sm 2, 21. y: Jgs 20, 1. z: Ex 25, 22. a: Ps 78, 61.
b: 1 Sm 2, 34. c: Jos 7, 6; 2 Sm 1, 2; Jer 7, 12.

sitting in his chair beside the gate, watching the road, for he was troubled at heart about the ark of God. The man, however, went into the city to divulge his news, which put the whole city in an uproar. *14*Hearing the outcry of the men standing near him, Eli inquired, "What does this commotion mean?" *15*(Eli was ninety-eight years old, and his eyes would not focus, so that he could not see.) *16*The man quickly came up to Eli and said, "It is I who have come from the battlefield; I fled from there today." He asked, "What happened, my son?" *17*And the messenger answered: "Israel fled from the Philistines; in fact, the troops suffered heavy losses. Your two sons, Hophni and Phinehas, are among the dead, and the ark of God has been captured." *18*At this mention of the ark of God, Eli fell backward from his chair into the gateway; since he was an old man and heavy, he died of a broken neck. He had judged Israel for forty years.

*19*His daughter-in-law, the wife of Phinehas, was with child and at the point of giving birth. When she heard the news concerning the capture of the ark and the deaths of her father-in-law and her husband, she was seized with the pangs of labor, and gave birth. *20*She was about to die when the women standing around her said to her, "Never fear! You have given birth to a son." Yet she neither answered nor paid any attention.*d 21*[She named the child Ichabod, saying, "Gone is the glory from Israel," with reference to the capture of the ark of God and to her father-in-law and her husband.] *22*She said, "Gone is the glory from Israel," because the ark of God had been captured.*e*

See RG 171-72

CHAPTER 5

The Ark in the Temple of Dagon. *1f*The Philistines, having captured the ark of God, transferred it from Ebenezer to Ashdod. *2*They then took the ark of God and brought it into the temple of Dagon, placing it beside Dagon. *3*When the people of Ashdod rose early the next morning, Dagon was lying prone on the ground before the ark of the LORD. So they picked Dagon up and replaced him. *4*But the next morning early, when they arose, Dagon lay prone on the ground before the ark of the LORD, his head and hands broken off and lying on the threshold, his trunk alone intact. *5*For this reason, neither the priests of Dagon nor any others who enter the temple of Dagon tread on the threshold of Dagon in Ashdod to this very day; they always step over it.

The Ark Is Carried About. *6*Now the LORD dealt severely with the people of Ashdod. He ravaged and afflicted the city and its vicinity with hemorrhoids; he brought upon the city a great and deadly plague of mice* that swarmed in their ships and overran their fields.*g 7*On seeing how matters stood, the men of Ashdod decided, "The ark of the God of Israel must not remain with us, for he is handling us and our god Dagon severely." *8*So they summoned all the Philistine lords and inquired of them, "What shall we do with the ark of the God of Israel?" The men of Gath replied, "Let them move the ark of the God of Israel on to us." *9*So they moved the ark of the God of Israel to Gath! But after it had been brought there, the LORD threw the city into utter turmoil: he afflicted its inhabitants, young and old, and hemorrhoids broke out on them. *10*The ark of God was next sent to Ekron; but as it entered that city, the people there cried out, "Why have they brought the ark of the God of Israel here to kill us and our kindred?" *11*Then they, too, sent a summons to all the Philistine lords and pleaded: "Send away the ark of the God of Israel. Let it return to its own place, that it may not kill us and our kindred." A deadly panic had seized the whole city, since the hand of God had been very heavy upon it. *12*Those who escaped death were afflicted with hemorrhoids, and the outcry from the city went up to the heavens.

CHAPTER 6

See RG 171-72

The Ark To Be Returned. *1*The ark of the LORD had been in the land of the Philis-

---

5, 6: Hemorrhoids . . . mice: a double calamity fell upon them—a plague of mice or rats, and a severe epidemic of pestilential tumors, probably the bubonic plague.

---

d: 1 Sm 14, 3; Gn 35, 16ff.   *e:* Ps 78, 61.   *f:* 1-5: Jgs 16, 23-30; Is 45, 5f. 20f.   *g:* Ps 78, 66.

tines seven months ²when they summoned priests and fortune-tellers to ask, "What shall we do with the ark of the LORD? Tell us what we should send back with it." ³They replied: "If you intend to send away the ark of the God of Israel, you must not send it alone, but must, by all means, make amends to him through a guilt offering.* Then you will be healed, and will learn why he continues to afflict you." ⁴When asked further, "What guilt offering should be our amends to him?", they replied:

"Five golden hemorrhoids and five golden mice to correspond to the number of Philistine lords, since the same plague has struck all of you and your lords. ⁵Therefore, make images of the hemorrhoids and of the mice that are infesting your land and give them as a tribute to the God of Israel. Perhaps then he will cease to afflict you, your gods, and your land. ⁶Why should you become stubborn, as the Egyptians and Pharaoh were stubborn? Was it not after he had dealt ruthlessly with them that the Israelites were released and departed?ʰ ⁷So now set to work and make a new cart. Then take two milch cows that have not borne the yoke; hitch them to the cart, but drive their calves indoors away from them.ⁱ ⁸You shall next take the ark of the LORD and place it on the cart, putting in a box beside it the golden articles that you are offering, as amends for your guilt. Start it on its way, and let it go. ⁹Then watch! If it goes up to Beth-shemesh along the route to his own territory, he has brought this great calamity upon us; if not, we will know it was not he who struck us, but that an accident happened to us."

The Ark in Beth-shemesh. ¹⁰They acted upon this advice. Taking two milch cows, they hitched them to the cart but shut up their calves indoors. ¹¹Then they placed the ark of the LORD on the cart, along with the box containing the golden mice and the images of the hemorrhoids. ¹²The cows went straight for the route to Beth-shemesh and continued along this road, mooing as they

went, without turning right or left. The Philistine lords followed them as far as the border of Beth-shemesh. ¹³The people of Beth-shemesh were harvesting the wheat in the valley. When they looked up and spied the ark, they greeted it with rejoicing. ¹⁴The cart came to the field of Joshua the Beth-shemite and stopped there. At a large stone in the field, the wood of the cart was split up and the cows were offered as a holocaust to the LORD.ʲ ¹⁵The Levites, meanwhile, had taken down the ark of God and the box beside it, in which the golden articles were, and had placed them on the great stone. The men of Beth-shemesh also offered other holocausts and sacrifices to the LORD that day. ¹⁶After witnessing this, the five Philistine lords returned to Ekron the same day.

Guilt Offering. ¹⁷The golden hemorrhoids the Philistines sent back as a guilt offering to the LORD were as follows: one for Ashdod, one for Gaza, one for Ashkelon, one for Gath, and one for Ekron. ¹⁸The golden mice, however, corresponded to the number of all the cities of the Philistines belonging to the five lords, including fortified cities and open villages. The large stone on which the ark of the LORD was placed is still in the field of Joshua the Beth-shemite at the present time.

Penalty for Irreverence. ¹⁹The descendants of Jeconiah did not join in the celebration with the inhabitants of Beth-shemesh when they greeted the ark of the LORD, and seventy of them were struck down. The people went into mourning at this great calamity with which the LORD had afflicted them. ²⁰The men of Beth-shemesh asked, "Who can stand in the presence of this Holy One? To whom shall he go from us?" ²¹They then sent messengers to the inhabitants of Kiriath-jearim, saying, "The Philistines have returned the ark of the LORD; come down and get it."

CHAPTER 7

See RG 171-73

¹So the inhabitants of Kiriath-jearim came for the ark of the LORD and brought it into the house of Abinadab on the hill, ap-

---

6, 3: A guilt offering: a propitiatory offering customary after unwitting transgression of the ordinances of God regarding holy things or property rights; cf Lv 6, 1ff.

h: Ex 7, 14; 8, 15; 9, 34.   *i:* Nm 19, 2; Dt 21, 3; 2 Sm 6, 3.   *j:* 2 Sm 24, 21ff.

pointing his son Eleazar as guardian of the ark of the LORD.

Religious Reform. ²From the day the ark came to rest in Kiriath-jearim a long time, twenty years, elapsed, and the whole Israelite population turned to the LORD. ³Samuel said to them: "If you wish with your whole heart to return to the LORD, put away your foreign gods and your Ashtaroth, devote yourselves to the LORD, and worship him alone. Then he will deliver you from the power of the Philistines."ᵏ ⁴So the Israelites put away their Baals and Ashtaroth, and worshiped the LORD alone. ⁵Samuel then gave orders, "Gather all Israel to Mizpah, that I may pray to the LORD for you."ˡ ⁶When they were gathered at Mizpah, they drew water and poured it out on the ground* before the LORD, and they fasted that day, confessing, "We have sinned against the LORD." It was at Mizpah that Samuel began to judge the Israelites.ᵐ

Rout of the Philistines. ⁷When the Philistines heard that the Israelites had gathered at Mizpah, their lords went up against Israel. Hearing this, the Israelites became afraid of the Philistines ⁸and said to Samuel, "Implore the LORD our God unceasingly for us, to save us from the clutches of the Philistines."ⁿ ⁹Samuel therefore took an unweaned lamb and offered it entire as a holocaust to the LORD.ᵒ He implored the LORD for Israel, and the LORD heard him. ¹⁰While Samuel was offering the holocaust, the Philistines advanced to join battle with Israel. That day, however, the LORD thundered loudly against the Philistines, and threw them into such confusion that they were defeated by Israel. ¹¹Thereupon the Israelites sallied forth from Mizpah and pursued the Philistines, harrying them down beyond Beth-car. ¹²Samuel then took a stone and placed it between Mizpah and Jeshanah; he named it Ebenezer,* explaining, "To this point has the LORD helped us." ¹³Thus were the Philistines subdued, never again to enter the territory of Israel, for the LORD was severe with them as long as Samuel lived.ᵖ ¹⁴The cities from Ekron to Gath which the Philistines had taken from Israel were restored to them. Israel also freed the territory of these cities from the dominion of the Philistines. Moreover there was peace between Israel and the Amorites.

¹⁵Samuel judged Israel as long as he lived. ¹⁶He made a yearly journey, passing through Bethel, Gilgal and Mizpah and judging Israel at each of these sanctuaries. ¹⁷Then he used to return to Ramah, for that was his home. There, too, he judged Israel and built an altar to the LORD.�q

II: Establishment of the Monarchy in Israel

CHAPTER 8*

See RG 172-73

Request for a King. ¹In his old age Samuel appointed his sons judges over Israel. ²His first-born was named Joel, his second son, Abijah; they judged at Beer-sheba. ³His sons did not follow his example but sought illicit gain and accepted bribes, perverting justice.ʳ ⁴Therefore all the elders of Israel came in a body to Samuel at Ramah ⁵and said to him, "Now that you are old, and your sons do not follow your example, appoint a king over us, as other nations have, to judge us."ˢ

God Grants the Request. ⁶Samuel was displeased when they asked for a king to judge them. He prayed to the LORD, however, ⁷who said in answer: "Grant the people's every request. It is not you they reject, they are rejecting me as their king.ᵗ ⁸As they

---

7, 6: Poured it out on the ground: for the symbolism, cf 2 Sm 14, 14.

7, 12: Ebenezer: or eben ha-ezer, means "stone of help."

8, 1: From this chapter on, the First Book of Samuel gives us two and sometimes three viewpoints on most of the events with which it is concerned, such as the appointment of Saul as king, the reasons for his downfall, his relationship with David, even the circumstances of Saul's death (1 Sm 31; 2 Sm 1). The choice of Saul as king is seen, in ch 8, followed by 10, 17-27 and ch 12, as motivated by the people's defection from the proper service of God; this later editorial approach incorporates not only narratives with which it is consistent, but also early traditions (9, 1-10. 16; ch 11) which portray the events and their motivation quite differently.

k: 1 Sm 12, 10. 20. 24; Jos 24, 23; Jgs 6, 6-10; 10, 10-16. l: 1 Sm 10, 17; Jgs 20, 1. m: Jgs 20, 26; Ps 22, 14; Lam 2, 19. n: Ex 17, 9-13. o: 9f: 2 Sm 22, 14f; Sir 46, 16ff. p: Jgs 3, 30; 8, 28; 11, 33. q: 1 Sm 9, 12; 14, 35. r: Ex 23, 8; Dt 16, 19; Prv 17, 23. s: 5f: Dt 17, 14f; Hos 13, 10; Acts 13, 21. t: 7f: 1 Sm 12, 1. 12f; Jgs 8, 22f; 10, 13; 1 Kgs 9, 9.

have treated me constantly from the day I brought them up from Egypt to this day, deserting me and worshiping strange gods, so do they treat you too. [9]Now grant their request; but at the same time, warn them solemnly and inform them of the rights of the king who will rule them."

The Rights of a King. [10]Samuel delivered the message of the LORD in full to those who were asking him for a king. [11]He told them: "The rights of the king who will rule you will be as follows: He will take your sons and assign them to his chariots and horses, and they will run before his chariot.[u] [12]He will also appoint from among them his commanders of groups of a thousand and of a hundred soldiers. He will set them to do his plowing and his harvesting, and to make his implements of war and the equipment of his chariots.[v] [13]He will use your daughters as ointment-makers, as cooks, and as bakers. [14]He will take the best of your fields, vineyards, and olive groves, and give them to his officials.[w] [15]He will tithe your crops and your vineyards, and give the revenue to his eunuchs and his slaves. [16]He will take your male and female servants, as well as your best oxen and your asses, and use them to do his work. [17]He will tithe your flocks and you yourselves will become his slaves.[x] [18]When this takes place, you will complain against the king whom you have chosen, but on that day the LORD will not answer you."

Persistent Demand. [19]The people, however, refused to listen to Samuel's warning and said, "Not so! There must be a king over us.[y] [20]We too must be like other nations, with a king to rule us and to lead us in warfare and fight our battles." [21]When Samuel had listened to all the people had to say, he repeated it to the LORD, [22]who then said to him, "Grant their request and appoint a king to rule them." Samuel thereupon said to the men of Israel, "Each of you go to his own city."

CHAPTER 9

See RG 173-74

[1]There was a stalwart man from Benjamin named Kish, who was the son of Abiel, son of Zeror, son of Becorath, son of Aphiah, a Benjaminite.[z] [2]He had a son named Saul, who was a handsome young man. There was no other Israelite handsomer than Saul; he stood head and shoulders above the people.[a]

The Lost Asses. [3]Now the asses of Saul's father, Kish, had wandered off. Kish said to his son Saul, "Take one of the servants with you and go out and hunt for the asses." [4]Accordingly they went through the hill country of Ephraim, and through the land of Shalishah. Not finding them there, they continued through the land of Shaalim without success. They also went through the land of Benjamin, but they failed to find the animals. [5]When they came to the land of Zuph, Saul said to the servant who was with him, "Come, let us turn back, lest my father forget about the asses and become anxious about us." [6]The servant replied, "Listen! There is a man of God in this city, a man held in high esteem; all that he says is sure to come true. Let us go there now! Perhaps he can tell us how to accomplish our errand." [7b]But Saul said to his servant, "If we go, what can we offer the man? There is no bread in our bags, and we have no present to give the man of God. What have we?" [8]Again the servant answered Saul, "I have a quarter of a silver shekel.* If I give that to the man of God, he will tell us our way." [10]Saul then said to his servant, "Well said! Come on, let us go!" And they went to the city where the man of God lived.

Quest for Samuel's Aid. [11c]As they were going up the ascent to the city, they met some girls coming out to draw water and inquired of them, "Is the seer in town?" [9d](In former times in Israel, anyone who sent to consult God used to say, "Come, let us go to the seer." For he who is now called prophet

---

9, 8: A quarter of a silver shekel: about a tenth of an ounce of silver.

u: 1 Sm 10, 25; Dt 17, 14-20; 1 Kgs 12.　*v:* 2 Sm 15, 1; 1 Kgs 1, 5.　*w:* 1 Sm 22, 7; 1 Kgs 21, 1-24; Ez 46, 18.　*x:* 1 Kgs 12, 4.
y: 1 Sm 10, 19.　*z:* 1 Sm 14, 51; 1 Chr 8, 33.　*a:* 1 Sm 10, 23.　*b:* 7f: Nm 22, 7; 1 Kgs 14, 3; 2 Kgs 4, 42; 5, 15; 8, 8f.　*c:* Gn 24, 11ff; Ex 2, 16.　*d:* Sir 46, 15.

was formerly called seer.)* *12e*The girls answered, "Yes, there—straight ahead. Hurry now; just today he came to the city, because the people have a sacrifice today on the high place.* *13*When you enter the city, you may reach him before he goes up to the high place to eat. The people will not eat until he arrives; only after he blesses the sacrifice will the invited guests eat. Go up immediately, for you should find him right now."

Samuel's Revelation about Saul. *14*So they went up to the city. As they entered it, Samuel was coming toward them on his way to the high place. *15*The day before Saul's arrival, the LORD had given Samuel the revelation:*f 16*"At this time tomorrow I will send you a man from the land of Benjamin whom you are to anoint as commander of my people Israel. He shall save my people from the clutches of the Philistines, for I have witnessed their misery and accepted their cry for help."*g 17*When Samuel caught sight of Saul, the LORD assured him, "This is the man of whom I told you; he is to govern my people." *18*Saul met Samuel in the gateway and said, "Please tell me where the seer lives." *19*Samuel answered Saul: "I am the seer. Go up ahead of me to the high place and eat with me today. In the morning, before dismissing you, I will tell you whatever you wish. *20*As for the asses you lost three days ago, do not worry about them, for they have been found. Whom does Israel desire ardently if not you and your father's family?" *21*Saul replied: "Am I not a Benjaminite, of one of the smallest tribes of Israel, and is not my clan the least among the clans of the tribe of Benjamin? Why say such things to me?"*h*

*22*Samuel then took Saul and his servant and brought them to the room, where he placed them at the head of the guests, of whom there were about thirty. *23*He said to the cook, "Bring the portion I gave you and told you to put aside." *24*So the cook took up the leg and what went with it,* and placed it before Saul. Samuel said: "This is a reserved portion that has been set before you. Eat, for it was kept for you until your arrival; I explained that I was inviting some guests." Thus Saul dined with Samuel that day. *25*When they came down from the high place into the city, a mattress was spread for Saul on the roof, *26*and he slept there.

Saul's Anointing. At daybreak Samuel called to Saul on the roof, "Get up, and I will start you on your journey." Saul rose, and he and Samuel went outside the city together. *27*As they were approaching the edge of the town, Samuel said to Saul, "Tell the servant to go on ahead of us, but stay here yourself for the moment, that I may give you a message from God."

CHAPTER 10

See RG 173–74

*1*Then, from a flask he had with him, Samuel poured oil on Saul's head; he also kissed him, saying: "The LORD anoints you commander over his heritage. You are to govern the LORD's people Israel, and to save them from the grasp of their enemies round-about.*i*

"This will be the sign for you that the LORD has anointed you commander over his heritage: *2*When you leave me today, you will meet two men near Rachel's tomb* at Zelzah in the territory of Benjamin, who will say to you, 'The asses you went to look for have been found. Your father is no longer worried about the asses, but is anxious about you and says, What shall I do about my son?'*j 3*Farther on, when you arrive at the

9, 9: This verse is a later explanation of the term seer, first used in the text in 1 Sm 9, 11.

9, 12: On the high place: the local sanctuary on the top of a hill, where the sacrifice was offered and the sacrificial meal eaten.

9, 24: And what went with it: a slight change would give "and the fatty tail" as perhaps the original reading. Sheep in the Near East are exceptionally fat-tailed, and such a portion would be thought a special delicacy by the Hebrews. However, the ritual legislation as we know it (Lv 3, 9) would require that the fat tail be burned on the altar. If this general rule

was later than the time of Samuel, the present text may have been retouched so as not to seem to contravene it. A Qumran text has "the festive (leg)" here.

10, 2: Here, as in Jer 31, 15, Rachel's tomb is placed north of Jerusalem. Later tradition understood Gn 35, 19f in the sense given by Mt 2, 16ff, and placed the tomb at Bethlehem, farther south.

e: 1 Sm 7, 17; 16, 2. 5; 20, 6. 29; Dt 12, 13; 1 Kgs 3, 2. 4. *f:* Acts 13, 21. *g:* 1 Sm 10, 1. *h:* 1 Sm 15, 17. *i:* 1 Sm 9, 16f; 24, 7; Jgs 9, 9; 1 Kgs 1, 39; Acts 13, 21. *j:* Jer 31, 15; Mk 14, 13.

terebinth of Tabor, you will be met by three men going up to God at Bethel; one will be bringing three kids, another three loaves of bread, and the third a skin of wine. [4]They will greet you and offer you two wave offerings of bread, which you will take from them. [5k]After that you will come to Gibeathelohim, where there is a garrison of the Philistines.* As you enter that city, you will meet a band of prophets, in a prophetic state, coming down from the high place preceded by lyres, tambourines, flutes and harps. [6]The spirit of the LORD will rush upon you, and you will join them in their prophetic state and will be changed into another man.[l] [7]When you see these signs fulfilled, do whatever you judge feasible, because God is with you. [8m]Now go down ahead of me to Gilgal, for I shall come down to you, to offer holocausts and to sacrifice peace offerings. Wait seven days until I come to you; I shall then tell you what you must do.'*

Fulfillment of the Signs. [9]As Saul turned to leave Samuel, God gave him another heart. That very day all these signs came to pass. . . . [10*]When they were going from there to Gibeah, a band of prophets met him, and the spirit of God rushed upon him, so that he joined them in their prophetic state.[n] [11]When all who had known him previously saw him in a prophetic state among the prophets, they said to one another, "What has happened to the son of Kish? Is Saul also among the prophets?"[o] [12]And someone from that district added, "And who is their father?" Thus the proverb arose, "Is Saul also among the prophets?" [13]When he came out of the prophetic state, he went home.

Silence about the Kingship. [14]Saul's uncle inquired of him and his servant, "Where have you been?" Saul replied, "To look for the asses. When we could not find them, we went to Samuel." [15]Then Saul's uncle said, "Tell me, then, what Samuel said to you." [16]Saul said to his uncle, "He assured us that the asses had been found." But he mentioned nothing to him of what Samuel had said about the kingship.

Saul Chosen King by Lot. [17]Samuel called the people together to the LORD at Mizpah[p] [18]and addressed the Israelites: "Thus says the LORD, the God of Israel, 'It was I who brought Israel up from Egypt and delivered you from the power of the Egyptians and from the power of all the kingdoms that oppressed you.'[q] [19]But today you have rejected your God, who delivers you from all your evils and calamities, by saying to him, 'Not so, but you must appoint a king over us.' Now, therefore, take your stand before the LORD according to tribes and families."[r] [20]So Samuel had all the tribes of Israel come forward, and the tribe of Benjamin was chosen. [21]Next he had the tribe of Benjamin come forward in clans, and the clan of Matri was chosen, and finally Saul, son of Kish, was chosen. But they looked for him in vain. [22s]Again they consulted the LORD, "Has he come here?" The LORD answered, "He is hiding among the baggage." [23]They ran to bring him from there; and when he stood among the people, he was head and shoulders above all the crowd.[t] [24]Samuel said to all the people, "Do you see the man whom the LORD has chosen? There is none like him among all the people!" Then all the people shouted, "Long live the king!"[u]

[25]Samuel next explained to the people the law of royalty* and wrote it in a book, which he placed in the presence of the LORD. This done, Samuel dismissed the people, each to his own place.[v] [26]Saul also went home to

---

10, 5: A garrison of the Philistines: the Hebrew word for "garrison" has been explained alternatively to mean a pillar erected to mark the Philistine occupation, or an inspector or officer for the collection of taxes. In a prophetic state: in an ecstatic condition due to strong feelings of religious enthusiasm induced by a communal observance, possibly accompanied by music and dancing.

10, 8: By inserting this verse, with its seven days, an editor has prepared for one narrative of the rejection of Saul (1 Sm 13, 8-15) in the very context of Saul's anointing.

10, 10: The story has here been abridged by omitting the fulfillment of the first two signs given by Samuel (1 Sm 10, 2ff).

10, 25: The law of royalty: the charter defining the rights of the king.

---

k: 5f: 1 Sm 13, 3; 16, 13; 19, 20f. *l:* 1 Sm 11, 6; 16, 13; Jgs 14, 6. 19; 15, 14; 2 Kgs 3, 15. *m:* 1 Sm 13, 8; Lv 3, 1. *n:* 1 Sm 19, 20-24; Nm 11, 25. *o:* 1 Sm 19, 24. *p:* 1 Sm 7, 5. *q:* Ex 20, 2; Lv 11, 45; 25, 38; Nm 15, 41; Dt 5, 6; Jgs 6, 8f. *r:* 1 Sm 8, 19. *s:* 1 Sm 30, 24. *t:* 1 Sm 9, 2; 16, 7. *u:* 2 Sm 16, 16; 1 Kgs 1, 25; 2 Kgs 11, 12. *v:* 1 Sm 8, 11; Dt 17, 14-20.

Gibeah, accompanied by warriors whose hearts the LORD had touched. [27]But certain worthless men said, "How can this fellow save us?" They despised him and brought him no present.[w]

See RG 173-74

CHAPTER 11

Defeat of the Ammonites. [1]About a month later,* Nahash the Ammonite went up and laid siege to Jabesh-gilead. All the men of Jabesh begged Nahash, "Make a treaty with us, and we will be your subjects."[x] [2]But Nahash the Ammonite replied, "This is my condition for a treaty with you: I must gouge out every man's right eye, that I may thus bring ignominy on all Israel." [3]The elders of Jabesh said to him: "Give us seven days to send messengers throughout the territory of Israel. If no one rescues us, we will surrender to you." [4]When the messengers arrived at Gibeah of Saul, they related the news to the people, all of whom wept aloud. [5]Just then Saul came in from the field, behind his oxen. "Why are the people weeping?" he asked. The message of the inhabitants of Jabesh was repeated to him. [6]As he listened to this report, the spirit of God rushed upon him and he became very angry.[y] [7]Taking a yoke of oxen, he cut them into pieces, which he sent throughout the territory of Israel by couriers with the message, "If anyone does not come out to follow Saul [and Samuel], the same as this will be done to his oxen!" In dread of the LORD, the people turned out to a man.[z] [8]When he reviewed them in Bezek, there were three hundred thousand Israelites and seventy thousand Judahites.

[9]To the messengers who had come he said, "Tell the inhabitants of Jabesh-gilead that tomorrow, while the sun is hot, they will be rescued." The messengers came and reported this to the inhabitants of Jabesh, who were jubilant, [10]and said to Nahash, "Tomorrow we will surrender to you, and you

may do whatever you please with us." [11]On the appointed day, Saul arranged his troops in three companies and invaded the camp during the dawn watch. They slaughtered Ammonites until the heat of the day; by then the survivors were so scattered that no two were left together.

Saul Accepted as King. [12]*The people then said to Samuel: "Who questioned whether Saul should rule over us? Hand over the men and we will put them to death."[a] [13]But Saul broke in to say, "No man is to be put to death this day, for today the LORD has saved Israel."[b] [14]Samuel said to the people, "Come, let us go to Gilgal to inaugurate the kingdom there." [15]So all the people went to Gilgal, where, in the presence of the LORD, they made Saul king. They also sacrificed peace offerings there before the LORD, and Saul and all the Israelites celebrated the occasion with great joy.

CHAPTER 12

See RG 173-74

Samuel's Integrity. [1]Samuel addressed all Israel: "I have granted your request in every respect," he said. "I have set a king over you[c] [2]and now the king is your leader. As for me, I am old and gray, and have sons among you. I have lived with you from my youth to the present day. [3]Here I stand! Answer me in the presence of the LORD and of his anointed. Whose ox have I taken? Whose ass have I taken? Whom have I cheated? Whom have I oppressed? From whom have I accepted a bribe and overlooked his guilt? I will make restitution to you."[d] [4]They replied, "You have neither cheated us, nor oppressed us, nor accepted anything from anyone." [5]So he said to them, "The LORD is witness against you this day, and his anointed as well, that you have found nothing in my possession." "He is witness," they agreed.

Samuel Upbraids the People. [6]Continuing, Samuel said to the people: "The LORD is wit-

---

11, 1: About a month later: there is ancient evidence for a longer introduction to this campaign. The time indication here may refer to its earlier stages rather than to the events of ch 10.

11, 12-14: With these verses, an editor has harmonized the account of the acknowledgment of Saul as king at Mizpah (1 Sm 10, 17-24) with the public acclamation at Gilgal (1 Sm 11, 15) after the defeat of the Ammonites (1 Sm 11, 1-11).

The Greek text of 1 Sm 11, 15 reads "and Samuel anointed Saul as king," instead of they made Saul king.

---

w: 1 Sm 11, 12.   x: 1 Sm 12, 12; 31, 11.   y: 1 Sm 16, 13; Jgs 14, 6. 19.   z: 1 Kgs 11, 30; 2 Kgs 13, 18.   a: 1 Sm 10, 27.   b: 2 Sm 19, 23.   c: 1 Sm 8, 7. 9. 22.   d: Ex 20, 17; 23, 8; Nm 16, 15; Dt 16, 19; Sir 46, 19.

ness, who appointed Moses and Aaron, and who brought your fathers up from the land of Egypt.*e* *7*Now, therefore, take your stand, and I shall arraign you before the LORD, and shall recount for you all the acts of mercy the LORD has done for you and your fathers. *8*When Jacob and his sons went to Egypt and the Egyptians oppressed them, your fathers appealed to the LORD, who sent Moses and Aaron to bring them out of Egypt, and he gave them this place to live in.*f* *9*But they forgot the LORD their God; and he allowed them to fall into the clutches of Sisera, the captain of the army of Jabin, king of Hazor, into the grasp of the Philistines, and into the grip of the king of Moab, who made war against them.*g* *10*Each time they appealed to the LORD and said, 'We have sinned in forsaking the LORD and worshiping Baals and Ashtaroth; but deliver us now from the power of our enemies, and we will worship you.'*h* *11*Accordingly, the LORD sent Jerubbaal, Barak, Jephthah, and Samson; he delivered you from the power of your enemies on every side, so that you were able to live in security.*i* *12*Yet, when you saw Nahash, king of the Ammonites, advancing against you, you said to me, 'Not so, but a king must rule us,' even though the LORD your God is your king.*j*

Warnings for People and King. *13*"Now you have the king you want, a king the LORD has given you.*k* *14*If you fear the LORD and worship him, if you are obedient to him and do not rebel against the LORD's command, if both you and the king who rules you follow the LORD your God—well and good. *15*But if you do not obey the LORD and if you rebel against his command, the LORD will deal severely with you and your king, and destroy you. *16*Now then, stand ready to witness the great marvel the LORD is about to accomplish before your eyes. *17*Are we not in the harvest time for wheat? Yet I shall call to the LORD,

and he will send thunder and rain. Thus you will see and understand how greatly the LORD is displeased that you have asked for a king."*l* *18*Samuel then called to the LORD, and the LORD sent thunder and rain that day.

Assistance Promised. As a result, all the people dreaded the LORD and Samuel. *19*They said to Samuel, "Pray to the LORD your God for us, your servants, that we may not die for having added to all our other sins the evil of asking for a king." *20*"Do not fear," Samuel answered them. "It is true you have committed all this evil; still, you must not turn from the LORD, but must worship him with your whole heart. *21*Do not turn to meaningless idols which can neither profit nor save; they are nothing.*m* *22*For the sake of his own great name the LORD will not abandon his people, since the LORD himself chose to make you his people.*n* *23*As for me, far be it from me to sin against the LORD by ceasing to pray for you and to teach you the good and right way.*o* *24*But you must fear the LORD and worship him faithfully with your whole heart; keep in mind the great things he has done among you. *25*If instead you continue to do evil, both you and your king shall perish."

III: Saul and David

CHAPTER 13

See RG 174

1[Saul was . . . years old when he became king and he reigned . . . . (two) years over Israel.]*

Saul Offers Sacrifice. *2*Saul chose three thousand men of Israel, of whom two thousand remained with him in Michmash and in the hill country of Bethel, and one thousand were with Jonathan in Gibeah of Benjamin. He sent the rest of the people back to their tents. *3*Now Jonathan overcame the Philistine garrison* which was in Gibeah, and the Philistines got word of it. Then Saul sounded

---

13, 1: A formula like that of 2 Sm 5, 4 was introduced here at some time; but the age of Saul when he became king remains a blank, and the two years assigned for his reign in the received text cannot be correct. Tradition (Acts 13, 21) offers the round number, "forty years."

13, 3-4: The Philistine garrison: see note on 1 Sm 10, 5. Let the Hebrews hear: a different reading of these verses, based on the Greek, would yield: "And the Philistines heard that the Hebrews (or: the slaves) had revolted. Saul in the

meantime sounded the trumpet throughout all the land (v 4), and all Israel heard that Saul. . . ."

e: Mi 6, 4. *f:* Gn 46, 5; Ex 1, 11; 2, 23ff. *g:* Jgs 3, 12ff; 4, 2f; 10, 7; 13, 1. *h:* 1 Sm 7, 3f. *i:* Jgs 6, 14. 32; 11, 1. *j:* 1 Sm 8, 6f. 19; 11, 1f; Jgs 8, 23. *k:* 1 Sm 8, 7. *l:* Ex 9, 23. 28ff; 1 Kgs 18, 1. *m:* Dt 32, 37ff. *n:* Jer 14, 21; Ex 20, 9; Dn 3, 34. *o:* Ex 32, 11.

0   10   20 Miles

0   10   20 Kilometers

- Baal-shalishah
- Aphek
- Ramah
- Bethel (Beth-aven)
- Ophrah
- Beth-horon
- Mizpah
- Gilgal
- Aijalon
- Migron
- Michmash
- Geba
- Gibeah
- Jerusalem
- Azekah
- Socoh
- Carmel

Mediterranean Sea

- Endor
- *V. of Jezreel*
- Jezreel
- *Mt. Gilboa*
- Beth-shan
- Jabesh-gilead
- Bezek

GILEAD

GAD

AMMON

Hill Country of Ephraim

BENJAMIN

- Ekron
- ?Gath
- Jerusalem

Dead Sea

PHILISTIA

MOAB

AMALEK

EDOM

33°

32°

31°

35°

36°

The Kingdom of Saul according to 1 Samuel

the horn throughout the land, with a proclamation, "Let the Hebrews hear!"*p* *4*Thus all Israel learned that Saul had overcome the garrison of the Philistines and that Israel had brought disgrace upon the Philistines; and the soldiers were called up to Saul in Gilgal. *5*The Philistines also assembled for battle, with three thousand chariots, six thousand horsemen, and foot soldiers as numerous as the sands of the seashore. Moving up against Israel, they encamped in Michmash, east of Beth-aven. *6*Some Israelites, aware of the danger and of the difficult situation, hid themselves in caves, in thickets, among rocks, in caverns, and in cisterns,*q* *7*and other Hebrews passed over the Jordan into the land of Gad and Gilead. Saul, however, held out at Gilgal, although all his followers were seized with fear.* *8*He waited seven days— the time Samuel had determined. When Samuel did not arrive at Gilgal, the men began to slip away from Saul.*r* *9*He then said, "Bring me the holocaust and peace offerings," and he offered up the holocaust.

King Saul Reproved. *10*He had just finished this offering when Samuel arrived. Saul went out to greet him, *11*and Samuel asked him, "What have you done?" Saul replied: "When I saw that the men were slipping away from me, since you had not come by the specified time, and with the Philistines assembled at Michmash, *12*I said to myself, 'Now the Philistines will come down against me at Gilgal, and I have not yet sought the LORD's blessing.' So in my anxiety I offered up the holocaust." *13*Samuel's response was: "You have been foolish! Had you kept the command the LORD your God gave you, the LORD would now establish your kingship in Israel as lasting; *14*but as things are, your kingdom shall not endure. The LORD has sought out a man after his own heart and has appointed him commander of his people, because you broke the LORD's command."*s*

Philistine Invasion. *15*Then Samuel set out from Gilgal and went his own way; but the rest of the people went up after Saul to meet the soldiers, going from Gilgal to Gibeah of Benjamin. Saul then numbered the soldiers he had with him, who were about six hundred.*t* *16*Saul, his son Jonathan, and the soldiers they had with them were now occupying Geba of Benjamin, and the Philistines were encamped at Michmash. *17*Meanwhile, raiders left the camp of the Philistines in three bands.*u* One band took the Ophrah road toward the district of Shual; *18*another turned in the direction of Beth-horon; and the third took the road for Geba that overlooks the Valley of the Hyenas toward the desert.

Disarmament of Israel. *19*Not a single smith was to be found in the whole land of Israel, for the Philistines had said, "Otherwise the Hebrews will make swords or spears."*v* *20*All Israel, therefore, had to go down to the Philistines to sharpen their plowshares, mattocks, axes, and sickles. *21*The price for the plowshares and mattocks was two-thirds of a shekel, and a third of a shekel for sharpening the axes and for setting the ox-goads. *22*And so on the day of battle neither sword nor spear could be found in the possession of any of the soldiers with Saul or Jonathan. Only Saul and his son Jonathan had them.

Jonathan's Exploit. *23*An outpost of the Philistines had pushed forward to the pass of Michmash.*w*

CHAPTER 14

See RG 174–75

*1*One day Jonathan, son of Saul, said to his armor-bearer, "Come, let us go over to the Philistine outpost on the other side." But he did not inform his father.*x* *2*(Saul's command post was under the pomegranate tree near the threshing floor on the outskirts of Geba; those with him numbered about six hundred men. *3*Ahijah, son of Ahitub, brother of Ichabod, who was the son of Phinehas, son of Eli, the priest of the LORD at Shiloh, was wearing the ephod.) Nor did the soldiers know that Jonathan had gone.*y* *4*Flanking the ravine through which Jona-

---

13, 7-15: These verses, like 1 Sm 10, 8, anticipate the rejection of Saul; a different occasion and motivation for this are given in ch 15, resumed in 1 Sm 28, 17f.

---

p: 1 Sm 14, 1-15; Jgs 3, 27; 6, 34; 2 Sm 20, 1f.   *q:* 1 Sm 14, 22.   *r:* 1 Sm 10, 8.   *s:* 1 Sm 25, 30; 2 Sm 7, 15f; Ps 78, 70; Acts 13, 22.
t: 1 Sm 14, 2.   *u:* 1 Sm 14, 15.   *v:* Jgs 5, 8.   *w:* 1 Sm 14, 15.   *x:* 1 Sm 13, 3.   *y:* 1 Sm 2, 28; 4, 21; 14, 18; 23, 9; 30, 7.

than intended to get over to the Philistine outpost there was a rocky crag on each side, one called Bozez, the other Seneh. ⁵One crag was to the north, toward Michmash, the other to the south, toward Geba. ⁶Jonathan said to his armor-bearer: "Come, let us go over to that outpost of the uncircumcised. Perhaps the LORD will help us, because it is no more difficult for the LORD to grant victory through a few than through many."ᶻ ⁷His armor-bearer replied, "Do whatever you are inclined to do; I will match your resolve." ⁸Jonathan continued: "We shall go over to those men and show ourselves to them. ⁹If they say to us, 'Stay there until we can come to you,' we shall stop where we are; we shall not go up to them. ¹⁰But if they say, 'Come up to us,' we shall go up, because the LORD has delivered them into our grasp. That will be our sign." ¹¹Accordingly, the two of them appeared before the outpost of the Philistines, who said, "Look, some Hebrews are coming out of the holes where they have been hiding." ¹²The men of the outpost called to Jonathan and his armor-bearer. "Come up here," they said, "and we will teach you a lesson." So Jonathan said to his armor-bearer, "Climb up after me, for the LORD has delivered them into the grasp of Israel." ¹³Jonathan clambered up with his armor-bearer behind him; as the Philistines turned to flee him, he cut them down, and his armor-bearer followed him and finished them off. ¹⁴In this first exploit Jonathan and his armor-bearer slew about twenty men within half a furlong. ¹⁵Then panic spread to the army and to the countryside, and all the soldiers, including the outpost and the raiding parties, were terror-stricken. The earth also shook, so that the panic was beyond human endurance.

Rout of the Philistines. ¹⁶The lookouts of Saul in Geba of Benjamin saw that the enemy camp had scattered and were running about in all directions. ¹⁷Saul said to those around him, "Count the troops and find out if any of us are missing." When they had investigated, they found Jonathan and his armor-bearer missing. ¹⁸Saul then said to Ahijah, "Bring the ephod* here." (Ahijah was wearing the ephod in front of the Israelites at that time.) ¹⁹While Saul was speaking to the priest, the tumult in the Philistine camp kept increasing. So he said to the priest, "Withdraw your hand." ²⁰And Saul and all his men shouted and rushed into the fight, where the Philistines, wholly confused, were thrusting swords at one another.ᵃ ²¹In addition, the Hebrews who had previously sided with the Philistines and had gone up with them to the camp, turned to join the Israelites under Saul and Jonathan.ᵇ ²²Likewise, all the Israelites who were hiding in the hill country of Ephraim, on hearing that the Philistines were fleeing, pursued them in the rout.ᶜ ²³Thus the LORD saved Israel that day.

Saul's Oath. The battle continued past Beth-horon;* ²⁴the whole people, about ten thousand combatants, were with Saul, and there was scattered fighting in every town in the hill country of Ephraim. And Saul swore a very rash oath that day, putting the people under this ban: "Cursed be the man who takes food before evening, before I am able to avenge myself on my enemies." So none of the people tasted food. ²⁵Indeed, there was a honeycomb lying on the ground, ²⁶and when the soldiers came to the comb the swarm had left it; yet no one would raise a hand to his mouth from it, because the people feared the oath.

Violation of the Oath. ²⁷Jonathan, who had not heard that his father had put the people under oath, thrust out the end of the staff he was holding and dipped it into the honey. Then he raised it to his mouth and his eyes lit up. ²⁸At this one of the soldiers spoke up: "Your father put the people under a strict oath, saying, 'Cursed be the man who takes food this day!' As a result the people are

---

14, 18: Ephod: to be used in consulting God; see note on v 41, and that on 1 Sm 2, 28 above.

14, 23: Past Beth-horon: this is a textual correction influenced by 1 Sm 13, 18; the received Hebrew text refers to Bethel (Bethaven), but the effect of the victory would seem to have been that the main ridge of mountains in the territories of Benjamin and Ephraim was cleared of Philistines.

z: 1 Sm 17, 26. 36. 47; Sir 39, 18; 1 Mc 3, 19. *a:* Jgs 7, 22. *b:* 1 Sm 29, 4. *c:* 1 Sm 13, 6.

weak." [29] Jonathan replied: "My father brings trouble to the land. Look how bright my eyes are from this small taste of honey I have had. [30] What is more, if the people had eaten freely today of their enemy's booty when they came across it, would not the slaughter of the Philistines by now have been the greater for it?"

Use of Flesh with Blood Forbidden. [31] After the Philistines were routed that day from Michmash to Aijalon, the people were completely exhausted. [32] So they pounced upon the spoil and took sheep, oxen and calves, slaughtering them on the ground and eating the flesh with blood.[d] [33] Informed that the people were sinning against the LORD by eating the flesh with blood, Saul said: "You have broken faith. Roll a large stone here for me." [34] He continued: "Mingle with the people and tell each of them to bring his ox or his sheep to me. Slaughter it here and then eat, but you must not sin against the LORD by eating the flesh with blood." So everyone brought to the LORD whatever ox he had seized, and they slaughtered them there; [35] and Saul built an altar to the LORD—this was the first time he built an altar to the LORD.[e]

Jonathan in Danger of Death. [36] Then Saul said, "Let us go down in pursuit of the Philistines by night, to plunder among them until daybreak and to kill them all off." They replied, "Do what you think best." But the priest said, "Let us consult God." [37] So Saul inquired of God: "Shall I go down in pursuit of the Philistines? Will you deliver them into the power of Israel?" But he received no answer on this occasion.[f] [38] Saul then said, "Come here, all officers of the army. We must investigate and find out how this sin was committed today. [39] As the LORD lives who has given victory to Israel, even if my son Jonathan has committed it, he shall surely die!" But none of the people answered him. [40] So he said to all Israel, "Stand on one side, and I and my son Jonathan will stand on the other." The people responded, "Do what you think best."[g] [41] And Saul said to the LORD, the God of Israel: "Why did you not answer your servant this time? If the blame for this resides in me or my son Jonathan, LORD, God of Israel, respond with Urim; but if this guilt is in your people Israel, respond with Thummim."* Jonathan and Saul were designated, and the people went free.[h] [42] Saul then said, "Cast lots between me and my son Jonathan." And Jonathan was designated. [43] Saul said to Jonathan, "Tell me what you have done." Jonathan replied, "I only tasted a little honey from the end of the staff I was holding. Am I to die for this?" [44] Saul said, "May God do thus and so to me if you do not indeed die, Jonathan!"[i]

Rescue of Jonathan. [45] But the army said to Saul: "Is Jonathan to die, though it was he who brought Israel this great victory? This must not be! As the LORD lives, not a single hair of his head shall fall to the ground, for God was with him in what he did today!" Thus the soldiers were able to rescue* Jonathan from death.[j] [46] After that Saul gave up the pursuit of the Philistines, who returned to their own territory.

Wars and Victories. [47] After taking over the kingship of Israel, Saul waged war on all their surrounding enemies—Moab, the Ammonites, Aram, Beth-rehob, the king of Zobah, and the Philistines. Wherever he turned, he was successful[k] [48] and fought bravely. He defeated Amalek and delivered Israel from the hands of those who were plundering them.

Saul's Family. [49] The sons of Saul were Jonathan, Ishvi,* and Malchishua; his two daughters were named, the elder, Merob, and the younger, Michal.[l] [50] Saul's wife, who was named Ahinoam, was the daughter of Ahim-

---

14, 41: The Urim and Thummim, or sacred lots, were a device for ascertaining the will of God; they ceased to be used after the time of David. The material and the shape of these objects, and the manner in which they were used, are unknown. They gave a "yes" or "no" answer to specific questions.

14, 45: Rescue: the Hebrew word used is that for the "redemption" of the first-born (Ex 13, 13ff).

14, 49: Ishvi: known also as Ishbaal, in 2 Sm 2, 8 and elsewhere. The name may once have read "Ishyo" here.

d: 1 Sm 15, 19. 21; Lv 3, 17; 7, 26f; 17, 10-14; Acts 15, 20. 29. *e:* 1 Sm 7, 17; Jgs 6, 24. *f:* 1 Sm 28, 6. 15. *g:* Jos 7, 13ff. *h:* 1 Sm 28, 6; Ex 28, 30; Dt 33, 8. *i:* 1 Sm 3, 17; Ru 1, 17. *j:* 2 Sm 14, 11; 1 Kgs 1, 52. *k:* 2 Sm 1, 22; 8, 2-5. *l:* 1 Sm 18, 20. 25; 31, 2; 1 Chr 8, 33; 9, 39; 10, 2.

aaz. The name of his general was Abner, son of Saul's uncle, Ner; [51]Kish, Saul's father, and Ner, Abner's father, were sons of Abiel.[m]

[52]An unremitting war was waged against the Philistines during Saul's lifetime. When Saul saw any strong or brave man, he took him into his service.

See RG 175

CHAPTER 15

[1]Samuel said to Saul: "It was I the LORD sent to anoint you king over his people Israel. Now, therefore, listen to the message of the LORD. [2]This is what the LORD of hosts has to say: 'I will punish what Amalek did to Israel when he barred his way as he was coming up from Egypt.[n] [3]Go, now, attack Amalek, and deal with him and all that he has under the ban.* Do not spare him, but kill men and women, children and infants, oxen and sheep, camels and asses.'"[o]

Disobedience of Saul. [4]Saul alerted the soldiers, and at Telaim reviewed two hundred thousand foot soldiers and ten thousand men of Judah.* [5]Saul went to the city of Amalek, and after setting an ambush in the wadi, [6p]warned the Kenites: "Come! Leave Amalek and withdraw, that I may not have to destroy you with them, for you were kind to the Israelites when they came up from Egypt." After the Kenites left, [7]Saul routed Amalek from Havilah to the approaches of Shur, on the frontier of Egypt.[q] [8]He took Agag, king of Amalek, alive, but on the rest of the people he put into effect the ban of destruction by the sword. [9]He and his troops spared Agag and the best of the fat sheep and oxen, and the lambs. They refused to carry out the doom on anything that was worthwhile, dooming only what was worthless and of no account.

Saul Is Reproved. [10]Then the LORD spoke to Samuel: [11]"I regret* having made Saul

king, for he has turned from me and has not kept my command." At this Samuel grew angry and cried out to the LORD all night. [12]Early in the morning he went to meet Saul, but was informed that Saul had gone to Carmel, where he erected a trophy in his own honor, and that on his return he had passed on and gone down to Gilgal. [13]When Samuel came to him, Saul greeted him: "The LORD bless you! I have kept the command of the LORD." [14]But Samuel asked, "What, then, is the meaning of this bleating of sheep that comes to my ears, and the lowing of oxen that I hear?" [15]Saul replied: "They were brought from Amalek. The men spared the best sheep and oxen to sacrifice to the LORD, your God; but we have carried out the ban on the rest." [16]Samuel said to Saul: "Stop! Let me tell you what the LORD said to me last night." "Speak!" he replied. [17]Samuel then said: "Though little in your own esteem, are you not leader of the tribes of Israel? The LORD anointed you king of Israel[r] [18]and sent you on a mission, saying, 'Go and put the sinful Amalekites under a ban of destruction. Fight against them until you have exterminated them.'[s] [19]Why then have you disobeyed the LORD? You have pounced on the spoil, thus displeasing the LORD."[t] [20]Saul answered Samuel: "I did indeed obey the LORD and fulfill the mission on which the LORD sent me. I have brought back Agag, and I have destroyed Amalek under the ban. [21]But from the spoil the men took sheep and oxen, the best of what had been banned, to sacrifice to the LORD their God in Gilgal."[u] [22v]But Samuel said:

"Does the LORD so delight in holocausts
    and sacrifices
  as in obedience to the command of the
    LORD?

15, 3: Under the ban: in such wars of extermination, all things (men, cities, beasts, etc.) were to be blotted out; nothing could be reserved for private use. The interpretation of God's will here attributed to Samuel is in keeping with the abhorrent practices of blood revenge prevalent among pastoral, seminomadic peoples such as the Hebrews had recently been. The slaughter of the innocent has never been in conformity with the will of God.

15, 4: The numbers here are not realistic; compare 1 Sm 14, 24 above.

15, 11: I regret: God manifests "regret" when, offended by men, he takes away his benefits, graces and favors. It is not God, but men, who change, to their own detriment.

m: 1 Sm 9, 1.   *n:* Ex 17, 8-10. 16; Dt 25, 17ff.   *o:* 1 Sm 27, 8; 30, 17; Ex 17, 16; Nm 24, 20.   *p:* Nm 24, 21.   *q:* 1 Sm 27, 8.   *r:* 1 Sm 9, 21.   *s:* 1 Sm 28, 18.   *t:* 1 Sm 14, 32.   *u:* Lv 27, 28.   *v:* Prv 21, 3; Hos 6, 6; Am 5, 21-25; Zec 10, 2; Mt 9, 13; 12, 7; Heb 10, 9.

Obedience is better than sacrifice,
and submission than the fat of rams.*
23 For a sin like divination is rebellion,
and presumption is the crime of
idolatry.
Because you have rejected the command
of the LORD,
he, too, has rejected you as ruler."

Saul Asks Forgiveness. 24 Saul replied to Samuel: "I have sinned, for I have disobeyed the command of the LORD and your instructions. In my fear of the people, I did what they said.w 25 Now forgive my sin, and return with me, that I may worship the LORD." 26 But Samuel said to Saul, "I will not return with you, because you rejected the command of the LORD and the LORD rejects you as king of Israel."x 27 As Samuel turned to go, Saul seized a loose end of his mantle, and it tore off.y 28 So Samuel said to him: "The LORD has torn the kingdom of Israel from you this day, and has given it to a neighbor of yours, who is better than you.z 29 The Glory of Israel neither retracts nor repents, for he is not man that he should repent."a 30 But he answered: "I have sinned, yet honor me now before the elders of my people and before Israel. Return with me that I may worship the LORD your God." 31 And so Samuel returned with him, and Saul worshiped the LORD.

Agag Is Cut Down. 32 Afterward Samuel commanded, "Bring Agag, king of Amalek, to me." Agag came to him struggling and saying, "So it is bitter death!" 33 And Samuel said,

"As your sword has made women
childless,
so shall your mother be childless
among women."

Then he cut Agag down before the LORD in Gilgal.b

34 Samuel departed for Ramah, while Saul went up to his home in Gibeah of Saul. 35 Never again, as long as he lived, did Samuel see Saul. Yet he grieved over Saul, because the LORD regretted having made him king of Israel.c

CHAPTER 16

See RG
175

Samuel Sent to Bethlehem. 1d The LORD said to Samuel: "How long will you grieve for Saul, whom I have rejected as king of Israel? Fill your horn with oil, and be on your way. I am sending you to Jesse of Bethlehem, for I have chosen my king from among his sons."* 2 But Samuel replied: "How can I go? Saul will hear of it and kill me." To this the LORD answered: "Take a heifer along and say, 'I have come to sacrifice to the LORD.' 3 Invite Jesse to the sacrifice, and I myself will tell you what to do; you are to anoint for me the one I point out to you."

4 Samuel did as the LORD had commanded him. When he entered Bethlehem, the elders of the city came trembling to meet him and inquired, "Is your visit peaceful, O seer?" 5 He replied: "Yes! I have come to sacrifice to the LORD. So cleanse yourselves and join me today for the banquet." He also had Jesse and his sons cleanse themselves and invited them to the sacrifice.e 6 As they came, he looked at Eliab and thought, "Surely the LORD's anointed is here before him." 7 But the LORD said to Samuel: "Do not judge from his appearance or from his lofty stature, because I have rejected him. Not as man sees does God see, because man sees the appearance but the LORD looks into the heart."f 8g Then Jesse called Abinadab and presented him before Samuel, who said, "The LORD has not chosen him." 9 Next Jesse presented Shammah, but Samuel said, "The LORD has not chosen this one either." 10 In the same way Jesse presented seven sons before Samuel, but Samuel said to Jesse, "The

15, 22: Samuel is disapproving, not of sacrifices in general, but of merely external sacrifices offered in defiance of God's commandment and without heartfelt obedience.

16, 1: The anointing here prepared for is unknown to David's brother Eliab in the next chapter (1 Sm 17, 28), and David is twice anointed after Saul's death (2 Sm 2, 4; 5, 3).

w: 1 Sm 26, 21.   x: 1 Kgs 11, 11. 30f.   y: 1 Sm 24, 6.   z: 1 Sm 28, 17; 2 Sm 7, 15f.   a: Nm 23, 19.   b: Ex 21, 23.   c: Gn 6, 6. d: 1 Kgs 1, 39; Ru 4, 17-22; 1 Chr 11, 3; Is 11, 1; Lk 2, 4.   e: 1 Sm 9, 12f; 20, 26; Ex 19, 10; Jb 1, 5.   f: 1 Sm 10, 23f; 1 Chr 28, 9; Prv 15, 11; Jer 17, 10; 20, 12; Lk 16, 15; Acts 1, 24.   g: 8ff: 1 Sm 17, 12f; 1 Chr 2, 13ff.

LORD has not chosen any one of these." [11] Then Samuel asked Jesse, "Are these all the sons you have?" Jesse replied, "There is still the youngest, who is tending the sheep." Samuel said to Jesse, "Send for him; we will not begin the sacrificial banquet until he arrives here."[h] [12] Jesse sent and had the young man brought to them. He was ruddy, a youth handsome to behold and making a splendid appearance. The LORD said, "There—anoint him, for this is he!"[i] [13] Then Samuel, with the horn of oil in hand, anointed him in the midst of his brothers; and from that day on, the spirit of the LORD rushed upon David. When Samuel took his leave, he went to Ramah.[j]

Saul's Spirit of Melancholy. [14k] The spirit of the LORD had departed from Saul, and he was tormented by an evil spirit sent by the LORD.* [15] So the servants of Saul said to him: "Please! An evil spirit from God is tormenting you. [16] If your lordship will order it, we, your servants here in attendance on you, will look for a man skilled in playing the harp. When the evil spirit from God comes over you, he will play and you will feel better." [17] Saul then told his servants, "Find me a skillful harpist and bring him to me." [18l] A servant spoke up to say: "I have observed that one of the sons of Jesse of Bethlehem is a skillful harpist. He is also a stalwart soldier, besides being an able speaker, and handsome. Moreover, the LORD is with him."*

David Made Armor-Bearer. [19] Accordingly, Saul dispatched messengers to ask Jesse to send him his son David, who was with the flock. [20] Then Jesse took five loaves of bread, a skin of wine, and a kid, and sent them to Saul by his son David.[m] [21] Thus David came to Saul and entered his service. Saul became very fond of him, made him his armor-bearer,[n] [22] and sent Jesse the message, "Allow David to remain in my service, for he meets with my approval." [23] Whenever the spirit from God seized Saul, David would take the harp and play, and Saul would be relieved and feel better, for the evil spirit would leave him.

CHAPTER 17

See RG 175-76

The Challenge of Goliath. [1] The Philistines rallied their forces for battle at Socoh in Judah and camped between Socoh and Azekah at Ephes-dammim. [2] Saul and the Israelites also gathered and camped in the Vale of the Terebinth, drawing up their battle line to meet the Philistines. [3] The Philistines were stationed on one hill and the Israelites on an opposite hill, with a valley between them.

[4] A champion named Goliath of Gath came out from the Philistine camp; he was six and a half feet tall. [5] He had a bronze helmet on his head and wore a bronze corselet of scale armor weighing five thousand shekels, [6] and bronze greaves, and had a bronze scimitar* slung from a baldric. [7] The shaft of his javelin was like a weaver's heddle-bar, and its iron head weighed six hundred shekels.* His shield-bearer went before him.[o] [8] He stood and shouted to the ranks of Israel: "Why come out in battle formation? I am a Philistine, and you are Saul's servants. Choose one of your men, and have him come down to me. [9] If he beats me in combat and kills me, we will be your vassals; but if I beat him and kill him, you shall be our vassals and serve us." [10] The Philistine continued: "I defy the ranks of Israel today. Give me a man and let us fight together." [11] Saul and all the men of Israel, when they heard this challenge of the Philistine, were dismayed and terror-stricken.

16, 14: An evil spirit sent by the Lord: the Lord permitted Saul to be tormented with violent fits of rage.

16, 18: Of the two traditions which describe the coming of David into Saul's service, the oldest Greek translation retains only the one comprised in 1 Sm 16, 14-23; 17, 1-11. 32-54. This effort at consistency is not in accord with the character of the rest of the book; see note on 1 Sm 8, 1. Though square brackets are used in this edition to indicate the passages lacking in the oldest translation, this is meant only to help the reader follow one account at a time. Both are equally a part of the inspired text, as are also the various amplifications and re-touchings of the narrative given within brackets in chs 18 and 19.

17, 6: Scimitar: the Hebrew word for this is rather rare, and the nature of the weapon was in doubt until recent years. It is not the same as the sword of v 45.

17, 7: Six hundred shekels: over 15 pounds.

h: 1 Sm 17, 15. 28. 34; 2 Sm 7, 8. i: 1 Sm 9, 2. j: 1 Sm 10, 6; 11, 6; Jgs 3, 10; 9, 9; Sir 46, 13. k: 1 Sm 18, 10f. l: 2 Sm 17, 8. m: 1 Sm 9, 7f; 10, 4. 27; 16, 1; 17, 27ff. n: 1 Sm 18, 2. o: 2 Sm 21, 19; 1 Chr 11, 23; 20, 5.

*David Comes to the Camp.** [12][David was the son of an Ephrathite named Jesse, who was from Bethlehem in Judah. He had eight sons, and in the days of Saul was old and well on in years.[p] [13]The three oldest sons of Jesse had followed Saul to war; these three sons who had gone off to war were named, the first-born Eliab, the second son Abinadab, and the third Shammah. [14]David was the youngest. While the three oldest had joined Saul, [15]David would go and come from Saul to tend his father's sheep at Bethlehem.[q]

[16][Meanwhile the Philistine came forward and took his stand morning and evening for forty days.

[17][Now Jesse said to his son David: "Take this ephah of roasted grain and these ten loaves for your brothers, and bring them quickly to your brothers in the camp. [18]Also take these ten cheeses for the field officer. Greet your brothers and bring home some token from them. [19]Saul, and they, and all Israel are fighting against the Philistines in the Vale of the Terebinth." [20]Early the next morning, having left the flock with a shepherd, David set out on his errand, as Jesse had commanded him. He reached the barricade of the camp just as the army, on their way to the battleground, were shouting their battle cry.[r] [21]The Israelites and the Philistines drew up opposite each other in battle array. [22]David entrusted what he had brought to the keeper of the baggage and hastened to the battle line where he greeted his brothers.[s] [23]While he was talking with them, the Philistine champion, by name Goliath of Gath, came up from the ranks of the Philistines and spoke as before, and David listened. [24]When the Israelites saw the man, they all retreated before him, very much afraid. [25]The Israelites had been saying: "Do you see this man coming up? He comes up to insult Israel. If anyone should kill him, the king would give him great wealth, and his daughter as well, and would grant exemp-

tion to his father's family in Israel."[t] [26]David now said to the men standing by: "What will be done for the man who kills this Philistine and frees Israel of the disgrace? Who is this uncircumcised Philistine in any case, that he should insult the armies of the living God?"[u] [27]They repeated the same words to him and said, "That is how the man who kills him will be rewarded." [28]When Eliab, his oldest brother, heard him speaking with the men, he grew angry with David and said: "Why did you come down? With whom have you left those sheep in the desert meanwhile? I know your arrogance and your evil intent. You came down to enjoy the battle!" [29]David replied, "What have I done now?—I was only talking." [30]Yet he turned from him to another and asked the same question; and everyone gave him the same answer as before. [31]The words that David had spoken were overheard and reported to Saul, who sent for him.]

David Fights Goliath. [32]Then David spoke to Saul: "Let your majesty not lose courage. I am at your service to go and fight this Philistine." [33]But Saul answered David, "You cannot go up against this Philistine and fight with him, for you are only a youth, while he has been a warrior from his youth." [34][v]Then David told Saul: "Your servant used to tend his father's sheep, and whenever a lion or bear came to carry off a sheep from the flock, [35]I would go after it and attack it and rescue the prey from its mouth. If it attacked me, I would seize it by the jaw, strike it, and kill it. [36]Your servant has killed both a lion and a bear, and this uncircumcised Philistine will be as one of them, because he has insulted the armies of the living God."

[37]David continued: "The LORD, who delivered me from the claws of the lion and the bear, will also keep me safe from the clutches of this Philistine." Saul answered David, "Go! the LORD will be with you."[w]

Preparation for the Encounter. [38]Then Saul clothed David in his own tunic, putting

---

17, 12-31: An alternative account of how David came to undertake the combat with the Philistine is here inserted; it is continued in 1 Sm 17, 55—18, 6. See note on 1 Sm 16, 18.

p: 1 Sm 16, 1. 10; Ru 1, 2.   *q:* 1 Sm 18, 2; 2 Sm 7, 8.   *r:* 1 Sm 26, 5.   *s:* 1 Sm 25, 13.   *t:* 1 Sm 18, 17; Jos 15, 16.   *u:* 1 Sm 18, 25; Jgs 15, 18; 2 Kgs 19, 4; Is 37, 4.   *v:* 34f: Jgs 14, 6; Sir 47, 3.   *w:* Prv 28, 1.

a bronze helmet on his head and arming him with a coat of mail. *39*David also girded himself with Saul's sword over the tunic. He walked with difficulty, however, since he had never tried armor before. He said to Saul, "I cannot go in these, because I have never tried them before." So he took them off. *40*Then, staff in hand, David selected five smooth stones from the wadi and put them in the pocket of his shepherd's bag. With his sling also ready to hand, he approached the Philistine.

David's Victory. *41*With his shield-bearer marching before him, the Philistine also advanced closer and closer to David. *42*When he had sized David up, and seen that he was youthful, and ruddy, and handsome in appearance, he held him in contempt. *43*The Philistine said to David, "Am I a dog that you come against me with a staff?" Then the Philistine cursed David by his gods *44*and said to him, "Come here to me, and I will leave your flesh for the birds of the air and the beasts of the field."*x* *45*David answered him: "You come against me with sword and spear and scimitar, but I come against you in the name of the LORD of hosts, the God of the armies of Israel that you have insulted. *46*Today the LORD shall deliver you into my hand; I will strike you down and cut off your head. This very day I will leave your corpse and the corpses of the Philistine army for the birds of the air and the beasts of the field; thus the whole land shall learn that Israel has a God. *47*All this multitude, too, shall learn that it is not by sword or spear that the LORD saves. For the battle is the LORD's, and he shall deliver you into our hands."*y*

*48*The Philistine then moved to meet David at close quarters, while David ran quickly toward the battle line in the direction of the Philistine. *49*David put his hand into the bag and took out a stone, hurled it with the sling, and struck the Philistine on the forehead. The stone embedded itself in his brow, and he fell prostrate on the ground. *50*[Thus David over-

came the Philistine with sling and stone; he struck the Philistine mortally, and did it without a sword.]*z* *51*Then David ran and stood over him; with the Philistine's own sword [which he drew from its sheath] he dispatched him and cut off his head.*a*

Flight of the Philistines. When they saw that their hero was dead, the Philistines took to flight. *52*Then the men of Israel and Judah, with loud shouts, went in pursuit of the Philistines to the approaches of Gath and to the gates of Ekron, and Philistines fell wounded along the road from Shaaraim as far as Gath and Ekron. *53*On their return from the pursuit of the Philistines, the Israelites looted their camp. *54b*David took the head of the Philistine and brought it to Jerusalem; but he kept Goliath's armor in his own tent.*

David Presented to Saul. *55*[When Saul saw David go out to meet the Philistine, he asked his general Abner, "Abner, whose son is that youth?" Abner replied, "As truly as your majesty is alive, I have no idea." *56*And the king said, "Find out whose son the lad is." *57*So when David returned from slaying the Philistine, Abner took him and presented him to Saul. David was still holding the Philistine's head. *58*Saul then asked him, "Whose son are you, young man?" David replied, "I am the son of your servant Jesse of Bethlehem."

CHAPTER 18

See RG
175–76

David and Jonathan. *1*[By the time David finished speaking with Saul, Jonathan had become as fond of David as if his life depended on him; he loved him as he loved himself.*c* *2*Saul laid claim to David that day and did not allow him to return to his father's house.*d* *3*And Jonathan entered into a bond with David, because he loved him as himself. *4*Jonathan divested himself of the mantle he was wearing and gave it to David, along with his military dress, and his sword, his bow and his belt.*e* *5*David then carried out successfully every mission on which

17, 54: At the time supposed by this narrative, Jerusalem was still Jebusite, and David had no military tent of his own; the verse is a later gloss.

x: Dt 28, 26; Is 18, 6; Jer 15, 3.   y: 1 Sm 14, 6; Ps 33, 16.   z: Sir 47, 4; 1 Mc 4, 30.   a: 1 Sm 21, 10.   b: 1 Sm 31, 9.   c: 1 Sm 19, 1-7; 20, 17; 23, 16; 2 Sm 1, 26; 9, 1.   d: 1 Sm 16, 21; 17, 15.   e: 2 Sm 1, 22.

Saul sent him. So Saul put him in charge of his soldiers, and this was agreeable to the whole army, even to Saul's own officers.]

Saul's Jealousy. 6At the approach of Saul and David (on David's return after slaying the Philistine), women came out from each of the cities of Israel to meet King Saul, singing and dancing, with tambourines, joyful songs, and sistrums.*f* 7The women played and sang:

"Saul has slain his thousands,
and David his ten thousands."*g*

8Saul was very angry and resentful of the song, for he thought: "They give David ten thousands, but only thousands to me. All that remains for him is the kingship." 9[And from that day on, Saul was jealous of David.

10[*h* The next day an evil spirit from God came over Saul, and he raged in his house. David was in attendance, playing the harp as at other times, while Saul was holding his spear. 11Saul poised the spear, thinking to nail David to the wall, but twice David escaped him.] 12Saul then began to fear David, [because the LORD was with him, but had departed from Saul himself.] 13Accordingly, Saul removed him from his presence by appointing him a field officer. So David led the people on their military expeditions, 14and prospered in all his enterprises, for the LORD was with him. 15Seeing how successful he was, Saul conceived a fear of David; 16on the other hand, all Israel and Judah loved him, since he led them on their expeditions.*i*

17[Saul said to David, "There is my older daughter, Merob, whom I will give you in marriage if you become my champion and fight the battles of the LORD." Saul had in mind, "I shall not touch him; let the Philistines strike him."*j* 18But David answered Saul: "Who am I? And who are my kin or my father's clan in Israel that I should become the king's son-in-law?" 19However, when it was time for Saul's daughter Merob to be given to David, she was given in marriage to Adriel the Meholathite instead.]*k*

20Now Saul's daughter Michal loved David, and it was reported to Saul, who was pleased at this,*l* 21for he thought, "I will offer her to him to become a snare for him, so that the Philistines may strike him." [Thus for the second time Saul said to David, "You shall become my son-in-law today."] 22Saul then ordered his servants to speak to David privately and to say: "The king is fond of you, and all his officers love you. You should become the king's son-in-law." 23But when Saul's servants mentioned this to David, he said: "Do you think it easy to become the king's son-in-law? I am poor and insignificant." 24When his servants reported to him the nature of David's answer, 25Saul commanded them to say this to David: "The king desires no other price for the bride than the foreskins of one hundred Philistines, that he may thus take vengeance on his enemies." Saul intended in this way to bring about David's death through the Philistines.*m* 26When the servants reported this offer to David, he was pleased with the prospect of becoming the king's son-in-law. [Before the year was up,] 27David made preparations and sallied forth with his men and slew two hundred Philistines. He brought back their foreskins and counted them out before the king, that he might thus become the king's son-in-law. So Saul gave him his daughter Michal in marriage. 28Saul thus came to recognize that the LORD was with David; besides, his own daughter Michal loved David. 29Therefore Saul feared David all the more [and was his enemy ever after].

30[The Philistine chiefs continued to make forays, but each time they took the field, David was more successful against them than any other of Saul's officers, and as a result acquired great fame.]

CHAPTER 19

See RG
176-77

Persecution of David. 1Saul discussed his intention of killing David with his son Jonathan and with all his servants. But Saul's son Jonathan, who was very fond of David,*n* 2told him: "My father Saul is trying

---

f: Ex 15, 20f; Jgs 11, 34; Jdt 15, 12.   *g:* 1 Sm 21, 12; 29, 5; Sir 47, 6f.   *h:* 10f: 1 Sm 16, 14; 19, 9f; 20, 33; 22, 6; 26, 8.   *i:* 2 Sm 5, 2.   *j:* 1 Sm 14, 49; 17, 25.   *k:* 1 Sm 21, 8; 24, 16.   *l:* 1 Sm 14, 49; 25, 44; 26, 23; 2 Sm 3, 13.   *m:* 1 Sm 17, 26; Gn 34, 12.   *n:* 1 Sm 18, 1; 20, 1ff.

to kill you. Therefore, please be on your guard tomorrow morning; get out of sight and remain in hiding. ³I, however, will go out and stand beside my father in the countryside where you are, and will speak to him about you. If I learn anything, I will let you know."

⁴Jonathan then spoke well of David to his father Saul, saying to him: "Let not your majesty sin against his servant David, for he has committed no offense against you, but has helped you very much by his deeds. ⁵When he took his life in his hands and slew the Philistine, and the LORD brought about a great victory for all Israel through him, you were glad to see it. Why, then, should you become guilty of shedding innocent blood by killing David without cause?"ᵒ ⁶Saul heeded Jonathan's plea and swore, "As the LORD lives, he shall not be killed." ⁷So Jonathan summoned David and repeated the whole conversation to him. Jonathan then brought David to Saul, and David served him as before.

⁸When war broke out again, David went out to fight against the Philistines and inflicted a great defeat upon them, putting them to flight. ⁹ᵖThen an evil spirit from the LORD came upon Saul as he was sitting in his house with spear in hand and David was playing the harp nearby. ¹⁰Saul tried to nail David to the wall with the spear, but David eluded Saul, so that the spear struck only the wall, and David got away safe.

¹¹The same night, Saul sent messengers to David's house to guard it, that he might kill him in the morning. David's wife Michal informed him, "Unless you save yourself tonight, tomorrow you will be killed."* ¹²Then Michal let David down through a window, and he made his escape in safety.�q ¹³Michal took the household idol and laid it in the bed, putting a net of goat's hair at its head and covering it with a spread.ʳ ¹⁴When Saul sent messengers to arrest David, she said, "He is sick." ¹⁵Saul, however, sent the messengers back to see David and commanded them, "Bring him up to me in the bed, that I may kill him." ¹⁶But when the messengers entered, they found the household idol in the bed, with the net of goat's hair at its head. ¹⁷Saul therefore asked Michal: "Why did you play this trick on me? You have helped my enemy to get away!" Michal answered Saul: "He threatened me, 'Let me go or I will kill you.'"

David and Samuel in Ramah. ¹⁸Thus David got safely away; he went to Samuel in Ramah, informing him of all that Saul had done to him. Then he and Samuel went to stay in the sheds. ¹⁹When Saul was told that David was in the sheds near Ramah, ²⁰he sent messengers to arrest David. But when they saw the band of prophets, presided over by Samuel, in a prophetic frenzy, they too fell into the prophetic state.ˢ ²¹Informed of this, Saul sent other messengers, who also fell into the prophetic state. For the third time Saul sent messengers, but they too fell into the prophetic state.

Saul among the Prophets. ²²Saul then went to Ramah himself. Arriving at the cistern of the threshing floor on the bare hilltop, he inquired, "Where are Samuel and David?", and was told, "At the sheds near Ramah." ²³As he set out from the hilltop toward the sheds, the spirit of God came upon him also, and he continued on in a prophetic condition until he reached the spot. At the sheds near Ramah ²⁴he, too, stripped himself of his garments and he, too, remained in the prophetic state in the presence of Samuel; all that day and night he lay naked. That is why they say, "Is Saul also among the prophets?"ᵗ

CHAPTER 20

See RG 176-77

David Consults with Jonathan. ¹David fled from the sheds near Ramah, and went to Jonathan. "What have I done?" he asked him. "What crime or what offense does your father hold against me that he seeks my life?"ᵘ ²Jonathan answered him:

19, 11: This story in all probability originally followed 1 Sm 18, 29, placing the episode of David's escape on the night of his marriage with Michal.

o: Dt 19, 10; Ps 119, 109.　*p:* 9f: 1 Sm 16, 14; 18, 10f.　*q:* Jos 2, 15; Acts 9, 25; 2 Cor 11, 33.　*r:* Gn 31, 19; Jgs 17, 5; 18, 14. 18. 20.
s: 1 Sm 10, 5f. 10; Nm 11, 25.　*t:* 1 Sm 10, 10ff.　*u:* 1 Sm 19, 1-7, 11-17

"Heaven forbid that you should die! My father does nothing, great or small, without disclosing it to me. Why, then, should my father conceal this from me? This cannot be so!" ³But David replied: "Your father is well aware that I am favored with your friendship, so he has decided, 'Jonathan must not know of this lest he be grieved.' Nevertheless, as the LORD lives and as you live, there is but a step between me and death." ⁴Jonathan then said to David, "I will do whatever you wish." ⁵David answered: "Tomorrow is the new moon, when I should in fact dine with the king. Let me go and hide in the open country until evening.ᵛ ⁶If it turns out that your father misses me, say, 'David urged me to let him go on short notice to his city Bethlehem, because his whole clan is holding its seasonal sacrifice there.' ⁷If he says, 'Very well,' your servant is safe. But if he becomes quite angry, you can be sure he has planned some harm. ⁸ʷDo this kindness for your servant because of the LORD's bond between us, into which you brought me: if I am guilty, kill me yourself! Why should you give me up to your father?" ⁹But Jonathan answered: "Not I! If ever I find out that my father is determined to inflict injury upon you, I will certainly let you know." ¹⁰David then asked Jonathan, "Who will tell me if your father gives you a harsh answer?"

Mutual Agreement. ¹¹[Jonathan replied to David, "Come, let us go out into the field." When they were out in the open country together, ¹²Jonathan said to David: "As the LORD, the God of Israel, lives, I will sound out my father about this time tomorrow. Whether he is well disposed toward David or not, I will send you the information. ¹³ˣShould it please my father to bring any injury upon you, may the LORD do thus and so to Jonathan if I do not apprise you of it and send you on your way in peace. May the LORD be with you even as he was with my father. ¹⁴Only this: if I am still alive, may you show me the kindness of the LORD. But if I die, ¹⁵never withdraw your kindness from my house. And when the LORD exterminates all the enemies of David from the surface of the earth, ¹⁶the name of Jonathan must never be allowed by the family of David to die out from among you, or the LORD will make you answer for it." ¹⁷And in his love for David, Jonathan renewed his oath to him, because he loved him as his very self.]

¹⁸Jonathan then said to him: "Tomorrow is the new moon; and you will be missed, since your place will be vacant. ¹⁹On the following day you will be missed all the more. Go to the spot where you hid on the other occasion and wait near the mound there.ʸ ²⁰On the third day of the month I will shoot arrows, as though aiming at a target. ²¹I will then send my attendant to go and recover the arrows. If in fact I say to him, 'Look, the arrow is this side of you; pick it up,' come, for you are safe. As the LORD lives, there will be nothing to fear. ²²But if I say to the boy, 'Look, the arrow is beyond you,' go, for the LORD sends you away. ²³However, in the matter which you and I have discussed, the LORD shall be between you and me forever." ²⁴So David hid in the open country.

On the day of the new moon, when the king sat at table to dine, ²⁵taking his usual place against the wall, Jonathan sat facing him, while Abner sat at the king's side, and David's place was vacant. ²⁶ᶻSaul, however, said nothing that day, for he thought, "He must have become unclean by accident, and not yet have been cleansed."* ²⁷On the next day, the second day of the month, David's place was vacant. Saul inquired of his son Jonathan, "Why has the son of Jesse not come to table yesterday or today?" ²⁸Jonathan answered Saul: "David urgently asked me to let him go to his city, Bethlehem. ²⁹'Please let me go,' he begged, 'for we are to have a clan sacrifice in our city, and my brothers insist on my presence. Now, therefore, if you think well of me, give me leave to visit my brothers.' That is why he has not

---

20, 26: The meal on the first day of the month would have religious overtones, and a ritual impurity (Lv 15, 16; Dt 23, 10ff) would bar David from sharing in it.

v: Nm 10, 10; 28, 11-15.   *w:* 8f: 1 Sm 23, 17f.   *x:* 13-16: 1 Sm 24, 22f; 2 Sm 9, 1-13; 21, 7.   *y:* 1 Sm 19, 1-7.   *z:* 1 Sm 16, 5; Lv 7, 20f; 15, 1ff.

come to the king's table." *30* But Saul was extremely angry with Jonathan and said to him: "Son of a rebellious woman, do I not know that, to your own shame and to the disclosure of your mother's shame, you are the companion of Jesse's son? *31* Why, as long as the son of Jesse lives upon the earth, you cannot make good your claim to the kingship! So send for him, and bring him to me, for he is doomed."*a* *32* But Jonathan asked his father Saul: "Why should he die? What has he done?" *33* At this Saul brandished his spear to strike him, and thus Jonathan learned that his father was resolved to kill David.*b* *34* Jonathan sprang up from the table in great anger and took no food that second day of the month, for he was grieved on David's account, since his father had railed against him.

Jonathan's Farewell. *35* The next morning Jonathan went out into the field with a little boy for his appointment with David. *36* There he said to the boy, "Run and fetch the arrow." And as the boy ran, he shot an arrow beyond him in the direction of the city. *37* When the boy made for the spot where Jonathan had shot the arrow, Jonathan called after him, "The arrow is farther on!" *38* Again he called to his lad, "Hurry, be quick, don't delay!" Jonathan's boy picked up the arrow and brought it to his master. *39* The boy knew nothing; only Jonathan and David knew what was meant. *40* Then Jonathan gave his weapons to this boy of his and said to him, "Go, take them to the city." *41* When the boy had left, David rose from beside the mound and prostrated himself on the ground three times before Jonathan in homage. They kissed each other and wept aloud together. *42c* At length Jonathan said to David, "Go in peace, in keeping with what we two have sworn by the name of the LORD: 'The LORD shall be between you and me, and between your posterity and mine forever.' "

CHAPTER 21

See RG 176-77

1 Then David departed on his way, while Jonathan went back into the city.

The Holy Bread. *2* David went to Ahimelech, the priest of Nob, who came trembling to meet him and asked, "Why are you alone? Is there no one with you?"*d* *3* David answered the priest: "The king gave me a commission and told me to let no one know anything about the business on which he sent me or the commission he gave me. For that reason I have arranged a meeting place with my men. *4e* Now what have you on hand? Give me five loaves, or whatever you can find." *5* But the priest replied to David, "I have no ordinary bread on hand, only holy bread; if the men have abstained from women, you may eat some of that."* *6* David answered the priest: "We have indeed been segregated from women as on previous occasions. Whenever I go on a journey, all the young men are consecrated—even for a secular journey. All the more so today, when they are consecrated at arms!" *7* So the priest gave him holy bread, for no other bread was on hand except the showbread which had been removed from the LORD's presence and replaced by fresh bread when it was taken away.*f* *8* One of Saul's servants was there that day, detained before the LORD; his name was Doeg the Edomite, and he was Saul's chief henchman.

The Sword of Goliath. *9* David then asked Ahimelech: "Do you have a spear or a sword on hand? I brought along neither my sword nor my weapons, because the king's business was urgent." *10* The priest replied: "The sword of Goliath the Philistine, whom you killed in the Vale of the Terebinth, is here [wrapped in a mantle] behind an ephod. If you wish to take that, take it; there is no sword here except that one." David said: "There is none to match it. Give it to me!"*g*

David a Fugitive. *11* That same day David

21, 5f: From women: the high priest, willing to distribute the holy bread to David and his men, requires that they be free from ritual uncleanness, associated in Old Testament times (Lv 15, 18) with the marriage act. David's answer supposes the discipline of a military campaign under the conditions of "holy war" (Dt 23, 10).

---

a: 2 Sm 12, 5.   *b:* 1 Sm 18, 11.   *c:* 2 Sm 9, 1; 21, 7.   *d:* Is 10, 32; Mk 2, 26.   *e:* Lv 24, 5. 9.   *f:* 1 Sm 22, 9; Lv 24, 5-9; Mt 12, 3f; Mk 2, 26; Lk 6, 3ff.   *g:* 1 Sm 17, 51. 54.

took to flight from Saul, going to Achish, king of Gath.[h] [12]But the servants of Achish said, "Is this not David, the king of the land? During their dances do they not sing,

> 'Saul has slain his thousands,
> but David his ten thousands'?"[i]

[13]David took note of these remarks and became very much afraid of Achish, king of Gath. [14]So, as they watched, he feigned insanity and acted like a madman in their hands, drumming on the doors of the gate and drooling onto his beard. [15]Finally Achish said to his servants: "You see the man is mad. Why did you bring him to me? [16]Do I not have enough madmen, that you bring in this one to carry on in my presence? Should this fellow come into my house?"

CHAPTER 22

See RG 176-77 [1]David left Gath and escaped to the cave of Adullam. When his brothers and the rest of his family heard about it, they came down to him there.[j] [2]He was joined by all those who were in difficulties or in debt, or who were embittered, and he became their leader. About four hundred men were with him.

[3]From there David went to Mizpeh of Moab and said to the king of Moab, "Let my father and mother stay with you, until I learn what God will do for me." [4]He left them with the king of Moab, and they stayed with him as long as David remained in the refuge.*

[5]But the prophet Gad said to David: "Do not remain in the refuge. Leave, and go to the land of Judah." And so David left and went to the forest of Hereth.

Doeg Betrays Ahimelech. [6]Now Saul heard that David and his men had been located. At the time he was sitting in Gibeah under a tamarisk tree on the high place, holding his spear, while all his servants were standing by.[k] [7]So he said to them: "Listen, men of Benjamin! Will the son of Jesse give all of you fields and vineyards? Will he make each of you an officer over a thousand

or a hundred men,[l] [8]that you have all conspired against me and no one tells me that my son has made an agreement with the son of Jesse? None of you shows sympathy for me or discloses to me that my son has stirred up my servant to be an enemy against me, as is the case today." [9m]Then Doeg the Edomite, who was standing with the officers of Saul, spoke up: "I saw the son of Jesse come to Ahimelech, son of Ahitub, in Nob. [10]He consulted the LORD for him and gave him supplies, and the sword of Goliath the Philistine as well."

Slaughter of the Priests. [11]At this the king sent a summons to Ahimelech the priest, son of Ahitub, and to all his family who were priests in Nob; and they all came to the king. [12]Then Saul said, "Listen, son of Ahitub!" He replied, "Yes, my lord." [13]Saul asked him, "Why did you conspire against me with the son of Jesse by giving him food and a sword and by consulting God for him, that he might rebel against me and become my enemy, as is the case today?" [14]Ahimelech answered the king: "And who among all your servants is as loyal as David, the king's son-in-law, captain of your bodyguard, and honored in your own house? [15]Is this the first time I have consulted God for him? No indeed! Let not the king accuse his servant or anyone in my family of such a thing. Your servant knows nothing at all, great or small, about the whole matter." [16]But the king said, "You shall die, Ahimelech, with all your family." [17]The king then commanded his henchmen standing by: "Make the rounds and kill the priests of the LORD, for they assisted David. They knew he was a fugitive and yet failed to inform me." But the king's servants refused to lift a hand to strike the priests of the LORD.[n]

[18]The king therefore commanded Doeg, "You make the rounds and kill the priests!" So Doeg the Edomite went from one to the next and killed the priests himself, slaying on that day eighty-five who wore the linen ephod. [19]Saul also put the priestly city of

22, 4-5: Refuge: seemingly connected with the cave complex spoken of in v 1.

h: 1 Sm 27, 2; 29, 5. *i:* 1 Sm 18, 7; 29, 5. *j:* 2 Sm 23, 13; Ps 63; Mi 1, 15. *k:* Ps 52. *l:* 1 Sm 8, 14. *m:* 9f: 1 Sm 21, 2-10. *n:* 1 Sm 2, 31. 33; 21, 7.

Nob to the sword, including men and women, children and infants, and oxen, asses and sheep.

Abiathar Escapes. [20]One son of Ahimelech, son of Ahitub, named Abiathar, escaped and fled to David.[o] [21]When Abiathar told David that Saul had slain the priests of the LORD, [22]David said to him: "I knew that day, when Doeg the Edomite was there, that he would surely tell Saul. I am responsible for the death of all your family. [23]Stay with me. Fear nothing; he that seeks your life must seek my life also. You are under my protection."

CHAPTER 23

See RG 176–77

Keilah Liberated. [1]David received information that the Philistines were attacking Keilah and plundering the threshing floors.[p] [2]So he consulted the LORD, inquiring, "Shall I go and defeat these Philistines?" The LORD answered, "Go, for you will defeat the Philistines and rescue Keilah."[q] [3]But David's men said to him: "We are afraid here in Judah. How much more so if we go to Keilah against the forces of the Philistines!" [4]Again David consulted the LORD, who answered, "Go down to Keilah, for I will deliver the Philistines into your power." [5]David then went with his men to Keilah and fought with the Philistines. He drove off their cattle and inflicted a severe defeat on them, and thus rescued the inhabitants of Keilah.

[6]Abiathar, son of Ahimelech, who had fled to David, went down with David to Keilah, taking the ephod with him.[r]

Flight from Keilah. [7]When Saul was told that David had entered Keilah, he said: "God has put him in my grip. Now he has shut himself in, for he has entered a city with gates and bars." [8]Saul then called all the people to war, in order to go down to Keilah and besiege David and his men. [9]When David found out that Saul was planning to harm him, he said to the priest Abiathar, "Bring forward the ephod."[s] [10]David then said: "O LORD God of Israel, your servant has heard a report that Saul plans to come to Keilah, to destroy the city on my account. [11]Will they hand me over? And now: will Saul come down as your servant has heard? O LORD God of Israel, tell your servant." The LORD answered, "He will come down." [12]David then asked, "Will the citizens of Keilah deliver me and my men into the grasp of Saul?" And the LORD answered, "Yes." [13]So David and his men, about six hundred in number, left Keilah and wandered from place to place. When Saul was informed that David had escaped from Keilah, he abandoned the expedition.

David and Jonathan in Horesh. [14]David now lived in the refuges in the desert, or in the barren hill country near Ziph. Though Saul sought him continually, the LORD did not deliver David into his grasp. [15]David was apprehensive because Saul had come out to seek his life; but while he was at Horesh in the barrens near Ziph, [16]Saul's son, Jonathan, came down there to David and strengthened his resolve in the LORD.[t] [17]He said to him: "Have no fear, my father Saul shall not lay a hand to you. You shall be king of Israel and I shall be second to you. Even my father Saul knows this." [18]They made a joint agreement before the LORD in Horesh, where David remained, while Jonathan returned to his home.[u]

Treachery of the Ziphites. [19]Some of the Ziphites went up to Saul in Gibeah and said, "David is hiding among us, now in the refuges, and again at Horesh, or on the hill of Hachilah, south of the wasteland.[v] [20]Therefore, whenever the king wishes to come down, let him do so. It will be our task to deliver him into the king's grasp." [21]Saul replied: "The LORD bless you for your sympathy toward me.[w] [22]Go now and make sure once more! Take note of the place where he sets foot" (for he thought, perhaps they are playing some trick on me). [23]"Look around and learn in which of all the various hiding places he is holding out. Then come back to me with sure information, and I will go with you. If he is in the region, I will search him out among all the families of Judah." [24]So

o: 1 Sm 23, 6; 30, 7; 1 Kgs 2, 28f.   p: Jos 15, 44.   q: 1 Sm 28, 6.   r: 1 Sm 22, 20; 30, 7.   s: 1 Sm 2, 28.   t: 1 Sm 18, 1.   u: 1 Sm 18, 3; 20, 8.   v: 1 Sm 26, 1-3; Ps 54.   w: 2 Sm 2, 5.

they went off to Ziph ahead of Saul. At this time David and his men were in the desert below Maon, in the Arabah south of the wasteland.*

Escape from Saul. 25When Saul and his men came looking for him, David got word of it and went down to the gorge in the desert below Maon. Saul heard of this and pursued David into the desert below Maon. 26As Saul moved along one rim of the gorge, David and his men took to the other. David was in anxious flight to escape Saul, and Saul and his men were attempting to outflank David and his men in order to capture them, 27when a messenger came to Saul, saying, "Come quickly, because the Philistines have invaded the land." 28Saul interrupted his pursuit of David and went to meet the Philistines. This is how that place came to be called the Gorge of Divisions.

See RG
176-77

CHAPTER 24

David Spares Saul. 1David then went up from there and stayed in the refuges behind Engedi. 2And when Saul returned from the pursuit of the Philistines, he was told that David was in the desert near Engedi. 3So Saul took three thousand picked men from all Israel and went in search of David and his men in the direction of the wild goat crags. 4When he came to the sheepfolds along the way, he found a cave, which he entered to ease nature. David and his men were occupying the inmost recesses of the cave.*

5David's servants said to him, "This is the day of which the LORD said to you, 'I will deliver your enemy into your grasp; do with him as you see fit.' " So David moved up and stealthily cut off an end of Saul's mantle. 6Afterward, however, David regretted that he had cut off an end of Saul's mantle.* 7He said to his men, "The LORD forbid that I should do such a thing to my master, the LORD's anointed, as to lay a hand on him, for he is the LORD's anointed."* 8With these words David restrained his men and would not permit them to attack Saul. Saul then left the cave and went on his way. 9David also

stepped out of the cave, calling to Saul, "My lord the king!" When Saul looked back, David bowed to the ground in homage 10and asked Saul: "Why do you listen to those who say, 'David is trying to harm you'? 11You see for yourself today that the LORD just now delivered you into my grasp in the cave. I had some thought of killing you, but I took pity on you instead. I decided, 'I will not raise a hand against my lord, for he is the LORD's anointed and a father to me.' 12Look here at this end of your mantle which I hold. Since I cut off an end of your mantle and did not kill you, see and be convinced that I plan no harm and no rebellion. I have done you no wrong, though you are hunting me down to take my life.* 13The LORD will judge between me and you, and the LORD will exact justice from you in my case. I shall not touch you. 14The old proverb says, 'From the wicked comes forth wickedness.' So I will take no action against you. 15Against whom are you on campaign, O king of Israel? Whom are you pursuing? A dead dog, or a single flea! 16The LORD will be the judge; he will decide between me and you. May he see this, and take my part, and grant me justice beyond your reach!"*

Saul's Remorse. 17When David finished saying these things to Saul, Saul answered, "Is that your voice, my son David?" And he wept aloud. 18Saul then said to David: "You are in the right rather than I; you have treated me generously, while I have done you harm. 19Great is the generosity you showed me today, when the LORD delivered me into your grasp and you did not kill me. 20For if a man meets his enemy, does he send him away unharmed? May the LORD reward you generously for what you have done this day. 21And now, since I know that you shall surely be king and that sovereignty over Israel shall come into your possession,* 22swear to me by the LORD that you will not destroy my descendants and that you will not blot out my name and family."* 23David gave Saul his oath and Saul returned home, while David and his men went up to the refuge.

x: 1 Sm 25, 2.   *y:* Ps 57.   *z:* 1 Sm 15, 27.   *a:* 1 Sm 10, 1; 31, 4; 2 Sm 1, 14.   *b:* Rom 12, 19.   *c:* 1 Sm 18, 19. 31; 26, 19; Pss 35, 1ff; 43, 1.   *d:* 1 Sm 26, 25.   *e:* 2 Sm 9, 1ff.

See RG
176–77

CHAPTER 25

Death of Samuel. [1]Samuel died, and all Israel gathered to mourn him; they buried him at his home in Ramah.*f*

Nabal and Abigail. [2]Then David went down to the desert of Maon. There was a man of Maon who had property in Carmel; he was very wealthy, owning three thousand sheep and a thousand goats. At this time he was present for the shearing of his flock in Carmel.*g* [3]The man was named Nabal, his wife, Abigail. The woman was intelligent and attractive, but Nabal himself, a Calebite, was harsh and ungenerous in his behavior.*h* [4]When David heard in the desert that Nabal was shearing his flock, [5]he sent ten young men, instructing them: "Go up to Carmel. Pay Nabal a visit and greet him in my name. [6]Say to him, 'Peace be with you, my brother, and with your family, and with all who belong to you. [7]I have just heard that shearers are with you. Now, when your shepherds were with us, we did them no injury, neither did they miss anything all the while they were in Carmel. [8]Ask your servants and they will tell you so. Look kindly on these young men, since we come at a festival time. Please give your servants and your son David whatever you can manage.' "

[9]When David's young men arrived, they delivered this message fully to Nabal in David's name, and then waited. [10]But Nabal answered the servants of David: "Who is David? Who is the son of Jesse? Nowadays there are many servants who run away from their masters. [11]Must I take my bread, my wine, my meat that I have slaughtered for my own shearers, and give them to men who come from I know not where?" [12]So David's young men retraced their steps and on their return reported to him all that had been said. [13]Thereupon David said to his men, "Let everyone gird on his sword." And so everyone, David included, girded on his sword. About four hundred men went up after David, while two hundred remained with the baggage.

[14]But Nabal's wife Abigail was informed of this by one of the servants, who said: "David sent messengers from the desert to greet our master, but he flew at them screaming. [15]Yet these men were very good to us. We were done no injury, neither did we miss anything all the while we were living among them during our stay in the open country. [16]For us they were like a rampart night and day the whole time we were pasturing the sheep near them. [17]Now, see what you can do, for you must realize that otherwise evil is in store for our master and for his whole family. He is so mean that no one can talk to him." [18]Abigail quickly got together two hundred loaves, two skins of wine, five dressed sheep, five seahs of roasted grain, a hundred cakes of pressed raisins, and two hundred cakes of pressed figs, and loaded them on asses. [19]She then said to her servants, "Go on ahead; I will follow you." But she did not tell her husband Nabal.

[20]As she came down through a mountain defile riding on an ass, David and his men were also coming down from the opposite direction. When she met them, [21]David had just been saying: "Indeed, it was in vain that I guarded all this man's possessions in the desert, so that he missed nothing. He has repaid good with evil. [22]May God do thus and so to David, if by morning I leave a single male alive among all those who belong to him."*i* [23]As soon as Abigail saw David, she dismounted quickly from the ass and, falling prostrate on the ground before David, did him homage. [24]As she fell at his feet she said:

"My lord, let the blame be mine. Please let your handmaid speak to you, and listen to the words of your handmaid. [25]Let not my lord pay attention to that worthless man Nabal, for he is just like his name. Fool is his name,* and he acts the fool. I, your handmaid, did not see the young men whom my lord sent. [26]Now, therefore, my lord, as the LORD lives, and as you live, it is the LORD who has kept you from shedding blood and from avenging yourself personally. May your enemies and those who seek to harm my lord become as Nabal!* [27]Accept this

25, 25: Fool is his name: Nabal in Hebrew means "a fool."
25, 26: Abigail anticipates that some misfortune will shortly overtake Nabal, as in fact it does (vv 37-38).

f: 1 Sm 28, 3; Sir 46, 13-20.   *g:* 1 Sm 23, 24; Jos 15, 55.   *h:* 1 Sm 27, 3; Jos 14, 6; 1 Chr 2, 42. 45.   *i:* 1 Kgs 16, 11; 21, 21; 2 Kgs 9, 8.

present, then, which your maidservant has brought for my lord, and let it be given to the young men who follow my lord. *28*Please forgive the transgression of your handmaid, for the LORD shall certainly establish a lasting dynasty for my lord, because your lordship is fighting the battles of the LORD, and there is no evil to be found in you your whole life long. *29*If anyone rises to pursue you and to seek your life, may the life of my lord be bound in the bundle of the living* in the care of the LORD your God; but may he hurl out the lives of your enemies as from the hollow of a sling.*j 30*And when the LORD carries out for my lord the promise of success he has made concerning you, and appoints you as commander over Israel,*k 31*you shall not have this as a qualm or burden on your conscience, my lord, for having shed innocent blood or for having avenged yourself personally. When the LORD confers this benefit on your lordship, remember your handmaid." *32*David said to Abigail: "Blessed be the LORD, the God of Israel, who sent you to meet me today. *33*Blessed be your good judgment and blessed be you yourself, who this day have prevented me from shedding blood and from avenging myself personally. *34*Otherwise, as the LORD, the God of Israel, lives, who has restrained me from harming you, if you had not come so promptly to meet me, by dawn Nabal would not have had a single man or boy left alive." *35*David then took from her what she had brought him and said to her: "Go up to your home in peace! See, I have granted your request as a personal favor."

*Nabal's Death. 36*When Abigail came to Nabal, there was a drinking party in his house like that of a king, and Nabal was merry because he was very drunk. So she told him nothing at all before daybreak the next morning. *37*But then, when Nabal had become sober, his wife told him what had happened. At this his courage died within him, and he

became like a stone. *38*About ten days later the LORD struck him and he died. *39*On hearing that Nabal was dead, David said: "Blessed be the LORD, who has requited the insult I received at the hand of Nabal, and who restrained his servant from doing evil, but has punished Nabal for his own evil deeds."

David Marries Abigail and Ahinoam. David then sent a proposal of marriage to Abigail. *40*When David's servants came to Abigail in Carmel, they said to her, "David has sent us to you that he may take you as his wife." *41*Rising and bowing to the ground, she answered, "Your handmaid would become a slave to wash the feet of my lord's servants." *42*She got up immediately, mounted an ass, and followed David's messengers, with her five maids following in attendance upon her. She became his wife, *43*and David also married Ahinoam of Jezreel. Thus both of them were his wives; but Saul gave David's wife Michal, Saul's own daughter, to Palti, son of Laish, who was from Gallim.*m*

CHAPTER 26

See RG 176–77

*Saul's Life Again Spared. 1n*Men from Ziph came to Saul in Gibeah, reporting that David was hiding on the hill of Hachilah at the edge of the wasteland. *2*So Saul went off down to the desert of Ziph with three thousand picked men of Israel, to search for David in the desert of Ziph. *3*Saul camped beside the road on the hill of Hachilah, at the edge of the wasteland. David, who was living in the desert, saw that Saul had come into the desert after him *4*and sent out scouts, who confirmed Saul's arrival. *5*David himself then went to the place where Saul was encamped and examined the spot where Saul and Abner, son of Ner, the general, had their sleeping quarters. Saul's were within the barricade, and all his soldiers were camped around him.*o 6*David asked Ahimelech the Hittite, and Abishai, son of Zeruiah and brother of Joab, "Who will go down into the

25, 29: The bundle of the living: the figure is perhaps taken from the practice of tying up valuables in a kerchief or bag for safekeeping. Abigail desires that David enjoy permanent peace and security, but that his enemies be subject to constant agitation and humiliation like a stone whirled about, cast out of the sling, and thereafter disregarded.

j: Ps 69, 28.   *k:* 1 Sm 13, 14; 2 Sm 3, 10.   *l:* 1 Sm 27, 3.   *m:* 1 Sm 18, 20; 27, 3; 30, 5; 2 Sm 3, 2. 13ff; 1 Chr 3, 1.   *n:* 1f: 1 Sm 23, 19f; Ps 54.   *o:* 1 Sm 17, 20.

camp with me to Saul?" Abishai replied, "I will."[p] [7]So David and Abishai went among Saul's soldiers by night and found Saul lying asleep within the barricade, with his spear thrust into the ground at his head and Abner and his men sleeping around him.

[8]Abishai whispered to David: "God has delivered your enemy into your grasp this day. Let me nail him to the ground with one thrust of the spear; I will not need a second thrust!"[q] [9]But David said to Abishai, "Do not harm him, for who can lay hands on the LORD's anointed and remain unpunished? [10]As the LORD lives," David continued, "it must be the LORD himself who will strike him, whether the time comes for him to die, or he goes out and perishes in battle. [11]But the LORD forbid that I touch his anointed! Now take the spear which is at his head and the water jug, and let us be on our way." [12]So David took the spear and the water jug from their place at Saul's head, and they got away without anyone's seeing or knowing or awakening. All remained asleep, because the LORD had put them into a deep slumber.

David Taunts Abner. [13]Going across to an opposite slope, David stood on a remote hilltop at a great distance from Abner, son of Ner, and the troops. [14]He then shouted, "Will you not answer, Abner?" And Abner answered, "Who is it that calls me?" [15]David said to Abner: "Are you not a man whose like does not exist in Israel? Why, then, have you not guarded your lord the king when one of his subjects went to kill the king, your lord? [16]This is no creditable service you have performed. As the LORD lives, you people deserve death because you have not guarded your lord, the LORD's anointed. Go, look: where are the king's spear and the water jug that was at his head?"

Saul Admits His Guilt. [17]Saul recognized David's voice and asked, "Is that your voice, my son David?" David answered, "Yes, my lord the king." [18]He continued: "Why does my lord pursue his servant? What have I done? What evil do I plan? [19]Please, now, let my lord the king listen to the words of his servant. If the LORD has incited you against me, let an offering appease him; but if men, may they be cursed before the LORD, because they have exiled me so that this day I have no share in the LORD's inheritance,* but am told: 'Go, serve other gods!'[r] [20]Do not let my blood flow to the ground far from the presence of the LORD. For the king of Israel has come out to seek a single flea as if he were hunting partridge in the mountains." [21]Then Saul said: "I have done wrong. Come back, my son David, I will not harm you again, because you have held my life precious today. Indeed, I have been a fool and have made a serious mistake." [22]But David answered: "Here is the king's spear. Let an attendant come over to get it. [23]The LORD will reward each man for his justice and faithfulness. Today, though the LORD delivered you into my grasp, I would not harm the LORD's anointed.[s] [24]As I valued your life highly today, so may the LORD value my life highly and deliver me from all difficulties." [25]Then Saul said to David: "Blessed are you, my son David! You shall certainly succeed in whatever you undertake." David went his way, and Saul returned to his home.[t]

CHAPTER 27

See RG 176–77

Refuge among Philistines. [1]But David said to himself: "I shall perish some day at the hand of Saul. I have no choice but to escape to the land of the Philistines; then Saul will give up his continuous search for me throughout the land of Israel, and I shall be out of his reach." [2]Accordingly, David departed with his six hundred men and went over to Achish, son of Maoch, king of Gath.[u] [3]David and his men lived in Gath with Achish; each one had his family, and David had his two wives, Ahinoam from Jezreel and Abigail, the widow of Nabal from Carmel.[v] [4]When Saul was told that David had fled to Gath, he no longer searched for him.

26, 19: The LORD's inheritance: the land of Israel (Dt 32, 8f), under the Lord's special protection, where he could be freely worshiped.

p: 1 Chr 2, 16. *q:* 1 Sm 18, 11; 19, 10. *r:* 1 Sm 24, 16. *s:* 1 Sm 18, 20. *t:* 1 Sm 24, 21. *u:* 1 Sm 21, 11-16. *v:* 1 Sm 25, 3. 44; 30, 3ff; 2 Sm 2, 3.

In Ziklag. [5]David said to Achish: "If I meet with your approval, let me have a place to live in one of the country towns. Why should your servant live with you in the royal city?" [6]That same day Achish gave him Ziklag, which has, therefore, belonged to the kings of Judah* up to the present time.[w] [7]In all, David lived a year and four months in the country of the Philistines.[x]

Raids on Israel's Foes. [8]David and his men went up and made raids on the Geshurites, Girzites, and Amalekites—peoples living in the land between Telam, on the approach to Shur, and the land of Egypt.[y] [9]In attacking the land David would not leave a man or woman alive, but would carry off sheep, oxen, asses, camels, and clothes. On his return he brought these to Achish, [10]who asked, "Whom did you raid this time?" And David answered, "The Negeb of Judah," or "The Negeb of Jarahmeel," or "The Negeb of the Kenites."[z] [11]But David would not leave a man or woman alive to be brought to Gath, fearing that they would betray him by saying, "This is what David did." This was his custom as long as he lived in the country of the Philistines. [12]And Achish trusted David, thinking, "He must certainly be detested by his people Israel. I shall have him as my vassal forever."

See RG
176–78

CHAPTER 28

[1]In those days the Philistines mustered their military forces to fight against Israel. So Achish said to David, "You realize, of course, that you and your men must go out on campaign with me to Jezreel." [2]David answered Achish, "Good! Now you shall learn what your servant can do." Then Achish said to David, "I shall appoint you my permanent bodyguard."

[3]Now Samuel had died and, after being mourned by all Israel, was buried in his city, Ramah. Meanwhile Saul had driven mediums and fortune-tellers out of the land.[a]

Saul in Dismay. [4]The Philistine levies advanced to Shunem and encamped. Saul, too, mustered all Israel; they camped on Gilboa. [5]When Saul saw the camp of the Philistines, he was dismayed and lost heart completely. [6]He therefore consulted the LORD; but the LORD gave no answer, whether in dreams or by the Urim or through prophets.[b] [7]Then Saul said to his servants, "Find me a woman who is a medium, to whom I can go to seek counsel through her." His servants answered him, "There is a woman in Endor who is a medium."[c]

The Witch of Endor. [8]So he disguised himself, putting on other clothes, and set out with two companions. They came to the woman by night, and Saul said to her, "Tell my fortune through a ghost; conjure up for me the one I ask you to."[d] [9]But the woman answered him, "You are surely aware of what Saul has done, in driving the mediums and fortune-tellers out of the land. Why, then, are you laying snares for my life, to have me killed?" [10]But Saul swore to her by the LORD, "As the LORD lives, you shall incur no blame for this." [11]Then the woman asked him, "Whom do you want me to conjure up?" and he answered, "Samuel."

Samuel Appears. [12]When the woman saw Samuel, she shrieked at the top of her voice and said to Saul, "Why have you deceived me? You are Saul!"* [13]But the king said to her, "Have no fear. What do you see?" The woman answered Saul, "I see a preternatural being rising from the earth." [14]"What does he look like?" asked Saul. And she replied, "It is an old man who is rising, clothed in a mantle." Saul knew that it was Samuel, and so he bowed face to the ground in homage.

Saul's Doom. [15]Samuel then said to Saul, "Why do you disturb me by conjuring me up?" Saul replied: "I am in great straits, for

27, 6: Has . . . belonged to the kings of Judah: as a personal holding, outside the system of tribal lands; Jerusalem, when taken by David, had a similar status (2 Sm 5, 7–9).

28, 12: Human beings cannot communicate at will with the souls of the dead. God may, however, permit a departed soul to appear to the living and even to disclose things unknown to them. Saul's own prohibition of necromancy and divination (v 3) was in keeping with the consistent teaching of the Old Testament. If we are to credit the reality of the apparition to Saul, it was due, not to the summons of the witch, but to God's will; the woman merely furnished the occasion.

the Philistines are waging war against me and God has abandoned me. Since he no longer answers me through prophets or in dreams, I have called you to tell me what I should do."*e* *16*To this Samuel said: "But why do you ask me, if the LORD has abandoned you and is with your neighbor?*f 17*The LORD has done to you what he foretold through me: he has torn the kingdom from your grasp and has given it to your neighbor David.

18"Because you disobeyed the LORD's directive and would not carry out his fierce anger against Amalek, the LORD has done this to you today.*g 19*Moreover, the LORD will deliver Israel, and you as well, into the clutches of the Philistines. By tomorrow you and your sons will be with me, and the LORD will have delivered the army of Israel into the hands of the Philistines."*h*

Saul's Despair. *20*Immediately Saul fell full length on the ground, for he was badly shaken by Samuel's message. Moreover, he had no bodily strength left, since he had eaten nothing all that day and night. *21*Then the woman came to Saul, and seeing that he was quite terror-stricken, said to him: "Remember, your maidservant obeyed you: I took my life in my hands and fulfilled the request you made of me. *22*Now you, in turn, please listen to your maidservant. Let me set something before you to eat, so that you may have strength when you go on your way." *23*But he refused, saying, "I will not eat." However, when his servants joined the woman in urging him, he listened to their entreaties, got up from the ground, and sat on a couch. *24*The woman had a stall-fed calf in the house, which she now quickly slaughtered. Then taking flour, she kneaded it and baked unleavened bread. *25*She set the meal before Saul and his servants, and they ate. Then they stood up and left the same night.

CHAPTER 29

See RG 177–78

David's Aid Rejected. *1*Now the Philistines had mustered all their forces in Aphek, and the Israelites were encamped at the spring of Harod near Jezreel.*i 2*As the Philistine lords were marching their groups of a hundred and a thousand, David and his men were marching in the rear guard with Achish. *3*The Philistine chiefs asked, "What are those Hebrews doing here?" And Achish answered them: "Why, that is David, the officer of Saul, king of Israel. He has been with me now for a year or two, and I have no fault to find with him from the day he came over to me until the present."*j 4*But the Philistine chiefs were angered at this and said to him: "Send that man back! Let him return to the place you picked out for him. He must not go down into battle with us, lest during the battle he become our enemy. For how else can he win back his master's favor, if not with the heads of these men of ours?*k 5*Is this not the David of whom they sing during their dances,

'Saul has slain his thousands,
    but David his ten thousands'?"*l*

*6*So Achish summoned David and said to him: "As the LORD lives, you are honest, and I should be pleased to have you active with me in the camp, for I have found nothing wrong with you from the day of your arrival to this day. But you are not welcome to the lords. *7*Withdraw peaceably, now, and do nothing that might displease the Philistine lords." *8*But David said to Achish: "What have I done? Or what have you against your servant from the first day I have been with you to this day, that I cannot go to fight against the enemies of my lord the king?" *9*"You know," Achish answered David, "that you are acceptable to me. But the Philistine chiefs have determined you are not to go up with us to battle. *10*So the first thing tomorrow, you and your lord's servants who came with you, go to the place I picked out for you. Do not decide to take umbrage at this; you are as acceptable to me as an angel of God. But make an early morning start, as soon as it grows light, and be on your way." *11*So David and his men left early in the morning to return to the land of the Philistines. The Philistines, however, went on up to Jezreel.

e: Sir 46, 20.   *f:* 1 Sm 15, 27f.   *g:* 1 Sm 15, 18f. 26.   *h:* 1 Sm 31, 2-6; Sir 46, 20.   *i:* 1 Sm 4, 1.   *j:* 1 Sm 27, 7.   *k:* 1 Chr 12, 19f.
l: 1 Sm 18, 6f; 21, 11.

CHAPTER 30

See RG
177–78

Ziklag in Ruins. [1]Before David and his men reached Ziklag on the third day, the Amalekites had raided the Negeb and Ziklag, had stormed the city, and had set it on fire.[m] [2]They had taken captive the women and all who were in the city, young and old, killing no one; they had carried them off when they left. [3]David and his men arrived at the city to find it burned to the ground and their wives, sons and daughters taken captive. [4]Then David and those who were with him wept aloud until they could weep no more. [5]David's two wives, Ahinoam of Jezreel and Abigail, the widow of Nabal from Carmel, had also been carried off with the rest.[n] [6]Now David found himself in great difficulty, for the men spoke of stoning him, so bitter were they over the fate of their sons and daughters. But with renewed trust in the LORD his God, [7o]David said to Abiathar, the priest, son of Ahimelech, "Bring me the ephod!" When Abiathar brought him the ephod, [8]David inquired of the LORD, "Shall I pursue these raiders? Can I overtake them?" The LORD answered him, "Go in pursuit, for you shall surely overtake them and effect a rescue."

Raid of the Amalekites. [9]So David went off with his six hundred men and came as far as the Wadi Besor, where those who were to remain behind halted. [10]David continued the pursuit with four hundred men, but two hundred were too exhausted to cross the Wadi Besor and remained behind. [11]An Egyptian was found in the open country and brought to David. He was provided with food, which he ate, and given water to drink; [12]a cake of pressed figs and two cakes of pressed raisins were also offered to him. When he had eaten, he revived; he had not taken food nor drunk water for three days and three nights. [13]Then David asked him, "To whom do you belong, and where do you come from?" He replied: "I am an Egyptian, the slave of an Amalekite. My master abandoned me because I fell sick three days ago today. [14]We raided the Negeb of the Cherethites, the territory of Judah, and the Negeb of Caleb; and we set Ziklag on fire."[p] [15]David then asked him, "Will you lead me down to this raiding party?" He answered, "Swear to me by God that you will not kill me or deliver me to my master, and I will lead you to the raiding party." [16]He did lead them, and there were the Amalekites scattered all over the ground, eating, drinking, and in a festive mood because of all the rich booty they had taken from the land of the Philistines and from the land of Judah.

The Booty Recovered. [17]From dawn to sundown David attacked them, putting them under the ban so that none escaped except four hundred young men, who mounted their camels and fled.[q] [18]David recovered everything the Amalekites had taken, and rescued his two wives. [19]Nothing was missing, small or great, booty or sons or daughters, of all that the Amalekites had taken. David brought back everything. [20]Moreover, David took all the sheep and oxen, and as they drove them before him, they shouted, "This is David's spoil."

Division of the Spoils. [21]When David came to the two hundred men who had been too exhausted to follow him, and whom he had left behind at the Wadi Besor, they came out to meet David and the men with him. On nearing them David greeted them. [22]But all the stingy and worthless men among those who had accompanied David spoke up to say, "Since they did not accompany us, we will not give them anything from the booty, except to each man his wife and children. Let them take those along and be on their way." [23]But David said: "You must not do this, my brothers, after what the LORD has given us. He has protected us and delivered into our grip the band that came against us. [24]Who could agree with this proposal of yours? Rather, the share of the one who goes down to battle and that of the one who remains with the baggage shall be the same; they shall share alike."[r] [25]And from that day forward he made it a law and a custom in Israel, as it still is today.[s]

---

m: 1 Sm 27, 6. 10; 1 Chr 12, 21.   *n:* 1 Sm 25, 42; 27, 3; 30, 5.   *o:* 7f: 1 Sm 2, 28; 23, 6; Ex 28, 30.   *p:* 1 Sm 27, 10; Ez 25, 16.
q: 1 Sm 15, 3; Jos 6, 17; Jgs 7, 12.   *r:* 1 Sm 17, 22; 25, 13.   *s:* Nm 31, 27.

David's Gifts to Judah. 26When David came to Ziklag, he sent part of the spoil to the elders of Judah, city by city, saying, "This is a gift to you from the spoil of the enemies of the LORD": 27to those in Bethel, to those in Ramoth-negeb, to those in Jattir, 28to those in Aroer, to those in Siphmoth, to those in Eshtemoa, 29to those in Racal, to those in the Jerahmeelite cities, to those in the Kenite cities,*t* 30to those in Hormah, to those in Borashan, to those in Athach, 31to those in Hebron, and to all the places frequented by David and his men.

CHAPTER 31

See RG 177–78

Death of Saul and His Sons. 1uAs they pressed their attack on Israel, with the Israelites fleeing before them and falling mortally wounded on Mount Gilboa, 2the Philistines pursued Saul and his sons closely, and slew Jonathan, Abinadab, and Malchishua, sons of Saul.*v* 3The battle raged around Saul, and the archers hit him; he was pierced through the abdomen. 4Then Saul said to his armor-bearer, "Draw your sword and run me through, lest these uncircumcised come and make sport of me." But his armor-bearer, badly frightened, refused to do it. So Saul took his own sword and fell upon it.*w* 5xWhen

the armor-bearer saw that Saul was dead, he too fell upon his sword and died with him.* 6Thus Saul, his three sons, and his armor-bearer died together on that same day.

7When the Israelites on the slope of the valley and those along the Jordan saw that the men of Israel had fled and that Saul and his sons were dead, they too abandoned their cities and fled. Then the Philistines came and lived in those cities.

8The day after the battle the Philistines came to strip the slain, and found Saul and his three sons lying on Mount Gilboa. 9They cut off Saul's head and stripped him of his armor, and then sent the good news throughout the land of the Philistines to their idols and to the people.*y* 10They put his armor in the temple of Astarte, but impaled his body on the wall of Beth-shan.

Burial of Saul. 11zWhen the inhabitants of Jabesh-gilead heard what the Philistines had done to Saul, 12all their warriors set out, and after marching throughout the night, removed the bodies of Saul and his sons from the wall of Beth-shan, and brought them to Jabesh, where they cremated them.* 13Then they took their bones and buried them under the tamarisk tree in Jabesh, and fasted for seven days.

31, 5: This report of the suicidal act of Saul is presented as a part of his downfall, to be judged accordingly.
31, 12: Cremated them: cremation was not normally practiced in Israel, though it was known in the country from pre-Israelite times.

t: 1 Sm 27, 10.   *u:* 1-13; 1 Chr 10, 1-12; 2 Sm 1, 1-16; 4, 4.   *v:* 1 Sm 14, 49; 28, 19; 1 Chr 10, 2f.   *w:* 1 Sm 24, 7; Jgs 9, 54; 1 Chr 10, 4.   *x:* 1 Sm 10, 1; 26, 9; 2 Mc 14, 42.   *y:* 1 Sm 17, 54; 2 Sm 1, 20; 2 Mc 15, 35.   *z:* 11ff: 1 Sm 11, 1-11; 2 Sm 2, 4-7.

See RG 177–83

The Second Book of Samuel

See RG 177–78
CHAPTER 1

Report of Saul's Death. 1After the death of Saul, David returned from his defeat of the Amalekites and spent two days in Ziklag.*a* 2On the third day a man came from Saul's camp, with his clothes torn and dirt on his head. Going to David, he fell to the ground in homage. 3David asked him, "Where do you come from?" He replied, "I have escaped from the Israelite camp."

4"Tell me what happened," David bade him. He answered that the soldiers had fled the battle and that many of them had fallen and were dead, among them Saul and his son Jonathan. 5Then David said to the youth who was reporting to him, "How do you know that Saul and his son Jonathan are dead?" 6bThe youthful informant replied: "It was by chance that I found myself on Mount Gilboa and saw Saul leaning on his spear, with chariots and horsemen closing in on

a: 1 Sm 30, 17-20; 31, 1-13.   *b:* 6-10: 2 Sm 4, 10; 1 Sm 31, 1-4; 1 Chr 10, 1-4.

him. [7]He turned around and, seeing me, called me to him. When I said, 'Here I am,' [8]he asked me, 'Who are you?' and I replied, 'An Amalekite.' [9]Then he said to me, 'Stand up to me, please, and finish me off, for I am in great suffering, yet fully alive.' [10]So I stood up to him and dispatched him, for I knew that he could not survive his wound. I removed the crown from his head and the armlet from his arm and brought them here to my lord."

[11]David seized his garments and rent them, and all the men who were with him did likewise.[c] [12]They mourned and wept and fasted until evening for Saul and his son Jonathan, and for the soldiers of the LORD of the clans of Israel, because they had fallen by the sword.[d] [13]Then David said to the young man who had brought him the information, "Where are you from?" He replied, "I am the son of an Amalekite immigrant." [14]David said to him, "How is it that you were not afraid to put forth your hand to desecrate the LORD's anointed?"[e] [15]David then called one of the attendants and said to him, "Come, strike him down"; and the youth struck him a mortal blow. [16]Meanwhile David said to him, "You are responsible for your own death, for you testified against yourself when you said, 'I dispatched the LORD's anointed.' "

Elegy for Saul and Jonathan. [17]Then David chanted this elegy for Saul and his son Jonathan, [18]which is recorded in the Book of Jashar to be taught to the Judahites. He sang:[f]

[19] "Alas! the glory of Israel, Saul,
 slain upon your heights;
 how can the warriors have fallen!

[20] "Tell it not in Gath,
 herald it not in the streets of Ashkelon,
 Lest the Philistine maidens rejoice,
 lest the daughters of the strangers
 exult![g]
[21] Mountains of Gilboa,

may there be neither dew nor rain
 upon you,
 nor upsurgings of the deeps!*
Upon you lie begrimed the warriors'
 shields,
 the shield of Saul, no longer anointed
 with oil.[h]

[22] "From the blood of the slain,
 from the bodies of the valiant,
The bow of Jonathan did not turn back,
 or the sword of Saul return unstained.[i]
[23] Saul and Jonathan, beloved and cherished,
 separated neither in life nor in death,
 swifter than eagles, stronger than lions!
[24] Women of Israel, weep over Saul,
 who clothed you in scarlet and in
 finery,
 who decked your attire with ornaments
 of gold.

[25] "How can the warriors have fallen—
 in the thick of the battle,
 slain upon your heights!
[26] "I grieve for you, Jonathan my brother!
 most dear have you been to me;
More precious have I held love for you
 than love for women.[j]

[27] "How can the warriors have fallen,
 the weapons of war have perished!"

CHAPTER 2

See RG 178–79

David Anointed King. [1]After this David inquired of the LORD, "Shall I go up into one of the cities of Judah?" The LORD replied to him, "Yes." Then David asked, "Where shall I go?" He replied, "To Hebron." [2]So David went up there accompanied by his two wives, Ahinoam of Jezreel and Abigail, the widow of Nabal of Carmel.[k] [3]David also brought up his men with their families, and they dwelt in the cities near Hebron. [4]Then the men of Judah came there and anointed David king of the Judahites.[l]

1, 21: Upsurgings of the deeps: this reading attempts to recover from an unintelligible Hebrew phrase the poetic parallel to dew and rain. The sense would be a wish that the mountain should have neither moisture from above nor water from springs or wells.

c: 2 Sm 13, 31. *d:* 1 Sm 31, 13. *e:* 1 Sm 10, 1; 24, 7; Ps. 105, 15. *f:* Jos 10, 13. *g:* Jgs 16, 23; 1 Sm 31, 9; Mi 1, 10. *h:* Gn 27, 28. *i:* 1 Sm 14, 47. *j:* 1 Sm 18, 1; 1 Mc 9, 21. *k:* 1 Sm 25, 42f. *l:* 1 Sm 31, 11ff.

A report reached David that the men of Jabesh-gilead had buried Saul. [5]So David sent messengers to the men of Jabesh-gilead and said to them: "May you be blessed by the LORD for having done this kindness to your lord Saul in burying him. [6]And now may the LORD be kind and faithful to you. I, too, will be generous to you for having done this. [7]Take courage, therefore, and prove yourselves valiant men, for though your lord Saul is dead, the Judahites have anointed me their king."

IV: The Reign of David

Ishbaal King of Israel. [8]Abner, son of Ner, Saul's general, took Ishbaal, son of Saul, and brought him over to Mahanaim,[m] [9]where he made him king over Gilead, the Ashurites, Jezreel, Ephraim, Benjamin, and the rest of Israel. [10]Ishbaal, son of Saul, was forty years old when he became king over Israel, and he reigned for two years. The Judahites alone followed David. [11]In all, David spent seven years and six months in Hebron as king of the Judahites.[n]

Combat near Gibeon. [12]Now Abner, son of Ner, and the servants of Ishbaal, Saul's son, left Mahanaim for Gibeon. [13]Joab, son of Zeruiah, and David's servants also set out and met them at the pool of Gibeon. And they sat down, one group on one side of the pool and the other on the opposite side. [14]Then Abner said to Joab, "Let the young men rise and perform for us." Joab replied, "All right!" [15]So they rose and were counted off: twelve of the Benjaminites of Ishbaal, son of Saul, and twelve of David's servants. [16]Then each one grasped his opponent's head and thrust his sword into his opponent's side, and all fell down together.[*] And so that place, which is in Gibeon, was named the Field of the Sides.

Death of Asahel. [17]After a very fierce battle that day, Abner and the men of Israel were defeated by David's servants. [18]The three sons of Zeruiah were there—Joab, Abishai, and Asahel. Asahel, who was as fleet of foot as a gazelle in the open field,[o]

[19]set out after Abner, turning neither right nor left in his pursuit.[p] [20]Abner turned around and said, "Is that you, Asahel?" He replied, "Yes." [21]Abner said to him, "Turn right or left; seize one of the young men and take what you can strip from him." But Asahel would not desist from his pursuit. [22]Once more Abner said to Asahel: "Stop pursuing me! Why must I strike you to the ground? How could I face your brother Joab?"[q] [23]Still he refused to stop. So Abner struck him in the abdomen with the heel of his javelin, and the weapon protruded from his back. He fell there and died on the spot. And all who came to the place where Asahel had fallen and died, came to a halt. [24]Joab and Abishai, however, continued the pursuit of Abner. The sun had gone down when they came to the hill of Ammah which lies east of the valley toward the desert near Geba.

Truce between Joab and Abner. [25]Here the Benjaminites rallied around Abner, forming a single group, and made a stand on the hilltop. [26]Then Abner called to Joab and said: "Must the sword destroy to the utmost? Do you not know that afterward there will be bitterness? How much longer will you refrain from ordering the people to stop the pursuit of their brothers?" [27]Joab replied, "As God lives, if you had not spoken, the soldiers would not have been withdrawn from the pursuit of their brothers until morning." [28]Joab then sounded the horn, and all the soldiers came to a halt, pursuing Israel no farther and fighting no more. [29]Abner and his men marched all night long through the Arabah, crossed the Jordan, marched all through the morning, and came to Mahanaim. [30]Joab, after interrupting the pursuit of Abner, assembled all the men. Besides Asahel, nineteen other servants of David were missing. [31]But David's servants had fatally wounded three hundred and sixty men of Benjamin, followers of Abner. [32]They took up Asahel and buried him in his father's tomb in Bethlehem. Joab and his men made an all-night march, and dawn found them in Hebron.

2, 16: The nature of this gruesome game is not clear, and the place name is variously given in the older texts.

m: 1 Sm 14, 50.   *n:* 2 Sm 5, 5; 1 Kgs 2, 11.   *o:* 2 Sm 23, 24: 1 Chr 2, 16.   *p:* 1 Chr 27, 7.   *q:* 2 Sm 3, 27f. 30.

CHAPTER 3

See RG
178–79

[1]There followed a long war between the house of Saul and that of David, in which David grew stronger, but the house of Saul weaker.

Sons Born in Hebron. [2r]Sons were born to David in Hebron: his first-born, Amnon, of Ahinoam from Jezreel; [3]the second, Chileab, of Abigail the widow of Nabal of Carmel; the third, Absalom, son of Maacah the daughter of Talmai, king of Geshur;[s] [4]the fourth, Adonijah, son of Haggith; the fifth, Shephatiah, son of Abital;[t] [5]and the sixth, Ithream, of David's wife Eglah. These were born to David in Hebron.

Ishbaal and Abner Quarrel. [6]During the war between the house of Saul and of David, Abner was gaining power in the house of Saul. [7]Now Saul had had a concubine, Rizpah, the daughter of Aiah. And Ishbaal, son of Saul, said to Abner, "Why have you been intimate with my father's concubine?"[u] [8]Enraged at the words of Ishbaal, Abner said, "Am I a dog's head in Judah? At present I am doing a kindness to the house of your father Saul, to his brothers and his friends, by keeping you out of David's clutches; yet this day you charge me with a crime involving a woman! [9]May God do thus and so to Abner if I do not carry out for David what the LORD swore to him[v]— [10]that is, take away the kingdom from the house of Saul and establish the throne of David over Israel and over Judah from Dan to Beer-sheba."[w] [11]In his fear of Abner, Ishbaal was no longer able to say a word to him.

Abner and David Reconciled. [12]Then Abner sent messengers to David in Telam, where he was at the moment, to say, "Make an agreement with me, and I will aid you by bringing all Israel over to you." [13]He replied, "Very well, I will make an agreement with you. But one thing I require of you. You must not appear before me unless you bring back Michal, Saul's daughter, when you come to present yourself to me."[x] [14]At the same time David sent messengers to Ishbaal,

son of Saul, to say, "Give me my wife Michal, whom I espoused by paying a hundred Philistine foreskins." [15]Ishbaal sent for her and took her away from her husband Paltiel, son of Laish,[y] [16]who followed her weeping as far as Bahurim. But Abner said to him, "Go back!" And he turned back.

[17]Abner then said in discussion with the elders of Israel: "For a long time you have been seeking David as your king. [18]Now take action, for the LORD has said of David, 'By my servant David I will save my people Israel from the grasp of the Philistines and from the grasp of all their enemies.' " [19]Abner also spoke personally to Benjamin, and then went to make his own report to David in Hebron concerning all that would be agreeable to Israel and to the whole house of Benjamin. [20]When Abner, accompanied by twenty men, came to David in Hebron, David prepared a feast for Abner and for the men who were with him. [21]Then Abner said to David, "I will now go to assemble all Israel for my lord the king, that they may make an agreement with you; you will then be king over all whom you wish to rule." So David bade Abner farewell, and he went away in peace.

Death of Abner. [22]Just then David's servants and Joab were coming in from an expedition, bringing much plunder with them. Abner, having been dismissed by David, was no longer with him in Hebron but had gone his way in peace. [23]When Joab and the whole force he had with him arrived, he was informed, "Abner, son of Ner, came to David; he has been sent on his way in peace." [24]So Joab went to the king and said: "What have you done? Abner came to you. Why did you let him go peacefully on his way? [25]Are you not aware that Abner came to deceive you and to learn the ins and outs of all that you are doing?" [26]Joab then left David, and without David's knowledge sent messengers after Abner, who brought him back from the cistern of Sirah. [27]When Abner returned to Hebron, Joab took him aside within the city gate as though to speak with

r: 2-5: 1 Chr 3, 14. s: 2 Sm 13, 37; 15, 8. t: 1 Kgs 1, 5. u: 2 Sm 21, 8ff. v: Ru 1, 17. w: 2 Sm 5, 2; 1 Sm 25, 30. x: 1 Sm 18, 20-27. y: 1 Sm 25, 44.

him privately. There he stabbed him in the abdomen, and he died in revenge for the killing of Joab's brother Asahel.^z ²⁸Later David heard of it and said: "Before the LORD, I and my kingdom are forever innocent.^a ²⁹May the full responsibility for the death of Abner, son of Ner, be laid to Joab and to all his family. May the men of Joab's family never be without one suffering from a discharge, or a leper, or one unmanly, one falling by the sword, or one in need of bread!" ³⁰[Joab and his brother Abishai had lain in wait for Abner because he killed their brother Asahel in battle at Gibeon.]

David Mourns Abner. ³¹Then David said to Joab and to all the people who were with him, "Rend your garments, gird yourselves with sackcloth, and mourn over Abner." King David himself followed the bier.^b ³²When they had buried Abner in Hebron, the king wept aloud at the grave of Abner, and the people also wept. ³³And the king sang this elegy over Abner:

"Would Abner have died like a fool?
³⁴ Your hands were not bound with chains,
    nor your feet placed in fetters;
    As men fall before the wicked, you fell."

And all the people continued to weep for him. ³⁵Then they went to console David with food while it was still day. But David swore, "May God do thus and so to me if I eat bread or anything else before sunset."^c ³⁶All the people noted this with approval, just as they were pleased with everything that the king did. ³⁷So on that day all the people and all Israel came to know that the king had no part in the killing of Abner, son of Ner. ³⁸The king then said to his servants: "You must recognize that a great general has fallen today in Israel. ³⁹Although I am the anointed king, I am weak this day, and these men, the sons of Zeruiah, are too ruthless for me. May the LORD requite the evildoer in accordance with his evil deed."^d

CHAPTER 4

See RG 178–79

Death of Ishbaal. ¹When Ishbaal, son of Saul, heard that Abner had died in Hebron, he ceased to resist and all Israel was alarmed. ²Ishbaal, son of Saul, had two company leaders named Baanah and Rechab, sons of Rimmon the Beerothite, of the tribe of Benjamin. [Beeroth, too, was ascribed to Benjamin:^e ³the Beerothites fled to Gittaim, where they have been resident aliens to this day.^f ⁴Jonathan, son of Saul, had a son named Meribbaal* with crippled feet. He was five years old when the news about Saul and Jonathan came from Jezreel, and his nurse took him up and fled. But in their hasty flight, he fell and became lame.]^g ⁵The sons of Rimmon the Beerothite, Rechab and Baanah, came into the house of Ishbaal during the heat of the day, while he was taking his siesta. ⁶The portress of the house had dozed off while sifting wheat, and was asleep. So Rechab and his brother Baanah slipped past ⁷and entered the house while Ishbaal was lying asleep in his bedroom. They struck and killed him, and cut off his head. Then, taking the head, they traveled on the Arabah road all night long.

The Murder Avenged. ⁸They brought the head of Ishbaal to David in Hebron and said to the king: "This is the head of Ishbaal, son of your enemy Saul, who sought your life. Thus has the LORD this day avenged my lord the king on Saul and his posterity." ⁹But David replied to Rechab and his brother Baanah, sons of Rimmon the Beerothite: "As the LORD lives, who rescued me from all difficulty, ¹⁰in Ziklag I seized and put to death the man who informed me of Saul's death, thinking himself the bearer of good news for which I ought to give him a reward.^h ¹¹How much more now, when wicked men have slain an innocent man in bed at home, must I hold you responsible for his death and destroy you from the earth!" ¹²So at a command from David, the young men killed

---

4, 4: Saul's grandson Meribbaal is the subject of ch 9 below. The text of this verse may owe its present place to the fact that pre-Christian copies of the Books of Samuel tended to confuse his name with that of his uncle Ishbaal, Saul's son and successor, a principal figure in chapters 2–4.

z: 1 Kgs 2, 5. 32.   a: 28. 30: 2 Sm 2, 22f.   b: 2 Sm 21, 10.   c: Ru 1, 17.   d: Ps 28, 4; Is 3, 11.   e: 2 Sm 9, 3; Jos 9, 17f.   f: Jos 18, 25.   g: 2 Sm 9, 3; 19, 25.   h: 2 Sm 1, 6-10. 14. 16.

them and cut off their hands and feet, hanging them up near the pool in Hebron. But he took the head of Ishbaal and buried it in Abner's grave in Hebron.[i]

See RG
178–79

CHAPTER 5

David King of Israel. [1][j]All the tribes of Israel came to David in Hebron and said: "Here we are, your bone and your flesh. [2]In days past, when Saul was our king, it was you who led the Israelites out and brought them back. And the LORD said to you, 'You shall shepherd my people Israel and shall be commander of Israel.' "[k] [3]When all the elders of Israel came to David in Hebron, King David made an agreement with them there before the LORD, and they anointed him king of Israel. [4]David was thirty years old when he became king, and he reigned for forty years: [5]seven years and six months in Hebron over Judah, and thirty-three years in Jerusalem over all Israel and Judah.[l]

*Capture of Zion.** [6][m]Then the king and his men set out for Jerusalem against the Jebusites who inhabited the region. David was told, "You cannot enter here: the blind and the lame will drive you away!" which was their way of saying, "David cannot enter here."[n] [7]But David did take the stronghold of Zion, which is the City of David. [8]On that day David said: "All who wish to attack the Jebusites must strike at them through the water shaft. The lame and the blind shall be the personal enemies of David." That is why it is said, "The blind and the lame shall not enter the palace."[o] [9]David then dwelt in the stronghold, which was called the City of David; he built up the area from Millo to the palace.[p] [10]David grew steadily more powerful, for the LORD of hosts was with him.[q] [11][r]Hiram, king of Tyre, sent ambassadors to David; he furnished cedar wood, as well as carpenters and masons, who built a palace for David.[s] [12]And David knew that the LORD had established him as king of Israel and had exalted his rule for the sake of his people Israel.

David's Family in Jerusalem. [13][t]David took more concubines and wives in Jerusalem after he had come from Hebron, and more sons and daughters were born to him in Jerusalem. [14]These are the names of those who were born to him in Jerusalem: Shammua, Shobab, Nathan, Solomon, [15]Ibhar, Elishua, Nepheg, Japhia, [16]Elishama, Baaliada, and Eliphelet.

Rout of the Philistines. [17]When the Philistines heard that David had been anointed king of Israel, they all took the field in search of him. On hearing this, David went down to the refuge.* [18]The Philistines came and overran the valley of Rephaim.* [19]David inquired of the LORD, "Shall I attack the Philistines—will you deliver them into my grip?" The LORD replied to David, "Attack, for I will surely deliver the Philistines into your grip." [20]David then went to Baal-perazim,* where he defeated them. He said, "The LORD has scattered my enemies before me like waters that have broken free." That is why the place is called Baal-perazim. [21]They abandoned their gods there, and David and his men carried them away. [22]But the Philistines came up again and overran the valley of Rephaim. [23]So David inquired of the LORD, who replied: "You must not attack frontally, but circle their rear and meet them before the mastic trees. [24]When you hear a sound of marching* in the tops of the mastic trees, act decisively, for the LORD will have gone forth before you to attack the camp of the Philistines." [25]David obeyed the LORD's command and routed the Philistines from Gibeon as far as Gezer.

5, 6-12: David's most important military exploit, the taking of Jerusalem, is here presented before his battles with the Philistines, vv 17-25, which were earlier in time. The sense of vv 6 and 8 is in doubt.

5, 17: Refuge: probably near Adullam (1 Sm 22, 1-5).

5, 18-25: The successive defeats of the Philistines in the valley of Rephaim southwest of Jerusalem had the effect of blocking their access to the mountain ridge near Gibeon, and confining them to their holdings on the coast and in the foothills beyond Gezer to the west and south.

5, 20: Baal-perazim: means approximately "the lord of scatterings."

5, 24: Sound of marching: the wind in the treetops suggestive of the Lord's footsteps.

---

i: Dt 21, 22f; 1 Sm 31, 10.   *j:* 1ff: 1 Chr 11, 1ff.   *k:* 2 Sm 3, 10; Dt 17, 15; 1 Sm 18, 16.   *l:* 2 Sm 2, 11; 1 Kgs 2, 11; 1 Chr 3, 4.   *m:* 6-10: 1 Chr 11, 4-9.   *n:* Jos 15, 63; Jgs 1, 19. 21; Is 29, 3.   *o:* Lv 21, 18; Mt 21, 14f.   *p:* 1 Kgs 3, 1; 11, 27.   *q:* Pss 78, 70ff. 89; 132, 13.   *r:* 11-25: 1 Chr 14, 1-16.   *s:* 11f: 1 Kgs 5, 15; 1 Chr 14, 1f.   *t:* 13-16: 1 Chr 3, 5-8; 14, 3-7.

The Kingdom of David according to 2 Samuel

Baal-hazor
Gilgal
Gezer
Gibeon
Geba
Ekron
Jerusalem
Gath?
Giloh
Tekoa
Hebron

Mediterranean
Sea

ZOBAH

ARAM (SYRIA)
Damascus

Tyre
Abel-beth-maacah

GESHUR

ISRAEL

Hill Country
of Ephraim

Mahanaim

AMMON

Rabbah

Ashdod
Jerusalem
Ashkelon
PHILISTIA
Gaza
JUDAH

MOAB

Valley of Salt

AMALEK

EDOM

0   25   50   75 Miles

0   40   80   120 Kilometers

See RG
179

CHAPTER 6

The Ark Brought to Jerusalem. *1u*David again assembled all the picked men of Israel, thirty thousand in number. *2*Then David and all the people who were with him set out for Baala of Judah to bring up from there the ark of God, which bears the name of the LORD of hosts enthroned above the cherubim.*v 3*The ark of God was placed on a new cart and taken away from the house of Abinadab on the hill. Uzzah and Ahio, sons of Abinadab, guided the cart,*w 4*with Ahio walking before it, *5*while David and all the Israelites made merry before the LORD with all their strength, with singing and with citharas, harps, tambourines, sistrums and cymbals.*x 6*When they came to the threshing floor of Nodan, Uzzah reached out his hand to the ark of God and steadied it, for the oxen were making it tip. *7*But the LORD was angry with Uzzah; God struck him on that spot, and he died there before God. *8*David was disturbed because the LORD had vented his anger on Uzzah. (The place has been called Perez-uzzah down to the present day.)*y 9*David feared the LORD that day and said, "How can the ark of the LORD come to me?" *10*So David would not have the ark of the LORD brought to him in the City of David, but diverted it to the house of Obed-edom the Gittite.

*11*The ark of the LORD remained in the house of Obed-edom the Gittite for three months, and the LORD blessed Obed-edom and his whole house.*z 12a*When it was reported to King David that the LORD had blessed the family of Obed-edom and all that belonged to him, David went to bring up the ark of God from the house of Obed-edom into the City of David amid festivities. *13*As soon as the bearers of the ark of the LORD had advanced six steps, he sacrificed an ox and a fatling. *14*Then David, girt with a linen apron, came dancing before the LORD with abandon,*b 15*as he and all the Israelites were bringing up the ark of the LORD with shouts of joy and to the sound of the horn. *16*As the ark of the LORD was entering the City of David, Saul's daughter Michal looked down through the window and saw King David leaping and dancing before the LORD, and she despised him in her heart. *17c*The ark of the LORD was brought in and set in its place within the tent David had pitched for it. Then David offered holocausts and peace offerings before the LORD. *18*When he finished making these offerings, he blessed the people in the name of the LORD of hosts. *19*He then distributed among all the people, to each man and each woman in the entire multitude of Israel, a loaf of bread, a cut of roast meat, and a raisin cake. With this, all the people left for their homes.

*20*When David returned to bless his own family, Saul's daughter Michal came out to meet him and said, "How the king of Israel has honored himself today, exposing himself to the view of the slave girls of his followers, as a commoner might do!"*d 21*But David replied to Michal: "I was dancing before the LORD. As the LORD lives, who preferred me to your father and his whole family when he appointed me commander of the LORD's people, Israel, not only will I make merry before the LORD,*e 22*but I will demean myself even more. I will be lowly in your esteem, but in the esteem of the slave girls you spoke of I will be honored." *23*And so Saul's daughter Michal was childless to the day of her death.

CHAPTER 7

See RG
179-80

David's Concern for the Ark. *1f*When King David was settled in his palace, and the LORD had given him rest from his enemies on every side,*g 2*he said to Nathan the prophet, "Here I am living in a house of cedar, while the ark of God dwells in a tent!"*h 3*Nathan answered the king, "Go, do whatever you have in mind, for the LORD is with you."*i 4*But that night the LORD spoke to Nathan and said: *5*"Go, tell my servant David, 'Thus says the LORD: Should you build me a house to dwell in?*j 6*I have not dwelt in a house from the day on which I led

u: 1-11: 1 Chr 13, 1-14.   *v:* Ex 25, 10; Jos 15, 9; Ps 132, 8ff; 1 Chr 1, 4.   *w:* 1 Sm 4, 3f; 6, 7f; 7, 1; Dn 3, 55.   *x:* Pss 68, 25f; 150, 3. 5.   *y:* 1 Kgs 8, 1.   *z:* 1 Chr 26, 4.   *a:* 12-23: 1 Chr 15, 1-29; Ps 24, 7-10.   *b:* 1 Sm 2, 18.   *c:* 17ff: Lv 1, 1-17; 3, 1-17; 1 Chr 16, 1ff.   *d:* 1 Chr 16, 43.   *e:* 1 Sm 13, 14; 15, 28.   *f:* 1-29: 1 Chr 17, 1-27.   *g:* 1 Kgs 5, 4.   *h:* Dt 12, 10; 25, 19.   *i:* Ps 132, 1-5.   *j:* 1 Kgs 5, 17; 8, 16. 27; 1 Chr 22, 8; 28, 3; Is 66, 1; Acts 7, 48.

the Israelites out of Egypt to the present, but I have been going about in a tent under cloth. [7]In all my wanderings everywhere among the Israelites, did I ever utter a word to any one of the judges whom I charged to tend my people Israel, to ask: Why have you not built me a house of cedar?'

The Lord's Promises. [8]"Now then, speak thus to my servant David, 'The LORD of hosts has this to say:* It was I who took you from the pasture and from the care of the flock to be commander of my people Israel.[k] [9]I have been with you wherever you went, and I have destroyed all your enemies before you. And I will make you famous like the great ones of the earth.[l] [10]I will fix a place for my people Israel; I will plant them so that they may dwell in their place without further disturbance. Neither shall the wicked continue to afflict them as they did of old, [11]since the time I first appointed judges over my people Israel. I will give you rest from all your enemies. The LORD also reveals to you that he will establish a house for you.[m] [12n]And when your time comes and you rest with your ancestors, I will raise up your heir after you, sprung from your loins, and I will make his kingdom firm. [13]It is he who shall build a house for my name. And I will make his royal throne firm forever. [14]I will be a father to him, and he shall be a son to me. And if he does wrong, I will correct him with the rod of men and with human chastisements; [15]but I will not withdraw my favor from him as I withdrew it from your predecessor Saul, whom I removed from my presence.[o] [16]Your house and your kingdom shall endure forever before me; your throne shall stand firm forever.' "[p] [17]Nathan reported all these words and this entire vision to David.

King David's Prayer. [18]Then King David went in and sat before the LORD and said, "Who am I, Lord GOD, and who are the members of my house, that you have brought me to this point?[q] [19]Yet even this you see as too little, Lord GOD; you have also spoken of the house of your servant for a long time to come: this too you have shown to man,* Lord GOD! [20]What more can David say to you? You know your servant, Lord GOD! [21]For your servant's sake and as you have had at heart, you have brought about this entire magnificent disclosure to your servant. [22]And so—

"Great are you, Lord GOD! There is none like you and there is no God but you, just as we have heard it told.[r] [23]What other nation on earth is there like your people Israel, which God has led, redeeming it as his people; so that you have made yourself renowned by doing this magnificent deed, and by doing awe-inspiring things as you have cleared nations and their gods out of the way of your people, which you redeemed for yourself from Egypt?[s] [24t]You have established for yourself your people Israel as yours forever, and you, LORD, have become their God. [25]And now, LORD God, confirm for all time the prophecy you have made concerning your servant and his house, and do as you have promised. [26]Your name will be forever great, when men say, 'The LORD of hosts is God of Israel,' and the house of your servant David stands firm before you. [27]It is you, LORD of hosts, God of Israel, who said in a revelation to your servant, 'I will build a house for you.' Therefore your servant now finds the courage to make this prayer to you. [28]And now, Lord GOD, you are God and your words are truth; you have made this generous promise to

---

7, 8-16: The prophecy to David contained in these verses is cited again, in poetic form, in Ps 89, 20-38, and alluded to in Ps 132. The promise regarding the people of Israel, vv 10-11, is a part of the promise to David at least as old as the composition of this chapter of Samuel, where it is anticipated in vv 6-7, and alluded to in David's thanksgiving, vv 23-24; it applies to the people an expression used of David in Ps 89, 23. The prophecy to David is the basis for Jewish expectation of a messiah, son of David, which Jesus Christ fulfilled in a transcendent way; cf Acts 2, 30; Heb 1, 5.

7, 19: This too you have shown to man: the text as transmitted has, rather, "and this is instruction for (or: the law of)

mankind." The author of Chronicles (1 Chr 17, 17) saw approximately the same phrase, which he endeavored to fit into the context in a quite different sense. The above is conjectural; cf Dt 5, 24.

---

k: 1 Sm 16, 13; 17, 15-20; Ps 78, 70f; Am 7, 14. *l:* Ps 89, 27. *m:* 2 Sm 23, 5; 1 Kgs 2, 4-24. *n:* 12ff; 1 Kgs 5, 19; 8, 19; 1 Chr 22, 10; 2 Chr 7, 18; Ps 89, 5. 27f. 30. 37f; Lk 1, 32; Heb 1, 5. *o:* 2 Sm 23, 5; 1 Sm 13, 14; 15, 26. 28; 2 Kgs 19, 34; 1 Chr 17, 11-14; Ps 89, 34. *p:* 2 Sm 23, 5; Dn 2, 45; 1 Mc 2, 57; Mk 11, 10; Lk 1, 32f; Heb 1, 8. *q:* 1 Chr 17, 16. *r:* Ex 15, 11; Is 45, 5. *s:* Dt 4, 7. 34. *t:* 24f; Ex 6, 7; Dt 7, 6; 26, 17; 29, 12.

your servant.[u] [29]Do, then, bless the house of your servant that it may be before you forever; for you, Lord GOD, have promised, and by your blessing the house of your servant shall be blessed forever."

See RG
180

CHAPTER 8

Summary of David's Wars. [1v]After this David attacked the Philistines and conquered them, wresting . . .* from the Philistines. [2]He also defeated Moab and then measured them with a line, making them lie down on the ground. He told off two lengths of line for execution, and a full length* to be spared. Thus the Moabites became tributary to David. [3w]Next David defeated Hadadezer, son of Rehob, king of Zobah, when he went to reestablish his dominion at the Euphrates River.[x] [4]David captured from him one thousand seven hundred horsemen and twenty thousand foot soldiers. And he hamstrung all the chariot horses, preserving only enough for a hundred chariots.[y] [5]When the Arameans of Damascus came to the aid of Hadadezer, king of Zobah, David slew twenty-two thousand of them. [6]David then placed garrisons in Aram of Damascus, and the Arameans became subjects, tributary to David. The LORD brought David victory in all his undertakings. [7]David also took away the golden shields used by Hadadezer's servants and brought them to Jerusalem. [These Shishak, king of Egypt, took away when he came to Jerusalem in the days of Rehoboam, son of Solomon.] [8]From Tebah and Berothai, towns of Hadadezer, King David removed a very large quantity of bronze. [9]When Toi, king of Hamath, heard that David had defeated all the forces of Hadadezer, [10]he sent his son Hadoram to King David to greet him and to congratulate him for his victory over Hadadezer in battle, because

Toi had been in many battles with Hadadezer. Hadoram also brought with him articles of silver, gold, and bronze. [11]These, too, King David consecrated to the LORD, together with the silver and gold he had taken from every nation he had conquered: [12]from Edom and Moab, from the Ammonites, from the Philistines, from the Amalekites, and from the plunder of Hadadezer, son of Rehob, king of Zobah.

[13]On his return,* David became famous for having slain eighteen thousand Edomites in the Salt Valley;[z] [14]after which he placed garrisons in Edom. Thus all the Edomites became David's subjects, and the LORD brought David victory in all his undertakings.

David's Officials. [15a]David reigned over all Israel, judging and administering justice to all his people. [16]Joab, son of Zeruiah, was in command of the army. Jehoshaphat, son of Ahilud, was chancellor. [17]Zadok, son of Ahitub, and Ahimelech, son of Abiathar, were priests. Shawsha was scribe. [18]Benaiah, son of Jehoiada, was in command of the Cherethites and Pelethites. And David's sons were priests.[b]

CHAPTER 9

See RG
180–82

David and Meribbaal. [1]David asked, "Is there any survivor of Saul's house to whom I may show kindness for the sake of Jonathan?"[c] [2]Now there was a servant of the family of Saul named Ziba. He was summoned to David, and the king asked him, "Are you Ziba?" He replied, "Your servant."[d] [3]Then the king inquired, "Is there any survivor of Saul's house to whom I may show God's kindness?" Ziba answered the king, "There is still Jonathan's son, whose feet are crippled."[e] [4]The king said to him, "Where is he?" and Ziba answered, "He is in the house of Machir, son of Ammiel, in

8, 1: Wresting . . . : the Hebrew text here gives "the bridle of the cubit"; 1 Chr 18, 1 understood "Gath and its dependent villages"; others implausibly read "dominion of the capital city."

8, 2: Two lengths . . . a full length: usually taken to mean that two-thirds of them were executed; but it could mean that two-thirds were spared, if the line was used full length in their case but doubled on itself to make "two lines" for those to be put to death.

8, 13: On his return: possibly to Jerusalem, after the revolt

of Absalom, a circumstance which this catalogue of victories would avoid mentioning. 1 Chr 18, 13 attributes the defeat of the Edomites to Abishai.

u: Nm 23, 19; Jn 17, 17. *v:* 1-18: 1 Chr 18, 1-17. *w:* 3-8: 2 Sm 10, 15-19. *x:* 2 Sm 10, 6; 1 Kgs 11, 23. *y:* Jos 11, 6. 9. *z:* 2 Kgs 14, 7. *a:* 15-18: 2 Sm 20, 23-26; 1 Kgs 4, 1-6; 1 Chr 18, 14-17. *b:* 2 Sm 15, 18; 20, 7. 23; 23, 20. *c:* 2 Sm 21, 7; 1 Sm 18, 1-4; 20, 8ff. 15f. 42. *d:* 2 Sm 16, 1-4; 19, 27. *e:* 2 Sm 4, 4.

Lodebar."*f 5*So King David sent for him and had him brought from the house of Machir, son of Ammiel, in Lodebar. *6*When Meribbaal, son of Jonathan, son of Saul, came to David, he fell prostrate in homage. David said, "Meribbaal," and he answered, "Your servant." *7*"Fear not," David said to him, "I will surely be kind to you for the sake of your father Jonathan. I will restore to you all the lands of your grandfather Saul, and you shall always eat at my table." *8*Bowing low, he answered, "What is your servant that you should pay attention to a dead dog like me?"*g* *9*The king then called Ziba, Saul's attendant, and said to him: "I am giving your lord's son all that belonged to Saul and to all his family. *10*You and your sons and servants must till the land for him. You shall bring in the produce, which shall be food for your lord's family to eat. But Meribbaal, your lord's son, shall always eat at my table." Ziba, who had fifteen sons and twenty servants, *11*said to the king, "Your servant shall do just as my lord the king has commanded him." And so Meribbaal ate at David's table like one of the king's sons.*h* *12*Meribbaal had a young son whose name was Mica; and all the tenants of Ziba's family worked for Meribbaal.*i* *13*But Meribbaal lived in Jerusalem, because he always ate at the king's table. He was lame in both feet.*j*

See RG 180-82

CHAPTER 10

Insult of the Ammonites. *1k*Some time later* the king of the Ammonites died, and his son Hanun succeeded him as king. *2*David thought, "I will be kind to Hanun, son of Nahash, as his father was kind to me." So David sent his servants with condolences to Hanun for the loss of his father. But when David's servants entered the country of the Ammonites, *3*the Ammonite princes said to their lord Hanun: "Do you think that David is honoring your father by sending men with condolences? Is it not rather to explore the city, to spy on it, and to overthrow it, that David has sent his messengers to you?" *4*Hanun, therefore, seized David's servants and, after shaving off half their beards and cutting away the lower halves of their garments at the buttocks, sent them away.*l* *5*When he was told of it, King David sent out word to them, since the men were quite ashamed. "Stay in Jericho until your beards grow," he said, "and then come back."

Ammonites Defeated. *6*In view of the offense they had given to David, the Ammonites sent for and hired twenty thousand Aramean foot soldiers from Beth-rehob and Zobah, as well as the king of Maacah with one thousand men, and twelve thousand men from Tob.*m* *7*On learning this, David sent out Joab with the entire levy of trained soldiers.*n* *8*The Ammonites came out and drew up in battle formation at the entrance of their city gate, while the Arameans of Zobah and Rehob and the men of Tob and Maacah remained apart in the open country. *9*When Joab saw the battle lines drawn up against him, both front and rear, he made a selection from all the picked troops of Israel and arrayed them against the Arameans. *10*He placed the rest of the soldiers under the command of his brother Abishai, who arrayed them against the Ammonites. *11*Joab said, "If the Arameans are stronger than I, you shall help me. But if the Ammonites are stronger than you, I will come to help you. *12*Be brave; let us prove our valor for the sake of our people and the cities of our God; the LORD will do what he judges best." *13*When Joab and the soldiers who were with him approached the Arameans for battle, they fled before him. *14*The Ammonites, seeing that the Arameans had fled, also fled from Abishai and withdrew into the city. Joab then ceased his attack on the Ammonites and returned to Jerusalem.

10, 1: Some time later: early in the reign of David, since Hanun's father had been ruling in Ammon at the beginning of Saul's reign (1 Sm 11) and Solomon was as yet unborn (2 Sm 11, 1; 12, 24).

10, 6-9: A Hebrew text from Qumran (4Q Samᵃ) comes closer in these verses to what is given in 1 Chr 19, 6-9. The scene of the conflict is more likely Rabbath-Ammon, with

Josephus (Ant., vii, 123), than Madeba, as in 1 Chr; compare ch 11.

f: 2 Sm 17, 27. *g*: 1 Sm 24, 15. *h*: 2 Sm 19, 29. *i*: 1 Chr 8, 34. *j*: 2 Sm 21, 7. *k*: 1-19: 1 Chr 19, 1-19. *l*: Is 20, 4. *m*: 2 Sm 8, 3; 1 Sm 14, 47. *n*: 2 Sm 11, 1.

Arameans Defeated. *15o*Then the Arameans responded to their defeat by Israel with a full mustering of troops; *16*Hadadezer sent for and enlisted Arameans from beyond the Euphrates. They came to Helam, with Shobach, general of Hadadezer's army, at their head. *17*On receiving this news, David assembled all Israel, crossed the Jordan, and went to Helam. The Arameans drew up in formation against David and fought with him. *18*But the Arameans gave way before Israel, and David's men killed seven hundred charioteers and forty thousand of the Aramean foot soldiers. Shobach, general of the army, was struck down and died on the field. *19*All of Hadadezer's vassal kings, in view of their defeat by Israel, then made peace with the Israelites and became their subjects. And the Arameans were afraid to give further aid to the Ammonites.

CHAPTER 11

See RG
180-82 ***David's Sin.*** *1*At the turn of the year,* when kings go out on campaign, David sent out Joab along with his officers and the army of Israel, and they ravaged the Ammonites and besieged Rabbah. David, however, remained in Jerusalem.*p* *2*One evening David rose from his siesta and strolled about on the roof of the palace. From the roof he saw a woman bathing, who was very beautiful. *3*David had inquiries made about the woman and was told, "She is Bathsheba, daughter of Eliam, and wife of [Joab's armor-bearer] Uriah the Hittite."*q* *4*Then David sent messengers and took her. When she came to him, he had relations with her, at a time when she was just purified after her monthly period. She then returned to her house.*r* *5*But the woman had conceived, and sent the information to David, "I am with child."

*6*David therefore sent a message to Joab, "Send me Uriah the Hittite." So Joab sent Uriah to David. *7*When he came, David questioned him about Joab, the soldiers, and how the war was going, and Uriah answered that all was well. *8*David then said to Uriah, "Go down to your house and bathe your feet." Uriah left the palace, and a portion was sent out after him from the king's table. *9*But Uriah slept at the entrance of the royal palace with the other officers of his lord, and did not go down to his own house. *10*David was told that Uriah had not gone home. So he said to Uriah, "Have you not come from a journey? Why, then, did you not go down to your house?" *11*Uriah answered David, "The ark and Israel and Judah are lodged in tents, and my lord Joab and your majesty's servants are encamped in the open field. Can I go home to eat and to drink and to sleep with my wife? As the LORD lives and as you live, I will do no such thing."*s* *12*Then David said to Uriah, "Stay here today also, I shall dismiss you tomorrow." So Uriah remained in Jerusalem that day. On the day following, *13*David summoned him, and he ate and drank with David, who made him drunk. But in the evening he went out to sleep on his bed among his lord's servants, and did not go down to his home. *14*The next morning David wrote a letter to Joab which he sent by Uriah. *15*In it he directed: "Place Uriah up front, where the fighting is fierce. Then pull back and leave him to be struck down dead." *16*So while Joab was besieging the city, he assigned Uriah to a place where he knew the defenders were strong. *17*When the men of the city made a sortie against Joab, some officers of David's army fell, and among them Uriah the Hittite died.

*18*Then Joab sent David a report of all the details of the battle, *19*instructing the messenger, "When you have finished giving the king all the details of the battle, *20*the king may become angry and say to you: 'Why did you go near the city to fight? Did you not know that they would shoot from the wall above? *21*Who killed Abimelech, son of Jerubbaal? Was it not a woman who threw a millstone down on him from the wall above, so that he died in Thebez? Why did you go near the wall?' Then you in turn shall say, 'Your servant Uriah the Hittite is also dead.' "*t* *22*The messenger set out, and on his arrival he relayed to David all the details as

11, 1: At the turn of the year: in the spring.

o: 15-19: 2 Sm 8, 3-8; 1 Chr 9, 16-19.   *p:* 2 Sm 10, 7; 1 Chr 20, 1.   *q:* 2 Sm 23, 39.   *r:* Lv 15, 19.   *s:* 1 Sm 4, 3f.   *t:* Jgs 9, 50-54.

Joab had instructed him.* [23]He told David: "The men had us at a disadvantage and came out into the open against us, but we pushed them back to the entrance of the city gate. [24]Then the archers shot at your servants from the wall above, and some of the king's servants died, among them your servant Uriah." [25]David said to the messenger: "This is what you shall convey to Joab: 'Do not be chagrined at this, for the sword devours now here and now there. Strengthen your attack on the city and destroy it.' Encourage him."

[26]When the wife of Uriah heard that her husband had died, she mourned her lord. [27]But once the mourning was over, David sent for her and brought her into his house. She became his wife and bore him a son. But the LORD was displeased with what David had done.

CHAPTER 12

See RG 180–82

Nathan's Parable. [1]*The LORD sent Nathan to David, and when he came to him, he said: "Judge this case for me! In a certain town there were two men, one rich, the other poor.[u] [2]The rich man had flocks and herds in great numbers. [3]But the poor man had nothing at all except one little ewe lamb that he had bought. He nourished her, and she grew up with him and his children. She shared the little food he had and drank from his cup and slept in his bosom. She was like a daughter to him. [4]Now, the rich man received a visitor, but he would not take from his own flocks and herds to prepare a meal for the wayfarer who had come to him. Instead he took the poor man's ewe lamb and made a meal of it for his visitor." [5]David grew very angry with that man and said to Nathan: "As the LORD lives, the man who has done this merits death! [6]He shall restore the ewe lamb fourfold because he has done this and has had no pity."[v]

David's Punishment. [7]Then Nathan said to David: "You are the man! Thus says the LORD God of Israel: 'I anointed you king of Israel. I rescued you from the hand of Saul.[w] [8]I gave you your lord's house and your lord's wives for your own. I gave you the house of Israel and of Judah. And if this were not enough, I could count up for you still more. [9]Why have you spurned the LORD and done evil in his sight? You have cut down Uriah the Hittite with the sword; you took his wife as your own, and him you killed with the sword of the Ammonites. [10]Now, therefore, the sword shall never depart from your house, because you have despised me and have taken the wife of Uriah to be your wife.'[x] [11]Thus says the LORD: 'I will bring evil upon you out of your own house. I will take your wives while you live to see it, and will give them to your neighbor. He shall lie with your wives in broad daylight.[y] [12]You have done this deed in secret, but I will bring it about in the presence of all Israel, and with the sun looking down.' "

David's Repentance. [13]Then David said to Nathan, "I have sinned against the LORD." Nathan answered David: "The LORD on his part has forgiven your sin: you shall not die.[z] [14]But since you have utterly spurned the LORD by this deed, the child born to you must surely die." [15]Then Nathan returned to his house.

The LORD struck the child that the wife of Uriah had borne to David, and it became desperately ill. [16]David besought God for the child. He kept a fast, retiring for the night to lie on the ground clothed in sackcloth. [17]The elders of his house stood beside him urging him to rise from the ground; but he would not, nor would he take food with them. [18]On the seventh day, the child died. David's servants, however, were afraid to tell him that the child was dead, for they said: "When the child was alive, we spoke to him, but he would not listen to what we said. How can we tell him the child is dead? He may do some harm!" [19]But David noticed his servants whispering among themselves

---

11, 22: After this verse, the Greek text, which is here the older form, has David, angry with Joab, repeat exactly the questions Joab had foreseen in vv 20ff. In v 24 of our oldest Greek text, the messenger specifies that about eighteen men were killed.

12, 1-4: This utterance of Nathan is in regular lines in Hebrew, resembling English blank verse.

u: Sir 47, 1.   *v:* Ex 21, 37; Lk 19, 8.   *w:* 1 Sm 16, 13.   *x:* 2 Sm 13, 28f; 18, 14.   *y:* 2 Sm 16, 11. 22.   *z:* 1 Kgs 21, 29; Pss 32, 5; 50, 6; Sir 47, 11.

and realized that the child was dead. He asked his servants, "Is the child dead?" They replied, "Yes, he is." [20]Rising from the ground, David washed and anointed himself, and changed his clothes. Then he went to the house of the LORD and worshiped. He returned to his own house, where at his request food was set before him, and he ate. [21]His servants said to him: "What is this you are doing? While the child was living, you fasted and wept and kept vigil; now that the child is dead you rise and take food." [22]He replied: "While the child was living, I fasted and wept, thinking, 'Perhaps the LORD will grant me the child's life.' [23]But now he is dead. Why should I fast? Can I bring him back again? I shall go to him, but he will not return to me."[a] [24]Then David comforted his wife Bathsheba. He went and slept with her; and she conceived and bore him a son, who was named Solomon. The LORD loved him [25]and sent the prophet Nathan to name him Jedidiah, on behalf of the LORD.

Ammonite War Ends. [26b]Joab fought against Rabbah of the Ammonites and captured this royal city. [27]He sent messengers to David with the word: "I have fought against Rabbah and have taken the water-city. [28]Therefore, assemble the rest of the soldiers, join the siege against the city and capture it, lest it be I that capture the city and it be credited to me." [29]So David assembled the rest of the soldiers and went to Rabbah. When he had fought against it and captured it, [30]he took the crown from Milcom's head. It weighed a talent,* of gold and precious stones; it was placed on David's head. He brought out immense booty from the city, [31]and also led away the inhabitants, whom he assigned to work with saws, iron picks, and iron axes, or put to work at the brickmold. This is what he did to all the Ammonite cities. David and all the soldiers then returned to Jerusalem.

CHAPTER 13

See RG
180–82

The Crime of Amnon. [1]Some time later the following incident occurred. David's son Absalom had a beautiful sister named Tamar, and David's son Amnon loved her.[c] [2]He was in such straits over his sister Tamar that he became sick; since she was a virgin, Amnon thought it impossible to carry out his designs toward her. [3]Now Amnon had a friend named Jonadab, son of David's brother Shimeah, who was very clever.[d] [4]He asked him, "Prince, why are you so dejected morning after morning? Why not tell me?" So Amnon said to him, "I am in love with Tamar, my brother Absalom's sister." [5]Then Jonadab replied, "Lie down on your bed and pretend to be sick. When your father comes to visit you, say to him, 'Please let my sister Tamar come and encourage me to take food. If she prepares something appetizing in my presence, for me to see, I will eat it from her hand.' " [6]So Amnon lay down and pretended to be sick. When the king came to visit him, Amnon said to the king, "Please let my sister Tamar come and prepare some fried cakes before my eyes, that I may take nourishment from her hand."

[7]David then sent home a message to Tamar, "Please go to the house of your brother Amnon and prepare some nourishment for him." [8]Tamar went to the house of her brother Amnon, who was in bed. Taking dough and kneading it, she twisted it into cakes before his eyes and fried the cakes. [9]Then she took the pan and set out the cakes before him. But Amnon would not eat; he said, "Have everyone leave me." When they had all left him, [10]Amnon said to Tamar, "Bring the nourishment into the bedroom, that I may have it from your hand." So Tamar picked up the cakes she had prepared and brought them to her brother Amnon in the bedroom. [11]But when she brought them to him to eat, he seized her and said to her, "Come! Lie with me, my sister!" [12]But she answered him, "No, my brother! Do not shame me! That is an intolerable crime in Israel. Do not commit this insensate deed.[e] [13]Where would I take my shame? And you would be a discredited man in Israel. So

---

12, 30: Weighed a talent: since this would be more than 75 pounds, some commentators picture the idol's crown as displaying a single precious stone of large size, which David took to wear; but the text does not say this.

a: Jb 7, 9.   *b:* 26-31: 1 Chr 20, 1-3.   *c:* 2 Sm 3, 2f; 1 Chr 3, 9.   *d:* 1 Sm 21, 21.   *e:* Lv 18, 9; 20, 17; Dt 27, 22.

please, speak to the king; he will not keep me from you."*f*

[14]Not heeding her plea, he overpowered her; he shamed her and had relations with her. [15]Then Amnon conceived an intense hatred for her, which far surpassed the love he had had for her. "Get up and leave," he said to her. [16]She replied, "No, brother, because to drive me out would be far worse than the first injury you have done me." He would not listen to her, [17]but called the youth who was his attendant and said, "Put her outside, away from me, and bar the door after her." [18]Now she had on a long tunic, for that is how maiden princesses dressed in olden days. When his attendant put her out and barred the door after her, [19]Tamar put ashes on her head and tore the long tunic in which she was clothed. Then, putting her hands to her head, she went away crying loudly. [20]Her brother Absalom said to her: "Has your brother Amnon been with you? Be still now, my sister; he is your brother. Do not take this affair to heart." But Tamar remained grief-stricken and forlorn in the house of her brother Absalom. [21]King David, who got word of the whole affair, became very angry. He did not, however, spark the resentment of his son Amnon, whom he favored because he was his first-born. [22]Absalom, moreover, said nothing at all to Amnon, although he hated him for having shamed his sister Tamar.

Absalom's Plot. [23]After a period of two years Absalom had shearers in Baal-hazor near Ephraim, and he invited all the princes. [24]Absalom went to the king and said: "Your servant is having shearers. Please, your majesty, come with all your retainers to your servant." [25]But the king said to Absalom, "No, my son, all of us should not go lest we be a burden to you." And though Absalom urged him, he refused to go and began to bid him goodbye. [26]Absalom then said, "If you will not come yourself, please let my brother Amnon come to us." The king asked him, "Why should he go to you?" [27]At Absalom's urging, however, he sent Amnon and all the other princes with him. Absalom prepared a banquet fit for royalty. [28]*g*But he had instructed his servants: "Now watch! When Amnon is merry with wine and I say to you, 'Kill Amnon,' put him to death. Do not be afraid, for it is I who order you to do it. Be resolute and act manfully."

Death of Amnon. [29]When the servants did to Amnon as Absalom had commanded, all the other princes rose, mounted their mules, and fled. [30]While they were still on the road, a report reached David that Absalom had killed all the princes and that not one of them had survived. [31]The king stood up, rent his garments, and then lay on the ground. All his servants standing by him also rent their garments.*h* [32]But Jonadab, son of David's brother Shimeah, spoke up: "Let not my lord think that all the young princes have been killed! Amnon alone is dead, for Absalom was determined on this ever since Amnon shamed his sister Tamar. [33]So let not my lord the king put faith in the report that all the princes are dead. Amnon alone is dead." [34]Meanwhile, Absalom had taken flight. Then the servant on watch looked about and saw a large group coming down the slope from the direction of Bahurim. He came in and reported this, telling the king that he had seen some men coming down the mountainside from the direction of Bahurim. [35]So Jonadab said to the king: "There! The princes have come. It is as your servant said." [36]No sooner had he finished speaking than the princes came in, weeping aloud. The king, too, and all his servants wept very bitterly. [37]But Absalom, who had taken flight, went to Talmai, son of Ammihud, king of Geshur,*i* [38]and stayed in Geshur for three years.

Efforts for Absalom's Return. [39]The king continued during all that time to mourn over his son; but his longing reached out for Absalom as he became reconciled to the death of Amnon.

CHAPTER 14

See RG 180–82

[1]When Joab, son of Zeruiah, observed how the king felt toward Absalom, [2]he sent to Tekoa and brought from there a gifted woman, to whom he said: "Pretend to be in

f: Gn 34, 7.   *g*: 28f: 2 Sm 12, 10.   *h*: 2 Sm 1, 11.   *i*: 2 Sm 3, 3; 15, 8.

353

mourning. Put on mourning apparel and do not anoint yourself with oil, that you may appear to be a woman who has been long in mourning for a departed one. ³Then go to the king and speak to him in this manner." And Joab instructed her what to say.

⁴So the woman of Tekoa went to the king and fell prostrate to the ground in homage, saying, "Help, your majesty!" ⁵ʲThe king said to her, "What do you want?" She replied: "Alas, I am a widow; my husband is dead. ⁶Your servant had two sons, who quarreled in the field. There being no one to part them, one of them struck his brother and killed him. ⁷Then the whole clan confronted your servant and demanded: 'Give up the one who killed his brother. We must put him to death for the life of his brother whom he has slain; we must extinguish the heir also.' Thus they will quench my remaining hope* and leave my husband neither name nor posterity upon the earth."ᵏ ⁸The king then said to the woman: "Go home. I will issue a command on your behalf." ⁹The woman of Tekoa answered him, "Let me and my family be to blame, my lord king; you and your throne are innocent." ¹⁰Then the king said, "If anyone says a word to you, have him brought to me, and he shall not touch you again." ¹¹But she went on to say, "Please, your majesty, keep in mind the LORD your God, that the avenger of blood may not go too far in destruction and that my son may not be done away with." He replied, "As the LORD lives, not a hair of your son shall fall to the ground."

¹²The woman continued, "Please let your servant say still another word to my lord the king." He replied, "Speak." ¹³So the woman said: "Why, then, do you think of this same kind of thing against the people of God? In pronouncing as he has, the king shows himself guilty, for not bringing back his own banished son. ¹⁴We must indeed die; we are then like water that is poured out on the ground and cannot be gathered up. Yet, though God does not bring back life, he does take thought how not to banish* anyone from him.ˡ ¹⁵And now, if I have presumed to speak of this matter to your majesty, it is because the people have given me cause to fear. And so your servant thought: 'Let me speak to the king. Perhaps he will grant the petition of his maidservant. ¹⁶For the king must surely consent to free his servant from the grasp of one who would seek to destroy me and my son as well from God's inheritance.' " ¹⁷And the woman concluded: "Let the word of my lord the king provide a resting place;* indeed, my lord the king is like an angel of God, evaluating good and bad. The LORD your God be with you."ᵐ

¹⁸The king answered the woman, "Now do not conceal from me anything I may ask you!" The woman said, "Let my lord the king speak." ¹⁹So the king asked, "Is Joab involved with you in all this?" And the woman answered: "As you live, my lord the king, it is just as your majesty has said, and not otherwise. It was your servant Joab who instructed me and told your servant all these things she was to say. ²⁰Your servant Joab did this to come at the issue in a roundabout way. But my lord is as wise as an angel of God, so that he knows all things on earth."

Absalom's Return. ²¹Then the king said to Joab: "I hereby grant this request. Go, therefore, and bring back young Absalom." ²²Falling prostrate to the ground in homage and blessing the king, Joab said, "This day I know that I am in good favor with you, my lord the king, since the king has granted the request of his servant." ²³Joab then went off to Geshur and brought Absalom to Jerusalem. ²⁴But the king said, "Let him go to his own house; he shall not appear before me." So Absalom went off to his house and did not appear before the king.

²⁵In all Israel there was not a man who could so be praised for his beauty as Absa-

14, 7: Hope: literally, "glowing coal." The image is similar to that of the lighted lamp, e.g., Ps 89, 17, to keep alive the ancestral name.

14, 14: How not to banish: a possible allusion to the religious institution of cities of refuge for involuntary murderers; see Nm 35, 9-15.

14, 17: A resting place: cf Ps 95, 11; Heb 3, 7–4, 11. The reference here is to a return home for Absalom to Israel.

j: 5f: 2 Kgs 6, 26f.   *k:* Nm 35, 19.   *l:* Jb 7, 9; 14, 7-12; Ps 88, 5. 11ff.   *m:* 17. 20: 1 Sm 29, 9.

lom, who was without blemish from the sole of his foot to the crown of his head. [26]When he shaved his head—which he used to do at the end of every year, because his hair became too heavy for him—the hair weighed two hundred shekels according to the royal standard. [27]Absalom had three sons born to him, besides a daughter named Tamar, who was a beautiful woman.[n]

Absalom Is Pardoned. [28]Absalom lived in Jerusalem for two years without appearing before the king. [29]Then he summoned Joab to send him to the king, but Joab would not come to him. Although he summoned him a second time, Joab refused to come. [30]He therefore instructed his servants: "You see Joab's field that borders mine, on which he has barley. Go, set it on fire." And so Absalom's servants set the field on fire.[o] Joab's farmhands came to him with torn garments and reported to him what had been done. [31]At this, Joab went to Absalom in his house and asked him, "Why have your servants set my field on fire?" [32]Absalom answered Joab: "I was summoning you to come here, that I may send you to the king to say: 'Why did I come back from Geshur? I would be better off if I were still there!' Now, let me appear before the king. If I am guilty, let him put me to death." [33]Joab went to the king and reported this. The king then called Absalom, who came to him and in homage fell on his face to the ground before the king. Then the king kissed him.

CHAPTER 15

See RG
180–82
Absalom's Plot. [1]After this Absalom provided himself with chariots, horses, and fifty henchmen.[p] [2]Moreover, Absalom used to rise early and stand alongside the road leading to the gate. If someone had a lawsuit to be decided by the king, Absalom would call to him and say, "From what city are you?" And when he replied, "Your servant is of such and such a tribe of Israel," [3]Absalom would say to him, "Your suit is good and just, but there is no one to hear you in the king's name." [4]And he would continue: "If only I could be appointed judge in the land! Then everyone who has a lawsuit to be decided might come to me and I would render him justice." [5]Whenever a man approached him to show homage, he would extend his hand, hold him, and kiss him. [6]By behaving in this way toward all the Israelites who came to the king for judgment, Absalom was stealing away the loyalties of the men of Israel.

Conspiracy in Hebron. [7]After a period of four years, Absalom said to the king: "Allow me to go to Hebron and fulfill a vow I made to the LORD. [8]For while living in Geshur in Aram, your servant made this vow: 'If the LORD ever brings me back to Jerusalem, I will worship him in Hebron.' "[q] [9]The king wished him a safe journey, and he went off to Hebron. [10]Then Absalom sent spies throughout the tribes of Israel to say, "When you hear the sound of the horn, declare Absalom king in Hebron." [11]Two hundred men had accompanied Absalom from Jerusalem. They had been invited and went in good faith, knowing nothing of the plan. [12]Absalom also sent to Ahithophel the Gilonite, David's counselor, an invitation to come from his town, Giloh, for the sacrifices he was about to offer. So the conspiracy gained strength, and the people with Absalom increased in numbers.[r]

David Flees Jerusalem. [13]An informant came to David with the report, "The Israelites have transferred their loyalty to Absalom."[s] [14]At this, David said to all his servants who were with him in Jerusalem: "Up! Let us take flight, or none of us will escape from Absalom. Leave quickly, lest he hurry and overtake us, then visit disaster upon us and put the city to the sword." [15]The king's officers answered him, "Your servants are ready, whatever our lord the king chooses to do." [16]Then the king set out, accompanied by his entire household, except for ten concubines whom he left behind to take care of the palace.[t] [17]As the king left the city, with all his officers accompanying him, they halted opposite the ascent of the Mount of Olives, at a distance, [18]while the whole army marched past him.[u]

n: 2 Sm 18, 18.   *o:* Jgs 15, 4f.   *p:* 1 Sm 8, 11; 1 Kgs 1, 5.   *q:* 2 Sm 3, 3; 13, 37.   *r:* 2 Sm 16, 23.   *s:* Ps 3.   *t:* 2 Sm 16, 21f; 20, 3. *u:* 2 Sm 8, 18.

David and Ittai. As all the Cherethites and Pelethites, and the six hundred men of Gath who had accompanied him from that city, were passing in review before the king, [19]he said to Ittai the Gittite: "Why should you also go with us? Go back and stay with the king, for you are a foreigner and you, too, are an exile from your own country. [20]You came only yesterday, and shall I have you wander about with us today, wherever I have to go? Return and take your brothers with you, and may the LORD be kind and faithful to you." [21]But Ittai answered the king, "As the LORD lives, and as my lord the king lives, your servant shall be wherever my lord the king may be, whether for death or for life."[v] [22]So the king said to Ittai, "Go, then, march on." And Ittai the Gittite, with all his men and all the dependents that were with him, marched on. [23]Everyone in the countryside wept aloud as the last of the soldiers went by, and the king crossed the Kidron Valley with all the soldiers moving on ahead of him by way of the Mount of Olives, toward the desert.

David and the Priests. [24]Zadok, too [with all the Levite bearers of the ark of the covenant of God], and Abiathar brought the ark of God to a halt until the soldiers had marched out of the city. [25]Then the king said to Zadok: "Take the ark of God back to the city. If I find favor with the LORD, he will bring me back and permit me to see it and its lodging. [26]But if he should say, 'I am not pleased with you,' I am ready; let him do to me as he sees fit."[w] [27]The king also said to the priest Zadok: "See to it that you and Abiathar return to the city in peace, and both your sons with you, your own son Ahimaaz, and Abiathar's son Jonathan. [28]Remember, I shall be waiting at the fords near the desert until I receive information from you." [29]So Zadok and Abiathar took the ark of God back to Jerusalem and remained there.

[30]As David went up the Mount of Olives, he wept without ceasing. His head was covered, and he was walking barefoot. All those who were with him also had their heads covered and were weeping as they went.[x] [31]When David was informed that Ahithophel was among the conspirators with Absalom, he said, "O LORD, turn the counsel of Ahithophel to folly!"[y]

David and Hushai. [32]When David reached the top, where men used to worship God, Hushai the Archite was there to meet him, with rent garments and dirt upon his head.[z] [33]David said to him: "If you come with me, you will be a burden to me. [34]But if you return to the city and say to Absalom, 'Let me be your servant, O king; I was formerly your father's servant, but now I will be yours,' you will undo for me the counsel of Ahithophel.[a] [35]You will have the priests Zadok and Abiathar there with you. If you hear anything from the royal palace, you shall report it to the priests Zadok and Abiathar, [36]who have there with them both Zadok's son Ahimaaz and Abiathar's son Jonathan. Through them you shall send on to me whatever you hear." [37]So David's friend Hushai went into the city of Jerusalem as Absalom was about to enter it.

CHAPTER 16

See RG 180-82

David and Ziba. [1]David had gone a little beyond the top when Ziba, the servant of Meribbaal, met him with saddled asses laden with two hundred loaves of bread, an ephah of cakes of pressed raisins, an ephah of summer fruits, and a skin of wine.[b] [2]The king said to Ziba, "What do you plan to do with these?" Ziba replied: "The asses are for the king's household to ride on. The bread and summer fruits are for your servants to eat, and the wine for those to drink who are weary in the desert." [3]Then the king said, "And where is your lord's son?" Ziba answered the king, "He is staying in Jerusalem, for he said, 'Now the Israelites will restore to me my father's kingdom.'"[c] [4]The king therefore said to Ziba, "So! Everything Meribbaal had is yours." Then Ziba said: "I pay you homage, my lord the king. May I find favor with you!"[d]

David and Shimei. [5]As David was approaching Bahurim, a man named Shimei,

v: Ru 1, 16.   *w:* 2 Sm 16, 10.   *x:* 2 Sm 19, 5; Mi 1, 8.   *y:* 2 Sm 16, 23; 17, 14. 23.   *z:* 2 Sm 16, 16.   *a:* 2 Sm 16, 19.   *b:* 2 Sm 4, 4; 9, 1-13; 19, 18. 25.   *c:* 2 Sm 19, 26f.   *d:* 2 Sm 19, 30.

the son of Gera of the same clan as Saul's family, was coming out of the place, cursing as he came.*[e] *6*He threw stones at David and at all the king's officers, even though all the soldiers, including the royal guard, were on David's right and on his left. *7*Shimei was saying as he cursed: "Away, away, you murderous and wicked man! *8*The LORD has requited you for all the bloodshed in the family of Saul,*[*] in whose stead you became king, and the LORD has given over the kingdom to your son Absalom. And now you suffer ruin because you are a murderer." *9*Abishai, son of Zeruiah, said to the king: "Why should this dead dog curse my lord the king? Let me go over, please, and lop off his head."*[f] *10*But the king replied: "What business is it of mine or of yours, sons of Zeruiah, that he curses? Suppose the LORD has told him to curse David; who then will dare to say, 'Why are you doing this?' "*[g] *11*Then the king said to Abishai and to all his servants: "If my own son, who came forth from my loins, is seeking my life, how much more might this Benjaminite do so? Let him alone and let him curse, for the LORD has told him to.*[h] *12*Perhaps the LORD will look upon my affliction and make it up to me with benefits for the curses he is uttering this day." *13*David and his men continued on the road, while Shimei kept abreast of them on the hillside, all the while cursing and throwing stones and dirt as he went.*[i] *14*The king and all the soldiers with him arrived at the Jordan tired out, and stopped there for a rest.

Absalom's Counselors. *15*In the meantime Absalom, accompanied by Ahithophel, entered Jerusalem with all the Israelites. *16*When David's friend Hushai the Archite came to Absalom, he said to him: "Long live the king! Long live the king!"*[j] *17*But Absalom asked Hushai: "Is this your devotion to your friend? Why did you not go with your friend?" *18*Hushai replied to Absalom: "On the contrary, I am his whom the LORD and all this people and all Israel have chosen, and with him I will stay. *19*Furthermore, as I was

in attendance upon your father, so will I be before you. Whom should I serve, if not his son?"*[k] *20*Then Absalom said to Ahithophel, "Offer your counsel on what we should do." *21*Ahithophel replied to Absalom: "Have relations with your father's concubines, whom he left behind to take care of the palace. When all Israel hears how odious you have made yourself to your father, all your partisans will take courage."*[l] *22*So a tent was pitched on the roof for Absalom, and he visited his father's concubines in view of all Israel.*[m]

Counsel of Ahithophel. *23*Now the counsel given by Ahithophel at that time was as though one had sought divine revelation. Such was all his counsel both to David and to Absalom.*[n]

CHAPTER 17

See RG
180–82

*1*Ahithophel went on to say to Absalom: "Please let me choose twelve thousand men, and be off in pursuit of David tonight. *2*If I come upon him when he is weary and discouraged, I shall cause him to panic. When all the people with him flee, I shall strike down the king alone. *3*Then I can bring back the rest of the people to you, as a bride returns to her husband. It is the death of only one man you are seeking; then all the people will be at peace." *4*This plan was agreeable to Absalom and to all the elders of Israel.

Counsel of Hushai. *5*Then Absalom said, "Now call Hushai the Archite also; let us hear what he too has to say." *6*When Hushai came to Absalom, Absalom said to him: "This is what Ahithophel proposed. Shall we follow his proposal? If not, speak up." *7*Hushai replied to Absalom, "This time Ahithophel has not given good counsel." *8*And he went on to say: "You know that your father and his men are warriors, and that they are as fierce as a bear in the wild robbed of her cubs. Moreover, since your father is skilled in warfare, he will not spend the night with the people.*[o] *9*Even now he lies hidden in one of the caves or in some other place. And if some of our soldiers should fall

16, 8: Bloodshed . . . Saul: refers to the episode recounted in 2 Sm 21, 1-14.

e: 2 Sm 3, 16; 19, 17. 22f; 1 Kgs 2, 8.   *f:* 2 Sm 19, 23. 29; 1 Sm 24, 15; 26, 6.   *g:* 2 Sm 15, 25f; 19, 23.   *h:* 2 Sm 12, 11.   *i:* 2 Sm 19, 19-24.   *j:* 2 Sm 15, 32-37.   *k:* 2 Sm 15, 34.   *l:* 2 Sm 15, 16; 20, 3.   *m:* 2 Sm 12, 11f.   *n:* 2 Sm 15, 12. 31; 17, 23.   *o:* Hos 13, 8.

at the first attack, whoever hears of it will say, 'Absalom's followers have been slaughtered.' [10]Then even the brave man with the heart of a lion will lose courage. For all Israel knows that your father is a warrior and that those who are with him are brave.

[11]"This is what I counsel: Let all Israel from Dan to Beer-sheba, who are as numerous as the sands by the sea, be called up for combat; and go with them yourself. [12]We can then attack him wherever we find him, settling down upon him as dew alights on the ground. None shall survive—neither he nor any of his followers. [13]And if he retires into a city, all Israel shall bring ropes to that city and we can drag it into the gorge, so that not even a pebble of it can be found." [14]Then Absalom and all the Israelites pronounced the counsel of Hushai the Archite better than that of Ahithophel. For the LORD had decided to undo Ahithophel's good counsel, in order thus to bring Absalom to ruin.[p]

David Told of the Plan. [15]Then Hushai said to the priests Zadok and Abiathar: "This is the counsel Ahithophel gave Absalom and the elders of Israel, and this is what I counseled. [16]So send a warning to David immediately, not to spend the night at the fords near the desert, but to cross over without fail. Otherwise the king and all the people with him will be destroyed." [17]Now Jonathan and Ahimaaz were staying at En-rogel, since they could not risk being seen entering the city. A maidservant was to come with information for them, and they in turn were to go and report to King David. [18]But an attendant saw them and informed Absalom. They sped on their way and reached the house of a man in Bahurim who had a cistern in his courtyard. They let themselves down into this, [19]and the housewife took the cover and spread it over the cistern, strewing ground grain on the cover so that nothing could be noticed. [20]When Absalom's servants came to the woman at the house, they asked, "Where are Ahimaaz and Jonathan?" The woman replied, "They went by a short while ago toward the water." They searched, but found no one, and so returned to Jerusalem. [21]As soon

as they left, Ahimaaz and Jonathan came up out of the cistern and went on to inform King David. They said to him: "Leave! Cross the water at once, for Ahithophel has given the following counsel in regard to you." [22]So David and all his people moved on and crossed the Jordan. By daybreak, there was no one left who had not crossed.

[23]When Ahithophel saw that his counsel was not acted upon, he saddled his ass and departed, going to his home in his own city. Then, having left orders concerning his family, he hanged himself. And so he died and was buried in his father's tomb.[q]

[24]Now David had gone to Mahanaim when Absalom crossed the Jordan accompanied by all the Israelites. [25]Absalom had put Amasa in command of the army in Joab's place. Amasa was the son of an Ishmaelite named Ithra, who had married Abigail, daughter of Jesse and sister of Joab's mother Zeruiah.[r] [26]Israel and Absalom encamped in the territory of Gilead.

[27]When David came to Mahanaim, Shobi, son of Nahash from Rabbah of the Ammonites, Machir, son of Ammiel from Lodebar, and Barzillai, the Gileadite from Rogelim,[s] [28]brought couches, coverlets, basins and earthenware, as well as wheat, barley, flour, roasted grain, beans, lentils,[t] [29]honey, butter and cheese from the flocks and herds, for David and those who were with him to eat; for they said, "The people have been hungry and tired and thirsty in the desert."

CHAPTER 18

See RG 180–82

Preparation for Battle. [1]After mustering the troops he had with him, David placed officers in command of groups of a thousand and groups of a hundred. [2]David then put a third part of the soldiers under Joab's command, a third under command of Abishai, son of Zeruiah and brother of Joab, and a third under command of Ittai the Gittite. The king then said to the soldiers, "I intend to go out with you myself." [3]But they replied: "You must not come out with us. For if we should flee, we shall not count; even if half of us should die, we shall not count. You are

p: 2 Sm 15, 31.   *q:* 2 Sm 15, 31; 16, 23.   *r:* 2 Sm 19, 14; 20, 4-13.   *s:* 2 Sm 9, 4; 19, 32; 1 Kgs 2, 7.   *t:* 2 Sm 19, 32; Ezr 2, 61.

equal to ten thousand of us. Therefore it is better that we have you to help us from the city." [4]So the king said to them, "I will do what you think best"; and he stood by the gate as all the soldiers marched out in units of a hundred and of a thousand. [5]But the king gave this command to Joab, Abishai and Ittai: "Be gentle with young Absalom for my sake." All the soldiers heard the king instruct the various leaders with regard to Absalom.

Defeat of Absalom. [6]David's army then took the field against Israel, and a battle was fought in the forest near Mahanaim. [7]The forces of Israel were defeated by David's servants, and the casualties there that day were heavy—twenty thousand men. [8]The battle spread out over that entire region, and the thickets consumed more combatants that day than did the sword.

Death of Absalom. [9]Absalom unexpectedly came up against David's servants. He was mounted on a mule, and, as the mule passed under the branches of a large terebinth, his hair caught fast in the tree. He hung between heaven and earth while the mule he had been riding ran off. [10]Someone saw this and reported to Joab that he had seen Absalom hanging from a terebinth. [11]Joab said to his informant: "If you saw him, why did you not strike him to the ground on the spot? Then it would have been my duty to give you fifty pieces of silver and a belt." [12]But the man replied to Joab: "Even if I already held a thousand pieces of silver in my two hands, I would not harm the king's son, for the king charged you and Abishai and Ittai in our hearing to protect the youth Absalom for his sake. [13]Had I been disloyal and killed him, the whole matter would have come to the attention of the king, and you would stand aloof." [14]Joab replied, "I will not waste time with you in this way." And taking three pikes in hand, he thrust for the heart of Absalom, still hanging from the tree alive.[u] [15]Next, ten of Joab's young armor-bearers closed in on Absalom, and killed him with further blows. [16]Joab then sounded the horn, and the soldiers turned back from the pursuit of the Israel-ites, because Joab called on them to halt.[v] [17]Absalom was taken up and cast into a deep pit in the forest, and a very large mound of stones was erected over him. And all the Israelites fled to their own tents.[w]

[18]During his lifetime Absalom had taken a pillar and erected it for himself in the King's Valley, for he said, "I have no son to perpetuate my name." The pillar which he named for himself is called Yad-abshalom to the present day.[x]

David Told of Absalom's Death. [19]Then Ahimaaz, son of Zadok, said, "Let me run to take the good news to the king that the LORD has set him free from the grasp of his enemies." [20]But Joab said to him: "You are not the man to bring the news today. On some other day you may take the good news, but today you would not be bringing good news, for in fact the king's son is dead." [21]Then Joab said to a Cushite, "Go, tell the king what you have seen." The Cushite bowed to Joab and sped away. [22]But Ahimaaz, son of Zadok, said to Joab again, "Come what may, permit me also to run after the Cushite." Joab replied: "Why do you want to run, my son? You will receive no reward." [23]But he insisted, "Come what may, I want to run." Joab said to him, "Very well." Ahimaaz sped off by way of the Jordan plain and outran the Cushite.

[24]Now David was sitting between the two gates, and a lookout mounted to the roof of the gate above the city wall, where he looked about and saw a man running all alone. [25]The lookout shouted to inform the king, who said, "If he is alone, he has good news to report." As he kept coming nearer, [26]the lookout spied another runner. From his place atop the gate he cried out, "There is another man running by himself." And the king responded, "He, too, is bringing good news." [27]Then the lookout said, "I notice that the first one runs like Ahimaaz, son of Zadok." The king replied, "He is a good man; he comes with good news."[y] [28]Then Ahimaaz called out and greeted the king. With face to the ground he paid homage to the king and said, "Blessed be the LORD your God, who has delivered up

u: 2 Sm 12, 10; 13, 28f.   v: 2 Sm 20, 23-26.   w: Jos 7, 26; 8, 29; 10, 27.   x: 2 Sm 14, 27.   y: 2 Kgs 9, 20.

the men who rebelled against my lord the king." [29]But the king asked, "Is the youth Absalom safe?" And Ahimaaz replied, "I saw a great disturbance when the king's servant Joab sent your servant on, but I do not know what it was." [30]The king said, "Step aside and remain in attendance here." So he stepped aside and remained there. [31]When the Cushite came in, he said, "Let my lord the king receive the good news that this day the LORD has taken your part, freeing you from the grasp of all who rebelled against you." [32]But the king asked the Cushite, "Is young Absalom safe?" The Cushite replied, "May the enemies of my lord the king and all who rebel against you with evil intent be as that young man!"

See RG
180–82

CHAPTER 19

[1]The king was shaken, and went up to the room over the city gate to weep. He said as he wept, "My son Absalom! My son, my son Absalom! If only I had died instead of you, Absalom, my son, my son!"

Joab Reproves David. [2]Joab was told that the king was weeping and mourning for Absalom; [3]and that day's victory was turned into mourning for the whole army when they heard that the king was grieving for his son. [4]The soldiers stole into the city that day like men shamed by flight in battle. [5]Meanwhile the king covered his face and cried out in a loud voice, "My son Absalom! Absalom! My son, my son!"[z] [6]Then Joab went to his residence and said: "Though they saved your life and your sons' and daughters' lives, also the lives of your wives and those of your concubines, you have put all your servants to shame today [7]by loving those who hate you and hating those who love you. For you have shown today that officers and servants mean nothing to you. Indeed I am now certain that if Absalom were alive today and all of us dead, you would think that more suitable. [8]Now then, get up! Go out and speak kindly to your servants. I swear by the LORD that if you do not go out, not a single man will remain with you overnight, and this will be a far greater disaster for you than

any that has afflicted you from your youth until now." [9]So the king stepped out and sat at the gate. When all the people were informed that the king was sitting at the gate, they came into his presence.

The Reconciliation. Now the Israelites had fled to their separate tents, [10]but throughout the tribes of Israel all the people were arguing among themselves, saying to one another: "The king delivered us from the clutches of our enemies, and it was he who rescued us from the grip of the Philistines. But now he has fled from the country before Absalom, [11]and Absalom, whom we anointed over us, died in battle. Why, then, should you remain silent about restoring the king to his palace?" When the talk of all Israel reached the king, [12]David sent word to the priests Zadok and Abiathar: "Say to the elders of Judah: 'Why should you be last to restore the king to his palace? [13]You are my brothers, you are my bone and flesh. Why should you be last to restore the king?' [14]Also say to Amasa: 'Are you not my bone and flesh? May God do thus and so to me, if you do not become my general permanently in place of Joab.' "[a] [15]He won over all the Judahites as one man, and so they summoned the king to return, with all his servants.

David and Shimei. [16]When the king, on his return, reached the Jordan, Judah had come to Gilgal to meet him and to escort him across the Jordan. [17]Shimei, son of Gera, the Benjaminite from Bahurim, hurried down with the Judahites to meet King David,[b] [18]accompanied by a thousand men from Benjamin. Ziba, too, the servant of the house of Saul, accompanied by his fifteen sons and twenty servants, hastened to the Jordan before the king.[c] [19d]They crossed over the ford to bring the king's household over and to do whatever he wished. When Shimei, son of Gera, crossed the Jordan, he fell down before the king [20]and said to him: "May my lord not hold me guilty, and may he not remember and take to heart the wrong that your servant did the day my lord the king left Jerusalem. [21]For your servant knows that he has done wrong. Yet realize that I have been

---

z: 2 Sm 15, 30.   *a:* 2 Sm 17, 25; 20, 4.   *b:* 2 Sm 16, 5-13.   *c:* 2 Sm 16, 1-4; 19, 25-31.   *d:* 19ff: 2 Sm 16, 13; Ex 22, 27; 1 Kgs 2, 8.

the first of the whole house of Joseph to come down today to meet my lord the king." [22]But Abishai, son of Zeruiah, countered: "Shimei must be put to death for this. He cursed the LORD's anointed." [23]David replied: "What has come between you and me, sons of Zeruiah, that you would create enmity for me this day? Should anyone die today in Israel? Am I not aware that today I am king of Israel?"[e] [24]Then the king said to Shimei, "You shall not die." And the king gave him his oath.

David and Meribbaal. [25]Meribbaal, son of Saul, also went down to meet the king. He had not washed his feet nor trimmed his mustache nor washed his clothes from the day the king left until he returned safely. [26]When he came from Jerusalem to meet the king, the king asked him, "Why did you not go with me, Meribbaal?"[f] [27]He replied: "My lord the king, my servant betrayed me. For your servant, who is lame, said to him, 'Saddle the ass for me, that I may ride on it and go with the king.'[g] [28]But he slandered your servant before my lord the king. But my lord the king is like an angel of God. Do what you judge best. [29]For though my father's entire house deserved only death from my lord the king, yet you placed your servant among the guests at your table. What right do I still have to make further appeal to the king?"[h] [30]But the king said to him: "Why do you go on talking? I say, 'You and Ziba shall divide the property.' "[i] [31]Meribbaal answered the king, "Indeed let him have it all, now that my lord the king has returned safely to his palace."

David and Barzillai. [32]Barzillai the Gileadite also came down from Rogelim and escorted the king to the Jordan for his crossing, taking leave of him there.[j] [33]It was Barzillai, a very old man of eighty and very wealthy besides, who had provisioned the king during his stay in Mahanaim. [34]The king said to Barzillai, "Cross over with me, and I will provide for your old age as my guest in Jerusalem." [35]But Barzillai answered the king: "How much longer have I to live, that I should go up to Jerusalem with the king? [36]I am now eighty years old. Can I distinguish between good and bad? Can your servant taste what he eats and drinks, or still appreciate the voices of singers and songstresses? Why should your servant be any further burden to my lord the king? [37]In escorting the king across the Jordan, your servant is doing little enough! Why should the king give me this reward? [38]Please let your servant go back to die in his own city by the tomb of his father and mother. Here is your servant Chimham. Let him cross over with my lord the king. Do for him whatever you will." [39]Then the king said to him, "Chimham shall come over with me, and I will do for him as you would wish. And anything else you would like me to do for you, I will do." [40]Then all the people crossed over the Jordan, but the king remained; he kissed Barzillai and bade him Godspeed as he returned to his own district. [41]Finally the king crossed over to Gilgal, accompanied by Chimham.

Israel and Judah Quarrel. All the people of Judah and half of the people of Israel had escorted the king across. [42]But all these Israelites began coming to the king and saying, "Why did our brothers the Judahites steal you away and escort the king and his household across the Jordan, along with all David's men?" [43]All the Judahites replied to the men of Israel: "Because the king is our relative. Why are you angry over this affair? Have we had anything to eat at the king's expense? Or have portions from his table been given to us?" [44]The Israelites answered the Judahites: "We have ten shares in the king. Also, we are the first-born rather than you. Why do you slight us? Were we not first to speak of restoring the king?" Then the Judahites in turn spoke even more fiercely than the Israelites.[k]

CHAPTER 20

See RG 180–82

Sheba's Rebellion. [1]Now a rebellious individual from Benjamin named Sheba, the son of Bichri, happened to be there. He sounded the horn and cried out,

---

e: 2 Sm 16, 9f; 1 Sm 11, 13; 1 Kgs 2, 8. 38. 46.   f: 2 Sm 16, 3.   g: 2 Sm 9, 2-13; Dt 21, 12f.   h: 2 Sm 9, 9ff.   i: 2 Sm 16, 4.   j: 2 Sm 17, 27ff; 1 Kgs 2, 7; Ezr 2, 61.   k: 1 Kgs 11, 31.

"We have no portion in David,
  nor any share in the son of Jesse.
  Every man to his tent, O Israel!"*l*

2 So all the Israelites left David for Sheba, son of Bichri. But from the Jordan to Jerusalem the Judahites remained loyal to their king. *3* When King David came to his palace in Jerusalem, he took the ten concubines whom he had left behind to take care of the palace and placed them in confinement. He provided for them, but had no further relations with them. And so they remained in confinement to the day of their death, lifelong widows.*m*

Amasa's Death. *4* Then the king said to Amasa: "Summon the Judahites for me within three days. Then present yourself here."*n* *5* Accordingly Amasa set out to summon Judah, but delayed beyond the time set for him by David. *6* Then David said to Abishai: "Sheba, son of Bichri, may now do us more harm than Absalom did. Take your lord's servants and pursue him, lest he find fortified cities and take shelter while we look on." *7* So Joab and the Cherethites and Pelethites and all the warriors marched out behind Abishai from Jerusalem to campaign in pursuit of Sheba, son of Bichri.*o* *8** They were at the great stone in Gibeon when Amasa met them. Now Joab had a belt over his tunic, from which was slung, in its sheath near his thigh, a sword that could be drawn with a downward movement.*p* *9* And Joab asked Amasa, "How are you, my brother?" With his right hand Joab held Amasa's beard as if to kiss him. *10* And since Amasa was not on his guard against the sword in Joab's other hand, Joab stabbed him in the abdomen with it, so that his entrails burst forth to the ground, and he died without receiving a second thrust. Then Joab and his brother Abishai pursued Sheba, son of Bichri.*q* *11* One of Joab's attendants stood by Amasa and said, "Let him who favors Joab and is for David follow Joab." *12* Amasa lay covered with blood in the middle of the high-road, and the man noticed that all the soldiers were stopping. So he removed Amasa from the road to the field and placed a garment over him, because all who came up to him were stopping. *13* When he had been removed from the road, everyone went on after Joab in pursuit of Sheba, son of Bichri.

Joab Pursues Sheba. *14* Sheba passed through all the tribes of Israel to Abel Beth-maacah. Then all the Bichrites assembled and they too entered the city after him. *15* So David's servants came and besieged him in Abel Beth-maacah. They threw up a mound against the city, and all the soldiers who were with Joab began battering the wall to throw it down. *16* Then a wise woman from the city stood on the outworks and called out, "Listen, listen! Tell Joab to come here, that I may speak with him." *17* When Joab had come near her, the woman said, "Are you Joab?" And he replied, "Yes." She said to him, "Listen to what your maidservant has to say." He replied, "I am listening." *18* Then she went on to say: "There is an ancient saying,* 'Let them ask if they will in Abel*r* *19* or in Dan whether loyalty is finished or ended in Israel.' You are seeking to beat down a city that is a mother in Israel. Why do you wish to destroy the inheritance of the LORD?" *20* Joab answered, "Not at all, not at all! I do not wish to destroy or to ruin anything. *21* That is not the case at all. A man named Sheba, son of Bichri, from the hill country of Ephraim has rebelled against King David. Surrender him alone, and I will withdraw from the city." Then the woman said to Joab, "His head shall be thrown to you across the wall." *22* She went to all the people with her advice, and they cut off the head of Sheba, son of Bichri, and threw it out to Joab. He then sounded the horn, and they scattered from the city to their own tents, while Joab returned to Jerusalem to the king.

David's Officials. *23* Joab was in command of the whole army of Israel. Banaiah, son of Jehoiada, was in command of the Cherethites and Pelethites.*s* *24* Adoram was in charge of

---

20, 8: The text of this verse is quite uncertain.
20, 18f: The proverbial expression here has been poorly transmitted, and its sense is doubtful.

l: 1 Kgs 12, 16. *m:* 2 Sm 15, 16; 16, 20ff. *n:* 2 Sm 17, 25; 19, 14. *o:* 2 Sm 8, 18. *p:* 2 Sm 2, 13. *q:* 1 Kgs 2, 5. *r:* Gn 49, 16.
s: 2 Sm 8, 16ff; 23, 20.

the forced labor. Jehoshaphat, son of Ahilud, was the chancellor. ²⁵Shawsha was the scribe. Zadok and Abiathar were priests.ᵗ ²⁶Ira the Jairite was also David's priest.

V: Appendixes

CHAPTER 21

See RG 182-83

Gibeonite Vengeance. ¹During David's reign there was a famine for three successive years. David had recourse to the Lord, who said, "There is bloodguilt on Saul and his family because he put the Gibeonites to death."ᵘ ²So the king called the Gibeonites and spoke to them. (Now the Gibeonites were not Israelites, but survivors of the Amorites; and although the Israelites had given them their oath, Saul had attempted to kill them off in his zeal for the men of Israel and Judah.)ᵛ ³David said to the Gibeonites, "What must I do for you and how must I make atonement, that you may bless the inheritance of the Lord?" ⁴The Gibeonites answered him, "We have no claim against Saul and his house for silver or gold, nor is it our place to put any man to death in Israel." Then he said, "I will do for you whatever you propose." ⁵They said to the king, "As for the man who was exterminating us and who intended to destroy us that we might have no place in all the territory of Israel, ⁶let seven men from among his descendants be given to us, that we may dismember them before the Lord in Gibeon, on the Lord's mountain." The king replied, "I will give them up." ⁷The king, however, spared Meribbaal, son of Jonathan, son of Saul, because of the Lord's oath that formed a bond between David and Saul's son Jonathan.ʷ ⁸But the king took Armoni and Meribbaal, the two sons that Aiah's daughter Rizpah had borne to Saul, and the five sons of Saul's daughter Merob that she had borne to Adriel, son of Barzillai the Meholathite,ˣ ⁹and surrendered them to the Gibeonites. They then dismembered them on the mountain before the Lord. The seven fell at the one time; they were put to death during the first days of the harvest—that is, at the beginning of the barley harvest.

¹⁰Then Rizpah, Aiah's daughter, took sackcloth and spread it out for herself on the rock from the beginning of the harvest until rain came down on them from the sky, fending off the birds of the sky from settling on them by day, and the wild animals by night.ʸ ¹¹When David was informed of what Rizpah, Aiah's daughter, the concubine of Saul, had done, ¹²he went and obtained the bones of Saul and of his son Jonathan from the citizens of Jabesh-gilead, who had carried them off secretly from the public square of Beth-shan, where the Philistines had hanged them at the time they killed Saul on Gilboa.ᶻ ¹³When he had brought up from there the bones of Saul and of his son Jonathan, the bones of those who had been dismembered were also gathered up. ¹⁴Then the bones of Saul and of his son Jonathan were buried in the tomb of his father Kish at Zela in the territory of Benjamin. After all that the king commanded had been carried out, God granted relief to the land.ᵃ

Exploits in Philistine Wars. ¹⁵There was another battle between the Philistines and Israel. David went down with his servants and fought the Philistines, but David grew tired. ¹⁶Dadu, one of the Rephaim, whose bronze spear weighed three hundred shekels, was about to take him captive. Dadu was girt with a new sword and planned to kill David, ¹⁷but Abishai, son of Zeruiah, came to his assistance and struck and killed the Philistine. Then David's men swore to him, "You must not go out to battle with us again, lest you quench the lamp of Israel."ᵇ

¹⁸ᶜAfter this there was another battle with the Philistines in Gob. On that occasion Sibbecai, from Husha, killed Saph, one of the Rephaim.ᵈ ¹⁹ᵉThere was another battle with the Philistines in Gob, in which Elhanan, son of Jair from Bethlehem, killed Goliath of Gath, who had a spear with a shaft like a weaver's heddle-bar. ²⁰There was another battle at Gath in which there was a man of

t: 2 Sm 8, 17f. u: 2 Sm 24, 13. v: Jos 9, 3-27. w: 2 Sm 9, 13; 1 Sm 18, 3; 20, 8ff. 15f. 42. x: 2 Sm 3, 7. y: 2 Sm 3, 31; 12, 16. z: 1 Sm 31, 10-13. a: 2 Sm 24, 25. b: 1 Kgs 11, 36; 15, 4; 2 Kgs 8, 19. c: 18-22: 1 Chr 20, 4-8. d: 2 Sm 23, 27. e: 19f: 1 Sm 17, 4. 7.

large stature with six fingers on each hand and six toes on each foot—twenty-four in all. He too was one of the Rephaim. *21* And when he insulted Israel, Jonathan, son of David's brother Shimei, killed him.*f* *22* These four were Rephaim in Gath, and they fell at the hands of David and his servants.

See RG 182-83

CHAPTER 22

*Song of Thanksgiving.** *1* David sang the words of this song to the LORD when the LORD had rescued him from the grasp of all his enemies and from the hand of Saul.*g* *2* This is what he sang:*h*

A

I

"O LORD, my rock, my fortress, my deliverer,
3   my God, my rock of refuge!
My shield, the horn of my salvation,*
   my stronghold, my refuge,
   my savior, from violence you keep me safe.*i*
4 'Praised be the LORD,' I exclaim,
   and I am safe from my enemies.

II

5 "The breakers of death surged round about me,*
   the floods of perdition overwhelmed me;
6 The cords of the nether world enmeshed me,
   the snares of death overtook me.
7 In my distress I called upon the LORD
   and cried out to my God;

From his temple* he heard my voice,
   and my cry reached his ears.

III

8 "The earth swayed and quaked;*
   the foundations of the heavens trembled
   and shook when his wrath flared up.
9 Smoke rose from his nostrils,
   and a devouring fire from his mouth;
   he kindled coals into flame.
10 He inclined the heavens and came down,
   with dark clouds under his feet.*j*

11 He mounted a cherub* and flew,
   borne on the wings of the wind.*k*
12 He made darkness the shelter about him,
   with spattering rain and thickening clouds.
13 From the brightness of his presence
   coals were kindled to flame.

14 "The LORD thundered from heaven;
   the Most High gave forth his voice.
15 He sent forth arrows to put them to flight;
   he flashed lightning and routed them.*l*
16 Then the wellsprings of the sea appeared,
   the foundations of the earth were laid bare,
At the rebuke of the LORD,
   at the blast of the wind of his wrath.

17 "He reached out from on high and grasped me;
   he drew me out of the deep waters.*m*
18 He rescued me from my mighty enemy,
   from my foes, who were too powerful for me.

22, 1-51: This song of thanksgiving is also given, with a few small variants, in Ps 18. In both places it is attributed to David. Two main sections can be distinguished. In the first part, after an introductory stanza of praise to God (2-4), David describes the peril he was in (5-7), and then poetically depicts, under the form of a theophany, God's intervention in his behalf (8-20), concluding with an acknowledgment of God's justice (21-31). In the second part, God is praised for having prepared the psalmist for war (32-35), given him victory over his enemies (36-39), whom he put to flight (40-43), and bestowed on him dominion over many peoples (44-46). The entire song ends with paean of grateful praise (47-51).

22, 3: The horn of my salvation: my strong savior. The horn, the dreadful weapon of an enraged bull, was a symbol of strength; cf Lk 1, 69.

22, 5f: These verses are to be understood figuratively.
22, 7: His temple: his heavenly abode.
22, 8ff: God's intervention is graphically portrayed under the figures of an earthquake (vv 8. 16) and a thunderstorm (vv 9-15); cf Jgs 5, 4f; Pss 29; 97, 2-6; Hb 3.
22, 11: He mounted a cherub: since God makes the winds his messengers, or "angels" (Ps 104, 4), he is spoken of poetically as riding on the clouds, or on the angelic creatures called "cherubim." His earthly throne above the ark of the covenant was likewise associated with two winged cherubim; cf Ex 37, 7ff. In both senses the Lord is enthroned upon the cherubim; cf Pss 79, 2; 99, 1.

f: 2 Sm 13, 3.   *g:* Ps 18, 1.   *h:* 2-51: Ps 18, 3-51.   *i:* 1 Sm 2, 1f.   *j:* Ps 144, 5.   *k:* Ex 25, 18.   *l:* Ps 144, 6.   *m:* Ps 144, 7.

[19] They attacked me on my day of calamity,
but the LORD came to my support.
[20] He set me free in the open,
and rescued me, because he loves me.

IV

[21] "The LORD rewarded me according to my
justice;
according to the cleanness of my
hands he requited me.
[22] For I kept the ways of the LORD
and was not disloyal to my God.
[23] For his ordinances were all present to
me,
and his statutes I put not from me;
[24] But I was wholehearted toward him,
and I was on my guard against guilt.
[25] And the LORD requited me according to
my justice,
according to my innocence in his
sight.

[26] n"Toward the faithful you are faithful;*
toward the wholehearted you are
wholehearted;
[27] Toward the sincere you are sincere;
but toward the crooked you are astute.
[28] You save lowly people,
though on the lofty your eyes look
down.
[29] You are my lamp,* O LORD!
O my God, you brighten the darkness
about me.
[30] For with your aid I run against an armed
band,
and by the help of my God I leap over
a wall.
[31] God's way is unerring;
the promise of the LORD is fire-tried;
he is a shield to all who take refuge in
him."o

B

I

[32] "For who is God except the LORD?
Who is a rock save our God?

[33] The God who girded me with strength
and kept my way unerring;
[34] Who made my feet swift as those of
hinds
and set me on the heights;*
[35] Who trained my hands for war
till my arms could bend a bow of
brass.

II

[36] "You have given me your saving shield,
and your help has made me great.
[37] You made room for my steps;
unwavering was my stride.
[38] I pursued my enemies and destroyed
them,
nor did I turn again till I made an end
of them.
[39] I smote them and they did not rise;
they fell beneath my feet.

III

[40] "You girded me with strength for war;
you subdued my adversaries beneath
me.
[41] My enemies you put to flight before me
and those who hated me I destroyed.
[42] They cried for help—but no one saved
them;
to the LORD—but he answered them
not.
[43] I ground them fine as the dust of the
earth;
like the mud in the streets I trampled
them down.

IV

[44] "You rescued me from the strife of my
people;
you made me head over nations.
A people I had not known became my
slaves;
[45] as soon as they heard me, they obeyed.
[46] The foreigners fawned and cringed
before me;
they staggered forth from their
fortresses."

22, 26f: Men are treated by God in the same way they treat
him and their fellow men.
22, 29: My lamp: a figure of life and happiness; cf 1 Kgs
11, 36.

22, 34: The heights: a natural stronghold safe from attack;
cf Ps 62, 3; Hb 3, 19.

n: 26f: 1 Sm 2, 30.   o: Prv 30, 5.

C

47 "The LORD live! And blessed be my
      Rock!
    Extolled be my God, Rock of my
      salvation.
48 O God, who granted me vengeance,
    who made peoples subject to me
49   and helped me escape from my
      enemies,
    Above my adversaries you exalt me
    and from the violent man you rescue
      me.
50 Therefore will I proclaim you, O LORD,
    among the nations,
    and I will sing praise to your name,[p]
51 You who gave great victories to your
      king
    and showed kindness to your anointed,
    to David and his posterity forever."

CHAPTER 23

See RG
182–83
The Last Words of David[*]

1 These are the last words of David:
  "The utterance of David, son of Jesse;
    the utterance of the man God raised up,
  Anointed of the God of Jacob,
    favorite of the Mighty One of Israel.[q]
2 The spirit of the LORD spoke through me;
    his word was on my tongue.[r]
3 The God of Israel spoke;
    of me the Rock of Israel said,
  'He that rules over men in justice,
    that rules in the fear of God,[s]
4 Is like the morning light at sunrise
    on a cloudless morning,
    making the greensward sparkle after
      rain.'[t]
5 Is not my house firm before God?
  He has made an eternal covenant
      with me,
    set forth in detail and secured.[u]
  Will he not bring to fruition
    all my salvation and my every desire?

6 But the wicked are all like thorns to be
    cast away;
  they cannot be taken up by hand.[v]
7 He who wishes to touch them
    must arm himself with iron and the
      shaft of a spear,
  and they must be consumed by fire."

David's Warriors. [8]These are the names of
David's warriors.[*] Ishbaal, son of Hachamoni, was the first of the Three. It was he who
brandished his battle-ax over eight hundred
slain in a single encounter.[w] [9]Next to him,
among the Three warriors, was Eleazar, son
of Dodo the Ahohite. He was with David at
Ephesdammim when the Philistines assembled there for battle. The Israelites had retreated,[x] [10]but he stood his ground and fought
the Philistines until his hand grew tired and
became cramped, holding fast to the sword.
The LORD brought about a great victory on
that day; the soldiers turned back after Eleazar, but only to strip the slain. [11]Next to him
was Shammah, son of Agee the Hararite. The
Philistines had assembled at Lehi, where
there was a plot of land full of lentils. When
the soldiers fled from the Philistines,[y] [12]he
took his stand in the middle of the plot and defended it. He slew the Philistines, and the
LORD brought about a great victory. Such
were the deeds of the Three warriors.

[13]During the harvest three of the Thirty
went down to David in the cave of Adullam,
while a Philistine clan was encamped in the
Vale of Rephaim.[z] [14]At that time David was in
the refuge, and there was a garrison of Philistines in Bethlehem. [15]Now David had a
strong craving and said, "Oh, that someone
would give me a drink of water from the cistern that is by the gate of Bethlehem!" [16]So
the Three warriors broke through the Philistine camp and drew water from the cistern
that is by the gate of Bethlehem. But when
they brought it to David he refused to drink it,

23, 1-7: The text of this short composition in the spirit of
the wisdom writers (Prv 30, 1-6) is difficult in places; it views
David's career in retrospect.

23, 8ff: There are thirty-seven warriors in all mentioned in
this list. First there are the Three warriors most noted for sin-
glehanded exploits (vv 8-12). Then comes the story of a daring adventure by three unnamed members of the larger group
(vv 13-17). Next come the commanders of the king's body-

guard, Abishai (vv 18-19) and Benaiah (vv 20-23), with
whom must be counted Asahel (v 24) and Joab (vv 18. 24.
37), and finally the group of the Thirty (vv 24-39).

---

p: Ps 22, 23; Rom 15, 9.   q: 1 Kgs 2, 3-9; Sir 47, 8.   r: Is 59, 21;
Jer 1, 9.   s: Ps 72, 1-4.   t: Jgs 5, 31; Ps 72, 6.   u: 2 Sm 7, 11.
15f; Ps 89, 30; Is 55, 3.   v: Dt 13, 14.   w: 8-39: 1 Chr 11, 41; 27,
1-15.   x: 1 Sm 17, 1.   y: Jgs 15, 9.   z: 1 Sm 22, 1; Mi 1, 15.

and instead poured it out to the LORD, [17]saying: "The LORD forbid that I do this! Can I drink the blood of these men who went at the risk of their lives?" So he refused to drink it.

[18]Abishai, brother of Joab, son of Zeruiah, was at the head of the Thirty. It was he who brandished his spear over three hundred slain. He was listed among the Thirty [19]and commanded greater respect than the Thirty, becoming their leader. However, he did not attain to the Three.

[20]Benaiah, son of Jehoiada, a stalwart from Kabzeel, was a man of great achievements. It was he who slew the two lions in Moab. He also went down and killed the lion in the cistern at the time of the snow.[a] [21]It was he, too, who slew an Egyptian of large stature. Although the Egyptian was armed with a spear, he went against him with a club and wrested the spear from the Egyptian's hand, then killed him with his own spear. [22]Such were the deeds performed by Benaiah, son of Jehoiada. He was listed among the Thirty warriors [23]and commanded greater respect than the Thirty. However, he did not attain to the Three. David put him in command of his bodyguard.[b] [24]Asahel,* brother of Joab. . . .[c]

Among the Thirty were: Elhanan, son of Dodo, from Bethlehem; [25]Shammah from En-harod; Elika from En-harod; [26]Helez from Beth-pelet; Ira, son of Ikkesh, from Tekoa; [27]Abiezer from Anathoth; Sibbekai from Hushah;[d] [28]Zalmon from Ahoh; Maharai from Netophah; [29]Heled, son of Baanath, from Netophah; Ittai, son of Ribai, from Gibeah of the Benjaminites; [30]Benaiah from Pirathon; Hiddai from Nahale-gaash; [31]Abibaal from Beth-arabah; Azmaveth from Bahurim; [32]Eliahba from Shaalbon; Jashen the Gunite; Jonathan, [33]son of Shammah the Hararite; Ahiam, son of Sharar the Hararite; [34]Eliphelet, son of Ahasbai, from Beth-maacah; Eliam, son of Ahithophel, from Gilo; [35]Hezrai from Carmel; Paarai the Arbite; [36]Igal, son of Nathan, from Zobah; Bani the

Gadite; [37]Zelek the Ammonite; Naharai from Beeroth, armor-bearer of Joab, son of Zeruiah; [38]Ira from Jattir; Gareb from Jattir; [39]Uriah the Hittite—thirty-seven in all.[e]

CHAPTER 24

Census of the People. [1]*The LORD's anger against Israel flared again,[f] and he incited David against the Israelites by prompting him to number Israel and Judah. [2]Accordingly the king said to Joab and the leaders of the army who were with him, "Tour all the tribes in Israel from Dan to Beer-sheba and register the people, that I may know their number." [3]But Joab said to the king: "May the LORD your God increase the number of people a hundredfold for your royal majesty to see it with his own eyes. But why does it please my lord the king to order a thing of this kind?" [4]The king, however, overruled Joab and the leaders of the army, so they left the king's presence in order to register the people of Israel. [5]Crossing the Jordan, they began near Aroer, south of the city in the wadi, and went in the direction of Gad, toward Jazer. [6]They continued on to Gilead and to the district below Mount Hermon. Then they proceeded to Dan; from there they turned toward Sidon, [7]going to the fortress of Tyre and to all the cities of the Hivites and Canaanites, and ending up at Beer-sheba in the Negeb of Judah. [8]Thus they toured the whole country, reaching Jerusalem again after nine months and twenty days. [9]Joab then reported to the king the number of people registered: in Israel, eight hundred thousand men fit for military service; in Judah, five hundred thousand.

The Pestilence. [10]Afterward, however, David regretted having numbered the people, and said to the LORD: "I have sinned grievously in what I have done.[g] But now, LORD, forgive the guilt of your servant, for I have been very foolish."* [11]When David rose in the morning, the LORD had spoken to

See RG 182–83

23, 24: A more complete notice about Asahel, who died early in his career (2 Sm 2, 16-23), is to be presumed lost at this point. Elhanan is the first of the Thirty.

24, 1ff: This story was probably joined at one time to 2 Sm 21, 1-14.

24, 10: The narrative supposes that since the people be-

longed to the Lord rather than to the king, only the Lord should know their exact number.

---

a: 2 Sm 8, 18; 20, 23; Jgs 14, 6; 1 Kgs 2, 29f.   *b:* 1 Sm 22, 14.
c: 2 Sm 2, 18-23.   *d:* 2 Sm 21, 18.   *e:* 2 Sm 11, 3f.   *f:* 1-25:
1 Chr 21, 1-27.   *g:* 1 Sm 24, 6; 1 Chr 21, 7.

the prophet Gad, David's seer, saying: *12*"Go and say to David, 'This is what the LORD says: I offer you three alternatives; choose one of them, and I will inflict it on you.' " *13*Gad then went to David to inform him. He asked: "Do you want a three years' famine to come upon your land, or to flee from your enemy three months while he pursues you, or to have a three days' pestilence in your land? Now consider and decide what I must reply to him who sent me."*h* *14*David answered Gad: "I am in very serious difficulty. Let us fall by the hand of God, for he is most merciful; but let me not fall by the hand of man." *15*Thus David chose the pestilence. Now it was the time of the wheat harvest when the plague broke out among the people. [The LORD then sent a pestilence over Israel from morning until the time appointed, and seventy thousand of the people from Dan to Beer-sheba died.] *16*But when the angel stretched forth his hand toward Jerusalem to destroy it, the LORD regretted the calamity and said to the angel causing the destruction among the people, "Enough now! Stay your hand." The angel of the LORD was then standing at the threshing floor of Araunah the Jebusite.*i* *17*When David saw the angel who was striking the people, he said to the LORD: "It is I who have sinned; it is I, the shepherd, who have done wrong. But these are sheep; what

have they done? Punish me and my kindred."*

Sacrifice of Atonement. *18*On the same day Gad went to David and said to him, "Go up and build an altar to the LORD on the threshing floor of Araunah the Jebusite." *19*Following Gad's bidding, David went up as the LORD had commanded. *20*Now Araunah looked down and noticed the king and his servants coming toward him while he was threshing wheat. So he went out and paid homage to the king, with face to the ground. *21*Then Araunah asked, "Why does my lord the king come to his servant?" David replied, "To buy the threshing floor from you, to build an altar to the LORD, that the plague may be checked among the people." *22j*But Araunah said to David: "Let my lord the king take and offer up whatever he may wish. Here are oxen for holocausts, and threshing sledges and the yokes of the oxen for wood. *23*All this does Araunah give to the king." Araunah then said to the king, "May the LORD your God accept your offering." *24*The king, however, replied to Araunah, "No, I must pay you for it, for I cannot offer to the LORD my God holocausts that cost nothing." So David bought the threshing floor and the oxen for fifty silver shekels. *25*Then David built an altar there to the LORD, and offered holocausts and peace offerings. The LORD granted relief to the country, and the plague was checked in Israel.

24, 17: Before this verse a Qumran manuscript (4Q Samᵃ) gives the fuller text of 1 Chr 21, 16, an alternative to the words "When David saw the angel who was striking the people."

h: 2 Sm 21, 1.   *i:* Ex 12, 23; 2 Kgs 19, 35.   *j:* 22f: 1 Sm 6, 14; 1 Kgs 19, 21.

See RG 183–98

The Books of Kings

The two Books of Kings were originally, like 1 and 2 Samuel, a single historical work. In conjunction with the Books of Samuel, they extend the consecutive history of Israel from the birth of Samuel to the destruction of Jerusalem in 587 B.C. This combined work is designed as a religious history; hence in Kings the temple, which is the chosen site for the worship of Yahweh, occupies the center of attention.

The Books of Kings show clearly the theological bent of a Deuteronomic editor. In them, as already in Judges, material from various sources, such as the "book of the acts of Solomon" (1 Kgs 11, 41) and the "book of the chronicles of the kings of Israel" (1 Kgs 14, 19), is forged into structural unity by an editor whose principal interest is in the fidelity to Yahweh of rulers and people. The reigns of individual kings are adapted to an editorial framework consisting of a presentation and an obituary notice for each, in stereotyped formulas. In between, the achievements of the king are reported—above all, his fidelity or lack of fidelity to Yahweh. The faithful prosper; the unfaithful pay for their defections. Since this is basically a narrative of sin and retribution, it would not be inappropriate to entitle the Books of Kings "The Rise and Fall of the Israelite Monarchy."

Without minimizing the complexity of the process by which this material was transmitted for many centuries, one may speak of two editions of the Books: the first at some time between 621 B.C. and 597 B.C., and the second, final edition during the Exile; probably shortly after Jehoiachin was released from his Babylonian prison (561 B.C.).

1 Kings carries the history of Israel from the last days and death of David to the accession in Samaria of Ahaziah, son of Ahab, near the end of the reign of Jehoshaphat, king of Judah. Judgment is passed on Ahaziah's reign but the details are given only later, in 2 Kings. We should note the two large cycles of traditions which grew up around the great prophetic figures of Elijah and Elisha, the former in 1 Kings and the latter chiefly in 2 Kings. These cycles, which interrupt the sequence of regnal chronicles, were very probably preserved and transmitted by the prophetic communities to which there are references in the same traditions. The Elijah cycle is the more important since it dramatically underscores Israel's critical struggle with the religion of Canaan.

The principal divisions of the Books of Kings are:

I: The Reign of Solomon (1 Kgs 1, 1—11, 43).

II: Judah and Israel to the Time of Ahab (1 Kgs 12, 1—16, 34).

III: Stories of the Prophets (1 Kgs 17, 1— 22, 54).

IV: The Kingdoms of Israel and Judah (2 Kgs 1, 1—17, 41).

V: The Kingdom of Judah after 721 B.C. (2 Kgs 18, 1—25, 30).

See RG 183–91

The First Book of Kings

I: The Reign of Solomon

See RG 184–85

CHAPTER 1

*1*When King David was old and advanced in years, though they spread covers over him he could not keep warm. *2*His servants therefore said to him, "Let a young virgin be sought to attend you, lord king, and to nurse you. If she sleeps with your royal majesty, you will be kept warm." *3*So they sought for a beautiful girl throughout the territory of Israel, and found Abishag the Shunamite, whom they brought to the king. *4*The maiden, who was very beautiful, nursed the king and cared for him, but the king did not have relations with her.

Ambition of Adonijah. *5*Adonijah, son of Haggith, began to display his ambition to be king. He acquired chariots, drivers, and fifty henchmen. *6*Yet his father never rebuked him or asked why he was doing this. Adonijah was also very handsome, and next in age to Absalom by the same mother. *7*He conferred with Joab, son of Zeruiah, and with Abiathar the priest, and they supported him. *8*However, Zadok the priest, Benaiah, son of Jehoiada, Nathan the prophet, and Shimei and his companions, the pick of David's army, did not side with Adonijah. *9*When he slaughtered sheep, oxen, and fatlings at the stone Zoheleth, near En-rogel,* Adonijah invited all his brothers, the king's sons, and all the royal officials of Judah. *10*But he did not invite the prophet Nathan, or Benaiah, or the pick of the army, or his brother Solomon.

Solomon Proclaimed King. *11*Then Nathan said to Bathsheba, Solomon's mother: "Have you not heard that Adonijah, son of Haggith, has become king without the knowledge of our lord David? *12*Come now, let me advise you so that you may save your life and that of your son Solomon. *13*Go, visit King David, and say to him, 'Did you not, lord king, swear to your handmaid: Your son Solomon shall be king after me and shall sit upon my throne? Why, then, has Adonijah become king?' *14*And while you are still

---

1, 9: En-rogel: the modern Job's Well southeast of Jerusalem. It marked the ancient boundary between the tribes of Benjamin and Judah (Jos 15, 7; 18, 16). Here David's men sought information about Absalom's revolt (2 Sm 17, 17).

there speaking to the king, I will come in after you and confirm what you have said."

[15]So Bathsheba visited the king in his room, while Abishag the Shunamite was attending him because of his advanced age. [16]Bathsheba bowed in homage to the king, who said to her, "What do you wish?" [17]She answered him: "My lord, you swore to me your handmaid by the LORD, your God, that my son Solomon should reign after you and sit upon your throne. [18]But now Adonijah has become king, and you, my lord king, do not know it. [19]He has slaughtered oxen, fatlings, and sheep in great numbers; he has invited all the king's sons, Abiathar the priest, and Joab, the general of the army, but not your servant Solomon. [20]Now, my lord king, all Israel is waiting for you to make known to them who is to sit on the throne after your royal majesty.* [21]If this is not done, when my lord the king sleeps with his fathers, I and my son Solomon will be considered criminals."

[22]While she was still speaking to the king, the prophet Nathan came in. [23]When he had been announced, the prophet entered the king's presence and, bowing to the floor, did him homage. [24]Then Nathan said: "Have you decided, my lord king, that Adonijah is to reign after you and sit on your throne? [25]He went down today and slaughtered oxen, fatlings, and sheep in great numbers; he invited all the king's sons, the commanders of the army, and Abiathar the priest, and they are eating and drinking in his company and saying, 'Long live King Adonijah!' [26]But me, your servant, he did not invite; nor Zadok the priest, nor Benaiah, son of Jehoiada, nor your servant Solomon. [27]Was this done by my royal master's order without my being told who was to succeed to your majesty's kingly throne?"

[28]King David answered, "Call Bathsheba here." When she re-entered the king's presence and stood before him, [29]the king swore, "As the LORD lives, who has delivered me from all distress, [30]this very day I will fulfill the oath I swore to you by the LORD, the God of Israel, that your son Solomon should reign after me and should sit upon my throne in my place." [31]Bowing to the floor in homage to the king, Bathsheba said, "May my lord, King David, live forever!" [32]Then King David summoned Zadok the priest, Nathan the prophet, and Benaiah, son of Jehoiada. When they had entered the king's presence, [33]he said to them: "Take with you the royal attendants. Mount my son Solomon upon my own mule and escort him down to Gihon. [34]There Zadok the priest and Nathan the prophet are to anoint him king of Israel, and you shall blow the horn and cry, 'Long live King Solomon!' [35]When you come back in his train, he is to go in and sit upon my throne and reign in my place. I designate him ruler of Israel and of Judah." [36]In answer to the king, Benaiah, son of Jehoiada, said: "So be it! May the LORD, the God of my lord the king, so decree! [37]As the LORD has been with your royal majesty, so may he be with Solomon, and exalt his throne even more than that of my lord, King David!"

[38]So Zadok the priest, Nathan the prophet, Benaiah, son of Jehoiada, and the Cherethites and Pelethites* went down, and mounting Solomon on King David's mule, escorted him to Gihon. [39]Then Zadok the priest took the horn of oil from the tent and anointed Solomon. They blew the horn and all the people shouted, "Long live King Solomon!" [40]Then all the people went up after him, playing flutes and rejoicing so much as to split open the earth with their shouting.

[41]Adonijah and all the guests who were with him heard it, just as they ended their banquet. When Joab heard the sound of the horn, he asked, "What does this uproar in the city mean?" [42]As he was speaking, Jonathan, son of Abiathar the priest, arrived. "Come," said Adonijah, "you are a man of worth and must bring good news." [43]"On the contrary!" Jonathan answered him. "Our lord, King David, has made Solomon king. [44]The king sent with him Zadok the priest, Nathan

---

1, 20: At this time, neither law nor the right of primogeniture, but the will of the ruling monarch, determined succession to the throne.

1, 38: Cherethites and Pelethites: mercenaries in David's bodyguard. They became part of his retinue after he defeated the Philistines and established himself in Jerusalem; cf 2 Sm 8, 18; 15, 18; 20, 23.

the prophet, Benaiah, son of Jehoiada, and the Cherethites and Pelethites, and they mounted him upon the king's own mule. [45]Zadok the priest and Nathan the prophet anointed him king at Gihon, and they went up from there rejoicing, so that the city is in an uproar. That is the noise you heard. [46]Besides, Solomon took his seat on the royal throne, [47]and the king's servants went in and paid their respects to our lord, King David, saying, 'May God make Solomon more famous than you and exalt his throne more than your own!' And the king in his bed worshiped God, [48]and this is what he said: 'Blessed be the LORD, the God of Israel, who has this day seated one of my sons upon my throne, so that I see it with my own eyes.' "

[49]All the guests of Adonijah left in terror, each going his own way. [50]Adonijah, in fear of Solomon, also left; he went and seized the horns of the altar.[*] [51]It was reported to Solomon that Adonijah, in his fear of King Solomon, had seized the horns of the altar and said, "Let King Solomon first swear that he will not kill me, his servant, with the sword." [52]Solomon answered, "If he proves himself worthy, not a hair shall fall from his head. But if he is found guilty of crime, he shall die." [53]King Solomon sent to have him brought down from the altar, and he came and paid homage to the king. Solomon then said to him, "Go to your home."

See RG 184-85

CHAPTER 2

David's Last Instructions and Death. [1]When the time of David's death drew near,[*] he gave these instructions to his son Solomon: [2]"I am going the way of all mankind. Take courage and be a man. [3]Keep the mandate of the LORD, your God, following his ways and observing his statutes, commands, ordinances, and decrees as they are written in the law of Moses, that you may succeed in whatever you do, wherever you turn,[a] [4]and the LORD may fulfill the promise he made on my behalf when he said, 'If your sons so conduct themselves that they remain faithful to me with their whole heart and with their whole soul, you shall always have someone of your line on the throne of Israel.'[b] [5]You yourself know what Joab, son of Zeruiah, did to me when he slew the two generals of Israel's armies, Abner, son of Ner, and Amasa, son of Jether. He took revenge for the blood of war in a time of peace, and put blood shed without provocation on the belt about my waist and on the sandal on my foot.[c] [6]Act with the wisdom you possess; you must not allow him to go down to the grave in peaceful old age.

[7]"But be kind to the sons of Barzillai the Gileadite, and have them eat at your table. For they received me kindly when I was fleeing your brother Absalom.[d]

[8]"You also have with you Shimei, son of Gera, the Benjaminite of Bahurim, who cursed me balefully when I was going to Mahanaim. Because he came down to meet me at the Jordan, I swore to him by the LORD that I would not put him to the sword.[e] [9]But you must not let him go unpunished. You are a prudent man and will know how to deal with him to send down his hoary head in blood to the grave."

[10]David rested with his ancestors and was buried in the City of David.[f] [11]The length of David's reign over Israel was forty years: he reigned seven years in Hebron and thirty-three years in Jerusalem.[g]

The Kingdom Made Secure. [12]When Solomon was seated on the throne of his father David, with his sovereignty firmly established, [13]Adonijah, son of Haggith, went to Bathsheba, the mother of Solomon. "Do you come as a friend?" she asked. "Yes," he answered, [14]and added, "I have something to say to you." She replied, "Say it." [15]So he said: "You know that the kingdom was mine,

---

1, 50: Horns of the altar: the protuberances on each of the four corners of the altar were surrounded with a special degree of holiness (Ex 27, 2; 29, 12), and constituted a place of asylum for transgressors of the law (Ex 21, 13f; 1 Kgs 2, 28).

2, 1-6. 8-9: Solomon is expected to remove from his father's family the imputation of blood guilt brought upon it by Joab in the unwarranted killings of Abner (2 Sm 3, 27-29) and Amasa (2 Sm 19, 9-10); and likewise to punish Shimei for his curse, the effects of which David had pledged himself not to avenge in person (2 Sm 19, 21-23). The standards of morality presumed in these verses are far from the Christian ones.

a: Dt 17, 19. b: 2 Sm 7, 11-16; Ps 132, 11f. c: 2 Sm 3, 27; 20, 10. d: 2 Sm 19, 33ff. e: 2 Sm 16, 5; 19, 19. f: Acts 2, 29. g: 1 Chr 29, 27.

and all Israel expected me to be king. But the kingdom escaped me and became my brother's, for the LORD gave it to him. [16]But now there is one favor I would ask of you. Do not refuse me." And she said, "Speak on." [17]He said, "Please ask King Solomon, who will not refuse you, to give me Abishag the Shunamite for my wife."* [18]"Very well," replied Bathsheba, "I will speak to the king for you."

[19]Then Bathsheba went to King Solomon to speak to him for Adonijah, and the king stood up to meet her and paid her homage. Then he sat down upon his throne, and a throne was provided for the king's mother, who sat at his right. [20]"There is one small favor I would ask of you," she said. "Do not refuse me." "Ask it, my mother," the king said to her, "for I will not refuse you." [21]So she said, "Let Abishag the Shunamite be given to your brother Adonijah for his wife." [22]"And why do you ask Abishag the Shunamite for Adonijah?" King Solomon answered his mother. "Ask the kingdom for him as well, for he is my elder brother and has with him Abiathar the priest and Joab, son of Zeruiah." [23]And King Solomon swore by the LORD: "May God do thus and so to me, and more besides, if Adonijah has not proposed this at the cost of his life. [24]And now, as the LORD lives, who has seated me firmly on the throne of my father David and made of me a dynasty as he promised, this day shall Adonijah be put to death." [25]Then King Solomon sent Benaiah, son of Jehoiada, who struck him dead.

[26]The king said to Abiathar the priest: "Go to your land in Anathoth. Though you deserve to die, I will not put you to death this time, because you carried the ark of the Lord GOD before my father David and shared in all the hardships my father endured." [27]So Solomon deposed Abiathar from his office of priest of the LORD, thus fulfilling the prophecy which the LORD had made in Shiloh about the house of Eli.[h]

[28]When the news came to Joab, who had sided with Adonijah, though not with Absalom, he fled to the tent of the LORD and seized the horns of the altar. [29]King Solomon was told that Joab had fled to the tent of the LORD and was at the altar. He sent Benaiah, son of Jehoiada, with the order, "Go, strike him down." [30]Benaiah went to the tent of the LORD and said to him, "The king says, 'Come out.' " But he answered, "No! I will die here." Benaiah reported to the king, "This is what Joab said to me in reply." [31]The king answered him: "Do as he has said. Strike him down and bury him, and you will remove from me and from my family the blood which Joab shed without provocation. [32]The LORD will hold him responsible for his own blood, because he struck down two men better and more just than himself, and slew them with the sword without my father David's knowledge: Abner, son of Ner, general of Israel's army, and Amasa, son of Jether, general of Judah's army.[i] [33]Joab and his descendants shall be responsible forever for their blood. But there shall be the peace of the LORD forever for David, and his descendants, and his house, and his throne." [34]Benaiah, son of Jehoiada, went back, struck him down and killed him; he was buried in his house in the desert. [35]The king appointed Benaiah, son of Jehoiada, over the army in his place, and put Zadok the priest in place of Abiathar.

[36]Then the king summoned Shimei and said to him: "Build yourself a house in Jerusalem and live there. Do not go anywhere else. [37]For if you leave, and cross the Kidron Valley, be certain you shall die without fail. You shall be responsible for your own blood." [38]Shimei answered the king: "I accept. Your servant will do just as the king's majesty has said." So Shimei stayed in Jerusalem for a long time. [39]But three years later, two of Shimei's servants ran away to Achish, son of Maacah, king of Gath, and Shimei was informed that his servants were in Gath. [40]So Shimei rose, saddled his ass, and went to Achish in Gath in search of his servants, whom he brought back. [41]When Solomon was informed that Shimei had gone

---

2, 17. 22-25: Abishag had been the concubine of King David (1 Kgs 1, 4). His successor, Solomon, inherited his father's harem. When Adonijah requested Abishag as his wife, he was subtly undermining the security of Solomon's throne and exposing himself to the suspicion of insurrection that would cost him his life; cf 2 Sm 3, 6-11; 16, 22.

h: 1 Sm 2, 31.   *i:* 2 Sm 3, 27; 20, 10.

from Jerusalem to Gath, and had returned, ⁴²the king summoned Shimei and said to him: "Did I not have you swear by the LORD to your clear understanding of my warning that, if you left and went anywhere else, you should die without fail? And you answered, 'I accept and obey.' ⁴³Why, then, have you not kept the oath of the LORD and the command that I gave you?" ⁴⁴And the king said to Shimei: "You know in your heart the evil that you did to my father David. Now the LORD requites you for your own wickedness. ⁴⁵But King Solomon shall be blessed, and David's throne shall endure before the LORD forever." ⁴⁶The king then gave the order to Benaiah, son of Jehoiada, who struck him dead as he left.

CHAPTER 3

See RG 185–86

Wisdom of Solomon. ¹With the royal power firmly in his grasp, Solomon allied himself by marriage with Pharaoh, king of Egypt. The daughter of Pharaoh, whom he married, he brought to the City of David, until he should finish building his palace, and the temple of the LORD, and the wall around Jerusalem.ʲ

²However, the people were sacrificing on the high places, for up to that time no temple had been built to the name of the LORD. ³Solomon loved the LORD, and obeyed the statutes of his father David; yet he offered sacrifice and burned incense on the high places.

⁴The king went to Gibeon to sacrifice there, because that was the most renowned high place. Upon its altar Solomon offered a thousand holocausts. ⁵In Gibeon the LORD appeared to Solomon in a dream at night. God said, "Ask something of me and I will give it to you." ⁶Solomon answered: "You have shown great favor to your servant, my father David, because he behaved faithfully toward you, with justice and an upright heart; and you have continued this great favor toward him, even today, seating a son of his on his throne. ⁷O LORD, my God, you have made me, your servant, king to succeed my father David; but I am a mere youth, not knowing at all how to act. ⁸I serve you in the midst of the people whom you have chosen, a people so vast that it cannot be numbered or counted. ⁹Give your servant, therefore, an understanding heart to judge your people and to distinguish right from wrong. For who is able to govern this vast people of yours?"ᵏ

¹⁰The LORD was pleased that Solomon made this request. ¹¹So God said to him: "Because you have asked for this—not for a long life for yourself, nor for riches, nor for the life of your enemies, but for understanding so that you may know what is right— ¹²I do as you requested. I give you a heart so wise and understanding that there has never been anyone like you up to now, and after you there will come no one to equal you. ¹³In addition, I give you what you have not asked for, such riches and glory that among kings there is not your like.ˡ ¹⁴And if you follow me by keeping my statutes and commandments, as your father David did, I will give you a long life."

¹⁵When Solomon awoke from his dream, he went to Jerusalem, stood before the ark of the covenant of the LORD, offered holocausts and peace offerings, and gave a banquet for all his servants.

Solomon's Judgment. ¹⁶Later, two harlots came to the king and stood before him. ¹⁷One woman said: "By your leave, my lord, this woman and I live in the same house, and I gave birth in the house while she was present. ¹⁸On the third day after I gave birth, this woman also gave birth. We were alone in the house; there was no one there but us two. ¹⁹This woman's son died during the night; she smothered him by lying on him. ²⁰Later that night she got up and took my son from my side, as I, your handmaid, was sleeping. Then she laid him in her bosom, after she had laid her dead child in my bosom. ²¹I rose in the morning to nurse my child, and I found him dead. But when I examined him in the morning light, I saw it was not the son whom I had borne."

²²The other woman answered, "It is not so! The living one is my son, the dead one is yours." But the first kept saying, "No, the dead one is your child, the living one is mine!" Thus they argued before the king.

ʲ: 1 Kgs 7, 8; 2 Chr 1, 1.   ᵏ: 2 Chr 1, 10.   ˡ: Wis 7, 11; Mt 6, 29.

²³Then the king said: "One woman claims, 'This, the living one, is my child, and the dead one is yours.' The other answers, 'No! The dead one is your child; the living one is mine.' " ²⁴The king continued, "Get me a sword." When they brought the sword before him, ²⁵he said, "Cut the living child in two, and give half to one woman and half to the other." ²⁶The woman whose son it was, in the anguish she felt for it, said to the king, "Please, my lord, give her the living child—please do not kill it!" The other, however, said, "It shall be neither mine nor yours. Divide it!" ²⁷The king then answered, "Give the first one the living child! By no means kill it, for she is the mother."

²⁸When all Israel heard the judgment the king had given, they were in awe of him, because they saw that the king had in him the wisdom of God for giving judgment.

See RG 186

CHAPTER 4

Chief Officers of the Kingdom. ¹Solomon was king over all Israel, ²and these were the officials he had in his service:

Azariah, son of Zadok, priest;
³ Elihoreph and Ahijah, sons of Shisha, scribes;
Jehoshaphat, son of Ahilud, chancellor;
⁴ [Benaiah, son of Jehoiada, commander of the army;
Zadok and Abiathar, priests;]
⁵ Azariah, son of Nathan, chief of the commissaries;
Zabud, son of Nathan, companion to the king;
⁶ Ahishar, major-domo of the palace; and Adoniram, son of Abda, superintendent of the forced labor.

Solomon's Royal State. ⁷*Solomon had twelve commissaries for all Israel who supplied food for the king and his household, each having to provide for one month in the year. ⁸Their names were:

the son of Hur in the hill country of Ephraim;
⁹ the son of Deker in Makaz, Shaalbim, Beth-shemesh, Elon and Beth-hanan;
¹⁰ the son of Hesed in Arubboth, as well as in Socoh and the whole region of Hepher;
¹¹ the son of Abinadab, who was married to Solomon's daughter Taphath, in all the Naphath-dor;
¹² Baana, son of Ahilud, in Taanach and Megiddo, and beyond Jokmeam, and in all Beth-shean, and in the country around Zarethan below Jezreel from Beth-shean to Abel-meholah;
¹³ the son of Geber in Ramoth-Gilead, having charge of the villages of Jair, son of Manasseh, in Gilead; and of the district of Argob in Bashan—sixty large walled cities with gates barred with bronze;
¹⁴ Ahinadab, son of Iddo, in Mahanaim;
¹⁵ Ahimaaz, who was married to Basemath, another daughter of Solomon, in Naphtali;
¹⁶ Baana, son of Hushai, in Asher and along the rocky coast;
¹⁷ Jehoshaphat, son of Paruah, in Issachar;
¹⁸ Shimei, son of Ela, in Benjamin;
¹⁹ Geber, son of Uri, in the land of Gilead, the land of Sihon, king of the Amorites, and of Og, king of Bashan.

There was one prefect besides, in the king's own land.*

CHAPTER 5

See RG 186

⁷These commissaries, one for each month, provided food for King Solomon and for all the guests at the royal table. They left nothing unprovided. ⁸For the chariot horses and draft animals also, each brought his quota of barley and straw to the required place.

4, 7-19: The administration of the kingdom thus initiated by Solomon continued in its main features for the duration of the monarchy in Israel and Judah.

4, 19: One prefect . . . in the king's own land: the royal territory of Judah had its own peculiar administration different from that of the twelve districts which had to supply the king and his household with a month's provisions of food each year (v 7).

*Mediterranean
Sea*

ASHER

NAPHTALI

BASHAN

33°

VIII

IX

NAPHATH-DOR

IV

ISSACHAR

X

Dor

Megiddo

Jezreel

Taanach

V

Beth-shean

GILEAD

VI

Ramoth-gilead

Hepher

Arubboth

Abel-meholah

Socoh

III

EPHRAIM

I

32°

VII

Mahanaim

XI

Shaalbim

Makaz

II

Elon

BENJAMIN

Beth-shemesh

JERUSALEM

XII

JUDAH

*Dead
Sea*

31°

| 0 | 10 | 20 Miles |

| 0 | 10 | 20 Kilometers |

35°

36°

Solomon's Twelve Administrative Districts

[20]*Judah and Israel were as numerous as the sands by the sea; they ate and drank and made merry. [1]Solomon ruled over all the kingdoms from the River to the land of the Philistines, down to the border of Egypt; they paid Solomon tribute and were his vassals as long as he lived.[m]

[2]Solomon's supplies for each day were thirty kors of fine flour, sixty kors of meal, [3]ten fatted oxen, twenty pasture-fed oxen, and a hundred sheep, not counting harts, gazelles, roebucks, and fatted fowl.

[4]He ruled over all the land west of the Euphrates, from Tiphsah to Gaza, and over all its kings, and he had peace on all his borders round about. [5]Thus Judah and Israel lived in security, every man under his vine or under his fig tree from Dan to Beer-sheba, as long as Solomon lived.

[6]Solomon had four thousand stalls for his twelve thousand chariot horses.[n]

[9o]Moreover, God gave Solomon wisdom and exceptional understanding and knowledge, as vast as the sand on the seashore. [10]Solomon surpassed all the Cedemites and all the Egyptians in wisdom. [11]He was wiser than all other men—than Ethan the Ezrahite, or Heman, Chalcol, and Darda, the musicians—and his fame spread throughout the neighboring nations. [12]Solomon also uttered three thousand proverbs, and his songs numbered a thousand and five.[p] [13]He discussed plants, from the cedar on Lebanon to the hyssop growing out of the wall, and he spoke about beasts, birds, reptiles, and fishes. [14]Men came to hear Solomon's wisdom from all nations, sent by all the kings of the earth who had heard of his wisdom.

Preparations for the Temple. [15]When Hiram, king of Tyre, heard that Solomon had been anointed king in place of his father, he sent an embassy to him; for Hiram had always been David's friend. [16]Solomon sent back this message to Hiram: [17]"You know that my father David, because of the enemies surrounding him on all sides, could not build a temple in honor of the LORD, his God, until such a time as the LORD should put these enemies under the soles of his feet. [18]But now the LORD, my God, has given me peace on all sides. There is no enemy or threat of danger. [19]So I propose to build a temple in honor of the LORD, my God, as the LORD predicted to my father David when he said: 'It is your son whom I will put upon your throne in your place who shall build the temple in my honor.'[q] [20]Give orders, then, to have cedars from the Lebanon cut down for me. My servants shall accompany yours, since you know that there is no one among us who is skilled in cutting timber like the Sidonians, and I will pay you whatever you say for your servants' salary."

[21]When he had heard the words of Solomon, Hiram was pleased and said, "Blessed be the LORD this day, who has given David a wise son to rule this numerous people." [22]Hiram then sent word to Solomon, "I agree to the proposal you sent me, and I will provide all the cedars and fir trees you wish. [23]My servants shall bring them down from the Lebanon to the sea, and I will arrange them into rafts in the sea and bring them wherever you say. There I will break up the rafts, and you shall take the lumber. You, for your part, shall furnish the provisions I desire for my household."

[24]So Hiram continued to provide Solomon with all the cedars and fir trees he wished; [25]while Solomon every year gave Hiram twenty thousand kors of wheat to provide for his household, and twenty thousand measures of pure oil. [26]The LORD, moreover, gave Solomon wisdom as he promised him, and there was peace between Hiram and Solomon, since they were parties to a treaty.

[27]King Solomon conscripted thirty thousand workmen from all Israel. [28]He sent them to the Lebanon each month in relays of ten thousand, so that they spent one month in the Lebanon and two months at home. Adoniram was in charge of the draft. [29]Solomon had seventy thousand carriers and eighty thousand stonecutters in the mountain, [30]in addition to three thousand three hundred overseers, answerable to Solomon's prefects

---

5, 20: This verse belongs to ch 4.

m: Sir 47, 15f; 2 Chr 9, 26.   n: 2 Chr 9, 25f.   o: 9-14; Sir 47, 16f.   p: 1 Kgs 3, 12.   q: 2 Sm 7, 13; 1 Chr 22, 10.

The Temple and Palace of Solomon

for the work, directing the people engaged in the work. ³¹By order of the king, fine, large blocks were quarried to give the temple a foundation of hewn stone. ³²Solomon's and Hiram's builders, along with the Gebalites, hewed them out, and prepared the wood and stones for building the temple.

CHAPTER 6

See RG
186-87   *Building of the Temple.* ¹In the four hundred and eightieth year from the departure of the Israelites from the land of Egypt, in the fourth year of Solomon's reign over Israel, in the month of Ziv, which is the second month, the construction of the temple of the LORD* was begun.ʳ

²The temple which King Solomon built for the LORD was sixty cubits long, twenty wide, and twenty-five high. ³The porch in front of the temple was twenty cubits from side to side, along the width of the nave, and ten cubits deep in front of the temple. ⁴Splayed windows with trellises were made for the temple, ⁵and adjoining the wall of the temple, which enclosed the nave and the sanctuary, an annex of several stories was built. ⁶Its lowest story was five cubits wide, the middle one six cubits wide, the third seven cubits wide, because there were offsets along the outside of the temple so that the beams would not be fastened into the walls of the temple. ⁷(The temple was built of stone dressed at the quarry, so that no hammer, axe, or iron tool was to be heard in the temple during its construction.) ⁸The entrance to the lowest floor of the annex was at the right side of the temple, and stairs with intermediate landings led up to the middle story and from the middle story to the

6, 1: Construction of the temple of the Lord is here paralleled in importance with the founding of the nation after the departure from Egypt. In both, God is the central figure who chose Israel as his people, and now chooses the place where his temple should be built (Dt 12, 4-18. 26). The year is given in a round number, 480, which corresponds to twelve generations. The fourth year of Solomon's reign: c. 968 B.C.

r: 2 Chr 3, 1.

third. [9]When the temple was built to its full height, it was roofed in with rafters and boards of cedar. [10]The annex, with its lowest story five cubits high, was built all along the outside of the temple, to which it was joined by cedar beams.

[11]This word of the LORD* came to Solomon: [12]"As to this temple you are building—if you observe my statutes, carry out my ordinances, keep and obey all my commands, I will fulfill toward you the promise I made to your father David.[s] [13]I will dwell in the midst of the Israelites and will not forsake my people Israel."

[14]When Solomon finished building the temple, [15]its walls were lined from floor to ceiling beams with cedar paneling, and its floor was laid with fir planking. [16]At the rear of the temple a space of twenty cubits was set off by cedar partitions from the floor to the rafters, enclosing the sanctuary, the holy of holies. [17]The nave, or part of the temple in front of the sanctuary, was forty cubits long. [18]The cedar in the interior of the temple was carved in the form of gourds and open flowers; all was of cedar, and no stone was to be seen.

[19]In the innermost part of the temple* was located the sanctuary to house the ark of the LORD's covenant, [20]twenty cubits long, twenty wide, and twenty high.* [21]Solomon overlaid the interior of the temple with pure gold. He made in front of the sanctuary a cedar altar, overlaid it with gold, and looped it with golden chains. [22]The entire temple was overlaid with gold so that it was completely covered with it; the whole altar before the sanctuary was also overlaid with gold. [23]In the sanctuary were two cherubim, each ten cubits high, made of olive wood. [24]Each wing of a cherub measured five cubits so that the space from wing tip to wing tip of each was ten cubits. [25]The cherubim were identical in size and shape, [26]and each was exactly ten cubits high. [27]The cherubim were placed in the inmost part of the temple, with their wings spread wide, so that one wing of each cherub touched a side wall while the other wing, pointing toward the middle of the room, touched the corresponding wing of the second cherub. [28]The cherubim, too, were overlaid with gold.

[29]The walls on all sides of both the inner and the outer rooms had carved figures of cherubim, palm trees, and open flowers. [30]The floor of both the inner and the outer rooms was overlaid with gold. [31]At the entrance of the sanctuary, doors of olive wood were made; the doorframes had beveled posts. [32]The two doors were of olive wood, with carved figures of cherubim, palm trees, and open flowers. The doors were overlaid with gold, which was also molded to the cherubim and the palm trees. [33]The same was done at the entrance to the nave, where the doorposts of olive wood were rectangular. [34]The two doors were of fir wood; each door was banded by a metal strap, front and back, [35]and had carved cherubim, palm trees, and open flowers, over which gold was evenly applied.

[36]The inner court was walled off by means of three courses of hewn stones and one course of cedar beams.

[37]The foundations of the LORD's temple were laid in the month of Ziv [38]in the fourth year, and it was completed in all particulars, exactly according to plan, in the month of Bul, the eighth month, in the eleventh year. Thus it took Solomon seven years to build it.

CHAPTER 7

See RG
187

Building of the Palace. [1]His own palace Solomon completed after thirteen years of construction.[u] [2]He built the hall called the Forest of Lebanon one hundred

---

6, 11ff: This word of the LORD . . . my people Israel: the oracle, which came as a climax at the completion of the work, was an expression of God's acceptance and approval. Nevertheless the fulfillment of God's promises to David and his royal descendants will depend on their observance of his ordinances and commands.

6, 19: The innermost part of the temple: the sanctuary or holy of holies reserved exclusively for the Lord. Here through his presence he dwelt as on a throne between the cherubim

above the ark of the covenant (2 Kgs 6, 23-28; 2 Chr 3, 10-13). See note on Ex 25, 18ff.

6, 20: Twenty (cubits) high: it is usually supposed that the holy of holies was of this height because it had a raised floor, five cubits above the floor level of the nave, rather than a dropped ceiling. The building was twenty-five cubits high (v 2) according to the reading here followed.

s: 2 Sm 7, 13.   t: 1 Chr 22, 9f.   u: 1 Kgs 9, 10.

cubits long, fifty wide, and thirty high; it was supported by four rows of cedar columns, with cedar capitals upon the columns. ³Moreover, it had a ceiling of cedar above the beams resting on the columns; these beams numbered forty-five, fifteen to a row. ⁴There were three window frames at either end, with windows in strict alignment. ⁵The posts of all the doorways were rectangular, and the doorways faced each other, three at either end. ⁶The porch of the columned hall he made fifty cubits long and thirty wide. The porch extended the width of the columned hall, and there was a canopy in front. ⁷He also built the vestibule of the throne where he gave judgment—that is, the tribunal; it was paneled with cedar from floor to ceiling beams. ⁸His living quarters were in another court, set in deeper than the tribunal and of the same construction. A palace like this tribunal was built for Pharaoh's daughter, whom Solomon had married.^v

⁹All these buildings were of fine stones, hewn to size and trimmed front and back with a saw, from the foundation to the bonding course. ¹⁰(The foundation was made of fine, large blocks, some ten cubits and some eight cubits. ¹¹Above were fine stones hewn to size, and cedar wood.) ¹²The great court was enclosed by three courses of hewn stones and a bonding course of cedar beams. So also were the inner court of the temple of the LORD and the temple porch.

Furnishing of the Temple. ¹³King Solomon had Hiram brought from Tyre. ¹⁴He was a bronze worker, the son of a widow from the tribe of Naphtali; his father had been from Tyre. He was endowed with skill, understanding, and knowledge of how to produce any work in bronze. He came to King Solomon and did all his metal work.

¹⁵Two hollow bronze columns* were cast, each eighteen cubits high and twelve cubits in circumference; their metal was of four fingers' thickness.^w ¹⁶There were also two capitals cast in bronze, to place on top of the columns, each of them five cubits high. ¹⁷Two pieces of network with a chainlike mesh were made to cover the (nodes of the) capitals on top of the columns, one for each capital. ¹⁸Four hundred pomegranates were also cast; two hundred of them in a double row encircled the piece of network on each of the two capitals. ¹⁹The capitals on top of the columns were finished wholly in a lotus pattern ²⁰above the level of the nodes and their enveloping network. ²¹The columns were then erected adjacent to the porch of the temple, one to the right, called Jachin, and the other to the left, called Boaz. ²²Thus the work on the columns was completed.

²³*The sea was then cast; it was made with a circular rim, and measured ten cubits across, five in height, and thirty in circumference.^x ²⁴Under the brim, gourds encircled it, ten to the cubit all the way around; the gourds were in two rows and were cast in one mold with the sea. ²⁵This rested on twelve oxen, three facing north, three facing west, three facing south, and three facing east, with their haunches all toward the center, where the sea was set upon them. ²⁶It was a handbreadth thick, and its brim resembled that of a cup, being lily-shaped. Its capacity was two thousand measures.

²⁷Ten stands were also made of bronze, each four cubits long, four wide, and three high. ²⁸When these stands were constructed, panels were set within the framework. ²⁹On the panels between the frames there were lions, oxen, and cherubim; and on the frames likewise, above and below the lions and oxen, there were wreaths in relief.

³⁰Each stand had four bronze wheels and bronze axles. ³²The four wheels were below the paneling, and the axletrees of the wheels and the stand were of one piece. Each wheel was a cubit and a half high. ³³The wheels were constructed like chariot wheels; their axles, fellies, spokes, and hubs were all cast.

The four legs of each stand had cast braces, which were under the basin; they had wreaths on each side. ³⁴These four braces,

---

7, 15-21: The two hollow bronze columns, Jachin and Boaz (2 Chr 3, 17), stood free to the right and left of the temple porch. The names are related to God's power (Boaz) founding (Jachin) the temple and his people.

7, 23-26: The sea . . . rested on twelve oxen: this was a large circular tank containing about twelve thousand gallons of water.

---

v: 1 Kgs 3, 1.   w: Jer 52, 21.   x: 2 Chr 4, 2.

extending to the corners of each stand, were of one piece with the stand.

³⁵On top of the stand there was a raised collar half a cubit high, with supports and panels which were of one piece with the top of the stand. ³¹This was surmounted by a crown one cubit high within which was a rounded opening to provide a receptacle a cubit and a half in depth. There was carved work at the opening, on panels that were angular, not curved. ³⁶On the surfaces of the supports and on the panels, wherever there was a clear space, cherubim, lions, and palm trees were carved, as well as wreaths all around. ³⁷This was how the ten stands were made, all of the same casting, the same size, the same shape. ³⁸Ten bronze basins were then made, each four cubits in diameter with a capacity of forty measures, one basin for the top of each of the ten stands. ³⁹The stands were placed, five on the south side of the temple and five on the north. The sea was placed off to the southeast from the south side of the temple.

⁴⁰When Hiram made the pots, shovels, and bowls, he therewith completed all his work for King Solomon in the temple of the LORD: ⁴¹two columns, two nodes for the capitals on top of the columns, two pieces of network covering the nodes for the capitals on top of the columns, ⁴²four hundred pomegranates in double rows on both pieces of network that covered the two nodes of the capitals where they met the columns, ⁴³ten stands, ten basins on the stands, ⁴⁴one sea, twelve oxen supporting the sea, ⁴⁵pots, shovels, and bowls. All these articles which Hiram made for King Solomon in the temple of the LORD were of burnished bronze. ⁴⁶The king had them cast in the neighborhood of the Jordan, in the clayey ground between Succoth and Zarethan. ⁴⁷Solomon did not weigh all the articles because they were so numerous; the weight of the bronze, therefore, was not determined.

⁴⁸Solomon had all the articles made for the interior of the temple of the LORD: the golden altar; the golden table on which the showbread lay; ⁴⁹the lampstands of pure gold, five to the right and five to the left before the sanctuary, with their flowers, lamps, and tongs of gold; ⁵⁰basins, snuffers, bowls, cups, and fire pans of pure gold; and hinges of gold for the doors of the inner room, or holy of holies, and for the doors of the outer room, the nave.

⁵¹When all the work undertaken by King Solomon in the temple of the LORD was completed, he brought in the dedicated offerings of his father David, putting the silver, gold, and other articles in the treasuries of the temple of the LORD.ʸ

CHAPTER 8

See RG 187

Dedication of the Temple. ¹At the order of Solomon, the elders of Israel and all the leaders of the tribes, the princes in the ancestral houses of the Israelites, came to King Solomon in Jerusalem, to bring up the ark of the LORD's covenant from the City of David [which is Zion].ᶻ ²All the men of Israel assembled before King Solomon during the festival in the month of Ethanim (the seventh month). ³When all the elders of Israel had arrived, the priests took up the ark; ⁴they carried the ark of the LORD and the meeting tent with all the sacred vessels that were in the tent. (The priests and Levites carried them.)

⁵King Solomon and the entire community of Israel present for the occasion sacrificed before the ark sheep and oxen too many to number or count. ⁶*The priests brought the ark of the covenant of the LORD to its place beneath the wings of the cherubim in the sanctuary, the holy of holies of the temple. ⁷The cherubim had their wings spread out over the place of the ark, sheltering the ark and its poles from above. ⁸The poles were so long that their ends could be seen from that part of the holy place adjoining the sanctuary; however, they could not be seen beyond. (They have remained there to this day.) ⁹There was nothing in the ark but the

---

8, 6-9: The transfer of the ark of the covenant into the newly constructed temple building, and the oracle of God's acceptance (1 Kgs 9, 3-9), and his act of possession (1 Kgs 8, 10-13), constituted the temple's solemn dedication, and made of it the abiding dwelling of God among his people for which David had hoped (2 Sm 6, 12-15; 7, 1-3). The concurrence of the feast of Booths marks an appropriate transition of God's dwelling among nomadic tribes to his permanent abode among a settled people.

y: 2 Chr 5, 1.   z: 2 Chr 5, 2.

two stone tablets which Moses had put there at Horeb, when the LORD made a covenant with the Israelites at their departure from the land of Egypt.*a*

*10*When the priests left the holy place, the cloud filled the temple of the LORD *11*so that the priests could no longer minister because of the cloud, since the LORD's glory had filled the temple of the LORD. *12*Then Solomon said, "The LORD intends to dwell in the dark cloud;*b* *13*I have truly built you a princely house, a dwelling where you may abide forever."

*14*The king turned and greeted the whole community of Israel as they stood. *15*He said to them: "Blessed be the LORD, the God of Israel, who with his own mouth made a promise to my father David and by his hand has brought it to fulfillment. It was he who said, *16*'Since the day I brought my people Israel out of Egypt, I have not chosen a city out of any tribe of Israel for the building of a temple to my honor; but I choose David to rule my people Israel.' *17*When my father David wished to build a temple to the honor of the LORD, the God of Israel,*c* *18*the Lord said to him, 'In wishing to build a temple to my honor, you do well. *19*It will not be you, however, who will build the temple; but the son who will spring from you, he shall build the temple to my honor.' *20*And now the LORD has fulfilled the promise that he made: I have succeeded my father David and sit on the throne of Israel, as the LORD foretold, and I have built this temple to honor the LORD, the God of Israel. *21*I have provided in it a place for the ark in which is the covenant of the LORD, which he made with our fathers when he brought them out of the land of Egypt."

Solomon's Prayer. *22*Solomon stood before the altar of the LORD in the presence of the whole community of Israel, and stretching forth his hands toward heaven, *23*he said, "LORD, God of Israel, there is no God like you in heaven above or on earth below; you keep your covenant of kindness with your servants who are faithful to you with their whole heart. *24*You have kept the promise you made to my father David, your servant. You who spoke that promise, have this day, by your own power, brought it to fulfillment. *25*Now, therefore, LORD, God of Israel, keep the further promise you made to my father David, your servant, saying, 'You shall always have someone from your line to sit before me on the throne of Israel, provided only that your descendants look to their conduct so that they live in my presence, as you have lived in my presence.'*d* *26*Now, LORD, God of Israel, may this promise which you made to my father David, your servant, be confirmed.

27"Can it indeed be that God dwells among men on earth? If the heavens and the highest heavens cannot contain you, how much less this temple which I have built! *28*Look kindly on the prayer and petition of your servant, O LORD, my God, and listen to the cry of supplication which I, your servant, utter before you this day. *29*May your eyes watch night and day over this temple, the place where you have decreed you shall be honored; may you heed the prayer which I, your servant, offer in this place. *30*Listen to the petitions of your servant and of your people Israel which they offer in this place. Listen from your heavenly dwelling and grant pardon.

31"If a man sins against his neighbor and is required to take an oath sanctioned by a curse, when he comes and takes the oath before your altar in this temple, *32*listen in heaven; take action and pass judgment on your servants. Condemn the wicked and punish him for his conduct, but acquit the just and establish his innocence.

*33**"If your people Israel sin against you and are defeated by an enemy, and if then they return to you, praise your name, pray to you, and entreat you in this temple, *34*listen in heaven and forgive the sin of your people Israel, and bring them back to the land you gave their fathers.

35"If the sky is closed, so that there is no rain, because they have sinned against you and you afflict them, and if then they repent

---

8, 33-34. 46-53: These references to deportation of Israelites to a hostile land are an expansion of Solomon's prayer dating from the Babylonian exile four centuries later.

a: Ex 34, 27; Heb 9, 4.   *b:* 2 Chr 6, 1.   *c:* 2 Sm 7, 5.   *d:* 2 Sm 7, 12.

of their sin, and pray, and praise your name in this place, [36]listen in heaven and forgive the sin of your servant and of your people Israel, teaching them the right way to live and sending rain upon this land of yours which you have given to your people as their heritage.

[37]"If there is famine in the land or pestilence; or if blight comes, or mildew, or a locust swarm, or devouring insects; if an enemy of your people besieges them in one of their cities; whatever plague or sickness there may be, [38]if then any one [of your entire people Israel] has remorse of conscience and offers some prayer or petition, stretching out his hands toward this temple, [39]listen from your heavenly dwelling place and forgive. You who alone know the hearts of all men, render to each one of them according to his conduct; knowing their hearts, so treat them [40]that they may fear you as long as they live on the land you gave our fathers.

[41]"To the foreigner, likewise, who is not of your people Israel, but comes from a distant land to honor you [42](since men will learn of your great name and your mighty hand and your outstretched arm), when he comes and prays toward this temple, [43]listen from your heavenly dwelling. Do all that the foreigner asks of you, that all the peoples of the earth may know your name, may fear you as do your people Israel, and may acknowledge that this temple which I have built is dedicated to your honor.

[44]"Whatever the direction in which you may send your people forth to war against their enemies, if they pray to you, O LORD, toward the city you have chosen and the temple I have built in your honor, [45]listen in heaven to their prayer and petition, and defend their cause.

[46]"When they sin against you (for there is no man who does not sin), and in your anger against them you deliver them to the enemy, so that their captors deport them to a hostile land, far or near,[e] [47]may they repent in the land of their captivity and be converted. If then they entreat you in the land of their captors and say, 'We have sinned and done wrong; we have been wicked'; [48]if with their whole heart and soul they turn back to you in the land of the enemies who took them captive, pray to you toward the land you gave their fathers, the city you have chosen, and the temple I have built in your honor, [49]listen from your heavenly dwelling. [50]Forgive your people their sins and all the offenses they have committed against you, and grant them mercy before their captors, so that these will be merciful to them. [51]For they are your people and your inheritance, whom you brought out of Egypt, from the midst of an iron furnace.

[52]"Thus may your eyes be open to the petition of your servant and to the petition of your people Israel. Hear them whenever they call upon you, [53]because you have set them apart among all the peoples of the earth for your inheritance, as you declared through your servant Moses when you brought our fathers out of Egypt, O Lord GOD."

[54]When Solomon finished offering this entire prayer of petition to the LORD, he rose from before the altar of the LORD, where he had been kneeling with his hands outstretched toward heaven. [55]He stood and blessed the whole community of Israel, saying in a loud voice: [56]"Blessed be the LORD who has given rest to his people Israel, just as he promised. Not a single word has gone unfulfilled of the entire generous promise he made through his servant Moses. [57]May the LORD, our God, be with us as he was with our fathers and may he not forsake us nor cast us off. [58]May he draw our hearts to himself, that we may follow him in everything and keep the commands, statutes, and ordinances which he enjoined on our fathers. [59]May this prayer I have offered to the LORD, our God, be present to him day and night, that he may uphold the cause of his servant and of his people Israel as each day requires, [60]that all the peoples of the earth may know the LORD is God and there is no other. [61]You must be wholly devoted to the LORD, our God, observing his statutes and keeping his commandments, as on this day."

[62]The king and all Israel with him offered sacrifices before the LORD. [63]Solomon of-

e: 2 Chr 6, 36; Eccl 7, 20; 1 Jn 1, 8.

fered as peace offerings to the LORD twenty-two thousand oxen and one hundred twenty thousand sheep. Thus the king and all the Israelites dedicated the temple of the LORD. ⁶⁴On that day the king consecrated the middle of the court facing the temple of the LORD; he offered there the holocausts, the cereal offerings, and the fat of the peace offerings, because the bronze altar before the LORD was too small to hold these offerings.

⁶⁵On this occasion Solomon and all the Israelites, who had assembled in large numbers from Labo of Hamath to the wadi of Egypt, celebrated the festival before the LORD, our God, for seven days. ⁶⁶On the eighth day he dismissed the people, who bade the king farewell and went to their homes, rejoicing and happy over all the blessings the LORD had given to his servant David and to his people Israel.

CHAPTER 9

See RG
187–88

Promise and Warning to Solomon.
¹After Solomon finished building the temple of the LORD, the royal palace, and everything else that he had planned, ²the LORD appeared to him a second time, as he had appeared to him in Gibeon.*f* ³The LORD said to him: "I have heard the prayer of petition which you offered in my presence. I have consecrated this temple which you have built; I confer my name upon it forever, and my eyes and my heart shall be there always. ⁴As for you, if you live in my presence as your father David lived, sincerely and uprightly, doing just as I have commanded you, keeping my statutes and decrees, ⁵I will establish your throne of sovereignty over Israel forever, as I promised your father David when I said, 'You shall always have someone from your line on the throne of Israel.'*g* ⁶But if you and your descendants ever withdraw from me, fail to keep the commandments and statutes which I set before you, and proceed to venerate and worship strange gods, ⁷I will cut off Israel from the land I gave them and repudiate the

temple I have consecrated to my honor. Israel shall become a proverb and a byword among all nations, ⁸and this temple shall become a heap of ruins. Every passerby shall catch his breath in amazement, and ask, 'Why has the LORD done this to the land and to this temple?'*h* ⁹Men will answer: 'They forsook the LORD, their God, who brought their fathers out of the land of Egypt; they adopted strange gods which they worshiped and served. That is why the LORD has brought down upon them all this evil.' "

Other Acts of the King. ¹⁰After the twenty years during which Solomon built the two houses, the temple of the LORD and the palace of the king— ¹¹Hiram, king of Tyre, supplying Solomon with all the cedar wood, fir wood, and gold he wished—King Solomon gave Hiram twenty cities in the land of Galilee. ¹²Hiram left Tyre to see the cities Solomon had given him, but was not satisfied with them. ¹³So he said, "What are these cities you have given me, my brother?" And he called them the land of Cabul, as they are called to this day. ¹⁴Hiram, however, had sent King Solomon one hundred and twenty talents of gold.*

¹⁵This is an account of the forced labor which King Solomon levied in order to build the temple of the LORD, his palace, Millo,* the wall of Jerusalem, Hazor, Megiddo, Gezer ¹⁶(Pharaoh king of Egypt, had come up and taken Gezer and, after destroying it by fire and slaying all the Canaanites living in the city, had given it as dowry to his daughter, Solomon's wife; ¹⁷Solomon then rebuilt Gezer), Lower Beth-horon, ¹⁸Baalath, Tamar in the desert of Judah, ¹⁹all his cities for supplies, cities for chariots and for horses, and whatever else Solomon decided should be built in Jerusalem, in Lebanon, and in the entire land under his dominion. ²⁰All the non-Israelite people who remained in the land, descendants of the Amorites, Hittites, Perizzites, Hivites, and Jebusites ²¹whose doom the Israelites had been unable to ac-

---

9, 14: One hundred and twenty talents of gold: approximately three million six hundred thousand dollars.

9, 15: Millo: probably means a filling, and may refer to an artificial earthwork or platform of stamped ground south of the temple area. It was begun by David (2 Sm 5, 9); cf 1 Kgs 9, 24; 11, 27.

f: 1 Kgs 3, 5; 11, 9; 2 Chr 7, 12.   *g:* 2 Sm 7, 12-16.   *h:* Dt 29, 23; Jer 22, 8.

complish, Solomon conscripted as forced laborers, as they are to this day. [22]But Solomon enslaved none of the Israelites, for they were his fighting force, his ministers, commanders, adjutants, chariot officers, and charioteers. [23]The supervisors of Solomon's works who policed the people engaged in the work numbered five hundred and fifty.

[24]As soon as Pharaoh's daughter went up from the City of David to her palace, which he had built for her, Solomon built Millo.

[25]Three times a year Solomon used to offer holocausts and peace offerings on the altar which he had built to the LORD, and to burn incense before the LORD; and he kept the temple in repair.

[26]King Solomon also built a fleet at Eziongeber, which is near Elath on the shore of the Red Sea in the land of Edom.* [27]In this fleet Hiram placed his own expert seamen with the servants of Solomon. [28]They went to Ophir, and brought back four hundred and twenty talents of gold to King Solomon.

CHAPTER 10

See RG
188

Visit of the Queen of Sheba. [1]The queen of Sheba,* having heard of Solomon's fame, came to test him with subtle questions.[i] [2]She arrived in Jerusalem with a very numerous retinue, and with camels bearing spices, a large amount of gold, and precious stones. She came to Solomon and questioned him on every subject in which she was interested. [3]King Solomon explained everything she asked about, and there remained nothing hidden from him that he could not explain to her.

[4]When the queen of Sheba witnessed Solomon's great wisdom, the palace he had built, [5]the food at his table, the seating of his ministers, the attendance and garb of his waiters, his banquet service, and the holocausts he offered in the temple of the LORD, she was breathless. [6]"The report I heard in my country about your deeds and your wisdom is true," she told the king. [7]"Though I

did not believe the report until I came and saw with my own eyes, I have discovered that they were not telling me the half. Your wisdom and prosperity surpass the report I heard. [8]Happy are your men, happy these servants of yours, who stand before you always and listen to your wisdom. [9]Blessed be the LORD, your God, whom it has pleased to place you on the throne of Israel. In his enduring love for Israel, the LORD has made you king to carry out judgment and justice."

[10]Then she gave the king one hundred and twenty gold talents, a very large quantity of spices, and precious stones. Never again did anyone bring such an abundance of spices as the queen of Sheba gave to King Solomon.

[11]Hiram's fleet, which used to bring gold from Ophir, also brought from there a large quantity of cabinet* wood and precious stones. [12]With the wood the king made supports for the temple of the LORD and for the palace of the king, and harps and lyres for the chanters. No more such wood was brought or seen to the present day.

[13]King Solomon gave the queen of Sheba everything she desired and asked for, besides such presents as were given her from Solomon's royal bounty. Then she returned with her servants to her own country.

Solomon's Wealth. [14]The gold that Solomon received every year weighed six hundred and sixty-six gold talents, [15]in addition to what came from the Tarshish fleet, from the traffic of merchants, and from all the kings of Arabia and the governors of the country. [16]Moreover, King Solomon made two hundred shields of beaten gold (six hundred gold shekels went into each shield)[j] [17]and three hundred bucklers of beaten gold (three minas of gold went into each buckler); and he put them in the hall of the Forest of Lebanon. [18]The king also had a large ivory throne made, and overlaid it with refined gold. [19]The throne had six steps, a back with a round top, and an arm on each side of the seat. Next to each arm stood a lion; [20]and twelve other li-

---

9, 26: Ezion-geber . . . Edom: the first mention of maritime commerce in the Israelite kingdom (to which the land of Edom was subject after its conquest by King David; cf 2 Sm 8, 14).

10, 1: Queen of Sheba: women rulers among the Arabs are recorded in eighth-century-B.C. Assyrian inscriptions. Sheba

was for centuries the leading principality in what is now the Yemen.

10, 11f: Cabinet: an unknown wood, probably fragrant.

i: 2 Chr 9, 1; Mt 12, 42; Lk 11, 31.   *j:* 1 Kgs 14, 26.

ons stood on the steps, two to a step, one on either side of each step. Nothing like this was produced in any other kingdom. [21]In addition, all King Solomon's drinking vessels were of gold, and all the utensils in the hall of the Forest of Lebanon were of pure gold. There was no silver, for in Solomon's time it was considered worthless. [22]The king had a fleet of Tarshish ships* at sea with Hiram's fleet. Once every three years the fleet of Tarshish ships would come with a cargo of gold, silver, ivory, apes, and monkeys. [23]Thus King Solomon surpassed in riches and wisdom all the kings of the earth. [24]And the whole world sought audience with Solomon, to hear from him the wisdom which God had put in his heart. [25]Each one brought his yearly tribute: silver or gold articles, garments, weapons, spices, horses and mules.

[26]Solomon collected chariots and drivers; he had one thousand four hundred chariots and twelve thousand drivers; these he allocated among the chariot cities and to the king's service in Jerusalem.[k] [27]The king made silver as common in Jerusalem as stones, and cedars as numerous as the sycamores of the foothills. [28]Solomon's horses were imported from Cilicia, where the king's agents purchased them. [29]A chariot imported from Egypt cost six hundred shekels, a horse one hundred and fifty shekels; they were exported at these rates to all the Hittite and Aramean kings.

CHAPTER 11

See RG 188

The Sins of Solomon. [1]*King Solomon loved many foreign women besides the daughter of Pharaoh (Moabites, Ammonites, Edomites, Sidonians, and Hittites),[l] [2]from nations with which the LORD had forbidden the Israelites to intermarry, "because," he

said, "they will turn your hearts to their gods."[m] [3]But Solomon fell in love with them. He had seven hundred wives of princely rank and three hundred concubines, and his wives turned his heart.

[4]When Solomon was old his wives had turned his heart to strange gods, and his heart was not entirely with the LORD, his God, as the heart of his father David had been. [5]By adoring Astarte, the goddess of the Sidonians, and Milcom, the idol of the Ammonites, [6]Solomon did evil in the sight of the LORD; he did not follow him unreservedly as his father David had done. [7]Solomon then built a high place to Chemosh, the idol of Moab, and to Molech, the idol of the Ammonites, on the hill opposite Jerusalem. [8]He did the same for all his foreign wives who burned incense and sacrificed to their gods. [9]The LORD, therefore, became angry with Solomon, because his heart was turned away from the LORD, the God of Israel, who had appeared to him twice[n] [10](for though the LORD had forbidden him this very act of following strange gods, Solomon had not obeyed him).

[11]So the LORD said to Solomon: "Since this is what you want, and you have not kept my covenant and my statutes which I enjoined on you, I will deprive you of the kingdom and give it to your servant. [12]I will not do this during your lifetime, however, for the sake of your father David; it is your son whom I will deprive.[o] [13]Nor will I take away the whole kingdom. I will leave your son one tribe for the sake of my servant David and of Jerusalem, which I have chosen."

[14]The LORD then raised up an adversary to Solomon: Hadad the Edomite, who was of the royal line in Edom. [15]Earlier, when David had conquered Edom, Joab, the general of the army, while going to bury the slain,

10, 22: Tarshish ships: large, strong vessels for long voyages. Tarshish was the ancient Tartessus, a Phoenician colony in southern Spain, the name of which denotes a center for smelting metallic ore.

11, 1-3. 7: The glorious rise of Solomon, his piety and wisdom, administrative skill and wealth, the extension of his kingdom, his prestige among neighboring rulers, his reign of peace, above all his friendship with God—these are now eclipsed by his sins of intermarriage with great numbers of pagan wives and the consequent forbidden worship of their gods (Ex 34, 11-16; Dt 7, 1-5). His construction of temples in

their honor merited the punishment of loss of a united kingdom to his posterity, and the opposition of adversaries to himself (vv 14. 23-27). Hadad the Edomite rebelled against Solomon at the beginning of his reign (v 25). Rezon of Syria established a new kingdom in Dàmascus; Jeroboam of Israel constituted the greatest threat because of his revolt from within. This threefold threat culminated in the breakup of Solomon's kingdom.

k: 2 Chr 1, 14. l: Dt 17, 17; Sir 47, 19f. m: Ex 34, 16.
n: 1 Kgs 9, 2. o: 1 Kgs 12, 15.

put to death every male in Edom.ᵖ ¹⁶Joab and all Israel remained there six months until they had killed off every male in Edom. ¹⁷Meanwhile, Hadad, who was only a boy, fled toward Egypt with some Edomite servants of his father. ¹⁸They left Midian and passing through Paran, where they picked up additional men, they went into Egypt to Pharaoh, king of Egypt, who gave Hadad a house, appointed him rations, and assigned him land.

¹⁹Hadad won great favor with Pharaoh, so that he gave him in marriage the sister of Queen Tahpenes, his own wife. ²⁰Tahpenes' sister bore Hadad a son, Genubath. After his weaning, the queen kept him in Pharaoh's palace, where he then lived with Pharaoh's own sons. ²¹When Hadad in Egypt heard that David rested with his ancestors and that Joab, the general of the army, was dead, he said to Pharaoh, "Give me leave to return to my own country." ²²Pharaoh said to him, "What do you lack with me, that you are seeking to return to your own country?" "Nothing," he said, "but please let me go!"

²³God raised up against Solomon another adversary, in Rezon, the son of Eliada, who had fled from his lord, Hadadezer, king of Zobah, ²⁴when David defeated them with slaughter. Rezon gathered men about him and became leader of a band, went to Damascus, settled there, and became king in Damascus. ²⁵He was an enemy of Israel as long as Solomon lived; this added to the harm done by Hadad, who made a rift in Israel by becoming king over Edom.

²⁶Solomon's servant Jeroboam, son of Nebat, an Ephraimite from Zeredah with a widowed mother, Zeruah, also rebelled against the king.�q ²⁷This is why he rebelled. King Solomon was building Millo, closing up the breach of his father's City of David. ²⁸Jeroboam was a man of means, and when Solomon saw that he was also an industrious young man, he put him in charge of the entire labor force of the house of Joseph. ²⁹At that time Jeroboam left Jerusalem, and the prophet Ahijah the Shilonite met him on the road. The two were alone in the area, and the prophet was wearing a new cloak.ʳ ³⁰Ahijah took off his new cloak, tore it into twelve pieces, ³¹and said to Jeroboam:

"Take ten pieces for yourself; the LORD, the God of Israel, says: 'I will tear away the kingdom from Solomon's grasp and will give you ten of the tribes.ˢ ³²One tribe shall remain to him for the sake of David my servant, and of Jerusalem, the city I have chosen out of all the tribes of Israel. ³³The ten I will give you because he has forsaken me and has worshiped Astarte, goddess of the Sidonians, Chemosh, god of Moab, and Milcom, god of the Ammonites; he has not followed my ways or done what is pleasing to me according to my statutes and my decrees, as his father David did. ³⁴Yet I will not take any of the kingdom from Solomon himself, but will keep him a prince as long as he lives for the sake of my servant David, whom I chose, who kept my commandments and statutes. ³⁵But I will take the kingdom from his son and will give it to you—that is, the ten tribes. ³⁶I will give his son one tribe, that my servant David may always have a lamp before me in Jerusalem, the city in which I choose to be honored. ³⁷I will take you; you shall reign over all that you desire and shall become king of Israel. ³⁸If, then, you heed all that I command you, follow my ways, and please me by keeping my statutes and my commandments like my servant David, I will be with you. I will establish for you, as I did for David, a lasting dynasty; I will give Israel to you. ³⁹I will punish David's line for this, but not forever.' "

⁴⁰When Solomon tried to have Jeroboam killed for his rebellion, he escaped to King Shishak, in Egypt, where he remained until Solomon's death.

⁴¹The rest of the acts of Solomon, with all his deeds and his wisdom, are recorded in the book of the chronicles of Solomon. ⁴²The time that Solomon reigned in Jerusalem over all Israel was forty years. ⁴³Solomon rested with his ancestors; he was buried in his father's City of David, and his son Rehoboam succeeded him as king.

p: 2 Sm 8, 14.   q: 2 Chr 13, 6.   r: 1 Kgs 14, 2; 2 Chr 10, 15.   s: 1 Kgs 12, 15.

II: Judah and Israel to the Time of Ahab

CHAPTER 12

See RG
188-89

Secession of Israel. ¹Rehoboam went to Shechem,* where all Israel had come to proclaim him king.ᵗ ³They said to Rehoboam: ⁴"Your father put on us a heavy yoke. If you now lighten the harsh service and the heavy yoke your father imposed on us, we will serve you." ⁵"Come back to me in three days," he answered them. When the people had departed, ⁶King Rehoboam consulted the elders who had been in his father's service while he was alive, and asked, "What answer do you advise me to give this people?" ⁷They replied, "If today you will be the servant of this people and submit to them, giving them a favorable answer, they will be your servants forever." ⁸But he ignored the advice the elders had given him, and consulted the young men who had grown up with him and were in his service. ⁹He said to them, "What answer do you advise me to give this people, who have asked me to lighten the yoke my father imposed on them?" ¹⁰The young men who had grown up with him replied, "This is what you must say to this people who have asked you to lighten the yoke your father put on them: 'My little finger is thicker than my father's body. ¹¹Whereas my father put a heavy yoke on you, I will make it heavier. My father beat you with whips, but I will beat you with scorpions.' "

¹²On the third day all Israel came back to King Rehoboam, as he had instructed them to do. ¹³Ignoring the advice the elders had given him, the king gave the people a harsh answer. ¹⁴He said to them, as the young men had advised: "My father put on you a heavy yoke, but I will make it heavier. My father beat you with whips, but I will beat you with scorpions." ¹⁵The king did not listen to the people, for the LORD brought this about to fulfill the prophecy he had uttered to Jeroboam, son of Nebat, through Ahijah the Shilonite.ᵘ

¹⁶When all Israel saw that the king did not listen to them, the people answered the king:

"What share have we in David?*
We have no heritage in the son of Jesse.
To your tents, O Israel!
Now look to your own house, David."

So Israel went off to their tents, ¹⁷but Rehoboam reigned over the Israelites who lived in the cities of Judah. ¹⁸King Rehoboam then sent out Adoram, superintendent of the forced labor, but all Israel stoned him to death. Rehoboam managed to mount his chariot to flee to Jerusalem, ¹⁹and Israel went into rebellion against David's house to this day. ²Jeroboam, son of Nebat, who was still in Egypt, where he had fled from King Solomon, returned from Egypt as soon as he learned this. ²⁰When all Israel heard that Jeroboam had returned, they summoned him to an assembly and made him king over all Israel. None remained loyal to David's house except the tribe of Judah alone.

²¹On his arrival in Jerusalem, Rehoboam gathered together all the house of Judah and the tribe of Benjamin—one hundred eighty thousand seasoned warriors—to fight against the house of Israel, to restore the kingdom to Rehoboam, son of Solomon. ²²ᵛHowever, the LORD spoke to Shemaiah, a man of God: ²³"Say to Rehoboam, son of Solomon, king of Judah, and to the house of Judah and to Benjamin, and to the rest of the people: ²⁴'Thus says the LORD: You must not march out to fight against your brother Israelites. Let every man return home, for I have brought this about.' " They accepted this message of the LORD and gave up the expedition accordingly.

²⁵Jeroboam built up Shechem in the hill country of Ephraim and lived there. Then he left it and built up Penuel.

12, 1: Shechem: chief city of the northern tribes, where a covenant of fidelity had previously been made between the Lord and his people and a stone of witness had been erected in memory of the event (Jos 24, 25ff).

12, 16: What share have we in David: even in David's time the northern tribes seemed ready to withdraw from Ju-

dah (2 Sm 20, 1). The unreasonable attitude of Rehoboam toward them intensified the discontent caused by the oppression of Solomon (v 4) and thus precipitated the establishment of a rival monarchy (v 20).

t: 2 Chr 10, 1.   *u:* 1 Kgs 11, 12. 31.   *v:* 22-24; 2 Chr 11, 2ff.

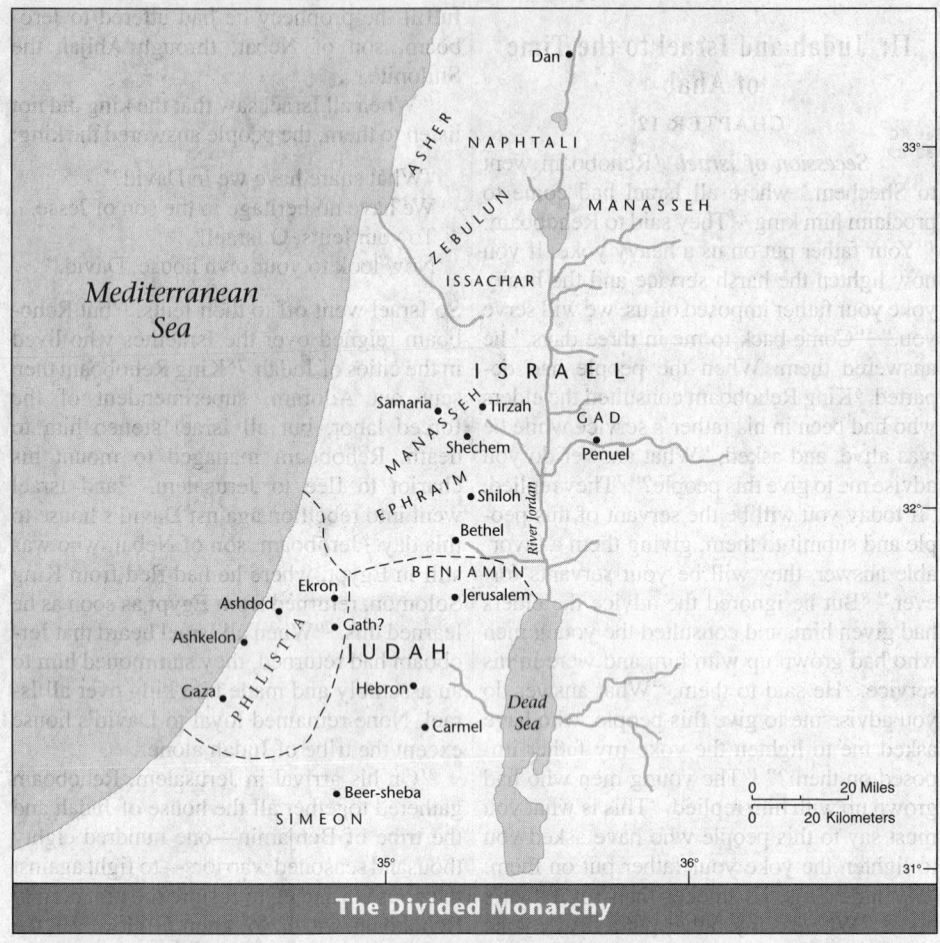

Dan

ASHER
NAPHTALI
ZEBULUN
MANASSEH
ISSACHAR

Mediterranean
Sea

I S R A E L

Samaria • • Tirzah
MANASSEH
Shechem
GAD
• Penuel
EPHRAIM
• Shiloh
River Jordan
Bethel •

B E N J A M I N
Ekron • • Jerusalem
Ashdod •
Ashkelon • • Gath?
PHILISTIA
J U D A H
Gaza • Hebron •
Dead
Sea
• Carmel

• Beer-sheba
S I M E O N

33°
32°
31°

35°   36°

0   20 Miles
0   20 Kilometers

The Divided Monarchy

Religious Rebellion.* [26]Jeroboam thought to himself: "The kingdom will return to David's house. [27]If now this people go up to offer sacrifices in the temple of the LORD in Jerusalem, the hearts of this people will return to their master, Rehoboam, king of Judah, and they will kill me." [28]After taking counsel, the king made two calves of gold and said to the people: "You have been going up to Jerusalem long enough. Here is your God, O Israel, who brought you up from the land of Egypt."[w] [29]And he put one in Bethel, the other in Dan.* [30]This led to sin, because the people frequented these calves in Bethel and in Dan. [31]He also built temples on the high places and made priests from among the people who were not Levites.[x] [32]Jeroboam established a feast in the eighth month on the fifteenth day of the month to duplicate in Bethel the pilgrimage feast of

12, 26-32: Jeroboam feared reunification of the divided kingdom through worship in the single temple in Jerusalem. To prevent this he encouraged shrines on the high places, and appointed false priests to supplement those of levitical descent. The golden bullocks he installed in two of his sanctuaries, though probably intended as bearers of the invisible Divine Majesty, quickly became occasions for idolatry. Thus Jeroboam caused Israel to sin, and

sealed his doom and that of his royal house (1 Kgs 13, 34; 14, 7-14).

12, 29: Bethel . . . Dan: at the southern and northern boundaries of the separate kingdom of Israel, where sanctuaries had existed in the past (Gn 12, 8; 13, 3; 18, 10-22; 25, 1-16; Jgs 18, 1-31).

w: Tb 1, 5; Ex 32, 8. x: 2 Chr 11, 15.

Judah, with sacrifices to the calves he had made; and he stationed in Bethel priests of the high places he had built.

Message of the Prophet from Judah. [33] Jeroboam ascended the altar he built in Bethel on the fifteenth day of the eighth month, the month in which he arbitrarily chose to establish a feast for the Israelites; he was going to offer sacrifice.

CHAPTER 13

See RG 189

[1] A man of God came from Judah to Bethel by the word of the LORD, while Jeroboam was standing at the altar to offer sacrifice. [2] He cried out against the altar the word of the LORD: "O altar, altar, the LORD says, 'A child shall be born to the house of David, Josiah by name, who shall slaughter upon you the priests of the high places who offer sacrifice upon you, and he shall burn human bones upon you.'" [y] [3] He gave a sign that same day and said: "This is the sign that the LORD has spoken: The altar shall break up and the ashes on it shall be strewn about."

[4] When King Jeroboam heard what the man of God was crying out against the altar, he stretched forth his hand from the altar and said, "Seize him!" But the hand he stretched forth against him withered, so that he could not draw it back. [5] Moreover, the altar broke up and the ashes from it were strewn about— the sign the man of God had given as the word of the LORD. [6] Then the king appealed to the man of God. "Entreat the LORD, your God," he said, "and intercede for me that I may be able to withdraw my hand." So the man of God entreated the LORD, and the king recovered the normal use of his hand. [7] "Come home with me for some refreshment," the king invited the man of God, "and I will give you a present." [8] "If you gave me half your kingdom," the man of God said to the king, "I would not go with you, nor eat bread or drink water in this place. [9] For I was instructed by the word of the LORD not to eat bread or drink water and not to return by the way I came." [10] So he departed by another road and did not go back the way he had come to Bethel.

[11] There was an old prophet living in the city, whose sons came and told him all that the man of God had done that day in Bethel. When they repeated to their father the words he had spoken to the king, [12] the father asked them, "Which way did he go?" And his sons pointed out to him the road taken by the man of God who had come from Judah. [13] Then he said to his sons, "Saddle the ass for me." When they had saddled it, he mounted [14] and followed the man of God, whom he found seated under a terebinth. When he asked him, "Are you the man of God who came from Judah?" he answered, "Yes." [15] Then he said, "Come home with me and have some bread." [16] "I cannot go back with you, and I cannot eat bread or drink water with you in this place," he answered, [17] "for I was told by the word of the LORD neither to eat bread nor drink water here, and not to go back the way I came." [18] But he said to him, "I, too, am a prophet like you, and an angel told me in the word of the LORD to bring you back with me to my house and to have you eat bread and drink water." He was lying to him, however.

[19] So he went back with him, and ate bread and drank water in his house. [20] But while they were sitting at table, the LORD spoke to the prophet who had brought him back, [21] and he cried out to the man of God who had come from Judah: "The LORD says, 'Because you rebelled against the command of the LORD and did not keep the command which the LORD, your God, gave you, [22] but returned and ate bread and drank water in the place where he told you to do neither, your corpse shall not be brought to the grave of your ancestors.'"

[23] After he had eaten bread and drunk water, the ass was saddled for him, and he again [24] set out. But a lion met him on the road, and killed him. His corpse lay sprawled on the road, and the ass remained standing by it, and so did the lion. [25] Some passers-by saw the body lying in the road, with the lion standing beside it, and carried the news to the city where the old prophet lived. [26] On hearing it, the prophet who had brought him back from his journey said: "It is the man of God who rebelled against the command of the LORD. He has delivered him to a lion, which man-

---

y: 2 Kgs 23, 16.

Chronology of the Two Kingdoms

Difficulties arise in comparing the chronology of the two kingdoms, Israel and Judah. Before the modern system of numbering years was adopted in the fifth century A.D., events were usually dated by the reigns of kings, beginning a new series with each new king. In some instances the remaining months of the year of a king's death were counted as the first year of his successor; in others the new series of numbers did not begin until the next full year. Frequently a king associated his son with him on the throne, so that the year could be designated by either king; in such cases one writer might begin the new king's reign when this occurred, whereas another writer might not begin the enumeration until after the father's death. Interest in precise chronology is comparatively recent. Until modern times the year was commenced at different dates in various countries. When these facts are recognized, most of the chronological discrepancies in the narratives of the two kingdoms can be resolved.

The total length of the kingdoms of Israel and Judah can be learned from events mentioned in the history of other countries. A much larger sum is reached by adding together the number of years of each king's reign, because fractions of a year would appear as full years in each reign.

From 1050–931 B.C. the united kingdom was ruled by Saul, David, and Solomon. The approximate dates of the reigns of the kings of Israel and Judah are shown in the table below:

Israel	Reign	Co-Regency	Judah	Reign	Co-Regency
Jeroboam I	931–910 B.C.		Rehoboam	931–913 B.C.	
			Abijah	913–911	
Nadab	910–909		Asa	911–870	
Baasha	909–886				
Elah	886–885				
Zimri	885				
Omri	885–874	885–880 B.C.			
Ahab	874–853		Jehoshaphat	870–848	873–870 B.C.
Ahaziah	853–852		Jehoram	848–841	853–848
Joram	852–841		Ahaziah	841	
Jehu	841–814		Athaliah	841–835	
Jehoahaz	814–798		Joash	835–796	
Jehoash	798–782		Amaziah	796–767	
Jeroboam II	782–753	793–782	Azariah	767–740	791–767
Zechariah	753–752				
Shallum	752				
Menahem	752–742		Jotham	740–732	750–740
Pekahiah	742–740				
Pekah	740–732	752–740	Ahaz	732–716	
Hoshea	732–721				
			Hezekiah	716–687	
			Manasseh	687–642	696–687
			Amon	642–640	
			Josiah	640–608	
			Jehoahaz	608	
			Jehoiakim	608–597	
			Jehoiachin	597	
			Zedekiah	597–586	

gled and killed him, as the LORD predicted to him." [27]Then he said to his sons, "Saddle the ass for me." When they had saddled it, [28]he went off and found the body lying in the road with the ass and the lion standing beside it. The lion had not eaten the body nor had it harmed the ass. [29]The prophet lifted up the body of the man of God and put it on the ass, and brought it back to the city to mourn over it and to bury it. [30]He laid the man's body in his own grave, and they mourned over it: "Alas, my brother!" [31]After he had buried him, he said to his sons, "When I die, bury me in the grave where the man of God is buried. Lay my remains beside his. [32]For the word of the LORD which he proclaimed against the altar in Bethel and against all the shrines on the high places in the cities of Samaria shall certainly come to pass."

[33]Jeroboam did not give up his evil ways after this event, but again made priests for the high places from among the common people. Whoever desired it was consecrated and became a priest of the high places. [34]This was a sin on the part of the house of Jeroboam for which it was to be cut off and destroyed from the earth.

See RG 189

CHAPTER 14

Death of Abijah. [1]At that time Abijah, son of Jeroboam, took sick. [2]So Jeroboam said to his wife, "Get ready and disguise yourself so that none will recognize you as Jeroboam's wife. Then go to Shiloh, where you will find the prophet Ahijah. It is he who predicted my reign over this people.[z] [3]Take along ten loaves, some cakes, and a jar of preserves, and go to him. He will tell you what will happen to the child." [4]The wife of Jeroboam obeyed. She made the journey to Shiloh and entered the house of Ahijah who could not see because age had dimmed his sight.

[5]The LORD had said to Ahijah: "Jeroboam's wife is coming to consult you about her son, for he is sick. This is what you must tell her. When she comes, she will be in disguise." [6]So Ahijah, hearing the sound of her footsteps as she entered the door, said, "Come in, wife of Jeroboam. Why are you in disguise? I have been commissioned to give you bitter news. [7]Go, tell Jeroboam, 'This is what the LORD, the God of Israel, says: I exalted you from among the people and made you ruler of my people Israel. [8]I deprived the house of David of the kingdom and gave it to you. Yet you have not been like my servant David, who kept my commandments and followed me with his whole heart, doing only what pleased me. [9]You have done worse than all who preceded you: you have gone and made for yourself strange gods and molten images to provoke me; but me you have cast behind your back. [10]Therefore, I am bringing evil upon the house of Jeroboam: I will cut off every male in Jeroboam's line, whether slave or freeman in Israel, and will burn up the house of Jeroboam completely, as though dung were being burned.[a] [11]When one of Jeroboam's line dies in the city, dogs will devour him; when one of them dies in the field, he will be devoured by the birds of the sky. For the LORD has spoken!'[b] [12]So leave; go home! As you step inside the city, the child will die, [13]and all Israel will mourn him and bury him, for he alone of Jeroboam's line will be laid in the grave, since in him alone of Jeroboam's house has something pleasing to the LORD, the God of Israel, been found. [14]Today, at this very moment, the LORD will raise up for himself a king of Israel who will destroy the house of Jeroboam. [15]The LORD will strike Israel like a reed tossed about in the water and will pluck out Israel from this good land which he gave their fathers, scattering them beyond the River, because they made sacred poles for themselves and thus provoked the LORD. [16]He will give up Israel because of the sins Jeroboam has committed and caused Israel to commit."

[17]So Jeroboam's wife started back; when she reached Tirzah and crossed the threshold of her house, the child died. [18]He was buried with all Israel mourning him, as the LORD had prophesied through his servant the prophet Ahijah.

[19]The rest of the acts of Jeroboam, with his warfare and his reign, are recorded in the book of the chronicles of the kings of Israel.

z: 1 Kgs 11, 29.   a: 1 Kgs 15, 29.   b: 1 Kgs 16, 4.

[20]The length of Jeroboam's reign was twenty-two years. He rested with his ancestors, and his son Nadab succeeded him as king.

Reign of Rehoboam. [21]Rehoboam, son of Solomon, reigned in Judah. He was forty-one years old when he became king, and he reigned seventeen years in Jerusalem, the city in which, out of all the tribes of Israel, the LORD chose to be honored. His mother was the Ammonite named Naamah.[c]

[22]Judah did evil in the sight of the LORD, and by their sins angered him even more than their fathers had done. [23]They, too, built for themselves high places, pillars, and sacred poles, upon every high hill and under every green tree. [24]There were also cult prostitutes in the land. Judah imitated all the abominable practices of the nations whom the LORD had cleared out of the Israelites' way.

[25]In the fifth year of King Rehoboam, Shishak, king of Egypt, attacked Jerusalem.* [26]He took everything, including the treasures of the temple of the LORD and those of the royal palace, as well as all the gold shields made under Solomon.[d] [27]To replace them, King Rehoboam had bronze shields made, which he entrusted to the officers of the guard on duty at the entrance of the royal palace. [28]Whenever the king visited the temple of the LORD, those on duty would carry the shields, and then return them to the guardroom.

[29]The rest of the acts of Rehoboam, with all that he did, are recorded in the book of the chronicles of the kings of Judah. [30]There was constant warfare between Rehoboam and Jeroboam. [31]Rehoboam rested with his ancestors; he was buried with them in the City of David. His mother was the Ammonite named Naamah. His son Abijam succeeded him as king.

See RG 189–90

CHAPTER 15

Reign of Abijam. [1]In the eighteenth year of King Jeroboam, son of Nebat, Abijam became king of Judah;[e] [2]he reigned three years in Jerusalem. His mother's name was Maacah, daughter of Abishalom. [3]He imitated all the sins his father had committed before him, and his heart was not entirely with the LORD, his God, like the heart of his grandfather David. [4]Yet for David's sake the LORD, his God, gave him a lamp in Jerusalem, raising up his son after him and permitting Jerusalem to endure; [5]because David had pleased the LORD and did not disobey any of his commands as long as he lived, except in the case of Uriah the Hittite.[f]

[7]The rest of Abijam's acts, with all that he did, are written in the book of the chronicles of the kings of Judah.[g] [6]There was war between Abijam and Jeroboam. [8]Abijam rested with his ancestors; he was buried in the City of David, and his son Asa succeeded him as king.

Reign of Asa. [9]In the twentieth year of Jeroboam, king of Israel, Asa, king of Judah, began to reign; [10]he reigned forty-one years in Jerusalem. His grandmother's name was Maacah, daughter of Abishalom. [11]Asa pleased the LORD like his forefather David, [12]banishing the temple prostitutes from the land and removing all the idols his father had made. [13]He also deposed his grandmother Maacah from her position as queen mother, because she had made an outrageous object for Asherah. Asa cut down this object and burned it in the Kidron Valley. [14]The high places did not disappear; yet Asa's heart was entirely with the LORD as long as he lived. [15]He brought into the temple of the LORD his father's and his own votive offerings of silver, gold, and various utensils.

[16]There was war between Asa and Baasha, king of Israel, as long as they both reigned. [17]Baasha, king of Israel, attacked Judah and fortified Ramah to prevent communication with Asa, king of Judah.[h] [18]Asa then took all the silver and gold remaining in the treasuries of the temple of the LORD and of the royal palace. Entrusting them to his

---

14, 25: In the fifth year . . . Shishak, king of Egypt, attacked Jerusalem: c. 926 B.C. According to 2 Chr 12, 1-12, the repentance of King Rehoboam and of the princes of Israel after the warning of the prophet Shemaiah diverted the actual attack on Jerusalem. Shishak, however, carried off the treasures of the temple of the Lord and of the king's palace (2 Chr

12, 9). A bas-relief of this Pharaoh in the temple of Aman at Karnak commemorates his conquest of some hundred and fifty Palestinian and Trans-Jordanian cities and towns.

c: 2 Chr 12, 13.   d: 1 Kgs 10, 16.   e: 2 Chr 13, 1f.   f: 2 Sm 11, 4.   g: 2 Chr 13, 2.   h: 2 Chr 16, 1.

ministers, King Asa sent them to Ben-hadad, son of Tabrimmon, son of Hezion, king of Aram,* resident in Damascus. He said: *19*"There is a treaty between you and me, as there was between your father and my father. I am sending you a present of silver and gold. Go, break your treaty with Baasha, king of Israel, that he may withdraw from me." *20*Ben-hadad agreed with King Asa and sent the leaders of his troops against the cities of Israel. They attacked Ijon, Dan, Abel-beth-maacah, and all Chinnereth, besides all the land of Naphtali. *21*When Baasha heard of it, he left off fortifying Ramah, and stayed in Tirzah. *22*Then King Asa summoned all Judah without exception, and they carried away the stones and beams with which Baasha was fortifying Ramah. With them King Asa built Geba of Benjamin and Mizpeh.

*23*The rest of the acts of Asa, with all his valor and accomplishments, and the cities he built, are written in the book of the chronicles of the kings of Judah. In his old age, Asa had an infirmity in his feet. *24*He rested with his ancestors; he was buried in his forefather's City of David, and his son Jehoshaphat succeeded him as king.*i*

Reign of Nadab. *25*In the second year of Asa, king of Judah, Nadab, son of Jeroboam, became king of Israel; he reigned over Israel two years. *26*He did evil in the LORD's sight, imitating his father's conduct and the sin which he had caused Israel to commit. *27*Baasha, son of Ahijah, of the house of Issachar, plotted against him and struck him down at Gibbethon of the Philistines, which Nadab and all Israel were besieging. *28*Baasha killed him in the third year of Asa, king of Judah, and reigned in his stead. *29*Once he was king, he killed off the entire house of Jeroboam, not leaving a single soul to Jeroboam but destroying him utterly, according to the warning which the LORD had pronounced through his servant, Ahijah the Shilonite,*j* *30*because of the sins Jeroboam committed and caused Israel to commit, by which he provoked the LORD, the God of Israel, to anger.

*31*The rest of the acts of Nadab, with all that he did, are written in the book of the chronicles of the kings of Israel. *32*[There was war between Asa and Baasha, king of Israel, as long as they lived.]

Reign of Baasha. *33*In the third year of Asa, king of Judah, Baasha, son of Ahijah, began his twenty-four-year reign over Israel in Tirzah. *34*He did evil in the LORD's sight, imitating the conduct of Jeroboam and the sin he had caused Israel to commit.

CHAPTER 16

See RG 190

*1*The LORD spoke against Baasha to Jehu, son of Hanani, and said: *2*"Inasmuch as I lifted you up from the dust and made you ruler of my people Israel, but you have imitated the conduct of Jeroboam and have caused my people Israel to sin, provoking me to anger by their sins, *3*I will destroy you, Baasha, and your house;*k* *4*I will make your house like that of Jeroboam, son of Nebat. If anyone of Baasha's line dies in the city, dogs shall devour him; if he dies in the field, he shall be devoured by the birds of the sky."*l*

*5*The rest of the acts of Baasha, with all his valor and accomplishments, are written in the book of the chronicles of the kings of Israel.*m* *6*Baasha rested with his ancestors; he was buried in Tirzah, and his son Elah succeeded him as king. *7*[Through the prophet Jehu, son of Hanani, the LORD had threatened Baasha and his house, because of all the evil Baasha did in the sight of the LORD, provoking him to anger by his evil deeds, so that he became like the house of Jeroboam; and because he killed Nadab.]

Reign of Elah. *8*In the twenty-sixth year of Asa, king of Judah, Elah, son of Baasha, began his two-year reign over Israel in Tirzah. *9*His servant Zimri, commander of half his chariots, plotted against him. As he was in Tirzah, drinking to excess in the house of Arza, superintendent of his palace in Tirzah, *10*Zimri entered; he struck and killed him in the twenty-seventh year of Asa, king of Judah, and reigned in his place.*n* *11*Once he was

---

15, 18: Ben-hadad . . . king of Aram: Ben-hadad I, third successor of Rezon, who had thrown off the yoke of the Israelites during the reign of Solomon and become king of Aram (11, 23f).

i: 2 Chr 17, 1.   *j:* 1 Kgs 14, 10; 21, 22.   *k:* 1 Kgs 21, 22.   *l:* 1 Kgs 14, 11.   *m:* 2 Chr 16, 1.   *n:* 2 Kgs 9, 31.

seated on the royal throne, he killed off the whole house of Baasha, not sparing a single male relative or friend of his. *12*Zimri destroyed the entire house of Baasha, as the LORD had prophesied to Baasha through the prophet Jehu, *13*because of all the sins which Baasha and his son Elah committed and caused Israel to commit, provoking the LORD, the God of Israel, to anger by their idols.

*14*The rest of the acts of Elah, with all that he did, are written in the book of the chronicles of the kings of Israel.

Reign of Zimri. *15*In the twenty-seventh year of Asa, king of Judah, Zimri reigned seven days in Tirzah. The army was besieging Gibbethon of the Philistines *16*when they heard that Zimri had formed a conspiracy and had killed the king. So that day in the camp all Israel proclaimed Omri, general of the army, king of Israel. *17*Omri marched up from Gibbethon, accompanied by all Israel, and laid siege to Tirzah. *18*When Zimri saw the city was captured, he entered the citadel of the royal palace and burned down the palace over him. He died *19*because of the sins he had committed, doing evil in the sight of the LORD by imitating the sinful conduct of Jeroboam, thus causing Israel to sin.

*20*The rest of the acts of Zimri, with the conspiracy he carried out, are written in the book of the chronicles of the kings of Israel.

*21*At that time the people of Israel were divided, half following Tibni, son of Ginath, to make him king, and half for Omri. *22*The partisans of Omri prevailed over those of Tibni, son of Ginath. Tibni died and Omri became king.

Reign of Omri. *23*In the thirty-first year of Asa, king of Judah, Omri became king; he reigned over Israel twelve years, the first six of them in Tirzah. *24*He then bought the hill of Samaria from Shemer for two silver talents and built upon the hill, naming the city he built Samaria after Shemer, the former owner. *25*But Omri did evil in the LORD's sight beyond any of his predecessors. *26*He closely imitated the sinful conduct of Jeroboam, son of Nebat, causing Israel to sin and to provoke the LORD, the God of Israel, to anger by their idols.

*27*The rest of the acts of Omri, with all his valor and accomplishments, are written in the book of the chronicles of the kings of Israel. *28*Omri rested with his ancestors; he was buried in Samaria, and his son Ahab succeeded him as king.

Reign of Ahab. *29*In the thirty-eighth year of Asa, king of Judah, Ahab, son of Omri, became king of Israel; he reigned over Israel in Samaria for twenty-two years. *30*Ahab, son of Omri, did evil in the sight of the LORD more than any of his predecessors. *31*It was not enough for him to imitate the sins of Jeroboam, son of Nebat. He even married Jezebel, daughter of Ethbaal, king of the Sidonians, and went over to the veneration and worship of Baal. *32*Ahab erected an altar to Baal in the temple of Baal which he built in Samaria, *33*and also made a sacred pole. He did more to anger the LORD, the God of Israel, than any of the kings of Israel before him.

*34o*During his reign, Hiel from Bethel rebuilt Jericho. He lost his first-born son, Abiram, when he laid the foundation, and his youngest son, Segub, when he set up the gates, as the LORD had foretold through Joshua, son of Nun.

III: Stories of the Prophets

CHAPTER 17

See RG 190

Drought Predicted by Elijah. *1*Elijah the Tishbite,* from Tishbe in Gilead, said to Ahab: "As the LORD, the God of Israel, lives, whom I serve, during these years there shall be no dew or rain except at my word."*p* *2*The LORD then said to Elijah: *3*"Leave here, go east and hide in the Wadi Cherith, east of the Jordan. *4*You shall drink of the stream, and I have commanded ravens to feed you there."

17, 1: Elijah the Tishbite: one of the most important figures in Old Testament history. As his name indicates ("Yahweh is my God"), Elijah was the successful leader in the struggle to preserve the knowledge and worship of Yahweh against the encroaching worship of Baal introduced into Israel by Jezebel, the Tyrian wife of Ahab. The Elijah cycle of narratives includes, besides the above struggle, miracle stories, denunciations of kings, and a preparation for the prophet's role as eschatological forerunner of the "great day of the Lord"; cf Mal 3, 23-24; Mt 17, 10-13; Lk 1, 17.

o: Jos 6, 26. *p:* Sir 48, 3; Jas 5, 17.

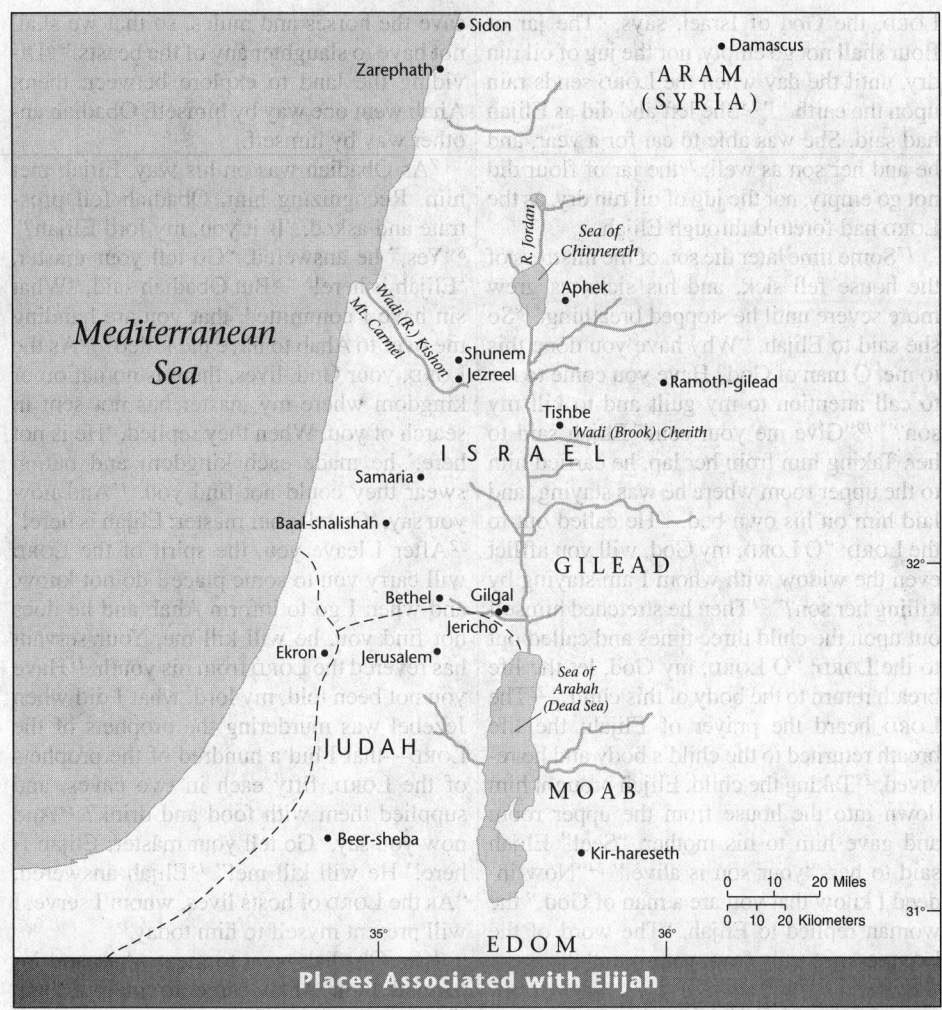

Places Associated with Elijah

⁵So he left and did as the LORD had commanded. He went and remained by the Wadi Cherith, east of the Jordan. ⁶Ravens brought him bread and meat in the morning, and bread and meat in the evening, and he drank from the stream.

Elijah and the Widow. ⁷After some time, however, the brook ran dry, because no rain had fallen in the land. ⁸So the LORD said to him: ⁹"Move on to Zarephath of Sidon and stay there. I have designated a widow there to provide for you." ¹⁰He left and went to Zarephath. As he arrived at the entrance of the city, a widow was gathering sticks there;

he called out to her, "Please bring me a small cupful of water to drink."*q* ¹¹She left to get it, and he called out after her, "Please bring along a bit of bread." ¹²"As the LORD, your God, lives," she answered, "I have nothing baked; there is only a handful of flour in my jar and a little oil in my jug. Just now I was collecting a couple of sticks, to go in and prepare something for myself and my son; when we have eaten it, we shall die." ¹³"Do not be afraid," Elijah said to her. "Go and do as you propose. But first make me a little cake and bring it to me. Then you can prepare something for yourself and your son. ¹⁴For the

q: Lk 4, 26.

LORD, the God of Israel, says, 'The jar of flour shall not go empty, nor the jug of oil run dry, until the day when the LORD sends rain upon the earth.' " [15]She left and did as Elijah had said. She was able to eat for a year, and he and her son as well; [16]the jar of flour did not go empty, nor the jug of oil run dry, as the LORD had foretold through Elijah.

[17]Some time later the son of the mistress of the house fell sick, and his sickness grew more severe until he stopped breathing. [18]So she said to Elijah, "Why have you done this to me, O man of God? Have you come to me to call attention to my guilt and to kill my son?" [19]"Give me your son," Elijah said to her. Taking him from her lap, he carried him to the upper room where he was staying, and laid him on his own bed. [20]He called out to the LORD: "O LORD, my God, will you afflict even the widow with whom I am staying by killing her son?" [21]Then he stretched himself out upon the child three times and called out to the LORD: "O LORD, my God, let the life breath return to the body of this child." [22]The LORD heard the prayer of Elijah; the life breath returned to the child's body and he revived. [23]Taking the child, Elijah brought him down into the house from the upper room and gave him to his mother. "See!" Elijah said to her, "your son is alive." [24]"Now indeed I know that you are a man of God," the woman replied to Elijah. "The word of the LORD comes truly from your mouth."

CHAPTER 18

See RG 190

Elijah and the Prophets of Baal.

[1]Long afterward, in the third year, the LORD spoke to Elijah. "Go, present yourself to Ahab," he said, "that I may send rain upon the earth." [2]So Elijah went to present himself to Ahab.

[3]Now the famine in Samaria was bitter, [4]and Ahab had summoned Obadiah, his vizier, who was a zealous follower of the LORD. When Jezebel was murdering the prophets of the LORD, Obadiah took a hundred prophets, hid them away fifty each in two caves, and supplied them with food and drink. [5]Ahab said to Obadiah, "Come, let us go through the land to all sources of water and to all the streams. We may find grass and save the horses and mules, so that we shall not have to slaughter any of the beasts." [6]Dividing the land to explore between them, Ahab went one way by himself, Obadiah another way by himself.

[7]As Obadiah was on his way, Elijah met him. Recognizing him, Obadiah fell prostrate and asked, "Is it you, my lord Elijah?" [8]"Yes," he answered. "Go tell your master, 'Elijah is here!' " [9]But Obadiah said, "What sin have I committed, that you are handing me over to Ahab to have me killed? [10]As the LORD, your God, lives, there is no nation or kingdom where my master has not sent in search of you. When they replied, 'He is not here,' he made each kingdom and nation swear they could not find you. [11]And now you say, 'Go tell your master: Elijah is here!' [12]After I leave you, the spirit of the LORD will carry you to some place I do not know, and when I go to inform Ahab and he does not find you, he will kill me. Your servant has revered the LORD from his youth. [13]Have you not been told, my lord, what I did when Jezebel was murdering the prophets of the LORD—that I hid a hundred of the prophets of the LORD, fifty each in two caves, and supplied them with food and drink? [14]And now you say, 'Go tell your master: Elijah is here!' He will kill me!" [15]Elijah answered, "As the LORD of hosts lives, whom I serve, I will present myself to him today."

[16]So Obadiah went to meet Ahab and informed him. Ahab came to meet Elijah, [17]and when he saw Elijah, said to him, "Is it you, you disturber of Israel?" [18]"It is not I who disturb Israel," he answered, "but you and your family, by forsaking the commands of the LORD and following the Baals. [19]Now summon all Israel to me on Mount Carmel, as well as the four hundred and fifty prophets of Baal and the four hundred prophets of Asherah who eat at Jezebel's table." [20]So Ahab sent to all the Israelites and had the prophets assemble on Mount Carmel.

[21]Elijah appealed to all the people and said, "How long will you straddle the issue? If the LORD is God, follow him; if Baal, follow him." The people, however, did not answer him. [22]So Elijah said to the people, "I am the only surviving prophet of the LORD,

and there are four hundred and fifty prophets of Baal. *23*Give us two young bulls. Let them choose one, cut it into pieces, and place it on the wood, but start no fire. I shall prepare the other and place it on the wood, but shall start no fire. *24*You shall call on your gods, and I will call on the LORD. The God who answers with fire is God." All the people answered, "Agreed!"

*25*Elijah then said to the prophets of Baal, "Choose one young bull and prepare it first, for there are more of you. Call upon your gods, but do not start the fire." *26*Taking the young bull that was turned over to them, they prepared it and called on Baal from morning to noon, saying, "Answer us, Baal!" But there was no sound, and no one answering. And they hopped around the altar they had prepared. *27*When it was noon, Elijah taunted them: "Call louder, for he is a god and may be meditating, or may have retired, or may be on a journey. Perhaps he is asleep and must be awakened." *28*They called out louder and slashed themselves with swords and spears, as was their custom, until blood gushed over them. *29*Noon passed and they remained in a prophetic state until the time for offering sacrifice. But there was not a sound; no one answered, and no one was listening.

*30*Then Elijah said to all the people, "Come here to me." When they had done so, he repaired the altar of the LORD which had been destroyed. *31*He took twelve stones, for the number of tribes of the sons of Jacob, to whom the LORD had said, "Your name shall be Israel." *32*He built an altar in honor of the LORD with the stones, and made a trench around the altar large enough for two seahs of grain. *33*When he had arranged the wood, he cut up the young bull and laid it on the wood. *34*"Fill four jars with water," he said, "and pour it over the holocaust and over the wood." "Do it again," he said, and they did it again. "Do it a third time," he said, and they did it a third time. *35*The water flowed around the altar, and the trench was filled with the water.

*36*At the time for offering sacrifice, the prophet Elijah came forward and said, "LORD, God of Abraham, Isaac, and Israel, let it be known this day that you are God in Israel and that I am your servant and have done all these things by your command. *37*Answer me, LORD! Answer me, that this people may know that you, LORD, are God and that you have brought them back to their senses." *38*The LORD's fire came down and consumed the holocaust, wood, stones, and dust, and it lapped up the water in the trench. *39*Seeing this, all the people fell prostrate and said, "The LORD is God! The LORD is God!" *40*Then Elijah said to them, "Seize the prophets of Baal. Let none of them escape!" They were seized, and Elijah had them brought down to the brook Kishon and there he slit their throats.

*41*Elijah then said to Ahab, "Go up, eat and drink, for there is the sound of a heavy rain." *42*So Ahab went up to eat and drink, while Elijah climbed to the top of Carmel, crouched down to the earth, and put his head between his knees. *43*"Climb up and look out to sea," he directed his servant, who went up and looked, but reported, "There is nothing." Seven times he said, "Go, look again!" *44*And the seventh time the youth reported, "There is a cloud as small as a man's hand rising from the sea." Elijah said, "Go and say to Ahab, 'Harness up and leave the mountain before the rain stops you.'" *45*In a trice, the sky grew dark with clouds and wind, and a heavy rain fell. Ahab mounted his chariot and made for Jezreel. *46*But the hand of the LORD was on Elijah, who girded up his clothing and ran before Ahab as far as the approaches to Jezreel.

CHAPTER 19

See RG 190–91

Flight to Horeb. *1*Ahab told Jezebel all that Elijah had done—that he had put all the prophets to the sword. *2*Jezebel then sent a messenger to Elijah and said, "May the gods do thus and so to me if by this time tomorrow I have not done with your life what was done to each of them." *3*Elijah was afraid and fled for his life, going to Beersheba of Judah. He left his servant there *4*and went a day's journey into the desert, until he came to a broom tree and sat beneath it. He prayed for death: "This is enough, O LORD! Take my life, for I am no better than my fathers." *5*He lay down and fell asleep under the broom tree, but then an angel touched him and ordered him to get up and eat. ⁶He looked and there at his head was a hearth cake and a jug of water. After he ate and drank, he lay down again, ⁷but the angel of the LORD came back a second time, touched him, and ordered, "Get up and eat, else the journey will be too long for you!" ⁸He got up, ate and drank; then strengthened by that food, he walked forty days and forty nights to the mountain of God, Horeb.

⁹There he came to a cave, where he took shelter. But the word of the LORD came to him, "Why are you here, Elijah?" ¹⁰He answered: "I have been most zealous for the LORD, the God of hosts, but the Israelites have forsaken your covenant, torn down your altars, and put your prophets to the sword. I alone am left, and they seek to take my life." ¹¹*Then the LORD said, "Go outside and stand on the mountain before the LORD; the LORD will be passing by." A strong and heavy wind was rending the mountains and crushing rocks before the LORD—but the LORD was not in the wind. After the wind there was an earthquake—but the LORD was not in the earthquake. ¹²After the earthquake there was fire—but the LORD was not in the fire. After the fire there was a tiny whispering sound. ¹³When he heard this, Elijah hid his face in his cloak and went and stood at the entrance of the cave. A voice said to him, "Elijah, why are you here?" ¹⁴He replied, "I have been most zealous for the LORD, the God of hosts. But the Israelites have forsaken your covenant, torn down your altars, and put your prophets to the sword. I alone am left, and they seek to take my life."ʳ ¹⁵*"Go, take the road back to the desert near Damascus,"

the LORD said to him. "When you arrive, you shall anoint Hazael as king of Aram. ¹⁶Then you shall anoint Jehu, son of Nimshi, as king of Israel, and Elisha, son of Shaphat of Abelmeholah, as prophet to succeed you.ˢ ¹⁷If anyone escapes the sword of Hazael, Jehu will kill him. If he escapes the sword of Jehu, Elisha will kill him. ¹⁸Yet I will leave seven thousand men in Israel—all those who have not knelt to Baal or kissed him."ᵗ

Call of Elisha. ¹⁹Elijah set out, and came upon Elisha, son of Shaphat, as he was plowing with twelve yoke of oxen; he was following the twelfth. Elijah went over to him and threw his cloak over him. ²⁰Elisha left the oxen, ran after Elijah, and said, "Please, let me kiss my father and mother goodbye, and I will follow you." "Go back!" Elijah answered. "Have I done anything to you?" ²¹Elisha left him and, taking the yoke of oxen, slaughtered them; he used the plowing equipment for fuel to boil their flesh, and gave it to his people to eat. Then he left and followed Elijah as his attendant.

CHAPTER 20

See RG 191

Ahab's Victories over Ben-hadad. ¹Ben-hadad, king of Aram, gathered all his forces, and accompanied by thirty-two kings with horses and chariotry, proceeded to invest and attack Samaria. ²He sent couriers to Ahab, king of Israel, within the city, ³and said to him, "This is Ben-hadad's message: 'Your silver and gold are mine, and your wives and your promising sons are mine.' " ⁴The king of Israel answered, "As you say, my lord king, I and all I have are yours." ⁵But the couriers came again and said, "This is Ben-hadad's message: 'I sent you word to

---

19, 11ff: Compare these divine manifestations to Elijah with those to Moses (Ex 19, 1-23; 33, 21ff; 34, 5) on the same Mount Horeb (Sinai) (Dt 4, 10-15). Though various phenomena, such as wind, storms, earthquakes, fire (Ex 19, 18f), herald the divine presence, they do not constitute the presence itself which, like the tiny whispering sound, is imperceptible and bespeaks the spirituality of God. It was fitting that Elijah, whose mission it was to reestablish the covenant and restore the pure faith, should have returned to Horeb where the covenant was revealed to Moses and through him to the Israelite people (Ex 3, 1-4. 17; 33, 18—34, 9). Moses and Elijah appeared with Christ at the time of his transfiguration (Mt 17, 1-9; Mk 9, 1-7; Lk 9, 28-36).

19, 15-17: Elijah himself carried out only the third of the commissions entrusted to him (vv 19-21); Elisha was deputed to perform the first in person (2 Kgs 8, 7-19), and the second through one of his followers (2 Kgs 9, 1-10).

19, 19-21: Elijah's act of throwing his mantle over the shoulders of Elisha expressed the divine call to share the prophetic mission. Elisha's prompt response through destruction of his plow and oxen is an example of total obedience and detachment from his former manner of living in order to promote the glory of God.

r: Rom 11, 3.   *s:* 2 Kgs 9, 2.   *t:* Rom 11, 4.

give me your silver and gold, your wives and your sons. *6*Now, however, at this time tomorrow I will send my servants to you, and they shall ransack your house and the houses of your servants. They shall seize and take away whatever they consider valuable.' "

*7*The king of Israel then summoned all the elders of the land and said: "Understand clearly that this man wants to ruin us. When he sent to me for my wives and sons, my silver and my gold, I did not refuse him." *8*All the elders and all the people said to him, "Do not listen. Do not give in." *9*Accordingly he directed the couriers of Ben-hadad, "Say to my lord the king, 'I will do all that you demanded of your servant the first time. But this I cannot do.' " The couriers left and reported this. *10*Ben-hadad then sent him the message, "May the gods do thus and so to me if there is enough dust in Samaria to make handfuls for all my followers." *11*The king of Israel replied, "Tell him, 'It is not for the man who is buckling his armor to boast as though he were taking it off.' " *12*Ben-hadad was drinking in the pavilions with the kings when he heard this reply. "Prepare the assault," he commanded his servants; and they made ready to storm the city.

*13*Then a prophet came up to Ahab, king of Israel, and said: "The LORD says, 'Do you see all this huge army? When I deliver it up to you today, you will know that I am the LORD.' " *14*But Ahab asked, "Through whom will it be delivered up?" He answered, "The LORD says, 'Through the retainers of the governors of the provinces.' " Then Ahab asked, "Who is to attack?" He replied, "You are." *15*So Ahab called up the retainers of the governors of the provinces, two hundred thirty-two of them. Behind them he mustered all the Israelite soldiery, who numbered seven thousand. *16*They marched out at noon, while Ben-hadad was drinking heavily in the pavilions with the thirty-two kings who were his allies. *17*When the retainers of the governors of the provinces marched out first, Ben-hadad received word that some men had marched out of Samaria. *18*He answered, "Whether they have come out for peace or for war, in any case take them alive." *19*But when these had come out of the city—the soldiers of the governors of the provinces with the army following them— *20*each of them struck down his man. The Arameans fled with Israel pursuing them, while Ben-hadad, king of Aram, escaped on a chariot steed. *21*The king of Israel went out, took the horses and chariots, and inflicted a severe defeat on Aram.

*22*Then the prophet went up to the king of Israel and said to him: "Go, regroup your forces. Mark well what you do, for at the beginning of the year* the king of Aram will attack you." *23*On the other hand, the servants of the king of Aram said to him: "Their gods are gods of mountains. That is why they defeated us. But if we fight them on level ground, we shall be sure to defeat them. *24*This is what you must do: Take the kings from their posts and put prefects in their places. *25*Mobilize an army as large as the army that has deserted you, horse for horse, chariot for chariot. Let us fight them on level ground, and we shall surely defeat them." He took their advice and did this.

*26*At the beginning of the year, Ben-hadad mobilized Aram and went up to Aphek to fight against Israel. *27*The Israelites, too, were called to arms and supplied with provisions; then they went out to engage the foe. The Israelites, encamped opposite them, seemed like a couple of small flocks of goats, while Aram covered the countryside. *28*A man of God came up and said to the king of Israel: "The LORD says, 'Because Aram has said the LORD is a god of mountains, not a god of plains, I will deliver up to you all this large army, that you may know I am the LORD.' " *29*They were encamped opposite each other for seven days. On the seventh day battle was joined, and the Israelites struck down one hundred thousand foot soldiers of Aram in one day. *30*The survivors, twenty-seven thousand of them, fled into the city of Aphek, and there the wall collapsed. Ben-hadad, too, fled, and took refuge within the city, in an inside room.

20, 22: At the beginning of the year: in the spring.

³¹His servants said to him: "We have heard that the kings of the land of Israel are merciful kings. Allow us, therefore, to garb ourselves in sackcloth, with cords around our heads, and go out to the king of Israel. Perhaps he will spare your life." ³²So they dressed in sackcloth girded at the waist, and wearing cords around their heads, they went to the king of Israel. "Your servant Ben-hadad pleads for his life," they said. "Is he still alive?" the king asked. "He is my brother." ³³Hearing this as a good omen, the men quickly took him at his word and said, "Benhadad is your brother." He answered, "Go and get him." When Ben-hadad came out to him, the king had him mount his chariot. ³⁴Ben-hadad said to him, "I will restore the cities which my father took from your father, and you may make yourself bazaars in Damascus, as my father did in Samaria." "On these terms," Ahab replied, "I will set you free." So he made an agreement with him and then set him free.

³⁵One of the guild prophets was prompted by the LORD to say to his companion, "Strike me." But he refused to strike him. ³⁶Then he said to him, "Since you did not obey the voice of the LORD, a lion will kill you when you leave me." When they parted company, a lion came upon him and killed him. ³⁷The prophet met another man and said, "Strike me." The man struck him a blow and wounded him. ³⁸The prophet went on and waited for the king on the road, having disguised himself with a bandage over his eyes. ³⁹As the king was passing, he called out to the king and said, "Your servant went into the thick of the battle, and suddenly someone turned and brought me a man and said, 'Guard this man. If he is missing, you shall have to pay for his life with your life or pay out a talent of silver.' ⁴⁰But while your servant was looking here and there, the man disappeared." The king of Israel said to him, "That is your sentence. You have decided it yourself." ⁴¹He immediately removed the bandage from his eyes, and the king of Israel recognized him as one of the prophets. ⁴²He said to him: "The LORD says, 'Because you have set free the man I doomed

to destruction, your life shall pay for his life, your people for his people.' " Disturbed and angry, the king of Israel went off homeward and entered Samaria.ᵘ

CHAPTER 21

See RG 191

Seizure of Naboth's Vineyard. ¹Some time after this, as Naboth the Jezreelite had a vineyard in Jezreel next to the palace of Ahab, king of Samaria, ²Ahab said to Naboth, "Give me your vineyard to be my vegetable garden, since it is close by, next to my house. I will give you a better vineyard in exchange, or, if you prefer, I will give you its value in money." ³"The LORD forbid," Naboth answered him, "that I should give you my ancestral heritage." ⁴Ahab went home disturbed and angry at the answer Naboth the Jezreelite had made to him: "I will not give you my ancestral heritage." Lying down on his bed, he turned away from food and would not eat.

⁵His wife Jezebel came to him and said to him, "Why are you so angry that you will not eat?" ⁶He answered her, "Because I spoke to Naboth the Jezreelite and said to him, 'Sell me your vineyard, or, if you prefer, I will give you a vineyard in exchange.' But he refused to let me have his vineyard." ⁷"A fine ruler over Israel you are indeed!" his wife Jezebel said to him. "Get up. Eat and be cheerful. I will obtain the vineyard of Naboth the Jezreelite for you."

⁸So she wrote letters in Ahab's name and, having sealed them with his seal, sent them to the elders and to the nobles who lived in the same city with Naboth. ⁹This is what she wrote in the letters: "Proclaim a fast and set Naboth at the head of the people. ¹⁰Next, get two scoundrels to face him and accuse him of having cursed God and king. Then take him out and stone him to death." ¹¹His fellow citizens—the elders and the nobles who dwelt in his city—did as Jezebel had ordered them in writing, through the letters she had sent them. ¹²They proclaimed a fast and placed Naboth at the head of the people. ¹³Two scoundrels came in and confronted him with the accusation, "Naboth has cursed God and king." And they led him out of the

u: 1 Kgs 22, 35.

city and stoned him to death. *14*Then they sent the information to Jezebel that Naboth had been stoned to death.

*15*When Jezebel learned that Naboth had been stoned to death, she said to Ahab, "Go on, take possession of the vineyard of Naboth the Jezreelite which he refused to sell you, because Naboth is not alive, but dead." *16*On hearing that Naboth was dead, Ahab started off on his way down to the vineyard of Naboth the Jezreelite, to take possession of it.

*17*But the LORD said to Elijah the Tishbite: *18*"Start down to meet Ahab, king of Israel, who rules in Samaria. He will be in the vineyard of Naboth, of which he has come to take possession. *19***v*This is what you shall tell him, 'The LORD says: After murdering, do you also take possession? For this, the LORD says: In the place where the dogs licked up the blood of Naboth, the dogs shall lick up your blood, too.' " *20**"Have you found me out, my enemy?" Ahab said to Elijah. "Yes," he answered. "Because you have given yourself up to doing evil in the LORD's sight, *21*I am bringing evil upon you: I will destroy you and will cut off every male in Ahab's line, whether slave or freeman, in Israel.*w* *22*I will make your house like that of Jeroboam, son of Nebat, and like that of Baasha, son of Ahijah, because of how you have provoked me by leading Israel into sin."*x* *23*(Against Jezebel, too, the LORD declared, "The dogs shall devour Jezebel in the district of Jezreel.")*y* *24*"When one of Ahab's line dies in the city, dogs will devour him; when one of them dies in the field, the birds of the sky will devour him." *25*Indeed, no one gave himself up to the doing of evil in the sight of the LORD as did Ahab, urged on by his wife Jezebel. *26*He became completely abominable by following idols, just as the Amorites had done, whom the LORD drove out before the Israelites.

*27*When Ahab heard these words, he tore his garments and put on sackcloth over his bare flesh. He fasted, slept in the sackcloth, and went about subdued. *28*Then the LORD said to Elijah the Tishbite, *29*"Have you seen that Ahab has humbled himself before me? Since he has humbled himself before me, I will not bring the evil in his time. I will bring the evil upon his house during the reign of his son."*z*

CHAPTER 22

See RG 191

Campaign against Ramoth-gilead.
*1*Three years passed without war between Aram and Israel.*a* *2*In the third year, however, King Jehoshaphat of Judah came down to the king of Israel, *3*who said to his servants, "Do you not know that Ramoth-gilead is ours and we are doing nothing to take it from the king of Aram?" *4*He asked Jehoshaphat, "Will you come with me to fight against Ramoth-gilead?" Jehoshaphat answered the king of Israel, "You and I are as one, and your people and my people, your horses and my horses as well." *5*Jehoshaphat also said to the king of Israel, "Seek the word of the LORD at once."

*6*The king of Israel gathered together the prophets, about four hundred of them, and asked, "Shall I go to attack Ramoth-gilead or shall I refrain?" "Go up," they answered. "The LORD will deliver it over to the king." *7*But Jehoshaphat said, "Is there no other prophet of the LORD here whom we may consult?" *8*The king of Israel answered, "There is one other through whom we might consult the LORD, Micaiah, son of Imlah; but I hate him because he prophesies not good but evil about me." Jehoshaphat said, "Let not your majesty speak of evil against you."

*9*So the king of Israel called an official and said to him, "Get Micaiah, son of Imlah, at once." *10*The king of Israel and King Jehoshaphat of Judah were seated, each on his

---

21, 19: The response of Ahab to this divine judgment is described in v 27, and the consequences are given in vv 28-29, and in 2 Kgs 9, 21-26.

21, 20-26: In these verses the Judean editor of the Books of Kings substitutes, for the message of Elijah prepared for in v 19, a sweeping and definitive judgment against the whole family of Ahab in the same terms as were used against the families of Jeroboam I (1 Kgs 14, 9-11) and Baasha (1 Kgs 16, 2-4). This judgment is the fruit of later theological reflec-

tion; it is not occasioned directly by the crime against Naboth, but by the idolatry of Ahab and Jezebel. The judgment on Jezebel herself (v 23) may have been uttered by Elijah during the Naboth episode; it finds its fulfillment in 2 Kgs 9, 36-37. Still another theological explanation for the death of Ahab is given by the north Israelite writer of 1 Kgs 20, 35-42 above.

v: 1 Kgs 22, 38. *w:* 2 Kgs 9, 8. *x:* 1 Kgs 15, 29; 16, 3. *y:* 2 Kgs 9, 36. *z:* 2 Kgs 9, 26. *a:* 2 Chr 18, 1.

throne, clothed in their robes of state on a threshing floor at the entrance of the gate of Samaria, and all the prophets were prophesying before them. [11]Zedekiah, son of Chenaanah, made himself horns of iron and said, "The LORD says, 'With these you shall gore Aram until you have destroyed them.' " [12]The other prophets prophesied in a similar vein, saying: "Go up to Ramoth-gilead; you shall succeed. The LORD will deliver it over to the king."

[13]The messenger who had gone to call Micaiah said to him, "Look now, the prophets are unanimously predicting good for the king. Let your word be the same as any of theirs; predict good." [14]"As the LORD lives," Micaiah answered, "I shall say whatever the LORD tells me."

[15]When he came to the king, the king said to him, "Micaiah, shall we go to fight against Ramoth-gilead, or shall we refrain?" "Go up," he answered, "you shall succeed! The LORD will deliver it over to the king." [16]But the king answered him, "How many times must I adjure you to tell me nothing but the truth in the name of the LORD?" [17]So Micaiah said:

"I see all Israel
scattered on the mountains,
like sheep without a shepherd,
and the LORD saying, 'These have no
master!
Let each of them go back home in
peace.' "

[18]The king of Israel said to Jehoshaphat, "Did I not tell you he prophesies not good but evil about me?" [19]*Micaiah continued: "Therefore hear the word of the LORD: I saw the LORD seated on his throne, with the whole host of heaven standing by to his right and to his left. [20]The LORD asked, 'Who will deceive Ahab, so that he will go up and fall at Ramoth-gilead?' And one said this, another that, [21]until one of the spirits came forth and presented himself to the LORD,

saying, 'I will deceive him.' The LORD asked, 'How?' [22]He answered, 'I will go forth and become a lying spirit in the mouths of all his prophets.' The LORD replied, 'You shall succeed in deceiving him. Go forth and do this.' [23]So now, the LORD has put a lying spirit in the mouths of all these prophets of yours, but the LORD himself has decreed evil against you."

[24]Thereupon Zedekiah, son of Chenaanah, came up and slapped Micaiah on the cheek, saying, "Has the spirit of the LORD, then, left me to speak with you?" [25]"You shall find out," Micaiah replied, "on that day when you retreat into an inside room to hide." [26]The king of Israel then said, "Seize Micaiah and take him back to Amon, prefect of the city, and to Joash, the king's son, [27]and say, 'This is the king's order: Put this man in prison and feed him scanty rations of bread and water until I return in safety.' " [28]But Micaiah said, "If ever you return in safety, the LORD has not spoken through me."*

[29]The king of Israel and King Jehoshaphat of Judah went up to Ramoth-gilead, [30]and the king of Israel said to Jehoshaphat, "I will disguise myself and go into battle, but you put on your own clothes." So the king of Israel disguised himself and entered the fray. [31]In the meantime the king of Aram had given his thirty-two chariot commanders the order, "Do not fight with anyone at all except the king of Israel." [32]When the chariot commanders saw Jehoshaphat, they cried out, "That must be the king of Israel!" and shifted to fight him. But Jehoshaphat shouted his battle cry, [33]and the chariot commanders, aware that he was not the king of Israel, gave up pursuit of him. [34]Someone, however, drew his bow at random, and hit the king of Israel between the joints of his breastplate. He ordered his charioteer, "Rein about and take me out of the ranks, for I am disabled." [35]The battle grew fierce during the day, and the king, who was propped up in his chariot facing the Arameans, died in the

22, 19-23: The prophet Micaiah uses as a last resort to deter Ahab from his foolhardy design of fighting against Ramoth-gilead the literary device of describing false prophets as messengers of a lying spirit which God, after holding counsel with his angels, permits to deceive them.

22, 28: A note in the Hebrew text after this verse attributes to Micaiah ben Imlah the first words of the book of a different Micaiah, the minor prophet of Moreshet.

evening. The blood from his wound flowed to the bottom of the chariot.[b] [36]At sunset a cry went through the army, "Every man to his city, every man to his land, [37]for the king is dead!" So they went to Samaria, where they buried the king. [38]When the chariot was washed at the pool of Samaria, the dogs licked up his blood and harlots bathed there, as the LORD had prophesied.[c]

[39]The rest of the acts of Ahab, with all that he did, including the ivory palace and all the cities he built, are recorded in the book of the chronicles of the kings of Israel. [40]Ahab rested with his ancestors, and his son Ahaziah succeeded him as king.

Reign of Jehoshaphat. [41]Jehoshaphat, son of Asa, began to reign over Judah in the fourth year of Ahab, king of Israel. [42]Jehoshaphat was thirty-five years old when he began to reign, and he reigned twenty-five years in Jerusalem. His mother's name was Azubah, daughter of Shilhi. [43]He followed all the ways of his father Asa unswervingly, doing what was right in the LORD's sight. [44]Nevertheless, the high places did not disappear, and the people continued to sacrifice and to burn incense on the high places. [45]Jehoshaphat also made peace with the king of Israel. [46]The rest of the acts of Jehoshaphat, with his prowess, what he did and how he fought, are recorded in the book of the chronicles of the kings of Judah.

[47]He removed from the land the rest of the cult prostitutes who had remained in the reign of his father Asa. [48]There was no king in Edom, but an appointed regent. [49]Jehoshaphat made Tarshish ships to go to Ophir for gold; but in fact the ships did not go, because they were wrecked at Ezion-geber. [50]Then Ahaziah, son of Ahab, said to Jehoshaphat, "Let my servants accompany your servants in the ships." But Jehoshaphat would not agree. [51]Jehoshaphat rested with his ancestors; he was buried in his forefathers' City of David. His son Jehoram succeeded him as king.

Reign of Ahaziah. [52]Ahaziah, son of Ahab, began to reign over Israel in Samaria in the seventeenth year* of Jehoshaphat, king of Judah; he reigned two years over Israel. [53]He did evil in the sight of the LORD, behaving like his father, his mother, and Jeroboam, son of Nebat, who caused Israel to sin. [54]He served and worshiped Baal, thus provoking the LORD, the God of Israel, just as his father had done.

22, 52: Seventeenth year: so the present Hebrew text. More consistent with 2 Kgs 1, 17 would be a date in the twenty-fourth year of Jehoshaphat for Ahab's death; see note on 2 Kgs 1, 1.

b: 1 Kgs 20, 42.   c: 1 Kgs 21, 19.

See RG 191–98

The Second Book of Kings

I: The Kingdoms of Israel and Judah

See RG 191

CHAPTER 1

Ahaziah Consults Baalzebub. [1]After Ahab's death, Moab rebelled against Israel.[a] [2]Ahaziah had fallen through the lattice of his roof terrace at Samaria and had been injured. So he sent out messengers with the instructions: "Go and inquire of Baalzebub,* the god of Ekron, whether I shall recover from this injury."

[3]Meanwhile, the angel of the LORD said to Elijah the Tishbite: "Go, intercept the messengers of Samaria's king, and ask them, 'Is it because there is no God in Israel that you are going to inquire of Baalzebub, the god of Ekron?' [4]For this, the LORD says: 'You shall not leave the bed upon which you lie; instead, you shall die.' " And with that, Elijah departed. [5]The messengers then returned to

---

1, 2: Baalzebub: in this form, "Baal of flies." The name in the Hebrew text is a derisive alteration of Baalzebul, "Prince Baal." The best New Testament evidence supports the latter form in Mt. 10, 25; Lk 11, 15. Later associations with Aramaic beeldebaba, "enemy," gave the ancient name its connotation of "devil."

a: 2 Kgs 3, 4-27.

403

Ahaziah, who asked them, "Why have you returned?" [6]"A man came up to us," they answered, "who said to us, 'Go back to the king who sent you and tell him: The LORD says, Is it because there is no God in Israel that you are sending to inquire of Baalzebub, the god of Ekron? For this you shall not leave the bed upon which you lie; instead, you shall die.' " [7]The king asked them, "What was the man like who came up to you and said these things to you?" [8]"Wearing a hairy garment,"* they replied, "with a leather girdle about his loins." "It is Elijah the Tishbite!" he exclaimed.[b]

Death of Two Captains. [9]Then the king sent a captain with his company of fifty men after Elijah. The prophet was seated on a hilltop when he found him. "Man of God," he ordered, "the king commands you to come down." [10]"If I am a man of God," Elijah answered the captain, "may fire come down from heaven and consume you and your fifty men." And fire came down from heaven and consumed him and his fifty men.[c] [11]Ahaziah sent another captain with his company of fifty men after Elijah. "Man of God," he called out to Elijah, "the king commands you to come down immediately." [12]"If I am a man of God," Elijah answered him, "May fire come down from heaven and consume you and your fifty men." And divine fire* came down from heaven, consuming him and his fifty men.

Death of the King. [13]Again, for the third time, Ahaziah sent a captain with his company of fifty men. When the third captain arrived, he fell to his knees before Elijah, pleading with him. "Man of God," he implored him, "let my life and the lives of these fifty men, your servants, count for something

in your sight! [14]Already fire has come down from heaven, consuming two captains with their companies of fifty men. But now, let my life mean something to you!" [15]Then the angel of the LORD said to Elijah, "Go down with him; you need not be afraid of him."

[16]So Elijah left and went down with him and stated to the king: "Thus says the LORD: 'Because you sent messengers to inquire of Baalzebub, the god of Ekron, you shall not leave the bed upon which you lie; instead you shall die.' "[d]

[17]Ahaziah died in fulfillment of the prophecy of the LORD spoken by Elijah. Since he had no son, his brother Joram* succeeded him as king, in the second year of Jehoram, son of Jehoshaphat, king of Judah. [18]The rest of the acts of Ahaziah are recorded in the book of chronicles of the kings of Israel.

CHAPTER 2

See RG
192

Elijah and Elisha. [1]When the LORD was about to take Elijah up to heaven in a whirlwind, he and Elisha were on their way from Gilgal.* [2]"Stay here, please," Elijah said to Elisha. "The LORD has sent me on to Bethel." "As the LORD lives, and as you yourself live," Elisha replied, "I will not leave you." So they went down to Bethel, [3]where the guild prophets went out to Elisha and asked him, "Do you know that the LORD will take your master from over you today?" "Yes, I know it," he replied. "Keep still."

[4]Then Elijah said to him, "Stay here, please, Elisha, for the LORD has sent me on to Jericho." "As the LORD lives, and as you yourself live," Elisha replied, "I will not leave you." [5]They went on to Jericho, where the guild prophets approached Elisha and

---

1, 8: Hairy garment: a sign of ascetical and prophetic calling, imitated by John the Baptizer; see Mt 3, 4; Mk 1, 6.

1, 12: Divine fire: literally, "fire of God," which in Hebrew sounds quite like man of God. The play on words is the basis for Elijah's alleged retort. This story was told among the people to enhance the dignity of the prophet and to reflect the power of God whom he served. The mercy which God extends even to the wicked is described in Wis 11, 17—12, 22, and the prophet Elijah was well aware of it (1 Kgs 21, 28f).

1, 17: Joram: in the Second Book of Kings the name Joram (yoram), alternately Jehoram (yehoram), appears in numerous passages to designate both the king of Judah, son and

successor of Jehoshaphat (848–841 B.C.), and the contemporary king of Israel, son of Ahab (852–841 B.C.). For the convenience of the reader in distinguishing these two kings, the longer form, Jehoram, is used to designate the king of Judah and the shorter form, Joram, to designate the king of Israel. See note on 2 Kgs 3, 1.

2, 1: Gilgal: commonly identified with Jiljulieh, about seven miles north of Bethel, and different from the Gilgal in Dt 11, 30 near Shechem, and that in Jos 4 and 5, passim, near Jericho.

b: Zec 13, 4.   c: Lv 10, 2; Sir 48, 3f; Lk 9, 54f.   d: Sir 48, 6.

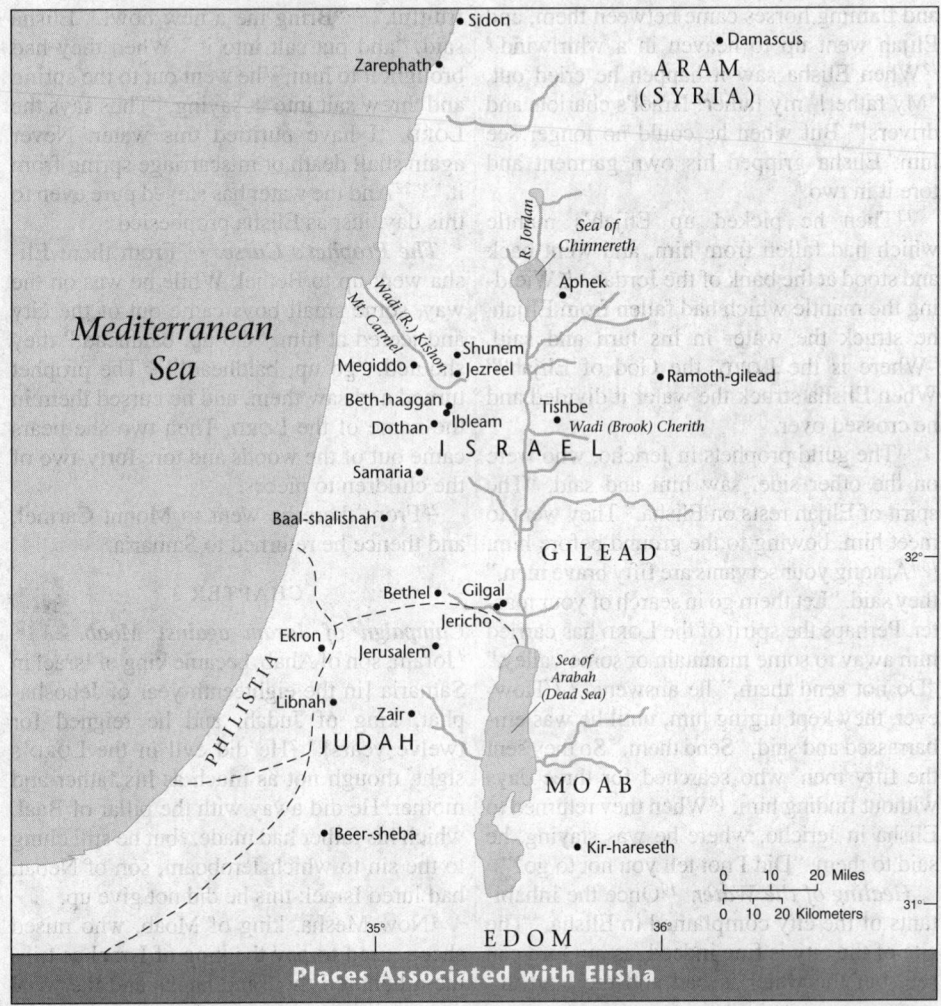

Places Associated with Elisha

asked him, "Do you know that the LORD will take your master from over you today?" "Yes, I know it," he replied. "Keep still."

[6] Elijah said to Elisha, "Please stay here; the LORD has sent me on to the Jordan." "As the LORD lives, and as you yourself live," Elisha replied, "I will not leave you." And so the two went on together. [7] Fifty of the guild prophets followed, and when the two stopped at the Jordan, stood facing them at a distance. [8] Elijah took his mantle, rolled it up and struck the water, which divided, and both crossed over on dry ground.[e]

Elisha Succeeds Elijah. [9] When they had crossed over, Elijah said to Elisha, "Ask for whatever I may do for you, before I am taken from you." Elisha answered, "May I receive a double portion of your spirit."* [10] "You have asked something that is not easy," he replied. "Still, if you see me taken up from you, your wish will be granted; otherwise not."[f] [11] As they walked on conversing, a flaming chariot

2, 9: *Double portion of your spirit:* as the first-born son inherited a double portion of his father's property (Dt 21, 17), so Elisha asks to inherit from Elijah his spirit of prophecy in the degree befitting his principal disciple. In Nm 11, 17. 25, God bestows some of the spirit of Moses on others.

e: Ex 14, 16. 22. *f:* Nm 11, 17. 25.

and flaming horses came between them, and Elijah went up to heaven in a whirlwind.[g] [12]When Elisha saw it happen he cried out, "My father![*] my father! Israel's chariots and drivers!" But when he could no longer see him, Elisha gripped his own garment and tore it in two.[h]

[13]Then he picked up Elijah's mantle which had fallen from him, and went back and stood at the bank of the Jordan.[i] [14]Wielding the mantle which had fallen from Elijah, he struck the water in his turn and said, "Where is the LORD, the God of Elijah?" When Elisha struck the water it divided and he crossed over.

[15]The guild prophets in Jericho, who were on the other side, saw him and said, "The spirit of Elijah rests on Elisha." They went to meet him, bowing to the ground before him. [16]"Among your servants are fifty brave men," they said. "Let them go in search of your master. Perhaps the spirit of the LORD has carried him away to some mountain or some valley." "Do not send them," he answered.[j] [17]However, they kept urging him, until he was embarrassed and said, "Send them." So they sent the fifty men, who searched for three days without finding him. [18]When they returned to Elisha in Jericho, where he was staying, he said to them, "Did I not tell you not to go?"

Healing of the Water. [19]Once the inhabitants of the city complained to Elisha, "The site of the city is fine indeed, as my lord can see, but the water is bad and the land un-

fruitful." [20]"Bring me a new bowl," Elisha said, "and put salt into it." When they had brought it to him, [21]he went out to the spring and threw salt into it, saying, "Thus says the LORD, 'I have purified this water. Never again shall death or miscarriage spring from it.' " [22]And the water has stayed pure even to this day, just as Elisha prophesied.

The Prophet's Curse. [23][*]From there Elisha went up to Bethel. While he was on the way, some small boys came out of the city and jeered at him. "Go up, baldhead," they shouted, "go up, baldhead!" [24]The prophet turned and saw them, and he cursed them in the name of the LORD. Then two she-bears came out of the woods and tore forty-two of the children to pieces.

[25]From there he went to Mount Carmel, and thence he returned to Samaria.

CHAPTER 3

See RG 192

Campaign of Joram against Moab. [1]Joram, son of Ahab, became king of Israel in Samaria [in the eighteenth year of Jehoshaphat, king of Judah, and he reigned for twelve years].[*] [2]He did evil in the LORD's sight, though not as much as his father and mother. He did away with the pillar of Baal, which his father had made, [3]but he still clung to the sin to which Jeroboam, son of Nebat, had lured Israel; this he did not give up.

[4]Now Mesha, king of Moab, who raised sheep, used to pay the king of Israel as tribute a hundred thousand lambs and the wool

2, 12: My father: a religious title accorded prophetic leaders; cf 2 Kgs 6, 21; 8, 9. Israel's chariots and drivers: Elijah was worth more than a whole army in defending Israel and the true religion. King Joash of Israel uses the same phrase of Elisha himself (2 Kgs 13, 14).

2, 23f: This story, like the one about Elijah and the captains (ch 1), is preserved for us in Scripture to convey a popular understanding of the dignity of the prophet. Told in popular vein, it becomes a caricature, in which neither Elisha nor the bears behave in character. See note on 2 Kgs 1, 12 and the contrasting narrative in ch 4.

3, 1: The sequence of the reigns between Ahab and Jehu of Israel may be reconstructed as follows: Jehoshaphat of Judah outlived Ahab by a short time, so that Ahaziah of Israel was his contemporary. Jehoram of Judah succeeded his father Jehoshaphat while Ahaziah of Israel was still alive. Jehoram (Joram) of Israel became king, following his brother Ahaziah, in the second year of Jehoram of Judah (2 Kgs 1, 17); this is one datum on which the earliest Greek evidence and the standard Hebrew text are in agreement.

The two Jehorams were contemporary for much of their reigns; Jehoram of Judah was succeeded by Ahaziah something more than a year before Jehu did away with the rulers of both kingdoms (2 Kgs 9, 1-29).

The Moabite campaign of 2 Kgs 3, 4-27 is thus best placed under the two Kings Jehoram, before the Edomite rebellion mentioned in 2 Kgs 8, 20. In the received Hebrew text, Jehoshaphat has been made the Judahite protagonist in the campaign against Moab as a tribute to his piety; this assimilates the story of 2 Kgs 3 to that of 1 Kgs 22, but creates difficulties in the chronology which the extant data leave partly unresolved. An older practice for stories of the Israelite kings was to leave them and their fellow kings without identification by name; cf 2 Kgs 6, 8—7, 20. The name of Jehoshaphat has been omitted from a number of places in 2 Kgs 3–8 in this translation; cf 1 Kgs 22, 51.

g: Gn 5, 24; 1 Mc 2, 58; Acts 1, 9.   h: 2 Kgs 13, 14; Sir 48, 9. 12.
i: 1 Kgs 19, 19.   j: 1 Kgs 18, 12.

of a hundred thousand rams. [5]But when Ahab died, the king of Moab had rebelled against the king of Israel. [6]Joram as king mustered all Israel, and when he set out on a campaign from Samaria, [7]he sent the king of Judah the message: "The king of Moab is in rebellion against me. Will you join me in battle against Moab?" "I will," he replied. "You and I shall be as one, your people and mine, and your horses and mine as well."[k] [8]They discussed the route for their attack, and settled upon the route through the desert of Edom.

[9]So the king of Israel set out, accompanied by the king of Judah and the king of Edom. After their roundabout journey of seven days the water gave out for the army and for the animals with them. [10]"Alas!" exclaimed the king of Israel. "The LORD has called together these three kings to put them in the grasp of Moab." [11]But the king of Judah asked, "Is there no prophet of the LORD here through whom we may inquire of the LORD?" One of the officers of the king of Israel replied, "Elisha, son of Shaphat, who poured water on the hands of Elijah, is here."[l] [12]"He has the word of the LORD," the king of Judah agreed. So the kings of Israel, Judah, and Edom went down to Elisha. [13]"What do you want with me?" Elisha asked the king of Israel. "Go to the prophets of your father and to the prophets of your mother." "No," the king of Israel replied. "The LORD has called these three kings together to put them in the grasp of Moab." [14]Then Elisha said, "As the LORD of hosts lives, whom I serve, were it not that I respect the king of Judah, I should neither look at you nor notice you at all."[m] [15]Now get me a minstrel."

When the minstrel played, the power of the LORD came upon Elisha [16]and he announced: "Thus says the LORD, 'Provide many catch basins in this wadi.' [17]For the LORD says, 'Though you will see neither wind nor rain, yet this wadi will be filled

with water for you, your livestock, and your pack animals to drink.' [18]And since the LORD does not consider this enough, he will also deliver Moab into your grasp. [19]You shall destroy every fortified city, fell every fruit tree, stop up all the springs, and ruin every fertile field with stones."[n]

[20]In the morning, at the time of the sacrifice, water came from the direction of Edom and filled the land.[o] [21]Meanwhile, all Moab heard that the kings had come to give them battle; every man capable of bearing arms was called up and stationed at the border. [22]Early that morning, when the sun shone on the water, the Moabites saw the water at a distance as red as blood.[*] [23]"This is blood!" they exclaimed. "The kings have fought among themselves and killed one another. Quick! To the spoils, Moabites!" [24]But when they reached the camp of Israel, the Israelites rose up and attacked the Moabites, who fled from them. They ranged through the countryside striking down the Moabites, and [25]destroying the cities; each of them cast stones onto every fertile field till they had loaded it down; all the springs they stopped up and every useful tree they felled. Finally only Kir-hareseth[*] was left behind its stone walls, and the slingers had surrounded it and were attacking it.[p] [26]When he saw that he was losing the battle, the king of Moab took seven hundred swordsmen to break through to the king of Aram, but he failed. [27]So he took his first-born, his heir apparent, and offered him as a holocaust upon the wall. The wrath against Israel[*] was so great that they gave up the siege and returned to their own land.[q]

CHAPTER 4

See RG 192

The Widow's Oil. [1]A certain woman, the widow of one of the guild prophets, complained to Elisha: "My husband, your servant, is dead. You know that he was a God-fearing man, yet now his creditor has come

---

3, 22: Red as blood: possibly caused by the red sandstone of the Wadi Zered (Dt 2, 13), south of Moab.

3, 25: Kir-hareseth: modern Kerak, east of the Dead Sea; cf Is 16, 7. 11; Jer 48, 31. 36.

3, 27: The wrath against Israel: probably the wrath of Chemosh, the Moabite god to whom the child was offered. He was feared by the Israelites who lost heart on foreign soil.

4, 1: His creditor . . . slaves: Hebrew law permitted the selling of wife and children as chattels for debt; cf Ex 21, 7; Am 2, 6; 8, 6; Is 50.

k: 1 Kgs 22, 4. l: 1 Kgs 22, 7. m: 1 Kgs 18, 15. n: Dt 20, 19. o: 1 Kgs 18, 29. p: Jb 5, 23. q: Jgs 11, 30f. r: 1 Kgs 17, 8-16.

to take my two children as his slaves.'"* [2]"How can I help you?" Elisha answered her. "Tell me what you have in the house." "This servant of yours has nothing in the house but a jug of oil," she replied. [3]"Go out," he said, "borrow vessels from all your neighbors—as many empty vessels as you can. [4]Then come back and close the door on yourself and your children; pour the oil into all the vessels, and as each is filled, set it aside." [5]She went and did so, closing the door on herself and her children. As they handed her the vessels, she would pour in oil. [6]When all the vessels were filled, she said to her son, "Bring me another vessel." "There is none left," he answered her. And then the oil stopped. [7]She went and told the man of God, who said, "Go and sell the oil to pay off your creditor; with what remains, you and your children can live."

Elisha and the Shunammite. [8]One day Elisha came to Shunem, where there was a woman of influence, who urged him to dine with her. Afterward, whenever he passed by, he used to stop there to dine. [9]So she said to her husband, "I know that he is a holy man of God. Since he visits us often, [10]let us arrange a little room on the roof and furnish it for him with a bed, table, chair, and lamp, so that when he comes to us he can stay there." [11]Some time later Elisha arrived and stayed in the room overnight. [12]Then he said to his servant Gehazi, "Call this Shunammite woman." He did so, and when she stood before Elisha, [13]he told Gehazi, "Say to her, 'You have lavished all this care on us; what can we do for you? Can we say a good word for you to the king or to the commander of the army?' " She replied, "I am living among my own people." [14]Later Elisha asked, "Can something be done for her?" "Yes!" Gehazi answered. "She has no son, and her husband is getting on in years." [15]"Call her," said Elisha. When she had been called, and stood at the door, [16]Elisha promised, "This time next year you will be fondling a baby son." "Please, my lord," she protested, "you are a man of God; do not deceive your servant."[s] [17]Yet the woman conceived, and by the same time the following year she had given birth to a son, as Elisha promised.

[18]The day came when the child was old enough to go out to his father among the reapers.[t] [19]"My head hurts!" he complained to his father. "Carry him to his mother," the father said to a servant. [20]The servant picked him up and carried him to his mother; he stayed with her until noon, when he died in her lap. [21]The mother took him upstairs and laid him on the bed of the man of God. Closing the door on him, she went out [22]and called to her husband, "Let me have a servant and a donkey. I must go quickly to the man of God, and I will be back." [23]"Why are you going to him today?" he asked. "It is neither the new moon nor the sabbath." But she bade him good-bye, [24]and when the donkey was saddled, said to her servant: "Lead on! Do not stop my donkey unless I tell you to." [25]She kept going till she reached the man of God on Mount Carmel. When he spied her at a distance, the man of God said to his servant Gehazi: "There is the Shunammite! [26]Hurry to meet her, and ask if all is well with her, with her husband, and with the boy." "Greetings,"* she replied. [27]But when she reached the man of God on the mountain, she clasped his feet. Gehazi came near to push her away, but the man of God said: "Let her alone, she is in bitter anguish; the LORD hid it from me and did not let me know." [28]"Did I ask my lord for a son?" she cried out. "Did I not beg you not to deceive me?" [29]"Gird your loins," Elisha said to Gehazi, "take my staff with you and be off; if you meet anyone, do not greet him,* and if anyone greets you, do not answer. Lay my staff upon the boy." [30]But the boy's mother cried out: "As the LORD lives and as you yourself live, I will not release you." So he started to go back with her.

4, 26: Greetings: the conventional answer to Gehazi's question, which tells him nothing.

4, 29: Do not greet him: the profuse exchange of compliments among Orientals meeting and greeting one another consumed time. Urgency necessitated their omission, as our Lord counseled his disciples (Lk 10, 4).

s: Gn 18, 10.   *t:* 1 Kgs 17, 17-24.

³¹ᵘMeanwhile, Gehazi had gone on ahead and had laid the staff upon the boy, but there was no sound or sign of life. He returned to meet Elisha and informed him that the boy had not awakened. ³²When Elisha reached the house, he found the boy lying dead. ³³He went in, closed the door on them both, and prayed to the LORD.ᵛ ³⁴Then he lay upon the child on the bed, placing his mouth upon the child's mouth, his eyes upon the eyes, and his hands upon the hands. As Elisha stretched himself over the child, the body became warm. ³⁵He arose, paced up and down the room, and then once more lay down upon the boy, who now sneezed seven times and opened his eyes.ʷ ³⁶Elisha summoned Gehazi and said, "Call the Shunammite." She came at his call, and Elisha said to her, "Take your son." ³⁷She came in and fell at his feet in gratitude; then she took her son and left the room.

The Poisoned Stew. ³⁸When Elisha returned to Gilgal, there was a famine in the land. Once, when the guild prophets were seated before him, he said to his servant, "Put the large pot on, and make some vegetable stew for the guild prophets." ³⁹Someone went out into the field to gather herbs and found a wild vine, from which he picked a clothful of wild gourds. On his return he cut them up into the pot of vegetable stew without anybody's knowing it. ⁴⁰The stew was poured out for the men to eat, but when they began to eat it, they exclaimed, "Man of God, there is poison in the pot!" And they could not eat it. ⁴¹"Bring some meal," Elisha said. He threw it into the pot and said, "Serve it to the people to eat." And there was no longer anything harmful in the pot.

Multiplication of Loaves. ⁴²A man came from Baal-shalishah bringing the man of God twenty barley loaves made from the first-fruits, and fresh grain in the ear. "Give it to the people to eat," Elisha said. ⁴³But his servant objected, "How can I set this before a hundred men?" "Give it to the people to eat," Elisha insisted. "For thus says the LORD, 'They shall eat and there shall be some left

over.' " ⁴⁴And when they had eaten, there was some left over, as the LORD had said.

CHAPTER 5

See RG 192

Cure of Naaman. ¹Naaman, the army commander of the king of Aram, was highly esteemed and respected by his master, for through him the LORD had brought victory to Aram. But valiant as he was, the man was a leper. ²Now the Arameans had captured from the land of Israel in a raid a little girl, who became the servant of Naaman's wife. ³"If only my master would present himself to the prophet in Samaria," she said to her mistress, "he would cure him of his leprosy." ⁴Naaman went and told his lord just what the slave girl from the land of Israel had said. ⁵"Go," said the king of Aram. "I will send along a letter to the king of Israel." So Naaman set out, taking along ten silver talents, six thousand gold pieces, and ten festal garments. ⁶To the king of Israel he brought the letter, which read: "With this letter I am sending my servant Naaman to you, that you may cure him of his leprosy."

⁷When he read the letter, the king of Israel tore his garments and exclaimed: "Am I a god with power over life and death, that this man should send someone to me to be cured of leprosy? Take note! You can see he is only looking for a quarrel with me!"ˣ ⁸When Elisha, the man of God, heard that the king of Israel had torn his garments, he sent word to the king: "Why have you torn your garments? Let him come to me and find out that there is a prophet in Israel."

⁹Naaman came with his horses and chariots and stopped at the door of Elisha's house. ¹⁰The prophet sent him the message: "Go and wash seven times in the Jordan, and your flesh will heal, and you will be clean."ʸ ¹¹But Naaman went away angry, saying, "I thought that he would surely come out and stand there to invoke the LORD his God, and would move his hand over the spot, and thus cure the leprosy. ¹²Are not the rivers of Damascus, the Abana and the Pharpar, better than all the waters of Israel? Could I not

---

u: 31-36; Acts 20, 10ff.   v: 1 Kgs 17, 21-23.   w: Heb 11, 35.   x: Gn 30, 2; 1 Sm 2, 6; Jn 5, 21.   y: Jn 9, 7.

wash in them and be cleansed?'"* With this, he turned about in anger and left.

¹³But his servants came up and reasoned with him. "My father," they said, "if the prophet had told you to do something extraordinary, would you not have done it? All the more now, since he said to you, 'Wash and be clean,' should you do as he said." ¹⁴So Naaman went down and plunged into the Jordan seven times at the word of the man of God. His flesh became again like the flesh of a little child, and he was clean.ᶻ

¹⁵He returned with his whole retinue to the man of God. On his arrival he stood before him and said, "Now I know that there is no God in all the earth, except in Israel. Please accept a gift from your servant."

¹⁶"As the LORD lives whom I serve, I will not take it," Elisha replied; and despite Naaman's urging, he still refused. ¹⁷Naaman said: "If you will not accept, please let me, your servant, have two mule-loads of earth,* for I will no longer offer holocaust or sacrifice to any other god except to the LORD. ¹⁸But I trust the LORD will forgive your servant this: when my master enters the temple of Rimmon to worship there, then I, too, as his adjutant, must bow down in the temple of Rimmon. May the LORD forgive your servant this." ¹⁹"Go in peace,"* Elisha said to him.

²⁰Naaman had gone some distance when Gehazi, the servant of Elisha, the man of God, thought to himself: "My master was too easy with this Aramean Naaman, not accepting what he brought. As the LORD lives, I will run after him and get something out of him." ²¹So Gehazi hurried after Naaman. Aware that someone was running after him, Naaman alighted from his chariot to wait for him. "Is everything all right?" he asked. ²²"Yes," Gehazi replied, "but my master sent me to say, 'Two young men have just come to me, guild prophets from the hill country of Ephraim. Please give them a talent of silver

and two festal garments.' " ²³"Please take two talents," Naaman said, and pressed them upon him. He tied up these silver talents in bags and gave them, with the two festal garments, to two of his servants, who carried them before Gehazi. ²⁴When they reached the hill, Gehazi took what they had, carried it into the house, and sent the men on their way.

²⁵He went in and stood before Elisha his master, who asked him, "Where have you been, Gehazi?" He answered, "Your servant has not gone anywhere." ²⁶But Elisha said to him: "Was I not present in spirit when the man alighted from his chariot to wait for you? Is this a time to take money or to take garments, olive orchards or vineyards, sheep or cattle, male or female servants? ²⁷The leprosy of Naaman shall cling to you and your descendants forever." And Gehazi left Elisha, a leper white as snow.ᵃ

CHAPTER 6

See RG 192-93

Recovery of the Lost Ax. ¹The guild prophets once said to Elisha: "There is not enough room for us to continue to live here with you. ²Let us go to the Jordan, where by getting one beam apiece we can build ourselves a place to live." "Go," Elisha said. ³"Please agree to accompany your servants," one of them requested. "Yes, I will come," he replied.

⁴So he went with them, and when they arrived at the Jordan they began to fell trees. ⁵While one of them was felling a tree trunk, the iron axhead slipped into the water. "O master," he cried out, "it was borrowed!" ⁶"Where did it fall?" asked the man of God. When he pointed out the spot, Elisha cut off a stick, threw it into the water, and brought the iron to the surface. ⁷"Pick it up," he said. And the man reached down and grasped it.

Aramean Ambush. ⁸When the king of Aram was waging war on Israel, he would make plans with his servants to attack a par-

---

5, 12: Wash in them and be cleansed: typical of the ambiguity in ritual healing or cleanliness. The muddy waters of the Jordan are no match hygienically for the mountain spring waters of Damascus; ritually, it is the other way around.

5, 17: Two mule-loads of earth: Israelite earth on which to erect in Aram an altar to the God of Israel.

5, 19: Go in peace: Elisha understands and approves the

situation of Naaman who, though a proselyte as regards belief in and worship of the God of Israel, is required by his office to assist his master, the king, worshiping in the pagan temple of Rimmon.

z: Lk 4, 27.   a: Ex 4, 6; Nm 12, 10.

ticular place. [9]But the man of God would send word to the king of Israel, "Be careful! Do not pass by this place, for Aram will attack there." [10]So the king of Israel would send word to the place which the man of God had indicated, and alert it; then they would be on guard. This happened several times.

[11]Greatly disturbed over this, the king of Aram called together his officers. "Will you not tell me," he asked them, "who among us is for the king of Israel?" [12]"No one, my lord king," answered one of the officers. "The Israelite prophet Elisha can tell the king of Israel the very words you speak in your bedroom." [13]"Go, find out where he is," he said, "so that I may take him captive."

Blinded Aramean Soldiers. Informed that Elisha was in Dothan, [14]he sent there a strong force with horses and chariots. They arrived by night and surrounded the city. [15]Early the next morning, when the attendant of the man of God arose and went out, he saw the force with its horses and chariots surrounding the city. "Alas!" he said to Elisha. "What shall we do, my lord?" [16]"Do not be afraid," Elisha answered. "Our side outnumbers theirs." [17]Then he prayed, "O LORD, open his eyes, that he may see." And the LORD opened the eyes of the servant, so that he saw the mountainside filled with horses and fiery chariots around Elisha.[b]

[18]When the Arameans came down to get him, Elisha prayed to the LORD, "Strike this people blind, I pray you." And in answer to the prophet's prayer the LORD struck them blind. [19]Then Elisha said to them: "This is the wrong road, and this is the wrong city. Follow me! I will take you to the man you want." And he led them to Samaria. [20]When they entered Samaria, Elisha prayed, "O LORD, open their eyes that they may see." The LORD opened their eyes, and they saw that they were inside Samaria. [21]When the king of Israel saw them, he asked, "Shall I kill them, my father?" [22]"You must not kill them," replied Elisha. "Do you slay those whom you have taken captive with your sword or bow?* Serve them bread and water. Let them eat and drink, and then go back to their master." [23]The king spread a great feast for them. When they had eaten and drunk he sent them away, and they went back to their master. No more Aramean raiders came into the land of Israel.

Siege of Samaria. [24]After this, Ben-hadad, king of Aram, mustered his whole army and laid siege to Samaria. [25]Because of the siege the famine in Samaria was so severe that an ass's head sold for eighty pieces of silver, and a fourth of a kab of wild onion for five pieces of silver.

[26]One day, as the king of Israel was walking on the city wall, a woman cried out to him, "Help, my lord king!" [27]"No," he replied, "the LORD help you! Where could I find help for you: from the threshing floor or the winepress?" [28]Then the king asked her, "What is your trouble?" She replied: "This woman said to me, 'Give up your son that we may eat him today; then tomorrow we will eat my son.'[c] [29]So we boiled my son and ate him. The next day I said to her, 'Now give up your son that we may eat him.' But she hid her son." [30]When the king heard the woman's words, he tore his garments. And as he was walking on the wall, the people saw that he was wearing sackcloth underneath, next to his skin.[d]

[31]"May God do thus and so to me," the king exclaimed, "if the head of Elisha, son of Shaphat, stays on him today!" [32]Meanwhile, Elisha was sitting in his house in conference with the elders. The king had sent a man ahead before he himself should come to him. Elisha had said to the elders: "Do you know that this son of a murderer is sending someone to cut off my head? When the messenger comes, see that you close the door and hold it fast against him. His master's footsteps are echoing behind him." [33]While Elisha was still speaking, the king came down to him and said, "This evil is from the LORD. Why should I trust in the LORD any longer?"

6, 22: With your sword or bow: since the king would not slay prisoners who had surrendered to his power, much less should he slay prisoners captured by God's power. By Oriental custom they became guests within Samaria's walls.

b: 2 Kgs 7, 6; Ps 67, 18.   *c:* Dt 28, 53-57.   *d:* 1 Kgs 20, 31; 21, 27.

See RG
193

CHAPTER 7

[1]Elisha said: "Hear the word of the LORD! Thus says the LORD, 'At this time tomorrow a seah of fine flour will sell for a shekel, and two seahs of barley for a shekel, in the market* of Samaria.' " [2]But the adjutant on whose arm the king leaned, answered the man of God, "Even if the LORD were to make windows in heaven, how could this happen?" "You shall see it with your own eyes," Elisha said, "but you shall not eat of it."[e]

The Lepers at the Gate. [3]At the city gate were four lepers who were deliberating, "Why should we sit here until we die?[f] [4]If we decide to go into the city, we shall die there, for there is famine in the city. If we remain here, we shall die too. Come, let us desert to the camp of the Arameans. If they spare us, we live; if they kill us, we die." [5]At twilight they left for the Arameans; but when they reached the edge of the camp, no one was there. [6g]The LORD had caused the army of the Arameans to hear the sound of chariots and horses, the din of a large army, and they had reasoned among themselves, "The king of Israel has hired the kings of the Hittites and the kings of the borderlands* to fight us." [7]Then in the twilight they fled, abandoning their tents, their horses, and their asses, the whole camp just as it was, and fleeing for their lives. [8]After the lepers reached the edge of the camp, they went first into one tent, ate and drank, and took silver, gold, and clothing from it, and went out and hid them. Back they came into another tent, took things from it, and again went out and hid them. [9]Then they said to one another: "We are not doing right. This is a day of good news, and we are keeping silent. If we wait until morning breaks, we shall be blamed. Come, let us go and inform the palace." [10]They came and summoned the city gatekeepers. "We went to the camp of the Arameans," they said, "but no one was there— not a human voice, only the horses and asses tethered, and the tents just as they were left."

[11]The gatekeepers announced this and it was reported within the palace. [12]Though it was night, the king got up; he said to his servants: "Let me tell you what the Arameans have done to us. Knowing that we are in famine, they have left their camp to hide in the field, hoping to take us alive and enter our city when we leave it." [13]One of his servants, however, suggested: "Since those who are left in the city are no better off than all the throng that has perished, let some of us take five of the abandoned horses and send scouts to investigate."

End of the Siege. [14]They took two chariots, and horses, and the king sent them to reconnoiter the Aramean army. "Go and find out," he ordered. [15]They followed the Arameans as far as the Jordan, and the whole route was strewn with garments and other objects that the Arameans had thrown away in their haste. The messengers returned and told the king.

[16]The people went out and plundered the camp of the Arameans; and then a seah of fine flour sold for a shekel and two seahs of barley for a shekel, as the LORD had said.

[17]The king put in charge of the gate the officer who was his adjutant; but the people trampled him to death at the gate, just as the man of God had predicted when the king visited him. [18]Thus was fulfilled the prophecy of the man of God to the king, "Two seahs of barley will sell for a shekel, and one seah of fine flour for a shekel at this time tomorrow at the gate of Samaria." [19]The adjutant had answered the man of God, "Even if the LORD were to make windows in heaven, how could this happen?" And Elisha had replied, "You shall see it with your own eyes, but you shall not eat of it." [20]And that is what happened to him, for the people trampled him to death at the gate.

CHAPTER 8

See RG
193

Prediction of Famine. [1]Elisha once said to the woman whose son he had restored to life: "Get ready! Leave with your family

7, 1: Market: literally "gate," the principal place of trading in ancient walled cities in time of peace.

7, 6: Kings of the borderlands: from Musur in Anatolia rather than Egypt.

e: 2 Kgs 7, 17; Ps 78, 23; Is 24, 18. *f:* Lv 13, 46. *g:* 6f: 2 Kgs 6, 17; 19, 35f; 2 Sm 5. 24.

and settle wherever you can, because the LORD has decreed a seven-year famine which is coming upon the land."[h] [2]The woman got ready and did as the man of God said, setting out with her family and settling in the land of the Philistines for seven years. [3]At the end of the seven years, the woman returned from the land of the Philistines and went out to the king to claim her house and her field. [4]The king was talking with Gehazi, the servant of the man of God. "Tell me," he said, "all the great things that Elisha has done." [5]Just as he was relating to the king how his master had restored a dead person to life, the very woman whose son Elisha had restored to life came to the king to claim her house and field. "My lord king," Gehazi said, "this is the woman, and this is that son of hers whom Elisha restored to life." [6]The king questioned the woman, and she told him her story. With that the king placed an official[*] at her disposal, saying, "Restore all her property to her, with all that the field produced from the day she left the land until now."

Death of Ben-hadad Foretold. [7]Elisha came to Damascus at a time when Ben-hadad, king of Aram, lay sick. When he was told that the man of God had come there, [8]the king said to Hazael, "Take a gift with you and go call on the man of God. Have him consult the LORD as to whether I shall recover from this sickness." [9]Hazael went to visit him, carrying a present, and with forty camel loads of the best goods of Damascus. On his arrival, he stood before the prophet and said, "Your son Ben-hadad, king of Aram, has sent me to ask you whether he will recover from his sickness." [10]"Go and tell him," Elisha answered, "that he will surely recover. However, the LORD has showed me that he will in fact die." [11]Then he stared him down until Hazael became ill at ease. The man of God wept, [12]and Hazael asked, "Why are you weeping, my lord?" Elisha replied, "Because

I know the evil that you will inflict upon the Israelites. You will burn their fortresses, you will slay their youth with the sword, you will dash their little children to pieces, you will rip open their pregnant women."[i]

[13]Hazael exclaimed, "How can a dog like me, your servant,[*] do anything so important?" "The LORD has showed you to me as king over Aram," replied Elisha.[j] [14]Hazael left Elisha and returned to his master. "What did Elisha tell you?" asked Ben-hadad. "He told me that you would surely recover," replied Hazael. [15]The next day, however, Hazael took a cloth, dipped it in water, and spread it over the king's face, so that he died. And Hazael reigned in his stead.

Reign of Jehoram of Judah. [16]In the fifth year of Joram, son of Ahab, king of Israel, Jehoram,[*] son of Jehoshaphat, king of Judah, became king. [17k]He was thirty-two years old when he began to reign, and he reigned eight years in Jerusalem. [18]He conducted himself like the kings of Israel of the line of Ahab, since the sister of Ahab was his wife; and he did evil in the LORD's sight. [19]Even so, the LORD was unwilling to destroy Judah, because of his servant David. For he had promised David that he would leave him a lamp in the LORD's presence for all time.[l] [20]During Jehoram's reign, Edom revolted against the sovereignty of Judah and chose a king of its own. [21]Thereupon Jehoram with all his chariots crossed over to Zair. He arose by night and broke through the Edomites when they had surrounded him and the commanders of his chariots. Then his army fled homeward. [22]To this day Edom has been in revolt against the rule of Judah. Libnah also revolted at that time.[m] [23]The rest of the acts of Jehoram, with all that he did, are recorded in the book of the chronicles of the kings of Judah. [24]Jehoram rested with his ancestors and was buried with them in the City of David. His son Ahaziah succeeded him as king.

8, 6: An official: Literally "eunuch," and perhaps actually so in this instance.

8, 13: A dog . . . your servant: Hazael feigns humility (1 Sm 24, 14; 2 Sm 9, 8), without attending to the crimes he would commit after usurping the royal power as the prophet predicts. Anything so important; literally "a great deed" for a patriotic Syrian.

8, 16: Jehoram of Judah succeeded his father Jehoshaphat during the reign of Ahaziah of Israel. See note on 2 Kgs 3, 1.

h: 2 Kgs 4, 36. i: 2 Kgs 13, 7. j: 2 Kgs 15, 16; 1 Kgs 19, 15. k: 17ff: 2 Chr 21, 5ff. l: 2 Sm 7, 11-16; 21, 17; 1 Kgs 11, 36; 15, 4; 2 Chr 21, 7. m: Gn 27, 40; 2 Chr 21, 8ff.

Accession of Ahaziah. [25]Ahaziah, son of Jehoram, king of Judah, became king in the twelfth year of Joram,[*] son of Ahab, king of Israel. [26]He was twenty-two years old when he began his reign, and he reigned one year in Jerusalem. His mother's name was Athaliah; she was the daughter of Omri, king of Israel. [27]He conducted himself like the house of Ahab, doing evil in the LORD's sight as they did, since he was related to them by marriage. [28]He joined Joram, son of Ahab, in battle against Hazael, king of Aram, at Ramoth-gilead, where the Arameans wounded Joram.[n] [29]King Joram returned to Jezreel to be healed of the wounds which the Arameans had inflicted on him at Ramah in his battle against Hazael, king of Aram. Then Ahaziah, son of Jehoram, king of Judah, went down to Jezreel to visit him there in his illness.

See RG
193–94

CHAPTER 9

Anointing of Jehu. [1]The prophet Elisha called one of the guild prophets and said to him: "Gird your loins, take this flask of oil with you, and go to Ramoth-gilead.[o] [2]When you get there, look for Jehu, son of Jehoshaphat, son of Nimshi. Enter and take him away from his companions into an inner chamber.[p] [3]From the flask you have, pour oil on his head, and say, 'Thus says the LORD: I anoint you king over Israel.' Then open the door and flee without delay."[q] [4]The young man (the guild prophet) went to Ramoth-gilead. [5]When he arrived, the commanders of the army were in session. "I have a message for you, commander," he said. "For which one of us?" asked Jehu. "For you, commander," he answered. [6]Jehu got up and went into the house. Then the young man poured the oil on his head and said, "Thus says the LORD, the God of Israel: 'I anoint you king over the people of the LORD, over Israel. [7*]You shall destroy the house of Ahab your master; thus will I avenge the blood of my servants the prophets, and the blood of all the other servants of the LORD shed by Jezebel, [8r]and by all the rest of the family of Ahab. I will cut off every male in Ahab's line, whether slave or freeman in Israel. [9]I will deal with the house of Ahab as I dealt with the house of Jeroboam, son of Nebat, and with the house of Baasha, son of Ahijah. [10]Dogs shall devour Jezebel at the confines of Jezreel, so that no one can bury her.' " Then he opened the door and fled.

[11]When Jehu rejoined his master's servants, they asked him, "Is all well? Why did that madman come to you?" "You know that kind of man and his talk," he replied. [12]But they said, "Not at all! Come, tell us." So he told them what the young man had said to him, and finally, "Thus says the LORD: 'I anoint you king over Israel.' " [13]At once each took his garment, spread it under Jehu on the bare steps, blew the trumpet, and cried out, "Jehu is king!"[s]

[14t]Thus Jehu, son of Jehoshaphat, son of Nimshi, formed a conspiracy against Joram. Joram, with all Israel, had been besieging Ramoth-gilead against Hazael, king of Aram, [15]but had returned to Jezreel to be healed of the wounds the Arameans had inflicted on him in the battle against Hazael, king of Aram.

Murder of Joram. "If you are truly with me," Jehu said, "see that no one escapes from the city to report in Jezreel." [16]Then Jehu mounted his chariot and drove to Jezreel, where Joram lay ill and Ahaziah, king of Judah, had come to visit him.

[17]The watchman standing on the tower in Jezreel saw the troop of Jehu coming and reported, "I see chariots." "Get a driver," Joram said, "and send him to meet them and to ask whether all is well." [18]So a driver went out to meet him and said, "The king asks whether all is well." "What does it matter to you how things are?" Jehu said. "Get behind me." The watchman reported to the king, "The messenger has reached them, but is not returning."

8, 25: Twelfth year of Joram: i.e., of Israel, who probably reigned only eight years.

9, 7-10: The editors of the Books of Kings have here added to the prophet's message the same type of indictment and sanctions against the family of Ahab as were invoked against the dynasties of Jeroboam (1 Kgs 14, 10f), Baasha

(1 Kgs 16, 3f), and Ahab on a previous occasion (1 Kgs 21, 21–24).

n: 2 Kgs 9, 14f. o: 1 Kgs 21, 29; Hos 1, 4. p: 1 Kgs 19, 16. q: 1 Kgs 19, 16. r: 8ff: 1 Kgs 14, 10f; 16, 3f; 21, 21-24. s: Mt 21, 8. t: 14f: 2 Kgs 8, 28f; 1 Kgs 22, 3f.

[19]Joram sent a second driver, who went to them and said, "The king asks whether all is well." "What does it matter to you how things are?" Jehu replied. "Get behind me."

[20]The watchman reported, "The messenger has reached them, but is not returning. The driving is like that of Jehu, son of Nimshi, in its fury." [21]"Prepare my chariot," said Joram. When they had done so, Joram, king of Israel, and Ahaziah, king of Judah, set out, each in his own chariot, to meet Jehu. They reached him near the field of Naboth the Jezreelite. [22]When Joram recognized Jehu, he asked, "Is all well, Jehu?" "How can all be well," Jehu replied, "as long as the many fornications and witchcrafts* of your mother Jezebel continue?" [23]Joram reined about and fled, crying to Ahaziah, "Treason, Ahaziah!" [24]But Jehu drew his bow and shot Joram between the shoulders, so that the arrow went through his heart and he collapsed in his chariot. [25u]Then Jehu said to his adjutant Bidkar, "Take him and throw him into the field of Naboth the Jezreelite. For I remember that when we were driving teams behind his father Ahab, the LORD delivered this oracle against him: [26]'As surely as I saw yesterday the blood of Naboth and the blood of his sons,' says the LORD, 'I will repay you for it in that very plot of ground, says the LORD.' So now take him into this plot of ground, in keeping with the word of the LORD."

Death of Ahaziah. [27v]Seeing what was happening, Ahaziah, king of Judah, fled toward Beth-haggan. Jehu pursued him, shouting, "Kill him too!" And they pierced him as he rode through the pass of Gur near Ibleam. He continued his flight as far as Megiddo and died there. [28]His servants brought him in a chariot to Jerusalem and buried him in the tomb of his ancestors in the City of David. [29]Ahaziah had become king of Judah in the eleventh year of Joram, son of Ahab.

Death of Jezebel. [30]When Jezebel learned that Jehu had arrived in Jezreel, she shadowed her eyes, adorned her hair, and looked down from her window. [31]As Jehu came through the gate, she cried out, "Is all well, Zimri, murderer of your master?"[w] [32]Jehu looked up to the window and shouted, "Who is on my side? Anyone?" At this, two or three eunuchs looked down toward him. [33]"Throw her down," he ordered. They threw her down, and some of her blood spurted against the wall and against the horses. Jehu rode in over her body [34]and, after eating and drinking, he said: "Attend to that accursed woman and bury her; after all, she was a king's daughter." [35]But when they went to bury her, they found nothing of her but the skull, the feet, and the hands. [36]They returned to Jehu, and when they told him, he said, "This is the sentence which the LORD pronounced through his servant Elijah the Tishbite: 'In the confines of Jezreel dogs shall eat the flesh of Jezebel.[x] [37]The corpse of Jezebel shall be like dung in the field in the confines of Jezreel, so that no one can say: This was Jezebel.'"

CHAPTER 10

See RG
194

Killing of Ahab's Descendants. [1]Ahab had seventy descendants in Samaria. Jehu prepared letters and sent them to the city rulers, to the elders, and to the guardians of Ahab's descendants in Samaria.[y] [2]"Since your master's sons are with you," he wrote, "and you have the chariots, the horses, a fortified city, and the weapons, when this letter reaches you [3]decide which is the best and the fittest of your master's offspring, place him on his father's throne, and fight for your master's house." [4]They were overcome with fright and said, "If two kings could not withstand him, how can we?" [5]So the vizier and the ruler of the city, along with the elders and the guardians, sent this message to Jehu: "We are your servants, and we will do everything you tell us. We will proclaim no one king; do whatever you think best." [6]So Jehu wrote them a second letter: "If you are on my side and will obey me, count the heads of your master's sons and come to me in Jezreel at this time tomorrow." [The seventy princes were in the care of prominent men of the city, who were rearing them.]

9, 22: Fornications and witchcrafts: the worship of foreign gods.

u: 25f: 1 Kgs 21, 9-16.   *v:* 27ff: 2 Chr 22, 7ff.   *w:* 1 Kgs 16, 9ff.   *x:* 1 Kgs 21, 23.   *y:* Jgs 9, 5; 1 Kgs 15, 29; 16, 11.

[7]When the letter arrived, they took the princes and slew all seventy of them, put their heads in baskets, and sent them to Jehu in Jezreel. [8]"They have brought the heads of the princes," a messenger came in and told him. "Pile them in two heaps at the entrance of the city until morning," he ordered. [9]Going out in the morning, he stopped and said to all the people: "You are not responsible, and although I conspired against my lord and slew him, yet who killed all these? [10]Know that not a single word which the LORD has spoken against the house of Ahab shall go unfulfilled. The LORD has accomplished all that he foretold through his servant Elijah."[z] [11]Thereupon Jehu slew all who were left of the family of Ahab in Jezreel, as well as all his powerful supporters, intimates, and priests, leaving him no survivor.[a]

Ahaziah's Kinsmen. [12b]Then he set out for Samaria, and at Beth-eked-haroim on the way, [13]he came across kinsmen of Ahaziah, king of Judah. "Who are you?" he asked. "We are kinsmen of Ahaziah," they replied. "We are going down to visit the princes and the family of the queen mother." [14]"Take them alive," Jehu ordered. They were taken alive, forty-two in number, then slain at the pit of Beth-eked. Not one of them was spared.

Jehu in Samaria. [15]When he had left there, Jehu met Jehonadab, son of Rechab, on the road. He greeted him and asked, "Are you sincerely disposed toward me, as I am toward you?" "Yes," replied Jehonadab. "If you are," continued Jehu, "give me your hand." Jehonadab gave him his hand, and Jehu drew him up into his chariot.[c] [16]"Come with me," he said, "and see my zeal for the LORD." And he took him along in his own chariot.

[17]When he arrived in Samaria, Jehu slew all who remained there of Ahab's line, doing away with them completely and thus fulfilling the prophecy which the LORD had spoken to Elijah.

Baal's Temple Destroyed. [18]Jehu gathered all the people together and said to them: "Ahab served Baal to some extent, but Jehu will serve him yet more.[d] [19]Now summon for me all Baal's prophets, all his worshipers, and all his priests. See that no one is absent, for I have a great sacrifice for Baal. Whoever is absent shall not live." This Jehu did as a ruse, so that he might destroy the worshipers of Baal. [20]Jehu said further, "Proclaim a solemn assembly in honor of Baal." They did so, [21]and Jehu sent word of it throughout the land of Israel. All the worshipers of Baal without exception came into the temple of Baal, which was filled to capacity. [22]Then Jehu said to the custodian of the wardrobe, "Bring out the garments for all the worshipers of Baal." When he had brought out the garments for them,[e] [23]Jehu, with Jehonadab, son of Rechab, entered the temple of Baal and said to the worshipers of Baal, "Search and be sure that there is no worshiper of the LORD here with you, but only worshipers of Baal." [24]Then they proceeded to offer sacrifices and holocausts. Now Jehu had stationed eighty men outside with this warning, "If one of you lets anyone escape of those whom I shall deliver into your hands, he shall pay life for life." [25]As soon as he finished offering the holocaust, Jehu said to the guards and officers, "Go in and slay them. Let no one escape." So the guards and officers put them to the sword and cast them out. Afterward they went into the inner shrine of the temple of Baal, [26]took out the stele of Baal, and burned the shrine. [27]Then they smashed the stele of Baal, tore down the building, and turned it into a latrine, as it remains today.

[28]Thus Jehu rooted out the worship of Baal from Israel. [29]However, he did not desist from the sins which Jeroboam, son of Nebat, had caused Israel to commit, as regards the golden calves at Bethel and at Dan.[f] [30]The LORD said to Jehu, "Because you have done well what I deem right, and have treated the house of Ahab as I desire, your sons to the fourth generation shall sit upon the throne of Israel."[g] [31]But Jehu was not careful to observe wholeheartedly the law of the LORD, the God of Israel, since he did not desist from the sins which Jeroboam caused Israel to commit.

z: 1 Kgs 21, 17-24. 29. a: Hos 1, 4. b: 12ff: 2 Chr 22, 8f. c: 1 Chr 2, 55; Jer 35, 1-11. d: 1 Kgs 16, 30ff. e: 1 Kgs 16, 32. f: 1 Kgs 12, 28f. g: 2 Kgs 15, 12ff.

[32h]At that time the LORD began to dismember Israel. Hazael defeated the Israelites throughout their territory [33]east of the Jordan (all the land of Gilead, of the Gadites, Reubenites and Manassehites), from Aroer on the river Arnon up through Gilead and Bashan.

[34]The rest of the acts of Jehu, his valor and all his accomplishments, are written in the book of the chronicles of the kings of Israel. [35]Jehu rested with his ancestors and was buried in Samaria. His son Jehoahaz succeeded him as king. [36]The length of Jehu's reign over Israel in Samaria was twenty-eight years.

CHAPTER 11

See RG 194

Rule of Athaliah. [1]When Athaliah, the mother of Ahaziah, saw that her son was dead, she began to kill off the whole royal family.[i] [2]But Jehosheba,* daughter of King Jehoram and sister of Ahaziah, took Joash, his son, and spirited him away, along with his nurse, from the bedroom where the princes were about to be slain. She concealed him from Athaliah, and so he did not die. [3]For six years he remained hidden in the temple of the LORD, while Athaliah ruled the land.

[4j]But in the seventh year, Jehoiada summoned the captains of the Carians and of the guards. He had them come to him in the temple of the LORD, exacted from them a sworn commitment, and then showed them the king's son. [5]He gave them these orders: "This is what you must do: the third of you who come on duty on the sabbath shall guard the king's palace; [6]another third shall be at the gate Sur; and the last third shall be at the gate behind the guards. [7]The two of your divisions who are going off duty that week shall keep guard over the temple of the LORD for the king. [8]You shall surround the king, each with drawn weapons, and if anyone tries to approach the cordon, kill him; stay with the king, whatever he may do."

[9k]The captains did just as Jehoiada the priest commanded. Each one with his men,

both those going on duty for the sabbath and those going off duty that week, came to Jehoiada the priest. [10l]He gave the captains King David's spears and shields, which were in the temple of the LORD. [11]And the guards, with drawn weapons, lined up from the southern to the northern limit of the enclosure, surrounding the altar and the temple on the king's behalf. [12]Then Jehoiada led out the king's son and put the crown and the insignia upon him. They proclaimed him king and anointed him, clapping their hands and shouting, "Long live the king!"[m]

[13n]Athaliah heard the noise made by the people, and appeared before them in the temple of the LORD. [14]When she saw the king standing by the pillar,* as was the custom, and the captains and trumpeters near him, with all the people of the land rejoicing and blowing trumpets, she tore her garments and cried out, "Treason, treason!" [15]Then Jehoiada the priest instructed the captains in command of the force: "Bring her outside through the ranks. If anyone follows her," he added, "let him die by the sword." He had given orders that she should not be slain in the temple of the LORD. [16]She was led out forcibly to the horse gate of the royal palace, where she was put to death.

[17o]Then Jehoiada made a covenant between the LORD as one party and the king and the people as the other, by which they would be the LORD's people; and another covenant, between the king and the people. [18]Thereupon all the people of the land went to the temple of Baal and demolished it. They shattered its altars and images completely, and slew Mattan, the priest of Baal, before the altars. After appointing a detachment for the temple of the LORD, Jehoiada [19]with the captains, the Carians, the guards, and all the people of the land, led the king down from the temple of the LORD through the guards' gate to the palace, where Joash took his seat on the royal throne. [20]All the people of the land rejoiced and the city was

---

11, 2: Jehosheba was the wife of Jehoida, the high priest; cf 2 Chr 22, 11.
11, 14: By the pillar: see note on 2 Chr 23, 13.

h: Am 1, 3.   *i:* Jgs 9, 5.   *j:* 4-8: 2 Chr 23, 1-7.   *k:* 9-12: 2 Chr 23, 8-11.   *l:* 10ff: 2 Sm 8, 7; 1 Kgs 1, 33f.   *m:* 2 Sm 1, 10.   *n:* 13-16: 2 Chr 23, 12-15.   *o:* 17-20: 2 Chr 23, 16-21.

quiet, now that Athaliah had been slain with the sword at the royal palace.

See RG 194

CHAPTER 12

Reign of Joash. [1]Joash was seven years old when he became king.[p] [2]Joash began to reign in the seventh year of Jehu, and he reigned forty years in Jerusalem. His mother, who was named Zibiah, was from Beer-sheba. [3]Joash did what was pleasing to the LORD as long as he lived, because the priest Jehoiada guided him. [4]Still, the high places did not disappear; the people continued to sacrifice and to burn incense there.

[5q]For the priests Joash made this rule: "All the funds for sacred purposes that are brought to the temple of the LORD—the census tax, personal redemption money, and whatever funds are freely brought to the temple of the LORD— [6]the priests may take for themselves, each from his own clients. However, they must make whatever repairs on the temple may prove necessary." [7]Nevertheless, as late as the twenty-third year of the reign of King Joash, the priests had not made needed repairs on the temple. [8]Accordingly, King Joash summoned the priest Jehoiada and the other priests. "Why do you not repair the temple?" he asked them. "You must no longer take funds from your clients, but you shall turn them over for the repairs." [9r]So the priests agreed that they would neither take funds from the people nor make the repairs on the temple.

[10]The priest Jehoiada then took a chest, bored a hole in its lid, and set it beside the stele, on the right as one entered the temple of the LORD. The priests who guarded the entry would put into it all the funds that were brought to the temple of the LORD. [11]When they noticed that there was a large amount of silver in the chest, the royal scribe [and the priest] would come up, and they would melt down all the funds that were in the temple of the LORD, and weigh them. [12]The amount thus realized they turned over to the master workmen in the temple of the LORD. They in turn would give it to the carpenters and builders working in the temple of the LORD,

[13]and to the lumbermen and stone cutters, and for the purchase of the wood and hewn stone used in repairing the breaches, and for any other expenses that were necessary to repair the temple. [14]None of the funds brought to the temple of the LORD were used there to make silver cups, snuffers, basins, trumpets, or any gold or silver article. [15]Instead, they were given to the workmen, and with them they repaired the temple of the LORD. [16]Moreover, no reckoning was asked of the men who were provided with the funds to give to the workmen, because they held positions of trust. [17]The funds from guilt-offerings and from sin-offerings, however, were not brought to the temple of the LORD; they belonged to the priests.

[18s]Then King Hazael of Aram mounted a siege against Gath. When he had taken it, Hazael decided to go on to attack Jerusalem.[t] [19]But King Jehoash of Judah took all the dedicated offerings presented by his forebears, Jehoshaphat, Jehoram, and Ahaziah, kings of Judah, as well as his own, and all the gold there was in the treasuries of the temple and the palace, and sent them to King Hazael of Aram, who then led his forces away from Jerusalem. [20]The rest of the acts of Joash, with all that he did, are recorded in the book of the chronicles of the kings of Judah. [21]Certain of his officials entered into a plot against him and killed him at Bethmillo. [22]Jozacar, son of Shimeath, and Jehozabad, son of Shomer, were the officials who killed him. He was buried in his forefathers' City of David, and his son Amaziah succeeded him as king.

CHAPTER 13

See RG 194

Reign of Jehoahaz of Israel. [1]In the twenty-third year of Joash, son of Ahaziah, king of Judah, Jehoahaz, son of Jehu, began his seventeen-year reign over Israel in Samaria. [2]He did evil in the LORD's sight, conducting himself like Jeroboam, son of Nebat, and not renouncing the sin he had caused Israel to commit. [3]The LORD was angry with Israel and for a long time left them in the power of Hazael, king of Aram, and of Ben-hadad,

p: 1f: 2 Chr 24, 1f.   *q:* 5-8: 2 Chr 24, 5-10.   *r:* 9-16: 2 Chr 24, 11-14.   *s:* 2 Kgs 8, 12.   *t:* 18-22: 2 Chr 24, 23-27.

418

son of Hazael. [4]Then Jehoahaz entreated the LORD, who heard him, since he saw the oppression to which the king of Aram had subjected Israel.[u] [5]So the LORD gave Israel a savior,[*] and the Israelites, freed from the power of Aram, dwelt in their own homes as formerly. [6]Nevertheless, they did not desist from the sins which the house of Jeroboam had caused Israel to commit, but persisted in them. The sacred pole[*] also remained standing in Samaria.[v] [7]No soldiers were left to Jehoahaz, except fifty horsemen with ten chariots and ten thousand foot soldiers, since the king of Aram had destroyed them and trampled them like dust. [8]The rest of the acts of Jehoahaz, with all his valor and accomplishments, are recorded in the book of the chronicles of the kings of Israel. [9]Jehoahaz rested with his ancestors and was buried in Samaria. His son Joash succeeded him as king.

Reign of Joash of Israel. [10]In the thirty-seventh year of Joash, king of Judah, Jehoash, son of Jehoahaz, began his sixteen-year reign over Israel in Samaria. [11]He did evil in the sight of the LORD; he did not desist from any of the sins which Jeroboam, son of Nebat, had caused Israel to commit, but persisted in them. [12]*[The rest of the acts of Joash, the valor with which he fought against Amaziah, king of Judah, and all his accomplishments, are recorded in the book of the chronicles of the kings of Israel.[w] [13]Joash rested with his ancestors, and Jeroboam occupied the throne. Joash was buried with the kings of Israel in Samaria.]

[14]When Elisha was suffering from the sickness of which he was to die, King Joash of Israel went down to visit him. "My father, my father!"[*] he exclaimed, weeping over him. "Israel's chariots and horsemen!"[x] [15]"Take a bow and some arrows," Elisha said to him. When he had done so, [16]*Elisha said to the

king of Israel, "Put your hand on the bow." As the king held the bow, Elisha placed his hands over the king's hands [17]and said, "Open the window toward the east." He opened it, Elisha said, "Shoot," and he shot. The prophet exclaimed, "The LORD's arrow of victory! The arrow of victory over Aram! You will completely conquer Aram at Aphec."

[18]Then he said to the king of Israel, "Take the arrows," which he did. Elisha said to him, "Strike the ground!" He struck the ground three times and stopped. [19]Angry with him, the man of God said: "You should have struck five or six times; you would have defeated Aram completely. Now, you will defeat Aram only three times."

[20]Elisha died and was buried. At the time, bands of Moabites used to raid the land each year. [21]Once some people were burying a man, when suddenly they spied such a raiding band. So they cast the dead man into the grave of Elisha, and everyone went off. But when the man came in contact with the bones of Elisha, he came back to life and rose to his feet.[y]

[22]King Hazael of Aram oppressed Israel during the entire reign of Jehoahaz. [23]But the LORD was merciful with Israel and looked on them with compassion because of his covenant with Abraham, Isaac, and Jacob. He was unwilling to destroy them or to cast them out from his presence.[z] [24]So when King Hazael of Aram died and his son Ben-hadad succeeded him as king, [25]Joash, son of Jehoahaz, took back from Ben-hadad, son of Hazael, the cities which Hazael had taken in battle from his father Jehoahaz. Joash defeated Ben-hadad three times, and thus recovered the cities of Israel.

CHAPTER 14

See RG 195

Amaziah of Judah.[*] [1]In the second year of Joash, son of Jehoahaz, king of Is-

---

13, 5: A savior: by this language, typical of the Book of Judges (Jgs 3, 9. 15), Jeroboam II of Israel is meant; cf 2 Kgs 14, 27.

13, 6: Sacred pole: see note on Ex 34, 13.

13, 12f: The conclusion to the reign of Joash is given again in 2 Kgs 14, 15f, where it is more appropriate.

13, 14: My father, my father: the king expresses here the same sentiments as those with which Elisha addressed Elijah.

13, 16-19: Symbolic acts similar to these are seen in Ex 17, 8ff; Jos 8, 18ff; Ez 4, 1ff.

14, 1f: In the second year . . . twenty-nine years in Jerusalem: the reigns of the kings of Judah between Athaliah and Ahaz are assigned too many years in all to correspond to the reigns in Israel from Jehu to the fall of Samaria. It seems probable that Amaziah was murdered as soon as his son Azaiah was old enough to rule, and that Amaziah's reign was nearer nineteen than twenty-nine years. The correlation, in

u: 2 Kgs 14, 26f.   *v:* Ex 34, 13.   *w:* 2 Kgs 14, 8-16.   *x:* 2 Kgs 2, 12.   *y:* Sir 48, 14.   *z:* Dt 9, 27.

rael, Amaziah, son of Joash, king of Judah, began to reign. ^{2a}He was twenty-five years old when he became king, and he reigned twenty-nine years in Jerusalem. His mother, whose name was Jehoaddin, was from Jerusalem. ³He pleased the LORD, yet not like his forefather David, since he did just as his father Joash had done. ⁴Thus the high places did not disappear, but the people continued to sacrifice and to burn incense on them. ^{5b}When Amaziah had the kingdom firmly in hand, he slew the officials who had murdered the king, his father. ⁶But the children of the murderers he did not put to death, obeying the LORD's command written in the book of the law of Moses, "Fathers shall not be put to death for their children, nor shall children be put to death for their fathers; each one shall die for his own sin."^c

⁷Amaziah slew ten thousand Edomites in the Salt Valley, and took Sela in battle. He renamed it Joktheel, the name it has to this day.^d

⁸Then Amaziah sent messengers to Jehoash, son of Jehoahaz, son of Jehu, king of Israel, with this challenge, "Come, let us meet face to face."^e ⁹King Jehoash of Israel sent this reply to the king of Judah: "The thistle of Lebanon sent word to the cedar of Lebanon, 'Give your daughter to my son in marriage,' but an animal of Lebanon passed by and trampled the thistle underfoot. ¹⁰You have indeed conquered Edom, and you have become ambitious. Enjoy your glory, but stay at home! Why involve yourself and Judah with you in misfortune and failure?"

¹¹But Amaziah would not listen. King Jehoash of Israel then advanced, and he and King Amaziah of Judah met in battle at Bethshemesh of Judah. ¹²Judah was defeated by Israel, and all the Judean soldiery fled homeward. ¹³King Jehoash of Israel captured Amaziah, son of Jehoash, son of Ahaziah, king of Judah, at Beth-shemesh. He went on to Jerusalem where he tore down four hundred cubits of the city wall, from the Gate of Ephraim to the Corner Gate. ¹⁴He took all the gold and silver and all the utensils there were in the temple of the LORD and in the treasuries of the palace, and hostages as well. Then he returned to Samaria. ¹⁵The rest of the acts of Jehoash, his valor, and how he fought Amaziah, king of Judah, are recorded in the book of the chronicles of the kings of Israel.^f ¹⁶Jehoash rested with his ancestors; he was buried in Samaria with the kings of Israel. His son Jeroboam succeeded him as king.

¹⁷Amaziah, son of Joash, king of Judah, survived Jehoash, son of Jehoahaz, king of Israel, by fifteen years.* ¹⁸The rest of the acts of Amaziah are written in the book of the chronicles of the kings of Judah. ¹⁹When a conspiracy was formed against him in Jerusalem, he fled to Lachish. But he was pursued to Lachish and killed there. ²⁰He was brought back on horses and buried with his ancestors in the City of David in Jerusalem. ²¹Thereupon all the people of Judah took the sixteen-year-old Azariah* and proclaimed him king to succeed his father Amaziah.^g ²²It was Azariah who rebuilt Elath and restored it to Judah, after King Amaziah rested with his ancestors.

Jeroboam II of Israel. ²³In the fifteenth year of Amaziah, son of Joash, king of Judah, Jeroboam, son of Joash, king of Israel, began his forty-one-year reign in Samaria. ²⁴He did evil in the sight of the LORD; he did not desist from any of the sins which Jeroboam, son of Nebat, had caused Israel to commit. ²⁵He restored the boundaries of Israel from Labo-of-Hamath to the sea of the Arabah,* just as the LORD, the God of Israel, had prophesied through his servant, the prophet Jonah, son of Amittai, from Gathhepher. ²⁶For the LORD saw the very bitter affliction of Israel, where there was neither slave nor freeman, no one at all to help Israel.^h ²⁷Since the LORD had not determined to blot out the name of Israel from under the heavens, he saved them through Jeroboam,

2 Kgs 15, 1, of the beginning of Azariah's reign with the 27th year of Jeroboam II can hardly be correct; and the sixteen-year reign of Jotham of Judah (2 Kgs 15, 33) consisted for the most part of a regency during the illness of his father (2 Kgs 15, 5).

14, 17: See note on 2 Kgs 14, 1f.

14, 21: Azariah: also called Uzziah in many texts.

14, 25: Sea of the Arabah: the Dead Sea. Jonah: see note on Jon 1, 1.

a: 2f: 2 Chr 25, 1f.   *b:* 5f: 2 Chr 25, 3f.   *c:* Dt 24, 16; Ez 18, 20.
d: 2 Sm 8, 13f; 2 Chr 25, 11.   *e:* 2 Kgs 13, 12; Jgs 9, 8-15.
f: 2 Kgs 13, 12f.   *g:* 2 Chr 26, 1f.   *h:* 2 Kgs 13, 4f; 1 Kgs 14, 10.

son of Joash. [28]The rest of the acts of Jeroboam, his valor and all his accomplishments, how he fought with Damascus and turned back Hamath from Israel, are recorded in the book of the chronicles of the kings of Israel. [29]Jeroboam rested with his ancestors, the kings of Israel, and his son Zechariah succeeded him as king.

CHAPTER 15

See RG 195

Azariah of Judah. [1i]Azariah, son of Amaziah, king of Judah, became king in the twenty-seventh year* of Jeroboam, king of Israel. [2]He was sixteen years old when he began to reign, and he reigned fifty-two years in Jerusalem. His mother, whose name was Jecholiah, was from Jerusalem. [3]He pleased the LORD just as his father Amaziah had done. [4]Yet the high places did not disappear; the people continued to sacrifice and to burn incense on them. [5j]The LORD afflicted the king, and he was a leper to the day of his death. He lived in a house apart, while Jotham, the king's son, was vizier and regent for the people of the land. [6]The rest of the acts of Azariah, and all his accomplishments, are recorded in the book of the chronicles of the kings of Judah. [7]Azariah rested with his ancestors, and was buried with them in the City of David. His son Jotham succeeded him as king.

Zechariah of Israel. [8]In the thirty-eighth year of Azariah, king of Judah, Zechariah, son of Jeroboam, was king of Israel in Samaria for six months. [9]He did evil in the sight of the LORD as his fathers had done, and did not desist from the sins which Jeroboam, son of Nebat, had caused Israel to commit. [10]Shallum, son of Jabesh, conspired against Zechariah, attacked and killed him at Ibleam, and reigned in his place. [11]The rest of the acts of Zechariah are recorded in the book of the chronicles of the kings of Israel. [12]Thus the LORD's promise to Jehu, "Your descendants to the fourth generation shall sit upon the throne of Israel," was fulfilled.[k]

Shallum of Israel. [13]Shallum, son of Jabesh, became king in the thirty-ninth year of Uzziah, king of Judah; he reigned one month in Samaria. [14]Menahem, son of Gadi, came up from Tirzah to Samaria, where he attacked and killed Shallum, son of Jabesh, and reigned in his place. [15]The rest of the acts of Shallum, and the fact of his conspiracy, are recorded in the book of the chronicles of the kings of Israel. [16]At that time, Menahem punished Tappuah, all the inhabitants of the town and of its whole district, because on his way from Tirzah they did not let him in. He punished them even to ripping open all the pregnant women.

Menahem of Israel. [17]In the thirty-ninth year of Azariah, king of Judah, Menahem, son of Gadi, began his ten-year reign over Samaria. [18]He did evil in the sight of the LORD, not desisting from the sins which Jeroboam, son of Nebat, had caused Israel to commit. During his reign, [19]Pul,* king of Assyria, invaded the land, and Menahem gave him a thousand talents of silver to have his assistance in strengthening his hold on the kingdom. [20]Menahem secured the money to give to the king of Assyria by exacting it from all the men of substance in the country, fifty silver shekels from each. The king of Assyria did not remain in the country but withdrew. [21]The rest of the acts of Menahem, and all his accomplishments, are recorded in the book of the chronicles of the kings of Israel. [22]Menahem rested with his ancestors, and his son Pekahiah succeeded him as king.

Pekahiah of Israel. [23]In the fiftieth year of Azariah, king of Judah, Pekahiah, son of Menahem, began his two-year reign over Israel in Samaria. [24]He did evil in the sight of the LORD, not desisting from the sins which Jeroboam, son of Nebat, had caused Israel to commit. [25]His adjutant Pekah, son of Remaliah, who had with him fifty men from Gilead, conspired against him, killed him within the palace stronghold in Samaria, and reigned in his place. [26]The rest of the acts of Pekahiah, and all his accomplishments, are

---

15, 1: Twenty-seventh year: see note on 2 Kgs 14, 1f.

15, 19: Pul: the Babylonian throne name of the Assyrian Tiglath-pileser III; cf 2 Kgs 15, 29.

---

i: 1ff: 2 Chr 26, 3f. *j:* 5ff: 2 Chr 26, 21ff. *k:* 2 Kgs 10, 30.

recorded in the book of the chronicles of the kings of Israel.

Pekah of Israel. [27]In the fifty-second year of Azariah, king of Judah, Pekah, son of Remaliah, began his twenty-year reign over Israel in Samaria.* [28]He did evil in the sight of the LORD, not desisting from the sins which Jeroboam, son of Nebat, had caused Israel to commit. [29]During the reign of Pekah, king of Israel, Tiglath-pileser, king of Assyria, came and took Ijon, Abel-beth-maacah, Janoah, Kedesh, Hazor, all the territory of Naphtali, Gilead, and Galilee, deporting the inhabitants to Assyria. [30]Hoshea, son of Elah, conspired against Pekah, son of Remaliah; he attacked and killed him, and reigned in his place [in the twentieth year of Jotham, son of Uzziah]. [31]The rest of the acts of Pekah, and all his accomplishments, are recorded in the book of the chronicles of the kings of Israel.

Jotham of Judah. [32]In the second year of Pekah, son of Remaliah, king of Israel, Jotham, son of Uzziah, king of Judah, began to reign. [33]He was twenty-five years old when he became king, and he reigned sixteen years in Jerusalem. His mother's name was Jerusha, daughter of Zadok. [34]He pleased the LORD, just as his father Uzziah had done. [35]Nevertheless the high places did not disappear and the people continued to sacrifice and to burn incense on them. It was he who built the Upper Gate* of the temple of the LORD. [36]The rest of the acts of Jotham, and all his accomplishments, are recorded in the book of the chronicles of the kings of Judah. [37]It was at that time that the LORD first loosed Rezin, king of Aram, and Pekah, son of Remaliah, against Judah. [38]Jotham rested with his ancestors and was buried with them in his forefather's City of David. His son Ahaz succeeded him as king.

CHAPTER 16

See RG 196

Ahaz of Judah. [1m]In the seventeenth year of Pekah, son of Remaliah, Ahaz, son of Jotham, king of Judah, began to reign. [2]Ahaz was twenty years old when he became king, and he reigned sixteen years in Jerusalem. He did not please the LORD, his God, like his forefather David, [3]but conducted himself like the kings of Israel, and even immolated his son by fire, in accordance with the abominable practice of the nations whom the LORD had cleared out of the way of the Israelites.[n] [4]Further, he sacrificed and burned incense on the high places, on hills, and under every leafy tree.[o]

[5]Then Rezin, king of Aram, and Pekah, son of Remaliah, king of Israel, came up to Jerusalem to attack it. Although they besieged Ahaz, they were unable to conquer him.[p] [6]At the same time the king of Edom recovered Elath for Edom, driving the Judeans out of it. The Edomites then entered Elath, which they have occupied until the present.[q]

[7]Meanwhile, Ahaz sent messengers to Tiglath-pileser, king of Assyria, with the plea: "I am your servant and your son. Come up and rescue me from the clutches of the king of Aram and the king of Israel, who are attacking me."[r] [8]Ahaz took the silver and gold that were in the temple of the LORD and in the palace treasuries and sent them as a present to the king of Assyria,[s] [9]who listened to him and moved against Damascus, which he captured. He deported its inhabitants to Kir and put Rezin to death.*

[10]King Ahaz went to Damascus to meet

15, 27: The twenty years here ascribed to Pekah are an impossibility; the calculation which made his reign, of five years at most, appear so long may have been based on the attempt to give Jotham of Judah a full sixteen-year reign independently of his regency. See 2 Kgs 16, 1 and the note on 2 Kgs 14, 1f.

15, 35: The Upper Gate: also the Gate of Benjamin; cf Jer 20, 2; Ez 9, 2.

16, 9: Firmly dated events bearing on chapters 16 through 20 are: the fall of Damascus (16, 9) in 732 B.C., the fall of Samaria (18, 9-11) in 721 B.C., and Sennacherib's invasion of Judah (18, 13) in 701 B.C., which is equated both in Kgs and in Is 36, 1 with the 14th year of Hezekiah. These data

make it necessary to credit Ahaz with at least a twenty-year reign, between 735 and c. 715 B.C., and to exclude the correlations between Hoshea of Israel and Hezekiah in chapter 18.

If the 14th-year correspondence for 701 B.C. is given up, other arrangements are possible. The alleged ages of Jotham (15, 33), Ahaz (16, 2), and Hezekiah (18, 2) at their successive accessions to the throne do not argue for an early date for Hezekiah; but one or more of these may be artificial. Azariah (15, 1-7; Is 6, 1) was still on the throne of Judah in 743 B.C.

---

l: 32-38: 2 Chr 27, 1-4. 7-9.   *m:* 1-4: 2 Chr 28, 1-4.   *n:* Lv 18, 21.   *o:* Dt 12, 2.   *p:* 2 Chr 28, 5f.   *q:* 2 Chr 28, 17.   *r:* 2 Chr 28, 16.   *s:* 2 Chr 28, 21.

Tiglath-pileser, king of Assyria. When he saw the altar in Damascus, King Ahaz sent to Uriah the priest a model of the altar and a detailed design of its construction. [11]Uriah the priest built an altar according to the plans which King Ahaz sent him from Damascus, and had it completed by the time the king returned home. [12]On his arrival from Damascus, the king inspected this altar, then went up to it and offered sacrifice on it, [13]burning his holocaust and cereal-offering, pouring out his libation, and sprinkling the blood of his peace-offerings on the altar.[t] [14]The bronze altar that stood before the LORD he brought from the front of the temple—that is, from the space between the new altar and the temple of the LORD—and set it on the north side of his altar. [15][u]"Upon the large altar," King Ahaz commanded Uriah the priest, "burn the morning holocaust and the evening cereal-offering, the royal holocaust and cereal-offering, as well as the holocausts, cereal-offerings, and libations of the people. You must also sprinkle on it all the blood of holocausts and sacrifices. But the old bronze altar shall be mine for consultation."[*] [16]Uriah the priest did just as King Ahaz had commanded. [17]King Ahaz detached the frames from the bases and removed the lavers from them; he also took down the bronze sea from the bronze oxen that supported it, and set it on a stone pavement.[v] [18]In deference to the king of Assyria he removed from the temple of the LORD the emplacement which had been built in the temple for a throne, and the outer entrance for the king.[*] [19]The rest of the acts of Ahaz are recorded in the book of the chronicles of the kings of Judah.[w] [20]Ahaz rested with his ancestors and was buried with them in the City of David. His son Hezekiah succeeded him as king.

See RG 196

CHAPTER 17

Hoshea of Israel. [1]In the twelfth year of Ahaz, king of Judah, Hoshea, son of Elah,

began his nine-year reign over Israel in Samaria. [2]He did evil in the sight of the LORD, yet not to the extent of the kings of Israel before him. [3]Shalmaneser,[*] king of Assyria, advanced against him, and Hoshea became his vassal and paid him tribute.[x] [4]But the king of Assyria found Hoshea guilty of conspiracy for sending envoys to the king of Egypt at Sais, and for failure to pay the annual tribute to his Assyrian overlord. [5]For this, the king of Assyria arrested and imprisoned Hoshea; he then occupied the whole land and attacked Samaria, which he besieged for three years. [6]In the ninth year of Hoshea, the king of Assyria[*] took Samaria, and deported the Israelites to Assyria, settling them in Halah, at the Habor, a river of Gozan, and in the cities of the Medes.[y]

[7]This came about because the Israelites sinned against the LORD, their God, who had brought them up from the land of Egypt, from under the domination of Pharaoh, king of Egypt, and because they venerated other gods. [8]They followed the rites of the nations whom the LORD had cleared out of the way of the Israelites [and the kings of Israel whom they set up]. [9]They adopted unlawful practices toward the LORD, their God. They built high places in all their settlements, the watchtowers as well as the walled cities. [10]They set up pillars and sacred poles for themselves on every high hill and under every leafy tree.[z] [11]There, on all the high places, they burned incense like the nations whom the LORD had sent into exile at their coming. They did evil things that provoked the LORD, [12]and served idols, although the LORD had told them, "You must not do this."

[13]And though the LORD warned Israel and Judah by every prophet and seer, "Give up your evil ways and keep my commandments and statutes, in accordance with the entire law which I enjoined on your fathers and which I sent you by my servants the prophets," [14a]they did not listen, but were as stiff-

16, 15: For consultation: perhaps the introduction into Judah of the Babylonian practice of omen sacrifices; cf Ez 21, 16.

16, 18: Emplacement . . . for a throne, and the outer entrance for the king: signs of sovereignty for the Hebrew kings.

17, 3: Shalmaneser: son and successor of Tiglath-pileser.

17, 6: The king of Assyria: Shalmaneser's successor and usurper, Sargon II.

t: 2 Chr 28, 23. *u:* Ex 29, 38f; Nm 28, 3f. *v:* 2 Chr 28, 24. *w:* 2 Chr 28, 26f. *x:* 2 Kgs 18, 9; Tb 1, 2. *y:* 2 Kgs 18, 10f. *z:* Ex 23, 24; 34, 13; Dt 12, 2. *a:* Jer 25, 5; Dt 9, 13.

Mediterranean
Sea

Damascus

Ijon

Kedesh

Abel-beth-
maacah

Janoah
Acco

Hazor

Dor

Ashtaroth

Megiddo

Ramoth-
gilead

Samaria

Joppa

Gezer

Jerusalem

Dead
Sea

Gaza

0   40 Mi.

0   40 Km.

Campaign of Tiglath-pileser III

of Israel. He afflicted them and delivered them over to plunderers, finally casting them out from before him. [21] When he tore Israel away from the house of David, they made Jeroboam, son of Nebat, king: he drove the Israelites away from the LORD, causing them to commit a great sin.[e] [22] The Israelites imitated Jeroboam in all the sins he committed, nor would they desist from them. [23] Finally, the LORD put Israel away out of his sight as he had foretold through all his servants, the prophets; and Israel went into exile from their native soil to Assyria, an exile lasting to the present.[f]

[24] The king of Assyria brought people from Babylon, Cuthah, Avva, Hamath, and Sepharvaim, and settled them in the cities of Samaria in place of the Israelites. They took possession of Samaria and dwelt in its cities. [25] When they first settled there, they did not venerate the LORD, so he sent lions among them that killed some of their number. [26] A report reached the king of Assyria: "The nations whom you deported and settled in the cities of Samaria do not know how to worship the God of the land, and he has sent lions among them that are killing them, since they do not know how to worship the God of the land." [27] The king of Assyria gave the order, "Send back one of the priests whom I deported, to go there and settle, to teach them how to worship the God of the land." [28] So one of the priests who had been deported from Samaria returned and settled in Bethel, and taught them how to venerate the LORD.

[29] But these peoples began to make their own gods in the various cities in which they were living; in the shrines on the high places which the Samaritans had made, each people set up gods.[g] [30] Thus the Babylonians made Marduk and his consort; the men of Cuth made Nergal; the men of Hamath made Ashima; [31] the men of Avva made Nibhaz and Tartak; and the men of Sepharvaim immolated their children by fire to their city gods, King Hadad and his consort Anath. [32] They also venerated the LORD, choosing from their number priests for the high

necked as their fathers, who had not believed in the LORD, their God. [15] They rejected his statutes, the covenant which he had made with their fathers, and the warnings which he had given them. The vanity they pursued, they themselves became: they followed the surrounding nations whom the LORD had commanded them not to imitate.[b] [16] They disregarded all the commandments of the LORD, their God, and made for themselves two molten calves; they also made a sacred pole and worshiped all the host of heaven, and served Baal.[c] [17][d] They immolated their sons and daughters by fire, practiced fortune-telling and divination, and sold themselves into evildoing in the LORD's sight, provoking him [18] till, in his great anger against Israel, the LORD put them away out of his sight. Only the tribe of Judah was left.

[19] Even the people of Judah, however, did not keep the commandments of the LORD, their God, but followed the rites practiced by Israel. [20] So the LORD rejected the whole race

b: Jer 2, 5.   c: 1 Kgs 12, 28; Ex 34, 13; Dt 4, 19; 17, 2f.   d: Lv 18, 21; Dt 18, 10.   e: 1 Kgs 12, 19f; 12, 26-33.   f: Jer 25, 9.   g: Jn 4, 9.

places, who officiated for them in the shrines on the high places.[h] [33]But, while venerating the LORD, they served their own gods, following the worship of the nations from among whom they had been deported.

[34]To this day they worship according to their ancient rites.* [They did not venerate the LORD nor observe the statutes and regulations, the law and commandments, which the LORD enjoined on the descendants of Jacob, whom he had named Israel.[i] [35]When he made a covenant with them, he commanded them: "You must not venerate other gods, nor worship them, nor serve them, nor offer sacrifice to them.[j] [36]The LORD, who brought you up from the land of Egypt with great power and outstretched arm: him shall you venerate, him shall you worship, and to him shall you sacrifice. [37]You must be careful to observe forever the statutes and regulations, the law and commandment, which he wrote for you, and you must not venerate other gods. [38]The covenant which I made with you, you must not forget; you must not venerate other gods. [39]But the LORD, your God, you must venerate; it is he who will deliver you from the power of all your enemies." [40]They did not listen, however, but continued in their earlier manner.] [41]Thus these nations venerated the LORD, but also served their idols. And their sons and grandsons, to this day, are doing as their fathers did.

II: The Kingdom of Judah after 721 B.C.

CHAPTER 18

See RG 196 *Hezekiah.* [1][k]In the third year of Hoshea, son of Elah, king of Israel, Hezekiah, son of Ahaz, king of Judah, began to reign. [2]He was twenty-five years old when he became king, and he reigned twenty-nine years in Jerusalem. His mother's name was Abi, daughter of Zechariah. [3]He pleased the LORD, just as his forefather David had done. [4]It was he who removed the high places, shattered the pillars, and cut down the sacred poles. He smashed the bronze serpent called Nehushtan which Moses had made, because up to that time the Israelites were burning incense to it.[l] [5]He put his trust in the LORD, the God of Israel; and neither before him nor after him was there anyone like him among all the kings of Judah. [6]Loyal to the LORD, Hezekiah never turned away from him, but observed the commandments which the LORD had given Moses. [7]The LORD was with him, and he prospered in all that he set out to do. He rebelled against the king of Assyria and did not serve him. [8]He also subjugated the watchtowers and walled cities of the Philistines, all the way to Gaza and its territory.

[9]In the fourth year of King Hezekiah, which was the seventh year of Hoshea, son of Elah, king of Israel, Shalmaneser, king of Assyria, attacked Samaria, laid siege to it,* [10][m]and after three years captured it. In the sixth year of Hezekiah, the ninth year of Hoshea, king of Israel, Samaria was taken. [11]The king of Assyria then deported the Israelites to Assyria and settled them in Halah, at the Habor, a river of Gozan, and in the cities of the Medes. [12]This came about because they had not heeded the warning of the LORD, their God, but violated his covenant, not heeding and not fulfilling the commandments of Moses, the servant of the LORD.[n]

Invasion of Sennacherib. [13]*In the fourteenth year of King Hezekiah, Sennacherib,* king of Assyria, went on an expedition against all the fortified cities of Judah and captured them.[o] [14]Hezekiah, king of Judah, sent this message to the king of Assyria at Lachish: "I have done wrong. Leave me, and I will pay whatever tribute you impose on me." The king of Assyria exacted three hundred talents of silver and thirty talents of gold from Hezekiah, king of Judah. [15]Hezekiah

---

17, 34-40: They did not . . . earlier manner: this passage is an adaptation of language denouncing the Israelites to make it applicable to the later Samaritan sect of postexilic times. The original bearing of the discourse (vv 13-15) can be seen by reading it between vv 22 and 23. Cf also 2 Kgs 18, 12.

18, 9: See note on 2 Kgs 16, 9.

18, 13—20, 11: Duplication of Is 36, 1—38, 8. 21. 22.

18, 13: Sennacherib succeeded Sargon II as king of As-

syria. His Judean campaign was waged in 701 B.C. See note on 2 Kgs 16, 9.

h: 1 Kgs 12, 31. i: Gn 32, 29. j: Ex 20, 3ff. k: 1ff: 2 Chr 28, 27; 29, 1f. l: Ex 23, 24; 34, 13; Nm 21, 9; Dt 12, 2; 2 Chr 31, 1; Wis 16, 6; Jn 3, 14. m: 10f: 2 Kgs 17. 6; Tb 1, 2. n: 2 Kgs 17, 7-18. o: 2 Chr 32, 1ff; Sir 48, 18; Is 36, 1.

paid him all the funds there were in the temple of the LORD and in the palace treasuries. [16]He broke up the door panels and the uprights of the temple of the LORD which he himself had ordered to be overlaid with gold, and gave the gold to the king of Assyria.[p]

[17]The king of Assyria sent the general, the lord chamberlain, and the commander* from Lachish with a great army to King Hezekiah at Jerusalem. They went up, and on their arrival in Jerusalem, stopped at the conduit of the upper pool on the highway of the fuller's field.[q] [18]They called for the king, who sent out to them Eliakim, son of Hilkiah, the master of the palace; Shebnah the scribe; and the herald Joah, son of Asaph.[r] [19]The commander said to them, "Tell Hezekiah, 'Thus says the great king, the king of Assyria: On what do you base this confidence of yours? [20]Do you think mere words substitute for strategy and might in war? On whom, then, do you rely, that you rebel against me? [21]This Egypt, the staff on which you rely, is in fact a broken reed which pierces the hand of anyone who leans on it. That is what Pharaoh, king of Egypt, is to all who rely on him.[s] [22]But if you say to me, We rely on the LORD, our God, is not he the one whose high places and altars Hezekiah has removed, commanding Judah and Jerusalem to worship before this altar in Jerusalem?'

[23]"Now, make a wager with my lord, the king of Assyria: I will give you two thousand horses if you can put riders on them. [24]How then can you repulse even one of the least servants of my lord, relying as you do on Egypt for chariots and horsemen? [25]Was it without the LORD's will that I have come up to destroy this place? The LORD said to me, 'Go up and destroy that land!' "

[26]Then Eliakim, son of Hilkiah, and Shebnah and Joah said to the commander: "Please speak to your servants in Aramaic; we understand it. Do not speak to us in Judean within earshot of the people who are on the wall."

[27]But the commander replied: "Was it to your master and to you that my lord sent me to speak these words? Was it not rather to the men sitting on the wall, who, with you, will have to eat their own excrement and drink their urine?" [28]Then the commander stepped forward and cried out in a loud voice in Judean, "Listen to the words of the great king, the king of Assyria. [29]Thus says the king: 'Do not let Hezekiah deceive you, since he cannot deliver you out of my hand. [30]Let not Hezekiah induce you to rely on the LORD, saying, The LORD will surely save us; this city will not be handed over to the king of Assyria. [31]Do not listen to Hezekiah, for the king of Assyria says: Make peace with me and surrender! Then each of you will eat of his own vine and of his own fig-tree, and drink the water of his own cistern, [32]until I come to take you to a land like your own, a land of grain and wine, of bread and orchards, of olives, oil and fruit syrup. Choose life, not death. Do not listen to Hezekiah when he would seduce you by saying, The LORD will rescue us. [33]Has any of the gods of the nations ever rescued his land from the hand of the king of Assyria? [34]Where are the gods of Hamath and Arpad? Where are the gods of Sepharvaim, Hena, and Avva? Where are the gods of the land of Samaria?[t] [35]Which of the gods for all these lands ever rescued his land from my hand? Will the LORD then rescue Jerusalem from my hand?' " [36]But the people remained silent and did not answer him one word, for the king had ordered them not to answer him.

[37]Then the master of the palace, Eliakim, son of Hilkiah, Shebnah the scribe, and the herald Joah, son of Asaph, came to Hezekiah with their garments torn, and reported to him what the commander had said.

CHAPTER 19

Hezekiah and Isaiah. [1u]When King Hezekiah heard this, he tore his garments, wrapped himself in sackcloth, and went into the temple of the LORD. [2]He sent Eliakim, the master of the palace, Shebnah the scribe, and the elders of the priests, wrapped in sack-

See RG
196

18, 17: General, the lord chamberlain . . . commander: the text lists three major functionaries by their Assyrian titles, of which only the first, more nearly "lord lieutenant," is military in origin; the commander was technically the king's chief butler.

---

p: 1 Kgs 6, 20-22.   *q:* 2 Chr 32, 9; Is 36, 1ff.   *r:* Is 22, 13-25.   *s:* Is 30, 1-7; 31, 1-3; Ez 29, 6-7.   *t:* 2 Kgs 17, 24.   *u:* 1-7: Is 37, 1-7.

cloth, to tell the prophet Isaiah, son of Amoz, ³"Thus says Hezekiah: 'This is a day of distress, of rebuke, and of disgrace. Children are at the point of birth, but there is no strength to bring them forth.* ⁴Perhaps the LORD, your God, will hear all the words of the commander, whom his master, the king of Assyria, sent to taunt the living God, and will rebuke him for the words which the LORD, your God, has heard. So send up a prayer for the remnant that is here.' " ⁵When the servants of King Hezekiah had come to Isaiah, ⁶he said to them, "Tell this to your master: 'Thus says the LORD: Do not be frightened by the words you have heard, with which the servants of the king of Assyria have blasphemed me.ᵛ ⁷I am about to put in him such a spirit that, when he hears a certain report, he will return to his own land, and there I will cause him to fall by the sword.' "

⁸When the commander, on his return, heard that the king of Assyria had withdrawn from Lachish, he found him besieging Libnah. ⁹The king of Assyria heard a report that Tirhakah, king of Ethiopia, had come out to fight against him. Again he sent envoys to Hezekiah with this message: ¹⁰"Thus shall you say to Hezekiah, king of Judah: 'Do not let your God on whom you rely deceive you by saying that Jerusalem will not be handed over to the king of Assyria. ¹¹You have heard what the kings of Assyria have done to all other countries: they doomed them! Will you, then, be saved? ¹²Did the gods of the nations whom my fathers destroyed save them? Gozan, Haran, Rezeph, or the Edenites in Telassar?ʷ ¹³Where are the king of Hamath, the king of Arpad, or the kings of the cities Sepharvaim, Hena and Avva?' "ˣ

¹⁴ʸHezekiah took the letter from the hand of the messengers and read it; then he went up to the temple of the LORD, and spreading it out before him, ¹⁵he prayed in the LORD's presence: "O LORD, God of Israel, enthroned upon the cherubim! You alone are God over all the kingdoms of the earth. You have made the heavens and the earth.ᶻ ¹⁶Incline your ear,

Campaign of Sennacherib

O LORD, and listen! Open your eyes, O LORD, and see! Hear the words of Sennacherib which he sent to taunt the living God. ¹⁷Truly, O LORD, the kings of Assyria have laid waste the nations and their lands, ¹⁸and cast their gods into the fire; they destroyed them because they were not gods, but the work of human hands, wood and stone.ᵃ ¹⁹Therefore, O LORD, our God, save us from the power of this man, that all the kingdoms of the earth may know that you alone, O LORD, are God."ᵇ

Punishment of Sennacherib. ²⁰Then Isaiah, son of Amoz, sent this message to Hezekiah: "Thus says the LORD, the God of Israel, in answer to your prayer for help against Sennacherib, king of Assyria: I have listened! ²¹This is the word the LORD has spoken concerning him:*

" 'She despises you, laughs you to scorn,
    the virgin daughter Zion!

19, 3: See note on Is 37, 3.

19, 21-31: vv 21-28 are addressed to Sennacherib, vv 29-31 to Judah.

v: Is 10, 5-19.   *w:* 2 Kgs 17, 6.   *x:* 2 Kgs 18, 34.   *y:* 14-19: 2 Chr 32, 20; Is 37, 14-20.   *z:* Ex 25, 18.   *a:* Jer 10, 3.   *b:* 1 Kgs 18, 24.

Behind you she wags her head,
daughter Jerusalem.
22 Whom have you insulted and blasphemed,
against whom have you raised your
voice
And lifted up your eyes on high?
Against the Holy One of Israel!
23 Through your servants you have insulted
the LORD.
You said: With my many chariots
I climbed the mountain heights,
the recesses of Lebanon;
I cut down its lofty cedars,
its choice cypresses;
I reached the remotest heights,
its forest park.
24 I dug wells and drank water in foreign
lands;
I dried up with the soles of my feet
all the rivers of Egypt.

25 " 'Have you not heard?
Long ago I prepared it,
From days of old I planned it.
Now I have brought it to pass:
That you should reduce fortified cities
into heaps of ruins,
26 While their inhabitants, shorn of power,
are dismayed and ashamed,
Becoming like the plants of the field, like
the green growth,
like the scorched grass on the
housetops.
27 I am aware whether you stand or sit;
I know whether you come or go,^{c}
28 and also your rage against me.
Because of your rage against me
and your fury which has reached my
ears,
I will put my hook in your nose
and my bit in your mouth,
and make you return the way you came.
29 " 'This shall be a sign for you:
this year you shall eat the aftergrowth,
next year, what grows of itself;
But in the third year, sow and reap,
plant vineyards and eat their fruit!

30 The remaining survivors of the house of
Judah
shall again strike root below
and bear fruit above.
31 For out of Jerusalem shall come a
remnant,
and from Mount Zion, survivors.
The zeal of the LORD of hosts shall do
this.'

32 "Therefore, thus says the LORD concerning the king of Assyria: 'He shall not reach this city, nor shoot an arrow at it, nor come before it with a shield, nor cast up siege-works against it. 33 He shall return by the same way he came, without entering the city, says the LORD. 34 I will shield and save this city for my own sake, and for the sake of my servant David.' "^{d}

35 That night the angel of the LORD went forth and struck down one hundred and eighty-five thousand men in the Assyrian camp. Early the next morning, there they were, all the corpses of the dead.^{e} 36 So Sennacherib, the king of Assyria, broke camp, and went back home to Nineveh.

37 When he was worshiping in the temple of his god Nisroch, his sons Adrammelech and Sharezer slew him with the sword and fled into the land of Ararat. His son Esarhaddon reigned in his stead.

CHAPTER 20

See RG
196

Hezekiah's Illness. ^{1f} In those days, when Hezekiah was mortally ill, the prophet Isaiah, son of Amoz, came and said to him: "Thus says the LORD: 'Put your house in order, for you are about to die; you shall not recover.' " 2 He turned his face to the wall and prayed to the LORD: 3 "O LORD, remember how faithfully and wholeheartedly I conducted myself in your presence, doing what was pleasing to you!" And Hezekiah wept bitterly.

4 Before Isaiah had left the central courtyard, the word of the LORD came to him: 5 "Go back and tell Hezekiah, the leader of my people: 'Thus says the LORD, the God of

---

c: Ps 139, 2f. *d*: 2 Sm 7, 12; Hos 1, 7. *e*: Sir 48, 21; 2 Chr 32, 21f; Is 37, 36-38; 1 Mc 7, 41; 2 Mc 8, 19. *f*: 1-9: 2 Chr 32, 24; Is 38, 1-8.

your forefather David: I have heard your prayer and seen your tears. I will heal you. In three days you shall go up to the LORD's temple; [6]I will add fifteen years to your life. I will rescue you and this city from the hand of the king of Assyria; I will be a shield to this city for my own sake, and for the sake of my servant David.'"

[7]Isaiah then ordered a poultice of figs to be brought and applied to the boil, that he might recover. [8]Then Hezekiah asked Isaiah, "What is the sign that the LORD will heal me and that I shall go up to the temple of the LORD on the third day?" [9]Isaiah replied, "This will be the sign for you from the LORD that he will do what he has promised: Shall the shadow go forward or back ten steps?"

[10]"It is easy for the shadow to advance ten steps," Hezekiah answered. "Rather, let it go back ten steps." [11]So the prophet Isaiah invoked the LORD, who made the shadow retreat the ten steps it had descended on the staircase to the terrace of Ahaz.

[12]*At that time, when Merodach-baladan, son of Baladan, king of Babylon, heard that Hezekiah had been ill, he sent letters and gifts to him.[g] [13]Hezekiah was pleased at this, and therefore showed the messengers his whole treasury, his silver, gold, spices and fine oil, his armory, and all that was in his storerooms; there was nothing in his house or in all his realm that Hezekiah did not show them.

[14]Then Isaiah the prophet came to King Hezekiah and asked him: "What did these men say to you? Where did they come from?" "They came from a distant land, from Babylon," replied Hezekiah. [15]"What did they see in your house?" the prophet asked. "They saw everything in my house," answered Hezekiah. "There is nothing in my storerooms that I did not show them."

[16]Then Isaiah said to Hezekiah: "Hear the word of the LORD: [17]The time is coming when all that is in your house, and everything that your fathers have stored up until this day, shall be carried off to Babylon; nothing shall be left, says the LORD. [18]Some of your own bodily descendants shall be taken and made servants in the palace of the king of Babylon."

[19]Hezekiah replied to Isaiah, "The word of the LORD which you have spoken is favorable." For he thought, "There will be peace and security in my lifetime."

[20]The rest of the acts of Hezekiah, all his valor, and his construction of the pool and conduit* by which water was brought into the city, are written in the book of the chronicles of the kings of Judah.[h] [21]Hezekiah rested with his ancestors and his son Manasseh succeeded him as king.

CHAPTER 21

See RG 196-97

Reign of Manasseh. [1][i]Manasseh was twelve years old when he began to reign, and he reigned fifty-five years in Jerusalem. His mother's name was Hephzibah. [2]He did evil in the sight of the LORD, following the abominable practices of the nations whom the LORD had cleared out of the way of the Israelites. [3]He rebuilt the high places which his father Hezekiah had destroyed. He erected altars to Baal, and also set up a sacred pole, as Ahab, king of Israel, had done. He worshiped and served the whole host of heaven.[j] [4]He built altars in the temple of the LORD, about which the LORD had said, "I will establish my name in Jerusalem"— [5]altars for the whole host of heaven, in the two courts of the temple.[k]

[6]He immolated his son by fire. He practiced soothsaying and divination, and reintroduced the consulting of ghosts and spirits. He did much evil in the LORD's sight and provoked him to anger.

[7]The Asherah idol he had made, he set up in the temple, of which the LORD had said to David and to his son Solomon: "In this temple and in Jerusalem, which I have chosen out of all the tribes of Israel, I shall place my name forever.[l] [8]I will not in future allow Israel to be driven off the land I gave their fathers, provided that they are careful to ob-

---

20, 12–19: Duplication of Is 39, 1–8.

20, 20: Pool and conduit: Hezekiah's tunnel; cf 2 Chr 32, 30.

g: 12f: Is 39, 1f; 2 Chr 32, 27ff.   h: 2 Chr 32, 30; Sir 48, 17.   i: 1-10: 2 Chr 33, 1-10.   j: 2 Kgs 17, 16; 1 Kgs 18, 4; 16, 32f.   k: Lv 18, 21.   l: 2 Sm 7, 13; 1 Kgs 8, 16: 9, 3.

serve all I have commanded them, the entire law which my servant Moses enjoined upon them." [9]But they did not listen, and Manasseh misled them into doing even greater evil than the nations whom the LORD had destroyed at the coming of the Israelites.

[10]Then the LORD spoke through his servants the prophets: [11]"Because Manasseh, king of Judah, has practiced these abominations and has done greater evil than all that was done by the Amorites before him, and has led Judah into sin by his idols,[m] [12]therefore thus says the LORD, the God of Israel: 'I will bring such evil on Jerusalem and Judah that, whenever anyone hears of it, his ears shall ring. [13]I will measure Jerusalem with the same cord as I did Samaria, and with the plummet I used for the house of Ahab. I will wipe Jerusalem clean as one wipes a dish, wiping it inside and out.[n] [14]I will cast off the survivors of my inheritance and deliver them into enemy hands, to become a prey and a booty for all their enemies, [15]because they have done evil in my sight and provoked me from the day their fathers came forth from Egypt until today.' "

[16]In addition to the sin which he caused Judah to commit, Manasseh did evil in the sight of the LORD, shedding so much innocent blood as to fill the length and breadth of Jerusalem. [17]The rest of the acts of Manasseh, the sin he committed and all that he did, are written in the book of the chronicles of the kings of Judah.[o] [18]Manasseh rested with his ancestors and was buried in his palace garden, the garden of Uzza. His son Amon succeeded him as king.

Reign of Amon. [19p]Amon was twenty-two years old when he began to reign, and he reigned two years in Jerusalem. His mother's name was Meshullemeth, daughter of Haruz of Jotbah. [20]He did evil in the sight of the LORD, as his father Manasseh had done. [21]He followed exactly the path his father had trod, serving and worshiping the idols his father had served. [22]He abandoned the LORD, the God of his fathers, and did not follow the path of the LORD. [23]Subjects of Amon conspired against him and slew the king in his palace, [24]but the people of the land then slew all who had conspired against King Amon, and proclaimed his son Josiah king in his stead. [25]The rest of the acts that Amon did are written in the book of the chronicles of the kings of Judah. [26]He was buried in his own grave in the garden of Uzza, and his son Josiah succeeded him as king.

CHAPTER 22

See RG 197

Reign of Josiah. [1q]Josiah was eight years old when he began to reign, and he reigned thirty-one years in Jerusalem. His mother's name was Jedidah, daughter of Adaiah of Bozkath. [2]He pleased the LORD and conducted himself unswervingly just as his ancestor David had done.

[3r]In his eighteenth year, King Josiah sent the scribe Shaphan,* son of Azaliah, son of Meshullam, to the temple of the LORD with orders to [4s]go to the high priest Hilkiah and have him smelt down the precious metals that had been donated to the temple of the LORD, which the doorkeepers had collected from the people. [5]They were to be consigned to the master workmen in the temple of the LORD, who should then pay them out to the carpenters, builders, and lumbermen making repairs on the temple, [6]and for the purchase of wood and hewn stone for the temple repairs. [7]No reckoning was asked of them regarding the funds consigned to them, because they held positions of trust.

The Book of the Law. [8]The high priest Hilkiah informed the scribe Shaphan, "I have found the book of the law in the temple of the LORD." Hilkiah gave the book to Shaphan, who read it. [9]Then the scribe Shaphan went to the king and reported, "Your servants have smelted down the metals available in the temple and have consigned them to the mas-

---

22, 3: Shaphan: head of a prominent family in the reign of Josiah, secretary to the king, bearer and reader of the newfound book of the law (vv 3-13; 2 Chr 34, 8f. 15-20). He and his sons favored the reform of King Josiah and supported the prophet Jeremiah; cf Jer 26, 24.

---

m: 1 Kgs 21, 26; Jer 15, 4.   n: Is 34, 11; Am 7, 7-9; Lam 2, 8.   o: 2 Chr 33, 18ff.   p: 19-26: 2 Chr 33, 21-25.   q: 1f: 2 Chr 34, 1f.
r: 3-13: 2 Chr 34, 8-21.   s: 4-7: 2 Kgs 12, 11-16.

ter workmen in the temple of the LORD." [10]The scribe Shaphan also informed the king that the priest Hilkiah had given him a book, and then read it aloud to the king. [11]When the king had heard the contents of the book of the law, he tore his garments[ᶠ] [12]and issued this command to Hilkiah the priest, Ahikam, son of Shaphan, Achbor, son of Micaiah, the scribe Shaphan, and the king's servant Asaiah: [13]"Go, consult the LORD for me, for the people, for all Judah, about the stipulations of this book that has been found, for the anger of the LORD has been set furiously ablaze against us, because our fathers did not obey the stipulations of this book, nor fulfill our written obligations."

[14]So Hilkiah the priest, Ahikam, Achbor, Shaphan, and Asaiah betook themselves to the Second Quarter in Jerusalem, where the prophetess Huldah resided. She was the wife of Shallum, son of Tikvah, son of Harhas, keeper of the wardrobe. When they had spoken to her, [15]she said to them, "Thus says the LORD, the God of Israel: 'Say to the man who sent you to me, [16]Thus says the LORD: I will bring upon this place and upon its inhabitants all the evil that is threatened in the book which the king of Judah has read. [17]Because they have forsaken me and have burned incense to other gods, provoking me by everything to which they turn their hands, my anger is ablaze against this place and it cannot be extinguished.'

[18]"But to the king of Judah who sent you to consult the LORD, give this response: 'Thus says the LORD, the God of Israel: As for the threats you have heard, [19]because you were heartsick and have humbled yourself before the LORD when you heard my threats that this place and its inhabitants would become a desolation and a curse; because you tore your garments and wept before me; I in turn have listened, says the LORD. [20]I will therefore gather you to your ancestors; you shall go to your grave in peace, and your eyes shall not see all the evil I will bring upon this place.' " This they reported to the king.

CHAPTER 23

See RG 197

[1]ᵘThe king then had all the elders of Judah and of Jerusalem summoned together before him. [2]The king went up to the temple of the LORD with all the men of Judah and all the inhabitants of Jerusalem: priests, prophets, and all the people, small and great. He had the entire contents of the book of the covenant that had been found in the temple of the LORD, read out to them. [3]Standing by the column, the king made a covenant before the LORD that they would follow him and observe his ordinances, statutes and decrees with their whole hearts and souls, thus reviving the terms of the covenant which were written in this book. And all the people stood as participants in the covenant.

[4]Then the king commanded the high priest Hilkiah, his vicar, and the doorkeepers to remove from the temple of the LORD all the objects that had been made for Baal, Asherah, and the whole host of heaven. He had these burned outside Jerusalem on the slopes of the Kidron and their ashes carried to Bethel.ᵛ [5]He also put an end to the pseudo-priests whom the kings of Judah had appointed to burn incense on the high places in the cities of Judah and in the vicinity of Jerusalem, as well as those who burned incense to Baal, to the sun, moon, and signs of the Zodiac, and to the whole host of heaven.ʷ [6]From the temple of the LORD he also removed the sacred pole, to the Kidron Valley, outside Jerusalem; there he had it burned and beaten to dust, which was then scattered over the common graveyard.ˣ [7]He tore down the apartments of the cult prostitutes* which were in the temple of the LORD, and in which the women wove garments for the Asherah.ʸ

[8]He brought in all the priests from the cities of Judah, and then defiled, from Geba to Beer-sheba, the high places where they had offered incense. He also tore down the high place of the satyrs, which was at the entrance of the Gate of Joshua, governor of the city, to the left as one enters the city gate.ᶻ [9]The

---

23, 7: Cult prostitutes: of both sexes; cf 1 Kgs 14, 24.

t: 11-20: 2 Chr 34, 19-28. *u:* 1-5: 2 Chr 34, 29-33. *v:* 2 Chr 34, 3-5; Sir 49, 3. *w:* Dt 17, 3ff. *x:* Dt 16, 21; 1 Kgs 14, 23. *y:* 1 Kgs 14, 24; Dt 23, 18f. *z:* Dt 12, 2f.

431

priests of the high places could not function at the altar of the LORD in Jerusalem; but they, along with their relatives, ate the unleavened bread.

¹⁰The king also defiled Topheth in the Valley of Ben-hinnom, so that there would no longer be any immolation of sons or daughters by fire* in honor of Molech.ᵃ ¹¹He did away with the horses which the kings of Judah had dedicated to the sun; these were at the entrance of the temple of the LORD, near the chamber of Nathan-melech the eunuch, which was in the large building.* The chariots of the sun he destroyed by fire. ¹²He also demolished the altars made by the kings of Judah on the roof (the roof terrace of Ahaz), and the altars made by Manasseh in the two courts of the temple of the LORD. He pulverized them and threw the dust into the Kidron Valley.ᵇ ¹³The king defiled the high places east of Jerusalem, south of the Mount of Misconduct,* which Solomon, king of Israel, had built in honor of Astarte, the Sidonian horror, of Chemosh, the Moabite horror, and of Milcom, the idol of the Ammonites.ᶜ ¹⁴He broke to pieces the pillars, cut down the sacred poles, and filled the places where they had been with human bones.ᵈ ¹⁵Likewise the altar which was at Bethel, the high place built by Jeroboam, son of Nebat, who caused Israel to sin—this same altar and high place he tore down, breaking up the stones and grinding them to powder, and burning the Asherah.ᵉ

¹⁶When Josiah turned and saw the graves there on the mountainside, he ordered the bones taken from the graves and burned on the altar, and thus defiled it in fulfillment of the word of the LORD which the man of God had proclaimed as Jeroboam was standing by the altar on the feast day. When the king looked up and saw the grave of the man of God who had proclaimed these words, ¹⁷he

asked, "What is that tombstone I see?" The men of the city replied, "It is the grave of the man of God who came from Judah and predicted the very things you have done to the altar of Bethel." ¹⁸ᶠ"Let him be," he said, "let no one move his bones." So they left his bones undisturbed together with the bones of the prophet who had come from Samaria.*

¹⁹Josiah also removed all the shrines on the high places near the cities of Samaria which the kings of Israel had erected, thereby provoking the LORD; he did the very same to them as he had done in Bethel.ᵍ ²⁰He slaughtered upon the altars all the priests of the high places that were at the shrines, and burned human bones upon them. Then he returned to Jerusalem.

²¹The king issued a command to all the people to observe the Passover of the LORD, their God, as it was prescribed in that book of the covenant.ʰ ²²No Passover such as this had been observed during the period when the Judges ruled Israel, or during the entire period of the kings of Israel and the kings of Judah, ²³until the eighteenth year of King Josiah, when this Passover of the LORD was kept in Jerusalem.

²⁴Further, Josiah did away with the consultation of ghosts and spirits, with the household gods, idols,* and all the other horrors to be seen in the land of Judah and in Jerusalem, so that he might carry out the stipulations of the law written in the book that the priest Hilkiah had found in the temple of the LORD.ⁱ

²⁵Before him there had been no king who turned to the LORD as he did, with his whole heart, his whole soul, and his whole strength, in accord with the entire law of Moses; nor could any after him compare with him.ʲ

²⁶Yet, because of all the provocations that Manasseh had given, the LORD did not desist

---

23, 10: Topheth . . . by fire: condemned by Deuteronomic law and denounced by Jeremiah (Dt 12, 31; Jer 7, 29ff; Jer 19).

23, 11: Large building: to the west of the temple area (1 Chr 26, 18), named in the Hebrew by an Egyptian name for a similar construction.

23, 13: Mount of Misconduct: a paranomasia on "Mount of Olives" (in Hebrew Maschit/mishchch) as suggested by the Targum. Cf Vulgate, "Mount of Offense." Horror . . . idol: in all three phrases here the Hebrew uses a pejorative desig-

nation meaning "abomination."

23, 18: From Samaria: more narrowly, from Bethel; cf 1 Kgs 13, 31f.

23, 24: Household gods . . . idols: teraphim. See note on Gn 31, 19.

a: Lv 18, 21.　b: 2 Kgs 21, 5.　c: 1 Kgs 11, 7.　d: Dt 16, 21f; 1 Kgs 14, 23.　e: 1 Kgs 12, 31f; 13, 32.　f: 1 Kgs 13, 31. g: 2 Chr 34, 6f.　h: Dt 16, 1-8; 2 Chr 35, 1ff. 18f.　i: 2 Kgs 21, 6; Gn 31, 19; Dt 18, 11; Jgs 18, 14.　j: Dt 6, 5.

from his fiercely burning anger against Judah. ²⁷The LORD said: "Even Judah will I put out of my sight as I did Israel. I will reject this city, Jerusalem, which I chose, and the temple of which I said, 'There shall my name be.' "ᵏ

²⁸The rest of the acts of Josiah, with all that he did, are written in the book of the chronicles of the kings of Judah.ˡ ²⁹In his time Pharaoh Neco, king of Egypt, went up toward the river Euphrates to the king of Assyria. King Josiah set out to confront him, but was slain at Megiddo at the first encounter.ᵐ ³⁰His servants brought his body on a chariot from Megiddo to Jerusalem, where they buried him in his own grave. Then the people of the land* took Jehoahaz, son of Josiah, anointed him, and proclaimed him king to succeed his father.

Reign of Jehoahaz. ³¹Jehoahaz was twenty-three years old when he began to reign, and he reigned three months in Jerusalem. His mother, whose name was Hamutal, daughter of Jeremiah, was from Libnah.ⁿ ³²He did evil in the sight of the LORD, just as his forebears had done. ³³Pharaoh Neco took him prisoner at Riblah in the land of Hamath, thus ending his reign in Jerusalem. He imposed a fine upon the land of a hundred talents of silver and a talent of gold.* ³⁴Pharaoh Neco then appointed Eliakim, son of Josiah, king in place of his father Josiah; he changed his name to Jehoiakim. Jehoahaz he took away with him to Egypt, where he died. ³⁵Jehoiakim gave the silver and gold to Pharaoh, but taxed the land to raise the amount Pharaoh demanded. He exacted the silver and gold from the people of the land, from each proportionately, to pay Pharaoh Neco.

Reign of Jehoiakim. ³⁶ᵒJehoiakim was twenty-five years old when he began to reign, and he reigned eleven years in Jerusalem. His mother's name was Zebidah, daughter of Pedaiah, from Rumah. ³⁷He did evil in the sight of the LORD, just as his forebears had done.

CHAPTER 24

See RG 197

¹ᵖDuring his reign Nebuchadnezzar, king of Babylon, moved against him, and Jehoiakim became his vassal for three years. Then Jehoiakim turned and rebelled against him. ²The LORD loosed against him bands of Chaldeans, Arameans, Moabites, and Ammonites; he loosed them against Judah to destroy it, as the LORD had threatened through his servants the prophets.ᵠ ³This befell Judah because the LORD had stated that he would inexorably put them out of his sight for the sins Manasseh had committed in all that he did; ⁴and especially because of the innocent blood he shed, with which he filled Jerusalem, the LORD would not forgive.ʳ

⁵The rest of the acts of Jehoiakim, with all that he did, are written in the book of the chronicles of the kings of Judah.ˢ ⁶Jehoiakim rested with his ancestors, and his son Jehoiachin succeeded him as king. ⁷The king of Egypt did not again leave his own land, for the king of Babylon had taken all that belonged to the king of Egypt from the wadi of Egypt to the Euphrates River.

Reign of Jehoiachin. ⁸Jehoiachin was eighteen years old when he began to reign, and he reigned three months* in Jerusalem. His mother's name was Nehushta, daughter of Elnathan of Jerusalem. ⁹He did evil in the sight of the LORD, just as his forebears had done.

¹⁰At that time the officials of Nebuchadnezzar, king of Babylon, attacked Jerusalem, and the city came under siege.ᵗ ¹¹Nebuchadnezzar, king of Babylon, himself arrived at the city while his servants were besieging it. ¹²Then Jehoiachin, king of Judah, together with his mother, his ministers, officers, and functionaries, surrendered to the king of Babylon, who, in the eighth year of his reign, took him captive. ¹³He carried off all the treasures of the temple of the LORD and those of the

---

23, 30. 35: People of the land: in this period, the phrase referred to "landed gentry"; in later times it meant "the poor." Cf 2 Kgs 24, 14.

23, 33: A talent of gold: some manuscripts of the Greek and Syriac texts have "ten talents."

24, 8: He reigned three months: in the year 597 B.C.

---

k: 2 Kgs 24, 2.   l: 2 Chr 35, 26f.   m: 2 Chr 35, 20-24.   n: 2 Chr 36, 2f.   o: 36f: 2 Chr 36, 4f.   p: 1-5: 2 Chr 36, 6ff.   q: 2 Kgs 23, 27.   r: 2 Kgs 21, 16.   s: 2 Chr 36, 8.   t: 2 Chr 36, 10; Dn 1, 1f.

palace, and broke up all the gold utensils that Solomon, king of Israel, had provided in the temple of the LORD, as the LORD had foretold.*u* *14*He deported all Jerusalem: all the officers and men of the army, ten thousand in number, and all the craftsmen and smiths. None were left among the people of the land except the poor. *15*He deported Jehoiachin to Babylon, and also led captive from Jerusalem to Babylon the king's mother and wives, his functionaries, and the chief men of the land.*v* *16*The king of Babylon also led captive to Babylon all seven thousand men of the army, and a thousand craftsmen and smiths, all of them trained soldiers. *17*In place of Jehoiachin, the king of Babylon appointed his uncle Mattaniah king, and changed his name to Zedekiah.

Reign of Zedekiah. *18*Zedekiah was twenty-one years old when he became king, and he reigned eleven years in Jerusalem. His mother's name was Hamutal, daughter of Jeremiah of Libnah.*w* *19*He also did evil in the sight of the LORD, just as Jehoiakim had done. *20*The LORD's anger befell Jerusalem and Judah till he cast them out from his presence. Thus Zedekiah rebelled against the king of Babylon.*x*

See RG 197–98

CHAPTER 25

*1**y*In the tenth month of the ninth year of Zedekiah's reign, on the tenth day of the month, Nebuchadnezzar, king of Babylon, and his whole army advanced against Jerusalem, encamped around it, and built siege walls on every side. *2*The siege of the city continued until the eleventh year of Zedekiah. *3*On the ninth day of the fourth month, when famine had gripped the city, and the people had no more bread, *4*the city walls were breached. Then the king and all the soldiers left the city by night through the gate between the two walls which was near the king's garden. Since the Chaldeans had the city surrounded, they went in the direction of the Arabah. *5*But the Chaldean army pursued

the king and overtook him in the desert near Jericho, abandoned by his whole army.

*6*The king was therefore arrested and brought to Riblah to the king of Babylon, who pronounced sentence on him. *7*He had Zedekiah's sons slain before his eyes. Then he blinded Zedekiah, bound him with fetters, and had him brought to Babylon.

*8*On the seventh day of the fifth month (this was in the nineteenth year of Nebuchadnezzar, king of Babylon), Nebuzaradan, captain of the bodyguard, came to Jerusalem as the representative of the king of Babylon. *9*He burned the house of the LORD, the palace of the king, and all the houses of Jerusalem; every large building was destroyed by fire.*z* *10*Then the Chaldean troops who were with the captain of the guard tore down the walls that surrounded Jerusalem.

*11*Then Nebuzaradan, captain of the guard, led into exile the last of the people remaining in the city, and those who had deserted* to the king of Babylon, and the last of the artisans. *12*But some of the country's poor, Nebuzaradan, captain of the guard, left behind as vinedressers and farmers.

*13*The bronze pillars that belonged to the house of the LORD, and the wheeled carts and the bronze sea in the house of the LORD, the Chaldeans broke into pieces; they carried away the bronze to Babylon.*a* *14*They took also the pots, the shovels, the snuffers, the bowls, the pans and all the bronze vessels used for service.*b* *15*The fire-holders and the bowls which were of gold or silver the captain of the guard also carried off. *16*The weight in bronze of the two pillars, the bronze sea, and the wheeled carts, all of them furnishings which Solomon had made for the house of the LORD, was never calculated. *17*Each of the pillars was eighteen cubits high; a bronze capital five cubits high surmounted each pillar, and a network with pomegranates encircled the capital, all of bronze; and so for the other pillar, as regards the network.*c*

25, 1-30: This chapter parallels Jer 39 and 52; see notes to those parts of Jeremiah.

25, 11: Those who had deserted: perhaps on the advice of Jeremiah; cf Jer 38, 2f.

u: 2 Kgs 20, 17; Is 39, 6.   *v:* Est A, 3; 2, 6.   *w:* 2 Chr 36, 9; Jer 37, 1f; 52, 1ff.   *x:* 2 Kgs 22, 17; 23, 27.   *y:* 1-21: Jer 39, 1-10; 52, 4-28.   *z:* 2 Chr 36, 19; Ps 74, 7.   *a:* 2 Kgs 16, 17; 1 Kgs 7, 15-39; 2 Chr 3, 15; 36, 18; Jer 27, 19.   *b:* 1 Kgs 7, 48ff.   *c:* 1 Kgs 7, 15; Jer 52, 21ff.

Nebuchadnezzar's Campaign

Governorship of Gedaliah. [22d]As for the people whom he had allowed to remain in the land of Judah, Nebuchadnezzar, king of Babylon, appointed as their governor Gedaliah, son of Ahikam, son of Shaphan. [23]Hearing that the king of Babylon had appointed Gedaliah governor, all the army commanders with their men came to him at Mizpah: Ishmael, son of Nethaniah, Johanan, son of Kareah, Seraiah, son of Tanhumeth the Netophathite, and Jaazaniah, from Beth-maacah. [24]Gedaliah gave the commanders and their men his oath. "Do not be afraid of the Chaldean officials," he said to them. "Remain in the country and serve the king of Babylon, and all will be well with you."

[25]But in the seventh month Ishmael, son of Nethaniah, son of Elishama, of royal descent, came with ten men, attacked Gedaliah and killed him, along with the Jews and Chaldeans who were in Mizpah with him. [26]Then all the people, great and small, left with the army commanders and went to Egypt for fear of the Chaldeans.

Release of Jehoiachin. [27e]In the thirty-seventh year of the exile of Jehoiachin, king of Judah, on the twenty-seventh day of the twelfth month, Evil-merodach, king of Babylon, in the inaugural year of his own reign, raised up Jehoiachin, king of Judah, from prison. [28]He spoke kindly to him and gave him a throne higher than that of the other kings who were with him in Babylon. [29]Jehoiachin took off his prison garb and ate at the king's table as long as he lived. [30]The allowance granted him by the king was a perpetual allowance, in fixed daily amounts, for as long as he lived.

[18]The captain of the guard also took Seraiah the high priest, Zephaniah the second priest, and the three keepers of the entry. [19]And from the city he took one courtier, a commander of soldiers, five men in the personal service of the king who were still in the city, the scribe of the army commander, who mustered the people of the land, and sixty of the common people still remaining in the city. [20]The captain of the guard, Nebuzaradan, arrested these and brought them to the king of Babylon at Riblah; [21]the king had them struck down and put to death in Riblah, in the land of Hamath. Thus was Judah exiled from her land.

d: 22-26: Jer 40, 5. 7-41, 1-3. e: 27-30: Jer 52, 31-34.

See RG 199–203

The First Book of Chronicles

Originally the two books of Chronicles formed, with the Books of Ezra and Nehemiah, a single historical work, uniform in style and basic ideas. The Greek title, *paraleipomena,* means "things omitted, or passed over (in Samuel and Kings)." The Books of Chronicles, however, are more than a supplement to Samuel and Kings; a comparison of the two histories discloses striking differences in scope and purpose. The Books of Chronicles record in some detail the lengthy span from the reign of Saul to the return from the Exile. Unlike the exact science of history today, wherein factual accuracy and impartiality of judgment are the standards for estimating what is of permanent worth, ancient biblical history, with rare exceptions, was less concerned with reporting in precise detail all the facts of a situation than with explaining the meaning of those facts. Such history was primarily interpretative and, in the Old Testament, its purpose was to disclose the action of the living God in the affairs of men. For this reason we speak of it as "sacred history"; its writer's first concern was to bring out the divine or supernatural dimension in history.

This is apparent when we examine the primary objective of the Chronicler in compiling his work. In view of the situation which confronted the Jewish people at this time (the end of the fifth century B.C.), the Chronicler realized that Israel's political greatness was a thing of the past. It would be a people under God, or nothing. Yet Israel's past held the key to her future. The Chronicler proposed to establish and defend the legitimate claims of the Davidic monarchy in Israel's history, and to underscore the place of Jerusalem and its divinely established temple worship as the center of religious life for the Jewish community of his day. If Judaism was to survive and prosper, it would have to heed the lessons of the past and devoutly serve Yahweh in the place where he had chosen to dwell, the temple of Jerusalem. From the Chronicler's point of view, David's reign was the ideal to which all subsequent rule in Judah must aspire.

The Chronicler was much more interested in David's religious and cultic influence than in his political power. There is little of royal messianism in his book. He apparently regarded as something of the distant past the prophet Zechariah's abortive attempt to have the Davidic kingdom reestablished in the time of Zerubbabel at the end of the sixth century B.C. (Zec 6, 9-15). He saw David's primary importance as deriving from the establishment of Jerusalem and its temple as the center of the true worship of the Lord. Furthermore, he presented David as the one who had authorized the elaborate ritual (which, in point of

fact, only gradually evolved in the temple built by Zerubbabel) and who had also appointed Levites to supervise the liturgical services there.

There are good reasons for believing that originally the Books of Ezra and Nehemiah formed the last part of a single literary work that began with 1 and 2 Chronicles. Some authors even regard Ezra himself as having been the anonymous Chronicler. In any case, the Chronicler's Hebrew as well as his religious and political outlook points to c. 400 B.C. as the time of composition of this work.

The Chronicler used sources in writing his history. Besides the canonical Books of Genesis, Exodus, Numbers, Joshua and Ruth, and especially the Books of Samuel and Kings, he cites the titles of many other works no longer extant. "The books of the kings of Israel," or "the books of the kings of Israel and Judah," "the history of Samuel the seer," "the history of Nathan the prophet," "the history of Gad the seer," "the commentary on the Books of Kings," are some of the documents mentioned as historical sources.

In addition, the Chronicler's work contains early preexilic material not found in the Books of Kings. At one time scholars discounted the value of this material, but modern research has shown that, even though the Chronicler may have at times treated the material rather freely, he derived it from authentic and reliable sources.

The principal divisions of 1 Chronicles are as follows:

I: Genealogical Tables (1, 1—9, 34).

II: The History of David (9, 35—29, 30).

I: Genealogical Tables

CHAPTER 1

See RG
200

From Adam to Abraham. 1a* Adam, Seth, Enosh, 2bKenan, Mahalalel, Jared, 3Enoch, Methuselah, Lamech,c 4Noah, Shem, Ham, and Japheth.d 5eThe descendants of Japheth were Gomer, Magog,

---

1, 1—9, 34: The Chronicler set as his task the retelling, from his particular viewpoint, of the story of God's people from the beginning to his own day. Since his primary interest was the history of David and the Davidic dynasty of Judah, he presents through mere genealogical lists a summary of what preceded the reign of Saul, David's predecessor in the kingdom. The sources for these genealogies are mostly the canon-

ical Hebrew Scriptures that were already in their present form in his time. The cross references in this book indicate in each case the scriptural sources used.

a: 1 Chr 4, 25f; Gn 5, 3. 6. 9. b: 2ff: Gn 5, 9-32; 10, 2ff. c: Gn 4, 25. d: Gn 5, 32; 6, 10; 9, 18. e: 5ff: Gn 10, 2ff.

Madai, Javan, Tubal, Meshech, and Tiras. ⁶The descendants of Gomer were Ashkenaz, Riphath, and Togarmah. ⁷The descendants of Javan were Elishah, Tarshis, the Kittim, and the Rodanim.

⁸ᶠThe descendants of Ham were Cush, Mesraim, Put, and Canaan. ⁹The descendants of Cush were Seba, Havilah, Sabta, Raama, and Sabteca. The descendants of Raama were Sheba and Dedan. ¹⁰Cush became the father of Nimrod, who was the first to be a conqueror on the earth. ¹¹ᵍMesraim became the father of the Ludim, Anamim, Lehabim, Naphtuhim, ¹²Pathrusim, Casluhim, and Caphtorim, from whom the Philistines sprang. ¹³Canaan became the father of Sidon, his first-born, and Heth, ¹⁴and the Jebusite, the Amorite, the Girgashite, ¹⁵the Hivite, the Arkite, the Sinite, ¹⁶the Arvadite, the Zemarite, and the Hamathite.

¹⁷ʰThe descendants of Shem were Elam, Asshur, Arpachshad, Lud, and Aram. The descendants of Aram were Uz, Hul, Gether, and Mash. ¹⁸Arpachshad became the father of Shelah, and Shelah became the father of Eber. ¹⁹Two sons were born to Eber; the first was named Peleg (for in his time the world was divided), and his brother was Joktan. ²⁰Joktan became the father of Almodad, Sheleph, Hazarmaveth, Jerah, ²¹Hadoram, Uzal, Diklah, ²²Ebal, Abimael, Sheba, ²³Ophir, Havilah, and Jobab; all these were the sons of Joktan.

²⁴ⁱShem, Arpachshad, Shelah, ²⁵Eber, Peleg, Reu, ²⁶Serug, Nahor, Terah, ²⁷Abram, who was Abraham.ʲ

From Abraham to Jacob. ²⁸The sons of Abraham were Isaac and Ishmael.ᵏ ²⁹These were their descendants:ˡ

Nebaioth, the first-born of Ishmael, then Kedar, Adbeel, Mibsam, ³⁰Mishma, Dumah, Massa, Hadad, Tema, ³¹Jetur, Naphish, and Kedemah. These were the descendants of Ishmael.

³²ᵐThe descendants of Keturah, Abraham's concubine: she bore Zimran, Jokshan, Medan, Midian, Ishbak, and Shuah. The sons of Jokshan were Sheba and Dedan. ³³The descendants of Midian were Ephah, Epher, Hanoch, Abida, and Eldaah. All these were the descendants of Keturah.

³⁴Abraham became the father of Isaac. The sons of Isaac were Esau and Israel.ⁿ

³⁵ᵒThe sons of Esau were Eliphaz, Reuel, Jeush, Jalam, and Korah. ³⁶The sons of Eliphaz were Teman, Omar, Zephi, Gatam, Kenaz, [Timna,] and Amalek. ³⁷The sons of Reuel were Nahath, Zerah, Shammah, and Mizzah.

³⁸ᵖThe descendants of Seir* were Lotan, Shobal, Zibeon, Anah, Dishon, Ezer, and Dishan. ³⁹The sons of Lotan were Hori and Homam; Timna was the sister of Lotan. ⁴⁰The sons of Shobal were Alian, Manahath, Ebal, Shephi, and Onam. The sons of Zibeon were Aiah and Anah. ⁴¹The sons of Anah: Dishon. The sons of Dishon were Hemdan, Eshban, Ithran, and Cheran. ⁴²The sons of Ezer were Bilhan, Zaavan, and Jaakan. The sons of Dishan were Uz and Aran.

⁴³�q The kings who reigned in the land of Edom before they had Israelite kings were the following: Bela, son of Beor, the name of whose city was Ninhabah. ⁴⁴When Bela died, Jobab, son of Zerah, from Bozrah, succeeded him.ʳ ⁴⁵When Jobab died, Husham, from the land of the Temanites, succeeded him.ˢ ⁴⁶Husham died and Hadad, son of Bedad, succeeded him. He overthrew the Midianites on the Moabite plateau, and the name of his city was Avith. ⁴⁷Hadad died and Samlah of Masrekah succeeded him. ⁴⁸Samlah died and Shaul from Rehoboth-han-nahar succeeded him. ⁴⁹When Shaul died, Baalhanan, son of Achbor, succeeded him. ⁵⁰Baalhanan died and Hadad succeeded him. The name of his city was Pai, and his wife's name was Mehetabel. She was the daughter of Matred, who was the daughter of Mezahab. ⁵¹ᵗAfter Hadad died. . . .

These were the chiefs of Edom: the chiefs

1, 38: Seir: another name for Esau (v 35) or Edom (v 43).

---

f: Gn 10, 8. *g:* 11-16: Gn 10, 13-18. *h:* 17-23: Gn 10, 22-29; 11, 10-18. *i:* 24-27: Gn 11, 10-26; Lk 3, 34ff. *j:* Gn 17, 5; Neh 9, 7. *k:* Gn 16, 11. 15; 21, 2f; Gal 4, 22f; Heb 11, 11. *l:* 29ff: Gn 25, 13-16. *m:* 32f: Gn 25, 1-4. *n:* Gn 21, 2f; 25, 19. 25f; 32, 28f; Mt 1, 2; Lk 3, 34. *o:* 35ff: Gn 36, 4f. 10-13. 15ff. *p:* 38-42; Gn 36, 20-28. *q:* 43-54: Gn 36, 31-43. *r:* Is 34, 6; 63, 1; Jer 49, 13. 22. *s:* Gn 36, 11; Jb 2, 11; Jer 49, 7. 20. *t:* 51-54: Gn 36, 40-43.

of Timna, Aliah, Jetheth, ⁵²Oholibamah, Elah, Pinon, ⁵³Kenaz, Teman, Mibzar, ⁵⁴Magdiel, and Iram were the chiefs of Edom.

See RG 200

CHAPTER 2

¹These were the sons of Israel: Reuben, Simeon, Levi, Judah, Issachar, Zebulun,^u ²Dan, Joseph, Benjamin, Naphtali, Gad, and Asher.^v

Judah. ³The sons of Judah* were: Er, Onan, and Shelah; these three were born to him of Bathshua, a Canaanite woman. But Judah's first-born, Er, was wicked in the sight of the LORD, so he killed him.^w ⁴Judah's daughter-in-law Tamar bore him Perez and Zerah, so that he had five sons in all.^x

⁵The sons of Perez were Hezron and Hamul.^y ⁶The sons of Zerah were Zimri, Ethan, Heman, Calcol, and Darda—five in all.^z ⁷The sons of Zimri: Carmi. The sons of Carmi: Achar, who brought trouble upon Israel by violating the ban.^a ⁸The sons of Ethan: Azariah. ⁹The sons born to Hezron were Jerahmeel, Ram, and Chelubai.^b *

¹⁰*Ram became the father of Amminadab, and Amminadab became the father of Nahshon, a prince of the Judahites.^c ¹¹d Nahshon became the father of Salma. Salma became the father of Boaz. ¹²Boaz became the father of Obed. Obed became the father of Jesse. ¹³e Jesse became the father of Eliab, his first-born, of Abinadab, the second son, Shimea, the third,^f ¹⁴Nethanel, the fourth, Raddai, the fifth, ¹⁵Ozem, the sixth, and David, the seventh. ¹⁶Their sisters were Zeruiah and Abigail. Zeruiah had three sons: Abishai, Joab, and Asahel.^g ¹⁷Abigail bore Amasa, whose father was Jether the Ishmaelite.^h

¹⁸*By his wife Azubah, Caleb, son of Hezron, became the father of a daughter, Jerioth. Her sons were Jesher, Shobab, and Ardon.ⁱ ¹⁹When Azubah died, Caleb married Ephrath, who bore him Hur.^j ²⁰Hur became the father of Uri, and Uri became the father of Bezalel.^k ²¹Then Hezron had relations with the daughter of Machir, the father of Gilead, having married her when he was sixty years old. She bore him Segub.^l ²²Segub became the father of Jair,^m who possessed twenty-three cities in the land of Gilead. ²³Geshur and Aram took from them the villages of Jair, that is, Kenath and its towns, sixty cities in all, which had belonged to the sons of Machir, the father of Gilead.ⁿ ²⁴After the death of Hezron, Caleb had relations with Ephrathah, the widow of his father Hezron, and she bore him Ashhur, the father of Tekoa.^o

²⁵The sons of Jerahmeel,* the first-born of Hezron, were Ram, the first-born, then Bunah, Oren, and Ozem, his brothers.^p ²⁶Jerahmeel also had another wife, Atarah by name, who was the mother of Onam. ²⁷The sons of Ram, the first-born of Jerahmeel, were Maaz, Jamin, and Eker. ²⁸The sons of Onam were Shammai and Jada. The sons of Shammai were Nadab and Abishur. ²⁹Abishur's wife, who was named Abihail, bore him Ahban and Molid. ³⁰The sons of Nadab were Seled and Appaim. Seled died without sons. ³¹The sons of Appaim: Ishi. The sons of Ishi: Sheshan. The sons of Sheshan: Ahlai.^q ³²The sons of Jada, the brother of Shammai, were Jether and Jonathan. Jether died without sons. ³³The sons of Jonathan were Peleth and Zaza. These were the descendants of

reckoned as part of the clan of the Hezronites.

2, 25-41: The Jerahmeelites were a clan in the Negeb of Judah.

2, 3—4, 23: For two reasons, the Chronicler places the genealogy of the tribe of Judah before that of the other tribes, giving it also at greater length than the others: because of his interest in David and because in the Chronicler's time the people of God were almost exclusively Jews. Both David and the Jews were of the tribe of Judah.

2, 9: Chelubai: a variant form of the name Caleb (vv 18. 42), distinct from Chelub of 1 Chr 4, 11.

2, 10-17: Immediate ancestors of David. A similar list is given in Ru 4, 19-22; each list, independent of the other, derives from a common source.

2, 18-24: Descendants of Caleb. In 1 Chr 4, 15, as is often the case in the Pentateuch (Nm 13, 6; 14, 6. 30: 26, 65; etc.), Caleb is called son of Jephunneh. Here he is called son of Hezron, perhaps because the Calebites were

u: Gn 29, 32-35; 30, 18. 20; 35, 23.   v: Gn 30, 6. 8. 11. 13. 24; 35, 18. 24ff.   w: 1 Chr 4, 21; Gn 38, 1-5; 46, 12.   x: Gn 38, 7. 13-30; 46, 12; Rv 4, 12. 18; Mt 1, 3.   y: Gn 46, 12.   z: 1 Kgs 5, 11.   a: Jos 7, 1. 18ff. 24f; 22, 20.   b: Rv 4, 19; Mt 1, 3.   c: Rv 4, 19; Mt 1, 4.   d: 11f; Nm 1, 7; Rv 4, 20f; Mt 1, 4f.   e: 13ff; 1 Sm 16, 6-13; 17, 13f.   f: 2 Chr 11, 18.   g: 2 Sm 2, 18. h: 2 Sm 17, 25; 19, 14; 20, 4-13.   i: 1 Chr 2, 24.   j: 1 Chr 2, 24. k: Ex 24, 14; 31, 2; 35, 30; 2 Chr 1, 5.   l: Nm 26, 29; 27, 1; 32, 32; Jos 13, 31; Jgs 5, 14.   m: Nm 32, 41; 1 Kgs 4, 13.   n: Dt 3, 14; Jos 13, 30; Jgs 10, 4.   o: 1 Chr 2, 19; 2 Sm 14, 2; 2 Chr 11, 6. p: 1 Sm 27, 10; 30, 29; Jb 32, 2.   q: 1 Chr 4, 20.

Jerahmeel. [34]Sheshan, who had no sons, only daughters, had an Egyptian slave named Jarha. [35]Sheshan gave his daughter in marriage to his slave Jarha, and she bore him Attai. [36]Attai became the father of Nathan. Nathan became the father of Zabad. [37]Zabad became the father of Ephlal. Ephlal became the father of Obed. [38]Obed became the father of Jehu. Jehu became the father of Azariah. [39]Azariah became the father of Helez. Helez became the father of Eleasah. [40]Eleasah became the father of Sismai. Sismai became the father of Shallum. [41]Shallum became the father of Jekamiah. Jekamiah became the father of Elishama.

[42]The descendants of Caleb,* the brother of Jerahmeel: [Mesha] his first-born, who was the father of Ziph. Then the sons of Mareshah, who was the father of Hebron. [43]The sons of Hebron were Korah, Tappuah, Rekem, and Shema. [44]Shema became the father of Raham, who was the father of Jorkeam. Rekem became the father of Shammai. [45]The sons of Shammai: Maon, who was the father of Beth-zur. [46]Ephah, Caleb's concubine, bore Haran, Moza, and Gazez. Haran became the father of Gazez. [47]The sons of Jahdai were Regem, Jotham, Geshan, Pelet, Ephah, and Shaaph. [48]Maacah, Caleb's concubine, bore Sheber and Tirhanah. [49]She also bore Shaaph, the father of Madmannah, Sheva, the father of Machbenah, and the father of Gibea. Achsah was Caleb's daughter.[r]

[50]These were descendants of Caleb, sons of Hur,* the first-born of Ephrathah: Shobal, the father of Kiriath-jearim, [51]Salma, the father of Bethlehem, and Hareph, the father of Beth-gader. [52]The sons of Shobal, the father of Kiriath-jearim, were Reaiah, half the Manahathites, [53]and the clans of Kiriath-jearim: the Ithrites, the Puthites, the Shumathites, and the Mishraites. From these the people of Zorah and the Eshtaolites derived.[s] [54]The descendants of Salma were Bethlehem, the Netophathites, Atroth-beth-Joab, half the Manahathites, and the Zorites. [55t]The clans of the Sopherim dwelling in Jabez were the Tirathites, the Shimeathites, and the Sucathites. They were the Kenites, who came from Hammath of the ancestor of the Rechabites.

CHAPTER 3

See RG 200

[1u]The following* were the sons of David who were born to him in Hebron: the first-born, Amnon, by Ahinoam of Jezreel; the second, Daniel,* by Abigail of Carmel; [2]the third, Absalom, son of Maacah, who was the daughter of Talmai, king of Geshur; the fourth, Adonijah, son of Haggith; [3]the fifth, Shephatiah, by Abital; the sixth, Ithream, by his wife Eglah. [4]Six in all were born to him in Hebron, where he reigned seven years and six months. Then he reigned thirty-three years in Jerusalem,[v] [5w]where the following were born to him: Shimea,* Shobab, Nathan, Solomon—four by Bathsheba, the daughter of Ammiel,[x] [6]Ibhar, Elishua, Eliphelet, [7]Nogah, Nepheg, Japhia, [8]Elishama, Eliada, and Eliphelet—nine. [9]All these were sons of David, in addition to other sons by concubines; and Tamar was their sister.[y]

[10z]* The son of Solomon was Rehoboam, whose son was Abijah, whose son was Asa, whose son was Jehoshaphat,[a] [11]whose son was Joram, whose son was Ahaziah, whose son was Joash,[b] [12]whose son was Amaziah, whose son was Azariah, whose son was Jotham,[c] [13]whose son was Ahaz, whose son was Hezekiah, whose son was Manasseh,[d] [14]whose son was Amon, whose son was Josiah.[e] [15]The sons of Josiah were: the first-born, Johanan; the second, Jehoiakim; the

---

2, 42-49: Another list, dating from preexilic times, of the Calebites, a clan that inhabited the south of Judah.

2, 50-55: The Hurites, a clan dwelling to the south and west of Jerusalem and related to the Calebites.

3, 1-9: David's sons.

3, 1: Daniel: called Chileab in 2 Sm 3, 3.

3, 5: Shimea: called Shammua in 2 Sm 5, 14. Ammiel: called Eliam in 2 Sm 11, 3.

3, 10-16: The kings of Judah from Solomon to the destruction of Jerusalem by the Babylonians.

r: Jos 15, 16; Jgs 1, 12. s: Jgs 18, 2. t: Nm 24, 21; Jgs 1, 16; 4, 11; 1 Sm 15, 6. u: 1-4; 2 Sm 3, 2-5. v: 2 Sm 2, 11; 5, 5. w: 5-8: 2 Sm 5, 14ff. x: 2 Sm 5, 5. y: 2 Sm 13, 1f. z: 10-17: Mt 1, 7-12. a: 1 Kgs 11, 43; 14, 31; 15, 1. 8. 24; 2 Chr 9, 31; 12, 16; 13, 23; 17, 1. b: 1 Kgs 22, 51; 2 Chr 21, 1; 22, 1; 24, 1. 27. c: 2 Kgs 12, 21; 14, 21; 15, 7; 2 Chr 25, 1; 26, 1. 23; 27, 1. d: 2 Kgs 15, 38; 16, 20; 20, 21; 2 Chr 28, 1. 27; 32, 33. e: 2 Kgs 21, 18. 26; 2 Chr 33, 20. 25.

third, Zedekiah; the fourth, Shallum.*f 16The sons of Jehoiakim were: Jeconiah, his son; Zedekiah, his son.g

17The sons of Jeconiah* the captive were: Shealtiel,h 18Malchiram, Pedaiah, Shenazzar,* Jekamiah, Shama, and Nedabiah. 19The sons of Pedaiah were Zerubbabel* and Shimei. The sons of Zerubbabel were Meshullam and Hananiah; Shelomith was their sister. 20The sons of Meshullam were Hashubah, Ohel, Berechiah, Hasadiah, Jushabhesed—five. 21The sons of Hananiah were Pelatiah, Jeshaiah, Rephaiah, Arnan, Obadiah, and Shecaniah. 22iThe sons of Shecaniah were Shemiah, Hattush, Igal, Bariah, Neariah, Shaphat—six. 23The sons of Neariah were Elioenai, Hizkiah, and Azrikam—three. 24The sons of Elioenai were Hodaviah, Eliashib, Pelaiah, Akkub, Johanan, Delaiah, and Anani—seven.

CHAPTER 4

See RG 200

1*The descendants of Judah were: Perez, Hezron, Carmi, Hur, and Shobal.j 2Reaiah, the son of Shobal, became the father of Jahath, and Jahath became the father of Ahumai and Lahad. These were the clans of the Zorathites.

3These were the descendants of Hareph, the father of Etam: Jezreel, Ishma, and Idbash; their sister was named Hazzelelponi. 4Penuel was the father of Gedor, and Ezer the father of Hushah. These were the descendants of Hur, the first-born of Ephrathah, the father of Bethlehem.

5Ashhur, the father of Tekoa, had two wives, Helah and Naarah.k 6Naarah bore him Ahuzzam, Hepher, the Temenites and the Ahashtarites. These were the descendants of Naarah. 7The sons of Helah were Zereth, Izhar, Ethnan, and Koz. 8Koz became the father of Anub and Zobebah, as well as of the clans of Aharhel, son of Harum. 9Jabez was the most distinguished of the brothers. His mother had named him Jabez, saying, "I bore him with pain." 10Jabez prayed to the God of Israel: "Oh, that you may truly bless me and extend my boundaries! Help me and make me free of misfortune, without pain!" And God granted his prayer.

11Chelub, the brother of Shuhah, became the father of Mehir, who was the father of Eshton. 12Eshton became the father of Betrapha, Paseah, and Tehinnah, the father of the city of Nahash. These were the men of Recah.

13The sons of Kenaz were Othniel and Seraiah. The sons of Othniel were Hathath and Meonothai;l 14Meonothai became the father of Ophrah. Seraiah became the father of Joab, the father of Geharashim, so called because they were craftsmen. 15The sons of Caleb, son of Jephunneh, were Ir, Elah, and Naam. The sons of Elah were . . . and Kenaz.m 16The sons of Jehallelel were Ziph, Ziphah, Tiria, and Asarel. 17The sons of Ezrah were Jether, Mered, Epher, and Jalon. Jether became the father of Miriam, Shammai, and Ishbah, the father of Eshtemoa. [. . . . . .]n 18His (Mered's) Egyptian wife bore Jared, the father of Gedor, Heber, the father of Soco, and Jekuthiel, the father of Zanoah. These were the sons of Bithiah, the daughter of Pharaoh, whom Mered married. 19The sons of his Jewish wife, the sister of Naham, the father of Keilah, were Shimon the Garmite and Ishi the Maacathite. 20The sons of Shimon were Amnon, Rinnah, Benhanan, and Tilon. The son of Ishi was Zoheth and the son of Zoheth. . . .

3, 15: Shallum: the same as Jehoahaz, Josiah's successor; cf Jer 22, 11.

3, 17-24: The descendants of King Jeconiah up to the time of the Chronicler. If twenty-five years are allowed to each generation, the ten generations between Jeconiah and Anani (the last name on the list) would bring the birth of the latter to about 405 B.C.—an important item in establishing the approximate date of the Chronicler.

3, 18: Shenazzar: presumably the same as Sheshbazzar of Ezr 1, 8. 11; 5, 14ff, the prince of Judah who was the first Jewish governor of Judah after the exile. Both forms of the name probably go back to the Babylonian name Sin-ab-ussar signifying, "O [god] Sin, protect [our] father!"

3, 19: Zerubbabel: here called the son of Pedaiah, though elsewhere (Hg 1, 12. 14; 2, 2. 23; Ezr 3, 2. 8; 5, 2; Neh 12, 1) called son of Shealtiel. The latter term may merely mean that Zerubbabel succeeded Shealtiel as head of the house of David.

4, 1-43: The southern tribes.

---

f: 2 Kgs 23, 34; 24, 17; 2 Chr 36, 4. 10.   g: 2 Kgs 24, 6. 17; 2 Chr 36, 8. 10.   h: 17. 19; Ezr 2, 2; 3, 2. 8; 5, 2; Sir 49, 11; Hg 1, 1. 12. 14; Mt 1, 12f; Lk 3, 27.   i: Neh 3, 29.   j: 1 Chr 2, 4f. 7. 9. 50; Gn 38, 29; 46, 12; Mt 1, 3.   k: 1 Chr 2, 24.   l: Jos 15, 17; Jgs 1, 13; 3, 9. 11.   m: Nm 13, 6; 14, 6; 32, 12; Jos 14, 6. 14.   n: 1 Sm 30, 28.

21 The descendants of Shelah, son of Judah, were: Er, the father of Lecah; Laadah, the father of Mareshah; the clans of the linen weavers' guild in Beth-ashbea;*o* *22* Jokim; the men of Cozeba; and Joash and Saraph, who held property in Moab, but returned to Bethlehem. [These are events of old.] *23* They were potters and inhabitants of Netaim and Gederah, where they lived in the king's service.

Simeon. *24* The sons of Simeon were Nemuel, Jamin, Jachin, Zerah, and Shaul,*p* *25* whose son was Shallum, whose son was Mibsam, whose son was Mishma. *26* The descendants of Mishma were his son Hammuel, whose son was Zaccur, whose son was Shimei. *27* Shimei had sixteen sons and six daughters. His brothers, however, did not have many sons, and as a result all their clans did not equal the number of the Judahites.

28q They dwelt in Beer-sheba, Moladah, Hazar-shual, *29* Bilhah, Ezem, Tolad, *30* Bethuel, Hormah, Ziklag, *31* Beth-marcaboth, Hazar-susim, Bethbiri, and Shaaraim. Until David came to reign, these were their cities *32* and their villages. Etam, also, and Ain, Rimmon, Tochen, and Ashan—five cities, *33* together with all their outlying villages as far as Baal. Here is where they dwelt, and so it was inscribed of them in their family records.

34 Meshobab, Jamlech, Joshah, son of Amaziah, *35* Joel, Jehu, son of Joshibiah, son of Seraiah, son of Asiel, *36* Elioenai, Jaakobath, Jeshohaiah, Asaiah, Adiel, Jesimiel, Benaiah, *37* Ziza, son of Shiphi, son of Allon, son of Jedaiah, son of Shimri, son of Shemaiah— *38* these just named were princes in their clans, and their ancestral houses spread out to such an extent*r* *39* that they went to the approaches of Gedor,* east of the valley, seeking pasture for their flocks. *40* They found abundant and good pastures, and the land was spacious, quiet, and peaceful. *41* They who have just been listed by name set out during the reign of Hezekiah, king of Judah, and attacked the tents of Ham (for

Hamites dwelt there formerly) and also the Meunites who were there. They pronounced against them the ban that is still in force and dwelt in their place because they found pasture there for their flocks.*s*

42 Five hundred of them (the Simeonites) went to Mount Seir under the leadership of Pelatiah, Neariah, Rephaiah, and Uzziel, sons of Ishi. *43* They attacked the surviving Amalekites who had escaped, and have resided there to the present day.*t*

CHAPTER 5

See RG 200

Reuben. *1* *The sons of Reuben, the first-born of Israel. (He was indeed the first-born, but because he disgraced the couch of his father his birthright was given to the sons of Joseph, son of Israel, so that he is not listed in the family records according to birthright.*u* *2* Judah, in fact, became powerful among his brothers, so that the ruler came from him, though the birthright had been Joseph's.)*v* *3* The sons of Reuben, the first-born of Israel, were Hanoch, Pallu, Hezron, and Carmi.*w* *4* His son was Joel, whose son was Shemaiah, whose son was Gog, whose son was Shimei, *5* whose son was Micah, whose son was Reaiah, whose son was Baal, *6* whose son was Beerah, whom Tiglath-pileser, the king of Assyria, took into exile; he was a prince of the Reubenites.*x* *7* His brothers who belonged to his clans, when they were listed in the family records according to their descendants, were: Jeiel, the chief, and Zechariah, *8* and Bela, son of Azaz, son of Shema, son of Joel. The Reubenites lived in Aroer and as far as Nebo and Baal-meon;*y* *9* toward the east they dwelt as far as the desert which extends from the Euphrates River, for they had much livestock in the land of Gilead.*z* *10* During the reign of Saul they waged war with the Hagrites, and when they had defeated them they occupied their tents throughout the region east of Gilead.*a*

4, 39: Gedor: in the Greek, Gerar, no doubt correct.
5, 1-26: The Transjordan tribes.

o: 1 Chr 2, 3; Gn 38, 5; 46, 12; Nm 26, 20.   *p:* Gn 46, 10; Ex 6, 15; Nm 26, 12f.   *q:* 28-32: Jos 19, 2-8.   *r:* Nm 1, 2.   *s:* 2 Kgs 18, 1f; 2 Chr 29, 1.   *t:* Ex 17, 8. 14; Dt 25, 17ff; 1 Sm 14, 48; 15, 3. 7f; 2 Sm 8, 12.   *u:* Gn 35, 22; 48, 5. 15-22; 49, 3f; Dt 33, 6.   *v:* 1 Chr 28, 4; Gn 49, 8ff.   *w:* Gn 46, 9; Ex 6, 14; Nm 26, 5f.   *x:* 2 Kgs 15, 29.   *y:* Jos 13, 9. 16f; Nm 32, 3. 38.   *z:* Jos 22, 9.   *a:* Ps 83, 6.

Gad. [11]The Gadites lived alongside them in the land of Bashan as far as Salecah.[b] [12]Joel was chief, Shapham was second in command, and Janai was judge in Bashan.[c] [13]Their brothers, corresponding to their ancestral houses, were: Michael, Meshullam, Sheba, Jorai, Jacan, Zia, and Eber—seven. [14]These were the sons of Abihail, son of Huri, son of Jaroah, son of Gilead, son of Michael, son of Jeshishai, son of Jahdo, son of Buz. [15]Ahi, son of Abdiel, son of Guni, was the head of their ancestral houses. [16]They dwelt in Gilead, in Bashan and its towns, and in all the pasture lands of Sirion to the borders. [17]All were listed in the family records in the time of Jotham, king of Judah, and of Jeroboam, king of Israel.

[18]The Reubenites, Gadites, and half-tribe of Manasseh were warriors, men who bore shield and sword and who drew the bow, trained in warfare—forty-four thousand seven hundred and sixty men fit for military service. [19]When they waged war against the Hagrites and against Jetur, Naphish, and Nodab,[d] [20]they received help so that they mastered the Hagrites and all who were with them. For during the battle they called on God, and he heard them because they had put their trust in him.[e] [21]Along with one hundred thousand men they also captured their livestock: fifty thousand camels, two hundred fifty thousand sheep, and two thousand asses. [22]Many had fallen in battle, for victory is from God; and they took over their dwelling place until the time of the exile.[f]

East Manasseh. [23]The numerous members of the half-tribe of Manasseh lived in the land of Bashan as far as Baal-hermon, Senir, and Mount Hermon. [24]The following were the heads of their ancestral houses: Epher, Ishi, Eliel, Azriel, Jeremiah, Hodaviah, and Jahdiel—men who were warriors, famous men, and heads over their ancestral houses.

[25]However, they offended the God of their fathers by lusting after the gods of the natives of the land, whom God had cleared out of their way.[g] [26]Therefore the God of Israel incited against them the anger of Pul,* king of Assyria, and of Tiglath-pileser, king of Assyria, who deported the Reubenites, the Gadites, and the half-tribe of Manasseh and brought them to Halah, Habor, and Hara, and to the river Gozan, where they have remained to this day.[h]

*Levi.** [27]The sons of Levi were Gershon, Kohath, and Merari.[i] [28]The sons of Kohath were Amram, Izhar, Hebron, and Uzziel.[j] [29]The children of Amram were Aaron, Moses, and Miriam. The sons of Aaron were Nadab, Abihu, Eleazar, and Ithamar.[k] [30]*Eleazar became the father of Phinehas. Phinehas became the father of Abishua. [31]Abishua became the father of Bukki. Bukki became the father of Uzzi. [32]Uzzi became the father of Zerahiah. Zerahiah became the father of Meraioth. [33]Meraioth became the father of Amariah. Amariah became the father of Ahitub. [34]Ahitub became the father of Zadok. Zadok became the father of Ahimaaz. [35]Ahimaaz became the father of Azariah. Azariah became the father of Johanan. [36]Johanan became the father of Azariah, who served as priest in the temple Solomon built in Jerusalem. [37]Azariah became the father of Amariah. Amariah became the father of Ahitub. [38]Ahitub became the father of Zadok. Zadok became the father of Shallum. [39]Shallum became the father of Hilkiah. Hilkiah became the father of Azariah. [40]Azariah became the father of Seraiah. Seraiah became the father of Jehozadak. [41]Jehozadak was one of those who went into the exile which the LORD inflicted on Judah and Jerusalem through Nebuchadnezzar.

5, 26: Pul: the name which the Assyrian king Tiglath-pileser III (745–727 B.C.) took as king of Babylon.

5, 27—6, 66: The tribe of Levi. The list gives special prominence to Levi's son Kohath, from whom were descended both the Aaronite priests (1 Chr 5, 28-41) and the leading group of temple singers (1 Chr 6, 18-23).

5, 30-41: The line of preexilic priests. The list seems to be confused in vv 36ff, which repeat the names, mostly in inverse order, that occur in vv 34f. A similar but shorter list is given, with variations, in Ezr 7, 1-5.

b: Jos 13, 11. 24-28.   c: Gn 46, 16.   d: 1 Chr 1, 31; 5, 10; Gn 25, 15; Ps 83, 6.   e: Dt 33, 20f.   f: Nm 32, 39; Dt 3, 8ff; Jgs 3, 3.   g: Ex 34, 14ff; 2 Kgs 17, 7.   h: 2 Kgs 15, 9. 29; 17, 6.   i: 1 Chr 6, 1; 23, 6; Gn 46, 11; Ex 6, 16; Nm 26, 57.   j: 1 Chr 6, 3; Ex 6, 18.   k: Ex 6, 20; Nm 26, 59f.

See RG
200

CHAPTER 6

[1]The sons of Levi were Gershon, Kohath, and Merari.[l] [2]The sons of Gershon were named Libni and Shimei.[m] [3]The sons of Kohath were Amram, Izhar, Hebron, and Uzziel.[n] [4o]The sons of Merari were Mahli and Mushi.

The following were the clans of Levi, distributed according to their ancestors: [5]of Gershon: his son Libni, whose son was Jahath, whose son was Zimmah, [6]whose son was Joah, whose son was Iddo, whose son was Zerah, whose son was Jetherai.

[7]The descendants of Kohath were: his son Amminadab, whose son was Korah, whose son was Assir, [8]whose son was Elkanah, whose son was Ebiasaph, whose son was Assir, [9]whose son was Tahath, whose son was Uriel, whose son was Uzziah, whose son was Shaul. [10]The sons of Elkanah were Amasai and Ahimoth, [11]whose son was Elkanah, whose son was Zophai, whose son was Nahath, [12]whose son was Eliab, whose son was Jeroham, whose son was Elkanah, whose son was Samuel. [13]The sons of Samuel were Joel, the first-born, and Abijah, the second.

[14]The descendants of Merari were Mahli, whose son was Libni, whose son was Shimei, whose son was Uzzah,[p] [15]whose son was Shimea, whose son was Haggiah, whose son was Asaiah.

[16]The following were entrusted by David with the choir services* in the LORD's house from the time when the ark had obtained a permanent resting place. [17]They served as singers before the Dwelling of the meeting tent until Solomon built the temple of the LORD in Jerusalem, and they performed their services in an order prescribed for them. [18]Those who so performed are the following, together with their descendants.

Among the Kohathites: Heman, the chanter, son of Joel, son of Samuel, [19]son of Elkanah, son of Jeroham, son of Eliel, son of Toah, [20]son of Zuth, son of Elkanah, son of Mahath, son of Amasi, [21]son of Elkanah, son of Joel, son of Azariah, son of Zephaniah, [22]son of Tahath, son of Assir, son of Ebiasaph, son of Korah,[q] [23]son of Izhar, son of Kohath, son of Levi, son of Israel.

[24]His brother Asaph stood at his right hand. Asaph was the son of Berechiah, son of Shimea, [25]son of Michael, son of Baaseiah, son of Malchijah, [26]son of Ethni, son of Zerah, son of Adaiah, [27]son of Ethan, son of Zimmah,[r] son of Shimei, [28]son of Jahath, son of Gershon, son of Levi.

[29]Their brothers, the Merarites, stood at the left: Ethan, son of Kishi, son of Abdi, son of Malluch, [30]son of Hashabiah, son of Amaziah, son of Hilkiah, [31]son of Amzi, son of Bani, son of Shemer, [32]son of Mahli, son of Mushi, son of Merari, son of Levi.[s]

[33]Their brother Levites were appointed to all other services of the Dwelling of the house of God.[t] [34]However, it was Aaron and his descendants who burnt the offerings on the altar of holocausts and on the altar of incense; they alone had charge of the holy of holies and of making atonement for Israel, as Moses, the servant of God, had ordained.[u]

[35]These were the descendants of Aaron: his son Eleazer, whose son was Phinehas, whose son was Abishua, [36]whose son was Bukki, whose son was Uzzi, whose son was Zerahiah, [37]whose son was Meraioth, whose son was Amariah, whose son was Ahitub, [38]whose son was Zadok, whose son was Ahimaaz.

[39*]The following were their dwelling places to which their encampment was limited. To the descendants of Aaron who belonged to the clan of the Kohathites, since the first lot fell to them, [40]was assigned Hebron with its adjacent pasture lands in the land of Judah, [41]although the open country and the villages belonging to the city had been given to Caleb, the son of Jephunneh. [42]There were assigned to the descendants of

---

6, 16-32: The origin of the choir services performed by the levitical families in the postexilic temple at the time of the Chronicler is here attributed to David, somewhat as all the laws in the Pentateuch are attributed to Moses.

6, 39-66: Regarding the nature of the rights of Levites in the cities assigned to them, see note on Jos 21, 1.

---

l: 1 Chr 5, 27; 23, 6; Gn 46, 11; Ex 6, 16; Nm 26, 57.   *m:* Ex 6, 17.   *n:* Ex 6, 18; Nm 3, 19; 26, 59.   *o:* 1 Chr 6, 14; Ex 6, 19; Nm 3, 20; 26, 58.   *p:* 1 Chr 6, 4; Ex 6, 19; Nm 3, 20; 26, 58.   *q:* Ex 6, 24.   *r:* 1 Chr 6, 2. 5.   *s:* Ex 6, 19; Nm 26, 58.   *t:* 1 Chr 15, 17. 19; 16, 41f; 2 Chr 5, 12.   *u:* 1 Chr 16, 39f.

Mediterranean
Sea

Dead
Sea

ASHER

NAPHTALI

Kedesh

Abdon •

Rehob •

Rimmon
(Dimnah)

Hammon

ZEBULUN

Daberath
Tabor

Hilkath • Joknean

• Kishion

ISSACHAR

Ramoth •

Taanach
Engannim •

Ibleam •

MANASSEH

MANASSEH

Ashtaroth •

• Golan

BASHAN

• Ramoth-gilead?

GILEAD

GAD

Shechem •

Mahanaim •

Gath-rimmon •

• Shiloh

D   A   N

EPHRAIM

Elteke? •

Beth-horon

Gibeon

Geba

Gibbethon •

Gezer •

Aijalon •

BENJAMIN

Almon

Anathoth •

Beth-shemesh •

• Holon?

Libnah •

Hebron
(Kiriath-arba)

JUDAH

Jetta •

Debir •

• Eshtemoa

• Jattir

• Ashan

SIMEON

Jazer •

Heshbon •

Kiriathaim •

• Bezer?

R   E   U   B   E   N

Jahzah ?

Kedemoth? •

0   10   20 Miles

0   10   20 Kilometers

33°

32°

31°

35°

36°

The Levitical Cities according to 1 Chronicles

444

Aaron: Hebron, a city of asylum, Libnah with its pasture lands, Jattir with its pasture lands, Eshtemoa with its pasture lands, 43Holon with its pasture lands, Debir with its pasture lands, 44Ashan with its pasture lands, Jetta with its pasture lands, and Beth-shemesh with its pasture lands. 45Also from the tribe of Benjamin: Gibeon with its pasture lands, Geba with its pasture lands, Almon with its pasture lands, Anathoth with its pasture lands. In all, they had thirteen cities with their pasture lands. 49The Israelites assigned these cities with their pasture lands to the Levites, 50designating them by name and assigning them by lot from the tribes of the Judahites, Simeonites, and Benjaminites.

46The other Kohathites obtained ten cities by lot for their clans from the tribe of Ephraim, from the tribe of Dan, and from the half-tribe of Manasseh. 47The clans of the Gershonites obtained thirteen cities from the tribes of Issachar, Asher, and Naphtali, and from the half-tribe of Manasseh in Bashan. 48The clans of the Merarites obtained twelve cities by lot from the tribes of Reuben, Gad, and Zebulun.

51The clans of the Kohathites obtained cities by lot from the tribe of Ephraim. 52They were assigned: Shechem in the mountain region of Ephraim, a city of asylum, with its pasture lands, Gezer with its pasture lands, 53Kibzaim with its pasture lands, and Bethhoron with its pasture lands. 54From the tribe of Dan: Elteke with its pasture lands, Gibbethon with its pasture lands, Aijalon with its pasture lands, and Gath-rimmon with its pasture lands. 55From the half-tribe of Manasseh: Taanach with its pasture lands and Ibleam with its pasture lands. These belonged to the rest of the Kohathite clan.

56The clans of the Gershonites received from the half-tribe of Manasseh: Golan in Bashan with its pasture lands and Ashtaroth with its pasture lands. 57From the tribe of Issachar: Kedesh with its pasture lands, Daberath with its pasture lands, 58Ramoth with its pasture lands, and Engannim with its pasture lands. 59From the tribe of Asher: Mashal with its pasture lands, Abdon with its pasture lands, 60Hilkath with its pasture lands, and Rehob with its pasture lands. 61From the tribe of Naphtali: Kedesh in Galilee with its pasture lands, Hammon with its pasture lands, and Kiriathaim with its pasture lands.

62The rest of the Merarites received from the tribe of Zebulun: Jokneam with its pasture lands, Kartah with its pasture lands, Rimmon with its pasture lands, and Tabor with its pasture lands. 63Across the Jordan at Jericho [that is, east of the Jordan] they received from the tribe of Reuben: Bezer in the desert with its pasture lands, Jahzah with its pasture lands, 64Kedemoth with its pasture lands, and Mephaath with its pasture lands. 65From the tribe of Gad: Ramoth in Gilead with its pasture lands, Mahanaim with its pasture lands, 66Heshbon with its pasture lands, and Jazer with its pasture lands.

CHAPTER 7

See RG 200

*Issachar.** 1The sons of Issachar were Tola, Puah, Jashub, and Shimron: four.v 2The sons of Tola were Uzzi, Rephaiah, Jeriel, Jahmai, Ibsam, and Shemuel, warrior heads of the ancestral houses of Tola. Their kindred numbered twenty-two thousand six hundred in the time of David.w 3The sons of Uzzi: Izarahiah. The sons of Izarahiah were Michael, Obadiah, Joel, and Isshiah. All five of these were chiefs. 4Their kindred, by ancestral houses, numbered thirty-six thousand men in organized military troops, since they had more wives and sons 5than their fellow tribesmen. In all the clans of Issachar there was a total of eighty-seven thousand warriors in their family records.

Benjamin. 6The sons of Benjamin were Bela, Becher, and Jediael—three.x 7The sons of Bela were Ezbon, Uzzi, Uzziel, Jerimoth, and Iri—five. They were heads of their ancestral houses and warriors. Their family records listed twenty-two thousand and thirty-four. 8The sons of Becher were Zemirah, Joash, Eliezer, Elioenai, Omri, Jeremoth, Abijah, Anathoth, and Alemeth—all these were sons of Becher.y 9Their family

7, 1-40: The northern tribes.

v: Gn 46, 13.   w: Nm 26, 23f; Jgs 10, 1.   x: 1 Chr 7, 6; Gn 46, 21; Nm 26, 38.   y: 1 Chr 7, 8.

records listed twenty thousand two hundred of their kindred who were heads of their ancestral houses and warriors. [10]The sons of Jediael: Bilhan. The sons of Bilhan were Jeush, Benjamin, Ehud, Chenaanah, Zethan, Tarshish, and Ahishahar. [11]All these were descendants of Jediael, heads of ancestral houses and warriors. They numbered seventeen thousand two hundred men fit for military service . . . Shupham and Hupham.[z]

Dan, Naphtali and Manasseh. [12a]The sons of Dan: Hushim. [13]The sons of Naphtali were Jahziel, Guni, Jezer, and Shallum. These were descendants of Bilhah. [14]The sons of Manasseh, whom his Aramean concubine bore:[b] she bore Machir, the father of Gilead.[c] [15]Machir took a wife whose name was Maacah; his sister's name was Molecheth. Manasseh's second son was named Zelophehad, but to Zelophehad only daughters were born.[d] [16]Maacah, Machir's wife, bore a son whom she named Peresh. He had a brother named Sheresh, whose sons were Ulam and Rakem. [17]The sons of Ulam: Bedan. These were the descendants of Gilead, the son of Machir, the son of Manasseh. [18]His sister Molecheth bore Ishhod, Abiezer, and Mahlah. [19]The sons of Shemida were Ahian, Shechem, Likhi, and Aniam.

Ephraim. [20e]The sons of Ephraim: Shuthelah, whose son was Bered, whose son was Tahath, whose son was Eleadah, whose son was Tahath, [21]whose son was Zabad. Ephraim's son Shuthelah, and Ezer and Elead, who were born in the land, were slain by the inhabitants of Gath because they had gone down to take away their livestock. [22]Their father Ephraim mourned a long time, but after his kinsmen had come and comforted him, [23]he visited his wife, who conceived and bore a son whom he named Beriah, since evil had befallen his house.[f] [24]He had a daughter, Sheerah, who built lower and upper Beth-horon and Uzzen-sheerah. [25]Zabad's son was Rephah, whose son was Resheph, whose son was Telah, whose son was Tahan, [26]whose

son was Ladan, whose son was Ammihud, whose son was Elishama,[g] [27]whose son was Nun, whose son was Joshua.

[28]Their property and their dwellings were in Bethel and its towns, Naaran to the east, Gezer and its towns to the west, and also Shechem and its towns as far as Ayyah and its towns.[h] [29]Manasseh, however, had possession of Beth-shean and its towns, Taanach and its towns, Megiddo and its towns, and Dor and its towns. In these dwelt the descendants of Joseph, the son of Israel.[i]

Asher. [30]The sons of Asher were Imnah, Iishvah, Ishvi, and Beriah; their sister was Serah.[j] [31]Beriah's sons were Heber and Malchiel, who was the father of Birzaith. [32]Heber became the father of Japhlet, Shomer, Hotham, and their sister Shua. [33]The sons of Japhlet were Pasach, Bimhal, and Ashvath; these were the sons of Japhlet. [34]The sons of Shomer were Ahi, Rohgah, Jehubbah, and Aram. [35]The sons of his brother Hotham were Zophah, Imna, Shelesh, and Amal. [36]The sons of Zophah were Suah, Harnepher, Shual, Beri, Imrah, [37]Bezer, Hod, Shamma, Shilshah, Ithran, and Beera. [38]The sons of Jether were Jephunneh, Pispa, and Ara. [39]The sons of Ulla were Arah, Hanniel, and Rizia. [40]All these were descendants of Asher, heads of ancestral houses, distinguished men, warriors, and chiefs among the princes. Their family records numbered twenty-six thousand men fit for military service.

CHAPTER 8

See RG 200

Benjamin.[*] [1]Benjamin became the father of Bela, his first-born, Ashbel, the second son, Aharah, the third,[k] [2]Nohah, the fourth, and Rapha, the fifth. [3]The sons of Bela were Addar and Gera, the father of Ehud. [4]The sons of Ehud were Abishua, Naaman, Ahoah,[l] [5]Gera, Shephuphan, and Huram. [6]These were the sons of Ehud, family heads over those who dwelt in Geba and were deported to Manahath. [7]Also Naaman,

8, 1-40: A second, variant list of the Benjaminites, with special prominence given to Saul's family (vv 33-40).

z: Nm 26, 39.   a: 12f: Gn 46, 24; Nm 26, 48f.   b: 14-19: Nm 26, 29-32.   c: Nm 26, 29; Jos 17, 1.   d: Nm 26, 33; Jos 17, 3.   e: Nm 26, 35.   f: 1 Chr 8, 13.   g: Nm 1, 10; 2, 18; 7, 48; 10, 22.   h: Gn 12, 8; 1 Kgs 9, 16.   i: Jos 17, 11.   j: Gn 46, 17; Nm 26, 44ff. k: 1 Chr 7, 6; Gn 46, 21; Nm 26, 38ff.   l: Jgs 3, 15.

Ahijah, and Gera. The last, who led them into exile, became the father of Uzza and Ahihud. [8]Shaharaim became a father on the Moabite plateau after he had put away his wives Hushim and Baara. [9]By his wife Hodesh he became the father of Jobab, Zibia, Mesha, Malcam, [10]Jeuz, Sachia, and Mirmah. These were his sons, family heads. [11]By Hushim he became the father of Abitub and Elpaal. [12]The sons of Elpaal were Eber, Misham, Shemed, who built Ono and Lod with its nearby towns,[m] [13]Beriah, and Shema. They were family heads of those who dwelt in Aijalon, and they put the inhabitants of Gath to flight. [14]Their brethren were Elpaal, Shashak, and Jeremoth. [15]Zebadiah, Arad, Eder, [16]Michael, Ishpah, and Joha were the sons of Beriah. [17]Zebadiah, Meshullam, Hizki, Heber, [18]Ishmerai, Izliah, and Jobab were the sons of Elpaal. [19]Jakim, Zichri, Zabdi, [20]Elienai, Zillethai, Eliel, [21]Adaiah, Beraiah, and Shimrath were the sons of Shimei. [22]Ishpan, Eber, Eliel, [23]Abdon, Zichri, Hanan, [24]Hananiah, Elam, Anthothijah, [25]Iphdeiah, and Penuel were the sons of Shashak. [26]Shamsherai, Shehariah, Athaliah, [27]Jaareshiah, Elijah, and Zichri were the sons of Jeroham. [28]These were family heads over their kindred, chiefs who dwelt in Jerusalem.

[29n]In Gibeon dwelt Jeiel, the founder of Gibeon, whose wife's name was Maacah; [30]also his first-born son, Abdon, and Zur, Kish, Baal, Ner, Nadab, [31]Gedor, Ahio, Zecher, and Mikloth. [32]Mikloth became the father of Shimeah. These, too, dwelt with their relatives in Jerusalem, opposite their fellow tribesmen. [33o]Ner became the father of Kish, and Kish became the father of Saul. Saul became the father of Jonathan, Malchishua, Abinadab, and Eshbaal.[p] [34]The son of Jonathan was Meribbaal, and Meribbaal became the father of Micah.[q] [35]The sons of Micah were Pithon, Melech, Tarea, and Ahaz. [36]Ahaz became the father of Jehoaddah, and Jehoaddah became the father of Alemeth, Azmaveth, and Zimri. Zimri became the father of Moza.[r] [37]Moza became the father of Binea, whose son was Raphah, whose son was Eleasah, whose son was Azel.[s] [38]Azel had six sons, whose names were Azrikam, his first-born, Ishmael, Sheariah, Azariah, Obadiah, and Hanan; all these were the sons of Azel. [39]The sons of Eshek, his brother, were Ulam, his first-born, Jeush, the second son, and Eliphelet, the third. [40]The sons of Ulam were combat archers, and many were their sons and grandsons: one hundred and fifty. All these were the descendants of Benjamin.

CHAPTER 9

See RG 200

[1]Thus all Israel was inscribed in its family records which are recorded in the book of the kings of Israel.[t]

Now Judah had been carried in captivity to Babylon because of its rebellion. [2u*]The first to settle again in their cities and dwell there were certain lay Israelites, the priests, the Levites, and the temple slaves.[v]

Jerusalemites. [3]In Jerusalem lived Judahites and Benjaminites; also Ephraimites and Manassehites. [4]Among the Judahites was Uthai, son of Ammihud, son of Omri, son of Imri, son of Bani, one of the descendants of Perez, son of Judah. [5]Among the Shelanites were Asaiah, the first-born, and his sons. [6]Among the Zerahites were Jeuel and six hundred and ninety of their brethren. [7]Among the Benjaminites were Sallu, son of Meshullam, son of Hodaviah, son of Hassenuah; [8]Ibneiah, son of Jeroham; Elah, son of Uzzi, son of Michri; Meshullam, son of Shephatiah, son of Reuel, son of Ibnijah. [9]Their kindred of various families were nine hundred and fifty-six. All those named were heads of their ancestral houses.

[10]Among the priests were Jedaiah; Jehoiarib; Jachin; [11]Azariah, son of Hilkiah, son of Meshullam, son of Zadok, son of Meraioth, son of Ahitub, the ruler of the house of God; [12]Adaiah, son of Jeroham, son of Pashhur, son of Malchijah; Maasai, son of

9, 2-34: The inhabitants of Jerusalem after the exile. A similar list, with many variants in the names, is given in Neh 11, 3-24.

m: Neh 11, 35.   *n:* 29-32: 1 Chr 9, 35-38.   *o:* 33-38: 1 Chr 9, 39-44.   *p:* 1 Chr 10, 2; 1 Sm 9, 1; 14, 49. 51; 31, 2.   *q:* 2 Sm 4, 4; 9, 6. 10. 12.   *r:* 1 Chr 9, 42.   *s:* 1 Chr 9, 43.   *t:* 2 Chr 16, 11; 20, 34; 25, 26; 27, 7; 33, 18; 36, 8.   *u:* 2-22: Neh 11, 3-19.   *v:* Ezr 2, 70; 7, 7; Neh 11, 3.

Adiel, son of Jahzerah, son of Meshullam, son of Meshillemith, son of Immer. ¹³Their brethren, heads of their ancestral houses, were one thousand seven hundred and sixty, valiant for the work of the service of the house of God.

¹⁴Among the Levites were Shemaiah, son of Hasshub, son of Azrikam, son of Hashabiah, one of the descendants of Merari; ¹⁵Bakbakkar; Heresh; Galal; Mattaniah, son of Mica, son of Zichri, a descendant of Asaph; ¹⁶Obadiah, son of Shemaiah, son of Galal, a descendant of Jeduthun; and Berechiah, son of Asa, son of Elkanah, whose family lived in the villages of the Netophathites.

¹⁷The gatekeepers were Shallum, Akkub, Talmon, Ahiman, and their brethren; Shallum was the chief. ¹⁸Previously they had stood guard at the king's gate on the east side; now they became gatekeepers for the encampments of the Levites. ¹⁹Shallum, son of Kore, son of Ebiasaph, a descendant of Korah, and his brethren of the same ancestral house of the Korahites had as their assigned task the guarding of the threshold of the tent, just as their fathers had guarded the entrance to the encampment of the LORD. ²⁰Phinehas, son of Eleazar, had been their chief in times past—the LORD be with him!ʷ ²¹Zechariah, son of Meshelemiah, guarded the gate of the meeting tent.ˣ ²²In all, those who were chosen for gatekeepers at the threshold were two hundred and twelve. They were inscribed in the family records of their villages. David and Samuel the seer had established them in their position of trust. ²³Thus they and their sons kept guard over the gates of the house of the LORD, the house which was then a tent. ²⁴The gatekeepers were stationed at the four sides, to the east, the west, the north, and the south.ʸ ²⁵Their kinsmen who lived in their own villages took turns in assisting them for seven-day periods,ᶻ ²⁶while the four chief gatekeepers were on constant duty. These were the Levites who also had charge of the chambers and treasures of the house of God.

²⁷At night they lodged about the house of God, for it was in their charge and they had the duty of opening it each morning.

²⁸Some of them had charge of the liturgical equipment, tallying it as it was brought in and taken out. ²⁹Others were appointed to take care of the utensils and all the sacred vessels, as well as the fine flour, the wine, the oil, the frankincense, and the spices. ³⁰It was the sons of priests, however, who mixed the spiced ointments.ᵃ ³¹ᵇMattithiah, one of the Levites, the first-born of Shallum the Koreite, was entrusted with preparing the cakes. ³²Benaiah the Kohathite, one of their brethren, was in charge of setting out the showbread each sabbath.ᶜ

³³These were the chanters and the gatekeepers, family heads over the Levites. They stayed in the chambers when free of duty, for day and night they had to be ready for service. ³⁴These were the levitical family heads over their kindred, chiefs who dwelt in Jerusalem.

II: The History of David

Genealogy of Saul. ³⁵ᵈIn Gibeon dwelt Jeiel, the founder of Gibeon, whose wife's name was Maacah. ³⁶His first-born son was Abdon; then came Zur, Kish, Baal, Ner, Nadab, ³⁷Gedor, Ahio, Zechariah, and Mikloth. ³⁸Mikloth became the father of Shimeam. These, too, with their brethren, dwelt opposite their brethren in Jerusalem. ³⁹Ner became the father of Kish, and Kish became the father of Saul. Saul became the father of Jonathan, Malchishua, Abinadab, and Eshbaal. ⁴⁰The son of Jonathan was Meribbaal, and Meribbaal became the father of Micah. ⁴¹The sons of Micah were Pithon, Melech, Tahrea, and Ahaz. ⁴²Ahaz became the father of Jehoaddah, and Jehoaddah became the father of Alemeth, Azmaveth, and Zimri. Zimri became the father of Moza. ⁴³Moza became the father of Binea, whose son was Rephaiah, whose son was Eleasah, whose son was Azel. ⁴⁴Azel had six sons, whose names were Azrikam, his first-born, Ishmael, Sheariah, Azariah, Obadiah, and Hanan; these were the sons of Azel.

w: Ex 6, 25; Nm 25, 7. 11; Jgs 20, 28.   *x:* 1 Chr 26, 2. 14.   *y:* 1 Chr 26, 13.   *z:* 2 Chr 23, 4f.   *a:* Ex 30, 22-33.   *b:* 31f: 1 Chr 23, 29; Lv 2, 1ff; 6, 13ff; 7, 11.   *c:* Ex 25, 30; Lv 24, 5-8.   *d:* 35-44: 1 Chr 8, 29-38.

CHAPTER 10

See RG 200–203

His Death and Burial. ¹ᵉNow the Philistines were at war with Israel; the Israelites fled before the Philistines, and a number of them fell, slain on Mount Gilboa. ²The Philistines pressed hard after Saul and his sons. When the Philistines had killed Jonathan, Abinadab, and Malchishua, sons of Saul, ³the whole fury of the battle descended upon Saul. Then the archers found him, and wounded him with their arrows.

⁴Saul said to his armor-bearer, "Draw your sword and thrust me through with it, that these uncircumcised may not come and maltreat me." But the armor-bearer, in great fear, refused. So Saul took his own sword and fell on it; ⁵and seeing him dead, the armor-bearer also fell on his sword and died. ⁶Thus, with Saul and his three sons, his whole house died at one time. ⁷When all the Israelites who were in the valley saw that Saul and his sons had died in the rout, they left their cities and fled; thereupon the Philistines came and occupied them.

⁸On the following day, when the Philistines came to strip the slain, they found Saul and his sons where they had fallen on Mount Gilboa. ⁹They stripped him, cut off his head, and took his armor; these they sent throughout the land of the Philistines to convey the good news to their idols and their people. ¹⁰His armor they put in the house of their gods, but his skull they impaled on the temple of Dagon.

¹¹When all the inhabitants of Jabesh-gilead had heard what the Philistines had done to Saul, ¹²its warriors rose to a man, recovered the bodies of Saul and his sons, and brought them to Jabesh. They buried their bones under the oak of Jabesh, and fasted seven days.ᶠ

¹³*Thus Saul died because of his rebellion against the LORD in disobeying his command, and also because he had sought counsel of a necromancer,ᵍ ¹⁴and had not rather inquired of the LORD. Therefore the LORD slew him, and transferred his kingdom to David, the son of Jesse.ʰ

CHAPTER 11

See RG 200–203

David Is Made King. ¹ⁱThen all Israel gathered about David in Hebron, and they said: "Surely, we are of the same bone and flesh as you. ²Even formerly, when Saul was still the king, it was you who led Israel in all its battles. And now the LORD, your God, has said to you, 'You shall shepherd my people Israel and be ruler over them.' "ʲ ³Then all the elders of Israel came to the king at Hebron, and there David made a covenant with them in the presence of the LORD; and they anointed him king over Israel, in accordance with the word of the LORD as revealed through Samuel.ᵏ

Jerusalem Captured. ⁴Then David and all Israel went to Jerusalem, that is, Jebus, where the natives of the land were called Jebusites.ˡ ⁵The inhabitants of Jebus said to David, "You shall not enter here." David nevertheless captured the fortress of Sion, which is the City of David. ⁶David said, "Whoever strikes the Jebusites first shall be made the chief commander." Joab, the son of Zeruiah, was the first to go up; and so he became chief.ᵐ ⁷David took up his residence in the fortress, which thenceforth was called the City of David. ⁸He rebuilt the city on all sides, from the Millo all the way around, while Joab restored the rest of the city.ⁿ ⁹David became more and more powerful, for the LORD of hosts was with him.

David's Warriors. ¹⁰ᵒThese were David's chief warriors who, together with all Israel, supported him in his reign in order to make him true king, even as the LORD had commanded concerning Israel. ¹¹Here is the list of David's warriors:

Ishbaal, the son of Hachamoni, chief of the Three.* He brandished his spear against

---

10, 13f: The Chronicler's comment on why Saul met his tragic end: he had disobeyed the Lord's command given through the prophet Samuel (1 Sm 15, 3-9), and had sought counsel of a necromancer (1 Sm 28, 6-19), contrary to the Mosaic law against necromancy (Dt 18, 10f).

11, 11f: The Three: the Chronicler names only two of them: Ishbaal and Eleazar. According to 2 Sm 23, 8-12, the Three were Ishbaal, Eleazar, and Shammah.

---

e: 1-12: 1 Sm 31, 1-13. *f:* 2 Sm 2, 5. *g:* Dt 18, 10ff; 1 Sm 13, 13f; 15, 3. 11. 26. *h:* 1 Sm 15, 28; 2 Sm 3, 9f. *i:* 1-9: 2 Sm 5, 1-10. *j:* 1 Sm 18, 5. 13-16. 30; 19, 8. *k:* 1 Sm 16, 1. 13; 2 Sm 2, 4. *l:* Jos 15, 8; Jgs 1, 21; 19, 10f. *m:* 2 Sm 2, 13ff; 8, 16. *n:* 1 Kgs 9, 15. 24; 11, 27; 2 Chr 32, 5. *o:* 10-41: 2 Sm 23, 8-39.

Baal-hazor
Gilgal
Gezer
Gibeon
Geba
Ekron
Jerusalem
Gath?
Giloh
Tekoa
Hebron

Mediterranean
Sea

ZOBAIT

ARAM (SYRIA)

Damascus

Tyre
Abel-beth-maacah

GESHUR

ISRAEL

AMMON

Mahanaim

Hill Country
of Ephraim

Rabbah

Ashdod
Jerusalem
Ashkelon

PHILISTIA
JUDAH
Gaza

MOAB

Valley of Salt

AMALEK

EDOM

0		25		50		75 Miles
0	40		80			120 Kilometers

The Kingdom of David according to 1 Chronicles

450

three hundred, whom he slew in a single encounter.

[12]Next to him Eleazar, the son of Dodo the Ahohite, one of the Three warriors.[p] [13]He was with David at Pasdammim, where the Philistines had massed for battle. The plowland was fully planted with barley, but its defenders were retreating before the Philistines.[q] [14]He made a stand on the sown ground, kept it safe, and cut down the Philistines. Thus the LORD brought about a great victory.

[15]Three of the Thirty chiefs went down to the rock, to David, who was in the cave of Adullam while the Philistines were encamped in the valley of Rephaim.[r] [16]David was then in the stronghold, and a Philistine garrison was at Bethlehem. [17]David expressed a desire: "Oh, that someone would give me a drink from the cistern that is by the gate at Bethlehem!" [18]Thereupon the Three broke through the encampment of the Philistines, drew water from the cistern by the gate at Bethlehem, and carried it back to David. But David refused to drink it. Instead, he poured it out as a libation to the LORD, [19]saying, "God forbid that I should do such a thing! Could I drink the blood of these men who risked their lives?" For at the risk of their lives they brought it; and so he refused to drink it. Such deeds as these the Three warriors performed.

[20s]Abishai, the brother of Joab. He was the chief of the Thirty;[*] he brandished his spear against three hundred, and slew them. Thus he had a reputation like that of the Three.[t] [21]He was twice as famous as any of the Thirty and became their commander, but he did not attain to the Three.

[22]Benaiah, the son of Jehoiada, a valiant man of mighty deeds, from Kabzeel. He killed the two sons of Ariel of Moab, and also, on a snowy day, he went down and killed the lion in the cistern. [23]He likewise slew the Egyptian, a huge man five cubits tall. The Egyptian carried a spear that was like a weaver's heddle-bar, but he came against him with a staff, wrested the spear from the Egyptian's hand, and killed him with his own spear. [24]Such deeds as these of Benaiah, the son of Jehoiada, gave him a reputation like that of the Three. [25]He was more famous than any of the Thirty, but he did not attain to the Three. David put him in charge of his bodyguard.[u]

[26]Also these warriors: Asahel, the brother of Joab; Elhanan, son of Dodo, from Bethlehem;[v] [27]Shammoth, from En-harod; Helez, from Palti; [28]Ira, son of Ikkesh, from Tekoa; Abiezer, from Anathoth; [29]Sibbecai, from Husha; Ilai, from Ahoh;[w] [30]Maharai, from Netophah; Heled, son of Baanah, from Netophah;[x] [31]Ithai, son of Ribai, from Gibeah of Benjamin; Benaiah, from Pirathon;[y] [32]Hurai, from the valley of Gaash; Abiel, from Betharabah; [33]Azmaveth, from Bahurim; Eliahba, from Shaalbon; [34]Jashen the Gunite; Jonathan, son of Shagee, from En-harod; [35]Ahiam, son of Sachar, from En-harod; Elipheleth, son of [36]Ahasabi, from Beth-maacah; Ahijah, from Gilo; [37]Hezro, from Carmel; Naarai, the son of Ezbai; [38]Joel, brother of Nathan, from Rehob, the Gadite; [39]Zelek the Ammonite; Naharai, from Beeroth, the armor-bearer of Joab, son of Zeruiah; [40]Ira, from Jattir; Gareb, from Jattir; [41]Uriah the Hittite; Zabad, son of Ahlai, [42]and, in addition to the Thirty, Adina, son of Shiza, the Reubenite, chief of the tribe of Reuben; [43]Hanan, from Beth-maacah; Joshaphat the Mithnite; [44]Uzzia, from Ashterath; Shama and Jeiel, sons of Hotham, from Aroer; [45]Jediael, son of Shimri, and Joha, his brother, the Tizite; [46]Eliel the Mahavite; Jeribai and Joshaviah, sons of Elnaam; Ithmah, from Moab; [47]Eliel, Obed, and Jaasiel the Mezobian.

CHAPTER 12

David's Early Followers. [1]The following men came to David in Ziklag while he was still under banishment from Saul, son of Kish; they, too, were among the warriors who

See RG
200–203

11, 20: The Thirty: listed by name in vv 26-47. The list given in 2 Sm 23, 8-39 often differs in names and spellings; for the numbers, see the note there.

p: 1 Chr 27, 4.   q: 1 Sm 17, 1.   r: 1 Chr 14, 9; 2 Sm 5, 18. 22.   s: 20f: 2 Sm 23, 18f.   t: 1 Chr 18, 12; 1 Sm 26, 6ff; 2 Sm 16, 9; 18, 2; 21, 17.   u: 2 Sm 8, 18; 20, 23.   v: 1 Chr 2, 16; 27, 7.   w: 1 Chr 27, 11.   x: 1 Chr 27, 13.   y: 1 Chr 27, 14.

helped him in his battles.[z] [2]They were archers who could use either the right or the left hand, both in slinging stones and in shooting arrows with the bow. They were some of Saul's kinsmen, from Benjamin. [3]Ahiezer was their chief, along with Joash, both sons of Shemaah of Gibeah; also Jeziel and Pelet, sons of Azmaveth; Beracah; Jehu, from Anathoth;[a] [4]Ishmaiah the Gibeonite, a warrior on the level of the Thirty, and in addition to their number: [5]Jeremiah; Jahaziel; Johanan; Jozabad, from Gederah; [6]Eluzai; Jerimoth; Bealiah; Shemariah; Shephatiah the Haruphite; [7]Elkanah, Isshiah, Azarel, Joezer, and Ishbaal, who were Korahites; [8]Joelah, finally, and Zebadiah, sons of Jeroham, from Gedor.

[9]Some of the Gadites also went over to David when he was at the stronghold in the wilderness. They were valiant warriors, experienced soldiers equipped with shield and spear, who bore themselves like lions, and were as swift as the gazelles on the mountains.[b] [10]Ezer was their chief, Obadiah was second, Eliab third, [11]Mishmannah fourth, Jeremiah fifth, [12]Attai sixth, Eliel seventh, [13]Johanan eighth, Elzabad ninth, [14]Jeremiah tenth, and Machbannai eleventh. [15]These Gadites were army commanders, the lesser placed over hundreds and the greater over thousands. [16]It was they who crossed over the Jordan when it was overflowing both its banks in the first month, and dispersed all who were in the valleys to the east and to the west.

[17]Some Benjaminites and Judahites also came to David at the stronghold. [18]David went out to meet them and addressed them in these words: "If you come peacefully, to help me, I am of a mind to have you join me. But if you have come to betray me to my enemies though my hands have done no wrong, may the God of our fathers see and punish you."

[19]Then spirit enveloped Amasai, the chief of the Thirty, who spoke:

"We are yours, O David,
    we are with you, O son of Jesse.

Peace, peace to you,
    and peace to him who helps you;
    your God it is who helps you."

So David received them and placed them among the leaders of his troops.

[20]Men from Manasseh also deserted to David when he came with the Philistines to battle against Saul. However, he did not help the Philistines, for their lords took counsel and sent him home, saying, "At the cost of our heads he will desert to his master Saul." [21]As he was returning to Ziklag, therefore, these deserted to him from Manasseh: Adnah, Jozabad, Jediael, Michael, Jozabad, Elihu, and Zillethai, chiefs of thousands of Manasseh. [22]They helped David by taking charge of his troops, for they were all warriors and became commanders of his army. [23]And from day to day men kept coming to David's help until there was a vast encampment, like an encampment of angels.

The Assembly at Hebron. [24]This is the muster of the detachments of armed troops that came to David at Hebron to transfer to him Saul's kingdom, as the LORD had ordained. [25]*Judahites bearing shields and spears: six thousand eight hundred armed troops. [26]Of the Simeonites, warriors fit for battle: seven thousand one hundred. [27]Of the Levites: four thousand six hundred, [28]along with Jehoiada, leader of the line of Aaron, with another three thousand seven hundred, [29]and Zadok, a young warrior, with twenty-two princes of his father's house. [30]Of the Benjaminites, the brethren of Saul: three thousand—until this time, most of them had held their allegiance to the house of Saul. [31]Of the Ephraimites: twenty thousand eight hundred warriors, men renowned in their ancestral houses. [32]Of the half-tribe of Manasseh: eighteen thousand, designated by name to come and make David king. [33]Of the Issacharites, their chiefs who were endowed with an understanding of the times and who knew what Israel had to do: two hundred

---

12, 25-38: The Chronicler fills out the pageantry of joyous occasions in keeping with his much later appreciation of the significance of the event in the history of God's people: the numbers in attendance at David's crowning in Hebron (cf 2 Sm 5, 1ff) are recounted in the same spirit of enthusiasm which in v 23 compares David's band of desert freebooters to a numerous encampment of angels.

z: 1 Sm 27, 1-7.   a: 1 Chr 27, 12.   b: Dt 33, 20.

chiefs, together with all their brethren under their command. ³⁴From Zebulun, men fit for military service, set in battle array with every kind of weapon for war: fifty thousand men rallying with a single purpose. ³⁵From Naphtali: one thousand captains, and with them, armed with shield and lance, thirty-seven thousand men. ³⁶Of the Danites, set in battle array: twenty-eight thousand six hundred. ³⁷From Asher, fit for military service and set in battle array: forty thousand. ³⁸From the other side of the Jordan, of the Reubenites, Gadites, and the half-tribe of Manasseh, men equipped with every kind of weapon of war: one hundred and twenty thousand.

³⁹All these soldiers, drawn up in battle order, came to Hebron with the resolute intention of making David king over all Israel. The rest of Israel was likewise of one mind to make David king. ⁴⁰They remained with David for three days, feasting and drinking, for their brethren had prepared for them. ⁴¹Moreover, their neighbors from as far as Issachar, Zebulun, and Naphtali came bringing food on asses, camels, mules, and oxen—provisions in great quantity of meal, pressed figs, raisins, wine, oil, oxen, and sheep. For there was rejoicing in Israel.

CHAPTER 13

See RG 200–203

Transfer of the Ark. ^{1c}After David had taken counsel with his commanders of thousands and of hundreds, that is to say, with every one of his leaders, ²he said to the whole assembly of Israel: "If it seems good to you, and is so decreed by the LORD our God, let us summon the rest of our brethren from all the districts of Israel, and also the priests and the Levites from their cities with pasture lands, that they may join us;^{d 3}and let us bring the ark of our God here among us, for in the days of Saul we did not visit it." ⁴And the whole assembly agreed to do this, for the idea was pleasing to all the people.

⁵Then David assembled all Israel, from Shihor of Egypt* to Labo of Hamath, to bring the ark of God from Kiriath-jearim.^{e 6}David and all Israel went up to Baalah, that is, to Kiriath-jearim, of Judah, to bring back the ark of God, which was known by the name "LORD enthroned upon the cherubim."^f ⁷They transported the ark of God on a new cart from the house of Abinadab; Uzzah and Ahio were guiding the cart, ⁸while David and all Israel danced before God with great enthusiasm, amid songs and music on lyres, harps, tambourines, cymbals, and trumpets.

⁹As they reached the threshing floor of Chidon,* Uzzah stretched out his hand to steady the ark, for the oxen were upsetting it. ¹⁰Then the LORD became angry with Uzzah and struck him; he died there in God's presence, because he had laid his hand on the ark. ¹¹David was disturbed because the LORD's anger had broken out against Uzzah. Therefore that place has been called Perez-uzza* even to this day.

¹²David was now afraid of God, and he said, "How can I bring the ark of God with me?" ¹³Therefore he did not take the ark back with him to the City of David, but he took it instead to the house of Obed-edom the Gittite. ¹⁴The ark of God remained in the house of Obed-edom with his family for three months, and the LORD blessed Obed-edom's household and all that he possessed.^g

CHAPTER 14

See RG 200–203

David in Jerusalem. ^{1h}Hiram, king of Tyre, sent envoys to David along with masons and carpenters, and cedar wood to build him a house.ⁱ ²David now understood that the LORD had truly confirmed him as king over Israel, for his kingdom was greatly exalted for the sake of his people Israel. ^{3 j}David took other wives in Jerusalem and became the father of more sons and daughters. ⁴These are the names of those who were born to him in Jerusalem: Shammua, Shobab, Nathan, Solomon, ⁵Ibhar, Elishua, El-

---

13, 5: Shihor of Egypt: the eastern branch of the Nile delta. Labo of Hamath: in southern Syria.

13, 9: Chidon: in 2 Sm 6, 6, Nodan.

13, 11: Perez-uzza: A Hebrew term meaning "the breaking out against Uzza."

---

c: 1-14: 2 Sm 6, 1-11.   *d:* Nm 35, 1ff; Jos 14, 4; 21, 2ff.   *e:* 1 Chr 15, 3; Jos 13, 3. 5; 1 Sm 6, 21; 7, 1f; 2 Sm 6, 1-11.   *f:* Jos 15, 9; 18, 14; 1 Sm 4, 4; 7, 1.   *g:* 1 Chr 26, 4f.   *h:* 1-16: 2 Sm 5, 11-25.   *i:* 1 Kgs 5, 1; 2 Chr 2, 3.   *j:* 3-7: 1 Chr 3, 5-8; 2 Sm 5, 13-16.

pelet, [6]Nogah, Nepheg, Japhia, [7]Elishama, Beeliada, and Eliphelet.

The Philistine Wars. [8]When the Philistines had heard that David was anointed king over all Israel, they went up in unison to seek him out. But when David heard of this, he marched out against them. [9]Meanwhile the Philistines had come and raided the valley of Rephaim.[k] [10]David inquired of God, "Shall I advance against the Philistines, and will you deliver them into my power?" The LORD answered him, "Advance, for I will deliver them into your power." [11]They advanced, therefore, to Baal-perazim, and David defeated them there. Then David said, "God has used me to break through my enemies just as water breaks through a dam." Therefore that place was called Baal-perazim. [12]The Philistines had left their gods there, and David ordered them to be burnt.[l]

[13]Once again the Philistines raided the valley, [14]and again David inquired of God. But God answered him: "Do not try to pursue them, but go around them and come upon them from the direction of the mastic trees. [15]When you hear the sound of marching in the tops of the mastic trees, then go forth to battle, for God has already gone before you to strike the army of the Philistines." [16]David did as God commanded him, and they routed the Philistine army from Gibeon to Gezer.

[17]Thus David's fame was spread abroad through every land, and the LORD made all the nations fear him.

CHAPTER 15

See RG
200–203

The Ark Brought to Jerusalem. [1]David built houses for himself in the City of David and prepared a place for the ark of God, pitching a tent for it there. [2]At that time he said, "No one may carry the ark of God except the Levites, for the LORD chose them to carry the ark of the LORD and to minister to him forever."[m] [3]Then David assembled all Israel in Jerusalem to bring the ark of the LORD to the place which he had prepared for

it.[n] [4]David also called together the sons of Aaron and the Levites: [5]of the sons of Kohath, Uriel, their chief, and one hundred and twenty of his brethren; [6]of the sons of Merari, Asaiah, their chief, and two hundred and twenty of his brethren; [7]of the sons of Gershon, Joel, their chief, and one hundred and thirty of his brethren; [8]of the sons of Elizaphan, Shemaiah, their chief, and two hundred of his brethren; [9]of the sons of Hebron, Eliel, their chief, and eighty of his brethren; [10]of the sons of Uzziel, Amminadab, their chief, and one hundred and twelve of his brethren.

[11]David summoned the priests Zadok and Abiathar, and the Levites Uriel, Asaiah, Joel, Shemaiah, Eliel, and Amminadab,[o] [12]and said to them: "You, the heads of the levitical families, must sanctify yourselves along with your brethren and bring the ark of the LORD, the God of Israel, to the place which I have prepared for it.[p] [13]Because you were not with us the first time, the wrath of the LORD our God burst upon us, for we did not seek him aright."[q] [14]Accordingly, the priests and the Levites sanctified themselves to bring up the ark of the LORD, the God of Israel. [15]The Levites bore the ark of God on their shoulders with poles, as Moses had ordained according to the word of the LORD.[r]

[16]David commanded the chiefs of the Levites to appoint their brethren as chanters, to play on musical instruments, harps, lyres, and cymbals, to make a loud sound of rejoicing.[s] [17]Therefore the Levites appointed Heman, son of Joel, and, among his brethren, Asaph, son of Berechiah; and among the sons of Merari, their brethren, Ethan, son of Kushaiah;[t] [18]and, together with these, their brethren of the second rank: the gatekeepers Zechariah, Uzziel, Shemiramoth, Jehiel, Unni, Eliab, Benaiah, Maaseiah, Mattithiah, Eliphelehu, Mikneiah, Obed-edom, and Jeiel. [19]The chanters, Heman, Asaph, and Ethan, sounded brass cymbals. [20]Zechariah, Uzziel, Shemiramoth, Jehiel, Unni, Eliab, Maaseiah, and Benaiah

---

k: 1 Chr 11, 15.   *l:* Dt 7, 5. 25.   *m:* Nm 1, 50; 7, 9; Dt 10, 8; 31, 25; 1 Sm 6, 15; Jos 3, 8.   *n:* 1 Chr 13, 5; 2 Sm 6, 15. 17.   *o:* 1 Chr 16, 39; 2 Sm 8, 17; 15, 29. 35.   *p:* 2 Chr 29, 5. 15. 34; 30, 3. 15. 24.   *q:* 1 Chr 13, 3.   *r:* Ex 25, 13ff; Nm 1, 50; 7, 9; 2 Chr 35, 3.   *s:* 1 Chr 13, 8; 16, 5; 2 Chr 5, 12; 29, 25; Neh 12, 27.   *t:* 1 Chr 6, 31-47; 25, 1-8.

played on harps set to "Alamoth."* [21]But Mattithiah, Eliphelehu, Mikneiah, Obed-edom, and Jeiel led the chant on lyres set to "the eighth." [22]Chenaniah was the chief of the Levites in the chanting; he directed the chanting, for he was skillful.[u] [23]Berechiah and Elkanah were gatekeepers before the ark. [24]The priests, Shebaniah, Joshaphat, Nethanel, Amasai, Zechariah, Benaiah, and Eliezer, sounded the trumpets before the ark of God. Obed-edom and Jeiel were also gatekeepers before the ark.[v]

[25w]Thus David, the elders of Israel, and the commanders of thousands went to bring up the ark of the covenant of the LORD with joy from the house of Obed-edom. [26]While the Levites, with God's help, were bearing the ark of the covenant of the LORD, seven bulls and seven rams were sacrificed.[x] [27]David was clothed in a robe of fine linen, as were all the Levites who carried the ark, the singers, and Chenaniah, the leader of the chant; David was also wearing a linen ephod.[y] [28]Thus all Israel brought back the ark of the covenant of the LORD with joyful shouting, and to the sound of horns, trumpets, and cymbals, and the music of harps and lyres. [29]But as the ark of the covenant of the LORD was entering the City of David, Michal, daughter of Saul, looked down from her window, and when she saw King David leaping and dancing, she despised him in her heart.[z]

CHAPTER 16

See RG 200–203 [1a]They brought in the ark of God and set it within the tent which David had pitched for it. Then they offered up holocausts and peace offerings to God.[b] [2]When David had finished offering up the holocausts and peace offerings, he blessed the people in the name of the LORD, [3]and distributed to every Israelite, to every man and to every woman, a loaf of bread, a piece of meat, and a raisin cake.

The Ministering Levites. [4]He now ap-pointed certain Levites to minister before the ark of the LORD, to celebrate, thank, and praise the LORD, the God of Israel.[c] [5]Asaph was their chief, and second to him were Zechariah, Uz-ziel, Shemira-moth, Jehiel, Mattithiah, Eliab, Benaiah, Obed-edom, and Jeiel. These were to play on harps and lyres, while Asaph was to sound the cymbals, [6]and the priests Benaiah and Jahaziel were to be the regular trumpeters before the ark of the covenant of God.

[7]Then, on that same day, David appointed Asaph and his brethren to sing for the first time these praises of the LORD:

[8] *Give thanks to the LORD, invoke his name;[d]
  make known among the nations his deeds.
[9] Sing to him, sing his praise,
  proclaim all his wondrous deeds.
[10] Glory in his holy name;
  rejoice, O hearts that seek the LORD!
[11] Look to the LORD in his strength;
  seek to serve him constantly.
[12] Recall the wondrous deeds that he has wrought,
  his portents, and the judgments he has uttered,
[13] You descendants of Israel, his servants,
  sons of Jacob, his chosen ones!

[14] He, the LORD, is our God;
  throughout the earth his judgments prevail.
[15] He remembers forever his covenant
  which he made binding for a thousand generations—
[16] Which he entered into with Abraham
  and by his oath to Isaac;
[17] Which he established for Jacob by statute,
  for Israel as an everlasting covenant,
[18] Saying, "To you will I give the land of Canaan
  as your allotted inheritance."

15, 20: Alamoth: a musical term (literally, "young women") of uncertain meaning, occurring also in Ps 46, 1, where it is rendered as virgins. Perhaps it may mean something like "soprano," whereas the term "eighth" (Hebrew sheminith, v 21) may then mean "bass"; cf Pss 6, 1; 12, 1.

16, 8-36: A hymn composed of parts, with textual variants, from several Psalms; vv 8-22 = Ps 105, 1-15; vv 23-33 = Ps 96, 1-13; vv 34-36 = Ps 106, 1. 47f.

u: 1 Chr 26, 29. v: Nm 10, 8; Jos 6, 4ff. w: 25-29: 2 Sm 6, 12-16. x: 2 Sm 6, 17; 2 Chr 29, 21. y: 1 Sm 2, 18; 2 Sm 6, 14. z: 2 Sm 6, 20ff. a: 1-3: 2 Sm 6, 17ff. b: 1 Chr 15, 1. c: Sir 47, 9. d: 8-22: Ps 105, 1-15.

19 When they were few in number,
   a handful, and strangers there,
20 Wandering from nation to nation,
   from one kingdom to another people,
21 He let no one oppress them,
   and for their sake he rebuked kings:
22 "Touch not my anointed,
   and to my prophets do no harm."

23 *e*Sing to the LORD, all the earth,
   announce his salvation, day after day.
24 Tell his glory among the nations;
   among all peoples, his wondrous
   deeds.
25 For great is the LORD and highly to be
   praised;
   and awesome is he, beyond all gods.
26 For all the gods of the nations are things
   of nought,
   but the LORD made the heavens.
27 Splendor and majesty go before him;
   praise and joy are in his holy place.

28 Give to the LORD, you families of
   nations,
   give to the LORD glory and praise;
29 Give to the LORD the glory due his name!
   Bring gifts, and enter his presence;
   worship the LORD in holy attire.
30 Tremble before him, all the earth;
   he has made the world firm, not to be
   moved.

31 Let the heavens be glad and the earth
   rejoice;
   let them say among the nations: The
   LORD is king.
32 Let the sea and what fills it resound;
   let the plains rejoice and all that is in
   them!
33 Then shall all the trees of the forest exult
   before the LORD, for he comes:
   he comes to rule the earth.

34 *f*Give thanks to the LORD, for he is good,
   for his kindness endures forever;
35 And say, "Save us, O God, our savior,
   gather us and deliver us from the
   nations,

That we may give thanks to your holy
   name
   and glory in praising you."
36 Blessed be the LORD, the God of Israel,
   through all eternity!
   Let all the people say, Amen! Alleluia.

37Then David left Asaph and his brethren there before the ark of the covenant of the LORD to minister before the ark regularly according to the daily ritual; 38he also left there Obed-edom and sixty-eight of his brethren, including Obed-edom, son of Jeduthun, and Hosah, to be gatekeepers.*g*

39But the priest Zadok and his priestly brethren he left before the Dwelling of the LORD on the high place at Gibeon,*h* 40to offer holocausts to the LORD on the altar of holocausts regularly, morning and evening, and to do all that is written in the law of the LORD which he has decreed for Israel.*i* 41With them were Heman and Jeduthun and the others who were chosen and designated by name to give thanks to the LORD, "because his kindness endures forever,"*j* 42with trumpets and cymbals for accompaniment, and instruments for the sacred chant. The sons of Jeduthun kept the gate.*k*

43Then all the people departed, each to his own home, and David returned to bless his household.*l*

CHAPTER 17

The Oracle of Nathan. 1*m*After David See RG 200–203 had taken up residence in his house, he said to Nathan the prophet, "See, I am living in a house of cedar, but the ark of the covenant of the LORD dwells under tentcloth."*n* 2Nathan replied to David, "Do, therefore, whatever you desire, for God is with you."

3But that same night the word of God came to Nathan: 4"Go and tell my servant David, Thus says the LORD: It is not you who are to build a house for me to dwell in.*o* 5For I have never dwelt in a house, from the time when I led Israel onward, even to this day, but I have been lodging in tent or pavilion

e: 23-33: Ps 96, 1-13. *f:* 34ff: Ps 106, 1. 47f. *g:* 1 Chr 15, 24. *h:* 1 Kgs 3, 4. *i:* Ex 29, 38-42; Lv 6, 9; Nm 28, 3. 6; 2 Chr 13, 11. *j:* 2 Chr 5, 12; 7, 3. 6; 20, 21; Ezr 3, 11. *k:* 2 Chr 29, 27. *l:* 2 Sm 6, 19f. *m:* 1-27: 2 Sm 7, 1-29. *n:* 1 Chr 15, 1; 2 Sm 5, 11. *o:* 1 Chr 28, 3; 1 Kgs 8, 19.

⁶as long as I have wandered about with all of Israel. Did I ever say a word to any of the judges of Israel whom I commanded to guide my people, such as, 'Why have you not built me a house of cedar?' ⁷Therefore, tell my servant David, Thus says the LORD of hosts: I took you from the pasture, from following the sheep, that you might become ruler over my people Israel.ᵖ ⁸I was with you wherever you went, and I cut down all your enemies before you. I will make your name great like that of the greatest on the earth. ⁹I will assign a place for my people Israel and I will plant them in it to dwell there henceforth undisturbed; nor shall wicked men ever again oppress them, as they did at first, ¹⁰and during all the time when I appointed judges over my people Israel. And I will subdue all your enemies. Moreover, I declare to you that I, the LORD, will build you a house; ¹¹so that when your days have been completed and you must join your fathers, I will raise up your offspring after you who will be one of your own sons, and I will establish his kingdom.�q ¹²He it is who shall build me a house, and I will establish his throne forever.ʳ ¹³I will be a father to him, and he shall be a son to me, and I will not withdraw my favor from him as I withdrew it from him who preceded you;ˢ ¹⁴but I will maintain him in my house and in my kingdom forever, and his throne shall be firmly established forever."

¹⁵All these words and this whole vision Nathan related exactly to David.

David's Thanksgiving. ¹⁶Then David came in and sat in the LORD's presence, saying: "Who am I, O LORD God, and what is my family, that you should have brought me as far as I have come? ¹⁷And yet, even this you now consider too little, O God! For you have made a promise regarding your servant's family reaching into the distant future, and you have looked on me as henceforth the most notable of men, O LORD God.ᵗ ¹⁸What more can David say to you? You know your servant. ¹⁹O LORD, for your servant's sake and in keeping with your purpose, you have

done this great thing. ²⁰O LORD, there is no one like you and there is no God but you, just as we have always understood.ᵘ

²¹"Is there, like your people Israel, whom you redeemed from Egypt, another nation on earth whom a god went to redeem as his people? You won for yourself a name for great and awesome deeds by driving out the nations before your people.ᵛ ²²You made your people Israel your own forever, and you, O LORD, became their God. ²³Therefore, O LORD, may the promise that you have uttered concerning your servant and his house remain firm forever. Bring about what you have promised, ²⁴that your renown as LORD of hosts, God of Israel, may be great and abide forever, while the house of David, your servant, is established in your presence.

²⁵"Because you, O my God, have revealed to your servant that you will build him a house, your servant has made bold to pray before you.ʷ ²⁶Since you, O LORD, are truly God and have promised this good thing to your servant, ²⁷and since you have deigned to bless the house of your servant, so that it will remain forever—since it is you, O LORD, who blessed it, it is blessed forever."ˣ

CHAPTER 18

See RG 200–203

David's Victories. ¹ʸAfter this, David defeated the Philistines and subdued them; and he took Gath and its towns away from the control of the Philistines. ²He also defeated Moab, and the Moabites became his subjects, paying tribute.

³David then defeated Hadadezer, king of Zobah toward Hamath, when the latter was on his way to set up his victory stele at the river Euphrates. ⁴David took from him twenty thousand foot soldiers, one thousand chariots, and seven thousand horsemen. Of the chariot horses, David hamstrung all but one hundred.ᶻ ⁵The Arameans of Damascus came to the aid of Hadadezer, king of Zobah, but David also slew twenty-two thousand of their men. ⁶Then David set up garrisons in the Damascus region of Aram, and the Arameans became his subjects, paying tribute.

p: 1 Sm 16, 11.   *q:* 2 Sm 7, 12f.   *r:* 1 Chr 22, 10; 28, 6. 10.   *s:* 2 Sm 7, 14.   *t:* 2 Sm 7, 19.   *u:* Sir 36, 4.   *v:* Dt 4, 7; 2 Sm 7, 23. *w:* 2 Sm 7, 27.   *x:* Nm 22, 6.   *y:* 1-13: 2 Sm 8, 1-14.   *z:* 2 Sm 8, 14; Jos 11, 6. 9.

Thus the LORD made David victorious in all his campaigns.

[7]David took the golden shields that were carried by Hadadezer's attendants and brought them to Jerusalem. [8]He likewise took away from Tibhath and Cun, cities of Hadadezer, large quantities of bronze, which Solomon later used to make the bronze sea and the pillars and the vessels of bronze.[a]

[9]When Tou, king of Hamath, heard that David had defeated the entire army of Hadadezer, king of Zobah, [10]he sent his son Hadoram to wish King David well and to congratulate him on having waged a victorious war against Hadadezer; for Hadadezer had been at war with Tou. He also sent David gold, silver and bronze utensils of every sort.[b] [11]These also King David consecrated to the LORD along with all the silver and gold that he had taken from the nations: from Edom, Moab, the Ammonites, the Philistines, and Amalek.

[12]Abishai, the son of Zeruiah, also slew eighteen thousand Edomites in the Valley of Salt.[c] [13]He set up garrisons in Edom, and all the Edomites became David's subjects. Thus the LORD made David victorious in all his campaigns.

David's Officials. [14d]David reigned over all Israel and dispensed justice and right to all his people. [15]Joab, son of Zeruiah, was in command of the army; Jehoshaphat, son of Ahilud, was herald;[e] [16]Zadok, son of Ahitub, and Ahimelech, son of Abiathar, were priests;* Shavsha was scribe;[f] [17]Benaiah, son of Jehoiada, was in command of the Cherethites and the Pelethites; and David's sons were the chief assistants to the king.*[g]

See RG 200–203

CHAPTER 19

Campaigns against Ammon. [1h]Afterward Nahash, king of the Ammonites, died and his son succeeded him as king. [2]David said, "I will show kindness to Hanun, the son of Nahash, for his father treated me with kindness." Therefore he sent envoys to him to comfort him over the death of his father. But when David's servants had entered the land of the Ammonites to comfort Hanun, [3]the Ammonite princes said to Hanun, "Do you think David is doing this—sending you these consolers—to honor your father? Have not his servants rather come to you to explore the land, spying it out for its overthrow?" [4]Thereupon Hanun seized David's servants and had them shaved and their garments cut off half-way at the hips. Then he sent them away. [5]When David was informed of what had happened to his men, he sent messengers to meet them, for the men had been greatly disgraced. "Remain at Jericho," the king told them, "until your beards have grown again; and then you may come back here."

[6]When the Ammonites realized that they had put themselves in bad odor with David, Hanun and the Ammonites sent a thousand talents of silver to hire chariots and horsemen from Aram Naharaim, from Aram-maacah, and from Zobah. [7]They hired thirty-two thousand chariots along with the king of Maacah and his army, who came and encamped before Medeba. The Ammonites also assembled from their cities and came out for war.

[8]When David heard of this, he sent Joab and his whole army of warriors against them. [9]The Ammonites marched out and lined up for battle at the gate of the city, while the kings who had come to their help remained apart in the open field. [10]When Joab saw that there was a battle line both in front of and behind him, he chose some of the best fighters among the Israelites and set them in array against the Arameans;[i] [11]the

---

18, 16: Zadok . . . and Ahimelech, son of Abiathar, were priests: as in the Chronicler's source, 2 Sm 8, 17. But according to 2 Sm 15, 24. 29. 35; 17, 15; 19, 11; 20, 25, and even 1 Chr 15, 11, it was Abiathar who shared the priestly office with Zadok, and he remained in this office even during the early years of Solomon's reign (1 Kgs 2, 26; 4, 4). Moreover, according to 1 Sm 22, 20; 23, 6; 30, 7, Ahimelech was the father, not the son, of Abiathar. If the text Ahimelech, son of Abiathar, is not due to a scribal change, one must assume that Abiathar had a son who was named after his grandfather and who shared the priestly office with his father during the last years of David's reign.

18, 17: David's sons were the chief assistants to the king: in the parallel passage, 2 Sm 8, 18, which was the Chronicler's source, David's sons were priests. The change is characteristic of the Chronicler, for whom only Aaron's descendants could be priests.

a: 2 Sm 8, 8; 1 Kgs 7, 15. 23. 27. *b:* 2 Sm 8, 10. *c:* 2 Sm 8, 13; 2 Kgs 14, 7. *d:* 14–17: 2 Sm 8, 15–18. *e:* 1 Chr 11, 6; 2 Sm 8, 16; 1 Kgs 4, 3. *f:* 1 Chr 24, 3. 6. 31; 2 Sm 8, 17. *g:* 1 Chr 11, 22; 2 Sm 8, 18; 1 Kgs 1, 38. 44. *h:* 1–19: 2 Sm 10, 1–19. *i:* 1 Chr 20, 23; 1 Kgs 2, 28. 34.

rest of the army, which he placed under the command of his brother Abishai, then lined up to oppose the Ammonites.*j* *12*And he said: "If the Arameans prove too strong for me, you must come to my help; and if the Ammonites prove too strong for you, I will save you. *13*Hold steadfast and let us show ourselves courageous for the sake of our people and the cities of our God; then may the LORD do what seems best to him." *14*Joab therefore advanced with his men to engage the Arameans in battle; but they fled before him. *15*And when the Ammonites saw that the Arameans had fled, they also took to flight before his brother Abishai, and reentered the city. Joab then returned to Jerusalem.

*16*Seeing themselves vanquished by Israel, the Arameans sent messengers to bring out the Arameans from the other side of the River, with Shophach, the general of Hadadezer's army, at their head. *17*When this was reported to David, he gathered all Israel together, crossed the Jordan, and met them. With the army of David drawn up to fight the Arameans, they gave battle. *18*But the Arameans fled before Israel, and David slew seven thousand of their chariot fighters and forty thousand of their foot soldiers; he also killed Shophach, the general of the army. *19*When the vassals of Hadadezer saw themselves vanquished by Israel, they made peace with David and became his subjects. After this, the Arameans refused to come to the aid of the Ammonites.

See RG 200–203

CHAPTER 20

*1*At the beginning of the following year, the time when kings go to war, Joab led the army out in force, laid waste the land of the Ammonites, and went on to besiege Rabbah, while David himself remained in Jerusalem. When Joab had attacked Rabbah and destroyed it, *2k*David took the crown of Milcom from the idol's head. It was found to weigh a talent of gold; and it contained precious stones, which David wore on his own head. He also brought out a great amount of booty from the city. *3*He deported the people of the city and set them to work with saws, iron picks, and axes. Thus David dealt with all the cities of the Ammonites. Then he and his whole army returned to Jerusalem.

Victories over the Philistines. *41*Afterward there was another battle with the Philistines, at Gezer. At that time, Sibbecai the Hushathite slew Sippai, one of the descendants of the Raphaim, and the Philistines were subdued.*m* *5*Once again there was war with the Philistines, and Elhanan, the son of Jair, slew Lahmi, the brother of Goliath* of Gath, whose spear shaft was like a weaver's heddle-bar.*n*

*6*In still another battle, at Gath, they encountered a giant, also a descendant of the Raphaim, who had six fingers to each hand and six toes to each foot; twenty-four in all. *7*He defied Israel, and Jonathan, the son of Shimea, David's brother, slew him. *8*These were the descendants of the Raphaim of Gath who died at the hands of David and his servants.

CHAPTER 21

See RG 200–203

David's Census; the Plague. *1o*A satan* rose up against Israel, and he enticed David into taking a census of Israel.*p* *2*David therefore said to Joab and to the other generals of the army, "Go, find out the number of the Israelites from Beer-sheba to Dan, and report back to me that I may know their number." *3*But Joab replied: "May the LORD increase his people a hundredfold! My lord king, are not all of them my lord's subjects? Why does my lord seek to do this thing? Why will he bring guilt upon Israel?" *4*However, the king's command prevailed over Joab, who departed and traversed all of Israel, and then returned to Jerusalem. *5*Joab reported the re-

---

20, 5: Elhanan . . . slew Lahmi, the brother of Goliath: the Chronicler thus solves the difficulty of the apparent contradiction between 1 Sm 17, 49ff (David killed Goliath) and 2 Sm 21, 19 (Elhanan killed Goliath).

21, 1: A satan: in the parallel passage of 2 Sm 24, 1, the Lord's anger. The change in the term reflects the changed theological outlook of postexilic Israel, when evil could no longer be attributed directly to God. At an earlier period the Hebrew word satan ("adversary," or, especially in a court of law, "ac-

cuser"), when not used of men, designated an angel who accused men before God (Jb 1, 6-12; 2, 1-7; Zec 3, 1f). Here, as in later Judaism (Wis 2, 24) and in the New Testament, satan, or the "devil" (from the Greek translation of the word), designates an evil spirit who tempts men to wrongdoing.

j: 1 Chr 23, 18f.   *k:* 2f: 2 Sm 12, 30f.   *l:* 4-8: 2 Sm 21, 18-22.   *m:* 1 Chr 11, 29; 27, 11.   *n:* 1 Chr 11, 26; 1 Sm 17, 4. 23.   *o:* 1-7: 2 Sm 24, 1-25.   *p:* Zec 3, 1f.

sult of the census to David: of men capable of wielding a sword, there were in all Israel one million one hundred thousand, and in Judah four hundred and seventy thousand. ⁶Levi and Benjamin, however, he did not include in the census, for the king's command was repugnant to Joab.�q ⁷This command displeased God, who began to punish Israel. ⁸Then David said to God, "I have sinned greatly in doing this thing. Take away your servant's guilt, for I have acted very foolishly."

⁹Then the LORD spoke to Gad, David's seer, in these words:ʳ ¹⁰"Go, tell David: Thus says the LORD: I offer you three alternatives; choose one of them, and I will inflict it on you." ¹¹Accordingly, Gad went to David and said to him: "Thus says the LORD: Decide now— ¹²will it be three years of famine; or three months of fleeing your enemies, with the sword of your foes ever at your back; or three days of the LORD's own sword, a pestilence in the land, with the LORD's destroying angel in every part of Israel? Therefore choose: What answer am I to give him who sent me?" ¹³Then David said to Gad: "I am in dire straits. But I prefer to fall into the hand of the LORD, whose mercy is very great, than into the hands of men."

¹⁴Therefore the LORD sent pestilence upon Israel, and seventy thousand men of Israel died. ¹⁵God also sent an angel to destroy Jerusalem; but as he was on the point of destroying it, the LORD saw and decided against the calamity, and said to the destroying angel, "Enough now! Stay your hand!"ˢ

Ornan's Threshing Floor. The angel of the LORD was then standing by the threshing floor of Ornan the Jebusite. ¹⁶When David raised his eyes, he saw the angel of the LORD standing between earth and heaven, with a naked sword in his hand stretched out against Jerusalem. David and the elders, clothed in sackcloth, prostrated themselves face to the ground, ¹⁷and David prayed to God: "Was it not I who ordered the census of the people? I am the one who sinned, I did this wicked thing. But these sheep, what have they done? O LORD, my God, strike me and my father's family, but do not afflict your people with this plague!"

¹⁸Then the angel of the LORD commanded Gad to tell David to go up and erect an altar to the LORD on the threshing floor of Ornan the Jebusite.ᵗ ¹⁹David went up at Gad's command, given in the name of the LORD. ²⁰While Ornan was threshing wheat, he turned around and saw the king, and his four sons who were with him, without recognizing them. ²¹But as David came on toward him, he looked up and saw that it was David. Then he left the threshing floor and bowed down before David, his face to the ground. ²²David said to Ornan: "Sell me the ground of this threshing floor, that I may build on it an altar to the LORD. Sell it to me at its full price, that the plague may be stayed from the people." ²³But Ornan said to David: "Take it as your own, and let my lord the king do what seems best to him. See, I also give you the oxen for the holocausts, the threshing sledges for the wood, and the wheat for the cereal offering. I give it all to you." ²⁴But King David replied to Ornan: "No! I will buy it from you properly, at its full price. I will not take what is yours for the LORD, nor offer up holocausts that cost me nothing." ²⁵So David paid Ornan six hundred shekels of gold* for the place.

Altar of Holocausts. ²⁶David then built an altar there to the LORD, and offered up holocausts and peace offerings. When he called upon the LORD, he answered him by sending down fire from heaven upon the altar of holocausts.ᵘ ²⁷Then the LORD gave orders to the angel to return his sword to its sheath.

²⁸Once David saw that the LORD had heard him on the threshing floor of Ornan the Jebusite, he continued to offer sacrifices there. ²⁹The Dwelling of the LORD, which Moses had built in the desert, and the altar of holocausts were at that time on the high place at

---

21, 25: Six hundred shekels of gold: about 10,000 dollars. According to 2 Sm 24, 24, David paid 50 shekels of silver, about 20 dollars, for Ornan's threshing floor; but for the Chronicler the site of the temple was much more precious than that.

q: 1 Chr 27, 24; Nm 1, 49.   *r:* 1 Chr 29, 29; 1 Sm 9, 9; 2 Chr 29, 25.   *s:* Gn 6, 6; Ex 32, 14; 2 Sm 24, 16; Jon 3, 10.   *t:* 2 Chr 3, 1. *u:* Lv 9, 24; Jgs 6, 21; 1 Kgs 18. 38; 2 Chr 7, 1; 2 Mc 2, 10ff.

Gibeon.ᵛ ³⁰But David could not go there to worship God, for he was fearful of the sword of the angel of the LORD. ¹Therefore David said, "This is the house of the LORD God, and this is the altar of holocausts for Israel."*ʷ

See RG
200–203

CHAPTER 22

Material for the Temple. ²*David then ordered that all the aliens who lived in the land of Israel be brought together, and he appointed them stonecutters to hew out stone blocks for building the house of God.ˣ ³He also laid up large stores of iron to make nails for the doors of the gates, and clamps, together with so much bronze that it could not be weighed,ʸ ⁴and cedar trees without number. The Sidonians and Tyrians brought great stores of cedar logs to David,ᶻ ⁵who said: "My son Solomon is young and immature; but the house that is to be built for the LORD must be made so magnificent that it will be renowned and glorious in all countries. Therefore I will make preparations for it." Thus before his death David laid up materials in abundance.ᵃ

Charge to Solomon. ⁶Then he called for his son Solomon and commanded him to build a house for the LORD, the God of Israel. ⁷ᵇDavid said to Solomon: "My son, it was my purpose to build a house myself for the honor of the LORD, my God. ⁸But this word of the LORD came to me: 'You have shed much blood, and you have waged great wars. You may not build a house in my honor, because you have shed too much blood upon the earth in my sight. ⁹However, a son is to be born to you. He will be a peaceful man, and I will give him rest from all his enemies on every side. For Solomon shall be his name,

and in his time I will bestow peace* and tranquility on Israel.ᶜ ¹⁰It is he who shall build a house in my honor; he shall be a son to me, and I will be a father to him, and I will establish the throne of his kingship over Israel forever.'ᵈ ¹¹Now, my son, the LORD be with you, and may you succeed in building the house of the LORD your God, as he has said you shall. ¹²May the LORD give you prudence and discernment when he brings you to rule over Israel, so that you keep the law of the LORD, your God. ¹³Only then shall you succeed, if you are careful to observe the precepts and decrees which the LORD gave Moses for Israel. Be brave and steadfast; do not fear or lose heart.ᵉ ¹⁴See, with great effort I have laid up for the house of the LORD a hundred thousand talents of gold,* a million talents of silver, and bronze and iron in such great quantities that they cannot be weighed. I have also stored up wood and stones, to which you must add.ᶠ ¹⁵Moreover, you have available an unlimited supply of workmen, stonecutters, masons, carpenters, and every kind of craftsman ¹⁶skilled in gold, silver, bronze, and iron. Set to work, therefore, and the LORD be with you!"

Charge to the Leaders. ¹⁷David also commanded all of Israel's leaders to help his son Solomon: ¹⁸"Is not the LORD your God with you? Has he not given you rest on every side? Indeed, he has delivered the occupants of the land into my power, and the land is subdued before the LORD and his people.ᵍ ¹⁹Therefore, devote your hearts and souls to seeking the LORD your God. Proceed to build the sanctuary of the LORD God, that the ark of the covenant of the LORD and God's

---

21, 1: This belongs to ch 22.

22, 2ff: According to 1 Kgs 5, 15-32, it was Solomon who made the material preparations for building the temple, even though David had wished to do so (1 Kgs 5, 17ff). The Chronicler, however, sought to have David, who was Israel's ideal king, more closely connected with Israel's most sacred sanctuary, the temple of Jerusalem.

22, 9: The Hebrew word for peace, shalom, is reflected in the name Solomon, in Hebrew, Shelomo. A contrast is drawn here between Solomon, the peaceful man, and David, who waged great wars (v 8). David was prevented from building the temple, not only because all his time was taken up in waging war (1 Kgs 5, 17), but also because he shed much blood (v 8), and in the eyes of the Chronicler this made him ritually unfit for the task.

22, 14: A hundred thousand talents of gold: about 3,775 tons of gold. A million talents of silver: about 37,750 tons of silver. The fantastically exaggerated figures are intended merely to stress the inestimable value of the temple as the center of Israelite worship. More modest figures are given in 1 Kgs 9, 14. 28; 10, 10. 14.

v: 1 Chr 16, 39; 1 Kgs 8, 4; 2 Chr 1, 8.   w: 1 Chr 21, 18. 26. 28; 2 Chr 3, 1.   x: 1 Kgs 5, 31f; 9, 20f; 2 Chr 2, 16f.   y: 1 Chr 18, 8; 1 Kgs 7, 47.   z: 1 Chr 10, 27; Ezr 3, 7.   a: 1 Chr 29, 1.   b: 7-10: 1 Chr 17, 1-14; 28, 2-7; 2 Sm 7, 1-16; 1 Kgs 5, 3ff; 8, 17-21.   c: 2 Sm 12, 24.   d: Heb 1, 5.   e: 1 Chr 28, 7. 20; Dt 31, 6. 23; Jos 1, 6f. 9; 1 Kgs 2, 2f.   f: 1 Chr 29, 2ff.   g: 1 Chr 23, 25; Jos 21, 44; 23, 1; 2 Sm 7, 1.

sacred vessels may be brought into the house built in honor of the LORD."[h]

See RG 200–203

CHAPTER 23

The Levitical Classes. [1]When David had grown old and was near the end of his days, he made his son Solomon king over Israel.[i] [2]He then gathered together all the leaders of Israel, together with the priests and the Levites.

[3]The Levites thirty years old and above were counted, and their total number was found to be thirty-eight thousand men.[j] [4]Of these, twenty-four thousand were to direct the service of the house of the LORD, six thousand were to be officials and judges, [5]four thousand were to be gatekeepers, and four thousand were to praise the LORD with the instruments which David had devised for praise.[k] [6]David divided them into classes according to the sons of Levi: Gershon, Kohath, and Merari.[l]

[7]To the Gershonites belonged Ladan and Shimei. [8]The sons of Ladan: Jehiel the chief, then Zetham and Joel; three in all.[m] [9]The sons of Shimei were Shelomoth, Haziel, and Haran; three. These were the heads of the families of Ladan. [10]The sons of Shimei were Jahath, Zizah, Jeush, and Beriah; these were the sons of Shimei, four in all. [11]Jahath was the chief and Zizah was second to him; but Jeush and Beriah had not many sons, and therefore they were classed as a single family, fulfilling a single office.

[12]The sons of Kohath: Amram, Izhar, Hebron, and Uzziel; four in all.[n] [13]The sons of Amran were Aaron and Moses. Aaron was set apart to be consecrated as most holy, he and his sons forever, to offer sacrifice before the LORD, to minister to him, and to bless his name forever.[o] [14]As for Moses, however, the man of God, his sons were counted as part of the tribe of Levi. [15]The sons of Moses were Gershon and Eliezer.[p] [16]The sons of Gershon: Shubael the chief.[q] [17]The sons of Eliezer were Rehabiah the chief—Eliezer had no other sons, but the sons of Rehabiah were

very numerous. [18]The sons of Izhar: Shelomith the chief. [19]The sons of Hebron: Jeriah, the chief, Amariah, the second, Jahaziel, the third, and Jekameam, the fourth.[r] [20]The sons of Uzziel: Micah, the chief, and Isshiah, the second.[s]

[21]The sons of Merari: Mahli and Mushi. The sons of Mahli: Eleazar and Kish.[t] [22]Eleazar died leaving no sons, only daughters; the sons of Kish, their kinsmen, married them.[u] [23]The sons of Mushi: Mahli, Eder, and Jeremoth; three in all.[v]

[24]These were the sons of Levi according to their ancestral houses, the family heads as they were enrolled one by one according to their names. They performed the work of the service of the house of the LORD from twenty years of age upward,[w] [27]for David's final orders were to enlist the Levites from the time they were twenty years old.

[25]David said: "The LORD, the God of Israel, has given rest to his people, and has taken up his dwelling in Jerusalem.[x] [26]Henceforth the Levites need not carry the Dwelling or any of its furnishings or equipment.[y] [28]Rather, their duty shall be to assist the sons of Aaron in the service of the house of the LORD, having charge of the courts, the chambers, and the preservation of everything holy: they shall take part in the service of the house of God. [29]They shall also have charge of the showbread, of the fine flour for the cereal offering, of the wafers of unleavened bread, and of the baking and mixing, and of all measures of quantity and size.[z] [30]They must be present every morning to offer thanks and to praise the LORD, and likewise in the evening;[a] [31]and at every offering of holocausts to the LORD on sabbaths, new moons, and feast days, in such numbers as are prescribed, they must always be present before the LORD.[b] [32]They shall observe what is prescribed for them concerning the meeting tent, the sanctuary, and the sons of Aaron, their brethren, in the service of the house of the LORD."[c]

h: 1 Kgs 8, 6. 21; 2 Chr 5, 7; 6, 11.   *i:* 1 Chr 28, 5; 1 Kgs 1, 30.   *j:* Nm 4, 3. 23. 30. 35. 39. 43. 47; 8, 23-26; 2 Chr 31, 17.   *k:* 1 Chr 9, 22.   *l:* 1 Chr 6, 1. 16-30; 26, 1-19; Ex 6, 16; Nm 3, 17; 26, 57.   *m:* 1 Chr 26, 21f; 29, 8.   *n:* 1 Chr 26, 23; Ex 6, 18; Nm 3, 19; 26, 23ff. *o:* 1 Chr 6, 49; Ex 6, 20; 28, 1; Nm 6, 23.   *p:* Ex 2, 22; 18, 3f.   *q:* 1 Chr 26, 24.   *r:* 1 Chr 24, 23.   *s:* 1 Chr 24, 24f.   *t:* 1 Chr 6, 29; 24, 26. 28f; Ex 6, 19; Nm 3, 20. 33.   *u:* 1 Chr 24, 28f.   *v:* 1 Chr 6, 47; 24, 30.   *w:* 2 Chr 31, 17; Ezr 3, 8.   *x:* 1 Chr 22, 18; Ps 132, 13. *y:* 1 Chr 15, 15; 2 Chr 35, 3.   *z:* 1 Chr 9, 29. 31f; Lv 2, 1. 4f; 24, 5-8.   *a:* Nm 28, 3-8.   *b:* Nm 28, 2-29. 39.   *c:* Nm 3, 6-9; 18, 2-5.

See RG
200–203

CHAPTER 24

The Priestly Classes. [1]The descendants of Aaron also were divided into classes. The sons of Aaron were Nadab, Abihu, Eleazar, and Ithamar.[d] [2]Nadab and Abihu died before their father, leaving no sons; therefore only Eleazar and Ithamar served as priests.[e] [3]David, with Zadok, a descendant of Eleazar, and Ahimelech, a descendant of Ithamar, assigned the functions for the priestly service.[f] [4]But since the descendants of Eleazar were found to be more numerous than those of Ithamar, the former were divided into sixteen groups, and the latter into eight groups, each under its family head. [5]Their functions were assigned impartially by lot, for there were officers of the holy place, and officers of the divine presence, descended both from Eleazar and from Ithamar. [6]The scribe Shemaiah, son of Nethanel, a Levite, made a record of it in the presence of the king, and of the leaders, of Zadok the priest, and of Ahimelech, son of Abiathar,* and of the heads of the ancestral houses of the priests and of the Levites, listing two successive family groups from Eleazar before each one from Ithamar.[g]

[7h]The first lot fell to Jehoiarib, the second to Jedaiah, [8]the third to Harim, the fourth to Seorim, [9]the fifth to Malchijah, the sixth to Mijamin, [10]the seventh to Hakkoz, the eighth to Abijah,[i] [11]the ninth to Jeshua, the tenth to Shecaniah, [12]the eleventh to Eliashib, the twelfth to Jakim, [13]the thirteenth to Huppah, the fourteenth to Ishbaal, [14]the fifteenth to Bilgah, the sixteenth to Immer, [15]the seventeenth to Hezir, the eighteenth to Happizzez, [16]the nineteenth to Pethahiah, the twentieth to Jehezkel, [17]the twenty-first to Jachin, the twenty-second to Gamul, [18]the twenty-third to Delaiah, the twenty-fourth to Maaziah. [19]This was the appointed order of their service when they functioned in the house of the

LORD in keeping with the precepts given them by Aaron, their father, as the LORD, the God of Israel, had commanded him.[j]

Other Levites. [20k]Of the remaining Levites, there were Shubael, of the descendants of Amram, and Jehdeiah, of the descendants of Shubael; [21]Isshiah, the chief, of the descendants of Rehabiah; [22]Shelomith of the Izharites, and Jahath of the descendants of Shelomith. [23]The descendants of Hebron were Jeriah, the chief, Amariah, the second, Jahaziel, the third, Jekameam, the fourth. [24]The descendants of Uzziel were Micah; Shamir, of the descendants of Micah; [25]Isshiah, the brother of Micah; and Zechariah, a descendant of Isshiah. [26]The descendants of Merari were Mahli, Mushi, and the descendants of his son Uzziah. [27]The descendants of Merari through his son Uzziah: Shoham, Zaccur, and Ibri. [28]Descendants of Mahli were Eleazar, who had no sons, [29]and Jerahmeel, of the descendants of Kish. [30]The descendants of Mushi were Mahli, Eder, and Jerimoth.

These were the descendants of the Levites according to their ancestral houses. [31]They too, in the same manner as their relatives, the descendants of Aaron, cast lots in the presence of King David, Zadok, Ahimelech, and the heads of the priestly and levitical families; the more important family did so in the same way as the less important one.[l]

CHAPTER 25

See RG
200–203

The Singers. [1]David and the leaders of the liturgical cult set apart for service the descendants of Asaph, Heman, and Jeduthun, as singers of inspired song to the accompaniment of lyres and harps and cymbals.[m]

This is the list of those who performed this service: [2*]Of the sons of Asaph: Zaccur, Joseph, Nethaniah, and Asharelah, sons of Asaph, under the direction of Asaph, who sang inspired songs under the guidance of

---

24, 6: Ahimelech, son of Abiathar: see note on 1 Chr 18, 16.

25, 2-31: This list of twenty-four classes of temple singers balances the list of the twenty-four classes of priests (1 Chr 24, 4-19). The last nine names in 1 Chr 25, 4, which seem to form a special group, appear to have been originally fragments or incipits of hymns. With some slight changes in the vocalization, the names would mean: "Have mercy on me, O Lord," "Have mercy on me," "You are my God," "I magnify,"

"I extol the help of . . . ," "Sitting in adversity," "I have fulfilled," "He made abundant," and "Visions."

d: Ex 6, 23; Nm 3, 2ff; 26, 60.   *e:* Lv 10, 1-7. 12; Nm 3, 2. 4.   *f:* 1 Chr 18, 16; 2 Sm 8, 17; 2 Chr 8, 14.   *g:* 1 Chr 18, 16; 2 Sm 8, 17.   *h:* 7-10: 1 Chr 9, 10ff; Ezr 2, 36ff; Neh 7, 39ff; 11, 10ff.   *i:* Lk 1, 5.   *j:* 2 Chr 23, 8.   *k:* 20-31: 1 Chr 23, 7-23.   *l:* 1 Chr 25, 8; 26, 13.   *m:* 1 Chr 6, 31ff; 15, 16f. 19; 16, 37; 2 Chr 5, 12; 35, 15; Neh 12, 27. 45.

the king. *3*Of Jeduthun, these sons of Jeduthun: Gedaliah, Zeri, Jeshaiah, Shimei, Hashabiah, and Mattithiah; six, under the direction of their father Jeduthun, who sang inspired songs to the accompaniment of a lyre, to give thanks and praise to the LORD. *4*Of Heman, these sons of Heman: Bukkiah, Mattaniah, Uzziel, Shubael, and Jerimoth; Hananiah, Hanani, Eliathah, Giddalti, Romamti-ezer, Joshbekashah, Mallothi, Hothir, and Mahazioth. *5*All these were the sons of Heman, the king's seer in divine matters; to enhance his prestige, God gave Heman fourteen sons and three daughters.*n* *6*All these, whether of Asaph, Jeduthun, or Heman, were under their fathers' direction in the singing in the house of the LORD to the accompaniment of cymbals, harps and lyres, serving in the house of God, under the guidance of the king.*o* *7*Their number, together with that of their brethren who were trained in singing to the LORD, all of them skilled men, was two hundred and eighty-eight. *8*They cast lots for their functions equally, young and old, master and pupil alike.*p*

*9*The first lot fell to Asaph, the family of Joseph; he and his sons and his brethren were twelve. Gedaliah was the second; he and his brethren and his sons were twelve. *10*The third was Zaccur, his sons, and his brethren: twelve. *11*The fourth fell to Izri, his sons, and his brethren: twelve. *12*The fifth was Nethaniah, his sons, and his brethren: twelve. *13*The sixth was Bukkiah, his sons, and his brethren: twelve. *14*The seventh was Jesarelah, his sons, and his brethren: twelve. *15*The eighth was Jeshaiah, his sons, and his brethren: twelve. *16*The ninth was Mattaniah, his sons, and his brethren: twelve. *17*The tenth was Shimei, his sons, and his brethren: twelve. *18*The eleventh was Uzziel, his sons, and his brethren: twelve. *19*The twelfth fell to Hashabiah, his sons, and his brethren: twelve. *20*The thirteenth was Shubael, his sons, and his brethren: twelve. *21*The fourteenth was Mattithiah, his sons, and his brethren: twelve. *22*The fifteenth fell to Jeremoth, his sons, and his brethren: twelve. *23*The sixteenth fell to Hananiah, his sons,

and his brethren: twelve. *24*The seventeenth fell to Joshbekashah, his sons, and his brethren: twelve. *25*The eighteenth fell to Hanani, his sons, and his brethren: twelve. *26*The nineteenth fell to Mallothi, his sons, and his brethren: twelve. *27*The twentieth fell to Eliathah, his sons, and his brethren: twelve. *28*The twenty-first fell to Hothir, his sons, and his brethren: twelve. *29*The twenty-second fell to Giddalti, his sons, and his brethren: twelve. *30*The twenty-third fell to Mahazioth, his sons, and his brethren: twelve. *31*The twenty-fourth fell to Romamti-ezer, his sons, and his brethren: twelve.

CHAPTER 26

See RG 200–203

Classes of Gatekeepers. *1q*As for the classes of gatekeepers. Of the Korahites was Meshelemiah, the son of Kore, one of the sons of Abiasaph. *2*Meshelemiah's sons: Zechariah, the first-born, Jediael, the second son, Zebadiah, the third, Jathniel, the fourth, *3*Elam, the fifth, Jehohanan, the sixth, Eliehoenai, the seventh. *4*Obed-edom's sons: Shemaiah, the first-born, Jehozabad, a second son, Joah, the third, Sachar, the fourth, Nethanel, the fifth, *5*Ammiel, the sixth, Issachar, the seventh, Peullethai, the eighth, for God blessed him. *6*To his son Shemaiah were born sons who ruled over their family, for they were warriors. *7*The sons of Shemaiah were Othni, Rephael, Obed, and Elzabad; also his brethren who were men of might, Elihu and Semachiah. *8*All these were of the sons of Obed-edom, who, together with their sons and their brethren, were mighty men, fit for the service. Of Obed-edom, sixty-two. *9*Of Meshelemiah, eighteen sons and brethren, mighty men.

*10*Hosah, a descendant of Merari, had these sons: Shimri, the chief (for though he was not the first-born, his father made him chief),*r* *11*Hilkiah, the second son, Tebaliah, the third, Zechariah, the fourth. All the sons and brethren of Hosah were thirteen.

*12*To these classes of gatekeepers, under their chief men, were assigned watches in the service of the house of the LORD, for each group in the same way. *13*They cast lots

---

n: 2 Chr 35, 15.   *o:* 1 Chr 15, 16.   *p:* 1 Chr 24, 31.   *q:* 1 Chr 9, 19; 2 Chr 8, 14; 23, 19; 35, 15; Neh 12, 45.   *r:* 1 Chr 16, 38.

for each gate, the small and the large families alike. [14]When the lot was cast for the east side, it fell to Meshelemiah. Then they cast lots for his son Zechariah, a prudent counselor, and the north side fell to his lot.[s] [15]To Obed-edom fell the south side, and to his sons the storehouse. [16]To Hosah fell the west side with the Shallecheth gate at the ascending highway. For each family, watches were established. [17]On the east, six watched each day, on the north, four each day, on the south, four each day, and at the storehouse they were two and two; [18]as for the large building* on the west, there were four at the highway and two at the large building. [19]These were the classes of the gatekeepers, descendants of Kore and Merari.

Treasurers. [20]Their brother Levites superintended the stores for the house of God and the stores of votive offerings.[t] [21]Among the descendants of Ladan the Gershonite, the family heads were descendants of Jehiel: the descendants of Jehiel,[u] [22][v]Zetham and his brother Joel, who superintended the treasures of the house of the LORD. [23]From the Amramites, Izharites, Hebronites, and Uzzielites, [24]Shubael, son of Gershon, son of Moses, was chief superintendent over the treasures. [25][w]His associate pertained to Eliezer, whose son was Rehabiah, whose son was Jeshaiah, whose son was Joram, whose son was Zichri, whose son was Shelomith. [26]This Shelomith and his brethren superintended all the stores of the votive offerings dedicated by King David, the heads of the families, the commanders of thousands and of hundreds, and the commanders of the army,[x] [27]from the booty they had taken in the wars, for the enhancement of the house of the LORD. [28]Also, whatever Samuel the seer, Saul, son of Kish, Abner, son of Ner, Joab, son of Zeruiah, and all others had consecrated, was under the charge of Shelomith and his brethren.

Magistrates. [29]Among the Izharites, Chananiah and his sons were in charge of Israel's civil affairs as officials and judges.[y] [30]Among the Hebronites, Hashabiah and his brethren, one thousand seven hundred police officers, had the administration of Israel on the western side of the Jordan in all the work of the LORD and in the service of the king.[z] [31]Among the Hebronites, Jerijah was their chief according to their family records. In the fortieth year of David's reign search was made, and there were found among them outstanding officers at Jazer of Gilead.[a] [32]His brethren were also police officers, two thousand seven hundred heads of families. King David appointed them to the administration of the Reubenites, the Gadites, and the half-tribe of Manasseh in everything pertaining to God and to the king.

CHAPTER 27

See RG 200–203

*Army Commanders.** [1]This is the list of the Israelite family heads, commanders of thousands and of hundreds, and other officers who served the king in all that pertained to the divisions, of twenty-four thousand men each, that came and went month by month throughout the year.

[2]Over the first division for the first month was Ishbaal, son of Zabdiel, and in his division were twenty-four thousand men; [3]a descendant of Perez, he was chief over all the commanders of the army for the first month. [4]Over the division of the second month was Eleazar, son of Dodo, from Ahoh, and in his division were twenty-four thousand men.[b] [5][c]The third army commander, chief for the third month, was Benaiah, son of Jehoiada the priest, and in his division were twenty-four thousand men. [6]This Benaiah was a warrior among the Thirty and over the Thirty. His son Ammizabad was over his division. [7]Fourth, for the fourth month, was

---

26, 18: The large building (in the Hebrew text Parbar): see note on 2 Kgs 23, 11.

27, 1-15: This list of army commanders is similar to, but distinct from, the list of David's warriors as given in 1 Chr 11, 10-47. The schematic enumeration of the soldiers as presented here is, no doubt, artificial and grossly exaggerated (12 × 24,000 = 288,000 men!), unless the Hebrew word (eleph) for thousand is understood as designating a military unit of much smaller size; see note on 1 Chr 12, 25-38.

---

s: 1 Chr 9, 24.   t: 1 Chr 28, 12; 1 Kgs 7, 51.   u: 1 Chr 23, 7f; 29, 8.   v: 22ff: 1 Chr 23, 8. 12. 16.   w: 1 Chr 23, 17f; 24, 21.   x: 2 Sm 8, 11.   y: 1 Chr 23, 4.   z: 1 Chr 27, 17; Neh 11, 15f.   a: 1 Chr 23, 19; 29, 27; Jos 13, 25.   b: 1 Chr 9, 37; 11, 12; 2 Sm 23, 9.   c: 5f: 1 Chr 11, 22ff; 18, 17; 2 Sm 23, 20ff.

Asahel, brother of Joab, and after him his son Zebadiah, and in his division were twenty-four thousand men.*d* *8*Fifth, for the fifth month, was the commander Shamhuth, a descendant of Zerah, and in his division were twenty-four thousand men. *9*Sixth, for the sixth month, was Ira, son of Ikkesh, from Tekoa, and in his division were twenty-four thousand men. *10*Seventh, for the seventh month, was Helles, from Beth-pheleth, of the sons of Ephraim, and in his division were twenty-four thousand men. *11*Eighth, for the eighth month, was Sibbecai the Hushathite, a descendant of Zerah, and in his division were twenty-four thousand men.*e* *12*Ninth, for the ninth month, was Abiezer from Anathoth, of Benjamin, and in his division were twenty-four thousand men. *13*Tenth, for the tenth month, was Maharai from Netophah, a descendant of Zerah, and in his division were twenty-four thousand men. *14*Eleventh, for the eleventh month, was Benaiah the Pirathonite, of Ephraim, and in his division were twenty-four thousand men. *15*Twelfth, for the twelfth month, was Heldai the Netophathite, of the family of Othniel, and in his division were twenty-four thousand men.

Tribal Heads. *16*Over the tribes of Israel, for the Reubenites the leader was Eliezer, son of Zichri; for the Simeonites, Shephatiah, son of Maacah; *17*for Levi, Hashabiah, son of Kemuel; for Aaron, Zadok; *18*for Judah, Eliab, one of David's brothers; for Issachar, Omri, son of Michael;*f* *19*for Zebulun, Ishmaiah, son of Obadiah; for Naphtali, Jeremoth, son of Azriel; *20*for the sons of Ephraim, Hoshea, son of Azaziah; for the half-tribe of Manasseh, Joel, son of Pedaiah; *21*for the half-tribe of Manasseh in Gilead, Iddo, son of Zechariah; for Benjamin, Jaasiel, son of Abner; *22*for Dan, Azarel, son of Jeroham. These were the commanders of the tribes of Israel.

*23*David did not count those who were twenty years of age or younger, for the LORD had promised to multiply Israel like the stars of the heavens.*g* *24*Joab, son of Zeruiah, began to take the census, but he did not complete it, for because of it wrath fell upon Israel. Therefore the number did not enter into the book of chronicles of King David.*h*

Overseers. *25*Over the treasures of the king was Azmaveth, the son of Adiel. Over the stores in the country, the cities, the villages, and the towers was Jonathan, son of Uzziah.*i* *26*Over the farm workers who tilled the soil was Ezri, son of Chelub. *27*Over the vineyards was Shimei from Ramah, and over their produce for the wine cellars was Zabdi the Shiphmite. *28*Over the olive trees and sycamores of the foothills was Baal-hanan the Gederite, and over the stores of oil was Joash. *29*Over the cattle that grazed in Sharon was Shitrai the Sharonite, and over the cattle in the valleys was Shaphat, the son of Adlai; *30*over the camels was Obil the Ishmaelite; over the she-asses was Jehdeiah the Meronothite; *31*and over the flocks was Jaziz the Hagrite. All these were the overseers of King David's possessions.

David's Court. *32*Jonathan, David's uncle and a man of intelligence, was counselor and scribe; he and Jehiel, the son of Hachmoni, were tutors of the king's sons. *33*Ahithophel was also the king's counselor, and Hushai the Archite was the king's confidant.*j* *34*After Ahithophel* came Jehoiada, the son of Benaiah, and Abiathar. The commander of the king's army was Joab.

CHAPTER 28

See RG 200–203

The Assembly at Jerusalem. *1*David assembled at Jerusalem all the leaders of Israel, the heads of the tribes, the commanders of the divisions who were in the service of king, the commanders of thousands and of hundreds, the overseers of all the king's estates and possessions, and his sons, together with the courtiers, the warriors, and every important man.*k* *2*King David rose to his feet and

---

27, 34: After Ahithophel: after his suicide (2 Sm 17, 23). Jehoiada then succeeded him as the king's counselor. Abiathar: the priest. The Chronicler does not mention his office because he regards only the Zadokites as legitimate high priests.

d: 2 Sm 2, 18; 23, 24. *e:* 1 Chr 11, 29; 20, 4; 2 Sm 21, 18. *f:* 1 Chr 2, 13. *g:* 1 Chr 22, 17. *h:* 2 Sm 24, 10. *i:* 2 Sm 23, 31. *j:* 2 Sm 15, 12. 32-37; 16, 16-19. 23; 17, 5-16. 23. *k:* 1 Chr 27, 2-22. 25-31; 11, 10ff. *l:* 2f: 1 Chr 17, 4; 22, 7ff; 2 Sm 7, 5; 1 Kgs 5, 3; Ps 132, 3-7.

said: "Hear me, my brethren and my people. It was my purpose to build a house of repose myself for the ark of the covenant of the LORD, the footstool for the feet of our God;* and I was preparing to build it. ³But God said to me, 'You may not build a house in my honor, for you are a man who fought wars and shed blood.' ⁴However, the LORD, the God of Israel, chose me from all my father's family to be king over Israel forever. For he chose Judah as leader, then one family of Judah, that of my father; and finally, among all the sons of my father, it pleased him to make me king over all Israel.ᵐ ⁵And of all my sons—for the LORD has given me many sons—he has chosen my son Solomon to sit on the LORD's royal throne over Israel.ⁿ ⁶For he said to me: 'It is your son Solomon who shall build my house and my courts, for I have chosen him for my son, and I will be a father to him.ᵒ ⁷I will establish his kingdom forever, if he perseveres in keeping my commandments and decrees as he keeps them now.' ⁸Therefore in the presence of all Israel, the assembly of the LORD, and in the hearing of our God, I exhort you to keep and to carry out all the commandments of the LORD, your God, that you may continue to possess this good land and afterward leave it as an inheritance to your children forever.ᵖ

⁹"As for you, Solomon, my son, know the God of your father and serve him with a perfect heart and a willing soul, for the LORD searches all hearts and understands all the mind's thoughts. If you seek him, he will let himself be found by you; but if you abandon him, he will cast you off forever.�q ¹⁰See, then! The LORD has chosen you to build a house as his sanctuary. Take courage and set to work."

Temple Plans Given to Solomon. ¹¹Then David gave to his son Solomon the pattern of the portico and of the building itself, with its storerooms, its upper rooms and inner chambers, and the room with the propitiatory.ʳ ¹²He provided also the pattern for all else that he had in mind by way of courts for the house of the LORD, with the surrounding compartments for the stores for the house of God and the stores of the votive offerings, ¹³as well as for the divisions of the priests and Levites, for all the work of the service of the house of the LORD, and for all the liturgical vessels of the house of the LORD. ¹⁴He specified the weight of gold to be used in the golden vessels for the various services and the weight of silver to be used in the silver vessels for the various services; ¹⁵likewise for the golden lampstands and their lamps he specified the weight of gold for each lampstand and its lamps, and for the silver lampstands he specified the weight of silver for each lampstand and its lamps, depending on the use to which each lampstand was to be put.ˢ ¹⁶He specified the weight of gold for each table to hold the showbread, and the silver for the silver tables; ¹⁷the pure gold to be used for the forks and pitchers; the amount of gold for each golden bowl and the silver for each silver bowl; ¹⁸the refined gold, and its weight, to be used for the altar of incense; and, finally, gold for what would suggest a chariot throne:* the cherubim that spread their wings and covered the ark of the covenant of the LORD.ᵗ ¹⁹He had successfully committed to writing the exact specifications of the pattern, because the hand of the LORD was upon him.

²⁰Then David said to his son Solomon: "Be firm and steadfast; go to work without fear or discouragement, for the LORD God, my God, is with you. He will not fail you or abandon you before you have completed all the work for the service of the house of the LORD.ᵘ ²¹The classes of the priests and Levites are ready for all the service of the house of God; they will help you in all your work with all those who are eager to show their skill in every kind of craftsmanship. Also the leaders and all the people will do everything that you command."ᵛ

28, 2: The ark . . . the footstool . . . of our God: the Lord, who was invisibly enthroned upon the cherubim that were associated with the ark of the covenant at Shiloh and later in the Jerusalem temple, had the ark as his footstool; cf Pss 99, 5; 132, 7. The propitiatory (1 Chr 28, 11) and the chariot throne (1 Chr 28, 18) reflect the different circumstances of the postexilic community, for whom only the place of the ark was a focal point of worship, though the ark itself was no longer present.

28, 18: Chariot throne: probably suggested by Ez 1, 4-24; 10, 1-22.

---

m: 1 Chr 17, 23; Gn 49, 8ff; 1 Sm 16, 6-13. *n:* 1 Chr 3, 1-9; 14, 3-7; 22, 9; 23, 1; Wis 9, 7. *o:* 1 Chr 17, 11ff; 22, 9f; 2 Sm 7, 12f. *p:* Dt 4, 5. *q:* 1 Chr 29, 17; 2 Chr 15, 2; 1 Kgs 8, 61. *r:* Ex 25, 9. 40; 26, 30. *s:* Ex 25, 31-37. *t:* Ex 25, 18-22; 30, 1-10; 1 Kgs 6, 23-28. *u:* 1 Chr 22, 13. 16; Jos 1, 5. *v:* Ex 36, 1-5.

CHAPTER 29

See RG
200–203

Offerings for the Temple. [1]King David then said to the whole assembly: "My son Solomon, whom alone God has chosen, is still young and immature; the work, however, is great, for this castle is not intended for man, but for the LORD God.[w] [2]For this reason I have stored up for the house of my God, as far as I was able, gold for what will be made of gold, silver for what will be made of silver, bronze for what will be made of bronze, iron for what will be made of iron, wood for what will be made of wood, onyx stones and settings for them, carnelian and mosaic stones, every other kind of precious stone, and great quantities of marble.[x] [3]But now, because of the delight I take in the house of my God, in addition to all that I stored up for the holy house, I give to the house of my God my personal fortune in gold and silver: [4]three thousand talents of Ophir gold, and seven thousand talents of refined silver, for overlaying the walls of the rooms,[y] [5]for the various utensils to be made of gold and silver, and for every work that is to be done by artisans. Now, who else is willing to contribute generously this day to the LORD?"[z]

[6]Then the heads of the families, the leaders of the tribes of Israel, the commanders of thousands and of hundreds, and the overseers of the king's affairs came forward willingly[a] [7]and contributed for the service of the house of God five thousand talents and ten thousand darics of gold, ten thousand talents of silver, eighteen thousand talents of bronze, and one hundred thousand talents of iron.[b] [8]Those who had precious stones gave them into the keeping of Jehiel the Gershonite for the treasury of the house of the LORD.[c] [9]The people rejoiced over these free-will offerings, which had been contributed to the LORD wholeheartedly. King David also rejoiced greatly.[d]

David's Prayer. [10]Then David blessed the LORD in the presence of the whole assembly, praying in these words:

"Blessed may you be, O LORD,
God of Israel our father,
from eternity to eternity.

[11] "Yours, O LORD, are grandeur and power,
majesty, splendor, and glory.
For all in heaven and on earth is yours;
yours, O LORD, is the sovereignty;
you are exalted as head over all.

[12] "Riches and honor are from you,
and you have dominion over all.
In your hand are power and might;
it is yours to give grandeur and
strength to all.[e]
[13] Therefore, our God, we give you thanks
and we praise the majesty of your
name."

[14]"But who am I, and who are my people, that we should have the means to contribute so freely? For everything is from you, and we only give you what we have received from you. [15]For we stand before you as aliens: we are only your guests, like all our fathers. Our life on earth is like a shadow that does not abide.[f] [16]O LORD our God, all this wealth that we have brought together to build you a house in honor of your holy name comes from you and is entirely yours. [17]I know, O my God, that you put hearts to the test and that you take pleasure in uprightness. With a sincere heart I have willingly given all these things, and now with joy I have seen your people here present also giving to you generously. [18]O LORD, God of our fathers Abraham, Isaac, and Israel, keep such thoughts in the hearts and minds of your people forever, and direct their hearts toward you.[g] [19]Give to my son Solomon a wholehearted desire to keep your commandments, precepts, and statutes, that he may carry out all these plans and build the castle for which I have made preparation."

[20]Then David besought the whole assembly, "Now bless the LORD your God!" And the whole assembly blessed the LORD, the

---

w: 1 Chr 22, 5; 28, 5.   *x:* 1 Chr 22, 14.   *y:* 2 Chr 9, 10; 1 Kgs 9, 28; 10, 11.   *z:* Ex 25, 2; 35, 5f.   *a:* 1 Chr 27, 1. 25-31; 28, 1.   *b:* Ezr 2, 69; 8, 27; Neh 7, 70ff.   *c:* 1 Chr 23, 8; 26, 21.   *d:* 2 Kgs 12, 4.   *e:* 2 Chr 20, 6; Wis 6, 3.   *f:* Lv 25, 23; Wis 2, 5; 5, 9.   *g:* Ex 3, 6. 15f; 4, 5; 1 Kgs 18, 36.

God of their fathers, bowing down and prostrating themselves before the LORD and before the king. ²¹On the following day they offered sacrifices and holocausts to the LORD, a thousand bulls, a thousand rams, and a thousand lambs, together with their libations and many other sacrifices for all Israel; ²²and on that day they ate and drank in the LORD's presence with great rejoicing.

Solomon Anointed. Then for a second time* they proclaimed David's son Solomon king, and they anointed him as the LORD's prince, and Zadok as priest. ²³Thereafter Solomon sat on the throne of the LORD as king in place of his father David; he prospered, and all Israel obeyed him.ʰ ²⁴All the leaders and warriors, and also all the other sons of King David, swore allegiance to King Solomon. ²⁵And the LORD exalted Solomon greatly in the eyes of all Israel, giving him a glorious reign such as had not been enjoyed by any king over Israel before him.ⁱ

Death of David. ²⁶Thus David, the son of Jesse, had reigned over all Israel. ²⁷The time that he reigned over Israel was forty years: in Hebron he reigned seven years, and in Jerusalem thirty-three.ʲ ²⁸He died at a ripe old age, rich in years and wealth and glory, and his son Solomon succeeded him as king.ᵏ

²⁹Now the deeds of King David, first and last, can be found written in the history of Samuel the seer, the history of Nathan the prophet, and the history of Gad the seer,ˡ ³⁰together with the particulars of his reign and valor, and of the events that affected him and all Israel and all the kingdoms of the surrounding lands.

29, 22: For a second time: the first time is referred to in 1 Chr 23, 1. Here there is a solemn public ratification of David's earlier appointment of Solomon as his successor.

h: 1 Chr 28, 5; 2 Chr 9, 8; 1 Kgs 2, 10ff. *i:* 2 Chr 1, 12; 1 Kgs 3, 13. *j:* 2 Sm 5, 5; 1 Kgs 2, 11. *k:* 1 Chr 23, 1. *l:* 1 Chr 21, 9; 1 Sm 22, 5.

See RG 203–7

The Second Book of Chronicles

The Second Book of Chronicles takes up the history of the monarchy where the First Book breaks off. It begins with the account of the reign of Solomon from the special viewpoint of the Chronicler. The portrait of Solomon is an idealized one; he appears as second only to David. The great achievement of the building of the temple and the magnificence of Solomon's court are described in detail while the serious defects of his reign are passed over without comment. All this is in keeping with the Chronicler's purpose of stressing the supreme importance of the temple and its worship. He wishes to impress on his readers the splendor of God's dwelling and the magnificence of the liturgy of sacrifice, prayer and praise offered there. Judah's kings are judged by their attitude toward the temple and its cult. To this ideal of one people, united in the worship of the one true God at the temple of Jerusalem founded by David and Solomon, the restored community would have to conform.

In treating the period of divided monarchy, the Chronicler gives practically all his attention to the kingdom of Judah. His omission of the northern Israelite kings is significant. In his view, the northern tribes of Israel were in religious schism as long as they worshiped Yahweh in a place other than the temple of Jerusalem. The Chronicler makes no mention of the important sanctuaries of Yahweh at Dan and Bethel—as though they had never existed. Nevertheless he retains the ancient ideal of "all Israel" (a phrase occuring forty-one times in Chronicles) as the people of God. The condition he places for a united people is that "the whole congregation of Israel" worship the Lord only in his temple at Jerusalem. This explains his praise of Kings Hezekiah and Josiah for striving, after the fall of Samaria, to unite the remnants of the northern tribes of Israel into the kingdom of Judah.

At the end of the fifth century B.C., during the Chronicler's own time, "the people of the land" were the descendants of the people of all the tribes (including Judah) who had not gone into exile. These had become intermingled with aliens and had evolved a religion of Yahweh very different from the Judaism that developed during the Babylonian exile. Thus, religious and political cooperation between the returned exiles and these "people of the land" was out of the question for the Chronicler. This he clearly shows in the last part of his work, the Books of Ezra and Nehemiah.

The Second Book of Chronicles is divided as follows:

——————

I: The Reign of Solomon

CHAPTER 1

See RG
203-7

Solomon at Gibeon. [1]Solomon, son of David, strengthened his hold on the kingdom, for the LORD, his God, was with him, constantly making him more renowned. [2]He sent a summons to all Israel, to the commanders of thousands and of hundreds, the judges, the princes of all Israel, and the family heads; [3a]and, accompanied by the whole assembly, he went to the high place at Gibeon, because the meeting tent of God, made in the desert by Moses, the LORD's servant, was there. [4](The ark of God, however, David had brought up from Kiriath-jearim to Jerusalem, where he had provided a place and pitched a tent for it.) [5]The bronze altar made by Bezalel, son of Uri, son of Hur, he put in front of the LORD's Dwelling* on the high place. There Solomon and the assembly consulted the LORD,[b] [6]and Solomon offered sacrifice in the LORD's presence on the bronze altar at the meeting tent; he offered a thousand holocausts upon it.

[7]That night God appeared to Solomon and said to him, "Make a request of me, and I will grant it to you." [8]Solomon answered God: "You have shown great favor to my father David, and you have allowed him to succeed him as king. [9]Now, LORD God, may your promise to my father David be fulfilled, for you have made me king over a people as numerous as the dust of the earth. [10]Give me, therefore, wisdom and knowledge to lead this people, for otherwise who could rule this great people of yours?" [11]God then replied to Solomon: "Since this has been your wish and you have not asked for riches, treasures and glory, nor for the life of those who hate you, nor even for a long life for yourself, but have asked for wisdom and knowledge in order to rule my people over whom I have made you king, [12]wisdom and knowledge are given you; but I will also give you riches, treasures and glory, such as kings before you never had, nor will those have them who come after you."

Solomon's Wealth. [13]Solomon returned to Jerusalem from the high place at Gibeon, from the meeting tent, and became king over Israel. [14]He gathered together chariots and drivers, so that he had one thousand four hundred chariots and twelve thousand drivers he could station in the chariot cities and with the king in Jerusalem.[c] [15]The king made silver and gold as common in Jerusalem as stones, while cedars became as numerous as the sycamores of the foothills.[d] [16]Solomon also imported horses from Egypt and Cilicia.[e] The king's agents would acquire them by purchase from Cilicia,* [17]and would then bring up chariots from Egypt and export them at six hundred silver shekels, with the horses going for a hundred and fifty shekels. At these rates they served as middlemen for all the Hittite and Aramean kings.[f]

Preparations for the Temple. [18]Solomon gave orders for the building of a house to

---

1, 5: The bronze altar . . . the Lord's Dwelling: the Chronicler justifies Solomon's worship at the high place of Gibeon. He pictures the Lord's Dwelling, i.e., the Mosaic meeting tent, and the bronze altar made at Moses' command (Ex 31, 1-9) as still at Gibeon after David had removed the ark of the covenant from there to a new tent in Jerusalem (1 Chr 15, 1. 25; 16, 1). The altar made by Bezalel is described as being of acacia wood plated with bronze (Ex 27, 1f). Solomon later made an all-bronze altar for the temple in Jerusalem (2 Chr 4, 1).

1, 16f: Egypt . . . Cilicia: it seems likely that the horses came from Cilicia and the chariots from Egypt. Some read the source of these data in 1 Kgs 10, 28f as containing the name (Musur) of a mountain district north of Cilicia, rather than of Egypt; but the author of Chronicles surely understood Egypt; cf 2 Chr 9, 28.

a: 3-12: 1 Kgs 3, 4-15; 1 Chr 21, 29. *b:* Ex 27, 1f; 31, 2; 1 Chr 2, 20. *c:* 2 Chr 9, 25; 10, 26-29. *d:* 1 Kgs 10, 27. *e:* 1 Kgs 10, 28. *f:* 1 Kgs 10, 29.

honor the LORD and also of a house for his own royal estate.

CHAPTER 2

See RG 203

*1*He conscripted seventy thousand men to carry stone and eighty thousand to cut the stone in the mountains, and over these he placed three thousand six hundred overseers.*g* *2h*Moreover, Solomon sent this message to Huram, king of Tyre: "As you dealt with my father David, sending him cedars to build a house for his dwelling, so deal with me. *3*I intend to build a house for the honor of the LORD, my God, and to consecrate it to him, for the burning of fragrant incense in his presence, for the perpetual display of the showbread, for holocausts morning and evening, and for the sabbaths, new moons, and festivals of the LORD, our God: such is Israel's perpetual obligation.*i* *4*And the house I intend to build must be large, for our God is greater than all other gods. *5*Yet who is really able to build him a house, since the heavens and even the highest heavens cannot contain him? And who am I that I should build him a house, unless it be to offer incense in his presence?*j* *6*Now, send me men skilled at work in gold, silver, bronze and iron, in purple, crimson, and violet fabrics, and who know how to do engraved work, to join the craftsmen who are with me in Judah and Jerusalem, whom my father David appointed. *7*Also send me boards of cedar, cypress and cabinet wood from Lebanon, for I realize that your servants know how to cut the wood of the Lebanon. My servants will labor with yours *8*in order to prepare for me a great quantity of wood, since the house I intend to build must be lofty and wonderful. *9*I will furnish as food for your servants, the hewers who cut the wood, twenty thousand kors of wheat, twenty thousand kors of barley, twenty thousand measures of wine, and twenty thousand measures of oil."*k*

*10*Huram, king of Tyre, wrote an answer which he sent to Solomon: "Because the LORD loves his people, he has placed you over them as king." *11*He added: "Blessed be the LORD, the God of Israel, who made heaven and earth, for having given King David a wise son of intelligence and understanding, who will build a house for the LORD and also a house for his royal estate.*l* *12*I am now sending you a craftsman of great skill, Huram-abi,*m* *13*son of a Danite woman* and of a father from Tyre; he knows how to work with gold, silver, bronze and iron, with stone and wood, with purple, violet, fine linen and crimson, and also how to do all kinds of engraved work and to devise every type of artistic work that may be given him and your craftsmen and the craftsmen of my lord David your father. *14n*And now, let my lord send to his servants the wheat, barley, oil and wine which he has promised. *15*For our part, we will cut trees on Lebanon, as many as you need, and float them down to you at the port of Joppa, whence you may take them up to Jerusalem."*o*

*16p*Thereupon Solomon took a census of all the alien men who were in the land of Israel (following the census David his father had taken of them), who were found to number one hundred fifty-three thousand six hundred. *17*Of these he made seventy thousand carriers and eighty thousand cutters in the mountains, and three thousand six hundred overseers to keep the people working.*q*

CHAPTER 3

See RG 203

Building of the Temple. *1r*Then Solomon began to build the house of the LORD in Jerusalem on Mount Moriah,* which had been pointed out to his father David, on the spot which David had selected, the threshing-floor of Ornan the Jebusite. *2*He began to build in the second month of the fourth year of his reign. *3*These were the specifications

---

2, 13: A Danite woman: a widow of the tribe of Naphtali (1 Kgs 7, 14). The Danites had settled in the northern section of Naphtali's territory (Jgs 18, 27ff). Bezalel's fellow craftsman was of the tribe of Dan (Ex 31, 6).

3, 1: Mount Moriah: the height in the land of Moriah (Gn 22, 2). This is the only place in the Bible where the temple mount is identified with the site where Abraham was to sacrifice Isaac.

---

g: 2 Chr 2, 17; 5, 29f.   *h:* 2-9: 1 Kgs 5, 15-20; 1 Chr 14, 1.   *i:* Lv 24, 5-8; Nm 28-29.   *j:* 2 Chr 6, 18.   *k:* 1 Kgs 5, 25; Ezr 3, 7.
l: 1 Kgs 5, 21.   *m:* 12f: 1 Kgs 7, 13f; Ex 31, 1-5.   *n:* 14f: 1 Kgs 5, 22-26.   *o:* Ezr 3, 7.   *p:* 16f: 1 Chr 22, 2.   *q:* 2 Chr 2, 1.   *r:* 1f: Gn 22, 2; 1 Kgs 6, 1; 1 Chr 21, 22-26.

The Temple of Solomon according to 2 Chronicles

laid down by Solomon for building the house of God: the length was sixty cubits according to the old measure, and the width was twenty cubits;^{s} ^{4}the porch which lay before the nave along the width of the house was also twenty cubits, and it was twenty cubits high.* He overlaid its interior with pure gold.^{t} ^{5}The nave he overlaid with cypress wood which he covered with fine gold, embossing on it palms and chains.^{u} ^{6}He also decorated the building with precious stones. ^{7}The house; its beams and thresholds, as well as its walls and its doors, he overlaid with gold, and he engraved cherubim upon the walls. (The gold was from Parvaim.) ^{8}He also made the room of the holy of holies. Its length corresponded to the width of the house, twenty cubits, and its width was also twenty cubits. He overlaid it with fine gold to the amount of six hundred talents.^{v} ^{9}The weight of the nails was fifty gold shekels. The upper chambers he likewise covered with gold.

^{10w}For the room of the holy of holies he made two cherubim of carved workmanship, which were then overlaid with gold. ^{11}The wings of the cherubim spanned twenty cubits: ^{12}one wing of each cherub, five cubits in length, extended to a wall of the building, while the other wing, also five cubits in length, touched the corresponding wing of the second cherub. ^{13}The combined wing-spread of the two cherubim was thus twenty cubits. They stood upon their own feet, facing toward the nave. ^{14}He made the veil* of violet, purple, crimson and fine linen, and had cherubim embroidered upon it.^{x}

^{15y}In front of the building he set two columns thirty-five cubits high; the capital topping each was of five cubits. ^{16}He worked out chains in the form of a collar with which he encircled the capitals of the columns, and he made a hundred pomegranates which he set on the chains. ^{17}He set up the columns to correspond with the nave, one for the right side and the other for the left, and he called the one to the right Jachin and the one to the left Boaz.

CHAPTER 4

^{1}Then he made a bronze altar twenty cubits long, twenty cubits wide and ten cubits high.^{z} ^{2a}He also made the molten sea. It was perfectly round, ten cubits in diameter, five in depth, and thirty in circumference; ^{3}below the rim a ring of figures of oxen* en-

See RG
203

3, 4: The porch . . . twenty cubits high: this measurement, not given in the Books of Kings, is here based on a variant Greek text that may be a later revision. The received Hebrew text says, "one hundred and twenty cubits high." The height of the two freestanding columns adjacent to the porch (1 Kgs 7, 15-16) is nearly doubled by the Chronicler (2 Chr 3, 15).

3, 14: The veil: at the entrance of the holy of holies, as also in the Mosaic meeting tent (Ex 26, 31f). Solomon's temple

had doors at this place (1 Kgs 6, 31). Apparently there was a veil here in the temple of the Chronicler's time as there was also in Herod's temple (Mt 27, 51; Mk 15, 38; Lk 23, 45).

s: 1 Kgs 6, 2; Ez 40, 5.   t: 1 Kgs 6, 3; Ez 40, 48.   u: 1 Kgs 6, 15; Ez 41, 1.   v: 1 Kgs 6, 16f. 20; Ez 41, 3.   w: 10-13: 1 Kgs 6, 23-27.   x: Mt 27, 51.   y: 15ff: 1 Kgs 7, 15-22; Ez 40, 49.   z: Ez 43, 13-17.   a: 2-5: 1 Kgs 7, 23-26; Ez 43, 13.

circled the sea, ten to the cubit, all the way around; there were two rows of these cast in the same mold with the sea. ⁴It rested on twelve oxen, three facing north, three west, three south, and three east, with their haunches all toward the center; the sea rested on their backs. ⁵It was a handbreadth thick, and its brim was made like that of a cup, being lily-shaped. It had a capacity of three thousand measures.*

⁶Then he made ten basins for washing, placing five of them to the right and five to the left. Here were cleansed the victims for the holocausts; but the sea was for the priests to wash in.ᵇ

⁷He made the lampstands of gold, ten of them as was prescribed, and placed them in the nave, five to the right and five to the left.ᶜ ⁸He made ten tables and had them set in the nave, five to the right and five to the left; and he made a hundred golden bowls.ᵈ ⁹He made the court of the priests and the great courtyard and the gates of the courtyard; the gates he overlaid with bronze.ᵉ ¹⁰The sea was placed off to the southeast from the right side of the temple.ᶠ

¹¹ᵍHuram also made the pots, the shovels and the bowls. Huram thus completed the work he had to do for King Solomon in the house of God: ¹²two columns, two nodes for the capitals topping these two columns, and two networks covering the nodes of the capitals topping the columns; ¹³also four hundred pomegranates for the two networks, with two rows of pomegranates to each network, to cover the two nodes of the capitals topping the columns. ¹⁴He made the stands, and the basins on the stands; ¹⁵one sea, and the twelve oxen under it; ¹⁶likewise the pots, the shovels and the forks. Huram-abi made all these articles for King Solomon from polished bronze for the house of the LORD. ¹⁷The king had them cast in the Jordan region, in the clayey ground between Succoth

and Zeredah. ¹⁸Solomon made all these vessels, so many in number that the weight of the bronze was not ascertained.

¹⁹Solomon had all these articles made for the house of God: the golden altar, the tables on which the showbread lay, ²⁰the lampstands and their lamps of pure gold which were to burn according to prescription before the sanctuary, ²¹flowers, lamps and gold tongs [this was the purest gold], ²²snuffers, bowls, cups and firepans of pure gold. As for the entry to the house, its inner doors to the holy of holies, as well as the doors to the nave, were of gold.

CHAPTER 5

See RG 203

Dedication of the Temple. ¹ʰWhen all the work undertaken by Solomon for the temple of the LORD had been completed, he brought in the dedicated offerings of his father David, putting the silver, the gold and all the other articles in the treasuries of the house of God. ²At Solomon's order the elders of Israel and all the leaders of the tribes, the princes of the Israelite ancestral houses, came to Jerusalem to bring up the ark of the LORD's covenant from the City of David (which is Zion). ³All the men of Israel assembled before the king during the festival of the seventh month. ⁴ⁱWhen all the elders of Israel had arrived, the Levites* took up the ark, ⁵and they carried the ark and the meeting tent with all the sacred vessels that were in the tent; it was the levitical priests who carried them.

⁶King Solomon and the entire community of Israel gathered about him before the ark were sacrificing sheep and oxen so numerous that they could not be counted or numbered. ⁷The priests brought the ark of covenant of the LORD to its place beneath the wings of the cherubim in the sanctuary, the holy of holies of the temple. ⁸The cherubim had their wings spread out over the place of

---

4, 3: Oxen: in 1 Kgs 7, 24 this double row of ornaments is described as being gourds. The text of Kings available to the Chronicler may have been faulty on this point as the words are similar in sound. In 2 Chr 4, 16 the forks correspond in a similar way to bowls in the text of 1 Kings (7, 40).

4, 5: Three thousand measures: according to 1 Kgs 7, 26, "two thousand measures."

5, 4: The Levites: The parallel passage in 1 Kgs 8, 3 has the priests; but see 2 Chr 5, 5, where the Deuteronomic term levitical priests is used, as also in 2 Chr 23, 18; 30, 27.

b: 1 Kgs 7, 38f; Ez 40, 38. *c:* 1 Kgs 7, 49. *d:* 1 Kgs 7, 50; 1 Chr 28, 16. *e:* 1 Kgs 7, 12. *f:* 1 Kgs 7, 39. *g:* 11-22; 1 Kgs 7, 40-51. *h:* 1-14: 1 Kgs 7, 51-8, 13. *i:* 4f: 2 Chr 35, 3.

the ark, sheltering the ark and its poles from above. [9]The poles were long enough so that their ends could be seen from that part of the holy place nearest the sanctuary; however, they could not be seen beyond. The ark has remained there to this day.* [10]There was nothing in it but the two tablets which Moses put there on Horeb, the tablets of the covenant which the LORD made with the Israelites at their departure from Egypt.

[11]When the priests came out of the holy place (all the priests who were present had purified themselves without reference to the rotation of their various classes), [12]the Levites who were singers, all who belonged to Asaph, Heman, Jeduthun, and their sons and brothers, clothed in fine linen, with cymbals, harps and lyres, stood east of the altar, and with them a hundred and twenty priests blowing trumpets.

[13]When the trumpeters and singers were heard as a single voice praising and giving thanks to the LORD, and when they raised the sound of the trumpets, cymbals and other musical instruments to "give thanks to the LORD, for he is good, for his mercy endures forever," the building of the LORD's temple was filled with a cloud. [14]The priests could not continue to minister because of the cloud, since the LORD's glory filled the house of God.[j]

See RG 203

CHAPTER 6

[1][k]Then Solomon said: "The LORD intends to dwell in the dark cloud. [2]I have truly built you a princely house and dwelling, where you may abide forever." [31]Turning about, the king greeted the whole community of Israel as they stood. [4]He said: "Blessed be the LORD, the God of Israel, who with his own mouth made a promise to my father David and by his own hands brought it to fulfillment. He said: [5]'Since the day I brought my people out of the land of Egypt, I have not chosen any city from among all the tribes of Israel for the building

of a temple to my honor, nor have I chosen any man to be commander of my people Israel; [6]but now I choose Jerusalem, where I shall be honored, and I choose David to rule my people Israel.' [7]My father David wished to build a temple to the honor of the LORD, the God of Israel, [8]but the LORD said to him: 'In wishing to build a temple to my honor, you do well. [9]However, you shall not build the temple; rather, your son whom you will beget shall build the temple to my honor.'

[10]"Now the LORD has fulfilled the promise that he made. I have succeeded my father David and have taken my seat on the throne of Israel, as the LORD foretold, and I have built the temple to the honor of the LORD, the God of Israel. [11]And I have placed there the ark, in which abides the covenant of the LORD which he made with the Israelites."

Solomon's Prayer. [12][m]Solomon then took his place before the altar of the LORD in the presence of the whole community of Israel and stretched forth his hands. [13]He had made a bronze platform five cubits long, five cubits wide, and three cubits high, which he had placed in the middle of the courtyard. Having ascended it, Solomon knelt in the presence of the whole of Israel and stretched forth his hands toward heaven.* [14]Thus he prayed: "LORD, God of Israel, there is no god like you in heaven or on earth; you keep your covenant and show kindness to your servants who are wholeheartedly faithful to you. [15]You have kept the promise you made to my father David, your servant. With your own mouth you spoke it, and by your own hand you have brought it to fulfillment this day. [16]Now, therefore, LORD, God of Israel, keep the further promise you made to my father David, your servant, when you said, 'You shall always have someone from your line to sit before me on the throne of Israel, provided only that your descendants look to their conduct so as always to live according to my law, even as you have lived in my

---

5, 9: The ark has remained there to this day: the Chronicler must have copied this from his source (1 Kgs 8, 8) without reflecting that the ark was lost in the Babylonian destruction of Jerusalem; cf 2 Mc 2, 4-8.

6, 13: This verse is not found in the Chronicler's source; cf 1 Kgs 8, 22f. He has Solomon praying on a bronze plat-

form . . . in the middle of the courtyard because at the time of the Chronicler only the priests prayed before the altar.

[j]: 2 Chr 7, 2; 1 Kgs 8, 10f.   [k]: 1f: 1 Kgs 8, 12f.   [l]: 3-11: 1 Kgs 8, 14-21.   [m]: 12-41: 1 Kgs 8, 22-53.

presence.' *17*Now, LORD, God of Israel, may this promise which you made to your servant David be confirmed.

18"Can it indeed be that God dwells with mankind on earth? If the heavens and the highest heavens cannot contain you, how much less this temple which I have built! *19*Look kindly on the prayer and petition of your servant, O LORD, my God, and listen to the cry of supplication your servant makes before you. *20*May your eyes watch day and night over this temple, the place where you have decreed you shall be honored; may you heed the prayer which I your servant offer toward this place. *21*Listen to the petitions of your servant and of your people Israel which they direct toward this place. Listen from your heavenly dwelling, and when you have heard, pardon.

22"When any man sins against his neighbor and is required to take an oath of execration against himself, and when he comes for the oath before your altar in this temple, *23*listen from heaven: take action and pass judgment on your servants, requiting the wicked man and holding him responsible for his conduct, but absolving the innocent and rewarding him according to his virtue. *24*When your people Israel have sinned against you and are defeated by the enemy, but afterward they return and praise your name, and they pray to you and entreat you in this temple, *25*listen from heaven and forgive the sin of your people Israel, and bring them back to the land which you gave them and their fathers. *26*When the sky is closed so that there is no rain, because they have sinned against you, but then they pray toward this place and praise your name, and they withdraw from sin because you afflict them, *27*listen in heaven and forgive the sin of your servants and of your people Israel. But teach them the right way to live, and send rain upon your land which you gave your people as their heritage. *28*When there is famine in the land, when there is pestilence, or blight, or mildew, or locusts, or caterpillars; when their enemies besiege them at any of their gates; whenever there is a plague or sickness of any kind; *29*when any Israelite of all your people offers a prayer or petition of any kind, and in awareness of his affliction and pain, stretches out his hands toward this temple, *30*listen from your heavenly dwelling place, and forgive. Knowing his heart, render to everyone according to his conduct, for you alone know the hearts of men. *31*So may they fear you and walk in your ways as long as they live on the land you gave our fathers.

32"For the foreigner, too, who is not of your people Israel, when he comes from a distant land to honor your great name, your mighty power, and your outstretched arm, when they come in prayer to this temple, *33*listen from your heavenly dwelling place, and do whatever the foreigner entreats you, that all the peoples of the earth may know your name, fearing you as do your people Israel, and knowing that this house which I have built is dedicated to your honor.

34"When your people go forth to war against their enemies, wherever you send them, and pray to you in the direction of this city and of the house I have built to your honor, *35*listen from heaven to their prayer and petition, and defend their cause. *36*When they sin against you (for there is no man who does not sin), and in your anger against them you deliver them to the enemy, so that their captors deport them to another land, far or near, *37*when they repent in the land where they are captive and are converted, when they entreat you in the land of their captivity and say, 'We have sinned and done wrong; we have been wicked,' *38*and with their whole heart and with their whole soul they turn back to you in the land of those who hold them captive, when they pray in the direction of their land which you gave their fathers, and of the city you have chosen, and of the house which I have built to your honor, *39*listen from your heavenly dwelling place, hear their prayer and petitions, and uphold their cause. Forgive your people who have sinned against you. *40*My God, may your eyes be open and your ears attentive to the prayer of this place. *41*And now,

"Advance, LORD God, to your resting
   place,
  you and the ark of your majesty.

May your priests, LORD God, be clothed
  with salvation,
  may your faithful ones rejoice in good
    things.
42 LORD God, reject not the plea of your
  anointed,
  remember the devotion of David, your
    servant."

CHAPTER 7

See RG
203

[1]n When Solomon had ended his
prayer, fire came down from heaven and
consumed the holocaust and the sacrifices,
and the glory of the LORD filled the house.
[2]But the priests could not enter the house of
the LORD, for the glory of the LORD had
filled the house of the LORD.[o] [3]All the Israelites looked on while the fire came down
and the glory of the LORD was upon the
house, and they fell down upon the pavement with their faces to the earth and adored,
praising the LORD, "for he is good, for his
mercy endures forever." [4]The king and all
the people were offering sacrifices before
the LORD.[p] [5]King Solomon offered as sacrifice twenty-two thousand oxen, and one
hundred twenty thousand sheep.[q]

End of the Dedication. [6]Thus the king
and all the people dedicated the house of
God. The priests were standing at their stations, as were the Levites, with the musical
instruments of the LORD which King David
had made for "praising the LORD, for his
mercy endures forever," when David used
them to accompany the hymns. Across from
them the priests blew the trumpets and all Israel stood.[r]

[7]Then Solomon consecrated the middle
part of the court which lay before the house
of the LORD; there he offered the holocausts
and the fat of the peace offerings, since the
bronze altar which Solomon had made could
not hold the holocausts, the cereal offerings
and the fat.[s]

[8]On this occasion Solomon and with him
all Israel, who had assembled in very large
numbers from Labo of Hamath to the Wadi
of Egypt, celebrated the festival for seven
days.[t] [9]u On the eighth day they held a special
meeting, for they had celebrated the dedication of the altar for seven days and the feast*
for seven days. [10]On the twenty-third day of
the seventh month he sent the people back to
their tents, rejoicing and glad at heart at the
good things the LORD had done for David,
for Solomon, and for his people Israel.
[11]v Solomon completed the house of the
LORD and the royal palace; he successfully
accomplished everything he had planned to
do in regard to the house of the LORD and his
own house.

God's Promise to Solomon. [12]The LORD
appeared to Solomon during the night and
said to him: "I have heard your prayer, and I
have chosen this place for my house of sacrifice. [13]If I close heaven so that there is no
rain, if I command the locust to devour the
land, if I send pestilence among my people,
[14]and if my people, upon whom my name has
been pronounced, humble themselves and
pray, and seek my presence and turn from
their evil ways, I will hear them from heaven
and pardon their sins and revive their land.
[15]Now my eyes shall be open and my ears attentive to the prayer of this place. [16]And now
I have chosen and consecrated this house that
my name may be there forever; my eyes and
my heart also shall be there always.

[17]"As for you, if you live in my presence
as your father David did, doing all that I
have commanded you and keeping my statutes and ordinances, [18]I will establish your
royal throne as I covenanted with your father
David when I said, 'There shall never be
lacking someone of yours as ruler in Israel.'
[19]But if you turn away and forsake my statutes and commands which I placed before
you, if you proceed to venerate and worship

7, 9f: The feast: of Booths, celebrated on the fifteenth day of the seventh month and followed by a solemn octave lasting
through the twenty-second day (Lv 23, 33-36; Nm 29, 12-35); the people are therefore sent home on the twenty-third day (v
10). The festival (v 8) for the dedication of the altar and of the temple lasted for seven days before the feast of Booths, from
the seventh to the fourteenth day. According to 1 Kgs 8, 65f, the people are dismissed at the end of these seven days.

n: 1-10: 1 Kgs 8, 54-66; Jgs 6, 21; 1 Chr 21, 26; 2 Mc 2, 10.   *o:* 2 Chr 5, 14; Ex 24, 16; 1 Kgs 8, 10f.   *p:* 2 Chr 5, 13; 1 Kgs 8, 62; Ps
136, 1.   *q:* 1 Kgs 8, 62f.   *r:* Nm 10, 8. 10; Ps 136, 1.   *s:* 1 Kgs 8, 64.   *t:* 1 Kgs 8, 65.   *u:* 9f: 1 Kgs 8, 66.   *v:* 11-22: 1 Kgs 9, 1-9.

strange gods, [20]then I will uproot the people from the land I gave them; I will cast from my sight this house which I have consecrated to my honor, and I will make it a proverb and a byword among all peoples. [21]This temple which is so exalted—everyone passing by it will be amazed and ask: 'Why has the LORD done this to this land and to this house?' [22]And men will answer: 'They forsook the LORD, the God of their fathers, who brought them out of the land of Egypt, and they adopted strange gods and worshiped them and served them. That is why he has brought down upon them all this evil.' "

CHAPTER 8

See RG 203

Public Works. [1w]After the twenty years during which Solomon built the house of the LORD and his own house, [2]he built up the cities which Huram had given him,* and settled Israelites there. [3]Then Solomon went to Hamath of Zoba and conquered it. [4]He built Tadmor* in the desert region and all the supply cities, which he built in Hamath. [5x]He built Upper Beth-horon and Lower Beth-horon, fortified cities with walls, gates and bars; [6]also Baalath, all the supply cities belonging to Solomon, and all the cities for the chariots, the cities for the horsemen, and whatever else Solomon decided should be built in Jerusalem, in the Lebanon, and in the entire land under his dominion. [7]All the people that remained of the Hittites, Amorites, Perizzites, Hivites, and Jebusites, who were not of Israel— [8]that is, their descendants remaining in the land, whom the Israelites had not destroyed—Solomon subjected to forced labor, as they continue to this day. [9]But Solomon did not enslave the Israelites for his works. They became soldiers, commanders of his warriors, and commanders of his chariots and his horsemen. [10]They were also King Solomon's two hundred and fifty overseers who had charge of the people.

Solomon's Piety. [11]Solomon brought the daughter of Pharaoh up from the City of David to the palace which he had built for her, for he said, "No wife of mine shall dwell in the house of David, king of Israel, for the places where the ark of the LORD has come are holy."

[12]In those times Solomon offered holocausts to the LORD upon the altar of the LORD which he had built in front of the porch, [13]as was required day by day according to the command of Moses, and in particular on the sabbaths, at the new moons, and on the fixed festivals three times a year: on the feast of the Unleavened Bread, the feast of Weeks and the feast of Booths.[y]

[14]And according to the ordinance of his father David he appointed the various classes of the priests for their service, and the Levites according to their functions of praise and ministry alongside the priests, as the daily duty required. The gatekeepers of the various classes stood guard at each gate, since such was the command of David, the man of God.[z] [15]There was no deviation from the king's command in any respect relating to the priests and Levites or the treasuries. [16]All of Solomon's work was carried out successfully from the day the foundation of the house of the LORD was laid until the house of the LORD had been completed in every detail.

Glories of the Court. [17]In those times Solomon went to Ezion-geber and to Elath on the seashore of the land of Edom.[a] [18]Huram, through his servants, sent him ships and crewmen acquainted with the sea, who accompanied Solomon's servants to Ophir and brought back from there four hundred and fifty talents of gold to King Solomon.[b]

CHAPTER 9

See RG 203

[1]When the queen of Sheba heard of Solomon's fame, she came to Jerusalem to test him with subtle questions, accompanied

---

8, 2: The cities which Huram had given him: according to 1 Kgs 9, 10-14, Solomon had ceded the cities as payment for the timber and gold received from Tyre. But since Huram was dissatisfied, he may have returned the cities to Solomon.

8, 4: Tadmor: later known as Palmyra, an important caravan city in the Syrian desert. The parallel passage in 1 Kgs 9,

18 has Tamar, in southern Judah; cf Ez 47, 19; 48, 28. But Solomon may well have fortified Tadmor against the Arameans.

---

w: 1f: 1 Kgs 9, 10f.   *x:* 5-12: 1 Kgs 9, 18-25.   *y:* 1 Kgs 9, 25; Ex 23, 14; Nm 28—29.   *z:* 1 Chr 23—26; Neh 12, 46.   *a:* 1 Kgs 9, 26; Mt 12, 42; Lk 11, 31.   *b:* 1 Kgs 9, 27f.

The Kingdom of Solomon according to 2 Chronicles

478

by a very numerous retinue and by camels bearing spices, much gold, and precious stones. She came to Solomon and questioned him on every subject in which she was interested.^{c} ^{2}Solomon explained to her everything she asked about, and there remained nothing hidden from Solomon that he could not explain to her.

^{3}When the queen of Sheba witnessed Solomon's wisdom, the palace he had built, ^{4}the food at his table, the seating of his ministers, the attendance of his servants and their dress, his cupbearers and their dress, and the holocausts he offered in the house of the LORD, it took her breath away. ^{5}"The account I heard in my country about your deeds and your wisdom is true," she told the king. ^{6}"Yet I did not believe the report until I came and saw with my own eyes. I have discovered that they did not tell me the half of your great wisdom; you have surpassed the stories I heard. ^{7}Happy are your men, happy these servants of yours, who stand before you always and listen to your wisdom. ^{8}Blessed be the LORD, your God, who has been so pleased with you as to place you on his throne as king for the LORD, your God. Because your God has so loved Israel as to will to make it last forever, he has appointed you over them as king to administer right and justice." ^{9}Then she gave the king one hundred and twenty gold talents and a very large quantity of spices, as well as precious stones. There was no other spice like that which the queen of Sheba gave to King Solomon.

^{10}The servants of Huram and of Solomon who brought gold from Ophir also brought cabinet wood and precious stones. ^{11}With the cabinet wood the king made stairs for the temple of the LORD and the palace of the king; also lyres and harps for the chanters. The like of these had not been seen before in the land of Judah.

^{12}King Solomon gave the queen of Sheba everything she desired and asked him for, more than she had brought to the king. Then she returned to her own country with her servants.

^{13d}The gold that Solomon received each year weighed six hundred and sixty-six gold talents, ^{14}in addition to what was collected from travelers and what the merchants brought. All the kings of Arabia also, and the governors of the country, brought gold and silver to Solomon.

^{15}Moreover, King Solomon made two hundred large shields of beaten gold, six hundred shekels of beaten gold going into each shield, ^{16}and three hundred bucklers of beaten gold, three hundred shekels of gold going into each buckler; these the king put in the hall of the Forest of Lebanon.

^{17}King Solomon also made a large ivory throne which he overlaid with fine gold. ^{18}The throne had six steps; a footstool of gold was fastened to it, and there was an arm on each side of the seat, with two lions standing beside the arms. ^{19}Twelve other lions also stood there, one on either side of each step. Nothing like this had ever been produced in any other kingdom. ^{20}Furthermore, all of King Solomon's drinking vessels were of gold, and all the utensils in the hall of the Forest of Lebanon were of pure gold; silver was not considered of value in Solomon's time. ^{21}For the king had ships that went to Tarshish with the servants of Huram. Once every three years the fleet of Tarshish would return with a cargo of gold and silver, ivory, apes and monkeys. ^{22}Thus King Solomon surpassed all the other kings of the earth in riches as well as in wisdom.

^{23}All the kings of the earth sought audience with Solomon, to hear from him the wisdom which God had put in his heart. ^{24}Year in and year out, each one would bring his tribute—silver and gold articles, garments, weapons, spices, horses and mules. ^{25}Solomon also had four thousand stalls of horses, chariots, and twelve thousand horsemen, which he assigned to the chariot cities and to the king in Jerusalem. ^{26}He was ruler over all the kings from the River to the land of the Philistines and down to the border of Egypt. ^{27}The king made silver as common in Jerusalem as stones, while cedars became as numerous as the sycamores of the foothills.

c: 1 Kgs 10, 1f; Mt 12, 42; Lk 11, 31.   d: 13-28: 1 Kgs 10, 14-28.

479

²⁸Horses were imported for Solomon from Egypt and from all the lands.*

The Death of Solomon. ²⁹ᵉThe rest of the acts of Solomon, first and last, are written, as is well known, in the acts of Nathan the prophet, in the prophecy of Ahijah the Shilonite, and in the visions of Iddo the seer which concern Jeroboam, son of Nebat. ³⁰Solomon reigned in Jerusalem over all Israel for forty years. ³¹He rested with his ancestors; he was buried in his father's City of David, and his son Rehoboam succeeded him as king.

II: The Monarchy before Hezekiah

CHAPTER 10

See RG
203–4

Division of the Kingdom. ¹ᶠRehoboam went to Shechem, for all Israel* had come to Shechem to proclaim him king. ²When Jeroboam, son of Nebat, heard of this in Egypt where he had fled from King Solomon, he returned from Egypt. ³Jeroboam was summoned to the assembly, and he and all Israel said to Rehoboam: ⁴"Your father laid a heavy yoke upon us. If you now lighten the harsh service and the heavy yoke that your father imposed on us, we will serve you." ⁵"In three days," he answered them, "come back to me."

When the people had departed, ⁶King Rehoboam consulted the elders who had been in the service of his father during Solomon's lifetime, asking, "What answer do you advise me to give this people?" ⁷They replied, "If you will deal kindly with this people and give in to them, acceding to their request, they will be your servants forever." ⁸But he ignored the advice the elders had given him and consulted the young men who had grown up with him and were in his service. ⁹He said to them, "What answer do you advise me to give this people, who have asked me to lighten the yoke my father imposed on them?" ¹⁰The young men who had grown up with him replied: "This is the answer you should give to this people who have said to you, 'Your father laid a heavy yoke upon us, but do you lighten our yoke'; this you should say to them: 'My little finger is thicker than my father's body. ¹¹Whereas my father put a heavy yoke on you, I will make it heavier! My father beat you with whips, but I will beat you with scorpions!"

¹²On the third day, Jeroboam and all the people came back to King Rehoboam as he had instructed them to do. ¹³Ignoring the advice the elders had given him, the king gave them a harsh answer, ¹⁴speaking to them according to the advice of the young men: "My father laid a heavy yoke on you, but I will make it heavier. My father beat you with whips, but I will beat you with scorpions." ¹⁵The king would not listen to the people, for this turn of events was divinely ordained to fulfill the prophecy the LORD had uttered to Jeroboam, the son of Nebat, through Ahijah the Shilonite.ᵍ

¹⁶ʰWhen all Israel saw that the king would not listen to them, the people answered the king,

"What share have we in David?
  We have no heritage in the son of
    Jesse.
Everyone to your tents, O Israel!
  Now look to your own house, David!"

So all Israel went off to their tents. ¹⁷Rehoboam, therefore, reigned over only those Israelites who lived in the cities of Judah. ¹⁸King Rehoboam then sent out Hadoram, who was superintendent of the forced labor, but the Israelites stoned him to death. Rehoboam himself managed to mount his chariot and flee to Jerusalem. ¹⁹Thus Israel has been in rebellion against David's house to this day.

CHAPTER 11

See RG
203–4

¹ⁱOn his arrival in Jerusalem Rehoboam gathered together the house of Judah and Benjamin, a hundred and eighty thousand seasoned warriors, to have them fight

9, 28: See note on 2 Chr 1, 16f.

10, 1: All Israel: as in the original source (1 Kgs 12, 1), the northern tribes, distinct from Judah and Benjamin. Contrast the Chronicler's own terms, those Israelites who lived in the cities of Judah (v 17), and all the Israelites [literally, all Israel] in Judah and Benjamin (2 Chr 11, 3).

e: 29ff: 1 Kgs 11, 41ff.   f: 1-14: 1 Kgs 12, 1-14.   g: 1 Kgs 11, 29-39; 12, 15.   h: 16-19: 1 Kgs 12, 16-19.   i: 1-4: 1 Kgs 12, 21-24.

against Israel and restore the kingdom to him. ²However, the word of the LORD came to Shemiah, a man of God: ³"Say to Rehoboam, son of Solomon, king of Judah, and to all the Israelites in Judah and Benjamin: ⁴'Thus says the LORD: You must not march out to fight against your brothers. Let every man return home, for what has occurred I have brought about.' " They obeyed this message of the LORD and gave up the expedition against Jeroboam.

Rehoboam's Works.* ⁵Rehoboam took up residence in Jerusalem and built fortified cities in Judah. ⁶He built up Bethlehem, Etam, Tekoa, ⁷Beth-zur, Soco, Adullam, ⁸Gath, Mareshah, Ziph, ⁹Adoraim, Lachish, Azekah, ¹⁰Zorah, Aijalon, and Hebron; these were fortified cities in Judah and Benjamin. ¹¹Then he strengthened the fortifications and put commanders in them, with supplies of food, oil and wine. ¹²In every city were shields and spears, and he made them very strong. Thus Judah and Benjamin remained his.

Refugees from the North. ¹³Now the priests and Levites throughout Israel presented themselves to him from all parts of their land, ¹⁴for the Levites left their assigned pasture lands and their holdings and came to Judah and Jerusalem, because Jeroboam and his sons repudiated them as priests of the LORD.ʲ ¹⁵In their place, he himself appointed priests for the high places and satyrs and calves he had made.ᵏ ¹⁶After them, all those of the Israelite tribes who firmly desired to seek the LORD, the God of Israel, came to Jerusalem to sacrifice to the LORD, the God of their fathers. ¹⁷Thus they strengthened the kingdom of Judah and made Rehoboam, son of Solomon, prevail for three years; for they walked in the way of David and Solomon three years.

Rehoboam's Family. ¹⁸Rehoboam took to himself as wife Mahalath, daughter of Jerimoth, son of David and of Abihail, daughter of Eliab, son of Jesse. ¹⁹She bore him sons: Jehush, Shemariah and Zaham. ²⁰After her,

he married Maacah, daughter of Absalom, who bore him Abijah, Attai, Ziza and Shelomith.ˡ ²¹Rehoboam loved Maacah, daughter of Absalom, more than all his other wives and concubines; he had taken eighteen wives and sixty concubines, and he fathered twenty-eight sons and sixty daughters. ²²Rehoboam constituted Abijah, son of Maacah, commander among his brothers, for he intended to make him king. ²³He acted prudently, distributing various of his sons throughout all the districts of Judah and Benjamin, in all the fortified cities; and he furnished them with copious provisions and sought an abundance of wives for them.

CHAPTER 12

See RG 203–4

His Apostasy. ¹After Rehoboam had consolidated his rule and had become powerful, he abandoned the law of the LORD, he and all Israel with him.ᵐ ²Thus it happened that in the fifth year of King Rehoboam, Shishak, king of Egypt, attacked Jerusalem, for they had been unfaithful to the LORD.ⁿ ³He came up with twelve hundred chariots and sixty thousand horsemen, and there was no counting the army that came with him from Egypt—Libyans, Sukkites* and Ethiopians. ⁴They captured the fortified cities of Judah and came as far as Jerusalem. ⁵Then Shemaiah the prophet came to Rehoboam and the commanders of Judah who had gathered at Jerusalem because of Shishak, and said to them: "Thus says the LORD: 'You have abandoned me, and therefore I have abandoned you to the power of Shishak.' "ᵒ

⁶However, the commanders of Israel and the king humbled themselves, saying, "The LORD is just." ⁷When the LORD saw that they had humbled themselves, the word of the LORD came to Shemaiah: "Because they have humbled themselves, I will not destroy them; I will give them some deliverance, and my wrath shall not be poured out upon Jerusalem through Shishak. ⁸But they shall be his servants, that they may know what it is to serve me and what it is to serve earthly

11, 5-12: These verses, though not found in 1 Kgs, are apparently based on a reliable, ancient source.
12, 3: Sukkites: foreign mercenaries in the Egyptian army.

j: 1 Kgs 12, 32. *k:* 1 Kgs 12, 32; Lv 17, 7. *l:* 1 Kgs 15, 2. *m:* 1 Kgs 11, 4; 14, 22. *n:* 1 Kgs 14, 25. *o:* 2 Chr 11, 2.

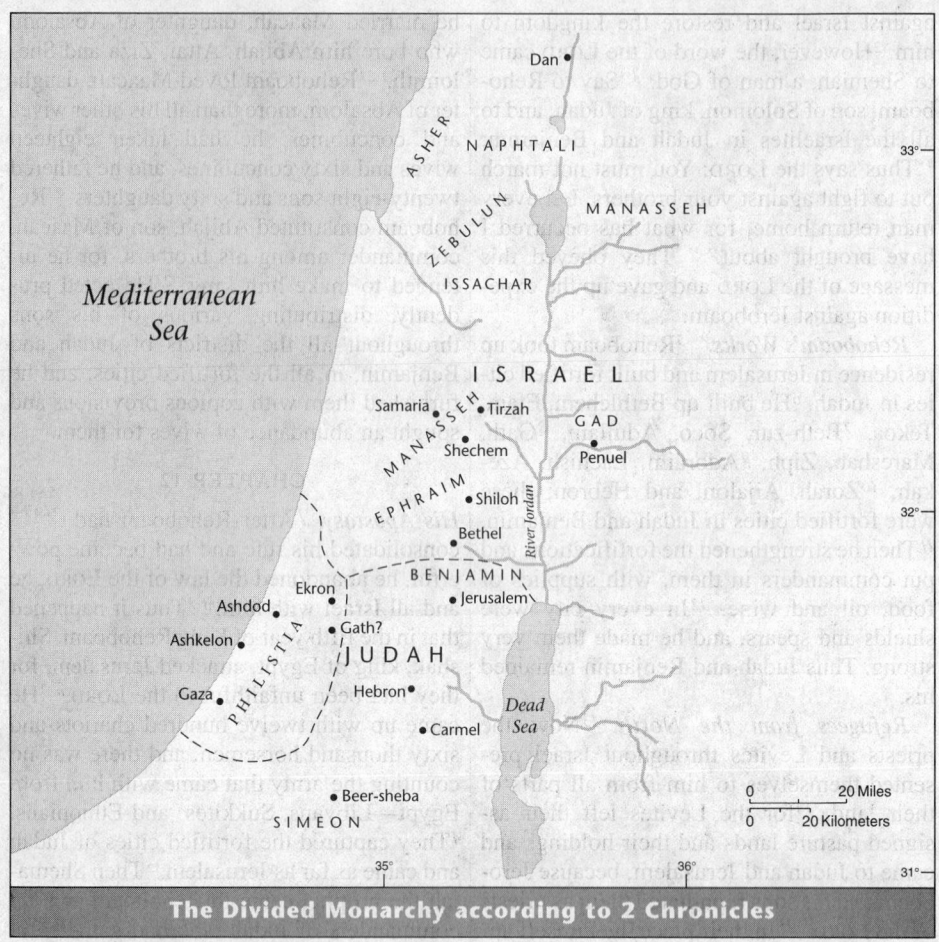

Mediterranean
Sea

The Divided Monarchy according to 2 Chronicles

kingdoms." ⁹^pTherefore Shishak, king of Egypt, attacked Jerusalem and carried off the treasures of the temple of the LORD and of the king's palace. He took everything, including the gold bucklers that Solomon had made. ¹⁰(To replace them, King Rehoboam made bronze bucklers, which he entrusted to the officers of the guard on duty at the entrance of the royal palace. ¹¹Whenever the king visited the temple of the LORD, the troops would come bearing them, and then they would return them to the guardroom.) ¹²Because he had humbled himself, the anger of the LORD turned from him so that it did not destroy him completely; and in Judah, moreover, good deeds were found.

¹³King Rehoboam consolidated his power in Jerusalem and continued to rule; he was forty-one years old when he became king, and he reigned seventeen years in Jerusalem, the city in which, out of all the tribes of Israel, the LORD chose to be honored. Rehoboam's mother was named Naamah, an Ammonite.^q ¹⁴He did evil, for he had not truly resolved to seek the LORD. ¹⁵^rThe acts of Rehoboam, first and last, are written, as is well known, in the history of Shemaiah the prophet and of Iddo the seer [his family record]. There was war continually between Rehoboam and Jeroboam. ¹⁶Rehoboam rested with his ancestors; he was buried in the City of David. His son Abijah succeeded him as king.

p: 9ff: 1 Kgs 14, 25-28.   q: 1 Kgs 14, 21.   r: 15f: 1 Kgs 14, 29ff.

482

See RG
203-4

CHAPTER 13

War between Abijah and Jeroboam.
¹ˢIn the eighteenth year of King Jeroboam, Abijah became king of Judah; ²he reigned three years in Jerusalem. His mother was named Michaiah, daughter of Uriel of Gibeah. There was war between Abijah and Jeroboam.

³Abijah joined battle with a force of four hundred thousand picked warriors, while Jeroboam lined up against him in battle with eight hundred thousand picked and valiant warriors. ⁴*Abijah stood on Mount Zemaraim, which is in the highlands of Ephraim, and said: "Listen to me, Jeroboam and all Israel! ⁵Do you not know that the LORD, the God of Israel, has given the kingdom of Israel to David forever, to him and to his sons, by a covenant made in salt? ⁶Yet Jeroboam, son of Nebat, the servant of Solomon, son of David, has stood up and rebelled against his lord!ᵗ ⁷Worthless men, scoundrels, joined him and overcame Rehoboam, son of Solomon, when Rehoboam was young and unthinking, and no match for them. ⁸But now, do you think you are a match for the kingdom of the LORD commanded by the sons of David, simply because you are a huge multitude and have with you the golden calves which Jeroboam made you for gods? ⁹"Have you not expelled the priests of the LORD, the sons of Aaron, and the Levites, and made for yourselves priests like the peoples of foreign lands? Everyone who comes to consecrate himself with a young bull and seven rams becomes a priest of no-gods. ¹⁰But as for us, the LORD is our God, and we have not forsaken him. The priests ministering to the LORD are sons of Aaron, and the Levites also have their offices. ¹¹They burn holocausts to the LORD and fragrant incense morning after morning and evening after evening; they display the showbread on the pure table, and the lamps of the golden lampstand burn evening after evening; for we observe our duties to the LORD, our God,

but you have abandoned him. ¹²See, God is with us, at our head, and his priests are here with trumpets to sound the attack against you. Do not battle against the LORD, the God of your fathers, O Israelites, for you will not succeed!"

¹³But Jeroboam had an ambush go around them to come at them from the rear; so that while his army faced Judah, his ambush lay behind them. ¹⁴When Judah turned and saw that they had to battle on both fronts, they cried out to the LORD and the priests sounded the trumpets. ¹⁵Then the men of Judah shouted; and when they did so, God defeated Jeroboam and all Israel before Abijah and Judah. ¹⁶The Israelites fled before Judah, and God delivered them into their hands. ¹⁷Abijah and his people inflicted a severe defeat upon them; five hundred thousand picked men of Israel fell slain. ¹⁸The Israelites were subdued on that occasion and the Judahites were victorious because they relied on the LORD, the God of their fathers. ¹⁹Abijah pursued Jeroboam and took cities from him: Bethel and its dependencies, Jeshanah and its dependencies, and Ephron and its dependencies. ²⁰Jeroboam did not regain power during the time of Abijah; the LORD struck him down and he died, ²¹while Abijah continued to grow stronger. He took to himself fourteen wives and fathered twenty-two sons and sixteen daughters.

Death of Abijah. ²²ᵘThe rest of Abijah's acts, his deeds and his words, are written in the midrash of the prophet Iddo. ²³Abijah rested with his ancestors; they buried him in the City of David. His son Asa succeeded him as king. During his time, ten years of peace began in the land.

CHAPTER 14

See RG
203-4

Asa the Reformer. ¹ᵛAsa did what was good and pleasing to the LORD, his God, ²removing the heathen altars and the high places, breaking to pieces the sacred pillars, and cutting down the sacred poles. ³He commanded Judah to seek the LORD, the God of

13, 4-12: This is a free composition of the Chronicler to show that this was a religious, rather than a political, war.

s: 1f: 1 Kgs 15, 1f. t: 1 Kgs 11, 26. u: 22f: 2 Chr 12, 15; 1 Kgs 7ff. v: 1f: 2 Chr 33, 15; Ex 23, 24; 34, 13; 1 Kgs 15, 11f.

their fathers, and to observe the law and its commands. *4*He removed the high places and incense stands from all the cities of Judah, and under him the kingdom had peace. *5*He built fortified cities in Judah, for the land had peace and no war was waged against him during these years, because the LORD had given him peace. *6*He said to Judah: "Let us build these cities and surround them with walls, towers, gates and bars. The land is still ours, for we have sought the LORD, our God; we sought him, and he has given us rest on every side." So they built and prospered.

The Ethiopian Invasion.* *7*Asa had an army of three hundred thousand shield- and lance-bearers from Judah, and two hundred and eighty thousand from Benjamin who carried bucklers and were archers, all of them valiant warriors. *8*Zerah the Ethiopian moved against them with a force of one million men and three hundred chariots, and he came as far as Mareshah.*w* *9*Asa went out to meet him and set himself in battle array in the valley of Zephathah, near Mareshah. *10*Asa called upon the LORD, his God, praying: "O LORD, there is none like you to help the powerless against the strong. Help us, O LORD, our God, for we rely on you, and in your name we have come against this multitude. You are the LORD, our God; let no man prevail against you."*x* *11*And so the LORD defeated the Ethiopians before Asa and Judah, and they fled.*y* *12*Asa and those with him pursued them as far as Gerar, and the Ethiopians fell until there were no survivors, for they were crushed before the LORD and his army, which carried away enormous spoils. *13*Then the Judahites conquered all the cities around Gerar, for the fear of the LORD was upon them; they despoiled all the cities, for there was much booty in them. *14*They attacked also the tents of the cattle-herders and carried off a great number of sheep and camels. Then they returned to Jerusalem.

CHAPTER 15

See RG 203–4

Cult Reform. *1*Upon Azariah, son of Oded, came the spirit of God. *2*He went forth to meet Asa and said to him: "Hear me, Asa and all Judah and Benjamin! The LORD is with you when you are with him, and if you seek him he will be present to you; but if you abandon him, he will abandon you.*z* *3*For a long time Israel had no true God, no priest-teacher and no law, *4*but when in their distress they turned to the LORD, the God of Israel, and sought him, he was present to them.*a* *5*In that former time there was no place for anyone to go or come, but there were many terrors upon the inhabitants of the lands. *6*Nation crushed nation and city crushed city, for God destroyed them by every kind of adversity.*b* *7*But as for you, be strong and do not relax, for your work shall be rewarded."*c*

*8*When Asa heard these words and the prophecy [Oded the prophet], he was encouraged to remove the detestable idols from the whole land of Judah and Benjamin and from the cities he had taken in the highlands of Ephraim, and to restore the altar of the LORD which was before the vestibule of the LORD. *9*Then he convened all Judah and Benjamin, together with those of Ephraim, Manasseh and Simeon who sojourned with them; for many had fled to him from Israel when they saw that the LORD, his God, was with him. *10**They gathered at Jerusalem in the third month of the fifteenth year of Asa's reign, *11*and sacrificed to the LORD at that time seven hundred oxen and seven thousand sheep of the booty they had brought. *12*They entered into a covenant to seek the LORD, the God of their fathers, with all their heart and soul; *13*and everyone who would not seek the LORD, the God of Israel, was to be put to death, whether small or great, whether man or woman.*d* *14*They swore to the LORD with a loud voice, with shouting

---

14, 7-14: An Ethiopian invasion of Judah is mentioned only in 1 Chronicles. This account may be a legend contrived to show how the pious King Asa was rewarded through divine assistance. There may, however, have been an incursion of nomads from the Negeb at this time; cf vv 13f.

15, 10ff: With this description of a covenant ceremony in the third month of a year beginning in the spring, the Chronicler lays a foundation for celebrating the ancient feast of

Pentecost (Weeks) as the time for a solemn renewal of the people's covenant with God on Mount Sinai; see Ex 19, 1ff; Lv 23, 16 and the note there. This is also the background for Pentecost as the "birthday of the Church."

w: 2 Chr 16, 8. *x:* 2 Chr 32, 8. *y:* Pss 20, 7f; 60, 11f. *z:* Jer 29, 13f; Hos 3, 4f. *a:* Dt 4, 29f. *b:* Is 19, 2. *c:* Is 7, 4; Jer 31, 16. *d:* Neh 10, 30.

and with trumpets and horns. *15* All Judah rejoiced over the oath, for they had sworn with their whole heart and sought him with complete desire, so that he was present to them. And the LORD gave them rest on every side.*e*

16f Maacah, the mother of King Asa, he deposed as queen mother because she had made an outrageous object for Asherah; Asa cut this down, smashed it, and burnt it in the Kidron Valley. *17* Although the high places did not disappear from Israel, yet Asa's heart was undivided as long as he lived. *18* He brought into the house of God his father's votive offerings and his own: silver, gold, and various utensils. *19* There was no war until the thirty-fifth year of Asa's reign.

CHAPTER 16

See RG
203-4

Asa's Infidelity. *18* In the thirty-sixth year of Asa's reign, Baasha, king of Israel, attacked Judah and fortified Ramah to prevent any communication with Asa, king of Judah. *2* Asa then brought out silver and gold from the treasuries of the temple of the LORD and of the royal palace and sent them to Ben-hadad, king of Aram, who lived in Damascus, with this message: *3* "There is a treaty between you and me, as there was between your father and my father. See, I am sending you silver and gold. Go, break your treaty with Baasha, king of Israel, that he may withdraw from me." *4* Ben-hadad agreed to King Asa's request and sent the leaders of his troops against the cities of Israel. They attacked Ijon, Dan, Abel-maim, and all the store cities of Naphtali. *5* When Baasha heard of it, he left off fortifying Ramah; he stopped his work. *6* Then King Asa commandeered all of Judah to carry away the stone and wood with which Baasha had been fortifying Ramah, and with them he fortified Geba and Mizpah.

7 At that time Hanani the seer came to Asa, king of Judah, and said to him: "Because you relied on the king of Aram and did not rely on the LORD, your God, the army of the king of Aram has escaped* your hand. *8* Were not the Ethiopians and Libyans a vast army, with great numbers of chariots and drivers? And yet, because you relied on the LORD, he delivered them into your power.*h* *9* The eyes of the LORD roam over the whole earth, to encourage those who are devoted to him wholeheartedly. You have acted foolishly in this matter, for from now on you will have wars."*i* *10* But Asa became angry with the seer and imprisoned him in the stocks, so greatly was he enraged at him over this. Asa also oppressed some of his people at this time.

11j Now the acts of Asa, first and last, can be found recorded in the book of the kings of Judah and Israel. *12* In the thirty-ninth year of his reign, Asa contracted a serious disease in his feet. But even in his sickness he did not seek the LORD, but only the physicians. *13* Asa rested with his ancestors; he died in the forty-first year of his reign. *14* They buried him in the tomb he had hewn for himself in the City of David, having laid him upon a couch which was filled with spices and various kinds of aromatics compounded into an ointment. They also burned a very great funeral pyre for him.

CHAPTER 17

See RG
203-4

Zeal of Jehoshaphat for the Law. *1* His son Jehoshaphat succeeded him as king and strengthened his hold against Israel.*k* *2* He placed armed forces in all the fortified cities of Judah, and put garrisons in the land of Judah and in the cities of Ephraim which his father Asa had taken. *3* The LORD was with Jehoshaphat,* for he walked in the ways his father had pursued in the beginning, and he did not consult the Baals. *4* Rather, he sought the God of his father and observed his commands, and not the practices of Israel. *5* As a result, the LORD made his kingdom secure, and all Judah gave Je-

---

16, 7: The king of Aram . . . escaped: according to the Lucianic recension, "the king of Israel escaped": this may well be the original reading; Asa was friendly with Aram.

17, 3: The Lord was with Jehoshaphat: along with Hezekiah and Josiah, Jehoshaphat was one of the Chronicler's favorite kings.

---

e: Dt 4, 29. *f:* 16ff: 1 Kgs 15, 13ff. *g:* 1-6: 1 Kgs 15, 16-21. *h:* 2 Chr 14, 8-14. *i:* Ps 33, 13ff. *j:* 11-14: 1 Kgs 15, 23f. *k:* 1 Kgs 15, 24.

hoshaphat gifts, so that he enjoyed great wealth and glory. [6]Thus he was encouraged to follow the LORD's ways, and again he removed the high places and the sacred poles from Judah.[l]

[7]In the third year of his reign he sent his leading men, Ben-hail, Obadiah, Zechariah, Nethanel and Micaiah, to teach in the cities of Judah. [8]With them he sent the Levites Shemaiah, Nethaniah, Zebadiah, Asahel, Shemiramoth, Jehonathan, Adonijah and Tobijah, together with the priests Elishama and Jehoram.[m] [9]They taught in Judah, having with them the book containing the law of the LORD; they traveled through all the cities of Judah and taught among the people.[n]

His Power. [10]Now the fear of the LORD was upon all the kingdoms of the countries surrounding Judah, so that they did not war against Jehoshaphat. [11]Some of the Philistines brought Jehoshaphat gifts and a tribute of silver; and the Arabs also brought him a flock of seven thousand seven hundred rams and seven thousand seven hundred he-goats.

[12]Jehoshaphat grew steadily greater. He built strongholds and store cities in Judah. [13]He carried out many works in the cities of Judah, and he had soldiers, valiant warriors, in Jerusalem. [14]This was their mustering according to their ancestral houses. Of Judah, the commanders of thousands: Adnah the commander, and with him three hundred thousand valiant warriors. [15]Next to him, Jehohanan the commander, and with him two hundred eighty thousand. [16]Next to him, Amasiah, son of Zichri, who offered himself to the LORD, and with him two hundred thousand valiant warriors. [17]From Benjamin: Eliada, a valiant warrior, and with him two hundred thousand armed with bow and buckler. [18]Next to him, Jozabad, and with him one hundred and eighty thousand equipped for war. [19]These were at the service of the king; in addition were those whom the king had placed in the fortified cities throughout all Judah.

CHAPTER 18

See RG 203-4

Alliance with Israel. [1o]Jehoshaphat therefore had wealth and glory in abundance; but he became related to Ahab by marriage. [2]After some years he went down to Ahab at Samaria; Ahab offered numerous sheep and oxen for him and the people with him, and persuaded him to go up against Ramoth-gilead. [3]Ahab, king of Israel, asked Jehoshaphat, king of Judah, "Will you come with me to Ramoth-gilead?" "You and I are as one," was his answer; "your people and my people as well. We will be with you in the battle." [4]But Jehoshaphat also said to the king of Israel, "Seek the word of the LORD at once."

The Prophets. [5]The king of Israel gathered his prophets, four hundred in number, and asked them, "Shall we go to attack Ramoth-gilead, or shall I refrain?" "Go up," they answered. "God will deliver it over to the king." [6]But Jehoshaphat said, "Is there no other prophet of the LORD here whom we may consult?" [7]The king of Israel answered Jehoshaphat, "There is still another through whom we may consult the LORD, but I hate him, for he prophesies not good but always evil about me. That is Micaiah, son of Imlah." Jehoshaphat said, "Let not your Majesty speak of evil against you." [8]So the king of Israel called an official, to whom he said, "Get Micaiah, son of Imlah, at once." [9]The king of Israel and King Jehoshaphat of Judah were seated each on his throne, clothed in their robes of state on a threshing floor at the entrance of the gate of Samaria, and all the prophets were prophesying before them.

[10]Zedekiah, son of Chenaanah, made iron horns for himself and said: "The LORD says, 'With these you shall gore Aram until you have destroyed them.'" [11]The other prophets prophesied in the same vein, saying: "Go up to Ramoth-gilead. You shall succeed; the LORD will deliver it over to the king." [12]*The messenger who had gone to call Micaiah said to him: "Look now, the prophets unanimously predict good for the king. Let your

18, 12-22: See note on 1 Kgs 22, 19-23.

l: 2 Chr 20, 33; Ex 34, 13.   *m:* 2 Chr 19, 8.   *n:* Ezr 7, 25.   *o:* 1-34: 1 Kgs 22, 1-35.

word, like each of theirs, predict good." [13]"As the LORD lives," Micaiah answered, "I will say what my God tells me."

[14]When he came to the king, the king said to him, "Micaiah, shall we go to fight against Ramoth-gilead, or shall I refrain?" "Go up," he answered, "and succeed; they will be delivered into your power." [15]But the king said to him, "How many times must I adjure you to tell me nothing but the truth in the name of the LORD?" [16]Then Micaiah answered:

"I see all Israel
    scattered on the mountains,
like sheep without a shepherd,
    and the LORD saying, 'These have no
        master!
Let each of them go back home in
    peace.' "

[17]The king of Israel said to Jehoshaphat, "Did I not tell you that he prophesies no good about me, but only evil?" [18]But Micaiah continued: "Therefore hear the word of the LORD: I saw the LORD seated on his throne, with the whole host of heaven standing by to his right and to his left. [19]The LORD asked, 'Who will deceive Ahab, king of Israel, so that he will go up and fall at Ramoth-gilead?' And one said this, another that, [20]until a spirit came forward and presented himself to the LORD, saying, 'I will deceive him.' The LORD asked, 'How?' [21]He answered, 'I will go forth and become a lying spirit in the mouths of all his prophets.' The LORD agreed: 'You shall succeed in deceiving him. Go forth and do this.' [22]So now the LORD has put a lying spirit in the mouths of these your prophets, but the LORD himself has decreed evil against you."

[23]Thereupon Zedekiah, son of Chenaanah, came up and slapped Micaiah on the cheek, saying, "Which way did the spirit of the LORD go when he left me to speak to you?" [24]"You shall find out," Micaiah replied, "on that day when you enter an in-

nermost chamber to hide." [25]The king of Israel then said: "Seize Micaiah and take him back to Amon, prefect of the city, and to Joash the king's son, [26]and say, 'This is the king's order: Put this man in prison and feed him scanty rations of bread and water until I return in safety!' " [27]But Micaiah said, "If ever you return in safety, the LORD has not spoken through me." And he said, "Hear, O peoples, all of you!"*

Ahab's Death. [28]The king of Israel and King Jehoshaphat of Judah went up to Ramoth-gilead [29]and the king of Israel said to Jehoshaphat, "I will go into battle disguised, but you put on your own clothes." So the king of Israel disguised himself and they entered the fray. [30]Meanwhile, the king of Aram had given his chariot commanders the order, "Fight with no one, small or great, except the king of Israel." [31]When the commanders saw Jehoshaphat, they exclaimed, "That must be the king of Israel!" and shifted to fight him. But Jehoshaphat cried out and the LORD helped him; God induced them to leave him. [32]The chariot commanders became aware that he was not the king of Israel and gave up their pursuit of him. [33]Someone, however, drew his bow at random and hit the king of Israel between the joints of his breastplate. He ordered his charioteer, "Rein about and take me out of the ranks, for I am disabled."*p* [34]The battle grew fierce during the day, and the king of Israel braced himself up on his chariot facing the Arameans until evening. He died as the sun was setting.

CHAPTER 19

See RG
203-4

Jehoshaphat Rebuked. [1]King Jehoshaphat of Judah returned in safety to his house in Jerusalem. [2]Jehu the seer, son of Hanani,* met King Jehoshaphat and said to him: "Should you help the wicked and love those who hate the LORD? For this reason, wrath is upon you from the LORD. [3]Yet some good things are to be found in you, since you

---

18, 27: "Hear, O peoples, all of you!": this quotation, which appears in some texts of 1 Kgs 22, 28, ascribes to the prophets Micaiah ben Imlah the opening words of the prophetic utterance of Micah of Moresheth (Mi 1, 2), a century later.

19, 2: Jehu the seer, son of Hanani: hardly the same seer as Jehu, son of Hanani, who prophesied against Baasha almost 50 years earlier (1 Kgs 16-1).

p: 2 Chr 35, 23; 1 Kgs 22, 34.

have removed the sacred poles from the land and have been determined to seek God."

Judges Appointed. ⁴Jehoshaphat dwelt in Jerusalem; but he went out again among the people from Beer-sheba to the highlands of Ephraim and brought them back to the LORD, the God of their fathers. ⁵He appointed judges in the land, in all the fortified cities of Judah, city by city, ⁶and he said to them: "Take care what you do, for you are judging, not on behalf of man, but on behalf of the LORD; he judges with you.⁹ ⁷And now, let the fear of the LORD be upon you. Act carefully, for with the LORD, our God, there is no injustice, no partiality, no bribe-taking."ʳ ⁸In Jerusalem also, Jehoshaphat appointed some Levites and priests and some of the family heads of Israel to judge in the name of the LORD and to settle quarrels among the inhabitants of Jerusalem.ˢ ⁹He gave them this command: "You shall act faithfully and wholeheartedly in the fear of the LORD. ¹⁰And in every dispute that your brethren living in their cities bring to you, whether it concerns bloodguilt or questions of law, command, statutes, or judgments, warn them lest they become guilty before the LORD and his wrath come upon you and your brethren. Do that and you shall be guiltless.ᵗ ¹¹See now, Amariah is high priest over you in everything that pertains to the LORD, and Zebadiah, son of Ishmael, is leader of the house of Judah in all that pertains to the king; and the Levites will be your officials. Act firmly, and the LORD will be with the good."

See RG 203-4

CHAPTER 20

Invasion from Edom.* ¹After this the Moabites, the Ammonites, and with them some Meunites came to fight against Jehoshaphat. ²The message was brought to Jehoshaphat: "A great multitude is coming against you from across the sea, from Edom; they are already in Hazazon-tamar" (which is En-gedi). ³Jehoshaphat was frightened,

and he hastened to consult the LORD. He proclaimed a fast for all Judah. ⁴Then Judah gathered to seek help from the LORD; from every one of the cities of Judah they came to seek the LORD.ᵘ

Prayer of Jehoshaphat. ⁵Jehoshaphat stood up in the assembly of Judah and Jerusalem in the house of the LORD before the new court, ⁶and he said: "LORD, God of our fathers, are you not the God in heaven, and do you not rule over all the kingdoms of the nations? In your hand is power and might, and no one can withstand you.ᵛ ⁷Was it not you, our God, who drove out the inhabitants of this land before your people Israel and gave it forever to the descendants of Abraham, your friend?ʷ ⁸They have dwelt in it and they built in it a sanctuary to your honor, saying, ⁹'When evil comes upon us, the sword of judgment, or pestilence, or famine, we will stand before this house and before you, for your name is in this house, and we will cry out to you in our affliction, and you will hear and save!' ¹⁰And now, see the Ammonites, Moabites, and those of Mount Seir whom you did not allow Israel to invade when they came from the land of Egypt, but instead they passed them by and did not destroy them.ˣ ¹¹See how they are now repaying us by coming to drive us out of the possession you have given us. ¹²O our God, will you not pass judgment on them? We are powerless before this vast multitude that comes against us. We are at a loss what to do, hence our eyes are turned toward you."

Victory Prophesied. ¹³All Judah was standing before the LORD, with their little ones, their wives, and their young sons. ¹⁴And the spirit of the LORD came upon Jahaziel, son of Zechariah, son of Benaiah, son of Jeiel, son of Mattaniah, a Levite of the clan of Asaph, in the midst of the assembly, ¹⁵and he said: "Listen, all of Judah, inhabitants of Jerusalem, and King Jehoshaphat! The LORD says to you: 'Do not fear or lose

---

20, 1-30: Although the account here seems to be a free composition of the Chronicler, there is probably a basis in fact for it; there could well have been a raid of nomads against Judah in the reign of Jehoshaphat, similar to Zerah's attack on Asa (2 Chr 14, 8-14). The story may also, in some way, be connected with the campaign of Israel and

Judah against Moab through the territory of Edom (2 Kgs 3, 4-27).

q: Dt 1, 16ff; 16, 19f. *r:* Dt 10, 17. *s:* 2 Chr 17, 8f; Dt 17, 8-13; Ps 122, 3ff. *t:* Nm 35, 19. *u:* Jer 36, 6; Jb 1, 14. *v:* 2 Chr 32, 7; Dt 4, 39. *w:* Dn 3, 35. *x:* Dt 2, 4f. 9f. 18f.

heart at the sight of this vast multitude, for the battle is not yours but God's. [16]Go down against them tomorrow. You will see them coming up by the ascent of Ziz, and you will come upon them at the end of the wadi which opens on the wilderness of Jeruel. [17]You will not have to fight in this encounter. Take your places, stand firm, and see how the LORD will be with you to deliver you, Judah and Jerusalem. Do not fear or lose heart. Tomorrow go out to meet them, and the LORD will be with you.' "[y] [18]Then Jehoshaphat knelt down with his face to the ground, and all Judah and the inhabitants of Jerusalem fell down before the LORD in worship. [19]Levites from among the Kohathites and Korahites rose to sing the praises of the LORD, the God of Israel, in a resounding chorus.

The Invaders Destroyed. [20]In the early morning they hastened out to the wilderness of Tekoa. As they were going out, Jehoshaphat halted and said: "Listen to me, Judah and inhabitants of Jerusalem! Trust in the LORD, your God, and you will be found firm. Trust in his prophets and you will succeed."[z] [21]After consulting with the people, he appointed some to sing to the LORD and some to praise the holy Appearance* as it went forth at the head of the army. They sang: "Give thanks to the LORD, for his mercy endures forever."[a] [22]At the moment they began their jubilant hymn, the LORD laid an ambush against the Ammonites, Moabites, and those of Mount Seir who were coming against Judah, so that they were vanquished. [23]For the Ammonites and Moabites set upon the inhabitants of Mount Seir and completely exterminated them. And when they had finished with the inhabitants of Seir, they began to destroy each other.[b]

[24]When Judah came to the watchtower of the desert and looked toward the throng, they saw only corpses fallen on the ground, with no survivors. [25]Jehoshaphat and his people came to take plunder, and they found an abundance of cattle and personal property, garments and precious vessels. They took so much that they were unable to carry it all; they were three days taking the spoil, so great was it. [26]On the fourth day they held an assembly in the Valley of Beracah—for there they blessed the LORD; therefore that place has ever since been called the Valley of Beracah.* [27]Then all the men of Judah and Jerusalem, with Jehoshaphat at their head, turned back toward Jerusalem celebrating the joyful victory the LORD had given them over their enemies. [28]They came to Jerusalem, to the house of the LORD, with harps, lyres and trumpets. [29]And the fear of God came upon all the kingdoms of the surrounding lands when they heard how the LORD had fought against the enemies of Israel. [30]Thereafter Jehoshaphat's kingdom enjoyed peace, for his God gave him rest on every side.

Jehoshaphat's Other Deeds. [31c]Thus Jehoshaphat reigned over Judah. He was thirty-five years old when he became king, and he reigned twenty-five years in Jerusalem. His mother was named Azubah, daughter of Shilhi. [32]He followed the path of his father Asa unswervingly, doing what was right in the LORD's sight. [33]But the high places were not removed, nor as yet had the people fixed their hearts on the God of their fathers.

[34]The rest of the acts of Jehoshaphat, first and last, can be found written in the chronicle of Jehu, son of Hanani, which is inserted in the book of the kings of Israel. [35]After this, King Jehoshaphat of Judah allied himself with King Ahaziah of Israel, who did evil. [36d]He joined with him in building ships to sail to Tarshish; the fleet was built at Ezion-geber. [37]But Eliezer, son of Dodavahu from Mareshah, prophesied against Jehoshaphat, saying, "Because you have joined with Ahaziah, the LORD will shatter your work." And the ships were wrecked and were unable to sail to Tarshish.

CHAPTER 21

See RG
203–4

[1]Jehoshaphat rested with his ancestors; he was buried with them in the City of

---

20, 21: Holy Appearance: the Lord, who is with the Israelite army (v 17), manifests himself (the same language is in Ps 29, 2) in bringing Israel the victory (Ex 14, 14. 24).

20, 26: Beracah: the Hebrew word for "blessing."

---

y: Is 8, 10.   z: Is 7, 9.   a: Ps 136, 1.   b: Jos 6, 17; Ez 38, 21.   c: 31-34: 1 Kgs 22, 41-45.   d: 36f: 1 Kgs 22, 48f.

David. Jehoram, his son, succeeded him as king.[e] [2]His brothers, sons of Jehoshaphat, were Azariah, Jehiel, Zechariah, Azariah, Michael and Shephatiah; all these were sons of King Jehoshaphat of Judah. [3]Their father gave them numerous gifts of silver, gold and precious objects, together with fortified cities in Judah, but the kingship he gave to Jehoram because he was the first-born.

Evil Deeds of Jehoram. [4]When Jehoram had come into his father's kingdom and had consolidated his power, he put to the sword all his brothers and also some of the princes of Israel. [5][f]Jehoram was thirty-two years old when he became king, and he reigned eight years in Jerusalem. [6]He conducted himself like the kings of Israel of the line of Ahab, because one of Ahab's daughters* was his wife. He did evil in the sight of the LORD, [7]but the LORD would not destroy the house of David because of the covenant he had made with David and because of his promise to give him and his sons a lamp for all time.[g]

[8][h]During his time Edom revolted against the sovereignty of Judah; they chose a king of their own. [9]Thereupon Jehoram crossed over with his officers and all the chariots he had. He arose by night and broke through the Edomites when they had surrounded him and the commanders of his chariots. [10]However, Edom has continued in revolt against the sovereignty of Judah down to the present time. Libnah also revolted at that time against Jehoram's sovereignty because he had forsaken the LORD, the God of his fathers. [11]He also set up high places in the mountains of Judah; he led the inhabitants of Jerusalem into idolatry and seduced Judah.

Retribution. [12]He received a letter from the prophet Elijah* with this message: Thus says the LORD, the God of your ancestor David: 'Because you have not followed the path of your father Jehoshaphat, nor of Asa, king of Judah, [13]but instead have walked in the way of the kings of Israel and have led

Judah and the inhabitants of Jerusalem into idolatry, as did the house of Ahab, and also because you have murdered your brothers of your father's house who were better than you, [14]the LORD will strike your people, your children, your wives, and all that is yours with a great plague; [15]and you shall have severe pains from a disease in your bowels, while your bowels issue forth because of the disease, day after day.' "

[16]Then the LORD stirred up against Jehoram the animosity of the Philistines and of the Arabs who bordered on the Ethiopians. [17]They came up against Judah, invaded it, and carried away all the wealth found in the king's palace, along with his sons and his wives; there was left to him only one son, Jehoahaz, his youngest. [18]After these events, the LORD afflicted him with an incurable disease of the bowels. [19]As time went on until a period of two years had elapsed, his bowels issued forth because of the disease and he died in great pain. His people did not make a pyre for him like that of his fathers. [20]He was thirty-two years old when he became king, and he reigned eight years in Jerusalem. He departed unloved and was buried in the City of David, but not in the tombs of the kings.[i]

CHAPTER 22

See RG 203–4

Ahaziah. [1][j]Then the inhabitants of Jerusalem made Ahaziah, his youngest son, king in his stead, since all the older sons had been slain by the band that had come into the fort with the Arabs. Thus Ahaziah, son of Jehoram, reigned as king of Judah. [2]He was twenty-two years old when he became king, and he reigned one year in Jerusalem. His mother was named Athaliah, daughter of Omri. [3]He, too, followed the ways of the house of Ahab, because his mother counseled him to act sinfully. [4]To his own destruction, he did evil in the sight of the LORD, as did the house of Ahab, since they were his counselors after the death of his father.

21, 6: One of Ahab's daughters: Athaliah. In 2 Chr 22, 2 (and its source, 2 Kgs 8, 26) she is called Omri's daughter; but this should probably be understood in the sense of granddaughter.

21, 12: Elijah: the only mention by the Chronicler of this prophet of the northern kingdom of Israel. It is doubtful that Elijah was still living in the reign of Jehoram of Judah; in any

case, the attribution of the letter to him is most likely an imaginative filling out of the narration.

e: 1 Kgs 22, 51. *f:* 5ff: 2 Kgs 8, 17ff. *g:* 1 Kgs 11, 36; 2 Kgs 8, 19. *h:* 8ff: Gn 27, 40; 2 Kgs 8, 20ff. *i:* 2 Kgs 8, 24. *j:* 1-6: 2 Kgs 8, 24-29.

⁵He was also following their counsel when he accompanied Jehoram, son of Ahab, king of Israel, to battle against Hazael, king of Aram, at Ramoth-gilead. There Jehoram was wounded by the Arameans. ⁶He returned to Jezreel to be healed of the wounds he had received at Rama in his battle against Hazael, king of Aram. Because of this illness, Ahaziah, son of Jehoram, king of Judah, went down to visit Jehoram, son of Ahab, in Jezreel. ⁷Now it was willed by God for Ahaziah's downfall that he should join Jehoram, for after his arrival he rode out with Jehoram to Jehu, son of Nimshi, whom the LORD had anointed to cut down the house of Ahab.ᵏ ⁸While Jehu was executing judgment on the house of Ahab, he also encountered the princes of Judah and the nephews of Ahaziah who were his attendants, and he slew them.ˡ ⁹Then he looked for Ahaziah himself. They caught him where he was hiding in Samaria and brought him to Jehu, who put him to death. They buried him, for they said, "He was the grandson of Jehoshaphat, who sought the LORD with his whole heart."ᵐ There remained in Ahaziah's house no one powerful enough to wield the kingship.*

Usurpation of Athaliah. ¹⁰ⁿWhen Athaliah, mother of Ahaziah, learned that her son was dead, she proceeded to kill off all the royal offspring of the house of Judah. ¹¹But Jehosheba, a royal princess, secretly took Ahaziah's son Joash from among the king's sons who were about to be slain, and put him and his nurse in a bedroom. In this way Jehosheba, who was the daughter of King Jehoram, a sister of Ahaziah, and wife of Jehoiada the priest, hid the child from Athaliah's sight, so that she did not put him to death. ¹²For six years he remained hidden with them in the house of God, while Athaliah ruled over the land.

See RG 203–4

CHAPTER 23

Athaliah Overthrown. ¹ᵒIn the seventh year, Jehoiada took courage and entered a conspiracy with certain captains: Azariah, son of Jehoram; Ishmael, son of Jehohanan; Azariah, son of Obed; Masseiah, son of Adaiah; and Elishaphat, son of Zichri. ²They journeyed about Judah, gathering the Levites from all the cities of Judah and also the heads of the Israelite families. When they had come to Jerusalem, ³the whole assembly made a covenant with the king in the house of God. Jehoiada said to them: "Here is the king's son who must reign, as the LORD promised concerning the sons of David. ⁴This is what you must do: a third of your number, both priests and Levites, who come in on the sabbath must guard the thresholds, ⁵another third must be at the king's palace, and the final third at the Foundation Gate, when all the people will be in the courts of the LORD's temple. ⁶Let no one enter the LORD's house except the priests and those Levites who are ministering. They may enter because they are holy; but all the other people must observe the prescriptions of the LORD. ⁷The Levites shall surround the king on all sides, each with his weapon drawn. Whoever tries to enter the house must be slain. Stay with the king wherever he goes."

⁸The Levites and all Judah did just as Jehoiada the priest commanded. Each brought his men, those who were to come in on the sabbath as well as those who were to depart on the sabbath, since Jehoiada the priest had not dismissed any of the divisions.ᵖ ⁹Jehoiada the priest gave the captains the spears, shields and bucklers of King David which were in the house of God. ¹⁰He stationed all the people, each with his spear in hand, from the southern to the northern extremity of the enclosure, around the altar and the temple on the king's behalf. ¹¹Then they brought out the king's son, set the crown and the insignia upon him, and made him king. Jehoiada and his sons anointed him, and they cried, "Long live the king!"

¹²When Athaliah heard the din of the people running and acclaiming the king, she went to the people in the temple of the LORD. ¹³She looked, and there was the king standing be-

---

22, 9: This account of the death of Ahaziah of Judah is not derived from 2 Kgs 9, 27f, with which it is at variance.

k: 2 Kgs 9, 21; 10, 12ff.   l: 2 Kgs 10, 12ff.   m: 2 Kgs 9, 27f.   n: 10ff: 2 Kgs 11, 1ff.   o: 1-17. 19ff: 2 Kgs 11, 4-20.   p: 2 Kgs 11, 9; 1 Chr 24, 19.

side his pillar* at the entrance, the officers and the trumpeters around him, and all the people of the land rejoicing and blowing trumpets, while the singers with their musical instruments were leading the acclaim. Athaliah tore her garments and cried out, "Treason! treason!" *14*Then Jehoiada the priest sent out the captains who were in command of the army; he said to them: "Take her outside through the ranks, and if anyone tries to follow her, let him die by the sword. For," the priest continued, "you must not put her to death in the LORD's temple." *15*So they seized her, and when she arrived at the entrance to the Horse Gate of the palace, they put her to death there.

*16*Then Jehoiada made a covenant between himself and all the people and the king, that they should be the LORD's people. *17*And all the people went to the temple of Baal and tore it down. They smashed its altars and images, and they slew Mattan, the priest of Baal, before the altars. *18*Then Jehoiada gave the charge of the LORD's temple into the hands of the levitical priests, to whom David had assigned turns in the temple for offering the holocausts of the LORD, as is written in the law of Moses, with rejoicing and song, as David had provided.*q* *19*Moreover, he stationed guards at the gates of the LORD's temple, so that no one unclean in any respect might enter. *20*Then he took the captains, the nobles, the rulers among the people, and all the people of the land, and led the king out of the LORD's house. When they had come within the upper gate of the king's house, they seated the king upon the royal throne. *21*All the people of the land rejoiced and the city was quiet, now that Athaliah had been put to death by the sword.

See RG 203-4

CHAPTER 24

The Temple Restored. *1r*Joash was seven years old when he became king, and he reigned forty years in Jerusalem. His mother, named Zibiah, was from Beersheba. *2*Joash did what was pleasing to the LORD as long as Jehoiada the priest lived. *3*Jehoiada provided him with two wives, and he became the father of sons and daughters.

*4*After some time, Joash decided to restore the LORD's temple. *5*He called together the priests and Levites and said to them: "Go out to all the cities of Judah and collect money* from all Israel that you may repair the house of your God over the years. You must hasten this affair." But the Levites did not hasten. *6*Then the king summoned Jehoiada, who was in charge, and said to him: "Why have you not required the Levites to bring in from Judah and Jerusalem the tax levied by Moses, the servant of the LORD, and by the assembly of Israel, for the tent of the testimony?"*s* *7*For the wicked Athaliah and her sons had damaged the house of God and had even turned over to the Baals the dedicated resources of the LORD's temple.

*8*At the king's command, therefore, they made a chest, which they put outside the gate of the LORD's temple.*t* *9*They had it proclaimed throughout Judah and Jerusalem that the tax which Moses, the servant of God, had imposed on Israel in the desert should be brought to the LORD.*u* *10*All the princes and the people rejoiced; they brought what was asked and cast it into the chest until it was filled. *11*Whenever the chest was brought to the royal officials by the Levites and they saw that it contained much money, the royal scribe and an overseer for the high priest came, emptied the chest, then took it back and returned it to its place. This they did day after day until they had collected a large sum of money. *12*Then the king and Jehoiada gave it to the workmen in charge of the labor on the LORD's temple, who hired masons and carpenters to restore the temple, and also iron- and bronze-smiths to repair it. *13*The workmen labored, and the task of restoration pro-

---

23, 13: Beside his pillar: the king had a special place in the eastern gateway of the temple court that contained the altar of holocausts. He occupied this place on feasts and sabbaths at the time of the statutory offerings, or when he made freewill offerings of his own; cf 2 Kgs 11, 4 and also Ez 46, 1-8 for a later reflection of this.

24, 5: Collect money: according to 2 Kgs 12, 5, the people themselves brought the money to the temple; it con-

sisted, at least in part, of voluntary contributions. At the time of the Chronicler (see Neh 10, 32) there was a fixed head tax for the upkeep of the temple (2 Chr 34, 9), based on Ex 30, 12-16. This was still in force in New Testament times (Mt 17, 24f).

q: 1 Chr 23, 13. *r:* 1-14: 2 Kgs 12, 1-13. *s:* Ex 25, 1-9; Neh 10, 33. *t:* 2 Chr 34, 9. *u:* Ex 30, 13.

gressed under their hands. They restored the house of God according to its original form, and reinforced it. [14] After they had finished, they brought the rest of the money to the king and to Jehoiada, who had it made into utensils for the LORD's temple, utensils for the service and the holocausts, and basins and other gold and silver utensils. They offered holocausts in the LORD's temple continually throughout the lifetime of Jehoiada. [15] Jehoiada lived to a ripe old age; he was a hundred and thirty years old when he died. [16] He was buried in the City of David with the kings, because he had done good in Israel, in particular with respect to God and his temple.

Apostasy of King Joash. [17] After the death of Jehoiada, the princes of Judah came and paid homage to the king, and the king then listened to them. [18] They forsook the temple of the LORD, the God of their fathers, and began to serve the sacred poles and the idols; and because of this crime of theirs, wrath came upon Judah and Jerusalem.[v] [19] Although prophets were sent to them to convert them to the LORD, the people would not listen to their warnings. [20] Then the spirit of God possessed Zechariah, son of Jehoiada the priest. He took his stand above the people and said to them: "God says, 'Why are you transgressing the LORD's commands, so that you cannot prosper? Because you have abandoned the LORD, he has abandoned you.'" [21] But they conspired against him, and at the king's order they stoned him to death in the court of the LORD's temple. [22] Thus King Joash was unmindful of the devotion shown him by Jehoiada, Zechariah's father, and slew his son. And as he was dying, he said, "May the LORD see and avenge."

Retribution. [23] At the turn of the year a force of Arameans came up against Joash. They invaded Judah and Jerusalem, did away with all the princes of the people, and sent all their spoil to the king of Damascus.[w] [24] Though the Aramean force came with few men, the LORD surrendered a very large force into their power, because Judah had abandoned the LORD, the God of their fathers. So

punishment was meted out to Joash.[x] [25][y] After the Arameans had departed from him, leaving him in grievous suffering, his servants conspired against him because of the murder of the son of Jehoiada the priest. They killed him on his sickbed. He was buried in the City of David, but not in the tombs of the kings. [26] These conspired against him: Zabad, son of Shimeath from Ammon, and Jehozabad, son of Shimrith from Moab. [27] Of his sons, and the great tribute imposed on him, and of his rebuilding of the house of God, there is a written account in the midrash of the book of the kings. His son Amaziah succeeded him as king.[z]

CHAPTER 25

See RG 203-4

Campaign in Edom. [1][a] Amaziah was twenty-five years old when he became king, and he reigned twenty-nine years in Jerusalem. His mother, named Jehoaddan, was from Jerusalem. [2] He did what was pleasing in the sight of the LORD, though not wholeheartedly. [3] After he had strengthened his hold on the kingdom, he slew those of his servants who had killed the king, his father; [4] but he did not put their children to death, for he acted according to what is written in the law, in the Book of Moses, as the LORD commanded: "Fathers shall not be put to death for their children, nor children for their fathers; but only for his own guilt shall a man be put to death."[b]

[5] Amaziah mustered Judah and placed them, out of all Judah and Benjamin according to their ancestral houses, under leaders of thousands and of hundreds. When he had counted those of twenty years and over, he found them to be three hundred thousand picked men fit for war, capable of handling lance and shield. [6] He also hired a hundred thousand valiant warriors from Israel for a hundred talents of silver. [7] But a man of God came to him and said: "O king, let not the army of Israel go with you, for the LORD is not with Israel, with any Ephraimite. [8] Instead, go on your own, strongly prepared for the conflict; otherwise the LORD will defeat

---

v: Ex 34, 13.   *w:* 2 Kgs 12, 17f.   *x:* Dt 32, 30.   *y:* 25f: 2 Kgs 12, 21f.   *z:* 2 Kgs 12, 19. 22.   *a:* 1-4: 2 Kgs 14, 1-6.   *b:* Dt 24, 16; 2 Kgs 14, 5f; Ez 18, 20.

you in the face of the enemy. It is God who has the power to reinforce or to defeat." [9]Amaziah answered the man of God, "But what is to be done about the hundred talents that I paid for the troops of Israel?" The man of God replied, "The LORD can give you much more than that." [10]Amaziah then disbanded the troops that had come to him from Ephraim, and sent them home. They, however, became furiously angry with Judah, and returned home blazing with resentment. [11]Amaziah now assumed command of his army. They proceeded to the Valley of Salt, and there they killed ten thousand men of Seir.[c] [12]The Judahites also brought back another ten thousand alive, whom they led to the summit of the Rock and then cast down, so that they were all crushed. [13]Meanwhile, the mercenaries whom Amaziah had dismissed from battle service with him raided the cities of Judah from Samaria to Beth-horon. They killed three thousand of the inhabitants and took away much booty.

Infidelity of Amaziah. [14]When Amaziah returned from his conquest of the Edomites he brought back with him the gods of the people of Seir, which he set up as his own gods; he bowed down before them and offered sacrifice to them. [15]Then the anger of the LORD blazed out against Amaziah, and he sent a prophet to him who said: "Why have you had recourse to this people's gods that could not save their own people from your hand?" [16]While he was still speaking, however, the king said to him: "Have you been made the king's counselor? Be silent! Why should it be necessary to kill you?" Therefore the prophet desisted. "I know, however," he said, "that God has let you take counsel to your own destruction, because you have done this thing and have refused to hear my counsel."

Retribution. [17d]Having taken counsel, King Amaziah of Judah sent messengers to Joash, son of Jehoahaz, son of Jehu, the king of Israel, saying, "Come, let us meet each other face to face." [18]King Joash of Israel sent this reply to King Amaziah of Judah: "The thistle of the Lebanon sent a message to the cedar of the Lebanon, saying, 'Give your daughter to my son for his wife.' But the wild beasts of the Lebanon passed by and trampled the thistle down.[e] [19]You are thinking, 'See, I have beaten Edom!', and thus ambition makes you proud. Remain at home. Why involve yourself, and Judah with you, in misfortune and failure?" [20]But Amaziah would not listen, for God had determined to hand them over because they had had recourse to the gods of Edom.

[21]Therefore King Joash of Israel advanced and he and King Amaziah met in battle at Beth-shemesh of Judah. [22]There Judah was defeated by Israel, and all the Judean soldiers fled homeward. [23]King Joash of Israel captured Amaziah, king of Judah, son of Joash, son of Jehoahaz, at Beth-shemesh and brought him to Jerusalem. Then he tore down the wall of Jerusalem from the Ephraim Gate to the Corner Gate, a distance of four hundred cubits. [24]He took away all the gold and silver and all the vessels he found in the house of God with Obed-edom,[*] together with the treasures of the palace, and hostages as well. Then he returned to Samaria.

[25f]Amaziah, son of Joash, king of Judah, survived Joash, son of Jehoahaz, king of Israel, by fifteen years. [26]The rest of the acts of Amaziah, first and last, can be found written, as is well known, in the book of the kings of Judah and Israel. [27]Now from the time that Amaziah ceased to follow the LORD, a conspiracy was formed against him in Jerusalem; hence he fled to Lachish. But they pursued him to Lachish and put him to death there. [28]They brought him back on horses and buried him with his ancestors in the City of Judah.[*]

25, 24: With Obed-edom: possibly a reference to the priest of an Edomite false worship (cf v 14), if not to a levitical family of gatekeepers; cf 1 Chr 15, 18; 26, 12-15.

25, 28: The city of Judah: in the parallel passage of 2 Kgs 14, 20, the City of David. The Chronicler is referring, by this term, to the capital of Judah, Jerusalem.

c: 2 Kgs 14, 7. *d:* 17-24: 2 Kgs 14, 8-14. *e:* Jgs 9, 7-15; 2 Kgs 14, 9. *f:* 25-28: 2 Kgs 14, 17-20.

See RG 203-4

CHAPTER 26

The Works of Uzziah. [1g]All the people of Judah chose Uzziah, though he was but sixteen years of age, and proclaimed him king to succeed his father Amaziah. [2]He rebuilt Elath and restored it to Judah; this was after King Amaziah had gone to rest with his ancestors. [3]Uzziah was sixteen years old when he became king, and he reigned fifty-two years in Jerusalem. His mother, named Jecoliah, was from Jerusalem. [4]He pleased the Lord, just as his father Amaziah had done.

[5]He was prepared to seek God as long as Zechariah* lived, who taught him to fear God; and as long as he sought the Lord, God made him prosper.[h] [6]He went out and fought the Philistines and razed the walls of Gath, Jabneh and Ashdod [and built cities in the district of Ashdod and in Philistia].[i] [7]God helped him against the Philistines, against the Arabs who dwelt in Gurbaal, and against the Meunites. [8]The Ammonites paid tribute to Uzziah and his fame spread as far as Egypt, for he grew stronger and stronger. [9]Moreover, Uzziah built towers in Jerusalem at the Corner Gate, at the Valley Gate, and at the Angle, and he fortified them. [10]He built towers in the desert and dug numerous cisterns, for he had many cattle. He had plowmen in the foothills and the plains, and vinedressers in the highlands and the garden land. He was a lover of the soil.

[11]Uzziah also had a standing army of fit soldiers divided into bands according to the number in which they were mustered by Jeiel the scribe and Maaseiah the recorder, under the command of Hananiah, one of the king's officials. [12]The entire number of family heads over these valiant warriors was two thousand six hundred, [13]and at their disposal was a mighty army of three hundred seven thousand five hundred fighting men of great valor to help the king against his enemies. [14]Uzziah provided for them—for the entire army—bucklers, lances, helmets, breastplates, bows

and slingstones. [15]He also built machines in Jerusalem, devices contrived to stand on the towers and at the angles of the walls to shoot arrows and cast large stones. His fame spread far and wide, and his power was ascribed to the marvelous help he had received.

Pride and Fall. [16]But after he had become strong, he became proud to his own destruction and broke faith with the Lord, his God. He entered the temple of the Lord to make an offering on the altar of incense. [17]But Azariah the priest, and with him eighty other priests of the Lord, courageous men, followed him. [18]They opposed King Uzziah, saying to him: "It is not for you, Uzziah, to burn incense to the Lord, but for the priests, the sons of Aaron, who have been consecrated for this purpose. Leave the sanctuary, for you have broken faith and no longer have a part in the glory that comes from the Lord God."[j] [19]Uzziah, who was holding a censer for burning the incense, became angry, but at the moment he showed his anger to the priests, while they were looking at him in the house of the Lord beside the altar of incense, leprosy broke out on his forehead.[k] [20]Azariah the chief priest and all the other priests examined him, and when they saw that his forehead was leprous, they expelled him from the temple. He himself fled willingly, for the Lord had afflicted him. [21l]King Uzziah remained a leper to the day of his death. As a leper he dwelt in a segregated house, for he was excluded from the house of the Lord. Therefore his son Jotham was regent of the palace and ruled the people of the land.

[22]The prophet Isaiah, son of Amos, wrote the rest of the acts of Uzziah, first and last. [23]Uzziah rested with his ancestors; he was buried with them in the field adjoining the royal cemetery, for they said, "He was a leper." His son Jotham succeeded him as king.

CHAPTER 27

See RG 203-4

Jotham. [1m]Jotham was twenty-five years old when he became king, and he

---

26, 5: Zechariah: this person, not otherwise identified, is referred to in language suggesting a pious layman rather than a priest or prophet; cf 2 Chr 29, 1.

---

g: 1-4: 2 Kgs 14, 21f; 15, 1ff. *h:* 2 Chr 24, 2. *i:* Am 1, 8. *j:* Ex 30, 7. *k:* Nm 12, 10. *l:* 21ff: 2 Kgs 15, 5ff; Lv 13, 46; Nm 19, 20. *m:* 1-3; 2 Kgs 15, 32-35.

reigned sixteen years in Jerusalem. His mother was named Jerusa, daughter of Zadok. [2]He pleased the LORD just as his father Uzziah had done, though he did not enter the temple of the LORD; the people, however, continued to act sinfully.

[3]He built the upper gate of the LORD's house and had much construction done on the wall of Ophel. [4]Moreover, he built cities in the hill country of Judah, and in the forest land he set up fortresses and towers. [5]He fought with the king of the Ammonites and conquered them. That year the Ammonites paid him one hundred talents of silver, together with ten thousand kors of wheat and ten thousand of barley. They brought the same to him also in the second and in the third year. [6]Thus Jotham continued to grow strong because he lived resolutely in the presence of the LORD, his God. [7][n]The rest of the acts of Jotham, his wars and his activities, can be found written in the book of the kings of Israel and Judah. [8]He was twenty-five years old when he became king, and he reigned sixteen years in Jerusalem. [9]Jotham rested with his ancestors and was buried in the City of David, and his son Ahaz succeeded him as king.

III: Reforms of Hezekiah and Josiah

CHAPTER 28

See RG 203-4

Impiety of Ahaz. [1][o]Ahaz was twenty years old when he became king, and he reigned sixteen years in Jerusalem. He did not please the LORD as his forefather David had done, [2]but conducted himself like the kings of Israel and even made molten idols of the Baals. [3]Moreover, he offered sacrifice in the Valley of Ben-hinnom, and immolated his sons by fire according to the abominable practice of the nations which the LORD had cleared out before the Israelites.[p] [4]He offered sacrifice and incense on the high places, on hills, and under every leafy tree.

Retribution. [5]Therefore the LORD, his God, delivered him into the power of the king of Aram. The Arameans defeated him

and carried away captive a large number of his people, whom they brought to Damascus. He was also delivered into the power of the king of Israel, who defeated him with great slaughter.[q] [6]For Pekah, son of Remaliah, slew one hundred and twenty thousand of Judah in a single day, all of them valiant men, because they had abandoned the LORD, the God of their fathers. [7]Zichri, an Ephraimite warrior, killed Maaseiah, the king's son, and Azrikam, the master of the palace, and also Elkanah, who was second to the king. [8]The Israelites took away as captives two hundred thousand of their brethren's wives, sons and daughters; they also took from them much plunder, which they brought to Samaria.

The Prophecy of Oded. [9]In Samaria there was a prophet of the LORD by the name of Oded. He went out to meet the army returning to Samaria and said to them: "It was because the LORD, the God of your fathers, was angry with Judah that he delivered them into your hands. You, however, have slaughtered them with a fury that has reached up to heaven. [10]And now you are planning to make the children of Judah and Jerusalem your slaves and bondwomen. Are not you yourselves, therefore, guilty of a crime against the LORD, your God? [11]Now listen to me: send back the captives you have carried off from among your brethren, for the burning anger of the LORD is upon you."

[12]At this, some of the Ephraimite leaders, Azariah, son of Johanan, Berechiah, son of Meshillemoth, Jehizkiah, son of Shallum, and Amasa, son of Hadlai, themselves stood up in opposition to those who had returned from the war. [13]They said to them: "Do not bring the captives here, for what you propose will make us guilty before the LORD and increase our sins and our guilt. Our guilt is already great, and there is a burning anger upon Israel." [14]Therefore the soldiers left their captives and the plunder before the princes and the whole assembly. [15]Then the men just named proceeded to help the captives. All of them who were naked they clothed from the booty; they clothed them, put sandals on their feet, gave them food and drink, anointed them, and all

---

n: 7-9: 2 Kgs 15, 36ff.   *o:* 1-4: 2 Kgs 16, 1-4.   *p:* 2 Kgs 16, 3; Lv 18, 21.   *q:* 2 Kgs 16, 5; Is 7, 1-9.

who were weak they set on asses. They brought them to Jericho, the city of palms, to their brethren. Then they returned to Samaria.[r]

Further Sins of Ahaz. [16]At that time King Ahaz sent an appeal for help to the kings of Assyria.[s] [17]The Edomites had returned, attacked Judah, and carried off captives.[t] [18]The Philistines too had raided the cities of the foothills and the Negeb of Judah; they captured Beth-shemesh, Aijalon, Gederoth, Soco and its dependencies, Timnah and its dependencies, and Gimzo and its dependencies, and occupied them. [19]For the LORD had brought Judah low because of Ahaz, king of Israel,* who let Judah go its own way and proved utterly faithless to the LORD. [20]Tilgath-pilneser, king of Assyria, did indeed come to him, but to oppress him rather than to help him.[u] [21]Though Ahaz plundered the LORD's house and the houses of the king and the princes to make payment to the king of Assyria, it availed him nothing.[v]

[22]While he was already in distress, the same King Ahaz became even more unfaithful to the LORD. [23]He sacrificed to the gods of Damascus who had defeated him, saying, "Since it was the gods of the kings of Aram who helped them, I will sacrifice to them that they may help me also." However, they only caused further disaster to him and to all Israel.[w] [24]Ahaz gathered up the utensils of God's house and broke them in pieces. He closed the doors of the LORD's house and had altars made for himself in every corner of Jerusalem.[x] [25]In every city throughout Judah he set up high places to offer sacrifice to other gods. Thus he angered the LORD, the God of his fathers.

[26y]The rest of his deeds and his activities, first and last, can be found written in the book of the kings of Judah and Israel. [27]Ahaz rested with his ancestors and was buried in Jerusalem—in the city, for they did not bring him to the tombs of the kings of Israel. His son Hezekiah succeeded him as king.

CHAPTER 29

See RG 203–4

Reforms of Hezekiah. [1z]Hezekiah was twenty-five years old when he became king, and he reigned twenty-nine years in Jerusalem. His mother was named Abia, daughter of Zechariah. [2]He pleased the LORD just as his forefather David had done. [3]It was he who, in the first month of the first year of his reign, opened the doors of the LORD's house and repaired them.[a] [4]He summoned the priests and Levites, gathered them in the open space to the east, [5]and said to them: "Listen to me, you Levites! Sanctify yourselves now and sanctify the house of the LORD, the God of your fathers, and clean out the filth from the sanctuary. [6]Our fathers acted faithlessly and did evil in the eyes of the LORD, our God. They abandoned him, turned away their faces from the LORD's dwelling, and turned their backs on him. [7]They also closed the doors of the vestibule, extinguished the lamps, and refused to burn incense and offer holocausts in the sanctuary to the honor of the God of Israel.[b] [8c]Therefore the anger of the LORD has come upon Judah and Jerusalem; he has made them an object of terror, astonishment and mockery, as you see with your own eyes. [9]For our fathers, as you know, fell by the sword, and our sons, our daughters and our wives have been taken captive because of this. [10]Now, I intend to make a covenant with the LORD, the God of Israel, that his burning anger may withdraw from us. [11]My sons, be not negligent any longer, for it is you whom the LORD has chosen to stand before him, to minister to him, to be his ministers and to offer incense."

[12]Then the Levites arose: Mahath, son of Amasai, and Joel, son of Azariah, descendants of the Kohathites; of the sons of Merari: Kish, son of Abdi, and Azariah, son of Jehallel; of the Gershonites: Joah, son of Zimmah, and Eden, son of Joah; [13]of the

---

28, 19: Ahaz, king of Israel: in the period of the divided kingdom the term king of Israel would elsewhere mean "king of the northern Kingdom of Israel."

[r]: Lk 10, 25-37.   [s]: 2 Kgs 16, 7.   [t]: 2 Kgs 16, 6.   [u]: 2 Kgs 16, 10; Is 7, 17-20; 8, 5-8.   [v]: 2 Kgs 16, 8.   [w]: 2 Kgs 16, 12f; Is 10, 20. [x]: 2 Chr 29, 3; 30, 14; 2 Kgs 16, 17.   [y]: 26f: 2 Kgs 16, 19f.   [z]: 1ff: 2 Kgs 18, 1ff.   [a]: 2 Chr 28, 24.   [b]: 2 Kgs 16, 15.   [c]: 8f: Lv 26, 32f; Dt 28, 25; Jer 25, 18.

sons of Elizaphan: Shimri and Jeuel; of the sons of Asaph: Zechariah and Mattaniah; [14]of the sons of Heman: Jehuel and Shimei; of the sons of Jeduthun: Shemiah and Uzziel. [15]They gathered their brethren together and sanctified themselves; then they came as the king had ordered, to cleanse the LORD's house in keeping with his words.

[16]The priests entered the interior of the LORD's house to cleanse it; and whatever they found in the LORD's temple that was unclean they brought out to the court of the LORD's house, where the Levites took it from them and carried it out to the Kidron Valley. [17]They began the work of consecration on the first day of the first month, and on the eighth day of the month they arrived at the vestibule of the LORD; they consecrated the LORD's house during eight days, and on the sixteenth day of the first month, they had finished.

[18]Then they went inside to King Hezekiah and said: "We have cleansed the entire house of the LORD, the altar of holocausts with all its utensils, and the table for the showbread with all its utensils. [19]All the articles which King Ahaz during his reign had thrown away because of his apostasy, we have restored and consecrated, and they are now before the LORD's altar."

The Rite of Expiation. [20]Then King Hezekiah hastened to convoke the princes of the city and went up to the LORD's house. [21]Seven bulls, seven rams, seven lambs and seven he-goats were brought for a sin offering for the kingdom, for the sanctuary, and for Judah, and he ordered the sons of Aaron, the priests, to offer them on the altar of the LORD. [22]They slaughtered the bulls, and the priests collected the blood and cast it on the altar. Then they slaughtered the rams and cast the blood on the altar; then they slaughtered the lambs and cast the blood on the altar. [23]Then the he-goats for the sin offering were led before the king and the assembly, who laid their hands upon them. [24]The priests then slaughtered them and offered their blood on the altar to atone for the sin of all Israel; for "The holocaust and the sin offering," the king had said, "is for all Israel."

[25]He stationed the Levites in the LORD's house with cymbals, harps and lyres according to the prescriptions of David, of Gad the king's seer, and of Nathan the prophet; for the prescriptions were from the LORD through his prophets. [26]The Levites were stationed with the instruments of David, and the priests with the trumpets. [27]Then Hezekiah ordered the holocaust to be sacrificed on the altar, and in the same instant that the holocaust began, they also began the song of the LORD, to the accompaniment of the trumpets and the instruments of David, king of Israel. [28]The entire assembly prostrated itself, and they continued to sing the song and to sound the trumpets until the holocaust had been completed. [29]As the holocaust was completed, the king and all who were with him knelt and prostrated themselves. [30]King Hezekiah and the princes then commanded the Levites to sing the praises of the LORD in the words of David and of Asaph the seer. They sang praises till their joy was full, then fell down and prostrated themselves.

[31]Hezekiah now spoke out this command: "You have undertaken a work for the LORD. Approach, and bring forward the sacrifices and thank offerings for the house of the LORD." Then the assembly brought forward the sacrifices and thank offerings and all the holocausts which were free-will offerings. [32]The number of holocausts that the assembly brought forward was seventy oxen, one hundred rams, and two hundred lambs: all of these as a holocaust to the LORD. [33]As consecrated gifts there were six hundred oxen and three thousand sheep. [34]Since the priests were too few in number to be able to skin all the victims for the holocausts, their brethren the Levites assisted them until the task was completed and the priests had sanctified themselves; the Levites, in fact, were more willing than the priests to sanctify themselves.[d] [35]Also, the holocausts were many, along with the fat of the peace offerings and the libations for the holocausts. Thus the service of the house of the LORD was reestablished. [36]Hezekiah and all the people rejoiced over what God had reestablished for the people, and at how suddenly this had been done.

d: 1 Chr 15, 12.

CHAPTER 30

See RG
203-4

Invitation to the Passover. [1]Hezekiah sent a message to all Israel and Judah, and even wrote letters to Ephraim and Manasseh saying that they should come to the house of the LORD in Jerusalem to celebrate the Passover in honor of the LORD, the God of Israel.[e] [2]The king, his princes, and the entire assembly in Jerusalem had agreed to celebrate the Passover during the second month, [3]for they could not celebrate it at the time of the restoration: the priests had not sanctified themselves in sufficient numbers, and the people were not gathered at Jerusalem. [4]When this proposal had been approved by the king and the entire assembly, [5]they issued a decree to be proclaimed throughout all Israel from Beer-sheba to Dan, that everyone should come to Jerusalem to celebrate the Passover in honor of the LORD, the God of Israel; for not many had kept it in the manner prescribed. [6]Accordingly the couriers, with the letters written by the king and his princes, traversed all Israel and Judah, and at the king's command they said: "Israelites, return to the LORD, the God of Abraham, Isaac and Israel, that he may return to you, the remnant left from the hands of the Assyrian kings. [7]Be not like your fathers and your brethren who proved faithless to the LORD, the God of their fathers, so that he delivered them over to desolation, as you yourselves now see.[g] [8]Be not obstinate, as your fathers were; extend your hands to the LORD and come to his sanctuary that he has consecrated forever, and serve the LORD, your God, that he may turn away his burning anger from you. [9]For when you return to the LORD, your brethren and your children will find mercy with their captors and return to this land; for merciful and compassionate is the LORD, your God, and he will not turn away his face from you if you return to him."[h]

[10]So the couriers passed from city to city in the land of Ephraim and Manasseh and as far as Zebulun, but they were derided and scoffed at. [11]Nevertheless, some from Asher, Manasseh and Zebulun humbled themselves and came to Jerusalem. [12]In Judah, however, the power of God brought it about that the people were of one mind to carry out the command of the king and the princes in accordance with the word of the LORD. [13]Thus many people gathered in Jerusalem to celebrate the feast of Unleavened Bread in the second month; it was a very great assembly.

The Passover Celebrated. [14]They proceeded to take down the altars that were in Jerusalem; also they removed all the altars of incense and cast them into the Kidron Valley.[i] [15]They slaughtered the Passover on the fourteenth day of the second month. The priests and Levites, touched with shame, sanctified themselves and brought holocausts into the house of the LORD. [16]They stood in the places prescribed for them according to the law of Moses, the man of God. The priests sprinkled the blood given them by the Levites; [17]for many in the assembly had not sanctified themselves, and the Levites were in charge of slaughtering the Passover victims for all who were unclean and therefore could not consecrate them to the LORD.[j] [18]The greater part of the people, in fact, chiefly from Ephraim, Manasseh, Issachar and Zebulun, had not cleansed themselves. Nevertheless they ate the Passover, contrary to the prescription; for Hezekiah prayed for them, saying, "May the LORD, who is good, grant pardon to [19]everyone who has resolved to seek God, the LORD, the God of his fathers, though he be not clean as holiness requires." [20]The LORD heard Hezekiah and spared the people.

[21]Thus the Israelites who were in Jerusalem celebrated the feast of Unleavened Bread with great rejoicing for seven days, and the Levites and the priests sang the praises of the LORD day after day with all their strength. [22]Hezekiah spoke encouragingly to all the Levites who had shown themselves well skilled in the service of the LORD. And when they had completed the seven days of festival, slaying peace offerings and singing praises to the LORD, the God of their fathers, [23]the whole assembly agreed to celebrate another seven days. With

e: Ex 12, 1-28.   *f:* 2ff: Nm 9, 6-13.   *g:* Acts 7, 51.   *h:* 1 Kgs 8, 50.   *i:* 2 Chr 28, 42f.   *j:* 2 Chr 35, 6.

joy, therefore, they continued the festivity seven days longer. [24]King Hezekiah of Judah had contributed a thousand bulls and seven thousand sheep to the assembly, and the princes had contributed to the assembly a thousand bulls and ten thousand sheep. The priests sanctified themselves in great numbers, [25]and the whole assembly of Judah rejoiced, together with the priests and Levites and the rest of the assembly that had come from Israel, as well as the sojourners from the land of Israel and those that lived in Judah. [26]There was great rejoicing in Jerusalem, for since the days of Solomon, son of David, king of Israel, there had not been the like in the city. [27]Then the levitical priests rose and blessed the people; their voice was heard and their prayer reached heaven, God's holy dwelling.

See RG
203-4

CHAPTER 31

Liturgical Reform. [1]After all this was over, those Israelites who had been present went forth to the cities of Judah and smashed the sacred pillars, cut down the sacred poles, and tore down the high places and altars throughout Judah, Benjamin, Ephraim and Manasseh, until all were destroyed. Then the Israelites returned to their various cities, each to his own possession.[k]

[2]Hezekiah reestablished the classes of the priests and the Levites according to their former classification, assigning to each priest and Levite his proper service, whether in regard to holocausts or peace offerings, thanksgiving or praise, or ministering in the gates of the encampment of the LORD. [3]From his own wealth the king allotted a portion for holocausts, those of morning and evening and those on sabbaths, new moons and festivals, as prescribed in the law of the LORD.[l] [4]He also commanded the people living in Jerusalem to provide the support of the priests and Levites, that they might devote themselves entirely to the law of the LORD.

[5]As soon as the order was promulgated, the Israelites brought, in great quantities, the best of their grain, wine, oil and honey, and all the produce of the fields; they gave a generous tithe of everything.[m] [6]Israelites and Judahites living in other cities of Judah also brought in tithes of oxen, sheep, and things that had been consecrated to the LORD, their God; these they brought in and set out in heaps.[n] [7]It was in the third month that they began to establish these heaps, and they completed them in the seventh month.* [8]When Hezekiah and the princes had come and seen the heaps, they blessed the LORD and his people Israel. [9]Then Hezekiah questioned the priests and the Levites concerning the heaps, [10]and the priest Azariah, head of the house of Zadoc, answered him, "Since they began to bring the offerings to the house of the LORD, we have eaten to the full and have had much left over, for the LORD has blessed his people. This great supply is what was left over."[o]

[11]Hezekiah then gave orders that chambers should be constructed in the house of the LORD. When this had been done, [12]the offerings, tithes and consecrated things were deposited there in safekeeping. The overseer of these things was Conaniah the Levite, and his brother Shimei was second in charge. [13]Jehiel, Azaziah, Nathan, Asahel, Jerimoth, Jozabad, Eliel, Ismachiah, Mahath and Benaiah were supervisors subject to Conaniah and his brother Shimei by appointment of King Hezekiah and of Azariah, the prefect of the house of God. [14]Kore, the son of Imnah, a Levite and the keeper of the eastern gate, was in charge of the free-will gifts made to God; he distributed the offerings made to the LORD and the most holy of the consecrated things. [15]Under him in the priestly cities were Eden, Miniamin, Jeshua, Shemaiah, Amariah and Shecaniah, who faithfully made the distribution to their brethren, great and small alike, according to their classes.

[16]There was also a register by ancestral houses of males thirty years of age and over, for all priests who were eligible to enter the

---

31, 7: Third month . . . seventh month: between the feast of Pentecost and that of Booths, an interval without rain in Palestine, at the end of which the problem of storage (v 11) would become more urgent.

---

k: 2 Chr 34, 3f; 2 Kgs 18, 4.   *l:* 1 Chr 29, 3; Ez 45, 17; Nm 28—29.   *m:* Nm 18, 8-24; Dt 14, 22f.   *n:* Nm 12, 44-47; 13, 10-13.
o: Lv 25, 19-22.

house of the LORD according to the daily rule to fulfill their service in the order of their classes.*p* *17*The priests were inscribed in their family records according to their ancestral houses, and the Levites of twenty years and over according to their various offices and classes.*q* *18*A distribution was also made to all who were inscribed in the family records, for their little ones, wives, sons and daughters—thus for the entire assembly, since they were to sanctify themselves by sharing faithfully in the consecrated things. *19*The sons of Aaron, the priests who lived on the lands attached to their cities, had in every city men designated by name to distribute portions to every male among the priests and to every Levite listed in the family records.

*20*This Hezekiah did in all Judah. He did what was good, upright and faithful before the LORD, his God. *21*Everything that he undertook, for the service of the house of God or for the law and the commandments, was to do the will of his God. He did this wholeheartedly, and he prospered.*r*

CHAPTER 32

See RG
203–4

Invasion of Sennacherib. *1*But after he had proved his fidelity by such deeds, Sennacherib, king of Assyria, came. He invaded Judah, besieged the fortified cities, and proposed to take them by storm.*s* *2*When Hezekiah saw that Sennacherib was coming with the intention of attacking Jerusalem, *3*he decided in counsel with his princes and warriors to stop the waters of the springs outside the city. When they had pledged him their support, *4t*a large crowd was gathered which stopped all the springs and also the running stream in the valley nearby. For they said, "Why should the kings of Assyria come and find an abundance of water?" *5*He then looked to his defenses: he rebuilt the wall where it was broken down, raised towers upon it, and built another wall outside. He strengthened the Millo of the City of David and had a great number of spears and shields prepared.*u* *6*Then he appointed army commanders over the people. He gathered

them together in his presence in the open space at the gate of the city and encouraged them with these words: *7*"Be brave and steadfast; do not be afraid or dismayed because of the king of Assyria and all the throng that is coming with him, for there is more with us than with him.*v* *8*For he has only an arm of flesh, but we have the LORD, our God, to help us and to fight our battles." And the people took confidence from the words of King Hezekiah of Judah.*w*

Threat of Sennacherib. *9x*After this, while Sennacherib, king of Assyria, himself remained at Lachish with all his forces, he sent his officials to Jerusalem with this message for King Hezekiah of Judah, and all the Judahites who were in Jerusalem: *10*"King Sennacherib of Assyria has this to say: On what are you relying, while you remain under siege in Jerusalem? *11*Has not Hezekiah deceived you, delivering you over to a death of famine and thirst, by his claim that 'the LORD, our God, will save us from the grasp of the king of Assyria'? *12*Has not this same Hezekiah removed his high places and altars and commanded Judah and Jerusalem, 'You shall prostrate yourselves before one altar only, and on it alone you shall offer incense'? *13*Do you not know what my fathers and I have done to all the peoples of other lands? Were the gods of the nations in those lands able to save their lands from my hand? *14*Who among all the gods of those nations which my fathers put under the ban was able to save his people from my hand? Will your god, then, be able to save you from my hand? *15*Let not Hezekiah mislead you further and deceive you in any such way. Do not believe him! Since no other god of any other nation or kingdom has been able to save his people from my hand or the hands of my fathers, how much the less shall your god save you from my hand!"

*16*His officials said still more against the LORD God and against his servant Hezekiah, *17*for he had written letters to deride the LORD, the God of Israel, speaking of him in these terms: "As the gods of the nations in

p: 1 Chr 23, 3f.   *q:* 1 Chr 23, 6-24.   *r:* Ps 119, 2f.   *s:* 2 Kgs 18, 13.   *t:* Is 22, 9. 11.   *u:* Neh 2, 17f.   *v:* 2 Chr 14, 10; 20, 6-12.
w: Is 31, 3.   *x:* 9-20: 2 Kgs 18, 17-37; Is 36, 1-22.

Exile of Northern Kingdom

other lands have not saved their people from my hand, neither shall Hezekiah's god save his people from my hand."[y] [18]In a loud voice they shouted in the Judean language to the people of Jerusalem who were on the wall, to frighten and terrify them so that they might capture their city. [19]They spoke of the God of Israel as though he were one of the gods of the other peoples of the earth, a work of human hands. [20]But because of this, King Hezekiah and the prophet Isaiah, son of Amos, prayed and called out to heaven.[z]

Defeat of Sennacherib. [21]Then the LORD sent an angel, who destroyed every valiant warrior, leader and commander in the camp of the Assyrian king, so that he had to return shamefaced to his own country. And when he entered the temple of his god, some of his own offspring struck him down there with the sword.[a] [22]Thus the LORD saved Hezekiah and the inhabitants of Jerusalem from the hand of Sennacherib, king of Assyria, as from every other power; he gave them rest on every side. [23]Many brought gifts for the LORD to Jerusalem and costly objects for King Hezekiah of Judah, who thereafter was exalted in the eyes of all the nations.[b]

Hezekiah's Other Deeds. [24]In those days Hezekiah became mortally ill. He prayed to the LORD, who answered him by giving him a sign.[c] [25]Hezekiah, however, did not then discharge his debt of gratitude, for he had become proud. Therefore anger descended upon him and upon Judah and Jerusalem. [26d]But then Hezekiah humbled himself for his pride—both he and the inhabitants of Jerusalem; and therefore the LORD did not vent his anger on them during the time of Hezekiah.

[27e]Hezekiah possessed very great wealth and glory. He had treasuries made for his silver, gold, precious stones, spices, jewels, and other precious things of all kinds; [28]also storehouses for the harvest of grain, for wine and oil, and barns for the various kinds of cattle and for the flocks. [29]He built cities for

y: 2 Kgs 19, 9-13; Is 37, 9-13.   *z:* 2 Kgs 19, 14-19; Is 37, 14-20.   *a:* 2 Kgs 19, 35ff; Is 37, 36ff.   *b:* 2 Chr 14, 6.   *c:* 2 Kgs 20, 1-11; Is 38, 1-8.   *d:* 26. 31: 2 Kgs 20, 12-19; Is 39, 1-8.   *e:* 27f: 2 Kgs 20, 13; Is 39, 2.

himself, and he acquired sheep and oxen in great numbers, for God gave him very great riches. *30*This same Hezekiah stopped the upper outflow of water from Gihon and led it underground westward to the City of David. Hezekiah prospered in all his undertakings.*f* *31*Nevertheless, in respect to the ambassadors [princes] sent to him from Babylon to investigate the sign that had occurred in the land, God forsook him to test him, that he might know all that was in his heart.

*32*The rest of Hezekiah's acts, including his pious works, can be found written in the Vision of the Prophet Isaiah, son of Amos, and in the book of the kings of Judah and Israel. *33*Hezekiah rested with his ancestors; he was buried at the approach to the tombs* of the descendants of David. All Judah and the inhabitants of Jerusalem paid him honor at his death. His son Manasseh succeeded him as king.

CHAPTER 33

See RG 203-4

Impiety of Manasseh. *1g*Manasseh was twelve years old when he became king, and he reigned fifty-five years in Jerusalem. *2*He did evil in the sight of the LORD, following the abominable practices of the nations whom the LORD had cleared out of the way of the Israelites. *3*He rebuilt the high places which his father Hezekiah had torn down, erected altars for the Baals, made sacred poles, and prostrated himself before the whole host of heaven and worshiped them. *4*He even built altars in the temple of the LORD, of which the LORD had said, "In Jerusalem shall my name be forever": *5*he built altars to the whole host of heaven in the two courts of the LORD's house. *6*It was he, too, who immolated his sons by fire in the Valley of Ben-hinnom. He practiced augury, divination and magic, and appointed necromancers and diviners of spirits, so that he provoked the LORD with the great evil that he did in his sight. *7*He placed

an idol that he had carved in the house of God, of which God had said to David and his son Solomon: "In this house and in Jerusalem which I have chosen from all the tribes of Israel I shall place my name forever. *8*I will not again allow Israel's feet to leave the land which I assigned to your fathers, provided they are careful to observe all that I commanded them, keeping the whole law and the statutes and the ordinances given by Moses." *9*Manasseh misled Judah and the inhabitants of Jerusalem into doing even greater evil than the nations which the LORD had destroyed at the coming of the Israelites. *10*The LORD spoke to Manasseh and his people, but they paid no attention.

His Conversion. *11h*Therefore the LORD brought against them the army commanders of the Assyrian king; they took Manasseh with hooks, shackled him with chains, and transported him to Babylon.* *12*In this distress, he began to appease the LORD, his God. He humbled himself abjectly before the God of his fathers *13*and prayed to him.* The LORD let himself be won over: he heard his prayer and restored him to his kingdom in Jerusalem. Then Manasseh understood that the LORD is indeed God.

*14*Afterward he built an outer wall for the City of David to the west of Gihon in the valley, extending to the Fish Gate and encircling Ophel; he built it very high. He stationed army officers in all the fortified cities of Judah. *15*He removed the foreign gods and the idol from the LORD's house and all the altars he had built on the mount of the LORD's house and in Jerusalem, and he cast them outside the city.*i* *16*He restored the altar of the LORD, and sacrificed on it peace offerings and thank offerings, and commanded Judah to serve the LORD, the God of Israel. *17*Though the people continued to sacrifice on the high places, they now did so to the LORD, their God.

32, 33: The approach to the tombs: literally, "the ascent of the tombs," which may mean "the upper section of the tombs," their most prominent and honored place.

33, 11: There is no evidence elsewhere for an imprisonment of King Manasseh in Babylon. However, according to the Assyrian inscriptions, he paid tribute to the Assyrian kings Esarhaddon (680–669 B.C.) and Asshurbanipal (668–627 B.C.). He may well have been obliged to go to Nineveh to

take the oath of allegiance as vassal to the king of Assyria.

33, 13: And prayed to him: these words led an unknown writer to compose the apocryphal "Prayer of Manasseh," which is added as an appendix to many editions of the Vulgate Bible and is used in the public prayers of the church.

---

f: 2 Kgs 20, 20f.   *g:* 1-10: 2 Kgs 21, 1-9.   *h:* Jb 36, 7f; Ez 19, 9. *i:* 2 Chr 14, 2.

[18] [j]The rest of the acts of Manasseh, his prayer to his God, and the words of the seers who spoke to him in the name of the LORD, the God of Israel, can be found written in the chronicles of the kings of Israel. [19]His prayer and how his supplication was heard, all his sins and his infidelity, the sites where he built high places and erected sacred poles and carved images before he humbled himself, all can be found written down in the history of his seers. [20]Manasseh rested with his ancestors and was buried in his own palace. His son Amon succeeded him as king.

Amon. [21] [k]Amon was twenty-two years old when he became king, and he reigned two years in Jerusalem. [22]He did evil in the sight of the LORD, just as his father Manasseh had done. Amon offered sacrifice to all the idols which his father Manasseh had made, and worshiped them. [23]Moreover, he did not humble himself before the LORD as his father Manasseh had done; on the contrary, Amon only increased his guilt. [24]His servants conspired against him and put him to death in his own house. [25]But the people of the land slew all those who had conspired against King Amon, and then they, the people of the land, made his son Josiah king in his stead.

CHAPTER 34

See RG
203–4

Reforms of Josiah. [1] [l]Josiah was eight years old when he became king, and he reigned thirty-one years in Jerusalem. [2]He pleased the LORD, following the path of his ancestor David. [3] [m]In the eighth year of his reign, while he was still a youth, he began to seek after the God of his forefather David, and in his twelfth year* he began to purge Judah and Jerusalem of the high places, the sacred poles and the carved and molten images. [4]In his presence, the altars of the Baals were destroyed; the incense stands erected above them were torn down; the sacred poles and the carved and molten images were shattered

and beaten into dust, which was strewn over the tombs of those who had sacrificed to them; [5]and the bones of the priests he burned upon their altars. Thus he purged Judah and Jerusalem. [6]He did likewise in the cities of Manasseh, Ephraim, Simeon, and in the ruined villages of the surrounding country as far as Naphtali; [7]he destroyed the altars, broke up the sacred poles and carved images and beat them into dust, and tore down the incense stands throughout the land of Israel. Then he returned to Jerusalem.

The Temple Restored. [8] [n]In the eighteenth year of his reign, in order to cleanse the temple as well as the land, he sent Shaphan, son of Azaliah, Maaseiah, the ruler of the city, and Joah, son of Joahaz, the chamberlain, to restore the house of the LORD, his God. [9]They came to Hilkiah the high priest and turned over the money brought to the house of God which the Levites, the guardians of the threshold, had collected from Manasseh, Ephraim, and all the remnant of Israel, as well as from all of Judah, Benjamin, and the inhabitants of Jerusalem.[o] [10]They turned it over to the master workmen in the house of the LORD, and these in turn used it to pay the workmen in the LORD's house who were restoring and repairing the temple. [11]They also gave it to the carpenters and the masons to buy hewn stone and timber for the tie beams and rafters of the buildings which the kings of Judah had allowed to fall into ruin. [12]The men worked faithfully at their tasks; their overseers were Jahath and Obadiah, Levites of the line of Merari, and Zechariah and Meshullam, of the Kohathites, who directed them. All those Levites who were skillful with musical instruments [13]were in charge of the men who carried the burdens, and they directed all the workers in every kind of labor. Some of the other Levites were scribes, officials and gatekeepers.

The Finding of the Law. [14] [p]When they

34, 3: In his twelfth year: c. 628 B.C., the year after Asshurbanipal's death, when Judah could free itself from Assyrian domination. From 2 Kgs 22, 1—23, 25 alone, one might think that Josiah's reform began only after the discovery of the book of the law in the temple, in the eighteenth year of his reign. But the Chronicler is no doubt right in placing the beginning of the reform at an earlier period.

The very repair of the temple, which led to the finding of the book of the law, must have been occasioned by a cultic reform.

j: 18. 20: 2 Kgs 21, 17f. k: 21-25: 2 Kgs 21, 19-26. l: 1f: 2 Kgs 22, 1f. m: 3-7: 2 Chr 14, 1-4; 31, 1; 2 Kgs 23, 4-20. n: 8-13: 2 Kgs 22, 3-7. o: 2 Chr 24, 8f. p: 14-28: 2 Kgs 22, 8-20.

brought out the money that had been deposited in the house of the LORD, Hilkiah the priest found the book of the law of the LORD given through Moses. ¹⁵He reported this to Shaphan the scribe, saying, "I have found the book of the law in the house of the LORD." Hilkiah gave the book to Shaphan, ¹⁶who brought it to the king at the same time that he was making his report to him. He said, "Your servants are doing everything that has been entrusted to them; ¹⁷they have turned into bullion the metals deposited in the LORD's house and have handed it over to the overseers and the workmen." ¹⁸Then Shaphan the scribe announced to the king, "Hilkiah the priest has given me a book." And Shaphan read from it before the king.

¹⁹When the king heard the words of the law, he tore his garments ²⁰and issued this command to Hilkiah, to Ahikam, son of Shaphan, to Abdon, son of Michah, to Shaphan the scribe, and to Asaiah, the king's servant: ²¹"On behalf of myself and those who are left in Israel and Judah, go, consult the LORD concerning the words of the book that has been found. For the anger of the LORD has been set furiously ablaze against us, since our fathers have not kept the word of the LORD and have not done all that is written in this book." ²²Then Hilkiah and the other men from the king went to the prophetess Huldah, the wife of Shallum, son of Tokhath, son of Hasrah, the guardian of the wardrobe; she dwelt in Jerusalem, in the new quarter. They spoke to her as they had been instructed, ²³and she said to them: "Thus says the LORD, the God of Israel: 'Tell the one who sent you to me, ²⁴The LORD says: I am prepared to bring evil upon this place and upon its inhabitants, all the curses written in the book that has been read before the king of Judah. ²⁵Because they have abandoned me and have offered incense to other gods, provoking me by every deed that they have performed, my anger is ablaze against this place and cannot be extinguished.' ²⁶"But to the king of Judah who sent you to consult the LORD, give this response: 'Thus

says the LORD, the God of Israel, concerning the threats you have heard: ²⁷Because you were heartsick and have humbled yourself before God on hearing his words spoken against this place and its inhabitants; because you have humbled yourself before me, have torn your garments, and have wept before me, I in turn have listened—so declares the LORD. ²⁸I will gather you to your ancestors and you shall be taken to your grave in peace. Your eyes shall not see all the evil I will bring upon this place and upon its inhabitants.' "

They brought back this message to the king.

Renewal of the Covenant. ²⁹�q The king now convened all the elders of Judah and Jerusalem. ³⁰He went up to the house of the LORD with all the men of Judah and the inhabitants of Jerusalem, the priests, the Levites, and all the people, great and small; and he had read aloud to them the entire text of the book of the covenant that had been found in the house of the LORD. ³¹Standing at his post,* the king made a covenant before the LORD to follow the LORD and to keep his commandments, decrees, and statutes with his whole heart and soul, thus observing the terms of the covenant written in this book. ³²He thereby committed all who were of Jerusalem and Benjamin, and the inhabitants of Jerusalem conformed themselves to the covenant of God, the God of their fathers. ³³Josiah removed every abominable thing from all the territory belonging to the Israelites, and he obliged all who were in Israel to serve the LORD, their God. During his lifetime they did not desert the LORD, the God of their fathers.ʳ

CHAPTER 35

See RG 203–4

The Passover. ¹ˢJosiah celebrated in Jerusalem a Passover to honor the LORD; the Passover sacrifice was slaughtered on the fourteenth day of the first month.ᵗ ²He reappointed the priests to their duties and encouraged them in the service of the LORD's house. ³He said to the Levites who were to instruct all Israel, and who were consecrated to the LORD: "Put the holy ark in the house built by

34, 31: Standing at his post: see note on 2 Chr 23, 13.

q: 29-32: 2 Kgs 23, 1ff.   *r:* 2 Kgs 23, 4-20.   *s:* 1-19: 2 Kgs 23, 21ff.   *t:* Ex 12, 1-28; 2 Kgs 23, 21.

Solomon, son of David, king of Israel. It shall no longer be a burden on your shoulders. Serve now the LORD, your God, and his people Israel.[u] [4]Prepare yourselves in your ancestral houses and your classes according to the prescriptions of King David of Israel and his son Solomon. [5]Stand in the sanctuary according to the divisions of the ancestral houses of your brethren, the common people, so that the distribution of the Levites and the families may be the same.[v] [6]Slay the Passover sacrifice, sanctify yourselves, and be at the disposition of your brethren, that all may be carried out according to the word of the LORD given through Moses."[w]

[7]Josiah contributed to the common people a flock of lambs and kids, thirty thousand in number, each to serve as a Passover victim for any who were present, and also three thousand oxen; these were from the king's property.[x] [8]His princes also gave a free-will gift to the people, the priests and the Levites. Hilkiah, Zechariah and Jehiel, prefects of the house of God, gave to the priests two thousand six hundred Passover victims together with three hundred oxen.[y] [9]Conaniah and his brothers Shemaiah, Nethanel, Hashabiah, Jehiel and Jozabad, the rulers of the Levites, contributed to the Levites five thousand Passover victims, together with five hundred oxen.

[10]When the service had been arranged, the priests took their places, as did the Levites in their classes according to the king's command. [11]The Passover sacrifice was slaughtered, whereupon the priests sprinkled some of the blood and the Levites proceeded to the skinning. [12]They separated what was destined for the holocaust and gave it to various groups of the ancestral houses of the common people to offer to the LORD, as is prescribed in the book of Moses. They did the same with the oxen. [13]They cooked the Passover on the fire as prescribed, and also cooked the sacred meals in pots, cauldrons and pans, then brought them quickly to all the common people.[z] [14]Afterward they prepared the Passover for themselves and for the priests. Indeed the priests, the sons of Aaron, were busy offering holocausts and the fatty portions until night; therefore the Levites prepared for themselves and for the priests, the sons of Aaron. [15]The singers, the sons of Asaph, were at their posts as prescribed by David: Asaph, Heman and Jeduthun, the king's seer. The gatekeepers were at every gate; there was no need for them to leave their stations, for their brethren, the Levites, prepared for them. [16]Thus the entire service of the Lord was arranged that day so that the Passover could be celebrated and the holocausts offered on the altar of the Lord, as King Josiah had commanded. [17]The Israelites who were present on that occasion kept the Passover and the feast of the Unleavened Bread for seven days. [18a]No such Passover had been observed in Israel since the time of the prophet Samuel, nor had any king of Israel kept a Passover like that of Josiah, the priests and Levites, all of Judah and Israel that were present, and the inhabitants of Jerusalem. [19]It was in the eighteenth year of Josiah's reign that this Passover was observed.

Josiah's Reign Ends. [20]After Josiah had done all this to restore the temple, Neco, king of Egypt, came up to fight at Carchemish on the Euphrates, and Josiah went out to intercept him. [21]Neco sent messengers to him, saying: "What quarrel is between us, king of Judah? I have not come against you this day, for my war is with another kingdom, and God has told me to hasten. Do not interfere with God who is with me, as otherwise he will destroy you." [22]But Josiah would not withdraw from him; for he had sought a pretext for fighting with him. Therefore he would not listen to the words of Neco that came from the mouth of God, but went out to fight in the plain of Megiddo. [23]Then the archers shot King Josiah, who said to his servants, "Take me away, for I am seriously wounded."[b] [24]His servants removed him from his own chariot, placed him in another he had in reserve, and brought him to Jerusalem, where he died. He was buried in the tombs of his ancestors, and

u: 2 Chr 5, 4; 1 Chr 15, 12. 15.   *v:* 1 Chr 24—26.   *w:* 2 Chr 30, 17.   *x:* Ex 12, 5.   *y:* Nm 7, 1-83.   *z:* Nm 12, 8f.   *a:* 18f: 2 Kgs 23, 22f.   *b:* 2 Chr 18, 33f.

all Judah and Jerusalem mourned him. [25]Jeremiah also composed a lamentation over Josiah,* which is recited to this day by all the male and female singers in their lamentations over Josiah. These have been made obligatory for Israel, and can be found written in the Lamentations.

[26c]The rest of the chronicle of Josiah, his pious deeds in regard to what is written in the law of the LORD, and his acts, first and last, can be found written in the book of the kings of Israel and Judah.

CHAPTER 36

See RG
203–4

[1d]The people of the land took Jehoahaz, son of Josiah, and made him king in Jerusalem in his father's stead.

IV: End of the Kingdom

Jehoahaz. [2]Jehoahaz was twenty-three years old when he became king, and he reigned three months in Jerusalem. [3]The king of Egypt deposed him in Jerusalem and fined the land one hundred talents of silver and a talent of gold. [4]Then the king of Egypt made his brother Eliakim king over Judah and Jerusalem, and changed his name to Jehoiakim. Neco took his brother Jehoahaz away and brought him to Egypt.

Jehoiakim. [5]Jehoiakim was twenty-five years old when he became king, and he reigned eleven years in Jerusalem. He did evil in the sight of the LORD, his God.[e] [6f]Nebuchadnezzar, king of Babylon, came up against him and bound him with chains to take him to Babylon.* [7]Nebuchadnezzar also carried away to Babylon some of the vessels of the house of the LORD and put them in his palace in Babylon. [8]The rest of the acts of Jehoiakim, the abominable things that he did, and what therefore happened to him, can be found written in the book of the kings of Israel and Judah. His son Jehoiachin succeeded him as king.[g]

Jehoiachin. [9]Jehoiachin was eighteen years old when he became king, and he reigned three months [and ten days] in Jerusalem. He did evil in the sight of the LORD.[h] [10]At the turn of the year, King Nebuchadnezzar sent for him and had him brought to Babylon, along with precious vessels from the temple of the LORD. He made his brother Zedekiah* king over Judah and Jerusalem.[i]

Zedekiah. [11]Zedekiah was twenty-one years old when he became king, and he reigned eleven years in Jerusalem.[j] [12]He did evil in the sight of the LORD, his God, and he did not humble himself before the prophet Jeremiah, who spoke the word of the LORD.[k] [13]He also rebelled against King Nebuchadnezzar, who had made him swear by God. He became stiff-necked and hardened his heart rather than return to the LORD, the God of Israel.[l] [14]Likewise all the princes of Judah, the priests and the people added infidelity to infidelity, practicing all the abominations of the nations and polluting the LORD's temple which he had consecrated in Jerusalem.

Dissolution of Judah. [15]Early and often did the LORD, the God of their fathers, send his messengers to them, for he had compassion on his people and his dwelling place.[m] [16]But they mocked the messengers of God, despised his warnings, and scoffed at his prophets, until the anger of the LORD against his people was so inflamed that there was no remedy.[n] [17]Then he brought up against them the king of the Chaldeans, who slew their young men in their own sanctuary building,

35, 25: The reference to a lamentation over Josiah composed by Jeremiah is not found either in 2 Kgs or Jer; but see note on Zec 12, 11. Their lamentations: probably a reference to the canonical Book of Lamentations.

36, 6: Nebuchadnezzar . . . bound him with chains to take him to Babylon: the Chronicler does not say that Jehoiakim was actually taken to Babylon. According to 2 Kgs 24, 1-6, Jehoiakim revolted after being Nebuchadnezzar's vassal for three years; he died in Jerusalem before the Babylonian king could reach the city. However, Dn 1, 1f, apparently based on 2 Chr 36, 6f, speaks of Jehoiakim's deportation to Babylon.

36, 10: His brother Zedekiah: Zedekiah was actually the brother of Jehoiakim and the uncle of Jehoiachin (2 Kgs 24, 17; Jer 37, 1), though scarcely older than his nephew (2 Kgs 24, 8. 18; 2 Chr 36, 9. 11).

c: 2 Kgs 23, 28. *d:* 1-4: 2 Kgs 23, 30-34; 1 Chr 3, 15f. *e:* 2 Kgs 23, 36f; Jer 22, 18f. *f:* 2 Kgs 24, 1f. *g:* 2 Kgs 24, 5. *h:* 2 Kgs 24, 8f. *i:* 2 Kgs 24, 10-16. *j:* 2 Kgs 24, 18ff; Jer 52, 1ff. *k:* Jer 37, 1ff. *l:* 2 Kgs 25, 1; Jer 52, 4; Ex 17, 13-16. *m:* Jer 7, 25; Heb 1, 1. *n:* Mt 23, 34ff.

Exile of Southern Kingdom

sparing neither young man nor maiden, neither the aged nor the decrepit; he delivered all of them over into his grip.[o] [18]All the utensils of the house of God, the large and the small, and the treasures of the LORD's house and of the king and his princes, all these he brought to Babylon.[p] [19]They burnt the house of God, tore down the walls of Jerusalem, set all its palaces afire, and destroyed all its precious objects.[q] [20]Those who escaped the sword he carried captive to Babylon, where they became his and his sons' servants until the kingdom of the Persians came to power. [21]All this was to fulfill the word of the LORD spoken by Jeremiah: "Until the land has retrieved its lost sabbaths, during all the time it lies waste it shall have rest while seventy years are fulfilled."

Decree of Cyrus. [22]*In the first year of Cyrus, king of Persia, in order to fulfill the word of the LORD spoken by Jeremiah, the LORD inspired King Cyrus of Persia to issue this proclamation throughout his kingdom, both by word of mouth and in writing:[r] [23]"Thus says Cyrus, king of Persia: 'All the kingdoms of the earth the LORD, the God of heaven, has given to me, and he has also charged me to build him a house in Jerusalem, which is in Judah. Whoever, therefore, among you belongs to any part of his people, let him go up, and may his God be with him!' "

36, 22f: The words of these verses are identical with those of Ezr 1, 1-3a. Originally Ezra-Nehemiah formed the last part of the single work of the Chronicler, of which 1 and 2 Chronicles formed the first part. But when Ezra-Nehemiah was regarded as a natural sequence to the Books of Samuel and of Kings, it was separated from 1 and 2 Chronicles and placed before them. Thus, 1 and 2 Chronicles became the last part of the Hebrew Bible. To prevent this work from ending on a note of doom, Ezr 1, 1-3a was repeated as 2 Chr 36, 22f.

o: Lam 1, 15; 5, 11-14.   p: 2 Kgs 25, 14f.   q: 2 Kgs 25, 9f; Lam 2, 8.   r: Ezr 1, 1ff.

See RG
207–11

The Book of Ezra

The last four books of the Hebrew canon are Ezra, Nehemiah, 1 and 2 Chronicles, in that order. Originally, however, Ezra and Nehemiah followed the Books of Chronicles, and formed with them a unified historical work so homogeneous in spirit that one usually speaks of a single author for the four books. He is called "the Chronicler." The treatment of Ezra-Nehemiah as a single book by the earliest chroniclers was undoubtedly due to the fact that in ancient times the two books were put under the one name—Ezra. The combined work Ezra-Nehemiah is our most important literary source for the formation of the Jewish religious community after the Babylonian exile. This is known as the period of the Restoration, and the two men most responsible for the reorganization of Jewish life at this time were Ezra and Nehemiah.

In the present state of the Ezra-Nehemiah text, there are several dislocations of large sections so that the chronological or logical sequence is disrupted. The major instances are pointed out in the footnotes. Although Ezra appears before Nehemiah in this work, it seems probable that Nehemiah's activity preceded his.

What is known of Ezra and his work is due almost exclusively to Ezra 7—10 (the "Ezra Memoirs") and to Neh 8—9. Strictly speaking, the term "Ezra Memoirs" should be used only of that section in which Ezra speaks in the first person, i.e., Ezr 7, 27—9, 15. Compare the "Nehemiah Memoirs" in Neh 1, 1—7, 72a; 11, 1f; 12, 27-43; 13, 4-31. The Chronicler combined this material with other sources at his disposal. The personality of Ezra is less known than that of Nehemiah. Ben Sirach, in his praise of the fathers, makes no mention of Ezra. The genealogy of Ezra (7, 1–5) traces his priesthood back to Aaron, brother of Moses. This was the accepted way of establishing the legality of one's priestly office. He is also called *a scribe, well-versed in the law of Moses* (7, 6), indicating Ezra's dedication to the study of the Torah, which he sought to make the basic rule of life in the restored community. It was in religious and cultic reform rather than in political affairs that Ezra made his mark as a postexilic leader. Jewish tradition holds him in great honor; the Talmud even regards him as a second Moses, claiming that the Torah would have been given to Israel through Ezra had not Moses preceded him.

Ezra is sometimes accused of having been a mere legalist who gave excessive attention to the letter of the law. His work, however, should be seen and judged within a specific historical context. He gave to his people a cohesion and spiritual unity which prevented the disintegration of the small Jewish community. Had it not been for the intransigence of Ezra and of those who adopted his ideal, it is doubtful that Judaism would have so effectively resisted Hellenism, then or in later centuries. Ezra set the tone of the postexilic community, and it was characterized by fidelity to the Torah, Judaism's authentic way of life. It is in this light that we can judge most fairly the work of Ezra during the Restoration.

The Book of Ezra is divided as follows:

I: The Return from Exile (1, 1—6, 22).

II: The Deeds of Ezra (7, 1—10, 44).

The following list of the kings of Persia, with the dates of their reigns, will be useful for dating the events mentioned in Ezra-Nehemiah:

Cyrus	538–529 B.C.
Cambyses	529–521 B.C.
Darius I	521–485 B.C.
Xerxes	485–464 B.C.
Artaxerxes I	464–423 B.C.
Darius II	423–404 B.C.
Artaxerxes II	404–358 B.C.
Artaxerxes III	358–337 B.C.
End of the Persian Empire	
(Defeat of Darius III)	331 B.C.

I: The Return from Exile

CHAPTER 1

See RG
208

The Decree of Cyrus. ¹ᵃIn the first year of Cyrus,* king of Persia, in order to ful-

---

1, 1: In the first year of Cyrus: as sovereign over the world empire which began with his conquest of Babylon; that is, 538 B.C.

---

a: 1ff: 2 Chr 36, 22f; Jer 25, 11f; 29, 10; Zec 1, 12.

509

The Kings of Persia					
Cyrus	538–529 B.C.	Xerxes	485–464 B.C.	Artaxerxes II	404–358 B.C.
Cambyses	529–521 B.C.	Artaxerxes I	464–423 B.C.	Artaxerxes III	358–337 B.C.
Darius I	521–485 B.C.	Darius II	423–404 B.C.	Darius III	336–330 B.C.

(Darius III was defeated by Alexander, and the Persian empire came to an end, in 331 B.C.)

fill the word of the LORD spoken by Jeremiah, the LORD inspired King Cyrus of Persia to issue this proclamation throughout his kingdom, both by word of mouth and in writing: ²"Thus says Cyrus, king of Persia: 'All the kingdoms of the earth the LORD, the God of heaven, has given to me, and he has also charged me to build him a house in Jerusalem, which is in Judah. ³Whoever, therefore, among you belongs to any part of his people, let him go up, and may his God be with him! ⁴Let everyone who has survived, in whatever place he may have dwelt, be assisted by the people of that place with silver, gold, goods, and cattle, together with free will offerings for the house of God in Jerusalem.'"

⁵Then the family heads of Judah and Benjamin and the priests and Levites—everyone, that is, whom God had inspired to do so—prepared to go up to build the house of the LORD in Jerusalem. ⁶All their neighbors gave them help in every way, with silver, gold, goods, and cattle, and with many precious gifts besides all their free-will offerings.ᵇ ⁷King Cyrus, too, had the utensils of the house of the LORD brought forth which Nebuchadnezzar had taken away from Jerusalem and placed in the house of his god. ⁸Cyrus, king of Persia, had them brought forth by the treasurer Mithredath, and counted out to Sheshbazzar,* the prince of Judah. ⁹This was the inventory: sacks of goldware, thirty; sacks of silverware, one thousand and twenty-nine; ¹⁰golden bowls, thirty; silver bowls, four hundred and ten; other ware, one thousand pieces. ¹¹Total of

the gold- and silverware: five thousand four hundred pieces.* All these Sheshbazzar took with him when the exiles were brought back from Babylon to Jerusalem.

CHAPTER 2

See RG 208-9

Census of the Province. ¹*These are the inhabitants of the province who returned from the captivity of the exiles, whom Nebuchadnezzar, king of Babylon, had carried away to Babylon,ᶜ and who came back to Jerusalem and Judah, each man in his own city ²(those who returned with Zerubbabel, Jeshua, Nehemiah, Seraiah, Reelaiah, Mordecai, Bilshan, Mispereth, Bigvai, Rehum, and Baanah):

The census of the men of Israel: ³sons of Parosh, two thousand one hundred and seventy-two; ⁴sons of Shephatiah, three hundred and seventy-two; ⁵sons of Arah, seven hundred and seventy-five; ⁶sons of Pahath-moab, who were sons of Jeshua and Joab, two thousand eight hundred and twelve; ⁷sons of Elam, one thousand two hundred and fifty-four; ⁸sons of Zattu, nine hundred and forty-five; ⁹sons of Zaccai, seven hundred and sixty; ¹⁰sons of Bani, six hundred and forty-two; ¹¹sons of Bebai, six hundred and twenty-three; ¹²sons of Azgad, one thousand two hundred and twenty-two; ¹³sons of Adonikam, six hundred and sixty-six; ¹⁴sons of Bigvai, two thousand and fifty-six; ¹⁵sons of Adin, four hundred and fifty-four; ¹⁶sons of Ater, who were sons of Hezekiah, ninety-eight; ¹⁷sons of Bezai, three hundred and twenty-three; ¹⁸sons of Jorah, one hundred

---

1, 8: Sheshbazzar: very probably the fourth son of Jehoiachin, king of Judah, taken captive to Babylon in 598 B.C., listed in 1 Chr 3, 18 as Senneser; if so, he was the uncle of Zerubbabel (Ezr 3, 2ff); see note on 1 Chr 3, 18.

1, 11: Total . . . five thousand four hundred pieces: either this figure or the figures given for one or more of the items listed (vv

9f) have been corrupted in the transmission of the text.

2, 1-67: As it now stands, this list is an expanded form of the lists of returned captives from the sixth century B.C.; see Neh 7, 6-72, where it reappears.

---

b: Ex 3, 22; 11, 2; 12, 35.   *c:* Neh 7, 6-67.

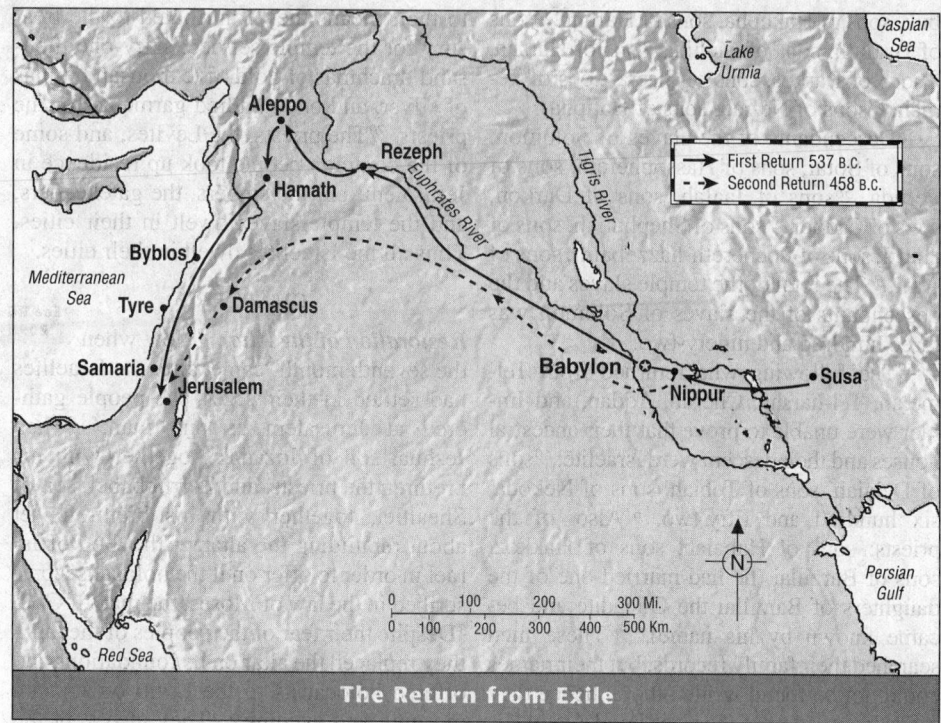

The Return from Exile

and twelve; [19]sons of Hashum, two hundred and twenty-three; [20]sons of Gibeon, ninety-five; [21]sons of Bethlehem, one hundred and twenty-three; [22]men of Netophah, fifty-six; [23]men of Anathoth, one hundred and twenty-eight; [24]men of Beth-azmaveth, forty-two; [25]men of Kiriath-jearim, Chephirah, and Beeroth, seven hundred and forty-three; [26]men of Ramah and Geba, six hundred and twenty-one; [27]men of Michmas, one hundred and twenty-two; [28]men of Bethel and Ai, two hundred and twenty-three; [29]sons of Nebo, fifty-two; [30]sons of Magbish, one hundred and fifty-six; [31]sons of the other Elam, one thousand two hundred and fifty-four; [32]sons of Harim, three hundred and twenty; [33]sons of Lod, Hadid, and Ono, seven hundred and twenty-five; [34]sons of Jericho, three hundred and forty-five; [35]sons of Senaah, three thousand six hundred and thirty.

[36]The priests: sons of Jedaiah, who were of the house of Jeshua, nine hundred and seventy-three; [37]sons of Immer, one thousand and fifty-two; [38]sons of Pashhur, one thousand two hundred and forty-seven; [39]sons of Harim, one thousand and seventeen.

[40]The Levites: sons of Jeshua, Kadmiel, Binnui, and Hodaviah, seventy-four.[d]

[41]The singers: sons of Asaph, one hundred and twenty-eight.

[42]The gatekeepers: sons of Shallum, sons of Ater, sons of Talmon, sons of Akkub, sons of Hatita, sons of Shobai, one hundred and thirty-nine in all.

[43]The temple slaves: sons of Ziha, sons of Hasupha, sons of Tabbaoth, [44]sons of Keros, sons of Siaha, sons of Padon, [45]sons of Lebanah, sons of Hagabah, sons of Akkub, [46]sons of Hagab, sons of Shamlai, sons of Hanan, [47]sons of Giddel, sons of Gahar, sons of Reaiah, [48]sons of Rezin, sons of Nekoda, sons of Gazzam, [49]sons of Uzza, sons of Paseah, sons of Besai, [50]sons of Asnah, sons of the Meunites, sons of the Nephusites, [51]sons of Bak-

d: Neh 12, 24.

buk, sons of Hakupha, sons of Harhur, [52]sons of Bazluth, sons of Mehida, sons of Harsha, [53]sons of Barkos, sons of Sisera, sons of Temah, [54]sons of Neziah, sons of Hatipha.

[55]Descendants of the slaves of Solomon: sons of Sotai, sons of Hassophereth, sons of Peruda, [56]sons of Jaalah, sons of Darkon, sons of Giddel, [57]sons of Shephatiah, sons of Hattil, sons of Pochereth-hazzebaim, sons of Ami. [58]The total of the temple slaves and the descendants of the slaves of Solomon was three hundred and ninety-two.

[59]The following who returned from Telmelah, Tel-harsha, Cherub, Addan, and Immer were unable to prove that their ancestral houses and their descent were Israelite: [60]sons of Delaiah, sons of Tobiah, sons of Nekoda, six hundred and fifty-two. [61]Also, of the priests: sons of Habaiah, sons of Hakkoz, sons of Barzillai (he had married one of the daughters of Barzillai the Gileadite and became known by his name).[e] [62]These men searched their family records, but their names could not be found written there; hence they were degraded from the priesthood, [63]and His Excellency* ordered them not to partake of the most holy foods until there should be a priest bearing the Urim and Thummim.

[64]The entire assembly taken together came to forty-two thousand three hundred and sixty, [65]not counting their male and female slaves, who were seven thousand three hundred and thirty-seven. They also had two hundred male and female singers. [66]Their horses were seven hundred and thirty-six, their mules two hundred and forty-five, [67]their camels four hundred and thirty-five, their asses six thousand seven hundred and twenty.

[68]When they arrived at the house of the LORD in Jerusalem, some of the family heads made free-will offerings for the house of God, to rebuild it in its place. [69]According

to their means they contributed to the treasury for the temple service: sixty-one thousand drachmas of gold, five thousand minas of silver, and one hundred garments for the priests. [70]The priests, the Levites, and some of the common people took up residence in Jerusalem; but the singers, the gatekeepers, and the temple slaves dwelt in their cities. Thus all the Israelites dwelt in their cities.

CHAPTER 3

See RG 209

Restoration of the Altar. [1]Now when the seventh month* came, after the Israelites had settled in their cities, the people gathered at Jerusalem as one man.[f] [2]Then Jeshua, son of Jozadak, together with his brethren the priests, and Zerubbabel, son of Shealtiel, together with his brethren, set about rebuilding the altar of the God of Israel in order to offer on it the holocausts prescribed in the law of Moses, the man of God. [3]Despite their fear of the peoples of the land, they replaced the altar on its foundations and offered holocausts to the LORD on it, both morning and evening.[g] [4]They also kept the feast of Booths in the manner prescribed, and they offered the daily holocausts in the proper number required for each day.[h] [5]Thereafter they offered the established holocaust, the sacrifices prescribed for the new moons and all the festivals sacred to the LORD, and those which anyone might offer as a free-will gift to the LORD. [6]From the first day of the seventh month they began to offer holocausts to the LORD, though the foundation of the temple of the LORD had not yet been laid.

Founding of the Temple. [7]Then they hired stonecutters and carpenters, and sent food and drink and oil to the Sidonians and Tyrians that they might ship cedar trees from the Lebanon to the port of Joppa, as Cyrus, king of Persia,

---

2, 63: His Excellency: the deputy of the Persian government; from the context, he was one of the Jewish exile leaders. Nehemiah as governor receives the same title (Neh 8, 9; 10, 2). Urim and Thummim: see note on Ex 28, 30.

3, 1f: The seventh month: Tishri (September–October), apparently of 538 B.C.; cf Ezr 1, 1; 4, 5. In this case, it was Sheshbazzar who erected the first altar, since he began the work on the foundations of the temple in Jerusalem; cf Ezr 5, 16. It was in the second year of Darius I, i.e., in 520 B.C., that Jeshua and Zerubbabel resumed the work on the temple that

had been temporarily interrupted (Ezr 4, 24—5, 1; Hg 1, 1; 2, 1). The Chronicler or a later editor of the text here attributes to them the beginning of the work which, in reality, they merely completed. Shealtiel: the oldest son of King Jehoiachin of Judah and the brother of Sheshbazzar (1 Chr 3, 18f); Zerubbabel was therefore the grandson of Jehoiachin; see note on Ezr 1, 8.

e: 2 Sm 17, 27; 19, 32f; 1 Kgs 2, 7. *f:* Neh 7, 73—8, 1. *g:* 1 Kgs 8, 64; Dn 9, 25. *h:* Ex 23, 16; Nm 28, 3-8.

had authorized.*[i]* *[8]*In the year after their coming to the house of God in Jerusalem, in the second month, Zerubbabel, son of Shealtiel, and Jeshua, son of Jozadak, together with the rest of their brethren, the priests and Levites and all who had come from the captivity to Jerusalem, began by appointing the Levites twenty years of age and over to supervise the work on the house of the LORD. *[9]*Jeshua and his sons and brethren, with Kadmiel and Binnui, son of Henadad, and their sons and their brethren, the Levites, stood as one man to supervise those who were engaged in the work on the house of God. *[10]*When the builders had laid the foundation of the LORD's temple, the vested priests with the trumpets and the Levites, sons of Asaph, were stationed there with the cymbals to praise the LORD in the manner laid down by David, king of Israel.*[j]* *[11]*They alternated in songs of praise and thanksgiving to the LORD, "for he is good, for his kindness to Israel endures forever"; and all the people raised a great shout of joy, praising the LORD because the foundation of the LORD's house had been laid.*[k]* *[12]*Many of the priests, Levites, and family heads, the old men who had seen the former house, cried out in sorrow as they watched the foundation of the present house being laid.*[l]* Many others, however, lifted up their voices in shouts of joy, *[13]*and no one could distinguish the sound of the joyful shouting from the sound of those who were weeping; for the people raised a mighty clamor which was heard afar off.*[m]*

CHAPTER 4

See RG 209

Samaritan Interference. *[1]*When the enemies of Judah and Benjamin heard that the exiles were building a temple for the LORD, the God of Israel, *[2]*they approached Zerubbabel and the family heads and said to them, "Let us build with you, for we seek

your God just as you do, and we have sacrificed to him since the days of Esarhaddon, king of Assyria, who had us brought here." *[3]*But Zerubbabel, Jeshua, and the rest of the family heads of Israel answered them, "It is not your responsibility to build with us a house for our God, but we alone must build it for the LORD, the God of Israel, as King Cyrus of Persia has commanded us." *[4]*Thereupon the people of the land set out to intimidate and dishearten the people of Judah so as to keep them from building. *[5]*They also suborned counselors to work against them and thwart their plans during the remaining years of Cyrus, king of Persia, and until the reign of Darius,* king of Persia.

Later Hostility. *[6]*Also at the beginning of the reign of Ahashuerus they prepared a written accusation against the inhabitants of Judah and Jerusalem.

*[7]*Again, in the time of Artaxerxes, Mithredath wrote in concert with Tabeel and the rest of his fellow officials to Artaxerxes, king of Persia. The document was written in Aramaic* and was accompanied by a translation. [Aramaic:]

*[8]*Then Rehum, the governor, and Shimshai, the scribe, wrote the following letter against Jerusalem to King Artaxerxes: *[9]*"Rehum, the governor, Shimshai, the scribe, and their fellow judges, officials, and agents from among the Persian, Urukian, Babylonian, Susian (that is, Elamite), *[10]*and the other peoples whom the great and illustrious Assurbanipal transported and settled in the city of Samaria and elsewhere in the province West-of-Euphrates, as follows. . . ." *[11]*This is a copy of the letter that they sent to him:

"To King Artaxerxes, your servants, the men of West-of-Euphrates, as follows: *[12]*Let it be known to the king that the Jews who came up from you to us have arrived at

---

4, 5: Darius: Darius I (521–485 B.C.). The temple-building narrative continues in Ezr 4, 24. In between (Ezr 4, 6-23) is a series of notes about the opposition to the returned exiles voiced at the Persian court in the early fifth century B.C., after the temple had been reestablished.

4, 7: Aramaic: this word in the original text seems to be a note indicating a change of language from Hebrew to Aramaic, which in fact takes place here. The Aramaic section ends with Ezr 6, 18, but again in Ezr 7, 12-26 a royal letter is cited in Aramaic.

4, 8-23: The central question here is the rebuilding of the fortification walls of Jerusalem, not the building of the temple. The interruption of work on the city wall some time before 445 B.C. was the occasion for the coming of Nehemiah to Palestine (Neh 1, 1-4; 2, 1-5). Artaxerxes: Artaxerxes I (464–423 B.C.).

i: 1 Chr 22, 4; 2 Chr 2, 9. *j:* Ezr 2, 41. *k:* Pss 100, 5; 136; Jer 33, 11. *l:* Hg 2, 3. *m:* Tb 14, 5.

Jerusalem and are now rebuilding this rebellious and evil city. They are raising up its walls, and the foundations have already been laid. [13]Now let it be known to the king that if this city is rebuilt and its walls are raised up again, they will no longer pay taxes, tributes, or tolls; thus it can only result in harm to the throne. [14]Now, since we partake of the salt of the palace, we ought not simply to look on while the king is being dishonored. Therefore we have sent this message to inform you, O king, [15]so that inquiry may be made in the historical records of your fathers. In the historical records you can discover and verify that this city is a rebellious city which has proved fatal to kings and provinces, and that sedition has been fostered there since ancient times. For that reason this city was destroyed. [16]We inform you, O king, that if this city is rebuilt and its walls are raised up again, by that very fact you will no longer own any part of West-of-Euphrates."

[17]The king sent this answer: "To Rehum, the governor, Shimshai, the scribe, and their fellow officials living in Samaria and elsewhere in the province West-of-Euphrates, greetings and the following: [18]The communication which you sent us has been read plainly in my presence. [19]When at my command inquiry was made, it was verified that from ancient times this city has risen up against kings and that rebellion and sedition have been fostered there. [20]Powerful kings were once in Jerusalem who ruled over all West-of-Euphrates, and taxes, tributes, and tolls were paid to them. [21]Give orders, therefore, that will stop the work of these men. This city may not be rebuilt until a further decree has been issued by me. [22]Take care that you do not neglect this matter, lest the evil grow to the detriment of the throne."

[23]As soon as a copy of King Artaxerxes' letter had been read before Rehum, the governor, Shimshai, the scribe, and their fellow officials, they went in all haste to the Jews in Jerusalem and stopped their work by force of arms.[n]

Rebuilding of the Temple. [24]Thus it was that the work on the house of God in Jerusalem was halted. This inaction lasted until the second year of the reign of Darius,[*] king of Persia.

CHAPTER 5

See RG 209

[1]Then the prophets Haggai and Zechariah,[*] son of Iddo, began to prophesy to the Jews in Judah and Jerusalem in the name of the God of Israel.[o] [2]Thereupon Zerubbabel, son of Shealtiel, and Jeshua, son of Jozadak, began again to build the house of God in Jerusalem, with the prophets of God giving them support. [3]At that time there came to them Tattenai, governor of West-of-Euphrates, and Shethar-bozenai, and their fellow officials, who asked of them: "Who issued the decree for you to build this house and raise this edifice? [4]What are the names of the men who are building this structure?" [5]But their God watched over the elders of the Jews so that they were not hindered, until a report could go to Darius and then a written order be sent back concerning this matter.

[6]A copy of the letter sent to King Darius by Tattenai, governor of West-of-Euphrates, and Shethar-bozenai, and their fellow officials from West-of-Euphrates; [7]they sent him a report in which was written the following:

"To King Darius, all good wishes! [8]Let it be known to the king that we have visited the province of Judah and the house of the great God: it is being rebuilt of cut stone and the walls are being reinforced with timber; the work is being carried on diligently and is making good progress under their hands. [9]We then questioned the elders, addressing to them the following words: 'Who issued the decree for you to build this house and raise this edifice?' [10]We also asked them their names, to report them to you in a list of the men who are their leaders. [11]This was their answer to us: 'We are the servants of the God of heaven and earth, and we are re-

---

4, 24: The second year . . . of Darius: 520 B.C.; it marks the beginning of the successful restoration of the temple, which was accomplished within the five years following (Ezr 5, 1—6, 18).

5, 1: The prophets Haggai and Zechariah: two of the Mi-

nor Prophets, whose books record their role in the encouragement of this work.

n: Neh 1, 3. o: Hg 1, 14—2, 9; Zec 4, 9.

building the house built here long years ago, which a great king of Israel built and finished. [12]But because our fathers provoked the wrath of the God of heaven, he delivered them into the power of the Chaldean, Nebuchadnezzar, king of Babylon, who destroyed this house and led the people captive to Babylon. [13]However, in the first year of Cyrus, king of Babylon, King Cyrus issued a decree for the rebuilding of this house of God. [14]Moreover, the gold and silver utensils of the house of God which Nebuchadnezzar had taken from the temple in Jerusalem and carried off to the temple in Babylon, King Cyrus ordered to be removed from the temple in Babylon and consigned to a certain Sheshbazzar, whom he named governor. [15]And he commanded him: Take these utensils and deposit them in the temple of Jerusalem, and let the house of God be rebuilt on its former site. [16]Then this same Sheshbazzar came and laid the foundations of the house of God in Jerusalem. Since that time the building has been going on, and it is not yet completed.' [17]Now, if it please the king, let a search be made in the royal archives of Babylon to discover whether a decree really was issued by King Cyrus for the rebuilding of this house of God in Jerusalem. And may the king's pleasure in this matter be communicated to us."

See RG 209

CHAPTER 6

The Decree of Darius. [1]Thereupon King Darius issued an order to search the archives in which the Babylonian records were stored away; [2]*p*and in Ecbatana, the stronghold in the province of Media, a scroll was found containing the following text: "Memorandum. [3]In the first year of King Cyrus, King Cyrus issued a decree: The house of God in Jerusalem. The house is to be rebuilt as a place for offering sacrifices and bringing burnt offerings. Its height is to be sixty cubits and its width sixty cubits. [4]It shall have three courses of cut stone for each one of timber. The costs are to be borne by the royal palace. [5]Also, the gold and silver utensils of the house of God which Nebuchadnezzar took

from the temple of Jerusalem and brought to Babylon are to be sent back: to be returned to their place in the temple of Jerusalem and deposited in the house of God.

[6]"Now, therefore, Tattenai, governor of West-of-Euphrates, and Shethar-bozenai, and you, their fellow officials in West-of-Euphrates, do not interfere in that place. [7]Let the governor and the elders of the Jews continue the work on that house of God; they are to rebuild it on its former site. [8]I also issue this decree concerning your dealing with these elders of the Jews in the rebuilding of that house of God: From the royal revenue, the taxes of West-of-Euphrates, let these men be repaid for their expenses, in full and without delay. [9]Whatever else is required— young bulls, rams, and lambs for holocausts to the God of heaven, wheat, salt, wine, and oil, according to the requirements of the priests who are in Jerusalem—is to be delivered to them day by day without fail, [10]that they may continue to offer sacrifices of pleasing odor to the God of heaven and pray for the life of the king and his sons. [11]I also issue this decree: If any man violates this edict, a beam is to be taken from his house, and he is to be lifted up and impaled on it; and his house is to be reduced to rubble for this offense. [12]And may the God who causes his name to dwell there overthrow every king or people who may undertake to alter this or to destroy this house of God in Jerusalem. I, Darius, have issued this decree; let it be carefully executed."

[13]Then Tattenai, the governor of West-of-Euphrates, and Shethar-bozenai, and their fellow officials carried out fully the instructions King Darius had sent them. [14]The elders of the Jews continued to make progress in the building, supported by the message of the prophets, Haggai and Zechariah, son of Iddo. They finished the building according to the command of the God of Israel and the decrees of Cyrus and Darius [and of Artaxerxes, king of Persia]. [15]They completed this house on the third day of the month Adar, in the sixth year of the reign of King Darius. [16]The Israelites—priests, Levites, and the

p: 2-12; Ezr 1, 4-11.

other returned exiles—celebrated the dedication of this house of God with joy. *¹⁷*For the dedication of this house of God, they offered one hundred bulls, two hundred rams, and four hundred lambs, together with twelve he-goats as a sin-offering for all Israel, in keeping with the number of the tribes of Israel. *¹⁸*Finally, they set up the priests in their classes and the Levites in their divisions for the service of God in Jerusalem, as is prescribed in the book of Moses.

The Passover. *¹⁹*ᵍThe exiles kept the Passover on the fourteenth day of the first month. *²⁰*The Levites, every one of whom had purified himself for the occasion, sacrificed the Passover for the rest of the exiles, for their brethren the priests, and for themselves. *²¹*The Israelites who had returned from the exile partook of it together with all those who had separated themselves from the uncleanness of the peoples of the land to join them in seeking the LORD, the God of Israel.ʳ *²²*They joyfully kept the feast of Unleavened Bread for seven days, for the LORD had filled them with joy by making the king of Assyria* favorable to them, so that he gave them help in their work on the house of God, the God of Israel.

II: The Deeds of Ezra

CHAPTER 7

See RG
209

Ezra the Scribe. *¹*After these events,* during the reign of Artaxerxes, king of Persia, Ezra, son of Seraiah, son of Azariah, son of Hilkiah, *²*son of Shallum, son of Zadok, son of Ahitub, *³*son of Amariah, son of Azariah, son of Meraioth, *⁴*son of Zerahiah, son of Uzzi, son of Bukki, *⁵*son of Abishua, son of Phinehas, son of Eleazar, son of the high priest Aaron— *⁶*this Ezra came up from Babylon. He was a scribe, well-versed in the law of Moses which was given by the LORD, the God of Israel. Because the hand of the

LORD, his God, was upon him, the king granted him all that he requested.ˢ

*⁷*Some of the Israelites and some priests, Levites, singers, gatekeepers, and temple slaves also came up to Jerusalem in the seventh year of King Artaxerxes. *⁸*Ezra came to Jerusalem in the fifth month of that seventh year of the king. *⁹*On the first day of the first month he resolved on the journey up from Babylon, and on the first day of the fifth month he arrived at Jerusalem, for the favoring hand of his God was upon him. *¹⁰*Ezra had set his heart on the study and practice of the law of the LORD and on teaching statutes and ordinances in Israel.ᵗ

The Decree of Artaxerxes. *¹¹*This is a copy of the rescript which King Artaxerxes gave to Ezra the priest-scribe, the scribe of the text of the LORD's commandments and statutes for Israel:

*¹²*ᵘ"Artaxerxes, king of kings, to Ezra the priest, scribe of the law of the God of heaven (then, after greetings): *¹³*I have issued this decree, that anyone in my kingdom belonging to the people of Israel, its priests or Levites, who is minded to go up to Jerusalem with you, may do so. *¹⁴*You are the envoy from the king and his seven counselors to supervise Judah and Jerusalem in respect of the law of your God which is in your possession, *¹⁵*and to bring with you the silver and gold which the king and his counselors have freely contributed to the God of Israel, whose dwelling is in Jerusalem, *¹⁶*as well as all the silver and gold which you may receive throughout the province of Babylon, together with the free-will offerings which the people and priests freely contribute for the house of their God in Jerusalem. *¹⁷*You must take care, therefore, to use this money to buy bulls, rams, lambs, and the cereal offerings and libations proper to these, and offer them on the altar of the house of your God in Jerusalem. *¹⁸*You and

---

6, 22: Assyria: used here in a broad sense for the Persian Empire.

7, 1-8: The date of Ezra's journey to Palestine is not known with certainty. The seventh year of King Artaxerxes I would be 458 B.C., and the present order of the text suggests that date. The narratives of Ezra and Nehemiah make it seem to many, however, that the arrival of Nehemiah in 445 B.C. should precede that of Ezra. If so, Ezra may be thought to

have come in 398 B.C., the seventh year of King Artaxerxes II. Others argue for the thirty-seventh year of Artaxerxes I, that is, 428 B.C.; this would suppose that the date given in the text has suffered in transmission.

q: 19-22; Ex 12, 1-20. *r:* Ps 47, 9. *s:* Ezr 7, 28; 8, 18; Neh 2, 8. 18. *t:* Ps 119, 45. *u:* 12-17: Ezr 1, 2ff.

your brethren may do whatever seems best to you with the remainder of the silver and gold, conformably to the will of your God. [19]The utensils consigned to you for the service of the house of your God you are to deposit before the God of Jerusalem. [20]Whatever else you may be required to supply for the needs of the house of your God, you may draw from the royal treasury. [21]I, Artaxerxes the king, issue this decree to all the treasurers of West-of-Euphrates: Whatever Ezra the priest, scribe of the law of the God of heaven, requests of you, dispense to him accurately, [22]within these limits: silver, one hundred talents; wheat, one hundred kors; wine, one hundred baths; oil, one hundred baths; salt, without limit. [23]Let everything that is ordered by the God of heaven be carried out exactly for the house of the God of heaven, that wrath may not come upon the realm of the king and his sons. [24]We also inform you that it is not permitted to impose taxes, tributes, or tolls on any priest, Levite, singer, gatekeeper, temple slave, or any other servant of that house of God.

[25]"As for you, Ezra, in accordance with the wisdom of your God* which is in your possession, appoint magistrates and judges to administer justice to all the people in West-of-Euphrates, to all, that is, who know the laws of your God. Instruct those who do not know these laws.[v] [26]Whoever does not obey the law of your God and the law of the king, let strict judgment be executed upon him, whether death, or corporal punishment, or a fine on his goods, or imprisonment."

Ezra and His Companions. [27]Blessed be the LORD, the God of our fathers, who thus disposed the mind of the king to glorify the house of the LORD in Jerusalem, [28]and who let me find favor with the king, with his counselors, and with all the most influential royal officials. I therefore took courage and, with the hand of the LORD, my God, upon me, I gathered together Israelite family heads to make the return journey with me.[w]

CHAPTER 8

See RG 209

[1]This is the list of the family heads who returned with me from Babylon during the reign of King Artaxerxes:

[2]Of the sons of Phinehas, Gershon; of the sons of Ithamar, Daniel; of the sons of David, Hattush, [3]son of Shecaniah; of the sons of Parosh, Zechariah, and with him one hundred and fifty males were enrolled; [4]of the sons of Pahath-moab, Eliehoenai, son of Zerahiah, and with him two hundred males; [5]of the sons of Zattu, Shecaniah, son of Jahaziel, and with him three hundred males; [6]of the sons of Adin, Ebed, son of Jonathan, and with him fifty males; [7]of the sons of Elam, Jeshaiah, son of Athaliah, and with him seventy males; [8]of the sons of Shephatiah, Zebadiah, son of Michael, and with him eighty males; [9]of the sons of Joab, Obadiah, son of Jehiel, and with him two hundred and eighteen males; [10]of the sons of Bani, Shelomith, son of Josiphiah, and with him one hundred and sixty males; [11]of the sons of Bebai, Zechariah, son of Bebai, and with him twenty-eight males; [12]of the sons of Azgad, Johanan, son of Hakkatan, and with him one hundred and ten males; [13]of the sons of Adonikam, younger sons, whose names were Eliphelet, Jeiel, and Shemaiah, and with them sixty males; [14]of the sons of Bigvai, Uthai, son of Zakkur, and with him seventy males.

The Journey to Jerusalem. [15]I had them assemble by the river that flows toward Ahava,* where we made camp for three days. There I perceived that both laymen and priests were present, but I could not discover a single Levite. [16]Therefore I sent Eliezer, Ariel, Shemaiah, Jarib, Elnathan, Nathan, Zechariah, and Meshullam, wise leaders, [17]with a command for Iddo, the leader in the place Casiphia, instructing them what to say to Iddo and his brethren, and to the temple slaves in Casiphia, in order to procure for us ministers for the house of our God. [18]They sent to us—for the favoring hand of our God was upon us—a well-instructed man, one of the sons of Mahli,

---

7, 25: The wisdom of your God: the Mosaic law; cf vv 6, 14.

8, 15: Ahava: a town at an unidentified site in Babylonia. The river that flowed toward it was probably a branch or canal of the Euphrates.

---

v: 2 Chr 17, 9.   *w:* Ezr 7, 6.

517

son of Levi, son of Israel, namely Sherebiah, with his sons and brethren, eighteen men.[x] [19]They also sent us Hashabiah, and with him Jeshaiah, sons of Merari, and their brethren and their sons, twenty men. [20]Of the temple slaves (those whom David and the princes appointed to serve the Levites) there were two hundred and twenty. All these men were enrolled by name.[y]

[21]Then I proclaimed a fast, there by the river of Ahava, that we might humble ourselves before our God to petition from him a safe journey for ourselves, our children, and all our possessions. [22]For I would have been ashamed to ask the king for troops and horsemen to protect us against enemies along the way, since we had said to the king, "The favoring hand of our God is upon all who seek him, but his mighty wrath is against all who forsake him."[z] [23]So we fasted, and prayed to our God for this, and our petition was granted. [24]Next I selected twelve of the priestly leaders along with Sherebiah, Hashabiah, and ten of their brethren, [25]and I weighed out before them the silver and the gold and the utensils offered for the house of our God by the king, his counselors, his officials, and all the Israelites of that region. I consigned it to them in these amounts: [26]silver, six hundred and fifty talents; silver utensils, one hundred; gold, one hundred talents; [27]twenty golden bowls valued at a thousand darics; two vases of excellent polished bronze, as precious as gold. [28]I addressed them in these words: "You are consecrated to the LORD, and the utensils are also consecrated; the silver and the gold are a freewill offering to the LORD, the God of your fathers. [29]Keep good watch over them till you weigh them out in Jerusalem in the presence of the chief priests and Levites and the family leaders of Israel, in the chambers of the house of the LORD." [30]The priests and the Levites then took over the silver, the gold, and the utensils that had been weighed out, to bring them to Jerusalem, to the house of our God.

[31]We set out for Jerusalem from the river of Ahava on the twelfth day of the first month.

The hand of our God remained upon us, and he protected us from enemies and bandits along the way. [32]Thus we arrived at Jerusalem, where we first rested for three days. [33]On the fourth day, the silver, the gold, and the utensils were weighed out in the house of our God and consigned to the priest Meremoth, son of Uriah, who was assisted by Eleazar, son of Phinehas; they were assisted by the Levites Jozabad, son of Jeshua, and Noadiah, son of Binnui. [34]Everything was in order as to number and weight, and the total weight was registered. At that same time, [35]those who had returned from the captivity, the exiles, offered as holocausts to the God of Israel twelve bulls for all Israel, ninety-six rams, seventy-seven lambs, and twelve goats as sin-offerings: all these as a holocaust to the LORD. [36]Finally, the orders of the king were presented to the king's satraps and to the governors in West-of-Euphrates, who gave their support to the people and to the house of God.[*]

CHAPTER 9

See RG 209–10

Denunciation of Mixed Marriages.

[1a]When these matters had been concluded, the leaders approached me with this report: "Neither the Israelite laymen nor the priests nor the Levites have kept themselves aloof from the peoples of the land and their abominations [Canaanites, Hittites, Perizzites, Jebusites, Ammonites, Moabites, Egyptians, and Amorites]; [2]for they have taken some of their daughters as wives for themselves and their sons, and thus they have desecrated the holy race with the peoples of the land. Furthermore, the leaders and rulers have taken a leading part in this apostasy!"

Ezra's Exhortation. [3]When I had heard this thing, I tore my cloak and my mantle, plucked hair from my head and beard, and sat there stupefied.[b] [4]Around me gathered all who were in dread of the sentence of the God of Israel on this apostasy of the exiles, while I remained motionless until the evening sacrifice.[c] [5]Then, at the time of the evening sacrifice, I rose in my wretchedness, and with

---

8, 36: The story of Ezra's mission is seemingly continued from this point by Neh 7, 72b—8, 18, which may be read before Ezr 9, 1.

---

x: Ezr 7, 6.   y: Ezr 2, 43.   z: Neh 2, 9.   a: 1f: Dt 7, 1; Neh 9, 2.   b: Ps 119, 136.   c: Is 66, 2.

cloak and mantle torn I fell on my knees, stretching out my hands to the LORD, my God.

⁶I said: "My God, I am too ashamed and confounded to raise my face to you, O my God, for our wicked deeds are heaped up above our heads and our guilt reaches up to heaven.ᵈ ⁷*From the time of our fathers even to this day great has been our guilt, and for our wicked deeds we have been delivered over, we and our kings and our priests, to the will of the kings of foreign lands, to the sword, to captivity, to pillage, and to disgrace, as is the case today.

⁸"And now, but a short time ago, mercy came to us from the LORD, our God, who left us a remnant and gave us a stake in his holy place; thus our God has brightened our eyes and given us relief in our servitude.ᵉ ⁹For slaves we are, but in our servitude our God has not abandoned us; rather, he has turned the good will of the kings of Persia toward us. Thus he has given us new life to raise again the house of our God and restore its ruins, and has granted us a fence in Judah and Jerusalem.ᶠ ¹⁰But now, O our God, what can we say after all this? For we have abandoned your commandments, ¹¹which you gave through your servants the prophets: the land which you are entering to take as your possession is a land unclean with the filth of the peoples of the land, with the abominations with which they have filled it from one end to the other in their uncleanness.ᵍ ¹²Do not, then, give your daughters to their sons in marriage, and do not take their daughters for your sons. Never promote their peace and prosperity; thus you will grow strong, enjoy the produce of the land, and leave it as an inheritance to your children forever.ʰ

¹³"After all that has come upon us for our evil deeds and our great guilt—though you, our God, have made less of our sinfulness than it deserved and have allowed us to survive as we do— ¹⁴shall we again violate your commandments by intermarrying with these abominable peoples? Would you not become so angered with us as to destroy us without remnant or survivor? ¹⁵O LORD, God of Israel, you are just; yet we have been spared, the remnant we are today. Here we are before you in our sins. Because of all this, we can no longer stand in your presence."

CHAPTER 10

See RG 209

The People's Response. ¹While Ezra prayed and acknowledged their guilt, weeping and prostrate before the house of God, a very large assembly of Israelites gathered about him, men, women, and children; and the people wept profusely. ²Then Shecaniah, the son of Jehiel, one of the sons of Elam, made this appeal to Ezra: "We have indeed betrayed our God by taking as wives foreign women of the peoples of the land. Yet even now there remains a hope for Israel. ³Let us therefore enter into a covenant before our God to dismiss all our foreign wives and the children born of them, in keeping with what you, my lord, advise, and those who fear the commandments of our God. Let the law be observed! ⁴Rise, then, for this is your duty! We will stand by you, so have courage and take action!"

⁵Ezra rose to his feet and demanded an oath from the chiefs of the priests, from the Levites and from all Israel that they would do as had been proposed; and they swore it. ⁶Then Ezra retired from his place before the house of God and entered the chamber of Johanan, son of Eliashib,* where he spent the night neither eating food nor drinking water, for he was in mourning over the betrayal by the exiles. ⁷A proclamation was made throughout Judah and Jerusalem that all the exiles should gather together in Jerusalem, ⁸and that whoever failed to appear within three days would, according to the judgment of the leaders and elders, suffer the confisca-

---

9, 7: After this verse, the next part of the prayer attributed to Ezra is perhaps to be found in Neh 9, 6-37, which may be read as leading up to Ezr 9, 8-15.

10, 6: Johanan, son of Eliashib: actually, the grandson of Eliashib; the father of Johanan was Eliashib's son Joiada (Neh 12, 10f. 22). Since Eliashib was high priest at the time of Nehemiah (Neh 3, 1. 20f; 13, 4. 7) and Johanan, if not yet

high priest, was at least old enough to have his own separate quarters (chamber) in the temple at the time of Ezra, it is practically certain that Nehemiah's activity in Jerusalem must have preceded that of Ezra.

---

d: Ps 38, 4.   *e:* Is 4, 3.   *f:* Ps 106, 46.   *g:* Lv 18, 24f; Ez 36, 17.   *h:* Dt 7, 3.

tion of all his possessions, and himself be excluded from the assembly of the exiles.

[9] All the men of Judah and Benjamin gathered together in Jerusalem within the three-day period: it was in the ninth month,* on the twentieth day of the month. All the people, standing in the open place before the house of God, were trembling both over the matter at hand and because it was raining. [10] Then Ezra, the priest, stood up and said to them: "Your unfaithfulness in taking foreign women as wives has added to Israel's guilt. [11] But now, give praise to the LORD, the God of your fathers, and do his will: separate yourselves from the peoples of the land and from these foreign women."[i] [12] In answer, the whole assembly cried out with a loud voice: "Yes, it is our duty to do as you say! [13] But the people are numerous and it is the rainy season, so that we cannot remain out-of-doors; besides, this is not a task that can be performed in a single day or even two, for those of us who have sinned in this regard are many. [14] Let our leaders represent the whole assembly; then let all those in our cities who have taken foreign women for wives appear at appointed times, accompanied by the elders and magistrates of each city in question, till we have turned away from us our God's burning anger over this affair." [15] Only Jonathan, son of Asahel, and Jahzeiah, son of Tikvah, were against this proposal, with Meshullam and Shabbethai the Levite supporting them.

The Guilty. [16]*The exiles did as agreed. Ezra appointed as his assistants men who were family heads, one for each family, all of them designated by name. They held sessions to examine the matter, beginning with the first day of the tenth month. [17] By the first day of the first month they had passed judgment on all the men who had taken foreign women for wives.

[18] Among the priests, the following were found to have taken foreign women for wives: Of the sons of Jeshua, son of Jozadak, and his brethren: Maaseiah, Eliezer, Jarib, and Gedaliah. [19] They pledged themselves to dismiss their wives, and as a guilt-offering for their guilt they gave a ram from the flock. [20] Of the sons of Immer: Hanani and Zebadiah; [21] of the sons of Harim: Maaseiah, Elijah, Shemaiah, Jehiel, and Uzziah; [22] of the sons of Pashhur: Elioenai, Maaseiah, Ishmael, Nethanel, Jozabad, and Elasah.

[23] Of the Levites: Jozabad, Shemei, Kelaiah (also called Kelita), Pethahiah, Judah, and Eliezer.[j]

[24] Of the singers: Eliashib and Zakkur; of the gatekeepers: Shallum, Telem, and Uri.

[25] Among the other Israelites: Of the sons of Parosh: Ramiah, Izziah, Malchijah, Mijamin, Eleazar, Malchijah, and Benaiah; [26] of the sons of Elam: Mattaniah, Zechariah, Jehiel, Abdi, Jeremoth, and Elijah; [27] of the sons of Zattu: Elioenai, Eliashib, Mattaniah, Jeremoth, Zabad, and Aziza; [28] of the sons of Bebai: Jehohanan, Hananiah, Zabbai, and Athlai; [29] of the sons of Bani: Meshullam, Malluch, Adaiah, Jashub, Sheal, and Jeremoth; [30] of the sons of Pahath-moab: Adna, Chelal, Benaiah, Maaseiah, Mattaniah, Bezalel, Binnui, and Manasseh; [31] of the sons of Harim: Eliezer, Isshijah, Malchijah, Shemaiah, Shimeon, [32] Benjamin, Malluch, Shemariah; [33] of the sons of Hashum: Mattenai, Mattattah, Zabad, Eliphelet, Jeremai, Manasseh, Shimei; [34] of the sons of Begui: Maadai, Amram, Uel, [35] Benaiah, Bedeiah, Cheluhi, [36] Vaniah, Meremoth, Eliashib, [37] Mattaniah, Mattenai, and Jaasu; [38] of the sons of Binnui: Shimei, [39] Shelemiah, Nathan, and Adaiah; [40] of the sons of Zachai: Shashai, Sharai, [41] Azarel, Shelemiah, Shemariah, [42] Shallum, Amariah, Joseph; [43] of the sons of Nebo: Jeiel, Mattithiah, Zabad, Zebina, Jaddai, Joel, Benaiah.

[44] All these had taken foreign wives; but they sent them away, both the women and their children.*

10, 9: Ninth month: Chislev (November–December), during the "early rains" in Palestine. Since the assembly took place in the open . . . all the people . . . were trembling . . . because it was raining.

10, 16f: The work of the committee lasted three months, from the first day of the tenth month, Tebet (December–January), to the first day of the first month, Nisan (March–April), of the following Jewish year.

10, 44: The account of the problem of mixed marriages at the time of Ezra is continued in Neh 9, 1-5; this may be read immediately after Ezr 10, 44, though the date given in Neh 9, 1 fits more precisely after Ezr 10, 15; cf Hg 2, 10-14.

i: Neh 9, 2.   *j:* Neh 8, 7; 10, 11.

The Book of Nehemiah

See RG
211–15

Problems common to the combined Books Ezra-Nehemiah have been pointed out in the Introduction to the Book of Ezra. The achievements of the two men were complementary; each helped to make it possible for Judaism to maintain its identity during the difficult days of the Restoration. Nehemiah was the man of action who rebuilt the walls of Jerusalem and introduced necessary administrative reforms. Ezra in turn was the great religious reformer who succeeded in establishing the Torah as the constitution of the returned community.

The biblical sources for Nehemiah's life and work are the autobiographical portions scattered through the book. They are called the "Memoirs of Nehemiah," and have been used more extensively and effectively by "the Chronicler" than the "Memoirs of Ezra." No competent scholar questions the authenticity of Nehemiah's memoirs. From these and other sources, the picture emerges of a man dedicated to the single purpose of the welfare of his people. Despite temperamental shortcomings, Nehemiah was a man of good practical sense combined with deep faith in God. In view of his selfless service to a community capable of severely testing any leader, we can be indulgent toward his numerous appeals to God to credit him with the work he had done. Nehemiah was a layman, and his generous dedication of talents to the service of God and of God's people remains an example of undiminished force for laymen today.

The Book of Nehemiah is divided as follows:

I: The Deeds of Nehemiah (1, 1—7, 72).
II: Promulgation of the Law (8, 1—13, 31).

———

I: The Deeds of Nehemiah

See RG
211–12

CHAPTER 1

Nehemiah's Vocation. *1*The words of Nehemiah, the son of Hacaliah.*

In the month Chislev of the twentieth year, I was in the citadel of Susa *2*when Hanani, one of my brothers, came with other men from Judah. I asked them about the Jews, the remnant preserved after the captivity, and about Jerusalem, *3*and they answered me: "The survivors of the captivity there in the province are in great distress and under reproach. Also, the wall of Jerusalem lies breached, and its gates have been gutted with fire." *4*When I heard this report, I began to weep and continued mourning for several days; I fasted and prayed before the God of heaven.

*5*I prayed: "O LORD, God of heaven, great and awesome God, you who preserve your covenant of mercy toward those who love you and keep your commandments,*a* *6*may your ear be attentive, and your eyes open, to heed the prayer which I, your servant, now offer in your presence day and night for your servants the Israelites, confessing the sins which we of Israel have committed against you, I and my father's house included.*b* *7*Grievously have we offended you, not keeping the commandments, the statutes, and the ordinances which you committed to your servant Moses.*c* *8*But remember, I pray, the promise which you gave through Moses, your servant, when you said:*d* 'Should you prove faithless, I will scatter you among the nations; *9*but should you return to me and carefully keep my commandments, even though your outcasts have been driven to the farthest corner of the world, I will gather them from there, and bring them back to the place which I have chosen as the dwelling place for my name.' *10*They are your servants, your people, whom you freed by your great might and your strong hand.*e* *11*O LORD, may your ear be attentive to my prayer and that of all your willing servants who revere your name. Grant success to your servant this day, and let him find favor

---

1, 1: The first mission of Nehemiah, from the twentieth year of Artaxerxes I, lasted from the spring (Neh 2, 1) of 445 B.C. until 433 B.C. (Neh 5, 14). It is recounted in Neh 1, 1—6, 15; 12, 27-43; 6, 16—7, 5; 11, 1-21, which may be read in that order.

———

a: Dt 7, 9. 12; Dn 9, 4.   *b:* 2 Chr 6, 40.   *c:* Dn 3, 29f.   *d:* 8f: Dt 30, 1-5.   *e:* Dt 9, 29.

The Four Stages of Return from Exile

THE CHRONOLOGY of Ezra and Nehemiah is not completely clear. The following list of stages outlines the possibilities.

STAGE 1:   Return of the people by permission of the Persian emperor Cyrus in 538 B.C. The leader of the people was Sheshbazzar, and the group he led began to rebuild the temple but abandoned the project when there was local opposition.

STAGE 2:   Return by permission of the Persian emperor Darius I (late 6th century/early 5th century). The leaders were Zerubbabel and Jeshua, and the group completed the rebuilding of the temple.

STAGE 3:   A group under the leadership of Ezra, in either 458 or 398 B.C. This group brought a copy of the Law of Moses.

STAGE 4:   A group returning by permission of the Persian emperor Artaxerxes I in 445 B.C. Nehemiah came as the governor with a retinue, and worked with other reurning groups to rebuild the walls of Jerusalem and re-establish worship and the Jewish community.

with this man"—for I was cupbearer to the king.*f

See RG 212

CHAPTER 2

Appointment by the King. ¹In the month Nisan of the twentieth year of King Artaxerxes, when the wine was in my charge, I took some and offered it to the king. As I had never before been sad in his presence, ²the king asked me, "Why do you look sad? If you are not sick, you must be sad at heart." Though I was seized with great fear, ³I answered the king: "May the king live forever! How could I not look sad when the city where my ancestors are buried lies in ruins, and its gates have been eaten out by fire?" ⁴The king asked me, "What is it, then, that you wish?" I prayed to the God of heaven ⁵and then answered the king: "If it please the king, and if your servant is deserving of your favor, send me to Judah, to

the city of my ancestors' graves, to rebuild it." ⁶Then the king, and the queen seated beside him, asked me how long my journey would take and when I would return. I set a date that was acceptable to him, and the king agreed that I might go.

⁷I asked the king further: "If it please the king, let letters be given to me for the governors of West-of-Euphrates, that they may afford me safe-conduct till I arrive in Judah; ⁸also a letter for Asaph, the keeper of the royal park, that he may give me wood for timbering the gates of the temple-citadel and for the city wall and the house that I shall occupy." The king granted my requests, for the favoring hand of my God was upon me.g ⁹Thus I proceeded to the governors of West-of-Euphrates and presented the king's letters to them. The king also sent with me army officers and cavalry.h

¹⁰When Sanballat the Horonite* and To-

1, 11: Cupbearer to the king: an important official in the royal household. Because Nehemiah could appear in the queen's presence (Neh 2, 6), it is commonly presumed that he was a eunuch; but this is not necessarily so.

2, 10: Sanballat the Horonite: the governor of the province of Samaria (Neh 3, 33f), apparently a native of one of the Bethhorons. A letter from the Jews living at Elephantine in southern Egypt, dated 408–407 B.C., mentions "Delayah and Shelemyah, the sons of Sanballat, the governor of Samaria." Although his own name was Babylonian—Sin-uballit, i.e., "Sin (the moon god) has given life"—two sons had names referring to Yahweh. Tobiah, the Ammonite slave: the governor

of the province of Ammon in Transjordan. His honorary title, "servant" (in Hebrew, ebed), i.e., of the king, could also be understood as slave, and Nehemiah no doubt meant it in this derogatory sense. The Tobiads remained a powerful family even in Maccabean times (2 Mc 3, 11). Sanballat and Tobiah together with Geshem the Arab (Neh 2, 19; 6, 1f), who was probably in charge of Edom and the regions to the south and southeast of Judah, opposed the rebuilding of Jerusalem's walls on political grounds; the city was the capital of a rival province.

f: Ps 118, 25.   g: Ezr 7, 6.   h: Ezr 8, 22.

biah the Ammonite slave had heard of this, they were very much displeased that someone had come to seek the welfare of the Israelites.

Circuit of the City. [11] When I had arrived in Jerusalem, I first rested there for three days. [12] Then I set out by night with only a few other men (for I had not told anyone what my God had inspired me to do for Jerusalem) and with no other animals but my own mount. [13*] I rode out at night by the Valley Gate, passed by the Dragon Spring, and came to the Dung Gate, observing how the walls of Jerusalem lay in ruins and its gates had been eaten out by fire. [14] Then I passed over to the Spring Gate and to the King's Pool. Since there was no room here for my mount to pass with me astride, [15] I continued on foot up the wadi by night, inspecting the wall all the while till I once more reached the Valley Gate, by which I went back in. [16] The magistrates knew nothing of where I had gone or what I was doing, for as yet I had disclosed nothing to the Jews, neither to the priests, nor to the nobles, nor to the magistrates, nor to the others who would be concerned about the matter.

Rebuilding Jerusalem's Walls. [17] Afterward I said to them: "You see the evil plight in which we stand: how Jerusalem lies in ruins and its gates have been gutted by fire. Come, let us rebuild the wall of Jerusalem, so that we may no longer be an object of derision!" [18] Then I explained to them how the favoring hand of my God had rested upon me, and what the king had said to me. They replied, "Let us be up and building!" And they undertook the good work with vigor.[i]

[19] On hearing of this, Sanballat the Horonite, Tobiah the Ammonite slave, and Geshem the Arab mocked us and ridiculed us. "What is this that you are about?" they asked. "Are you rebelling against the king?" [20] My answer to them was this: "It is the God of heaven who will grant us success. We, his servants, shall set about the rebuilding; but for you there is to be neither share nor claim nor memorial* in Jerusalem."

CHAPTER 3

See RG 212

*List of Workers.** [1] Eliashib the high priest and his priestly brethren took up the task of rebuilding the Sheep Gate. They timbered it and set up its doors, its bolts, and its bars, then continued the rebuilding to the Tower of Hananel.[j] [2] At their side the men of Jericho were rebuilding, and next to them was Zaccur, son of Imri. [3] The Fish Gate was rebuilt by the sons of Hassenaah; they timbered it and set up its doors, its bolts, and its bars.[k] [4] At their side Meremoth, son of Uriah, son of Hakkoz, carried out the work of repair; next to him was Meshullam, son of Berechiah, son of Meshezabel; and next to him was Zadok, son of Baana. [5] Next to him the Tekoites carried out the work of repair; however, some of their outstanding men would not submit to the labor asked by their lords. [6] The New City Gate was repaired by Joiada, son of Paseah; and Meshullam, son of Besodeiah; they timbered it and set up its doors, its bolts, and its bars. [7] At their side were Melatiah the Gibeonite, Jadon the Meronothite, and the men of Gibeon and of Mizpah, who were under the jurisdiction of the governor of West-of-Euphrates. [8] Next to them the work of repair was carried out by Uzziel, son of Harhaiah, a member of the goldsmiths' guild, and at his side was Hananiah, one of the perfumers' guild. They restored Jerusalem as far as the wall of the public square.* [9] Next to them the work of repair was carried out by Rephaiah,

---

2, 13ff: Nehemiah left Jerusalem by the Valley Gate near the northwestern end of the old City of David and went south down the Tyropoean Valley toward the Dragon Spring (or the En-rogel of Jos 15, 7; 18, 16; 2 Sm 17, 17; 1 Kgs 1, 9, now known as Job's Well) at the juncture of the Valley of Hinnom and the Kidron Valley; he then turned north at the Dung Gate (or the Potsherd Gate of Jer 19, 2) at the southern end of the city and proceeded up the wadi, that is, the Kidron Valley, passing the Spring Gate (at the Spring of Gihon) and the King's Pool (unidentified); finally he turned west and then south to his starting point.

2, 20: Neither share nor claim nor memorial: although Sanballat and Tobiah were Yahwist, Nehemiah would not let

them participate in any of the rights of the religious community in Jerusalem.

3, 1-32: The construction work on the gates and walls of the city is described in counterclockwise direction, beginning and ending at the Sheep Gate (to the north of the temple). The exact sites of many of the topographical points mentioned are uncertain.

3, 8: Wall of the public square: that is, the section of wall bounding the place of assembly outside the Gate of Ephraim, or New City Gate; cf Neh 3, 6; 8, 16.

---

i: Ezr 7, 6.   j: Jer 31, 38.   k: Ezr 2, 35; Zep 1, 10.

son of Hur, leader of half the district of Jerusalem, [10] and at his side was Jedaiah, son of Harumaph, who repaired opposite his own house. Next to him Hattush, son of Hashabneiah, carried out the work of repair. [11] The adjoining sector, as far as the Oven Tower, was repaired by Malchijah, son of Harim, and Hasshub, of Pahath-moab. [12] At their side the work of repair was carried out by Shallum, son of Hallohesh, leader of half the district of Jerusalem, by himself and his daughters. [13] The Valley Gate was repaired by Hanun and the inhabitants of Zanoah; they rebuilt it and set up its doors, its bolts, and its bars. They also repaired a thousand cubits of the wall up to the Dung Gate. [14] The Dung Gate was repaired by Malchijah, son of Rechab, leader of the district of Beth-haccherem; he rebuilt it and set up its doors, its bolts, and its bars. [15] The Spring Gate was repaired by Shallum, son of Colhozeh, leader of the district of Mizpah; he rebuilt it, roofed it over, and set up its doors, its bolts, and its bars. He also repaired the wall of the Aqueduct Pool near the king's garden as far as the steps that lead down from the City of David. [16] After him, the work of repair was carried out by Nehemiah, son of Azbuk, leader of half the district of Beth-zur, to a place opposite the tombs of David, as far as the artificial pool and the barracks.

[17] After him, the Levites carried out the work of repair: Rehum, son of Bani. Next to him, for his own district, was Hashabiah, leader of half the district of Keilah. [18] After him, their brethren carried out the work of repair: Binnui, son of Henadad, leader of half the district of Keilah; [19] next to him Ezer, son of Jeshua, leader of Mizpah, who repaired the adjoining sector, the Corner, opposite the ascent to the arsenal. [20] After him, Baruch, son of Zabbai, repaired the adjoining sector from the Corner to the entrance of the house of Eliashib, the high priest. [21] After him, Meremoth, son of Uriah, son of Hakkoz, repaired the adjoining sector from the entrance of Eliashib's house to the end of the house.

[22] After him, the work of repair was carried out by the priests, men of the surrounding country. [23] After them, Benjamin and Hasshub carried out the repair in front of their houses; after them, Azariah, son of Maaseiah, son of Ananiah, made the repairs alongside his house. [24] After him, Binnui, son of Henadad, repaired the adjoining sector from the house of Azariah to the Corner [that is, to the Angle]. [25] After him, Palal, son of Uzai, carried out the work of repair opposite the Corner and the tower projecting from the Upper Palace at the quarters of the guard. After him, Pedaiah, son of Parosh, carried out the work of repair [26] to a point opposite the Water Gate on the east, and the projecting tower. [27] After him, the Tekoites repaired the adjoining sector opposite the great projecting tower, to the wall of Ophel [the temple slaves were dwelling on Ophel].

[28] Above the Horse Gate the priests carried out the work of repair, each before his own house. [29] After them Zadok, son of Immer, carried out the repair before his house, and after him the repair was carried out by Shemaiah, son of Shecaniah, keeper of the East Gate.[1] [30] After him, Hananiah, son of Shelemiah, and Hanun, the sixth son of Zalaph, repaired the adjoining sector; after them, Meshullam, son of Berechiah, repaired the place opposite his own lodging. [31] After him, Malchijah, a member of the goldsmiths' guild, carried out the work of repair as far as the quarters of the temple slaves and the merchants, before the Gate of Inspection and as far as the upper chamber of the Angle. [32] Between the upper chamber of the Angle and the Sheep Gate, the goldsmiths and the merchants carried out the work of repair.

Opposition from Judah's Foes. [33] When Sanballat heard that we were rebuilding the wall, it roused his anger and he became very much incensed. He ridiculed the Jews, [34] saying in the presence of his brethren and the troops of Samaria: "What are these miserable Jews trying to do? Will they complete their restoration in a single day? Will they recover these stones, burnt as they are, from the heaps of dust?" [35] Tobiah the Ammonite was beside him, and he said: "It is a rubble heap they are building. Any fox that attacked it would breach their wall of stones!" [36] Take

l: Ezr 40, 6.

note, O our God, how we were mocked! Turn back their derision upon their own heads and let them be carried away to a land of captivity! [37]Hide not their crime and let not their sin be blotted out in your sight, for they insulted the builders to their face![m] [38]We, however, continued to build the wall, which was soon filled in and completed up to half its height. The people worked with a will.

CHAPTER 4

See RG 212

[1]When Sanballat, Tobiah, the Arabs, the Ammonites, and the Ashdodites heard that the restoration of the walls of Jerusalem was progressing—for the gaps were beginning to be closed up—they became extremely angry. [2]Thereupon they all plotted together to come and fight against Jerusalem and thus to throw us into confusion. [3]We prayed to our God and posted a watch against them day and night for fear of what they might do. [4]Meanwhile the Judahites were saying:

"Slackened is the bearers' strength,
    there is no end to the rubbish;
Never shall we be able
    the wall to rebuild."

[5]Our enemies thought, "Before they are aware of it or see us, we shall come into their midst, kill them, and put an end to the work."

[6]When the Jews who lived near them had come to us from one place after another, and had told us ten times over that they were about to attack us, [7]I stationed guards down below, behind the wall, near the exposed points, assigning them by family groups with their swords, their spears, and their bows. [8]I made an inspection, then addressed these words to the nobles, the magistrates, and the rest of the people: "Have no fear of them! Keep in mind the LORD, who is great and to be feared, and fight for your brethren, your sons and daughters, your wives and your homes." [9]When our enemies became aware that we had been warned and that God had upset their plan, we all went back, each to his own task at the wall.

[10]From that time on, however, only half my able men took a hand in the work, while the other half, armed with spears, bucklers, bows, and breastplates, stood guard behind the whole house of Judah[n] [11]as they rebuilt the wall. The load carriers, too, were armed; each did his work with one hand and held a weapon with the other. [12]Every builder, while he worked, had his sword girt at his side. Also, a trumpeter stood beside me, [13]for I had said to the nobles, the magistrates, and the rest of the people: "Our work is scattered and extensive, and we are widely separated from one another along the wall; [14]wherever you hear the trumpet sound, join us there; our God will fight with us." [15]Thus we went on with the work, half of the men with spears at the ready, from daybreak till the stars came out.

[16]At the same time I told the people to spend the nights inside Jerusalem, each man with his own attendant, so that they might serve as a guard by night and a working force by day. [17]Neither I, nor my kinsmen, nor any of my attendants, nor any of the bodyguard that accompanied me took off his clothes; everyone kept his weapon at his right hand.

CHAPTER 5

See RG 212

Antisocial Conduct. [1o]Then there rose a great outcry of the common people and their wives against certain of their fellow Jews. [2]Some said: "We are forced to pawn our sons and daughters in order to get grain to eat that we may live." [3]Others said: "We are forced to pawn our fields, our vineyards, and our houses, that we may have grain during the famine." [4]Still others said: "To pay the king's tax we have borrowed money on our fields and our vineyards. [5]And though these are our own kinsmen and our children are as good as theirs, we have had to reduce our sons and daughters to slavery, and violence has been done to some of our daughters! Yet we can do nothing about it, for our fields and our vineyards belong to others."[p]

Nehemiah's Action. [6]I was extremely angry when I heard the reasons they had for complaint. [7]After some deliberation, I called

m: Jer 18, 23.   n: Ps 149, 6.   o: 1f: Jer 34, 8-22.   p: Ez 21, 7; Lv 25, 39.

the nobles and magistrates to account, saying to them, "You are exacting interest from your own kinsmen!"* I then rebuked them severely, [8]saying to them: "As far as we were able, we bought back our fellow Jews who had been sold to Gentiles; you, however, are selling your own brothers, to have them bought back by us." They remained silent, for they could find no answer.[q] [9]I continued: "What you are doing is not good. Should you not walk in the fear of our God, and put an end to the derision of our Gentile enemies? [10]I myself, my kinsmen, and my attendants have lent the people money and grain without charge. Let us put an end to this usury! [11]I ask that you return to them this very day their fields, their vineyards, their olive groves, and their houses, together with the interest on the money, the grain, the wine, and the oil that you have lent them." [12]They answered: "We will return everything and exact nothing further from them. We will do just what you ask." Then I called for the priests and had them administer an oath to these men that they would do as they had promised. [13]I also shook out the folds of my garment, saying, "Thus may God shake from his home and his fortune every man who fails to keep this promise, and may he thus be shaken out and emptied!" And the whole assembly answered, "Amen," and praised the LORD. Then the people did as they had promised.

Nehemiah's Lack of Self-Interest. [14]Moreover, from the time that King Artaxerxes appointed me governor in the land of Judah, from his twentieth to his thirty-second year—during these twelve years neither I nor my brethren lived from the governor's allowance. [15]The earlier governors, my predecessors, had laid a heavy burden on the people, taking from them each day forty silver shekels for their food; then too, their men oppressed the people. But I, because I feared God, did not act thus. [16]Moreover, though I had acquired no land of my own, I did my part in this work on the wall, and all my men were gathered there for the work. [17]Though I set my table for a hundred and fifty persons, Jews and magistrates, as well as those who came to us from the nations round about, [18]and though the daily preparations were made at my expense—one beef, six choice muttons, poultry—besides all kinds of wine in abundance every ten days, despite this I did not claim the governor's allowance, for the labor lay heavy upon this people. [19]Keep in mind, O my God, in my favor all that I did for this people.

CHAPTER 6

See RG 212

Plots against Nehemiah. [1]When it had been reported to Sanballat, Tobiah, Geshem the Arab, and our other enemies that I had rebuilt the wall and that there was no breach left in it (though up to that time I had not yet set up the doors in the gates), [2]Sanballat and Geshem sent me this message: "Come, let us hold council together at Caphirim in the plain of Ono." They were planning to do me harm. [3]However, I sent messengers to them with this reply: "I am engaged in a great enterprise and am unable to come down; why should the work stop, while I leave it to come down to you?" [4]Four times they sent me this same proposal, and each time I gave the same reply. [5]Then, the fifth time, Sanballat sent me the same message by one of his servants, who bore an unsealed letter [6]containing this text: "Among the nations it has been reported—Geshem is witness to this—that you and the Jews are planning a rebellion; that for this reason you are rebuilding the wall; and that you are to be their king"—and so on. [7]"Also, that you have set up prophets in Jerusalem to proclaim you king of Judah. Now, since matters like these must reach the ear of the king, come, let us hold council together." [8]I sent him this answer: "Nothing of what you report has taken place; rather, it is the invention of your own mind." [9]They were all trying to frighten us, thinking, "Their hands will slacken in the work, and it will never be completed." But instead, I now redoubled my efforts.

[10]I went to the house of Shemaiah, son of Delaiah, son of Mehetabel, who was unable to go about, and he said:

5, 7: You are exacting interest from your own kinsmen!: contrary to the Mosaic law (Dt 23, 20).

q: Lv 25, 48.

"Let us meet in the house of God,
　inside the temple building;
let us lock the doors of the temple.
For men are coming to kill you;
　by night they are coming coming to
　　kill you."

[11] My answer was: "A man like me take flight? Can a man like me enter the temple to save his life? I will not go!" [12] For on consideration it was plain to me that God had not sent him; rather, because Tobiah and Sanballat had bribed him, he voiced this prophecy concerning me [13] that I might act on it out of fear and commit this sin. Then they would have had a shameful story with which to discredit me. [14] Keep in mind Tobiah and Sanballat, O my God, because of these things they did; keep in mind as well Noadiah the prophetess and the other prophets who were trying to frighten me.[r]

Conclusion of the Work. [15] The wall was finished on the twenty-fifth day of Elul;* it had taken fifty-two days. [16] When all our enemies had heard of this, and all the nations round about had taken note of it, our enemies lost much face in the eyes of the nations, for they knew that it was with our God's help that this work had been completed.[s] [17]* At that same time, however, many letters were going to Tobiah from the nobles of Judah, and Tobiah's letters were reaching them, [18] for many in Judah were in league with him, since he was the son-in-law of Shecaniah, son of Arah, and his son Jehohanan had married the daughter of Meshullam, son of Berechiah. [19] Thus they would praise his good deeds in my presence and relate to him whatever I said; and Tobiah sent letters trying to frighten me.

CHAPTER 7

See RG 212

[1] When the wall had been rebuilt, I had the doors set up, and the gatekeepers [and the singers and the Levites] were put in charge of them. [2] Over Jerusalem I placed Hanani, my brother, and Hananiah, the commander of the citadel, who was a more trustworthy and God-fearing man than most. [3] I said to them: "The gates of Jerusalem are not to be opened until the sun is hot, and while the sun is still shining they shall shut and bar the doors. Appoint as watchmen the inhabitants of Jerusalem, some at their watch posts, and others before their own houses."

Census of the Province. [4] Now the city was quite wide and spacious, but its population was small, and none of the houses had been rebuilt. [5] When my God had put it into my mind to gather together the nobles, the magistrates, and the common people, and to examine their family records, I came upon the family list of those who had returned in the earliest period. There I found the following written:

[6]t* These are the inhabitants of the province who returned from the captivity of the exiles whom Nebuchadnezzar, king of Babylon, had carried away, and who came back to Jerusalem and Judah, each man to his own city [7] (those who returned with Zerubbabel, Jeshua, Nehemiah, Azariah, Raamiah, Nahamani, Mordecai, Bilshan, Mispereth, Bigvai, Nehum, and Baanah).

The census of the men of Israel: [8] sons of Parosh, two thousand one hundred and seventy-two; [9] sons of Shephatiah, three hundred and seventy-two; [10] sons of Arah, six hundred and fifty-two; [11] sons of Pahath-moab who were sons of Jeshua and Joab, two thousand eight hundred and eighteen; [12] sons of Elam, one thousand two hundred and fifty-four; [13] sons of Zattu, eight hundred and forty-five; [14] sons of Zaccai, seven hundred and sixty; [15] sons of Binnui, six hundred and forty-eight; [16] sons of Bebai, six hundred and twenty-eight; [17] sons of Azgad, two thousand three hundred and twenty-two; [18] sons of Adonikam, six hundred and sixty-seven; [19] sons of Bigvai, two thousand and

6, 15: Elul: the sixth month (August–September). Fifty-two days: according to Josephus (Antiquities XI, v 8), the rebuilding of the walls of Jerusalem by Nehemiah took two years and four months, which seems more probable.

6, 17ff: These verses should be read immediately after v 14.

7, 6-72a: See note on Ezr 2, 1-67.

r: Jer 23, 9-40; Zec 13, 3.　s: Ps 118, 22f; 127, 1.　t: 6-72: Ezr 2, 1-70.

sixty-seven; [20]sons of Adin, six hundred and fifty-five; [21]sons of Ater who were sons of Hezekiah, ninety-eight; [22]sons of Hashum, three hundred and twenty-eight; [23]sons of Bezai, three hundred and twenty-four; [24]sons of Hariph, one hundred and twelve; [25]sons of Gibeon, ninety-five; [26]men of Bethlehem and Netophah, one hundred and eighty-eight; [27]men of Anathoth, one hundred and twenty-eight; [28]men of Beth-azmaveth, forty-two; [29]men of Kiriath-jearim, Chephirah, and Beeroth, seven hundred and forty-three; [30]men of Ramah and Geba, six hundred and twenty-one; [31]men of Michmas, one hundred and twenty-two; [32]men of Bethel and Ai, one hundred and twenty-three; [33]men of Nebo, fifty-two; [34]sons of another Elam, one thousand two hundred and fifty-four; [35]sons of Harim, three hundred and twenty; [36]sons of Jericho, three hundred and forty-five; [37]sons of Lod, Hadid, and Ono, seven hundred and twenty-one; [38]sons of Senaah, three thousand nine hundred and thirty.

[39]The priests: sons of Jedaiah who were of the house of Jeshua, nine hundred and seventy-three; [40]sons of Immer, one thousand and fifty-two; [41]sons of Pashhur, one thousand two hundred and forty-seven; [42]sons of Harim, one thousand and seventeen.

[43]The Levites: sons of Jeshua, Kadmiel, Binnui, Hodeviah, seventy-four.

[44]The singers: sons of Asaph, one hundred and forty-eight.

[45]The gatekeepers: sons of Shallum, sons of Ater, sons of Talmon, sons of Akkub, sons of Hatita, sons of Shobai, one hundred and thirty-eight.

[46]The temple slaves: sons of Ziha, sons of Hasupha, sons of Tabbaoth, [47]sons of Keros, sons of Sia, sons of Padon, [48]sons of Lebana, sons of Hagaba, sons of Shalmai, [49]sons of Hanan, sons of Giddel, sons of Gahar, [50]sons of Reaiah, sons of Rezin, sons of Nekoda, [51]sons of Gazzam, sons of Uzza, sons of Paseah, [52]sons of Besai, sons of the Meunites, sons of the Nephusites, [53]sons of Bakbuk, sons of Hakupha, sons of Harhur, [54]sons of Bazlith, sons of Mehida, sons of Harsha, [55]sons of Barkos, sons of Sisera, sons of Temah, [56]sons of Neziah, sons of Hatipha.

[57]Descendants of the slaves of Solomon: sons of Sotai, sons of Sophereth, sons of Perida, [58]sons of Jaala, sons of Darkon, sons of Giddel, [59]sons of Shephatiah, sons of Hattil, sons of Pochereth-hazzebaim, sons of Amon. [60]The total of the temple slaves and the descendants of the slaves of Solomon was three hundred and ninety-two.

[61]The following who returned from Tel-melah, Tel-harsha, Cherub, Addon, and Immer were unable to prove that their ancestral houses and their descent were Israelite: [62]sons of Delaiah, sons of Tobiah, sons of Nekoda, six hundred and forty-two. [63]Also, of the priests: sons of Hobaiah, sons of Hakkoz, sons of Barzillai (he had married one of the daughters of Barzillai the Gileadite and became known by his name). [64]These men searched their family records, but their names could not be found written there; hence they were degraded from the priesthood, [65]and His Excellency* ordered them not to partake of the most holy foods until there should be a priest bearing the Urim and Thummim.

[66]The entire assembly taken together came to forty-two thousand three hundred and sixty, [67]not counting their male and female slaves, who were seven thousand three hundred and thirty-seven. They also had two hundred male and female singers. Their horses were seven hundred and thirty-six, their mules two hundred and forty-five, [68]their camels four hundred and thirty-five, their asses six thousand seven hundred and twenty.

[69]Certain of the family heads contributed to the service. His Excellency put into the treasury one thousand drachmas of gold, fifty basins, thirty garments for priests, and five hundred minas of silver. [70]Some of the family heads contributed to the treasury for the temple service: twenty thousand drachmas of gold and two thousand two hundred minas of silver. [71]The contributions of the rest of the people amounted to twenty thousand drachmas of gold, two thousand minas of silver, and sixty-seven garments for priests.

7, 65. 69: His Excellency: see note on Ezr 2, 63.

⁷²The priests, the Levites, the gatekeepers, the singers, the temple slaves, and all Israel took up residence in their cities.

II: Promulgation of the Law

CHAPTER 8

See RG
212-14

Ezra Reads the Law. Now when the seventh month came, ¹the whole people gathered as one man in the open space before the Water Gate, and they called upon Ezra the scribe to bring forth the book of the law of Moses which the LORD prescribed for Israel.ᵘ ²On the first day of the seventh month, therefore, Ezra the priest brought the law before the assembly, which consisted of men, women, and those children old enough to understand. ³Standing at one end of the open place that was before the Water Gate, he read out of the book from daybreak till midday, in the presence of the men, the women, and those children old enough to understand; and all the people listened attentively to the book of the law. ⁴Ezra the scribe stood on a wooden platform that had been made for the occasion; at his right side stood Mattithiah, Shema, Anaiah, Uriah, Hilkiah, and Maaseiah, and on his left Pedaiah, Mishael, Malchijah, Hashum, Hashbaddanah, Zechariah, Meshullam. ⁵Ezra opened the scroll so that all the people might see it (for he was standing higher up than any of the people); and, as he opened it, all the people rose. ⁶Ezra blessed the LORD, the great God, and all the people, their hands raised high, answered, "Amen, amen!" Then they bowed down and prostrated themselves before the LORD, their faces to the ground. ⁷[The Levites Jeshua, Bani, Sherebiah, Jamin, Akkub, Shabbethai, Hodiah, Maaseiah, Kelita, Azariah, Jozabad, Hanan, and Pelaiah explained the law to the people, who remained in their places.]ᵛ ⁸Ezra read plainly from the book of the law of God, interpreting it so that all could understand what was read.ʷ ⁹Then [Nehemiah, that is, His Excellency, and]

Ezra the priest-scribe [and the Levites who were instructing the people] said to all the people: "Today is holy to the LORD your God. Do not be sad, and do not weep"—for all the people were weeping as they heard the words of the law. ¹⁰He said further: "Go, eat rich foods and drink sweet drinks, and allot portions to those who had nothing prepared; for today is holy to our LORD. Do not be saddened this day, for rejoicing in the LORD must be your strength!"ˣ ¹¹[And the Levites quieted all the people, saying, "Hush, for today is holy, and you must not be saddened."] ¹²Then all the people went to eat and drink, to distribute portions, and to celebrate with great joy, for they understood the words that had been expounded to them.

The Feast of Booths. ¹³On the second day, the family heads of the whole people and also the priests and the Levites gathered around Ezra the scribe and examined the words of the law more closely. ¹⁴They found it written in the law prescribed by the LORD through Moses that the Israelites must dwell in booths during the feast of the seventh month;ʸ ¹⁵and that they should have this proclamation made throughout their cities and in Jerusalem: "Go out into the hill country and bring in branches of olive trees, oleasters, myrtle, palm, and other leafy trees, to make booths, as the law prescribes."ᶻ ¹⁶The people went out and brought in branches with which they made booths for themselves, on the roofs of their houses, in their courtyards, in the courts of the house of God, and in the open spaces of the Water Gate and the Gate of Ephraim. ¹⁷Thus the entire assembly of the returned exiles made booths and dwelt in them. Now the Israelites had done nothing of this sort from the days of Jeshua, son of Nun, until this occasion; therefore there was very great joy. ¹⁸Ezra read from the book of the law of God day after day, from the first day to the last. They kept the feast for seven days, and the solemn assembly on the eighth day, as was required.

7, 72b—8, 18: to be read after Ezr 8, 36. The gloss mentioning Nehemiah in v 9 was inserted in this Ezra section after the dislocation of several parts of Ezra-Nehemiah had occurred. There is no clear evidence of a simultaneous presence of Nehemiah and Ezra in Jerusalem; Neh. 12, 26 and 12, 36 are also scribal glosses.

---

u: Ezr 3, 1.   *v:* Neh 10, 11.   *w:* Ezr 7, 6.   *x:* Est 9, 19.   *y:* Ex 23, 14; Lv 23, 33-36.   *z:* Ps 118, 27.

CHAPTER 9

Confession of the People. ¹ᵃ* On the twenty-fourth day of this month, the Israelites gathered together fasting and in sackcloth, their heads covered with dust. ²Those of Israelite descent separated themselves from all who were of foreign extraction, then stood forward and confessed their sins and the guilty deeds of their fathers.ᵇ ³When they had taken their places, they read from the book of the law of the LORD their God, for a fourth part of the day, and during another fourth part they made their confession and prostrated themselves before the LORD their God. ⁴Standing on the platform of the Levites were Jeshua, Binnui, Kadmiel, Shebaniah, Bunni, Sherebiah, Bani, and Chenani, who cried out to the LORD their God with a loud voice. ⁵The Levites Jeshua, Kadmiel, Bani, Hashabneiah, Sherebiah, Hodiah, Shebaniah, and Pethahiah said,

"Arise, bless the LORD, your God,
    from eternity to eternity!"

The Israelites answered with the blessing,

"Blessed is your glorious name,
    and exalted above all blessing and
        praise."ᶜ

⁶*Then Ezra said: "It is you, O LORD, you are the only one; you made the heavens, the highest heavens and all their host, the earth and all that is upon it, the seas and all that is in them. To all of them you give life, and the heavenly hosts bow down before you. ⁷You, O LORD, are the God who chose Abram, who brought him out from Ur of the Chaldees, and named him Abraham.ᵈ ⁸When you had found his heart faithful in your sight, you made the covenant with him to give to him and his posterity the land of the Canaanites, Hittites, Amorites, Perizzites, Jebusites, and Girgashites. These promises of yours you fulfilled, for you are just.ᵉ

⁹ "You saw the affliction of our fathers in
        Egypt,
    you heard their cry by the Red Sea;ᶠ
¹⁰ You worked signs and wonders against
        Pharoah,
    against all his servants and the people
        of his land,
Because you knew of their insolence
        toward them;
    thus you made for yourself a name
        even to this day.ᵍ
¹¹ The sea you divided before them,
    on dry ground they passed through the
        midst of the sea;
Their pursuers you hurled into the
        depths,
    like a stone into the mighty waters.ʰ
¹² With a column of cloud you led them by
        day,
    and by night with a column of fire,
To light the way of their journey,
    the way in which they must travel.ⁱ
¹³ On Mount Sinai you came down,
    you spoke with them from heaven;
You gave them just ordinances, firm
        laws,
    good statutes, and commandments;ʲ
¹⁴ Your holy sabbath you made known to
        them,
    commandments, statutes, and law you
        prescribed for them,
    by the hand of Moses your servant.ᵏ
¹⁵ Food from heaven you gave them in their
        hunger,
    water from a rock you sent them in
        their thirst.
You bade them enter and occupy the land
    which you had sworn with upraised
        hand to give them.ˡ

¹⁶"But they, our fathers, proved to be insolent; they held their necks stiff and would not obey your commandments. ¹⁷They refused to obey and no longer remembered the miracles you had worked for them. They stiffened their necks and turned their heads

9, 1-5: This is a continuation of the account concerning the problem of mixed marriages at the time of Ezra; it should be read immediately after Ezr 10, 44.

9, 6-37: The prayer of Ezra which began in Ezr 9, 6f is here continued; see note on Ezr 9, 7.

a: Dn 9, 3.   b: Ezr 9, 1f; 10, 11.   c: Dn 2, 20; 3, 52.   d: Gn 12, 1; 17, 5.   e: Gn 15, 18f.   f: Ex 2, 23f.   g: Ex 7—11; 14.   h: Ex 15, 5. 10.   i: Ex 13, 21f.   j: Ex 19—20.   k: Ex 20, 8.   l: Ex 16, 4; 17, 1f.

to return to their slavery in Egypt. But you are a God of pardons, gracious and compassionate, slow to anger and rich in mercy; you did not forsake them.*m* *18*Though they made for themselves a molten calf, and proclaimed, 'Here is your God who brought you up out of Egypt,' and were guilty of great effronteries,*n* *19*yet in your great mercy you did not forsake them in the desert. The column of cloud did not cease to lead them by day on their journey, nor did the column of fire by night cease to light for them the way by which they were to travel.

20"Your good spirit you bestowed on them, to give them understanding; your manna you did not withhold from their mouths, and you gave them water in their thirst.*o* *21*Forty years in the desert you sustained them: they did not want; their garments did not become worn, and their feet did not become swollen.*p* *22*You gave them kingdoms and peoples, which you divided up among them as border lands. They possessed the land of Sihon, king of Heshbon, and the land of Og, king of Bashan.*q*

23"You made their children as numerous as the stars of the heavens, and you brought them into the land which you had commanded their fathers to enter and possess.*r* *24*The sons went in to take possession of the land, and you humbled before them the Canaanite inhabitants of the land and delivered them over into their power, their kings as well as the peoples of the land, to do with them as they would. *25*They captured fortified cities and fertile land; they took possession of houses filled with all good things, cisterns already dug, vineyards, olive groves, and fruit trees in abundance. They could eat and have their fill, fatten and feast themselves on your immense good gifts.*s*

26"But they were contemptuous and rebellious: they cast your law behind their backs, they slew your prophets who bore witness against them in order to bring them back to you, and they were guilty of great effronteries.*t* *27*Therefore you delivered them into the power of their enemies, who oppressed

them. But in the time of their oppression they would cry out to you, and you would hear them from heaven, and according to your great mercy give them saviors to deliver them from the power of their enemies.*u*

28"As soon as they had relief, they would go back to doing evil in your sight. Then again you abandoned them to the power of their enemies, who crushed them. Then they cried out to you, and you heard them from heaven and delivered them according to your mercy, many times over. *29*You bore witness against them, in order to bring them back to your law. But they were insolent and would not obey your commandments; they sinned against your ordinances, from which men draw life when they practice them. They turned stubborn backs, stiffened their necks, and would not obey.*v* *30*You were patient with them for many years, bearing witness against them through your spirit, by means of your prophets; still they would not listen. Thus you delivered them over into the power of the peoples of the lands. *31*Yet in your great mercy you did not completely destroy them and you did not forsake them, for you are a kind and merciful God.

32"Now, therefore, O our God, great, mighty, and awesome God, you who in your mercy preserve the covenant, take into account all the disasters that have befallen us, our kings, our princes, our priests, our prophets, our fathers, and your entire people, from the time of the kings of Assyria until this day!*w* *33*In all that has come upon us you have been just, for you kept faith while we have done evil.*x* *34*Yes, our kings, our princes, our priests, and our fathers have not kept your law; they paid no attention to your commandments and the obligations of which you reminded them. *35*While they were yet in their kingdom, in the midst of the many good things that you had given them and in the wide and fertile land that you had spread out before them, they did not serve you nor did they turn away from their evil deeds. *36*But, see, we today are slaves; and as for the land which you gave our fathers that

m: Nm 14, 1-4; Ex 34, 6; Dn 9, 9.   n: Ex 32, 4.   o: Dt 2, 7.   p: Dt 8, 4.   q: Nm 21, 21—35; Dt 1, 4; 2, 26—3, 11.   r: Dt 1, 10.
s: Dt 3, 5; 6, 10f; 11, 11; 32, 15.   t: Wis 2, 10-20.   u: Dn 9, 19.   v: Lv 18, 5; Dt 30, 16; 32, 47.   w: Lam 5.   x: Dn 3, 27; 9, 14.

they might eat its fruits and good things—see, we have become slaves upon it! [37]Its rich produce goes to the kings whom you set over us because of our sins, who rule over our bodies and our cattle as they please. We are in great distress!"

See RG 212-14

CHAPTER 10

Agreement of the People. [1]*In view of all this, we are entering into a firm pact, which we are putting into writing. On the sealed document appear the names of our princes, our Levites, and our priests.[y]

[2]On the sealed document: His Excellency Nehemiah, son of Hacaliah, and Zedekiah.

[3]Seraiah, Azariah, Jeremiah, [4]Pashhur, Amariah, Malchijah, [5]Hattush, Shebaniah, Malluch, [6]Harim, Meremoth, Obadiah, [7]Daniel, Ginnethon, Baruch, [8]Meshullam, Abijah, Mijamin, [9]Maaziah, Bilgai, Shemaiah: these are the priests.

[10]The Levites: Jeshua, son of Azaniah; Binnui, of the sons of Henadad; Kadmiel; [11]and their brethren Shebaniah, Hodiah, Kelita, Pelaiah, Hanan,[z] [12]Mica, Rehob, Hashabiah, [13]Zaccur, Sherebiah, Shebaniah, [14]Hodiah, Bani, Beninu.

[15]The leaders of the people: Parosh, Pahath-moab, Elam, Zattu, Bani, [16]Bunni, Azgad, Bebai, [17]Adonijah, Bigvai, Adin, [18]Ater, Hezekiah, Azzur, [19]Hodiah, Hashum, Bezai, [20]Hariph, Anathoth, Nebai, [21]Magpiash, Meshullam, Hazir, [22]Meshezabel, Zadok, Jaddua, [23]Pelatiah, Hanan, Anaiah, [24]Hoshea, Hananiah, Hasshub, [25]Hallohesh, Pilha, Shobek, [26]Rehum, Hashabnah, Maaseiah, [27]Ahiah, Hanan, Anan, [28]Malluch, Harim, Baanah.

Provisions of the Pact. [29]The rest of the people, priests, Levites, gatekeepers, singers, temple slaves, and all others who have separated themselves from the peoples of the lands in favor of the law of God, with their wives, their sons, their daughters, all who are of the age of discretion, [30]join with their brethren who are their princes, and with the sanction of a curse take this oath to follow the law of God which was given through Moses, the servant of God, and to observe carefully all the commandments of the LORD, our Lord, his ordinances and his statutes.[a]

[31]Agreed, that we will not marry our daughters to the peoples of the land, and that we will not take their daughters for our sons.[b]

[32]When the peoples of the land bring in merchandise or any kind of grain for sale on the sabbath day, we will not buy from them on the sabbath or on any other holy day. We will forgo the seventh year, as well as every kind of debt.[c]

[33]We impose these commandments on ourselves: to give a third of a shekel each year for the service of the house of our God,[d] [34]for the showbread, for the daily cereal offering, for the daily holocaust, for the sabbaths, new moons, and festivals, for the holy offerings, for sin offerings to make atonement for Israel, and for every service of the house of our God. [35]We, priests, Levites, and people, have determined by lot concerning the procurement of wood: it is to be brought to the house of our God by each of our family houses at stated times each year, to be burnt on the altar of the LORD, our God, as the law prescribes.[e] [36f]We have agreed to bring each year to the house of the LORD the first fruits of our fields and of our fruit trees, of whatever kind; [37]also, as is prescribed in the law, to bring to the house of our God, to the priests who serve in the house of our God, the first-born of our children and our animals, including the first-born of our flocks and herds. [38]The first batch of our dough, and our offerings of the fruit of every tree, of wine and of oil, we will bring to the priests, to the chambers of the house of our God. The tithe of our fields we will bring to the Levites; they, the Levites, shall take the tithe in all the cities of our service.[g] [39]An Aaronite priest shall be with the Levites when they take the tithe, and the Levites shall bring the tithe of the tithes to the house

---

10, 1-40: This section belongs to the Nehemiah narrative rather than to that of Ezra. It is best read after Neh 13, 31. In view of all this: considering the situation described in Neh 13, 4-31.

---

y: Neh 12, 12-26. *z:* Ezr 10, 23. *a:* Neh 13, 23-27. *b:* Neh 13, 15-22. *c:* Neh 5, 1-13; Ex 20, 8; Lv 25, 2-7. *d:* 2 Chr 24, 6. 9f; Lv 24, 5-9. *e:* Neh 13, 31. *f:* 36f: Ex 13, 1. 11ff; Dt 26, 1. *g:* Neh 13, 10-14; Nm 18, 21. 24ff.

of our God, to the chambers of the treasury. ⁴⁰For to these chambers the Israelites and Levites bring the offerings of grain, wine, and oil; there also are housed the utensils of the sanctuary, and the ministering priests, the gatekeepers, and the singers. We will not neglect the house of our God.

See RG
214

CHAPTER 11

Repeopling of Jerusalem. ¹*The leaders of the people took up residence in Jerusalem, and the rest of the people cast lots to bring one man in ten to reside in Jerusalem, the holy city, while the other nine would remain in the other cities.^h ²The people applauded all those men who willingly agreed to take up residence in Jerusalem.

The Residents of Jerusalem. ³ⁱThese are the heads of the province who took up residence in Jerusalem. (In the cities of Judah dwelt lay Israelites, priests, Levites, temple slaves, and the descendants of the slaves of Solomon, each man on the property he owned in his own city.)

⁴In Jerusalem dwelt both Judahites and Benjaminites. Of the Judahites: Athaiah, son of Uzziah, son of Zechariah, son of Amariah, son of Shephatiah, son of Mehallalel, of the sons of Perez; ⁵Maaseiah, son of Baruch, son of Colhozeh, son of Hazaiah, son of Adaiah, son of Joiarib, son of Zechariah, a son of the Shelanites. ⁶The total of the sons of Perez who dwelt in Jerusalem was four hundred and sixty-eight valiant men.

⁷These were the Benjaminites: Sallu, son of Meshullam, son of Joed, son of Pedaiah, son of Kolaiah, son of Maaseiah, son of Ithiel, son of Jeshaiah, ⁸and his brethren, warriors, nine hundred and twenty-eight in number. ⁹Joel, son of Zichri, was their commander, and Judah, son of Hassenuah, was second in charge of the city.

¹⁰Among the priests were: Jedaiah; Joiarib; Jachin; ¹¹Seraiah, son of Hilkiah, son of Meshullam, son of Zadok, son of Meraioth, son of Ahitub, the ruler of the house of God, ¹²and their brethren who carried out the temple ser-

vice, eight hundred and twenty-two; Adaiah, son of Jeroham, son of Pelaliah, son of Amzi, son of Zechariah, son of Pashhur, son of Malchijah, ¹³and his brethren, family heads, two hundred and forty-two; and Amasai, son of Azarel, son of Ahzai, son of Meshillemoth, son of Immer, ¹⁴and his brethren, warriors, one hundred and twenty-eight. Their commander was Zabdiel, son of Haggadol.

¹⁵Among the Levites were Shemaiah, son of Hasshub, son of Azrikam, son of Hashabiah, son of Bunni; ¹⁶Shabbethai and Jozabad, levitical chiefs who were placed over the external affairs of the house of God; ¹⁷Mattaniah, son of Micah, son of Zabdi, son of Asaph, director of the psalms, who led the thanksgiving at prayer; Bakbukiah, second in rank among his brethren; and Abda, son of Shammua, son of Galal, son of Jeduthun. ¹⁸The total of the Levites in the holy city was two hundred and eighty-four.

¹⁹The gatekeepers were Akkub, Talmon, and their brethren, who kept watch over the gates; one hundred and seventy-two in number.

²⁰The rest of Israel, including priests and Levites, were in all the other cities of Judah, each man in his inheritance. ²¹The temple slaves lived on Ophel. Ziha and Gishpa were in charge of the temple slaves.

²²The prefect of the Levites in Jerusalem was Uzzi, son of Bani, son of Hashabiah, son of Mattaniah, son of Mica; he was one of the sons of Asaph, the singers appointed to the service of the house of God^j — ²³for they had been appointed by royal decree, and there was a fixed schedule for the singers assigning them their daily duties.

²⁴Pethahiah, son of Meshezabel, a descendant of Zerah, son of Judah, was royal deputy in all affairs that concerned the people.

The Other Cities. ²⁵As concerns their villages in the country: Judahites lived in Kiriath-arba and its dependencies, in Dibon and its dependencies, in Jekabzeel and its vil-

---

11, 1-19: This list of the family heads who lived in Jerusalem at the time of Nehemiah is best read after Neh 7, 72a. It is basically the same as that given in 1 Chr 9, 2-17, but there are many differences between the two lists.

h: Neh 7, 4. *i:* 3-19: 1 Chr 9, 2-34. *j:* 2 Chr 20, 14.

lages, ^{26}in Jeshua, Moladah, Beth-pelet, ^{27}in Hazar-shual, in Beer-sheba and its dependencies, ^{28}in Ziklag, in Meconah and its dependencies, ^{29}in En-rimmon, Zorah, Jarmuth, ^{30}Zanoah, Adullam, and their villages, Lachish and its countryside, Azekah and its dependencies. They were settled from Beer-sheba to Ge-hinnom.

^{31}Benjaminites were in Geba, Michmash, Aija, Bethel and its dependencies, ^{32}Anathoth, Nob, Ananiah, ^{33}Hazor, Ramah, Gittaim, ^{34}Hadid, Zeboim, Neballat, ^{35}Lod, Ono, and the Valley of the Artisans.

^{36}Some sections of the Levites from Judah settled in Benjamin.

See RG 214

CHAPTER 12

Priests and Levites under Zerubbabel.

^{1k}The following are the priests and Levites who returned with Zerubbabel, son of Shealtiel, and Jeshua: Seraiah, Jeremiah, Ezra, ^{2}Amariah, Malluch, Hattush, ^{3}Shecaniah, Rehum, Meremoth, ^{4}Iddo, Ginnethon, Abijah, ^{5}Mijamin, Maadiah, Bilgah, ^{6}Shemaiah, and Joiarib, Jedaiah, ^{7}Sallu, Amok, Hilkiah, Jedaiah. These were the priestly heads and their brethren in the days of Jeshua.

^{8}The Levites were Jeshua, Binnui, Kadmiel, Sherebiah, Judah, Mattaniah; the last-mentioned, together with his brethren, was in charge of the hymns, ^{9}while Bakbukiah and Unno and their brethren ministered opposite them by turns.

High Priests.*

^{10}Jeshua became the father of Joiakim, Joiakim became the father of Eliashib, and Eliashib became the father of Joiada. ^{11}Joiada became the father of Johanan, and Johanan became the father of Jaddua.

Priests and Levites under Joiakim.

^{12l}In the days of Joiakim these were the priestly family heads: for Seraiah, Meraiah; for Jere-miah, Hananiah; ^{13}for Ezra, Meshullam; for Amariah, Jehohanan; ^{14}for Malluch, Jonathan; for Shebaniah, Joseph; ^{15}for Harim, Adna; for Meremoth, Helkai; ^{16}for Iddo, Zechariah; for Ginnethon, Meshullam; ^{17}for Abijah, Zichri; for Miamin, . . . ; for Maadiah, Piltai; ^{18}for Bilgah, Shammua; for Shemaiah, Jehonathan; ^{19}and for Joiarib, Mattenai; for Jedaiah, Uzzi; ^{20}for Sallu, Kallai; for Amok, Eber; ^{21}for Hilkiah, Hashabiah; for Jedaiah, Nethanel.

^{22}In the time of Eliashib, Joiada, Johanan, and Jaddua, the family heads of the priests were written down in the Book of Chronicles, up until the reign of Darius the Persian. ^{23}The sons of Levi: the family heads were written down in the Book of Chronicles, up until the time of Johanan, the son of Eliashib.

^{24}The heads of the Levites were Hashabiah, Sherebiah, Jeshua, Binnui, Kadmiel. Their brethren who stood opposite them to sing praises and thanksgiving in fulfillment of the command of David, the man of God, one section opposite the other,^{m} ^{25}were Mattaniah, Bakbukiah, Obadiah.

Meshullam, Talmon, and Akkub were gatekeepers. They kept watch over the storerooms at the gates.^{n}

^{26}All these lived in the time of Joiakim, son of Jeshua, son of Jozadak [and in the time of Nehemiah the governor and of Ezra the priest-scribe].

Dedication of the City Wall.

^{27}*At the dedication of the wall of Jerusalem, the Levites were sought out wherever they lived and were brought to Jerusalem to celebrate a joyful dedication with thanksgiving hymns and the music of cymbals, harps, and lyres. ^{28}The levitical singers gathered together from the region about Jerusalem, from the villages of the Netophathites, ^{29}from Beth-gilgal, and

12, 10f: Jeshua, the high priest when Zerubbabel was governor, i.e., the last decades of the sixth century B.C. (Hg 1, 1. 12. 14; 2, 2. 4). He was the grandfather of Eliashib, the high priest at least in the early period of Nehemiah's governorship, i.e., 445–433 B.C. (Ezr 10, 6; Neh 3, 1. 20f; 13, 4. 7). Eliashib, in turn, was the grandfather of Johanan, a grown man, if not yet a high priest, at the time of Ezra, i.e., c. 400 B.C. (Ezr 10, 6, and note). According to Josephus (Antiquities XI, v), whose testimony here is doubtful, Jaddua, son of Johanan, died as an old man about the same time that Alexander the Great died, i.e., 323 B.C. If this list of the postexilic high priests, at least as far as Johanan, comes, as seems probable (cf v 23), from the Chronicler himself and not from a later scribe, it is of prime importance for dating the Chronicler's work in the first decades of the fourth century B.C.

12, 27-43: The dedication of the wall of Jerusalem took place, no doubt, soon after the restoration of the wall and its gates had been completed. Therefore, this section is best read after Neh 6, 15.

k: 1-6: Neh 12, 12-22. l: 12-22: Neh 10, 3-9; 12, 1-6. m: Ezr 2, 40. n: Neh 11, 17.

from the plains of Geba and Azmaveth (for the singers had built themselves settlements about Jerusalem). *30*The priests and Levites first purified themselves, then they purified the people, the gates, and the wall.

*31*I had the princes of Judah mount the wall, and I arranged two great choirs. The first of these proceeded to the right, along the top of the wall, in the direction of the Dung Gate, *32*followed by Hoshaiah and half the princes of Judah, *33*along with Azariah, Ezra, Meshullam, *34*Judah, Benjamin, She-maiah, and Jeremiah, *35*priests with the trumpets, and also Zechariah, son of Jona-than, son of Shemaiah, son of Mattaniah, son of Micaiah, son of Zaccur, son of Asaph, *36*and his brethren Shemaiah, Azarel, Mila-lai, Gilalai, Maai, Nethanel, Judah, and Ha-nani, with the musical instruments of David, the man of God. [Ezra the scribe was at their head.] *37*At the Spring Gate they went straight up by the steps of the City of David and continued along the top of the wall above the house of David until they came to the Water Gate on the east.

*38*The second choir proceeded to the left, followed by myself and the other half of the princes of the people, along the top of the wall past the Oven Tower as far as the Broad Wall, *39*then past the Ephraim Gate [the New City Gate], the Fish Gate, the Tower of Han-anel, and the Hundred Tower, as far as the Sheep Gate [and they came to a halt at the Prison Gate].

*40*The two choirs took up a position in the house of God; I, too, who had with me half the magistrats, *41*the priests Eliakim, Maase-iah, Minjamin, Micaiah, Elioenai, Zechariah, Hananiah, with the trumpets, *42*and Maaseiah, Shemaiah, Eleazar, Uzzi, Jehohanan, Malchi-jah, Elam, and Ezer. The singers were heard under the leadership of Jezrahiah. *43*Great sacrifices were offered on that day, and there

was rejoicing over the great feast of the LORD in which they shared. The women and the children joined in, and the rejoicing at Jerusalem could be heard from afar off.

*Offerings for Priests and Levites.** *44o*At that time men were appointed over the chambers set aside for stores, offerings, first fruits, and tithes; in them they were to col-lect from the fields of the various cities the portions legally assigned to the priests and Levites. For Judah rejoiced in its appointed priests and Levites *45*who carried out the ministry of their God and the ministry of pu-rification (as did the singers and the gate-keepers) in accordance with the prescrip-tions of David and of Solomon, his son. *46*For the heads of the families of the singers and the hymns of praise and thanksgiving to God came down from the days of David and Asaph in times of old.*p* *47*Thus all Israel, in the days of Zerubbabel [and in the days of Nehemiah], gave the singers and the gate-keepers their portions, according to their daily needs. They made their consecrated of-fering to the Levites, and the Levites made theirs to the sons of Aaron.*q*

CHAPTER 13

See RG 214

Separation from Aliens. *1r*At that time, when there was reading from the book of Moses in the hearing of the people, it was found written there that "no Ammonite or Moabite may ever be admitted into the as-sembly of God; *2*for they would not succor the Israelites with food and water, but they hired Balaam to curse them, though our God turned the curse into a blessing."*s* *3*When they had heard the law, they separated from Israel every foreign element.*t*

Reform in the Temple. *4*Before this, the priest Eliashib, who had been placed in charge of the chambers of the house of our God and who was an associate of Tobiah,

---

12, 44-47: This account of the provisions made for the temple services is apparently a composition of the Chronicler. At that time: a mere connective; no particular time is meant, but the account fits best after that of the restoration of the temple (Ezr 6, 13-18) in the days of Zerubbabel (v 47). The gloss mentioning Nehemiah is not in the ancient Greek version.

13, 1ff: These verses were composed by the Chronicler to serve as an introduction to the reforms that Nehemiah insti-

tuted during his second mission in Jerusalem (vv 4-31). The part of the book of Moses read to the people is freely quoted here from Dt 23, 3-6.

13, 4-31: This is part of the "Memoirs of Nehemiah"; it is continued in Neh 10, 1-40.

o: 44f: 1 Chr 23—26; 2 Chr 8, 14. *p:* 2 Chr 29, 30; 35, 15. *q:* Neh 13, 10f; 10, 39; Nm 18, 26. *r:* 1ff: Dt 23, 3-6. *s:* Nm 22—24. *t:* Neh 13, 23-28.

[5]had set aside for the latter's use a large chamber in which had previously been stored the cereal offerings, incense and utensils, the tithes in grain, wine, and oil allotted to the Levites, singers, and gatekeepers, and the offerings due the priests.[u] [6]During all this time I had not been in Jerusalem, for in the thirty-second year of Artaxerxes, king of Babylon, I had gone back to the king. After due time,* however, I asked leave of the king [7]and returned to Jerusalem, where I discovered the evil thing that Eliashib had done for Tobiah, in setting aside for him a chamber in the courts of the house of God. [8]This displeased me very much, and I had all of Tobiah's household goods thrown outside the chamber. [9]Then I gave orders to purify the chambers, and I had them replace there the utensils of the house of God, the cereal offerings, and the incense.

[10]I learned, too, that the portions due the Levites were no longer being given, so that the Levites and the singers who should have been carrying out the services had deserted, each man to his own field. [11]I took the magistrates to task, demanding, "Why is the house of God abandoned?" Then I brought the Levites together and had them resume their stations. [12]All Judah once more brought in the tithes of grain, wine, and oil to the storerooms;[v] [13]and in charge of the storerooms I appointed the priest Shelemiah, Zadok the scribe, and Pedaiah, one of the Levites, together with Hanan, son of Zaccur, son of Mattaniah, as their assistant; for these men were held to be trustworthy. It was their duty to make the distribution to their brethren. [14]Remember this to my credit, O my God! Let not the devotion which I showed for the house of my God and its services be forgotten!

Sabbath Observance. [15]In those days I perceived that men in Judah were treading the winepresses on the sabbath; that they were bringing in sheaves of grain, loading them on their asses, together with wine, grapes, figs, and every other kind of burden, and bringing them to Jerusalem on the sabbath day. I warned them to sell none of these victuals.[w] [16]In Jerusalem itself the Tyrians who were resident there were importing fish and every other kind of merchandise and selling it to the Judahites on the sabbath. [17]I took the nobles of Judah to task, demanding of them: "What is this evil thing that you are doing, profaning the sabbath day? [18]Did not your fathers act in this same way, with the result that our God has brought all this evil upon us and upon this city? Would you add to the wrath against Israel by once more profaning the sabbath?"

[19]When the shadows were falling on the gates of Jerusalem before the sabbath, I ordered the doors to be closed and forbade them to be reopened till after the sabbath. I posted some of my own men at the gates so that no burden might enter on the sabbath day. [20]The merchants and sellers of various kinds of merchandise spent the night once or twice outside Jerusalem, [21]but then I warned them, saying to them: "Why do you spend the night alongside the wall? If you keep this up, I will lay hands on you!" From that time on, they did not return on the sabbath. [22]Then I ordered the Levites to purify themselves and to go and watch the gates, so that the sabbath day might be kept holy. This, too, remember in my favor, O my God, and have mercy on me in accordance with your great mercy!

Mixed Marriages. [23]Also in those days I saw Jews who had married Ashdodite, Ammonite, or Moabite wives.[x] [24]Of their children, half spoke Ashdodite,* and none of them knew how to speak Jewish; and so it was in regard to the languages of the various other peoples. [25]I took them to task and cursed them; I had some of them beaten and their hair pulled out; and I adjured them by God: "You shall not marry your daughters to their sons nor take any of their daughters for your sons or for yourselves! [26]Did not Solo-

---

13, 6: After due time: It is not known when Nehemiah returned to Jerusalem or how long his second period of activity there lasted, but it probably ended before Ezra came to Palestine; see note on Ezr 7, 1-8.

13, 24: Ashdodite: the language spoken at Ashdod, more likely an Aramaic rather than a Philistine dialect. Jewish: Hebrew as spoken in postexilic Judah.

u: Neh 12, 44. *v:* Neh 10, 38f; 12, 44f. 47; 2 Chr 31, 6. *w:* Neh 10, 32; Ex 20, 8. *x:* Neh 10, 31; 13, 1ff; Dt 23, 3.

mon, the king of Israel, sin because of them? Though among the many nations there was no king like him, and though he was beloved of his God and God had made him king over all Israel, yet even he was made to sin by foreign women.[y] [27]Must it also be heard of you that you have done this same very great evil, betraying our God by marrying foreign women?"

[28]One of the sons of Joiada, son of Eliashib the high priest, was the son-in-law of Sanballat the Horonite! I drove him from my presence.[z] [29]Remember against them, O my God, how they defiled the priesthood and the covenant of the priesthood and the Levites!

[30]Thus I cleansed them of all foreign contamination. I established the various functions for the priests and Levites, so that each had his appointed task. [31]I also provided for the procurement of wood at stated times and for the first fruits. Remember this in my favor, O my God![a]

y: 1 Kgs 11, 1-13.   z: Neh 2, 10; 13, 4f. 7ff.   a: Neh 10, 35f.

See RG
215–18

The Book of Tobit

The Book of Tobit, named after its principal hero, combines specifically Jewish piety and morality with oriental folklore in a fascinating story that has enjoyed wide popularity in both Jewish and Christian circles. Prayers, psalms, and words of wisdom, as well as the skillfully constructed story itself, provide valuable insights into the faith and the religious milieu of its unknown author. The book was probably written early in the second century B.C.; it is not known where.

Tobit, a devout and wealthy Israelite living among the captives deported to Nineveh, from the northern kingdom of Israel in 721 B.C., suffers severe reverses and is finally blinded. Because of his misfortunes he begs the Lord to let him die. But recalling the large sum he had formerly deposited in far-off Media, he sends his son Tobiah there to bring back the money. In Media, at this same time, a young woman, Sarah, also prays for death, because she has lost seven husbands, each killed in turn on his wedding night by the demon Asmodeus. God hears the prayers of Tobit and Sarah, and sends the angel Raphael in disguise to aid them both.

Raphael makes the trip to Media with Tobiah. When Tobiah is attacked by a large fish as he bathes, Raphael orders him to seize it and to remove its gall, heart, and liver because they make "useful medicines." Later, at Raphael's urging, Tobiah marries Sarah, and uses the fish's heart and liver to drive Asmodeus from the bridal chamber. Returning to Nineveh with his wife and his father's money, Tobiah rubs the fish's gall into his father's eyes and cures them. Finally, Raphael reveals his true identity and returns to heaven. To-

bit then utters his beautiful hymn of praise. Before dying, Tobit tells his son to leave Nineveh because God will destroy that wicked city. After Tobiah buries his father and mother, he and his family depart for Media, where he later learns that the destruction of Nineveh has taken place.

The inspired author of the book used the literary form of religious novel (as in Jonah and Judith) for the purpose of instruction and edification. There may have been a historical nucleus around which the story was composed, but this possibility has nothing to do with the teaching of the book. The seemingly historical data—names of kings, cities, etc.—are used merely as vivid details to create interest and charm.

Although the Book of Tobit is usually listed with the historical books, it more correctly stands midway between them and the wisdom literature. It contains numerous maxims like those found in the wisdom books (cf 4, 3-19. 21; 12, 6-10; 14, 7. 9) as well as the customary sapiential themes: fidelity to the law, the intercessory function of angels, piety toward parents, the purity of marriage, reverence for the dead, and the value of almsgiving, prayer, and fasting. The book makes Tobit a relative of *Ahiqar*, a hero of ancient Near Eastern folklore.

Written in Aramaic, the original of the book was lost for centuries. The Greek translation, existing in three different recensions, is our primary source. In 1955, fragments of the book in Aramaic and in Hebrew were recovered from Cave IV at Qumran. These texts are in substantial agreement with the Greek recension that has served as the basis for the present translation.

The divisions of the Book of Tobit are:

_____

CHAPTER 1

See RG
215

Tobit. ¹This book tells the story of Tobit,* son of Tobiel, son of Hananiel, son of Aduel, son of Gabael of the family of Asiel, of the tribe of Naphtali, ²who during the reign of Shalmaneser,* king of Assyria, was taken captive from Thisbe, which is south of Kedesh Naphtali in upper Galilee, above and to the west of Asser, north of Phogor.^a

I: Tobit's Ordeals

His Virtue. ³I, Tobit, have walked all the days of my life on the paths of truth and righteousness. I performed many charitable works for my kinsmen and my people who had been deported with me to Nineveh, in Assyria. ⁴When I lived as a young man in my own country, Israel, the entire tribe of my forefather Naphtali had broken away from the house of David and from Jerusalem. This city had been singled out of all Israel's tribes, so that they all might offer sacrifice in the place where the temple, God's dwelling, had been built and consecrated for all generations to come. ^{5b}All my kinsmen, like the rest of the tribe of my forefather Naphtali, used to offer sacrifice on all the mountains of Galilee as well as to the young bull which Jeroboam, king of Israel, had made in Dan.*

^{6c}I, for my part, would often make the pilgrimage alone to Jerusalem for the festivals, as is prescribed for all Israel by perpetual decree.* Bringing with me the first fruits of the field and the firstlings of the flock, together with a tenth of my income and the first shearings of the sheep,^d I would hasten to Jerusalem ^{7e}and present them to the priests, Aaron's sons, at the altar. To the Levites who were doing service in Jerusalem I would give the tithe of grain, wine, olive oil, pomegranates, figs, and other fruits. And except for sabbatical years, I used to give a second tithe in money, which each year I would go and disburse in Jerusalem. ⁸The third tithe I gave to orphans and widows, and to converts who were living with the Israelites. Every third year I would bring them this offering, and we ate it in keeping with the decree of the Mosaic law and the commands of Deborah, the mother of my father Tobiel; for when my father died, he left me an orphan.

⁹When I reached manhood, I married Anna, a woman of our own lineage. By her I had a son whom I named Tobiah. ¹⁰Now after I had been deported to Nineveh, all my brothers and relatives ate the food of heathens,^f ¹¹but I refrained from eating that kind of food. ¹²Because of this wholehearted service of God, ¹³the Most High granted me favor and status with Shalmaneser, so that I became purchasing agent for all his needs.^g ¹⁴Every now and then until his death I would go to Media to buy goods for him. I also deposited several

1, 1: Tobit: in the fragments of the book found at Qumran, is given as Tobi, an abbreviated form of Tobiyah (v 9; Ezr 2, 60) or of Tobiyahu (2 Chr 17, 8), a name which means "Yahweh is good." Tobiel, "God is good"; Hananiel, "God is merciful." The book abounds in theophoric names.

1, 2: Shalmaneser V (727–722 B.C.): began the siege of Samaria; the inhabitants of the northern kingdom were taken into captivity by his successor, Sargon II (722–705). Thisbe and Phogor: towns of Galilee that have not been identified; Thisbe in Gilead was perhaps the birthplace of Elijah. Kedesh: cf Jos 20, 7. Asser: Hazor (Jos 11, 1).

1, 5: Jeroboam established sanctuaries in Dan and Bethel so that the people would no longer go to Jerusalem for the festivals. The gold statues of bulls which he placed in the sanctuaries were considered the throne of Yahweh; but the people soon came to worship the images themselves. Jeroboam also encouraged the high places or hilltop shrines (1 Kgs 12, 26-33).

1, 6ff: Perpetual decree: Dt 12, 11. 13-14. Refusing to worship at Jeroboam's shrines, the faithful Tobit continued to bring his offerings to Jerusalem; see 2 Chr 11, 16. For the various tithes, cf Nm 18, 20-32; 2 Chr 31, 4-6; Dt 14, 22-29; 26, 12f.

a: 2 Kgs 17, 3; 18, 9ff. *b:* 1 Kgs 12, 26-32. *c:* Ex 23, 14f. 17; 34, 23. *d:* Dt 16, 16. *e:* 7f: Nm 18, 12f. Lv 14, 22-29; 18, 4f. *f:* Lv 11: Dt 14, 3-21; Acts 15, 29; 1 Cor 8, 7ff. *g:* Dn 2, 48f.

538

pouches containing a great sum of money* with my kinsman Gabael, son of Gabri, who lived at Rages, in Media. *15*But when Shalmaneser died and his son Sennacherib* succeeded him as king, the roads to Media became unsafe, so I could no longer go there.

Courage in Burying the Dead. *16*During Shalmaneser's reign I performed many charitable works for my kinsmen and my people. *17h*I would give my bread to the hungry and my clothing to the naked. If I saw one of my people who had died and been thrown outside the walls of Nineveh, I would bury him.* *18*I also buried anyone whom Sennacherib slew when he returned as a fugitive from Judea during the days of judgment decreed against him by the heavenly King because of the blasphemies he had uttered. In his rage he killed many Israelites, but I used to take their bodies by stealth and bury them; so when Sennacherib looked for them, he could not find them. *19*But a certain citizen of Nineveh informed the king that it was I who buried the dead. When I found out that the king knew all about me and wanted to put me to death, I went into hiding; then in my fear I took to flight. *20*Afterward, all my property was confiscated; I was left with nothing. All that I had was taken to the king's palace, except for my wife Anna and my son Tobiah.

*21*But less than forty days later the king was assassinated by two of his sons, who then escaped into the mountains of Ararat. His son Esarhaddon,* who succeeded him as king, placed Ahiqar, my brother Anael's son, in charge of all the accounts of his kingdom, so that he took control over the entire administration.*i* *22*Then Ahiqar interceded on my behalf, and I was able to return to Nineveh. For under Sennacherib, king of Assyria, Ahiqar had been chief cupbearer, keeper of the seal, administrator, and treasurer; and Esarhaddon reappointed him. He was a close relative—in fact, my nephew.

CHAPTER 2

See RG 216

*1*Thus under King Esarhaddon I returned to my home, and my wife Anna and my son Tobiah were restored to me. Then on our festival of Pentecost, the feast of Weeks,* a fine dinner was prepared for me, and I reclined to eat.*j* *2*The table was set for me, and when many different dishes were placed before me, I said to my son Tobiah: "My son, go out and try to find a poor man from among our kinsmen exiled here in Nineveh. If he is a sincere worshiper of God, bring him back with you, so that he can share this meal with me. Indeed, son, I shall wait for you to come back."*

*3*Tobiah went out to look for some poor kinsman of ours. When he returned he exclaimed, "Father!" I said to him, "What is it, son?" He answered, "Father, one of our people has been murdered! His body lies in the market place where he was just strangled!" *4*I sprang to my feet, leaving the dinner untouched; and I carried the dead man from the street and put him in one of the rooms, so that I might bury him after sunset. *5*Returning to my own quarters, I washed myself* and ate my food in sorrow.*k* *6*I was reminded of the oracle pronounced by the prophet Amos against Bethel:*l*

1, 14: A great sum of money: literally, "ten silver talents," about ten thousand dollars. Rages: modern Rai, about five miles southeast of Teheran. Media: the northwestern part of modern Iran.

1, 15: Sennacherib (705–681 B.C.): the son of Sargon (722–705 B.C.); neither was descended from Shalmaneser. Inconsistencies such as this point to the fact that the Book of Tobit is a religious novel (see Introduction; also notes on 5, 6 and 14, 15).

1, 17-18: Tobit risked his own life to bury the dead. Deprivation of burial was viewed with horror by the Jews. Cf Tb 4, 3-4; 6, 15; 14, 12-13.

1, 21: Esarhaddon: 681–669 B.C. Ahiqar: a hero of an ancient folklore, known for his outstanding wisdom. The Story (or Wisdom) of Ahiqar was very popular in antiquity and is extant in many different forms: Aramaic, Syriac, Armenian, Arabic (Arabian Nights), Greek (Aesop's Fables), Slavonic, Ethiopic, and Romanian. The sacred author makes Tobit the uncle of the famous Ahiqar in order to enhance Tobit's own prestige. See note on Tb 14, 10.

2, 1: The feast of Weeks: also called by its Greek name Pentecost, was celebrated fifty days after the Passover. Cf Lv 23, 15-21; Dt 16, 9-12.

2, 2: Almsgiving and charity to the poor are important virtues taught by the book (Tb 4, 7-11. 16f; 12, 8f; 14, 10f).

2, 5: I washed myself: because of ritual defilement from touching a corpse (Nm 19, 11-13).

---

h: Jb 31, 16-20. i: 2 Kgs 19, 37; 2 Chr 32, 21; Sir 48, 21; Is 37, 38; 2 Mc 8, 19. j: Lv 23, 15-21; Nm 28, 26-31; Dt 16, 9-12. k: Nm 19, 11-22. l: Am 8, 10; 1 Mc 1, 39.

"Your festivals shall be returned into
          mourning,
    And all your songs into lamentation."

[7]And I wept. Then at sunset I went out, dug a grave, and buried him.

[8]The neighbors mocked me, saying to one another: "Will this man never learn! Once before he was hunted down for execution because of this very thing; yet now that he has escaped, here he is again burying the dead!"

Tobit's Blindness. [9]That same night I bathed, and went to sleep next to the wall of my courtyard. Because of the heat I left my face uncovered. [10]I did not know there were birds perched on the wall above me, till their warm droppings settled in my eyes, causing cataracts.* I went to see some doctors for a cure, but the more they anointed my eyes with various salves, the worse the cataracts became, until I could see no more. For four years I was deprived of eyesight, and all my kinsmen were grieved at my condition. Ahiqar, however, took care of me for two years, until he left for Elymais.

[11]At that time my wife Anna worked for hire at weaving cloth, the kind of work women do. [12]When she sent back the goods to their owners, they would pay her. Late in winter* she finished the cloth and sent it back to the owners. They paid her the full salary, and also gave her a young goat for the table. [13]On entering my house the goat began to bleat. I called to my wife and said: "Where did this goat come from? Perhaps it was stolen! Give it back to its owners; we have no right to eat stolen food!" [14m]But she said to me, "It was given to me as a bonus over and above my wages." Yet I would not believe her; and told her to give it back to its owners. I became very angry with her over this. So she retorted:

"Where are your charitable deeds now? Where are your virtuous acts? See! Your true character is finally showing itself!"*

CHAPTER 3

[1]Grief-stricken in spirit, I groaned and wept aloud. Then with sobs I began to pray:

Tobit's Prayer for Death

[2] "You are righteous, O Lord,
    and all your deeds are just;
All your ways are mercy and truth;
    you are the judge of the world.[n]
[3] And now, O Lord, may you be mindful
        of me,
    and look with favor upon me.
Punish me not for my sins,
    nor for my inadvert offenses,
    nor for those of my fathers.[o]

"They sinned against you,
[4]   and disobeyed your commandments.
So you handed us over to plundering,
        exile, and death,
    till we were an object lesson, a
        byword, a reproach
    in all the nations among whom you
        scattered us.[p]

[5] "Yes, your judgments are many and true
    in dealing with me as my sins
    and those of my fathers deserve.
For we have not kept your
        commandments,
    nor have we trodden the paths of truth
        before you.

[6] "So now, deal with me as you please,
    and command my life breath to be
        taken from me,
    that I may go from the face of the earth
        into dust.

2, 10: Cataracts: literally, "white scales, or films." Elymais: the Greek name of ancient Elam, a district northeast of the head of the Persian Gulf.

2, 12: Late in winter: literally, "seventh of Dystros," the Macedonian month which corresponds to the Jewish month of Shebat (January–February). For the table: literally, "for the hearth"; the gift had probably been made in view of some springtime festival like the Jewish Purim.

2, 14: Anna's sharp rebuke calls to mind the words of Job's wife (Jb 2, 9).

3, 6: It is better for me to die than to live: in his distress To-

bit uses the words of the petulant Jonah (Jon 4, 3. 8), who wished to die because God did not destroy the hated Ninevites. In similar circumstances, Moses (Nm 11, 15), Elijah (1 Kgs 19, 4), and Job (Jb 7, 15) also prayed for death. Everlasting abode: a reference to Sheol, the dismal abode of the dead from which no one returns (Jb 7, 9-10; 14, 12; Is 26, 14). The revelation of a blessed immortality had not yet been made. See note on Tb 4, 6.

---

m: Jb 2, 9. *n:* Pss 25, 10; 119, 137; Dn 3, 27. *o:* Ex 34, 7.
p: Dt 28, 15; Bar 1, 16-22; 2, 4f; 3, 8; Dn 9, 5f.

It is better for me to die than to live,*
  because I have heard insulting
    calumnies,
  and I am overwhelmed with grief.*q*

"Lord, command me to be delivered
      from such anguish;
  let me go to the everlasting abode;
  Lord, refuse me not.
For it is better for me to die
  than to endure so much misery in life,
  and to hear these insults!'"

II: Sarah's Plight

Sarah Falsely Accused. [7]*On the same day, at
Ecbatana in Media, it so happened that
Raguel's daughter Sarah also had to listen to
abuse, from one of her father's maids. [8]For
she had been married to seven husbands, but
the wicked demon Asmodeus* killed them off
before they could have intercourse with her,
as it is prescribed for wives. So the maid said
to her: "You are the one who strangles your
husbands! Look at you! You have already
been married seven times, but you have had
no joy with any one of your husbands. [9]Why
do you beat us? Because your husbands are
dead? Then why not join them! May we never
see a son or daughter of yours!"

[10]That day she was deeply grieved in
spirit. She went in tears to an upstairs room
in her father's house with the intention of
hanging herself. But she reconsidered, saying to herself: "No! People would level this
insult against my father: 'You had only one
beloved daughter, but she hanged herself because of ill fortune!' And thus would I cause
my father in his old age to go down to the
nether world laden with sorrow. It is far better for me not to hang myself, but to beg the
Lord to have me die, so that I need no longer
live to hear such insults."*r*

[11]At that time, then, she spread out her
hands, and facing the window,* poured out
this prayer:

Sarah's Prayer for Death

"Blessed are you, O Lord, merciful God!
  Forever blessed and honored is your
    holy name;
  may all your works forever bless you.*s*
[12] And now, O Lord, to you I turn my face
  and raise my eyes.
[13] Bid me to depart from the earth,
    never again to hear such insults.

[14] "You know, O Master, that I am innocent
  of any impure act with a man,
[15] And that I have never defiled my own
    name
  or my father's name in the land of my
    exile.

"I am my father's only daughter,
  and he has no other child to make his
    heir,
Nor does he have a close kinsman or
    other relative
  whom I might bide my time to marry.
I have already lost seven husbands;
  why then should I live any longer?
But if it please you, Lord, not to slay me,
  look favorably upon me and have pity
    on me;
  never again let me hear these insults!"

An Answer to Prayer. [16]At that very time,
the prayer of these two suppliants was heard in
the glorious presence of Almighty God. [17]*t*So
Raphael was sent to heal them both: to remove
the cataracts from Tobit's eyes, so that he
might again see God's sunlight; and to marry
Raguel's daughter Sarah to Tobit's son Tobiah,
and then drive the wicked demon Asmodeus
from her. For Tobiah had the right* to claim her
before any other who might wish to marry her.

3, 7: From here on, the story is told in the third person. V
7 relates one of the several marvelous coincidences which the
story-teller uses to heighten interest; see also vv 16. 17; 4, 1;
5, 4. Ecbatana: Hamadan in modern Iran; this was the capital
of ancient Media. Raguel: "friend of God."

3, 8: Asmodeus: in Persian *aeshma daeva,* "demon of
wrath," adopted into Aramaic with the sense of "the Destroyer."
He will be subdued (Tb 8, 3) by Raphael (v 17), "God heals."

3, 11: Facing the window: that is, looking toward Jerusalem;

cf Dn 6, 11. Blessed are you and "Blessed be God" are traditional openings of Jewish prayers (Tb 8, 5. 15; 11, 14; 13, 1).

3, 17: Tobiah had the right: according to the patriarchal custom of marriage within the family group. Tobiah was Sarah's
closest eligible relative (Tb 6, 12). Cf Tb 4, 12-13; Gn 24.

q: Nm 11, 15; 1 Kgs 19, 4; Jb 7, 15; Jon 4, 3. 8.   *r:* Tb 6, 15; Gn
37, 35; 42, 38; 44, 29. 31.   *s:* 1 Kgs 8, 44, 48; Pss 28, 2; 134, 2;
Dn 6, 11.   *t:* Tb 4, 12f; 6, 12f; Gn 24, 3f.

In the very moment that Tobit returned from the courtyard to his house, Raguel's daughter Sarah came downstairs from her room.

III: Tobiah's Journey and Marriage to Sarah

CHAPTER 4

See RG 217

A Father's Instruction. [1]That same day Tobit remembered the money he had deposited with Gabael at Rages in Media, and he thought, [2]"Now that I have asked for death, why should I not call my son Tobiah and let him know about this money before I die?" [3]So he called his son Tobiah; and when he came, he said to him:* "My son, when I die, give me a decent burial. Honor your mother, and do not abandon her as long as she lives. Do whatever pleases her, and do not grieve her spirit in any way.[u] [4]Remember, my son, that she went through many trials for your sake while you were in her womb. And when she dies, bury her in the same grave with me.

[5]"Through all your days, my son, keep the Lord in mind, and suppress every desire to sin or to break his commandments. Perform good works all the days of your life, and do not tread the paths of wrongdoing. [6v]For if you are steadfast in your service, your good works will bring success, not only to you, but also to all those who live uprightly.*

[7]"Give alms from your possessions. Do not turn your face away from any of the poor, and God's face will not be turned away from you.[w] [8]Son, give alms in proportion to what you own. If you have great wealth, give alms out of your abundance; if you have but little, distribute even some of that. But do not hesitate to give alms; [9]you will be storing up a goodly treasure for yourself

against the day of adversity.[x] [10]Almsgiving frees one from death, and keeps one from going into the dark abode. [11]Alms are a worthy offering in the sight of the Most High for all who give them.[y]

[12]"Be on your guard, son, against every form of immorality, and above all, marry a woman of the lineage of your forefathers. Do not marry a stranger who is not of your father's tribe, because we are sons of the prophets. My boy, keep in mind Noah, Abraham, Isaac, and Jacob, our fathers from of old: all of them took wives from among their own kinsmen and were blessed in their children. Remember that their posterity shall inherit the land.[z] [13]Therefore, my son, love your kinsmen. Do not be so proudhearted toward your kinsmen, the sons and daughters of your people, as to refuse to take a wife for yourself from among them. For in such arrogance there is ruin and great disorder. Likewise, in worthlessness there is decay and dire poverty, for worthlessness is the mother of famine.

[14]"Do not keep with you overnight the wages of any man who works for you, but pay him immediately. If you thus behave as God's servant, you will receive your reward. Keep a close watch on yourself, my son, in everything you do, and discipline yourself in all your conduct.[a] [15]Do to no one what you yourself dislike. Do not drink wine till you become drunk, nor let drunkenness accompany you on your way.[b]

[16c]"Give to the hungry some of your bread, and to the naked some of your clothing. Whatever you have left over, give away as alms; and do not begrudge the alms you give. [17d]Be lavish with your bread and wine at the burial of the virtuous, but do not share them with sinners.*

[18]"Seek counsel from every wise man,

4, 3-19: A collection of maxims which parallel those in the wisdom literature, especially Prv and Sir (see Introduction): duties toward parents (3-4); cf also Tb 14, 13; perseverance in virtue and avoidance of evil (5-6. 14b); necessity and value of almsgiving and charity (7-11. 16-17); marriage to a kinsman (12-13a); industry (13b); prompt payment of wages (14a); the golden rule (15a); temperance (15b); docility (18); prayer (19).

4, 6: Before the revelation of retribution for all men in the afterlife—a doctrine taught in the Book of Wisdom—Old Testament man believed that virtue guaranteed earthly prosperity, and sin earthly disaster (cf Dt 28).

4, 17: Tobit counsels his son either to give alms in honor of the dead, or, more probably, to give the "bread of consolation" to the family of the deceased. Cf Jer 16, 7; Ez 24, 17.

---

u: Ex 20, 12; Prv 23, 22; Sir 7, 27. *v:* Tb 13, 6; Jn 3, 21; Eph 4, 15. *w:* 7f: Tb 12, 8ff; Dt 15, 7f. 11; Prv 19, 17; Sir 4, 1-6; 14, 13; Lk 14, 13; 1 Jn 3, 17. *x:* Mt 6, 20f. *y:* Sir 3, 30; 29, 12. *z:* Tb 3, 15. 17; 6, 12; Gn 11, 29. 31; 25, 20; 28, 1-4; 29, 15-30; Ex 34, 16; Dt 7, 3; Jgs 14, 3. *a:* Lv 19, 13; Dt 24, 15. *b:* Mt 7, 12; Lk 6, 31. *c:* Dt 15, 10; Is 58, 7; Mt 25, 35f; 2 Cor 9, 7. *d:* Jer 16, 7; Lk 14, 13.

and do not think lightly of any advice that can be useful. [19e]At all times bless the Lord God, and ask him to make all your paths straight and to grant success to all your endeavors and plans. For no pagan nation possesses good counsel, but the Lord himself gives all good things. If the Lord chooses, he raises a man up; but if he should decide otherwise, he casts him down to the deepest recesses of the nether world. So now, my son, keep in mind my commandments, and never let them be erased from your heart.*

[20]"And now, son, I wish to inform you that I have deposited a great sum of money with Gabri's son Gabael at Rages in Media. [21]Do not be discouraged, my child, because of our poverty. You will be a rich man if you fear God, avoid all sin, and do what is right before the Lord your God."[f]

See RG 217

CHAPTER 5

The Angel Raphael. [1]Then Tobiah replied to his father Tobit: "Everything that you have commanded me, father, I will do. [2]But how shall I be able to obtain the money from him, since he does not know me nor do I know him? What can I show him to make him recognize me and trust me, so that he will give me the money? I do not even know which roads to take for the journey into Media!" [3]Tobit answered his son Tobiah: "We exchanged signatures on a document* written in duplicate; I divided it into two parts, and each of us kept one; his copy I put with the money. Think of it, twenty years have already passed since I deposited that money! So now, my son, find yourself a trustworthy man who will make the journey with you. We will, of course, give him a salary when you return; but get back that money from Gabael."

[4]Tobiah went to look for someone acquainted with the roads who would travel with him to Media. As soon as he went out, he found the angel Raphael standing before him, though he did not know* that this was an angel of God.[g] [5]Tobiah said to him, "Who are you, young man?" He replied, "I am an Israelite, one of your kinsmen. I have come here to work." Tobiah said, "Do you know the way to Media?" [6]The other replied: "Yes, I have been there many times. I know the place well and I know all the routes. I have often traveled to Media; I used to stay with our kinsman Gabael, who lives at Rages in Media. It is a good two days' travel from Ecbatana to Rages,* for Rages is situated at the mountains, Ecbatana out on the plateau." [7]Tobiah said to him, "Wait for me, young man, till I go back and tell my father; for I need you to make the journey with me. I will, of course, pay you."[h] [8]Raphael replied, "Very well, I will wait for you; but do not be long." [9]Tobiah went back to tell his father Tobit what had happened. He said to him, "I have just found a man who is one of our own Israelite kinsmen!" Tobit said, "Call the man, so that I may find out what family and tribe he comes from, and whether he is trustworthy enough to travel with you, son." Tobiah went out to summon the man saying, "Young man, my father would like to see you."

[10]When Raphael entered the house, Tobit greeted him first. Raphael said, "Hearty greetings* to you!" Tobit replied: "What joy is left for me any more? Here I am, a blind man who cannot see God's sunlight, but must remain in darkness, like the dead who no longer see the light! Though alive, I am among the dead. I can hear a man's voice, but I cannot see him." Raphael said, "Take

4, 19: Prayer is the foundation of a moral life.

5, 3: Document: in Greek cheirographon. In the Middle Ages, notably in England, a deed and its duplicate were written on one piece of parchment, with the Latin word chirographum inscribed across the top of the sheet or between the two copies of the text. The document was then cut in two in either a straight or a wavy line, the parts being given to the persons concerned. Perhaps this procedure derived from the present verse of Tobit. Duplicate documents, usually one open and the other sealed, are well known from the ancient Near East.

5, 4: He did not know: the theme of an angel in disguise

occurs frequently in folklore as well as in the Old Testament (Gn 18; cf Heb 13, 2).

5, 6: It is a good two days' travel from Echatana to Rages: Alexander's army took eleven days in forced marches to cover this distance, about 180 miles. The author is merely using popular impressions about faraway places; he is not teaching geography. (See notes on Tb 1, 15; 3, 7 and Introduction.)

5, 10: Hearty greetings and what joy form a wordplay on the Greek verb chairein, "to greet" and "to be joyful."

e: Dt 4, 6; Ps 119, 10.   *f:* 1 Tm 6, 6ff.   *g:* Heb 13, 2.   *h:* Tb 12, 2.

courage! God has healing in store for you; so take courage!" Tobit then said: "My son Tobiah wants to go to Media. Can you go with him to show him the way? I will of course pay you, brother." Raphael answered: "Yes, I can go with him, for I know all the routes. I have often traveled to Media and crossed all its plains and mountains; so I know every road well." *11*Tobit asked, "Brother, tell me, please, what family and tribe are you from?" *12*Raphael said: "Why? Do you need a tribe and a family? Or are you looking for a hired man to travel with your son?" Tobit replied, "I wish to know truthfully whose son you are, brother, and what your name is."*i*

*13*Raphael answered, "I am Azariah,* son of Hananiah the elder, one of your own kinsmen." *14*Tobit exclaimed: "Welcome! God save you, brother! Do not be provoked with me, brother, for wanting to learn the truth about your family. So it turns out that you are a kinsman, and from a noble and good line! I knew Hananiah and Nathaniah, the two sons of Shemaiah the elder; with me they used to make the pilgrimage to Jerusalem, where we would worship together. No, they did not stray from the right path; your kinsmen are good men. You are certainly of good lineage, and welcome!"

*15*Then he added: "For each day you are away I will give you the normal wages,* plus expenses for you and for my son. If you go with my son, *16*I will even add a bonus to your wages!" Raphael replied: "I will go with him; have no fear. In good health we shall leave you, and in good health we shall return to you, for the way is safe." *17*Tobit said, "God bless you, brother." Then he called his son and said to him: "My son, prepare whatever you need for the journey, and set out with your kinsman. May God in heaven protect you on the way and bring you back to me safe and sound; and may his angel accompany you for safety, my son."

Before setting out on his journey, Tobiah kissed his father and mother. Tobit said to him, "Have a safe journey." *18*But his mother began to weep. She said to Tobit: "Why have you decided to send my child away? Is he not the staff to which we cling, ever there with us in all that we do? *19*I hope more money is not your chief concern! Rather let it be a ransom for our son! *20*What the Lord has given us to live on is certainly enough for us." *21*Tobit reassured her: "Have no such thought. Our son will leave in good health and come back to us in good health. Your own eyes will see the day when he returns to you safe and sound. *22*So, no such thought; do not worry about them, my love.* For a good angel will go with him, his journey will be successful, and he will return unharmed." *1*Then she stopped weeping.*

CHAPTER 6

See RG 216

Journey to Rages. *2*When the boy left home, accompanied by the angel, the dog followed Tobiah out of the house and went with him. The travelers walked till nightfall, and made camp beside the Tigris River. *3*Now when the boy went down to wash his feet in the river, a large fish suddenly leaped out of the water and tried to swallow his foot. He shouted in alarm. *4*But the angel said to him, "Take hold of the fish and don't let it get away!" The boy seized the fish and hauled it up on the shore. *5*The angel then told him: "Cut the fish open and take out its gall, heart, and liver, and keep them with you; but throw away the entrails. Its gall, heart, and liver make useful medicines."* *6*After the lad had cut the fish open, he put aside the gall, heart, and liver. Then he broiled and ate part of the fish; the rest he salted and kept for the journey.

Raphael's Instructions. *7*Afterward they traveled on together till they were near Media. The boy asked the angel this question:

5, 13-14: Azariah, "Yahweh helps"; Hananiah, "Yahweh is merciful"; Nathaniah, "Yahweh gives"; Shemaiah, "Yahweh hears."

5, 15: The normal wages: literally, "a drachma," about seventeen cents, a day's wage for a workingman.

5, 22: My love: literally, "sister," a term of endearment applied to one's wife; cf Tb 7, 11. 15; 8, 4. 21; 10, 6. 13; Song 4, 9. 10. 12; 5, 1f. A good angel: a reference to the guardian angel, though Tobit does not know, of course, that Raphael himself, disguised as Azariah, is the good angel in this case.

5, 1: Then . . . weeping: this verse belongs to ch 6.

6, 5: Its gall . . . medicines: belief in the healing power of these organs was common among even the physicians of antiquity.

i: Jgs 13, 17f.

"Brother Azariah, what medicinal value is there in the fish's heart, liver, and gall?" [8]He answered: "As regards the fish's heart and liver, if you burn them so that the smoke surrounds a man or a woman who is afflicted by a demon or evil spirit, the affliction will leave him completely, and no demons will ever return to him again. [9]And as for the gall, if you rub it on the eyes of a man who has cataracts, blowing into his eyes right on the cataracts, his sight will be restored."

[10]When they had entered Media and were getting close to Ecbatana, [11]Raphael said to the boy, "Brother Tobiah!" He answered, "Yes, what is it?" Raphael continued: "Tonight we must stay with Raguel, who is a relative of yours. He has a daughter named Sarah, [12]but no other child. Since you are Sarah's closest relative, you before all other men have the right to marry her. Also, her father's estate is rightfully yours to inherit. Now the girl is sensible, courageous, and very beautiful; and her father loves her dearly."[j] [13]He continued: "Since you have the right to marry her, listen to me, brother. Tonight I will ask the girl's father to let us have her as your bride. When we return from Rages, we will hold the wedding feast for her. I know that Raguel cannot keep her from you or let her become engaged to another man; that would be a capital crime according to the decree in the Book of Moses,* and he knows that it is your right, before all other men, to marry his daughter. So heed my words, brother; tonight we must speak for the girl, so that we may have her engaged to you. And when we return from Rages, we will take her and bring her back with us to your house."

[14]Tobiah objected, however: "Brother Azariah, I have heard that this woman has already been married seven times, and that her husbands died in their bridal chambers. On the very night they approached her, they dropped dead. And I have heard it said that it was a demon who killed them. [15]So now I too am afraid of this demon. Because he loves her, he does not harm her; but he does slay any man who wishes to come close to her. I am my father's only child. If I should die, I would bring my father and mother down to their grave in sorrow over me. And they have no other son to bury them!"[k]

[16]Raphael said to him: "Do you not remember your father's orders? He commanded you to marry a woman from your own family. So now listen to me, brother; do not give another thought to this demon, but marry Sarah. I know that tonight you shall have her for your wife! [17]When you go into the bridal chamber, take the fish's liver and heart, and place them on the embers for the incense. [18]As soon as the demon smells the odor they give off, he will flee and never again show himself near her. Then when you are about to have intercourse with her, both of you first rise up to pray.* Beg the Lord of heaven to show you mercy and grant you deliverance. But do not be afraid, for she was set apart for you before the world existed. You will save her, and she will go with you. And I suppose that you will have children by her, who will take the place of brothers for you. So do not worry."

When Tobiah heard Raphael say that she was his kinswoman, of his own family's lineage, he fell deeply in love with her, and his heart became set on her.

CHAPTER 7

See RG
215-18

At the House of Raguel. [1]When they entered Ecbatana, Tobiah said, "Brother Azariah, lead me straight to our kinsman Raguel." So he brought him to the house of Raguel, whom they found seated by his courtyard gate. They greeted him first. He said to them, "Greetings to you too, brothers! Good health to you, and welcome!" When he brought them into his home, [2]he said to his wife Edna, "This young man looks just like my kinsman Tobit!" [3]So Edna asked them, "Who are you, brothers?" They answered, "We are of the exiles from Naphtali at Nin-

6, 13: Raguel . . . Book of Moses: Nm 36, 6-8 prescribed marriage within the ancestral tribe, but no death penalty is mentioned.

6, 18: Rise up to pray: prayer is needed to drive out the demon.

j: Tb 4, 12f; Nm 36, 8.   *k:* Tb 3, 10.

eveh." [4] She said, "Do you know our kinsman Tobit?" They answered, "Indeed we do!" She asked, "Is he well?" [5] They answered, "Yes, he is alive and well." Then Tobiah exclaimed, "He is my father!" [6] Raguel sprang up and kissed him, shedding tears of joy. [7] But when he heard that Tobit had lost his eyesight, he was grieved and wept aloud. He said to Tobiah: "My child, God bless you! You are the son of a noble and good father. But what a terrible misfortune that such a righteous and charitable man should be afflicted with blindness!" He continued to weep in the arms of his kinsman Tobiah. [8] His wife Edna also wept for Tobit; and even their daughter Sarah began to weep.

Marriage of Tobiah and Sarah. [9] Afterward, Raguel slaughtered a ram from the flock and gave them a cordial reception. When they had bathed and reclined to eat, Tobiah said to Raphael, "Brother Azariah, ask Raguel to let me marry my kinswoman Sarah." [10] Raguel overheard the words; so he said to the boy: "Eat and drink and be merry tonight, for no man is more entitled to marry my daughter Sarah than you, brother. Besides, not even I have the right to give her to anyone but you, because you are my closest relative. But I will explain the situation to you very frankly. [11] I have given her in marriage to seven men, all of whom were kinsmen of ours, and all died on the very night they approached her. But now, son, eat and drink. I am sure the Lord will look after you both." Tobiah answered, "I will eat or drink nothing until you set aside what belongs to me."

Raguel said to him: "I will do it. She is yours according to the decree of the Book of Moses. Your marriage to her has been decided in heaven! Take your kinswoman; from now on you are her love, and she is your beloved. She is yours today and ever after. And tonight, son, may the Lord of heaven prosper you both. May he grant you mercy and peace." [12] Then Raguel called his daughter Sarah, and she came to him. He took her by the hand and gave her to Tobiah with the words: "Take her according to the law. According to the decree written in the Book of Moses she is your wife. Take her and bring her back safely to your father. And may the God of heaven grant both of you peace and prosperity." [l] [13] He then called her mother and told her to bring a scroll, so that he might draw up a marriage contract stating that he gave Sarah to Tobiah as his wife according to the decree of the Mosaic law. Her mother brought the scroll, and he drew up the contract, to which they affixed their seals. [m]

[14] Afterward they began to eat and drink. [15] Later Raguel called his wife Edna and said, "My love, prepare the other bedroom and bring the girl there." [16] She went and made the bed in the room, as she was told, and brought the girl there. After she had cried over her, she wiped away the tears and said: [17] "Be brave, my daughter. May the Lord of heaven grant you joy in place of your grief. Courage, my daughter." Then she left.

CHAPTER 8

See RG 216

Expulsion of the Demon. [1] When they had finished eating and drinking, the girl's parents wanted to retire. They brought the young man out of the dining room and led him into the bedroom. [2] At this point Tobiah, mindful of Raphael's instructions, took the fish's liver and heart from the bag which he had with him, and placed them on the embers for the incense.* [3] The demon, repelled by the odor of the fish, fled into Upper Egypt;* Raphael pursued him there and bound him hand and foot. Then Raphael returned immediately.

[4] When the girl's parents left the bedroom and closed the door behind them, Tobiah arose from bed and said to his wife, "My love, get up. Let us pray and beg our Lord to have mercy on us and to grant us deliverance." [5] She got up, and they started to pray

---

8, 2f: The manner of coping with demonic influences among the ancients seems quaint to us. However, the fish here is part of the story, and not a recipe for exorcism. It is clear that the author places primary emphasis on the value of prayer to God (Tb 6, 18; 8, 4-8), on the role of the angel as God's agent, and on the pious dispositions of Tobiah.

8, 3: Into Upper Egypt: to the desert there. The desert was considered the dwelling place of demons. Cf Is 13, 21; 34, 14; Mt 4, 1; 12, 43.

l: Gn 24, 50f. *m:* Tb 6, 12.

and beg that deliverance might be theirs. He began with these words:

"Blessed are you, O God of our fathers;
   praised be your name forever and ever.
Let the heavens and all your creation
   praise you forever.[n]
⁶ You made Adam and you gave him his
     wife Eve
   to be his help and support;
   and from these two the human race
     descended.
You said, 'It is not good for the man to be
     alone;
   let us make him a partner like
     himself.'[o]
⁷ Now, Lord, you know that I take this
     wife of mine
   not because of lust,
   but for a noble purpose.
Call down your mercy on me and on her,
   and allow us to live together to a
     happy old age."

⁸They said together, "Amen, amen," ⁹and went to bed for the night.

But Raguel got up and summoned his servants. With him they went out to dig a grave, ¹⁰for he said, "I must do this, because if Tobiah should die, we would be subjected to ridicule and insult." ¹¹When they had finished digging the grave, Raguel went back into the house and called his wife, ¹²saying, "Send one of the maids in to see whether Tobiah is alive or dead, so that if necessary we may bury him without anyone's knowing about it." ¹³She sent the maid, who lit a lamp, opened the bedroom door, went in, and found them sound asleep together. ¹⁴The maid went out and told the girl's parents that Tobiah was alive, and that there was nothing wrong. ¹⁵Then Raguel praised the God of heaven in these words:

"Blessed are you, O God, with every
     holy and pure blessing!
Let all your chosen ones praise you;
   let them bless you forever!

¹⁶ Blessed are you, who have made me
     glad;
   what I feared did not happen.
Rather you have dealt with us
   according to your great mercy.
¹⁷ Blessed are you, for you were merciful
   toward two only children.
Grant them, Master, mercy and
     deliverance,
   and bring their lives to fulfillment
   with happiness and mercy."

¹⁸Then he told his servants to fill in the grave before dawn.

Wedding Feast. ¹⁹He asked his wife to bake many loaves of bread; he himself went out to the herd and picked out two steers and four rams which he ordered to be slaughtered. So the servants began to prepare the feast. ²⁰He summoned Tobiah and made an oath in his presence, saying: "For fourteen days* you shall not stir from here, but shall remain here eating and drinking with me; and you shall bring joy to my daughter's sorrowing spirit. ²¹Take, to begin with, half of whatever I own when you go back in good health to your father; the other half will be yours when I and my wife die. Be of good cheer, my son! I am your father, and Edna is your mother; and we belong to you and to your beloved now and forever. So be happy, son!"

CHAPTER 9

The Money Recovered. ¹Then Tobiah called Raphael and said to him: ²"Brother Azariah, take along with you four servants and two camels and travel to Rages. Go to Gabael's house and give him this bond. Get the money and then bring him along with you to the wedding celebration, ⁴For you know that my father is counting the days. If I should delay my return by a single day, I would cause him intense grief. ³You witnessed the oath that Raguel has sworn; I cannot violate his oath." ⁵So Raphael, together with the four servants and two camels, traveled to Rages in Media, where they stayed at

See RG
215-18

8, 20: For fourteen days: because of the happy, and unexpected, turn of events, Raguel doubles the time of the wedding feast. When Tobiah returns home, the usual seven-day feast is held (Tb 11, 18). Cf Jgs 14, 12.

n: Dn 3, 26. *o:* Gn 2, 18-23.

Gabael's house. Raphael gave Gabael his bond and told him about Tobit's son Tobiah, and that he had married and was inviting him to the wedding celebration. Gabael promptly checked over the sealed money-bags, and they placed them on the camels.

⁶The following morning they got an early start and traveled to the wedding celebration. When they entered Raguel's house, they found Tobiah reclining at table. He sprang up and greeted Gabael, who wept and blessed him, exclaiming: "O noble and good child, son of a noble and good, upright and charitable man, may the Lord grant heavenly blessing to you and to your wife, and to your wife's father and mother. Blessed be God, because I have seen the very image of my cousin Tobit!"

IV: Tobiah's Return; Cure of Tobit's Blindness

CHAPTER 10

See RG 215–18

Anxiety of the Parents. ¹Meanwhile, day by day, Tobit was keeping track of the time Tobiah would need to go and to return. When the number of days was reached and his son did not appear, ²he said, "I wonder what has happened. Perhaps he has been detained there; or perhaps Gabael is dead, and there is no one to give him the money." ³And he began to worry. ⁴His wife Anna said, "My son has perished and is no longer among the living!" And she began to weep aloud and to wail over her son: ⁵"Alas, my child, light of my eyes, that I let you make this journey!" ⁶But Tobit kept telling her: "Hush, do not think about it, my love; he is safe! Probably they have to take care of some unexpected business there. The man who is traveling with him is trustworthy, and is one of our own kinsmen. So do not worry over him, my love. He will be here soon." ⁷But she retorted, "Stop it, and do not lie to me! My child has perished!" She would go out and keep watch all day at the road her son had taken, and she ate nothing. At sunset she would go back home to wail and cry the whole night through, getting no sleep at all.ᵖ

Departure from Ecbatana. Now at the end of the fourteen-day wedding celebration which Raguel had sworn to hold for his daughter, Tobiah went to him and said: "Please let me go, for I know that my father and mother do not believe they will ever see me again. So I beg you, father, let me go back to my father. I have already told you how I left him." ⁸Raguel said to Tobiah: "Stay, my child, stay with me. I am sending messengers to your father Tobit, and they will give him news of you." ⁹But Tobiah insisted, "No, I beg you to let me go back to my father."

¹⁰Raguel then promptly handed over to Tobiah Sarah his wife, together with half of all his property: male and female slaves, oxen and sheep, asses and camels, clothing, money, and household goods. ¹¹Bidding them farewell, he let them go. He embraced Tobiah and said to him: "Good-bye, my son. Have a safe journey. May the Lord of heaven grant prosperity to you and to your wife Sarah. And may I see children of yours before I die!" ¹²Then he kissed his daughter Sarah and said to her: "My daughter, honor your father-in-law and your mother-in-law, because from now on they are as much your parents as the ones who brought you into the world. Go in peace, my daughter; let me hear good reports about you as long as I live." Finally he said good-bye to them and sent them away.

¹³Then Edna said to Tobiah: "My child and beloved kinsman, may the Lord bring you back safely, and may I live long enough to see children of you and of my daughter Sarah before I die. Before the Lord, I entrust my daughter to your care. Never cause her grief at any time in your life. Go in peace, my child. From now on I am your mother, and Sarah is your beloved. May all of us be prosperous all the days of our lives." She kissed them both and sent them away in peace.

¹⁴When Tobiah left Raguel, he was full of happiness and joy, and he blessed the Lord of heaven and earth, the King of all, for making his journey so successful. Finally he said good-bye to Raguel and his wife Edna, and added, "May I honor you all the days of my life!"

p: Gn 45, 26.

548

CHAPTER 11

See RG 216

Homeward Journey. ¹Then they left and began their return journey. When they were near Kaserin, just before Nineveh, ²Raphael said: "You know how we left your father. ³Let us hurry on ahead of your wife to prepare the house while the rest of the party are still on the way." ⁴So they both went on ahead and Raphael said to Tobiah, "Have the gall in your hand!" And the dog ran along behind them.

⁵Meanwhile, Anna sat watching the road by which her son was to come. ⁶When she saw him coming, she exclaimed to his father, "Tobit, your son is coming, and the man who traveled with him!"

⁷Raphael said to Tobiah before he reached his father: "I am certain that his eyes will be opened. ⁸Smear the fish gall on them. This medicine will make the cataracts shrink and peel off from his eyes; then your father will again be able to see the light of day."

Sight Restored. ⁹Then Anna ran up to her son, threw her arms around him, and said to him, "Now that I have seen you again, son, I am ready to die!" And she sobbed aloud.*q* ¹⁰Tobit got up and stumbled out through the courtyard gate. Tobiah went up to him ¹¹with the fish gall in his hand, and holding him firmly, blew into his eyes. "Courage, father," he said. ¹²Next he smeared the medicine on his eyes, ¹³and it made them smart. Then, beginning at the corners of Tobit's eyes, Tobiah used both hands to peel off the cataracts. When Tobit saw his son, he threw his arms around him ¹⁴and wept. He exclaimed, "I can see you, son, the light of my eyes!" Then he said:

"Blessed be God,
    and praised be his great name,
    and blessed be all his holy angels.
May his holy name be praised
    throughout all the ages,
¹⁵ Because it was he who scourged me,
    and it is he who has had mercy on me.
Behold, I now see my son Tobiah!"

Then Tobit went back in, rejoicing and praising God with full voice. Tobiah told his father that his journey had been a success; that he had brought back the money; and that he had married Raguel's daughter Sarah, who would arrive shortly, for she was approaching the gate of Nineveh.*r*

¹⁶Rejoicing and praising God, Tobit went out to the gate of Nineveh to meet his daughter-in-law. When the people of Nineveh saw him walking along briskly, with no one leading him by the hand, they were amazed. ¹⁷Before them all Tobit proclaimed how God had mercifully restored sight to his eyes. When Tobit reached Sarah, the wife of his son Tobiah, he greeted her: "Welcome, my daughter! Blessed be your God for bringing you to us, daughter! Blessed are your father and your mother. Blessed is my son Tobiah, and blessed are you, daughter! Welcome to your home with blessing and joy. Come in, daughter!" That day there was joy for all the Jews who lived in Nineveh. ¹⁸Ahiqar and his nephew Nadab also came to rejoice with Tobit. They celebrated Tobiah's wedding feast for seven happy days, and he received many gifts.

V: Raphael Reveals His Identity

CHAPTER 12

See RG 216-17

*Raphael's Wages.** ¹When the wedding celebration came to an end, Tobit called his son Tobiah and said to him, "Son, see to it that you give what is due to the man who made the journey with you; give him a bonus too." ²Tobiah said: "Father, how much shall I pay him? It would not hurt me at all to give him half of all the wealth he brought back with me.*s* ³He led me back safe and sound; he cured my wife; he brought the money back with me; and he cured you. How much of a bonus should I give him?" ⁴Tobit answered, "It is only fair, son, that he should receive half of all that he brought back." ⁵So Tobiah called Raphael and said, "Take as your wages half of all that you have brought back, and go in peace."

12, 1-5: Tobit and his son generously agree to give Azariah far more than the wages agreed upon in Tb 5, 15-16.

q: Gn 33, 4; 45, 14; 46, 29f; Lk 15, 20. *r:* Tb 13, 2; Dt 32, 39; 1 Sm 2, 6. *s:* Tb 5, 3. 7. 15f.

*Exhortation.** [6]Raphael called the two men aside privately and said to them: "Thank God! Give him the praise and the glory. Before all the living, acknowledge the many good things he has done for you, by blessing and extolling his name in song. Before all men, honor and proclaim God's deeds, and do not be slack in praising him.* [7]A king's secret it is prudent to keep, but the works of God are to be declared and made known. Praise them with due honor. Do good, and evil will not find its way to you. [8]Prayer and fasting are good, but better than either is almsgiving accompanied by righteousness.* A little with righteousness is better than abundance with wickedness. It is better to give alms than to store up gold;[t] [9]for almsgiving saves one from death and expiates every sin. Those who regularly give alms shall enjoy a full life;[u] [10]but those habitually guilty of sin are their own worst enemies.

Raphael's Identity. [11]"I will now tell you the whole truth; I will conceal nothing at all from you. I have already said to you, 'A king's secret it is prudent to keep, but the works of God are to be made known with due honor.' [12v]I can now tell you that when you, Tobit, and Sarah prayed, it was I who presented and read the record of your prayer before the Glory of the Lord; and I did the same thing when you used to bury the dead.* [13]When you did not hesitate to get up and leave your dinner in order to go and bury the dead, [14]I was sent to put you to the test.* At the same time, however, God commissioned me to heal you and your daughter-in-law Sarah. [15]I am Raphael, one of the seven angels who enter and serve before the Glory of the Lord."[w]

[16]Stricken with fear, the two men fell to the ground. [17]But Raphael said to them: "No need to fear; you are safe. Thank God now and forever. [18]As for me, when I came to you it was not out of any favor on my part, but because it was God's will. So continue to thank him every day; praise him with song. [19]Even though you watched me eat and drink, I did not really do so; what you were seeing was a vision. [20]So now get up from the ground and praise God. Behold, I am about to ascend to him who sent me; write down all these things that have happened to you."[x] [21]When Raphael ascended, they rose to their feet and could no longer see him. [22]They kept thanking God and singing his praises; and they continued to acknowledge these marvelous deeds which he had done when the angel of God appeared to them.

VI: Tobit's Song of Praise

CHAPTER 13

See RG 217-18

[1]Then Tobit composed this joyful prayer:*

Blessed be God who lives forever,
  because his kingdom lasts for all ages.[y]
[2] For he scourges and then has mercy;
  he casts down to the depths of the
    netherworld,
  and he brings up from the great abyss.
No one can escape his hand.[z]

[3] Praise him, you Israelites, before the
    Gentiles,
  for though he has scattered you among
    them,
[4] he has shown you his greatness even
    there.

12, 6-10: In the fashion of a wisdom teacher, Raphael gives the two men a short exhortation similar to the one Tobit gave his son in Tb 4, 3-19.

12, 6f: The Jews considered the duty of praising God their most esteemed privilege. Without praise of God, life was meaningless. Cf Is 38, 16-20.

12, 8: Prayer . . . fasting . . . almsgiving . . . righteousness: these, together with the proper attitude toward wealth, are treated in great detail by Christ our Lord in the Sermon on the Mount (Mt 6).

12, 12. 15: Raphael is one of the seven specially designated intercessors who present man's prayers to God. Angelology was developing in this period. The names of two other angels are given in the Bible: Gabriel (Dn 8, 16; 9, 21; Lk 1, 19. 26)

and Michael (Dn 10, 13. 21; 12, 1; Jude 9; Rv 12, 7).

12, 14: I was sent . . . test: God often sends trials to purify his faithful servants further. Cf Jb 1—2.

13, 1-18: Tobit's hymn of praise (cf Ex 15, 1-18; Jdt 16, 1-17) is divided into two parts. The first part (vv 1-8) is a song of praise that echoes themes from the hymns and psalms of the kingdom; the second (vv 9-18) is addressed to Jerusalem in the style of the prophets who spoke of a new and ideal Jerusalem (Is 60); cf Rv 21.

t: Tb 4, 7-11; Sir 29, 8-13. *u:* Dn 4, 24. *v:* Jb 33, 23f; Acts 10, 4; Rv 8, 3f. *w:* Lk 1, 19; Rv 8, 2. *x:* Jgs 13, 20. *y:* Tb 3, 11; 8, 5. 15; 1 Chr 29, 10; Dn 3, 26. *z:* Tb 11, 15; 13, 9; Dt 32, 39; 1 Sm 2, 6; Wis 16, 13.

Exalt him before every living being,
because he is the Lord our God,
our Father and God forever.
5 He scourged you for your iniquities,
but will again have mercy on you all.
He will gather you from all the Gentiles
among whom you have been
scattered.*a*

6 When you turn back to him with all your
heart,
to do what is right before him,
Then he will turn back to you,
and no longer hide his face from you.*b*

So now consider what he has done for
you,
and praise him with full voice.
Bless the Lord of righteousness,
and exalt the King of the ages.

In the land of my exile I praise him,
and show his power and majesty to a
sinful nation.
"Turn back, you sinners! do the right
before him:
perhaps he may look with favor upon
you
and show you mercy.

7 "As for me, I exalt my God,
and my spirit rejoices in the King of
heaven.
8 Let all men speak of his majesty,
and sing his praises in Jerusalem."

9 O Jerusalem, holy city,
he scourged you for the works of your
hands,*
but will again pity the children of the
righteous.*c*
10 Praise the Lord for his goodness,
and bless the King of the ages,
so that his tent may be rebuilt in you
with joy.
May he gladden within you all who were
captives;

all who were ravaged may he cherish
within you
for all generations to come.*d*

11 A bright light will shine to all parts of the
earth;
many nations shall come to you from
afar,
And the inhabitants of all the limits of
the earth,
drawn to you by the name of the Lord
God,
Bearing in their hands their gifts for the
King of heaven.
Every generation shall give joyful praise
in you,
and shall call you the chosen one,
through all ages forever.*e*

12 Accursed are all who speak a harsh word
against you;
accursed are all who destroy you
and pull down your walls,
And all who overthrow your towers
and set fire to your homes;
but forever blessed are all those who
build you up.*f*

13 Go, then, rejoice over the children of the
righteous,
who shall all be gathered together
and shall bless the Lord of the ages.
14 Happy are those who love you,
and happy those who rejoice in your
prosperity.

Happy are all the men who shall grieve
over you,
over all your chastisements,
For they shall rejoice in you
as they behold all your joy forever.*g*

15 My spirit blesses the Lord, the great King;
16 Jerusalem shall be rebuilt as his home
forever.
Happy for me if a remnant of my
offspring survive

13, 9: Works of your hands: idols.

a: Dt 30, 3; Neh 1, 9.   *b:* Dt 30, 2.   *c:* Tb 11, 15; Mi 7, 19; Rv 21.
60, 1; Mi 4, 2; Zec 8, 22.   *f:* Bar 4, 31f.   *g:* Ps 122, 6; Is 66, 10.   *d:* Is 44, 26, 28; Am 9, 11; Zec 1, 16.   *e:* Is 2, 3f; 9, 1; 49, 6;

to see your glory and to praise the
    King of heaven!

The gates of Jerusalem shall be built with
    sapphire and emerald,
and all your walls with precious
    stones.
The towers of Jerusalem shall be built
    with gold,
and their battlements with pure gold.[h]
[17] The streets of Jerusalem shall be paved
    with rubies and stones of Ophir;
[18] The gates of Jerusalem shall sing hymns
    of gladness,
and all her houses shall cry out,
    "Alleluia!"

"Blessed be God who has raised you up!
    may he be blessed for all ages!"
For in you they shall praise his holy
    name forever.

The end of Tobit's hymn of praise

VII: Epilogue

CHAPTER 14

See RG
215-16
Parting Advice. [1]Tobit died peacefully at the age of a hundred and twelve, and received an honorable burial in Nineveh. [2]He was sixty-two years old when he lost his eyesight, and after he recovered it he lived in prosperity, giving alms and continually blessing God and praising the divine Majesty.

[3]Just before he died, he called his son Tobiah and Tobiah's seven sons, and gave him this command: "Son, take your children[i] [4]and flee into Media, for I believe God's word which was spoken by Nahum[*] against Nineveh. It shall all happen, and shall overtake Assyria and Nineveh; indeed, whatever was said by Israel's prophets, whom God

commissioned, shall occur. Not one of all the oracles shall remain unfulfilled, but everything shall take place in the time appointed for it. So it will be safer in Media than in Assyria or Babylon. For I know and believe that whatever God has spoken will be accomplished. It shall happen, and not a single word of the prophecies shall prove false.

"As for our kinsmen who dwell in Israel, they shall all be scattered and led away into exile from the Good Land. The entire country of Israel shall become desolate; even Samaria and Jerusalem shall become desolate! God's temple there shall be burnt to the ground and shall be desolate for a while.[j] [5]But God will again have mercy on them and bring them back to the land of Israel. They shall rebuild the temple, but it will not be like the first one, until the era when the appointed times shall be completed.[*] Afterward all of them shall return from their exile, and they shall rebuild Jerusalem with splendor. In her the temple of God shall also be rebuilt; yes, it will be rebuilt for all generations to come, just as the prophets of Israel said of her.[k] [6]All the nations of the world shall be converted and shall offer God true worship; all shall abandon their idols which have deceitfully led them into error,[*] [7]and shall bless the God of the ages in righteousness. Because all the Israelites who are to be saved in those days will truly be mindful of God, they shall be gathered together and go to Jerusalem; in security shall they dwell forever in the land of Abraham, which will be given over to them. Those who sincerely love God shall rejoice, but those who become guilty of sin shall completely disappear from the land.[m]

[9]"Now, children, I give you this command: serve God faithfully and do what is right before him; you must tell your children to do what is upright and to give alms, to be

14, 4f: Nahum: one of the minor prophets, whose book contains oracles of doom against Nineveh. Here, in keeping with the period to which he assigns his story, the sacred author makes Tobit speak as if the punishment of Nineveh, the destruction of Jerusalem (587 B.C.), the exile from Judah and the return, would all take place in the future. The technique of using the facts of past history as seemingly future predictions, is a frequent device of apocalyptic writers. The Good Land: a favorite name for the promised land. Cf Dt 1, 35; 3, 25; 4, 21. 22.

14, 5: Until the era . . . completed: a reference to the advent of messianic times, in which a new, more perfect temple was to be expected. Cf Heb 9, 1-14.
14, 6: Conversion of the Gentiles is also to come in the messianic era.

h: Tb 14, 5; Is 54, 11-13; 62, 2; Rv 21, 10-21. i: Gn 47, 29f. j: Na 2, 2—3, 19. k: Neh 12, 27; Jer 31, 38. l: Tb 45, 14; Is 60, 1-4. m: Is 60, 21; Jer 32, 37; Ex 34, 28; 37, 25; 39, 26.

mindful of God and at all times to bless his name sincerely and with all their strength.

[8]"Now, as for you, my son, depart from Nineveh; do not remain here. [10]The day you bury your mother next to me, do not even stay overnight within the confines of the city. For I see that people here shamelessly commit all sorts of wickedness and treachery. Think, my son, of all that Nadab* did to Ahiqar, the very one who brought him up: Ahiqar went down alive into the earth! Yet God made Nadab's disgraceful crime rebound against him. Ahiqar came out again into the light, but Nadab went into the everlasting darkness, for he had tried to kill Ahiqar. Because Ahiqar had given alms to me, he escaped from the deadly trap Nadab had set for him. But Nadab himself fell into the deadly trap, and it destroyed him.[n] [11]So, my children, note well what almsgiving does, and also what wickedness does—it kills! But now my spirit is about to leave me."

Death of Tobit and Tobiah. [12]They placed him on his bed and he died; and he received an honorable burial. When Tobiah's mother died, he buried her next to his father. He then departed with his wife and children for Media, where he settled in Ecbatana with his father-in-law Raguel.[o] [13]He took respectful care of his aging father-in-law and mother-in-law; and he buried them at Ecbatana in Media. Then he inherited Raguel's estate as well as that of his father Tobit. [14]He died at the venerable age of a hundred and seventeen. [15]But before he died, he heard of the destruction of Nineveh and saw its effects. He witnessed the exile of the city's inhabitants when Cyaxares,* king of Media, led them captive into Media. Tobiah praised God for all that he had done against the citizens of Nineveh and Assyria. Before dying he rejoiced over Nineveh's destruction, and he blessed the Lord God forever and ever. Amen.

14, 10: Nadab: In the story of Ahiqar, the hero Ahiqar, chancellor under the Assyrian kings Sennacherib and Esarhaddon, adopts his nephew Nadab and prepares him to become his successor. But Nadab treacherously plots to have his uncle put to death. Ahiqar hides in a friend's house, and is finally vindicated (came out again into the light) when Nadab's scheme is discovered. Thereupon Nadab is thrown into a dungeon where he dies (went into everlasting darkness). It

was Ahiqar's almsgiving that delivered him from death; see note on Tb 2, 2.

14, 15: Cyaxares: Nabopolassar, king of Babylon, and Cyaxares conquered and destroyed Nineveh in 612 B.C.; see note on Tb 1, 15.

_____

n: Tb 1, 21f.   *o:* Tb 4, 4.

See RG 218–22

The Book of Judith

The Book of Judith is a vivid story relating how, in a grave crisis, God delivered the Jewish people through the instrumentality of a woman. The unknown author composed this edifying narrative of divine providence at the end of the second or the beginning of the first century B.C. The original was almost certainly written in Hebrew, but the Greek text shows so much freedom in adapting from the Septuagint the language of older biblical books that it must be regarded as having a literary character of its own. It is this Greek form of the book, accepted as canonical by the Catholic Church, which is translated here. St. Jerome, who prepared (with some reluctance) a Latin text of Judith, based his work on a secondary Aramaic text available to him in Palestine, combined with an older Latin rendering from the Greek. The long hymn of chapter 16 he took in its entirety from that earlier Latin text.

Since it is no longer possible to determine with any precision the underlying events which may have given rise to this narrative, it is enough to note that the author sought to strengthen the faith of his people in God's abiding presence among them. The Book of Judith is a tract for difficult times; the reader, it was hoped, would take to heart the lesson that God was still the Master of history, who could save Israel from her enemies. Note the parallel with the time of the Exodus: as God had delivered his people by the hand of Moses, so he could deliver them by the hand of the pious widow Judith (see note on 2, 12).

The story can be divided into two parts. In the first (cc 1—7), Holofernes, commander-in-chief of the armies of Nebuchadnezzar, leads an overwhelming Assyrian force in a punitive campaign against the vassals who refused to help in the Assyrian war against the Medes. The Jewish people stubbornly resist the enemy at Bethulia, guarding the route of access to Jerusalem. Despite the warning of Achior that the Jews cannot be conquered unless they sin against God, the proud general lays siege to the town and cuts off its water supply. After a siege of thirty-four days, the exhausted defenders are desperate and ready to surrender.

At this point, the climax of the story, Judith (the name means "Jewess") appears and promises to defeat the Assyrians. The rest of the story is too well known to repeat in detail. Having fasted and prayed, Judith dresses in her finest garments and proceeds to the Assyrian camp, where she succeeds in killing Holofernes while he lies in a drunken stupor. The Assyrians panic when they discover this, and the Jews are able to rout and slaughter them. The beautiful hymn of the people honoring Judith (15, 9-10) is often applied to Mary in the liturgy.

Any attempt to read the book directly against the backdrop of Jewish history in relation to the empires of the ancient world is bound to fail. The story was written as a pious reflection on the meaning of the yearly Passover observance. It draws its inspiration from the Exodus narrative (especially Ex 14, 31) and from the texts of Isaiah and the Psalms portraying the special intervention of God for the preservation of Jerusalem. The theme of God's hand as the agent of this providential activity, reflected of old in the hand of Moses and now in the hand of Judith, is again exemplified at a later time in Jewish synagogue art. God's hand reaching down from heaven appears as part of the scene at Dura-Europos (before A.D. 256) in paintings of the Exodus, of the sacrifice of Isaac (Gn 22), and of Ezekiel's valley of dry bones (Ez 37).

The Book of Judith is divided as follows:

I: Peril of the Jews (1, 1—7, 32).

II: Deliverance of the Jews (8, 1—14, 10).

III: Victory (14, 11—16, 25).

I: Peril of the Jews

CHAPTER 1

See RG 219

War against the Medes. [1]It was the twelfth year of the reign of Nebuchadnezzar, king of the Assyrians in the great city of Nineveh. At that time Arphaxad ruled over the Medes in Ecbatana. [2]Around this city he built a wall of blocks of stone, each three cubits in height and six in length. He made the wall seventy cubits high and fifty thick. [3]At the gates he raised towers of a hundred cubits, with a thickness of sixty cubits at the base. [4]The gateway he built to a height of seventy cubits, with an opening forty cubits wide for the passage of his chariot forces and the marshaling of his infantry. [5]Then King Nebuchadnezzar waged war against King Arphaxad in the vast plain, in the district of Ragae. [6]To him there rallied all the inhabitants of the mountain region, all who dwelt along the Euphrates, the Tigris, and the Hydaspes, and King Arioch of the Elamites, in the plain. Thus many nations came together to resist the people of Cheleoud.*

Ultimatum to the West. [7]Now Nebuchadnezzar, king of the Assyrians, sent messengers to all the inhabitants of Persia, and to all those who dwelt in the West: to the inhabitants of Cilicia and Damascus, Lebanon and Anti-Lebanon, to all who dwelt along the seacoast, [8]to the peoples of Carmel, Gilead, Upper Galilee, and the vast plain of Esdraelon, [9]to all those in Samaria and its cities, and west of the Jordan as far as Jerusalem, Bethany, Chelous, Kadesh, and the River of Egypt; to Tahpanhes, Raamses, all the land of Goshen, [10]Tanis, Memphis and beyond, and to all the inhabitants of Egypt as far as the borders of Ethiopia.

[11]But the inhabitants of all that land disregarded the summons of Nebuchadnezzar, king of the Assyrians, and would not go with him to the war. They were not afraid of him but regarded him as a lone individual opposed to them, and turned away his envoys empty-handed, in disgrace. [12]Then Nebuchadnezzar fell into a violent rage against all that land, and swore by his throne and his kingdom that he would avenge himself on all the territories of Cilicia and Damascus and Syria, and also destroy with his sword all the inhabitants of Moab, Ammon, the whole of Judea, and those living anywhere

---

1, 6: Cheleoud: probably the Chaldeans are meant.

in Egypt as far as the borders of the two seas.*

Defeat of Arphaxad. [13] In the seventeenth year he proceeded with his army against King Arphaxad, and was victorious in his campaign. He routed the whole force of Arphaxad, his entire cavalry and all his chariots, [14] and took possession of his cities. He pressed on to Ecbatana and took its towers, sacked its marketplaces, and turned its glory into shame. [15] Arphaxad himself he overtook in the mountains of Ragae, ran him through with spears, and utterly destroyed him. [16] Then he returned home with all his numerous, motley horde of warriors; and there he and his army relaxed and feasted for a hundred and twenty days.[a]

See RG
219

CHAPTER 2

Council of War against the West. [1] In the eighteenth year, on the twenty-second day of the first month, there was a discussion in the palace of Nebuchadnezzar, king of the Assyrians, about taking revenge on the whole world, as he had threatened. [2] He summoned all his ministers and nobles, laid before them his secret plan, and urged the total destruction of those countries. [3] They decided to do away with all those who had refused to comply with the order he had issued.

[4] When he had completed his plan, Nebuchadnezzar, king of the Assyrians, summoned Holofernes, general in chief of his forces, second to himself in command, and said to him: [5b] "Thus says the great king, the lord of all the earth: Go forth from my presence, take with you men of proven valor, a hundred and twenty thousand infantry and twelve thousand cavalry, [6] and proceed against all the land of the West, because they did not comply with the order I issued. [7] Tell them to have earth and water* ready, for I will come against them in my wrath; I will cover all the land with the feet of my sol-

diers, to whom I will deliver them as spoils. [8] Their slain shall fill their ravines and wadies, the swelling torrent shall be choked with their dead; [9] and I will deport them as exiles to the very ends of the earth.

[10] "You go before me and take possession of all their territories for me. If they surrender to you, guard them for me till the day of their punishment. [11] As for those who resist, show them no quarter, but deliver them up to slaughter and plunder in each country you occupy. [12] For as I live,* and by the strength of my kingdom, what I have spoken I will accomplish by my power. [13] Do not disobey a single one of the orders of your lord; fulfill them exactly as I have commanded you, and do it without delay."

Campaign of Holofernes. [14] So Holofernes left the presence of his lord, and summoned all the princes, and the generals and officers of the Assyrian army. [15] He mustered a hundred and twenty thousand picked troops, as his lord had commanded, and twelve thousand mounted archers, [16] and grouped them into a complete combat force. [17] He took along a very large number of camels, asses, and mules for their baggage; innumerable sheep, cattle, and goats for their food supply; [18] abundant provisions for each man, and much gold and silver from the royal palace.

[19] Then he and his whole army proceeded on their expedition in advance of King Nebuchadnezzar, to cover all the western region with their chariots and cavalry and regular infantry. [20] A huge, irregular force, too many to count, like locusts or the dust of the earth, went along with them.[c]

[21] After a three-day march from Nineveh, they reached the plain of Bectileth, and from Bectileth they next encamped near the mountains to the north of Upper Cilicia. [22] From there Holofernes took his whole force, the infantry, calvary, and chariots, and

---

1, 12: The two seas: the ancient rulers in Mesopotamia often designated the limits of their realm as extending from the Upper Sea (the Mediterranean) to the Lower Sea (the Persian Gulf).

2, 7: Earth and water: in the Persian period, the offering of these to a conqueror was a symbolic gesture of unconditional surrender.

2, 12: As I live: in the Old Testament, an oath proper to di-

vinity; cf Dt 32, 40. Nebuchadnezzar is making himself equal to God; see Jdt 6, 2. By my power: literally "by my hand." The hand of Nebuchadnezzar raised in opposition to God and to his people is the occasion for Judith's intervention by a woman's hand; cf Jdt 9, 9f; Is 10, 5-14.

---

a: Est 1, 3f.   *b:* 5f: Est 3, 8f.   *c:* Jgs 7, 12.

marched into the mountain region. [23]He devastated Put and Lud,* and plundered all the Rassisites and the Ishmaelites on the border of the desert toward the south of Chaldea.

[24]Then, following the Euphrates, he went through Mesopotamia, and battered down every fortified city along the Wadi Abron, until he reached the sea. [25]He seized the territory of Cilicia, and cut down everyone who resisted him. Then he proceeded to the southern borders of Japheth, toward Arabia. [26]He surrounded all the Midianites, burned their tents, and plundered their sheepfolds. [27]Descending to the plain of Damascus at the time of the wheat harvest, he set fire to all their fields, destroyed their flocks and herds, despoiled their cities, devastated their plains, and put all their youths to the sword.

[28]The fear and dread of him fell upon all the inhabitants of the coastland, upon those in Sidon and Tyre, and those who dwelt in Sur and Ocina, and the inhabitants of Jamnia. Those in Azotus and Ascalon also feared him greatly.

CHAPTER 3

See RG 219

Submission of the West. [1]They therefore sent messengers to him to sue for peace in these words: [2]"We, the servants of Nebuchadnezzar the great king, lie prostrate before you; do with us as you will. [3]Our dwellings and all our wheat fields, our flocks and herds, and all our encampments are at your disposal; make use of them as you please. [4]Our cities and their inhabitants are also at your service; come and deal with them as you see fit."

[5]After the spokesmen had reached Holofernes and given him this message, [6]he went down with his army to the seacoast, and stationed garrisons in the fortified cities; from them he impressed picked troops as auxiliaries. [7]The people of these cities and all the inhabitants of the countryside received him with garlands and dancing to the sound of timbrels. [8]Nevertheless, he devastated their whole territory and cut down their sacred groves, for he had been commissioned to destroy all the gods of the earth, so that every nation might worship Nebuchadnezzar alone, and every people and tribe invoke him as a god.[d] [9]At length Holofernes reached Esdraelon in the neighborhood of Dothan, the approach to the main ridge of the Judean mountains; [10]he set up his camp between Geba* and Scythopolis, and stayed there a whole month to refurbish all the equipment of his army.

CHAPTER 4

See RG 219

Israelite Defense. [1]When the Israelites who dwelt in Judea heard of all that Holofernes, commander in chief of Nebuchadnezzar, king of the Assyrians, had done to the nations, and how he had despoiled all their temples and destroyed them, [2]they were in extreme dread of him, and greatly alarmed for Jerusalem and the temple of the LORD, their God. [3]Now, they had lately returned from exile, and only recently had all the people of Judea been gathered together, and the vessels, the altar, and the temple been purified from profanation.* [4]So they sent word to the whole region of Samaria, to Kona, Beth-horon, Belmain, and Jericho, to Choba and Aesora, and to the valley of Salem. [5]The people there posted guards on all the summits of the high mountains, fortified their villages, and since their fields had recently been harvested, stored up provisions in preparation for war.

[6]Joakim, who was high priest* in Jerusalem in those days, wrote to the inhabitants of Bethulia [and Betomesthaim], which is on the way to Esdraelon, facing the plain near Dothan, [7]and instructed them to keep firm hold of the mountain passes, since

---

2, 23: Put and Lud: the same as the "Put and Lud" mentioned in Ez 30, 5 as allies of Egypt, and in Ez 27, 10 as supplying mercenary soldiers to Tyre. Here they seem inserted to embellish the narrative with assonance and prophetic associations rather than to indicate definite localities.

3, 10: Geba: perhaps originally "Gelboe," the mountain range near the eastern end of which lay Scythopolis, the Greek name for ancient Beth-shean (Jos 17, 11).

4, 3: Returned from exile . . . profanation: these allusions

are variously attributed—to the Persian period (538-323 B.C.), or even to a condition in the days of Antiochus Epiphanes (175-164 B.C.).

4, 6: Joakim, who was high priest: see Bar 1, 7 and the footnote on Bar 1, 8f; this name for a high priest cannot be used in dating the events in Jdt.

---

d: Ex 34, 13.

these offered access to Judea. It would be easy to ward off the attacking forces, as the defile was only wide enough for two abreast. [8]The Israelites carried out the orders given them by Joakim, the high priest, and the senate of the whole people of Israel, which met in Jerusalem.*

Prayer and Penance. [9]All the men of Israel cried to God with great fervor and did penance— [10e]they, along with their wives, and children, and domestic animals.* All their resident aliens, hired laborers, and slaves also girded themselves with sackcloth. [11]And all the Israelite men, women, and children who lived in Jerusalem prostrated themselves in front of the temple building,* with ashes strewn on their heads, displaying their sackcloth covering before the LORD. [12]The altar, too, they draped in sackcloth; and with one accord they cried out fervently to the God of Israel not to allow their children to be seized, their wives to be taken captive, the cities of their inheritance to be ruined, or the sanctuary to be profaned and mocked for the nations to gloat over.[f]

[13]The LORD heard their cry and had regard for their distress. For the people observed a fast of many days' duration throughout Judea, and before the sanctuary of the LORD Almighty in Jerusalem.[g] [14]The high priest Joakim, and all the priests in attendance on the LORD who served his altar, were also girded with sackcloth as they offered the daily holocaust, the votive offerings, and the free-will offerings of the people. [15]With ashes upon their turbans, they cried to the LORD with all their strength to look with favor on the whole house of Israel.

CHAPTER 5

See RG 219

Council against the Israelites. [1]It was reported to Holofernes, commander in chief of the Assyrian army, that the Israelites were ready for battle, and had blocked the mountain passes, fortified the summits of all the higher peaks, and placed roadblocks in the plains. [2]In great anger he summoned all the rulers of the Moabites, the generals of the Ammonites, and all the satraps of the seacoast [3]and said to them: "Now tell me, you Canaanites, what sort of people is this that dwells in the mountains? Which cities do they inhabit? How large is their army? In what does their power and strength consist? Who has set himself up as their king and the leader of their army? [4]Why have they refused to come out to meet me along with all the other inhabitants of the West?"

Achior's Speech. [5]Then Achior, the leader of all the Ammonites, said to him: "My lord, hear this account from your servant; I will tell you the truth about this people that lives near you [that inhabits this mountain region]; no lie shall escape your servant's lips.[h]

[6*]"These people are descendants of the Chaldeans. [7]They formerly dwelt in Mesopotamia, for they did not wish to follow the gods of their forefathers who were born in the land of the Chaldeans.[i] [8]Since they abandoned the way of their ancestors, and acknowledged with divine worship the God of heaven, their forefathers expelled them from the presence of their gods. So they fled to Mesopotamia and dwelt there a long time. [9]Their God bade them leave their abode and proceed to the land of Canaan. Here they settled, and grew very rich in gold, silver, and a great abundance of livestock.[j] [10]Later, when famine had gripped the whole land of Canaan, they went down into Egypt. They stayed there as long as they found sustenance, and grew into such a great multitude that the number of their race could not be counted.[k] [11]The king of Egypt, however, rose up against them, shrewdly forced them

---

4, 8: The organization of the Jewish nation as subject to a high priest and a senate, or council of elders, was proper to the Greek period (after 323 B.C.), and is reflected in the coinage of John Hyrcanus (135–104 B.C.).

4, 10: Domestic animals: see note on Jon 3, 8.

4, 11: Prostrated themselves in front of the temple building: for a parallel to this ceremony of entreaty, see Jl 1, 13f; 2, 15ff, and the note on Jl 2, 17.

5, 6-9: Achior outlines the early history of the Hebrews,

whose forefather, Abraham, first lived in Ur of the Chaldeans (Gn 11, 28) and then migrated to Haran (Gn 11, 31) in Aram Naharaim (Gn 24, 10), which was called Mesopotamia by the Greeks. The gods of their forefathers were the pagan deities worshiped by Abraham's relatives (Jos 24, 2).

e: 10f: Jon 3, 7f. *f:* Est 4, 1f. *g:* Est 4, 16. *h:* Jdt 11, 9-19. *i:* Gn 11, 31. *j:* Gn 11, 31—12, 5. *k:* Gn 42, 1-5; 46, 1-7; Ex 1, 7. *l:* 11f: Ex 5, 4-21; 7, 1-9.

to labor at brickmaking, oppressed and enslaved them. [12]But they cried to their God, and he struck the land of Egypt with plagues for which there was no remedy. When the Egyptians expelled them, [13m]God dried up the Red Sea before them, [14]and led them along the route to Sinai and Kadesh-barnea. First they drove out all the inhabitants of the desert; [15]then they settled in the land of the Amorites, destroyed all the Heshbonites by main force, crossed the Jordan, and took possession of the whole mountain region.[n] [16]They expelled the Canaanites, the Perizzites, the Jebusites, the Shechemites, and all the Gergesites; and they lived in these mountains a long time.[o]

[17p]"As long as the Israelites did not sin in the sight of their God, they prospered, for their God, who hates wickedness, was with them. [18]But when they deviated from the way he prescribed for them, they were ground down steadily, more and more, by frequent wars, and finally taken as captives into foreign lands. The temple of their God was razed to the ground, and their cities were occupied by their enemies.[q] [19]But now that they have returned to their God, they have come back from the Dispersion wherein they were scattered, and have repossessed Jerusalem, where their sanctuary is, and have settled again in the mountain region which was unoccupied.

[20r]"So now, my lord and master, if these people are at fault, and are sinning against their God, and if we verify this offense of theirs, then we shall be able to go up and conquer them. [21]But if they are not a guilty nation, then your lordship should keep his distance; otherwise their LORD and God will shield them, and we shall become the laughingstock of the whole world."

[22]Now when Achior had concluded his recommendation, all the people standing round about the tent murmured; and the officers of Holofernes and all the inhabitants of the seacoast and of Moab alike said he should be cut to pieces. [23]"We are not afraid of the Israelites," they said, "for they are a powerless people, incapable of a strong defense. [24]Let us therefore attack them; your great army, Lord Holofernes, will swallow them up."[s]

CHAPTER 6

See RG 219

Holofernes' Answer. [1]When the noise of the crowd surrounding the council had subsided, Holofernes, commander in chief of the Assyrian army, said to Achior, in the presence of the whole throng of coastland peoples, of the Moabites, and of the Ammonite mercenaries: [2]"Who are you, Achior, to prophesy among us as you have done today, and to tell us not to fight against the Israelites because their God protects them? What god is there beside Nebuchadnezzar? He will send his force and destroy them from the face of the earth. Their God will not save them;[t] [3]but we, the servants of Nebuchadnezzar, will strike them down as one man, for they will be unable to withstand the force of our cavalry.[u] [4]We will overwhelm them with it, and the mountains shall be drunk with their blood, and their plains filled with their corpses. Not a trace of them shall survive our attack: they shall utterly perish, says King Nebuchadnezzar, lord of all the earth; for he has spoken, and his words shall not remain unfulfilled.[v] [5]As for you, Achior, you Ammonite mercenary, for saying these things in a moment of perversity you shall not see my face after today, until I have taken revenge on this race of people from Egypt. [6]Then at my return, the sword of my army or the spear of my servants will pierce your sides, and you shall fall among their slain.[w] [7]My servants will now conduct you to the mountain region, and leave you at one of the towns along the ascent. [8]You shall not die till you are destroyed together with them. [9]If you still cherish the hope that they will not be taken, then there is no need for you to be downcast. I have spoken, and my words shall not prove false in any respect."

Achior in Bethulia. [10]Then Holofernes ordered the servants who were standing by in his tent to seize Achior, conduct him to Bethulia, and hand him over to the Israelites. [11]So

m: 13f: Ex 14, 21f. 29.   n: Nm 21, 21-32; Jos 2, 10.   o: Dt 7, 1.   p: 17f: Dt 28—30; Ps 106, 40-46; Is 59, 7.   q: 2 Kgs 25.   r: 20f: Jdt 8, 18ff; 11, 10.   s: Jdt 6. 2; 9, 7; 16, 2.   t: Jdt 3, 8; 9, 7.   u: Is 36, 18ff.   v: Jdt 6, 17.   w: Jdt 5, 22.

the servants took him in custody and brought him out of the camp into the plain. From there they led him into the mountain region till they reached the springs below Bethulia. *12*When the men of the city saw them, they seized their weapons and ran out of the city to the crest of the ridge; and all the slingers blocked the ascent of Holofernes' servants by hurling stones upon them. *13*So they took cover below the mountain, where they bound Achior and left him lying at the foot of the mountain; then they returned to their lord.

*14*The Israelites came down to him from their city, loosed him, and brought him into Bethulia. They haled him before the rulers of the city, *15*who in those days were Uzziah, son of Micah of the tribe of Simeon, Chabris, son of Gothoniel, and Charmis, son of Melchiel. *16*They then convened all the elders of the city; and all their young men, as well as the women, gathered in haste at the place of assembly. They placed Achior in the center of the throng, and Uzziah questioned him about what had happened. *17*He replied by giving them an account of what was said in the council of Holofernes, and of all his own words among the Assyrian officers, and of all the boasting threats of Holofernes against the house of Israel.

*18*At this the people fell prostrate and worshiped God; and they cried out: *19*"LORD, God of heaven, behold their arrogance! Have pity on the lowliness of our people, and look with favor this day on those who are consecrated to you."* *20*Then they reassured Achior and praised him highly. *21*Uzziah brought him from the assembly to his home, where he gave a banquet for the elders. That whole night they called upon the God of Israel for help.

See RG
219

CHAPTER 7

Siege of Bethulia. *1*The following day Holofernes ordered his whole army, and all the allied troops that had come to his support, to move against Bethulia, seize the mountain passes, and engage the Israelites in battle. *2*That same day all their fighting men went into action. Their forces numbered a hundred and seventy thousand infantry and twelve thousand horsemen, not counting the baggage train or the men who accompanied it on foot—a very great army. *3*They encamped at the spring in the valley near Bethulia, and spread out in breadth toward Dothan as far as Balbaim, and in length from Bethulia to Cyamon, which faces Esdraelon.

*4*When the Israelites saw how many there were, they said to one another in great dismay: "Soon they will devour the whole country. Neither the high mountains nor the valleys and hills can support the mass of them." *5*Yet they all seized their weapons, lighted fires on their bastions,* and kept watch throughout the night.

*6*On the second day Holofernes led out all his cavalry in the sight of the Israelites who were in Bethulia. *7*He reconnoitered the approaches to their city and located their sources of water; these he seized, stationing armed detachments around them, while he himself returned to his troops.

*8*All the commanders of the Edomites and all the leaders of the Ammonites, together with the generals of the seacoast, came to Holofernes and said: *9*"Sir, listen to what we have to say, that there may be no losses among your troops. *10*These Israelites do not rely on their spears, but on the height of the mountains where they dwell; it is not easy to reach the summit of their mountains.*x* *11*Therefore, sir, do not attack them in regular formation; thus not a single one of your troops will fall. *12*Stay in your camp, and spare all your soldiers. Have some of your servants keep control of the source of water that flows out at the base of the mountain, *13*for that is where the inhabitants of Bethulia

---

6, 19: The Latin Vulgate (6, 15) has a longer form of this prayer: "Lord, God of heaven and earth, behold their arrogance; regard our lowliness and look with favor on your holy ones; show that you do not abandon those who trust in you, but that you humble those who trust in themselves and glory in their own strength."

7, 5: Lighted fires on their bastions: to serve as signals for

alerting the neighboring towns. Reference to fire signals in time of siege is made in the Lachish ostraca at the beginning of the sixth century B.C. Kept watch throughout the night: to prevent a surprise attack.

---

x: 1 Kgs 20, 23. 28.

get their water. Then thirst will begin to carry them off, and they will surrender their city. Meanwhile, we and our men will go up to the summits of the nearby mountains, and encamp there to guard against anyone's leaving the city.*^y* ^14^ They and their wives and children will languish with hunger, and even before the sword strikes them they will be laid low in the streets of their city. ^15^ Thus you will render them dire punishment for their rebellion and their refusal to meet you peacefully."

^16^ Their words pleased Holofernes and all his ministers, and he ordered their proposal to be carried out. ^17^ Thereupon the Moabites moved camp, together with five thousand Assyrians. They encamped in the valley, and held the water supply and the springs of the Israelites. ^18^ The Edomites and the Ammonites went up and encamped in the mountain region opposite Dothan; and they sent some of their men to the south and to the east opposite Egrebel, near Chusi, which is on Wadi Mochmur. The rest of the Assyrian army was encamped in the plain, covering the whole countryside. Their enormous store of tents and equipment was spread out in profusion everywhere.

^19^ The Israelites cried to the LORD, their God, for they were disheartened, since all their enemies had them surrounded, and there was no way of slipping through their lines.*^z* ^20^ The whole Assyrian camp, infantry, chariots, and cavalry, kept them thus surrounded for thirty-four days. All the reservoirs of water failed the inhabitants of Bethulia, ^21^ and the cisterns ran dry, so that on no day did they have enough to drink, but their drinking water was rationed. ^22^ Their children fainted away, and the women and youths were consumed with thirst and were collapsing in the streets and gateways of the city, with no strength left in them.

^23^ All the people, therefore, including youths, women, and children, went in a crowd to Uzziah and the rulers of the city. They set up a great clamor and said before the elders: ^24^ "God judge between you and us! You have done us grave injustice in not making peace with the Assyrians. ^25^ There is no help for us now! Instead, God has sold us into their power by laying us prostrate before them in thirst and utter exhaustion. ^26^ Therefore, summon them and deliver the whole city as booty to the troops of Holofernes and to all his forces; ^27^ we would be better off to become their prey. We should indeed be made slaves, but at least we should live, and not have to behold our little ones dying before our eyes and our wives and children breathing out their souls. ^28^ We adjure you by heaven and earth, and by our God, the LORD of our forefathers, who is punishing us for our sins and those of our forefathers, to do as we have proposed, this very day."

^29^ All in the assembly with one accord broke into shrill wailing and loud cries to the LORD their God. ^30^ But Uzziah said to them, "Courage, my brothers! Let us wait five days more for the LORD our God, to show his mercy toward us; he will not utterly forsake us. ^31^ But if those days pass without help coming to us, I will do as you say." ^32^ Then he dispersed the men to their posts, and they returned to the walls and towers of the city; the women and children he sent to their homes. Throughout the city they were in great misery.

II: Deliverance of the Jews

CHAPTER 8

See RG
219

Judith. ^1^ Now in those days Judith, daughter of Merari, son of Joseph, son of Oziel, son of Elkiah, son of Ananias, son of Gideon, son of Raphain, son of Ahitob, son of Elijah, son of Hilkiah, son of Eliab, son of Nathanael, son of Salamiel, son of Sarasadai,* son of Simeon, son of Israel, heard of this. ^2^ Her husband, Manasseh, of her own tribe and clan, had died at the time of the barley harvest. ^3^ While he was in the field supervising those who bound the sheaves, he suffered sunstroke; and he died of this illness in Bethulia, his native city. He was buried with his forefathers in the field between Dothan and Balamon. ^4^ The widowed

---

8, 1: Salamiel, son of Sarasadai: head of the tribe of Simeon during the wanderings of the Israelites in the desert (Nm 1, 6).

y: Ex 5, 21.   *z:* Ps 106, 6.

Judith remained three years and four months at home, [5]where she set up a tent* for herself on the roof of her house. She put sackcloth about her loins and wore widow's weeds. [6]She fasted all the days of her widowhood, except sabbath eves and sabbaths, new moon eves and new moons, feastdays and holidays of the house of Israel.[a] [7]She was beautifully formed and lovely to behold. Her husband, Manasseh, had left her gold and silver, servants and maids, livestock and fields, which she was maintaining. [8]No one had a bad word to say about her, for she was a very God-fearing woman.

Her Words to the Elders. [9]When Judith, therefore, heard of the harsh words which the people, discouraged by their lack of water, had spoken against their ruler, and of all that Uzziah had said to them in reply, swearing that he would hand over the city to the Assyrians at the end of five days, [10]she sent the maid who was in charge of all her things to ask Uzziah, Chabris, and Charmis, the elders of the city, to visit her. [11]When they came, she said to them: "Listen to me, you rulers of the people of Bethulia. What you said to the people today is not proper. When you promised to hand over the city to our enemies at the end of five days unless within that time the LORD comes to our aid, you interposed between God and yourselves this oath which you took. [12]Who are you, then, that you should have put God to the test this day, setting yourselves in the place of God in human affairs?[b] [13]It is the LORD Almighty for whom you are laying down conditions; will you never understand anything? [14]You cannot plumb the depths of the human heart or grasp the workings of the human mind; how then can you fathom God, who has made all these things, discern his mind, and understand his plan?[c]

"No, my brothers, do not anger the LORD our God. [15]For if he does not wish to come to our aid within the five days, he has it equally within his power to protect us at such time as he pleases, or to destroy us in the face of our enemies. [16]It is not for you to make the LORD our God give surety for his plans.

"God is not man that he should be moved by threats,
nor human, that he may be given an ultimatum.

[17]"So while we wait for the salvation that comes from him, let us call upon him to help us, and he will hear our cry if it is his good pleasure. [18]For there has not risen among us in recent generations, nor does there exist today, any tribe, or clan, or town, or city of ours that worships gods made by hands, as happened in former days.[d] [19]It was for such conduct that our forefathers were handed over to the sword and to pillage, and fell with great destruction before our enemies.[e] [20]But since we acknowledge no other god but the LORD, we hope that he will not disdain us or any of our people. [21]If we are taken, all Judea will fall, our sanctuary will be plundered, and God will make us pay for its profanation with our life's blood. [22]For the slaughter of our kinsmen, for the taking of exiles from the land, and for the devastation of our inheritance, he will lay the guilt on our heads. Wherever we shall be enslaved among the nations, we shall be a mockery and a reproach in the eyes of our masters. [23]Our enslavement will not be turned to our benefit, but the LORD our God will maintain it to our disgrace.

[24]"Therefore, my brothers, let us set an example for our kinsmen. Their lives depend on us, and the defense of the sanctuary, the temple, and the altar rests with us. [25]Besides all this, we should be grateful to the LORD our God, for putting us to the test, as he did our forefathers. [26]Recall how he dealt with Abraham, and how he tried Isaac, and all that happened to Jacob in Syrian Mesopotamia while he was tending the flocks of Laban, his mother's brother. [27]Not for vengeance did the LORD put them in the crucible to try their hearts, nor has he done so with us. It is by way of admonition that he chastises those who are close to him."[g]

8, 5: A tent: erected by Judith on the roof of her house (v 5); it was here that the elders came to confer with her (v 11).

a: Lk 2, 37.   b: Jb 38, 2; 40, 2. 7f; 42, 3.   c: Jb 41, 3; Prv 14, 10; Wis 9, 13; Is 40, 13; Rom 11, 33f; 1 Cor 2, 11   d: Jdt 5, 20f; 11, 10.   e: Pss 78, 56f; 106, 13f; Jer 7, 16-20; 14, 7.   f: 25f: Gn 22, 1-12; 29, 22-30.   g: Dt 4, 7.

Uzziah's Response. ²⁸Then Uzziah said to her: "All that you have said was spoken with good sense, and no one can gainsay your words. ²⁹Not today only is your wisdom made evident, but from your earliest years all the people have recognized your prudence, which corresponds to the worthy dispositions of your heart. ³⁰The people, however, were so tortured with thirst that they forced us to speak to them as we did, and to bind ourselves by an oath that we cannot break. ³¹But now, God-fearing woman that you are, pray for us that the LORD may send rain to fill up our cisterns, lest we be weakened still further."

³²Then Judith said to them: "Listen to me! I will do something that will go down from generation to generation among the descendants of our race. ³³Stand at the gate tonight to let me pass through with my maid; and within the days you have specified before you will surrender the city to our enemies, the LORD will rescue Israel by my hand. ³⁴You must not inquire into what I am doing, for I will not tell you until my plan has been accomplished." ³⁵Uzziah and the rulers said to her, "Go in peace, and may the LORD God go before you to take vengeance upon our enemies!" ³⁶Then they withdrew from the tent and returned to their posts.

See RG
219

CHAPTER 9

The Prayer of Judith. ¹Judith threw herself down prostrate, with ashes strewn upon her head, and wearing nothing over her sackcloth. While the incense was being offered in the temple of God in Jerusalem that evening, Judith prayed to the LORD with a loud voice:^h ²"LORD, God of my forefather Simeon! You put a sword into his hand to take revenge upon the foreigners who had immodestly loosened the maiden's* girdle, shamefully exposed her thighs, and disgracefully violated her body. This they did, though you forbade it.ⁱ ³Therefore you had their rulers slaughtered; and you covered with their blood the bed in which they lay deceived, the same bed that had felt the shame of their own deceiving. You smote the slaves together with their princes, and the princes together with their servants.* ⁴Their wives you handed over to plunder, and their daughters to captivity; and all the spoils you divided among your favored sons, who burned with zeal for you, and in their abhorrence of the defilement of their kinswoman, called on you for help.

⁵"O God, my God, hear me also, a widow. It is you who were the author of those events and of what preceded and followed them. The present, also, and the future you have planned. Whatever you devise comes into being;^j ⁶the things you decide on come forward and say, 'Here we are!' All your ways are in readiness, and your judgment is made with foreknowledge.^k

⁷"Here are the Assyrians, a vast force, priding themselves on horse and rider, boasting of the power of their infantry, trusting in shield and spear, bow and sling. They do not know that

⁸ " 'You, the LORD, crush warfare;
Lord is your name.'

"Shatter their strength in your might, and crush their force in your wrath; for they have resolved to profane your sanctuary, to defile the tent where your glorious name resides, and to overthrow with iron the horns of your altar. ⁹See their pride, and send forth your wrath upon their heads. Give me, a widow, the strong hand to execute my plan.^m ¹⁰With the guile of my lips, smite the slave together with the ruler, the ruler together with his servant; crush their pride by the hand of a woman.

¹¹"Your strength is not in numbers, nor does your power depend upon stalwart men; but you are the God of the lowly, the helper of the oppressed, the supporter of the weak, the protector of the forsaken, the savior of those without hope.

9, 2: The maiden's: Dinah, Jacob's daughter, who was violated by Shechem, the Hivite (Gn 34, 2).

9, 3: Because Shechem had deceived and violated Dinah, her brothers, Simeon and Levi, tricked Shechem and the men of his city into being circumcised, and then slew them while they were confined to bed from the circumcision; cf Gn 34, 13-29.

h: Ex 30, 7f; Ps 141, 2.   *i:* Gn 34.   *j:* Is 44, 7.   *k:* Jb 38, 35; Is 46, 9-13; Bar 3, 35.   *l:* 7f: Jdt 5, 23; 6, 2; 16, 2.   *m:* Ps 33, 16.

[12]"Please, please, God of my forefather, God of the heritage of Israel, LORD of heaven and earth, Creator of the waters, King of all you have created, hear my prayer! [13]Let my guileful speech bring wound and wale on those who have planned dire things against your covenant, your holy temple, Mount Zion, and the homes your children have inherited.[n] [14]Let your whole nation and all the tribes know clearly that you are the God of all power and might, and that there is no other who protects the people of Israel but you alone."

See RG 219

CHAPTER 10

Judith's Departure. [1]As soon as Judith had thus concluded, and ceased her invocation to the God of Israel, [2]she rose from the ground. She called her maid and they went down into the house, which she used only on sabbaths and feast days. [3]She took off the sackcloth she had on, laid aside the garments of her widowhood, washed her body with water, and anointed it with rich ointment. She arranged her hair and bound it with a fillet, and put on the festive attire she had worn while her husband, Manasseh, was living.[o] [4]She chose sandals for her feet, and put on her anklets, bracelets, rings, earrings, and all her other jewelry. Thus she made herself very beautiful, to captivate the eyes of all the men who should see her.[p]

[5]She gave her maid a leather flask of wine and a cruse of oil. She filled a bag with roasted grain, fig cakes, bread and cheese; all these provisions she wrapped up and gave to the maid to carry.[q]

[6]Then they went out to the gate of the city of Bethulia and found Uzziah and the elders of the city, Chabris and Charmis, standing there. [7]When these men saw Judith transformed in looks and differently dressed, they were very much astounded at her beauty and said to her, [8]"May the God of our fathers bring you to favor, and make your undertaking a success, for the glory of the Israelites and the exaltation of Jerusalem."

Judith bowed down to God. Then she said to them, [9]"Order the gate of the city opened for me, that I may go to carry out the business we discussed." So they ordered the youths to open the gate for her as she requested. [10]When they did so, Judith and her maid went out. The men of the city kept her in view as she went down the mountain and crossed the valley; then they lost sight of her.

Judith Captured. [11]As Judith and her maid walked directly across the valley, they encountered the Assyrian outpost. [12]The men took her in custody and asked her, "To what people do you belong? Where do you come from, and where are you going?" She replied: "I am a daughter of the Hebrews, and I am fleeing from them, because they are about to be delivered up to you as prey.* [13]I have come to see Holofernes, the general in chief of your forces, to give him a trustworthy report; I will show him the route by which he can ascend and take possession of the whole mountain district without a single one of his men suffering injury or loss of life."[r]

[14]When the men heard her words and gazed upon her face, which appeared wondrously beautiful to them, they said to her, [15]"By coming down thus promptly to see our master, you have saved your life. Now go to his tent; some of our men will accompany you to present you to him. [16]When you stand before him, have no fear in your heart; give him the report you speak of, and he will treat you well." [17]So they detailed a hundred of their men as an escort for her and her maid, and these conducted them to the tent of Holofernes.

[18]When the news of her arrival spread among the tents, a crowd gathered in the camp. They came and stood around her as she waited outside the tent of Holofernes, while he was being informed about her. [19]They marveled at her beauty, regarding the Israelites with wonder because of her, and they said to one another, "Who can despise this people that has such women among them? It is not wise to leave one man of them alive, for if any were to be spared they could beguile the whole world."

10, 12f: The deceitful means used by Judith against Holofernes, here and in Jdt 11, 5-19, are to be judged in the light of the moral concepts of Old Testament times; cf Gn 27, 1-25; 34, 13-29; 37, 32ff; Jos 2, 1-7; Jgs 4, 17-22.

---

n: Jdt 10, 4; 11, 20. 23; 16, 6. 9. *o:* Jdt 8, 6ff. *p:* Jdt 9, 13. *q:* Jdt 12, 2. *r:* Jdt 11, 5f.

Judith Meets Holofernes. [20]The guard of Holofernes and all his servants came out and ushered her into the tent. [21]Now Holofernes was reclining on his bed under a canopy with a netting of crimson and gold, emeralds and other precious stones. [22]When they announced her to him, he came out to the antechamber, preceded by silver lamps; [23]and when Holofernes and his servants beheld Judith, they all marveled at the beauty of her face. She threw herself down prostrate before him, but his servants raised her up.

CHAPTER 11

See RG 219

[1]Then Holofernes said to her: "Take courage, lady; have no fear in your heart! Never have I harmed anyone who chose to serve Nebuchadnezzar, king of all the earth. [2]Nor would I have raised my spear against your people who dwell in the mountain region, had they not despised me and brought this upon themselves. [3]But now tell me why you fled from them and came to us. In any case, you have come to safety. Take courage! Your life is spared tonight and for the future. [4]No one at all will harm you. Rather, you will be well treated, as are all the servants of my lord, King Nebuchadnezzar."

[5]s Judith answered him: "Listen to the words of your servant, and let your handmaid speak in your presence! I will tell no lie to my lord this night, [6]and if you follow out the words of your handmaid, God will give you complete success, and my lord will not fail in any of his undertakings. [7]By the life of Nebuchadnezzar, king of all the earth, and by the power of him who has sent you to set all creatures aright! not only do men serve him through you; but even the wild beasts and the cattle and the birds of the air, because of your strength, will live for Nebuchadnezzar and his whole house.[t] [8]Indeed, we have heard of your wisdom and sagacity, and all the world is aware that throughout the kingdom you alone are competent, rich in experience, and distinguished in military strategy.

[9]u "As for Achior's speech in your council, we have heard of it. When the men of Bethulia spared him, he told them all he had said to you. [10]So then, my lord and master, do not disregard his word, but bear it in mind, for it is true. For our people are not punished, nor does the sword prevail against them, except when they sin against their God.[v] [11]But now their guilt has caught up with them by which they bring the wrath of their God upon them whenever they do wrong; so that my lord will not be repulsed and fail, but death will overtake them. [12]Since their food gave out and all their water ran low, they decided to kill their animals, and determined to consume all the things which God in his laws forbade them to eat. [13]They decreed that they would use up the first fruits of grain and the tithes of wine and oil which they had sanctified and reserved for the priests who minister in the presence of our God in Jerusalem: things which no layman should even touch with his hands. [14]They have sent messengers to Jerusalem to bring back to them authorization from the council of the elders; for the inhabitants there have also done these things. [15]On the very day when the response reaches them and they act upon it, they will be handed over to you for destruction.

[16]"As soon as I, your handmaid, learned all this, I fled from them. God has sent me to perform with you such deeds that people throughout the world will be astonished on hearing of them. [17]Your handmaid is, indeed, a God-fearing woman, serving the God of heaven night and day. Now I will remain with you, my lord; but each night your handmaid will go out to the ravine and pray to God. He will tell me when the Israelites have committed their crimes. [18]Then I will come and let you know, so that you may go out with your whole force, and not one of them will be able to withstand you. [19]I will lead you through Judea, till you come to Jerusalem, and there I will set up your judgment seat. You will drive them like sheep that have no shepherd, and not even a dog will growl at you. This was told me, and announced to me in advance, and I in turn have been sent to tell you."

[20]Her words pleased Holofernes and all his servants; they marveled at her wisdom

s: 5f: Jdt 10, 13.   *t:* Jer 27, 6; Bar 3, 16f; Dn 2, 38.   *u:* 9f: Jdt 5, 5.   *v:* Jdt 5, 21; 8, 18.

and exclaimed,^{w} ^{21}"No other woman from one end of the world to the other looks so beautiful and speaks so wisely!" ^{22}Then Holofernes said to her: "God has done well in sending you ahead of your people, to bring victory to our arms, and destruction to those who have despised my lord. ^{23}You are fair to behold, and your words are well spoken. If you do as you have said, your God will be my God; you shall dwell in the palace of King Nebuchadnezzar, and shall be renowned throughout the earth."^{x}

See RG 219

CHAPTER 12

Judith's Conduct. ^{1}Then he ordered them to lead her into the room where his silverware was kept, and bade them set a table for her with his own delicacies to eat and his own wine to drink. ^{2}But Judith said, "I will not partake of them, lest it be an occasion of sin; but I shall be amply supplied from the things I brought with me."^{y} ^{3}Holofernes asked her: "But if your provisions give out, where shall we get more of the same to provide for you? None of your people are with us." ^{4}Judith answered him, "As surely as you, my lord, live, your handmaid will not use up her supplies till the Lord accomplishes by my hand what he has determined."

^{5}Then the servants of Holofernes led her into the tent, where she slept till midnight. In the night watch just before dawn, she rose ^{6}and sent this message to Holofernes, "Give orders, my lord, to let your handmaid go out for prayer." ^{7}So Holofernes ordered his bodyguard not to hinder her. Thus she stayed in the camp three days. Each night she went out to the ravine of Bethulia, where she washed herself at the spring of the camp. ^{8}After bathing, she besought the Lord, the God of Israel, to direct her way for the triumph of his people. ^{9}Then she returned purified to the tent, and remained there until her food was brought to her toward evening.

Holofernes' Banquet. ^{10}On the fourth day Holofernes gave a banquet for his servants alone, to which he did not invite any of the officers.* ^{11}And he said to Bagoas, the eunuch in charge of his household: "Go and persuade this Hebrew woman in your care to come and to eat and drink with us. ^{12}It would be a disgrace for us to have such a woman with us without enjoying her company. If we do not entice her, she will laugh us to scorn."

^{13}So Bagoas left the presence of Holofernes, and came to Judith and said, "So fair a maiden should not be reluctant to come to my lord to be honored by him, to enjoy drinking wine with us, and to be like one of the Assyrian women who live in the palace of Nebuchadnezzar." ^{14}She replied, "Who am I to refuse my lord? Whatever is pleasing to him I will promptly do. This will be a joy for me till the day of my death."

^{15}Thereupon she proceeded to put on her festive garments and all her feminine adornments. Meanwhile her maid went ahead and spread out on the ground for her in front of Holofernes the fleece Bagoas had furnished for her daily use in reclining at her dinner. ^{16}Then Judith came in and reclined on it. The heart of Holofernes was in rapture over her, and his spirit was shaken. He was burning with the desire to possess her, for he had been biding his time to seduce her from the day he saw her. ^{17}Holofernes said to her, "Drink and be merry with us!" ^{18}Judith replied, "I will gladly drink, my lord, for at no time since I was born have I ever enjoyed life as much as I do today." ^{19}She then took the things her maid had prepared, and ate and drank in his presence. ^{20}Holofernes, charmed by her, drank a great quantity of wine, more than he had ever drunk on one single day in his life.

CHAPTER 13

See RG 219

^{1}When it grew late, his servants quickly withdrew. Bagoas closed the tent from the outside and excluded the attendants from their master's presence. They went off to their beds, for they were all tired from the prolonged banquet. ^{2}Judith was left alone in the tent with Holofernes, who lay prostrate on his bed, for he was sodden with wine.

12, 10: Banquet for his servants alone . . . officers: Holofernes invited the officials of his household, but not the officers of his army who were needed for military duty.

---

w: Jdt 9, 13.   *x:* Jdt 9, 13.   *y:* Jdt 10, 5; Dn 1, 8.

³She had ordered her maid to stand outside the bedroom and wait, as on the other days, for her to come out; she said she would be going out for her prayer. To Bagoas she had said this also.

Beheading of Holofernes. ⁴When all had departed, and no one, small or great, was left in the bedroom, Judith stood by Holofernes' bed and said within herself: "O LORD, God of all might, in this hour look graciously on my undertaking for the exaltation of Jerusalem; ⁵now is the time for aiding your heritage and for carrying out my design to shatter the enemies who have risen against us." ⁶She went to the bedpost near the head of Holofernes, and taking his sword from it, ⁷drew close to the bed, grasped the hair of his head, and said, "Strengthen me this day, O God of Israel!" ⁸Then with all her might she struck him twice in the neck and cut off his head.ᶻ ⁹She rolled his body off the bed and took the canopy from its supports. Soon afterward, she came out and handed over the head of Holofernes to her maid, ¹⁰who put it into her food pouch; and the two went off together as they were accustomed to do for prayer.

The Return to Bethulia. They passed through the camp, and skirting the ravine, reached Bethulia on the mountain. As they approached its gates, ¹¹Judith shouted to the guards from a distance: "Open! Open the gate! God, our God, is with us. Once more he has made manifest his strength in Israel and his power against our enemies; he has done it this very day." ¹²When the citizens heard her voice, they quickly descended to their city gate and summoned the city elders. ¹³All the people, from the least to the greatest, hurriedly assembled, for her return seemed unbelievable. They opened the gate and welcomed the two women. They made a fire for light; and when they gathered around the two, ¹⁴Judith urged them with a loud voice: "Praise God, praise him! Praise God, who has not withdrawn his mercy from the house of Israel, but has shattered our enemies by my hand this very night." ¹⁵Then she took the head out of the pouch, showed it to them, and said: "Here is the head of Holofernes, general in charge of the Assyrian army, and here is the canopy under which he lay in his drunkenness. The LORD struck him down by the hand of a woman.ᵃ ¹⁶As the LORD lives, who has protected me in the path I have followed, I swear that it was my face that seduced Holofernes to his ruin, and that he did not sin with me to my defilement or disgrace."

¹⁷All the people were greatly astonished. They bowed down and worshiped God, saying with one accord, "Blessed are you, our God, who today have brought to nought the enemies of your people." ¹⁸Then Uzziah said to her: "Blessed are you, daughter, by the Most High God, above all the women on earth; and blessed be the LORD God, the creator of heaven and earth, who guided your blow at the head of the chief of our enemies.ᵇ ¹⁹Your deed of hope will never be forgotten by those who tell of the might of God. ²⁰May God make this redound to your everlasting honor, rewarding you with blessings, because you risked your life when your people were being oppressed, and you averted our disaster, walking uprightly before our God." And all the people answered, "Amen! Amen!"

CHAPTER 14

See RG 219

Judith's Counsel. ¹Then Judith said to them: "Listen to me, my brothers. Take this head and hang it on the parapet of your wall. ²At daybreak, when the sun rises on the earth, let each of you seize his weapons, and let all the able-bodied men rush out of the city under command of a captain, as if about to go down into the plain against the advance guard of the Assyrians, but without going down. ³They will seize their armor and hurry to their camp to awaken the generals of the Assyrian army. When they run to the tent of Holofernes and do not find him, panic will seize them, and they will flee before you. ⁴Then you and all the other inhabitants of the whole territory of Israel will pursue them and strike them down in their tracks. ⁵But before doing this, summon for me Achior the Ammonite, that he may see and recognize the one who despised the

z: Jgs 4, 21.   a: Jdt 14, 18.   b: Jgs 5, 24; Lk 1, 28. 42.

house of Israel and sent him here to meet his death."

Achior Summoned.* ⁶So they called Achior from the house of Uzziah. When he came and saw the head of Holofernes in the hand of one of the men in the assembly of the people, he fell forward in a faint. ⁷Then, after they lifted him up, he threw himself at the feet of Judith in homage, saying: "Blessed are you in every tent of Judah; and in every foreign nation, all who hear of you will be struck with terror. ⁸But now, tell me all that you did during these days." So Judith told him, in the presence of the people, all that she had been doing from the day she left till the time she began speaking to them. ⁹When she finished her account, the people cheered loudly, and their city resounded with shouts of joy. ¹⁰Now Achior, seeing all that the God of Israel had done, believed firmly in him. He had the flesh of his foreskin circumcised, and he has been united with the house of Israel to the present day.

III: Victory

Consternation in the Camp. ¹¹At daybreak they hung the head of Holofernes on the wall. Then all the Israelite men took up their arms and went to the slopes of the mountain. ¹²When the Assyrians saw them, they notified their captains; these, in turn, went to the generals and division leaders and all their other commanders. ¹³They came to the tent of Holofernes and said to the one in charge of all his things, "Waken our master, for the slaves have dared come down to give us battle, to their utter destruction." ¹⁴Bagoas went in, and knocked at the entry of the tent, presuming that he was sleeping with Judith. ¹⁵As no one answered, he parted the curtains, entered the bedroom, and found him lying on the floor, a headless corpse. ¹⁶He broke into a loud clamor of weeping, groaning, and howling, and rent his garments. ¹⁷Then he entered the tent where Judith had her quarters; and, not finding her, he rushed out to the

troops and cried: ¹⁸"The slaves have duped us! A single Hebrew woman has brought disgrace on the house of King Nebuchadnezzar. Here is Holofernes headless on the ground!"ᶜ ¹⁹When the commanders of the Assyrian army heard these words, they rent their tunics and were seized with consternation. Loud screaming and howling arose in the camp.

CHAPTER 15

See RG 219

¹On hearing what had happened, those still in their tents were amazed, ²and overcome with fear and trembling. No one kept ranks any longer; they scattered in all directions, and fled along every road, both through the valley and in the mountains. ³Those also who were stationed in the mountain district around Bethulia took to flight. Then all the Israelite warriors overwhelmed them.

Pursuit. ⁴Uzziah sent messengers to Betomasthaim, to Choba and Kona, and to the whole country of Israel to report what had happened, that all might fall upon the enemy and destroy them. ⁵On hearing this, all the Israelites, with one accord, attacked them and cut them down as far as Choba. Even those from Jerusalem and the rest of the mountain region took part in this, for they too had been notified of the happenings in the camp of their enemies. The Gileadites and the Galileans struck the enemy's flanks with great slaughter, even beyond Damascus and its territory. ⁶The remaining inhabitants of Bethulia swept down on the camp of the Assyrians, plundered it, and acquired great riches. ⁷The Israelites who returned from the slaughter took possession of what was left, till the towns and villages in the mountains and on the plain were crammed with the enormous quantity of booty they had seized.ᵈ

⁸The high priest Joakim and the elders of the Israelites, who dwelt in Jerusalem, came to see for themselves the good things that the LORD had done for Israel, and to meet and congratulate Judith.ᵉ ⁹When they had visited her, all with one accord blessed her, saying:

14, 6-10: In recognizing the head of Holofernes, whom he had known personally, Achior was so overcome with the evidence of the Lord's power exerted through a woman that he believed in the God of Israel.

c: Jdt 13, 15; 16, 5-9; Jgs 9, 54.   *d:* Est 9, 5. 16.   *e:* Est 9, 10.

"You are the glory of Jerusalem,
  the surpassing joy of Israel;
  you are the splendid boast of our
    people.*
[10] With your own hand you have done all
    this;
  you have done good to Israel,
  and God is pleased with what you
    have wrought.
  May you be blessed by the LORD
    Almighty
  forever and ever!"

And all the people answered, "Amen!"

[11] For thirty days the whole populace plundered the camp, giving Judith the tent of Holofernes, with all his silver, his couches, his dishes, and all his furniture, which she accepted. She harnessed her mules, hitched her wagons to them, and loaded these things on them.

[12] All the women of Israel gathered to see her; and they blessed her and performed a dance in her honor. She took branches in her hands and distributed them to the women around her,[f] [13] and she and the other women crowned themselves with garlands of olive leaves. At the head of all the people, she led the women in the dance, while the men of Israel followed in their armor, wearing garlands and singing hymns.

Hymn of Praise. [14] Judith led all Israel in this song of thanksgiving, and the people swelled this hymn of praise:

CHAPTER 16

See RG
219

[1] "Strike up the instruments,
  a song to my God with timbrels,
  chant to the LORD with cymbals;
  Sing to him a new song,
  exalt and acclaim his name.[g]
[2] For the LORD is God; he crushes warfare,
  and sets his encampment among his
    people;
  he snatched me from the hands of my
    persecutors.[h]

[3] "The Assyrian came from the mountains
    of the north,
  with the myriads of his forces he
    came;
  Their numbers blocked the torrents, their
    horses covered the hills.
[4] He threatened to burn my land,
  put my youths to the sword,
  Dash my babes to the ground,
  make my children a prey,
  and seize my virgins as spoil.

[5] "But the LORD Almighty thwarted them,
  by a woman's hand he confounded
    them.[i]
[6] Not by youths was their mighty one
    struck down,
  nor did titans bring him low,
  nor huge giants attack him;
  But Judith, the daughter of Merari,
  by the beauty of her countenance
    disabled him.[j]
[7] She took off her widow's garb
  to raise up the afflicted in Israel.
  She anointed her face with fragrant oil;
[8]   with a fillet she fastened her tresses
  and put on a linen robe to beguile him.
[9] Her sandals caught his eyes,
  and her beauty captivated his mind.
  The sword cut through his neck.[k]

[10] "The Persians were dismayed at her
    daring,
  the Medes appalled at her boldness.
[11] When my lowly ones shouted, they were
    terrified;
  when my weaklings cried out, they
    trembled;
  at the sound of their war cry, they took
    to flight.
[12] The sons of slave girls pierced them
    through;
  the supposed sons of rebel mothers cut
    them down;
  they perished before the ranks of my
    LORD.

15, 9: You are the glory of Jerusalem, the surpassing joy of Israel; you are the splendid boast of our people: these words are used in the liturgy of the Church in regard to the Blessed Virgin Mary.

f: Ex 15, 20f; Jgs 11, 34; 1 Sm 18, 6; Jer 31, 4. 13. g: Pss 81, 2f; 135, 1ff; 149, 1ff. h: Jdt 5, 23; 6, 2; 9. 7f; Ex 15, 3; Ps 46, 10.
i: Jdt 14, 8. j: Jdt 9, 13. k: Jdt 9, 13.

[13] "A new hymn I will sing to my God.
O LORD, great are you and glorious,
  wonderful in power and
    unsurpassable.[l]
[14] Let your every creature serve you;
  for you spoke, and they were made,
You sent forth your spirit, and they were
    created;
  no one can resist your word.[m]
[15] The mountains to their bases, and the
    seas, are shaken;
  the rocks, like wax, melt before your
    glance.[n]

"But to those who fear you,
  you are very merciful.
[16] Though the sweet odor of every sacrifice
    is a trifle,
  and the fat of all holocausts but little in
    your sight,
  one who fears the LORD is forever
    great.[o]

[17] "Woe to the nations that rise against my
    people!
  The LORD Almighty will requite them;
  in the day of judgment he will punish
    them:
He will send fire and worms into their
    flesh,[*]
  and they shall burn and suffer
    forever."[p]

Thanksgiving. [18]The people then went to Jerusalem to worship God; when they were purified, they offered their holocausts, free-will offerings, and gifts. [19]Judith dedicated, as a votive offering to God, all the things of Holofernes that the people had given her, as well as the canopy that she herself had taken from his bedroom.[q] [20]For three months the people continued their celebration in Jerusalem before the sanctuary, and Judith remained with them.

Judith's Renown. [21]When those days were over, each one returned to his inheritance. Judith went back to Bethulia and remained on her estate. For the rest of her life she was renowned throughout the land. [22]Many wished to marry her, but she gave herself to no man all the days of her life from the time of the death and burial of her husband, Manasseh. [23]She lived to be very old in the house of her husband, reaching the advanced age of a hundred and five. She died in Bethulia, where they buried her in the tomb of her husband, Manasseh;[r] [24]and the house of Israel mourned her for seven days. Before she died, she distributed her goods to the relatives of her husband, Manasseh, and to her own relatives; and to the maid she gave her freedom.

[25s]During the life of Judith and for a long time after her death, no one again disturbed the Israelites.[*]

16, 17: Fire and worms into their flesh: see footnote on Is 66, 24.

16, 25: The Vulgate adds: "The feast day of this victory was adopted by the Hebrews into the calendar of their holy days, and has been celebrated by the Jews from that time to the present." However, there is no other evidence of such a festivity; and it is the ancient feast of Passover to which the narrative is especially suited.

---

l: Ps 144, 9.   *m:* Pss 33, 9; 104, 30; 148, 5.   *n:* Jgs 5, 5; Ps 97, 5.   *o:* Ps 86, 11; Sir 34, 13-17.   *p:* Is 66, 24.   *q:* Nm 31, 48-54; Dt 13, 13-18; Jos 6, 18f.   *r:* Gn 23, 19; 49, 29-32.   *s:* Jgs 3, 11. 30; 5, 31; 8, 28.

See RG
222-26

The Book of Esther

The Book of Esther is named after its Jewish hero-ine. It tells the story of the plot of Haman the Ag-agite, jealous and powerful vizier of King Xerxes (Ahasuerus) of Persia (485–464 B.C.), to destroy in a single day all the Jews living in the Persian Empire. He is moved to this out of hatred for the Jewish servant Mordecai, who for religious mo-tives refuses to render him homage. The day of the proposed massacre is determined by lot. Mean-

while Esther, niece and adopted daughter of Mor-decai, is chosen queen by King Xerxes in place of Vashti. She averts the pogrom planned against her people and has the royal decree of extermination reversed against Haman and the enemies of the Jews. Mordecai replaces Haman, and together with Esther, works for the welfare of their people. The event is celebrated with feasting and great joy, and the memory of it is to be perpetuated by the annual observance of the feast of Purim (lots), when the lot of destruction for the Jews was reversed for one of deliverance and triumph by Queen Esther and her uncle Mordecai.

The purpose of the book is didactic: the glorification of the Jewish people and the explanation of the origin, significance and date of the feast of Purim on the fourteenth and fifteenth of Adar (February–March). The book was intended as a consolation for Israel, a reminder that God's providence continually watches over them, never abandoning them when they serve him faithfully or turn to him in sincere repentance. There is no justification for interpreting the story in mythological or cultic terms, as though Mordecai and Esther represented Marduk and Ishtar in their mythological triumph over two Elamite deities.

The Hebrew text of Esther is found in the Hebrew Bible, where it is the last of the five megilloth (scrolls) read on special feasts of the Jewish liturgical year.

The book is a free composition—not a historical document, despite the Achaemenian coloring of the narrative. Its time of composition may well have been at the end of the Persian Empire, toward the close of the fourth century B.C. The author shows skill in developing his story and in using the art of contrast for instruction and edification. The solution to the difficulties of the book is to be found in its literary presentation rather than in a forced attempt to square detailed data of the narrative with facts. The evident literary motif of the reversal of fortune of the prosperous wicked and the oppressed virtuous through eventual punishment of the former and triumph of the latter finds parallels in the story of Joseph (Gn 37; 39—45) and of Judith (8—16). The book is vindictive, but it should be remembered that the precept of love of enemies had not yet been taught by the word and example of Christ.

The text of Esther, written originally in Hebrew, was transmitted in two forms: a short Hebrew form and a longer Greek version. The latter contains 107 additional verses, inserted at appropriate places

within the Hebrew form of the text. A few of these seem to have a Hebrew origin while the rest are Greek in original composition. It is possible that the Hebrew form of the text is original throughout. If it systematically omits reference to God and his Providence over Israel, this is perhaps due to fear of irreverent response (see note on 4, 14). The Greek text with the above-mentioned additions is probably a later literary paraphrase in which the author seeks to have the reader share his sentiments. This standard Greek text is pre-Christian in origin. The church has accepted the additions as equally inspired with the rest of the book.

In the present translation, the portions preceded by the letters A through F indicate the underlying Greek additions referred to above. The regular chapter numbers apply to the Hebrew text.

The book may be divided as follows:

I: Prologue (A, 1-17).

II: Elevation of Esther (1, 1—2, 23).

III: Haman's Plot against the Jews (3, 1-13; B, 1-7; 3, 14—4, 8; B, 8; 4, 9-16; C, 1—D, 16; 5, 1-14).

IV: Vindication of the Jews (6, 1—8, 12; E, 1-24; 8, 13—10, 3).

V: Epilogue (F, 1-11).

The order of the Vulgate text in relation to the order of the Greek text is as follows:

Vulg. 11, 2—12, 6 = A, 1—17 at the beginning of the book.

13, 1-7 = B, 1-7 after 3, 13.

13, 8—15, 3-19 = C, 1—D, 16 after 4, 16.

15, 1-2 = B, 8. 9 after 4, 8.

16, 1-24 = E, 1-24 after 8, 12.

10, 4—10, 13 = F, 1-10 after 10, 3.

I: Prologue

CHAPTER A

See RG 222-26

Dream of Mordecai. [1]In the second year of the reign of the great King Ahasuerus,* on the first day of Nisan, Mordecai,

---

A, 1: King Ahasuerus: Xerxes I (485–464 B.C.). Mordecai: a Babylonian name, after the God Marduk. The genealogy of Mordecai is designed to reflect opposition to Israel's enemy, as narrated in 1 Sm 15, 7ff, where Saul (whose father's name was Kish, of the Tribe of Benjamin) conquered Agag the Amalekite; in A, 17 Haman is said to be the son of an Agagite. Further emphasis on the

Benjaminite-Agagite opposition can be seen in Shimei, the Benjaminite who reviled David (2 Sm 16, 5ff). Jair appears to be the minor Judge, a Transjordan Manassehite (Jgs 10, 3). The chronology of the book would make Mordecai well over one hundred years old, since he was deported with Jehoiachin about 598 B.C.; cf Est 2, 5f.

son of Jair, son of Shimei, son of Kish, of the tribe of Benjamin, had a dream.*a* *2*He was a Jew residing in the city of Susa, a prominent man who served at the king's court, *3*and one of the captives whom Nebuchadnezzar, king of Babylon, had taken from Jerusalem with Jeconiah, king of Judah.*b*

*4c*This was his dream.* There was noise and tumult, thunder and earthquake—confusion upon the earth. *5*Two great dragons came on, both poised for combat. They uttered a mighty cry, *6*and at their cry every nation prepared for war, to fight against the race of the just. *7*It was a dark and gloomy day. Tribulation and distress, evil and great confusion, lay upon the earth. *8*The whole race of the just were dismayed with fear of the evils to come upon them, and were at the point of destruction. *9d*Then they cried out to God, and as they cried, there appeared to come forth a great river, a flood of water from a little spring. *10*The light of the sun broke forth; the lowly were exalted and they devoured the nobles.

*11*Having seen this dream and what God intended to do, Mordecai awoke. He kept it in mind, and tried in every way, until night, to understand its meaning.

The Plot Discovered. *12e*Mordecai lodged at the court with Bagathan and Thares, two eunuchs of the king who were court guards. *13*He overheard them plotting, investigated their plans, and discovered that they were preparing to lay hands on King Ahasuerus. So he informed the king about them, *14*and the king had the two eunuchs questioned and, upon their confession, put to death. *15*Then the king had these things recorded; Mordecai, too, put them into writing. *16*The king also appointed Mordecai to serve at the court, and rewarded him* for his actions.*f*

*17*Haman, however, son of Hammedatha the Agagite,* who was in high honor with the king, sought to harm Mordecai and his people because of the two eunuchs of the king.*g*

II: Elevation of Esther

CHAPTER 1

See RG 222-26

The Banquet of Ahasuerus. *1*During the reign of Ahasuerus—this was the Ahasuerus who ruled over a hundred and twenty-seven provinces from India to Ethiopia*— *2*while he was occupying the royal throne in the stronghold of Susa,* *3*in the third year of his reign, he presided over a feast for all his officers and ministers: the Persian and Median aristocracy, the nobles, and the governors of the provinces.*h* *4*For as many as a hundred and eighty days, he displayed the glorious riches of his kingdom and the resplendent wealth of his royal estate.

*5*At the end of this time the king gave a feast of seven days in the garden court of the royal palace for all the people, great and small, who were in the stronghold of Susa. *6*There were white cotton draperies and violet hangings, held by cords of crimson byssus from silver rings on marble pillars. Gold and silver couches were on the pavement, which was of porphyry, marble, mother-of-pearl, and colored stones. *7*Liquor was served in a variety of golden cups, and the royal wine flowed freely, as befitted the king's munificence. *8*By ordinance of the king the drinking was unstinted, for he had instructed all the stewards of his household to comply with the good pleasure of everyone.

*9*Queen Vashti* also gave a feast for the women inside the royal palace of King Ahasuerus.

A, 4: The interpretation of this dream is given in Est F, 1-6.

A, 16: Rewarded him: this reward comes only later; see the sequence of events from the Hebrew text of Esther at 2, 22f, and 6, 3, below.

A, 17: Haman . . . the Agagite: opposed Mordecai the Benjaminite, by whom, however, he was overcome (Est 7, 9f), just as King Agag the Amalekite, was conquered by King Saul ancestor of Mordecai (1 Sm 15, 7ff).

1, 1: From India to Ethiopia: from western India to Upper Egypt, the greatest extent of the Persian Empire achieved under Darius the Great, father of Ahasuerus.

1, 2: Susa: ancient capital of Elam (Gn 14, 1); under the Achamenid kings, one of the two capitals of the Persian Empire. The other was Persepolis, the summer palace of the kings.

1, 9: Queen Vashti: Herodotus (Histories 7, 61) relates that the wife of Ahasuerus was Amestris.

---

a: Est 2, 5. *b:* Est 2, 6; 2 Kgs 24, 15; 2 Chr 36, 9f; Jer 22, 24ff; 24, 1; 29, 1f. *c:* 4ff: Est F, 2. 4ff. *d:* gf: Est F, 3. *e:* 12-15: Est 2, 21ff; 6, 1ff. *f:* Est 6, 3. *g:* Est 3, 1-15; B, 1-7; E, 13. *h:* Jdt 1, 16.

The Persian Empire

Deposal of Vashti. [10]On the seventh day, when the king was merry with wine, he instructed Mehuman, Biztha, Harbona, Bigtha, Abagtha, Zethar, and Carkas, the seven eunuchs who attended King Ahasuerus,[i] [11]to bring Queen Vashti into his presence wearing the royal crown, that he might display her beauty to the populace and the officials, for she was lovely to behold. [12]But Queen Vashti refused to come at the royal order issued through the eunuchs. At this the king's wrath flared up, and he burned with fury. [13]He conferred with the wise men versed in the law, because the king's business was conducted in general consultation with lawyers and jurists. [14]He summoned Carshena, Shethar, Admatha, Tarshish, Meres, Marsena and Memucan, the seven Persian and Median officials who were in the king's personal service and held first rank in the realm,[j] [15]and asked them, "What is to be done by law with Queen Vashti for disobeying the order of King Ahasuerus issued through the eunuchs?"

[16]In the presence of the king and of the officials, Memucan answered: "Queen Vashti has not wronged the king alone, but all the officials and the populace throughout the provinces of King Ahasuerus. [17]For the queen's conduct will become known to all the women, and they will look with disdain upon their husbands when it is reported, 'King Ahasuerus commanded that Queen Vashti be ushered into his presence, but she would not come.' [18]This very day the Persian and Median ladies who hear of the queen's conduct will rebel against all the royal officials, with corresponding disdain and rancor. [19]If it please the king, let an irrevocable royal decree* be issued by him and inscribed among the laws of the Persians and Medes, forbidding Vashti to come into the presence

1, 19: Irrevocable royal decree: the historian Siculus indicates that such a concept of irrevocable laws existed in the time of Darius III (335–331 B.C.), the last of the Persian kings, cf Est 8, 8.

i: Dn 5, 1.   *j*: Ezr 7, 14.

of King Ahasuerus and authorizing the king to give her royal dignity to one more worthy than she.[k] [20]Thus, when the decree which the king will issue is published throughout his realm, vast as it is, all wives will honor their husbands, from the greatest to the least."

[21]This proposal found acceptance with the king and the officials, and the king acted on the advice of Memucan. [22]He sent letters to all the royal provinces, to each province in its own script and to each people in its own language,[*] to the effect that every man should be lord in his own home.

See RG 222-26

CHAPTER 2

Esther Made Queen. [1]After this, when King Ahasuerus' wrath had cooled, he thought over what Vashti had done and what had been decreed against her. [2]Then the king's personal attendants suggested: "Let beautiful young virgins be sought for the king. [3]Let the king appoint commissaries in all the provinces of his realm to bring together all beautiful young virgins to the harem in the stronghold of Susa. Under the care of the royal eunuch Hegai, custodian of the women, let cosmetics be given them. [4]Then the girl who pleases the king shall reign in place of Vashti." This suggestion pleased the king, and he acted accordingly.

[5]There was in the stronghold of Susa a certain Jew named Mordecai, son of Jair, son of Shimei, son of Kish, a Benjaminite, [6]who had been exiled from Jerusalem with the captives taken with Jeconiah, king of Judah, whom Nebuchadnezzar, king of Babylon, had deported.[l] [7]He was foster father to Hadassah,[*] that is, Esther, his cousin; for she had lost both father and mother. The girl was beautifully formed and lovely to behold. On the death of her father and mother, Mordecai had taken her as his own daughter.[m]

[8]When the king's order and decree had been obeyed and many maidens brought together to the stronghold of Susa under the care of Hegai, Esther also was brought in to the royal palace under the care of Hegai, custodian of the women. [9]The girl pleased him and won his favor. So he promptly furnished her with cosmetics and provisions. Then picking out seven maids for her from the royal palace, he transferred both her and her maids to the best place in the harem. [10]Esther did not reveal her nationality or family, for Mordecai had commanded her not to do so.

[11]Day by day Mordecai would walk about in front of the court of the harem, to learn how Esther was faring and what was to become of her.

[12]Each girl went in turn to visit King Ahasuerus after the twelve months' preparation decreed for the women. Of this period of beautifying treatment, six months were spent with oil of myrrh, and the other six months with perfumes and cosmetics. [13]Then, when the girl was to visit the king, she was allowed to take with her from the harem to the royal palace whatever she chose. [14]She would go in the evening and return in the morning to a second harem under the care of the royal eunuch Shaashgaz, custodian of the concubines. She could not return to the king unless he was pleased with her and had her summoned by name.[n]

[15]As for Esther, daughter of Abihail and adopted daughter of his nephew Mordecai, when her turn came to visit the king, she did not ask for anything but what the royal eunuch Hegai, custodian of the women, suggested. Yet she won the admiration of all who saw her. [16]Esther was led to King Ahasuerus in his palace in the tenth month, Tebeth, in the seventh year of his reign. [17]The king loved Esther more than all other women, and of all the virgins she won his favor and benevolence. So he placed the royal diadem on her head and made her queen in place of Vashti. [18]Then the king gave a great feast in honor of Esther to all his

---

1, 22: To each province . . . script and to each people . . . language: many languages were spoken in the Persian Empire, the principal ones being Persian, Elamite, Babylonian, Aramaic, Phoenician, Egyptian, and Greek. Each of them had its own script.

2, 7: Hadassah (the feminine form of hadas, myrtle), was the name by which this woman would be known among her Jewish compatriots. Esther is a variant of the name of the Babylonian goddess Ishtar.

k: Est 8, 5. 8; Dn 6, 8f.   *l:* Est A, 3; 2 Kgs 24, 15; 2 Chr 36, 9f; Jer 22, 24ff; 24, 1; 29, 1f.   *m:* Est 2, 15.   *n:* Est 2, 19f; 4, 11. 16.

officials and ministers, granting a holiday* to the provinces and bestowing gifts with royal bounty.

The Plot Discovered.* 19o*[To resume: From the time the virgins had been brought together, and while Mordecai was passing his time at the king's gate, 20Esther had not revealed her family or nationality, because Mordecai had told her not to; and Esther continued to follow Mordecai's instructions, just as she had when she was being brought up by him. 21pAnd during the time that Mordecai spent at the king's gate,* Bagathan and Thares, two of the royal eunuchs who guarded the entrance, had plotted in anger to lay hands on King Ahasuerus. 22When the plot became known to Mordecai, he told Queen Esther, who in turn informed the king for Mordecai. 23The matter was investigated and verified, and both of them were hanged on a gibbet.* This was written in the annals for the king's use.]

III: Haman's Plot Against the Jews
CHAPTER 3

See RG 222-26 ***Mordecai Refuses To Honor Haman.*** 1After these events King Ahasuerus raised Haman, son of Hammedatha the Agagite, to high rank, seating him above all his fellow officials.q 2All the king's servants who were at the royal gate would kneel and bow down to Haman, for that is what the king had ordered in his regard.r Mordecai, however, would not kneel and bow down.* 3The king's servants who were at the royal gate said to Mordecai, "Why do you disobey the king's order?"s 4When they had reminded him day after day and he would not listen to them,

they informed Haman, to see whether Mordecai's explanation was acceptable, since he had told them that he was a Jew.

Haman's Reprisal. 5When Haman observed that Mordecai would not kneel and bow down to him, he was filled with anger. 6Moreover, he thought it was not enough to lay hands on Mordecai alone. Since they had told Haman of Mordecai's nationality, he sought to destroy all the Jews, Mordecai's people, throughout the realm of King Ahasuerus. 7In the first month, Nisan, in the twelfth year of King Ahasuerus, the pur,* or lot, was cast in Haman's presence, to determine the day and the month for the destruction of Mordecai's people on a single day, and the lot fell on the thirteenth day of the twelfth month, Adar.t

Decree against the Jews. 8Then Haman said to King Ahasuerus: "Dispersed among the nations throughout the provinces of your kingdom, there is a certain people living apart, with laws differing from those of every other people. They do not obey the laws of the king, and so it is not proper for the king to tolerate them.u 9If it please the king, let a decree be issued to destroy them; and I will deliver to the procurators ten thousand silver talents for deposit in the royal treasury."v 10The king took the signet ring* from his hand and gave it to Haman, son of Hammedatha the Agagite, the enemy of the Jews.w 11"The silver you may keep," the king said to Haman, "but as for this people, do with them whatever you please."

12So the royal scribes were summoned; and on the thirteenth day of the first month they wrote, at the dictation of Haman, an order to the royal satraps, the governors of every province, and the officials of every people, to each

---

2, 18: A holiday: or perhaps, "a remission of taxes."

2, 19-23: This is a resumption, in a slightly different form, of the story already told in Est A, 12-15.

2, 21: Mordecai . . . at the king's gate: to exercise watchful care for Esther. Some understand this to mean that Mordecai was stationed at the gate to render royal service; cf Est A, 2.

2, 23: Hanged on a gibbet: impaled, perhaps, after the Babylonian manner.

3, 2: Mordecai . . . would not kneel and bow down: in order not to render to man, the homage which he regarded as belonging to God alone; cf Est C, 5ff.

3, 7: Pur: a Babylonian word which the Hebrew translates

as goral, "lot." This word is preserved in the text because its plural, purim, became the name of the feast of Purim commemorating the deliverance of the Jews; cf Est 9, 24. 26.

3, 10: Signet ring: a ring containing a seal which was impressed on documents to authenticate them. By giving this ring to Haman, the king bestowed on him the power to authenticate royal decrees.

o: 19f: Est 2, 14. p: 21ff: Est A, 12-15; 6, 1ff. q: Est B, 3; 5, 11; E, 11. r: Est C, 5; 5, 9. 13; 6, 10. 12. s: Est 4, 16. t: Est 9, 24ff; F, 10. u: Est 3, 13; B, 4; E, 24; Dn 3, 8-12; Wis 2, 14f. v: Est 7, 4. w: Gn 41, 42.

their ancestors, as a lasting heritage, and that you fulfilled all your promises to them.[i] [17]But now we have sinned in your sight, and you have delivered us into the hands of our enemies, [18]because we worshiped their gods. You are just, O LORD. [19]But now they are not satisfied with our bitter servitude, but have undertaken [20]to do away with the decree you have pronounced, and to destroy your heritage; to close the mouths of those who praise you, and to extinguish the glory of your temple and your altar; [21]to open the mouths of the heathen to acclaim their false gods, and to extol an earthly king forever.

[22]"O LORD, do not relinquish your scepter to those that are nought. Let them not gloat over our ruin, but turn their own counsel against them and make an example of our chief enemy. [23]Be mindful of us, O LORD. Manifest yourself in the time of our distress and give me courage, King of gods and Ruler of every power. [24]Put in my mouth persuasive words in the presence of the lion and turn his heart to hatred for our enemy, so that he and those who are in league with him may perish. [25]Save us by your power, and help me, who am alone and have no one but you, O LORD.

"You know all things. [26]You know that I hate the glory of the pagans, and abhor the bed of the uncircumcised or of any foreigner. [27]You know that I am under constraint, that I abhor the sign of grandeur which rests on my head when I appear in public; abhor it like a polluted rag, and do not wear it in private. [28]I, your handmaid, have never eaten at the table of Haman, nor have I graced the banquet of the king or drunk the wine of libations.* [29]From the day I was brought here till now, your handmaid has had no joy except in you, O LORD, God of Abraham. [30]O God, more powerful than all, hear the voice of those in despair. Save us from the power of the wicked, and deliver me from my fear."

CHAPTER D

See RG 222–26

Esther Is Received by the King.
[1]On the third day, putting an end to her prayers,

she took off her penitential garments and arrayed herself in her royal attire. [2]In making her state appearance, after invoking the all-seeing God and savior, she took with her two maids; [3]on the one she leaned gently for support, [4]while the other followed her, bearing her train. [5]She glowed with the perfection of her beauty and her countenance was as joyous as it was lovely, though her heart was shrunk with fear. [6]She passed through all the portals till she stood face to face with the king, who was seated on his royal throne, clothed in full robes of state, and covered with gold and precious stones, so that he inspired great awe. [7]As he looked up, his features ablaze with the height of majestic anger, the queen staggered, changed color, and leaned weakly against the head of the maid in front of her. [8]But God changed the king's anger to gentleness. In great anxiety he sprang from his throne, held her in his arms until she recovered, and comforted her with reassuring words. [9]"What is it, Esther?" he said to her. "I am your brother. Take courage! [10]You shall not die because of this general decree of ours. [11]Come near!" [12]Raising the golden scepter, he touched her neck with it, embraced her, and said, "Speak to me."[j]

[13]She replied: "I saw you, my lord, as an angel of God, and my heart was troubled with fear of your majesty. [14]For you are awesome, my lord, though your glance is full of kindness." [15]As she said this, she fainted. [16]The king became troubled and all his attendants tried to revive her.

CHAPTER 5

See RG 222–26

[1]*[Now on the third day, Esther put on her royal garments and stood in the inner courtyard, looking toward the royal palace, while the king was seated on his royal throne in the audience chamber, facing the palace doorway. [2]He saw Queen Esther standing in the courtyard, and made her welcome by extending toward her the golden staff which he

---

C, 28: Wine of libations: offered in sacrifice to the gods.

5, 1f: The Hebrew text here translated is a short form of the account already given in Greek.

i: Dt 4, 20; 7, 6; 9, 29; 14, 2; 26, 18; 32, 9. *j:* Est 4, 11.

held. She came up to him, and touched the top of the staff.]

³Then the king said to her, "What is it, Queen Esther? What is your request? Even if it is half of my kingdom, it shall be granted you."^k ⁴"If it please your majesty," Esther replied, "come today with Haman to a banquet I have prepared." ⁵And the king ordered, "Have Haman make haste to fulfill the wish of Esther."

First Banquet of Esther. So the king went with Haman to the banquet Esther had prepared. ⁶During the drinking of the wine, the king said to Esther, "Whatever you ask for shall be granted, and whatever request you make shall be honored, even if it is for half my kingdom."^l ⁷Esther replied: "This is my petition and request: ⁸if I have found favor with the king and if it pleases your majesty to grant my petition and honor my request, come with Haman tomorrow to a banquet which I shall prepare for you; and then I will do as you ask."

Haman's Plot against Mordecai. ⁹That day Haman left happy and in good spirits. But when he saw that Mordecai at the royal gate did not rise, and showed no fear of him, he was filled with anger toward him.^m ¹⁰Haman restrained himself, however, and went home, where he summoned his friends and his wife Zeresh. ¹¹He recounted the greatness of his riches, the large number of his sons, and just how the king had promoted him and placed him above the officials and royal servants.ⁿ ¹²"Moreover," Haman added, "Queen Esther invited no one but me to the banquet with the king; again tomorrow I am to be her guest, with the king. ¹³Yet none of this satisfies me as long as I continue to see the Jew Mordecai sitting at the royal gate."^o ¹⁴His wife Zeresh and all his friends said to him, "Have a gibbet set up, fifty cubits in height, and in the morning ask the king to have Mordecai hanged on it. Then go to the banquet with the king in good cheer." This suggestion pleased Haman, and he had the gibbet erected.^p

IV: Vindication of the Jews

CHAPTER 6

See RG 222–26

Mordecai's Reward from the King. ¹That night the king, unable to sleep, asked that the chronicle of notable events be brought in. While this was being read to him, ²the passage occurred in which Mordecai reported Bagathan and Teresh, two of the royal eunuchs who guarded the entrance, for seeking to lay hands on King Ahasuerus.^q ³The king asked, "What was done to reward and honor Mordecai for this?" The king's attendants replied, "Nothing was done for him."^r

⁴"Who is in the court?" the king asked. Now Haman had entered the outer court of the king's palace to suggest to the king that Mordecai should be hanged on the gibbet he had raised for him.^s ⁵The king's servants answered him, "Haman is waiting in the court." "Let him come in," the king said. ⁶When Haman entered, the king said to him, "What should be done for the man whom the king wishes to reward?" Now Haman thought to himself, "Whom would the king more probably wish to reward than me?" ⁷So he replied to the king: "For the man whom the king wishes to reward ⁸there should be brought the royal robe which the king wore and the horse on which the king rode when the royal crown was placed on his head. ⁹The robe and the horse should be consigned to one of the noblest of the king's officials, who must clothe the man the king wishes to reward, have him ride on the horse in the public square of the city, and cry out before him, 'This is what is done for the man whom the king wishes to reward.' "^t ¹⁰Then the king said to Haman: "Hurry! Take the robe and horse as you have proposed, and do this for the Jew Mordecai, who is sitting at the royal gate. Do not omit anything you proposed."^u ¹¹So Haman took the robe and horse, clothed Mordecai, had him ride in the public square of the city, and cried out before him, "This is what is done for the man whom the king wishes to reward."

k: Est 5, 6; 7, 2; 9, 12. l: Est 5, 3. m: Est 3, 2f; C, 5ff; 6, 10. 12. n: Est 3, 1; B, 3; E, 11; 9, 6-10. o: Est 3, 2f; 6, 10, 12. p: Est 6, 4; 7, 9f. q: Est A, 12ff; 2, 21ff. r: Est A, 16. s: Est 5, 14; 7, 9f. t: Gn 41, 42f; 1 Kgs 1, 33; Dn 5, 29. u: Est 2, 21; 3, 2f; 5, 9. 13.

[12]Mordecai then returned to the royal gate, while Haman hurried home, his head covered in grief.[v] [13]When he told his wife Zeresh and all his friends everything that had happened to him, his advisers and his wife Zeresh said to him, "If Mordecai, before whom you are beginning to decline, is of the Jewish race, you will not prevail against him, but will surely be defeated by him."

Esther's Second Banquet. [14]While they were speaking with him, the king's eunuchs arrived and hurried Haman off to the banquet Esther had prepared.

CHAPTER 7

See RG
222-26

[1]So the king and Haman went to the banquet with Queen Esther. [2]Again, on this second day, during the drinking of the wine, the king said to Esther, "Whatever you ask, Queen Esther, shall be granted you. Whatever request you make shall be honored, even for half the kingdom."[w] [3]Queen Esther replied: "If I have found favor with you, O king, and if it pleases your majesty, I ask that my life be spared, and I beg that you spare the lives of my people. [4]For my people and I have been delivered to destruction, slaughter, and extinction. If we were to be sold into slavery I would remain silent, but as it is, the enemy will be unable to compensate for the harm done to the king."[x] [5]"Who and where," said King Ahasuerus to Queen Esther, "is the man who has dared to do this?"[y] [6]Esther replied, "The enemy oppressing us is this wicked Haman." At this, Haman was seized with dread of the king and queen.

[7]The king left the banquet in anger and went into the garden of the palace, but Haman stayed to beg Queen Esther for his life, since he saw that the king had decided on his doom. [8]When the king returned from the garden of the palace to the banquet hall, Haman had thrown himself on the couch on which Esther was reclining; and the king exclaimed, "Will he also violate the queen while she is with me in my own house!" Scarcely had the king spoken, when the face of Haman was covered over.

Punishment of Haman. [9z]Harbona, one of the eunuchs who attended the king, said, "At the house of Haman stands a gibbet fifty cubits high. Haman prepared it for Mordecai, who gave the report that benefited the king." The king answered, "Hang him on it." [10]So they hanged Haman on the gibbet which he had made ready for Mordecai, and the anger of the king abated.

CHAPTER 8

See RG
222-26

[1]That day King Ahasuerus gave the house of Haman, enemy of the Jews, to Queen Esther; and Mordecai was admitted to the king's presence, for Esther had revealed his relationship to her.[a] [2]The king removed his signet ring from Haman, and transferred it into the keeping of Mordecai; and Esther put Mordecai in charge of the house of Haman.[b]

The Second Royal Decree. [3]In another audience with the king, Esther fell at his feet and tearfully implored him to revoke the harm done by Haman the Agagite, and the plan he had devised against the Jews. [4]The king stretched forth the golden scepter to Esther. So she rose and, standing in his presence, [5]said: "If it pleases your majesty and seems proper to you, and if I have found favor with you and you love me, let a document be issued to revoke the letters which that schemer Haman, son of Hammedatha the Agagite, wrote for the destruction of the Jews in all the royal provinces.[c] [6]For how can I witness the evil that is to befall my people, and how can I behold the destruction of my race?"

[7]King Ahasuerus then said to Queen Esther and to the Jew Mordecai: "Now that I have given Esther the house of Haman, and they have hanged him on the gibbet because he attacked the Jews, [8d]you in turn may write in the king's name what you see fit concerning the Jews and seal the letter with the royal signet ring." For whatever is writ-

v: Est 2, 21; 3, 2f; 5, 9. 13.   w: Est 5, 3.   x: Est 3, 13; B, 6.   y: Est 3, 8f.   z: 9f: Est 5, 14; 6, 4.   a: Est 9, 1; Prv 11, 8; 26, 27; Mt 7, 2.   b: Prv 13, 22; Dn 2, 48f.   c: Est 1, 19.   d: Est 1, 19.

ten in the name of the king and sealed with the royal signet ring cannot be revoked.*

⁹At that time, on the twenty-third day of the third month, Sivan, the royal scribes were summoned. Exactly as Mordecai dictated, they wrote to the Jews and to the satraps, governors, and officials of the hundred and twenty-seven provinces from India to Ethiopia: to each province in its own script and to each people in its own language, and to the Jews in their own script and language. ¹⁰These letters, which he wrote in the name of King Ahasuerus and sealed with the royal signet ring, he sent by mounted couriers riding thoroughbred royal steeds. ¹¹ᵉIn these letters the king authorized the Jews in each and every city to group together and defend their lives, and to kill, destroy, wipe out, along with their wives and children, every armed group of any nation or province which should attack them, and to seize their goods as spoil ¹²throughout the provinces of King Ahasuerus, on a single day, the thirteenth of the twelfth month, Adar.

CHAPTER E

See RG
222-26 ¹The following is a copy of the letter:

"King Ahasuerus the Great to the governors of the provinces in the hundred and twenty-seven satrapies from India to Ethiopia, and to those responsible for our interests: Greetings!

²"Many have become the more ambitious the more they were showered with honors through the bountiful generosity of their patrons. ³Not only do they seek to do harm to our subjects; incapable of bearing such greatness, they even begin plotting against their own benefactors. ⁴Not only do they drive out gratitude from among men; with the arrogant boastfulness of those to whom goodness has no meaning, they suppose they will escape the vindictive judgment of the all-seeing God. ⁵"Often, too, the fair speech of friends en-

trusted with the administration of affairs has induced many placed in authority to become accomplices in the shedding of innocent blood, and has involved them in irreparable calamities ⁶by deceiving with malicious slander the sincere good will of rulers. ⁷This can be verified in the ancient stories that have been handed down to us, but more fully when one considers the wicked deeds perpetrated in your midst by the pestilential influence of those undeserving of authority. ⁸ᶠWe must provide for the future, so as to render the kingdom undisturbed and peaceful for all men, ⁹taking advantage of changing conditions and deciding always with equitable treatment matters coming to our attention.

¹⁰"For instance, Haman, son of Hammedatha, a Macedonian,* certainly not of Persian blood, and very different from us in generosity, was hospitably received by us. ¹¹He so far enjoyed the good will which we have toward all peoples that he was proclaimed 'father of the king,' before whom everyone was to bow down; he attained the rank second to the royal throne.ᵍ ¹²But, unequal to this dignity, he strove to deprive us of kingdom and of life; ¹³and by weaving intricate webs of deceit, he demanded the destruction of Mordecai, our savior and constant benefactor, and of Esther, our blameless royal consort, together with their whole race.ʰ ¹⁴For by such measures he hoped to catch us defenseless and to transfer the rule of the Persians to the Macedonians. ¹⁵But we find that the Jews, who were doomed to extinction by this arch-criminal, are not evildoers, but rather are governed by very just laws ¹⁶and are the children of the Most High, the living God of majesty, who has maintained the kingdom in a flourishing condition for us and for our forebears.

¹⁷"You will do well, then, to ignore the letter sent by Haman, son of Hammedatha, ¹⁸for he who composed it has been hanged,

---

8, 8: Whatever is written . . . cannot be revoked: the king cannot directly grant Esther's request (v 5) to revoke the previous decree against the Jews because of the irreparable character of the laws of the Medes and Persians (Est 1, 19; Dn 6, 9); but he empowers Esther to issue a new decree in his name which renders the earlier decree without effect; cf Est 3, 12f.

E, 10: Macedonian: a redactor of the book in the Hel-

lenistic period used the designation Macedonian, here and in v 14, to express, after Macedonia's conquest of Persia, the most odious kind of man that a Persian ruler could be supposed to think of; the Hebrew text, for a similar reason, called Haman an Agagite. See note on Est A, 17.

e: 11f: Est 9, 1-4.   *f:* 8f: Est B, 2.   *g:* Est B, 3. 6.   *h:* Est A, 17.

together with his entire household, before the gates of Susa. Thus swiftly has God, who governs all, brought just punishment upon him.*i*

19"You shall exhibit a copy of this letter publicly in every place, to certify that the Jews may follow their own laws, *20*and that you may help them on the day set for their ruin, the thirteenth day of the twelfth month, Adar, to defend themselves against those who attack them. *21*For God, the ruler of all, has turned that day for them from one of destruction of the chosen race into one of joy. *22*Therefore, you too must celebrate this memorable day among your designated feasts with all rejoicing, *23*so that both now and in the future it may be, for us and for loyal Persians, a celebration of victory, and for those who plot against us a reminder of destruction.

24"Every city and province, without exception, that does not observe this decree shall be ruthlessly destroyed with fire and sword, so that it will be left not merely untrodden by men, but even shunned by wild beasts and birds forever."*j*

(CHAPTER 8)

See RG 222–26

*13*A copy of the letter to be promulgated as law in each and every province was published among all the peoples, so that the Jews might be prepared on that day to avenge themselves on their enemies.* *14*Couriers mounted on royal steeds sped forth in haste at the king's order, and the decree was promulgated in the stronghold of Susa.

*15*Mordecai left the king's presence clothed in a royal robe of violet and of white cotton, with a large crown of gold and a cloak of crimson byssus. The city of Susa shouted with joy,*k* *16*and there was splendor and merriment for the Jews, exultation and triumph. *17*In each and every province and in each and every city, wherever the king's order arrived, there was merriment and exultation, banqueting and feasting for the Jews.

And many of the peoples of the land embraced Judaism, for they were seized with a fear of the Jews.*l*

CHAPTER 9

See RG 222–26

Victory of the Jews. *1m*When the day arrived on which the order decreed by the king was to be carried out, the thirteenth day of the twelfth month, Adar, on which the enemies of the Jews had expected to become masters of them, the situation was reversed: the Jews became masters of their enemies. *2*The Jews mustered in their cities throughout the provinces of King Ahasuerus to attack those who sought to do them harm, and no one could withstand them, but all peoples were seized with a fear of them. *3*Moreover, all the officials of the provinces, the satraps, governors, and royal procurators supported the Jews from fear of Mordecai; *4*for Mordecai was powerful in the royal palace, and the report was spreading through all the provinces that he was continually growing in power.

*5*The Jews struck down all their enemies with the sword, killing and destroying them; they did to their enemies as they pleased.*n* *6o*In the stronghold of Susa, the Jews killed and destroyed five hundred men. *7*They also killed Parshandatha, Dalphon, Aspatha, *8*Porathai, Adalia, Aridatha, *9*Parmashta, Arisai, Aridai, and Vaizatha, *10p*the ten sons of Haman, son of Hammedatha, the foe of the Jews. However, they did not engage in plundering.*

*11*On the same day, when the number of those killed in the stronghold of Susa was reported to the king, *12*he said to Queen Esther: "In the stronghold of Susa the Jews have killed and destroyed five hundred men, as well as the ten sons of Haman. What must they have done in the other royal provinces! You shall again be granted whatever you ask, and whatever you request shall be honored." *13*So Esther said, "If it pleases your majesty, let the Jews in Susa be permitted again to-

---

8, 13: Avenge themselves on their enemies: partly in self-defense (Est E, 20), and partly to express the fact that the extreme cruelty designed against the Jews by their enemies now recoiled upon the latter as a punishment. Cf 9, 1f.

9, 10: They did not engage in plundering: in contrast to the Israelites who fought Agag (1 Sm 15, 9); cf also vv 15f.

i: Est 7, 10; 9, 14.   *j:* Est 3, 8f; B, 4.   *k:* Dn 5, 7.   *l:* Est 9, 27.   *m:* 1f: Est 8, 11f.   *n:* Jdt 15, 6.   *o:* 6-10: Est 5, 11; B, 3; E, 11.
p: Est 9, 15; Jdt 15, 7. 11.

morrow to act according to today's decree, and let the ten sons of Haman be hanged on gibbets." *14*The king then gave an order to this effect, and the decree was published in Susa. So the ten sons of Haman were hanged,*q* *15*and the Jews in Susa mustered again on the fourteenth of the month of Adar and killed three hundred men in Susa.* However, they did not engage in plundering.*r*

*16*The other Jews, who dwelt in the royal provinces, also mustered and defended themselves, and obtained rest from their enemies. They killed seventy-five thousand* of their foes, without engaging in plunder,*s* *17*on the thirteenth day of the month of Adar. On the fourteenth of the month they rested, and made it a day of feasting and rejoicing.

18(The Jews in Susa, however, mustered on the thirteenth and fourteenth of the month. But on the fifteenth they rested, and made it a day of feasting and rejoicing.) *19*That is why the rural Jews, who dwell in villages, celebrate the fourteenth of the month of Adar as a day of rejoicing and feasting, a holiday on which they send gifts of food to one another.

The Feast of Purim. *20*Mordecai recorded these events and sent letters to all the Jews, both near and far, in all the provinces of King Ahasuerus. *21*He ordered them to celebrate every year both the fourteenth and the fifteenth of the month of Adar *22*as the day on which the Jews obtained rest from their enemies and as the month which was turned for them from sorrow into joy, from mourning into festivity. They were to observe these days with feasting and gladness, sending food to one another and gifts to the poor. *23*The Jews took upon themselves for the future this observance which they instituted at the written direction of Mordecai.*t*

*24u*Haman, son of Hammedatha the Agagite, the foe of all the Jews, had planned to de-

stroy them and had cast the pur, or lot, for the time of their defeat and destruction. *25*Yet, when Esther entered the royal presence, the king ordered in writing that the wicked plan Haman had devised against the Jews should instead be turned against Haman and that he and his sons should be hanged on gibbets.*v* *26*And so these days have been named Purim after the word pur.

Thus, because of all that was contained in this letter, and because of what they had witnessed and experienced in this affair, *27*the Jews established and took upon themselves, their descendants, and all who should join them, the inviolable obligation of celebrating these two days every year in the manner prescribed by this letter, and at the time appointed.*w* *28*These days were to be commemorated and kept in every generation, by every clan, in every province, and in every city. These days of Purim were never to fall into disuse among the Jews, nor into oblivion among their descendants.

*29*Queen Esther, daughter of Abihail and of Mordecai* the Jew, wrote to confirm with full authority this second letter about Purim, *30*when Mordecai sent documents concerning peace and security to all the Jews in the hundred and twenty-seven provinces of Ahasuerus' kingdom.*x* *31*Thus were established, for their appointed time, these days of Purim which Mordecai the Jew and Queen Esther had designated for the Jews, just as they had previously enjoined upon themselves and upon their race the duty of fasting and supplication.* *32*The command of Esther confirmed these prescriptions for Purim and was recorded in the book.

CHAPTER 10

See RG 222-26

*1*King Ahasuerus laid tribute on the land and on the islands of the sea. *2*All the acts of his power and valor, as well as a de-

---

9, 15: This second slaughter explains the two dates (13th and 14th) of the Purim celebration by Jews in Susa (v 18).

9, 16: Seventy-five thousand: according to the Greek text this number was fifteen thousand.

9, 29: Queen Esther, daughter of Abihail and of Mordecai: the natural offspring of Abihail and adopted daughter of Mordecai; cf Est 2, 15. This second letter: for the burden of this letter see Est 9, 20ff. It was endorsed by Queen Esther. The first letter, written in the king's name, is referred to in Est 8, 9.

9, 31: Fasting and supplication: as the Jews had previously undertaken the duty of fasting and supplication to prevent the impending disaster, they now observe days of festival to commemorate their deliverance—in both cases (cf Est 4, 3. 15f) at the request of Mordecai and Esther.

q: Est 7, 10; E, 18.   *r:* Est 9, 10.   *s:* Jdt 15, 6.   *t:* Est 9, 29.   *u:* 24ff: Est 3, 7; F, 10.   *v:* Est 6, 5-13.   *w:* Est 8, 12. 17.   *x:* Est 9, 23-26.

tailed account of the greatness of Mordecai, whom the king promoted, are recorded in the chronicles of the kings of Media and Persia. [3]The Jew Mordecai was next in rank to King Ahasuerus, in high standing among the Jews, and was regarded with favor by his many brethren, as the promoter of his people's welfare and the herald of peace for his whole race.[y]

V: Epilogue

See RG
222-26

CHAPTER F

Mordecai's Dream Fulfilled. [1z]Then Mordecai said: "This is the work of God. [2]I recall the dream I had about these very things, and not a single detail has been left unfulfilled— [3]the tiny spring that grew into a river, the light of the sun, the many waters. The river is Esther, whom the king married

and made queen. [4]The two dragons are myself and Haman. [5]The nations are those who assembled to destroy the name of the Jews, [6]but my people is Israel, who cried to God and was saved.

"The LORD saved his people and delivered us from all these evils. God worked signs and great wonders, such as have not occurred among the nations. [7]For this purpose he arranged two lots:[*] one for the people of God, the second for all the other nations. [8]These two lots were fulfilled in the hour, the time, and the day of judgment before God and among all the nations. [9]God remembered his people and rendered justice to his inheritance.[a]

[10]"Gathering together with joy and happiness before God, they shall celebrate these days on the fourteenth and fifteenth of the month Adar throughout all future generations of his people Israel."[*]

F, 7: Two lots: in this passage of the Greek text, which gives a more religious interpretation of the feast, the two lots are drawn by God to determine, respectively, the destiny of Israel and that of the nations. In Est 3, 7 above, translated from the Hebrew text, the feast is called Purim because of the lots which Aman cast to determine the day for the extinction of the Jews.

F, 10: The Greek text of Esther contains a postscript as follows: In the fourth year of the reign of Ptolemy and

Cleopatra, Dositheus, who said he was a priest and Levite, and his son Ptolemy brought the present letter of Purim, saying that it was genuine and that Lysimachus, son of Ptolemy, of the community of Jerusalem, had translated it. The date referred to in this postscript is most probably 78-77 B.C., in the reign of Ptolemy XII and Cleopatra V.

y: 2 Mc 15, 14. *z:* 1-6: Est A, 4-10. *a:* Est 3, 7; 9, 17f. 21. 24-28.

See RG
226-31

The First Book of Maccabees

The name Maccabee, probably meaning "hammer," is actually applied in the Books of Maccabees to only one man, Judas, third son of the priest Mattathias and first leader of the revolt against the Seleucid kings who persecuted the Jews (1 Mc 2, 4. 66; 2 Mc 8, 5. 16; 10, 1. 16). Traditionally the name has come to be applied to the brothers of Judas, his supporters, and even to other Jewish heroes of the period, such as the seven brothers (2 Mc 7).

The two Books of Maccabees, placed last in the Douai version of the Old Testament, contain independent accounts of events in part identical which accompanied the attempted suppression of Judaism in Palestine in the second century B.C. The vigorous reaction to this attempt established for a time the religious and political independence of the Jews.

1 Maccabees was written about 100 B.C., in Hebrew, but the original has not come down to us. In-

stead, we have an early, pre-Christian, Greek translation full of Hebrew idioms. The author, probably a Palestinian Jew, is unknown. He was familiar with the traditions and sacred books of his people and had access to much reliable information on their recent history (from 175 to 134 B.C.). He may well have played some part in it himself in his youth. His purpose in writing is to record the salvation of Israel which God worked through the family of Mattathias (5, 62)—especially through his three sons, Judas, Jonathan, and Simon, and his grandson, John Hyrcanus. Implicitly the writer compares their virtues and their exploits with those of the ancient heroes, the Judges, Samuel, and David.

There are seven poetic sections in the book which imitate the style of classical Hebrew poetry: four laments (1, 25-28. 36-40; 2, 8-13; 3, 45), and three hymns of praise of "our fathers" (2, 51-64), of Judas (3, 3-9), and of Simon (14, 4-15).

The doctrine expressed in the book is the customary belief of Israel, without the new developments which appear in 2 Maccabees and Daniel. The people of Israel have been specially chosen by the one true God as his covenant-partner, and they alone are privileged to know him and worship him. He is their eternal benefactor and their unfailing source of help. The people, in turn, must be loyal to his exclusive worship and must observe exactly the precepts of the law he has given them.

There is no doctrine of individual immortality except in the survival of one's name and fame, nor does the book express any messianic expectation, though messianic images are applied historically to "the days of Simon" (14, 4–17). In true deuteronomic tradition, the author insists on fidelity to the law as the expression of Israel's love for God. The contest which he describes is a struggle, not simply between Jew and Gentile, but between those who would uphold the law and those, Jews or Gentiles, who would destroy it. His severest condemnation goes, not to the Seleucid politicians, but to the lawless apostates among his own people, adversaries of Judas and his brothers, who are models of faith and loyalty.

1 Maccabees has importance also for the New Testament. Salvation is paralleled with Jewish national aspirations (1 Mc 4, 46—14, 41), in contrast to the universal reign of God taught by Christ in the Gospel (Mt 13, 47-50; 22, 1-14). Also, destruction of the wall of the temple separating Jew from Gentile is an act of desecration in 1 Mc 9, 54 but in Eph 2, 14, an act of redemption and unification of both through Christ. On the other hand, association, in 1 Mc 2, 52, of Abraham's offering up of Isaac (Gn 22) with his justification by God (Gn 15, 6) is reflected in Jn 2, 21f, just as the Scriptures are regarded as a source of consolation in 1 Mc 12, 9 and in Rom 15, 4.

The Books of Maccabees, though regarded by Jews and Protestants as apocryphal, i.e., not inspired Scripture, because not contained in the Palestinian Canon or list of books drawn up at the end of the first century A.D., have nevertheless always been accepted by the Catholic Church as inspired, on the basis of apostolic tradition.

1 Maccabees is divided as follows:
I: Introduction: Hellenism in Asia Minor (1, 1-9).
II: The Maccabean Revolt (1, 10—2, 70).
III: Leadership of Judas Maccabeus (3, 1—9, 22).
IV: Leadership of Jonathan (9, 23—12, 54).
V: Simon, High Priest and Ethnarch (13, 1—16, 24).

I: Introduction: Hellenism in Asia Minor

CHAPTER 1

See RG 227

Conquests and Death of Alexander. [1a]After Alexander the Macedonian, Philip's son, who came from the land of Kittim,* had defeated Darius, king of the Persians and Medes, he became king in his place, having first ruled in Greece. [2]He fought many campaigns, captured fortresses, and put kings to death. [3]He advanced to the ends of the earth, gathering plunder from many nations; the earth fell silent before him, and his heart became proud and arrogant. [4]He collected a very strong army and conquered provinces, nations, and rulers, and they became his tributaries. [5]But after all this he took to his bed, realizing that he was going to die. [6]He therefore summoned his officers, the nobles, who had been brought up with him from his youth, to divide his kingdom among them while he was still alive. [7]Alexander had reigned twelve years* when he died.

[8]So his officers took over his kingdom, each in his own territory, [9]and after his death they all put on royal crowns, and so did their sons after them for many years, causing much distress over the earth.

II: The Maccabean Revolt

Pact between Jews and Gentiles. [10]There sprang from these a sinful offshoot, Antiochus Epiphanes, son of King Antiochus,

---

1, 1: Land of Kittim: Greece. The name referred originally to inhabitants of Kiti, capital of the isle of Cyprus, then to any Cypriots (Is 23, 1; Jer 2, 10), later to Greeks in general, and finally even to Romans. See note on Dn

11, 30. Darius: Darius III, Codoman (336–331 B.C.).
1, 7: Twelve years: 336–323 B.C.

a: 1-10: Dn 8, 20ff; 11, 3f. 21.

once a hostage at Rome. He became king in the year one hundred and thirty-seven* of the kingdom of the Greeks.[b]

[11] In those days there appeared in Israel men who were breakers of the law, and they seduced many people, saying: "Let us go and make an alliance with the Gentiles all around us; since we separated from them, many evils have come upon us."[c] [12] The proposal was agreeable; [13][d] some from among the people promptly went to the king, and he authorized them to introduce the way of living of the Gentiles. [14] Thereupon they built a gymnasium* in Jerusalem according to the Gentile custom. [15] They covered over the mark of their circumcision and abandoned the holy covenant; they allied themselves with the Gentiles and sold themselves to wrongdoing.[e]

Egyptian Campaign of Antiochus. [16] When his kingdom seemed secure, Antiochus proposed to become king of Egypt, so as to rule over both kingdoms. [17] He invaded Egypt with a strong force, with chariots and elephants,* and with a large fleet,[f] [18] to make war on Ptolemy, king of Egypt. Ptolemy was frightened at his presence and fled, leaving many casualties. [19] The fortified cities in the land of Egypt were captured, and Antiochus plundered the land of Egypt.

Persecution of the Jews. [20][g] After Antiochus had defeated Egypt in the year one hundred and forty-three,* he returned and went up to Israel and to Jerusalem with a strong force. [21] He insolently invaded the sanctuary and took away the golden altar, the lampstand for the light with all its fixtures,

[22] the offering table, the cups and the bowls, the golden censers, the curtain, the crowns, and the golden ornament on the façade of the temple. He stripped off everything, [23] and took away the gold and silver and the precious vessels; he also took all the hidden treasures he could find. [24] Taking all this, he went back to his own country, after he had spoken with great arrogance and shed much blood.

[25] And there was great mourning for Israel,
　　in every place where they dwelt,
[26] 　and the rulers and the elders groaned.
　Virgins and young men languished,
　　and the beauty of the women was
　　　disfigured.
[27] Every bridegroom took up lamentation,
　　she who sat in the bridal chamber
　　　mourned,
[28] And the land was shaken on account of
　　its inhabitants,
　and all the house of Jacob was covered
　　with shame.

[29][h] Two years later, the king sent the Mysian commander to the cities of Judah, and he came to Jerusalem with a strong force. [30] He spoke to them deceitfully in peaceful terms, and won their trust. Then he attacked the city suddenly, in a great onslaught, and destroyed many of the people in Israel. [31] He plundered the city and set fire to it, demolished its houses and its surrounding walls, [32] took captive the women and children, and seized the cattle. [33] Then they built up the City of David* with a high, massive wall and strong towers, and it became their

---

1, 10: The year one hundred and thirty-seven: Antiochus IV seized the throne in September, 175 B.C. Dates are given in this book according to the Seleucid era, which however was reckoned in two different ways. Antiochians considered this date to be October, 312 B.C. (Syrian calendar), while Babylonians and Jewish priests accepted April, 311 B.C. as the commencement of the era (temple calendar). The author of 1 Mc dates political events by the Syrian calendar but religious events by the temple calendar. Accordingly, the civil New Year occurred variously in September or October, the religious New Year in March or April.

1, 14: Gymnasium: symbol and center of athletic and intellectual life, it was the chief instrument of Hellenistic propaganda. Jewish youth were attracted by sports and encouraged to join youth clubs. They received training in military skills and in the duties of citizens. Through participation in the intellectual life, many were gradually won over to paganism.

1, 17: Elephants: an important part of Seleucid armament. About 300 B.C. Seleucus I, founder of the dynasty, procured five hundred of them from India; cf 1 Mc 6, 34-37.

1, 20: Defeated Egypt in the year one hundred and forty-three: 169 B.C. No mention is made in 1 Mc of the second expedition to Egypt a year later, described in 2 Mc 5, 1. 11. Dn 11, 25. 29 records both.

1, 33: City of David: not Mount Zion on the eastern hill of Jerusalem, which David captured from the Jebusites (2 Sm 5, 7), but a new fortress built on the western hill and overlooking the temple and its courts on Mount Zion. It was occupied for twenty-six years by the Syro-Macedonian garrison, together with apostate Jews, and was a continual

b: 2 Mc 4, 7.　c: 2 Mc 4, 9-17.　d: 13ff: 2 Mc 4, 7-17.　e: 1 Cor 7, 18.　f: 2 Mc 5, 1; Dn 11, 25-28.　g: 20-24: 2 Mc 5, 11-21.　h: 29-32: 2 Mc 5, 24ff.

citadel.[i] [34]There they installed a sinful race, perverse men, who fortified themselves inside it, [35]storing up weapons and provisions, and depositing there the plunder they had collected from Jerusalem. And they became a great threat.

[36] The citadel became an ambush against
the sanctuary,
and a wicked adversary to Israel at all
times.
[37] And they shed innocent blood around the
sanctuary;
they defiled the sanctuary.
[38] Because of them the inhabitants of
Jerusalem fled away,
and she became the abode of strangers.
She became a stranger to her own
offspring,
and her children forsook her.
[39] Her sanctuary was as desolate as a
wilderness;[j]
her feasts were turned into mourning,
Her sabbaths to shame,
her honor to contempt.
[40] Her dishonor was as great as her glory
had been,
and her exaltation was turned into
mourning.

Prohibitions against Religion. [41]Then the king wrote to his whole kingdom that all should be one people, [42]each abandoning his particular customs. All the Gentiles conformed to the command of the king, [43]and many Israelites were in favor of his religion; they sacrificed to idols and profaned the sabbath.

[44k]The king sent messengers with letters to Jerusalem and to the cities of Judah, ordering them to follow customs foreign to their land: [45]to prohibit holocausts, sacrifices, and libations in the sanctuary, to profane the sabbaths and feast days, [46 l]to desecrate the sanctuary and the sacred ministers, to build pagan altars and temples and shrines, [47]to sacrifice swine and unclean animals, [48]to leave their sons uncircumcised, and to let themselves be defiled with every kind of impurity and abomination, [49]so that they might forget the law and change all their observances. [50]Whoever refused to act according to the command of the king should be put to death.[m]

[51]Such were the orders he published throughout his kingdom. He appointed inspectors over all the people, and he ordered the cities of Judah to offer sacrifices, each city in turn. [52]Many of the people, those who abandoned the law, joined them and committed evil in the land. [53]Israel was driven into hiding, wherever places of refuge could be found.

[54]On the fifteenth day of the month Chislev, in the year one hundred and forty-five,[*] the king erected the horrible abomination upon the altar of holocausts, and in the surrounding cities of Judah they built pagan altars.[n] [55]They also burnt incense at the doors of houses and in the streets. [56]Any scrolls of the law[*] which they found they tore up and burnt. [57]Whoever was found with a scroll of the covenant, and whoever observed the law, was condemned to death by royal decree.[o] [58]So they used their power against Israel, against those who were caught, each month, in the cities. [59]On the twenty-fifth day of each month they sacrificed on the altar erected over the altar of holocausts. [60p]Women who had had their children circumcised were put to death, in keeping with the decree, [61]with the babies hung from their necks; their families also and those who had circumcised them were killed. [62]But many in Israel were determined and resolved in their hearts not to eat anything unclean; [63]they preferred to die rather than to be defiled with unclean food or to profane the holy covenant; and they did die. Terrible affliction was upon Israel.[q]

threat to the temple and the Jewish people (v 36); cf 1 Mc 13, 49ff.

1, 54: Fifteenth day of the month Chislev in the year one hundred and forty-five: early December, 167 B.C. Horrible abomination: in the original Hebrew, a contemptuous pun on the title "Lord of heaven" given to the god Zeus Olympios, to whom an image or perhaps an altar was erected upon the altar of holocausts in the temple of Jerusalem; cf Dn 9, 27; 11, 31.

1, 56f: Scrolls of the law: one or more of the first five books of the Old Testament.

i: 1 Mc 6, 18. j: 39f: Tb 2, 6; Am 8, 10. k: 44-63: 2 Mc 6, 1-11. l: 2 Mc 6, 2; Dn 9, 27. m: 2 Mc 6, 18—7, 41. n: 1 Mc 6, 7; Dn 9, 27; 11, 31. o: 2 Mc 2, 14. p: 60f: 2 Mc 6, 10. q: 2 Mc 6, 10.

CHAPTER 2

See RG
227–28

Mattathias and His Sons. [1]In those days Mattathias, son of John, son of Simeon, a priest of the family of Joarib, left Jerusalem and settled in Modein.* [2]He had five sons: John, who was called Gaddi;[r] [3]Simon, who was called Thassi; [4]Judas, who was called Maccabeus; [5]Eleazar, who was called Avaran; and Jonathan, who was called Apphus. [6]When he saw the sacrileges that were being committed in Judah and in Jerusalem, [7]he said: "Woe is me! Why was I born to see the ruin of my people and the ruin of the holy city, and to sit idle while it is given into the hands of enemies, and the sanctuary into the hands of strangers?

[8] "Her temple has become like a man
        disgraced,
[9]   her glorious ornaments have been
            carried off as spoils,
    Her infants have been murdered in her
            streets,
        her young men by the sword of the
            enemy.[s]
[10] What nation has not taken its share of her
        realm,
    and laid its hand on her possessions?
[11] All her adornment has been taken away.
    From being free, she has become a
        slave.
[12] We see our sanctuary and our beauty
    and our glory laid waste,
And the Gentiles have defiled them!
[13]   Why are we still alive?"

[14]Then Mattathias and his sons tore their garments, put on sackcloth, and mourned bitterly.

Pagan Worship Refused. [15]The officers of the king in charge of enforcing the apostasy came to the city of Modein to organize the sacrifices. [16]Many of Israel joined them, but Mattathias and his sons gathered in a group apart. [17]Then the officers of the king addressed Mattathias: "You are a leader, an honorable and great man in this city, supported by sons and kinsmen. [18]Come now, be the first to obey the king's command, as all the Gentiles and the men of Judah and those who are left in Jerusalem have done. Then you and your sons shall be numbered among the King's Friends,* and shall be enriched with silver and gold and many gifts." [19]But Mattathias answered in a loud voice: "Although all the Gentiles in the king's realm obey him, so that each forsakes the religion of his fathers and consents to the king's orders, [20]yet I and my sons and my kinsmen will keep to the covenant of our fathers. [21]God forbid that we should forsake the law and the commandments. [22]We will not obey the words of the king nor depart from our religion in the slightest degree."

[23]As he finished saying these words, a certain Jew came forward in the sight of all to offer sacrifice on the altar in Modein according to the king's order. [24]When Mattathias saw him, he was filled with zeal; his heart was moved and his just fury was aroused; he sprang forward and killed him upon the altar. [25]At the same time, he also killed the messenger of the king who was forcing them to sacrifice, and he tore down the altar. [26]Thus he showed his zeal for the law, just as Phinehas did with Zimri, son of Salu.[t]

[27]Then Mattathias went through the city shouting, "Let everyone who is zealous for the law and who stands by the covenant follow after me!" [28]Thereupon he fled to the mountains with his sons, leaving behind in the city all their possessions.[u] [29]Many who sought to live according to righteousness and religious custom went out into the desert* to settle there, [30]they and their sons, their wives and their cattle, because misfortunes pressed so hard on them.

[31]It was reported to the officers and soldiers of the king who were in the City of David, in Jerusalem, that certain men who had

---

2, 1: Modein: a village twenty miles northwest of Jerusalem.

2, 18: The King's Friends: a regular order of nobility at Hellenistic courts. The various grades are frequently mentioned in this book: Friends, Chief Friends, Kinsmen.

2, 29: The desert: the sparsely inhabited mountain country southward from Jerusalem and west of the Dead Sea. It was an arid region with some perennial springs and a fair amount of rain in winter.

r: 1 Chr 24, 7. *s:* Lam 2, 11. 21. *t:* 1 Mc 2, 54; Nm 25, 6-14. *u:* 2 Mc 5, 27.

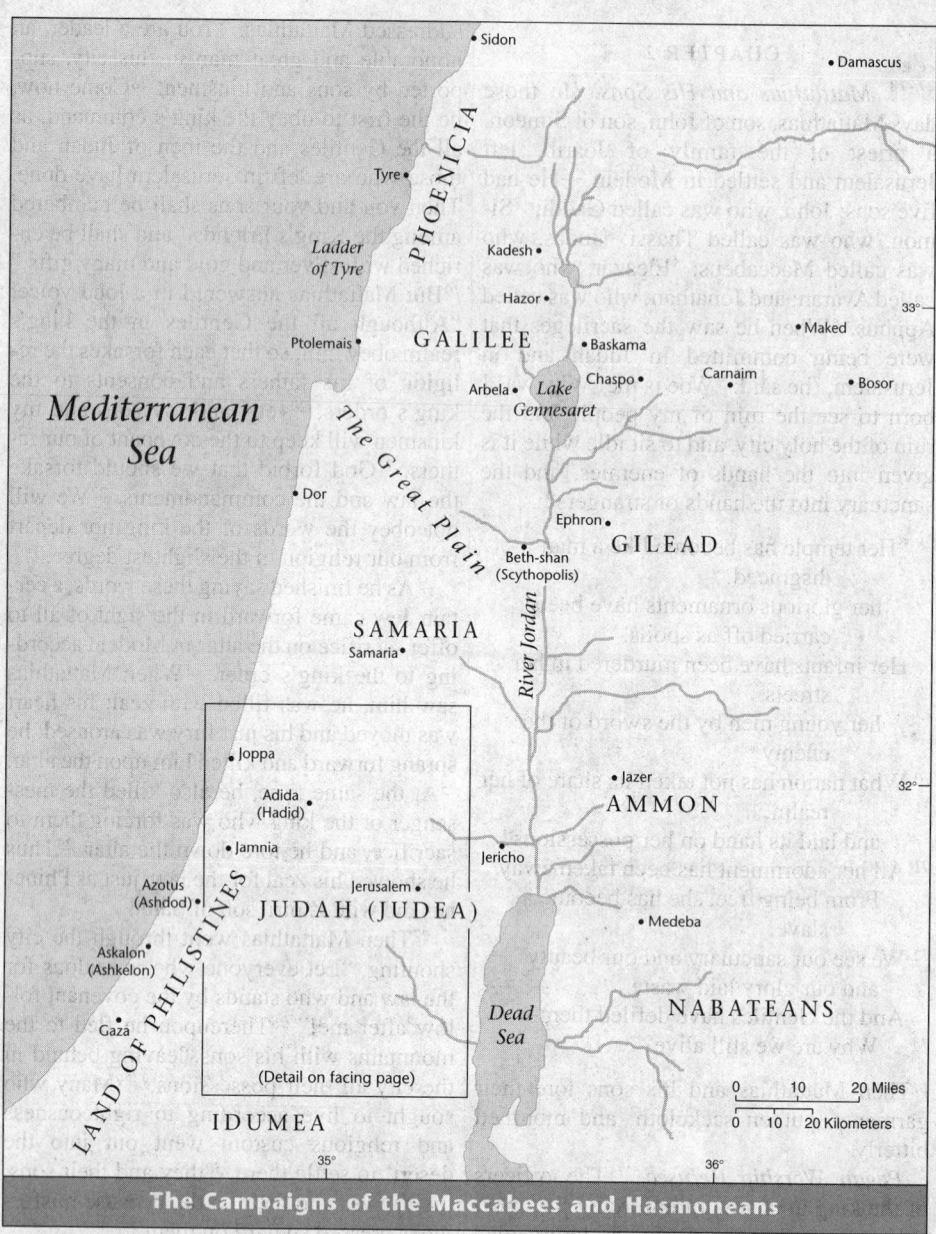

The Campaigns of the Maccabees and Hasmoneans

flouted the king's order had gone out to the hiding places in the desert. ³²ᵛMany hurried out after them, and having caught up with them, camped opposite and prepared to attack them on the sabbath. ³³"Enough of this!" the pursuers said to them. "Come out and obey the king's command, and your lives will be spared." ³⁴But they replied, "We will not come out, nor will we obey the king's command to profane the sabbath." ³⁵Then the enemy attacked them at once; ³⁶but they did not retaliate; they neither threw stones, nor blocked up their own hiding places. ³⁷They said, "Let us all die without reproach; heaven

v: 32-38: 2 Mc 6, 11.

588

The Jerusalem Vicinity

an army and struck down sinners in their anger and lawbreakers in their wrath, and the survivors fled to the Gentiles for safety.[w] [45]Mattathias and his friends went about and tore down the pagan altars; [46]they also forcibly circumcised any uncircumcised boys whom they found in the territory of Israel. [47]They put to flight the arrogant, and the work prospered in their hands. [48]They saved the law from the hands of the Gentiles and of the kings and did not let the sinner triumph.

Death of Mattathias. [49]When the time came for Mattathias to die, he said to his sons: "Arrogance and scorn have now grown strong; it is a time of disaster and violent anger. [50]Therefore, my sons, be zealous for the law and give your lives for the covenant of our fathers.

[51] "Remember the deeds that our fathers did
    in their times,
  and you shall win great glory and an
    everlasting name.
[52] Was not Abraham found faithful in trial,
  and it was reputed to him as
    uprightness?[x]
[53] Joseph, when in distress, kept the
    commandment,
  and he became master of Egypt.[y]
[54] Phinehas our father, for his burning zeal,
  received the covenant of an everlasting
    priesthood.[z]
[55] Joshua, for executing his commission,
  became a judge in Israel.[a]
[56] Caleb, for bearing witness before the
    assembly,
  received an inheritance in the land.[b]
[57] David, for his piety,
  received as a heritage a throne of
    everlasting royalty.[c]
[58] Elijah, for his burning zeal for the law,
  was taken up to heaven.[d]
[59] Hananiah, Azariah and Mishael, for their
    faith,
  were saved from the fire.[e]

and earth are our witnesses that you destroy us unjustly." [38]So the officers and soldiers attacked them on the sabbath, and they died with their wives, their children and their cattle, to the number of a thousand persons.

[39]When Mattathias and his friends heard of it, they mourned deeply for them. [40]"If we all do as our kinsmen have done," they said to one another, "and do not fight against the Gentiles for our lives and our traditions, they will soon destroy us from the earth." [41]On that day they came to this decision: "Let us fight against anyone who attacks us on the sabbath, so that we may not all die as our kinsmen died in the hiding places."

[42]Then they were joined by a group of Hasideans,* valiant Israelites, all of them devout followers of the law. [43]And all those who were fleeing from the disaster joined them and supported them. [44]They gathered

2, 42: Hasideans: in Hebrew hasidim, "pious ones," a religious group devoted to the strict observance of the law. They were the forerunners of both the Pharisees and the Essenes. They first supported the Maccabean movement, but subsequently opposed it, regarding it as too political.

w: Is 63, 3.   x: Gn 15, 6; 22, 1ff.   y: Gn 39, 7-10; 41, 39-43.   z: Nm 25, 10-13; Sir 45, 28ff.   a: Jos 1, 2, 5.   b: Nm 13, 30; 14, 6-9. 24; Jos 14, 14.   c: 2 Sm 2, 4; 7, 16.   d: 1 Kgs 19, 10. 14; 2 Kgs 2, 11.   e: Dn 3, 50.

⁶⁰ Daniel, for his innocence,
   was delivered from the jaws of lions.ᶠ
⁶¹ And so, consider this from generation to
      generation,
   that none who hope in him shall fail in
      strength.
⁶² Do not fear the words of a sinful man,
   for his glory ends in corruption and
      worms.
⁶³ Today he is exalted, and tomorrow he is
      not to be found,
   because he has returned to his dust,
   and his schemes have perished.
⁶⁴ Children! be courageous and strong in
      keeping the law,
   for by it you shall be glorified.

⁶⁵"Here is your brother Simeon who I know
is a wise man; listen to him always, and he
will be a father to you. ⁶⁶ And Judas Maccabeus, a warrior from his youth, shall be the
leader of your army and direct the war
against the nations. ⁶⁷ You shall also gather
about you all who observe the law, and you
shall avenge the wrongs of your people.
⁶⁸ Pay back the Gentiles what they deserve,
and observe the precepts of the law."

⁶⁹ Then he blessed them, and he was
united with his fathers. ⁷⁰ He died in the year
one hundred and forty-six,* and was buried
in the tombs of his fathers in Modein, and all
Israel mourned him greatly.

III: Leadership of Judas Maccabeus

CHAPTER 3

See RG
229

Defeat of Apollonius and Seron.
¹ Then his son Judas, who was called Maccabeus, took his place. ² All his brothers and
all who had joined his father supported him,
and they carried on Israel's war joyfully.

³ He spread abroad the glory of his people,
   and put on his breastplate like a giant.
   He armed himself with weapons of war;

he planned battles and protected the
   camp with his sword.ᵍ
⁴ In his actions he was like a lion,
   like a young lion roaring for prey.
⁵ He pursued the wicked, hunting them
      out,
   and those who troubled his people he
      destroyed by fire.
⁶ The lawbreakers were cowed by fear of
      him,
   and all evildoers were dismayed.
By his hand redemption was happily
      achieved,
⁷   and he afflicted many kings;
He made Jacob glad by his deeds,
   and his memory is blessed forever.
⁸ He went about the cities of Judah
   destroying the impious there.
He turned away wrath from Israel
⁹   and was renowned to the ends of the
      earth;
   he gathered together those who were
      perishing.

¹⁰ Then Apollonius* gathered the Gentiles,
together with a large army from Samaria, to
fight against Israel. ¹¹ When Judas learned of
it, he went out to meet him and defeated and
killed him. Many fell wounded, and the rest
fled. ¹² Their possessions were seized and the
sword of Apollonius was taken by Judas,
who fought with it the rest of his life.

¹³ But Seron, commander of the Syrian
army, heard that Judas had gathered many
about him, an assembly of faithful men
ready for war. ¹⁴ So he said, "I will make a
name for myself and win glory in the kingdom by defeating Judas and his followers,
who have despised the king's command."
¹⁵ And again a large company of renegades
advanced with him to help him take revenge
on the Israelites. ¹⁶ When he reached the ascent of Beth-horon,* Judas went out to meet
him with a few men. ¹⁷ But when they saw
the army coming against them, they said to
Judas: "How can we, few as we are, fight

2, 70: In the year one hundred and forty-six: 166 B.C.
3, 10: Apollonius: the Mysian commander mentioned in 1 Mc 1, 29 and in 2 Mc 5, 24.
3, 16: Beth-horon: the famous pass leading up from the coastal plain to the Judean hill country. Here Joshua won an important battle (Jos 10, 10f), and in 66 A.D. a Roman force under Cestius was trapped and massacred.

f: Dn 6, 23; 14, 31-42. *g:* 2 Mc 8, 5.

such a mighty host as this? Besides, we are weak today from fasting." [18]But Judas said: "It is easy for many to be overcome by a few; in the sight of Heaven there is no difference between deliverance by many or by few; [19]for victory in war does not depend upon the size of the army, but on strength that comes from Heaven.[h] [20]With great presumption and lawlessness they come against us to destroy us and our wives and children and to despoil us; [21]but we are fighting for our lives and our laws. [22]He himself* will crush them before us; so do not be afraid of them." [23]When he finished speaking, he rushed suddenly upon Seron and his army, who were crushed before him. [24]He pursued Seron down the descent of Beth-horon into the plain. About eight hundred* of their men fell, and the rest fled to the country of the Philistines.[i] [25]Then Judas and his brothers began to be feared, and dread fell upon the Gentiles about them. [26]His fame reached the king, and all the Gentiles talked about the battles of Judas.

Regency of Lysias. [27]When Antiochus heard about these events, he was angry; so he ordered a muster of all the forces of his kingdom, a very strong army. [28]He opened his treasure chests, gave his soldiers a year's pay, and commanded them to be prepared for anything. [29]He then found that this exhausted the money in his treasury; moreover the income from the province was small, because of the dissension and distress he had brought upon the land by abolishing the laws which had been in effect from of old. [30]He feared that, as had happened more than once, he would not have enough for his expenses and for the gifts that he had previously given with a more liberal hand than the preceding kings. [31]Greatly perplexed, he decided to go to Persia and levy tribute on those provinces,

and so raise a large sum of money. [32]He left Lysias, a nobleman of royal blood, in charge of the king's affairs from the Euphrates River to the frontier of Egypt, [33]and commissioned him to take care of his son Antiochus until his own return. [34]He entrusted to him half of the army, and the elephants, and gave him instructions concerning everything he wanted done. As for the inhabitants of Judea and Jerusalem, [35]Lysias was to send an army against them to crush and destroy the power of Israel and the remnant of Jerusalem and efface their memory from the land. [36]He was to settle foreigners in all their territory and distribute their land by lot.

[37]The king took the remaining half of the army and set out from Antioch, his capital, in the year one hundred and forty-seven; he crossed the Euphrates River and advanced inland.*

The Victories of Judas. [38][j]Lysias chose Ptolemy, son of Dorymenes, and Nicanor* and Gorgias, capable men among the King's Friends,[k] [39]and with them he sent forty thousand men and seven thousand cavalry to invade the land of Judah and ravage it according to the king's orders. [40]Setting out with all their forces, they came and pitched their camp near Emmaus* in the plain. [41]When the merchants of the country heard of their fame, they came to the camp, bringing fetters and a large sum of silver and gold, to buy the Israelites as slaves. A force from Idumea and from Philistia joined with them.

[42]Judas and his brothers saw that the situation had become critical now that armies were encamped within their territory; they knew of the orders which the king had given to destroy and utterly wipe out the people. [43]So they said to one another, "Let us restore our people from their ruined estate, and fight for our people and our sanctuary!"

3, 22: He himself: out of reverence for God, the author of 1 Mc prefers to use this and other expressions, such as "Heaven," instead of the divine name. Cf 1 Mc 3, 50.

3, 24: About eight hundred: the figures given in this book for strength of armies and number of casualties are not to be taken literally. In accordance with biblical usage, they indicate rather the importance of the battle described or the greatness of the victory.

3, 37: This expedition, in the spring of 165 B.C., resulted in failure; cf ch 6.

3, 38: Nicanor: the leader of another attack against the Jews four years later. He was finally killed by Judas; cf 1 Mc 7, 26-46.

3, 40: Emmaus: probably not the village mentioned in Lk 24, 13, but a settlement about twenty miles west of Jerusalem at the edge of the hill country.

h: 1 Sm 14, 16. i: Jos 10, 10. j: 38-44: 2 Mc 8, 8-15. k: 38f: 1 Mc 7, 26; 2 Mc 4, 45; 8, 8f; 10, 14.

[44]The assembly gathered together to prepare for battle and to pray and implore mercy and compassion.

[45] Jerusalem was uninhabited, like a desert;
    not one of her children entered or
        came out.
The sanctuary was trampled on,
    and foreigners were in the citadel;
        it was a habitation of Gentiles.
Joy had disappeared from Jacob,
    and the flute and the harp were silent.

[46]*l*Thus they assembled and went to Mizpah near Jerusalem, because there was formerly at Mizpah a place of prayer for Israel.* [47]That day they fasted and wore sackcloth; they sprinkled ashes on their heads and tore their clothes. [48]They unrolled the scroll of the law, to learn about the things for which the Gentiles consulted the images of their idols.* [49]They brought with them the priestly vestments, the first fruits, and the tithes; and they brought forward the nazirites* who had completed the time of their vows.*m* [50]And they cried aloud to Heaven: "What shall we do with these men, and where shall we take them? [51]For your sanctuary has been trampled on and profaned, and your priests are in mourning and humiliation. [52]Now the Gentiles are gathered together against us to destroy us. You know what they plot against us. [53]How shall we be able to resist them unless you help us?" [54]Then they blew the trumpets and cried out loudly.

[55]After this Judas appointed officers among the people, over thousands, over hundreds, over fifties, and over tens. [56]He proclaimed that those who were building houses, or were just married, or were planting vineyards, and those who were afraid, could each return to his home, according to the law.*n* [57]Then the army moved off, and they camped to the south of Emmaus. [58]Judas said: "Arm yourselves and be brave; in the morning be ready to fight these Gentiles who have assembled against us to destroy us and our sanctuary. [59]It is better for us to die in battle than to witness the ruin of our nation and our sanctuary. Whatever Heaven wills, he will do."*o*

CHAPTER 4

See RG 229

[1]Now Gorgias took five thousand infantry and a thousand picked cavalry, and this detachment set out at night [2]in order to attack the camp of the Jews and take them by surprise. Some men from the citadel were their guides. [3]Judas heard of it, and himself set out with his soldiers to attack the king's army at Emmaus, [4]while the latter's forces were still scattered away from the camp. [5]During the night Gorgias came into the camp of Judas, and found no one there; so he began to hunt for them in the mountains, saying, "They are fleeing from us."

[6]But at daybreak Judas appeared in the plain with three thousand men, who lacked such armor and swords as they would have wished. [7]They saw the army of the Gentiles, strong and breastplated, flanked with cavalry, and made up of expert soldiers. [8]Judas said to the men with him: "Do not be afraid of their numbers or dread their attack. [9]Remember how our fathers were saved in the Red Sea, when Pharaoh pursued them with an army.*p* [10]So now let us cry to Heaven in the hope that he will favor us, remember his covenant with our fathers, and destroy this army before us today.*q* [11]All the Gentiles shall know that there is One who redeems and delivers Israel."

[12]When the foreigners looked up and saw them marching toward them, [13]they came out of their camp for battle, and the men with Judas blew the trumpet. [14]The battle was joined and the Gentiles were defeated and fled toward the plain. [15]Their whole rearguard fell by the sword, and they were pursued as far as Gazara* and the plains of Ju-

---

3, 46: . . . Mizpah a place of prayer for Israel: a holy place established of old eight miles north and slightly west of Jerusalem. It was here that Samuel began to judge the Israelites (1 Sm 7, 5-11; 10, 17).
3, 48: To learn . . . idols: favorable omens for the coming battle. A contrast is intended between the idol worship of the pagans and the consultation of the word of God by the Jews; cf 2 Mc 8, 23.

3, 49: Nazirites: see note on Nm 6, 1ff.
4, 15: Gazara: Gezer of the Hebrew Bible, five miles northwest of Emmaus; Azotus, Hebrew Ashdod, lay to the southwest; and Jamnia, Hebrew Jabneel (Jos 15, 11) or Jabneh (2 Chr 26, 6), to the west of Gazara.

l: 46ff; 1 Sm 7, 5f; 2 Mc 8, 16-23. *m:* Nm 6, 2-5. *n:* Dt 20, 5-8; Jgs 7, 3. *o:* 1 Mc 2, 21f. *p:* Ex 14, 21ff. *q:* 1 Mc 2, 21.

dea, to Azotus and Jamnia. About three thousand of their men fell.

[16]When Judas and the army returned from the pursuit, [17]he said to the people: "Do not be greedy for the plunder, for there is a fight ahead of us, [18]and Gorgias and his army are near us on the mountain. But now stand firm against our enemies and overthrow them. Afterward you can freely take the plunder."

[19]As Judas was finishing this speech, a detachment appeared, looking down from the mountain. [20]They saw that their army had been put to flight and their camp was being burned. The smoke that could be seen indicated what had happened. [21]When they realized this, they were terrified; and when they also saw the army of Judas in the plain ready to attack, [22]they all fled to Philistine territory.[*]

[23]Then Judas went back to plunder the camp, and his men collected much gold and silver, violet and crimson cloth, and great treasure. [24]As they returned, they were singing hymns and glorifying Heaven, "for he is good, for his mercy endures forever."[r] [25]Thus Israel had a great deliverance that day.

Victory over Lysias. [26s]But those of the foreigners who had escaped went and told Lysias all that had occurred. [27]When he heard it he was disturbed and discouraged, because things in Israel had not turned out as he intended and as the king had ordered. [28]So the following year he gathered together sixty thousand picked men and five thousand cavalry, to subdue them. [29]They came into Idumea and camped at Beth-zur,[*] and Judas met them with ten thousand men. [30]Seeing that the army was strong, he prayed thus:

"Blessed are you, O Savior of Israel, who broke the rush of the mighty one by the hand of your servant David and delivered the camp of the Philistines into the hand of Jonathan, the son of Saul, and his armor-bearer.[t] [31]Give this army into the hands of your people Israel; make them ashamed of their troops and their cavalry. [32]Strike them with fear, weaken the boldness of their strength, and let them tremble at their own destruction. [33]Strike them down by the sword of those who love you, that all who know your name may hymn your praise."

[34]Then they engaged in battle, and about five thousand of Lysias' men fell in hand-to-hand fighting. [35]When Lysias saw his ranks beginning to give way, and the increased boldness of Judas, whose men were ready either to live or to die bravely, he withdrew to Antioch and began to recruit mercenaries so as to return to Judea with greater numbers.[*]

Purification of the Temple. [36u]Then Judas and his brothers said, "Now that our enemies have been crushed, let us go up to purify the sanctuary[*] and rededicate it." [37]So the whole army assembled, and went up to Mount Zion. [38]They found the sanctuary desolate, the altar desecrated, the gates burnt, weeds growing in the courts as in a forest or on some mountain, and the priests' chambers demolished.[v] [39]Then they tore their clothes and made great lamentation; they sprinkled their heads with ashes [40]and fell with their faces to the ground. And when the signal was given with trumpets, they cried out to Heaven.

[41]Judas appointed men to attack those in the citadel, while he purified the sanctuary. [42]He chose blameless priests, devoted to the law; [43]these purified the sanctuary and carried away the stones of the Abomination to an unclean place. [44]They deliberated what ought to be done with the altar of holocausts that had been desecrated.[w] [45]The happy thought came to them to tear it down, lest it be a lasting shame to them that the Gentiles had defiled it; so they tore down the altar.[x] [46]They stored the stones in a suitable place on the temple hill, until a prophet should come and decide what to do with them. [47]Then they took uncut stones, according to

---

4, 22: Philistine territory: the coastal cities of southern Palestine, traditionally hostile to Jerusalem. Jamnia in particular was an important base for the Seleucid power.

4, 29: Beth-zur: an important frontier city in the mountain area, fifteen miles southwest of Jerusalem. Its inhabitants were sympathetic to the Maccabees and refused to receive Lysias.

4, 35: According to 2 Mc 11, 13-15, peace negotiations followed between Lysias and Judas.

4, 36: The sanctuary: the whole temple area with its walls, courts and outbuildings, to be distinguished from the temple proper, the oblong edifice with porch, main room and inner shrine.

r: Ps 118, 1ff. 29.   *s:* 26-35: 2 Mc 11, 1-12.   *t:* 1 Sm 17, 48ff. *u:* 36-59: 2 Mc 10, 1-8.   *v:* Ps 74, 2-7.   *w:* 1 Kgs 8, 64. *x:* 1 Mc 6, 7.

the law, and built a new altar like the former one.*y* *48*They also repaired the sanctuary and the interior of the temple and purified the courts. *49*They made new sacred vessels and brought the lampstand, the altar of incense, and the table into the temple.*z* *50*Then they burned incense on the altar and lighted the lamps on the lampstand, and these illuminated the temple.*a* *51*They also put loaves on the table and hung up the curtains. Thus they finished all the work they had undertaken.

*52*Early in the morning on the twenty-fifth day of the ninth month, that is, the month of Chislev, in the year one hundred and forty-eight,* *53*they arose and offered sacrifice according to the law on the new altar of holocausts that they had made.*b* *54*On the anniversary of the day on which the Gentiles had defiled it, on that very day it was reconsecrated with songs, harps, flutes, and cymbals. *55*All the people prostrated themselves and adored and praised Heaven, who had given them success.

*56*For eight days they celebrated the dedication of the altar and joyfully offered holocausts and sacrifices of deliverance and praise. *57*They ornamented the façade of the temple with gold crowns and shields; they repaired the gates and the priests' chambers and furnished them with doors. *58*There was great joy among the people now that the disgrace of the Gentiles was removed. *59*Then Judas and his brothers and the entire congregation of Israel decreed that the days of the dedication* of the altar should be observed with joy and gladness on the anniversary every year for eight days, from the twenty-fifth day of the month Chislev.*c*

*60*At that time they built high walls and strong towers around Mount Zion, to prevent the Gentiles from coming and trampling over it as they had done before. *61*Judas also placed a garrison there to protect it, and likewise fortified Beth-zur, that the people might have a stronghold facing Idumea.

CHAPTER 5*

Punishment of Hostile Acts. *1d*When the Gentiles round about heard that the altar had been rebuilt and the sanctuary consecrated as before, they were very angry. *2*So they decided to destroy the descendants of Jacob who were among them, and they began to massacre and persecute the people. *3e*Then Judas attacked the sons of Esau at Akrabattene* in Idumea, because they were blockading Israel; he defeated them heavily, overcame and despoiled them. *4*He also remembered the malice of the sons of Baean,* who had become a snare and a stumblingblock to the people by ambushing them along the roads. *5*He forced them to take refuge in towers, which he besieged; he vowed their annihilation and burned down the towers along with all the persons in them. *6*Then he crossed over to the Ammonites, where he found a strong army and a large body of people with Timothy as their leader. *7*He fought many battles with them, routed them, and struck them down. *8*After seizing Jazer and its villages, he returned to Judea.

Liberation of Galilean Jews. *9*The Gentiles in Gilead assembled to attack and destroy the Israelites who were in their territory; these then fled to the stronghold of Dathema. *10*They sent a letter to Judas and his brothers saying: "The Gentiles around us have combined against us to destroy us, *11*and they are preparing to come and seize this stronghold to which we have fled. Timothy is the leader of their army. *12*Come at once and rescue us from them, for many of us have fallen. *13*All our kinsmen who were among the Tobiads have been killed; the

---

4, 52: Twenty-fifth day of the ninth month . . . in the year one hundred and forty-eight: December 14, 164 B.C.

4, 59: Days of the dedication . . . Chislev: institution of the feast of Hanukkah, also called the feast of Dedication (Jn 10, 22). Josephus Flavius calls it the feast of Lights.

5, 1: The events of this chapter occurred within the year 163 B.C.

5, 3: Akrabattene: a district southwest of the Dead Sea.

5, 4: Sons of Baean: 2 Mc 10, 15-23 calls them simply Idumeans.

5, 6ff: This summary anticipates the order of events and would fit better between vv 36 and 37. It corresponds to 2 Mc 12, 17-23. The action was probably a reprisal for the massacre referred to in v 13. Timothy was the Seleucid governor of Transjordan. Jazer: a town on the road from the Jordan to Amman.

y: Ex 20, 25. *z:* Ex 25, 23-39; 30, 1-6. *a:* Ex 30, 7ff. *b:* 53. 56: Ex 30, 10; Ez 43, 18-27. *c:* Jn 10, 22. *d:* 1f: 1 Mc 13, 6. *e:* 3ff: 2 Mc 10, 15-23.

Gentiles have carried away their wives and children and their goods, and they have slain there about a thousand men."[f]

[14]While they were reading this letter, suddenly other messengers, in torn clothes, arrived from Galilee to deliver a similar message: [15]that the inhabitants of Ptolemais,* Tyre, and Sidon, and the whole of Gentile Galilee had joined forces to destroy them. [16]When Judas and the people heard this, a great assembly convened to consider what they should do for their unfortunate kinsmen who were being attacked by enemies.

[17]Judas said to his brother Simon: "Choose men for yourself, and go, rescue your kinsmen in Galilee; I and my brother Jonathan will go to Gilead." [18]In Judea he left Joseph, son of Zechariah, and Azariah, leader of the people, with the rest of the army to guard it. [19]"Take charge of these people," he commanded them, "but do not fight against the Gentiles until we return." [20]Three thousand men were allotted to Simon, to go into Galilee, and eight thousand men to Judas, for Gilead.

[21]Simon went into Galilee and fought many battles with the Gentiles. They were crushed before him, [22]and he pursued them to the very gate of Ptolemais. About three thousand men of the Gentiles fell, and he gathered their spoils. [23]He took with him the Jews who were in Galilee and in Arbatta, with their wives and children and all that they had, and brought them to Judea with great rejoicing.

Rescue in Gilead. [24][g]Judas Maccabeus and his brother Jonathan crossed the Jordan and marched for three days through the desert. [25]There they met some Nabateans,* who received them peacefully and told them all that had happened to the Jews in Gilead: [26]"Many of them have been imprisoned in Bozrah, in Bosor near Alema, in Chaspho, Maked, and Carnaim"—all of these are large, fortified cities— [27]"and some have been imprisoned in the other cities of Gilead. Tomorrow their en-

emies plan to attack the strongholds and to seize and destroy all these people in one day."

[28]Thereupon Judas suddenly changed direction with his army, marched across the desert to Bozrah, and captured the city. He slaughtered all the male population, took all their possessions, and set fire to the city. [29]He led his army from that place by night, and they marched toward the stronghold of Dathema. [30]When morning came, they looked ahead and saw a countless multitude of people, with ladders and devices for capturing the stronghold, and beginning to attack the people within. [31]When Judas perceived that the struggle had begun and that the noise of the battle was resounding to heaven with trumpet blasts and loud shouting, [32]he said to the men of his army, "Fight for our kinsmen today."

[33]He came up behind them with three columns blowing their trumpets and shouting in prayer. [34]When the army of Timothy realized that it was Maccabeus, they fell back before him, and he inflicted on them a crushing defeat. About eight thousand of their men fell that day. [35]Then he turned toward Alema and attacked and captured it; he killed all the male population, plundered the place, and burned it down. [36]From there he moved on and took Chaspho, Maked, Bosor, and the other cities of Gilead.

[37][h]After these events Timothy assembled another army and camped opposite Raphon, on the other side of the stream. [38]Judas sent men to spy on the camp, and they reported to him: "All the Gentiles around us have rallied to him, making a very large force; [39]they have also hired Arabs to help them, and have camped beyond the stream, ready to attack you." So Judas went forward to attack them. [40]As Judas and his army were approaching the running stream, Timothy said to the officers of his army: "If he crosses over to us first, we shall not be able to resist him; he will certainly defeat us.[i] [41]But if he is afraid

---

5, 15: Ptolemais: Hebrew Acco (Jgs 1, 31), modern Acre, on the coast north of Haifa.

5, 25: Nabateans: an Arab people who acquired wealth and power as caravan merchants in the final two centuries B.C. They settled down, established Petra as their capital, and for a time controlled all of Transjordan, even as far as Da-

mascus. It was from a Nabatean governor that St. Paul escaped about 38 A.D. (2 Cor 11, 32f).

---

f: 2 Mc 12, 17.   g: 24-36: 2 Mc 12, 10ff.   h: 37-44; 2 Mc 12, 20-26.   i: 1 Sm 14, 9f.

and camps on the other side of the river, we will cross over to him and defeat him."

⁴²But when Judas reached the running stream, he stationed the officers of the people beside the stream and gave them this order: "Do not allow any man to pitch a tent; all must go into battle." ⁴³He was the first to cross to the attack, with all the people behind him, and the Gentiles were crushed before them; they threw away their arms and fled to the temple enclosure at Carnaim. ⁴⁴The Jews captured that city and burnt the enclosure with all who were in it. So Carnaim was subdued, and Judas met with no more resistance.ʲ

⁴⁵Then he assembled all the Israelites, great and small, who were in Gilead, with their wives and children and their goods, a great crowd of people, to go into the land of Judah. ⁴⁶ᵏWhen they reached Ephron,* a large and strongly fortified city along the way, they found it impossible to encircle it on either the right or the left; they would have to march right through it. ⁴⁷But the men in the city shut them out and blocked up the gates with stones.ˡ ⁴⁸Then Judas sent them his peaceful message: "We wish to cross your territory in order to reach our own; no one will harm you; we will only march through." But they would not open to him.

⁴⁹So Judas ordered a proclamation to be made in the camp that everyone make an attack from the place where he was. ⁵⁰When the men of the army took up their positions, he assaulted the city all that day and night, and it was delivered to him. ⁵¹He slaughtered every male, razed and plundered the city, and passed through it over the slain.

⁵²Then they crossed the Jordan to the great plain in front of Beth-shan; ⁵³and Judas kept rounding up the stragglers and encouraging the people the whole way, until he reached the land of Judah. ⁵⁴They ascended Mount Zion in joy and gladness and offered holocausts, because not one of them had fallen; they returned in safety.

Joseph and Azariah Defeated. ⁵⁵During the time that Judas and Jonathan were in the land of Gilead, and Simon his brother was in Galilee opposite Ptolemais, ⁵⁶Joseph, son of Zechariah, and Azariah, the leaders of the army, heard about the brave deeds and the fighting that they were doing. ⁵⁷They said, "Let us also make a name for ourselves by going out and fighting against the Gentiles around us."

⁵⁸They gave orders to the men of their army who were with them, and marched toward Jamnia. ⁵⁹But Gorgias and his men came out of the city to meet them in battle. ⁶⁰Joseph and Azariah were beaten, and were pursued to the frontiers of Judea, and about two thousand Israelites fell that day. ⁶¹It was a bad defeat for the people, because they had not obeyed Judas and his brothers, thinking that they would do brave deeds. ⁶²But they did not belong to the family of those men to whom it was granted to achieve Israel's salvation. ⁶³The valiant Judas and his brothers were greatly renowned in all Israel and among all the Gentiles, wherever their name was heard; ⁶⁴and men gathered about them and praised them.

⁶⁵Then Judas and his brothers went out and attacked the sons of Esau* in the country toward the south; he took Hebron and its villages, and he destroyed its strongholds and burned the towers around it. ⁶⁶He then set out for the land of the Philistines and passed through Marisa. ⁶⁷At that time some priests fell in battle who had gone out rashly to fight in their desire to distinguish themselves. ⁶⁸Judas then turned toward Azotus in the land of the Philistines. He destroyed their altars and burned the statues of their gods; and after plundering their cities he returned to the land of Judah.

CHAPTER 6

See RG
229

Defeat and Death of Antiochus IV.

¹ᵐAs King Antiochus was traversing the inland provinces, he heard that in Persia there was a city called Elymais,* famous for its

---

5, 46: Ephron: a city in Trans-jordan opposite Beth-shan, about five miles east of the Jordan River. Situated on a height, it dominated the valleys of the two tributaries of the Jordan.

5, 65: Sons of Esau: Idumeans.

6, 1: Elymais: the mountainous region of Elam, north of the Persian Gulf. This section continues the story from 1 Mc 3, 37 and pertains to events preceding those in 1 Mc 4, 37ff.

j: 2 Mc 12, 21.   k: 46-54; 2 Mc 12, 27-31.   l: Nm 20, 17-21; 21, 21-25.   m: 1-13: 2 Mc 1, 12-17; 9, 1-29.

wealth in silver and gold, [2]and that its temple was very rich, containing gold helmets, breastplates, and weapons left there by Alexander, son of Philip, king of Macedon, the first king of the Greeks. [3]He went therefore and tried to capture and pillage the city. But he could not do so, because his plan became known to the people of the city [4]who rose up in battle against him. So he retreated and in great dismay withdrew from there to return to Babylon.

[5]While he was in Persia, a messenger brought him news that the armies sent into the land of Judah had been put to flight; [6]that Lysias had gone at first with a strong army and been driven back by the Israelites; that they had grown strong by reason of the arms, men, and abundant possessions taken from the armies they had destroyed; [7]that they had pulled down the Abomination which he had built upon the altar in Jerusalem; and that they had surrounded with high walls both the sanctuary, as it had been before, and his city of Beth-zur.[n]

[8]When the king heard this news, he was struck with fear and very much shaken. Sick with grief because his designs had failed, he took to his bed. [9]There he remained many days, overwhelmed with sorrow, for he knew he was going to die.

[10]So he called in all his Friends and said to them: "Sleep has departed from my eyes, for my heart is sinking with anxiety. [11]I said to myself: 'Into what tribulation have I come, and in what floods of sorrow am I now! [12]Yet I was kindly and beloved in my rule.' But I now recall the evils I did in Jerusalem, when I carried away all the vessels of gold and silver that were in it, and for no cause gave orders that the inhabitants of Judah be destroyed. [13]I know that this is why these evils have overtaken me; and now I am dying, in bitter grief, in a foreign land."

[14]Then he summoned Philip, one of his Friends, and put him in charge of his whole kingdom. [15]He gave him his crown, his robe, and his signet ring, so that he might guide the king's son Antiochus and bring him up to be king. [16]King Antiochus died in Persia in the year one hundred and forty-nine.[*]

The Citadel Besieged. [17]When Lysias learned that the king was dead, he set up the king's son Antiochus,[*] whom he had reared as a child, to be king in his place; and he gave him the title Eupator.[o]

[18]The men in the citadel were hemming in Israel around the sanctuary, continually trying to harm them and to strengthen the Gentiles.[p] [19]But Judas planned to destroy them, and called all the people together to besiege them. [20]So in the year one hundred and fifty[*] they assembled and stormed the citadel, for which purpose he constructed catapults and other devices. [21]Some of the besieged escaped, joined by impious Israelites; [22]they went to the king and said:

"How long will you fail to do justice and avenge our kinsmen? [23]We agreed to serve your father and to follow his orders and obey his edicts. [24]And for this the sons of our people have become our enemies; they have put to death as many of us as they could find and have plundered our estates. [25]They have acted aggressively not only against us, but throughout their whole territory. [26]Look! They have now besieged the citadel in Jerusalem in order to capture it, and they have fortified the sanctuary and Beth-zur. [27]Unless you quickly forestall them, they will do even worse things than these, and you will not be able to stop them."

Campaign against Judas. [28q]When the king heard this he was angry, and he called together all his Friends, the officers of his army, and the commanders of the cavalry.[r] [29]Mercenary forces also came to him from other kingdoms and from the islands of the seas. [30]His army numbered a hundred thou-

---

6, 16: The year one hundred and forty-nine: September 22, 164, to October 9, 163 B.C. A Babylonian list of the Seleucid kings indicates that Antiochus died in November or early December of 164.

6, 17: The king's son Antiochus: Antiochus V Eupator, then about nine years old. He was in Antioch, still in the charge of Lysias, who proceeded to govern and wage wars in his name. Both were put to death two years later, when

Demetrius, brother of Antiochus IV, arrived to claim the kingship; cf 1 Mc 7, 1ff.

6, 20: The year one hundred and fifty: October, 163, to September, 162 B.C.

n: 1 Mc 1, 54; 4, 41ff.60f. o: 2 Mc 10, 10f. p: 1 Mc 1, 33ff. q: 28-54: 2 Mc 13, 1-23. r: 28ff: 2 Mc 13, 1f.

sand foot-soldiers, twenty thousand cavalry, and thirty-two elephants trained for war. [31]They passed through Idumea and camped before Beth-zur. For many days they attacked it; they constructed siege-devices, but the besieged made a sortie and burned these, and they fought bravely.

[32]Then Judas marched away from the citadel and moved his camp to Beth-zechariah, on the way to the king's camp. [33]The king, rising before dawn, moved his force hastily along the road to Beth-zechariah; and the armies prepared for battle, while the trumpets sounded. [34]They made the elephants drunk on grape and mulberry wine to provoke them to fight. [35]The beasts were distributed along the phalanxes, each elephant having assigned to it a thousand men in coats of mail, with bronze helmets, and five hundred picked cavalry. [36]These anticipated the beast wherever it was; and wherever it moved, they moved too and never left it. [37]A strong wooden tower covering each elephant, and fastened to it by a harness, held, besides the Indian mahout, three soldiers who fought from it. [38]The remaining cavalry were stationed on one or the other of the two flanks of the army, to harass the enemy and to be protected from the phalanxes. [39]When the sun shone on the gold and bronze shields, the mountains gleamed with their brightness and blazed like flaming torches. [40]Part of the king's army extended over the heights, while some were on low ground, but they marched forward steadily and in good order. [41]All who heard the noise of their numbers, the tramp of their marching, and the clashing of the arms, trembled; for the army was very great and strong.

[42]Judas with his army advanced to fight, and six hundred men of the king's army fell. [43]Eleazar, called Avaran, saw one of the beasts bigger than any of the others and covered with royal armor, and he thought the king must be on it.[s] [44]So he gave up his life to save his people and win an everlasting name for himself. [45]He dashed up to it in the middle of the phalanx, killing men right and left, so that they fell back from him on both sides. [46]He ran right under the elephant and stabbed it in the belly, killing it. The beast fell to the ground on top of him, and he died there.

[47]When the Jews saw the strength of the royal army and the ardor of its forces, they retreated from them. [48t]A part of the king's army went up to Jerusalem to attack them, and the king established camps in Judea and at Mount Zion. [49u]He made peace with the men of Beth-zur, and they evacuated the city, because they had no food there to enable them to stand a siege, for that was a sabbath year in the land.* [50]The king took Beth-zur and stationed a garrison there to hold it. [51]For many days he besieged the sanctuary, setting up artillery and machines, fire-throwers, catapults and mechanical bows for shooting arrows and slingstones. [52]The Jews countered by setting up machines of their own, and kept up the fight a long time. [53]But there were no provisions in the storerooms, because it was the seventh year, and the tide-over provisions had been eaten up by those who had been rescued from the Gentiles and brought to Judea. [54]Few men remained in the sanctuary; the rest scattered, each to his own home, for the famine was too much for them.

Peace Treaty. [55v]Lysias heard that Philip, whom King Antiochus, before his death, had appointed to train his son Antiochus to be king, [56]had returned from Persia and Media with the army that accompanied the king, and that he was seeking to take over the government. [57]So he hastily resolved to withdraw. He said to the king, the leaders of the army, and the soldiers: "We are growing weaker every day, our provisions are scanty, the place we are besieging is strong, and it is our duty to take care of the affairs of the kingdom.[w] [58]Therefore let us now come to terms with these men, and make peace with them and all their nation. [59]Let us grant them freedom to live according to their own laws as formerly; it was on account of their laws,

---

6, 49: A sabbath year in the land: when sowing and reaping were prohibited (Ex 23, 10f; Lv 25, 2-7). The year without a harvest (autumn of 164 to autumn of 163) was followed by a food shortage.

s: 2 Mc 13, 15.   *t:* 48f: 2 Mc 13, 22-23.   *u:* Lv 25, 2.   *v:* 55-63: 2 Mc 13, 23-26.   *w:* 2 Mc 11, 13ff.

which we abolished, that they became angry and did all these things."

⁶⁰The proposal found favor with the king and the leaders; he sent peace terms to the Jews, and they accepted. ⁶¹So the king and the leaders swore an oath to them, and on these terms they evacuated the fortification. ⁶²But when the king entered Mount Zion and saw how the place was fortified, he broke the oath he had sworn and gave orders for the encircling wall to be destroyed. ⁶³Then he departed in haste and returned to Antioch, where he found Philip in possession of the city. He fought against him and took the city by force.

See RG 229

CHAPTER 7

Expedition of Bacchides and Alcimus.

¹ˣIn the year one hundred and fifty-one,* Demetrius, son of Seleucus, set out from Rome, arrived with a few men in a city on the seacoast, and began to rule there. ²As he was preparing to enter the royal palace of his ancestors, the soldiers seized Antiochus and Lysias to bring them to him. ³When he was informed of this, he said, "Do not show me their faces." ⁴So the soldiers killed them, and Demetrius sat on the royal throne.

⁵Then all the lawless and impious men of Israel came to him. They were led by Alcimus,* who desired to be high priest. ⁶They made this accusation to the king against the people: "Judas and his brothers have destroyed all your friends and have driven us out of our country. ⁷So now, send a man whom you trust to go and see all the havoc Judas has done to us and to the king's land, and let him punish them and all their supporters."

⁸Then the king chose Bacchides, one of the King's Friends, governor of West-of-Euphrates, a great man in the kingdom, and faithful to the king. ⁹ʸHe sent him and the impious Alcimus, to whom he granted the high priesthood, with orders to take revenge on the Israelites. ¹⁰They set out and, on arriving in the land of Judah with a great army, sent messengers who spoke deceitfully to Judas and his brothers in peaceful terms. ¹¹But these paid no attention to their words, seeing that they had come with a great army. ¹²A group of scribes, however, gathered about Alcimus and Bacchides to ask for a just agreement. ¹³ᶻThe Hasideans were the first among the Israelites to seek peace with them, ¹⁴for they said, "A priest of the line of Aaron has come with the army, and he will not do us any wrong." ¹⁵He spoke with them peacefully and swore to them, "We will not try to injure you or your friends." ¹⁶So they trusted him. But he arrested sixty of them and killed them in one day, according to the text of Scripture:

¹⁷ "The flesh of your saints they have
    strewn,
  and their blood they have shed round
    about Jerusalem,
  and there was no one to bury them."ᵃ

¹⁸Then fear and dread of them came upon all the people, who said: "There is no truth or justice among them; they violated the agreement and the oath that they swore."

¹⁹Bacchides withdrew from Jerusalem and pitched his camp in Beth-zaith.* He had many of the men arrested who deserted to him, throwing them into the great pit. ²⁰He handed the province over to Alcimus, leaving troops to help him, while he himself returned to the king.

²¹Alcimus spared no pains to maintain his high priesthood, ²²and all those who were disturbing their people gathered about him. They took possession of the land of Judah and caused great distress in Israel. ²³When Judas

---

7, 1ff: The year one hundred and fifty-one: the spring of 161 B.C. Demetrius, son of Seleucus, was the lawful heir to the kingdom; but when only nine years old, he was taken as a hostage at Rome in place of his uncle, who ruled as Antiochus IV Epiphanes. At the age of twenty-five Demetrius fled secretly from Rome and, with the support of the Syrians, overcame his rival Antiochus V and put him to death. The royal palace: at Antioch.

7, 5f: Alcimus: a renegade Jew hostile to the Maccabees, who became high priest after the death of Menelaus (2 Mc 14,

3). He received confirmation in his office from the new King Demetrius (v 9), and brought malicious charges against Judas and his brothers and the people (v 6). He wrought more evils on the Israelites than the Gentiles had done (v 23).

7, 19: Beth-zaith: about three miles north of Beth-zur and twelve miles south of Jerusalem.

---

x: 1-7: 2 Mc 14, 1-11.   y: 9ff: 2 Mc 14, 46.   z: 13f: 1 Mc 2, 42.
a: Ps 79, 1ff.

saw all the evils that Alcimus and his men were bringing upon the Israelites, more than even the Gentiles had done, [24]he went about all the borders of Judea and took revenge on the men who had deserted, preventing them from going out into the country. [25]But when Alcimus saw that Judas and his followers were gaining strength and realized that he could not oppose them, he returned to the king and accused them of grave crimes.

Defeat of Nicanor. [26b]Then the king sent Nicanor, one of his famous officers, who was a bitter enemy of Israel, with orders to destroy the people. [27]Nicanor came to Jerusalem with a large force and deceitfully sent to Judas* and his brothers this peaceable message: [28]"Let there be no fight between me and you. I will come with a few men to meet you peaceably." [29]So he came to Judas, and they greeted one another peaceably. But Judas' enemies were prepared to seize him. [30]When he became aware that Nicanor had come to him with treachery in mind, Judas was afraid and would not meet him again.[c] [31]When Nicanor saw that his plan had been discovered, he went out to fight Judas near Caphar-salama.* [32]About five hundred men of Nicanor's army fell; the rest fled to the City of David.

[33d]After this, Nicanor went up to Mount Zion. Some of the priests from the sanctuary and some of the elders of the people came out to greet him peaceably and to show him the holocaust that was being offered for the king. [34]But he mocked and ridiculed them, defiled them,* and spoke disdainfully. [35]In a rage he swore: "If Judas and his army are not delivered to me at once, when I return victorious I will burn this temple down." He went away in great anger. [36]The priests, however, went in and stood before the altar and the sanctuary.[e] They wept and said: [37]"You have chosen this house to bear your name, to be a house of prayer and petition for your people. [38]Take revenge on this man and his army, and let them fall by the sword. Remember their blasphemies, and do not let them continue."

[39]Nicanor left Jerusalem and pitched his camp at Beth-horon, where the Syrian army joined him. [40]But Judas camped in Adasa* with three thousand men. Here Judas uttered this prayer: [41]"When they who were sent by the king blasphemed, your angel went out and killed a hundred and eighty-five thousand of them.[f] [42]In the same way, crush this army before us today, and let the rest know that Nicanor spoke wickedly against your sanctuary; judge him according to his wickedness."[g]

[43]The armies met in battle on the thirteenth day of the month Adar. Nicanor's army was crushed, and he himself was the first to fall in the battle.[h] [44]When his army saw that Nicanor was dead, they threw down their arms and fled. [45]The Jews pursued them a day's journey, from Adasa to near Gazara, blowing the trumpets behind them as signals. [46]From all the surrounding villages of Judea people came out and closed in on them. They hemmed them in, and all the enemies fell by the sword; not a single one escaped.

[47]Then the Jews collected the spoils and the booty; they cut off Nicanor's head and his right arm, which he had lifted up so arrogantly. These they brought to Jerusalem and displayed there. [48]The people rejoiced greatly, and observed that day as a great festival. [49]They decreed that it should be observed every year on the thirteenth of Adar.* [50]And for a short time* the land of Judah was quiet.

CHAPTER 8

See RG 229

*Treaty with the Romans.** [1]Judas had heard of the reputation of the Romans. They

---

7, 27: Nicanor . . . deceitfully sent to Judas: a more favorable picture of Nicanor, as an honest man who became a personal friend of Judas, is given in 2 Mc 14, 17-25. Their friendship was broken by the intrigues of Alcimus (2 Mc 14, 26-30).

7, 31: Caphar-salama: a village seven miles north-northwest of Jerusalem, on the road leading to Beth-horon.

7, 34: Defiled them: spitting on the priests caused them to become legally defiled.

7, 40: Adasa: a village southeast of Caphar-salama.

7, 49: The thirteenth of Adar: March 27, 160 B.C. This

day in the Jewish calendar was called the "Day of Nicanor" (2 Mc 15, 36), but it was not long celebrated by the Jews.

7, 50: A short time: about one month following the death of Nicanor. After that began the attack of Bacchides resulting in the death of Judas (1 Mc 9, 1-18).

8, 1: This chapter contains the account of the embassy which Judas sent to Rome, probably before the death of Ni-

b: 26f: 1 Mc 3, 38; 2 Mc 8, 9; 14, 12f.   *c:* 2 Mc 14, 30.   *d:* 33-38: 2 Mc 14, 31-36.   *e:* Jl 2, 17.   *f:* 41f: 2 Mc 8, 19; 15, 22ff.   *g:* Is 37, 36ff.   *h:* 2 Mc 15, 25-35.

were valiant fighters and acted amiably to all who took their side. They established a friendly alliance with all who applied to them. ²He was also told of their battles and the brave deeds that they had performed against the Gauls,* conquering them and forcing them to pay tribute. ³They had gotten possession of the silver and gold mines in Spain, ⁴and by planning and persistence had conquered the whole country, although it was very remote from their own. They had crushed the kings who had come against them from the far corners of the earth and had inflicted on them severe defeat, and the rest paid tribute to them every year. ⁵Philip* and Perseus, king of the Macedonians, and the others who opposed them in battle had been overwhelmed and subjugated. ⁶Antiochus* the Great, king of Asia, who had fought against them with a hundred and twenty elephants and with cavalry and chariots and a very great army, had been defeated by them. ⁷They had taken him alive and obliged him and the kings who succeeded him to pay a heavy tribute, to give hostages and a section of ⁸Lycia, Mysia,* and Lydia from among their best provinces. The Romans took these from him and gave them to King Eumenes. ⁹*When the men of Greece had planned to come and destroy them, ¹⁰the Romans discovered it, and sent against the Greeks a sin-

gle general who made war on them. Many were wounded and fell, and the Romans took their wives and children captive. They plundered them, took possession of their land, tore down their strongholds and reduced them to slavery even to this day. ¹¹All the other kingdoms and islands that had ever opposed them they destroyed and enslaved; ¹²with their friends, however, and those who relied on them, they maintained friendship. They had conquered kings both far and near, and all who heard of their fame were afraid of them. ¹³In truth, those whom they desired to help to a kingdom became kings, and those whom they wished to depose they deposed; and they were greatly exalted. ¹⁴Yet with all this, none of them put on a crown or wore purple as a display of grandeur. ¹⁵They had made for themselves a senate house, and every day three hundred and twenty men took counsel, deliberating on all that concerned the people and their well-being. ¹⁶They entrusted their government to one man* every year, to rule over their entire country, and they all obeyed that one, and there was no envy or jealousy among them.

¹⁷So Judas chose Eupolemus, son of John, son of Accos, and Jason, son of Eleazar, and sent them to Rome to establish an alliance of friendship with them.ⁱ ¹⁸He did this to get rid of the yoke, for it was obvious that the king-

---

canor, to conclude a treaty of alliance between Rome and the Jewish nation. Without precise chronology, the pertinent data are gathered into a unified theme.

The image of the Roman Republic greatly impressed the smaller Eastern peoples seeking support against their overlords (1-16), because of Roman success in war (2-11) and effective aid to their allies (12-13). Numerous interventions by Rome in the politics of the Near East bear witness to its power and prestige in the second century B.C. Cf 1 Mc 1, 10; 7, 2; 12, 3; 15, 15-24; 2 Mc 11, 34. With the Roman control of Palestine in 63 B.C., the Republic and later the Empire became heartily detested. The eulogy of Rome in this chapter is one of the reasons why 1 Maccabees was not preserved by the Palestinian Jews of the century that followed.

8, 2: Gauls: probably the Celts of northern Italy and southern France, subdued by the Romans in 222 B.C., and again in 200–191 B.C.; but perhaps also those in Asia Minor (the Galatians), whom the Romans defeated in 189 B.C.

8, 5: Philip: Philip V of Macedonia, defeated by a Graeco-Roman alliance at Cynoscephalae in 197 B.C. Perseus, his son, was defeated at Pydna in 168 B.C., and died a prisoner. With this, the kingdom of Macedonia came to an end.

8, 6: Antiochus: Antiochus III, greatest of the Seleucid

kings. He was defeated at Magnesia in 190 B.C. By the Treaty of Apamea in 189, he was obliged to pay Rome a crushing indemnity of 15,000 talents. It was the weakening of Antiochene power and the growing military and economic influence of Rome that led Antiochus IV to adopt the policy of political, religious and cultural unification of Syria and Palestine.

8, 8: Lycia, Mysia: regions in western Asia Minor, These names are restored here by conjectural emendation; the Greek text has "India, Media," most likely through scribal error. Eumenes: Eumenes II (197–158), king of Pergamum, an ally of Rome who benefited greatly from Antiochus' losses.

8, 9f: The revolt of the Achaean League, inserted here, occurred in 146 B.C., after Judas' time. It was crushed by the Roman consul Lucius Mummius and marked the end of Greek independence. The author regards all Greeks as the enemies of God.

8, 16: They entrusted their government to one man: actually the Roman Republic always had two consuls as joint heads of the government. Presumably, a single one dealt with embassies and answered letters, hence the impression the Jews received; cf 1 Mc 15, 16.

i: 1 Mc 12, 1f; 15, 15-22.

dom of the Greeks was subjecting Israel to slavery. [19]After making a very long journey to Rome, the envoys entered the senate and spoke as follows: [20]"Judas, called Maccabeus, and his brothers, with the Jewish people, have sent us to you to make a peaceful alliance with you, and to enroll ourselves among your allies and friends." [21]The proposal pleased the Romans, [22]and this is a copy of the reply they inscribed on bronze tablets and sent to Jerusalem,* to remain there with the Jews as a record of peace and alliance:[j]

[23]"May it be well with the Romans and the Jewish nation at sea and on land forever; may sword and enemy be far from them. [24]But if war is first made on Rome, or any of its allies in any of their dominions, [25]the Jewish nation will help them wholeheartedly, as the occasion shall demand; [26]and to those who wage war they shall not give nor provide grain, arms, money, or ships; this is Rome's decision. They shall fulfill their obligations without receiving any recompense. [27]In the same way, if war is made first on the Jewish nation, the Romans will help them willingly, as the occasion shall demand, [28]and to those who are attacking them there shall not be given grain, arms, money, or ships; this is Rome's decision. They shall fulfill their obligations without deception. [29]On these terms the Romans have made an agreement with the Jewish people. [30]But if both parties hereafter decide to add or take away anything, they shall do as they choose, and whatever they shall add or take away shall be valid.

[31]"Moreover, concerning the wrongs that King Demetrius has done to them, we have written to him thus: 'Why have you made your yoke heavy upon our friends and allies the Jews? [32]If they complain about you again, we will do them justice and make war on you by land and sea.' "

CHAPTER 9

See RG 229

Invasion of Judah. [1]When Demetrius heard that Nicanor and his army had fallen in battle, he again sent Bacchides and Alcimus into the land of Judah, along with the right wing of his army. [2]They took the road to Galilee, and camping opposite the ascent at Arbela, they captured it* and killed many people. [3]In the first month of the year one hundred and fifty-two,* they encamped against Jerusalem. [4]Then they set out for Berea with twenty thousand men and two thousand cavalry. [5]Judas, with three thousand picked men, had camped at Elasa. [6]When his men saw the great number of the troops, they were very much afraid, and many slipped away from the camp, until only eight hundred men remained.

[7]As Judas saw that his army was melting away just when the battle was imminent, he was panic-stricken, because he had no time to gather them together. [8]But in spite of his discouragement, he said to those who remained: "Let us go forward to meet our enemies; perhaps we can put up a good fight against them." [9]They tried to dissuade him, saying: "We certainly cannot. Let us save our lives now, and come back with our kinsmen, and then fight against them. Now we are too few." [10]But Judas said: "Far be it from me to do such a thing as to flee from them! If our time has come, let us die bravely for our kinsmen and not leave a stain upon our glory!"

Death of Judas. [11]Then the army of Bacchides moved out of camp and took its position for combat. The cavalry were divided into two squadrons, and the slingers and the archers came on ahead of the army, and all the valiant men were in the front line. [12]Bacchides was on the right wing. Flanked by the

---

8, 22: The reply . . . on bronze tablets and sent to Jerusalem: the decree of the Senate would be inscribed on bronze and kept in the Roman Capitol, with only a copy in letter form sent to Jerusalem. The translation of the decree into Hebrew and then into Greek, as found here in 1 Mc, may have occasioned this error.

9, 2: They took the road . . . Arbela, they captured it: this passage is restored, in part, by conjectural emendation. The present Greek text could be translated, "They took the road to Gilgal, and camping opposite Mesaloth at Arbela, they cap-

tured it." But Arbela (modern Khirbet Irbid) was in Galilee—on a high hill overlooking the western shore of the Sea of Galilee. Gilgal, on the contrary, was in the Jordan valley near Jericho. "Mesaloth" is probably a corrupt form of a Hebrew word meaning "steps, ascent."

9, 3: The first month of the year one hundred and fifty-two: April/May 160 B.C., by the temple calendar.

j: 1 Mc 14, 18.

two squadrons, the phalanx attacked as they blew their trumpets. Those who were on Judas' side also blew their trumpets. [13]The earth shook with the noise of the armies, and the battle raged from morning until evening. [14]Seeing that Bacchides was on the right, with the main force of his army, Judas, with all the most stouthearted rallying to him, [15]drove back the right wing and pursued them as far as the mountain slopes.* [16]But when the men on the left wing saw that the right wing was driven back, they turned and followed Judas and his men, taking them in the rear. [17]The battle was fought desperately, and many on both sides fell wounded. [18]Then Judas fell, and the rest fled.

[19]Jonathan and Simon took their brother Judas and buried him in the tomb of their fathers at Modein. [20]All Israel bewailed him in great grief. They mourned for him many days, and they said, [21]"How the mighty one has fallen, the savior of Israel!"[k] [22]The other acts of Judas, his battles, the brave deeds he performed, and his greatness have not been recorded; but they were very many.

IV: Leadership of Jonathan

Bacchides and Jonathan. [23]After the death of Judas, the transgressors of the law raised their heads in every part of Israel, and all kinds of evildoers appeared. [24]In those days there was a very great famine, and the country deserted to them. [25]Bacchides chose impious men and made them masters of the country. [26]These sought out and hunted down the friends of Judas and brought them to Bacchides, who punished and derided them. [27]There had not been such great distress in Israel since the time prophets ceased to appear among the people.

[28]Then all the friends of Judas came together and said to Jonathan: [29]"Since your brother Judas died, there has been no one like him to oppose our enemies, Bacchides and those who are hostile to our nation. [30]Now therefore we have chosen you today to be our ruler and leader in his place, and to fight our battle." [31]From that moment Jonathan accepted the leadership, and took the place of Judas his brother.

[32]When Bacchides learned of it, he sought to kill him. [33]But Jonathan and his brother Simon and all the men with him discovered this, and they fled to the desert of Tekoa* and camped by the waters of the pool of Asphar.*

[35]Jonathan sent his brother* as leader of the convoy to ask permission of his friends, the Nabateans, to deposit with them their great quantity of baggage.[l] [36]But the sons of Jambri from Medaba* made a raid and seized and carried off John and everything he had. [37]After this, word was brought to Jonathan and his brother Simon: "The sons of Jambri are celebrating a great wedding, and with a large escort they are bringing the bride, the daughter of one of the great princes of Canaan, from Nadabath." [38]Remembering the blood of John their brother, they went up and hid themselves under cover of the mountain. [39]They watched, and suddenly saw a noisy crowd with baggage; the bridegroom and his friends and kinsmen had come out to meet the bride's party with tambourines and musicians and much equipment. [40]The Jews rose up against them from their ambush and killed them. Many fell wounded, and after the survivors fled toward the mountain, all their spoils were taken. [41]Thus the wedding was turned into mourning, and the sound of music into lamentation. [42]Having taken their revenge for the blood of their brother, the Jews returned to the marshes of the Jordan.

[43]When Bacchides heard of it, he came on the sabbath to the banks of the Jordan with a large force. [44]Then Jonathan said to his companions, "Let us get up now and fight for our lives, for today is not like yesterday and the day before. [45]The battle is before us, and behind us are the waters of the Jordan on one

---

9, 15: As far as the mountain slopes: conjectural emendation. The Greek text has "as far as Mount Azotus"; this is most unlikely. Apparently the Greek translator mistook the Hebrew word ashdot, "slopes," for asdod, "Azotus."

9, 33: Tekoa: Home of the prophet Amos in the wild country above the Dead Sea, southeast of Jerusalem.

9, 34: Omitted, it is a dittography of verse 43.

9, 35: Jonathan sent his brother: this was John who was called Gaddi (1 Mc 2, 2; cf 9, 36. 38).

9, 36: Medaba: northeast of the Dead Sea.

k: 2 Sam 1, 27.   l: 1 Mc 5, 25.

side, marsh and thickets on the other, and there is no way of escape.* ⁴⁶Cry out now to Heaven for deliverance from our enemies." ⁴⁷When they joined battle, Jonathan raised his arm to strike Bacchides, but Bacchides backed away from him. ⁴⁸Jonathan and his men jumped into the Jordan and swam across to the other side, but the enemy did not pursue them across the Jordan. ⁴⁹A thousand men on Bacchides' side fell that day.

⁵⁰On returning to Jerusalem, Bacchides built strongholds in Judea: the Jericho fortress, as well as Emmaus, Beth-horon, Bethel, Timnath, Pharathon, and Tephon, with high walls and gates and bars.* ⁵¹In each he put a garrison to oppose Israel. ⁵²He fortified the city of Beth-zur, Gazara and the citadel, and put soldiers in them and stores of provisions. ⁵³He took as hostages the sons of the leaders of the country and put them in custody in the citadel at Jerusalem.ᵐ

⁵⁴In the year one hundred and fifty-three, in the second month,* Alcimus ordered the wall of the inner court of the sanctuary to be torn down, thus destroying the work of the prophets. But he only began to tear it down. ⁵⁵Just at that time he had a stroke, and his work was interrupted; his mouth was closed and he was paralyzed, so that he could no longer utter a word to give orders concerning his house. ⁵⁶Finally he died in great agony. ⁵⁷Seeing that Alcimus was dead, Bacchides returned to the king, and the land of Judah was quiet for two years.

⁵⁸Then all the transgressors of the law held a council and said: "Jonathan and his companions are living in peace and security. Now then, let us have Bacchides return, and he will capture all of them in a single night." ⁵⁹So they went and took counsel with him. ⁶⁰When Bacchides was setting out with a large force, he sent letters secretly to all his allies in Judea, telling them to seize Jonathan and his companions. They were not able to do this, however, because their plot became known. ⁶¹In fact, Jonathan's men seized about fifty of the men of the country who were ringleaders in the mischief and put them to death. ⁶²Then Jonathan and Simon and their companions withdrew to Bethbasi* in the desert; they rebuilt and strengthened its fortifications that had been demolished. ⁶³When Bacchides learned of this, he gathered together his whole force and sent word to those who were in Judea. ⁶⁴He came and pitched his camp before Bethbasi, and constructing siege-machines, he fought against it for many days.

⁶⁵Leaving his brother Simon in the city, Jonathan, accompanied by a small group of men, went out into the field. ⁶⁶He struck down Odomera and his kinsmen and the sons of Phasiron in their encampment; these men had set out to go up to the siege with their forces. ⁶⁷Simon and his men then sallied forth from the city and set fire to the machines. ⁶⁸They fought against Bacchides, and he was beaten. This caused him great distress. Because the enterprise he had planned came to naught, ⁶⁹he was angry with the lawless men who had advised him to invade the province. He killed many of them and resolved to return to his own country.

⁷⁰Jonathan learned of this and sent ambassadors to make peace with him and to obtain the release of the prisoners. ⁷¹He agreed to do as Jonathan had asked. He swore an oath to him that he would never try to injure him for the rest of his life; ⁷²and he released the prisoners he had previously taken from the land of Judah. He returned to his own country and never came into their territory again.

⁷³Then the sword ceased in Israel. Jonathan settled in Michmash; he began to judge* the people, and he destroyed the impious in Israel.

9, 45: Jonathan's force was apparently trapped in one of the many oxbows of the lower Jordan. Bacchides had crossed and caught them still on the east bank.

9, 50: These sites constitute a ring on the edges of the province of Judea.

9, 54: In the year . . . second month: May 159 B.C.

9, 62: Bethbasi: two miles east of Bethlehem, and six miles north of Tekoa.

9, 73: Began to judge: exercise the governing authority as in the book of Judges. With Jerusalem and the garrison towns (v 50) firmly in Seleucid hands, Jonathan's freedom of action was greatly restricted. Michmash, southeast of Bethel, famous for the exploit of the former Jonathan, son of Saul; cf 1 Sm 14.

m: 1 Mc 10, 9.

See RG
229

CHAPTER 10

Revolt of Alexander. [1] In the year one hundred and sixty,* Alexander, who was called Epiphanes, son of Antiochus, came up and took Ptolemais. He was accepted and began to reign there. [2] When King Demetrius heard of it, he mustered a very large army and marched out to engage him in combat. [3] Demetrius sent a letter to Jonathan written in peaceful terms, to pay him honor; [4] for he said: "Let us be the first to make peace with him, before he makes peace with Alexander against us, [5] since he will remember all the wrongs we have done to him, his brothers, and his nation."

[6] So Demetrius authorized Jonathan, as his ally, to gather an army and procure arms; and he ordered that the hostages in the citadel be released to him. [7] Accordingly Jonathan went up to Jerusalem and read the letter to all the people. The men in the citadel [8] were struck with fear when they heard that the king had given him authority to gather an army. [9] They released the hostages to Jonathan, and he gave them back to their parents.[n] [10] Thereafter Jonathan dwelt in Jerusalem, and began to build and restore the city. [11] He ordered the workmen to build the walls and encircle Mount Zion with square stones for its fortification, which they did. [12] The foreigners in the strongholds that Bacchides had built, took flight; [13] each one of them left his place and returned to his own country. [14] Only in Beth-zur did some remain of those who had abandoned the law and the commandments, for they used it as a place of refuge.

Jonathan Supports Alexander. [15] King Alexander heard of the promises that Demetrius had made to Jonathan; he was also told of the battles and valiant deeds of Jonathan and his brothers and the troubles that they

had endured. [16] He said, "Shall we ever find another man like him? Let us now make him our friend and ally." [17] So he sent Jonathan a letter written in these terms: [18] "King Alexander sends greetings to his brother Jonathan. [19] We have heard of you, that you are a mighty warrior and worthy to be our friend. [20] We have therefore appointed you today to be high priest of your nation; you are to be called the King's Friend, and you are to look after our interests and preserve amity with us." He also sent him a purple robe and a crown of gold.[o]

[21] Jonathan put on the sacred vestments in the seventh month of the year one hundred and sixty at the feast of Booths,* and he gathered an army and procured many arms. [22] When Demetrius heard of these things, he was distressed and said: [23] "Why have we allowed Alexander to get ahead of us by gaining the friendship of the Jews and thus strengthening himself? [24] I too will write them conciliatory words and offer dignities and gifts, so that they may be an aid to me." [25] So he sent them this message: "King Demetrius sends greetings to the Jewish nation. [26] We have heard how you have kept the treaty with us and continued in our friendship and not gone over to our enemies, and we are glad. [27] Continue, therefore, to keep faith with us, and we will reward you with favors in return for what you do in our behalf. [28] We will grant you many exemptions and will bestow gifts on you.

[29] "I now free you, as I also exempt all the Jews, from the tribute, the salt tax, and the crown levies.[p] [30] Instead of collecting the third of the grain and the half of the fruit of the trees that should be my share, I renounce the right from this day forward. Neither now nor in the future will I collect them from the land of Judah or from the three districts annexed from Samaria.* [31] Let Jerusalem and

---

10, 1: The year one hundred and sixty: 152 B.C. Alexander . . . Antiochus: Alexander Balas claimed to be a son of Antiochus IV. He had the backing of the Romans, who had never forgiven Demetrius for becoming king without their permission. The latter meanwhile had become unpopular with his own people as well as with the Jews.

10, 21: Jonathan . . . feast of Booths: Jonathan began to discharge the office of high priest October 23-30, 152 B.C. For seven years after the death of Alcimus there had been no high priest in Jerusalem. It was taken for granted that the

king, though a Gentile, had the power to appoint one. The Maccabees, though a priestly family, were not of the line of Zadok, and some in Israel regarded Jonathan's tenure as a usurpation.

10, 30: The three districts annexed from Samaria: mentioned by name in 1 Mc 11, 34. The present Greek text, by a scribal error, has added "and Galilee" after "Samaria."

n: 1 Mc 9, 53. *o:* 1 Mc 2, 18. *p:* 1 Mc 11, 28f. 35. *q:* 1 Mc 11, 28, 34.

her territory, her tithes and her tolls, be sacred and free from tax. [32]I also yield my authority over the citadel in Jerusalem, and I transfer it to the high priest, that he may put in it such men as he shall choose to guard it. [33]Every one of the Jews who has been carried into captivity from the land of Judah into any part of my kingdom I set at liberty without ransom; and let all their taxes, even those on their cattle, be canceled. [34]Let all feast days, sabbaths, new moon festivals, appointed days, and the three days that precede each feast day, and the three days that follow, be days of immunity and exemption for every Jew in my kingdom. [35]Let no man have authority to exact payment from them or to molest any of them in any matter.

[36]"Let thirty thousand Jews be enrolled in the king's army and allowances be given them, as is due to all the king's soldiers. [37]Let some of them be stationed in the king's principal strongholds, and of these let some be given positions of trust in the affairs of the kingdom. Let their superiors and their rulers be taken from among them, and let them follow their own laws, as the king has commanded in the land of Judah.

[38]"Let the three districts that have been added to Judea from the province of Samaria be incorporated with Judea so that they may be under one man and obey no other authority than the high priest. [39]Ptolemais and its confines I give as a present to the sanctuary in Jerusalem for the necessary expenses of the sanctuary. [40]I make a yearly personal grant of fifteen thousand silver shekels out of the royal revenues, from appropriate places. [41]All the additional funds that the officials did not hand over as they had done in the first years, shall henceforth be handed over for the services of the temple. [42]Moreover, the dues of five thousand silver shekels that used to be taken from the revenue of the sanctuary every year shall be canceled, since these funds belong to the priests who perform the services. [43]Whoever takes refuge in the temple of Jerusalem or in any of its precincts, because of money he owes the king, or because of any other debt, shall be released, together with all the goods he possesses in my kingdom. [44]The cost of rebuilding and restoring the structures of the sanctuary shall be covered out of the royal revenue. [45]Likewise the cost of building the walls of Jerusalem and fortifying it all around, and of building walls in Judea, shall be donated from the royal revenue."

[46]When Jonathan and the people heard these words, they neither believed nor accepted them, for they remembered the great evil that Demetrius had done in Israel, and how sorely he had afflicted them. [47]They therefore decided in favor of Alexander, for he had been the first to address them peaceably, and they remained his allies for the rest of his life.

[48]King Alexander gathered together a large army and encamped opposite Demetrius. [49]The two kings joined battle, and when the army of Demetrius fled, Alexander pursued him, and overpowered his soldiers. [50]He pressed the battle hard until sunset, and Demetrius fell that day.

Treaty of Ptolemy and Alexander. [51]Alexander sent ambassadors to Ptolemy, king of Egypt, with this message: [52]"Now that I have returned to my realm, taken my seat on the throne of my fathers, and established my rule by crushing Demetrius and gaining control of my country— [53]for I engaged him in battle, defeated him and his army, and recovered the royal throne— [54]let us now establish friendship with each other. Give me your daughter for my wife; and as your son-in-law, I will give to you and to her gifts worthy of you."

[55]King Ptolemy answered in these words: "Happy the day on which you returned to the land of your fathers and took your seat on their royal throne! [56]I will do for you what you have written; but meet me in Ptolemais, so that we may see each other, and I will become your father-in-law as you have proposed."

[57]So Ptolemy with his daughter Cleopatra* set out from Egypt and came to Ptolemais in the year one hundred and sixty-two.

10, 57: Cleopatra: Cleopatra Thea, then about fifteen years old. She later married Demetrius II, and later still, his brother Antiochus VII. The year one hundred and sixty-two. 151/150 B.C.

⁵⁸There King Alexander met him, and Ptolemy gave him his daughter Cleopatra in marriage. Their wedding was celebrated at Ptolemais with great splendor according to the custom of kings.

⁵⁹King Alexander also wrote to Jonathan to come and meet him. ⁶⁰So he went with pomp to Ptolemais, where he met the two kings and gave them and their friends silver and gold and many gifts and thus won their favor.ʳ ⁶¹Some pestilent Israelites, transgressors of the law, united against him to accuse him, but the king paid no heed to them. ⁶²He ordered Jonathan to be divested of his ordinary garments and to be clothed in royal purple; and so it was done. ⁶³The king also had him seated at his side. He said to his magistrates: "Go with him to the center of the city and make a proclamation that no one is to bring charges against him on any grounds or be troublesome to him in any way."

⁶⁴ˢWhen his accusers saw the honor paid to him in the proclamation, and the purple with which he was clothed, they all fled. ⁶⁵The king also honored him by numbering him among his Chief Friends and made him military commander and governor of the province. ⁶⁶So Jonathan returned in peace and happiness to Jerusalem.

Victory over Apollonius. ⁶⁷In the year one hundred and sixty-five,* Demetrius, son of Demetrius, came from Crete to the land of his fathers. ⁶⁸When King Alexander heard of it he was greatly troubled, and returned to Antioch. ⁶⁹Demetrius appointed Apollonius governor of Coelesyria. Having gathered a large army, Apollonius pitched his camp at Jamnia. From there he sent this message to Jonathan the high priest:

⁷⁰"You are the only one who resists us. I am laughed at and put to shame on your account. Why are you displaying power against us in the mountains? ⁷¹If you have confidence in your forces, come down now to us in the plain, and let us test each other's strength there; the city forces are on my side.

⁷²Inquire and learn who I am and who the others are who are helping me. Men say that you cannot make a stand against us because your fathers were twice put to flight in their own land. ⁷³Now you too will be unable to withstand our cavalry and such a force as this in the plain, where there is not a stone or a pebble or a place to flee."

⁷⁴When Jonathan heard the message of Apollonius, he was roused. Choosing ten thousand men, he set out from Jerusalem, and Simon his brother joined him to help him. ⁷⁵He pitched camp near Joppa, but the men in the city shut him out because Apollonius had a garrison there. When the Jews besieged it, ⁷⁶the men of the city became afraid and opened the gates, and so Jonathan took possession of Joppa.*

⁷⁷When Apollonius heard of it, he drew up three thousand horsemen and an innumerable infantry. He marched on Azotus as though he were going on through the country, but at the same time he advanced into the plain, because he had such a large number of horsemen to rely on. ⁷⁸Jonathan followed him to Azotus, and they engaged in battle. ⁷⁹Apollonius, however, had left a thousand cavalry in hiding behind them. ⁸⁰When Jonathan discovered that there was an ambush behind him, his army was surrounded. From morning until evening they showered his men with arrows. ⁸¹But his men held their ground, as Jonathan had commanded, whereas the enemy's horses became tired out. ⁸²When the horsemen were exhausted, Simon attacked the phalanx, overwhelmed it and put it to flight. ⁸³The horsemen too were scattered over the plain. The enemy fled to Azotus and entered Beth-dagon, the temple of their idol, to save themselves. ⁸⁴But Jonathan burned and plundered Azotus with its neighboring towns, and destroyed by fire both the temple of Dagon and the men who had taken refuge in it.ᵗ ⁸⁵Those who fell by the sword, together with those who were burned alive, came to about eight thousand

---

10, 67: The year one hundred and sixty-five: 147 B.C. Demetrius: Demetrius II Nicator.

10, 76: Joppa: about forty miles northwest of Jerusalem. For the first time the Maccabees took possession of a seaport; nominally it was on behalf of King Alexander.

---

r: 1 Mc 2, 18. *s:* 64f: 1 Mc 2, 18; 11, 27. *t:* 1 Mc 11, 4; 1 Sm 5, 2-5.

men. [86]Then Jonathan left there and pitched his camp at Ashkalon, and the people of that city came out to meet him with great pomp. [87]He and his men then returned to Jerusalem, laden with much booty. [88]When King Alexander heard of these events, he accorded new honors to Jonathan. [89]He sent him a gold buckle, such as is usually given to King's Kinsmen;[*] he also gave him Ekron and all its territory as a possession.

See RG
229

CHAPTER 11

Alliance of Demetrius and Ptolemy. [1]The king of Egypt gathered his forces, as numerous as the sands of the seashore, and many ships; and he sought by deceit to take Alexander's kingdom and add it to his own. [2]He entered Syria with peaceful words, and the people in the cities opened their gates to welcome him, as King Alexander had ordered them to do, since Ptolemy was his father-in-law. [3]But when Ptolemy entered the cities, he stationed garrison troops in each one. [4]When he reached Azotus, he was shown the temple of Dagon destroyed by fire, Azotus and its suburbs demolished, corpses lying about, and the charred bodies of those burned by Jonathan in the war and stacked up along his route.[u] [5]To prejudice the king against Jonathan, he was told what the latter had done; but the king said nothing. [6]Jonathan met the king with pomp at Joppa, and they greeted each other and spent the night there. [7]Jonathan accompanied the king as far as the river called Eleutherus[*] and then returned to Jerusalem.

[8]Plotting evil against Alexander, King Ptolemy took possession of the cities along the seacoast as far as Seleucia-by-the-Sea.[*] [9]He sent ambassadors to King Demetrius, saying: "Come, let us make a pact with each other; I will give you my daughter whom Alexander has married, and you shall reign over your father's kingdom. [10]I regret that I gave him my daughter, for he has sought to kill me."[*] [11]His real reason for accusing Alexander, however, was that he coveted Alexander's kingdom. [12]After taking his daughter away and giving her to Demetrius, Ptolemy broke with Alexander; their enmity became open. [13]Then Ptolemy entered Antioch and assumed the crown of Asia; he thus wore two crowns on his head, that of Egypt and that of Asia.

Deaths of Alexander and Ptolemy. [14]King Alexander was in Cilicia at that time, because the people of that region had revolted. [15]When Alexander heard the news, he came to challenge Ptolemy in battle. Ptolemy marched out and met him with a strong force and put him to flight. [16]Alexander fled to Arabia to seek protection. King Ptolemy's triumph was complete [17]when the Arab Zabdiel cut off Alexander's head and sent it to Ptolemy. [18]But three days later King Ptolemy himself died, and his men in the fortified cities were killed by the inhabitants of the strongholds. [19]Thus Demetrius became king in the year one hundred and sixty-seven.[*]

Pact with Demetrius. [20]At that time Jonathan gathered together the men of Judea to attack the citadel in Jerusalem, and they set up many machines against it. [21]Some transgressors of the law, enemies of their own nation, went to the king and informed him that Jonathan was besieging the citadel. [22]When Demetrius heard this, he was furious, and set out immediately for Ptolemais. He wrote to Jonathan to discontinue the siege and to meet him for a conference at Ptolemais as soon as possible.

[23]On hearing this, Jonathan ordered the siege to continue. He selected some elders and priests of Israel and exposed himself to danger [24]by going to the king at Ptolemais. He brought with him silver, gold apparel, and many other presents, and found favor with

---

10, 89: Kinsmen: a class higher than Chief Friends:

11, 7: Eleutherus: modern Nahr el-Kebir, the northern border of modern Lebanon; in the second century B.C. the northern limit of Coelesyria.

11, 8: Seleucia-by-the-Sea: at the mouth of the Orontes, the port city of Antioch.

11, 10: I regret . . . to kill me: according to Josephus, Ammonius, a friend of Alexander, had tried to assassinate

Ptolemy, and the latter claimed that Alexander was the instigator, thus calumniating him to gain his kingdom (v 11).

11, 19: The year one hundred and sixty-seven: 146/145 B.C. The two deaths (vv 17-18) occurred in the summer of 145 B.C.

---

u: 1 Mc 10, 84.

the king. [25]Although some impious men of his own nation brought charges against him, [26]the king treated him just as his predecessors had done and showed him great honor in the presence of all his Friends. [27]He confirmed him in the high priesthood and in all the honors he had previously held, and had him enrolled among his Chief Friends.

[28]Jonathan asked the king to exempt Judea and the three districts of Samaria from tribute, promising him in return three hundred talents.[v] [29]The king agreed and wrote the following letter to Jonathan about all these matters:

[30w]"King Demetrius sends greetings to his brother[*] Jonathan and to the Jewish nation. [31]We are sending you, for your information, a copy of the letter that we wrote to Lasthenes[*] our kinsman concerning you. [32]'King Demetrius sends greetings to his father Lasthenes. [33]Because of the good will they show us, we have decided to bestow benefits on the Jewish nation, who are our friends and who observe their obligations to us. [34x]Therefore we confirm their possession, not only of the territory of Judea, but also of the three districts of Aphairema,[*] Lydda, and Ramathaim. These districts, together with all their dependencies, were transferred from Samaria to Judea in favor of all those who offer sacrifices for us in Jerusalem instead of paying the royal taxes that formerly the king received from them each year from the produce of the soil and the fruit of the trees. [35]From this day on we grant them release from payment of all other things that would henceforth be due to us, that is, of tithes and tribute and of the tax on the salt pans and the crown tax. [36]Henceforth none of these provisions shall ever be revoked. [37]Be sure, therefore, to have a copy of these instructions made and given to Jonathan, that it may be displayed in a conspicuous place on the holy hill.' "

The Intrigue of Trypho. [38]When King Demetrius saw that the land was peaceful under his rule and that he had no opposition, he dismissed his entire army, every man to his home, except the foreign troops which he had hired from the islands of the nations. So all the soldiers who had served under his predecessors hated him. [39]When a certain Trypho, who had previously belonged to Alexander's party, saw that all the troops were grumbling at Demetrius, he went to Imalkue the Arab, who was bringing up Alexander's young son Antiochus.[y] [40]Trypho kept urging Imalkue to hand over the boy to him, that he might make him king in his father's place. During his stay there of many days, he told him of all that Demetrius had done and of the hatred that his soldiers had for him.

Jonathan Aids Demetrius. [41]Meanwhile Jonathan sent the request to King Demetrius to withdraw his troops from the citadel of Jerusalem and from the other strongholds, for they were constantly hostile to Israel. [42]Demetrius, in turn, sent this word to Jonathan: "I will not only do this for you and your nation, but I will greatly honor you and your nation when I find the opportunity. [43]Do me the favor, therefore, of sending men to fight for me, because all my troops have revolted."

[44]So Jonathan sent three thousand good fighting men to him at Antioch. When they came to the king, he was delighted over their arrival, [45]for the populace, one hundred and twenty thousand strong, had massed in the center of the city in an attempt to kill him. [46]But he took refuge in the palace, while the populace gained control of the main streets and began to fight. [47]So the king called the Jews to his aid. They all rallied around him and spread out through the city. On that day they killed about a hundred thousand men in the city, [48]which, at the same time, they set on fire and plundered on a large scale. Thus they

---

11, 30: Brother: this title and father in v 32 are honorific titles used of the Kinsmen.

11, 31: Lasthenes: leader of the mercenary troops who had come with Demetrius from Crete. He was now the young king's chief minister and was apparently responsible for the disastrous policy (v 38) of disbanding the national army.

11, 34: Aphairema: the Ophrah of Jos 18, 23; 1 Sm 23, 6; the Ephron of 2 Chr 13, 19; and the Ephraim of Jn 11, 54—modern et-Taiyibeh, five miles northeast of Bethel. Lydda:

the Lod of the post-exilic Jews (Ez 2, 33; Neh 11, 35) and the hometown of Aeneas, who was cured by Peter (Acts 9, 32ff). It is ten miles southeast of Joppa. Ramathaim: the Ramathaim-zophim of 1 Sm 1, 1, and the Arimathea of Mt 27, 57—modern Rentis, nine miles northeast of Lydda.

---

v: 1 Mc 10, 29; 11, 34.   *w:* 30-37: 1 Mc 10, 26-45.   *x:* 34f: 1 Mc 10, 29; 11, 28.   *y:* 1 Mc 12, 39.

saved the king's life. ⁴⁹When the populace saw that the Jews held the city at their mercy, they lost courage and cried out to the king in supplication, ⁵⁰"Give us your terms and let the Jews stop attacking us and our city." So they threw down their arms and made peace. ⁵¹The Jews thus gained glory in the eyes of the king and all his subjects, and they became renowned throughout his kingdom. Finally they returned to Jerusalem with much spoil.

⁵²But when King Demetrius was sure of his royal throne, and the land was peaceful under his rule, ⁵³he broke all his promises and became estranged from Jonathan. Instead of rewarding Jonathan for all the favors he had received from him, he caused him much trouble.

Alliance with Trypho. ⁵⁴After this, Trypho returned and brought with him the young boy Antiochus, who became king and wore the royal crown.ᶻ ⁵⁵All the soldiers whom Demetrius had discharged rallied around Antiochus and fought against Demetrius, who was routed and fled. ⁵⁶Trypho captured the elephants and occupied Antioch. ⁵⁷Then young Antiochus wrote to Jonathan: "I confirm you in the high priesthood and appoint you ruler over the four districts and wish you to be one of the King's Friends." ⁵⁸He also sent him gold dishes and a dinner service, gave him the right to drink from gold cups, to dress in royal purple, and to wear a gold buckle.ᵃ ⁵⁹Likewise, he made Jonathan's brother Simon governor of the region from the Ladder of Tyre* to the frontier of Egypt.

⁶⁰Jonathan set out and traveled through West-of-Euphrates* and its cities, and all the forces of Syria espoused his cause as allies. When he arrived at Ashkalon, the citizens welcomed him with pomp. ⁶¹But when he set out for Gaza, the people of Gaza locked their gates against him. So he besieged it and burned and plundered its suburbs. ⁶²Then the people of Gaza appealed to him for mercy, and he granted them peace. He took the sons of their chief men as hostages and sent them to Jerusalem. He then traveled on through the province as far as Damascus.

War with Demetrius. ⁶³Jonathan heard that the generals of Demetrius had come with a strong force to Kadesh in Galilee, intending to remove him from office. ⁶⁴So he went to meet them, leaving his brother Simon in the province. ⁶⁵Simon besieged Beth-zur, attacked it for many days, and blockaded the inhabitants. ⁶⁶When they sued for peace, he granted it to them. He expelled them from the city, took possession of it, and put a garrison there.

⁶⁷Meanwhile, Jonathan and his army pitched their camp near the waters of Gennesaret, and at daybreak they went to the plain of Hazor.* ⁶⁸There, in front of him on the plain, was the army of the foreigners. This army attacked him in the open, having first detached an ambush against him in the mountains. ⁶⁹Then the men in ambush rose out of their places and joined in the battle. ⁷⁰All of Jonathan's men fled; no one stayed except the army commanders Mattathias, son of Absalom, and Judas, son of Chalphi. ⁷¹Jonathan tore his clothes, threw earth on his head, and prayed. ⁷²Then he went back to the combat and so overwhelmed the enemy that they took to flight. ⁷³Those of his men who were running away saw it and returned to him; and with him they pursued the enemy as far as their camp in Kadesh, where they pitched their own camp. ⁷⁴Three thousand of the foreign troops fell on that day. Then Jonathan returned to Jerusalem.

CHAPTER 12

See RG 229

Alliances with Rome and Sparta. ¹When Jonathan saw that the times favored him, he sent selected men to Rome to confirm and renew his friendship with the Romans.ᵇ ²He also sent letters to Sparta and other places for the same purpose.

³After reaching Rome, the men entered

11, 59: Ladder of Tyre: modern Ras en-Naqurah, on the border between Lebanon and Israel, where the mountains reach the sea, so that the coastal road must ascend in a series of steps.

11, 60: West-of-Euphrates: refers here to the territory of Palestine and Coelesyria, but not Upper Syria; cf 1 Mc 3, 32; 7, 8.

11, 67: Plain of Hazor: the site of the ancient Canaanite city (Jos 11, 10), ten miles north of the Lake of Gennesaret.

---

z: 1 Mc 11, 39; 12, 39.   a: 1 Mc 2, 18.   b: 1 Mc 8, 17.

the senate chamber and said, "The high priest Jonathan and the Jewish people have sent us to renew the earlier friendship and alliance between you and them." *4*The Romans gave them letters addressed to the authorities in the various places, requesting them to provide the envoys with safe conduct to the land of Judah.

*5*This is a copy of the letter that Jonathan wrote to the Spartans: *6*"Jonathan the high priest, the senate of the nation, the priests, and the rest of the Jewish people send greetings to their brothers the Spartans. *7*Long ago a letter was sent to the high priest Onias* from Arius, who then reigned over you, stating that you are our brothers, as the attached copy shows.*c* *8*Onias welcomed the envoy with honor and received the letter, which clearly referred to alliance and friendship. *9d*Though we have no need of these things, since we have for our encouragement the sacred books that are in our possession,* *10*we have ventured to send word to you for the renewal of brotherhood and friendship, so as not to become strangers to you altogether; a long time has passed since your mission to us. *11*We, on our part, have never ceased to remember you in the sacrifices and prayers that we offer on our feasts and other appropriate days, as it is right and proper to remember brothers. *12*We likewise rejoice in your renown. *13*But many hardships and wars have beset us, and the kings around us have attacked us. *14*We did not wish to be troublesome to you and to the rest of our allies and friends in these wars; *15*with the help of Heaven for our support, we have been saved from our enemies, and they have been humbled. *16*So we have chosen Numenius, son of Antiochus, and Antipater, son of Jason, and we have sent them to the Romans to renew our former friendship and alliance with them.*e* *17*We have also ordered them to come to you and greet you, and to deliver to you our letter about the renewal of our brotherhood.

*18*Therefore kindly send us an answer on this matter."

*19*This is a copy of the letter that was sent to Onias: *20f*"Arius, king of the Spartans, sends greetings to Onias the high priest. *21*A document has been found stating that the Spartans and the Jews are brothers; both nations descended from Abraham. *22*Now that we have learned this, kindly write to us about your welfare. *23*We, on our part, are informing you that your cattle and your possessions are ours, and ours are yours. We have, therefore, given orders that you should be told of this."

Demetrius Repelled. *24*Jonathan heard that the generals of Demetrius had returned to attack him with a stronger army than before. *25*He set out from Jerusalem and went into the country of Hamath* to meet them, giving them no time to enter his province. *26*The spies he had sent into their camp came back and reported that the enemy had made ready to attack the Jews that very night. *27*Therefore, when the sun set, Jonathan ordered his men to be on guard and to remain armed, ready for combat, throughout the night. He also set outposts all around the camp. *28*When the enemy heard that Jonathan and his men were ready for battle, their hearts sank with fear and dread. They lighted fires and then withdrew. *29*But because Jonathan and his men were watching the lights burning, they did not know what had happened until morning. *30*Then Jonathan pursued them, but he could not overtake them, for they had crossed the river Eleutherus. *31*So Jonathan turned aside against the Arabs who are called Zabadeans, overwhelming and plundering them. *32*Then he marched on to Damascus and traversed that whole region.

*33*Simon also set out and went as far as Ashkalon and its neighboring strongholds. He then turned to Joppa and occupied it, *34*for he heard that its men had intended to hand over this stronghold to the supporters

---

12, 7: Onias: Onias I, high priest from 323–300 or 290 B.C. Arius: Arius I, king from 309 to 265 B.C. The letter was sent long ago, i.e., a century and a half before.

12, 9: The sacred books . . . in our possession: a reference to "the law, the prophets and other books," as mentioned in the Prologue to Sirach (v 1), after 132 B.C.

12, 25: Country of Hamath: the Seleucid territory of Up-

per Syria northeast of Coelesyria and separated from it by the Eleutherus River. The latter territory was under the command of Jonathan (1 Mc 11, 59f).

c: 1 Mc 12, 20-23. *d:* Rom 15, 4. *e:* 1 Mc 14, 22; 15, 15.
f: 20-23: 1 Mc 12, 6f.

of Demetrius. He left a garrison there to guard it.

35 When Jonathan returned, he assembled the elders of the people, and with them he made plans for building strongholds in Judea, 36 for making the walls of Jerusalem still higher, and for erecting a high barrier between the citadel and the city, that would isolate the citadel and so prevent its garrison from commerce with the city. 37 The people therefore worked together on building up the city, for part of the east wall above the ravine had collapsed. The quarter called Chaphenatha was also repaired. 38 Simon likewise built up Adida in the Shephelah, and strengthened its fortifications by providing them with gates and bars.

Capture of Jonathan. 39 Trypho was determined to become king of Asia, assume the crown, and do away with King Antiochus.g 40 But he was afraid that Jonathan would not permit him, but would fight against him. Looking for a way to seize and kill him, he set out and reached Beth-shan. 41 Jonathan marched out against him with forty thousand picked fighting men and came to Beth-shan. 42 But when Trypho saw that Jonathan had arrived with a large army, he was afraid to offer him violence. 43 Instead, he received him with honor, introduced him to all his friends, and gave him presents. He also ordered his friends and soldiers to obey him as they would himself. 44 Then he said to Jonathan: "Why have you put all your soldiers to so much trouble when we are not at war? 45 Pick out a few men to stay with you, send the rest back home, and then come with me to Ptolemais. I will hand it over to you together with other strongholds and their garrisons, as well as the officials, then I will leave and go home. That is why I came here."

46 Jonathan believed him and did as he said. He dismissed his troops, and they returned to the land of Judah. 47 But he kept with him three thousand men, of whom he sent two thousand to Galilee while one thousand accompanied him. 48 Then as soon as Jonathan had entered Ptolemais, the men of the city closed the gates and seized him; all who had entered him, they killed with the sword.

49 Trypho sent soldiers and cavalry to Galilee and the Great Plain* to destroy all Jonathan's men. 50 These, upon learning that Jonathan had been captured and his companions killed, encouraged one another and went out in compact body ready to fight. 51 As their pursuers saw that they were ready to fight for their lives, they turned back. 52 Thus all these men of Jonathan came safely into the land of Judah. They mourned over Jonathan and his men, and were in great fear, and all Israel fell into deep mourning.

53 All the nations round about sought to destroy them. They said, "Now that they have no leader to help them, let us make war on them and wipe out their memory from among men."h

V: Simon, High Priest and Ethnarch

CHAPTER 13

Simon, Leader of the Jews. 1 When Simon heard that Trypho was gathering a large army to invade and ravage the land of Judah, 2 and saw that the people were in dread and terror, he went up to Jerusalem. There he assembled the people 3 and exhorted them in these words: "You know what I, my brothers, and my father's house have done for the laws and the sanctuary; what battles and disasters we have been through. 4 It was for the sake of these, for the sake of Israel, that all my brothers have perished, and I alone am left. 5 Far be it from me, then, to save my own life in any time of distress, for I am not better than my brothers. 6 Rather will I avenge my nation and the sanctuary, as well as your wives and children, for all the nations out of hatred have united to destroy us."i

7 As the people heard these words, their spirit was rekindled. 8 They shouted in reply: "You are our leader in place of your brothers Judas and Jonathan. 9 Fight our battles, and we will do everything that you tell us." 10 So

---

12, 49: The Great Plain: of Beth-shan (v 41), where Jonathan's disbanded troops remained.

g: 1 Mc 11, 39f. 54f.   h: 1 Mc 5, 2; 13, 6.   i: 1 Mc 5, 2; 12, 53.

Simon mustered all the men able to fight, and quickly completing the walls of Jerusalem, fortified it on every side. [11]He sent Jonathan, son of Absalom, to Joppa with a large force; Jonathan drove out the occupants and remained there.

Deceit and Treachery of Trypho. [12]Then Trypho moved from Ptolemais with a large army to invade the land of Judah, bringing Jonathan with him as prisoner. [13]But Simon pitched his camp at Adida, facing the plain. [14]When Trypho learned that Simon had succeeded his brother Jonathan, and that he intended to fight him, he sent envoys to him with this message: [15]"We have detained your brother Jonathan on account of the money that he owed the royal treasury in connection with the offices that he held. [16]Therefore, if you send us a hundred talents of silver, and two of his sons as hostages to guarantee that when he is set free he will not revolt against us, we will release him."

[17]Although Simon knew that they were speaking deceitfully to him, he gave orders to get the money and the boys, for fear of provoking much hostility among the people, who might say [18]that Jonathan perished because Simon would not send Trypho the money and the boys. [19]So he sent the boys and the hundred talents; but Trypho broke his promise and would not let Jonathan go. [20]*Next he began to invade and ravage the country. His troops went around by the road that leads to Adora, but Simon and his army moved along opposite him everywhere he went. [21]The men in the citadel sent messengers to Trypho, urging him to come to them by way of the desert, and to send them provisions. [22]Although Trypho got all his cavalry ready to go, there was a heavy fall of snow that night, and he could not go. So he left for Gilead. [23]When he was approaching Baskama,* he had Jonathan killed and buried there. [24]Then Trypho returned to his own country.

Jonathan's Tomb. [25]Simon sent for the remains of his brother Jonathan, and buried him in Modein, the city of his fathers. [26]All Israel bewailed him with solemn lamentation, mourning over him for many days. [27]Then Simon erected over the tomb of his father and his brothers a monument of stones, polished front and back, and raised high enough to be seen at a distance. [28]He set up seven pyramids facing one another for his father and his mother and his four brothers. [29]For the pyramids he devised a setting of big columns, on which he carved suits of armor as a perpetual memorial, and next to the armor he placed carved ships, which could be seen by all who sailed the sea. [30]This tomb which he built at Modein is there to the present day.

Pact between Simon and Demetrius. [31]Trypho dealt treacherously with the young King Antiochus. He killed him [32]and assumed the kingship in his place, putting on the crown of Asia. Thus he brought much evil on the land. [33]Simon, on his part, built up the strongholds of Judea, strengthening their fortifications with high towers, thick walls, and gates with bars, and he stored up provisions in the fortresses. [34]Simon also sent chosen men to King Demetrius with the request that he grant the land a release from taxation, for all that Trypho did was to plunder the land. [35]In reply, King Demetrius sent him the following letter: [36]"King Demetrius sends greetings to Simon the high priest, the friend of kings, and to the elders and the Jewish people. [37]We have received the gold crown and the palm branch that you sent. We are willing to be on most peaceful terms with you and to write to our official to grant you release from tribute. [38]Whatever we have guaranteed to you remains in force, and the strongholds that you have built shall remain yours. [39]We remit any oversights and defaults incurred up to now, as well as the crown tax that you owe. Any other tax that may have been collected in Jerusalem shall no longer be collected there. [40]If any of you are qualified for enrollment in our service, let them be enrolled. Let there be peace between us."

[41]Thus in the year one hundred and seventy,* the yoke of the Gentiles was removed

---

13, 20f: The invaders made a wide flanking movement to invade Judea from the south. Adora was a few miles southwest of Beth-zur. They would avoid Beth-zur itself and other strongholds of the Maccabees by following the way of the desert.

13, 23: Baskama: northeast of the Sea of Galilee.

13, 41: The year one hundred and seventy: March, 142, to April, 141 B.C., by the temple calendar.

from Israel, [42] and the people began to write in their records and contracts, "In the first year of Simon, high priest, governor, and leader of the Jews."

Capture of Gazara and the Citadel. [43] In those days Simon besieged Gazara[*] and surrounded it with troops. He made a siege machine, pushed it up against the city, and attacked and captured one of the towers.[j] [44] The men who had been on the siege machine jumped down into the city and caused a great tumult there. [45] The men of the city, joined by their wives and children, went up on the wall, with their garments rent, and cried out in loud voices, begging Simon to grant them peace. [46] "Do not treat us according to our evil deeds," they said, "but according to your mercy."

[47] So Simon came to terms with them and did not destroy them. He made them leave the city, however, and he purified the houses in which there were idols. Then he entered the city with hymns and songs of praise. [48] After removing from it everything that was impure, he settled there men who observed the law. He improved its fortifications and built himself a residence.

[49] The men in the citadel in Jerusalem were prevented from going out into the country and back for the purchase of food; they suffered greatly from hunger, and many of them died of starvation. [50] They finally cried out to Simon for peace, and he gave them peace. He expelled them from the citadel and cleansed it of impurities. [51] On the twenty-third day of the second month,[*] in the year one hundred and seventy-one, the Jews entered the citadel with shouts of jubilation, waving of palm branches, the music of harps and cymbals and lyres, and the singing of hymns and canticles, because a great enemy of Israel had been destroyed.[k] [52] Simon decreed that this day should be celebrated every year with rejoicing. He also strengthened the fortifications of the temple hill alongside the citadel, and he and his companions dwelt there. [53] Seeing that his son John[*] was now a grown man, Simon made him commander of all his soldiers, with his residence in Gazara.

CHAPTER 14

See RG 229-30

Capture of Demetrius. [1] In the year one hundred and seventy-two,[*] King Demetrius assembled his army and marched into Media to obtain help so that he could fight Trypho. [2] When Arsaces,[*] king of Persia and Media, heard that Demetrius had invaded his territory, he sent one of his generals to take him alive. [3] The general went forth and defeated the army of Demetrius; he captured him and brought him to Arsaces, who put him in prison.

Glory of Simon

[4] The land was at rest all the days of
    Simon,
  who sought the good of his nation.
His people were delighted with his power
  and his magnificence throughout his
    reign.[l]
[5] As his crowning glory he captured the
    port of Joppa
  and made it a gateway to the isles of
    the sea.
[6] He enlarged the borders of his nation
  and gained control of the country.[m]
[7] He took many enemies prisoners of war
  and made himself master of Gazara,
    Beth-zur, and the citadel.

He cleansed the citadel of its impurities;
  there was no one to withstand him.
[8] The people cultivated their land in peace;
  the land yielded its produce
  and the trees of the field their fruit.[n]

13, 43: Gazara: a key position in the Shephelah, fortified by Bacchides in 160 B.C.; cf 1 Mc 9, 52.

13, 51: The twenty-third day of the second month: June 3, 141 B.C.

13, 53: John: John Hyrcanus, who was to succeed his father as ruler and high priest; cf 1 Mc 16, 23f.

14, 1: The year one hundred and seventy-two: 141-140 B.C. The expedition began most probably in the spring of 140.

14, 2: Arsaces: Arsaces VI, also called Mithridates I, the Parthian king (171-138 B.C.). Parthians had overrun Persia and now held Babylonia, both of which had hitherto belonged to the Seleucid empire. The Greeks and Macedonians in these countries had appealed to Demetrius for help.

j: 2 Mc 10, 32-38. k: 1 Mc 1, 36. l: 1 Mc 3, 3-9. m: Ex 34, 24. n: Zec 8, 12.

⁹ Old men sat in the squares,
    all talking about the good times,
    while the young men wore the glorious
        apparel of war.ᵒ
¹⁰ He supplied the cities with food
    and equipped them with means of
        defense,
    till his glorious name reached the ends
        of the earth.
¹¹ He brought peace to the land,
    and Israel was filled with happiness.ᵖ
¹² Every man sat under his vine and his fig
        tree,
    with no one to disturb him. q
¹³ No one was left to attack them in their
        land;
    the kings in those days were crushed.
¹⁴ He strengthened all the lowly among his
        people
    and was zealous for the law;
    he suppressed all the lawless and the
        wicked.
¹⁵ He made the temple splendid
    and enriched its equipment.

Alliance with Rome and Sparta. ¹⁶When
people heard in Rome and even in Sparta that
Jonathan had died, they were deeply grieved.*
¹⁷But when the Romans heard that his brother
Simon had been made high priest in his place
and was master of the country and the cities,
¹⁸they sent him inscribed tablets of bronze to
renew with him the friendship and alliance
that they had established with his brothers Judas and Jonathan.ʳ ¹⁹These were read before
the assembly in Jerusalem.

²⁰This is a copy of the letter that the Spartans sent: "The rulers and the citizens of
Sparta send greetings to Simon the high
priest, the elders, the priests, and the rest of
the Jewish people, our brothers. ²¹The envoys you sent to our people have informed us
of your glory and fame, and we were happy
that they came. ²²In accordance with what
they said we have recorded the following in
the public decrees: Since Numenius, son of

Antiochus, and Antipater, son of Jason, envoys of the Jews, have come to us to renew
their friendship with us,ˢ ²³the people have
voted to receive the men with honor, and to
deposit a copy of their words in the public archives, so that the people of Sparta may have
a record of them. A copy of this decree has
been made for Simon the high priest."

²⁴After this, Simon sent Numenius to
Rome with a great gold shield weighing a
thousand minas, to confirm the alliance with
the Romans.ᵗ

Decree of Honor. ²⁵When the people
heard of these things, they said, "How can
we thank Simon and his sons? ²⁶He and his
brothers and his father's house have stood
firm and repulsed Israel's enemies. They
have thus preserved its liberty." So they
made an inscription on bronze tablets, which
they affixed to pillars on Mount Zion. ²⁷The
following is a copy of the inscription:

"On the eighteenth day of Elul,* in the
year one hundred and seventy-two, that is,
the third year under Simon the high priest in
Asaramel, ²⁸in a great assembly of priests,
people, rulers of the nation, and elders of the
country, the following proclamation was
made:

²⁹" 'Since there have often been wars in
our country, Simon, son of the priest Mattathias, descendant of Joarib, and his brothers have put themselves in danger and resisted the enemies of their nation, so that
their sanctuary and law might be maintained,
and they have thus brought great glory to
their nation. ³⁰After Jonathan had rallied his
nation and become their high priest, he was
gathered to his kinsmen. ³¹When the enemies
of the Jews sought to invade and devastate
their country and to lay hands on their temple, ³²Simon rose up and fought for his nation, spending large sums of his own money
to equip the men of his nation's armed forces
and giving them their pay. ³³He fortified the
cities of Judea, especially the frontier city of
Beth-zur, where he stationed a garrison of

14, 16: The embassy to Rome and Sparta was sent soon
after Simon's accession to power, and the replies were received before Demetrius' expedition (vv 1-3)—probably in
142 B.C.

14, 27: Eighteenth day of Elul: September 13, 140 B.C.

Asaramel: a Hebrew name meaning "court of the people of
God."

o: Zec 8, 4f.   p: Lv 26, 6.   q: Mi 4, 4; Zec 3, 10.   r: Mc 8, 22.
s: 1 Mc 12, 16; 15, 15.   t: 1 Mc 12, 16; 15, 15.

Jewish soldiers, and where previously the enemy's arms had been stored. [34]He also fortified Joppa by the sea and Gazara on the border of Azotus, a place previously occupied by the enemy; these cities he resettled with Jews, and furnished them with all that was necessary for their restoration. [35]When the Jewish people saw Simon's loyalty and the glory he planned to bring to his nation, they made him their leader and high priest because of all he had accomplished and the loyalty and justice he had shown his nation. In every way he sought to exalt his people.

[36]" 'In his time and under his guidance they succeeded in driving the Gentiles out of their country, especially those in the City of David in Jerusalem, who had built for themselves a citadel from which they used to sally forth to defile the environs of the temple and inflict grave injury on its purity. [37]In this citadel he stationed Jewish soldiers, and he strengthened its fortifications for the defense of the land and the city, while he also raised the wall of Jerusalem to a greater height. [38]Consequently, King Demetrius confirmed him in the high priesthood, [39u]made him one of his Friends, and conferred the highest honors on him. [40]He had indeed heard that the Romans had addressed the Jews as friends, allies, and brothers and that they had received Simon's envoys with honor.

[41]" 'The Jewish people and their priest have, therefore, made the following decisions. Simon shall be their permanent leader and high priest until a true prophet arises. [42]He shall act as governor general over them, and shall have charge of the temple, to make regulations concerning its functions and concerning the country, its weapons and strongholds; [43]he shall be obeyed by all. All contracts made in the country shall be dated by his name. He shall have the right to wear royal purple and gold ornaments. [44]It shall not be lawful for any of the people or priests to nullify any of these decisions, or to contradict the orders given by him, or to con-

vene an assembly in the country without his consent, to be clothed in royal purple or wear an official gold brooch. [45]Whoever acts otherwise or violates any of these prescriptions shall be liable to punishment.

[46]" 'All the people approved of granting Simon the right to act in accord with these decisions, [47]and Simon accepted and agreed to act as high priest, governor general, and ethnarch* of the Jewish people and priests and to exercise supreme authority over all.' "

[48]It was decreed that this inscription should be engraved on bronze tablets, to be set up in a conspicuous place in the precincts of the temple, [49]and that copies of it should be deposited in the treasury, where they would be available to Simon and his sons.

CHAPTER 15

See RG 229–30

Letter of Antiochus. [1]Antiochus,* son of King Demetrius, sent a letter from the islands of the sea to Simon, the priest and ethnarch of the Jews, and to all the nation, [2]which read as follows:

"King Antiochus sends greetings to Simon, the priest and ethnarch, and to the Jewish nation. [3]Whereas certain villains have gained control of the kingdom of my ancestors, I intend to reclaim it, that I may restore it to its former state. I have recruited a large number of mercenary troops and equipped warships [4]to make a landing in my country and take revenge on those who have ruined it and laid waste many cities in my realm.

[5]"Now, therefore, I confirm to you all the tax exemptions that the kings before me granted you and whatever other privileges they conferred on you. [6]I authorize you to coin your own money, as legal tender in your country. [7]Jerusalem and its temple shall be free. All the weapons you have prepared and all the strongholds you have built and now occupy shall remain in your possession. [8]All debts, present or future, due to the royal treasury shall be canceled for you, now and for all time. [9]When we recover our kingdom,

---

14, 47: Ethnarch: a subaltern ruler over a racial group whose office needed confirmation by a higher authority within the empire.

15, 1: Antiochus: Antiochus VII Sidetes, son of Demetrius I, and younger brother of Demetrius II, now a prisoner of the

Parthians. At the age of twenty he set out from the island of Rhodes to take his brother's place and drive out the usurper Trypho.

u: 39f: 1 Mc 2, 18.

we will greatly honor you and your nation and the temple, so that your glory will be manifest in all the earth."

[10] In the year one hundred and seventy-four,[*] Antiochus invaded the land of his ancestors, and all the troops rallied to him, so that few were left with Trypho. [11] Pursued by Antiochus, Trypho fled to Dor, by the sea,[*] [12] realizing what a mass of troubles had come upon him now that his soldiers had deserted him. [13] Antiochus encamped before Dor with a hundred and twenty thousand infantry and eight thousand horsemen. [14] While he invested the city, his ships closed in along the coast, so that he blockaded it by land and sea and let no one go in or out.

Roman Alliance Renewed. [15] Meanwhile, Numenius and his companions left Rome with letters such as this addressed to various kings and countries:[v]

[16] "Lucius,[*] Consul of the Romans, sends greetings to King Ptolemy. [17] Certain envoys of the Jews, our friends and allies, have come to us to renew their earlier alliance of friendship. They had been sent by Simon the high priest and the Jewish people, [18] and they brought with them a gold shield worth a thousand minas.[w] [19] Therefore we have decided to write to various kings and countries, that they are not to harm them, or wage war against them or their cities or their country, and are not to assist those who fight against them. [20] We have also decided to accept the shield from them. [21] If, then, any troublemakers from their country take refuge with you, hand them over to Simon the high priest, so that he may punish them according to their law."

[22] The consul sent similar letters to Kings Demetrius, Attalus,[*] Ariarthes and Arsaces; [23] to all the countries—Sampsames, Sparta, Delos, Myndos, Sicyon, Caria, Samos, Pamphylia, Lycia, Halicarnassus, Rhodes, Phaselis, Cos, Side, Aradus, Gortyna, Cnidus, Cyprus, and Cyrene. [24] A copy of the letter was also sent to Simon the high priest.

Hostility of Antiochus. [25] When King Antiochus was encamped before Dor, he assaulted it continuously both with troops and with the siege machines he had made. He blockaded Trypho by preventing anyone from going in or out. [26] Simon sent to Antiochus' support two thousand elite troops, together with gold and silver and much equipment. [27] But he refused to accept the aid; in fact, he broke all the agreements he had previously made with Simon and became hostile toward him.

[28] He sent Athenobius, one of his Friends, to confer with Simon and say: "You are occupying Joppa and Gazara and the citadel of Jerusalem; these are cities of my kingdom. [29] You have laid waste their territories, done great harm to the land, and taken possession of many districts in my realm. [30] Therefore, give up the cities you have seized and the tribute money of the districts outside the territory of Judea of which you have taken possession; [31] or instead, pay me five hundred talents of silver for the devastation you have caused and five hundred talents more for the tribute money of the cities. If you do not do this, we will come and make war on you."

[32] So Athenobius, the king's Friend, came to Jerusalem, and on seeing the splendor of Simon's court, the gold and silver plate on the sideboard, and the rest of his rich display, he was amazed. When he gave him the king's message, [33] Simon said to him in reply:

"We have not seized any foreign land; what we took is not the property of others, but our ancestral heritage which for a time had been unjustly held by our enemies. [34] Now that we have the opportunity, we are holding on to the heritage of our ancestors. [35] As for Joppa and Gazara, which you demand, the men of these cities were doing great harm to our people and laying waste our country; however, we are willing to pay you a hundred talents for these cities."

[36] Athenobius made no reply, but returned

15, 10: The year one hundred and seventy-four: 138 B.C.

15, 11: Dor, by the sea: a fortress on the Palestinian coast, fifteen miles south of Carmel.

15, 16: Lucius: perhaps Lucius Caecilius Metellus, consul in 142 B.C., or Lucius Calpurnicus Piso, consul in 140–139 B.C. This document pertains to Simon's first year as leader.

15, 22: Attalus: Attalus II of Pergamum, reigned 159–138 B.C. Ariarthes: Ariarthes V of Cappadocia, reigned 162–130 B.C. Arsaces: see note on 1 Mc 14, 2.

v: 1 Mc 8, 17; 12, 16; 14, 22, 24.   w: 1 Mc 14, 24.

to the king in anger. When he told him of Simon's words, of his splendor, and of all he had seen, the king fell into a violent rage.

Victory over Cendebeus. [37] Trypho had gotten aboard a ship and escaped to Orthosia.* [38] Then the king appointed Cendebeus commander in chief of the seacoast, and gave him infantry and cavalry forces. [39] He ordered him to move his troops against Judea and to fortify Kedron* and strengthen its gates, so that he could launch attacks against the Jewish people. Meanwhile the king went in pursuit of Trypho. [40] When Cendebeus came to Jamnia, he began to harass the people and to make incursions into Judea, where he took people captive or massacred them. [41] As the king ordered, he fortified Kedron and stationed horsemen and infantry there, so that they could go out and patrol the roads of Judea.

See RG
229-30

CHAPTER 16

[1] John then went up from Gazara and told his father Simon what Cendebeus was doing. [2] Simon called his two oldest sons, Judas and John, and said to them: "I and my brothers and my father's house have fought the battles of Israel from our youth until today, and many times we succeeded in saving Israel. [3] I have now grown old, but you, by the mercy of Heaven, have come to man's estate. Take my place and my brother's, and go out and fight for our nation; and may the help of Heaven be with you!"

[4] John then mustered in the land twenty thousand warriors and horsemen. Setting out against Cendebeus, they spent the night at Modein, [5] rose early, and marched into the plain. There, facing them, was an immense army of foot soldiers and horsemen, and between the two armies was a stream. [6] John and his men took their position against the enemy. Seeing that his men were afraid to cross the stream, John crossed first. When his men saw this, they crossed over after him. [7] Then he divided his infantry into two corps and put his cavalry between them, for the enemy's horsemen were very numerous. [8] They blew the trumpets, and Cendebeus and his army were put to flight; many of them fell wounded, and the rest fled toward the stronghold. [9] It was then that John's brother Judas fell wounded; but John pursued them until Cendebeus reached Kidron, which he had fortified. [10] Some took refuge in the towers on the plain of Azotus, but John set fire to these, and about two thousand of the enemy perished. He then returned to Judea in peace.

Murder of Simon and His Sons. [11] Ptolemy, son of Abubus, had been appointed governor of the plain of Jericho, and he had much silver and gold, [12] being the son-in-law of the high priest. [13] But he became ambitious and sought to get control of the country. So he made treacherous plans to do away with Simon and his sons. [14] As Simon was inspecting the cities of the country and providing for their needs, he and his sons Mattathias and Judas went down to Jericho in the year one hundred and seventy-seven, in the eleventh month* (that is, the month Shebat). [15] The son of Abubus gave them a deceitful welcome in the little stronghold called Dok* which he had built. While serving them a sumptuous banquet, he had his men hidden there. [16] Then, when Simon and his sons had drunk freely, Ptolemy and his men sprang up, weapons in hand, rushed upon Simon in the banquet hall, and killed him, his two sons, and some of his servants. [17] By this vicious act of treason he repaid good with evil.

[18] Then Ptolemy wrote an account of this and sent it to the king, asking that troops be sent to help him and that the country be turned over to him. [19] He sent other men to Gazara to do away with John. To the army officers he sent letters inviting them to come to him so that he might present them with silver, gold, and gifts. [20] He also sent others to seize Jerusalem and the mount of the tem-

---

15, 37: Orthosia: a port between Tripoli and the Eleutherus River.

15, 39: Kedron: a few miles southeast of Jamnia and facing the fortress of Gazara held by John Hyrcanus.

16, 14: In the year one hundred and seventy-seven, in the eleventh month: January-February, 134 B.C., by the temple calendar.

16, 15: Dok: a fortress built on a cliff three miles northwest of Jericho, near modern Ain Duq.

ple. *21* But someone ran ahead and brought word to John at Gazara that his father and his brothers had perished, and that Ptolemy had sent men to kill him also. *22* On hearing this, John was utterly astounded. When the men came to kill him, he had them arrested and put to death, for he knew what they meant to do. *23* *Now the rest of the history of John, his wars and the brave deeds he performed, his rebuilding of the walls, and his other achievements— *24* these things are recorded in the chronicle of his pontificate, from the time that he succeeded his father as high priest.

16, 23f: John Hyrcanus was ruler and high priest from 134 B.C. till his death in 104 B.C. These verses suggest that the book was written, or at least completed, only after he died.

See RG 231-34

The Second Book of Maccabees

Although this book, like the preceding one, receives its title from its protagonist, Judas Maccabee (or Maccabeus), it is not a sequel to 1 Maccabees. The two differ in many respects. Whereas the first covers the period from the beginning of the reign of Antiochus IV (175 B.C.) to the accession of John Hyrcanus I (134 B.C.), this present book treats of the events in Jewish history from the time of the high priest Onias III and King Seleucus IV (c. 180 B.C.) to the defeat of Nicanor's army (161 B.C.).

The author of 2 Maccabees states (2, 23) that his one-volume work is an abridgment of a certain five-volume work by Jason of Cyrene; but since this latter has not survived, it is difficult to determine its relationship to the present epitome. One does not know how freely the anonymous epitomizer may have rewritten his shorter composition, or how closely he may have followed the wording of the original in the excerpts he made. Some parts of the text here, clearly not derived from Jason's work, are the Preface (2, 19-32), the Epilogue (15, 37-39), and probably also certain moralizing reflections (e. g., 5, 17-20; 6, 12-17). It is certain, however, that both works were written in Greek, which explains why the Second Book of Maccabees was not included in the canon of the Hebrew Bible.

The book is not without genuine historical value in supplementing I Maccabees, and it contains some apparently authentic documents (11, 16-38). Its purpose, whether intended by Jason himself or read into it by the compiler, is to give a theological interpretation to the history of the period. There is less interest, therefore, in the actual exploits of Judas Maccabeus than in God's marvelous interventions. These direct the course of events, both to punish the sacrilegious and blasphemous pagans, and to purify God's holy temple and restore it to his faithful people. The author sometimes effects his purpose by transferring events from their proper chronological order, and giving exaggerated figures for the size of armies and the numbers killed in battle; he also places long, edifying discourses and prayers in the mouths of his heroes, and inclines to elaborate descriptions of celestial apparitions (3, 24-34; 5, 2ff; 10, 29f; 15, 11-16). He is the earliest known composer of stories that glorify God's holy martyrs (6, 18—7, 42; 14, 37-46).

Of theological importance are the author's teachings on the resurrection of the just on the last day (7, 9. 11. 14. 23; 14, 46), the intercession of the saints in heaven for people living on earth (15, 11-16), and the power of the living to offer prayers and sacrifices for the dead (12, 39-46).

The beginning of 2 Maccabees consists of two letters sent by the Jews of Jerusalem to their co-religionists in Egypt. They deal with the observance of the feast commemorating the central event of the book, the purification of the temple. It is uncertain whether the author or a later scribe prefixed these letters to the narrative proper. If the author is responsible for their insertion, he must have written his book some time after 124 B.C., the date of the more recent of the two letters. In any case, Jason's five-volume work very likely continued the history of the Jews well into the Hasmonean period, so that 2 Maccabees would probably not have been produced much before the end of the second century B.C.

The main divisions of 2 Maccabees are:

I: Letters to the Jews In Egypt

CHAPTER 1

See RG
231

First Letter 124 B.C. ¹The Jews in Jerusalem and in the land of Judea send greetings to their brethren, the Jews in Egypt, and wish them true peace! ²May God bless you and remember his covenant with his faithful servants, Abraham, Isaac and Jacob. ³May he give to all of you a heart to worship him and to do his will readily and generously. ⁴May he open your heart to his law and his commandments and grant you peace. ⁵May he hear your prayers, and be reconciled to you, and never forsake you in time of adversity. ⁶Even now we are praying for you here.

⁷In the reign of Demetrius,* the year one hundred and sixty-nine, we Jews wrote to you during the trouble and violence that overtook us in those years after Jason and his followers had revolted against the holy land and the kingdom,*a* ⁸setting fire to the gatehouse and shedding innocent blood. But we prayed to the LORD, and our prayer was heard;* we offered sacrifices and fine flour; we lighted the lamps and set out the loaves of bread.*b* ⁹We are now reminding you to celebrate the feast of Booths in the month of Chislev.* ¹⁰Dated in the year one hundred and eighty-eight.*

Festival Letter 164 B.C. The people of Jerusalem and Judea, the senate, and Judas send greetings and good wishes to Aristobulus, counselor of King Ptolemy and member of the family of the anointed priests, and to the Jews in Egypt. ¹¹Since we have been saved by God from grave dangers, we give him great thanks for having fought on our side against the king;* ^{12c}it was he who drove out those who fought against the holy city. ¹³When their leader arrived in Persia with his seemingly irresistible army, they were cut to pieces in the temple of the goddess Nanea* through a deceitful stratagem employed by Nanea's priests. ¹⁴*On the pretext of marrying the goddess, Antiochus with his Friends had come to the place to get its great treasures by way of dowry. ¹⁵When the priests of the Nanaeon had displayed the treasures, Antiochus with a few attendants came to the temple precincts. As soon as he entered the temple, the priests locked the doors. ¹⁶Then they opened a hidden trapdoor in the ceiling, hurled stones at the leader and his companions and struck them down. They dismembered the bodies, cut off their heads and tossed them to the people outside. ¹⁷Forever blessed be our God, who has thus punished the wicked!

¹⁸*We shall be celebrating the purification of the temple on the twenty-fifth day of the

---

1, 7: Demetrius: Demetrius II, king of Syria (145–139, 129–125 B.C.). The year one hundred and sixty-nine of the Seleucid era, 143 B.C. Regarding the dates in 1 and 2 Mc, see note on 1 Mc 1, 10. On the troubles caused by Jason and his revolt against the kingdom, i.e., the rule of the legitimate high priest, see 2 Mc 4, 7-22.

1, 8: Our prayer was heard: in the ultimate victory of the Maccabees.

1, 9: Feast of Booths in the month of Chislev: really the feast of the Dedication of the temple (2 Mc 10, 1-8), celebrated on the twenty-fifth of Chislev (Nov.-Dec.). Its solemnity resembles that of the true feast of Booths (Lv 23, 33-43), celebrated on the fifteenth of Tishri (Sept.-Oct.); cf 2 Mc 1, 18.

1, 10: 124 B.C. The date pertains to the preceding, not the following letter. King Ptolemy: Ptolemy VI Philometor, ruler of Egypt from 180 to 145 B.C.; he is mentioned also in 1 Mc 1, 18; 10, 51-59.

1, 11f: The king: Antiochus IV of Syria, the bitter persecutor of the Jews, who, as leader of the Syrian army that invaded Persia, perished there in 164 B.C.

1, 13: Nanea: an oriental goddess comparable to Artemis of the Greeks.

1, 14-17: A different account of the death of Antiochus IV is given in 2 Mc 9, 1-29, and another variant account in 1 Mc 6, 1-16. The writer of this letter had probably heard a distorted rumor of the king's death. This fact and other indications show that the letter was written very soon after Antiochus IV died, hence in 164 B.C.

1, 18-36: This purely legendary account of Nehemiah's miraculous fire is incorporated in the letter because of its connection with the temple and its rededication.

a: 2 Mc 4, 7-20. *b:* 1 Mc 4, 38. *c:* 12-17: 2 Mc 9, 1-29; 1 Mc 6, 1-13.

month Chislev, so we thought it right to inform you that you too may celebrate the feast of Booths and of the fire that appeared when Nehemiah, the rebuilder of the temple[*] and the altar, offered sacrifices. [19]When our fathers were being exiled to Persia,[*] devout priests of the time took some of the fire from the altar and hid it secretly in the hollow of a dry cistern, making sure that the place would be unknown to anyone. [20]Many years later, when it so pleased God, Nehemiah, commissioned by the king of Persia, sent the descendants of the priests who had hidden the fire to look for it. [21]When they informed us that they could not find any fire, but only muddy water, he ordered them to scoop some out and bring it. After the material for the sacrifices had been prepared, Nehemiah ordered the priests to sprinkle with the water the wood and what lay on it. [22]When this was done and in time the sun, which had been clouded over, began to shine, a great fire blazed up, so that everyone marveled. [23]While the sacrifice was being burned, the priests recited a prayer, and all present joined in with them, Jonathan leading and the rest responding with Nehemiah.

[24]The prayer was as follows: "LORD, LORD God, creator of all things, awesome and strong, just and merciful, the only king and benefactor, [25]who alone are gracious, just, almighty, and eternal, Israel's savior from all evil, who chose our forefathers and sanctified them: [26]accept this sacrifice on behalf of all your people Israel and guard and sanctify your heritage. [27]Gather together our scattered people, free those who are the slaves of the Gentiles, look kindly on those who are despised and detested, and let the Gentiles know that you are our God. [28]Punish those who tyrannize over us and arrogantly mistreat us. [29]Plant your people in your holy place, as Moses promised."[d]

[30]Then the priests began to sing hymns. [31]After the sacrifice was burned, Nehemiah ordered the rest of the liquid to be poured upon large stones. [32]As soon as this was done, a flame blazed up, but its light was lost in the brilliance cast from a light on the altar. [33]When the event became known and the king of the Persians was told that, in the very place where the exiled priests had hidden the fire, a liquid was found with which Nehemiah and his people had burned the sacrifices, [34]the king, after verifying the fact, fenced the place off and declared it sacred. [35]To those on whom the king wished to bestow favors he distributed the large revenues he received there. [36]Nehemiah and his companions called the liquid nephthar, meaning purification, but most people name it naphtha.[*]

CHAPTER 2

See RG 231-33

[1][*]You will find in the records, not only that Jeremiah the prophet ordered the deportees to take some of the aforementioned fire with them, [2]but also that the prophet, in giving them the law, admonished them not to forget the commandments of the LORD or be led astray in their thoughts, when seeing the gold and silver idols and their ornaments.[e] [3]With other similar words he urged them not to let the law depart from their hearts. [4][f]The same document also tells how the prophet, following a divine revelation, ordered that the tent and the ark should accompany him and how he went off to the mountain[*] which Moses climbed to see God's inheritance. [5]When Jeremiah arrived there, he found a room in a cave in which he put the tent, the ark, and the altar of incense; then he blocked up the entrance. [6]Some of those who followed him came up intending to mark the path, but they could not find it. [7]When Jeremiah heard of this, he reproved them: "The place is to remain unknown until God gathers his people

---

1, 18: Nehemiah, the rebuilder of the temple: he rebuilt the walls of Jerusalem, but the temple had been rebuilt by Zerubbabel almost a century before.

1, 19: Persia: actually Babylonia, which later became part of the Persian Empire.

1, 36: By a play on words, the Greek term naphtha (petroleum) is assimilated to some Semitic word, perhaps nephthar, meaning "loosened."

2, 1-8: This legendary account of how Jeremiah hid the sa-

cred tent (which was not mentioned after the time of Solomon!), the ark and the altar is given for the purpose of explaining why the postexilic temple was the legitimate place of worship even without these sacred objects.

2, 4: The mountain: Nebo; cf Dt 34, 1.

---

d: 2 Mc 2, 18; Dt 30, 3ff. *e:* Bar 6, 3-72. *f:* 4f: Dt 32, 49; 34, 1; Rv 11, 19.

together again and shows them mercy. [8]Then the LORD will disclose these things, and the glory of the LORD will be seen in the cloud, just as it appeared in the time of Moses and when Solomon prayed that the Place* might be gloriously sanctified."[g]

[9]It is also related how Solomon in his wisdom offered a sacrifice at the dedication and the completion of the temple. [10]Just as Moses prayed to the LORD and fire descended from the sky and consumed the sacrifices, so Solomon also prayed and fire came down and burned up the holocausts.[h] [11]Moses had said,[i] "Because it had not been eaten, the sin offering was burned up."* [12]Solomon also celebrated the feast in the same way for eight days.

[13]Besides these things, it is also told in the records and in Nehemiah's Memoirs* how he collected the books about the kings, the writings of the prophets and of David, and the royal letters about sacred offerings. [14]In like manner Judas also collected for us the books that had been scattered because of the war, and we now have them in our possession.[j] [15]If you need them, send messengers to get them for you.

[16]As we are about to celebrate the feast of the purification of the temple, we are writing to you requesting you also to please celebrate the feast. [17]It is God who has saved all his people and has restored to all of them their heritage, the kingdom, the priesthood, and the sacred rites, [18]as he promised through the law. We trust in God, that he will soon have mercy on us and gather us together from everywhere under the heavens to his holy Place, for he has rescued us from great perils and has purified his Place.[k]

II: Author's Preface

[19]This is the story of Judas Maccabeus and his brothers, of the purification of the great temple, the dedication of the altar, [20]the campaigns against Antiochus Epiphanes and his son Eupator,* [21]and of the heavenly manifestations accorded to the heroes who fought bravely for Judaism, so that, few as they were, they seized the whole land, put to flight the barbarian hordes, [22]regained possession of the world-famous temple, liberated the city, and reestablished the laws that were in danger of being abolished, while the LORD favored them with all his generous assistance. [23]All this, which Jason of Cyrene set forth in detail in five volumes, we will try to condense into a single book.

Purpose and Method. [24]In view of the flood of statistics, and the difficulties encountered by those who wish to plunge into historical narratives where the material is abundant, [25]we have aimed to please those who prefer simple reading, as well as to make it easy for the studious who wish to commit things to memory, and to be helpful to all. [26]For us who have taken upon ourselves the labor of making this digest, the task, far from being easy, is one of sweat and of sleepless nights, [27]just as the preparation of a festive banquet is no light matter for one who thus seeks to give enjoyment to others. Similarly, to win the gratitude of many we will gladly endure these inconveniences, [28]while we leave the responsibility for exact details to the original author, and confine our efforts to giving only a summary outline. [29]As the architect of a new house must give his attention to the whole structure, while the man who undertakes the decoration and the frescoes has only to concern himself with what is needed for ornamentation, so I think it is with us. [30]To enter into questions and examine them thoroughly from all sides is the task of the professional historian; [31]but the man who is making an adaptation should be allowed to aim at brevity of expression and to omit detailed treatment of the matter. [32]Here, then, we shall begin our account without further ado; it would be nonsense to write a long preface to a story and then abbreviate the story itself.

2, 8: The place: the temple of Jerusalem.

2, 11: The statement attributed here to Moses seems to be based on Lv 10, 16-20.

2, 13: Nehemiah's Memoirs: a lost apocryphal work.

2, 20: For the account of the campaigns against Antiochus IV Epiphanes, see 2 Mc 4, 7—10, 9; and for the account of

those against his son Antiochus V Eupator, see 2 Mc 10, 10—13, 26.

3, 1-40: This legendary episode about Heliodorus is re-

g: 1 Kgs 8, 11. h: Lv 9, 23f; 2 Chr 7, 1. i: Lv 10, 16-20. j: 1 Mc 1, 57. k: Dt 30, 3ff.

III: Heliodorus' Attempt to Profane the Temple*

CHAPTER 3

See RG
233

Treachery of Simon. [1]While the holy city lived in perfect peace and the laws were strictly observed because of the piety of the high priest Onias* and his hatred of evil, [2]the kings themselves honored the Place and glorified the temple with the most magnificent gifts. [3]Thus Seleucus,* king of Asia, defrayed from his own revenues all the expenses necessary for the sacrificial services. [4]But a certain Simon, of the priestly course of Bilgah,* who had been appointed superintendent of the temple, had a quarrel with the high priest about the supervision of the city market.[m] [5]Since he could not prevail against Onias, he went to Apollonius of Tarsus, who at that time was governor of Coelesyria and Phoenicia, [6]and reported to him that the treasury in Jerusalem was so full of untold riches that the total sum of money was incalculable and out of all proportion to the cost of the sacrifices, and that it would be possible to bring it all under the control of the king.

Mission of Heliodorus. [7]When Apollonius had an audience with the king, he informed him about the riches that had been reported to him. The king chose his minister Heliodorus and sent him with instructions to expropriate the aforesaid wealth. [8]So Heliodorus immediately set out on his journey, ostensibly to visit the cities of Coelesyria and Phoenicia, but in reality to carry out the king's purpose. [9]When he arrived in Jerusalem and had been graciously received by the high priest of the city, he told him about the information that had been given, and explained the reason for his presence, and he asked if these things were really true. [10]The high priest explained that part of the money was a care fund for widows and orphans,[n] [11]and a part was the property of

Hyrcanus, son of Tobias,* a man who occupied a very high position. Contrary to the calumnies of the impious Simon, the total amounted to four hundred talents of silver and two hundred of gold. [12]He added that it was utterly unthinkable to defraud those who had placed their trust in the sanctity of the Place and in the sacred inviolability of a temple venerated all over the world. [13]But because of the orders he had from the king, Heliodorus said that in any case the money must be confiscated for the royal treasury. [14]So on the day he had set he went in to take an inventory of the funds.

Anguish of the Faithful. There was great distress throughout the city. [15]Priests prostrated themselves in their priestly robes before the altar, and loudly begged him in heaven who had given the law about deposits to keep the deposits safe for those who had made them. [16]Whoever saw the appearance of the high priest was pierced to the heart, for the changed color of his face manifested the anguish of his soul. [17]The terror and bodily trembling that had come over the man clearly showed those who saw him the pain that lodged in his heart. [18]People rushed out of their houses in crowds to make public supplication, because the Place was in danger of being profaned. [19]Women, girded with sackcloth below their breasts, filled the streets; maidens secluded indoors ran together, some to the gates, some to the walls, others peered through the windows, [20]all of them with hands raised toward heaven, making supplication. [21]It was pitiful to see the populace variously prostrated in prayer and the high priest full of dread and anguish.

Divine Intervention. [22]While they were imploring the almighty LORD to keep the deposits safe and secure for those who had placed them in trust, [23]Heliodorus went on with his plan. [24]But just as he was approach-

counted here for the purpose of stressing the inviolability of the temple of Jerusalem; its later profanation was allowed by God because of the people's sins; cf 2 Mc 5, 17f.

3, 1: The high priest Onias: Onias III, who was priest from 196 to 175 B.C., and died in 171 B.C. He was the son of Simon, whose praises are sung in Sir 50, 1-21.

3, 3: Seleucus: Seleucus IV Philopator, who reigned from 187 to 175 B.C.

3, 4: Bilgah: a priestly family mentioned in Neh 12, 5. 18.

3, 11: Son of Tobias: a member of the Tobiad family of Transjordan (Neh 2, 10; 6, 17ff; 13, 4-8). Hyrcanus' father was Joseph, whose mother was the sister of the high priest Onias II.

---

l: 1ff: 2 Mc 5, 19f; 15, 12.   *m:* 2 Mc 4, 23.   *n:* Dt 14, 29.

ing the treasury with his bodyguards, the LORD of spirits who holds all power manifested himself in so striking a way that those who had been bold enough to follow Heliodorus were panic-stricken at God's power and fainted away in terror. *25*There appeared to them a richly caparisoned horse, mounted by a dreadful rider. Charging furiously, the horse attacked Heliodorus with its front hoofs. The rider was seen to be wearing golden armor. *26*Then two other young men, remarkably strong, strikingly beautiful, and splendidly attired, appeared before him. Standing on each side of him, they flogged him unceasingly until they had given him innumerable blows. *27*Suddenly he fell to the ground, enveloped in great darkness. Men picked him up and laid him on a stretcher. *28*The man who a moment before had entered that treasury with a great retinue and his whole bodyguard was carried away helpless, having clearly experienced the sovereign power of God. *29*While he lay speechless and deprived of all hope of aid, due to an act of God's power, *30*the Jews praised the LORD who had marvelously glorified his holy Place; and the temple, charged so shortly before with fear and commotion, was filled with joy and gladness, now that the almighty LORD had manifested himself.

*31*Soon some of the companions of Heliodorus begged Onias to invoke the Most High, praying that the life of the man who was about to expire might be spared. *32*Fearing that the king might think that Heliodorus had suffered some foul play at the hands of the Jews, the high priest offered a sacrifice for the man's recovery. *33*While the high priest was offering the sacrifice of atonement, the same young men in the same clothing again appeared and stood before Heliodorus. "Be very grateful to the high priest Onias," they told him. "It is for his sake that the LORD has spared your life. *34*Since you have been scourged by Heaven, proclaim to all men the majesty of God's power." When they had said this, they disappeared.

Testimony of Heliodorus. *35*After Heliodorus had offered a sacrifice to the LORD and made most solemn vows to him who had spared his life, he bade Onias farewell, and returned with his soldiers to the king. *36*Before all men he gave witness to the deeds of the most high God that he had seen with his own eyes. *37*When the king asked Heliodorus who would be a suitable man to be sent to Jerusalem next, he answered: *38*"If you have an enemy or a plotter against the government, send him there, and you will receive him back well-flogged, if indeed he survives at all; for there is certainly some special divine power about the Place. *39*He who has his dwelling in heaven watches over that Place and protects it, and he strikes down and destroys those who come to harm it." *40*This was how the matter concerning Heliodorus and the preservation of the treasury turned out.

IV: Profanation and Persecution

CHAPTER 4

See RG 233

Onias Appeals to the King. *1*The Simon mentioned above as the informer about the funds against his own country, made false accusations that it was Onias who threatened Heliodorus and instigated the whole miserable affair. *2*He dared to brand as a plotter against the government the man who was a benefactor of the city, a protector of his compatriots, and a zealous defender of the laws. *3*When Simon's hostility reached such a point that murders were being committed by one of his henchmen, *4*Onias saw that the opposition was serious and that Apollonius, son of Menestheus, the governor of Coelesyria and Phoenicia, was abetting Simon's wickedness. *5*So he had recourse to the king, not as an accuser of his countrymen, but as a man looking to the general and particular good of all the people. *6*He saw that, unless the king intervened, it would be impossible to have a peaceful government, and that Simon would not desist from his folly.

Jews Led by Jason To Apostatize. *7*But Seleucus died,* and when Antiochus surnamed Epiphanes succeeded him on the throne,

---

4, 7: Seleucus died: he was murdered by Heliodorus. Antiochus Epiphanes was his younger brother. Onias' brother showed his love for the Greek way of life (v 10) by changing his Hebrew name Joshua, or Jesus, to the Greek name Jason.

Onias' brother Jason obtained the high priest-hood by corrupt means:*o* *8*in an interview, he promised the king three hundred and sixty talents of silver, as well as eighty talents from another source of income. *9*Besides this he agreed to pay a hundred and fifty more, if he were given authority to establish a gymna-sium and a youth club* for it and to enroll men in Jerusalem as Antiochians.

*10*When Jason received the king's approval and came into office, he immediately initiated his countrymen into the Greek way of life. *11*He set aside the royal concessions granted to the Jews through the mediation of John, father of Eupolemus* (that Eupolemus who would later go on an embassy to the Romans to es-tablish a treaty of friendship with them); he abrogated the lawful institutions and intro-duced customs contrary to the law.*p* *12*He quickly established a gymnasium* at the very foot of the acropolis, where he induced the noblest young men to wear the Greek hat.*q* *13*The craze for Hellenism and foreign cus-toms reached such a pitch, through the outra-geous wickedness of the ungodly pseudo-high-priest Jason, *14*that the priests no longer cared about the service of the altar. Disdaining the temple and neglecting the sacrifices, they hastened, at the signal for the discus-throw-ing, to take part in the unlawful exercises on the athletic field. *15*They despised what their ancestors had regarded as honors, while they highly prized what the Greeks esteemed as glory. *16*Precisely because of this, they found themselves in serious trouble: the very people whose manner of life they emulated, and whom they desired to imitate in everything, became their enemies and oppressors. *17*It is no light matter to flout the laws of God, as the following period will show.

*18*When the quinquennial games were held at Tyre in the presence of the king, *19*the vile Jason sent envoys as representatives of the Antiochians of Jerusalem, to bring there three hundred silver drachmas for the sacrifice to Hercules. But the bearers themselves decided that the money should not be spent on a sac-rifice, as that was not right, but should be used for some other purpose. *20*So the contribution destined by the sender for the sacrifice to Her-cules was in fact applied, by those who brought it, to the construction of triremes.*

*21*When Apollonius, son of Menestheus, was sent to Egypt for the coronation of King Philometor,* Antiochus learned that the king was opposed to his policies; so he took mea-sures for his own security. *22*After going to Joppa, he proceeded to Jerusalem. There he was received with great pomp by Jason and the people of the city, who escorted him with torchlights and acclamations; following this, he led his army into Phoenicia.

Menelaus Supplants Jason. *23*Three years later Jason sent Menelaus,* brother of the aforementioned Simon, to deliver the money to the king, and to obtain decisions on some important matters. *24*When he had been intro-duced to the king, he flattered him with such an air of authority that he secured the high priesthood for himself, outbidding Jason by three hundred talents of silver. *25*He returned with the royal commission, but with nothing that made him worthy of the high priesthood; he had the temper of a cruel tyrant and the rage of a wild beast. *26*Then Jason, who had cheated his own brother and now saw himself cheated by another man, was driven out as a fugitive to the country of the Ammonites.

*27*Although Menelaus had obtained the of-fice, he did not make any payments of the money he had promised to the king, *28*in spite of the demand of Sostratus, the commandant

---

4, 9: Youth club: an educational institution in which young men were trained both in Greek intellectual culture and in physical fitness. Antiochians: honorary citizens of An-tioch, a Hellenistic city of the Seleucid Kingdom that had a corporation of such Antiochians, who enjoyed certain politi-cal and commercial privileges.

4, 11: Eupolemus: one of the two envoys sent to Rome by Judas Maccabeus (1 Mc 8, 17).

4, 12: Since the gymnasium, where the youth exercised naked (Greek gymnos), lay in the Tyropoeon Valley to the east of the citadel, it was directly next to the temple on its

eastern side. The Greek hat: a wide-brimmed hat, traditional headgear of Hermes, the patron god of athletic contests; it formed part of the distinctive costume of the members of the "youth club."

4, 20: Triremes: war vessels with three banks of oars.

4, 21: Philometor: Ptolemy VI, king of Egypt, c. 172 to c. 145 B.C.

4, 23: Menelaus: Jewish high priest from c. 172 to his ex-ecution in 162 B.C. (2 Mc 13, 3-8).

---

o: 2 Mc 1, 7; 1 Mc 1, 10.   *p:* 1 Mc 8, 17.   *q:* 1 Mc 1, 14.

of the citadel, whose duty it was to collect the taxes. For this reason, both were summoned before the king. [29]Menelaus left his brother Lysimachus as his substitute in the high priesthood, while Sostratus left Crates, commander of the Cypriots, as his substitute.

Murder of Onias. [30]While these things were taking place, the people of Tarsus and Mallus* rose in revolt, because their cities had been given as a gift to Antiochis, the king's mistress. [31]The king, therefore, went off in haste to settle the affair, leaving Andronicus, one of his nobles, as his deputy. [32]Then Menelaus, thinking this a good opportunity, stole some gold vessels from the temple and presented them to Andronicus; he had already sold some other vessels in Tyre and in the neighboring cities. [33]When Onias had clear evidence of the facts, he made a public protest, after withdrawing to the inviolable sanctuary at Daphne, near Antioch. [34]Thereupon Menelaus approached Andronicus privately and asked him to lay hands on Onias. So Andronicus went to Onias, and by treacherously reassuring him through sworn pledges with right hands joined, persuaded him, in spite of his suspicions, to leave the sanctuary. Then, without any regard for justice, he immediately put him to death.

[35]As a result, not only the Jews, but many people of other nations as well, were indignant and angry over the unjust murder of the man. [36]When the king returned from the region of Cilicia, the Jews of the city,* together with the Greeks who detested the crime, went to see him about the murder of Onias. [37]Antiochus was deeply grieved and full of pity; he wept as he recalled the prudence and noble conduct of the deceased. [38]Inflamed with anger, he immediately stripped Andronicus of his purple robe, tore off his other garments, and had him led through the whole city to the very place where he had committed the outrage against Onias; and there he put the murderer to death. Thus the LORD rendered him the punishment he deserved.

Riot against Lysimachus. [39]Many sacrilegious thefts had been committed by Lysimachus in the city* with the connivance of Menelaus. When word was spread that a large number of gold vessels had been stolen, the people assembled in protest against Lysimachus. [40]As the crowds, now thoroughly enraged, began to riot, Lysimachus launched an unjustified attack against them with about three thousand armed men under the leadership of Auranus, a man as advanced in folly as he was in years. [41]Reacting against Lysimachus' attack, the people picked up stones or pieces of wood or handfuls of the ashes lying there and threw them in wild confusion at Lysimachus and his men. [42]As a result, they wounded many of them and even killed a few, while they put all the rest to flight. The sacrilegious thief himself they slew near the treasury.

[43]Charges about this affair were brought against Menelaus. [44]When the king came to Tyre, three men sent by the senate* presented to him the justice of their cause. [45]But Menelaus, seeing himself on the losing side, promised Ptolemy, son of Dorymenes, a substantial sum of money if he would win the king over.[r] [46]So Ptolemy retired with the king under a colonnade, as if to get some fresh air, and persuaded him to change his mind. [47]Menelaus, who was the cause of all the trouble, the king acquitted of the charges, while he condemned to death those poor men who would have been declared innocent even if they had pleaded their case before Scythians. [48]Thus, those who had prosecuted the case for the city, for the people, and for the sacred vessels, quickly suffered unjust punishment. [49]For this reason, even some Tyrians were indignant over the crime and provided sumptuously for their burial. [50]But Menelaus, thanks to the covetousness of the men in power, remained in office, where he grew in wickedness and became the chief plotter against his fellow citizens.

4, 30: Mallus: a city of Cilicia (v 36) in southeastern Asia Minor, about thirty miles east of Tarsus.

4, 36: The city: Antioch. But some understand the Greek to mean "each city."

4, 39: The city: Jerusalem. Menelaus was still in Syria.

4, 44: The senate: the council of Jewish elders at Jerusalem; cf 1 Mc 12, 6.

r: 2 Mc 8, 8; 1 Mc 3, 38.

See RG
233

CHAPTER 5

Sedition and Death of Jason. [1]About this time Antiochus sent his second expedition* into Egypt.[s] [2]It then happened that all over the city, for nearly forty days, there appeared horsemen charging in midair, clad in garments interwoven with gold—companies fully armed with lances [3]and drawn swords; squadrons of cavalry in battle array, charges and countercharges on this side and that, with brandished shields and bristling spears, flights of arrows and flashes of gold ornaments, together with armor of every sort. [4]Therefore all prayed that this vision might be a good omen.

[5]But when a false rumor circulated that Antiochus was dead, Jason* gathered fully a thousand men and suddenly attacked the city. As the defenders on the walls were forced back and the city was finally being taken, Menelaus took refuge in the citadel. [6]Jason then slaughtered his fellow citizens without mercy, not realizing that triumph over one's own kindred was the greatest failure, but imagining that he was winning a victory over his enemies, not his fellow countrymen. [7]Even so, he did not gain control of the government, but in the end received only disgrace for his treachery, and once again took refuge in the country of the Ammonites. [8]At length he met a miserable end. Called to account before Aretas,* king of the Arabs, he fled from city to city, hunted by all men, hated as a transgressor of the laws, abhorred as the butcher of his country and his countrymen. After being driven into Egypt, [9]he crossed the sea to the Spartans, among whom he hoped to find protection because of his relations with them. There he who had exiled so many from their country perished in exile; [10]and he who had cast out

so many to lie unburied went unmourned himself with no funeral of any kind or any place in the tomb of his ancestors.

The City Ravaged. [11][u]When these happenings were reported to the king, he thought that Judea was in revolt. Raging like a wild animal, he set out from Egypt and took Jerusalem by storm. [12]He ordered his soldiers to cut down without mercy those whom they met and to slay those who took refuge in their houses. [13]There was a massacre of young and old, a killing of women and children, a slaughter of virgins and infants. [14]In the space of three days, eighty thousand were lost, forty thousand meeting a violent death, and the same number being sold into slavery. [15]Not satisfied with this, the king dared to enter the holiest temple in the world; Menelaus, that traitor both to the laws and to his country, served as guide. [16]He laid his impure hands on the sacred vessels and gathered up with profane hands the votive offerings made by other kings for the advancement, the glory, and the honor of the Place. [17]Puffed up in spirit, Antiochus did not realize that it was because of the sins of the city's inhabitants that the LORD was angry for a little while and hence disregarded the holy Place.[v] [18]If they had not become entangled in so many sins, this man, like Heliodorus, who was sent by King Seleucus to inspect the treasury, would have been flogged and turned back from his presumptuous action as soon as he approached. [19][w]The LORD, however, had not chosen the people for the sake of the Place, but the Place for the sake of the people.* [20]Therefore, the Place itself, having shared in the people's misfortunes, afterward participated in their good fortune; and what the Almighty had forsaken in his anger was restored in all its glory, once the great Sovereign became reconciled.

5, 1: Second expedition: the first invasion of Egypt by Antiochus in 169 B.C. (1 Mc 1, 16-20) is not mentioned in 2 Mc, unless the coming of the Syrian army to Palestine (2 Mc 4, 21f) is regarded as the first invasion. The author of 2 Mc apparently combines the first pillage of Jerusalem in 169 B.C. after Antiochus' first invasion of Egypt (1 Mc 1, 20-28; cf 2 Mc 5, 5ff) with the second pillage of the city two years later (167 B.C.), following the king's second invasion of Egypt in 168 B.C. (1 Mc 1, 29-35; cf 2 Mc 5, 24ff).

5, 5: Jason: brother of Onias III, was claimant of the high

priesthood (2 Mc 4, 7-10). Later he was supplanted by Menelaus who drove him into Transjordan (2 Mc 4, 26).

5, 8: Aretas: King Aretas I of the Nabateans; cf 1 Mc 5, 25.

5, 19: Man is more important than even the most sacred institutions; cf Mk 2, 27.

---

s: 1 Mc 1, 17.   *t:* 2f: 2 Mc 3, 24ff; 10, 29f; 11, 8.   *u:* 11-21: 1 Mc 1, 20-24.   *v:* 2 Mc 6, 12-16; 7, 16-19. 32-38.   *w:* 19ff: 2 Mc 3, 1ff; 1 Chr 17, 9; Mk 2, 27.

²¹Antiochus carried off eighteen hundred talents from the temple, and hurried back to Antioch. In his arrogance he planned to make the land navigable and the sea passable on foot, so carried away was he with pride.ˣ ²²But he left governors to harass the nation: at Jerusalem, Philip, a Phrygian by birth,* and in character more cruel than the man who appointed him; ²³at Mount Gerizim,* Andronicus; and besides these, Menelaus, who lorded it over his fellow citizens worse than the others did. Out of hatred for the Jewish citizens, ²⁴ʸthe king sent Apollonius,* commander of the Mysians, at the head of an army of twenty-two thousand men, with orders to kill all the grown men and sell the women and young men into slavery. ²⁵When this man arrived in Jerusalem, he pretended to be peacefully disposed and waited until the holy day of the sabbath; then, finding the Jews refraining from work, he ordered his men to parade fully armed. ²⁶All those who came out to watch, he massacred, and running through the city with armed men, he cut down a large number of people.

²⁷But Judas Maccabeus with about nine others withdrew to the wilderness where he and his companions lived like wild animals in the hills, continuing to eat what grew wild to avoid sharing the defilement.ᶻ

CHAPTER 6

See RG 233

The Temple Desecrated. ¹ᵃNot long after this the king sent an Athenian senator to force the Jews to abandon the customs of their ancestors and live no longer by the laws of God; ²also to profane the temple in Jerusalem and dedicate it to Olympian Zeus,* and that on Mount Gerizim to Zeus the Hospitable, as the inhabitants of the place requested.ᵇ ³This intensified the evil in an intolerable and utterly disgusting way. ⁴The Gentiles filled the temple with debauchery and revelry; they amused themselves with prostitutes* and had intercourse with women even in the sacred court. They also brought into the temple things that were forbidden, ⁵so that the altar was covered with abominable offerings prohibited by the laws.

Abolition of the Law. ⁶A man could not keep the sabbath or celebrate the traditional feasts, nor even admit that he was a Jew. ⁷Moreover, at the monthly celebration of the king's birthday the Jews had, from bitter necessity, to partake of the sacrifices, and when the festival of Dionysus* was celebrated, they were compelled to march in his procession, wearing wreaths of ivy.

⁸At the suggestion of the citizens of Ptolemais, a decree was issued ordering the neighboring Greek cities to act in the same way against the Jews: oblige them to partake of the sacrifices, ⁹and put to death those who would not consent to adopt the customs of the Greeks. It was obvious, therefore, that disaster impended. ¹⁰Thus, two women who were arrested for having circumcised their children were publicly paraded about the city with their babies hanging at their breasts and then thrown down from the top of the city wall.ᶜ ¹¹Others, who had assembled in nearby caves to observe the sabbath in secret, were betrayed to Philip and all burned to death. In their respect for the holiness of that day, they had scruples about defending themselves.ᵈ

Purpose of Divine Judgment. ¹²ᵉNow I beg those who read this book not to be disheartened by these misfortunes, but to consider that these chastisements were meant not for the ruin but for the correction of our nation. ¹³It is, in fact, a sign of great kindness to punish sinners promptly instead of letting them go for long. ¹⁴ᶠThus, in dealing with other nations, the LORD patiently waits until they

---

5, 22: Philip, a Phrygian by birth: the Philip of 2 Mc 6, 11 and 8, 8, but probably not the same as Philip the regent of 2 Mc 9, 29 and 1 Mc 6, 14.

5, 23: Mount Gerizim: the sacred mountain of the Samaritans at Shechem; cf 2 Mc 6, 2.

5, 24: Apollonius: the Mysian commander of 1 Mc 1, 29; mentioned also in 2 Mc 3, 5; 4, 4.

6, 2: Olympian Zeus: equated with the Syrian Baal shomem ("the lord of the heavens"), a term which the Jews rendered as "Shiqqus shomem," horrible abomina-

tion (Dn 9, 27; 11, 31; 12, 11; 1 Mc 1, 54).

6, 4: Amused themselves with prostitutes: as in the fertility cults of the ancient Near East; see notes on Bar 6, 10. 42f.

6, 7: Dionysus: called also Bacchus the god of the grape harvest and of wine; ivy was one of his symbols.

x: 1 Mc 1, 23f. *y:* 24ff: 1 Mc 1, 29f. *z:* 1 Mc 2, 28. *a:* 1-11: 1 Mc 1, 44-63. *b:* 1 Mc 1, 46; Dn 9, 27. *c:* 1 Mc 1, 60f. *d:* 1 Mc 2, 32-38. *e:* 12-16: 2 Mc 5, 17; 7, 16-19. 32-38. *f:* Wis 11, 9f; 12, 2, 22.

reach the full measure of their sins before he punishes them; but with us he has decided to deal differently, *15*in order that he may not have to punish us more severely later, when our sins have reached their fullness. *16*He never withdraws his mercy from us. Although he disciplines us with misfortunes, he does not abandon his own people. *17*Let these words suffice for recalling this truth. Without further ado we must go on with our story.

Martyrdom of Eleazar.* *18*Eleazar, one of the foremost scribes, a man of advanced age and noble appearance, was being forced to open his mouth to eat pork.*g* *19*But preferring a glorious death to a life of defilement, he spat out the meat, and went forward of his own accord to the instrument of torture, *20*as men ought to do who have the courage to reject the food which it is unlawful to taste even for love of life. *21*Those in charge of that unlawful ritual meal took the man aside privately, because of their long acquaintance with him, and urged him to bring meat of his own providing, such as he could legitimately eat, and to pretend to be eating some of the meat of the sacrifice prescribed by the king; *22*in this way he would escape the death penalty, and be treated kindly because of their old friendship with him. *23*But he made up his mind in a noble manner, worthy of his years, the dignity of his advanced age, the merited distinction of his gray hair, and of the admirable life he had lived from childhood; and so he declared that above all he would be loyal to the holy laws given by God.

He told them to send him at once to the abode of the dead, explaining: *24*"At our age it would be unbecoming to make such a pretense; many young men would think the ninety-year-old Eleazar had gone over to an alien religion. *25*Should I thus dissimulate for the sake of a brief moment of life, they would be led astray by me, while I would bring shame and dishonor on my old age. *26*Even if, for the time being, I avoid the punishment of men, I shall never, whether alive or dead, escape the hands of the Almighty.

*27*Therefore, by manfully giving up my life now, I will prove myself worthy of my old age, *28*and I will leave to the young a noble example of how to die willingly and generously for the revered and holy laws."

He spoke thus, and went immediately to the instrument of torture. *29*Those who shortly before had been kindly disposed, now became hostile toward him because what he had said seemed to them utter madness. *30*When he was about to die under the blows, he groaned and said: "The LORD in his holy knowledge knows full well that, although I could have escaped death, I am not only enduring terrible pain in my body from this scourging, but also suffering it with joy in my soul because of my devotion to him." *31*This is how he died, leaving in his death a model of courage and an unforgettable example of virtue not only for the young but for the whole nation.

CHAPTER 7

See RG 233

Martyrdom of a Mother and Her Sons. *1*It also happened that seven brothers with their mother were arrested and tortured with whips and scourges by the king, to force them to eat pork in violation of God's law.*h* *2*One of the brothers, speaking for the others, said: "What do you expect to achieve by questioning us? We are ready to die rather than transgress the laws of our ancestors." *3*At that the king, in a fury, gave orders to have pans and caldrons heated. *4*While they were being quickly heated, he commanded his executioners to cut out the tongue of the one who had spoken for the others, to scalp him and cut off his hands and feet, while the rest of his brothers and his mother looked on. *5*When he was completely maimed but still breathing, the king ordered them to carry him to the fire and fry him. As a cloud of smoke spread from the pan, the brothers and their mother encouraged one another to die bravely, saying such words as these: *6*"The LORD God is looking on, and he truly has compassion on us, as Moses declared in his canticle, when he protested

---

6, 18—7, 42: The stories of Eleazar and of the mother and her seven sons, among the earliest models of "martyrology," were understandably popular among the Christians of the early centuries. Written originally to encourage God's people in times of persecution, they add gruesome details to the record of tortures, and place long speeches in the mouths of the martyrs.

g: Lv 11, 7f; Heb 11, 35.   h: Jer 15, 9.

openly with the words, 'And he will have pity on his servants.' "[i]

[7]When the first brother had died in this manner, they brought the second to be made sport of. After tearing off the skin and hair of his head, they asked him, "Will you eat the pork rather than have your body tortured limb by limb?" [8]Answering in the language of his forefathers, he said, "Never!" So he too in turn suffered the same tortures as the first. [9]At the point of death he said: "You accursed fiend, you are depriving us of this present life, but the King of the world will raise us up* to live again forever. It is for his laws that we are dying."[j]

[10]After him the third suffered their cruel sport. He put out his tongue at once when told to do so, and bravely held out his hands, [11]as he spoke these noble words: "It was from Heaven that I received these; for the sake of his laws I disdain them; from him I hope to receive them again."[k] [12]Even the king and his attendants marveled at the young man's courage, because he regarded his sufferings as nothing.

[13]After he had died, they tortured and maltreated the fourth brother in the same way. [14]When he was near death, he said, "It is my choice to die at the hands of men with the God-given hope of being restored to life by him; but for you, there will be no resurrection to life."

[15]They next brought forward the fifth brother and maltreated him. [16]Looking at the king, he said:[l] "Since you have power among men, mortal though you are, do what you please. But do not think that our nation is forsaken by God. [17]Only wait, and you will see how his great power will torment you and your descendants."

[18]After him they brought the sixth brother. When he was about to die, he said: "Have no vain illusions. We suffer these things on our own account, because we have sinned against our God; that is why such astonishing things have happened to us. [19]Do not

think, then, that you will go unpunished for having dared to fight against God."[m]

[20]Most admirable and worthy of everlasting remembrance was the mother, who saw her seven sons perish in a single day, yet bore it courageously because of her hope in the LORD. [21]Filled with a noble spirit that stirred her womanly heart with manly courage, she exhorted each of them in the language of their forefathers with these words: [22]"I do not know how you came into existence in my womb; it was not I who gave you the breath of life, nor was it I who set in order the elements of which each of you is composed. [23]Therefore, since it is the Creator of the universe who shapes each man's beginning, as he brings about the origin of everything, he, in his mercy, will give you back both breath and life, because you now disregard yourselves for the sake of his law."

[24]Antiochus, suspecting insult in her words, thought he was being ridiculed. As the youngest brother was still alive, the king appealed to him, not with mere words, but with promises on oath, to make him rich and happy if he would abandon his ancestral customs: he would make him his Friend and entrust him with high office. [25]When the youth paid no attention to him at all, the king appealed to the mother, urging her to advise her boy to save his life. [26]After he had urged her for a long time, she went through the motions of persuading her son. [27]In derision of the cruel tyrant, she leaned over close to her son and said in their native language: "Son, have pity on me, who carried you in my womb for nine months, nursed you for three years, brought you up, educated and supported you to your present age. [28]I beg you, child, to look at the heavens and the earth and see all that is in them; then you will know that God did not make them out of existing things;* and in the same way the human race came into existence. [29]Do not be afraid of this executioner, but be worthy of your brothers and accept death, so that in the

---

7, 9: The King of the world will raise us up: here, and in vv 11. 14. 23. 29. 36, belief in the future resurrection of the body, at least for the just, is clearly stated; cf also 2 Mc 12, 44; 14, 46; Dn 12, 2.

7, 28: God did not make them out of existing things: that

is, God made all things solely by his omnipotent will and his creative word; cf Heb 11, 3.

i: Dt 32, 36. *j:* 2 Mc 12, 44; 14, 46. *k:* 2 Mc 12, 43ff. *l:* 16-19: 2 Mc 5, 17; 6, 12-16. *m:* Acts 5, 39.

time of mercy I may receive you again with them."

³⁰She had scarcely finished speaking when the youth said: "What are you waiting for? I will not obey the king's command. I obey the command of the law given to our forefathers through Moses. ³¹But you, who have contrived every kind of affliction for the Hebrews, will not escape the hands of God. ³²ⁿWe, indeed, are suffering because of our sins. ³³Though our living LORD treats us harshly for a little while to correct us with chastisements, he will again be reconciled with his servants. ³⁴But you, wretch, vilest of all men! do not, in your insolence, concern yourself with unfounded hopes, as you raise your hand against the children of Heaven. ³⁵You have not yet escaped the judgment of the almighty and all-seeing God. ³⁶My brothers, after enduring brief pain, have drunk of never-failing life, under God's covenant, but you, by the judgment of God, shall receive just punishments for your arrogance. ³⁷Like my brothers, I offer up my body and my life for our ancestral laws, imploring God to show mercy soon to our nation, and by afflictions and blows to make you confess that he alone is God. ³⁸Through me and my brothers, may there be an end to the wrath of the Almighty that has justly fallen on our whole nation." ³⁹At that, the king became enraged and treated him even worse than the others, since he bitterly resented the boy's contempt. ⁴⁰ºThus he too died undefiled, putting all his trust in the LORD. ⁴¹The mother was last to die, after her sons.

⁴²Enough has been said about the sacrificial meals and the excessive cruelties.

V: Victories of Judas and Purification of the Temple

See RG 233

CHAPTER 8

Judas Maccabeus. ¹ᵖJudas Maccabeus and his companions entered the vil-

lages secretly, summoned their kinsmen, and by also enlisting others who remained faithful to Judaism, assembled about six thousand men. ²They implored the LORD to look kindly upon his people, who were being oppressed on all sides; to have pity on the temple, which was profaned by godless men; ³to have mercy on the city, which was being destroyed and about to be leveled to the ground; to hearken to the blood that cried out to him; ⁴to remember the criminal slaughter of innocent children and the blasphemies uttered against his name; and to manifest his hatred of evil. ⁵�q Once Maccabeus got his men organized, the Gentiles could not withstand him, for the LORD's wrath had now changed to mercy. ⁶Coming unexpectedly upon towns and villages, he would set them on fire. He captured strategic positions, and put to flight a large number of the enemy. ⁷He preferred the nights as being especially helpful for such attacks. Soon the fame of his valor spread everywhere.

*First Victory over Nicanor.*ᵃ ⁸When Philip saw that Judas was gaining ground little by little and that his successful advances were becoming more frequent, he wrote to Ptolemy, governor of Coelesyria and Phoenicia, to come to the aid of the king's government.ʳ ⁹Ptolemy promptly selected Nicanor, son of Patroclus, one of the Chief Friends, and sent him at the head of at least twenty thousand armed men of various nations to wipe out the entire Jewish race. With him he associated Gorgias, a professional military commander, well-versed in the art of war.ˢ ¹⁰Nicanor planned to raise the two thousand talents of tribute owed by the king to the Romans by selling captured Jews into slavery. ¹¹So he immediately sent word to the coastal cities, inviting them to buy Jewish slaves and promising to deliver ninety slaves for a talent—little did he dream of the punishment that was to fall upon him from the Almighty.

¹²When Judas learned of Nicanor's advance and informed his companions about

---

8, 8-29. 34ff: This account of the campaign of Nicanor and Gorgias against Judas is paralleled, with certain differences, in 1 Mc 3, 38—4, 24.

---

n: 32. 38: 2 Mc 5, 17; 6, 12-16; 17, 16-19.   *o:* 40f: Heb 11, 35.   *p:* 1-7: 2 Mc 5, 27; 1 Mc 3, 10-26.   *q:* 5ff: 1 Mc 3, 3-9.   *r:* 2 Mc 4, 45; 1 Mc 3, 38.   *s:* 1 Mc 7, 26.

the approach of the army, [13]the cowardly and those who lacked faith in God's justice deserted and got away. [14]But the others sold everything they had left, and at the same time besought the LORD to deliver those whom the ungodly Nicanor had sold before even meeting them. [15]They begged the LORD to do this, if not for their sake, at least for the sake of the covenants made with their forefathers, and because they themselves bore his holy, glorious name. [16]Maccabeus assembled his men, six thousand strong, and exhorted them not to be panic-stricken before the enemy, nor to fear the large number of the Gentiles attacking them unjustly, but to fight courageously, [17]keeping before their eyes the lawless outrage perpetrated by the Gentiles against the holy Place and the affliction of the humiliated city, as well as the subversion of their ancestral way of life. [18]"They trust in weapons and acts of daring," he said, "but we trust in almighty God, who can by a mere nod destroy not only those who attack us, but the whole world." [19]He went on to tell them of the times when help had been given their ancestors: both the time of Sennacherib, when a hundred and eighty-five thousand of his men were destroyed,[t] [20]and the time of the battle in Babylonia against the Galatians, when only eight thousand Jews fought along with four thousand Macedonians; yet when the Macedonians were hard pressed, the eight thousand routed one hundred and twenty thousand and took a great quantity of booty, because of the help they received from Heaven. [21]With such words he encouraged them and made them ready to die for their laws and their country.

Then Judas divided his army into four, [22]placing his brothers, Simon, Joseph,* and Jonathan, each over a division, assigning to each fifteen hundred men. [23](There was also Eleazar.) After reading to them from the holy book and giving them the watchword, "The Help of God," he himself took charge of the first division and joined in battle with Nicanor.[u] [24]With the Almighty as their ally, they killed more than nine thousand of the enemy, wounded and disabled the greater part of Nicanor's army, and put all of them to flight. [25]They also seized the money of those who had come to buy them as slaves. When they had pursued the enemy for some time, [26]they were obliged to return by reason of the late hour. It was the day before the sabbath, and for that reason they could not continue the pursuit. [27]They collected the enemy's arms and stripped them of their spoils, and then observed the sabbath with fervent praise and thanks to the LORD who kept them safe for that day on which he let descend on them the first dew of his mercy. [28]After the sabbath, they gave a share of the booty to the persecuted and to widows and orphans; the rest they divided among themselves and their children. [29]When this was done, they made supplication in common, imploring the merciful LORD to be completely reconciled with his servants.

Timothy and Bacchides Defeated. [30]They also challenged the forces of Timothy and Bacchides, killed more than twenty thousand of them, and captured some very high fortresses. They divided the enormous plunder, allotting half to themselves and the rest to the persecuted, to orphans, widows, and the aged. [31]They collected the enemies' weapons and carefully stored them in suitable places; the rest of the spoils they carried to Jerusalem. [32]They also killed the commander of Timothy's forces, a most wicked man, who had done great harm to the Jews. [33]While celebrating the victory in their ancestral city, they burned both those who had set fire to the sacred gates and Callisthenes, who had taken refuge in a little house; so he received the reward his wicked deeds deserved.

Humiliation of Nicanor. [34v]The accursed Nicanor, who had brought the thousand slave dealers to buy the Jews, [35]after being humbled through the LORD's help by those whom he had thought of no account, laid

8, 22: Joseph: called John in 1 Mc 2, 2; 9, 36. 38. This paragraph interrupts the story of Nicanor's defeat, which is resumed in v 34. The purpose of the author apparently is to group together the defeats suffered by the Syrians on various occasions. Battles against Timothy are recounted in 1 Mc 5, 37-44 and 2 Mc 12, 10-25; against Bacchides in 1 Mc 7, 8-20.

t: 2 Mc 15, 22; 2 Kgs 19, 35; Is 37, 36. u: 1 Mc 3, 48. v: 34f: 2 Mc 8, 23f; 1 Mc 7, 26.

aside his fine clothes and fled alone across country like a runaway slave, until he reached Antioch. He was eminently successful in destroying his own army. [36]So he who had promised to provide tribute for the Romans by the capture of the people of Jerusalem testified that the Jews had a champion, and that they were invulnerable for the very reason that they followed the laws laid down by him.

CHAPTER 9

See RG
233

Punishment and Death of Antiochus.*

[1w]About that time Antiochus retreated in disgrace from the region of Persia. [2]He had entered the city called Persepolis and attempted to rob the temple and gain control of the city. Thereupon the people had swift recourse to arms, and Antiochus' men were routed, so that in the end Antiochus was put to flight by the natives and forced to beat a shameful retreat. [3]On his arrival in Ecbatana, he learned what had happened to Nicanor and to Timothy's forces. [4]Overcome with anger, he planned to make the Jews suffer for the injury done by those who had put him to flight. Therefore he ordered his charioteer to drive without stopping until he finished the journey.

Yet the condemnation of Heaven rode with him, since he said in his arrogance, "I will make Jerusalem the common graveyard of the Jews as soon as I arrive there." [5]So the all-seeing LORD, the God of Israel, struck him down with an unseen but incurable blow; for scarcely had he uttered those words when he was seized with excruciating pains in his bowels and sharp internal torment,[x] [6]a fit punishment for him who had tortured the bowels of others with many barbarous torments. [7]Far from giving up his insolence, he was all the more filled with arrogance. Breathing fire in his rage against the Jews, he gave orders to drive even faster. As a result he hurtled from the dashing chariot, and every part of his body was racked by the violent fall. [8y]Thus he who previously, in his superhuman presumption, thought he could command the waves of the sea, and imagined he could weigh the mountaintops in his scales, was now thrown to the ground and had to be carried on a litter, clearly manifesting to all the power of God. [9z]The body of this impious man swarmed with worms, and while he was still alive in hideous torments, his flesh rotted off, so that the entire army was sickened by the stench of his corruption. [10]Shortly before, he had thought that he could reach the stars of heaven, and now, no one could endure to transport the man because of this intolerable stench.

[11]At last, broken in spirit, he began to give up his excessive arrogance, and to gain some understanding, under the scourge of God, for he was racked with pain unceasingly. [12]When he could no longer bear his own stench, he said, "It is right to be subject to God, and not to think one's mortal self divine." [13]Then this vile man vowed to the LORD, who would no longer have mercy on him, [14]that he would set free the holy city, toward which he had been hurrying with the intention of leveling it to the ground and making it a common graveyard; [15]he would put on perfect equality with the Athenians all the Jews, whom he had judged not even worthy of burial, but fit only to be thrown out with their children to be eaten by vultures and wild animals; [16]he would adorn with the finest offerings the holy temple which he had previously despoiled; he would restore all the sacred vessels many times over; and would provide from his own revenues the expenses required for the sacrifices. [17]Besides all this, he would become a Jew himself and visit every inhabited place to proclaim there the power of God. [18]But since God's punishment had justly come upon him, his sufferings were not lessened, so he lost hope for himself and wrote the following letter to the Jews in the form of a supplication. It read thus:

9, 1-28: In order to keep together the various accounts of God's punishment of the persecutors of his people, the author places here the stories of Antiochus' illness and death (in actuality the king died only after the purification of the temple; cf 1 Mc 4, 36-59; 6, 1-16; 2 Mc 10, 1-8); of Judas' campaigns in Idumea and Transjordan (cf 2 Mc 5, 1-51; 2 Mc 10, 14-38); and of the first expedition of Lysias (1 Mc 4, 26-35; 2 Mc 11, 1-15).

w: 1-29: 2 Mc 1, 12-17; 1 Mc 6, 1-13.   x: Acts 12, 20-23.   y: Jb 38, 8-11; Ps 65, 6f; Is 40, 12.   z: Acts 12, 23.

19*"To my esteemed Jewish citizens, Antiochus, their king and general, sends hearty greetings and best wishes for their health and happiness. 20If you and your children are well and your affairs are going as you wish, I thank God very much, for my hopes are in heaven. 21Now that I am ill, I recall with affection the esteem and good will you bear me. On returning from the regions of Persia, I fell victim to a troublesome illness; so I thought it necessary to form plans for the general welfare of all. 22Actually, I do not despair about my health, since I have great hopes of recovering from my illness. 23Nevertheless, I know that my father, whenever he went on campaigns in the hinterland, would name his successor, 24so that, if anything unexpected happened or any unwelcome news came, the people throughout the realm would know to whom the government had been entrusted, and so not be disturbed. 25I am also bearing in mind that the neighboring rulers, especially those on the borders of our kingdom, are on the watch for opportunities and waiting to see what will happen. I have therefore appointed as king my son Antiochus, whom I have often before entrusted and commended to most of you, when I made hurried visits to the outlying provinces. I have written to him the letter copied below.* 26Therefore I beg and entreat each of you to remember the general and individual benefits you have received, and to continue to show good will toward me and my son. 27I am confident that, following my policy, he will treat you with mildness and kindness in his relations with you."

28So this murderer and blasphemer, after extreme sufferings, such as he had inflicted on others, died a miserable death in the mountains of a foreign land. 29His foster brother Philip brought the body home; but fearing Antiochus' son, he later withdrew into Egypt, to Ptolemy Philometor.

CHAPTER 10

See RG 233

Purification of Temple and City. 1aWhen Maccabeus and his companions, under the LORD's leadership, had recovered the temple and the city, 2they destroyed the altars erected by the Gentiles in the marketplace and the sacred enclosures. 3After purifying the temple, they made a new altar. Then, with fire struck from flint, they offered sacrifice for the first time in two years,* burned incense, and lighted lamps. They also set out the showbread. 4When they had done this, they prostrated themselves and begged the LORD that they might never again fall into such misfortunes, and that if they should sin at any time, he might chastise them with moderation and not hand them over to blasphemous and barbarous Gentiles. 5On the anniversary of the day on which the temple had been profaned by the Gentiles, that is, the twenty-fifth of the same month Chislev, the purification of the temple took place. 6The Jews celebrated joyfully for eight days as on the feast of Booths, remembering how, a little while before, they had spent the feast of Booths living like wild animals in caves on the mountains. 7Carrying rods entwined with leaves, green branches and palms, they sang hymns of grateful praise to him who had brought about the purification of his own Place. 8By public edict and decree they prescribed that the whole Jewish nation should celebrate these days every year.

VI: Renewed Persecution

Death of Ptolemy. 9Such was the end of Antiochus surnamed Epiphanes.b 10Now we shall relate what happened under Antiochus Eupator, the son of that godless man, and shall give a summary of the chief evils caused by the wars. 11When Eupator suc-

---

9, 19-27: Despite the statement in v 18, this letter is not really a supplication. It is rather a notification to all the king's subjects of the appointment of his son as his successor and a request that they be loyal to the new king. Apparently the same letter, which has every appearance of being authentic, was sent to the various peoples throughout the kingdom, with only a few words of address changed for each group.

9, 25: The letter copied below: not included in the text of 2 Mc.

10, 3: Two years: three years according to 1 Mc 1, 54 and 4, 52.

a: 1-8: 1 Mc 4, 36-59. b: 2 Mc 2, 21; 1 Mc 6, 17.

ceeded to the kingdom, he put a certain Lysias in charge of the government as commander in chief of Coelesyria and Phoenicia. [12]Ptolemy, surnamed Macron,* had taken the lead in treating the Jews fairly because of the previous injustice that had been done them, and he endeavored to have peaceful relations with them. [13]As a result, he was accused before Eupator by the King's Friends. In fact, on all sides he heard himself called a traitor for having abandoned Cyprus, which Philometor had entrusted to him, and for having gone over to Antiochus Epiphanes. Since he could not command the respect due to his high office, he ended his life by taking poison.

*Victory over the Idumeans.** [14]When Gorgias became governor of the region, he employed foreign troops and used every opportunity to attack the Jews. [15c]At the same time the Idumeans, who held some important strongholds, were harassing the Jews; they welcomed fugitives from Jerusalem and endeavored to continue the war. [16]Maccabeus and his companions, after public prayers asking God to be their ally, moved quickly against the strongholds of the Idumeans. [17]Attacking vigorously, they gained control of the places, drove back all who manned the walls, and cut down those who opposed them, killing as many as twenty thousand men. [18]When at least nine thousand took refuge in two very strong towers, containing everything necessary to sustain a siege, [19]Maccabeus left Simon and Joseph, along with Zacchaeus and his men, in sufficient numbers to besiege them, while he himself went off to places where he was more urgently needed. [20]But some of the men in Simon's force who were money lovers let themselves be bribed by some of the men in the towers; on receiving seventy thousand drachmas, they allowed a number of them to escape. [21]When Maccabeus was told what had happened, he assembled the rulers of the people and accused those men of having sold their kinsmen for money by setting their enemies free to fight against them. [22]So he put them to death as traitors, and without delay captured the two towers. [23]As he was successful at arms in all his undertakings, he destroyed more than twenty thousand men in the two strongholds.

Victory over Timothy. [24]Timothy, who had previously been defeated by the Jews,* gathered a tremendous force of foreign troops and collected a large number of cavalry from Asia; then he appeared in Judea, ready to conquer it by force. [25]At his approach, Maccabeus and his men made supplication to God, sprinkling earth upon their heads and girding their loins in sackcloth. [26]Lying prostrate at the foot of the altar, they begged him to be gracious to them, and to be an enemy to their enemies, and a foe to their foes, as the law declares.[d]

[27]After the prayer, they took up their arms and advanced a considerable distance from the city, halting when they were close to the enemy. [28]As soon as dawn broke,* the armies joined battle, the one having as pledge of success and victory not only their valor but also their reliance on the LORD, and the other taking fury as their leader in the fight.

[29e]In the midst of the fierce battle, there appeared to the enemy from the heavens five majestic men riding on golden-bridled horses, who led the Jews on. [30]They surrounded Maccabeus, and shielding him with their own armor, kept him from being wounded. They shot arrows and hurled thunderbolts at the enemy, who were bewildered and blinded, thrown into confusion and routed. [31]Twenty-five hundred of their foot soldiers and six hundred of their horsemen were slain. [32]Timothy, however, fled to a well-fortified stronghold called Gazara, where Chaereas was in command.[f] [33]For four days Maccabeus and his men eagerly besieged the fortress. [34]Those inside, relying

---

10, 12: Ptolemy, surnamed Macron: son of Dorymenes (2 Mc 4, 45), was formerly hostile to the Jews (2 Mc 6, 8).

10, 14-23: Probably the same campaign of Judas against the Idumeans that is mentioned in 1 Mc 5, 1-3.

10, 24: Timothy . . . previously . . . defeated by the Jews: as recounted in 2 Mc 8, 30ff.

10, 28: As soon as dawn broke: the same battle at dawn as in 1 Mc 5, 30-34.

---

c: 15-23: 1 Mc 5, 3ff. *d:* Ex 23, 22. *e:* 29f: 2 Mc 3, 24ff; 5, 2f: 10, 29f; 11, 8. *f:* 1 Mc 13, 43-48.

on the strength of the place, kept repeating outrageous blasphemies and uttering abominable words. [35]When the fifth day dawned, twenty young men in the army of Maccabeus, angered over such blasphemies, bravely stormed the wall and with savage fury cut down everyone they encountered. [36]Others who climbed up the same way swung around on the defenders, taking the besieged in the rear; they put the towers to the torch, spread the fire and burned the blasphemers alive. Still others broke down the gates and let in the rest of the troops, who took possession of the city. [37]Timothy had hidden in a cistern, but they killed* him, along with his brother Chaereas, and Apollophanes. [38]On completing these exploits, they blessed, with hymns of grateful praise, the LORD who shows great kindness to Israel and grants them victory.

CHAPTER 11

See RG 233

*Defeat of Lysias.** [1]Very soon afterward, Lysias, guardian and kinsman of the king and head of the government, being greatly displeased at what had happened, [2]mustered about eighty thousand infantry and all his cavalry and marched against the Jews. His plan was to make Jerusalem a Greek settlement; [3]to levy tribute on the temple, as he did on the sanctuaries of the other nations; and to put the high priesthood up for sale every year. [4]He did not take God's power into account at all, but felt exultant confidence in his myriads of foot soldiers, his thousands of horsemen, and his eighty elephants. [5]So he invaded Judea, and when he reached Beth-zur, a fortified place about twenty miles from Jerusalem, launched a strong attack against it. [6]When Maccabeus and his men learned that Lysias was besieging the strongholds, they and all the people begged the LORD with lamentations and tears to send a good angel to save Israel.[h] [7]Maccabeus himself was the first to take up arms, and he exhorted the others to join him in risk-

ing their lives to help their kinsmen. Then they resolutely set out together. [8]Suddenly, while they were still near Jerusalem, a horseman appeared at their head, clothed in white garments and brandishing gold weapons.[i] [9]Then all of them together thanked God for his mercy, and their hearts were filled with such courage that they were ready to assault not only men, but the most savage beasts, yes, even walls of iron. [10]Now that the LORD had shown his mercy toward them, they advanced in battle order with the aid of their heavenly ally. [11]Hurling themselves upon the enemy like lions, they laid low eleven thousand foot soldiers and sixteen hundred horsemen, and put all the rest to flight. [12]Most of those who got away were wounded and stripped of their arms, while Lysias himself escaped only by shameful flight.

Peace with the Syrians. [13][j]But Lysias was not a stupid man. He reflected on the defeat he had suffered, and came to realize that the Hebrews were invincible because the mighty God was their ally. He therefore sent a message [14]persuading them to settle everything on just terms, and promising to persuade the king also, and to induce him to become their friend. [15]Maccabeus, solicitous for the common good, agreed to all that Lysias proposed; and the king, on his part, granted in behalf of the Jews all the written requests of Maccabeus to Lysias.

Official Letters. [16]These are the terms of the letter which Lysias wrote to the Jews: "Lysias sends greetings to the Jewish people. [17]John and Absalom, your envoys, have presented your signed communication and asked about the matters contained in it. [18]Whatever had to be referred to the king I called to his attention, and the things that were acceptable he has granted. [19]If you maintain your loyalty to the government, I will endeavor to further your interests in the future. [20]On the details of these matters I have authorized my representatives, as well as your envoys, to confer with you.

10, 37: Timothy . . . they killed: apparently, the same Timothy is still alive in 2 Mc 12, 2. 18-25. The present passage is not in chronological order, Gazara, v 32 (Gezer) was not captured by the Jews until much later (cf 1 Mc 9, 50ff; 13, 53).

11, 1-12: The defeat of Lysias at Beth-zur probably occurred before the purification of the temple; cf 1 Mc 4, 26-35.

g: 1-12: 1 Mc 4, 26-35.   *h:* Ex 23, 20.   *i:* 2 Mc 3, 24ff; 5, 2f; 10, 29f.   *j:* 13-33: 1 Mc 6, 57-61.

²¹Farewell." The year one hundred and forty-eight,* the twenty-fourth of Dioscorinthius.

²²The king's letter read thus: "King Antiochus sends greetings to his brother Lysias. ²³Now that our father has taken his place among the gods, we wish the subjects of our kingdom to be undisturbed in conducting their own affairs. ²⁴We understand that the Jews do not agree with our father's policy concerning Greek customs but prefer their own way of life. They are petitioning us to let them retain their own customs. ²⁵Since we desire that this people too should be undisturbed, our decision is that their temple be restored to them and that they live in keeping with the customs of their ancestors. ²⁶Accordingly, please send them messengers to give them our assurances of friendship, so that, when they learn of our decision, they may have nothing to worry about but may contentedly go about their own business."

²⁷The king's letter to the people was as follows: "King Antiochus sends greetings to the Jewish senate and to the rest of the Jews. ²⁸If you are well, it is what we desire. We too are in good health. ²⁹Menelaus has told us of your wish to return home and attend to your own affairs. ³⁰Therefore, those who return by the thirtieth of Xanthicus will have our assurance of full permission ³¹to observe their dietary laws and other laws, just as before, and none of the Jews shall be molested in any way for faults committed through ignorance. ³²I have also sent Menelaus to reassure you. ³³Farewell." In the year one hundred and forty-eight, the fifteenth of Xanthicus.*

³⁴The Romans also sent them a letter as follows: "Quintus Memmius and Titus Manius, legates of the Romans, send greetings to the Jewish people. ³⁵Whatever Lysias, kinsman of the king, has granted you, we also approve. ³⁶But the matters on which he passed judgment should be submitted to the king. As soon as you have considered them,

send someone to us with your decisions so that we may present them to your advantage, for we are on our way to Antioch. ³⁷Make haste, then, to send us those who can inform us of your intentions. ³⁸Farewell." In the year one hundred and forty-eight, the fifteenth of Xanthicus.*

CHAPTER 12

See RG 233-34

Persecution Renewed. ¹After these agreements were made, Lysias returned to the king, and the Jews went about their farming. ²But some of the local governors, Timothy and Apollonius, son of Gennaeus,* as also Hieronymus and Demophon, to say nothing of Nicanor, the commander of the Cyprians, would not allow them to live in peace.

³Some people of Joppa also committed this outrage: they invited the Jews who lived among them, together with their wives and children, to embark on boats which they had provided. There was no hint of enmity toward them: ⁴this was done by public vote of the city. When the Jews, not suspecting treachery and wishing to live on friendly terms, accepted the invitation, the people of Joppa took them out to sea and drowned at least two hundred of them.

Activity of Judas. ⁵As soon as Judas heard of the barbarous deed perpetrated against his countrymen, he summoned his men; ⁶and after calling upon God, the just judge, he marched against the murderers of his kinsmen. In a night attack he set the harbor on fire, burnt the boats, and put to the sword those who had taken refuge there. ⁷When the gates of the town were shut, he withdrew, intending to come back later and wipe out the entire population of Joppa.

⁸On hearing that the men of Jamnia planned to give like treatment to the Jews who lived among them, ⁹he attacked the Jamnian populace by night, setting fire to the harbor and the fleet, so that the glow of

---

11, 21: The year one hundred and forty-eight: 164 B.C. The reading of the name of the month and its position in the calendar are uncertain.

11, 33: The date, which is the same as the date of the Romans' letter (v 38) cannot be correct. The king's letter must be connected with the peace treaty of the year 149 of the Seleucid era, i.e., 163 B.C. Perhaps the mention of the month of

Xanthicus in the body of the letter (v 30) caused the date of the Romans' letter to be transferred to this one.

11, 38: The date is April 12, 164 B.C.

12, 2: Apollonius, son of Gennaeus: not the Apollonius who was the son of Menestheus (2 Mc 4, 21). Nicanor: probably distinct from the Nicanor of 2 Mc 14, 2.

the flames was visible as far as Jerusalem, thirty miles away.

[10k]When the Jews had gone about a mile from there* in the campaign against Timothy, they were attacked by Arabs numbering at least five thousand foot soldiers, and five hundred horsemen. [11]After a hard fight, Judas and his companions, with God's help, were victorious. The defeated nomads begged Judas to make friends with them and promised to supply the Jews with cattle and to help them in every other way. [12]Realizing that they could indeed be useful in many respects, Judas agreed to make peace with them. After the pledge of friendship had been exchanged, the Arabs withdrew to their tents.

[13]He also attacked a certain city called Caspin, fortified with earthworks and ramparts and inhabited by a mixed population of Gentiles. [14]Relying on the strength of their walls and their supply of provisions, the besieged treated Judas and his men with contempt, insulting them and even uttering blasphemies and profanity. [15]But Judas and his men invoked the aid of the great Sovereign of the world, who, in the day of Joshua, overthrew Jericho without battering-ram or siege machine; then they furiously stormed the ramparts.[l] [16]Capturing the city by the will of God, they inflicted such indescribable slaughter on it that the adjacent pool, which was about a quarter of a mile wide, seemed to be filled with the blood that flowed into it.

[17m]When they had gone on some ninety miles, they reached Charax,[n] where there were certain Jews known as Toubiani.* [18]But they did not find Timothy in that region, for he had already departed from there without having done anything except to leave behind in one place a very strong garrison. [19]But Dositheus and Sosipater, two of Maccabeus' captains, marched out and destroyed the force of more than ten thousand men that Timothy had left in the stronghold. [20]Meanwhile, Maccabeus divided his army into cohorts, with a commander over each cohort, and went in pursuit of Timothy, who had a force of a hundred and twenty thousand foot soldiers and twenty-five hundred horsemen. [21]When Timothy learned of the approach of Judas, he sent on ahead of him the women and children, as well as the baggage, to a place called Karnion, which was hard to besiege and even hard to reach because of the difficult terrain of that region. [22]But when Judas' first cohort appeared, the enemy was overwhelmed with fear and terror at the manifestation of the All-seeing. Scattering in every direction, they rushed away in such headlong flight that in many cases they wounded one another, pierced by the swords of their own men. [23]Judas pressed the pursuit vigorously, putting the sinners to the sword and destroying as many as thirty thousand men.

[24]Timothy himself fell into the hands of the men under Dositheus and Sosipater; but with great cunning, he asked them to spare his life and let him go, because he had in his power the parents and relatives of many of them, and could make these suffer. [25]When he had fully confirmed his solemn pledge to restore them unharmed, they let him go for the sake of saving their brethren.

Further Successes. [26]Judas then marched to Karnion and the shrine of Atargatis,* where he killed twenty-five thousand people. [27o]After the defeat and destruction of these, he moved his army to Ephron, a fortified city inhabited by people of many nationalities. Robust young men took up their posts in defense of the walls, from which they fought valiantly; inside were large supplies of machines and missiles. [28]But the Jews, invoking the Sovereign who forcibly shatters the might of his enemies, got possession of the city and slaughtered twenty-five thousand of the people in it. [29]Then they set out from there and hastened on to Scythopolis,* seventy-five miles from Jerusa-

12, 10: From there: not from the aforesaid Jamnia (vv 8f) or Joppa (vv 3-7), but from a place in Transjordan; vv 10-26 parallel the account given in 1 Mc 5, 9-13. 24-54 of Judas' campaign in northern Transjordan.

12, 17: Certain Jews known as Toubiani: because they lived "in the land of Tob" (1 Mc 5, 13).

12, 26: Atargatis: a Syrian goddess, represented by the body of a fish.

12, 29: Scythopolis: the Greek name of the city of Beth-shan; cf 1 Mc 5, 52.

k: 10-16: 1 Mc 5, 24-36.   *l:* Jos 6, 1-21.   *m:* 17-26: 1 Mc 5, 37-44.   *n:* 1 Mc 5, 13.   *o:* 27-31: 2 Mc 5, 45-54.

lem. [30]But when the Jews who lived there testified to the good will shown by the Scythopolitans and to their kind treatment even in times of adversity, [31]Judas and his men thanked them and exhorted them to be well disposed to their race in the future also. Finally they arrived in Jerusalem, shortly before the feast of Weeks.

[32]After this feast called Pentecost, they lost no time in marching against Gorgias, governor of Idumea, [33]who opposed them with three thousand foot soldiers and four hundred horsemen. [34]In the ensuing battle, a few of the Jews were slain. [35]A man called Dositheus, a powerful horseman and one of Bacenor's men,* caught hold of Gorgias, grasped his military cloak and dragged him along by main strength, intending to capture the vile wretch alive, when a Thracian horseman attacked Dositheus and cut off his arm at the shoulder. Then Gorgias fled to Marisa. [36]After Esdris and his men had been fighting for a long time and were weary, Judas called upon the LORD to show himself their ally and leader in the battle. [37]Then, raising a battle cry in his ancestral language, and with songs, he charged Gorgias' men when they were not expecting it and put them to flight.

Expiation for the Dead. [38]Judas rallied his army and went to the city of Adullam. As the week was ending, they purified themselves according to custom and kept the sabbath there. [39]On the following day, since the task had now become urgent, Judas and his men went to gather up the bodies of the slain and bury them with their kinsmen in their ancestral tombs. [40]But under the tunic of each of the dead they found amulets sacred to the idols of Jamnia, which the law forbids the Jews to wear. So it was clear to all that this was why these men had been slain.p [41]They all therefore praised the ways of the LORD, the just judge who brings to light the things that are hidden. [42]*Turning to supplication, they prayed that the sinful deed might be fully blotted out. The noble Judas warned the soldiers to keep themselves free from sin, for they had seen with their own eyes what had happened because of the sin of those who had fallen. [43]He then took up a collection among all his soldiers, amounting to two thousand silver drachmas, which he sent to Jerusalem to provide for an expiatory sacrifice. In doing this he acted in a very excellent and noble way, inasmuch as he had the resurrection of the dead in view; [44]for if he were not expecting the fallen to rise again, it would have been useless and foolish to pray for them in death. [45]But if he did this with a view to the splendid reward that awaits those who had gone to rest in godliness, it was a holy and pious thought. [46]Thus he made atonement for the dead that they might be freed from this sin.

CHAPTER 13

The Syrians Invade Judea. [1]In the year one hundred and forty-nine,* Judas and his men learned that Antiochus Eupator was invading Judea with a large force, [2]and that with him was Lysias, his guardian, who was in charge of the government. They led* a Greek army of one hundred and ten thousand foot soldiers, fifty-three hundred horsemen, twenty-two elephants, and three hundred chariots armed with scythes.q

Death of Menelaus. [3]Menelaus also joined them, and with great duplicity kept urging Antiochus on, not for the welfare of his country, but in the hope of being established in office. [4]But the King of kings aroused the anger of Antiochus against the scoundrel. When the king was shown by Lysias that Menelaus was to blame for all the trouble, he ordered him to be taken to Beroea* and exe-

See RG 233-34

12, 35: One of Bacenor's men: certain ancient witnesses to the text have "one of the Toubiani"; cf v 17.

12, 42-46: This is the earliest statement of the doctrine that prayers (v 42) and sacrifices (v 43) for the dead are beneficial. The statement is made here, however, only for the purpose of proving that Judas believed in the resurrection of the just (2 Mc 7, 9. 14. 23. 36). That is, he believed that expiation could be made for certain sins of otherwise good men—soldiers who had given their lives for God's cause. Thus, they could share in the resurrection. His belief was similar to, but not quite the same as, the Catholic doctrine of purgatory.

13, 1: In the year one hundred and forty-nine: 163–162 B.C.

13, 2: They led: the Greek means literally "Each (of them) led," but it is unlikely that the author meant the already immense numbers to be doubled; the numbers are similar to those in 1 Mc 6, 30.

13, 4: Beroea: the Greek name of Aleppo.

p: Dt 7, 25.   q: 1 Mc 6, 30.

cuted there in the customary local method.[r] [5]There is at that place a tower seventy-five feet high, full of ashes,* with a circular rim sloping down steeply on all sides toward the ashes. [6]A man guilty of sacrilege or notorious for certain other crimes is brought up there and then hurled down to destruction. [7]In such a manner was Menelaus, the transgressor of the law, fated to die; he was deprived even of decent burial. [8]It was altogether just that he who had committed so many sins against the altar with its pure fire and ashes should meet his death in ashes.

Skirmish near Modein. [9]The king was advancing, his mind full of savage plans for inflicting on the Jews worse things than those they suffered in his father's time. [10]When Judas learned of this, he urged the people to call upon the LORD night and day, to help them now, if ever, [11]when they were about to be deprived of their law, their country, and their holy temple; and not to allow this nation, which had just begun to revive, to be subjected again to blasphemous Gentiles. [12]When they had all joined in doing this, and had implored the merciful LORD continuously with weeping and fasting and prostrations for three days, Judas encouraged them and told them to stand ready. [13]After a private meeting with the elders, he decided that, before the king's army could invade Judea and take possession of the city, the Jews should march out and settle the matter with God's help. [14]Leaving the outcome to the Creator of the world, and exhorting his followers to fight nobly to death for the laws, the temple, the city, the country, and the government, he pitched his camp near Modein. [15]Giving his men the battle cry "God's Victory," he made a night attack on the king's pavilion with a picked force of the bravest young men and killed about two thousand in the camp. They also slew* the lead elephant

and its rider.[s] [16]Finally they withdrew in triumph,* having filled the camp with terror and confusion. [17]Day was just breaking when this was accomplished with the help and protection of the LORD.

Treaty with Antiochus V. [18t]The king, having had a taste of the Jews' daring, tried to take their positions by a stratagem. [19]So he marched against Beth-zur, a strong fortress of the Jews; but he was driven back, checked, and defeated. [20]Judas then sent supplies to the men inside, [21]but Rhodocus, of the Jewish army, betrayed military secrets* to the enemy. He was found out, arrested, and imprisoned. [22]The king made a second attempt by negotiating with the men of Beth-zur. After giving them his pledge and receiving theirs, he withdrew [23]and attacked Judas and his men. But he was defeated. Next he heard that Philip, who was left in charge of the government in Antioch, had rebelled. Dismayed, he parleyed with the Jews, submitted to their terms, and swore to observe their rights. Having come to this agreement, he offered a sacrifice, and honored the temple with a generous donation. [24]He approved of Maccabeus and left him as military and civil governor of the territory from Ptolemais to the region of the Gerrenes.* [25]When he came to Ptolemais, the people of that city were angered by the peace treaty; in fact they were so indignant that they wanted to annul its provisions. [26]But Lysias took the platform, defended the treaty as well as he could, and won them over by persuasion. After calming them and gaining their good will, he returned to Antioch.

That is how the king's attack and withdrawal went.

CHAPTER 14

See RG 233-34

Antagonism of Alcimus. [1u]Three years later,* Judas and his men learned that Demetrius, son of Seleucus, had sailed into

---

13, 5: Ashes: probably smoldering ashes; the tower resembles the ancient Persian fire towers.

13, 15: Slew: literally "stabbed"; the deed was done by Eleazar (1 Mc 6, 43-46).

13, 16: They withdrew in triumph: according to 1 Mc 6, 47 they fled.

13, 21: Military secrets: probably about the lack of provisions in the besieged city; cf 1 Mc 6, 49.

13, 24: The Greek text is uncertain and may be rendered:

"He approved of Maccabeus, then left Hegemonides as governor of the territory . . ." Gerrenes: probably the inhabitants of Gerar, southeast of Gaza.

14, 1: Three years later: actually, Demetrius (I Soter), son of Seleucus (IV), landed at Tripolis in the year 151 of the Seleucid era (v 4), i.e., 162–161 B.C.; cf 1 Mc 7, 1-7.

r: 1 Tm 6, 15; Rv 17, 14; 19, 16. s: 1 Mc 6, 43-46. t: 18-23: 1 Mc 6, 48-53. u: 1-11: 1 Mc 7, 1-7.

the port of Tripolis with a powerful army and a fleet, [2]and that he had occupied the country, after doing away with Antiochus and his guardian Lysias.

[3]A certain Alcimus, a former high priest, who had willfully incurred defilement at the time of the revolt, realized that there was no way for him to salvage his position and regain access to the holy altar. [4]So he went to King Demetrius in the year one hundred and fifty-one and presented him with a gold crown and a palm branch, as well as some of the customary olive branches from the temple. On that occasion he kept quiet.[v] [5]But he found an opportunity to further his mad scheme when he was invited to the council by Demetrius and questioned about the dispositions and intentions of the Jews. He replied: [6]"Those Jews called Hasideans, led by Judas Maccabeus, are warmongers, who stir up sedition and keep the kingdom from enjoying peace and quiet. [7]For this reason, now that I am deprived of my ancestral dignity, that is to say, the high priesthood, I have come here— [8]first, out of my genuine concern for the king's interests, and secondly, out of consideration for my own countrymen, since our entire nation is suffering great affliction from the unreasonable conduct of the people just mentioned. [9]When you have informed yourself in detail on these matters, O king, act in the interest of our country and its hard-pressed people with the same gracious consideration that you show toward all. [10]As long as Judas is around, it is impossible for the state to enjoy peace." [11]When he had said this, the other Friends who were hostile to Judas quickly added fuel to Demetrius' indignation.

Dealings with Nicanor. [12w]The king immediately chose Nicanor, who had been in command of the elephants, and appointed him governor of Judea. He sent him off [13]with orders to put Judas to death, to disperse his followers, and to set up Alcimus as high priest of the great temple. [14]The Gentiles from Judea, who would have banished Judas,* came flocking to Nicanor, thinking that the misfortunes and calamities of the Jews would mean prosperity for themselves. [15x]When the Jews heard of Nicanor's coming, and that the Gentiles were rallying to him, they sprinkled themselves with earth and prayed to him who established his people forever, and who always comes to the aid of his heritage. [16]At their leader's command, they set out at once and came upon the enemy at the village of Adasa. [17]Judas' brother Simon had engaged Nicanor, but because of the sudden appearance of the enemy suffered a slight repulse. [18]However, when Nicanor heard of the valor of Judas and his men, and the great courage with which they fought for their country, he shrank from deciding the issue by bloodshed. [19]So he sent Posidonius, Theodotus and Mattathias to arrange an agreement. [20]After a long discussion of the terms, each leader communicated them to his troops; and when general agreement was expressed, they assented to the treaty. [21]A day was set on which the leaders would meet by themselves. From each side a chariot came forward and thrones were set in place. [22]Judas had posted armed men in readiness at suitable points for fear that the enemy might suddenly carry out some treacherous plan. But the conference was held in the proper way. [23]Nicanor stayed on in Jerusalem, where he did nothing out of place. He got rid of the throngs of ordinary people who gathered around him; [24]but he always kept Judas in his company, for he had a cordial affection for the man. [25]He urged him to marry and have children; so Judas married, settled down, and shared the common life.

Threats against Judas. [26]When Alcimus saw their friendship for each other, he took the treaty that had been made, went to Demetrius, and said that Nicanor was plotting against the state, and that he had appointed Judas, the conspirator against the kingdom, to be his successor. [27]Stirred up by the villain's calumnies, the king became enraged. He wrote to Nicanor, stating that he was displeased with the treaty, and ordering him to send Maccabeus as a prisoner to An-

14, 14: Who would have banished Judas: the meaning of the Greek is uncertain; some render it: "who had fled before Judas."

v: 1 Mc 7, 7. 25.   w: 12f: 2 Mc 8, 9; 1 Mc 3, 38f.   x: 15-19: 1 Mc 7, 26-32.

tioch without delay. ²⁸When this message reached Nicanor he was dismayed, for he hated to break his agreement with a man who had done no wrong. ²⁹However, there was no way of opposing the king, so he watched for an opportunity to carry out this order by a stratagem. ³⁰But Maccabeus noticed that Nicanor was becoming cool in his dealings with him, and acting with unaccustomed rudeness when they met; he concluded that this coldness betokened no good. So he gathered together a large number of his men, and went into hiding from Nicanor.

^{31y}When Nicanor realized that he had been disgracefully outwitted by the man, he went to the great and holy temple, at a time when the priests were offering the customary sacrifices, and ordered them to surrender Judas. ³²As they declared under oath that they did not know where the wanted man was, ³³he raised his right hand toward the temple and swore this oath: "If you do not hand Judas over to me as prisoner, I will level this shrine of God to the ground; I will tear down the altar, and erect here a splendid temple to Dionysus." ³⁴With these words he went away. The priests stretched out their hands toward heaven, calling upon the unfailing defender of our nation in these words: ³⁵"LORD of all, though you are in need of nothing, you have approved of a temple for your dwelling place among us.^z ³⁶Therefore, O holy One, LORD of all holiness, preserve forever undefiled this house, which has been so recently purified."

The Story of Razis. * ³⁷A certain Razis, one of the elders of Jerusalem, was denounced to Nicanor as a patriot. A man highly regarded, he was called a father of the Jews because of his love for them. ³⁸In the early days of the revolt, he had been convicted of Judaism, and had risked body and life in his ardent zeal for it. ³⁹Nicanor, to show his detestation of the Jews, sent more than five hundred soldiers to arrest him. ⁴⁰He thought that by arresting such a man he would deal the Jews a hard blow. ⁴¹But when

these troops, on the point of capturing the tower, were forcing the outer gate and calling for fire to set the door ablaze, Razis, now caught on all sides, turned his sword against himself, ⁴²preferring to die nobly rather than fall into the hands of vile men and suffer outrages unworthy of his noble birth. ⁴³In the excitement of the struggle he failed to strike exactly. So while the troops rushed in through the doors, he gallantly ran up to the top of the wall and with manly courage threw himself down into the crowd. ⁴⁴But as they quickly drew back and left an opening, he fell into the middle of the empty space. ⁴⁵Still breathing, and inflamed with anger, he got up and ran through the crowd, with blood gushing from his frightful wounds. ⁴⁶Then, standing on a steep rock, as he lost the last of his blood, he tore out his entrails and flung them with both hands into the crowd, calling upon the LORD of life and of spirit to give these back to him again. Such was the manner of his death.^a

CHAPTER 15

See RG 233-34

Nicanor's Blasphemy. ¹When Nicanor learned that Judas and his companions were in the territory of Samaria, he decided to attack them in all safety on the day of rest. ²The Jews who were forced to follow him pleaded, "Do not massacre them in that way, like a savage barbarian, but show respect for the day which the All-seeing has exalted with holiness above all other days." ³At this the thrice-sinful wretch asked if there was a ruler in heaven who prescribed the keeping of the sabbath day.^b ⁴When they replied that there was indeed such a ruler in heaven, the living LORD himself, who commanded the observance of the sabbath day, ⁵he said, "I, on my part, am ruler on earth, and my orders are that you take up arms and carry out the king's business." Nevertheless he did not succeed in carrying out his cruel plan.

Fresh Hope. ⁶In his utter boastfulness and arrogance Nicanor had determined to erect a public monument of victory* over Ju-

---

14, 37-46: The story of Razis belongs to the "martyrology" class of literature; it is similar to the stories in 2 Mc 6, 18—7, 42.
15, 6: Public monument of victory: a heap of stones covered with the arms and armor of the fallen enemy.

y: 31-36: 1 Mc 7, 33-38. z: Acts 17, 25. a: 2 Mc 7, 9ff. b: 1 Mc 7, 34.

das and his men. [7]But Maccabeus remained confident, fully convinced that he would receive help from the LORD. [8]He urged his men not to fear the enemy, but mindful of the help they had received from Heaven in the past, to expect that now, too, victory would be given them by the Almighty. [9]By encouraging them with words from the law and the prophets,* and by reminding them of the battles they had already won, he filled them with fresh enthusiasm. [10]Having stirred up their courage, he gave his orders and pointed out at the same time the perfidy of the Gentiles and their violation of oaths. [11]When he had armed each of them, not so much with the safety of shield and spear as with the encouragement of noble words, he cheered them all by relating a dream, a kind of vision, worthy of belief.

[12]What he saw was this: Onias, the former high priest,* a good and virtuous man, modest in appearance, gentle in manners, distinguished in speech, and trained from childhood in every virtuous practice, was praying with outstretched arms for the whole Jewish community.[c] [13]Then in the same way another man appeared, distinguished by his white hair and dignity, and with an air about him of extraordinary, majestic authority. [14]Onias then said of him, "This is God's prophet Jeremiah,* who loves his brethren and fervently prays for his people and their holy city." [15]Stretching out his right hand, Jeremiah presented a gold sword to Judas. As he gave it to him he said, [16]"Accept this holy sword as a gift from God; with it you shall crush your adversaries."

Defeat and Death of Nicanor. [17]Encouraged by Judas' noble words, which had power to instill valor and stir young hearts to courage, the Jews determined not to delay, but to charge gallantly and decide the issue by hand-to-hand combat with the utmost courage, since their city and its temple with the sacred vessels were in danger. [18]They were not so much concerned about their wives and children or their brothers and kinsmen; their first and foremost fear was for the consecrated sanctuary.[d] [19]Those who remained in the city suffered a like agony, anxious as they were about the battle in the open country.

[20]Everyone now awaited the decisive moment. The enemy were already drawing near with their troops drawn up in battle line, their elephants placed in strategic positions, and their cavalry stationed on the flanks. [21]Maccabeus, contemplating the hosts before him, their elaborate equipment, and the fierceness of their elephants, stretched out his hands toward heaven and called upon the LORD who works miracles; for he knew that it is not through arms but through the LORD's decision that victory is won by those who deserve it. [22][e]He prayed to him thus: "You, O LORD, sent your angel in the days of King Hezekiah of Judea, and he slew a hundred and eighty-five thousand men of Sennacherib's army. [23]Sovereign of the heavens, send a good angel now to spread fear and dread before us. [24]By the might of your arm may those be struck down who have blasphemously come against your holy people!" With this he ended his prayer.

[25][f]Nicanor and his men advanced to the sound of trumpets and battle songs. [26]But Judas and his men met the army with supplication and prayers. [27]Fighting with their hands and praying to God with their hearts, they laid low at least thirty-five thousand, and rejoiced greatly over this manifestation of God's power. [28]When the battle was over and they were joyfully departing, they discovered Nicanor lying there in all his armor; [29]so they raised tumultuous shouts in their native tongue in praise of the divine Sovereign.

[30]Then Judas, who was ever in body and soul the chief defender of his fellow citizens, and had maintained from youth his affection for his countrymen, ordered Nicanor's head

---

15, 9: The law and the prophets: the first of the three parts of the Hebrew Scriptures, called the sacred books (1 Mc 12, 9).

15, 12: Onias, the former high priest: Onias III (2 Mc 3, 1-40). Evidently the author believed that the departed just were in some way alive even before the resurrection.

15, 14: Jeremiah: regarded by the postexilic Jews as one of the greatest figures in their history; cf 2 Mc 2, 1; Mt 16, 14. Who . . . prays for his people: a clear belief in the intercession of the saints.

c: 2 Mc 3, 1ff. *d:* 1 Mc 4, 36. *e:* 22f: 2 Mc 8, 19; 2 Kgs 19, 35; Is 37, 36; 1 Mc 7, 40f. *f:* 25-36: 2 Mc 8, 39-50.

and whole right arm to be cut off and taken to Jerusalem. *31*When he arrived there, he assembled his countrymen, stationed the priests before the altar, and sent for those in the citadel.* *32*He showed them the vile Nicanor's head and the wretched blasphemer's arm that had been boastfully stretched out against the holy dwelling of the Almighty. *33*He cut out the tongue of the godless Nicanor, saying he would feed it piecemeal to the birds and would hang up the other wages of his folly opposite the temple. *34*At this, everyone looked toward heaven and praised the LORD who manifests his divine power, saying, "Blessed be he who has kept his own Place undefiled!"

*35*Judas hung up Nicanor's head on the wall of the citadel, a clear and evident proof to all of the Lord's help.*g* *36*By public vote it was unanimously decreed never to let this day pass unobserved,*h* but to celebrate it on the thirteenth day of the twelfth month, called Adar in Aramaic, the eve of Mordecai's Day.*

VII: Epilogue

Author's Apology. *37*Since Nicanor's doings ended in this way, with the city remaining in possession of the Hebrews from that time on, I will bring my own story to an end here too. *38*If it is well written and to the point, that is what I wanted; if it is poorly done and mediocre, that is the best I could do. *39*Just as it is harmful to drink wine alone or water alone, whereas mixing wine with water makes a more pleasant drink that increases delight, so a skillfully composed story delights the ears of those who read the work. Let this, then, be the end.

15, 31: Those in the citadel: presumably Jewish soldiers; actually, the citadel was still in the possession of the Syrians.
15, 36: Mordecai's Day: the feast of Purim, celebrated on the fourteenth and fifteenth days of Adar (Est 9, 17-22).

---

g: 1 Sm 31, 9f.   *h*: 1 Mc 7, 49.

THE WISDOM BOOKS

The Books of Job, Psalms, Proverbs, Ecclesiastes, the Song of Songs, Wisdom, and Sirach, are all versified by the skillful use of parallelism, that is, of the balanced and symmetrical phrases peculiar to Hebrew poetry. With the exception of the Psalms, the majority of which are devotional lyrics, and the Song of Songs, a nuptial hymn, these books belong to the general class of wisdom or didactic literature, strictly so called because their chief purpose is instruction.

The wisdom literature of the Bible is the fruit of a movement among ancient oriental people to gather, preserve and express, usually in aphoristic style, the results of human experience as an aid toward understanding and solving the problems of life. In Israel especially, the movement concerned itself with such basic and vital problems as man's origin and destiny, his quest for happiness, the problem of suffering, of good and evil in human conduct, of death, and the state beyond the grave. Originating with oral tradition, these formulations found their way into the historical books of the Old Testament in the shape of proverbs, odes, chants, epigrams, and also into those psalms intended for instruction.

The developed compositions of this literature form the sapiential books. The Book of Proverbs is a collection of sentences or practical norms for moral conduct. The Book of Job is an artistic dialogue skillfully handling the problem of suffering though only from the standpoint of temporal life. Ecclesiastes examines a wide range of human experience only to conclude that all things are vanity except the fear of the Lord and observance of his commandments, and that God requites man in his own good time. Sirach gathers

and presents the fruits of past experience, thus preparing for the Book of Wisdom, which sees for the just man seeking happiness the full hope of immortality (Wis 3, 4).

Those who cultivated wisdom were called sages. Men of letters, scribes, skilled in the affairs of government, and counselors to rulers, they were instructors of the people, especially of youth (Sir 51, 13-30). In times of crisis they guided the people by revaluating tradition, thus helping to preserve unity, peace and good will. The most illustrious of the sages, and the originator of wisdom literature in Israel, was Solomon. Because of his fame, some of the wisdom books of which he was not the author bear his name.

Despite numerous resemblances, sometimes exaggerated, between the sapiential literature of pagan nations and the wisdom books of the Bible, the former are often replete with vagaries and abound in polytheistic conceptions; the latter remained profoundly human, universal, fundamentally moral, and essentially religious and monotheistic. Under the influence of the law and the prophets, wisdom became piety and virtue; impiety and vice were folly. The teachers of wisdom were regarded as men of God, and their books were placed beside the law and the prophets. The highest wisdom became identified with the spirit of God through which the world was created and preserved (Prv 8, 22-31), and mankind was enlightened.

The limitations of Old Testament wisdom served to crystalize the problems of human life and destiny, thus preparing for their solution through New Testament revelation. Ecclesiastes' vain search for success and happiness on earth

645

ends when the Savior assures these things to his followers, not in this world but in the bliss of heaven. The anxiety in the Book of Job over reconciling God's justice and wisdom with the suffering of the innocent is relieved by the account of the crucified and risen Redeemer in the gospel. By fulfilling all that the Psalms foretold concerning him, Jesus makes the Psalter his prayer book and that of the Church for all time. The love of God for the chosen people which underlies the Song of Songs is perfected in the union of Christ with his Church. The personification of the wisdom of Proverbs, Wisdom and Sirach shines forth in resplendent reality in the Word who was with God, and who was God, and who became incarnate to dwell among us; cf Jn 1, 2. 14.

See RG 236–43

The Book of Job

The Book of Job, named after its protagonist, is an exquisite dramatic poem which treats the problem of the suffering of the innocent, and of retribution. The contents of the book, together with its artistic structure and elegant style, place it among the literary masterpieces of all time.

Job, an oriental chieftain, pious and upright, richly endowed in his own person and in domestic prosperity, suffers a sudden and complete reversal of fortune. He loses his property and his children; a loathsome disease afflicts his body; and sorrow oppresses his soul. Nevertheless, Job does not complain against God. When some friends visit him to condole with him, Job protests his innocence and does not understand why he is afflicted. He curses the day of his birth and longs for death to bring an end to his sufferings. The debate which ensues consists of three cycles of speeches. Job's friends insist that his plight can only be a punishment for personal wrongdoing and an invitation from God to repentance. Job rejects their inadequate explanation and calls for a response from God himself. At this point the speeches of a youth named Elihu (chs 32—37) interrupt the development.

In response to Job's plea that he be allowed to see God and hear from him the cause of his suffering, God answers, not by justifying his action before men, but by referring to his own omniscience and almighty power. Job is content with this. He recovers his attitude of humility and trust in God, which is deepened now and strengthened by his experience of suffering.

The author of the book is not known; it was composed some time between the 7th and 5th centuries B.C. Its literary form, with speeches, prologue and epilogue disposed according to a studied plan, indicates that the purpose of the writing is didactic. The lesson is that even the just may suffer here, and their sufferings are a test of their fidelity. They shall be rewarded in the end. Man's finite mind cannot probe the depths of the divine omniscience that governs the world. The problems we encounter can be solved by a broader and deeper awareness of God's power, presence (42, 5) and wisdom.

The divisions of the Book of Job are as follows:

I: Prologue (1, 1—2, 13).
II: First Cycle of Speeches (3, 1—14, 22).
III: Second Cycle of Speeches (15, 1—21, 34).
IV: Third Cycle of Speeches (22, 1—28, 28).
V: Job's Final Summary of His Cause (29, 1—31, 37).
VI: Elihu's Speeches (32, 1—37, 24).
VII: The Lord's Speech (38, 1—42, 6).
VIII: Epilogue (42, 7-17).

I: Prologue

CHAPTER 1

See RG 236–43

Job's Wealth and Piety. *¹*In the land of Uz* there was a blameless and upright man named Job,*ᵃ* who feared God and avoided evil. ²*Seven sons and three daughters were born to him; ³and he had seven thousand sheep, three thousand camels, five hundred yoke of oxen, five hundred she-asses, and a great number of work animals,

---

1, 1: Uz: somewhere in Edom or Arabia. Job: a not uncommon name in ancient Semitic circles; its original meaning was "enemy."

1, 2f: The numbers mentioned here indicate Job's great wealth and happiness, external proof of God's friendship.

a: Jb 2, 3.

so that he was greater than any of the men of the East.* ⁴His sons used to take turns giving feasts, sending invitations to their three sisters to eat and drink with them. ⁵And when each feast had run its course, Job would send for them and sanctify them, rising early and offering holocausts for every one of them. For Job said, "It may be that my sons have sinned and blasphemed God in their hearts." This Job did habitually.

⁶ᵇOne day, when the sons of God* came to present themselves before the LORD, Satan also came among them.ᶜ ⁷And the LORD said to Satan, "Whence do you come?" Then Satan answered the LORD and said,ᵈ "From roaming the earth and patrolling it." ⁸And the LORD said to Satan, "Have you noticed my servant Job, and that there is no one on earth like him, blameless and upright, fearing God and avoiding evil?" ⁹But Satan answered the LORD and said, "Is it for nothing that Job is God-fearing? ¹⁰Have you not surrounded him and his family and all that he has with your protection? You have blessed the work of his hands, and his livestock are spread over the land. ¹¹ᵉBut now put forth your hand and touch anything that he has, and surely he will blaspheme you to your face." ¹²And the LORD said to Satan, "Behold, all that he has is in your power; only do not lay a hand upon his person." So Satan went forth from the presence of the LORD.

The First Trial. ¹³And so one day, while his sons and his daughters were eating and drinking wine in the house of their eldest brother, ¹⁴a messenger came to Job and said, "The oxen were plowing and the asses grazing beside them, ¹⁵and the Sabeans* carried them off in a raid. They put the herdsmen to the sword, and I alone have escaped to tell you." ¹⁶While he was yet speaking, another came and said, "Lightning* has fallen from heaven and struck the sheep and their shepherds and consumed them; and I alone have

escaped to tell you." ¹⁷While he was yet speaking, another came and said, "The Chaldeans formed three columns, seized the camels, carried them off, and put those tending them to the sword, and I alone have escaped to tell you." ¹⁸While he was yet speaking, another came and said, "Your sons and daughters were eating and drinking wine in the house of their eldest brother, ¹⁹when suddenly a great wind came across the desert and smote the four corners of the house. It fell upon the young people and they are dead; and I alone have escaped to tell you." ²⁰Then Job began to tear his cloak and cut off his hair. He cast himself prostrate upon the ground, ²¹and said,

"Naked I came forth from my mother's
    womb,ᶠ
and naked shall I go back again.*
The LORD gave and the LORD has taken
    away;
blessed be the name of the LORD!"

²²In all this Job did not sin,ᵍ nor did he say anything disrespectful of God.

CHAPTER 2

See RG 236–43

The Second Trial. ¹Once again the sons of Godʰ came to present themselves before the LORD, and Satan also came with them. ²And the LORD said to Satan, "Whence do you come?" And Satan answered the LORD and said, "From roaming the earth and patrolling it." ³And the LORD said to Satan, "Have you noticed my servant Job, and that there is no one on earth like him, faultless and upright, fearing God and avoiding evil?ⁱ He still holds fast to his innocence although you incited me against him to ruin him without cause." ⁴And Satan answered the LORD and said, "Skin for skin!* All that a man has will he give for his life. ⁵ʲBut now put forth your hand and touch his bone and his flesh, and surely he will blaspheme you to your

---

1, 3: Men of the East: that is, east of Palestine.
1, 6: Sons of God: angels. Satan: literally, "adversary."
1, 15: Sabeans: from southern Arabia.
1, 16: Lightning: literally, "God's fire."
1, 21: Go back again: to the earth; cf Gn 2, 7; Sir 40, 1.
2, 4: Skin for skin: an expression which, as applied to Job, means that he has borne his suffering patiently thus far only

because he seeks to avoid greater suffering and to receive greater favors from God.

b: 6ff: Jb 2. 1ff.   c: Gn 6, 2, 4; Zec 3, 1; Lk 22, 31; Rv 12, 9.
d: 1 Pt 5, 8.   e: Jb 2, 5.   f: Eccl 5, 14; 1 Tm 6, 7.   g: Jb 2, 10;
Jas 5, 11.   h: Jb 1, 6.   i: Jb 1, 1.   j: Jb 1, 11.

face." [6] And the LORD said to Satan, "He is in your power; only spare his life." [7] So Satan went forth from the presence of the LORD and smote Job with severe boils from the soles of his feet to the crown of his head. [8] And he took a potsherd to scrape himself, as he sat among the ashes. [9] Then his wife said to him,[k] "Are you still holding to your innocence? Curse God and die."* [10] But he said to her, "Are even you going to speak as senseless women do? We accept good things from God; and should we not accept evil?" Through all this, Job said nothing sinful.[l]

Job's Three Friends. [11] Now when three of Job's friends heard of all the misfortune that had come upon him, they set out each one from his own place: Eliphaz from Teman, Bildad from Shuh, and Zophar from Naamath.* They met and journeyed together to give him sympathy and comfort. [12] But when, at a distance, they lifted up their eyes and did not recognize him, they began to weep aloud; they tore their cloaks and threw dust upon their heads. [13] Then they sat down upon the ground with him seven days and seven nights, but none of them spoke a word to him; for they saw how great was his suffering.

II: First Cycle of Speeches

CHAPTER 3

See RG
236–43 *Job's Plaint.* [1] After this, Job opened his mouth and cursed his day. [2] Job spoke out and said:

[3] Perish the day on which I was born,[m]
  the night when they said, "The child is
    a boy!"
[4] May that day be darkness:
  let not God above call for it,
  nor light shine upon it!

[5] May darkness and gloom claim it,
  clouds settle upon it,
  the blackness of night affright it!
[6] May obscurity seize that day;
  let it not occur among the days of the
    year,
  nor enter into the count of the months!
[7] May that night be barren;
  let no joyful outcry greet it!
[8] Let them curse it who curse the sea,
  the appointed disturbers of Leviathan!*
[9] May the stars of its twilight be darkened;
  may it look for daylight, but have
    none,
  nor gaze on the eyes of the dawn,
[10] Because it kept not shut the doors of the
    womb
  to shield my eyes from trouble!
[11] Why did I not perish at birth,[n]
  come forth from the womb and expire?
[16] Or why was I not buried away like an
    untimely birth,*
  like babes that have never seen the
    light?
[12] Wherefore did the knees receive me?
  or why did I suck at the breasts?
[13] For then I should have lain down and
    been tranquil;
  had I slept, I should then have been at
    rest
[14] With kings and counselors of the earth
  who built where now there are ruins
[15] Or with princes who had gold
  and filled their houses with silver.
[17] There* the wicked cease from troubling,
  there the weary are at rest.
[18] There the captives are at ease together,
  and hear not the voice of the slave
    driver.
[19] Small and great are there the same,
  and the servant is free from his master.

2, 9: Curse God and die: you have nothing to hope for from God and therefore nothing to live for.

2, 11: The names of Job's friends suggest Edomite origin. The Edomites (Ob 8f) and more specifically the Temanites (Jer 49, 7) enjoyed a reputation for wisdom.

3, 8: Leviathan: in Jb 40, 25, the crocodile; here the reference is probably to a mythological sea monster symbolizing primeval chaos. Cf Jb 9, 13; 26, 13; Pss 74, 13f; 104, 26; Is 27, 1.

3, 16: This verse has been placed between vv 11 and 12 where it probably stood originally. There is reason to believe that here, as well as in several other places in Job, the origi-

nal order of the poetic lines was accidentally disturbed in the early transmission of the text; so in chapters 12-15; 19-21; 24-31; 34; 36; 38-42. The verse numbers given in such cases are always those of the current Hebrew text, though the arrangement may differ. The footnotes will advise the reader of the difficulties and provide him with further indications for following the progress of thought in the book.

3, 17: There: in death.

k: Jb 19, 17. *l:* Jb 1, 22; Sir 2, 4; Jas 5, 11. *m:* Jer 20, 14. *n:* Jb 10, 18f.

20 Why is light given to the toilers,
and life to the bitter in spirit?
21 They wait for death and it comes not;
they search for it rather than for hidden
treasures,
22 Rejoice in it exultingly,
and are glad when they reach the
grave:
23 Men whose path is hidden from them,
and whom God has hemmed in!
24 For sighing comes more readily to me
than food,
and my groans well forth like water.
25 For what I fear overtakes me,
and what I shrink from comes upon me.
26 I have no peace nor ease;
I have no rest, for trouble comes!

See RG
236-43

CHAPTER 4

Eliphaz's First Speech. ¹Then spoke
Eliphaz the Temanite, who said:

2 If someone attempts a word with you,
will you mind?
For how can anyone refrain from
speaking?
3 Behold, you have instructed many,
and have made firm their feeble hands.
4 Your words have upheld the stumbler;
you have strengthened his faltering
knees.
5 But now that it comes to you, you are
impatient;
when it touches yourself, you are
dismayed.
6 Is not your peity a source of confidence,
and your integrity of life your hope?
7 Reflect now, what innocent person
perishes?ᵒ
Since when are the upright destroyed?
8 As I see it, those who plow for mischief
and sow trouble, reap the same.
9 By the breath of God they perish,ᵖ
and by the blast of his wrath they are
consumed.

10 Though the lion* roars, though the king
of beasts cries out,
yet the teeth of the young lions are broken;
11 The old lion perishes for lack of prey,
and the cubs of the lioness are scattered.
12 For a word was stealthily brought to me,*
and my ear caught a whisper of it.
13 In my thoughts during visions of the night,�q
when deep sleep falls on men,
14 Fear came upon me, and shuddering,
that terrified me to the bones.
15 Then a spirit passed before me,
and the hair of my flesh stood up.
16 It paused, but its likeness I could not
discern;
a figure was before my eyes,
and I heard a still voice:
17 "Can a man be righteous as against God?ʳ
Can a mortal be blameless against his
Maker?
18 Lo, he puts no trust in his servants,ˢ
and with his angels he can find fault.
19 How much more with those that dwell in
houses of clay,
whose foundation is in the dust,
who are crushed more easily than the
moth!
20 Morning or evening they may be shattered;
with no heed paid to it, they perish
forever.
21 The pegs of their tent are plucked up;
they die without knowing wisdom."

CHAPTER 5

See RG
236-43

1 Call now! Will anyone respond to
you?
To which of the holy ones will you
appeal?
2 Nay, impatience kills the fool
and indignation slays the simpleton.
3 I have seen a fool spreading his roots,ᵗ
but his household suddenly decayed.
4 His children shall be far from safety;
they shall be crushed at the gate*
without a rescuer.

4, 10: The lion: used figuratively here for the violent, rapacious sinner who cannot prevail against God.
4, 12-21: A dramatic presentation of the idea of man's nothingness in contrast to God's greatness.
5, 4: At the gate: of the city, where justice was administered.

o: Ps 37, 25. *p:* Ps 18, 16; Is 11, 4; 2; Thes 2, 8. *q:* Jb 33, 15. *r:* Jb 9, 2; 15, 14ff; 25, 4; Pss 130, 3; 143, 2. *s:* Jb 15, 15; 2 Pt 2, 4; Jude 6. *t:* Ps 37, 35f.

649

5 What they have reaped the hungry shall
eat up;
[or God shall take it away by blight;]
and the thirsty shall swallow their
substance.
6 For mischief comes not out of the earth,
nor does trouble spring out of the
ground;
7 But man himself begets mischief,
as sparks* fly upward.
8 In your place, I would appeal to God,
and to God I would state my plea.*
10 He gives rain upon the earth
and sends water upon the fields;
11 ᵘHe sets up on high the lowly,
and those who mourn he exalts to
safety.
12 He frustrates the plans of the cunning,
so that their hands achieve no success;
13 He catches the wise in their own ruses,ᵛ
and the designs of the crafty are routed.
14 They meet with darkness in the daytime,
and at noonday they grope as though it
were night.
15 But the poor from the edge of the sword
and from the hand of the mighty, he
saves.
16 Thus the unfortunate have hope,
and iniquity closes her mouth.
17 Happy is the man whom God reproves!
The Almighty's chastening do not
reject.
18 For he wounds, but he binds up;ʷ
he smites, but his hands give healing.
19 Out of six troubles he will deliver you,
and at the seventh* no evil shall touch
you.
20 In famine he will deliver you from death,
and in war from the threat of the
sword;
21 From the scourge of the tongue you shall
be hidden,
and shall not fear approaching ruin.
22 At destruction and want you shall laugh;

the beasts of the earth you need not
dread.
23 You shall be in league with the stones of
the field,
and the wild beasts shall be at peace
with you.
24 And you shall know that your tent is
secure;
taking stock of your household, you
shall miss nothing.
25 You shall know that your descendants are
many,
and your offspring as the grass of the
earth.
26 You shall approach the grave in full vigor,
as a shock of grain comes in at its
season.
27 Lo, this we have searched out; so it is!
This we have heard, and you should
know.

CHAPTER 6

See RG
236–43

Job's First Reply. ¹Then Job answered
and said:

2 Ah, could my anguish but be measured
and my calamity laid with it in the
scales,
3 They would now outweigh the sands of
the sea!
Because of this I speak without
restraint.
4 For the arrows of the Almighty pierce
me,ˣ
and my spirit drinks in their poison;
the terrors of God are arrayed against
me.
5 Does the wild ass bray when he has
grass?*
Does the ox low over his fodder?
6 Can a thing insipid be eaten without salt?
Is there flavor in the white of an egg?
7 I refuse to touch them;
they are loathsome food to me.

5, 7: Sparks: in Hebrew, "sons of resheph," which the ancient versions took as the name of a bird.

5, 9: Omitted here; it is a duplicate of Jb 9, 10.

5, 19: Six . . . the seventh: proverbial expression for any
large number; cf Prv 24, 16; Lk 17, 4.

6, 5f: Job would not complain if his life were as pleasant
to him as fodder to a hungry animal; but his life is as dis-

agreeable as insipid food. White of an egg: thus the obscure
Hebrew has been understood in Jewish tradition; some render
it "mallow juice."

u: 1 Sm 2, 7f; Ps 113, 7; Lk 1, 52.   *v:* 1 Cor 3, 19.   *w:* Hos 6, 1f.
x: Ps 88, 17.

8 Oh, that I might have my request,
and that God would grant what I long
for:
9 Even that God would decide to crush me,
that he would put forth his hand and
cut me off!
10 Then I should still have consolation
and could exult through unremitting
pain,
because I have not transgressed the
commands of the Holy One.
11 What strength have I that I should endure,
and what is my limit that I should be
patient?
12 Have I the strength of stones,
or is my flesh of bronze?
13 Have I no helper,y
and has advice deserted me?
14 A friend owes kindness to one in despair,
though he have forsaken the fear of the
Almighty.
15 My brethren are undependable as a brook,
as watercourses that run dry in the
wadies;
16 Though they may be black with ice,
and with snow heaped upon them,
17 Yet once they flow, they cease to be;
in the heat, they disappear from their
place.
18 Caravans turn aside from their routes;
they go into the desert and perish.
19 The caravans of Tema* search,
the companies of Sheba have hopes;
20 They are disappointed, though they were
confident;
they come there and are frustrated.
21 It is thus that you have now become for
me;
you see a terrifying thing and are
afraid.
22 Have I asked you to give me anything,
to offer a gift for me from your
possessions,
23 Or to deliver me from the enemy,
or to redeem me from oppressors?
24 Teach me, and I will be silent;
prove to me wherein I have erred.

25 How agreeable are honest words;
yet how unconvincing is your
argument!
26 Do you consider your words as proof,
but the sayings of a desperate man as
wind?
27 You would even cast lots for the orphan,
and would barter away your friend!
28 Come, now, give me your attention;
surely I will not lie to your face.
29 Think it over; let there be no injustice.
Think it over; I still am right.
30 Is there insincerity on my tongue,
or cannot my taste discern falsehood?

CHAPTER 7

See RG 236–43

1 zIs not man's life on earth a
drudgery?*
Are not his days those of a hireling?
2 He is a slave who longs for the shade,
a hireling who waits for his wages.
3 So I have been assigned months of misery,
and troubled nights have been told off
for me.
4 If in bed I say, "When shall I arise?"
then the night drags on;
I am filled with restlessness until the
dawn.
5 My flesh is clothed with worms and scabs;a
my skin cracks and festers;
6 My days are swifter than a weaver's
shuttle;
they come to an end without hope.
7 Remember that my life is like the wind;b
I shall not see happiness again.
8 The eye that now sees me shall no more
behold me;
as you look at me, I shall be gone.
9 As a cloud dissolves and vanishes,c
so he who goes down to the nether
world shall come up no more.
10 He shall not again return to his house;
his place shall know him no more.
11 My own utterance I will not restrain;
I will speak in the anguish of my spirit;
I will complain in the bitterness of my
soul.

6, 19: Tema: in northwest Arabia. Sheba: see note on Jb 1, 15.
7, 1: Drudgery: taken by some to refer to military service; cf also Jb 14, 14.

y: Jb 19, 14f. z: Jb 14, 14. a: Jb 2, 7f. b: Pss 8, 5; 144, 3. c: 9f: Jb 10. 21; 14, 10ff; 2 Sm 12, 23; 14, 14; Wis 2, 1.

¹² *Am I the sea, or a monster of the deep,
    that you place a watch over me?*
  Why have you set me up as an object of
    attack?
    or why should I be a target for you?
¹³ When I say, "My bed shall comfort me,
    my couch shall ease my complaint,"
¹⁴ Then you affright me with dreams
    and with visions terrify me,
¹⁵ So that I should prefer choking
    and death rather than my pains.
¹⁶ I waste away: I cannot live forever;ᵈ
    let me alone, for my days are but a
    breath.
¹⁷ What is man, that you make much of
    him,
    or pay him any heed?
¹⁸ You observe him with each new dayᵉ
    and try him at every moment!
¹⁹ How long will it be before you look
    away from me,
    and let me alone long enough to
    swallow my spittle?
²⁰ Though I have sinned, what can I do to you,
    O watcher of men?
²¹ Why do you not pardon my offense,
    or take away my guilt?
  For soon I shall lie down in the dust;
    and should you seek me I shall then be
    gone.

See RG
236–43

CHAPTER 8

Bildad's First Speech. ¹Bildad the
Shuhite spoke out and said:

² How long will you utter such things?
    The words from your mouth are like a
    mighty wind!
³ Does God pervert judgment,ᶠ
    and does the Almighty distort justice?
⁴ If your children have sinned against him
    and he has left them in the grip of their
    guilt,
⁵ Still, if you yourself have recourse to
    God

and make supplication to the
    Almighty,
⁶ Should you be blameless and upright,
    surely now he will awake for you
    and restore your rightful domain;
⁷ Your former state will be of little
    moment,
    for in time to come you will flourish
    indeed.
⁸ If you inquire of the former generations,
    and give heed to the experience of the
    fathersᵍ
⁹ (As we are but of yesterday and have no
    knowledge,
    because our days on earth are but a
    shadow),ʰ
¹⁰ Will they not teach you and tell you
    and utter their words of
    understanding?
¹¹ Can the papyrus grow up without mire?*
    Can the reed grass flourish without
    water?
¹² While it is yet green and uncut,
    it withers quicker than any grass.
¹³ So is the end of everyone who forgets
    God,
    and so shall the hope of the godless
    man perish.
¹⁴ His confidence is but a gossamer thread
    and his trust is a spider's web.
¹⁵ He shall rely upon his family, but it shall
    not last;
    he shall cling to it, but it shall not
    endure.
¹⁶ He is full of sap before sunrise,
    and beyond his garden his shoots go
    forth;
¹⁷ About a heap of stones are his roots
    entwined;
    among the rocks he takes hold.
¹⁸ Yet if one tears him from his place,
    it will disown him: "I have never seen
    you!"
¹⁹ There he lies rotting beside the road,
    and out of the soil another sprouts.

7, 12: An allusion in poetic imagery to primeval chaos as a monstrous ocean vanquished by God at the world's creation.
7, 12-21: Job now speaks, not to his friends, but to God.
  8, 11ff: As marsh plants need water, so man needs God. These verses are taken by some as a quotation from the teaching
of the forefathers; cf v 10.

d: Jb 14, 1ff, 5. *e:* Ps 17, 3. *f:* Jb 34, 10ff. *g:* Dt 4, 32; 32, 7. *h:* Jb 14, 2; Pss 102, 12; 109, 23; 144, 4; Wis 2, 5.

20 Behold, God will not cast away the upright;
  neither will he take the hand of the
      wicked.
21 Once more will he fill your mouth with
      laughter,
  and your lips with rejoicing.
22 They that hate you shall be clothed with
      shame,
  and the tent of the wicked shall be no
      more.

See RG
236–43

CHAPTER 9

Job's Second Reply. 1 Then Job answered and said:

2 I know well that it is so;
  but how can a man be justified before
      God?
3 Should one wish to contend with him,
  he could not answer him once in a
      thousand times.
4 God is wise in heart and mighty in
      strength;
  who has withstood him and remained
      unscathed?
5 He removes the mountains before they
      know it;
  he overturns them in his anger.
6 He shakes the earth out of its place,*i*
  and the pillars beneath it tremble.
7 He commands the sun, and it rises not;
  he seals up the stars.
8 He alone stretches out the heavens*j*
  and treads upon the crests of the sea.
9 He made the Bear and Orion,
  the Pleiades and the constellations of
      the south;
10 He does great things past finding out,
  marvelous things beyond reckoning.
11 Should he come near me, I see him not;
  should he pass by, I am not aware of
      him;
12 Should he seize me forcibly, who can say
      him nay?
  Who can say to him, "What are you
      doing?"
13 He is God and he does not relent;

the helpers of Rahab* bow beneath him.
14 How much less shall I give him any
      answer,
  or choose out arguments against him!
15 Even though I were right, I could not
      answer him,*k*
  but should rather beg for what was due
      me.
16 If I appealed to him and he answered my
      call,
  I could not believe that he would
      hearken to my words;
17 With a tempest he might overwhelm me,
  and multiply my wounds without
      cause;
18 He need not suffer me to draw breath,
  but might fill me with bitter griefs.
19 If it be a question of strength, he is
      mighty;
  and if of judgment, who will call him
      to account?
20 Though I were right, my own mouth
      might condemn me;*l*
  were I innocent, he might put me in
      the wrong.
21 Though I am innocent, I myself cannot
      know it;
  I despise my life.
22 It is all one! therefore I say:
  Both the innocent and the wicked he
      destroys.*m*
23 When the scourge slays suddenly,
  he laughs at the despair of the innocent.
24 The earth is given into the hands of the
      wicked;
  he covers the faces of its judges.
  If it is not he, who then is it?
25 My days are swifter than a runner,
  they flee away; they see no happiness;*n*
26 They shoot by like skiffs of reed,
  like an eagle swooping upon its prey.
27 If I say: I will forget my complaining,
  I will lay aside my sadness and be of
      good cheer,
28 Then I am in dread of all my pains;
  I know that you* will not hold me
      innocent.

9, 13: Rahab: cf Jb 26, 12. See note on Ps 89, 11.
9, 28-31: You: refers to God.

i: Jb 26, 11.   *j*: Ps 104, 2; Is 40, 22.   *k*: Jb 10, 15.   *l*: Jb 15, 6.   *m*: Eccl 9, 2.   *n*: Jb 7, 6.

²⁹ If I must be accounted guilty,
    why then should I strive in vain?
³⁰ If I should wash myself with snow
    and cleanse my hands with lye,
³¹ Yet you would plunge me in the ditch,
    so that my garments would abhor me.
³² For he is not a man like myself, that I
        should answer him,
    that we should come together in
        judgment.
³³ Would that there were an arbiter between
        us,
    who could lay his hand upon us both
³⁴   and withdraw his rod from me.
    Would that his terrors did not frighten
        me;
³⁵   that I might speak without being afraid
        of him.
    Since this is not the case with me,
¹   *I loathe my life.ᵒ

See RG 236–43

CHAPTER 10

    I will give myself up to complaint;
    I will speak from the bitterness of my
        soul.
² I will say to God: Do not put me in the
        wrong!
    Let me know why you oppose me.
³ Is it a pleasure for you to oppress,
    to spurn the work of your hands,
    and smile on the plan of the wicked?
⁴ Have you eyes of flesh?
    Do you see as man sees?
⁵ Are your days as the days of a mortal,ᵖ
    and are your years as a man's lifetime,
⁶ That you seek for guilt in me
    and search after my sins,
⁷ Even though you know that I am not
        wicked,�q
    and that none can deliver me out of
        your hand?
⁸ Your hands have formed me and
        fashioned me;
    will you then turn and destroy me?
⁹ Oh, remember that you fashioned me
        from clay!ʳ

Will you then bring me down to dust
        again?
¹⁰ Did you not pour me out as milk,
    and thicken me like cheese?
¹¹ With skin and flesh you clothed me,
    with bones and sinews knit me
        together.
¹² Grace and favor you granted me,
    and your providence has preserved my
        spirit.
¹³ Yet these things you have hidden in your
        heart;
    I know that they are your purpose:
¹⁴ If I should sin, you would keep a watch
        against me,
    and from my guilt you would not
        absolve me.
¹⁵ If I should be wicked, alas for me!
    if righteous, I dare not hold up my
        head,
    filled with ignominy and sodden with
        affliction!
¹⁶ Should it lift up, you hunt me like a lion:
    repeatedly you show your wondrous
        power against me,
¹⁷ You renew your attack upon me
    and multiply your harassment of me;
    in waves your troops come against me.
¹⁸ Why then did you bring me forth from
        the womb?ˢ
    I should have died and no eye have
        seen me.
¹⁹ I should be as though I had never lived;
    I should have been taken from the
        womb to the grave.
²⁰ Are not the days of my life few?
    Let me alone, that I may recover a
        little
²¹ Before I go whence I shall not return,ᵗ
    to the land of darkness and of gloom,
²² The black, disordered land
    where darkness is the only light.

CHAPTER 11

Zophar's First Speech. ¹And Zophar
the Naamathite spoke out and said:

See RG 236–43

10, 1: I loathe my life: this is the first verse of ch 10.

o: Jb 9, 21.   p: Jb 36, 26.   q: Jb 2, 3. 9; Dt 32, 39; Wis 16, 15.   r: Jb 4, 19; 33, 6; Gn 2, 7; 3, 19; Ps 146, 4.   s: Jb 3, 3, 11.   t: Jb 7, 9f; 16, 22.

2 Should not the man of many words be
   answered,
   or must the garrulous man necessarily
   be right?
3 Shall your babblings keep men silent,
   and shall you deride and no one give
   rebuke?
4 Shall you say: "My teaching is pure,
   and I am clean in your sight"?
5 But oh, that God would speak,
   and open his lips against you,
6 And tell you that the secrets of wisdom
   are twice as effective:
So you might learn that God
   will make you answer for your guilt.
7 Can you penetrate the designs of God?[u]
   Dare you vie with the perfection of the
   Almighty?
8 It is higher than the heavens; what can
   you do?
   It is deeper than the nether world; what
   can you know?
9 It is longer than the earth in measure,
   and broader than the sea.
10 If he seize and imprison
   or call to judgment, who then can say
   him nay?
11 For he knows the worthlessness of men
   and sees iniquity; will he then ignore
   it?
12 Will empty man then gain understanding,
   and the wild jackass[v] be made docile?
13 If you set your heart aright
   and stretch out your hands toward him,
14 If you remove all iniquity from your
   conduct,
   and let not injustice dwell in your tent,
15 Surely then you may lift up your face in
   innocence;
   you may stand firm and unafraid.
16 For then you shall forget your misery,
   or recall it like waters that have ebbed
   away.
17 Then your life shall be brighter than the
   noonday;
   its gloom shall become as the
   morning,

18 And you shall be secure, because there is
   hope;
   you shall look round you and lie down
   in safety,[w]
19 and you shall take your rest with none
   to disturb.
Many shall entreat your favor,
20 but the wicked, looking on, shall be
   consumed with envy.
Escape shall be cut off from them,
   they shall wait to expire.

CHAPTER 12

See RG
236-43

Job's Third Reply. [1]Then Job replied
and said:

2 No doubt you are the intelligent folk,
   and with you wisdom shall die!
3 But I have intelligence as well as you;[x]
   for who does not know such things as
   these?
4 I have become the sport of my neighbors:*
   "The one whom God answers when he
   calls upon him,
   the just, the perfect man," is a
   laughingstock;[y]
5 The undisturbed esteem my downfall a
   disgrace
   such as awaits unsteady feet;
6 Yet the tents of robbers are prosperous,
   and those who provoke God are
   secure.
7 But now ask the beasts to teach you,
   and the birds of the air to tell you;
8 Or the reptiles on earth to instruct you,
   and the fish of the sea to inform you.
9 Which of all these does not know
   that the hand of God has done this?
10 In his hand is the soul of every living
   thing,[z]
   and the life breath of all mankind.
11 Does not the ear judge words
   as the mouth tastes food?[a]
12 So with old age is wisdom,[b]
   and with length of days understanding.
13 With him are wisdom and might;
   his are counsel and understanding.

12, 4f: The Hebrew is somewhat obscure, but the general sense is that the wicked mock at the pious when the latter appear to be abandoned by God; cf Ps 22, 7ff; Mt 27, 39-43.

u: Rom 11, 33. *v:* Jb 39, 5-8. *w:* Lv 26, 6; Ps 4, 9. *x:* Jb 13, 2; 15, 9. *y:* Jb 21, 3; 30, 1. *z:* Acts 17, 28. *a:* Jb 34, 3. *b:* Jb 32, 7.

14 If he breaks a thing down, there is no
  rebuilding;*c*
  if he imprisons a man, there is no
  release.
15 He holds back the waters and there is
  drought;*d*
  he sends them forth and they
  overwhelm the land.
18 He loosens the bonds imposed by kings
  and leaves but a waistcloth to bind the
  king's own loins.*
21 He breaks down the barriers of the
  streams
19 and lets their never-failing waters flow
  away.
16 With him are strength and prudence;
  the misled and the misleaders are his.
17 He sends counselors away barefoot,
  and of judges he makes fools.
20 He silences the trusted adviser,
  and takes discretion from the aged.
22 The recesses of the darkness he
  discloses,
  and brings the gloom forth to the light.
23 He makes nations great and he destroys
  them;
  he spreads peoples abroad and he
  abandons them.
24 He takes understanding from the leaders
  of the land,
25 till they grope in the darkness without
  light;
  he makes them stagger like drunken
  men.

CHAPTER 13

See RG
236–43
1 Lo, all this my eye has seen;
  my ear has heard and perceived it.
2 What you know, I also know;*e*
  I fall not short of you.
3 But I would speak with the Almighty;*f*
  I wish to reason with God.
4 You are glossing over falsehoods
  and offering vain remedies, every one
  of you!

5 Oh, that you would be altogether silent!
  This for you would be wisdom.
6 Hear now the rebuke I shall utter
  and listen to the reproof from my lips.
7 Is it for God that you speak falsehood?
  Is it for him that you utter deceit?
8 Is it for him that you show partiality?
  Do you play advocate on behalf of God?
9 Will it be well when he shall search you
  out?
  Would you impose on him as one does
  on men?
10 He will openly rebuke you
  if even in secret you show partiality.
11 Surely will his majesty affright you
  and the dread of him fall upon you.
12 Your reminders are ashy maxims,
  your fabrications are mounds of clay.
13 Be silent, let me alone! that I may speak
  and give vent to my feelings.
14 I will carry my flesh between my teeth,
  and take my life in my hand.*
15 Slay me though he might,*g* I will wait for
  him;
  I will defend my conduct before him.
16 And this shall be my salvation,
  that no impious man can come into his
  presence.
17 Pay careful heed to my speech,
  and give my statement a hearing.
18 Behold, I have prepared my case,*h*
  I know that I am in the right.
19 If anyone can make a case against me,
  then I shall be silent and die.
20 These things only do not use against me,*
  then from your presence I need not
  hide:
21 Withdraw your hand far from me,
  and let not the terror of you frighten
  me.
22 Then call me, and I will respond;
  or let me speak first, and answer me.
23 What are my faults and my sins?
  My misdeeds and my sins make
  known to me!

12, 18: Waistcloth . . . loins: he reduces kings to the condition of slaves, who wear only a cloth wrapped about the waist.
  13, 14: The second half of the verse is a common biblical expression for risking one's life; cf Jgs 12, 3; 1 Sm 19, 5; 28, 21; Ps 119, 109; the first half of the verse must have a similar meaning. Job is so confident of his innocence that he is willing to risk his life by going to judgment with God.
  13, 20: From here to the end of chapter 14, Job pleads his case, addressing God rather than his three friends.

c: Rv 3, 7. *d:* Gn 7, 11-24. *e:* Jb 12, 3; 15, 9. *f:* Jb 23, 4. *g:* Jb 27, 5. *h:* Jb 33, 9.

24 Why do you hide your face[i]
  and consider me your enemy?
25 Will you harass a wind-driven leaf,
  or pursue a withered straw?
26 For you draw up bitter indictments
    against me,
  and punish in me the faults of my youth.
27 You put my feet in the stocks;
  you watch all my paths
  and trace out all my footsteps.

See RG 236–43

CHAPTER 14

1 Man born of woman
  is short-lived and full of trouble,[j]
2 Like a flower that springs up and fades,[k]
  swift as a shadow that does not abide.
3 Upon such a one will you cast your eyes
  so as to bring him into judgment
    before you,
28 Though he wears out like a leather bottle,
  like a garment that the moth has
    consumed?*
4 Can a man be found who is clean of
    defilement?[l]
  There is none, 5however short his
    days.
  You know the number of his months;
  you have fixed the limit which he
    cannot pass.
6 Look away from him and let him be,
  while, like a hireling, he completes his
    day.
7 For a tree there is hope,
  if it be cut down, that it will sprout
    again
  and that its tender shoots will not cease.
8 Even though its root grow old in the
    earth,
  and its stump die in the dust,
9 Yet at the first whiff of water it may
    flourish again
  and put forth branches like a young
    plant.
10 But when a man dies, all vigor leaves
    him;[m]
  when man expires, where then is he?

11 As when the waters of a lake fail,
  or a stream grows dry and parches,
12 So men lie down and rise not again.
  Till the heavens are no more, they
    shall not awake,
  nor be roused out of their sleep.[n]
13 Oh, that you would hide me in the nether
    world
  and keep me sheltered till your wrath
    is past;
  would fix a time for me, and then
    remember me!
14 When a man has died, were he to live
    again,
  all the days of my drudgery I would wait,[o]
  until my relief should come.
15 You would call, and I would answer you;
  you would esteem the work of your
    hands.
16 Surely then you would count my steps,[p]
  and not keep watch for sin in me.
17 My misdeeds would be sealed up in a
    pouch,*
  and you would cover over my guilt.
18 But as a mountain falls at last
  and its rock is moved from its place,
19 As waters wear away the stones
  and floods wash away the soil of the
    land,
  so you destroy the hope of man.
20 You prevail once for all against him and
    he passes on;
  with changed appearance you send
    him away.
21 If his sons are honored, he is not aware
    of it;
  if they are in disgrace, he does not
    know about them.
22 Only his own flesh pains him,
  and his soul grieves for him.

III: Second Cycle of Speeches

CHAPTER 15

Second Speech of Eliphaz. 1Then Eliphaz the Temanite spoke and said:

See RG 236–43

14, 28: This verse has been transposed from ch 13.
14, 17: Sealed up in a pouch: hidden away and forgotten.

i: Jb 19, 11; 33, 10. j: Jb 10, 20; 15, 14; Pss 39, 5f; 89, 46; Wis 2, 1. k: Jb 8, 9; Pss 90:6; 102, 12; 103, 15; 109, 23; 144, 4; Is 40, 6f; Jas 1, 10. l: Ps 51, 4, 7. m: Jb 20, 7. n: Jb 7, 10. o: Jb 7, 1. p: Jb 31, 4; 34, 21.

2 Should a wise man answer with airy
   opinions,
   or puff himself up with wind?
3 Should he argue in speech which does
   not avail,
   and in words which are to no profit?
4 You in fact do away with piety,
   and you lessen devotion toward God,
5 Because your wickedness instructs your
   mouth,
   and you choose to speak like the
   crafty.
6 Your own mouth condemns you, not I;q
   your own lips refute you.
7 Are you indeed the first-born of
   mankind,
   or were you brought forth before the
   hills?
8 Are you privy to the counsels of God,r
   and do you restrict wisdom to
   yourself?
9 What do you know that we do not know?s
   What intelligence have you which we
   have not?
10 There are gray-haired old men among us
   more advanced in years than your
   father.
11 Are the consolations of God not enough
   for you,
   and speech that deals gently with you?
12 Why do your notions carry you away,
   and why do your eyes blink,
13 So that you turn your anger against God
   and let such words escape your mouth!
14 What is a man that he should be
   blameless,t
   one born of woman that he should be
   righteous?u
15 If in his holy ones God places no
   confidence,v
   and if the heavens are not clean in his
   sight,
16 How much less so is the abominable, the
   corrupt:
   man, who drinks in iniquity like water!
17 I will show you, if you listen to me;
   what I have seen I will tell—
18 What wise men relate

and have not contradicted since the
   days of their fathers,
19 To whom alone the land was given,
   when no foreigner moved among
   them.
20 The wicked man is in torment all his days,
   and limited years are in store for the
   tyrant;
21 The sound of terrors is in his ears;
   when all is prosperous, the spoiler
   comes upon him.
22 He despairs of escaping the darkness,
   and looks ever for the sword;
23 A wanderer, food for the vultures,
   he knows that his destruction is
   imminent.
24 By day the darkness fills him with dread;
   distress and anguish overpower him.
25 Because he has stretched out his hand
   against God
   and bade defiance to the Almighty,
26 One shall rush sternly upon him
   with the stout bosses of his shield,
   like a king prepared for the charge.
27 Because he has blinded himself with his
   crassness,
   padding his loins with fat,
28 He shall dwell in ruinous cities,
   in houses that are deserted,
   That are crumbling into clay
29 with no shadow to lengthen over the
   ground.
   He shall not be rich, and his possessions
   shall not endure;
31 for vain shall be his bartering.
30 A flame shall wither him up in his early
   growth,
   and with the wind his blossoms shall
   disappear.
32 His stalk shall wither before its time,
   and his branches shall be green no
   more.
33 He shall be like a vine that sheds its
   grapes unripened,
   and like an olive tree casting off its
   bloom.
34 For the breed of the impious shall be
   sterile,w

q: Jb 9, 20.   r: Jb 11, 7; Wis 9, 13; Jer 23, 18; Rom 11, 34; 1 Cor 2, 11, 16.   s: Jb 12, 3; 13, 2.   t: 14ff: Jb 25, 4ff.   u: Jb 14, 4.   v: Jb
4, 18f.   w: Wis 3, 11, 18.

and fire shall consume the tents of
extortioners.

³⁵ They conceive malice and bring forth
emptiness;ˣ
they give birth to failure.*

CHAPTER 16

Job's Fourth Reply. ¹Then Job answered and said:

² I have heard this sort of thing many
times.ʸ
Wearisome comforters are you all!

³ Is there no end to windy words?
Or what sickness have you that you
speak on?

⁴ I also could talk as you do,
were you in my place.
I could declaim over you,
or wag my head at you;

⁵ I could strengthen you with talk,
or shake my head with silent lips.

⁶ If I speak, this pain I have will not be
checked;
if I leave off, it will not depart from
me.

⁷ But now that I am exhausted and stunned,
all my company has closed in on me.

⁸ As a witness there rises up
my traducer, speaking openly against
me;

⁹ I am the prey his wrath assails,
he gnashes his teeth against me.
My enemies lord it over me;

¹⁰ their mouths are agape to bite me.
They smite me on the cheek insultingly;
they are all enlisted against me.

¹¹ God has given me over to the impious;
into the clutches of the wicked he has
cast me.

¹² I was in peace, but he dislodged me;
he seized me by the neck and dashed
me to pieces.
He has set me up for a target;

¹³ his arrows strike me from all
directions,

He pierces my sides without mercy,
he pours out my gall upon the ground.

¹⁴ He pierces me with thrust upon thrust;
he attacks me like a warrior.

¹⁵ I have fastened sackcloth over my skin,
and have laid my brow in the dust.

¹⁶ My face is inflamed with weeping
and there is darkness over my eyes,

¹⁷ Although my hands are free from
violence,
and my prayer is sincere.

¹⁸ O earth, cover not my blood,
nor let my outcry come to rest!*

¹⁹ Even now, behold, my witness* is in
heaven,
and my spokesman is on high.

²⁰ My friends it is who wrong me;
before God my eyes drop tears,

²¹ That he may do justice for a mortal in his
presence
and decide between a man and his
neighbor.

²² For my years are numbered now,
and I am on a journey from which I
shall not return.

CHAPTER 17

¹ My spirit is broken, my lamp of
life extinguished;
my burial is at hand.

² I am indeed mocked,
and, as their provocation mounts, my
eyes grow dim.

³ Grant me one to offer you a pledge on
my behalf:*
who is there that will give surety for
me?

⁴ You darken their minds to knowledge;
therefore they do not understand.

⁵ My lot is described as evil,

⁶ and I am made a byword of the
people;ᶻ
their object lesson I have become.

⁷ My eye has grown blind with anguish,
and all my frame is shrunken to a
shadow.

15, 35: They give birth to failure: their wicked plans yield
nothing but futile results. Cf Ps 7, 15; Is 59, 4.

16, 18: As the blood of those who were unjustly slain cries
to heaven for vengeance (Gn 4, 10; Ez 24, 6-9), so Job's sufferings demand redress.

16, 19: Witness: refers either to God or, more probably, to
Job's prayer.

17, 3: Addressed to God; v 10 to Job's friends.

---

x: Ps 7, 15; Is 59, 4.   *y:* Jb 12, 3.   *z:* Jb 30, 9.

8 Upright men are astonished at this,
    and the innocent aroused against the
        wicked.
9 Yet the righteous shall hold to his way,
    and he who has clean hands increase in
        strength.
10 But turn now, and come on again;
    for I shall not find a wise man among
        you!
11 My days are passed away, my plans are
        at an end,
    the cherished purposes of my heart.
12 Such men change the night into day;
    where there is darkness they talk of
        approaching light.
13 If I look for the nether world as my
        dwelling,
    if I spread my couch in the darkness,
14 If I must call corruption "my father,"
    and the maggot "my mother" and "my
        sister,"
15 Where then is my hope,
    and my prosperity, who shall see?
16 Will they descend with me into the
        nether world?
    Shall we go down together into the
        dust?

CHAPTER 18

See RG
236–43

Bildad's Second Speech. ¹Then Bildad the Shuhite replied and said:

2 When will you put an end to words?
    Reflect, and then we can have
        discussion.
3 Why are we accounted like the beasts,
    their equals in your sight?
4 You who tear yourself in your anger,*
    shall the earth be neglected on your
        account
    [or the rock be moved out of its
        place]?
5 Truly, the light of the wicked is
        extinguished;
    no flame brightens his hearth.
6 The light is darkened in his tent;

in spite of him, his lamp goes out.*a*
7 His vigorous steps are hemmed in,
    and his own counsel casts him down.
8 For he rushes headlong into a net,
    and he wanders into a pitfall.
9 A trap seizes him by the heel,
    and a snare lays hold of him.
10 A noose for him is hid on the ground,
    and the toils for him on the way.
11 On every side terrors affright him;*b*
    they harry him at each step.
12 Disaster is ready at his side,
13   the first-born of death* consumes his
        limbs.
14 Fiery destruction lodges in his tent,
    and marches him off to the king of
        terrors.*
He is plucked from the security of his
        tent;
15   over his abode brimstone is scattered.
16 Below, his roots dry up,
    and above, his branches wither.
17 His memory perishes from the land,*c*
    and he has no name on the earth.
18 He is driven from light into darkness,
    and banished out of the world.
19 He has neither son nor grandson among
        his people,
    nor any survivor where once he dwelt.
20 They who come after shall be appalled at
        his fate;
    they who went before are struck with
        horror.
21 So is it then with the dwelling of the
        impious man,
    and such is the place of him who
        knows not God!

CHAPTER 19

Job's Fifth Reply. ¹Then Job answered See RG
236–43 and said:

2 How long will you vex my soul,
    grind me down with words?
3 These ten times you have reviled me,
    have assailed me without shame!

18, 4: Job himself is portrayed as having the heedless rage of wild beasts, despite which God does not forsake the usual course of Divine Providence.

18, 13: First-born of death: that is, disease, plague.

18, 14: The king of terrors: of the nether world, death; however, the Hebrew is obscure.

a: Jb 21, 17; Prv 13, 9; 24, 20.   *b:* Jb 15, 20-24; 27, 20.   *c:* Ps 34, 17; Prv 2, 22; 10, 7.

⁴ Be it indeed that I am at fault
    and that my fault remains with me.
⁵ Even so, if you would vaunt yourselves
    against me
    and cast up to me my reproach,
⁶ Know then that God has dealt unfairly
    with me,
    and compassed me round with his net.
⁷ If I cry out "Injustice!" I am not heard.ᵈ
    I cry for help, but there is no redress.
⁸ He has barred my way and I cannot pass;
    he has veiled my path in darkness;
⁹ He has stripped me of my glory,
    and taken the diadem from my brow.
¹⁰ He breaks me down on every side, and I
    am gone;
    my hope he has uprooted like a tree.
¹¹ His wrath he has kindled against me;
    he counts me among his enemies.ᵉ
¹² His troops advance as one man;
    they build up their road to attack me,
    and they encamp around my tent.
¹³ My brethren have withdrawn from me,ᶠ
    and my friends are wholly estranged.
¹⁴ My kinsfolk and companions neglect me,
    and my guests have forgotten me.
¹⁵ Even my handmaids treat me as a
    stranger;
    I am an alien in their sight.
¹⁶ I call my servant, but he gives no answer,
    though in my speech I plead with him.
¹⁷ My breath is abhorred by my wife;ᵍ
    I am loathsome to the men of my
    family.
¹⁸ The young children, too, despise me;
    when I appear, they speak against me.
¹⁹ All my intimate friends hold me in horror;
    those whom I loved have turned
    against me!ʰ
²⁰ My bones cleave to my skin,
    and I have escaped with my flesh
    between my teeth.*

²¹ Pity me, pity me, O you my friends,
    for the hand of God has struck me!
²² Why do you hound me as though you
    were divine,*
    and insatiably prey upon me?
²³ Oh, would that my words were written
    down!ⁱ
    Would that they were inscribed in a
    record:*
²⁴ That with an iron chisel and with lead
    they were cut in the rock forever!
²⁵ But as for me, I know that my Vindicator
    lives,*
    and that he will at last stand forth upon
    the dust;ʲ
²⁷ Whom I myself shall see:
    my own eyes, not another's, shall
    behold him,
²⁶ And from my flesh I shall see God;
    my inmost being is consumed with
    longing.
²⁸ But you who say, "How shall we
    persecute him,
    seeing that the root of the matter is
    found in him?"
²⁹ Be afraid of the sword for yourselves,
    for these crimes deserve the sword;
    that you may know that there is a
    judgment.

CHAPTER 20

Zophar's Second Speech. ¹Then Zophar the Naamathite spoke and said:

See RG
236–43

³ A rebuke which puts me to shame I hear,
²   and because of this I am disturbed.
So now my thoughts provide me with an
    answer,
    and from my understanding a spirit
    gives me a reply.
⁴ Do you not know this from olden time,
    since man was placed upon the earth,

19, 20: With my flesh between my teeth: meaning perhaps that Job has been reduced to such an extremity that he scarcely has thin lips over his teeth. But the current Hebrew text of this line is probably corrupt.

19, 22: Divine: possessing God's attributes of judgment and authority to punish.

19, 23f: Job regards what he is about to say as so important that he wishes it recorded in a permanent manner.

19, 25. 27: The meaning of this passage is obscure because the original text has been poorly preserved and the

ancient versions do not agree among themselves. It is certain that Job expresses his belief in a future vindication by God (called here in the Hebrew "Goel"), but the time and manner of this vindication are undefined. In the Vulgate Job is made to indicate a belief in physical resurrection after death, but the Hebrew and the other ancient versions are less specific.

d: Jb 30, 20. e: Jb 13, 24; 33, 10. f: Jb 6, 13. g: Jb 2, 9.
h: Sir 6, 8. i: Jb 31, 35. j: 25ff: Phil 3, 20; Ti 2, 13.

5 That the triumph of the wicked is short
    and the joy of the impious but for a
        moment?k
6 Though his pride mount up to the
        heavens
    and his head reach to the clouds,
7 Yet he perishes forever like the fuel of
        his fire,
    and the onlookers say, "Where is he?"l
8 Like a dream he takes flight and is not
        found again;
    he fades away like a vision of the
        night.
9 The eye which saw him does so no more;
    nor shall his dwelling again behold
        him.
11 Though his frame is full of youthful
        vigor,
    this shall lie with him in the dust.
12 Though wickedness is sweet in his
        mouth,
    and he hides it under his tongue,
13 Though he retains it and will not let it go
    but keeps it still within his mouth,
14 Yet in his stomach the food shall turn;
    it shall be venom of asps inside him.
15 The riches he swallowed he shall
        disgorge;
    God shall compel his belly to disown
        them.
16 The poison of asps he shall drink in;
    the viper's fangs shall slay him.
17 He shall see no streams of oil,*
    no torrents of honey or milk.
18 Restoring his gains, he shall not enjoy
        them;
    though his wealth increases, he shall
        not rejoice.
19 Because he has oppressed the poor,
    and stolen a patrimony he had not built
        up,
21 Therefore his prosperity shall not endure,
10   and his hands shall yield up his
        riches.m
20 Though he has known no quiet in his
        greed,
    his treasures shall not save him.n

22 oWhen he abounds to overflowing, he
        shall be brought into straits,
    and nought shall be left of his goods.
23 God shall send against him the fury of
        his wrath
    and rain down his missiles of war
        upon him.
24 Should he escape the iron weapon,
    the bow of bronze shall pierce him
        through;
25 The dart shall come out of his back;
    terrors shall fall upon him.
26 Complete darkness is in store for him;
    the fire which shall consume him
        needs not to be fanned.p
27 The heavens shall reveal his guilt,
    and the earth shall rise up against him.
28 The flood shall sweep away his house
    with the waters that run off in the day
        of God's anger.
29 This is the portion of a wicked man,
    and the heritage appointed him by
        God.q

CHAPTER 21

Job's Sixth Reply. 1Then Job said in
reply:

2 At least listen to my words,r
    and let that be the consolation you offer.
3 Bear with me while I speak;
    and after I have spoken, you can
        mock!
4 Is my complaint toward man?
    And why should I not be impatient?
5 Look at me and be astonished,
    put your hands over your mouths.
6 When I think of it, I am dismayed,
    and horror takes hold on my flesh.

7 Why do the wicked survive,
    grow old, become mighty in power?s
8 Their progeny is secure in their sight;
    they see before them their kinsfolk and
        their offspring.
9 Their homes are safe and without fear,
    nor is the scourge of God upon them.

20, 17: Oil: olive oil, one of the main agricultural products of Palestine, a land proverbially rich in honey and milk.

k: Jb 21, 13; Ps 37, 35f.   l: Jb 14, 10; Ps 37, 10, 36.   m: Jb 27, 14.   n: Eccl 5, 9; Lk 12, 20.   o: Jb 15, 20-35.   p: Dt 32, 22.   q: Jb
27, 13.   r: Jb 13, 17.   s: Jb 12, 6; Pss 37, 35; 73, 3; Eccl 8, 14; Jer 12, 1f; Mal 3, 14f.

¹⁰ Their bulls gender without fail;
    their cows calve and do not miscarry.
¹¹ These folk have infants numerous as
        lambs,
    and their children dance.
¹² They sing to the timbrel and harp,
    and make merry to the sound of the
        flute.
¹³ They live out their days in prosperity,
    and tranquilly go down to the nether
        world.ᵗ
¹⁴ Yet they say to God, "Depart from us,ᵘ
    for we have no wish to learn your
        ways!
¹⁵ What is the Almighty that we should
        serve him?
    And what gain shall we have if we
        pray to him?"ᵛ
¹⁶ If their happiness is not in their own
        hands
    and if the counsel of the wicked is
        repulsive to God,ʷ
¹⁷ How often is the lamp of the wicked put
        out?
    How often does destruction come
        upon them,
    the portion he allots in his anger?

¹⁸ Let them be like straw before the wind,
    and like chaff which the storm
        snatches away!
¹⁹ May God not store up the man's misery
        for his children;
    let him requite the man himself so that
        he feels it,
²⁰ Let his own eyes see the calamity,
    and the wrath of the Almighty let him
        drink!
²¹ For what interest has he in his family
        after him,
    when the number of his months is
        finished?

²³ One dies in his full vigor,
    wholly at ease and content;
²⁴ His figure is full and nourished,
    and his bones are rich in marrow.
²⁵ Another dies in bitterness of soul,

having never tasted happiness.
²⁶ Alike they lie down in the dust,
    and worms cover them both.

²⁷ Behold, I know your thoughts,
    and the arguments you rehearse
        against me.
²⁸ For you say, "Where is the house of the
        magnate,
    and where the dwelling place of the
        wicked?"
²⁹ Have you not asked the wayfarers
    and do you not recognize their
        monuments?
³⁰ Nay, the evil man is spared calamity
        when it comes;
³² and on the day he is carried to the grave
³¹ Who will charge him with his conduct to
        his face,
    and for what he has done who will
        repay him?
³³ Sweet to him are the clods of the valley,
    and over him the funeral mound keeps
        watch,
    While all the line of mankind follows him,
    and the countless others who have
        gone before.
³⁴ How then can you offer me vain comfort,
    while in your answers perfidy remains?

IV: Third Cycle of Speeches
CHAPTER 22

See RG 236–43

Eliphaz's Third Speech. ¹Then Eliphaz the Temanite answered and said:

² Can a man be profitable to God?ˣ
    Though to himself a wise man be
        profitable!
²² Can anyone teach God knowledge,
    seeing that he judges those on high?*
³ Is it of advantage to the Almighty if you
        are just?ʸ
    Or is it a gain to him if you make your
        ways perfect?
⁴ Is it because of your piety that he
        reproves you—
    that he enters with you into judgment?

21, 22: Those on high: the angels. (This verse has been transposed from ch 21.)

t: Jb 34, 20. *u:* Jb 22, 17. *v:* Mal 3, 14. *w:* Jb 22, 18. *x:* Jb 9, 2. *y:* Jb 35, 7.

5 Is not your wickedness manifold?
  Are not your iniquities endless?

6 You have unjustly kept your kinsmen's
      goods in pawn,*
  left them stripped naked of their
      clothing.ᶻ

7 To the thirsty you have given no water to
      drink,
  and from the hungry you have
      withheld bread;

8 As if the land belonged to the man of
      might,
  and only the privileged were to dwell
      in it.

9 You have sent widows away empty-
      handed,
  and the resources of orphans you have
      destroyed.ᵃ

10 Therefore snares are round about you,ᵇ
   and a sudden terror causes you dismay,

11 Or darkness, in which you cannot see;
   a deluge of waters covers you.

12 Does not God, in the heights of the
       heavens,ᶜ
   behold the stars, high though they are?

13 Yet you say, "What does God know?ᵈ
   Can he judge through the thick
       darkness?

14 Clouds hide him so that he cannot see;
   he walks upon the vault of the
       heavens!"

15 Do you indeed keep to the ancient way
   trodden by worthless men,

16 Who were snatched away before their
       time;
   whose foundations a flood swept
       away?

17 These men said to God, "Depart from us!"
   and, "What can the Almighty do
       to us?"

18 [Yet he had filled their houses with good
       things!ᵉ
   But far be from me the mind of the
       impious!]*

19 The just look on and are gladdened,
   and the innocent deride them:ᶠ

20 "Truly these have been destroyed where
       they stood,
   and such as were left, fire has
       consumed!"

21 Come to terms with him to be at peace.
   In this shall good come to you:

22 Receive instruction from his mouth,
   and lay up his words in your heart.

23 If you return to the Almighty, you will
       be restored;
   if you put iniquity far from your tent,

24 And treat raw gold like dust,
   and the fine gold of Ophir* as pebbles
       from the brook,

25 Then the Almighty himself shall be your
       gold
   and your sparkling silver.

26 For then you shall delight in the
       Almighty
   and you shall lift up your face toward
       God.

27 You shall entreat him and he will hear
       you,ᵍ
   and your vows you shall fulfill.

28 When you make a decision, it shall
       succeed for you,
   and upon your ways the light shall
       shine.

29 For he brings down the pride of the
       haughty,
   but the man of humble mien he
       saves.ʰ

30 God delivers him who is innocent;
   you shall be delivered through
       cleanness of hands.ⁱ

22, 6ff: This criticism of Job by Eliphaz is altogether untrue, but it is made to dramatize the latter's argument that God always acts justly when he causes someone to suffer. Verse 8 is misplaced.

22, 18: A gloss, taken partly from Jb 21, 16.

22, 24: Ophir: cf note to Ps 45, 10.

---

z: Jb 24, 3; Dt 24, 6, 17; Ez 18, 12, 16. a: Dt 24, 17; 27, 19. b: Jb 18, 8ff. c: Jb 11, 8. d: 13f; Pss 10, 11; 73, 11; 94, 7; Is 29, 15; Ez 8, 12: 9, 9. e: Jb 21, 16. f: Ps 107, 42. g: Jb 33, 26. h: Ps 138, 6; Prv 29, 23; Mt 23, 12; Lk 1, 52; Jas 4, 10; 1 Pt 5, 5. i: Jb 17.9; Ps 18, 21, 25.

CHAPTER 23

See RG
236-43

Job's Seventh Reply. [1] Again Job answered and said:

[2] Though I know my complaint is bitter,
    his hand is heavy upon me in my
        groanings.
[3] Oh, that today I might find him,
    that I might come to his judgment
        seat!
[4] I would set out my cause before him,
    and fill my mouth with arguments;
[5] I would learn the words with which he
        would answer,
    and understand what he would reply to
        me.
[6] Even should he contend against me with
        his great power,
    yet, would that he himself might heed
        me!
[7] There the upright man might reason with
        him,
    and I should once and for all preserve
        my rights.

[8] But if I go to the east, he is not there;
    or to the west, I cannot perceive him;
[9] Where the north enfolds him, I behold
        him not;
    by the south he is veiled, and I see him
        not.
[10] Yet he knows my way;
    if he proved me, I should come forth
        as gold.[j]
[11] My foot has always walked in his steps;
    his way I have kept and have not
        turned aside.
[12] From the commands of his lips I have not
        departed;
    the words of his mouth I have
        treasured in my heart.
[13] But he has decided, and who can say him
        nay?
    What he desires, that he does.[k]
[14] For he will carry out what is appointed
        for me;

and many such things may yet be in
    his mind.

[15] Therefore am I dismayed before him;
    when I take thought, I fear him.
[16] Indeed God has made my courage fail;
    the Almighty has put me in dismay.
[17] Yes, would that I had vanished in
        darkness,
    and that thick gloom were before me
        to conceal me.

CHAPTER 24

See RG
236-43

[1] Why are not times set by the
        Almighty,
    and why do his friends not see his days?*
[2] The wicked remove landmarks;
    they steal away herds and pasture
        them.
[3] The asses of orphans they drive away;
    they take the widow's ox for a
        pledge.
[4] They force the needy off the road;
    all the poor of the land are driven into
        hiding.
[5] Like wild asses in the desert, these go
        forth
    to their task of seeking food;
The steppe provides food for the young
        among them;
[6]   they harvest at night in the untilled
        land.
[7] They pass the night naked, without
        clothing,
    for they have no covering against the
        cold;
[8] They are drenched with the rain of the
        mountains,
    and for want of shelter they cling to
        the rock.
[11] Between the rows they press out the oil;
    they glean in the vineyard of the
        wicked.
They tread the wine presses, yet suffer
        thirst,
[10]   and famished are those who carry the
        sheaves.

24, 1: Why does not God favor his friends by the speedy punishment of his enemies? (The text and order of verses in this chapter are not certain; note the omission of v 9 which duplicates words of vv 2-4.)

j: Ps 66, 10; Prv 17, 3; Mal 3, 3; 1 Pt 1, 7. *k:* Jb 42, 2; Pss 115, 3; 135, 6.

12 From the dust the dying groan,
  and the souls of the wounded cry out
  [yet God does not treat it as
    unseemly].

13 There are those who are rebels against
    the light;[l]
  they know not its ways;
  they abide not in its paths.

14 When there is no light the murderer rises,
  to kill the poor and needy.

15 The eye of the adulterer watches for the
    twilight;[m]
  he says, "No eye will see me."
  In the night the thief roams about,
  and he puts a mask over his face;

16 in the dark he breaks into houses.
  By day they shut themselves in;
  none of them know the light,

17 for daylight they regard as darkness.*

* * *

18 Their portion in the land is accursed,

20 and wickedness is splintered like
    wood.

19.21 . . . .

22 To him who rises without assurance of
    his life

23 he gives safety and support.
  He sustains the mighty by his strength,
  and his eyes are on their ways.

24 They are exalted for a while, and then
    they are gone;
  they are laid low and, like all others,
    are gathered up;
  like ears of grain they shrivel.

* * *

25 If this be not so, who will confute me,
  and reduce my argument to nought?

CHAPTER 25

See RG 236–43

Bildad's Third Speech. [1]Then Bildad
the Shuhite answered and said:

2 Dominion and awesomeness are his
  who brings about harmony in his
    heavens.

3 Is there any numbering of his troops?*
  Yet to which of them does not his light
    extend?

4 How can a man be just in God's sight,[n]
  or how can any woman's child be
    innocent?

5 Behold, even the moon is not bright
  and the stars are not clear in his sight.

6 How much less man, who is but a
    maggot,
  the son of man, who is only a worm?[o]

CHAPTER 26

See RG 236–43

Job's Reply. [1]Then Job spoke again
and said:*

2 What help you give to the powerless,
  what strength to the feeble arm!

3 How you counsel, as though he had no
    wisdom;
  how profuse is the advice you offer!

4 With whose help have you uttered those
    words,
  and whose is the breath that comes
    forth from you?[p]

5 The shades* beneath writhe in terror,[q]
  the waters, and their inhabitants.

6 Naked before him is the nether world,*
  and Abaddon has no covering.[r]

7 He stretches out the North* over empty
    space,
  and suspends the earth over nothing at all;

those who are rebels against the light.

24, 17: The asterisks which follow this verse mark off a
passage (vv 18-24) which cannot be ascribed to Job with certainty. Vv 17-24 are in general poorly preserved; and much of
vv 18-21 has not been translated because these verses are obscure. St. Jerome renders them as follows: (18) "He is light
upon the face of the water, cursed be his portion on the earth;
let him not walk by the way of vineyards. (19) Let him pass
from the snow waters to excessive heat, and his sin even to
hell. (20) Let mercy forget him; may worms be his sweetness;
let him be remembered no more, but be broken in pieces as an
unfruitful tree. (21) For he has fed the barren that bears not,
and to the widow he has done no good."

25, 3: His troops: the heavenly hosts, the stars or
the angels. His light: compare the wording in Jb 24, 13:

26, 1-14: Probably to be read as Job's reply to Bildad's
short speech. Some, however, would make it the reply to Zophar (Jb 27, 13-21); it would thus lead up to the poem of ch 28.

26, 5: Shades: the dead in Sheol, the nether world; cf Pss
6, 6; 88, 11.

26, 6: Nether world: cf note to Ps 6, 6. Abaddon: Hebrew
for "(place of) destruction," a synonym for nether world: cf
Jb 28, 22; Rv 9, 11.

26, 7: The North: used here as a synonym for the firmament, the heavens; cf Is 14, 13.

l: Jn 3, 19f. *m:* Prv 7, 9f. *n:* Jb 4, 17ff; 9, 2. *o:* Jb 4, 19; 15,
16. *p:* Gn 2, 7. *q:* Prv 9, 18. *r:* Ps 139, 7-12.

8 He binds up the waters in his clouds,
  yet the cloud is not rent by their weight;
9 He holds back the appearance of the full moon
  by spreading his clouds before it.

10 He has marked out a circle* on the surface of the deep^s
  as the boundary of light and darkness.
11 The pillars of the heavens tremble^t
  and are stunned at his thunderous rebuke;
12 By his power he stirs up the sea,
  and by his might he crushes Rahab;*
13 With his angry breath he scatters the water,
  and he hurls the lightning against it relentlessly;
  His hand pierces the fugitive dragon*
  as from his hand it strives to flee.^u
14 Lo, these are but the outlines of his ways,
  and how faint is the word we hear!

CHAPTER 27

See RG 236-43

Job's Reply

1^1 I will teach you the manner of God's dealings,
  and the way of the Almighty I will not conceal.
2 As God lives,* who withholds my deserts,^v
  the Almighty, who has made bitter my soul,
3 So long as I still have life in me
  and the breath of God is in my nostrils,
4 My lips shall not speak falsehood,
  nor my tongue utter deceit!
5 Far be it from me to account you right;
  till I die I will not renounce my innocence.^w
6 My justice I maintain and I will not relinquish it;
  my heart does not reproach me for any of my days.

7 Let my enemy be as the wicked
  and my adversary as the unjust!
8 For what can the impious man expect when he is cut off,
  when God requires his life?
9 Will God then attend to his cry
  when calamity comes upon him?
10 Will he then delight in the Almighty
  and call upon him constantly?
12 Behold, you yourselves have all seen it;
  why then do you spend yourselves in idle words!

* * *

13 *This is the portion of a wicked man from God,
  the inheritance an oppressor receives from the Almighty:^x
14 Though his children be many, the sword is their destiny.
  His offspring shall not be filled with bread.
15 His survivors, when they die, shall have no burial,
  and their widows shall not be mourned.
16 Though he heap up silver like dust
  and store away mounds of clothing,
17 What he has stored the just man shall wear,
  and the innocent shall divide the silver.
18 He builds his house as of cobwebs,
  or like a booth put up by the vinekeeper.
19 He lies down a rich man, one last time;
  he opens his eyes and nothing remains to him.^y
20 Terrors rush upon him by day;
  at night the tempest carries him off.
21 The storm wind seizes him and he disappears;
  it sweeps him out of his place.*

* * *

26, 10: Circle: the horizon of the ocean which serves as the boundary for the activity of light and darkness.

26, 12: Rahab: cf Jb 9, 13; see note on Ps 89, 11.

26, 13: The fugitive dragon: the same term occurs in Is 27, 1 in apposition to Leviathan; see note on Jb 3, 8. This is actually Jb 27, 22.

27, 2-12: This is probably to be read as Job's reply to Zophar's speech of Jb 27, 13-21. In the current Hebrew text the heading for this chapter (Jb 27, 1, here omitted) is identical with Jb 29, 1; we should expect rather such a heading as is Jb 21, 1; 23, 1; 26, 1.

27, 13-21: This is probably to be read as Zophar's third speech. The asterisks are present to indicate it is not likely that the sacred writer intended these words to be ascribed to Job.

27, 21: The Hebrew has two more verses: v 22 (read above with Jb 26, 13); and v 23, which is a variant form of v 21.

s: Jb 38, 8-11; Prv 8, 29.   t: Jb 9, 6.   u: Is 27, 1.   v: Jb 34, 5.
w: Jb 2, 3, 9; 13, 15; 33, 9.   x: Jb 20, 4-29.   y: Pss 49, 18; 76, 6.

See RG
236–43

CHAPTER 28

The Inaccessibility of Wisdom

1 There is indeed a mine for silver,*
  and a place for gold which men refine.
2 Iron is taken from the earth,
  and copper is melted out of stone.
4 . . . .
5 The earth, though out of it comes forth
    bread,
  is in fiery upheaval underneath.
6 Its stones are the source of sapphires,
  and there is gold in its dust.

12 But whence can wisdom be obtained,
  and where is the place of
    understanding?ᶻ
13 Man knows nothing to equal it,
  nor is it to be had in the land of the
    living.
15 Solid gold cannot purchase it,
  nor can its price be paid with silver.ᵃ
16 It cannot be bought with gold of Ophir,*
  with the precious onyx or the sapphire.
17 Gold or crystal cannot equal it,
  nor can golden vessels reach its worth.
18 Neither coral nor jasper should be
    thought of;
  it surpasses pearls and 19 Arabian
  topaz.

20 Whence, then, comes wisdom,
  and where is the place of
    understanding?
21 It is hid from the eyes of any beast;
  from the birds of the air it is
    concealed.
7 The path to it no bird of prey knows,
  nor has the hawk's eye seen that path.
8 The proud beasts have not trodden it,
  nor has the lion gone that way.
14 The abyss declares, "It is not in me";
  and the sea says, "I have it not."

22 Abaddon* and Death say,
  "Only by rumor have we heard of it."
23 God knows the way to it;ᵇ
  it is he who is familiar with its place.ᶜ
24 For he beholds the ends of the earth
  and sees all that is under the heavens.
3 He has set a boundary for the darkness;
  to the farthest confines he penetrates.
9 He sets his hand to the flinty rock,
  and overturns the mountains at their
    foundations.
10 He splits channels in the rocks;
  his eyes behold all that is precious.
11 He probes the wellsprings of the streams,
  and brings hidden things to light.
25 He has weighed out the wind,
  and fixed the scope of the waters;
26 When he made rules for the rain
  and a path for the thunderbolts,ᵈ
27 Then he saw wisdom and appraised it,
  gave it its setting, knew it through and
    through.
28 And to man he said:
  Behold, the fear of the LORD is wisdom;
  and avoiding evil is understanding.ᵉ

V: Job's Final Summary
of His Cause

CHAPTER 29

See RG
236–43

1 Job took up his theme anew and said:

2 Oh, that I were as in the months
    past!
  as in the days when God watched over
    me,ᶠ
3 While he kept his lamp shining above my
    head,
  and by his light I walked through
    darkness;
4 As I was in my flourishing days,
  when God sheltered my tent;

28, 1-28: Note the changed order of verses; v 4 is uncertain.

This chapter contains a beautifully vivid description of that Wisdom which is beyond the attainment of creatures; known only to God, it is reflected in the order and majesty of his creation. Man, however, can, in a way, participate in this Wisdom by fearing the Lord and avoiding evil. Scholars are not agreed regarding the authorship of this poem, though it is altogether worthy of the author of the Book of Job. Used here as a counterpoise to ch 3 at the beginning of the dialogue, it may have been first conceived as an independent poem.

28, 16: Ophir: cf note to Ps 45, 10.
28, 22: Abaddon: cf note to Jb 26, 6.

---

z: Eccl 7, 24f; Bar 3, 14f. 29-33. a: Prv 3, 14; 8, 10f, 19; 16, 16; Wis 7, 7-11. b: 23-27: Prv 8, 22-31. c: Prv 2, 6; Sir 1, 1; Jas 1, 5. d: Jb 38, 25; Prv 3, 20. e: Ps 111, 10; Prv 1, 7; 9, 10; Sir 1, 16. f: Jb 1, 10.

5 When the Almighty was yet with me,
  and my children were round about me;
6 When my footsteps were bathed in milk,
  and the rock flowed with streams of
    oil;*
7 When I went forth to the gate of the city
  and set up my seat in the square—

8 Then the young men saw me and
    withdrew,
  while the elders rose up and stood;
9 The chief men refrained from speaking
  and covered their mouths with their
    hands;*
10 The voice of the princes was silenced,
  and their tongues stuck to the roofs of
    their mouths.

21 For me they listened and waited;
  they were silent for my counsel.
22 Once I spoke, they said no more,
  but received my pronouncement drop
    by drop.
23 They waited for me as for the rain;
  they drank in my words like the spring
    rains.

24 When I smiled on them they were
    reassured;
25 mourners took comfort from my
    cheerful glance.
  I chose out their way and presided;
  I took a king's place in the armed
    forces.
11 Whoever heard of me blessed me;
  those who saw me commended me.

12 For I rescued the poor who cried out for
    help,
  the orphans, and the unassisted;
13 The blessing of those in extremity came
    upon me,
  and the heart of the widow I made
    joyful.

14 I wore my honesty like a garment;
  justice was my robe and my turban.
15 I was eyes to the blind,
  and feet to the lame was I;
16 I was a father to the needy;
  the rights of the stranger I studied,
17 And I broke the jaws of the wicked man;
  from his teeth I forced the prey.

18 Then I said: "In my own nest I shall grow
    old;
  I shall multiply years like the
    phoenix.*
19 My root is spread out to the waters;
  the dew rests by night on my branches.
20 My glory is fresh within me,
  and my bow is renewed in my hand!"

CHAPTER 30

See RG
236–43

1 But now they hold me in derision
  who are younger in years than I;*
  Whose fathers I should have disdained
  to rank with the dogs of my flock.
2 Such strength as they had, to me meant
    nought;
  they were utterly destitute.

3 In want and hunger was their lot,*
  they who fled to the parched
    wastelands:
4 They plucked saltwort* and shrubs;
  the roots of the broom plant were their
    food.
5 They were banished from among men,
  with an outcry like that against a
    thief—
6 To dwell on the slopes of the wadies,
  in caves of sand and stone;
7 Among the bushes they raised their
    raucous cry;
  under the nettles they huddled
    together.
8 Irresponsible, nameless men,
  they were driven out of the land.

29, 6: Hyperbole to express abundance; see note on Jb 20, 17.
29, 18: Phoenix: a legendary bird which, after several centuries of life, consumed itself in fire, then rose from its ashes in youthful freshness. This meaning, originally intended in the Greek, later came to mean "palm tree." Some render the Hebrew as "sand."

30, 4: Saltwort: found in salt marshes and very sour to the taste; eaten by the extremely poor as a cooked vegetable. Broom plant: the juniper or brushwood; cf Ps 120, 4; a figure of bitterness and poverty, because of its bitter-tasting roots which are practically inedible.

g: Wis 8, 10ff. h: Jb 12, 4; 19, 18. i: 3-8: Jb 24, 5f.

9 Yet now they sing of me in mockery;
  I am become a byword among them.*j*

10 They abhor me, they stand aloof from
  me,
  they do not hesitate to spit in my face!

11 Indeed, they have loosed their bonds;
  they lord it over me,
  and have thrown off restraint in my
  presence.

12 To subvert my paths they rise up;
  they build their approaches for my
  ruin.

13 To destroy me, they attack with none to
  stay them;

14 as through a wide breach they
  advance.
  Amid the uproar they come on in waves;

15 over me rolls the terror.
  My dignity is borne off on the wind,
  and my welfare vanishes like a cloud.

18 One with great power lays hold of my
  clothing;*
  by the collar of my tunic he seizes me:

19 He has cast me into the mire;
  I am leveled with the dust and ashes.

20 I cry to you, but you do not answer me;*k*
  you stand off and look at me,

21 Then you turn upon me without mercy
  and with your strong hand you buffet
  me.

22 You raise me up and drive me before the
  wind;
  I am tossed about by the tempest.

23 Indeed I know you will turn me back in
  death
  to the destined place of everyone alive.*l*

24 Yet should not a hand be held out
  to help a wretched man in his
  calamity?

25 Or have I not wept for the hardships of
  others;
  was not my soul grieved for the
  destitute?*m*

26 Yet when I looked for good, then evil
  came;

when I expected light, then came
  darkness.

16 My soul ebbs away from me;

27 days of affliction have overtaken me.

17 My frame takes no rest by night;
  my inward parts seethe and will not be
  stilled.

28 I go about in gloom, without the sun;
  I rise up in public to voice my grief.

29 I have become the brother of jackals,
  companion to the ostrich.

30 My blackened skin falls away from me;
  the heat scorches my very frame.

31 My harp is turned to mourning,
  and my reed pipe to sounds of
  weeping.

CHAPTER 31

See RG
236–43

2 But what is man's lot from God
  above,
  his inheritance from the Almighty on
  high?

3 Is it not calamity for the unrighteous,
  and woe for evildoers?

4 Does he not see my ways,
  and number all my steps?*n*

6 Let God weigh me in the scales of justice;
  thus will he know my innocence!*o*

5 If I have walked in falsehood*
  and my foot has hastened to deceit;

7 If my steps have turned out of the way,
  and my heart has followed my eyes,
  or any stain clings to my hands,

8 Then may I sow, but another eat of it,
  or may my planting be rooted up!

38 If my land has cried out against me
  till its very furrows complained;

39 If I have eaten its produce without
  payment
  and grieved the hearts of its tenants;

40 Then let the thistles grow instead of
  wheat
  and noxious weeds instead of barley!

30, 18-23: Job here refers to God's stern treatment of him.
31, 5-34: Job's final protestation of his innocence.

j: Jb 17, 6. *k:* Jb 19, 7. *l:* Heb 9, 27. *m:* Jb 29, 12-16. *n:* Jb 14, 16; 34, 21; Ps 139, 3; Prv 5, 21. *o:* Jb 23, 10.

¹ If I have made an agreement with my
  eyes*
  and entertained any thoughts against a
  maiden;
⁹ If my heart has been enticed toward a
  woman,
  and I have lain in wait at my
  neighbor's door;
¹⁰ Then may my wife grind for another,
  and may others cohabit with her!

¹¹ For that would be heinous,
  a crime to be condemned;ᵖ
¹² A fire that should burn down to the abyss
  till it consumed all my possessions to
  the roots.�q
¹³ Had I refused justice to my manservant
  or to my maid, when they had a claim
  against me,
¹⁴ What then should I do when God rose
  up;
  what could I answer when he
  demanded an account?
¹⁵ Did not he who made me in the womb
  make him?
  Did not the same One fashion us
  before our birth?

¹⁶ If I have denied anything to the poor,ʳ
  or allowed the eyes of the widow to
  languish
¹⁷ While I ate my portion alone,
  with no share in it for the fatherless,
¹⁸ Though like a father God has reared me
  from my youth,
  guiding me even from my mother's
  womb—
¹⁹ If I have seen a wanderer without clothing,
  or a poor man without covering,
²⁰ Whose limbs have not blessed me
  when warmed with the fleece of my
  sheep;
²¹ If I have raised my hand against the
  innocent

because I saw that I had supporters at
  the gate—*
²² Then may my arm fall from the shoulder,
  my forearm be broken at the elbow!
²³ For the dread of God will be upon me,
  and his majesty will overpower me.
²⁴ Had I put my trust in gold
  or called fine gold my security;
²⁵ Or had I rejoiced that my wealth was great,
  or that my hand had acquired
  abundance—
²⁶ Had I looked upon the sun as it shone,ˢ
  or the moon in the splendor of its
  progress,*
²⁷ And had my heart been secretly enticed
  to waft them a kiss with my hand;
²⁸ This too would be a crime for
  condemnation,
  for I should have denied God above.ᵗ

²⁹ Had I rejoiced at the destruction of my
  enemy
  or exulted when evil fell upon him,ᵘ
³⁰ Even though I had not suffered my
  mouth to sin
  by uttering a curse against his life—

³¹ Had not the men of my tent exclaimed,
  "Who has not been fed with his meat!"*
³² Because no stranger lodged in the street,
  but I opened my door to wayfarers—

³³ Had I, out of human weakness, hidden
  my sins
  and buried my guilt in my bosom*
³⁴ Because I feared the noisy multitude
  and the scorn of the tribes terrified
  me—
  then I should have remained silent,
  and not come out of doors!

³⁵ Oh, that I had one to hear my case,
  and that my accuser would write out
  his indictment!ᵛ

31, 1. 9: Note the gradation: avoidance of sinful glances and thoughts against a maiden; desire for another's wife.

31, 21: Gate: cf notes on Jb 5, 4; Ru 4, 1.

31, 26ff: Job never sinned by worshiping the sun or the moon; waft them a kiss: an act of idolatrous worship.

31, 31: The members of his household will testify to his hospitality.

31, 33f: Job's present protest is made, not in spite of hidden sins which he had been unwilling to disclose, but out of genuine innocence.

p: Ex 20, 14; Lv 20, 10; Dt 22, 22.   q: Sir 9, 8f.   r: 16-23: Jb 29, 12-16.   s: 26f: Dt 4, 19.   t: Dt 17, 2-7.   u: Prv 24, 17.   v: Jb 19, 23; 23, 3-7.

³⁶ Surely, I should wear it on my shoulder*
  or put it on me like a diadem;
³⁷ Of all my steps I should give him an
  account;
    like a prince* I should present myself
    before him.

This is my final plea; let the Almighty answer me!
The words of Job are ended.

VI: Elihu's Speeches

CHAPTER 32

See RG
236–43

¹Then the three men ceased to answer Job, because he was righteous^w in his own eyes. ²*But the anger of Elihu,* son of Barachel the Buzite, of the family of Ram, was kindled. He was angry with Job for considering himself rather than God to be in the right. ³^yHe was angry also with the three friends because they had not found a good answer and had not condemned Job. ⁴But since these men were older than he, Elihu bided his time before addressing Job. ⁵When, however, Elihu saw that there was no reply in the mouths of the three men, his wrath was inflamed. ⁶So Elihu, son of Barachel the Buzite, spoke out and said:

  I am young and you are very old;
    therefore I held back and was afraid
    to declare to you my knowledge.
⁷ Days should speak, I thought,
    and many years teach wisdom!^z
⁸ But it is a spirit in man,^a
    the breath of the Almighty, that gives
    him understanding.
⁹ It is not those of many days who are
    wise,
    nor the aged who understand the
    right.
¹⁰ Therefore I say, hearken to me;
    let me too set forth my knowledge!

¹¹ Behold, I have waited for your
    discourses,
    and have given ear to your arguments.
¹² Yes, I followed you attentively
    as you searched out what to say;
  And behold, there is none who has
    convicted Job,
    not one of you who could refute his
    statements.
¹³ Yet do not say, "We have met wisdom.*
    God may vanquish him but not man!"
¹⁴ For had he addressed his words to me,
    I should not then have answered him
    as you have done.

¹⁵ They are dismayed, they make no more
    reply;
    words fail them.
¹⁶ Must I wait? Now that they speak no
    more,
    and have ceased to make reply,
¹⁷ I too will speak my part;
    I also will show my knowledge!
¹⁸ For I am full of matters to utter;
    the spirit within me compels me.
¹⁹ Like a new wineskin with wine under
    pressure,
    my bosom is ready to burst.
²⁰ Let me speak and obtain relief;
    let me open my lips, and make reply.
²¹ I would not be partial to anyone,
    nor give flattering titles to any.
²² For I know nought of flattery;
    if I did, my Maker would soon take me
    away.

CHAPTER 33

See RG
236–43

¹ Therefore, O Job, hear my discourse,
    and hearken to all my words.
² Behold, now I open my mouth;
    my tongue and my voice form words.
³ I will state directly what is in my mind,

31, 36: On my shoulder: i.e., boldly, proudly.

31, 37: Like a prince: not as a frightened criminal. Final plea: literally, "tau," the last letter of the Hebrew alphabet; in the current Hebrew text this line is in v 35, while the following one ends v 40.

32, 2: Elihu means "My God is he." This speaker was from Buz, which, according to Jer 25, 23, was near Tema and Dedan. A young man, he impetuously and impatiently upbraids Job for his boldness toward God, and the three friends

for not successfully answering Job. He undertakes to defend God's absolute justice and to explain more clearly why there is suffering. While fundamentally his position is the same as that of the three friends, he does locate more definitely, though not perfectly, the place of suffering in the divine plan.

32, 13: Met wisdom: in Job's arguments.

w: Jb 33, 9.   x: Jb 13, 18; 27, 6; 34, 5; 35, 2.   y: Jb 22, 5.   z: Jb 12, 12.   a: Jb 33, 4.

my lips shall utter knowledge
  sincerely;
4 For the spirit of God has made me,
  the breath of the Almighty keeps me
  alive.b

5 If you are able, refute me;
  draw up your arguments and stand
  forth.
6 Behold I, like yourself, have been taken
  from the same clay by God.c
7 Therefore no fear of me should dismay
  you,
  nor should my presence weigh heavily
  upon you.

8 But you have said in my hearing,
  as I listened to the sound of your
  words:
9 "I am clean and without transgression;
  I am innocent; there is no guilt in me.d
10 Yet he invents pretexts against me
  and reckons me as his enemy.e
11 He puts my feet in the stocks;
  he watches all my ways!"f

12 In this you are not just, let me tell you;
  for God is greater than man.
13 Why, then, do you make complaint
  against him
  that he gives no account of his
  doings?g
14 For God does speak, perhaps once,
  or even twice, though one perceive it
  not.

15 In a dream, in a vision of the night,
  [when deep sleep falls upon men]
  as they slumber in their beds,
16 It is then he opens the ears of men
  and as a warning to them, terrifies
  them;
17 By turning man from evil
  and keeping pride away from him,
18 He withholds his soul from the pit
  and his life from passing to the grave.

19 Or a man is chastened on his bed by pain
  and unceasing suffering within his
  frame,
20 So that to his appetite food becomes
  repulsive,
  and his senses reject the choicest
  nourishment.h
21 His flesh is wasted so that it cannot be
  seen,
  and his bones, once invisible, appear;
22 His soul draws near to the pit,
  his life to the place of the dead.

23 If then there be for him an angel,*
  one out of a thousand, a mediator,
  To show him what is right for him
  and bring the man back to justice,
24 He will take pity on him and say,
  "Deliver him from going down to the
  pit;
  I have found him a ransom."
25 Then his flesh shall become soft as a boy's;
  he shall be again as in the days of his
  youth.
26 He shall pray and God will favor him;
  he shall see God's face with rejoicing.i
27 He shall sing before men and say,
  "I sinned and did wrong,
  yet he has not punished me
  accordingly.
28 He delivered my soul from passing to the
  pit,
  and I behold the light of life."

29 Lo, all these things God does,
  twice, or thrice, for a man,
30 Bringing back his soul from the pit
  to the light, in the land of the living.
31 Be attentive, O Job; listen to me!
  Be silent and I will speak.
32 If you have aught to say, then answer me.
  Speak out! I should like to see you
  justified.
33 If not, then do you listen to me;
  be silent while I teach you wisdom.

33, 23: Angel: one of the thousands who stand between God and man as intermediaries, reminding man of his duties and giving God an account of their fulfillment.

b: Jb 32, 8.   c: Jb 31, 15.   d: Jb 10, 7; 13, 18; 27, 5f; 29, 14; 32, 1; 34, 5.   e: Jb 13, 24; 19, 11.   f: Jb 13, 27; 31, 4.   g: Jb 31, 35.
h: Jb 6, 7.   i: Jb 22, 26-29.

CHAPTER 34

See RG
236-43

¹Then Elihu continued and said:

² Hear, O wise men, my discourse,
and you that have knowledge, hear
me!
³ For the ear tests words,
as the taste does food.ʲ
⁴ Let us discern for ourselves what is
right;
let us learn between us what is good.
⁵ For Job has said, "I am innocent,
but God has taken what is my due.ᵏ
⁶ Notwithstanding my right I am set at
nought;
in my wound the arrow rankles, sinless
though I am."ˡ

⁷ What man is like Job?
He drinks in blasphemies like water,
⁸ Keeps company with evildoers
and goes along with wicked men,
⁹ When he says, "It profits a man nought
that he is pleasing to God."ᵐ

¹⁰ Therefore, men of understanding,
hearken to me:
far be it from God to do wickedness;
far from the Almighty to do wrong!ⁿ
¹¹ Rather, he requites men for their conduct,
and brings home to a man his way of
life.ᵒ
¹² Surely, God cannot act wickedly,
the Almighty cannot violate justice.ᵖ
¹³ Who gave him government over the
earth,
or who else set all the land in its
place?�q
¹⁴ If he were to take back his spirit to
himself,
withdraw to himself his breath,
¹⁵ All flesh would perish together,
and man would return to the dust.ʳ

¹⁶ Now, do you, O Job, hear this!
Hearken to the words I speak!

¹⁷ Can an enemy of justice indeed be in
control,
or will you condemn the supreme Just
One,
¹⁸ Who says to a king, "You are worthless!"
and to nobles, "You are wicked!"
¹⁹ Who neither favors the person of princes,
nor respects the rich more than the
poor?
For they are all the work of his hands;ˢ
²⁰ in a moment they die, even at
midnight.ᵗ
He brings on nobles, and takes them
away,
removing the powerful without lifting
a hand;
²¹ For his eyes are upon the ways of man,
and he beholds all his steps.

²² There is no darkness so dense
that evildoers can hide in it.
²⁵ Therefore he discerns their works;
he turns at night and crushes them.
²³ For he forewarns no man of his time
to come before God in judgment.
²⁴ Without a trial he breaks the mighty,ᵘ
and sets others in their stead,
²⁷ Because they turned away from him
and heeded none of his ways,
²⁸ But caused the cries of the poor to reach
him,
so that he heard the plea of the
afflicted.

²⁹ If he remains tranquil, who then can
condemn?*
If he hides his face, who then can
behold him?
³⁰ . . . .
³¹ When anyone says to God,
"I was misguided; I will offend no
more.
³² Teach me wherein I have sinned;
if I have done wrong, I will do so no
more,"

34, 26. 29f: The extant Hebrew text of these verses contains several added phrases which either represent duplication or are very obscure.

---

j: Jb 12, 11.   *k:* Jb 33, 9f.   *l:* Jb 9, 20.   *m:* Jb 9, 22f. 30f; 21, 15; 35, 3.   *n:* Jb 36, 23.   *o:* Ps 62, 13; Prv 24, 12; Mt 16, 27; Rom 2, 6; 2 Cor 5, 10; Rv 22, 12.   *p:* Jb 8, 3.   *q:* Jb 38, 4-7.   *r:* Jb 10, 9.   *s:* Dt 10, 17; 2 Chr 19, 7; Wis 6, 7; Acts 10, 34; Rom 2, 11; Eph 6, 9; Col 3, 25; 1 Pt 1, 17.   *t:* Jb 21, 3.   *u:* Ps 2, 9.

33 Would you then say that God must
punish,
since you reject what he is doing?
It is you who must choose, not I;
speak, therefore, what you know.

34 Men of understanding will say to me,
every wise man who hears my views:
35 "Job speaks without intelligence,
and his words are without sense."[v]
36 Let Job be tried to the limit,
since his answers are those of the
impious;
37 For he is adding rebellion to his sin
by brushing off our arguments
and addressing many words to God.

CHAPTER 35

See RG 236–43

1 Then Elihu proceeded and said:

2 Do you think it right to say,
"I am just rather than God"?[w]
3 To say, "What does it profit me;
what advantage have I more than if I
had sinned?"[x]
4 I have words for a reply to you*
and your three companions as well.
5 Look up to the skies and behold;
regard the heavens high above you.
6 If you sin, what injury do you do to God?
Even if your offenses are many, how
do you hurt him?
7 If you are righteous, what do you give
him,
or what does he receive from your
hand?[y]
8 Your wickedness can affect only a man
like yourself;
and your justice only a fellow human
being.

9 In great oppression men cry out;
they call for help because of the power
of the mighty,

10 Saying, "Where is God, my Maker,
who has given visions in the night,
11 Taught us rather than the beasts of the
earth,
and made us wise rather than the birds
of the heavens?"
12 Though thus they cry out, he answers not
against the pride of the wicked.
13 But it is idle to say God does not hear
or that the Almighty does not take
notice.
14 Even though you say that you see him
not,*
the case is before him; with trembling
should you wait upon him.
15 But now that you have done otherwise,
God's anger punishes,
nor does he show concern that a man
will die.
16 Yet Job to no purpose opens his mouth,
and without knowledge multiplies
words.[z]

CHAPTER 36

See RG 236–43

1 Elihu proceeded further and said:

2 Wait yet a little and I will instruct you,
for there are still words to be said on
God's behalf.
3 I will bring my knowledge from afar,
and to my Maker I will accord the
right.
4 For indeed, my theme cannot fail me:
the one perfect in knowledge I set
before you.

5 Behold, God rejects the obstinate in
heart;*
he preserves not the life of the wicked,
6 He withholds not the just man's rights,
but grants vindication to the
oppressed[a]
7 And with kings upon thrones
he sets them, exalted forever.[b]

35, 4: A reply to you: Elihu refers to Job's statement that the innocent suffer as much as the wicked, and especially to Eliphaz's words in Jb 22, 2f.

35, 14f: The text here is uncertain. It seems to indicate that Job should have realized God's indifference is only apparent, and that, because he has not done so, God will punish him.

36, 5-21: Perhaps this section should be read between vv 6 and 7 of chapter 34.

v: Jb 35, 16; 38, 2; 42, 3. w: Jb 32, 2. x: Jb 34, 9. y: Jb 22, 3; 41, 2; Lk 17, 10; Rom 11, 35. z: Jb 34, 35; 38, 2; 42, 3. a: Ps 72, 4. 12f. b: Ps 113, 7f.

⁸ Or if they are bound with fetters
 and held fast by bonds of affliction,
⁹ Then he makes known to them what they
  have done
 and their sins of boastful pride.
¹⁰ He opens their ears to correction
 and exhorts them to turn back from
  evil.

¹¹ If they obey and serve him,
 they spend their days in prosperity,
 their years in happiness.
¹² But if they obey not, they perish;
 they die for lack of knowledge.*

¹³ The impious in heart lay up anger for
  themselves;
 they cry not for help when he enchains
  them;
¹⁴ Therefore they expire in youth,
 and perish among the reprobate.*
¹⁵ But he saves the unfortunate through
  their affliction,
 and instructs them through distress.
¹⁶⁻²⁰ . . . .*
²¹ Take heed, turn not to evil;
 for you have preferred carousal to
  affliction.

²² Behold, God is sublime in his power.
 What teacher is there like him?
²³ Who prescribes for him his conduct,
 or who can say, "You have done
  wrong"?ᶜ
²⁴ Remember, you should extol his work,
 which men have praised in song.
²⁵ All men contemplate it;
 man beholds it from afar.

²⁶ Lo, God is great beyond our knowledge;

the number of his years is past
 searching out.
²⁷ He holds in check the waterdrops
 that filter in rain through his mists,
²⁸ Till the skies run with them
 and the showers rain down on
  mankind.
³¹ For by these* he nourishes the nations,
 and gives them food in abundance.
²⁹·³⁰Lo! he spreads the clouds in layers
 as the carpeting of his tent.*
³² In his hands he holds the lightning,
 and he commands it to strike the mark.
³³ His thunder speaks for him
 and incites the fury of the storm.

CHAPTER 37

See RG
236–43

¹ At this my heart trembles
 and leaps out of its place,
² To hear his angry voice*
 as it rumbles forth from his mouth!
³ Everywhere under the heavens he sends
  it,
 with his lightning, to the ends of the
  earth.
⁴ Again his voice roars—
 the majestic sound of his thunder.
⁵ He does great things beyond our
  knowing;
 wonders past our searching out.
⁶ For he says to the snow, "Fall to the
  earth";
 likewise to his heavy, drenching rain.
⁷ He shuts up all mankind indoors;
⁸ the wild beasts take to cover
 and remain quietly in their dens.

⁹ Out of its chamber* comes forth the
  tempest;
 from the north winds, the cold.

36, 12: Knowledge: practical wisdom in serving God, which they lack because they refused it when warned (cf v 10).

36, 14: Reprobate: cf Dt 23, 18f.

36, 16-20: The Hebrew text here is in disorder. The Vulgate has: "(16) Therefore he will give you most ample salvation from the narrow mouth which has no foundations beneath it; but the repose of your table will be filled with fatness. (17) Your case has been judged as that of the wicked; case and judgment you will receive. (18) Let no wrath, then, overcome you, that you oppress anyone; nor let numerous gifts mislead you. (19) Lay down your greatness without

tribulation, and all who are mighty in strength. (20) Do not draw out the night, that people may go in place of them."

36, 31: These: refers to the showers of v 28, if the verse order indicated above is correct.

36, 29f: Because of the uncertainty of the text, no translation of these verses has received unanimous approval from exegetes.

37, 2: Voice: the thunder.

37, 9: Chamber: where it was popularly believed storms were kept enclosed.

___

c: Jb 34, 10; Is 40, 13.

[10] With his breath God brings the frost,
and the broad waters become
congealed.[d]
[11] With hail, also, the clouds are laden,
as they scatter their flashes of light.
[12] He it is who changes their rounds,*
according to his plans,
in their task upon the surface of the earth,
[13] whether for punishment or mercy, as
he commands.

[14] Hearken to this, O Job!
Stand and consider the wondrous
works of God!
[15] Do you know how God lays his
commands upon them,
and makes the light shine forth from
his clouds?
[16] Do you know how the clouds are banked,
the wondrous work of him who is
perfect in knowledge?
[17] You, whom the streams of water fail
when a calm from the south comes
over the land,
[18] Do you spread out with him the
firmament of the skies,
hard as a brazen mirror?*

[19] Teach us then what we shall say to him;
we cannot, for the darkness, make our
plea.
[20] Will he be told about it when I speak,
or when a man says he is being
destroyed?*
[21] Nay, rather, it is as the light which men
see not
while it is obscured among the clouds,
till the wind comes by and sweeps the
clouds away.*

[22] From the North the splendor comes,*
surrounding God's awesome majesty!
[23] The Almighty! we cannot discover him,
pre-eminent in power and judgment;
his great justice owes no one an
accounting.
[24] Therefore men revere him,
though none can see him, however
wise their hearts.

VII: The Lord's Speech

CHAPTER 38

See RG 236-43

[1] Then the LORD* addressed Job out of
the storm and said:

[2] Who is this that obscures divine plans
with words of ignorance?
[3] Gird up your loins* now, like a man;
I will question you, and you tell me the
answers![e]
[4] Where were you when I founded the
earth?
Tell me, if you have understanding.
[5] Who determined its size; do you know?
Who stretched out the measuring line
for it?
[6] Into what were its pedestals sunk,
and who laid the cornerstone,
[7] While the morning stars sang in chorus
and all the sons of God* shouted for
joy?

[8] And who shut within doors the sea,
when it burst forth from the womb;[f]
[9] When I made the clouds its garment
and thick darkness its swaddling bands?
[10] When I set limits for it
and fastened the bar of its door,

37, 12: Their rounds: of rain (Jb 36, 27), of clouds (Jb 36, 29f), of lightning and thunder (Jb 36, 32f), of snow (Jb 37, 6), of winds (Jb 37, 9).

37, 18: The firmament . . . mirror: the ancients thought of the sky as a ceiling above which were the "upper waters" (cf Gn 1, 6f; 7, 11); when this ceiling became as hard as metal, the usual rain failed to fall on the earth (cf Lv 26, 19; Dt 28, 23).

37, 20: Will an angel bring this to God's attention?

37, 21: Even though God seems not to know our circumstances, he does know them, just as surely as the sun shines, unseen by man, behind the clouds.

37, 22: Now the storms of doubt and ignorance disappear, and from the North, used here as a symbol for God's myste-

rious abode, comes the splendor of the manifestation of God's majestic ways.

38, 1: Now the Lord enters the debate and addresses two discourses (38—39 and 40—41) to Job, in which he speaks of his wisdom and power, which are altogether beyond the capacity of Job, who therefore should never dare to demand a reason for the divine actions. Out of the storm: frequently the background of the appearances of the Lord in the Old Testament; cf Pss 18; 50; Na 1, 3; Hb 3.

38, 3: Gird up your loins: prepare for combat—figuratively, be ready to defend yourself in debate.

38, 7: Sons of God: angels; cf Jb 1, 6.

d: Ps 148, 17.   e: Jb 40, 1.   f: Gn 1, 9.

¹¹ And said: Thus far shall you come but no
   farther,
   and here shall your proud waves be
   stilled!

¹² Have you ever in your lifetime
   commanded the morning
   and shown the dawn its place
¹³ For taking hold of the ends of the earth,
   till the wicked are shaken from its
   surface?
¹⁴ The earth is changed as is clay by the
   seal,
   and dyed as though it were a garment;
¹⁵ But from the wicked the light is withheld,
   and the arm of pride is shattered.

¹⁶ Have you entered into the sources of the
   sea,
   or walked about in the depths of the
   abyss?
¹⁷ Have the gates of death been shown to
   you,
   or have you seen the gates of
   darkness?
¹⁸ Have you comprehended the breadth of
   the earth?
   Tell me, if you know all:
¹⁹ Which is the way to the dwelling place of
   light,
   and where is the abode of darkness,
²⁰ That you may take them to their
   boundaries
   and set them on their homeward paths?
²¹ You know, because you were born before
   them,
   and the number of your years is great!*
²² Have you entered the storehouse of the
   snow,
   and seen the treasury of the hail
²³ Which I have reserved for times of stress,
   for the days of war* and of battle?
²⁴ Which way to the parting of the winds,
   whence the east wind spreads over the
   earth?

²⁵ Who has laid out a channel for the
   downpour
   and for the thunderstorm a path
²⁶ To bring rain to no man's land,
   the unpeopled wilderness;
²⁷ To enrich the waste and desolate ground
   till the desert blooms with verdure?
²⁸ Has the rain a father;
   or who has begotten the drops of dew?
²⁹ Out of whose womb comes the ice,
   and who gives the hoarfrost its birth in
   the skies,
³⁰ When the waters lie covered as though
   with stone
   that holds captive the surface of the
   deep?

³¹ Have you fitted a curb to the Pleiades,*
   or loosened the bonds of Orion?
³² Can you bring forth the Mazzaroth in
   their season,
   or guide the Bear with its train?
³³ Do you know the ordinances of the
   heavens;
   can you put into effect their plan on
   the earth?

³⁴ Can you raise your voice among the
   clouds,
   or veil yourself in the waters of the
   storm?*
³⁵ Can you send forth the lightnings on
   their way,
   or will they say to you, "Here we
   are"?*
³⁷ Who counts the clouds in his wisdom?
   Or who tilts the water jars of heaven
³⁸ So that the dust of earth is fused into a
   mass
   and its clods made solid?
³⁹ Do you hunt the prey for the lioness
   or appease the hunger of her cubs,
⁴⁰ While they crouch in their dens,
   or lie in wait in the thicket?
³⁶ Who puts wisdom in the heart,

38, 21: Divine irony.
38, 22f: Hail . . . of war: thus God used a hailstorm to rout Joshua's foes in the battle of Gibeon; cf Jos 10, 11; Sir 46, 5.
38, 31f: Pleiades . . . Orion . . . Bear: cf Jb 9, 9. Mazzaroth: it is uncertain what astronomical group is meant by this Hebrew word; perhaps a southern constellation (cf Jb 9, 9).
38, 34: Veil yourself . . . storm: wrap yourself in a cloud, as God comes in a theophany; cf Ps 18, 12.
38, 35: Here we are: at your service.

and gives the cock its understanding?*

[41] Who provides nourishment for the ravens
when their young ones cry out to
God,[g]
and they rove abroad without food?

See RG
236–43

CHAPTER 39

[1] Do you know about the birth of the
mountain goats,
watch for the birth pangs of the hinds,
[2] Number the months that they must fulfill,
and fix the time of their bringing
forth?
[3] They crouch down and bear their young;
they deliver their progeny in the desert.
[4] When their offspring thrive and grow,
they leave and do not return.

[5] Who has given the wild ass his freedom,
and who has loosed him from bonds?
[6] I have made the wilderness his home
and the salt flats his dwelling.
[7] He scoffs at the uproar of the city,
and hears no shouts of a driver.
[8] He ranges the mountains for pasture,
and seeks out every patch of green.

[9] Will the wild ox consent to serve you,
and to pass the nights by your manger?
[10] Will a rope bind him in the furrow,
and will he harrow the valleys after you?
[11] Will you trust him for his great strength
and leave to him the fruits of your toil?
[12] Can you rely on him to thresh out your
grain
and gather in the yield of your
threshing floor?
[13] The wings of the ostrich* beat idly;
her plumage is lacking in pinions.
[14] When she leaves her eggs on the ground*
and deposits them in the sand,
[15] Unmindful that a foot may crush them,
that the wild beasts may trample them,
[16] She cruelly disowns her young
and ruthlessly makes nought of her
brood;

[17] For God has withheld wisdom from her
and has given her no share in
understanding.
[18] Yet in her swiftness of foot
she makes sport of the horse and his
rider.

[19] Do you give the horse his strength,*
and endow his neck with splendor?
[20] Do you make the steed to quiver
while his thunderous snorting spreads
terror?
[21] He jubilantly paws the plain
and rushes in his might against the
weapons.
[22] He laughs at fear and cannot be deterred;
he turns not back from the sword.
[23] Around him rattles the quiver,
flashes the spear and the javelin.
[24] Frenzied and trembling he devours the
ground;
he holds not back at the sound of the
trumpet,
[25] but at each blast he cries, "Aha!"
Even from afar he scents the battle,
the roar of the chiefs and the shouting.

[26] Is it by your discernment that the hawk
soars,
that he spreads his wings toward the
south?
[27] Does the eagle fly up at your command
to build his nest aloft?
[28] On the cliff he dwells and spends the
night,
on a spur of the cliff or the fortress.
[29] From thence he watches for his prey;
his eyes behold it afar off.
[30] His young ones greedily drink blood;
where the slain are, there is he.[h]

CHAPTER 40

See RG
236–43

[1] The LORD then said to Job:

[2] Will we have arguing with the Almighty
by the critic?

38, 36: Understanding: the reflection of divine Wisdom discernible in the created animal instincts of the cock.

39, 13: The wings of the ostrich cannot raise her from the ground, but they help her to run swiftly.

39, 14ff: It was popularly believed that, because the os-

trich laid her eggs on the sand, she was thereby cruelly abandoning them; cf Lam 4, 3.

39, 19-25: The famous description of a war horse.

g: Ps 147, 9.   h: Mt 24, 28; Lk 17, 37.

Let him who would correct God give
    answer!*i*

³Then Job answered the LORD and said:

⁴ Behold, I am of little account; what can I
    answer you?
  I put my hand over my mouth.
⁵ Though I have spoken once, I will not do
    so again;
  though twice, I will do so no more.

⁶Then the LORD addressed Job out of the
storm and said:

⁷ Gird up your loins now, like a man.
  I will question you, and you tell me the
    answers!
⁸ Would you refuse to acknowledge my
    right?
  Would you condemn me that you may
    be justified?

⁹ Have you an arm like that of God,
  or can you thunder with a voice like
    his?
¹⁰ Adorn yourself with grandeur and majesty,
  and array yourself with glory and
    splendor.
¹¹ Let loose the fury of your wrath;
¹²   tear down the wicked and shatter
    them.
  Bring down the haughty with a glance;
¹³   bury them in the dust together;
  in the hidden world imprison them.
¹⁴ Then will I too acknowledge
  that your own right hand can save you.

¹⁵ See, besides you I made Behemoth,*
  that feeds on grass like an ox.
¹⁶ Behold the strength in his loins,
  and his vigor in the sinews of his belly.
¹⁷ He carries his tail like a cedar;
  the sinews of his thighs are like cables.
¹⁸ His bones are like tubes of bronze;
  his frame is like iron rods.

¹⁹ He came at the beginning of God's ways,
  and was made the taskmaster of his
    fellows;
²⁰ For the produce of the mountains is
    brought to him,
  and of all wild animals he makes sport.
²¹ Under the lotus trees he lies,
  in coverts of the reedy swamp.
²² The lotus trees cover him with their
    shade;
  all about him are the poplars on the
    bank.
²³ If the river grows violent, he is not
    disturbed;
  he is tranquil though the torrent surges
    about his mouth.
²⁴ Who can capture him by his eyes,
  or pierce his nose* with a trap?

²⁵ Can you lead about Leviathan* with a
    hook,
  or curb his tongue with a bit?
²⁶ Can you put a rope into his nose,
  or pierce through his cheek with a gaff?
²⁷ Will he then plead with you, time after
    time,
  or address you with tender words?
²⁸ Will he make an agreement with you
  that you may have him as a slave
    forever?
²⁹ Can you play with him, as with a bird?
  Can you put him in leash for your
    maidens?
³⁰ Will the traders bargain for him?
  Will the merchants* divide him up?

³¹ Can you fill his hide with barbs,
  or his head with fish spears?
³² Once you but lay a hand upon him,
  no need to recall any other conflict!

CHAPTER 41

² Is he not relentless when aroused;
  who then dares stand before him?*

40, 15: Behemoth: the hippopotamus.

40, 24: Eyes . . . nose: the only exposed parts of the submerged beast.

40, 25: Leviathan here is the crocodile. But cf Jb 3, 8.

40, 30: Merchants: literally, "Canaanites," whose reputation for trading was so widespread that their name came to be
used for merchants; cf Prv 31, 24. The meaning of this verse

is that the crocodile is too powerful a creature to be sold like
common fish.

41, 2: Before him: some read, "before me," i.e., God; also
in v 3.

41, 17: The text here is uncertain.

---

i: Jb 38, 3.

¹ Whoever might vainly hope to do so
   need only see him to be overthrown.
³ Who has assailed him and come off
   safe—
   who under all the heavens?

⁴ I need hardly mention his limbs,
   his strength, and the fitness of his
   armor.
⁵ Who can strip off his outer garment,
   or penetrate his double corselet?
⁶ Who can force open the doors of his
   mouth,
   close to his terrible teeth?
⁷ Rows of scales are on his back,
   tightly sealed together;
⁸ They are fitted each so close to the next
   that no space intervenes;
⁹ So joined one to another
   that they hold fast and cannot be parted.

¹⁰ When he sneezes, light flashes forth;
   his eyes are like those of the dawn.
¹¹ Out of his mouth go forth firebrands;
   sparks of fire leap forth.
¹² From his nostrils issues steam,
   as from a seething pot or bowl.
¹³ His breath sets coals afire;
   a flame pours from his mouth.
¹⁴ Strength abides in his neck,
   and terror leaps before him.

¹⁵,¹⁶ His heart is hard as stone:
   his flesh, as the lower millstone.
¹⁷ When he rises up, the mighty are afraid;
   the waves of the sea fall back.*
¹⁸ Should the sword reach him, it will not
   avail;
   nor will the spear, nor the dart, nor the
   javelin.
¹⁹ He regards iron as straw,
   and bronze as rotten wood.
²⁰ The arrow will not put him to flight;
   slingstones used against him are but
   straws.

²¹ Clubs he esteems as splinters;
   he laughs at the crash of the spear.
²² His belly is sharp as pottery fragments;
   he spreads like a threshing sledge upon
   the mire.
²³ He makes the depths boil like a pot;
   the sea he churns like perfume in a
   kettle.
²⁴ Behind him he leaves a shining path;
   you would think the deep had the
   hoary head of age.
²⁵ Upon the earth there is not his like,
   intrepid he was made.
²⁶ All, however lofty, fear him;
   he is king over all proud beasts.

CHAPTER 42

See RG 236-43

¹Then Job answered the LORD and said:

² I know that you can do all things,*
   and that no purpose of yours can be
   hindered.
³ I have dealt with great things that I do
   not understand;
   things too wonderful for me, which I
   cannot know.ʲ
⁵ I had heard of you by word of mouth,
   but now my eye has seen you.
⁶ Therefore I disown what I have said,
   and repent in dust and ashes.

VIII: Epilogue

Job's Restoration. ⁷And it came to pass after the LORD had spoken these words to Job, that the LORD said to Eliphaz the Temanite, "I am angry with you and with your two friends;* for you have not spoken rightly concerning me, as has my servant Job. ⁸Now, therefore, take seven bullocks and seven rams, and go to my servant Job, and offer up a holocaust for yourselves; and let my servant Job pray for you;* for his prayer I will accept, not to punish you severely. For you have not spoken rightly con-

42, 2-6: In the current Hebrew text, this final utterance of Job is interrupted by words ascribed to God (vv 3f) which are in large part a duplication of Jb 38, 2f.

42, 7: The three friends of Job (Elihu is ignored in the Epilogue) are criticized by the Lord because they had (even though in good faith) leveled false charges against him.

42, 8: Job becomes the intercessor for his friends, as were other great Old Testament characters, e.g., Abraham and Moses, and as our Lord would be, whom he prefigured. Seven: a symbolic number.

j: Jb 34, 35; 35, 16; 38, 2.

cerning me, as has my servant Job." ⁹Then Eliphaz the Temanite, and Bildad the Shuhite,
and Zophar the Naamathite, went and did as
the LORD had commanded them. And the
LORD accepted the intercession of Job.

¹⁰Also, the LORD restored the prosperity
of Job, after he had prayed for his friends;
the LORD even gave to Job twice as much as
he had before. ¹¹Then all his brethren and his
sisters came to him, and all his former acquaintances, and they dined with him in his
house. They condoled with him and comforted him for all the evil which the LORD
had brought upon him; and each one gave
him a piece of money* and a gold ring.

¹²ᵏThus the LORD blessed the latter days
of Job more than his earlier ones. For he had
fourteen thousand sheep, six thousand
camels, a thousand yoke of oxen, and a thousand she-asses. ¹³And he had seven sons and
three daughters, ¹⁴of whom* he called the
first Jemimah, the second Keziah, and the
third Keren-happuch. ¹⁵In all the land no
other women were as beautiful as the daughters of Job; and their father gave them an inheritance* among their brethren. ¹⁶After this,
Job lived a hundred and forty years;* and he
saw his children, his grandchildren, and
even his great-grandchildren.ˡ ¹⁷Then Job
died, old and full of years.

42, 11: A piece of money: the term is the same as that used in Gn 33, 19; Jos 24, 32. Gold ring: for the nose or ear.

42, 14: Job's daughters had names symbolic of their charms: Jemimah, dove; Keziah, precious perfume (cf Ps 45, 9); Kerenhappuch, cosmetic jar—more precisely, a container for a black powder that was used like modern mascara.

42, 15: Ordinarily daughters did not inherit property unless there were no sons; cf Nm 27, 1-11.

42, 16: As his other rewards were twice as much as he had before (v 10), so Job's hundred and forty years were double the expected span of human life; cf Ps 90, 10.

k: Jb 1, 3. *l:* Jb 5, 25f.

See RG
243–54

The Book of Psalms

The Hebrew Psalter numbers 150 songs. The corresponding number in the LXX differs because of
a different division of certain psalms. Hence the
numbering in the Greek Psalter (which was followed by the Latin Vulgate) is usually one digit
behind the Hebrew. In *The New American Bible*
the numbering of the verses follows the Hebrew
numbering; many of the traditional English translations are often a verse number behind the Hebrew because they do not count the superscriptions as a verse.

The superscriptions derive from pre-Christian
Jewish tradition, and they contain technical
terms, many of them apparently liturgical, which
are no longer known to us. Seventy-three psalms
are attributed to David, but there is no sure way
of dating any psalm. Some are preexilic (before
587), and others are postexilic (after 539), but not
as late as the Maccabean period (ca. 165). The
psalms are the product of many individual collections (e.g., Songs of Ascents, Pss 120—134),
which were eventually combined into the present
work in which one can detect five "books," because of the doxologies which occur at 41, 14;
72, 18-19; 89, 53; 106, 48.

Two important features of the psalms deserve
special notice. First, the majority were composed
originally precisely for liturgical worship. This is
shown by the frequent indication of liturgical
leaders interacting with the community (e.g., Ps
118, 1-4). Secondly, they follow certain distinct
patterns or literary forms. Thus, the hymn is a
song of praise, in which a community is urged
joyfully to sing out the praise of God. Various reasons are given for this praise (often introduced by
"for" or "because"): the divine work of creation
and sustenance (Pss 8; 104), or the divine acts in
Israel's favor (Pss 135, 1-12; 136). Some of the
hymns have received a more specific classification, based on content. The "Songs of Zion" are so
called because they exalt Zion, the city in which
God dwells among the people (Pss 46; 48). Others
are termed "enthronement" psalms because they
re-enact or re-present in the liturgy the kingship of
the Lord (Pss 47; 96—99). Characteristic of the
songs of praise is the joyful summons to get involved in the activity; Ps 104 is an exception to
this, although it remains universal in its thrust.

Another type of psalm is similar to the hymn:
the thanksgiving psalm. This too is a song of

praise acknowledging the Lord as the rescuer of the psalmist from a desperate situation. Very often the psalmist will give a flash-back, recounting the past distress, and the plea that was uttered (Pss 30; 116). The setting for such prayers seems to have been the offering of a *todah* (a "praise" sacrifice) with friends in the Temple.

There are more psalms of lament than of any other type. They may be individual (e.g., Pss 3—7; 22) or communal (e.g., Ps 44). Although they usually begin with a cry for help, they develop in various ways. The description of the distress is couched in the broad imagery typical of the Bible (one is in Sheol, the Pit, or is afflicted by enemies or wild beasts, etc.)—in such a way that one cannot pinpoint the exact nature of the psalmist's plight. However, Ps 51 (cf also Ps 130) seems to refer clearly to deliverance from sin. Several laments end on a note of certainty that the Lord has heard the prayer (cf Ps 7, but contrast Ps 88), and the Psalter has been characterized as a movement from lament to praise. If this is somewhat of an exaggeration, it serves at least to emphasize the frequent expressions of trust which characterize the lament. In some cases it would seem as if the theme of trust has been lifted out to form a literary type all its own; cf Pss 23; 62; 91. Among the communal laments can be counted Pss 74 and 79. They complain to the Lord about some national disaster, and try to motivate God to intervene in favor of the suffering people.

Other psalms are clearly classified on account of content, and they may be in themselves laments or psalms of thanksgiving. Among the "royal" psalms, that deal directly with the currently reigning king, are Pss 20; 21 and 72. Many of the royal psalms were given a messianic interpretation by Christians. In Jewish tradition they were preserved, even after kingship had disappeared, because they were read in the light of the Davidic covenant reported in 2 Samuel 7. Certain psalms are called wisdom psalms because they seem to betray the influence of the concerns of

the ages (cf. Pss 37; 49), but there is no general agreement as to the number of these prayers. Somewhat related to the wisdom psalms are the "torah" psalms, in which the torah (instruction or law) of the Lord is glorified (Pss 1; 19, 8-14; 119). Pss 78; 105 and 106 can be considered as "historical" psalms. Although the majority of the psalms have a liturgical setting, there are certain prayers that may be termed "liturgies," so clearly does their structure reflect a liturgical incident (e.g., Pss 15; 24).

It is obvious that not all of the psalms can be pigeon-holed into neat classifications, but even a brief sketch of these types helps us to catch the structure and spirit of the psalms we read. It has been rightly said that the psalms are "a school of prayer." They not only provide us with models to follow, but inspire us to voice our own deepest feelings and aspirations.

First Book: Psalms 1—41

PSALM 1[*]

True Happiness in God's Law

See RG 245–46

I

¹ Happy those[*] who do not follow
  the counsel of the wicked,
Nor go the way[*] of sinners,
  nor sit in company with scoffers.[a]
² Rather, the law of the LORD[*] is their joy;
  God's law they study day and night.[b]
³ They are like a tree[c]
  planted near streams of water,
  that yields its fruit in season;
Its leaves never wither;
  whatever they do prospers.

II

⁴ But not the wicked![*]
  They are like chaff driven by the wind.[d]
⁵ Therefore the wicked will not survive
  judgment,

Ps 1: A preface to the whole Book of Psalms, contrasting with striking similes the destiny of the good and the wicked. The psalm views life as activity, as choosing either the good or the bad. Each "way" brings its inevitable consequences. The wise through their good actions will experience rootedness and life, and the wicked, rootlessness and death.

1, 1: Those: literally, "the man." That word is used here and in many of the Psalms as typical, and therefore is translated "they." The way: a common biblical term for manner of living

or moral conduct (Pss 32, 8; 101, 2. 6; Prv 2, 20; 1 Kgs 8, 36).

1, 2: The law of the LORD: either the Torah, the first five books of the Bible, or, more probably, divine teaching or instruction.

1, 4: The wicked: those who by their actions distance themselves from God's life-giving presence.

a: Pss 26, 4-5; 40, 5. *b:* Jos 1, 8; Ps 119; Sir 39, 1. *c:* Pss 52, 10; 92, 13-15; Jer 17, 8. *d:* Pss 35, 5; 83, 14-16; Jb 21, 18.

nor will sinners in the assembly of the
just.

[6] The LORD watches over the way of the
just,[e]

but the way of the wicked leads to ruin.

See RG
245, 250,
251

PSALM 2[*]

A Psalm for a Royal Coronation

[1] Why do the nations protest
and the peoples grumble in vain?[f]

[2] Kings on earth rise up
and princes plot together
against the LORD and his anointed:[g] [*]

[3] "Let us break their shackles
and cast off their chains!"[h]

[4] The one enthroned in heaven laughs;
the LORD derides them,[i]

[5] Then speaks to them in anger,
terrifies them in wrath:

[6] "I myself have installed my king
on Zion, my holy mountain."

[7] I will proclaim the decree of the LORD,
who said to me, "You are my son;
today I am your father.[j]

[8] Only ask it of me,
and I will make your inheritance the
nations,
your possession the ends of the earth.

[9] With an iron rod you shall shepherd
them,
like a clay pot you will shatter them."[k]

[10] And now, kings, give heed;
take warning, rulers on earth.

[11] Serve the LORD with fear;
with trembling bow down in homage,
Lest God be angry and you perish from
the way

in a sudden blaze of anger.
Happy are all who take refuge in
God![l]

PSALM 3[*]

See RG
244

Threatened but Trusting

[1] A psalm of David, when he fled from his
son Absalom.[m] [*]

I

[2] How many are my foes, LORD!
How many rise against me!

[3] How many say of me,
"God will not save that one."[n]   Selah[*]

[4] But you, LORD, are a shield around me;
my glory, you keep my head high.[o]

II

[5] Whenever I cried out to the LORD,
I was answered from the holy
mountain.   Selah

[6] Whenever I lay down and slept,
the LORD preserved me to rise again.[p]

[7] I do not fear, then, thousands of people
arrayed against me on every side.

III

[8] Arise, LORD! Save me, my God!
You will shatter the jaws of all my
foes;
you will break the teeth of the
wicked.[q]

[9] Safety comes from the LORD!
Your blessing for your people![r]   Selah

PSALM 4[*]

See RG
244

Trust in God

[1] For the leader;[*] with stringed instruments.
A psalm of David.

I

[2] Answer when I call, my saving God.

Ps 2: A royal psalm. To rebellious kings (1-3) God responds vigorously (4-6). A speaker proclaims the divine decree (in the legal adoption language of the day), making the Israelite king the earthly representative of God (7-9) and warning kings to obey (10-11). The psalm has a messianic meaning for the Church; the New Testament understands it of Christ (Acts 4, 25-27; 13, 33; Heb 1, 5).

2, 2: Anointed: in Hebrew *mashiah*, "anointed"; in Greek *christos*, whence English Messiah and Christ. In Israel kings (Jgs 9, 8; 1 Sm 9, 16; 16, 12-13) and high priests (Lv 8, 12; Nm 3, 3) received the power of their office through anointing.

Ps 3: An individual lament complaining of enemies who deny that God will come to the rescue (2-3). Despite such taunts the psalmist hopes for God's protection even in sleep (4-7). The psalm prays for an end to the enemies' power to speak mali-

ciously (8) and closes peacefully with an expression of trust (9).

3, 1: The superscription, added later, relates the psalm to an incident in the life of David.

3, 3. 5. 9: Selah: the term is generally considered a direction to the cantor or musicians but its exact meaning is not known. It occurs 71 times in 39 psalms.

Ps 4: An individual lament emphasizing trust in God. The petition is based upon the psalmist's vivid experience of God

e: Ps 37, 18.   *f:* Rv 11, 18.   *g:* Ps 83, 6.   *h:* Ps 149, 8.
i: Pss 37, 13; 59, 9; Wis 4, 18.   *j:* Pss 89, 27; 110, 2-3; Is 49, 1.
k: Rv 2, 27; 12, 5; 19, 15.   *l:* Pss 34, 9; 146, 5; Prv 16, 20.
m: 2 Sm 15, 13ff.   *n:* Ps 71, 11.   *o:* Pss 7, 11; 18, 3; 62, 7-8;
Dt 33, 29; Is 60, 19.   *p:* Ps 4, 9; Prv 3, 24.   *q:* Ps 58, 7.
r: Ps 28, 9; Jon 2, 10.

The Structure of the Book of Psalms

P SALMS IS DIVIDED into five "books," each of which ends with a verse or song of praise (a doxology).

Book 1, Psalms 1—41   Doxology is 41, 14
Book 2, Psalms 42—72   Doxology is 72, 18–19
Book 3, Psalms 73—89   Doxology is 89, 53
Book 4, Psalms 90—106   Doxology is 106, 48
Book 5, Psalms 107—150   Doxology is Psalm 150

Books 1, 4, and 5 tend to use "LORD" ("Yahweh") as the name of God; books 2 and 3 use "God" ("Elohim"). This indicates that there may have been two centers of collection for Psalms, and in one case—Psalms 14 and 53—we have a nearly identical Psalm with the different names for God.

In my troubles, you cleared a way;
show me favor; hear my prayer.[s]

II

3 How long will you people mock my
        honor,
    love what is worthless, chase after
        lies?[t]   *Selah*
4 Know that the LORD works wonders for
        the faithful;
    the LORD hears when I call out.
5 Tremble* and do not sin;
    upon your beds ponder in silence.[u]
6 Offer fitting sacrifice
    and trust in the LORD.[v]

III

7 Many say, "May we see better times!
    LORD, show us the light of your
        face!"[w]   *Selah*
8 But you have given my heart more joy
    than they have when grain and wine
        abound.
9 In peace I shall both lie down and
        sleep,[x]
    for you alone, LORD, make me
        secure.

PSALM 5*

Prayer for Divine Help

See RG
244

1 For the leader; with wind instruments.
        A psalm of David.

I

2 Hear my words, O LORD;
    listen to my sighing.[y]
3 Hear my cry for help,
    my king, my God!
To you I pray, O LORD;
4   at dawn you will hear my cry;
    at dawn I will plead before you and
        wait.[z]

II

5 You are not a god who delights in evil;
    no wicked person finds refuge with you;
6   the arrogant cannot stand before you.
You hate all who do evil;
7   you destroy all who speak falsely.[a]
Murderers and deceivers
    the LORD abhors.

III

8 But I can enter your house
    because of your great love.

as savior (2). That experience of God is the basis for the warning to the wicked: revere God who intervenes on the side of the faithful (3-6). The faithful psalmist exemplifies the blessings given to the just (7-9).

4, 1: For the leader: many psalm headings contain this rubric. Its exact meaning is unknown but may signify that such psalms once stood together in a collection of "the choirmaster." Cf 1 Chr 15, 21.

4, 5: Tremble: be moved deeply with religious awe. The Greek translation understood the emotion to be

anger, and it is so cited in Eph 4, 26.

Ps 5: A lament contrasting the security of the house of God (8-9. 12-13) with the danger of the company of evildoers (5-7. 10-11). The psalmist therefore prays that God will hear (2-4) and grant the protection and joy of the temple.

s: Ps 118, 5.   *t:* Ps 62, 4.   *u:* Eph 4, 26.   *v:* Ps 51, 19.   *w:* Pss 31, 17; 44, 4; 67, 1; 80, 4; Jb 13, 24; Nm 6, 25; Dn 9, 17.   *x:* Ps 3, 6.   *y:* Pss 86, 6; 130, 1-2.   *z:* Wis 16, 28.   *a:* Ps 101, 7; Wis 14, 9; Hb 1, 13.

I can worship in your holy temple
　　because of my reverence for you,
　　LORD.[b]
[9] Guide me in your justice because of my
　　foes;
　　make straight your way before me.[c]

IV

[10] For there is no sincerity in their mouths;
　　their hearts are corrupt.
Their throats[*] are open graves;[d]
　　on their tongues are subtle lies.
[11] Declare them guilty, God;
　　make them fall by their own devices.[e]
Drive them out for their many sins;
　　they have rebelled against you.

V

[12] Then all who take refuge in you will be
　　glad
　　and forever shout for joy.[f]
Protect them that you may be the joy
　　of those who love your name.
[13] For you, LORD, bless the just;
　　you surround them with favor like a
　　shield.

See RG
244

PSALM 6[*]

Prayer in Distress

[1] For the leader; with stringed instruments,
　　"upon the eighth."[*] A psalm of David.

I

[2] Do not reprove me in your anger,
　　LORD,
　　nor punish me in your wrath.[g]
[3] Have pity on me, LORD, for I am weak;

heal me, LORD, for my bones are
　　trembling.[h]
[4] In utter terror is my soul—
　　and you, LORD, how long . . . ?[i][*]
[5] Turn, LORD, save my life;
　　in your mercy[*] rescue me.
[6] For who among the dead remembers
　　you?
　　Who praises you in Sheol?[j][*]

II

[7] I am wearied with sighing;
　　all night long tears drench my bed;
　　my couch is soaked with
　　weeping.
[8] My eyes are dimmed with sorrow,
　　worn out because of all my foes.[k]

III

[9] Away from me, all who do evil![l]
　　The LORD has heard my weeping.
[10] The LORD has heard my prayer;
　　the LORD takes up my plea.
[11] My foes will be terrified and
　　disgraced;
　　all will fall back in sudden shame.[m]

PSALM 7[*]

God the Vindicator

See RG
244

[1] A plaintive song of David, which he sang
　　to the LORD concerning Cush,
　　the Benjaminite.

I

[2] LORD my God, in you I take refuge;
　　rescue me; save me from all who
　　pursue me,[n]

5, 10: Their throats: their speech brings harm to their hearers (cf Jer 5, 16). The verse mentions four parts of the body, each a source of evil to the innocent.

Ps 6: The first of the seven Penitential Psalms (Pss 6; 32; 38; 51; 102; 130; 143), a designation dating from the seventh century A.D. for psalms suitable to express repentance. The psalmist does not, as in many laments, claim to be innocent but appeals to God's mercy (5). Sin here, as often in the Bible, is both the sinful act and its injurious consequences; here it is physical sickness (3-4. 7-8) and the attacks of enemies (8. 9. 11). The psalmist prays that the effects of personal and social sin be taken away.

6, 1: Upon the eighth: apparently a musical notation, now lost.

6, 4: How long?: elliptical for "How long will it be before you answer my prayer?" Cf Ps 13, 2-3.

6, 5: Mercy: Hebrew *hesed*, translated as "mercy" or "love", describes God's affectionate fidelity to human beings, which is rooted in divine and not human integrity.

6, 6: A motive for God to preserve the psalmist from

death: in the shadowy world of the dead no one offers you praise. Sheol is the biblical term for the underworld where the insubstantial souls of dead human beings dwelt. It was similar to the Hades of Greek and Latin literature. In the second century B.C., biblical books begin to speak positively of life with God after death (Dn 12, 1-3; Wis 3).

Ps 7: An individual lament. The psalmist flees to God's presence in the sanctuary for justice and protection (2-3) and takes an oath that only the innocent can swear (4-6). The innocent psalmist can thus hope for the just God's protection (7-14) and be confident that the actions of the wicked will come back upon their own heads (15-17). The justice of God leads the psalmist to praise (18).

b: Ps 138, 2; Jon 2, 5.　c: Ps 23, 3; Prv 4, 11; Is 26, 7.　d: Rom 3, 13.　e: Ps 141, 10.　f: Ps 64, 11.　g: Ps 38, 2.　h: Jer 17, 14-15.　i: Ps 13, 2-3; 74, 10; 89, 47.　j: Pss 30, 10; 88, 11; 115, 17; Is 38, 18.　k: Pss 31, 10; 38, 11; 40, 13.　l: Ps 119, 115; Mt 7, 23; Lk 13, 27.　m: Pss 35, 4. 26; 40, 15; 71, 13.　n: Pss 6, 5; 22, 21.

³ Lest they maul me like lions,
　　tear me to pieces with none to save.

II

⁴ LORD my God, if I am at fault in this,*
　　if there is guilt on my hands,
⁵ If I have repaid my friend with evil—
　　I spared even those who hated me
　　　　without cause—
⁶ Then let my enemy pursue and
　　　　overtake me,
　　trample my life to the ground,
　　and leave me dishonored in the dust.ᵒ
　　　　　　　　　　　　　Selah

III

⁷ Rise up, LORD, in your anger;
　　rise against the fury of my foes.ᵖ
　　Wake to judge as you have decreed.
⁸ Have the assembly of the peoples gather
　　　　about you;
　　sit on your throne high above them,
⁹ O LORD, judge of the nations.
　　Grant me justice, LORD, for I am
　　　　blameless,
　　free of any guilt.
¹⁰ Bring the malice of the wicked to an end;
　　uphold the innocent,
　　O God of justice,
　　who tries hearts and minds.�q

IV

¹¹ A shield before me is God
　　who saves the honest heart.ʳ
¹² God is a just judge,
　　who rebukes in anger every day.
¹³ If sinners do not repent,
　　God sharpens his sword,
　　strings and readies the bow,ˢ
¹⁴ Prepares his deadly shafts,
　　makes arrows blazing thunderbolts.ᵗ

V

¹⁵ Sinners conceive iniquity;
　　pregnant with mischief,
　　they give birth to failure.ᵘ
¹⁶ They open a hole and dig it deep,
　　but fall into the pit they have dug.ᵛ
¹⁷ Their mischief comes back upon
　　　　themselves;
　　their violence falls on their own heads.

VI

¹⁸ I praise the justice of the LORD;
　　I celebrate the name of the LORD Most
　　　　High.ʷ

PSALM 8*

*Divine Majesty and
Human Dignity*

**See RG
244, 249**

¹ For the leader; "upon the *gittith*."* A psalm
of David.

² O LORD, our Lord,
　　how awesome is your name through
　　　　all the earth!
　　You have set your majesty above the
　　　　heavens!
³ Out of the mouths of babesˣ and infants*
　　you have drawn a defense* against
　　　　your foes,
　　to silence enemy and avenger.*
⁴ When I see your heavens, the work of
　　　　your fingers,
　　the moon and stars that you set in
　　　　place—
⁵ What are humans that you are mindful of
　　　　them,ʸ
　　mere mortals* that you care for them?ᶻ
⁶ Yet you have made them little less than a
　　　　god,*

7, 4: At fault in this: in the accusation the enemies have
made against the psalmist.

Ps 8: While marvelling at the limitless grandeur of God
(2-3), the psalmist is struck first by the smallness of human
beings in creation (4-5), and then by the royal dignity and
power that God has graciously bestowed upon them (6-10).

8, 1: Upon the gittith: probably the title of the melody to
which the psalm was to be sung or a musical instrument.

8, 3: Babes and infants: the text is obscure. Some join
this line to the last line of 2 (itself obscure) to read: "(you)
whose majesty is exalted above the heavens / by the mouths
of babes and infants." **Drawn a defense**: some prefer the
Septuagint's "fashioned praise," which is quoted in Mt 21,
16. **Enemy and avenger**: probably cosmic enemies. The
primeval powers of watery chaos are often personified in po-

etic texts (Pss 74, 13-14; 89, 11; Jb 9, 13; 26, 12-13; Is 51, 9).

8, 5: Humans . . . mere mortals: literally, "(mortal) person" . . . . "son of man (in sense of a human being, Hebrew
'adam)." The emphasis is on the fragility and mortality of human beings to whom God has given great dignity.

8, 6: Little less than a god: Hebrew *'elohim*, the ordinary
word for "God" or "the gods" or members of the heavenly
court. The Greek version translated *'elohim* by "angel, messenger"; several ancient and modern versions so translate.

---

o: Ps 143, 3.　　*p:* Pss 9, 4; 19, 20.　　*q:* Pss 17, 3; 26, 2; 35, 24; 43,
1; 139, 23; Jer 17, 10; 20, 12.　　*r:* Ps 3, 4.　　*s:* Ps 11, 2.　　*t:* Is 50,
11.　　*u:* Jb 15, 35; Is 59, 4.　　*v:* Pss 9, 16; 35, 8; 57, 7; Prv 26,
27; Eccl 10, 8; Sir 27, 26.　　*w:* Pss 18, 50; 30, 5; 135, 3; 146, 2.
x: Mt 21, 16; Wis 10, 21.　　*y:* Ps 144, 3; Jb 7, 17.　　*z:* Heb 2, 6ff.

crowned them with glory and honor.

7 You have given them rule over the works
of your hands,*a*
put all things at their feet:

8 All sheep and oxen,
even the beasts of the field,

9 The birds of the air, the fish of the sea,
and whatever swims the paths of the
seas.

10 O LORD, our Lord,
how awesome is your name through
all the earth!

See RG
245

PSALMS 9—10*

*Thanksgiving for Victory and
Prayer for Justice*

1 For the leader; according to *Muth Labben.**
A psalm of David.

A

I

2 I will praise you, LORD, with all my heart;
I will declare all your wondrous deeds.

3 I will delight and rejoice in you;
I will sing hymns to your name, Most
High.

4 For my enemies turn back;
they stumble and perish before you.

II

5 You upheld my right and my cause,
seated on your throne, judging justly.

6 You rebuked the nations, you destroyed
the wicked;
their name you blotted out for all time.*b*

7 The enemies have been ruined forever;
you destroyed their cities;
their memory has perished.

III

8 The LORD rules forever,
has set up a throne for judgment.

9 It is God who governs the world with
justice,*c*
who judges the peoples with fairness.

10 The LORD is a stronghold for the
oppressed,
a stronghold in times of trouble.*d*

11 Those who honor your name trust in you;
you never forsake those who seek you,
LORD.

IV

12 Sing hymns to the LORD enthroned on
Zion;
proclaim God's deeds among the
nations!

13 For the avenger of bloodshed remembers,
does not forget the cry of the
afflicted.*e*

V

14 Have mercy on me, LORD;
see how my foes afflict me!
You alone can raise me from the gates
of death.*f*

15 Then I will declare all your praises,
sing joyously of your salvation
in the gates of daughter Zion.*

VI

16 The nations fall into the pit they dig;
in the snare they hide, their own foot is
caught.

17 The LORD is revealed in this divine rule:
by the deeds they do the wicked are
trapped.*g** *Higgaion. Selah*

VII

18 To Sheol the wicked will depart,
all the nations that forget God.

19 The needy will never be forgotten,
nor will the hope of the afflicted ever
fade.*h*

20 Arise, LORD, let no mortal prevail;

The meaning seems to be that God created human beings almost at the level of the beings in the heavenly world. Heb 2,
9 finds the eminent fulfillment of this verse in Jesus Christ,
who was humbled before being glorified. Cf also 1 Cor 15,
27, where St. Paul applies to Christ the closing words of v 7.

Pss 9—10: Pss 9 and 10 in the Hebrew text have been
transmitted as separate poems but they actually form a single
acrostic poem and are so transmitted in the Greek and Latin
tradition. Each verse of the two psalms begins with a successive letter of the Hebrew alphabet (though several letters have
no corresponding stanza). The psalm states loosely connected
themes: the rescue of the helpless poor from their enemies,
God's worldwide judgment and rule over the nations, the

psalmist's own concern for rescue (14-15).

9, 1: Muth Labben: probably the melodic accompaniment of the psalm, now lost.

9, 15: Daughter Zion: an ancient Near Eastern city could
sometimes be personified as a woman or a queen, the spouse
of the god of the city.

9, 17: The LORD is revealed in this divine rule: God has
so made the universe that the wicked are punished by the very
actions they perform.

a: 7ff: Gn 1, 26. 28; Wis 9, 2; 1 Cor 15, 27. *b:* Jb 18, 17. *c:* Pss
96, 10; 98, 9. *d:* Ps 37, 39; Is 25, 4. *e:* Jb 16, 18. *f:* Wis 16,
13. *g:* Sir 27, 26. *h:* Prv 23, 18.

let the nations be judged in your
    presence.
[21] Strike them with terror, LORD;
    show the nations they are mere
        mortals.   *Selah*

B

I

[1] Why, LORD, do you stand at a distance
    and pay no heed to these troubled
        times?
[2] Arrogant scoundrels pursue the poor;
    they trap them by their cunning
        schemes.*i*

II

[3] The wicked even boast of their greed;
    these robbers curse and scorn the
        LORD.*j*
[4] In their insolence the wicked boast:
    "God doesn't care, doesn't even
        exist."*k*
[5] Yet their affairs always succeed;
    they ignore your judgment on high;
    they sneer at all who oppose them.
[6] They say in their hearts, "We will never
        fall;
    never will we see misfortune."
[7] Their mouths are full of oaths, violence,
        and lies;
    discord and evil are under their
        tongues.*l*
[8] They wait in ambush near towns;
    their eyes watch for the helpless,
    to murder the innocent in secret.*m*
[9] They lurk in ambush like lions in a
        thicket,
    hide there to trap the poor,
    snare them and close the net.*n*
[10] The helpless are crushed, laid low;
    they fall into the power of the
        wicked,
[11] Who say in their hearts, "God pays no
        attention,
    shows no concern, never bothers to
        look."*o*

III

[12] Rise up, LORD God! Raise your arm!
    Do not forget the poor!
[13] Why should the wicked scorn God,
    say in their hearts, "God doesn't care"?
[14] But you do see;
    you do observe this misery and
        sorrow;*p*
    you take the matter in hand.
To you the helpless can entrust their cause;
    you are the defender of orphans.*q*
[15] Break the arms of the wicked and
        depraved;
    make them account for their crimes;
    let none of them survive.

IV

[16] The LORD is king forever;*r*
    the nations have vanished from God's
        land.
[17] You listen, LORD, to the needs of the poor;
    you encourage them and hear their
        prayers.
[18] You win justice for the orphaned and
        oppressed;*s*
    no one on earth will cause terror again.

PSALM 11*

Confidence in the Presence of God

[1] For the leader. Of David.

See RG
245

I

In the LORD I take refuge;
    how can you say to me,
    "Flee like a bird to the mountains!*t*
[2] See how the wicked string their bows,
    fit their arrows to the string
    to shoot from the shadows at the
        upright.*u*
[3] When foundations* are being destroyed,
    what can the upright do?"

II

[4] The LORD is in his holy temple;
    the LORD's throne is in heaven.*v*
God's eyes keep careful watch;

Ps 11: A song of trust. Though friends counsel flight to the mountain country (a traditional hideout) to escape trouble (1-3), the innocent psalmist reaffirms confidence in God, who protects those who seek asylum in the temple (4-7).

11, 3: Foundations: usually understood of public order. Cf Ps 82, 5.

---

i: Is 32, 7. *j:* Ps 36, 2. *k:* Ps 14, 1; Jb 22, 13; Is 29, 15; Jer 5, 12; Zep 1, 12. *l:* Is 32, 7; Rom 3, 14. *m:* Ps 11, 2; Jb 24, 14. *n:* Ps 17, 12; Prv 1, 11; Jer 5, 26. *o:* Pss 44, 25; 64, 6; 73, 11; 94, 7; Ez 9, 9. *p:* Pss 31, 8; 56, 9; 2 Kgs 20, 5; Is 25, 8; Rv 7, 17. *q:* Ex 22, 21-22. *r:* Ps 145, 13; Jer 10, 10. *s:* Dt 10, 18. *t:* Pss 55, 7; 91, 4. *u:* Pss 7, 13; 37, 14; 57, 5; 64, 4. *v:* Pss 14, 2; 102, 20; Hb 2, 20; Dt 26, 15; Is 66, 1; Mt 5, 34.

they test all peoples.
5 The LORD tests the good and the bad,
  hates those who love violence,
6 And rains upon the wicked
  fiery coals and brimstone,
  a scorching wind their allotted cup.[w] *
7 The LORD is just and loves just deeds;
  the upright shall see his face.

PSALM 12*

See RG 244

Prayer against Evil Tongues

1 For the leader; "upon the eighth."
  A psalm of David.

I

2 Help, LORD, for no one loyal remains;
  the faithful have vanished from the
    human race.[x]
3 Those who tell lies to one another
  speak with deceiving lips and a double
    heart.[y]

II

4 May the LORD cut off all deceiving lips,
  and every boastful tongue,
5 Those who say, "By our tongues we
    prevail;
  when our lips speak, who can lord it
    over us?"[z]

III

6 "Because they rob the weak, and the
    needy groan,
  I will now arise," says the LORD;
  "I will grant safety to whoever longs
    for it."[a]

IV

7 The promises of the LORD are sure,
  silver refined in a crucible,*
  silver purified seven times.[b]

8 LORD, protect us always;
  preserve us from this generation.
9 On every side the wicked strut;
  the shameless are extolled by all.

PSALM 13*

See RG 244

Prayer in Time of Illness

1 For the leader. A psalm of David.

I

2 How long, LORD? Will you utterly forget
    me?
  How long will you hide your face
    from me?[c]
3 How long must I carry sorrow in my soul,
  grief in my heart day after day?
  How long will my enemy triumph over
    me?

II

4 Look upon me, answer me, LORD, my
    God!
  Give light to my eyes lest I sleep in
    death,
5 Lest my enemy say, "I have prevailed,"
  lest my foes rejoice at my downfall.[d]

III

6 I trust in your faithfulness.
  Grant my heart joy in your help,
  That I may sing of the LORD,
  "How good our God has been to me!"[e]

PSALM 14*

See RG 244, 250

A Lament over
Widespread Corruption

1 For the leader. Of David.

I

Fools* say in their hearts,
  "There is no God."[f]

11, 6: Their allotted cup: the cup that God gives people to drink is a common figure for their destiny. Cf Pss 16, 5; 75, 9; Mt 20, 22; 26, 39; Rv 14, 10.

Ps 12: A lament. The psalmist, thrown into a world where lying and violent people persecute the just (2-3), prays that the wicked be punished (4-5). The prayer is not simply for vengeance but arises from a desire to see God's justice appear on earth. V 6 preserves the word of assurance spoken by the priest to the lamenter; it is not usually transmitted in such psalms. In vv 7-9 the psalmist affirms the intention to live by the word of assurance.

12, 7: A crucible: literally "in a crucible in the ground." The crucible was placed in the ground for support.

Ps 13: A lament in which the psalmist, seriously ill (4), expresses fear that enemies will interpret his or her death as a divine judgment. Hence the heartfelt prayer (2-3) is for heal-

ing that will signal to those enemies that the psalmist enjoys God's favor (4-5). The poem ends with a confession of trust in God and a statement of praise (6).

Ps 14: The lament (duplicated in Ps 53) depicts the world as consisting of two types of people: "the fools" (= the wicked, 1-3) and "the company of the just" (4-6; also called "my people," and "the poor"). The wicked persecute the just, but the psalm expresses the hope that God will punish the wicked and reward the good.

14, 1: Fools: literally, "the fool." The singular is used

w: Pss 120, 4; 140, 11; Prv 16, 27; Ez 38, 22; Rv 8, 5; 20, 10. x: Pss 14, 3; 116, 11; Is 59, 15; Mi 7, 2. y: Pss 28, 3; 55, 22; Is 59, 3-4; Jer 9, 7. z: Sir 5, 3. a: Is 33, 10. b: Pss 18, 31; 19, 8; Prv 30, 5. c: Pss 6, 4; 44, 25; 77, 8; 79, 5; 89, 47; 94, 3; Lam 5, 20. d: Ps 38, 17. e: Ps 116, 7. f: Pss 10, 4; 36, 2; Is 32, 6; Jer 5, 12.

Their deeds are loathsome and corrupt;
   not one does what is right.
[2] The LORD looks down from heaven
   upon the human race,[g]
To see if even one is wise,[h]
   if even one seeks God.
[3] All have gone astray;
   all alike are perverse.
Not one does what is right,
   not even one.[i]

II

[4] Will these evildoers never learn?
   They devour my people as they
      devour bread;[j]
   they do not call upon the LORD.[k]
[5] They have good reason, then, to fear;
   God is with the company of the just.
[6] They would crush the hopes of the
      poor,
   but the poor have the LORD as their
      refuge.

III

[7] Oh, that from Zion might come
   the deliverance of Israel,
That Jacob may rejoice, and Israel be
      glad
when the LORD restores his people![l] *

See RG
246

PSALM 15*

The Righteous Israelite

[1] A psalm of David.

I

LORD, who may abide in your tent?
Who may dwell on your holy
      mountain?[m] *

II

[2] Whoever walks without blame,[n]

doing what is right,
   speaking truth from the heart;
[3] Who does not slander a neighbor,
   does no harm to another,
   never defames a friend;
[4] Who disdains the wicked,
   but honors those who fear the LORD;
Who keeps an oath despite the cost,
[5]   lends no money at interest,*
   accepts no bribe against the
      innocent.[o]

III

Whoever acts like this
   shall never be shaken.

PSALM 16*

God the Supreme Good

See RG
245

[1] A miktam* of David.

I

Keep me safe, O God;
   in you I take refuge.[p]
[2] I say to the LORD,
   you are my Lord,
   you are my only good.
[3] Worthless are all the false gods of the
      land.
   Accursed are all who delight in
      them.
[4] They multiply their sorrows
   who court other gods.
Blood libations to them I will not pour
      out,
   nor will I take their names* upon my
      lips.
[5] LORD, my allotted portion and my
      cup,
   you have made my destiny secure.[q]

---

typically, hence the plural translation.

14, 7: Israel . . . Jacob . . . his people: the righteous poor are identified with God's people.

Ps 15: The psalm records a liturgical scrutiny at the entrance to the temple court (cf Ps 24, 3-6; Is 33, 14b-16). The Israelite wishing to be admitted had to ask the temple official what conduct was appropriate to God's precincts. Note the emphasis on virtues relating to one's neighbor.

15, 1: Your tent . . . your holy mountain: the temple could be referred to as "tent" (Ps 61, 5; Is 33, 20), a reference to the tent of the wilderness period and the tent of David (2 Sm 6, 17; 7, 2), predecessors of the temple. **Holy mountain**: a venerable designation of the divine abode (Pss 2, 6; 3, 5; 43, 3; 48, 2, etc.).

15, 5: Lends no money at interest: lending money in the Old Testament was often seen as assistance to the poor in

their distress, not as an investment; making money off the poor by charging interest was thus forbidden (Ex 22, 24; Lv 25, 36-37; Dt 23, 20).

Ps 16: In the first section, the psalmist rejects the futile worship of false gods (2-5), preferring Israel's God (1), the giver of the land (6). The second section reflects on the wise and life-giving presence of God (7-11).

16, 1: Miktam: a term occurring six times in psalm superscriptions, always with "David." Its meaning is unknown.

16, 4: Take their names: to use the gods' names in oaths and hence to affirm them as one's own gods.

---

g: Pss 11, 4; 102, 20. h: 2b-3: Rom 3, 11-12. i: Ps 12, 1. j: Ps 27, 2; Is 9, 11. k: Ps 79, 6. l: Ps 85, 2. m: Is 56, 7. n: Ps 119, 1. o: Ex 22, 24; 23, 8. p: Ps 25, 20. q: Pss 23, 5; 73, 26; Nm 18, 20; Lam 3, 24.

6 Pleasant places were measured out for
me;*
  fair to me indeed is my inheritance.

II

7 I bless the LORD who counsels me;
  even at night my heart exhorts me.
8 I keep the LORD always before me;
  with the Lord at my right, I shall
  never be shaken.ʳ
9 Therefore my heart is glad, my soul
  rejoices;
  my body also dwells secure,
10 For you will not abandon me to Sheol,
  nor let your faithful servant see the pit.ˢ *
11 You will show me the path to life,
  abounding joy in your presence,
  the delights at your right hand forever.

See RG
244

PSALM 17*

*Prayer for Rescue from
Persecutors*

1 A prayer of David.

I

Hear, LORD, my plea for justice;
  pay heed to my cry;
Listen to my prayer
  spoken without guile.
2 From you let my vindication come;
  your eyes see what is right.
3 You have tested my heart,
  searched it in the night.ᵗ
You have tried me by fire,
  but find no malice in me.
My mouth has not transgressed
4   as humans often do.
As your lips have instructed me,
  I have kept the way of the law.

5 My steps have kept to your paths;
  my feet have not faltered.ᵘ

II

6 I call upon you; answer me, O God.
  Turn your ear to me; hear my prayer.
7 Show your wonderful love,
  you who deliver with your right arm
  those who seek refuge from their
  foes.
8 Keep me as the apple of your eye;
  hide me in the shadow of your wings*
9   from the violence of the wicked.ᵛ

III

My ravenous enemies press upon me;ʷ
10   they close their hearts,*
  they fill their mouths with proud
  roaring.
11 Their steps even now encircle me;
  they watch closely, keeping low to
  the ground,
12 Like lions eager for prey,
  like young lions lurking in ambush.
13 Rise, O LORD, confront and cast them
  down;
  rescue me so from the wicked.
14 Slay them with your sword;
  with your hand, LORD, slay them;
  snatch them from the world in their
  prime.
Their bellies are being filled with your
  friends;
  their children are satisfied too,
  for they share what is left with their
  young.
15 I am just—let me see your face;
  when I awake,* let me be filled with
  your presence.ˣ

16, 6: **Pleasant places were measured out for me**: the
psalmist is pleased with the plot of land measured out to the
family, which was to be passed on to succeeding generations
("my inheritance").

16, 10: **Nor let your faithful servant see the pit**: Hebrew
shahath means here the pit, a synonym for Sheol, the underworld. The Greek translation derives the word here and elsewhere from the verb *shahath*, "to be corrupt." On the basis of
the Greek, Acts 2, 25-32 and 13, 35-37 apply the verse to
Christ's resurrection, "Nor will you suffer your holy one to
see corruption."

Ps 17: A lament of an individual unjustly attacked who
has taken refuge in the temple. Confident of being found innocent, the psalmist cries out for God's just judgment (1-5)
and requests divine help against enemies (6-9a). Those ravenous lions (9b-12) should be punished (13-14). The psalm

ends with a serene statement of praise (15). The Hebrew text
of vv 3-4 and 14 is uncertain.

17, 8: **Apple of your eye . . . shadow of your wings**: images of God's special care. Cf Dt 32, 10; Prv 7, 2; Is 49, 2.

17, 10-12. 14: An extended metaphor: the enemies are lions.

17, 15: **When I awake**: probably the psalmist has spent
the night in the sanctuary (cf 3) and hopes to wake to an oracle assuring God's protective presence.

r: Pss 73, 23; 121, 5. 8-12; Acts 2, 25-28.   s: Pss 28, 1; 30, 4; 49,
16; 86, 13; Jon 2, 7; Acts 13, 35.   t: Pss 26, 2; 139, 23.   u: Ps 18,
36; Jb 23, 11-12.   v: Pss 36, 8; 57, 2; 61, 5; 63, 8; 91, 4; Dt 32,
10; Ru 2, 12; Zec 2, 12; Mt 23, 37.   w: 9b-12: Pss 10, 9; 22, 14.
22; 35, 17; 58, 7; Jb 4, 10-11.   x: Pss 4, 7; 31, 17; 67, 2; 80, 4;
Nm 6, 25; Dn 9, 17.

See RG
245

PSALM 18*

*A King's Thanksgiving
for Victory*

1 For the leader. Of David, the servant of the
LORD, who sang to the LORD the words of
this song after the LORD had rescued him
from the clutches of all his enemies and
from the hand of Saul. *2* He said:

I

I love you, LORD, my strength,
3   LORD, my rock, my fortress, my
        deliverer,*y*
My God, my rock of refuge,
    my shield, my saving horn,* my
    stronghold!*z*
4 Praised be the LORD, I exclaim!
    I have been delivered from my
        enemies.

II

5 The breakers of death surged round
        about me;
    the menacing floods terrified me.
6 The cords* of Sheol tightened;
    the snares of death lay in wait for me.*a*
7 In my distress I called out: LORD!
    I cried out to my God.*b*
From his temple* he heard my voice;
    my cry to him reached his ears.
8 The earth rocked and shook;*
    the foundations of the mountains
        trembled;
    they shook as his wrath flared up.*c*
9 Smoke rose in his nostrils,
    a devouring fire poured from his
        mouth;
    it kindled coals into flame.

10 He parted the heavens and came down,
    a dark cloud under his feet.*d*
11 Mounted on a cherub* he flew,
    borne along on the wings of the wind.
12 He made darkness the cover about him;
    his canopy, heavy thunderheads.
13 Before him scudded his clouds,
    hail and lightning too.*e*
14 The LORD thundered from heaven;
    the Most High made his voice
        resound.*f*
15 He let fly his arrows* and scattered them;
    shot his lightning bolts and dispersed
        them.*g*
16 Then the bed of the sea appeared;
    the world's foundations lay bare,*h*
At the roar of the LORD,
    at the storming breath of his nostrils.
17 He reached down from on high and
        seized me;
    drew me out of the deep waters.*i*
18 He rescued me from my mighty enemy,
    from foes too powerful for me.
19 They attacked me on a day of distress,
    but the LORD came to my support.
20 He set me free in the open;
    he rescued me because he loves me.

III

21 The LORD acknowledged my
        righteousness,
    rewarded my clean hands.*j*
22 For I kept the ways of the LORD;
    I was not disloyal to my God.
23 His laws were all before me,
    his decrees I did not cast aside.
24 I was honest toward him;
    I was on guard against sin.

Ps 18: A royal thanksgiving for a military victory, duplicated in 2 Sm 22. Thanksgiving psalms are in essence reports
of divine rescue. The psalm has two parallel reports of rescue,
the first told from a heavenly perspective (5-20), and the second from an earthly perspective (36-46). The first report
adapts old mythic language of a cosmic battle between sea
and rainstorm in order to depict God's rescue of the Israelite
king from his enemies. Each report has a short hymnic introduction (2-4. 32-35) and conclusion (21-31. 47-51).

18, 3: My saving horn: my strong savior. The horn referred to is the weapon of a bull and the symbol of fertility. Cf
1 Sm 2, 10; Ps 132, 17; Lk 1, 69.

18, 6: Cords: hunting imagery, the cords of a snare.

18, 7: His temple: his heavenly abode.

18, 8-16: God appears in the storm, which in Palestine
comes from the west. The introduction to the theophany (vv

8-9) is probably a description of a violent, hot, and dry east-
wind storm. In the fall transition period from the rainless
summer to the rainy winter, such storms regularly precede the
rains. Cf Ex 14, 21-22.

18, 11: Cherub: a winged creature, derived from myth, in
the service of the deity (Gn 3, 24; Ex 25, 18-20; 37, 6-9).
Cherubim were the throne bearers of the deity (Pss 80, 2; 99,
1; 1 Kgs 6, 23-28; 8, 6-8).

18, 15: Arrows: lightning.

y: 2-51: 2 Sm 22, 2-51. *z:* Pss 3, 4; 31, 3-4; 42, 10; Gn 49, 24;
Dt 32, 4. *a:* Pss 88, 8; 93, 3-4; 116, 3-4. *b:* Jon 2, 3. *c:* Pss
97, 3-4; 99, 1; Jgs 5, 4-5; Is 64, 1; Hab 3, 9-11. *d:* Pss 104, 3;
144, 5; Is 63, 19. *e:* Ex 13, 21; 19, 16. *f:* Pss 29; 77, 19; Ex 19,
19; Jb 37, 3-4. *g:* Ps 144, 6; Wis 5, 21. *h:* Ps 77, 17; Zec 9, 14.
i: Ps 144, 7. *j:* Ps 26; 1 Sm 26, 23.

²⁵ So the LORD rewarded my righteousness,
  the cleanness of my hands in his sight.
²⁶ Toward the faithful you are faithful;
  to the honest you are honest;*k*
²⁷ Toward the sincere, sincere;
  but to the perverse you are devious.
²⁸ Humble people you save;
  haughty eyes you bring low.*l*
²⁹ You, LORD, give light to my lamp;
  my God brightens the darkness about
  me.*m*
³⁰ With you I can rush an armed band,
  with my God to help I can leap a wall.
³¹ God's way is unerring;
  the LORD's promise is tried and true;
  he is a shield for all who trust in him.*n*

IV

³² Truly, who is God except the LORD?
  Who but our God is the rock?*o*
³³ This God who girded me with might,
  kept my way unerring,
³⁴ Who made my feet swift as a deer's,
  set me safe on the heights,*p*
³⁵ Who trained my hands for war,
  my arms to bend even a bow of
  bronze.*q**

V

³⁶ You have given me your protecting
  shield;
  your right hand has upheld me;
  you stooped to make me great.
³⁷ You gave me room to stride;
  my feet never stumbled.*r*
³⁸ I pursued my enemies and overtook
  them;
  I did not turn back till I destroyed
  them.
³⁹ I struck them down; they could not rise;
  they fell dead at my feet.
⁴⁰ You girded me with strength for war,
  subdued adversaries at my feet.
⁴¹ My foes you put to flight before me;
  those who hated me I destroyed.

⁴² They cried for help, but no one saved
  them;
  cried to the LORD but got no answer.
⁴³ I ground them fine as dust in the wind;
  like mud in the streets I trampled them
  down.
⁴⁴ You rescued me from the strife of
  peoples;
  you made me head over nations.
  A people I had not known became my
  slaves;
⁴⁵ as soon as they heard of me they
  obeyed.
  Foreigners cringed before me;
⁴⁶ their courage failed;
  they came trembling from their
  fortresses.*s*

VI

⁴⁷ The LORD lives! Blessed be my rock!*t*
  Exalted be God, my savior!
⁴⁸ O God who granted me vindication,
  made peoples subject to me,*u*
⁴⁹ and preserved me from my enemies,
  Truly you have exalted me above my
  adversaries,
  from the violent you have rescued me.
⁵⁰ Thus I will proclaim you, LORD, among
  the nations;
  I will sing the praises of your name.*v*
⁵¹ You have given great victories to your
  king,
  and shown kindness to your anointed,
  to David and his posterity forever.*w*

PSALM 19*

God's Glory in the Heavens
and in the Law

| See RG 244 |

¹ For the leader. A psalm of David.

I

² The heavens declare the glory of God;
  the sky proclaims its builder's craft.*x*
³ One day to the next conveys that
  message;

18, 35: Bow of bronze: hyperbole for a bow difficult to bend and therefore capable of propelling an arrow with great force.
  Ps 19: The heavenly elements of the world, now beautifully arranged, bespeak the power and wisdom of their creator (2-7). The creator's wisdom is available to human beings in the law (8-11), toward which the psalmist prays to be open (12-15). The themes of light and speech unify the poem.

k: Ps 125, 4. *l*: Jb 22, 29; Prv 3, 34. *m*: Pss 27, 1; 36, 10; 43, 3; 119, 105; Jb 29, 3; Mi 7, 8. *n*: Pss 12, 6; 77, 13; Prv 30, 5. *o*: Is 44, 8; 45, 21. *p*: Hb 3, 19. *q*: Ps 144, 1. *r*: Ps 17, 5. *s*: Mi 7, 17. *t*: Ps 144, 1. *u*: Ps 144, 2. *v*: Pss 7, 18; 30, 5; 57, 9; 135, 3; 146, 2; Rom 15, 9. *w*: Pss 89, 28-37; 144, 10; 1 Sm 2, 10. *x*: Pss 8, 1; 50, 6; 97, 6.

one night to the next imparts that
knowledge.

4 There is no word or sound;*
no voice is heard;

5 Yet their report goes forth through all the
earth,
their message, to the ends of the world.
God has pitched there a tent for the sun;*

6 it comes forth like a bridegroom from
his chamber,
and like an athlete joyfully runs its
course.

7 From one end of the heavens it comes
forth;
its course runs through to the other;
nothing escapes its heat.

II

8 The law of the LORD is perfect,
refreshing the soul.
The decree of the LORD is trustworthy,
giving wisdom to the simple.*y*

9 The precepts of the LORD are right,
rejoicing the heart.
The command of the LORD is clear,
enlightening the eye.

10 The fear of the LORD is pure,
enduring forever.
The statutes of the LORD are true,
all of them just;

11 More desirable than gold,
than a hoard of purest gold,
Sweeter also than honey
or drippings from the comb.*z*

12 By them your servant is instructed;*
obeying them brings much reward.

III

13 Who can detect heedless failings?
Cleanse me from my unknown faults.

14 But from willful sins keep your servant;

let them never control me.
Then shall I be blameless,
innocent of grave sin.

15 Let the words of my mouth meet with
your favor,
keep the thoughts of my heart before
you,
LORD, my rock and my redeemer.

PSALM 20*

Prayer for the King in Time of War

See RG 245

1 For the leader. A psalm of David.

I

2 The LORD answer you in time of distress;
the name of the God of Jacob defend
you!

3 May God send you help from the temple,
from Zion be your support.*a*

4 May God remember* your every offering,
graciously accept your
holocaust,   *Selah*

5 Grant what is in your heart,
fulfill your every plan.

6 May we shout for joy at your victory,*
raise the banners in the name of our
God.
The LORD grant your every prayer!

II

7 Now I know victory is given
to the anointed of the LORD.*b*
God will answer him from the holy
heavens
with a strong arm that brings victory.

8 Some rely on chariots, others on horses,
but we on the name of the LORD our
God.*c*

9 They collapse and fall,
but we stand strong and firm.*d*

19, 4: No word or sound: the regular functioning of the heavens and the alternation of day and night inform humans without words of the creator's power and wisdom.

19, 5: The sun: in other religious literature the sun is a judge and lawgiver since it sees all in its daily course; 5b-7 form a transition to the law in 8-11. The six synonyms for God's revelation (8-11) are applied to the sun in comparable literature.

19, 12: Instructed: the Hebrew verb means both to shine and to teach. Cf Dn 12, 3.

Ps 20: The people pray for the king before battle. The people ask for divine help (2-6) and express confidence that such help will be given (7-10). A solemn assurance of divine

help may well have been given between the two sections in the liturgy, something like the promises of Pss 12, 6 and 21, 9-13. The final verse (10) echoes the opening verse.

20, 4: Remember: God's remembering implies readiness to act. Cf Gn 8, 1; Ex 2, 24.

20, 6: Victory: the Hebrew root is often translated "salvation," "to save," but in military contexts it can have the specific meaning of "victory."

y: Pss 12, 7; 119.   *z:* Sir 24, 19.   *a:* Pss 128, 5; 134, 3.   *b:* Pss 18, 51; 144, 10; 1 Sm 2, 10.   *c:* Ps 147, 10-11; 2 Chr 14, 10; Prv 21, 31; 1 Sm 17, 45; Is 31, 1; 36, 9.   *d:* Is 40, 30.

[10] LORD, grant victory to the king;
     answer when we call upon you.

See RG
245

PSALM 21[*]

Thanksgiving and Assurances
for the King

[1] For the leader. A psalm of David.

I

[2] LORD, the king finds joy in your power;[e]
    in your victory how greatly he
        rejoices!
[3] You have granted him his heart's desire;
    you did not refuse the prayer of his
        lips.   *Selah*
[4] For you welcomed him with goodly
        blessings;
    you placed on his head a crown of
        pure gold.
[5] He asked life of you;
    you gave it to him,
    length of days forever.[f]
[6] Great is his glory in your victory;
    majesty and splendor you confer upon
        him.
[7] You make him the pattern of blessings
        forever,
    you gladden him with the joy of your
        presence.
[8] For the king trusts in the LORD,
    stands firm through the love of the
        Most High.

II

[9] Your hand will reach all your enemies;
    your right hand will reach your foes!
[10] At the time of your coming
     you will drive them into a furnace.
     Then the LORD's anger will consume
         them,
     devour them with fire.

[11] Even their descendants you will wipe out
         from the earth,
     their offspring from the human race.
[12] Though they intend evil against you,
     devising plots, they will not succeed,
[13] For you will put them to flight;
     you will aim at them with your bow.

III

[14] Arise, LORD, in your power![g]
     We will sing and chant the praise of
         your might.

PSALM 22[*]

See RG
245, 251

The Prayer of an
Innocent Person

[1] For the leader; according to "The deer of
    the dawn."[*] A psalm of David.

I

[2] My God, my God, why have you
        abandoned me?
    Why so far from my call for help,
    from my cries of anguish?[h]
[3] My God, I call by day, but you do not
        answer;
    by night, but I have no relief.[i]
[4] Yet you are enthroned as the Holy One;
    you are the glory of Israel.[j]
[5] In you our ancestors trusted;
    they trusted and you rescued them.
[6] To you they cried out and they
        escaped;
    in you they trusted and were not
        disappointed.[k]
[7] But I am a worm, hardly human,[*]
    scorned by everyone, despised by the
        people.[l]
[8] All who see me mock me;
    they curl their lips and jeer;
    they shake their heads at me:[m]

Ps 21: The first part of this royal psalm is a thanksgiving (2-8), and the second is a promise that the king will triumph over his enemies (9-14). The king's confident prayer (3. 5) and trust in God (8) enable him to receive the divine gifts of vitality, peace, and military success. V 14 reprises v 1. When kings ceased in Israel after the sixth century B.C., the psalm was sung of a future Davidic king.

Ps 22: A lament unusual in structure and in intensity of feeling. The psalmist's present distress is contrasted with God's past mercy in vv 2-12. In vv 13-22 enemies surround the psalmist. The last third is an invitation to praise God (23-27), becoming a universal chorus of praise (28-32). The psalm is important in the New Testament. Its opening words

occur on the lips of the crucified Jesus (Mk 15, 34; Mt 27, 46), and several other verses are quoted, or at least alluded to, in the accounts of Jesus' passion (Mt 27, 35. 43; Jn 19, 24).

22, 1: The deer of the dawn: apparently the title of the melody.

22, 7: I am a worm, hardly human: the psalmist's sense of isolation and dehumanization, an important motif of Ps 22, is vividly portrayed here.

e: Ps 63, 12.   *f:* 1 Kgs 3, 14.   *g:* Nm 10, 35.   *h:* Is 49, 14; 54, 7; Mt 27, 46; Mk 15, 34.   *i:* Sir 2, 10.   *j:* Is 6, 3.   *k:* Ps 25, 3; Is 49, 23; Dn 3, 40.   *l:* Is 53, 3.   *m:* Ps 109, 25; Mt 27, 39; Mk 15, 29; Lk 23, 35.

⁹ "You relied on the LORD—let him deliver
  you;
  if he loves you, let him rescue you."ⁿ
¹⁰ Yet you drew me forth from the womb,
  made me safe at my mother's breast.
¹¹ Upon you I was thrust from the womb;
  since birth you are my God.ᵒ
¹² Do not stay far from me,
  for trouble is near,
  and there is no one to help.ᵖ

II

¹³ Many bulls* surround me;
  fierce bulls of Bashan* encircle me.
¹⁴ They open their mouths against me,
  lions that rend and roar.�q
¹⁵ Like water my life drains away;
  all my bones grow soft.
  My heart has become like wax,
  it melts away within me.
¹⁶ As dry as a potsherd is my throat;
  my tongue sticks to my palate;
  you lay me in the dust of death.*
¹⁷ Many dogs surround me;
  a pack of evildoers closes in on me.
  So wasted are my hands and feet
¹⁸   that I can count all my bones.ʳ
  They stare at me and gloat;
¹⁹   they divide my garments among
    them;
  for my clothing they cast lots.ˢ
²⁰ But you, LORD, do not stay far off;
  my strength, come quickly to help me.
²¹ Deliver me from the sword,
  my forlorn life from the teeth of the
    dog.
²² Save me from the lion's mouth,
  my poor life from the horns of wild
    bulls.ᵗ

III

²³ Then I will proclaim your name to the
  assembly;
  in the community I will praise you:ᵘ *
²⁴ "You who fear the LORD, give praise!
  All descendants of Jacob, give
    honor;
  show reverence, all descendants of
    Israel!
²⁵ For God has not spurned or disdained
  the misery of this poor wretch,
  Did not turn away* from me,
  but heard me when I cried out.
²⁶ I will offer praise in the great assembly;
  my vows I will fulfill before those
    who fear him.
²⁷ The poor* will eat their fill;
  those who seek the LORD will offer
    praise.
  May your hearts enjoy life forever!"ᵛ

IV

²⁸ All the ends of the earth
  will worship and turn to the LORD;
  All the families of nations
  will bow low before you.ʷ
²⁹ For kingship belongs to the LORD,
  the ruler over the nations.ˣ
³⁰ All who sleep in the earth
  will bow low before God;
  All who have gone down into the dust*
  will kneel in homage.
³¹ And I will live for the LORD;
  my descendants will serve you.
³² The generation to come will be told of
  the Lord,
  that they may proclaim to a people yet
    unborn
  the deliverance you have brought.ʸ

22, 13-14: Bulls: the enemies of the psalmist are also portrayed in less-than-human form, as wild animals (cf 17. 21-22). **Bashan**: a grazing land east of the Jordan, famed for its cattle. Cf Dt 32, 14; Ez 39, 18; Am 4, 1.

22, 16: The dust of death: the netherworld, the domain of the dead.

22, 23: In the community I will praise you: the person who offered a thanksgiving sacrifice in the temple recounted to the other worshipers the favor received from God and invited them to share in the sacrificial banquet. The final section (24-32) may be a summary or a citation of the psalmist's poem of praise.

22, 25: Turn away: literally, "hides his face from me," an important metaphor for God withdrawing from someone, e.g., Mi 3, 4; Is 8, 17; Pss 27, 9; 69, 18; 88, 15.

22, 27: The poor: originally the poor, who were dependent on God; the term ('*anawim*) came to include the religious sense of "humble, pious, devout."

22, 30: Hebrew unclear. The translation assumes that all on earth (28-29) and under the earth (30) will worship God.

n: Ps 71, 11; Wis 2, 18-20; Mt 27, 43. *o:* Ps 71, 6; Is 44, 2; 46, 3. *p:* Pss 35, 22; 38, 22; 71, 12. *q:* Ps 17, 12; Jb 4, 10; 1 Pt 5, 8. *r:* Ps 109, 24. *s:* Mt 27, 35; Mk 15, 24; Lk 23, 34; Jn 19, 24. *t:* Pss 7, 2-3; 17, 12; 35, 17; 57, 5; 58, 7; 2 Tm 4, 17. *u:* Pss 26, 12; 35, 18; 40, 10; 109, 30; 149, 1; 2 Sm 22, 50; Heb 2, 12. *v:* Pss 23, 5; 69, 33. *w:* Ps 86, 9; Tb 13, 11; Is 45, 22; 52, 10; Zec 14, 16. *x:* Ps 103, 19; Ob 21; Zec 14, 9. *y:* Pss 48, 14-15; 71, 18; 78, 6; 102, 19; Is 53, 10.

See RG
245, 249

PSALM 23*

The Lord, Shepherd and Host

1 A psalm of David.

I

The LORD is my shepherd;*
  there is nothing I lack.*z*

2 In green pastures you let me graze;
  to safe waters you lead me;
3   you restore my strength.
You guide me along the right path*
  for the sake of your name.*a*

4 Even when I walk through a dark
    valley,*b* *
  I fear no harm for you are at my side;
  your rod and staff give me courage.

II

5 You set a table before me*
  as my enemies watch;*
You anoint my head with oil;*c* *
  my cup overflows.*d*

6 Only goodness and love* will pursue me
  all the days of my life;
I will dwell in the house of the LORD*e*
  for years to come.

See RG
246

PSALM 24*

*The Glory of God in
Procession to Zion*

1 A psalm of David.

I

The earth is the LORD's and all it holds,*f*
  the world and those who live there.

2 For God founded it on the seas,
  established it over the rivers.*g*

II

3 Who may go up the mountain of the
    LORD?*h*
  Who can stand in his holy
    place?

4 "The clean of hand and pure of
    heart,*
  who are not devoted to idols,
  who have not sworn falsely.

5 They will receive blessings from the
    LORD,
  and justice from their saving God.

6 Such are the people that love the
    LORD,
  that seek the face of the God of
    Jacob."   *Selah*

III

7 Lift up your heads, O gates;
  rise up, you ancient portals,*
  that the king of glory may
    enter.*i*

8 Who is this king of glory?
  The LORD, a mighty warrior,
  the LORD, mighty in battle.

9 Lift up your heads, O gates;
  rise up, you ancient portals,
  that the king of glory may
    enter.

10 Who is this king of glory?
  The LORD of hosts is the king of
    glory.   *Selah*

Ps 23: God's loving care for the psalmist is portrayed under the figures of a shepherd for the flock (1-4) and a host's generosity toward a guest (5-6). The imagery of both sections is drawn from traditions of the exodus (Is 40, 11; 49, 10; Jer 31, 10).

23, 1: My shepherd: God as good shepherd is common in both the Old Testament and the New Testament (Ez 34, 11-16 and Jn 10, 11-18).

23, 3: The right path: connotes "right way" and "way of righteousness."

23, 4: A dark valley: a different division of the Hebrew consonants yields the translation "the valley of the shadow of death."

23, 5: You set a table before me: this expression occurs in an exodus context in Ps 78, 19. **As my enemies watch:** my enemies see that I am God's friend and guest. **Oil:** a perfumed ointment made from olive oil, used especially at banquets (Ps 104, 15; Mt 26, 7; Lk 7, 37. 46; Jn 12, 2).

23, 6: Goodness and love: the blessings of God's covenant with Israel.

Ps 24: The psalm apparently accompanied a ceremony of

the entry of God (invisibly enthroned upon the ark), followed by the people, into the temple. The temple commemorated the creation of the world (1-2). The people had to affirm their fidelity before being admitted into the sanctuary (3-6; cf Ps 15). A choir identifies the approaching God and invites the very temple gates to bow down in obeisance (7-10).

24, 4-5: Literally, "the one whose hands are clean." The singular is used for the entire class of worshipers, hence the plural translation.

24, 7. 9: Lift up your heads, O gates . . . you ancient portals: the literal meaning is impossible since the portcullis (a gate that moves up and down) was unknown in the ancient world. Extra-biblical parallels suggest a full personification of the circle of gate towers: they are like a council of elders, bowed down and anxious, awaiting the return of the army and the Great Warrior gone to battle.

z: Pss 80, 2; 95, 7; 100, 3; Dt 2, 7. *a:* Prv 4, 11. *b:* Jb 10, 21-22; Is 50, 10. *c:* Ps 92, 11. *d:* Ps 16, 5. *e:* Ps 27, 4. *f:* Pss 50, 12; 89, 12; Dt 10, 14; 1 Cor 10, 26. *g:* Ps 136, 6; Is 42, 5. *h:* Ps 15, 1. *i:* Ps 118, 19-20.

See RG
244, 245

PSALM 25*

Confident Prayer for Forgiveness and Guidance

¹ Of David.

I

I wait for you, O LORD;
  I lift up my soul ² to my God.ʲ
In you I trust; do not let me be
  disgraced;ᵏ
  do not let my enemies gloat over me.
³ No one is disgraced who waits for you,ˡ
  but only those who lightly break faith.
⁴ Make known to me your ways, LORD;
  teach me your paths.ᵐ
⁵ Guide me in your truth and teach me,
  for you are God my savior.
For you I wait all the long day,
  because of your goodness, LORD.*
⁶ Remember your compassion and love,
  O LORD;
  for they are ages old.ⁿ
⁷ Remember no more the sins of my
  youth;ᵒ
  remember me only in light of your
  love.

II

⁸ Good and upright is the LORD,
  who shows sinners the way,
⁹ Guides the humble rightly,
  and teaches the humble the way.
¹⁰ All the paths of the LORD are faithful
  love
  toward those who honor the covenant
  demands.
¹¹ For the sake of your name, LORD,
  pardon my guilt, though it is great.
¹² Who are those who fear the LORD?
  God shows them the way to choose.ᵖ

¹³ They live well and prosper,
  and their descendants inherit the land.�q
¹⁴ The counsel of the LORD belongs to the
  faithful;
  the covenant instructs them.
¹⁵ My eyes are ever upon the LORD,
  who frees my feet from the snare.ʳ

III

¹⁶ Look upon me, have pity on me,
  for I am alone and afflicted.ˢ
¹⁷ Relieve the troubles of my heart;
  bring me out of my distress.
¹⁸ Put an end to my affliction and suffering;
  take away all my sins.
¹⁹ See how many are my enemies,
  see how fiercely they hate me.
²⁰ Preserve my life and rescue me;
  do not let me be disgraced, for I trust
  in you.
²¹ Let honesty and virtue preserve me;
  I wait for you, O LORD.
²² Redeem Israel, God,*
  from all its distress!

PSALM 26*

Prayer of Innocence

¹ Of David.

See RG
244

I

Grant me justice, LORD!
  I have walked without blame.ᵗ
In the LORD I have trusted;
  I have not faltered.
² Test me, LORD, and try me;
  search my heart and mind.ᵘ
³ Your love is before my eyes;
  I walk guided by your faithfulness.ᵛ

II

⁴ I do not sit with deceivers,
  nor with hypocrites do I mingle.

Ps 25: A lament. Each verse begins with a successive letter of the Hebrew alphabet. Such acrostic psalms are often a series of statements only loosely connected. The psalmist mixes ardent pleas (1-2. 16-22) with expressions of confidence in God who forgives and guides.
25, 5: Because of your goodness, LORD: these words have been transposed from the end of 7 to preserve the pattern of two lines per letter of the Hebrew alphabet in the acrostic poem.
25, 22: A final verse beginning with the Hebrew letter *pe* is added to the normal 22-letter alphabet. Thus the letters *aleph, lamed,* and *pe* open the first, middle (v 11), and last lines of the psalm. Together, they spell *aleph*, the first letter

of the alphabet.
Ps 26: Like a priest washing before approaching the altar (Ex 30, 17-21), the psalmist seeks God's protection upon entering the temple. 1-3, matched by 11-12, remind God of past integrity while asking for purification; 4-5, matched by 9-10, pray for inclusion among the just; 6-8, the center of the poem, express the joy in God at the heart of all ritual.

j: Pss 86, 4; 143, 8. *k*: Ps 71, 1. *l*: Ps 22, 6; Is 49, 23; Dn 3, 40.
m: Pss 27, 11; 86, 11; 119, 12. 35; 143, 8. 10. *n*: Sir 51, 8. *o*: Jb 13, 26; Is 64, 8. *p*: Prv 19, 23. *q*: Ps 37, 9. 29. *r*: Pss 123, 1. 2; 141, 8. *s*: Pss 86, 16; 119, 132. *t*: Ps 7, 9. *u*: Pss 17, 3; 139, 23. *v*: Ps 86, 11.

⁵ I hate the company of evildoers;
  with the wicked I do not sit.
⁶ I will wash my hands* in innocence^w
  and walk round your altar, LORD,
⁷ Lifting my voice in thanks,
  recounting all your wondrous deeds.
⁸ LORD, I love the house where you dwell,
  the tenting-place of your glory.^x

III

⁹ Do not take me away with sinners,
  nor my life with the violent.^y
¹⁰ Their hands carry out their schemes;
  their right hands are full of bribes.
¹¹ But I walk without blame;^z
  redeem me, be gracious to me!^a
¹² My foot stands on level ground;*
  in assemblies* I will bless the LORD.^b

See RG 244

PSALM 27*

Trust in God

¹ Of David

A

I

The LORD is my light and my salvation;^c
  whom do I fear?
The LORD is my life's refuge;
  of whom am I afraid?
² When evildoers come at me
  to devour my flesh,^d *
These my enemies and foes
  themselves stumble and fall.
³ Though an army encamp against me,
  my heart does not fear;
Though war be waged against me,
  even then do I trust.

II

⁴ One thing I ask of the LORD;
  this I seek:

To dwell in the LORD's house
  all the days of my life,
To gaze on the LORD's beauty,
  to visit his temple.^e
⁵ For God will hide me in his shelter
  in time of trouble,^f
Will conceal me in the cover of his tent;
  and set me high upon a rock.
⁶ Even now my head is held high
  above my enemies on every side!
I will offer in his tent
  sacrifices with shouts of joy;
I will sing and chant praise to the LORD.

B

I

⁷ Hear my voice, LORD, when I call;
  have mercy on me and answer me.
⁸ "Come," says my heart, "seek God's
  face";*
  your face, LORD, do I seek!^g
⁹ Do not hide your face from me;
  do not repel your servant in anger.
You are my help; do not cast me off;
  do not forsake me, God my savior!
¹⁰ Even if my father and mother forsake me,
  the LORD will take me in.^h

II

¹¹ LORD, show me your way;
  lead me on a level path
  because of my enemies.^i
¹² Do not abandon me to the will of my foes;
  malicious and lying witnesses have
    risen against me.
¹³ But I believe I shall enjoy the LORD's
    goodness
  in the land of the living.^j *
¹⁴ Wait for the LORD, take courage;
  be stouthearted, wait for the LORD!

26, 6: I will wash my hands: the washing of hands was a liturgical act (Ex 30, 19. 21; 40, 31-32), symbolic of inner as well as outer cleanness. Cf Is 1, 16.

26, 12: On level ground: in safety, where there is no danger of tripping and falling. **In assemblies**: at the temple. Having walked around the altar, the symbol of God's presence, the psalmist blesses God.

Ps 27: Tradition has handed down the two sections of the psalm (1-6 and 7-14) as one psalm, though each part could be understood as complete in itself. Asserting boundless hope that God will bring rescue (1-3), the psalmist longs for the presence of God in the temple, protection from all enemies (4-6). In part B there is a clear shift in tone (7-12); the climax of the poem comes with "I believe" (13), echoing "I trust" (3).

27, 2: To devour my flesh: the psalmist's enemies are ra-

pacious beasts (Pss 7, 3; 17, 12; 22, 14. 17).

27, 8: Seek God's face (literally: "to seek his face"): to commune with God in the temple. The idiom is derived from the practice of journeying to sacred places. Cf Hos 5, 15; 2 Sm 21, 1; Ps 24, 6.

27, 13: In the land of the living: or "in the land of life," an epithet of the Jerusalem temple (Pss 52, 7; 116, 9; Is 38, 11), where the faithful had access to the life-giving presence of God.

w: Ps 73, 13. x: Pss 29, 9; 63, 3; Ex 24, 16; 25, 8. y: Ps 28, 3.
z: Ps 101, 6. a: Ps 25, 16. b: Pss 22, 23; 35, 18; 149, 1. c: Pss
18, 29; 36, 10; 43, 3; Is 10, 17; Mi 7, 8. d: Ps 14, 4. e: Pss 23,
6; 61, 5. f: Ps 31, 21. g: Ps 24, 6; Hos 5, 15. h: Is 49, 15.
i: Pss 25, 4; 86, 11. j: Ps 116, 9; Is 38, 11.

See RG
244

PSALM 28*

Petition and Thanksgiving
¹ Of David.

I

To you, LORD, I call;
    my Rock, do not be deaf to me.*ᵏ*
If you fail to answer me,
    I will join those who go down to the
        pit.*ˡ* *
² Hear the sound of my pleading when I
        cry to you,
    lifting my hands toward your holy
        place.*ᵐ* *
³ Do not drag me off with the wicked,
    with those who do wrong,*ⁿ*
Who speak peace to their neighbors
    though evil is in their hearts.*ᵒ*
⁴ Repay them for their deeds,
    for the evil that they do.
For the work of their hands repay them;
    give them what they deserve.*ᵖ*
⁵ They pay no heed to the LORD's works,
    to the deeds of God's hands.*�q*
God will tear them down,
    never to be rebuilt.

II

⁶ Blessed be the LORD,
    who has heard the sound of my
        pleading.*
⁷ The LORD is my strength and my shield,
    in whom my heart trusted and found
        help.
So my heart rejoices;

with my song I praise my God.

III

⁸ LORD, you are the strength of your
        people,*
    the saving refuge of your anointed
        king.
⁹ Save your people, bless your inheritance;
    feed and sustain them forever!

PSALM 29*

The Lord of Majesty
Acclaimed as King of the World
¹ A psalm of David.

See RG
244, 250

I

Give to the LORD, you heavenly beings,*
    give to the LORD glory and might;
² Give to the LORD the glory due God's
        name.
Bow down before the LORD's holy
        splendor!*ʳ*

II

³ The voice of the LORD* is over the
        waters;
    the God of glory thunders,
    the LORD, over the mighty waters.
⁴ The voice of the LORD is power;
    the voice of the LORD is splendor.*ˢ*
⁵ The voice of the LORD cracks the cedars;
    the LORD splinters the cedars of
        Lebanon,
⁶ Makes Lebanon leap like a calf,
    and Sirion* like a young bull.
⁷ The voice of the LORD strikes with fiery
        flame;

Ps 28: A lament asking that the psalmist, who has taken refuge in the temple (2), not be punished with the wicked, who are headed inevitably toward destruction (1. 3-5). The statement of praise is exceptionally lengthy and vigorous (6-7). The psalm ends with a prayer (8-9).
28, 1: The pit: a synonym for Sheol, the shadowy place of the dead.
28, 2: Your holy place: the innermost part of the temple, the holy of holies, containing the ark. Cf 1 Kgs 6, 16. 19-23; 8, 6-8.
28, 6: The psalmist shifts to fervent thanksgiving, probably responding to a priestly or prophetic oracle in 5cd (not usually transmitted) assuring the worshiper that the prayer has been heard.
28, 8: Your people . . . your anointed king: salvation is more than individual, affecting all the people and their God-given leader.
Ps 29: The hymn invites the members of the heavenly court to acknowledge God's supremacy by ascribing glory and might to God alone (1-2a. 9b). Divine glory and might

are dramatically visible in the storm (3-9a). The storm apparently comes from the Mediterranean onto the coast of Syria-Palestine and then moves inland. In 10 the divine beings acclaim God's eternal kingship. The psalm concludes with a prayer that God will impart the power just displayed to the Israelite king and through the king to Israel.
29, 1: You heavenly beings: literally "sons of God," i.e., members of the heavenly court who served Israel's God in a variety of capacities.
29, 3: The voice of the LORD: the sevenfold repetition of the phrase imitates the sound of crashing thunder and may allude to God's primordial slaying of Leviathan, the seven-headed sea monster of Canaanite mythology.
29, 6: Sirion: the Phoenician name for Mount Hermon. Cf Dt 3, 9.

k: Ps 18, 2.   *l:* Pss 30, 4; 88, 5; 143, 7; Prv 1, 12.   *m:* Ps 134, 2.   *n:* Ps 26, 9.   *o:* Pss 12, 2; 55, 22; 62, 5; Prv 26, 24-28.   *p:* 2 Sm 3, 39.   *q:* Is 5, 12.   *r:* Pss 68, 35; 96, 7-9.   *s:* Pss 46, 7; 77, 18-19; Jb 37, 4; Is 30, 30.

8 the voice of the LORD rocks the
    desert;
  the LORD rocks the desert of Kadesh.*
9 The voice of the LORD twists the oaks
    and strips the forests bare.
  All in his palace say, "Glory!"*

III

10 The LORD sits enthroned above the
    flood!*
  The LORD reigns as king forever!
11 May the LORD give might to his people;*
    may the LORD bless his people with
    peace!*

See RG
245
PSALM 30*

Thanksgiving for Deliverance

1 A psalm. A song for the dedication of the
    temple.* Of David.

I

2 I praise you, LORD, for you raised
    me up
  and did not let my enemies rejoice
    over me.
3 O LORD, my God,
  I cried out to you and you healed* me.
4 LORD, you brought me up from Sheol;
  you kept me from going down to the
    pit.*

II

5 Sing praise to the LORD, you faithful;
    give thanks to God's holy name.
6 For divine anger lasts but a moment;
    divine favor lasts a lifetime.
  At dusk weeping comes for the night;
    but at dawn there is rejoicing.

III

7 Complacent,* I once said,
  "I shall never be shaken."
8 LORD, when you showed me favor
  I stood like the mighty mountains.
  But when you hid your face
  I was struck with terror.*
9 To you, LORD, I cried out;
  with the Lord I pleaded for mercy:
10 "What gain is there from my lifeblood,
  from my going down to the grave?
  Does dust give you thanks
  or declare your faithfulness?*
11 Hear, O LORD, have mercy on me;
  LORD, be my helper."

IV

12 You changed my mourning into dancing;
  you took off my sackcloth
  and clothed me with gladness.*
13 With my whole being I sing
  endless praise to you.
  O LORD, my God,
  forever will I give you thanks.

PSALM 31*

Prayer in Distress and
Thanksgiving for Escape

1 For the leader. A psalm of David.

I

2 In you, LORD, I take refuge;*
  let me never be put to shame.
  In your justice deliver me;
3   incline your ear to me;
    make haste to rescue me!
  Be my rock of refuge,

See RG
244

29, 8: The desert of Kadesh: probably north of Palestine in the neighborhood of Lebanon and Hermon.

29, 9b-10: Having witnessed God's supreme power (3-9a), the gods acknowledge the glory that befits the king of the divine and human world.

29, 10: The flood: God defeated the primordial waters and made them part of the universe. Cf Pss 89, 10-13 and 93, 3-4.

29, 11: His people: God's people, Israel.

Ps 30: An individual thanksgiving in four parts: praise and thanks for deliverance and restoration (2-4); an invitation to others to join in (5-6); a flashback to the time before deliverance (7-11); a return to praise and thanks (12-13). Two sets of images recur: 1) going down, death, silence; 2) coming up, life, praising. God has delivered the psalmist from one state to the other.

30, 1: For the dedication of the temple: a later adaptation of the psalm to celebrate the purification of the temple in 164 B.C. during the Maccabean Revolt.

30, 3: Healed: for God as healer, see also Pss 103, 3; 107, 20; Hos 6, 1; 7, 1; 11, 3; 14, 5.

30, 4: Sheol . . . pit: the shadowy underworld residence of the spirits of the dead, here a metaphor for near death.

30, 7: Complacent: untroubled existence is often seen as a source of temptation to forget God. Cf Dt 8, 10-18; Hos 13, 6; Prv 30, 9.

30, 10: In the stillness of Sheol no one gives you praise; let me live and be among your worshipers. Cf Pss 6, 6; 88, 11-13; 115, 17; Is 38, 18.

Ps 31: A lament (2-19) with a strong emphasis on trust (4. 6. 15-16), ending with an anticipatory thanksgiving (20-25). As is usual in laments, the affliction is couched in general terms. The psalmist feels overwhelmed by evil people but trusts in the "faithful God" (6).

t: Bar 3, 3.   *u:* Ps 68, 36.   *v:* Ps 28, 1; Jon 2, 7.   *w:* Ps 104, 29.
x: Is 61, 3; Jer 31, 13.   *y:* 2-4: Ps 71, 1-3.

a stronghold to save me.

[4] You are my rock and my fortress;[z]
  for your name's sake lead and guide me.

[5] Free me from the net they have set for me,
  for you are my refuge.

[6] Into your hands I commend my spirit;[a]*
  you will redeem me, LORD, faithful
    God.

[7] You hate those who serve worthless idols,
  but I trust in the LORD.

[8] I will rejoice and be glad in your love,
  once you have seen my misery,
  observed my distress.[b]

[9] You will not abandon me into enemy
    hands,
  but will set my feet in a free and open
    space.

II

[10] Be gracious to me, LORD, for I am in
    distress;
  with grief my eyes are wasted,
  my soul and body spent.

[11] My life is worn out by sorrow,
  my years by sighing.
  My strength fails in affliction;
  my bones are consumed.[c]

[12] To all my foes I am a thing of scorn,
  to my neighbors, a dreaded sight,
  a horror to my friends.
  When they see me in the street,
  they quickly shy away.[d]

[13] I am forgotten, out of mind like the dead;
  I am like a shattered dish.*

[14] I hear the whispers of the crowd;
  terrors are all around me.*
  They conspire against me;
  they plot to take my life.

[15] But I trust in you, LORD;
  I say, "You are my God."[e]

[16] My times are in your hands;

rescue me from my enemies,
  from the hands of my pursuers.

[17] Let your face shine on your servant;[f]
  save me in your kindness.

[18] Do not let me be put to shame,
  for I have called to you, LORD.
  Put the wicked to shame;
  reduce them to silence in Sheol.

[19] Strike dumb their lying lips,
  proud lips that attack the just
  in contempt and scorn.[g]

III

[20] How great is your goodness, LORD,
  stored up for those who fear you.
  You display it for those who trust you,
  in the sight of all the people.

[21] You hide them in the shelter of your
    presence,
  safe from scheming enemies.
  You keep them in your abode,
  safe from plotting tongues.[h]

[22] Blessed be the LORD,
  who has shown me wondrous love,
  and been for me a city most secure.

[23] Once I said in my anguish,
  "I am shut out from your sight."[i]
  Yet you heard my plea,
  when I cried out to you.

[24] Love the LORD, all you faithful.
  The LORD protects the loyal,
  but repays the arrogant in full.

[25] Be strong and take heart,
  all you who hope in the LORD.

PSALM 32*

Remission of Sin

See RG
245

[1] Of David. A *maskil.*

I

Happy the sinner whose fault is removed,
  whose sin is forgiven.[j]

31, 6: Into your hands I commend my spirit: in Lk 23, 46 Jesus breathes his last with this psalm verse. Stephen in Acts 7, 59 alludes to these words as he is attacked by enemies. The verse is used as an antiphon in the Divine Office at Compline, the last prayer of the day.

31, 13: Like a shattered dish: a common comparison for something ruined and useless. Cf Is 30, 14; Jer 19, 11; 22, 28.

31, 14: Terrors are all around: a cry used in inescapable danger. Cf Jer 6, 25; 20, 10; 46, 5; 49, 29.

Ps 32: An individual thanksgiving and the second of the seven Penitential Psalms (cf Ps 6). The opening declaration—the forgiven are blessed (1-2)—arises from the psalmist's

own experience. At one time the psalmist was stubborn and closed, a victim of sin's power (3-4), and then became open to the forgiving God (5-7). Sin here, as often in the Bible, is not only the personal act of rebellion against God but also the consequences of that act—frustration and waning of vitality. Having been rescued, the psalmist can teach others the joys of justice and the folly of sin (8-11).

z: Ps 18, 2. *a:* Lk 23, 46; Acts 7, 59. *b:* Ps 10, 14. *c:* Pss 32, 3; 38, 10-11. *d:* Jb 19, 13-19. *e:* Ps 140, 7; Is 25, 1. *f:* Ps 67, 1; Nm 6, 24. *g:* Ps 12, 4. *h:* Ps 27, 5. *i:* Jon 2, 5. *j:* Is 1, 18; Ps 65, 3; Rom 4, 7-8.

2 Happy those to whom the LORD imputes
    no guilt,
  in whose spirit is no deceit.

II

3 As long as I kept silent,* my bones
    wasted away;
  I groaned all the day.[k]
4 For day and night your hand was heavy
    upon me;
  my strength withered as in dry
    summer heat.   *Selah*
5 Then I declared my sin to you;
  my guilt I did not hide.[l]
  I said, "I confess my faults to the
    LORD,"
  and you took away the guilt of my
    sin.   *Selah*
6 Thus should all your faithful pray
  in time of distress.
  Though flood waters* threaten,
    they will never reach them.[m]
7 You are my shelter; from distress you
    keep me;
  with safety you ring me round.   *Selah*

III

8 I will instruct you and show you the way
    you should walk,
  give you counsel and watch over you.
9 Do not be senseless like horses or
    mules;
  with bit and bridle their temper is
    curbed,
  else they will not come to you.

IV

10 Many are the sorrows of the wicked,
  but love surrounds those who trust in
    the LORD.
11 Be glad in the LORD and rejoice, you
    just;
  exult, all you upright of heart.[n]

PSALM 33*

*Praise of the Lord's Power
and Providence*

See RG
244

I

1 Rejoice, you just, in the LORD;
  praise from the upright is fitting.[o]
2 Give thanks to the LORD on the harp;
  on the ten-stringed lyre offer praise.[p]
3 Sing to God a new song;
  skillfully play with joyful chant.
4 For the LORD's word is true;
  all his works are trustworthy.
5 The LORD loves justice and right
  and fills the earth with goodness.[q]

II

6 By the LORD's word the heavens were
    made;
  by the breath of his mouth all their
    host.[r]*
7 The waters of the sea were gathered as in
    a bowl;*
  in cellars the deep was confined.[s]

III

8 Let all the earth fear the LORD;
  let all who dwell in the world show
    reverence.
9 For he spoke, and it came to be,
  commanded, and it stood in place.[t]
10 The LORD foils the plan of nations,
  frustrates the designs of peoples.
11 But the plan of the LORD stands forever,
  wise designs through all generations.[u]
12 Happy the nation whose God is the LORD,
  the people chosen as his very own.[v]

IV

13 From heaven the LORD looks down
  and observes the whole human race,[w]
14 Surveying from the royal throne
  all who dwell on earth.

32, 3: I kept silent: did not confess the sin before God.
32, 6: Flood waters: the untamed waters surrounding the earth, a metaphor for danger.
Ps 33: A hymn in which the just are invited (1-3) to praise God, who by a mere word (4-5) created the three-tiered universe of the heavens, the cosmic waters, and the earth (6-9). Human words, in contrast, effect nothing (10-11). The greatness of human beings consists in God's choosing them as a special people and their faithful response (12-22).
33, 6: All their host: the stars of the sky are commonly viewed as a vast army, e.g., Neh 9, 6; Is 40, 26; 45, 12; Jer 33, 22.

33, 7: The waters . . . as in a bowl: ancients sometimes attributed the power keeping the seas from overwhelming land to a primordial victory of the storm-god over personified Sea. God confines the seas as easily as one puts water in a bowl.

---

k: Ps 31, 11. l: Pss 38, 19; 51, 5. m: Ps 18, 5. n: Ps 33, 1.
o: Pss 32, 11; 147, 1. p: Pss 92, 4; 144, 9. q: Ps 119, 64.
r: Gn 2, 1. s: Ps 78, 13; Gn 1, 9-10; Ex 15, 8. t: Ps 148, 5; Gn
1, 3f; Jdt 16, 14. u: Prv 19, 21; Is 40, 8. v: Ps 144, 15; Ex 19,
6; Dt 7, 6. w: Jb 34, 21; Sir 15, 19; Jer 16, 17; 32, 19.

15 The one who fashioned the hearts of
them all
knows all their works.

V

16 A king is not saved by a mighty army,
nor a warrior delivered by great
strength.

17 Useless is the horse for safety;
its great strength, no sure escape.

18 But the LORD's eyes are upon the
reverent,
upon those who hope for his gracious
help,

19 Delivering them from death,
keeping them alive in times of
famine.

VI

20 Our soul waits for the LORD,
who is our help and shield.*x*

21 For in God our hearts rejoice;
in your holy name we trust.

22 May your kindness, LORD, be upon us;
we have put our hope in you.

PSALM 34*

**See RG
245–46**

*Thanksgiving to God
Who Delivers the Just*

1 Of David, when he feigned madness before
Abimelech,* who forced him to depart.

I

2 I will bless the LORD at all times;
praise shall be always in my mouth.*y*

3 My soul will glory in the LORD
that the poor may hear and be glad.

4 Magnify the LORD with me;
let us exalt his name together.

II

5 I sought the LORD, who answered me,
delivered me from all my fears.

6 Look to God that you may be radiant
with joy
and your faces may not blush for
shame.

7 In my misfortune I called,
the LORD heard and saved me from all
distress.

8 The angel of the LORD, who encamps
with them,
delivers all who fear God.*z*

9 Learn to savor how good the LORD is;
happy are those who take refuge in
him.*a*

10 Fear the LORD, you holy ones;
nothing is lacking to those who fear
him.*b*

11 The powerful* grow poor and hungry,
but those who seek the LORD lack no
good thing.

III

12 Come, children,* listen to me;*c*
I will teach you the fear of the LORD.

13 Who among you loves life,*d*
takes delight in prosperous days?

14 Keep your tongue from evil,
your lips from speaking lies.

15 Turn from evil and do good;*e*
seek peace and pursue it.

16 The LORD has eyes for the just*f*
and ears for their cry.

17 The LORD's face is against evildoers
to wipe out their memory from the
earth.

18 When the just cry out, the LORD hears
and rescues them from all distress.

19 The LORD is close to the brokenhearted,
saves those whose spirit is crushed.

20 Many are the troubles of the just,
but the LORD delivers from them all.

21 God watches over all their bones;
not a one shall be broken.*g*

22 Evil will slay the wicked;
those who hate the just are
condemned.

23 The LORD redeems loyal servants;
no one is condemned whose refuge is
God.

Ps 34: A thanksgiving in acrostic form, each line beginning with a successive letter of the Hebrew alphabet. In this
psalm one letter is missing and two are in reverse order. The
psalmist, fresh from the experience of being rescued (5. 7),
can teach the "poor," those who are defenseless, to trust in
God alone (4. 12). God will make them powerful (5-11) and
give them protection (12-23).

34, 1: Abimelech: a scribal error for Achish. In 1 Sm 21,
13-16, David feigned madness before Achish, not Abimelech.

34, 11: The powerful: literally, "lions." Fierce animals
were sometimes metaphors for influential people.

34, 12: Children: the customary term for students in Wisdom literature.

x: Ps 115, 9.   *y:* Ps 145, 2.   *z:* Ex 14, 19.   *a:* Ps 2, 12.   *b:* Prv
3, 7.   *c:* Prv 1, 8; 4, 1.   *d:* 13-17: 1 Pt 3, 10-12.   *e:* Ps 37, 27.
f: Ps 33, 18.   *g:* Jn 19, 36.

See RG
244

PSALM 35*

*Prayer for Help against
Unjust Enemies*

¹ Of David.

I

Oppose, LORD, those who oppose me;*
  war upon those who make war upon
    me.
² Take up the shield and buckler;
  rise up in my defense.
³ Brandish lance and battle-ax
  against my pursuers.
Say to my heart,
  "I am your salvation."
⁴ Let those who seek my life
  be put to shame and disgrace.
Let those who plot evil against me[h]
  be turned back and confounded.
⁵ Make them like chaff before the wind,[i]
  with the angel of the LORD driving
    them on.
⁶ Make their way slippery and dark,
  with the angel of the LORD pursuing
    them.

II

⁷ Without cause they set their snare for me;
  without cause they dug a pit for me.
⁸ Let ruin overtake them unawares;
  let the snare they have set catch
    them;
  let them fall into the pit they have
    dug.[j]
⁹ Then I will rejoice in the LORD,
  exult in God's salvation.
¹⁰ My very bones shall say,
  "O LORD, who is like you,[k]
Who rescue the afflicted from the
    powerful,
  the afflicted and needy from the
    despoiler?"

III

¹¹ Malicious witnesses come forward,
  accuse me of things I do not know.
¹² They repay me evil for good
  and I am all alone.[l]
¹³ Yet I, when they were ill, put on
    sackcloth,*
  afflicted myself with fasting,
  sobbed my prayers upon my bosom.
¹⁴ I went about in grief as for my brother,
  bent in mourning as for my mother.
¹⁵ Yet when I stumbled they gathered with
    glee,
  they gathered against me like
    strangers.
They slandered me without ceasing;
¹⁶ without respect they mocked me,
  gnashed their teeth against me.

IV

¹⁷ LORD, how long will you look on?
  Save me from roaring beasts,
  my precious life from lions![m]
¹⁸ Then I will thank you in the great
    assembly;
  I will praise you before the mighty
    throng.[n]
¹⁹ Do not let lying foes smirk at me,
  my undeserved enemies wink
    knowingly.[o]
²⁰ They speak no words of peace,
  but against the quiet in the land
  they fashion deceitful speech.[p]
²¹ They open wide their mouths against me.
  They say, "Aha! Good!
  Our eyes relish the sight!"[q]
²² You see this, LORD; do not be silent;[r]
  Lord, do not withdraw from me.
²³ Awake, be vigilant in my defense,
  in my cause, my God and my Lord.
²⁴ Defend me because you are just, LORD;
  my God, do not let them gloat over me.

Ps 35: A lament of a person betrayed by friends. The psalmist prays that the evildoers be publicly exposed as unjust (1-8), and gives thanks in anticipation of vindication (9-10). Old friends are the enemies (11-16). May their punishment come quickly (17-21)! The last part (22-26) echoes the opening in praying for the destruction of the psalmist's persecutors. The psalm may appear vindictive, but one must keep in mind that the psalmist is praying for *public* redress now of a *public* injustice. There is at this time no belief in an afterlife in which justice will be redressed.

35, 1-6: The mixture of judicial, martial, and hunting im-

ages shows that the language is figurative. The actual injustice is false accusation of serious crimes (11. 15. 20-21). The psalmist seeks lost honor through a trial before God.

35, 13. 15-17: The Hebrew is obscure.

h: Pss 40, 15; 71, 13. *i:* Pss 1, 4; 83, 14; Jb 21, 18. *j:* Pss 7, 16; 9, 16; 57, 7; Prv 26, 27; Eccl 10, 8; Sir 27, 26. *k:* Ps 86, 8; 89, 7. 9; Ex 15, 11. *l:* Pss 27, 12; 38, 20-21; 109, 5; Jer 18, 20. *m:* Pss 17, 12; 22, 22; 58, 7. *n:* Pss 22, 23; 26, 12; 35, 18; 40, 10; 149, 1. *o:* Ps 38, 17. *p:* Ps 120, 6-7. *q:* Ps 40, 16; Lam 2, 16. *r:* Pss 22, 12; 38, 21; 109, 1.

²⁵ Do not let them say in their hearts,
   "Aha! Just what we wanted!"
Do not let them say,
   "We have devoured that one!"
²⁶ Put to shame and confound
   all who relish my misfortune.
Clothe with shame and disgrace
   those who lord it over me.
²⁷ But let those who favor my just cause
   shout for joy and be glad.
May they ever say, "Exalted be the
      LORD
   who delights in the peace of his loyal
      servant."
²⁸ Then my tongue shall recount your
      justice,
   declare your praise, all the day long.^s

See RG
244, 249

PSALM 36*

Human Wickedness and
Divine Providence

¹ For the leader. Of David, the servant
^v   of the LORD.

I

² Sin directs the heart of the wicked;
   their eyes are closed to the fear of
      God.^t
³ For they live with the delusion:
   their guilt will not be known and
      hated.*
⁴ Empty and false are the words of their
      mouth;
   they have ceased to be wise and do
      good.
⁵ In their beds they hatch plots;
   they set out on a wicked way;
   they do not reject evil.^u

II

⁶ LORD, your love reaches to heaven;
   your fidelity, to the clouds.^v
⁷ Your justice is like the highest
      mountains;
   your judgments,* like the mighty deep;
   all living creatures you sustain, LORD.
⁸ How precious is your love, O God!
   We take refuge in the shadow of your
      wings.^w *
⁹ We feast on the rich food of your house;
   from your delightful stream^x you give
      us drink.
¹⁰ For with you is the fountain of life,^y
   and in your light we see light.^z
¹¹ Continue your kindness toward your
      friends,
   your just defense of the honest heart.
¹² Do not let the foot of the proud overtake
      me,
   nor the hand of the wicked disturb me.
¹³ There make the evildoers fall;
   thrust them down, never to rise.

PSALM 37*

See RG
245-46,
251

The Fate of Sinners and
the Reward of the Just

¹ Of David.

ALEPH
Do not be provoked by evildoers;
   do not envy those who do wrong.^a
² Like grass they wither quickly;
   like green plants they wilt away.^b
BETH
³ Trust in the LORD and do good
   that you may dwell in the land* and
      live secure.^c

Ps 36: A psalm with elements of wisdom (2-5), the hymn (6-10), and the lament (11-13). The rule of sin over the wicked (2-5) is contrasted with the rule of divine love and mercy over God's friends (6-10). The psalm ends with a prayer that God's guidance never cease (11-13).

36, 3: Hated: punished by God.

36, 6-7: Love . . . judgments: God actively controls the entire world.

36, 8: The shadow of your wings: metaphor for divine protection. It probably refers to the winged cherubim in the holy of holies in the temple. Cf 1 Kgs 6, 23-28. 32; 2 Chr 3, 10-13; Ez 1, 4-9.

Ps 37: The psalm responds to the problem of evil, which the Old Testament often expresses as a question: Why do the wicked prosper and the good suffer? The psalm answers that the situation is only temporary. God will reverse things, re-

warding the good and punishing the wicked here on earth. The perspective is concrete and earthbound: people's very actions place them among the ranks of the good or wicked. Each group or "way" has its own inherent dynamism—eventual frustration for the wicked, eventual reward for the just. The psalm is an acrostic, i.e., each section begins with a successive letter of the Hebrew alphabet. Each section has its own imagery and logic.

37, 3. 9. 11. 22. 27. 29. 34: The land: the promised land, Israel, which became for later interpreters a type or figure of heaven. Cf Heb 11, 9-10. 13-16. The New Testament

s: Ps 71, 15-16.   *t:* Rom 3, 18.   *u:* Mi 2, 1.   *v:* Pss 57, 11; 71, 19.   *w:* Ps 17, 8.   *x:* Gn 2, 8. 10.   *y:* Is 55, 1; Jn 4, 14.   *z:* Ps 80, 4. 8. 20.   *a:* Prv 3, 31; 23, 17; 24, 1. 19.   *b:* Pss 90, 5-6; 102, 12; 103, 15-16; Jb 14, 2; Is 40, 7.   *c:* Ps 128, 2.

4 Find your delight in the LORD
    who will give you your heart's desire.*d*

GIMEL

5 Commit your way to the LORD;
    trust that God will act*e*

6 And make your integrity shine like the
    dawn,
    your vindication like noonday.*f*

DALETH

7 Be still before the LORD;
    wait for God.

Do not be provoked by the prosperous,
    nor by malicious schemers.

HE

8 Give up your anger, abandon your wrath;
    do not be provoked; it brings only
    harm.

9 Those who do evil will be cut off,
    but those who wait for the LORD will
    possess the land.*g*

WAW

10 Wait a little, and the wicked will be no
    more;
    look for them and they will not be
    there.

11 But the poor will possess the land,*h*
    will delight in great prosperity.

ZAYIN

12 The wicked plot against the just
    and grind their teeth at them;

13 But the LORD laughs at them,*i*
    knowing their day is coming.

HETH

14 The wicked draw their swords;
    they string their bows

To fell the poor and oppressed,
    to slaughter those whose way is
    honest.*j*

15 Their swords will pierce their own
    hearts;
    their bows will be broken.

TETH

16 Better the poverty of the just
    than the great wealth of the wicked.*k*

17 The arms of the wicked will be broken;

the LORD will sustain the just.

YODH

18 The LORD watches over the days of the
    blameless;
    their heritage lasts forever.

19 They will not be disgraced when times
    are hard;
    in days of famine they will have
    plenty.

KAPH

20 The wicked perish,
    the enemies of the LORD;

Like the beauty of meadows they vanish;
    like smoke they disappear.*l*

LAMEDH

21 The wicked borrow but do not repay;
    the just are generous in giving.

22 For those blessed by the Lord will
    possess the land,
    but those accursed will be cut off.

MEM

23 Those whose steps are guided by the
    LORD;*m*
    whose way God approves,

24 May stumble, but they will never fall,
    for the LORD holds their hand.

NUN

25 Neither in my youth, nor now in old age
    have I ever seen the just abandoned*n*
    or their children begging bread.

26 The just always lend generously,
    and their children become a blessing.

SAMEKH

27 Turn from evil and do good,
    that you may inhabit the land forever.*o*

28 For the LORD loves justice
    and does not abandon the faithful.

AYIN

When the unjust are destroyed,
    and the children of the wicked cut off,

29 The just will possess the land
    and live in it forever.*p*

PE

30 The mouths of the just utter wisdom;*q*
    their tongues speak what is right.

Beatitudes (Mt 5, 3-12; Lk 6, 20-26) have been influenced by the psalm, especially their total reversal of the present and their interpretation of the happy future as possession of the land.

---

d: Prv 10, 24. e: Ps 55, 23; Prv 3, 5; 16, 3. f: Wis 5, 6; Is 58, 10. g: Ps 25, 13; Prv 2, 21; Is 57, 13. h: Mt 5, 4. i: Pss 2, 4; 59, 9; Wis 4, 18. j: Pss 11, 2; 57, 5; 64, 4. k: Prv 15, 16; 16, 8. l: Wis 5, 14. m: Prv 20, 24. n: Jb 4, 7; Sir 2, 10. o: Ps 34, 14-15; Am 5, 14. p: Ps 25, 13; Prv 2, 21; Is 57, 13. q: Prv 10, 31.

³¹ God's teaching is in their hearts;ʳ
their steps do not falter.

SADHE

³² The wicked spy on the just
and seek to kill them.

³³ But the LORD does not leave the just in
their power,
nor let them be condemned when tried.

QOPH

³⁴ Wait eagerly for the LORD,
and keep to the way;ˢ
God will raise you to possess the land;
you will gloat when the wicked are cut
off.

RESH

³⁵ I have seen ruthless scoundrels,
strong as flourishing cedars.ᵗ

³⁶ When I passed by again, they were gone;
though I searched, they could not be
found.

SHIN

³⁷ Observe the honest, mark the upright;
those at peace with God have a future.ᵘ

³⁸ But all sinners will be destroyed;
the future of the wicked will be cut off.

TAW

³⁹ The salvation of the just is from the LORD,
their refuge in time of distress.ᵛ

⁴⁰ The LORD helps and rescues them,
rescues and saves them from the
wicked,
because in God they take refuge.

PSALM 38*

See RG 244

Prayer of an Afflicted Sinner

¹ A psalm of David. For remembrance.

I

² LORD, punish me no more in your anger;
in your wrath do not chastise me!ʷ

³ Your arrows have sunk deep in me;ˣ
your hand has come down upon me.

⁴ My flesh is afflicted because of your
anger;
my frame aches because of my sin.ʸ

⁵ My iniquities overwhelm me,
a burden beyond my strength.ᶻ

II

⁶ Foul and festering are my sores
because of my folly.

⁷ I am stooped and deeply bowed;ᵃ
all day I go about mourning.

⁸ My loins burn with fever;
my flesh is afflicted.

⁹ I am numb and utterly crushed;
I wail with anguish of heart.ᵇ

¹⁰ My Lord, my deepest yearning is before
you;
my groaning is not hidden from you.

¹¹ My heart shudders, my strength forsakes
me;
the very light of my eyes has failed.ᶜ

¹² Friends and companions shun my pain;
my neighbors stand far off.

¹³ Those who seek my life lay snares for
me;
they seek my misfortune, they speak
of ruin;
they plot treachery all the day.

III

¹⁴ But I am like the deaf, hearing nothing,
like the dumb, saying nothing,

¹⁵ Like someone who does not hear,
who has no answer ready.

¹⁶ LORD, I wait for you;
O Lord, my God, answer me.ᵈ

¹⁷ For I fear they will gloat,
exult over me if I stumble.

IV

¹⁸ I am very near to falling;
my pain is with me always.

¹⁹ I acknowledge my guilt
and grieve over my sin.ᵉ

²⁰ But many are my foes without cause,
a multitude of enemies without reason,

²¹ Repaying me evil for good,
harassing me for pursuing good.ᶠ

²² Forsake me not, O LORD;
my God, be not far from me!ᵍ

Ps 38: In this lament, one of the Penitential Psalms (cf Ps 6), the psalmist acknowledges the sin that has brought physical and mental sickness and social ostracism. There is no one to turn to for help; only God can undo the past and restore the psalmist.

---

r: Ps 40, 9; Dt 6, 6; Is 51, 7; Jer 31, 33.   s: Ps 31, 24.   t: Ps 92, 8-9; Is 2, 13; Ez 31, 10-11.   u: Prv 23, 18; 24, 14.   v: Ps 9, 10; Is 25, 4.   w: Ps 6, 2.   x: Jb 6, 4; Lam 3, 12; Pss 31, 11; 64, 7.   y: Is 1, 5-6.   z: Ps 40, 13; Ezr 9, 6.   a: Ps 35, 14.   b: Ps 102, 4-6.   c: Pss 6, 8; 31, 10.   d: Ps 13, 4.   e: Pss 32, 5; 51, 5.   f: Ps 109, 5.   g: Pss 22, 2. 12. 20; 35, 22.

²³ Come quickly to help me,*h*
 my Lord and my salvation!

PSALM 39*

See RG
244, 250

The Vanity of Life

¹ For the leader, for Jeduthun.*i*
 A psalm of David.

I

² I said, "I will watch my ways,
 lest I sin with my tongue;
I will set a curb on my mouth."
³ Dumb and silent before the wicked,
 I refrained from any speech.
But my sorrow increased;
⁴ my heart smoldered within me.*j*
In my thoughts a fire blazed up,
 and I broke into speech:

II

⁵ LORD, let me know my end, the number
 of my days,
 that I may learn how frail I am.
⁶ You have given my days a very short
 span;
 my life is as nothing before you.
All mortals are but a breath.*k*   Selah
⁷ Mere phantoms, we go our way;
 mere vapor, our restless pursuits;
 we heap up stores without knowing for
 whom.
⁸ And now, Lord, what future do I have?
 You are my only hope.
⁹ From all my sins deliver me;
 let me not be the taunt of fools.

III

¹⁰ I was silent and did not open my mouth
 because you were the one who did
 this.
¹¹ Take your plague away from me;
 I am ravaged by the touch of your hand.

¹² You rebuke our guilt and chasten us;
 you dissolve all we prize like a
 cobweb.
All mortals are but a breath.   Selah
¹³ Listen to my prayer, LORD, hear my
 cry;
 do not be deaf to my weeping!
I sojourn with you like a passing
 stranger,
 a guest, like all my ancestors.*l*
¹⁴ Turn your gaze from me, that I may find
 peace
 before I depart to be no more.

PSALM 40*

Gratitude and Prayer for Help

See RG
244

¹ For the leader. A psalm of David.

A
I

² I waited, waited for the LORD;
 who bent down and heard my cry,*m*
³ Drew me out of the pit of destruction,
 out of the mud of the swamp,*n*
Set my feet upon rock,
 steadied my steps,
⁴ And put a new song* in my mouth,*o*
 a hymn to our God.
Many shall look on in awe
 and they shall trust in the LORD.

II

⁵ Happy those whose trust is the LORD,
 who turn not to idolatry
 or to those who stray after falsehood.*p*
⁶ How numerous, O LORD, my God,
 you have made your wondrous deeds!
And in your plans for us
 there is none to equal you.*q*
Should I wish to declare or tell them,
 too many are they to recount.*r*

Ps 39: The lament of a mortally ill person who at first had resolved to remain silently submissive (2-4). But the grief was too much and now the psalmist laments the brevity and vanity of life (5-7), yet remaining hopeful (8-10). The psalmist continues to express both acceptance of the illness and hope for healing in 11-14.

Ps 40: A thanksgiving (2-13) has been combined with a lament (14-18), that appears also in Ps 70. The psalmist describes the rescue in spatial terms—being raised up from the swampy underworld to firm earth where one can praise God (2-4). All who trust God will experience like protection (5-6)! The psalm stipulates the precise mode of thanksgiving: not animal sacrifice but open and enthusiastic proclamation of

the salvation just experienced (7-11). A prayer for protection concludes (12-18).

40, 4: A new song: a song in response to the new action of God (cf Pss 33, 3; 96, 1; 144, 9; 149, 1; Is 42, 10). Giving thanks is not purely a human response but is itself a divine gift.

h: Ps 40, 14. *i:* 1 Chr 16, 41; Pss 62, 1; 77, 1. *j:* Jer 20, 9.
k: Pss 62, 10; 90, 9-10; 144, 4; Jb 7, 6. 16; 14, 1. 5; Eccl 6, 12; Wis 2, 5. *l:* Ps 119, 19; Gn 23, 4; Heb 11, 13; 1 Pt 2, 11. *m:* Lam 3, 25. *n:* Pss 28, 1; 30, 4; 69, 3. 15-16; 88, 5; Prv 1, 12; Jon 2, 7.
o: Ps 33, 3. *p:* Ps 1, 1; Prv 16, 20; Jer 17, 7. *q:* Ps 35, 10.
r: Pss 71, 15; 139, 17-18.

III

7 Sacrifice and offering you do not want;[s]*
   but ears open to obedience you gave
      me.
   Holocausts and sin-offerings you do not
      require;
8 so I said, "Here I am;
   your commands for me are written in
      the scroll.
9 To do your will is my delight;
   my God, your law is in my heart!"[t]
10 I announced your deed to a great
      assembly;
   I did not restrain my lips;
   you, LORD, are my witness.[u]
11 Your deed I did not hide within my heart;
   your loyal deliverance I have
      proclaimed.
   I made no secret of your enduring
      kindness
   to a great assembly.

B
I

12 LORD, do not withhold your compassion
      from me;
   may your enduring kindness ever
      preserve me.[v]
13 For all about me are evils beyond count;
   my sins so overcome me I cannot see.
   They are more than the hairs of my head;
   my courage fails me.[w]

II

14 LORD, graciously rescue me![x]
   Come quickly to help me, LORD!
15 Put to shame and confound
   all who seek to take my life.
   Turn back in disgrace
   those who desire my ruin.[y]
16 Let those who say "Aha!"[z]
   know dismay and shame.

17 But may all who seek you
   rejoice and be glad in you.
   May those who long for your help
   always say, "The LORD be glorified."[a]
18 Though I am afflicted and poor,
   the Lord keeps me in mind.
   You are my help and deliverer;
   my God, do not delay!

PSALM 41*

Thanksgiving after Sickness
1 For the leader. A psalm of David.

See RG
245, 250

I

2 Happy those concerned for the lowly and
      poor;*
   when misfortune strikes, the LORD
      delivers them.[b]
3 The LORD keeps and preserves them,
   makes them happy in the land,
   and does not betray them to their
      enemies.
4 The LORD sustains them on their sickbed,
   allays the malady when they are ill.

II

5 Once I prayed, "LORD, have mercy on me;
   heal me, I have sinned against you.
6 My enemies say the worst of me:
   'When will that one die and be
      forgotten?'
7 When people come to visit me,
   they speak without sincerity.
   Their hearts store up malice;
   they leave and spread their vicious
      lies.[c]
8 My foes all whisper against me;
   they imagine the worst about me:
9 I have a deadly disease, they say;
   I will never rise from my sickbed.
10 Even the friend who had my trust,
   who shared my table, has scorned me.[d]*

40, 7-9: Obedience is better than sacrifice (cf 1 Sm 15, 22; Is 1, 10-20; Hos 6, 6; Am 5, 22-25; Mi 6, 6-8; Acts 7, 42-43 [quoting Am 5, 25-26 LXX]). Heb 10, 5-9 quotes the somewhat different Greek version and interprets it as Christ's self-oblation.

Ps 41: A thanksgiving for rescue from illness (4. 5. 9). Many people, even friends, have interpreted the illness as a divine punishment for sin and have ostracized the psalmist (5-11). The healing shows the return of God's favor and rebukes the psalmist's detractors (12-13).

41, 2: Happy those concerned for the lowly and poor: other psalms use the same formula ("Happy those") for those

whom God favors. Cf Pss 32, 1-2; 34, 9; 40, 5; 65, 5. The psalmist's statement about God's love of the poor is based on the experience of being rescued (1-3).

41, 10: Even the friend . . . has scorned me: Jn 13, 18 cites this verse to characterize Judas as a false friend.

s: 7-9: Heb 10, 5-7; Ps 51, 18-19; Am 5, 22; Hos 6, 6; Is 1, 11-15. *t:* Ps 37, 31. *u:* Pss 22, 23; 26, 12; 35, 18; 149, 1. *v:* Ps 89, 34. *w:* Ps 38, 5. 11; Ezr 9, 6. *x:* 14-18: Pss 70, 2-6; 71, 12. *y:* Ps 35, 4. 26. *z:* Ps 35, 21. 25. *a:* Ps 35, 27. *b:* Tb 4, 7-11. *c:* Pss 31, 12; 38, 12-13; 88, 8; Jb 19, 13-19; Jer 20, 10. *d:* Ps 55, 14-15; Jn 13, 18.

11 But you, LORD, have mercy and raise
me up
that I may repay them as they
deserve."*

III

12 By this I know you are pleased with me,
that my enemy no longer jeers at me.
13 For my integrity you have supported me
and let me stand in your presence
forever.

* * *

14 Blessed be the LORD, the God of
Israel,
from all eternity and forever.
Amen. Amen.*e* *

Second Book: Psalms 42—72

See RG
244

PSALMS 42—43*

*Longing for God's Presence
in the Temple*

1 For the leader. A *maskil* of the Korahites.*

I

2 As the deer longs for streams of water,*f*
so my soul longs for you, O God.
3 My being thirsts for God, the living God.
When can I go and see the face of
God?*g* *
4 My tears have been my food day and
night,*h*
as they ask daily, "Where is your
God?"*i*
5 Those times I recall
as I pour out my soul,*j*

When I went in procession with the
crowd,
I went with them to the house of God,
Amid loud cries of thanksgiving,
with the multitude keeping festival.*k*
6 Why are you downcast, my soul;
why do you groan within me?
Wait for God, whom I shall praise again,
my savior and my God.

II

7 My soul is downcast within me;
therefore I will remember you
From the land of the Jordan* and Hermon,
from the land of Mount Mizar.*l*
8 Here deep calls to deep* in the roar of
your torrents.
All your waves and breakers sweep
over me.*m*
9 At dawn may the LORD bestow faithful
love
that I may sing praise through the
night,
praise to the God of my life.
10 I say to God, "My rock,
why do you forget me?*n*
Why must I go about mourning
with the enemy oppressing me?"
11 It shatters my bones, when my
adversaries reproach me.
They say to me daily: "Where is your
God?"
12 Why are you downcast, my soul,
why do you groan within me?
Wait for God, whom I shall praise again,
my savior and my God.

Scorned me: an interpretation of the unclear Hebrew, "made great the heel against me."

41, 11: That I may repay them as they deserve: the healing itself is an act of judgment through which God decides for the psalmist and against the false friends. The prayer is not necessarily for strength to punish enemies.

41, 14: The doxology, not part of the psalm, marks the end of the first of the five books of the Psalter. Compare Pss 72, 18-20; 89, 53; 106, 48.

Pss 42—43: Pss 42—43 form a single lament of three sections, each section ending in an identical refrain (42, 6. 12; 43, 5). The psalmist is in the extreme north of Israel, far from Jerusalem, and longs for the divine presence that Israel experienced in the temple liturgy. Despite sadness, the psalmist hopes once again to join the worshiping crowds.

42, 1: The Korahites: a major guild of temple singers (2 Chr 20, 19) whose name appears in the superscriptions of Pss 42; 44-49; 84-85; 87-88.

42, 3: See the face of God: "face" designates a personal presence (Gn 33, 10; Ex 10, 28-29; 2 Sm 17, 11). The expressions "see God/God's face" occur elsewhere (Pss 11, 7; 17, 15; 63, 3; cf Ex 24, 10; 33, 7-11; Jb 33, 26) for the presence of God in the temple.

42, 7: From the land of the Jordan: the sources of the Jordan are in the foothills of Mount Hermon in present-day southern Lebanon. Mount Mizar is presumed to be a mountain in the same range.

42, 8: Here deep calls to deep: to the psalmist, the waters arising in the north are overwhelming and far from God's presence, like the waters of chaos (Pss 18, 5; 69, 2-3. 15; Jon 2, 3-6).

---

e: Neh 9, 5. *f*: 2-3: Pss 63, 2; 84, 3; 143, 6; Is 26, 9. *g*: Ps 27, 4. *h*: Pss 80, 6; 102, 10. *i*: Ps 79, 10; Jl 2, 17. *j*: Lam 3, 20. *k*: Ps 122, 5. *l*: Ps 43, 3. *m*: Pss 18, 5; 32, 6; 69, 2; 88, 8; Jon 2, 4. *n*: Pss 18, 2; 31, 3-4.

III

¹ Grant me justice, God;
  defend me from a faithless people;
  from the deceitful and unjust rescue me.ᵒ
² You, God, are my strength.
  Why then do you spurn me?
  Why must I go about mourning,
  with the enemy oppressing me?
³ Send your light and fidelity,*
  that they may be my guideᵖ
  And bring me to your holy mountain,
  to the place of your dwelling,�q
⁴ That I may come to the altar of God,
  to God, my joy, my delight.
  Then I will praise you with the harp,
  O God, my God.
⁵ Why are you downcast, my soul?
  Why do you groan within me?
  Wait for God, whom I shall praise again,
  my savior and my God.

PSALM 44*

See RG
244, 247 *God's Past Favor and Israel's
       Present Need*

¹ For the leader. A *maskil* of the Korahites.

I

² O God, we have heard with our own ears;
  our ancestors have told usʳ
  The deeds you did in their days,
  with your own hand in days of old:
³ You rooted out nations to plant them,ˢ
  crushed peoples to make room for
    them.
⁴ Not with their own swords did they
    conquer the land,ᵗ
  nor did their own arms bring victory;
  It was your right hand, your own arm,
  the light of your face, for you favored
    them.ᵘ
⁵ You are my king and my God,ᵛ
  who bestows victories on Jacob.

⁶ Through you we batter our foes;
  through your name, trample our
    adversaries.
⁷ Not in my bow do I trust,
  nor does my sword bring me victory.
⁸ You have brought us victory over our
    enemies,
  shamed those who hate us.
⁹ In God we have boasted all the day long;
  your name we will praise forever.

                                    Selah

II

¹⁰ But now you have rejected and
    disgraced us;ʷ
  you do not march out with our armies.ˣ
¹¹ You make us retreat* before the foe;
  those who hate us plunder us at will.ʸ
¹² You hand us over like sheep to be
    slaughtered,
  scatter us among the nations.ᶻ
¹³ You sell your people for nothing;
  you make no profit from their sale.ᵃ
¹⁴ You make us the reproach of our
    neighbors,ᵇ
  the mockery and scorn of those around
    us.
¹⁵ You make us a byword among the nations;
  the peoples shake their heads at us.
¹⁶ All day long my disgrace is before me;
  shame has covered my face
¹⁷ At the sound of those who taunt and
    revile,
  at the sight of the spiteful enemy.

III

¹⁸ All this has come upon us,
  though we have not forgotten you,
  nor been disloyal to your covenant.
¹⁹ Our hearts have not turned back,*
  nor have our steps strayed from your
    path.
²⁰ Yet you have left us crushed,

43, 3: Your light and fidelity: a pair of divine attributes personified as guides for the pilgrimage. The psalmist seeks divine protection for the journey to Jerusalem.

Ps 44: In this lament the community reminds God of past favors which it has always acknowledged (2-9). But now God has abandoned Israel to defeat and humiliation (10-17), though the people are not conscious of any sin against the covenant (18-23). They struggle with being God's special people amid divine silence; yet they continue to pray (24-27).

44, 11: You make us retreat: the corollary of v 4.

Defeat, like victory, is God's doing; neither Israel norits enemies can claim credit (23).

44, 19: Our hearts have not turned back: Israel's defeat was not caused by its lack of fidelity.

o: Ps 119, 154.   *p:* Pss 18, 29; 27, 1; 36, 10; Mi 7, 8.   *q:* Ps 122, 1.   *r:* Ps 78, 3.   *s:* Pss 78, 55; 80, 9f.   *t:* Dt 8, 17f; Jos 24, 12.   *u:* Pss 4, 7; 31, 17; 67, 2; 80, 4; Nm 6, 25; Dn 9, 17.   *v:* Ps 145, 1.   *w:* 10-27: Ps 89, 39-52.   *x:* Ps 60, 12.   *y:* Lv 26, 17; Dt 28, 25.   *z:* Lv 26, 33; Dt 28, 64.   *a:* Dt 32, 30; Is 52, 3.   *b:* 14-17: Pss 79, 4; 80, 7; 123, 3-4; Jb 12, 4; Dn 9, 16.

desolate in a place of jackals;[c]*
you have covered us with darkness.
21 If we had forgotten the name of our
God,
stretched out our hands to another god,
22 Would not God have discovered this,
God who knows the secrets of the
heart?
23 For you we are slain all the day long,
considered only as sheep to be
slaughtered.[d]

IV
24 Awake! Why do you sleep, O Lord?
Rise up! Do not reject us forever![e]
25 Why do you hide your face;[f]
why forget our pain and misery?
26 We are bowed down to the ground;[g]
our bodies are pressed to the earth.
27 Rise up, help us!
Redeem us as your love demands.

See RG
245

PSALM 45*
Song for a Royal Wedding
1 For the leader; according to "Lilies."
A maskil of the Korahites. A love song.
I
2 My heart is stirred by a noble theme,
as I sing my ode to the king.
My tongue is the pen of a nimble
scribe.
II
3 You are the most handsome of men;
fair speech has graced your lips,
for God has blessed you forever.[h]
4 Gird your sword upon your hip, mighty
warrior!

In splendor and majesty ride on
triumphant![i]
5 In the cause of truth and justice
may your right hand show you
wondrous deeds.
6 Your arrows are sharp;
peoples will cower at your feet;
the king's enemies will lose heart.
7 Your throne, O god,* stands forever;[j]
your royal scepter is a scepter for
justice.
8 You love justice and hate wrongdoing;
therefore God, your God, has anointed
you
with the oil of gladness above your
fellow kings.
9 With myrrh, aloes, and cassia
your robes are fragrant.
From ivory-paneled palaces*
stringed instruments bring you joy.
10 Daughters of kings are your lovely wives;
a princess arrayed in Ophir's gold*
comes to stand at your right hand.
III
11 Listen, my daughter, and understand;
pay me careful heed.
Forget your people and your father's
house,*
12 that the king might desire your beauty.
He is your lord;
13 honor him, daughter of Tyre.
Then the richest of the people
will seek your favor with gifts.[k]
14 All glorious is the king's daughter as she
enters,[l]
her raiment threaded with gold;

44, 20: A place of jackals: following Israel's defeat and exile (11-12), the land lies desolate, inhabited only by jackals. Cf Is 13, 22; Jer 9, 10; 10, 22. Others take *tannim* as "sea monster" (cf Ez 29, 3; 32, 2) and render: "you crushed us as you did the sea monster."

Ps 45: A song for the Davidic king's marriage to a foreign princess from Tyre in Phoenicia. The court poet sings (2. 18) of God's choice of the king (3. 8), of his role in establishing divine rule (4-8), and of his splendor as he waits for his bride (9-10). The woman is to forget her own house when she becomes wife to the king (11-13). Her majestic beauty today is a sign of the future prosperity of the royal house (14-18). The psalm was retained in the collection when there was no reigning king, and came to be applied to the king who was to come, the messiah.

45, 7: O god: the king, in courtly language, is called "god," i.e., more than human, representing God to the people. Heb 1, 8-9 applies 7-8 to Christ.

45, 9: Ivory-paneled palaces: literally, "palaces of ivory." Ivory paneling and furniture decoration have been found in Samaria and other ancient Near Eastern cities. Cf Am 3, 15.

45, 10: Ophir's gold: uncertain location, possibly a region on the coast of southern Arabia or eastern Africa, famous for its gold. Cf 1 Kgs 9, 28; 10, 11; Jb 22, 24.

45, 11: Forget your people and your father's house: the bride should no longer consider herself a daughter of her father's house, but the wife of the king—the queen.

Ps 46: A song of confidence in God's protection of Zion with close parallels to Ps 48. The dominant note in Ps 46 is

c: Jer 9, 10.   d: Rom 8, 36.   e: Pss 10, 1; 74, 1; 77, 8; 79, 5; 83, 2.   f: Pss 10, 11; 89, 47; Jb 13, 24.   g: Ps 119, 25.   h: Song 5, 10-16.   i: Ps 21, 5.   j: 7-8: Heb 1, 8-9.   k: Ps 72, 10-11; Is 60, 5f.   l: 14-16: Ez 16, 10-13.

15 In embroidered apparel she is led to the
  king.
  The maids of her train are presented to
  the king.
16 They are led in with glad and joyous
  acclaim;
  they enter the palace of the king.

IV

17 The throne of your fathers your sons will
  have;
  you shall make them princes through
  all the land.*m*
18 I will make your name renowned through
  all generations;
  thus nations shall praise you forever.*n*

See RG
245

PSALM 46*

God, the Protector of Zion

1 For the leader. A song of the Korahites.
  According to *alamoth.**

I

2 God is our refuge and our strength,
  an ever-present help in distress.*o*
3 Thus we do not fear, though earth be
  shaken*
  and mountains quake to the depths of
  the sea,
4 Though its waters rage and foam
  and mountains totter at its surging.*p*
The LORD of hosts is with us;*
  our stronghold is the God of Jacob.

  Selah

II

5 Streams of the river gladden the city of
  God,
  the holy dwelling of the Most High.*q **
6 God is in its midst; it shall not be shaken;
  God will help it at break of day.*r*

7 Though nations rage and kingdoms totter,
  God's voice thunders and the earth
  trembles.*s*

III

8 The LORD of hosts is with us;
  our stronghold is the God of Jacob.

  Selah

III

9 Come and see the works of the LORD,
  who has done fearsome deeds on
  earth;*t*
10 Who stops wars to the ends of the earth,
  breaks the bow, splinters the spear,
  and burns the shields with fire;*u*
11 Who says:
  "Be still and confess that I am God!
  I am exalted among the nations,
  exalted on the earth."*v*
12 The LORD of hosts is with us;
  our stronghold is the God of Jacob.

  Selah

PSALM 47*

The Ruler of All the Nations

See RG
245, 249

1 For the leader. A psalm of the Korahites.

I

2 All you peoples, clap your hands;
  shout to God with joyful cries.*w*
3 For the LORD, the Most High, inspires
  awe,
  the great king over all the earth,*x*
4 Who made people subject to us,
  brought nations under our feet,*y*
5 Who chose a land for our heritage,
  the glory* of Jacob, the beloved.*z Selah*

II

6 God mounts the throne* amid shouts of
  joy;
  the LORD, amid trumpet blasts.*a*

---

sounded by the refrain, **The LORD of hosts is with us** (4. 8.
12). The first strophe (2-4) sings of the security of God's
presence even in utter chaos; the second (5-8), of divine protection of the city from its enemies; the third (9-12), of God's
imposition of imperial peace.

46, 1: Alamoth: the melody of the psalm, now lost.

46, 3-4: Figurative ancient Near Eastern language to describe social and political upheavals.

46, 4b: The first line of the refrain is similar in structure
and meaning to Isaiah's name for the royal child, Immanuel,
With us is God (Is 7, 14; 8, 8. 10).

46, 5: Jerusalem is not situated on a river. This description
derives from mythological descriptions of the divine abode
and symbolizes the divine presence as the source of all life
(cf Is 33, 21; Ez 47, 1-12; Jl 4, 18; Zec 14, 8; Rv 22, 1-2).

Ps 47: A hymn calling on the nations to acknowledge the
universal rule of Israel's God (2-5) who is enthroned as king
over Israel and the nations (6-10).

47, 5: Our heritage ... the glory: the land of Israel (cf Is
58, 14), which God has given Israel in an act of sovereignty.

47, 6: God mounts the throne: "has gone up to the
throne," according to the context (9). Christian liturgical tradition has applied the verse to the ascension of Christ.

m: Gn 17, 6. *n:* Is 60, 15. *o:* Ps 48, 4; Is 33, 2. *p:* Ps 93, 3-4;
Jb 9, 5-6; Is 24, 18-20; 54, 10. *q:* Pss 48, 2-3; 76, 3. *r:* Is 7, 14.
s: Pss 2, 1-5; 48, 5-8; 76, 7-9; Is 17, 12-14. *t:* Ps 48, 9-10. *u:* Ps
76, 4. *v:* Ps 48, 11. *w:* Pss 89, 16; Zep 3, 14. *x:* Ps 95, 3; Ex
15, 18; Is 24, 23; 52, 7. *y:* Ps 2, 8. *z:* Is 58, 14. *a:* Pss 24, 8.
10; 68, 18-19; 98, 6.

⁷ Sing praise to God, sing praise;
  sing praise to our king, sing praise.

III

⁸ God is king over all the earth;*ᵇ*
  sing hymns of praise.
⁹ God rules over the nations;
  God sits upon his holy throne.
¹⁰ The princes of the peoples assemble
  with the people of the God of Abraham.
  For the rulers of the earth belong to God,
  who is enthroned on high.*ᶜ*

See RG
245

PSALM 48*

*The Splendor of the
Invincible City*

¹ A psalm of the Korahites.* A song.

I

² Great is the LORD and highly praised
  in the city of our God:*ᵈ*
  The holy mountain, ³ fairest of heights,
  the joy of all the earth,*ᵉ*
  Mount Zion, the heights of Zaphon,*ᶠ**
  the city of the great king.

II

⁴ God is its citadel,
  renowned as a stronghold.
⁵ See! The kings assembled,
  together they invaded.
⁶ When they looked* they were astounded;
  terrified, they were put to flight!*ᵍ*
⁷ Trembling seized them there,

anguish, like a woman's labor,*ʰ*
⁸ As when the east wind wrecks
  the ships of Tarshish!*

III

⁹ What we had heard we now see*
  in the city of the LORD of hosts,
  In the city of our God,
  founded to last forever.   *Selah*
¹⁰ O God, within your temple
  we ponder your steadfast love.
¹¹ Like your name, O God,
  your praise reaches the ends of the
    earth.*ⁱ*
  Your right hand is fully victorious.
¹² Mount Zion is glad!
  The cities of Judah rejoice
  because of your saving deeds!*ʲ*

IV

¹³ Go about Zion, walk all around it,
  note the number of its towers.
¹⁴ Consider the ramparts, examine its
    citadels,
  that you may tell future generations:*ᵏ*
¹⁵ "Yes, so mighty is God,*
  our God who leads us always!"

PSALM 49*

See RG
245, 251

*Confidence in God
rather than in Riches*

¹ For the leader. A psalm of
    the Korahites.*

Ps 48: A Zion hymn, praising the holy city as the invincible dwelling place of God. Unconquerable, it is an apt symbol of God who has defeated all enemies. After seven epithets describing the city (2-3), the psalm describes the victory by the Divine Warrior over hostile kings (4-8). The second half proclaims the dominion of the God of Zion over all the earth (9-12) and invites pilgrims to announce that God is eternally invincible like Zion itself (13-15).

48, 1: Korahites: see note on Ps 42, 1.

48, 3: The heights of Zaphon: the mountain abode of the Canaanite storm-god Baal in comparable texts. To speak of Zion as if it were Zaphon was to claim for Israel's God what Canaanites claimed for Baal. Though topographically speaking Zion is only a hill, viewed religiously it towers over other mountains as the home of the supreme God (cf Ps 68, 16-17).

48, 6: When they looked: the kings are stunned by the sight of Zion, touched by divine splendor. The language is that of holy war, in which the enemy panics and flees at the sight of divine glory.

48, 8: The ships of Tarshish: large ships, named after the distant land or port of Tarshish, probably ancient Tartessus in southern Spain, although other identifications have been proposed. Cf Is 2, 16; 60, 9; Jon 1, 3.

48, 9: What we had heard we now see: the glorious things that new pilgrims had heard about the holy city—its beauty and awesomeness—they now see with their own eyes. The seeing here contrasts with the seeing of the hostile kings in 6.

48, 15: So mighty is God: Israel's God is like Zion in being eternal and invincible. The holy city is therefore a kind of "sacrament" of God.

Ps 49: The psalm affirms confidence in God (cf Pss 23; 27, 1-6; 62) in the face of the apparent good fortune of the unjust rich. Cf Pss 37; 73. Reliance on wealth is misplaced (8-10) for it is of no avail in the face of death (18-20). After inviting all to listen to this axiom of faith (2-5), the psalmist depicts the self-delusion of the ungodly (6-13), whose destiny is to die like ignorant beasts (13. 18; cf Prv 7, 21-23). Their wealth should occasion no alarm, for they will come to nought, whereas God will save the just (14-21).

49, 1: Korahites: see note on Ps 42, 1.

---

b: 8-9: Pss 72, 11; 93, 1; 96, 10; 97, 1; 99, 1; Jer 10, 7. *c:* Ps 89, 19; Ex 3, 6; Is 2, 2-4. *d:* Pss 96, 4; 145, 3. *e:* Ps 50, 2; Lam 2, 15. *f:* Is 14, 13. *g:* Jgs 5, 19. *h:* Ex 15, 14; Jer 4, 31. *i:* Mal 1, 11. *j:* Ps 97, 8. *k:* Pss 22, 31-32; 71, 18.

[2] Hear this, all you peoples!
Give ear, all who inhabit the world,
[3] You of lowly birth or high estate,
rich and poor alike.
[4] My mouth shall speak wisdom,
my heart shall offer insight.[l]
[5] I will turn my attention to a problem,*
expound my question* to the music of
a lyre.

I

[6] Why should I fear in evil days,
when my wicked pursuers ring me
round,
[7] Those who trust in their wealth
and boast of their abundant riches?[m]
[8] One cannot redeem oneself,*
pay to God a ransom.[n]
[9] Too high the price to redeem a life;
one would never have enough
[10] To stay alive forever
and never see the pit.
[11] Anyone can see that the wisest die,
the fool and the senseless pass away
too,[o]
and must leave their wealth to others.[p]
[12] Tombs are their homes forever,
their dwellings through all generations,
though they gave their names to their
lands.
[13] For all their riches
mortals do not abide;
they perish like the beasts.[q]

II

[14] This is the destiny of those who trust in
folly,
the end of those so pleased with their
wealth.   *Selah*
[15] Like sheep they are herded into Sheol,
where death will be their shepherd.

Straight to the grave they descend,
where their form will waste away,
Sheol will be their palace.
[16] But God will redeem my life,   *Selah*
will take me* from the power of
Sheol.[r]
[17] Do not fear when others become rich,
when the wealth of their houses grows
great.
[18] When they die they will take nothing
with them,
their wealth will not follow them
down.[s]
[19] When living, they congratulate
themselves and say:
"All praise you, you do so well."
[20] But they will join the company of their
forebears,
never again to see the light.[t]
[21] For all their riches,
if mortals do not have wisdom,
they perish like the beasts.

PSALM 50*

The Acceptable Sacrifice

See RG 246

[1] A psalm of Asaph.

I

The LORD, the God of gods,
has spoken and summoned the earth
from the rising of the sun to its
setting.[u]
[2] From Zion God shines forth,[v]
perfect in beauty.
[3] Our God comes and will not be silent!
Devouring fire precedes,
storming fiercely round about.[w]
[4] God summons the heavens above
and the earth to the judgment of his
people:

49, 5: Problem: the psalmist's personal solution to the perennial biblical problem of the prosperity of the wicked. **Question**: parallel in meaning to **problem**; in Wisdom literature it means the mysterious way of how the world works.

49, 8: One cannot redeem oneself: an axiom. For the practice of redemption, cf Jb 6, 21-23. A play on the first Hebrew word of v 8 and v 16 relates the two verses.

49, 16: Will take me: the same Hebrew verb is used of God "taking up" a favored servant: Enoch in Gn 5, 24; Elijah in 2 Kgs 2, 11-12; the righteous person in Ps 73, 24. The verse apparently states the hope that God will rescue the faithful psalmist in the same manner.

Ps 50: A covenant lawsuit stating that the sacrifice God

really wants is the sacrifice of praise accompanied by genuine obedience (cf Mi 6, 1-8). It begins with a theophany and the summoning of the court (1-6). Then in direct address God explains what is required of the faithful (7-15), rebukes the hypocritical worshiper (16-21), and concludes with a threat and a promise (22-23; cf Is 1, 19-20).

---

l: Ps 78, 2; Mt 13, 35.   *m:* Jb 31, 24.   *n:* Prv 10, 15; 11, 4; Ez 7, 19; Mt 16, 26.   *o:* Eccl 2, 16.   *p:* Ps 39, 7; Sir 11, 18-19.   *q:* Eccl 3, 18-21.   *r:* Pss 16, 10; 86, 13; 103, 4; 116, 8.   *s:* Sir 11, 18-19; Eccl 5, 15; 1 Tm 6, 7.   *t:* Jb 10, 21-22.   *u:* Dt 10, 17; Jos 22, 22.   *v:* Ps 48, 2.   *w:* Ps 97, 3; Dn 7, 10.

5 "Gather my faithful ones before me,
    those who made a covenant with me
      by sacrifice."
6 The heavens proclaim divine justice,
    for God alone is the judge.[x]   *Selah*

II

7 "Listen, my people, I will speak;
    Israel, I will testify against you;
    God, your God, am I.
8 Not for your sacrifices do I rebuke you,
    nor for your holocausts, set before me
      daily.
9 I need no bullock from your house,
    no goats from your fold.[y]
10 For every animal of the forest is mine,
    beasts by the thousands on my
      mountains.
11 I know every bird of the heavens;
    the creatures of the field belong to me.
12 Were I hungry, I would not tell you,
    for mine is the world and all that
      fills it.[z]
13 Do I eat the flesh of bulls
    or drink the blood of goats?
14 Offer praise as your sacrifice to God;[a]
    fulfill your vows to the Most High.
15 Then call on me in time of distress;[b]
    I will rescue you, and you shall honor
      me."

III

16 But to the wicked God says:
    "Why do you recite my commandments
    and profess my covenant with your
      lips?
17 You hate discipline;
    you cast my words behind you!
18 When you see thieves, you befriend them;
    with adulterers you throw in your lot.
19 You give your mouth free rein for evil;

you harness your tongue to deceit.
20 You sit maligning your own kin,
    slandering the child of your own
      mother.
21 When you do these things should I be
    silent?
    Or do you think that I am like you?
    I accuse you, I lay the charge before
      you."

IV

22 "Understand this, you who forget God,
    lest I attack you with no one to rescue.
23 Those who offer praise as a sacrifice
    honor me;
    to the obedient I will show the
      salvation of God."[c]

PSALM 51[*]

The Miserere:
Prayer of Repentance

See RG 244

1 For the leader. A psalm of David, 2 when
Nathan the prophet came to him after his
affair with Bathsheba.[d]

I

3 Have mercy on me, God, in your
    goodness;
    in your abundant compassion blot out
      my offense.
4 Wash away all my guilt;
    from my sin cleanse me.
5 For I know my offense;
    my sin is always before me.[e]
6 Against you alone have I sinned;
    I have done such evil in your sight
    That you are just in your sentence,
    blameless when you condemn.[f]
7 True, I was born guilty,
    a sinner, even as my mother conceived
      me.[g][*]

Ps 51: A lament, the most famous of the seven Penitential Psalms, prays for the removal of the personal and social disorders that sin has brought. The poem has two parts of approximately equal length: 3-10 and 11-19, and a conclusion in 20-21. The two parts interlock by repetition of "blot out" in the first verse of each section (3. 11), of "wash (away)" just after the first verse of each section (4) and just before the last verse (9) of the first section, and of "heart," "God," and "spirit" in 12 and 19. The first part (3-10) asks deliverance from sin, which is not just a past act but its emotional, physical, and social consequences. The second part (11-19) seeks something more profound than wiping the slate clean: nearness to God, living by the spirit of God (12-13), like the rela-

tion between God and people described in Jer 31, 33-34. Nearness to God brings joy and the authority to teach sinners (15-16). Such proclamation is better than offering sacrifice (17-19). The last two verses ask for the rebuilding of Jerusalem (20-21).

51, 7: A sinner, even as my mother conceived me: literally, "In iniquity was I conceived," an instance of hyperbole: at no time was the psalmist ever without sin. Cf Ps 88, 16, "I

---

x: Pss 19, 2; 97, 6.   y: Ps 69, 32; Am 5, 21-22.   z: Pss 24, 1; 89, 12; Dt 10, 14; 1 Cor 10, 26.   a: Heb 13, 15.   b: Ps 77, 3. c: Ps 91, 16.   d: 2 Sm 12.   e: Pss 32, 5; 38, 19; Is 59, 12. f: Rom 3, 4.   g: Jb 14, 4.

8 Still, you insist on sincerity of heart;
    in my inmost being teach me wisdom.
9 Cleanse me with hyssop,* that I may be
    pure;
    wash me, make me whiter than snow.*h*
10 Let me hear sounds of joy and gladness;
    let the bones you have crushed rejoice.

II

11 Turn away your face from my sins;
    blot out all my guilt.
12 A clean heart create for me, God;
    renew in me a steadfast spirit.*i*
13 Do not drive me from your presence,
    nor take from me your holy spirit.*j*
14 Restore my joy in your salvation;
    sustain in me a willing spirit.
15 I will teach the wicked your ways,
    that sinners may return to you.
16 Rescue me from death, God, my saving
    God,
    that my tongue may praise your
    healing power.*k*
17 Lord, open my lips;
    my mouth will proclaim your praise.
18 For you do not desire sacrifice;*
    a burnt offering you would not accept.*l*
19 My sacrifice, God, is a broken spirit;
    God, do not spurn a broken, humbled
    heart.

III

20 Make Zion prosper in your good
    pleasure;*
    rebuild the walls of Jerusalem.*m*
21 Then you will be pleased with proper
    sacrifice,
    burnt offerings and holocausts;
    then bullocks will be offered on your
    altar.

PSALM 52*

See RG 244

The Deceitful Tongue

1 For the leader. A *maskil* of David,
2 when Doeg the Edomite went and
    told Saul, "David went to the house
    of Ahimelech."*n*

I

3 Why do you glory in evil,
    you scandalous liar?
    All day long 4 you plot destruction;
    your tongue is like a sharpened
    razor,
    you skillful deceiver.*o*
5 You love evil rather than good,
    lies rather than honest speech.*p*   *Selah*
6 You love any word that destroys,
    you deceitful tongue.*q*

II

7 Now God will strike you down,
    leave you crushed forever,
    Pluck you from your tent,
    uproot you from the land of the
    living.*r*   *Selah*
8 The righteous will look on with awe;
    they will jeer and say:*s*
9 "That one did not take God as a
    refuge,
    but trusted in great wealth,
    relied on devious plots."*t*

III

10 But I, like an olive tree in the house of
    God,*u*
    trust in God's faithful love forever.
11 I will praise you always
    for what you have done.
    I will proclaim before the faithful*v*
    that your name is good.

am mortally afflicted since youth," i.e., I have always been afflicted. The verse does not imply that the sexual act of conception is sinful.

51, 9: Hyssop: a small bush whose many woody twigs make a natural sprinkler. It was prescribed in the Mosaic law as an instrument for sprinkling sacrificial blood or lustral water for cleansing. Cf Ex 12, 22; Lv 14, 4; Nm 19, 18.

51, 18: For you do not desire sacrifice: the mere offering of the ritual sacrifice apart from good dispositions is not acceptable to God. Cf Ps 50.

51, 20-21: Most scholars think that these verses were added to the psalm some time after the destruction of the temple in 587 B.C. The verses assume that the rebuilt temple will be an ideal site for national reconciliation.

Ps 52: A condemnation of the powerful and arrogant (3-6),

who bring down upon themselves God's judgment (7). The just, those who trust in God alone, are gladdened and strengthened by the downfall of their traditional enemies (8-11).

52, 10: Like an olive tree: the righteous will flourish in the house of God like a well-watered olive tree. Cf Pss 92, 14; 128, 3.

h: Jb 9, 30; Is 1, 18; Ez 36, 25.   *i:* Ez 11, 19.   *j:* Wis 1, 5; 9, 17; Is 63, 11; Hg 2, 5; Rom 8, 9.   *k:* Ps 30, 10.   *l:* Pss 40, 7; 50, 8; Am 5, 21-22; Hos 6, 6; Is 1, 11-15; Heb 10, 5-7.   *m:* Jer 31, 4; Ez 36, 33.   *n:* 1 Sm 21, 8; 22, 6ff.   *o:* Pss 12, 3; 59, 8; 120, 2-3; Sir 51, 3.   *p:* Jer 4, 22; Jn 3, 19-20.   *q:* Jer 9, 4.   *r:* Pss 27, 13; 28, 5; 56, 14; Jb 18, 14; Prv 2, 22; Is 38, 11.   *s:* Pss 44, 14; 64, 9.   *t:* Jb 31, 24; Prv 11, 28.   *u:* Pss 1, 3; 92, 12-14; Jer 11, 16; 17, 8.   *v:* Pss 22, 23; 26, 12; 35, 18; 149, 1.

PSALM 53[*]

A Lament over Widespread Corruption

[1] For the leader; according to *Mahalath.*
A *maskil* of David.

I

[2] Fools say in their hearts,[w]
"There is no God."[x]
Their deeds are loathsome and
corrupt;
not one does what is right.
[3] God looks down from heaven
upon the human race,[y]
To see if even one is wise,[z]
if even one seeks God.
[4] All have gone astray;
all alike are perverse.
Not one does what is right, not even
one.[a]

II

[5] Will these evildoers never learn?
They devour my people as they
devour bread;[b]
they do not call upon God.[c]
[6] They have good reason to fear,
though now they do not fear.
For God will certainly scatter
the bones of the godless.
They will surely be put to shame,
for God has rejected them.

III

[7] Oh, that from Zion might come
the deliverance of Israel,
That Jacob may rejoice and Israel be
glad[d]
when God restores the
people!

PSALM 54[*]

Confident Prayer in Great Peril

[1] For the leader. On stringed instruments.
A *maskil* of David, [2] when the Ziphites came
and said to Saul, "David is hiding
among us."[e]

I

[3] O God, by your name[*] save me.
By your strength defend my cause.
[4] O God, hear my prayer.
Listen to the words of my mouth.
[5] The arrogant have risen against me;
the ruthless seek my life;
they do not keep God before them.[f]

Selah

II

[6] God is present as my helper;[g]
the Lord sustains my life.
[7] Turn back the evil upon my foes;
in your faithfulness, destroy them.[h]
[8] Then I will offer you generous sacrifice
and praise your gracious name, LORD,
[9] Because it has rescued me from every
trouble,
and my eyes look down on my foes.[i]

PSALM 55[*]

A Lament over Betrayal

[1] For the leader. On stringed instruments.
A *maskil* of David.

I

[2] Listen, God, to my prayer;[j]
do not hide from my pleading;
[3]   hear me and give answer.
I rock with grief; I groan
[4]   at the uproar of the enemy,

Ps 53: A lament of an individual, duplicated in Ps 14, except that "God" is used for "the LORD," and v 6 is different. See under Ps 14.

Ps 54: A lament in which the person under attack calls directly upon God for help (3-5). Refusing to despair, the psalmist hopes in God, who is active in history and just (6-7). The psalm ends with a serene promise to return thanks (8-9).

54, 3: By your name: one is present in one's name, hence God as revealed to humans.

Ps 55: The psalmist, betrayed by intimate friends (14-15, 21-22), prays that God punish those oath breakers and thus be acknowledged as the protector of the wronged. The sufferings of the psalmist include both ostracism (4) and mental turmoil (5-6), culminating in the wish to flee society (7-9). The wish for a sudden death for one's enemies (16) occurs elsewhere in

the psalms; an example of such a death is the earth opening under the wicked Dathan and Abiram (Nm 16, 31-32). The psalmist, confident of vindication, exhorts others to a like trust in the God of justice (23-24). The psalm is not so much for personal vengeance as for a public vindication of God's righteousness now. There was no belief in an afterlife where such vindication could take place.

w: 2-6a: Ps 14, 1-5a. x: Pss 10, 4; 36, 2; Is 32, 6; Jer 5, 12.
y: Pss 11, 4; 102, 20. z: 2b-3: Rom 3, 11-12. a: Ps 12, 2.
b: Ps 27, 2; Is 9, 11. c: Ps 79, 6. d: Ps 85, 2. e: 1 Sm 23, 19;
26, 1. f: Ps 86, 14. g: Ps 118, 7. h: Ps 143, 12. i: Pss 59, 11;
91, 8; 92, 12. j: 2-3: Pss 5, 2-3; 55; 2-3; 86, 6; 130, 1-2; Lam 3,
56; Jon 2, 3.

the clamor of the wicked.
They heap trouble upon me,
    savagely accuse me.
5 My heart pounds within me;
    death's terrors fall upon me.
6 Fear and trembling overwhelm me;
    shuddering sweeps over me.
7 I say, "If only I had wings like a dove
    that I might fly away and find rest.*k*
8 Far away I would flee;
    I would stay in the desert.*l*   *Selah*
9 I would soon find a shelter
    from the raging wind and storm."

II

10 Lord, check and confuse their scheming.
    I see violence and strife in the city
11   making rounds on its walls day and
      night.
Within are mischief and evil;
12   treachery is there as well;
    oppression and fraud never leave its
      streets.*m*
13 If an enemy had reviled me,
    that I could bear;
If my foe had viewed me with contempt,
    from that I could hide.
14 But it was you, my other self,
    my comrade and friend,*n*
15 You, whose company I enjoyed,
    at whose side I walked
    in procession in the house of God.

III

16 Let death take them by surprise;
    let them go down alive to Sheol,*o*
for evil is in their homes and hearts.
17 But I will call upon God,
    and the LORD will save me.
18 At dusk, dawn, and noon
    I will grieve and complain,
    and my prayer will be heard.*p*
19 God will give me freedom and peace
    from those who war against me,
    though there are many who oppose me.

20 God, who sits enthroned forever,*q*
    will hear me and humble them.
For they will not mend their ways;
    they have no fear of God.
21 They strike out at friends
    and go back on their promises.
22 Softer than butter is their speech,
    but war is in their hearts.
Smoother than oil are their words,
    but they are unsheathed swords.*r*
23 Cast your care upon the LORD,
    who will give you support.
God will never allow
    the righteous to stumble.*s*
24 But you, God, will bring them down
    to the pit of destruction.*t*
These bloodthirsty liars
    will not live half their days,
    but I put my trust in you.*u*

PSALM 56*

Trust in God

See RG 244

1 For the director. According to *Yonath elem
    rehoqim.* A *miktam* of David, when the
    Philistines seized him at Gath.*v*

I

2 Have mercy on me, God,
    for I am treated harshly;
    attackers press me all the day.
3 My foes treat me harshly all the day;
    yes, many are my attackers.
O Most High, 4 when I am afraid,
    in you I place my trust.
5 God, I praise your promise;
    in you I trust, I do not fear.*w*
    What can mere flesh do to me?*x*

II

6 All the day they foil my plans;
    their every thought is of evil against me.
7 They hide together in ambush;
    they watch my every step;
    they lie in wait for my life.*y*
8 They are evil; watch them, God!

Ps 56: Beset physically (2-3) and psychologically (6-7), the psalmist maintains a firm confidence in God (5. 9-10). Nothing will prevent the psalmist from keeping the vow to give thanks for God's gift of life (13-14). A refrain (5. 11-12) divides the psalm in two equal parts.

56, 1: Yonath elem rehoqim: Hebrew words probably designating the melody to which the psalm was to be sung.

---

k: Ps 11, 1. *l:* Jer 9, 1; Rv 12, 6. *m:* Jer 5, 1; 6, 6; Ez 22, 2; Hb 1, 3; Zep 3, 1. *n:* Ps 41, 10; Jer 9, 3; Mt 26, 21-24 par. *o:* Ps 49, 15; Nm 16, 33; Prv 1, 2; Is 5, 14. *p:* Dn 6, 11. *q:* Pss 29, 10; 93, 2; Bar 3, 3. *r:* Pss 12, 3; 28, 3; 57, 5; 62, 5; 64, 4; Prv 26, 24-28; Jer 9,7. *s:* Ps 37, 5; Prv 3, 5; 16, 3; 1 Pt 5, 7. *t:* Pss 28, 1; 30, 4; 40, 3; 88, 5; 143, 7; Prv 1, 12; Jon 2, 7. *u:* Pss 25, 2; 56, 4; 130, 5. *v:* 1 Sm 21, 10. *w:* Ps 130, 5. *x:* Ps 118, 6; Heb 13, 6. *y:* Ps 140, 5-6.

Cast the nations down in your anger!
9 My wanderings you have noted;
  are my tears not stored in your vial,*
  recorded in your book?z
10 My foes turn back when I call on you.
  This I know: God is on my side.
11 God, I praise your promise;
12   in you I trust, I do not fear.
  What can mere mortals do to me?

III

13 I have made vows to you, God;
  with offerings I will fulfill them,a
14 Once you have snatched me from death,
  kept my feet from stumbling,
  That I may walk before God
  in the light of the living.

See RG
244

PSALM 57*

Confident Prayer for Deliverance

1 For the director. Do not destroy.* A *miktam*
  of David, when he fled from Saul into
  a cave.b

I

2 Have mercy on me, God,
  have mercy on me.
  In you I seek shelter.
  In the shadow of your wings* I seek shelter
  till harm pass by.c
3 I call to God Most High,
  to God who provides for me.
4 May God send help from heaven to save me,
  shame those who trample upon me.
  May God send fidelity and love. *Selah*

5 I must lie down in the midst of lions
  hungry for human prey.d
  Their teeth are spears and arrows;
  their tongue, a sharpened sword.e
6 Show yourself over the heavens, God;
  may your glory appear above all the
  earth.f

II

7 They have set a trap for my feet;
  my soul is bowed down;
  They have dug a pit before me.
  May they fall into it
  themselves!g   *Selah*
8 My heart is steadfast, God,
  my heart is steadfast.
  I will sing and chant praise.h
9 Awake, my soul;
  awake, lyre and harp!
  I will wake the dawn.i *
10 I will praise you among the peoples, Lord;
  I will chant your praise among the
  nations.j
11 For your love towers to the heavens;
  your faithfulness, to the skies.k
12 Show yourself over the heavens, God;
  may your glory appear above all the
  earth.

PSALM 58*

The Dethroning of Unjust Rulers

See RG
244

1 For the leader. Do not destroy.* A *miktam*
  of David.

I

2 Do you indeed pronounce justice, O gods;*

56, 9: Are my tears not stored in your vial: a unique saying in the Old Testament. The context suggests that the tears are saved because they are precious; God puts a high value on each of the psalmist's troubles.

Ps 57: Each of the two equal strophes contains a prayer for rescue from enemies, accompanied by joyful trust in God (2-5, 7-11). The refrain prays that God be manifested as saving (6, 12). Ps 108 is nearly identical to part of this psalm (57, 8-12 = 108, 2-6).

57, 1: Do not destroy: Probably the title of the melody to which the psalm was to be sung.

57, 2: The shadow of your wings: probably refers to the wings of the cherubim (powerful winged animals) whose wings spread over the ark in the inner chamber of the temple (1 Kgs 6, 23-28).

57, 9: I will wake the dawn: by a bold figure the psalmist imagines the sound of music and singing will waken a new day.

Ps 58: A lament expressing trust in God's power to de-

throne all powers obstructing divine rule of the world. First condemned are "the gods," the powers that were popularly imagined to control human destinies (2-3), then "the wicked," the human instruments of these forces (4-6). The psalmist prays God to prevent them from harming the just (7-10). The manifestation of justice will gladden the just; they will see that their God is with them (11-12). The psalm is less concerned with personal vengeance than with public vindication of God's justice now.

58, 1: Do not destroy: probably the title of the melody to which the psalm was to be sung.

58, 2: Gods: the Bible sometimes understands pagan gods

z: Ps 10, 14; 2 Kgs 20, 5; Is 25, 8; Rv 7, 17. a: Nm 30, 3.
b: 1 Sm 22, 1. c: Pss 17, 8; 36, 8. d: Pss 17, 11-12; 22, 22; 58,
7. e: Pss 11, 2; 64, 4. f: Ps 72, 19; Nm 14, 21. g: Ps 7, 15;
140, 5-6. h: Ps 108, 2. i: Jb 38, 12. j: Pss 9, 12; 18, 50.
k: Pss 36, 6; 71, 19.

do you judge mortals fairly?[l]

[3] No, you freely engage in crime;
  your hands dispense violence to the
    earth.

II

[4] The wicked have been corrupt since
    birth;
  liars from the womb, they have gone
    astray.
[5] Their poison is like the poison of a
    snake,[*]
  like that of a serpent stopping its
    ears,[m]
[6] So as not to hear the voice of the
    charmer
  who casts such cunning spells.

III

[7] O God, smash the teeth in their
    mouths;
  break the jaw-teeth of these lions,
    LORD![n]
[8] Make them vanish like water flowing
    away;[o]
  trodden down, let them wither like
    grass.[p]
[9] Let them dissolve like a snail that oozes
    away,[*]
  like an untimely birth that never sees
    the sun.[q]
[10] Suddenly, like brambles or thistles,
  have the whirlwind snatch them
    away.[r]
[11] Then the just shall rejoice to see the
    vengeance
  and bathe their feet in the blood of the
    wicked.[s]
[12] Then it will be said:
  "Truly there is a reward for the just;
  there is a God who is judge on
    earth!"

PSALM 59[*]

Complaint against
Bloodthirsty Enemies

[1] For the director. Do not destroy.[*] A miktam
  of David, when Saul sent people to watch
    his house and kill him.[t]

I

[2] Rescue me from my enemies, my God;
  lift me out of reach of my foes.
[3] Deliver me from evildoers;
  from the bloodthirsty save me.
[4] They have set an ambush for my life;
  the powerful conspire against me.
For no offense or misdeed of mine,
  LORD,
[5] for no fault they hurry to take up
    arms.
Come near and see my plight!
[6] You, LORD of hosts, are the God of
    Israel!
Awake! Punish all the nations.
Have no mercy on these worthless
    traitors.   Selah
[7] Each evening they return,
  growling like dogs, prowling the city.[u]
[8] Their mouths pour out insult;
  sharp words are on their lips.
  They say: "Who is there to hear?"[*]
[9] You, LORD, laugh at them;
  you deride all the nations.[v]
[10] My strength, for you I watch;
  you, God, are my fortress, [11] my loving
    God.

II

May God go before me,
  and show me my fallen foes.
[12] Slay them, God,
  lest they deceive my people.
Shake them by your power;

See RG
244

to be lesser divine beings who are assigned by Israel's God to
rule the foreign nations. Here they are accused of injustice,
permitting the human judges under their patronage to abuse
the righteous. Cf Ps 82.

58, 5-6: The image is that of a poisonous snake that is controlled by the voice or piping of its trainer.

58, 9: A snail that oozes away: empty shells suggested to
ancients that snails melted away as they left a slimy trail.

Ps 59: A lament in two parts (2-9. 11b-17), each ending in
a refrain (10. 18). Both parts alternate prayer for vindication
(2-3. 5b-6. 11b-14) with vivid depictions of the psalmist's enemies (4-5a. 7-8. 15-16). The near curse in 12-13 is not a

crude desire for revenge but a wish that God's just rule over
human affairs be recognized now.

59, 1: Do not destroy: probably the title of the melody to
which the psalm was to be sung.

59, 8: Who is there to hear?: a sample of the enemies'
godless reflection. The answer is that God hears their blasphemies.

l: Ps 82, 2; Dt 16, 19.   m: Pss 64, 4; 140, 3; Rom 3, 13.   n: Ps 3,
7.   o: Wis 16, 29.   p: Ps 37, 2.   q: Jb 3, 16.   r: Jb 21, 18; Hos
13, 3; Na 1, 10.   s: Ps 68, 24; Is 63, 1-6.   t: 1 Sm 19, 11.   u: Ps
55, 11.   v: Pss 2, 4; 37, 13; Wis 4, 18.

Lord, our shield, bring them down.
13 For the sinful words of their mouths
    and lips
let them be caught in their pride.
For the lies they have told under oath[w]
14   destroy them in anger,
    destroy till they are no more.
Then people will know God rules over
    Jacob,
    yes, even to the ends of the
        earth.[x]   Selah
15 Each evening they return,
    growling like dogs, prowling the
        city.
16 They roam about as scavengers;
    if they are not filled, they howl.

III

17 But I shall sing of your strength,
    extol your love at dawn,
For you are my fortress,
    my refuge in time of trouble.
18 My strength, your praise I will sing;
    you, God, are my fortress, my loving
        God.

PSALM 60[*]

See RG 244, 252

Lament after Defeat in Battle

1 For the leader; according to "The Lily
of . . . ." A *miktam* of David (for teaching),
2 when he fought against Aram-Naharaim
and Aram-Zobah; and Joab, coming back,
killed twelve thousand Edomites in the
Valley of Salt.[y]

I

3 O God, you rejected us, broke our
    defenses;
you were angry but now revive us.
4 You rocked the earth, split it open;[z]
repair the cracks for it totters.

5 You made your people go through
    hardship,
    made us stagger from the wine you
        gave us.[a]
6 Raise up a flag for those who revere you,
    a refuge for them out of
        bowshot.   Selah
7 Help with your right hand and answer us[*]
    that your loved ones may escape.

II

8 In the sanctuary God promised:
    "I will exult, will apportion Shechem;
    the valley of Succoth[*] I will measure
        out.[*]
9 Gilead is mine, mine is Manasseh;
    Ephraim is the helmet for my head,
    Judah, my own scepter.[*]
10 Moab is my washbowl;[*]
    upon Edom I cast my sandal.[b *]
    I will triumph over Philistia."

III

11 Who will bring me to the fortified city?[*]
    Who will lead me into Edom?
12 Was it not you who rejected us, God?
    Do you no longer march with our
        armies?[c]
13 Give us aid against the foe;
    worthless is human help.
14 We will triumph with the help of God,
    who will trample down our foes.

PSALM 61[*]

See RG 244

Prayer of the King in Time of Danger

1 For the leader; with stringed instruments.
Of David.

I

2 Hear my cry, O God,
    listen to my prayer!

Ps 60: The community complains that God has let the enemy win the battle (3-5) and asks for an assurance of victory (6-7). In the oracle God affirms ownership of the land; the invasion of other nations is not permanent and will be reversed ultimately (8-10). With renewed confidence, the community resolves to fight again (11). The opening lament is picked up again (12-14), but this time with new awareness of God's power and human limitation.

60, 7-14: These verses occur again as the second half of Ps 108.

60, 8: I . . . will apportion . . . measure out: God lays claim to these places. The valley of Succoth: probably the lower stretch of the Jabbok valley.

60, 9: Judah, my own scepter: an allusion to the

Testament of Jacob, Gn 49, 10.

60, 10: Moab is my washbowl: Moab borders the Dead Sea, hence a metaphor for the country. Upon Edom I cast my sandal: an ancient legal gesture of taking possession of land.

60, 11: The fortified city: perhaps Bozrah, the fortified capital of Edom. Cf Is 34, 6; 63, 1; Am 1, 12.

Ps 61: A lament of the king who feels himself at the brink of death (3) and cries out for the strong and saving presence of God (3b-5). The king cites the prayer being made for him (7-8), and promises to give thanks to God.

w: Prv 12, 13; 18, 7.   x: Ps 83, 18-19; Ez 5, 13.   y: 2 Sm 8, 2. 3. 13; 1 Chr 18, 2. 3. 12.   z: Ps 75, 4; Is 24, 19.   a: Ps 75, 9; Is 51, 17. 21-22; Jer 25, 15.   b: Ru 4, 7-8.   c: Ps 44, 10.

3 From the brink of Sheol* I call;
  my heart grows faint.
  Raise me up, set me on a rock,
4 for you are my refuge,
  a tower of strength against the foe.*d*
5 Then I will ever dwell in your tent,
  take refuge in the shelter of your
      wings.*e*   *Selah*

II

6 O God, when you accept my vows
  and hear the plea of those
  who revere your name in prayer:*
7 "Add to the days of the king's life;
  may his years be many generations;*f*
8 May he reign before God forever;*g*
  may your love and fidelity preserve
      him"— *h*
9 Then* I will sing your name forever,
  fulfill my vows day after day.

See RG
245

PSALM 62*

Trust in God Alone

1 For the leader; *'al Jeduthun.*
  A psalm of David.

I

2 My soul rests in God alone,*i*
  from whom comes my salvation.
3 God alone is my rock and salvation,
  my secure height; I shall never fall.
4 How long will you set upon people,
  all of you beating them down,
  As though they were a sagging fence
  or a battered wall?
5 Even from my place on high
  they plot to dislodge me.
  They delight in lies;

they bless with their mouths,
  but inwardly they curse.*j*   *Selah*

II

6 My soul, be at rest in God alone,
  from whom comes my hope.
7 God alone is my rock and my salvation,
  my secure height; I shall not fall.
8 My safety and glory are with God,*k*
  my strong rock and refuge.
9 Trust God at all times, my people!
  Pour out your hearts to God our
      refuge!   *Selah*

III

10 Mortals are a mere breath,
   the powerful but an illusion;*l*
  On a balance they rise;*
   together they are lighter than air.
11 Do not trust in extortion;
   in plunder put no empty hope.
  Though wealth increase,
   do not set your heart upon it.*m*
12 One thing God has said;
   two things* I have heard:*n*
  Power belongs to God;
13   so too, Lord, does kindness,
  And you render to each of us
   according to our deeds.*o*

PSALM 63*

Ardent Longing for God

See RG
244

1 A psalm of David, when he was in the
   wilderness of Judah.*p*

I

2 O God, you are my God—
   for you I long!
  For you my body yearns;

61, 3: Brink of Sheol: literally, "edge of the earth," "earth" being taken in its occasional meaning "the underworld." Cf Jon 2, 3.

61, 6: In prayer: added for sense. Vv 7-8 express the plea of v 6.

61, 9: Then: Hebrew "just as," i.e., in accord with the vows referred to in v 6.

Ps 62: A song of trust displaying serenity from experiencing God's power (the refrains of 2-3 and 6-7) and anger toward unjust enemies (4-5). From the experience of being rescued, the psalmist can teach others to trust in God (10-13).

62, 1: 'Al Jeduthun: apparently the Hebrew name for the melody.

62, 10: On a balance they rise: precious objects were weighed by balancing two pans suspended from a beam. The lighter pan rises.

62, 12: One thing . . . two things: parallelism of numbers

for the sake of variation, a common device in Semitic poetry. One should not literally add up the numbers. Cf Am 1, 3; Prv 6, 16-19; 30, 15. 18. 21.

Ps 63: A psalm expressing the intimate relationship between God and the worshiper. Separated from God (2), the psalmist longs for the divine life given in the temple (3-6), which is based on a close relationship with God (7-9). May all my enemies be destroyed and God's true worshipers continue in giving praise (10-12)!

d: Ps 46, 2. *e:* Pss 17, 8; 36, 8; 57, 2. *f:* Ps 21, 5. *g:* Pss 72, 5; 89, 5. 30. 37. *h:* Pss 85, 11; 89, 15. 25; Prv 20, 28. *i:* 2-3. 6-7: Pss 18, 3; 31, 3-4; 42, 10; 118, 8; 146, 3. *j:* Pss 12, 3; 28, 3; 55, 22; Prv 26, 24-25. *k:* Ps 3, 3; Is 26, 4; 60, 19. *l:* Pss 39, 6-7; 144, 4; Jb 7, 16; Wis 2, 5. *m:* Jb 31, 25; Eccl 5, 9; Jer 17, 11; Mt 6, 19-21. 24. *n:* Jb 40, 5. *o:* Pss 28, 4; 31, 24; 2 Sm 3, 39; Jb 34, 11; Jer 17, 10; Mt 16, 27; Rom 2, 6; 2 Tm 4, 14. *p:* 1 Sm 24.

for you my soul thirsts,
Like a land parched, lifeless,
and without water.[q]
[3] So I look to you in the sanctuary
to see your power and glory.
[4] For your love is better than life;[*]
my lips offer you worship!

II

[5] I will bless you as long as I live;
I will lift up my hands, calling on your
name.
[6] My soul shall savor the rich banquet of
praise,
with joyous lips my mouth shall honor
you!
[7] When I think of you upon my bed,
through the night watches I will recall
[8] That you indeed are my help,
and in the shadow of your wings I
shout for joy.[r]
[9] My soul clings fast to you;
your right hand upholds me.

III

[10] But those who seek my life will come to
ruin;
they shall go down to the depths of the
earth!
[11] They shall be handed over to the sword
and become the prey of jackals!
[12] But the king shall rejoice in God;
all who swear by the Lord[*] shall exult,
for the mouths of liars will be shut![s]

See RG
244

PSALM 64[*]

Treacherous Conspirators
Punished by God

[1] For the leader. A psalm of David.

I

[2] O God, hear my anguished voice;

from the foes I dread protect my life.
[3] Hide me from the malicious crowd,
the mob of evildoers.
[4] They sharpen their tongues like swords,
ready their bows for arrows of poison
words.[t]
[5] They shoot at the innocent from ambush,
shoot without risk, catch them
unawares.[*]
[6] They resolve on their wicked plan;
they conspire to set snares;
they say: "Who will see us?"
[7] They devise wicked schemes,
conceal the schemes they devise;
the designs of their hearts are hidden.[u]

II

[8] But God will shoot arrows at them
and strike them unawares.[v]
[9] They will be brought down by their own
tongues;
all who see them will shake their
heads.[w]
[10] Then all will fear and proclaim God's
deed,
pondering what has been done.
[11] The just will rejoice and take refuge in
the LORD;
all the upright will glory in their God.[x]

PSALM 65[*]

See RG
245, 250

Thanksgiving for God's
Blessings

[1] For the leader. A psalm of David. A song.

I

[2] To you we owe our hymn of praise,
O God on Zion;
To you our vows[*] must be fulfilled,
[3] you who hear our prayers.
To you all flesh must come[y][*]

63, 4: **For your love is better than life**: only here in the
Old Testament is anything prized above life—in this case
God's love.

63, 12: **All who swear by the Lord**: to swear by a particular god meant that one was a worshiper of that god (Is 45,
23; 48, 1; Zep 1, 5).

Ps 64: A lament of a person overwhelmed by the malice of
the wicked who are depicted in the psalms as the enemies of
the righteous (2-7). When people see God bringing upon the
wicked the evil they intended against others, they will know
who is the true ruler of the world (8-10). The final verse is a
vow of praise (11).

64, 5: **Catch them unawares**: literally, "suddenly," i.e.,
"unexpectedly."

Ps 65: The community, aware of its unworthiness (3-4),
gives thanks for divine bounty (5), a bounty resulting from
God's creation victory (6-9). At God's touch the earth comes
alive with vegetation and flocks (10-14).

65, 2: **Vows**: the Israelites were accustomed to promising
sacrifices in the temple if their prayers were heard.

65, 3: **To you all flesh must come**: all must have recourse
to God's mercy.

q: Pss 42, 2; 143, 6; Is 26, 9.   r: Pss 17, 8; 36, 8.   s: Ps 107, 42.
t: Pss 11, 2; 37, 14; 55, 22; 57, 5.   u: Ps 140, 3; Prv 6, 14.   v: Pss
7, 13-14; 38, 3; Dt 32, 42.   w: Pss 5, 11; 44, 14; 52, 6.   x: Pss
36, 8; 57, 2.   y: Is 66, 23.

4 with its burden of wicked deeds.
We are overcome by our sins;
only you can pardon them.[z]
5 Happy the chosen ones you bring
to dwell in your courts.
May we be filled with the good things of
your house,
the blessings of your holy temple!

II

6 You answer us with awesome deeds* of
justice,
O God our savior,
The hope of all the ends of the earth
and of far distant islands.[a]
7 You are robed in power,
you set up the mountains by your
might.
8 You still the roaring of the seas,[b]
the roaring of their waves,
the tumult of the peoples.[c]
9 Distant peoples stand in awe of your
marvels;
east and west you make resound with
joy.
10 You visit the earth and water it,*
make it abundantly fertile.[d]
God's stream* is filled with water;
with it you supply the world with
grain.
Thus do you prepare the earth:
11 you drench plowed furrows,
and level their ridges.
With showers you keep the ground soft,
blessing its young sprouts.
12 You adorn the year with your bounty;
your paths* drip with fruitful rain.
13 The untilled meadows also drip;

the hills are robed with joy.
14 The pastures are clothed with flocks,
the valleys blanketed with grain;
they cheer and sing for joy.[e]

PSALM 66*

Praise of God,
Israel's Deliverer

See RG
245, 249

1 For the leader. A song; a psalm.

I

Shout joyfully to God, all you on earth;
2 sing of his glorious name;
give him glorious praise.[f]
3 Say to God: "How awesome your deeds!
Before your great strength your
enemies cringe.
4 All on earth fall in worship before you;[g]
they sing of you, sing of your name!"
Selah

II

5 Come and see the works of God,*
awesome in the deeds done for us.
6 He changed the sea to dry land;
through the river they passed on foot.[h]
Therefore let us rejoice in him,
7 who rules by might forever,
Whose eyes are fixed upon the nations.
Let no rebel rise to challenge! *Selah*
8 Bless our God, you peoples;
loudly sound his praise,
9 Who has kept us alive
and not allowed our feet to slip.[i]
10 You tested us, O God,
tried us as silver tried by fire.[j]
11 You led us into a snare;
you bound us at the waist as captives.
12 You let captors set foot on our neck;*

65, 6: **Awesome deeds**: the acts of creating—installing mountains, taming seas, restraining nations (7-8)—that are visible worldwide (6. 9).

65, 10-14: Apparently a description of the agricultural year, beginning with the first fall rains that soften the hard sun-baked soil (10-11).

65, 10: **God's stream**: the fertile waters of the earth derive from God's fertile waters in the heavenly world.

65, 12: **Paths**: probably the tracks of God's storm chariot dropping rain upon earth.

Ps 66: In the first part (1-12), the community praises God for powerful acts for Israel, both in the past (the exodus from Egypt and the entry into the land [6]) and in the present (deliverance from a recent but unspecified calamity [8-12]). In the second part (13-20), an individual from the rescued community fulfills a vow to offer a sacrifice of thanksgiving. As

often in thanksgivings, the rescued person steps forward to teach the community what God has done (16-20).

66, 5-6: Cf the events described in Ex 14, 1—15, 21; Jos 3, 11—4, 24, and Ps 114.

66, 12: **You let captors set foot on our neck**: literally, "you let men mount our head." Conquerors placed their feet on the neck of their enemies as a sign of complete defeat. Cf Jos 10, 24. A ceremonial footstool of the Egyptian king Tutankhamen portrays bound and prostrate bodies of enemies

z: Pss 32, 1-2; 78, 38; Is 1, 18. a: Is 66, 19. b: Pss 89, 10; 107, 29; Jb 38, 11; Mt 8, 26. c: Is 17, 12. d: Lv 26, 4; Is 30, 23. 25; Jl 2, 22-23. e: Is 44, 23. f: Ps 65, 14; Is 44, 23. g: 3-4: Ps 18, 45; Mi 7, 17. h: Pss 74, 15; 114, 3; Ex 14, 21f; Jos 3, 14ff; Is 44, 27; 50, 2. i: Pss 91, 12; 121, 3; 1 Sm 2, 9; Prv 3, 23. j: Is 48, 10.

we went through fire and water;
then you led us out to freedom.[k]

III

13 I will bring holocausts* to your house;
to you I will fulfill my vows,
14 The vows my lips pronounced
and my mouth spoke in distress.
15 Holocausts of fatlings I will offer you
and burnt offerings of rams;
I will sacrifice oxen and goats.   *Selah*
16 Come and hear, all you who fear God,
while I recount what has been done for
me.
17 I called to the Lord with my mouth;
praise was upon my tongue.
18 Had I cherished evil in my heart,
the Lord would not have heard.
19 But God did hear
and listened to my voice in prayer.
20 Blessed be God, who did not refuse me
the kindness I sought in prayer.

PSALM 67*

See RG 245

Harvest Thanks and Petition

1 For the leader; with stringed instruments.
A psalm; a song.

I

2 May God be gracious to us* and bless us;
may God's face shine upon us.[l]   *Selah*
3 So shall your rule be known upon the
earth,
your saving power among all the
nations.[m]

4 May the peoples praise you, God;
may all the peoples praise you!

II

5 May the nations be glad and shout for joy;
for you govern the peoples justly,
you guide the nations upon the
earth.[n]   *Selah*
6 May the peoples praise you, God;
may all the peoples praise you!

III

7 The earth has yielded its harvest;
God, our God, blesses us.[o]
8 May God bless us still;
that the ends of the earth may revere
our God.

PSALM 68*

See RG 245, 250

The Exodus and Conquest,
Pledge of Future Help

1 For the leader. A psalm of David, a song.

I

2 God will arise for battle;*
the enemy will be scattered;
those who hate God will flee.[p]
3 The wind will disperse them like smoke;
as wax is melted by fire,
so the wicked will perish before God.[q]
4 Then the just will be glad;
they will rejoice before God;
they will celebrate with great joy.

II

5 Sing to God, praise the divine name;
exalt the rider of the clouds.*

---

ready for the king's feet on their heads, and one of Tut-ankhamen's ceremonial chariots depicts the king as a sphinx standing with paw atop the neck of an enemy.

66, 13: Holocausts: wholly burnt offerings. Cf Lv 1, 3-13; 6, 1-4; 22, 17-20.

Ps 67: A petition for a bountiful harvest (7), made in the awareness that Israel's prosperity will persuade the nations to worship its God.

67, 2: May God be gracious to us: the people's petition echoes the blessing pronounced upon them by the priests. Cf Nm 6, 22-27.

Ps 68: The psalm is extremely difficult because the Hebrew text is badly preserved and the ceremony that it describes is uncertain. The translation assumes the psalm accompanied the early autumn Feast of Tabernacles (Sukkoth), which included a procession of the tribes (25-28). Israel was being oppressed by a foreign power, perhaps Egypt (31-32)—unless Egypt stands for any oppressor. The psalm may have been composed from segments of ancient poems, which would explain why the transitions are implied rather than explicitly stated. At any rate, v 2 is based on Nm 10, 35-

36, and vv 8-9 are derived from Jgs 5, 4-5.

The argument develops in nine stanzas (each of three to five poetic lines): 1) confidence that God will destroy Israel's enemies (2-4); 2) call to praise God as savior (5-7); 3) God's initial rescue of Israel from Egypt (8), the Sinai encounter (9), and the settlement in Canaan (10-11); 4) the defeat of the Canaanite kings (12-15); 5) the taking of Jerusalem, where Israel's God will rule the world (16-19); 6) praise for God's past help and for the future interventions that will be modeled on the ancient exodus-conquest (20-24); 7) procession at the Feast of Tabernacles (25-28); 8) prayer that the defeated enemies bring tribute to the temple (29-32); 9) invitation for all kingdoms to praise Israel's God (33-36).

68, 2: The opening line alluding to Nm 10, 35 makes clear that God's assistance in the period of the exodus and conquest is the model and assurance of all future divine help.

68, 5: Exalt the rider of the clouds: God's intervention is

k: Is 43, 2. *l:* Pss 4, 7; 31, 17; 44, 4; 80, 4; Dn 9, 17. *m:* Jer 33, 9. *n:* Ps 98, 9. *o:* Ps 85, 13; Lv 26, 4; Ez 34, 27; Hos 2, 23-24.
p: Nm 10, 35. *q:* Ps 97, 5; Jdt 16, 15; Wis 5, 14; Mi 1, 4.

Rejoice before this God
whose name is the LORD.*r*

6 Father of the fatherless, defender of
widows— *s*
this is the God whose abode is holy,

7 Who gives a home to the forsaken,
who leads prisoners out to prosperity,
while rebels live in the desert.*

III

8 God, when you went forth before your
people,*t*
when you marched through the
desert,   *Selah*

9 The earth quaked, the heavens shook,
before God, the One of Sinai,
before God, the God of Israel.

10 You claimed a land as your own, O God;

11   your people settled there.
There you poured abundant rains, God,
graciously given to the poor in their
need.

IV

12a The Lord announced the news of victory:*

13a   "The kings and their armies are in
desperate flight.*u*

12b All you people so numerous,

14a   will you stay by the sheepfolds?*v*

13b Every household will share the booty,

14b   perhaps a dove sheathed with silver,

14c   its wings covered with yellow gold."

15 When the Almighty routed the kings
there,
the spoils were scattered like snow on
Zalmon.*

V

16 You high mountains of Bashan,
you rugged mountains of Bashan,

17 You rugged mountains, why look with
envy
at the mountain* where God has
chosen to dwell,
where the LORD resides forever?*w*

18 God's chariots were myriad, thousands
upon thousands;
from Sinai the Lord entered the holy
place.

19 You went up to its lofty height;
you took captives, received slaves as
tribute.*x*
No rebels can live in the presence of
God.

VI

20 Blessed be the Lord day by day,
God, our salvation, who carries
us.*y*   *Selah*

21 Our God is a God who saves;
escape from death is in the LORD
God's hands.

22 God will crush the skulls of the enemy,
the hairy heads of those who walk in
sin.*z*

23 The Lord has said:
"Even from Bashan I will fetch them,
fetch them even from the depths of the
sea.*

24 You will wash your feet in your enemy's
blood;
the tongues of your dogs will lap it
up."*a*

VII

25 Your procession* comes into view,
O God,
your procession into the holy place,
my God and king.

---

in the imagery of Canaanite myth in which the storm-god
mounted the storm clouds to ride to battle. Such theophanies
occur throughout the psalm: 2-3. 8-10. 12-15. 18-19. 22-24.
29-32. 34-35. See Dt 33, 26; Ps 18, 8-16; Is 19, 1.

68, 7: **While rebels live in the desert**: rebels must live in
the arid desert, whereas God's people will live in the well-watered land (vv 8-11).

68, 12-15: The Hebrew text upon which the translation is
based has apparently suffered dislocation and has been substantially rearranged for sense. The version of the defeat of
the kings differs from that in the Book of Joshua, where the
people play a significant role. Here God alone is responsible
for the victory (though the actual battle is not described); Israel only gathers the spoils. God alone is the source of Israel's
success; human effort is not important.

68, 15: **Zalmon**: generally taken as the name of a moun-

tain where snow is visible in winter, perhaps to be located in
the Golan Heights or in the mountains of Bashan or Hauran
east of the Sea of Galilee.

68, 17: **The mountain**: Mount Zion, the site of the temple.

68, 23: **Even from Bashan . . . from the depths of the
sea**: the heights and the depths, the farthest places where enemies might flee.

68, 25-28: **Your procession**: the procession renews God's
original taking up of residence on Zion, described in 16-19.

r: Pss 18, 10; 104, 3; Dt 33, 26; Is 19, 1.   *s:* 6-7: Pss 103, 6; 146,
7. 9; Ex 22, 20-22; Bar 6, 37.   *t:* 8-9: Pss 44, 10; 114, 4. 7; Jgs 5,
4-5; Heb 12, 26.   *u:* Jgs 5, 19. 22.   *v:* Jgs 5, 16.   *w:* Ps 132, 13-
14; Ez 43, 7.   *x:* Ps 47, 8; Eph 4, 8-10.   *y:* Pss 34, 2; 145, 2; Is
46, 3-4; 63, 9.   *z:* Dt 32, 42.   *a:* Pss 58, 11; 1 Kgs 21, 19; 22, 38;
Is 63, 1-6.

26 The singers go first, the harpists follow;
   in their midst girls sound the timbrels.[b]
27 In your choirs, bless God;
   bless the LORD, you from Israel's
   assemblies.
28 In the lead is Benjamin, few in number;
   there the princes of Judah, a large
   throng,
   the princes of Zebulun, the princes of
   Naphtali, too.[c]

VIII

29 Summon again, O God, your power,
   the divine power you once showed for
   us.
30 Show it from your temple on behalf of
   Jerusalem,
   that kings may bring you tribute.
31 Roar at the wild beast of the reeds,*
   the herd of mighty bulls, the lords of
   nations;
   scatter the nations that delight in war.
32 Exact rich tribute from lower Egypt,[d]
   from upper Egypt,* gold and silver;
   make Ethiopia* extend its hands to
   God.[e]

IX

33 You kingdoms of the earth, sing to God;[f]
   chant the praises of the Lord,   *Selah*
34 Who rides the heights of the ancient
   heavens,
   whose voice is thunder, mighty
   thunder.
35 Confess the power of God,
   whose majesty protects Israel,
   whose power is in the sky.
36 Awesome is God in his holy place,
   the God of Israel,

who gives power and strength to his
people.[g]
Blessed be God!

PSALM 69*

*A Cry of Anguish in
Great Distress*

See RG
244, 251

1 For the leader; according to "Lilies."*
   Of David.

I

2 Save me, God,
   for the waters* have reached my neck.[h]
3 I have sunk into the mire of the deep,
   where there is no foothold.
I have gone down to the watery depths;
   the flood overwhelms me.[i]
4 I am weary with crying out;
   my throat is parched.
My eyes have failed,
   looking for my God.[j]
5 More numerous than the hairs of my
   head
   are those who hate me without cause.[k]
Too many for my strength
   are my treacherous enemies.
Must I now restore
   what I did not steal?*

II

6 God, you know my folly;
   my faults are not hidden from you.
7 Let those who wait for you, LORD of
   hosts,
   not be shamed through me.
Let those who seek you, God of Israel,[l]
   not be disgraced through me.
8 For your sake I bear insult,
   shame covers my face.[m]

68, 31: The wild beast of the reeds: probably the Nile crocodile, a symbol for Egypt; see 32 and Ez 29, 2-5.

68, 31-32: Lower Egypt is the delta area north of Cairo. **Upper Egypt** is the Nile Valley from Cairo to Aswan. **Ethiopia** is still further south.

Ps 69: A lament complaining of suffering in language both metaphorical (2-3 and 15-16, the waters of chaos) and literal (4. 5. 9. 11-13, exhaustion, alienation from family and community, false accusation). In the second part the psalmist prays with special emphasis that the enemies be punished for all to see (23-29). Despite the pain, the psalmist does not lose hope that all be set right, and promises public praise (30-37). The psalm, which depicts the suffering of the innocent just person vividly, is cited often by the New Testament especially in the passion accounts, e.g., v 5 in Jn 15, 25; v 22 in Mk 15, 23. 36 and parallels and in Jn 19, 29. The psalm prays not so

much for personal vengeance as for public vindication of God's justice. There was, at this time, no belief in an afterlife where such vindication could take place. Redress had to take place now, in the sight of all.

69, 1: "Lilies": apparently the name of the melody.

69, 2: Waters: the waters of chaos from which God created the world are a common metaphor for extreme distress. Cf Pss 18, 5; 42, 8; 88, 8; Jon 2, 3-6.

69, 5: What I did not steal: the psalmist, falsely accused of theft, is being forced to make restitution.

b: Pss 81, 2-3; 87, 7; 149, 3; 150, 3-5; 2 Sm 6, 5.   *c:* Is 8, 23.
d: Ez 29, 2ff,   *e:* Is 18, 7; 45, 14.   *f:* Ps 138, 4.   *g:* Pss 28, 8; 29,
11.   *h:* Pss 18, 5; 93, 3-4; Jb 22, 11.   *i:* Pss 40, 2; 124, 4-5.
j: Pss 25, 15; 119, 82; 123, 2; 141, 8; Is 38, 14.   *k:* Ps 40, 13; Lam
3, 52; Jn 15, 25.   *l:* Ps 40, 17.   *m:* Jer 15, 15.

⁹ I have become an outcast to my kin,
a stranger to my mother's children.ⁿ
¹⁰ Because zeal for your house consumes
me,*
I am scorned by those who scorn
you.ᵒ*
¹¹ I have wept and fasted,ᵖ
but this led only to scorn.
¹² I clothed myself in sackcloth;
I became a byword for them.
¹³ They who sit at the gate gossip about me;
drunkards make me the butt of their
songs.

III

¹⁴ But I pray to you, LORD,
for the time of your favor.
God, in your great kindness answer me
with your constant help.�q
¹⁵ Rescue me from the mire;ʳ
do not let me sink.
Rescue me from my enemies
and from the watery depths.
¹⁶ Do not let the floodwaters overwhelm
me,
nor the deep swallow me,
nor the mouth of the pit close over me.
¹⁷ Answer me, LORD, in your generous
love;
in your great mercy turn to me.
¹⁸ Do not hide your face from your servant;
in my distress hasten to answer me.ˢ
¹⁹ Come and ransom my life;
because of my enemies redeem me.
²⁰ You know my reproach, my shame, my
disgrace;
before you stand all my foes.
²¹ Insult has broken my heart, and I am
weak;
I looked for compassion, but there was
none,
for comforters, but found none.ᵗ
²² Instead they put gall in my food;
for my thirst they gave me vinegar.ᵘ

IV

²³ Make their own table a snare for them,
a trap for their friends.ᵛ
²⁴ Make their eyes so dim they cannot see;
keep their backs ever feeble.
²⁵ Pour out your wrath upon them;
let the fury of your anger overtake
them.
²⁶ Make their camp desolate,
with none to dwell in their tents.ʷ
²⁷ For they pursued the one you struck,
added to the pain of the one you
wounded.
²⁸ Add that to their crimes;
let them not attain to your reward.
²⁹ Strike them from the book of the living;
do not count them among the just!ˣ

V

³⁰ But I am afflicted and in pain;
let your saving help protect me, God,
³¹ That I may praise God's name in song*
and glorify it with thanksgiving.
³² My song will please the LORD more than
oxen,
more than bullocks with horns and
hooves:ʸ
³³ "See, you lowly ones, and be glad;
you who seek God, take heart!ᶻ
³⁴ For the LORD hears the poor,
does not spurn those in bondage.
³⁵ Let the heavens and the earth sing
praise,
the seas and whatever moves in
them!"

VI

³⁶ God will rescue Zion,
rebuild the cities of Judah.ᵃ
God's servants shall dwell in the land
and possess it;
³⁷ it shall be the heritage of their
descendants;
those who love God's name shall
dwell there.ᵇ

69, 10: Zeal for your house consumes me: the psalmist's commitment to God's cause brings only opposition. Cf Jn 2, 17.
I am scorned by those who scorn you: Rom 15, 3 uses the verse as an example of Jesus' unselfishness.

69, 31: That I may praise God's name in song: the actual song is cited in 33-35, the word "praise" in 35 referring back to "praise" in 31.

---

n: Jb 19, 13-15. o: Ps 119, 139; Jn 2, 17; Rom 15, 3. p: 11-13: Ps 109, 24-25; Jb 30, 9; Lam 3, 14. q: Is 49, 8. r: 15-16: Pss 28, 1; 30, 4; 32, 6; 40, 3; 88, 5; Prv 1, 12. s: Pss 102, 3; 143, 7. t: Lam 1, 2. u: Lam 3, 15; Mt 27, 34. 48; Mk 15, 23. v: Rom 11, 9-10. w: Acts 1, 20. x: Ps 139, 16; Ex 32, 32; Is 4, 3; Dn 12, 1; Mal 3, 16; Rv 3, 5. y: Pss 40, 7; 50, 8-9. 14; 51, 18; Is 1, 11-15; Hos 6, 6; Am 5, 21-22; Heb 10, 5-8. z: Pss 22, 27; 35, 27; 70, 5. a: Is 44, 26; Ez 36, 10. b: Ps 102, 29; Is 65, 9.

PSALM 70[*]

See RG 244

Prayer for Divine Help

[1] For the leader; of David. For remembrance.

[2] Graciously rescue me, God![c]
　Come quickly to help me, LORD![d]
[3] Confound and put to shame
　those who seek my life.[e]
Turn back in disgrace
　those who desire my ruin.
[4] Let those who say "Aha!"[f]
　turn back in their shame.
[5] But may all who seek you
　rejoice and be glad in you.
May those who long for your help
　always say, "God be glorified!"[g]
[6] Here I am, afflicted and poor.
　God, come quickly!
You are my help and deliverer.
LORD, do not delay!

See RG 244

PSALM 71[*]

Prayer in Time of Old Age

I

[1] In you, LORD, I take refuge;[h]
　let me never be put to shame.[i]
[2] In your justice rescue and deliver me;
　listen to me and save me!
[3] Be my rock and refuge,
　my secure stronghold;
　for you are my rock and fortress.[j]
[4] My God, rescue me from the power of
　the wicked,
　from the clutches of the violent.[k]
[5] You are my hope, Lord;
　my trust, GOD, from my youth.
[6] On you I depend since birth;
　from my mother's womb you are my
　strength;[l]
　my hope in you never wavers.

[7] I have become a portent to many,[*]
　but you are my strong refuge!
[8] My mouth shall be filled with your praise,
　shall sing your glory every day.

II

[9] Do not cast me aside in my old age;
　as my strength fails, do not forsake me.
[10] For my enemies speak against me;
　they watch and plot against me.[m]
[11] They say, "God has abandoned that one.
　Pursue, seize the wretch!
　No one will come to the rescue!"
[12] God, do not stand far from me;
　my God, hasten to help me.[n]
[13] Bring to a shameful end
　those who attack me;
Cover with contempt and scorn
　those who seek my ruin.[o]
[14] I will always hope in you
　and add to all your praise.
[15] My mouth shall proclaim your just deeds,
　day after day your acts of deliverance,
　though I cannot number them all.[p]
[16] I will speak of the mighty works of the
　Lord;
　O GOD, I will tell of your singular
　justice.

III

[17] God, you have taught me from my youth;
　to this day I proclaim your wondrous
　deeds.
[18] Now that I am old and gray,[q]
　do not forsake me, God,
That I may proclaim your might
　to all generations yet to come,[r]
Your power [19] and justice, God,
　to the highest heaven.
You have done great things;[s]
　O God, who is your equal?[t]
[20] You have sent me many bitter afflictions,
　but once more revive me.
From the watery depths of the earth

Ps 70: A lament of a poor and afflicted person (6) who has no resource except God, and who cries out to be saved from the enemy. The psalm is almost identical to Ps 40, 14–18.

Ps 71: A lament of an old person (9. 18) whose afflictions are interpreted by enemies as a divine judgment (11). The first part of the psalm pleads for help (1–4) on the basis of a hope learned from a lifetime's experience of God; the second part describes the menace (9–13) yet remains buoyant (14–16); the third develops the theme of hope and praise.

71, 7: A portent to many: the afflictions of the sufferer are taken as a manifestation of God's anger. Cf Dt 28, 46; Ps 31, 12.

---

c: 2–6: Ps 40, 14–18.　d: Ps 71, 12.　e: Ps 35, 4. 26.　f: Ps 35, 21. 25.　g: Ps 35, 27.　h: 1–3: Ps 31, 2–4.　i: Ps 25, 2.　j: Ps 18, 3.　k: Ps 140, 2.　l: Ps 22, 11.　m: Pss 3, 2; 22, 8.　n: Ps 22, 20.　o: Pss 35, 4; 40, 15; 70, 3.　p: Ps 35, 28.　q: Is 46, 3–4.　r: Pss 22, 31–32; 48, 14–15; 145, 4.　s: Ps 72, 18.　t: Ps 86, 8.

once more raise me up.
²¹ Restore my honor;
    turn and comfort me,
²² That I may praise you with the lyre
    for your faithfulness, my God,
And sing to you with the harp,
    O Holy One of Israel!
²³ My lips will shout for joy as I sing your
        praise;
    my soul, too, which you have redeemed.
²⁴ Yes, my tongue shall recount
    your justice day by day.
For those who sought my ruin
    will have been shamed and disgraced.

See RG 245

PSALM 72*

A Prayer for the King
¹ Of Solomon.

I

O God, give your judgment to the king;
    your justice to the son of kings;ᵘ*
² That he may govern your people with
        justice,
    your oppressed with right judgment,ᵛ
³ That the mountains may yield their
        bounty for the people,
    and the hills great abundance,ʷ
⁴ That he may defend the oppressed among
        the people,
    save the poor and crush the oppressor.

II

⁵ May he live as long as the sun endures,
    like the moon, through all
        generations.ˣ
⁶ May he be like rain coming down upon
        the fields,
    like showers watering the earth,ʸ
⁷ That abundance may flourish in his days,

great bounty, till the moon be no more.

III

⁸ May he rule from sea to sea,
    from the river to the ends of the
        earth.ᶻ*
⁹ May his foes kneel before him,
    his enemies lick the dust.ᵃ
¹⁰ May the kings of Tarshish and the
        islands* bring tribute,
    the kings of Arabia and Seba* offer
        gifts.ᵇ
¹¹ May all kings bow before him,
    all nations serve him.ᶜ
¹² For he rescues the poor when they cry
        out,
    the oppressed who have no one to
        help.
¹³ He shows pity to the needy and the
        poorᵈ
    and saves the lives of the poor.
¹⁴ From extortion and violence he frees
        them,
    for precious is their blood* in his sight.

IV

¹⁵ Long may he live, receiving gold from
        Arabia,
    prayed for without cease, blessed day
        by day.
¹⁶ May wheat abound in the land,
    flourish even on the mountain heights.
May his fruit increase like Lebanon's,
    his wheat like the grasses of the
        land.ᵉ*
¹⁷ May his name be blessed forever;
    as long as the sun, may his name
        endure.ᶠ
May the tribes of the earth give blessings
    with his name;*

Ps 72: A royal psalm in which the Israelite king, as the representative of God, is the instrument of divine justice (1-4. 12-14) and blessing (5-7. 15-17) for the whole world. The king is human, giving only what he has received from God. Hence intercession must be made for him. The extravagant language is typical of oriental royal courts.

72, 1: The king . . . the son of kings: the crown prince is the king's son; the prayer envisages the dynasty.

72, 8: From sea to sea . . . the ends of the earth: the boundaries of the civilized world known at the time: from the Mediterranean Sea (the western sea) to the Persian Gulf (the eastern sea), and from the Euphrates (the river) to the islands and lands of southwestern Europe, "the ends of the earth." The words may also have a mythic nuance—the earth surrounded by cosmic waters, hence everywhere.

72, 10: Tarshish and the islands: the far west (Ps 48, 6); Arabia and Seba: the far south (1 Kgs 10, 1).
72, 14: Their blood: cf Ps 116, 15.
72, 16: The translation of the difficult Hebrew is tentative.
72, 17: May the tribes of the earth give blessing with his name: an echo of the promise to the ancestors (Gn 12, 3; 26, 4; 28, 14), suggesting that the monarchy in Israel fulfilled the promise to Abraham, Isaac, and Jacob.

u: Ps 99, 4; Jer 23, 5. v: Prv 31, 8-9. w: Is 52, 7; 55, 12. x: Ps 89, 37-38; Jer 31, 35. y: Dt 32, 2; Is 45, 8; Hos 6, 3. z: Dt 11, 24; Zec 9, 10. a: Is 49, 23; Mi 7, 17. b: Ps 68, 30; Is 60, 5-6; 1 Kgs 10, 1ff. c: Pss 47, 5. d: Prv 31, 9. e: Is 27, 6; Hos 14, 6-8; Am 9, 13. f: Ps 21, 7.

may all the nations regard him as
favored.*g*

* * *

18 Blessed be the LORD, the God of Israel,*
who alone does wonderful deeds.*h*
19 Blessed be his glorious name forever;
may all the earth be filled with the
LORD's glory.*i*
Amen and amen.

20 The end of the psalms of David, son of
Jesse.

Third Book: Psalms 73—89

See RG
245

PSALM 73*

The Trial of the Just

1 A psalm of Asaph.

How good God is to the upright,
the Lord, to those who are clean of
heart!

I
2 But, as for me, I lost my balance;
my feet all but slipped,
3 Because I was envious of the arrogant
when I saw the prosperity of the
wicked.*j*
4 For they suffer no pain;
their bodies are healthy and sleek.
5 They are free of the burdens of life;
they are not afflicted like others.
6 Thus pride adorns them as a necklace;
violence clothes them as a robe.
7 Out of their stupidity comes sin;
evil thoughts flood their hearts.*k*
8 They scoff and spout their malice;
from on high they utter threats.*l*
9 They set their mouths against the heavens,*

their tongues roam the earth.
10 So my people turn to them
and drink deeply of their words.*
11 They say, "Does God really know?"
"Does the Most High have any
knowledge?"*m*
12 Such, then, are the wicked,
always carefree, increasing their wealth.

II
13 Is it in vain that I have kept my heart
clean,
washed my hands in innocence?*n*
14 For I am afflicted day after day,
chastised every morning.
15 Had I thought, "I will speak as they do,"
I would have betrayed your people.
16 Though I tried to understand all this,
it was too difficult for me,
17 Till I entered the sanctuary of God
and came to understand their end.*

III
18 You set them, indeed, on a slippery
road;
you hurl them down to ruin.
19 How suddenly they are devastated;
undone by disasters forever!
20 They are like a dream after waking,
Lord,
dismissed like shadows when you
arise.*o*

IV
21 Since my heart was embittered
and my soul deeply wounded,
22 I was stupid and could not understand;
I was like a brute beast in your
presence.
23 Yet I am always with you;
you take hold of my right hand.*p*
24 With your counsel you guide me,

72, 18-19: A doxology marking the end of Book II of the
Psalter.

Ps 73: The opening verse of this probing poem (cf Pss 37,
49) is actually the psalmist's hard-won conclusion from personal experience: God is just and good! The psalmist describes near loss of faith (2-3), occasioned by observing the
wicked who blasphemed God with seeming impunity (4-12).
Feeling abandoned despite personal righteousness, the
psalmist could not bear the injustice until an experience of
God's nearness in the temple made clear how deluded the
wicked were. Their sudden destruction shows their impermanence (13-20). The just can thus be confident, for, as the
psalmist now knows, their security is from God (1, 23-28).

73, 9: They set their mouths against the heavens: in an
image probably derived from mythic stories of half-divine giants, the monstrous speech of the wicked is likened to enormous jaws gaping wide, devouring everything in sight.

73, 10: The Hebrew is obscure.

73, 17: And came to understand their end: the psalmist
receives a double revelation in the temple: 1) the end of the
wicked comes unexpectedly (18-20); 2) God is with me.

---

g: Gn 12, 3; Zec 8, 13. *h:* Pss 41, 14; 89, 53; 106, 48; 136, 4.
i: Ps 57, 5; Nm 14, 21. *j:* Ps 37, 1; Jb 21, 13. *k:* Jb 15, 27.
l: Ps 17, 10. *m:* Ps 10, 11; Jb 22, 13. *n:* Ps 26, 6; Mal 3, 14.
o: Jb 20, 8. *p:* Ps 121, 5.

and at the end receive me with honor.*

25 Whom else have I in the heavens?
None beside you delights me on earth.

26 Though my flesh and my heart fail,
God is the rock of my heart, my
portion forever.

27 But those who are far from you perish;
you destroy those unfaithful to you.

28 As for me, to be near God is my good,
to make the Lord GOD my refuge.
I shall declare all your works
in the gates of daughter Zion.

See RG
244, 247

PSALM 74*

Prayer at the Destruction
of the Temple

1 A *maskil* of Asaph.

I

Why, God, have you cast us off
forever?q *
Why does your anger burn against the
sheep of your pasture?r

2 Remember your flock that you gathered
of old,
the tribe you redeemed as your very
own.
Remember Mount Zion where you
dwell.s

3 Turn your steps toward the utter ruins,
toward the sanctuary devastated by the
enemy.

4 Your foes roared triumphantly in your
shrine;
they set up their own tokens of victory.

5 They hacked away like foresters
gathering boughs,
swinging their axes in a thicket of trees.

6 They smashed all your engraved work,
pounded it with hammer and pick.

7 They set your sanctuary on fire;
the abode of your name they razed and
profaned.t

8 They said in their hearts, "Destroy them
all!
Burn all the shrines of God in the
land!"

9 Now we see no signs,*
we have no prophets,u
no one who knows how long.

10 How long, O God, shall the enemy jeer?v
Shall the foe revile your name forever?

11 Why draw back your right hand,
why keep it idle beneath your cloak?

II

12 Yet you, God, are my king from of old,*
winning victories throughout the earth.

13 You stirred up the sea in your might;w
you smashed the heads of the dragons
on the waters.x

14 You crushed the heads of Leviathan,y
tossed him for food to the sharks.

15 You opened up springs and torrents,
brought dry land out of the primeval
waters.

16 Yours the day and yours the night;
you set the moon and sun in place.

17 You fixed all the limits of the earth;
summer and winter you made.z

73, 24: And at the end receive me with honor: a perhaps deliberately enigmatic verse. It is understood by some commentators as reception into heavenly glory, hence the traditional translation, "receive me into glory." The Hebrew verb can indeed refer to mysterious divine elevation of a righteous person into God's domain: Enoch in Gn 5, 24; Elijah in 2 Kgs 2, 11-12; the righteous psalmist in Ps 49, 16. Personal resurrection in the Old Testament, however, is clearly attested only in the second century B.C. The verse is perhaps best left unspecified as a reference to God's nearness and protection.

Ps 74: A communal lament sung when the enemy invaded the temple; it would be especially appropriate at the destruction of Jerusalem in 587 B.C. Israel's God is urged to look upon the ruined sanctuary and remember the congregation who worshiped there (1-11). People and sanctuary are bound together; an attack on Zion is an attack on Israel. In the second half of the poem, the community brings before God the story of their origins—their creation (12-17)—in order to move God to reenact that deed of creation now. Will God allow a lesser power to destroy the divine project (18-23)?

74, 1: Forever: the word implies that the disaster is already of long duration. Cf 74, 9 and note.

74, 9: Now we see no signs: ancients often asked prophets to say for how long a divine punishment was to last. Cf 2 Sm 24, 13. Here no prophet has arisen to indicate the duration.

74, 12-17: Comparable Canaanite literature describes the storm-god's victory over all-encompassing Sea and its allies (dragons and Leviathan) and the subsequent peaceful arrangement of the universe, sometimes through the placement of paired cosmic elements (day and night, sun and moon). Cf Ps 89, 12-13. The psalm apparently equates the enemies attacking the temple with the destructive cosmic forces already tamed by God. Why then are those forces now raging untamed against your own people?

q: Pss 10, 1; 44, 24; 77, 8. r: Ps 80, 5. s: Pss 68, 17; 132, 13; Ex 15, 17; Jer 10, 16; 51, 19. t: Is 64, 10; Ps 79, 1. u: Lam 2, 9. v: Ps 89, 47. w: Ps 89, 10. x: Is 51, 9-10. y: Jb 3, 8; 40, 25; Is 27, 1. z: 16-17: Gn 1.

18 Remember how the enemy has jeered,
O LORD,
how a foolish people has reviled your
name.
19 Do not surrender to beasts those who
praise you;
do not forget forever the life of your
afflicted.
20 Look to your covenant,
for the land is filled with gloom;
the pastures, with violence.
21 Let not the oppressed turn back in shame;
may the poor and needy praise your
name.
22 Arise, God, defend your cause;
remember the constant jeers of the
fools.
23 Do not ignore the clamor of your foes,
the unceasing uproar of your enemies.

PSALM 75*

See RG
245, 250

God the Judge of the World

1 For the leader. Do not destroy! A psalm of
Asaph; a song.

I

2 We thank you, God, we give thanks;
we call upon your name,
declare your wonderful deeds.
You said:*
3 "I will choose the time;
I will judge fairly.
4 The earth and all its inhabitants will
quake,
but I have firmly set its pillars."a Selah

II

5 So I say to the boastful: "Do not boast!"b
to the wicked: "Do not raise your
horns!*

6 Do not raise your horns against heaven!
Do not speak arrogantly against the
Rock!"c
7 For judgment comes not from east or
from west,
not from the desert or from the
mountains,d
8 But from God who decides,
who brings some low and raises others
high.e
9 Yes, a cup* is in the LORD's hand,
foaming wine, fully spiced.*
When God pours it out,
they will drain it even to the dregs;
all the wicked of the earth must drink.f
10 But I will rejoice forever;
I will sing praise to the God of Jacob,
11 Who has said:
"I will break off all the horns of the
wicked,
but the horns of the just shall be lifted
up."g

PSALM 76*

See RG
245, 249

God Defends Zion

1 For the leader; a psalm with stringed
instruments. A song of Asaph.

I

2 Renowned in Judah is God,h
whose name is great in Israel.
3 On Salem* is God's tent, a shelter on Zion.
4 There the flashing arrows were
shattered,
shield, sword, and weapons of war.i
Selah

II

5 Terrible and awesome are you,
stronger than the ancient mountains.*

Ps 75: The psalmist gives thanks and rejoices (2. 10) for
the direct intervention of God, which is promised in two oracles (3-4. 11). Expecting that divine intervention, the psalmist
warns evildoers to repent (5-9).

75, 2: You said: supplied for clarity here and in v 11. The
translation assumes in both places that the psalmist is citing
an oracle of God.

75, 5: Do not raise your horns!: the horn is the symbol of
strength; to raise one's horn is to exalt one's own power as v
6 explains.

75, 9: A cup: "the cup of God's wrath" is the punishment
inflicted on the wicked. Cf Is 51, 17; Jer 25, 15-29; 49, 12; Ez
23, 31-33. Spiced: literally, "a mixed drink"; spices or drugs
were added to wine. Cf Prv 9, 2. 5.

Ps 76: A song glorifying Zion, the mountain of Jerusalem

where God destroyed Israel's enemies. Zion is thus the appropriate site to celebrate the victory (3-4), a victory described in parallel scenes (5-7. 8-11). Israel is invited to worship its powerful patron deity (12-13).

76, 3: Salem: an ancient name for Jerusalem, used here
perhaps on account of its allusion to the Hebrew word for
peace, shalom. Cf Gn 14, 18; Heb 7, 1-3.

76, 5: Ancient mountains: conjectural translation of a
difficult Hebrew phrase on the basis of Gn 49, 26. The mountains are part of the structure of the universe (Ps 89, 12-13).

a: Pss 46, 3; 60, 4; 93, 1; 96, 10; 104, 5; 1 Sm 2, 8; Is 24, 19.
b: 1 Sm 2, 3; Zec 2, 1-4. c: Jb 15, 25. d: Mt 24, 23-27. e: Jb 5,
11; 1 Sm 2, 7. f: Ps 60, 5; Jb 21, 20; Is 51, 17. 21-22; Jer 25, 15ff;
Hb 2, 16. g: Ps 92, 11. h: Hb 3, 2. i: Pss 46, 10; 122, 6-9.

⁶ Despoiled are the bold warriors;
   they sleep their final sleep;
   the hands of all the mighty have
     failed.*ʲ*
⁷ At your roar, O God of Jacob,
   chariots and steeds lay still.
⁸ So terrible and awesome are you;
   who can stand before you and your
     great anger?*ᵏ*
⁹ From the heavens you pronounced
    sentence;
   the earth was terrified and reduced to
    silence,
¹⁰ When you arose, O God, for judgment
   to deliver the afflicted of the
    land.   *Selah*
¹¹ Even wrathful Edom praises you;
   the remnant of Hamath* keeps your
    feast.

III

¹² Make and keep vows to the LORD your
   God.*ˡ*
   May all present bring gifts to this
    awesome God,
¹³ Who checks the pride of princes,
   inspires awe among the kings of earth.

See RG 244

PSALM 77*

Confidence in God during National Distress

¹ For the leader; 'al Jeduthun. A psalm
   of Asaph.

I

² I cry aloud to God,
   cry to God to hear me.
³ On the day of my distress I seek the
    Lord;
   by night my hands are raised
    unceasingly;*ᵐ*
   I refuse to be consoled.
⁴ When I think of God, I groan;
   as I ponder, my spirit grows
    faint.*ⁿ*   *Selah*
⁵ My eyes cannot close in sleep;
   I am troubled and cannot speak.
⁶ I consider the days of old;
   the years long past ⁷ I remember.*ᵒ*
   In the night I meditate in my heart;
   I ponder and my spirit broods:
⁸ "Will the Lord reject us forever,*ᵖ*
   never again show favor?
⁹ Has God's love ceased forever?
   Has the promise failed for all ages?
¹⁰ Has God forgotten mercy,
   in anger withheld compassion?" *Selah*
¹¹ I conclude:* "My sorrow is this,
   the right hand of the Most High has
    left us."*�q*

II

¹² I will remember* the deeds of the LORD;
   yes, your wonders of old I will
    remember.*ʳ*
¹³ I will recite all your works;
   your exploits I will tell.
¹⁴ Your way, O God, is holy;
   what god is as great as our God?*ˢ*
¹⁵ You alone are the God who did wonders;
   among the peoples you revealed your
    might.*ᵗ*
¹⁶ With your arm you redeemed your
    people,
   the descendants of Jacob and
    Joseph.*ᵘ*   *Selah*
¹⁷ The waters saw you, God;
   the waters saw you and lashed about,
   trembled even to their depths.*ᵛ*
¹⁸ The clouds poured down their rains;
   the thunderheads rumbled;
   your arrows flashed back and forth.*ʷ*
¹⁹ The thunder of your chariot wheels
    resounded;
   your lightning lit up the world;

76, 11: Edom . . . Hamath: conjectural translation. Israel's neighbors to the southeast and north.

Ps 77: A community lament in which the speaker ("I") describes the anguish of Israel at God's silence when its very existence is at stake (2-11). In response the speaker recites the story of how God brought the people into existence (12-21). The question is thus posed to God: Will you allow the people you created to be destroyed?

77, 11: I conclude: literally, "I said." The psalmist, after pondering the present distress and God's promises to Israel, has decided that God has forgotten the people.

77, 12: I will remember: the verb sometimes means to make present the great deeds of Israel's past by reciting them. Cf Pss 78, 42; 105, 5; 106, 7.

j: 2 Kgs 19, 35; Jer 51, 39; Na 3, 18. *k:* Dt 7, 21; 1 Sm 6, 20; Na 1, 6; Mal 3, 2. *l:* Nm 30, 3. *m:* Pss 50, 15; 88, 2. *n:* Jon 2, 8. *o:* Ps 143, 5; Dt 32, 7. *p:* 8-10: Pss 13, 2; 44, 24; 74, 1; 80, 5; 89, 47; Lam 3, 31. *q:* Ex 15, 6. 12; Pss 17, 7; 18, 36. *r:* Ps 143, 5. *s:* Ps 18, 31; Ex 15, 11. *t:* Pss 86, 10; 89, 6. *u:* Gn 46, 26-27; Neh 1, 10. *v:* Pss 18, 16; 114, 3; Na 1, 4. *w:* Pss 18, 14-15; 29; 144, 6; Jb 37, 3-4; Wis 5, 21; Hb 3, 10-11; Zec 9, 14.

the earth trembled and quaked.[x]

20 Through the sea was your path;
  your way, through the mighty waters,
  though your footsteps were unseen.[y]

21 You led your people like a flock
  under the care of Moses and Aaron.[z]

See RG
246

PSALM 78[*]

A New Beginning in Zion
and David

1 A maskil of Asaph.

I

Attend, my people, to my teaching;
  listen to the words of my mouth.

2 I will open my mouth in story,[*]
  drawing lessons from of old.[a]

3 We have heard them, we know them;
  our ancestors have recited them to us.[b]

4 We do not keep them from our children;
  we recite them to the next generation,
The praiseworthy and mighty deeds of
    the LORD,
  the wonders that he performed.[c]

5 God set up a decree in Jacob,
  established a law in Israel:[d]
What he commanded our ancestors,
  they were to teach their children;

6 That the next generation might come to
    know,
  children yet to be born.[e]
In turn they were to recite them to their
    children,

7 that they too might put their trust in
    God,
And not forget the works of God,

keeping his commandments.

8 They were not to be like their ancestors,
  a rebellious and defiant generation,[f]
A generation whose heart was not
    constant,[g]
  whose spirit was not faithful to God,

9 Like the ranks of Ephraimite archers,[*]
  who retreated on the day of battle.

10 They did not keep God's covenant;
  they refused to walk by his law.

11 They forgot his works,
  the wondrous deeds he had shown
    them.

II
A

12 In the sight of their ancestors God did
    wonders,
  in the land of Egypt, the plain of
    Zoan.[h][*]

13 He split the sea and led them across,[i]
  piling up the waters rigid as walls.[j]

14 God led them with a cloud by day,
  all night with the light of fire.[k]

15 He split rock in the desert,
  gave water to drink, abounding as the
    deep.[l]

16 He made streams flow from crags,
  drew out rivers of water.

B

17 But they went on sinning against him,
  rebelling against the Most High in the
    desert.[m]

18 They tested God in their hearts,
  demanding the food they craved.[n]

19 They spoke against God, and said,

Ps 78: A recital of history to show that past generations did not respond to God's gracious deeds and were punished by God making the gift into a punishment. Will Israel now fail to appreciate God's new act—the choosing of Zion and of David? The tripartite introduction invites Israel to learn the lessons hidden in its traditions (1-4. 5-7. 8-11); each section ends with the mention of God's acts. There are two distinct narratives of approximately equal length: the wilderness events (12-39) and the movement from Egypt to Canaan (40-72). The structure of both is parallel: gracious act (12-16. 40-55), rebellion (17-20. 56-58), divine punishment (21-31. 59-64), God's readiness to forgive and begin anew (32-39. 65-72). The psalm may reflect the reunification program of either King Hezekiah (late eighth century) or King Josiah (late seventh century) in that the Northern Kingdom (Ephraim, Joseph) is especially invited to accept Zion and the Davidic king.

78, 2: Story: Hebrew *mashal* literally means "compari-

son" and can signify a story with a hidden meaning. Mt 13, 35 cites the verse to explain Jesus' use of parables.

78, 9: Ephraimite archers: Ephraim was the most important tribe of the Northern Kingdom. Its military defeat (here unspecified) demonstrates its infidelity to God, who otherwise would have protected it.

78, 12. 43: Zoan: a city on the arm of the Nile, a former capital of Egypt.

---

x: Pss 18, 8; 97, 4; 99, 1; Ex 19, 16; Jgs 5, 4-5. y: Neh 9, 11; Wis 14, 3; Is 51, 10; Hb 3, 15. z: Ps 78, 52; Is 63, 11-14; Hos 12, 14; Mi 6, 4. a: Ps 49, 5; Mt 13, 35. b: Ps 44, 2. c: Ex 10, 2; Dt 4, 9; Jb 8, 8. d: Ps 147, 19; Dt 33, 4. e: Ps 22, 31-32; Dt 4, 9; 6, 7. f: Dt 31, 27; 32, 5. g: Ps 95, 10. h: Ps 106, 7. i: 13-14: Ex 14-15; Ps 136, 13. j: Ex 14, 22; 15, 8. k: Ps 105, 39; Ex 13, 21; Wis 18, 3. l: Pss 105, 41; 114, 8; Ex 17, 1-7; Nm 20, 2-13; Dt 8, 15; Wis 11, 4; Is 48, 21. m: Dt 9, 7; Ez 20, 13. n: Ps 106, 14; Ex 16, 2-36.

"Can God spread a table in the
   desert?[o]
[20] True, when he struck the rock,
      water gushed forth,
      the wadis flooded.
   But can he also provide bread,
      give meat to his people?"

C

[21] The LORD heard and grew angry;[p]
      fire blazed up against Jacob;
      anger flared up against Israel.
[22] For they did not believe in God,
      did not trust in his saving power.
[23] So he commanded the skies above;[*]
      the doors of heaven he opened.
[24] God rained manna upon them for food;
      bread from heaven he gave them.[q]
[25] All ate a meal fit for heroes;
      food he sent in abundance.
[26] He stirred up the east wind in the
      heavens;
   by his power God brought on the south
      wind.
[27] He rained meat upon them like dust,
      winged fowl like the sands of the sea,
[28] Brought them down in the midst of the
      camp,
      round about their tents.
[29] They ate and were well filled;
      he gave them what they had craved.
[30] But while they still wanted more,
      and the food was still in their mouths,
[31] God's anger attacked them,
      killed their best warriors,
      laid low the youth of Israel.[r]
[32] In spite of all this they went on sinning,
      they did not believe in his wonders.

D

[33] God ended their days abruptly,
      their years in sudden death.
[34] When he slew them, they began to seek
      him;
      they again inquired of their God.[s]

[35] They remembered[*] that God was their
      rock,
      God Most High, their redeemer.
[36] But they deceived him with their mouths,
      lied to him with their tongues.
[37] Their hearts were not constant toward
      him;
      they were not faithful to his covenant.[t]
[38] But God is merciful and forgave their
      sin;
      he did not utterly destroy them.
   Time and again he turned back his anger,
      unwilling to unleash all his rage.[u][*]
[39] He was mindful that they were flesh,
      a breath that passes and does not
      return.

III

A

[40] How often they rebelled against God in
      the desert,
      grieved him in the wasteland.
[41] Again and again they tested God,
      provoked the Holy One of Israel.
[42] They did not remember his power,
      the day he redeemed them from the
      foe,[v]
[43] When he displayed his wonders in
      Egypt,[*]
      his marvels in the plain of Zoan.[w]
[44] God changed their rivers to blood;
      their streams they could not drink.
[45] He sent insects that devoured them,[x]
      frogs that destroyed them.
[46] He gave their harvest to the caterpillar,
      the fruits of their labor to the locust.
[47] He killed their vines with hail,[y]
      their sycamores with frost.
[48] He exposed their flocks to deadly hail,
      their cattle to lightning.[z]
[49] He unleashed against them his fiery
      breath,
      roar, fury, and distress,
      storming messengers of death.

78, 23-31: On the manna and the quail, see Ex 16 and Nm 11. Unlike Ex 16, here both manna and quail are instruments of punishment, showing that a divine gift can become deadly because of Israel's apostasy.

78, 35: Remembered: invoked God publicly in worship. Their words were insincere (36).

78, 38: God is always ready to forgive and begin anew, as in choosing Zion and David (65-72).

78, 43-55: Ex 7—12 records ten plagues. Here there are

six divine attacks upon Egypt; the seventh climactic act is God's bringing Israel to the holy land.

o: Ps 23, 5.   *p*: 21f; Nm 11; Dt 32, 22.   *q*: Ps 105, 40; Ex 16, 4. 14; Dt 8, 3; Wis 16, 20; Jn 6, 31.   *r*: Nm 14, 29.   *s*: Dt 32, 15. 18; Is 26, 16.   *t*: Ps 95, 10; Is 29, 13.   *u*: Ps 85, 4; Ex 32, 14; Is 48, 9; Ez 20, 22.   *v*: Ps 106, 21.   *w*: 43f: Pss 105, 27-36; 135, 9; Ex 7, 14-11, 10; 12, 29-36; Wis 16-18.   *x*: Ex 8, 17.   *y*: Wis 16, 16.   *z*: Ex 9, 3.

50 He cleared a path for his anger;
  he did not spare them from death;
  he delivered their beasts to the plague.
51 He struck all the firstborn of Egypt,*a*
  love's first child in the tents of Ham.
52 God led forth his people like sheep;
  he guided them through the desert like
    a flock.*b*
53 He led them on secure and unafraid,
  but the sea enveloped their enemies.*c*
54 He brought them to his holy land,
  the mountain his right hand had won.*d*
55 God drove out the nations before them,
  apportioned them a heritage by lot,
  settled the tribes of Israel in their
    tents.

B

56 But they tested, rebelled against God
    Most High,
  his decrees they did not observe.
57 They turned back, deceitful like their
    ancestors;
  they proved false like a bow with no
    tension.
58 They enraged him with their high
    places;
  with their idols they goaded him.*e*

C

59 God heard and grew angry;
  he rejected Israel completely.
60 He forsook the shrine at Shiloh,*f*
  the tent where he dwelt with humans.
61 He gave up his might into captivity,
  his glorious ark into the hands of the
    foe.*g*
62 God abandoned his people to the sword;
  he was enraged against his heritage.
63 Fire consumed their young men;
  their young women heard no wedding
    songs.*h*

64 Their priests fell by the sword;
  their widows made no lamentation.

D

65 Then the Lord awoke as from sleep,
  like a warrior from the effects of wine.
66 He put his enemies to flight;
  everlasting shame he dealt them.
67 He rejected the tent of Joseph,
  chose not the tribe of Ephraim.
68 God chose the tribe of Judah,*
  Mount Zion which he favored.*i*
69 He built his shrine like the heavens,
  like the earth which he founded
    forever.
70 He chose David his servant,
  took him from the sheepfold.*j*
71 From tending sheep God brought him,
  to shepherd Jacob, his people,
  Israel, his heritage.*k*
72 He shepherded them with a pure heart;
  with skilled hands he guided them.

PSALM 79*

A Prayer for Jerusalem

See RG 244

1 A psalm of Asaph.

I

O God, the nations have invaded your
    heritage;
  they have defiled your holy temple,
  have laid Jerusalem in ruins.*l*
2 They have left the corpses of your
    servants
  as food for the birds of the heavens,
  the flesh of your faithful for the beasts
    of the earth.*m*
3 They have spilled their blood like water
  all around Jerusalem,
  and no one is left to bury them.*n*
4 We have become the reproach of our
    neighbors,

78, 60: Shiloh: an important shrine in the north prior to Jerusalem. Despite its holy status, it was destroyed (60-64; cf Jer 7, 12. 14).

78, 68. 70: God's ultimate offer of mercy to the sinful helpless people is Zion and the Davidic king.

Ps 79: A communal lament complaining that the nations have defiled the temple and murdered the holy people, leaving their corpses unburied (1-4). The occasion is probably the destruction of Jerusalem by the Babylonian army in 587 B.C. The people ask how long the withdrawal of divine favor will last (5), pray for action now (6-7), and admit that their own sins have brought about the catastrophe (8-9). They seek to

persuade God to act for reasons of honor: the nations who do not call upon the Name are running amok (6); the divine honor is compromised (1. 10. 12); God's own servants suffer (2-4. 11).

a: Pss 105, 36; 136, 10; Ex 12, 29.   *b:* Ps 77, 21.   *c:* Ex 14, 26-28.   *d:* Ex 15, 17.   *e:* Dt 32, 16. 21.   *f:* Jos 18, 1; 1 Sm 1, 3; Jer 7, 12; 26, 6.   *g:* 1 Sm 4, 11. 22.   *h:* Dt 32, 25; Jer 7, 34.   *i:* Pss 48, 2; 50, 2; Lam 2, 15.   *j:* Ps 89, 21; Ez 34, 23; 37, 24; 2 Chr 6, 6.   *k:* 1 Sm 16, 11-13; 2 Sm 7, 8.   *l:* 2 Kgs 25, 9-10; Lam 1, 10.   *m:* Jer 7, 33.   *n:* 1 Mc 7, 17; Jer 14, 16.

the scorn and derision of those
 around us.[o]

II

[5] How long, LORD? Will you be angry
 forever?
Will your rage keep burning like
 fire?[p]
[6] Pour out your wrath on nations that
 reject you,
on kingdoms that do not call on your
 name,[q]
[7] For they have devoured Jacob,
 laid waste his home.
[8] Do not hold past iniquities against us;
may your compassion come quickly,
for we have been brought very low.[r]

III

[9] Help us, God our savior,
 for the glory of your name.
Deliver us, pardon our sins
 for your name's sake.[s]
[10] Why should the nations say,
 "Where is their God?"[t]
Before our eyes make clear to the
 nations
that you avenge the blood of your
 servants.[u]

IV

[11] Let the groans of prisoners come before
 you;
by your great power free those
 doomed to death.[v]
[12] Lord, inflict on our neighbors
 sevenfold
the disgrace they inflicted on you.[w]
[13] Then we, your people, the sheep of your
 pasture,
will give thanks to you forever;
through all ages we will declare your
 praise.

PSALM 80[*]

Prayer to Restore God's
Vineyard

See RG
244, 247

[1] For the leader; according to "Lilies."
 Eduth.[*] A psalm of Asaph.

I

[2] Shepherd of Israel, listen,
 guide of the flock of Joseph!
From your throne upon the cherubim
 reveal yourself[x]
[3] to Ephraim, Benjamin, and Manasseh.
Stir up your power, come to save us.
[4] O LORD of hosts, restore us;
Let your face shine upon us,
that we may be saved.[y]

II

[5] LORD of hosts,
 how long will you burn with anger
 while your people pray?[z]
[6] You have fed them the bread of tears,
 made them drink tears in abundance.[a]
[7] You have left us to be fought over by our
 neighbors;
 our enemies deride us.[b]
[8] O LORD of hosts, restore us;
 let your face shine upon us,
 that we may be saved.

III

[9] You brought a vine[*] out of Egypt;
 you drove away the nations and
 planted it.
[10] You cleared the ground;
 it took root and filled the land.
[11] The mountains were covered by its
 shadow,
 the cedars of God by its branches.
[12] It sent out boughs as far as the sea,[*]
 shoots as far as the river.[*]
[13] Why have you broken down the walls,

Ps 80: A community lament in time of military defeat. Using the familiar image of Israel as a vineyard, the people complain that God has broken down the wall protecting the once splendid vine brought from Egypt (9-14). They pray that God will again turn to them and use the Davidic king to lead them to victory (15-20).

80, 1: Lilies . . . . Eduth: the first term is probably the title of the melody to which the psalm was to be sung; the second is unexplained.

80, 9: A vine: a frequent metaphor for Israel. Cf Is 5, 1-7; 27, 2-5; Jer 2, 21; Hos 10, 1; Mt 21, 33.

80, 12: The sea: the Mediterranean. The river: the Eu-
phrates. Cf Gn 15, 18; 1 Kgs 5, 1. The terms may also have a mythic nuance—the seas that surround the earth; sea and river are sometimes paralleled in poetry.

---

o: Pss 44, 14; 80, 7; 123, 3-4; Jb 12, 4; Dn 9, 16; Zep 2, 8. p: Pss 13, 2; 44, 24; 89, 47; Dt 4, 24. q: Ps 14, 4; Jer 10, 25. r: Ps 142, 7. s: Ez 20, 44; 36, 22. t: Pss 42, 4; 115, 2; Jl 2, 17. u: Jl 4, 21. v: Ps 102, 21. w: Ps 89, 51-52. x: Pss 23, 1-3; 95, 7; 100, 3; Gn 48, 15; Ex 25, 22; 1 Sm 4, 4; 2 Sm 6, 2; Mi 7, 14. y: 4. 8. 20: Pss 4, 7; 31, 17; 67, 2; 85, 5; Nm 6, 25; Dn 9, 17. z: Pss 13, 2; 44, 24; 74, 1; 79, 5; 89, 47; Dt 4, 24. a: Pss 42, 4; 102, 10. b: Pss 44, 14; 79, 4; 123, 3-4; Jb 12, 4; Dn 9, 16; Zep 2, 8.

so that all who pass by pluck its fruit?[c]

[14] The boar from the forest strips the vine;
the beast of the field feeds upon it.[d]

[15] Turn again, LORD of hosts;
look down from heaven and see;
Attend to this vine,

[16] the shoot your right hand has planted.

[17] Those who would burn or cut it down—
may they perish at your rebuke.

[18] May your help be with the man at your
right hand,
with the one[*] whom you once made
strong.

[19] Then we will not withdraw from you;
revive us, and we will call on your
name.

[20] LORD of hosts, restore us;
let your face shine upon us,
that we may be saved.

PSALM 81[*]

See RG 246

An Admonition to Fidelity

[1] For the leader; "upon the *gittith*."[*]
Of Asaph.

I

[2] Sing joyfully to God our strength;[e]
shout in triumph to the God of Jacob!

[3] Take up a melody, sound the timbrel,
the sweet-sounding harp and lyre.

[4] Blow the trumpet at the new moon,
at the full moon,[*] on our solemn feast.[f]

[5] For this is a law in Israel,
an edict of the God of Jacob,[g]

[6] Who made it a decree for Joseph
when he came out of the land of Egypt.

II

I hear a new oracle:[*]

[7] "I relieved their shoulders of the
burden;[*]
their hands put down the basket.[h][*]

[8] In distress you called and I rescued you;
unseen, I spoke to you in thunder;
At the waters of Meribah[*] I tested you
and said:[i]   *Selah*

[9] 'Listen, my people, I give you warning!
If only you will obey me, Israel![j]

[10] There must be no foreign god among
you;[k][*]
you must not worship an alien god.

[11] I, the LORD, am your God,
who brought you up from the land of
Egypt.
Open wide your mouth that I may fill
it.'

[12] But my people did not listen to my
words;
Israel did not obey me.

[13] So I gave them over to hardness of heart;
they followed their own designs.[l]

[14] But even now if my people would listen,
if Israel would walk in my paths,[m]

[15] In a moment I would subdue their foes,
against their enemies unleash my
hand.[n]

[16] Those who hate the LORD would tremble,
their doom sealed forever.

[17] But Israel I would feed with the finest
wheat,
satisfy them with honey from the
rock."[o]

80, 18: The man at your right hand . . . the one: the Davidic king who will lead the army in battle.

Ps 81: At a pilgrimage feast, probably harvest in the fall, the people assemble in the temple in accord with the Sinai ordinances (2-6a). They hear a divine word (mediated by a temple speaker) telling how God rescued them from slavery in Egypt (7-9), gave them the fundamental commandment of fidelity (9-11), which would bring punishment if they refused to obey (12-13). But if Israel repents, God will be with them once again, bestowing protection and fertility (14-17).

81, 1: Upon the gittith: probably the title of the melody to which the psalm was to be sung or a muscial instrument.

81, 4: New moon . . . full moon: the pilgrimage feast of harvest began with a great assembly (Lv 23, 24; Nm 29, 1), used the new moon as a sign (Nm 29, 6), and included trumpets (Lv 23, 24).

81, 6: I hear a new oracle: literally, "a tongue I do not know I hear." A temple official speaks the word of God (6b-

17), which is authoritative and unlike merely human words (cf Nm 24, 4. 16).

81, 7: I relieved their shoulders of the burden: literally, "his [Israel's] shoulder," hence the plural translation. A reference to the liberation of Israel from salvery in Egypt. **The basket**: for carrying clay to make bricks. Cf Ex 1, 14.

81, 8: Meribah: place of rebellion in the wilderness; cf Ex 17, 7; Nm 20, 13.

81, 10: There must be no foreign god among you: as in Pss 50 and 95, Israel is challenged to obey the first commandment of fidelity to God after the proclamation of the exodus.

c: Ps 89, 41.   d: Hos 2, 14.   e: Pss 43, 4; 68, 26; 149, 3; 150, 3-4; Jdt 16, 1.   f: Lev 23, 24; Nm 29, 1.   g: Ex 23, 14ff.   h: Ex 1, 14; 6, 6.   i: Ps 95, 8; Ex 2, 23ff; 17, 7; 19, 16; Nm 20, 13; 27, 14.   j: Ex 1, 14; 6, 6.   k: 10-11: Ex 20, 2-6; Dt 5, 6-10.   l: Jer 3, 17; 7, 24.   m: Is 48, 18.   n: Lv 26, 7-8.   o: Ps 147, 14; Dt 32, 13-14.

See RG 246

PSALM 82*

The Downfall of Unjust Gods

¹ A psalm of Asaph.

I

God rises in the divine council,
  gives judgment in the midst of the
  gods.ᵖ
² "How long will you judge unjustly
  and favor the cause of the
  wicked?�q *Selah*
³ Defend the lowly and fatherless;
  render justice to the afflicted and needy.
⁴ Rescue the lowly and poor;
  deliver them from the hand of the
  wicked."ʳ

II

⁵ The gods neither know nor understand,
  wandering about in darkness,
  and all the world's foundations shake.*
⁶ I declare: "Gods though you be,*
  offspring of the Most High all of you,
⁷ Yet like any mortal you shall die;
  like any prince you shall fall."
⁸ Arise, O God, judge the earth,*
  for yours are all the nations.

See RG 244, 246

PSALM 83*

Prayer against a Hostile Alliance

¹ A song; a psalm of Asaph.

I

² God, do not be silent;

God, be not still and unmoved!ˢ
³ See how your enemies rage;
  your foes proudly raise their heads.
⁴ They conspire against your people,
  plot against those you protect.ᵗ
⁵ They say, "Come, let us wipe out their
  nation;
  let Israel's name be mentioned no
  more!"
⁶ They scheme with one mind,
  in league against you:ᵘ
⁷ The tents of Ishmael and Edom,*
  the people of Moab and Hagar,ᵛ*
⁸ Gebal,* Ammon, and Amalek,ʷ
  Philistia and the inhabitants of Tyre.ˣ
⁹ Assyria, too, in league with them
  gives aid to the descendants of Lot.* *Selah*

II

¹⁰ Deal with them as with Midian;*
  as with Sisera and Jabin at the torrent
  Kishon,ʸ
¹¹ Those destroyed at Endor,
  who became dung for the ground.ᶻ
¹² Make their nobles like Oreb and Zeeb,
  all their princes like Zebah and
  Zalmunna,
¹³ Who made a plan together,
  "Let us seize the pastures of God."
¹⁴ My God, turn them into withered grass,
  into chaff flying before the wind.ᵃ
¹⁵ As a fire raging through a forest,
  a flame setting mountains ablaze,ᵇ

Ps 82: As in Ps 58, the pagan gods are seen as subordinate divine beings to whom Israel's God had delegated oversight of the foreign countries in the beginning (Dt 32, 8-9 LXX). Now God arises in the heavenly assembly (1) to rebuke the unjust "gods" (2-4), who are stripped of divine status and reduced in rank to mortals (5-7). They are accused of misruling the earth by not upholding the poor. A short prayer for universal justice concludes the psalm (8).

82, 5: The gods are blind and unable to declare what is right. Their misrule shakes earth's foundations (cf Pss 11, 3; 75, 4), which God made firm in creation (Ps 96, 10).

82, 6: I declare: "Gods though you be": in Jn 10, 34 Jesus uses the verse to prove that those to whom the word of God is addressed can fittingly be called "gods."

82, 8: Judge the earth: according to Dt 32, 8-9 LXX, Israel's God had originally assigned jurisdiction over the foreign nations to the subordinate deities, keeping Israel as a personal possession. Now God will directly take over the rulership of the whole world.

Ps 83: The community lament complains to God of the nations' attempts to wipe out the name of Israel (2-9). The psalmist sees all Israel's enemies throughout its history united in a conspiracy (3-9). May God destroy the current crop of enemies as the enemies of old were destroyed (10-13), and may they be pursued until they acknowledge the name of Israel's God (14-19).

83, 7-9: Apart from the Assyrians, all the nations listed here were neighbors of Israel. **The people of . . . Hagar:** a tribe of the desert regions east of **Ammon** and **Moab** (1 Chr 5, 10. 19-22). **Gebal** is the Phoenician city of Byblos or perhaps a mountain region south of the Dead Sea. **The descendants of Lot** are Moab and Edom (Gn 19, 36-38 and Dt 2, 9). These nations were never united against Israel in the same period; the psalm has lumped them all together.

83, 10-13: For the historical events, see Jgs 4—8.

p: Is 3, 13-14. *q:* Ps 58, 2. *r:* Dt 1, 17. *s:* Pss 10, 1; 44, 24; 109, 1. *t:* Jer 11, 9. *u:* Ps 2, 2. *v:* Nm 20, 23; 1 Chr 5, 10. 19. *w:* Ex 17, 8. *x:* Jos 13, 2. *y:* Ex 2, 15; Is 9, 3; 10, 26. *z:* Jer 8, 2. *a:* Pss 1, 4; 35, 5; 58, 10; Is 5, 24; 10, 17; 17, 13; 29, 5; Ez 21, 3. *b:* Ps 50, 3.

[16] Pursue them with your tempest;
    terrify them with your storm.[c]
[17] Cover their faces with shame,
    till they pay you homage, LORD.
[18] Let them be dismayed and shamed
    forever;
    let them perish in disgrace.
[19] Show them you alone are the LORD,
    the Most High over all the earth.[d]

See RG
245

PSALM 84[*]

Prayer of a Pilgrim to Jerusalem

[1] For the leader; "upon the *gittith*." A psalm
    of the Korahites.

I

[2] How lovely your dwelling,
    O LORD of hosts![e]
[3] My soul yearns and pines
    for the courts of the LORD.[f]
    My heart and flesh cry out
    for the living God.
[4] As the sparrow finds a home
    and the swallow a nest to settle her
    young,[*]
    My home is by your altars,
    LORD of hosts, my king and my God![g]
[5] Happy are those who dwell in your
    house!
    They never cease to praise you. Selah

II

[6] Happy are those who find refuge in you,
    whose hearts are set on pilgrim roads.
[7] As they pass through the Baca valley,[*]
    they find spring water to drink.
    Also from pools the Lord provides water
    for those who lose their way.
[8] They pass through outer and inner wall
    and see the God of gods on Zion.

III

[9] LORD of hosts, hear my prayer;
    listen, God of Jacob. Selah
[10] O God, look kindly on our shield;
    look upon the face of your anointed.[h][*]

IV

[11] Better one day in your courts
    than a thousand elsewhere.
    Better the threshold of the house of my
    God
    than a home in the tents of the wicked.
[12] For a sun and shield is the LORD God,
    bestowing all grace and glory.
    The LORD withholds no good thing
    from those who walk without
    reproach.
[13] O LORD of hosts,
    happy are those who trust in you!

PSALM 85[*]

See RG
244, 250

Prayer for Divine Favor

[1] For the leader. A psalm of the Korahites.

I

[2] You once favored, LORD, your land,
    restored the good fortune of Jacob.[i]
[3] You forgave the guilt of your people,
    pardoned all their sins. Selah
[4] You withdrew all your wrath,
    turned back your burning anger.[j]

II

[5] Restore us once more, God our savior;
    abandon your wrath against us.[k]
[6] Will you be angry with us forever,
    drag out your anger for all
    generations?[l]
[7] Please give us life again,
    that your people may rejoice in you.
[8] Show us, LORD, your love;
    grant us your salvation.

Ps 84: Israelites celebrated three pilgrimage feasts in Jerusalem annually. The psalm expresses the sentiments of the pilgrims eager to enjoy the divine presence.

84, 4: The desire of a restless bird for a secure home is an image of the desire of a pilgrim for the secure house of God. Cf Ps 42, 2-3, where the image for the desire of the pilgrim is the thirst of the deer for water.

84, 7: Baca valley: Hebrew obscure; probably a valley on the way to Jerusalem.

84, 10: Our shield ... your anointed: the king had a role in the liturgical celebration. For the king as shield, cf Ps 89, 19.

Ps 85: A national lament reminding God of past favors and forgiveness (2-4) and begging for forgiveness and grace now (5-8). A speaker represents the people who wait humbly with open hearts (9-10): God will be active on their behalf (11-14). The situation suggests the conditions of Judea during the early postexilic period, the fifth century B.C.; the thoughts are similar to those of postexilic prophets (Hg 1, 5-11; 2, 6-9).

c: Jb 25, 32; 27, 21. *d:* Ps 97, 9; Dt 4, 39; Dn 3, 45. *e:* Pss 43, 3-4; 122, 1. *f:* Pss 42, 2-3; 63, 2-3; 143, 6; Is 26, 9. *g:* Ps 5, 3. *h:* Ps 89, 19. *i:* Pss 14, 7; 126, 4. *j:* Ps 78, 38; Ex 32, 14; Is 48, 9. *k:* Ps 80, 4. *l:* Pss 79, 5; 89, 47.

III

9 I will listen for the word of God;
  surely the LORD will proclaim peace
To his people, to the faithful,
  to those who trust in him.*

10 Near indeed is salvation for the loyal;
  prosperity will fill our land.

11 Love and truth will meet;*
  justice and peace will kiss.m

12 Truth will spring from the earth;
  justice will look down from heaven.n

13 The LORD will surely grant abundance;
  our land will yield its increase.o

14 Prosperity will march before the LORD,
  and good fortune will follow behind.

See RG
244, 250

PSALM 86*

Prayer in Time of Distress

1 A prayer of David.

I

Hear me, LORD, and answer me,
  for I am poor and oppressed.

2 Preserve my life, for I am loyal;
  save your servant who trusts in you.

3 You are my God; pity me, Lord;
  to you I call all the day.

4 Gladden the soul of your servant;
  to you, Lord, I lift up my soul.p

5 Lord, you are kind and forgiving,
  most loving to all who call on you.q

6 LORD, hear my prayer;
  listen to my cry for help.r

7 In this time of trouble I call,
  for you will answer me.

II

8 None among the gods can equal you,
  O Lord;
  nor can their deeds compare to yours.s

9 All the nations you have made shall
  come
  to bow before you, Lord,

and give honor to your name.t

10 For you are great and do wondrous
  deeds;
  and you alone are God.

III

11 Teach me, LORD, your way
  that I may walk in your truth;u
  single-hearted and revering your
  name.

12 I will praise you with all my heart,
  glorify your name forever, Lord my
  God.

13 Your love for me is great;
  you have rescued me from the depths
  of Sheol.v

14 O God, the arrogant have risen against
  me;
  a ruthless band has sought my life;
  to you they pay no heed.

15 But you, Lord, are a merciful and
  gracious God,
  slow to anger, most loving and true.w

16 Turn to me, have pity on me;
  give your strength to your servant;
  save this child of your handmaid.x

17 Give me a sign of your favor:
  make my enemies see, to their
  confusion,
  that you, LORD, help and comfort me.

PSALM 87*

Zion the True Birthplace of
Diaspora Pilgrims

See RG
245

1 A psalm of the Korahites. A song.

I

The LORD loves the cityy
  founded on holy mountains,

2 Loves the gates* of Zion
  more than any dwelling in Jacob.

3 Glorious things are said of you,
  O city of God!   *Selah*

85, 9: The prophet listens to God's revelation. Cf Hb 2, 1.
85, 11-14: Divine activity is personified as pairs of virtues.
Ps 86: An individual lament. The psalmist, "poor and oppressed" (1), "devoted" (2), "your servant" (2. 4. 16), "rescued from the depths of Sheol" (13), attacked by the ruthless (14), desires only God's protection (1-7. 11-17).
Ps 87: A song of Zion, like Psalms 46, 48, 76, and 132. After the exile of the sixth century B.C., diaspora Jews from all over the world (4) made the long pilgrimage to Jerusalem, the city of God (1-3). Such Jews may have hailed from distant lands, but the psalm sees them as children of Zion (5-7). The

original occasion may have been Pentecost, which always attracted a large number of diaspora Jews.

87, 2: The gates: the city itself, a common Hebrew idiom.

m: Pss 89, 15; 97, 2.   n: Is 45, 8.   o: Ps 67, 7; Lv 26, 4; Ez 34, 27; Hos 2, 23-24; Zec 8, 12.   p: Pss 25, 1; 143, 8.   q: Jl 2, 13.
r: Pss 5, 2; 130, 1-2.   s: Pss 35, 10; 89, 9; Ex 15, 11; Dt 3, 24; Jer 10, 6.   t: Ps 22, 28; Zec 14, 16; Rv 15, 4.   u: Pss 25, 4; 26, 3; 27, 11; 119, 12. 35; 143, 8. 10.   v: Pss 30, 4; 40, 3; Jon 2, 7.   w: Pss 103, 8; 130, 7; 145, 8; Ex 34, 6.   x: Pss 25, 16; 116, 16; Wis 9, 5.
y: 1-2: Pss 76, 2-3; 78, 68-69.

II

4 From Babylon and Egypt I count
    those who acknowledge the LORD.
Philistia, Ethiopia, Tyre,
    of them it can be said:
    "This one was born there."
5 But of Zion it must be said:*
    "They all were born here."*z*
The Most High confirms this;*a*
6   the LORD notes in the register of the
    peoples:
    "This one was born here."*b*   *Selah*
7 So all sing in their festive dance:
    "Within you is my true home."*c*

See RG 244

PSALM 88*

A Despairing Lament

1 A song; a psalm of the Korahites. For the
leader; according to *Mahalath*. For singing;
a *maskil* of Heman the Ezrahite.

I

2 LORD, my God, I call out by day;
    at night I cry aloud in your presence.*d*
3 Let my prayer come before you;
    incline your ear to my cry.*e*
4 For my soul is filled with troubles;*f**
    my life draws near to Sheol.
5 I am reckoned with those who go down
      to the pit;
    I am weak, without strength.
6 My couch is among the dead,
    with the slain who lie in the grave.
You remember them no more;
    they are cut off from your care.
7 You plunged me into the bottom of the pit,
    into the darkness of the abyss.
8 Your wrath lies heavy upon me;
    all your waves crash over me.*g*   *Selah*
9 Because of you my friends shun me;

you make me loathsome to them;*h*
Caged in, I cannot escape;
10   my eyes grow dim from trouble.

II

All day I call on you, LORD;
    I stretch out my hands to you.
11 Do you work wonders for the dead?*
    Do the shades arise and praise
      you?*i*   *Selah*
12 Is your love proclaimed in the grave,
    your fidelity in the tomb?
13 Are your marvels declared in the
      darkness,
    your righteous deeds in the land of
      oblivion?

III

14 But I cry out to you, LORD;
    in the morning my prayer comes
      before you.
15 Why do you reject me, LORD?
    Why hide your face from me?
16 I am mortally afflicted since youth;
    lifeless, I suffer your terrible blows.
17 Your wrath has swept over me;
    your terrors have reduced me to
      silence.*j*
18 All the day they surge round like a flood;
    from every side they close in on me.
19 Because of you companions shun me;*k*
    my only friend is darkness.

PSALM 89*

A Lament over God's Promise to David

See RG 244, 250

1 A *maskil* of Ethan the Ezrahite.

I

2 The promises of the LORD I will sing
    forever,*l*
    proclaim your loyalty through all ages.

87, 5-6: The bond between the exile and the holy city was so strong as to override the exile's citizenship of lesser cities.

Ps 88: A lament in which the psalmist prays for rescue from the alienation of approaching death. Each of the three stanzas begins with a call to God (2. 10b. 14) and complains of the death that separates one from God. The tone is persistently grim.

88, 4-8: In imagination the psalmist already experiences the alienation of Sheol.

88, 11-13: The psalmist seeks to persuade God to act out of concern for divine honor: the shades give you no worship, so keep me alive to offer you praise.

Ps 89: The community laments the defeat of the Davidic

king, to whom God promised kingship as enduring as the heavens (2-5). The psalm narrates how God became king of the divine beings (6-9) and how the Davidic king became king of earthly kings (20-38). Since the defeat of the king calls into question God's promise, the community ardently prays God to be faithful to the original promise to David (39-52).

z: Gal 4, 26.   *a:* Ps 48, 9.   *b:* Is 4, 3.   *c:* Pss 68, 26; 149, 3. *d:* Ps 77, 3.   *e:* Ps 119, 170.   *f:* 4-7: Pss 28, 1; 30, 4; 40, 3; 86, 13; 143, 7; Nm 16, 33; Jb 17, 1; Jon 2, 7.   *g:* Pss 18, 5; 32, 6; 42, 8; 69, 2; Jon 2, 4.   *h:* Pss 38, 12; 79, 4; 80, 7; 123, 3-4; 142, 8; Jb 12, 4; 19, 13; Lam 3, 7; Dn 9, 16.   *i:* Pss 6, 6; 30, 10; 38, 18; 115, 17.   *j:* Jb 6, 4; 20, 25.   *k:* Jb 19, 13.   *l:* Is 63, 7.

3 For you said, "My love is established
   forever;*
   my loyalty will stand as long as the
   heavens.
4 I have made a covenant with my chosen
   one;
   I have sworn to David my servant:
5 I will make your dynasty stand forever
   and establish your throne through all
   ages."*m*   *Selah*

II

6 The heavens praise your marvels, LORD,
   your loyalty in the assembly of the
   holy ones.*n*
7 Who in the skies ranks with the LORD?
   Who is like the LORD among the
   gods?*o* *
8 A God dreaded in the council of the holy
   ones,
   greater and more awesome than all
   who sit there!
9 LORD, God of hosts, who is like you?
   Mighty LORD, your loyalty is always
   present.
10 You rule the raging sea;*p*
   you still its swelling waves.
11 You crushed Rahab* with a mortal blow;
   your strong arm scattered your foes.
12 Yours are the heavens, yours the earth;
   you founded the world and everything
   in it.*q*
13 Zaphon and Amanus* you created;
   Tabor* and Hermon* rejoice in your
   name.
14 Mighty your arm, strong your hand,
   your right hand is ever exalted.

15 Justice and judgment are the foundation
   of your throne;
   love and loyalty march before you.*r*
16 Happy the people who know you, LORD,
   who walk in the radiance of your face.
17 In your name they sing joyfully all the
   day;
   at your victory they raise the festal
   shout.*s*
18 You are their majestic strength;
   by your favor our horn* is exalted.*t*
19 Truly the LORD is our shield,
   the Holy One of Israel, our king!*u*

III

20 Once you spoke in vision;*v*
   to your faithful ones you said:
   "I have set a leader over the warriors;
   I have raised up a hero from the army.
21 I have chosen David, my servant;
   with my holy oil I have anointed him.
22 My hand will be with him;*w*
   my arm will make him strong.
23 No enemy shall outwit him,
   nor shall the wicked defeat him.
24 I will crush his foes before him,
   strike down those who hate him.
25 My loyalty and love will be with him;
   through my name his horn will be
   exalted.
26 I will set his hand upon the sea,
   his right hand upon the rivers.*
27 He shall cry to me, 'You are my father,*x*
   my God, the Rock that brings me
   victory!'
28 I myself make him firstborn,
   Most High* over the kings of the earth.

89, 3-5: David's dynasty is to be as long-lasting as the heavens, a statement reinforced by using the same verbs (establish, stand) both of the divine love and loyalty and of the Davidic dynasty and throne. Cf 29-30.

89, 7: The gods: literally, "the sons of gods," "the holy ones" and "courtiers" of 6 and 8. These heavenly spirits are members of God's court.

89, 11: Rahab: a mythological sea monster whose name is used in the Bible mainly as a personification of primeval chaos. Cf Jb 9, 13; 26, 12; Ps 74, 13-14; Is 51, 9.

89, 13: Zaphon and Amanus: two sacred mountains in northern Syria. Tabor: a high hill in the valley of Jezreel in northern Israel. Hermon: a mountain in Lebanon, forming the southern spur of the Anti-Lebanon range.

89, 18. 25: Horn: a concrete noun for an abstract quality; horn is a symbol of strength.

89, 26: The sea . . . the rivers: geographically the limits

of the Davidic Empire (the Mediterranean and the Euphrates); mythologically, the traditional forces of chaos. See note on v 11.

89, 28: Most High: a divine title, which is here extended to David as God's own king. Cf Ps 2, 7-9; Is 9, 5. As God rules over the members of the heavenly council (6-9), so David, God's surrogate, rules over earthly kings.

m: Pss 61, 7-8; 132, 11; 2 Sm 7, 8-16.   *n:* Pss 29, 1; 82, 1; Jb 1, 6; 5, 1.   *o:* 7-9: Pss 35, 10; 86, 8; 113, 5; Ex 15, 11; Jer 10, 6.   *p:* 10-11: Pss 65, 8; 74, 13-15; 107, 29; Jb 7, 12; Is 51, 9-10.   *q:* Pss 24, 1-2; 50, 12; Dt 10, 14; 1 Cor 10, 26.   *r:* Pss 85, 11-12; 97, 2.   *s:* Ps 47, 2; Zep 3, 14.   *t:* Pss 112, 9; 148, 14.   *u:* Pss 47, 9; 96, 10; 97, 1; 99, 1; Is 6, 3.   *v:* 20-21: Pss 78, 70; 132, 11-12; 2 Sm 7, 4. 8-16; 1 Chr 17, 3. 7-14; Is 42, 1; Acts 13, 22   *w:* 22-25: 1 Sm 2, 9-10.   *x:* 27-28: Pss 2, 7; 110, 2-3; 2 Sm 7, 9. 14; Col 1, 15. 18; Rv 1, 5.

29 Forever I will maintain my love for him;[y]
    my covenant with him stands firm.
30 I will establish his dynasty forever,
    his throne as the days of the heavens.
31 If his descendants forsake my law,[z]
    do not follow my decrees,
32 If they fail to observe my statutes,
    do not keep my commandments,
33 I will punish their crime with a rod
    and their guilt with lashes.
34 But I will not take my love from him,
    nor will I betray my bond of loyalty.[a]
35 I will not violate my covenant;
    the promise of my lips I will not alter.[b]
36 By my holiness I swore once for all:[c]
    I will never be false to David.
37 His dynasty will continue forever,[d]
    his throne, like the sun before me.
38 Like the moon it will stand eternal,
    forever firm like the sky!"*   Selah

IV

39 But now you have rejected and spurned,[e]
    been enraged at your anointed.
40 You renounced the covenant with your
        servant,
    defiled his crown in the dust.
41 You broke down all his defenses,[f]
    left his strongholds in ruins.
42 All who pass through seize plunder;
    his neighbors deride him.
43 You have exalted the right hand of his
        foes,
    have gladdened all his enemies.[g]
44 You turned back his sharp sword,
    did not support him in battle.
45 You brought to an end his splendor,
    hurled his throne to the ground.
46 You cut short the days of his youth,
    covered him with shame.   Selah

47 How long, LORD?
    Will you stay hidden forever?
    Must your wrath smolder like fire?[h]
48 Remember how brief is my life,
    how frail the race you created![i]
49 What mortal can live and not see death?
    Who can escape the power of
        Sheol?[j]   Selah
50 Where are your promises of old, Lord,
    the loyalty sworn to David?
51 Remember, Lord, the insults to your
        servants,
    how I bear all the slanders of the
        nations.[k]
52 Your enemies, LORD, insult your
        anointed;
    they insult my every endeavor.

* * *

53 Blessed be the LORD forever! Amen and
        amen![l] *

Fourth Book: Psalms 90—106

PSALM 90*

God's Eternity and
Human Frailty

See RG
244, 247

1 A prayer of Moses, the man of God.

I

Lord, you have been our refuge
    through all generations.
2 Before the mountains were born,
    the earth and the world brought forth,
    from eternity to eternity you are God.[m]
4* A thousand years in your eyes
    are merely a yesterday,[n]
3 But humans you return to dust,
    saying, "Return,* you mortals!"[o]
4c Before a watch passes in the night,*

89, 37-38: **Like the sun before me . . . like the sky**: as enduring as the heavenly lights. Cf 2-5 and Ps 72, 5. 17.

89, 53: The doxology at the end of the third book of the Psalms; it is not part of Ps 89.

Ps 90: A communal lament that describes only in general terms the cause of the community's distress. After confidently invoking God (1), the psalm turns to a complaint contrasting God's eternity with the brevity of human life (2-6) and sees in human suffering the punishment for sin (7-12). The psalm concludes with a plea for God's intervention (13-17).

90, 3: **Return**: one word of God is enough to return mortals to the dust from which they were created. Humans were created from earth in Gn 2, 7; 3, 19.

90, 4: The translation reverses the order of the difficult

Hebrew verses 3 and 4 to get the probable original order. **A watch . . . in the night**: the night was divided into three sentry periods or watches. Cf Jgs 7, 19.

---

y: 29-30: Pss 18, 51; 61, 8; 144, 10; 2 Sm 7, 11; Is 55, 3. z: 31-33: Lv 26, 14-33. a: Ps 40, 12; Sir 47, 22. b: Jer 33, 20-21. c: Am 4, 2. d: 37-38: Pss 61, 8; 72, 5; Sir 43, 6. e: 39-47: Ps 44, 10-25. f: 41-42: Ps 80, 13-14. g: Lam 1, 5. h: Pss 13, 2; 44, 25; 74, 10; 79, 5; Dt 4, 24. i: Pss 39, 5-6; 62, 10; 90, 9-10; 144, 4; Jb 7, 6. 16; 14, 1. 5; Eccl 6, 12; Wis 2, 5. j: Ps 90, 3. k: Ps 79, 12. l: Pss 41, 14; 72, 18; 106, 48. m: Pss 48, 15; 55, 20; 93, 2; 102, 13; Hb 1, 12. n: 2 Pt 3, 8. o: Pss 103, 14; 104, 29; 146, 4; Gn 3, 19; 1 Mc 2, 63; Jb 34, 14-15; Eccl 3, 20; 12, 7; Sir 40, 11.

5 you have brought them to their
end;[p]*
They disappear like sleep at dawn;
they are like grass that dies.
6 It sprouts green in the morning;
by evening it is dry and withered.[q]*

II

7 Truly we are consumed by your anger,
filled with terror by your wrath.
8 You have kept our faults before you,
our hidden sins exposed to your
sight.[r]
9 Our life ebbs away under your wrath;[s]
our years end like a sigh.
10 Seventy is the sum of our years,
or eighty, if we are strong;
Most of them are sorrow and toil;
they pass quickly, we are all but
gone.
11 Who comprehends your terrible anger?
Your wrath matches the fear it
inspires.
12 Teach us to count our days aright,
that we may gain wisdom of heart.
13 Relent, O LORD! How long?
Have pity on your servants!
14 Fill us at daybreak with your love,[t]
that all our days we may sing for joy.
15 Make us glad as many days as you
humbled us,
for as many years as we have seen
trouble.[u]
16 Show your deeds to your servants,
your glory to their children.
17 May the favor of the Lord our God be
ours.[v]
Prosper the work of our hands!
Prosper the work of our hands!

PSALM 91*

Security Under God's
Protection

See RG
245

I

1 You who dwell in the shelter of the Most
High,*
who abide in the shadow of the
Almighty,*
2 Say to the LORD, "My refuge and
fortress,
my God in whom I trust."[w]
3 God will rescue you from the fowler's
snare,
from the destroying plague,
4 Will shelter you with pinions,
spread wings that you may take
refuge;[x]
God's faithfulness is a protecting
shield.
5 You shall not fear the terror of the night
nor the arrow that flies by day,[y]
6 Nor the pestilence that roams in
darkness,
nor the plague that ravages at noon.[z]
7 Though a thousand fall at your side,
ten thousand at your right hand,
near you it shall not come.
8 You need simply watch;
the punishment of the wicked you will
see.[a]
9 You have the LORD for your refuge;
you have made the Most High your
stronghold.
10 No evil shall befall you,
no affliction come near your tent.[b]
11 For God commands the angels[c]*
to guard you in all your ways.[d]

90, 5: You have brought them to their end: an interpretation of the unclear Hebrew.
90, 6: It is dry and withered: the transitory nature of the
grass under the scorching sun was proverbial. Cf Ps 129, 6; Is
40, 6-8.
Ps 91: A prayer of someone who has taken refuge in the
security of the temple (1-2). The psalmist is confident that
God's presence will protect the people in every dangerous situation (3-13). The final verses are an oracle of salvation
promising salvation to those who trust in God (14-16).
91, 1: The shelter of the Most High: basically "hiding
place" but in the psalms a designation for the protected temple precincts. Cf Pss 27, 5; 31, 21; 61, 5. **The shadow of the
Almighty**: literally, "the shadow of the wings of the
Almighty." Cf Pss 17, 8; 36, 8; 57, 2; 63, 8. V 4 makes clear

that the shadow is an image of the safety afforded by the outstretched wings of the cherubim in the holy of holies.
91, 11-12: The words are cited in Mt 4, 6; Lk 4, 10-11, as
Satan tempts Jesus in the desert.

p: Ps 89, 48.   q: Pss 37, 2; 102, 11; 103, 15-16; Jb 14, 1-2; Is 40,
6-8.   r: Ps 109, 14-15; Hos 7, 2.   s: 9-10: Pss 39, 5-7; 62, 10;
102, 24-25; 144, 4; Gn 6, 3; Jb 7, 6. 16; 14, 5; Prv 10, 27; Eccl 6,
12; Wis 2, 5; Sir 18, 8; Is 65, 20.   t: Ps 17, 15.   u: Nm 14, 34;
Jer 31, 13.   v: Ps 33, 22.   w: Pss 18, 3; 31, 3-4; 42, 10; 142,
6; 2 Sm 22, 3.   x: Pss 17, 8; 36, 8; 57, 2; 63, 8; Dt 32, 11; Ru 2,
12; Mt 23, 37.   y: Prv 3, 25; Song 3, 8.   z: Dt 32, 24.   a: Ps
92, 12.   b: Prv 12, 21; Dt 7, 15.   c: 11-12: Mt 4, 6; Lk 4, 10f.
d: Heb 1, 14.

¹² With their hands they shall support you,
  lest you strike your foot against a
    stone.ᵉ
¹³ You shall tread upon the asp and the
    viper,
  trample the lion and the dragon.ᶠ

II

¹⁴ Whoever clings to me I will deliver;
  whoever knows my name I will set on
    high.ᵍ
¹⁵ All who call upon me I will answer;ʰ
  I will be with them in distress;ⁱ
  I will deliver them and give them
    honor.
¹⁶ With length of days I will satisfy them
  and show them my saving power.ʲ

See RG 245

PSALM 92*

A Hymn of Thanksgiving for God's Fidelity

¹ A psalm. A sabbath song.

I

² It is good to give thanks to the LORD,
  to sing praise to your name, Most
    High,ᵏ
³ To proclaim your love in the morning,
  your faithfulness in the night,
⁴ With the ten-stringed harp,
  with melody upon the lyre.ˡ
⁵ For you make me jubilant, LORD, by your
    deeds;
  at the works of your hands I shout for
    joy.

II

⁶ How great are your works, LORD!ᵐ
  How profound your purpose!
⁷ A senseless person cannot know this;

a fool cannot comprehend.
⁸ Though the wicked flourish like grass
  and all sinners thrive,ⁿ
They are destined for eternal destruction;
⁹ for you, LORD, are forever on high.
¹⁰ Indeed your enemies, LORD,
  indeed your enemies shall perish;
  all sinners shall be scattered.ᵒ

III

¹¹ You have given me the strength of a wild
    bull;ᵖ
  you have poured rich oil upon me.�q
¹² My eyes look with glee on my wicked
    enemies;
  my ears delight in the fall of my foes.ʳ
¹³ The just shall flourish like the palm tree,
  shall grow like a cedar of Lebanon.ˢ
¹⁴ Planted* in the house of the LORD,
  they shall flourish in the courts of our
    God.
¹⁵ They shall bear fruit even in old age,
  always vigorous and sturdy,
¹⁶ As they proclaim: "The LORD is just;
  our rock, in whom there is no wrong."ᵗ

PSALM 93*

God is a Mighty King

See RG 245

¹ The LORD is king,* robed with majesty;
  the LORD is robed, girded with might.ᵘ
The world will surely stand in place,
  never to be moved.ᵛ
² Your throne stands firm from of old;
  you are from everlasting, LORD.ʷ
³ The flood* has raised up, LORD;
  the flood has raised up its roar;
  the flood has raised its pounding waves.

Ps 92: A hymn of praise and thanks for God's faithful deeds (2-5). The wicked, deluded by their prosperity (6-9), are punished (10), whereas the psalmist has already experienced God's protection (11-16).

92, 14: Planted: the just are likened to trees growing in the sacred precincts of the temple, which is often seen as the source of life and fertility because of God's presence. Cf Ps 36, 9. 10; Ez 47, 1-12.

Ps 93: A hymn celebrating the kingship of God, who created the world (1-2) by defeating the sea (3-4). In the ancient myth that is alluded to here, Sea completely covered the land, making it impossible for the human community to live. Sea, or Flood, roars in anger against God, who is personified in the storm. God's utterances or decrees are given authority by the victory over Sea (5).

93, 1: The LORD is king: literally, "the LORD reigns." This

psalm, and Pss 47 and 96—99, are sometimes called enthronement psalms. They may have been used in a special liturgy during which God's ascent to the throne was ritually reenacted. They have also been interpreted eschatologically, pointing to the coming of God as king at the end-time.

93, 3: The flood: the primordial sea was tamed by God in the act of creation. It is a figure of chaos and rebellion. Cf Ps 46, 4.

e: Ps 121, 3; Prv 3, 23. f: Is 11, 8; Lk 10, 19. g: Pss 9, 11; 119, 132. h: Jer 33, 3; Zec 13, 9. i: Is 43, 2. j: Prv 3, 2. k: Pss 33, 1; 147, 1. l: Pss 33, 2; 144, 9. m: 6-7: Pss 131, 1; 139, 6. 17; Wis 13, 1; 17, 1. n: Ps 37, 35. o: Pss 68, 1-2; 125, 5. p: Ps 75, 10; Dt 33, 17. q: Ps 23, 5. r: Ps 91, 8. s: Pss 1, 3; 52, 10; Jer 17, 8. t: Dt 32, 4. u: Pss 47, 8; 96, 10; 97, 1; 99, 1. v: Pss 75, 2-3; 104, 5. w: Pss 55, 20; 90, 2; 102, 13; Hb 1, 12.

⁴ More powerful than the roar of many
waters,
more powerful than the breakers of the
sea,
powerful in the heavens is the LORD.
⁵ Your decrees are firmly established;
holiness belongs to your house, LORD,
for all the length of days.

PSALM 94[*]

See RG
244-45

*A Prayer for Deliverance
from the Wicked*

I

¹ LORD, avenging God,
avenging God, shine forth!^x
² Rise up, judge of the earth;
give the proud what they deserve.^y

II

³ How long, LORD, shall the wicked,
how long shall the wicked glory?^z
⁴ How long will they mouth haughty
speeches,
go on boasting, all these evildoers?^a
⁵ They crush your people, LORD,
torment your very own.
⁶ They kill the widow and alien;
the fatherless they murder.^b
⁷ They say, "The LORD does not see;
the God of Jacob takes no notice."^c

III

⁸ Understand, you stupid people!
You fools, when will you be wise?^d
⁹ Does the one who shaped the ear not
hear?
The one who formed the eye not see?^e
¹⁰ Does the one who guides nations not
rebuke?
The one who teaches humans not have
knowledge?
¹¹ The LORD does know human plans;
they are only puffs of air.^f

IV

¹² Happy those whom you guide, LORD,^g
whom you teach by your instruction.
¹³ You give them rest from evil days,
while a pit is being dug for the wicked.
¹⁴ You, LORD, will not forsake your people,
nor abandon your very own.^h
¹⁵ Judgment shall again be just,
and all the upright of heart will
follow it.

V

¹⁶ Who will rise up for me against the
wicked?
Who will stand up for me against
evildoers?
¹⁷ If the LORD were not my help,
I would long have been silent in the
grave.ⁱ
¹⁸ When I say, "My foot is slipping,"
your love, LORD, holds me up.^j
¹⁹ When cares increase within me,
your comfort gives me joy.

VI

²⁰ Can unjust judges be your allies,
those who create burdens in the name
of law,
²¹ Those who conspire against the just
and condemn the innocent to death?
²² No, the LORD is my secure height,
my God, the rock where I find refuge,
²³ Who will turn back their evil upon them^k
and destroy them for their wickedness.
Surely the LORD our God will destroy
them!^l

PSALM 95[*]

See RG
246

*A Call to Praise and
Obedience*

I

¹ Come, let us sing joyfully to the LORD;
cry out to the rock of our salvation.^m

Ps 94: A lament of an individual who is threatened by wicked people. The danger affects the whole community. Calling upon God as judge (1-2), the psalm complains about oppression of the holy community by people within (3-7). Bold declarations of faith follow: denunciation of evildoers (8-11) and assurance to the just (12-15). The psalm continues with further lament (16-19) and ends with strong confidence in God's response (20-23).

Ps 95: Twice the psalm calls the people to praise and worship God (1-2. 6), the king of all creatures (3-5) and shepherd of the flock (7ab). The last strophe warns the people to be

more faithful than were their ancestors in the journey to the promised land (7c-11). This invitation to praise God regularly opens the Church's official prayer, the Liturgy of the Hours.

x: Na 1, 2.   *y:* Jer 51, 56; Lam 3, 64.   *z:* Pss 13, 2; 75, 5; Jer 12, 1.   *a:* Ps 73; Mal 2, 17; 3, 14.   *b:* Ex 22, 21-22; Dt 24, 17-22.   *c:* Pss 10, 11; 64, 6; 73, 11; Jb 22, 13-14; Ez 9, 9.   *d:* Prv 1, 22; 8, 5.   *e:* Ex 4, 11; Prv 20, 12.   *f:* Ps 33, 15; 1 Cor 3, 20.   *g:* Ps 119, 71; Jb 5, 17.   *h:* 1 Sm 12, 22; Sir 47, 22.   *i:* Ps 115, 17.   *j:* Ps 145, 14.   *k:* Pss 7, 16; 9, 16; 35, 8; 57, 7; Prv 26, 27; Eccl 10, 8; Sir 27, 26.   *l:* Ps 107, 42.   *m:* Dt 32, 15.

2 Let us greet him with a song of praise,
   joyfully sing out our psalms.
3 For the LORD is the great God,
   the great king over all gods,[n]
4 Whose hand holds the depths of the earth;
   who owns the tops of the mountains.
5 The sea and dry land belong to God,
   who made them, formed them by
   hand.[o]

II

6 Enter, let us bow down in worship;
   let us kneel before the LORD who
   made us.
7 For this is our God,
   whose people we are,
   God's well-tended flock.[p]

III

Oh, that today you would hear his voice:[q]
8   Do not harden your hearts as at
    Meribah,*
   as on the day of Massah* in the desert.
9 There your ancestors tested me;
   they tried me though they had seen
   my works.[r]
10 Forty years I loathed that generation;
   I said: "This people's heart goes
   astray;
   they do not know my ways."[s]
11 Therefore I swore in my anger:
   "They shall never enter my rest."*

See RG
245, 248,
250

PSALM 96*

God of the Universe

I

1 Sing to the LORD a new song;[t]
   sing to the LORD, all the earth.
2 Sing to the LORD, bless his name;
   announce his salvation day after day.
3 Tell God's glory among the nations;
   among all peoples, God's marvelous
   deeds.[u]

II

4 For great is the LORD and highly to be
   praised,
   to be feared above all gods.[v]*
5 For the gods of the nations all do
   nothing,
   but the LORD made the heavens.[w]
6 Splendor and power go before him;
   power and grandeur are in his holy
   place.

III

7 Give to the LORD, you families of nations,
   give to the LORD glory and might;
8   give to the LORD the glory due his
    name![x]
Bring gifts and enter his courts;
9   bow down to the LORD, splendid in
    holiness.
Tremble before God, all the earth;
10   say among the nations: The LORD is
    king.[y]
The world will surely stand fast, never to
   be moved.
God rules the peoples with fairness.[r]

IV

11 Let the heavens be glad and the earth
   rejoice;
   let the sea and what fills it resound;[z]
12   let the plains be joyful and all that is
    in them.
Then let all the trees of the forest rejoice
13   before the LORD who comes,
   who comes to govern the earth,[a]
To govern the world with justice
   and the peoples with faithfulness.

PSALM 97*

The Divine Ruler of All

See RG
245

I

1 The LORD is king; let the earth rejoice;
   let the many islands be glad.[b]

95, 8: **Meribah**: literally, "contention"; the place where
the Israelites quarreled with God. **Massah**: "testing," the
place where they put God to the trial. Cf Ex 17, 7; Nm 20, 13.

95, 11: **My rest**: the promised land as in Dt 12, 9. Heb 4
applies the verse to the eternal rest of heaven.

Ps 96: A hymn inviting all humanity to praise the glories
of Israel's God (1-3), who is the sole God (4-6). To the just
ruler of all belongs worship (7-10); even inanimate creation
is to offer praise (11-13). This psalm has numerous verbal
and thematic contacts with Is 40-55, as does Ps 98. Another
version of the psalm is 1 Chr 16, 23-33.

96, 4: For references to other gods, see comments on Pss
58 and 82.

Ps 97: The hymn begins with God appearing in a storm, a
traditional picture of some ancient Near Eastern gods (1-6);

n: Pss 47, 2; 135, 5. o: Ps 24, 1-2. p: Pss 23, 1-3; 100, 3; Mi 7,
14. q: 7c-11: Pss 81, 8; 106, 32; Heb 3, 7-11. 15; 4, 3. 5. 7. r: Nm
14, 22; 20, 2-13; Dt 6, 16; 33, 8. s: Ps 78, 8; Nm 14, 34; Dt 32, 5.
t: Ps 98, 1; Is 42, 10. u: Pss 98, 4; 105, 1. v: Pss 48, 2; 95, 3; 145,
3. w: Ps 97, 7; Is 40, 17; 1 Cor 8, 4. x: Ps 29, 2. y: Pss 75, 4;
93, 1. z: Ps 98, 7. a: Ps 98, 9. b: Pss 75, 4; 93, 1; 96, 10.

2 Cloud and darkness surround the Lord;
  justice and right are the foundation of
    his throne.*c*
3 Fire goes before him;
  everywhere it consumes the foes.
4 Lightning illumines the world;
  the earth sees and trembles.*d*
5 The mountains melt like wax before the
    LORD,
  before the Lord of all the earth.*e*
6 The heavens proclaim God's justice;
  all peoples see his glory.*f*

II

7 All who serve idols are put to shame,
  who glory in worthless things;
  all gods* bow down before you.*g*
8 Zion hears and is glad,
  and the cities of Judah rejoice
  because of your judgments, O LORD.*h*
9 You, LORD, are the Most High over all
    the earth,*i*
  exalted far above all gods.
10 The LORD loves those who hate evil,
  protects the lives of the faithful,*j*
  rescues them from the hand of the
    wicked.
11 Light dawns for the just;
  gladness, for the honest of heart.*k*
12 Rejoice in the LORD, you just,
  and praise his holy name.*l*

See RG
245, 248

PSALM 98*

The Coming of God

1 A psalm.

I

Sing a new song to the LORD,
  who has done marvelous deeds,*m*

Whose right hand and holy arm*
  have won the victory.*n**
2 The LORD has made his victory known;
  has revealed his triumph for the
    nations to see,
3 Has remembered faithful love
  toward the house of Israel.
All the ends of the earth have seen
  the victory of our God.

II

4 Shout with joy to the LORD, all the earth;
  break into song; sing praise.
5 Sing praise to the LORD with the harp,
  with the harp and melodious song.
6 With trumpets and the sound of the horn
  shout with joy to the King, the LORD.*o*

III

7 Let the sea and what fills it resound,*p*
  the world and those who dwell there.
8 Let the rivers clap their hands,
  the mountains shout with them for joy,*q*
9 Before the LORD who comes,
  who comes to govern the earth,*r*
To govern the world with justice
  and the peoples with fairness.*s*

PSALM 99*

The Holy King

See RG
245

I

1 The LORD is king, the peoples tremble;
  God is enthroned on the cherubim,*
  the earth quakes.*t*
2 The LORD is great on Zion,
  exalted above all the peoples.
3 Let them praise your great and awesome
    name:
  holy is God!*u*

cf Ps 18, 8-16; Mi 1, 3-4; Hb 3, 3-15. Israel rejoices in the
overthrowing of idol worshipers and their gods (7-9) and the
rewarding of the faithful righteous (10-12).

97, 7: All gods: divine beings thoroughly subordinate to
Israel's God. The Greek translates "angels," an interpretation
adopted by Heb 1, 6.

Ps 98: A hymn, similar to Ps 96, extolling God for Israel's
victory (1-3). All nations (4-6) and even inanimate nature (7-
8) are summoned to welcome God's coming to rule over the
world (9).

98, 1: Marvelous deeds . . . victory: the conquest of all
threats to the peaceful existence of Israel, depicted in the
psalms variously as a cosmic force such as Sea, or nations
bent on Israel's destruction, or evildoers seemingly triumphant. **Whose right hand and holy arm**: God is pictured
as a powerful warrior.

Ps 99: A hymn to God as the king whose grandeur is most
clearly seen on Mount Zion (2) and in the laws given to Israel
(4). Israel is special because of God's word of justice, which
was mediated by the revered speakers, Moses, Aaron, and
Samuel (6-8). The poem is structured by the threefold statement that God is holy (3. 5. 9) and by the twice-repeated
command to praise (5. 9).

99, 1: Enthroned on the cherubim: cherubim were

c: Pss 85, 11; 89, 15; Ex 19, 6; Dt 4, 11; 5, 22; 1 Kgs 8, 12.   *d:* Pss
18, 8; 50, 3; 77, 18; 99, 1; Jgs 5, 4-5.   *e:* Jdt 16, 15; Mi 1, 4.   *f:* Ps
50, 6.   *g:* Ps 96, 5.   *h:* Ps 48, 12.   *i:* Ps 83, 19.   *j:* Ps 121, 7.
k: Ps 112, 4.   *l:* Ps 30, 5.   *m:* Ps 96, 1; Is 42, 10.   *n:* Is 59, 16;
63, 5.   *o:* Ps 47, 6-7.   *p:* Ps 96, 11.   *q:* Is 44, 23; 55, 12.   *r:* Ps
96, 13.   *s:* Ps 67, 5.   *t:* Pss 18, 8-11; 80, 2; 93, 1; Ex 25, 22; 1 Sm
4, 4; 2 Sm 6, 2.   *u:* Is 6, 3.

II

4 O mighty king, lover of justice,
    you alone have established fairness;
    you have created just rule in Jacob.*v*

5 Exalt the LORD, our God;
    bow down before his footstool;*w* *
    holy is God!

III

6 Moses and Aaron were among his priests,
    Samuel among those who called on
        God's name;
    they called on the LORD, who
        answered them.*x*

7 From the pillar of cloud God spoke to
        them;
    they kept the decrees, the law they
        received.*y*

8 O LORD, our God, you answered them;
    you were a forgiving God,
    though you punished their offenses.*z*

9 Exalt the LORD, our God;
    bow down before his holy mountain;
    holy is the LORD, our God.

See RG
244

PSALM 100*

Processional Hymn

1 A psalm of thanksgiving.

Shout joyfully to the LORD, all you lands;
2   worship the LORD with cries of
        gladness;
    come before him with joyful song.
3 Know that the LORD is God,
    our maker to whom we belong,
    whose people we are, God's well-
        tended flock.*a* *

4 Enter the temple gates with praise,
    its courts with thanksgiving.

Give thanks to God, bless his name;*b*
5   good indeed is the LORD,
    Whose love endures forever,
        whose faithfulness lasts through every
        age.

PSALM 101*

See RG
245

Norm of Life for Rulers

1 A psalm of David.

I

I sing of love and justice;
    to you, LORD, I sing praise.
2 I follow the way of integrity;*c*
    when will you come to me?
I act with integrity of heart
    within my royal court.*d* *
3 I do not allow into my presence
    anyone who speaks perversely.
Whoever acts shamefully I hate;
    no such person can be my friend.*e*
4 I shun the devious of heart;
    the wicked I do not tolerate.
5 Whoever slanders another in secret
    I reduce to silence.*f*
Haughty eyes and arrogant hearts*g*
    I cannot endure.

II

6 I look to the faithful of the land;*
    they alone can be my companions.
Those who follow the way of integrity,*h*
    they alone can enter my service.
7 No one who practices deceit
    can hold a post in my court.
No one who speaks falsely
    can be among my advisors.*i*
8 Each morning* I clear the wicked from
        the land,*
    and rid the LORD's city of all evildoers.

---

composite beings with animal and human features, common in ancient Near Eastern art. Two cherubim were placed on the ark (or box) of the covenant in the holy of holies. Upon them God was believed to dwell invisibly. Cf Ex 25, 20-22; 1 Sm 4, 4; 2 Sm 6, 2; Ps 80, 2.

99, 5: Footstool: a reference to the ark. Cf 1 Chr 28, 2; Ps 132, 7.

Ps 100: A hymn inviting the people to enter the temple courts with thank offerings for the God who created them.

100, 3: Although the people call on all the nations of the world to join in their hymn, they are conscious of being the chosen people of God.

Ps 101: The king, grateful at being God's chosen (1), promises to be a ruler after God's own heart (2-3), allowing into the royal service only the God-fearing (3-8).

101, 2: Within my royal court: the king promises to make his own household a model for Israel, banning all officials who abuse their power.

101, 6: I look to the faithful of the land: the king seeks companions only among those faithful to God.

101, 8: Each morning: the normal time for the administration of justice (2 Sm 15, 2; Jer 21, 12) and for the arrival of divine aid (Pss 59, 17; 143, 8; Is 33, 2). **I clear the wicked**

---

v: Pss 72, 1; 99, 4; Jer 23, 5.   *w:* Ps 132, 7.   *x:* Jer 15, 1.   *y:* Ex 33, 9; Nm 12, 5.   *z:* Ex 32, 11; Nm 20, 12.   *a:* Pss 23, 1; 95, 7; Mi 7, 14; Is 64, 7.   *b:* 4-5: Pss 106, 1; 107, 1; 118, 1; 136, 1; 138, 8; Jer 33, 11.   *c:* Ps 26, 11.   *d:* 1 Kgs 9, 4; Is 33, 15.   *e:* Prv 11, 20.   *f:* Prv 17, 20; 30, 10.   *g:* Prv 21, 4.   *h:* Ps 26, 11; Prv 20, 7.   *i:* Ps 5, 5; Prv 25, 5.

See RG 244

PSALM 102[*]

Prayer in Time of Distress

1 The prayer of one afflicted and wasting away whose anguish is poured out before the LORD.

I

[2] LORD, hear my prayer;
let my cry come to you.

[3] Do not hide your face from me
now that I am in distress.[j]
Turn your ear to me;
when I call, answer me quickly.

[4] For my days vanish like smoke;[k]
my bones burn away as in a furnace.

[5] I am withered, dried up like grass,
too wasted to eat my food.

[6] From my loud groaning
I become just skin and bones.

[7] I am like a desert owl,
like an owl among the ruins.

[8] I lie awake and moan,
like a lone sparrow on the roof.

[9] All day long my enemies taunt me;
in their rage, they make my name a curse.[*]

[10] I eat ashes like bread,
mingle my drink with tears.[l]

[11] Because of your furious wrath,
you lifted me up just to cast me down.

[12] My days are like a lengthening shadow;[m]
I wither like the grass.[n]

II

[13] But you, LORD, are enthroned forever;
your renown is for all generations.[o]

[14] You will again show mercy to Zion;
now is the time for pity;
the appointed time has come.

[15] Its stones are dear to your servants;
its dust moves them to pity.

[16] The nations shall revere your name, LORD,
all the kings of the earth, your glory,[p]

[17] Once the LORD has rebuilt Zion
and appeared in glory,

[18] Heeding the plea of the lowly,
not scorning their prayer.

[19] Let this be written for the next generation,
for a people not yet born,
that they may praise the LORD:[q]

[20] "The LORD looked down from the holy heights,[*]
viewed the earth from heaven,[r]

[21] To attend to the groaning of the prisoners,
to release those doomed to die."[s]

[22] Then the LORD's name will be declared on Zion,
the praise of God in Jerusalem,

[23] When all peoples and kingdoms gather
to worship the LORD.[t]

III

[24] God has shattered my strength in mid-course,
has cut short my days.

[25] I plead, O my God,
do not take me in the midst of my days.[u][*]
Your years last through all generations.

[26] Of old you laid the earth's foundations;[v]
the heavens are the work of your hands.

[27] They perish, but you remain;
they all wear out like a garment;
Like clothing you change them and they are changed,

[28] but you are the same, your years have no end.

[29] May the children of your servants live on;
may their descendants live in your presence.[w]

---

from the land: the king, as God's servant, is responsible for seeing that divine justice is carried out.

Ps 102: A lament, one of the Penitential Psalms. The psalmist, experiencing psychic and bodily disintegration (4-12), cries out to God (1-3). In the temple precincts where God has promised to be present, the psalmist recalls God's venerable promises to save the poor (13-23). The final part (24-29) restates the original complaint and prayer, and emphasizes God's eternity.

102, 9: They make my name a curse: enemies use the psalmist's name in phrases such as, "May you be as wretched as this person!"

102, 20-23: Both 20-21 and 22-23 depend on 19.

102, 25: In the midst of my days: when the normal span of life is but half completed. Cf Is 38, 10; Jer 17, 11.

---

j: Pss 69, 18; 143, 7. *k*: 4-6: Ps 38, 7-9. *l*: Pss 42, 4; 80, 6. *m*: Pss 109, 23; 144, 4; Jb 8, 9; 14, 2; Eccl 6, 12; Wis 2, 5. *n*: Ps 90, 5-6. *o*: Pss 55, 20; 90, 2; 93, 2; 102, 13; 135, 13; 145, 13; Lam 5, 19; Hb 1, 12. *p*: Is 59, 19; 66, 18. *q*: Ps 22, 31-32. *r*: Pss 11, 4; 14, 2. *s*: Ps 79, 11. *t*: Is 60, 3-4; Zec 2, 15; 8, 22. *u*: Pss 39, 5; 90, 10; Jb 14, 5. *v*: 26-28: Heb 1, 10-12. *w*: Ps 69, 36-37.

See RG
244, 250

PSALM 103*

Praise of Divine Goodness

¹ Of David.

I

Bless the LORD, my soul;
  all my being, bless his holy name!
² Bless the LORD, my soul;
  do not forget all the gifts of God,
³ Who pardons all your sins,
  heals all your ills,
⁴ Delivers your life from the pit,ˣ
  surrounds you with love and
    compassion,
⁵ Fills your days with good things;
  your youth is renewed like the
    eagle's.*

II

⁶ The LORD does righteous deeds,
  brings justice to all the oppressed.ʸ
⁷ His ways were revealed to Moses,
  mighty deeds to the people of Israel.
⁸ Merciful and gracious is the LORD,
  slow to anger, abounding in kindness.ᶻ
⁹ God does not always rebuke,
  nurses no lasting anger,
¹⁰ Has not dealt with us as our sins merit,
  nor requited us as our deeds deserve.

III

¹¹ As the heavens tower over the earth,
  so God's love towers over the
    faithful.ᵃ
¹² As far as the east is from the west,
  so far have our sins been removed
    from us.
¹³ As a father has compassion on his
    children,
  so the LORD has compassion on the
    faithful.

¹⁴ For he knows how we are formed,
  remembers that we are dust.ᵇ
¹⁵ Our days are like the grass;
  like flowers of the field we blossom.ᶜ
¹⁶ The wind sweeps over us and we are
    gone;
  our place knows us no more.
¹⁷ But the LORD's kindness is forever,
  toward the faithful from age to age.
  He favors the children's children
¹⁸   of those who keep his covenant,
  who take care to fulfill its precepts.

IV

¹⁹ The LORD's throne is established in
    heaven;
  God's royal power rules over all.
²⁰ Bless the LORD, all you angels,ᵈ
  mighty in strength and attentive,
  obedient to every command.
²¹ Bless the LORD, all you hosts,
  ministers who do God's will.
²² Bless the LORD, all creatures,
  everywhere in God's domain.
  Bless the LORD, my soul!

PSALM 104*

Praise of God the Creator

See RG
244, 250

I

¹ Bless the LORD, my soul!
  LORD, my God, you are great indeed!
  You are clothed with majesty and glory,
²   robed in light as with a cloak.
  You spread out the heavens like a tent;ᵉ
³   you raised your palace upon the
    waters.*
  You make the clouds your chariot;
  you travel on the wings of the wind.
⁴ You make the winds your messengers;
  flaming fire, your ministers.ᶠ

Ps 103: The speaker in this hymn begins by praising God for personal benefits (1-5), then moves on to God's mercy toward all the people (6-18). Even sin cannot destroy that mercy (11-13), for the eternal God is well aware of the people's human fragility (14-18). The psalmist invites the heavenly beings to join in praise (19-22).

103, 5: Your youth is renewed like the eagle's: because of the eagle's long life it was a symbol of perennial youth and vigor. Cf Is 40, 31.

Ps 104: A hymn praising God who easily and skillfully made rampaging waters and primordial night into a world vibrant with life. The psalmist describes God's splendor in the heavens (1-4), how the chaotic waters were tamed to fertilize and feed the world (5-18), and how primordial night was

made into a gentle time of refreshment (19-23). The picture is like Gn 1, 1-2: a dark and watery chaos is made dry and lighted so that creatures might live. The psalmist reacts to the beauty of creation with awe (24-34). May sin not deface God's work (35)!

104, 3: Your palace upon the waters: God's heavenly dwelling above the upper waters of the sky. Cf Gn 1, 6-7; Ps 29, 10.

x: Pss 28, 1; 30, 4; 40, 3; 69, 16; 88, 5; 143, 7; Prv 1, 12; Jon 2, 7. *y:* Ps 146, 6-7. *z:* Pss 86, 15; 145, 8; Ex 34, 6-7; Nm 14, 18; Jer 3, 12; Jl 2, 13; Jon 4, 2. *a:* Is 55, 9. *b:* Ps 90, 3. *c:* Pss 37, 2; 90, 5-6; Is 40, 7. *d:* Ps 148, 2; Dn 3, 58. *e:* Prv 8, 27-28; Jb 9, 8; Is 40, 22; Gn 1, 6-7; Am 9, 6. *f:* Heb 1, 7.

II

5 You fixed the earth on its foundation,*
never to be moved.
6 The ocean covered it like a garment;
above the mountains stood the waters.
7 At your roar they took flight;
at the sound of your thunder they fled.g
8 They rushed up the mountains, down the
valleys
to the place you had fixed for them.
9 You set a limit they cannot pass;
never again will they cover the earth.h

III

10 You made springs flow into channels
that wind among the mountains.
11 They give drink to every beast of the
field;i
here wild asses quench their thirst.
12 Beside them the birds of heaven nest;
among the branches they sing.
13 You water the mountains from your
palace;
by your labor the earth abounds.
14 You raise grass for the cattle
and plants for our beasts of burden.
You bring bread from the earth,
15   and wine to gladden our hearts,
Oil to make our faces gleam,
food to build our strength.
16 The trees of the LORD drink their fill,*
the cedars of Lebanon, which you
planted.
17 There the birds build their nests;
junipers are the home of the stork.j
18 The high mountains are for wild goats;
the rocky cliffs, a refuge for badgers.

IV

19 You made the moon to mark the seasons,k
the sun that knows the hour of its
setting.
20 You bring darkness and night falls,
then all the beasts of the forest roam
abroad.

21 Young lions roar for prey;
they seek their food from God.l
22 When the sun rises, they steal away
and rest in their dens.
23 People go forth to their work,
to their labor till evening falls.

V

24 How varied are your works, LORD!
In wisdom you have wrought them all;
the earth is full of your creatures.m
25 Look at the sea, great and wide!
It teems with countless beings,
living things both large and small.n
26 Here ships ply their course;
here Leviathan,* your creature, plays.o

VI

27 All of these look to you
to give them food in due time.p
28 When you give to them, they gather;
when you open your hand, they are
well filled.
29 When you hide your face, they are lost.*
When you take away their breath, they
perish
and return to the dust from which they
came.q
30 When you send forth your breath, they
are created,
and you renew the face of the earth.

VII

31 May the glory of the LORD endure forever;
may the LORD be glad in these works!
32 If God glares at the earth, it trembles;
if God touches the mountains, they
smoke!r
33 I will sing to the LORD all my life;
I will sing praise to my God while I
live.s
34 May my theme be pleasing to God;
I will rejoice in the LORD.
35 May sinners vanish from the earth,
and the wicked be no more.
Bless the LORD, my soul! Hallelujah!*

104, 5-9: God places the gigantic disk of the earth securely on its foundation and then, as a warrior, chases away the enveloping waters and confines them under, above, and around the earth.

104, 16-18: Even the exotic flora and fauna of the high mountains of the Lebanon range receive adequate water.

104, 26: Leviathan: a sea monster symbolizing primeval chaos. Cf Ps 74, 14; Is 27, 1; Jb 40, 25. God does not destroy chaos but makes it part of the created order.

104, 29-30: On one level, the spirit (or wind) of God is the fall and winter rains that provide food for all creatures. On another, it is the breath (or spirit) of God that makes beings live.

104, 35: Hallelujah: a frequent word in the last third of

g: Ps 29, 3.   h: Jer 5, 22; Gn 9, 11-15.   i: 11-14: Ps 147, 8-9.
j: Ez 31, 6.   k: Sir 43, 6.   l: Jb 38, 39.   m: Ps 92, 6; Sir 39, 16.
n: Sir 43, 26.   o: Jb 3, 8; 40, 25.   p: Pss 136, 25; 145, 15-16.
q: Jb 34, 14-15; Eccl 3, 20; Ps 90, 3.   r: Ps 144, 5.   s: Ps 146, 2.

See RG
246, 247

PSALM 105*

God's Fidelity to the Promise

I

¹ Give thanks to the LORD, invoke his
    name;[t]
  make known among the peoples his
    deeds![u]
² Sing praise, play music;
  proclaim all his wondrous deeds!
³ Glory in his holy name;
  rejoice, O hearts that seek the LORD!
⁴ Rely on the mighty LORD;
  constantly seek his face.[v]
⁵ Recall the wondrous deeds he has done,
  his signs and his words of judgment,
⁶ You descendants of Abraham his
    servant,
  offspring of Jacob the chosen one!

II

⁷ The LORD is our God
  who rules the whole earth.
⁸ He remembers forever his covenant,
  the pact imposed for a thousand
    generations,
⁹ Which was made with Abraham,
  confirmed by oath to Isaac,[w]
¹⁰ And ratified as binding for Jacob,
  an everlasting covenant for Israel:
¹¹ "To you I give the land of Canaan,
  your own allotted heritage."[x]

III

¹² When they were few in number,[y]
  a handful, and strangers there,
¹³ Wandering from nation to nation,
  from one kingdom to another,
¹⁴ He let no one oppress them;
  for their sake he rebuked kings:*

¹⁵ "Do not touch my anointed,
  to my prophets* do no harm."

IV

¹⁶ Then he called down a famine on the
    land,
  destroyed the grain that sustained
    them.[z]
¹⁷ He had sent a man ahead of them,
  Joseph, sold as a slave.[a]
¹⁸ They shackled his feet with chains;
  collared his neck in iron,[b]
¹⁹ Till his prediction came to pass,
  and the word of the LORD proved him
    true.[c]
²⁰ The king sent and released him;
  the ruler of peoples set him free.[d]
²¹ He made him lord over his palace,
  ruler over all his possessions,[e]
²² To instruct his princes by his word,
  to teach his elders wisdom.

V

²³ Then Israel entered Egypt;[f]
  Jacob lived in the land of Ham.*
²⁴ God greatly increased his people,
  made them too many for their foes.[g]
²⁵ He turned their hearts to hate his
    people,
  to treat his servants unfairly.[h]
²⁶ He sent his servant Moses,
  Aaron whom he had chosen.[i]
²⁷ They worked his signs in Egypt[j]*
  and wonders in the land of Ham.
²⁸ He sent darkness and it grew dark,
  but they rebelled against his word.
²⁹ He turned their waters into blood
  and killed all their fish.
³⁰ Their land swarmed with frogs,
  even the chambers of their kings.

---

the Psalter. The word combines the plural imperative of praise (*hallelu*) with an abbreviated form of the divine name Yah(weh).

Ps 105: A hymn to God who promised the land of Canaan to the holy people. Cf Pss 78; 106; 136. Israel is invited to praise and seek the presence of God (1-6), who is faithful to the promise of land to the ancestors (7-11). In every phase of the national story—the ancestors in the land of Canaan (12-15), Joseph in Egypt (16-22), Israel in Egypt (23-38), Israel in the desert on the way to Canaan (39-45)—God remained faithful, reiterating the promise of the land to successive servants.

105, 14: Kings: Pharaoh and Abimelech of Gerar. Cf Gn 12, 17; 20, 6-7.

105, 15: My anointed . . . my prophets: the patriarchs

Abraham, Isaac, and Jacob, who were "anointed" in the sense of being consecrated and recipients of God's revelation.

105, 23. 27: The land of Ham: a synonym for Egypt. Cf Gn 10, 6.

105, 27-38: This psalm and Ps 78, 43-51 have an account of the plagues differing in number or in order from Ex 7, 14—12, 30. Several versions of the exodus story were current.

t: 1-15: 1 Chr 16, 8-22. *u:* Pss 18, 50; 96, 3; 145, 5; Is 12, 4-5. *v:* Pss 24, 6; 27, 8. *w:* Gn 15, 1ff; 26, 3. *x:* Gn 12, 7; 15, 18. *y:* 12-13: Dt 4, 27; 26, 5. *z:* Gn 41, 54. 57. *a:* Gn 37, 28. 36; 45, 5. *b:* Gn 39, 20. *c:* Gn 40-41. *d:* Gn 41, 14. *e:* Gn 41; 41-44. *f:* Gn 46, 1-47, 12; Acts 7, 15. *g:* Ex 1, 7; Acts 7, 17. *h:* Ex 1, 8-14. *i:* Ex 3, 10; 4, 27. *j:* 27-36: Ps 78, 43-51; Ex 7-12.

³¹ He spoke and there came swarms of flies,
    gnats through all their country.
³² For rain he gave them hail,
    flashes of lightning throughout their
        land.
³³ He struck down their vines and fig trees,
    shattered the trees of their country.
³⁴ He spoke and the locusts came,
    grasshoppers without number.ᵏ
³⁵ They devoured every plant in the land;
    they ravaged the crops of their fields.
³⁶ He struck down every firstborn in the
        land,
    the first fruits of all their vigor.
³⁷ He brought his people out,
    laden with silver and gold;ˡ
    no stragglers among the tribes.
³⁸ Egypt rejoiced when they left,
    for panic had seized them.

VI

³⁹ He spread a cloud as a cover,
    and made a fire to light up the night.ᵐ
⁴⁰ They asked and he brought them quail;
    with bread from heaven he filled
        them.ⁿ
⁴¹ He split the rock and water gushed
        forth;
    it flowed through the desert like a
        river.ᵒ
⁴² For he remembered his sacred word
    to Abraham his servant.
⁴³ He brought his people out with joy,
    his chosen ones with shouts of
        triumph.
⁴⁴ He gave them the lands of the nations,
    the wealth of the peoples to own,ᵖ
⁴⁵ That they might keep his laws
    and observe his teachings.�q
Hallelujah!

PSALM 106*

Israel's Confession of Sin

See RG
244, 247

¹ Hallelujah!

A

Give thanks to the LORD, who is good,
    whose love endures forever.ʳ
² Who can tell the mighty deeds of the
        LORD,
    proclaim in full God's praise?
³ Happy those who do what is right,
    whose deeds are always just.ˢ
⁴ Remember me, LORD, as you favor your
        people;
    come to me with your saving help,ᵗ
⁵ That I may see the prosperity of your
        chosen,
    rejoice in the joy of your people,
    and glory with your heritage.

B

⁶ We have sinned like our ancestors;ᵘ
    we have done wrong and are guilty.

I

⁷ Our ancestors in Egypt
    did not attend to your wonders.
They did not remember your great
        love;
    they defied the Most High at the Red
        Sea.
⁸ Yet he saved them for his name's sake
    to make his power known.ᵛ
⁹ He roared at the Red Sea and it dried up.
    He led them through the deep as
        through a desert.ʷ
¹⁰ He rescued them from hostile hands,
    freed them from the power of the
        enemy.
¹¹ The waters covered their oppressors;
    not one of them survived.

Ps 106: Israel is invited to praise the God whose mercy
has always tempered judgment of Israel (1-3). The speaker,
on behalf of all, seeks solidarity with the people, who can always count on God's fidelity despite their sin (4-5). Confident of God's mercy, the speaker invites national repentance
(6) by reciting from Israel's history eight instances of sin,
judgment, and forgiveness. The sins are the rebellion at the
Red Sea (6-12; see Ex 14-15), the craving for meat in the
desert (13-15; see Nm 11), the challenge to Moses' authority
(16-18; see Nm 16), the golden calf episode (19-23; see Ex
32-34), the refusal to take Canaan by the southern route (24-
27; see Nm 13-14 and Dt 1-2), the rebellion at Baal-Peor (28-
31; see Nm 25, 1-10), the anger of Moses (32-33; see Nm 20,
1-13), and mingling with the nations (34-47). The last, as sug-

gested by its length and generalized language, may be the sin
that invites the repentance of the present generation. The text
gives the site of each sin: Egypt (7), the desert (14), the camp
(16), Horeb (19), in their tents (25), Baal-Peor (28), the waters of Meribah (32), Canaan (38).

---

k: Jl 1, 4. *l:* Ex 12, 33-36. *m:* Ps 78, 14; Ex 13, 21-22; Wis 18,
3. *n:* Ps 78, 24-28; Ex 16, 13-15; Nm 11, 31ff; Wis 16, 20.
o: Ps 78, 15-16; Ex 17, 1-7; Nm 20, 11. *p:* Dt 4, 37-40. *q:* Dt
6, 20-25; 7, 8-11. *r:* Pss 100, 5; 107, 1; 1 Chr 16, 34; Jer 33, 11;
Dn 3, 89. *s:* Is 56, 1-2. *t:* Ps 25, 7; Neh 5, 19. *u:* 6-7: Ps 78,
11-17; Ex 14, 11; Lv 26, 40; 1 Kgs 8, 47; Bar 2, 12; Dn 9, 5.
v: Ez 36, 20-22. *w:* Ex 14, 21-31; Is 50, 2; 63, 11-14; Na 1, 4.

¹² Then they believed his words
and sang songs of praise.*

II

¹³ But they soon forgot all he had done;
they had no patience for his plan.
¹⁴ In the desert they gave way to their
cravings,
tempted God in the wasteland.*
¹⁵ So he gave them what they asked
and sent among them a wasting
disease.*

III

¹⁶ In the camp they challenged Moses*
and Aaron, the holy one of the LORD.
¹⁷ The earth opened and swallowed Dathan,
it closed on the followers of Abiram.
¹⁸ Against that company the fire blazed;
flames consumed the wicked.

IV

¹⁹ At Horeb they fashioned a calf,*
worshiped a metal statue.
²⁰ They exchanged their glorious God
for the image of a grass-eating bull.
²¹ They forgot the God who saved them,
who did great deeds in Egypt,*
²² Amazing deeds in the land of Ham,
fearsome deeds at the Red Sea.
²³ He would have decreed their destruction,
had not Moses, the chosen leader,
Withstood him in the breach*
to turn back his destroying anger.*

V

²⁴ Next they despised the beautiful land;*
they did not believe the promise.
²⁵ In their tents they complained;
they did not obey the LORD.
²⁶ So with raised hand he swore
to destroy them in the desert,
²⁷ To scatter their descendants among the
nations,
disperse them in foreign lands.

VI

²⁸ They joined in the rites of Baal of Peor,*
ate food sacrificed to dead gods.
²⁹ They provoked him by their actions,
and a plague broke out among them.
³⁰ Then Phinehas rose to intervene,
and the plague was brought to a halt.
³¹ This was counted for him as a righteous
deed
for all generations to come.

VII

³² At the waters of Meribah they angered
God,*
and Moses suffered because of them.*
³³ They so embittered his spirit
that rash words crossed his lips.

VIII

³⁴ They did not destroy the peoples
as the LORD had commanded them,*
³⁵ But mingled with the nations
and imitated their ways.*
³⁶ They worshiped their idols
and were ensnared by them.*
³⁷ They sacrificed to the gods*
their own sons and daughters,
³⁸ Shedding innocent blood,
the blood of their own sons and
daughters,
Whom they sacrificed to the idols of
Canaan,
desecrating the land with bloodshed.
³⁹ They defiled themselves by their
actions,
became adulterers by their conduct.
⁴⁰ So the LORD grew angry with his
people,
abhorred his own heritage.
⁴¹ He handed them over to the nations,
and their adversaries ruled them.*
⁴² Their enemies oppressed them,
kept them under subjection.

106, 23: Withstood him in the breach: the image is that
of Moses standing in a narrow break made in the wall to keep
anyone from entering.

106, 32: Moses suffered because of them: Moses was
not allowed to enter the promised land because of his rash
words (Nm 20, 12). According to Dt 1, 37, Moses was not allowed to cross because of the people's sin, not his own.

106, 37: The gods: Hebrew **shedim**, customarily translated "demons," occurs in parallelism with "gods" in an important inscription from Transjordan and hence is translated
"gods."

x: Ex 15, 1-21.   y: Ps 78, 18; Ex 15, 24; 16, 3; Nm 11, 1-6.   z: Ps
78, 26-31; Nm 11, 33.   a: 16-18: Nm 16; Dt 11, 6; Is 26, 11.
b: 19-20: Ex 32; Dt 9, 8-21; Jer 2, 11; Acts 7, 41; Rom 1, 23.
c: Ps 78, 42-58; Dt 32, 18; Jer 2, 32.   d: Ex 32, 11; Dt 9, 25; Ez
22, 30.   e: 24-27: Lv 26, 33; Nm 14; Dt 1, 25-36; Ez 20, 15. 23.
f: 28-31; Nm 25; Dt 26, 14; Sir 45, 23-24.   g: 32-33: Ps 95, 8-9;
Ex 17, 1-7; Nm 20, 2-13; Dt 6, 16; 33, 8.   h: Dt 7, 1; Jgs 2, 1-5.
i: Lv 18, 3; Jgs 1, 27-35; 3, 5.   j: 36-38: Lv 18, 21; Nm 35, 33;
Dt 32, 17; Jgs 2, 11-13. 17. 19; 2 Kgs 16, 3; Bar 4, 7; 1 Cor 10, 20.
k: Jgs 2, 14-23.

43 Many times did he rescue them,
     but they kept rebelling and scheming
     and were brought low by their own
     guilt.*l*

44 Still God had regard for their affliction
     when he heard their wailing.

45 For their sake he remembered his
     covenant
     and relented in his abundant love,*m*

46 Winning for them compassion
     from all who held them captive.

C

47 Save us, LORD, our God;
     gather us from among the nations
   That we may give thanks to your holy
     name
     and glory in praising you.*n*

* * *

48 Blessed be the LORD, the God of
     Israel,
     from everlasting to everlasting!
   Let all the people say, Amen!*o*
   Hallelujah!*

Fifth Book: Psalms 107—150

See RG
244

PSALM 107*

*God the Savior of Those
in Distress*

1 "Give thanks to the LORD who is good,
     whose love endures forever!"*p*

2 Let that be the prayer of the LORD's
     redeemed,
     those redeemed from the hand of the
     foe,*q*

3 Those gathered from foreign lands,
     from east and west, from north and
     south.*r*

I

4 Some had lost their way in a barren
     desert;

found no path toward a city to live in.

5 They were hungry and thirsty;
     their life was ebbing away.*s*

6 In their distress they cried to the LORD,
     who rescued them in their peril,

7 Guided them by a direct path*t*
     so they reached a city to live in.*u*

8 Let them thank the LORD for such
     kindness,
     such wondrous deeds for mere mortals.

9 For he satisfied the thirsty,
     filled the hungry with good things.*v*

II

10 Some lived in darkness and gloom,
     in prison, bound with chains,

11 Because they rebelled against God's
     word,
     scorned the counsel of the Most High,*w*

12 Who humbled their hearts through
     hardship;
     they stumbled with no one to help.*x*

13 In their distress they cried to the LORD,
     who saved them in their peril,

14 Led them forth from darkness and gloom
     and broke their chains asunder.*y*

15 Let them thank the LORD for such
     kindness,
     such wondrous deeds for mere mortals.

16 For he broke down the gates of bronze
     and snapped the bars of iron.

III

17 Some fell sick from their wicked ways,
     afflicted because of their sins.

18 They loathed all manner of food;*z*
     they were at the gates of death.

19 In their distress they cried to the LORD,
     who saved them in their peril,

20 Sent forth the word to heal them,*a*
     snatched them from the grave.

21 Let them thank the LORD for such
     kindness,
     such wondrous deeds for mere mortals.

106, 48: A doxology ending Book IV of the Psalter. It is not part of the psalm.

Ps 107: A hymn inviting those who have been rescued by God to give praise (1-3). Four archetypal divine rescues are described, each ending in thanksgiving: from the sterile desert (4-9), from imprisonment in gloom (10-16), from mortal illness (17-22), and from the angry sea (23-32). The number four connotes totality, all the possible varieties of rescue. The same saving activity of God is shown in Israel's history (33-41); whenever the people were endangered God rescued

them. The last verses invite people to ponder the persistent saving acts of God (42-43).

l: Is 63, 7-9. m: Lv 26, 42. n: 1 Chr 16, 35. o: Pss 41, 14; 72, 18; 89, 53; 1 Chr 16, 36; Neh 9, 5. p: Pss 100, 4-5; 106, 1; Jer 33, 11. q: Is 63, 12. r: Is 43, 5-6; 49, 12; Zec 8, 7. s: Dt 8, 15; 32, 10; Is 49, 10. t: Is 35, 8; 40, 3; 43, 19. u: Dt 6, 10. v: Lk 1, 53. w: Is 42, 7. 22; Jb 36, 8-9; Prv 1, 25. x: Ps 106, 43. y: Is 42, 7; 49, 9; 51, 14. z: Jb 6, 6-7; 33, 20. a: Ps 147, 15; Wis 16, 12; Is 55, 11; Mt 8, 8.

²² Let them offer a sacrifice in thanks,
  declare his works with shouts of joy.

IV

²³ Some went off to sea in ships,
  plied their trade on the deep waters.*b*
²⁴ They saw the works of the LORD,
  the wonders of God in the deep.
²⁵ He spoke and roused a storm wind;
  it tossed the waves on high.*c*
²⁶ They rose up to the heavens, sank to the
    depths;
  their hearts trembled at the danger.
²⁷ They reeled, staggered like drunkards;
  their skill was of no avail.*d*
²⁸ In their distress they cried to the LORD,
  who brought them out of their peril,
²⁹ Hushed the storm to a murmur;
  the waves of the sea were stilled.*e*
³⁰ They rejoiced that the sea grew calm,
  that God brought them to the harbor
    they longed for.
³¹ Let them thank the LORD for such
    kindness,
  such wondrous deeds for mere
    mortals.
³² Let them praise him in the assembly of
    the people,
  give thanks in the council of the elders.

V

³³ God changed rivers into desert,*
  springs of water into thirsty ground,*f*
³⁴ Fruitful land into a salty waste,
  because of the wickedness of its
    people.*g*
³⁵ He changed the desert into pools of water,
  arid land into springs of water,*h*
³⁶ And settled the hungry there;
  they built a city to live in.*i*
³⁷ They sowed fields and planted vineyards,
  brought in an abundant harvest.*j*
³⁸ God blessed them, they became very
    many,
  and their livestock did not decrease.*k*

⁴⁰ But he poured out contempt on princes,
  made them wander the trackless
    wastes,*l*
³⁹ Where they were diminished and brought
    low
  through misery and cruel oppression,
⁴¹ While the poor were released from their
    affliction;
  their families increased like their
    flocks.*m*
⁴² The upright saw this and rejoiced;*n*
  all wickedness shut its mouth.
⁴³ Whoever is wise will take note of these
    things,*o*
  will ponder the merciful deeds of the
    LORD.

PSALM 108*

Prayer for Victory

¹ A song; a psalm of David.

I

² My heart is steadfast, God;*p*
  my heart is steadfast.
  I will sing and chant praise.
³ Awake, my soul; awake, lyre and harp!
  I will wake the dawn.*q*
⁴ I will praise you among the peoples,
    LORD;
  I will chant your praise among the
    nations.*r*
⁵ For your love towers to the heavens;
  your faithfulness, to the skies.*s*
⁶ Appear on high over the heavens, God;
  may your glory appear above all the
    earth.
⁷ Help with your right hand and answer
    us
  that your loved ones may escape.

II

⁸ God promised in the sanctuary:*t*
  "I will exult, I will apportion Shechem;
  the valley of Succoth I will measure
    out.

See RG
246

107, 33-41: God destroyed Sodom and Gomorrah in Gn 18-19, which the psalm sees as the destruction of the wicked inhabitants of Canaan to prepare the way for Israel (33-34). God then led Israel through the desert to give them a fertile land (35-38) and protected them from every danger (39-41).

Ps 108: A prayer compiled from two other psalms: 2-6 are virtually the same as Ps 57, 8-12; 7-14 are the same as Ps 60, 7-14. An old promise of salvation (8-10) is combined with a

confident assurance (1-6. 14) and petition (7. 12-13).

b: Sir 43, 25. *c:* Jon 1, 4. *d:* Is 29, 9. *e:* Pss 65, 8; 89, 10; Mt 8, 26 par. *f:* Is 35, 7; 42, 15; 50, 2. *g:* Gn 19, 23-28; Dt 29, 22; Sir 39, 23. *h:* Ps 114, 8; Is 41, 8. *i:* Ez 36, 35. *j:* Is 65, 21; Jer 31, 5. *k:* Dt 7, 13-14. *l:* Jb 12, 23-25. *m:* Ps 113, 7. *n:* Pss 58, 11; 63, 12. *o:* Hos 14, 10. *p:* 2-6: Pss 57, 8-12. *q:* Jb 38, 12. *r:* Pss 9, 12; 18, 50; 148, 13. *s:* Pss 36, 6; 71, 19. *t:* 8-14: Ps 60, 8-14.

⁹ Gilead is mine, mine is Manasseh;
    Ephraim is the helmet for my head,
    Judah, my own scepter.
¹⁰ Moab is my washbowl;
    upon Edom I cast my sandal;ᵘ
    I will triumph over Philistia."

III

¹¹ Who will bring me to the fortified city?
    Who will lead me into Edom?
¹² Was it not you who rejected us, God?
    Do you no longer march with our
        armies?ᵛ
¹³ Give us aid against the foe;
    worthless is human help.
¹⁴ We will triumph with the help of God,
    who will trample down our foes.

See RG
244

PSALM 109*

Prayer of a Person Falsely Accused

¹ For the leader. A psalm of David.

I

O God, whom I praise, do not be silent,ʷ
²   for wicked and treacherous mouths
        attack me.
They speak against me with lying tongues;
³   with hateful words they surround me,
        attacking me without cause.
⁴ In return for my love they slander me,
    even though I prayed for them.
⁵ They repay me evil for good,
    hatred for my love.ˣ

II

My enemies say of me:
⁶ "Find a lying witness,
    an accuser* to stand by his right hand,
⁷ That he may be judged and found guilty,
    that his plea may be in vain.
⁸ May his days be few;
    may another take his office.ʸ

⁹ May his children be fatherless,
    his wife, a widow.ᶻ
¹⁰ May his children be vagrant beggars,
    driven from their hovels.
¹¹ May the usurer snare all he owns,
    strangers plunder all he earns.
¹² May no one treat him kindly
    or pity his fatherless children.
¹³ May his posterity be destroyed,ᵃ
    his name cease in the next generation.
¹⁴ May the LORD remember his fathers'
        guilt;
    his mother's sin not be canceled.ᵇ
¹⁵ May their guilt be always before the
        LORD,ᶜ
    till their memory is banished from the
        earth,ᵈ
¹⁶ For he did not remember to show
        kindness,
    but hounded the wretched poor
    and brought death to the brokenhearted.
¹⁷ He loved cursing; may it come upon him;
    he hated blessing; may none come to
        him.
¹⁸ May cursing clothe him like a robe;
    may it enter his belly like water,
    seep into his bones like oil.
¹⁹ May it be near as the clothes he wears,
    as the belt always around him."

III

²⁰ May the LORD bring all this* upon my
        accusers,
    upon those who speak evil against me.
²¹ But you, LORD, my God,
    deal kindly with me for your name's
        sake;
    in your great mercy rescue me.
²² For I am sorely in need;
    my heart is pierced within me.
²³ Like a lengthening shadow I near my end,

Ps 109: A lament notable for the length and vehemence of its prayer against evildoers (6-20); the cry to God (1) and the complaint (22-25) are brief in comparison. The psalmist is apparently the victim of a slander campaign, potentially devastating in a society where reputation and honor are paramount. In the emotional perspective of the psalm, there are only two types of people: the wicked and their poor victims. The psalmist is a poor victim (22. 31) and by that fact a friend of God and enemy of the wicked. The psalmist seeks vindication not on the basis of personal virtue but because of God's promise to protect the poor.

109, 6: An accuser: Hebrew *satan*, a word occurring in Jb

1-2 and Zec 3, 1-2. In the latter passage Satan stands at the right hand of the high priest to bring false accusations against him before God. Here the accuser is human.

109, 20: May the LORD bring all this: the psalmist prays that God ratify the curses of 6-19 and bring them upon the wicked.

---

u: Ru 4, 7-8. *v*: Ps 44, 10. *w*: Pss 35, 22; 83, 1. *x*: Pss 35, 12; 38, 21; Prv 17, 13; Jer 18, 20. *y*: Acts 1, 20. *z*: Ex 22, 23; Jer 18, 21. *a*: Ps 21, 11; Prv 10, 7. *b*: Ex 20, 5. *c*: Ps 90, 8. *d*: Ps 34, 16.

all but swept away like the locust.

24 My knees totter from fasting;*e*
  my flesh has wasted away.
25 I have become a mockery to them;
  when they see me, they shake their
    heads.
26 Help me, LORD, my God;
  save me in your kindness.
27 Make them know this is your hand,
  that you, LORD, have acted.
28 Though they curse, may you bless;
  shame my foes, that your servant may
    rejoice.
29 Clothe my accusers with disgrace;
  make them wear shame like a mantle.
30 I will give fervent thanks to the LORD;
  before all I will praise my God.*f*
31 For God stands at the right hand of the
    poor
  to defend them against unjust accusers.

PSALM 110*

See RG 245, 251

God Appoints the King both King and Priest

1 A psalm of David.

The LORD says to you, my lord:*
  "Take your throne at my right hand,
  while I make your enemies your
    footstool."*g* *

2 The scepter of your sovereign might
  the LORD will extend from Zion.

The LORD says: "Rule over your enemies!
3   Yours is princely power from the day
    of your birth.
In holy splendor before the daystar,*
  like the dew I begot you."*h* *
4 The LORD has sworn and will not waver:
  "Like Melchizedek* you are a priest
    forever."*i*
5 At your right hand is the Lord,
  who crushes kings on the day of wrath,*j*
6 Who, robed in splendor, judges nations,
  crushes heads across the wide earth,
7 Who drinks from the brook by the
    wayside*
  and thus holds high his head.*k*

PSALM 111*

See RG 244, 246

Praise of God for Goodness to Israel

1 Hallelujah.

I will praise the LORD with all my heart*l*
  in the assembled congregation of the
    upright.*
2 Great are the works of the LORD,
  to be treasured for all their delights.
3 Majestic and glorious is your* work,
  your wise design endures forever.
4 You won renown for your wondrous
    deeds;
  gracious and merciful is the LORD.*m*
5 You gave food to those who fear you,*

Ps 110: A royal psalm in which a court singer recites three oracles in which God assures the king that his enemies are conquered (1-2), makes the king "son" in traditional adoption language (3), gives priestly status to the king and promises to be with him in future military ventures (4-7).

110, 1: The LORD says to you, my lord: literally, "The LORD says to my lord," a polite form of address of an inferior to a superior. Cf 1 Sm 25, 25; 2 Sm 1, 10. The court singer refers to the king. Jesus in the synoptic gospels (Mt 22, 41-46 and parallels) takes the psalmist to be David and hence "my lord" refers to the messiah, who must be someone greater than David. **Your footstool:** in ancient times victorious kings put their feet on the prostrate bodies of their enemies.

110, 3: Before the daystar: possibly an expression for before the world began (Prv 8, 22). **Like the dew I begot you:** an adoption formula as in Pss 2, 7; 89, 27-28.

110, 4: Like Melchizedek: Melchizedek was the ancient king of Salem (Jerusalem) who blessed Abraham (Gn 14, 18-20); like other kings of the time he performed priestly functions. Heb 7 sees in Melchizedek a type of Christ.

110, 7: Who drinks from the brook by the wayside: the meaning is uncertain. Some see an allusion to a rite of royal

consecration at the Gihon spring (cf 1 Kgs 1, 33. 38). Others find here an image of the divine warrior (or king) pursuing enemies so relentlessly that he does not stop long enough to eat and drink.

Ps 111: A temple singer (1) tells how God is revealed in Israel's history (2-10). The deeds reveal God's very self, powerful, merciful, faithful. The poem is an acrostic, each verse beginning with a successive letter of the Hebrew alphabet.

111, 1: In the assembled congregation of the upright: in the temple. Cf Ps 149, 1.

111, 3: Your: the psalm refers to God in the third person throughout; the shift to the second person is for the sake of inclusive language.

111, 5: Food to those who fear you: probably a reference to the manna in the desert, which elsewhere is seen as a type of the Eucharist. Cf Jn 6, 31-33. 49-51.

e: 24-25: Ps 69, 11-13. *f:* Ps 111, 1. *g:* Mt 22, 44; Acts 2, 34-35; 1 Cor 15, 25; Heb 1, 13; 8, 1; 10, 12-13; 1 Pt 3, 22. *h:* Pss 2, 7; 89, 27; Is 49, 1. *i:* Pss 89, 35; 132, 11; Gn 14, 18; Heb 5, 6; 7, 21. *j:* Ps 2, 9; Rv 2, 27; 12, 5; 19, 15. *k:* Ps 3, 4. *l:* Ps 138, 1. *m:* Ps 103, 8; 112, 4.

mindful of your covenant forever.
6 You showed powerful deeds to your
people,
giving them the lands* of the nations.
7 The works of your hands are right and
true,
reliable all your decrees,
8 Established forever and ever,
to be observed with loyalty and care.
9 You sent deliverance to your people,
ratified your covenant forever;
holy and awesome is your name.
10 The fear of the LORD* is the beginning of
wisdom;ⁿ
prudent are all who live by it.
Your praise endures forever.

See RG
245-46

PSALM 112*

The Blessings of the Just

1 Hallelujah!

Happy are those* who fear the LORD,
who greatly delight in God's
commands.ᵒ
2 Their descendants shall be mighty in the
land,
a generation upright and blessed.
3 Wealth and riches shall be in their
homes;
their prosperity* shall endure forever.
4 They shine through the darkness, a light
for the upright;ᵖ
they are gracious, merciful, and just.
5 All goes well for those gracious in
lending,
who conduct their affairs with justice.
6 They shall never be shaken;
the just shall be remembered forever.�q

7 They shall not fear an ill report;
their hearts are steadfast, trusting the
LORD.
8 Their hearts are tranquil, without fear,
till at last they look down on their foes.
9 Lavishly they give to the poor;
their prosperity shall endure forever;ʳ
their horn* shall be exalted in honor.
10 The wicked shall be angry to see this;
they will gnash their teeth and waste
away;
the desires of the wicked come to
nothing.

PSALM 113*

Praise of God's Care of the Poor

See RG
244

1 Hallelujah!

I

Praise, you servants of the LORD,
praise the name of the LORD.ˢ
2 Blessed be the name of the LORD
both now and forever.
3 From the rising of the sun to its setting
let the name of the LORD be praised.

II

4 High above all nations is the LORD;
above the heavens God's glory.ᵗ
5 Who is like the LORD,
our God enthroned on high,
6 looking down on heaven and earth?ᵘ
7 The LORD raises the needy from the dust,
lifts the poor from the ash heap,ᵛ
8 Seats them with princes,
the princes of the people,
9 Gives the childless wife a home,
the joyful mother of children.ʷ
Hallelujah!

111, 6: Lands: literally, "inheritance, heritage."
111, 10: The fear of the LORD: reverence for God, the Hebrew term for religion.
Ps 112: An acrostic poem detailing the blessings received by those who remain close to God by obedience to the commandments. Among their blessings are children (2), wealth that enables them to be magnanimous (3. 5. 9), and virtue by which they encourage others (4). The just person is an affront to the wicked, whose hopes remain unfulfilled (10). The logic resembles Pss 1 and 111.
112, 1: Happy are those: literally, "Happy the person." "Person" is used typically, hence the plural translation.
112, 3: Prosperity: literally, "justice." In the Second Temple Period the word acquired the nuance of liberality

and almsgiving. Cf Sir 3, 30; 7, 10; Mt 6, 1-4.
112, 9: Their horn: the symbol for vitality and honor.
Ps 113: A hymn exhorting the congregation to praise God's name, i.e., the way in which God is present in the world; the name is mentioned three times in 1-3. The divine name is especially honored in the temple (1) but its recognition is not limited by time (2) and space (3), for God is everywhere active (4-5) especially in rescuing the lowly faithful (7-9).

Prv 1, 7; 9, 10; Sir 1, 16. *o:* Pss 1, 1-2; 119, 1-2; 128, 1.
p: Pss 37, 6; 97, 11; Prv 13, 9; Is 58, 10. *q:* Prv 10, 7; Wis 8, 13.
r: Prv 22, 9; 2 Cor 9, 9. *s:* Ps 135, 1. *t:* Ps 148, 13. *u:* Ps 89,
7-9. *v:* Ps 107, 41; 1 Sm 2, 7-8. *w:* 1 Sm 2, 5; Is 54, 1.

See RG
244,
247, 250

PSALM 114[*]

The Lord's Wonders at the Exodus

[1] When Israel came forth from Egypt,
the house of Jacob from an alien people,

[2] Judah became God's holy place,
Israel, God's domain.[x]

[3] The sea beheld and fled;[*]
the Jordan turned back.[y]

[4] The mountains skipped like rams;
the hills, like lambs of the flock.[z]

[5] Why was it, sea, that you fled?
Jordan, that you turned back?

[6] You mountains, that you skipped like rams?
You hills, like lambs of the flock?

[7] Tremble, earth, before the Lord,[a]
before the God of Jacob,

[8] Who turned rock into pools of water,
stone into flowing springs.[b][*]

PSALM 115[*]

See RG
245

The Greatness of the True God

I

[1] Not to us, LORD, not to us
but to your name give glory
because of your faithfulness and love.[c]

[2] Why should the nations say,
"Where is their God?"[d][*]

[3] Our God is in heaven;
whatever God wills is done.[e]

II

[4] Their idols are silver and gold,[f]
the work of human hands.[g]

[5] They have mouths but do not speak,
eyes but do not see.

[6] They have ears but do not hear,
noses but do not smell.

[7] They have hands but do not feel,
feet but do not walk,
and no sound rises from their throats.

[8] Their makers shall be like them,
all who trust in them.

III

[9] The house of Israel trusts in the LORD,[h]
who is their help and shield.[i]

[10] The house of Aaron trusts in the LORD,
who is their help and shield.

[11] Those who fear the LORD[*] trust in the LORD,
who is their help and shield.

[12] The LORD remembers us and will bless us,
will bless the house of Israel,
will bless the house of Aaron,

[13] Will bless those who fear the LORD,
small and great alike.

[14] May the LORD increase your number,
you and your descendants.

[15] May you be blessed by the LORD,
who made heaven and earth.

[16] The heavens[*] belong to the LORD,
but the earth is given to us.[j]

[17] The dead do not praise the LORD,
all those gone down into silence.[k][*]

Ps 114: A hymn celebrating Israel's escape from Egypt, journey through the wilderness, and entry into the promised land, and the miracles of nature that bore witness to God's presence in their midst. In the perspective of the psalm, the people proceed directly from Egypt into the promised land (1-2). Sea and Jordan, which stood like soldiers barring the people from their land, flee before the mighty God as the earth recoils from the battle (3-4). The poet taunts the natural elements as one taunts defeated enemies (5-6).

114, 3-4: Pairs of cosmic elements such as sea and rivers, mountains and hills, are sometimes mentioned in creation accounts. Personified here as warriors, the pairs tremble in fear before the Divine Warrior. The quaking also recalls the divine appearance in the storm at Sinai (Ex 19, 16-19) and elsewhere (Jgs 5, 4-5; Ps 18, 8-16).

114, 8: The miracles of giving drink to the people in the arid desert. Cf Ex 17, 1-7; Is 41, 17-18.

Ps 115: A response to the enemy taunt, "Where is your God?" This hymn to the glory of Israel's God (1-3) ridicules the lifeless idols of the nations (4-8), expresses in a litany the trust of the various classes of the people in God (9-11), in-

vokes God's blessing on them as they invoke the divine name (12-15), and concludes as it began with praise of God. Ps 135, 15-18 similarly mocks the Gentile gods and has a similar litany and hymn (Ps 135, 19-21).

115, 2: Where is their God?: implies that God cannot help them.

115, 9-11: The house of Israel ... the house of Aaron ... those who fear the LORD: the laity of Israelite birth, the priests, and the converts to Judaism. Cf Pss 118, 2-4; 135, 19-21. In the New Testament likewise "those who fear the Lord" means converts to Judaism (cf Acts 10, 2. 22. 35; 13, 16. 26).

115, 16: The heavens: literally "the heaven of heavens" or "the highest heavens," i.e., above the firmament. See note on Ps 148, 4.

115, 17: See note on Ps 6, 6.

---

x: Ex 19, 6.   y: Ex 14, 21f; Jos 3, 14ff; Pss 66, 6; 74, 15.   z: Ps 29, 6; Wis 19, 9.   a: Ps 68, 9.   b: Ex 17, 6; Nm 20, 11.   c: Ez 36, 22-23.   d: Ps 79, 10.   e: Ps 135, 6.   f: 4-10: Ps 135, 15-19; Wis 15, 15-16; Is 44, 9f; Jer 10, 1-5.   g: Is 40, 19.   h: Ps 118, 2-4.   i: Ps 33, 20.   j: Gn 1, 28.   k: Pss 6, 6; 88, 11ff; Sir 17, 22f; Is 38, 18.

18 It is we who bless the LORD,
   both now and forever.
Hallelujah!

See RG
245

PSALM 116*

Thanksgiving to God Who Saves from Death

I

1 I love the LORD, who listened
   to my voice in supplication,
2 Who turned an ear to me
   on the day I called.
3 I was caught by the cords of death;*l**
   the snares of Sheol had seized me;
   I felt agony and dread.
4 Then I called on the name of the LORD,
   "O LORD, save my life!"

II

5 Gracious is the LORD and just;
   yes, our God is merciful.*m*
6 The LORD protects the simple;
   I was helpless, but God saved me.
7 Return, my soul, to your rest;
   the LORD has been good to you.*n*
8 For my soul has been freed from death,
   my eyes from tears, my feet from
   stumbling.*o*
9 I shall walk before the LORD
   in the land of the living.*p**

III

10 I kept faith, even when I said,*
   "I am greatly afflicted!"*q*
11 I said in my alarm,
   "No one can be trusted!"*r*

12 How can I repay the LORD
   for all the good done for me?
13 I will raise the cup of salvation*
   and call on the name of the LORD.
14 I will pay my vows to the LORD
   in the presence of all his people.
15 Too costly in the eyes of the LORD*
   is the death of his faithful.*s*
16 LORD, I am your servant,
   your servant, the child of your
   maidservant;*t*
   you have loosed my bonds.
17 I will offer a sacrifice of thanksgiving
   and call on the name of the LORD.*u*
18 I will pay my vows to the LORD*v*
   in the presence of all his people,
19 In the courts of the house of the LORD,
   in your midst, O Jerusalem.
Hallelujah!

PSALM 117*

The Nations Called to Praise

See RG
244, 250

1 Praise the LORD, all you nations!
   Give glory, all you peoples!*w*
2 The LORD's love for us is strong;
   the LORD is faithful forever.
Hallelujah!

PSALM 118*

Hymn of Thanksgiving

See RG
245, 252

I

1 Give thanks to the LORD, who is good,*x*
   whose love endures forever.

Ps 116: A thanksgiving in which the psalmist responds to divine rescue from mortal danger (3-4) and from near despair (10-11) with vows and temple sacrifices (13-14. 17-19). The Greek and Latin versions divide the psalm into two parts: 1-9 and 10-19, corresponding to its two major divisions.

116, 3: The cords of death: death is personified here; it attempts to capture the psalmist with snares and nets. Cf Ps 18, 6.

116, 9: The land of the living: the phrase elsewhere is an epithet of the Jerusalem temple (cf Pss 27, 13; 52, 7; Is 38, 11). Hence the psalmist probably refers to being present to God in the temple.

116, 10: I kept faith, even when I said: even in the days of despair, the psalmist did not lose all hope.

116, 13: The cup of salvation: probably the libation of wine poured out in gratitude for rescue. Cf Ex 25, 29; Nm 15, 5. 7. 10.

116, 15: Too costly in the eyes of the LORD: the meaning is that the death of God's faithful is grievous to God, not that God is pleased with the death. Cf Ps 72, 14. In Wis 3, 5-6 God

accepts the death of the righteous as a sacrificial burnt offering.

Ps 117: This shortest of hymns calls on the nations to acknowledge God's supremacy. The supremacy of Israel's God has been demonstrated to them by the people's secure existence, which is owed entirely to God's gracious fidelity.

Ps 118: A thanksgiving liturgy accompanying a victory procession of the king and the people into the temple precincts. After an invocation in the form of a litany (1-4), the psalmist (very likely speaking in the name of the community) describes how the people confidently implored God's help (5-9) when hostile peoples threatened its life (10-14); vividly God's rescue is recounted (15-18). Then follows a dialogue at the temple gates between the priests and the psalmist as the latter enters to offer the thanksgiving sacrifice (19-25).

l: Ps 18, 5; Jon 2, 3.   *m:* Ex 34, 6.   *n:* Ps 13, 6.   *o:* Ps 56, 14; Is 25, 8; Rv 21, 4.   *p:* Pss 27, 13; 56, 14; Is 38, 11.   *q:* 2 Cor 4, 13.   *r:* Ps 12, 2.   *s:* Ps 72, 14; Is 43, 4.   *t:* Pss 86, 16; 143, 12; Wis 9, 5.   *u:* Lv 7, 12ff.   *v:* Jon 2, 10.   *w:* Rom 15, 11.   *x:* Pss 100, 5; 136, 1f.

² Let the house of Israel say:
  God's love endures forever.
³ Let the house of Aaron say,
  God's love endures forever.
⁴ Let those who fear the LORD say,ʸ
  God's love endures forever.

II

⁵ In danger I called on the LORD;
  the LORD answered me and set me free.
⁶ The LORD is with me; I am not afraid;
  what can mortals do against me?ᶻ
⁷ The LORD is with me as my helper;
  I shall look in triumph on my foes.
⁸ Better to take refuge in the LORDᵃ
  than to put one's trust in mortals.
⁹ Better to take refuge in the LORD
  than to put one's trust in princes.

III

¹⁰ All the nations surrounded me;
  in the LORD's name I crushed them.
¹¹ They surrounded me on every side;
  in the LORD's name I crushed them.
¹² They surrounded me like bees;ᵇ
  they blazed like fire among thorns;
  in the LORD's name I crushed them.
¹³ I was hard pressed and falling,
  but the LORD came to my help.ᶜ
¹⁴ The LORD, my strength and might,
  came to me as savior.ᵈ

IV

¹⁵ The joyful shout of deliverance
  is heard in the tents of the victors:
  "The LORD's right hand strikes with
    power;
¹⁶ the LORD's right hand is raised;
  the LORD's right hand strikes with
    power."
¹⁷ I shall not die but live
  and declare the deeds of the LORD.

¹⁸ The LORD chastised me harshly,
  but did not hand me over to death.

V

¹⁹ Open the gates of victory;
  I will enter and thank the LORD.ᵉ
²⁰ This is the LORD's own gate,
  where the victors enter.*
²¹ I thank you for you answered me;
  you have been my savior.
²² The stone the builders rejected*
  has become the cornerstone.ᶠ
²³ By the LORD has this been done;
  it is wonderful in our eyes.
²⁴ This is the day the LORD has made;
  let us rejoice in it and be glad.
²⁵ LORD, grant salvation!*
  LORD, grant good fortune!

VI

²⁶ Blessed is he
  who comes in the name of the LORD.ᵍ
  We bless you from the LORD's house.
²⁷ The LORD is God and has given us
    light.
  Join in procession with leafy branches
  up to the horns of the altar.

VII

²⁸ You are my God, I give you thanks;
  my God, I offer you praise.
²⁹ Give thanks to the LORD, who is good,
  whose love endures forever.

PSALM 119*

A Prayer to God, the Lawgiver

See RG 245-46

ALEPH

¹ Happy those whose way is blameless,
  who walk by the teaching of the
    LORD.ʰ
² Happy those who observe God's decrees,
  who seek the LORD with all their heart.ⁱ

Finally, the priests impart their blessing (26-27), and the psalmist sings in gratitude (28-29).

118, 20: Where the victors enter: their victory has demonstrated that God favors them; they are "just" in the biblical sense.

118, 22: The stone the builders rejected: a proverb: what is insignificant to human beings has become great through divine election. The "stone" may originally have meant the foundation stone or capstone of the temple. The New Testament interpreted the verse as referring to the death and resurrection of Christ (Mt 21, 42; Acts 4, 11; cf Is 28, 16 and Rom 9, 33; 1 Pt 2, 7).

118, 25: Grant salvation: the Hebrew for this cry has come into English as "Hosanna." This cry and the words in 26

were used in the gospels to welcome Jesus entering the temple on Palm Sunday (Mk 11, 9-10).

Ps 119: This psalm, the longest by far in the Psalter, praises God for giving such splendid laws and instruction for people to live by. The author glorifies and thanks God for the Torah, prays for protection from sinners enraged by others' fidelity to the law, laments the cost of obedience, delights in the law's consolations, begs for wisdom to understand the precepts, and asks for the rewards of keeping them. Several expected ele-

y: Ps 115, 9-11. z: Ps 27, 1; Heb 13, 6. a: 8f: Ps 146, 3. b: Dt 1, 44. c: Ps 129, 1-2. d: Ex 15, 2; Is 12, 2. e: Is 26, 2. f: Mt 21, 42; Lk 20, 17; Acts 4, 11; Rom 9, 33; 1 Pt 2, 7. g: Mt 21, 9; 23, 39. h: Pss 1, 1-2; 15, 2; 112, 1. i: Dt 4, 29.

3 They do no wrong;
    they walk in God's ways.
4 You have given them the command
    to keep your precepts with care.
5 May my ways be firm
    in the observance of your laws!
6 Then I will not be ashamed
    to ponder all your commands.
7 I will praise you with sincere heart
    as I study your just edicts.
8 I will keep your laws;
    do not leave me all alone.

BETH

9 How can the young walk without fault?
    Only by keeping your words.
10 With all my heart I seek you;
    do not let me stray from your
        commands.
11 In my heart I treasure your promise,
    that I may not sin against you.
12 Blessed are you, O LORD;
    teach me your laws.[j]
13 With my lips I recite
    all the edicts you have spoken.
14 I find joy in the way of your decrees
    more than in all riches.
15 I will ponder your precepts
    and consider your paths.
16 In your laws I take delight;
    I will never forget your word.

GIMEL

17 Be kind to your servant that I may live,
    that I may keep your word.
18 Open my eyes to see clearly
    the wonders of your teachings.
19 I am a sojourner in the land;[k] *
    do not hide your commands from me.
20 At all times my soul is stirred
    with longing for your edicts.
21 With a curse you rebuke the proud

who stray from your commands.
22 Free me from disgrace and contempt,
    for I observe your decrees.
23 Though princes meet and talk against
        me,
    your servant studies your laws.
24 Your decrees are my delight;
    they are my counselors.

DALETH

25 I lie prostrate in the dust;[l]
    give me life in accord with your word.
26 I disclosed my ways and you answered
        me;
    teach me your laws.
27 Make me understand the way of your
        precepts;
    I will ponder your wondrous deeds.
28 I weep in bitter pain;
    in accord with your word to strengthen
        me.
29 Lead me from the way of deceit;
    favor me with your teaching.
30 The way of loyalty I have chosen;
    I have set your edicts before me.
31 I cling to your decrees, LORD;
    do not let me come to shame.
32 I will run the way of your commands,
    for you open my docile heart.*

HE

33 LORD, teach me the way of your laws;
    I shall observe them with care.[m]
34 Give me insight to observe your
        teaching,
    to keep it with all my heart.
35 Lead me in the path of your commands,[n]
    for that is my delight.
36 Direct my heart toward your decrees
    and away from unjust gain.
37 Avert my eyes from what is worthless;
    by your way give me life.

---

ments do not appear in the psalm: Mount Sinai with its story of God's revelation and gift to Israel of instruction and commandments, the temple and other institutions related to revelation and laws (frequent in other psalms). The psalm is fascinated with God's word directing and guiding human life.

The poem is an acrostic; its twenty-two stanzas (of eight verses each) are in the order of the Hebrew alphabet. Each of the eight verses within a stanza begins with the same letter. Each verse contains one word for "instruction." The translation here given attempts to translate each Hebrew word for "instruction" with the same English word. There are, however, nine words for "instruction," not eight, so the principle

of a different word for "instruction" in each verse cannot be maintained with perfect consistency. The nine words for "instruction" in the translation are: law, edict, command, precept, word, utterance, way, decree, and teaching.

119, 19: A sojourner in the land: like someone without the legal protection of a native inhabitant, the psalmist has a special need for the guidance of God's teaching.

119, 32: For you open my docile heart: literally, "you make broad my heart."

j: Pss 25, 4; 27, 11; 86, 11; 143, 8. 10.   *k:* Ps 39, 13.   *l:* Ps 44, 26.   *m:* Ps 19, 12.   *n:* Pss 25, 4; 27, 11; 86, 11; 143, 8. 10.

³⁸ For your servant fulfill your promise
    made to those who fear you.
³⁹ Turn away from me the taunts I dread,
    for your edicts bring good.
⁴⁰ See how I long for your precepts;
    in your justice give me life.
    WAW
⁴¹ Let your love come to me, LORD,
    salvation in accord with your promise.
⁴² Let me answer my taunters with a word,
    for I trust in your word.
⁴³ Do not take the word of truth from my
    mouth,
    for in your edicts is my hope.
⁴⁴ I will keep your teachings always,
    for all time and forever.
⁴⁵ I will walk freely in an open space
    because I cherish your precepts.
⁴⁶ I will speak openly of your decrees
    without fear even before kings.
⁴⁷ I delight in your commands,
    which I dearly love.
⁴⁸ I lift up my hands to your commands;*
    I study your laws, which I love.
    ZAYIN
⁴⁹ Remember your word to your servant
    by which you give me hope.
⁵⁰ This is my comfort in affliction,
    your promise that gives me life.
⁵¹ Though the arrogant utterly scorn me,
    I do not turn from your teaching.
⁵² When I recite your edicts of old
    I am comforted, LORD.
⁵³ Rage seizes me because of the wicked;
    they forsake your teaching.
⁵⁴ Your laws become my songs
    wherever I make my home.
⁵⁵ Even at night I remember your name
    in observance of your teaching, LORD.
⁵⁶ This is my good fortune,
    for I have observed your precepts.
    HETH
⁵⁷ My portion is the LORD;
    I promise to keep your words.
⁵⁸ I entreat you with all my heart:
    have mercy on me in accord with your
    promise.

⁵⁹ I have examined my ways
    and turned my steps to your decrees.
⁶⁰ I am prompt, I do not hesitate
    in keeping your commands.
⁶¹ Though the snares of the wicked
    surround me,
    your teaching I do not forget.
⁶² At midnight I rise to praise you
    because your edicts are just.
⁶³ I am the friend of all who fear you,
    of all who keep your precepts.
⁶⁴ The earth, LORD, is filled with your love;^o
    teach me your laws.
    TETH
⁶⁵ You have treated your servant well,
    according to your word, O LORD.
⁶⁶ Teach me wisdom and knowledge,
    for in your commands I trust.
⁶⁷ Before I was afflicted I went astray,
    but now I hold to your promise.
⁶⁸ You are good and do what is good;
    teach me your laws.
⁶⁹ The arrogant smear me with lies,
    but I observe your precepts with all
    my heart.
⁷⁰ Their hearts are gross and fat;^p
    as for me, your teaching is my delight.
⁷¹ It was good for me to be afflicted,
    in order to learn your laws.
⁷² Teaching from your lips is more precious
    to me
    than heaps of silver and gold.
    YODH
⁷³ Your hands made me and fashioned me;
    give me insight to learn your
    commands.
⁷⁴ Those who fear you rejoice to see me,
    because I hope in your word.
⁷⁵ I know, LORD, that your edicts are just;
    though you afflict me, you are faithful.
⁷⁶ May your love comfort me
    in accord with your promise to your
    servant.
⁷⁷ Show me compassion that I may live,
    for your teaching is my delight.
⁷⁸ Shame the proud for oppressing me
    unjustly,

119, 48: I lift up my hands to your commands: to lift up the hands was an ancient gesture of reverence to God. Here the picture is applied to God's law.

o: Ps 33, 5.   *p:* Pss 17, 10; 73, 7; Jb 15, 27.

that I may study your precepts.

⁷⁹ Let those who fear you turn to me,
those who acknowledge your decrees.

⁸⁰ May I be wholehearted toward your
laws,
that I may not be put to shame.

KAPH

⁸¹ My soul longs for your salvation;
I put my hope in your word.^q

⁸² My eyes long to see your promise.^r
When will you comfort me?

⁸³ I am like a wineskin shriveled by smoke,^s
but I have not forgotten your laws.

⁸⁴ How long can your servant survive?
When will your edict doom my foes?

⁸⁵ The arrogant have dug pits for me;
defying your teaching.

⁸⁶ All your commands are steadfast.
Help me! I am pursued without cause.

⁸⁷ They have almost ended my life on earth,
but I do not forsake your precepts.

⁸⁸ In your kindness give me life,
to keep the decrees you have spoken.

LAMEDH

⁸⁹ Your word, LORD, stands forever;^t*
it is firm as the heavens.

⁹⁰ Through all generations your truth
endures;
fixed to stand firm like the earth.

⁹¹ By your edicts they stand firm to this
day,
for all things are your servants.

⁹² Had your teaching not been my delight,
I would have perished in my affliction.

⁹³ I will never forget your precepts;
through them you give me life.

⁹⁴ I am yours; save me,
for I cherish your precepts.

⁹⁵ The wicked hope to destroy me,
but I pay heed to your decrees.

⁹⁶ I have seen the limits of all perfection,
but your command is without bounds.

MEM

⁹⁷ How I love your teaching, LORD!
I study it all day long.

⁹⁸ Your command makes me wiser than my
foes,

for it is always with me.

⁹⁹ I have more understanding than all my
teachers,
because I ponder your decrees.

¹⁰⁰I have more insight than my elders,
because I observe your precepts.^u

¹⁰¹I keep my steps from every evil path,
that I may obey your word.

¹⁰²From your edicts I do not turn,
for you have taught them to me.

¹⁰³How sweet to my tongue is your
promise,
sweeter than honey to my mouth!^v

¹⁰⁴Through your precepts I gain insight;
therefore I hate all false ways.

NUN

¹⁰⁵Your word is a lamp for my feet,
a light for my path.^w

¹⁰⁶I make a solemn vow
to keep your just edicts.

¹⁰⁷I am very much afflicted, LORD;
give me life in accord with your word.

¹⁰⁸Accept my freely offered praise;^x
LORD, teach me your decrees.

¹⁰⁹My life is always at risk,
but I do not forget your teaching.

¹¹⁰The wicked have set snares for me,
but from your precepts I do not stray.

¹¹¹Your decrees are my heritage forever;
they are the joy of my heart.

¹¹²My heart is set on fulfilling your laws;
they are my reward forever.

SAMEKH

¹¹³I hate every hypocrite;
your teaching I love.

¹¹⁴You are my refuge and shield;
in your word I hope.

¹¹⁵Depart from me, you wicked,^y
that I may observe the commands of
my God.

¹¹⁶Sustain me by your promise that I may
live;
do not disappoint me in my hope.

¹¹⁷Strengthen me that I may be safe,
ever to contemplate your laws.

¹¹⁸You reject all who stray from your laws,
for vain is their deceit.

119, 89-91: God's word creates the world, which manifests that word by its permanence and reliability.

q: Ps 130, 6.   *r:* Pss 25, 15; 123, 1-2; 141, 8.   *s:* Jb 30, 30.   *t:* Is 40, 8.   *u:* Jb 32, 6; Wis 4, 8-9.   *v:* Ps 19, 11.   *w:* Ps 18, 29; Prv 6, 23.   *x:* Ps 50, 14. 23; Heb 13, 15.   *y:* Pss 6, 9; 139, 19; Jb 21, 14.

¹¹⁹Like dross you regard all the wicked on
earth;
therefore I love your decrees.
¹²⁰My flesh shudders with dread of you;
I hold your edicts in awe.

AYIN

¹²¹I have fulfilled your just edict;
do not abandon me to my oppressors.
¹²²Guarantee your servant's welfare;
do not let the arrogant oppress me.
¹²³My eyes long to see your salvation
and the justice of your promise.
¹²⁴Act with kindness toward your servant;
teach me your laws.
¹²⁵I am your servant; give me discernment
that I may know your decrees.
¹²⁶It is time for the LORD to act;
they have disobeyed your teaching.
¹²⁷Truly I love your commands
more than the finest gold.
¹²⁸Thus I follow all your precepts;
every wrong way I hate.

PE

¹²⁹Wonderful are your decrees;
therefore I observe them.
¹³⁰The revelation of your words sheds light,
gives understanding to the simple.
¹³¹I sigh with open mouth,
yearning for your commands.
¹³²Turn to me and be gracious,ᶻ
your edict for lovers of your name.
¹³³Steady my feet in accord with your
promise;
do not let iniquity lead me.
¹³⁴Free me from human oppression,
that I may keep your precepts.
¹³⁵Let your face shine upon your servant;
teach me your laws.
¹³⁶My eyes shed streams of tears
because your teaching is not followed.

SADHE

¹³⁷You are righteous, LORD,
and just are your edicts.ᵃ
¹³⁸You have issued your decrees in justice
and in surpassing faithfulness.
¹³⁹I am consumed with rage,
because my foes forget your words.
¹⁴⁰Your servant loves your promise;
it has been proved by fire.

¹⁴¹Though belittled and despised,
I do not forget your precepts.
¹⁴²Your justice is forever right,
your teaching forever true.
¹⁴³Though distress and anguish come upon
me,
your commands are my delight.
¹⁴⁴Your decrees are forever just;
give me discernment that I may live.

QOPH

¹⁴⁵I call with all my heart, O LORD;
answer me that I may observe your
laws.
¹⁴⁶I call to you to save me
that I may keep your decrees.
¹⁴⁷I rise before dawn and cry out;
I put my hope in your words.
¹⁴⁸My eyes greet the night watches
as I meditate on your promise.ᵇ
¹⁴⁹Hear my voice in your love, O LORD;
by your edict give me life.
¹⁵⁰Malicious persecutors draw near me;
they are far from your teaching.
¹⁵¹You are near, O LORD;
reliable are all your commands.
¹⁵²Long have I known from your decrees
that you have established them forever.

RESH

¹⁵³Look at my affliction and rescue me,
for I have not forgotten your teaching.
¹⁵⁴Take up my cause and redeem me;ᶜ
for the sake of your promise give me
life.
¹⁵⁵Salvation is far from sinners
because they do not cherish your laws.
¹⁵⁶Your compassion is great, O LORD;
in accord with your edicts give me life.
¹⁵⁷Though my persecutors and foes are
many
I do not turn from your decrees.
¹⁵⁸I view the faithless with loathing,ᵈ
because they do not heed your promise.
¹⁵⁹See how I love your precepts, LORD;
in your kindness give me life.
¹⁶⁰Your every word is enduring;
all your just edicts are forever.

SHIN

¹⁶¹Princes persecute me without reason,
but my heart reveres only your word.

z: Pss 25, 16; 86, 16.   a: Tb 3, 2.   b: Pss 63, 7; 77, 7.   c: Ps 43, 1.   d: Ps 139, 22.

162I rejoice at your promise,
    as one who has found rich spoil.
163Falsehood I hate and abhor;
    your teaching I love.
164Seven times a day I praise you
    because your edicts are just.
165Lovers of your teaching have much
        peace;e
    for them there is no stumbling block.
166I look for your salvation, LORD,
    and I fulfill your commands.
167I observe your decrees;
    I love them very much.
168I observe your precepts and decrees;
    all my ways are before you.

TAW

169Let my cry come before you, LORD;f
    in keeping with your word give me
        discernment.
170Let my prayer come before you;
    rescue me according to your
        promise.
171May my lips pour forth your praise,
    because you teach me your laws.
172May my tongue sing of your promise,
    for all your commands are just.
173Keep your hand ready to help me,
    for I have chosen your precepts.
174I long for your salvation, LORD;
    your teaching is my delight.
175Let me live to praise you;
    may your edicts give me help.
176I have wandered like a lost sheep;

seek out your servant,
    for I do not forget your commands.g

PSALM 120*

Prayer of a Returned Exile

See RG
244

1 A song of ascents.*

I

The LORD answered me
    when I called in my distress:h
2 LORD, deliver me from lying lips,
    from treacherous tongues.i

II

3 What will the Lord inflict on you,
    O treacherous tongue,
    and what more besides?*
4 A warrior's sharpened arrows
    and fiery coals of brushwood!j *

III

5 Alas, I was an alien in Meshech,*
    I lived near the tents of Kedar!
6 Too long did I live
    among those who hated peace.
7 When I spoke of peace,
    they were for war.k

PSALM 121*

The Lord My Guardian

See RG
245, 250

1 A song of ascents.

I

I raise my eyes toward the mountains.*
    From where will my help come?l
2 My help comes from the LORD,
    the maker of heaven and earth.m

Ps 120: A thanksgiving, reporting divine rescue (1) yet with fervent prayer for further protection against lying attackers (2-4). The psalmist is acutely conscious of living away from God's own land where divine peace prevails (5-7).

120, 1: Song of ascents: Pss 120—134 all begin with this superscription. Most probably these fifteen psalms once formed a collection of psalms sung when pilgrims went to Jerusalem, since one "ascended" to Jerusalem (1 Kgs 12, 28; Pss 24, 3; 122, 4; Lk 2, 42) or to the house of God or to an altar (1 Kgs 12, 33; 2 Kgs 23, 2; Ps 24, 3). Less probable is the explanation that these psalms were sung by the exiles when they "ascended" to Jerusalem from Babylonia (cf Ezr 7, 9). The idea, found in the Mishnah, that the fifteen steps on which the Levites sang corresponded to these fifteen psalms (*Middot* 2, 5) must underlie the Vulgate translation *canticum graduum*, "song of the steps" or "gradual song."

120, 3: More besides: a common curse formula in Hebrew was "May the Lord do such and such evils to you [the evils being specified], and add *still more* to them." Cf 1 Sm 3, 17; 14, 44; 25, 22. Here the psalmist is at a loss for a suitable malediction.

120, 4: Coals of brushwood: coals made from the stalk of the broom plant burn with intense heat. The psalmist thinks of lighted coals cast at his enemies.

120, 5: Meshech was in the far north (Gn 10, 2) and **Kedar** was a tribe of the north Arabian desert (Gn 25, 13). The psalmist may be thinking generally of all aliens living among inhospitable peoples.

Ps 121: A blessing given to someone embarking on a dangerous journey, whether a soldier going on a campaign or a pilgrim returning home from the temple. People look anxiously at the wooded hills. Will God protect them on their journey (1)? The speaker declares that God is not confined to a place or a time (2), that every step is guarded (3-4); night and day (5-6) God watches over their every movement (7-8).

121, 1: The mountains: possibly Mount Zion, the site of the temple and hence of safety, but more probably mountains as a place of dangers, causing anxiety to the psalmist.

---

e: Ps 72, 7.   f: Ps 88, 3.   g: Is 53, 6; Jer 50, 6; Lk 15, 1-7.   h: Jon 2, 3.   i: Ps 12, 3-5; Sir 51, 3.   j: Pss 11, 6; 140, 11; Prv 16, 27.   k: Pss 35, 20; 140, 3-4.   l: Jer 3, 23.   m: Pss 124, 8; 146, 6.

II

[3] God will not allow your foot to slip;[n]
    your guardian does not sleep.
[4] Truly, the guardian of Israel
    never slumbers nor sleeps.
[5] The LORD is your guardian;[*]
    the LORD is your shade
    at your right hand.[o]
[6] By day the sun cannot harm you,
    nor the moon by night.[p]
[7] The LORD will guard you from all evil,
    will always guard your life.[q]
[8] The LORD will guard your coming and
      going
    both now and forever.[r]

See RG
245

PSALM 122[*]

A Pilgrim's Prayer for
Jerusalem

[1] A song of ascents. Of David.

I

I rejoiced when they said to me,
    "Let us go to the house of the LORD."[s]
[2] And now our feet are standing
    within your gates, Jerusalem.
[3] Jerusalem, built as a city,
    walled round about.[t][*]
[4] Here the tribes have come,
    the tribes of the LORD,
As it was decreed for Israel,
    to give thanks to the name of the LORD.[u]
[5] Here are the thrones of justice,
    the thrones of the house of David.

II

[6] For the peace of Jerusalem pray:
    "May those who love you prosper!
[7] May peace be within your ramparts,

prosperity within your towers."[v]
[8] For family and friends I say,
    "May peace be yours."
[9] For the house of the LORD, our God, I pray,
    "May blessings be yours."

PSALM 123[*]

Reliance on the Lord
See RG
244

[1] A song of ascents.

To you I raise my eyes,
    to you enthroned in heaven.[w]
[2] Yes, like the eyes of a servant
    on the hand of his master,
Like the eyes of a maid
    on the hand of her mistress,
So our eyes are on the LORD our God,
    till we are shown favor.
[3] Show us favor, LORD, show us favor,
    for we have our fill of contempt.[x]
[4] We have our fill of insult from the
      insolent,
    of disdain from the arrogant.

PSALM 124[*]

God, the Rescuer of the People
See RG
245

[1] A song of ascents. Of David.

I

Had not the LORD been with us,
    let Israel say,[y]
[2] Had not the LORD been with us,
    when people rose against us,
[3] They would have swallowed us alive,[z]
    for their fury blazed against us.
[4] The waters would have engulfed us,
    the torrent overwhelmed us;[a]
[5]   seething waters would have drowned us.

121, 5-6: The image of shade, a symbol of protection, is apt: God as shade protects from the harmful effects that ancients believed were caused by the sun and moon.

Ps 122: A song of Zion, sung by pilgrims obeying the law to visit Jerusalem three times on a journey. The singer anticipates joining the procession into the city (1-3). Jerusalem is a place of encounter, where the people praise God (4) and hear the divine justice mediated by the king (5). The very buildings bespeak God's power (cf Ps 48, 13-15). May the grace of this place transform the people's lives (6-9)!

122, 3: Walled round about: literally, "which is joined to it," probably referring both to the density of the buildings and to the dense population.

Ps 123: A lament that begins as a prayer of an individual (1), who expresses by a touching comparison exemplary confidence in God (2). The psalm ends in prayer that God relieve

the people's humiliation at the hands of the arrogant (3-4).

Ps 124: A thanksgiving which teaches that Israel's very existence is owed to God who rescues them. In the first part Israel's enemies are compared to the mythic sea dragon (2b-3a; cf Jer 51, 34) and Flood (3b-5; cf Is 51, 9-10). The psalm heightens the malice of human enemies by linking them to the primordial enemies of God's creation. Israel is a bird freed from the trapper's snare (6-8)—freed originally from Pharaoh and now from the current danger.

---

n: Pss 66, 9; 91, 12; 1 Sm 2, 9; Prv 3, 23.   *o:* Pss 16, 8; 73, 23.
p: Wis 18, 3; Is 25, 4; 49, 10.   *q:* Ps 97, 10.   *r:* Dt 28, 6.   *s:* Pss 43, 3-4; 84, 2-5.   *t:* Ps 48, 13-14.   *u:* Dt 16, 16.   *v:* Ps 128, 5.
w: Pss 25, 15; 119, 82; 141, 8.   *x:* Ps 44, 13-14; Jb 12, 4.   *y:* Ps 129, 1.   *z:* Prv 1, 12.   *a:* Pss 18, 5; 69, 2.

II

6 Blessed be the LORD, who did not leave us
to be torn by their fangs.
7 We escaped with our lives
like a bird from the fowler's snare;
the snare was broken and we escaped.
8 Our help is the name* of the LORD,
the maker of heaven and earth.[b]

PSALM 125*

See RG 245

Israel's Protector

1 A song of ascents.

I

Like Mount Zion are they
who trust in the LORD,
unshakable, forever enduring.[c]
2 As mountains surround Jerusalem,
the LORD surrounds his people
both now and forever.[d]

II

3 The scepter of the wicked will not prevail
in the land given to the just,*
Lest the just themselves
turn their hands to evil.

III

4 Do good, LORD, to the good,
to those who are upright of heart.[e]
5 But those who turn aside to crooked ways
may the LORD send down with the
wicked.[f]
Peace upon Israel![g]

PSALM 126*

See RG 244

The Reversal of Zion's Fortunes

1 A song of ascents.

I

When the LORD restored the fortunes of
Zion,[h]

then we thought we were dreaming.
2 Our mouths were filled with laughter;
our tongues sang for joy.[i]
Then it was said among the nations,
"The LORD has done great things for
them."
3 The LORD had done great things for us;
Oh, how happy we were!
4 Restore again our fortunes, LORD,
like the dry stream beds of the Negeb.*

II

5 Those who sow in tears
will reap with cries of joy.[j]
6 Those who go forth weeping,
carrying sacks of seed,
Will return with cries of joy,
carrying their bundled sheaves.

PSALM 127*

See RG 245

The Need of God's Blessing

1 A song of ascents. Of Solomon.

I

Unless the LORD build the house,
they labor in vain who build.
Unless the LORD guard the city,
in vain does the guard keep watch.
2 It is vain for you to rise early
and put off your rest at night,
To eat bread earned by hard toil—
all this God gives to his beloved in
sleep.[k]

II

3 Children too are a gift from the LORD,
the fruit of the womb, a reward.[l]
4 Like arrows in the hand of a warrior
are the children born in one's youth.
5 Blessed are they whose quivers are
full.

124, 8: **Our help is the name**: for the idiom, see Ex 18, 4.

Ps 125: In response to exilic anxieties about the ancient promises of restoration, the psalm expresses confidence that God will surround the people as the mountains surround Zion (1-2). The just will not be contaminated by the wicked (3). May God judge between the two groups (4-5).

125, 3: **The land given to the just**: literally, "the lot of the just." The promised land was divided among the tribes of Israel by lot (Nm 26, 55; Jos 18). **The just** are the members of the people who are obedient to God. If the domination of the wicked were to continue in the land, even the just would be infected by their evil attitudes.

Ps 126: A lament probably sung shortly after Israel's return from exile. The people rejoice that they are in Zion (1-3) but mere presence in the holy city is not enough; they must

pray for the prosperity and the fertility of the land (4). The last verses are probably an oracle of promise: the painful work of sowing will be crowned with life (5-6).

126, 4: **Like the dry stream beds of the Negeb**: the psalmist prays for rain in such abundance that the dry riverbeds will run.

Ps 127: The psalm puts together two proverbs (1-2 and 3-5) on God establishing "houses" or families. The prosperity of human groups is not the work of humans but the gift of God.

---

b: Pss 121, 2; 146, 6.   c: Prv 10, 25.   d: Dt 32, 11.   e: Ps 18, 25ff.   f: Prv 3, 32.   g: Ps 128, 6.   h: Ps 14, 7.   i: Jb 8, 21. j: Bar 4, 23; Is 65, 19.   k: Eccl 2, 24.   l: Pss 115, 14; 128, 3; Dt 28, 11; Prv 17, 6.

They will never be shamed
contending with foes at the gate.*

See RG
245

PSALM 128*

The Happy Home of the Just

1 A song of ascents.

I

Happy are all who fear the LORD,*
who walk in the ways of God.*m*
2 What your hands provide you will
enjoy;
you will be happy and prosper:*n*
3 Like a fruitful vine
your wife within your home,
Like olive plants
your children around your table.*o*
4 Just so will they be blessed
who fear the LORD.

II

5 May the LORD bless you from Zion,
all the days of your life*p*
That you may share Jerusalem's joy
6 and live to see your children's
children.*q*
Peace upon Israel!*r*

See RG
245

PSALM 129*

Against Israel's Enemies

1 A song of ascents.

I

Much have they oppressed me from my
youth,
now let Israel say.*s*

2 Much have they oppressed me from my
youth,*t*
yet they have not prevailed.
3 Upon my back the plowers plowed,
as they traced their long furrows.*u*
4 But the just LORD cut me free
from the ropes of the yoke of the
wicked.*

II

5 May they be scattered in disgrace,
all who hate Zion.
6 May they be like grass on the rooftops*
withered in early growth,*v*
7 Never to fill the reaper's hands,
nor the arms of the binders of
sheaves,
8 With none passing by to call out:
"The blessing of the LORD be upon
you!"*
We bless you in the name of the
LORD!"*w*

PSALM 130*

Prayer for Pardon and Mercy

See RG
244

1 A song of ascents.

I

Out of the depths* I call to you,
LORD;
2   Lord, hear my cry!
May your ears be attentive
to my cry for mercy.*x*
3 If you, LORD, mark our sins,
Lord, who can stand?*y*

127, 5: At the gate: the reference is not to enemies besieging the walls of a city but to adversaries in litigation. Law courts functioned in the open area near the main city gate. The more adult sons a man had, the more forceful he would appear in disputes. Cf Prv 31, 23.

Ps 128: A statement that the ever-reliable God will bless the reverent (1). God's blessing is concrete: satisfaction and prosperity, a fertile spouse and abundant children (2-4). The perspective is that of the adult male, ordinarily the ruler and representative of the household to the community. The last verses extend the blessing to all the people for generations to come (5-6).

128, 1: All who fear the LORD: literally, singular: "the one fearing," is used in a typical sense and so is translated by the plural.

Ps 129: A psalm giving thanks for God's many rescues of Israel over the long course of their history (1-4); the people pray that their oppressors never know the joy of harvest (5-8).

129, 4: The ropes of the yoke of the wicked: usually understood as the rope for yoking animals to the plow. If it is severed, the plowing (cf 3) comes to a halt.

129, 6: Like grass on the rooftops: after the spring rains, grass would sprout from the coat of mud with which the flat roofs of simple houses were covered, but when the dry summer began there was no moisture in the thin roof-covering to sustain the grass.

129, 8: The blessing of the LORD be upon you: harvesters greeted one another with such blessings. Cf Ru 2, 4.

Ps 130: This lament, a Penitential Psalm, is the *De profundis* used in liturgical prayers for the faithful departed. In deep sorrow the psalmist cries to God (1-2), asking for mercy (3-4). The psalmist's trust (5-6) becomes a model for the people (7-8).

130, 1: The depths: Sheol here is a metaphor of total misery. Deep anguish makes the psalmist feel "like those descending to the pit" (Ps 143, 7).

m: Ps 112, 1.   *n:* Ps 112, 3.   *o:* Jb 29, 5; Ps 144, 12.   *p:* Pss 20, 3; 134, 3.   *q:* Jb 42, 16; Prv 17, 6.   *r:* Ps 125, 5.   *s:* Ps 124, 1.   *t:* Ps 118, 13.   *u:* Is 51, 23.   *v:* Is 37, 27.   *w:* Ps 118, 26.   *x:* Pss 5, 2-3; 55, 2-3; 86, 6; Lam 3, 55-56; Jon 2, 3.   *y:* Na 1, 6.

⁴ But with you is forgiveness
  and so you are revered.*

II

⁵ I wait with longing for the LORD,
  my soul waits for his word.ᶻ
⁶ My soul looks for the Lord
  more than sentinels for daybreak.ᵃ
More than sentinels for daybreak,
⁷   let Israel look for the LORD,
For with the LORD is kindness,
  with him is full redemption,ᵇ
⁸ And God will redeem Israel
  from all their sins.ᶜ

See RG
245

PSALM 131*

Humble Trust in God

¹ A song of ascents. Of David.

LORD, my heart is not proud;
  nor are my eyes haughty.
I do not busy myself with great matters,
  with things too sublime for me.ᵈ
² Rather, I have stilled my soul,
  hushed it like a weaned child.
Like a weaned child on its mother's lap,
  so is my soul within me.ᵉ
³ Israel, hope in the LORD,
  now and forever.

See RG
245, 260

PSALM 132*

*The Covenant between
David and God*

¹ A song of ascents.

I

LORD, remember David
  and all his anxious care;*
² How he swore an oath to the LORD,

vowed to the Mighty One of Jacob:*
³ "I will not enter the house where I live,ᶠ
  nor lie on the couch where I sleep;
⁴ I will give my eyes no sleep,
  my eyelids no rest,
⁵ Till I find a home for the LORD,
  a dwelling for the Mighty One of
    Jacob."
⁶ "We have heard of it in Ephrathah;*
  we have found it in the fields of Jaar.*
⁷ Let us enter God's dwelling;
  let us worship at God's footstool."ᵍ
⁸ "Arise, LORD, come to your resting place,ʰ
  you and your majestic ark.
⁹ Your priests will be clothed with justice;
  your faithful will shout for joy."
¹⁰ For the sake of David your servant,
  do not reject your anointed.

II

¹¹ The LORD swore an oath to David,
  a pledge never to be broken:ⁱ
"Your own offspringʲ I will set upon
    your throne.
¹² If your sons observe my covenant,
  the laws I shall teach them,
Their sons, in turn,
  shall sit forever on your throne."
¹³ Yes, the LORD has chosen Zion,
  desired it for a dwelling:
¹⁴ "This is my resting place forever;
  here I will dwell, for I desire it.
¹⁵ I will bless Zion with meat;
  its poor I will fill with bread.
¹⁶ I will clothe its priests with blessing;
  its faithful shall shout for joy.ᵏ
¹⁷ There I will make a horn sprout for
    David's line;ˡ*

130, 4: **And so you are revered**: the experience of God's mercy leads one to a greater sense of God.

Ps 131: A song of trust, in which the psalmist gives up self-sufficiency (1), like a babe enjoying the comfort of its mother's lap (2), thus providing a model for Israel's faith (3).

Ps 132: A song for a liturgical ceremony in which the ark, the throne of Israel's God, was carried in procession to the temple. The singer asks that David's care for the proper housing of the ark be regarded with favor (1-5), and tells how it was brought to Jerusalem (6-10). There follows God's promise of favor to the Davidic dynasty (11-12) and to Zion (13-17). The transfer of the ark to the tent in Jerusalem is described in 2 Sm 6.

132, 1: All his anxious care: to build the temple. Cf 2 Sm 7, 1-17 and 1 Kgs 8, 17.

132, 2. 5: Mighty One of Jacob: one of the titles of

Israel's God. Cf Gn 49, 24; Is 49, 26; 60, 16.

132, 6: Ephrathah: the homeland of David. Cf Ru 4, 11. **The fields of Jaar**: poetic for Kiriath-jearim, a town west of Jerusalem, where the ark remained for several generations. Cf 1 Sm 7, 1-2 ; 2 Sm 6, 2; 1 Chr 13, 5-6.

132, 17: A horn sprout for David's line: the image of the horn, a symbol of strength, is combined with that of a "sprout," a term used for the Davidic descendant (cf Jer 23, 5; 33, 15; Zec 3, 8; 6, 12). Early Christians referred the

z: Ps 119, 81. a: Is 21, 11; 26, 9. b: Pss 86, 15; 100, 5; 103, 8. c: Ps 25, 22; Mt 1, 21. d: Ps 139, 6. e: Is 66, 12-13. f: 2 Sm 7; 1 Chr 28, 2. g: Ps 99, 5. h: 8-10: Pss 2, 2; 89, 21; 95, 11; Nm 10, 35; 2 Chr 6, 41-42; Sir 24, 7. i: Ps 110, 4; 2 Sm 7, 12. j: 11-14: Ps 68, 17; 1 Kgs 8, 13; Sir 24, 7. k: 2 Chr 6, 41; Is 61, 10. l: Is 11, 1; Jer 33, 15; Ez 29, 21; Zec 3, 8; Lk 1, 69.

I will set a lamp for my anointed.
[18] His foes I will clothe with shame,
  but on him my crown shall gleam."

See RG 246

PSALM 133[*]

A Vision of a Blessed Community

[1] A song of ascents. Of David.

How good it is, how pleasant,
  where the people[*] dwell as one!
[2] Like precious ointment[*] on the head,[m]
  running down upon the beard,
Upon the beard of Aaron,
  upon the collar of his robe.
[3] Like dew[*] of Hermon[*] coming down
  upon the mountains of Zion.[n]
There the Lord has lavished blessings,
  life for evermore![o]

See RG 246

PSALM 134[*]

Exhortation to the Night Watch to Bless God

[1] A song of ascents.

Come, bless the Lord,
  all you servants of the Lord[*]
Who stand in the house of the Lord
  through the long hours of night.[p]
[2] Lift up your hands toward the sanctuary,[q]
  and bless the Lord.
[3] May the Lord who made heaven and earth[r]
  bless you from Zion.

PSALM 135[*]

See RG 244, 247

Praise of God, the Ruler and Benefactor of Israel

[1] Hallelujah!

I

Praise the name of the Lord!
  Praise, you servants of the Lord,[s]
[2] Who stand in the house of the Lord,
  in the courts of the house of our God![t]
[3] Praise the Lord; the Lord is good!
  Sing to God's name; it is gracious!
[4] For the Lord has chosen Jacob,
  Israel as a treasured possession.[u][*]

II

[5] I know that the Lord is great,
  our Lord is greater than all gods.[v]
[6] Whatever the Lord wishes
  he does in heaven and on earth,
  in the seas and in all the deeps.[w]
[7] He raises storm clouds from the end of the earth,
  makes lightning and rain,
  brings forth wind from the storehouse.[x]

III

[8] He struck down Egypt's firstborn,[y]
  human and beast alike,
[9] And sent signs and portents against you, Egypt,
  against Pharaoh and all his servants.
[10] The Lord struck down many nations,[z]
  slew mighty kings—

---

latter designation to Christ as son of David (Lk 1, 69).

Ps 133: A benediction over a peaceful community, most probably the people Israel, but appropriate too for Israelite families (1). The history of Israel, whether of its ancestors in the book of Genesis or of later periods, was a history of distinct groups struggling to live in unity. Here that unity is declared blessed, like the holy oils upon the priest Aaron or the dew of the rainless summer that waters the crops (2-3).

133, 1: The people: literally, "brothers," i.e., male and female members of a kin group or people—most probably, the people Israel.

133, 2: Ointment: oil was used at the consecration of the high priest (Ex 30, 22-33).

133, 3: Dew: dew was an important source of moisture in the dry climate (Gn 27, 28; Hos 14, 6). **Hermon:** the majestic snow-capped mountain visible in the north of Palestine.

Ps 134: A brief liturgy exhorting the temple singers to acknowledge the great deeds of God at a night service (cf Is 30, 29). Mount Zion is the place from which blessings affect the lives of humans, for there Israel's God dwells.

134, 1: Servants of the Lord: priests and Levites. Cf Dt 10, 8; Pss 113, 1; 135, 1; Dn 3, 84-85.

Ps 135: The hymn begins and ends with an invitation to praise God (1-3. 19-20) for the great act of choosing Israel (4). The story of Israel's emergence as a people is told in 5-14; God created and redeemed the people, easily conquering all opposition. God's defeat of hostile powers means that the powers themselves and their images are useless (15-18). The last three verses appear also in Ps 115, 4-8.

135, 4: Though all nations are God's, Israel has a special status as God's "treasured" people: Ex 19, 5; Dt 7, 6; 14, 2; 26, 18; Mal 3, 17.

m: Ex 30, 25. 30. *n:* Hos 14, 6. *o:* Dt 28, 8; 30, 20. *p:* Ps 135, 1-2; 1 Chr 9, 33. *q:* Pss 28, 2; 141, 2. *r:* Pss 20, 3; 128, 5; Nm 6, 24. *s:* Ps 113, 1. *t:* Ps 134, 1. *u:* Pss 33, 12; 144, 15; Ex 19, 6; Dt 7, 6. *v:* Ps 95, 3; Ex 18, 11. *w:* Ps 115, 3. *x:* Ps 148, 8; Jer 10, 13; 51, 16; Jb 37, 9. *y:* 8-9: Pss 78, 51; 105, 27. 36; 136, 10; Ex 12, 29. *z:* 10-12: Nm 21, 21-35; Dt 2, 24-3, 17; Ps 136, 17-22.

¹¹ Sihon, king of the Amorites,
  Og, king of Bashan,
  all the kings of Canaan—
¹² And made their land a heritage,
  a heritage for Israel his people.
¹³ O LORD, your name is forever,
  your renown, from age to age!ᵃ
¹⁴ For the LORD defends his people,
  shows mercy to his servants.ᵇ

IV

¹⁵ The idols of the nations are silver and
  gold,ᶜ
  the work of human hands.
¹⁶ They have mouths but speak not;
  they have eyes but see not;
¹⁷ They have ears but hear not;
  no breath is in their mouths.
¹⁸ Their makers shall be like them,
  all who trust in them.

V

¹⁹ House of Israel, bless the LORD!ᵈ
  House of Aaron, bless the LORD!
²⁰ House of Levi, bless the LORD!
  You who fear the LORD, bless the
  LORD!
²¹ Blessed from Zion be the LORD,
  who dwells in Jerusalem!
Hallelujah!

See RG 244

PSALM 136*

Hymn of Thanksgiving for God's Everlasting Love

I

¹ Praise the LORD, who is so good;ᵉ
  God's love endures forever;
² Praise the God of gods;
  God's love endures forever;
³ Praise the Lord of lords;
  God's love endures forever;

II

⁴ Who alone has done great wonders,ᶠ
  God's love endures forever;
⁵ Who skillfully made the heavens,ᵍ

God's love endures forever;
⁶ Who spread the earth upon the waters,ʰ
  God's love endures forever;
⁷ Who made the great lights,
  God's love endures forever;
⁸ The sun to rule the day,
  God's love endures forever;
⁹ The moon and stars to rule the night,ⁱ
  God's love endures forever;

III

¹⁰ Who struck down the firstborn of Egypt,ʲ
  God's love endures forever;
¹¹ And led Israel from their midst,
  God's love endures forever;
¹² With mighty hand and outstretched arm,ᵏ
  God's love endures forever;
¹³ Who split in two the Red Sea
  God's love endures forever;
¹⁴ And led Israel through,
  God's love endures forever;
¹⁵ But swept Pharaoh and his army into the
  Red Sea,ˡ
  God's love endures forever;
¹⁶ Who led the people through the desert,ᵐ
  God's love endures forever;

IV

¹⁷ Who struck down great kings,ⁿ
  God's love endures forever;
¹⁸ Slew powerful kings,
  God's love endures forever;
¹⁹ Sihon, king of the Amorites,
  God's love endures forever;
²⁰ Og, king of Bashan,
  God's love endures forever;
²¹ And made their lands a heritage,
  God's love endures forever;
²² A heritage for Israel,* God's servant,
  God's love endures forever.

V

²³ The LORD remembered us in our misery,
  God's love endures forever;
²⁴ Freed us from our foes,
  God's love endures forever;

Ps 136: The hymn praises Israel's God ("the God of gods," 2), who has created the world in which Israel lives. The refrain occurring after every line suggests that a speaker and chorus sang the psalm in antiphonal fashion. A single act of God is described in 4-25: God arranges the heavens and the earth as the environment for human community, and then creates the community by freeing them and giving them land. In the final section (23-25) God, who created the people and gave them land, continues to protect and nurture them.

136, 22: A heritage for Israel: the land was given to Israel by God to be handed on to future generations.

a: Ps 102, 13; Ex 3, 15. b: Dt 32, 36. c: 15-18: Ps 115, 4-6. 8.
d: 19-20: Ps 118, 2-4. e: Pss 100, 5; 118, 1. f: Ps 72, 18.
g: Gn 1, 9-19. h: Ps 24, 2. i: Jer 31, 35. j: Ex 12, 29. 51; 14,
22. 27; 15, 22; Pss 78, 51-52; 135, 8. k: Dt 4, 34. l: Ex 14, 21f.
m: Dt 8, 2. 15. n: 17-22: Ps 135, 10-12.

²⁵ And gives food to all flesh,
    God's love endures forever.

VI

²⁶ Praise the God of heaven,
    God's love endures forever.

See RG
244

PSALM 137*

Sorrow and Hope in Exile

I

¹ By the rivers of Babylon
    we sat mourning and weeping
    when we remembered Zion.°

² On the poplars* of that land
    we hung up our harps.ᵖ

³ There our captors asked us
    for the words of a song;
Our tormentors, for a joyful song:
    "Sing for us a song of Zion!"

⁴ But how could we sing a song of the
    LORD
    in a foreign land?

II

⁵ If I forget you, Jerusalem,
    may my right hand wither.�q

⁶ May my tongue stick to my palate
    if I do not remember you,
If I do not exalt Jerusalem
    beyond all my delights.

III

⁷ Remember, LORD, against Edom
    that day at Jerusalem.
They said: "Level it, level it
    down to its foundations!"ʳ

⁸ Fair Babylon, you destroyer,
    happy those who pay you back
    the evil you have done us!ˢ

⁹ Happy those who seize your
    children
    and smash them against a rock.ᵗ*

PSALM 138*

Hymn of a Grateful Heart

See RG
245, 246

¹ Of David.

I

I thank you, LORD, with all my heart;ᵘ
    before the gods* to you I sing.

² I bow low toward your holy temple;
    I praise your name for your fidelity
    and love.

For you have exalted over all
    your name and your promise.

³ When I cried out, you answered;
    you strengthened my spirit.

II

⁴ All the kings of earth will praise you,
    LORD,
    when they hear the words of your
    mouth.

⁵ They will sing of the ways of the LORD:
    "How great is the glory of the LORD!"

⁶ The LORD is on high, but cares for the
    lowlyᵛ
    and knows the proud from afar.

⁷ Though I walk in the midst of dangers,
    you guard my life when my enemies
    rage.

You stretch out your hand;
    your right hand saves me.

⁸ The LORD is with me to the end.
    LORD, your love endures forever.
    Never forsake the work of your hands!

PSALM 139*

The All-knowing and
Ever-present God

See RG
250

¹ For the leader. A psalm of David.

I

LORD, you have probed me, you know me:

Ps 137: A temple singer refuses to sing the people's sacred songs in an alien land despite demands from Babylonian captors (1-4). The singer swears an oath by what is most dear to a musician—hands and tongue—to exalt Jerusalem always (5-6). The psalm ends with a prayer that the old enemies of Jerusalem, Edom and Babylon, be destroyed (7-9).

137, 2: Poplars: sometimes incorrectly translated "willow." The Euphrates poplar is a high tree common on riverbanks in the Orient.

137, 9: Happy those who seize your children and smash them against a rock: the infants represent the future generations, and so must be destroyed if the enemy is truly to be eradicated.

Ps 138: A thanksgiving to God, who came to the rescue of

the psalmist. Divine rescue was not the result of the psalmist's virtues but of God's loving fidelity (1-3). The act is not a private transaction but a public act that stirs the surrounding nations to praise God's greatness and care for the people (4-6). The psalmist, having experienced salvation, trusts that God will always be there in moments of danger (7-8).

138, 1: Before the gods: i.e., heavenly beings, who were completely subordinate to Israel's God. The earthly temple represents the heavenly palace of God.

Ps 139: A hymnic meditation on God's omnipresence and

---

o: Ez 3, 15; Lam 3, 48. p: Is 24, 8; Lam 5, 14. q: Jer 51, 50.
r: Jer 49, 7; Lam 4, 21-22; Ez 25, 12-14. s: Is 47, 1-3; Jer 50-51.
t: Hos 14, 1. u: Ps 9, 1. v: Lk 1, 51-52.

2 you know when I sit and stand;[w]*
   you understand my thoughts from afar.
3 My travels and my rest you mark;
   with all my ways you are familiar.
4 Even before a word is on my tongue,
   LORD, you know it all.
5 Behind and before you encircle me
   and rest your hand upon me.
6 Such knowledge is beyond me,
   far too lofty for me to reach.[x]

II

7 Where can I hide from your spirit?
   From your presence, where can I flee?
8 If I ascend to the heavens, you are there;
   if I lie down in Sheol, you are there
   too.[y]
9 If I fly with the wings of dawn*
   and alight beyond the sea,*
10 Even there your hand will guide me,
   your right hand hold me fast.
11 If I say, "Surely darkness shall hide me,
   and night shall be my light"—*
12 Darkness is not dark for you,
   and night shines as the day.
   Darkness and light are but one.[z]

III

13 You formed my inmost being;
   you knit me in my mother's womb.[a]
14 I praise you, so wonderfully you made
   me;
   wonderful are your works!
   My very self you knew;
15   my bones were not hidden from you,
   When I was being made in secret,
   fashioned as in the depths of the earth.*
16 Your eyes foresaw my actions;
   in your book all are written down;[b]

my days were shaped, before one
   came to be.

IV

17 How precious to me are your designs,
   O God;
   how vast the sum of them!
18 Were I to count, they would outnumber
   the sands;
   to finish, I would need eternity.[c]
19 If only you would destroy the wicked,
   O God,
   and the bloodthirsty would depart
   from me![d]
20 Deceitfully they invoke your name;
   your foes swear faithless oaths.
21 Do I not hate, LORD, those who hate you?
   Those who rise against you, do I not
   loathe?[e]
22 With fierce hatred I hate them,
   enemies I count as my own.

V

23 Probe me, God, know my heart;
   try me, know my concerns.[f]
24 See if my way is crooked,
   then lead me in the ancient paths.*

PSALM 140*

Prayer for Deliverance from the Wicked

1 For the leader. A psalm of David.

I

2 Deliver me, LORD, from the wicked;
   preserve me from the violent,[g]
3 From those who plan evil in their hearts,
   who stir up conflicts every day,
4 Who sharpen their tongues like serpents,
   venom of asps upon their lips.[h]* *Selah*

See RG 244

omniscience. The psalmist is keenly aware of God's all-knowing gaze (1-6), of God's presence in every part of the universe (7-12), and of God's control over the psalmist's very self (13-16). Summing up 1-16. 17-18 express wonder. There is only one place hostile to God's rule—wicked people. The psalmist prays to be removed from their company (19-24).

139, 2: When I sit and stand: in all my physical movement.
139, 9: Fly with the wings of dawn: go to the extremities of the east. **Beyond the sea:** uttermost bounds of the west; the sea is the Mediterranean.
139, 11: Night shall be my light: night to me is what day is to others.
139, 15: The depths of the earth: figurative language for the womb, stressing the hidden and mysterious operations that occur there.
139, 24: My way ... the ancient paths: the manner of liv-

ing of our ancestors, who were faithful to God's will. Cf Jer 6, 16.
Ps 140: A lament seeking rescue from violent and treacherous foes (2-6). The psalmist remains trusting (7-8), vigorously praying that the plans of the wicked recoil upon themselves (9-12). A serene statement of praise ends the psalm (13-14). The psalmist is content to be known as one of "the needy," "the poor," "the just," "the upright" (13-14), a class of people expecting divine protection.
140, 4: Similar metaphors for a wicked tongue are used in Pss 52, 4; 55, 22; 58, 5.

w: 2 Kgs 19, 27; Jb 12, 3. x: Ps 131, 1. y: Jb 23, 8-9; Jer 23, 23-24. z: Jb 12, 22. a: Wis 7, 1; Eccl 11, 5; Jb 1, 21. b: Mal 3, 16. c: Jb 11, 7. d: Jb 21, 14. e: Ps 119, 158. f: Pss 17, 3; 26, 2. g: Ps 71, 4. h: Ps 64, 4; Rom 3, 13.

II

⁵ Keep me, LORD, from the clutches of the
    wicked;
  preserve me from the violent,
  who plot to trip me up.ⁱ
⁶ The arrogant have set a trap for me;
  villains have spread a net,*
  laid snares for me by the
    wayside.   *Selah*
⁷ I say to the LORD: You are my God;ʲ
  listen, LORD, to the words of my prayer.
⁸ My revered LORD, my strong helper,
  my helmet on the day of battle.
⁹ LORD, do not grant the desires of the
    wicked;
  do not let their plots succeed.   *Selah*
¹⁰ Around me they raise their proud heads;
  may the mischief they threaten
    overwhelm them.
¹¹ May God rain burning coals upon them,ᵏ
  cast them into the grave never more to
    rise.

III

¹² Slanderers will not survive on earth;
  evil will quickly entrap the violent.
¹³ For I know the LORD will secure
  justice for the needy, their rights for
    the poor.
¹⁴ Then the just will give thanks to your
    name;
  the upright will dwell in your presence.ˡ

See RG
244

PSALM 141*

*Prayer for Deliverance from
the Wicked*

¹ A psalm of David.

LORD, I call to you;
  come quickly to help me;

listen to my plea when I call.
² Let my prayer be incense* before you;
  my uplifted hands* an evening
    sacrifice.ᵐ
³ Set a guard, LORD, before my mouth,
  a gatekeeper at my lips.ⁿ
⁴ Do not let my heart incline to evil,
  or yield to any sin.
  I will never feast upon
    the fine food of evildoers.
⁵ Let the just strike me; that is kindness;*
  let them rebuke me; that is oil for my
    head.ᵒ
  All this I shall not refuse,
    but will pray despite these trials.
⁶ When their leaders are cast over the cliff,
  all will learn that my prayers were
    heard.
⁷ As when a farmer plows a field into
    broken clods,
  so their bones will be strewn at the
    mouth of Sheol.
⁸ My eyes are upon you, O GOD, my Lord;ᵖ
  in you I take refuge; do not strip me of
    life.
⁹ Guard me from the trap they have set for
    me,
  from the snares of evildoers.�q
¹⁰ Into their own nets let all the wicked fall,
  while I make good my own escape.

PSALM 142*

A Prayer in Time of Trouble

See RG
244

¹ A *maskil* of David, when he was in the
    cave.* A prayer.

² With full voice I cry to the LORD;
  with full voice I beseech the LORD.
³ Before God I pour out my complaint,

140, 6: Have set a trap . . . have spread a net: the same
figure, of hunters setting traps, occurs in Pss 9, 16; 31, 5; 35,
7; 64, 6. Cf Mt 22, 15; Lk 11, 54.

Ps 141: A lament of an individual (1-2) who is keenly
aware that only the righteous can worship God properly and
who therefore prays to be protected from the doomed wicked
(3-10).

141, 2: Incense: literally, "smoke," i.e., the fragrant fumes
arising from the altar at the burning of sacrificial animals or
of aromatic spices; also used in Rv 5, 8 as a symbol of prayer.
My uplifted hands: the gesture of supplication. Cf Pss 28, 2;
63, 5; 88, 10; 119, 48; 134, 2; 143, 6.

141, 5-7: The Hebrew text is obscure.

Ps 142: In this lament imploring God for help (2-4b), the
psalmist tells how enemies have set a trap (4c-5), and prays
for rescue (6-8). The speaker feels utterly alone (5), exhausted (7), and may even be imprisoned (8a). Prison is possibly a metaphor for general distress. The last two verses are
the vow of praise, made after receiving an assurance of divine
help (8cd).

142, 1: In the cave: cf 1 Sm 22, 1; 24, 1-3; Ps 57, 1.

---

i: Jer 18, 22; Pss 56, 7; 57, 7. *j:* Ps 31, 15. *k:* Pss 11, 6; 120, 4;
Gn 19, 24. *l:* Pss 11, 7; 16, 11; 17, 15. *m:* Ps 134, 2; Ex 30, 8.
n: Sir 22, 27. *o:* Prv 9, 8; 25, 12. *p:* Pss 25, 15; 123, 1-2.
q: Ps 142, 4.

lay bare my distress.
4 My spirit is faint within me,*r*
but you know my path.*s*
Along the way I walk
they have hidden a trap for me.*t*
5 I look to my right hand,*u*
but no friend is there.
There is no escape for me;
no one cares for me.
6 I cry out to you, LORD,
I say, You are my refuge,*v*
my portion in the land of the living.*w*
7 Listen to my cry for help,
for I am brought very low.*x*
Rescue me from my pursuers,
for they are too strong for me.
8 Lead me out of my prison,
that I may give thanks to your name.
Then the just shall gather around me*
because you have been good to me.

See RG 244

PSALM 143*

A Prayer in Distress
1 A psalm of David.

LORD, hear my prayer;
in your faithfulness listen to my
pleading;
answer me in your justice.
2 Do not enter into judgment with your
servant;
before you no living being can be just.*y*
3 The enemy has pursued me;
they have crushed* my life to the
ground.*z*
They have left me in darkness
like those long dead.*a*

4 My spirit is faint within me;
my heart is dismayed.*b*
5 I remember the days of old;
I ponder all your deeds;
the works of your hands I recall.*c*
6 I stretch out my hands to you;
I thirst for you like a parched
land.*d*   *Selah*
7 Hasten to answer me, LORD;
for my spirit fails me.
Do not hide your face from me,
lest I become like those descending to
the pit.*e*
8 At dawn let me hear of your kindness,
for in you I trust.
Show me the path I should walk,
for to you I entrust my life.*f*
9 Rescue me, LORD, from my foes,
for in you I hope.
10 Teach me to do your will,
for you are my God.
May your kind spirit guide me
on ground that is level.
11 For your name's sake, LORD, give me life;
in your justice lead me out of distress.
12 In your kindness put an end to my foes;
destroy all who attack me,
for I am your servant.*g*

PSALM 144*

A Prayer for Victory
and Prosperity
1 Of David.

See RG 245, 250

I

Blessed be the LORD, my rock,*
who trains my hands for battle,
my fingers for war;

142, 8: Then the just shall gather around me: in the temple, when the psalmist offers a thanksgiving sacrifice.

Ps 143: One of the Church's seven Penitential Psalms, this lament is a prayer to be freed from death-dealing enemies. The psalmist addresses God, aware that there is no equality between God and humans; salvation is a gift (1-2). Victimized by evil people (3-4), the psalmist recites ("remembers") God's past actions on behalf of the innocent (5-6). The psalm continues with fervent prayer (7-9) and a strong desire for guidance and protection (10-12).

143, 3: They have crushed: literally, "he crushed"; the singular is used typically, hence the plural translation.

Ps 144: The psalm may reflect a ceremony in which the king, as leader of the army, asked God's help (1-8). In 9 the poem shifts abruptly from pleading to thanksgiving, and (except for 11) shifts again to prayer for the people. The first sec-

tion (1-2) is a prayer of thanks for victory; the second (3-7a), a humble acknowledgment of human nothingness and a supplication that God show forth saving power; the third (9-11), a promise of future thanksgiving; the fourth (12-15), a wish for prosperity and peace. A prayer for deliverance from treacherous foes serves as a refrain after the second and third sections (7b-8. 11). Except for its final section, the psalm is made up almost entirely of verses from other psalms.

144, 1-2: Composed of phrases from Ps 18, 3. 35. 47-48.

r: Ps 143, 4.   *s*: Ps 139, 24.   *t*: Ps 141, 9.   *u*: Pss 16, 8; 73, 23; 121, 5.   *v*: Ps 91, 2. 9.   *w*: Pss 16, 5; 27, 13; 116, 9; Is 38, 11. *x*: Ps 79, 8.   *y*: Ecc 7, 20; Jb 4, 17; Rom 3, 20.   *z*: Ps 7, 6. *a*: Lam 3, 6.   *b*: Ps 142, 4; Jb 17, 1.   *c*: Ps 77, 6. 12.   *d*: Pss 42, 2; 63, 2.   *e*: Pss 28, 1; 30, 4; 88, 5; Prv 1, 12.   *f*: Pss 25, 4; 27, 11; 86, 11; 119, 12. 35.   *g*: Ps 116, 16.

2 My safeguard and my fortress,
  my stronghold, my deliverer,
My shield, in whom I trust,
  who subdues peoples under me.

II

3 LORD, what are mortals that you notice
    them;
  human beings, that you take thought of
    them?[h]*
4 They are but a breath;
  their days are like a passing shadow.[i]*
5 LORD, incline your heavens and come;*
  touch the mountains and make them
    smoke.[j]
6 Flash forth lightning and scatter my foes;
  shoot your arrows and rout them.
7 Reach out your hand from on high;
  deliver me from the many waters;
  rescue me from the hands of foreign
    foes.
8 Their mouths speak untruth;
  their right hands are raised in lying
    oaths.*
9 O God, a new song I will sing to you;
  on a ten-stringed lyre I will play for
    you.[k]
10 You give victory to kings;
  you delivered David your servant.[l]
  From the menacing sword 11 deliver me;
  rescue me from the hands of foreign
    foes.
  Their mouths speak untruth;
  their right hands are raised in lying
    oaths.

III

12 May our sons be like plants[m]
  well nurtured from their youth,
Our daughters, like carved columns,
  shapely as those of the temple.
13 May our barns be full
  with every kind of store.

May our sheep increase by thousands,
  by tens of thousands in our fields;
  may our oxen be well fattened.
14 May there be no breach in the walls,
  no exile, no outcry in our streets.[n]
15 Happy the people so blessed;
  happy the people whose God is the
    LORD.[o]

PSALM 145*

*The Greatness and Goodness
of God*

1 Praise. Of David.

See RG
244, 246

I will extol you, my God and king;
  I will bless your name forever.
2 Every day I will bless you;
  I will praise your name forever.[p]
3 Great is the LORD and worthy of high
    praise;[q]
  God's grandeur is beyond
    understanding.
4 One generation praises your deeds to the
    next
  and proclaims your mighty works.[r]
5 They speak of the splendor of your
    majestic glory,
  tell of your wonderful deeds.[s]
6 They speak of your fearsome power
  and attest to your great deeds.[t]
7 They publish the renown of your
    abounding goodness
  and joyfully sing of your justice.
8 The LORD is gracious and merciful,
  slow to anger and abounding in love.[u]
9 The LORD is good to all,
  compassionate to every creature.[v]
10 All your works give you thanks, O LORD
  and your faithful bless you.[w]
11 They speak of the glory of your reign
  and tell of your great works,

144, 3: Similar to Ps 8, 5.

144, 4: Composed of phrases from Pss 39, 6; 102, 12.

144, 5-7: Adapted in large part from Pss 18, 10. 15. 17;
104, 32.

**144, 8b. 11b: Their right hands are raised in lying
oaths:** the psalmist's enemies give false testimony.

Ps 145: A hymn in acrostic form; every verse begins with
a successive letter of the Hebrew alphabet. Acrostic poems
usually do not develop ideas but consist rather of loosely connected statements. The singer invites all to praise God (1-3.
21). The "works of God" make God present and invite human

praise (4-7); they climax in a confession (8-9). God's mighty
acts show forth divine kingship (10-20), a major theme in the
literature of early Judaism and in Christianity.

---

h: Jb 7, 17.   i: Pss 62, 10; 90, 9-10; Jb 7, 16; Eccl 6, 12; Wis 2, 5.
j: Is 63, 19.   k: Ps 33, 2-3.   l: Ps 18, 51.   m: Ps 128, 3.   n: Is
65, 19.   o: Ps 33, 12.   p: Ps 34, 2.   q: Pss 48, 2; 95, 3; 96, 4; Jb
36, 26.   r: Pss 22, 31-32; 48, 14-15; 71, 18; 78, 4; Ex 10, 2; Dt 4,
9.   s: Pss 96, 3; 105, 2.   t: Ps 66, 3.   u: Pss 86, 5. 15; 103, 8; Ex
34, 6; Sir 2, 11.   v: Ps 103, 13; Wis 11, 24.   w: Dn 3, 57.

¹² Making known to all your power,
 the glorious splendor of your rule.
¹³ Your reign is a reign for all ages,
 your dominion for all generations.ˣ
The LORD is trustworthy in every word,
 and faithful in every work.
¹⁴ The LORD supports all who are falling
 and raises up all who are bowed down.ʸ
¹⁵ The eyes of all look hopefully to you;
 you give them their food in due season.ᶻ
¹⁶ You open wide your hand
 and satisfy the desire of every living
 thing.
¹⁷ You, LORD, are just in all your ways,
 faithful in all your works.ᵃ
¹⁸ You, LORD, are near to all who call upon
 you,
 to all who call upon you in truth.ᵇ
¹⁹ You satisfy the desire of those who fear
 you;
 you hear their cry and save them.ᶜ
²⁰ You, LORD, watch over all who love you,
 but all the wicked you destroy.ᵈ
²¹ My mouth will speak your praises, LORD;
 all flesh will bless your holy name
 forever.ᵉ

See RG 244

PSALM 146*

Trust in God the Creator and Redeemer

¹ Hallelujah!

² Praise the LORD, my soul;
 I shall praise the LORD all my life,
 sing praise to my God while I live.ᶠ

I

³ Put no trust in princes,
 in mere mortals powerless to save.ᵍ
⁴ When they breathe their last, they return
 to the earth;

that day all their planning comes to
 nothing.ʰ

II

⁵ Happy those whose help is Jacob's God,
 whose hope is in the LORD, their God,
⁶ The maker of heaven and earth,
 the seas and all that is in them,ⁱ
Who keeps faith forever,
⁷ secures justice for the oppressed,ʲ
 gives food to the hungry.
The LORD sets prisoners free;ᵏ
⁸ the LORD gives sight to the blind.
The LORD raises up those who are bowed
 down;ˡ
 the LORD loves the righteous.
⁹ The LORD protects the stranger,
 sustains the orphan and the widow,ᵐ
 but thwarts the way of the wicked.
¹⁰ The LORD shall reign forever,
 your God, Zion, through all
 generations!ⁿ
Hallelujah!

PSALM 147*
See RG 244, 250

God's Word Restores Jerusalem

¹ Hallelujah!

I

How good to celebrate our God in song;
 how sweet to give fitting praise.ᵒ
² The LORD rebuilds Jerusalem,
 gathers the dispersed of Israel,ᵖ
³ Heals the brokenhearted,
 binds up their wounds,�q
⁴ Numbers all the stars,
 calls each of them by name.ʳ
⁵ Great is our Lord, vast in power,
 with wisdom beyond measure.ˢ
⁶ The LORD sustains the poor,
 but casts the wicked to the ground.ᵗ

Ps 146: A hymn of someone who has learned there is no other source of strength except the merciful God. Only God, not mortal humans (3-4), can help vulnerable and oppressed people (5-9). The first of the five hymns that conclude the Psalter.

Ps 147: The hymn is divided into three sections by the calls to praise in 1, 7 and 12. The first section praises the powerful creator who restores exiled Judah (1-6); the second section, the creator who provides food to animals and humans; the third and climactic section exhorts the holy city to recognize it has been re-created and made the place of disclosure for God's word, a word as life-giving as water.

x: Pss 10, 16; 102, 13; 146, 10; Lam 5, 19; Dn 3, 100; Rv 11, 15. *y:* Pss 94, 18; 146, 8. *z:* Pss 136, 25; 104, 27-28; Mt 6, 25-26. *a:* Dt 32, 4. *b:* Dt 4, 7; Is 55, 6; 58, 9. *c:* Ps 34, 18. *d:* Jgs 5, 31. *e:* Sir 40, 35. *f:* Pss 103, 1; 104, 33. *g:* Ps 118, 8-9. *h:* Pss 90, 3; 104, 29; 1 Mc 2, 63; Jb 34, 14-15; Eccl 3, 20; 12, 7; Sir 40, 11; Is 2, 22. *i:* Ex 20, 11; Pss 121, 2; 124, 8; Acts 14, 15; Rv 14, 7. *j:* Ps 103, 6. *k:* Ps 68, 7; Is 49, 9; 61, 1. *l:* Ps 145, 14. *m:* Ps 68, 6; Dt 10, 18. *n:* Ps 145, 13; Lam 5, 19. *o:* Pss 33, 1; 92, 2. *p:* Is 11, 12; 56, 8; Jer 31, 10. *q:* Jb 5, 18; Is 30, 26; 61, 1; Jer 33, 6. *r:* Is 40, 26. *s:* Jdt 16, 13; Jer 51, 15. *t:* Ps 146, 9; 1 Sm 2, 7-8.

II

7 Sing to the LORD with thanksgiving;
with the lyre celebrate our God,[u]

8 Who covers the heavens with clouds,*
provides rain for the earth,
makes grass sprout on the
mountains,[v]

9 Who gives animals their food
and ravens what they cry for.[w]

10 God takes no delight in the strength of
horses,*
no pleasure in the runner's stride.[x]

11 Rather the LORD takes pleasure in the
devout,
those who await his faithful care.

III

12 Glorify the LORD, Jerusalem;
Zion, offer praise to your God,

13 Who has strengthened the bars of your
gates,
blessed your children within you,[y]

14 Brought peace to your borders,
and filled you with finest wheat.[z]

15 The LORD sends a command to earth;*
his word runs swiftly![a]

16 Thus snow is spread like wool,
frost is scattered like ash,[b]

17 Hail is dispersed like crumbs;
before such cold the waters freeze.

18 Again he sends his word and they melt;
the wind is unleashed and the waters
flow.

19 The LORD also proclaims his word to
Jacob,
decrees and laws to Israel.[c]

20 God has not done this for other
nations;
of such laws they know nothing.
Hallelujah!

PSALM 148*

All Creation Summoned
to Praise

See RG 244, 250

1 Hallelujah!

I

Praise the LORD from the heavens;
give praise in the heights.

2 Praise him, all you angels;
give praise, all you hosts.[d]

3 Praise him, sun and moon;
give praise, all shining stars.

4 Praise him, highest heavens,*
you waters above the heavens.

5 Let them all praise the LORD's name;
for the LORD commanded and they
were created,[e]

6 Assigned them duties forever,
gave them tasks that will never
change.

II

7 Praise the LORD from the earth,
you sea monsters and all deep
waters;[f]

8 You lightning and hail, snow and clouds,
storm winds that fulfill his command;

9 You mountains and all hills,
fruit trees and all cedars;[g]

10 You animals wild and tame,
you creatures that crawl and fly;[h]

11 You kings of the earth and all peoples,
princes and all who govern on earth;

12 Young men and women too,
old and young alike.

13 Let them all praise the LORD's name,
for his name alone is exalted,
majestic above earth and heaven.[i]

14 The LORD has lifted high the horn of his
people,*

147, 8-9: God clothes the fields and feeds the birds. Cf Mt 6, 26. 30.

147, 10-11: Acknowledging one's dependence upon God rather than claiming self-sufficiency pleases God. Cf Pss 20, 8; 33, 16-19.

147, 15-19: God speaks through the thunder of nature and the word of revealed law. Cf Is 55, 10-11. The weather phenomena are well known in Jerusalem: a blizzard of snow and hail followed by a thunderstorm that melts the ice.

Ps 148: A hymn inviting the beings of heaven (1-6) and of earth (7-14) to praise God. The hymn does not distinguish between inanimate and animate (and rational) nature.

148, 4: Highest heavens: literally, "the heavens of the heavens," i.e., the space above the firmament, where the "up-

per waters" are stored. Cf Gn 1, 6-7; Dt 10, 14; 1 Kgs 8, 27; Ps 104, 3. 13.

148, 14: The LORD has lifted high the horn of his people: horn = strength, the concrete noun for the abstract. Of all peoples God has chosen Israel to return praise and thanks in a special way.

---

u: Ps 71, 22.   v: Ps 104, 13f; Jb 5, 10; Jer 14, 22; Jl 2, 23.   w: Jb 38, 41; Mt 6, 26.   x: Pss 20, 8; 33, 16-18.   y: Ps 48, 14.   z: Ps 81, 17.   a: Ps 33, 9.   b: Jb 6, 16; 37, 10; 38, 22.   c: Ps 78, 5; Bar 3, 37; Dt 4, 7-8.   d: Dn 3, 58-63; Ps 103, 20f.   e: Ps 33, 9; Gn 1, 3f; Jdt 16, 14.   f: Gn 1, 21; Ps 135, 6.   g: Is 44, 23.   h: Gn 1, 21. 24f; Ps 30, 5. Dt 4, 7.   i: Ps 30, 5; Dt 4, 7.

to the glory of all the faithful,
of Israel, the people near to their God.
Hallelujah!

See RG
244

PSALM 149*

*Praise God with Song
and Sword*

1 Hallelujah!

Sing to the LORD a new song,
a hymn in the assembly of the faithful.*j*
2 Let Israel be glad in their maker,
the people of Zion rejoice in their king.
3 Let them praise his name in festive dance,
make music with tambourine and lyre.*k**
4 For the LORD takes delight in his people,
honors the poor with victory.
5 Let the faithful rejoice in their glory,
cry out for joy at their banquet,*
6 With the praise of God in their mouths,
and a two-edged sword in their hands,*l*
7 To bring retribution on the nations,
punishment on the peoples,*m*
8 To bind their kings with chains,

shackle their nobles with irons,
9 To execute the judgments decreed for
them—
such is the glory* of all God's faithful.
Hallelujah!

See RG
244

PSALM 150*

Final Doxology

1 Hallelujah!

Praise God in his holy sanctuary;*n**
give praise in the mighty dome of
heaven.*
2 Give praise for his mighty deeds,*o*
praise him for his great majesty.
3 Give praise with blasts upon the horn,*p*
praise him with harp and lyre.
4 Give praise with tambourines and dance,
praise him with flutes and strings.*q*
5 Give praise with crashing cymbals,
praise him with sounding cymbals.
6 Let everything that has breath
give praise to the LORD!*r*
Hallelujah!

Ps 149: A hymn inviting the people of Israel to celebrate their God in song and festive dance (1-3. 5) because God has chosen them and given them victory (4). The exodus and conquest are the defining acts of Israel; the people must be ready to do again those acts in the future at the divine command (6-9).

149, 3: Make music with tambourine and lyre: the verse recalls the great exodus hymn of Ex 15, 20.

149, 5: At their banquet: literally, "upon their couches." The people reclined to banquet.

149, 9: The glory: what brings honor to the people is their readiness to carry out the divine will, here conceived as punishing injustice done by the nations.

Ps 150: The psalm is a closing doxology both for the fifth book of the Psalms (107—149) and for the Psalter as a whole.

Temple musicians and dancers are called to lead all beings on earth and in heaven in praise of God. The psalm proclaims to whom praise shall be given, and where (1); what praise shall be given, and why (2); how praise shall be given (3-5), and by whom (6).

150, 1: His holy sanctuary: God's temple on earth. **The mighty dome of heaven:** literally, "[God's] strong vault"; heaven is here imagined as a giant plate separating the inhabited world from the waters of the heavens.

j: Pss 22, 23; 26, 12; 35, 18; 40, 10; Jdt 16, 1. *k:* Pss 68, 26; 81, 2-3; 87, 7; 150, 3-4. *l:* Neh 4, 10-12; 2 Mc 15, 27. *m:* Wis 3, 8. *n:* Dn 3, 53. *o:* Dt 3, 24. *p:* 3ff: Pss 81, 3-4; 149, 3; 2 Sm 6, 5; 1 Chr 13, 8; 16, 5. 42; 2 Chr 5, 12-13; 7, 6. *q:* Ps 68, 26; Ex 15, 20. *r:* Rv 5, 13.

See RG
254, 262

The Book of Proverbs

The first word of this book, *MISHLE*, has provided the title by which it is generally designated in Jewish and Christian circles. The name "Proverbs," while not an exact equivalent of *MISHLE*, describes the main contents satisfactorily, even though it is hardly an adequate designation for such parts as 1, 1—9, 18 or 31, 10-31. Among some early Christian writers the book was also known by the name of "Wisdom," and in the Roman Missal it was referred to as a "Book of Wisdom."

The Book of Proverbs is an anthology of didactic poetry forming part of the sapiential literature of the Old Testament. Its primary purpose, indicated in the first sentence (1, 2f), is to teach wisdom. It is thus directed particularly to the young and inexperienced (1, 4); but also to those who desire advanced training in wisdom (1, 5). The wisdom which the book teaches covers a wide field of human and divine activity, ranging from matters purely secular to most lofty moral and religious truths, such as God's omniscience (5, 21; 15, 3-11), power (19, 21; 21, 30), providence (20, 1-24), goodness (15, 29), and the joy and strength resulting from abandonment to him (3, 5; 16, 20; 18, 10). The teaching of the entire book is placed on a firm religious foundation by the principle that "the fear of the LORD is the beginning of knowledge" (1, 7; cf 9, 10).

To Solomon are explicitly ascribed parts II and V of the book; he is the patron of Hebrew wisdom. Of Agur (part VI) and Lemuel (part VIII), nothing further is known. Parts III and IV are attributed to "the wise." The remaining parts are anonymous.

The manner of compilation is conjectural. Parts II and V may have circulated first as independent collections, compiled before the fall of Jerusalem, as the references to Solomon (10, 1) and Hezekiah (25, 1) suggest. Parts III, IV and VII would seem to belong together as a third collection of a similar kind. The author of the first nine chapters, a religious sage familiar with the earlier sacred books, was the editor of the whole as we have it, probably in the early part of the fifth century B.C.

Christ and the Apostles often expressly quoted the Proverbs (Jn 7, 38; Rom 12, 20; Jas 4, 6) or repeated their teaching; compare Lk 10, 14, and Prv 25, 7; 1 Pe 4, 8; Jas 5, 20 and Prv 10, 12. The book has an important place in the Latin and Greek liturgies.

On the basis of titles, subject matter, and poetic structure the Book of Proverbs may be divided as follows:

I: Introduction: The Value of Wisdom (1, 1—9, 18).

II: First Collection of the Proverbs of Solomon (10, 1—22, 16).

III: Sayings of the Wise (22, 17—24, 22).

IV: Other Sayings of the Wise (24, 23-34).

V: Second Collection of the Proverbs of Solomon (25, 1—29, 27).

VI: The Words of Agur (30, 1-6).

VII: Numerical Proverbs (30, 7-33).

VIII: The Words of Lemuel (31, 1-9).

IX: The Ideal Wife (31, 10-31).

I: Introduction: The Value of Wisdom

CHAPTER 1

See RG 254-61

Purpose of the Proverbs of Solomon*

¹ The proverbs of Solomon,ᵃ the son of David,
   king of Israel:

² That men may appreciate wisdom and discipline,*
   may understand words of intelligence;

³ May receive training in wise conduct,
   in what is right, just and honest;

⁴ That resourcefulness may be imparted to the simple,*
   to the young man knowledge and discretion.

⁵ A wise man by hearing them will advance in learning,
   an intelligent man will gain sound guidance,

⁶ That he may comprehend proverb and parable,
   the words of the wise and their riddles.

⁷ The fear of the LORD* is the beginning of knowledge;ᵇ
   wisdom and instruction fools despise.

The Path of the Wicked: Greed and Violence*

⁸ Hear, my son, your father's instruction,
   and reject not your mother's teaching;

⁹ A graceful diadem will they be for your head;

1, 1-6: This prologue explains the purpose of the book: to educate the inexperienced in knowledge and right conduct, and to increase the learning of the wise man by proverbs, parables and riddles.

1, 2: Discipline: education or formation which dispels ignorance and corrects vice.

1, 4: Simple: immature and inexperienced, hence easily influenced for good or evil.

1, 7: Fear of the LORD: reverential fear and respect for God on account of his sovereignty, goodness and justice to-

ward men. This is the foundation of religion.

1, 8-19: A warning against association with the greedy and the violent who seek to destroy the honest man and to steal his possessions (11-14). The trap which the wicked set for the innocent (11), in the end (19) takes away the life of the wicked themselves.

 a: Prv 10, 1; 25, 1; 1 Kgs 4, 32.   b: Prv 9, 10; Jb 28, 28; Ps 111, 10; Sir 1, 16.

a torque for your neck.

[10] My son, should sinners entice you, [11] and say,

"Come along with us!

Let us lie in wait for the honest man,

let us, unprovoked, set a trap for the innocent;

[12] Let us swallow them up, as the nether world does, alive,

in the prime of life, like those who go down to the pit!

[13] All kinds of precious wealth shall we gain,

we shall fill our houses with booty;

[14] Cast in your lot with us,

we shall all have one purse!"—

[15] My son, walk not in the way with them,

hold back your foot from their path!

[16] [For their feet run to evil,

they hasten to shed blood.[c]]

[17] It is in vain that a net is spread*

before the eyes of any bird—

[18] These men lie in wait for their own blood,

they set a trap for their own lives.

[19] This is the fate of everyone greedy of loot:

unlawful gain takes away the life of him who acquires it.

Wisdom in Person Gives Warning*

[20] Wisdom cries aloud in the street,

in the open squares she raises her voice;[d]

[21] Down the crowded ways she calls out,

at the city gates she utters her words:

[22] "How long, you simple ones, will you love inanity,

[23] how long will you turn away at my reproof?

Lo! I will pour out to you my spirit,

I will acquaint you with my words.

[24] "Because I called and you refused,

I extended my hand and no one took notice;[e]

[25] Because you disdained all my counsel,

and my reproof you ignored—

[26] I, in my turn, will laugh at your doom;

I will mock when terror overtakes you;

[27] When terror comes upon you like a storm,

and your doom approaches like a whirlwind;

when distress and anguish befall you.

[28] "Then they call me, but I answer not;

they seek me, but find me not;*

[29] Because they hated knowledge,

and chose not the fear of the LORD;

[30] They ignored my counsel,

they spurned all my reproof;

And in their arrogance they preferred arrogance,

and like fools they hated knowledge:

[31] "Now they must eat the fruit of their own way,

and with their own devices be glutted.*

[32] For the self-will of the simple kills them,

the smugness of fools destroys them.

[33] But he who obeys me dwells in security,

in peace, without fear of harm."[f]

CHAPTER 2*

The Blessings of Wisdom*

See RG
254–62

[1] My son, if you receive my words

and treasure my commands,

1, 17: Instructed by the wise man, the youth (of v 4) will recognize the invitation of the wicked (11-14) as a net spread before him, and he will thus, like the bird, be protected against falling into it.

1, 20-33: Wisdom is here personified: with divine authority she sets forth and proclaims the moral order, instructing and threatening (24-33) the multitudes in the streets and places of assembly.

1, 28: Overtaken by doom, the foolish seek wisdom, but in vain because they do so too late. Cf Jn 7, 34; 8, 21.

1, 31: Sinners are punished by the bad fruits which their sins produce. Cf Wis 11, 16.

2—7: These chapters form an ordered discourse in seven "columns" of twenty-two verses each. Chapter 2 introduces

the four topics about which the sage instructs his pupil: the service of God (3, 1-12. 25-34), the search for wisdom (3, 13-24. 35; 4, 1-9), the avoidance of evil companions among men (4, 10-27; 5, 21-23), and among women (5, 1-20; 6, 20—7, 27). The last topic is treated at a length equal to the first three because the discourse is meant especially for youths (cf Prv 1, 4).

2, 1-22: The search for wisdom (1-4) leads to the protection of God (5-8) and of wisdom herself (9ff; cf Prv 1, 20-33) and to deliverance from evil men (12-15) and evil women (16-19), and so to lasting happiness (20ff).

c: Is 59, 7.   d: Prv 8, 1-3; 9, 3.   e: Is 65, 2. 12; 66, 4; Jer 7, 13.
f: Prv 8, 33f.

2 Turning your ear to wisdom,*
   inclining your heart to understanding;
3 Yes, if you call to intelligence,
   and to understanding raise your voice;
4 If you seek her like silver,
   and like hidden treasures search her
      out:

5 Then will you understand the fear of the
      LORD;
   the knowledge of God you will find;
6 For the LORD gives wisdom,
   from his mouth come knowledge and
      understanding;^g
7 He has counsel in store for the upright,
   he is the shield of those who walk
      honestly,
8 Guarding the paths of justice,
   protecting the way of his pious ones.

9 Then you will understand rectitude and
      justice,
   honesty, every good path;
10 For wisdom will enter your heart,
   knowledge will please your soul,
11 Discretion will watch over you,
   understanding will guard you;

12 Saving you from the way of evil men,
   from men of perverse speech,
13 Who leave the straight paths
   to walk in ways of darkness,
14 Who delight in doing evil,
   rejoice in perversity;
15 Whose ways are crooked,
   and devious their paths;

16 Saving you from the wife of another,
   from the adulteress with her smooth
      words,^h
17 Who forsakes the companion of her youth
   and forgets the pact with her God;
18 For her path sinks down to death,
   and her footsteps lead to the shades;ⁱ

19 None who enter thereon come back
      again,
   or gain the paths of life.

20 Thus you may walk in the way of good
      men,
   and keep to the paths of the just.
21 For the upright will dwell in the land,^j
   the honest will remain in it;
22 But the wicked will be cut off from the
      land,
   the faithless will be rooted out of it.

CHAPTER 3

*Attitude toward the Lord**

See RG
254–62

1 My son, forget not my teaching,
   keep in mind my commands;
2 For many days, and years of life,^k
   and peace, will they bring you.

3 Let not kindness and fidelity leave you;
   bind them around your neck;
4 Then will you win favor and good
      esteem
   before God and man.

5 Trust in the LORD with all your heart,
   on your own intelligence rely not;
6 In all your ways be mindful of him,
   and he will make straight your paths.

7 Be not wise in your own eyes,^l
   fear the LORD and turn away from evil;
8 This will mean health for your flesh
   and vigor for your bones.

9 Honor the LORD with your wealth,
   with first fruits of all your produce;^m
10 Then will your barns be filled with grain,
   with new wine your vats will
      overflow.
11 The discipline of the LORD, my son,
   disdain not;ⁿ
   spurn not his reproof;

2, 2f: Wisdom, understanding, intelligence: various names or aspects of the same gift.
3, 1-12: Many are the rewards for fidelity and trust in God, and for diffidence of self (1-8). Cf Dt 30, 20; Is 38, 19. The offering of material things for divine worship is blessed by an increase of such goods (9f). Even correction and chastisement
are a mark of God's love and favor (11f).

---

g: Jb 32, 8; Wis 7, 25; Sir 1, 1; Jas 1, 5.   h: Prv 5, 3. 20; 6, 24; 7, 5; 22, 14.   i: Prv 5, 5f; 7, 27.   j: 21f: Prv 10, 7, 30; Jb 18, 17; Pss
21, 9-13; 37, 22. 28.   k: Prv 4, 10; 9, 11; 10, 27.   l: Rom 11, 25; 12, 16.   m: Ex 34, 26; Lv 27, 30; Dt 26, 2; Sir 7, 31; 35, 7.   n: Heb
12, 5f.

[12] For whom the LORD loves he reproves,
and he chastises the son he favors.*o*

The Value of Wisdom*

[13] Happy the man who finds wisdom,
the man who gains understanding!*p*
[14] For her profit is better than profit in
silver,
and better than gold is her revenue;
[15] She is more precious than corals,*
and none of your choice possessions
can compare with her.*q*

[16] Long life is in her right hand,
in her left are riches and honor;
[17] Her ways are pleasant ways,
and all her paths are peace;
[18] She is a tree of life* to those who grasp
her,*r*
and he is happy who holds her fast.

[19] The LORD by wisdom founded the earth,
established the heavens by
understanding;
[20] By his knowledge the depths break open,
and the clouds drop down dew.*
[21] My son, let not these slip out of your
sight:
keep advice and counsel in view;
[22] So will they be life to your soul,
and an adornment for your neck.
[23] Then you may securely go your way;
your foot will never stumble;
[24] When you lie down, you need not be
afraid,
when you rest, your sleep will be
sweet.
[35] Honor is the possession of wise men,
but fools inherit shame.

Attitude toward Fellow Men*

[25] Be not afraid of sudden terror,
of the ruin of the wicked* when it
comes;
[26] For the LORD will be your confidence,
and will keep your foot from the
snare.

[27] Refuse no one the good on which he has
a claim
when it is in your power to do it for him.
[28] Say not to your neighbor, "Go, and come
again,
tomorrow I will give," when you can
give at once.
[29] Plot no evil against your neighbor,
against him who lives at peace with
you.
[30] Quarrel not with a man without cause,
with one who has done you no harm.
[31] Envy not the lawless man
and choose none of his ways:*s*
[32] To the LORD the perverse man is an
abomination,
but with the upright is his friendship.

[33] The curse of the LORD is on the house of
the wicked,
but the dwelling of the just he blesses;
[34] When he is dealing with the arrogant, he
is stern,*t*
but to the humble he shows kindness.

CHAPTER 4

Wisdom: the Supreme
Guide of Men*

See RG
254–62

[1] Hear, O children, a father's instruction,
be attentive, that you may gain
understanding!

3, 13-24: Wisdom, or understanding, is more valuable than silver and gold. Its fruit is long life, riches, honor and happiness (13-18). Even the creation of the universe and its adornment (Gn 1) were not done without wisdom (19f). It is the life of the soul and gives security in work and in repose (21-24).

3, 15: Corals: some precious stone may be intended.

3, 18: A tree of life: cf Prv 11, 30; 13, 12; Gn 2, 9.

3, 20: For the Hebrews, the depths enclosed the great subterranean ocean; the rain and dew descended from the celestial ocean above the firmament; cf Gn 1, 6-10; Jb 26, 8. 12; Pss 18, 16; 24, 2.

3, 25-34: Serving God with confidence in him (25f) re-

quires serving one's neighbor through kindness (27f), peace with the good (29ff), no envy of the wicked (31), because the Lord's friendship and kindness are with the just; his curse is with the wicked.

3, 25: The ruin of the wicked: i.e., the ruin that comes upon the wicked.

4, 1-9: The sage speaks as a father admonishing his children to secure wisdom at any cost.

---

o: Jdt 8, 27; Rv 3, 19.   *p:* Prv 8, 34f.   *q:* Prv 8, 11. 19; Wis 7, 8-11.   *r:* Prv 4, 13; 8, 35; 11, 30; Gn 2, 9; 3, 22.   *s:* Prv 23, 17; 24, 1. 19; Ps 37, 1.   *t:* Prv 1, 26.

2 Yes, excellent advice I give you;
   my teaching do not forsake.
3 When I was my father's child,
   frail, yet the darling of my mother,
4 He taught me, and said to me:
   "Let your heart hold fast my words:*u*
   keep my commands, that you may
      live!

5 "Get wisdom, get understanding!
   Do not forget or turn aside from the
      words I utter.
6 Forsake her not, and she will preserve
      you;
   love her, and she will safeguard you;
7 The beginning of wisdom is: get wisdom;
   at the cost of all you have, get
      understanding.
8 Extol her, and she will exalt you;
   she will bring you honors if you
      embrace her;
9 She will put on your head a graceful
      diadem;
   a glorious crown will she bestow on
      you."

*The Good and the Evil Way**

10 Hear, my son, and receive my words,
   and the years of your life shall be
      many.*v*
11 On the way of wisdom I direct you,
   I lead you on straightforward paths.
12 When you walk, your step will not be
      impeded,
   and should you run, you will not
      stumble.
13 Hold fast to instruction, never let her go;
   keep her, for she is your life.

14 The path of the wicked enter not,
   walk not on the way of evil men;
15 Shun it, cross it not,
   turn aside from it, and pass on.

16 For they cannot rest unless they have
      done evil;
   to have made no one stumble steals
      away their sleep.
17 For they eat the bread of wickedness
   and drink the wine of violence.
19 The way of the wicked is like darkness;
   they know not on what they stumble.
18 But the path of the just is like shining
      light,
   that grows in brilliance till perfect
      day.*

20 My son, to my words be attentive,
   to my sayings incline your ear;
21 Let them not slip out of your sight,
   keep them within your heart;
22 For they are life to those who find them,*w*
   to man's whole being they are health.

23 With closest custody, guard your heart,
   for in it are the sources of life.
24 Put away from you dishonest talk,
   deceitful speech put far from you.
25 Let your eyes look straight ahead
   and your glance be directly forward.
26 Survey the path for your feet,
   and let all your ways be sure.
27 Turn neither to right nor to left,
   keep your foot far from evil.

CHAPTER 5

See RG
254-62

*Warning against Adultery**

1 My son, to my wisdom be attentive,
   to my knowledge incline your ear,
2 That discretion may watch over you,
   and understanding may guard you.
3 The lips of an adulteress drip with
      honey,
   and her mouth is smoother than oil;*x*
4 But in the end she is as bitter as
      wormwood,
   as sharp as a two-edged sword.

4, 10-27: The way of wisdom leads directly to life (10-13); it is a light that grows brighter (18). The wise man is bound to shun (14-17) the dark and violent path of the wicked (19). Singleness of purpose and right conduct proceed from the heart of a wise man as from the source of life (23-26); they save him from destruction on evil paths (4, 27; 5, 21ff).

4, 18: Till perfect day: literally, "till the day is established"; this may refer to full daylight or to noonday.

5, 1-20: Understanding and discretion guard a man against the wiles of an adulteress, which lead astray and beget bitterness, bloodshed and death (1-6). They destroy honor, waste the years of life, despoil hard-earned wealth, consume the flesh, and bring remorse in the end (7-14). Conjugal fidelity and love for one wife only bring happiness and security (15-20). Cf Prv 6, 20—7, 27.

u: 1 Kgs 2, 2ff.   *v:* Prv 3, 2.   *w:* Prv 8, 35.   *x:* Prv 7, 5.

Hebrew Poetry

MOST READERS NOTICE a particular feature of Hebrew poetry, and one that is particularly prevalent in the Book of Proverbs. This is the use of "parallelism," or the statement of an idea in two (or more) different ways.

Parallelism can be simple, as in Proverbs 3, 12:

> For whom the LORD loves he reproves,
> and he chastises the son he favors.

Here the idea is simply restated in different words. A second type of parallelism is the antithesis, as in Proverbs 2, 21-22:

> For the upright will dwell in the land,
> the honest will remain in it;
> But the wicked will be cut off from the land,
> the faithless will be rooted out of it.

The ideas in the first verse are echoed as negatives in the second.

Finally, the restatement of the idea may serve to advance the thought in some way. Proverbs 4, 1 says:

> Hear, O children, a father's instruction,
> be attentive, that you may gain understanding!

The exhortation to hear is explained in the second line: "you will benefit from paying attention."

Parallelism seems to have served several functions. It allowed Hebrew poetry to be very terse; if the idea was obscure the first time it was stated, perhaps the second time would make things clearer. In addition, it was a substitute for grammatical links between different parts of a line. Hebrew poetry tends to avoid subordinate clauses, connectives (such as "so that"), and other means of leading the reader on from one line to the next. Instead, the lines seem almost detached from one another. But the parallel structure serves to link lines together, and sometimes leads on to larger units as well. In this way, parallelism unites the structure and the content of much Hebrew poetry.

---

⁵ Her feet go down to death,
  to the nether world her steps attain;ʸ
⁶ Lest you see before you the road to life,
  her paths will ramble, you know not where.

⁷ So now, O children, listen to me,
  go not astray from the words of my mouth.
⁸ Keep your way far from her,ᶻ

approach not the door of her house,
⁹ Lest you give your honor* to others,ᵃ
  and your years to a merciless one;
¹⁰ Lest strangers have their fill of your wealth,
  your hard-won earnings go to an alien's house;
¹¹ And you groan in the end,
  when your flesh and your body are consumed;

5, 9: Honor: the words "life" and "wealth" have also been read in this place. A merciless one: the offended husband; cf Prv 6, 34f.

y: Prv 2, 18; 7, 27.   z: Prv 7, 25.   a: 9f: Sir 9, 6.

¹² And you say, "Oh, why did I hate
instruction,
and my heart spurn reproof!
¹³ Why did I not listen to the voice of my
teachers,
nor to my instructors incline my ear!
¹⁴ I have all but come to utter ruin,
condemned by the public
assembly!"

¹⁵ Drink water from your own cistern,
running water from your own well.
¹⁶ How may your water sources be
dispersed abroad,
streams of water in the streets?
¹⁷ Let your fountain be yours alone,
not one shared with strangers;
¹⁸ And have joy of the wife of your
youth,
¹⁹   your lovely hind, your graceful doe.*
Her love will invigorate you always,
through her love you will flourish
continually,
²² When you lie down she will watch over
you,
and when you wake, she will share
your concerns;
wherever you turn, she will guide
you.*
²⁰ Why then, my son, should you go astray
for another's wife
and accept the embraces of an
adulteress?

²¹ For each man's ways are plain to the
LORD's sight;*
all their paths he surveys;^b
²² By his own iniquities the wicked man
will be caught,
in the meshes of his own sin he will be
held fast;
²³ He will die from lack of discipline,
through the greatness of his folly he
will be lost.

CHAPTER 6

See RG
254-62

Miscellaneous Proverbs*

¹ My son, if you have become surety to
your neighbor,^c
given your hand in pledge* to another,
² You have been snared by the utterance of
your lips,
caught by the words of your mouth;
³ So do this, my son, to free yourself,
since you have fallen into your
neighbor's power:
Go, hurry, stir up your neighbor!
⁴ Give no sleep to your eyes,
nor slumber to your eyelids;
⁵ Free yourself as a gazelle from the snare,
or as a bird from the hand of the
fowler.

⁶ Go to the ant,^d O sluggard,
study her ways and learn wisdom;
⁷ For though she has no chief,
no commander or ruler,
⁸ She procures her food in the summer,
stores up her provisions in the harvest.
⁹ How long, O sluggard, will you rest?
when will you rise from your sleep?
¹⁰ A little sleep, a little slumber,
a little folding of the arms to rest—*
¹¹ Then will poverty come upon you like a
highwayman,
and want like an armed man.

¹² A scoundrel, a villain, is he
who deals in crooked talk.
¹³ He winks his eyes,
shuffles his feet,
makes signs with his fingers;
¹⁴ He has perversity in his heart,
is always plotting evil,
sows discord.
¹⁵ Therefore suddenly ruin comes upon
him;
in an instant he is crushed beyond cure.

5, 19: Lovely hind . . . graceful doe: oriental symbols of
feminine beauty and charm; cf Song 2, 7. 9. 17.

5, 22: This is transposed from chapter 6, 22.

5, 21-23: These verses are best read after Prv 4, 27.

6, 1-19: These verses interrupt the discourse of chapters
2—7, which should be read apart from them; they contain
four shorter proverbs akin to those in chapter 30.

6, 1: Given your hand in pledge: literally, "struck your

hands"; this was probably the legal method for closing a contract.

6, 10: This verse may be regarded as the sluggard's reply
or as a continuation of the remonstrance.

b: Jb 14, 16; 31, 4; 34, 21.   *c:* 1f: Prv 11, 15; 22, 26; Sir 8, 13; 29,
19.   *d:* Prv 30, 25.

[16] There are six things the LORD hates,
yes, seven are an abomination to him;*
[17] Haughty eyes, a lying tongue,
and hands that shed innocent blood;
[18] A heart that plots wicked schemes,
feet that run swiftly to evil,
[19] The false witness who utters lies,
and he who sows discord among
brothers.

Warning against Adultery*

[20] Observe, my son, your father's bidding,
and reject not your mother's
teaching;
[21] Keep them fastened over your heart
always,
put them around your neck;
[23] For the bidding is a lamp, and the
teaching a light,
and a way to life are the reproofs of
discipline;
[24] To keep you from your neighbor's wife,
from the smooth tongue of the
adulteress.[e]

[25] Lust not in your heart after her beauty,
let her not captivate you with her
glance![f]
[26] For the price of a loose woman
may be scarcely a loaf of bread,
But if she is married,
she is a trap for your precious life.*
[27] Can a man take fire to his bosom,
and his garments not be burned?
[28] Or can a man walk on live coals,
and his feet not be scorched?
[29] So with him who goes in to his
neighbor's wife—
none who touches her shall go
unpunished.[g]

[30] Men despise not the thief if he steals
to satisfy his appetite when he is
hungry;

[31] Yet if he be caught he must pay back
sevenfold;
all the wealth of his house he may
yield up.
[32] But he who commits adultery is a fool;
he who would destroy himself does it.
[33] A degrading beating will he get,
and his disgrace will not be wiped
away;
[34] For vindictive is the husband's wrath,
he will have no pity on the day of
vengeance;
[35] He will not consider any restitution,
nor be satisfied with the greatest gifts.

CHAPTER 7

See RG
254-62

[1] My son, keep my words,
and treasure my commands.
[2] Keep my commands and live,
my teaching as the apple of your eye;
[3] Bind them on your fingers,
write them on the tablet of your heart.[h]
[4] Say to Wisdom, "You are my sister!"
call Understanding, "Friend!"
[5] That they may keep you from another's
wife,
from the adulteress with her smooth
words.[i]
[6] For at the window of my house,
through my lattice I looked out—

[7] And I saw among the simple ones,
I observed among the young men,
a youth with no sense,
[8] Going along the street near the corner,
then walking in the direction of her
house—
[9] In the twilight, at dusk of day,
at the time of the dark of night.
[10] And lo! the woman comes to meet him,
robed like a harlot, with secret
designs—
[11] She is fickle and unruly,
in her home her feet cannot rest;

6, 16-19: The seven vices symbolized for the most part by
bodily organs are pride, lying, murder, intrigue, readiness to
do evil, false witness, and the stirring up of discord.

6, 20—7, 27: Parental training and the love of wisdom are
an invaluable and constant help for the young (6, 20-23; 7, 1-
4). They are the best defense against adultery (6, 24; 7, 5.
24f), which involves the guilty in many dangers and punishments (6, 26-35; 7, 6-27). Cf Prv 5, 1-20.

6, 26: Some interpret the verse in a progressive sense, i.e.,
to satisfy the increasing demands of a courtesan a man is reduced to poverty; if the woman is married, even his very life
is endangered.

e: Prv 2, 16; 7, 5.   f: Ex 20, 17; Dt 5, 21; Sir 9, 8; 25, 20; Mt 5,
28.   g: Sir 9, 9.   h: Dt 6, 8.   i: Prv 2, 16; 6, 24.

12 Now she is in the streets, now in the open
	squares,
	and at every corner she lurks in
	ambush—
13 When she seizes him, she kisses him,
	and with an impudent look says to
	him:

14 "I owed peace offerings,
	and today I have fulfilled my vows;*
15 So I came out to meet you,
	to look for you, and I have found you!
16 With coverlets I have spread my couch,
	with brocaded cloths of Egyptian
	linen;
17 I have sprinkled my bed with myrrh,
	with aloes, and with cinnamon.

18 "Come, let us drink our fill of love,
	until morning, let us feast on love!
19 For my husband is not at home,
	he has gone on a long journey;
20 A bag of money he took with him,
	not till the full moon will he return
	home."

21 She wins him over by her repeated
	urging,
	with her smooth lips she leads him
	astray;j
22 He follows her stupidly,
	like an ox that is led to slaughter;
	Like a stag that minces toward the net,
23	till an arrow pierces its liver;
	Like a bird that rushes into a snare,
	unaware that its life is at stake.

24 So now, O children, listen to me,
	be attentive to the words of my
	mouth!
25 Let not your heart turn to her ways,
	go not astray in her paths;

26 For many are those she has struck down
	dead,
	numerous, those she has slain.
27 Her house is made up of ways to the
	nether world,
	leading down into the chambers of
	death.k

CHAPTER 8

The Discourse of Wisdom*

See RG
254–62

1 Does not Wisdom call,
	and Understanding raise her voice?l
2 On the top of the heights along the road,
	at the crossroads she takes her stand;
3 By the gates at the approaches of the city,
	in the entryways she cries aloud:
4 "To you, O men, I call;
	my appeal is to the children of men.
5 You simple ones, gain resource,
	you fools,* gain sense.
6 "Give heed! for noble things I speak;
	honesty opens my lips.
7 Yes, the truth my mouth recounts,*
	but wickedness my lips abhor.
8 Sincere are all the words of my mouth,
	no one of them is wily or crooked;
9 All of them are plain to the man of
	intelligence,
	and right to those who attain
	knowledge.
10 Receive my instruction in preference to
	silver,
	and knowledge rather than choice gold.
11 [For Wisdom is better than corals,
	and no choice possession can compare
	with her.m]

12 "I, Wisdom, dwell with experience,
	and judicious knowledge I attain.
13 [The fear of the LORD is to hate evil;]
	Pride, arrogance, the evil way,
	and the perverse mouth I hate.n

7, 14: "Peace offerings . . . vows": a portion of the sacrifice reverted to the donor and had to be eaten on the same day
at a family festival (Lv 7, 11-15). In this figure, the adulteress
offers to share with the foolish young man the deadly feast of
her sensuality.
8, 1-36: Wisdom is here personified as in Prv 1, 20-33, to
confirm the words of the teacher of wisdom. She exalts her
grandeur and origin, and invites all (1-11) to be attentive to
her salutary influence in human society (12-21), for she was
privileged to be present at the creation of the world (22-31).

Finally, she promises life and the favor of God to those who
find her, death to those who despise her.
8, 5: Simple ones . . . fools: see note on Prv 1, 4.
8, 7f: The truth and sincerity of wisdom are absolute because they are divine. They can neither deceive nor tolerate
deception. An intelligent man understands and accepts
them.

j: Prv 5, 3; 6, 24. k: Prv 2, 18f; 5, 5. l: Prv 1, 20f; 9, 3. m: Prv
3, 15; Wis 7, 8. n: Prv 6, 16f; 16, 5.

[14] Mine are counsel and advice;
  mine is strength; I am understanding.*
[15] By me kings reign,
  and lawgivers establish justice;
[16] By me princes govern,
  and nobles; all the rulers of earth.

[17] "Those who love me I also love,
  and those who seek me find me.
[18] With me are riches and honor,[o]
  enduring wealth and prosperity.
[19] My fruit is better than gold, yes, than
  pure gold,
  and my revenue than choice
  silver.[p]
[20] On the way of duty I walk,
  along the paths of justice,
[21] Granting wealth to those who love me,
  and filling their treasuries.

[22] "The LORD begot me, the first-born of his
  ways,*
  the forerunner of his prodigies of long
  ago;[q]
[23] From of old I was poured forth,*
  at the first, before the earth.[r]
[24] When there were no depths I was brought
  forth,*
  when there were no fountains or
  springs of water;
[25] Before the mountains were settled into
  place,
  before the hills, I was brought
  forth;
[26] While as yet the earth and the fields were
  not made,
  nor the first clods of the world.

[27] "When he established the heavens I was
  there,[s]
  when he marked out the vault over the
  face of the deep;
[28] When he made firm the skies above,
  when he fixed fast the foundations of
  the earth;
[29] When he set for the sea its limit,
  so that the waters should not transgress
  his command;
[30] Then was I beside him as his craftsman,*
  and I was his delight day by day,[t]
  Playing before him all the while,
[31] playing on the surface of his earth;
  and I found delight in the sons of men.

[32] "So now, O children, listen to me;
[33] instruction and wisdom do not reject!
  Happy the man who obeys me,
  and happy those who keep my ways,
[34] Happy the man watching daily at my
  gates,
  waiting at my doorposts;
[35] For he who finds me finds life,[u]
  and wins favor from the LORD;
[36] But he who misses me harms himself;
  all who hate me love death."

CHAPTER 9

The Two Banquets*

See RG
254–62

[1] Wisdom has built her house,
  she has set up her seven columns;
[2] She has dressed her meat, mixed her
  wine,
  yes, she has spread her table.
[3] She has sent out her maidens; she calls*
  from the heights out over the city:[v]

8, 14: What is here predicated of wisdom is elsewhere attributed to God (Jb 12, 13-16).

8, 22-31: Wisdom is of divine origin. It is here represented as a being which existed before all things (22-26) and concurred with God when he planned and executed the creation of the universe, adorned it with beauty and variety, and established its wonderful order (27-30). Here that plurality of divine Persons is foreshadowed which was afterward to be fully revealed when Wisdom in the Person of Jesus Christ became incarnate.

8, 23: Poured forth: the exact meaning of the Hebrew is uncertain; the expression must imply the equivalent of "born." The Hebrews likened the movement of air and of spirit to that of liquids.

8, 24-26: The formless mass from which God created the heavens and the earth; cf Gn 1, 1f; 2, 4ff.

8, 30: His craftsman: furnishing God with the plan, as it were, for the creation of all things; cf Jb 38, 1f; Wis 7, 22—8, 1. I was his delight: the ever-present object of God's complacency.

9, 1-6. 13-18: Wisdom and folly are represented as matrons, each inviting people to her banquet. Wisdom offers the food and drink of divine doctrine and virtue which give life (1-6). Unstable and senseless folly furnishes the stolen bread and water of deceit and vice which bring death to her guests.

9, 3: She calls: i.e., indirectly, through her maidens; but the text could also mean that wisdom herself publicly proclaims her invitation.

o: Prv 3, 16. p: Prv 3, 14. q: Wis 9, 9; Sir 1, 1; 24, 9. r: Sir 1, 4. s: Prv 3, 19; Sir 24, 4f. t: Wis 9, 9. u: Prv 3, 13-18; 4, 22. v: Prv 8, 1f.

⁴ "Let whoever is simple turn in here;
   to him who lacks understanding, I
      say,
⁵ Come, eat of my food,
   and drink of the wine I have mixed!
⁶ Forsake foolishness that you may live;
   advance in the way of understanding.
¹¹ For by me your days will be multiplied
   and the years of your life increased."ʷ

⁷ He who corrects an arrogant man earns
      insult;
   and he who reproves a wicked man
      incurs opprobrium.
⁸ Reprove not an arrogant man, lest he hate
      you;
   reprove a wise man, and he will love
      you.ˣ
⁹ Instruct a wise man, and he becomes still
      wiser;
   teach a just man, and he advances in
      learning.

¹⁰ The beginning of wisdom is the fear of
      the LORD,
   and knowledge of the Holy One is
      understanding.ʸ
¹² If you are wise, it is to your own
      advantage;
   and if you are arrogant, you alone shall
      bear it.

¹³ The woman Folly is fickle,ᶻ
   she is inane, and knows nothing.
¹⁴ She sits at the door of her house
   upon a seat on the city heights,
¹⁵ Calling to passers-by
   as they go on their straight way:
¹⁶ "Let whoever is simple turn in here,
   or who lacks understanding; for to him
      I say,
¹⁷ Stolen water is sweet,
   and bread gotten secretly is pleasing!"*
¹⁸ Little he knows that the shades are there,

that in the depths of the nether world
   are her guests!*

II: First Collection of the Proverbs of Solomon*

CHAPTER 10

¹The Proverbs of Solomon:

A wise son makes his father glad,
   but a foolish son is a grief to his
      mother.ᵃ

² Ill-gotten treasures profit nothing,
   but virtue saves from death.ᵇ

³ The LORD permits not the just to hunger,
   but the craving of the wicked he
      thwarts.

⁴ The slack hand impoverishes,
   but the hand of the diligent enriches.ᶜ

⁵ A son who fills the granaries in summer
      is a credit;
   a son who slumbers during harvest, a
      disgrace.

⁶ Blessings are for the head of the just,
   but a rod for the back of the fool.

⁷ The memory of the just will be blessed,
   but the name of the wicked will rot.

⁸ A wise man heeds commands,
   but a prating fool will be overthrown.

⁹ He who walks honestly walks securely,
   but he whose ways are crooked will
      fare badly.

¹⁰ He who winks at a fault causes trouble,
   but he who frankly reproves promotes
      peace.

9, 17: The secrecy implies wrongdoing.

9, 18: The banquet chamber of folly is a tomb from which no one who enters it is released.

10, 1—22, 16: The varied contents of this first collection of Solomon's proverbs apply mostly to individual life. Each of its three hundred and seventy-five proverbs is meant to be distinct from the others, developing one idea through con-

trasting parallelism in chapters 10—15, and a climactic treatment in 16—22.

w: Prv 3, 2. 16; 4, 10; 10, 27.   x: Sir 10, 27.   y: Prv 1, 7; Jb 28, 28; Ps 111, 10; Sir 1, 16.   z: 13-18; Prv, 7, 7-27.   a: Prv 1, 1; 15, 20; 17, 25; 19, 13; 25, 1; 29, 15.   b: Prv 11, 4. 6.   c: Prv 6, 11; 12, 24; 13, 4; 20, 13; 28, 19.

11 A fountain of life is the mouth of the just,
  but the mouth of the wicked conceals
    violence.

12 Hatred stirs up disputes,
  dbut love covers all offenses.*

13 On the lips of the intelligent is found
    wisdom,
  [but the mouth of the wicked conceals
    violence].

14 Wise men store up knowledge,
  but the mouth of a fool is imminent
    ruin.

15 The rich man's wealth is his strong city;
  the ruination of the lowly is their
    poverty.*

16 The just man's recompense leads to life,
  the gains of the wicked, to sin.e

17 A path to life is his who heeds
    admonition,
  but he who disregards reproof goes
    astray.f

18 It is the lips of the liar that conceal
    hostility;
  but he who spreads accusations is a fool.

19 Where words are many, sin is not
    wanting;
  but he who restrains his lips does
    well.g

20 Like choice silver is the just man's
    tongue;
  the heart of the wicked is of little
    worth.

21 The just man's lips nourish many,
  but fools die for want of sense.

22 It is the LORD's blessing that brings
    wealth,h
  and no effort can substitute for it.*

23 Crime is the entertainment of the fool;
  so is wisdom for the man of sense.

24 What the wicked man fears will befall
    him,
  but the desire of the just will be
    granted.

25 When the tempest passes, the wicked
    man is no more;
  but the just man is established
    forever.

26 As vinegar to the teeth, and smoke to the
    eyes,
  is the sluggard to those who use him as
    a messenger.

27 The fear of the LORD prolongs life,
  but the years of the wicked are brief.i

28 The hope of the just brings them joy,
  but the expectation of the wicked
    comes to nought.

29 The LORD is a stronghold to him who
    walks honestly,
  but to evildoers, their downfall.

30 The just man will never be disturbed,
  but the wicked will not abide in the
    land.

31 The mouth of the just yields wisdom,
  but the perverse tongue will be cut
    off.

32 The lips of the just know how to please,
  but the mouth of the wicked, how to
    pervert.

10, 12: Love covers all offenses: a favorite maxim of the Apostles; cf 1 Cor 13, 7; Jas 5, 20; 1 Pt 4, 8; also Prv 17, 9.

10, 15: The inspired author reflects upon the reality of the power of money and the defeat of poverty, without approving these things.

10, 22: The blessing of God rather than our own industry crowns our efforts with success; cf Ps 127, 1f; Mt 6, 25-34.

---

d: 1 Cor 13, 4-7; 1 Pt 4, 8. *e:* Prv 11, 18f. *f:* Prv 15, 10. *g:* Prv 17, 27; Sir 20, 17; Jas 1, 19. *h:* Sir 11, 22. *i:* Prv 3, 2; 4, 10; 9, 11; 14, 27.

See RG
254–62

CHAPTER 11

¹ False scales are an abomination to
the LORD,
but a full weight is his delight.ʲ

² When pride comes, disgrace comes;
but with the humble is wisdom.

³ The honesty of the upright guides them;
the faithless are ruined by their
duplicity.

⁴ Wealth is useless on the day of wrath,ᵏ
but virtue saves from death.*

⁵ The honest man's virtue makes his way
straight,
but by his wickedness the wicked man
falls.ˡ

⁶ The virtue of the upright saves them,
but the faithless are caught in their
own intrigue.

⁷ When a wicked man dies his hope
perishes,ᵐ
and what is expected from strength
comes to nought.

⁸ The just man escapes trouble,
and the wicked man falls into it in his
stead.

⁹ With his mouth the impious man would
ruin his neighbor,ⁿ
but through their knowledge the just
make their escape.

¹⁰ When the just prosper, the city rejoices;ᵒ
and when the wicked perish, there is
jubilation.

¹¹ Through the blessing of the righteous the
city is exalted,
but through the mouth of the wicked it
is overthrown.

¹² He who reviles his neighbor has no sense,
but the intelligent man keeps silent.

¹³ A newsmonger reveals secrets,ᵖ
but a trustworthy man keeps a
confidence.

¹⁴ For lack of guidance a people falls;
security lies in many counselors.�q

¹⁵ He is in a bad way who becomes surety
for another,ʳ
but he who hates giving pledges is safe.

¹⁶ A gracious woman wins esteem,
but she who hates virtue is covered
with shame.

[The slothful become impoverished,
but the diligent gain wealth.]

¹⁷ A kindly man benefits himself,
but a merciless man harms himself.

¹⁸ The wicked man makes empty profits,
but he who sows virtue has a sure
reward.ˢ

¹⁹ Virtue directs toward life,
but he who pursues evil does so to his
death.

²⁰ The depraved in heart are an abomination
to the LORD,
but those who walk blamelessly are his
delight.

²¹ Truly the evil man shall not go
unpunished,
but those who are just shall escape.

²² Like a golden ring in a swine's snout
is a beautiful woman with a rebellious
disposition.

²³ The desire of the just ends only in good;
the expectation of the wicked is wrath.

11, 4: Wealth . . . death: not what a man is worth but what he is, counts before God.

ʲ: Prv 16, 11; 20, 10; Lv 19, 35f.   ᵏ: Prv 10, 2.   ˡ: Prv 28, 18.   ᵐ: Prv 10, 28; Wis 3, 18.   ⁿ: Prv 29, 5.   ᵒ: Prv 28, 12; 29, 2.   ᵖ: Prv 20, 19.   q: Prv 15, 22; 20, 18; 24, 6.   ʳ: Prv 6, 1f.   ˢ: Prv 10, 16.

²⁴ One man is lavish yet grows still richer;
   another is too sparing, yet is the
   poorer.

²⁵ He who confers benefits will be amply
   enriched,
   and he who refreshes others will
   himself be refreshed.

²⁶ Him who monopolizes grain, the people
   curse—
   but blessings upon the head of him
   who distributes it!

²⁷ He who seeks the good commands favor,
   but he who pursues evil will have evil
   befall him.

²⁸ He who trusts in his riches will fall,
   but like green leaves the just flourish.ᵗ

²⁹ He who upsets his household has empty
   air for a heritage;
   and the fool will become slave to the
   wise man.

³⁰ The fruit of virtue is a tree of life,
   but violence takes lives away.

³¹ If the just man is punished on earth,
   how much more the wicked and the
   sinner!ᵘ

CHAPTER 12

See RG
254–62

¹He who loves correction loves
   knowledge,
   but he who hates reproof is stupid.ᵛ

² The good man wins favor from the LORD,
   but the schemer is condemned by him.

³ No man is built up by wickedness,
   but the root of the just will never be
   disturbed.

⁴ A worthy wife is the crown of her
   husband,ʷ

but a disgraceful one is like rot in his
   bones.

⁵ The plans of the just are legitimate;
   the designs of the wicked are
   deceitful.

⁶ The words of the wicked are a deadly
   ambush,
   but the speech of the upright saves
   them.

⁷ The wicked are overthrown and are no
   more,
   but the house of the just stands firm.

⁸ According to his good sense a man is
   praised,
   but one with a warped mind is
   despised.

⁹ Better a lowly man who supports
   himself
   than one of assumed importance who
   lacks bread.ˣ

¹⁰ The just man takes care of his beast,
   but the heart of the wicked is
   merciless.

¹¹ He who tills his own land has food in
   plenty,
   but he who follows idle pursuits is a
   fool.ʸ

¹² The stronghold of evil men will be
   demolished,
   but the root of the just is enduring.

¹³ In the sin of his lips the evil man is
   ensnared,
   but the just comes free of trouble.

¹⁴ From the fruit of his words a man has his
   fill of good things,ᶻ
   and the work of his hands comes back
   to reward him.*

12, 14: Cf Mt 7, 17; Gal 6, 8.

t: Ps 52, 9f.   u: 1 Pt 4, 18.   v: Prv 15, 5. 10; 29, 1; Sir 19, 5; 21, 6.   w: Sir 26, 1. 16.   x: Sir 10, 26.   y: Prv 28, 19; Sir 20, 27.
z: Prv 13, 2; 18, 20.

¹⁵ The way of the fool seems right in his
    own eyes,
  but he who listens to advice is wise.

¹⁶ The fool immediately shows his anger,
  but the shrewd man passes over an
    insult.

¹⁷ He tells the truth who states what he is
    sure of,
  but a lying witness speaks deceitfully.ᵃ

¹⁸ The prating of some men is like sword
    thrusts,
  but the tongue of the wise is healing.

¹⁹ Truthful lips endure forever,
  the lying tongue, for only a moment.

²⁰ Deceit is in the hands of those who plot
    evil,
  but those who counsel peace have joy.

²¹ No harm befalls the just,
  but the wicked are overwhelmed with
    misfortune.

²² Lying lips are an abomination to the Lord,ᵇ
  but those who are truthful are his
    delight.

²³ A shrewd man conceals his knowledge,
  but the hearts of fools gush forth folly.

²⁴ The diligent hand will govern,
  but the slothful will be enslaved.ᶜ

²⁵ Anxiety in a man's heart depresses it,
  but a kindly word makes it glad.ᵈ

²⁶ The just man surpasses his neighbor,
  but the way of the wicked leads them
    astray.

²⁷ The slothful man catches not his prey,
  but the wealth of the diligent man is
    great.

²⁸ In the path of justice there is life,
  but the abominable way leads to death.

CHAPTER 13

See RG
254–62

¹ A wise son loves correction,
  but the senseless one heeds no rebuke.

² From the fruit of his words a man eats
    good things,ᵉ
  but the treacherous one craves
    violence.

³ He who guards his mouth protects his
    life;
  to open wide one's lips brings
    downfall.ᶠ

⁴ The soul of the sluggard craves in vain,
  but the diligent soul is amply satisfied.

⁵ Anything deceitful the just man hates,
  but the wicked brings shame and
    disgrace.

⁶ Virtue guards one who walks honestly,
  but the downfall of the wicked is sin.ᵍ

⁷ One man pretends to be rich, yet has
    nothing;
  another pretends to be poor, yet has
    great wealth.

⁸ A man's riches serve as ransom for his
    life,
  but the poor man heeds no rebuke.

⁹ The light of the just shines gaily,
  but the lamp* of the wicked goes out.ʰ

¹⁰ The stupid man sows discord by his
    insolence,
  but with those who take counsel is
    wisdom.

¹¹ Wealth quickly gotten dwindles away,
  but amassed little by little, it
    grows.ⁱ

13, 9: Light . . . lamp: symbols of life and prosperity; cf Prv 4, 18f.

a: Prv 14, 5. b: Prv 6, 17. c: Prv 10, 4; 13, 4. d: Prv 15, 13; 17, 22. e: Prv 12, 14; 18, 20. f: Prv 18, 7; 21, 23. g: Prv 11, 3.
5f. h: Prv 24, 20. i: Prv 28, 20. 22.

¹² Hope deferred makes the heart sick,
but a wish fulfilled is a tree of life.

¹³ He who despises the word* must pay for
it,
but he who reveres the commandment
will be rewarded.

¹⁴ The teaching of the wise is a fountain of
life,
that a man may avoid the snares of
death.

¹⁵ Good sense brings favor,
but the way of the faithless is their ruin.

¹⁶ The shrewd man does everything with
prudence,
but the fool peddles folly.

¹⁷ A wicked messenger brings on disaster,
but a trustworthy envoy is a healing
remedy.

¹⁸ Poverty and shame befall the man who
disregards correction,
but he who heeds reproof is honored.

¹⁹ Lust indulged starves the soul,
but fools hate to turn from evil.

²⁰ Walk with wise men and you will
become wise,
but the companion of fools will fare
badly.^j

²¹ Misfortune pursues sinners,
but the just shall be recompensed with
good.

²² The good man leaves an inheritance to
his children's children,
but the wealth of the sinner is stored
up for the just.

²³ A lawsuit devours the tillage of the poor,
but some men perish for lack of a law
court.

13, 13: Word: advice, or God's law.

²⁴ He who spares his rod hates his son,
but he who loves him takes care to
chastise him.^k

²⁵ When the just man eats, his hunger is
appeased;
but the belly of the wicked suffers
want.

CHAPTER 14

See RG
254-62

¹ Wisdom builds her house,
but Folly tears hers down with her
own hands.

² He who walks uprightly fears the LORD,
but he who is devious in his ways
spurns him.

³ In the mouth of the fool is a rod for his
back,
but the lips of the wise preserve them.

⁴ Where there are no oxen, the crib
remains empty;
but large crops come through the
strength of the bull.

⁵ A truthful witness does not lie,
but a false witness utters lies.^l

⁶ The senseless man seeks in vain for
wisdom,
but knowledge is easy to the man of
intelligence.

⁷ To avoid the foolish man, take steps!
But knowing lips one meets with by
surprise.

⁸ The shrewd man's wisdom gives him
knowledge of his way,
but the folly of fools is their deception.

⁹ Guilt lodges in the tents of the arrogant,
but favor in the house of the just.

¹⁰ The heart knows its own bitterness,
and in its joy no one else shares.

j: Sir 6, 34; 8, 8. 17.   k: Prv 19, 18; 22, 15; 23, 13f; 29, 15; Sir 30, 1. 8-13.   l: Prv 12. 17.

¹¹ The house of the wicked will be
  destroyed,
    but the tent of the upright will
      flourish.^m

¹² Sometimes a way seems right to a man,
    but the end of it leads to death!ⁿ

¹³ Even in laughter the heart may be sad
    and the end of joy may be sorrow.

¹⁴ The scoundrel suffers the consequences
  of his ways,
    and the good man reaps the fruit of his
      paths.

¹⁵ The simpleton believes everything,
    but the shrewd man measures his
      steps.

¹⁶ The wise man is cautious and shuns evil;
    the fool is reckless and sure of himself.

¹⁷ The quick-tempered man makes a fool of
  himself,
    but the prudent man is at peace.

¹⁸ The adornment of simpletons is folly,
    but shrewd men gain the crown of
      knowledge.

¹⁹ Evil men must bow down before the
  good,
    and the wicked, at the gates of the just.

²⁰ Even by his neighbor the poor man is
  hated,
    but the friends of the rich are many.^o

²¹ He sins who despises the hungry;
    but happy is he who is kind to the
      poor!

²² Do not those who plot evil go astray?
    But those intent on good gain kindness
      and constancy.

²³ In all labor there is profit,
    but mere talk tends only to penury.

²⁴ The crown of the wise is resourcefulness;
    the diadem of fools is folly.

²⁵ The truthful witness saves lives,
    but he who utters lies is a betrayer.

²⁶ In the fear of the LORD is a strong
  defense;
    even for one's children he will be a
      refuge.

²⁷ The fear of the LORD is a fountain of
  life,
    that a man may avoid the snares of
      death.

²⁸ In many subjects lies the glory of the
  king;
    but if his people are few, it is the
      prince's ruin.

²⁹ The patient man shows much good
  sense,
    but the quick-tempered man displays
      folly at its height.^p

³⁰ A tranquil mind gives life to the body,
    but jealousy rots the bones.

³¹ He who oppresses the poor blasphemes
  his Maker,
    but he who is kind to the needy
      glorifies him.^q

³² The wicked man is overthrown by his
  wickedness,
    but the just man finds a refuge in his
      honesty.

³³ In the heart of the intelligent wisdom
  abides,
    but in the bosom of fools it is
      unknown.

³⁴ Virtue exalts a nation,
    but sin is a people's disgrace.

³⁵ The king favors the intelligent servant,
    but the worthless one incurs his wrath.

m: Prv 3, 33; 12, 7; 15, 25.   n: Prv 16, 25.   o: Prv 19, 4. 7; Sir 6, 8, 12.   p: Prv 16, 32; 19, 11; Jas 1, 19.   q: Prv 17, 5.

CHAPTER 15

See RG 254–62

¹ A mild answer calms wrath,ʳ
but a harsh word stirs up anger.

² The tongue of the wise pours out
knowledge,
but the mouth of fools spurts forth folly.

³ The eyes of the LORD are in every place,
keeping watch on the evil and the
good.

⁴ A soothing tongue is a tree of life,
but a perverse one crushes the spirit.

⁵ The fool spurns his father's admonition,
but prudent is he who heeds reproof.ˢ

⁶ In the house of the just there are ample
resources,
but the earnings of the wicked are in
turmoil.

⁷ The lips of the wise disseminate
knowledge,
but the heart of fools is perverted.

⁸ The sacrifice of the wicked is an
abomination to the LORD,ᵗ
but the prayer of the upright is his
delight.

⁹ The way of the wicked is an abomination
to the LORD,
but he loves the man who pursues
virtue.ᵘ

¹⁰ Severe punishment is in store for the man
who goes astray;
he who hates reproof will die.

¹¹ The nether world and the abyss* lie open
before the LORD;
how much more the hearts of men!

¹² The senseless man loves not to be
reproved;
to wise men he will not go.

¹³ A glad heart lights up the face,
but by mental anguish the spirit is
broken.ᵛ

¹⁴ The mind of the intelligent man seeks
knowledge,
but the mouth of fools feeds on folly.

¹⁵ Every day is miserable for the
depressed,
but a lighthearted man has a continual
feast.

¹⁶ Better a little with fear of the LORD*
than a great fortune with anxiety.

¹⁷ Better a dish of herbs where love is
than a fatted ox and hatred with it.

¹⁸ An ill-tempered man stirs up strife,ʷ
but a patient man allays discord.

¹⁹ The way of the sluggard is hemmed in as
with thorns,
but the path of the diligent is a
highway.

²⁰ A wise son makes his father glad,
but a fool of a man despises his
mother.ˣ

²¹ Folly is joy to the senseless man,
but the man of understanding goes the
straight way.

²² Plans fail when there is no counsel,
but they succeed when counselors are
many.ʸ

²³ There is joy for a man in his utterance;
a word in season, how good it is!ᶻ

15, 11: Nether world . . . abyss: the abode of the dead, signifying the profound obscurity which is open nevertheless to the sight and power of God.

15, 16f: Not the amount of temporal goods but the virtue of their possessor makes them a source of happiness.

---

r: Prv 25, 15; Sir 6, 5.   s: Prv 12, 1; 13, 18.   t: Prv 21, 27; Eccl 4, 17; Sir 34, 18ff; Is 1, 11-15.   u: Prv 11, 20; 21, 21.   v: Prv 12, 25; 17, 22; Sir 30, 22.   w: Prv 26, 21; 29, 22; Sir 28, 11.   x: Prv 10, 1; 29, 3.   y: Prv 11, 14.   z: Prv 25, 11; Sir 20, 6.

²⁴ The path of life leads the prudent man
  upward,
  that he may avoid the nether world
  below.

²⁵ The LORD overturns the house of the
  proud,
  but he preserves intact the widow's
  landmark.

²⁶ The wicked man's schemes are an
  abomination to the LORD,ᵃ
  but the pure speak what is pleasing to
  him.

²⁷ He who is greedy of gain brings ruin on
  his own house,
  but he who hates bribes will live.

²⁸ The just man weighs well his utterance,
  but the mouth of the wicked pours out
  evil.

²⁹ The LORD is far from the wicked,
  but the prayer of the just he hears.

³⁰ A cheerful glance brings joy to the heart;
  good news invigorates the bones.

³¹ He who listens to salutary reproofᵇ
  will abide among the wise.

³² He who rejects admonition despises his
  own soul,
  but he who heeds reproof gains
  understanding.

³³ The fear of the LORD is training for
  wisdom,
  and humility goes before honors.ᶜ

CHAPTER 16

See RG
254–62

¹ Man may make plans in his heart,
  but what the tongue utters is from the
  LORD.*

² All the ways of a man may be pure in his
  own eyes,
  but it is the LORD who proves the spirit.ᵈ

³ Entrust your works to the LORD,
  and your plans will succeed.

⁴ The LORD has made everything for his
  own ends,
  even the wicked for the evil day.*

⁵ Every proud man is an abomination to
  the LORD;ᵉ
  I assure you that he will not go
  unpunished.

⁶ By kindness and piety guilt is expiated,
  and by the fear of the LORD man
  avoids evil.

⁷ When the LORD is pleased with a man's
  ways,
  he makes even his enemies be at peace
  with him.

⁸ Better a little with virtue,
  than a large income with injustice.

⁹ In his mind a man plans his course,
  but the LORD directs his steps.ᶠ

¹⁰ The king's lips are an oracle;
  no judgment he pronounces is false.*

¹¹ Balance and scales belong to the LORD;
  all the weights used with them are his
  concern.ᵍ

¹² Kings have a horror of wrongdoing,
  for by righteousness the throne
  endures.ʰ

¹³ The king takes delight in honest lips,
  and the man who speaks what is right
  he loves.ⁱ

16, 1: Words, like actions, often produce results different from those which were planned.
16, 4: Even the wicked, in their punishment, cannot escape glorifying God's justice.
16, 10: Decisions of supreme judicial authority were presumed disinterested and correct.

---

a: Prv 6, 18. *b:* Prv 25, 12. *c:* Prv 1, 7; Sir 1, 24. *d:* Prv 21, 2. *e:* Prv 6, 16f; 8, 13. *f:* Prv 19, 21; 20, 24. *g:* Prv 11, 1. *h:* Prv 25, 5. *i:* Prv 14, 35; 22, 11.

[14] The king's wrath is like messengers of
death,[j]
but a wise man can pacify it.

[15] In the light of the king's countenance is
life,
and his favor is like a rain cloud in
spring.

[16] How much better to acquire wisdom than
gold!
To acquire understanding is more
desirable than silver.[k]

[17] The path of the upright avoids
misfortune;
he who pays attention to his way
safeguards his life.

[18] Pride goes before disaster,
and a haughty spirit before a fall.

[19] It is better to be humble with the meek
than to share plunder with the proud.[l]

[20] He who plans a thing will be successful;
happy is he who trusts in the LORD!

[21] The wise man is esteemed for his
discernment,
yet pleasing speech increases his
persuasiveness.

[22] Good sense is a fountain of life to its
possessor,
but folly brings chastisement on fools.

[23] The mind of the wise man makes him
eloquent,
and augments the persuasiveness of
his lips.

[24] Pleasing words are a honeycomb,
sweet to the taste and healthful to the
body.

[25] Sometimes a way seems right to a man,
but the end of it leads to death![m]

[26] The laborer's appetite labors for him,
for his mouth urges him on.[n]

[27] A scoundrel is a furnace of evil,
and on his lips there is a scorching fire.

[28] An intriguer sows discord,
and a talebearer separates bosom
friends.[o]

[29] A lawless man allures his neighbor,
and leads him into a way that is not
good.

[30] He who winks his eye is plotting
trickery;
he who compresses his lips has
mischief ready.

[31] Gray hair is a crown of glory;[p]
it is gained by virtuous living.

[32] A patient man is better than a warrior,
and he who rules his temper, than he
who takes a city.[q]

[33] When the lot is cast into the lap,
its decision depends entirely on the
LORD.*

CHAPTER 17

See RG
254-62

[1] Better a dry crust with peace
than a house full of feasting with strife.

[2] An intelligent servant will rule over a
worthless son,
and will share the inheritance with the
brothers.*

[3] The crucible for silver, and the furnace
for gold,
but the tester of hearts is the LORD.

16, 33: The favorable or unfavorable result of chance depends on God. Deciding strifes and doubts by lot was practiced
by the ancient Hebrews; cf Ex 28, 15-30; Lv 16, 8; Jos 7, 14; 1 Sm 10, 20f.

17, 2: Intelligence and ability are esteemed more highly than nobility of blood.

---

j: Prv 19, 12; 20, 2.   *k:* Prv 8, 10f. 19.   *l:* Prv 11, 2.   *m:* Prv 14, 12.   *n:* Prv 10, 4.   *o:* Prv 6, 14. 19; 17, 9; 26, 22; Sir 28, 15.   *p:* Prv
20, 29.   *q:* Prv 14, 29.

⁴ The evil man gives heed to wicked lips,
and listens to falsehood from a
mischievous tongue.*

⁵ He who mocks the poor blasphemes his
Maker;ʳ
he who is glad at calamity will not go
unpunished.

⁶ Grandchildren are the crown of old men,
and the glory of children is their
parentage.

⁷ Fine words are out of place in a fool;
how much more, lying words in a
noble!

⁸ A man who has a bribe to offer rates it a
magic stone;
at every turn it brings him success.

⁹ He who covers up a misdeed fosters
friendship,
but he who gossips about it separates
friends.

¹⁰ A single reprimand does more for a man
of intelligence
than a hundred lashes for a fool.

¹¹ On rebellion alone is the wicked man
bent,
but a merciless messenger will be sent
against him.

¹² Face a bear robbed of her cubs,
but never a fool in his folly!

¹³ If a man returns evil for good,
from his house evil will not depart.ˢ

¹⁴ The start of strife is like the opening of a
dam;
therefore, check a quarrel before it
begins!

¹⁵ He who condones the wicked,ᵗ he who
condemns the just,
are both an abomination to the LORD.

¹⁶ Of what use in the fool's hand are the
means
to buy wisdom, since he has no mind
for it?

¹⁷ He who is a friend is always a friend,
and a brother is born for the time of
stress.ᵘ

¹⁸ Senseless is the man who gives his hand
in pledge,
who becomes surety for his neighbor.ᵛ

¹⁹ He who loves strife loves guilt;ʷ
he who builds his gate high* courts
disaster.

²⁰ He who is perverse in heart finds no
good,
and a double-tongued man falls into
trouble.

²¹ To be a fool's parent is grief for a man;
the father of a numskull has no joy.

²² A joyful heart is the health of the body,
but a depressed spirit dries up the
bones.ˣ

²³ The wicked man accepts a concealed
bribe
to pervert the course of justice.

²⁴ The man of intelligence fixes his gaze on
wisdom,ʸ
but the eyes of a fool are on the ends
of the earth.

²⁵ A foolish son is vexation to his father,
and bitter sorrow to her who bore
him.ᶻ

17, 4: To justify his own evil ways, a wicked man judges evil of others. Cf Mt 7, 1-5.
17, 19: Builds . . . high: a symbol of arrogance.

---

r: Prv 14, 31.   *s:* Mt 5, 39; Rom 12, 17; 1 Thes 5, 15; 1 Pt 3, 9.   *t:* Prv 24, 24; Is 5, 23.   *u:* Prv 18, 24.   *v:* Prv 6, 1f; 11, 15.   *w:* Prv 15, 18.   *x:* Prv 12, 25; 15, 13.   *y:* Eccl 8, 1.   *z:* Prv 10, 1; 29, 15.

²⁶ It is wrong to fine an innocent man,
     but beyond reason to scourge princes.

²⁷ He who spares his words is truly wise,
     and he who is chary of speech is a man
         of intelligence.ᵃ

²⁸ Even a fool, if he keeps silent, is
         considered wise;
     if he closes his lips, intelligent.

CHAPTER 18

See RG
254-62

¹In estrangement one seeks pretexts:
     with all persistence he picks a
         quarrel.

² The fool takes no delight in
         understanding,
     but rather in displaying what he thinks.

³ With wickedness comes contempt,
     and with disgrace comes scorn.

⁴ The words from a man's mouth are deep
         waters,
     but the source of wisdom is a flowing
         brook.ᵇ

⁵ It is not good to be partial to the guilty,
     and so to reject a rightful claim.ᶜ

⁶ The fool's lips lead him into strife,
     and his mouth provokes a beating.

⁷ The fool's mouth is his ruin;
     his lips are a snare to his life.ᵈ

⁸ The words of a talebearer are like dainty
         morsels
     that sink into one's inmost being.ᵉ

⁹ The man who is slack in his work
     is own brother to the man who is
         destructive.

¹⁰ The name of the LORD is a strong tower;*
     the just man runs to it and is safe.

¹¹ The rich man's wealth is his strong city;ᶠ
     he fancies it a high wall.

¹² Before his downfall a man's heart is
         haughty,ᵍ
     but humility goes before honors.*

¹³ He who answers before he hearsʰ —
     his is the folly and the shame.*

¹⁴ A man's spirit sustains him in infirmity—
     but a broken spirit who can bear?

¹⁵ The mind of the intelligent gains
         knowledge,
     and the ear of the wise seeks
         knowledge.

¹⁶ A man's gift clears the way for him,
     and gains him access to great men.ⁱ

¹⁷ The man who pleads his case first seems
         to be in the right;
     then his opponent comes and puts him
         to the test.

¹⁸ The lot puts an end to disputes,
     and is decisive in a controversy
         between the mighty.*

¹⁹ A brother is a better defense than a strong
         city,
     and a friend is like the bars of a castle.

²⁰ From the fruit of his mouth a man has his
         fill;*
     with the yield of his lips he sates
         himself.ʲ

²¹ Death and life are in the power of the
         tongue;ᵏ

18, 10f: Religion is a strong support and sure refuge in the struggle of life. The rich foolishly rely on their wealth for such support.

18, 12: Compare the Savior's words: "Whoever exalts himself shall be humbled, but whoever humbles himself shall be exalted" (Mt 23, 12).

18, 13: To speak without first listening is characteristic of a fool; cf Prv 10, 14; Sir 11, 8.

18, 18: See note on Prv 16, 33.

18, 20f: Everyone must accept the consequences, of benefit or harm to himself, which his words produce.

a: Prv 10, 19; Sir 1, 21; Jas 1, 19. b: Prv 20, 5; Jn 7, 38. c: Prv 24, 23; 28, 21. d: Prv 10, 14; 12, 13; 13, 3; Eccl 10, 12. e: Prv 26, 22. f: Prv 10, 15. g: Prv 11, 2; 16, 18; Sir 10, 15. h: Sir 11, 8. i: Prv 21, 14. j: Prv 12, 14; 13, 2. k: Sir 37, 18.

those who make it a friend shall eat its fruit.

22 He who finds a wife finds happiness;
it is a favor he receives from the LORD.[l]

23 The poor man implores,
but the rich man answers harshly.

24 Some friends bring ruin on us,
but a true friend is more loyal than a brother.[m]

CHAPTER 19

See RG 254-62

1 Better a poor man who walks in his integrity
than he who is crooked in his ways and rich.[n]

2 Without knowledge even zeal is not good;
and he who acts hastily, blunders.

3 A man's own folly upsets his way,
but his heart is resentful against the LORD.

4 Wealth adds many friends,
but the friend of the poor man deserts him.[o]

5 The false witness will not go unpunished,
and he who utters lies will not escape.[p]

6 Many curry favor with a noble;
all are friends of the man who has something to give.

7 All the poor man's brothers hate him;
how much more do his friends shun him!

8 He who gains intelligence is his own best friend;
he who keeps understanding will be successful.

9 The false witness will not go unpunished,
and he who utters lies will perish.

10 Luxury is not befitting a fool;
much less should a slave rule over princes.

11 It is good sense in a man to be slow to anger,
and it is his glory to overlook an offense.

12 The king's wrath is like the roaring of a lion,
but his favor, like dew on the grass.[q]

13 The foolish son is ruin to his father,[r]
and the nagging of a wife is a persistent leak.

14 Home and possessions are an inheritance from parents,
but a prudent wife is from the LORD.[s]

15 Laziness plunges a man into deep sleep,
and the sluggard must go hungry.[t]

16 He who keeps the precept keeps his life,
but the despiser of the word will die.[u]

17 He who has compassion on the poor lends to the LORD,[v]
and he will repay him for his good deed.[*]

18 Chastise your son, for in this there is hope;
but do not desire his death.[w]

19 The man of violent temper pays the penalty;
even if you rescue him, you will have it to do again.

20 Listen to counsel and receive instruction,
that you may eventually become wise.

19, 17: Cf Mt 25, 34-40.

---

l: Prv 12, 4; 19, 14; Sir 7, 26.   m: Prv 17, 17.   n: Prv 28, 6.   o: Prv 14, 20; Sir 13, 20ff.   p: Dt 19, 16-20; Dn 13, 61.   q: Prv 20, 2.
r: Prv 10, 1; 17, 25.   s: Prv 18, 22.   t: Prv 6, 9ff.   u: Prv 13, 13; 16, 17.   v: Prv 14, 21; 22, 9; 28, 27.   w: Prv 13, 24; 23, 13f.

21 Many are the plans in a man's heart,
  but it is the decision of the LORD that
  endures.[x]

22 From a man's greed comes his shame;
  rather be a poor man than a liar.

23 The fear of the LORD is an aid to life;
  one eats and sleeps without being
  visited by misfortune.

24 The sluggard loses his hand in the dish;
  he will not even lift it to his mouth.[y]

25 If you beat an arrogant man, the simple
  learn a lesson;
  if you rebuke an intelligent man, he
  gains knowledge.[z]

26 He who mistreats his father, or drives
  away his mother,
  is a worthless and disgraceful son.[a]

27 If a son ceases to hear instruction,
  he wanders from words of knowledge.

28 An unprincipled witness perverts justice,
  and the mouth of the wicked pours out
  iniquity.

29 Rods are prepared for the arrogant,
  and blows for the backs of fools.[b]

CHAPTER 20

See RG
254–62

1 Wine is arrogant, strong drink is
  riotous;
  none who goes astray for it is wise.[c]

2 The dread of the king is as when a lion
  roars;[d]
  he who incurs his anger forfeits his life.

3 It is honorable for a man to shun strife,
  while every fool starts a quarrel.

4 In seedtime the sluggard plows not;
  when he looks for the harvest, it is not
  there.

5 The intention in the human heart is like
  water far below the surface,
  but the man of intelligence draws it
  forth.[e]

6 Many are declared to be men of virtue:
  but who can find one worthy of trust?

7 When a man walks in integrity and
  justice,
  happy are his children after him!

8 A king seated on the throne of judgment
  dispels all evil with his glance.

9 Who can say, "I have made my heart
  clean,[f]
  I am cleansed of my sin"?*

10 Varying weights, varying measures,
  are both an abomination to the LORD.[g]

11 Even by his manners the child betrays
  whether his conduct is innocent and
  right.

12 The ear that hears, and the eye that
  sees—
  the LORD has made them both.

13 Love not sleep, lest you be reduced to
  poverty;
  eyes wide open mean abundant food.

14 "Bad, bad!" says the buyer;
  but once he has gone his way, he
  boasts.*

15 Like gold or a wealth of corals,
  wise lips are a precious ornament.

20, 9: Man can be free of sin only by the power of God. Cf 1 Kgs 8, 46ff; Jb 4, 17; 14, 4; Pss 51, 2ff; 130, 3f; Rom 3, 23f; 1 Jn 1, 8.
20, 14: What one wishes to buy is valued cheaply in order that it may be obtained at a low price; once purchased, it is deemed more valuable.

x: Prv 16, 9. y: Prv 26, 15. z: Prv 17, 10; 21, 11. a: Sir 3, 16. b: Prv 26, 3. c: Prv 23, 29-35. d: Prv 19, 12. e: Prv 18, 4.
f: 1 Kgs 8, 46; 2 Chr 6, 36; Eccl 7, 20; 1 Jn 1, 8. g: Prv 11, 1; 20, 23.

16 Take his garment who becomes surety
   for another,[h]
   and for strangers yield it up!*

17 The bread of deceit is sweet to a man,
   but afterward his mouth will be filled
   with gravel.

18 Plans made after advice succeed;
   so with wise guidance wage your war.

19 A newsmonger reveals secrets;
   so have nothing to do with a babbler!

20 If one curses his father or mother,
   his lamp will go out* at the coming of
   darkness.[i]

21 Possessions gained hastily at the outset
   will in the end not be blessed.

22 Say not, "I will repay evil!"
   Trust in the LORD and he will help you.[j]

23 Varying weights are an abomination to
   the LORD,
   and false scales are not good.[k]

24 Man's steps are from the LORD;[l]
   how, then, can a man understand his
   way?*

25 Rashly to pledge a sacred gift is a trap for
   a man,
   or to regret a vow once made.*

26 A wise king winnows the wicked,
   and threshes them under the cartwheel.

27 A lamp from the LORD is the breath of
   man;
   it searches through all his inmost
   being.

28 Kindness and piety safeguard the king,
   and he upholds his throne by justice.[m]

29 The glory of young men is their strength,
   and the dignity of old men is gray
   hair.[n]

30 Evil is cleansed away by bloody lashes,
   and a scourging to the inmost being.

CHAPTER 21

See RG
254–62

1 Like a stream is the king's heart in
   the hand of the Lord;
   wherever it pleases him, he directs it.

2 All the ways of a man may be right in his
   own eyes,
   but it is the LORD who proves hearts.[o]

3 To do what is right and just[p]
   is more acceptable to the LORD than
   sacrifice.*

4 Haughty eyes and a proud heart—
   the tillage of the wicked is sin.

5 The plans of the diligent are sure of
   profit,
   but all rash haste leads certainly to
   poverty.

6 He who makes a fortune by a lying
   tongue
   is chasing a bubble over deadly
   snares.

7 The oppression of the wicked will sweep
   them away,
   because they refuse to do what is right.

8 The way of the culprit is crooked,
   but the conduct of the innocent is
   right.

20, 16: Caution is again advised in the matter of becoming surety; cf Prv 6, 1ff.

20, 20: His lamp will go out: misfortune, even death, awaits him; cf Prv 13, 9; Ex 21, 17.

20, 24: Man is dependent upon God and cannot fully foresee his own course.

20, 25: This verse cautions against making vows without proper reflection; cf Dt 23, 22ff; Eccl 5, 4f.

21, 3: External rites or sacrifices do not please God unless accompanied by internal worship and right moral conduct; cf Prv 15, 8; 21, 27; Is 1, 11-15; Am 5, 22; Mal 1, 12.

h: Prv 27, 13. i: Prv 30, 11. 17; Ex 21, 17; Lv 20, 9; Mt 15, 4. j: Prv 24, 29; Sir 28, 1; Mt 5, 39; Rom 12, 17. 19; 1 Thes 5, 15; 1 Pt 3, 9. k: Prv 11, 1; 20, 10. l: Prv 16, 9. m: Prv 16, 12. n: Prv 16, 31. o: Prv 16, 2. p: 1 Sm 15, 22; Hos 6, 6.

⁹ It is better to dwell in a corner of the
  housetop
  than in a roomy house with a
  quarrelsome woman.�q

¹⁰ The soul of the wicked man desires evil;
  his neighbor finds no pity in his eyes.

¹¹ When the arrogant man is punished, the
  simple are the wiser;
  when the wise man is instructed, he
  gains knowledge.ʳ

¹² The just man appraises the house of the
  wicked:
  there is one who brings down the
  wicked to ruin.

¹³ He who shuts his ear to the cry of the
  poor
  will himself also call and not be heard.

¹⁴ A secret gift allays anger,
  and a concealed present, violent wrath.

¹⁵ To practice justice is a joy for the just,
  but terror for evildoers.ˢ

¹⁶ The man who strays from the way of
  good sense
  will abide in the assembly of the
  shades.*

¹⁷ He who loves pleasure will suffer want;
  he who loves wine and perfume will
  not be rich.

¹⁸ The wicked man serves as ransom for the
  just,*
  and the faithless man for the righteous.ᵗ

¹⁹ It is better to dwell in a wilderness
  than with a quarrelsome and vexatious
  wife.

²⁰ Precious treasure remains in the house of
  the wise,
  but the fool consumes it.

²¹ He who pursues justice and kindness
  will find life and honor.

²² The wise man storms a city of the mighty,
  and overthrows the stronghold in
  which it trusts.

²³ He who guards his mouth and his tongue
  keeps himself from trouble.ᵘ

²⁴ Arrogant is the name for the man of
  overbearing pride
  who acts with scornful effrontery.

²⁵ The sluggard's propensity slays him,
  for his hands refuse to work.

²⁶ Some are consumed with avarice all the
  day,
  but the just man gives unsparingly.

²⁷ The sacrifice of the wicked is an
  abomination,
  the more so when they offer it with a
  bad intention.ᵛ

²⁸ The false witness will perish,ʷ
  but he who listens will finally have his
  say.

²⁹ The wicked man is brazenfaced,
  but the upright man pays heed to his
  ways.

³⁰ There is no wisdom, no understanding,
  no counsel, against the LORD.

³¹ The horse is equipped for the day of
  battle,
  but victory is the LORD's.

21, 16: Assembly of the shades: cf note on Jb 26, 5.

21, 18: Wicked . . . ransom for the just: exemplified in the history of God's chosen people whom he ransomed from Egypt at the cost of the life of Pharaoh and his army (Ex 14, 23-31), and from Babylon by giving to Cyrus, the Persian conqueror, Egypt, Ethiopia and Seba, the richest lands of the world (Is 43, 1ff).

q: Prv 21, 19; 25, 24; 27, 15; Sir 25, 23.   r: Prv 19, 25.   s: Prv 10, 29.   t: Prv 11, 8.   u: Prv 13, 3.   v: Prv 15, 8; Sir 34, 18ff.   w: Prv 19, 5. 9.

CHAPTER 22

[1] A good name is more desirable than
     great riches,
     and high esteem, than gold and silver.[x]

[2] Rich and poor have a common bond:
     the LORD is the maker of them all.[y]

[3] The shrewd man perceives evil and hides,
     while simpletons continue on and
     suffer the penalty.[z]

[4] The reward of humility and fear of the
     LORD
     is riches, honor and life.

[5] Thorns and snares are on the path of the
     crooked;
     he who would safeguard his life will
     shun them.

[6] Train a boy in the way he should go;
     even when he is old, he will not
     swerve from it.

[7] The rich rule over the poor,
     and the borrower is the slave of the
     lender.

[8] He who sows iniquity reaps calamity,[a]
     and the rod destroys his labors.

[9] The kindly man will be blessed,
     for he gives of his sustenance to the poor.

[10] Expel the arrogant man and discord goes
     out;
     strife and insult cease.

[11] The LORD loves the pure of heart;[b]
     the man of winning speech has the
     king for his friend.

[12] The eyes of the LORD safeguard
     knowledge,
     but he defeats the projects of the
     faithless.

[13] The sluggard says, "A lion is outside;[c]
     in the streets I might be slain."*

[14] The mouth of the adulteress is a deep pit;[d]
     he with whom the LORD is angry will
     fall into it.

[15] Folly is close to the heart of a child,
     but the rod of discipline will drive it
     far from him.

[16] He who oppresses the poor to enrich
     himself
     will yield up his gains to the rich as
     sheer loss.*

III: Sayings of the Wise*

[17] The sayings of the wise:*

     Incline your ear, and hear my words,[e]
     and apply your heart to my doctrine;
[18] For it will be well if you keep them in
     your bosom,
     if they all are ready on your lips.
[19] That your trust may be in the LORD,
     I make known to you the words of
     Amen-em-Ope.*
[20] Have I not written for you the "Thirty,"
     with counsels and knowledge,
[21] To teach you truly

22, 13: To avoid the effort required for doing good, the sluggard exaggerates the difficulties that must be overcome.

22, 16: Money gained by exploiting the poor is in turn lost to those who are more wealthy.

22, 17—24, 22: This collection of proverbs, introduced as sayings of the wise, is given in the more intimate and personal form of an address to a pupil called the son and is arranged in strophes instead of couplets.

22, 17—23, 35: The maxims warn against: oppression of the poor and defenseless (22, 22f), anger (24f), giving surety for debts (26f), bad manners at a king's table (23, 1f), anxiety for riches (4f), a grudging host (6ff), intemperance in food and drink (19ff. 29-35), and adultery (26ff). They exhort

to: careful workmanship (22, 29), respect for the rights of orphans (23, 10f), correction of the young (13f), filial piety (15f. 22-25), and fear of the Lord (17f).

22, 19f: Amen-em-Ope: an Egyptian scribe to whom is attributed a collection of maxims in Thirty chapters (v 20) composed for the instruction of his children and addressed to a young man who wishes to enter upon a career. The inspired editor of Proverbs does not translate these, but uses their materials in constructing a similar collection of proverbs.

x: Eccl 7, 1.   y: Prv 29, 13.   z: Prv 27, 12.   a: Jb 4, 8; Sir 7, 3; Hos 8, 7.   b: Mt 5, 8.   c: Prv 26, 13.   d: Prv 23, 27.   e: Prv 5, 1.

how to give a dependable report to one
who sends you?

22 Injure not the poor because they are poor,
nor crush the needy at the gate;
23 For the LORD will defend their cause,*f*
and will plunder the lives of those who
plunder them.

24 Be not friendly with a hotheaded man,
nor the companion of a wrathful man,
25 Lest you learn his ways,
and get yourself into a snare.

26 Be not one of those who give their hand
in pledge,
of those who become surety for debts;*g*
27 For if you have not the means to pay,
your bed will be taken from under you.

28 Remove not the ancient landmark
which your fathers set up.*h*

29 You see a man skilled at his work?
He will stand in the presence of kings;
he will not stand in the presence of
obscure men.

CHAPTER 23

**See RG
254–62**

1 When you sit down to dine with a
ruler,
keep in mind who is before you;
2 And put a knife to your throat*
if you have a ravenous appetite.
3 Do not desire his delicacies;
they are deceitful food.
4 Toil not to gain wealth,
cease to be concerned about it;
5 While your glance flits to it, it is gone!
for assuredly it grows wings,
like the eagle that flies toward heaven.

6 Do not take food with a grudging man,
and do not desire his dainties;
7 For in his greed he is like a storm.
"Eat and drink," he says to you,
though his heart is not with you;

8 The little you have eaten you will vomit
up,
and you will have wasted your
agreeable words.
9 Speak not for the fool's hearing;
he will despise the wisdom of your
words.*i*

10 Remove not the ancient landmark,*j*
nor invade the fields of orphans;
11 For their redeemer is strong;
he will defend their cause against you.*k*

12 Apply your heart to instruction,
and your ears to words of knowledge.

13 Withhold not chastisement from a boy;
if you beat him with the rod, he will
not die.*l*
14 Beat him with the rod,*m*
and you will save him from the nether
world.

15 My son, if your heart be wise,
my own heart also will rejoice;
16 And my inmost being will exult,
when your lips speak what is right.

17 Let not your heart emulate sinners,*n*
but be zealous for the fear of the LORD
always;
18 For you will surely have a future,
and your hope will not be cut off.*o*

19 Hear, my son, and be wise,
and guide your heart in the right way.
20 Consort not with winebibbers,
nor with those who eat meat to
excess;
21 For the drunkard and the glutton come to
poverty,
and torpor clothes a man in rags.

22 Listen to your father who begot you,
and despise not your mother when she
is old.
23 Get the truth, and sell it not—

23, 2: Put a knife to your throat: a proverbial metaphor for self-restraint.

---

f: Prv 23, 11.   *g:* Prv 6, 1f; 11, 15; 17, 18.   *h:* Prv 23, 10; Dt 19, 14; 27, 17.   *i:* Prv 9, 7.   *j:* Prv 22, 28.   *k:* Prv 22, 23.   *l:* Prv 13,
24; 19, 18; Sir 30, 1.   *m:* Prv 29, 15. 17.   *n:* Prv 3, 31; 24, 1.19.   *o:* Prv 24, 14.

wisdom, instruction and
understanding.
24 The father of a just man will exult with
glee;
he who begets a wise son will have joy
in him.*p*
25 Let your father and mother have joy;
let her who bore you exult.

26 My son, give me your heart,
and let your eyes keep to my ways.
27 For the harlot is a deep ditch,
and the adulteress a narrow pit;
28 Yes, she lies in wait like a robber,*q*
and increases the faithless among men.

29 Who scream? Who shriek?*
Who have strife? Who have anxiety?
Who have wounds for nothing?
Who have black eyes?
30 Those who linger long over wine,
those who engage in trials of blended
wine.*r*
31 Look not on the wine when it is red,
when it sparkles in the glass.
It goes down smoothly;
32 but in the end it bites like a serpent,
or like a poisonous adder.
33 Your eyes behold strange sights,
and your heart utters disordered
thoughts;
34 You are like one now lying in the depths
of the sea,
now sprawled at the top of the mast.
35 "They struck me, but it pained me not;
they beat me, but I felt it not;
When shall I awake
to seek wine once again?"*

CHAPTER 24

See RG
254–62

1 Be not emulous of evil men,*
and desire not to be with them;*s*

2 For their hearts plot violence,
and their lips speak of foul play.

3 By wisdom is a house built,
by understanding is it made firm;
4 And by knowledge are its rooms filled
with every precious and pleasing
possession.
5 A wise man is more powerful than a
strong man,
and a man of knowledge than a man of
might;*t*
6 For it is by wise guidance that you wage
your war,
and the victory is due to a wealth of
counselors.*u*
7 For a fool, to be silent is wisdom;*v*
not to open his mouth at the gate.*
8 He who plots evil doing—
men call him an intriguer.
9 Beyond intrigue and folly and sin,
it is arrogance that men find
abominable.

10 If you remain indifferent* in time of
adversity,
your strength will depart from you.
11 Rescue those who are being dragged to
death,*
and from those tottering to execution
withdraw not.
12 If you say, "I know not this man!"
does not he who tests hearts perceive
it?
He who guards your life knows it,
and he will repay each one according
to his deeds.*w*

13 If you eat honey, my son, because it is
good,
if virgin honey is sweet to your taste;

23, 29-35: A vivid description of the evil effects, physical and psychological, of drunkenness.

23, 35: Wine makes the drunkard insensible to bodily and moral harm. His one desire is to indulge again.

24, 1-22: These verses continue an exhortation to wisdom (vv 3-7. 13f), and against: violence (1f), pride and intrigue (8f), callousness (10-12), injustice (15f), joy in the failure of others (17f) or scandal at their success (19f), and rebellion against authority (21f).

24, 7: At the gate: of the city, where justice was adminis-

tered and public affairs discussed; see note on Ru 4, 1. Cf also Pss 69, 13; 127, 5; Prv 22, 22; 31, 23. 31.

24, 10: Indifferent: to those who suffer unjustly.

24, 11: Rescue . . . death: most probably refers to the legal rescue of those unjustly condemned to death.

p: Prv 10, 1. *q:* Prv 7, 10-27. *r:* Prv 20, 1; Sir 19, 2; Hos 4, 11. *s:* Prv 3, 31; 23, 17. *t:* Prv 21, 22. *u:* Prv 20, 18. *v:* Sir 6, 21. *w:* Ps 62, 13; Sir 16, 12; Mt 16, 27; Rom 2, 6.

[14] Such, you must know, is wisdom to your
soul.
If you find it, you will have a future,
and your hope will not be cut off.[x]

[15] Lie not in wait against the home of the
just man,
ravage not his dwelling place;
[16] For the just man* falls seven times and
rises again,
but the wicked stumble to ruin.

[17] Rejoice not when your enemy falls,
and when he stumbles, let not your
heart exult,
[18] Lest the LORD see it, be displeased with
you,
and withdraw his wrath from your
enemy.

[19] Be not provoked with evildoers,
nor envious of the wicked;
[20] For the evil man has no future,
the lamp of the wicked will be put out.[y]

[21] My son, fear the LORD and the king;*
have nothing to do with those who
rebel against them;
[22] For suddenly arises the destruction they
send,
and the ruin from either one, who can
measure?

IV: Other Sayings of the Wise*

[23]These also are sayings of the wise:

To show partiality in judgment is not good.[z]
[24] He who says to the wicked man, "You
are just"—
men will curse him, people will
denounce him;

[25] But those who convict the evildoer will
fare well,
and on them will come the blessing of
prosperity.
[26] He gives a kiss on the lips*
who makes an honest reply.

[27] Complete your outdoor tasks,
and arrange your work in the field;
afterward you can establish your house.*

[28] Be not a witness against your neighbor
without just cause,[a]
thus committing folly with your lips.
[29] Say not, "As he did to me, so will I do to
him;[b]
I will repay the man according to his
deeds."*

[30] I passed by the field of the sluggard,
by the vineyard of the man without
sense;
[31] And behold! it was all overgrown with
thistles;
its surface was covered with nettles,
and its stone wall broken down.
[32] And as I gazed at it, I reflected;
I saw and learned the lesson:
[33] A little sleep, a little slumber,[c]
a little folding of the arms to rest—
[34] Then will poverty come upon you like a
highwayman,
and want like an armed man.

V: Second Collection of the Proverbs of Solomon

CHAPTER 25

See RG
254–62

[1]These also are proverbs of Solomon.[d] The men of Hezekiah,* king of Judah,
transmitted them.

24, 16: The just man overcomes every misfortune which
oppresses him, Seven times: i.e., an indefinite number; cf Mt
18, 21f; Lk 17, 4.
24, 21f: One owes obedience to God and to supreme civil
authority (Mt 22, 21; Rom 13, 1ff; 1 Pt 2, 13f). The punishments for failure in either duty transcend the limits of private
justice.
24, 23-34: This collection of sayings continues in the
same vein as the preceding: it instructs in fairness (23-26) and
preparation for the future (27); and warns against vengeance
(28f) and slothfulness (30-34).

24, 26: He gives a kiss on the lips: shows himself a true friend.
24, 27: This verse is commonly interpreted as advocating
careful and practical preparation for marriage.
24, 29: This verse indicates great progress from the principle on the law of Talion (see note on Ex 21, 23ff) toward the
teaching found in Rom 12, 17ff. Cf also Prv 25, 21ff.
25, 1: The men of Hezekiah: literary men at the royal

x: Prv 23, 18.   y: Prv 13, 9.   z: Prv 18, 5; 28, 21; Lv 19, 15; Dt
1, 17; 16, 19.   a: Prv 19, 5; 25, 18.   b: Prv 20, 22.   c: 33f: Prv
6, 10f.   d: Prv 1, 1.

2 God has glory in what he conceals,
    kings have glory in what they
        fathom.
3 As the heavens in height, and the earth in
        depth,
    the heart of kings is unfathomable.

4 Remove the dross from silver,
    and it comes forth perfectly purified;
5 Remove the wicked from the presence of
        the king,
    and his throne is made firm through
        righteousness.

6 Claim no honor in the king's presence,*
    nor occupy the place of great men;
7 For it is better that you be told, "Come
        up closer!"
    than that you be humbled before the
        prince.*

8 What your eyes have seen
    bring not forth hastily against an
        opponent;
For what will you do later on
    when your neighbor puts you to
        shame?
9 Discuss your case with your neighbor,
    but another man's secret do not
        disclose;
10 Lest, hearing it, he reproach you,
    and your ill repute cease not.

11 Like golden apples in silver settings
    are words spoken at the proper time.

12 Like a golden earring, or a necklace of
        fine gold,
    is a wise reprover to an obedient ear.

13 Like the coolness of snow in the heat of
        the harvest
    is a faithful messenger for the one who
        sends him.
    [He refreshes the soul of his master.]

14 Like clouds and wind when no rain
        follows
    is the man who boastfully promises
        what he never gives.

15 By patience is a ruler persuaded,*f*
    and a soft tongue will break a bone.

16 If you find honey, eat only what you
        need,
    lest you become glutted with it and
        vomit it up.

17 Let your foot be seldom in your
        neighbor's house,
    lest he have more than enough of you,
        and hate you.

18 Like a club, or a sword, or a sharp
        arrow,
    is the man who bears false witness
        against his neighbor.

19 Like an infected tooth or an unsteady
        foot
    is [dependence on] a faithless man in
        time of trouble.

20 Like a moth in clothing, or a maggot in
        wood,
    sorrow gnaws at the human heart.*g*

21 If your enemy be hungry, give him food
        to eat,*
    if he be thirsty, give him to drink;*h*

22 For live coals you will heap on his head,
    and the LORD will vindicate you.

23 The north wind brings rain,
    and a backbiting tongue an angry
        countenance.

24 It is better to dwell in a corner of the
        housetop

---

court of Hezekiah who are represented as transcribing the proverbs from other collections. Hezekiah was a reformer of national religious life (2 Chr 29, 25-30).

25, 6f: Compare the lesson on humility which was taught by Christ (Lk 14, 7-11).

25, 21f: Charity is invaluable in resolving enmities and

restoring peace. Live coals: i.e., either remorse and embarrassment for the harm done, or increased punishment for refusing reconciliation. Cf Mt 5, 44; Rom 12, 20.

e: Lk 14, 8ff.   *f:* Prv 15, 1. 4.   *g:* Sir 30, 24.   *h:* Rom 12, 20.

than in a roomy house with a
quarrelsome woman.*i*

25 Like cool water to one faint from
thirst
is good news from a far country.

26 Like a troubled fountain or a polluted
spring
is a just man who gives way before the
wicked.

27 To eat too much honey is not good;
nor to seek honor after honor.*

28 Like an open city with no defenses
is the man with no check on his
feelings.

CHAPTER 26*

See RG
254-62
1 Like snow in summer, or rain in
harvest,
honor for a fool is out of place.

2 Like the sparrow in its flitting, like the
swallow in its flight,
a curse uncalled-for arrives nowhere.

3 The whip for the horse, the bridle for the
ass,
and the rod for the back of fools.*j*

4 Answer not the fool according to his
folly,*
lest you too become like him.

5 Answer the fool according to his folly,
lest he become wise in his own eyes.

6 He cuts off his feet, he drinks down
violence,
who sends messages by a fool.

7 A proverb in the mouth of a fool*
hangs limp, like crippled legs.

8 Like one who entangles the stone in the
sling
is he who gives honor to a fool.

9 Like a thorn stick brandished by the hand
of a drunkard
is a proverb in the mouth of fools.

10 Like an archer wounding all who
pass by
is he who hires a drunken fool.

11 As the dog returns to his vomit,
so the fool repeats his folly.*k*

12 You see a man wise in his own eyes?
There is more hope for a fool than for
him.

13 The sluggard says, "There is a lion in the
street,
a lion in the middle of the square!"*l*

14 The door turns on its hinges,
the sluggard, on his bed!

15 The sluggard loses his hand in the
dish;
he is too weary to lift it to his mouth.*m*

16 The sluggard imagines himself wiser
than seven men who answer with good
sense.

17 Like the man who seizes a passing dog
by the ears
is he who meddles in a quarrel not his
own.

18 Like a crazed archer
scattering firebrands and deadly
arrows

19 Is the man who deceives his neighbor,
and then says, "I was only joking."

25, 27: Nor . . . honor after honor: the text is uncertain.

26, 1-28: Concrete images describe the vices of fools (1-12), of sluggards (13-16), of meddlers (17-19), of talebearers (20ff), and of flatterers (23-28).

26, 4f: There is no contradiction between these two proverbs. In any answer the wise man gives he must

protect his own interest against the fool.

26, 7ff: The fool abuses whatever knowledge he possesses.

i: Prv 21, 9. *j:* Pv 19, 29; Sir 33, 25. *k:* 2 Pt 2, 22. *l:* Prv 22, 13. *m:* Prv 19, 24.

20 For lack of wood, the fire dies out;
and when there is no talebearer, strife
subsides.

21 What a bellows is to live coals, what
wood is to fire,
such is a contentious man in
enkindling strife.ⁿ

22 The words of a talebearer are like dainty
morsels
that sink into one's inmost being.ᵒ

23 Like a glazed finish on earthenware
are smooth lips with a wicked heart.

24 With his lips an enemy pretends,
but in his inmost being he maintains
deceit;

25 When he speaks graciously, trust him
not,ᵖ
for seven abominations* are in his
heart.

26 A man may conceal hatred under
dissimulation,
but his malice will be revealed in the
assembly.

27 He who digs a pit falls into it;
and a stone comes back upon him who
rolls it.�q

28 The lying tongue is its owner's enemy,
and the flattering mouth works ruin.

CHAPTER 27

See RG
254-62

1 Boast not of tomorrow,
for you know not what any day may
bring forth.

2 Let another praise you—not your own
mouth;
someone else—not your own lips.

3 Stone is heavy, and sand a burden,

but a fool's provocation is heavier than
both.ʳ

4 Anger is relentless, and wrath
overwhelming—
but before jealousy who can stand?

5 Better is an open rebuke
than a love that remains hidden.

6 Wounds from a friend may be accepted
as well meant,
but the greetings of an enemy one
prays against.

7 One who is full, tramples on virgin
honey;
but to the man who is hungry, any
bitter thing is sweet.

8 Like a bird that is far from its nest
is a man who is far from his home.

9 Perfume and incense gladden the heart,
but by grief the soul is torn asunder.

10 Your own friend and your father's friend
forsake not;
but if ruin befalls you, enter not a
kinsman's house.
Better is a neighbor near at hand
than a brother far away.

11 If you are wise, my son, you will gladden
my heart,
and I will be able to rebut him who
taunts me.

12 The shrewd man perceives evil and
hides;
simpletons continue on and suffer the
penalty.ˢ

13 Take his garment who becomes surety
for another,ᵗ
and for the sake of a stranger, yield it
up!*

26, 25: Seven abominations: many evil intentions.
27, 13: See note on Prv 20, 16.

n: Prv 15, 18; 29, 22.   o: Prv 18, 8.   p: Sir 12, 10; 27, 23.   q: Eccl 10, 8; Sir 27, 25f.   r: Sir 22, 14f.   s: Prv 22, 3.   t: Prv 20, 16.

¹⁴ When one greets his neighbor with a
loud voice in the early morning,
a curse can be laid to his charge.*

¹⁵ For a persistent leak on a rainy day
the match is a quarrelsome woman.ᵘ

¹⁶ He who keeps her stores up a stormwind;
he cannot tell north from south.

¹⁷ As iron sharpens iron,
so man sharpens his fellow man.

¹⁸ He who tends a fig tree eats its fruit,
and he who is attentive to his master
will be enriched.

¹⁹ As one face differs from another,
so does one human heart from another.

²⁰ The nether world and the abyss are never
satisfied;ᵛ
so too the eyes of men.

²¹ As the crucible tests silver and the
furnace gold,
so a man is tested by the praise he
receives.

²² Though you should pound the fool to bits
with the pestle, amid the grits in a
mortar,
his folly would not go out of him.

²³ Take good care of your flocks,*
give careful attention to your herds;

²⁴ For wealth lasts not forever,
nor even a crown from age to age.

²⁵ When the grass is taken away and the
aftergrowth appears,
and the mountain greens are gathered
in,

²⁶ The lambs will provide you with clothing,
and the goats will bring the price of a
field,

²⁷ And there will be ample goat's milk to
supply you,
to supply your household,
and maintenance for your maidens.

CHAPTER 28

See RG 254–62

¹ The wicked man flees although no
one pursues him;
but the just man, like a lion, feels sure
of himself.

² If a land is rebellious, its princes will be
many;
but with a prudent man it knows
security.*

³ A rich man who oppresses the poor
is like a devastating rain that leaves no
food.

⁴ Those who abandon the law* praise the
wicked man,
but those who keep the law war
against him.

⁵ Evil men understand nothing of justice,
but those who seek the LORD
understand all.

⁶ Better a poor man who walks in his
integrity
than he who is crooked in his ways
and rich.ʷ

⁷ He who keeps the law is a wise son,
but the gluttons' companion disgraces
his father.

⁸ He who increases his wealth by interest
and overcharge*

27, 14: The loud voice suggests hypocrisy in the greeting.

27, 23-27: The land of Palestine was very suitable for flocks and herds, which formed the principal source of wealth for their owners.

28, 2: The meaning of this poorly preserved verse seems to be that frequent changes of rulers often result from moral corruption and political disorder.

28, 4: The law: religious and moral teaching.

28, 8: Interest and overcharge were strictly forbidden in the old law among Israelites because it was presumed that the borrower was in distress; cf Ex 22, 25; Lv 25, 35ff; Dt 23, 19; Ps 15, 5; Ez 18, 8. Civil and divine law will take the offender's wealth from him.

---

u: Prv 21, 9; 25, 24.   *v:* Prv 30, 16; Eccl 4, 8.   *w:* Prv 19, 1.

gathers it for him who is kind to the poor.

9 When one turns away his ear from hearing the law,[x]
   even his prayer is an abomination.*

10 He who seduces the upright into an evil way
   will himself fall into his own pit.
   [And blameless men will gain prosperity.]

11 The rich man is wise in his own eyes,
   but a poor man who is intelligent sees through him.

12 When the just are triumphant, there is great jubilation;
   but when the wicked gain pre-eminence, people hide.

13 He who conceals his sins prospers not,
   but he who confesses and forsakes them obtains mercy.

14 Happy the man who is always on his guard;
   but he who hardens his heart will fall into evil.

15 Like a roaring lion or a ravenous bear
   is a wicked ruler over a poor people.

16 The less prudent the prince, the more his deeds oppress.
   He who hates ill-gotten gain prolongs his days.

17 Though a man burdened with human blood
   were to flee to the grave, none should support him.

18 He who walks uprightly is safe,
   but he whose ways are crooked falls into the pit.

19 He who cultivates his land will have plenty of food,
   but from idle pursuits a man has his fill of poverty.[y]

20 The trustworthy man will be richly blessed;
   he who is in haste to grow rich will not go unpunished.[z]

21 To show partiality is never good:[a]
   for even a morsel of bread a man may do wrong.

22 The avaricious man is perturbed about his wealth,
   and he knows not when want will come upon him.

23 He who rebukes a man gets more thanks in the end
   than one with a flattering tongue.

24 He who defrauds father or mother and calls it no sin,[b]
   is a partner of the brigand.

25 The greedy man stirs up disputes,
   but he who trusts in the LORD will prosper.

26 He who trusts in himself is a fool,
   but he who walks in wisdom is safe.

27 He who gives to the poor suffers no want,[c]
   but he who ignores them gets many a curse.

28 When the wicked gain pre-eminence, other men hide;
   but at their fall the just flourish.

CHAPTER 29

See RG 254–62

1 The man who remains stiff-necked and hates rebuke
   will be crushed suddenly beyond cure.

28, 9: Prayers offered in bad faith are displeasing to God.

---

x: Prv 21, 27.   y: Prv 12, 11.   z: Prv 13, 11.   a: Prv 24, 23.   b: Mk 7, 11ff.   c: Prv 19, 17; Sir 4, 3-8.

2 When the just prevail, the people rejoice;
  but when the wicked rule, the people
  groan.*d*

3 He who loves wisdom makes his father
  glad,
  but he who consorts with harlots
  squanders his wealth.*e*

4 By justice a king gives stability to the
  land;
  but he who imposes heavy taxes ruins
  it.

5 The man who flatters his neighbor
  is spreading a net under his feet.

6 The wicked man steps into a snare,
  but the just man runs on joyfully.

7 The just man has a care for the rights of
  the poor;
  the wicked man has no such concern.

8 Arrogant men set the city ablaze,
  but wise men calm the fury.*f*

9 If a wise man disputes with a fool,
  he may rage or laugh but can have no
  peace.

10 Bloodthirsty men hate the honest man,
   but the upright show concern for his
   life.

11 The fool gives vent to all his anger;
   but by biding his time, the wise man
   calms it.*g*

12 If a ruler listens to lying words,
   his servants all become wicked.

13 The poor and the oppressor* have a
   common bond:*h*
   the Lord gives light to the eyes of both.

14 If a king is zealous for the rights of the
   poor,
   his throne stands firm forever.

15 The rod of correction gives wisdom,
   but a boy left to his whims disgraces
   his mother.*i*

16 When the wicked prevail, crime increases;
   but their downfall the just will behold.

17 Correct your son, and he will bring you
   comfort,
   and give delight to your soul.

18 Without prophecy the people become
   demoralized;
   but happy is he who keeps the law.

19 By words no servant can be trained;*j*
   for he understands what is said, but
   obeys not.

20 Do you see a man hasty in his words?*k*
   More can be hoped for from a fool!

21 If a man pampers his servant from
   childhood,
   he will turn out to be stubborn.

22 An ill-tempered man stirs up disputes,
   and a hotheaded man is the cause of
   many sins.*l*

23 Man's pride causes his humiliation,
   but he who is humble of spirit obtains
   honor.*m*

24 The accomplice of a thief is his own
   enemy:*
   he hears himself put under a curse, yet
   discloses nothing.

25 The fear of man brings a snare,
   but he who trusts in the Lord is safe.

29, 13: God gives life to all classes of people; cf Prv 22, 2.
  29, 24: Is his own enemy: because he not only incurs guilt as an accomplice but, by his silence, brings down on himself
the curse invoked on the unknown guilty partner.

d: Prv 11, 10. *e:* Prv 5, 10; 10, 1. *f:* Prv 11, 11. *g:* Prv 12, 16; 25, 28; Sir 21, 26. *h:* Prv 22, 2. *i:* Prv 13, 24; 22, 15; 23, 13f; Sir
22. 6; 30, 1. *j:* Sir 33, 25f. *k:* Eccl 5, 1. *l:* Prv 15, 18; 26, 21. *m:* Prv 11, 2; 16, 18; 18, 12; Jb 22, 29.

26 Many curry favor with the ruler,
　　but the rights of each are from the
　　　LORD.

27 The evildoer is an abomination to the
　　just,
　　and he who walks uprightly is an
　　　abomination to the wicked.

VI: The Words of Agur

CHAPTER 30

See RG
254–62 1The words of Agur,* son of Jakeh the
Massaite:

The pronouncement of mortal man: "I
　　am not God;*
I am not God, that I should prevail.
2 Why, I am the most stupid of men,
　　and have not even human intelligence;
3 Neither have I learned wisdom,
　　nor have I the knowledge of the Holy
　　　One.
4 Who has gone up to heaven and come
　　down again—
who has cupped the wind in his hands?
Who has bound up the waters in a
　　cloak—
who has marked out all the ends of the
　　earth?
What is his name, what is his son's name,
　　if you know it?"
5 Every word of God is tested;n
　　he is a shield to those who take refuge
　　　in him.
6 Add nothing to his words,o
　　lest he reprove you, and you be
　　　exposed as a deceiver.

VII: Numerical Proverbs

7 Two things I ask of you,
　　deny them not to me before I die:

8 Put falsehood and lying far from me,
　　give me neither poverty nor riches;
　　[provide me only with the food I need;]
9 Lest, being full, I deny you,
　　saying, "Who is the Lord?"
Or, being in want, I steal,
　　and profane the name of my God.

10 Slander not a servant to his master,
　　lest he curse you, and you have to pay
　　　the penalty.

11 There is a group of people that curses its
　　father,*
　　and blesses not its mother.p
12 There is a group that is pure in its own
　　eyes,
　　yet is not purged of its filth.
13 There is a group—how haughty their eyes!
　　how overbearing their glance!
14 There is a group whose incisors are
　　swords,
　　whose teeth are knives,
Devouring the needy from the earth,
　　and the poor from among men.

15 The two daughters of the leech are,
　　"Give, Give."*
Three things are never satisfied,
　　four never say, "Enough!"
16 The nether world, and the barren womb;q
　　the earth, that is never saturated with
　　　water,
　　and fire, that never says, "Enough!"
17 The eye that mocks a father,
　　or scorns an aged mother,
Will be plucked out by the ravens in the
　　valley;
　　the young eagles will devour it.

18 Three things are too wonderful for me,*
　　yes, four I cannot understand:

30, 1: Agur: an unknown person. Massaite: from Massa in
northern Arabia, elsewhere referred to as an encampment of
the Ishmaelites (Gn 25, 14). But the word may not be intended as a place name; it might signify "an oracle," "a
prophecy."

30, 1ff: Agur wishes to stress man's insignificance when
he is compared to God; cf Jb 38—39.

30, 11-14: Perverted people are here classified as unfilial
(11), self-righteous (12), proud (13) and rapacious (14).

30, 15f: The two daughters . . . "Give, Give": the text is

obscure but the sense seems to be that the leech is insatiable
in its desire for blood, just as are the nether world for victims,
the barren womb for offspring, the parched earth for water,
and fire for fuel (16).

30, 18f: The soaring flight of the eagle, the mysterious
movement upon a rock of the serpent which has no feet, the
path of the ship through the trackless deep, and the marvelous
procreation of human life, excite great wonderment.

---

n: Ps 12, 7.　o: Dt 4, 2.　p: Prv 20. 20.　q: Prv 27, 20.

¹⁹ The way of an eagle in the air,
  the way of a serpent upon a rock,
The way of a ship on the high seas,
  and the way of a man with a maiden.
²⁰ Such is the way of an adulterous woman:
  she eats, wipes her mouth,
  and says, "I have done no wrong."*

²¹ Under three things the earth trembles,
  yes, under four it cannot bear up:
²² Under a slave when he becomes king,
  and a fool when he is glutted with
    food;*
²³ Under an odious woman when she is
    wed,
  and a maidservant when she displaces
    her mistress.

²⁴ Four things are among the smallest on
    the earth,
  and yet are exceedingly wise:
²⁵ Ants—a species not strong,
  yet they store up their food in the
    summer;
²⁶ Rock-badgers*—a species not mighty,
  yet they make their home in the crags;
²⁷ Locusts—they have no king,
  yet they migrate all in array;
²⁸ Lizards—you can catch them with your
    hands,
  yet they find their way into kings'
    palaces.

²⁹ Three things are stately in their stride,
  yes, four are stately in their carriage:
³⁰ The lion, mightiest of beasts,
  who retreats before nothing;
³¹ The strutting cock, and the he-goat,
  and the king at the head of his people.

³² If you have foolishly been proud*
  or presumptuous—put your hand on
    your mouth;
³³ For the stirring of milk brings forth
    curds,

and the stirring of anger brings forth
  blood.

VIII: The Words of Lemuel

CHAPTER 31

¹The words of Lemuel, king of
Massa. The advice which his mother gave
him:

² What, my son, my first-born!
  what, O son of my womb;
  what, O son of my vows!
³ Give not your vigor to women,
  nor your strength to those who ruin
    kings.*
⁴ It is not for kings, O Lemuel,
  not for kings to drink wine;
  strong drink is not for princes!*
⁵ Lest in drinking they forget what the law
    decrees,
  and violate the rights of all who are in
    need.
⁶ Give strong drink to one who is
    perishing,
  and wine to the sorely depressed;
⁷ When they drink, they will forget their
    misery,
  and think no more of their burdens.
⁸ Open your mouth in behalf of the dumb,
  and for the rights of the destitute;
⁹ Open your mouth, decree what is just,
  defend the needy and the poor!

IX: The Ideal Wife

¹⁰ When one finds a worthy wife,*
  her value is far beyond pearls.
¹¹ Her husband, entrusting his heart to her,
  has an unfailing prize.
¹² She brings him good, and not evil,*
  all the days of her life.
¹³ She obtains wool and flax
  and makes cloth with skillful hands.
¹⁴ Like merchant* ships,
  she secures her provisions from afar.

See RG
254-62

30, 20: This verse portrays the indifference of an adulterous woman who thinks there is no trace of her wicked act.

30, 26: Rock-badgers: cf note on Ps 104, 18.

30, 32f: The anger aroused by overweening pride threatens an awesome punishment.

31, 12: Good, and not evil: i.e., prosperity, not adversity.

31, 14: Merchant: literally, "Canaanite" (cf v 24), probably because the merchant class had been composed chiefly of Canaanites.

r: Prv 19, 10; Eccl 10, 6f. s: Prv 5, 9. t: Prv 20, 1. u: 10-31:
Sir 26, 1ff. 13-18.

¹⁵ She rises while it is still night,
 and distributes food to her household.
¹⁶ She picks out a field to purchase;
 out of her earnings she plants a
 vineyard.
¹⁷ She is girt about with strength,
 and sturdy are her arms.
¹⁸ She enjoys the success of her dealings;
 at night her lamp is undimmed.*
¹⁹ She puts her hands to the distaff,
 and her fingers ply the spindle.
²⁰ She reaches out her hands to the poor,
 and extends her arms to the needy.
²¹ She fears not the snow for her household;
 all her charges are doubly clothed.
²² She makes her own coverlets;
 fine linen and purple are her clothing.
²³ Her husband is prominent at the city
 gates
 as he sits with the elders of the land.

²⁴ She makes garments and sells them,
 and stocks the merchants with belts.
²⁵ She is clothed with strength and
 dignity,
 and she laughs at the days to come.*
²⁶ She opens her mouth in wisdom,
 and on her tongue is kindly counsel.
²⁷ She watches the conduct of her
 household,
 and eats not her food in idleness.
²⁸ Her children rise up and praise her;
 her husband, too, extols her:
²⁹ "Many are the women of proven worth,
 but you have excelled them all."
³⁰ Charm is deceptive and beauty fleeting;
 the woman who fears the LORD is to be
 praised.*
³¹ Give her a reward of her labors,
 and let her works praise her at the city
 gates.

31, 18: Her lamp is undimmed: indicates abundance of productive work and its accompanying prosperity; cf Prv 20, 20; Jb 18, 6.

31, 25: Laughs at the days to come: anticipates the future with gladness free from anxiety.

31, 30: The true charm of the ideal wife is her religious spirit, for she fears the Lord; cf note on Prv 1, 7.

See RG
261–67

The Book of Ecclesiastes

The title ECCLESIASTES given to this book is the Greek translation of the Hebrew name QOHELETH meaning, perhaps, "one who convokes an assembly." The book, however, does not consist of public addresses, but is a treatise, more or less logically developed, on the vanity of all things. Reflections in prose and aphorisms in verse are intermingled in Ecclesiastes, which contains, besides, an introduction and an epilogue.

The book is concerned with the purpose and value of human life. While admitting the existence of a divine plan, it considers such a plan to be hidden from man, who seeks happiness without ever finding it here below (3, 11; 8, 7. 17). Ecclesiastes applies his "Vanity of vanities" to everything "under the sun," even to that wisdom which seeks to find at last a semblance of good in the things of the world. Merit does not yield happiness for it is often tried by suffering. Riches and pleasures do not avail. Existence is monotonous, enjoyment fleeting and vain; darkness quickly follows. Life, then, is an enigma beyond human ability to solve.

While Ecclesiastes concedes that there is an advantage for man in the enjoyment of certain legitimate pleasures lest he lapse into pessimism and despair, he nevertheless considers this indulgence also vanity unless man returns due thanks to the Creator who has given him all. Under this aspect, earthly wisdom would rise to the higher level of true spiritual wisdom. This true wisdom is not found "under the sun" but is perceived only by the light of faith, inasmuch as it rests with God, who is the final Judge of the good and the bad, and whose reign endures forever. The Epilogue gives the clue to this thought (12, 13f).

The moral teaching of the book is imperfect, like the Old Testament itself (Heb 7, 19), yet it marks an advance in the development of the doctrine of divine retribution. While rejecting the older solution of earthly rewards and punishments, Ecclesiastes looks forward to a more lasting one. The clear answer to the problem was to come with the light of Christ's teaching concerning future life.

The author of the book was a teacher of popular wisdom (12, 9). Qoheleth was obviously only his literary name. Because he is called "David's son, king in Jerusalem," it was commonly thought that he was King Solomon. Such personation, however, was but a literary device to lend greater dignity and authority to the book—a circumstance which does not in any way impugn its inspired character. The Epilogue seems to have been written by an editor, probably a disciple of Qoheleth. The entire work differs considerably in language and style from earlier books of the Old Testament. It reflects a late period of Hebrew, and was probably written about three centuries before Christ.

See RG
261-67

CHAPTER 1

¹The words of David's son, Qoheleth,* king in Jerusalem:ª

Vanity of Toil without Profit

² Vanity of vanities,* says Qoheleth,
  vanity of vanities! All things are vanity!ᵇ
³ What profit has man from all the laborᶜ
  which he toils at under the sun?*
⁴ One generation passes and another
      comes,
  but the world forever stays.
⁵ The sun rises and the sun goes down;
  then it presses on to the place where it
      rises.
⁶ Blowing now toward the south, then
      toward the north,
  the wind turns again and again,
      resuming its rounds.
⁷ All rivers go to the sea,
  yet never does the sea become full.
 To the place where they go,
  the rivers keep on going.
⁸ All speech is labored;
  there is nothing man can say.*
 The eye is not satisfied with seeing
  nor is the ear filled with hearing.ᵈ

⁹What has been, that will be; what has been done, that will be done. Nothing is new under the sun.ᵉ ¹⁰Even the thing of which we say, "See, this is new!" has already existed in the ages that preceded us.ᶠ ¹¹There is no remembrance of the men of old;ᵍ nor of those to come will there be any remembrance among those who come after them.*

I: Qoheleth's Investigation of Life

Twofold Introduction. ¹²I, Qoheleth, was king over Israel in Jerusalem, ¹³and I applied my mind to search and investigate in wisdom all things that are done under the sun.ʰ

 A thankless task God has appointed
  for men to be busied about.

¹⁴I have seen all things that are done under the sun,ⁱ and behold, all is vanity and a chase after wind.*

¹⁵ What is crooked cannot be made straight,
  and what is missing cannot be supplied.

¹⁶ʲThough I said to myself, "Behold, I have become great and stored up wisdom beyond all who were before me in Jerusalem, and my mind has broad experience of wisdom and knowledge"; ¹⁷yet when I applied my mind to know wisdom and knowledge, madness and folly, I learned that this also is a chase after wind.ᵏ

¹⁸ For in much wisdom there is much sorrow,
  and he who stores up knowledge stores
      up grief.

CHAPTER 2

See RG
261-67

Study of Pleasure-seeking. ¹I said to myself,* "Come, now, let me try you with pleasure and the enjoyment of good things."ˡ

1, 1: Qoheleth: see Introduction.
1, 2: Vanity of vanities: a Hebrew superlative expressing the supreme degree of futility and emptiness.
1, 3: Under the sun: used throughout this book to signify "on the earth."
1, 8: All speech . . . man can say: or "All things are wearisome beyond man's power to tell."
1, 11: Men remember nothing long; God, however, never forgets.
1, 14: Chase after wind: futility, like an attempt to corral

the winds. Cf Hos 12, 2. The ancient versions understood "affliction of spirit." These words are used to conclude sections of the discourse, as far as Eccl 6, 9.
2, 1-11: The author here assumes the role of Solomon.

---

a: Eccl 7, 27; 12, 8f. b: Eccl 12, 8. c: Eccl 2, 11. 22; 3, 9; 5, 15. d: Eccl 8, 17. e: Eccl 3, 15; 6, 10. f: Eccl 3, 15. g: Eccl 2, 16. h: Eccl 8, 9. i: Eccl 2, 11. 17. j: Eccl 2, 9. k: Eccl 2, 3; 7, 25. l: Wis 2, 6.

But behold, this too was vanity. [2]Of laughter I said: "Mad!" and of mirth: "What good does this do?" [3]I thought of beguiling my senses with wine, though my mind was concerned with wisdom,* and of taking up folly, until I should understand what is best for men to do under the heavens during the limited days of their life.

[4]I undertook great works; I built myself houses and planted vineyards; [5]I made gardens and parks, and set out in them fruit trees of all sorts. [6]And I constructed for myself reservoirs to water a flourishing woodland. [7]I acquired male and female slaves, and slaves were born in my house. I also had growing herds of cattle and flocks of sheep, more than all who had been before me in Jerusalem. [8]I amassed for myself silver and gold, and the wealth of kings and provinces. I got for myself male and female singers and all human luxuries. [9]I became great, and I stored up more than all others before me in Jerusalem; my wisdom, too, stayed with me. [10m]Nothing that my eyes desired did I deny them, nor did I deprive myself of any joy, but my heart rejoiced in the fruit of all my toil. This was my share for all my toil. [11n]But when I turned to all the works that my hands had wrought, and to the toil at which I had taken such pains, behold! all was vanity and a chase after wind, with nothing gained under the sun. [12]For what will the man do who is to come after the king? What men have already done!

Study of Wisdom and Folly. I went on to the consideration of wisdom, madness and folly. [13]And I saw that wisdom has the advantage over folly as much as light has the advantage over darkness.

[14] The wise man has eyes in his head, but the fool walks in darkness.[o]

Yet I knew that one lot befalls both of them. [15]So I said to myself, if the fool's lot is to befall me also, why then should I be wise? Where is the profit for me? And I concluded in my heart that this too is vanity. [16p]Neither of the wise man nor of the fool will there be an abiding remembrance, for in days to come both will have been forgotten. How is it that the wise man dies as well as the fool! [17]Therefore I loathed life, since for me the work that is done under the sun is evil; for all is vanity and a chase after wind.

Study of the Fruits of Toil

To Others the Profits. [18]And I detested all the fruits of my labor under the sun, because I must leave them to a man who is to come after me. [19]And who knows whether he will be a wise man or a fool? Yet he will have control over all the fruits of my wise labor under the sun. This also is vanity. [20]So my feelings turned to despair of all the fruits of my labor under the sun. [21]For there is a man who has labored with wisdom and knowledge and skill, and to another, who has not labored over it, he must leave his property. This also is vanity and a great misfortune. [22q]For what profit comes to a man from all the toil and anxiety of heart with which he has labored under the sun? [23]All his days sorrow and grief are his occupation; even at night his mind is not at rest. This also is vanity.

[24r]There is nothing better for man than to eat and drink and provide himself with good things by his labors. Even this, I realized, is from the hand of God.* [25]For who can eat or drink apart from him? [26s]For to whatever man he sees fit he gives wisdom and knowledge and joy; but to the sinner he gives the task of gathering possessions to be given to whatever man God sees fit. This also is vanity and a chase after wind.

CHAPTER 3

Man Cannot Hit on the Right Time To Act

See RG 261-67

[1] There is an appointed time for everything,

2, 3: Though my mind ... wisdom: while indulging in pleasure the author hopes to discover wherein man's true happiness consists.

2, 24: Unrestrained indulgence is not advocated here, but legitimate pleasure and the cheerfulness it begets.

m: Eccl 3, 22; 5, 18. *n:* Eccl 1, 17; Sir 44, 9. *o:* 14f: Eccl 6, 8; 9, 2f. *p:* Eccl 1, 11; Wis 2, 4. *q:* Eccl 1, 3. *r:* Eccl 3, 12f. 22; 5, 17f; 8, 15. *s:* Prv 13, 22.

and a time for every affair under the
heavens.
2 A time to be born, and a time to die;
a time to plant, and a time to uproot
the plant.
3 A time to kill, and a time to heal;
a time to tear down, and a time to build.
4 A time to weep, and a time to laugh;
a time to mourn, and a time to dance.
5 A time to scatter stones, and a time to
gather them;
a time to embrace, and a time to be far
from embraces.
6 A time to seek, and a time to lose;
a time to keep, and a time to cast away.
7 A time to rend, and a time to sew;
a time to be silent, and a time to speak.
8 A time to love, and a time to hate;
a time of war, and a time of peace.

*9t*What advantage has the worker from his
toil? *10*I have considered the task which God
has appointed for men to be busied about.
*11u*He has made everything appropriate to its
time, and has put the timeless into their
hearts, without men's ever discovering, from
beginning to end, the work which God has
done. *12*I recognized that there is nothing better than to be glad and to do well during life.
*13v*For every man, moreover, to eat and drink
and enjoy the fruit of all his labor is a gift of
God. *14*I recognized that whatever God does
will endure forever; there is no adding to it,
or taking from it. Thus has God done that he
may be revered. *15w*What now is has already
been; what is to be, already is; and God restores* what would otherwise be displaced.

The Problem of Retribution. *16x*And still
under the sun in the judgment place I saw
wickedness, and in the seat of justice, iniquity. *17y*And I said to myself, both the just and
the wicked God will judge, since there is a
time for every affair and on every work a
judgment. *18*I said to myself: As for the children of men, it is God's way of testing them

and of showing that they are in themselves
like beasts. *19*For the lot of man and of beast
is one lot; the one dies as well as the other.
Both have the same life-breath, and man has
no advantage over the beast; but all is vanity.
*20z*Both go to the same place; both were made
from the dust, and to the dust they both return. *21a*Who knows if the life-breath of the
children of men goes upward and the life-
breath of beasts goes earthward? *22b*And I
saw that there is nothing better for a man than
to rejoice in his work; for this is his lot. Who
will let him see what is to come after him?

CHAPTER 4

See RG
261-67

Vanity of Toil. *1*Again I considered all
the oppressions that take place under the
sun: the tears of the victims with none to
comfort them! From the hand of their oppressors comes violence, and there is none
to comfort them!*c* *2*And those now dead, I
declared more fortunate in death than are the
living to be still alive.*d* *3*And better off than
both is the yet unborn, who has not seen the
wicked work that is done under the sun.
*4*Then I saw that all toil and skillful work is
the rivalry of one man for another. This also
is vanity and a chase after wind.

5 "The fool folds his arms
and consumes his own flesh"*—
6 Better is one handful with tranquility
than two with toil and a chase after
wind!

Companions and Successors. *7*Again I
found this vanity under the sun: *8*a solitary
man with no companion; with neither son
nor brother. Yet there is no end to all his toil,
and riches do not satisfy his greed. "For
whom do I toil and deprive myself of good
things?" This also is vanity and a worthless
task. *9*Two are better than one: they get a
good wage for their labor. *10*If the one falls,
the other will lift up his companion. Woe to
the solitary man! For if he should fall, he has

3, 15: God restores: the meaning is probably that God allows no part of his creation to drop out of existence.

4, 5: Consumes his own flesh: refuses to work for the necessities of life and consequently suffers hunger and impairs his
bodily health.

t: Eccl 1, 3. *u:* Eccl 8, 17; 11, 5; Gn 1, 31. *v:* Eccl 2, 24. *w:* Eccl 1, 9. *x:* Eccl 4, 1. *y:* Eccl 12, 14. *z:* Eccl 12, 7; Gn 2, 7; 3,
19; Ps 103, 14; Wis 2, 3; Sir 10, 9; 17, 1; 40, 11. *a:* Wis 2, 2. *b:* Eccl 8, 7; 10, 14. *c:* Eccl 5, 7. *d:* Eccl 7, 2.

no one to lift him up. ¹¹So also, if two sleep together, they keep each other warm. How can one alone keep warm? ¹²Where a lone man may be overcome, two together can resist. A three-ply cord is not easily broken.

¹³Better is a poor but wise youth than an old but foolish king who no longer knows caution; ¹⁴for from a prison house* one comes forth to rule, since even in his royalty he was poor at birth. ¹⁵Then I saw all those who are to live and move about under the sun with the heir apparent who will succeed to his place.* ¹⁶There is no end to all these people, to all over whom he takes precedence; yet the later generations will not applaud him. This also is vanity and a chase after wind.

Vanity of Many Words. ¹⁷ᵉGuard your step when you go to the house of God. Let your approach be obedience, rather than the fools' offering of sacrifice;* for they know not how to keep from doing evil.

See RG 261-67

CHAPTER 5

¹Be not hasty in your utterance and let not your heart be quick to make a promise in God's presence. God is in heaven and you are on earth; therefore let your words be few.

² For nightmares* come with many cares,
    and a fool's utterance with many
        words.

³ᶠWhen you make a vow to God, delay not its fulfillment. For God has no pleasure in fools; fulfill what you have vowed. ⁴You had better not make a vow than make it and not fulfill it. ⁵Let not your utterances make you guilty, and say not before his representative, "It was a mistake," lest God be angered by such words and destroy the works of your hands. ⁶ᵍRather, fear God!

Gain and Loss of Goods. ⁷ʰIf you see oppression of the poor, and violation of rights and justice in the realm, do not be shocked

by the fact, for the high official has another higher than he watching him and above these are others higher still—. ⁸Yet an advantage for a country in every respect is a king for the arable land.*

⁹ⁱThe covetous man is never satisfied with money, and the lover of wealth reaps no fruit from it; so this too is vanity. ¹⁰Where there are great riches, there are also many to devour them. Of what use are they to the owner except to feast his eyes upon? ¹¹Sleep is sweet to the laboring man, whether he eats little or much, but the rich man's abundance allows him no sleep.

¹²ʲThis is a grievous evil which I have seen under the sun: riches kept by their owner to his hurt. ¹³Should the riches be lost through some misfortune, he may have a son when he is without means. ¹⁴ᵏAs he came forth from his mother's womb, so again shall he depart, naked as he came, having nothing from his labor that he can carry in his hand. ¹⁵This too is a grievous evil, that he goes just as he came. What then does it profit him to toil for wind? ¹⁶All the days of his life are passed in gloom and sorrow, under great vexation, sickness and wrath.

¹⁷ˡHere is what I recognize as good: it is well for a man to eat and drink and enjoy all the fruits of his labor under the sun during the limited days of the life which God gives him; for this is his lot. ¹⁸Any man to whom God gives riches and property, and grants power to partake of them, so that he receives his lot and finds joy in the fruits of his toil, has a gift from God. ¹⁹For he will hardly dwell on the shortness of his life, because God lets him busy himself with the joy of his heart.*

CHAPTER 6

See RG 261-67

Limited Worth of Enjoyment. ¹There is another evil which I have seen under the sun, and it weighs heavily upon man: ²ᵐthere is the man to whom God gives riches

---

4, 14: Prison house: probably his mother's womb, from which the king issues without possessions. Cf Eccl 5, 14.

4, 15: The king is no sooner dead than the people transfer their allegiance to his successor.

4, 17: The fools' . . . sacrifice: unacceptable to God because of their disobedience; cf 1 Sm 15, 22; Hos 6, 6.

5, 2: Nightmares: literally, "dreams."

5, 8: The wording of this verse has perhaps never been

adequately explained.

5, 19: The meaning is that the joys of life, though temporary, keep a man from dwelling on the ills which afflict humanity.

---

e: 1 Sm 15, 22; Hos 6, 6. *f:* Nm 30, 3; Dt 23, 23; Ps 50, 14. *g:* Eccl 12, 13; Dt 10, 12. *h:* Eccl 3, 16; 4, 1. *i:* Prv 28, 22. *j:* Jb 20, 20. *k:* Jb 1, 21; 1 Tm 6, 7. *l:* 17f; Eccl 2, 24. *m:* Eccl 2, 18f.

and property and honor, so that he lacks none of all the things he craves; yet God does not grant him power to partake of them, but a stranger devours them. This is vanity and a dire plague. ³Should a man have a hundred children and live many years, no matter to what great age, still if he has not the full benefit of his goods, or if he is deprived of burial, of this man I proclaim that the child born dead is more fortunate than he.* ⁴Though it came in vain and goes into darkness and its name is enveloped in darkness; ⁵though it has not seen or known the sun, yet the dead child is at rest rather than such a man. ⁶Should he live twice a thousand years and not enjoy his goods, do not both go to the same place?*

⁷All man's toil is for his mouth,* yet his desire is not fulfilled. ⁸For what advantage has the wise man over the fool, or what advantage has the poor man in knowing how to conduct himself in life? ⁹"What the eyes see is better than what the desires wander after."* This also is vanity and a chase after wind.

II: Qoheleth's Conclusions

¹⁰Whatever is, was long ago given its name, and the nature of man is known, and that he cannot contend in judgment with one who is stronger than he.* ¹¹For though there are many sayings that multiply vanity, what profit is there for a man? ¹²ⁿFor who knows what is good for a man in life, the limited days of his vain life (which God has made like a shadow)? Because—who is there to tell a man what will come after him under the sun?

A. Man Cannot Find Out What Is Good for Him To Do

CHAPTER 7

See RG 261-67

Critique of Sages on the Day of Adversity

¹ A good name is better than good ointment,* and the day of death than the day of birth.ᵒ
² It is better to go to the house of mourning than to the house of feasting,
For that is the end of every man,
    and the living should take it to heart.ᵖ
³ Sorrow is better than laughter,
    because when the face is sad the heart grows wiser.
⁴ The heart of the wise is in the house of mourning,
    but the heart of fools is in the house of mirth.
⁵ It is better to hearken to the wise man's rebuke
    than to hearken to the song of fools;
⁶ For as the crackling of thorns under a pot,
    so is the fool's laughter.
    This also is vanity,
⁷ For oppression can make a fool of a wise man,
    and a bribe corrupts the heart.
⁸ Better is the end of speech than its beginning;
    better is the patient spirit than the lofty spirit.
⁹ Do not in spirit become quickly discontented,
    for discontent lodges in the bosom of a fool.

¹⁰Do not say: How is it that former times were better than these? For it is not in wisdom that you ask about this.

¹¹ Wisdom and an inheritance are good,
    and an advantage to those that see the sun.

¹²For the protection of wisdom is as the protection of money; and the advantage of knowledge is that wisdom preserves the life of its owner.
    ¹³Consider the work of God. Who can make straight what he has made crooked?

6, 3: A large family, a long life, an honorable burial, all were highly esteemed by the Hebrews, and it was considered a great misfortune to be deprived of them.

6, 6: Same place: the grave.

6, 7: Mouth: appetite, and therefore, body.

6, 9: Better . . . wander after: the good that is present to us is better than that which is absent and, perhaps, unattainable.

6, 10: The one who is stronger than man is God.

7, 1: Ointment: applied to the child at birth; a good name remains even after death.

---

n: Jb 8, 9; 14, 2; Ps 102, 12.   o: Eccl 4, 2; Prv 22, 1; Sir 41, 13.   p: Eccl 4, 2.

*14*On a good day enjoy good things, and on an evil day consider: Both the one and the other God has made, so that man cannot find fault with him in anything.

Critique of Sages on Justice and Wickedness. *15*I have seen all manner of things in my vain days: a just man perishing in his justice, and a wicked one surviving in his wickedness. *16q*"Be not just to excess, and be not overwise, lest you be ruined.* *17*Be not wicked to excess, and be not foolish. Why should you die before your time?"* *18*It is good to hold to this rule, and not to let that one* go; but he who fears God will win through at all events.

*19*Wisdom is a better defense for the wise man than would be ten princes in the city, *20r*yet there is no man on earth so just as to do good and never sin.* *21s*Do not give heed to every word that is spoken lest you hear your servant speaking ill of you, *22*for you know in your heart that you have many times spoken ill of others.

*23*All these things I probed in wisdom. I said, "I will acquire wisdom"; but it was beyond me. *24*What exists is far-reaching; it is deep, very deep: who can find it out? *25t*I turned my thoughts toward knowledge; I sought and pursued wisdom and reason, and I recognized that wickedness is foolish and folly is madness.

Critique of Sages on Women. *26u*More bitter than death I find the woman who is a hunter's trap, whose heart is a snare and whose hands are prison bonds. He who is pleasing to God will escape her, but the sinner will be entrapped by her. *27*Behold, this have I found, says Qoheleth, adding one thing to another that I might discover the answer *28*which my soul still seeks and has not found: One man out of a thousand have I come upon, but a woman among them all I have not found.* *29*Behold, only this have I found out: God made mankind straight, but men have had recourse to many calculations.*

CHAPTER 8

Critique of Sages on the Wise Man and the King

1 Who is like the wise man,
and who knows the explanation of things?
A man's wisdom illumines his face,
but an impudent look is resented.

*2*Observe the precept of the king, and in view of your oath to God, *3*be not hasty to withdraw from the king; do not join in with a base plot, for he does whatever he pleases, *4*because his word is sovereign, and who can say to him, "What are you doing?"

5"He who keeps the commandment experiences no evil, and the wise man's heart knows times and judgments; *6*for there is a time and a judgment for everything."—Yet it is a great affliction for man *7v*that he is ignorant of what is to come; for who will make known to him how it will be? *8*There is no man who is master of the breath of life so as to retain it, and none has mastery of the day of death. There is no exemption from the struggle, nor are the wicked saved by their wickedness. *9w*All these things I considered and I applied my mind to every work that is done under the sun, while one man tyrannizes over another to his hurt.

The Problem of Retribution. *10*Meanwhile I saw wicked men approach and enter; and as they left the sacred place, they were praised in the city for what they had done. This also is vanity.* *11*Because the sentence

---

7, 16: St. Jerome explains the warning against excessive justice in reference to the self-righteous man who is so stern that he is never willing to forgive sin in others; cf vv 20ff.

7, 17: Untimely death was traditionally recognized as a divine punishment of the wicked; cf 1 Sm 2, 31-34; Jer 17, 11; Ps 55, 24; Prv 10, 27. This warning against presumptuous wickedness is not an endorsement of any lesser degree of misconduct.

7, 18: This rule . . . that one: the sayings cited in vv 16f. Others refer this and that to riches and wisdom (cf 7, 12), justice and wisdom, or justice and wickedness. This last supposition makes the author's thought hard to follow.

7, 20: This is to be understood in the sense of Rom 5, 12.

See note there.

7, 28: The author found sincerity rare among men, but among women still more rare.

7, 29: Calculations: the many vain attempts and schemes of men to attain happiness by their own efforts.

8, 10: The text is obscure. The Latin has "wicked men buried, who, while still alive, were in the holy place, and were praised in the city as if their works were just."

q: 16f: Eccl 8, 12ff. *r:* Jb 25, 4; Prv 20, 9; 1 Kgs 8, 46; Rom 3, 23; Jas 3, 2; 1 Jn 1, 8. *s:* 21f: 1 Kgs 8, 46. *t:* Eccl 1, 17. *u:* Prv 5, 4. *v:* Eccl 3, 22; 10, 14. *w:* Eccl 1, 13f.

against evildoers is not promptly executed, therefore the hearts of men are filled with the desire to commit evil— [12]because the sinner does evil a hundred times and survives. Though indeed I know that it shall be well with those who fear God, for their reverence toward him; [13]and that it shall not be well with the wicked man, and he shall not prolong his shadowy* days, for his lack of reverence toward God.

[14]This is a vanity which occurs on earth: there are just men treated as though they had done evil and wicked men treated as though they had done justly. This, too, I say is vanity. [15x]Therefore I commend mirth, because there is nothing good for man under the sun except eating and drinking and mirth: for this is the accompaniment of his toil during the limited days of the life which God gives him under the sun.*

[16y]When I applied my heart to know wisdom and to observe what is done on earth, [17z]I recognized that man is unable to find out all God's work that is done under the sun, even though neither by day nor by night do his eyes find rest in sleep. However much man toils in searching, he does not find it out; and even if the wise man says that he knows, he is unable to find it out.

B. Man Does Not Know What Is To Come

See RG 261–67

CHAPTER 9

[1]All this I have kept in mind and recognized:* the just, the wise, and their deeds are in the hand of God. Love from hatred* man cannot tell; both appear equally vain, [2a]in that there is the same lot for all, for the just and the wicked, for the good and the bad, for the clean and the unclean, for him who offers sacrifice and him who does not. As it is for the good man, so it is for the sinner; as it is for him who swears rashly, so it is for him who fears an oath. [3]Among all the things that happen under the sun, this is the worst, that things turn out the same for all. Hence the minds of men are filled with evil, and madness is in their hearts during life; and afterward they go to the dead.

[4]Indeed, for any among the living there is hope; a live dog is better off than a dead lion. [5b]For the living know that they are to die, but the dead no longer know anything. There is no further recompense for them, because all memory of them is lost. [6]For them, love and hatred and rivalry have long since perished. They will never again have part in anything that is done under the sun.

[7c]Go, eat your bread with joy and drink your wine with a merry heart, because it is now that God favors your works. [8]At all times let your garments be white, and spare not the perfume for your head. [9]Enjoy life with the wife whom you love, all the days of the fleeting life that is granted you under the sun. This is your lot in life, for the toil of your labors under the sun. [10]Anything you can turn your hand to, do with what power you have; for there will be no work, nor reason, nor knowledge, nor wisdom in the nether world where you are going.

The Evil Time Not Known. [11]Again I saw under the sun that the race is not won by the swift, nor the battle by the valiant, nor a livelihood by the wise, nor riches by the shrewd, nor favor by the experts; for a time of calamity comes to all alike. [12]Man no more knows his own time* than fish taken in the fatal net, or birds trapped in the snare; like these the children of men are caught when the evil time falls suddenly upon them.

The Uncertain Future and the Sages. [13]On the other hand I saw this wise deed under the sun, which I thought sublime. [14]Against a small city with few men in it advanced a mighty king, who surrounded it and threw up great siegeworks about it. [15]But in the city lived a man who, though poor, was wise, and he delivered it through his wisdom. Yet no one remembered this

---

8, 13: Shadowy: perhaps an addition here; cf Eccl 6, 12.

8, 15: See notes on Eccl 2, 24; 5, 19.

9, 1-10: These statements are based on a very imperfect concept of life beyond the grave. With Christian revelation about the future life came the only satisfactory solution of the problem which so perplexed the author.

9, 1: Love from hatred: divine favor or disfavor.

9, 12: His own time: the time of death or sudden disaster.

---

x: Eccl 2, 24; 9, 7.   y: Eccl 1, 13; 3, 10.   z: Eccl 3, 11.   a: Eccl 2, 14.   b: Eccl 1, 11.   c: Eccl 2, 1. 24; 8, 15; 11, 9.

poor man. [16d]Though I had said, "Wisdom is better than force," yet the wisdom of the poor man is despised and his words go unheeded.

[17] "The quiet words of the wise are better heeded
than the shout of a ruler of fools"—!

[18] "A fly that dies can spoil the perfumer's ointment,
and a single slip can ruin much that is good."

CHAPTER 10

See RG 261-67

[1]More weighty than wisdom or wealth is a little folly!
[2] The wise man's understanding turns him to his right;
the fool's understanding turns him to his left.*

[3]When the fool walks through the street, in his lack of understanding he calls everything foolish.
[4]Should the anger of the ruler burst upon you, forsake not your place; for mildness abates great offenses.
[5]I have seen under the sun another evil, like a mistake that proceeds from the ruler: [6]a fool put in lofty position while the rich sit in lowly places. [7]I have seen slaves on horseback, while princes walked on the ground like slaves.

[8] He who digs a pit may fall into it,[e]
and he who breaks through a wall may be bitten by a serpent.

[9] He who moves stones may be hurt by them,
and he who chops wood is in danger from it.

[10]If the iron becomes dull, though at first he made easy progress, he must increase his efforts; but the craftsman has the advantage of his skill.

[11] If the serpent bites because it has not been charmed,
then there is no advantage for the charmer.

[12] Words from the wise man's mouth win favor,
but the fool's lips consume him.[f]
[13] The beginning of his words is folly,
and the end of his talk is utter madness;
[14] yet the fool multiplies words.
Man knows not what is to come,
for who can tell him what is to come after him?[g]
[15] When will the fool be weary of his labor,
he who knows not the way to the city?*

Man Does Not Know What Evil Will Come
[16] Woe to you, O land, whose king was a servant,
and whose princes dine in the morning!
[17] Blessed are you, O land, whose king is of noble birth,
and whose princes dine at the right time
(for vigor and not in drinking bouts).
[18] When hands are lazy, the rafters sag;
when hands are slack, the house leaks.
[19] Bread and oil call forth merriment
and wine makes the living glad,
but money answers for everything.
[20] Even in your thoughts do not make light of the king,
nor in the privacy of your bedroom revile the rich,
Because the birds of the air may carry your voice,
a winged creature may tell what you say.

CHAPTER 11

See RG 261-67

[1] Cast your bread upon the waters;*
after a long time you may find it again.

10, 2: It is doubtful whether the author is endorsing either direction; cf Prv 4, 25ff.

10, 15: He who . . . city: perhaps a proverbial expression for supreme stupidity.

11, 1: This may refer to a spirit of adventure in business or to generosity in almsgiving. Waters: of the ocean, which sometimes carry lost treasures to the shore.

---

d: Prv 24, 5.   e: 8f: Prv 26, 27; Sir 27, 29.   f: Sir 21, 19.   g: Eccl 5, 2; 8, 7.

[2] Make seven or eight portions;*
    you know not what misfortune may
        come upon the earth.

Man Does Not Know What Good Will Come

[3] When the clouds are full,
    they pour out rain upon the earth.
Whether a tree falls to the south or to the
        north,
    wherever it falls, there shall it lie.
[4] One who pays heed to the wind will not
        sow,
    and one who watches the clouds will
        never reap.
[5] Just as you know not how the breath of
        life
    fashions the human frame in the
        mother's womb,
So you know not the work of God
    which he is accomplishing in the
        universe.[h]
[6] In the morning sow your seed,
    and at evening let not your hand be
        idle:
For you know not which of the two will
        be successful,
    or whether both alike will turn out
        well.

Poem on Youth and Old Age. [7]Light is sweet! and it is pleasant for the eyes to see the sun. [8]However many years a man may live, let him, as he enjoys them all, remember that the days of darkness will be many. All that is to come is vanity.

[9] Rejoice, O young man, while you are
        young,
    and let your heart be glad in the days
        of your youth.
Follow the ways of your heart,
    the vision of your eyes;

Yet understand that as regards all this
    God will bring you to judgment.
[10] Ward off grief from your heart
    and put away trouble from your
        presence,
    though the dawn of youth is fleeting.*

CHAPTER 12

See RG 261–67

[1] Remember your Creator in the
        days of your youth,
    before the evil days come
And the years approach of which you
        will say,
    I have no pleasure in them;
[2] Before the sun is darkened,
    and the light, and the moon, and the
        stars,
    while the clouds return* after the rain;
[3] When the guardians* of the house
        tremble,
    and the strong men are bent,
And the grinders are idle because they
        are few,
    and they who look through the
        windows grow blind;
[4] When the doors* to the street are shut,
    and the sound of the mill is low;
When one waits for the chirp of a bird,
    but all the daughters of song are
        suppressed;
[5] And one fears heights,
    and perils in the street;
When the almond tree blooms,*
    and the locust grows sluggish
    and the caper berry is without effect,
Because man goes to his lasting home,
    and mourners go about the streets;
[6] Before the silver cord is snapped
    and the golden bowl* is broken,
And the pitcher is shattered at the spring,
    and the broken pulley falls into the
        well,

11, 2: This verse refers either to almsgiving or to the wisdom of not putting all one's cargo into a single vessel.

11, 10: Dawn . . . fleeting: literally, "youth and the dawn [of life] are vanity."

12, 2: The sun . . . return: the cloudy and rainy Palestinian winter, a natural symbol of old age.

12, 3: Guardians: the arms; strong men: the legs; grinders: the teeth; they who . . . windows: the eyes.

12, 4: Doors: the tightly compressed lips; sound of the mill: perhaps the sound of mastication; daughters of song: the voice.

12, 5: The almond tree blooms: resembling the white hair of age. The locust . . . sluggish: an image of the stiffness in movement of the aged. The caper berry: a stimulant for appetite.

12, 6: The golden bowl suspended by the silver cord was a symbol of life; the snapping of the cord and the breaking of the bowl, a symbol of death. The pitcher . . . the broken pulley: another pair of metaphors for life and its ending.

h: Eccl 8, 17.

⁷ And the dust returns to the earth as it
      once was,
  and the life breath returns to God who
      gave it.ⁱ

⁸ Vanity of vanities, says Qoheleth,
  all things are vanity!ʲ

Epilogue. ⁹Besides being wise, Qoheleth
taught the people knowledge, and weighed,
scrutinized and arranged many proverbs.
¹⁰Qoheleth sought to find pleasing sayings,
and to write down true sayings with precision. ¹¹The sayings of the wise are like
goads; like fixed spikes are the topics given
by one collector.* ¹²ᵏAs to more than these,
my son, beware. Of the making of many
books there is no end, and in much study
there is weariness for the flesh.

¹³ˡThe last word, when all is heard: Fear
God and keep his commandments, for this is
man's all;* ¹⁴ᵐbecause God will bring to
judgment every work, with all its hidden
qualities, whether good or bad.

12, 11: Goads . . . one collector: the sayings were stimulants to thought and also spikes or centers around which to group correlated pronouncements of the wise.

12, 13: Man's all: St. Jerome explains: "Unto this is every man born, that, knowing his Maker, he may revere him in fear, honor, and the observance of his commandments."

i: Eccl 3, 20f; Jb 34, 15.   *j:* Eccl 1, 2.   *k:* Eccl 1, 18.   *l:* Eccl 5, 6.   *m:* Eccl 11, 9.

See RG
267–71

The Song of Songs

The Song of Songs, meaning the greatest of songs (1, 1), contains in exquisite poetic form the sublime portrayal and praise of the mutual love of the Lord and his people. The Lord is the Lover and his people are the beloved. Describing this relationship in terms of human love, the author simply follows Israel's tradition. Isaiah (5, 1-7; 54, 4-8), Jeremiah (2, 2f. 32), and Ezekiel (16; 23) all characterize the covenant between the Lord and Israel as a marriage. Hosea the prophet sees the idolatry of Israel in the adultery of Go-mer (1—3). He also represents the Lord speak-ing to Israel's heart (2, 16) and changing her into a new spiritual people, purified by the Babyloni-an captivity and betrothed anew to her divine Lover "in justice and uprightness, in love and mercy" (2, 21).

The author of the Song, using the same literary figure, paints a beautiful picture of the ideal Is-rael, the chosen people of the Old and New Tes-taments, whom the Lord led by degrees to an ex-alted spiritual union with himself in the bond of perfect love. When the Song is thus interpreted there is no reason for surprise at the tone of the poem, which employs in its descriptions the courtship and marriage customs of the author's time. Moreover, the poem is not an allegory in which each remark, e. g., in the dialogue of the lovers, has a higher meaning. It is a parable in which the true meaning of mutual love comes from the poem as a whole.

While the Song is thus commonly understood by most Catholic scholars, it is also possible to see in it an inspired portrayal of ideal human love. Here we would have from God a description of the sacredness and the depth of married union.

Although the poem is attributed to Solomon in the traditional title (1, 1), the language and style of the work, among other considerations, point to a time after the end of the Babylonian Exile (538 B.C.) as that in which an unknown poet com-posed this masterpiece. The structure of the Song is difficult to analyze; here it is regarded as a lyric dialogue, with dramatic movement and interest.

The use of marriage as a symbol, characteristic of the Song, is found extensively also in the New Testament (Mt 9, 15; 25, 1-13; Jn 3, 29; 2 Cor 11, 2; Eph 5, 23-32; Rv 19, 7ff; 21, 9ff). In Chris-tian tradition, the Song has been interpreted in terms of the union between Christ and the Church and, particularly by St. Bernard, of the union be-tween Christ and the individual soul. Throughout the liturgy, especially in the Little Office, there is a consistent application of the Song of Songs to the Blessed Virgin Mary.

I: The Song of Songs by Solomon*

CHAPTER 1

See RG
267–71

Love's Desires

2 B Let him kiss me with kisses of his
mouth!*

More delightful is your love than wine!*a*
3 Your name spoken is a spreading
perfume—
that is why the maidens love you.
4 Draw me!—
D We will follow you eagerly!
B Bring me, O king, to your chambers.

D With you we rejoice and exult,
we extol your love; it is beyond wine:*b*
how rightly you are loved!

Love's Boast

5 B I am as dark—but lovely,
O daughters of Jerusalem*—
As the tents of Kedar,
as the curtains of Salma.
6 Do not stare at me because I am swarthy,*
because the sun has burned me.
My brothers have been angry with me;
they charged me with the care of the
vineyards:
my own vineyard I have not cared for.

Love's Inquiry

7 B Tell me, you whom my heart loves,*
where you pasture your flock,

where you give them rest at midday,
Lest I be found wandering
after the flocks of your companions.

8 G If you do not know,
O most beautiful among women,
Follow the tracks of the flock
and pasture the young ones
near the shepherds' camps.

Love's Vision

9 G To the steeds of Pharaoh's chariots*
would I liken you, my beloved:
10 Your cheeks lovely in pendants,
your neck in jewels.
11 We will make pendants of gold for you,
and silver ornaments.

Love's Union

12 B For the king's banquet
my nard* gives forth its fragrance.
13 My lover is for me a sachet of myrrh*
to rest in my bosom.
14 My lover is for me a cluster of henna*
from the vineyards of Engedi.

15 G Ah, you are beautiful, my beloved,*c*
ah, you are beautiful; your eyes are
doves!*

16 B Ah, you are beautiful, my lover—
yes, you are lovely.
Our couch, too, is verdant;*
17 the beams of our house are cedars,
our rafters, cypresses.

1, 1: This title is actually the first verse of chapter 1.

1, 2ff: The marginal letters indicate the speaker of the verses: B—Bride; D—Daughters of Jerusalem; G—Bridegroom. In vv 2-7 the bride and the daughters address the bridegroom who appears here as a king, but more often in the poem as a shepherd. King and shepherd are familiar figures of the Lord in the Sacred Scriptures. Cf Ps 23, 1; Is 40, 11; Jn 10, 1-16.

1, 5: Daughters of Jerusalem: the chorus whom the bride addresses and who ask her questions (Song 5, 9; 6, 1), thus developing action within the poem. Kedar: a Syrian desert region whose name suggests blackness; tents were often made of black goat hair. Curtains: tent coverings of Salma, a region close to Kedar.

1, 6: Swarthy: tanned by the sun from working in her brothers' vineyards. My own vineyard: the bride herself; cf Is 5, 1-7, where Israel is designated as the vineyard and the Lord is the Lover.

1, 7: Here and elsewhere in the Song (3, 1; 5, 8; 6, 1), the bride expresses her desire to be in the company of her lover. These verses point to a certain tension in the poem. Only at the end (Song 8, 5ff) does mutual possession of the lovers become final.

1, 9ff: The bridegroom compares the girl's beauty to the rich adornment of the royal chariot of Pharaoh.

1, 12: Nard: a precious perfume, a figure of the bride; cf Song 4, 14.

1, 13: Myrrh: produced from aromatic resin of balsam or roses.

1, 14: Henna: a plant which bears white scented flowers.

1, 15: Doves: suggesting innocence and charm.

1, 16f: Though the meeting place of the lovers is but a shepherd's hut of green branches, it becomes a palace with beams of cedar and rafters of cypress when adorned with their love.

---

a: 2f: Song 4, 10.   *b:* Song 4, 10.   *c:* Song 4, 1. 7.

See RG
267–71

CHAPTER 2

1 I am a flower of Sharon,*
a lily of the valley.

2 G As a lily among thorns,
so is my beloved among women.
3 B As an apple tree among the trees of
the woods,
so is my lover among men.
I delight to rest in his shadow,
and his fruit is sweet to my mouth.
4 He brings me into the banquet hall*
and his emblem over me is love.*d*
5 Strengthen me with raisin cakes,
refresh me with apples,
for I am faint with love.*e*
6 His left hand is under my head
and his right arm embraces me.*f*
7 I adjure you, daughters of Jerusalem,*g*
by the gazelles and hinds* of the field,
Do not arouse, do not stir up love
before its own time.

A Tryst in the Spring

8 B Hark! my lover—here he comes*
springing across the mountains,
leaping across the hills.
9 My lover is like a gazelle
or a young stag.
Here he stands behind our wall,
gazing through the windows,
peering through the lattices.
10 My lover speaks; he says to me,
"Arise, my beloved, my beautiful one,
and come!
11 "For see, the winter is past,
the rains are over and gone.
12 The flowers appear on the earth,

the time of pruning the vines has come,
and the song of the dove is heard in
our land.
13 The fig tree puts forth its figs,
and the vines, in bloom, give forth
fragrance.
Arise, my beloved, my beautiful one,
and come!

14 "O my dove in the clefts of the rock,*
in the secret recesses of the cliff,
Let me see you,
let me hear your voice,
For your voice is sweet,
and you are lovely."

15 B Catch us the foxes, the little foxes*
that damage the vineyards; for our
vineyards are in bloom!

16 My lover belongs to me and I to him;
he browses among the lilies.*h*
17 Until the day breathes cool* and the
shadows lengthen,
roam, my lover,
Like a gazelle or a young stag
upon the mountains of Bether.*i*

CHAPTER 3

See RG
267–71

Loss and Discovery

1 B On my bed at night I sought him*
whom my heart loves—
I sought him but I did not find him.*j*
2 I will rise then and go about the city;
in the streets and crossings I will seek
Him whom my heart loves.
I sought him but I did not find him.
3 The watchmen came upon me,
as they made their rounds of the city:

2, 1: Flower of Sharon: probably the narcissus, which grows in the fertile Plain of Sharon lying between Mount Carmel and Jaffa on the Mediterranean coast.

2, 4ff: The banquet hall, the sweet things of the table, the embrace of the bride and bridegroom, express the delicacy of their affection and the intimacy of their love.

2, 7: By the gazelles and hinds: the swiftness of these animals and the luster and soft expression of their eyes are suggestive of love; cf Prv 5, 19.

2, 8ff: In this sudden change of scene, the bride pictures her lover hastening toward her dwelling until his voice is heard bidding her come to him.

2, 14: The bride is addressed as though she were a dove in

a mountain fastness out of sight and reach.

2, 15: A snatch of song in answer to the request of v 14; cf Song 8, 13f. Foxes: all who threaten to disturb the security of love symbolized by the vineyard; cf v 16.

2, 17: Breathes cool: in the evening when the sun is going down. Cf Gn 3, 8. Bether: a very obscure word; some interpret it in the sense of ruggedness; others, of spices; still others, of sacrifice (Gn 15, 10).

3, 1ff: See the parallel in Song 5, 2-8.

---

d: Song 1, 4.   *e:* Song 5, 8.   *f:* Song 8, 3.   *g:* Song 3, 5; 8, 4.
h: Song 6, 3; 7, 10.   *i:* Song 4, 6; 8, 14.   *j:* 1ff: Song 5, 2ff.

Have you seen him whom my heart
loves?
⁴ I had hardly left them
when I found him whom my heart
loves.
I took hold of him and would not let him
go
till I should bring him to the home of
my mother,ᵏ
to the room of my parent.
⁵ I adjure you, daughters of Jerusalem,
by the gazelles and hinds of the field,
Do not arouse, do not stir up love
before its own time.ˡ

Regal State of the Bridegroom

⁶ **D** What is this coming up from the
desert,*
like a column of smoke
Laden with myrrh, with frankincense,
and with the perfume of every exotic
dust?ᵐ
⁷ Ah, it is the litter of Solomon;
sixty valiant men surround it,
of the valiant men of Israel:
⁸ All of them expert with the sword,
skilled in battle,
Each with his sword at his side
against danger in the watches of the
night.

⁹ King Solomon made himself a carriage
of wood from Lebanon.
¹⁰ He made its columns of silver,
its roof of gold,
Its seat of purple cloth,
its framework inlaid with ivory.
¹¹ Daughters of Jerusalem, come forth
and look upon King Solomon
In the crown with which his mother has
crowned him

on the day of his marriage,
on the day of the joy of his heart.

CHAPTER 4

The Charms of the Beloved

See RG 267–71

¹ **G** Ah, you are beautiful, my beloved,ⁿ
ah, you are beautiful!
Your eyes are dovesᵒ
behind your veil.
Your hair is like a flock of goats
streaming down the mountains of
Gilead.
² Your teeth* are like a flock of ewes to be
shorn,
which come up from the washing,
All of them big with twins,
none of them thin and barren.
³ Your lips are like a scarlet strand;
your mouth is lovely.
Your cheek is like a half-pomegranate*
behind your veil.

⁴ Your neck is like David's towerᵖ
girt with battlements;
A thousand bucklers hang upon it,
all the shields of valiant men.*
⁵ Your breasts are like twin fawns,�q
the young of a gazelle
that browse among the lilies.
⁶ Until the day breathes cool and the
shadows lengthen,ʳ
I will go to the mountain of myrrh,
to the hill of incense.*
⁷ You are all-beautiful, my beloved,
and there is no blemish in you.*

⁸ Come from Lebanon, my bride,
come from Lebanon, come!
Descend from the top of Amana,
from the top of Senir and
Hermon,*

3, 6ff: The lover is portrayed as King Solomon, escorted by sixty armed men, coming in royal procession to meet his bride.

4, 2: Teeth: praised for whiteness and regularity.

4, 3: Pomegranate: a fruit somewhat like an orange, with a firm skin and deep red color. The girl's cheek is compared, in roundness and tint, to a half-pomegranate.

4, 4: The ornaments about her neck are compared to the trophies on the city walls. Cf 1 Kgs 10, 10; 14, 26ff; Ez 27, 10.

4, 6: Mountain of myrrh . . . hill of incense: spoken figu-

ratively of the bride; cf Song 8, 14.

4, 7: Cf St. Paul's description of the church in Eph 5, 27. This verse is also applied to Our Lady, especially in the liturgy of the feast of the Immaculate Conception.

4, 8: Amana . . . Senir and Hermon: these rugged heights symbolize obstacles that would separate the lovers; cf Song 2, 14.

k: Song 8, 2. *l:* Song 2, 7; 8, 4. *m:* Song 6, 10; 8, 5. *n:* Song 1, 15. *o:* 1ff: Song 6, 5ff. *p:* Song 7, 5. *q:* Song 7, 4. *r:* Song 2, 17.

From the haunts of lions,
from the leopards' mountains.
[9] You have ravished my heart, my sister,*
my bride;[s]
you have ravished my heart with one
glance of your eyes,
with one bead of your necklace.
[10] How beautiful is your love, my sister, my
bride,[t]
how much more delightful is your love
than wine,
and the fragrance of your ointments
than all spices!
[11] Your lips drip honey,* my bride,
sweetmeats and milk are under your
tongue;
And the fragrance of your garments
is the fragrance of Lebanon.

The Lover and His Garden

[12] G You are an enclosed garden, my sister,
my bride,[u]
an enclosed garden, a fountain
sealed.*
[13] You are a park that puts forth
pomegranates,
with all choice fruits;
[14] Nard and saffron, calamus and
cinnamon,
with all kinds of incense;
Myrrh and aloes,
with all the finest spices.*
[15] You are a garden fountain, a well of
water
flowing fresh from Lebanon.
[16] Arise, north wind! Come, south
wind!
blow upon my garden*
that its perfumes may spread
abroad.
B Let my lover come to his garden
and eat its choice fruits.

CHAPTER 5

See RG
267–71

[1] G I have come to my garden, my sister,
my bride;[v]
I gather my myrrh and my spices,
I eat my honey and my sweetmeats,
I drink my wine and my milk.

D Eat, friends; drink!* Drink freely of
love!

A Fruitless Search

[2] B I was sleeping, but my heart kept
vigil;*
I heard my lover knocking:
"Open to me, my sister, my beloved,
my dove, my perfect one![w]
For my head is wet with dew,
my locks with the moisture of the
night."
[3] I have taken off my robe,*
am I then to put it on?
I have bathed my feet,
am I then to soil them?

[4] My lover put his hand through the
opening;
my heart trembled within me,
and I grew faint when he spoke.
[5] I rose to open to my lover,
with my hands dripping myrrh:
With my fingers dripping choice myrrh
upon the fittings of the lock.
[6] I opened to my lover—
but my lover had departed, gone.[x]
I sought him but I did not find him;
I called to him but he did not answer
me.*

[7] The watchmen came upon me[y]
as they made their rounds of the city;
They struck me, and wounded me,

4, 9: Sister: a term of endearment; it forms part of the conventional language of love used in this canticle.

4, 11: Honey: sweet words. Cf Prv 5, 3.

4, 12: Enclosed garden . . . fountain sealed: reserved for
the bridegroom alone. The bride's fidelity is implied. Cf Prv
5, 15-19.

4, 14: These plants are all known for their sweet scent.

4, 16: The last two lines of the verse are spoken by the girl,
inviting her lover to herself, the garden.

5, 1: Eat, friends; drink!: the lovers are encouraged to

enjoy the delights of their love, symbol of Christ's union
with the church.

5, 2-8: A trial similar to that in Song 3, 1ff.

5, 3f: The bride's hesitation is due, not to levity, but to
strong emotion.

5, 6: The disappearance of the lover seems to be a deliberate trial and test inflicted on the girl.

---

s: Song 6, 5.   t: Song 1, 2f.   u: Song 6, 2. 11.   v: Song 6, 2.
w: 2ff: Song 3, 1f.   x: Song 3, 1.   y: Song 3, 3.

and took my mantle from me,
  the guardians of the walls.*
[8] I adjure you, daughters of Jerusalem,[z]
  if you find my lover—
  What shall you tell him?—
  that I am faint with love.

The Charms of the Lost Lover
[9] D How does your lover differ from any
  other,
  O most beautiful among women?
How does your lover differ from any
  other,
  that you adjure us so?

[10] B My lover is radiant and ruddy;*
  he stands out among thousands.
[11] His head is pure gold;
  his locks are palm fronds,
  black as the raven.
[12] His eyes are like doves
  beside running waters,
His teeth would seem bathed in
  milk,
  and are set like jewels.
[13] His cheeks are like beds of spice
  with ripening aromatic herbs.
His lips are red blossoms;
  they drip choice myrrh.
[14] His arms are rods of gold
  adorned with chrysolites.
His body is a work of ivory
  covered with sapphires.
[15] His legs are columns of marble
  resting on golden bases.
His stature is like the trees on
  Lebanon,
  imposing as the cedars.
[16] His mouth is sweetness itself;
  he is all delight.
Such is my lover, and such my friend,
  O daughters of Jerusalem.

CHAPTER 6

Discovery

See RG
267-71

[1] D Where has your lover gone,
  O most beautiful among women?
Where has your lover gone
  that we may seek him with you?*
[2] B My lover has come down to his
  garden,*
  to the beds of spice,
To browse in the garden[a]
  and to gather lilies.
[3] My lover belongs to me and I to him;
  he browses among the lilies.[b]

The Charms of the Beloved
[4] G You are as beautiful as Tirzah, my
  beloved,*
  as lovely as Jerusalem,
  as awe-inspiring as bannered troops.
[5] Turn your eyes from me,[c]
  for they torment me.
Your hair is like a flock of goats
  streaming down from Gilead.
[6] Your teeth are like a flock of ewes[d]
  which come up from the washing,
All of them big with twins,
  none of them thin and barren.
[7] Your cheek is like a half-pomegranate
  behind your veil.

[8] There are sixty queens, eighty
  concubines,
  and maidens without number—
[9] One alone is my dove, my perfect one,
  her mother's chosen,
  the dear one of her parent.
The daughters saw her and declared her
  fortunate,
  the queens and concubines, and they
  sang her praises;
[10] D Who is this that comes forth like the
  dawn,[e]

5, 7: The watchmen do not know the reason for the girl's appearance in the city streets; cf Song 3, 2ff.

5, 10f: In answer to the question of v 9, the girl sings her lover's praises (vv 10-16). Gold: indicates how precious the lover is. Palm fronds: his thick, luxuriant growth of hair.

6, 1: The daughters of Jerusalem are won by this description of the lover and offer their aid in seeking him.

6, 2f: Determined to share her lover with no one, the girl

refuses the aid offered by the daughters in seeking him. She implies that she had never really lost him, for he has come down to his garden.

6, 4-9: The lover again celebrates her beauty. Tirzah: probably meaning "pleasant"; it was the early capital of the northern kingdom of Israel (1 Kgs 16).

z: Song 2, 5. a: Song 4, 12; 5, 1. b: Song 2, 16; 7, 11. c: Song 4, 9. d: 6f: Song 4, 1ff. e: Song 3, 6; 8, 5.

as beautiful as the moon, as
resplendent as the sun,
as awe-inspiring as bannered troops?

Love's Meeting

[11] **B** I came down to the nut garden[f]
to look at the fresh growth of the
valley,
To see if the vines were in bloom,
if the pomegranates had blossomed.
[12] Before I knew it, my heart had made me
the blessed one of my kinsmen.*

See RG
267-71

CHAPTER 7

The Beauty of the Bride

[1] **D** Turn, turn, O Shulammite,*
turn, turn, that we may look at you!

B Why would you look at the
Shulammite
as at the dance of the two companies?

[2] **D** How beautiful are your feet in
sandals,*
O prince's daughter!
Your rounded thighs are like jewels,
the handiwork of an artist.
[3] Your navel is a round bowl
that should never lack for mixed wine.
Your body is a heap of wheat
encircled with lilies.
[4] Your breasts are like twin fawns,
the young of a gazelle.[g]
[5] Your neck is like a tower of ivory.[h]
Your eyes are like the pools in
Heshbon
by the gate of Bath-rabbim.

Your nose is like the tower on Lebanon
that looks toward Damascus.*
[6] Your head rises like Carmel;
your hair is like draperies of purple;
a king is held captive in its tresses.

Love's Desires

[7] **G** How beautiful you are, how pleasing,
my love, my delight!
[8] Your very figure is like a palm tree,*
your breasts are like clusters.
[9] I said: I will climb the palm tree,
I will take hold of its branches.
Now let your breasts be like clusters of
the vine
and the fragrance of your breath like
apples,
[10] And your mouth like an excellent wine—

Love's Union

B that flows smoothly for my lover,
spreading over the lips and the teeth.*
[11] I belong to my lover*
and for me he yearns.[i]
[12] Come, my lover, let us go forth to the
fields
and spend the night among the villages.
[13] Let us go early to the vineyards, and see
if the vines are in bloom,
If the buds have opened,
if the pomegranates have blossomed;[j]
There will I give you my love.
[14] The mandrakes* give forth fragrance,
and at our doors are all choice fruits;
Both fresh and mellowed fruits, my
lover,
I have kept in store for you.

6, 12: The text is obscure in Hebrew and in the ancient versions. The Vulgate reads: "I did not know; my soul disturbed me because of the chariots of Aminadab."

7, 1: Shulammite: so called either because the girl is considered to be from Shulam in the plain of Esdraelon (cf 1 Kgs 1, 3) or because the name may mean "the peaceful one," and thus recall the name of Solomon. As at the dance of the two companies: the meaning is uncertain. The question in this verse could be construed as a refusal to dance; more probably, however, the girl accedes, as the following verses suggest.

7, 2-6: A flattering description of the girl's charms. Rounded . . . jewels: the meaning of these Hebrew words is not certain. Wine and wheat are symbolic of fertility; they are here associated with parts of the body which have a close relation to fruitfulness.

7, 5: The comparison emphasizes the stateliness and

whiteness of the neck, and the limpidity of the eyes. Bath-rabbim: a proper name which occurs only here; there was a city of Rabbah northeast of Heshbon in Transjordan. Cf Jer 49, 3.

7, 8f: Palm tree: a figure of stateliness. The bridegroom is eager to enjoy the possession of his bride.

7, 10: The bride delicately turns his compliment into an expression of the love and tenderness she feels for him.

7, 11-14: The girl's answer assures him of her affection and invites him to return with her to the rural delights which are associated with their love and which recall the meeting described in Song 6, 11f.

7, 14: Mandrakes: herbs believed to have power to arouse love and promote fertility; cf Gn 30, 14ff.

---

f: Song 4, 12ff; 7, 13.   *g:* Song 4, 5.   *h:* Song 4, 4.   *i:* Song 2, 16; 6, 3.   *j:* Song 6, 11.

See RG
267–71

CHAPTER 8

¹Oh, that you were my brother,
    nursed at my mother's breasts!
If I met you out of doors, I would kiss you
    and none would taunt me.
² I would lead you, bring you in
    to the home of my mother.ᵏ
There you would teach me to give you
    spiced wine to drink, and pomegranate
        juice.

³ His left hand is under my head
    and his right arm embraces me.ˡ
⁴ I adjure you, daughters of Jerusalem,
    by the gazelles and hinds of the field,
Do not arouse, do not stir up love,
    before its own time.ᵐ

Homecoming

⁵ D Who is this coming up from the
        desert,ⁿ
    leaning upon her lover?*
G Under the apple tree I awakened you;
    it was there that your mother
        conceived you,
    it was there that your parent
        conceived.

True Love

⁶ B Set me as a seal* on your heart,
    as a seal on your arm;
For stern as death is love,
    relentless as the nether world is
        devotion;
    its flames are a blazing fire.
⁷ Deep waters cannot quench love,
    nor floods sweep it away.

Were one to offer all he owns to purchase
        love,
    he would be roundly mocked.

Chastity and Its Welcome

⁸ "Our sister is little*
    and she has no breasts as yet.
What shall we do for our sister
    when her courtship begins?
⁹ If she is a wall,
    we will build upon it a silver parapet;
If she is a door,
    we will reinforce it with a cedar plank."

¹⁰ I am a wall,
    and my breasts are like towers.
So now in his eyes I have become
    one to be welcomed.

The Bride and Her Dowry

¹¹ B Solomon had a vineyard at Baalhamon;*
    he gave over the vineyard to caretakers.
For its fruit one would have to pay
    a thousand silver pieces.
¹² My vineyard is at my own disposal;
    the thousand pieces are for you,
        O Solomon,
    and two hundred for the caretakers of
        its fruit.

Life Together

¹³ G O garden-dweller,*
    my friends are listening for your voice,
    let me hear it!

¹⁴ B Be swift, my lover,
    like a gazelle or a young stag
    on the mountains of spices!ᵒ

8, 5: The lovers are pictured walking homeward, enjoying the fulfillment of the desire which the girl expressed in vv 1f. The groom speaks of their first meeting.

8, 6f: Seal: this could be worn bound to the arm, as here, or suspended at the neck, or as a ring (Jer 22, 24). It was used for identification and signatures. Stern . . . relentless: in human experience, death and the nether world are inevitable, unrelenting; in the end they always triumph. Love, which is just as certain of its victory, matches its strength against the natural enemies of life; waters cannot extinguish it nor floods carry it away. It is more priceless than all riches.

8, 8ff: The bride affirms her chastity. In 8, 9 she quotes the course of action which her elder brothers had decided on. While she is yet immature, they will shelter her in view of eventual marriage. If she is virtuous, she will be honored; if

she is unchaste, she will be kept under strict vigilance. In reply to this she proclaims her virtue and boasts of having found welcome from her lover.

8, 11f: These enigmatic verses have been variously interpreted. In v 11 the girl alludes to a vineyard of great value which is compared to her own self in v 12. Her enormous dowry, a thousand silver pieces, is in keeping with her intrinsic worth. She has been the generous lover, giving herself and a dowry to her lover, referred to as Solomon, and also smaller gifts to her brothers, the caretakers (cf vv 8ff).

8, 13f: As in Song 2, 14f, her lover asks for a word or a song and she replies in words similar to those found in Song 2, 17.

---

k: Song 3, 4. l: Song 2, 6. m: Song 2, 7; 3, 5. n: Song 3, 6; 6, 10. o: Song 2, 9. 17; 4, 6.

See RG
272–76

The Book of Wisdom

The Book of Wisdom was written about a hundred years before the coming of Christ. Its author, whose name is not known to us, was a member of the Jewish community at Alexandria, in Egypt. He wrote in Greek, in a style patterned on that of Hebrew verse. At times he speaks in the person of Solomon, placing his teachings on the lips of the wise king of Hebrew tradition in order to emphasize their value. His profound knowledge of the earlier Old Testament writings is reflected in almost every line of the book, and marks him, like Ben Sira, as an outstanding representative of religious devotion and learning among the sages of postexilic Judaism.

The primary purpose of the sacred author was the edification of his co-religionists in a time when they had experienced suffering and oppression, in part at least at the hands of apostate fellow Jews. To convey his message he made use of the most popular religious themes of his time, namely the splendor and worth of divine wisdom (6, 22—11, 1), the glorious events of the Exodus (11, 2-16; 12, 23-27; 15, 18—19, 22), God's mercy (11, 17—12, 22), the folly of idolatry (13, 1—15, 17), and the manner in which God's justice is vindicated in rewarding or punishing the individual soul (1, 1—6, 21). The first ten chapters especially form a preparation for the fuller teachings of Christ and his Church. Many passages from this section of the book, notably 3, 1-8, are used by the Church in her liturgy.

The principal divisions of the Book of Wisdom are:

I: Reward of Justice (1, 1—6, 21).

II: Praise of Wisdom by Solomon (6, 22—11, 1).

III: Special Providence of God during the Exodus (11, 2-16; 12, 23-27; 15, 18—19, 22) with digressions on God's mercy (11, 17—12, 22) and on the folly and shame of idolatry (13, 1—15, 17).

I: The Reward of Justice

CHAPTER 1

See RG
273–74

Exhortation to Justice,
the Key to Life

1 Love justice,* you who judge the
earth;[a]
think of the LORD in goodness,
and seek him in integrity of heart;[b]
2 Because he is found by those who test
him not,
and he manifests himself to those who
do not disbelieve him.[c]
3 For perverse counsels separate a man
from God,
and his power, put to the proof,
rebukes the foolhardy;[d]
4 Because into a soul that plots evil
wisdom enters not,
nor dwells she in a body under debt of
sin.[e]
5 For the holy spirit of discipline* flees
deceit
and withdraws from senseless
counsels;
and when injustice occurs it is
rebuked.[f]
6 For wisdom is a kindly spirit,
yet she acquits not the blasphemer of
his guilty lips;
Because God is the witness of his inmost
self[g]
and the sure observer of his heart
and the listener to his tongue.[h]
7 For the spirit of the LORD fills the world,[i]
is all-embracing, and knows what man
says.*
8 Therefore no one who utters wicked
things can go unnoticed,

1, 1: Justice: not merely the cardinal virtue of that name (cf Wis 8, 7), but the universal moral quality which is the application of Wisdom to moral conduct.

1, 5: Discipline: here and elsewhere, another name for Wisdom; injustice: the opposite of the virtue in Wis 1, 1.

1, 7: This verse is applied to the Holy Spirit in the liturgy at Pentecost.

a: 1 Chr 29, 17; Ps 2, 10; Is 26, 9.   *b:* 1f: Sir 1, 25.   *c:* 1 Chr 28, 9.   *d:* Is 59, 2.   *e:* Sir 15, 7f; Rom 7, 14.   *f:* Is 63, 10.   *g:* Jer 17, 10.   *h:* 6f: Jer 23, 24f.   *i:* Wis 12, 1.

nor will chastising condemnation pass
him by.*j*

[9] For the devices of the wicked man shall
be scrutinized,
and the sound of his words shall reach
the LORD,
for the chastisement of his
transgressions;

[10] Because a jealous ear hearkens to
everything,*k*
and discordant grumblings are no
secret.

[11] Therefore guard against profitless
grumbling,
and from calumny* withhold your
tongues;
For a stealthy utterance does not go
unpunished,
and a lying mouth slays the soul.

[12] Court not death by your erring way of
life,
nor draw to yourselves destruction by
the works of your hands.

[13] Because God did not make death,*l*
nor does he rejoice in the destruction
of the living.

[14] For he fashioned all things that they
might have being;
and the creatures of the world are
wholesome,
And there is not a destructive drug
among them
nor any domain of the nether world on
earth,

[15] For justice is undying.*m*

The Wicked Reject Immortality and Justice Alike

[16] It was the wicked who with hands and
words invited death,
considered it a friend, and pined
for it,
and made a covenant with it,
Because they deserve to be in its
possession,*n*

CHAPTER 2

See RG
273–74

[1]   they who said among
themselves, thinking not aright:
"Brief and troublous is our lifetime;*o*
neither is there any remedy for man's
dying,
nor is anyone known to have come
back from the nether world.

[2] For haphazard were we born,
and hereafter we shall be as though we
had not been;
Because the breath in our nostrils is a
smoke
and reason is a spark at the beating of
our hearts,

[3] And when this is quenched, our body
will be ashes
and our spirit will be poured abroad
like unresisting air.*p*

[4] Even our name will be forgotten in time,
and no one will recall our deeds.
So our life will pass away like the traces
of a cloud,
and will be dispersed like a mist
pursued by the sun's rays
and overpowered by its heat.

[5] For our lifetime is the passing of a
shadow;
and our dying cannot be deferred
because it is fixed with a seal; and no
one returns.*q*

[6] Come, therefore, let us enjoy the good
things that are real,
and use the freshness of creation avidly.*r*

[7] Let us have our fill of costly wine and
perfumes,
and let no springtime blossom pass us
by;

[8]   let us crown ourselves with rosebuds
ere they wither.

[9] Let no meadow be free from our
wantonness;*
everywhere let us leave tokens of our
rejoicing,

1, 11: Calumny: speech against God and his providence is meant.

2, 9: Let no meadow . . . wantonness: the extant Greek Mss have "Let none of us be without part in our wanton doings."
Most Latin Mss have both forms of this line.

---

j: Prv 19, 5.   *k:* 10f: Nm 14, 27f.   *l:* 13f: Ez 18, 32; 33, 11; 2 Pt 3, 9.   *m:* Is 51, 6ff.   *n:* Is 28, 15.   *o:* Jb 14, 1; 7, 9.   *p:* Jb 7, 9; Jas
4, 14.   *q:* Ps 144, 4.   *r:* Is 22, 13; 1 Cor 15, 32.

for this our portion is, and this our lot.[s]

10 Let us oppress the needy just man;
  let us neither spare the widow
  nor revere the old man for his hair
  grown white with time.[t]

11 But let our strength be our norm of
  justice;
  for weakness proves itself useless.

12 *Let us beset the just one, because he is
  obnoxious to us;
  he sets himself against our doings,
  Reproaches us for transgressions of the
  law*
  and charges us with violations of our
  training.[u]

13 He professes to have knowledge of God
  and styles himself a child of the
  LORD.[v]

14 To us he is the censure of our thoughts;
  merely to see him is a hardship for us,[w]

15 Because his life is not like other men's,
  and different are his ways.

16 He judges us debased;
  he holds aloof from our paths as from
  things impure.
  He calls blest the destiny of the just
  and boasts that God is his Father.[x]

17 Let us see whether his words be true;
  let us find out what will happen to him.[y]

18 For if the just one be the son of God, he
  will defend him
  and deliver him from the hand of his
  foes.[z]

19 With revilement and torture let us put
  him to the test
  that we may have proof of his
  gentleness
  and try his patience.

20 Let us condemn him to a shameful death;
  for according to his own words, God
  will take care of him."[a]

21 These were their thoughts, but they
  erred;
  for their wickedness blinded them,[b]

22 And they knew not the hidden counsels
  of God;
  neither did they count on a
  recompense of holiness
  nor discern the innocent souls' reward.[c]

23 For God formed man to be imperishable;
  the image of his own nature he made
  him.[d]

24 But by the envy of the devil, death
  entered the world,
  and they who are in his possession
  experience it.[e]

CHAPTER 3

The Hidden Counsels of God

See RG
273-74

A. ON SUFFERING

1 But the souls of the just are in the hand of
  God,[f]
  and no torment shall touch them.*

2 They seemed, in the view of the foolish,
  to be dead;
  and their passing away was thought an
  affliction

3 and their going forth from us, utter
  destruction.
  But they are in peace.[g]

4 For if before men, indeed, they be
  punished,
  yet is their hope full of immortality;

5 Chastised a little, they shall be greatly
  blessed,
  because God tried them
  and found them worthy of himself.[h]

6 As gold in the furnace, he proved them,
  and as sacrificial offerings* he took
  them to himself.[i]

7 In the time of their visitation* they shall
  shine,

2, 12-20: Often applied to the Passion of our Lord; many have understood these verses as a direct prophecy. Cf Mt 27, 41-44.

2, 12: Law: the law of Moses; training has the same meaning.

3, 1-8: Verses frequently applied to the martyrs.

3, 6: Offerings: the image is that of the holocaust, in which the victim is completely consumed by fire.

3, 7: Visitation: God's loving judgment of those who have been faithful to him; the same word is used in Wis 14, 11 for the punishment of the wicked at God's final judgment. Cf also Wis 3, 13.

s: Jer 13, 25.   t: Ex 22, 22ff; Lv 19, 32.   u: Hos 8, 1.   v: Mt 27, 43; Jn 8, 55; 10, 36-39.   w: Mt 9, 4.   x: Jer 6, 30.   y: Gn 37, 20.
z: Ps 22, 9; Is 42, 1; Mt 27, 43; Jn 5, 18.   a: Jas 5, 6.   b: Rom 1, 21.   c: Ps 18, 24f; Prv 11, 18; Mt 11, 25.   d: Gn 1, 26f; Is 54, 16
LXX.   e: Gn 3, 1-24; Rom 5, 12.   f: Jb 12, 10; 5, 19.   g: Is 57, 2.   h: Tb 12, 13; 2 Cor 4, 17; 1 Pt 1, 6f.   i: Ps 51, 19; Prv 17, 3; Sir
2, 5; Is 48, 10.

and shall dart about as sparks through stubble;*j*

⁸ They shall judge nations and rule over peoples,

and the LORD shall be their King forever.*k*

⁹ Those who trust in him shall understand truth,

and the faithful shall abide with him in love:

Because grace and mercy are with his holy ones,*l*

and his care is with his elect.

¹⁰ But the wicked shall receive a punishment to match their thoughts,*

since they neglected justice and forsook the LORD.

¹¹ For he who despises wisdom and instruction is doomed.*m*

Vain is their hope, fruitless are their labors,

and worthless are their works.*n*

¹² Their wives are foolish and their children wicked;

accursed is their brood.*o*

B. ON CHILDLESSNESS

¹³ Yes, blessed is she who, childless and undefiled,

knew not transgression of the marriage bed;

she shall bear fruit at the visitation of souls.*

¹⁴ So also the eunuch whose hand wrought no misdeed,

who held no wicked thoughts against the LORD—

For he shall be given fidelity's choice reward*

and a more gratifying heritage in the LORD's temple.*p*

¹⁵ For the fruit of noble struggles is a glorious one;

and unfailing is the root of understanding.*q*

¹⁶ But the children of adulterers will remain without issue,

and the progeny of an unlawful bed will disappear.*r*

¹⁷ For should they attain long life, they will be held in no esteem,

and dishonored will their old age be at last;

¹⁸ While should they die abruptly, they have no hope

nor comfort in the day of scrutiny;

¹⁹ for dire is the end of the wicked generation.*s*

CHAPTER 4

See RG 273–74

¹ Better is childlessness with virtue;

for immortal is its memory:*

because both by God is it acknowledged, and by men.*t*

² When it is present men imitate it,

and they long for it when it is gone;

And forever it marches crowned in triumph,

victorious in unsullied deeds of valor.

³ But the numerous progeny of the wicked shall be of no avail;

their spurious offshoots shall not strike deep root

nor take firm hold.*u*

⁴ For even though their branches flourish for a time,

they are unsteady and shall be rocked by the wind

and, by the violence of the winds, uprooted;*v*

⁵ Their twigs shall be broken off untimely,

and their fruit be useless, unripe for eating,

and fit for nothing.

⁶ For children born of lawless unions

3, 10: To match their thoughts: a fate as empty as that which they describe; cf Wis 2, 1-5.

3, 13: Visitation of souls: that is, the last judgment. Cf Wis 3, 7-9.

3, 14: Fidelity's choice reward: cf Is 56, 1-8. More gratifying: better than sons and daughters; cf Is 56, 5.

4, 1: The Latin form of this line, "Oh, how fair is the chaste generation in its glory!" is a later adaptation, which is applied in the liturgy to the splendor of virginity.

j: Dn 12, 3; Ob 18; Mal 3, 3; Mt 13, 43. *k:* Wis 8, 14; Prv 8, 16; Dn 7, 22; 1 Cor 6, 2; Rv 20, 4. *l:* Wis 3, 9; 4, 15; Jb 10, 12; Jn 15, 10. *m:* Prv 1, 7. *n:* 11f: Sir 41, 8. *o:* Dt 28, 18ff. *p:* Is 56, 2-5. *q:* Sir 1, 18. *r:* 2 Sm 12, 14. *s:* Ps 34, 22. *t:* Sir 16, 1ff; Prv 3, 3f. *u:* Sir 23, 25. *v:* Sir 40, 15; Is 40, 24.

give evidence of the wickedness of
their parents, when they are
examined.

C. ON EARLY DEATH

7 But the just man, though he die early,
shall be at rest.w

8 For the age that is honorable comes not
with the passing of time,x

nor can it be measured in terms of
years.

9 Rather, understanding is the hoary crown
for men,

and an unsullied life, the attainment of
old age.

10 He who pleased God was loved;y

he who lived among sinners was
transported—*

11 Snatched away, lest wickedness pervert
his mind

or deceit beguile his soul;z

12 For the witchery of paltry things
obscures what is right

and the whirl of desire transforms the
innocent mind.a

13 Having become perfect in a short while,
he reached the fullness of a long
career;

14 for his soul was pleasing to the LORD,
therefore he sped him out of the midst
of wickedness.b

But the people saw and did not
understand,

nor did they take this into account.*

16 Yes, the just man dead condemns the
sinful who live,

and youth swiftly completed
condemns the many years of the
wicked man grown old.c

17 For they see the death of the wise man
and do not understand what the LORD
intended for him,

or why he made him secure.

18 They see, and hold him in contempt;
but the LORD laughs them to scorn.d

19 And they shall afterward become
dishonored corpsese

and an unceasing mockery among the
dead.

For he shall strike them down speechless
and prostratef

and rock them to their foundations;
They shall be utterly laid waste
and shall be in grief
and their memory shall perish.

The Final Judgment of the Wicked

20 Fearful shall they come, at the counting
up* of their sins,

and their lawless deeds shall convict
them to their face.

CHAPTER 5

1 Then shall the just one with great
assurance confrontg

his oppressors who set at nought his
labors.h

2 Seeing this, they shall be shaken with
dreadful fear,

and amazed at the unlooked-for
salvation.

3 They shall say among themselves,
rueful

and groaning through anguish of
spirit:

"This is he whom once we held as a
laughingstock

and as a type for mockery, 4fools that
we were!

His life we accounted madness,
and his death dishonored.

5 See how he is accounted among the sons
of God;

how his lot is with the saints!i

6 We, then, have strayed from the way of
truth,j

and the light of justice did not shine
for us,

and the sun did not rise for us.k

**See RG
273-74**

4, 10f: There are allusions here to Enoch (Gn 5, 21-24), who was young by patriarchal standards, and to Lot (Gn 19, 10f;
2 Pt 2, 7f). Cf also Is 57, 1f.

4, 15: The verse here omitted repeats the last two lines of Wis 3, 9.

4, 20: Counting up: the last judgment.

---

w: Wis 3, 3.   x: 8f: Jb 12, 12; 32, 9; Sir 25, 4ff.   y: Gn 5, 24; Sir 44, 16; Heb 11, 5.   z: Is 57, 1f.   a: Wis 2, 21; Dn 13, 9.   b: Gn
19, 22. 29; 2 Pt 2, 7.   c: Mt 12, 41f.   d: Ps 37, 13.   e: Neh 1, 10 LXX; Ps 18, 8; Is 14, 19; Jer 23, 39f.   f: 2 Mc 3, 29.   g: 1f: 2 Thes
1, 6f.   h: Col 2, 15.   i: Acts 26, 18; Col 1, 12.   j: Prv 4, 18f; Jn 12, 35.   k: 6f. Is 59, 6-14.

⁷ We had our fill of the ways of mischief
    and of ruin;
  we journeyed through impassable
    deserts,
  but the way of the LORD we knew not.
⁸ What did our pride avail us?
  What have wealth and its boastfulness
    afforded us?ˡ
⁹ All of them passed like a shadow
  and like a fleeting rumor;ᵐ
¹⁰ Like a ship traversing the heaving
    water,
  of which, when it has passed, no trace
    can be found,
  no path of its keel in the waves.
¹¹ Or like a bird flying through the air;
  no evidence of its course is to be
    found—
  But the fluid air, lashed by the beat of
    pinions,
  and cleft by the rushing force
  Of speeding wings, is traversed:
  and afterward no mark of passage can
    be found in it.
¹² Or as, when an arrow has been shot at a
    mark,
  the parted air straightway flows
    together again
  so that none discerns the way it went
    through—
¹³ Even so we, once born, abruptly came to
    nought
  and held no sign of virtue to display,
  but were consumed in our
    wickedness."ⁿ
¹⁴ Yes, the hope of the wicked is like
    thistledown borne on the wind,
  and like fine, tempest-driven foam;
  Like smoke scattered by the wind,
  and like the passing memory of the
    nomad camping for a single day.ᵒ
¹⁵ But the just live forever,
  and in the LORD is their recompense,
  and the thought of them is with the
    Most High.ᵖ
¹⁶ Therefore shall they receive the splendid
    crown,

  the beauteous diadem, from the hand
    of the LORD—
  For he shall shelter them with his right
    hand,
  and protect them with his arm.�q
¹⁷ He shall take his zeal for armorʳ
  and he shall arm creation to requite the
    enemy;
¹⁸ He shall don justice for a breastplate
  and shall wear sure judgment for a
    helmet;
¹⁹ He shall take invincible rectitude as a
    shieldˢ
²⁰ and whet his sudden anger for a sword,
  And the universe shall war with him
    against the foolhardy.
²¹ Well-aimed shafts of lightnings shall go
    forth
  and from the clouds as from a well-
    drawn bow shall leap to the mark;ᵗ
²² and as from his sling, wrathful
    hailstones shall be hurled.
  The water of the sea shall be enraged
    against them
  and the streams shall abruptly
    overflow;ᵘ
²³ A mighty wind shall confront them
  and a tempest winnow them out;
  Thus lawlessness shall lay the whole
    earth waste
  and evildoing overturn the thrones of
    potentates.ᵛ

CHAPTER 6

Exhortation to Seek Wisdom

See RG 274–75

¹ Hear, therefore, kings, and
    understand;ʷ
  learn, you magistrates of the earth's
    expanse!
² Hearken, you who are in power over the
    multitude
  and lord it over throngs of peoples!
³ Because authority was given you by the
    LORD
  and sovereignty by the Most High,
  who shall probe your works and
    scrutinize your counsels!ˣ

---

l: Ps 49, 7; Prv 10, 2. m: 9ff. 1 Chr 20, 15; Ps 144, 4; Jb 9, 25f LXX. n: Ez 33, 10. o: Jb 21, 18; Ps 1, 4; 37, 20; Is 17, 13. p: Is 62, 11; Ez 18, 9. q: Ex 33, 22; Is 62, 3; 2 Tm 4, 8; 1 Pt 5, 4. r: 17: Is 59, 16. s: 19f: Dt 32, 40ff. t: Hb 3, 9ff. u: Dt 11, 4. v: Wis 11, 20; Sir 10, 13f. w: 1f: Wis 1, 1; Sir 33, 19; Mi 3, 1. 9. x: 2 Chr 36, 23; Prv 8, 15f; Jn 19, 11; Rom 13, 1ff.

[4] Because, though you were ministers of his
kingdom, you judged not rightly,
and did not keep the law,*
nor walk according to the will of
God,
[5] Terribly and swiftly shall he come
against you,
because judgment is stern for the
exalted—
[6] For the lowly may be pardoned out of
mercy[y]
but the mighty shall be mightily put to
the test.
[7] For the Lord of all shows no partiality,
nor does he fear greatness,[z]
Because he himself made the great as
well as the small,
and he provides for all alike;
[8] but for those in power a rigorous
scrutiny impends.
[9] To you, therefore, O princes, are my
words addressed[a]
that you may learn wisdom and that
you may not sin.
[10] For those who keep the holy precepts
hallowed shall be found holy,
and those learned in them will have
ready a response.*
[11] Desire therefore my words;
long for them and you shall be
instructed.
[12] Resplendent and unfading is Wisdom,
and she is readily perceived by those
who love her,
and found by those who seek her.[b]
[13] She hastens to make herself known in
anticipation of men's desire;[c]
[14] he who watches for her at dawn shall
not be disappointed,
for he shall find her sitting by his
gate.
[15] For taking thought of her is the
perfection of prudence,
and he who for her sake keeps vigil
shall quickly be free from care;

[16] Because she makes her own rounds,
seeking those worthy of her,
and graciously appears to them in the
ways,
and meets them with all solicitude.[d]
[17] For the first step toward discipline is a
very earnest desire for her;[e]
then, care for discipline is love of her;
[18] love means the keeping of her laws;
To observe her laws is the basis for
incorruptibility;
[19] and incorruptibility makes one close to
God;
[20] thus the desire for Wisdom leads up to
a kingdom.
[21] If, then, you find pleasure in throne and
scepter, you princes of the peoples,
honor Wisdom, that you may reign as
kings forever.

II: Praise of Wisdom by Solomon

Introduction

[22] Now what Wisdom is, and how she came
to be, I shall relate;
and I shall hide no secrets from you,
But from the very beginning I shall
search out
and bring to light knowledge of her,
nor shall I diverge from the truth.[f]
[23] Neither shall I admit consuming jealousy
to my company,
because that can have no fellowship
with Wisdom.[g]
[24] A great number of wise men is the safety
of the world,
and a prudent king, the stability of his
people;[h]
[25] so take instruction from my words, to
your profit.

CHAPTER 7

See RG
274-75

Solomon Is Like All
Other Men

[1] I too am a mortal man, the same as all the
rest,[i]

6, 4: Law: that of Moses; cf v 10; Wis 2, 12.
6, 10: Response: a suitable plea before the great Judge. Cf
Prv 22, 21; Jb 31, 14; Hb 2, 1; Sir 8, 9.

y: 6ff; Lk 12, 48.   z: Dt 1, 17; Prv 22, 2.   a: 9ff: Dt 4, 10; Ps 2,
12; Sir 32, 14; 1 Jn 3, 7.   b: Wis 7, 10; Prv 8, 17; Jer 29, 13.
c: 13ff: Prv 8, 3. 17. 34.   d: Prv 8, 20f; Sir 15, 1ff.   e: 17-21; Ps
2, 10ff; Prv 4, 4-9; 7, 1-4; 8, 15f; Dn 7, 27; Jn 14, 15. 21; 1 Jn 5,
3.   f: Tb 12, 7. 11; Mt 13, 11; Jn 15, 15.   g: Wis 7, 13; Jas 3, 14f.
h: Prv 24, 6; 29, 4; Sir 10, 1ff.   i: 1f: Wis 10, 1; Gn 2, 7; Jb 10, 9-
12; 33, 6; 1 Cor 15, 47ff.

and a descendant of the first man formed of earth.*

And in my mother's womb I was molded into flesh

2 in a ten-months' period*—body and blood,

from the seed of man, and the pleasure that accompanies marriage.

3 And I too, when born, inhaled the common air,

and fell upon the kindred earth;

wailing, I uttered that first sound common to all.

4 In swaddling clothes and with constant care I was nurtured.

5 For no king has any different origin or birth,

6 but one is the entry into life for all; and in one same way they leave it.*j*

Solomon Prayed and Wisdom and Riches Came to Him

7 Therefore I prayed, and prudence was given me;

I pleaded, and the spirit of Wisdom came to me.*k*

8 I preferred her to scepter and throne,*l*

And deemed riches nothing in comparison with her,

9 nor did I liken any priceless gem to her;

Because all gold, in view of her, is a little sand,

and before her, silver is to be accounted mire.

10 Beyond health and comeliness I loved her,

And I chose to have her rather than the light,

because the splendor of her never yields to sleep.*m*

11 Yet all good things together came to me in her company,*n*

and countless riches at her hands;

12 And I rejoiced in them all, because Wisdom is their leader,

though I had not known that she is the mother of these.*o*

Solomon Prays for Help To Speak of Wisdom

13 Simply I learned about her, and ungrudgingly do I share—

her riches I do not hide away;*p*

14 For to men she is an unfailing treasure;

those who gain this treasure win the friendship of God,

to whom the gifts they have from discipline* commend them.

15 Now God grant I speak suitably and value these endowments at their worth:

For he is the guide of Wisdom and the director of the wise.

16 For both we and our words are in his hand,

as well as all prudence and knowledge of crafts.*q*

17 For he gave me sound knowledge of existing things,

that I might know the organization of the universe and the force of its elements,

18 The beginning and the end and the midpoint of times,

the changes in the sun's course and the variations of the seasons.

19 Cycles of years, positions of the stars,

20 natures of animals, tempers of beasts,

Powers of the winds and thoughts of men,

uses of plants and virtues of roots—

21 Such things as are hidden I learned, and such as are plain;

22 for Wisdom, the artificer of all, taught me.*r*

7, 1: First man formed of earth: Adam. The author omits throughout the book the proper names of the characters in sacred history of whom he speaks; see especially chapter 10.

7, 2: In a ten-months' period: thus the ancients were accustomed to reckon the period of pregnancy.

7, 14: Discipline: cf note on Wis 1, 5.

---

j: Jb 1, 21; 1 Tm 6, 7f.   *k:* 1 Kgs 3, 5-15; Prv 2, 3-11.   *l:* 8f: Wis 8, 5; 1 Kgs 10, 21; Prv 3, 14ff; 8, 10. 18f; Jb 28, 15-19.   *m:* Prv 6, 23.   *n:* Prv 8, 21.   *o:* Prv 8, 14f.   *p:* Wis 6, 23.   *q:* Wis 3, 1.   *r:* Wis 14, 2; Prv 8, 30.

Nature and Incomparable Dignity of Wisdom

For in her is a spirit
intelligent, holy, unique,
Manifold, subtle, agile,
clear, unstained, certain,
Not baneful, loving the good, keen,[s]
unhampered, beneficent, [23]kindly,
Firm, secure, tranquil,
all-powerful, all-seeing,
And pervading all spirits,
though they be intelligent, pure and
very subtle.

[24] For Wisdom is mobile beyond all motion,
and she penetrates and pervades all
things by reason of her purity.[t]

[25] For she is an aura of the might of God
and a pure effusion of the glory of the
Almighty;
therefore nought that is sullied enters
into her.

[26] For she is the refulgence of eternal light,
the spotless mirror of the power of God,
the image of his goodness.[u]

[27] And she, who is one, can do all things,
and renews everything while herself
perduring;
And passing into holy souls from age to
age,
she produces friends of God and
prophets.[v]

[28] For there is nought God loves, be it not
one who dwells with Wisdom.

[29] For she is fairer than the sun[w]
and surpasses every constellation of
the stars.
Compared to light, she takes precedence;

[30] for that, indeed, night supplants,
but wickedness prevails not over
Wisdom.

CHAPTER 8

See RG 274-75

[1]Indeed, she reaches from end to
end* mightily
and governs all things well.[x]

Solomon Sought Wisdom, the Source of Blessings

[2] Her I loved and sought after from my
youth;
I sought to take her for my bride
and was enamored of her beauty.[y]

[3] She adds to nobility the splendor of
companionship with God;
even the LORD of all loved her.

[4] For she is instructress in the
understanding of God,
the selector of his works.[z]

[5] And if riches be a desirable possession in
life,
what is more rich than Wisdom, who
produces all things?[a]

[6] And if prudence renders service,[b]
who in the world is a better craftsman
than she?

[7] Or if one loves justice,
the fruits of her works are virtues;
For she teaches moderation and
prudence,
justice and fortitude,*
and nothing in life is more useful for
men than these.

[8] Or again, if one yearns for copious
learning,
she knows the things of old, and infers
those yet to come.
She understands the turns of phrases and
the solutions of riddles;
signs and wonders she knows in
advance
and the outcome of times and ages.[c]

Solomon Sought Wisdom as His Counselor and Comfort

[9] So I determined to take her to live with
me,
knowing that she would be my
counselor while all was well,
and my comfort in care and grief.

[10] For her sake I should have glory among
the masses,[d]

8, 1: End to end: from one end of the heavens to the other.
8, 7: Moderation . . . fortitude: what are now known as the cardinal virtues.

---

s: 22f; Heb 4, 12f; Jas 3, 17.   t: Wis 8, 1.   u: 2 Cor 4, 4; Col 1, 15; Heb 1, 3.   v: Ex 33, 11; Jb 42, 2; Ps 104, 29; Jl 3, 1.   w: 29f; Song 6, 3. 9.   x: Wis 7, 24; 15, 1.   y: 1 Kgs 3, 7ff; Ps 45, 12; Prv 5, 18; 8, 17.   z: Prv 8, 27-31.   a: Prv 8, 18f.   b: 6f; Prv 8, 14f. c: Prv 1, 6; Sir 39, 1ff; 42, 19f; Dn 2, 21.   d: 10ff; 1 Kgs 3, 28; Jb 29, 8ff. 21f.

and esteem from the elders, though I
be but a youth.

11 I should become keen in judgment,
and should be a marvel before
rulers.

12 They would abide my silence and attend
my utterance;
and as I spoke on further,
they would place their hands upon
their mouths.*

13 For her sake I should have immortality
and leave to those after me an
everlasting memory.*e*

14 I should govern peoples, and nations
would be my subjects—*f*

15 terrible princes, hearing of me, would
be afraid;
in the assembly I should appear noble,
and in war courageous.

16 Within my dwelling, I should take my
repose beside her;
For association with her involves no
bitterness
and living with her no grief,
but rather joy and gladness.*g*

Solomon Realizes That Wisdom Is a Gift of God

17 Thinking thus within myself,
and reflecting in my heart
That there is immortality in kinship with
Wisdom,*h*

18 and good pleasure in her friendship,
and unfailing riches in the works of
her hands,
And that in frequenting her society there
is prudence,
and fair renown in sharing her
discourses,
I went about seeking to take her for
my own.

19 Now, I was a well-favored child,*
and I came by a noble nature;

20 or rather, being noble, I attained an
unsullied body.

21 And knowing that I could not otherwise
possess her* except God gave it—
and this, too, was prudence, to know
whose is the gift—
I went to the LORD and besought him,*i*
and said with all my heart:

CHAPTER 9

Solomon's Prayer

1 God of my fathers, LORD of mercy,*j*
you who have made all things by your
word*k*

2 And in your wisdom have established
man
to rule the creatures produced by you,*l*

3 To govern the world in holiness and
justice,
and to render judgment in integrity of
heart:*m*

4 Give me Wisdom, the attendant at your
throne,
and reject me not from among your
children;*n*

5 For I am your servant, the son of your
handmaid,
a man weak and short-lived
and lacking in comprehension of
judgment and of laws.*o*

6 Indeed, though one be perfect among the
sons of men,
if Wisdom, who comes from you, be
not with him,
he shall be held in no esteem.*p*

7 You have chosen me king over your
people
and magistrate for your sons and
daughters.*q*

8 You have bid me build a temple on your
holy mountain
and an altar in the city that is your
dwelling place,

See RG
274-75

8, 12: Hands upon their mouths: an oft-mentioned sign of respect among the ancients for unanswerable wisdom; cf Jb 40, 4.

8, 19f: Here the sacred writer mentions first bodily, then spiritual, excellence. To make it plain that the latter is the governing factor in the harmonious development of the human person, he then reverses the order.

8, 21: Possess her: in the Latin, "be continent." Though this verse has often been cited in connection with the virtue

of chastity, the original must certainly mean "be possessed of Wisdom."

---

e: Sir 15, 6; 41, 12f; Is 56, 5. *f:* Wis 3, 8; Ps 18, 48; 47, 4.
g: Prv 29, 6; Sir 15, 6; Bar 3, 38. *h:* Prv 3, 18. *i:* 1 Kgs 3, 9; 4,
29; Prv 2, 6; Jas 1, 5. *j:* Ps 86, 15. *k:* 1f: Gn 1; Ps 33, 6; Prv 3,
19; Jer 10, 12; Jn 1, 3. 10. *l:* Ps 8, 7ff; Sir 17, 2ff. *m:* 1 Kgs 3,
6; 9 4f; Ps 9, 8f. *n:* 2 Chr 1, 10. *o:* 1 Kgs 3, 7; Ps 116, 16.
p: Wis 3, 17; 1 Kgs 11, 4; 1 Cor 3, 18ff. *q:* 1 Chr 28, 5.

a copy of the holy tabernacle which
    you had established from of old.*r*
9 Now with you is Wisdom, who knows
    your works
    and was present when you made the
      world;
Who understands what is pleasing in
    your eyes
    and what is conformable with your
      commands.*s*
10 Send her forth from your holy heavens
    and from your glorious throne dispatch
      her
That she may be with me and work with
    me,
    that I may know what is your
      pleasure,*t*
11 For she knows and understands all
    things,
    and will guide me discreetly in my
      affairs
    and safeguard me by her glory;*u*
12 Thus my deeds will be acceptable,
    and I shall judge your people justly
    and be worthy of my father's throne.*v*
13 For what man knows God's counsel,
    or who can conceive what the LORD
      intends?*w*
14 For the deliberations of mortals are
    timid,
    and unsure are our plans.
15 For the corruptible body burdens the
    soul
    and the earthen shelter weighs down
      the mind that has many
      concerns.*x*
16 And scarce do we guess the things on
    earth,
    and what is within our grasp we find
      with difficulty;
    but when things are in heaven, who
      can search them out?*y*

17 Or who ever knew your counsel, except
    you had given Wisdom
    and sent your holy spirit from on
      high?*z*
18 And thus were the paths of those on earth
    made straight,
    and men learned what was your
      pleasure,
    and were saved by Wisdom.*a*

CHAPTER 10*

Wisdom Preserves Her
Followers

See RG
274-75

1 She preserved the first-formed father* of
    the world*b*
    when he alone had been created;*c*
    And she raised him up from his fall,
2   and gave him power to rule all things.*d*
3 But when the unjust man* withdrew from
    her in his anger,
    he perished through his fratricidal
      wrath.*e*
4 When on his account the earth was
    flooded, Wisdom again saved it,
    piloting the just man* on frailest
      wood.*f*
5 She, when the nations were sunk in
    universal wickedness,
    knew the just man,* kept him
      blameless before God,
    and preserved him resolute against
      pity for his child.*g*
6 She delivered the just man* from among
    the wicked who were being
      destroyed,*h*
    when he fled as fire descended upon
      Pentapolis—
7 Where as a testimony to its wickedness,
    there yet remain a smoking desert,
    Plants bearing fruit that never ripens,
    and the tomb of a disbelieving soul,*
    a standing pillar of salt.*i*

10, 1-21: This chapter prepares for the following section (11, 2—19, 22) on the history of Israel in the Exodus, by reviewing the dealings of Wisdom with the patriarchs. It has a parallel in Sir 44—50; cf also Wis 18, 9.
  10, 1f: Adam.
  10, 3: Cain.
  10, 4: Noah.
  10, 5: Abraham.
  10, 6: Lot. Pentapolis: the five cities, including Sodom; cf Gn 14, 2.

10, 7: Disbelieving soul: Lot's wife; cf Gn 19, 26.

r: Ex 25, 8f; 2 Sm 7, 13; 1 Chr 28, 5; 2 Chr 6, 1f; 7, 7; Tb 1, 4; Pss 15. 1; 48, 2f. *s:* Dt 6, 17f; Prv 8, 22-31; Jn 1, 1ff. 10. *t:* Wis 18, 15; Mt 5, 34; Jn 3, 17; 20, 21. *u:* Wis 8, 8. *v:* 1 Kgs 3, 6-9. *w:* Is 40, 13; Bar 3, 31. *x:* Jb 4, 19. *y:* Sir 1. 3; Jn 3, 12. *z:* Jn 14, 26. *a:* Wis 10, 9; Prv 28, 26. *b:* 1-16: Heb 11, 17-27. *c:* Wis 7, 1. *d:* Gn 1, 28. *e:* Gn 4, 1-16. *f:* Wis 14, 5f; Gn 6, 5-9. *g:* Gn 22, 7-10. *h:* Gn 18, 22-33; 19, 15-25; 2 Pt 2, 6f. *i:* Gn 19, 26; Lk 17, 32.

8 For those who forsook Wisdom
   first were bereft of knowledge of the
      right,
And then they left mankind a memorial
   of their folly—
so that they could not even be hidden
   in their fall.
9 But Wisdom delivered from tribulations
   those who served her.ʲ
10 She, when the just man fled from his
      brother's anger,ᵏ
   guided him in direct ways,*
Showed him the kingdom of God
   and gave him knowledge of holy
      things;
She prospered him in his labors
   and made abundant the fruit of his
      works,
11 Stood by him against the greed of his
      defrauders,
   and enriched him;ˡ
12 She preserved him from foes,
   and secured him against ambush,
And she gave him the prize for his stern
      struggle
   that he might know that devotion to
      God* is mightier than all else.ᵐ
13 She did not abandon the just man* when
      he was sold,ⁿ
   but delivered him from sin.ᵒ
14 She went down with him into the
      dungeon,
   and did not desert him in his bonds,
Until she brought him the scepter of
      royalty
   and authority over his oppressors,
Showed those who had defamed him
      false,
   and gave him eternal glory.
15 The holy people and blameless race—it
      was she

who delivered them from the nation
   that oppressed them.ᵖ
16 She entered the soul of the LORD's
      servant,*
   and withstood fearsome kings with
      signs and portents;�q
17   she gave the holy ones the recompense
      of their labors,ʳ
Conducted them by a wondrous road,
   and became a shelter for them by day
   and a starry flame by night.
18 She took them across the Red Sea
   and brought them through the deep
      waters—
19 But their enemies she overwhelmed,
   and cast them up* from the bottom of
      the depths.
20 Therefore the just despoiled the wicked;
   and they sang, O LORD, your holy
      name
   and praised in unison your conquering
      handˢ—
21 Because Wisdom opened the mouths of
      the dumb,
   and gave ready speech to infants.ᵗ

CHAPTER 11

See RG
275-76

1 She made their affairs prosper
   through the holy prophet.ᵘ

III: Special Providence of God
During the Exodus

Introduction
2 They journeyed through the uninhabited
      desert,*
   and in solitudes they pitched their tents;ᵛ
3   they withstood enemies and took
      vengeance on their foes.ʷ
4 When they thirsted, they called upon
      you,

10, 10ff: Jacob.
10, 12: Devotion to God: in the Greek this signifies "piety" or "religion," and is the equivalent of the Hebrew "fear of the Lord"; cf Prv 1, 7.
10, 13f: Joseph.
10, 16: Moses.
10, 19: Cast them up: their bodies, on the shore.
11, 2ff: Few verses in these later chapters can be fully understood without consulting the passages in the Mosaic books which are indicated in the cross references. The theme of this part of the book is expressed in Wis 11, 5, and is illustrated in

the following chapters by five examples drawn from Exodus events.

j: Wis 16, 8. k: Gn 27, 43ff; 28, 12-15. l: Gn 30, 29f; 31, 5-12. m: Gn 32, 24-29; 1 Tm 4, 8. n: 13f: Gn 37-45. o: Gn 39, 7-10. p: Ex 3, 9; 14, 30; 19, 6. q: Wis 1, 4; 7, 27; Ex 4, 10; Ps 76, 13. r: 17ff; Wis 14, 3; 19, 7; Ex 13, 21f; 14—15; Pss 77, 20f; 78, 13. 53; Is 4, 5f. s: Ex 12, 35f; 15, 1-21. t: Ex 4, 10-15; Ps 8, 3; Mt 11, 25. u: Dt 2, 7; Hos 12, 14. v: 2ff: Ex 17, 2-6; Nm 20, 1-13; Pss 63, 2; 107, 4-7; Jer 2, 6. w: Ex 17, 8-16; Nm 21, 1ff. 21-35; 31, 1-12; Ps 118, 10ff.

and water was given them from the
    sheer rock,
assuagement for their thirst from the
    hard stone.
[5] For by the things through which their
    foes were punished
they in their need were benefited.[x]

First Example: Water Punishes the Egyptians and Benefits the Israelites

[6] Instead of a spring, when the perennial
    river*
was troubled with impure blood[y]
[7] as a rebuke to the decree for the
    slaying of infants,
You gave them abundant water in an
    unhoped-for way,
[8] once you had shown by the thirst they
    then had
how you punished their
    adversaries.
[9] For when they had been tried, though
    only mildly chastised,[z]
they recognized how the wicked,
    condemned in anger, were being
    tormented.
[11] Both those afar off and those close by
    were afflicted:[a]
[10] the latter you tested, admonishing
    them as a father;
the former as a stern king you probed
    and condemned.
[12] For a twofold grief took hold of them[b]
and a groaning at the remembrance of
    the ones who had departed.
[13] For when they heard that the cause of
    their own torments
was a benefit to these others, they
    recognized the LORD.
[14] Him who of old had been cast out in
    exposure they indeed mockingly
    rejected;
but in the end of events, they marveled
    at him,

since their thirst proved unlike that of
    the just.[c]

Second Example: Animals Punish the Egyptians and Benefit the Israelites

[15] And in return for their senseless, wicked
    thoughts,
which misled them into worshiping
    dumb* serpents and worthless
    insects,
You sent upon them swarms of dumb
    creatures for vengeance;[d]
[16] that they might recognize that a man is
    punished by the very things
    through which he sins.[e]

Digression on God's Mercy

[17] For not without means was your
    almighty hand,[f]
that had fashioned the universe from
    formless matter,
to send upon them a drove of bears or
    fierce lions,
[18] Or new-created, wrathful, unknown
    beasts
to breathe forth fiery breath,
Or pour out roaring smoke,
or flash terrible sparks from their eyes.
[19] Not only could these attack and
    completely destroy them;
even their frightful appearance itself
    could slay.
[20] Even without these, they could have been
    killed at a single blast,
pursued by retribution
and winnowed out by your mighty
    spirit;
But you have disposed all things by
    measure and number and weight.[g]
[21] For with you great strength abides
    always;
who can resist the might of your arm?[h]
[22] Indeed, before you the whole universe is
    as a grain from a balance,*

11, 6ff: The perennial river: the Nile; the contrast is between the first plague of Egypt (Ex 7, 17-24) and the water drawn from the rock in Horeb (Ex 17, 5-7; Nm 20, 8-11).

11, 15: Dumb: that is, irrational.

11, 22: Grain from a balance: a tiny particle used for weighing on sensitive scales.

x: Wis 16, 1f. y: 6ff: Wis 18, 5; Ex 1, 22; 7, 17-24. z: 9ff: Wis 3, 5; 16, 3f; Dt 8, 2-5; Ps 6, 2; Prv 3, 12; 2 Mc 6, 12-11.11 a: Ps 6, 2. b: 12f: Wis 16, 8; Ex 14, 4. 18. c: Ex 2, 3. d: Wis 12, 23f; 15, 18—16, 1; Ex 7, 26ff. e: Wis 12, 23. 27; Ex 10, 16; Prv 1, 31f; 26, 27. f: 17ff: Wis 12, 8f; 16, 1. 5; Gn 1, 1f; Dt 32, 24; 2 Kgs 17, 25f; Hos 13, 4-8. g: Jb 4, 9. h: Wis 12, 12; 2 Chr 20, 6.

or a drop of morning dew come down
upon the earth.[i]

23 But you have mercy on all, because you
can do all things;

and you overlook the sins of men that
they may repent.[j]

24 For you love all things that are
and loathe nothing that you have
made;

for what you hated, you would not
have fashioned.[k]

25 And how could a thing remain, unless
you willed it;

or be preserved, had it not been called
forth by you?[l]

26 But you spare all things, because they are
yours, O LORD and lover of
souls,[m]

CHAPTER 12

See RG
275–76

1 for your imperishable spirit is in all
things![n]

2 Therefore you rebuke offenders little by
little,

warn them, and remind them of the
sins they are committing,

that they may abandon their
wickedness and believe in you, O
LORD!

3 For, truly, the ancient inhabitants of your
holy land,[o]

4 whom you hated for deeds most
odious—

Works of witchcraft and impious
sacrifices;

5 a cannibal feast of human flesh
and of blood, from the midst of . . .*—

These merciless murderers of children,

6 and parents who took with their own
hands defenseless lives,[p]

You willed to destroy by the hands of our
fathers,

7 that the land that is dearest of all to
you

might receive a worthy colony of
God's children.[q]

8 But even these, as they were men, you
spared,

and sent wasps as forerunners of your
army

that they might exterminate them by
degrees.[r]

9 Not that you were without power to have
the wicked vanquished in battle
by the just,

or wiped out at once by terrible beasts
or by one decisive word;[s]

10 But condemning them bit by bit, you
gave them space for repentance.

You were not unaware that their race was
wicked

and their malice ingrained,[t]

And that their dispositions would never
change;

11 for they were a race accursed from the
beginning.

Neither out of fear for anyone
did you grant amnesty for their sins.[u]

12 For who can say to you, "What have you
done?"

or who can oppose your decree?

Or when peoples perish, who can
challenge you, their maker;

or who can come into your presence as
vindicator of unjust men?[v]

13 For neither is there any god besides you
who have the care of all,

that you need show you have not
unjustly condemned;[w]

14 Nor can any king or prince confront you
on behalf of those you have
punished.[x]

15 But as you are just, you govern all things
justly;

you regard it as unworthy of your
power

to punish one who has incurred no
blame.[y]

12, 5: And of blood, from the midst of . . . : this line is obscure in the current Greek text and in all extant translations. Either one or two words would complete it. The horrible crimes here spoken of (cf Wis 14, 23) were not unheard of in the ancient pagan world.

i: Hos 13, 3. j: Wis 12, 10; Dt 9, 27; Acts 17, 30; Rom 2, 4; 11, 32; 2 Pt 3, 9. k: Ps 145, 9. l: Is 41, 4. m: Wis 12, 16; Is 63, 9. n: Wis 1, 7. o: 3ff: Wis 14, 23; Dt 18, 9-12; Pss 5, 6; 106, 28. 34-39; Jer 19, 4f; Ez 21, 3. 20f. 36. p: Nm 33, 52. q: Dt 11, 12. r: Ex 23, 28ff; Dt 7, 17-24. s: Wis 11, 18; 18, 15; Nm 16, 21. t: Wis 11, 23; Ps 55, 20; Sir 16, 9. u: Gn 9, 25. v: 2 Sm 16, 10; Eccl 8, 4; Sir 46, 19; Is 45, 9; Dn 4, 32; Rom 9, 19ff. w: Wis 6, 7; Dt 3, 24; 32, 39; Is 44, 6. 8. x: Jer 49, 19; 50, 44. y: Gn 18, 23ff; Dt 32, 4.

16 For your might is the source of justice;
  your mastery over all things makes
    you lenient to all.z
17 For you show your might when the
    perfection of your power is
    disbelieved;*
  and in those who know you, you
    rebuke temerity.a
18 But though you are master of might, you
    judge with clemency,
  and with much lenience you govern
    us;
  for power, whenever you will, attends
    you.
19 And you taught your people, by these
    deeds,b
  that those who are just must be kind;
  And you gave your sons good ground for
    hope
  that you would permit repentance for
    their sins.
20 For these were enemies of your servants,
    doomed to death;
  yet, while you punished them with
    such solicitude and pleading,
  granting time and opportunity to
    abandon wickedness,
21 With what exactitude you judged your
    sons,
  to whose fathers you gave the sworn
    covenants of goodly promises!c
22 Us, therefore, you chastise, and our
    enemies with a thousand blows
    you punish,
  that we may think earnestly of your
    goodness when we judge,
  and, when being judged, may look for
    mercy.

Second Example Resumed

23 Hence those unjust also, who lived a life
    of folly,
  you tormented through their own
    abominations.d

24 For they went far astray in the paths of
    error,
  taking for gods the worthless and
    disgusting among beasts,
  deceived like senseless infants.e
25 Therefore as though upon unreasoning
    children,
  you sent your judgment on them as a
    mockery;f
26 But they who took no heed of
    punishment which was but child's
    play
  were to experience a condemnation
    worthy of God.
27 For in the things through which they
    suffered distress,
  since they were tortured by the very
    things they deemed gods,
  They saw and recognized the true God
  whom before they had refused to know;
  with this, their final condemnation
    came upon them.g

Digression on False Worship

CHAPTER 13

See RG
275-76

A. NATURE WORSHIP

1 For all men were by nature foolish who
    were in ignorance of God,
  and who from the good things seen did
    not succeed in knowing him who
    is,*
  and from studying the works did not
    discern the artisan;h
2 But either fire, or wind, or the swift air,
  or the circuit of the stars, or the mighty
    water,
  or the luminaries of heaven,* the
    governors of the world, they
    considered gods.i
3 Now if out of joy in their beauty they
    thought them gods,
  let them know how far more excellent
    is the Lord than these;

12, 17: The brunt of God's anger and vindictive justice is borne by those who know him and yet defy his authority and might. Cf Wis 1, 2; 15, 2, but also Wis 12, 27; 18, 13.

13, 1: Him who is: the Hebrew sacred name of God; cf Ex 3, 14.

13, 2: Luminaries of heaven: the Latin interprets, "sun and moon"; governors: cf Gn 1, 16.

---

z: Wis 2, 11; 11, 26; Ps 103, 19. a: Wis 15, 2f; Ex 9, 16. b: 19f: Wis 11, 23; Sir 17, 24. c: Wis 18, 22; Gn 50, 24; Dt 7, 6-14; Ps 105, 8ff. d: Wis 11, 16; 16, 1. e: Dt 11, 28; Jer 5, 28; Rom 1, 23. f: Jer 4, 22. g: Wis 16, 16; Ex 14, 4. 28. h: Acts 14, 17; Eph 4, 17ff. i: Gn 1, 14-19; Dt 4, 19; Jb 31, 26ff.

for the original source of beauty
fashioned them.*j*

4 Or if they were struck by their might and
energy,
let them from these things realize how
much more powerful is he who
made them.*k*

5 For from the greatness and the beauty of
created things
their original author, by analogy, is
seen.

6 But yet, for these the blame is less;*
For they indeed have gone astray
perhaps,
though they seek God and wish to find
him.

7 For they search busily among his
works,
but are distracted by what they see,
because the things seen are fair.

8 But again, not even these are pardonable.

9 For if they so far succeeded in
knowledge
that they could speculate about the
world,
how did they not more quickly find its
LORD?

B. IDOLATRY

10 But doomed are they, and in dead things
are their hopes,
who termed gods things made by
human hands:
Gold and silver, the product of art, and
likenesses of beasts,
or useless stone, the work of an
ancient hand.*l*

The Carpenter and Wooden Idols

11 A carpenter may saw out a suitable
tree*m*
and skillfully scrape off all its bark,
And deftly plying his art,
produce something fit for daily use,*n*

12 and use up the refuse from his
handiwork in preparing his food,
and have his fill;

13 Then the good-for-nothing refuse from
these remnants,
crooked wood grown full of knots,
he takes and carves to occupy his spare
time.*o*
This wood he models with listless skill,
and patterns it on the image of a man

14 or makes it resemble some worthless
beast.
When he has daubed it with red and
crimsoned its surface with red
stain,
and daubed over every blemish in it,*p*

15 He makes a fitting shrine for it
and puts it on the wall, fastening it
with a nail.*q*

16 Thus lest it fall down he provides for it,
knowing that it cannot help itself;
for, truly, it is an image and needs help.*r*

17 But when he prays about his goods or
marriage or children,*s*
he is not ashamed to address the thing
without a soul.
And for vigor he invokes the powerless;

18 and for life he entreats the dead;
And for aid he beseeches the wholly
incompetent,
and about travel, something that
cannot even walk.

19 And for profit in business and success
with his hands
he asks facility of a thing with hands
completely inert.

CHAPTER 14

See RG
275-76

1 Again, one preparing for a voyage
and about to traverse the wild
waves
cries out to wood more unsound than
the boat that bears him.*t*

2 For the urge for profits devised this latter,
and Wisdom the artificer produced it.

3 But your providence, O Father! guides it,
for you have furnished even in the sea
a road,
and through the waves a steady path,*u*

13, 6: The blame is less: the greater blame is incurred by those mentioned in Wis 13, 10 and 15, 14ff.

j: Ps 8, 4.   *k:* Jer 10, 2; Bar 6, 39.   *l:* Wis 3, 11; 15, 5. 17; Dt 4, 25-28; 7, 25; 27, 15; Ps 115, 4; Hos 14, 4; Acts 17, 29.   *m:* 11-19: Is
44, 9-20.   *n:* Wis 15, 7; Bar 6, 58.   *o:* Dt 4, 16.   *p:* Jer 10, 9.   *q:* Is 40, 20; 41, 7; 44, 13.   *r:* 1 Sm 5, 3ff; Bar 6, 57.   *s:* 17ff: Wis
15, 15.   *t:* Is 46, 7.   *u:* Ps 107, 23-30; Is 43, 16.

4 Showing that you can save from any
    danger,
  so that even one without skill may
    embark.*y*

5 But you will that the products of your
    Wisdom be not idle;
  therefore men trust their lives even to
    frailest wood,
  and have been safe crossing the surge
    on a raft.*w*

6 For of old, when the proud giants were
    being destroyed,
  the hope of the universe, who took
    refuge on a raft,*
  left to the world a future for his race,
    under the guidance of your hand.*x*

7 For blest is the wood through which
    justice comes about;*

8   but the handmade idol is accursed, and
    its maker as well:
  he for having produced it, and it,
    because though corruptible, it
    was termed a god.*y*

9 Equally odious to God are the evildoer
    and his evil deed;

10   and the thing made shall be punished
    with its contriver.

11 Therefore upon even the idols of the
    nations shall a visitation come,
  since they have become abominable
    amid God's works,
  Snares for the souls of men
  and a trap for the feet of the senseless.*z*

The Origin and Evils of Idolatry

12 For the source of wantonness is the
    devising of idols;
  and their invention was a corruption of
    life.*a*

13 For in the beginning they were not,
  nor shall they continue forever;*b*

14   for by the vanity of men they came
    into the world,
  and therefore a sudden end is devised
    for them.

15 For a father, afflicted with untimely
    mourning,
  made an image of the child so quickly
    taken from him,
  And now honored as a god what was
    formerly a dead man
  and handed down to his subjects
    mysteries and sacrifices.

16 Then, in time, the impious practice
    gained strength and was observed
    as law,
  and graven things were worshiped by
    princely decrees.*c*

17 Men who lived so far away that they
    could not honor him in his
    presence
  copied the appearance of the distant
    king
  And made a public image of him they
    wished to honor,
  out of zeal to flatter him when absent,
    as though present.

18 And to promote this observance among
    those to whom it was strange,
  the artisan's ambition provided a
    stimulus.

19 For he, mayhap in his determination to
    please the ruler,
  labored over the likeness to the best of
    his skill;*d*

20 And the masses, drawn by the charm of
    the workmanship,
  soon thought he should be worshiped
    who shortly before was honored
    as a man.*e*

21 And this became a snare for mankind,
    that men enslaved to either grief or
    tyranny
  conferred the incommunicable Name
    on stocks and stones.

22 Then it was not enough for them to err in
    their knowledge of God;*f*
  but even though they live in a great
    war of ignorance,
  they call such evils peace.*g*

14, 6: Noah.
14, 7: Often applied to the Cross of our Lord.

v: Wis 16, 8.   *w:* Wis 10, 4.   *x:* Gn 6, 4; 17, 1ff. 21f.   *y:* Rom 1, 23.   *z:* Wis 3, 7; 23, 33; Nm 33, 4; Jos 23, 13; Ps 115, 4; Jer 6, 15; 10, 15; 46, 25; Hos 9, 15.   *a:* Rom 1, 23ff.   *b:* Is 2, 18.   *c:* Dn 3, 4ff; 1 Mc 1, 47-50.   *d:* Is 44, 12f LXX.   *e:* Wis 15, 4.   *f:* 22-31: Jer 2, 20; 3, 1-25; Hos 4, 1f. 9-19; Rom 1, 26-31; Gal 5, 19ff; 1 Tm 1, 9f.   *g:* Jer 6, 14; Ez 13, 10.

23 For while they celebrate either child-
      slaying sacrifices or clandestine
      mysteries,
   or frenzied carousals in unheard-of
      rites,*h*

24 They no longer safeguard either lives or
      pure wedlock;
   but each either waylays and kills his
      neighbor, or aggrieves him by
      adultery.

25 And all is confusion—blood and murder,
      theft and guile,*i*
   corruption, faithlessness, turmoil,
      perjury,

26 Disturbance of good men, neglect of
      gratitude,
   besmirching of souls, unnatural lust,
   disorder in marriage, adultery and
      shamelessness.

27 For the worship of infamous idols
   is the reason and source and extremity
      of all evil.*j*

28 For they either go mad with enjoyment,
      or prophesy lies,
   or live lawlessly or lightly forswear
      themselves.*k*

29 For as their trust is in soulless idols,
   they expect no harm when they have
      sworn falsely.

30 But on both counts shall justice overtake
      them:
   because they thought ill of God and
      devoted themselves to idols,*l*
   and because they deliberately swore
      false oaths, despising piety.*

31 For not the might of those that are sworn
      by
   but the retribution of sinners
   ever follows upon the transgression of
      the wicked.*

CHAPTER 15

See RG
275–76

1 But you, our God, are good and true,
   slow to anger, and governing all with
      mercy.*m*

2 For even if we sin, we are yours, and
      know your might;
   but we will not sin, knowing that we
      belong to you.*n*

3 For to know you well is complete justice,
   and to know your might is the root of
      immortality.*o*

4 For neither did the evil creation of men's
      fancy deceive us,
   nor the fruitless labor of painters,*p*
   A form smeared with varied colors,

5 the sight of which arouses yearning in
      the senseless man,
   till he longs for the inanimate form of
      a dead image.

6 Lovers of evil things, and worthy of such
      hopes
   are they who make them and long for
      them and worship them.*q*

The Potter's Clay Idols

7 For truly the potter, laboriously working
      the soft earth,
   molds for our service each several
      article:
   Both the vessels that serve for clean
      purposes
   and their opposites, all alike;
   As to what shall be the use of each vessel
      of either class
   the worker in clay is the judge.*r*

8 And with misspent toil he molds a
      meaningless god from the
      selfsame clay;
   though he himself shortly before was
      made from the earth
   And after a little, is to go whence he was
      taken,
   when the life that was lent him is
      demanded back.*s*

9 But his concern is not that he is to die
   nor that his span of life is brief;
   Rather, he vies with goldsmiths and
      silversmiths
   and emulates molders of bronze,

14, 30: Piety: the sanctity of oaths.

14, 31: Perjury is a form of deceit which calls for punishment even though it be practiced in the name of a lifeless idol.

h: Wis 12, 4f; 14, 15; Is 57, 5.   *i:* 25f; Jer 7, 8f; 22, 17.   *j:* Ex 23, 13.   *k:* Jer 5, 31; 29, 26.   *l:* Wis 1, 1. 8; 11, 20; Jer 5, 2. 7.   *m:* Ex 34, 6f; Pss 86, 5. 15; 145, 8. 9. 14.   *n:* Jb 10, 14f LXX.   *o:* Wis 3, 15; Jn 17, 3.   *p:* Wis 13, 14.   *q:* Ps 115, 8.   *r:* Wis 13, 11; Jer 18, 3f; Rom 9, 21; 2 Tm 2, 20f.   *s:* Gn 3, 19; Eccl 12, 7.

and takes pride in modeling counterfeits.[t]

[10] Ashes his heart is! more worthless than earth is his hope,[u]
and more ignoble than clay his life;

[11] Because he knew not the one who fashioned him,
and breathed into him a quickening soul,
and infused a vital spirit.[v]

[12] Instead, he esteemed our life a plaything,
and our span of life a holiday for gain;
"For one must," says he, "make profit every way, be it even out of evil."[w]

[13] For this man more than any knows that he is sinning,
when out of earthen stuff he creates fragile vessels and idols alike.

[14] But all quite senseless, and worse than childish in mind,
are the enemies of your people who enslaved them.[x]

[15] For they esteemed all the idols of the nations, gods,
which have no use of the eyes for vision,
nor nostrils to snuff the air,
Nor ears to hear,
nor fingers on their hands for feeling;
even their feet are useless to walk with.[y]

[16] For a man made them;[z]
one whose spirit has been lent him fashioned them.
For no man succeeds in fashioning a god like himself;

[17] being mortal, he makes a dead thing with his lawless hands.
For he is better than the things he worships;
he at least lives, but never they.

Second Example Resumed

[18] And besides, they worship* the most loathsome beasts—[a]
for compared as to folly, these are worse than the rest,*

[19] Nor for their looks are they good or desirable beasts,
but they have escaped both the approval of God and his blessing.[b]

CHAPTER 16

See RG 275–76

[1] Therefore they* were fittingly punished by similar creatures,
and were tormented by a swarm of insects.[c]

[2] Instead of this punishment, you benefited your people
with a novel dish, the delight they craved,
by providing quail for their food;[d]

[3] That those others, when they desired food,
since the creatures sent to plague them were so loathsome,
should be turned from even the craving of necessities,
While these, after a brief period of privation,
partook of a novel dish.[e]

[4] For upon those oppressors, inexorable want had to come;
but these needed only be shown how their enemies were being tormented.[f]

[5] For when the dire venom of beasts came upon them[g]
and they were dying from the bite of crooked serpents,
your anger endured not to the end.

[6] But as a warning, for a short time they were terrorized,

15, 18ff: The author here returns to the main theme of chapters 11—19, which was interrupted by the digression 13, 1—15, 17.

15, 18: For . . . rest: this may mean that the creatures worshiped by the Egyptians (e.g., crocodiles, serpents, scarabs, etc.) were more patently lacking in intelligence than the general run of beasts; cf Wis 11, 15; 12, 24.

16, 1: They: the Egyptian idolaters.

---

t: Bar 6, 46. u: Jb 13, 12 LXX. v: Gn 2, 7; Zec 12, 1. w: Jas 4, 13f. x: Ex 1, 13. y: Wis 14, 11; Dt 4, 28; Pss 115, 4-7; 135, 15ff. z: 16f: Wis 13. 10. a: Wis 11, 15; 12, 24. b: Gn 1, 25; 3, 14. c: Wis 11, 15f; 12, 23. 27; Ex 7, 27; 8, 12. 17. d: Wis 11, 13; 19, 11f; Ex 16, 13; Nm 11, 31f; Ps 105, 40. e: Wis 11, 15; Ex 8, 10; 16, 3. f: Wis 11, 8f. g: 5f: Nm 21, 4-9; Dt 32, 24; Jer 8, 7 LXX.

though they had a sign* of salvation, to
remind them of the precept of
your law.

7 For he who turned toward it was saved,
not by what he saw,
but by you, the savior of all.

8 And by this also you convinced our foes
that you are he who delivers from all
evil.[h]

9 For the bites of locusts and of flies slew
them,
and no remedy was found to save their
lives
because they deserved to be punished
by such means;[i]

10 But not even the fangs of poisonous
reptiles overcame your sons,
for your mercy brought the antidote to
heal them.[j]

11 For as a reminder of your injunctions,
they were stung,
and swiftly they were saved,
Lest they should fall into deep
forgetfulness
and become unresponsive to your
beneficence.[k]

12 For indeed, neither herb nor application
cured them,
but your all-healing word, O LORD![l]

13 For you have dominion over life and
death;[m]
you lead down to the gates of the
nether world, and lead back.

14 Man, however, slays in his malice,
but when the spirit has come away, it
does not return,
nor can he bring back the soul once it
is confined.*

15 But your hand none can escape.

Third Example: A Rain of Manna for Israel instead of the Plague of Storms

16 For the wicked who refused to know you
were punished by the might of your arm,

Pursued by unwonted rains and
hailstorms and unremitting
downpours,
and consumed by fire.[n]

17 For against all expectation, in water
which quenches anything,
the fire grew more active;
For the universe fights on behalf of the
just.[o]

18 For now the flame was tempered[p]
so that the beasts might not be burnt
up that were sent upon the
wicked,
but that these might see and know they
were struck by the judgment of
God;

19 And again, even in the water, fire blazed
beyond its strength
so as to consume the produce of the
wicked land.

20 Instead of this, you nourished your
people with food of angels
and furnished them bread from
heaven, ready to hand, untoiled-
for,
endowed with all delights and
conforming to every taste.[q]

21 For this substance of yours revealed your
sweetness toward your children,
and serving the desire of him who
received it,
was blended to whatever flavor each
one wished.[r]

22 Yet snow and ice* withstood fire and
were not melted,
that they might know that their
enemies' fruits
Were consumed by a fire that blazed in
the hail
and flashed lightning in the rain.[s]

23 But this fire, again, that the just might be
nourished,
forgot even its proper strength;[t]

24 For your creation, serving you, its maker,

16, 6: Sign: the brazen serpent; cf Nm 21, 9.
16, 14: Confined: in the nether world, in limbo.
16, 22: Snow and ice: the manna; cf Wis 16, 27; 19, 21.

h: Gn 48, 16; 2 Mc 1, 24f.   *i:* Ex 8, 16-28; 10, 4-19; Pss 78, 45f; 105, 31. 34; Rv 9, 1-11.   *j:* Dt 32, 33.   *k:* Ps 78, 11.   *l:* Ex 15, 26.
m: 13ff: Dt 32, 39; 1 Sm 2, 6; Tb 13, 2; Ps 78, 34. 39; Eccl 8, 8; Dn 5, 19; 2 Mc 6, 26; 7, 23.   *n:* Wis 11, 21; 12, 27; Ex 5, 2; 9, 29-34.
o: Wis 10, 20; 19, 20; Ex 9, 23-28; 2 Mc 8, 36; 14, 34.   *p:* 18f: Wis 19, 20f.   *q:* Ex 16, 4; Nm 11, 8; Ps 78, 24f; Jn 6, 31.   *r:* Ps 34,
9.   *s:* Ex 9, 25-31; 10, 12; Ps 148, 8.   *t:* Wis 19, 21.

grows tense for punishment against the
wicked,
but is relaxed in benefit for those who
trust in you.*u*

25 Therefore at that very time, transformed
in all sorts of ways,
it was serving your all-nourishing
bounty
according to what they needed and
desired;

26 That your sons whom you loved might
learn, O LORD,
that it is not the various kinds of fruits
that nourish man,
but it is your word that preserves those
who believe you!*v*

27 For what was not destroyed by fire,
when merely warmed by a momentary
sunbeam, melted;*w*

28 So that men might know that one must
give you thanks before the
sunrise,
and turn to you at daybreak.*x*

29 For the hope of the ingrate melts like a
wintry frost
and runs off like useless water.*y*

CHAPTER 17

See RG
275-76

Fourth Example: Darkness
Afflicts the Egyptians, While
the Israelites Have Light

1 For great are your judgments, and hardly
to be described;
therefore the unruly souls were wrong.*z*

2 For when the lawless thought to enslave
the holy nation,
shackled with darkness, fettered by the
long night,
they lay confined beneath their own
roofs as exiles from the eternal
providence.*a*

3 For they who supposed their secret sins
were hid*b*
under the dark veil of oblivion
Were scattered in fearful trembling,
terrified by apparitions.

4 For not even their inner chambers kept
them fearless,
for crashing sounds on all sides
terrified them,
and mute phantoms with somber looks
appeared.

5 No force, even of fire, was able to give
light,
nor did the flaming brilliance of the
stars
succeed in lighting up that gloomy
night.*c*

6 But only intermittent, fearful fires*
flashed through upon them;
And in their terror they thought
beholding these was worse
than the times when that sight was no
longer to be seen.*d*

7 And mockeries of the magic art were in
readiness,
and a jeering reproof of their vaunted
shrewdness.*e*

8 For they who undertook to banish fears
and terrors from the sick soul
themselves sickened with a ridiculous
fear.

9 For even though no monstrous thing
frightened them,
they shook at the passing of insects
and the hissing of reptiles,*f*

10 And perished trembling,
reluctant to face even the air that they
could nowhere escape.

11 For wickedness, of its nature cowardly,
testifies in its own condemnation,
and because of a distressed
conscience, always magnifies
misfortunes.*g*

12 For fear is nought but the surrender of
the helps that come from reason;

13 and the more one's expectation is of
itself uncertain,
the more one makes of not knowing
the cause that brings on torment.

14 So they, during that night, powerless
though it was,

17, 6: Fires: that is, lightnings.

u: Wis 5, 17. 20; 19, 6; Sir 39, 25ff.   *v:* Dt 8, 3; Mt 4, 4.   *w:* Ex 16, 21.   *x:* Pss 57, 9f; 92, 3.   *y:* Wis 5, 14; 2 Sm 14, 14.   *z:* Ex 6,
6 LXX.   *a:* Wis 18, 4; Ex 1, 13f; 19, 6; 10, 21ff.   *b:* 3f: Wis 1, 7f; 10, 8; 18, 17.   *c:* Wis 10, 17; Jer 23, 24 LXX.   *d:* Ex 9, 23f.
e: Wis 12, 25f; Ex 7, 11f. 22; 8, 3; 9, 11; 10, 2.   *f:* Wis 16, 1; Jer 26, 22 LXX.   *g:* Wis 4, 6; 10, 7; Rom 2, 15.

that had come upon them from the
    recesses of a powerless* nether
    world,
    while all sleeping the same sleep,
15 Were partly smitten by fearsome
    apparitions
    and partly stricken by their soul's
    surrender;
    for fear came upon them, sudden and
    unexpected.^{h}
16 Thus, then, whoever was there fell
    into that unbarred prison and was kept
    confined.^{i}
17 For whether one was a farmer, or a
    shepherd,
    or a worker at tasks in the
    wasteland,
    Taken unawares, he served out the
    inescapable sentence;
18   for all were bound by the one bond of
    darkness.^{j}
    And were it only the whistling wind,
    or the melodious song of birds in the
    spreading branches,
    Or the steady sound of rushing water,
19   or the rude crash of overthrown
    rocks,
    Or the unseen gallop of bounding
    animals,
    or the roaring cry of the fiercest beasts,
    Or an echo resounding from the hollow
    of the hills,
    these sounds, inspiring terror,
    paralyzed them.
20 For the whole world shone with brilliant
    light^k
    and continued its works without
    interruption;
21 Over them alone was spread oppressive
    night,
    an image of the darkness that next
    should come upon them;
    yet they were to themselves more
    burdensome than the darkness.

CHAPTER 18

See RG
275-76

1 But your holy ones had very great
    light;
    And those others, who heard their voices
    but did not see their forms,
    since now they themselves had
    suffered, called them blest;
2 And because they who formerly had been
    wronged did not harm them, they
    thanked them,
    and pleaded with them, for the sake of
    the difference between them.*
3 Instead of this, you furnished the flaming
    pillar
    which was a guide on the unknown
    way,
    and the mild sun for an honorable
    migration.^{l}
4 For those deserved to be deprived of
    light and imprisoned by darkness,
    who had kept your sons confined
    through whom the imperishable light
    of the law was to be given to the
    world.^{m}

Fifth Example: Death of the Egyptian First-born; the Israelites Are Spared

5 When they determined to put to death the
    infants of the holy ones,
    and when a single boy* had been cast
    forth but saved,
    As a reproof you carried off their
    multitude of sons
    and made them perish all at once in the
    mighty water.^{n}
6 That night was known beforehand to our
    fathers,
    that, with sure knowledge of the oaths
    in which they put their faith, they
    might have courage.^{o}
7 Your people awaited
    the salvation of the just and the
    destruction of their foes.^{p}

17, 14: Powerless: the nether world, the home of darkness, has no power against God, nor even against such men as do not submit to it of themselves; cf Wis 1, 14ff.

18, 2: The difference between them: God's distinctive manner of treating the Israelites and the Egyptians according to their respective merits.

18, 5: Single boy: Moses.

h: Ex 11, 9f.   *i:* Wis 18, 4; Ex 10, 23.   *j:* 18f: Lv 26, 36.   *k:* 20f: Ex 10, 23; Is 9, 1; 60, 1ff; 2 Pt 2, 17.   *l:* Ex 13, 21.   *m:* Wis 17, 2; Ps 119, 105; Is 2, 3. 5.   *n:* Wis 11, 7. 14; Ex 1, 16. 22; 2, 3. 6-10; 15, 10; Neh 9, 11.   *o:* Wis 12, 21; Ex 6, 8; 13, 5.   *p:* Ex 14, 13.

⁸ For when you punished our adversaries,
in this you glorified us whom you had
summoned.�q

⁹ For in secret the holy children of the
good were offering sacrifice
and putting into effect with one accord
the divine institution,
That your holy ones should share alike the
same good things and dangers,ʳ
having previously sung the praises of
the fathers.*

¹⁰ But the discordant cry of their enemies
responded,
and the piteous wail of mourning for
children was borne to them.ˢ

¹¹ And the slave was smitten with the same
retribution as his master;
even the plebeian suffered the same as
the king.ᵗ

¹² And all alike by a single death
had countless dead;
For the living were not even sufficient
for the burial,
since at a single instant their nobler
offspring were destroyed.ᵘ

¹³ For though they disbelieved at every turn
on account of sorceries,
at the destruction of the first-born they
acknowledged that the people*
was God's son.ᵛ

¹⁴ For when peaceful stillness compassed
everything
and the night in its swift course was
half spent,

¹⁵ Your all-powerful word from heaven's
royal throne
bounded, a fierce warrior, into the
doomed land,ʷ

¹⁶ bearing the sharp sword of your
inexorable decree.
And as he alighted, he filled every place
with death;

he still reached to heaven, while he
stood upon the earth.ˣ

¹⁷ Then, forthwith, visions in horrible
dreams perturbed themʸ
and unexpected fears assailed them;

¹⁸ And cast half-dead, one here, another there,
each was revealing the reason for his
dying.

¹⁹ For the dreams that disturbed them had
proclaimed this beforehand,
lest they perish unaware of why they
suffered ill.

²⁰ But the trial of death touched at one time
even the just,
and in the desert a plague struck the
multitude;
Yet not for long did the anger last.ᶻ

²¹ For the blameless man* hastened to be
their champion,
bearing the weapon of his special office,
prayer and the propitiation of incense;
He withstood the wrath and put a stop to
the calamity,
showing that he was your servant.ᵃ

²² And he overcame the bitterness
not by bodily strength, not by force of
arms;
But by word he overcame the smiter,*
recalling the sworn covenants with
their fathers.ᵇ

²³ For when corpses had already fallen one
on another in heaps,
he stood in the midst and checked the
anger,
and cut off the way to the living.ᶜ

²⁴ For on his full-length robe was the whole
world,
and the glories of the fathers were
carved in four rows upon the
stones,
and your grandeur* was on the crown
upon his head.ᵈ

18, 9: Praises of the fathers: cf Sir 44—50; Wis 10.
18, 13: People: the Hebrews.
18, 21: Blameless man: Aaron acting according to his office of high priest and intercessor.
18, 22: Smiter: the destroying angel; cf v 25.
18, 24: Glories . . . grandeur: the name of God and the names of the tribes were inscribed on the high priest's apparel.

q: Wis 19, 22; Ex 3, 18; Is 43, 3f.   r: Ex 12, 21-28; Sir 44—50.   s: Ex 12, 30; Jer 9, 17. 19.   t: Ex 11, 5; 12, 29.   u: Nm 33, 4.
v: Wis 17, 7; Ex 4, 22f; 12, 12. 29; 13, 2. 13. 15.   w: Wis 9, 10; Ex 15, 3.   x: 1 Chr 21, 16; Heb 4, 12; Rv 1, 16.   y: 17ff; Wis 17, 3f.
z: Wis 16, 5; Nm 17, 9-15.   a: Wis 12, 21; Ex 32, 12f; Ps 20, 8.   b: 12, 21; Ex 32, 12f.   c: Nm 14, 29f.   d: Ex 28, 15-21. 31-38; Sir
45, 8-12; 50, 11.

²⁵ To these names the destroyer yielded,
    and these he feared;
for the mere trial of anger was
    enough.^e

CHAPTER 19

See RG
275–76

¹ But the wicked, merciless wrath
    assailed until the end.
For he* knew beforehand what they
    were yet to do:^f
² That though they themselves had agreed
    to the departure
and had anxiously sent them* on their
    way,
they would regret it and pursue them.^g
³ For while they* were still engaged in
    funeral rites
and were mourning at the burials of
    the dead,
They adopted another senseless plan;
    and those whom they had sent away
    with entreaty,
they pursued as fugitives.^h
⁴ For a compulsion suited to this ending
    drew them on,
and made them forgetful of what had
    befallen them,
That they might fill out the torments of
    their punishment,
⁵ and your people might experience a
    glorious* journey
while those others met an
    extraordinary death.
⁶ For all creation, in its several kinds, was
    being made over anew,
    serving its natural laws,
that your children might be preserved
    unharmed.ⁱ
⁷ The cloud overshadowed their camp;
    and out of what had before been water,
    dry land was seen emerging:
Out of the Red Sea an unimpeded road,

and a grassy plain out of the mighty
    flood.^j
⁸ Over this crossed the whole nation
    sheltered by your hand,
after they beheld stupendous wonders.
⁹ For they ranged about like horses,
    and bounded about like lambs,
praising you, O Lord! their deliverer.^k
¹⁰ For they were still mindful of what had
    happened in their sojourn:
how instead of the young of animals
    the land brought forth gnats,
and instead of fishes the river swarmed
    with countless frogs.^l
¹¹ And later they saw also a new kind of
    bird^m
when, prompted by desire, they asked
    for pleasant foods;
¹² For to appease them quail came to them
    from the sea.
¹³ And the punishments came upon the
    sinners
only after forewarnings from the
    violence of the thunderbolts.
For they justly suffered for their own
    misdeeds,
since indeed they treated their guests
    with the more grievous* hatred.ⁿ
¹⁴ For those others did not receive
    unfamiliar visitors,^o
but these were enslaving beneficent
    guests.
¹⁵ And not that only; but what punishment
    was to be theirs*
since they received strangers
    unwillingly!
¹⁶ Yet these, after welcoming them with
    festivities,
oppressed with awful toils
those who now shared with them the
    same rights.^p
¹⁷ And they were struck with blindness,

19, 1: He: i.e., God.
19, 2: Them: the Hebrews.
19, 3: They: the Egyptians.
19, 5: Glorious: more precisely, "wondrous," but the word reflects glorified in Wis 18, 8 and 19, 22.
19, 13: More grievous: than that of the people of Sodom; cf Gn 19.
19, 15: Theirs: the people of Sodom.

e: 1 Chr 21, 15. *f*: Ex 14, 4. *g*: Ex 12, 33; 14, 5. 8. *h*: Wis 18, 10. 12; Ex 12, 30ff. *i*: Wis 5, 17; 16, 24. *j*: Ex 14, 21-29. *k*: Wis 10, 20; 16, 8; Ex 15, 1-18; Ps 114, 4-6. *l*: Ex 7, 27ff; 8, 12-15; Ps 105, 30f. *m*: 11f: Wis 16, 2; Ps 78, 18. *n*: 2 Mc 7, 18. 32. *o*: 14f: Gn 15, 13; Ex 2, 22. *p*: Gn 45, 17-20; 47, 4ff; Ex 1, 11.

as those others had been at the portals
of the just—
When, surrounded by yawning darkness,
each sought the entrance of his own
gate.*q*
18 For the elements, in variable harmony
among themselves,
like strings of the harp, produce new
melody,
while the flow of music steadily
persists.
And this can be perceived exactly from a
review of what took place.
19 For land creatures were changed into
water creatures,

and those that swam went over on to
the land.
20 Fire in water maintained its own
strength,*r*
and water forgot its quenching nature;
21 Flames, by contrast, neither consumed
the flesh
of the perishable animals that went
about in them,
nor melted the icelike, quick-melting
kind of ambrosial food.
22 For every way, O LORD! you magnified
and glorified your people;
unfailing, you stood by them in every
time and circumstance.*s*

q: Wis 17, 2; Gn 19, 11.   *r:* 20f: Wis 16, 17ff. 22f. 27.   *s:* Wis 18, 8; Lv 26, 44; Ps 126, 3.

See RG
276–79

The Book of Sirach (Ecclesiasticus)

The Book of Sirach derives its name from the author, Jesus, son of Eleazar, son of Sirach (Sir 50, 27). Its earliest title seems to have been "Wisdom of the Son of Sirach." The designation "Liber Ecclesiasticus," meaning "Church Book," appended to some Greek and Latin manuscripts was due to the extensive use which the church made of this book in presenting moral teaching to catechumens and to the faithful.

The author, a sage who lived in Jerusalem, was thoroughly imbued with love for the law, the priesthood, the temple, and divine worship. As a wise and experienced observer of life he addressed himself to his contemporaries with the motive of helping them to maintain religious faith and integrity through study of the holy books, and through tradition.

The book contains numerous maxims formulated with care, grouped by affinity, and dealing with a variety of subjects such as the individual, the family, and the community in their relations with one another and with God. It treats of friendship, education, poverty and wealth, the law, religious worship, and many other matters which reflect the religious and social customs of the time.

Written in Hebrew between 200 and 175 B.C., the text was translated into Greek sometime after 132 B.C. by the author's grandson, who also wrote a Foreword which contains information about the book, the author, and the translator himself. Until the close of the nineteenth century Sirach was known only in translations, of which this Greek rendering was the most important. From it the Latin version was made. Between 1896 and 1900, again in 1931, and several times since 1956, manuscripts were discovered containing in all about two thirds of the Hebrew text, which agrees substantially with the Greek. One such text, from Masada, is pre-Christian in date.

Though not included in the Hebrew Bible after the first century A.D., nor accepted by Protestants, the Book of Sirach has always been recognized by the Catholic Church as divinely inspired and canonical. The Foreword, though not inspired, is placed in the Bible because of its antiquity and importance.

The contents of Sirach are of a discursive nature, not easily divided into separate parts. Chapters 1—43 deal largely with moral instruction; 44, 1—50, 24 contain a eulogy of the heroes of Israel and some of the patriarchs. There are two appendices in which the author expresses his gratitude to God, and appeals to the unlearned to acquire true wisdom.

The church uses the Book of Sirach extensively in her liturgy.

FOREWORD

Many important truths have been handed down to us through the law, the prophets, and the later authors; and for these the instruction and wisdom of Israel merit praise. Now, those who are familiar with these truths must not only understand them themselves but, as lovers of wisdom, be able, in speech and in writing, to help others less familiar. Such a one was my grandfather, Jesus, who, having devoted himself for a long time to the diligent study of the law, the prophets, and the rest of the books of our ancestors, and having developed a thorough familiarity with them, was moved to write something himself in the nature of instruction and wisdom, in order that those who love wisdom might, by acquainting themselves with what he too had written, make even greater progress in living in conformity with the divine law.

You therefore are now invited to read it in a spirit of attentive good will, with indulgence for any apparent failure on our part, despite earnest efforts, in the interpretation of particular passages. For words spoken originally in Hebrew are not as effective when they are translated into another language. That is true not only of this book but of the law itself, the prophets and the rest of the books, which differ no little when they are read in the original.

I arrived in Egypt in the thirty-eighth year of the reign of King Euergetes,[2] and while there, I found a reproduction of our valuable teaching.[3] I therefore considered myself in duty bound to devote some diligence and industry to the translation of this book. Many sleepless hours of close application have I devoted in the interval to finishing the book for publication, for the benefit of those living abroad who wish to acquire wisdom

and are disposed to live their lives according to the standards of the law.

The Wisdom of Sirach

CHAPTER 1

See RG 276–79

*Praise of Wisdom**

[1] All wisdom* comes from the LORD
   and with him it remains forever.[a]
[2] The sand of the seashore, the drops of rain,
   the days of eternity: who can number these?
[3] Heaven's height, earth's breadth,
   the depths of the abyss: who can explore these?
[4] Before all things else wisdom was created;
   and prudent understanding, from eternity.
[5] To whom has wisdom's root been revealed?
   Who knows her subtleties?[b]
[6] There is but one, wise and truly awe-inspiring,
   seated upon his throne:
[7] It is the LORD; he created her,
   has seen her and taken note of her.[c]
[8] He has poured her forth upon all his works,
   upon every living thing according to his bounty;
   he has lavished her upon his friends.
[9] *Fear of the LORD* is glory and splendor,
   gladness and a festive crown.
[10] Fear of the LORD warms the heart,
   giving gladness and joy and length of days.

---

[1] The law, the prophets, and the rest of the books: the Sacred Scriptures of the Old Testament written before the time of Sirach, according to the threefold division of the present Hebrew Bible.

[2] Thirty-eighth . . . Euergetes: 132 B.C. The reference is to Ptolemy VII, Physkon Euergetes II (170–163; 145, 117 B.C.).

[3] Reproduction . . . teaching: may refer to the Septuagint (Greek) translation of Hebrew wisdom writings predating Sirach.

1, 1-8: The Lord is the source and preserver of wisdom (1); he created her from eternity, before all things else (4-7); all his works reflect wisdom (2f. 8).

1, 1: Wisdom: here the author speaks of true wisdom, namely God's external revelation of himself. Throughout the book he describes in great detail just what wisdom is; sometimes it is divine; sometimes it is a synonym for God's law; sometimes it is human. But the author makes clear that even human wisdom, properly understood, comes from God.

1, 9-18: Here are described the spiritual and temporal blessings that come during the lifetime of him who fears the Lord, i.e. practices true religion.

1, 9: Fear of the Lord: see note on Ps 111, 10.

a: 1 Kgs 3, 9.   *b:* Bar 3, 15.   *c:* Jb 28, 27.

¹¹ He who fears the LORD will have a happy
end;
even on the day of his death he will be
blessed.

¹² The beginning of wisdom is fear of the
LORD,
which is formed with the faithful in
the womb.ᵈ

¹³ With devoted men was she created from
of old,
and with their children her beneficence
abides.

¹⁴ Fullness of wisdom is fear of the LORD;
she inebriates men with her fruits.ᵉ

¹⁵ Her entire house she fills with choice
foods,
her granaries with her harvest.

¹⁶ Wisdom's garland is fear of the LORD,
with blossoms of peace and perfect
health.ᶠ

¹⁷ Knowledge and full understanding she
showers down;
she heightens the glory of those who
possess her.

¹⁸ The root of wisdom is fear of the LORD;
her branches are length of days.

¹⁹ One cannot justify unjust anger;*
anger plunges a man to his downfall.

²⁰ A patient man need stand firm but for a
time,
and then contentment comes back to
him.

²¹ For a while he holds back his words,
then the lips of many herald his
wisdom.

²² Among wisdom's treasures is the
paragon of prudence;
but fear of the LORD is an abomination
to the sinner.

²³ If you desire wisdom, keep the
commandments,
and the LORD will bestow her upon you;

²⁴ For fear of the LORD is wisdom and
culture;
loyal humility is his delight.

²⁵ Be not faithless to the fear of the LORD,*
nor approach it with duplicity of
heart.

²⁶ Play not the hypocrite before men;
over your lips keep watch.

²⁷ Exalt not yourself lest you fall
and bring upon you dishonor;

²⁸ For then the LORD will reveal your
secrets
and publicly cast you down,

²⁹ Because you approached the fear of the
LORD
with your heart full of guile.

CHAPTER 2

See RG
276–79

Duties toward God

¹ My son, when you come to serve the
LORD,*
prepare yourself for trials.ᵍ

² Be sincere of heart and steadfast,
undisturbed in time of adversity.

³ Cling to him, forsake him not;
thus will your future be great.

⁴ Accept whatever befalls you,
in crushing misfortune be patient;

⁵ For in fire gold is tested,
and worthy men in the crucible of
humiliation.ʰ

⁶ Trust God and he will help you;
make straight your ways and hope in
him.

⁷ You who fear the LORD, wait for his
mercy,
turn not away lest you fall.

⁸ You who fear the LORD, trust him,
and your reward will not be lost.

⁹ You who fear the LORD, hope for good
things,
for lasting joy and mercy.

1, 19-22: The disciple of wisdom shuns unjust anger
which brings downfall. By patience and self-control he preserves calm, recovers contentment, and receives public
praise. The sinner, on the contrary, despises the restraints
which religion imposes.

1, 25-29: Infidelity to religion, or the use of it for any but
the single purpose of serving God, is hypocrisy and self-exal-
tation, deserving of public disgrace.

2, 1-11: Serving God is not without its trials (1); more-

over, it must be done with sincerity, steadfastness and fidelity
(2f). Misfortune and humiliation merely purify man and
prove his worth (4f). Patience and unwavering trust in God
are always rewarded with the benefits of God's mercy and of
lasting joy (6-11).

---

d: Jb 28, 28; Ps 111, 10; Prv 1, 7; 9, 10.   e: Eccl 12, 13.   f: Sir
21, 11.   g: 2 Tm 3, 12.   h: Prv 17, 3; Wis 3, 6; 1 Pt 1, 7.

¹⁰ Study the generations long past and
understand;
has anyone hoped in the LORD and
been disappointed?
Has anyone persevered in his fear and
been forsaken?
has anyone called upon him and been
rebuffed?ⁱ

¹¹ Compassionate and merciful is the LORD;
he forgives sins, he saves in time of
trouble.

¹² Woe to craven hearts and drooping
hands,*
to the sinner who treads a double path!

¹³ Woe to the faint of heart who trust not,
who therefore will have no shelter!

¹⁴ Woe to you who have lost hope!
what will you do at the visitation of
the LORD?

¹⁵ Those who fear the LORD disobey not his
words;
those who love him keep his ways.ʲ

¹⁶ Those who fear the LORD seek to please
him,
those who love him are filled with his
law.

¹⁷ Those who fear the LORD prepare their
hearts
and humble themselves before him.

¹⁸ Let us fall into the hands of the LORD
and not into the hands of men,
For equal to his majesty
is the mercy that he shows.ᵏ

**See RG
276–79**

CHAPTER 3

Duties toward Parents*

¹ Children, pay heed to a father's right;
do so that you may live.

² For the LORD sets a father in honor over
his children;
a mother's authority he confirms over
her sons.

³ He who honors his father atones for sins;

⁴ he stores up riches who reveres his
mother.

⁵ He who honors his father is gladdened by
children,
and when he prays he is heard.

⁶ He who reveres his father will live a long
life;
he obeys the LORD who brings comfort
to his mother.

⁷ He who fears the LORD honors his
father,
and serves his parents as rulers.

⁸ In word and deed honor your father
that his blessing may come upon
you;ˡ

⁹ For a father's blessing gives a family
firm roots,
but a mother's curse uproots the
growing plant.ᵐ

¹⁰ Glory not in your father's shame,
for his shame is no glory to you!

¹¹ His father's honor is a man's glory;
disgrace for her children, a mother's
shame.

¹² My son, take care of your father when he
is old;
grieve him not as long as he lives.ⁿ

¹³ Even if his mind fail, be considerate with
him;
revile him not in the fullness of your
strength.

¹⁴ For kindness to a father will not be
forgotten,
it will serve as a sin offering—it will
take lasting root.

¹⁵ In time of tribulation it will be recalled to
your advantage,
like warmth upon frost it will melt
away your sins.

¹⁶ A blasphemer is he who despises his
father;
accursed of his Creator, he who angers
his mother.ᵒ

2, 12-18: A warning to those who compromise their religion in time of affliction; they fail in courage and trust and
therefore have no security (12ff). But those who fear the Lord
through obedience, reverence, love and humility find his
mercy equal to his majesty (15-18).

3, 1-16: Besides the virtues that must characterize our
conduct toward God, special duties toward our neighbor are
enjoined, such as honor and respect toward parents, with cor-

responding blessings (1-9). Even to old and infirm parents
this respect is due (10-13); through it, the sins of children are
pardoned (14f). Failure to render respect is blasphemy and
merits a curse from God (16). Cf Ex 20, 12; Eph 6, 2f.

i: Pss 31, 2; 145, 18f. j: Jn 14, 23. k: Sir 18, 3. l: Ex 20, 12;
Dt 5, 16; Mt 15, 4; Mk 7, 10; Eph 6, 2. m: Gn 27, 29; 49, 2-27.
n: Prv 23, 22. o: Prv 19, 26; 30, 11. 14. 17.

Humility*

17 My son, conduct your affairs with
    humility,
    and you will be loved more than a
    giver of gifts.
18 Humble yourself the more, the greater
    you are,
    and you will find favor with God.p
19 For great is the power of God;
    by the humble he is glorified.*
20 What is too sublime for you, seek not,
    into things beyond your strength
    search not.q
21 What is committed to you, attend to;
    for what is hidden is not your concern.
22 With what is too much for you meddle
    not,
    when shown things beyond human
    understanding.
23 Their own opinion has misled many,
    and false reasoning unbalanced their
    judgment.
24 Where the pupil of the eye is missing,
    there is no light,
    and where there is no knowledge,
    there is no wisdom.

25 A stubborn man will fare badly in the
    end,
    and he who loves danger will perish in
    it.
26 A stubborn man will be burdened with
    sorrow;
    a sinner will heap sin upon sin.
27 For the affliction of the proud man there
    is no cure;
    he is the offshoot of an evil plant.r
28 The mind of a sage appreciates proverbs,
    and an attentive ear is the wise man's
    joy.

Alms for the Poor*

29 Water quenches a flaming fire,
    and alms atone for sins.s
30 He who does a kindness is remembered
    afterward;
    when he falls, he finds a support.

CHAPTER 4

See RG
276–79

1 My son, rob not the poor man of
    his livelihood:
    force not the eyes of the needy* to turn
    away.t
2 A hungry man grieve not,
    a needy man anger not;
3 Do not exasperate the downtrodden;
    delay not to give to the needy.
4 A beggar in distress do not reject;
    avert not your face from the poor.
5 From the needy turn not your eyes,
    give no man reason to curse you;
6 For if in the bitterness of his soul he
    curse you,
    his Creator will hear his prayer.
7 Endear yourself to the assembly;
    before a ruler bow your head.
8 Give a hearing to the poor man,
    and return his greeting with courtesy;
9 Deliver the oppressed from the hand of
    the oppressor;
    let not justice be repugnant to you.
10 To the fatherless be as a father,
    and help their mother as a husband
    would;
    Thus will you be like a son to the Most
    High,
    and he will be more tender to you than
    a mother.

The Rewards of Wisdom*

11 Wisdom instructs her children

3, 17-27: Humility gives a true estimate of self (17ff).
Through it a man performs duty, avoids what is beyond his
understanding and strength (20ff). Pride, however, begets
false greatness, misjudgment, stubbornness, sorrow, affliction and perdition (23-27).

3, 19: An alternate or additional line would read: "For
though many have been great in the course of time, it is to the
humble he reveals his secrets." Cf Mt 11, 25f; 1 Cor 1, 26-29.

3, 29—4, 10: Mercy and kindness toward those in misfortune atone for sin and endear a man to God and to his fellow
men.

4, 1: Eyes of the needy: when they look for help; cf Sir 18, 17.

4, 11-19: The Hebrew text presents wisdom speaking in
the first person, as in ch 24. The precious fruits of wisdom:
life, favor, glory, blessings, God's love, are intended to arouse
desire for her (11-14). Her disciples are like priests (14) and
judges (15), even partners who possess her for themselves
and their descendants (16). They enjoy happiness and penetrate her profound secrets after surviving her tests (17f).
Those who fail her are abandoned to destruction (19).

---

p: Mt 23, 12.   q: Ps 131, 1.   r: Dt 32, 32; Wis 12, 10.   s: Dn 4,
27.   t: Tb 4, 7-11.

and admonishes those who seek her.

¹² He who loves her loves life;
    those who seek her out win her favor.
¹³ He who holds her fast inherits glory;
    wherever he dwells, the LORD bestows
      blessings.
¹⁴ Those who serve her serve the Holy One;
    those who love her the LORD loves.ᵘ
¹⁵ He who obeys her judges nations;
    he who hearkens to her dwells in her
      inmost chambers.
¹⁶ If one trusts her, he will possess her;
    his descendants too will inherit her.
¹⁷ She walks with him as a stranger,
    and at first she puts him to the test;
  Fear and dread she brings upon him
    and tries him with her discipline;
  With her precepts she puts him to the
      proof,
    until his heart is fully with her.
¹⁸ Then she comes back to bring him
      happiness
    and reveal her secrets to him.
¹⁹ But if he fails her, she will abandon him
    and deliver him into the hands of
      despoilers.

Sincerity and Justice*

²⁰ Use your time well; guard yourself from
      evil,
  and bring upon yourself no shame.
²¹ There is a sense of shame laden with
      guilt,
    and a shame that merits honor and
      respect.
²² Show no favoritism to your own
      discredit;
    let no one intimidate you to your own
      downfall.
²³ Refrain not from speaking at the proper
      time,
    and hide not away your wisdom;
²⁴ For it is through speech that wisdom
      becomes known,

and knowledge through the tongue's
    rejoinder.
²⁵ Never gainsay the truth,
    and struggle not against the rushing
      stream.
²⁶ Be not ashamed to acknowledge your guilt,
    but of your ignorance rather be
      ashamed.
²⁷ Do not abase yourself before an impious
      man,
    nor refuse to do so before rulers.
²⁸ Even to the death fight for truth,
    and the LORD your God will battle for
      you.
²⁹ Be not surly in your speech,
    nor lazy and slack in your deeds.
³⁰ Be not a lion at home,
    nor sly and suspicious at work.
³¹ Let not your hand be open to receive
    and clenched when it is time to give.

CHAPTER 5

Against Presumption*

See RG
276-79

¹ Rely not on your wealth;
    say not: "I have the power."ᵛ
² Rely not on your strength
    in following the desires of your heart.
³ Say not: "Who can prevail against me?"
    for the LORD will exact the
      punishment.
⁴ Say not: "I have sinned, yet what has
      befallen me?"
    for the LORD bides his time.
⁵ Of forgiveness be not overconfident,
    adding sin upon sin.
⁶ Say not: "Great is his mercy;
    my many sins he will forgive."
⁷ For mercy and anger alike are with him;
    upon the wicked alights his wrath.
⁸ Delay not your conversion to the LORD,
    put it not off from day to day;
⁹ For suddenly his wrath flames forth;
    at the time of vengeance, you will be
      destroyed.

4, 20-31: Besides the interior trials of discipline and precept, the disciple of wisdom is warned against external dangers to his sincerity and justice, namely evil, human respect (20f), compromise of liberty in speech and action (22-25), false shame, and ignorance (26). He must fight for the truth (28), and avoid cynicism and laziness (29), and inconsistency in his conduct (30).

5, 1-10: The vices of the rich are pride and independence (1f), presumption (3), false security (4-7), and impenitence (8), which cannot escape the divine wrath (9f). Cf Prv 18, 23; 19, 1; 28, 6.

---

u: Wis 7, 28.   *v:* Lk 12, 19.

¹⁰ Rely not upon deceitful wealth,
  for it will be no help on the day of
    wrath.ʷ

Sincerity in Speech

¹¹ Winnow not in every wind,
  and start not off in every direction.*
¹² Be consistent in your thoughts;
  steadfast be your words.*
¹³ Be swift to hear,
  but slow to answer.ˣ
¹⁴ If you have the knowledge, answer your
    neighbor;
  if not, put your hand over your mouth.
¹⁵ Honor and dishonor through talking!
  A man's tongue can be his downfall.
¹⁶ Be not called a detractor;
  use not your tongue for calumny;
¹⁷ For shame has been created for the thief,
  and the reproach of his neighbor for
    the double-tongued.

CHAPTER 6

See RG
276-79
¹ Say nothing harmful, small or great;
  be not a foe instead of a friend;
A bad name and disgrace will you
    acquire:
  "That for the evil man with double
    tongue!"*

² Fall not into the grip of desire,ʸ
  lest, like fire, it consume your strength;
³ Your leaves it will eat, your fruits destroy,
  and you will be left a dry tree,
⁴ For contumacious desire destroys its
    owner
  and makes him the sport of his enemies.

True Friendship*

⁵ A kind mouth multiplies friends,
  and gracious lips prompt friendly
    greetings.

⁶ Let your acquaintances be many,
  but one in a thousand your confidant.
⁷ When you gain a friend, first test him,ᶻ
  and be not too ready to trust him.
⁸ For one sort of friend is a friend when it
    suits him,
  but he will not be with you in time of
    distress.
⁹ Another is a friend who becomes an
    enemy,
  and tells of the quarrel to your shame.
¹⁰ Another is a friend, a boon companion,
  who will not be with you when sorrow
    comes.
¹¹ When things go well, he is your other self,
  and lords it over your servants;
¹² But if you are brought low, he turns
    against you
  and avoids meeting you.
¹³ Keep away from your enemies;
  be on your guard with your friends.
¹⁴ A faithful friend is a sturdy shelter;
  he who finds one finds a treasure.
¹⁵ A faithful friend is beyond price,
  no sum can balance his worth.
¹⁶ A faithful friend is a life-saving remedy,
  such as he who fears God finds;
¹⁷ For he who fears God behaves
    accordingly,
  and his friend will be like himself.

Blessings of Wisdom*

¹⁸ My son, from your youth embrace
    discipline;
  thus will you find wisdom with
    graying hair.
¹⁹ As though plowing and sowing, draw
    close to her;
  then await her bountiful crops.
²⁰ For in cultivating her you will labor but
    little,
  and soon you will eat of her fruits.

5, 11: A proverbial expression condemning inconstancy and advocating sincerity and honesty.

5, 12—6, 1: Proper use of the tongue requires constancy in speech (5, 12), prudence (13f), reserve (15), charity (6, 1), as well as the avoidance of detraction, calumny (16) and double talk, which bring shame and disgrace (5, 17; 6, 1).

6, 1: "That . . . double tongue!": people will say this against the man whose deceitful tongue has brought him to disgrace.

6, 5-17: True friends are discerned not by prosperity (11)

but through the trials of adversity: distress, quarrels (9), sorrow (10) and misfortune (12). Such friends are rare and their value is beyond estimation, a gift from God (14-17).

6, 18-37: The various figures in each of the three strophes urge the search for wisdom through patience (19-23), docility (32-37), and perseverance in trials (25ff), promising rich rewards (28-31). Cf 4, 11-19.

w: Prv 10, 2; 11, 4. 28.   x: Prv 29, 20; Jas 1, 19.   y: 2-3: Sir 9, 8; 23, 17; Jb 31, 12; Is 56, 3.   z: 7ff: Sir 12, 8f; 37, 1-5; Prv 19, 4.

²¹ How irksome she is to the unruly!
    The fool cannot abide her.
²² She will be like a burdensome stone to
        test him,
    and he will not delay in casting her
        aside.
²³ For discipline* is like her name,
    she is not accessible to many.

²⁴ Listen, my son, and heed my advice;
    refuse not my counsel.
²⁵ Put your feet into her fetters,
    and your neck under her yoke.
²⁶ Stoop your shoulders and carry her
    and be not irked at her bonds.
²⁷ With all your soul draw close to her;
    with all your strength keep her ways.
²⁸ Search her out, discover her; seek her
        and you will find her.
    Then when you have her, do not let her
        go;
²⁹ Thus will you afterward find rest in her,
    and she will become your joy.
³⁰ Her fetters will be your throne of
        majesty;
    her bonds, your purple cord.
³¹ You will wear her as your robe of glory,ᵃ
    bear her as your splendid crown.*

³² My son, if you wish, you can be taught;
    if you apply yourself, you will be
        shrewd.
³³ If you are willing to listen, you will learn;
    if you give heed, you will be wise.
³⁴ Frequent the company of the elders;
    whoever is wise, stay close to him.
³⁵ Be eager to hear every godly discourse;
    let no wise saying escape you.ᵇ
³⁶ If you see a man of prudence, seek him
        out;
    let your feet wear away his doorstep!
³⁷ Reflect on the precepts of the LORD,
    let his commandments be your
        constant meditation;

Then he will enlighten your mind,
    and the wisdom you desire he will
        grant.ᶜ

CHAPTER 7

Conduct in Public Life*

See RG 276–79

¹ Do no evil, and evil will not overtake
        you;
² avoid wickedness, and it will turn
        aside from you.
³ Sow not in the furrows of injustice,
    lest you harvest it sevenfold.ᵈ
⁴ Seek not from the LORD authority,
    nor from the king a place of honor.
⁵ Parade not your justice before the
        LORD,
    and before the king flaunt not your
        wisdom.ᵉ
⁶ Seek not to become a judge
    if you have not strength to root out
        crime,
    Or you will show favor to the ruler
        and mar your integrity.
⁷ Be guilty of no evil before the city's
        populace,
    nor disgrace yourself before the
        assembly.
⁸ Do not plot to repeat a sin;
    not even for one will you go
        unpunished.
⁹ Say not: "He will appreciate my many
        gifts;
    the Most High will accept my
        offerings."ᶠ
¹⁰ Be not impatient in prayers,
    and neglect not the giving of alms.
¹¹ Laugh not at an embittered man;
    be mindful of him who exalts and
        humbles.*
¹² Plot no mischief against your brother,
    nor against your friend and
        companion.
¹³ Delight not in telling lie after lie,
    for it never results in good.

6, 23: Discipline (musar, in the sense of wisdom) is a perfect homonym for musar, "removed, withdrawn"; thus the path of discipline is inaccessible to many.

6, 31: Some forms of the text speak also of the "yoke" of wisdom under the imagery of golden ornaments.

7, 1-17: In the conduct of social relations wisdom forbids evil and injustice (1ff), pride (5. 15ff), ambition and human respect (4, 6), public disorder (7), presumption and impatience toward God (9f), ridicule (11), mischief and deceit toward one's neighbor (8, 12f).

7, 11: Him who exalts and humbles: God; cf 1 Sm 2, 7; Ps 75, 8; Lk 1, 52.

a: Is 62, 3. b: Sir 8, 9. c: Ps 1, 2. d: Prv 22, 8. e: Jb 9, 2; Ps 143, 2; Prv 25, 6; 1 Cor 4, 4. f: Sir 34, 18; 35, 12.

14 Thrust not yourself into the deliberations
        of princes,^{g}
    and repeat not the words of your
        prayer.*
15 Hate not laborious tasks,
    nor farming, which was ordained by
        the Most High.^{h}
16 Do not esteem yourself better than your
        fellows;
    remember, his wrath will not delay.
17 More and more, humble your pride;
    what awaits man is worms.^{i}

Duties of Family Life, Religion and Charity*
18 Barter not a friend for money,
    nor a dear brother for the gold of
        Ophir.*
19 Dismiss not a sensible wife;
    a gracious wife is more precious than
        corals.
20 Mistreat not a servant who faithfully
        serves,
    nor a laborer who devotes himself to
        his task.^{j}
21 Let a wise servant be dear to you as your
        own self;
    refuse him not his freedom.*
22 If you have livestock, look after them;
    if they are dependable, keep them.
23 If you have sons, chastise them;
    bend their necks* from childhood.^{k}
24 If you have daughters, keep them chaste,
    and be not indulgent to them.^{l}
25 Giving your daughter in marriage ends a
        great task;
    but give her to a worthy man.^{m}

26 If you have a wife, let her not seem
        odious to you;
    but where there is ill-feeling, trust her
        not.
27 With your whole heart honor your father;
    your mother's birthpangs forget not.^{n}
28 Remember, of these parents you were born;
    what can you give them for all they
        gave you?
29 With all your soul, fear God,
    revere his priests.
30 With all your strength, love your Creator,
    forsake not his ministers.
31 Honor God and respect the priest;
    give him his portion as you have been
        commanded:^{o}
    First fruits and contributions,
        due sacrifices and holy offerings.*
32 To the poor man also extend your hand,
    that your blessing may be complete;
33 Be generous to all the living,
    and withhold not your kindness from
        the dead.*
34 Avoid not those who weep,
    but mourn with those who mourn;^{p}
35 Neglect not to visit the sick—
    for these things you will be loved.^{q}
36 In whatever you do, remember your last
        days,
    and you will never sin.

CHAPTER 8

~ See RG
276–79

**Prudence in Dealing
with Other Men***
1 Contend not with an influential man,
    lest you fall into his power.

7, 14: Repeat not . . . prayer: brevity of speech in dealings
with superiors and more especially with God is a sign of reverence and respect; cf Eccl 5, 1; Mt 6, 7.

7, 18-36: The duties of respect and appreciation, justice
and kindness should characterize relations toward members
of the household (18-28), and also toward God and his priests
(29ff), the poor and afflicted, the living and the dead (32-36).

7, 18: Ophir was the port, at present unidentified, to which
the ships of Solomon sailed and from which they brought
back gold and silver; cf note on Ps 45, 10.

7, 21: After six years of service a Hebrew slave was entitled to freedom; cf Ex 21, 2; Dt 15, 12-15.

7, 23: Bend their necks: keep them from rebellious pride;
so with the Greek. Cf Sir 30, 12. The present Hebrew text,
which is probably not original here, reads: "Choose wives for
them while they are young."

7, 31: First fruits . . . holy offerings: cf Ex 29, 27; Lv 7, 31-

34; Nm 18, 8-20; Dt 18, 1-5.

7, 33: This seems to refer to the observances ordained toward the dead, that is, proper mourning and burial. Cf 2 Sm
21, 12ff; Tb 1, 20; 12, 12. When this verse is read in the light
of later teaching, prayers for the souls of the deceased would
also be recommended. Cf 2 Mc 12, 43ff.

8, 1-19: A prudent man will be circumspect, avoiding conflict with the powerful, the rich and insolent, the impious, the
irascible, and with judges (1ff. 10ff. 14. 16). He will seek
friendship not with the undisciplined (4. 12f) and the ruthless
(15), nor with fools and strangers (17ff), but with the wise
and the ancients of the people (8f).

g: Sir 32, 7ff; Mt 6, 7.   *h:* Gn 2, 15; 3, 17.   *i:* Is 66, 24.   *j:* Lv
19, 13; Dt 24, 14f; Jas 5, 4.   *k:* Sir 30, 8-13; Prv 13, 24.   *l:* Sir
42, 9ff.   *m:* 1 Cor 7, 36ff.   *n:* Ex 20, 12.   *o:* Lv 7, 31; Nm 18,
18.   *p:* Rom 12, 15.   *q:* Mt 25, 36.

² Quarrel not with a rich man,
    lest he pay out the price of your
      downfall;
  For gold has dazzled many,
    and perverts the character of princes.ʳ
³ Dispute not with a man of railing speech,
    heap no wood upon his fire.ˢ
⁴ Be not too familiar with an unruly man,
    lest he speak ill of your forebears.
⁵ Shame not a repentant sinner;ᵗ
    remember, we all are guilty.*
⁶ Insult no man when he is old,
    for some of us, too, will grow old.
⁷ Rejoice not when a man dies;
    remember, we are all to die.
⁸ Spurn not the discourse of the wise,ᵘ
    but acquaint yourself with their
      proverbs;
  From them you will acquire the training
    to serve in the presence of princes.
⁹ Reject not the tradition of old men
    which they have learned from their
      fathers;
  From it you will obtain the knowledge
    how to answer in time of need.
¹⁰ Kindle not the coals of a sinner,
    lest you be consumed in his flaming
      fire.
¹¹ Let not the impious man intimidate you;
    it will set him in ambush against you.*
¹² Lend not to one more powerful than
      yourself;
  and whatever you lend, count it as lost.ᵛ
¹³ Go not surety beyond your means;
    think any pledge a debt you must pay.
¹⁴ Contend not at law with a judge,
    for he will settle it according to his
      whim.
¹⁵ Travel not with a ruthless man,
    lest he weigh you down with calamity;
  For he will go his own way straight,
    and through his folly you will perish
      with him.

¹⁶ Provoke no quarrel with a quick-
      tempered man
  nor ride with him through the desert;
  For bloodshed is nothing to him;
    when there is no one to help you, he
      will destroy you.
¹⁷ Take no counsel with a fool,
    for he can keep nothing to himself.
¹⁸ Before a stranger do nothing that should
      be kept secret,
  for you know not what it will
      engender.ʷ
¹⁹ Open your heart to no man,
    and banish not your happiness.

CHAPTER 9

*Advice concerning Women**

See RG 276–79

¹ Be not jealous of the wife of your
      bosom,
  lest you teach her to do evil against
      you.*
² Give no woman power over you
    to trample upon your dignity.ˣ
³ Be not intimate with a strange woman,
    lest you fall into her snares.
⁴ With a singing girl be not familiar,
    lest you be caught in her wiles.
⁵ Entertain no thoughts against a virgin,
    lest you be enmeshed in damages for
      her.*
⁶ Give not yourself to harlots,
    lest you surrender your inheritance.ʸ
⁷ Gaze not about the lanes of the city
    and wander not through its squares;
⁸ Avert your eyes from a comely woman;
    gaze not upon the beauty of another's
      wife—
  Through woman's beauty many perish,
    for lust for it burns like fire.ᶻ
⁹ With a married woman dine not,
    recline not at table to drink by her side,
  Lest your heart be drawn to her
    and you go down in blood to the grave.

8, 5: We all are guilty: cf 1 Kgs 8, 46; 2 Chr 6, 36; Eccl 7, 20; Rom 3, 9f; 1 Jn 1, 8.

8, 11: To give in to the wicked in one instance becomes an occasion of sin for the future.

9, 1-9: Prudence and reserve in dealing with women are the best defense of morality. To preserve the liberty and dignity of his person and the integrity of his possessions, a man must avoid jealousy toward his own wife and familiarity toward all other women. Cf Sir 25, 12—26, 18.

9, 1: Unjust suspicions often engender hatred between husband and wife and may prompt a wife to commit those faults of which heretofore she had been innocent.

9, 5: Cf Ex 22, 15f; Dt 22, 28f; Jb 31, 1.

ʳ: Sir 31, 6; Dt 16, 19. ˢ: Prv 26, 20. ᵗ: 1 Kgs 8, 46; 1 Jn 1, 8.
ᵘ: 8f; Sir 6, 35. ᵛ: Sir 29, 4-7; Prv 17, 18. ʷ: Prv 25, 9f.
ˣ: Sir 25, 21. ʸ: Prv 5, 3-11; 6, 24; 29, 3. ᶻ: Sir 25, 20; 41, 21.

Choice of Friends*

10 Discard not an old friend,
   for the new one cannot equal him.
   A new friend is like new wine
   which you drink with pleasure only
      when it has aged.
11 Envy not a sinner's fame,
   for you know not what disaster awaits
      him.
12 Rejoice not at a proud man's
      success;
   remember he will not reach death
      unpunished.
13 Keep far from the man who has power to
      kill,
   and you will not be filled with the
      dread of death.
   But if you approach him, offend him
      not,
   lest he take away your life;
   Know that you are stepping among
      snares
   and walking over a net.
14 As best you can, take your neighbors'
      measure,
   and associate with the wise.
15 With the learned be intimate;
   let all your conversation be about the
      law of the LORD.
16 Have just men for your table
      companions;
   in the fear of God be your glory.

Concerning Rulers*

17 Skilled artisans are esteemed for their
      deftness;
   but the ruler of his people is the skilled
      sage.
18 Feared in the city is the man of railing
      speech,
   and he who talks rashly is hated.

CHAPTER 10

See RG
276–79

1 A wise magistrate lends stability to
      his people,
   and the government of a prudent man
      is well ordered.[a]
2 As the people's judge, so are his
      ministers;[b]
   as the head of a city, its inhabitants.
3 A wanton king destroys his people,
   but a city grows through the wisdom
      of its princes.[c]
4 Sovereignty over the earth is in the hand
      of God,
   who raises up on it the man of the
      hour;
5 Sovereignty over every man is in the
      hand of God,
   who imparts his majesty to the ruler.

The Sin of Pride*

6 No matter the wrong, do no violence to
      your neighbor,
   and do not walk the path of
      arrogance.[d]
7 Odious to the LORD and to men is
      arrogance,
   and the sin of oppression they both
      hate.
8 Dominion is transferred from one people
      to another
   because of the violence of the
      arrogant.
9 Why are dust and ashes proud?*
   even during life man's body decays;
10 A slight illness—the doctor jests,
   a king today—tomorrow he is dead.
11 When a man dies, he inherits corruption;
   worms and gnats and maggots.[e]
12 The beginning of pride is man's
      stubbornness

9, 10-16: In social relations, adherence to the law of the Lord should serve as a guide (15). Associate with true friends (10), with the just and the learned (14ff); avoid the company of the mighty and of sinners doomed to punishment (11ff). Cf Sir 8, 1-19.

9, 17—10, 5: Public office as conducted justly, or unjustly benefits or destroys the people, according to the axiom, "as the prince, so the people." Cf Is 24, 2. God, however, has sovereignty over both.

10, 6-18: Glory displayed through arrogance and pride is false and displeasing to God and men, because founded on dust and ashes (6-11). It is the denial of the glory due to God, and therefore the source of all sin (12f). Even the memory of the proud is destroyed and God transfers their power to the lowly (14-18).

10, 9f: The text is uncertain. Its general implication is that man deteriorates physically even while alive: a slight illness today may be followed by death tomorrow. The uncertainty of life leaves no room for pride.

a: Wis 6, 24.   b: 2f: Prv 29, 12.   c: Prv 29, 4. 8.   d: Lv 19, 18.   e: Jb 17, 14.

in withdrawing his heart from his
 Maker;
13 For pride is the reservoir of sin,
 a source which runs over with vice;
Because of it God sends unheard-of
 afflictions
 and brings men to utter ruin.*f*
14 The thrones of the arrogant God
 overturns
 and establishes the lowly in their stead.
15 The roots of the proud God plucks up,
 to plant the humble in their place:
16 He breaks down their stem to the level of
 the ground,
 then digs their roots from the earth.
17 The traces of the proud God sweeps
 away
 and effaces the memory of them from
 the earth.
18 Insolence is not allotted to a man,
 nor stubborn anger to one born of
 woman.

True Glory*

19 Whose offspring can be in honor? Those
 of men.
Which offspring are in honor? Those
 who fear God.
Whose offspring can be in disgrace?
 Those of men.
Which offspring are in disgrace?
 Those who transgress the
 commandments.
20 Among brethren their leader is in honor;
 he who fears God is in honor among
 his people.
21 Be it tenant or wayfarer, alien or pauper,
 his glory is the fear of the LORD.
22 It is not just to despise a man who is wise
 but poor,
 nor proper to honor any sinner.*g*
23 The prince, the ruler, the judge are in
 honor;
 but none is greater than he who fears
 God.

24 When free men serve a prudent slave,
 the wise man does not complain.*h*
25 Flaunt not your wisdom in managing
 your affairs,
 and boast not in your time of need.
26 Better the worker who has plenty of
 everything
 than the boaster who is without bread.*i*
27 My son, with humility have self-esteem;
 prize yourself as you deserve.
28 Who will acquit him who condemns
 himself?
 who will honor him who discredits
 himself?
29 The poor man is honored for his wisdom
 as the rich man is honored for his
 wealth;
30 Honored in poverty, how much more so
 in wealth!
 Dishonored in wealth, in poverty how
 much the more!

CHAPTER 11

See RG
276–79

1 The poor man's wisdom lifts his
 head high
 and sets him among princes.
2 Praise not a man for his looks;
 despise not a man for his appearance.
3 Least is the bee among winged things,
 but she reaps the choicest of all
 harvests.
4 Mock not the worn cloak
 and jibe at no man's bitter day:
For strange are the works of the LORD,
 hidden from men his deeds.
5 The oppressed often rise to a throne,
 and some that none would consider
 wear a crown.*
6 The exalted often fall into utter disgrace;
 the honored are given into enemy
 hands.

Moderation*

7 Before investigating, find no fault;
 examine first, then criticize.

10, 19—11, 6: Regardless of social barriers, genuine
honor among men comes from fear of the Lord and a true estimate of self. The Lord exalts the lowly and oppressed; transgressors of the commandments merit dishonor and disgrace.
 11, 5: Cf 1 Sm 2, 8; Ps 105, 17-22; Lk 1, 52.
 11, 7-25: Discretion regulates a man's conduct toward

others and their affairs (7ff); as regards his own interests, a
man should avoid solicitude for the passing external benefits
of life and property (10-14. 18f. 21. 23ff), and cultivate the
lasting inward gifts of wisdom and virtue (15. 17. 20. 22).

---

f: Prv 18, 12. *g:* Jas 2, 1-4. *h:* Prv 17, 2. *i:* Prv 12, 9.

8 Before hearing, answer not,
    and interrupt no one in the middle of
        his speech.*j*
9 Dispute not about what is not your
        concern;
    in the strife of the arrogant take no
        part.
10 My son, why increase your cares,
    since he who is avid for wealth will
        not be blameless?
Even if you run after it, you will never
        overtake it;
    however you seek it, you will not find
        it.
11 One may toil and struggle and drive,
    and fall short all the more.*k*
12 Another goes his way a weakling and a
        failure,
    with little strength and great misery—
Yet the eyes of the LORD look favorably
        upon him;
    he raises him free of the vile dust,
13 Lifts up his head and exalts him
    to the amazement of the many.
14 Good and evil, life and death,*l*
    poverty and riches, are from the
        LORD.*
15 Wisdom and understanding and
        knowledge of affairs,*
    love and virtuous paths are from the
        LORD.
16 Error and darkness were formed with
        sinners from their birth,
    and evil grows old with evildoers.
17 The LORD's gift remains with the just;
    his favor brings continued success.
18 A man may become rich through a
        miser's life,
    and this is his allotted reward:
19 When he says: "I have found rest,*m*
    now I will feast on my possessions,"
He does not know how long it will be
    till he dies and leaves them to others.*
20 My son, hold fast to your duty, busy
        yourself with it,

grow old while doing your task.
21 Admire not how sinners live,
    but trust in the LORD and wait for his
        light;
For it is easy with the LORD
    suddenly, in an instant, to make a poor
        man rich.
22 God's blessing is the lot of the just man,
    and in due time his hopes bear fruit.
23 Say not: "What do I need?
    What further pleasure can be mine?"
24 Say not: "I am independent.
    What harm can come to me now?"
25 The day of prosperity makes one forget
        adversity;
    the day of adversity makes one forget
        prosperity.*n*
26 For it is easy with the LORD on the day of
        death*
    to repay man according to his deeds.
27 A moment's affliction brings
        forgetfulness of past delights;
    when a man dies, his life is revealed.
28 Call no man happy before his death,
    for by how he ends, a man is known.

Care in Choosing Friends

29 Bring not every man into your house,
    for many are the snares of the crafty
        one;
30 Though he seem like a bird confined in a
        cage,
    yet like a spy he will pick out the weak
        spots.
31 The talebearer turns good into evil;
    with a spark he sets many coals afire.
32 The evil man lies in wait for blood,
    and plots against your choicest
        possessions.
33 Avoid a wicked man, for he breeds only
        evil,
    lest you incur a lasting stain.
34 Lodge a stranger with you, and he will
        subvert your course,
    and make a stranger of you to your
        own household.

11, 14: Divine Providence ultimately governs the lives of men. Evil: misfortune and calamity sent by God either in punishment or as an incentive to repentance or to greater virtue.
11, 15f: Some ancient witnesses omit these two verses.
11, 19: Cf the parable of the rich man, Lk 12, 16-21.

11, 26ff: Sirach, writing before Christian revelation, did not go beyond the hour of death to find full divine retribution.

j: Prv 18, 13.   *k:* Ps 127, 2; Eccl 4, 8.   *l:* Jb 1, 21; 2, 10.
m: Eccl 4, 8; 6, 2; Lk 12, 19.   *n:* Sir 18, 25.

CHAPTER 12

See RG
276-79

¹ If you do good, know for whom you
are doing it,*
and your kindness will have its effect.
² Do good to the just man and reward will
be yours,
if not from him, from the LORD.
³ No good comes to him who gives
comfort to the wicked,*
nor is it an act of mercy that he does.
⁴ Give to the good man, refuse the sinner;ᵒ
refresh the downtrodden, give nothing
to the proud man.
⁵ No arms for combat should you give
him,
lest he use them against yourself;
⁶ With twofold evil you will meet
for every good deed you do for him.
⁷ The Most High himself hates sinners,
and upon the wicked he takes
vengeance.

⁸ In our prosperity we cannot know our
friends;*
in adversity an enemy will not remain
concealed.ᵖ
⁹ When a man is successful even his
enemy is friendly;
in adversity even his friend
disappears.�q
¹⁰ Never trust your enemy,
for his wickedness is like corrosion in
bronze.
¹¹ Even though he acts humbly and
peaceably toward you,
take care to be on your guard against
him.
Rub him as one polishes a brazen
mirror,*
and you will find that there is still
corrosion.
¹² Let him not stand near you,
lest he oust you and take your place.

Let him not sit at your right hand,
lest he then demand your seat,
And in the end you appreciate my advice,
when you groan with regret, as I
warned you.
¹³ Who pities a snake charmer when he is
bitten,
or anyone who goes near a wild beast?
¹⁴ So is it with the companion of the proud
man,
who is involved in his sins:
¹⁵ While you stand firm, he makes no bold
move;
but if you slip, he cannot hold back.
¹⁶ With his lips an enemy speaks sweetly,
but in his heart he schemes to plunge
you into the abyss.
Though your enemy has tears in his eyes,
if given the chance, he will never have
enough of your blood.
¹⁷ If evil comes upon you, you will find him
at hand;
feigning to help, he will trip you up,
¹⁸ Then he will nod his head and clap his
hands
and hiss repeatedly, and show his true
face.

CHAPTER 13

Caution Regarding Associates*

See RG
276-79

¹ He who touches pitch blackens his
hand;
he who associates with an impious
man learns his ways.
² Bear no burden too heavy for you;
go with no one greater or wealthier
than yourself.
How can the earthen pot go with the
metal cauldron?
When they knock together, the pot will
be smashed:
³ The rich man does wrong and boasts of it,
the poor man is wronged and begs
forgiveness.

12, 1-7: The limitations to the practice of charity here reflected were removed by Christ, who requires that good be done even to enemies and to those who hate, persecute and calumniate us (Mt 5, 43-48).

12, 3ff: The author advises against generosity to those who would abuse it.

12, 8-18: Through adversity friends are distinguished from enemies; to trust the latter or permit them intimacy

is to invite disaster. Cf note on Sir 6, 5-17.

12, 11: Brazen mirror: see note on Ex 38, 8.

13, 1—14, 2: By means of various figures Sirach indicates the practical impossibility of genuine and sincere companionship between the poor and the proud rich. He lays down the principle of associating with equals (13, 15).

o: 4f: Gal 6, 10.   *p:* Prv 17, 17.   *q:* Prv 19, 4-7.

⁴ As long as the rich man can use you he
    will enslave you,
  but when you are exhausted, he will
    abandon you.
⁵ As long as you have anything he will
    speak fair words to you,
  and with smiles he will win your
    confidence;
⁶ When he needs something from you he
    will cajole you,
  then without regret he will impoverish
    you.
⁷ While it serves his purpose he will
    beguile you,
  then twice or three times he will terrify
    you;
  When later he sees you he will pass you by,
    and shake his head over you.
⁸ Guard against being presumptuous;
  be not as those who lack sense.
⁹ When invited by a man of influence,
    keep your distance;
  then he will urge you all the more.
¹⁰ Be not bold with him lest you be rebuffed,
    but keep not too far away lest you be
    forgotten.
¹¹ Engage not freely in discussion with him,
    trust not his many words;
  For by prolonged talk he will test you,
    and though smiling he will probe you.
¹² Mercilessly he will make of you a
    laughingstock,
  and will not refrain from injury or
    chains.
¹³ Be on your guard and take care
    never to accompany men of violence.

¹⁴ Every living thing loves its own kind,
    every man a man like himself.
¹⁵ Every being is drawn to its own kind;
    with his own kind every man
    associates.
¹⁶ Is a wolf ever allied with a lamb?
    So it is with the sinner and the just.ʳ
¹⁷ Can there be peace between the hyena
    and the dog?

Or between the rich and the poor can
    there be peace?*
¹⁸ Lion's prey are the wild asses of the desert;
    so too the poor are feeding grounds for
    the rich.
¹⁹ A proud man abhors lowliness;
    so does the rich man abhor the poor.
²⁰ When a rich man stumbles he is
    supported by a friend;
  when a poor man trips he is pushed
    down by a friend.
²¹ Many are the supporters for a rich man
    when he speaks;
  though what he says is odious, it wins
    approval.
  When a poor man speaks they make
    sport of him;
  he speaks wisely and no attention is
    paid him.
²² A rich man speaks and all are silent,
    his wisdom they extol to the clouds.
  A poor man speaks and they say: "Who
    is that?"
  If he slips they cast him down.
²³ Wealth is good when there is no sin;
    but poverty is evil by the standards of
    the proud.
²⁴ The heart of a man changes his
    countenance,
    either for good or for evil.ˢ
²⁵ The sign of a good heart is a cheerful
    countenance;
    withdrawn and perplexed is the
    laborious schemer.

CHAPTER 14

See RG
276-79

¹ Happy the man whose mouth
    brings him no grief,
  who is not stung by remorse for sin.ᵗ
² Happy the man whose conscience does
    not reproach him,
  who has not lost hope.

The Use of Wealth

³ Wealth ill becomes the mean man;*
    and to the miser, of what use is gold?

13, 17: The hostility between the dogs which guard the
flocks at night and the rapacious hyenas is proverbial in
Palestine.

14, 3-16: The miser does no good even to himself (3-10);
wealth should be wisely used during life, for it must be left
behind at death (11-16). In the light of the gospel, generosity
has a higher motivation and promise of reward than the Old
Testament writer could propose. Cf Mt 6, 19ff; Lk 12, 32ff.

r: 2 Cor 6, 14ff.   s: Prv 15, 13.   t: Sir 19, 15; 25, 8; Jas 3, 2.

⁴ What he denies himself he collects for
others,
and in his possessions a stranger will
revel.ᵘ
⁵ To whom will he be generous who is
stingy with himself
and does not enjoy what is his own?
⁶ None is more stingy than he who is
stingy with himself;
he punishes his own miserliness.
⁷ If ever he is generous, it is by mistake;
and in the end he displays his greed.
⁸ In the miser's opinion his share is too
small;
⁹ he refuses his neighbor and brings ruin
on himself.
¹⁰ The miser's eye is rapacious for bread,
but on his own table he sets it stale.
¹¹ My son, use freely whatever you have
and enjoy it as best you can;ᵛ
¹² Remember that death does not tarry,
nor have you been told the grave's
appointed time.
¹³ Before you die, be good to your friend,
and give him a share in what you
possess.ʷ
¹⁴ Deprive not yourself of present good
things,
let no choice portion escape you.
¹⁵ Will you not leave your riches to others,
and your earnings to be divided by lot?
¹⁶ Give, take, and treat yourself well,
for in the nether world there are no
joys to seek.
¹⁷ All flesh grows old, like a garment;
the age-old law is: All must die.ˣ
¹⁸ As with the leaves that grow on a
vigorous tree:
one falls off and another sprouts—
So with the generations of flesh and
blood:
one dies and another is born.ʸ
¹⁹ All man's works will perish in decay,
and his handiwork will follow after
him.

The Search for Wisdom and Its Blessings*

²⁰ Happy the man who meditates on
wisdom,
and reflects on knowledge;ᶻ
²¹ Who ponders her ways in his heart,
and understands her paths;
²² Who pursues her like a scout,
and lies in wait at her entry way;
²³ Who peeps through her windows,
and listens at her doors;
²⁴ Who encamps near her house,
and fastens his tent pegs next to her
walls;
²⁵ Who pitches his tent beside her,
and lives as her welcome neighbor;
²⁶ Who builds his nest in her leafage,
and lodges in her branches;
²⁷ Who takes shelter with her from the heat,
and dwells in her home.

CHAPTER 15

See RG
276–79

¹ He who fears the LORD will do this;
he who is practiced in the law will
come to wisdom.
² Motherlike she will meet him,
like a young bride she will embrace
him,
³ Nourish him with the bread of
understanding,
and give him the water of learning to
drink.ᵃ
⁴ He will lean upon her and not fall,
he will trust in her and not be put to
shame.
⁵ She will exalt him above his fellows;
in the assembly she will make him
eloquent.
⁶ Joy and gladness he will find,
an everlasting name inherit.ᵇ
⁷ Worthless men will not attain to her,
haughty men will not behold her.
⁸ Far from the impious is she,
not to be spoken of by liars.
⁹ Unseemly is praise on a sinner's lips,
for it is not accorded to him by God.

14, 20—15, 20: From his social teaching the sage now turns
to consider individual responsibility. Happiness is to be found
in the pursuit and possession of wisdom (14, 20—15, 5). Joy
and honor are given, not to the sinner (7ff), but to him who
fears God and observes his law (1-6. 10). The sinner is fully responsible for his conduct because God, who sees all things

(18f), is not the author of wickedness (11ff. 20): he gives to
every man the liberty to choose between good and evil (14-17).

ᵘ: Eccl 6, 2.   ᵛ: Prv 3, 9.   ʷ: Sir 4, 1; Tb 4, 7.   ˣ: Ps 103; 14ff;
Is 40, 6; Jas 1, 10; 1 Pt 1, 24.   ʸ: Eccl 1, 4.   ᶻ: Ps 1, 2.   ᵃ: Jn 4,
10; 6, 31ff.   ᵇ: Sir 6, 29-32.

10 But praise is offered by the wise man's
    tongue;
        its rightful steward will proclaim it.

Man's Free Will

11 Say not: "It was God's doing that I fell
    away";
        for what he hates he does not do.
12 Say not: "It was he who set me astray";
        for he has no need of wicked man.[c]
13 Abominable wickedness the LORD hates,
    he does not let it befall those who fear
    him.
14 When God, in the beginning, created
    man,
        he made him subject to his own free
        choice.[d]
15 If you choose you can keep the
    commandments;
        it is loyalty to do his will.
16 There are set before you fire and water;
        to whichever you choose, stretch forth
        your hand.
17 Before man are life and death,
        whichever he chooses shall be given
        him.[e]
18 Immense is the wisdom of the LORD;
        he is mighty in power, and all-seeing.
19 The eyes of God see all he has made;
        he understands man's every deed.[f]
20 No man does he command to sin,
        to none does he give strength for lies.

See RG 276–79

CHAPTER 16

God's Punishment of Sinners*

1 Desire not a brood of worthless children,
        nor rejoice in wicked offspring.
2 Many though they be, exult not in them
        if they have not the fear of the LORD.
3 Count not on their length of life,[g]
        have no hope in their future.
    For one can be better than a thousand;

rather die childless than have godless
children!
4 Through one wise man can a city be
    peopled;
        through a clan of rebels it becomes
        desolate.
5 Many such things has my eye seen,
        even more than these has my ear
        heard.
6 Against a sinful band fire is enkindled,[h]
        upon a godless people wrath flames
        out.*
7 He forgave not the leaders of old*
        who rebelled long ago in their
        might;[i]
8 He spared not the neighbors of Lot[j]
        whom he detested for their pride;*
9 Nor did he spare the doomed people*
        who were uprooted because of their
        sin;
10 Nor the six hundred thousand foot
    soldiers[k]
        who perished for the impiety of their
        hearts.*
11 And had there been but one stiffnecked
    man,
        it were a wonder had he gone
        unpunished.
    For mercy and anger alike are with him
        who remits and forgives, though on the
        wicked alights his wrath.
12 Great as his mercy is his punishment;
        he judges men, each according to his
        deeds.
13 A criminal does not escape with his
    plunder;
        a just man's hope God does not leave
        unfulfilled.
14 Whoever does good has his reward,
        which each receives according to his
        deeds.
15 Say not: "I am hidden from God;
        in heaven who remembers me?

16, 1-21: Sinful offspring are a great misfortune (1-4), for
history and experience show how God punishes sin (5-10).
He judges everyone according to his deeds (11ff); no one is
hidden from him or escapes retribution at his hand (15-21).

16, 6: For Korah and his band (6a), see Nm 16, 35; Ps 106,
18; for the disgruntled Israelites (6b), Ps 78, 21f.

16, 7: The leaders of flood: the "mighty men of old" who
were destroyed by the flood: Gn 6, 4; Wis 14, 6; Bar 3, 26ff.

16, 8: The people of Sodom and Gomorrah: Gn 19, 24f;
Ez 16, 49f.

16, 9: The Canaanites: Ex 23, 23f. 27-31; 33, 2; Dt 7, 1;
Wis 12, 3.

16, 10: The Israelites who murmured against Moses: Nm
11, 20; 14, 12. 22ff.

c: Jas 1, 13.   d: Gn 1, 27.   e: Dt 30, 15.   f: Pss 33, 18; 34, 16;
Heb 4, 13.   g: 3f: Wis 4, 1f.   h: Sir 21, 9.   i: Gn 6, 4; Wis 14,
6; Bar 3, 26ff.   j: Gn 19, 24ff.   k: Nm 14, 29.

Among so many people I cannot be
  known;
  what am I in the world of spirits?
16 Behold, the heavens, the heaven of
  heavens,
  the earth and the abyss tremble at his
    visitation;
17 The roots of the mountains, the earth's
  foundations,
  at his mere glance, quiver and quake.
18 Of me, therefore, he will take no thought;
  with my ways who will concern
    himself?
19 If I sin, no eye will see me;
  if all in secret I am disloyal, who is to
    know?[l]
20 Who tells him of just deeds
  and what could I expect for doing my
    duty?"
21 Such are the thoughts of senseless men,
  which only the foolish knave will
    think.

Divine Wisdom Seen in Creation*

22 Hearken to me, my son, take my advice,
  apply your mind to my words,
23 While I propose measured wisdom,
  and impart accurate knowledge.
24 When at the first God created his works
  and, as he made them, assigned their
    tasks,[m]
25 He ordered for all time what they were to
    do
  and their domains from generation to
    generation.
  They were not to hunger, nor grow
    weary,
  nor ever cease from their tasks.
26 Not one should ever crowd its neighbor,
  nor should they ever disobey his
    word.
27 Then the LORD looked upon the earth,
  and filled it with his blessings.[n]

28 Its surface he covered with all manner of
  life
  which must return into it again.

CHAPTER 17

See RG
276-79

1 The LORD from the earth created
  man,
  and in his own image he made him.[o]
2 Limited days of life he gives him[p]
  and makes him return to earth again.
3 He endows man with a strength of his
    own,
  and with power over all things else on
    earth.
4 He puts the fear of him in all flesh,
  and gives him rule over beasts and
    birds.
5 He forms men's tongues and eyes and ears,
  and imparts to them an understanding
    heart.
6 With wisdom and knowledge he fills
    them;
  good and evil he shows them.
7 He looks with favor upon their hearts,
  and shows them his glorious works,
8 That they may describe the wonders of
    his deeds
  and praise his holy name.
9 He has set before them knowledge,
  a law of life as their inheritance;
10 An everlasting covenant* he has made
    with them,
  his commandments he has revealed to
    them.
11 His majestic glory their eyes beheld,
  his glorious voice their ears heard.
12 He says to them, "Avoid all evil";
  each of them he gives precepts about
    his fellow men.
13 Their ways are ever known to him,
  they cannot be hidden from his eyes.
14 Over every nation he places a ruler,*
  but the LORD's own portion is Israel.[q]

16, 22—17, 18: In harmony with Gn 1—2, the author describes God's wisdom in creating the universe and all things in it (22-28), endowing man with a moral nature, with wisdom and knowledge and freedom of will according to his own image (17, 1. 6), so that man may govern the earth (3f), praise God's name (8), obey his law (9-12), and render to him an account of his deeds (18). Cf Pss 19; 104.

17, 10: An everlasting covenant . . . his commandments: the various covenants which God entered into with mankind, e.g.,

Gn 2, 15ff; 17, 1-22, especially on Mount Sinai where the people saw God's glory and heard his voice (Ex 19, 16—24, 18).

17, 14: Ruler: this may refer to civil authority or to angels placed over nations as guardians; see note on Dt 32, 8, and the cross references above.

---

l: Sir 23, 18.   *m:* Gn 1, 4ff.   *n:* Gn 1, 20ff.   *o:* Gn 2, 7; 3, 19.
p: 2ff; Gn 1, 26ff; Ps 8, 4-8.   *q:* Ex 19, 5; Dt 4, 19f; 32, 8f; Dn 10, 13-21; 12, 1; Rom 13, 1.

15 All their actions are clear as the sun to
him,
his eyes are ever upon their ways.
16 Their wickedness cannot be hidden from
him;
all of their sins are before the LORD.
17 A man's goodness God cherishes like a
signet ring,
a man's virtue, like the apple of his
eye.
18 Later he will rise up and repay them,
and requite each one of them as they
deserve.[r]

Appeal for a Return to God*
19 But to the penitent he provides a way
back,
he encourages those who are losing
hope!
20 Return to the LORD and give up sin,
pray to him and make your offenses
few.
21 Turn again to the Most High and away
from sin,
hate intensely what he loathes;
22 Who in the nether world can glorify the
Most High[s]
in place of the living who offer their
praise?
23 No more can the dead give praise than
those who have never lived;
they glorify the LORD who are alive
and well.
24 How great the mercy of the LORD,
his forgiveness of those who return to
him!
25 The like cannot be found in men,
for not immortal is any son of man.
26 Is anything brighter than the sun? Yet it
can be eclipsed.
How obscure* then the thoughts of
flesh and blood!

27 God watches over the hosts of highest
heaven,
while all men are dust and ashes.

CHAPTER 18

The Divine Power and Mercy*

See RG
276–79

1 The Eternal is the judge of all things
without exception;
the LORD alone is just.
2 Whom has he made equal to describing
his works,
and who can probe his mighty deeds?
3 Who can measure his majestic power,
or exhaust the tale of his mercies?
4 One cannot lessen, nor increase,
nor penetrate the wonders of the LORD.
5 When a man ends he is only beginning,
and when he stops he is still
bewildered.
6 What is man, of what worth is he?
the good, the evil in him, what are these?
7 The sum of a man's days is great
if it reaches a hundred years:[t]
8 Like a drop of sea water, like a grain of
sand,
so are these few years among the days
of eternity.
9 That is why the LORD is patient with men
and showers upon them his mercy.
10 He sees and understands that their death
is grievous,
and so he forgives them all the more.
11 Man may be merciful to his fellow man,
but the LORD's mercy reaches all flesh,
12 Reproving, admonishing, teaching,
as a shepherd guides his flock;[u]
13 Merciful to those who accept his guidance,
who are diligent in his precepts.

The Necessity of Prudence
14 My son, to your charity add no reproach,*
nor spoil any gift by harsh words.

17, 19-27: Exhorting the sinner to return to God (19ff. 24ff), the author implies that the Lord will postpone death for a repentant sinner so that he may fulfill his destiny of praising God on earth (22f). In the light of Christian teaching, the gift of final penitence extends this divine purpose into life everlasting. See note on Ps 6, 6; cf also Ez 18, 23; 33, 11-16.

17, 26: Obscure: literally, evil; compare Gn 6, 5. Though moral fault is not excluded, the thought here is the inability to understand the merciful designs of God. Cf Wis 9, 14-18.

18, 1-13: Not only are God's justice and power beyond man's understanding (1-5), his mercy also is boundless and surpasses all human compassion (6-13).

18, 14-27: The practice of charity is an art which avoids every offense to the recipient (14-18). Prudence directs the changing circumstances of daily life toward the attainment of its reward at the time of visitation, i.e., the day of reckoning (19-27).

r: Jb 19, 25; Jl 3, 4.   s: 22f: Pss 6, 6; 115, 17; Is 38, 18.   t: Ps 90, 10.   u: Jn 10, 11.

¹⁵ Like dew that abates a burning wind,
  so does a word improve a gift.
¹⁶ Sometimes the word means more than
    the gift;
  both are offered by a kindly man.
¹⁷ Only a fool upbraids before giving;
  a grudging gift wears out the expectant
    eyes.ᵛ
¹⁸ Be informed before speaking;
  before sickness prepare the cure.
¹⁹ Before you are judged, seek merit for
    yourself,
  and at the time of visitation you will
    have a ransom.*
²⁰ Before you have fallen, humble
    yourself;
  when you have sinned, show
    repentance.
²¹ Delay not to forsake sins,
  neglect it not till you are in distress.
²² Let nothing prevent the prompt payment
    of your vows;*
  wait not to fulfill them when you are
    dying.ʷ
²³ Before making a vow have the means to
    fulfill it;
  be not one who tries the LORD.
²⁴ Think of wrath and the day of death,
  the time of vengeance when he will
    hide his face.ˣ
²⁵ Remember the time of hunger in the time
    of plenty,
  poverty and want in the day of wealth.ʸ
²⁶ Between morning and evening the
    weather changes;
  before the LORD all things are fleeting.
²⁷ A wise man is circumspect in all things;
  when sin is rife he keeps himself from
    wrongdoing.

²⁸ Any learned man should make wisdom
    known,*
  and he who attains to her should
    declare her praise;
²⁹ Those trained in her words must show
    their wisdom,
  dispensing sound proverbs like life-
    giving waters.

Self-Control*

³⁰ Go not after your lusts,ᶻ
  but keep your desires in check.
³¹ If you satisfy your lustful appetites
  they will make you the sport of your
    enemies.
³² Have no joy in the pleasures of a moment
  which bring on poverty redoubled;
³³ Become not a glutton and a winebibber
  with nothing in your purse.

CHAPTER 19

See RG
276-79

¹ He who does so grows no richer;
  he who wastes the little he has will be
    stripped bare.
² Wine and women make the mind giddy,
  and the companion of harlots becomes
    reckless.ᵃ
⁴ He who lightly trusts in them has no sense,
  and he who strays after them sins
    against his own life.
³ Rottenness and worms will possess him,
  for contumacious desire destroys its
    owner.

The Proper Use of Speech*

⁵ He who gloats over evil will meet with
    evil,
  and he who repeats an evil report has
    no sense.

18, 19: Merit . . . ransom: almsgiving is often portrayed in the Bible as a means of approach to the forgiving mercy of God. Cf Sir 3, 29f; 29, 11f; Tb 12, 12f; Dn 4, 24; Lk 16, 9; Acts 10, 31.

18, 22f: The usual object of a vow in Old Testament times was the offering of a bloody sacrifice.

18, 28f: A general statement on the teaching of wisdom, serving either as a conclusion to the preceding section or as an introduction to the following one. The neighbors of the wise man are regarded as the field into which he channels the waters of wisdom to encourage growth. Cf Sir 24, 28-31.

18, 30—19, 4: Inordinate gratification of the senses makes a man unreasonable, the slave of passion, the sport of his ene-

mies. In the end it destroys him physically and spiritually.

19, 5-16: An excellent commentary on the eighth commandment of the Decalogue, forbidding intemperance in speech through calumny, rash judgment, and detraction (5f), and inculcating discreet silence in defense of self and of neighbor (7-11). Justice requires that an accused neighbor be given a hearing, and charity urges fraternal correction; both together fulfill the law of the Most High (12-16); cf Mt 7, 1f; 18, 15f.

---

v: Sir 20, 13. w: Nm 30, 3; Dt 23, 22; Ps 50, 14; Prv 20, 25; Eccl 5, 4. x: Sir 7, 16. y: Sir 11, 25. z: Rom 6, 12; 13, 14. a: Prv 20, 1; 23, 20ff.

6 Never repeat gossip,
  and you will not be reviled.*b*
7 Tell nothing to friend or foe;
  if you have a fault, reveal it not,*c*
8 For he who hears it will hold it against
  you,
  and in time become your enemy.
9 Let anything you hear die within you;
  be assured it will not make you burst.
10 When a fool hears something, he is in
  labor,
  like a woman giving birth to a child.
11 Like an arrow lodged in a man's thigh
  is gossip in the breast of a fool.
12 Admonish your friend—he may not have
  done it;
  and if he did, that he may not do it
  again.*d*
13 Admonish your neighbor—he may not
  have said it;
  and if he did, that he may not say it
  again.
14 Admonish your friend—often it may be
  slander;
  every story you must not believe.
15 Then, too, a man can slip and not mean
  it;
  who has not sinned with his tongue?*e*
16 Admonish your neighbor before you
  break with him;
  thus will you fulfill the law of the
  Most High.*f*

How To Recognize True Wisdom*

17 All wisdom is fear of the LORD;
  perfect wisdom is the fulfillment of the
  law.*g*
18 The knowledge of wickedness is not
  wisdom,
  nor is there prudence in the counsel of
  sinners.
19 There is a shrewdness that is detestable,
  while the simple man may be free
  from sin.

20 There are those with little understanding
  who fear God,
  and those of great intelligence who
  violate the law.
21 There is a shrewdness keen but
  dishonest,
  which by duplicity wins a judgment.
22 There is the wicked man who is bowed in
  grief,
  but is full of guile within;
23 He bows his head and feigns not to
  hear,
  but when not observed, he will take
  advantage of you:
24 Even though his lack of strength keeps
  him from sinning,
  when he finds the opportunity, he will
  do harm.
25 One can tell a man by his appearance;
  a wise man is known as such when
  first met.
26 A man's attire, his hearty laughter and his
  gait,
  proclaim him for what he is.

CHAPTER 20

*Conduct of the Wise and
the Foolish*

See RG
276–79

1 An admonition can be inopportune,*
  and a man may be wise to hold his
  peace.
2 It is much better to admonish than to lose
  one's temper,
  for one who admits his fault will be
  kept from disgrace.
3 Like a eunuch lusting for intimacy with a
  maiden
  is he who does right under
  compulsion.*
4 One man is silent and is thought wise,
  another is talkative and is disliked.
5 One man is silent because he has nothing
  to say;
  another is silent, biding his time.*h*

19, 17-26: True and false wisdom as here described are
synonymous with virtue and vice, with the fulfillment of the
law and the violation of it.

20, 1-7: Wisdom indicates the proper times for speech and
silence, that is, the occasions when the most benefit can be
gained from them.

20, 3: The sense is that violence or force against a person

can prevent an external act of sin or compel a good deed without eliminating the internal sin or desire of wrongdoing. Cf
Sir 20, 20.

b: Prv 25, 10. *c:* Sir 8, 18f. *d:* Lv 19, 17; Mt 18, 15; Lk 17, 3.
e: Sir 14, 1; Jas 3, 2. *f:* Lv 19, 17. *g:* Sir 1, 1. 12. 14; Jb 28, 28;
Ps 111, 10; Prv 1, 7; 9, 10. *h:* Sir 20, 1; Prv 10, 19; 17, 28.

⁶ A wise man is silent till the right time
    comes,
  but a boasting fool ignores the proper
    time.
⁷ He who talks too much is detested;
  he who pretends to authority is hated.

⁸ Some misfortunes bring success;*
  some things gained are a man's loss.
⁹ Some gifts do one no good,
  and some must be paid back double.*
¹⁰ Humiliation can follow fame,
  while from obscurity a man can lift up
    his head.
¹¹ A man may buy much for little,
  but pay for it seven times over.
¹² A wise man makes himself popular by a
    few words,
  but fools pour forth their
    blandishments in vain.
¹³ A gift from a rogue will do you no good,
  for in his eyes his one gift is equal to
    seven.
¹⁴ He gives little and criticizes often,
  and like a crier he shouts aloud.
  He lends today, he asks it back
    tomorrow;
  hateful indeed is such a man.
¹⁵ A fool has no friends,
  nor thanks for his generosity;
¹⁶ Those who eat his bread have an evil
    tongue.
  How many times they laugh him to
    scorn!

¹⁷ A fall to the ground is less sudden than a
    slip of the tongue;*
  that is why the downfall of the wicked
    comes so quickly.
¹⁸ Insipid food is the untimely tale;
  the unruly are always ready to offer it.

¹⁹ A proverb when spoken by a fool is
    unwelcome,
  for he does not utter it at the proper
    time.
²⁰ A man through want may be unable to
    sin,
  yet in this tranquility he cannot rest.
²¹ One may lose his life through shame,
  and perish through a fool's
    intimidation.
²² A man makes a promise to a friend out of
    shame,
  and has him for his enemy needlessly.
²³ A lie is a foul blot in a man,
  yet it is constantly on the lips of the
    unruly.
²⁴ Better a thief than an inveterate liar,
  yet both will suffer disgrace;
²⁵ A liar's way leads to dishonor,
  his shame remains ever with him.
²⁶ A wise man advances himself by his
    words,*
  a prudent man pleases the great.
²⁷ He who works his land has abundant
    crops,
  he who pleases the great is pardoned
    his faults.
²⁸ Favors and gifts blind the eyes;
  like a muzzle over the mouth they
    silence reproof.ⁱ
²⁹ Hidden wisdom and unseen treasure—
  of what value is either?
³⁰ Better the man who hides his folly
  than the one who hides his wisdom.

CHAPTER 21

Sin Must Be Avoided*

See RG
276–79

¹ My son, if you have sinned, do so no
    more,
  and for your past sins pray to be
    forgiven.

20, 8-16: In a series of paradoxes the author indicates how much true and lasting values differ from apparent ones.
20, 9: And some . . . double: or perhaps, "but some are doubly precious."
20, 17-25: The ill-timed speech of the wicked, the unruly and a fool is repulsive (17ff); human respect exposes one to intimidation, rash promises and enmity (21f); lies bring dishonor and lasting disgrace (23ff).
20, 26-30: Unlike the fool who invites disaster through misuse of his tongue, the sage through prudent speech gains in honor and esteem among the great (26f). He must beware,

however, of accepting bribes, lest he share in evil through silence when he should reprove (28ff).
21, 1-10: Under various figures the consequences of sin are described as destructive of wealth, and even of bodily life, and deserving of death and a place in the depths of the nether world (2ff. 6a. 8ff). Through prayer, forgiveness can be sought (1), and through fear of the Lord, repentance is achieved (1, 5. 6b).

i: Ex 23, 8; Dt 16, 19.

2 Flee from sin as from a serpent
     that will bite you if you go near it;
   Its teeth are lion's teeth,
     destroying the souls of men.
3 Every offense is a two-edged sword;
     when it cuts, there can be no healing.
4 Violence and arrogance wipe out wealth;
     so too a proud man's home is
       destroyed.
5 Prayer from a poor man's lips is heard at
       once,
     and justice is quickly granted him.
6 He who hates correction walks the
       sinner's path,
     but he who fears the LORD repents in
       his heart.
7 Widely known is the boastful speaker,
     but the wise man knows his own
       faults.
8 He who builds his house with another's
       money
     is collecting stones for his funeral
       mound.
9 A band of criminals is like a bundle of
       tow;
     they will end in a flaming fire.*j*
10 The path of sinners is smooth stones
     that end in the depths of the nether
       world.*

The Wise and the Foolish Differ*

11 He who keeps the law controls his
       impulses;
     he who is perfect in fear of the LORD
       has wisdom.
12 He can never be taught who is not
       shrewd,
     but one form of shrewdness is
       thoroughly bitter.
13 A wise man's knowledge wells up in a
       flood,
     and his counsel, like a living spring;*k*
14 A fool's mind is like a broken jar—

no knowledge at all can it hold.
15 When an intelligent man hears words of
       wisdom,
     he approves them and adds to them;
   The wanton hears them with scorn
     and casts them behind his back.
16 A fool's chatter is like a load on a
       journey,
     but there is charm to be found upon
       the lips of the wise.
17 The views of a prudent man are sought in
       an assembly,
     and his words are considered with
       care.
18 Like a house in ruins is wisdom to a fool;
     the stupid man knows it only as
       inscrutable words.
19 Like fetters on the legs is learning to a
       fool,
     like a manacle on his right hand.
20 A fool raises his voice in laughter,
     but a prudent man at the most smiles
       gently.*l*
21 Like a chain of gold is learning to a wise
       man,
     like a bracelet on his right arm.

22 The fool steps boldly into a house,
     while the well-bred man remains
       outside;*m*
23 A boor peeps through the doorway of a
       house,
     but a cultured man keeps his glance
       cast down.
24 It is rude for one to listen at a door;
     a cultured man would be overwhelmed
       by the disgrace of it.
25 The lips of the impious talk of what is
       not their concern,
     but the words of the prudent are
       carefully weighed.
26 Fools' thoughts are in their mouths,
     wise men's words are in their hearts.

21, 10: The path of sinners . . . nether world: eternal retribution is not yet proposed in this reference. It became clearly
revealed through the teaching of Christ; cf Mt 7, 13f; 25, 41-
46; Lk 16, 19-31.
21, 11-28: The mind of the wise man is a fountain of
knowledge (13. 15); his will is trained to keep the law (11);
his words are gracious, valued, carefully weighed, sincere
(16f. 25f); his conduct is respectful, cultured and restrained

(20. 22ff). The fool's mind is devoid of knowledge and impenetrable to it (12. 14. 18f); his will rejects it (15); his talk
is burdensome (16), his laughter unrestrained (20), his conversation shallow and meddlesome (25f); his conduct is bold
and rude (22ff); his abuse of others redounds on himself
(27f).

j: Ps 21, 9.   *k:* Prv 13, 14; 16, 22.   *l:* Eccl 7, 6.   *m:* Prv 25, 17.

27 When a godless man curses his
adversary,*
he really curses himself.
28 A slanderer besmirches himself,
and is hated by his neighbors.

CHAPTER 22

See RG
276–79

On Laziness and Foolishness

1 The sluggard is like a stone in the mud;*
everyone hisses at his disgrace.
2 The sluggard is like a lump of dung;
whoever touches him wipes his hands.
3 An unruly child is a disgrace to its
father;
if it be a daughter, she brings him to
poverty.ⁿ
4 A thoughtful daughter becomes a
treasure to her husband,
a shameless one is her father's grief.
5 A hussy shames her father and her
husband;
by both she is despised.
6 Like a song in time of mourning is
inopportune talk,*
but lashes and discipline are at all
times wisdom.
7 Teaching a fool is like gluing a broken pot,ᵒ
or like disturbing a man in the depths
of sleep;
8 He talks with a slumberer who talks with
a fool,
for when it is over, he will say, "What
was that?"
9 Weep over the dead man, for his light has
gone out;
weep over the fool, for sense has left
him.
10 Weep but a little over the dead man, for
he is at rest;

but worse than death is the life of a
fool.
11 Seven days of mourning for the dead,
but for the wicked fool a whole
lifetime.ᵖ
12 Speak but seldom with the stupid man,
be not the companion of a brute;
13 Beware of him lest you have trouble
and be spattered when he shakes
himself;
Turn away from him and you will find
rest
and not be wearied by his lack of
sense.
14 What is heavier than lead,
and what is its name but "Fool"?
15 Sand and salt and an iron mass
are easier to bear than a stupid man.�q
16 Masonry bonded with wooden beams*
is not loosened by an earthquake;
Neither is a resolve constructed with
careful deliberation
shaken in a moment of fear.
17 A resolve that is backed by prudent
understanding
is like the polished surface of a smooth
wall.
18 Small stones lying on an open height
will not remain when the wind blows;
Neither can a timid resolve based on
foolish plans
withstand fear of any kind.

The Preservation of Friendship*

19 One who jabs the eye brings tears:
he who pierces the heart bares its
feelings.

21, 27: Adversary: this can be understood in the sense
that, if a man curses one who led him into sin, he implicitly
curses himself for having yielded to the sin; or in the sense
that the enemy is the man's own sinful nature; or even in
the sense that the enemy is the devil, since the Hebrew
word used here is satan. Cf 1 Chr 21, 1; Zec 3, 2; 2 Pt 2,
12f; Jude 9.

22, 1-15: To Sirach, a lazy person and an unruly child are
a cause of shame and disgrace; everyone wishes to be rid of
them (1-5). A wicked fool is as senseless as a man asleep or
dead, but the grief he causes others lasts a lifetime (7-11). He
is like a brute, troublesome and intolerable (12-15).

22, 6: Like a song . . . is . . . talk: some understand talk in
the sense of a rebuke unheeded by the unruly as a joyful song

is out of place among mourners. Corporal punishment, however, is always effective.

22, 16ff: A prudent mind firmly resolved is undisturbed
by violent and conflicting thoughts, whereas a foolish person
is tossed about by the winds of fear, like small stones whipped
about by high winds.

22, 19-26: As disputes and violence weaken friendship,
and disloyalty and abuse of confidence destroy it utterly (19-
22. 24. 26), so kindness to a poor man in time of poverty and
adversity builds up friendship and merits a share in his prosperity and inheritance (23. 25).

n: Prv 17, 21; 19, 13.　o: 7-11: Prv 23, 9.　p: Gn 50, 10.　q: Prv
27, 3.

20 He who throws stones at birds drives
  them away,
  and he who insults a friend breaks up
  the friendship.
21 Should you draw a sword against a
  friend,
  despair not, it can be undone.
22 Should you speak sharply to a friend,
  fear not, you can be reconciled.
  But a contemptuous insult, a confidence
  broken,
  or a treacherous attack will drive away
  any friend.

23 Make fast friends with a man while he is
  poor;
  thus will you enjoy his prosperity with
  him.
  In time of trouble remain true to him,
  so as to share in his inheritance when
  it comes.
24 Before flames burst forth an oven
  smokes;
  so does abuse come before bloodshed.
25 From a friend in need of support
  no one need hide in shame;
26 But from him who brings harm to his
  friend
  all will stand aloof who hear of it.

Prayer*

27 Who will set a guard over my mouth,
  and upon my lips an effective seal,
  That I may not fail through them,
  that my tongue may not destroy me?*r*

CHAPTER 23

See RG
276–79
1 LORD, Father and Master of my life,*
  permit me not to fall by them!
2 Who will apply the lash to my thoughts,
  to my mind the rod of discipline,
  That my failings may not be spared,

nor the sins of my heart overlooked;
3 Lest my failings increase,
  and my sins be multiplied;
  Lest I succumb to my foes,
  and my enemy rejoice over me?
4 LORD, Father and God of my life,
  abandon me not into their control!
5 A brazen look allow me not;
  ward off passion from my heart,
6 Let not the lustful cravings of the flesh
  master me,
  surrender me not to shameless desires.

The Proper Use of the Tongue*

7 Give heed, my children, to the instruction
  that I pronounce,
  for he who keeps it will not be
  enslaved.
8 Through his lips is the sinner ensnared;
  the railer and the arrogant man fall
  thereby.
9 Let not your mouth form the habit of
  swearing,
  or becoming too familiar with the
  Holy Name.*s*
10 Just as a slave that is constantly under
  scrutiny*
  will not be without welts,
  So one who swears continually by the
  Holy Name
  will not remain free from sin.
11 A man who often swears heaps up
  obligations;
  the scourge will never be far from his
  house.
  If he swears in error, he incurs guilt;
  if he neglects his obligation, his sin is
  doubly great.*t*
  If he swears without reason he cannot be
  found just,
  and all his house will suffer affliction.
12 There are words which merit death;

22, 27—23, 6: The sage implores the divine assistance to preserve him through stern discipline from sins of the tongue (22, 27; 23, 1); ignorance of mind and weakness of will (2f); and inclinations of the senses and the flesh, lest he fall into the hands of his enemies, or become a prey of shameful desires (3-6).

23, 1: LORD, Father and Master of my life: these words express the tender personal relationship between the author's soul and God, the need of his assistance, and the truth of his providence.

23, 7-15: A warning against sins of the tongue through misuse of the Holy Name, thoughtless swearing which involves obligation and incurs guilt (7-11), blasphemy (12), talk that is coarse and blundersome (13f), and the incorrigible habit of abusive language (15).

23, 10: As a slave . . . under scrutiny, so is he who calls on God to witness the truth of what he says.

r: Ps 141, 3.   *s:* Ex 20, 7; Lv 19, 12; Dt 5, 11; Mt 5, 33ff.   *t:* Lv 5, 4ff.

may they never be heard among
  Jacob's heirs.
For all such words are foreign to the
  devout,
who do not wallow in sin.
[13] Let not your mouth become used to
  coarse talk,
for in it lies sinful matter.
[14] Keep your father and mother in mind
  when you sit among the mighty,
Lest in their presence you commit a
  blunder
and disgrace your upbringing,
By wishing you had never been born
  or cursing the day of your birth.[u]
[15] A man who has the habit of abusive
  language
will never mature in character as long
  as he lives.

Sins of the Flesh[*]

[16] Two types of men multiply sins,
  a third[*] draws down wrath;
For burning passion is a blazing fire,
  not to be quenched till it burns itself
  out:
A man given to sins of the flesh,
  who never stops until the fire breaks
  forth;
[17] The rake to whom all bread is sweet
  and who is never through till he dies;[v]
[18] And the man who dishonors his marriage
  bed
and says to himself, "Who can see me?
Darkness surrounds me, walls hide me;
  no one sees me; why should I fear to
  sin?"[w]
Of the Most High he is not mindful,
[19] fearing only the eyes of men;
He does not understand that the eyes of
  the LORD,

ten thousand times brighter than the
  sun,
Observe every step a man takes
  and peer into hidden corners.
[20] He who knows all things before they
  exist
still knows them all after they are
  made.
[21] Such a man will be punished in the
  streets of the city;[x]
when he least expects it, he will be
  apprehended.[*]

[22] So also with the woman who is
  unfaithful to her husband
and offers as heir her son by a stranger.
[23] First, she has disobeyed the law of the
  Most High;
secondly, she has wronged her
  husband;
Thirdly, in her wanton adultery
  she has borne children by another
  man.[*]
[24] Such a woman will be dragged before the
  assembly,[*]
and her punishment will extend to her
  children;
[25] Her children will not take root;
  her branches will not bring forth
  fruit.
[26] She will leave an accursed memory;
  her disgrace will never be blotted
  out.
[27] Thus all who dwell on the earth shall
  know,
and all who inhabit the world shall
  understand,
That nothing is better than the fear of the
  LORD,
nothing more salutary than to obey his
  commandments.[y]

23, 16-27: From sins of the tongue the author proceeds to treat of sins of the flesh and their dire consequences. The passion of lust tyrannizes over its victims and, like fire, consumes and utterly destroys them (16f. 22-26). The false security of the adulterer serves but to aggravate his inevitable fate (18-21). Only the fear of the Lord and observance of his commandments can assure moral safety (27).

23, 16: Two types . . . a third: three kinds of sins of impurity, with increasing degrees of gravity: solitary sins (16), fornication (17) and adultery (18-21).

23, 21: Cf Lv 20, 19; Dt 22, 22.

23, 23: The detailed evil of adultery includes disobedience to God's law (Ex 20, 14), injustice to a partner in marriage, and disgraceful offspring.

23, 24f: The judgment of the assembly determined the illegitimacy of children born of adultery or incest and excluded them from the "community of the Lord" (Dt 23, 3). Cf Wis 3, 16-19; 4, 3-6.

u: Sir 7, 27; Ex 20, 12; Dt 5, 16.   v: Prv 9, 17.   w: Is 29, 15.   x: 21f: Lv 20, 10; Dt 22, 21.   y: Sir 1, 10-18. 24; Prv 3, 1f.

See RG
276-79

CHAPTER 24

Praise of Wisdom

1 Wisdom sings her own praises,*
  before her own people she proclaims
    her glory;
2 In the assembly of the Most High she
    opens her mouth,
  in the presence of his hosts she
    declares her worth:
3 "From the mouth of the Most High I
    came forth,ᶻ
  and mistlike covered the earth.
4 In the highest heavens did I dwell,
  my throne on a pillar of cloud.
5 The vault of heaven I compassed alone,
  through the deep abyss I wandered.
6 Over waves of the sea, over all the land,
  over every people and nation I held
    sway.
7 Among all these I sought a resting place;
  in whose inheritance should I abide?

8 "Then the Creator of all gave me his
    command,
  and he who formed me chose the spot
    for my tent,
  Saying, 'In Jacob make your dwelling,
    in Israel your inheritance.'
9 Before all ages, in the beginning, he
    created me,
  and through all ages I shall not cease
    to be.
10 In the holy tent I ministered before him,
  and in Zion I fixed my abode.
11 Thus in the chosen city he has given me
    rest,
  in Jerusalem is my domain.
12 I have struck root among the glorious
    people,
  in the portion of the LORD, his heritage.

13 "Like a cedar on Lebanon I am raised
    aloft,
  like a cypress on Mount Hermon,
14 Like a palm tree in Engedi,
  like a rosebush in Jericho,
  Like a fair olive tree in the field,
    like a plane tree growing beside the
    water.
15 Like cinnamon, or fragrant balm, or
    precious myrrh,
  I give forth perfume;ᵃ
  Like galbanum and onycha and sweet
    spices,
  like the odor of incense in the holy
    place.*
16 I spread out my branches like a terebinth,
  my branches so bright and so graceful.
17 I bud forth delights like the vine,
  my blossoms become fruit fair and
    rich.
18 Come to me, all you that yearn for me,
  and be filled with my fruits;*
19 You will remember me as sweeter than
    honey,
  better to have than the honeycomb.
20 He who eats of me will hunger still,*
  he who drinks of me will thirst for
    more;ᵇ
21 He who obeys me will not be put to
    shame,
  he who serves me will never fail."

22 All this is true of the book of the Most
    High's covenant,ᶜ
  the law which Moses commanded us
  as an inheritance for the community of
    Jacob.*
23 It overflows, like the Pishon, with
    wisdom—ᵈ
  like the Tigris in the days of the new
    fruits.

24, 1-27: In this chapter Wisdom speaks in the first person, describing her origin, her dwelling place in Israel, and the reward she gives her followers. As in Prv 8, Wisdom is described as a being who comes from God and is distinct from him. While we do not say with certainty that this description applies to a personal being, it does foreshadow the beautiful doctrine of the Word of God later developed in St. John's Gospel (Jn 1, 1-14). In the liturgy this chapter is applied to the Blessed Virgin because of her constant and intimate association with Christ, the Incarnate Wisdom.

24, 15: These substances were associated with worship, being mentioned in Ex 30, 22f. 34 as the ingredients of the anointing oil and the sacred incense. Israel was a priestly nation.

24, 18: Compare the words of the Savior in Mt 11, 28ff.

24, 20: So pleasing is wisdom to man that, far from being satiated, he will always desire more.

24, 22: Here the author begins to speak once more, Wisdom having ended her discourse in the preceding verse. Wisdom and the law of Moses are now identified.

---

z: 3ff: Sir 1, 1; Prv 2, 6; 8, 22-36; Wis 7, 24f. *a:* Ex 30, 22-25.
b: Is 55, 1; Jn 6, 35. *c:* Ex 24, 7. *d:* 23ff: Gn 2, 11-14.

24 It runs over, like the Euphrates, with
        understanding,
    like the Jordan at harvest time.
25 It sparkles like the Nile with knowledge,
    like the Gihon* at vintage time.
26 The first man never finished
        comprehending wisdom,
    nor will the last succeed in fathoming
        her.
27 For deeper than the sea are her thoughts;
    her counsels, than the great abyss.

28 Now I, like a rivulet from her stream,*
    channeling the waters into a garden,
29 Said to myself, "I will water my plants,
    my flower bed I will drench";
    And suddenly this rivulet of mine
        became a river,
    then this stream of mine, a sea.
30 Thus do I send my teachings forth
        shining like the dawn,
    to become known afar off.
31 Thus do I pour out instruction like
        prophecy
    and bestow it on generations to come.

See RG
276–79

CHAPTER 25

Those Who Are Worthy
of Praise*

1 With three things I am delighted,
    for they are pleasing to the LORD and
        to men:
    Harmony among brethren, friendship
        among neighbors,
    and the mutual love of husband and
        wife.
2 Three kinds of men I hate;
    their manner of life I loathe indeed:
    A proud pauper, a rich dissembler,
    and an old man lecherous in his dotage.

3 What you have not saved in your
        youth,
    how will you acquire in your old age?
4 How becoming to the gray-haired is
        judgment,
    and a knowledge of counsel to those
        on in years!
5 How becoming to the aged is wisdom,
    understanding and prudence to the
        venerable!
6 The crown of old men is wide
        experience;
    their glory, the fear of the LORD.

7 There are nine who come to my mind as
        blessed,
    a tenth whom my tongue proclaims:
    The man who finds joy in his children,
    and he who lives to see his enemies'
        downfall.
8 Happy is he who dwells with a sensible
        wife,
    and he who plows not like a donkey
        yoked with an ox.*
    Happy is he who sins not with his
        tongue,
    and he who serves not his inferior.
9 Happy is he who finds a friend
    and he who speaks to attentive ears.
10 He who finds wisdom is great indeed,
    but not greater than he who fears the
        LORD.
11 Fear of the LORD surpasses all else,
    its possessor is beyond compare.

Wicked and Virtuous Women*

12 Worst of all wounds is that of the heart,
    worst of all evils is that of a woman.
13 Worst of all sufferings is that from one's
        foes,

24, 25: Gihon: understood by some to have been a name for the Nile; cf Gn 2, 13.

24, 28-31: Spoken by the author. He had at first drawn a small portion of the water of wisdom for his own private benefit, but finding it so useful, he soon began to let others share in this boon by teaching them the lessons of wisdom.

25, 1-11: While praising brotherly love, love of neighbor, and conjugal love, the sage condemns their opposites in the arrogant pauper who despises his brother, the fraudulent rich man who cheats his neighbor, and the lecherous old man unfaithful to his wife (1f). This last, sensual from his youth, lacks the mature blessings of judgment and wisdom in old age

(3-6), and the joy of a peaceful household, where honesty and dignity, friendship, wisdom and fear of God prevail (7-11).

25, 8: Like a donkey yoked with an ox: incompatibility between husband and wife.

25, 12-25: Wickedness in a woman is most grievous, painful and bitter to her husband. Through it she becomes vengeful, dangerous and intolerable, jealous, talkative, intemperate and unchaste. Even her very appearance is changed (12-17). The worst of all evils, a source of grief, a snare and a disgrace to her husband, she depresses his mind, saddens and breaks his heart, destroys his strength (18-22). She must not be indulged but made obedient or punished (24f).

worst of all vengeance is that of one's
enemies:

[14] No poison worse than that of a serpent,
no venom greater than that of a
woman.

[15] With a dragon or a lion I would rather
dwell
than live with an evil woman.

[16] Wickedness changes a woman's looks,
and makes her sullen as a female bear.

[17] When her husband sits among his
neighbors,
a bitter sigh escapes him unawares.

[18] There is scarce any evil like that in a
woman;
may she fall to the lot of the sinner!

[19] Like a sandy hill to aged feet
is a railing wife to a quiet man.

[20] Stumble not through woman's beauty,
nor be greedy for her wealth;

[21] The man is a slave, in disgrace and
shame,
when a wife supports her husband.

[22] Depressed mind, saddened face,
broken heart—this from an evil wife.
Feeble hands and quaking knees—
from a wife who brings no happiness
to her husband.

[23] In woman was sin's beginning,
and because of her we all die.*

[24] Allow water no outlet,
and be not indulgent to an erring wife.

[25] If she walks not by your side,
cut her away from you.

CHAPTER 26

See RG
276-79

[1] Happy the husband of a good wife,*
twice-lengthened are his days;e

[2] A worthy* wife brings joy to her
husband,
peaceful and full is his life.

[3] A good wife is a generous gift

bestowed upon him who fears the
Lord;f

[4] Be he rich or poor, his heart is content,
and a smile is ever on his face.

[5] There are three things at which my heart
quakes,
a fourth before which I quail:
Though false charges in public, trial
before all the people,
and lying testimony are harder to bear
than death,

[6] A jealous wife is heartache and
mourning*
and a scourging tongue like the other
three.

[7] A bad wife is a chafing yoke;
he who marries her seizes a scorpion.

[8] A drunken wife arouses great anger,
for she does not hide her shame.

[9] By her eyelids and her haughty stare
an unchaste wife can be recognized.

[10] Keep a strict watch over an unruly wife,
lest, finding an opportunity, she make
use of it;g

[11] Follow close if her eyes are bold,
and be not surprised if she betrays
you:

[12] As a thirsty traveler with eager mouth
drinks from any water that he finds,
So she settles down before every tent peg
and opens her quiver for every arrow.

[13] A gracious wife delights her husband,
her thoughtfulness puts flesh on his
bones;

[14] A gift from the Lord is her governed
speech,
and her firm virtue is of surpassing
worth.

[15] Choicest of blessings is a modest wife,
priceless her chaste person.

[16] Like the sun rising in the Lord's
heavens,

25, 23: According to the account in Gn 3, to which Ben
Sirach refers, sin, the cause of death, originated in woman:
Eve, the first human being to sin, induced Adam to follow her
example. But it is through Adam, as head of the race, that
original sin and its punishment of spiritual death are presented by St. Paul (Rom 5) as having entered the world, to become the occasion for the redemptive work of Christ our
Lord.

26, 1-4. 13-18: A good wife is as a gift from God, bring-

ing joy and peace, happiness and contentment to her husband
(1-4) through her thoughtfulness, reserve, modesty and
chastity, beauty, grace and virtue (13-18).

26, 2: Worthy: gifted spiritually, mentally and physically.
Cf Prv 31, 10.

26, 6-12: A repetition of the thought expressed in Sir 25,
12-25.

e: Sir 25, 8; Prv 18, 22; 31, 10ff.   f: Sir 36, 24.   g: Sir 42, 11.

the beauty of a virtuous wife is the
  radiance of her home.
17 Like the light which shines above the
  holy lampstand,*
  are her beauty of face and graceful
    figure.
18 Golden columns on silver bases
  are her shapely limbs and steady feet.*

Dangers to Integrity and Friendship

19 These two bring grief to my heart,
  and the third arouses my horror:
A wealthy man reduced to want;
  illustrious men held in contempt;
And the man who passes from justice to
    sin,
  for whom the LORD makes ready the
    sword.*h*

20 A merchant can hardly remain upright,*
  nor a shopkeeper free from sin;

See RG
276-79

CHAPTER 27

1 For the sake of profit many sin,
  and the struggle for wealth blinds the
    eyes.*i*
2 Like a peg driven between fitted stones,
  between buying and selling sin is
    wedged in.
3 Unless you earnestly hold fast to the fear
    of the LORD,
  suddenly your house will be thrown
    down.
4 When a sieve is shaken, the husks
    appear;
  so do a man's faults when he speaks.

5 As the test of what the potter molds is in
    the furnace,
  so in his conversation is the test of a
    man.*j*
6 The fruit of a tree shows the care it has
    had;
  so too does a man's speech disclose
    the bent of his mind.*k*
7 Praise no man before he speaks,
  for it is then that men are tested.
8 If you strive after justice you will attain it,
  and put it on like a splendid robe.
9 Birds nest with their own kind,
  and fidelity comes to those who live
    by it.
10 As a lion crouches in wait for prey,
  so do sins for evildoers.
11 Ever wise are the discourses of the
    devout,
  but the godless man, like the moon,
    is inconstant.
12 Limit the time you spend among fools,
  but frequent the company of
    thoughtful men.
13 The conversation of the wicked is
    offensive,
  their laughter is wanton guilt.
14 Their oath-filled talk makes the hair
    stand on end,
  their brawls make one stop one's ears.
15 Wrangling among the haughty ends in
    bloodshed,
  their cursing is painful to hear.*l*
16 He who betrays a secret cannot be
    trusted,*
  he will never find an intimate friend.*m*

26, 17f: The holy lampstand and the golden columns
stood in the holy place of the ancient Tabernacle (Ex 25, 31-
40; 26, 32).

26, 18: Among the additions found here in some manuscripts are the following lines:
"My son, take care in the prime of life
  not to surrender your strength to strangers;
Single out from the land a goodly field
  and there with confidence sow the seed of your increase;
So shall you have your offspring around you,
  and in confidence shall they grow up.

"Though a woman for hire be thought of as a trifle,
  a married woman is a deadly snare for those who
  embrace her. [Cf Prv 6, 26.]

"A wife's complaint should be made in meekness,
  and show itself in a slight flush;

But a loud-mouthed, scolding wife
  is a trumpet signaling for battle:
Any human being who answers that challenge
  will spend his life amid the turbulence of war."

26, 20—27, 15: From proper conduct in family life, the
author proceeds to social morality, warning especially against
injustice in commerce (26, 20—27, 3), and perversity of
speech in business (4-7). The pursuit of justice in these matters is all the more meritorious as it is difficult (8ff). The discourses of the devout are marked with wisdom, but the conversations of the wicked, with offense, swearing, cursing,
quarrels and even bloodshed (11-15).

27, 16—28, 11: Betrayal of confidence through indiscre-
tion destroys friendship and does irreparable harm (16-21); cf

h: Ez 18, 24ff. *i:* Sir 7, 18; 31, 6; Prv 30, 8f. *j:* 1 Pt 1, 7. *k:* Mt
7, 20. *l:* Sir 23, 9-15. *m:* Prv 11, 13; 20, 19.

17 Cherish your friend, keep faith with him;
  but if you betray his confidence,
    follow him not;
18 For as an enemy might kill a man,
  you have killed your neighbor's
    friendship.
19 Like a bird released from the hand,
  you have let your friend go and cannot
    recapture him;
20 Follow him not, for he is far away,
  he has fled like a gazelle from the trap.
21 A wound can be bound up, and an insult
    forgiven,
  but he who betrays secrets does
    hopeless damage.ⁿ

Malice, Anger and Vengeance

22 He who has shifty eyes plots mischief
  and no one can ward him off;
23 In your presence he uses honeyed talk,
  and admires your every word,
But later he changes his tone
  and twists your words to your ruin.ᵒ
24 There is nothing that I hate so much,
  and the LORD hates him as well.ᵖ
25 As a stone falls back on him who throws
    it up,�q
  so a blow struck in treachery injures
    more than one.
26 As he who digs a pit falls into it,
  and he who lays a snare is caught in it,
27 Whoever does harm will be involved in it
  without knowing how it came upon him.

28 Mockery and abuse will be the lot of the
    proud,
  and vengeance lies in wait for them
    like a lion.
29 The trap seizes those who rejoice in
    pitfalls,
  and pain will consume them before
    they die;
30 Wrath and anger are hateful things,
  yet the sinner hugs them tight.

CHAPTER 28

See RG
276-79

1 The vengeful will suffer the
    LORD's vengeance,
  for he remembers their sins in detail.ʳ
2 Forgive your neighbor's injustice;
  then when you pray, your own sins
    will be forgiven.ˢ
3 Should a man nourish anger against his
    fellows
  and expect healing from the LORD?ᵗ
4 Should a man refuse mercy to his fellows,
  yet seek pardon for his own sins?
5 If he who is but flesh cherishes wrath,
  who will forgive his sins?
6 Remember your last days, set enmity
    aside;
  remember death and decay, and cease
    from sin!ᵘ
7 Think of the commandments, hate not
    your neighbor;
  of the Most High's covenant, and
    overlook faults.

8 Avoid strife and your sins will be fewer,
  for a quarrelsome man kindles
    disputes,
9 Commits the sin of disrupting friendship
  and sows discord among those at
    peace.ᵛ
10 The more wood, the greater the fire,ʷ
  the more underlying it, the fiercer the
    fight;
The greater a man's strength, the sterner
    his anger,
  the greater his power, the greater his
    wrath.
11 Pitch and resin make fires flare up,
  and insistent quarrels provoke
    bloodshed.

The Evil Tongue*

12 If you blow upon a spark, it quickens into
    flame,

Sir 22, 22. False friendship based on hypocrisy and deceit is
hateful to God and man (22ff); it soon becomes a victim of its
own treachery (25ff). The same fate awaits the malicious and
vengeful (27, 28—28, 1). They can obtain mercy and forgiveness only by first forgiving their neighbor, being mindful
of death and of the commandments of the Most High (28, 2-
7). And they must avoid quarrels and strife (8-11).

28, 12-26: Further treatment of sins of the tongue and their

havoc; cf Sir 5, 12—6, 1; 19, 5-16; 20, 17-25; 23, 7-15. Gossips and the double-tongue destroy domestic peace (12-16).
The whip, the sword, chains, even the nether world, are not so

n: Sir 22, 20.   o: Prv 26, 24ff.   p: Prv 6, 13. 16.   q: 25f: Ps 7,
16f; Prv 26, 27: Eccl 10, 8.   r: Dt 32, 35; Rom 12, 19.   s: Mt 6,
14.   t: Mt 18, 23ff.   u: Sir 7, 36; 38, 20.   v: Prv 15, 18.
w: 10ff: Prv 26, 20f.

if you spit on it, it dies out;
yet both you do with your mouth!

[13] Cursed be gossips and the double-tongued,
for they destroy the peace of many.[x]

[14] A meddlesome tongue subverts many,
and makes them refugees among the peoples;
It destroys walled cities,
and overthrows powerful dynasties.

[15] A meddlesome tongue can drive virtuous women from their homes
and rob them of the fruit of their toil;

[16] Whoever heeds it has no rest,
nor can he dwell in peace.

[17] A blow from a whip raises a welt,
but a blow from the tongue smashes bones;

[18] Many have fallen by the edge of the sword,
but not as many as by the tongue.[y]

[19] Happy he who is sheltered from it,
and has not endured its wrath;
Who has not borne its yoke
nor been fettered with its chains;

[20] For its yoke is a yoke of iron
and its chains are chains of bronze!

[21] Dire is the death it inflicts,
besides which even the nether world is a gain;

[22] It will not take hold among the just
nor scorch them in its flame,

[23] But those who forsake the LORD will fall victims to it,
as it burns among them unquenchably!
It will hurl itself against them like a lion;
like a panther, it will tear them to pieces.

[24] As you hedge round your vineyard with thorns,
set barred doors over your mouth;[z]

[25] As you seal up your silver and gold,
so balance and weigh your words.

[26] Take care not to slip by your tongue
and fall victim to your foe waiting in ambush.

CHAPTER 29

Loans, Alms and Surety*

See RG
276–79

[1] He does a kindness who lends to his neighbor,
and he fulfills the precepts who holds out a helping hand.[a]

[2] Lend to your neighbor in his hour of need,
and pay back your neighbor when a loan falls due;[b]

[3] Keep your promise, be honest with him,
and you will always come by what you need.

[4] Many a man who asks for a loan
adds to the burdens of those who help him;

[5] When he borrows, he kisses the lender's hand
and speaks with respect of his creditor's wealth;
But when payment is due he disappoints him
and says he is helpless to meet the claim.

[6] If the lender is able to recover barely half,
he considers this an achievement;
If not, he is cheated of his wealth
and acquires an enemy at no extra charge;
With curses and insults the borrower pays him back,
with abuse instead of honor.

[7] Many refuse to lend, not out of meanness,
but from fear of being cheated.

[8] To a poor man, however, be generous;
keep him not waiting for your alms;

[9] Because of the precept, help the needy,

---

cruel as the suffering inflicted by an evil tongue (17-21). Not the just but those who forsake the Lord are victims of their evil tongues (22f). Therefore, guard your mouth and tongue as you would guard treasure against an enemy (24ff).

29, 1-20: Some practical maxims concerning the use of wealth. Give to a poor man (8f), lend to a needy neighbor, but repay when a loan falls due lest the lender's burden be increased (1-5) and his kindness abused (6f); through charity

build up defense against evil (10-13). Go surety for your neighbor according to your means, but take care (20) not to fall, for the shameless play false and bring their protectors and themselves to misfortune and ruin (14-19).

x: Sir 5, 16f.   y: Jas 3, 5ff.   z: Sir 22, 27; Ps 141, 3.   a: Dt 15, 8; Ps 112, 5; Prv 19, 17.   b: Ex 22, 24ff; Lv 25, 36; Mt 5, 42.

and in their want, do not send them
    away empty-handed.*c*

10 Spend your money for your brother and
    friend,
    and hide it not under a stone to perish;
11 Dispose of your treasure as the Most
    High commands,
    for that will profit you more than the
    gold.*d*
12 Store up almsgiving in your treasure
    house,
    and it will save you from every evil;
13 Better than a stout shield and a sturdy
    spear
    it will fight for you against the foe.

14 A good man goes surety for his neighbor,
    and only the shameless would play
    him false;*e*
15 Forget not the kindness of your backer,
    for he offers his very life for you.
16 The wicked turn a pledge on their behalf
    into misfortune,
    and the ingrate abandons his protector;
17 Going surety has ruined many
    prosperous men
    and tossed them about like waves of
    the sea.*f*
18 Has exiled men of prominence
    and sent them wandering through
    foreign lands.
19 The sinner through surety comes to grief,
    and he who undertakes too much falls
    into lawsuits.
20 Go surety for your neighbor according to
    your means,
    but take care lest you fall thereby.

*Frugality and Its Rewards**

21 Life's prime needs are water, bread, and
    clothing,
    a house, too, for decent privacy.*g*

22 Better a poor man's fare under the
    shadow of one's own roof
    than sumptuous banquets among
    strangers.*h*
23 Be it little or much, be content with what
    you have,
    and pay no heed to him who would
    disparage your home;
24 A miserable life it is to go from house to
    house,
    for as a guest you dare not open your
    mouth.
25 The visitor has no thanks for filling the
    cups;
    besides, you will hear these bitter
    words:
26 "Come here, stranger, set the table,
    give me to eat the food you have!
27 Away, stranger, for one more worthy;
    for my brother's visit I need the
    room!"
28 Painful things to a sensitive man
    are abuse at home and insults from his
    creditors.

CHAPTER 30

*The Training of Children**

See RG 276-79

1 He who loves his son chastises him
    often,
    that he may be his joy when he grows
    up.*i*
2 He who disciplines his son will benefit
    from him,
    and boast of him among his
    intimates.
3 He who educates his son makes his
    enemy jealous,
    and shows his delight in him among
    his friends.
4 At the father's death, he will seem not
    dead,
    since he leaves after him one like
    himself,

29, 21-28: The man who provides his own basic needs of food, clothing and dwelling, and is content with what he has, preserves his freedom and self-respect (21ff). But if he lives as a guest, even among the rich, he exposes himself to insult and abuse (24-28).

30, 1-13: Sound discipline and careful education of children correct frivolity and stubbornness, prevent remorse and humiliation, and bring to parents lasting joy and delight, pres-

tige among friends, jealousy of enemies, perpetuation and vindication of themselves through their offspring (1-6). Lack of discipline and overindulgence of children bring sorrow and disappointment, terror and grief (7-13).

c: Sir 4, 1ff; Lv 19, 9f; 23, 22; Dt 15, 8.   *d:* Sir 17, 17; Tb 4, 7ff.
e: Sir 8, 13.   *f:* Prv 6, 1f; 11, 15.   *g:* Sir 39, 26.   *h:* Sir 40, 29.
i: Prv 13, 24; 23, 13; 29, 15; Heb 12, 7.

⁵ Whom he looks upon through life with
joy,
and even in death, without regret:
⁶ The avenger he leaves against his foes,
and the one to repay his friends with
kindness.

⁷ He who spoils his son will have wounds
to bandage,
and will quake inwardly at every outcry.
⁸ A colt untamed turns out stubborn;
a son left to himself grows up unruly.
⁹ Pamper your child and he will be a terror
for you,
indulge him and he will bring you grief.
¹⁰ Share not in his frivolity lest you share in
his sorrow,
when finally your teeth are clenched in
remorse.
¹¹ Give him not his own way in his youth,
and close not your eyes to his follies.
¹² Bend him to the yoke when he is young,
thrash his sides while he is still small,
Lest he become stubborn, disobey you,
and leave you disconsolate.ʲ
¹³ Discipline your son, make heavy his yoke,
lest his folly humiliate you.

Health of Soul and Body*

¹⁴ Better a poor man strong and robust,
than a rich man with wasted frame.
¹⁵ More precious than gold is health and
well-being,
contentment of spirit than coral.
¹⁶ No treasure greater than a healthy body;
no happiness, than a joyful heart!
¹⁷ Preferable is death to a bitter life,ᵏ
unending sleep to constant illness.*
¹⁸ Dainties set before one who cannot eat
are like the offerings placed before a
tomb.ˡ
¹⁹ What good is an offering to an idol

that can neither taste nor smell?
²⁰ So it is with the afflicted man
who groans at the good things his eyes
behold!

²¹ Do not give in to sadness,
torment not yourself with brooding;ᵐ
²² Gladness of heart is the very life of man,
cheerfulness prolongs his days.
²³ Distract yourself, renew your courage,
drive resentment far away from you;
For worry has brought death to many,
nor is there aught to be gained from
resentment.ⁿ
²⁴ Envy and anger shorten one's life,
worry brings on premature old age.
²⁵ One who is cheerful and gay while at
table
benefits from his food.ᵒ

CHAPTER 31

The Proper Attitude toward Riches*

See RG 276-79

¹ Keeping watch over riches wastes the
flesh,
and the care of wealth drives away
rest.
² Concern for one's livelihood banishes
slumber;
more than a serious illness it disturbs
repose.*
³ The rich man labors to pile up wealth,
and his only rest is wanton pleasure;
⁴ The poor man toils for a meager
subsistence,
and if ever he rests, he finds himself in
want.
⁵ The lover of gold will not be free from
sin,
for he who pursues wealth is led astray
by it.
⁶ Many have been ensnared by gold,

30, 14-25: Health of mind and body and joy of heart are
judged more precious than wealth (14ff); bitterness, constant
illness and affliction more difficult to bear than death (17-20).
Sadness, resentment, anxiety, envy and anger shorten . . . life;
they should be dispelled by cheerfulness and gladness of
heart, which help to prolong one's days (21-25).

30, 17: Preferable is death . . . constant illness: the true
value of human suffering was revealed through the passion
and death of Christ. It serves as reparation for sin, and when
united with Christ's suffering, as merit for eternal life.

31, 1-11: Solicitude for acquiring wealth and anxiety over
preserving it disturb repose and easily lead to sin and ruin (1-
7). Cf Mt 6, 25-34. A rich man who has not sinned or been seduced by wealth is worthy of praise (8-11).

31, 2: The Hebrew adds a verse that seems out of place
here: "A faithful comrade drives away reproach, and the
friend who keeps secrets is as dear as life."

j: Sir 7, 23. k: Sir 41, 2. l: Tb 4, 17. m: Sir 38, 20; Prv 12, 25;
15, 13; 17, 22. n: Sir 38, 18f. o: Prv 15, 15.

though destruction lay before their eyes;*p*

7 It is a stumbling block to those who are avid for it,
a snare for every fool.

8 Happy the rich man found without fault,*
who turns not aside after gain!*q*

9 Who is he, that we may praise him?
he, of all his kindred, has done wonders,

10 For he has been tested by gold and come off safe,
and this remains his glory;
He could have sinned but did not,
could have done evil but would not,

11 So that his possessions are secure,
and the assembly recounts his praises.*r*

Table Etiquette*

12 If you are dining with a great man,
bring not a greedy gullet to his table,
Nor cry out, "How much food there is here!"

13 Remember that gluttony is evil.
No creature is greedier than the eye:
therefore it weeps for any cause.*s*

15 Recognize that your neighbor feels as you do,
and keep in mind your own dislikes:

14 Toward what he eyes, do not put out a hand;
nor reach when he does for the same dish.

16 Behave at table like a favored guest,
and be not greedy, lest you be despised.

17 Be the first to stop, as befits good manners;
gorge not yourself, lest you give offense.*t*

18 If there are many with you at table,
be not the first to reach out your hand.

19 Does not a little suffice for a well-bred man?
When he lies down, it is without discomfort.*u*

20 Distress and anguish and loss of sleep,
and restless tossing for the glutton!
Moderate eating ensures sound slumber
and a clear mind next day on rising.

21 If perforce you have eaten too much,
once you have emptied your stomach,*
you will have relief.

22 Listen to me, my son, and scorn me not;
later you will find my advice good.
In whatever you do, be moderate,
and no sickness will befall you.

23 On a man generous with food, blessings are invoked,
and this testimony to his goodness is lasting;*v*

24 He who is miserly with food is denounced in public,
and this testimony to his stinginess is lasting.

25 Let not wine-drinking be the proof of your strength,
for wine has been the ruin of many.

26 As the furnace probes the work of the smith,
so does wine the hearts of the insolent.

27 Wine is very life to man
if taken in moderation.
Does he really live who lacks the wine
which was created for his joy?*w*

28 Joy of heart, good cheer and merriment
are wine drunk freely at the proper time.

29 Headache, bitterness and disgrace
is wine drunk amid anger and strife.

30 More and more wine is a snare for the fool;
it lessens his strength and multiplies his wounds.

31, 8ff: The church in her liturgy applies this passage to holy confessors of the Faith.

31, 12—32, 13: A man observing etiquette at table avoids greed and selfishness (31, 12f), is considerate of a neighbor's likes and dislikes and generous toward him (14f. 23f), observes proper manners (16ff), is moderate in eating and drinking (19-22. 25-30). A good host makes himself one with his guests, is solicitous for them (32, 1f), provides conversation and diversion (3-6), is modest in speech (7f. 10), is re-spectful of elders (9), polite in comportment and grateful to God for his favors (11ff).

31, 21: Emptied your stomach: the practice of induced vomiting, well-known among pagan Romans, and less well-known among the Jews, seems to be referred to here.

p: Sir 8, 2.   *q:* Sir 5, 1. 10.   *r:* Prv 29, 14.   *s:* Sir 37, 28ff; Prv 23, 1f.   *t:* Sir 37, 29.   *u:* Eccl 5, 11.   *v:* Prv 22, 9.   *w:* Ps 104, 15; 1 Tm 5, 23.

³¹ Rebuke not your neighbor when wine is
   served,

   nor put him to shame while he is merry;
Use no harsh words with him
   and distress him not in the presence of
   others.

See RG
276-79

CHAPTER 32

¹ If you are chosen to preside at
   dinner, be not puffed up,
but with the guests be as one of
   themselves;
Take care of them first before you sit
   down;
² when you have fulfilled your duty,
   then take your place,
To share in their joy
   and win praise for your hospitality.
³ Being older, you may talk; that is only
   your right,
   but temper your wisdom, not to disturb
   the singing.
⁴ When wine is present, do not pour out
   discourse,
   and flaunt not your wisdom at the
   wrong time.
⁵ Like a seal of carnelian in a setting of gold
   is a concert when wine is served.
⁶ Like a gold mounting with an emerald
   seal
   is string music with delicious wine.
⁷ Young man, speak only when necessary,ˣ
   when they have asked you more than
   once;
⁸ Be brief, but say much in those few words,
   be like the wise man, taciturn.
⁹ When among your elders be not forward,
   and with officials be not too insistent.
¹⁰ Like the lightning that flashes before a
   storm
   is the esteem that shines on modesty.
¹¹ When it is time to leave, tarry not;
   be off for home! There take your ease,
¹² And there enjoy doing as you wish,
   but without sin or words of pride.

¹³ Above all, give praise to your Creator,
   who showers his favors upon you.

The Providence of God

¹⁴ He who would find God must accept
   discipline;*
   he who seeks him obtains his request.ʸ
¹⁵ He who studies the law masters it,
   but the hypocrite finds it a trap.ᶻ
¹⁶ His judgment is sound who fears the
   LORD;
   out of obscurity he draws forth a clear
   plan.ᵃ
¹⁷ The sinner turns aside reproof
   and distorts the law to suit his purpose.ᵇ
¹⁸ The thoughtful man will not neglect
   direction;
   the proud and insolent man is deterred
   by nothing.
¹⁹ Do nothing without counsel,
   and then you need have no regrets.ᶜ
²⁰ Go not on a way that is set with snares,
   and let not the same thing trip you
   twice.
²¹ Be not too sure even of smooth roads,
²² be careful on all your paths.
²³ Whatever you do, be on your guard,
   for in this way you will keep the
   commandments.
²⁴ He who keeps the law preserves himself;
   and he who trusts in the LORD shall not
   be put to shame.

CHAPTER 33

See RG
276-79

¹ No evil can harm the man who
   fears the LORD;
   through trials, again and again he is
   safe.ᵈ
² He who hates the law is without wisdom,
   and is tossed about like a boat in a
   storm.
³ The prudent man trusts in the word of the
   LORD,
   and the law is dependable for him as a
   divine oracle.*

32, 14—33, 4: God is shown to reveal himself through the discipline of his law, a clear and safe plan of life for the pious Jew of old. Direction and counsel are aids in following it (14ff. 18-24); 33, 1. 3f). Sinners and hypocrites, hating the law or distorting it, fail in wisdom and are devoid of security (32, 15. 17f; 33, 2).

33, 3: Oracle: as the answer given through the Urim and Thummim to the high priest is true, so the law proves itself true to him who obeys it. Cf Ex 28, 30; Nm 27, 21.

x: 7ff: Sir 7, 14.   y: Sir 4, 13.   z: Sir 2, 16.   a: Ps 37, 6.   b: Sir 21, 6; Prv 12, 1.   c: Sir 37, 16; Tb 4, 18.   d: Ps 91, 10.

⁴ Prepare your words and you will be
listened to;
draw upon your training, and then give
your answer.

⁵ Like the wheel of a cart is the mind of a
fool;*
his thoughts revolve in circles.
⁶ A fickle friend is like the stallion
that neighs, no matter who the rider.
⁷ Why is one day more important than
another,
when it is the sun that lights up every
day?
⁸ It is due to the LORD's wisdom that they
differ;
it is through him the seasons and feasts
come and go.ᵉ
⁹ Some he dignifies and sanctifies,
and others he lists as ordinary days.ᶠ
¹⁰ So too, all men are of clay,
for from earth man was formed;ᵍ
¹¹ Yet with his great knowledge the LORD
makes men unlike;
in different paths he has them walk.
¹² Some he blesses and makes great,
some he sanctifies and draws to
himself.
Others he curses and brings low,
and expels them from their place.
¹³ Like clay in the hands of a potter,
to be molded according to his pleasure,
So are men in the hands of their Creator,
to be assigned by him their function.ʰ
¹⁴ As evil contrasts with good, and death
with life,
so are sinners in contrast with the just;ⁱ
¹⁵ See now all the works of the Most High:
they come in pairs, the one the
opposite of the other.

¹⁶ Now I am the last to keep vigil,*
like a gleaner after the vintage;

¹⁷ Since by the LORD's blessing I have
made progress
till like a vintager I have filled my
winepress,
¹⁸ I would inform you that not for myself
only have I toiled,
but for every seeker after wisdom.

Property and Servants*

¹⁹ Listen to me, O leaders of the
multitude;
O rulers of the assembly, give ear!ʲ
²⁰ Let neither son nor wife, neither brother
nor friend,
have power over you as long as you
live.
²¹ While breath of life is still in you,
let no man have dominion over you.
Give not to another your wealth,
lest then you have to plead with him;
²² Far better that your children plead with
you
than that you should look to their
generosity.
²³ Keep control over all your affairs;
let no one tarnish your glory.
²⁴ When your few days reach their limit,
at the time of death distribute your
inheritance.

²⁵ Fodder and whip and loads for an ass;
the yoke and harness and the rod of his
master.
²⁷ Food, correction and work for a slave;
and for a wicked slave, punishment in
the stocks.
²⁶ Make a slave work and he will look for
his rest;
let his hands be idle and he will seek to
be free.ᵏ
²⁸ Force him to work that he be not idle,
for idleness is an apt teacher of
mischief.

33, 5-15: Contrasts observable in the physical universe as
well as in the moral order serve the purposes of divine wisdom (5-9). All creatures are like clay . . . in the hands of their
Creator—the fool and the wise man, the sinner, and the just
(10-15). This does not imply that man is created to be a sinner: God is not the author of wickedness. Cf Jas 1, 13f.

33, 16ff: Here the author refers to himself as the most recent of the writers who have endeavored to present true wisdom to their readers.

33, 19-33: Public officials should reject every influence that
would restrict their freedom in the management of their affairs.
They must make their own household subservient to them
rather than be subservient to it (19-24). Slaves are to be given
food and work and correction but never to be treated unjustly
(25-29). Great care should be taken of good slaves (30-33).

e: Gn 1, 14. *f:* Ex 20, 11. *g:* Gn 2, 7. *h:* Wis 15, 7; Jer 18, 1-
6; Rom 9, 20f. *i:* Sir 42, 25. *j:* Wis 6, 1f. *k:* Prv 29, 19.

²⁹ Put him to work, for that is what befits him;

if he becomes unruly, load him with chains.

³⁰ But never lord it over any human being, and do nothing unjust.

³¹ If you have but one slave, treat him like yourself,

for you have acquired him with your life's blood;*l*

³² If you have but one slave, deal with him as a brother,

for you need him as you need your life:

³³ If you mistreat him and he runs away, in what direction will you look for him?

See RG 276–79

CHAPTER 34

*Trust in the Lord and Not in Dreams**

¹ Empty and false are the hopes of the senseless,

and fools are borne aloft by dreams.

² Like a man who catches at shadows or chases the wind,

is the one who believes in dreams.

³ What is seen in dreams is to reality what the reflection of a face is to the face itself.

⁴ Can the unclean produce the clean?

can the liar ever speak the truth?*m*

⁵ Divination, omens and dreams all are unreal;

what you already expect, the mind depicts.

⁶ Unless it be a vision specially sent by the Most High,

fix not your heart on it;

⁷ For dreams have led many astray, and those who believed in them have perished.

⁸ The law is fulfilled without fail,

and perfect wisdom is found in the mouth of the faithful man.

⁹ A man with training gains wide knowledge;

a man of experience speaks sense.

¹⁰ One never put to the proof knows little,

whereas with travel a man adds to his resourcefulness.

¹¹ I have seen much in my travels,

learned more than ever I could say.

¹² Often I was in danger of death,

but by these attainments I was saved.

¹³ Lively is the courage of those who fear the LORD,

for they put their hope in their savior;

¹⁴ He who fears the LORD is never alarmed,

never afraid; for the LORD is his hope.*n*

¹⁵ Happy the soul that fears the LORD!

In whom does he trust, and who is his support?

¹⁶ The eyes of the LORD are upon those who love him;

he is their mighty shield and strong support,

A shelter from the heat, a shade from the noonday sun,

a guard against stumbling, a help against falling.*o*

¹⁷ He buoys up the spirits, brings a sparkle to the eyes,

gives health and life and blessing.

*True Worship of God**

¹⁸ Tainted his gifts who offers in sacrifice ill-gotten goods!

Mock presents from the lawless win not God's favor.*p*

¹⁹ The Most High approves not the gifts of the godless,

nor for their many sacrifices does he forgive their sins.

²⁰ Like the man who slays a son in his father's presence

is he who offers sacrifice from the possessions of the poor.

34, 1-17: Confidence placed in dreams, divinations and omens is false because these are devoid of reality (1-8). True confidence is founded on knowledge and experience (9-12), and above all on the fear of the Lord, with its accompanying blessings of divine assistance and protection (13-17).

34, 18-26: To be acts of true religion, sacrifice and penance must be accompanied by the proper moral disposi-tions. To offer to God goods taken from the poor (18-22), or to practice penance without interior reform, is a mockery, worthless in the sight of God (23-26). Cf Mt 15, 4-7; Mk 7, 9-13.

l: Sir 7, 21.   *m:* Jb 14, 4.   *n:* Pss 23, 4; 112, 7f; Prv 3, 23ff; 28, 1.   *o:* Pss 33, 18; 34, 16.   *p:* Sir 35, 11; Prv 21, 27.

21 The bread of charity is life itself for the
needy;*q*

he who withholds it is a man of blood.

22 He slays his neighbor who deprives him
of his living;

he sheds blood who denies the laborer
his wages.

23 If one man builds up and another tears
down,

what do they gain but trouble?

24 If one man prays and another curses,
whose voice will the LORD hear?

25 If a man again touches a corpse after he
has bathed,

what did he gain by the purification?*r*

26 So with a man who fasts for his sins,
but then goes and commits them again:

Who will hear his prayer,

and what has he gained by his
mortification?

See RG
276-79

CHAPTER 35*

1 To keep the law is a great oblation,*s*
and he who observes the

commandments sacrifices a peace
offering.

2 In works of charity one offers fine flour,*
and when he gives alms he presents

his sacrifice of praise.

3 To refrain from evil pleases the LORD,
and to avoid injustice is an atonement.

4 Appear not before the LORD empty-
handed,

for all that you offer is in fulfillment of
the precepts.*t*

5 The just man's offering enriches the altar
and rises as a sweet odor before the

Most High.

6 The just man's sacrifice is most pleasing,
nor will it ever be forgotten.

7 In generous spirit pay homage to the
LORD,

be not sparing of freewill gifts.*u*

8 With each contribution show a cheerful
countenance,

and pay your tithes in a spirit of joy.*v*

9 Give to the Most High as he has given to
you,

generously, according to your means.

10 For the LORD is one who always repays,
and he will give back to you

sevenfold.*w*

11 But offer no bribes, these he does not
accept!

Trust not in sacrifice of the fruits of
extortion,*x*

12 For he is a God of justice,
who knows no favorites.*y*

13 Though not unduly partial toward the
weak,

yet he hears the cry of the oppressed.*

14 He is not deaf to the wail of the orphan,*z*
nor to the widow when she pours out

her complaint;

15 Do not the tears that stream down her
cheek

cry out against him that causes them to
fall?

16 He who serves God willingly is heard;
his petition reaches the heavens.

17 The prayer of the lowly pierces the
clouds;

it does not rest till it reaches its goal,

18 Nor will it withdraw till the Most High
responds,

judges justly and affirms the right.

19 God indeed will not delay,
and like a warrior, will not be still*a*

20 Till he breaks the backs of the merciless
and wreaks vengeance upon the proud;

21 Till he destroys the haughty root and
branch,

and smashes the scepter of the wicked;

35, 1-24: Keeping the commandments of the law and
avoiding injustice constitute sacrifice pleasing and acceptable to God (1ff). Offerings also should be made to him,
cheerfully and generously; these he repays . . . sevenfold (4-
10). Extortion from widows and orphans is injustice, which
God quickly repays (11-18). Punishing the proud and the
merciless and coming to the aid of the distressed, he requites
all according to their deeds (19-24).

35, 2: Fine flour, together with oil and frankincense, was

a prescribed offering to God; cf Lv 2, 1ff.

35, 13: Cf Lv 19, 15.

q: 21f: Lv 19, 13; Dt 24, 14f; Tb 4, 14. *r*: Nm 19, 11f; Prv 26,
11; 2 Pt 2, 22. *s*: 1ff: 1 Sm 15, 22; Ps 51, 18f; Is 1, 11-18; Hos 6,
6; Am 5, 21-24. *t*: Ex 23, 15; 34, 20; Dt 16, 16. *u*: Sir 7, 31.
v: 2 Cor 9, 7. *w*: Prv 19, 17. *x*: Sir 34, 18f; Prv 21, 27. *y*: Dt
10, 17; 2 Chr 19, 7; Jb 34, 19; Wis 6, 7; Acts 10, 34; Rom 2, 11;
Gal 2, 6; 1 Pt 1, 17. *z*: 14f: Ex 22, 22. *a*: Is 42, 13ff; 2 Pt 3, 9.

²² Till he requites mankind according to its
deeds,
and repays men according to their
thoughts;
²³ Till he defends the cause of his people,
and gladdens them by his mercy.
²⁴ Welcome is his mercy in time of distress
as rain clouds in time of drought.

See RG
276-79

CHAPTER 36

A Prayer for God's People*

¹ Come to our aid, O God of the universe,
and put all the nations in dread of you!
² Raise your hand against the heathen,
that they may realize your power.
³ As you have used us to show them your
holiness,
so now use them to show us your glory.
⁴ Thus they will know, as we know,
that there is no God but you.

⁵ Give new signs and work new wonders;
show forth the splendor of your right
hand and arm;
⁶ Rouse your anger, pour out wrath,
humble the enemy, scatter the foe.ᵇ
⁷ Hasten the day, bring on the time;
⁹ crush the heads of the hostile rulers.
⁸ Let raging fire consume the fugitive,
and your people's oppressors meet
destruction.
¹⁰ Gather all the tribes of Jacob,
that they may inherit the land as
of old.
¹¹ Show mercy to the people called by your
name;
Israel, whom you named your first-
born.ᶜ
¹² Take pity on your holy city,
Jerusalem, your dwelling place.ᵈ
¹³ Fill Zion with your majesty,
your temple with your glory.

¹⁴ Give evidence of your deeds of old;
fulfill the prophecies spoken in your
name,
¹⁵ Reward those who have hoped in you,
and let your prophets be proved true.
¹⁶ Hear the prayer of your servants,
for you are ever gracious to your
people;
¹⁷ Thus it will be known to the very ends of
the earth
that you are the eternal God.

Choice of Associates*

¹⁸ The throat can swallow any food,
yet some foods are more agreeable
than others;
¹⁹ As the palate tests meat by its savor,
so does a keen mind insincere words.
²⁰ A deceitful character causes grief,
but an experienced man can turn the
tables on him.
²¹ Though any man may be accepted as a
husband,
yet one girl will be more suitable than
another:
²² A woman's beauty makes her husband's
face light up,
for it surpasses all else that charms the
eye;ᵉ
²³ And if, besides, her speech is kindly,
his lot is beyond that of mortal men.
²⁴ A wife is her husband's richest treasure,
a helpmate, a steadying column.ᶠ
²⁵ A vineyard with no hedge will be
overrun;
a man with no wife becomes a
homeless wanderer.
²⁶ Who will trust an armed band
that shifts from city to city?
²⁷ Or a man who has no nest,
but lodges where night overtakes
him?ᵍ

36, 1-17: Making an act of faith and hope in the supreme Lord of the universe, the author begs God to continue manifesting his holiness and mercy through Israel, his people (1ff. 10-13), and his power and justice through the punishment of the nations (2. 5-9), that all the earth may acknowledge him the eternal God (4. 14-17).

36, 18—37, 15: In the choice of wife, friend or associate, experience is a discerner of character (18-21). Beauty and kindly speech make a woman desirable as wife (22f). The good wife becomes her husband's richest treasure, his help-

mate in establishing his household (24-27). A true friend fights for his comrade and shares his spoils with him (37, 5f); a false one deceives and abandons him in time of need (1-4). A true counselor and associate should be sought among those who keep the commandments, not among those who break them and seek their own advantage (7-12). In all things pray to God for light and follow conscience (13ff).

b: Ps 79, 6.   c: Ex 4, 22.   d: 2 Chr 6, 41; Ps 132, 8. 14; Is 2, 1ff; Mi 4, 1ff.   e: Sir 26, 13ff.   f: Gn 2, 18; Prv 18, 22.   g: Prv 27, 8.

See RG
276–79

CHAPTER 37

1 Every friend declares his friendship,
   but there are friends who are friends in
      name only.[h]
2 Is it not a sorrow unto death
   when your bosom companion becomes
      your enemy?
3 "Alas, my companion! Why were you
      created
   to blanket the earth with deceit?"
4 A false friend will share your joys,
   but in time of trouble he stands afar off.
5 A true friend will fight with you against
      the foe,
   against your enemies he will be your
      shield-bearer.
6 Forget not your comrade during the battle,
   and neglect him not when you
      distribute your spoils.

7 Every counselor points out a way,
   but some counsel ways of their own;
8 Be on the alert when one proffers advice,
   find out first of all what he wants.
   For he may be thinking of himself alone;
   why should the profit fall to him?
9 He may tell you how good your way will
      be,
   and then stand by to watch your
      misfortune.
10 Seek no advice from one who regards
      you with hostility;
    from those who envy you, keep your
      intentions hidden.
11 Speak not to a woman about her rival,
    nor to a coward about war,
    to a merchant about business,
    to a buyer about value,
    to a miser about generosity,
    to a cruel man about mercy,
    to a lazy man about work,
    to a seasonal laborer about the harvest,
    to an idle slave about a great task:
    pay no attention to any advice they give.

12 Instead, associate with a religious man,
    who you are sure keeps the
      commandments;
    Who is like-minded with yourself
    and will feel for you if you fall.
13 Then, too, heed your own heart's counsel;
    for what have you that you can depend
      on more?
14 A man's conscience can tell him his
      situation
    better than seven watchmen in a lofty
      tower.
15 Most important of all, pray to God
    to set your feet in the path of truth.

Wisdom and Temperance

16 A word is the source of every deed;*
    a thought, of every act.[i]
17 The root of all conduct is the mind;
    four branches it shoots forth:
18 Good and evil, death and life,
    their absolute mistress is the tongue.[j]
19 A man may be wise and benefit many,
    yet be of no use to himself.
20 Though a man may be wise, if his words
      are rejected
    he will be deprived of all enjoyment.
21 When a man is wise to his own advantage,
    the fruits of his knowledge are seen in
      his own person;
22 When a man is wise to his people's
      advantage,
    the fruits of his knowledge are
      enduring:[k]
23 Limited are the days of one man's life,
    but the life of Israel is days without
      number.
24 One wise for himself has full enjoyment,
    and all who see him praise him;
25 One wise for his people wins a heritage
      of glory,
    and his name endures forever.[l]

26 My son, while you are well, govern your
      appetite*

37, 16-25: Thoughts determine action. Wisdom is the source of good and life; folly, of evil and death (16ff). If the fruits of a man's wisdom benefit himself, he may be praised in his own lifetime; if they benefit his people, his praise endures after him, in their lives (19-25).

37, 26-30: Temperance and self-control should govern a

man's appetite for food, which is intended not to destroy but to preserve life.

---

h: Sir 6, 7ff.   i: Sir 32, 19.   j: Prv 18, 21.   k: Sir 15, 1ff.   l: Sir 39, 9; 44, 13f.

so that you allow it not what is bad for
you;

27 For not every food is good for everyone,
nor is everything suited to every
taste.*m*

28 Be not drawn after every enjoyment,*n*
neither become a glutton for choice
foods,

29 For sickness comes with overeating,
and gluttony brings on biliousness.

30 Through lack of self-control many have
died,
but the abstemious man prolongs his
life.

See RG
276–79

CHAPTER 38

Sickness and Death

1 Hold the physician in honor, for he is
essential to you,*
and God it was who established his
profession.

2 From God the doctor has his wisdom,
and the king provides for his
sustenance.

3 His knowledge makes the doctor
distinguished,
and gives him access to those in
authority.

4 God makes the earth yield healing
herbs
which the prudent man should not
neglect;

5 Was not the water sweetened by a twig
that men might learn his power?*o*

6 He endows men with the knowledge
to glory in his mighty works,

7 Through which the doctor eases pain
and the druggist prepares his
medicines;

8 Thus God's creative work continues
without cease
in its efficacy on the surface of the
earth.

9 My son, when you are ill, delay not,
but pray to God, who will heal you:*p*

10 Flee wickedness; let your hands be just,
cleanse your heart of every sin;

11 Offer your sweet-smelling oblation and
petition,
a rich offering according to your
means.*q*

12 Then give the doctor his place
lest he leave; for you need him too.

13 There are times that give him an
advantage,

14 and he too beseeches God
That his diagnosis may be correct
and his treatment bring about a cure.

15 He who is a sinner toward his Maker
will be defiant toward the doctor.

16 My son, shed tears for one who is dead*
with wailing and bitter lament;
As is only proper, prepare the body,
absent not yourself from his burial:*r*

17 Weeping bitterly, mourning fully,
pay your tribute of sorrow, as he
deserves,

18 One or two days, to prevent gossip;
then compose yourself after your grief,

19 For grief can bring on an extremity
and heartache destroy one's health.*s*

20 Turn not your thoughts to him again;
cease to recall him; think rather of the
end.*t*

21 Recall him not, for there is no hope of his
return;
it will not help him, but will do you
harm.*u*

22 Remember that his fate will also be
yours;
for him it was yesterday, for you
today.*v*

23 With the departed dead, let memory fade;
rally your courage, once the soul has
left.

38, 1-15: The profession of medicine comes from God,
who makes the earth yield healing herbs and gives the physician knowledge of their virtue (1-8). In illness the sick man
should cleanse his soul from sin and petition God for help
through an offering of sacrifice; the physician, too, does well
to invoke God that he may understand the illness and apply
the proper remedy (9-14). The sinner, in contrast, defies both
his Maker and the doctor (15).

38, 16-23: A period of mourning for the deceased and care

for their burial is becoming (16ff). But grief should not be excessive, for it neither helps the dead, who cannot return, nor
fails to harm the living. The mourner's own end will quickly
follow, and the time to prepare for it is now (19-23).

---

m: 1 Cor 6, 12; 10, 23.   *n:* 28f: Sir 31, 13. 16ff.   *o:* Ex 15, 25.
p: Is 38, 2f.   *q:* Lv 2, 1ff.   *r:* Sir 22, 9f.   *s:* Prv 12, 25; 15, 13;
17, 22.   *t:* Sir 7, 36; 18, 24; 30, 21.   *u:* 2 Sm 12, 23; Wis 2, 1.
v: Jas 4, 13ff.

Vocations of the Craftsman and the Scribe*

24 The scribe's profession increases his
  wisdom;
    whoever is free from toil can become a
    wise man.
25 How can he become learned who guides
  the plow,
    who thrills in wielding the goad like a
    lance,
  Who guides the ox and urges on the
  bullock,
    and whose every concern is for cattle?
26 His care is for plowing furrows,
    and he keeps a watch on the beasts in
    the stalls.

27 So with every engraver and designer
  who, laboring night and day,
  Fashions carved seals,
    and whose concern is to vary the
    pattern.
  His care is to produce a vivid impression,
    and he keeps watch till he finishes his
    design.

28 So with the smith standing near his anvil,
  forging crude iron.
  The heat from the fire sears his flesh,
    yet he toils away in the furnace heat.
  The clang of the hammer deafens his
    ears,
    his eyes are fixed on the tool he is
    shaping.
  His care is to finish his work,
    and he keeps watch till he perfects it in
    detail.

29 So with the potter sitting at his labor
  revolving the wheel with his feet.
  He is always concerned for his products,
    and turns them out in quantity.
30 With his hands he molds the clay,
    and with his feet softens it.
  His care is for proper coloring,
    and he keeps watch on the fire of his
    kiln.

31 All these men are skilled with their
  hands,
    each one an expert at his own task;
32 Without them no city could be lived in,
    and wherever they stay, they need not
    hunger.
33 They do not occupy the judge's bench,
    nor are they prominent in the
    assembly;
  They set forth no decisions or judgments,
    nor are they found among the rulers;
34 Yet they maintain God's ancient
    handiwork,
    and their concern is for exercise of
    their skill.

CHAPTER 39

See RG
276–79

1 How different the man who
    devotes himself
  to the study of the law of the Most
    High!
  He explores the wisdom of the men of old
    and occupies himself with the
    prophecies;
2 He treasures the discourses of famous
    men,
    and goes to the heart of involved
    sayings;
3 He studies obscure parables,
    and is busied with the hidden
    meanings of the sages.
4 He is in attendance on the great,
    and has entrance to the ruler.
5 He travels among the peoples of foreign
    lands
    to learn what is good and evil among
    men.
6 His care is to seek the LORD, his Maker,
    to petition the Most High,
  To open his lips in prayer,
    to ask pardon for his sins.
  Then, if it pleases the LORD Almighty,
    he will be filled with the spirit of
    understanding;
  He will pour forth his words of wisdom
    and in prayer give thanks to the LORD,

38, 24—39, 11: More excellent than the useful service of craftsmen—farmer, engraver, smith, potter (25-34)—is the profession of the scribe (24), who studies and meditates on the law of the Most High, seeks him in prayer of thanksgiving, petition and repentance for sin (39, 1. 6f), explores the wisdom of the past and present, travels abroad to observe the conduct of many peoples, and attends rulers and great men. Through the spirit of understanding granted by God, he will show forth his wisdom to the glory of God's law, gaining renown for generations to come (2-5. 8-11).

7 Who will direct his knowledge and his
counsel,
as he meditates upon his mysteries.
8 He will show the wisdom of what he has
learned
and glory in the law of the LORD's
covenant.
9 Many will praise his understanding;
his fame can never be effaced;
Unfading will be his memory,
through all generations his name will
live;[w]
10 Peoples will speak of his wisdom,
and in assembly sing his praises.
11 While he lives he is one out of a thousand,
and when he dies his renown will not
cease.

Praise of God the Creator*

12 Once more I will set forth my theme
to shine like the moon in its fullness!
13 Listen, my faithful children: open up
your petals,
like roses planted near running waters;
14 Send up the sweet odor of incense,
break forth in blossoms like the lily.
Send up the sweet odor of your hymn of
praise;
bless the LORD for all he has done!
15 Proclaim the greatness of his name,
loudly sing his praises,
With music on the harp and all stringed
instruments;
sing out with joy as you proclaim:

16 The works of God are all of them good;
in its own time every need is supplied.[x]
17 At his word the waters become still as in
a flask;
he had but to speak and the reservoirs
were made.[y]
18 He has but to command and his will is
done;
nothing can limit his achievement.

19 The works of all mankind are present to
him;
not a thing escapes his eye.[z]
20 His gaze spans all the ages;
to him there is nothing unexpected.
21 No cause then to say: "What is the
purpose of this?"
Everything is chosen to satisfy a need.
22 His blessing overflows like the Nile;
like the Euphrates it enriches the
surface of the earth.
23 Again, his wrath expels the nations
and turns fertile land into a salt
marsh.[a]
24 For the virtuous his paths are level,
to the haughty they are steep;
25 Good things for the good he provided
from the beginning,
but for the wicked good things and
bad.
26 Chief of all needs for human life
are water and fire, iron and salt,
The heart of the wheat, milk and honey,
the blood of the grape, and oil, and
cloth;[b]
27 For the good all these are good,
but for the wicked they turn out evil.
28 There are storm winds created to punish,
which in their fury can dislodge
mountains;
When destruction must be, they hurl all
their force
and appease the anger of their Maker.
29 In his treasury also, kept for the proper
time,
are fire and hail, famine, disease,
30 Ravenous beasts, scorpions, vipers,
and the avenging sword to exterminate
the wicked;
31 In doing his bidding they rejoice,
in their assignments they disobey not
his command.
32 So from the first I took my stand,
and wrote down as my theme:

39, 12-35: The sage invites his disciples to join him in
joyfully proclaiming his favorite theme: The works of God
are all of them good; in its own time every need is supplied
(12-16. 32-35). He describes God's omniscience, supreme
power and wisdom, whereby all created things, good in
themselves, are ever present to him, obey him, and fulfill
their intended purpose (17-21), bringing blessing to the virtuous, but evil and punishment to the wicked who misuse
them (22-31). Cf similar hymns of praise, Sir 36, 1-17; 42,
15—43, 35.

w: Sir 37, 25; 44, 14.   *x:* Gn 1, 31; Eccl 3, 11.   *y:* Gn 1, 6-10; Ex
14, 21f; Jos 3, 16.   *z:* Sir 15, 19; 42, 20.   *a:* Jos 1, 2-6.   *b:* Sir
29, 21.

³³ The works of God are all of them good;
   every need when it comes he fills.^c
³⁴ No cause then to say: "This is not as
      good as that";
   for each shows its worth at the proper
      time.
³⁵ So now with full joy of heart proclaim
   and bless the name of the Holy One.

See RG
276-79

CHAPTER 40

Joys and Miseries of Life

¹ A great anxiety has God allotted,*
   and a heavy yoke, to the sons of men;^d
From the day one leaves his mother's
      womb
   to the day he returns to the mother of
      all the living,*
² His thoughts, the fear in his heart,
   and his troubled forebodings till the
      day he dies—
³ Whether he sits on a lofty throne
   or grovels in dust and ashes,
⁴ Whether he bears a splendid crown
   or is wrapped in the coarsest of
      cloaks—
⁵ Are of wrath and envy, trouble and
      dread,
   terror of death, fury and strife.
Even when he lies on his bed to rest,
   his cares at night disturb his sleep.
⁶ So short is his rest it seems like none,
   till in his dreams he struggles as he did
      by day,
Terrified by what his mind's eye sees,
   like a fugitive being pursued;
⁷ As he reaches safety, he wakes up
   astonished that there was nothing to
      fear.
⁸ So it is with all flesh, with man and with
      beast,
   but for sinners seven times more.

⁹ Plague and bloodshed, wrath and the
      sword,
   plunder and ruin, famine and death:^e
¹⁰ For the wicked, these were created evil,
   and it is they who bring on
      destruction.

¹¹ All that is of earth returns to earth,
   and what is from above returns above.*
¹² All that comes from bribes or injustice
   will be wiped out,
   but loyalty remains for ages.
¹³ Wealth out of wickedness is like a wadi
      in spate:
   like a mighty stream with lightning
      and thunder,
¹⁴ Which, in its rising, rolls along the
      stones,
   but suddenly, once and for all, comes
      to an end.^f
¹⁵ The offshoot of violence will not
      flourish,
   for the root of the godless is on sheer
      rock;
¹⁶ Or they are like reeds on the riverbank,
   withered before all other plants.
¹⁷ But goodness will never be cut off,
   and justice endures forever.

Wealth or wages can make life sweet,*
   but better than either is finding a
      treasure.
¹⁸ A child or a city will preserve one's
      name,
   but better than either, attaining
      wisdom.^g
¹⁹ Sheepfolds and orchards bring
      flourishing health;
   but better than either, a devoted wife;
²⁰ Wine and music delight the soul,
   but better than either, conjugal love.^h

40, 1-16: The former idyllic description of the universe is contrasted with the picture of the evils afflicting humanity. Every man, high or low, is burdened from birth to death with fears, anxieties and troubles, by day and often by night, the time appointed for rest (1-7). For sinners, the suffering is much greater (8ff). What they gained by violence and injustice is quickly destroyed; but justice endures forever (14ff).

40, 1: Mother of all the living: the earth from which man was taken. Cf Gn 2, 7; 3, 19f; Jb 1, 21; Ps 139, 15.

40, 11: All that is of earth . . . returns above: a reference to bodily mortality and to the divine origin of life from the Spirit

of God. Cf Sir 41, 10; Gn 2, 7; 3, 19; Jb 34, 14f; Pss 104, 29f; 146, 4; Eccl 12, 7. The Greek and the Latin render the second half of the verse: "all waters shall return to the sea."

40, 17-27: Of the many treasures making life sweet, such as health, children, friends, music, vigor, the best are called true conjugal love, wisdom, and above all, fear of God; cf Sir 25, 6-11.

c: Sir 39, 16; Gn 1, 31; Eccl 3, 11.   *d:* Gn 3, 17; Jb 7, 1; 14, 1; Eccl 2, 23.   *e:* Sir 39, 28ff.   *f:* Sir 23, 25; Wis 4, 3ff.   *g:* Prv 19, 14.   *h:* Ps 104, 15.

21 The flute and the harp offer sweet
  melody,
  but better than either, a voice that is
    true.
22 Charm and beauty delight the eye,
  but better than either, the flowers of
    the field.*i*
23 A friend, a neighbor, are timely guides,
  but better than either, a prudent wife.
24 A brother, a helper, for times of stress;
  but better than either, charity that
    rescues.
25 Gold and silver make one's way secure,
  but better than either, sound judgment.
26 Wealth and vigor build up confidence,
  but better than either, fear of God.
  Fear of the LORD leaves nothing wanting;
  he who has it need seek no other
    support:
27 The fear of God is a paradise of
    blessings;
  its canopy, all that is glorious.*j*

28 My son, live not the life of a beggar,*
  better to die than to beg;
29 When one has to look to another's table,
  his life is not really a life.
  His neighbor's delicacies bring revulsion
    of spirit
  to one who understands inward
    feelings:*k*
30 In the mouth of the shameless man
    begging is sweet,
  but within him it burns like fire.

**See RG
276-79**

CHAPTER 41

1 O death! how bitter the thought of
    you*
  for the man at peace amid his
    possessions,
  For the man unruffled and always
    successful,
  who still can enjoy life's pleasures.
2 O death! how welcome your sentence

to the weak man of failing strength,
Tottering and always rebuffed,
  with no more sight, with vanished
    hope.*l*
3 Fear not death's decree for you;
  remember, it embraces those before
    you, and those after.*m*
4 Thus God has ordained for all flesh;
  why then should you reject the will of
    the Most High?
  Whether one has lived a thousand years,
    a hundred, or ten,
  in the nether world he has no claim on
    life.

5 A reprobate line are the children of
    sinners,*n*
  and witless offspring are in the homes
    of the wicked.
6 Their dominion is lost to sinners'
    children,
  and reproach abides with their
    descendants.
7 Children curse their wicked father,
  for they suffer disgrace through him.
8 Woe to you, O sinful men,
  who forsake the law of the Most High.
9 If you have children, calamity will seize
    them;
  you will beget them only for groaning.
  When you stumble, there is lasting joy;
  at death, you become a curse.
10 Whatever is of nought returns to nought,
  so too the godless from void to void.*o*
11 Man's body is a fleeting thing,
  but a virtuous name will never be
    annihilated.*p*
12 Have a care for your name, for it will
    stand by you
  better than precious treasures in the
    thousands;*q*
13 The boon of life is for limited days,
  but a good name, for days without
    number.*

40, 28ff: Among the Jews, beggary was considered degrading to human dignity; it was agreeable only to the shameless, who had lost their sense of honor. Cf Sir 29, 22f.

41, 1-13: Whether death seems bitter to one who enjoys peace, success and pleasure, or welcome to one who is weak and in despair, it comes to all and must be accepted as the will of God (1-4). As the human body passes away (11), so do those who have sinned through the body and their offspring

alike, who, needy and accursed, pass on with their parents as if they had never been (5-10). Only the good name of the virtuous endures (11ff).

41, 13: After this verse many texts repeat Sir 20, 29f.

i: Mt 6, 28f. *j*: Is 4, 5. *k*: Sir 29, 24. *l*: Sir 30, 17. *m*: Sir 38,
20ff. *n*: 5ff: Sir 3, 9ff; Wis 3, 16-19. *o*: Sir 40, 11; Wis 4, 19.
p: Prv 10, 7. *q*: Prv 22, 1; Eccl 7, 1.

True and False Shame*

14 My children, heed my instruction about
    shame;
    judge of disgrace only according to my
    rules,
    For it is not always well to be ashamed,
    nor is it always the proper thing to
    blush:
15 Before father and mother be ashamed of
    immorality,
    before master and mistress, of
    falsehood;
16 Before prince and ruler, of flattery;
    before the public assembly, of crime;
17 Before friend and companion, of
    disloyalty,
    and of breaking an oath or agreement.
18 Be ashamed of theft from the people
    where you settle,
    and of stretching out your elbow when
    you dine;
19 Of refusing to give when asked,
    of defrauding another of his appointed
    share,
20 Of failing to return a greeting,
    and of rebuffing a friend;
21 Of gazing at a married woman,
    and of entertaining thoughts about
    another's wife;ʳ
    Of trifling with a servant girl you have,
    and of violating her couch;
22 Of using harsh words with friends,
    and of following up your gifts with
    insults;ˢ
23 Of repeating what you hear,
    and of betraying secrets—ᵗ
24 These are the things you should rightly
    avoid as shameful
    if you would be looked upon by
    everyone with favor.

CHAPTER 42

See RG
276-79

1 But of these things be not ashamed,
    lest you sin through human respect:ᵘ
2 Of the law of the Most High and his
    precepts,
    or of the sentence to be passed upon
    the sinful;
3 Of sharing the expenses of a business or
    a journey,
    or of dividing an inheritance or
    property;
4 Of accuracy of scales and balances,
    or of tested measures and weights;ᵛ
5 Of acquiring much or little,
    or of bargaining in dealing with a
    merchant;
    Of constant training of children,
    or of beating the sides of a disloyal
    servant;ʷ
6 Of a seal to keep an erring wife at home,
    or of a lock placed where there are
    many hands;
7 Of numbering every deposit,
    or of recording all that is given or
    received;
8 Of chastisement of the silly and the
    foolish,
    or of the aged and infirm answering
    for wanton conduct.
    Thus you will be truly cautious
    and recognized by all men as discreet.

A Father's Care for His Daughter*

9 A daughter is a treasure that keeps her
    father wakeful,
    and worry over her drives away rest:ˣ
    Lest she pass her prime unmarried,
    or when she is married, lest she be
    disliked;
10 While unmarried, lest she be seduced,
    or, as a wife, lest she prove
    unfaithful;
    Lest she conceive in her father's home,
    or be sterile in that of her husband.
11 Keep a close watch on your daughter,
    lest she make you the sport of your
    enemies,

41, 14—42, 8: The author illustrates the subject of true
and false shame with numerous and detailed examples of sin
(14-24) and virtue (42, 1-8), following the norm of the commandments.
  42, 9-14: The author considers a daughter to be a source
of anxiety to her father, lest she fail to marry, or be seduced,
or lest, marrying, she be disliked, prove unfaithful, or find

herself sterile (9f). He is advised to keep a close watch on her
at home, and on her companionship while abroad, lest he suffer on her account among the people (11-14).

r: Sir 9, 8; Mt 5, 28. s: Sir 18, 14; 20, 13. t: Sir 27, 16. u: Prv
24, 23; Jas 2, 1. v: Prv 11, 1. w: Sir 30, 1-13; 33, 25-33.
x: Sir 7, 24f.

A byword in the city, a reproach among
the people,
an object of derision in public
gatherings.
See that there is no lattice in her room,
no place that overlooks the approaches
to the house.*y*

12 Let her not parade her charms before
men,*z*
or spend her time with married
women;

13 For just as moths come from garments,
so harm to women comes from
women:

14 Better a man's harshness than a woman's
indulgence,
and a frightened daughter than any
disgrace.

The Works of God in Nature*

15 Now will I recall God's works;
what I have seen, I will describe.
At God's word were his works brought
into being;
they do his will as he has ordained for
them.*a*

16 As the rising sun is clear to all,
so the glory of the LORD fills all his
works;

17 Yet even God's holy ones must fail
in recounting the wonders of the
LORD,
Though God has given these, his hosts,
the strength
to stand firm before his glory.

18 He plumbs the depths and penetrates the
heart;
their innermost being he understands.
The Most High possesses all knowledge,
and sees from of old the things that are
to come:

19 He makes known the past and the future,
and reveals the deepest secrets.

20 No understanding does he lack;
no single thing escapes him.*b*

21 Perennial is his almighty wisdom;
he is from all eternity one and the
same,

22 With nothing added, nothing taken away;
no need of a counselor for him!*c*

23 How beautiful are all his works!
even to the spark and fleeting vision!

24 The universe lives and abides forever;
to meet each need, each creature is
preserved.

25 All of them differ, one from another,
yet none of them has he made in vain,
For each in turn, as it comes, is good;
can one ever see enough of their
splendor?*d*

CHAPTER 43

See RG 276-79

1 The clear vault of the sky shines
forth*e*
like heaven itself, a vision of glory.

2 The orb of the sun, resplendent at its
rising:
what a wonderful work of the Most
High!

3 At noon it seethes the surface of the
earth,
and who can bear its fiery heat?

4 Like a blazing furnace of solid metal,
it sets the mountains aflame with its
rays;
By its fiery darts the land is consumed;
the eyes are dazzled by its light.

5 Great indeed is the LORD who made it,
at whose orders it urges on its steeds.

6 The moon, too, that marks the changing
times,
governing the seasons, their lasting
sign,*f*

7 By which we know the feast days and
fixed dates,
this light-giver which wanes in its
course:

8 As its name says, each month it renews
itself;
how wondrous in this change!

42, 15—43, 35: These verses comprise a new section. In them the author contemplates God's power, beauty and goodness as manifested in the mighty work of creating and preserving the universe (42, 15ff. 23. 25; 43, 1-27), his omniscience (42, 18ff), his perfect wisdom (21f), his eternity (24). The conclusion is a fervent hymn of praise (43, 28-35). Cf Sir 16, 22—18, 13.

y: Sir 26, 10. *z:* 12f: Sir 9, 1-9. *a:* Ps 77, 12f. *b:* Sir 39, 19; Wis 1, 6-10. *c:* Is 40, 13; Rom 11, 34. *d:* Sir 33, 15. *e:* 1ff: Ps 19, 2f. *f:* Lv 23, 5; Nm 28, 11-14; Ps 81, 4.

9 The beauty, the glory, of the heavens are
the stars
that adorn with their sparkling the
Heights of God,[g]

10 At whose command they keep their place
and never relax in their vigils.
A weapon against the flood waters stored
on high,
lighting up the firmament by its
brilliance,

11 Behold the rainbow! Then bless its Maker,
for majestic indeed is its splendor;[h]

12 It spans the heavens with its glory,
this bow bent by the mighty hand of
God.

13 His rebuke marks out the path for the
lightning,
and speeds the arrows of his judgment
to their goal.

14 At it the storehouse is opened,
and like vultures the clouds hurry forth.

15 In his majesty he gives the storm its
power
and breaks off the hailstones.

16 The thunder of his voice makes the earth
writhe;
before his might the mountains quake.

17 A word from him drives on the south
wind,
the angry north wind, the hurricane
and the storm.

18 He sprinkles the snow like fluttering
birds;
it comes to settle like swarms of
locusts.

19 Its shining whiteness blinds the eyes,
the mind is baffled by its steady fall.

20 He scatters frost like so much salt;
it shines like blossoms on the
thornbush.

21 Cold northern blasts he sends
that turn the ponds to lumps of ice.
He freezes over every body of water,
and clothes each pool with a coat of
mail.

22 When the mountain growth is scorched
with heat,
and the flowering plains as though by
flames,

23 The dripping clouds restore them all,
and the scattered dew enriches the
parched land.

24 His is the plan that calms the deep,
and plants the islands in the sea.

25 Those who go down to the sea tell part of
its story,
and when we hear them we are
thunderstruck;[i]

26 In it are his creatures, stupendous,
amazing,
all kinds of life, and the monsters of
the deep.

27 For him each messenger succeeds,
and at his bidding accomplishes his
will.[j]

28 More than this we need not add;
let the last word be, he is all in all!*

29 Let us praise him the more, since we
cannot fathom him,
for greater is he than all his works;

30 Awful indeed is the LORD's majesty,
and wonderful is his power.

31 Lift up your voices to glorify the LORD,
though he is still beyond your power
to praise;

32 Extol him with renewed strength,
and weary not, though you cannot
reach the end:

33 For who can see him and describe him?
or who can praise him as he is?[k]

34 Beyond these, many things lie hid;
only a few of his works have we seen.

35 It is the LORD who has made all things,
and to those who fear him he gives
wisdom.[l]

CHAPTER 44

Praise of Israel's Great Ancestors

1 Now will I praise those godly men,*
our ancestors, each in his own time:*

See RG
276–79

43, 28: All in all: the perfections reflected in creation are
found in a transcendent way in God, who alone is their
source.

44, 1—50, 24: As in the previous section God's wisdom
shone forth in the works of nature, so in these chapters it is
also revealed through the history of God's people as seen in
the lives of their patriarchs, prophets, priests and rulers. The

g: Ps 8, 4.   h: Gn 9, 13.   i: Ps 104, 25-30.   j: Ps 33, 6.   k: Ps
106, 2.   l: Jb 28, 28.

2 The abounding glory of the Most High's
   portion,
   his own part, since the days of old.
   Subduers of the land in kingly fashion,
   men of renown for their might,*m*
3 Or counselors in their prudence,
   or seers of all things in prophecy;*n*
4 Resolute princes of the folk,
   and governors with their staves;
   Authors skilled in composition,
   and forgers of epigrams with their
   spikes;
5 Composers of melodious psalms,
   or discoursers on lyric themes;
6 Stalwart men, solidly established
   and at peace in their own estates—
7 All these were glorious in their time,
   each illustrious in his day.
8 Some of them have left behind a name
   and men recount their praiseworthy
   deeds;
9 But of others there is no memory,
   for when they ceased, they ceased.
   And they are as though they had not
   lived,
   they and their children after them.
10 Yet these also were godly men
   whose virtues have not been forgotten;
11 Their wealth remains in their families,
   their heritage with their descendants;
12 Through God's covenant with them their
   family endures,
   their posterity for their sake.
13 And for all time their progeny will
   endure,
   their glory will never be blotted out;
14 Their bodies are peacefully laid away,
   but their name lives on and on.*o*
15 At gatherings their wisdom is retold,
   and the assembly proclaims their praise.

The Early Patriarchs

16 [ENOCH* walked with the LORD and was
   taken up,*p*
   that succeeding generations might
   learn by his example.]
17 NOAH, found just and perfect,
   renewed the race in the time of
   devastation.*q*
   Because of his worth there were
   survivors,
   and with a sign to him the deluge
   ended;
18 A lasting agreement was made with him,
   that never should all flesh be
   destroyed.
19 ABRAHAM, father of many peoples,
   kept his glory without stain:*r*
20 He observed the precepts of the Most
   High,
   and entered into an agreement with
   him;
   In his own flesh he incised the
   ordinance,*
   and when tested he was found loyal.*s*
21 For this reason, God promised him with
   an oath
   that in his descendants the nations
   would be blessed,
   That he would make him numerous as
   the grains of dust,
   and exalt his posterity like the stars;
   That he would give them an inheritance
   from sea to sea,
   and from the River* to the ends of the
   earth.
22 And for ISAAC he renewed the same
   promise
   because of Abraham, his father.
   The covenant with all his forebears was
   confirmed,

example of these great men, whose virtues are here recalled,
constitutes a high point of the author's teaching and illustrates
his belief in the canonical Scriptures.

44, 1-15: The reader is here introduced to those men of Israel, later mentioned by name, who through various achievements and beneficial social activities have acquired great
renown (1-8. 14f); and also to those who, though forgotten,
endure through the fruit of their virtues and through their
families because of God's covenant with them (9-13).

44, 16: Enoch: because of his friendship with God and
also by reason of his unusual disappearance from the earth,
this prophet's renown was great among the chosen people,

particularly in the two centuries just before the coming of
Christ; cf Gn 5, 21-24; Heb 11, 5. The present verse is an expansion of the original text; cf Sir 49, 14.

44, 20: In his own flesh . . . ordinance: the covenant of circumcision; cf Gn 17, 10-14. And when tested . . . loyal: Abraham's willingness to sacrifice his son Isaac at the Lord's command; cf Gn 22, 9-12.

44, 21: The River: the Euphrates; cf Gn 2, 14.

m: Dt 32, 8f. *n:* Sir 39, 1. *o:* Wis 3, 3. *p:* Sir 49, 14; Gn 5, 18-
24; Heb 11, 5. *q:* Gn 6, 8—9, 29; Heb 11, 7. *r:* Gn 12, 1—25,
10; Gal 3, 6; Heb 11, 8-19. *s:* Gn 17, 10; 22, 1.

and the blessing rested upon the head
   of JACOB.[t]
23 God acknowledged him as the firstborn,
   and gave him his inheritance.
He fixed the boundaries for his tribes,
   and their division into twelve.

See RG
276-79

CHAPTER 45

Praise of Moses, Aaron and Phinehas

1 From him was to spring the man[*]
   who won the favor of all:[u]
Dear to God and men,
   MOSES, whose memory is held in
      benediction.
2 God's honor[v] devolved upon him,[*]
   and the Lord strengthened him with
      fearful powers;[w]
3 God wrought swift miracles at his words
   and sustained him in the king's
      presence.
He gave him the commandments for his
   people,
   and revealed to him his glory.[x]
4 For his trustworthiness and meekness
   God selected him from all mankind;[y]
5 He permitted him to hear his voice,
   and led him into the cloud,
Where, face to face,[*] he gave him the
   commandments,
   the law of life and understanding,
That he might teach his precepts to Jacob,
   his judgments and decrees to Israel.

6 He raised up also, like Moses in
   holiness,[*]
   his brother AARON, of the tribe of
      Levi.[z]

7 He made him perpetual in his office
   when he bestowed on him the
      priesthood[*] of his people;
He established him in honor
   and crowned him with lofty majesty;
8 He clothed him with splendid apparel,
   and adorned him with the glorious
      vestments:
Breeches and tunic and robe
   with pomegranates around the hem,
9 And a rustle of bells round about,
   through whose pleasing sound at each
      step
He would be heard within the sanctuary,
   and the children of his race would be
      remembered;
10 The sacred vestments of gold, of violet,
   and of crimson, wrought with
      embroidery;
The breastpiece for decision, the ephod
   and cincture
11 with scarlet yarn, the work of the
   weaver;
Precious stones with seal engravings
   in golden settings, the work of the
      jeweler,
To commemorate in incised letters
   each of the tribes of Israel;
12 On his turban the diadem of gold,
   its plate wrought with the insignia of
      holiness,
Majestic, glorious, renowned for
   splendor,
   a delight to the eyes, beauty supreme.
13 Before him, no one was adorned with
   these,
   nor may they ever be worn by any
Except his sons and them alone,

45, 1-5: Moses manifested God's power through miracles (1ff), God's authority through the promulgation of the commandments and the law (5), and God's mercy through the intimacy granted him by the Lord for his own faithfulness and meekness (4f). The very personification of the old covenant, Moses was also a type of Christ, the Prophet and Legislator of the new; cf Dt 18, 15.

45, 2: God's honor devolved upon him: Moses was actually God's substitute in dealing with Pharaoh, hence God entrusted his own honor to Moses.

45, 5: Face to face: on God's intimacy with Moses, see Ex 33, 11; Nm 12, 8. St. Paul alluded to this in 1 Cor 13, 12.

45, 6-21: The author here expresses his reverence and esteem for the priesthood of the old covenant. He recalls God's choice of Aaron and his sons for this sublime office (6f), and

describes in detail the beauty of the high priest's vestments (8-13). He relates the ordination of Aaron at the hands of Moses, his brother (15), and describes the priestly functions, of offering sacrifice to God (16), and of blessing (15), teaching, governing and judging the people (17); the inheritance of the high priest (20ff); the punishment of those families who were jealous of Aaron (18f); and the confirmation of the covenant of the priesthood with Aaron's descendants through Phinehas (23ff).

45, 7: The priesthood of Aaron was superseded by the priesthood of Christ; cf Heb 7, 18-28.

---

t: Gn 26, 3. 5. 24; 27, 28f; 28, 14.   *u:* Ex 2, 2; 11, 3; 33, 11; Nm 12, 7.   *v:* Ex 7, 1—13, 22.   *w:* 2-5: Ex 7—Dt 34.   *x:* Ex 4, 17; 7, 1.   *y:* Nm 12, 3. 7.   *z:* 6ff: Ex 28f; Wis 18, 24.

generation after generation, for all
time.

¹⁴ His cereal offering is wholly burnt
with the established sacrifice twice
each day;

¹⁵ For Moses ordained him
and anointed him with the holy oil,
In a lasting covenant with him
and with his family, as permanent as
the heavens,
That he should serve God in his
priesthood
and bless his people in his name.

¹⁶ He chose him from all mankind
to offer holocausts and choice
offerings,
To burn sacrifices of sweet odor for a
memorial,
and to atone for the people of Israel.

¹⁷ He gave to him his laws,
and authority to prescribe and to
judge:
To teach the precepts to his people,
and the ritual to the descendants of
Israel.

¹⁸ Men of other families were inflamed
against him,
were jealous of him in the desert,
The followers of Dathan and Abiram,
and the band of Korah in their
defiance.ᵃ

¹⁹ But the LORD saw this and became angry,
he destroyed them in his burning wrath.
He brought down upon them a miracle,
and consumed them with his flaming
fire.

²⁰ Then he increased the glory of Aaronᵇ
and bestowed upon him his
inheritance:
The sacred offerings he allotted to him,
with the showbread as his portion;

²¹ The oblations of the LORD are his food,
a gift to him and his descendants.

²² But he holds no land among the people
nor shares with them their heritage;

For the LORD himself is his portion,
his inheritance in the midst of Israel.

²³ PHINEHAS too, the son of Eleazar,
was the courageous third of his line
When, zealous for the God of all,
he met the crisis of his people ᶜ
And, at the prompting of his noble heart,
atoned for the children of Israel.

²⁴ Therefore on him again God conferred
the right,
in a covenant of friendship, to provide
for the sanctuary,
So that he and his descendants
should possess the high priesthood
forever.

²⁵ For even his covenant with David,
the son of Jesse of the tribe of Judah,
Was an individual heritage through one
son alone;
but the heritage of Aaron is for all his
descendants.ᵈ

²⁶ And now bless the LORD
who has crowned you with glory!
May he grant you wisdom of heart
to govern his people in justice,
Lest their welfare should ever be forgotten,
or your authority, throughout all time.

CHAPTER 46
Joshua, Caleb and the Judges

See RG 276-79

¹ Valiant leader was JOSHUA, son of Nun*
assistant to Moses in the prophetic
office,
Formed to be, as his name implies,
the great savior of God's chosen ones,
To punish the enemy
and to win the inheritance for Israel.ᵉ

² What glory was his when he raised his
arm,
to brandish his javelin against
the city!ᶠ

³ And who could withstand him
when he fought the battles of the LORD?*

46, 1-6: Joshua: whose name means "the LORD is savior" (1), was the instrument through which God delivered his people in miraculous ways (2-6) by destroying their enemies, whose land he gave to the Israelites as an inheritance (1).
46, 3: The battles of the LORD: cf Jos 6—10.

---

a: Nm 16, 1ff.   b: 20f: Nm 18, 11-21; Dt 10, 9.   c: Nm 25, 7-13; Ps 106, 30f; 1 Mc 2, 26. 54.   d: 2 Sm 7, 12-16.   e: Ex 17, 9; Nm 27, 18; Dt 34, 9; Jos 1, 1-4.   f: Jos 8, 18.

⁴ Did he not by his power stop the sun,
    so that one day became two?ᵍ
⁵ He called upon the Most High God
    when his enemies beset him on all
      sides,
And God Most High gave answer to him
    in hailstones of tremendous power,
⁶ Which he rained down upon the hostile
      army
    till on the slope he destroyed the foe;
That all the doomed nations might know
    that the LORD was watching over his
      people's battles.
And because he was a devoted follower
    of God
⁷   and in Moses' lifetime showed himself
      loyal,
He and CALEB,* son of Jephunneh,
    when they opposed the rebel assembly,
Averted God's anger from the people
    and suppressed the wicked
      complaint—ʰ
⁸ Because of this, they were the only two
      spared
    from the six hundred thousand
      infantry,
To lead the people into their
      inheritance,
    the land flowing with milk and
      honey.ⁱ
⁹ And the strength he gave to Caleb
    remained with him even in his old age
Till he won his way onto the summits of
      the land;
    his family too received an inheritance,ʲ
¹⁰ That all the people of Jacob might know
    how good it is to be a devoted follower
      of the LORD.
¹¹ The JUDGES,* too, each one of them,
    whose hearts were not deceived,
Who did not abandon God:
    may their memory be ever blessed,ᵏ

¹² Their bones return to life from their
      resting place,
    and their names receive fresh luster in
      their children!
¹³ Beloved of his people, dear to his Maker,
    dedicated from his mother's womb,
Consecrated to the LORD as a prophet,
    was SAMUEL, the judge and priest.
At God's word he established the
      kingdom
    and anointed princes to rule the
      people.ˡ
¹⁴ By the law of the LORD he judged the
      nation,
    when he visited the encampments of
      Jacob.
¹⁵ As a trustworthy prophet he was sought
      out
    and his words proved him true as a
      seer.
¹⁶ He, too, called upon God,
    and offered him a suckling lamb;ᵐ
¹⁷ Then the LORD thundered forth from
      heaven,
    and the tremendous roar of his voice
      was heard.ⁿ
¹⁸ He brought low the rulers of the enemy
    and destroyed all the lords of the
      Philistines.
¹⁹ When Samuel approached the end of his
      life,
    he testified before the LORD and his
      anointed prince,
"No bribe or secret gift have I taken from
      any man!"
    and no one dared gainsay him.ᵒ
²⁰ Even when he lay buried, his guidance
      was sought;
    he made known to the king his fate,
And from the grave he raised his voice
    as a prophet, to put an end to
      wickedness.ᵖ

46, 7-10: Caleb, who with Joshua advised Moses and the people in the desert to conquer Canaan, despite the counsel of their companion scouts and the rebellion of the people, merited to lead the Israelites of the succeeding generation into the Promised Land. Caleb in his old age received as his inheritance a portion of land which he himself had previously conquered; cf Jos 15, 13f.

46, 11-20: Of the Judges praised and blessed for their fidelity to God in opposing idolatry, Samuel, a man of spotless integrity, was the greatest (11f. 19). He was judge of the en-tire nation, and was also a prophet and priest who through his sacrificial offering obtained victory over the Philistines. He established the kingdom, anointed kings (13-18), and even after his death foretold the king's fate and put an end to wickedness (20).

g: Jos 10, 13.   *h:* Nm 13, 30; 14, 6.   *i:* Nm 14, 22-38.   *j:* Jos 14, 6; 15, 13.   *k:* Jgs 1, 1—16, 31.   *l:* 1 Sm 1, 10ff; 8, 4ff; 10, 1; 16, 13.   *m:* 1 Sm 7, 9.   *n:* Sir 12, 18.   *o:* 1 Sm 12, 3.   *p:* 1 Sm 28, 14.

See RG
276–79

CHAPTER 47

Nathan, David and Solomon

¹ After him came NATHAN*
    who served in the presence of David.�q
² Like the choice fat of the sacred
    offerings,
    so was DAVID in Israel.ʳ
³ He made sport of lions as though they
    were kids,
    and of bears, like lambs of the flock.ˢ
⁴ As a youth he slew the giant
    and wiped out the people's disgrace,
When his hand let fly the slingstone
    that crushed the pride of Goliath.ᵗ
⁵ Since he called upon the Most High God,
    who gave strength to his right arm
To defeat the skilled warrior
    and raise up the might of his people,
⁶ Therefore the women sang his praises
    and ascribed to him tens of thousands.
When he assumed the royal crown, he
    battledᵘ
⁷   and subdued the enemy on every side.
He destroyed the hostile Philistines
    and shattered their power till our own
    day.ᵛ
⁸ With his every deed he offered thanks
    to God Most High, in words of praise.
With his whole being he loved his
    Maker
    and daily had his praises sung;
⁹ He added beauty to the feasts
    and solemnized the seasons of each
    year
With string music before the altar,
    providing sweet melody for the
    psalmsʷ
¹⁰ So that when the Holy Name was praised,

before daybreak the sanctuary would
    resound.
¹¹ The LORD forgave him his sins
    and exalted his strength forever;
He conferred on him the rights of royalty
    and established his throne in Israel.ˣ

¹² Because of his merits he had as his
    successor*
    a wise son, who lived in security:ʸ
¹³ SOLOMON reigned during an era of peace,
    for God made tranquil all his borders.
He built a house to the name of God,
    and established a lasting sanctuary.ᶻ
¹⁴ How wise you were when you were
    young,
    overflowing with instruction, like the
    Nile in flood!ᵃ
¹⁵ Your understanding covered the whole
    earth,
    and, like a sea, filled it with
    knowledge.
¹⁶ Your fame reached distant coasts,
    and their peoples came to hear you;
¹⁷ With song and story and riddle,
    and with your answers, you astounded
    the nations.
¹⁸ You were called by that glorious name
    which was conferred upon Israel.*
Gold you gathered like so much iron,
    you heaped up silver as though it were
    lead;
¹⁹ But you abandoned yourself to women
    and gave them dominion over your
    body.ᵇ
²⁰ You brought dishonor upon your
    reputation,
    shame upon your marriage,
Wrath upon your descendants,

47, 1-11: David, a youthful and fearless warrior, the favorite of all Israel, by defeating Goliath, the boastful Philistine giant, removed the people's disgrace and greatly strengthened their power (1-7). With his whole being he loved and praised God, and his devotion to divine worship led him to develop liturgical cult. David fell into sin, but repenting, received pardon from God and the promise of an everlasting kingdom (8-11).

47, 12-24: Solomon, son and successor of David, inherited peace through his father's conquests. He built the magnificent temple of Jerusalem (12f) and received from God the favor of unparalleled wisdom, through which he obtained great fame (14-17). Luxury and sensuality, however, brought

disgrace upon him, and because of his oppressive burdens, he disposed the kingdom for division after his death (19-21. 23f). Nevertheless God did not withdraw his promise of establishing his throne in the descendants of David (22).

47, 18: Cf 2 Sm 12, 25, where Solomon is called Jedidiah, "beloved of the Lord." The same term is used of Israel in Jer 11, 15.

---

q: 2 Sm 7, 2.   r: 1 Sm 16, 11.   s: 1 Sm 17, 35.   t: 1 Sm 17, 49.
u: 1 Sm 18, 7.   v: 2 Sm 5, 6-25.   w: 1 Chr 16, 4ff; 23, 2ff; 25, 1-
7.   x: 2 Sm 12, 13; 7, 12-16.   y: 1 Kgs 2, 12.   z: 1 Kgs 5, 1. 5.
a: 14-18: 1 Kgs 5, 9-14; 10, 14-28.   b: 1 Kgs 11, 1ff.

and groaning upon your domain;

21 Thus two governments came into being,
   when in Ephraim kingship was
      usurped.*c*

22 But God does not withdraw his mercy,
   nor permit even one of his promises to
      fail.
He does not uproot the posterity of his
   chosen one,
   nor destroy the offspring of his friend.
So he gave to Jacob a remnant,
   to David a root from his own family.*d*

23 Solomon finally slept with his fathers,
   and left behind him one of his sons,
Expansive* in folly, limited in sense,
   REHOBOAM, who by his policy made
      the people rebel;
Until one arose who should not be
   remembered,
   the sinner who led Israel into sin,*e*
Who brought ruin to Ephraim

24 and caused them to be exiled from
      their land.

Elijah and Elisha

Their sinfulness grew more and more,
25 and they lent themselves to every evil,*

CHAPTER 48

See RG
276-79 1 Till like a fire there appeared the
   prophet
whose words were as a flaming
   furnace.*f*

2 Their staff of bread he shattered,
   in his zeal he reduced them to straits;

3 By God's word he shut up the heavens
   and three times brought down fire.*g*

4 How awesome are you, ELIJAH!
   Whose glory is equal to yours?

5 You brought a dead man back to life

from the nether world, by the will of
   the LORD.*h*

6 You sent kings down to destruction,
   and nobles, from their beds of sickness.*i*

7 You heard threats at Sinai,
   at Horeb avenging judgments.*j*

8 You anointed kings who should inflict
   vengeance,
   and a prophet as your successor.*k*

9 You were taken aloft in a whirlwind,
   in a chariot with fiery horses.*l*

10 You are destined, it is written, in time to
   come
   to put an end to wrath before the day
      of the LORD,
To turn back the hearts of fathers toward
   their sons,
   and to re-establish the tribes of Jacob.*m*

11 Blessed is he who shall have seen you
   before he dies,

12 O Elijah, enveloped in the whirlwind!*n*

Then ELISHA, filled with a twofold
   portion of his spirit,*
   wrought many marvels by his mere
      word.
During his lifetime he feared no one,
   nor was any man able to intimidate his
      will.

13 Nothing was beyond his power;*o*
   beneath him flesh was brought back
      into life.

14 In life he performed wonders,
   and after death, marvelous deeds.

15 Despite all this the people did not repent,
   nor did they give up their sins,
Until they were rooted out of their land
   and scattered all over the earth.
But Judah remained, a tiny people,
   with its rulers from the house of David.*p*

47, 23: Expansive: the name Rehoboam means "the people is expansive," that is, widespread. The sinner: Jeroboam; cf 1 Kgs 12, 2. 20. 26-32.

47, 25—48, 11: The prophetic ministry of Elijah amid widespread idolatry is here described as a judgment by fire (47, 25f). Through his preaching, miracles and vengeance against God's enemies within and without Israel, the prophet succeeded for a time in destroying idols and in restoring faith and the worship of the true God (48, 2-8). His miraculous departure from this life gave rise to the belief that he did not die but would return before the end of the world to put an end to wrath and restore the tribes of Israel (9ff). Cf Mt 17, 9-13.

48, 12-16: Elisha fearlessly continued the work of his predecessor by numerous miracles (12ff), but the obstinacy of the people eventually brought on the destruction of the kingdom of Israel and the dispersion of its subjects. Judah, however, survived under the rule of Davidic kings, both good and bad (15f).

c: 1 Kgs 12, 1ff. *d:* 2 Sm 7, 15; Ps 89, 34ff. *e:* 1 Kgs 11, 43; 12, 13. 21; 13, 34; 2 Kgs 17, 6ff. *f:* 1 Kgs 17, 1. *g:* 1 Kgs 17, 1; 2 Kgs 1, 9-14. *h:* 1 Kgs 17, 22. *i:* 1 Kgs 21, 19; 2 Kgs 1, 17. *j:* 1 Kgs 19, 8ff. *k:* 1 Kgs 19, 15ff. *l:* 2 Kgs 2, 11. *m:* Mal 3, 23f; Mt 17, 10. *n:* 2 Kgs 2, 9; 3, 13. *o:* 13f; 2 Kgs 13, 21. *p:* 2 Kgs 15, 29; 18, 11.

16 Some of these did what was right,
   but others were extremely sinful.

Hezekiah and Isaiah*

17 HEZEKIAH fortified his city
   and had water brought into it;*q*
With iron tools he cut through the rock
   and he built reservoirs for water.
18 During his reign Sennacherib led an
      invasion,
   and sent his adjutant;
He shook his fist at Zion
   and blasphemed God in his pride.*r*
19 The people's hearts melted within them,
   and they were in anguish like that of
      childbirth.
20 But they called upon the Most High God
   and lifted up their hands to him;
He heard the prayer they uttered,
   and saved them through ISAIAH.*s*
21 God struck the camp of the Assyrians
   and routed them with a plague.*t*
22 For Hezekiah did what was right
   and held fast to the paths of David,
As ordered by the illustrious prophet
   Isaiah, who saw the truth in visions.
23 In his lifetime he turned back the sun
   and prolonged the life of the king.*u*
24 By his powerful spirit he looked into the
      future*v*
   and consoled the mourners of Zion;
25 He foretold what should be till the end of
      time,
   hidden things yet to be fulfilled.

See RG
276-79

CHAPTER 49

Josiah and the Prophets*

1 The name JOSIAH is like blended
      incense,
   made lasting by a skilled perfumer.*w*

Precious is his memory, like honey to the
      taste,
   like music at a banquet.
2 For he grieved over our betrayals
   and destroyed the abominable idols.
3 He turned to God with his whole heart,
   and, though times were evil, he
      practiced virtue.
4 Except for David, Hezekiah and Josiah,
   they all were wicked;
They abandoned the law of the Most High,
   these kings of Judah, right to the very
      end.
5 So he gave over their power to others,
   their glory to a foolish foreign nation
6 Who burned the holy city
   and left its streets desolate,
As JEREMIAH had foretold;*x* 7for they had
      treated him badly
   who even in the womb had been made
      a prophet,
To root out, pull down, and destroy,
   and then to build and to plant.*y*
8 EZEKIEL beheld the vision
   and described the different creatures of
      the chariot;*z*
9 He also referred to JOB,
   who always persevered in the right
      path.*a*
10 Then, too, the TWELVE PROPHETS—
   may their bones return to life from
      their resting place!—
Gave new strength to Jacob
   and saved him by their faith and hope.

The Heroes after the Exile

11 How can we fittingly praise
      ZERUBBABEL,*
   who was like a signet ring on God's
      right hand,*b*

48, 17-25: The fidelity, trust and courage of King Hezekiah (17. 22), the zeal of the prophet Isaiah, and the prayer of the people (20) availed with God. The Assyrian oppressors were routed (18f. 21), the king's life was prolonged, and consolations were granted the people through Isaiah's prophecies concerning the future (23ff), especially the coming of the Messiah and the establishment of his kingdom; cf Is 7, 14; 9, 6f; 40—65.

49, 1-10: The author's praise of King Josiah (1-3), of the prophets Jeremiah and Ezekiel and likewise the minor prophets (7-10) derives from their spirit of fidelity to the Lord and his law amid the infidelity of kings and people (4ff. 10).

49, 11ff: Zerubbabel and Jeshua, in rebuilding the temple, and Nehemiah, the governor, in repairing the walls of the Holy City, also restored what these constructions signify, namely, religious worship and civil authority as prescribed in the law.

q: 2 Kgs 20, 20; 2 Chr 32, 3ff. 30.   *r:* 2 Kgs 18, 13ff; Is 36, 1ff.
s: 2 Kgs 19, 20.   *t:* 2 Kgs 19, 35; Is 37, 36.   *u:* 2 Kgs 20, 11; Is 38, 8.   *v:* 24f: 2 Kgs 20, 17; Is 40, 1ff; 42, 9; 46, 10; 48, 6; 61, 2.
w: 2 Kgs 22, 1; 2 Chr 34, 1.   *x:* 2 Kgs 25, 9; 2 Chr 36, 19.   *y:* Jer 1, 5. 10.   *z:* Ez 1, 4ff.   *a:* Ez 14, 14. 20.   *b:* 11f: Ezr 3, 2; Hg 1, 12; Zec 3, 1.

¹² And Jeshua, Jozadak's son?
　　In their time they built the house of
　　　God;
　　They erected the holy temple,
　　　destined for everlasting glory.
¹³ Extolled be the memory of NEHEMIAH!
　　He rebuilt our ruined walls,
　　Restored our shattered defenses,
　　　and set up gates and bars.ᶜ

The Earliest Patriarchs

¹⁴ Few on earth have been made the equal
　　　of ENOCH,*
　　for he was taken up bodily.ᵈ
¹⁵ Was ever a man born like JOSEPH?
　　Even his dead body was provided for.ᵉ
¹⁶ Glorious, too, were SHEM and SETH and
　　　ENOS;
　　but beyond that of any living being
　　was the splendor of ADAM.ᶠ

See RG 276–79

CHAPTER 50

Simon, Son of Jochanan

¹The greatest among his brethren, the glory
　　　of his people,
　　was SIMON the priest, son of Jochanan,*
　　In whose time the house of God was
　　　renovated,
　　in whose days the temple was
　　　reinforced.
² In his time also the wall was built
　　with powerful turrets for the temple
　　　precincts;
³ In his time the reservoir was dug,
　　the pool with a vastness like the sea's.
⁴ He protected his people against brigands
　　and strengthened his city against the
　　　enemy.
⁵ How splendid he was as he appeared
　　from the tent,

as he came from within the veil!
⁶ Like a star shining among the clouds,
　　like the full moon at the holyday
　　　season;
⁷ Like the sun shining upon the temple,
　　like the rainbow appearing in the
　　　cloudy sky;
⁸ Like the blossoms on the branches in
　　　springtime,
　　like a lily on the banks of a stream;
　　Like the trees of Lebanon in summer,
⁹　　like the fire of incense at the sacrifice;
　　Like a vessel of beaten gold,
　　　studded with precious stones;
¹⁰ Like a luxuriant olive tree thick with fruit,
　　like a cypress standing against the
　　　clouds;
¹¹ Vested in his magnificent robes,
　　and wearing his garments of splendor,ᵍ
　　As he ascended the glorious altar
　　and lent majesty to the court of the
　　　sanctuary.

¹² When he received the sundered victims
　　　from the priests
　　while he stood before the sacrificial
　　　wood,
　　His brethren ringed him about like a
　　　garland,
　　like a stand of cedars on Lebanon;
¹³ All the sons of Aaron in their dignity
　　clustered around him like poplars,
　　With the offerings to the LORD in their
　　　hands,
　　in the presence of the whole assembly
　　　of Israel.
¹⁴ Once he had completed the services at
　　　the altar
　　with the arranging of the sacrifices for
　　　the Most High,

49, 14ff: The patriarchs here mentioned were glorious because of their spirit of religion, i.e., their profound reverence for God and obedience to him. The splendor of Adam, moreover, was due to his direct origin from God.

50, 1-21: The son of Jochanan here mentioned was Simon II, in whose time as high priest (219-196 B.C.) great works were accomplished for the benefit of public worship and welfare (1-4). The author, a contemporary of this high priest, describes in great detail and by numerous comparisons the impression of awful majesty received, the lofty joy aroused, at sight of the high priest fully vested entering the sanctuary, ascending the altar (6-11), and, in the presence of the whole as-

sembly of Israel, encircled by assistant priests bearing offerings, sacrificing the burnt offering on the Day of Atonement, while the trumpets blast and the people bow down in adoration of the Most High (12-17). The hymnody, the joyful shouts of the multitude, and finally the high priest's blessing, in which he pronounces—once only in the year, on this occasion—the holy name of Yahweh, climax the description of this most solemn Jewish liturgical function (18-21).

c: Neh 1, 1; 3, 1.　*d:* Sir 44, 16; Gn 5, 18-24.　*e:* Gn 37—50; Ex 13, 19; Jos 24, 32.　*f:* Gn 1, 27; 4, 25f.　*g:* Sir 45, 8-12; Ex 28, 2-5; 39, 1-21.

¹⁵ And had stretched forth his hand for the
    cup,^h
  to offer blood of the grape,
  And poured it out at the foot of the altar,
    a sweet-smelling odor to the Most
      High God,
¹⁶ The sons of Aaron would sound a blast,
    the priests, on their trumpets of beaten
      metal;
  A blast to resound mightily
    as a reminder before the Most High.ⁱ
¹⁷ Then all the people with one accord
    would quickly fall prostrate to the
      ground
  In adoration before the Most High,
    before the Holy One of Israel.

¹⁸ Then hymns would re-echo,
    and over the throng sweet strains of
      praise resound.
¹⁹ All the people of the land would shout
    for joy,
  praying to the Merciful One,
  As the high priest completed the services
    at the altar
  by presenting to God the sacrifice due;
²⁰ Then coming down he would raise his
    hands
  over all the congregation of Israel.^j
  The blessing of the LORD would be upon
    his lips,
    the name of the LORD would be his
      glory.
²¹ Then again the people would lie prostrate
    to receive from him the blessing of the
      Most High.

²² And now, bless the God of all,*
    who has done wondrous things on earth;
  Who fosters men's growth from their
    mother's womb,

and fashions them according to his will!
²³ May he grant you joy of heart
    and may peace abide among you;
²⁴ May his goodness toward us endure in
    Israel
  as long as the heavens are above.

Epilogue and Canticles
²⁵ My whole being loathes two nations,*
    the third is not even a people:*
²⁶ Those who live in Seir* and Philistia,
    and the degenerate folk who dwell in
      Shechem.^k

²⁷ Wise instruction, appropriate proverbs,*
    I have written in this book,
  I, Jesus, son of Eleazar, son of Sirach,
    as they gushed forth from my heart's
      understanding.
²⁸ Happy the man who meditates upon
    these things,
  wise the man who takes them to heart!
²⁹ If he puts them into practice, he can cope
    with anything,
  for the fear of the LORD is his lamp.

CHAPTER 51

See RG
276–79

¹ I give you thanks, O God of my
    father;*
  I praise you, O God my savior!
  I will make known your name, refuge of
    my life;^l
²   you have been my helper against my
      adversaries.
  You have saved me from death,
    and kept back my body from the pit,
  From the clutches of the nether world
    you have snatched my feet;^m
³   you have delivered me, in your great
      mercy,
  From the scourge of a slanderous tongue,

50, 22ff: Praise and thanksgiving are given to God for his wondrous works, and a blessing is invoked on man that he may enjoy peace and gladness of heart and the abiding goodness of the Most High.

50, 25f: The author's abhorrence of the pagan Edomites (Idumeans), Philistines and Samaritans can be understood in the light of Old Testament thinking, which does not always distinguish between hatred of evildoers and hatred of the evil they do.

50, 25: Not even a people: the Samaritans.

50, 26: Seir: Mount Seir in the territory of the Edomites.

Shechem: a city in Samaria.

50, 27ff: These verses contain the subscription of the author, Jesus, son of Eleazar, son of Sirach, to his long and beautiful treatise on wisdom as applying to all of human life, integrating it under the direction of the fear of the Lord.

51, 1-12: A canticle of praise and thanks to God for delivering the author from slander, dangers, destruction, death, the nether world, and evil of every kind.

---

h: 15f: Nm 15, 5; 28, 7.   *i:* Nm 10, 10.   *j:* Nm 6, 23-26.
k: 2 Kgs 17, 24; Jn 4, 9.   *l:* Ps 138, 1.   *m:* Ps 91, 3.

and from lips that went over to
falsehood;
From the snare of those who watched for
my downfall,
and from the power of those who
sought my life;[n]
From many a danger you have saved me,
4 from flames that hemmed me in on
every side;[o]
From the midst of unremitting fire,
5 from the deep belly of the nether
world;
From deceiving lips and painters of lies,
6 from the arrows of dishonest tongues.
I was at the point of death,
my soul was nearing the depths of the
nether world;[p]
7 I turned every way, but there was no one
to help me,
I looked for one to sustain me, but
could find no one.[q]
8 But then I remembered the mercies of the
LORD,
his kindness through ages past;
For he saves those who take refuge in
him,
and rescues them from every evil.
9 So I raised my voice from the very earth,

from the gates of the nether world, my
cry.
10 I called out: O Lord, you are my father,
you are my champion and my savior;
Do not abandon me in time of trouble,
in the midst of storms and dangers.[r]
11 I will ever praise your name
and be constant in my prayers to you.
Thereupon the LORD heard my voice,
he listened to my appeal;
12 He saved me from evil of every kind
and preserved me in time of trouble.
For this reason I thank him and I praise
him;
I bless the name of the LORD.*
13 *When I was young and innocent,
I sought wisdom.[s]
14 She came to me in her beauty,
and until the end I will cultivate her.
15 As the blossoms yielded to ripening
grapes,
the heart's joy,
My feet kept to the level path
because from earliest youth I was
familiar with her.
16 In the short time I paid heed,
I met with great instruction.

51, 12: After this verse the Hebrew text gives the litany of praise contained below. It is similar to Ps 136. Though not found in any versions, and therefore of doubtful authenticity, the litany seems from internal evidence to go back to the time of Sirach:

Give thanks to the Lord, for he is good, for his mercy endures forever;

Give thanks to the God of glory, for his mercy endures forever;

Give thanks to the guardian of Israel, for his mercy endures forever;

Give thanks to the creator of the universe, for his mercy endures forever;

Give thanks to the redeemer of Israel, for his mercy endures forever;

Give thanks to him who gathers the dispersed of Israel, for his mercy endures forever;

Give thanks to him who builds his city and his sanctuary, for his mercy endures forever;

Give thanks to him who makes a horn to sprout forth, for the house of David, for his mercy endures forever;

Give thanks to him who has chosen for his priests the sons of Zadok, for his mercy endures forever;

Give thanks to the shield of Abraham, for his mercy endures forever;

Give thanks to the rock of Isaac, for his mercy endures forever;

Give thanks to the mighty one of Jacob, for his mercy endures forever;

Give thanks to him who has chosen Zion, for his mercy endures forever;

Give thanks to the king over kings of kings, for his mercy endures forever;

He has lifted up the horn of his people, be this his praise from all his faithful ones,

From the children of Israel, the people close to him. Alleluia! (Cf Ps 148, 14.)

51, 13-30: An alphabetic canticle describing: a) the approach to wisdom through prayer, persistent study and instruction (13-17), purification from sin, enlightenment and ardent desire; b) the possession of wisdom (18-22). The author concludes with an urgent invitation to men to receive instruction in wisdom from him, and to live by it, because wisdom gives herself to those who seek her (23-26); and for their labor. God will reward them in the end (27-30). Cf Mt 11, 28; Eccl 12, 14.

In the Greek of 13f there is an expansion introducing Solomon as the speaker. This deviates from the original author's intent. It reads, "Publicly, in my prayer, facing the temple, I asked for her."

n: Pss 40, 5; 91, 3.   o: Ps 66, 12.   p: Pss 88, 4; 94, 17.   q: Pss 22, 12; 142, 5.   r: Ps 89, 27.   s: Sir 34, 11.

¹⁷ Since in this way I have profited,
  I will give my teacher grateful praise.

¹⁸ I became resolutely devoted to her—
  the good I persistently strove for.
¹⁹ I burned with desire for her,
  never turning back.
I became preoccupied with her,
  never weary of extolling her.
My hand opened her gate
  and I came to know her secrets.
²⁰ For her I purified my hands;
  in cleanness I attained to her.
At first acquaintance with her, I gained
  understanding
  such that I will never forsake her.^t
²¹ My whole being was stirred as I learned
  about her;
  therefore I have made her my prize
  possession.
²² The LORD has granted me my lips as a
  reward,
  and my tongue will declare his praises.

²³ Come aside to me, you untutored,
  and take up lodging in the house of
  instruction;^u

²⁴ How long will you be deprived of
  wisdom's food,
  how long will you endure such bitter
  thirst?
²⁵ I open my mouth and speak of her:
  gain, at no cost, wisdom for
  yourselves.^v
²⁶ Submit your neck to her yoke,
  that your mind may accept her
  teaching.
For she is close to those who seek
  her,
  and the one who is in earnest finds
  her.^w
²⁷ See for yourselves! I have labored only a
  little,
  but have found much.
²⁸ Acquire but a little instruction;
  you will win silver and gold through
  her.
²⁹ Let your spirits rejoice in the mercy of
  God,
  and be not ashamed to give him
  praise.
³⁰ Work at your tasks in due season,
  and in his own time God will give you
  your reward.^x

t: Prv 4, 6.   u: Prv 8, 5.   v: Sir 6, 20.   w: Sir 6, 25.   x: Sir 2, 8; Jb 34, 11; Jn 9, 4.

See RG
280-370

THE PROPHETIC BOOKS

The prophetic books bear the names of the four major and twelve minor prophets, besides Lamentations and Baruch. The terms "major" and "minor" refer merely to the length of the respective compositions and not to any distinction in the prophetic office. Jonah is a story of the mission of the prophet rather than a collection of prophecies. Lamentations and Daniel are listed among the hagiographa in the Hebrew Bible, not among the prophetic books. The former contains a series of elegies on the fate of Jerusalem; the latter is apocalyptic in character. Daniel, who lived far removed from Palestine, was not called by God to preach; yet the book is counted as prophecy. Baruch, though excluded from the Hebrew canon, is found in the Septuagint version, and the church has always acknowledged it to be sacred and inspired.

The prophetic books, together with the oral preaching of the prophets, were the result of the institution of prophetism, in which a succession of Israelites chosen by God and appointed by him to be prophets received communications from him and transmitted them to the people in his name (Dt 18, 15-20). The prophets were spokesmen of God, intermediaries between him and his people. The communications they received from God came through visions, dreams, and ecstasies and were transmitted to the people through sermons, writings, and symbolic actions.

The office of prophet was due to a direct call from God. It was not the result of heredity, just as it was not a permanent gift but a transient one, subject entirely to the divine will. The prophets preserved and developed revealed religion (1 Sm 12, 6-25), denounced idolatry (1 Kgs 14, 1-13),

defended the moral law (2 Sm 12, 1-15), gave counsel in political matters (Is 31, 1ff), and often also in matters of private life (1 Sm 9, 6-9). At times miracles confirmed their preaching, and their predictions of the future intensified the expectation of the Messiah and of his kingdom.

The prophetic literature in this volume contains the substance of the prophets' authentic preaching, résumés, and genuine samples of such preaching. Some parts were recorded by the prophets themselves, some by persons other than the prophets who uttered them.

The prophecies express judgments of the people's moral conduct, on the basis of the Mosaic alliance between God and Israel. They teach sublime truths and lofty morals. They contain exhortations, threats, announcements of punishment, promises of deliverance, made with solemn authority and in highly imaginative language. In the affairs of men, their prime concern is the interests of God, especially in what pertains to the chosen people through whom the Messiah is to come; hence their denunciations of idolatry and of that externalism in worship which excludes the interior spirit of religion. They are concerned also with the universal nature of the moral law, with personal responsibility, with the person and office of the Messiah, and with the conduct of foreign nations.

In content, the literary genre of prophecy uses warning and threat besides exhortation and promise to declare in God's name events of the near and distant future (Is 8—9). In form, the divine source of prophetic declaration appears in: "The word (or oracle) of the LORD," or "Thus says the LORD," followed by the announcement of a coming event and its moral cause (Hos 4, 7-10). Divine exhortation and promise are introduced by such forms as: "Hear this word, O men of Israel, that the LORD pronounces over you" (Am 3, 1). Kindly and persuasive tones pervade the promises of reward and even the threats of punishment (Am 5, 14-15).

Disregard for exact chronological perspective in the prophecies is an additional characteristic. Predictions of the immediate and distant future are often interrelated, not on the basis of years separating the events but on the analogy of the pattern joining present with very distant, though similar, conditions and circumstances. This is prophetic compenetration, idealization in which persons and things of the more immediate present, in the prophet's day, fade into a wider and more perfect order of persons and things of the future; the former are figures and types of the latter. Thus, some details of what the Psalmist said of the kingdom of David and Solomon (Ps 72) went beyond what was fulfilled in these men, as St. Thomas points out, and found their realization only in the kingdom of Christ. St. Jerome before him, and still earlier the apostles themselves—Peter (Acts 2, 14-36) and Paul (Gal 4, 21-31)—taught us that through anticipation in types we discover in Sacred Scripture the truth of things to come.

Thus the universal blessing for mankind, often promised by God through the mouths of his prophets in figures and types, was in time to become personalized and to confer its full benefit on us through the Word made flesh, who became for us the New Covenant through his life, death, and resurrection, as the prophets had foretold.

The Book of Isaiah

See RG 280-95

The greatest of the prophets appeared at a critical moment of Israel's history. The second half of the eighth century B.C. witnessed the collapse of the northern kingdom under the hammerlike blows of Assyria (722), while Jerusalem itself saw the army of Sennacherib drawn up before its walls (701). In the year that Uzziah, king of Judah, died (742), Isaiah received his call to the prophetic office in the Temple of Jerusalem. Close attention should be given to chapter 6, where this divine summons to be the ambassador of the Most High is circumstantially described.

The vision of the Lord enthroned in glory stamps an indelible character on Isaiah's ministry and provides the key to the understanding of his message. The majesty, holiness and glory of the Lord took possession of his spirit and, conversely, he gained a new awareness of human pettiness and sinfulness. The enormous abyss between God's sovereign holiness and man's sin overwhelmed the prophet. Only the purifying coal of the seraphim could cleanse his lips and prepare him for acceptance of the call: "Here I am, send me!"

The ministry of Isaiah may be divided into three periods, covering the reigns of Jotham (742–735), Ahaz (735–715), and Hezekiah (715–687). To the first period belong, for the most part, the early oracles (1—5) which exposed the moral breakdown of Judah and its capital, Jerusalem. With the accession of Ahaz, the prophet became adviser to the king, whose throne was threatened by the Syro-Ephraimite coalition. Rejecting the plea of Isaiah for faith and courage, the weak Ahaz turned to Assyria for help. From this period came the majority of messianic oracles found in the section of Immanuel prophecies (6—12).

Hezekiah succeeded his father and undertook a religious reform which Isaiah undoubtedly supported. But the old intrigues began again, and the king was soon won over to the pro-Egyptian party. Isaiah denounced this "covenant with death" and again summoned Judah to faith in Yahweh as her only hope. But it was too late; the revolt had already begun. Assyria acted quickly and her army, after ravaging Judah, laid siege to Jerusalem (701). "I shut up Hezekiah like a bird in his cage," boasts the famous inscription of Sennacherib. But Yahweh delivered the city, as Isaiah had promised: God is the Lord of history, and Assyria but an instrument in his hands.

Little is known about the last days of this great religious leader, whose oracles, of singular poetic beauty and power constantly reminded his wayward people of their destiny and the fidelity of Yahweh to his promises.

The complete Book of Isaiah is an anthology of poems composed chiefly by the great prophet, but also by disciples, some of whom came many years after Isaiah. In 1—39 most of the oracles come from Isaiah and faithfully reflect the situation in eighth-century Judah. To disciples deeply influenced by the prophet belong sections such as the Apocalypse of Isaiah (24—27), the oracles against Babylon (13—14), and probably the poems of 34—35.

Chapters 40—55, sometimes called the Deutero-Isaiah, are generally attributed to an anonymous poet who prophesied toward the end of the Babylonian exile. From this section come the great messianic oracles known as the songs of the Servant, whose mysterious destiny of suffering and glorification is fulfilled in the passion and glorification of Christ. Chapters 56—66 contain oracles from a later period and were composed by disciples who inherited the spirit and continued the work of the great prophet.

The principal divisions of the Book of Isaiah are the following:

A: The Book of Judgment:
I: Indictment of Israel and Judah (1, 1—5, 30).
II: Immanuel Prophecies (6, 1—12, 6).
III: Oracles against the Pagan Nations (13, 1—23, 18).
IV: Apocalypse of Isaiah (24, 1—27, 13).
V: The Lord Alone, Israel's and Judah's Salvation (28, 1—33, 24).
VI: The Lord, Zion's Avenger (34, 1—35, 10).
VII: Historical Appendix (36, 1—39, 8).
B: The Book of Consolation:
I: The Lord's Glory in Israel's Liberation (40, 1—48, 21).
II: Expiation of Sin, Spiritual Liberation of Israel (49, 1—55, 13).
III: Return of the First Captives (56, 1—66, 24).

A. The Book of Judgment

I: Indictment of Israel and Judah

CHAPTER 1

Israel's Sinfulness. [1]The vision* which Isaiah, son of Amoz, had concerning Judah and Jerusalem in the days of Uzziah, Jotham, Ahaz and Hezekiah, kings of Judah.

See RG 280-95

2 Hear, O heavens, and listen, O earth,
 for the LORD speaks:
Sons have I raised and reared,
 but they have disowned me![a]
3 An ox knows its owner,
 and an ass, its master's manger;
But Israel* does not know,
 my people has not understood.
4 Ah! sinful nation, people laden with
  wickedness,
 evil race, corrupt children!
They have forsaken the LORD,
 spurned the Holy One of Israel,*
  apostatized.[b]
5 Where would you yet be struck,*
 you that rebel again and again?
The whole head is sick,
 the whole heart faint.
6 From the sole of the foot to the head
 there is no sound spot:
Wound and welt and gaping gash,
 not drained, or bandaged,
 or eased with salve.
7 Your country is waste,
 your cities burnt with fire;
Your land before your eyes
 strangers devour
 [a waste, like Sodom overthrown]—
8 And daughter Zion* is left
 like a hut in a vineyard,
Like a shed in a melon patch,
 like a city blockaded.

1, 1: The title of the book: an editorial addition. Isaiah: meaning "the salvation of the Lord," or "The Lord is salvation." Amoz: not the minor prophet. Judah: The southern kingdom of the tribes of Judah and Benjamin. Uzziah: also called Azariah; cf 2 Kgs 15, 1; 2 Chr 26, 1.

1, 3: Israel, not the northern kingdom, as in Is 9, 11, exclusively, which Isaiah usually calls "Ephraim" from the tribe bordering on the southern kingdom, but the entire chosen people; cf Is 8, 14.

1, 4: Holy One of Israel: a title used frequently by Isaiah, rarely by other writers.

1, 5-8: Sufferings inflicted upon God's people for their sins.

1, 8: Daughter Zion: Jerusalem. Hut . . . shed: for the shelter of watchmen and laborers.

---

a: Dt 32, 1. 5f.   b: Is 5, 24; Dt 32, 15.

⁹ Unless the LORD of hosts*
 had left us a scanty remnant,
We had become as Sodom,
 we should be like Gomorrah.ᶜ
¹⁰ Hear the word of the LORD,
 princes of Sodom!
Listen to the instruction of our God,
 people of Gomorrah!
¹¹ What care I for the number of your
  sacrifices?*
 says the LORD.
I have had enough of whole-burnt rams
 and fat of fatlings;
In the blood of calves, lambs and goats
 I find no pleasure.ᵈ

¹² When you come in to visit me,
 who asks these things of you?
¹³ Trample my courts no more!
 Bring no more worthless offerings;
 your incense is loathsome to me.
New moon and sabbath, calling of
  assemblies,
 octaves with wickedness:* these I
  cannot bear.ᵉ
¹⁴ Your new moons and festivals I detest;
 they weigh me down, I tire of the load.
¹⁵ When you spread out your hands,*
 I close my eyes to you;
Though you pray the more,
 I will not listen.
Your hands are full of blood!ᶠ
¹⁶ Wash yourselves clean!
Put away your misdeeds from before my
  eyes;
 cease doing evil; ¹⁷learn to do good.
Make justice your aim: redress the
  wronged,
 hear the orphan's plea, defend the
  widow.ᵍ

¹⁸ Come now, let us set things right,
 says the LORD:
Though your sins be like scarlet,
 they may become white as snow;
Though they be crimson red,
 they may become white as wool.ʰ
¹⁹ If you are willing, and obey,
 you shall eat the good things of the land;
²⁰ But if you refuse and resist,
 the sword shall consume you:
 for the mouth of the LORD has spoken!

²¹ How has she turned adulteress,
 the faithful city, so upright!*
Justice used to lodge within her,
 but now, murderers.ⁱ
²² Your silver is turned to dross,
 your wine is mixed with water.
²³ Your princes are rebels
 and comrades of thieves;
Each one of them loves a bribe
 and looks for gifts.
The fatherless they defend not,
 and the widow's plea does not reach
  them.ʲ
²⁴ Now, therefore, says the Lord,
 the LORD of hosts, the Mighty One of
  Israel:
Ah! I will take vengeance on my foes
 and fully repay my enemies!ᵏ
²⁵ I will turn my hand against you,
 and refine your dross in the furnace,
 removing all your alloy.
²⁶ I will restore your judges as at first,
 and your counselors as in the beginning;
After that you shall be called
 city of justice, faithful city.ˡ

²⁷ Zion shall be redeemed by judgment,
 and her repentant ones by justice.*

1, 9: Lord of hosts: God, who is the Creator and Ruler of the heavenly armies of the angels, stars, etc. Remnant: St. Paul uses this text in Rom 9, 29, where he speaks of God's saving mercy toward the Jews and Gentiles. Sodom . . . Gomorrah: cf Gn 19.

1, 11: The number of your sacrifices: however numerous, they are not acceptable without the right dispositions on the part of the worshipers.

1, 13: Octaves with wickedness: the solemnity of the feasts marred by evil deeds.

1, 15: Spread out your hands: in prayer.

1, 21: A picture of Jerusalem, once so faithful to God.

Apostasy from the covenant is often likened by the prophets to unfaithfulness to the marriage vow.

1, 27: This verse is the key to the whole Book of Isaiah. Zion's defiant persistence in sin has demanded a divine judgment, by which her survivors will be cleansed and will return to God in justice; cf Is 40, 2.

c: Rom 9, 29.   d: Ps 50, 8-13; Sir 34, 19; Mi 6, 7.   e: Prv 15, 8; Jer 6, 20.   f: Prv 1, 28; Sir 34, 21-25.   g: Ex 23, 6; Dt 24, 17; Sir 4, 9f; Jer 22, 3; Ez 22, 7; Zec 7, 9f.   h: Ps 51, 9.   i: Jer 3, 8; Hos 2, 7.   j: Ex 23, 8; Dt 16, 19.   k: Dt 32, 41.   l: Jer 33, 7ff; Zec 8, 3.

28 Rebels and sinners alike shall be crushed,
   those who desert the LORD shall be
      consumed.
29 You shall be ashamed of the terebinths
      which you prized,
   and blush for the groves which you
      chose.*
30 You shall become like a tree with falling
      leaves,
   like a garden that has no water.
31 The strong man shall turn to tow,
   and his work shall become a spark;
   Both shall burn together,
   and there shall be none to quench the
      flames.

CHAPTER 2

See RG
280–95

Zion, the Messianic Capital. [1]This is
what Isaiah, son of Amoz, saw concerning
Judah and Jerusalem.*

2   In days to come,*
   The mountain of the LORD's house[m]
      shall be established as the highest
         mountain
   and raised above the hills.
   All nations shall stream toward it;[n]
3   many peoples shall come and say:
   "Come, let us climb the LORD's mountain,
      to the house of the God of Jacob,
   That he may instruct us in his ways,
      and we may walk in his paths."[o]
   For from Zion shall go forth instruction,
      and the word of the LORD from
         Jerusalem.*
4 He shall judge between the nations,
   and impose terms on many peoples.
   They shall beat their swords into
      plowshares
   and their spears into pruning hooks;

One nation shall not raise the sword
      against another,
   nor shall they train for war again.[p]

5 O house of Jacob, come,
   let us walk in the light of the LORD!

The Lord's Judgment against Idols

6 You have abandoned your people,
   the house of Jacob,
   Because they are filled with
      fortune-tellers
   and soothsayers,* like the Philistines;
   they covenant with strangers.[q]
7 Their land is full of silver and gold,
   and there is no end to their treasures;
   Their land is full of horses,
   and there is no end to their chariots.
8 Their land is full of idols;
   they worship the works of their hands,
   that which their fingers have made.[r]

9 But man is abased,
   each one brought low.
   [Do not pardon them!]
10 Get behind the rocks,
   hide in the dust,
   From the terror of the LORD
   and the splendor of his majesty![s]
11 The haughty eyes of man will be
      lowered,
   the arrogance of men will be abased,
   and the LORD alone will be exalted, on
      that day.*
12 For the LORD of hosts will have his day
   against all that is proud and arrogant,
   all that is high, and it will be brought
      low;
13 Yes, against all the cedars of Lebanon*
   and all the oaks of Bashan,

1, 29: Terebinths which you prized . . . groves which you chose: as popular shrines for idolatrous worship.

2, 1: An editorial addition introducing chapters 2—5.

2, 2-4: The messianic destiny which ensures Judah's later restoration. In the messianic kingdom the prophets generally see the Lord's house as the seat of authority and the source of clear and certain doctrine; also, its rule willingly accepted by all peoples, maintained by spiritual sanctions, and tending to universal peace. This passage is found substantially unchanged in Mi 4, 1-3; it probably, although not certainly, has Isaiah as its author.

2, 3: Zion . . . Jerusalem: types of the earthly center of the messianic kingdom.

2, 6: Fortune-tellers and soothsayers: divination was strictly forbidden; cf Dt 18, 9-14.

2, 11: That day: the day of the Lord, a day of retribution, often referred to, especially by the minor prophets, and described in terms of natural phenomena: earthquake, fire, storm.

2, 13: Lebanon: Mount Lebanon in Syria, famed for its cedars. Bashan: the wooded uplands east of the Jordan River.

m: 2ff: Mi 4, 1ff.   n: Is 56, 7.   o: Zec 8, 20-23.   p: Is 9, 7; 11, 4; Ps 72, 3f; Zec 9, 10.   q: Is 8, 19; 19, 3.   r: Is 31, 1ff.
s: 2 Thes 1, 9.

14 Against all the lofty mountains
  and all the high hills,
15 Against every lofty tower
  and every fortified wall,
16 Against all the ships of Tarshish*
  and all stately vessels.
17 Human pride will be abased,
  the arrogance of men brought low,
And the LORD alone will be exalted, on
  that day.

18   The idols will perish forever.

19 Men will go into caves in the rocks
  and into holes in the earth,
From the terror of the LORD
  and the splendor of his majesty,
  when he arises to overawe the
  earth.

20 On that day men will throw to the moles
and the bats the idols of silver and gold
which they made for worship.

21 They go into caverns in the rocks
  and into crevices in the cliffs,
From the terror of the LORD
  and the splendor of his majesty,
  when he arises to overawe the earth.

22 As for you, let man alone,
  in whose nostrils is but a breath;
  for what is he worth?

CHAPTER 3

See RG
280-95

Judgment of Judah and Jerusalem

1 The Lord, the LORD of hosts,*
  shall take away from Jerusalem and
    from Judah
  support and prop [all supplies of bread
    and water]:¹
2 Hero and warrior,
  judge and prophet, fortune-teller and
    elder,
3 The captain of fifty and the nobleman,
  counselor, skilled magician, and expert
    charmer.
4 I will make striplings their princes;

  the fickle shall govern them,
5 And the people shall oppress one
    another,
  yes, every man his neighbor.
The child shall be bold toward the elder,
  and the base toward the honorable.
6 When a man seizes his brother
  in his father's house, saying,
"You have clothes! Be our ruler,
  and take in hand this ruin!"—
7   Then shall he answer in that day:
"I will not undertake to cure this,
  when in my own house there is no
    bread or clothing!
You shall not make me ruler of the
    people."

8 Jerusalem is crumbling, Judah is falling;
  for their speech and their deeds are
    before the LORD,
  a provocation in the sight of his
    majesty.
9 Their very look bears witness against
    them;
  their sin like Sodom they vaunt,
They hide it not. Woe to them!
  they deal out evil to themselves.
10 Happy the just, for it will be well with
    them,
  the fruit of their works they will eat.
11 Woe to the wicked man! All goes ill,
  with the work of his hands he will be
    repaid.
12 My people—a babe in arms will be their
    tyrant,
  and women will rule them!
O my people, your leaders mislead,
  they destroy the paths you should
    follow.

13 The LORD rises to accuse,
  standing to try his people.
14 The Lord enters into judgment
  with his people's elders and princes:
It is you who have devoured the
    vineyard;

2, 16: Tarshish: cf note on Ps 48, 8.

3, 1-12: Anarchy will reign in Jerusalem and Judah. In the prevailing desperation, even the most unworthy and the least qualified will be sought as rulers.

t: Lv 26, 26; Ez 4, 16.

the loot wrested from the poor is in
    your houses.
¹⁵ What do you mean by crushing my
    people,
and grinding down the poor when they
    look to you?
says the Lord, the God of hosts.^u
¹⁶ The LORD said:^v
Because the daughters of Zion are
    haughty,
and walk with necks outstretched
Ogling and mincing as they go,
    their anklets tinkling with every step,
¹⁷ The Lord shall cover the scalps of Zion's
    daughters with scabs,
and the LORD shall bare their heads.[*]

¹⁸On that day the LORD will do away with
the finery of the anklets, sunbursts, and crescents; ¹⁹the pendants, bracelets, and veils;
²⁰the headdresses, bangles, cinctures, per-
fume boxes, and amulets; ²¹the signet rings,
and the nose rings;[*] ²²the court dresses,
wraps, cloaks, and purses; ²³the mirrors,
linen tunics, turbans, and shawls.

²⁴ Instead of perfume there will be stench,
    instead of the girdle, a rope,
And for the coiffure, baldness;
    for the rich gown, a sackcloth skirt.
        Then, instead of beauty:
²⁵ Your men will fall by the sword,
    and your champions, in war;
²⁶ Her gates will lament and mourn,
    as the city sits desolate on the ground.

CHAPTER 4

See RG
280-95
¹Seven women will take hold of one
    man[*]
on that day, saying:
"We will eat our own food
    and wear our own clothing;
Only let your name be given us,
    put an end to our disgrace!"

The Messianic Branch

²   On that day,
The branch of the LORD[*] will be luster
    and glory,
and the fruit of the earth will be honor
    and splendor
for the survivors of Israel.^w
³ He who remains in Zion
    and he that is left in Jerusalem
Will be called holy:
    every one marked down for life[*] in
    Jerusalem.^x
⁴ When the Lord washes away
    the filth of the daughters of Zion,
And purges Jerusalem's blood from her
    midst
    with a blast of searing judgment,
⁵ Then will the LORD create,
    over the whole site of Mount Zion
    and over her place of assembly,
A smoking cloud by day
    and a light of flaming fire by night.^y
⁶ For over all, his glory will be shelter and
    protection:
    shade from the parching heat of day,
    refuge and cover from storm and rain.

CHAPTER 5

See RG
280-95

The Vineyard Song

¹ Let me now sing of my friend,
    my friend's song concerning his
    vineyard.
My friend had a vineyard[*]
    on a fertile hillside;
² He spaded it, cleared it of stones,
    and planted the choicest vines;
Within it he built a watchtower,
    and hewed out a wine press.
Then he looked for the crop of grapes,
    but what it yielded was wild grapes.

³ Now, inhabitants of Jerusalem and men
    of Judah,

3, 17: Bare their heads: a mark of social disgrace; cf Nm
5, 18.

3, 21: Nose rings: of gold, a feminine ornament in the
East; cf note on Gn 24, 22.

4, 1: Seven women . . . one man: the disproportion of the
sexes due to war leaves the female population almost without
male partners. The women are eager to marry, not for support,
but to avoid the disgrace of being childless.

4, 2: Branch of the Lord: divine blessings in general,

which later culminated in the Messiah; cf Jer 23, 5; Zec 3, 8;
6, 12.

4, 3: Marked down for life: in God's list of his elect; cf Ex
32, 32.

5, 1: My friend had a vineyard: the Lord and his chosen
people.

---

u: Lv 25, 42. 55.   v: 16ff: Is 32, 11f.   w: Is 11, 1; Jer 23, 5; 33,
15.   x: Is 6, 13; 10, 20; Ob 17.   y: Ex 13, 21.

judge between me and my vineyard:

⁴ What more was there to do for my
        vineyard
    that I had not done?
Why, when I looked for the crop of grapes,
    did it bring forth wild grapes?

⁵ Now, I will let you know
    what I mean to do to my vineyard:
Take away its hedge, give it to grazing,
    break through its wall, let it be
        trampled!

⁶ Yes, I will make it a ruin:
    it shall not be pruned or hoed,
    but overgrown with thorns and briers;
I will command the clouds
    not to send rain upon it.

⁷ The vineyard of the LORD of hosts is the
        house of Israel,
    and the men of Judah are his cherished
        plant;
He looked for judgment, but see,
        bloodshed!
    for justice, but hark, the outcry!*

Doom of the Unjust

⁸ Woe to you who join house to house,*
    who connect field with field,
Till no room remains, and you are left to
        dwell
    alone in the midst of the land!ᶻ

⁹ In my hearing the LORD of hosts has
        sworn:
    Many houses shall be in ruins,
    large ones and fine, with no one to live
        in them.ᵃ

¹⁰ Ten acres* of vineyard
    shall yield but one liquid measure,
And a homer of seed
    shall yield but an ephah.

¹⁷ Lambs shall graze there at pasture,
    and kids shall eat in the ruins of the
        rich.

¹¹ Woe to those who demand strong drink
    as soon as they rise in the morning,

And linger into the night
    while wine inflames them!

¹² With harp and lyre, timbrel and flute,
    they feast on wine;
But what the LORD does, they regard not,
    the work of his hands they see not.ᵇ

¹³ Therefore my people go into exile,
    because they do not understand;
Their nobles die of hunger,
    and their masses are parched with
        thirst.

¹⁴ Therefore the nether world* enlarges its
        throat
    and opens its maw without limit;
Down go their nobility and their masses,
    their throngs and their revelry.ᶜ

¹⁵ Men shall be abased, each one brought
        low,
    and the eyes of the haughty lowered,

¹⁶ But the LORD of hosts shall be exalted by
        his judgment,
    and God the Holy shall be shown holy
        by his justice.

¹⁸ Woe to those who tug at guilt with cords
        of perversity,
    and at sin as if with cart ropes!

¹⁹ To those who say, "Let him make haste
    and speed his work, that we may see it;
On with the plan of the Holy One of
        Israel!
    let it come to pass, that we may know
        it!"ᵈ

²⁰ Woe to those who call evil good, and
        good evil,
    who change darkness into light, and
        light into darkness,
    who change bitter into sweet, and
        sweet into bitter!

²¹ Woe to those who are wise in their own
        sight,
    and prudent in their own esteem!ᵉ

²² Woe to the champions at drinking wine,
    the valiant at mixing strong drink!ᶠ

²³ To those who acquit the guilty for bribes,

5, 7: Judgment . . . bloodshed . . . justice . . . outcry: in Hebrew, these adversative terms constitute a play on words.

5, 8-10: Land-grabbers who unjustly acquire property will be impoverished instead of enriched.

5, 10: Ten acres: a field requiring ten days of plowing by a yoke of oxen. Liquid measure: in Hebrew, a "bath," i.e.,

about ten gallons. Homer: a dry measure of about ten bushels. Ephah: a dry measure of about one bushel.

5, 14: Nether world: cf note on Ps 6, 6.

z: Mi 2, 2.   a: Is 6, 12.   b: Am 6, 5f.   c: Hb 2, 5.   d: Jer 5, 12; 2 Pt 3, 4.   e: Prv 3, 7; Rom 12, 16.   f: Sir 31, 3.

and deprive the just man of his rights!*g*

24 Therefore, as the tongue of fire licks up
   stubble,
   as dry grass shrivels in the flame,
Even so their root shall become rotten
   and their blossom scatter like dust;
For they have spurned the law of the
   LORD of hosts,
   and scorned the word of the Holy One
   of Israel.

25 Therefore the wrath of the LORD blazes
   against his people,
   he raises his hand to strike them;
When the mountains quake,
   their corpses shall be like refuse in the
   streets.
For all this, his wrath is not turned back,
   and his hand is still outstretched.

Invasion*

26 He will give a signal to a far-off nation,
   and whistle to them from the ends of
   the earth;
   speedily and promptly will they come.

27 None of them will stumble with
   weariness,
   none will slumber and none will sleep.
None will have his waist belt loose,
   nor the thong of his sandal broken.

28 Their arrows are sharp,
   and all their bows are bent.
The hoofs of their horses seem like flint,
   and their chariot wheels like the
   hurricane.

29 Their roar is that of the lion,
   like the lion's whelps they roar;
They growl and seize the prey,
   they carry it off and none will rescue it.

30 [They will roar over it, on that day,
   with a roaring like that of the sea.]*h*

II: Immanuel Prophecies

CHAPTER 6

See RG
280-95

Call of Isaiah. [1]In the year king Uzziah died,* I saw the Lord seated on a high and
lofty throne,*i* with the train of his garment filling the temple.* [2]Seraphim were stationed
above; each of them had six wings: with two
they veiled their faces, with two they veiled
their feet, and with two they hovered aloft.*j*

[3]"Holy, holy, holy is the LORD of hosts!"
they cried one to the other. "All the earth is
filled with his glory!" [4k]At the sound of that
cry, the frame of the door shook and the
house was filled with smoke.*

[5]Then I said, "Woe is me, I am doomed!"*
For I am a man of unclean lips, living among
a people of unclean lips; yet my eyes have
seen the King, the LORD of hosts!"*l* [6]Then
one of the seraphim flew to me, holding an
ember which he had taken with tongs from
the altar.

[7]He touched my mouth with it. "See," he
said, "now that this has touched your lips,*
your wickedness is removed, your sin
purged."*m*

[8]Then I heard the voice of the Lord saying, "Whom shall I send? Who will go for
us?" "Here I am;" I said; "send me!" [9]And
he replied: Go and say to this people:*

Listen carefully, but you shall not
   understand!
Look intently, but you shall know
   nothing!*n*

5, 26-30: A description of the invading Assyrian army,
God's instrument for punishing his people.

6, 1: In the year King Uzziah died: 742 B.C.

6, 1ff: Temple: the holy place, just in front of the holy of
holies. Seraphim: literally "the burning ones," are celestial
beings who surround the throne of God. Each has six wings.
Reverence for the divine majesty causes them to veil their
faces with two wings; modesty, to veil their extremities in
similar fashion; alacrity in God's service, to extend two wings
in preparation for flight. Holy, holy, holy: God's perfect interior holiness whose exterior manifestation is his glory. These
words are found in the Roman liturgy just before the Canon
of the Mass.

6, 4: Smoke: reminiscent of the clouds which surrounded
God at Mount Sinai; cf Ex 19, 16-19; Dt 4, 11f.

6, 5: Doomed: it was popularly believed that to see God
would lead to one's death; cf Gn 32, 31; Ex 33, 20; Jgs 13, 22.

6, 7: Touched your lips: Isaiah is thus symbolically purified to be worthy of his vocation as God's prophet. In the Roman liturgy, the celebrant at Mass makes reference to this incident just before he reads the gospel.

6, 9f: The truth that the nation will remain impenitent is
vividly foretold, as if its obstinacy would be caused, instead
of merely occasioned, by the prophet's warning. Cf Mt 13,
13ff; Mk 4, 12; Lk 8, 10.

---

g: Ex 23, 8; Prv 17, 15. *h:* Is 8, 22. *i:* Jn 12, 41. *j:* Rv 4, 8.
k: 1 Kgs 8, 10f; Rv 15, 8. *l:* Gn 32, 3; Ex 20, 19; 33, 20; Jgs 6,
22; 13, 22. *m:* Jer 1, 9; Dn 10, 16. *n:* Mt 13, 14f; Mk 4, 12; Lk
8, 10; Acts 28, 26f.

10 You are to make the heart of this people sluggish,

to dull their ears and close their eyes;
Else their eyes will see, their ears hear,
their heart understand,
and they will turn and be healed.*o*

11 "How long, O Lord?" I asked. And he replied:

Until the cities are desolate,
without inhabitants,
Houses, without a man,
and the earth is a desolate waste.
12 Until the LORD removes men far away,
and the land is abandoned more and
more.*
13 If there be still a tenth part in it,
then this in turn shall be laid waste;
As with a terebinth or an oak
whose trunk remains when its leaves
have fallen.
[Holy offspring is the trunk.]*p*

See RG 280-95

CHAPTER 7

Birth of Immanuel. *1* In the days of Ahaz,* king of Judah, son of Jotham, son of Uzziah, Rezin, king of Aram, and Pekah, king of Israel, son of Remaliah, went up to attack Jerusalem,*q* but they were not able to conquer it. *2* When word came to the house of David that Aram was encamped in Ephraim, the heart of the king and the heart of the people trembled, as the trees of the forest tremble in the wind.

3r Then the LORD said to Isaiah: Go out to meet Ahaz, you and your son Shear-jashub,* at the end of the conduit of the upper pool, on the highway of the fuller's field, *4* and say to him: Take care you remain tranquil and do not fear; let not your courage fail before these two stumps of smoldering brands [the blazing anger of Rezin and the Arameans, and of the son of Remaliah], *5* because of the mischief that Aram [Ephraim and the son of Remaliah] plots against you, saying, *6* "Let us go up and tear Judah asunder, make it our own by force, and appoint the son of Tabeel* king there."

7 Thus says the LORD:

This shall not stand, it shall not be!
8 Damascus is the capital of Aram,
and Rezin the head of Damascus;
Samaria is the capital of Ephraim,
and Remaliah's son the head of
Samaria.
9 But within sixty years and five,*
Ephraim shall be crushed, no longer a
nation.
Unless your faith is firm
you shall not be firm!*s*

10 Again the LORD spoke to Ahaz: *11* Ask for a sign from the LORD, your God; let it be deep as the nether world, or high as the sky!* *12* But Ahaz answered, "I will not ask! I will not tempt the LORD!"* *13* Then he said: Listen, O house of David! Is it not enough for you to weary men, must you also weary my God? *14* Therefore the Lord himself will give you this sign:* the virgin shall be with child, and

6, 12: Several limited deportations in the time of Isaiah would later culminate in the Babylonian Exile.

7, 1: Days of Ahaz: who ruled from 735 to 715 B.C. This attack against Jerusalem by the kings of Aram (Syria) and Israel was occasioned by Ahaz' refusal to enter with them into an anti-Assyrian alliance; cf 2 Kgs 16.

7, 3: Shear-jashub: this name means "a remnant will return."

7, 6: Son of Tabeel: an adherent of Jerusalem's enemies. His appointment would interrupt the lawful succession from David.

7, 9: Within sixty years and five: if the text is correct, its reference is unknown.

7, 11: Deep . . . sky: an extraordinary or miraculous sign that would prove God's firm will to save the royal house of David from its oppressors.

7, 12: Tempt the Lord: Ahaz expresses in this hypocritical way his preference for depending upon the might of Assyria rather than upon God.

7, 14: The sign proposed by Isaiah was concerned with the preservation of Judah in the midst of distress (cf Is 7, 15. 17), but more especially with the fulfillment of God's earlier promise to David (2 Sm 7, 12-16) in the coming of Immanuel (meaning, "With us is God") as the ideal king (cf Is 9, 5-6; 11, 1-5). The church has always followed St. Matthew in seeing the transcendent fulfillment of this verse in Christ and his Virgin Mother. The prophet need not have known the full force latent in his own words; and some Catholic writers have sought a preliminary and partial fulfillment in the conception and birth of the future King Hezekiah, whose mother, at the time Isaiah spoke, would have been a young, unmarried woman (Hebrew, almah). The Holy Spirit was preparing, however, for another Nativity which alone could fulfill the divinely given terms of Immanuel's mission, and in which the perpetual virginity of the Mother of God was to fulfill also the words of this prophecy in the integral sense intended by the divine Wisdom.

o: Jer 5, 21; Jn 12, 40. *p:* Is 10, 22. *q:* 2 Kgs 16, 5; 2 Chr 28, 5-15. *r:* Is 36, 2; 2 Chr 32, 3. *s:* Is 8, 6ff.

bear a son, and shall name him Immanuel. [15]He shall be living on curds and honey* by the time he learns to reject the bad and choose the good. [16]For before the child learns to reject the bad and choose the good, the land of those two kings whom you dread shall be deserted.

[17]The LORD shall bring upon you and your people and your father's house days worse than any since Ephraim seceded from Judah. [This means the king of Assyria.] [18]On that day

The LORD shall whistle
    for the fly that is in the farthest
        streams of Egypt,
    and for the bee in the land of Assyria.
[19] All of them shall come and settle
    in the steep ravines and in the rocky
        clefts,
    on all thornbushes and in all pastures.

[20]On that day the LORD shall shave with the razor hired from across the River [with the king of Assyria] the head, and the hair between the legs. It shall also shave off the beard.* [21]On that day a man shall keep a heifer or a couple of sheep, [22]and from their abundant yield of milk he shall live on curds; curds and honey shall be the food of all who remain in the land. [23]On that day every place where there used to be a thousand vines, worth a thousand pieces of silver, shall be turned to briers and thorns. [24]Men shall go there with bow and arrows; for all the country shall be briers and thorns. [25]For fear of briers and thorns you shall not go upon any mountainside which used to be hoed with the mattock; they shall be grazing land for cattle and shall be trampled upon by sheep.

CHAPTER 8

See RG 280–95

The Son of Isaiah. [1]The LORD said to me: Take a large cylinder-seal, and inscribe on it in ordinary letters:* "Belonging to Maher-shalal-hash-baz." [2]And I took reliable witnesses,* Uriah the priest, and Zechariah, son of Jeberechiah. [3]Then I went to the prophetess* and she conceived and bore a son. The LORD said to me: Name him Maher-shalal-hash-baz, [4]for before the child knows how to call his father or mother by name, the wealth of Damascus and the spoil of Samaria shall be carried off by the king of Assyria.

[5]Again the LORD spoke to me:

[6] Because this people* has rejected
    the waters of Shiloah that flow gently,[t]
And melts with fear before the loftiness
    of Rezin and Remaliah's son,
[7] Therefore the LORD raises against them
    the waters of the River, great and
        mighty
    [the king of Assyria and all his power].
It shall rise above all its channels,
    and overflow all its banks;
[8] It shall pass into Judah, and flood it all
        throughout:
    up to the neck it shall reach;
It shall spread its wings
    the full width of your land, Immanuel!
[9] Know, O peoples, and be appalled!
    Give ear, all you distant lands!
    Arm, but be crushed! Arm, but be
        crushed!
[10] Form a plan,* and it shall be thwarted;
    make a resolve, and it shall not be
        carried out,
    for "With us is God!"

7, 15: Curds and honey: the restricted diet of those who remain after devastation has changed the once fertile fields of Judah into grazing land; cf Is 7, 21-25.

7, 20: God will use the Assyrians from across the River (the Euphrates) as his instrument (razor) to inflict disgrace and suffering upon his people.

8, 1: Ordinary letters: easily read by all. Maher-shalal-hash-baz: a symbolic name to be given to another son of Isaiah (v 3); it means "quick spoils; speedy plunder," and describes what the Assyrians will do.

8, 2: Reliable witnesses: who would testify that Isaiah had indeed prophesied the future destruction. Uriah the priest: cf 2 Kgs 16, 10.

8, 3: The prophetess: wife of Isaiah.

8, 6ff: This people: Judah. Waters of Shiloah: the stream that flows into the pool of Shiloah in Jerusalem, its slow current symbolizing the silent, divine protection which Judah has rejected. God will therefore summon the mighty Assyrian army, symbolized by the River (Euphrates), to devastate Judah, which, however, will not be entirely destroyed, because it is the land of Immanuel.

8, 10: The plan of Israel's enemies will be thwarted because, as the name "Immanuel" signifies, With us is God.

t: Jn 9. 7. 11.

Disciples of Isaiah. [11] For thus said the LORD to me, taking hold of me and warning me not to walk in the way of this people:[u]

[12] Call not alliance what this people calls alliance,
  and fear not, nor stand in awe of what they fear.
[13] But with the LORD of hosts make your alliance—
  for him be your fear and your awe.
[14] Yet he shall be a snare, an obstacle and a stumbling stone
  to both the houses of Israel,
A trap and a snare
  to those who dwell in Jerusalem;[v]
[15] And many among them shall stumble and fall,
  broken, snared, and captured.

[16] The record is to be folded and the sealed instruction kept among my disciples.[*] [17] For I will trust in the LORD, who is hiding his face from the house of Jacob; yes, I will wait for him. [18] Look at me and the children whom the Lord has given me: we are signs[*] and portents in Israel from the LORD of hosts who dwells on Mount Zion. [19w] And when they say to you, "Inquire of mediums and fortune-tellers (who chirp and mutter!*); should not a people inquire of their gods, apply to the dead on behalf of the living!"— [20] then this document will furnish its instruction. That kind of thing they will surely say.[*]

The Prince of Peace. [23] First he degraded the land of Zebulun and the land of Naphtali;[*] but in the end he has glorified the seaward road, the land west of the Jordan, the District of the Gentiles.

Anguish has taken wing, dispelled is darkness:
  for there is no gloom where until now there was distress.

CHAPTER 9

See RG 280–95

[1] The people who walked in darkness[x]
  have seen a great light;
Upon those who dwelt in the land of gloom
  a light has shone.
[2] You have brought them abundant joy
  and great rejoicing,
As they rejoice before you as at the harvest,
  as men make merry when dividing spoils.
[3] For the yoke that burdened them,
  the pole on their shoulder,
And the rod of their taskmaster
  you have smashed, as on the day of Midian.
[4] For every boot that tramped in battle,
  every cloak rolled in blood,
  will be burned as fuel for flames.[y]
[5] For a child[*] is born to us, a son is given us;
  upon his shoulder dominion rests.
They name him Wonder-Counselor, God-Hero,
  Father-Forever, Prince of Peace.[z]
[6] His dominion is vast
  and forever peaceful,
From David's throne, and over his kingdom,
  which he confirms and sustains
By judgment and justice,
  both now and forever.
The zeal of the LORD of hosts will do this![a]

8, 16: Kept among my disciples: for preservation and transmission.

8, 18: Signs: Isaiah and his sons had symbolic names.

8, 19: Chirp and mutter: a mocking reference to the sounds uttered by necromancers, as if the dead were speaking; all such practices were forbidden.

8, 21f: These verses have been transposed and placed within Is 14, 25, which affords the context in which they can be understood.

8, 23: Zebulun . . . Naphtali: northern Palestine, which was first to be attacked by the Assyrians; God, however, redeems it, as he redeems all his people. Seaward road; from Damascus, across southern Galilee to the Mediterranean Sea. District of the Gentiles: northern Galilee, inhabited by pagans; cf Jos 20, 7; Is 9, 1. Mt 4, 15f refers to this, since Jesus began his public mission in Galilee.

9, 5: A child: the Immanuel of Is 7, 14 and 8, 8; cf Is 11, 1. 2. 9. In Christian tradition and liturgy, this passage is used to refer to Christ. Upon his shoulder dominion rests: authority. Wonder-Counselor: remarkable for his wisdom and prudence. God-Hero: a warrior and a defender of his people, like God himself. Father-Forever: ever devoted to his people. Prince of Peace: his reign will be characterized by peace.

u: Ez 3, 14. *v:* Rom 9, 33; 1 Pt 2, 8. *w:* Lv 19, 31; Dt 18, 10ff. *x:* 1f: Mt 4, 15f. *y:* Sir 39, 9. *z:* Ps 72, 7; Lk 2, 11. 14. *a:* Jer 23, 5; Lk 1, 32f.

Fall of the Northern Kingdom

7 The Lord has sent word against Jacob,
   it falls upon Israel;
8 And all the people know it,
   Ephraim and those who dwell in
      Samaria,
   those who say in arrogance and pride
      of heart,
9 "Bricks have fallen,
   but we will build with cut stone;
Sycamores are felled,
   but we will replace them with cedars."
10 But the LORD raises up their foes against
      them
   and stirs up their enemies to action:
11 Aram* on the east and the Philistines on
      the west
   devour Israel with open mouth.
For all this, his wrath is not turned
      back,
   and his hand is still outstretched!

12 The people do not turn to him who struck
      them,
   nor seek the LORD of hosts.
13 So the LORD severs from Israel head and
      tail,
   palm branch and reed in one day.
14 [The elder and the noble are the head,
   the prophet who teaches falsehood is
      the tail.]
15 The leaders of this people mislead them
   and those to be led are engulfed.b
16 For this reason, the Lord does not spare
      their young men,
   and their orphans and widows he does
      not pity;
They are wholly profaned and sinful,
   and every mouth gives vent to folly.
For all this, his wrath is not turned back,
   his hand is still outstretched!

17 For wickedness burns like fire,
   devouring brier and thorn;
It kindles the forest thickets,
   which go up in columns of smoke.

18 At the wrath of the LORD of hosts the
      land quakes,
   and the people are like fuel for fire;
No man spares his brother,
   each devours the flesh of his
      neighbor.
19 Though they hack on the right, they are
      hungry;
   though they eat on the left, they are not
      filled.
20 Manasseh devours Ephraim,* and
      Ephraim Manasseh;
   together they turn on Judah.
For all this, his wrath is not turned back,
   his hand is still outstretched!

CHAPTER 10

See RG
280-95

Social Injustice

1 Woe to those who enact unjust statutes
   and who write oppressive decrees,c
2 Depriving the needy of judgment
   and robbing my people's poor of their
      rights.
Making widows their plunder,
   and orphans their prey!d
3 What will you do on the day of
      punishment,
   when ruin comes from afar?
To whom will you flee for help?
   Where will you leave your wealth,
4 Lest it sink beneath the captive
   or fall beneath the slain?
For all this, his wrath is not turned back,
   his hand is still outstretched!

Assyria the Unconscious Instrument of God

5 Woe to Assyria! My rod in anger,
   my staff in wrath.
6 Against an impious nation* I send him,
   and against a people under my wrath I
      order him
To seize plunder, carry off loot,
   and tread them down like the mud of
      the streets.
7 But this is not what he intends,
   nor does he have this in mind;

9, 11: Aram: the Syrian kingdom, with its capital at Damascus.
9, 20: Manasseh . . . Ephraim: two of the leading tribes of the northern kingdom.
10, 6f: Impious nation: Israel. It was God's intention to use Assyria merely to punish, not to destroy, his people.

b: Is 28, 7; Jer 2, 8; 5, 31; 20, 6; 23, 13f; 29, 30ff; Ez 13, 1-7; 22, 28; Mi 3, 11.   c: Jer 8, 8.   d: Is 1, 23.

Rather, it is in his heart to destroy,
to make an end of nations not a few.
8 "Are not my commanders all kings?" he says,
9 "Is not Calno like Carchemish,*e*
Or Hamath like Arpad,
or Samaria like Damascus?"*
10 Just as my hand reached out to idolatrous kingdoms
that had more images than Jerusalem and Samaria,
11 Just as I treated Samaria and her idols,
shall I not do to Jerusalem and her graven images?"*f*

12*[But when the LORD has brought to an end all his work on Mount Zion and in Jerusalem,

I will punish the utterance
of the king of Assyria's proud heart,
13 and the boastfulness of his haughty eyes.
For he says:]

"By my own power I have done it,
and by my wisdom, for I am shrewd.
I have moved the boundaries of peoples,
their treasures I have pillaged,
and, like a giant, I have put down the enthroned.
14 My hand has seized like a nest
the riches of nations;
As one takes eggs left alone,
so I took in all the earth;
No one fluttered a wing,
or opened a mouth, or chirped!"

15 Will the axe boast against him who hews with it?
Will the saw exalt itself above him who wields it?
As if a rod could sway him who lifts it,
or a staff him who is not wood!
16 Therefore the Lord, the LORD of hosts,
will send among his fat ones* leanness,

And instead of his glory there will be kindling
like the kindling of fire.
17 The Light of Israel will become a fire,
Israel's Holy One a flame,
That burns and consumes his briers
and his thorns in a single day.
18 His splendid forests and orchards
will be consumed, soul and body;
19 And the remnant of the trees in his forest
will be so few,
Like poles set up for signals,
that any boy can record them.
20 On that day
The remnant of Israel,
the survivors of the house of Jacob,
will no more lean upon him who struck them;
But they will lean upon the LORD,
the Holy One of Israel, in truth.
21 A remnant will return,* the remnant of Jacob,
to the mighty God.
22 For though your people, O Israel,
were like the sand of the sea,
Only a remnant of them will return;
their destruction is decreed
as overwhelming justice demands.*g*

23 Yes, the destruction he has decreed, the Lord, the GOD of hosts, will carry out within the whole land. 24 Therefore thus says the Lord, the GOD of hosts: O my people, who dwell in Zion, do not fear the Assyrian, though he strikes you with a rod, and raises his staff against you. 25 For only a brief moment more, and my anger shall be over; but them I will destroy in wrath. 26 Then the LORD of hosts will raise against them a scourge such as struck Midian at the rock of Oreb; and he will raise his staff over the sea as he did against Egypt.*h* 27 On that day,*

His burden shall be taken from your shoulder,
and his yoke shattered from your neck.

10, 9: Calno . . . Damascus: cities captured by the Assyrians.

10, 16: His fat ones: the strong men of the king of Assyria.

10, 21: A remnant will return: in Hebrew, shear-jashub, an allusion to the name of Isaiah's son, Shear-jashub; cf Is 7, 3.

10, 27-32: A poetic description of the progress of the Assyrian army, advancing from the north through Judah to the gates of Jerusalem.

e: Is 36, 19; Am 6, 2.   *f:* Is 36, 20.   *g:* Rom 9, 27f.   *h:* Jgs 7, 25.

Sennacherib's Invasion

He has come up from the direction of
Rimmon,

28 he has reached Aiath, passed through
Migron,

at Michmash his supplies are stored.

29 They cross the ravine:

"We will spend the night at Geba."

Ramah is in terror,

Gibeah of Saul has fled.

30 Cry and shriek, O daughter of Gallim!

Hearken, Laishah! Answer her,
Anathoth!

31 Madmenah is in flight,

the inhabitants of Gebim seek refuge.

32 Even today he will halt at Nob,*

he will shake his fist at the mount of
daughter Zion,

the hill of Jerusalem!

33 Behold, the Lord, the LORD of hosts,

lops off the boughs with terrible
violence;

The tall of stature are felled,

and the lofty ones brought low;

34 The forest thickets are felled with the axe,

and Lebanon in its splendor falls.

CHAPTER 11

See RG
280-95

The Rule of Immanuel

1 But a shoot shall sprout from the stump of
Jesse,*

and from his roots a bud shall blossom.i

2 The spirit of the LORD shall rest upon
him:j

a spirit of wisdom and of understanding,

A spirit of counsel and of strength,

a spirit of knowledge and of fear of the
LORD,*

3 and his delight shall be the fear of the
LORD.

Not by appearance shall he judge,

nor by hearsay shall he decide,

4 But he shall judge the poor with justice,

and decide aright for the land's
afflicted.k

He shall strike the ruthless with the rod
of his mouth,

and with the breath of his lips he shall
slay the wicked.

5 Justice shall be the band around his waist,

and faithfulness a belt upon his hips.

6 Then the wolf shall be a guest of the
lamb,*

and the leopard shall lie down with the
kid;

The calf and the young lion shall browse
together,

with a little child to guide them.l

7 The cow and the bear shall be neighbors,

together their young shall rest;

the lion shall eat hay like the ox.

8 The baby shall play by the cobra's den,

and the child lay his hand on the
adder's lair.

9 There shall be no harm or ruin on all my
holy mountain;

for the earth shall be filled with
knowledge of the LORD,

as water covers the sea.m

Union of Ephraim and Judah

10 On that day,

The root of Jesse,

set up as a signal for the nations,

The Gentiles shall seek out,

for his dwelling shall be glorious.n

11 On that day,

The Lord shall again take it in hando

to reclaim the remnant of his people

that is left from Assyria and Egypt,

Pathros, Ethiopia, and Elam,

Shinar, Hamath, and the isles of the
sea.*

10, 32ff: Just when the enemy is about to capture
Jerusalem, God intervenes and destroys the hostile army.

11, 1: Jesse: David's father. Shoot . . . stump: after the
Babylonian exile only a stump of the Davidic dynasty will remain; from it will arise the new shoot, the messianic King.

11, 2f: The source of the traditional names of the gifts of
the Holy Spirit. The Septuagint and the Vulgate read "piety"
for fear of the Lord in its first occurrence, thus listing seven
gifts.

11, 6-9: This picture of the idyllic harmony of paradise is
a dramatic symbol of the universal peace and justice of messianic times.

11, 11: Pathros . . . sea: where God's people lived in exile.
Pathros: upper Egypt. Elam: east of Babylonia. Shinar: Babylonia. Hamath: on the Orontes River in Syria. Isles: or coastlands, in the Mediterranean.

---

i: Lk 3, 32. *j:* Mt 3, 16; Mk 1, 10. *k:* Pss 72, 2. 4; 98, 9; 2 Thes
2, 8. *l:* Is 65, 25. *m:* Hb 2, 14. *n:* Is 49, 22; Rom 15, 12.
o: Is 27, 13; Mi 7, 12; Zec 10, 10.

¹² He shall raise a signal to the nations
  and gather the outcasts of Israel;
The dispersed of Judah he shall assemble
  from the four corners of the earth.
¹³ The envy of Ephraim shall pass away,
  and the rivalry of Judah be removed;
Ephraim shall not be jealous of Judah,
  and Judah shall not be hostile to
    Ephraim;*p*
¹⁴ But they shall swoop down on the
    foothills
  of the Philistines to the west,
together they shall plunder the
    Kedemites;*
Edom and Moab shall be their possessions,
  and the Ammonites their subjects.
¹⁵ The LORD shall dry up the tongue of the
    Sea of Egypt,*
  and wave his hand over the Euphrates
    in his fierce anger
And shatter it into seven streamlets,
  so that it can be crossed in sandals.*q*
¹⁶ There shall be a highway for the remnant
    of his people
  that is left from Assyria,
As there was for Israel
  when he came up from the land of
    Egypt.

See RG
280-95

CHAPTER 12

*Song of Thanksgiving**

¹   On that day, you will say:
I give you thanks, O LORD;
  though you have been angry with me,
  your anger has abated, and you have
    consoled me.
² God indeed is my savior;
  I am confident and unafraid.
My strength and my courage is the LORD,
  and he has been my savior.*r*

³ With joy you will draw water
  at the fountain of salvation, ⁴and say
    on that day:

Give thanks to the LORD, acclaim his
    name;
  among the nations make known his
    deeds,
  proclaim how exalted is his name.
⁵ Sing praise to the LORD for his glorious
    achievement;
  let this be known throughout all the
    earth.*s*
⁶ Shout with exultation, O city of Zion,
  for great in your midst
  is the Holy One of Israel!*t*

III: Oracles Against the Pagan Nations

CHAPTER 13

See RG
280-95

Babylon. ¹An oracle concerning Babylon; a vision of Isaiah, son of Amoz.

² Upon the bare mountains set up a signal;
  cry out to them,*
Wave for them to enter
  the gates of the volunteers.*u*

³ I have commanded my dedicated
    soldiers,*
  I have summoned my warriors,
  eager and bold to carry out my anger.
⁴ Listen! the rumble on the mountains:
  that of an immense throng!
Listen! the noise of kingdoms,
  nations assembled!
The LORD of hosts is mustering
  an army for battle.*v*
⁵ They come from a far-off country,
  and from the end of the heavens,
The LORD and the instruments of his
    wrath,
  to destroy all the land.

⁶ Howl, for the day of the LORD* is near;
  as destruction from the Almighty it
    comes.*w*

11, 14: Kedemites: tribes in the Arabian Desert.
11, 15: Tongue . . . Egypt: the body of water between
Egypt and Palestine.
12, 1-6: Israel's thanksgiving to the Lord, expressed in
language like that of the Psalms.
13, 2: To them: the Medes (v 17) and Persians, who would
destroy Babylon. Gates of the volunteers: the mustering
places of Babylon's enemies for war against her.

13, 3: Dedicated soldiers: in the sense that they will wage
a "holy war" and carry out God's plan.
13, 6ff: Day of the LORD: described often in prophetical
writings, it generally signified the coming of the Lord in

p: Ex 37, 16-17.   *q:* Ex 14, 29.   *r:* Ex 15, 2; Ps 118, 14.   *s:* Ex
15, 1.   *t:* Is 41, 14. 16; 54, 1; Zep 3, 14; Zec 2, 10.   *u:* Is 5, 26.
v: Jer 50, 9.   *w:* Jer 46, 10; Jl 1, 15.

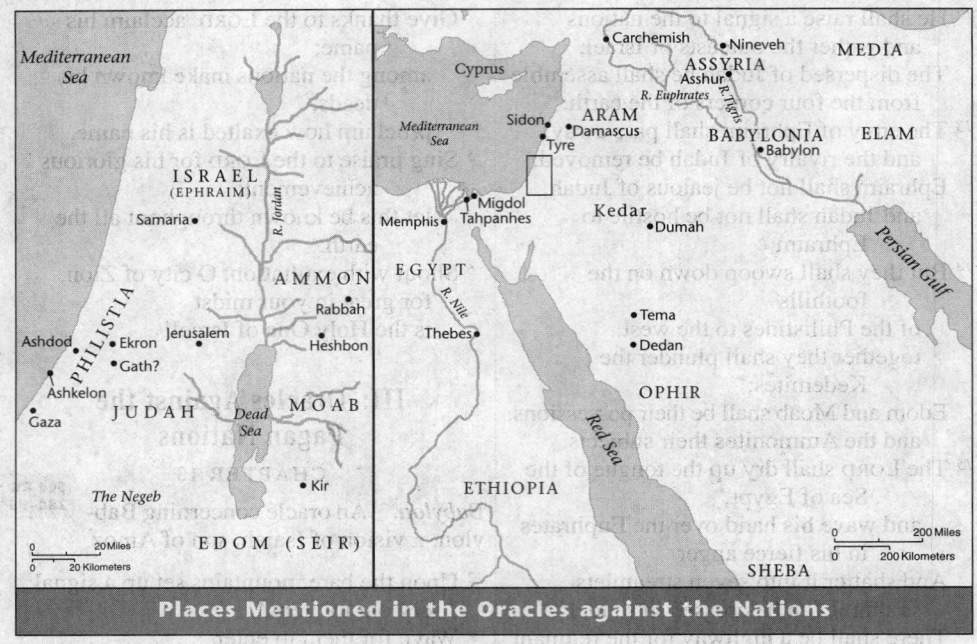

Places Mentioned in the Oracles against the Nations

7 Therefore all hands fall helpless,[x]
  the bows of the young men fall from
    their hands.
Every man's heart melts [8] in terror.
  Pangs and sorrows take hold of them,
  like a woman in labor they writhe;
They look aghast at each other,
  their faces aflame.[y]
9 Lo, the day of the LORD comes,
  cruel, with wrath and burning anger;
To lay waste the land
  and destroy the sinners within it!
10 The stars and constellations of the
    heavens
  send forth no light;
The sun is dark when it rises,
  and the light of the moon does not
    shine.[z]
11 Thus I will punish the world for its evil
  and the wicked for their guilt.
I will put an end to the pride of the
    arrogant,

the insolence of tyrants I will humble.[a]
12 I will make mortals more rare than pure
    gold,
  men, than gold of Ophir.*
13 For this I will make the heavens
    tremble
  and the earth shall be shaken from its
    place,
At the wrath of the LORD of hosts
  on the day of his burning anger.
14 Like a hunted gazelle,
  or a flock that no one gathers,
Every man shall turn to his kindred
  and flee to his own land.[b]
15 Everyone who is caught shall be run
    through;
  to a man, they shall fall by the sword.
16 Their infants shall be dashed to pieces in
    their sight;
  their houses shall be plundered
  and their wives ravished.[c]

power and majesty to destroy his enemies and inaugurate his kingdom. Here it refers to the overthrow of Babylon. The figures used convey the idea of horror and destruction. Read vv 6-8 with vv 14-16.

13, 12: Ophir: cf note to Ps 45, 10.

x: Ez 7, 17.   y: Is 21, 3; Ps 48, 7; Mi 4, 9.   z: Is 24, 23.   a: Is 2, 17; Jer 50. 32.   b: Jer 50, 16.   c: Na 3, 10.

[17] I am stirring up against them the Medes,
who think nothing of silver
and take no delight in gold.[d]
[18] The fruit of the womb they shall not
spare,
nor shall they have eyes of pity for
children.
[19] And Babylon, the jewel of kingdoms,
the glory and pride of the Chaldeans,
Shall be overthrown by God
like Sodom and like Gomorrah.
[20] She shall never be inhabited,
nor dwelt in, from age to age;
The Arab shall not pitch his tent there,
nor shepherds couch their flocks.[e]
[21] But wildcats shall rest there
and owls shall fill the houses;
There ostriches shall dwell,
and satyrs* shall dance.[f]
[22] Desert beasts shall howl in her castles,
and jackals in her luxurious palaces.
Her time is near at hand
and her days shall not be prolonged.

CHAPTER 14

See RG 280-95

The King of Babylon. [1]When the
LORD has pity on Jacob and again chooses
Israel and settles them on their own soil, the
aliens will join them and be counted with the
house of Jacob.[g] [2]The house of Israel will
take them and bring them along to its place,
and possess them as male and female slaves
on the Lord's soil, making captives of its
captors and ruling over its oppressors.[h] [3]On
the day the LORD relieves you of sorrow and
unrest and the hard service in which you
have been enslaved,[i] [4]you will take up this
taunt-song* against the king of Babylon:[j]

How the oppressor has reached his end!
how the turmoil is stilled!
[5] The LORD has broken the rod of the
wicked,
the staff of the tyrants
[6] That struck the peoples in wrath

relentless blows;
That beat down the nations in anger,
with oppression unchecked.
[7] The whole earth rests peacefully,
song breaks forth;
[8] The very cypresses rejoice over you,
and the cedars of Lebanon:
"Now that you are laid to rest,
there will be none to cut us down."[k]

[9] The nether world below is all astir
preparing for your coming;
It awakens the shades to greet you,
all the leaders of the earth;
It has the kings of all nations
rise from their thrones.
[10] All of them speak out
and say to you,
"You too have become weak like us,
you are the same as we.
[11] Down to the nether world your pomp is
brought,
the music of your harps.
The couch beneath you is the maggot,
your covering, the worm."[l]

[12] How have you fallen from the heavens,
O morning star,* son of the dawn!
How are you cut down to the ground,
you who mowed down the nations!
[13] You said in your heart:[m]
"I will scale the heavens;
Above the stars of God
I will set up my throne;
I will take my seat on the Mount of
Assembly,
in the recesses of the North.*
[14] I will ascend above the tops of the
clouds;
I will be like the Most High!"[n]

[15] Yet down to the nether world you go
to the recesses of the pit!
[16] When they see you they will stare,
pondering over you:

13, 21: Satyrs: in the popular mind, demons of goatlike
form dwelling in ruins, symbols of immorality; cf Lv 17, 7.

14, 4-21: This taunt-song, or satire, is one of the finest in
the Bible.

14, 12: Morning star: the king of Babylon. The Vulgate
has "Lucifer," a name applied by the church Fathers to Satan.

14, 13: Recesses of the North: see note on Ps 48, 3.

d: Is 21, 2; Jer 51, 11. 28.　e: Jer 51, 62.　f: Is 34, 13f; 35, 7.
g: Is 56, 3; 60, 4; Ps 102, 14; Jer 24, 6; Zec 1, 17.　h: Is 66, 20.
i: Jer 30, 10.　j: Hb 2, 6.　k: Ez 31, 16.　l: Sir 10, 13.　m: Jer
51, 53; Am 9, 2.　n: Ez 28, 2.

"Is this the man who made the earth
  tremble,
  and kingdoms quake?
17 Who made the world a desert,
  razed its cities,
  and gave his captives no release?
18 All the kings of the nations lie in glory,
  each in his own tomb;
19 But you are cast forth without burial,
  loathsome and corrupt,
Clothed as those slain at sword-point,
  a trampled corpse.
Going down to the pavement of the pit,
20 you will never be one with them in the
  grave."
For you have ruined your land,
  you have slain your people!

Let him not be named forever,
  that scion of an evil race!
21 Make ready to slaughter his sons
  for the guilt of their fathers;
Lest they rise and possess the earth,
  and fill the breadth of the world with
  tyrants.

22I will rise up against them, says the
LORD of hosts, and cut off from Babylon
name and remnant, progeny and offspring,
says the LORD.o 23I will make it a haunt of
hoot owls and a marshland; I will sweep it
with the broom of destruction, says the
LORD of hosts.

Assyria

24   The LORD of hosts has sworn:
As I have resolved,
  so shall it be;
As I have proposed,
  so shall it stand:
25 I will break the Assyrian in my land
  and trample him on my mountains;
21*He shall pass through it hard-pressed and
  hungry,
  and in his hunger he shall become
  enraged,

and curse his king and his gods.
He shall look upward,
  but there shall be strict darkness
  without any dawn;
22 He shall gaze at the earth,
  but there shall be distress and
  darkness,
  with the light blacked out by its
  clouds.
(25)Then his yoke shall be removed from
  them,
  and his burden from their
  shoulder.
26 This is the plan proposed for the whole
  earth.
  and this the hand outstretched over all
  nations.
27 The LORD of hosts has planned;
  who can thwart him?
His hand is stretched out;
  who can turn it back?

Philistia. 28In the year that King Ahaz
died,* there came this oracle:

29 Rejoice not, O Philistia, not a man of
  you,
  that the rod* which smote you is
  broken;
For out of the serpent's root shall come
  an adder,
  its fruit shall be a flying saraph.
30 In my pastures the poor shall eat,
  and the needy lie down in safety;
But I will kill your root with famine
  that shall slay even your
  remnant.
31 Howl, O gate; cry out, O city!
  Philistia, all of you melts away!
For there comes a smoke from the north,
  without a straggler in the ranks.
32 What will one answer the messengers of
  the nation?
  "The LORD has established Zion,
  and in her the afflicted of his people
  find refuge."p

14, 21f: He . . . clouds: the two verses have been transposed from chap. 8.
14, 28: The year that King Ahaz died: 715 B.C.
14, 29: Rod: an Assyrian oppressor whose identity is uncertain. Flying saraph: a poisonous serpent, distinguished by its speedy movement; cf note on Nm 21, 6.

o: Jer 51, 62. *p:* Pss 87, 5; 102, 17f; Zep 3, 12.

11 Though you make them grow the day
you plant them
and make your sprouts blossom on the
next morning.
The harvest shall disappear on the day of
the grievous blow,
the incurable blight.
12 Ah! the roaring of many peoples*
that roar like the roar of the seas!
The surging of nations
that surge like the surging of mighty
waves!
13 But God shall rebuke them,
and they shall flee far away;
Windswept, like chaff on the mountains,
like tumbleweed in a storm.
14 In the evening, they spread terror,
before morning, they are gone!
Such is the portion of those who despoil
us,
the lot of those who plunder us.

See RG
280-95 ## CHAPTER 18

Ethiopia

1 Ah, land of buzzing insects,*
beyond the rivers of Ethiopia,
2 Sending ambassadors by sea,
in papyrus boats* on the waters!
Go, swift messengers,
to a nation tall and bronzed,
To a people dreaded near and far,
a nation strong and conquering,
whose land is washed by rivers.*h*
3 All you who inhabit the world,
who dwell on earth,
When the signal is raised on the
mountain, look!
When the trumpet blows, listen!
4 For thus says the LORD to me:
I will quietly look on from where I
dwell,
Like the glowing heat of sunshine,
like a cloud of dew at harvest time.

5 Before the vintage, when the flowering is
ended,
and the blooms are succeeded by
ripening grapes,
Then comes the cutting of branches with
pruning hooks
and the discarding of the lopped-off
shoots.
6 They shall all be left to the mountain
birds of prey,
and to the beasts in the land;
The birds of prey shall summer on them
and on them all the beasts of the earth
shall winter.

7 Then will gifts be brought to the LORD of
hosts from a people tall and bronzed, from a
people dreaded near and far, a nation strong
and conquering, whose land is washed by
rivers—to Mount Zion where dwells the
name of the LORD of hosts.*i*

CHAPTER 19

Egypt

See RG
280-95

1 Oracle on Egypt:
See, the LORD is riding on a swift cloud
on his way to Egypt;
The idols of Egypt tremble before him,
the hearts of the Egyptians melt within
them.
2 I will rouse Egypt against Egypt:
brother will war against brother,
Neighbor against neighbor,
city against city, kingdom against
kingdom.
3 The courage of the Egyptians ebbs away
within them,
and I will bring to nought their counsel;
They shall consult idols and charmers,
ghosts and spirits.*j*
4 I will deliver Egypt
into the power of a cruel master,*
A harsh king who shall rule over them,
says the Lord, the LORD of hosts.*k*

17, 12f: Many peoples: the hordes that accompanied the invading Assyrians, whom God repels just as he vanquished the primeval waters of chaos; see notes on Jb 3, 8; 7, 12; Ps 89, 11.

18, 1: Land of buzzing insects: the region of the Upper Nile where these multiplied with great rapidity.

18, 2: Papyrus boats: light and serviceable vessels made of bundles of papyrus stalks and sealed with pitch. Egypt,

ruled by a dynasty from Ethiopia, had invited Judah to join a coalition against Assyria, but Isaiah bade the ambassadors return to their own people.

19, 4: Cruel master: the king of Assyria.

---

h: Is 18, 7. *i:* Is 45, 14; Zep 3, 10; Mal 1, 11. *j:* Is 44, 25. *k:* Ez 29, 19; 30, 10.

5 The waters shall be drained from the sea,
   the river shall shrivel and dry up;[l]
6 Its streams shall become foul,
   and the canals of Egypt shall dwindle
      and dry up.
Reeds and rushes shall wither away,
7   and bulrushes on the bank of the Nile;
All the sown land along the Nile
   shall dry up and blow away, and be no
      more.
8 The fishermen shall mourn and lament,
   all who cast hook in the Nile;
Those who spread their nets in the water
   shall pine away.
9 The linen-workers shall be disappointed,
   the combers and weavers shall turn
      pale;[m]
10 The spinners shall be crushed,
   all the hired laborers shall be despondent.
11 Utter fools are the princes of Zoan!*
   the wisest of Pharaoh's advisers give
      stupid counsel.
How can you say to Pharaoh,
   "I am a disciple of wise men, of
      ancient kings"?
12 Where then are your wise men?
   Let them tell you and make known
What the LORD of hosts has planned
   against Egypt.
13 The princes of Zoan have become fools,
   the princes of Memphis have been
      deceived.
The chiefs of her tribes
   have led Egypt astray.
14 The LORD has prepared among them
   a spirit of dizziness,
And they have made Egypt stagger in
      whatever she does,
   as a drunkard staggers in his vomit.
15 Egypt shall have no work to do[n]
   for head or tail, palm branch or reed.*

16 On that day the Egyptians shall be like
women, trembling with fear, because of the
LORD of hosts shaking his fist at them.[o]
17 And the land of Judah shall be a terror to
the Egyptians. Every time they remember
Judah, they shall stand in dread because of
the plan which the LORD of hosts has in mind
for them.[p]
18 On that day there shall be five cities* in
the land of Egypt speaking the language of
Canaan and swearing by the LORD of hosts;
one shall be called "City of the Sun."
19 On that day there shall be an altar to the
LORD in the land of Egypt, and a sacred pillar to the LORD near the boundary. 20 It shall
be a sign and a witness to the LORD of hosts
in the land of Egypt, when they cry out to the
LORD against their oppressors, and he sends
them a savior to defend and deliver them.
21 The LORD shall make himself known to
Egypt, and the Egyptians shall know the
LORD in that day; they shall offer sacrifices
and oblations, and fulfill the vows they
make to the LORD.[q] 22 Although the LORD
shall smite Egypt severely, he shall heal
them; they shall turn to the LORD and he
shall be won over and heal them.
23 On that day there shall be a highway
from Egypt to Assyria; the Assyrians shall
enter Egypt, and the Egyptians enter Assyria, and Egypt shall serve Assyria.
24 On that day Israel shall be a third party
with Egypt and Assyria, a blessing in the
midst of the land,[r] 25 when the LORD of hosts
blesses it: "Blessed be my people Egypt, and
the work of my hands Assyria, and my inheritance, Israel."

CHAPTER 20

See RG
280-95

Captivity of Egypt and Ethiopia. 1 In
the year the general sent by Sargon, king of
Assyria, fought against Ashdod and captured
it, 2 the LORD gave a warning through Isaiah,*
the son of Amoz: Go and take off the sackcloth from your waist, and remove the sandals from your feet. This he did, walking

19, 11. 13: Zoan: later known as Tanis, and Memphis (in
Hebrew Noph) were the key cities of the Nile Delta.
19, 15: Head or tail, palm branch or reed: the leaders or the
people; cf Is 9, 13f.
19, 18: Five cities: colonies of Jews living together and
speaking their languages, Hebrew and Aramaic; cf Jer, chap.
43. City of the Sun: the meaning is uncertain, but the reference seems to be to the city known later as Heliopolis.

20, 2-6: The symbolic act of the prophet conveyed the
idea that Assyria would lead captive the Egyptians and Ethiopians. The Judeans and their allies would then realize the
folly of having trusted in them.

l: Ez 30, 12; 32, 2. m: Ez 27, 7. n: Is 9, 14. o: Na 3, 13.
p: Ex 14, 25. q: Zec 14, 16. 18. r: Gn 12, 2.

naked and barefoot. ³Then the LORD said: Just as my servant Isaiah has gone naked and barefoot for three years as a sign and portent against Egypt and Ethiopia, ⁴so shall the king of Assyria lead away captives from Egypt, and exiles from Ethiopia, young and old, naked and barefoot, with buttocks uncovered [the shame of Egypt]. ⁵They shall be dismayed and ashamed because of Ethiopia, their hope, and because of Egypt, their boast.ˢ ⁶The inhabitants of this coastland shall say on that day, "Look at our hope! We have fled here for help and deliverance from the king of Assyria; where can we flee now?"ᵗ

CHAPTER 21

See RG 280–95

Fall of Babylon

1 Oracle on the wastelands by the sea:*

Like whirlwinds sweeping in waves
       through the Negeb,
   there comes from the desert,
   from the fearful land,
² A cruel sight, revealed to me:
   the traitor betrays,
   the despoiler spoils.
"Go up, Elam; besiege, O Media;*
   I will put an end to all groaning!"ᵘ
³ Therefore my loins are filled with anguish,
   pangs have seized me like those of a
       woman in labor;
   I am too bewildered to hear,
   too dismayed to look.ᵛ
⁴ My mind reels,
   shuddering assails me;
   My yearning for twilight
   has turned into dread.
⁵ They set the table,
   spread out the rugs;
   they eat, they drink.*
Rise up, O princes,
   oil the shield!

⁶ For thus says my Lord to me:
   Go, station a watchman,
   let him tell what he sees.
⁷ If he sees a chariot,
   a pair of horses,
Someone riding an ass,
   someone riding a camel,
Then let him pay heed,
   very close heed.
⁸   Then the watchman cried,
"On the watchtower, O my Lord,
   I stand constantly by day;
And I stay at my post
   through all the watches of the night.ʷ
⁹ Here he comes now:
   a single chariot,
   a pair of horses;
He calls out and says,
   'Fallen, fallen is Babylon,
And all the images of her gods
   are smashed to the ground.' "ˣ

¹⁰ O my people who have been threshed,
   beaten on my threshing floor!
What I have heard
   from the LORD of hosts,
The God of Israel,
   I have announced to you.ʸ

Edom

¹¹   Oracle on Edom:
They call to me from Seir,*
   "Watchman, how much longer the
       night?
Watchman, how much longer the
       night?"
¹²   The watchman replies,
"Morning has come, and again night.
   If you will ask, ask; come back again."

Arabia

¹³   Oracle on Arabia:*

21, 1: Wastelands by the sea: Babylonia. Negeb: the desert south of Judah.

21, 2: Elam . . . Media: nations which, under the leadership of Cyrus, captured Babylon in 538 B.C. End to all groaning: those who were captives of Babylon shall be freed.

21, 5: Babylon is destroyed while its leaders are feasting; cf Dn 5. Oil the shield: shields were oiled and greased so as to divert blows more easily.

21, 11f: Seir: another name for Edom. The Edomites ask the prophet how much longer they must suffer (the night of

suffering); he answers ambiguously: "Liberation (morning) and further suffering (night)," but perhaps they will later receive a more encouraging answer (ask; come back again).

21, 13f: Arabia: that is, the nomad country. Dedanites: an Arab tribe associated with Edom and Tema, and living east of the Red Sea; cf Gn 10, 7; 25, 3; Jer 25, 23.

s: Is 30, 3. 5.   t: Is 31, 3; 36. 6.   u: Is 13, 17.   v: Ps 38, 8. w: Hb 2, 1.   x: Is 46, 1; Jer 50, 2: 51, 8; Rv 14, 8.   y: Is 51, 23.

In the thicket in the nomad country spend
the night,
O caravans of Dedanites.
[14] Meet the thirsty, bring them water;
you who dwell in the land of Tema,
greet the fugitives with bread.
[15] They flee from the sword,
from the whetted sword;
From the taut bow,
from the fury of battle.

[16] For thus says the Lord to me: In another
year, like those of a hireling,* all the glory of
Kedar shall come to an end. [17]Few of Kedar's stalwart archers shall remain, for the
LORD, the God of Israel, has spoken.

See RG
280-95

CHAPTER 22

Jerusalem

[1]
Oracle of the Valley of Vision:*
What is the matter with you now, that
you have gone up,
all of you, to the housetops,
[2] O city full of noise and chaos,
O wanton town!
Your slain are not slain with the sword,
nor killed in battle.
[3] All your leaders fled away together,
fled afar off;
All who were in you were captured
together,
captured without the use of a bow.[a]
[4] At this I say: Turn away from me,
let me weep bitterly;
Do not try to comfort me
for the ruin of the daughter of my
people.[b]
[5] It is a day of panic, rout and confusion,
from the Lord, the GOD of hosts, in the
Valley of Vision.
Walls crash;
they cry for help to the mountains.[c]
[6] Elam* takes up the quivers,
Aram mounts the horses,

and Kir uncovers the shields.
[7] Your choice valleys are filled with
chariots,
and horses are posted at the gates,
[8]   and shelter over Judah is removed.

*On that day you looked to the weapons in
the House of the Forest; [9]you saw that the
breaches in the City of David were many;
you collected the water of the lower pool.
[10]You numbered the houses of Jerusalem,
tearing some down to strengthen the wall;
[11]you made a reservoir between the two
walls for the water of the old pool. But you
did not look to the city's Maker, nor did you
consider him who built it long ago.

[12] On that day the Lord,
the GOD of hosts, called on you
To weep and mourn,
to shave your head and put on
sackcloth.[d]
[13] But look! you feast and celebrate,
you slaughter oxen and butcher sheep,
You eat meat and drink wine:
"Eat and drink, for tomorrow we die!"[e]
[14] This reaches the ears of the LORD of
hosts—
You shall not be pardoned this
wickedness till you die,
says the Lord, the GOD of hosts.

Shebna and Eliakim
[15] Thus says the Lord, the GOD of hosts:
Up, go to that official,
Shebna,* master of the palace,
[16] Who has hewn for himself a sepulcher on
a height
and carved his tomb in the rock:
"What are you doing here, and what
people have you here,
that here you have hewn for yourself a
tomb?"
[17] The LORD shall hurl you down headlong,
mortal man!

21, 16: Year . . . of a hireling: see note on Is 16, 14. Kedar:
a nomad tribe in Arabia; cf Is 42, 11; 60, 7; Ps 120, 5.

22, 1-8: Valley of Vision: while the people live in revelry and
disorder, the prophet foresees the impending doom of the city.

22, 6: Elam, Aram, Kir: all allies of Assyria. Kir: perhaps
the same people referred to in Am 1, 5.

22, 8-11: Defense measures, in which the inhabitants of

Jerusalem placed their trust instead of relying on God. House
of the Forest: an armory built by Solomon; its columns of
wood suggested the trees of a forest; cf 1 Kgs 7, 2; 10, 17.

22, 15: Shebna: referred to as the scribe in Is 36, 3.

z: Is 32, 13. *a:* 2 Kgs 25, 4. *b:* Jer 6, 26; 9, 1; 14, 17. *c:* Is 37,
3. *d:* Jl 2, 17. *e:* Is 56, 12; Wis 2, 6; 1 Cor 15, 32.

He shall grip you firmly

18 And roll you up and toss you like a ball
     into an open land
   To perish there, you and the chariots you
        glory in,
     you disgrace to your master's house!

19 I will thrust you from your office
     and pull you down from your station.

20 On that day I will summon my servant
     Eliakim,* son of Hilkiah;*f*

21 I will clothe him with your robe,
     and gird him with your sash,
     and give over to him your authority.
   He shall be a father to the inhabitants of
        Jerusalem,
     and to the house of Judah.

22 I will place the key* of the House of
        David on his shoulder;
     when he opens, no one shall shut,
     when he shuts, no one shall open.*g*

23 I will fix him like a peg in a sure spot,
     to be a place of honor for his family;

24 On him shall hang all the glory of his
        family:*
     descendants and offspring,
     all the little dishes, from bowls to jugs.

25 On that day, says the LORD of hosts, the
peg fixed in a sure spot shall give way, break
off and fall, and the weight that hung on it
shall be done away with; for the LORD has
spoken.

See RG
280-95

CHAPTER 23

Tyre and Sidon

1   Oracle on Tyre:
   Wail, O ships of Tarshish,*
     for your port is destroyed;
   From the land of the Kittim*
     the news reaches them.

2 Silence! you who dwell on the coast,
     you merchants of Sidon,
   Whose messengers crossed the sea

3   over the deep waters.
   The grain of Shihor,* the harvest of the
        Nile, was her revenue,
     and she the merchant among nations.

4 Shame, O Sidon, fortress on the sea,
     for the sea has spoken:*
   "I have not been in labor, nor given birth,
     nor raised young men,
     nor reared virgins."

5 When it is heard in Egypt
     they shall be in anguish at the news of
        Tyre.

6 Pass over to Tarshish, wailing,
     you who dwell on the coast!

7 Is this your wanton city,
     whose origin is from of old,
   Whose feet have taken her
     to dwell in distant lands?

8 Who has planned such a thing
     against Tyre, the bestower of crowns,
   Whose merchants are princes,
     whose traders are the earth's honored
        men?

9 The LORD of hosts has planned it,
     to disgrace all pride of majesty,
     to degrade all the earth's honored men.*h*

10 Cross to your own land,
     O ship of Tarshish;
     the harbor is no more.

11 His hand he stretches out over the sea,
     he shakes kingdoms;
   The LORD has ordered the destruction
     of Canaan's strongholds.*

12 You shall exult no more, he says,
     you who are now oppressed, virgin
        daughter Sidon.
   Arise, pass over to the Kittim,
     even there you shall find no rest.*i*

13 *[This people is the land of the Chaldeans,
not Assyria.]
   She whom the impious founded,
     setting up towers for her,
   Has had her castles destroyed,

22, 20: Eliakim: also referred to in Is 36, 3; he is described
as loyal to God.

22, 22: Key: symbol of authority; cf Mt 16, 19; Rv 3, 7.

22, 24f: If Eliakim should anger God, he and his family
(compared here to dishes, bowls and jugs) will suffer disaster.

23, 1-4. 12ff: These verses refer to Sidon, vv 5-11 to Tyre.

23, 1: Kittim: Cyprus.

23, 3: Shihor: a synonym for the Nile.

23, 4: The sea brings to distant coasts the news that Sidon
must disown her children; her people are dispersed.

23, 11: Canaan's strongholds: the fortresses of Phoenicia.

23, 13: The gloss here identifies she whom the impious
founded with the land of the Chaldeans.

f: 2 Kgs 18, 18. 37.   *g:* Rv 3, 7.   *h:* Ez 28, 7.   *i:* Ez 28, 21f.

and has been turned into a ruin.[j]

[14] Lament, O ships of Tarshish,
for your haven is destroyed.

[15]On that day, Tyre shall be forgotten for seventy years. With the days of another king, at the end of seventy years,[*] it shall be for Tyre as in the song about the harlot:[k]

[16] Take a harp, go about the city,
O forgotten harlot;
Pluck the strings skillfully, sing many
songs,
that they may remember you.

[17]At the end of the seventy years the LORD shall visit Tyre. She shall return to her hire and deal with all the world's kingdoms on the face of the earth.[l] [18]But her merchandise and her hire shall be sacred to the LORD. It shall not be stored up or laid away, but from her merchandise those who dwell before the LORD shall eat their fill and clothe themselves in choice attire.[*]

IV: Apocalypse of Isaiah[*]

CHAPTER 24

See RG 280-95

Devastation of the World:
A Remnant Saved

[1]Lo, the LORD empties the land and lays it
waste;
he turns it upside down,
scattering its inhabitants:[m]
[2] Layman and priest alike,
servant and master,
The maid as her mistress,
the buyer as the seller,
The lender as the borrower,
the creditor as the debtor.
[3] The earth is utterly laid waste, utterly
stripped,
for the LORD has decreed this thing.
[4] The earth mourns and fades,
the world languishes and fades;

both heaven and earth languish.
[5] The earth is polluted because of its
inhabitants,
who have transgressed laws, violated
statutes,
broken the ancient covenant.[*]
[6] Therefore a curse devours the earth,
and its inhabitants pay for their guilt;
Therefore they who dwell on earth turn
pale,
and few men are left.
[7] The wine mourns, the vine languishes,
all the merry-hearted groan.[n]
[8] Stilled are the cheerful timbrels,
ended the shouts of the jubilant,
stilled is the cheerful harp.[o]
[9] They cannot sing and drink wine;
strong drink is bitter to those who
partake of it.
[10] Broken down is the city of chaos,[*]
shut against entry, every house.[p]
[11] In the streets they cry out for lack of
wine;
all joy has disappeared
and cheer has left the land.[q]
[12] In the city nothing remains but ruin;
its gates are battered and desolate.
[13] Thus it is within the land,
and among the peoples,
As with an olive tree after it is beaten,
as with a gleaning when the vintage is
done.[r]
[14] These[*] lift up their voice in acclaim;
from the sea they proclaim the majesty
of the LORD:
[15] "For this, in the coastlands,
give glory to the LORD!
In the coastlands of the sea,
to the name of the LORD, the God of
Israel!"[s]
[16] From the end of the earth we hear songs:
"Splendor to the Just One!"
But I said, "I am wasted, wasted away.
Woe is me! The traitors betray:

23, 15: Seventy years: a conventional period of time indicating simply a long disaster; cf Jer 25, 11 and 29, 10.

23, 18: Describes the conversion of Tyre.

24, 1—27, 13: This section, probably composed at a later date, contains oracles on the day of the Lord, combined with hymns of thanksgiving and of supplication.

24, 5: Ancient covenant: God's commandments to all mankind.

24, 10: City of chaos: a symbol of godlessness as opposed to Jerusalem, the city of God.

24, 14: These: the saved.

j: Ez 26, 7. *k:* Jer 25, 11. *l:* Ez 27, 12. *m:* Is 13, 9; Hos 4, 9. *n:* Jl 1, 10. *o:* Jer 7, 34; Hos 2, 13. *p:* Is 25, 2. *q:* Jer 48, 33; Lam 5, 14f. *r:* Is 17, 6; Mi 7, 1. *s:* Is 42. 10. 12; Zep 2, 11.

with treachery have the traitors
    betrayed!
[17] Terror, pit, and trap[t]
    are upon you, inhabitant of the earth;
[18] He who flees at the sound of terror
    will fall into the pit;
He who climbs out of the pit
    will be caught in the trap.
For the windows on high will be opened
    and the foundations of the earth will
    shake.
[19] The earth will burst asunder,
    the earth will be shaken apart,
    the earth will be convulsed.
[20] The earth will reel like a drunkard,
    and it will sway like a hut;
Its rebellion will weigh it down,
    until it falls, never to rise again."[u]

[21] On that day the LORD will punish
    the host of the heavens* in the
    heavens,
    and the kings of the earth on the earth.[v]
[22] They will be gathered together
    like prisoners into a pit;
They will be shut up in a dungeon,
    and after many days they will be
    punished.
[23] Then the moon will blush[w]
    and the sun grow pale,
For the LORD of hosts will reign
    on Mount Zion and in Jerusalem,
    glorious in the sight of his elders.*

CHAPTER 25

See RG
280–95

[1] O LORD, you are my God,*
    I will extol you and praise your name;
For you have fulfilled your wonderful
    plans of old,
    faithful and true.[x]
[2] For you have made the city a heap,
    the fortified city a ruin;
The castle of the insolent is a city no
    more,

nor ever to be rebuilt.[y]
[3] Therefore a strong people will honor
    you,
    fierce nations will fear you.
[4] For you are a refuge to the poor,
    a refuge to the needy in distress;
Shelter from the rain,
    shade from the heat.[z]
As with the cold rain,
[5]   as with the desert heat,
    even so you quell the uproar of the
    wanton.
[6] On this mountain* the LORD of hosts
    will provide for all peoples
A feast of rich food and choice wines,
    juicy, rich food and pure, choice
    wines.
[7] On this mountain he will destroy
    the veil that veils all peoples,
The web that is woven over all nations;[a]
[8]   he will destroy death forever.
The Lord GOD will wipe away
    the tears from all faces;
The reproach of his people he will
    remove
    from the whole earth; for the LORD has
    spoken.

[9]   On that day it will be said:
"Behold our God, to whom we looked to
    save us!
    This is the LORD for whom we looked;
    let us rejoice and be glad that he has
    saved us!"[b]
[10] For the hand of the LORD will rest on this
    mountain,
    but Moab* will be trodden down
    as a straw is trodden down in the
    mire.[c]
[11] He will stretch forth his hands in Moab
    as a swimmer extends his hands to
    swim;
He will bring low their pride
    as his hands sweep over them.[d]

24, 21: Host of the heavens: the stars, which were regarded by the pagans as gods; cf Dt 4, 19; Jer 8, 2.
24, 23: His elders: the heavenly courtiers surrounding the throne of God.
25, 1-8: Victory in messianic times.
25, 6: This mountain: Zion, symbol of the heavenly Jerusalem.
25, 10: Moab: symbol of God's enemies.

t: 17f. Jer 48, 43f. u: Is 9, 14. v: Ps 76, 13. w: Is 13, 10; Jl 3, 3f; 4, 15. x: Ex 15, 2. y: Jer 9, 11. z: Is 14, 32; 32, 2; Na 1, 7.
a: Is 60, 1. 3; 1 Cor 15, 53ff; Rv 7, 17; 21, 4. b: Is 30, 18f. c: Zep 2, 9f. d: Is 16, 6f. 14.

[12] The high-walled fortress he will raze,
and strike it down level with the earth,
with the very dust.[e]

See RG 280-95

CHAPTER 26

The Divine Vindicator. [1]On that day
they will sing this song in the land of Judah:

"A strong city have we;
he sets up walls and ramparts to
protect us.
[2] Open up the gates
to let in a nation that is just,
one that keeps faith.[f]
[3] A nation of firm purpose you keep in
peace;
in peace, for its trust in you."[g]

[4] Trust in the LORD forever!
For the LORD is an eternal Rock.[h]
[5] He humbles those in high places,
and the lofty city he brings down;
He tumbles it to the ground,
levels it with the dust.[i]
[6] It is trampled underfoot by the needy,
by the footsteps of the poor.
[7] The way of the just is smooth;
the path of the just you make level.[j]
[8] Yes, for your way and your judgments,
O LORD,
we look to you;
Your name and your title
are the desire of our souls,
[9] My soul yearns for you in the night,
yes, my spirit within me keeps vigil
for you;
When your judgment dawns upon the
earth,
the world's inhabitants learn justice.[k]
[10] The wicked man, spared, does not learn
justice;
in an upright land he acts perversely,
and sees not the majesty of the
LORD.[l]
[11] O LORD, your hand is uplifted,
but they behold it not;

Let them be shamed when they see your
zeal for your people:
let the fire prepared for your enemies
consume them.
[12] O LORD, you mete out peace to us,
for it is you who have accomplished
all we have done.[m]
[13] O LORD, our God, other lords than you
have ruled us;
it is from you only that we can call
upon your name.

[14] Dead they are, they have no life,
shades that cannot rise;
For you have punished and destroyed
them,
and wiped out all memory of them.
[15] You have increased the nation, O LORD,
increased the nation to your own glory,
and extended far all the borders of the
land.[n]
[16] O LORD, oppressed by your punishment,
we cried out in anguish under your
chastising.[o]
[17] As a woman about to give birth
writhes and cries out in her pains,
so were we in your presence,
O LORD.[p]
[18] We conceived and writhed in pain,
giving birth to wind;
Salvation we have not achieved for the
earth,
the inhabitants of the world cannot
bring it forth.
[19] But your dead shall live, their corpses
shall rise;
awake and sing, you who lie in the
dust.[q]
For your dew is a dew of light,
and the land of shades gives birth.*

Day of the Lord: Reward and Punishment

[20] Go, my people, enter your chambers,
and close your doors behind you;
Hide yourselves for a brief moment,
until the wrath is past.

26, 19: This verse refers to the restoration of Israel in messianic times under the figure of the resurrection of the dead; cf
Ez, chap. 37.

e: Is 26, 5.   *f:* Ps 118, 19f.   *g:* Is 32, 17f; 54, 13.   *h:* Is 30, 29; Ps 62, 8.   *i:* Is 25, 12; 32, 19.   *j:* Ps 23, 3f; Prv 11, 3. 5.   *k:* Ps 94,
15.   *l:* Is 5, 12.   *m:* Jer 29, 11.   *n:* Is 54, 2f; Neh 9, 23.   *o:* Hos 6, 1.   *p:* Mi 4, 10.   *q:* Ez 37, 5f; Dn 12. 2; Hos 6, 2.

[21] See, the LORD goes forth from his place,
to punish the wickedness of the earth's
inhabitants;
The earth will reveal the blood upon her,
and no longer conceal her slain.[r]

CHAPTER 27

See RG 280-95

[1] On that day,
The LORD will punish with his sword
that is cruel, great, and strong,
Leviathan the fleeing serpent,
Leviathan the coiled serpent;
and he will slay the dragon* that is in
the sea.[s]
[2] On that day—
The pleasant vineyard, sing about it![t]
[3] I, the LORD, am its keeper,
I water it every moment;
Lest anyone harm it,
night and day I guard it.[u]
[4] I am not angry,
but if I were to find briers and thorns,
In battle I should march against them;
I should burn them all.[v]
[8] Expunging and expelling, I should strive
against them,
carrying them off with my cruel wind
in time of storm.[w]
[6] In days to come Jacob shall take root,
Israel shall sprout and blossom,
covering all the world with fruit.
[7] Is he to be smitten as his smiter was
smitten?
or slain as his slayer was slain?*
[5] Or shall he cling to me for refuge?*
He must make peace with me;
peace shall he make with me![x]
[9] This, then, shall be the expiation of
Jacob's guilt,
this the whole fruit of the removal of
his sin:

He shall pulverize all the stones of the
altars
like pieces of chalk;
no sacred poles or incense altars shall
stand.
[10] For the fortified city* shall be desolate,
an abandoned pasture, a forsaken
wilderness,
where calves shall browse and lie.[y]
Its boughs shall be destroyed,
[11] its branches shall wither and be broken
off,
and women shall come to build a fire
with them.
This is not an understanding people;
therefore their maker shall not spare
them,
nor shall he who formed them have
mercy on them.[z]
[12] On that day,
The LORD shall beat out the grain
between the Euphrates and the Wadi of
Egypt,*
and you shall be gleaned one by one,
O sons of Israel.
[13] On that day,*
A great trumpet shall blow,
and the lost in the land of Assyria
and the outcasts in the land of
Egypt
Shall come and worship the LORD
on the holy mountain, in Jerusalem.[a]

V: The Lord Alone, Israel's and Judah's Salvation

CHAPTER 28

The Fate of Samaria

See RG 280-95

[1] Woe to the majestic garland
of the drunkard Ephraim,*

27, 1: Leviathan . . . dragon: symbols of the forces of evil
which God vanquishes even as he overcame primeval chaos;
cf notes on Jb 3, 8; 7, 12.

27, 7: God's people will not be treated as sternly as were
their enemies.

27, 5. 9: Israel will make peace with God and destroy all
signs of idolatrous worship.

27, 10f: The fortified city: symbol of the powers of evil;
see note on Is 24, 10.

27, 12: The Euphrates and the Wadi of Egypt: the ideal
borders of Israel; cf Gn 15, 18; 2 Kgs 24, 7.

27, 13: The triumph of God's people is described in eschatological language; they will gather in Jerusalem from Assyria and Egypt.

28, 1: Ephraim: the northern kingdom. Its capital,
Samaria, was built upon a hill, suggestive of a majestic garland adorning the head of the drunken kingdom.

r: Mi 1, 3.   *s:* Jb 40, 25-32; Ez 32, 2.   *t:* Is 5, 1.   *u:* Is 5, 2ff; Ps
121, 4f.   *v:* Is 10, 17.   *w:* Jer 18, 17.   *x:* Is 37, 31; Rom 11, 12.
y: Is 6, 11.   *z:* Jer 4, 22.   *a:* Hos 11, 11.

To the fading blooms of his glorious
beauty,
on the head of him who is stupefied
with wine.*b*
2 Behold, the LORD has a strong one and a
mighty,*
who, like a downpour of hail, a
destructive storm,
Like a flood of water, great and
overflowing,
levels to the ground with violence;*c*
3 With feet that will trample
the majestic garland of the drunkard
Ephraim.
4 The fading blooms of his glorious beauty
on the head of the fertile valley
Will be like an early fig before summer:
when a man sees it,
he picks and swallows it at once.
5 On that day the LORD of hosts
will be a glorious crown
And a brilliant diadem
to the remnant of his people,
6 A spirit of justice
to him who sits in judgment,
And strength to those
who turn back the battle at the gate.

Against Judah
7 But these also stagger from wine
and stumble from strong drink:
Priest and prophet stagger from strong
drink,
overpowered by wine;
Led astray by strong drink,
staggering in their visions,
tottering when giving judgment.*d*
8 Yes, all the tables
are covered with filthy vomit,
with no place left clean.

9 "To whom would he impart knowledge?*
To whom would he convey the message?
To those just weaned from milk,
those taken from the breast? *10*For he
says,
'Command on command, command on
command,
rule on rule, rule on rule,
here a little, there a little!' "
11 Yes, with stammering lips and in a
strange language*
he will speak to this people*e*
12 to whom he said:
This is the resting place,
give rest to the weary;
Here is repose—
but they would not listen.
13 So for them the word of the LORD shall be:
"Command on command, command
on command,
Rule on rule, rule on rule,
here a little, there a little!"
So that when they walk, they stumble
backward,
broken, ensnared, and captured.

14 Therefore, hear the word of the LORD,
you arrogant,
who rule this people in Jerusalem:
15 Because you say, "We have made a
covenant with death,
and with the nether world* we have
made a pact;
When the overwhelming scourge passes,
it will not reach us;
For we have made lies our refuge,
and in falsehood we have found a
hiding place,"—*f*
16   Therefore, thus says the Lord GOD:
See, I am laying a stone in Zion,*

28, 2: A strong one and a mighty: Assyria.

28, 9f: The words of those who ridicule Isaiah. The Hebrew of v 10, by its very sound, conveys the idea of mocking imitation of what the prophet says, as though he spoke like a stammering child: SAU LASAU, SAU LASAU, CAU LACAU, CAU LACAU, ZE'ER SHAM, ZE'ER SHAM. But in v 13 God repeats these words in deadly earnest, putting them in the mouth of the victorious pagan army.

28, 11: God will answer the mockers and defend Isaiah. Strange language: spoken by the invading army.

28, 15. 18: A covenant with death, and with the nether world: an alliance with foreign powers, such as Egypt and

Babylon, to prevent death and destruction. Have made lies . . . a hiding place: this confidence in human aid proves to be false and deceitful, incapable of averting the dreaded disaster. Overwhelming scourge: the flood of the Assyrian invasion; cf Is 8, 7f.

28, 16: A stone in Zion: the true and sure foundation of salvation promised by God to the Davidic dynasty (cf Is 7, 13-16; 9, 1-6), which the Apostles saw fulfilled in Christ the universal Savior; cf 1 Pt 2, 6-8; Rom 9, 33; 10, 9ff. Corner-

b: Hos 7, 5; Am 6, 6.   *c:* Is 30, 30.   *d:* Is 56, 10. 12.   *e:* Jer 5, 15; 1 Cor 14, 21; Dt 28, 49; Bar 4, 15.   *f:* Wis 1, 16; Jer 5, 12.

a stone that has been tested,
A precious cornerstone as a sure
foundation;
he who puts his faith in it shall
not be shaken.[g]

17 I will make of right a measuring
line,
of justice a level.—
Hail shall sweep away the refuge of lies,
and waters shall flood the hiding
place.

18 Your covenant with death shall be
canceled
and your pact with the nether world
shall not stand.
When the overwhelming scourge passes,
you shall be trampled down by it.

19 Whenever it passes, it shall take you;
morning after morning it shall pass,
By day and by night;
terror alone shall convey the message.

20 For the bed shall be too short to stretch
out in,
and the cover too narrow to wrap in.

21 For the LORD shall rise up as on Mount
Perazim,*
bestir himself as in the Valley of
Gibeon,
To carry out his work, his singular work,
to perform his deed, his strange deed.[h]

22 Now, be arrogant no more
lest your bonds be tightened,
For I have heard from the Lord, the GOD
of hosts,
the destruction decreed for the whole
earth.[i]

23 Give ear and hear my voice,*
pay attention and listen to what I say:

24 Is the plowman forever plowing,
always loosening and harrowing his
land for planting?

25 When he has leveled the surface,
does he not scatter gith and sow cumin,*
Put in wheat and barley,
with spelt as its border?

26 He has learned this rule,
instructed by his God.

27 Gith is not threshed with a sledge,
nor does a cartwheel roll over cumin.
But gith is beaten out with a staff,
and cumin crushed for food with a rod.

28 No, he does not thresh it unendingly,
nor does he crush it
with his noisy cartwheels and horses.

29 This too comes from the LORD of hosts;
wonderful is his counsel and great his
wisdom.

CHAPTER 29

The Fall of Jerusalem

See RG 280–95

1 Woe to Ariel, Ariel,*
the city where David encamped!
Add year to year,
let the feasts come round.[j]

2 But I will bring distress upon Ariel,
with mourning and grief.
You shall be to me like Ariel,[k]

3 I will encamp like David against you;
I will encircle you with outposts
and set up siege works against you.[l]

4 Prostrate you shall speak from the earth,
and from the base dust your words
shall come.
Your voice shall be like a ghost's from
the earth,
and your words like chirping* from the
dust.

5 The horde of your arrogant shall be like
fine dust,
the horde of the tyrants like flying
chaff.
Then suddenly, in an instant,[m]

stone: the assurance of salvation rejected by Israel in the
prophet's time, is reflected by the psalmist (Ps 118, 22) and
fulfilled in the Person of Christ; cf Mt 21, 42; Lk 20, 17; Acts
4, 11; Rom 9. 33; 1 Pt 2, 7.

28, 21: Mount Perazim . . . Valley of Gibeon: where David
defeated the Philistines; cf 2 Sm 5, 20. 25; 1 Chr 14, 11. 16.

28, 23-29: The practical variation of the farmer's work
taught him by God reflects God's dealing with his people,
wisely adapted to circumstances; he does not crush their
weakness altogether; cf ch 29.

28, 25: Gith . . . cumin: herbs used in seasoning food.

Spelt: a variety of wheat.

29, 1f: Ariel: variously interpreted to mean "lion of God"
or "hearth (altar) of God," a poetic name for Jerusalem; or
perhaps to be read as Uru-el, "foundation of God," an archaic
name for the Jebusite city of Jerusalem; like that Ariel,
against which David encamped, it will be besieged by God.

29, 4: Chirping: see note on Is 8, 19.

g: Ps 118, 22; Mt 21, 42; Acts 4, 11; Rom 9, 33; 1 Pt 2, 6. h: Jos
10, 10; 2 Sm 5, 20; 1 Chr 14, 11. i: Is 10, 23. j: 2 Sm 5, 9. k: Is
33, 7. l: 2 Kgs 25, 1; Ez 4, 2. m: Is 17, 13; Ps 18, 43; Jb 21, 18.

⁶ you shall be visited by the LORD of
    hosts,
With thunder, earthquake, and great
    noise,
    whirlwind, storm, and the flame of
        consuming fire.

⁷ Then like a dream,*
    a vision in the night,
Shall be the horde of all the nations
    who war against Ariel
    with all the earthworks of her
        besiegers.
⁸ As when a hungry man dreams he is
        eating
    and awakens with an empty stomach,
Or when a thirsty man dreams he is
        drinking
    and awakens faint and dry,
So shall the horde of all the nations be,
    who make war against Zion.

Blindness and Perversity

⁹ Be irresolute, stupefied;*
    blind yourselves and stay blind!
Be drunk, but not from wine,
    stagger, but not from strong drink!ⁿ
¹⁰ For the LORD has poured out on you
    a spirit of deep sleep.
He has shut your eyes [the prophets]
    and covered your heads [the seers].^o

¹¹ For you the revelation of all this has be-
come like the words of a sealed scroll. When
it is handed to one who can read, with the request, "Read this," he replies, "I cannot; it is
sealed."^p ¹² When it is handed to one who
cannot read, with the request, "Read this,"
he replies, "I cannot read."

¹³   The Lord said:
Since this people draws near with words
        only
    and honors me with their lips alone,

though their hearts are far from me,
And their reverence for me has become
    routine observance of the precepts of
    men,^q
¹⁴ Therefore I will again deal with this
        people
    in surprising and wondrous fashion:
The wisdom of its wise men shall perish
    and the understanding of its prudent
        men be hid.^r
¹⁵ Woe to those who would hide their plans
    too deep for the LORD!
Who work in the dark, saying,
    "Who sees us, or who knows us?"^s
¹⁶ Your perversity is as though the potter
    were taken to be the clay:
As though what is made should say of its
        maker,
    "He made me not!"
Or the vessel should say of the potter,
    "He does not understand."^t

Redemption*

¹⁷ But a very little while,
    and Lebanon shall be changed into an
        orchard,
    and the orchard be regarded as a forest!^u
¹⁸ On that day the deaf shall hear
    the words of a book;
And out of gloom and darkness,
    the eyes of the blind shall see.^v
¹⁹ The lowly will ever find joy in the LORD,
    and the poor rejoice in the Holy One
        of Israel.^w
²⁰ For the tyrant will be no more
    and the arrogant will have gone;
All who are alert to do evil will be cut
        off,^x
²¹   those whose mere word condemns a
        man,
Who ensnare his defender at the gate,
    and leave the just man with an empty
        claim.^y

29, 7f: Just when the Assyrians think their capture of
Jerusalem to be certain, the Lord will snatch victory from
their hands and save his city.

29, 9-12: Jerusalem in her blindness refuses to believe
God's revelation that she will be saved.

29, 17-24: The prophet presents God's plan of redemption in terms of unheard-of natural phenomena as if such
changes in nature took place, e. g., the change of the

cedars of Lebanon into an orchard (v 17).

n: Is 19, 14; 28, 7f. *o:* Is 6, 10; Rom 11, 8. *p:* Dn 12, 4. *q:* Ez
33, 31; Mt 15, 8f; Mk 7, 6f. *r:* Jer 49, 7; 1 Cor 1, 19. *s:* Is 30,
1; Ez 8, 12; Jn 3, 19f. *t:* Is 45, 9; Jer 18, 6; Rom 9, 20. *u:* Is 32,
15. *v:* Is 35, 5; 42, 6f. *w:* Is 61, 1. *x:* Is 28, 22. *y:* Am 5, 10.
12.

22 Therefore thus says the LORD,
the God of the house of Jacob,
who redeemed Abraham:*
Now Jacob shall have nothing to be
ashamed of,
nor shall his face grow pale.ᶻ
23 When his children see
the work of my hands in his midst,
They shall keep my name holy;
they shall reverence the Holy One of
Jacob,
and be in awe of the God of Israel.
24 Those who err in spirit shall acquire
understanding,
and those who find fault shall receive
instruction.

See RG
280-95

CHAPTER 30

Futile Alliance with Egypt

1Woe to the rebellious children,
says the LORD,
Who carry out plans that are not
mine,
who weave webs that are not inspired
by me,
adding sin upon sin.ᵃ
2 They go down to Egypt,
but my counsel they do not seek.
They find their strength in Pharaoh's
protection
and take refuge in Egypt's shadow;ᵇ
3 Pharaoh's protection shall be your
shame,
and refuge in Egypt's shadow your
disgrace.ᶜ
4 When their princes are at Zoan
and their messengers reach Hanes,ᵈ
5 All shall be ashamed
of a people that gain them nothing,
Neither help nor benefit,
but only shame and reproach.ᵉ

6   [Oracle on the Beasts of the
Negeb]

Through the distressed and troubled
land
of the lioness and roaring lion,
of the viper and flying saraph,*
They carry their riches on the backs of
asses
and their treasures on the humps of
camels
To a people good for nothing,
7 to Egypt whose help is futile and vain.
Therefore I call her
"Rahab* quelled."
8 Now come, write it on a tablet they can
keep,
inscribe it in a record;*
That it may be in future days
an eternal witness:ᶠ
9 This is a rebellious people,
deceitful children,
Children who refuse
to obey the law of the LORD.ᵍ
10 They say to the seers, "Have no visions";
to the prophets, "Do not descry for us
what is right;
speak flatteries to us, conjure up
illusions.ʰ
11 Out of the way! Out of our path!
Let us hear no more
of the Holy One of Israel."ⁱ
12 Therefore, thus says the Holy One of
Israel:
Because you reject this word,
And put your trust in what is crooked and
devious,
and depend on it,
13 This guilt of yours shall be
like a descending rift
Bulging out in a high wall
whose crash comes suddenly, in an
instant.ʲ
14 It crashes like a potter's jar
smashed beyond rescue,
And among its fragments cannot be
found

29, 22: Who redeemed Abraham: by freeing him from the idolatry of his native land.

30, 6: Flying saraph: see note on Nm 21, 6.

30, 7: Rahab: Egypt, here as elsewhere (cf Ps 87, 4), is compared to the stormy, impetuous sea monster (cf Is 51, 9; Jb 26, 12; Ps 89, 11), which yet, when asked for aid by Judah, becomes silent, quelled.

30, 8: Isaiah will write down his condemnation of the people so that (vv 12-18) its fulfillment may afterward be admitted.

---

z: Is 45, 17.   a: Is 1, 4.   b: Is 31, 1; 36, 6.   c: Is 20, 5; Jer 2, 26f.   d: Is 19, 11.   e: 36, 6.   f: Is 8, 1. 16; Jer 36, 2; Heb 2, 2.   g: Is 1, 4; Jer 7, 28.   h: Jer 5, 31.   i: Jb 21, 14f.   j: Ez 13, 14.

a sherd to scoop fire from the hearth
  or dip water from the cistern.*k*

15 For thus said the Lord GOD,
  the Holy One of Israel:
By waiting and by calm you shall be
    saved,
  in quiet and in trust your strength lies.
  But this you did not wish.*l*
16 "No," you said,
  "Upon horses we will flee."
  —Very well, flee!
  "Upon swift steeds we will ride."
  —Not so swift as your pursuers.*m*
17 A thousand shall tremble at the threat of
    one;
  if five threaten you, you shall flee,
Until you are left like a flagstaff on the
    mountaintop,
  like a flag on the hill.
18 Yet the LORD is waiting to show you
    favor,
  and he rises to pity you;
For the LORD is a God of justice:
  blessed are all who wait for him!*n*

19 O people of Zion, who dwell in
    Jerusalem,
  no more will you weep;
He will be gracious to you when you cry
    out,
  as soon as he hears he will answer
    you.*o*
20 The Lord will give you the bread you
    need
  and the water for which you thirst.
No longer will your Teacher* hide
    himself,
  but with your own eyes you shall see
    your Teacher,
21 While from behind, a voice shall sound
    in your ears:
  "This is the way; walk in it,"
  when you would turn to the right or to
    the left.*p*

22 And you shall consider unclean your
    silver-plated idols
  and your gold-covered images;
You shall throw them away like filthy
    rags
  to which you say, "Begone!"*q*

Zion's Future Prosperity
23 He will give rain for the seed
  that you sow in the ground,
And the wheat that the soil produces
  will be rich and abundant.
On that day your cattle will graze
  in spacious meadows;*r*
24 The oxen and the asses that till the
    ground
  will eat silage tossed to them
  with shovel and pitchfork.
25 Upon every high mountain and lofty hill
  there will be streams of running water.
On the day of the great slaughter,
  when the towers fall,*s*
26 The light of the moon will be like that of
    the sun
  and the light of the sun will be seven
    times greater
  [like the light of seven days].
On the day the LORD binds up the
    wounds of his people,
  he will heal the bruises left by his
    blows.*t*

Divine Judgment on Assyria*
27 See the name of the LORD coming from
    afar
  in burning wrath, with lowering
    clouds!
His lips are filled with fury,
  his tongue is like a consuming fire;
28 His breath, like a flood in a ravine
  that reaches suddenly to the neck,
Will winnow the nations with a
    destructive winnowing,
  and with repeated winnowings will he
    battle against them

30, 20: Teacher: God, who in the past taught in a veiled manner through his prophets, will in future help them to understand his teaching clearly. This was eminently true when the Son of God became Man.

30, 27-33: God's punishment of Assyria. The name of the Lord: God himself; cf Ps 20, 2.

---

k: Jer 19, 11.   *l:* Is 7, 4; Mi 7, 7.   *m:* Is 31, 3.   *n:* Ps 34, 9; Jer 17, 7.   *o:* Is 58, 9.   *p:* Jer 31, 33f.   *q:* Is 31, 7.   *r:* Lv 26, 3. 5.   *s:* Jl 4, 18.   *t:* Jer 30, 17.

[and a bridle on the jaws of the
 peoples to send them astray].
30 The LORD will make his glorious voice
 heard,
 and let it be seen how his arm
 descends
In raging fury and flame of consuming
 fire,
 in driving storm and hail.
31 When the LORD speaks, Assyria will be
 shattered,
 as he strikes with the rod;
32 While at every sweep of the rod
 which the LORD will bring down on
 him in punishment,
29 You will sing
 as on a night when a feast is observed,
And be merry of heart,
 as one marching along with a flute
Toward the mountain of the LORD,
 toward the Rock of Israel,
 accompanied by the timbrels and lyres.
33 For the pyre* has long been ready,
 prepared for the king;
Broad and deep it is piled
 with dry grass and wood in abundance,
And the breath of the LORD, like a stream
 of sulphur,
 will set it afire.

CHAPTER 31

See RG
280-95

Against the Egyptian Alliance

1Woe to those who go down to Egypt for
 help,
 who depend upon horses;
Who put their trust in chariots because of
 their number,
 and in horsemen because of their
 combined power,
But look not to the Holy One of Israel
 nor seek the LORD!u
2 Yet he too is wise and will bring disaster;
 he will not turn from what he has
 threatened to do.
He will rise up against the house of the
 wicked

and against those who help evildoers.
3 The Egyptians are men, not God,
 their horses are flesh, not spirit;
When the LORD stretches forth his hand,
 the helper shall stumble, the one
 helped shall fall,
 and both of them shall perish together.v
4 Thus says the LORD to me:
As a lion or a lion cub
 growling over its prey,
With a band of shepherds
 assembled against it,
Is neither frightened by their shouts
 nor disturbed by their noise,
So shall the LORD of hosts come down
 to wage war upon the mountain and
 hill of Zion.
5 Like hovering birds, so the LORD of hosts
 shall shield Jerusalem,
To protect and deliver,
 to spare and rescue it.w

6Return, O children of Israel, to him
whom you have utterly deserted.x 7On that
day each one of you shall spurn his sinful
idols of silver and gold, which he made with
his hands.y

Downfall of Assyria

8 Assyria shall fall by a sword not wielded
 by man,
 no mortal sword shall devour him;
He shall flee before the sword,
 and his young men shall be impressed
 as laborers.z
9 He shall rush past his crag* in panic,
 and his princes shall flee in terror from
 his standard,
Says the LORD who has a fire in Zion
 and a furnace in Jerusalem.

CHAPTER 32

See RG
280-95

The Kingdom of Justice

1 See, a king will reign justly
 and princes will rule rightly.a

30, 29-33: Pyre: on which the corpse of the king of Assyria is burned. This is the occasion of festal rejoicing for the Israelites, who are now free from his yoke.

31, 9: Crag: the king as the rallying point of the princes.

---

u: Is 30, 2; 36, 6.   v: Ps 146, 3ff.   w: Ps 91, 4.   x: Jer 3, 12.   y: Is 30, 22.   z: Is 37, 36.   a: Is 16, 5; Ps 72, 2ff; Jer 23, 5.

2 Each of them will be a shelter from the
     wind,
  a retreat from the rain.
  They will be like streams of water in a
     dry country,
  like the shade of a great rock in a
     parched land.[b]
3 The eyes of those who see will not be
     closed;
  the ears of those who hear will be
     attentive.
4 The flighty will become wise and
     capable,
  and the stutterers will speak fluently
     and clearly.
5 No more will the fool be called noble,
  nor the trickster be considered
     honorable.
6 For the fool speaks foolishly,
  planning evil in his heart:
  How to do wickedness,
    to speak perversely against the LORD,
  To let the hungry go empty
    and the thirsty be without drink.[c]
7 And the trickster uses wicked trickery,
     planning crimes:
  How to ruin the poor with lies,
    and the needy when they plead their
     case.
8 But the noble man plans noble things,
  and by noble things he stands.

The Women of Jerusalem
9 O complacent ladies, rise up and hear my
     voice,
  overconfident women, give heed to my
     words.
10 In a little more than a year
   you overconfident ones will be
      shaken;
  The vintage will fail,
    there will be no harvest.[d]
11 Tremble, you who are complacent!
   Shudder, you who are overconfident!
  Strip yourselves bare,

  with only a loincloth to cover you.[e]
12 Beat your breasts
   for the pleasant fields, the fruitful vine,
13 And the soil of my people,
   overgrown with thorns and briers;
  For all the joyful houses,
    the wanton city.[f]
14 Yes, the castle* will be forsaken,
   the noisy city deserted;[g]
19 Down it comes, as trees come down in
      the forest!
  The city will be utterly laid low.
  Hill and tower will become wasteland
     forever
  for wild asses to frolic in, and flocks to
     pasture,
15 Until the spirit from on high*
   is poured out on us.
  Then will the desert become an orchard
    and the orchard be regarded as a
     forest.[h]
16 Right will dwell in the desert
   and justice abide in the orchard.
17 Justice will bring about peace;
    right will produce calm and security.[i]
18 My people will live in peaceful country,
   in secure dwellings and quiet resting
     places.[j]
20 Happy are you who sow beside every
      stream,
  and let the ox and the ass go freely![k]

CHAPTER 33
Overthrow of Assyria

See RG 280-95

1 Woe, O destroyer never destroyed,
   O traitor never betrayed!
  When you finish destroying, you will be
      destroyed;
  when wearied with betraying, you will
      be betrayed.
2 O LORD, have pity on us, for you we
      wait.
  Be our strength every morning,
    our salvation in time of trouble![l]

32, 14. 19: The castle: the citadel of Jerusalem. Hill and tower: the fortified hill, in Hebrew Ophel, with its stronghold
called "the great projecting tower" in Neh 3, 27.

32, 15-18. 20: Extraordinary peace and prosperity will come to Israel under just rulers.

---

b: Is 4, 6; 25, 4.   c: Prv 10, 32; Eccl 10, 12f.   d: Zep 1, 13.   e: Jer 4, 8.   f: Is 7, 23; 34, 13.   g: Is 27, 10.   h: Is 35, 1; 44, 3.   i: Is
54, 13f; Ps 72, 7; Jas 3, 18.   j: Mi 4, 4.   k: Is 30, 23.   l: Is 25, 9.

3 At the roaring sound, peoples flee;
  when you rise in your majesty, nations
    are scattered.
4 Men gather spoil as caterpillars are
    gathered up;
  they rush upon it like the onrush of
    locusts.*m*
5 The LORD is exalted, enthroned on high;
  he fills Zion with right and justice.*n*
6 That which makes her seasons lasting,
  the riches that save her, are wisdom
    and knowledge;
  the fear of the LORD is her treasure.*o*

7 See, the men of Ariel cry out in the
    streets,
  the messengers of Shalem* weep
    bitterly.
8 The highways are desolate,
  travelers have quit the paths,
  Covenants are broken, their terms are
    spurned;
  yet no man gives it a thought.*p*
9 The country languishes in mourning,
  Lebanon withers with shame;
  Sharon* is like the steppe,
  Bashan and Carmel are stripped bare.*q*
10 Now will I rise up, says the LORD,
  now will I be exalted, now be lifted up.
11 You conceive dry grass, bring forth
    stubble;
  my spirit shall consume you like fire.
12 The peoples shall be as in a limekiln,
  like brushwood cut down for burning
    in the fire.*r*
13 Hear, you who are far off, what I have
    done;
  you who are near, acknowledge my
    might.
14 On Zion sinners are in dread,
  trembling grips the impious:
  "Who of us can live with the consuming
    fire?
  who of us can live with the everlasting
    flames?"*s*

15 He who practices virtue and speaks
    honestly,
  who spurns what is gained by
    oppression,
  Brushing his hands free of contact with a
    bribe,
  stopping his ears lest he hear of
    bloodshed,
  closing his eyes lest he look on evil—*t*
16 He shall dwell on the heights,
  his stronghold shall be the rocky
    fastness,
  his food and drink in steady supply.

Restoration of Zion
17 Your eyes will see a king* in his
    splendor,
  they will look upon a vast land.
18 Your mind will dwell on the terror:
  "Where is he who counted, where is he
    who weighed?
  Where is he who counted the towers?"
19 To the people of alien tongue you will
    look no more,
  the people of obscure speech,
  stammering in a language not
    understood.
20 Look to Zion, the city of our festivals;
  let your eyes see Jerusalem
  as a quiet abode, a tent not to be
    struck,
  Whose pegs will never be pulled up,
  nor any of its ropes severed.
21 Indeed the LORD will be there with us,
    majestic;
  yes, the LORD our judge, the LORD our
    lawgiver,
  the LORD our king, he it is who will
    save us.
22 In a place of rivers and wide streams
  on which no boat is rowed,
  where no majestic ship* passes,
23 The rigging hangs slack;
  it cannot hold the mast in place,
  nor keep the sail spread out.

33, 7: Ariel . . . Shalem: Jerusalem; cf Is 29, 1; Gn 14, 18.
33, 9: Sharon: the fertile plain near the Mediterranean.
33, 17: King: the messianic King, or God; cf v 22.
33, 21. 23: Boat . . . majestic ship: of a foreign oppressor.

m: 2 Chr 20, 25. *n:* Is 1, 26. *o:* Prv 9, 10. *p:* Jgs 5, 6. *q:* Na 1, 4. *r:* Is 10, 17. *s:* Na 1, 6. *t:* Pss 15, 2-6; 24, 4f.

Then the blind will divide great spoils
and the lame will carry off the loot.
²⁴ No one who dwells there will say, "I am
sick";
the people who live there will be
forgiven their guilt.

VI: The Lord, Zion's Avenger

CHAPTER 34

See RG
280-95

Judgment upon Edom

¹ Come near, O nations, and hear;
be attentive, O peoples!
Let the earth and what fills it listen,
the world and all it produces.ᵘ
² The LORD is angry with all the nations
and is wrathful against all their host;
he has doomed them and given them
over to slaughter.
³ Their slain shall be cast out,
their corpses shall send up a stench;
The mountains shall run with their
blood,ʸ
⁴ and all the hills shall rot;
The heavens shall be rolled up like a
scroll,
and all their host shall wither away,
As the leaf wilts on the vine,
or as the fig withers on the tree.ʷ

⁵ When my sword has drunk its fill in the
heavens,
lo, it shall come down in judgment
upon Edom, a people I have doomed.ˣ
⁶ The LORD has a sword filled with blood,ʸ
greasy with fat,
With the blood of lambs and goats,
with the fat of rams' kidneys;
For the LORD has a sacrifice in Bozrah,
a great slaughter in the land of Edom.
⁷ Wild oxen shall be struck down with
fatlings,
and bullocks with bulls;
Their land shall be soaked with blood,
and their earth greasy with fat.

⁸ For the LORD has a day of vengeance,
a year of requital by Zion's defender.ᶻ
⁹ Edom's streams shall be changed into
pitch
and her earth into sulphur,
and her land shall become burning
pitch;
¹⁰ Night and day it shall not be quenched,
its smoke shall rise forever.
From generation to generation she shall
lie waste,
never again shall anyone pass through
her.
¹¹ But the desert owl and hoot owl shall
possess her,
the screech owl and raven shall dwell
in her.
The LORD will measure her with line and
plummet
to be an empty waste
for satyrs* to dwell in.ᵃ

¹² Her nobles shall be no more,
nor shall kings be proclaimed there;
all her princes are gone.ᵇ
¹³ Her castles shall be overgrown with
thorns,
her fortresses with thistles and briers.
She shall become an abode for jackals
and a haunt for ostriches.ᶜ
¹⁴ Wildcats shall meet with desert beasts,
satyrs shall call to one another;
There shall the lilith* repose,
and find for herself a place to rest.
¹⁵ There the hoot owl shall nest and lay
eggs,
hatch them out and gather them in her
shadow;
There shall the kites assemble,
none shall be missing its mate.

¹⁶ Look in the book of the LORD* and read:
No one of these shall be lacking,
For the mouth of the LORD has ordered it,
and his spirit shall gather them there.ᵈ

34, 11: Satyrs: see note on Is 13, 21; cf Is 34, 14.
34, 14: Lilith: a female demon thought to roam about the desert.
34, 16: Book of the Lord: God's list of all his creatures; cf Ps 69, 29, "the book of the living"; Ps 139, 16, "your book."

u: Dt 32, 1.   v: Ez 32, 4. 6.   w: Is 13, 10; Ez 32, 7f; 4, 15.   x: Jer 46, 10.   y: 6f: Jer 49, 12f.   z: Is 13, 9; 63, 4.   a: Is 14, 23; Zep 2, 14.   b: Ob 18.   c: Is 13, 21; Hos 9, 6.   d: Jos 18, 10; Ps 78, 55.

[17] It is he who casts the lot for them,
and with his hand he marks off their
shares of her;
They shall possess her forever,
and dwell there from generation to
generation.

CHAPTER 35

See RG
280-95

Israel's Deliverance*

[1] The desert and the parched land will
exult;
the steppe will rejoice and bloom.[e]
[2] They will bloom with abundant flowers,
and rejoice with joyful song.
The glory of Lebanon will be given to
them,
the splendor of Carmel and Sharon;
They will see the glory of the LORD,
the splendor of our God.[f]
[3] Strengthen the hands that are feeble,
make firm the knees that are weak,[g]
[4] Say to those whose hearts are frightened:
Be strong, fear not!
Here is your God,
he comes with vindication;
With divine recompense
he comes to save you.[h]
[5] Then will the eyes of the blind be
opened,
the ears of the deaf be cleared;[i]
[6] Then will the lame leap like a stag,
then the tongue of the dumb will sing.[j]

Streams will burst forth in the desert,
and rivers in the steppe.
[7] The burning sands will become pools,
and the thirsty ground, springs of
water;
The abode where jackals lurk
will be a marsh for the reed and
papyrus.
[8] A highway will be there,
called the holy way;

No one unclean may pass over it,
nor fools go astray on it.
[9] No lion will be there,
nor beast of prey go up to be met upon
it.
It is for those with a journey to make,
and on it the redeemed will walk.[k]
[10] Those whom the LORD has ransomed will
return
and enter Zion singing,
crowned with everlasting joy;
They will meet with joy and gladness,
sorrow and mourning will flee.[l]

VII: Historical Appendix

CHAPTER 36

See RG
280-95

Invasion of Sennacherib. [1]In the
fourteenth year of King Hezekiah, Sennacherib, king of Assyria, went on an expedition against all the fortified cities of Judah
and captured them.[m] [2]From Lachish the king
of Assyria sent his commander with a great
army to King Hezekiah in Jerusalem. When
he stopped at the conduit of the upper pool, on
the highway of the fuller's field, [3]there came
out to him the master of the palace, Eliakim,
son of Hilkiah, and Shebna the scribe, and the
herald Joah, son of Asaph. [4]The commander
said to them, "Tell King Hezekiah: Thus says
the great king, the king of Assyria, 'On what
do you base this confidence of yours? [5]Do
you think mere words substitute for strategy
and might in war? On whom, then, do you
rely, that you rebel against me? [6]This Egypt,
the staff on which you rely, is in fact a broken
reed which pierces the hand of anyone who
leans on it. That is what Pharaoh, king of
Egypt, is to all who rely on him.[n] [7]But if you
say to me: "We rely on the LORD, our God,"
is not he the one whose high places and altars
Hezekiah removed,* commanding Judah and
Jerusalem to worship before this altar?'[o]

35, 1-10: Similar to the description of the return from the
Exile, as found in chaps. 40—55.

36, 1—39, 8: Except for 38, 9-20, this historical appendix
describing the siege, etc., is paralleled in 2 Kgs 18, 13—20,
19, which, however, has certain details proper to itself. The
events are also recorded in substantially the same way in the
cuneiform inscriptions of Sennacherib.

36, 7: The Assyrians pretend that Hezekiah's removal of
the high places and altars (illegal sanctuaries) was taken by

the Lord as an insult. They declare to Jerusalem's emissaries
that the city therefore no longer has a right to the Lord's protection and that they are the ones who truly carry out his will
(cf v 10).

e: Is 55, 12f. *f:* Is 60, 13; Ps 96, 12. *g:* Jb 4, 3f; Heb 12, 12.
h: Is 41, 10; Zec 8, 13. *i:* Is 29, 18; 32, 3. *j:* Is 41, 18; 43, 10.
19. *k:* Is 62, 10; Lv 26, 6. *l:* Is 51, 11. *m:* 2 Kgs 18, 13; 2 Chr
32, 1. *n:* Is 30, 2. *o:* 2 Kgs 18, 4.

The Assyrian Empire

⁸"Now, make a wager with my lord the king of Assyria: 'I will give you two thousand horses, if you can put riders on them.' ⁹How then can you repulse even one of the least servants of my lord? And yet you rely on Egypt for chariots and horsemen! ¹⁰'Was it without the LORD's will that I have come up to destroy this land? The LORD said to me, "Go up and destroy that land!" ' "ᵖ

¹¹Then Eliakim and Shebna and Joah said to the commander, "Please speak to your servants in Aramaic; we understand it. Do not speak to us in Judean within earshot of the people who are on the wall."* ¹²But the commander replied, "Was it to you and your master that my lord sent me to speak these words? Was it not rather to the men sitting on the wall, who, with you, will have to eat their own excrement and drink their own urine?" ¹³Then the commander stepped forward and cried out in a loud voice in Judean, "Listen to the words of the great king, the king of Assyria. ¹⁴Thus says the king: 'Do not let Hezekiah deceive you, since he cannot deliver you. ¹⁵Let not Hezekiah induce you to rely on the LORD, saying, "The LORD will surely save us; this city will not be handed over to the king of Assyria." ' ¹⁶Do not listen to Hezekiah, for the king of Assyria says: 'Make peace with me and surrender! Then each of you will eat of his own vine and of his own fig tree, and drink the water of his own cistern,�q ¹⁷until I come to take you to a land like your own, a land of grain and wine, of bread and vineyards. ¹⁸Do not let Hezekiah seduce you by saying, "The LORD will save us." Has any of the gods of the nations ever rescued his land from the hand of the king of Assyria?ʳ ¹⁹Where are the gods of Hamath and Arpad? Where are the gods of Sepharvaim? Where are the gods of Samaria? Have they saved Samaria from my hand?ˢ ²⁰Which of all the gods of these lands ever rescued his land from my hand?

36, 11: The Jewish emissaries ask that the conversation be carried on in Aramaic, not in Judean, for they fear the effect of the Assyrian claims upon the morale of the people.

p: Is 10, 5f.   *q:* 1 Kgs 4, 25; Zec 3, 10.   *r:* Is 37, 11.   *s:* Is 10, 9; 37, 13.

Will the LORD then save Jerusalem from my hand?' " [21]But they remained silent and did not answer him one word, for the king had ordered them not to answer him.

[22]Then the master of the palace, Eliakim, son of Hilkiah, Shebna the scribe, and the herald Joah, son of Asaph, came to Hezekiah with their garments torn, and reported to him what the commander had said.

CHAPTER 37

See RG
280–95
[1]When King Hezekiah heard this, he tore his garments, wrapped himself in sackcloth, and went into the temple of the LORD. [2]He sent Eliakim, the master of the palace, and Shebna the scribe, and the elders of the priests, wrapped in sackcloth, to tell the prophet Isaiah, son of Amoz: [3]"Thus says Hezekiah: 'This is a day of distress, of rebuke, and of disgrace. Children are at the point of birth, but there is no strength to bring them forth.* [4]Perhaps the LORD, your God, will hear the words of the commander, whom his master, the king of Assyria, sent to taunt the living God, and will rebuke him for the words which the LORD, your God, has heard. Send up a prayer for the remnant that is here.' "

[5]When the servants of King Hezekiah had come to Isaiah, [6]he said to them: "Tell this to your master: 'Thus says the LORD: Do not be frightened by the words you have heard, with which the servants of the king of Assyria have blasphemed me.[t] [7]I am about to put in him such a spirit that, when he hears a certain report, he will return to his own land, and there I will cause him to fall by the sword.' "

[8]When the commander returned to Lachish and heard that the king of Assyria had left there, he found him besieging Libnah. [9]The king of Assyria heard a report that Tirhakah,* king of Ethiopia, had come out to fight against him. Again he sent envoys to Hezekiah with this message: "Thus shall you say to Hezekiah, king of Judah: [10]'Do not let your God on whom you rely deceive you by saying that Jerusalem will not be handed over to the king of Assyria.[u] [11]You yourself have heard what the kings of Assyria have done to all the countries: They doomed them! Will you, then, be saved? [12]Did the gods of the nations whom my fathers destroyed save them? Gozen, Haran, Rezeph, and the Edenites in Telassar? [13]Where is the king of Hamath, the king of Arpad, or a king of the cities of Sepharvaim, Hena or Ivvah?' "

[14]Hezekiah took the letter from the hand of the messengers and read it; then he went up to the temple of the LORD, and spreading it out before him, [15]he prayed to the LORD: [16]"O LORD of hosts, God of Israel, enthroned upon the cherubim! You alone are God over all the kingdoms of the earth. You have made the heavens and the earth.* [17]Incline your ear, O LORD, and listen! Open your eyes, O LORD, and see! Hear all the words of the letter that Sennacherib sent to taunt the living God. [18]Truly, O LORD, the kings of Assyria have laid waste all the nations and their lands, [19]and cast their gods into the fire; they destroyed them because they were not gods but the work of human hands, wood and stone.[v] [20]Therefore, O LORD, our God, save us from his hand, that all the kingdoms of the earth may know that you, O LORD, alone are God."

Punishment of Sennacherib. [21]Then Isaiah, son of Amoz, sent this message to Hezekiah: Thus says the LORD, the God of Israel: In answer to your prayer for help against Sennacherib, king of Assyria, [22]this is the word the LORD has spoken concerning him:[w]

She despises you, laughs you to scorn,
   the virgin daughter Zion;
Behind you she wags her head,
   daughter Jerusalem.

37, 3: A proverbial expression. In the Bible the pangs of childbirth often typify extreme anguish; cf Is 13, 8; Jer 6, 24; Mi 4, 9f. In this instance there is reference to the desperate situation of Hezekiah from which he was scarcely able to free himself.

37, 9: Tirhakah: may have been general of the Egyptian army in 701 B.C.; later he became king, one of the Ethiopian dynasty of Egyptian kings (c. 690–664 B.C.). Many consider that this account in Isaiah combines features of two originally distinct sieges of Jerusalem by Sennacherib.

37, 16: In contrast to the empty boasting of the Assyrians, Hezekiah proclaims the Lord as God over all the kingdoms of the earth.

---

t: Is 41, 10-14; 51, 7. u: Is 36, 14. v: Jer 16, 20. w: 2 Kgs 19, 21.

23 Whom have you insulted and blasphemed,
  against whom have you raised your
    voice
  And lifted up your eyes on high?
  Against the Holy One of Israel!ˣ
24 Through your servants you have insulted
    the Lord:
  You said, "With my many chariots
  I climbed the mountain heights,
    the recesses of Lebanon;
  I cut down its lofty cedars,
    its choice cypresses;
  I reached the remotest heights,
    its forest park.
25 I dug wells and drank water in foreign
    lands;
  I dried up with the soles of my feet
  all the rivers of Egypt."

26 Have you not heard?
  Long ago I prepared it,
  From days of old I planned it,
    now I have brought it to pass:
  That you should reduce fortified cities
    into heaps of ruins,
27 While their inhabitants, shorn of power,
  are dismayed and ashamed,
  Becoming like the plants of the field,
    like the green growth,
    like the scorched grass on the
      housetops.
28 I am aware whether you stand or sit;
  I know whether you come or go,
  and also your rage against me.
29 Because of your rage against me
  and your fury which has reached my
    ears,
  I will put my hook in your nose
  and my bit in your mouth,
  and make you return the way you
    came.

30 This shall be a sign for you:*
  this year you shall eat the aftergrowth,
  next year, what grows of itself;
  But in the third year, sow and reap,
  plant vineyards and eat their fruit!
31 The remaining survivors of the house of
    Judah
  shall again strike root below
  and bear fruit above.ʸ
32 For out of Jerusalem shall come a
    remnant,
  and from Mount Zion, survivors.
  The zeal of the LORD of hosts shall do
    this.

33 Therefore, thus says the LORD concerning the king of Assyria: He shall not reach this city, nor shoot an arrow at it, nor come before it with a shield, nor cast up siege-works against it. 34 He shall return by the same way he came, without entering the city, says the LORD.ᶻ 35 I will shield and save this city for my own sake, and for the sake of my servant David.ᵃ

36 The angel of the LORD went forth and struck down one hundred and eighty-five thousand in the Assyrian camp.ᵇ Early the next morning, there they were, all the corpses of the dead.* 37 So Sennacherib, the king of Assyria, broke camp and went back home to Nineveh.ᶜ

38 When he was worshiping in the temple of his god Nisroch, his sons Adrammelech and Sharezer slew him with the sword and fled into the land of Ararat.* His son Esarhaddon reigned in his stead.

CHAPTER 38

*Sickness and Recovery of Hezekiah.**

See RG
280–95

1 In those days,* when Hezekiah was mortally ill, the prophet Isaiah, son of Amoz, came and

---

37, 30: You: Hezekiah. A sign: it is difficult to know the nature of this sign. Either it is merely a proverbial expression to signify that prosperity follows adversity, or it indicates that after two years the normal conditions of life will be resumed.

37, 36: The destruction of Sennacherib's army is also recorded by Herodotus, a Greek historian of the fifth century B.C. It was probably due to the bubonic plague, but the sacred author attributes it to its ultimate cause, God through his angel.

37, 38: The violent death of Sennacherib (681 B.C.) is also mentioned in non-biblical sources. It occurred twenty

years after his invasion of Judea.

38, 1—39, 8: The events of this section—sickness and recovery of Hezekiah, embassy of Merodach-baladan—point forward to Babylon (cc 40—66). They occurred prior to the events of Is 36, 1—37, 38, which point back to Assyria (Is 1, 1—35, 10).

38, 1: In those days: a time prior to the siege of Jerusalem in 701 B.C.

x: Is 1, 4. *y:* Is 27, 6. *z:* Is 37, 29. *a:* 1 Kgs 15, 4f. *b:* Is 10, 12; 17, 14. *c:* 2 Kgs 19, 35f.

said to him: "Thus says the LORD: Put your house in order, for you are about to die; you shall not recover."[d] [2]Then Hezekiah turned his face to the wall and prayed to the LORD:

["3]O LORD, remember how faithfully and wholeheartedly I conducted myself in your presence, doing what was pleasing to you!" And Hezekiah wept bitterly.[e]

[4]Then the word of the LORD came to Isaiah: [5]"Go, tell Hezekiah:* Thus says the LORD, the God of your father David: I have heard your prayer and seen your tears. I will heal you: in three days you shall go up to the LORD's temple; I will add fifteen years to your life. [6]I will rescue you and this city from the hand of the king of Assyria; I will be a shield to this city."[f]

[21]Isaiah then ordered a poultice of figs to be taken and applied to the boil, that he might recover. [22]Then Hezekiah asked, "What is the sign that I shall go up to the temple of the LORD?"

[7][Isaiah answered:] "This will be the sign for you from the LORD that he will do what he has promised: [8]See, I will make the shadow cast by the sun on the stairway to the terrace of Ahaz* go back the ten steps it has advanced." So the sun came back the ten steps it had advanced.[g]

Hezekiah's Hymn of Thanksgiving. [9]The song of Hezekiah, king of Judah, after he had been sick and had recovered from his illness:

[10] Once I said,
"In the noontime of life* I must depart!
To the gates of the nether world I shall be
consigned

for the rest of my years."[h]
[11] I said, "I shall see the LORD* no more
in the land of the living.
No longer shall I behold my fellow men
among those who dwell in the world."
[12] My dwelling, like a shepherd's tent,
is struck down and borne away from
me;
You have folded up my life, like a
weaver
who severs the last thread.*
Day and night you give me over to
torment;[i]
[13] I cry out until the dawn.
Like a lion he breaks all my bones;
[day and night you give me over to
torment].
[14] Like a swallow I utter shrill cries;
I moan like a dove.
My eyes grow weak, gazing heavenward:
O Lord, I am in straits; be my surety!
[15] What am I to say or tell him?*
He has done it!
I shall go on through all my years
despite the bitterness of my soul.
[16] Those live whom the LORD protects;
yours . . . the life of my spirit.*
You have given me health and life;
[17] thus is my bitterness transformed into
peace.
You have preserved my life
from the pit of destruction,
When you cast behind your back
all my sins.*
[18] For it is not the nether world that gives
you thanks,*
nor death that praises you;

38, 5: Since Hezekiah died in 687 B.C. this sickness of his seems to have been in 702 B.C., that is, fifteen years before.

38, 8: Stairway to the terrace of Ahaz: this interpretation is based on a reading of the Hebrew text revised according to the Dead Sea Scroll of Isaiah; cf 2 Kgs 23, 12. Many translate the phrase as "steps of Ahaz" and understand this as referring to a sundial.

38, 10: In the noontime of life: long before the end of a full span of life; cf Pss 55, 24; 102, 25.

38, 11: See the Lord: go to the temple and take part in its service.

38, 12: These two metaphors emphasize the suddenness and finality of death.

38, 15: What am I to say or tell him?: a rhetorical question, as if the poet were at a loss in giving fitting expression

to his gratitude; cf Ps 116, 12. He has done it: accomplished the cure. Despite the bitterness: even though the one praying was previously so dejected.

38, 16: Yours . . . the life of my spirit: the current Hebrew text is corrupt. The revised Latin psalter renders it: "You have revived my soul."

38, 17: You cast behind your back all my sins: figurative language to express the divine forgiveness of sins, as if God no longer saw or cared about them. This expression is ordinarily used of men forgetting God; cf 1 Kgs 14, 9; Ez 23, 35; Ps 50, 17.

38, 18f: See note on Ps 6, 6.

d: 2 Kgs 20, 1. e: 2 Kgs 18, 5f. f: Is 37, 35. g: 2 Kgs 20, 9. 11. h: Jb 17, 11; Ps 102, 25. i: Jb 7, 6.

Neither do those who go down into the
pit
await your kindness.[j]

[19] The living, the living give you thanks,
as I do today.
Fathers declare to their sons,
O God, your faithfulness.
[20] The LORD is our savior;
we shall sing to stringed instruments
In the house of the LORD
all the days of our life.

CHAPTER 39

See RG
280-95

Embassy from Merodach-baladan.
[1]At that time when Merodach-baladan,* son
of Baladan, king of Babylon, heard that Hezekiah had recovered from his sickness, he
sent letters and gifts to him.[k] [2]Hezekiah was
pleased at this, and therefore showed the
messengers his treasury, the silver and gold,
the spices and fine oil, his whole armory, and
everything that was in his storerooms; there
was nothing in his house or in his whole
realm that he did not show them.[l]

[3]Then Isaiah the prophet came to King
Hezekiah and asked him, "What did these
men say to you? Where did they come
from?" Hezekiah answered, "They came to
me from a distant land, from Babylon."
[4]"What did they see in your house?" he
asked. Hezekiah replied, "They saw everything in my house; there is nothing in my
storerooms that I did not show them."
[5]Then Isaiah said to Hezekiah, "Hear the
word of the LORD of hosts: [6]Behold, the days
shall come when all that is in your house, and
everything that your fathers have stored up
until this day, shall be carried off to Babylon;*
nothing shall be left, says the LORD.[m] [7]Some
of your own bodily descendants shall be
taken and made servants in the palace of the
king of Babylon."[n] [8]Hezekiah replied to Isa-

iah, "The word of the LORD which you have
spoken is favorable."* For he thought, "There
will be peace and security in my lifetime."[o]

B. The Book of Consolation

I: The Lord's Glory in Israel's Liberation

CHAPTER 40

Promise of Salvation See RG
280-95

[1] Comfort, give comfort to my people,
says your God.
[2] Speak tenderly to Jerusalem, and
proclaim to her
that her service* is at an end,
her guilt is expiated;
Indeed, she has received from the hand
of the LORD
double for all her sins.[p]

[3]   A voice cries out:*
In the desert prepare the way of the
LORD!
Make straight in the wasteland a
highway for our God![q]
[4] Every valley shall be filled in,
every mountain and hill shall be made
low;
The rugged land shall be made a plain,
the rough country, a broad valley.
[5] Then the glory of the LORD shall be
revealed,
and all mankind shall see it together;
for the mouth of the LORD has
spoken.

[6] A voice says, "Cry out!"
I answer, "What shall I cry out?"
"All mankind is grass,
and all their glory like the flower of
the field.[r]

39, 1: Merodach-baladan: twice king of Babylon, probably from 721 to 710 B.C., and again for nine months, in
704–703. This visit of his messengers, certainly before 701,
was in reality a political one. Babylon hoped to lead an anti-
Assyrian confederation composed of neighboring states.

39, 6: Because Judah preferred to follow a pro-Bab-
ylonian policy, instead of trusting in God, it would later be exiled to Babylon.

39, 8: Favorable: for the Exile would not occur in his lifetime.

40, 2: Service: servitude and exile.

40, 3-5: The figurative language here describes the actual return of the exiles from Babylon to Jerusalem. It is the Lord who
leads them; their road is made easy for them. Mt 3, 3 and parallels see in these verses a prophecy of the Baptizer and Christ.

---

j: Pss 6, 6; 88, 11-13. *k:* 1-8: 2 Kgs 20, 12. *l:* 2 Chr 32, 25ff.
m: 2 Kgs 24, 13; 25, 13ff. *n:* 2 Chr 33, 11; Dn 1, 2f. *o:* 2 Chr
32, 26. *p:* Is 50, 21. *q:* Mt 3, 3; Jn 1, 23. *r:* Jb 8, 12; 14, 2; Ps
37, 2; Sir 14, 18; Jas 1, 10; 1 Pt 1, 24.

7 The grass withers, the flower wilts,
  when the breath of the LORD blows
    upon it.
  [So then, the people is the grass.]
8 Though the grass withers and the flower
    wilts,
  the word of our God stands forever."

9 Go up onto a high mountain,
  Zion, herald of glad tidings;
  Cry out at the top of your voice,
  Jerusalem, herald of good news!
  Fear not to cry out
  and say to the cities of Judah:
  Here is your God!
10 Here comes with power
  the Lord GOD,
  who rules by his strong arm;
  Here is his reward with him,
  his recompense before him.
11 Like a shepherd he feeds his flock;
  in his arms he gathers the lambs,
  Carrying them in his bosom,
  and leading the ewes with care.[s]

Power of the Creator To Save His People

12 Who has cupped in his hand the waters
    of the sea,
  and marked off the heavens with a
    span?[*]
  Who has held in a measure the dust of
    the earth,
  weighed the mountains in scales
  and the hills in a balance?
13 Who has directed the spirit of the LORD,
  or has instructed him as his
    counselor?[t]
14 Whom did he consult to gain knowledge?
  Who taught him the path of judgment,
  or showed him the way of
    understanding?

15 Behold, the nations count as a drop of the
    bucket,

as dust on the scales;
  the coastlands weigh no more than
    powder.
16 Lebanon would not suffice for fuel,[*]
  nor its animals be enough for
    holocausts.
17 Before him all the nations are as nought,
  as nothing and void he accounts them.

18 To whom can you liken God?[u]
  With what equal can you confront
    him?
19 An idol, cast by a craftsman,
  which the smith plates with gold
  and fits with silver chains?[v]
20 Mulberry wood, the choice portion
  which a skilled craftsman picks out for
    himself,
  Choosing timber that will not rot,
  to set up an idol that will not be
    unsteady?[w]
6 One man helps another,[*]
  one says to the other, "Keep on!"
7 The craftsman encourages the goldsmith,
  the one who beats with the hammer,
    him who strikes on the anvil;
  He says the soldering is good,
  and he fastens it with nails to steady it.

21 Do you not know? Have you not heard?
  Was it not foretold you from the
    beginning?
  Have you not understood? Since the
    earth was founded
22 He sits enthroned above the vault of the
    earth,
  and its inhabitants are like
    grasshoppers;
  He stretches out the heavens like a veil,
  spreads them out like a tent to dwell
    in.[x]
23 He brings princes to nought
  and makes the rulers of the earth as
    nothing.

40, 12: Span: the distance between the extended little finger and the thumb. Measure: literally, "third"; here a small container.

40, 16: Lebanon . . . fuel: the famed cedars would not be enough to keep the fires of sacrifice burning.

40, 6-7: These two verses have been transposed from chap. 41.

s: Is 49, 9f; 63, 11; Ez 34, 23; 37, 24; Jn 10, 11.   t: Wis 9, 13; Rom 11, 34; 1 Cor 2, 16; Jb 38, 1ff.   u: 18f: Acts 17, 29.   v: Ps 115, 4-7.   w: Is 44, 13.   x: Ps 104, 2.

²⁴ Scarcely are they planted or sown,
    scarcely is their stem rooted in the
       earth,
When he breathes upon them and they
      wither,
    and the stormwind carries them away
      like straw.

²⁵ To whom can you liken me as an equal?
    says the Holy One.

²⁶ Lift up your eyes on high
    and see who has created* these:
He leads out their army and numbers
    them,
    calling them all by name.
By his great might and the strength of his
    power
    not one of them is missing!^y

²⁷ Why, O Jacob, do you say,*
    and declare, O Israel,
"My way is hidden from the LORD,
    and my right is disregarded by my
      God"?

²⁸ Do you not know
    or have you not heard?
The LORD is the eternal God,
    creator of the ends of the earth.
He does not faint nor grow weary,
    and his knowledge is beyond
      scrutiny.

²⁹ He gives strength to the fainting;
    for the weak he makes vigor abound.

³⁰ Though young men faint and grow
      weary,
    and youths stagger and fall,

³¹ They that hope in the LORD will renew
      their strength,
    they will soar as with eagles' wings;
They will run and not grow weary,
    walk and not grow faint.

CHAPTER 41

See RG 280-95

The Liberator of Israel

¹ Keep silence before me, O coastlands;*
    you peoples, wait for my words!

Let them draw near and speak;
    let us come together for judgment.

² Who has stirred up from the East the
      champion of justice,*
    and summoned him to be his
      attendant?
To him he delivers the nations
    and subdues the kings;
With his sword he reduces them to dust,
    with his bow, to driven straw.

³ He pursues them, passing on without
      loss,
    by a path his feet do not even tread.

⁴ Who has performed these deeds?
    He who has called forth the
      generations since the beginning.^z

I, the LORD, am the first,
    and with the last I will also be.

⁵ The coastlands see, and fear;
    the ends of the earth tremble:
    these things are near, they come to
      pass.

⁸ But you, Israel, my servant,^a
    Jacob, whom I have chosen,
    offspring of Abraham my friend—

⁹ You whom I have taken from the ends of
      the earth
    and summoned from its far-off places,
You whom I have called my servant,
    whom I have chosen and will not cast
      off—

¹⁰ Fear not, I am with you;
    be not dismayed; I am your God.
I will strengthen you, and help you,
    and uphold you with my right hand of
      justice.

¹¹ Yes, all shall be put to shame and
      disgrace
    who vent their anger against you;
Those shall perish and come to nought
    who offer resistance.

¹² You shall seek out, but shall not find,

40, 26: Created: see note on Gn 1, 1. By name: for he is their Creator.

40, 27f: God's people, here called Jacob and Israel, must not give way to discouragement: their Lord is the eternal God.

41, 1-4: It is generally agreed that these verses describe the vocation and victory of Cyrus, whom the Lord used as his instrument to redeem Israel.

41, 2: Cyrus is the champion of justice and God's attendant.

y: Ps 147, 4f.   z: Is 44, 7; 46, 10.   a: 8f: Is 44, 1f. 21; 45, 4.

those who strive against you;
They shall be as nothing at all
who do battle with you.

¹³ For I am the LORD, your God,
who grasp your right hand;
It is I who say to you, "Fear not,
I will help you."
¹⁴ Fear not, O worm Jacob,
O maggot Israel;
I will help you, says the LORD;
your redeemer* is the Holy One of
Israel.
¹⁵ I will make of you a threshing sledge,
sharp, new, and double-edged,
To thresh the mountains and crush them,
to make the hills like chaff.
¹⁶ When you winnow them, the wind shall
carry them off
and the storm shall scatter them.
But you shall rejoice in the LORD,
and glory in the Holy One of Israel.
¹⁷ The afflicted and the needy seek water in
vain,
their tongues are parched with thirst.
I, the LORD, will answer them;
I, the God of Israel, will not forsake
them.
¹⁸ I will open up rivers on the bare heights,
and fountains in the broad valleys;
I will turn the desert into a marshland,
and the dry ground into springs of
water.
¹⁹ I will plant in the desert the cedar,
acacia, myrtle, and olive;
I will set in the wasteland the cypress,
together with the plane tree and the pine,
²⁰ That all may see and know,
observe and understand,
That the hand of the LORD has done this,
the Holy One of Israel has created it.

²¹ Present your case, says the LORD;*
bring forward your reasons, says the
King of Jacob.

²² Let them come near and foretell to us
what it is that shall happen!
What are the things of long ago?
Tell us, that we may reflect on them
And know their outcome;
or declare to us the things to come!
²³ Foretell the things that shall come
afterward,
that we may know that you are gods!
Do something, good or evil,
that will put us in awe and in fear.
²⁴ Why, you are nothing and your work is
nought!
To choose you is an abomination.

²⁵ I have stirred up one from the north, and
he comes;
from the east I summon him* by name;
He shall trample the rulers down like red
earth,
as the potter treads the clay.
²⁶ Who announced this from the beginning,
that we might know;
beforehand, that we might say it is
true?
Not one of you foretold it, not one spoke;
no one heard you say,
²⁷ "The first news for Zion: they are coming
now,"
or, "For Jerusalem I will pick out a
bearer of the glad tidings."
²⁸ When I look, there is not one,
no one of them to give counsel,
to make an answer when I question
them.
²⁹ Ah, all of them are nothing,
their works are nought,
their idols are empty wind!

CHAPTER 42

The Servant of the Lord

See RG
280-95

¹ Here is my servant* whom I uphold,
my chosen one with whom I am
pleased,
Upon whom I have put my spirit;

41, 14: Redeemer: in Hebrew, goel, one who frees another from slavery and avenges his sufferings; cf Lv 25, 48: Dt 19. 6, 12.

41, 21-24: An indictment of idols.

41, 25: I summon him: Cyrus.

42, 1-4: Servant: there are three other "Servant-of-the-Lord" oracles, Is 49, 1-7; 50, 4-11; 52, 13—53, 12. Many identifications have been proposed, e.g., historical Israel, ideal Israel, an Old Testament historical character before or during the lifetime of the prophet, the prophet himself. The New Testament and Christian tradition, however, have seen a fulfillment of these prophecies in Jesus Christ.

he shall bring forth justice to the
    nations,[b]
[2] Not crying out, not shouting,
    not making his voice heard in the
        street.
[3] A bruised reed he shall not break,
    and a smoldering wick he shall not
        quench,*
[4] Until he establishes justice on the earth;
    the coastlands* will wait for his
        teaching.

[5] Thus says God, the LORD,
    who created the heavens and stretched
        them out,
    who spreads out the earth with its
        crops,
    Who gives breath to its people
    and spirit to those who walk on it:
[6] I, the LORD, have called you for the
        victory of justice,
    I have grasped you by the hand;
    I formed you, and set you
        as a covenant of the people,
        a light for the nations,[c]
[7] To open the eyes of the blind,
    to bring out prisoners from
        confinement,
    and from the dungeon, those who live
        in darkness.
[8] I am the LORD, this is my name;
    my glory I give to no other,
    nor my praise to idols.
[9] See, the earlier things have come to pass,
    new ones I now foretell;
    Before they spring into being,
    I announce them to you.

The Salvation of Israel despite Its Sins
[10] Sing to the LORD a new song,
    his praise from the end of the earth:
    Let the sea and what fills it resound,
    the coastlands, and those who dwell in
        them.
[11] Let the steppe and its cities cry out,

the villages where Kedar* dwells;
Let the inhabitants of Sela exult,
    and shout from the top of the
        mountains.
[12] Let them give glory to the LORD,
    and utter his praise in the coastlands.
[13] The LORD goes forth like a hero,
    like a warrior he stirs up his ardor;
He shouts out his battle cry,
    against his enemies he shows his
        might:[d]
[14] I have looked away, and kept silence,
    I have said nothing, holding myself in;
But now, I cry out as a woman in labor,
    gasping and panting.
[15] I will lay waste mountains and hills,
    all their herbage I will dry up;
I will turn the rivers into marshes,
    and the marshes I will dry up.[e]
[16] I will lead the blind on their journey;
    by paths unknown I will guide them.
I will turn darkness into light before
        them,
    and make crooked ways straight.
These things I do for them,
    and I will not forsake them.[f]
[17] They shall be turned back in utter shame
    who trust in idols;
Who say to molten images,
    "You are our gods."
[18] You who are deaf, listen,*
    you who are blind, look and see!
[19] Who is blind but my servant,
    or deaf like the messenger I send?
[20] You see many things without taking note;
    your ears are open, but without
        hearing.
[21] Though it pleased the LORD in his justice
    to make his law great and glorious,
[22] This is a people* despoiled and
        plundered,
    all of them trapped in holes,
    hidden away in prisons.
They are taken as booty, with no one to
        rescue them,

42, 3: A reference to the mercy of Christ.
42, 4: Coastlands: the lands of the Mediterranean. In the
Old Testament the word often refers to the pagan lands of the
west.
  42, 11: Kedar: cf footnote to Is 21, 16. Sela: Petra, the capital of Edom.

42, 18-20: Because of their unbelief, the Lord rebukes his
people, whom he calls his servant, his messenger.
42, 22: A people: Israel in exile.

b: Is 45, 6; 49, 6. *c:* Is 45, 13. *d:* Ex 14, 3. *e:* Ex 9, 25; 10,
15; 14, 21; Ps 105, 33ff. *f:* Ex 13, 21.

as spoil, with no one to demand their
return.

²³ Who of you gives ear to this?
Who listens and pays heed for the time
to come?

²⁴ Who was it that gave Jacob to be
plundered,
Israel to the despoilers?*
Was it not the LORD, against whom we
have sinned?
In his ways they refused to walk,
his law they disobeyed.

²⁵ So he poured out wrath upon them,
his anger, and the fury of battle;
It blazed round about them, yet they did
not realize,
it burned them, but they took it not to
heart.

CHAPTER 43

See RG
280–95

*Promises of Redemption
and Restoration*

¹But now, thus says the LORD,
who created you, O Jacob, and formed
you, O Israel:
Fear not, for I have redeemed you;
I have called you by name: you are
mine.

² When you pass through the water, I will
be with you;
in the rivers you shall not drown.
When you walk through fire, you shall
not be burned;
the flames shall not consume you.

³ For I am the LORD, your God,
the Holy One of Israel, your savior.
I give Egypt as your ransom,
Ethiopia and Seba* in return for you.

⁴ Because you are precious in my eyes
and glorious, and because I love you.
I give men in return for you
and peoples in exchange for your life.ᵍ

⁵ Fear not, for I am with you;
from the east I will bring back your
descendants,
from the west I will gather you.

⁶ I will say to the north: Give them up!
and to the south: Hold not back!
Bring back my sons from afar,
and my daughters from the ends of the
earth:ʰ

⁷ Everyone who is named as mine,
whom I created for my glory,
whom I formed and made.

⁸ Lead out the people who are blind
though they have eyes,
who are deaf though they have ears.

⁹ Let all the nations gather together,
let the peoples assemble!
Who among them could have revealed
this,
or foretold to us the earlier things?*
Let them produce witnesses to prove
themselves right,
that one may hear and say, "It is true!"

¹⁰ You are my witnesses, says the LORD,
my servants whom I have chosen
To know and believe in me
and understand that it is I.
Before me no god was formed,
and after me there shall be none.

¹¹ It is I, I the LORD;
there is no savior but me.

¹² It is I who foretold, I who saved;
I made it known, not any strange god
among you;
You are my witnesses, says the LORD.
I am God, ¹³yes, from eternity I am He;
There is none who can deliver from my
hand:
who can countermand what I do?ⁱ

¹⁴ Thus says the LORD, your redeemer,*
the Holy One of Israel:
For your sakes I send to Babylon;
I will lower all the bars,
and the Chaldeans shall cry out in
lamentation.

¹⁵ I am the LORD, your Holy One,
the creator of Israel, your King.

42, 24: Despoilers: the Assyrians and Babylonians.

43, 3f: Egypt . . . Ethiopia and Seba: countries which God
permitted the Persians to conquer in return for having given
Israel its freedom.

43, 9: Only God can know and predict future events; cf Is

41, 1-5. 21-29.

43, 14-17: The destruction of Babylon.

g: Dt 4, 37; Hos 11, 1.   h: Is 49, 22; Ez 16, 20.   i: Is 41, 4.

16 Thus says the LORD,
   who opens a way in the sea
   and a path in the mighty waters,[j]
17 Who leads out chariots and horsemen,
   a powerful army,
   Till they lie prostrate together, never to
      rise,
   snuffed out and quenched like a wick.[k]
18 Remember not the events of the past,
   the things of long ago consider not;*
19 See, I am doing something new!
   Now it springs forth, do you not
      perceive it?
   In the desert I make a way,
   in the wasteland, rivers.
20 Wild beasts honor me,
   jackals and ostriches,
   For I put water in the desert
   and rivers in the wasteland
   for my chosen people to drink,
21 The people whom I formed for myself,
   that they might announce my praise.

22 Yet you did not call upon me, O Jacob,*
   for you grew weary of me, O Israel.
23 You did not bring me sheep for your
      holocausts,
   nor honor me with your sacrifices.
   I did not exact from you the service of
      offerings,
   nor weary you for frankincense.[l]
24 You did not buy me sweet cane* for
      money,
   nor fill me with the fat of your
      sacrifices;
   Instead, you burdened me with your sins,
   and wearied me with your crimes.
25 It is I, I, who wipe out,
   for my own sake, your offenses;
   your sins I remember no more.
26 Would you have me remember, have us
      come to trial?
   Speak up, prove your innocence!

27 Your first father* sinned;
   your spokesmen rebelled against me
28 Till I repudiated the holy gates,
   put Jacob under the ban,
   and exposed Israel to scorn.

CHAPTER 44

See RG
280-95

1 Hear then, O Jacob, my servant,
   Israel, whom I have chosen.
2 Thus says the LORD who made you,
   your help, who formed you from the
      womb:
   Fear not, O Jacob, my servant,
   the darling* whom I have chosen.
3 I will pour out water upon the thirsty
      ground,
   and streams upon the dry land;
   I will pour out my spirit upon your
      offspring,
   and my blessing upon your descendants.
4 They shall spring up amid the verdure
   like poplars beside the flowing waters.[m]
5 One shall say, "I am the LORD's,"
   another shall be named after Jacob,
   And this one shall write on his hand,*
      "The LORD's,"
   and Israel shall be his surname.[n]

The True God and False Gods

6 Thus says the LORD, Israel's King
   and redeemer, the LORD of hosts:
   I am the first and I am the last;
   there is no God but me.[o]
7 Who is like me? Let him stand up and
      speak,
   make it evident, and confront me with
      it.
   Who of old announced future events?
   Let them foretell to us the things to
      come.
8 Fear not, be not troubled:
   did I not announce and foretell it long
      ago?

43, 18: No need to think solely of the past wonders of the exodus from Egypt; equally great is the exodus from Babylon.

43, 22-28: The reason for the liberation of the Israelites is not their fidelity but rather God's mercy.

43, 24: Sweet cane: a fragrant substance used in making incense and the sacred anointing oil; cf Ex 30, 23; Jer 6, 20.

43, 27: First father: Adam or Jacob, or collectively "early ancestors." Spokesmen: leaders, priests, prophets.

44, 2: The darling: see note on Dt 32, 15; cf also Dt 33, 5. 26.

44, 5: Write on his hand: an allusion to the Babylonian custom of tatooing the owner's name on the hand of his slave; cf also Rv 13, 16.

j: Is 51, 10f; Ex 14, 21.   k: Ex 15, 4.   l: Jer 6, 20.   m: Is 54, 1ff.
n: Is 43, 7; 45, 14.   o: Is 41, 44; 43, 15; 45, 21; 48, 3. 12; 51, 15;
54, 5.

You are my witnesses! Is there a God
or any Rock* besides me?*p*

⁹*Idol makers all amount to nothing, and
their precious works are of no avail, as they
themselves give witness. To their shame,
they neither see nor know anything; and they
are more deaf than men are.*q* ¹⁰Indeed, all
the associates of anyone who forms a god, or
casts an idol to no purpose, will be put to
shame; ¹¹they will all assemble and stand
forth, to be reduced to fear and shame.

¹²The smith fashions an iron image,
works it over the coals, shapes it with hammers, and forges it with his strong arm. He is
hungry and weak, drinks no water and becomes exhausted.*r*

¹³The carpenter stretches a line and marks
with a stylus the outline of an idol. He
shapes it with a plane and measures it off
with a compass, making it like a man in appearance and dignity, to occupy a shrine.
¹⁴He cuts down cedars, takes a holm or an
oak, and lays hold of other trees of the forest, which the Lord had planted and the rain
made grow ¹⁵to serve man for fuel. With a
part of their wood he warms himself, or
makes a fire for baking bread; but with another part he makes a god which he adores,
an idol which he worships. ¹⁶Half of it he
burns in the fire, and on its embers he roasts
his meat; he eats what he has roasted until he
is full, and then warms himself and says,
"Ah! I am warm, I feel the fire." ¹⁷Of what
remains he makes a god, his idol, and prostrate before it in worship, he implores it,
"Rescue me, for you are my god."

¹⁸The idols have neither knowledge nor
reason; their eyes are coated so that they
cannot see, and their hearts so that they cannot understand. ¹⁹Yet he does not reflect, nor
have the intelligence and sense to say, "Half
of the wood I burned in the fire, and on its
embers I baked bread and roasted meat
which I ate. Shall I then make an abomination out of the rest, or worship a block of

wood?" ²⁰He is chasing ashes*—a thing that
cannot save itself when the flame consumes
it; yet he does not say, "Is not this thing in
my right hand a fraud?"

²¹ Remember this, O Jacob,
   you, O Israel, who are my servant!
 I formed you to be a servant to me;
   O Israel, by me you shall never be
     forgotten:
²² I have brushed away your offenses like a
     cloud,
   your sins like a mist;
   return to me, for I have redeemed you.

²³ Raise a glad cry, you heavens: the Lord
     has done this;
   shout, you depths of the earth.
 Break forth, you mountains, into song,
   you forest, with all your trees.
 For the Lord has redeemed Jacob,
   and shows his glory through Israel.

Cyrus, Anointed of the Lord, Liberator of Israel

²⁴ Thus says the Lord, your redeemer,
   who formed you from the womb:
 I am the Lord, who made all things,
   who alone stretched out the heavens;
   when I spread out the earth, who was
     with me?*s*
²⁵ It is I who bring to nought the omens of
     liars,
   who make fools of diviners;
 I turn wise men back
   and make their knowledge foolish.
²⁶ It is I who confirm the words of my
     servants,
   I carry out the plan announced by my
     messengers;
 I say to Jerusalem: Be inhabited;
   to the cities of Judah: Be rebuilt;
   I will raise up their ruins.
²⁷ It is I who said to the deep: Be dry;
   I will dry up your wellsprings.*t*
²⁸ I say of Cyrus:* My shepherd,

44, 8: Rock: place of refuge; said of God in Dt 32, 4. 18;
1 Sm 2, 2; etc.

44, 9-20: Satire on the makers and worshipers of idols.

44, 20: Chasing ashes: exerting efforts in vain; cf Hos 12,
2; Eccl 1, 14; 2, 11. 17.

44, 28: Cyrus: king of Persia (559–529 B.C.) and conqueror of Babylon (538 B.C.), who liberated the Jews, permitting them to return to their native land and to rebuild
Jerusalem and the Temple.

---

p: Is 43, 10. 12; Dt 32, 4.   *q:* Is 48, 5. 7.   *r:* Wis 13, 11ff.   *s:* Is
40, 22; Jb 9, 8.   *t:* Is 42, 15; 51, 10.

who fulfills my every wish;
He shall say of Jerusalem, "Let her be
rebuilt,"
and of the temple, "Let its foundations
be laid."^{u}

CHAPTER 45

See RG
280-95 ^{1}Thus says the LORD to his anointed,*
Cyrus,
whose right hand I grasp,
Subduing nations before him,
and making kings run in his service,
Opening doors before him
and leaving the gates unbarred:
^{2} I will go before you
and level the mountains;
Bronze doors* I will shatter,
and iron bars I will snap.^{v}
^{3} I will give you treasures out of the
darkness,
and riches that have been hidden away,
That you may know that I am the LORD,
the God of Israel, who calls you by
your name.
^{4} For the sake of Jacob, my servant,
of Israel my chosen one,
I have called you by your name,
giving you a title, though you knew
me not.^{w}
^{5} I am the LORD and there is no other,
there is no God besides me.
It is I who arm you, though you know me
not,
^{6} so that toward the rising and the
setting of the sun
men may know that there is none
besides me.*

I am the LORD, there is no other;
^{7} I form the light, and create the
darkness,

I make well-being and create woe;*
I, the LORD, do all these things.
^{8} Let justice descend, O heavens, like dew
from above,
like gentle rain let the skies drop it
down.
Let the earth open and salvation bud forth;
let justice also spring up!*
I, the LORD, have created this.^{x}
^{9} Woe to him who contends with his
Maker;^{y}
a potsherd among potsherds of the
earth!*
Dare the clay say to its modeler, "What
are you doing?"
or, "What you are making has no
hands"?
^{10} Woe to him who asks a father, "What are
you begetting?"
or a woman, "What are you giving
birth to?"
^{11} Thus says the LORD,
the Holy One of Israel, his maker:
You question me about my children,
or prescribe the work of my hands for
me!
^{12} It was I who made the earth
and created mankind upon it;
It was my hands that stretched out the
heavens;
I gave the order to all their host.
^{13} It was I who stirred up one* for the
triumph of justice;
all his ways I make level.
He shall rebuild my city
and let my exiles go free
Without price or ransom,
says the LORD of hosts.
^{14} Thus says the LORD:
The earnings of Egypt, the gain of
Ethiopia,

45, 1: Anointed: in Hebrew, meshiah, from which the word "Messiah" is derived; from its Greek translation, Christos, we have the name "Christ." Applied to kings, "anointed" originally referred only to those of Israel, but it is here given to Cyrus because he is the agent of the Lord.

45, 2: Bronze doors: of Babylon.

45, 6: The Gentiles will come to know the true God; cf also vv 20-25.

45, 7: Create woe: God permits evil for the sake of a greater good.

45, 8: The Vulgate rendering gives a more precise Mes-

sianic sense to this verse, using "just one" and "savior" in place of justice and salvation. The Advent liturgy uses the Vulgate form, Rorate coeli desuper . . . , to express the world's longing for the coming of Christ.

45, 9: No one may challenge God's freedom of action, exemplified here by the selection of Cyrus as his anointed.

45, 13: One: Cyrus, called by God for the deliverance and restoration of Israel.

u: Jer 3, 15; Ez 34, 23. v: Ps 107, 16. w: Is 40, 26. x: Pss 72, 6; 85, 11. y: Jer 18, 6; Rom 9, 20.

and the Sabeans,* tall of stature,
Shall come over to you and belong to
    you;
they shall follow you, coming in
    chains.
Before you they shall fall prostrate,
    saying in prayer:
"With you only is God, and nowhere
    else;
    the gods are nought.*

15 Truly with you God is hidden,*
    the God of Israel, the savior!*

16 Those are put to shame and disgrace
    who vent their anger against him;
Those go in disgrace
    who carve images.

17 Israel, you are saved by the LORD,
    saved forever!
You shall never be put to shame or
    disgrace
    in future ages."

18   For thus says the LORD,
The creator of the heavens,
    who is God,
The designer and maker of the earth
    who established it,
Not creating it to be a waste,*
    but designing it to be lived in:
I am the LORD, and there is no other.

19   I have not spoken from hiding
    nor from some dark place of the earth,
And I have not said to the descendants of
    Jacob,
    "Look for me in an empty waste."
I, the LORD, promise justice,
    I foretell what is right.

20 Come and assemble, gather together,
    you fugitives from among the gentiles!
They are without knowledge who bear
    wooden idols*
    and pray to gods that cannot save.

21 Come here and declare

in counsel together:
Who announced this from the beginning
    and foretold it from of old?
Was it not I, the LORD,
    besides whom there is no other God?
There is no just and saving God but me.

22 Turn to me and be safe,
    all you ends of the earth,
    for I am God; there is no other!

23 By myself I swear,
    uttering my just decree
    and my unalterable word:
To me every knee shall bend;
    by me every tongue shall swear,*

24 Saying, "Only in the LORD
    are just deeds and power.
Before him in shame shall come
    all who vent their anger against him.

25 In the LORD shall be the vindication and
    the glory
    of all the descendants of Israel."

CHAPTER 46

The Gods of Babylon

See RG
280-95

1 Bel bows down, Nebo* stoops,
    their idols are upon beasts and cattle;
They must be borne up on shoulders,
    carried as burdens by the weary.

2 They stoop and bow down together;
    unable to save those who bear them,
    they too go into captivity.

3 Hear me, O house of Jacob,
    all who remain of the house of Israel,
My burden since your birth,
    whom I have carried from your infancy.*

4 Even to your old age I am the same,
    even when your hair is gray I will bear
    you;
It is I who have done this, I who will
    continue,
    and I who will carry you to safety.

45, 14: Egypt . . . Ethiopia . . . Sabeans: the Egyptians and their allies who, when conquered by Cyrus, are seen as acknowledging the God of Israel to be the one true God; cf Is 43, 3.

45, 15: God is hidden: he dwells invisibly in the holy of holies.

45, 18: Waste: an allusion to the beginning of creation, when the earth was waste and void (Gn 1, 2), the same Hebrew word, tohu, being used in both passages. The further reference here is to Palestine, which God wishes again to be in-

habited by the returning exiles.

45, 20: Who bear wooden idols: in their religious processions. The gods of the pagans have feet but cannot walk; cf Ps 115, 7; Bar 6, 25.

46, 1: Bel . . . Nebo: gods of Babylon; their complete helplessness is here contrasted with God's omnipotence.

z: Is 43, 3. *a:* Is 55, 8; Prv 25, 2. *b:* Rom 14, 11; Phil 2, 10. *c:* Is 44, 2.

5 Whom would you compare me with, as
	an equal,
	or match me against, as though we
		were alike?
6 There are those who pour out gold from a
		purse
	and weigh out silver on the scales;
Then they hire a goldsmith to make it
		into a god
	before which they fall down in worship.
7 They lift it to their shoulders to carry;
	when they set it in place again, it stays,
	and does not move from the spot.
Although they cry out to it, it cannot
		answer;
	it delivers no one from distress.

8 Remember this and be firm,
	bear it well in mind, you rebels;
	remember the former things, those
		long ago:
9 I am God, there is no other;
	I am God, there is none like me.
10 At the beginning I foretell the outcome;
	in advance, things not yet done.
I say that my plan shall stand,
	I accomplish my every purpose.

11 I call from the east a bird of prey,*
	from a distant land, one to carry out
		my plan.
Yes, I have spoken, I will accomplish it;
	I have planned it, and I will do it.
12 Listen to me, you fainthearted,
	you who seem far from the victory of
		justice:
13 I am bringing on my justice, it is not far
		off,
	my salvation shall not tarry;
I will put salvation within Zion,
	and give to Israel my glory.

CHAPTER 47

The Fall of Babylon*

See RG 280-95

1 Come down, sit in the dust,
	O virgin daughter Babylon;

Sit on the ground, dethroned,
	O daughter of the Chaldeans.
No longer shall you be called
	dainty and delicate.
2 Take the millstone and grind flour,
	remove your veil;
Strip off your train, bare your legs,
	pass through the streams.
3 Your nakedness shall be uncovered
	and your shame be seen;
I will take vengeance,
	I will yield to no entreaty,
	says our redeemer.
4 Whose name is the LORD of hosts,
	the Holy One of Israel.

5 Go into darkness and sit in silence,
	O daughter of the Chaldeans,
No longer shall you be called
	sovereign mistress of kingdoms.
6 Angry at my people,
	I profaned my inheritance,
And I gave them into your hand;
	but you showed them no mercy,
And upon old men
	you laid a very heavy yoke.
7 You said, "I shall remain always,
	a sovereign mistress forever!"
But you did not lay these things to heart,
	you disregarded their outcome.d
8 Now hear this, voluptuous one,
	enthroned securely,
Saying to yourself,
	"I, and no one else!
I shall never be a widow,
	or suffer the loss of my children"—e
9 Both these things shall come to you
	suddenly, in a single day:
Complete bereavement and widowhood
	shall come upon you
For your many sorceries
	and the great number of your spells;*
10 Because you felt secure in your
		wickedness,
	and said, "No one sees me."
Your wisdom and your knowledge

46, 11: From the east a bird of prey: Cyrus; cf Is 41, 2-4.

47, 1-15: A taunt-song, mocking Babylon, once queen of the nations, now made a slave girl.

47, 9. 13. 15: Babylon was known for its sorcery and astrology.

d: Is 14, 13f.   e: Zep 2, 15; Rv 18, 7.

led you astray,
And you said to yourself,
"I, and no one else!"

[11] But upon you shall come evil
you will not know how to predict;
Disaster shall befall you
which you cannot allay.
Suddenly there shall come upon you
ruin which you will not expect.

[12] Keep up, now, your spells
and your many sorceries;
Perhaps you can make them avail,
perhaps you can strike terror!

[13] You wearied yourself with many
consultations,
at which you toiled from your youth;
Let the astrologers stand forth to save
you,
the stargazers who forecast at each
new moon
what would happen to you.

[14] Lo, they are like stubble,
fire consumes them;
They cannot save themselves
from the spreading flames.
This is no warming ember,
no fire to sit before.

[15] Thus do your wizards serve you
with whom you have toiled from your
youth;
Each wanders his own way,
with none to save you.

CHAPTER 48

Exhortations to the Exiles

See RG 280–95

[1] Hear this, O house of Jacob
called by the name Israel,
sprung from the stock of Judah,
You who swear by the name of the LORD
and invoke the God of Israel
without sincerity or justice,

[2] Though you are named after the holy city
and rely on the God of Israel,
whose name is the LORD of hosts.

[3] Things of the past I foretold long ago,
they went forth from my mouth, I let
you hear of them;
then suddenly I took action and they
came to be.

[4] Because I know that you are stubborn
and that your neck is an iron sinew
and your forehead bronze,

[5] I foretold them to you of old;
before they took place I let you hear of
them,
That you might not say, "My idol did
them,
my statue, my molten image
commanded them."

[6] Now that you have heard, look at all
this;
must you not admit it?[f]

From now on I announce new things to
you,
hidden events of which you knew not.

[7] Now, not long ago, they are brought into
being,
and beforetime you did not hear of
them,
so that you cannot claim to have
known them;

[8] You neither heard nor knew,
they did not reach your ears
beforehand.
Yes, I know you are utterly treacherous,
a rebel you were called from birth.[g]

[9] For the sake of my name I restrain my
anger,
for the sake of my renown I hold it
back from you,
lest I should destroy you.

[10] See, I have refined you like silver,
tested you in the furnace of affliction.[h]

[11] For my sake, for my own sake, I do
this;
why should I suffer profanation?
My glory I will not give to another.

[12] Listen to me, Jacob,
Israel, whom I named!
I, it is I who am the first,
and also the last am I.[i]

[13] Yes, my hand laid the foundations of the
earth;
my right hand spread out the heavens.
When I call them,
they stand forth at once.[j]

f: Is 42, 9.   *g:* Is 43, 22ff.   *h:* Is 1, 25; Jer 6, 29f; Zec 13, 9; Mal 3, 2.   *i:* Is 41, 4; 44, 6; 48, 12; Rv 1, 8. 17.   *j:* Is 40, 22. 26; 45, 12. 18.

14 All of you assemble and listen:
    Who among you foretold these things?
    The LORD's friend* shall do his will
        against Babylon and the progeny of
            Chaldea.
15 I myself have spoken, I have called him,
    I have brought him, and his way
        succeeds!
16 Come near to me and hear this!
    Not from the beginning did I speak it
        in secret;
    At the time it comes to pass, I am
        present:
    "Now the Lord* GOD has sent me, and
        his spirit."
17 Thus says the LORD, your redeemer,
    the Holy One of Israel:
    I, the LORD, your God,
        teach you what is for your good,
        and lead you on the way you should go.
18 If you would hearken to my
        commandments,
    your prosperity would be like a river,
        and your vindication like the waves of
            the sea;
19 Your descendants would be like the sand,
    and those born of your stock like its
        grains,
    Their name never cut off
        or blotted out from my presence.
20 Go forth from Babylon, flee from
        Chaldea!
    With shouts of joy proclaim this, make
        it known;
    Publish it to the ends of the earth, and say,
    "The LORD has redeemed his servant
        Jacob.
21 They did not thirst
    when he led them through dry lands;
    Water from the rock he set flowing for
        them;
    he cleft the rock, and waters welled
        forth."k

22 [There is no peace for the wicked,
    says the LORD.]

II: Expiation of Sin, Spiritual Liberation of Israel

CHAPTER 49

The Servant of the Lord*

See RG
280-95

1 Hear me, O coastlands,
    listen, O distant peoples.l
    The LORD called me from birth,
        from my mother's womb he gave me
            my name.*
2 He made of me a sharp-edged sword
    and concealed me in the shadow of his
        arm.
    He made me a polished arrow,
        in his quiver he hid me.*
3 You are my servant, he said to me,
    Israel,* through whom I show my
        glory.

4 Though I thought I had toiled in vain,
    and for nothing, uselessly, spent my
        strength,
    Yet my reward is with the LORD,
        my recompense is with my God.m
5 For now the LORD has spoken
    who formed me as his servant from the
        womb,
    That Jacob may be brought back to him
        and Israel gathered to him;
    And I am made glorious in the sight of
        the LORD,
        and my God is now my strength!
6 It is too little, he says, for you to be my
        servant,
    to raise up the tribes of Jacob,
        and restore the survivors of Israel;n
    I will make you a light to the nations,
        that my salvation may reach to the
            ends of the earth.*

48, 14: The Lord's friend: Cyrus, who carries out God's plans.
48, 16: "Now the Lord . . . spirit": said by Cyrus; cf v 14.
49, 1-7: The second of the four "Servant-of-the-Lord" oracles.
49, 1: Gave me my name: designated me for a special office (cf Jer 1, 5), or perhaps, made me renowned (cf Ps 45, 18).
49, 2: The servant was made ready and fit for the preaching of God's word.

49, 3: Israel: the Servant is identified with the people of Israel as their ideal representative; however, since vv 5f seem to distinguish the Servant from Israel, some regard the word Israel here as a gloss.
49, 6: The Servant's vocation will be not only the restoration of Israel but the conversion of the world; cf Lk 2, 32.

k: Ex 17, 6; Nm 20, 11. l: Is 41, 9; 43, 1; 44, 2. 24; 46, 3. m: Is 40, 27. n: Is 42, 1-6; 44, 5; 45, 14; Lk 2, 32; Acts 13, 46f.

⁷ Thus says the LORD,
    the redeemer and the Holy One of
        Israel,
To the one despised, whom the nations
        abhor,
    the slave of rulers:
When kings see you, they shall stand up,
    and princes shall prostrate themselves
Because of the LORD who is faithful,
    the Holy One of Israel who has chosen
        you.^o

The Liberation and Restoration of Zion

⁸   Thus says the LORD:
In a time of favor I answer you,
    on the day of salvation I help you,
To restore the land
    and allot the desolate heritages,^p
⁹ Saying to the prisoners: Come out!
To those in darkness: Show yourselves!
Along the ways they shall find pasture,
    on every bare height shall their
        pastures be.^q
¹⁰ They shall not hunger or thirst,
    nor shall the scorching wind or the sun
        strike them;
For he who pities them leads them
    and guides them beside springs of
        water.^r
¹¹ I will cut a road through all my
        mountains,
    and make my highways level.^s
¹² See, some shall come from afar,
    others from the north and the west,
    and some from the land of Syene.[*]

¹³ Sing out, O heavens, and rejoice,
    O earth,
    break forth into song, you mountains.
For the LORD comforts his people
    and shows mercy to his afflicted.

¹⁴ But Zion said, "The LORD has forsaken
        me;
    my Lord has forgotten me."^t
¹⁵ Can a mother forget her infant,

    be without tenderness for the child of
        her womb?
Even should she forget,
    I will never forget you.^u
¹⁶ See, upon the palms of my hands I have
        written your name;[*]
    your walls are ever before me.
¹⁷ Your rebuilders make haste,
    as those who tore you down and laid
        you waste
    go forth from you;
¹⁸ Look about and see,
    they are all gathering and coming to
        you.
As I live, says the LORD,
    you shall be arrayed with them all as
        with adornments,
    like a bride you shall fasten them on
        you.

¹⁹ Though you were waste and desolate,
    a land of ruins,
Now you shall be too small for your
        inhabitants,
    while those who swallowed you up
        will be far away.
²⁰ The children whom you had lost
    shall yet say to you,
"This place is too small for me,
    make room for me to live in."
²¹ You shall ask yourself:
    "Who has borne me these?
I was bereft and barren
    [exiled and repudiated];
    who has reared them?
I was left all alone;
    where then do these come from?"^v

²²   Thus says the Lord GOD:
See, I will lift up my hand to the nations,
    and raise my signal to the peoples;
They shall bring your sons in their arms,
    and your daughters shall be carried on
        their shoulders.^w
²³ Kings shall be your foster fathers,
    their princesses your nurses;

49, 12: Syene: now called Aswan, at the first cataract of the Nile in southern Egypt.
49, 16: Upon the palms . . . name: for continual remembrance; cf Ex 13, 9. 16; Dt 6, 6-9.

o: Is 49, 23; 55, 5.   *p:* 2 Cor 6, 2.   *q:* Is 42, 7. 18ff.   *r:* Is 51, 14; Rv 7, 16.   *s:* Is 40, 3f.   *t:* Is 40, 27.   *u:* Is 43, 4; 44, 21; 46, 3f.
v: Is 54, 1ff.   *w:* Is 5, 26; 13, 2.

Bowing to the ground, they shall worship
you
and lick the dust at your feet.
Then you shall know that I am the LORD,
and those who hope in me shall never
be disappointed.

24   Thus says the LORD:
Can booty be taken from a warrior?
or captives be rescued from a tyrant?
25 Yes, captives can be taken from a
warrior,
and booty be rescued from a tyrant;
Those who oppose you I will oppose,
and your sons I will save.
26 I will make your oppressors eat their own
flesh,
and they shall be drunk with their own
blood
as with the juice of the grape.
All mankind shall know
that I, the LORD, am your savior,
your redeemer, the mighty one of
Jacob.x

See RG
280-95

CHAPTER 50

Salvation Only through the Lord's Servant

1   Thus says the LORD:
Where is the bill of divorce
with which I dismissed your mother?*
Or to which of my creditors
have I sold you?
It was for your sins that you were sold,
for your crimes that your mother was
dismissed.y

2 Why was no one there when I came?
Why did no one answer when I called?*
Is my hand too short to ransom?
Have I not the strength to deliver?
Lo, with my rebuke I dry up the sea,

I turn rivers into a desert;
Their fish rot for lack of water,
and die of thirst.z
3 I clothe the heavens in mourning,
and make sackcloth their vesture.

4 The Lord GOD has given me*
a well-trained tongue,
That I might know how to speak to the
weary
a word that will rouse them.
Morning after morning
he opens my ear that I may hear;
5 And I have not rebelled,
have not turned back.*
6 I gave my back to those who beat me,
my cheeks to those who plucked my
beard;*
My face I did not shield
from buffets and spitting.a

7 The Lord GOD is my help,
therefore I am not disgraced;
I have set my face like flint,
knowing that I shall not be put to
shame.b
8 He is near who upholds my right;
if anyone wishes to oppose me,
let us appear together.
Who disputes my right?
Let him confront me.
9 See, the Lord GOD is my help;
who will prove me wrong?
Lo, they will all wear out like cloth,
the moth will eat them up.c

10 Who among you fears the LORD,*
heeds his servant's voice,
And walks in darkness
without any light,
Trusting in the name of the LORD
and relying on his God?d

50, 1: Responding to the people's complaint of utter abandonment by God, the prophet shows that their sins were responsible for their banishment. Since there was no bill of divorce, the bond between the Lord and his people still exists and he will ultimately save them.

50, 2: Israel's faith in God is weak; she does not answer his call, nor believe in his promises of deliverance.

50, 4-11: The third of the four "Servant-of-the-Lord" oracles; in vv 4-9 the Servant speaks; in vv 10f God reproves the people for not following the Servant.

50, 5: The Servant does not refuse the divine vocation.

50, 6: He willingly submits to insults and beatings. Plucked my beard: a grave insult.

50, 10f: Instead of trusting in the Lord and his Servant, the people rely on their own devices, to their own destruction.

x: Is 19, 2; Ez 38, 21; Zec 14, 13.   y: Dt 24, 1-4; Mt 19, 3; Mk 10, 2ff; Is 54, 6ff.   z: Ex 7, 18; Ps 105, 29.   a: 2 Sm 10, 4ff; Mt 26, 67; 27, 30.   b: Ez 3, 9.   c: Is 51, 6-8; Ps 102, 27.   d: Is 43, 1f; 44, 1f.

[11] All of you kindle flames
and carry about you fiery darts;
Walk by the light of your own fire
and by the flares you have burnt!
This is your fate from my hand:
you shall lie down in a place of pain.

See RG
280-95

CHAPTER 51

Exhortation To Trust
in the Lord

[1] Listen to me, you who pursue justice,
who seek the LORD;
Look to the rock from which you were
hewn,
to the pit* from which you were
quarried;*e*
[2] Look to Abraham, your father,
and to Sarah, who gave you birth;
When he was but one I called him,
I blessed him and made him many.*f*
[3] Yes, the LORD shall comfort Zion
and have pity on all her ruins;
Her deserts he shall make like Eden,
her wasteland like the garden of the
LORD;
Joy and gladness shall be found in her,
thanksgiving and the sound of song.

[4] Be attentive to me, my people;*
my folk, give ear to me.
For law shall go forth from my presence,
and my judgment, as the light of the
peoples.*g*
[5] I will make my justice come speedily;
my salvation shall go forth
[and my arm shall judge the nations];
In me shall the coastlands hope,
and my arm they shall await.

[6] Raise your eyes to the heavens,
and look at the earth below;
Though the heavens grow thin like smoke,
the earth wears out like a garment
and its inhabitants die like flies,
My salvation shall remain forever

and my justice shall never be
dismayed.*
[7] Hear me, you who know justice,
you people who have my teaching at
heart:
Fear not the reproach of men,
be not dismayed at their revilings.
[8] They shall be like a garment eaten by
moths,
like wool consumed by grubs;
But my justice shall remain forever
and my salvation, for all generations.*h*

[9] Awake, awake, put on strength,
O arm of the LORD!
Awake as in the days of old,
in ages long ago!
Was it not you who crushed Rahab,*
you who pierced the dragon?*i*
[10] Was it not you who dried up the sea,
the waters of the great deep,*
Who made the depths of the sea into a way
for the redeemed to pass over?
[11] Those whom the LORD has ransomed will
return
and enter Zion singing,
crowned with everlasting joy;
They will meet with joy and gladness,
sorrow and mourning will flee.
[12] I, it is I who comfort you.
Can you then fear mortal man,
who is human only, to be looked upon
as grass,
[13] And forget the LORD, your maker,
who stretched out the heavens
and laid the foundations of the earth?
All the day you are in constant dread
of the fury of the oppressor;
But when he sets himself to destroy,
what is there of the oppressor's fury?

[14] The oppressed shall soon be released;
they shall not die and go down into the
pit,
nor shall they want for bread.

51, 1: Rock . . . pit: your glorious ancestry.
51, 4f: The conversion of the Gentiles.
51, 6: God's salvation and justice are eternal, in contrast to
the impermanence of the heavens and the earth: cf Mt 24, 35.
51, 9: Rahab: see note on Is 30, 7. The dragon: see notes
on Is 27, 1; Ps 74, 13.

51, 10: Great deep: another reference to the primeval
chaos of Gn 1, 2.

e: Rom 9, 30f. *f:* Ez 33, 24; Gn 12, 2ff; 22, 17. *g:* Is 2, 3. *h:* Is
50, 9. *i:* Ex 15, 16; Jb 9, 13; 26, 12; Pss 74, 13; 89, 11.

¹⁵ For I am the LORD, your God,
    who stirs up the sea so that its waves
        roar;
    the LORD of hosts by name.ʲ
¹⁶ I have put my words into your mouth
    and shielded you in the shadow of my
        hand,
  I, who stretched out the heavens,
    who laid the foundations of the earth,
    who say to Zion: You are my people.

The Cup of the Lord

¹⁷ Awake, awake!
    Arise, O Jerusalem,
  You who drank at the LORD's hand
    the cup of his wrath;
  Who drained to the dregs
    the bowl of staggering!ᵏ
¹⁸ She has no one to guide her
    of all the sons she bore;
  She has no one to grasp her by the hand,
    of all the sons she reared!—
¹⁹ Your misfortunes are double;
    who is there to condole with you?
  Desolation and destruction, famine and
        sword!
  Who is there to comfort you?
²⁰ Your sons lie helpless
    at every street corner
    like antelopes in a net.
  They are filled with the wrath of the
    LORD,
    the rebuke of your God.

²¹ But now, hear this, O afflicted one,
    drunk, but not with wine,ˡ
²² Thus says the LORD, your Master,
    your God, who defends his people:
  See, I am taking from your hand
    the cup of staggering;
  The bowl of my wrath
    you shall no longer drink.
²³ I will put it into the hands of your
        tormentors,
    those who ordered you
    to bow down, that they might walk
        over you,

While you offered your back like the
        ground,
    like the street for them to walk on.

CHAPTER 52

Let Zion Rejoice

See RG
280–95

¹ Awake, awake!
    Put on your strength, O Zion;
  Put on your glorious garments,
    O Jerusalem, holy city.
  No longer shall the uncircumcised
    or the unclean enter you.
² Shake off the dust,
    ascend to the throne, Jerusalem;
  Loose the bonds from your neck,
    O captive daughter Zion!
³   For thus says the LORD:
  You were sold for nothing,
    and without money you shall be
        redeemed.
⁴   Thus says the Lord GOD:
  To Egypt in the beginning my people
        went down,
    to sojourn there;
  Assyria, too, oppressed them for
        nought.
⁵ But now, what am I to do here?
    says the LORD.
  My people have been taken away without
        redress;
    their rulers make a boast of it, says the
        LORD;
    all the day my name is constantly
        reviled.
⁶ Therefore on that day my people shall
        know my renown,
    that it is I who have foretold it. Here I
        am!
⁷ How beautiful upon the mountains*
    are the feet of him who brings glad
        tidings,
  Announcing peace, bearing good news,
    announcing salvation, and saying to
        Zion,
    "Your God is King!"ᵐ
⁸ Hark! Your watchmen raise a cry,
    together they shout for joy,

52, 7-10: God leads his people back from Babylon to Zion, from whose ruined walls watchmen … shout for joy; cf Rom
10, 15.

ʲ: Jer 31, 35. ᵏ: Jer 25, 15ff; Ez 23, 32ff. ˡ: Is 29, 9. ᵐ: Is 40, 9; Rom 10, 15.

For they see directly, before their eyes,
the LORD restoring Zion.[n]

[9] Break out together in song,
O ruins of Jerusalem!
For the LORD comforts his people,
he redeems Jerusalem.

[10] The LORD has bared his holy arm
in the sight of all the nations;
All the ends of the earth will behold
the salvation of our God.

[11] Depart, depart, come forth from there,
touch nothing unclean!
Out from there!* Purify yourselves,
you who carry the vessels of the LORD.

[12] Yet not in fearful haste will you come
out,
nor leave in headlong flight,
For the LORD comes before you,
and your rear guard is the God of Israel.[o]

Suffering and Triumph of the Servant of the Lord*

[13] See, my servant shall prosper,
he shall be raised high and greatly
exalted.

[14] Even as many were amazed at him—
so marred was his look beyond that of
man,
and his appearance beyond that of
mortals—[p]

[15] So shall he startle many nations,
because of him kings shall stand
speechless;
For those who have not been told shall see,
those who have not heard shall ponder
it.[q]

CHAPTER 53

See RG 280-95

[1] Who would believe what we have
heard?
To whom has the arm of the LORD
been revealed?[r]

[2] He grew up like a sapling before him,[s]
like a shoot from the parched earth;
There was in him no stately bearing to
make us look at him,
nor appearance that would attract us to
him.*

[3] He was spurned* and avoided by men,
a man of suffering, accustomed to
infirmity,
One of those from whom men hide their
faces,
spurned, and we held him in no
esteem.[t]

[4] Yet it was our infirmities that he bore,*
our sufferings that he endured,
While we thought of him as stricken,
as one smitten by God and afflicted.[u]

[5] But he was pierced for our offenses,
crushed for our sins,
Upon him was the chastisement that
makes us whole,
by his stripes we were healed.[v]

[6] We had all gone astray like sheep,
each following his own way;
But the LORD laid upon him
the guilt of us all.[w]

[7] Though he was harshly treated, he
submitted
and opened not his mouth;
Like a lamb led to the slaughter
or a sheep before the shearers,
he was silent and opened not his
mouth.[x]

[8] Oppressed and condemned, he was taken
away,
and who would have thought any more
of his destiny?
When he was cut off from the land of the
living,
and smitten for the sin of his people,

[9] A grave was assigned him among the
wicked

52, 11: From there: from Babylon. Vessels of the Lord: taken to Babylon by Nebuchadnezzar, now carried back by the exiled priests returning in procession to Zion; cf Ezr 1, 7.

52, 13—53, 12: The last of the four "Servant-of-the-Lord" oracles. An extraordinary description of the sinless Servant, who by his voluntary suffering atones for the sins of his people, and saves them from just punishment at the hands of God. Only in Jesus Christ is the prophecy perfectly fulfilled.

53, 2: Only God appreciated his Servant's true greatness.

53, 3: Because he suffered, he was regarded as a sinner and therefore as one to be spurned.

53, 4ff: He did indeed suffer but it was for the sins of mankind, and through his sufferings men are healed.

n: 1 Is 62, 6. o: Ex 12, 11. p: Ps 69, 8. q: Mi 7, 16. r: Is 52, 10; Jn 12, 38; Rom 10, 16. s: Is 11, 1. t: Jb 19, 18; Ps 31, 11ff; Mk 9, 11. u: Jer 10, 19; Mt 8, 17. v: 1 Cor 15, 3; 1 Pt 2, 24. w: Lv 16, 21ff. x: Mt 26, 63; Acts 8, 32.

and a burial place with evildoers,
Though he had done no wrong
nor spoken any falsehood.*y*
10 [But the LORD was pleased*
to crush him in infirmity.]

If he gives his life as an offering for sin,
he shall see his descendants in a long
life,
and the will of the LORD shall be
accomplished through him.
11 Because of his affliction
he shall see the light in fullness of
days;
Through his suffering, my servant shall
justify many,
and their guilt he shall bear.
12 Therefore I will give him his portion
among the great,
and he shall divide the spoils with the
mighty,
Because he surrendered himself to death
and was counted among the wicked;
And he shall take away the sins of many,
and win pardon for their offenses.*z*

CHAPTER 54

See RG
280-95

The New Zion

1 Raise a glad cry, you barren one* who did
not bear,
break forth in jubilant song, you who
were not in labor,
For more numerous are the children of
the deserted wife
than the children of her who has a
husband,
says the LORD.*a*
2 Enlarge the space for your tent,
spread out your tent cloths
unsparingly;
lengthen your ropes and make firm
your stakes.*b*
3 For you shall spread abroad to the right
and to the left;

your descendants shall dispossess the
nations
and shall people the desolate cities.
4 Fear not, you shall not be put to shame;
you need not blush, for you shall not
be disgraced.
The shame of your youth you shall
forget,
the reproach of your widowhood no
longer remember.
5 For he who has become your husband is
your Maker;
his name is the LORD of hosts;
Your redeemer* is the Holy One of Israel,
called God of all the earth.
6 The LORD calls you back,
like a wife forsaken and grieved in
spirit,
A wife married in youth and then cast
off,
says your God.*c*
7 For a brief moment I abandoned you,
but with great tenderness I will take
you back.
8 In an outburst of wrath, for a moment
I hid my face from you;
But with enduring love I take pity on you,
says the LORD, your redeemer.

9 This is for me like the days of Noah,
when I swore that the waters of Noah
should never again deluge the earth;
So I have sworn not to be angry with
you,
or to rebuke you.*d*
10 Though the mountains leave their place
and the hills be shaken,
My love shall never leave you
nor my covenant of peace be shaken,
says the LORD, who has mercy on you.*e*

11 O afflicted one, storm-battered and
unconsoled,*
I lay your pavements in carnelians,

53, 10ff: Because he fulfilled the divine will by suffering
for the sins of others, the Servant will be rewarded by the
Lord. See the light: enjoy happiness. This line may originally
have read, "he shall drink and eat to the full"—at the thanksgiving sacrifice at which he shall divide the spoils (v 12).

54, 1: Jerusalem, pictured as a wife who had been barren
and deserted, now suddenly finds herself with innumerable
children (the returning exiles); cf Gal 4, 27 for the application

of this text to the church, the New Zion.

54, 5: Redeemer: cf note on Is 41, 14.

54, 11f: Cf Rv 21. Afflicted one: Jerusalem; camelians:
reddish quartz, hard and durable; carbuncles: another precious stone of red color.

y: 1 Pt 2, 22f; 1 Jn 3, 5.   *z:* Mk 15, 28; Lk 22, 37.   *a:* Gal 4, 27.
b: Is 49, 20.   *c:* Mal 2, 14f.   *d:* Gn 9, 15.   *e:* Pss 76, 5; 46, 3.

and your foundations in sapphires;*f*

12 I will make your battlements of rubies,
   your gates of carbuncles,
   and all your walls of precious stones.
13 All your sons shall be taught by the
   LORD,
   and great shall be the peace of your
   children.
14 In justice shall you be established,
   far from the fear of oppression,
   where destruction cannot come near
   you.
15 Should there be any attack, it shall not be
   of my making;
   whoever attacks you shall fall before
   you.
16 Lo, I have created the craftsman
   who blows on the burning coals
   and forges weapons as his work;
   It is I also who have created
   the destroyer to work havoc.
17 No weapon fashioned against you shall
   prevail;
   every tongue you shall prove false
   that launches an accusation against
   you.
   This is the lot of the servants of the LORD,
   their vindication from me, says the
   LORD.

See RG
280-95

CHAPTER 55

An Invitation to Grace

1 All you who are thirsty,*
   come to the water!
   You who have no money,
   come, receive grain and eat;
   Come, without paying and without cost,
   drink wine and milk!*g*
2 Why spend your money for what is not
   bread;
   your wages for what fails to satisfy?
   Heed me, and you shall eat well,
   you shall delight in rich fare.
3 Come to me heedfully,
   listen, that you may have life.
   I will renew with you the everlasting
   covenant,

the benefits assured to David.*h*

4 As I made him a witness to the peoples,
   a leader and commander of nations,
5 So shall you summon a nation you knew
   not,
   and nations that knew you not shall
   run to you,
   Because of the LORD, your God,
   the Holy One of Israel, who has
   glorified you.*i*

6 Seek the LORD while he may be found,
   call him while he is near.
7 Let the scoundrel forsake his way,
   and the wicked man his thoughts;
   Let him turn to the LORD for mercy;
   to our God, who is generous in
   forgiving.
8 For my thoughts are not your thoughts,
   nor are your ways my ways, says the
   LORD.
9 As high as the heavens are above the
   earth,
   so high are my ways above your ways
   and my thoughts above your
   thoughts.
10 For just as from the heavens
   the rain and snow come down
   And do not return there
   till they have watered the earth,
   making it fertile and fruitful,
   Giving seed to him who sows
   and bread to him who eats,
11 So shall my word be
   that goes forth from my mouth;
   It shall not return to me void,
   but shall do my will,
   achieving the end for which I sent it.

12 Yes, in joy you shall depart,
   in peace you shall be brought back;
   Mountains and hills shall break out in
   song before you,
   and all the trees of the countryside
   shall clap their hands.
13 In place of the thornbush, the cypress
   shall grow,

55, 1ff: God's salvation is freely extended to his people and to all nations; through him will the benefits assured to David
be renewed; cf Is 12, 3; Jn 7, 37.

f: Rv 21, 18-21.   *g*: Jn 4, 10ff; 6, 35; 7, 37ff; Rv 21, 6; 22, 17.   *h*: 2 Sm 7, 12-16.   *i*: Acts 13, 34.

instead of nettles,* the myrtle.
This shall be to the LORD's renown,
an everlasting imperishable sign.

III: Return of the First Captives

CHAPTER 56

See RG
280-95

The Lord's House Open to All*

1 Thus says the LORD:
Observe what is right, do what is just;
for my salvation is about to come,
my justice, about to be revealed.
2 Happy is the man who does this,
the son of man who holds to it;
Who keeps the sabbath free from
profanation,
and his hand from any evildoing.
3 Let not the foreigner say,
when he would join himself to the LORD,
"The LORD will surely exclude me
from his people";
Nor let the eunuch say,
"See, I am a dry tree."*
4 For thus says the LORD:
To the eunuchs who observe my sabbaths
and choose what pleases me
and hold fast to my covenant,ʲ
5 I will give, in my house
and within my walls, a monument and
a name*
Better than sons and daughters;
an eternal, imperishable name will I
give them.

6 And the foreigners who join themselves
to the LORD,
ministering to him,
Loving the name of the LORD,
and becoming his servants—
All who keep the sabbath free from
profanation

and hold to my covenant,
7 Them I will bring to my holy mountain
and make joyful in my house of
prayer;
Their holocausts and sacrifices
will be acceptable on my altar,
For my house shall be called
a house of prayer for all peoples.ᵏ
8 Thus says the Lord GOD,
who gathers the dispersed of Israel:
Others will I gather to him
besides those already gathered.

Blind Leaders

9 *All you wild beasts* of the field,
come and eat,
all you beasts in the forest!ˡ
10 My watchmen are blind,
all of them unaware;
They are all dumb dogs,
they cannot bark;
Dreaming as they lie there,
loving their sleep.
11 They are relentless dogs,
they know not when they have enough.
These are the shepherds
who know no discretion;
Each of them goes his own way,
every one of them to his own gain:
12 "Come, I will fetch some wine;
let us carouse with strong drink,
And tomorrow will be like today,
or even greater."ᵐ

CHAPTER 57

See RG
280-95

1 The just man perishes,
but no one takes it to heart;
Devout men are swept away,
with no one giving it a thought.
Though he is taken away from the
presence of evil,

55, 13: Thornbush . . . nettles: suggestive of the desert and therefore symbolic of suffering and hardship; cypress, myrtle: suggestive of fertile land and therefore symbolic of joy and strength.

56, 1-8: Participation in the future messianic salvation is offered to all who believe in the Lord and keep his commandments, regardless of origin or social condition.

56, 3: Eunuchs had originally been excluded from the community of the Lord; cf Dt 23, 2; Wis 3, 14. Dry tree: unable to produce the fruit of offspring.

56, 5: A monument and a name: a memorial inscription to

prevent oblivion for one who had no children; cf 2 Sm 18, 18; Neh 7, 15; 13, 14.

56, 9—57, 13: This section is apparently preexilic, written in the manner of the older prophets who condemned the pagan rites of Baal worship.

56, 9: Wild beasts: foreign nations, which are invited to come and ravage Israel.

---

j: Wis 3, 14f.   k: 1 Kgs 8, 29f; Mt 21, 13.   l: Ez 34, 5.   m: Is 28, 7ff; Wis 2, 7.

the just man [2]enters into peace;
There is rest on his couch
for the sincere, straightforward man.

Faithless People

[3] But you, draw near,
you sons of a sorceress,
adulterous, wanton race!
[4] Of whom do you make sport,
at whom do you open wide your
mouth,
and put out your tongue?
Are you not rebellious children,
a worthless race;
[5] You who are in heat among the
terebinths,
under every green tree;
You who immolate children in the
wadies,
behind the crevices in the cliffs?[n]

[6] Among the smooth stones* of the wadi is
your portion,
these are your lot;
To these you poured out libations,
and brought offerings.
Should I decide not to punish these
things?
[7] Upon a high and lofty mountain
you made your bed,
and there you went up to offer
sacrifice.[o]
[8] Behind the door and the doorpost
you placed your indecent symbol.
Deserting me, you spread out
your high, wide bed;
And of those whose embraces you love
you carved the symbol and gazed
upon it
[9] While you approached the king* with
scented oil,
and multiplied your perfumes;
While you sent your ambassadors far
away,

down even to the nether world.
[10] Though worn out by your many
misdeeds,
you never said, "It is hopeless";
New strength you found,
and so you did not weaken.

[11] Of whom were you afraid? Whom did
you fear,
that you became false
And did not remember me
or give me any thought?
Was I to remain silent and unseeing,
so that you would not have me to
fear?
[12] I will expose your justice*
and your works;
[13] They shall not help you when you cry
out,
nor save you in your distress.
All these* the wind shall carry off,
the breeze shall bear away;
But he who takes refuge in me shall
inherit the land,
and possess my holy mountain.

Comfort for the Afflicted

[14] Build up, build up, prepare the way,
remove the stumbling blocks from my
people's path.[p]
[15] For thus says he who is high and exalted,
living eternally, whose name is the
Holy One:
On high I dwell, and in holiness,
and with the crushed and dejected in
spirit,
To revive the spirits of the dejected,
to revive the hearts of the crushed.[q]
[16] I will not accuse forever,
nor always be angry;
For their spirits would faint before me,
the souls that I have made.
[17] Because of their wicked avarice I was
angry,

57, 6: Smooth stones: the Hebrew word for this expression has the same consonants as the word for "portion"; instead of making the Lord their portion (cf Ps 16, 5), the people adored slabs of stone which they took from the streambeds in valleys and set up as idols; cf Jer 3, 9. Therefore, it is implied, they will be swept away as by a sudden torrent of waters carrying them down the rocky-bottomed gorge to destruction and death without burial.

57, 9: The king: the pagan god Moloch. Ambassadors: children sent to him through a sacrificial death.
57, 12: Justice: here used ironically.
57, 13: All these: the wicked mentioned in Is 57, 3-10.

n: Jer 7, 31; 19, 5; Ez 20, 28. 31. o: Hos 4, 13; Jer 2, 20; Ez 6, 13. p: Is 40, 3f. q: Is 61, 2f.

and struck them, hiding myself in
 wrath,
 as they went their own rebellious way.*r*
[18] I saw their ways,
 but I will heal them and lead them;
 I will give full comfort
 to them and to those who mourn for
 them,
[19] I, the Creator, who gave them life.

Peace, peace to the far and the near,
 says the LORD; and I will heal them.
[20] But the wicked are like the tossing sea
 which cannot be calmed,
 And its waters cast up mud and filth.
[21] No peace for the wicked! says my
 God.*s*

See RG
280-95

CHAPTER 58

True Fasting

[1] Cry out full-throated and unsparingly,
 lift up your voice like a trumpet blast;
 Tell my people their wickedness,
 and the house of Jacob their sins.*
[2] They seek me day after day,*
 and desire to know my ways,
 Like a nation that has done what is just
 and not abandoned the law of their
 God;
 They ask me to declare what is due them,
 pleased to gain access to God.
[3] "Why do we fast, and you do not see it?
 afflict ourselves, and you take no note
 of it?"

Lo, on your fast day you carry out your
 own pursuits,
 and drive all your laborers.
[4] Yes, your fast ends in quarreling and
 fighting,
 striking with wicked claw.
 Would that today you might fast
 so as to make your voice heard on
 high!
[5] Is this the manner of fasting I wish,
 of keeping a day of penance:
 That a man bow his head like a reed,

and lie in sackcloth and ashes?
 Do you call this a fast,
 a day acceptable to the LORD?*t*
[6] This, rather, is the fasting that I wish:
 releasing those bound unjustly,
 untying the thongs of the yoke;
 Setting free the oppressed,
 breaking every yoke;
[7] Sharing your bread with the hungry,
 sheltering the oppressed and the
 homeless;
 Clothing the naked when you see them,
 and not turning your back on your
 own.*u*
[8] Then your light shall break forth like the
 dawn,
 and your wound shall quickly be
 healed;
 Your vindication shall go before you,
 and the glory of the LORD shall be
 your rear guard.
[9] Then you shall call, and the LORD will
 answer,
 you shall cry for help, and he will say:
 Here I am!
 If you remove from your midst
 oppression,
 false accusation and malicious speech;
[10] If you bestow your bread on the hungry
 and satisfy the afflicted;
 Then light shall rise for you in the
 darkness,
 and the gloom shall become for you
 like midday;
[11] Then the LORD will guide you always
 and give you plenty even on the
 parched land.
 He will renew your strength,
 and you shall be like a watered garden,
 like a spring whose water never fails.*v*
[12] The ancient ruins shall be rebuilt for your
 sake,
 and the foundations from ages past
 you shall raise up;
 "Repairer of the breach," they shall call
 you,
 "Restorer of ruined homesteads."*w*

58, 1: This command is directed to the prophet.
58, 2-14: Merely external worship does not avail with God; it must be joined to internal sincerity.

r: Is 56, 11.   *s:* Is 48, 21.   *t:* Zec 7, 5.   *u:* Ez 18, 7. 16; Mt 25, 35.   *v:* Is 51, 3; Ps 24.   *w:* Is 61, 4.

[13] If you hold back your foot on the sabbath
  from following your own pursuits on
    my holy day;
If you call the sabbath a delight,
  and the LORD's holy day honorable;
If you honor it by not following your
    ways,
  seeking your own interests, or
    speaking with malice—
[14] Then you shall delight in the LORD,
  and I will make you ride on the heights
    of the earth;
I will nourish you with the heritage of
    Jacob, your father,
  for the mouth of the LORD has spoken.

See RG
280-95

CHAPTER 59

Sin and Confession

[1] Lo, the hand of the LORD is not too short
    to save,
  nor his ear too dull to hear.[x]
[2] Rather, it is your crimes
  that separate you from your God,
It is your sins that make him hide his face
  so that he will not hear you.
[3] For your hands are stained with blood,
  your fingers with guilt;
Your lips speak falsehood,
  and your tongue utters deceit.[y]
[4] No one brings suit justly,
  no one pleads truthfully;
They trust in emptiness* and tell lies;
  they conceive mischief and bring forth
    malice.
[5] They hatch adders' eggs,*
  and weave spiders' webs:
Whoever eats their eggs will die,
  if one of them is pressed, it will hatch
    as a viper;[z]
[6] Their webs cannot serve as clothing,
  nor can they cover themselves with
    their works.
Their works are evil works,
  and deeds of violence come from their
    hands.

[7] Their feet run to evil,
  and they are quick to shed innocent
    blood;
Their thoughts are destructive thoughts,
  plunder and ruin are on their
    highways.[a]
[8] The way of peace they know not,
  and there is nothing that is right in
    their paths;
Their ways they have made crooked,
  whoever treads them knows no peace.
[9] That is why right is far from us*
  and justice does not reach us.
We look for light, and lo, darkness;
  for brightness, but we walk in gloom!
[10] Like blind men we grope along the wall,
  like people without eyes we feel our
    way.
We stumble at midday as at dusk,
  in Stygian darkness, like the dead.
[11] We all growl like bears,
  like doves we moan without ceasing.
We look for right, but it is not there;
  for salvation, and it is far from us.[b]
[12] For our offenses before you are many,
  our sins bear witness against us.
Yes, our offenses are present to us,
  and our crimes we know:
[13] Transgressing, and denying the LORD,
  turning back from following our God,
Threatening outrage, and apostasy,
  uttering words of falsehood the heart
    has conceived.
[14] Right is repelled,
  and justice stands far off;
For truth stumbles in the public square,
  uprightness cannot enter.
[15] Honesty is lacking,
  and the man who turns from evil is
    despoiled.

The Redeemer in Zion

The LORD saw this, and was aggrieved
  that right did not exist.

59, 4: Emptiness: things having no value.

59, 5f: A proverb signifying evil works—adders' eggs—and useless devices—spiders' webs; the former do positive harm to oneself and others, the latter serve no useful purpose.

59, 9-15: Spoken by the people through the mouth of the prophet.

---

x: Is 50, 2; Nm 11, 23.   y: Is 1, 15.   z: Jb 20, 12-16.   a: Rom 3, 15.   b: Is 38, 14.

[16] He saw that there was no one,
  and was appalled that there was none
      to intervene;
So his own arm brought about the
    victory,
  and his justice lent him its support.
[17] He put on justice as his breastplate,
  salvation, as the helmet on his head;
He clothed himself with garments of
    vengeance,
  wrapped himself in a mantle of zeal.[c]
[18] He repays his enemies their deserts,
  and requites his foes with wrath.
[19] Those in the west shall fear the name of
    the LORD,
  and those in the east, his glory;
For it shall come like a pent-up river
  which the breath of the LORD drives
    on.
[20] He shall come to Zion a redeemer
  to those of Jacob who turn from sin,
    says the LORD.[d]
[21] This is the covenant with them
  which I myself have made, says the
    LORD:
My spirit which is upon you
  and my words that I have put into your
    mouth
Shall never leave your mouth,
  nor the mouths of your children
Nor the mouths of your children's
    children
  from now on and forever, says the
    LORD.

CHAPTER 60

See RG
280-95

Glory of the New Zion

[1] Rise up in splendor! Your light has
    come,[*]
  the glory of the Lord shines upon you.
[2] See, darkness covers the earth,
  and thick clouds cover the peoples;
But upon you the LORD shines,
  and over you appears his glory.
[3] Nations shall walk by your light,
  and kings by your shining radiance.[e]

[4] Raise your eyes and look about;
  they all gather and come to you:
Your sons come from afar,
  and your daughters in the arms of their
    nurses.[f]

[5] Then you shall be radiant at what you
    see,
  your heart shall throb and overflow,
For the riches of the sea shall be emptied
    out before you,
  the wealth of nations shall be brought
    to you.
[6] Caravans of camels shall fill you,
  dromedaries from Midian and Ephah;
All from Sheba shall come
  bearing gold and frankincense,
  and proclaiming the praises of the
    LORD.
[7] All the flocks of Kedar shall be gathered
    for you,
  the rams of Nebaioth shall be your
    sacrifices;
They will be acceptable offerings on my
    altar,
  and I will enhance the splendor of my
    house.

[8] What are these that fly along like clouds,
  like doves[*] to their cotes?
[9] All the vessels of the sea are assembled,
  with the ships of Tarshish in the lead,
To bring your children from afar
  with their silver and gold,
In the name of the LORD, your God,
  the Holy One of Israel, who has
    glorified you.

[10] Foreigners shall rebuild your walls,
  and their kings shall be your
    attendants;
Though I struck you in my wrath,
  yet in my good will I have shown you
    mercy.
[11] Your gates shall stand open constantly;
  day and night they shall not be closed

60, 1-6: The Church makes use of these verses for the first reading of the Mass on the feast of Epiphany, for she sees in them symbols of her universality.

60, 8f: Like clouds, like doves: the white sails of the ships of Tarshish; cf note on Ps 48, 8.

c: Wis 5, 17ff; Eph 6, 14; 1 Thes 5, 8.   *d:* Rom 11, 26f.   *e:* Is 42. 6; 45, 14; 49, 6.   *f:* Is 49, 18.

But shall admit to you the wealth of
    nations,
    and their kings, in the vanguard.[g]
[12] For the people or kingdom shall perish
    that does not serve you;
    those nations shall be utterly
    destroyed.
[13] The glory of Lebanon* shall come to you:
    the cypress, the plane and the pine,
To bring beauty to my sanctuary,
    and glory to the place where I set my
    feet.[h]
[14] The children of your oppressors shall
    come,
    bowing low before you;
All those who despised you
    shall fall prostrate at your feet.
They shall call you "City of the LORD,"
    "Zion of the Holy One of Israel."

[15] Once you were forsaken,
    hated and unvisited,
Now I will make you the pride of the
    ages,
    a joy to generation after generation.[i]
[16] You shall suck the milk of nations,
    and be nursed at royal breasts;
You shall know that I, the LORD, am your
    savior,
    your redeemer, the mighty one of
    Jacob.
[17] In place of bronze I will bring gold,
    instead of iron, silver;
In place of wood, bronze,
    instead of stones, iron;
I will appoint peace your governor,
    and justice your ruler.
[18] No longer shall violence be heard of in
    your land,
    or plunder and ruin within your
    boundaries.
You shall call your walls "Salvation"
    and your gates "Praise."
[19] No longer shall the sun
    be your light by day,
Nor the brightness of the moon

shine upon you at night;
The LORD shall be your light forever,
    your God shall be your glory.[j]
[20] No longer shall your sun go down,
    or your moon withdraw,
For the LORD will be your light forever,
    and the days of your mourning shall be
    at an end.
[21] Your people shall all be just,
    they shall always possess the land,
They, the bud of my planting,
    my handiwork to show my glory.
[22] The smallest shall become a thousand,
    the youngest, a mighty nation;
I, the LORD, will swiftly accomplish
    these things
    when their time comes.[k]

CHAPTER 61

*See RG
280-95*

The Mission to the Afflicted

[1] The spirit of the Lord GOD is upon me,*
    because the LORD has anointed me;
He has sent me to bring glad tidings to
    the lowly,
    to heal the brokenhearted,
To proclaim liberty to the captives
    and release to the prisoners,[l]
[2] To announce a year of favor from the
    LORD
    and a day of vindication by our God,
    to comfort all who mourn;[m]
[3] To place on those who mourn in Zion
    a diadem instead of ashes,
To give them oil of gladness in place of
    mourning,
    a glorious mantle instead of a listless
    spirit.
They will be called oaks of justice,
    planted by the LORD to show his
    glory.

The Reward of Israel

[4] They shall rebuild the ancient ruins,
    the former wastes they shall raise up
And restore the ruined cities,
    desolate now for generations.[n]

60, 13: Glory of Lebanon: the cedars, together with the cypress, the plane and the pine, all precious, durable wood.
61, 1f: This was spoken by the prophet in regard to the restoration of Zion, but quoted by Christ as referring to his mission; cf Lk 4, 18f. Year of favor . . . day of vindication: the time of God's salvation.

---

g: Rv 21, 25.   *h:* Is 35, 2.   *i:* Ez 16.   *j:* Rv 21,23; 22, 5.   *k:* Gn 12, 2; 17, 6.   *l:* Is 42, 1; 48, 16; Lk 4, 18f.   *m:* Mt 5, 5.   *n:* Is 58, 12.

5 Strangers shall stand ready to pasture
your flocks,
foreigners shall be your farmers and
vinedressers.
6 You yourselves shall be named priests of
the LORD,
ministers of our God you shall be
called.
You shall eat the wealth of the
nations
and boast of riches from them.

7 Since their shame was double
and disgrace and spittle were their
portion,
They shall have a double inheritance in
their land,
everlasting joy shall be theirs.°
8 For I, the LORD, love what is right,
I hate robbery and injustice;
I will give them their recompense
faithfully,
a lasting covenant I will make with
them.ᵖ
9 Their descendants shall be renowned
among the nations,
and their offspring among the
peoples;
All who see them shall acknowledge
them
as a race the LORD has blessed.

10 I rejoice heartily in the LORD,
in my God is the joy of my soul;
For he has clothed me with a robe of
salvation,
and wrapped me in a mantle of justice,
Like a bridegroom adorned with a
diadem,
like a bride bedecked with her jewels.
11 As the earth brings forth its plants,
and a garden makes its growth spring
up,
So will the Lord GOD make justice and
praise
spring up before all the nations.

CHAPTER 62

See RG
280-95

Jerusalem the Lord's Bride

1 For Zion's sake I will not be silent,
for Jerusalem's sake I will not be
quiet,
Until her vindication shines forth like the
dawn
and her victory like a burning torch.

2 Nations shall behold your vindication,
and all kings your glory;
You shall be called by a new name*
pronounced by the mouth of the LORD.�q
3 You shall be a glorious crown in the hand
of the LORD,
a royal diadem held by your God.
4 No more shall men call you "Forsaken,"
or your land "Desolate,"
But you shall be called "My Delight,"
and your land "Espoused."
For the LORD delights in you,
and makes your land his spouse.ʳ
5 As a young man marries a virgin,
your Builder shall marry you;
And as a bridegroom rejoices in his bride
so shall your God rejoice in you.

Restoration of Zion

6 Upon your walls, O Jerusalem,
I have stationed watchmen;
Never, by day or by night,
shall they be silent.
O you who are to remind the LORD,*
take no rest
7 And give no rest to him,
until he re-establishes Jerusalem
And makes of it
the pride of the earth.

8 The LORD has sworn by his right hand
and by his mighty arm:
No more will I give your grain
as food to your enemies;
Nor shall foreigners drink your wine,
for which you toiled.ˢ

62, 2: New name: figurative expression for a new state of happiness; cf Rv 2, 17; 3, 12.
62, 6f: Remind the LORD . . . give no rest to him: figuratively, as though to make certain that the Lord will remember his pledge to Jerusalem. Cf Lk 11, 7f.

o: Is 40, 2. *p:* Is 55, 3; 59, 21. *q:* Rv 2, 17; 3, 12. *r:* Is 49, 15f; 54, 1ff. *s:* Is 52, 10.

9 But you who harvest the grain shall eat it,
  and you shall praise the LORD;
You who gather the grapes shall drink the
  wine
  in the courts of my sanctuary.*

10 Pass through, pass through the gates,
  prepare the way for the people;*
Build up, build up the highway,
  clear it of stones,
  raise up a standard over the nations.*

11 See, the LORD proclaims
  to the ends of the earth:
Say to daughter Zion,
  your savior comes!
Here is his reward with him,
  his recompense before him.*

12 They shall be called the holy people,
  the redeemed of the LORD,
And you shall be called "Frequented,"
  a city that is not forsaken.*

See RG
280-95

CHAPTER 63

Punishment of Edom*

1 Who is this that comes from Edom,
  in crimsoned garments, from Bozrah—
This one arrayed in majesty,
  marching in the greatness of his
  strength?
"It is I, I who announce vindication,
  I who am mighty to save."

2 Why is your apparel red,
  and your garments like those of the
  wine presser?*

3 "The wine press I have trodden alone,
  and of my people there was no one
  with me.
I trod them in my anger,
  and trampled them down in my wrath;
Their blood spurted on my garments;
  all my apparel I stained.

4 For the day of vengeance was in my
  heart,

my year for redeeming was at hand.*

5 I looked about, but there was no one to
  help,
  I was appalled that there was no one to
  lend support;
So my own arm brought about the victory
  and my own wrath lent me its support.*

6 I trampled down the peoples in my anger,
  I crushed them in my wrath,
  and I let their blood run out upon the
  ground."

Prayer for the Return of God's Favor*

7 The favors of the LORD I will recall,
  the glorious deeds of the LORD,
Because of all he has done for us;
  for he is good to the house of Israel,
He has favored us according to his mercy
  and his great kindness.*

8 He said: They are indeed my people,
  children who are not disloyal;
So he became their savior
9   in their every affliction.
It was not a messenger or an angel,
  but he himself who saved them.
Because of his love and pity
  he redeemed them himself,
Lifting them and carrying them
  all the days of old.*

10 But they rebelled, and grieved
  his holy spirit;
So he turned on them like an enemy,
  and fought against them.

11 Then they remembered the days of old
  and Moses, his servant;
Where is he who brought up out of the
  sea
  the shepherd of his flock?
Where is he who put his holy spirit
  in their midst;

12 Whose glorious arm
  was the guide at Moses' right;
Who divided the waters before them,

62, 10: The command is given to the workmen to begin the reconstruction of the city.

63, 1-6: In a dramatic dialogue between God and the prophet, the Lord is portrayed as the sole avenger of justice against his enemies.

63, 7—64, 11: A prayer probably composed toward the end of the exile, in which the prophet, after recalling God's blessings on Israel in its past history (63, 7-10), especially at

the Exodus (11-14), begs the Lord to come once more to the aid of his people (63, 15—64, 3), who now humbly confess their sins (4-11).

t: Dt 12, 17f; 14, 23. u: Is 58, 14. v: Is 40, 10. w: Is 62, 4.
x: Rv 19, 13. y: Is 34, 8; 61, 2. z: Is 59, 16. a: Is 26, 15.
b: Dt 4, 37f.

winning for himself eternal renown;

[13] Who led them without stumbling through
the depths
like horses in the open country,

[14] Like cattle going down into the plain,
the spirit of the LORD guiding them?
Thus you led your people,
bringing glory to your name.

[15] Look down from heaven and regard us
from your holy and glorious palace!
Where is your zealous care and your
might,
your surge of pity and your mercy?[c]
O Lord, hold not back,
[16]   for you are our father.
Were Abraham not to know us,
nor Israel to acknowledge us,
You, LORD, are our father,
our redeemer you are named forever.

[17] Why do you let us wander, O LORD, from
your ways,
and harden our hearts so that we fear
you not?
Return for the sake of your servants,
the tribes of your heritage.

[18] Why have the wicked invaded your holy
place,
why have our enemies trampled your
sanctuary?

[19] Too long have we been like those you do
not rule,
who do not bear your name.

Oh, that you would rend the heavens and
come down,
with the mountains quaking before you,

See RG
280-95

CHAPTER 64

[1] As when brushwood is set ablaze,
or fire makes the water boil!
Thus your name would be made known
to your enemies
and the nations would tremble before
you,

[2] While you wrought awesome deeds we
could not hope for,

[3]   such as they had not heard of from of
old.

No ear has ever heard, no eye ever seen,
any God but you
doing such deeds for those who wait
for him.[d]

[4] Would that you might meet us doing
right,
that we were mindful of you in our
ways!
Behold, you are angry, and we are sinful;
[5]   all of us have become like unclean
men,
all our good deeds are like polluted
rags;
We have all withered like leaves,
and our guilt carries us away like the
wind.

[6] There is none who calls upon your name,
who rouses himself to cling to you;
For you have hidden your face from us
and have delivered us up to our guilt.

[7] Yet, O LORD, you are our father;
we are the clay and you the potter:
we are all the work of your hands.

[8] Be not so very angry, LORD,
keep not our guilt forever in mind;
look upon us, who are all your people.

[9] Your holy cities have become a desert,
Zion is a desert, Jerusalem a waste.[e]

[10] Our holy and glorious temple
in which our fathers praised you
Has been burned with fire;
all that was dear to us is laid waste.

[11] Can you hold back, O LORD, after all
this?
Can you remain silent, and afflict us so
severely?

CHAPTER 65

See RG
280-95

Necessity of Punishment

[1] I was ready to respond to those who
asked me not,
to be found by those who sought me
not.
I said: Here I am! Here I am!
To a nation that did not call upon my
name.[f]

[2] I have stretched out my hands all the day
to a rebellious people,
Who walk in evil paths

c: Dt 26, 15; Bar 2, 16.   d: 1 Cor 2, 9.   e: Ps 79, 1.   f: Rom 10, 20.

and follow their own thoughts,[g]

³ People who provoke me
   continually, to my face,
Offering sacrifices in the groves
   and burning incense on bricks,
⁴ Living among the graves
   and spending the night in caverns,
Eating swine's flesh,
   with carrion broth in their dishes,
⁵ Crying out, "Hold back,
   do not touch me; I am too sacred for
      you!" *

These things enkindle my wrath,
   a fire that burns all the day.
⁶ Lo, before me it stands written;
   I will not be quiet until I have paid in full
⁷ Your crimes and the crimes of your
      fathers as well,
says the LORD.
Since they burned incense on the
      mountains,
   and disgraced me on the hills,
I will at once pour out in full measure
   their recompense into their laps.

Fate of the Good and the Bad in Israel
⁸   Thus says the LORD:
When the juice is pressed from grapes,
   men say, "Do not discard them,
   for there is still good in them";
Thus will I do with my servants:
   I will not discard them all;
⁹ From Jacob I will save offspring,
   from Judah, those who are to inherit
      my mountains;
My chosen ones shall inherit the land,
   my servants shall dwell there.
¹⁰ Sharon shall be a pasture for the flocks
   and the valley of Achor a resting place
      for the cattle
   of my people who have sought me.

¹¹ But you who forsake the LORD,
   forgetting my holy mountain,
You who spread a table for Fortune

and fill cups of blended wine for
      Destiny,*
¹² You I will destine for the sword;
   you shall all go down in slaughter.
Since I called and you did not answer,
   I spoke and you did not listen,
But did what was evil in my sight
   and preferred things which displease
      me,[h]
¹³   therefore thus says the Lord GOD:
Lo, my servants shall eat,
   but you shall go hungry;
My servants shall drink,
   but you shall be thirsty;
My servants shall rejoice,
   but you shall be put to shame;
¹⁴ My servants shall shout
   for joy of heart,
But you shall cry out for grief of heart
   and howl for anguish of spirit.
¹⁵ The Lord GOD shall slay you,
   and the name you leave
Shall be used by my chosen ones for
      cursing;
   but my servants shall be called by
      another name
¹⁶ By which he will be blessed
   on whom a blessing is invoked in the
      land;
He who takes an oath in the land
   shall swear by the God of truth;
For the hardships of the past shall be
      forgotten,
   and hidden from my eyes.

The World Renewed
¹⁷ Lo, I am about to create new heavens
   and a new earth;
The things of the past shall not be
      remembered
   or come to mind.[i]
¹⁸ Instead, there shall always be rejoicing
   and happiness
   in what I create;
For I create Jerusalem to be a joy
   and its people to be a delight;

65, 5: I am too sacred for you: the uncleanness of pork, obvious to a Semite, is what these people claim has made them sacred! The prophet ridicules them. Some translate: "I will render you sacred," and understand this as referring to the concept of sacredness as something contagious.

65, 11f: Destiny: the Hebrew also has a play on the words: Destiny and destine; meni and manithi.

g: Rom 10, 21.   *h:* Is 66, 4; Prv 1, 24; Jer 7, 13.   *i:* Is 66, 22; Rv 21, 1.

[19] I will rejoice in Jerusalem
  and exult in my people.
No longer shall the sound of weeping be
    heard there,
  or the sound of crying;
[20] No longer shall there be in it
    an infant who lives but a few days,
  or an old man who does not round out
    his full lifetime;
He dies a mere youth who reaches but a
    hundred years,
  and he who fails of a hundred shall be
    thought accursed.

[21] They shall live in the houses they build,
  and eat the fruit of the vineyards they
    plant;
[22] They shall not build houses for others to
    live in,
  or plant for others to eat.
As the years of a tree, so the years of my
    people;
  and my chosen ones shall long enjoy
  the produce of their hands.
[23] They shall not toil in vain,
  nor beget children for sudden
    destruction;
For a race blessed by the LORD
  are they and their offspring.
[24] Before they call, I will answer;
  while they are yet speaking, I will
    hearken to them.
[25] The wolf and the lamb shall graze alike,
  and the lion shall eat hay like the ox
  [but the serpent's food shall be dust].[j]
None shall hurt or destroy
  on all my holy mountain, says the
  LORD.[*]

See RG
280-95

CHAPTER 66

True and False Worship

[1]   Thus says the LORD:
The heavens are my throne,
  the earth is my footstool.
What kind of house can you build for me;

what is to be my resting place?[k]
[2] My hand made all these things
  when all of them came to be, says the
  LORD.
This is the one whom I approve:
  the lowly and afflicted man who
  trembles at my word.

[3] Merely slaughtering an ox is like slaying
    a man;
  sacrificing a lamb, like breaking a
    dog's neck;
Bringing a cereal offering, like offering
    swine's blood;
  burning incense, like paying homage
    to an idol.
Since these have chosen their own ways
  and taken pleasure in their own
    abominations,[l]
[4] I in turn will choose ruthless treatment
    for them[*]
  and bring upon them what they fear.

Because, when I called, no one
    answered,
  when I spoke, no one listened;
Because they did what was evil in my
    sight,
  and chose what gave me displeasure,[m]
[5] Hear the word of the LORD,
  you who tremble at his word:
Your brethren who, because of my
    name,
  hate and reject you, say,
"Let the LORD show his glory
  that we may see your joy";
  but they shall be put to shame.
[6] A sound of roaring from the city,
  a sound from the temple,
The sound of the LORD
  repaying his enemies their deserts![n]

Mother Zion

[7] Before she comes to labor,[*]
  she gives birth;[o]

65, 25: See note on Is 11, 6-9.

66, 4f: Worship which is merely external is as evil as though it were idolatry.

66, 7-9: The absence of labor in Zion's childbearing is a symbol of the joyful begetting of the new people of God.

j: Is 11, 6-9.   *k:* 2 Sm 7, 4ff; 1 Kgs 8, 27; Acts 7, 49; 17, 24.   *l:* Lv 11, 7.   *m:* Is 65, 12; Prv 1, 24; Jer 7, 13.   *n:* Jl 4, 16; Am 1, 2.
o: 7-9: Is 49, 18-21; 54, 1.

Before the pains come upon her,
    she safely delivers a male child.
[8] Who ever heard of such a thing,
    or saw the like?
Can a country be brought forth in one day,
    or a nation be born in a single
      moment?
Yet Zion is scarcely in labor
    when she gives birth to her children.
[9] Shall I bring a mother to the point of
      birth,
    and yet not let her child be born? says
      the LORD;
Or shall I who allow her to conceive,
    yet close her womb? says your God.

[10] Rejoice with Jerusalem and be glad
      because of her,
    all you who love her;
Exult, exult with her,
    all you who were mourning over her!
[11] Oh, that you may suck fully
    of the milk of her comfort,
That you may nurse with delight
    at her abundant breasts!
[12]   For thus says the LORD:
Lo, I will spread prosperity over her like
      a river,
    and the wealth of the nations like
    an overflowing torrent.
As nurslings, you shall be carried in her
      arms,
    and fondled in her lap;
[13] As a mother comforts her son,
    so will I comfort you;
    in Jerusalem you shall find your
      comfort.

[14] When you see this, your heart shall rejoice,
    and your bodies flourish like the grass;
The LORD's power shall be known to his
      servants,
    but to his enemies, his wrath.

[15] Lo, the LORD shall come in fire,
    his chariots like the whirlwind,

To wreak his wrath with burning heat
    and his punishment with fiery flames.
[16] For the LORD shall judge all mankind
    by fire and sword,
    and many shall be slain by the LORD.

[17] They who sanctify and purify themselves to go to the groves, as followers of one who stands within, they who eat swine's flesh, loathsome things and mice, shall all perish with their deeds and their thoughts, says the LORD.[p]

Gathering of the Nations. [18] I come to gather nations of every language; they shall come and see my glory.* [19] I will set a sign among them; from them I will send fugitives to the nations: to Tarshish, Put and Lud, Mosoch, Tubal and Javan, to the distant coastlands that have never heard of my fame, or seen my glory; and they shall proclaim my glory among the nations. [20] They shall bring all your brethren from all the nations as an offering to the LORD, on horses and in chariots, in carts, upon mules and dromedaries, to Jerusalem, my holy mountain, says the LORD, just as the Israelites bring their offering to the house of the LORD in clean vessels. [21] Some of these I will take as priests and Levites, says the LORD.

Lasting Reward and Punishment
[22] As the new heavens and the new earth
    which I will make
Shall endure before me, says the LORD,
    so shall your race and your name
      endure.[q]
[23] From one new moon to another,
    and from one sabbath to another,
All mankind shall come to worship
    before me, says the LORD.
[24] They shall go out and see the corpses[r]
    of the men who rebelled against me;
Their worm shall not die,
    nor their fire be extinguished;
    and they shall be abhorrent to all
      mankind.*

66, 18-21: God summons the neighboring nations to Zion and from among them will send some to far distant lands to proclaim his glory. All your brethren: Jews in exile.

66, 24: God's enemies lie dead outside the walls of the New Jerusalem; just as in the past, corpses, filth and refuse lay in the Valley of Hinnom outside the city, where huge fires were constantly burning; cf Jos 15, 8; 2 Chr 28, 3; Mk 9, 45-48.

p: Lv 11, 29.   *q:* Is 65, 17; Rv 21, 1.   *r:* Mk 9, 45.

See RG
296-309

The Book of Jeremiah

The Book of Jeremiah combines history, biography, and prophecy. It portrays a nation in crisis and introduces the reader to an extraordinary leader upon whom the Lord placed the heavy burden of the prophetic office. Jeremiah was born about 650 B.C. of a priestly family from the little village of Anathoth, near Jerusalem. While still very young he was called to his task in the thirteenth year of King Josiah (628), whose reform, begun with enthusiasm and hope, ended with his death on the battlefield of Megiddo (609) as he attempted to stop the northward march of the Egyptian Pharaoh Neco.

The prophet heartily supported the reform of the pious King Josiah, which began in 629 B.C. Nineveh, the capital of Assyria, fell in 612, preparing the way for the new colossus, Babylon, which was soon to put an end to Judean independence.

After the death of Josiah the old idolatry returned. Jeremiah opposed it with all his strength. Arrest, imprisonment, and public disgrace were his lot. Jeremiah saw in the nation's impenitence the sealing of its doom. Nebuchadnezzar captured Jerusalem and carried King Jehoiachin into exile (22, 24).

During the years 598–587, Jeremiah attempted to counsel Zedekiah in the face of bitter opposition. The false prophet Hananiah proclaimed that the yoke of Babylon was broken and a strong pro-Egyptian party in Jerusalem induced Zedekiah to revolt. Nebuchadnezzar took swift and terrible vengeance; Jerusalem was destroyed in 587 and its leading citizens sent into exile. About this time Jeremiah uttered the great oracle of the "New Covenant" (31, 31-34) sometimes called "The Gospel before the Gospel." This passage contains his most sublime teaching and is a landmark in Old Testament theology.

The prophet remained amidst the ruins of Jerusalem, but was later forced into Egyptian exile by a band of conspirators. There, according to an old tradition, he was murdered by his own countrymen. The influence of Jeremiah was greater after his death than before. The exiled community read and meditated on the lessons of the prophet, and his influence can be seen in Ezekiel, certain of the psalms, and the second part of Isaiah. Shortly after the exile, the Book of Jeremiah as we have it today was published in a final edition.

It is divided as follows:

I: Oracles in the Days of Josiah (1, 1—6, 30).

II: Oracles Mostly in the Days of Jehoiakim (7, 1—20, 18).

III: Oracles in the Last Years of Jerusalem (21, 1—33, 26).

IV: Fall of Jerusalem (34, 1—45, 5).

V: Oracles against the Nations (46, 1—51, 64).

VI: Historical Appendix (52, 1-34).

I: Oracles in the Days of Josiah

CHAPTER 1

See RG
302

¹The words of Jeremiah, son of Hilkiah, of a priestly family in Anathoth,* in the land of Benjamin. ²The word of the LORD first came to him in the days of Josiah, son of Amon, king of Judah, in the thirteenth year of his reign,*ᵃ ³and continued through the reign of Jehoiakim, son of Josiah, king of Judah, and until the downfall* and exile of Jerusalem in the fifth month of the eleventh year of Zedekiah, son of Josiah, king of Judah.ᵇ

Call of Jeremiah

⁴ The word of the LORD came to me thus:

1, 1: Anathoth: a village about three miles northeast of Jerusalem, where Solomon exiled Abiathar (1 Kgs 2, 26f); it is probable that Jeremiah belonged to the priestly family of Abiathar.

1, 3: Until the downfall: these words were originally prefixed as a title to a collection of Jeremiah's prophecies which lacked chapters 40—44. The new title in Jer 40, 1 and the oracles that follow clearly show that Jeremiah continued to prophesy after the destruction of Jerusalem in 587 B.C.

a: Jer 25, 3.   b: Jer 25, 1.

⁵ Before I formed you in the womb I knew
you,*
before you were born I dedicated you,
a prophet to the nations I appointed you.ᶜ
⁶ "Ah, Lord Goᴅ!" I said,
"I know not how to speak; I am too
young."*
⁷ But the Lᴏʀᴅ answered me,

Say not, "I am too young."
To whomever I send you, you shall go;
whatever I command you, you shall
speak.
⁸ Have no fear before them,
because I am with you to deliver you,
says the Lᴏʀᴅ.

⁹Then the Lᴏʀᴅ extended his hand and
touched my mouth, saying,

See, I place my words in your mouth!ᵈ
¹⁰   This day I set you
over nations and over kingdoms,
To root up and to tear down,
to destroy and to demolish,
to build and to plant.

¹¹The word of the Lᴏʀᴅ came to me with
the question: What do you see, Jeremiah? "I
see a branch of the watching-tree,"* I
replied. ¹²Then the Lᴏʀᴅ said to me: Well
have you seen, for I am watching to fulfill
my word. ¹³ᵉA second time the word of the
Lᴏʀᴅ came to me with the question: What
do you see? "I see a boiling cauldron," I
replied, "that appears from the north."*
¹⁴And from the north, said the Lᴏʀᴅ to
me, evil will boil over upon all who dwell in
the land.ᶠ

¹⁵ Lo, I am summoning
all the kingdoms of the north, says the
Lᴏʀᴅ;
Each king shall come and set up his
throne
at the gateways of Jerusalem,
Opposite her walls all around
and opposite all the cities of Judah.ᵍ
¹⁶ I will pronounce my sentence against
them
for all their wickedness in forsaking me,
And in burning incense to strange gods
and adoring their own handiwork.ʰ

¹⁷ But do you gird your loins;
stand up and tell them
all that I command you.
Be not crushed on their account,
as though I would leave you crushed
before them;
¹⁸ For it is I this day
who have made you a fortified city,
A pillar of iron, a wall of brass,
against the whole land:
Against Judah's kings and princes,
against its priests and people.ⁱ
¹⁹ They will fight against you, but not
prevail over you,
for I am with you to deliver you, says
the Lᴏʀᴅ.

CHAPTER 2

Infidelity of Israel.* ¹This word of the
Lᴏʀᴅ came to me: ²Go, cry out this message
for Jerusalem to hear!

See RG
302

I remember the devotion* of your youth,
how you loved me as a bride,

1, 5: Jeremiah was destined to the office of prophet before
his birth; cf Is 49, 1. 5; Lk 1, 15; Gal 1, 15f. I knew you: I
loved you and chose you. I dedicated you: I set you apart to
be a prophet. Some Fathers and later theologians understand
this to mean that Jeremiah was freed from original sin before
his birth. The context does not justify this conclusion. The nations: the pagan neighbors of Judah, besides the great world
powers—Assyria, Babylonia, Egypt—intimately associated
with Judah's destiny.

1, 6: I am too young: Jeremiah's youth (he was less than
thirty years old) must not be an obstacle to the responsibilities of the prophetic office; God will supply for his human defects (cf vv 7f).

1, 11: The watching-tree: the almond tree, which is the
first to blossom in the springtime as though it had not slept.

The Hebrew name contains a play on words with "I am
watching."

1, 13: Boiling cauldron . . . the north: symbol of an invasion from the north; cf vv 14f.

2, 1—3, 5: These verses probably contain the earliest of
Jeremiah's preachings. The covenant relationship, symbolized by the figure of a marriage, was frequently broken by Israel, seen here as an unfaithful wife unworthy of reconciliation with God (Jer 3, 1-5).

2, 2: Devotion: Israel's gratitude, fidelity, and love for
God.

ᶜ: Jer 49, 1; Gal 1, 15f.   ᵈ: Is 6, 7.   ᵉ: Ez 11, 3. 7; 24, 3.   ᶠ: Jer
4, 6; 6, 1.   ᵍ: Jer 6, 22.   ʰ: Is 2, 8.   ⁱ: Jer 6, 27; 15, 20; Ex 3, 8.

Following me in the desert,
in a land unsown.*ʲ*
³ Sacred to the LORD was Israel,
the first fruits* of his harvest;
Should anyone presume to partake of them,
evil would befall him, says the LORD.*ᵏ*

⁴ Listen to the word of the LORD, O house
of Jacob!
All you clans of the house of Israel,
⁵ thus says the LORD:
What fault did your fathers find in me
that they withdrew from me,
Went after empty idols,
and became empty themselves?*ˡ*
⁶ They did not ask, "Where is the LORD
who brought us up from the land of
Egypt,
Who led us through the desert,
through a land of wastes and gullies,
Through a land of drought and
darkness,
through a land which no one crosses,
where no man dwells?"*ᵐ*
⁷ When I brought you into the garden land
to eat its goodly fruits,
You entered and defiled my land,
you made my heritage loathsome.*ⁿ*
⁸ The priests asked not,
"Where is the LORD?"
Those who dealt with the law* knew me
not:
the shepherds rebelled against me.
The prophets prophesied by Baal,
and went after useless idols.*ᵒ*
⁹ Therefore will I yet accuse you, says the
LORD,
and even your children's children I
will accuse.*ᵖ*

¹⁰ Pass over to the coast of the Kittim* and
see,
send to Kedar and carefully inquire:
Where has the like of this been done?
¹¹ Does any other nation change its gods?—
yet they are not gods at all!
But my people have changed their glory
for useless things.*�q*
¹² Be amazed at this, O heavens,
and shudder with sheer horror, says the
LORD.
¹³ Two evils have my people done:
they have forsaken me, the source of
living waters;
They have dug themselves cisterns,
broken cisterns, that hold no water.*ʳ*

¹⁴ Is Israel a slave, a bondman by birth?*
Why then has he become booty?
¹⁵ Against him lions roar
full-throated cries.
They have made his land a waste;
his cities are charred ruins, without
inhabitant.*ˢ*
¹⁶ Yes, the people of Memphis* and
Tahpanhes
shave the crown of your head.
¹⁷ Has not the forsaking of the LORD, your
God,
done this to you?*ᵗ*
¹⁸ And now, why go to Egypt,*
to drink the waters of the Nile?
Why go to Assyria,
to drink the waters of the Euphrates?
¹⁹ Your own wickedness chastises you,
your own infidelities punish you.
Know then, and see, how evil and bitter
is your forsaking the LORD, your God,
And showing no fear of me,
says the Lord, the GOD of hosts.*ᵘ*

2, 3: First fruits: an offering to God which became his exclusive property, and could therefore not be put to profane use; cf Lv 22, 1.

2, 8: Those who dealt with the law: the priests. The shepherds: the kings and nobles.

2, 10: Kittim: a Phoenician colony in Cyprus. Kedar: a nomad tribe of the Syrian desert. These two names represent West and East.

2, 14: Bondman by birth: a perpetual slave, different from the debt-slave, who was to be freed after six years; cf Ex 21, 2.

2, 16: Memphis: the capital of Lower Egypt. Tahpanhes: a frontier city of Egypt, east of the Delta. Shave the crown of your head: the spoliation of Judah at the hands of the Egyptians.

2, 18: Egypt and Assyria were the protecting foreign powers favored by rival parties within Judah. The desire for such foreign alliances is a further desertion of the Lord, the source of living waters (v 13), in favor of the above-named powers, symbolized by the Nile and the Euphrates rivers.

j: Dt 2, 7; 32, 9-12; Mi 6, 4. *k:* Jer 12, 14; Ex 4, 22; Dt 7, 6; 14, 2. *l:* Is 5, 4; Mi 6, 3. *m:* Ex 20, 2f; Dt 8, 14; Is 63, 11ff. *n:* Lv 18, 24f; Dt 8, 7-10; 32, 13f. *o:* Jer 8, 8ff; 23, 1. 13. *p:* Ex 20, 5. *q:* Jer 16, 20; Ps 106, 20. *r:* Jer 17, 13; Ps 36, 9; Is 1, 4. *s:* Jer 9, 11. *t:* Jer 4, 18; 30, 15. *u:* Prv 5, 22; Hos 5, 5.

20 Long ago you broke your yoke,^{v}
  you tore off your bonds.
  "I will not serve," you said.
  On every high hill, under every green
    tree,
  you gave yourself to harlotry.*
21 I had planted you, a choice vine
  of fully tested stock;
  How could you turn out obnoxious to
    me,
  a spurious vine?^{w}
22 Though you scour it with soap,
  and use much lye,
  The stain of your guilt is still before me,
  says the Lord GOD.^{x}
23 How can you say, "I am not defiled,
  I have not gone after the Baals"?
  Consider your conduct in the Valley,*
  recall what you have done:
  A frenzied she-camel, coursing near and
    far,
24   breaking away toward the desert,
  Snuffing the wind in her ardor—
    who can restrain her lust?
  No beasts need tire themselves seeking
    her;
  in her month they will meet her.

25 Stop wearing out your shoes
  and parching your throat!
  But you say, "No use! no!
  I love these strangers,
  and after them I must go."^{y}
26 As the thief is shamed when caught,
  so shall the house of Israel be shamed:
  They, their kings and their princes,
  their priests and their prophets;^{z}
27 They who say to a piece of wood, "You
    are my father,"
  and to a stone, "You gave me birth."
  They turn to me their backs, not their
    faces;
  yet, in their time of trouble they cry
    out,
  "Rise up and save us!"

28 Where are the gods you made for
    yourselves?
  Let them rise up!
  Will they save you in your time of
    trouble?
  For as numerous as your cities
  are your gods, O Judah!
  And as many as the streets of Jerusalem
  are the altars you have set up for Baal.^{a}

29 How dare you still plead with me?
  You have all rebelled against me, says
    the LORD.
30 In vain I struck your children;
  the correction they did not take.
  Your sword devoured your prophets
  like a ravening lion.^{b}
31 You, of this generation,
  take note of the word of the Lord:
  Have I been a desert to Israel,
  a land of darkness?
  Why do my people say, "We have moved
    on,
  we will come to you no more"?
32 Does a virgin forget her jewelry,
  a bride her sash?
  Yet my people have forgotten me
  days without number.^{c}

33 How well you pick your way
  when seeking love!
  You who, in your wickedness,
  have gone by ways unclean!
34 You, on whose clothing there is
  the life-blood of the innocent,
  whom you found committing no
    burglary;
35 Yet withal you say, "I am innocent;
  at least, his anger is turned away from
    me."
  Behold, I will judge you
  on that word of yours, "I have not
    sinned."
36 How very base you have become
  in changing your course!

2, 20: Harlotry: idolatry (because Israel is the bride of God).
  2, 23: The Valley: of Ben-hinnom, south of Jerusalem, site of the infamous sanctuary of Topheth where children were sacrificed to Molech; cf Jer 7, 31.

v: Jer 3, 6. 13; Jgs 10, 6.   w: Ex 15, 17; Ps 80, 9; Is 5, 4.   x: Jb 9, 30.   y: Jer 18, 12.   z: Jer 48, 27; Rom 6, 21.   a: Jer 11, 13; Dt 32, 38; Jgs 10, 14.   b: Jer 5, 3; Neh 9, 26.   c: Jer 13, 25; Dt 32, 18.

By Egypt will you be shamed,
    as you were shamed by Assyria.[d]
[37] From there also shall you go away
    with hands upon your head;
For the LORD has rejected those in whom
    you trust,
    with them you will have no success.[e]

See RG
302

CHAPTER 3

[1] If a man sends away his wife[f]
    and, after leaving him,
    she marries another man,
Does the first husband come back to her?
    Would not the land be wholly defiled?
But you have sinned with many lovers,
    and yet you would return to me! says
        the LORD.*

[2] Lift your eyes to the heights, and see,
    where have men not lain with you?
By the waysides you waited for them
    like an Arab* in the desert.
You defiled the land
    by your wicked harlotry.[g]
[3] Therefore the showers were withheld,
    the spring rain failed.
But because you have a harlot's brow,
    you refused to blush.[h]

[4] Even now do you not call me, "My
        father,
    you who are the bridegroom of my
        youth"?
[5] "Will he keep his wrath forever,
    will he hold his grudge to the end?"
This is what you say; yet you do
    all the evil you can.

Judah and Israel. [6] The LORD said to me in the days of King Josiah: See now what rebellious Israel has done! She has gone up every high mountain, and under every green tree she has played the harlot.[i] [7] And I thought, after she has done all this she will return to me. But she did not return. Then, even though her traitor sister Judah saw [8] that for all the adulteries rebellious Israel had committed, I put her away and gave her a bill of divorce, nevertheless her traitor sister Judah was not frightened; she too went off and played the harlot.[j] [9] Eager to sin, she polluted the land, committing adultery with stone and wood.[k] [10] With all this, the traitor sister Judah did not return to me wholeheartedly, but insincerely, says the LORD.

Restoration of Israel. [11] Then the LORD said to me: Rebel Israel is inwardly more just than traitorous Judah.[l] [12] Go, proclaim these words toward the north, and say:

Return, rebel Israel, says the LORD,
    I will not remain angry with you;
For I am merciful, says the LORD,
    I will not continue my wrath forever.[m]
[13] Only know your guilt:
    how you rebelled against the LORD,
        your God,
How you ran hither and yon to strangers
    [under every green tree]
    and would not listen to my voice, says
        the LORD.[n]
[14] Return, rebellious children, says the
        LORD,*
    for I am your Master;
I will take you, one from a city, two from
        a clan,
    and bring you to Zion.[o]
[15] I will appoint over you shepherds after
        my own heart,
    who will shepherd you wisely and
        prudently.[p]
[16] When you multiply and become fruitful
        in the land,
    says the LORD,
They will in those days no longer say,
    "The ark of the covenant of the
        LORD!"

3, 1: Such remarriage of divorced spouses was forbidden by Dt 24, 1-4. Under this figure the prophet sees the presumption of Judah, the unfaithful spouse, who thinks she can return to the Lord after uniting herself to other gods.

3, 2: An Arab: a marauding nomad who lay in wait for caravans.

3, 14-18: A remnant of Israel (14) will reunite with Judah (18). The elementary cult of the Lord represented by the ark of the covenant will now be replaced by a more deeply spiritual and universal alliance, symbolized by his throne in the ideal Jerusalem around which all nations will be gathered together (17).

d: 2 Chr 28, 16-21. e: 2 Sm 13, 19. f: Dt 24, 1-4. g: Ex 16, 24f. h: Jer 6, 15; 8, 12. i: Jer 2, 20; Dt 12, 2. j: 2 Kgs 17, 6. 18-23; Ez 23, 11. k: Jer 2, 27. l: Ez 16, 51; 23, 11. m: Dt 4, 29ff. n: Jer 2, 20. 25; Lv 26, 40. o: Jer 23, 3; Is 10, 21f. p: Ez 34, 23; Jn 21, 15.

They will no longer think of it, or
    remember it,
    or miss it, or make another.

[17] At that time they will call Jerusalem the
LORD's throne; there all nations will be gathered together to honor the name of the LORD
at Jerusalem, and they will walk no longer in
their hardhearted wickedness.[q] [18] In those
days the house of Judah will join the house
of Israel; together they will come from the
land of the north to the land which I gave to
your fathers as a heritage.[r]

Conditions for Forgiveness

[19] I had thought:
    How I should like to treat you as sons,
And give you a pleasant land,
    a heritage most beautiful among the
      nations!
You would call me, "My Father," I
      thought,
    and never cease following me.[s]
[20] But like a woman faithless to her lover,
    even so have you been faithless to me,
    O house of Israel, says the LORD.[t]
[21] A cry is heard on the heights!
    the plaintive weeping of Israel's
      children,
Because they have perverted their ways
    and forgotten the LORD, their God.
[22] Return, rebellious children,
    and I will cure you of your rebelling.
"Here we are, we now come to you
    because you are the LORD, our God.[u]
[23] Deceptive indeed are the hills,
    the thronging mountains;
In the LORD, our God, alone
    is the salvation of Israel.[v]
[24] The shame-god* has devoured
    our fathers' toil from our youth,
Their sheep and their cattle,
    their sons and their daughters.
[25] Let us lie down in our shame,
    let our disgrace cover us,

for we have sinned against the LORD,
    our God,
From our youth to this day, we and our
      fathers also;
    we listened not to the voice of the
      LORD, our God."[w]

CHAPTER 4

See RG
302

[1] If you wish to return, O Israel,
    says the LORD,
    return to me.
If you put your detestable things out of
      my sight,
    and do not stray,[x]
[2] Then you can swear, "As the LORD lives,"*
    in truth, in judgment, and in justice;
Then shall the nations use his name in
      blessing,
    and glory in him.[y]

[3] For to the men of Judah and to Jerusalem,
thus says the LORD:

Till your untilled ground,
    sow not among thorns.[z]
[4] For the sake of the LORD, be
      circumcised,*
    remove the foreskins of your hearts,
    O men of Judah and citizens of
      Jerusalem;
Lest my anger break out like fire,
    and burn till none can quench it,
    because of your evil deeds.[a]

The Invasion from the North
[5] Proclaim it in Judah,
    make it heard in Jerusalem;
Blow the trumpet through the land,
    summon the recruits!
Say, "Fall in, let us march
    to the fortified cities."
[6] Bear the standard to Zion,
    seek refuge without delay!
Evil I bring from the north,
    and great destruction.

3, 24: Shame-god: literally, shame, a term commonly substituted for Baal, the Canaanite god with many local shrines.

4, 2: As the LORD lives: this oath, made sincerely, implies
Israel's return to God and loyal adherence to him. Thus the
ancient promises are fulfilled; cf Gn 12, 3; 18, 18; 22, 18; 26,
4; Ps 72, 17.

4, 4: The mere external rite of circumcision avails nothing

unless accompanied by the removal of blindness and obstinacy
of heart; cf Rom 2, 25. 29; 1 Cor 7, 19; Gal 5, 6; 6, 13. 15.

q: Is 2, 2. *r:* Jer 30, 3; 31, 8. *s:* Jer 31, 9. 20; Is 63, 16. *t:* Jer
5, 11. *u:* Hos 3, 5. *v:* Jer 14, 8. *w:* Jer 16, 11f; 22, 21. *x:* Jer
25, 5. *y:* Jer 12, 16; Dt 10, 20; Is 65, 16. *z:* Hos 10, 12; Mt 13,
7. 22. *a:* Jer 9, 24.

7 Up comes the lion from his lair,
    the destroyer of nations has set out,
    has left his place,
To turn your land into desolation,
    till your cities lie waste and empty.*b*
8 So gird yourselves with sackcloth,
    mourn and wail:
"The blazing wrath of the LORD
    is not turned away from us."*c*

9   In that day, says the LORD,
The king will lose heart, and the
    princes;
    the priests will be amazed,
    and the prophets stunned.
10 "Alas! Lord GOD," they will say,
    "You only deceived us*
When you said: Peace shall be yours;
    for the sword touches our very soul."*d*
11 At that time it will be said
    of this people and of Jerusalem,
"From the glaring heights through the
    desert
    a wind comes toward the daughter of
    my people."
Not to winnow, not to cleanse,
12   does this wind from the heights come
    at my bidding;
And I myself now pronounce
    sentence upon them.*e*

13 See! like storm clouds he advances,
    like a hurricane his chariots;
Swifter than eagles are his steeds:
    "Woe to us! we are ruined."
14 Cleanse your heart of evil, O Jerusalem,
    that you may be saved.
How long must your pernicious thoughts
    lodge within you?
15 Listen! They proclaim it from Dan,
    from Mount Ephraim they announce
    destruction:
16 "Make this known to the nations,
    announce it to Jerusalem:
The besiegers are coming from the
    distant land,

    shouting their war cry against the
    cities of Judah."*f*
17 Like watchmen of the fields they
    surround her,
    for she has rebelled against me, says
    the LORD.*g*
18 Your conduct, your misdeeds, have done
    this to you;
    how bitter is this disaster of yours,
    how it reaches to your very heart!*h*

19 My breast! my breast! how I suffer!*
    The walls of my heart!
My heart beats wildly,
    I cannot be still;
For I have heard the sound of the
    trumpet,
    the alarm of war.
20 Ruin after ruin is reported;
    the whole earth is laid waste.
In an instant my tents are ravaged;
    in a flash, my shelters.*i*
21 How long must I see that signal,
    hear that trumpet sound!

22 Fools my people are,
    they know me not;
Senseless children they are,
    having no understanding;
They are wise in evil,
    but know not how to do good.*j*
23 I looked at the earth, and it was waste
    and void;
    at the heavens, and their light had gone
    out!*k*
24 I looked at the mountains, and they were
    trembling,
    and all the hills were crumbling!
25 I looked and behold, there was no man;
    even the birds of the air had flown
    away!
26 I looked and behold, the garden land was
    a desert,
    with all its cities destroyed
    before the LORD, before his blazing
    wrath.*l*

4, 10: You only deceived us: the false prophets blame their deception on God; cf Jer 14, 13-16.
4, 19ff: Probably the prophet's own anguish at the coming destruction of Judah.

b: Jer 2, 15; 5, 6. *c:* Jer 6, 26; Is 5, 25. *d:* Jer 6, 14. *e:* Jer 1, 16. *f:* Jer 5, 15. *g:* Jer 6, 3. *h:* Jer 2, 17. 19. *i:* Jer 10, 20. *j:* Dt
32, 5f. 28. *k:* Is 24, 1. 3. *l:* Lv 26, 31.

27 For thus says the LORD:
Waste shall the whole land be;
I will [not] wholly destroy it.[m]
28 Because of this the earth shall mourn,
the heavens above shall darken;
I have spoken, I will not repent,
I have resolved, I will not turn back.[n]
29 At the shout of horseman and
bowman
each city takes to flight;
They shrink into the thickets,
they scale the rocks:
All the cities are abandoned,
and no one dwells in them.
30 You now who are doomed, what do you
mean
by putting on purple,
bedecking yourself with gold,
Shading your eyes with cosmetics,
beautifying yourself in vain?
Your lovers spurn you,
they seek your life.
31 Yes, I hear the moaning, as of a woman
in travail,
like the anguish of a mother with her
first child—
The cry of daughter Zion gasping,
as she stretches forth her hands:
"Ah, woe is me! I sink exhausted
before the slayers!"[o]

CHAPTER 5

See RG
302

Universal Corruption

1 Roam the streets of Jerusalem,
look about and observe,
Search through her public places,
to find even one
Who lives uprightly
and seeks to be faithful,
and I will pardon her!
2 Though they say, "As the LORD lives,"
they swear falsely.
3 O LORD, do your eyes not look for
honesty?
You struck them, but they did not cringe;
you laid them low, but they refused
correction;

They set their faces harder than stone,
and refused to return to you.[p]
4 It is only the lowly, I thought,
who are foolish;
For they know not the way of the LORD,
their duty to their God.[q]
5 I will go to the great ones
and speak with them;
For they know the way of the LORD,
their duty to their God.
But, one and all, they had broken the yoke,
torn off the harness.[r]
6 Therefore lions from the forest slay them,
wolves of the desert ravage them,
Leopards keep watch round their cities:
all who come out are torn to pieces
For their many crimes
and their numerous rebellions.

7 Why should I pardon you these things?
Your sons have forsaken me,
they swear by gods that are not.
I fed them, but they committed adultery;
to the harlot's house they throng.
8 Lustful stallions they are,
each neighs after another's wife.[s]
9 Shall I not punish them for these things?
says the LORD;
On a nation such as this shall I not take
vengeance?
10 Climb to her terraces, and ravage them,
destroy them [not] wholly.
Tear away her tendrils,
they do not belong to the LORD.[t]
11 For they have openly rebelled against me,
both the house of Israel and the house
of Judah,
says the LORD,[u]
12 They denied the LORD,[*]
saying, "Not he—
No evil shall befall us,
neither sword nor famine shall we
see.[v]
13 The prophets have become wind,
and the word is not in them.
May their threats be carried out against
themselves!"

5, 12: They denied the LORD: the people act as though God does not exist and will not interfere.

m: Jer 5, 18.   n: Is 24, 4.   o: Jer 6, 24.   p: Jer 2, 30.   q: Jer 8, 7.   r: Jer 6, 13.   s: Jer 13, 27.   t: Jer 2, 21.   u: Jer 3, 20.   v: Jer 14, 13; Is 28, 15.

[14] Now, for this that you have said,
  says the LORD, the God of hosts—
Behold, I make my words
  in your mouth, a fire,
And this people is the wood
  that it shall devour!—
[15] Beware, I will bring against you
  a nation from afar,
  O house of Israel, says the LORD;
A long-lived nation, an ancient nation,
  a people whose language you know not,
  whose speech you cannot understand.[w]
[16] Their quivers are like open graves;
  all of them are warriors.
[17] They will devour your harvest and your
    bread,
  devour your sons and your daughters,
Devour your sheep and cattle,
  devour your vines and fig trees;
They will beat flat with the sword
  the fortified city in which you trust.[x]

[18] Yet even in those days, says the LORD, I
will not wholly destroy you.[y] [19] And when
they ask, "Why has the LORD done all these
things to us?" say to them, "As you have forsaken me to serve strange gods in your own
land, so shall you serve strangers in a land
not your own."

[20] Announce this to the house of Jacob,
  proclaim it in Judah:
[21] Pay attention to this,
  foolish and senseless people
Who have eyes and see not,
  who have ears and hear not.[z]
[22] Should you not fear me, says the LORD,
  should you not tremble before me?
I made the sandy shore the sea's limit,
  which by eternal decree it may not
    overstep.
Toss though it may, it is to no avail;
  though its billows roar, they cannot
    pass.[a]
[23] But this people's heart is stubborn and
    rebellious;

they turn and go away,
[24] And say not in their hearts,
  "Let us fear the LORD, our God,
Who gives us rain
  early and late,* in its time;
Who watches for us
  over the appointed weeks of harvest."[b]
[25] Your crimes have prevented these things,
  your sins have turned back these
    blessings from you.[c]
[26] For there are among my people
    criminals;
  like fowlers they set traps,
  but it is men they catch.[d]
[27] Their houses are as full of treachery
  as a bird-cage is of birds;
Therefore they grow powerful and rich,
[28] fat and sleek.
They go their wicked way;
  justice they do not defend
By advancing the claim of the fatherless
  or judging the cause of the poor.[e]
[29] Shall I not punish these things? says the
    LORD;
  on a nation such as this shall I not take
    vengeance?
[30] A shocking, horrible thing
  has happened in the land:
[31] The prophets prophesy falsely,
  and the priests teach as they wish;
Yet my people will have it so;
  what will you do when the end comes?[f]

CHAPTER 6

The Enemy at the Gates

[1] Flee, sons of Benjamin,
  out of Jerusalem!
Blow the trumpet in Tekoa,
  raise a signal over Beth-haccherem;
For evil threatens from the north,
  and mighty destruction.[g]
[2] O lovely and delicate
  daughter Zion, you are ruined!
[3] Against her, shepherds come with their
    flocks;*

5, 24: Rain early and late: autumn and spring rains respectively. Appointed weeks of harvest: the seven weeks between the Passover (Dt 16, 9f) and Pentecost, during which it ordinarily did not rain.

6, 3: Shepherds . . . with their flocks: foreign invaders with their armies.

---

w: Dt 28, 49.   x: Dt 28, 31.   y: Jer 4, 27.   z: Is 6, 9.   a: Jb 38, 10f.   b: Gn 8, 22; Dt 11, 14.   c: Jer 2, 17. 19.   d: Prv 1, 11.   e: Jer 12, 1; Is 1, 23.   f: Jer 14, 14; Mi 2, 11.   g: Jer 1, 14f.

all around, they pitch their tents,
  each one grazes his portion.[h]
[4] "Prepare for war against her,
  Up! let us rush upon her at midday!
Alas! the day is waning,
  evening shadows lengthen;
[5] Up! let us rush upon her by night,
  destroy her palaces!"[i]

[6]   For thus says the LORD of hosts:
Hew down her trees,
  throw up a siege mound against
    Jerusalem.
Woe to the city marked for punishment;
  nought but oppression within her![j]
[7] As the well gushes out its waters,
  so she gushes out her wickedness.
Violence and destruction resound in her;
  ever before me are wounds and blows.[k]
[8] Be warned, O Jerusalem,
  lest I be estranged from you;
Lest I turn you into a desert,
  a land where no man dwells.

[9]   Thus says the LORD of hosts:
Glean, glean like a vine
  the remnant of Israel;
Pass your hand, like a vintager,
  repeatedly over the tendrils.
[10] To whom shall I speak?
  whom shall I warn, and be heard?
See! their ears are uncircumcised,
  they cannot give heed;
See, the word of the LORD has become
    for them
  an object of scorn, which they will not
    have.[l]
[11] Therefore my wrath brims up within me,
  I am weary of holding it in;
I will pour it out upon the child in the
    street,
  upon the young men gathered together.
Yes, all will be taken, husband and wife,
  graybeard with ancient.[m]

[12] Their houses will fall to strangers,
  their fields and their wives as well;
For I will stretch forth my hand
  against those who dwell in this land,
    says the LORD.[n]
[13] Small and great alike, all are greedy for
    gain;
  prophet and priest, all practice fraud.[o]
[14] They would repair, as though it were
    nought,*
  the injury to my people:
"Peace, peace!" they say,
  though there is no peace.[p]
[15] They are odious; they have done
    abominable things,
  yet they are not at all ashamed,
  they know not how to blush.
Hence they shall be among those who fall;
  in their time of punishment they shall
    go down,
    says the LORD.[q]

[16]   Thus says the LORD:
Stand beside the earliest roads,
  ask the pathways of old*
Which is the way to good, and walk it;
  thus you will find rest for your souls.
But they said, "We will not walk it."[r]
[17] When I raised up watchmen* for them:
  "Hearken to the sound of the trumpet!"
  they said, "We will not hearken."
[18] Therefore hear, O nations,
  and know, O earth,
  what I will do with them:
[19] See, I bring evil upon this people,
  the fruit of their own schemes,
Because they heeded not my words,
  because they despised my law.[s]
[20] Of what use to me incense that comes
    from Sheba,
  or sweet cane from far-off lands?
Your holocausts find no favor with me,
  your sacrifices please me not.[t]
[21]   Therefore, thus says the LORD:

6, 14: As though it were nought: the false assurance of well-being given by priest and prophet cannot reduce the harm which universal materialism and corruption have done to the people.

6, 16: Earliest roads . . . pathways of old: history and the lessons to be learned from it.

6, 17: Watchmen: the prophets who, like Jeremiah, had upheld God's moral law.

h: Jer 4, 17. *i:* 2 Chr 36, 19. *j:* Jer 32, 24; Zep 3, 1-4. *k:* Is 57, 20. *l:* Jer 7, 26; 20, 8. *m:* Ez 9, 6. *n:* Jer 8, 10; Dt 28, 30ff.
o: Jer 8, 10; 23, 11. *p:* Jer 8, 11. *q:* Jer 3, 3; 8, 12. *r:* Jer 7, 23f; 18, 15. *s:* Prv 1, 31. *t:* Is 1, 11; 43, 24.

See, I will place before this people
  obstacles to bring them down;
Fathers and sons alike,
  neighbors and friends shall perish.*u*

22 Thus says the LORD:
See, a people comes from the land of the
  north,
  a great nation, roused from the ends of
    the earth.*v*
23 Bow and javelin they wield;
  cruel and pitiless are they.
They sound like the roaring sea
  as they ride forth on steeds,
Each in his place, for battle
  against you, daughter Zion.
24 We hear the report of them;
  helpless fall our hands,
Anguish takes hold of us,
  throes like a mother's in childbirth.*w*
25 Go not forth into the field,
  step not into the street,
Beware of the enemy's sword;
  terror on every side!
26 O daughter of my people, gird on
    sackcloth,
  roll in the ashes.
Mourn as for an only child
  with bitter wailing,
For sudden upon us
  comes the destroyer.*x*

27 A tester among my people I have
    appointed you,
  to search and test their way.*y*
28 Arch-rebels are they all,
  dealers in slander,
  all of them corrupt.
29 The bellows roars,
  the lead is consumed by the fire;
In vain has the smelter refined,
  the wicked are not drawn off.
30 "Silver rejected" they shall be called,
  for the LORD has rejected them.

II: Oracles Mostly in the Days of Jehoiakim

CHAPTER 7

See RG 302

The Temple Sermon.* *1*The following
message came to Jeremiah from the LORD:
*2*Stand at the gate of the house of the LORD,
and there proclaim this message: Hear the
word of the LORD, all you of Judah who enter these gates to worship the LORD! *3*Thus
says the LORD of hosts, the God of Israel:
Reform your ways and your deeds, so that I
may remain with you in this place.*z* *4*Put not
your trust in the deceitful words: "This is the
temple of the LORD! The temple of the
LORD! The temple of the LORD!"*a* *5*Only if
you thoroughly reform your ways and your
deeds; if each of you deals justly with his
neighbor; *6*if you no longer oppress the resident alien,* the orphan, and the widow; if
you no longer shed innocent blood in this
place, or follow strange gods to your own
harm,*b* *7*will I remain with you in this place,
in the land which I gave your fathers long
ago and forever.*c*

*8*But here you are, putting your trust in deceitful words to your own loss! *9*Are you to
steal and murder, commit adultery and perjury, burn incense to Baal, go after strange
gods that you know not,*d* *10*and yet come to
stand before me in this house which bears
my name, and say: "We are safe; we can
commit all these abominations again"?*e*
*11*Has this house which bears my name become in your eyes a den of thieves? I too see
what is being done, says the LORD.*f* *12*You
may go to Shiloh,* which I made the
dwelling place of my name in the beginning.
See what I did to it because of the wickedness of my people Israel.*g* *13*And now, because you have committed all these misdeeds, says the LORD, because you did not
listen, though I spoke to you untiringly; be-

7, 1-15: The temple of the Lord will not serve as a place
of refuge for the Jews against their enemies if they fail to reform their evil ways.

7, 6: The resident alien: specially protected by law; cf Ex
20, 10; Nm 9, 14; 15, 14; Dt 5, 14; 28, 43.

7, 12: Shiloh: original place of worship from the time of
Joshua to that of Samuel. The sanctuary was later rejected by

God and destroyed by the Philistines; cf 1 Sm 1, 9; 4, 3f; Ps
78, 60. 68f.

u: Is 8, 14f. *v:* Jer 1, 15; 5, 15. *w:* Jer 4, 31. *x:* Jer 25, 34; Am
8, 10. *y:* Jer 1, 18. *z:* Jer 18, 11; 26, 13. *a:* Mi 3, 11. *b:* Ex
22, 21-24. *c:* Dt 4, 40. *d:* Jer 44, 17. *e:* Jer 32, 34. *f:* Mt 21,
13. *g:* Jos 18, 1.

cause you did not answer, though I called you, [14]I will do to this house named after me, in which you trust, and to this place which I gave to you and your fathers, just as I did to Shiloh.[h] [15]I will cast you away from me, as I cast away all your brethren, all the offspring of Ephraim.[i]

Abuses in Worship. [16]You, now, do not intercede for this people; raise not in their behalf a pleading prayer![j] Do not urge me, for I will not listen to you. [17]Do you not see what they are doing in the cities of Judah, in the streets of Jerusalem? [18]The children gather wood, their fathers light the fire, and the women knead dough to make cakes for the queen of heaven,* while libations are poured out to strange gods in order to hurt me.[k] [19]Is it I whom they hurt, says the LORD; is it not rather themselves, to their own confusion?[l] [20]See now, says the Lord GOD, my anger and my wrath will pour out upon this place, upon man and beast, upon the trees of the field and the fruits of the earth; it will burn without being quenched.[m]

[21]Thus says the LORD of hosts, the God of Israel: Heap your holocausts upon your sacrifices; eat up the flesh! [22]In speaking to your fathers on the day I brought them out of the land of Egypt, I gave them no command* concerning holocaust or sacrifice. [23]This rather is what I commanded them: Listen to my voice; then I will be your God and you shall be my people. Walk in all the ways that I command you, so that you may prosper.[n]

[24]But they obeyed not, nor did they pay heed. They walked in the hardness of their evil hearts and turned their backs, not their faces, to me.[o] [25]From the day that your fathers left the land of Egypt even to this day, I have sent you untiringly all my servants the prophets.[p] [26]Yet they have not obeyed me nor paid heed; they have stiffened their necks and done worse than their fathers.[q]

[27]When you speak all these words to them, they will not listen to you either; when you call to them, they will not answer you. [28]Say to them: This is the nation which does not listen to the voice of the LORD, its God, or take correction. Faithfulness has disappeared; the word itself is banished from their speech.

[29] Cut off your dedicated hair* and throw it away!
on the heights intone an elegy;
For the LORD has rejected and cast off
the generation that draws down his wrath.[r]

[30]The people of Judah have done what is evil in my eyes, says the LORD. They have defiled the house which bears my name by setting up in it their abominable idols.[s] [31]In the Valley of Ben-hinnom they have built the high place of Topheth to immolate in fire their sons and their daughters, such a thing as I never commanded or had in mind. [32]Therefore, beware! days will come, says the LORD, when Topheth and the Valley of Ben-hinnom will no longer be called such, but rather the Valley of Slaughter. For lack of space, Topheth will be a burial place.[t] [33]The corpses of this people will be food for the birds of the sky and for the beasts of the field, which no one will drive away.[u] [34]In the cities of Judah and in the streets of Jerusalem I will silence the cry of joy, the cry of gladness, the voice of the bridegroom and the voice of the bride; for the land will be turned to rubble.[v]

CHAPTER 8

See RG 302

[1]At that time, says the LORD, the bones of the kings and princes of Judah, the bones of the priests and the prophets, and the bones of the citizens of Jerusalem will be emptied out of their graves[w] [2]and spread out

---

7, 18: Queen of heaven: the Assyro-Babylonian Ishtar, goddess of fertility, whose worship was introduced under King Manasseh and was revived after Josiah's death. Cakes shaped like stars (Ishtar was identified with the planet Venus) were offered in her honor.

7, 22: I gave them no command: right conduct rather than mere external cult was God's will concerning his people (v 23).

7, 29: Dedicated hair: the unshorn hair of the nazirite, regarded as sacred because of a vow, temporary or permanent,

to abstain from cutting or shaving the hair, from contact with a corpse, and from all products of the vine; cf Nm 6, 4-8. The cutting of this hair was a sign of extreme mourning.

---

h: Jer 26, 9. *i:* 1 Kgs 9, 7; 2 Kgs 17, 23. *j:* Jer 11, 14; 14, 11. *k:* Jer 44, 17. 19. *l:* Jb 35, 6. *m:* Jer 36, 29; 2 Kgs 22, 17. *n:* Jer 11, 4; Lv 26, 3. 12. *o:* Jer 17, 23. *p:* 2 Chr 36, 15f; Bar 1, 19. *q:* Jer 19, 15; 2 Chr 30, 8. *r:* Jer 9, 17-21. *s:* Jer 32, 34. *t:* Jer 19, 6; 32, 35. *u:* Jer 16, 4; 34, 20. *v:* Jer 16, 9. *w:* Bar 2, 24.

before the sun and the moon and the whole army of heaven,* which they loved and served, which they followed, consulted, and worshiped. They will not be gathered up for burial, but will lie like dung upon the ground.x ³Death will be preferred to life by all the survivors of this wicked race who remain in any of the places to which I banish them, says the LORD of hosts.

Israel's Conduct Incomprehensible

⁴   Tell them: Thus says the LORD:
When someone falls, does he not rise
     again?
if he goes astray, does he not turn back?
⁵ Why do these people rebel
     with obstinate resistance?
Why do they cling to deceptive idols,
     refuse to turn back?ʸ
⁶ I listen closely:
     they speak what is not true;
No one repents of his wickedness,
     saying "What have I done!"
Everyone keeps on running his course,
     like a steed dashing into battle.ᶻ
⁷ Even the stork in the air
     knows its seasons;
Turtledove, swallow and thrush
     observe their time of return,
But my people do not know
     the ordinance of the LORD.ᵃ
⁸ How can you say, "We are wise,ᵇ
     we have the law of the LORD"?
Why, that has been changed into falsehood
     by the lying pen of the scribes!*
⁹ The wise are confounded,
     dismayed and ensnared;
Since they have rejected the word of the
     LORD,
     of what avail is their wisdom?ᶜ

Shameless in Their Crimes

¹⁰ Therefore, I will give their wives to
     strangers,

their fields to spoilers.
Small and great alike, all are greedy for
     gain,
     prophet and priest, all practice fraud.ᵈ
¹¹ They would repair, as though it were
     nought,
     the injury to the daughter of my
     people:*
"Peace, peace!" they say,
     though there is no peace.ᵉ
¹² They are odious; they have done
     abominable things,
     yet they are not at all ashamed,
     they know not how to blush.
Hence they shall be among those who
     fall;
     in their time of punishment they shall
     go down,
     says the LORD.ᶠ

Threats of Punishment

¹³ I will gather them all in, says the LORD:
     no grapes on the vine,
No figs on the fig trees,
     foliage withered!
¹⁴ Why do we remain here?
     Let us form ranks and enter the walled
     cities,
     to perish there;
For the LORD has wrought our
     destruction,
he has given us poison to drink,
     because we have sinned against the
     LORD.ᵍ
¹⁵ We wait for peace to no avail;
     for a time of healing, but terror comes
     instead.ʰ
¹⁶ From Dan is heard
     the snorting of his steeds;
The neighing of his stallions
     shakes the whole land.
They come devouring the land and all it
     contains,
     the city and those who dwell in it.

8, 2: Army of heaven: the stars, worshiped by the pagan nations and even by the inhabitants of Jerusalem during the reigns of Manasseh and Amon.
8, 8f: Lying pen of the scribes: because the interpretations and ordinances of the scribes ran counter to the word of the Lord.
8, 11: Daughter of my people: the people itself personified as a woman.

x: Dt 4, 19. y: Jer 5, 3; 7, 24. 26. z: Jb 34, 31f. a: Is 1, 3. b: Mal 2, 8; Rom 2, 17-23. c: 1 Cor 3, 20. d: Jer 6, 13; Dt 28, 30.
e: Jer 6, 14. f: Jer 6, 15. g: Jer 9, 14; 23, 15. h: Jer 14, 19.

17 Yes, I will send against you
poisonous snakes,
Against which no charm will work
when they bite you, says the LORD.*i*

The Prophet's Grief over the People's Suffering

18 My grief is incurable,
my heart within me is faint.
19 Listen! the cry of the daughter of my
people,
far and wide in the land!
Is the LORD no longer in Zion,
is her King no longer in her midst?
[Why do they provoke me with their
idols,
with their foreign nonentities?]*j*
20 "The harvest has passed, the summer is
at an end,
and yet we are not safe!"
21 I am broken by the ruin of the daughter
of my people.
I am disconsolate; horror has seized
me.*k*
22 Is there no balm in Gilead,*
no physician there?
Why grows not new flesh
over the wound of the daughter of my
people?*l*
23 Oh, that my head were a spring of water,
my eyes a fountain of tears,
That I might weep day and night
over the slain of the daughter of my
people!

See RG 302

CHAPTER 9

The Corruption of the People

1 Would that I had in the desert
a travelers' lodge!
That I might leave my people
and depart from them.
They are all adulterers,
a faithless band.
2 They ready their tongues like a drawn
bow;
with lying, and not with truth,

they hold forth in the land.
They go from evil to evil,
but me they know not, says the
LORD.
3 Be on your guard, everyone against his
neighbor;
put no trust in any brother.
Every brother apes Jacob, the
supplanter,*
every friend is guilty of slander.
4 Each one deceives the other,
no one speaks the truth.
They have accustomed their tongues to
lying,
and are perverse, and cannot repent.*m*
5 Violence upon violence,
deceit upon deceit:
They refuse to recognize me,
says the LORD.

6 Therefore, thus says the LORD of
hosts:
I will smelt them and test them;
how else should I deal with their
wickedness?
7 A murderous arrow is his tongue,
his mouth utters deceit;
He speaks cordially with his friends,
but in his heart he lays an ambush!*n*
8 For these things, says the LORD,
shall I not punish them?
On a nation such as this
shall I not take vengeance?*o*

Dirge over the Ravaged Land

9 Over the mountains, break out in cries of
lamentation,
over the pasture lands, intone a dirge:
They are scorched, and no man crosses
them,
unheard is the bleat of the flock;
Birds of the air as well as beasts,
all have fled, and are gone.*p*
10 I will turn Jerusalem into a heap of
ruins,
a haunt of jackals;

8, 22: Gilead: noted for its healing balm but unable to heal the moral wound of the people.
9, 3: Jacob, the supplanter: in Hebrew, a play on words. Jacob, as his name indicates ("he supplants"), deprived his brother Esau of his birthright; cf Gn 25, 26. 33.

i: Dt 32, 24. *j:* Dt 32, 21; Mi 4, 9. *k:* Jer 14, 17. *l:* Jer 46, 11. *m:* Jer 12, 6. *n:* Pss 28, 3; 62, 4. *o:* Jer 5, 9. 29. *p:* Jer 4, 25; 12, 4.

The cities of Judah I will make into a
waste,
where no one dwells.*q*

[11] Who is so wise that he can understand
this? Let him to whom the mouth of the
LORD has spoken make it known:

Why is the land ravaged,
scorched like a wasteland
untraversed?*r*

[12] The LORD answered: Because they have
abandoned my law, which I set before them,
and have not followed it or listened to my
voice, [13] but followed rather the hardness of
their hearts and the Baals, as their fathers
had taught them;*s* [14] therefore, thus says the
LORD of hosts, the God of Israel: See now, I
will give them wormwood to eat and poison
to drink.*t* [15] I will scatter them among nations
whom neither they nor their fathers have
known; I will send the sword to pursue them
until I have completely destroyed them.*u*

[16]   Thus says the LORD of hosts:
Attention! tell the wailing women to
come,
summon the best of them;
[17] Let them come quickly
and intone a dirge for us,
That our eyes may be wet with weeping,
our cheeks run with tears.*v*
[18] The dirge is heard from Zion:
Ruined we are, and greatly ashamed;
We must leave the land,
give up our homes!
[19] Hear, you women, the word of the LORD,
let your ears receive his message.
Teach your daughters this dirge,
and each other this lament.
[20] Death has come up through our
windows,
has entered our palaces;
It cuts down the children in the street,
young people in the squares.*w*
[21] The corpses of the slain

lie like dung on a field,
Like sheaves behind the harvester,
with no one to gather them.

True Glory

[22]   Thus says the LORD:
Let not the wise man glory in his
wisdom,
nor the strong man glory in his
strength,
nor the rich man glory in his riches;*x*
[23] But rather, let him who glories, glory in
this,
that in his prudence he knows me,
Knows that I, the LORD, bring about
kindness,
justice and uprightness on the earth;
For with such am I pleased, says the
LORD.

Circumcision Worthless. [24] See, days are
coming, says the LORD, when I will demand
an account of all those circumcised in their
flesh:*y* [25] Egypt and Judah, Edom and the
Ammonites, Moab and the desert dwellers
who shave their temples.* For all these nations, like the whole house of Israel, are uncircumcised in heart.

CHAPTER 10

See RG
302

The Folly of Idolatry. [1] Hear the word
which the LORD speaks to you, O house of
Israel. [2] Thus says the LORD:

Learn not the customs of the nations,
and have no fear of the signs of the
heavens,*
though the nations fear them.*z*
[3] For the cult idols of the nations are
nothing,
wood cut from the forest,
Wrought by craftsmen with the adze,*a*
[4]   adorned with silver and gold.
With nails and hammers they are fastened,
that they may not totter.*b*
[5] Like a scarecrow in a cucumber field are
they,

9, 25: Desert dwellers . . . temples: Arab tribesmen who cut off their hair and shaved their temples in honor of the pagan
god of Dushara. This was forbidden the Israelites (Lv 19, 27).
10, 2: Signs of the heavens: phenomena in the sky superstitiously regarded by the pagans as dire omens.

q: Is 13, 22. *r:* Ps 107, 43; Hos 14, 10. *s:* Jer 7, 24; 19, 4f. *t:* Jer 23, 15. *u:* Lv 26, 33; Dt 28, 36. 64. *v:* Jer 14, 17. *w:* Jer 14,
16. *x:* Prv 21, 30. *y:* Jer 4, 4. *z:* Bar 6, 6. *a:* Wis 13, 11; Is 44, 9. *b:* Is 40, 19; 41, 7.

but far from their inmost thoughts.[x]
[3] You, O Lord, know me, you see me,
  you have found that at heart I am with
    you.[y]
Pick them out like sheep for the
    slaughter,
  set them apart for the day of carnage.*
[4] How long must the earth mourn,
  the green of the whole countryside
    wither?
For the wickedness of those who dwell
    in it
  beasts and birds disappear,
  because they say, "God does not see
    our ways."

[5] If running against men has wearied you,
  how will you race against horses?
And if in a land of peace you fall
    headlong,
  what will you do in the thickets of the
    Jordan?

[6]For even your own brothers, the members
of your father's house, betray you; they have
recruited a force against you. Do not believe
them, even if they are friendly to you in their
words.[z]

[19]*Yet I, like a trusting lamb led to slaughter, had not realized that they were hatching
plots against me: "Let us destroy the tree in
its vigor; let us cut him off from the land of
the living, so that his name will be spoken no
more."[a]

[20] But, you, O LORD of hosts, O just Judge,
    searcher of mind and heart,
  Let me witness the vengeance you take
    on them,
  for to you I have entrusted my cause![b]

[21]Therefore, thus says the LORD concerning the men of Anathoth who seek your life,
saying, "Do not prophesy in the name of the
LORD; else you shall die by our hand."[c]
[22]Therefore, thus says the LORD of hosts: I

am going to punish them. The young men
shall die by the sword; their sons and daughters shall die by famine.[d] [23]None shall be
spared among them, for I will bring misfortune upon the men of Anathoth, the year of
their punishment.[e]

The Lord's Complaint
[7] I abandon my house,
  cast off my heritage;
The beloved of my soul I deliver
  into the hand of her foes.[f]
[8] My heritage has turned on me
  like a lion in the jungle;
Because she has roared against me,
  I treat her as an enemy.[g]
[9] My heritage is a prey for hyenas,
  is surrounded by vultures;
Come, gather together, all you beasts of
    the field,
  come and eat![h]
[10] Many shepherds have ravaged my
    vineyard,
  have trodden my heritage underfoot;
The portion that delighted me they have
    turned
  into a desert waste.[i]
[11] They have made it a mournful waste,
  desolate it lies before me,
Desolate, all the land,
  because no one takes it to heart.
[12] Upon every desert height
  brigands have come up.
The LORD has a sword which consumes
  the land, from end to end:
  no peace for all mankind.[j]
[13] They have sown wheat and reaped
    thorns,
  they have tired themselves out to no
    purpose;
They recoil before their harvest,
  the flaming anger of the LORD.
Judah's Neighbors. [14]Thus says the LORD
against all my evil neighbors* who plunder

12, 3: Jeremiah does not seek private vengeance but the punishment of the wicked by the Lord; cf Jer 20, 12. Nevertheless, the prophet's reaction to persecution shows the difference between the spirit of the Old Testament and the New.
12, 19-23: These verses have been transposed from ch 11.
12, 14: My evil neighbors: nations surrounding Israel, the land belonging to the Lord; cf Is 8, 8.

x: Is 29, 13. y: Jer 17, 18; Jb 23, 10. z: Jer 9, 4. a: Jer 18, 18; 20, 10; Wis 2, 20. b: Jer 15, 15. c: Am 7, 13. 16. d: Jer 18, 21f.
e: Jer 23, 12. f: Ps 78, 62; Lam 2, 1f. g: Ps 106, 40. h: 2 Kgs 24, 2; Is 56, 9. i: Jer 6, 3; Is 63, 18. j: Is 42, 25; 57, 21.

the heritage which I gave my people Israel as their own: See, I will pluck them up from their land; the house of Judah I will pluck up in their midst.*k* 15But after plucking them up, I will pity them again and bring them back, each to his heritage, each to his land.*l* 16And if they carefully learn my people's custom of swearing by my name, "As the LORD lives," they who formerly taught my people to swear by Baal shall be built up in the midst of my people.*m* 17But if they do not obey, I will uproot and destroy that nation entirely, says the LORD.*n*

See RG
302

CHAPTER 13

Judah's Corruption.* 1The LORD said to me: Go buy yourself a linen loincloth; wear it on your loins, but do not put it in water. 2I bought the loincloth, as the LORD commanded, and put it on. 3A second time the word of the LORD came to me thus: 4Take the loincloth which you bought and are wearing, and go now to the Parath; there hide it in a cleft of the rock. 5Obedient to the LORD's command, I went to the Parath and buried the loincloth. 6After a long interval, he said to me: Go now to the Parath and fetch the loincloth which I told you to hide there. 7Again I went to the Parath, sought out and took the loincloth from the place where I had hid it. But it was rotted, good for nothing! 8Then the message came to me from the LORD: 9Thus says the LORD: So also I will allow the pride of Judah to rot, the great pride of Jerusalem.*o* 10This wicked people who refuse to obey my words, who walk in the stubbornness of their hearts, and follow strange gods to serve and adore them, shall be like this loincloth which is good for nothing.*p* 11For, as close as the loincloth clings to a man's loins, so had I made the whole house of Israel and the whole house of Judah cling to me, says the LORD; to be my people, my renown, my praise, my beauty. But they did not listen.*q*

The Broken Wineflask. 12Now speak to them this word: Thus says the LORD, the God of Israel: Every wineflask is meant to be filled with wine. If they reply, "Do we not know that every wineflask is meant to be filled with wine?" 13say to them: Thus says the LORD: Beware! I am filling with drunkenness all the inhabitants of this land, the kings who succeed to David's throne, the priests and prophets, and all the citizens of Jerusalem.*r* 14I will dash them against each other, fathers and sons together, says the LORD; I will show no compassion, I will not spare or pity, but will destroy them.*s*

A Last Warning

15 Give ear, listen humbly,
    for the LORD speaks.
16 Give glory to the LORD, your God,
    before it grows dark;
Before your feet stumble
    on darkening mountains;
Before the light you look for turns to
    darkness,
    changes into black clouds.*t*
17 If you do not listen to this in your pride,
    I will weep in secret many tears;
My eyes will run with tears
    for the LORD's flock, led away to
    exile.*u*

Exile

18 Say to the king and to the queen mother:
    come down from your throne;
From your heads fall
    your magnificent crowns.*v*
19 The cities of the Negeb are besieged,
    with no one to relieve them;
All Judah is banished
    in universal exile.

Jerusalem's Disgrace

20 Lift up your eyes and see
    men coming from the north.
Where is the flock entrusted to you,

13, 1-11: This is probably a vision of the prophet symbolizing the religious corruption of Judah at the hands of the Babylonians, represented here by the river Parath, the Euphrates; though a spring of the same name, northeast of Anathoth, may be directly meant.

k: 2 Kgs 24, 2.   *l:* Am 9, 14.   *m:* Dt 6, 13.   *n:* Is 60, 12.   *o:* Prv 16, 18.   *p:* Jer 2, 20; 7, 24; 16, 11.   *q:* Ex 19, 5; Dt 26, 18f.   *r:* Jer 25, 15-18; Is 51, 17.   *s:* Jer 19, 10f.   *t:* Prv 4, 18f; Is 5, 30; Am 8, 9.   *u:* Jer 14, 17; Ps 119, 136.   *v:* Jer 22, 26; 2 Kgs 24, 12. 15.

the sheep that were your glory?[w]

²¹ What will you say when they place as
rulers over you
those whom you taught to be your
lovers?
Will not pangs seize you
like those of a woman giving birth?[x]

²² If you ask in your heart
why these things befall you:
For your great guilt your skirts are
stripped away
and you are violated.[y]

²³ Can the Ethiopian change his skin?
the leopard his spots?
As easily would you be able to do good,
accustomed to evil as you are.[z]

²⁴ I will scatter them like chaff that flies
when the desert wind blows.[a]

²⁵ This is your lot, the portion measured out
to you
from me, says the LORD.
Because you have forgotten me,
and trusted in the lying idol,[b]

²⁶ I now will strip off your skirts from
you,
so that your shame will appear.[c]

²⁷ Your adulteries, your neighings,
your shameless prostitutions:
On the hills in the highlands
I see these horrible crimes of yours.
Woe to you, Jerusalem, how long will it
yet be
before you become clean![d]

See RG
302

CHAPTER 14

The Great Drought. ¹The word of the
LORD that came to Jeremiah concerning the
drought:[e]

² Judah mourns,
her gates are lifeless;
Her people sink down in mourning:
from Jerusalem ascends a cry of
anguish.[f]

³ The nobles send their servants for water,
but when they come to the cisterns
They find no water
and return with empty jars.[g]

Ashamed, despairing, they cover their
heads

⁴ because of the stricken soil;
Because there is no rain in the land
the farmers are ashamed, they cover
their heads.[h]

⁵ Even the hind in the field deserts her
offspring
because there is no grass.

⁶ The wild asses stand on the bare heights,
gasping for breath like jackals;
Their eyes grow dim,
because there is no vegetation to be
seen.

⁷ Even though our crimes bear witness
against us,
take action, O LORD, for the honor of
your name—
Even though our rebellions are many,
though we have sinned against you.[i]

⁸ O Hope of Israel, O LORD,
our savior in time of need!
Why should you be a stranger in this
land,
like a traveler who has stopped but for
a night?

⁹ Why are you like a man dumbfounded,
a champion who cannot save?
You are in our midst, O LORD,
your name we bear:
do not forsake us![j]

¹⁰ Thus says the LORD of this
people:
They so love to wander
that they do not spare their feet.
The LORD has no pleasure in them;
now he remembers their guilt,
and will punish their sins.[k]

¹¹Then the LORD said to me: Do not intercede for this people.[l] ¹²If they fast, I will not
listen to their supplication. If they offer
holocausts or cereal offerings, I will not accept them. Rather, I will destroy them with
the sword, famine, and pestilence.[m]

¹³Ah! Lord GOD, I replied, it is the prophets who say to them, "You shall not see the

---

w: Jer 6, 22f.   x: 2 Kgs 16, 7.   y: Is 47, 2f.   z: Ps 55, 20.   a: Pss 1, 4; 83, 14.   b: Jb 20, 29.   c: Ez 16, 32.   d: Jer 2, 20.   e: Lv
26, 19f.   f: Is 3, 26.   g: Am 4, 8.   h: Dt 28, 23.   i: Dn 9, 4-14.   j: Is 59, 1f; 63, 19.   k: Jer 2, 25.   l: Jer 11, 14; Ex 32, 10.   m: Jer
6, 20; Is 1, 11. 13.

sword; famine shall not befall you. Indeed, I will give you lasting peace in this place."[n]

[14]Lies these prophets utter in my name, the LORD said to me. I did not send them; I gave them no command nor did I speak to them. Lying visions, foolish divination, dreams of their own imagination, they prophesy to you.[o] [15]Therefore, thus says the LORD: Concerning the prophets who prophesy in my name, though I did not send them; who say, "Sword and famine shall not befall this land": by the sword and famine shall these prophets meet their end.[p] [16]The people to whom they prophesy shall be cast out into the streets of Jerusalem by famine and the sword. No one shall bury them, their wives, their sons, or their daughters, for I will pour out upon them their own wickedness.[q] [17]Speak to them this word:

Let my eyes stream with tears
 day and night, without rest,
Over the great destruction which
   overwhelms
 the virgin daughter of my people,
 over her incurable wound.[r]
[18] If I walk out into the field,
 look! those slain by the sword;
If I enter the city,
 look! those consumed by hunger.
Even the prophet and the priest
 forage in a land they know not.

[19] Have you cast Judah off completely?
 Is Zion loathsome to you?
Why have you struck us a blow
 that cannot be healed?
We wait for peace, to no avail;
 for a time of healing, but terror comes
   instead.[s]
[20] We recognize, O LORD, our wickedness,
 the guilt of our fathers;
 that we have sinned against you.[t]
[21] For your name's sake spurn us not,
 disgrace not the throne of your glory;
 remember your covenant with us, and
   break it not.[u]

[22] Among the nations' idols is there any that
   gives rain?
 Or can the mere heavens send
   showers?
Is it not you alone, O LORD,
 our God, to whom we look?
 You alone have done all these things.[v]

CHAPTER 15

See RG
302

[1]The LORD said to me: Even if Moses and Samuel stood before me, my heart would not turn toward this people. Send them away from me.[w] [2]If they ask you where they should go, tell them, Thus says the LORD: Whoever is marked for death, to death; whoever is marked for the sword, to the sword; whoever is marked for famine, to famine; whoever is marked for captivity, to captivity.[x] [3]Four kinds of scourge I have decreed against them, says the LORD: the sword to slay them; dogs to drag them about; the birds of the sky and the beasts of the earth to devour and destroy them.[y] [4]And I will make them an object of horror to all the kingdoms of the earth because of what Manasseh, son of Hezekiah, king of Judah, did in Jerusalem.[z]

Scene of Tragedy
[5] Who will pity you, Jerusalem,
 who will console you?
Who will stop to ask
 about your welfare?[a]
[6] You have disowned me, says the LORD,
 turned your back upon me;
And so I stretched out my hand to
   destroy you,
 I was weary of sparing you.[b]
[7] I winnowed them with the fan
 in every city gate.
I destroyed my people through
   bereavement;
 they returned not from their evil
   ways.[c]
[8] Their widows were more numerous
   before me
 than the sands of the sea.

n: Jer 4, 10; 5, 12. o: Jer 5, 31; 23, 16. p: Jer 5, 12f. q: Jer 7, 33; 19, 7. r: Jer 9, 17. s: Jer 8, 15; 2 Chr 36, 16. t: Ps 106, 6; Dn 9, 5. 8. u: Jer 14, 7; Lv 26, 44; Ps 25, 11. v: Jer 5, 24; Zec 10, 1. w: Ps 99, 6; Ez 14, 14. 16. x: Jer 14, 12; Ez 5, 12. y: Ez 14, 21. z: Jer 24, 9; 2 Kgs 21, 11-16; 23, 26; 24, 3f. a: Is 51, 19. b: Am 7, 8. c: Is 41, 16.

I brought against the mother of youths
  the spoiler at midday;
Suddenly I struck her
  with anguish and terror.
⁹ The mother of seven swoons away,
  gasping out her life;
Her sun sets in full day,
  she is disgraced, despairing.
Their survivors I will give to the sword
  before their enemies, says the LORD.ᵈ

Jeremiah's Complaint

¹⁰ Woe to me, mother, that you gave me
  birth!
  a man of strife and contention to all
    the land!
I neither borrow nor lend,
  yet all curse me.ᵉ
¹¹ Tell me, LORD, have I not served you for
  their good?
Have I not interceded with you
  in the time of misfortune and anguish?ᶠ*
¹⁵   You know I have.
Remember me, LORD, visit me,
  and avenge me on my persecutors.
Because of your long-suffering banish
  me not;
  know that for you I have borne insult.ᵍ
¹⁶ When I found your words, I devoured
  them;
  they became my joy and the happiness
    of my heart,
Because I bore your name,
  O LORD, God of hosts.
¹⁷ I did not sit celebrating
  in the circle of merrymakers;
Under the weight of your hand I sat alone
  because you filled me with
    indignation.ʰ
¹⁸ Why is my pain continuous,
  my wound incurable, refusing to be
    healed?
You have indeed become for me a
  treacherous brook,*

whose waters do not abide!ⁱ
¹⁹   Thus the LORD answered me:
If you repent, so that I restore you,
  in my presence you shall stand;
If you bring forth the precious without
    the vile,
  you shall be my mouthpiece.
Then it shall be they who turn to you,
  and you shall not turn to them;
²⁰ And I will make you toward this people
  a solid wall of brass.
Though they fight against you,
  they shall not prevail,
For I am with you,
  to deliver and rescue you, says the
    LORD.ʲ
²¹ I will free you from the hand of the
  wicked,
  and rescue you from the grasp of the
    violent.

CHAPTER 16

See RG 302

Jeremiah's Life a Warning. ¹This message came to me from the LORD: ²Do not marry any woman; you shall not have sons or daughters in this place, ³for thus says the LORD concerning the sons and daughters who will be born in this place, the mothers who will give them birth, the fathers who will beget them in this land: ⁴Of deadly disease they shall die. Unlamented and unburied they will lie like dung on the ground. Sword and famine will make an end of them, and their corpses will become food for the birds of the sky and the beasts of the field.ᵏ

⁵Go not into a house of mourning, the LORD continued: go not there to lament or offer sympathy. For I have withdrawn my friendship from this people, says the LORD, my kindness and my pity.ˡ ⁶They shall die, the great and the lowly, in this land, and shall go unburied and unlamented.* No one will gash himself or shave his head for them.ᵐ ⁷They will not break bread with the be-

---

15, 12-14: These verses are omitted because v 12 is a dittography of 17, 1. Verses 13-14 are a dittography of 17, 3 f.

15, 18: A treacherous brook: that dries up when its waters are needed. The prophet complains that he cannot rely on God with unfailing assurance of his assistance.

16, 6f: These verses refer to popular mourning practices, sometimes connected with pagan superstition; cf Dt 14, 1f.

---

d: 1 Sm 2, 5. *e:* Jer 20, 14. *f:* Jer 39, 11-14. *g:* Jer 11, 20; 12, 3; Ps 69, 8. *h:* Ps 25, 4. *i:* Jer 14, 19; 30, 15. *j:* Jer 1, 18; 6, 27.
k: Jer 7, 33; 22, 18. *l:* Ez 24, 16f. *m:* Lv 19, 28; Dt 14, 1.

reaved to console them in their bereavement; they will not give them the cup of consolation to drink over the death of father or mother.[n]

[8]Enter not a house where people are celebrating, to sit with them eating and drinking. [9]For thus says the LORD of hosts, the God of Israel: Before your very eyes and during your lifetime I will silence from this place the cry of joy and the cry of gladness, the voice of the bridegroom and the voice of the bride.[o]

[10]When you proclaim all these words to this people and they ask you: "Why has the LORD pronounced all these great evils against us? What is our crime? What sin have we committed against the LORD, our God?"[p] — [11q]you shall answer them: It is because your fathers have forsaken me, says the LORD, and followed strange gods, which they served and worshiped; but me they have forsaken, and my law they have not observed. [12]And you have done worse than your fathers. Here you are, every one of you, walking in the hardness of his evil heart instead of listening to me.[r] [13]I will cast you out of this land into a land that neither you nor your fathers have known; there you can serve strange gods day and night, because I will not grant you my mercy.

Return from Exile. [14]However, days will surely come, says the LORD, when it will no longer be said, "As the LORD lives, who brought the Israelites out of Egypt";[s] [15]but rather, "As the LORD lives, who brought the Israelites out of the land of the north and out of all the countries to which he had banished them." I will bring them back to the land which I gave their fathers.[t]

Double Punishment. [16]Look! I will send many fishermen, says the LORD, to catch them. After that, I will send many hunters to hunt them out from every mountain and hill and from the clefts of the rocks.[u] [17]For my eyes are upon all their ways; they are not hidden from me, nor does their guilt escape my view.[v] [18]I will at once repay them double for their crime and their sin of profaning my land with their detestable corpses of idols, and filling my heritage with their abominations.[w]

Conversion of the Heathen

[19] O LORD, my strength, my fortress,
  my refuge in the day of distress!
To you will the nations come
  from the ends of the earth, and say,
"Mere frauds are the heritage of our
    fathers,
  empty idols of no use."[x]
[20] Can man make for himself gods?
  These are not gods.[y]
[21] Look, then: I will give them knowledge;
  this time I will leave them in no doubt
Of my strength and my power:
  they shall know that my name is LORD.[z]

CHAPTER 17

See RG
302

The Sin of Judah and
Its Punishment

[1] The sin of Judah is written
  with an iron stylus,
Engraved with a diamond point
  upon the tablets of their hearts.[a]

[And the horns of their altars, [2]when their sons remember their altars and their sacred poles, beside the green trees, on the high hills, [3]the peaks in the highland.]

Your wealth and all your treasures
  I will give as spoil.
In recompense for all your sins
  throughout your borders,
[4] You will relinquish your hold on your
    heritage
  which I have given you.
I will enslave you to your enemies
  in a land that you know not:
For a fire has been kindled by my wrath
  that will burn forever.[b]

True Wisdom

[5]   Thus says the LORD:
Cursed is the man who trusts in human
    beings,

---

n: Ez 24, 17. o: Jer 7, 34; 25, 10. p: Jer 2, 35; 5, 19; 13, 22. q: Jer 22, 9; Dt 29, 25. r: Jer 7, 24ff. s: Jer 23, 7f. t: Jer 24, 6. u: 2 Kgs 24, 2; Lam 4, 19. v: Jer 32, 19; Jb 34, 21. w: Is 40, 2. x: Jer 2, 11; Is 2, 2f. y: Jer 2, 11; Gal 4, 8. z: Am 5, 8. a: Jb 19, 24. b: Jer 5, 19; Dt 32, 22.

who seeks his strength in flesh,
whose heart turns away from the
LORD.^c

⁶ He is like a barren bush in the desert
that enjoys no change of season,
But stands in a lava waste,
a salt and empty earth.

⁷ Blessed is the man who trusts in the
LORD,
whose hope is the LORD.^d

⁸ He is like a tree planted beside the waters
that stretches out its roots to the
stream:
It fears not the heat when it comes,
its leaves stay green;
In the year of drought it shows no
distress,
but still bears fruit.^e

⁹ More tortuous than all else is the human
heart,
beyond remedy; who can understand
it?

¹⁰ I, the LORD, alone probe the mind
and test the heart,
To reward everyone according to his ways,
according to the merit of his deeds.^f

¹¹ A partridge that mothers a brood not her
own
is the man who acquires wealth
unjustly:
In midlife it will desert him;
in the end he is only a fool.^g

The Source of Life

¹² A throne of glory, exalted from the
beginning,
such is our holy place.^h

¹³ O hope of Israel, O LORD!
all who forsake you shall be in
disgrace;
The rebels in the land shall be put to
shame;
they have forsaken the source of living
waters
[the LORD].ⁱ

Prayer for Vengeance

¹⁴ Heal me, LORD, that I may be healed;
save me, that I may be saved,
for it is you whom I praise.

¹⁵ See how they say to me,
"Where is the word of the LORD?
Let it come to pass!"^j

¹⁶ Yet I did not press you to send calamity;
the day without remedy I have not
desired.
You know what passed my lips;
it is present before you.

¹⁷ Do not be my ruin,
you, my refuge in the day of
misfortune.^k

¹⁸ Let my persecutors, not me, be
confounded;
let them, not me, be broken.
Bring upon them the day of misfortune,
crush them with repeated destruction.^l

Observance of the Sabbath.
¹⁹Thus said the LORD to me: Go, stand at the Gate of Benjamin,* where the kings of Judah enter and leave, and at the other gates of Jerusalem.^m ²⁰There say to them: Hear the word of the LORD, you kings of Judah, and all Judah, and all you citizens of Jerusalem who enter these gates! ²¹Thus says the LORD: As you love your lives, take care not to carry burdens on the sabbath day, to bring them in through the gates of Jerusalem.ⁿ ²²Bring no burden from your homes on the sabbath. Do no work whatever, but keep holy the sabbath, as I commanded your fathers,^o ²³though they did not listen or give ear, but stiffened their necks so as not to hear or take correction.^p ²⁴If you obey me wholeheartedly, says the LORD, and carry no burden through the gates of this city on the sabbath, keeping the sabbath holy and abstaining from all work on it,^q ²⁵then, through the gates of this city, kings who sit upon the throne of David will continue to enter, riding in their chariots or upon their horses, along with their princes, and the men

---

17, 19: The Gate of Benjamin: probably the northern gate of the temple area and city wall of Jerusalem; cf Jer 20, 2; 37, 12; 38, 7.

c: Ps 146, 2f.   d: Ps 1, 3.   e: Is 58, 11.   f: Jer 32, 19; 1 Sm 16, 7; Eccl 12, 14.   g: Prv 13, 11; Lk 12, 20.   h: Jer 14, 21.   i: Jer 2, 13.   j: Is 5, 19; 2 Pt 3, 4.   k: Jer 16, 19.   l: Jer 15, 15; 18, 20-23; Ps 35, 5f.   m: Jer 7, 2.   n: Neh 13, 15-19.   o: Ex 20, 8; 23, 12.   p: Jer 5, 3; 7, 24.   q: Is 58, 14.

of Judah, and the citizens of Jerusalem. This city will remain inhabited forever.*r* *26*To it people will come from the cities of Judah and the neighborhood of Jerusalem, from the land of Benjamin and from the foothills, from the hill country and the Negeb, to bring holocausts and sacrifices, cereal offerings and incense and thank offerings to the house of the LORD.*s* *27*But if you do not obey me and keep holy the sabbath, if you carry burdens and come through the gates of Jerusalem on the sabbath, I will set unquenchable fire to its gates, which will consume the palaces of Jerusalem.*t*

CHAPTER 18

See RG 302

The Potter's Vessel.* *1*This word came to Jeremiah from the LORD: *2*Rise up, be off to the potter's house; there I will give you my message. *3*I went down to the potter's house and there he was, working at the wheel. *4*Whenever the object of clay which he was making turned out badly in his hand, he tried again, making of the clay another object of whatever sort he pleased.*u* *5*Then the word of the Lord came to me: *6*Can I not do to you, house of Israel, as this potter has done? says the LORD. Indeed, like clay in the hand of the potter, so are you in my hand, house of Israel.*v* *7w*Sometimes I threaten to uproot and tear down and destroy a nation or a kingdom. *8*But if that nation which I have threatened turns from its evil, I also repent of the evil which I threatened to do.*x* *9*Sometimes, again, I promise to build up and plant a nation or a kingdom. *10*But if that nation does what is evil in my eyes, refusing to obey my voice, I repent of the good with which I promised to bless it.*y*

*11*And now, tell this to the men of Judah and the citizens of Jerusalem: Thus says the LORD: Take care! I am fashioning evil against you and making a plan. Return, each of you, from his evil way; reform your ways

and your deeds.*z* *12*But they will say, "No use! We will follow our own devices; each one of us will behave according to the stubbornness of his evil heart!"*a*

Judah's Apostasy Unnatural

13 Therefore thus says the LORD:
Ask among the nations—
  who has ever heard the like?
Truly horrible things
  has virgin Israel done!*b*
14 Does the snow of Lebanon*
  desert the rocky heights?
Do the gushing waters dry up
  that flow fresh down the mountains?
15 Yet my people have forgotten me:
  they burn incense to a thing that does
    not exist.
They stumble out of their ways,
  the paths of old,
To travel on bypaths,
  not the beaten track.*c*
16 Their land shall be turned into a desert,
  an object of lasting ridicule:
All passers-by will be amazed,
  will shake their heads.*d*
17 Like the east wind, I will scatter them
  before their enemies;
I will show them my back, not my face,
  in their day of disaster.*e*

Another Prayer for Vengeance. *18*"Come," they said, "let us contrive a plot against Jeremiah. It will not mean the loss of instruction from the priests, nor of counsel from the wise, nor of messages from the prophets. And so, let us destroy him by his own tongue; let us carefully note his every word."*f*

19 Heed me, O LORD,
  and listen to what my adversaries say.
20 Must good be repaid with evil
  that they should dig a pit to take my
    life?
Remember that I stood before you

18, 1-12: The lesson of the potter is not that God deals arbitrarily with his people, but that he is almighty to destroy or restore, accordingly as they disobey him or fulfill his plans.

18, 14: Lebanon: here apparently including Mount Hermon, whose snow-capped peak can be seen from parts of Palestine all year round. The prophet contrasts the certainties of nature with Israel's unnatural desertion of the Lord for idols (v 15).

r: Jer 22, 4. *s:* Jer 32, 44. *t:* Ez 22, 8. *u:* Rom 9, 20f. *v:* Wis 15, 7; Is 45, 9. *w:* Jer 1, 10. *x:* Jer 26, 3; Is 55, 7; Ez 18, 21. 27. *y:* Nm 14, 22f. *z:* Jer 7, 3; 25, 5; 35, 15. *a:* Jer 2, 25; 7, 24. *b:* Jer 2, 10f; 5, 30. *c:* Jer 2, 13. 32. *d:* Jer 19, 8; Lv 26, 32; 1 Kgs 9, 8. *e:* Prv 1, 24-31. *f:* Jer 11, 19; Ps 35, 15f.

to speak in their behalf,
to turn away your wrath from them.g

21 So now, deliver their children to famine,h
do away with them by the sword.
Let their wives be made childless and
widows;
let their men die of pestilence,
their young men be slain by the sword
in battle.*

22 May cries be heard from their homes,
when suddenly you send plunderers
against them.
For they have dug a pit to capture me,
they have hid snares for my feet;

23 But you, O LORD, know
all their plans to slay me.
Forgive not their crime,
blot not out their sin in your sight!
Let them go down before you,
proceed against them in the time of
your anger.i

See RG
302

CHAPTER 19

Symbol of the Potter's Flask. 1Thus said the LORD: Go, buy a potter's earthen flask. Take along some of the elders of the people and of the priests, 2and go out toward the Valley of Ben-hinnom, at the entrance of the Potsherd Gate;* there proclaim the words which I will speak to you: 3Listen to the word of the LORD, kings of Judah and citizens of Jerusalem: Thus says the LORD of hosts, the God of Israel: I am going to bring such evil upon this place that all who hear of it will feel their ears tingle. 4This is because they have forsaken me and alienated this place by burning in it incense to strange gods which neither they nor their fathers knew; and the kings of Judah have filled this place with the blood of the innocent.j 5They have built high places for Baal to immolate their sons in fire as holocausts to Baal: such a thing as I neither commanded nor spoke of, nor did it ever enter my mind.k 6Therefore, days will come, says the

LORD, when this place will no longer be called Topheth, or the Valley of Ben-hinnom, but rather, the Valley of Slaughter.l 7In this place I will foil the plan of Judah and Jerusalem; I will make them fall by the sword before their enemies, by the hand of those that seek their lives. Their corpses I will give as food to the birds of the sky and the beasts of the field.m 8I will make this city an object of amazement and derision. Because of all its wounds, every passer-by will be amazed and will catch his breath. 9I will have them eat the flesh of their sons and daughters; they shall eat one another's flesh during the strict siege by which their enemies and those who seek their lives will confine them.n

10And you shall break the flask in the sight of the men who went with you, 11and say to them: Thus says the LORD of hosts: Thus will I smash this people and this city, as one smashes a clay pot so that it cannot be repaired. And Topheth shall be a burial place, for lack of place to bury elsewhere.o 12Thus I will do to this place and to its inhabitants, says the LORD; I will make this city like Topheth.p 13And the houses of Jerusalem and the palaces of the kings of Judah shall be defiled like the place of Topheth, all the houses upon whose roofs they burnt incense to the whole host of heaven and poured out libations to strange gods.q

14When Jeremiah returned from Topheth, where the LORD had sent him to prophesy, he stood in the court of the house of God and said to all the people:r 15Thus says the LORD of hosts, the God of Israel: I will surely bring upon this city all the evil with which I threatened it, because they have stiffened their necks and have not obeyed my words.s

CHAPTER 20

See RG
302

1Jeremiah was heard prophesying these things by the priest Pashhur,t son of Immer, chief officer in the house of the LORD.*

18, 21: In the Old Testament a man's family was regarded as part of his personality, to be rewarded or punished along with him; cf Jos 7, 24ff.

19, 2: Potsherd Gate: in the south wall of Jerusalem, through which potsherds and other refuse were carried to the Valley of Ben-hinnom.

20, 1: Chief officer in the house of the LORD: head of the temple police; cf Jer 29, 26. By entering the temple court (Jer 19, 14), Jeremiah had put himself under Pashhur's jurisdiction.

g: Ps 35, 12. h: Ps 109, 9f. i: Neh 4, 5; Pss 35, 4; 37, 32f.
j: Jer 1, 16; 2 Kgs 21, 16; 24, 4. k: Jer 7, 31f; 32, 35. l: Jer 7, 32. m: Jer 7, 33. n: Lv 26, 29. o: Jer 7, 32. p: 2 Kgs 23, 10.
q: Jer 32, 29. r: Jer 26, 2. s: Jer 7, 26; Prv 29, 1. t: Jer 21, 1.

²So he had the prophet scourged and placed in the stocks at the upper Gate of Benjamin in the house of the LORD.ᵘ ³The next morning, after Pashhur had released Jeremiah from the stocks, the prophet said to him:ᵛ Instead of Pashhur, the LORD will name you "Terror on every side."* ⁴For thus says the LORD: Indeed, I will deliver you to terror, you and all your friends. Your own eyes shall see them fall by the sword of their enemies. All Judah I will deliver to the king of Babylon,* who shall take them captive to Babylon or slay them with the sword. ⁵All the wealth of this city, all it has toiled for and holds dear, all the treasures of the kings of Judah, I will give as plunder into the hands of their foes, who shall seize it and carry it away to Babylon.ʷ ⁶You, Pashhur, and all the members of your household shall go into exile. To Babylon you shall go, you and all your friends; there you shall die and be buried, because you have prophesied lies to them.ˣ

Jeremiah's Interior Crisis

⁷ You duped me,* O LORD, and I let myself be duped;
   you were too strong for me, and you triumphed.
All the day I am an object of laughter;
   everyone mocks me.
⁸ Whenever I speak, I must cry out,
   violence and outrage is my message;
The word of the LORD has brought me
   derision and reproach all the day.
⁹ I say to myself, I will not mention him,
   I will speak in his name no more.
But then it becomes like fire burning in my heart,
   imprisoned in my bones;
I grow weary holding it in,
   I cannot endure it.ʸ
¹⁰ Yes, I hear the whisperings of many:

"Terror on every side!
   Denounce! let us denounce him!"
All those who were my friends
   are on the watch for any misstep of mine.
"Perhaps he will be trapped; then we can prevail,
   and take our vengeance on him."ᶻ
¹¹ But the LORD is with me, like a mighty champion:
   my persecutors will stumble, they will not triumph.
In their failure they will be put to utter shame,
   to lasting, unforgettable confusion.ᵃ
¹² O LORD of hosts, you who test the just,
   who probe mind and heart,
Let me witness the vengeance you take on them,
   for to you I have entrusted my cause.ᵇ
¹³ Sing to the LORD,
   praise the LORD,
For he has rescued the life of the poor
   from the power of the wicked!ᶜ

¹⁴ Cursed be the day*
   on which I was born!
May the day my mother gave me birth
   never be blessed!ᵈ
¹⁵ Cursed be the man who brought the news
   to my father, saying,
"A child, a son, has been born to you!"
   filling him with great joy.
¹⁶ Let that man be like the cities
   which the LORD relentlessly overthrew;
Let him hear war cries in the morning,
   battle alarms at noonday,ᵉ
¹⁷   because he did not dispatch me in the womb!
Then my mother would have been my grave,
   her womb confining me forever.ᶠ

20, 3: Terror on every side: Pashhur will share the fate of doomed Jerusalem and will experience personally all that the people as a whole have had to endure.

20, 4: Babylon: mentioned here for the first time as the land of exile. The prophecy probably dates from after 605 B.C., when Nebuchadnezzar defeated Egypt and made the Chaldean empire dominant in Syria and Palestine.

20, 7: You duped me: to be understood in the light of Jeremiah's intimate dealings with God; cf Jer 15, 18.

20, 14-18: Deception, sorrow and terror have brought the prophet close to the point of despair; nevertheless he has expressed his utmost confidence in the triumph of God's will (vv 11ff); cf Jb 3, 3-12.

u: Jer 29, 26. v: Jer 6, 25. w: 2 Kgs 20, 17; 24, 12-16. x: Jer 14, 13f; 28, 15. y: Jer 6, 11; Jb 32, 18. z: Jb 19, 19; Ps 31, 13; Lk 20, 20. a: Jer 1, 8; 15, 20. b: Jer 11, 20. c: Pss 35, 9f; 109, 30f. d: Jer 15, 10; Jb 3, 1-10; 10, 18. e: Gn 19, 25; Is 13, 19. f: Jb 3, 10f; 10, 19.

[18] Why did I come forth from the womb,
to see sorrow and pain,
to end my days in shame?[g]

III: Oracles in the Last Years of Jerusalem

See RG 302–3

CHAPTER 21

Fate of Zedekiah and Jerusalem. [1]The message which came to Jeremiah from the LORD when King Zedekiah* sent him Pashhur, son of Malchiah, and the priest Zephaniah, son of Maaseiah, with this request: [2]Inquire for us of the LORD, because Nebuchadnezzar, king of Babylon, is attacking us. Perhaps the LORD will deal with us according to all his wonderful works, so that he will withdraw from us. [3]But Jeremiah answered them: This is what you shall report to Zedekiah: [4]Thus says the LORD, the God of Israel: I will turn back in your hands the weapons with which you intend to fight the king of Babylon and the Chaldeans who besiege you outside the walls. These weapons I will pile up in the midst of this city,[h] [5]and I myself will fight against you with outstretched hand and mighty arm, in anger, and wrath, and great rage![i] [6]I will strike the inhabitants of this city, both man and beast; they shall die in a great pestilence.[j] [7]After that, says the LORD, I will hand over Zedekiah, king of Judah, and his ministers and the people in this city who survive pestilence, sword, and famine, into the hand of Nebuchadnezzar, king of Babylon, into the hands of their enemies and those who seek their lives. He shall strike them with the edge of the sword, without quarter, without

pity or mercy.[k] [8]And to this people you shall say: Thus says the LORD: See, I am giving you a choice between life and death.[l] [9]Whoever remains in this city shall die by the sword or famine or pestilence. But whoever leaves and surrenders to the besieging Chaldeans shall live and have his life as booty. [10]For I have turned against this city, for its woe and not for its good, says the LORD. It shall be given into the power of the king of Babylon who shall burn it with fire.*

Oracles regarding the Kings

[11] To the royal house of Judah:*
Hear the word of the LORD, [12]O house of David!
Thus says the LORD:
Each morning dispense justice,
rescue the oppressed from the hand of the oppressor,
Lest my fury break out like fire
which burns without being quenched,
because of the evil of your deeds.[m]
[13] Beware! I am against you, Valley-site,
Rock of the Plain,* says the LORD.
You who say, "Who will attack us,
who can penetrate our retreats?"
[14] I will punish you, says the LORD,
as your deeds deserve!
I will kindle a fire in its forest*
that shall devour all its surroundings.[n]

CHAPTER 22

See RG 302–3

[1]The LORD told me this: Go down to the palace of the king of Judah and there deliver this message: [2]You shall say: Listen to the word of the LORD, king of Judah, who sit on the throne of David, you, your ministers, and your people that enter by these gates![o]

21, 1: Zedekiah: brother of Jehoiakim, appointed king by Nebuchadnezzar after he had carried Jehoiachin away to captivity (2 Kgs 24, 17). Pashhur: different from the one in Jer 20, 1ff but also one of Jeremiah's enemies; cf Jer 38, 1. 4.

21, 10: Jeremiah consistently pointed out the uselessness of resistance to Babylon, since the Lord had delivered Judah to Nebuchadnezzar (Jer 27, 6). Because of this the prophet was denounced and imprisoned as a traitor (Jer 37, 13f).

21, 11—23, 8: This section contains an editor's collection of Jeremiah's oracles against the kings of Judah. They are placed in the chronological order of the kings, and are prefaced by the oracles against the kings of Judah in general (Jer 21, 11—22, 9).

21, 13: Valley-site, Rock of the Plain: Mount Zion, surrounded by valleys, was regarded by the royal house as impregnable. Despite this natural fortification, God shows derisively that it is no more than a rock rising from the plain, undefendable against the attack of his fury.

21, 14: Its forest: probably the royal palace, built of cedar wood; cf Jer 22, 14; in 1 Kgs 7, 2 the armory of Solomon's palace is called "the house of the forest of Lebanon."

g: Jb 14, 1. h: Jer 37, 8ff. i: Is 63, 10; Lam 2, 4f. j: Jer 16, 4.
k: Jer 24, 8ff; Dt 28, 49f. l: Jer 21, 9; Dt 30, 15. 19. m: Jer 4, 4; 22, 3; Zec 7, 9. n: 2 Kgs 25, 9; 2 Chr 36, 19. o: Jer 17, 20.

³Thus says the LORD: Do what is right and just. Rescue the victim from the hand of his oppressor. Do not wrong or oppress the resident alien, the orphan, or the widow, and do not shed innocent blood in this place.ᵖ ⁴If you carry out these commands, kings who succeed to the throne of David will continue to enter the gates of this palace, riding in chariots or mounted on horses, with their ministers, and their people. ⁵But if you do not obey these commands, I swear by myself, says the LORD: this palace shall become rubble. ⁶For thus says the LORD concerning the palace of the king of Judah:

Though you be to me like Gilead,
    like the peak of Lebanon,*
I will turn you into a waste,
    a city uninhabited.
⁷ Against you I will send destroyers,
    each with his axe:
They shall cut down your choice
        cedars,
    and cast them into the fire.�q

⁸Many people will pass by this city and ask one another: "Why has the LORD done this to so great a city?"ʳ ⁹And the answer will be given: "Because they have deserted their covenant with the LORD, their God, by worshiping and serving strange gods."ˢ

Jehoahaz
¹⁰ Weep not for him who is dead,*
    mourn not for him!
Weep rather for him who is going away;
    never again will he see
    the land of his birth.ᵗ

¹¹Thus says the LORD concerning Shallum,* son of Josiah, king of Judah, who succeeded his father as king. He has left this place never to return. ¹²Rather, he shall die in the place where they exiled him; this land he shall not see again.

Jehoiakim
¹³ Woe to him who builds his house on
        wrong,
    his terraces on injustice;
Who works his neighbor without pay,*
    and gives him no wages.ᵘ
¹⁴ Who says, "I will build myself a spacious
        house,
    with airy rooms,"
Who cuts out windows for it,
    panels it with cedar,
    and paints it with vermillion.
¹⁵ Must you prove your rank among
        kings*
    by competing with them in cedar?
Did not your father eat and drink?
    He did what was right and just,
    and it went well with him.ᵛ
¹⁶ Because he dispensed justice to the weak
        and the poor,
    it went well with him.
Is this not true knowledge of me?
    says the LORD.ʷ
¹⁷ But your eyes and heart are set on
        nothing
    except on your own gain,
On shedding innocent blood,
    on practicing oppression and
        extortion.ˣ

¹⁸Therefore, thus says the LORD concerning Jehoiakim, son of Josiah, king of Judah:

They shall not lament him,
    "Alas! my brother"; "Alas! sister."*
They shall not lament him,
    "Alas, Lord! alas, Majesty!"ʸ

22, 6: Gilead . . . Lebanon: both were known for their trees; cf v 7.

22, 10: Him who is dead: Josiah. His successor, Jehoahaz, who is going away, was deported by Pharaoh Neco to Egypt, where he died (2 Kgs 23, 33f).

22, 11: Shallum: Jehoahaz is called this only here. Presumably it was his name at birth, while Jehoahaz was his royal name.

22, 13: Without pay: either by forced labor in public works, or in as much as workers were defrauded of their hire. Despite the impoverishment caused in Judah by the payment of foreign tribute, Jehoiakim embarked on a program of lav-ish building in Jerusalem (v 14). Social injustice is the cause of much of the prophetic condemnation of the kings (v 17).

22, 15f: Josiah, the reforming king, prospered materially without oppressing his people; he embodied all the ideals of kingship.

22, 18: "Alas! my brother"; "Alas! sister": customary cries of mourning.

p: Jer 21, 12; Ex 22, 21-24; Dt 24, 17.   q: Jer 21, 14.   r: Dt 29, 24ff.   s: Jer 19, 4; 40, 2f.   t: 2 Chr 35, 23ff.   u: Lv 19, 13; Dt 24, 14; Hb 2, 9. 12.   v: 2 Kgs 23, 25.   w: Prv 31, 9.   x: Ez 22, 13. 27.   y: Jer 16, 4ff; 1 Kgs 13, 30.

¹⁹ The burial of an ass* shall he be given,
  dragged forth and cast out
  beyond the gates of Jerusalem.ᶻ

Jeconiah

²⁰ Scale Lebanon and cry out,*
  in Bashan lift up your voice;
Cry out from Abarim,
  for all your lovers are crushed.ᵃ
²¹ I spoke to you when you were secure,
  but you answered, "I will not listen."
This has been your way from your youth,
  not to listen to my voice.
²² The wind shall shepherd all your
    shepherds,
  your lovers shall go into exile.
Surely then you shall be ashamed and
    confounded
  because of all your wickedness.
²³ You who dwell on Lebanon,
  who nest in the cedars,
How you shall groan when pains come
    upon you,
  like the pangs of a woman in travail!

²⁴As I live, says the LORD, if you, Coniah,* son of Jehoiakim, king of Judah, are a
signet ring on my right hand, I will snatch
you from it. ²⁵I will deliver you into the
hands of those who seek your life; the hands

of those whom you fear; the hands of Nebuchadnezzar, king of Babylon, and the
Chaldeans.ᵇ ²⁶I will cast you out, you and the
mother who bore you,* into a different land
from the one you were born in; and there you
shall die.ᶜ ²⁷Neither of them shall come back
to the land for which they yearn.ᵈ

²⁸ Is this man Coniah a vessel despised, to
    be broken up,
  an instrument that no one wants?
Why are he and his descendants cast out?
  why thrown into a land they know
    not?
²⁹ O land, land, land,
  hear the word of the LORD—
³⁰   Thus says the LORD:
ᵉWrite this man down as one childless,*
  who will never thrive in his lifetime!
No descendant of his shall achieve
  a seat on the throne of David
  as ruler again over Judah.

CHAPTER 23

See RG 302-3

Messianic Reign.* ¹ᶠWoe to the shepherds who mislead and scatter the flock of
my pasture, says the LORD. ²Therefore, thus
says the LORD, the God of Israel, against the
shepherds who shepherd my people: You
have scattered my sheep and driven them

22, 19: The burial of an ass: no burial at all, except to be cast outside the city as refuse. This prophecy regards the popular feeling toward Jehoiakim rather than the actual circumstances of his burial. According to 2 Kgs 24, 5 he was buried with his fathers in Jerusalem. However, his grave may have been profaned by Nebuchadnezzar.

22, 20-23: The prophet first apostrophizes Jerusalem, which is bidden to scale Lebanon, Bashan, and Abarim, i.e., the highest surrounding mountains to the north, northeast, and southeast, to gaze on the ruin of its lovers, i.e., the false leaders of Judah, called its shepherds (22); cf Jer 2, 8. The year is 597 B.C., after Nebuchadnezzar's deportation of Jehoiachin. Jerusalem still stands (23), apparently as secure as the heights of Lebanon, but destruction is to follow (cf v 6).

22, 24: Coniah: a shortened form of Jeconiah, the name which Jeremiah gives the king called elsewhere in the Bible Jehoiachin. A signet ring: the seal used by important men—in a sense, their most valuable possession—mounted in a ring worn constantly on the hand. The Lord says that even were Jehoiachin such a precious possession, he would reject him. The words in vv 24-30 date from the short three-month reign of Jehoiachin, before he was carried away by Nebuchadnezzar.

22, 26: You and the mother who bore you: the queen mother held a special position in the monarchy of Judah, and in the Books of Kings she is invariably mentioned by name

along with the king (1 Kgs 15, 2; 2 Kgs 18, 2). Jehoiachin did indeed die in Babylon.

22, 30: Childless: Jehoiachin is so considered because none of his descendants will be king. From the Book of Ezekiel, who dates his oracles according to Jehoiachin's fictitious regnal years, it is evident that the people expected Jehoiachin to return. The above prophecy of Jeremiah was uttered to dispel this hope (Jer 28, 4). Of the seven sons born to Jehoiachin in exile, none became king. His grandson Zerubbabel presided for a time over the Jewish community after the return from exile, but not as king.

23, 1-8: With the false rulers who have governed his people the Lord contrasts himself, the good shepherd, who will in the times of restoration appoint worthy rulers (1-4). A messianic King will arise from the line of David who will rule over Judah and Israel with the justice of the Lord, fulfilling all the kingly ideals (5f). "The Lord our justice" is probably an ironic wordplay on the name of the weak King Zedekiah ("The Lord is justice"); the messianic King will be in reality what Zedekiah's name falsely proclaims him. The final verses, 7-8, were probably added during the exile.

z: Jer 36, 30. a: Jer 30, 14f; Dt 32, 49. b: Jer 21, 7; 34, 20. c: 2 Kgs 24, 15. d: Jer 44, 14. e: Jer 36, 30; 1 Chr 3, 16f; Mt 1, 12. f: Jer 22, 22.

away. You have not cared for them, but I will take care to punish your evil deeds.*g* *3*I myself will gather the remnant of my flock from all the lands to which I have driven them and bring them back to their meadow; there they shall increase and multiply.*h* *4*I will appoint shepherds for them who will shepherd them so that they need no longer fear and tremble; and none shall be missing, says the Lord.*i*

5 Behold, the days are coming, says the
     Lord,
   when I will raise up a righteous shoot
     to David;
   As king he shall reign and govern wisely,
     he shall do what is just and right in the
       land.*j*
6 In his days Judah shall be saved,
     Israel shall dwell in security.
   This is the name they give him:
     "The Lord our justice."*k*

7l Therefore, the days will come, says the Lord, when they shall no longer say, "As the Lord lives, who brought the Israelites out of the land of Egypt"; *8*but rather, "As the Lord lives, who brought the descendants of the house of Israel up from the land of the north"—and from all the lands to which I banished them; they shall again live on their own land.

The False Prophets*

9   Concerning the prophets:
   My heart within me is broken,
     my bones all tremble;
   I am like a man who is drunk,
     overcome by wine,
   Because of the Lord,
     because of his holy words.
10 With adulterers the land is filled;
     on their account the land mourns,
     the pasture ranges are seared.*m*

   Theirs is an evil course,
     theirs is unjust power.
11 Both prophet and priest are godless!
     In my very house I find their
       wickedness,
     says the Lord.*n*
12 Hence their way shall become for them
       slippery ground.
   In the darkness they shall lose their
       footing,
     and fall headlong;
   Evil I will bring upon them:
     the year of their punishment, says the
       Lord.*o*
13 Among Samaria's prophets
     I saw unseemly deeds:
   They prophesied by Baal
     and led my people Israel astray.*p*
14 But among Jerusalem's prophets
     I saw deeds still more shocking:
   Adultery, living in lies,
     siding with the wicked,
     so that no one turns from evil;
   To me they are all like Sodom,
     its citizens like Gomorrah.*q*

*15*Therefore, thus says the Lord of hosts against the prophets:

   Behold, I will give them wormwood to
       eat,
     and poison to drink;
   For from Jerusalem's prophets
     ungodliness has gone forth into the
       whole land.*r*
16   Thus says the Lord of hosts:
   Listen not to the words of your
       prophets,
     who fill you with emptiness;
   Visions of their own fancy they speak,
     not from the mouth of the Lord.*s*
17 They say to those who despise the word
       of the Lord,*
     "Peace shall be yours";

23, 9–40: After the collection of oracles against the kings, the editor of the book placed this collection of oracles against the false prophets. With them are associated the priests, for both have betrayed their trust as instructors in the religion of the Lord; cf Jer 2, 8; 4, 9; 6, 13f.

23, 17–20: Not only are the false prophets personally immoral, but they encourage immorality by prophesying good of those who do evil. The true prophet, on the other hand, sees the inevitable consequences of sin.

g: Ez 34, 4ff; Zec 11, 16f.   *h:* Jer 29, 14; 32, 37.   *i:* Jer 3, 15; Ez 34, 11f.   *j:* Jer 33, 14ff; Is 4, 2; 9, 5f; 11, 1–5.   *k:* Dn 9, 24.   *l:* 7f: Jer 16, 14f.   *m:* Jer 4, 22; 5, 7f; 9, 2. 10.   *n:* Jer 6, 13.   *o:* Ps 35, 6.   *p:* 1 Kgs 18, 19.   *q:* Jer 29, 21ff; Is 1, 9f.   *r:* Jer 8, 14; 9, 14. *s:* Jer 14, 14.

And to everyone who walks in hardness
of heart,
"No evil shall overtake you."[t]
[18] Now, who has stood in the council of the
LORD,
to see him and to hear his word?
Who has heeded his word, so as to
announce it?[u]
[19] See, the storm of the LORD!
His wrath breaks forth
In a whirling storm
that bursts upon the heads of the
wicked.[v]
[20] The anger of the LORD shall not abate
until he has done and fulfilled
what he has determined in his heart.
When the time comes,
you shall fully understand.
[21] I did not send these prophets,
yet they ran;
I did not speak to them,
yet they prophesied.[w]
[22] Had they stood in my council,
and did they but proclaim to my
people my words,
They would have brought them back
from evil ways
and from their wicked deeds.
[23] Am I a God near at hand only, says the
LORD,[x]
and not a God far off?*
[24] Can a man hide in secret
without my seeing him? says the
LORD.
Do I not fill
both heaven and earth? says the LORD.

[25] I have heard the prophets who prophesy
lies in my name say, "I had a dream! I had a
dream!" [26] How long will this continue? Is
my name in the hearts of the prophets who
prophesy lies and their own deceitful fan-
cies? [27] By their dreams which they recount

to each other, they think to make my people
forget my name, just as their fathers forgot
my name for Baal.[y] [28] Let the prophet who
has a dream recount his dream; let him who
has my word speak my word truthfully!

What has straw to do with the wheat?*
says the LORD.[z]
[29] Is not my word like fire, says the LORD,
like a hammer shattering rocks?

[30] Therefore I am against the prophets,
says the LORD, who steal my words from
each other.[a] [31] Yes, I am against the prophets,
says the LORD, who borrow speeches to pronounce oracles. [32] Yes, I am against the
prophets who prophesy lying dreams, says
the LORD, and who lead my people astray by
recounting their lies and by their empty
boasting. From me they have no mission or
command, and they do this people no good
at all, says the LORD.[b]

[33]* And when this people, or a prophet or a
priest asks you, "What is the burden of the
LORD?" you shall answer, "You are the burden, and I cast you off, says the LORD." [34] If
a prophet or a priest or anyone else mentions
"the burden of the LORD," I will punish that
man and his house. [35] Thus you shall ask,
when speaking to one another, "What answer did the LORD give?" or, "What did the
LORD say?" [36] But the burden of the LORD
you shall mention no more. For each man his
own word becomes the burden so that you
pervert the words of the living God, the
LORD of hosts, our God. [37] Thus shall you ask
the prophet, "What answer did the LORD
give?" or, "What did the LORD say?" [38] But if
you ask about "the burden of the LORD,"
then thus says the LORD: Because you use
this phrase, "the burden of the LORD,"
though I forbade you to use it, [39] therefore I
will lift you on high and cast you from my
presence, you and the city which I gave to

23, 23: Near at hand only . . . far off: God knows not
merely the present but also the future.

23, 28f: Straw . . . wheat: such is the contrast between
false and true prophecy. True prophecy is like fire (cf Jer 5,
14; 20, 9), producing violent results (v 29); Jeremiah's own
life is a testimony of this.

23, 33-40: A wordplay on massa, which means both oracle (usually of woe) and burden. In 34ff it appears that the
word massa itself is forbidden the people in the meaning of a

divine oracle. Doubtless this was because of some association
unknown to us. In Hos 2, 18 it is forbidden to call God "Baal"
("master"), because of the association of this title with the
Canaanite god.

t: Jer 5, 12; Ez 13, 10; Mi 3, 11; Zec 10, 2.   u: Jb 15, 8; Is 40, 13;
1 Cor 2, 16.   v: Jer 30, 23.   w: Jer 29, 9.   x: Jer 16; 17; Ps 139,
8.   y: Jgs 3, 7; 8, 33.   z: Nm 12, 6.   a: Dt 18, 20.   b: Jer 28,
15ff.

you and your fathers. [40]And I will bring upon you eternal reproach, eternal, unforgettable shame.[c]

CHAPTER 24

See RG
302-3

The Two Baskets of Figs.[*] [1]The LORD showed me two baskets of figs placed before the temple of the LORD.[d] —This was after Nebuchadnezzar, king of Babylon, had exiled from Jerusalem Jeconiah, son of Jehoiakim, king of Judah, and the princes of Judah, the artisans and the skilled workers, and brought them to Babylon.— [2]One basket contained excellent figs, the early-ripening kind. But the other basket contained very bad figs, so bad they could not be eaten. [3]Then the LORD said to me: What do you see, Jeremiah?[e] "Figs," I replied; "the good ones are very good, but the bad ones very bad, so bad they cannot be eaten." [4]Thereupon this word of the LORD came to me: [5]Thus says the LORD, the God of Israel: Like these good figs, even so will I regard with favor Judah's exiles whom I sent away from this place into the land of the Chaldeans.[f] [6]I will look after them for their good, and bring them back to this land, to build them up, not to tear them down; to plant them, not to pluck them out.[g] [7]I will give them a heart with which to understand that I am the LORD. They shall be my people and I will be their God, for they shall return to me with their whole heart.[h] [8]And like the figs that are bad, so bad they cannot be eaten—yes, thus says the LORD— even so will I treat Zedekiah, king of Judah, and his princes, the remnant of Jerusalem remaining in this land and those who have settled in the land of Egypt.[i] [9]I will make them an object of horror to all the kingdoms of the earth, a reproach and a byword, a taunt and a curse, in all the places to which I will drive them.[j] [10]I will send upon them the sword,

famine, and pestilence, until they have disappeared from the land which I gave them and their fathers.[k]

CHAPTER 25

See RG
302-3

Seventy Years of Exile.[*] [1]The word that came to Jeremiah concerning all the people of Judah, in the fourth year of Jehoiakim,[*] son of Josiah, king of Judah (the first year of Nebuchadnezzar, king of Babylon).[l] [2]This word the prophet Jeremiah spoke to all the people of Judah and all the citizens of Jerusalem: [3]Since the thirteenth year of Josiah, son of Amon, king of Judah, to this day—these three and twenty years—the word of the LORD has come to me and I spoke to you untiringly, but you would not listen.[m] [4]Though you refused to listen or pay heed, the LORD has sent you without fail all his servants the prophets[n] [5]with this message: Turn back, each of you, from your evil way and from your evil deeds; then you shall remain in the land which the LORD gave you and your fathers, from of old and forever. [6]Do not follow strange gods to serve and adore them, lest you provoke me with your handiwork, and I bring evil upon you.[o] [7]But you would not listen to me, says the LORD, and so you provoked me with your handiwork to your own harm.[p] [8]Hence, thus says the LORD of hosts: Since you would not listen to my words, [9]lo! I will send for and fetch all the tribes of the north, says the LORD (and I will send to Nebuchadnezzar, king of Babylon, my servant); I will bring them against this land, against its inhabitants, and against all these neighboring nations. I will doom them, making them an object of horror, of ridicule, of everlasting reproach.[q] [10]Among them I will bring to an end the song of joy and the song of gladness, the voice of the bridegroom and the voice of the bride, the

24, 1-10: Jeremiah, like Ezekiel, saw that no good could be expected from the people who had been left in Judah under Zedekiah or who had fled into Egypt; good was to be hoped for only from those who would pass through the purifying experience of the exile to form the new Israel.

25, 1-14: The fourth year of Jehoiakim: 605 B.C. Officially, the first year of Nebuchadnezzar began the following year; but as early as his victory over Egypt at Carchemish in 605, Nebuchadnezzar was the dominant power in the Near East, in whom Jeremiah now saw the fulfillment of his proph-

ecy of the enemy to come from the north (cf Jer 1, 13; 6 22ff). In vv 11f occurs for the first time the prophecy of the seventy years' exile; cf Jer 29, 10. This Jeremiah intends as a round number, to signify that the present generation must die out.

c: Jer 20, 11. *d:* Am 8, 1f. *e:* Jer 1, 11. *f:* Jer 29, 11; Lv 26, 44f. *g:* Jer 12, 15; Am 9, 15. *h:* Jer 30, 22; 31, 1; 32, 37; Bar 2, 31. *i:* Jer 29, 18. *j:* Jer 15, 4; Dt 28, 37. *k:* Jer 14, 12. *l:* Jer 36, 1. *m:* Jer 1, 2. *n:* 2 Chr 36, 15. *o:* Jer 7, 6f. *p:* Jer 7, 17ff. *q:* Jer 1, 15; 43, 10.

sound of the millstone and the light of the lamp. [11]This whole land shall be a ruin and a desert. Seventy years these nations shall be enslaved to the king of Babylon;[r] [12]but when the seventy years have elapsed, I will punish the king of Babylon and the nation and the land of the Chaldeans for their guilt, says the LORD. Their land I will turn into everlasting desert.[s] [13]Against that land I will fulfill all the words I have spoken against it [all that is written in this book, which Jeremiah prophesied against all the nations]. [14]They also shall be enslaved to great nations and mighty kings, and thus I will repay them according to their own deeds and according to their own handiwork.[t]

The Cup of Judgment on the Nations. [15]For thus said the LORD, the God of Israel, to me:* Take this cup of foaming wine from my hand, and have all the nations to whom I will send you drink it.[u] [16]They shall drink, and be convulsed, and go mad, because of the sword I will send among them.[v] [17]I took the cup from the hand of the LORD and gave drink to all the nations to which the LORD sent me: [18][Jerusalem, the cities of Judah, her kings and her princes, to make them a ruin and a desert, an object of ridicule and cursing, as they are today;] [19]Pharaoh, king of Egypt, and his servants, his princes, all the people under him, native [20]and foreign; all the kings of the land of Uz;* all the kings of the land of the Philistines: Ashkelon, Gaza, Ekron, and the remnant of Ashdod; [21]Edom, Moab, and the Ammonites; [22]all the kings of Tyre, of Sidon, and of the shores beyond the sea;* [23]Dedan and Tema and Buz,* all the desert dwellers who shave their temples; [24][all the kings of Arabia;] [25]all the kings of Zimri, of Elam, of the Medes; [26]all the kings of the north, near and far, one after the other; all the kingdoms upon the face of the earth [and after them the king of Sheshach* shall drink].

[27]Tell them: Thus says the LORD of hosts, the God of Israel: Drink! become drunk and vomit; fall, never to rise, before the sword that I will send among you![w] [28]If they refuse to take the cup from your hand and drink, say to them: Thus says the LORD of hosts: You must drink![x] [29]For since with this city, which is called by my name, I begin to inflict evil, how can you possibly be spared? You shall not be spared! I will call down the sword upon all who inhabit the earth, says the LORD of hosts.

[30]Prophesy against them all these things and say to them:

> The LORD roars from on high,
>> from his holy dwelling he raises his voice;
> Mightily he roars over the range,
>> a shout like that of vintagers over the grapes.[y]
> [31] To all who inhabit the earth to its very ends the uproar spreads;
> For the LORD has an indictment against the nations,
>> he is to pass judgment upon all mankind:
> The godless shall be given to the sword, says the LORD.
> [32]   Thus says the LORD of hosts:
> Lo! calamity stalks
>> from nation to nation;
> A great storm is unleashed
>> from the ends of the earth.

[33]On that day, those whom the LORD has slain will be strewn from one end of the earth to the other. None will mourn them, none will gather them for burial; they shall lie like dung on the field.[z]

> [34] Howl, you shepherds, and wail!
>> roll in the dust, leaders of the flock!
> The time for your slaughter has come;
>> like choice rams you shall fall.

25, 15ff: Jeremiah is a prophet to the nations (cf 1, 5) as well as to his own people. All the nations mentioned here appear again in the more extensive collection of Jeremiah's oracles against the nations in chapters 46—51.

25, 20: Uz: the homeland of Job, in Edomite or Arabian territory.

25, 22: The shores beyond the sea: Phoenician commercial colonies planted throughout the Mediterranean world.

25, 23: Dedan and Tema and Buz: North Arabian tribes.

25, 26: Sheshach: Babylon. The word is formed from babel by substituting letters of the Hebrew alphabet in inverse order.

r: Lv 26, 32-35.   s: Is 13, 20ff.   t: Jer 27, 7; 50, 9. 41f; 51, 6. 24. u: Rv 14, 10.   v: Jer 51, 7.   w: Ob 1, 16.   x: Jer 49, 12.   y: Jer 51, 14.   z: Jer 8, 2; 16, 4. 6.

35 There is no flight for the shepherds,
no escape for the leaders of the flock.*a*
36 Listen! Wailing from the shepherds,
howling by the leaders of the flock!
For the LORD lays waste their grazing
place,
37 desolate lie the peaceful pastures;
38 The lion leaves his lair,
and their land is made desolate
By the sweeping sword,
by the burning wrath of the LORD.*b*

See RG
303

CHAPTER 26

Jeremiah Threatened with Death. 1 In
the beginning of the reign* of Jehoiakim, son
of Josiah, king of Judah, this message came
from the LORD: 2 Thus says the LORD: Stand
in the court of the house of the LORD and
speak to the people of all the cities of Judah
who come to worship in the house of the
LORD; whatever I command you, tell them,
and omit nothing.*c* 3 Perhaps they will listen
and turn back, each from his evil way, so that
I may repent of the evil I have planned to inflict upon them for their evil deeds.*d* 4 Say to
them: Thus says the LORD: If you disobey
me, not living according to the law I placed
before you 5 and not listening to the words of
my servants the prophets, whom I send you
constantly though you do not obey them,*e* 6 I
will treat this house like Shiloh, and make
this the city which all the nations of the earth
shall refer to when cursing another.*f*

7 Now the priests, the prophets, and all the
people heard Jeremiah speak these words in
the house of the LORD. 8 When Jeremiah finished speaking all that the LORD bade him
speak to all the people, the priests and
prophets laid hold of him, crying, "You must
be put to death! 9 Why do you prophesy in
the name of the LORD: 'This house shall be
like Shiloh,' and 'This city shall be desolate
and deserted'?" And all the people gathered
about Jeremiah in the house of the LORD.
10 When the princes of Judah were informed of these things, they came up from
the king's palace to the house of the LORD
and held court at the New Gate of the house
of the LORD. 11 The priests and prophets said
to the princes and to all the people, "This
man deserves death; he has prophesied
against this city, as you have heard with your
own ears."*g* 12 Jeremiah gave this answer to
the princes and all the people: "It was the
LORD who sent me to prophesy against this
house and city all that you have heard.
13 Now, therefore, reform your ways and your
deeds; listen to the voice of the LORD your
God, so that the LORD will repent of the evil
with which he threatens you.*h* 14 As for me, I
am in your hands; do with me what you think
good and right. 15 But mark well: if you put
me to death, it is innocent blood you bring on
yourselves, on this city and its citizens. For in
truth it was the LORD who sent me to you, to
speak all these things for you to hear."

16 Thereupon the princes and all the people
said to the priests and the prophets, "This
man does not deserve death; it is in the name
of the LORD, our God, that he speaks to us."
17 At this, some of the elders of the land came
forward and said to all the people assembled, 18 "Micah of Moresheth* used to prophesy in the days of Hezekiah, king of Judah,
and he told all the people of Judah: Thus
says the LORD of hosts:

Zion shall become a plowed field,
Jerusalem a heap of ruins,
and the temple mount a forest ridge.*i*

19 Did Hezekiah, king of Judah, and all Judah
condemn him to death? Did they not rather
fear the LORD and entreat the favor of the
LORD, so that he repented of the evil with
which he had threatened them? But we are
on the point of committing this great evil to
our own undoing."*j*

The Fate of Uriah. 20 There was another
man who prophesied in the name of the
LORD, Uriah, son of Shemaiah, from Kiri-

26, 1: The beginning of the reign: a technical expression for the time between a king's accession to the throne and the beginning of his first official (calendar) year as king. Jehoiakim's first regnal year was 608 B.C.
26, 18: Micah of Moresheth: the prophet Micah, who appears among the canonical minor prophets (cf Mi 1, 1).

a: Jer 32, 4. *b:* Jer 4, 7. *c:* Jer 7, 2. *d:* Jer 18, 3. *e:* Jer 25, 4. *f:* Jer 7, 12. 14. *g:* Jer 38, 4. *h:* Jer 7, 3. *i:* Mi 1, 1; 3, 12.
j: 2 Chr 32, 26.

ath-jearim; he prophesied the same things against this city and land as Jeremiah did. [21]When King Jehoiakim and all his officers and princes were informed of his words, the king sought to kill him. But Uriah heard of it and fled in fear to Egypt. [22]Thereupon King Jehoiakim sent Elnathan, son of Achbor, and others with him into Egypt [23]to bring Uriah back to the king, who had him slain by the sword and his corpse cast into the common grave. [24]But Ahikam, son of Shaphan,* protected Jeremiah, so that he was not handed over to the people to be put to death.

See RG 303

CHAPTER 27

*Serve Babylon or Perish.** [1][In the beginning of the reign of Jehoiakim, son of Josiah, king of Judah,]* . . . this message came to Jeremiah from the LORD: [2]Thus said the LORD to me: Make for yourself bands and yoke bars and put them over your shoulders. [3]Send to the kings of Edom, of Moab, of the Ammonites, of Tyre, and of Sidon, through the ambassadors who have come to Jerusalem to Zedekiah, king of Judah, [4]and charge them thus: Tell your masters: Thus says the LORD of hosts, the God of Israel: [5]It was I who made the earth, and man and beast on the face of the earth, by my great power, with my outstretched arm; and I can give them to whomever I think fit.[k] [6]Now I have given all these lands into the hand of Nebuchadnezzar, king of Babylon, my servant; even the beasts of the field I have given him for his use.[l] [7]All nations shall serve him and his son and his grandson, until the time of his land, too, shall come. Then it in turn shall serve great nations and mighty kings.[m] [8]Meanwhile, if any nation or kingdom will not serve Nebuchadnezzar, king of Babylon, or will not bend its neck under the yoke of the king of Babylon, I will

punish that nation with sword, famine, and pestilence, says the LORD, until I give them into his hand.[n]

[9]You, however, must not listen to your prophets,* to your diviners and dreamers, to your soothsayers and sorcerers, who say to you, "You need not serve the king of Babylon."[o] [10]For they prophesy lies to you, in order to drive you far from your land, to make me banish you so that you will perish.[p] [11]The people that submits its neck to the yoke of the king of Babylon to serve him I will leave in peace on its own land, says the LORD, to till it and dwell in it.[q] [12]To Zedekiah, king of Judah, I spoke the same words: Submit your necks to the yoke of the king of Babylon; serve him and his people, so that you may live.[r] [13]Why should you and your people die by sword, famine, and pestilence, with which the LORD has threatened the nation that will not serve the king of Babylon?[s] [14]Do not listen to the words of those prophets who say, "You need not serve the king of Babylon," for they prophesy lies to you.[t] [15]I did not send them, says the LORD, but they prophesy falsely in my name, with the result that I must banish you, and you will perish, you and the prophets who are prophesying to you.[u]

[16v]To the priests and to all the people I spoke as follows: Thus says the LORD: Do not listen to the words of your prophets who prophesy to you: "The vessels of the house of the LORD will be brought back from Babylon soon now," for they prophesy lies to you. [17]Do not listen to them! Serve the king of Babylon that you may live; else this city will become a heap of ruins. [18]If they were prophets, if the word of the LORD were with them, they would intercede with the LORD of hosts, that the vessels which remain in the

---

26, 24: Ahikam, son of Shaphan: one of Josiah's officials (2 Kgs 22, 12) and father of Gedaliah, Jeremiah's friend, who was governor of Judah after Zedekiah's deportation (cf Jer 39, 14; 40, 5ff).

27, 1—29, 32: A special collection of Jeremiah's prophecies dealing with false prophets. From stylistic peculiarities, quite evident in the Hebrew, it is plain that these three chapters once existed independently of the other prophecies of Jeremiah.

27, 1: [In the beginning of the reign of Jehoiakim . . . Judah]: this gloss cannot be correct because according to Jer 28,

1 the time is the fourth year of Zedekiah, 594 B.C., the occasion of an embassy of the neighboring states (v 3), doubtless for the purpose of laying plans against Nebuchadnezzar.

27, 9: Your prophets: seers and diviners served the Gentile kings as the professional prophets served the kings of Judah.

k: Jer 32, 17. *l:* Jer 25, 9; 43, 10; Ez 30, 21. 25. *m:* Jer 25, 11; 2 Chr 36, 20. *n:* Jer 25, 9; Bar 2, 22. *o:* Jer 29, 8. *p:* Jer 14, 13-16. *q:* Bar 2, 21. *r:* Jer 38, 17. *s:* Jer 24, 8ff. *t:* Jer 14, 14; 23, 21. *u:* Jer 20, 6. *v:* Jer 28, 3; 2 Chr 36, 7. 10. 18.

house of the LORD and in the palace of the king of Judah and in Jerusalem might not be taken to Babylon. *19**For thus says the LORD of hosts concerning the pillars, the bronze sea, the stands, and the rest of the vessels that remain in this city, *20*which Nebuchadnezzar, king of Babylon, did not take when he exiled Jeconiah, son of Jehoiakim, king of Judah, from Jerusalem to Babylon, along with all the nobles of Judah and Jerusalem— *21*yes, thus says the LORD of hosts, the God of Israel, concerning the vessels that remain in the house of the LORD, in the palace of the king of Judah, and in Jerusalem:*w* *22*To Babylon they shall be brought, and there they shall remain, until the day I look for them, says the LORD; then I will bring them back and restore them to this place.

CHAPTER 28

See RG 303

The Two Yokes. *1*That same year, in [the beginning of] the reign of Zedekiah, king of Judah, in the fifth month of the fourth year, the prophet Hananiah, son of Azzur, from Gibeon, said to me in the house of the LORD in the presence of the priests and all the people: *2*"Thus says the LORD of hosts, the God of Israel: 'I will break the yoke of the king of Babylon. *3*Within two years I will restore to this place all the vessels of the temple of the LORD which Nebuchadnezzar, king of Babylon, took away from this place to Babylon. *4*And I will bring back to this place Jeconiah, son of Jehoiakim, king of Judah, and all the exiles of Judah who went to Babylon,' says the LORD, 'for I will break the yoke of the king of Babylon.' "

*5*The prophet Jeremiah answered the prophet Hananiah in the presence of the priests and all the people assembled in the house of the LORD, *6*and said: Amen! thus may the LORD do! May he fulfill the things you have prophesied by bringing the vessels of the house of the LORD and all the exiles back from Babylon to this place! *7*But now, listen to what I am about to state in your hearing and the hearing of all the people. *8*From of old, the prophets who were before you and me prophesied war, woe, and pestilence against many lands and mighty kingdoms. *9*But the prophet who prophesies peace is recognized as truly sent by the LORD only when his prophetic prediction is fulfilled.*x*

*10*Thereupon the prophet Hananiah took the yoke from the neck of the prophet Jeremiah, broke it, *11*and said in the presence of all the people: "Thus says the LORD: 'Even so, within two years I will break the yoke of Nebuchadnezzar, king of Babylon, from off the neck of all the nations.' " At that, the prophet Jeremiah went away.

*12*Some time after the prophet Hananiah had broken the yoke from off the neck of the prophet Jeremiah, the word of the LORD came to Jeremiah: *13*Go tell Hananiah this: Thus says the LORD: By breaking a wooden yoke, you forge an iron yoke! *14*For thus says the LORD of hosts, the God of Israel: A yoke of iron I will place on the necks of all these nations serving Nebuchadnezzar, king of Babylon, and they shall serve him; even the beasts of the field I give him.*y*

*15*To the prophet Hananiah the prophet Jeremiah said: Hear this, Hananiah! The LORD has not sent you, and you have raised false confidence in this people. *16*For this, says the LORD, I will dispatch you from the face of the earth; this very year you shall die, because you have preached rebellion against the LORD.*z* *17*That same year, in the seventh month, Hananiah the prophet died.

CHAPTER 29

See RG 303

Letter to the Exiles in Babylon. *1*This is the contents of the letter which the prophet Jeremiah sent from Jerusalem to the remaining elders among the exiles, to the priests, the prophets, and all the people who were exiled by Nebuchadnezzar from Jerusalem to Babylon. *2*This was after King Jeconiah and the queen mother, the courtiers, the princes of Judah and Jerusalem, the artisans and the skilled workmen had left Jerusalem.*a* *3*Delivered in Babylon by Elasah,* son of

---

27, 19-22: This prophecy was fulfilled after Zedekiah's disastrous defeat; cf 2 Kgs 25, 13ff.

29, 3: Elasah: possibly the brother of Ahikam (cf Jer 26, 24). Gemariah; perhaps the son of the high priest Hilkiah; cf 2 Kgs

w: 21f: 2 Kgs 25, 13-17; 2 Chr 36, 18. 22.　*x:* Dt 18, 22.　*y:* Jer 27, 6f; Dt 28, 48.　*z:* Dt 13, 6.　*a:* 2 Kgs 24, 15.

Shaphan, and by Gemariah, son of Hilkiah, whom Zedekiah, king of Judah, sent to the king of Babylon, the letter read:

[4]Thus says the LORD of hosts, the God of Israel, to all the exiles whom I exiled from Jerusalem to Babylon: [5]Build houses to dwell in; plant gardens, and eat their fruits. [6]Take wives and beget sons and daughters; find wives for your sons and give your daughters husbands, so that they may bear sons and daughters. There you must increase in number, not decrease. [7]Promote the welfare of the city to which I have exiled you; pray for it to the LORD, for upon its welfare depends your own.[b]

[10]Thus says the LORD: Only after seventy years have elapsed for Babylon will I visit you and fulfill for you my promise to bring you back to this place.[c] [11]For I know well the plans I have in mind for you, says the LORD, plans for your welfare, not for woe! plans to give you a future full of hope. [12]When you call me, when you go to pray to me, I will listen to you.[d] [13]When you look for me, you will find me. Yes, when you seek me with all your heart, [14]you will find me with you, says the LORD, and I will change your lot; I will gather you together from all the nations and all the places to which I have banished you, says the LORD, and bring you back to the place from which I have exiled you.[e]

[16]Thus says the LORD concerning the king who sits on David's throne, and all the people who remain in this city, your brethren who did not go with you into exile; [17]thus says the LORD of hosts: I am sending against them sword, famine and pestilence. I will make them like rotten figs, too bad to be eaten. [18]I will pursue them with sword, famine, and pestilence, and make them an object of horror to all the kingdoms of the earth, of malediction, astonishment, ridicule, and reproach to all the nations among which I will banish them.[f] [19]For they did not listen to my words, says the LORD, though I kept sending them my servants the prophets, only to have them go unheeded, says the LORD.[g]

[20]You, now, listen to the word of the LORD, all you exiles whom I sent away from Jerusalem to Babylon. [15]As for your saying, "The LORD has raised up for us prophets here in Babylon"— [8]thus says the LORD of hosts, the God of Israel: Do not let yourselves be deceived by the prophets and diviners who are among you; do not listen to those among you who dream dreams.[h] [9]For they prophesy lies to you in my name; I did not send them, says the LORD.[i] [21]This is what the LORD of hosts, the God of Israel, has to say about those who prophesy lies to you in my name, Ahab, son of Kolaiah, and Zedekiah, son of Maaseiah: I am handing them over to Nebuchadnezzar, king of Babylon, who will slay them before your eyes.[j] [22]All the exiles of Judah in Babylon will pattern a curse after them: "May the LORD make you like Zedekiah and Ahab, whom the king of Babylon roasted in the flames." [23]For they are criminals in Israel, committing adultery with their neighbors' wives, and alleging in my name things I did not command. I know, I am witness, says the LORD.[k]

The False Prophet Shemaiah. [24]Say this to Shemaiah, the Nehelamite: [25]Thus says the LORD of hosts, the God of Israel: Because you sent letters on your own authority to all the people of Jerusalem, to all the priests and to Zephaniah, the priest, son of Maaseiah, with this message: [26]*"The LORD has appointed you priest in place of the priest Jehoiada, so that there may be police officers in the house of the LORD, to take action against all madmen and those who pose as prophets, by putting them into the stocks or the pillory. [27]Why, then, do you not rebuke Jeremiah of Anathoth who poses as a prophet among you? [28]For he sent us in Bab-

---

22, 4. Zedekiah had dispatched these men to Nebuchadnezzar for some other purpose, possibly the payment of tribute, but Jeremiah took advantage of their mission to send his letter by them.

29, 26-29: The words of Jeremiah to the false prophet Shemaiah are not fully preserved in the current Hebrew text, as is seen in the incomplete sentence of this translation (vv 25-28). In his letter to Zephaniah Shemaiah reminds him of

his authority, as Pashhur's successor, to imprison Jeremiah. Zephaniah, however, merely reads the letter to Jeremiah but does not imprison him.

b: 1 Tm 2, 1f.   c: Jer 25, 11; 2 Chr 36, 21f; Ezr 1, 1; Dn 9, 2; Zec 1, 12; 7, 5.   d: Jer 33, 3.   e: Jer 23, 3. 8.   f: Jer 15, 4; 24, 9; 34, 17f.   g: Jer 25, 4.   h: Jer 27, 9. 14.   i: Jer 5, 31.   j: Jer 14, 14.   k: Jer 23, 14.

ylon this message: It will be a long time; build houses to live in; plant gardens and eat their fruits. . . ."

²⁹When the priest Zephaniah read this letter to the prophet, ³⁰the word of the LORD came to Jeremiah: ³¹Send the message to all the exiles: Thus says the LORD concerning Shemaiah, the Nehelamite: Because Shemaiah prophesies to you without a mission from me, and raises false confidence, ³²says the LORD, I will therefore punish Shemaiah, the Nehelamite, and his offspring. None of them shall survive among this people to see the good I will do to this people, says the LORD, because he preached rebellion against the LORD.

CHAPTER 30

See RG 303

*The Restoration.** ¹The following message came to Jeremiah from the LORD: ²Thus says the LORD, the God of Israel: Write all the words I have spoken to you in a book.ˡ ³For behold, the days will come, says the LORD, when I will change the lot of my people (of Israel and Judah, says the LORD), and bring them back to the land which I gave to their fathers; they shall have it as their possession.ᵐ

⁴These are the words which the LORD spoke to Israel and to Judah: ⁵thus says the LORD:

A cry of dismay we hear;
    fear reigns, not peace.
⁶ Inquire, and see:
    since when do men bear children?
Why, then, do I see all these men,
    with their hands on their loins
    like women in childbirth?
Why have all their faces turned deathly
        pale?ⁿ
⁷ How mighty is that day—

none like it!
A time of distress for Jacob,
    though he shall be saved from it.ᵒ

⁸On that day, says the LORD of hosts, "I will break his yoke from off your necks and snap your bonds." Strangers shall no longer enslave them;ᵖ ⁹instead, they shall serve the LORD, their God, and David, their king,* whom I will raise up for them.�q

¹⁰ But you, my servant Jacob, fear not, says
        the LORD,
    be not dismayed, O Israel!
Behold, I will deliver you from the far-
        off land,
    your descendants, from their land of
        exile;
Jacob shall again find rest,
    shall be tranquil and undisturbed,ʳ
¹¹   for I am with you, says the LORD, to
        deliver you.
I will make an end of all the nations
    among which I have scattered you;
    but of you I will not make an end.
I will chastise you as you deserve,
    I will not let you go unpunished.ˢ

¹²   For thus says the LORD:
Incurable is your wound,
    grievous your bruise;ᵗ
¹³ There is none to plead your cause,
    no remedy for your running sore,
    no healing for you.
¹⁴ All your lovers have forgotten you,
    they do not seek you.
I struck you as an enemy would strike,
    punished you cruelly;ᵘ
¹⁵ Why cry out over your wound?
    your pain is without relief.
Because of your great guilt,
    your numerous sins,
    I have done this to you.ᵛ

30, 1—31, 40: These two chapters do not belong chronologically to those that precede or follow. They contain mainly oracles of salvation which Jeremiah originally uttered on behalf of the conquered remnants of the northern kingdom; then, after Judah began to share Samaria's fate, the oracles were extended to include Judah. Their composition is to be placed early in Jeremiah's ministry, probably after the fall of Nineveh (612 B.C.), when Josiah assumed power over the North; cf 2 Kgs 23, 15ff.

30, 9: David, their king: the messianic King of the Davidic line, often called David by the prophets; cf Ez 34, 23f; 37, 24f; Hos 3, 5.

l: Jer 36, 2; Hb 2, 2; Rv 1, 11. *m:* Jer 29, 14; 31, 8. 10. 23; 32, 37. 44; Ez 39, 25; Am 9, 14. *n:* Jer 6, 24; 50, 43. *o:* Am 5, 18; Zep 1, 14f. *p:* Is 14, 5f; Ez 34, 27. *q:* Ez 34, 23; 37, 24; Hos 3, 5; Lk 1, 69. *r:* Jer 46, 27; Is 43, 5. *s:* Jer 46, 28; Ez 11, 16f; Am 9, 8f. *t:* Jer 10, 19; 14, 17; 15, 18. *u:* Jer 22, 22; Lam 1, 19. *v:* Jer 15, 18.

16 Yet all who devour you shall be
  devoured,
  all your enemies shall go into exile.
All who plunder you shall be plundered,
  all who pillage you I will hand over to
  pillage.*w*
17 For I will restore you to health;
  of your wounds I will heal you, says
  the LORD.
"The outcast" they have called you,
  "with no avenger."*x*
18   Thus says the LORD:
See! I will restore the tents of Jacob,
  his dwellings I will pity;
City shall be rebuilt upon hill,
  and palace restored as it was.*y*
19 From them will resound songs of praise,
  the laughter of happy men.
I will make them not few, but many;
  they will not be tiny, for I will glorify
  them.*z*
20 His sons shall be as of old,
  his assembly before me shall stand
  firm;
  I will punish all his oppressors.*a*
21 His leader* shall be one of his own,
  and his rulers shall come from his kin.
When I summon him, he shall approach
  me;
  how else should one take the deadly
  risk
  of approaching me? says the LORD.
22 You shall be my people,
  and I will be your God.*b*

23 See, the storm of the LORD!
  His wrath breaks forth
In a whirling storm
  that bursts upon the heads of the
  wicked.*c*
24 The anger of the LORD will not abate
  until he has done and fulfilled

what he has determined in his heart.
When the time comes,
  you will fully understand.*d*

CHAPTER 31

Good News of the Return

See RG 303

1 At that time, says the LORD,
  I will be the God of all the tribes of
  Israel,
  and they shall be my people.*e*
2   Thus says the LORD:
The people that escaped the sword*
  have found favor in the desert.
As Israel comes forward to be given his
  rest,
3   the LORD appears to him from afar:
With age-old love I have loved you;
  so I have kept my mercy toward you.*f*
4 Again I will restore you, and you shall be
  rebuilt,
  O virgin Israel;
Carrying your festive tambourines,
  you shall go forth dancing with the
  merrymakers.
5 Again you shall plant vineyards
  on the mountains of Samaria;
  those who plant them shall enjoy the
  fruits.*g*
6 Yes, a day will come when the watchmen
  will call out on Mount Ephraim:
"Rise up, let us go to Zion,
  to the LORD, our God."*h*

The Road of Return

7   For thus says the LORD:
Shout with joy for Jacob,
  exult at the head of the nations;
  proclaim your praise and say:
The LORD has delivered his people,
  the remnant of Israel.*i*
8 Behold, I will bring them back
  from the land of the north;

30, 21: His leader: probably not the messianic King, but simply any one of the rulers of the restored Israel, who will no longer be foreigners, and with whom the Lord will be on terms of intimacy, as with the whole people. The deadly risk of approaching me: to approach God unsummoned brings death; cf Lv 16, 1f.

31, 2: The people that escaped the sword: the exiles who were not killed but deported; they have found favor in the desert, across which they were driven into captivity. The prophet alludes to the first desert wandering of Israel (Ex

16ff), in which the people found the Lord. His rest: the land of promise. The perfect fulfillment of this promised rest is found only in the New Testament (Heb chapters 3 and 4).

w: Jer 2, 3. *x:* Jer 33, 6. *y:* Jer 33, 7. 11; Ezr 6, 3-15; Ez 36, 10. *z:* Is 35, 10; 51, 11. *a:* Is 49, 26. *b:* Jer 24, 7; 31, 1. 33; 32, 38; Lv 26, 12; Ez 11, 20; 36, 28. *c:* Jer 23, 19. *d:* Jer 23, 20. *e:* Jer 30, 22. *f:* Dt 7, 8; 10, 15; Is 43, 4; 63, 9; Hos 11, 1. 4. *g:* Is 65, 21; Am 9, 14. *h:* Is 2, 3; 27, 13; Mi 4, 2. *i:* Is 12, 6.

I will gather them from the ends of the
world,
with the blind and the lame in their
midst,
The mothers and those with child;
they shall return as an immense
throng.[j]
[9] They departed in tears,
but I will console them and guide
them;
I will lead them to brooks of water,
on a level road, so that none shall
stumble.
For I am a father to Israel,
Ephraim is my first-born.[k]
[10] Hear the word of the LORD, O nations,
proclaim it on distant coasts, and
say:
He who scattered Israel, now gathers
them together,
he guards them as a shepherd his
flock.
[11] The LORD shall ransom Jacob,
he shall redeem him from the hand of
his conqueror.[l]
[12] Shouting, they shall mount the heights of
Zion,
they shall come streaming to the
LORD's blessings:
The grain, the wine, and the oil,
the sheep and the oxen;
They themselves shall be like watered
gardens,
never again shall they languish.[m]
[13] Then the virgins shall make merry and
dance,
and young men and old as well.
I will turn their mourning into joy,
I will console and gladden them after
their sorrows.
[14] I will lavish choice portions upon the
priests,
and my people shall be filled with my
blessings,
says the LORD.

End of Rachel's Mourning

[15] Thus says the LORD:
In Ramah* is heard the sound of
moaning,
of bitter weeping!
Rachel mourns her children,
she refuses to be consoled
because her children are no more.[n]
[16] Thus says the LORD:
Cease your cries of mourning,
wipe the tears from your eyes.
The sorrow you have shown shall have
its reward,
says the LORD,
they shall return from the enemy's
land.
[17] There is hope for your future, says the
LORD;
your sons shall return to their own
borders.[o]

[18] I hear, I hear Ephraim pleading:
You chastised me, and I am chastened;
I was an untamed calf.
If you allow me, I will return,
for you are the LORD, my God.[p]
[19] I turn in repentance;
I have come to myself, I strike my
breast;
I blush with shame,
I bear the disgrace of my youth.[q]
[20] Is Ephraim not my favored son,
the child in whom I delight?
Often as I threaten him,
I still remember him with favor;
My heart stirs for him,
I must show him mercy, says the LORD.[r]

Summons To Return Home

[21] Set up road markers,
put up guideposts;
Turn your attention to the highway,
the road by which you went.
Turn back, O virgin Israel,
turn back to these your cities.

31, 15: Ramah: a village about five miles north of Jerusalem, where Rachel was buried (1 Sm 10, 2). Rachel: said to mourn for her children since she was the ancestress of Ephraim, the chief of the northern tribes. Mt 2, 18 applies this verse to the slaughter of the innocents by Herod.

j: Jer 3, 18; 23, 3. 8; Is 35, 5f.   *k:* Ex 4, 22.   *l:* Is 44, 23; 48, 20.   *m:* Is 58, 11.   *n:* Mt 2, 18.   *o:* Jer 29, 10-14.   *p:* Lv 26, 40ff.
q: Dt 30, 1ff.   *r:* Hos 11, 8.

22 How long will you continue to stray,
   rebellious daughter?
The LORD has created a new thing upon
      the earth:
   the woman must encompass the man*
      with devotion.

23 Thus says the LORD of hosts, the God of
Israel: When I change their lot in the land of
Judah and her cities, they shall again repeat
this greeting: "May the LORD bless you, holy
mountain, abode of justice!"s 24 Judah and all
her cities, the farmers and those who lead the
flock, shall dwell there together. 25 For I will
refresh the weary soul; every soul that languishes I will replenish. 26 Upon this I awoke
and opened my eyes; but my sleep was
sweet to me.*

27 The days are coming, says the LORD,
when I will seed the house of Israel and the
house of Judah with the seed of man and the
seed of beast. 28 As I once watched over them
to uproot and pull down, to destroy, to ruin,
and to harm, so I will watch over them to
build and to plant, says the LORD.t 29 In those
days they shall no longer say,

"The fathers ate unripe grapes,u
   and the children's teeth are set on
      edge,"*

30 but through his own fault only shall anyone die: the teeth of him who eats the unripe
grapes shall be set on edge.

The New Covenant. * 31 The days are coming, says the LORD, when I will make a new
covenant with the house of Israel and the
house of Judah.v 32 It will not be like the covenant I made with their fathers the day I took
them by the hand to lead them forth from the
land of Egypt; for they broke my covenant
and I had to show myself their master, says
the LORD.w 33 But this is the covenant which I
will make with the house of Israel after those
days, says the LORD. I will place my law
within them, and write it upon their hearts; I
will be their God, and they shall be my peo-
ple.x 34 No longer will they have need to teach
their friends and kinsmen how to know the
LORD. All, from least to greatest, shall know
me, says the LORD, for I will forgive their
evildoing and remember their sin no more.y

Certainty of God's Promise
35   Thus says the LORD,
He who gives the sun to light the day,
   moon and stars to light the night;
Who stirs up the sea till its waves roar,
   whose name is LORD of hosts:z
36 If ever these natural laws give way
   in spite of me, says the LORD,
Then shall the race of Israel cease
   as a nation before me forever.a
37   Thus says the LORD:
If the heavens on high can be measured,
   or the foundations below the earth be
      sounded,
Then will I cast off the whole race of
      Israel

31, 22: The woman must encompass the man: the words
"with devotion," not in the Hebrew, are added for the sense.
No fully satisfactory explanation has been given this text.
Among the more probable are these: (a) Formerly the man
(the Lord) encompassed the woman (Israel) with mercy and
devotion; now in the spiritual religion of Israel which will follow on the restoration, this order will be reversed. (b) So secure will Israel be after the restoration that women will no
longer need the natural protection of their husbands, but even
weak women can protect men. (c) St. Jerome in his commentary on this verse understood it of Mary's virginal conception
of Christ. "The Lord has created a new thing on earth; without seed of man, without carnal union and conception, 'a
woman will encompass a man' within her womb—One who,
though He will later appear to advance in wisdom and age
through the stages of infancy and childhood, yet, while confined for the usual number of months in his mother's womb,
will already be perfect man."

31, 26: I awoke . . . sweet to me: probably said by the
prophet himself.

31, 29: "The fathers . . . on edge": a proverb used in Israel,
expressing the idea that children suffer for the sins of their
parents (cf Ez 18, 2). The Israel of the restoration will be
characterized instead by personal responsibility and retribution for one's acts (v 30; cf vv 31-34).

31, 31-34: The new covenant to be made with Israel is a
common theme of the prophets, beginning with Hosea. According to Jeremiah, the qualities of the new covenant that
make it different from the old are: (a) It will not be broken,
but will last forever; (b) Its law will be written in the heart,
not merely on tablets of stone; (c) The knowledge of God will
be so generally shown forth in the life of the people that it will
no longer be necessary to put it into words of instruction. In
the fullest sense, this prophecy was fulfilled only through the
work of Jesus Christ; cf Lk 22, 20; 1 Cor 11, 25.

s: Jer 30, 3; Ps 122, 8. t: Jer 1, 10; 18, 7. u: Dt 24, 16; Ez 18,
2. v: Jer 32, 40; Heb 9, 15. w: Ex 24, 7f; Dt 5, 2. x: Jer 32,
40; Ez 37, 26; Heb 10, 16. y: Is 54, 13. z: Gn 1, 14-18.
a: Jer 33, 20f.

because of all they have done, says the LORD.

Rebuilding of Jerusalem. *38*The days are coming, says the LORD, when the city shall be rebuilt as the LORD's,*b* from the Tower of Hananel to the Corner Gate.* *39*The measuring line shall be stretched from there straight to the hill Gareb and then turn to Goah. *40*The whole valley of corpses and ashes,* all the slopes toward the Kidron Valley, as far as the corner of the Horse Gate at the east, shall be holy to the LORD. Never again shall the city be rooted up or thrown down.

CHAPTER 32

See RG 303

Pledge of Restoration.* *1*This message came to Jeremiah from the LORD in the tenth year of Zedekiah,* king of Judah, the eighteenth year of Nebuchadnezzar. *2*At that time the army of the king of Babylon was besieging Jerusalem, and the prophet Jeremiah was imprisoned in the quarters of the guard, at the king's palace.*c* *3*Zedekiah, king of Judah, had imprisoned him there, remonstrating: "How dare you prophesy: Thus says the LORD: I am handing over this city to the king of Babylon, who will capture it.*d* *4*Neither shall Zedekiah, king of Judah, escape the hands of the Chaldeans; rather shall he be handed over to the king of Babylon. They shall meet and speak face to face,*e* *5*and Zedekiah shall be taken to Babylon. There he shall remain, until I attend to him, says the LORD; in fighting the Chaldeans, you cannot win!"*f*

*6*This message came to me from the LORD, said Jeremiah: *7*Hanamel, son of your uncle Shallum, will come to you with the offer:*8* "Buy for yourself my field in Anathoth, since you, as nearest relative, have the first right of purchase."* *8*Then, as the LORD foretold, Hanamel, my uncle's son, came to me to the quarters of the guard and said, "Please buy my field in Anathoth, in the district of Benjamin; as nearest relative, you have the first claim to possess it; make it yours." I knew this was what the LORD meant, *9*so I bought the field in Anathoth from my cousin Hanamel, paying him the money, seventeen silver shekels.

*10*When I had written and sealed the deed, called witnesses and weighed out the silver on the scales, *11*I accepted the deed of purchase, both the sealed copy, containing title and conditions, and the open one.* *12*This deed of purchase I gave to Baruch, son of Neriah, son of Mahseiah, in the presence of my cousin Hanamel and of the witnesses who had signed the deed, and before all the men of Judah who happened to be in the quarters of the guard.*h*

*13*In their presence I gave Baruch this charge: *14*Thus says the LORD of hosts, the God of Israel: Take these deeds, both the sealed and the open deed of purchase, and put them in an earthen jar,* so that they can be kept there a long time. *15*For thus says the LORD of hosts, the God of Israel: Houses and fields and vineyards shall again be bought in this land.

*16*After giving the deed of purchase to Baruch, son of Neriah, I prayed thus to the

---

31, 38: From the Tower of Hananel to the Corner Gate: from the northeast to the northwest.

31, 40: Valley of corpses and ashes: the Valley of Benhinnom, which joins the Kidron at the southeast of ancient Jerusalem. The Horse Gate: in the eastern city wall, at the southeast corner of the temple area.

32, 1-44: This chapter recounts a prophecy "in action." At the Lord's command, Jeremiah fulfills his family duty to purchase the land of his cousin, carrying out all the legal forms, including records, to testify that Judah will be restored and that the life of the past will be resumed.

32, 1: The tenth year of Zedekiah: 588 B.C. The eighteenth year of Nebuchadnezzar: dating his reign from his victory at Carchemish; see note on Jer 25, 1-14.

32, 6-9: Jeremiah's imprisonment by the weak-willed Zedekiah was a technical custody that did not deprive him of all freedom of action. The siege maintained by the Chaldeans

(v 2) was only now beginning (v 24), and could be bypassed by individual persons going to and fro between Jerusalem and nearby Anathoth.

32, 7: The first right of purchase: the obligation of the closest relative to redeem the property of one in economic distress, so that the ancestral land might remain within the family (Lv 25, 25-28); see note on Ru 2, 20.

32, 11: The sealed copy . . . and the open one: the legal deed of sale was written on a scroll, which was then rolled up and sealed; about it was rolled another scroll, left unsealed, containing a copy or a summary of the first.

32, 14: In an earthen jar: the first of the Dead Sea Scrolls were found in such a jar.

b: Neh 12, 38; Zec 14, 10f. *c:* Jer 33, 1; 37, 20; 38, 6; 39, 14. *d:* Jer 26, 9; 34, 2; 37, 6-10. *e:* Jer 34, 3; 38, 18. 23; 39, 4-7. *f:* Jer 39, 7; 52, 11. *g:* Lv 25, 24-34; Ru 4, 4. *h:* Jer 36, 4.

LORD: ¹⁷Ah, Lord GOD, you have made heaven and earth by your great might, with your outstretched arm; nothing is impossible to you.ⁱ ¹⁸You continue your kindness through a thousand generations; and you repay the fathers' guilt, even into the lap of their sons who follow them. O God, great and mighty, whose name is LORD of hosts,^j ¹⁹great in counsel, mighty in deed, whose eyes are open to all the ways of men, giving to each according to his ways, according to the fruit of his deeds:^k ²⁰you have wrought signs and wonders in the land of Egypt and to this day, both in Israel and among all other men, until now you have gained renown.^l ²¹With strong hand and outstretched arm you brought your people Israel out of the land of Egypt amid signs and wonders and great terror. ²²This land you gave them, as you had promised their fathers under oath, a land flowing with milk and honey.^m ²³They entered and took possession of it, but they did not listen to your voice; by your law they did not live, and what you commanded they failed to do. Hence you let all these evils befall them.ⁿ ²⁴See, the siegeworks have arrived at this city to breach it; the city will be handed over to the Chaldeans who are attacking it, amid sword, famine, and pestilence. What you threatened has happened, you see it yourself;^o ²⁵and yet you tell me, O Lord GOD: Buy the field with money, call in witnesses. But the city has already been handed over to the Chaldeans!

²⁶Then this word of the LORD came to Jeremiah: ²⁷I am the LORD, the God of all mankind! Is anything impossible to me? ²⁸This now is what the LORD says: I will hand over this city to the Chaldeans, for Nebuchadnezzar, king of Babylon, to take. ²⁹The Chaldeans who are attacking it shall enter this city and set fire to it, burning it and its houses, on the roofs of which incense was burned to Baal and libations were poured out to strange gods as a provocation to me.^p

³⁰The Israelites and the Judeans from their youth have done only what is evil in my eyes; the Israelites did nothing but provoke me with the works of their hands, says the LORD.^q ³¹From the day it was built to this day, this city has excited my anger and wrath, ³²so that I must put it out of my sight for all the wickedness the Israelites and Judeans, with their kings and their princes, their priests and their prophets, the men of Judah and the citizens of Jerusalem, have done to provoke me.^r ³³They turned their backs to me, not their faces; though I kept teaching them, they would not listen to my correction.^s ³⁴They defiled the house named after me by the horrid idols they set up in it.^t ³⁵They built high places to Baal in the Valley of Ben-hinnom, and immolated their sons and daughters to Molech,* bringing sin upon Judah; this I never commanded them, nor did it even enter my mind that they should practice such abominations.^u

³⁶Now, therefore, thus says the LORD, the God of Israel, concerning this city, which as you say is handed over to the king of Babylon amid sword, famine, and pestilence: ³⁷Behold, I will gather them together from all the lands to which in anger, wrath, and great rage I banish them; I will bring them back to this place and settle them here in safety.^v ³⁸They shall be my people, and I will be their God.^w ³⁹One heart and one way I will give them, that they may fear me always, to their own good and that of their children after them. ⁴⁰I will make with them an eternal covenant, never to cease doing good to them; into their hearts I will put the fear of me, that they may never depart from me.^x ⁴¹I will take delight in doing good to them: I will replant them firmly in this land, with all my heart and soul.^y

⁴²For thus says the LORD: Just as I brought upon this people all this great evil, so I will bring upon them all the good I promise them.^z ⁴³Fields shall again be bought in this land,

---

32, 35: Molech: the god to whom human sacrifice was offered in the Valley of Ben-hinnom. Here, as in Jer 19, 5, he is given the name Baal; see note on Lv 18, 21.

i: 2 Kgs 19, 15; Jb 42, 2.   *j:* Ex 20, 5f; Dt 5, 9.   *k:* Jb 34, 21; Ps 33, 13ff.   *l:* Ex 6, 6; Dt 4, 34; Ps 135, 9.   *m:* Jer 11, 5; Gn 15, 18; 17, 8; 26, 3.   *n:* Jer 7, 24ff; Dn 9, 10-14.   *o:* Jer 21, 5; 33, 4.   *p:* Jer 21, 10; 37, 8ff.   *q:* Jer 3, 25; 44, 8.   *r:* Jer 2, 26; Is 3, 8.   *s:* Jer 7, 24.   *t:* Jer 7, 30; 2 Kgs 21, 4f.   *u:* Jer 7, 31; 19, 5; Ps 106, 37f.   *v:* Jer 23, 3; 29, 14; Is 11, 12; Ez 11, 17.   *w:* Jer 24, 7; 31, 33. *x:* Jer 31, 31ff.   *y:* Dt 30, 9.   *z:* Jer 33, 10-14; Zec 8, 13.

which you call a desert, without man or beast, handed over to the Chaldeans.ª ⁴⁴Fields shall be bought with money, deeds written and sealed, and witnesses shall be used in the land of Benjamin, in the suburbs of Jerusalem, in the cities of Judah and of the hill country, in the cities of the foothills and of the Negeb, when I change their lot, says the LORD.ᵇ

See RG 303

CHAPTER 33

Restoration of Jerusalem. ¹The word of the LORD came to Jeremiah a second time while he was still imprisoned in the quarters of the guard; ²Thus says the LORD who made the earth and gave it form and firmness, whose name is LORD: ³Call to me, and I will answer you; I will tell to you things great beyond reach of your knowledge.ᶜ ⁴Thus says the LORD, the God of Israel, concerning the houses of this city and the palaces of Judah's kings, which are being destroyed in the face of siegeworks and the sword:ᵈ ⁵men come to battle the Chaldeans, and these houses will be filled with the corpses of those whom I slay in my anger and wrath, when I hide my face from this city for all their wickedness.ᵉ

⁶Behold, I will treat and assuage the city's wounds; I will heal them, and reveal to them an abundance of lasting peace.ᶠ ⁷I will change the lot of Judah and the lot of Israel, and rebuild them as of old.ᵍ ⁸I will cleanse them of all the guilt they incurred by sinning against me; all their offenses by which they sinned and rebelled against me, I will forgive.ʰ ⁹Then Jerusalem shall be my joy, my praise, my glory, before all the nations of the earth, as they hear of all the good I will do among them. They shall be in fear and trembling over all the peaceful benefits I will give her.

¹⁰Thus says the LORD: In this place of which you say, "How desolate it is, without man, without beast!" and in the cities of Ju-

dah, in the streets of Jerusalem that are now deserted, without man, without citizen, without beast, there shall yet be heardⁱ ¹¹the cry of joy, the cry of gladness, the voice of the bridegroom, the voice of the bride, the sound of those who bring thank offerings to the house of the LORD, singing, "Give thanks to the LORD of hosts, for the LORD is good; his mercy endures forever." For I will restore this country as of old, says the LORD.ʲ

¹²Thus says the LORD of hosts: In this place, now desolate, without man or beast, and in all its cities there shall again be sheepfolds for the shepherds to couch their flocks. ¹³In the cities of the hill country, of the foothills, and of the Negeb, in the land of Benjamin and the suburbs of Jerusalem, and in the cities of Judah, flocks will again pass under the hands of the one who counts them, says the LORD.

¹⁴*The days are coming, says the LORD, when I will fulfill the promise I made to the house of Israel and Judah. ¹⁵In those days, in that time, I will raise up for David a just shoot; he shall do what is right and just in the land.ᵏ ¹⁶In those days Judah shall be safe and Jerusalem shall dwell secure; this is what they shall call her: "The LORD our justice." ¹⁷For thus says the LORD: Never shall David lack a successor on the throne of the house of Israel,ˡ ¹⁸nor shall priests of Levi ever be lacking, to offer holocausts before me, to burn cereal offerings, and to sacrifice victims.ᵐ

This word of the LORD also came to Jeremiah: ¹⁹Thus says the LORD: ²⁰If you can break my covenant with day,ⁿ and my covenant with night, so that day and night no longer alternate in sequence, ²¹then can my covenant with my servant David also be broken, so that he will not have a son to be king upon his throne, and my covenant with the priests of Levi who minister to me. ²²Like the host of heaven which cannot be num-

---

33, 14-26: This is the longest continuous passage in the Book of Jeremiah that is lacking in the Greek. It appears to be the postexilic composition of an inspired writer who used parts of the prophecies of Jeremiah—often, however, in a sense different from the prophet's. The prediction of an eternal Davidic dynasty (14-17) to fulfill the prophecy of Nathan (2 Sm 7, 11-16), and of a perpetual priesthood and sacrifice (18), was not to be realized in the restoration of the Jewish nation. It finds its fulfillment only in Jesus of Nazareth, who

combined with his messianic Davidic kingship an eternal priesthood; cf Heb 6, 20; 7, 24f.

---

a: Jer 33, 10.   *b:* Jer 17, 26; 33, 7.   *c:* Is 48, 6.   *d:* Jer 32, 24.
e: Jer 21, 4ff.   *f:* Is 57, 18.   *g:* Jer 30, 3; 32, 44.   *h:* Ez 36, 25.
i: Jer 32, 43.   *j:* 1 Chr 16, 34; Ezr 3, 11; Ps 136, 1.   *k:* Jer 23, 5;
Ps 72, 1-4. 12ff; Is 11.1.   *l:* 2 Sm 7, 16; 1 Kgs 2, 4; Ps 89, 4f. 29.
36f.   *m:* Ez 44, 15f.   *n:* 20f: Jer 31, 36f; Ps 89, 37f.

bered, and the sands of the sea which cannot be counted, I will multiply the descendants of my servant David and the Levites who minister to me.

²³This word of the LORD came to Jeremiah: ²⁴Have you not noticed what these people are saying: "The LORD has rejected the two tribes which he had chosen"? They spurn my people as if it were no longer a nation in their eyes.ᵒ ²⁵ᵖThus says the LORD: When I have no covenant with day and night, and have given no laws to heaven and earth, ²⁶then too will I reject the descendants of Jacob and of my servant David, so as not to take from his descendants rulers for the race of Abraham, Isaac, and Jacob. For I will change their lot and show them mercy.

IV: Fall of Jerusalem

CHAPTER 34

See RG
303

Fate of Zedekiah. ¹This word came to Jeremiah from the LORD while Nebuchadnezzar, king of Babylon, and his armies and the earth's kingdoms subject to him, as well as the other peoples, were all attacking Jerusalem and all her cities:�q ²Thus says the LORD, the God of Israel: Go to Zedekiah, king of Judah, and tell him: Thus says the LORD: I am handing this city over to the king of Babylon; he will destroy it with fire.ʳ ³Neither shall you escape his hand; rather you will be captured and fall into his hands. You shall see the king of Babylon and speak to him face to face. Then you shall be taken to Babylon.ˢ

⁴But if you obey the word of the LORD, Zedekiah, king of Judah, then, says the LORD to you, you shall not die by the sword. ⁵You shall die in peace, and they will lament you as their lord, and burn spices for your

burial as they did for your fathers, the kings who preceded you from the first; it is I who make this promise, says the LORD.

⁶The prophet Jeremiah told all these things to Zedekiah, king of Judah, in Jerusalem, ⁷while the armies of the king of Babylon were attacking Jerusalem and the remaining cities of Judah, Lachish, and Azekah,* since these alone were left of the fortified cities of Judah.

The Pact Broken.* ⁸This is the word that came to Jeremiah from the LORD after King Zedekiah had made an agreement with all the people in Jerusalem to issue an edict of emancipation. ⁹Everyone was to free his Hebrew slaves, male and female, so that no one should hold a man of Judah, his brother, in slavery.ᵗ ¹⁰All the princes and the others who entered the agreement consented to set free their male and female servants, so that they should be slaves no longer. But though they agreed and freed them, ¹¹afterward they took back their male and female slaves whom they had set free and again forced them into service.

¹²Then this word of the LORD came to Jeremiah: ¹³Thus says the LORD, the God of Israel: The day I brought your fathers out of the land of Egypt, out of the place where they were slaves, I made this covenant with them: ¹⁴Every seventh year each of you shall set free his Hebrew brother who has sold himself to you; six years he shall serve you, but then you shall let him go free. Your fathers, however, did not heed me or obey me. ¹⁵Today you indeed repented and did what is right in my eyes by proclaiming the emancipation of your brethren and making an agreement before me in the house that is named after me. ¹⁶But then you changed your mind and profaned my name by taking back your male and female slaves to whom

34, 7: Lachish and Azekah: fortress towns to the southwest of Jerusalem which Nebuchadnezzar besieged to prevent help coming to Jerusalem from Egypt. Between 1935 and 1938, archaeologists found at Lachish several letters written on pottery fragments which date from 598 or 588 B.C., and which mention both Lachish and Azekah.

34, 8-22: While the Chaldean siege of Jerusalem was in progress, the citizens of Jerusalem made a covenant at Zedekiah's instigation to free their brother Judeans who were in slavery. Doubtless this was both to provide additional free defenders for the city and to offer reparation for past violations

of the law, according to which Hebrew slaves were to serve no longer than six years (Dt 15, 12-15). But when the siege was temporarily lifted, probably because of the help promised by Pharaoh Hophra (cf Jer 37, 5), the inhabitants of Jerusalem broke the covenant and once more pressed their brethren into slavery (v 11).

o: Rom 11, 1f.   *p:* 25f: Jer 31, 36f; 32, 44.   *q:* Jer 52, 4; 2 Kgs 25, 1.   *r:* Jer 21, 10; 32, 3. 28.   *s:* Jer 32, 4; 52, 11.   *t:* Ex 21, 2ff; Lv 25, 39. 46; Dt 15, 12-15.

you had given their freedom; you forced them once more into slavery.^u ¹⁷Therefore, thus says the LORD: You did not obey me by proclaiming your neighbors and kinsmen free. I now proclaim you free, says the LORD, for the sword, famine, and pestilence. I will make you an object of horror to all the kingdoms of the earth. ¹⁸*The men who violated my covenant and did not observe the terms of the agreement which they made before me, I will make like the calf which they cut in two, between whose two parts they passed. ¹⁹The princes of Judah and of Jerusalem, the courtiers, the priests, and the common people, who passed between the parts of the calf, ²⁰I will hand over, all of them, to their enemies, to those who seek their lives: their corpses shall be food for the birds of the air and the beasts of the field.^v

²¹Zedekiah, too, king of Judah, and his princes, I will hand over to their enemies, to those who seek their lives, to the soldiers of the king of Babylon who have at present withdrawn from you.^w ²²I will give the command, says the LORD, and bring them back to this city. They shall attack and capture it, and destroy it with fire; the cities of Judah I will turn into a desert where no man dwells.^x

CHAPTER 35

See RG 303

The Faithful Rechabites. ¹This word came to Jeremiah from the LORD in the days of Jehoiakim, son of Josiah, king of Judah: ²Approach the Rechabites* and speak to them; bring them into the house of the LORD, to one of the rooms, and give them wine to drink. ³So I went and brought Jaazaniah, son of Jeremiah, son of Habazziniah, his brothers and all his sons, the whole company of the Rechabites, ⁴into the house of the LORD,

to the room of the sons of Hanan,* son of Igdaliah, the man of God, next to the princes' room, above the room of Maaseiah, son of Shallum, keeper of the doorway. ⁵I set before these Rechabite men bowls full of wine and offered them cups to drink the wine.

⁶"We do not drink wine," they said to me: "Jonadab,* Rechab's son, our father, forbade us in these words: 'Neither you nor your children shall ever drink wine. ⁷Build no house and sow no seed; neither plant nor own a vineyard. You shall dwell in tents all your life, so that you may live long on the earth where you are wayfarers.' ⁸Now we have heeded Jonadab, Rechab's son, our father, in all his prohibitions. All our lives have not drunk wine, neither we, nor our wives, nor our sons, nor our daughters. ⁹We build no houses to live in; we own no vineyards or fields or crops, ¹⁰and we live in tents; we obediently do everything our father Jonadab commanded us. ¹¹But when Nebuchadnezzar, king of Babylon, invaded this land, we decided to come into Jerusalem to escape the army of the Chaldeans and the army of Aram;* that is why we are now living in Jerusalem."

¹²Then this word of the LORD came to Jeremiah: ¹³Thus says the LORD of hosts, the God of Israel: Go, say to the men of Judah and to the citizens of Jerusalem: Will you not take correction and obey my words? says the LORD.^y ¹⁴The advice of Jonadab, Rechab's son, by which he forbade his children to drink wine, has been followed: to this day they have not drunk it; they obeyed their father's command. Me, however, you have not obeyed, although I spoke to you untiringly and insistently.^z ¹⁵I kept sending you all my servants the prophets, telling you to

---

34, 18f: As the Bible (Gn 15, 10-17) and also contemporary inscriptions make clear, agreements were sometimes ratified by walking between the divided pieces of animals while the contracting parties invoked on themselves a fate similar to that of the slaughtered beast if they should fail to keep their word. The agreement: that mentioned in vv 10. 15.

35, 2: The Rechabites: reactionaries who believed that the Lord could not be well served except by maintaining the original nomadic conditions of Israel's life. Without sharing their convictions, the prophet holds up their fidelity to their ideals as an example to put to shame his faithless countrymen. In the days of Jehoiakim: probably in 599 or 598 B.C.

35, 4: The sons of Hanan: probably the disciples of this man of God or prophet. Maaseiah: possibly the father of the priest Zephaniah (Jer 29, 25; 37, 3). Keeper of the doorway: a priestly function of responsibility; cf Jer 52, 24.

35, 6: Jonadab: a contemporary of King Jehu; cf 2 Kgs 10, 15ff.

35, 11: The army of Aram; Nebuchadnezzar enlisted the help of Judah's foreign neighbors in his assault on Jerusalem.

---

u: Lv 19, 12. v: Jer 7, 33; 16, 4; 19, 7. w: Jer 37, 5. 11. x: Jer 37, 8; 52, 7-13; 2 Chr 36, 17. 19. y: Jer 32, 33. z: Jer 7, 13; 25, 3; 2 Chr 36, 15f.

turn back, all of you, from your evil way; to reform your conduct, and not follow strange gods or serve them, if you would remain on the land which I gave you and your fathers; but you did not heed me or obey me.*a* *16*Yes, the children of Jonadab, Rechab's son, observed the command which their father laid on them; but this people does not obey me! *17*Now, therefore, says the LORD God of hosts, the God of Israel: I will bring upon Judah and all the citizens of Jerusalem every evil that I threatened; because when I spoke they did not obey, when I called they did not answer.*b*

*18*But to the company of the Rechabites Jeremiah said: Thus says the LORD of hosts, the God of Israel: Since you have obeyed the command of Jonadab, your father, kept all his commands and done everything he commanded you, *19*thus therefore says the LORD of hosts, the God of Israel: Never shall there fail to be a descendant of Jonadab, Rechab's son, standing in my service.

See RG 303

CHAPTER 36

Baruch Writes the Prophecies of Jeremiah. *1*In the fourth year of Jehoiakim, son of Josiah, king of Judah, this word came to Jeremiah from the LORD: *2*Take a scroll and write on it all the words I have spoken to you against Israel, Judah, and all the nations, from the day I first spoke to you, in the days of Josiah, until today. *3*Perhaps, when the house of Judah hears all the evil I have in mind to do to them, they will turn back each from his evil way, so that I may forgive their wickedness and their sin.*c* *4*So Jeremiah called Baruch, son of Neriah, who wrote down on a scroll, as Jeremiah dictated, all the words which the LORD had spoken to him.

*9*In the ninth month, in the fifth year of Jehoiakim, son of Josiah, king of Judah, a fast to placate the LORD was proclaimed for all the people of Jerusalem and all who came from Judah's cities to Jerusalem. *5*Then Jer-

emiah charged Baruch: I cannot go to the house of the LORD; I am prevented* from doing so. *6*Do you go on the fast day and read publicly in the LORD's house the LORD's words from the scroll you wrote at my dictation; read them also to all the men of Judah who come up from their cities. *7*Perhaps they will lay their supplication before the LORD and will all turn back from their evil way; for great is the fury of anger with which the LORD has threatened this people.*d*

*8*Baruch, son of Neriah, did everything the prophet Jeremiah commanded; from the book-scroll he read the LORD's words in the LORD's house. *10*It was in the room of Gemariah,* son of the scribe Shaphan, in the upper court of the LORD's house, at the entrance of the New Temple-Gate, that Baruch publicly read the words of Jeremiah from his book.

*11*Now Micaiah, son of Gemariah, son of Shaphan, heard all the words of the LORD read from the book. *12*So he went down to the king's palace, into the scribe's chamber,* where the princes were just then in session: Elishama, the scribe, Delaiah, son of Shemaiah, Elnathan, son of Achbor, Gemariah, son of Shaphan, Zedekiah, son of Hananiah, and the other princes. *13*To them Micaiah reported all that he had heard Baruch read publicly from his book. *14*Thereupon the princes sent Jehudi, son of Nethaniah, son of Shelemiah, son of Cushi, to Baruch with the order: "Come, and bring with you the scroll you read publicly to the people." Scroll in hand, Baruch, son of Neriah, went to them. *15*"Sit down," they said to him, "and read it to us." Baruch read it to them, *16*and when they heard all its words, they were frightened and said to one another, "We must certainly tell the king all these things." *17*Then they asked Baruch: "Tell us, please, how you came to write down all these words." *18*"Jeremiah dictated all these words to me," Baruch answered them, "and I wrote them down with ink in the book." *19*At this the princes

---

36, 5: I am prevented: probably because of his temple sermon (Jer 7, 1-15), or because of temporary ritual uncleanness.

36, 10: Gemariah: member of a family friendly to Jeremiah, which had rights to a room in the fortress of the temple gateway overlooking the court of the temple; from a window in this room Baruch read Jeremiah's prophetic sermon to the people.

36, 12: The scribe's chamber: the office of the royal secretary.

a: Jer 25, 4f. 7. *b:* Jer 11, 8f. *c:* Jer 26, 3; Is 55, 6f. *d:* 2 Kgs 22, 13.

said to Baruch, "Go into hiding, you and Jeremiah; let no one know where you are."

20Leaving the scroll in safekeeping in the room of Elishama the scribe, they entered the room where the king was. When they told him everything that had happened, 21he sent Jehudi to fetch the scroll. Jehudi brought it from the room of Elishama the scribe, and read it to the king and to all the princes who were in attendance on the king. 22Now the king was sitting in his winter house, since it was the ninth month, and fire was burning in a brazier before him. 23Each time Jehudi finished reading three or four columns, the king would cut off the piece with a scribe's knife* and cast it into the fire in the brazier, until the entire roll was consumed in the fire. 24Hearing all these words did not frighten the king and his ministers or cause them to rend their garments. 25And though Elnathan, Delaiah, and Gemariah urged the king not to burn the scroll, he would not listen to them, 26but commanded Jerahmeel, a royal prince, and Seraiah, son of Azriel, and Shelemiah, son of Abdeel, to arrest Baruch, the secretary, and the prophet Jeremiah. But the LORD kept them concealed.

27This word of the LORD came to Jeremiah, after the king burned the scroll with the text Jeremiah had dictated to Baruch: 28Take another scroll, and write on it everything that the first scroll contained, which Jehoiakim, king of Judah, burned up. 29And against Jehoiakim, king of Judah, say this: Thus says the LORD: You burned that scroll, saying, "Why did you write on it: Babylon's king shall surely come and lay waste this land and empty it of man and beast?" 30The LORD now says of Jehoiakim, king of Judah:e No descendant of his shall succeed to David's throne; his corpse shall be cast out, exposed to the heat of day, to the cold of night.* 31I will punish him and his descendants and his ministers for their wickedness;

against them and the citizens of Jerusalem and the men of Judah I will fulfill all the threats of evil which went unheeded.

32Jeremiah took another scroll, and gave it to his secretary, Baruch, son of Neriah; he wrote on it at Jeremiah's dictation all the words contained in the book which Jehoiakim, king of Judah, had burned in the fire, and many others of the same kind in addition.

CHAPTER 37

See RG 303

Jeremiah in the Dungeon. 1Coniah, son of Jehoiakim, was succeeded by King Zedekiah, son of Josiah; he was made king over the land of Judah by Nebuchadnezzar, king of Babylon.f 2Neither he, nor his ministers, nor the people of the land would listen to the words of the LORD spoken by Jeremiah the prophet. 3Yet King Zedekiah sent Jehucal, son of Shelemiah, and Zephaniah, son of Maaseiah the priest, to the prophet Jeremiah with this request: "Pray to the LORD, our God, for us."g 4At this time Jeremiah had not yet been put into prison;* he still came and went freely among the people. 5Also, Pharaoh's army* had set out from Egypt, and when the Chaldeans who were besieging Jerusalem heard this report they marched away from the city.h

6This word of the LORD then came to the prophet Jeremiah: 7Thus says the LORD, the God of Israel: Give this answer to the king of Judah who sent you to me to consult me: Pharaoh's army which has set out to help you will return to its own land, Egypt.i 8The Chaldeans shall return to the fight against this city; they shall capture it and destroy it with fire.j

9Thus says the LORD: Do not deceive yourselves with the thought that the Chaldeans will leave you for good, because they shall not leave! 10Even if you were to defeat the whole Chaldean army now attack-

---

36, 23: A scribe's knife: used to sharpen the reeds which were employed as pens.

36, 30: Jehoiakim's son Jehoiachin was named king, but reigned only three months; he was known better for his thirty-seven-year exile in Babylon. His corpse shall be cast out: see note on Jer 22, 19.

37, 4: Put into prison: as described in Jer 32, 1ff. Chrono-

logically, the present episode follows Jer 34, 1-7.

37, 5: Pharaoh's army: the force sent by Pharaoh Hophra which caused the Chaldeans momentarily to lift the siege of Jerusalem (cf Jer 34, 21).

e: Jer 22, 19. f: Jer 52, 1; 2 Kgs 24, 17; 2 Chr 36, 10. g: Jer 21, 1. h: Ez 17, 15; 29, 6f. i: Ez 17, 17. j: Jer 34, 22.

ing you, and only the wounded remained, each in his tent, these would rise up and destroy the city with fire.^k

^11When the Chaldean army lifted the siege of Jerusalem at the threat of the army of Pharaoh,^l ^12Jeremiah set out from Jerusalem for the district of Benjamin, to take part with his family in the division of an inheritance. ^13But when he reached the Gate of Benjamin, he met the captain of the guard, a man named Irijah, son of Shelemiah, son of Hananiah; he seized the prophet Jeremiah, saying, "You are deserting to the Chaldeans!" ^14"That is a lie!" Jeremiah answered, "I am not deserting to the Chaldeans." Without listening, Irijah kept Jeremiah in custody and brought him to the princes.

^15The princes were enraged, and had Jeremiah beaten and thrown into prison in the house of Jonathan the scribe, which they were using as a jail.^m ^16And so Jeremiah entered the vaulted dungeon, where he remained a long time.

^17Once King Zedekiah had him brought to his palace and he asked him secretly whether there was any message from the LORD. Yes! Jeremiah answered: you shall be handed over to the king of Babylon.^n ^18Jeremiah then asked King Zedekiah: In what have I wronged you, or your ministers, or this people, that you should put me in prison?^o ^19And where are your own prophets now, ^20who prophesied to you that the king of Babylon would not attack you or this land? Hear now, my lord king, and grant my petition: do not send me back into the house of Jonathan the scribe, or I shall die there.

^21King Zedekiah ordered that Jeremiah be confined in the quarters of the guard, and given a loaf of bread each day from the bakers' shop until all the bread in the city was eaten up. Thus Jeremiah remained in the quarters of the guard.^p

CHAPTER 38

See RG 303

Jeremiah in the Miry Cistern. ^1Shephatiah, son of Mattan, Gedaliah, son of Pashhur, Jucal, son of Shelemiah, and Pashhur, son of Malchiah, heard Jeremiah speaking these words to all the people:* ^2Thus says the LORD: He who remains in this city shall die by sword, or famine, or pestilence; but he who goes out to the Chaldeans shall live; his life shall be spared him as booty, and he shall live.^q ^3Thus says the LORD: This city shall certainly be handed over to the army of the king of Babylon; he shall capture it.

^4"This man ought to be put to death," the princes said to the king; "he demoralizes the soldiers* who are left in this city, and all the people, by speaking such things to them; he is not interested in the welfare of our people, but in their ruin."^r ^5King Zedekiah answered: "He is in your power"; for the king could do nothing with them. ^6And so they took Jeremiah and threw him into the cistern of Prince Malchiah, which was in the quarters of the guard, letting him down with ropes. There was no water in the cistern, only mud, and Jeremiah sank into the mud.^s

^7Now Ebed-melech, a Cushite,* a courtier in the king's palace, heard that they had put Jeremiah into the cistern. The king happened just then to be at the Gate of Benjamin, ^8and Ebed-melech went there from the palace and said to him, ^9"My lord king, these men have been at fault in all they have done to the prophet Jeremiah, casting him into the cistern. He will die of famine on the spot, for there is no more food in the city."^t ^10Then the king ordered Ebed-melech the Cushite to take three men along with him, and draw the prophet Jeremiah out of the cistern before he should die. ^11Ebed-melech took the men along with him, and went first to the linen closet in the palace, from which he took some old, tattered rags; these he sent down

---

38, 1: Jeremiah enjoyed sufficient liberty in the quarters of the guard (Jer 37, 21) to speak to the people; cf Jer 32, 6-9. Gedaliah, son of Pashhur: the latter is possibly the Pashhur of Jer 20, 1. Pashhur, son of Malchiah; mentioned in Jer 21, 1.

38, 4: He demoralizes the soldiers: literally, "he weakens their hands." One of the Lachish ostraca (see note on Jer 34, 7) uses the same expression of the princes in Jerusalem.

38, 7: A Cushite: an Ethiopian. Ebed-melech evidently held a position of some authority at court.

k: Jer 21, 4. *l:* Zec 14, 10. *m:* Jer 38, 6-13. *n:* Jer 21, 7; 32, 3; 34, 21. *o:* Jer 26, 19. *p:* Jer 32, 2; 38, 28. *q:* Jer 21, 9f; 39, 18; 45, 5. *r:* Jer 26, 11. *s:* Jer 37, 14f. *t:* Jer 52, 6.

to Jeremiah in the cistern, with ropes. [12] Then he said to Jeremiah, "Put the old, tattered rags between your armpits and the ropes." Jeremiah did so, [13] and they drew him up with the ropes out of the cistern. But Jeremiah remained in the quarters of the guard.

[14] Once King Zedekiah summoned the prophet Jeremiah to come to him at the third entrance to the house of the LORD. "I have a question to ask you," the king said to Jeremiah; "hide nothing from me."[u] Jeremiah answered Zedekiah: [15] If I tell you anything, you will have me killed, will you not? If I counsel you, you will not listen to me![v] [16] But King Zedekiah swore to Jeremiah secretly: "As the LORD lives who gave us the breath of life, I will not kill you; nor will I hand you over to these men who seek your life."

[17] Thereupon Jeremiah said to Zedekiah: Thus says the LORD God of hosts, the God of Israel: If you surrender to the princes of Babylon's king, you shall save your life; this city shall not be destroyed with fire, and you and your family shall live.[w] [18] But if you do not surrender to the princes of Babylon's king, this city shall fall into the hands of the Chaldeans, who shall destroy it with fire, and you shall not escape their hands.[x]

[19] King Zedekiah, however, said to Jeremiah, "I am afraid of the men of Judah who have deserted to the Chaldeans; I may be handed over to them, and they will mistreat me."[y] [20] You will not be handed over, Jeremiah answered. Please obey the voice of the LORD and do as I tell you; then it shall go well with you, and your life will be spared.[z] [21] But if you refuse to surrender, this is what the LORD shows me: [22] All the women left in the house of Judah's king shall be brought out to the princes of Babylon's king, and they shall taunt you thus:

"They betrayed you, outdid you,
   your good friends!
Now that your feet are stuck in the mud,
   they slink away."[a]

[23] All your wives and sons shall be led forth to the Chaldeans, and you shall not escape their hands; you shall be handed over to the king of Babylon, and this city shall be destroyed with fire.[b] [24] Then Zedekiah said to Jeremiah, "Let no one know about this conversation, or you shall die. [25] If the princes hear I spoke to you, if they come and ask you, 'Tell us what you said to the king; do not hide it from us, or we will kill you,' or, 'What did the king say to you?' [26] give them this answer: 'I petitioned the king not to send me back to Jonathan's house to die there.' " [27] When all the princes came to Jeremiah, they questioned him, and he answered them in the very words the king had commanded. They said no more to him, for nothing had been heard of the earlier conversation. [28] Thus Jeremiah stayed in the quarters of the guard till the day Jerusalem was taken.[c]

CHAPTER 39

See RG 303

Jeremiah and Gedaliah. When Jerusalem was taken. . . . [1] In the tenth month of the ninth year* of Zedekiah,[d] king of Judah, Nebuchadnezzar, king of Babylon, and all his army marched against Jerusalem and besieged it. [2] On the ninth day of the fourth month, in the eleventh year* of Zedekiah, a breach was made in the city's defenses. [3] All the princes of the king of Babylon came and occupied the middle gate: Nergal-sharezer, of Simmagir, the chief officer, Nebushazban, the high dignitary, and all the other princes of the king of Babylon. . . . [4] When Zedekiah, king of Judah, saw them, he and all his warriors fled by night, leaving the city on the Royal Garden Road* through the gate

---

39, 1: The tenth month of the ninth year: the month Tebet (mid-December to mid-January) of the year 589/8 B.C.

39, 2: The ninth day of the fourth month, in the eleventh year: in July of 587 B.C.

39, 4: The Royal Garden Road: along the southeast side of the city; the royal garden was in the Kidron Valley. The gate between the two walls: the southernmost city gate, at the end of the Tyropoean Valley. The Arabah: the Jordan Valley. Zed-

ekiah was attempting to escape across the Jordan when he was captured near Jericho.

---

u: Jer 37, 16. *v:* Lk 22, 67f. *w:* Jer 27, 12f; 2 Kgs 24, 12. *x:* Jer 32, 4. *y:* 1 Sm 31, 4. *z:* 2 Chr 20, 20. *a:* Jb 6, 15; 19, 13f. 19. *b:* Jer 41, 10. *c:* Jer 39, 14. *d:* 1f: Jer 52, 4-16; 2 Kgs 25, 1-12; Ez 24, 1.

between the two walls. He went in the direction of the Arabah,*e* *5*but the Chaldean army pursued them, and overtook and captured Zedekiah in the desert near Jericho. He was brought to Riblah,* in the land of Hamath, where Nebuchadnezzar, king of Babylon, pronounced sentence upon him.*f* *6*As Zedekiah looked on, his sons were slain at Riblah by order of the king of Babylon, who slew also all the nobles of Judah.*g* *7*He then blinded Zedekiah and bound him in chains to bring him to Babylon.*h*

*8*The Chaldeans set fire to the king's palace and the houses of the people, and demolished the walls of Jerusalem.*i* *9*Nebuzaradan, chief of the bodyguard, deported to Babylon the rest of the people left in the city, those who had deserted to him, and the rest of the workmen.*j* *10*But some of the poor who had no property were left in the land of Judah by Nebuzaradan, chief of the bodyguard, and were given at the same time vineyards and farms.*k*

*11*Concerning Jeremiah, Nebuchadnezzar, king of Babylon, gave the following orders through Nebuzaradan, chief of the bodyguard: *12*"Take him and look after him; let no harm befall him, but treat him as he himself requests."*l* *13*Thereupon Nebuzaradan, chief of the bodyguard, and Nebushazban, the high dignitary, and Nergal-sharezer, the chief officer, and all the nobles of the king of Babylon, *14*had Jeremiah taken out of the quarters of the guard, and entrusted to Gedaliah, son of Ahikam, son of Shaphan, to be brought home. And so he remained among the people.*m*

A Word of Comfort for Ebed-melech. *15*While Jeremiah was still imprisoned in the quarters of the guard, the word of the LORD came to him: *16*Go, tell this to Ebed-melech the Cushite: Thus says the LORD of hosts, the God of Israel: Behold, I am now fulfilling the words I spoke against this city, for evil and not for good; and this before your very eyes.*n* *17*But on that day I will rescue you, says the LORD; you shall not be handed over to the men of whom you are afraid. *18*I will make certain that you escape and do not fall by the sword. Your life shall be spared as booty, because you trusted in me, says the LORD.*o*

CHAPTER 40

See RG 303

Jeremiah Still in Judah. *1*This word* came to Jeremiah from the LORD, after Nebuzaradan, captain of the bodyguard, had released him in Ramah, where he had found him a prisoner in chains, among the captives of Jerusalem and Judah who were being exiled to Babylon.*p* *2*When the captain of the bodyguard took charge of Jeremiah, he said to him, "The LORD, your God, foretold the ruin of this place. *3*Now he has brought about in deed what he threatened; because you sinned against the LORD and did not obey his voice, this fate has befallen you. *4*And now, I am freeing you today from the fetters that bind your hands; if it seems good to you to come with me to Babylon, you may come: I will look after you well. But if it does not please you to come to Babylon, you need not come. See, the whole land is before you; go wherever you think good and proper";*q* *5*and then, before he left—"or go to Gedaliah, son of Ahikam, son of Shaphan, whom the king of Babylon has appointed ruler over the cities of Judah; stay with him among the people, or go wherever you please." The captain of the bodyguard gave him food and gifts and let him go.*r* *6*Jeremiah went to Gedaliah, son of Ahikam, in Mizpah,* and stayed with him among the people left in the land.*s*

*7*When the army leaders who were still in the field with all their men heard that the king of Babylon had given Gedaliah, son of Ahikam, charge of the land, of men, women, and children, and of those poor who had not been

---

39, 5: Riblah: Nebuchadnezzar's headquarters in Syria, which had also been used by Pharaoh Neco (2 Kgs 23, 33).

40, 1: This word: actually, no further word of the Lord is recorded until Jer 42, 7ff. This is a title affixed to the following chapters after they were attached to an earlier form of the book ending with chapter 39.

40, 6: Mizpah: some five miles northwest of Jerusalem, where Israel chose its first king (1 Sm 10, 17-24). Presumably

Jerusalem had been damaged too much by the Chaldean conquest to remain a seat of government.

e: Jer 52, 7.   *f:* Jer 32, 4f; 38, 18.   *g:* Jer 34, 21.   *h:* Jer 32, 4f;
Ez 12, 13.   *i:* Jer 21, 10; 34, 2; 52, 13.   *j:* 2 Kgs 25, 11.
k: 2 Kgs 25, 12. 22.   *l:* Jer 40, 4.   *m:* Jer 26, 24; 38, 28.   *n:* Jer
21, 10; Dn 9, 12.   *o:* Jer 45, 5; Pss 25, 3; 36, 40.   *p:* Jer 39, 14.
q: Jer 39, 12.   *r:* Jer 39, 14; 2 Kgs 25, 22.   *s:* Jer 39, 14.

led captive to Babylon, [8]they came with their men to Gedaliah in Mizpah: Ishmael, son of Nethaniah; Johanan, son of Kareah; Seraiah, son of Tanhumeth; the sons of Ephai of Netophah; and Jezaniah* of Beth-maacah. [9]Gedaliah, son of Ahikam, son of Shaphan, adjured them and their men not to be afraid to serve the Chaldeans: to stay in the land and submit to the king of Babylon, for their own welfare,[t] [10]saying that he himself would remain in Mizpah, as their intermediary with the Chaldeans who should come to them. They were to collect the wine, the fruit, and the oil, to store them in jars, and to settle in the cities they occupied. [11]When the people of Judah in Moab, those among the Ammonites, those in Edom, and those in all other lands heard that the king of Babylon had left a remnant in Judah, and had appointed over them Gedaliah, son of Ahikam, son of Shaphan, [12]they all returned to the land of Judah from the places to which they had scattered. They went to Gedaliah at Mizpah and had a rich harvest of wine and fruit.

Assassination of Gedaliah. [13]Now Johanan, son of Kareah, and all the leaders of the armies in the field came to Gedaliah in Mizpah [14]and asked him whether he did not know that Baalis, the king of the Ammonites,* had sent Ishmael, son of Nethaniah, to assassinate him.[u] [15]But Gedaliah, son of Ahikam, would not believe them. Then Johanan, son of Kareah, said secretly to Gedaliah in Mizpah: "Let me go and kill Ishmael, son of Nethaniah; no one will know it. Why should he be allowed to kill you? All the Jews who have now rallied to you will be dispersed and the remnant of Judah will perish." [16]Nevertheless, Gedaliah, son of Ahikam, answered Johanan, son of Kareah, "You shall do nothing of the kind; you have lied about Ishmael."

See RG
303

CHAPTER 41

[1]In the seventh month Ishmael, son of Nethaniah, son of Elishama, of royal descent, one of the king's nobles, came with ten men to Gedaliah, son of Ahikam, at Mizpah.[v] And while they were together at table in Mizpah, [2]Ishmael, son of Nethaniah, and the ten who were with him, rose up and attacked with swords Gedaliah, son of Ahikam, son of Shaphan, whom the king of Babylon had made ruler over the land; and they killed him. [3]Ishmael also slew all the men of Judah of military age who were with Gedaliah and the Chaldean soldiers who were there.

[4]The second day after the murder of Gedaliah, before anyone knew of it, [5]eighty men with beards shaved off, clothes in rags, and with gashes on their bodies came from Shechem, Shiloh, and Samaria, bringing food offerings and incense for the house of the LORD. [6]Ishmael, son of Nethaniah, went out from Mizpah to meet them, weeping as he went. [7]"Come to Gedaliah, son of Ahikam," he said as he met them. When they were once inside the city, Ishmael, son of Nethaniah, and his men slew them and threw them into the cistern. [8]But there were ten among them who pleaded with Ishmael: "Do not kill us; we have stores buried in the field: wheat and barley, oil and honey." And so he spared them and did not kill them, as he had killed their companions. [9]The cistern into which Ishmael threw all the corpses of the men he had killed was the large one made by King Asa to defend himself against Baasha, king of Israel; this cistern Ishmael, son of Nethaniah, filled with the slain.[w]

[10]Ishmael, son of Nethaniah, led away the remnant of the people left in Mizpah and the princesses,* whom Nebuzaradan, captain of the bodyguard, had confided to Gedaliah, son of Ahikam. With these captives, Ishmael, son of Nethaniah, set out to make his way to the Ammonites.

Flight to Egypt. [11]But when Johanan, son of Kareah, and the other army leaders with him heard of the crimes Ishmael, son of Nethaniah, had committed, [12]they took all

---

40, 8: Jezaniah: the seal ring of a high official of this name was discovered in 1932 at the site usually identified with Mizpah, Tell en-Nasbe.

40, 14: The Ammonites: they resented the survival of their ancient enemy, Judah. Ishmael: their willing tool, who doubtless aspired to rule over Judah himself, as he was of the house of David; cf Jer 41, 1.

41, 10: The princesses: of the royal house of Judah. They had not been deported to Babylon with the men of this house.

t: Jer 27, 12f; 2 Kgs 25, 24.   *u:* Jer 41, 1ff. 10.   *v:* Jer 40, 14ff; 2 Kgs 25, 25.   *w:* 1 Kgs 15, 16; 2 Chr 16, 6.

their men and set out to attack Ishmael, son of Nethaniah. They overtook him at the Great Waters in Gibeon.* ¹³At the sight of Johanan, son of Kareah, and the other army leaders, the people who were Ishmael's captives rejoiced. ¹⁴All of those whom Ishmael had brought away from Mizpah went over to Johanan, son of Kareah. ¹⁵But Ishmael, son of Nethaniah, escaped from Johanan and fled to the Ammonites with eight men. ¹⁶Then Johanan, son of Kareah, and all his army leaders took charge of the remnant of the people, both the soldiers and the women and children with their guardians, whom Ishmael, son of Nethaniah, had brought away from Mizpah after he killed Gedaliah, son of Ahikim. From Gibeon, ¹⁷they retreated to the lodging place of Chimham near Bethlehem, where they stopped, intending to flee into Egypt. ¹⁸They were afraid of the Chaldeans, because Ishmael, son of Nethaniah, had slain Gedaliah, son of Ahikam, whom the king of Babylon had made ruler in the land of Judah.

CHAPTER 42

See RG 303

¹Then all the army leaders, Johanan, son of Kareah, Azariah, son of Hoshaiah, and all the people, high and low, approached the prophet Jeremiah ²and said, "Grant our petition; pray for us to the LORD, your God, for all this remnant. We are now few who once were many, as you well see. ³Let the LORD, your God, show us what way we should take and what we should do." ⁴Very well! the prophet Jeremiah answered them: I will pray to the LORD, your God, as you desire; whatever the LORD answers you, I will tell you; I will withhold nothing from you.ˣ ⁵And they said to Jeremiah, "May the LORD be our witness: we will truly and faithfully follow all the instructions the LORD, your God, will send us.ʸ ⁶Whether it is pleasant or difficult, we will obey the command of the LORD, our God, to whom we are sending you, so that it will go well with us for obeying the command of the LORD, our God."ᶻ

⁷Ten days passed before the word of the LORD came to Jeremiah. ⁸Then he called Johanan, son of Kareah, his army leaders, and all the people, high and low, ⁹and said to them: Thus says the LORD, the God of Israel, to whom you sent me to offer your prayer: ¹⁰If you remain quietly in this land I will build you up, and not tear you down; I will plant you, not uproot you; for I regret the evil I have done you.ᵃ ¹¹Do not fear the king of Babylon, before whom you are now afraid; do not fear him, says the LORD, for I am with you to save you, to rescue you from his power.ᵇ ¹²I will grant you mercy, so that he will be sorry for you and let you return to your land.ᶜ ¹³But if you disobey the voice of the LORD, your God, and decide not to remain in this land, ¹⁴saying, "No, we will go to Egypt, where we will see no more of war, hear the trumpet alarm no longer, nor hunger for bread; there we will live";ᵈ ¹⁵then listen to the word of the LORD, remnant of Judah: Thus says the LORD of hosts, the God of Israel: If you are determined to go to Egypt, when you arrive there to stay, ¹⁶the sword you fear shall reach you in the land of Egypt; the hunger you dread shall cling to you no less in Egypt, and there you shall die.ᵉ ¹⁷All those men who determine to go to Egypt to stay, shall die by the sword, famine, and pestilence; not one shall survive or escape the evil that I will bring upon them.ᶠ ¹⁸For thus says the LORD of hosts, the God of Israel: Just as my furious anger was poured out upon the citizens of Jerusalem, so shall my anger be poured out on you when you reach Egypt. You shall become an example of malediction and horror, a curse and a reproach, and you shall never see this place again.ᵍ

¹⁹It is the LORD who has spoken to you, remnant of Judah; do not go to Egypt! You can never say that I did not warn you this day. ²⁰At the cost of your lives you have deceived me, sending me to the LORD, your God, saying, "Pray for us to the LORD, our God; make known to us all that the LORD,

---

41, 12: Gibeon: today called El-Jib; it is northwest of Jerusalem. The most recent excavations have revealed the extensive dimensions of the city spring and well, called here the Great Waters; cf 2 Sm 2, 12ff.

x: 1 Sm 3, 18.   y: Jgs 11, 10.   z: Jer 7, 23; Dt 5, 33; 6, 3.   a: Jer 31, 28; 32, 41.   b: Jer 30, 10f.   c: Ps 106, 45f; Prv 16, 7.   d: Dt 28, 68.   e: Jer 44, 13f. 27.   f: Jer 29, 17f; 44, 14. 28.   g: Jer 44, 12.

our God, shall say, and we will do it." [21]Today I proclaim his message, but you obey the voice of the LORD, your God, in nothing that he has commissioned me to make known to you.[h] [22]Have no doubt of this, you shall die by the sword, famine, and pestilence in the place where you wish to go and settle.[i]

CHAPTER 43

See RG 303

[1]When Jeremiah finished speaking to the people all these words of the LORD, their God, with which the LORD had sent him to them, [2]Azariah, son of Hoshaiah, Johanan, son of Kareah, and all the insolent men shouted to Jeremiah: "You lie; it was not the LORD, our God, who sent you to tell us not to go to Egypt to settle. [3]It is Baruch, son of Neriah, who stirs you up against us, to hand us over to the Chaldeans to be killed or exiled to Babylon."[j]

[4]Johanan, son of Kareah, and the rest of the leaders and the people did not obey the LORD's command to stay in the land of Judah.[k] [5]Instead, Johanan, son of Kareah, and all the army leaders took along the whole remnant of Judah that had been dispersed among the nations and had returned thence to dwell again in the land of Judah: [6]men, women, and children, the princesses and everyone whom Nebuzaradan, captain of the bodyguard, had entrusted to Gedaliah, son of Ahikam, son of Shaphan; also Jeremiah, the prophet, and Baruch, son of Neriah.[l] [7]Against the LORD's command they went to Egypt, and arrived at Tahpanhes. . . .[m]

Jeremiah in Egypt. [8]This word of the LORD came to Jeremiah in Tahpanhes: [9]Take with you large stones and sink them in mortar in the brickyard at the entrance to the royal building* in Tahpanhes, while the men of Judah look on, [10]and then say to them: Thus says the LORD of hosts, the God of Israel: I will send for my servant Nebuchadnezzar, king of Babylon, and bring him here. He will set his throne upon these stones

which I, Jeremiah, have sunk, and stretch his canopy over them.[n] [11]He shall come and strike the land of Egypt: with death, whoever is marked for death; with exile, everyone destined for exile; with the sword, all who are intended for the sword.[o] [12]He shall set fire to the temples of Egypt's gods, and burn the gods or carry them off. As a shepherd delouses his cloak, he shall delouse the land of Egypt and depart victorious.[p] [13]He shall smash the obelisks of the temple of the sun in the land of Egypt and destroy with fire the temples of the Egyptian gods.

CHAPTER 44

See RG 303

[1]This word came to Jeremiah for all the people of Judah who were living in Egypt, at Migdol, Tahpanhes, and Memphis, and in Upper Egypt: [2]*Thus says the LORD of hosts, the God of Israel: You have seen all the evil I brought on Jerusalem and the other cities of Judah. Today they are ruins and uninhabited,[q] [3]because of the evil they did to provoke me, going after strange gods, serving them and sacrificing to them, gods which neither they, nor you, nor your fathers knew.[r] [4]Though I kept sending to you all my servants the prophets, with the plea not to commit this horrible deed which I hate, [5]they would not listen or accept the warning to turn away from the evil of sacrificing to strange gods.[s] [6]Therefore the fury of my anger poured forth in flame over the cities of Judah and the streets of Jerusalem, so that they became the ruinous waste they are today.

[7]Now thus says the LORD God of hosts, the God of Israel: Why do you inflict so great an evil upon yourselves? Will you root out from Judah man and wife, child and nursling, and not leave yourselves even a remnant? [8]Will you go on provoking me by the works of your hands, by sacrificing to strange gods here in the land of Egypt where you have come to live? Will you be rooted out and become a curse and a disgrace

---

43, 9: The royal building: residence of the Egyptian governor.

44, 2-30: Chronologically, this is the last of Jeremiah's prophecies to his countrymen. The narrative leaves him an old man nearing seventy, rejected by his people. According to tradition, he was murdered in Egypt by fellow Judeans.

h: Zec 7, 11f.   *i:* Jer 44, 12; Hos 9, 6.   *j:* Jer 38, 4.   *k:* Jer 41, 16.   *l:* Jer 41, 10.   *m:* Jer 42, 13f; 44, 1.   *n:* Jer 27, 6; Ez 29, 19.
o: Jer 46, 13; Ez 30, 10.   *p:* Jer 46, 25; Ez 30, 13f.   *q:* Jer 34, 22; Lv 26, 32f.   *r:* Jer 11, 17; Dt 32, 17.   *s:* Jer 7, 24. 26; 19, 4.

Jeremiah's Journey to Egypt

among all the nations of the earth?ᵗ ⁹Have you forgotten the evil deeds which your fathers, and the kings of Judah and their wives, and you yourselves and your wives have done in the land of Judah and the streets of Jerusalem?ᵘ ¹⁰To this day they have not been crushed; they do not fear or follow the law and the statutes which I set before you and your fathers.ᵛ

¹¹Hence, thus says the LORD of hosts, the God of Israel: I have determined evil against you; and I will uproot all Judah. ¹²I will take away the remnant of Judah who insisted on coming to dwell in Egypt, so that they shall be wholly destroyed. In the land of Egypt they shall fall by the sword or be consumed by hunger. High and low, they shall die by the sword, or by hunger, and become an example of malediction, a horror, a curse and a reproach.ʷ ¹³Thus will I punish those who live in Egypt, just as I punished Jerusalem with sword, hunger, and pestilence. None of the remnant of Judah that have come to set-tle in the land of Egypt shall escape or survive.ˣ ¹⁴None shall return to the land of Judah, though they yearn to return and live there. Only scattered refugees shall return.

¹⁵From all the men who knew that their wives were burning incense to strange gods, from all the women who were present in the immense crowd, and from all the people who lived in Lower and Upper Egypt, Jeremiah received this answer: ¹⁶"We will not listen to what you say in the name of the LORD.ʸ ¹⁷Rather will we continue doing what we had proposed; we will burn incense to the queen of heaven and pour out libations to her, as we and our fathers, our kings and princes have done in the cities of Judah and the streets of Jerusalem. Then we had enough food to eat and we were well off; we suffered no misfortune.ᶻ ¹⁸But since we stopped burning incense to the queen of heaven and pouring out libations to her, we are in need of everything and are being destroyed by the sword and by hunger. ¹⁹And

t: Jer 25, 6f.   *u:* 1 Kgs 11, 1. 8; Ezr 9, 7. 14.   *v:* Jer 7, 24.   *w:* Jer 42, 15. 18. 22.   *x:* Jer 43, 11.   *y:* Jer 6, 16f.   *z:* Jer 5, 3; 7, 18.

when we burned incense to the queen of heaven and poured out libations to her, was it without our husbands' consent that we baked for her cakes in her image and poured out libations to her?"*a*

*20*To all the people, men and women, who gave him this answer, Jeremiah said: *21*Was it not this that the LORD remembered and brought to mind, that you burned incense in the cities of Judah and the streets of Jerusalem: you, your fathers, your kings and princes, and the people generally?*b* *22*The LORD could no longer bear your evil deeds, the horrible things which you were doing; and so your land became a waste, a desert, a thing accursed and without inhabitants, as it is today.*c* *23*Because you burned incense and sinned against the LORD, not obeying the voice of the LORD, not living by his law, his statutes, and his decrees, this evil has befallen you at the present day.*d*

*24*Jeremiah said further to all the people, including the women: Hear the word of the LORD, all you Judeans in the land of Egypt: *25*Thus says the LORD of hosts, the God of Israel: You and your wives have stated your intentions, and kept them in fact: "We will continue to fulfill the vows we have made to burn incense to the queen of heaven and to pour out libations to her." Very well! keep your vows, carry out your resolutions! *26*But listen then to the word of the LORD, all you people of Judah who live in Egypt; I swear by my own great name, says the LORD, in the whole land of Egypt no man of Judah shall henceforth pronounce my name, saying, "As the Lord GOD lives." *27*I am watching over them to do evil, not good. All the men of Judah in Egypt shall perish by the sword or famine until they are utterly destroyed.*e* *28*Those who escape the sword to return from the land of Egypt to the land of Judah shall be few in number. The whole remnant of Judah who came to settle in Egypt shall know whose word stands, mine or theirs.*f*

*29*That you may know how surely my threats of punishment for you shall be fulfilled, this shall be a sign to you, says the LORD, that I will punish you in this place. *30*Thus says the LORD: See! I will hand over Pharaoh Hophra,* king of Egypt, to his enemies, to those who seek his life, just as I handed over Zedekiah, king of Judah, to his enemy and mortal foe, Nebuchadnezzar, king of Babylon.*g*

CHAPTER 45

See RG 303

*A Message to Baruch.** *1*This is the message that the prophet Jeremiah gave to Baruch, son of Neriah, when he wrote in a book the prophecies that Jeremiah dictated in the fourth year of Jehoiakim, son of Josiah, king of Judah:*h* *2*Thus says the LORD, God of Israel, to you, Baruch, *3*because you said, "Alas! the LORD adds grief to my pain;*i* I am weary from groaning, and can find no rest": *4*say this to him, says the LORD: What I have built, I am tearing down; what I have planted, I am uprooting: even the whole land.*j* *5*And do you seek great things for yourself? Seek them not! I am bringing evil on all mankind, says the LORD, but your life I will leave you as booty, wherever you may go.*k*

V: Oracles against the Nations*

CHAPTER 46

See RG 303

*1*This is the word of the LORD that came to the prophet Jeremiah against the nations.

44, 30: Hophra: killed by his own people. The ruler of Egypt at the time of its conquest by Nebuchadnezzar was Hophra's successor Amasis, who was also slain by his enemies.

45, 1-5: At the conclusion of his narrative, Baruch appends a prophecy given him personally by Jeremiah when he first wrote down Jeremiah's words (cf chap. 36). The future revealed by the prophet had depressed Baruch; this prophecy was to assure him of his personal safety, while repeating the Lord's determination to destroy Judah.

46—51: In these chapters most of Jeremiah's oracles against the foreign nations have been gathered together and placed at the end of his book; in the Greek text they appear with the other oracles against the nations, in chap. 25. In general, they are in chronological order: 46, 1—49, 33, from the fourth year of Jehoiakim; 49, 34-39, at the beginning of Zedekiah's reign; 50, 1—51, 64, from the fourth year of Zedekiah.

a: Jer 7, 18. *b:* Jer 11, 13. *c:* Jer 15, 6. *d:* 2 Kgs 17, 15; Dn 9, 11f. *e:* Ez 7, 3-7. *f:* Dt 28, 62; Is 10, 22. *g:* Jer 39, 5ff; 46, 25f; Ez 29, 3f; 30, 21. *h:* Jer 36, 4. 18. 32. *i:* Lam 1, 3; 5, 5. *j:* Jer 18, 7; Is 5, 5f. *k:* Jer 25, 26-29.

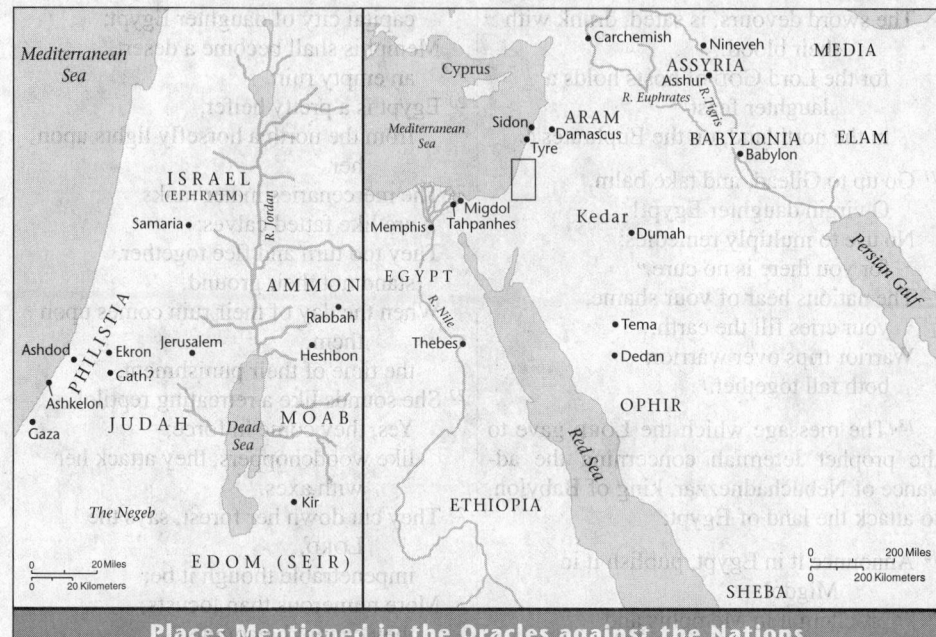

Places Mentioned in the Oracles against the Nations

Against Egypt. ²Concerning Egypt. Against the army of Pharaoh Neco, king of Egypt, which was defeated at Carchemish on the Euphrates* by Nebuchadnezzar, king of Babylon, in the fourth year of Jehoiakim, son of Josiah, king of Judah:

³ Prepare shield and buckler!
   march to battle!
⁴ Harness the horses,
   mount, charioteers
Fall in with your helmets;
   polish your spears, put on your
      breastplates.
⁵ What do I see?
   With broken ranks
They fall back;
   their heroes are routed,
They flee headlong
   without making a stand.
Terror on every side,
   says the LORD!*ˡ*
⁶ The swift cannot flee,

nor the hero escape:
There in the north, on the Euphrates'
      bank,
   they stumble and fall.

⁷ Who is this that surges forward like the
      Nile,
   like rivers of billowing waters?
⁸ Egypt surges like the Nile,
   like rivers of billowing waters.
"I will surge forward," he says, "and
      cover the earth,
   destroying the city and its people.*ᵐ*
⁹ Forward, horses!
   drive madly, chariots!
Set out, warriors,
   Cush and Put, bearing your shields,
   Men of Lud, stretching your
      bows!"
¹⁰ But this is the day of the Lord GOD of
      hosts,
   a day of vengeance, vengeance on his
      foes!

46, 2: Carchemish on the Euphrates: the western terminus of the Mesopotamian trade route, where Nebuchadnezzar defeated Neco in 605 B.C., thus gaining undisputed control of Syria and Palestine.

l: Jer 6, 25; 49, 29.   *m:* Ez 29, 3; 32, 2.

The sword devours, is sated, drunk with
their blood:
for the Lord GOD of hosts holds a
slaughter feast
in the northland, on the Euphrates.[n]

[11] Go up to Gilead, and take balm,
O virgin daughter Egypt!
No use to multiply remedies;
for you there is no cure.[o]
[12] The nations hear of your shame,
your cries fill the earth.
Warrior trips over warrior,
both fall together.[p]

[13][q]The message which the LORD gave to
the prophet Jeremiah concerning the advance of Nebuchadnezzar, king of Babylon,
to attack the land of Egypt:[*]

[14] Announce it in Egypt, publish it in
Migdol,
proclaim it in Memphis and
Tahpanhes!
Say: Take your stand, prepare yourselves,
the sword has already devoured your
neighbors.[r]
[15] Why has Apis[*] fled,
your mighty one failed to stand?
The LORD thrust him down;
[16]   he stumbled repeatedly, and fell.
They said one to another,
"Up! let us return to our own people,
To the land of our birth,
away from the destroying sword."[s]

[17] Call Pharaoh, king of Egypt, by the
name
"The noise that let its time go by."[*]
[18] As I live, says the King
whose name is LORD of hosts,
Like Tabor among the mountains he shall
come,
like Carmel[*] above the sea.
[19] Pack your baggage for exile,

capital city of daughter Egypt;
Memphis shall become a desert,
an empty ruin.
[20] Egypt is a pretty heifer,
from the north a horsefly lights upon
her.
[21] The mercenaries in her ranks
are like fatted calves;
They too turn and flee together,
stand not their ground,
When the day of their ruin comes upon
them,
the time of their punishment.
[22] She sounds like a retreating reptile!
Yes, they come in force;
like woodchoppers, they attack her
with axes.
[23] They cut down her forest, says the
LORD,
impenetrable though it be;
More numerous than locusts,
they cannot be counted.
[24] Disgraced is daughter Egypt,
handed over to the people of the
north.

[25]The LORD of hosts, the God of Israel,
has said: See! I will punish Amon[*] of
Thebes, and Egypt, her gods and her kings,
Pharaoh, and those who trust in him.[t] [26]I will
hand them over to those who seek their lives,
to Nebuchadnezzar, king of Babylon, and
his ministers. But later on Egypt shall be inhabited again, as in times past, says the
LORD.[u]

[27] But you, my servant Jacob, fear not;
be not dismayed, O Israel.
Behold, I will deliver you from the faroff
land,
your descendants, from their land of
exile.
Jacob shall again find rest,
shall be tranquil and undisturbed.[v]

46, 13: In 601 B.C. Nebuchadnezzar advanced against Egypt and even entered the country, but finally had to withdraw to Syria.

46, 15: Apis: the chief god of Memphis, venerated in the form of a black bull.

46, 17: "The noise . . . go by": in Hebrew there is wordplay here on the name Hophra, who still made a pretense of power though his career was at an end.

46, 18: Tabor . . . Carmel: outstanding mountains of Pales-

tine, symbols of strength, to which Nebuchadnezzar is compared.

46, 25: Amon: the sun-god worshiped at Thebes, in Upper Egypt.

n: Dt 32, 42; Is 13, 9; Ez 39, 17-20. o: Jer 8, 22; 51, 8; Ez 30, 21f. p: Ez 32, 9-12. q: Jer 43, 10f; 44, 30; Is 19, 1. r: Jer 44, 1. s: Lv 26, 37. t: Ez 30, 15f. u: Jer 44, 30; Ez 30, 4; 32, 11f. v: Jer 30, 10; 43, 5.

[28] You, my servant Jacob, never fear, says
the LORD,
for I am with you;
I will make an end of all the nations
to which I have driven you,
But of you I will not make an end:
I will chastise you as you deserve,
I will not let you go unpunished.[w]

CHAPTER 47

See RG
303

Against the Philistines. [1]This is the
word that came from the LORD to the
prophet Jeremiah concerning the Philistines,
before Pharaoh attacked Gaza:[x] [2]Thus says
the LORD:

*Behold: waters are rising from the north,
a torrent in flood;
It shall flood the land and all that is in it,
the cities and their people.
All the people of the land
set up a wailing cry.
[3] They hear the stamping hooves of his
steeds,
the rattling chariots, the rumbling
wheels.
Fathers turn not to save their children;
their hands fall helpless
[4] Because of the day which has come
to ruin all the Philistines,
And cut off from Tyre and Sidon*
the last of their allies.
Yes, the LORD is destroying the
Philistines,
the remnant from the coasts of
Caphtor.[y]
[5] Gaza is shaved bald,[z]
Ashkelon is reduced to silence;
Ashdod, the remnant of their strength,
how long will you gash yourself?*
[6] Alas, sword of the LORD!
how long till you find rest?

Return into your scabbard;
stop, be still!*
[7] How can it find rest
when the LORD has commanded it?
Against Ashkelon and the seashore
he has appointed it.[a]

CHAPTER 48

See RG
303

Against Moab. [1]Concerning Moab,
thus says the LORD of hosts, the God of Israel:

Woe to Nebo, it is laid waste;
Kiriathaim is disgraced and captured,
Disgraced and overthrown is the
stronghold:
[2] Moab's glory is no more.
Evil they plan against Heshbon:
"Come, let us put an end to her as a
people."
You, too, Madmen, shall be reduced to
silence;
behind you stalks the sword.
[3] Listen! a cry from Horonaim[b]
of ruin and great destruction!
[4] Moab is crushed,
their outcry is heard in Zoar.
[5] The ascent of Luhith
they climb weeping;
On the descent to Horonaim
the cry of destruction is heard.
[6] "Flee, save your lives,
to survive like the wild ass in the
desert!"
[7] Because you trusted in your works and
your treasures,
you also shall be captured.
Chemosh* shall go into exile,
his priests and princes with him.[c]
[8] The destroyer comes upon every city,
not a city escapes;
Ruined is the valley,
wasted the plain, as the LORD has said.

47, 2-7: This prophecy was fulfilled in 605/4 B.C.
47, 4: Tyre and Sidon: Phoenician cities associated commercially with the Philistines, and enemies of Nebuchadnezzar; cf Jer 27, 1-4. Nebuchadnezzar carried out a thirteen-year siege of Tyre which was only partially successful. Caphtor: probably the island of Crete, the traditional place of origin of the Philistines; cf Am 9, 7.
47, 5: Of the ancient Philistine cities, neither Gath nor Ekron (Jer 25, 20) is mentioned in this period of waning independence of the seacoast.

47, 6: Words of the Philistines.
48, 1-47: Moab was one of the Israelites' bitterest enemies. According to Flavius Josephus, Moab and Ammon were conquered by Nebuchadnezzar in this twenty-third year, 582 B.C., five years after the destruction of Jerusalem.
48, 7: Chemosh: chief god of the Moabites.

w: Jer 30, 11. *x:* Ez 25, 15f; Zep 2, 4. *y:* Jer 25, 22; Ez 25, 16f;
Am 1, 8; 9, 7. *z:* Am 1, 7. *a:* Zep 2, 5f. *b:* 3ff: Is 15, 5.
c: Nm 21, 29.

9 Set up a memorial for Moab,
  for it is an utter wasteland;
Its cities are turned into ruins
  where no one dwells.
10 [Cursed be he who does the LORD's work
    remissly,
  cursed he who holds back his sword
    from blood.]
11 Moab has been tranquil from his youth,
  has rested upon his lees;
He was not poured from one flask to
    another,
  he went not into exile.
Thus he kept his taste,
  and his scent was not lost.d

12Hence, the days shall come, says the
LORD, when I will send him coopers to turn
him over; they shall empty his flasks and
break his jars. 13Chemosh shall disappoint
Moab, as Israel was disappointed by Bethel
in which they trusted.e

14 How can you say, "We are heroes,
  men valiant in war"?
15 The ravager of Moab and his cities
    advances,
  the flower of his youth goes down to
    be slaughtered,
  says the King, the LORD of hosts by
    name.
16 Near at hand is Moab's ruin,
  his disaster hastens apace.
17 Mourn for him, all you his neighbors,
  all you who knew him well!
Say: How the strong staff is broken,
  the glorious rod!
18 Come down from glory, sit on the
    ground,
  you that dwell in Dibon;
Moab's ravager has come up against you,
  he has ruined your strongholds.f
19 Stand by the wayside, watch closely,
  you that dwell in Aroer;
Ask the man who flees, the woman who
    tries to escape:
  say to them, "What has happened?"g
20 Moab is disgraced, yes, destroyed,
  howl and cry out;

Publish it at the Arnon,
  Moab is ruined!h

21For judgment has come on the land of
the plateau: on Holon, Jahzah, and Mephaath,i 22on Dibon, Nebo, and Beth-dibla-
thaim, 23on Kiriathaim, Beth-gamul, and
Beth-meon, 24on Kerioth and on Bozrah: on
all the cities of Moab, far and near.

25 Moab's strength is broken,
  his might is shattered, says the LORD.

26Because he boasted against the LORD,
make Moab drunk so that he retches and
vomits, and he too becomes a laughingstock.
27Is Israel a laughingstock to you? Was she
caught among thieves, that you shake your
head whenever you speak of her?j

28 Leave the cities, dwell in the crags,
  you that dwell in Moab.
Be like a dove that nests
  out of reach on the edge of a chasm.
29 We have heard of the pride of Moab,k
  pride beyond bounds;
His loftiness, his pride, his scorn,
  his insolence of heart.
30 I know, says the LORD, his arrogance;
  liar in boast, liar in deed.
31 And so I wail over Moab,
  over all Moab I cry,
  over the men of Kir-heres I moan.l
32 More than for Jazer I weep over you,
  vineyard of Sibmah.
Your tendrils trailed down to the sea,
  as far as Jazer they stretched.
Upon your harvest, upon your vintage,
  the ravager has fallen.m
33 Joy and jubilation are at an end
  in the fruit gardens of the land of
    Moab.
I drain the wine from the wine vats,
  the treader treads no more,
  the vintage shout is stilled.

34The cry of Heshbon and Elealeh is heard
as far as Jahaz; they call from Zoar to Horonaim, and to Eglath-shelishiyah, for even the
waters of Nimrim turn into a desert.n 35I will
leave no one in Moab, says the LORD, to of-

d: Zep 1, 12.   e: Is 16, 12.   f: Nm 21, 30.   g: Dt 2, 36.   h: Is 16, 7.   i: Is 15, 4.   j: Zep 2, 8ff.   k: 29f: Is 16, 6.   l: Is 16, 7.   m: Is 16, 8f.   n: Is 15, 4f.

fer a holocaust on the high place, or to burn incense to his gods. ³⁶Hence the wail of flutes for Moab is in my heart; for the men of Kir-heres the wail of flutes is in my heart: the wealth they acquired has perished.ᵒ ³⁷Every head has been made bald, every beard shaved; every hand is gashed, and the loins of all are clothed in sackcloth.ᵖ ³⁸On every roof of Moab and in all his squares there is mourning; I have shattered Moab like a pot that no one wants, says the LORD. ³⁹How terror seizes Moab, and wailing! How he turns his back in shame! Moab has become a laughingstock and a horror to all his neighbors! ⁴⁰For thus says the LORD:

Behold, like an eagle he soars,
 spreads his wings over Moab.�q
⁴¹ Cities are taken,
 strongholds seized:
On that day the hearts of Moab's heroes
 are like the heart of a woman in travail.ʳ
⁴² Moab shall be destroyed, no more a
 people,
 because he boasted against the LORD.ˢ
⁴³ Terror, pit, and trap be upon you,
 people of Moab, says the LORD.ᵗ
⁴⁴ He who flees from the terror
 falls into the pit;
He who climbs from the pit
 is caught in the trap;
For I will bring these things upon Moab
 in the year of their punishment, says
 the LORD.
⁴⁵ In Heshbon's shadow stop short
 the exhausted refugees;
For fire breaks forth from Heshbon,
 and a blaze from the house of Sihon:
It consumes the brow of Moab,
 the skull of the noisemakers.ᵘ
⁴⁶ Woe to you, O Moab,
 you are ruined, O people of Chemosh!
Your sons are taken into exile,
 your daughters into captivity.
⁴⁷ But I will change the lot of Moab

in the days to come, says the LORD.ᵛ
Thus far the judgment of Moab.

CHAPTER 49

See RG 303

Against the Ammonites. ¹Concerning the Ammonites, thus says the LORD:

Has Israel no sons?
 has he no heir?
Why then has Milcom* disinherited Gad,
 why have his people settled in Gad's
 cities?
² But the days are coming, says the LORD,
 when against Rabbah of the Ammonites*
 I will sound the battle alarm;
She shall become a mound of ruins,
 and her daughter cities shall be
 destroyed by fire.
Israel shall inherit those who disinherited
 her,
 says the LORD.ʷ
³ Howl, Heshbon, for the ravager
 approaches,
 shriek, daughters of Rabbah!
Put on sackcloth and mourn,
 run to and fro, gashing yourselves;
For Milcom goes into exile
 along with his priests and captains.ˣ
⁴ Why do you glory in your strength,
 your ebbing strength, rebellious
 daughter?
You who trust in your treasures, saying,
 "Who can come against me?"
⁵ I am bringing terror upon you,
 says the Lord GOD of hosts,
 from all round about you;
You shall be scattered, each man in
 headlong flight,
 with no one to rally the fugitives.ʸ
⁶ But afterward I will change the lot
 of the Ammonites, says the LORD.

Against Edom.* ⁷Concerning Edom, thus says the LORD of hosts:

Is there no more wisdom in Teman,*

49, 1: Milcom: chief god of the Ammonites. The Transjordan tribe of Gad bordered on Ammon, and after the collapse of the northern kingdom the Ammonites occupied its territory.

49, 2: Rabbah of the Ammonites: or Rabbath-Ammon, capital of the Ammonite kingdom. The modern Amman is the capital of the kingdom of Jordan.

49, 7-22: Edom: this implacable enemy from ancient

times profited from Judah's downfall; cf Ob 11f.

49, 7: Teman: a district of Edom, used here for the whole country; it was famous for its wise men; cf Jb 2, 11.

o: Is 16, 11. *p:* Jer 47, 5; Is 15, 2f; Ez 7, 18. *q:* Jer 49, 22. *r:* Jer 6, 24; 30, 6. *s:* Zep 2, 9f. *t:* Is 24, 17f. *u:* Nm 21, 28f. *v:* Jer 49, 39. *w:* Am 1, 14. *x:* Is 15, 2ff. *y:* Jer 48, 47.

has counsel perished from the prudent,
has their wisdom become corrupt?
8 Flee, retreat, hide in deep holes,
 you who live in Dedan:
For I will bring destruction upon Esau*
 when I come to punish him.*z*
9 If vintagers came upon you,
 they would leave no gleanings;
If thieves by night,
 they would destroy as they pleased.*a*
10 So I myself will strip Esau;
 I will uncover his retreats so that he
 cannot hide.
He is ruined: sons, and brothers,
 and neighbors, so that he is no more.*b*
11 Leave your orphans behind, I will keep
 them alive;
 your widows, let them trust in me.*c*

12 For thus says the LORD: Even those not
sentenced to drink the cup must drink it!
Shall you then go unpunished? You shall not
go unpunished; you shall surely drink it.*d*
13 By my own self I have sworn, says the
LORD: Bozrah* shall become an object of
horror and a disgrace, a desolation and a
curse; she and all her cities shall become ruins forever.*e*

14 I have heard a report from the LORD,
 a herald has been sent among the
 nations:
Gather together, move against her,
 rise up for battle.
15 Small will I make you among the
 nations,
 despised among men!*f*
16 The terror you spread beguiled you,
 and your presumption of heart;
You that live in rocky crags,
 that hold the heights of the hill:
Though you build your nest high as the
 eagle,
 from there I will drag you down, says
 the LORD.*g*

17 Edom shall become an object of horror.
Every passer-by shall be appalled and catch
his breath at all her wounds. 18 As when
Sodom, Gomorrah, and their neighbors were
overthrown, says the LORD, not a man shall
dwell there: no one shall visit there.*h*

19 As when a lion comes up from the
 thicket of Jordan
 to the permanent feeding grounds,
So I, in an instant, will drive men off;
 and whom I choose I will establish
 there!
For who is like me? who can call me to
 account?
 What shepherd can stand against me?*i*
20 Therefore, hear the counsel of the LORD,
 which he has taken against Edom;
Hear the plans he has made
 against those that live in Teman:
They shall be dragged away, even the
 smallest sheep,
 their own pasture shall be aghast
 because of them.
21 At the noise of their fall the earth quakes,
 to the Red Sea the outcry is heard!
22 See! like an eagle he soars aloft,
 and spreads his wings over Bozrah;
On that day the hearts of Edom's heroes
 shall be
 like the heart of a woman in travail.*j*

Against Damascus. Concerning Damascus:
23 Hamath and Arpad* are covered with
 shame,
 they have heard bad news;
Worried, they toss like the sea
 which cannot rest.*k*
24 Damascus is weakened, she turns to flee,
 panic has seized her.
Distress and pangs take hold of her,
 like those of a woman in travail.
25 How can the city of glory be forsaken,
 the town of delight!

49, 8: Esau: Jacob's brother, the traditional ancestor of the Edomites; cf Gn 36.
49, 13: Bozrah: capital of Edom, southeast of the Dead Sea.
49, 23: Hamath and Arpad: independent Aramean states to the north of Damascus; the invasion is conceived as coming from the north. The situation is of the eighth century B.C. Cf Is 10, 9ff.

z: Ez 25, 13. *a:* Ob 5. *b:* Mal 1, 3. *c:* Dt 10, 18; Ps 68, 6. *d:* Jer 25, 15. 28; Lam 4, 21f. *e:* Is 34, 6; Ez 35, 3-9; Ob 16. *f:* Ob 2. *g:* Jer 48, 29f. *h:* Jer 50, 40; Dt 29, 23. *i:* Jer 12, 5; 25, 9; 50, 44f. *j:* Jer 4, 13. *k:* Is 36, 19; 37, 13.

26 But now her young men shall fall in her
    streets,
  and all her warriors shall be stilled.
  On that day, says the LORD of hosts,
27 I will set fire to the wall of Damascus,
  and it shall devour the palaces of Ben-
    hadad.*

Against Arabia. 28Of Kedar and the kingdoms of Hazor, defeated by Nebuchadnezzar, king of Babylon, thus says the LORD:

  Rise up, attack Kedar,
    ravage the Easterners.*l*
29 Their tents and herds shall be taken
    away,
  their tent curtains and all their goods;
  Their camels they shall carry off for
    themselves,
  and shout from upon them, "Terror on
    every side!"*m*
30 Flee! leave your homes, hide in deep
    holes,
  you that live in Hazor, says the LORD;
  For counsel has been taken against you,
  a plan has been formed against you
  [Nebuchadnezzar, king of Babylon].
31 Rise up! set out against a nation that is at
    peace,
  that lives secure, says the LORD,
  That has no gates or bars,
  and dwells alone.
32 Their camels shall be your booty,
  their many herds your spoil;
  I will scatter to the winds those who
    shave their temples,
  from all sides I will bring ruin upon
    them,
  says the LORD.*n*
33 Hazor shall become a haunt of jackals,
  a desert forever,
  Where no man lives,
  no human being stays.

Against Elam. 34The following word of

the LORD against Elam* came to the prophet
Jeremiah at the beginning of the reign of
Zedekiah, king of Judah: 35Thus says the
LORD of hosts:

  Behold, I will break the bow of Elam,
  the mainstay of their might.
36 I will bring upon Elam the four winds
  from the four ends of the heavens:
  I will scatter them to all these winds, till
    there is no nation
  to which the outcasts of Elam shall not
    come.
37 I will break Elam before their foes,
  before those who seek their life;
  I will bring evil upon them,
  my burning wrath, says the LORD.
  I will send the sword to pursue them
  until I have completely made an end of
    them;
38 My throne I will set up in Elam
  and destroy from there king and
    princes,
  says the LORD.
39 But in the days to come I will change
  the lot of Elam, says the LORD.

CHAPTER 50

See RG
303

The First Prophecy against Babylon.
1The word which the LORD spoke against
Babylon,* against the land of the Chaldeans,
through the prophet Jeremiah:*o*

 2 Announce and publish it among the
    nations;
  publish it, hide it not, but say:
  Babylon is taken, Bel* confounded,
    Merodach shattered;
  her images are put to shame, her idols
    shattered.
 3 A people from the north advances against
    her
  to turn her land into a desert,
  So that no one shall live there,

49, 27: The palaces of Ben-hadad: the royal palaces in Damascus where at least three kings bore this name; cf 1 Kgs 15,
18. 20.

49, 34: Elam: the ancient kingdom to the east of Babylonia.

50, 1—51, 58: A collection of miscellaneous prophecies
against Babylon which now stands as the introduction to the
story in Jer 51, 59-64. The Greek text of Jer 50, 1 omits through
the prophet Jeremiah, and it is in fact likely that these oracles

are not Jeremiah's, but were composed by other inspired writers after the fall of Jerusalem, who may have used some of Jeremiah's texts. Babylon fell to the Persians in 538 B.C.

50, 2: Bel: originally the name of the god of Nippur in
Mesopotamia, then identified with Merodach (Marduk),
chief god of Babylon.

---

l: Is 21, 16. *m:* Jer 4, 20. *n:* Jer 9, 25. *o:* Jer 51, 1; Is 13, 1-
14; 21, 1-10.

because man and beast have fled
away.[p]

4 In those days, at that time, says the LORD,
the men of Israel and of Judah shall
come,

Weeping as they come, to seek the LORD,
their God;[q]

5 to their goal in Zion they shall ask the
way.

"Come, let us join ourselves to the LORD
with covenant everlasting, never to be
forgotten."[r]

6 Lost sheep were my people,
their shepherds misled them,
straggling on the mountains;

From mountain to hill they wandered,
losing the way to their fold.[s]

7 Whoever came upon them devoured
them,
and their enemies said, "We incur no
guilt,

Because they sinned against the LORD,
the hope of their fathers, their abode of
justice."[t]

8 Flee from Babylon, leave the land of the
Chaldeans,
be like the rams at the head of the
flock.[u]

9 See, I am stirring up against Babylon
a band of great nations from the north;
from there they advance, and she shall
be taken.

Their arrows are arrows of the skilled
warrior;
none shall return without effect.[v]

10 Chaldea shall be their plunder,
and all her plunderers shall be
enriched,
says the LORD.

11 Yes, rejoice and exult,
you that plunder my portion;
Frisk like calves on the green,
snort like stallions!

12 Your mother shall be sorely put to shame,

she that bore you shall be abashed;
See, the last of the nations,
a desert, dry and waste.[w]

13 Because of the LORD's wrath she shall be
empty,
and become a total desert;

Everyone who passes by Babylon will be
appalled
and catch his breath, at all her
wounds.[x]

14 Take your posts encircling Babylon,
you who bend the bow;
Shoot at her, spare not your arrows,[y]

15 raise the war cry against her on all
sides.

She surrenders, her bastions fall,
her walls are torn down:[*]

Vengeance of the LORD is this! Take
revenge on her,
as she has done, do to her;
for she sinned against the LORD.[z]

16 Cut off from Babylon the sower
and him who wields the sickle in
harvest time!

Before the destroying sword,
each of them turns to his own
people,
everyone flees to his own land.[a]

17 A stray sheep was Israel
that lions pursued;

Formerly the king of Assyria devoured
her,
now Nebuchadnezzar of Babylon
gnaws her bones.[b]

18 Therefore, thus says the LORD of hosts,
the God of Israel:

I will punish the king of Babylon and his
land,
as once I punished the king of
Assyria;[c]

19 But I will bring back Israel to her fold,
to feed on Carmel and Bashan,
And on Mount Ephraim and Gilead,
till she has her fill.[d]

50, 15: *Her walls are torn down:* the prophet is not predicting the details of Babylon's downfall, but describing such a downfall in conventional language. Actually, Babylon was surrendered peaceably, without destruction.

p: Jer 51, 48; Is 13, 17.   q: Jer 3, 18; Ps 126, 6.   r: Jer 31, 31; 32, 40.   s: Is 53, 6; 1 Pt 2, 25.   t: Jer 31, 23.   u: Jer 51, 6. 45; Is 48, 20.   v: Jer 51, 27.   w: Jer 51, 43; Is 13, 20ff.   x: Jer 25, 12.   y: Jer 51, 11; Is 21, 2.   z: Jer 51, 11. 44, 58; Ps 137, 8.   a: Is 13, 14.   b: 2 Kgs 17, 24; 18, 14.   c: Is 10, 12; 14, 24f.   d: Jer 23, 3; Ez 34, 13f.

^{20}In those days, at that time, says the LORD:

> They shall seek Israel's guilt, but it shall be no more,
> and Judah's sins, but these shall no longer be found;
> for I will forgive the remnant I preserve.^{e}

^{21} Attack the land of Merathaim,*
> and those who live in Pekod;
> Slaughter and doom them, says the LORD,
> do all I have commanded you.
^{22} Battle alarm in the land,
> dire destruction!
^{23} How has the hammer of the whole earth been broken and shattered!
> What an object of horror
> Babylon has become among the nations.^{f}
^{24} You ensnared yourself, and were caught, O Babylon, before you knew it!
> You were discovered and seized,
> because you challenged the LORD.^{g}
^{25} The LORD opens his armory
> and brings forth the weapons of his wrath;
> For the Lord GOD of hosts has work to do in the land of the Chaldeans.^{h}

^{26} Come upon her from every side,
> open her granaries,
> Pile up her goods in heaps and doom it, leave not a remnant.
^{27} Slay all her oxen,
> let them go down to the slaughter;
> Woe to them! their day has come,
> the time of their punishment.
^{28} Listen! the fugitives, the escaped from the land of Babylon:
> They announce in Zion
> the vengeance of the LORD, our God.^{i}
^{29} Call up against Babylon archers,
> all who bend the bow;

> Encamp around her,
> let no one escape.
> Repay her for her deeds;
> as she has done, do to her,
> For she insulted the LORD,
> the Holy One of Israel.^{j}
^{30} Therefore her young men shall fall in her streets,
> all her warriors shall perish on that day;
> says the LORD.^{k}

^{31} I am against you, man of insolence,
> says the Lord GOD of hosts;
> For your day has come,
> the time for me to punish you.
^{32} Insolence stumbles and falls;
> there is no one to raise him up.
> I will kindle in his cities a fire
> that shall devour everything around him.
^{33} Thus says the LORD of hosts:
> Oppressed are the men of Israel,
> and with them the men of Judah;
> All their captors hold them fast
> and refuse to let them go.
^{34} Strong is their avenger,
> whose name is LORD of hosts;
> He will defend their cause with success,
> and give rest to the earth,
> but unrest to those who live in Babylon.^{l}

^{35} A sword upon the Chaldeans, says the LORD,
> upon Babylon's people, her princes and wise men!
^{36} A sword upon the soothsayers,
> that they may become fools!
> A sword upon her warriors,
> that they may tremble;
^{37} A sword upon her motley throng,
> that they may become women!
> A sword upon her treasures,
> that they may be plundered;^{m}
^{38} A sword upon her waters,

50, 21: Merathaim, "twice bitter," and Pekod, "punishment," are here symbolic terms for Babylonia, though probably they suggest also the names of regions in that country.

e: Jer 31, 34; Is 43, 25; Mi 7, 19. *f:* Jer 51, 20; Is 14, 6. *g:* Jer 51, 57. *h:* Jer 51, 11; Is 13, 5. *i:* Jer 51, 10f. *j:* Jer 51, 56. *k:* Jer 49, 26; 51, 4. *l:* Jer 51, 36. *m:* Jer 51, 30; Na 3, 13.

that they may dry up!
For it is a land of idols,
   and they shall be made frantic by
     fearful things.ⁿ
³⁹ Hence, wildcats and desert beasts shall
     dwell there,
   and ostriches shall occupy it;
Never again shall it be peopled, or lived in,
   from age to age.ᵒ
⁴⁰ As when God overturned Sodom
   and Gomorrah, with their neighbors,
     says the LORD,
Not a man shall dwell there,
   no human being shall tarry there.ᵖ
⁴¹ See! a people comes from the north,
   a great nation, and mighty kings
   roused from the ends of the earth.�q
⁴² Bow and javelin they wield,
   cruel and pitiless are they;
They sound like the roaring sea,
   as they ride forth on steeds,
Each in his place for battle
   against you, daughter Babylon.
⁴³ The king of Babylon hears news of them,
   and helpless fall his hands;
Anguish seizes him,
   throes like a mother's in childbirth.ʳ
⁴⁴ As when a lion comes up from the
     Jordan's thicket
   to the permanent feeding grounds,
So I, in one instant, will drive them off,
   and whom I choose I will establish
     there;
For who is like me? who calls me to
     account?
   what shepherd can stand against me?ˢ
⁴⁵ Therefore hear the counsel of the LORD
   which he has taken against Babylon;
Hear the plans he has made
   against the land of the Chaldeans:
They shall be dragged away, even the
     smallest sheep;
   their own pasture shall be aghast
     because of them.ᵗ
⁴⁶ At the cry "Babylon is captured!" the
     earth quakes;
   the outcry is heard among the nations.ᵘ

CHAPTER 51

See RG
303

The Second Prophecy
against Babylon

¹   Thus says the LORD:
See! I rouse against Babylon,
   and against those who live in Chaldea,
   a destroying wind.
² Against Babylon I will send winnowers
   to winnow her and lay waste her land;
They shall besiege her from all sides
   on the day of affliction.ᵛ
³ Let the bowman draw his bow,
   and flaunt his coat of mail;
Spare not her young men,
   doom her entire army.ʷ
⁴ The slain shall fall in the land of
     Chaldea,
   the transfixed, in her streets;ˣ
⁵ For Israel and Judah are not widowed
   of their God, the LORD of hosts,
And the Chaldean land is full of guilt
   to be punished by the Holy One of
     Israel.

⁶ Flee out of Babylon;
   let each one save his life,
   perish not for her guilt;
This is a time of vengeance for the LORD,
   he pays her her due.ʸ
⁷ Babylon was a golden cup in the hand of
     the LORD
   which made the whole earth drunk;
The nations drank its wine,
   with this they have become mad.ᶻ
⁸ Babylon suddenly falls and is crushed:
   howl over her!
Bring balm for her wounds,
   in case she can be healed.ᵃ
⁹ "We have tried to heal Babylon,
   but she cannot be healed.
   Leave her, let us go, each to his own
     land."
Her judgment reaches heaven,
   it touches the clouds.ᵇ
¹⁰ The LORD has brought to light our just
     cause;

---

n: Jer 51, 32. 36. o: Jer 51, 37; Is 13, 21f. p: Jer 51, 43. q: Jer 51, 27f. r: Is 13, 7. s: Jer 49, 19. t: Jer 51, 12. 29. u: Jer 51,
29. v: Jer 15, 7; Is 41, 16. w: Jer 50, 14. 29. x: Jer 50, 30. y: Jer 50, 8. 15. 29; Is 48, 20. z: Rv 14, 8; 17, 4. a: Rv 18, 9-18.
b: Is 13, 14; Rv 18, 5.

come, let us tell in Zion
  what the LORD, our God, has done.*c*

11 Sharpen the arrows,
  fill the quivers;
The LORD has stirred up the spirit of
    Media's kings;*
Babylon he is resolved to destroy.
Yes, it is the vengeance of the LORD,
  vengeance for his temple.*d*
12 Against the walls of Babylon raise a
    signal,
  make strong the watch;
Post sentries,
  arrange ambushes!
For the LORD has planned and he will
    carry out
  his threat against the inhabitants of
    Babylon.
13 You who dwell by mighty waters,
  rich in treasure,
Your end has come,
  the term at which you shall be cut off!*e*
14 The LORD of hosts has sworn by himself:
  I will fill you with men as numerous as
    locusts,
  who shall raise over you the vintage
    shout!
15 He has sworn who made the earth by his
    power,
  and established the world by his
    wisdom,
  and stretched out the heavens by his
    skill.*f*
16 When he thunders, the waters in the
    heavens roar,
  and he brings up clouds from the end
    of the earth;
He makes the lightning flash in the rain,
  and releases stormwinds from their
    chambers.
17 Every man is stupid, ignorant;
  every artisan is put to shame by his idol:
He molded a fraud,
  without breath of life.

18 Nothingness are they, a ridiculous work,
  that will perish in their time of
    punishment.
19 Not like these is the portion of Jacob,
  he is the creator of all things;
Israel is his very own tribe,
  LORD of hosts is his name.

20 You are my hammer,
  my weapon for war;
With you I shatter nations,
  with you I destroy kingdoms.
21 With you I shatter horse and rider,
  with you I shatter chariot and driver.*g*
22 With you I shatter man and wife,
  with you I shatter old and young,
  with you I shatter youth and maiden.*h*
23 With you I shatter the shepherd and his
    flock,
  with you I shatter the farmer and his
    team,
  with you I shatter satraps and prefects.
24 Thus will I repay Babylon,
  and all who live in Chaldea
All the evil they did to Zion,
  as you shall see with your own eyes,
    says the LORD.*i*
25 Beware! I am against you,
  destroying mountain,
  destroyer of the entire earth, says the
    LORD;
I will stretch forth my hand against you,
  roll you down over the cliffs,
  and make you a burnt mountain:*j*
26 They will not take from you a
    cornerstone,
  or a foundation stone;
Ruins forever shall you be,
  say the LORD.*k*

27 Raise a signal on the earth,
  blow the trumpet among the nations;
Dedicate peoples to war against her,
  summon against her the kingdoms,
  Ararat, Minni, and Ashkenaz;*

51, 11: Media's kings: the Medes dwelt with the Persians in the land now known as Iran. At the time these words were written the Medes were the dominant people of the two, but within a short time the Persians had gained the ascendancy.
51, 27: Ararat, Minni, and Ashkenaz: regions or people in what is now Armenia, subject at this time to Media.

c: Jer 50, 28. *d:* 2 Kgs 17, 6; Is 13, 17. *e:* Na 2, 1. *f:* Jer 10, 12. *g:* Dn 7, 7. 19. 23. *h:* Is 13, 16. 18. *i:* Jer 25, 14; 50, 29; Ps 137, 8. *j:* Rv 8, 7; 18, 8f. *k:* Jer 25, 12; Ps 118, 22.

Appoint recruiting officers against her,
send up horses like bristling locusts.[l]

28 Dedicate peoples to war against her:
the king of Media,
Its governors and all its prefects,
every land in his domain.

29 The earth quakes and writhes,
the LORD's plan against Babylon is
carried out,
Turning the land of Babylon
into a desert where no one lives.

30 Babylon's warriors have ceased to
fight,
they remain in their strongholds;
Dried up is their strength,
they have become women.
Burned are their homes,
and broken their bars.

31 One runner meets another,
herald meets herald,
Telling the king of Babylon
that all his city is taken.[m]

32 The fords have been seized,
and the fortresses set on fire,
while warriors are in panic.

33 For thus says the LORD of hosts, the God
of Israel:

Daughter Babylon is like a threshing
floor
at the time it is trodden;
Yet a little while,
and the harvest time will come for her.[n]

34 He has consumed me,* routed me,
[Nebuchadnezzar, king of Babylon,]
he has left me as an empty vessel;
He has swallowed me like a dragon:
filled his belly with my delights, and
cast me out.

35 My torn flesh be upon Babylon,
says the city on Zion;
My blood upon the people of Chaldea,
says Jerusalem.

36 But now, thus says the LORD:
Surely I will defend your cause,
I will avenge you;
I will dry up her sea,
and drain her fountain.

37 Babylon shall become a heap of ruins,
a haunt of jackals;
A place of horror and ridicule,
where no one lives.[o]

38 They all roar like lions,
growl like lion cubs.[p]

39 When they are parched, I will set a drink
before them
to make them drunk, that they may be
overcome
with perpetual sleep, never to awaken,
says the LORD.

40 I will bring them down like lambs to the
slaughter,
like rams and goats.

41 How has she been seized, made captive,
the glory of the whole world!
What a horror has Babylon become
among nations:[q]

42 against Babylon the sea rises,
she is overwhelmed by the roaring
waves!

43 Her cities have become a desert,
parched and arid land
Where no man lives,
and no one passes through.

44 I will punish Bel in Babylon,
and make him disgorge what he
swallowed;
peoples shall stream to him no more.
The wall of Babylon falls!

45 Leave her, my people, let each one
save himself
from the burning wrath of the LORD.

46 Be not discouraged for fear of rumors
spread in the land; this year the rumor
comes, then violence in the land, tyrant
against tyrant.[r] 47 But behold, the days are
coming when I will punish the idols of Babylon; her whole land shall be put to shame,
and all her slain shall lie fallen within her.
48 Then heaven, and earth, and everything in
them shall shout over Babylon with joy,
when the destroyers come against her from
the north, says the LORD.[s] 49 Babylon, too,
must fall, O slain of Israel, as at the hands of
Babylon have fallen the slain of all the earth.

51, 34: Me, my: refers to Jerusalem.

l: Na 3, 17.   m: 2 Chr 30, 6; Jb 1, 14-18.   n: Rv 14, 15.   o: Is 25, 2.   p: Na 2, 11f.   q: Is 13, 19.   r: Mt 24, 6f.   s: Rv 18, 20.

⁵⁰ You who have escaped the sword,
    go on, stand not still;
  Remember the LORD from afar,
    let Jerusalem come to your
      minds.
⁵¹ We are ashamed because we have heard
    taunts,
  confusion covers our faces; strangers
    have entered
  the holy places of the house of the
    LORD.ᵗ
⁵² But behold, the days are coming, says the
    LORD,
  when I will punish her idols,
  and in her whole land the wounded
    will groan.
⁵³ Though Babylon scale the heavens,
  and make her strong heights
    inaccessible,
  destroyers from me shall reach her,
    says the LORD.ᵘ
⁵⁴ Hear! loud cries from Babylon,
  dire destruction from the land of the
    Chaldeans;
⁵⁵ For the LORD lays Babylon waste,
  stills her loud cry,
  Though her waves were roaring like
    mighty waters,
  and their clamor was heard afar.
⁵⁶ For the destroyer comes upon her,
    [Babylon,]
  her heroes are captured, their bows
    broken;
  The LORD is a God who requites,
    he will surely repay.ᵛ

⁵⁷I will make her princes and her wise men drunk, her governors, her prefects, and her warriors, so that they sleep an eternal sleep, never to awaken, says the King, whose name is the LORD of hosts. ⁵⁸Thus says the LORD of hosts:

The walls of spacious Babylon shall be
    leveled utterly;
  her lofty gates shall be destroyed by
    fire.
The toil of the nations is for nothing;
  for the flames the peoples weary
    themselves.ʷ

The Prophecy Sent to Babylon. ⁵⁹This was the errand given by the prophet Jeremiah to Seraiah,* son of Neriah, son of Mahseiah, when he went to Babylon for the king in the fourth year of the reign of Zedekiah; Seraiah was chief quartermaster. ⁶⁰Jeremiah had written all the misfortune that was to befall Babylon in a single book:* all these words that were written against Babylon. ⁶¹And Jeremiah said to Seraiah: When you reach Babylon, see that you read aloud all these words,ˣ ⁶²and then say: O LORD, you yourself threatened to destroy this place, so that neither man nor beast should dwell in it, since it would remain an everlasting desert. ⁶³When you have finished reading this book, tie a stone to it and throw it in the Euphrates,ʸ ⁶⁴and say: Thus shall Babylon sink. Never shall she rise, because of the evil I am bringing upon her. [To "weary themselves" are the words of Jeremiah.]*

VI: Historical Appendix*

CHAPTER 52

See RG
303

Capture of Jerusalem. ¹Zedakiah was twenty-one years old when he became king, and he reigned eleven years in Jerusalem.ᶻ His mother's name was Hamutal, daughter of Jeremiah of Libnah. ²He did what was evil in the eyes of the LORD, just as Jehoiakim had done. ³Indeed, what was done in Jerusalem and in Judah so angered the

---

51, 59: Seraiah: the brother of Baruch; cf Jer 32, 12. The king: Zedekiah. Perhaps Seraiah went to Babylon to explain away the presence of foreign ambassadors in Jerusalem that same year; cf Jer 27, 3.

51, 60: Jeremiah prophesied against Babylon, even as he foretold Judah's release from Babylon's power (Jer 3, 14-18; 32, 15; 33, 6-9. 12f); but his book against Babylon was thrown in the Euphrates (v 63). The preceding oracles were composed by later writers; see note on Jer 50, 1—51, 58.

51, 64: [To "weary themselves" are the words of Jere-

miah]: an editorial remark concerning the end of v 58.

52, 1-34: This supplement to the Book of Jeremiah was taken by the final editor from 2 Kgs 24, 18—25, 30 and placed here in order to show the fulfillment of Jeremiah's prophecies. In part this repeats the history given in Jer 39—41; the history of Gedaliah in 2 Kgs 25, 22-26, however, has not been reproduced here.

t: Pss 44, 16f; 78, 1-4.   *u:* Is 14, 13.   *v:* Na 1, 2.   *w:* Hb 2, 13.
x: Jer 50, 1-51.   *y:* Rv 18, 21.   *z:* 1-27: 2 Kgs 24, 18—25, 21.

LORD that he cast them out from his presence.

Zedekiah rebelled against the king of Babylon. [4a]In the tenth month of the ninth year of his reign, on the tenth day of the month,* Nebuchadnezzar, king of Babylon, and his whole army advanced against Jerusalem, encamped around it, and built siege walls on every side. [5]The siege of the city continued until the eleventh year of King Zedekiah.

[6]On the ninth day of the fourth month, when famine had gripped the city and the people had no more bread, [7]the city walls were breached. Then all the soldiers took to flight and left the city by night through the gate between the two walls which was near the king's garden. With the Chaldeans surrounding the city, they went in the direction of the Arabah. [8]But the Chaldean army pursued the king and overtook Zedekiah in the desert near Jericho, while his whole army fled from him.

[9]The king, therefore, was arrested and brought to Riblah, in the land of Hamath, to the king of Babylon, who pronounced sentence on him. [10]As Zedekiah looked on, the king of Babylon slew his sons as well as all the princes of Judah at Riblah. [11]Then he blinded Zedekiah, bound him with fetters, and had him brought to Babylon and kept in prison until the day of his death.

Destruction of Jerusalem. [12]On the tenth day of the fifth month (this was in the nineteenth year* of Nebuchadnezzar, king of Babylon), Nebuzaradan, captain of the bodyguard, came to Jerusalem as the representative of the king of Babylon. [13]He burned the house of the LORD, the palace of the king, and all the houses of Jerusalem; every large building he destroyed with fire. [14]And the Chaldean troops who were with the captain of the guard tore down all the walls that surrounded Jerusalem.

[15]Then Nebuzaradan, captain of the guard, led into exile the rest of the people left in the city, and those who had deserted to the king of Babylon, and the rest of the artisans. [16]But some of the country's poor, Nebuzaradan, captain of the guard, left behind as vinedressers and farmers.

[17]The bronze pillars that belonged to the house of the LORD, and the wheeled carts and the bronze sea in the house of the LORD, the Chaldeans broke into pieces; they carried away all the bronze to Babylon. [18]They took also the pots, the shovels, the snuffers, the bowls, the pans, and all the bronze vessels used for service. [19]The basins also, the fire holders, the bowls, the pots, the lampstands, the pans, the sacrificial bowls which were of gold or silver, these too the captain of the guard carried off, [20]as well as the two pillars, the one sea, and the twelve oxen of bronze under the sea, and the wheeled carts which King Solomon had made for the house of the LORD. The bronze of all these furnishings could not be weighed.

[21]Each of the pillars was eighteen cubits high and twelve cubits in diameter; each was four fingers thick, and hollow inside. [22]A bronze capital five cubits high surmounted the one pillar, and a network with pomegranates encircled the capital, all of brass; and so for the other pillar. The pomegranates . . . [23]there were ninety-six pomegranates. There were a hundred pomegranates, all around the network.

[24]The captain of the guard also took Seraiah, the high priest, Zephaniah, the second priest, and the three keepers of the entry. [25]And from the city he took one courtier, a commander of soldiers, and seven men in the personal service of the king who were present in the city, and the scribe of the army commander who mustered the people of the land, and sixty of the common people who were in the city. [26]The captain of the guard, Nebuzaradan, arrested these and brought them to the king of Babylon at Riblah, [27]who had them struck down and put to death in Riblah, in the land of Hamath.

Thus was Judah exiled from her land. [28]*This is the number of the people whom

---

52, 4: In the tenth month of the ninth year of his reign, on the tenth day of the month: January 15, 588 B.C. Cf Jer 39, 1.

52, 12: On the tenth day of the fifth month . . . nineteenth year: the tenth of Ab—July/August in 587 B.C.

52, 28-30: These verses are missing in the Greek text and have not been taken from 2 Kgs 25, but from some other

a: 4-16: Jer 39, 1-10.

Nebuchadnezzar led away captive: in his seventh year, three thousand and twenty-three people of Judah; [29]in the eighteenth year of Nebuchadnezzar, eight hundred and thirty-two persons from Jerusalem; [30]in the twenty-third year of Nebuchadnezzar, Nebuzaradan, captain of the guard, exiled seven hundred and forty-five people of Judah: four thousand six hundred persons in all.

Favor Shown to Jehoiachin.* [31b]In the thirty-seventh year of the exile of Jehoiachin, king of Judah, on the twenty-fifth

day of the twelfth month, Evil-merodach, king of Babylon, in the inaugural year of his reign, took up the case of Jehoiachin, king of Judah, and released him from prison. [32]He spoke kindly to him and gave him a throne higher than that of the other kings* who were with him in Babylon. [33]Jehoiachin took off his prison garb and ate at the king's table as long as he lived. [34]The allowance given him by the king of Babylon was a perpetual allowance, in fixed daily amounts, all the days of his life until the day of his death.

source using a different system of chronology. Besides the deportations of 598 and 587 B.C., mention is made here of a final one that took place in the year 582/1, possibly as a sequel to the murder of Gedaliah; cf Jer 41, 2.

52, 31-34: In the year 561/0 B.C., Jehoiachin was released from prison by Nebuchadnezzar's successor Awel-Marduk (Evil-merodach), who reigned only two years. Babylonian

records confirm the fact that Jehoiachin and his family were supported at public expense.

52, 32: The other kings: who had also been brought as captives to Babylon.

b: 31-34: 2 Kgs 25, 27-30.

See RG 310–14

The Book of Lamentations

The sixth century B.C. was an age of crisis, a turning point in the history of Israel. With the destruction of the temple and the interruption of its ritual, the exile of the leaders and loss of national sovereignty, an era came to an end. Not long after the fall of Jerusalem (587) an eyewitness of the national humiliation composed these five laments. They combine confession of sin, grief over the suffering and humiliation of Zion, submission to merited chastisement, and strong faith in the constancy of Yahweh's love and power to restore. The union of poignant grief and unquenchable hope reflects the constant prophetic vision of the weakness of man and the strength of God's love; it also shows how Israel's faith in Yahweh could survive the shattering experience of national ruin.

As a literary work, the Book of Lamentations is carefully constructed according to a familiar structural device. The first four poems are acrostics in which the separate stanzas begin with successive letters of the Hebrew alphabet from the first to the last. Far from destroying the spontaneous pathos of the songs, this literary feature permits a symbolic and disciplined ex-

pression of the profound grief, the sinful responsibility, and the enduring hope of the suffering community. The figure of Israel as the bride of Yahweh, familiar from the prophets, appears here again; but now Zion is a desolate widow, the *Judaea Capta* of Titus' memorial coins, sustained only by the faith that God's chastisement will eventually give place to his infinite compassion.

CHAPTER 1

Jerusalem Abandoned and Disgraced*

See RG 310–14

[1] How lonely she is now,
the once crowded city!
Widowed is she
who was mistress over nations;
The princess among the provinces
has been made a toiling slave.

[2] Bitterly she weeps at night,
tears upon her cheeks,
With not one to console her
of all her dear ones;

1, 1-22: In this poem the poet first describes Jerusalem's miserable state after the destruction wrought by the Chaldeans (vv 1-11a); in v 11b the city itself takes up the lament.

Her friends have all betrayed her
  and become her enemies.*a*

3 Judah has fled into exile
  from oppression and cruel slavery;
Yet where she lives among the nations
  she finds no place to rest:
All her persecutors come upon her
  where she is narrowly confined.*b*

4 The roads to Zion mourn
  for lack of pilgrims going to her feasts;
All her gateways are deserted,
  her priests groan,
Her virgins sigh;
  she is in bitter grief.*c*

5 Her foes are uppermost,
  her enemies are at ease;
The LORD has punished her
  for her many sins.
Her little ones have gone away,
  captive before the foe.

6 Gone from daughter Zion
  is all her glory:
Her princes, like rams
  that find no pasture,
Have gone off without strength
  before their captors.

7 Jerusalem is mindful of the days
  of her wretched homelessness,
When her people fell into enemy hands,
  and she had no one to help her;
When her foes gloated over her,
  laughed at her ruin.

8 Through the sin of which she is guilty,
  Jerusalem is defiled;
All who esteemed her think her vile
  now that they see her nakedness;
She herself groans
  and turns away.*d*

9 Her filth is on her skirt;
  she gave no thought how she would end.

Astounding is her downfall,
  with no one to console her.
Look, O LORD, upon her misery,
  for the enemy has triumphed!

10 The foe stretched out his hand
  to all her treasures;
She has seen those nations
  enter her sanctuary
Whom you forbade to come
  into your assembly.*e*

11 All her people groan,
  searching for bread;
They give their treasures for food,
  to retain the breath of life.
"Look, O LORD, and see
  how worthless I have become!*f*

12 "Come, all you who pass by the way,
  look and see
Whether there is any suffering like my
    suffering,
  which has been dealt me
When the LORD afflicted me
  on the day of his blazing wrath.

13 "From on high he sent fire
  down into my very frame;
He spread a net for my feet,
  and overthrew me.
He left me desolate,
  in pain all the day.*g*

14 "He has kept watch over my sins;
  by his hand they have been plaited:
They have settled about my neck,*
  he has brought my strength to its
    knees;
The Lord has delivered me into their
    grip,
  I am unable to rise.

15 "All the mighty ones in my midst
  the Lord has cast away;
He summoned an army against me
  to crush my young men;

1, 14: They have been plaited . . . my neck: the sins of the people have been bound together and laid as a yoke on their back; cf Mt 23, 4.

a: Jer 30, 14; Ez 16, 37. *b:* Dt 28, 65; Jer 45, 3. *c:* Jer 14, 2. *d:* Is 47, 2; Jer 13, 22. 26. *e:* Jer 51, 51. *f:* Jer 52, 6. *g:* Ez 12, 13.

The LORD has trodden in the wine press
  virgin daughter Judah.[h]

16 "At this I weep,
  my eyes run with tears:
Far from me are all who could console me,
  any who might revive me;
My sons were reduced to silence
  when the enemy prevailed."[i]

17 Zion stretched out her hands,
  but there was no one to console her;
The LORD gave orders against Jacob
  for his neighbors to be his foes;
Jerusalem has become in their midst
  a thing unclean.[j]

18 "The LORD is just;
  I had defied his command.
Listen, all you peoples,
  and behold my suffering:
My maidens and my youths
  have gone into captivity.[k]

19 "I cried out to my lovers,*
  but they failed me.
My priests and my elders
  perished in the city;
Where they sought food for themselves,
  they found it not.[l]

20 "Look, O LORD, upon my distress:
  all within me is in ferment,
My heart recoils within me
  from my monstrous rebellion.
In the streets the sword bereaves,
  at home death stalks.[m]

21 "Give heed to my groaning;
  there is no one to console me.
All my enemies rejoice at my misfortune:
  it is you who have wrought it.
Bring on the day you have proclaimed,
  that they may be even as I.

22 "Let all their evil come before you;*
  deal with them
As you have dealt with me
  for all my sins;
My groans are many,
  and I am sick at heart."[n]

CHAPTER 2

The Lord's Wrath against Zion

See RG
310–14

1 How the Lord in his wrath
  has detested daughter Zion!
He has cast down from heaven to earth
  the glory of Israel,*
Unmindful of his footstool
  on the day of his wrath.

2 The Lord has consumed without pity
  all the dwellings of Jacob;
He has torn down in his anger
  the fortresses of daughter Judah;
He has brought to the ground in dishonor
  her king and her princes.

3 He broke off, in fiery wrath,
  the horn* that was Israel's whole
    strength;
He withheld the support of his right hand
  when the enemy approached;
He blazed up in Jacob like a flaming fire
  devouring all about it.[o]

4 Like an enemy he made taut his bow;
  with his arrows in his right hand
He took his stand as a foe, and slew
  all on whom the eye doted;
Over the tent of daughter Zion
  he poured out his wrath like fire.[p]

5 The Lord has become an enemy,
  he has consumed Israel:
Consumed all her castles
  and destroyed her fortresses;
For daughter Judah he has multiplied
  moaning and groaning.

1, 19: My lovers: Zion's foreign allies, who failed to help her, as the prophets had warned.

1, 22: Zion fully acknowledges her guilt and the justness of divine punishment; nevertheless, she pleads that her enemies also be punished for their guilt.

2, 1: The glory of Israel: the temple. His footstool: the ark of the covenant (1 Chr 28, 2; Pss 99, 5; 132, 7); or again, the temple (Ez 43, 7).

2, 3: Horn: symbol of power and strength; cf Lam 2, 17; 1 Sm 2, 10; Lk 1, 69; etc.

h: Jer 8, 16.   i: Jer 13, 17; 14, 17.   j: Ps 74, 7.   k: Dt 28, 41.
l: Jer 30, 14.   m: Lam 2, 11.   n: Lam 3, 64.   o: Lam 1, 12.
p: Jer 30, 14.

Acrostic Poems in Hebrew

A N ACROSTIC POEM is one in which the initial letters of each line of poetry follow some sort of pattern. In the Hebrew Bible, all of the acrostic poems are alphabetical acrostics: that is, the first letters of each line (or each group of lines) form the Hebrew alphabet of twenty-two letters.

The following passages in the Bible are acrostics: Psalms 9—10, 25, 34, 37, 111, 112, 119, 145; Proverbs 31, 10–31; each chapter in Lamentations except chapter 5, which nevertheless has twenty-two lines; Nahum 1, 2–8 (or perhaps 2–10; the acrostic is incomplete). The Hebrew text of Sirach 51, 13–30 is also an acrostic. Psalms 34, 37, 112, 119, Proverbs 31, and Sirach 51 are all examples of wisdom literature, and if these texts were used in schools, the acrostic feature may have been an aid to memorization.

Although this kind of pattern in a poem may seem strange to us, we can compare it to the use of rhyme in English poetry. Rhyme is a pattern involving similar sounds at the ends of lines; it is therefore like an acrostic in combining a pattern of sound and meaning. We can admire the artistry involved in such a combination, and perhaps that will give us insight into the enjoyment that acrostic poems may have provided to their original audiences.

In the case of Lamentations, where chapters 1—4 are acrostics, and chapter 5 continues the pattern with its twenty-two lines, there may be a deeper meaning. By expressing grief in a pattern that completes the alphabet, the poet may be expressing two things: the completeness of grief—covering it "from A to Z," as we might say—and also its end. The poetical form helps the poet to channel and contain grief, as mourning rituals can do in other social settings.

6 He has demolished his shelter like a
    garden booth,
he has destroyed his dwelling;
In Zion the LORD has made
    feast and sabbath to be forgotten;
He has scorned in fierce wrath
    both king and priest.*q*

7 The Lord has disowned his altar,
    rejected his sanctuary;
The walls of her towers
    he has handed over to the enemy,
Who shout in the house of the LORD
    as on a feast day.*r*

8 The LORD marked for destruction
    the wall of daughter Zion:
He stretched out the measuring line;*
    his hand brought ruin, yet he did not
    relent—

He brought grief on wall and rampart
    till both succumbed.*s*

9 Sunk into the ground are her gates;
    he has removed and broken her bars.
Her king and her princes are among the
    pagans;
    priestly instruction is wanting,
And her prophets have not received
    any vision from the LORD.*t*

10 On the ground in silence sit
    the old men of daughter Zion;
They strew dust* on their heads
    and gird themselves with sackcloth;
The maidens of Jerusalem
    bow their heads to the ground.*u*

11 Worn out from weeping are my eyes,
    within me all is in ferment;

2, 8: The measuring line: used not only in building, but in deciding what must be destroyed; cf Is 34, 11; 2 Kgs 21, 13.
2, 10: They strew dust: as a sign of penance; cf Jb 2, 12.
2, 11: My gall is poured out on the ground: I am afflicted with bitter sorrow; cf Jb 16, 13.

q: Lam 1, 4; Is 1, 13; 5, 5.　*r:* Ez 24, 21.　*s:* Jer 52, 13.　*t:* Dt 28, 36.　*u:* Is 3, 26.

My gall is poured out on the ground*
    because of the downfall of the
        daughter of my people,
As child and infant faint away
    in the open spaces of the town.ᵛ

12 They ask their mothers,
    "Where is the cereal?"—in vain,
As they faint away like the wounded
    in the streets of the city,
And breathe their last
    in their mothers' arms.ʷ

13 To what can I liken or compare you,
    O daughter Jerusalem?
What example can I show you for your
        comfort,
    virgin daughter Zion?
For great as the sea is your downfall;
    who can heal you?ˣ

14 Your prophets had for you
    false and specious visions;
They did not lay bare your guilt,
    to avert your fate;
They beheld for you in vision
    false and misleading portents.ʸ

15 All who pass by
    clap their hands at you;
They hiss and wag their heads
    over daughter Jerusalem:
"Is this the all-beautiful city,
    the joy of the whole earth?"ᶻ

16 All your enemies
    open their mouths against you;
They hiss and gnash their teeth.
    They say, "We have devoured her.
This at last is the day we hoped for;
    we have lived to see it!"ᵃ

17 The LORD has done as he decreed:
    he has fulfilled the threat
He set forth from days of old;

he has destroyed and had no pity,
Letting the enemy gloat over you
    and exalting the horn of your foes.ᵇ

18 Cry out to the Lord;
    moan, O daughter Zion!
Let your tears flow like a torrent
    day and night;
Let there be no respite for you,
    no repose for your eyes.

19 Rise up, shrill in the night,
    at the beginning of every watch;
Pour out your heart like water
    in the presence of the Lord;
Lift up your hands to him
    for the lives of your little ones
[Who faint from hunger
    at the corner of every street].

20 "Look, O LORD, and consider:
    whom have you ever treated thus?
Must women eat their offspring,*
    their well-formed children?
Are priest and prophet to be slain
    in the sanctuary of the LORD?ᶜ

21 "Dead in the dust of the streets
    lie young and old;
My maidens and young men
    have fallen by the sword;
You have slain on the day of your wrath,
    slaughtered without pity.ᵈ

22 "You summoned as for a feast day
    terrors against me from all sides;
There was not, on the day of your wrath,
    either fugitive or survivor;
Those whom I bore and reared
    my enemy has utterly destroyed."ᵉ

CHAPTER 3

See RG
310-14

Sufferings of the Prophet and His People

1 I am a man who knows affliction*

2, 20: Must women eat their offspring: extreme famine in a besieged city sometimes led to this form of cannibalism; cf Lam 4, 10; 2 Kgs 6, 28f; Bar 2, 3; Ez 5, 10.

3, 1-21: The author identifies Zion's sufferings with his own.

ᵛ: Lam 3, 48.   ʷ: Lam 1, 11.   ˣ: Lam 1, 12.   ʸ: Is 58, 1; Jer 2, 8; 23, 16.   ᶻ: Jer 18, 16.   ᵃ: Lam 3, 46.   ᵇ: Dt 28, 15.   ᶜ: Lam 4, 10.   ᵈ: Lam 3, 43; 2 Chr 36, 17; Jer 6, 11.   ᵉ: Jer 42, 17.

from the rod of his anger,[f]

2 One whom he has led and forced to walk
in darkness, not in the light;

3 Against me alone he brings back his
hand
again and again all the day.

4 He has worn away my flesh and my skin,
he has broken my bones;[g]

5 He has beset me round about
with poverty and weariness;

6 He has left me to dwell in the dark
like those long dead.[h]

7 He has hemmed me in with no escape
and weighed me down with chains;

8 Even when I cry out for help,
he stops my prayer;[i]

9 He has blocked my ways with fitted
stones,
and turned my paths aside.

10 A lurking bear he has been to me,
a lion in ambush![j]

11 He deranged my ways, set me astray,
left me desolate.[k]

12 He bent his bow, and set me up
as the target for his arrow.[l]

13 He pierces my sides
with shafts from his quiver.[m]

14 I have become a laughingstock for all
nations,
their taunt all the day long;[n]

15 He has sated me with bitter food,
made me drink my fill of wormwood.[o]

16 He has broken my teeth with gravel,
pressed my face in the dust;

17 My soul is deprived of peace,
I have forgotten what happiness is;

18 I tell myself my future is lost,
all that I hoped for from the LORD.

19 The thought of my homeless poverty
is wormwood and gall;

20 Remembering it over and over
leaves my soul downcast within me.

21 But I will call this to mind,
as my reason to have hope:

22 The favors of the LORD are not
exhausted,
his mercies are not spent;[p]

23 They are renewed each morning,
so great is his faithfulness.

24 My portion is the LORD, says my soul;
therefore will I hope in him.[q]

25 Good is the LORD to one who waits for
him,
to the soul that seeks him;[r]

26 It is good to hope in silence
for the saving help of the LORD.

27 It is good for a man to bear
the yoke* from his youth.

28 Let him sit alone and in silence,
when it is laid upon him.

29 Let him put his mouth to the dust;*
there may yet be hope.[s]

30 Let him offer his cheek to be struck,
let him be filled with disgrace.[t]

31 For the Lord's rejection
does not last forever;[u]

32 Though he punishes, he takes pity,
in the abundance of his mercies;[v]

33 He has no joy in afflicting
or grieving the sons of men.[w]

34 When anyone tramples underfoot
all the prisoners in the land,

35 When he distorts men's rights
in the very sight of the Most High,

36 When he presses a crooked claim,
the Lord does not look on
unconcerned.

37 Who commands, so that it comes to pass,
except the Lord ordains it;

3, 27: To bear the yoke: to do God's will; cf Jer 2, 20.
3, 29: Let him put his mouth to the dust: in humble submission; cf Ps 72, 9.

f: Jer 20, 18.   g: Jb 30, 30; Is 38, 13.   h: Ps 143, 3.   i: Ps 22, 2.   j: Jb 10, 16; Hos 13, 8.   k: Lam 1, 13.   l: Lam 2, 4; Jb 16, 12.
m: Jb 6, 4; Ps 38, 3.   n: Jb 30, 9; Ps 69, 13.   o: Jer 9, 14; 23, 15.   p: Neh 9, 31.   q: Pss 16, 5; 73, 26.   r: Ps 130, 6; Is 30, 18.   s: Jb
42, 6.   t: Is 50, 6; Mt 5, 39.   u: Ps 103, 9.   v: Is 54, 8f.   w: Heb 12, 10f.

38 Except it proceeds from the mouth of the
    Most High,
  whether the thing be good or bad!x
39 Why should any living man complain,
  any mortal, in the face of his sins?y

40 Let us search and examine our ways
  that we may return to the LORD!z
41 Let us reach out our hearts
  toward God in heaven!
42 We have sinned and rebelled;
  you have not forgiven us.

43 You veiled yourself in wrath and pursued
    us,
  you slew us and took no pity;a
44 You wrapped yourself in a cloud
  which prayer could not pierce.
45 You have made us offscourings and refuse
  among the nations.b

46 All our enemies
  have opened their mouths against us;
47 Terror and the pit have been our lot,
  desolation and destruction;c
48 My eyes run with streams of water
  over the downfall of the daughter of
    my people.d

49 My eyes flow without ceasing,
  there is no respite,
50 Till the LORD from heaven
  looks down and sees.
51 My eyes torment my soul
  at the sight of all the daughters of my
    city.

52 Those who were my enemies without
    cause
  hunted me down like a bird;
53 They struck me down alive in the pit,
  and sealed me in with a stone.e
54 The waters flowed over my head,
  and I said, "I am lost!"

55 I called upon your name, O LORD,f
  from the bottom of the pit;

56 You heard me call, "Let not your ear
  be deaf to my cry for help!"
57 You came to my aid when I called to
    you;
  you said, "Have no fear!"

58 You defended me in mortal danger,
  you redeemed my life.
59 You see, O LORD, how I am wronged;
  do me justice!g
60 You see all their vindictiveness,
  all their plots against me.

61 You hear their insults, O LORD,
  [all their plots against me],
62 The whispered murmurings of my foes,
  against me all the day;
63 Whether they sit or stand,
  see, I am their taunt song.

64 Requite them as they deserve, O LORD,
  according to their deeds;
65 Give them hardness of heart,
  as your curse upon them;h
66 Pursue them in wrath and destroy them
  from under your heavens!

CHAPTER 4

Miseries of the Besieged City

See RG
310-14

1 How tarnished is the gold,
  how changed the noble metal;
  How the sacred stones lie strewn
  at every street corner!

2 Zion's precious sons,
  fine gold their counterpart,
  Now worth no more than earthen jars
  made by the hands of a potter!i

3 Even the jackals bare their breasts
  and suckle their young;
  The daughter of my people has become
    as cruel
  as the ostrich* in the desert.j

4 The tongue of the suckling cleaves
  to the roof of its mouth in thirst;

4, 3: Cruel as the ostrich: see note on Jb 39, 14ff. Jerusalem, in her distress, had abandoned her children.

x: Is 45, 7.   y: Prv 19, 3.   z: Jl 2, 12f.   a: Lam 2, 21.   b: 1 Cor 4, 13.   c: Is 24, 17; Jer 48, 43.   d: Ps 119, 136.   e: Jer 37, 16; 38,
6-9.   f: 55f: Ps 130, 1f.   g: Ps 35, 23.   h: Jer 11, 20; 2 Tm 4, 14.   i: Jer 19, 11.   j: Jb 39, 16.

The babes cry for food,
   but there is no one to give it to them.

5 Those accustomed to dainty food
   perish in the streets;
Those brought up in purple
   now cling to the ash heaps.*k*

6 The punishment of the daughter of my
      people
   is greater than the penalty of Sodom,
Which was overthrown in an instant
   without the turning of a hand.*l*

7 Brighter than snow were her princes,
   whiter than milk,
More ruddy than coral,
   more precious than sapphire.

8 Now their appearance is blacker than soot,
   they are unrecognized on the streets;
Their skin shrinks on their bones,
   as dry as wood.*m*

9 Better for those who perish by the sword
   than for those who die of hunger,
Who waste away, as though pierced
      through,
   lacking the fruits of the field!

10 The hands of compassionate women
      boiled their own children,
To serve them as mourners' food
   in the downfall of the daughter of my
      people.*n*

11 The LORD has spent his anger,
   poured out his blazing wrath;
He has kindled a fire in Zion
   that has consumed her foundations.*o*

12 The kings of the earth did not believe,
   nor any of the world's inhabitants,

That enemy or foe could enter
   the gates of Jerusalem.

13 Because of the sins of her prophets*
   and the crimes of her priests,
Who shed in her midst
   the blood of the just!—*p*

14 They staggered blindly in the streets,
   soiled with blood,
So that people could not touch
   even their garments:*q*

15 "Away, you unclean!" they cried to them,
   "Away, away, do not draw near!"
If they left and wandered among the
      nations,
   nowhere could they remain.

16 The LORD himself has dispersed them,
   he regards them no more;
He does not receive the priests with favor,
   nor show kindness to the elders.

17 Our eyes ever wasted away,
   looking in vain for aid;
From our watchtower we watched
   for a nation* that could not save us.

18 Men dogged our steps
   so that we could not walk in our
      streets;
Our end drew near, and came;
   our time had expired.

19 Our pursuers were swifter
   than eagles in the air,
They harassed us on the mountains
   and waylaid us in the desert.*r*

20 The anointed one of the LORD, our breath
      of life,*
   was caught in their snares,

4, 13ff: The priests and the false prophets lulled the people into an illusory security (Jer 2, 8; 5, 31; 6, 13; etc.), condoning and entering into their crimes so that they themselves became unclean.

4, 17: A nation: Egypt, which failed to give effective aid against Babylon.

4, 20: Our breath of life: the king. This is a royal epithet borrowed from Egyptian usage, while the anointed one of the Lord is Israelite. After the disaster of 598 B.C. (2 Kgs 24, 1-17), Jerusalem could have hoped to live in peace amidst her neighbors; but they (vv 21f) as well as Babylon turned against her to ensure her total devastation in 587 B.C.

---

k: Dt 28, 56.   *l:* Gn 19, 23-29; 2 Pt 2, 6; Jude 1, 7.   *m:* Lam 3, 4.   *n:* Lam 2, 20; Dt 28, 56f; 2 Kgs 6, 29.   *o:* Jer 7, 20; Ez 5, 13.
p: Jer 6, 13.   *q:* Is 59, 10.   *r:* Jer 4, 13; Hb 1, 8.

He in whose shadow we thought
    we could live on among the nations.[s]

21 Though you rejoice and are glad, O
    daughter Edom,
  you who dwell in the land of Uz,[*]
To you also shall the cup be passed;
  you shall become drunk and naked.[t]

22 Your chastisement is completed, O
    daughter Zion,
  he will not prolong your exile;
But your wickedness, O daughter Edom,
  he will punish,
  he will lay bare your sins.[u]

**See RG
310–14**

CHAPTER 5

*The Prophet's Lament
and Supplication*

1 Remember, O LORD, what has befallen
    us,
  look, and see our disgrace:
2 Our inherited lands have been turned
    over to strangers,
  our homes to foreigners.[v]
3 We have become orphans, fatherless;
  widowed are our mothers.
4 The water we drink we must buy,
  for our own wood we must pay.
5 On our necks is the yoke of those who
    drive us;
  we are worn out, but allowed no rest.

6 To Egypt we submitted,
  and to Assyria, to fill our need of
    bread.[*]
7 Our fathers,[*] who sinned, are no more;
  but we bear their guilt.
8 Slaves rule over us;
  there is no one to rescue us from their
    hands.[*]

9 At the peril of our lives we bring in our
    sustenance,
  in the face of the desert heat;[w]
10 Our skin is shriveled up, as though by a
    furnace,
  with the searing blasts of famine.[x]
11 The wives in Zion were ravished by the
    enemy,
  the maidens in the cities of Judah;[y]
12 Princes were gibbeted by them,
  elders shown no respect.[z]
13 The youths carry the millstones,
  boys stagger under their loads of
    wood;
14 The old men have abandoned the
    gate,[*]
  the young men their music.

15 The joy of our hearts has ceased,
  our dance has turned into
    mourning;[a]
16 The garlands have fallen from our
    heads:
  woe to us, for we have sinned!
17 Over this our hearts are sick,
  at this our eyes grow dim:
18 That Mount Zion should be desolate,
  with jackals roaming there!

19 You, O LORD, are enthroned forever;
  your throne stands from age to age.[b]
20 Why, then, should you forget us,
  abandon us so long a time?[c]
21 Lead us back to you, O LORD, that we
    may be restored:
  give us anew such days as we had of
    old.[d]
22 For now you have indeed rejected us,
  and in full measure turned your wrath
    against us.[e]

4, 21: Uz: see note on Jer 25, 20.

5, 6: In its state of abjection, Judah was forced to depend on its traditional enemies to the west and the east for subsistence. Mesopotamia is here called by the name it had long borne, Assyria, though in these times the power of the Assyrians had been superseded by that of the Chaldeans.

5, 7: Our fathers: collective responsibility, for good and for evil, was recognized in the Old Testament; cf Jer 31, 29. But the present generation is also personally guilty of sin (v 16).

5, 8: Administrations imposed by foreign powers were notoriously corrupt and inept. The Hebrew word for "slave"

is the same as that used for an official (servant of the ruler); the author doubtless intends the double meaning here.

5, 14: The gate: the place of assembly, where city decisions were made and judgment given by the elders and other notables; see note on Ru 4, 1.

s: Lam 2, 9; Ez 19, 4. 8. *t:* Lam 1, 21; Jer 25, 15. *u:* Is 40, 2.
v: Ps 79, 1. *w:* Jer 6, 25. *x:* Lam 4, 8. *y:* Zec 14, 2. *z:* Lam 4, 16. *a:* Jer 16, 9; 25, 10; Am 8, 10. *b:* Pss 9, 8; 45, 7; 102, 13. 27. *c:* Pss 13, 1; 42, 10. *d:* Ps 80, 19f. *e:* Jer 14, 19.

See RG
315–19

The Book of Baruch

The opening verses of this book ascribe it, or at least its first part, to Baruch, the well-known secretary of the prophet Jeremiah. It contains five very different compositions, the first and the last in prose, the others in poetic form. The prose sections were certainly composed in Hebrew, though the earliest known form of the book is in Greek.

An observance of the feast of Booths with a public prayer of penitence and petition (1, 15—3, 8), such as is supposed by the introduction (1, 1-14), would not have been possible during the lifetime of Baruch after the fall of Jerusalem; this indeed is suggested in the prayer itself (2, 26). The prayer is therefore to be understood as the pious reflection of a later Jewish writer upon the circumstances of the exiles in Babylon as he knew them from the Book of Jeremiah. He expresses in their name sentiments called for by the prophet, and ascribes the wording of these sentiments to the person most intimately acquainted with Jeremiah's teaching, namely, Baruch. The purpose of this literary device is to portray for his own and later generations the spirit of repentance which prompted God to bring the exile to an end.

The lesson thus gained is followed by a hymn in praise of Wisdom (3, 9—4, 4), exalting the law of Moses as the unique gift of God to Israel, the observance of which is the way to life and peace. The ideal city of Jerusalem is then represented (4, 5-29) as the solicitous mother of all exiles, who is assured in the name of God that all her children will be restored to her (4, 30—5, 9).

The final chapter is really a separate work, with a title of its own (6, 1). It is patterned after the earlier letter of Jeremiah (Jer 29), in the spirit of the warnings against idolatry contained in Jer 10 and Is 44. Its earnestness is impressive, but in restating previous inspired teachings at a later day, it does so with no special literary grace.

Thus the principal divisions of the book are seen to be:

I: Prayer of the Exiles (1, 1—3, 8).

II: Praise of Wisdom in the Law of Moses (3, 9—4, 4).

III: Jerusalem Bewails and Consoles Her Captive Children (4, 5-29).

IV: Jerusalem Consoled: The Captivity about To End (4, 30—5, 9).

V: The Letter of Jeremiah against Idolatry (6, 1-72).

I: Prayer of the Exiles

CHAPTER 1

See RG
316–17

Meeting in Babylon. *1*Now these are the words of the scroll which Baruch, son of Neriah, son of Mahseiah, son of Zedekiah, son of Hasadiah, son of Hilkiah, wrote in Babylon,*a 2*in the fifth year [on the seventh day of the month,* at the time when the Chaldeans took Jerusalem and burnt it with fire].*b 3c*And Baruch read the words of this scroll for Jeconiah, son of Jehoiakim, king of Judah, to hear it, as well as all the people who came to the reading:*d 4*the nobles, the kings' sons, the elders, and the whole people, small and great alike—all who lived in Babylon by the river Sud.*

*5*They wept and fasted and prayed before the LORD, *6*and collected such funds as each could furnish.*e 7*These they sent to Jerusalem, to Jehoiakim, son of Hilkiah, son of Shallum, the priest, and to the priests and the whole people who were with him in Jerusalem. *8*[This was when he* received the vessels of the house of the LORD that had

---

1, 2: In the fifth year on the seventh day of the month: Jerusalem fell on the seventh day of the fifth month; cf 2 Kgs 25, 8; Jer 52, 12. Either the text read originally "the fifth month," or it refers to the observance of an anniversary of the fall of Jerusalem in 587 B.C.

1, 4: The river Sud: one of the Babylonian canals, not otherwise identified. In ancient non-Biblical Hebrew fragments discovered in 1952, there is reference to

a river "Sur" in a similar context.

1, 8f: He: possibly Baruch; less likely Jehoiakim . . . the priest (v 7), a member of the high-priestly family not mentioned elsewhere. The silver vessels here described are distinct from the vessels referred to in 2 Kgs 25, 14 and Ezr 1,

a: Jer 32, 12; 36, 4; 45, 1-5. *b:* 2 Kgs 25, 8ff. *c:* 2 Kgs 24, 8-17; Jer 22, 24-30; 51, 59-64. *d:* 3-4; 2 Kgs 23, 1-2. *e:* Dt 16, 17.

been removed from the temple, to restore them to the land of Judah, on the tenth of Sivan. These silver vessels Zedekiah, son of Josiah, king of Judah, had had made ⁹after Nebuchadnezzar, king of Babylon, carried off Jeconiah, and the princes, and the skilled workers, and the nobles, and the people of the land from Jerusalem, as captives, and brought them to Babylon.]

¹⁰Their message was: "We send you funds, with which you are to procure holocausts, sin offerings, and frankincense, and to prepare cereal offerings; offer these on the altar of the LORD our God,ᶠ ¹¹and pray for the life of Nebuchadnezzar, king of Babylon, and that of Belshazzar, his son,* that their lifetimes may equal the duration of the heavens above the earth;ᵍ ¹²and that the LORD may give us strength, and light to our eyes, that we may live under the protective shadow of Nebuchadnezzar, king of Babylon, and that of Belshazzar, his son, and serve them long, finding favor in their sight.

Confession of Guilt. ¹³"Pray for us also to the LORD, our God; for we have sinned against the LORD, our God, and the wrath and anger of the LORD have not yet been withdrawn from us at the present day. ¹⁴And read out publicly this scroll which we send you, in the house of the LORD, on the feast day and during the days of assembly:ʰ

¹⁵"Justice is with the LORD, our God; and we today are flushed with shame, we men of Judah and citizens of Jerusalem,ⁱ ¹⁶that we, with our kings and rulers and priests and prophets, and with our fathers, ¹⁷have sinned in the LORD's sight ¹⁸and disobeyed him. We have neither heeded the voice of the LORD, our God, nor followed the precepts which the LORD set before us. ¹⁹From the time the LORD led our fathers out of the land of Egypt until the present day, we have been disobedient to the LORD, our God, and only too ready to disregard his voice. ²⁰And the evils

and the curse which the LORD enjoined upon Moses, his servant, at the time he led our fathers forth from the land of Egypt to give us the land flowing with milk and honey, cling to us even today.ʲ ²¹For we did not heed the voice of the LORD, our God, in all the words of the prophets whom he sent us, ²²but each one of us went off after the devices of our own wicked hearts, served other gods, and did evil in the sight of the LORD, our God.

CHAPTER 2

See RG 317

¹"And the LORD fulfilled the warning he had uttered against us: against our judges, who governed Israel, against our kings and princes, and against the men of Israel and Judah. ²He brought down upon us evils so great that there has not been done anywhere under heaven what has been done in Jerusalem, as was written in the law of Moses:ᵏ ³that one after another of us should eat* the flesh of his son or of his daughter. ⁴He has made us subject to all the kingdoms round about us, a reproach and a horror among all the nations round about to which the LORD has scattered us.ˡ ⁵We are brought low, not raised up, because we sinned against the LORD, our God, not heeding his voice.

⁶"Justice is with the LORD, our God; and we, like our fathers, are flushed with shame even today.ᵐ ⁷All the evils of which the LORD had warned us have come upon us; ⁸and we did not plead before the LORD, or turn, each from the figments of his evil heart. ⁹And the LORD kept watch over the evils, and brought them home to us; for the LORD is just in all the works he commanded us to do,ⁿ ¹⁰but we did not heed his voice, or follow the precepts of the LORD which he set before us.

Prayer for Deliverance. ¹¹"And now, LORD, God of Israel, you who led your people out of the land of Egypt with your mighty hand, with signs and wonders and great might, and with your upraised arm, so

---

7ff. The author of this note may have thought of the fifth year (v 1) of Zedekiah, in view of Jer 28, 1; 29, 1ff. A "fifth year," again with no month mentioned, is given in Ez 1, 2 for the inaugural vision of Ezekiel's prophetic career.

  1, 11: Nebuchadnezzar . . . Belshazzar, his son: as in Dn 5, 1f. Later Jewish tradition seems to have simplified the history of the past by making the last Chaldean ruler of Babylon the son of the conqueror of Jerusalem.

2, 3: One after another of us should eat: see note on Lam 2, 20.

f: Jer 17, 26. g: Dt 11, 21; Jer 29, 7; Dn 5, 1-2; 1 Tm 2, 1f. h: Ex 23, 14ff; Lv 23, 35f; Hos 9, 5; Sir 50, 6. i: Bar 2, 6; 3, 8; Neh 9, 6-37; Ezr 9, 6-15; Dn 9, 4-19. j: Lv 26, 14-39; Dt 28, 15-68. k: 2f: 2 Kgs 6, 28f; Jer 19, 9; Lam 2, 20; 4, 10; Ez 5, 10. l: Jer 29, 18. m: Bar 1, 15. n: Jer 1, 12; 31, 28; 44, 27.

that you have made for yourself a name till the present day:*o* *12*we have sinned, been impious, and violated, O LORD, our God, all your statutes.*p* *13*Let your anger be withdrawn from us, for we are left few in number among the nations to which you scattered us. *14*Hear, O LORD, our prayer of supplication, and deliver us for your own sake: grant us favor in the presence of our captors, *15*that the whole earth may know that you are the LORD, our God, and that Israel and his descendants bear your name.*q* *16*O LORD, look down from your holy dwelling and take thought of us; turn, O LORD, your ear to hear us.*r* *17*Look directly at us, and behold: it is not the dead in the nether world, whose spirits have been taken from within them, who will give glory and vindication to the LORD.*s* *18*He whose soul is deeply grieved, who walks bowed and feeble, with failing eyes and famished soul, will declare your glory and justice, LORD!*t*

19"Not on the just deeds of our fathers and our kings do we base our plea for mercy in your sight, O LORD, our God. *20*You have brought your wrath and anger down upon us, as you had warned us through your servants the prophets: *21*'Thus says the LORD: Bend your shoulders to the service of the king of Babylon, that you may continue in the land I gave your fathers:*u* *22*for if you do not hear the LORD's voice so as to serve the king of Babylon,

23 I will make to cease from the cities of
  Judah
and from the streets of Jerusalem
The sounds of joy and the sounds of
  gladness,
  the voice of the bridegroom
  and the voice of the bride;
And all the land shall be deserted,
  without inhabitants.'*v*

*24*But we did not heed your voice, or serve the king of Babylon, and you fulfilled the threats you had made through your servants the prophets, to have the bones of our kings and the bones of our fathers brought out from their burial places.*w* *25*And indeed, they lie exposed* to the heat of day and the frost of night. They died in dire anguish, by hunger and the sword and plague.*x* *26*And you reduced the house which bears your name* to what it is today, for the wickedness of the kingdom of Israel and the kingdom of Judah.*y*

God's Promises Recalled. *27*"But with us, O Lord, our God, you have dealt in all your clemency and in all your great mercy. *28*This was your warning through your servant Moses, the day you ordered him to write down your law in the presence of the Israelites: *29*If you do not heed my voice, surely this great and numerous throng will dwindle away among the nations to which I will scatter them. *30*For I know they will not heed me, because they are a stiff-necked people. But in the land of their captivity they shall have a change of heart;*z* *31*they shall know that I, the LORD, am their God. I will give them hearts, and heedful ears;*a* *32*and they shall praise me in the land of their captivity, and shall invoke my name.*b* *33*Then they shall turn back from their stiff-necked stubbornness, and from their evil deeds, because they shall remember the fate of their fathers who sinned against the LORD.*c* *34*And I will bring them back to the land which with my oath I promised to their fathers, to Abraham, Isaac and Jacob; and they shall rule it. I will make them increase; they shall not then diminish. *35*And I will establish for them, as an eternal covenant, that I will be their God, and they shall be my people; and I will not again remove my people Israel from the land I gave them.*d*

CHAPTER 3

See RG
317

1"LORD Almighty, God of Israel, afflicted souls and dismayed spirits call to you. *2*Hear, O LORD, for you are a God of

---

2, 25: They lie exposed: probably an allusion to Jer 36, 30; see note on Jer 22, 19.
2, 26: The house which bears your name: the temple of Jerusalem. What it is today: during the exile it lay in ruins.

---

o: Dt 6, 21-22. *p:* Ps 106, 6. *q:* Sir 36, 11; Jer 14, 9. *r:* Dt 26, 15. *s:* Ps 6, 6; Is 38, 18. *t:* Zep 2, 3. *u:* Jer 27, 12. *v:* Jer 7, 34. *w:* Jer 8, 1f. *x:* Jer 7, 34; 14,12; 31, 30. *y:* Jer 7, 10-15. *z:* Dt 30, 1f; 31, 27. *a:* Jer 24, 7; Ez 36, 26; Ps 40, 7. *b:* Tb 13, 7. *c:* 33ff: Dt 30, 1-10. *d:* Jer 31, 31; Lam 4, 22.

mercy; and have mercy on us, who have sinned against you: ³for you are enthroned forever, while we are perishing forever.ᵉ ⁴LORD Almighty, God of Israel, hear the prayer of Israel's few, the sons of those who sinned against you; they did not heed the voice of the LORD, their God, and the evils cling to us. ⁵Remember at this time not the misdeeds of our fathers, but your own hand and name: ⁶for you are the LORD our God; and you, O LORD, we will praise! ⁷For this, you put into our hearts the fear of you: that we may call upon your name, and praise you in our captivity, when we have removed from our hearts all the wickedness of our fathers who sinned against you.ᶠ ⁸Behold us today in our captivity, where you scattered us, a reproach, a curse, and a requital for all the misdeeds of our fathers, who withdrew from the LORD, our God."

II: Praise of Wisdom in the Law of Moses

⁹ Hear, O Israel, the commandments of life: listen, and know prudence!ᵍ
¹⁰ How is it, Israel,
that you are in the land of your foes,
grown old in a foreign land,
Defiled with the dead,
¹¹ accounted with those destined for the nether world?ʰ
¹² You have forsaken the fountain of wisdom!ⁱ
¹³ Had you walked in the way of God,
you would have dwelt in enduring peace.ʲ
¹⁴ Learn where prudence is,
where strength, where understanding;
That you may know also
where are length of days, and life,
where light of the eyes, and peace.ᵏ

¹⁵ Who has found the place of wisdom,ˡ
who has entered into her treasures?

¹⁶ Where are the rulers of the nations,
they who lorded it over the wild beasts of the earth,ᵐ
¹⁷ and made sport of the birds of the heavens:
They who heaped up the silver
and the gold in which men trust;
of whose possessions there was no end?
¹⁸ They schemed anxiously for money,
but there is no trace of their work:
¹⁹ They have vanished down into the nether world,
and others have risen up in their stead.
²⁰ Later generations have seen the light,
have dwelt in the land,
But the way to understanding they have not known,
²¹ they have not perceived her paths, or reached her;
their offspring were far from the way to her.
²² She has not been heard of in Canaan,*
nor seen in Teman.ⁿ
²³ The sons of Hagar who seek knowledge on earth,
the merchants of Midian and Teman,
the phrasemakers seeking knowledge,
These have not known the way to wisdom,
nor have they her paths in mind.
²⁴ O Israel, how vast is the house of God,*
how broad the scope of his dominion:
²⁵ Vast and endless,
high and immeasurable!
²⁶ In it were born the giants,
renowned at the first,
stalwarts, skilled in war.ᵒ
²⁷ Not these did God choose,
nor did he give them the way of understanding;ᵖ
²⁸ They perished for lack of prudence,
perished through their folly.�q
²⁹ Who has gone up to the heavens and taken her,

3, 22f: Despite the renown for wisdom of the peoples of Canaan or Phoenicia (Ez 28, 3f), of Teman (Jer 49, 7), of the sons of Hagar or the Arabians, they did not possess true wisdom, which is found only in the law of God.
3, 24: The house of God: here, the created universe.

e: Pss 29, 10; 102, 12f. *f:* Jer 31, 33. *g:* Prv 4, 20ff. *h:* Ps 88, 5. *i:* Jer 2, 13; Jn 4, 10. 14. *j:* Is 48, 18. *k:* Prv 3, 2; 8, 14. *l:* 15ff; Jb 28, 1-28. *m:* Jer 27, 6. *n:* Jer 49, 7; Ez 28, 4-5; Zec 9, 2; Jb 2, 11. *o:* Gn 6, 4; Wis 14, 6. *p:* 1 Sm 16, 7-10. *q:* Sir 10, 8.

or brought her down from the clouds?[r]

³⁰ Who has crossed the sea and found her,
  bearing her away rather than choice
    gold?

³¹ None knows the way to her,
  nor has any understood her paths.

³² Yet he who knows all things knows her;
  he has probed her by his knowledge—
He who established the earth for all time,
  and filled it with four-footed beasts;

³³ He who dismisses the light, and it
    departs,
  calls it, and it obeys him trembling;

³⁴ Before whom the stars at their posts
    shine and rejoice;

³⁵ When he calls them, they answer, "Here
    we are!"
  shining with joy for their Maker.[s]

³⁶ Such is our God;
  no other is to be compared to him:

³⁷ He has traced out all the way of
    understanding,
  and has given her to Jacob, his servant,
to Israel, his beloved son.[t]

³⁸ Since then she has appeared on earth,
  and moved among men.[u]

CHAPTER 4

See RG
317-18

¹ She is the book of the precepts of
    God,
  the law that endures forever;
All who cling to her will live,
  but those will die who forsake her.[v]

² Turn, O Jacob, and receive her:
  walk by her light toward splendor.[w]

³ Give not your glory to another,
  your privileges to an alien race.

⁴ Blessed are we, O Israel;
  for what pleases God is known to us![x]

III: Jerusalem Bewails and Consoles Her Captive Children

⁵ Fear not, my people!
  Remember, Israel,

⁶ You were sold to the nations
  not for your destruction;
It was because you angered God
  that you were handed over to your
    foes.[y]

⁷ For you provoked your Maker[z]
  with sacrifices to demons, to no-gods;

⁸ You forsook the Eternal God who
    nourished you,
  and you grieved Jerusalem who
    fostered you.

⁹ She indeed saw coming upon you
  the anger of God; and she said:

"Hear, you neighbors of Zion!
  God has brought great mourning upon
    me,

¹⁰ For I have seen the captivity
  that the Eternal God has brought
upon my sons and daughters.

¹¹ With joy I fostered them;
  but with mourning and lament I let
    them go.

¹² Let no one gloat over me, a widow,
  bereft of many:
For the sins of my children I am left
    desolate,
  because they turned from the law of
    God,[a]

¹³ and did not acknowledge his statutes;
In the ways of God's commandments
    they did not walk,
  nor did they tread the disciplined paths
    of his justice.

¹⁴ "Let Zion's neighbors come,
  to take note of the captivity of my sons
    and daughters,
  brought upon them by the Eternal
    God.

¹⁵ He has brought against them a nation
    from afar,
  a nation ruthless and of alien speech,
That has neither reverence for age
  nor tenderness for childhood:[b]

¹⁶ They have led away this widow's
    cherished sons,

r: Dt 30, 12f; Sir 24, 4; Rom 10, 6f. s: Jb 38, 7; Ps 147, 4; Is 40, 26. t: Ps 147, 19; Sir 24, 8-12. u: Wis 9, 18; Jn 1, 14. v: Dt 4,
6-8; Prv 8, 35f; Sir 24, 22. w: Prv 4, 13. 19. x: Dt 4, 32-37; 33, 29. y: Jgs 2, 14; Is 50, 1; 52, 3. z: 7-8: Dt 32, 13-18; 1 Cor 10,
20. a: Lam 1, 1. 2. 7. b: Dt 28, 49f; Jer 5, 15; 6, 22f.

have left me solitary, without
        daughters.

[17] What can I do to help you?

[18]   He who has brought this evil upon you
        must himself deliver you from your
        enemies' hands.[c]

[19] Farewell, my children, farewell:
        I am left desolate.

[20] I have taken off the garment of peace,
        have put on sackcloth for my prayer of
        supplication,
        and while I live I will cry out to the
        Eternal God.[d]

[21] "Fear not, my children; call upon God,
        who will deliver you from oppression
        at enemy hands.[e]

[22] I have trusted in the Eternal God for your
        welfare,
        and joy has come to me from the Holy
        One
    Because of the mercy that will swiftly
        reach you
        from your eternal savior.

[23] With mourning and lament I sent you
        forth,
        but God will give you back to me
        with enduring gladness and joy.[f]

[24] As Zion's neighbors lately saw you taken
        captive,
        so shall they soon see God's salvation
        come to you,
        with great glory and the splendor of
        the Eternal God.[g]

[25] "My children, bear patiently the anger[h]
        that has come from God upon you;
    Your enemies have persecuted you,
        and you will soon see their destruction
        and trample upon their necks.*

[26] My pampered children have trodden
        rough roads,
        carried off by their enemies like sheep
        in a raid.[i]

[27] Fear not, my children; call out to God!

He who brought this upon you will
        remember you.[j]

[28] As your hearts have been disposed to
        stray from God,
        turn now ten times the more to seek
        him;

[29] For he who has brought disaster upon
        you
        will, in saving you, bring you back
        enduring joy."[k]

IV: Jerusalem Consoled: The Captivity About to End

[30] Fear not, Jerusalem!
        He who gave you your name is your
        encouragement.[l]

[31] Fearful are those who harmed you,
        who rejoiced at your downfall;

[32] Fearful are the cities where your children
        were enslaved,
        fearful the city that took your sons.[m]

[33] As that city rejoiced at your collapse,[n]
        and made merry at your downfall,
        so shall she grieve over her own
        desolation.

[34] I will take from her the joyous
        throngs,
        and her exultation shall be turned to
        mourning:

[35] For fire shall come upon her[o]
        from the Eternal God, for a long
        time,
        and demons shall dwell in her from
        that time on.*

[36] Look to the east, Jerusalem!
        behold the joy that comes to you from
        God.[p]

[37] Here come your sons whom you once let
        go,
        gathered in from the east and from the
        west
    By the word of the Holy One,
        rejoicing in the glory of God.

4, 25: Trample upon their necks: love of enemies was not an Old Testament ideal. The Babylonians are considered here, however, to be God's enemies as well as Israel's.
4, 35: Deserts and desolate places were looked upon as the special habitations of demons; Tb 8, 3; Lk 11, 24.

---

c: Jer 32, 42.   d: Jdt 9, 1; Est 4, 16.   e: Jer 51, 5.   f: Jer 31, 12f.   g: Is 60, 1ff.   h: Is 51, 23.   i: Lam 2, 22.   j: Is 40, 1.   k: Is 35,
10.   l: Ps 46, 5; Is 60, 14.   m: Jer 51, 43.   n: 33f: Is 13, 20ff; 47, 1-11; Jer 50, 13.   o: Is 34, 9-14.   p: Is 60, 4f.

CHAPTER 5

See RG
318

¹ Jerusalem, take off your robe of
  mourning and misery;
  put on the splendor of glory from God
  forever:*q*

² Wrapped in the cloak of justice from God,
  bear on your head the mitre
  that displays the glory of the eternal
  name.*r*

³ For God will show all the earth your
  splendor:

⁴ you will be named by God forever
  the peace of justice, the glory of God's
  worship.*s*

⁵ Up, Jerusalem! stand upon the heights;
  look to the east and see your children
  Gathered from the east and the west
  at the word of the Holy One,
  rejoicing that they are remembered by
  God.

⁶ Led away on foot by their enemies they
  left you:
  but God will bring them back to you
  borne aloft in glory as on royal thrones.*t*

⁷ For God has commanded
  that every lofty mountain be made low,
  And that the age-old depths and gorges
  be filled to level ground,
  that Israel may advance secure in the
  glory of God.*u*

⁸ The forests and every fragrant kind of tree
  have overshadowed Israel at God's
  command;*v*

⁹ For God is leading Israel in joy
  by the light of his glory,
  with his mercy and justice for company.

V: The Letter of Jeremiah
Against Idolatry

CHAPTER 6

See RG
318

¹ A copy of the letter which Jeremiah
sent to those who were being led captive to

Babylon by the king of the Babylonians, to
convey to them what God had commanded
him:*w*

For the sins you committed before God,
you are being led captive to Babylon by
Nebuchadnezzar, king of the Babylonians.
²When you reach Babylon you will be there
many years, a period seven generations*
long; after which I will bring you back from
there in peace. ³And now in Babylon you
will see borne upon men's shoulders gods of
silver and gold and wood, which cast fear
upon the pagans.*x* ⁴Take care that you yourselves do not imitate their alien example and
stand in fear of them, ⁵when you see the
crowd before them and behind worshiping
them. Rather, say in your hearts, "You, O
LORD, are to be worshiped!"; ⁶for my angel
is with you, and he is the custodian of your
lives.*y*

⁷Their tongues are smoothed by woodworkers; they are covered with gold and silver—but they are a fraud, and cannot speak.*z*
⁸People bring gold, as to a maiden in love
with ornament, ⁹and furnish crowns for the
heads of their gods. Then sometimes the
priests take the silver and gold from their
gods and spend it on themselves, ¹⁰or give
part of it to the harlots on the terrace.* They
trick them out in garments like men, these
gods of silver and gold and wood; ¹¹but
though they are wrapped in purple clothing,
they are not safe from corrosion or insects.
¹²They wipe their faces clean of the house
dust which is thick upon them. ¹³Each has a
scepter, like the human ruler of a district; but
none does away with those that offend
against it. ¹⁴Each has in its right hand an axe
or dagger, but it cannot save itself from war
or pillage. Thus it is known they are not
gods; do not fear them.

¹⁵As useless as one's broken tools ¹⁶are
their gods, set up in their houses; their eyes
are full of dust from the feet of those who enter. ¹⁷Their courtyards are walled in like

---

6, 2: Seven generations: possibly an indication of the date of this composition by an author writing for his contemporaries
for whom the conditions of the exile were still realities. He has multiplied the seventy years of Jer 29, 10 by three or four.

6, 10: Harlots on the terrace: cult prostitutes, common in the idolatrous religions of the Gentiles.

---

q: Is 52, 1.   *r:* Ex 39, 30; Wis 18, 24; Is 61. 10; 62, 3.   *s:* Is 1, 26; 32, 17; Jer 33, 16.   *t:* Is 49, 22.   *u:* Is 40, 3f.   *v:* Is 41, 19.   *w:* Jer
29, 1.   *x:* Is 46, 7; Jer 10, 1-16.   *y:* Ex 23, 20.   *z:* Ps 135, 16.

those of a man brought to execution for a crime against the king; the priests reinforce their houses with gates and bars and bolts, lest they be carried off by robbers. *18*They light more lamps for them than for themselves, yet not one of these can they see. *19*They are like any beam in the house; it is said their hearts are eaten away. Though the insects out of the ground consume them and their garments, they do not feel it. *20*Their faces are blackened by the smoke of the house. *21*Bats and swallows alight on their bodies and on their heads; and cats as well as birds. *22*Know, therefore, that they are not gods, and do not fear them.

*23*Despite the gold that covers them for adornment, unless someone wipes away the corrosion, they do not shine; nor did they feel anything when they were molded. *24*They are bought at any price, and there is no spirit in them. *25*Having no feet, they are carried on men's shoulders, displaying their shame to all; and those who worship them are put to confusion*a* *26*because, if they fall to the ground, the worshipers must raise them up. They neither move of themselves if one sets them upright, nor come upright if they fall; but one puts gifts beside them as beside the dead. *27**Their priests resell their sacrifices for their own advantage. Even their wives cure parts of the meat, but do not share it with the poor and the weak;*b* *28*the menstruous and women in childbed handle their sacrifices. Knowing from this that they are not gods, do not fear them.

*29*How can they be called gods? For women bring the offerings to these gods of silver and gold and wood; *30*and in their temples the priests squat with torn tunic and with shaven hair and beard, and with their heads uncovered.*c* *31*They shout and wail before their gods as others do at a funeral banquet. *32*The priests take some of their clothing and put it on their wives and children.

*33**Whether they are treated well or ill by anyone, they cannot requite it; they can neither set up a king nor remove him.*d* *34*Similarly, they cannot give anyone riches or coppers; if one fails to fulfill a vow to them, they cannot exact it of him. *35*They neither save a man from death, nor deliver the weak from the strong.*e* *36*To no blind man do they restore his sight, nor do they save any man in an emergency. *37*They neither pity the widow nor benefit the orphan. *38*These gilded and silvered wooden statues are like stones from the mountains; and their worshipers will be put to shame. *39*How then can it be thought or claimed that they are gods?

*40*Even the Chaldeans themselves have no respect for them; for when they see a deaf mute, incapable of speech, they bring forward Bel* and ask the god to make noise, as though the man could understand; *41*and they are themselves unable to reflect and abandon these gods, for they have no sense. *42**And their women, girt with cords, sit by the roads, burning chaff for incense;*f* *43*and whenever one of them is drawn aside by some passerby who lies with her, she mocks her neighbor who has not been dignified as she has, and has not had her cord broken. *44*All that takes place around these gods is a fraud: how then can it be thought or claimed that they are gods?

*45*They are produced by woodworkers and goldsmiths, and they are nothing else than what these craftsmen wish them to be. *46*Even those who produce them are not long-lived; *47*how then can what they have produced be gods? They have left frauds and opprobrium to their successors. *48*For when war or disaster comes upon them, the priests deliberate among themselves where they can hide with them. *49*How then can one not know that these are no-gods, which do not save themselves either from war or from disaster? *50*They are wooden, gilded and sil-

---

6, 27-31: From the point of view of Jewish ritual law, the practices named here were grotesque and depraved; cf Lv 12, 2ff; 15, 19-23.

6, 33-39: All that the gods cannot do, the true God does; cf 1 Sm 2, 7; Dt 23, 22; Pss 68, 6; 146, 7-9; Is 35, 4f.

6, 40: Bel: cf note on Jer 50, 2.

6, 42f: This seems to refer to the obligation of Bab-

ylonian women to serve once in their lives as cult prostitutes. The unbroken cord was a sign that this duty had not yet been fulfilled. Chaff: burnt as an aphrodisiac or for use in erotic rites.

a: Wis 13, 16.   *b:* Lv 12. 4; 15, 19f; Dt 14, 28f.   *c:* Lv 10, 6; 21, 5. 10.   *d:* Dn 2, 21.   *e:* Pss 68, 6; 146, 7ff.   *f:* 42-43: Jer 3, 2.

vered; they will later be known for frauds. To all peoples and kings it will be clear that they are not gods, but human handiwork; and that God's work is not in them.

⁵¹Who does not know that they are not gods? ⁵²They set no king over the land, nor do they give men rain. ⁵³They neither vindicate their own rights, nor do they recover what is unjustly taken, for they are unable; ⁵⁴they are like crows between heaven and earth. For when fire breaks out in the temple of these wooden or gilded or silvered gods, though the priests flee and are safe, they themselves are burnt up in the fire like beams. ⁵⁵They cannot resist a king, or enemy forces. ⁵⁶How then can it be admitted or thought that they are gods?

They are safe from neither thieves nor bandits, these wooden and silvered and gilded gods; ⁵⁷those who seize them strip off the gold and the silver, and go away with the clothing that was on them, and they cannot help themselves. ⁵⁸How much better to be a king displaying his valor, or a handy tool in a house, the joy of its owner, than these false gods; or the door of a house, that keeps safe those who are within, rather than these false gods; or a wooden post in a palace, rather than these false gods!ᵍ ⁵⁹The sun and moon and stars are bright, and obedient in the service for which they are sent. ⁶⁰Likewise the lightning, when it flashes, is a goodly sight;

g: Wis 13, 10-15; 15, 7ff.

and the same wind blows over all the land. ⁶¹The clouds, too, when commanded by God to proceed across the whole world, fulfill the order; ⁶²and fire, sent from on high to burn up the mountains and the forests, does what has been commanded. But these false gods are not their equal, whether in beauty or in power; ⁶³so that it is unthinkable, and cannot be claimed, that they are gods. They can neither execute judgment, nor benefit man. ⁶⁴Know, therefore, that they are not gods, and do not fear them.

⁶⁵Kings they neither curse nor bless. ⁶⁶They show the nations no signs in the heavens, nor are they brilliant like the sun, nor shining like the moon. ⁶⁷The beasts which can help themselves by fleeing to shelter are better than they are. ⁶⁸Thus in no way is it clear to us that they are gods; so do not fear them. ⁶⁹For like a scarecrow in a cucumber patch, that is no protection, are their wooden, gilded, silvered gods. ⁷⁰Just like a thornbush in a garden on which perches every kind of bird, or like a corpse hurled into darkness, are their silvered and gilded wooden gods. ⁷¹From the rotting of the purple and the linen upon them, it can be known that they are not gods; they themselves will in the end be consumed, and be a disgrace in the land. ⁷²The better for the just man who has no idols: he shall be far from disgrace!

See RG
320–35

The Book of Ezekiel

Ezekiel's complex character makes him one of the most interesting figures in Israelite prophecy. In many ways he resembles the more primitive type of prophet represented by Elijah and Elisha; yet he clearly depends on all his predecessors in prophecy, and his teaching is a development of theirs. His unique contribution to the history of prophetism lies in his manifest interest in the temple and the liturgy, an interest paralleled in no other prophet—not even Jeremiah who, like Ezekiel, was also a priest. Particularly because of this interest, Ezekiel's influence on postexilic religion was enormous, and not without reason has

he been called "the father of Judaism." This has resulted in his prophecies reaching us with the evident marks of editing and addition by the postexilic circles that shared his intense interest. However, we may be sure that in this book we have throughout what is in substance the prophet's own work.

Ezekiel became a prophet in Babylon—the first prophet to receive the call to prophesy outside the Holy Land. As one of the exiles deported by Nebuchadnezzar in 597 B.C., his first task was to prepare his fellow countrymen in Babylon for the final destruction of Jerusalem, which they believed to be inviolable. Accordingly, the first part of his book consists of reproaches for Israel's past and present sins and the confident prediction of yet a further devastation of the land of promise and a more general exile. In 587 B.C., when Nebuchadnezzar destroyed Jerusalem, Ezekiel was vindicated before his unbelieving compatriots.

After this time, Ezekiel's message changes. From now on his prophecy is characterized by the promise of salvation in a new covenant, and he is anxious to lay down the conditions necessary to obtain it. Even as Jeremiah had believed, Ezekiel thought that the exiles were the hope of Israel's restoration, once God's allotted time for the Exile had been accomplished. His final eight chapters are a utopian vision of the Israel of the future, rid of its past evils and reestablished firmly under the rule of the Lord. The famous vision of the dry bones in chapter 37 expresses his firm belief in a forthcoming restoration, Israel rising to new life from the graveyard of Babylon. But Ezekiel's new covenant, like Jeremiah's, was to see its true fulfillment only in the New Testament.

Perhaps no other prophet has stressed the absolute majesty of God as Ezekiel does. This appears not only in the tremendous vision by the river Chebar with which his prophecy opens, but throughout the book. Ultimately, says Ezekiel, whatever God does to or for man is motivated by zeal for his own holy name. The new heart and the new spirit which must exist under the new covenant cannot be the work of man; they too must be the work of God. By such teachings he helped prepare for the New Testament doctrine of salvation through grace.

The Book of Ezekiel is divided as follows:

I: Call of the Prophet (1, 1—3, 27).

II: Before the Siege of Jerusalem (4, 1—24, 27).

III: Prophecies against Foreign Nations (25, 1—32, 32).

IV: Salvation for Israel (33, 1—39, 29).

V: The New Israel (40, 1—48, 35).

I: Call of the Prophet

CHAPTER 1

See RG 325-32

The Vision: God on the Cherubim. [1]In the thirtieth year,* on the fifth day of the fourth month, while I was among the exiles by the river Chebar, the heavens opened, and I saw divine visions.[a] — [2]On the fifth day of the month, the fifth year,* that is, of King Jehoiachin's exile, [3]the word of the LORD came to the priest Ezekiel, the son of Buzi, in the land of the Chaldeans by the river Chebar.—There the hand of the LORD came upon me.

[4]As I looked, a stormwind came from the North,* a huge cloud with flashing fire [enveloped in brightness], from the midst of which [the midst of the fire] something gleamed like electrum. [5]Within it were figures resembling four living creatures* that looked like this: their form was human, [6]but each had four faces and four wings, [7]and their legs went straight down; the soles of their feet were round. They sparkled with a gleam like burnished bronze.

[10]*Their faces were like this:[b] each of the four had the face of a man, but on the right side was the face of a lion, and on the left side the face of an ox, and finally each had the face of an eagle. [9]Their faces [and their wings] looked out on all their four sides; they did not turn when they moved, but each went straight forward. [12][Each went straight forward; wherever the spirit wished to go, there they went; they did not turn when they moved.]

[8]Human hands were under their wings, and the wings of one touched those of another.

1, 1: The thirtieth year, which corresponds to the fifth year of exile (v 2), has never been satisfactorily explained; possibly it refers to the prophet's age. The river Chebar: probably a canal near Nippur, southeast of Babylon, one of the sites on which the Jewish exiles were settled.

1, 2: The fifth day of the fourth month, the fifth year: July 31, 593 B.C.; cf v 1.

1, 4: The North: the abode of God; see notes on Jb 37, 22; Ps 48, 3. Electrum: an alloy of gold and silver,

used here for some undetermined bright metal.

1, 5: Four living creatures: identified as cherubim in Ez 10, 20f.

1, 10-22: Note the changed order of the verses and the omission of the textually uncertain verses 14 and 21. Such changes also occur elsewhere in this book.

---

a: Ez 3, 23; 10, 20; 43, 3.   *b:* Rv 4, 6f.

1093

[11]Each had two wings spread out above so that they touched one another's, while the other two wings of each covered his body. [13]In among the living creatures something like burning coals of fire could be seen; they seemed like torches, moving to and fro among the living creatures. The fire gleamed, and from it came forth flashes of lightning.

[15]As I looked at the living creatures, I saw wheels on the ground, one beside each of the four living creatures. [16]The wheels had the sparkling appearance of chrysolite, and all four of them looked the same: they were constructed as though one wheel were within another. [17]They could move in any of the four directions they faced, without veering as they moved. [18c]The four of them had rims, and I saw that their rims were full of eyes all around. [19]When the living creatures moved, the wheels moved with them; and when the living creatures were raised from the ground, the wheels also were raised. [20]Wherever the spirit wished to go, there the wheels went, and they were raised together with the living creatures; for the spirit of the living creatures was in the wheels.

[22*]Over the heads of the living creatures, something like a firmament could be seen, seeming like glittering crystal, stretched straight out above their heads. [23]Beneath the firmament their wings were stretched out, one toward the other. [Each of them had two covering his body.] [24]Then I heard the sound of their wings, like the roaring of mighty waters, like the voice of the Almighty. When they moved, the sound of the tumult was like the din of an army. [And when they stood still, they lowered their wings.]

[26]Above the firmament over their heads something like a throne could be seen, looking like sapphire. Upon it was seated, up above, one who had the appearance of a man.* [27]Upward from what resembled his waist I saw what gleamed like electrum; downward from what resembled his waist I saw what looked like fire; he was surrounded with splendor. [28]Like the bow which appears in the clouds on a rainy day was the splendor that surrounded him. Such was the vision of the likeness of the glory of the LORD.

CHAPTER 2

See RG 325-32

Eating of the Scroll. When I had seen it, I fell upon my face and heard a voice that said to me: [1]Son of man,* stand up! I wish to speak with you. [2]As he spoke to me, spirit* entered into me and set me on my feet, and I heard the one who was speaking [3]say to me: Son of man, I am sending you to the Israelites, rebels who have rebelled against me; they and their fathers have revolted against me to this very day. [4]Hard of face and obstinate of heart are they to whom I am sending you. But you shall say to them: Thus says the Lord GOD! [5]And whether they heed or resist—for they are a rebellious house—they shall know that a prophet has been among them. [6]But as for you, son of man, fear neither them nor their words when they contradict you and reject you, and when you sit on scorpions.* Neither fear their words nor be dismayed at their looks, for they are a rebellious house. [7][But speak my words to them, whether they heed or resist, for they are rebellious.] [8]As for you, son of man, obey me when I speak to you: be not rebellious like this house of rebellion, but open your mouth and eat what I shall give you.

[9d]It was then I saw a hand stretched out to me, in which was a written scroll [10]which he unrolled before me. It was covered with writing front and back, and written on it was: Lamentation and wailing and woe!

CHAPTER 3

See RG 325-32

[1]He said to me: Son of man, eat what is before you; eat this scroll, then go, speak to the house of Israel. [2]So I opened my

---

1, 22f. 26: This symbolic description of God's throne is similar to that in Ex 24, 9f.

1, 26: One who had the appearance of a man: God appearing in human form (v 28); cf Ex 33, 18-23.

2, 1: Son of man: a formal way of saying simply "man"; God's habitual way of addressing the prophet throughout this book. Probably the title is used to emphasize the separation of the divine and the human.

2, 2: Spirit: vital power, coming from God, which enables the prophet to hear the word of God; cf Ez 8, 3; 9, 24; 11, 1.

2, 6: When you sit on scorpions: the prophet must be prepared for the bitterest opposition.

c: Ez 10, 12; Rv 4, 6. 8.   d: Rv 5, 1.

mouth and he gave me the scroll to eat. ^{3e}Son of man, he then said to me, feed your belly and fill your stomach with this scroll I am giving you. I ate it, and it was as sweet as honey* in my mouth. He said: ^{4}Son of man, go now to the house of Israel, and speak my words to them.

^{5}Not to a people with difficult speech and barbarous language am I sending you, ^{6}nor to the many peoples [with difficult speech and barbarous language] whose words you cannot understand. If I were to send you to these, they would listen to you; ^{7}but the house of Israel will refuse to listen to you, since they will not listen to me. For the whole house of Israel is stubborn of brow and obstinate in heart. ^{8}But I will make your face as hard as theirs, and your brow as stubborn as theirs, ^{9}like diamond, harder than flint. Fear them not, nor be dismayed at their looks, for they are a rebellious house.

^{10}Son of man, he said to me, take into your heart all my words that I speak to you; hear them well. ^{11}Now go to the exiles, to your countrymen, and say to them: Thus says the Lord GOD!—whether they heed or resist!

^{12}Then spirit lifted me up, and I heard behind me the noise of a loud rumbling as the glory of the LORD* rose from its place: ^{13}the noise made by the wings of the living creatures striking one another, and by the wheels alongside them, a loud rumbling. ^{14}The spirit which had lifted me up seized me, and I went off spiritually stirred, while the hand of the LORD rested heavily upon me. ^{15}Thus I came to the exiles who lived at Tel-abib* by the river Chebar, and for seven days I sat among them distraught.

The Prophet as Watchman. ^{17}Thus the word of the LORD came to me: Son of man, I have appointed you a watchman for the

house of Israel.^{f} When you hear a word from my mouth, you shall warn them for me.

^{18}If I say to the wicked man, You shall surely die; and you do not warn him or speak out to dissuade him from his wicked conduct so that he may live: that wicked man shall die for his sin, but I will hold you responsible for his death. ^{19}If, on the other hand, you have warned the wicked man, yet he has not turned away from his evil nor from his wicked conduct, then he shall die for his sin, but you shall save your life.

^{20}If a virtuous man turns away from virtue and does wrong when I place a stumbling block before him, he shall die. He shall die for his sin, and his virtuous deeds shall not be remembered; but I will hold you responsible for his death if you did not warn him. ^{21}When, on the other hand, you have warned a virtuous man not to sin, and he has in fact not sinned, he shall surely live because of the warning, and you shall save your own life.

Ezekiel's Dumbness. ^{22}The hand of the Lord came upon me, and he said to me: Get up and go out into the plain, where I will speak with you. ^{23g}So I got up and went out into the plain, and I saw that the glory of the LORD was in that place, like the glory I had seen by the river Chebar. I fell prone, ^{24}but then spirit entered into me and set me on my feet, and he spoke with me.

He said to me: Go shut yourself up in your house. ^{25}[As for you, son of man, they will put cords upon you and bind you with them, so that you cannot go out among them.] ^{26}I will make your tongue stick to your palate so that you will be dumb* and unable to rebuke them for being a rebellious house. ^{27}Only when I speak with you and open your mouth, shall you say to them: Thus says the Lord GOD! Let him heed who will, and let him resist who will, for they are a rebellious house.

3, 3: As sweet as honey: though the prophet must foretell terrible things the word of God is sweet to him who receives it.

3, 12: The glory of the LORD: the divine presence, manifested here in visible form.

3, 15: Tel-abib: one of the sites where the exiles were settled, probably near Nippur.

3, 17-21: This passage refers to one of the prophet's most characteristic qualities. It was placed here by an editor, though it properly belongs to a later stage in

Ezekiel's ministry; cf chapter 33.

3, 22-27: This passage also belongs to a later period, with Ez 24, 25ff and 33, 21f, during the time of the final siege of Jerusalem, when Ezekiel's prophecies consisted mainly of symbolic actions rather than words.

3, 26: Dumb: unwilling to speak to the people in exile while Jerusalem was being besieged; cf Ez 24, 27.

e: Rv 10, 9f.　f: Ez 33, 7.　g: Ez 1, 3; 10. 15. 20. 22; 43, 3.

II: Before the Siege of Jerusalem

CHAPTER 4

See RG
325-32

Acts Symbolic of Siege and Exile. *16* At the end of seven days . . . :* *1* As for you, son of man, take a clay tablet; lay it in front of you, and draw on it a city [Jerusalem]. *2* Raise a siege against it: build a tower, lay out a ramp, pitch camps, and set up battering rams all around. *3* Then take an iron griddle and set it up as an iron wall between you and the city. Fix your gaze on it: it shall be in the state of siege, and you shall besiege it. This shall be a sign for the house of Israel. *4* Then you shall lie on your left side, while I place the sins of the house of Israel upon you. As many days as you lie thus, you shall bear their sins. *5* For the years of their sins I allot you the same number of days, three hundred and ninety, during which you will bear the sins of the house of Israel. *6* When you finish this, you are to lie down again, but on your right side, and bear the sins of the house of Judah forty days;* one day for each year I have allotted you. *7* Fixing your gaze on the siege of Jerusalem, with bared arm* you shall prophesy against it. *8* See, I will bind you with cords so that you cannot turn from one side to the other until you have completed the days of your siege.

9 *Again, take wheat and barley, and beans and lentils, and millet and spelt; put them in a single vessel and make bread out of them. Eat it for as many days as you lie upon your side, three hundred and ninety. *10* The food you eat shall be twenty shekels a day by weight; each day the same. *11* And the water you drink shall be the sixth of a hin by measure; each day the same. *16h* Then he said to me: Son of man, I am breaking the staff of bread* in Jerusalem.

They shall eat bread which they have weighed out anxiously, and they shall drink water which they have measured out fearfully, *17* so that, owing to the scarcity of bread and water, everyone shall be filled with terror and waste away because of his sins.

12 For your food you must bake barley loaves over human excrement in their sight, said the LORD. *13* Thus the Israelites shall eat their food unclean among the nations where I scatter them.*i* *14* "Oh no, Lord GOD!" I protested. "Never have I been made unclean, and from my youth till now, never have I eaten carrion flesh or that torn by wild beasts: never has any unclean meat entered my mouth." *15* Very well, he replied, I allow you cow's dung in place of human excrement; bake your bread on that.

CHAPTER 5

See RG
325-32

1 As for you, son of man, take a sharp sword and use it like a barber's razor, passing it over your head and beard. Then take a set of scales and divide the hair you have cut. *2* Burn a third in the fire, within the city,* when the days of your siege are completed; place another third around the city and strike it with the sword; the final third strew in the wind, and pursue it with the sword. *3* [But of the last take a small number and tie them in the hem of your garment. *4* Then take some of these and throw them in the midst of the fire and burn them.]

Say to the whole house of Israel: *5* Thus says the Lord GOD: This is Jerusalem! In the midst of the nations I placed her, surrounded by foreign countries. *6* But she rebelled against my ordinances more wickedly than the nations, and against my statutes more than the foreign countries surrounding her;

3, 16: At the end of seven days . . . : the incomplete sentence probably contained some such words as "the word of the Lord came to me." For seven days, see v 15. (This verse has been transposed from ch 3.)

4, 5f: Three hundred and ninety . . . forty days: symbolically representing the respective lengths of the periods of exile of northern Israelites and Judahites. Northern Israel had already fallen to Assyria in 722 B.C. The letters in the Hebrew phrase for the days of your siege (v 8), each of which has its own numerical value, add up to three hundred and ninety. Forty years represent one generation.

4, 7: Bared arm: a symbol of unrestrained power.

4, 9-17: This action represents the scarcity of food during the siege of Jerusalem, and the consequent need to eat whatever is at hand. Twenty shekels: about nine ounces. The sixth of a hin: about one quart.

4, 16: Breaking the staff of bread: reducing the supply of bread which sustains the life of man as the walking staff sustains the traveler on his journey; cf Ez 5, 16; 14, 13; Lv 26, 26; Ps 105, 16; Is 3, 1.

5, 2: The city: the one drawn on the tablet.

---

h: Ez 5, 16; 14, 13. i: Hos 9, 4.

she has spurned my ordinances and has not lived by my statutes. [7]Therefore thus says the Lord God: Because you have been more rebellious than the nations surrounding you, not living by my statutes nor fulfilling my ordinances, but acting according to the ordinances of the surrounding nations; [8]therefore thus says the Lord God: see, I am coming at you!* I will inflict punishments in your midst while the nations look on. [9]Because of all your abominations I will do with you what I have never done before, the like of which I will never do again. [10]This means that fathers within you shall eat sons, and sons shall eat fathers.* I will inflict punishments upon you and scatter all that remain of your people in every direction.

[11]Therefore, as I live, says the Lord God, because you have defiled my sanctuary with all your detestable abominations, I swear to cut you down. I will not look upon you with pity nor have mercy. [12]A third of your people shall die of pestilence and perish of hunger within you; another third shall fall by the sword all around you; and a third I will scatter in every direction, and I will pursue them with the sword. [16j]When I loose against you the cruel, destructive arrows of hunger, I will break your staff of bread; [17]I will send famine against you, and wild beasts that shall rob you of your children. Pestilence and bloodshed shall stalk through you, and I will bring the sword upon you. I, the Lord, have spoken!

[13]Thus shall my anger spend itself, and I will wreak my fury upon them till I am appeased; they shall know that I, the Lord, have spoken in my jealousy when I spend my fury upon them. [14]I will make you a waste and a reproach among the nations that surround you, which every passer-by may see. [15]When I execute judgment upon you in anger and fury and with furious chastisements, you shall be a reproach and an object of scorn, a terrible warning to the nations that surround you. I, the Lord, have spoken!

CHAPTER 6

See RG 325-32

Against the Mountains of Israel. [1]Thus the word of the Lord came to me: [2]Son of man, turn toward the mountains of Israel, and prophesy against them: [3]Mountains of Israel, hear the word of the Lord God. Thus says the Lord God [to the mountains and hills, the ravines and valleys]:[k] See, I am bringing a sword against you, and I will destroy your high places.* [4]Your altars shall be laid waste, your incense stands shall be broken, and I will cast down your slain ones before your idols; [5]I will scatter their bones all around your altars.* [6]In all your dwelling places cities shall be made desolate and high places laid waste, so that your altars will be made desolate and laid waste, your idols broken and removed, and your incense stands smashed to bits. [7][The slain shall fall in your midst, and you shall know that I am the Lord. [8]I have warned you.]

When some of your people have escaped to other nations from the sword, and have been scattered over the foreign lands, [9]then those who have escaped will remember me among the nations to which they have been exiled, after I have broken their adulterous hearts that turned away from me [and their eyes which lusted after idols]. They shall loathe themselves because of their evil deeds, all their abominations. [10]Then they shall know that it was not in vain that I, the Lord, threatened to inflict this calamity upon them.

[11]Thus says the Lord God: Clap your hands, stamp your feet,* and cry "Alas!" because of all the abominations of the house of Israel, for which they shall fall by the sword, by famine, and by pestilence. [12]He that is far off shall die of pestilence, he that is near shall fall by the sword, and he that is besieged

---

5, 8: I am coming at you: an expression borrowed from the language of warfare in which enemies attacked one another with the sword. You in vv 8-17 is Jerusalem.

5, 10: Fathers . . . shall eat sons, and sons . . . fathers: see note on Lam 2, 20.

6, 3: High places: the sanctuaries on the mountaintops where illegal worship, whether of the Lord or of Canaanite deities, was performed.

6, 5: Scatter their bones . . . altars: dead men's bones defiled a place; cf 2 Kgs 23, 14.

6, 11: Clap your hands, stamp your feet: here evidently signs of mourning; in Ez 25, 6, signs of joy.

---

j: Ez 4, 16; 14, 13.   k: Ez 36, 1.

shall perish by famine; so will I spend my fury upon them. [13]Then shall they know that I am the LORD, when their slain shall lie amid their idols, all about their altars, on every high hill and mountaintop, beneath every green tree and leafy oak,* wherever they offered appeasing odors to any of their gods. [14]I will stretch out my hand against them, and wherever they live I will make the land a desolate waste, from the desert to Riblah;* thus shall they know that I am the LORD.

See RG 325–32

CHAPTER 7

The End Has Come. [1]Thus the word of the LORD came to me: [2]Son of man, now say: Thus says the Lord GOD to the land of Israel: An end! The end has come upon the four corners of the land! [3]Now the end is upon you; I will unleash my anger against you and judge you according to your conduct and lay upon you the consequences of all your abominations. [4]I will not look upon you with pity nor have mercy; I will bring your conduct down upon you, and the consequences of your abominations shall be in your midst; then shall you know that I am the LORD.

[5]Thus says the Lord GOD: Disaster upon disaster! See it coming! [6]An end is coming, the end is coming upon you! See it coming! [7]The climax has come for you who dwell in the land! The time has come, near is the day: a time of consternation, not of rejoicing. [8]Soon now I will pour out my fury upon you and spend my anger upon you; I will judge you according to your conduct and lay upon you the consequences of all your abominations. [9]I will not look upon you with pity nor have mercy; I will deal with you according to your conduct, and the consequences of your abominations shall be in your midst; then shall you know that it is I, the LORD, who strike.

[10]See, the day of the LORD! See, the end is coming! Lawlessness is in full bloom, insolence flourishes, [11]violence has risen to support wickedness. It shall not be long in coming, nor shall it delay. [12]*The time has come, the day dawns. Let not the buyer rejoice nor the seller mourn, for wrath shall be upon all the throng. [13]The seller shall not regain what he sold as long as he lives, for wrath shall be upon all the throng. Because of his sins, no one shall preserve his life. [14]They shall sound the trumpet and make everything ready, yet no one shall go to war, for my wrath is upon all the throng.

[15]The sword is outside; pestilence and hunger are within. He that is in the country shall die by the sword; pestilence and famine shall devour those in the city. [16]Even those who escape and flee to the mountains like the doves of the valleys—I will put them all to death, each one for his own sins. [17]All their hands shall be limp, and all their knees shall run with water. [18]lThey shall put on sackcloth, and horror shall cover them; shame shall be on all their faces and baldness* on all their heads. [19]They shall fling their silver into the streets, and their gold shall be considered refuse.m Their silver and gold cannot save them on the day of the LORD's wrath. They shall not be allowed to satisfy their craving or fill their bellies, for this has been the occasion of their sin. [20]In the beauty of their ornaments they put their pride: they made of them their abominable images [their idols]. For this reason I make them refuse. [21]I will hand them over as booty to foreigners, to be spoiled and defiled by the wicked of the earth. [22]I will turn away my face from them, and my treasure* shall be profaned: robbers shall enter and profane it.

[23]They shall wreak slaughter, for the land is filled with bloodshed and the city full of violence. [24]I will bring in the worst of the nations, who shall take possession of their houses. I will put an end to their proud strength, and their sanctuaries shall be profaned. [25]When anguish comes they shall seek peace, but there will be none. [26]There shall

---

6, 13: Every green tree and leafy oak: sacred groves had a long history in Palestine as places of worship; cf Dt 12, 2; note on Gn 12, 6.

6, 14: From the desert to Riblah: the whole land, from the far south to the far north.

7, 12f: Mundane affairs will cease to have any meaning in view of the disaster that is to come.

7, 18: Baldness: shaving the head was a sign of mourning.

7, 22: My treasure: the temple of Jerusalem.

l: Is 15, 2; Jer 48, 37.   *m:* Prv 11, 4; Sir 5, 10; Zep 1, 18.

be disaster after disaster, rumor after rumor. Prophetic vision shall fade; instruction shall be lacking to the priest, and counsel to the elders, [27]while the prince shall be enveloped in terror, and the hands of the common people shall tremble. I will deal with them according to their conduct, and according to their judgments I will judge them; thus they shall know that I am the LORD.

CHAPTER 8

See RG 325–32

Vision of Abominations in the Temple.

[3]Spirit lifted me up in the air and brought me in divine visions to Jerusalem,[n] to the entrance of the north gate, where stood the statue of jealousy which stirs up jealousy.* [5]He* said to me: Son of man, look toward the north! I looked toward the north and saw northward of the gate the altar of the statue of jealousy. [6]Son of man, he asked me, do you see what they are doing? Do you see the great abominations that the house of Israel is practicing here, so that I must depart from my sanctuary? But you shall see still greater abominations!

[7]Then he brought me to the entrance of the court, where I saw there was a hole in the wall. [8]Son of man, he ordered, dig through the wall. I dug through the wall and saw a door. [9]Enter, he said to me, and see the abominable evils which they are doing here. [10]I entered and saw that all around upon the wall were pictured the figures of all kinds of creeping things and loathsome beasts* [all the idols of the house of Israel]. [11]Before these stood seventy of the elders of the house of Israel, among whom stood Jaazaniah, son of Shaphan, each of them with his censer in his hand, and the fragrance of the incense was rising upward. [12]Then he said to me: Do you see, son of man, what each of these elders of the house of Israel is doing in his idol room? They think: "The LORD cannot see us; the LORD has forsaken the land." [13]He continued: You shall see still greater abominations that they are practicing.

[14]Then he brought me to the entrance of the north gate of the temple, and I saw sitting there the women who were weeping for Tammuz.* [15]Then he said to me: Do you see this, son of man? You shall see other abominations, greater than these!

[16]Then he brought me into the inner court of the LORD's house, and there at the door of the LORD's temple, between the vestibule and the altar, were about twenty-five men with their backs to the LORD's temple and their faces toward the east; they were bowing down to the sun.* [17]Do you see, son of man? he asked me. Is it such a trivial matter for the house of Judah to do the abominable things they have done here—for they have filled the land with violence, and again and again they have provoked me—that now they must also put the branch to my nose?* [18]Therefore I in turn will act furiously: I will not look upon them with pity nor will I show mercy.

CHAPTER 9

Slaughter of the Idolaters.

See RG 325–32

[1]Then he cried loud for me to hear: Come, you scourges of the city! [2]With that I saw six men coming from the direction of the upper gate which faces the north, each with a destroying weapon in his hand. In their midst was a man dressed in linen, with a writer's case at his waist. They entered and stood beside the bronze altar. [3]Then he called to the

---

8, 3: The statue of jealousy which stirs up jealousy: the statue which provokes the Lord's jealousy for his honor. This was probably the statue of the goddess Asherah erected by the wicked King Manasseh (cf 2 Kgs 21, 7; 2 Chr 33, 7. 15). Though it had been removed by King Josiah (2 Kgs 23, 6), it had no doubt been set up again in the repaganizing of Jerusalem that followed on Josiah's death.

8, 5: He: an angel accompanies Ezekiel in these visions and represents the voice of the Lord; cf Ez 40, 3f.

8, 10: Creeping things and loathsome beasts: probably Egyptian deities, which were represented in animal form. During the last days of Jerusalem King Zedekiah was allied with Egypt, trusting in it for protection against the Chaldeans.

8, 14: Weeping for Tammuz: the withering of trees and plants in autumn was thought to be due to the descent of Tammuz, the Babylonian god of fertility, to the nether world of the dead; this descent was bewailed by the women.

8, 16: Bowing down to the sun: sun worship had been made an important part of Judahite idolatry by the impious kings; cf 2 Kgs 23, 11.

8, 17: Put the branch to my nose: the meaning is uncertain. Perhaps it refers to an Egyptian practice imported into Judah; the Egyptian sun god Re is pictured with a vine branch at his nose, signifying the transfer of creative power (divine breath) to living things. Such rites were abominable to the Lord.

n: Dn 14, 6.

man dressed in linen with the writer's case at his waist, [4c]saying to him:* Pass through the city [through Jerusalem] and mark an X on the foreheads of those who moan and groan over all the abominations that are practiced within it. [5]To the others I heard him say: Pass through the city after him and strike! Do not look on them with pity nor show any mercy! [6]Old men, youths and maidens, women and children—wipe them out! But do not touch any marked with the X; begin at my sanctuary. So they began with the men [the elders] who were in front of the temple. [7]Defile the temple, he said to them, and fill the courts with the slain; then go out and strike in the city.

[8]As they began to strike, I was left alone. I fell prone, crying out, "Alas, Lord GOD! Will you destroy all that is left of Israel when you pour out your fury on Jerusalem?" [9]He answered me: The sins of the house of Israel are great beyond measure; the land is filled with bloodshed, the city with lawlessness. They think that the LORD has forsaken the land, that he does not see them. [10]I, however, will not look upon them with pity, nor show any mercy. I will bring down their conduct upon their heads.

[11]Then I saw the man dressed in linen with the writing case at his waist make his report: "I have done as you ordered."

[24]*Spirit lifted me up and brought me back to the exiles in Chaldea [in a vision, by God's spirit]. Then the vision I had seen left me, [25]and I told the exiles everything the LORD had shown me.

See RG 325–32

CHAPTER 10

God's Glory Leaves Jerusalem. [8, 1]*On the fifth day of the sixth month, in the sixth year,* as I was sitting in my house, and the elders of Judah sat before me, the hand of the Lord GOD fell upon me there. [2]I looked up and saw a form that looked like a man. Downward from what seemed to be his waist, there was fire; from his waist upward there seemed to be a brightness like the sheen of electrum. He stretched out what appeared to be a hand and seized me by the hair of my head. . . .*

[4]I saw there the glory of the God of Israel, like the vision I had seen in the plain. The cherubim were stationed to the right of the temple; [20]these were the living creatures I had seen beneath the God of Israel by the river Chebar,[p] whom I now recognized to be cherubim. [21]Each had four faces and four wings; something like human hands were under their wings. [22]Their faces looked just like those I had seen by the river Chebar; each one went straight forward. [14q]Each had four faces: the first face was that of an ox, the second that of a man, the third that of a lion, and the fourth that of an eagle. [15]Such were the living creatures I had seen by the river Chebar.

[9r]I also saw four wheels beside them, one wheel beside each cherub; the wheels appeared to have the luster of chrysolite stone. [10]All four of them seemed to be made the same, as though there were a wheel within a wheel. [11]When they moved, they went in any one of their four directions without veering as they moved; for in whichever direction they were faced, they went straight towards it without veering as they moved. [12s]The rims of the four wheels were full of eyes all around. [13]I heard the wheels given the name "wheelwork." [16t]When the cherubim moved, the wheels went beside them; when the cherubim lifted their wings to rise from the earth, even then the wheels did not leave

---

9, 4: Ezekiel is preeminently the prophet of personal retribution; the innocent inhabitants of Jerusalem are to be spared when the idolatrous are punished. An X: literally, the Hebrew letter taw, which had the form of a cross.

9, 24f: These verses have been transposed from ch 11.

10, 1: In chapters 8, 1—11, 25 of the current Hebrew text, several visions involving the temple of Jerusalem were combined to form a single continuous vision. The redistribution of verses in this translation is an attempt to separate the original visions. (10, 1. 2. 4. have been transposed from ch 8)

10, 1: The fifth day of the sixth month, in the sixth year: September 17, 592 B.C.

10, 2: The dots suppose the omission of some words describing the prophet's being transported in his visions to the court of the temple.

10, 2: The burning coals within the wheelwork under God's throne, a sign of the divine presence (cf Ez 28, 14; Ps 18, 13), symbolize the judgment to be visited on the city.

o: Ex 12, 7; Rv 7, 3.   *p:* Ez 1, 1. 3.   *q:* Ez 1, 10.   *r:* Ez 1, 15f.   *s:* Ez 1, 18.   *t:* Ez 1, 19.

their sides. ¹⁷When they stood still, the wheels stood still; when they rose, the wheels rose with them; for the living creatures' spirit was in them.

¹I looked and saw in the firmament above the cherubim what appeared to be sapphire stone; something like a throne could be seen upon it. ²He said to the man dressed in linen: Go within the wheelwork under the cherubim; fill both your hands with burning coals* from among the cherubim, then scatter them over the city. As I looked on, he entered.

The glory of the God of Israel had gone up from the cherubim, upon which it had been, to the threshold of the temple. ³As the man entered, the cloud filled the inner court, ⁴and the glory of the LORD rose from over the cherubim to the threshold of the temple; the temple was filled with the cloud, and all the court was bright with the glory of the LORD. ⁵The noise of the wings of the cherubim could be heard as far as the outer court; it was like the voice of God the Almighty when he speaks.

⁶When he had commanded the man dressed in linen to take fire from within the wheelwork, among the cherubim, the man entered and stood by one of the wheels. ⁷Thereupon its cherub stretched out his hand toward the fire that was among the cherubim. He took up some of it and put it in the hands of the one dressed in linen, who took it and came out. ⁸[Something like human hands could be seen under the wings of the cherubim.]

¹⁸Then the glory of the LORD left the threshold of the temple and rested upon the cherubim. ¹⁹These lifted their wings, and I saw them rise from the earth, the wheels rising along with them. They stood at the entrance of the eastern gate of the LORD's house, and the glory of the God of Israel was up above them. ²²*Then the cherubim lifted their wings, and the wheels went along with them, while up above them was the glory of the God of Israel. ²³And the glory of the LORD rose from the city and took a stand on the mountain which is to the east of the city.

CHAPTER 11

See RG 325–32

Judgment of the Princes. ¹Spirit lifted me up and brought me to the east gate of the temple. At the entrance of the gate I saw twenty-five men, among whom were Jaazaniah, son of Azzur, and Pelatiah, son of Benaiah, princes of the people. ²The LORD said to me: Son of man, these are the men who are planning evil and giving wicked counsel in this city. ³"Shall we not," they say, "be building houses soon? The city is the kettle, and we are the meat."* ⁴Therefore prophesy against them, son of man, prophesy! ⁵Then the spirit of the LORD fell upon me, and he told me to say: Thus says the LORD: This is the way you talk, house of Israel, and what you are plotting I well know. ⁶You have slain many in this city and have filled its streets with your slain. ⁷Therefore thus says the Lord GOD: Your slain whom you have placed within it, they are the meat, and the city is the kettle; but you I will take out of it. ⁸You fear the sword, but the sword I will bring upon you, says the Lord GOD. ⁹I will bring you out of the city, and hand you over to foreigners, and inflict punishments upon you. ¹⁰By the sword you shall fall; at the boundaries of Israel I will judge you; thus you shall know that I am the LORD. ¹¹The city shall not be a kettle for you, nor shall you be the meat within it. At the boundaries of Israel I will judge you, ¹²and you shall know that I am the LORD, by whose statutes you have not lived, and whose ordinances you have not kept; rather, you have acted according to the ordinances of the nations around you.

¹³While I was prophesying, Pelatiah, the son of Benaiah, died. I fell prone and cried out in a loud voice: "Alas, Lord GOD! will you utterly wipe out what remains of Israel?"

Restoration of the Exiles. ¹⁴Thus the word of the LORD came to me: ¹⁵*Son of man, it is about your kinsmen, your fellow exiles, and

---

10, 22f: These verses have been transposed from ch 11.

11, 3: These words reflect the false confidence of the inhabitants of Jerusalem in the face of the Chaldean invasion. Jerusalem, they think, is like an iron kettle protecting the meat within it from harm; but cf Ez 24, 3-6.

11, 15-21: Like Jeremiah (cf chapter 29), Ezekiel knows that no reform is to be expected from the men of Judah who remained in Palestine; but the exiles will be the ones to form the new Israel. The new, spiritual covenant will replace the former covenant; cf Jer 24, 7.

the whole house of Israel that the inhabitants of Jerusalem say, "They are far away from the LORD; to us the land of Israel has been given as our possession." [16]Therefore say: Thus says the Lord GOD: Though I have removed them far among the nations and scattered them over foreign countries—and was for a while their only sanctuary in the countries to which they had gone— [17]I will gather you from the nations and assemble you from the countries over which you have been scattered, and I will restore to you the land of Israel. [18]They shall return to it and remove from it all its detestable abominations. [19u]I will give them a new heart and put a new spirit within them; I will remove the stony heart from their bodies, and replace it with a natural heart, [20]so that they will live according to my statutes, and observe and carry out my ordinances; thus they shall be my people and I will be their God. [21]But as for those whose hearts are devoted to their detestable abominations, I will bring down their conduct upon their heads, says the Lord GOD.

CHAPTER 12

See RG 325-32

Acts Symbolic of the Exile. [1]Thus the word of the LORD came to me: [2]Son of man, you live in the midst of a rebellious house; they have eyes to see but do not see, and ears to hear but do not hear, for they are a rebellious house. [3]Now, son of man, during the day while they are looking on, prepare your baggage as though for exile, and again while they are looking on, migrate from where you live to another place; perhaps they will see that they are a rebellious house. [4]You shall bring out your baggage like an exile in the daytime while they are looking on; in the evening, again while they are looking on, you shall go out like one of those driven into exile; [5]while they look on, dig a hole in the wall* and pass through it; [6]while they look on, shoulder the burden and set out in the darkness; cover your face that you may not see the land, for I have made you a sign for the house of Israel.

[7]I did as I was told. During the day I brought out my baggage as though it were that of an exile, and at evening I dug a hole through the wall with my hand and, while they looked on, set out in the darkness, shouldering my burden.

[8]Then, in the morning, the word of the LORD came to me: [9]Son of man, did not the house of Israel, that rebellious house, ask you what you were doing? [10]Tell them: Thus says the Lord GOD: This oracle concerns Jerusalem and the whole house of Israel within it. [11]I am a sign for you: as I have done, so shall it be done to them; as captives they shall go into exile. [12]The prince who is among them shall shoulder his burden and set out in darkness, going through a hole that he has dug in the wall, and covering his face lest he be seen by anyone. [13v]But I will spread my net over him, and he shall be taken in my snare. I will bring him to Babylon, into the land of the Chaldeans—but he shall not see it*—and there he shall die. [14]All his retinue, his aides, and his troops I will scatter in every direction, and pursue them with the sword. [15]Then shall they know that I am the LORD, when I disperse them among the nations and scatter them over foreign lands. [16]Yet I will leave a few of them to escape the sword, famine and pestilence, so that they may tell of all their abominations among the nations to which they will come; thus they shall know that I am the LORD.

[17]Thus the word of the LORD came to me: [18]Son of man, eat your bread trembling, and drink your water shaking with anxiety. [19]Then say to the people of the land: Thus says the Lord GOD of the inhabitants of Jerusalem [to the land of Israel]: They shall eat their bread in anxiety and drink their water in horror, that their land may be emptied of the violence of all its inhabitants that now fills it. [20]Inhabited cities shall be in ruins, and the land shall be a waste; thus you shall know that I am the LORD.

Prophecy Ridiculed. [21]Thus the word of the LORD came to me: [22]Son of man, what is

---

12, 5: Dig a hole in the wall: the exiles are to leave Jerusalem through the broken walls of the ruined city.

12, 13: But he shall not see it: Zedekiah was blinded by Nebuchadnezzar before being deported to Babylonia; cf 2 Kgs 25, 7.

u: Ez 36, 26; Jer 31, 33.   v: Ez 17, 20; 32, 3.

this proverb that you have in the land of Israel: "The days drag on, and no vision ever comes to anything"?* [23] Say to them therefore: Thus says the Lord GOD: I will put an end to this proverb; they shall never quote it again in Israel. Rather, say to them: The days are at hand, and also the fulfillment of every vision. [25] Whatever I speak is final, and it shall be done without further delay. In your days, rebellious house, whatever I speak I will bring about, says the Lord GOD.

[24] There shall no longer be any false visions or deceitful divinations within the house of Israel, because it is I, the LORD, who will speak.

[26] Thus the word of the LORD came to me: [27] Son of man, listen to the house of Israel saying, "The vision he sees is a long way off; he prophesies of the distant future!" [28] Say to them therefore: Thus says the Lord GOD: None of my words shall be delayed any longer; whatever I speak is final, and it shall be done, says the Lord GOD.

See RG 325-32

CHAPTER 13

Against the Prophets of Peace. [1] Thus the word of the LORD came to me: [2] Son of man, prophesy against the prophets of Israel, prophesy! Say to those who prophesy their own thought: Hear the word of the LORD:* [5] You did not step into the breach, nor did you build a wall about the house of Israel that would stand firm against attack on the day of the LORD. [7] Was not the vision you saw false, and your divination lying? [8] Therefore thus says the Lord GOD: Because you have spoken falsehood and have seen lying visions, therefore see! I am coming at you, says the Lord GOD.

[10] For the very reason that they led my people astray, saying, "Peace!" when there was no peace, and that, as one built a wall, they would cover it with whitewash,* [11] say then to the whitewashers: I will bring down a flooding rain; hailstones shall fall, and a stormwind shall break out. [12] And when the

wall has fallen, will you not be asked: Where is the whitewash you spread on?

[13] Therefore thus says the Lord GOD: In my fury I will let loose stormwinds; because of my anger there shall be a flooding rain, and hailstones shall fall with destructive wrath. [14] I will tear down the wall that you have whitewashed and level it to the ground, laying bare its foundations. When it falls, you shall be crushed beneath it; thus you shall know that I am the LORD. [15] When I have spent my fury on the wall and its whitewashers, I tell you there shall be no wall, nor shall there be whitewashers— [16] those prophets of Israel who prophesied to Jerusalem and saw for it visions of peace when there was no peace, says the Lord GOD.

Against False Prophets in Chaldea. [3w] Thus says the Lord GOD: Woe to those prophets who are fools, who follow their own spirit and have seen no vision. [4] Like foxes among ruins are your prophets, O Israel! [6] Their visions are false and their divination lying. They say, "Thus says the LORD!" though the LORD did not send them; then they wait for him to fulfill their word! [9] But I will stretch out my hand against the prophets who have false visions and who foretell lies. They shall not belong to the community of my people, nor be recorded in the register of the house of Israel, nor enter the land of Israel; thus you shall know that I am the LORD.

Against False Prophetesses. [17] Now, son of man, turn toward the daughters of your people who prophesy their own thoughts; against these, prophesy: Thus says the Lord GOD: [22] Because you have disheartened the upright man with lies when I did not wish him grieved, and have encouraged the wicked man not to turn from his evil conduct and save his life; [23] therefore you shall no longer see false visions and practice divination, but I will rescue my people from your power. Thus you shall know that I am the LORD.

12, 22. 27: These words used against Ezekiel because of the apparent failure of his prophecies; cf Jer 20, 7ff.

13, 3-23: These verses have been transposed according to the following order: 7-8. 10-16. 3-4. 6. 9. 17. 22-23. 18-21.

13, 10: To the confidence which the people had in their de-

fenses against the Chaldeans, the false prophets contributed the illusion of security by predictions of peace, like men who whitewash a wall rather than allow its defects to be seen.

w: Ez 14, 9; 34, 2; Jer 23, 1.

Against Sorceresses. [18]Woe to those who sew bands for everyone's wrists and make veils* for every size of head so as to entrap their owners. Do you think to entrap the lives of my people, yet keep yourselves alive? [19]You dishonor me before my people with handfuls of barley and crumbs of bread,* killing those who should not die and keeping alive those who should not live, lying to my people who willingly hear lies. [20]Therefore thus says the Lord GOD: See! I am coming at those bands of yours in which you entrap men's lives: I will tear them from their arms and set free those you have caught. [21]I will tear off your veils and rescue my people from your power, so that they shall no longer be prey to your hands. Thus you shall know that I am the LORD.

CHAPTER 14

See RG 325-32 ***Prophecy Useless for Idolaters.*** [1]When certain elders of Israel came and sat down before me, [2]the word of the LORD came to me: [3]Son of man, these men have the memory of their idols fresh in their hearts, and they keep the occasion of their sin before them. Why should I allow myself to be consulted by them? [4]Therefore speak with them, and say to them: Thus says the Lord GOD: If anyone of the house of Israel, holding the memory of his idols in his heart and keeping the occasion of his sin before him, has recourse to a prophet, I, the LORD, will be his answer in person because of his many idols. [5]Thus would I bring back to their senses the house of Israel, who have become estranged from me through all their idols.

[6]Therefore say to the house of Israel: Thus says the Lord GOD: Return and be converted from your idols; turn yourselves away from all your abominations. [7]For if anyone of the house of Israel or any alien resident in Israel is estranged from me, and holds the memory of his idols in his heart and keeps the occasion of his sin before him, yet asks a prophet to consult me for him, I, the LORD, will be his answer in person. [8]I will turn against that man, and make of him an example and a byword. I will cut him off from the midst of my people. Thus you shall know that I am the LORD.

[9x]As for the prophet, if he is beguiled into speaking a word, I, the LORD, shall have beguiled that prophet;* I will stretch out my hand against him and root him out of my people Israel. [10]Each shall receive punishment for his sin, the inquirer and the prophet shall be punished alike, [11]so that the house of Israel may no longer stray from me and may no longer be defiled by all their sins. Thus they shall be my people, and I will be their God, says the Lord GOD.

Personal Responsibility.* [12]Thus the word of the LORD came to me: [13y]Son of man, when a land sins against me by breaking faith, I stretch out my hand against it and break its staff of bread, I let famine loose upon it and cut off from it both man and beast; [14]and even if these three men were in it, Noah, Daniel, and Job,* they could save only themselves by their virtue, says the Lord GOD. [15]If I were to cause wild beasts to prowl the land, depopulating it so that it became a waste, traversed by none because of the wild beasts, [16]and these three men were in it, as I live, says the Lord GOD, I swear they could save neither sons nor daughters; they alone would be saved, and the land would be a waste. [17]Or if I brought the sword upon this country, commanding the sword to pass through the land cutting off from it man and beast, [18]and these three men were in it, as I live, says the Lord GOD, they would be unable to save either sons or daughters; they

---

13, 18: Sew bands . . . make veils: magical practices believed to give to the sorceresses power over those on whom they placed these objects.

13, 19: Handfuls of barley and crumbs of bread: used in divination and forecasting the future.

14, 9: I, the Lord, shall have beguiled that prophet: the ancient Israelites attributed to God every action, good or evil; cf 1 Sm 18, 10; 2 Sm 24, 1ff. We would say, rather, that God permitted this deceit.

14, 12-23: The doctrine of personal responsibility before

God was not new (cf Ez 3, 16-21; 18; 33, 1-20); but it had not been emphasized by the prophets before the Exile, who mostly predicted national retribution and called for national repentance.

14, 14: Noah, Daniel, and Job: proverbially virtuous men. The Daniel named here may be the traditional just judge of the ancient past, celebrated in Canaanite literature, who is possibly reflected in Dn 13, but is not the hero of Dn 1—12.

x: 1 Kgs 22, 23.   y: Ez 4, 16.

alone would be saved. [19]Or if I were to send pestilence into this land, pouring out upon it my bloodthirsty fury, cutting off from it man and beast, [20]even if Noah, Daniel, and Job were in it, as I live, says the Lord GOD, I swear that they could save neither son nor daughter; they would save only themselves by their virtue.

[21]Thus says the Lord GOD: Even though I send Jerusalem my four cruel punishments, the sword, famine, wild beasts, and pestilence, to cut off from it man and beast, [22]still some survivors shall be left in it who will bring out sons and daughters; when they come out to you, you shall see their conduct and their actions and be consoled regarding the evil I have brought on Jerusalem [all that I have brought upon it]. [23]They shall console you when you see their conduct and actions, for you shall then know that it was not without reason that I did to it what I did, says the Lord GOD.

CHAPTER 15

See RG 325-32

Parable of the Vine. [1]Thus the word of the LORD came to me: [2]Son of man, what makes the wood of the vine better than any other wood? That branch among the trees of the forest! [3]Can you use its wood to make anything worthwhile? Can you make even a peg from it, to hang on it any kind of vessel? [4]If you throw it on the fire as fuel and the fire devours both ends and even the middle is scorched, is it still good for anything? [5]Why, even when it was whole it was good for nothing; how much less, when the fire has devoured and scorched it, can it be used for anything! [6]Therefore, thus says the Lord GOD: Like the wood of the vine among the trees of the forest, which I have destined as fuel for the fire, do I make the inhabitants of Jerusalem. [7]I will set my face against them; they have escaped from the fire, but the fire shall devour them. Thus you shall know that I am the LORD, when I turn my face against them. [8]I will make the land a waste, because they have broken faith, says the Lord God.

CHAPTER 16

See RG 325-32

The Faithless Spouse. [1]Thus the word of the LORD came to me: [2]Son of man, make known to Jerusalem her abominations. [3]Thus says the Lord GOD to Jerusalem: By origin and birth you are of the land of Canaan; your father was an Amorite and your mother a Hittite.* [4]As for your birth, the day you were born your navel cord was not cut; you were neither washed with water nor anointed, nor were you rubbed with salt, nor swathed in swaddling clothes. [5]No one looked on you with pity or compassion to do any of these things for you. Rather, you were thrown out on the ground as something loathsome, the day you were born.

[6]Then I passed by and saw you weltering in your blood. I said to you: Live in your blood [7]and grow like a plant in the field. You grew and developed, you came to the age of puberty; your breasts were formed, your hair had grown, but you were still stark naked. [8]Again I passed by you and saw that you were now old enough for love. So I spread the corner of my cloak over you to cover your nakedness;* I swore an oath to you and entered into a covenant with you; you became mine, says the Lord GOD. [9]Then I bathed you with water, washed away your blood, and anointed you with oil. [10]I clothed you with an embroidered gown, put sandals of fine leather on your feet; I gave you a fine linen sash and silk robes to wear. [11]I adorned you with jewelry: I put bracelets on your arms, a necklace about your neck, [12]a ring in your nose, pendants in your ears, and a glorious diadem upon your head. [13]Thus you were adorned with gold and silver; your garments were of fine linen, silk, and embroidered cloth. Fine flour, honey, and oil were your food. You were exceedingly beautiful, with the dignity of a queen. [14]You were renowned among the nations for your beauty, perfect as it was, because of my splendor which I had bestowed on you, says the Lord God.

16, 3f: By origin and birth . . . Canaan . . . Amorite . . . Hittite: the inhabitants of Jerusalem and Judah absorbed not only pre-Israelite racial strains, but also many elements of the country's pagan cult and customs.

16, 8: I spread the corner of my cloak over you to cover your nakedness: and also to signify the intention of marriage; cf Ru 3, 9.

¹⁵But you were captivated by your own beauty, you used your renown to make yourself a harlot, and you lavished your harlotry on every passer-by, whose own you became. ¹⁶*You took some of your gowns and made for yourself gaudy high places, where you played the harlot. . . . ¹⁷You took the splendid gold and silver ornaments that I had given you and made for yourself male images, with which also you played the harlot. ¹⁸You took your embroidered gowns to cover them; my oil and my incense you set before them; ¹⁹the food that I had given you, the fine flour, the oil, and the honey with which I fed you, you set before them as an appeasing odor, says the Lord God. ²⁰ᶻThe sons and daughters you had borne me you took and offered as sacrifices* to be devoured by them! Was it not enough that you had become a harlot? ²¹ᵃYou slaughtered and immolated my children to them, making them pass through fire. ²²And through all your abominations and harlotries you remembered nothing of when you were a girl, stark naked and weltering in your blood.

²³Then after all your evildoing—woe, woe to you! says the Lord God— ²⁴you raised for yourself a platform and a dais* in every public place. ²⁵ᵇAt every street corner you built a dais for yourself to use your beauty obscenely, spreading your legs for every passer-by, playing the harlot countless times. ²⁶You played the harlot with the Egyptians, your lustful neighbors, so many times that I was provoked to anger. ²⁷Therefore I stretched out my hand against you, I diminished your allowance and delivered you over to the will of your enemies, the Philistines, who revolted at your lewd conduct. ²⁸You also played the harlot with the Assyrians, because you were not satisfied; and after playing the harlot with them, you were still not satisfied. ²⁹Again and again you played the harlot, now going to Chaldea, the land of the traders; but despite this, you were still not satisfied.

³⁰How wild your lust! says the Lord God, that you did all these things, acting like a shameless prostitute, ³¹building your platform at every street corner and erecting your dais in every public place! Yet you were unlike a prostitute, since you disdained payment. ³²The adulterous wife receives, instead of her husband, payment. ³³All harlots receive gifts. But you rather bestowed your gifts on all your lovers, bribing them to come to you from all sides for your harlotry. ³⁴Thus in your harlotry you were different from all other women. No one sought you out for prostitution. Since you gave payment instead of receiving it, how different you were!

³⁵Therefore, harlot, hear the word of the Lord! ³⁶Thus says the Lord God: Because you poured out your lust and revealed your nakedness in your harlotry with your lovers and abominable idols, and because you sacrificed the life-blood of your children to them, ³⁷ᶜI will now gather together all your lovers whom you tried to please, whether you loved them or loved them not; I will gather them against you from all sides and expose you naked for them to see. ³⁸I will inflict on you the sentence of adulteresses and murderesses; I will wreak fury and jealousy upon you. ³⁹I will hand you over to them to tear down your platform and demolish your dais; they shall strip you of your garments and take away your splendid ornaments, leaving you stark naked. ⁴⁰They shall lead an assembly against you to stone you and hack you with their swords. ⁴¹ᵈThey shall burn your apartments with fire and inflict punishments on you while many women look on. Thus I will put an end to your harlotry, and you shall never again give payment. ⁴²When I have wreaked my fury upon you I will cease to be jealous of you, I will be quiet and no longer vexed. ⁴³Because you did not re-

16, 16: Fine robes were used to cover a couch for harlotry; cf Prv 7, 16f. In the allegory of this chapter the viewpoint often shifts from the figure (harlotry) to the reality (idolatry).

16, 20f: Human sacrifice was introduced under Judah's impious kings; cf 2 Kgs 16, 3; 17, 17; Jer 7, 31.

16, 24: A platform and a dais: associated with ritual prostitution, which the Israelites borrowed from Canaanite practice.

z: Ez 20, 26. 31; 23, 37ff; Lv 18, 21; 20, 2; Dt 12, 31; 18, 10; 2 Kgs 21, 6; 23, 10; 24. 4; Jer 7, 31; 19, 5; 32, 34; Mi 6, 7. a: 2 Kgs 16, 3; 17, 17; 21, 6; 23, 10. b: Ez 23, 8; Is 57, 7; Jer 2, 20; 3, 2; 5, 7; 13, 27; Hos 2, 4; 4, 13. c: Ez 23, 10. d: 2 Kgs 25, 9.

member what happened when you were a girl, but enraged me with all these things, therefore in return I am bringing down your conduct upon your head, says the Lord GOD. For did you not add lewdness to the rest of your abominable deeds?

⁴⁴See, everyone who is fond of proverbs will say of you, 'Like mother, like daughter.' ⁴⁵Yes, you are the true daughter of the mother* who spurned her husband and children, and you are a true sister to those who spurned their husbands and children—your mother was a Hittite and your father an Amorite. ⁴⁶Your elder sister was Samaria* with her daughters, living to the north of you; and your younger sister, living to the south of you, was Sodom with her daughters. ⁴⁷Yet not only in their ways did you walk, and act as abominably as they did; in a very short time you became more corrupt in all your ways than they. ⁴⁸As I live, says the Lord GOD, I swear that your sister Sodom, with her daughters, has not done as you and your daughters have done! ⁴⁹ᵉAnd look at the guilt of your sister Sodom: she and her daughters were proud, sated with food, complacent in their prosperity, and they gave no help to the poor and needy. ⁵⁰Rather, they became haughty and committed abominable crimes in my presence; then, as you have seen, I removed them. ⁵¹Samaria did not commit half your sins! You have done more abominable things than they, and have even made your sisters appear just, with all the abominable deeds you have done. ⁵²You, then, bear your shame; you are an argument in favor of your sisters! In view of your sinful deeds, more abominable than theirs, they appear just in comparison with you. Blush for shame, and bear the shame of having made your sisters appear just.

⁵³I will restore their fortunes, the fortune of Sodom and her daughters and of Samaria and her daughters [and I will restore your fortune along with them], ⁵⁴that you may bear your shame and be disgraced for all the comfort you brought them. ⁵⁵Yes, your sisters, Sodom and her daughters, Samaria and her daughters, shall return to their former state [you and your daughters shall return to your former state]. ⁵⁶Was not your sister Sodom kept in bad repute by you while you felt proud of yourself, ⁵⁷before your wickedness became evident? Now you are like her, reproached by the Edomites and all your neighbors, despised on all sides by the Philistines. ⁵⁸The penalty of your lewdness and your abominations—you must bear it all, says the LORD.

⁵⁹For thus speaks the Lord GOD: I will deal with you according to what you have done, you who despised your oath, breaking a covenant. ⁶⁰Yet I will remember the covenant I made with you when you were a girl, and I will set up an everlasting covenant with you. ⁶¹Then you shall remember your conduct and be ashamed when I take your sisters, those older and younger than you, and give them to you as daughters, even though I am not bound by my covenant with you. ⁶²For I will re-establish my covenant with you, that you may know that I am the LORD, ⁶³that you may remember and be covered with confusion, and that you may be utterly silenced for shame when I pardon you for all you have done, says the Lord GOD.

CHAPTER 17

The Eagles and the Vine. ¹Thus the word of the LORD came to me: ²Son of man, propose a riddle, and speak this proverb to the house of Israel: ³Thus speaks the Lord GOD:

See RG 325-32

The great eagle, with great wings, with
    long pinions,
  with thick plumage, many-hued, came
    to Lebanon.
He took the crest of the cedar,
⁴   tearing off its topmost branch,
And brought it to a land of tradesmen,
    set it in a city of merchants.

16, 45: True daughter of the mother: Jerusalem has followed in the footsteps of its heathen forebears; cf v 3.

16, 46: Your elder sister was Samaria: Samaria can be called an elder sister in view of the relatively greater importance of the northern kingdom, Israel, during most of Old Testament history. Also, the relatively insignificant Sodom of ancient history can be called your younger sister.

e: Gn 19, 24.

⁵ Then he took some seed of the land,
   and planted it in a seedbed;
A shoot by plentiful waters,
   like a willow he placed it,
⁶ To sprout and grow up a vine,
   dense and low-lying,
Its branches turned toward him,
   its roots lying under him.
Thus it became a vine, produced
   branches
   and put forth shoots.
⁷ But there was another great eagle,
   great of wing, rich in plumage;
To him this vine bent its roots,
   sent out its branches,
That he might water it more freely
   than the bed where it was planted.
⁸ In a fertile field by plentiful waters it was
   planted,
   to grow branches, bear fruit,
   and become a majestic vine.

⁹Say: Thus says the Lord GOD: Can it prosper? Will he not rather tear it out by the roots and strip off its fruit, so that all its green growth will wither when he pulls it up by the roots? [No need of a mighty arm or many people to do this.] ¹⁰True, it is planted, but will it prosper? Will it not rather wither, when touched by the east wind, in the bed where it grew?

¹¹*Thus the word of the LORD came to me: ¹²Son of man, say now to the rebellious house: Do you not understand what this means? It is this: The king of Babylon came to Jerusalem and took away its king and princes with him to Babylon. ¹³Then he selected a man of the royal line with whom he made a covenant, binding him under oath, while removing the nobles of the land, ¹⁴so that the kingdom would remain a modest one, without aspirations, and would keep his covenant and obey him. ¹⁵But this man rebelled against him, sending envoys to Egypt to obtain horses and a great army. Can he prosper? Can who does such things escape? Can he break a covenant and still go free? ¹⁶As I live, says the Lord GOD, in the home of the king who set him up to rule, whose oath he spurned, whose covenant with him he broke, there in Babylon I swear he shall die! ¹⁷When ramps are cast up and siege towers are built for the destruction of many lives, he shall not be saved in the conflict by Pharaoh with a great army and numerous troops. ¹⁸He spurned his oath, breaking his covenant. Though he gave his hand in pledge, he did all these things. He shall not escape!

¹⁹Therefore say: Thus says the Lord GOD: As I live, my oath which he spurned, my covenant which he broke, I swear to bring down upon his head. ²⁰I will spread my net over him, and he shall be taken in my snare. I will bring him to Babylon and enter into judgment with him there over his breaking faith with me. ²¹All the crack troops among his forces shall fall by the sword, and the survivors shall be scattered in every direction. Thus you shall know that I, the LORD, have spoken.

²²Therefore say: Thus says the Lord GOD:

I, too, will take from the crest of the
   cedar,
   from its topmost branches tear off a
      tender shoot,
And plant it on a high and lofty
      mountain;
²³   on the mountain heights of Israel I will
         plant it.*
It shall put forth branches and bear fruit,
   and become a majestic cedar.
Birds of every kind shall dwell beneath it,
   every winged thing in the shade of its
      boughs.
²⁴ And all the trees of the field shall know
      that I, the LORD,
Bring low the high tree,
   lift high the lowly tree,
Wither up the green tree,
   and make the withered tree bloom.

As I, the LORD, have spoken, so will I do.

17, 11-21: These verses explain the foregoing allegory. In 597 B.C. Nebuchadnezzar removed King Jehoiachin and took him into exile; in his place he set Zedekiah, Jehoiachin's uncle, on the throne and received from him the oath of loyalty. But Zedekiah was beguiled into rebellion by Pharaoh Hophra of Egypt, and thereby merited punishment; cf 2 Kgs 24, 10—25, 7.

17, 22f: I, too, will take from the crest of the cedar . . . plant it: the Lord will restore Israel under a messianic King from the same Davidic dynasty.

f: Ez 12, 13; 32, 3.

CHAPTER 18

See RG 325–32

Personal Responsibility. [1]Thus the word of the LORD came to me: Son of man, [2]what is the meaning of this proverb that you recite in the land of Israel:

> "Fathers have eaten green grapes,[g]
>   thus their children's teeth are on
>   edge"?[*]

[3]As I live, says the Lord GOD: I swear that there shall no longer be anyone among you who will repeat this proverb in Israel. [4]For all lives are mine; the life of the father is like the life of the son, both are mine; only the one who sins shall die.

[5]If a man is virtuous—if he does what is right and just, [6]if he does not eat on the mountains,[*] nor raise his eyes to the idols of the house of Israel; if he does not defile his neighbor's wife, nor have relations with a woman in her menstrual period; [7h]if he oppresses no one, gives back the pledge received for a debt, commits no robbery; if he gives food to the hungry and clothes the naked; [8]if he does not lend at interest nor exact usury; if he holds off from evildoing, judges fairly between a man and his opponent; [9]if he lives by my statutes and is careful to observe my ordinances, that man is virtuous—he shall surely live, says the Lord GOD.

[10]But if he begets a son who is a thief, a murderer, or who does any of these things [11](though the father does none of them), a son who eats on the mountains, defiles the wife of his neighbor, [12]oppresses the poor and needy, commits robbery, does does not give back a pledge, raises his eyes to idols, does abominable things, [13]lends at interest and exacts usury—this son certainly shall not live. Because he practiced all these abominations, he shall surely die; his death shall be his own fault.

[14]On the other hand, if a man begets a son who, seeing all the sins his father commits, yet fears and does not imitate him; [15]a son who does not eat on the mountains, or raise his eyes to the idols of the house of Israel, or defile his neighbor's wife; [16]who does not oppress anyone, or exact a pledge, or commit robbery; who gives his food to the hungry and clothes the naked; [17]who holds off from evildoing, accepts no interest or usury, but keeps my ordinances and lives by my statutes—this one shall not die for the sins of his father, but shall surely live. [18]Only the father, since he violated rights, and robbed, and did what was not good among his people, shall in truth die for his sins. [19]You ask: "Why is not the son charged with the guilt of his father?" Because the son has done what is right and just, and has been careful to observe all my statutes, he shall surely live. [20i]Only the one who sins shall die. The son shall not be charged with the guilt of his father, nor shall the father be charged with the guilt of his son. The virtuous man's virtue shall be his own, as the wicked man's wickedness shall be his.

[21]But if the wicked man turns away from all the sins he committed, if he keeps all my statutes and does what is right and just, he shall surely live, he shall not die. [22]None of the crimes he committed shall be remembered against him; he shall live because of the virtue he has practiced. [23j]Do I indeed derive any pleasure from the death of the wicked? says the Lord GOD. Do I not rather rejoice when he turns from his evil way that he may live?

[24]And if the virtuous man turns from the path of virtue to do evil, the same kind of abominable things that the wicked man does, can he do this and still live? None of his virtuous deeds shall be remembered, because he has broken faith and committed sin; because of this, he shall die. [25k]You say, "The LORD's way is not fair!" Hear now, house of Israel: Is it my way that is unfair, or rather, are not your ways unfair? [26]When a virtuous man turns away from virtue to commit iniquity, and dies, it is because of the iniquity he committed that he must die. [27]But

---

18, 2: Fathers . . . on edge: a proverb by which the people claimed that they were being punished for their ancestors' sins rather than for their own; cf Jer 31, 29.

18, 6: Eat on the mountains: partake of ritual meals at the heathen high places.

g: Jer 13, 29.   *h:* Is 58, 7; Mt 25, 35.   *i:* Dt 24, 16; 2 Kgs 14, 6; 2 Chr 25, 4.   *j:* Ez 33, 11; 2 Pt 3, 9.   *k:* Ez 33, 20.

if a wicked man, turning from the wickedness he has committed, does what is right and just, he shall preserve his life; ²⁸since he has turned away from all the sins which he committed, he shall surely live, he shall not die. ²⁹And yet the house of Israel says, "The LORD's way is not fair!" Is it my way that is not fair, house of Israel, or rather, is it not that your ways are not fair?

³⁰ᴵTherefore I will judge you, house of Israel, each one according to his ways, says the Lord GOD. Turn and be converted from all your crimes, that they may be no cause of guilt for you. ³¹Cast away from you all the crimes you have committed, and make for yourselves a new heart and a new spirit. Why should you die, O house of Israel? ³²ᵐFor I have no pleasure in the death of anyone who dies, says the Lord GOD. Return and live!

See RG 325–32

CHAPTER 19

¹As for you, son of man, raise a lamentation over the prince of Israel:

Allegory of the Lions*

² What a lioness was your mother,
  a lion of lions!
Among young lions she couched
  to rear her whelps.
³ One whelp she raised up,
  a young lion he became;
He learned to seize prey,
  men he devoured.
⁴ Then nations raised cries against him,
  in their pit he was caught;
They took him away with hooks
  to the land of Egypt.
⁵ Then she saw that in vain she had waited,
  her hope was destroyed.
She took another of her whelps,
  him she made a young lion.
⁶ He prowled among the lions,
  a young lion he became;
He learned to seize prey,
  men he devoured;

⁷ He ravaged their strongholds,
  their cities he wasted.
The land and all in it were appalled
  at the noise of his roar.
⁸ Nations laid out against him
  snares all about him;
They spread their net to take him,
  in their pit he was caught.
⁹ They put him in a cage and took him away
  to the king of Babylon,
So that his voice would not be heard
  on the mountains of Israel.

Allegory of the Vine Branch

¹⁰ Your mother was like a vine*
  planted by the water;
Fruitful and branchy was she
  because of the abundant water.
¹¹ One strong branch she put out
  as a royal scepter.
Stately was her height
  amid the dense foliage;
Notably tall was she
  with her many clusters.
¹² But she was torn up in fury
  and flung to the ground;
The east wind withered her up,
  her fruit was torn off;
Then her strong branch withered up,
  fire devoured it.ⁿ
¹³ So now she is planted in the desert,
  in a land dry and parched,
¹⁴ For fire came out of the branch
  and devoured her shoots;
She is now without a strong branch,
  a ruler's scepter.

This is a lamentation and serves as a lamentation.

CHAPTER 20

See RG 325–32

Israel's History of Infidelity. ¹In the seventh year, on the tenth day of the fifth month,* some of the elders of Israel came to consult the LORD and sat down before me.

19, 2-9: The meaning of this allegory is uncertain. Probably the two young lions are Jehoahaz and Zedekiah, sons of the same mother, who were deported to Egypt and Babylonia respectively. Cf 2 Kgs 23, 31-34; 24, 18ff.

19, 10-14: A vine: Judah. One strong branch: the Davidic king.

20, 1: The seventh year, on the tenth day of the fifth month: August 14, 591 B.C.

---

l: Mt 3, 2; Lk 3, 3.　*m:* Ez 18, 23; 33, 11; 2 Pt 3, 9.　*n:* Hos 13, 15.

²Then the word of the LORD came to me: ³Son of man, speak with the elders of Israel and say to them: Thus says the Lord GOD: Have you come to consult me? As I live! I swear I will not allow myself to be consulted by you, says the Lord GOD.

⁴Will you judge them? Will you judge, son of man? Make known to them the abominations of their ancestors ⁵in these words: Thus speaks the Lord GOD: The day I chose Israel, I swore to the decendants of the house of Jacob; in the land of Egypt I revealed myself to them and swore: I am the LORD, your God. ⁶That day I swore to bring them out of the land of Egypt to the land I had scouted for them, a land flowing with milk and honey, a jewel among all lands. ⁷Then I said to them: Throw away, each of you, the detestable things that have held your eyes; do not defile yourselves with the idols of Egypt: I am the LORD, your God.

⁸But they rebelled against me and refused to listen to me; none of them threw away the detestable things that had held their eyes, they did not abandon the idols of Egypt. Then I thought of pouring out my fury on them and spending my anger on them there in the land of Egypt; ⁹but I acted for my name's sake, that it should not be profaned in the sight of the nations among whom they were, in whose presence I had made myself known to them, revealing that I would bring them out of the land of Egypt. ¹⁰Therefore I led them out of the land of Egypt and brought them into the desert. ¹¹ᵒThen I gave them my statutes and made known to them my ordinances, which everyone must keep, to have life through them. ¹²ᵖI also gave them my sabbaths to be a sign between me and them, to show that it was I, the LORD, who made them holy.

¹³But the house of Israel rebelled against me in the desert. They did not observe my statutes, and they despised my ordinances that bring life to those who keep them. My sabbaths, too, they desecrated grievously. Then I thought of pouring out my fury on them in the desert to put an end to them, ¹⁴but I acted for my name's sake, that it should not be profaned in the sight of the nations in whose presence I had brought them out. ¹⁵Nevertheless I swore to them in the desert not to bring them to the land I had given them, a land flowing with milk and honey, a jewel among all lands. ¹⁶So much were their hearts devoted to their idols, they had not lived by my statutes, but despised my ordinances and desecrated my sabbaths. ¹⁷But I looked on them with pity, not wanting to destroy them, so I did not put an end to them in the desert.

¹⁸Then I said to their children in the desert: Do not observe the statutes of your parents or keep their ordinances; do not defile yourselves with their idols. ¹⁹I am the LORD, your God: observe my statutes and be careful to keep my ordinances; ²⁰keep holy my sabbaths, as a sign between me and you to show that I am the LORD, your God. ²¹But their children rebelled against me: they did not observe my statutes or keep my ordinances that bring life to those who observe them, and my sabbaths they desecrated. Then I thought of pouring out my fury on them, of spending my anger on them in the desert; ²²but I stayed my hand, acting for my name's sake, lest it be profaned in the sight of the nations in whose presence I brought them out. ²³Nevertheless I swore to them in the desert that I would disperse them among the nations and scatter them over foreign lands; ²⁴for they did not keep my ordinances, but despised my statutes and desecrated my sabbaths with eyes only for the idols of their fathers. ²⁵Therefore I gave them statutes that were not good,* and ordinances through which they could not live. ²⁶I let them become defiled by their gifts, by their immolation of every first-born, so as to make them an object of horror.

²⁷Therefore speak to the house of Israel, son of man, and tell them: Thus says the Lord GOD: In this way also your fathers blasphemed me, breaking faith with me: ²⁸when I had brought them to the land I had sworn to give them, and they saw all its high

---

20, 25f: I gave them statutes that were not good: the Lord permitted them to adopt pagan practices, including the abominable sacrifice of their newborn infants, which could only merit their destruction. See note on Ez 14, 9.

o: Lv 18, 5; Rom 10, 5.   *p:* Ex 20, 8; 31, 13; Dt 5, 12.

hills and leafy trees, there they offered their sacrifices [there they brought their offensive offerings], there they sent up appeasing odors, and there they poured out their libations. ²⁹I asked them: To what sort of high place do you betake yourselves?—and so they call it a high place even to the present day. ³⁰Therefore say to the house of Israel: Thus says the Lord GOD: Will you defile yourselves like your fathers? Will you lust after their detestable idols? ³¹By offering your gifts, by making your children pass through the fire, you defile yourselves with all your idols even to this day. Shall I let myself be consulted by you, house of Israel? As I live! says the Lord GOD: I swear I will not let myself be consulted by you.

³²What you are thinking of shall never happen: "We shall be like the nations, like the peoples of foreign lands, serving wood and stone." ³³As I live, says the Lord GOD, with a mighty hand and outstretched arm, with poured-out wrath, I swear I will be king over you! ³⁴With a mighty hand and outstretched arm, with poured-out wrath, I will bring you out from the nations and gather you from the countries over which you are scattered; ³⁵*then I will lead you to the desert of the peoples, where I will enter into judgment with you face to face. ³⁶Just as I entered into judgment with your fathers in the desert of the land of Egypt, so will I enter into judgment with you, says the Lord GOD. ³⁷I will count you with the staff and bring back but a small number. ³⁸I will separate from you those who have rebelled and transgressed against me; from the land where they sojourned as aliens I will bring them out, but they shall not return to the land of Israel. Thus you shall know that I am the LORD.

³⁹As for you, house of Israel, thus says the Lord GOD: Come, each one of you, destroy your idols! Then listen to me, and never again profane my holy name with your gifts and your idols. ⁴⁰For on my holy mountain, on the mountain height of Israel, says the Lord GOD, there the whole house of Israel without ex-

ception shall worship me; there I will accept them, and there I will claim your tributes and the first fruits of your offerings, and all that you dedicate. ⁴¹As a pleasing odor I will accept you, when I have brought you from among the nations and gathered you out of the countries over which you were scattered; and by means of you I will manifest my holiness in the sight of the nations. ⁴²Thus you shall know that I am the LORD, when I bring you back to the land of Israel, the land which I swore to give to your fathers. ⁴³There you shall recall your conduct and all the deeds by which you defiled yourselves; and you shall loathe yourselves because of all the evil things you did. ⁴⁴And you shall know that I am the LORD when I deal with you thus, for my name's sake, and not according to your evil conduct and corrupt actions, O house of Israel, says the Lord GOD.

CHAPTER 21

See RG 325-32

The Sword of the Lord. ¹Thus the word of the LORD came to me: ²*Son of man, look southward, preach toward the south, and prophesy against the forest of the southern land. ³Hear the word of the LORD! you shall say to the southern forest. Thus says the Lord GOD: See! I am kindling a fire in you that shall devour all trees, the green as well as the dry. The blazing flame shall not be quenched, but from south to north every face shall be scorched by it. ⁴Everyone shall see that I, the LORD, have kindled it, and it shall not be quenched.

⁵But I said, "Alas! Lord GOD, they say to me, 'Is not this the one who is forever spinning parables?' " ⁶Then the word of the LORD came to me: ⁷Son of man, look toward Jerusalem, preach against their sanctuary, and prophesy against the land of Israel, ⁸saying to the land of Israel: Thus says the LORD: See! I am coming at you; I will draw my sword from its sheath and cut off from you the virtuous and the wicked.* ⁹Thus my sword shall leave its sheath against everyone from south to north, ¹⁰and everyone shall

---

20, 35-38: Exile in the pagan lands will serve the same purpose as the desert journey after the Exodus from Egypt: the rebellious will be eliminated, and only a remnant will survive.

21, 2ff: The southern kingdom, Judah, is likened to a for-

est about to be burned; cf Jer 21, 14.

21, 8: Cut off from you the virtuous and the wicked: a more complete devastation of Jerusalem than that described in Ez 9, 6.

know that I, the LORD, have drawn my sword from its sheath, and it shall not be sheathed again.

Act Symbolic of the City's Fall. [11]As for you, son of man, groan! with shattered strength groan bitterly while they look on. [12]And when they ask you, "Why are you groaning?", you shall say: Because of a report;* when it comes every heart shall fail, every hand shall fall helpless, every spirit shall be daunted, and every knee shall run with water. See, it is coming, it is here! says the Lord GOD.

Song of the Sword. [13]Thus the word of the LORD came to me: [14]Son of man, prophesy! say: Thus says the LORD:

A sword, a sword has been sharpened,
  a sword, a sword has been burnished:
[15] To work slaughter has it been sharpened,
  to flash lightning has it been
    burnished.
Why should I now withdraw it?
  You have spurned the rod and every
    judgment!
[16] I have given it over to the burnisher
  that he might hold it in his hand,
A sword sharpened and burnished
  to be put in the hand of a slayer.
[17] Cry out and wail, son of man,
  for it is destined for my people;
It is for all the princes of Israel,
  victims of the sword with my people.

Therefore, slap your thigh,* [18]for the sword has been tested; and why should it not be so? says the Lord GOD, since you have spurned the rod.

[19] As for you, son of man, prophesy,
  brushing one hand against the other:
While the sword is doubled and tripled,
  this sword of slaughter,
This great sword of slaughter
  which threatens all around,

[20] That every heart may tremble;
  for many will be the fallen.
At all their gates
  I have appointed the sword for
    slaughter,
Fashioned to flash lightning,
  burnished for slaughter.
[21] Cleave to the right! destroy!
  to the left! wherever your edge is
    turned.

[22]Then I, too, shall brush one hand against the other* and wreak my fury. I, the LORD, have spoken.

Nebuchadnezzar at the Crossroads. [23]Thus the word of the LORD came to me: [24]Son of man, make for yourself two roads over which the sword of the king of Babylon can come. Both roads shall lead out from the same land. Then put a signpost at the head of each road, [25]so that the sword can come to Rabbah of the Ammonites or to Judah's capital, Jerusalem. [26]For at the fork where the two roads divide stands the king of Babylon, divining;* he has shaken the arrows, inquired of the teraphim, inspected the liver. [27]In his right hand is the divining arrow marked "Jerusalem,"* bidding him to give the order for slaying, to raise his voice in the battle cry, to post battering rams at the gates, to cast up a ramp, to build a siege tower. [28]In their eyes this is but a lying oracle; yet they are bound by the oaths they have sworn, and the arrow taken in hand marks their guilt.

[29]Therefore thus says the Lord GOD: Because you have drawn attention to your guilt, with your crimes laid bare and your sinfulness in all your wicked deeds revealed (because attention has been drawn to you), you shall be taken in hand. [30]And as for you, depraved and wicked prince of Israel, whose day is coming when your life of crime will be ended, [31]thus says the Lord GOD: Off with the turban and away with the crown! Noth-

---

21, 12: A report: the news of the fall of Jerusalem; cf Ez 33, 21f.

21, 17: Slap your thigh: a gesture signifying grief and dread.

21, 22: Brush one hand against the other: a gesture signifying the rejection of responsibility; cf Ez 22, 13; Nm 24, 10.

21, 26: Three forms of divination are mentioned: arrow divination, consisting in the use of differently marked arrows extracted or shaken from a case at random; the consultation of the teraphim or household idols; and liver divination, scrutiny of the configurations of the livers of newly slaughtered animals, a common form of divination in Mesopotamia.

21, 27f: An arrow marked "Jerusalem" is picked out, which marks the guilt of the city's inhabitants for having broken their oath of allegiance to Nebuchadnezzar.

ing shall be as it was! Up with the low and down with the high! *32*Twisted, twisted, twisted will I leave it; it shall not be the same until he comes who has the claim against the city; and to him I will hand it over.

*Against the Ammonites** *33*As for you, son of man, prophesy: Thus says the Lord GOD against the Ammonities and their insults: A sword, a sword is drawn for slaughter, burnished to consume and to flash lightning, *34*because you planned with false visions and lying divinations to lay it on the necks of depraved and wicked men whose day has come when their crimes are at an end. *35*Return it to its sheath! In the place where you were created, in the land of your origin, I will judge you. *36*I will pour out my indignation upon you, breathing my fiery wrath upon you; I will hand you over to ravaging men, artisans of destruction. *37*You shall be fuel for the fire, your blood shall flow throughout the land. You shall not be remembered, for I, the LORD, have spoken.

CHAPTER 22

See RG
325–32

Crimes of Jerusalem. *1*Thus the word of the LORD came to me: *2*You, son of man, would you judge, would you judge the bloody city? Then make known all her abominations, *3*and say: Thus says the Lord GOD: Woe to the city which sheds blood within herself so that her time has come, and which has made idols for her own defilement. *4*By the blood which you shed you have been made guilty, and with the idols you made you have become defiled; you have brought on your day, so that the end of your years has come. Therefore I make you an object of scorn to the nations and a laughingstock to all foreign lands. *5*Those near you and those far off shall deride you because of your foul reputation and your great perversity. *6*See! the princes of Israel, family by family, are in you only for bloodshed. *7*Within you, father and mother are despised; in your midst, they extort from the resident alien; within you, they oppress orphans and widows. *8*What is holy

to me you have spurned, and my sabbaths you have desecrated. *9*There are those in you who slander to cause bloodshed; within you are those who feast on the mountains; in your midst are those who do lewd things. *10*In you are those who uncover the nakedness of their fathers, and in you those who coerce women in their menstrual period. *11q*There are those in you who do abominable things with the wives of their neighbors, men who defile their daughters-in-law by incest, men who coerce their sisters, the daughters of their own fathers. *12*There are those in you who take bribes to shed blood. You exact interest and usury; you despoil your neighbors violently; and me you have forgotten, says the Lord GOD.

*13*See, I am brushing one hand against the other because of the unjust profits you have made and because of the blood shed in your midst. *14*Can your heart remain firm, will your hands be strong, in the days when I deal with you? I, the LORD, have spoken, and I will act. *15*I will disperse you among the nations and scatter you over foreign lands, so that I may purge your uncleanness. *16*In you I will allow myself to be profaned in the eyes of the nations; thus you shall know that I am the LORD.

*17*Thus the word of the LORD came to me: *18*Son of man, the house of Israel has become dross for me. All of them are bronze and tin, iron and lead [in the midst of a furnace]: dross from silver have they become. *19*Therefore thus says the Lord GOD: Because all of you have become dross, therefore I must gather you together within Jerusalem. *20*Just as silver, bronze, iron, lead, and tin are gathered into a furnace and smelted in the roaring flames, so I will gather you together in my furious wrath, put you in, and smelt you. *21*When I have assembled you, I will blast you with the fire of my anger and smelt you with it. *22*You shall be smelted by it just as silver is smelted in a furnace. Thus you shall know that I, the Lord, have poured out my fury on you.

21, 33-37: In the preceding section Nebuchadnezzar is represented as deciding whether to attack Jerusalem or Rabbath-Ammon. As it happened, Jerusalem was chosen for attack; later, however, the Chaldeans also invaded Ammon. The present ora-

cle against Ammon is inserted here, rather than in chapters 25—32, in order to complement the oracle against Jerusalem.

q: Jer 5, 7f.

²³Thus the word of the LORD came to me: ²⁴Son of man, say to her: You are a land unrained on [that is, not rained on] at the time of my fury. ²⁵Her princes are like roaring lions that tear prey; they devour people, seizing their wealth and precious things, and make widows of many within her. ²⁶Her priests violate my law and profane what is holy to me; they do not distinguish between the sacred and the profane, nor teach the difference between the unclean and the clean; they pay no attention to my sabbaths, so that I have been profaned in their midst. ²⁷ʳHer nobles within her are like wolves that tear prey, shedding blood and destroying lives to get unjust gain. ²⁸Her prophets cover them with whitewash, pretending to visions that are false and performing lying divinations, saying, "Thus says the Lord GOD," although the LORD has not spoken. ²⁹The people of the land practice extortion and commit robbery; they afflict the poor and the needy, and oppress the resident alien without justice. ³⁰Thus I have searched among them for someone who could build a wall or stand in the breach before me to keep me from destroying the land; but I found no one. ³¹Therefore I have poured out my fury upon them; with my fiery wrath I have consumed them; I have brought down their conduct upon their heads, says the Lord GOD.

CHAPTER 23

See RG
325-32

The Two Sisters. ¹Thus the word of the LORD came to me: ²Son of man, there were two women, daughters of the same mother, ³who even as young girls played the harlot in Egypt. There the Egyptians caressed their bosoms and fondled their virginal breasts. ⁴Oholah was the name of the elder, and the name of her sister was Oholibah.* They became mine and bore sons and daughters. [As for their names: Samaria is Oholah, and Jerusalem is Oholibah.] ⁵Oholah became a harlot faithless to me; she lusted after her lovers, the Assyrians, warriors ⁶dressed in purple, governors and officers, all of them attractive young men, knights mounted on horses. ⁷Thus she gave herself as a harlot to them, to all the elite of the Assyrians, and she defiled herself with all those for whom she lusted [with all their idols]. ⁸She did not give up the harlotry which she had begun in Egypt, when they had lain with her as a young girl, fondling her virginal breasts and pouring out their impurities on her. ⁹Therefore I handed her over to her lovers, the Assyrians for whom she had lusted. ¹⁰ˢThey exposed her nakedness, her sons and daughters they took away, and herself they slew with the sword. Thus she became a byword for women, for they punished her grievously.

¹¹Though her sister Oholibah saw all this, her lust was more depraved than her sister's, and she outdid her in harlotry. ¹²She too lusted after the Assyrians, governors and officers, warriors impeccably clothed, knights mounted on horses, all of them attractive young men. ¹³I saw that she had defiled herself. Both had gone down the same path, ¹⁴yet she went further in her harlotry. When she saw men drawn on the wall, the images of Chaldeans drawn with vermillion, ¹⁵with sashes girded about their waists, flowing turbans on their heads, all looking like chariot warriors, the portraits of Babylonians, natives of Chaldea, ¹⁶she lusted for them; no sooner had she set eyes on them than she sent messengers to them in Chaldea. ¹⁷Then the Babylonians came to her, to the love couch, and defiled her with their intercourse. As soon as she was defiled by them, she became disgusted with them. ¹⁸Her harlotry was discovered and her shame was revealed, and I became disgusted with her as I had become disgusted with her sister. ¹⁹But she played the harlot all the more, recalling the days of her girlhood, when she had been a harlot in the land of Egypt. ²⁰She lusted for the lechers of Egypt, whose members are like that of an ass, and whose heat is like those of stallions.

²¹You yearned for the lewdness of your girlhood, when the Egyptians fondled your breasts, caressing your bosom. ²²Therefore,

---

23, 4: Oholah . . . Oholibah: symbolic names. The first, standing for Samaria, may be read to mean "her own tent"; the latter, standing for Jerusalem, means "My tent is in her." The references seem to be to the schismatic temple and cult of the Lord in Samaria, as opposed to their authentic counterpart in Jerusalem.

r: Mi 3, 11; Zep 3, 3.   *s:* Ez 16, 37.

Oholibah, thus says the Lord GOD: I will now stir up your lovers against you, those with whom you are disgusted, and I will bring them against you from every side: *23*the men of Babylon and all of Chaldea, Pekod, Shoa and Koa,* along with all those of Assyria, attractive young men, all of them governors and officers, charioteers and warriors, all of them horsemen. *24*They shall come against you from the north with chariots and wagons and many peoples. Shields, bucklers, and helmets they shall array against you everywhere. *25*I will leave it to them to judge, and they will judge you by their own ordinances. I will let loose my jealousy against you, so that they shall deal with you in fury, cutting off your nose and ears; and what is left of you shall fall by the sword. They shall take away your sons and daughters, and what is left of you shall be devoured by fire. *26*They shall strip off your clothes and seize your splendid ornaments. *27*I will put an end to your lewdness and to the harlotry you began in Egypt; you shall no longer look toward it, nor shall you remember Egypt again.

*28*For thus says the Lord GOD: I am now handing you over to those whom you hate, to those who fill you with disgust. *29*They shall deal with you in hatred, seizing all that you have worked for and leaving you stark naked, so that your indecent nakedness is exposed. Your lewdness and harlotry *30*have brought these things upon you, because you played the harlot with the nations by defiling yourself with their idols.

*31*Because you followed in the path of your sister, I will hand you her cup. *32*Thus says the Lord GOD:

The cup of your sister you shall drink,
   so wide and deep, which holds so
         much,
33 Filled with destruction and grief,
   a cup of dismay, the cup of your sister.

*34*You shall drain it dry, and gnaw at the very sherds of the cup, and you shall tear out your breasts; for I have spoken, says the Lord GOD. *35*Therefore thus says the Lord GOD:

Because you have forgotten me and cast me behind your back, it is for you to bear the penalty of your lewdness and harlotry.

*36*Then the LORD said to me: Son of man, would you judge Oholah and Oholibah? Then make known to them their abominations. *37*For they committed adultery, and blood is on their hands. They committed adultery with their idols; to feed them they immolated the children they had borne me. *38*[This, too, they did to me: they defiled my sanctuary and desecrated my sabbaths. *39*On the very day they slew their children for their idols, they entered my sanctuary to desecrate it. Thus they acted within my house.] *40*Moreover, they sent for men who had to come from afar,* to whom messengers were sent. And so they came—and for them you bathed yourself, painted your eyes, and put on ornaments. *41*You sat on a couch prepared for them, with a table spread before it, on which you had set my incense and oil. *42*Then was heard the shout of a carefree mob in the city, and these were men brought in from the desert, who put bracelets on the women's arms and splendid diadems on their heads. *43*So I said: "Oh, this woman jaded with adulteries! Now they will commit whoredom with her, and as for her. . . ." *44*And indeed they did come to her as men come to a harlot. Thus they came to Oholah and Oholibah, the lewd women. *45*But just men shall punish them with the sentence meted out to adulteresses and murderesses, for they have committed adultery, and blood is on their hands.

*46*Thus says the Lord GOD: Summon an assembly against them, and deliver them over to terror and plunder. *47*The assembly shall stone them and hack them to pieces with their swords. They shall slay their sons and daughters, and burn their houses with fire. *48*Thus I will put an end to lewdness in the land, and all the women will be warned not to imitate your lewdness. *49*They shall inflict on you the penalty of your lewdness, and you shall pay for your sins of idolatry. Thus you shall know that I am the LORD.

23, 23: Pekod, Shoa and Koa: peoples living about the Tigris, part of "greater Babylonia."
23, 40: Men who had to come from afar: ambassadors from Assyria and Babylon. Alliances with these countries aided in the corruption of both Israel and Judah.

CHAPTER 24

See RG 325–32

Allegory of the Pot. ¹On the tenth day of the tenth month, in the ninth year,* the word of the LORD came to me: ²Son of man, write down this date today, for this very day the king of Babylon has invested Jerusalem. ³Propose this parable to the rebellious house: Thus says the Lord GOD:

*Set up the pot, set it up,
then pour in some water.
⁴ Put in it pieces of meat,
all good pieces: thigh and shoulder;
Fill it with the choicest joints
⁵ taken from the pick of the flock.
Then pile the wood beneath it;
bring to a boil these pieces
and the joints that are in it.
⁶ Take out its pieces, one by one,
without casting lots for it.

Therefore, thus says the Lord GOD: Woe to the bloody city,ᵗ a pot containing rust, whose rust has not been removed. ⁷For the blood she shed is in her midst; she poured it on the bare rock; she did not pour it out on the earth, to be covered with dust.* ⁸To work up my wrath, to excite my vengeance, she put her blood on the bare rock, not to be covered. ⁹Therefore, thus says the Lord GOD:

I, too, will heap up a great bonfire,
¹⁰ piling on wood and kindling the fire,
Till the meat has been cooked,
till the broth has boiled.

¹¹Then I will set the pot empty on the coals till its metal glows red hot, till the impurities in it melt, and its rust disappears. ¹²Yet not even with fire will its great rust be removed. ¹³Because you have sullied yourself with lewdness when I would have purified you, and you refused to be purified of your uncleanness, therefore you shall not be purified until I wreak my fury on you. ¹⁴I, the LORD,

have spoken; it is coming, for I will bring it about without fail. I will not have pity nor repent. By your conduct and your deeds you shall be judged, says the Lord GOD.

Symbol of the Destruction of the Temple. ¹⁵Thus the word of the LORD came to me: ¹⁶Son of man, by a sudden blow I am taking away from you the delight of your eyes, but do not mourn or weep or shed any tears. ¹⁷Groan in silence, make no lament for the dead, bind on your turban, put your sandals on your feet, do not cover your beard, and do not eat the customary bread.* ¹⁸That evening my wife died, and the next morning I did as I had been commanded. ¹⁹Then the people asked me, "Will you not tell us what all these things that you are doing mean for us?" I therefore spoke to the people that morning, ²⁰saying to them: Thus the word of the LORD came to me: ²¹Say to the house of Israel: Thus says the Lord GOD: I will now desecrate my sanctuary, the stronghold of your pride, the delight of your eyes, the desire of your soul. The sons and daughters you left behind shall fall by the sword. ²⁴Ezekiel shall be a sign for you: all that he did you shall do when it happens. Thus you shall know that I am the LORD. ²²*You shall do as I have done, not covering your beards nor eating the customary bread. ²³Your turbans shall remain on your heads, your sandals on your feet. You shall not mourn or weep, but you shall rot away because of your sins and groan one to another.

End of Ezekiel's Dumbness. ²⁵ᵘAs for you, son of man, truly, on the day I take away from them their bulwark, their glorious joy, the delight of their eyes, the desire of their soul, and the pride of their hearts, their sons and daughters, ²⁶that day the fugitive will come to you, that you may hear it for yourself; ²⁷that day your mouth shall be opened and you shall be dumb no longer. Thus you shall be a sign to them, and they shall know that I am the LORD.

24, 1: The tenth day of the tenth month, in the ninth year: January 15, 588 B.C. The same date is given in Jer 52, 4.

24, 3ff: This present comparison of the inhabitants of Jerusalem to meat boiled in a pot symbolizes their punishment rather than their supposed protection as in Ez 11, 3.

24, 7: Blood . . . to be covered with dust: since blood is sacred to God, it had to be covered with earth (Lv 17, 13); the blood of a murdered man that was left uncovered cried to

heaven for vengeance; cf Jb 16, 18; Gn 4, 10.

24, 17: The customary bread: eaten as a mourning observance; cf Jer 16, 7. The other gestures here forbidden were also popular mourning customs.

24, 22f: The fall of the city will be so sudden and final that the exiles will have no time to go into mourning.

t: Na 3, 1; Hb 2, 12.   u: 25ff: Ez 3, 22-27.

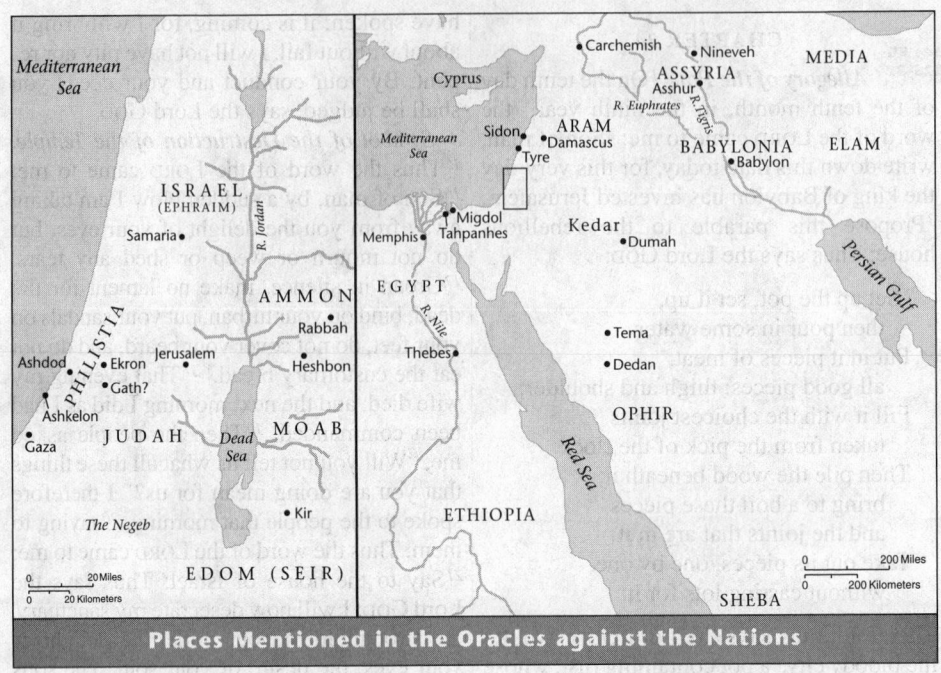

Places Mentioned in the Oracles against the Nations

III: Prophecies Against Foreign Nations

CHAPTER 25

See RG 325-32

Against Ammon. ¹Thus the word of the LORD came to me: ²Son of man, turn toward the Ammonites and prophesy against them. ³ᵛSay to the Ammonites: Hear the word of the LORD! Thus says the Lord GOD: Because you cried out your joy over the desecration of my sanctuary, the devastation of the land of Israel, and the exile of the house of Judah, ⁴therefore I will deliver you into the possession of the Easterners.* They shall set up their encampments among you and pitch their tents; they shall eat your fruits and drink your milk. ⁵I will make Rabbah a pasture for camels, and the villages of the Ammonites a resting place for flocks. Thus you shall know that I am the LORD.

⁶For thus says the Lord GOD: Because you clapped your hands and stamped your feet, rejoicing most maliciously in your heart over the land of Israel, ⁷therefore I will stretch out my hand against you. I will make you plunder for the nations, I will cut you off from the peoples, and remove you from the lands. I will destroy you, and thus you shall know that I am the LORD.

Against Moab. ⁸ʷThus says the Lord GOD: Because Moab said, "See! the house of Judah is like all other nations," ⁹therefore I will clear the shoulder of Moab* totally of its cities, the jewels of the land: Beth-jesimoth, Baalmeon, and Kiriathaim. ¹⁰I will hand her over, along with the Ammonites, into the possession of the Easterners, that she may not be remembered among the peoples. ¹¹Thus I will execute judgment upon Moab, that they may know that I am the LORD.

Against Edom. ¹²ˣThus says the Lord GOD: Because Edom has taken vengeance on the house of Judah and has made itself

---

25, 4: The Easterners: nomadic tribes to the east of Ammon and Moab.

25, 9: The shoulder of Moab: the edge of the Moabite plateau.

v: Jer 40, 14; 41, 10: 49, 2; Am 1, 13ff: Zep 2, 8ff.   *w:* Sir 50, 26; Is 15, 1-9; 16, 1-14; Jer 48, 1-47; Am 2, 1ff; Zep 2, 8f.   *x:* 12ff: Ez 35, 1ff; Is 34, 5; Jer 49, 7-22; Jl 4, 19; Am 1, 11f; Ob 1, 1-21.

grievously guilty by taking vengeance on them, [13]therefore thus says the Lord GOD: I will stretch out my hand against Edom and cut off from it man and beast. I will make it a waste from Teman to Dedan; they shall fall by the sword. [14]My vengeance upon Edom I will entrust to my people Israel, who will deal with Edom in accordance with my anger and my fury; thus they shall know my vengeance, says the Lord GOD.

Against the Philistines. [15]Thus says the Lord GOD: Because the Philistines have acted revengefully, and have taken vengeance with destructive malice in their hearts, with an undying enmity, [16]therefore thus says the Lord GOD: See! I am stretching out my hand against the Philistines; I will cut off the Cherethites* and wipe out the remnant on the seacoast. [17]I will execute great acts of vengeance on them, punishing them furiously. Thus they shall know that I am the LORD, when I wreak my vengeance on them.

See RG 325–32

CHAPTER 26

Against the City of Tyre. [1]On the first day of the . . . month in the eleventh year, the word of the LORD came to me: [2]Son of man, because of what Tyre said of Jerusalem:

"Aha! it is broken, the gateway to the
    peoples;
    now that it is ruined, its wealth reverts
        to me!"
[3] therefore thus says the Lord GOD:
    See! I am coming at you, Tyre;
    I will churn up against you many
        nations,
    even as the sea churns up its waves;[y]
[4] They shall destroy the walls of Tyre
    and raze her towers.
    I will scrape the ground from her
    and leave her a bare rock;*
[5] She shall be a drying place for nets
    in the midst of the sea.

I have spoken, says the Lord GOD: and she

shall be booty for the nations. [6]And her daughters* on the mainland shall be slaughtered by the sword; thus they shall know that I am the LORD.

[7]For thus says the Lord GOD: I am now bringing up against Tyre from the north Nebuchadnezzar the king of Babylon, the king of kings, with horses and chariots, with cavalry and a great and mighty army.

[8] Your daughters on the mainland
        he shall slay with the sword;
    He shall place a siege tower against you,
        cast up a ramp about you,
        and raise his shields against you.
[9] He shall pound your walls with battering-
            rams
        and break down your towers with his
            weapons.
[10] The surge of his horses shall cover you
            with dust,
        amid the noise of steeds, of wheels and
            of chariots.
    Your walls shall shake as he enters your
            gates,
        even as one enters a city that is
            breached.
[11] With the hoofs of his horses
        he shall trample all your streets;
    Your people he shall slay by the sword;
        your mighty pillars he shall pull to the
            ground.
[12] Your wealth shall be plundered,
        your merchandise pillaged;
    Your walls shall be torn down,
        your precious houses demolished;
    Your stones, your timber, and your clay
        shall be cast into the sea.
[13] I will put an end to the noise of your
            songs,
        and the sound of your lyres shall be
            heard no more.
[14] I will make you a bare rock;
        a drying place for nets shall you be.

Never shall you be rebuilt, for I have spoken, says the Lord GOD.

25, 16: Cherethites: a people forming part of the Philistine nation; cf Zep 2, 5.

26, 4f: A bare rock: the Tyre of Ezekiel's time was situated on a rocky island just off the Phoenician coast; it was not until the time of Alexander the Great that it was connected by a causeway to the mainland.

26, 6: Her daughters: tributary towns and villages on the mainland.

y: Is 26, 1-21; 47, 4; Jl 4, 4f; Zec 9, 2ff.

[15]Thus says the Lord GOD to Tyre: At the noise of your fall, at the groaning of the wounded, when the sword slays in your midst, shall not the isles quake? [16]All the princes of the sea* shall step down from their thrones, lay aside their robes, and strip off their embroidered garments. They shall be clothed in mourning and, sitting on the ground, they shall tremble at every moment and be horrified at you. [17]Then they shall utter a lament over you:

How have you perished, gone from the
      seas,
   city most prized!
Once she was mighty on the sea,
   she and her dwellers,
Who spread terror into all
   that dwelt by the sea.
[18] On this, the day of your fall,
   the islands quake!

The isles in the sea are terrified at your passing.

[19]For thus says the Lord GOD: When I make you a city desolate like cities that are no longer inhabited, when I churn up the abyss against you, and its mighty waters cover you, [20]then I will thrust you down with those who descend into the pit,* those of the bygone age; and I will make you dwell in the nether lands, in the everlasting ruins, with those who go down to the pit, so that you may never return to take your place in the land of the living. [21]I will make you a devastation, and you shall be no more; you shall be sought, but never again found, says the Lord GOD.

CHAPTER 27

See RG
325–32

The Ship Tyre. [1]Thus the word of the LORD came to me: [2]As for you, son of man, utter a lament over Tyre, [3]and say to Tyre that is situated at the approaches of the sea, that brought the trade of the peoples to many a coastland: Thus says the Lord GOD:

Tyre, you said, "I am a ship,
   perfect in beauty."
[4] In the midst of the sea your builders
      placed you,
   perfected your beauty.
[5] With cypress from Senir* they built for
      you
   all of your decks;
Cedar from Lebanon they took
   to make you a mast;
[6] From the highest oaks of Bashan*
   they made your oars;
Your bridge they made of cypress wood
   from the coasts of Kittim.
[7] Fine embroidered linen from Egypt
   became your sail [to serve you as a
      banner].
Purple and scarlet from the coasts of
      Elishah*
   covered your cabin.
[8] Citizens of Sidon and Arvad
   served as your oarsmen;
Skilled men of Zemer were in you
   to be your mariners;
[9] The elders and experts of Gebal* were in
      you
   to caulk your seams.

Every ship and sailor on the sea came to you to carry trade. [10]Persia and Lud and Put were in your army as warriors; shield and helmet they hung upon you, increasing your splendor. [11]The men of Arvad were all about your walls, and the Gamadites were in your towers; they hung their bucklers all around on your walls, and made perfect your beauty. [12]Tarshish traded with you, so great was your wealth, exchanging silver, iron, tin, and lead for your wares. [13]Javan, Tubal, and Meshech were also traders with you, exchanging slaves and articles of bronze for your goods. [14]From Beth-togarmah horses, steeds, and mules were exchanged for your wares. [15]The Rhodanites trafficked with you; many coastlands traded with you; ivory tusks and ebony

---

26, 16: The princes of the sea: the rulers of the islands and coastal cities leagued commercially with Tyre.

26, 20: Those who descend into the pit: the dead, pictured as dwelling in a place or cave of darkness.

27, 5: Senir: another name for Mount Hermon; cf Dt 3, 9.

27, 6: Bashan: northern Transjordan, which, like Leba-

non, was noted for its great forests. Kittim: probably Cyprus.

27, 7: Elishah: probably another term for Cyprus.

27, 8f: Sidon . . . Arvad . . . Zemer . . . Gebal: Phoenician cities in Tyre's orbit of influence; the last-named is the classical Byblos.

wood they gave you for payment. [16]Edom traded with you, so many were your products, exchanging garnets, purple, embroidered cloth, fine linen, coral, and rubies for your wares. [17]Judah and the land of Israel trafficked with you, exchanging Minnith wheat, figs, honey, oil, and balm for your goods. [18]Damascus traded with you, so great was your wealth, exchanging Helbon wine and Zahar wool. [19]Javan exchanged wrought iron, cassia, and aromatic cane from Uzal for your wares. [20]Dedan traded with you for riding gear. [21]The trade of Arabia and of all the sheikhs of Kedar belonged to you; they dealt in lambs, rams, and goats. [22]The merchants of Sheba and Raamah also traded with you, exchanging for your wares the very choicest spices, all kinds of precious stones, and gold. [23]Haran, Canneh, and Eden, the merchants of Sheba, Asshur, and Chilmad [24]traded with you, marketing with you rich garments, violet mantles, embroidered cloth, varicolored carpets, and firmly woven cords. [25]Ships of Tarshish journeyed for you in your merchandising.

You were full and heavily laden
  in the heart of the sea.
[26] Through the deep waters your oarsmen
    brought you home,
  But the east wind smashed you
    in the heart of the sea.
[27] Your wealth, your goods, your wares,
    your sailors, and your crew,

[the caulkers of your seams, those who traded for your goods, all your warriors who were in you, and all the great crowd within you]

  Sank into the heart of the sea
    on the day of your shipwreck.
[28] Hearing the shouts of your mariners,
    the shores begin to quake.
[29] Down from their ships
    come all who ply the oar;
  The sailors, all the mariners of the sea,
    stand on the shore,
[30] Making their voice heard on your behalf,
    shouting bitter cries,

Strewing dust on their heads,
    rolling in the ashes.
[31] For you they shave their heads
    and put on sackcloth,
  For you they weep in anguish,
    with bitter lament.
[32] In their mourning they utter a lament
    over you;
  thus they wail over you:
  Who was ever destroyed like Tyre
    in the midst of the sea?
[33] With your goods which you drew from
    the seas
  you filled many peoples;
  With your great wealth and merchandise
    you enriched the kings of the earth.
[34] Now you are wrecked in the sea,
    in the watery depths;
  Your wares and all your crew
    have gone down with you.
[35] All who dwell on the coastlands
    are aghast over you,
  Their kings are terrified,
    their faces convulsed.
[36] The traders among the peoples
    now hiss at you;
  You have become a horror,
    and you shall be no more.

CHAPTER 28

See RG 325–32

The Prince of Tyre. [1]Thus the word of the LORD came to me: [2]Son of man, say to the prince of Tyre: Thus says the Lord GOD:

Because you are haughty of heart,
    you say, "A god am I!
  I occupy a godly throne
    in the heart of the sea!"—
  And yet you are a man, and not a god,
    however you may think yourself like a
      god.
[3] Oh yes, you are wiser than Daniel,*
    there is no secret that is beyond you.
[4] By your wisdom and your intelligence
    you have made riches for yourself;
  You have put gold and silver
    into your treasuries.
[5] By your great wisdom applied to your
      trading

28, 3: Wiser than Daniel: see note on Ez 14, 14.

you have heaped up your riches;
your heart has grown haughty from
your riches—
6 therefore thus says the Lord GOD:
Because you have thought yourself
to have the mind of a god,
7 Therefore I will bring against you
foreigners, the most barbarous of
nations.
They shall draw their swords
against your beauteous wisdom,
they shall run them through your
splendid apparel.
8 They shall thrust you down to the pit,
there to die
a bloodied corpse, in the heart of the
sea.
9 Will you then say, "I am a god!"
when you face your murderers?
No, you are a man, not a god,
handed over to those who will slay
you.
10 You shall die the death of the
uncircumcised
at the hands of foreigners,
for I have spoken,
says the Lord GOD.

11 Thus the word of the LORD came to me:
12 Son of man, utter a lament over the king of
Tyre, saying to him: Thus says the Lord
GOD:

*You were stamped with the seal of
perfection,
of complete wisdom and perfect
beauty.
13 In Eden, the garden of God, you were,
and every precious stone was your
covering

[carnelian, topaz, and beryl, chrysolite,
onyx, and jasper, sapphire, garnet, and emer-
ald];

Of gold your pendants and jewels
were made, on the day you were
created.

14 With the Cherub I placed you;
you were on the holy mountain of God,*
walking among the fiery stones.
15 Blameless you were in your conduct
from the day you were created,
Until evil was found in you,
16 the result of your far-flung trade;
violence was your business, and you
sinned.
Then I banned you from the mountain of
God;
the Cherub drove you from among the
fiery stones.
17 You became haughty of heart because of
your beauty;
for the sake of splendor you debased
your wisdom.
I cast you to the earth, so great was your
guilt;
I made you a spectacle in the sight of
kings.
18 Because of your guilt, your sinful trade,
I have profaned your sanctuaries,
And I have brought out fire from your
midst
which will devour you.
I have reduced you to dust on the earth
in the sight of all who should see you.
19 Among the peoples, all who knew you
stand aghast at you;
You have become a horror,
you shall be no more.

Against Sidon. 20 z Thus the word of the
LORD came to me: Son of man, look toward
Sidon, 21a and prophesy against it: 22 Thus
says the Lord GOD:b See! I am coming at
you, Sidon; I will be glorified in your midst.
Then they shall know that I am the LORD,
when I inflict punishments upon it and use it
to manifest my holiness.

23 Into it I will send pestilence,
and blood shall flow in its streets.
Within it shall fall those slain
by the sword that comes against it
from every side.

28, 12-19: This picture of Tyre and its fall recalls images
of the earthly paradise portraying the creation of man in perfection and his fall (Gn, chapters 2—3).
28, 14: The holy mountain of God: the residence of God
was sometimes designated as a mountain; cf Is 14, 13. The

fiery stones: associated with the divine presence; cf Ez 1, 13;
Ps 18, 13.

z: Is 23, 1-18.   a: Jer 47, 4.   b: Jl 4, 4; Zec 9, 2ff.

Thus they shall know that I am the LORD. [24]Sidon shall no longer be a tearing thorn for the house of Israel, a brier that scratches them more than all the others about them who despise them; thus they shall know that I am the LORD.

[25]Thus says the Lord GOD: When I gather the house of Israel from the peoples among whom they are scattered, then I will manifest my holiness through them in the sight of the nations. Then they shall live on their land which I gave to my servant Jacob; [26]they shall live on it in security, building houses and planting vineyards. They shall dwell secure while I inflict punishments on all their neighbors who despised them; thus they shall know that I, the LORD, am their God.

See RG 325-32

CHAPTER 29

Egypt the Crocodile. [1]On the twelfth day of the tenth month in the tenth year,[*] the word of the LORD came to me: [2]Son of man, set your face against Pharaoh, king of Egypt, and prophesy against him and against all Egypt.[*] [3]Say this to him: Thus says the Lord GOD:

See! I am coming at you, Pharaoh,
    king of Egypt,
Great crouching monster
    amidst your Niles:[*]
Who say, "The Niles are mine;
    it is I who made them!"

[4]I will put hooks in your jaws and make the fish of your Niles stick to your scales, then draw you up from the midst of your Niles along with all the fish of your Niles sticking to your scales.

[5] I will cast you into the desert,
    you and all the fish of your Niles;
You shall fall upon the open field,
    you shall not be taken up or buried;
To the beasts of the earth and the birds of
    the air

I give you as food,
[6] That all who dwell in Egypt may know
    that I am the LORD.
Because you have been a reed staff
    for the house of Israel:[c]
[7] When they held you in hand, you
    splintered,
    throwing every shoulder out of joint;
When they leaned on you, you broke,
    bringing each one of them down
    headlong;

[8]therefore thus says the Lord GOD: See! I will bring the sword against you, and cut off from you both man and beast. [9]The land of Egypt shall become a desolate waste; thus they shall know that I am the LORD.

Because you said, "The Niles are mine; it is I who made them," [10]therefore see! I am coming at you and against your Niles; I will make the land of Egypt a waste and a desolation from Migdol to Syene,[*] and even to the frontier of Ethiopia. [11]No foot of man or beast shall pass through it; they shall not pass through it, and it will be uninhabited for forty years. [12]I will make the land of Egypt the most desolate of lands, and its cities shall be the most deserted of cities for forty years; and I will scatter the Egyptians among the nations and strew them over foreign lands. [13]Yet thus says the Lord GOD: At the end of forty years I will gather the Egyptians from the peoples among whom they are scattered, [14]and I will restore Egypt's fortune, bringing them back to the land of Pathros, the land of their origin,[*] where it will be the lowliest [15]of kingdoms, never more to set itself above the nations. I will make them few, that they may not dominate the nations. [16]No longer shall they be for the house of Israel to trust in, but the living reminder of its guilt for having turned to follow after them. Thus they shall know that I am the LORD.

The Wages of Nebuchadnezzar. [17]On the first day of the first month in the twenty-sev-

29, 1: The twelfth day of the tenth month in the tenth year: January 7, 587 B.C. The siege of Jerusalem had begun a year earlier; cf Ez 24, 1.

29, 2: Egypt was allied with Judah against the Chaldeans.

29, 3: Niles: the many rivulets of the Nile as it branches out into the Delta.

29, 10: From Migdol to Syene: from the northern to the southern extremity of Egypt. Syene is the modern Assuan.

29, 14: Pathros, the land of their origin: upper Egypt, that is, southern Egypt, where the Egyptians were thought to have originated; Is 11, 11; Jer 44, 1. 15.

---

c: Is 36, 6.

1123

enth year,* the word of the LORD came to me: *18*Son of man, Nebuchadnezzar, the king of Babylon, has led his army in an exhausting campaign against Tyre.* Their heads became bald and their shoulders were galled; but neither he nor his army received any wages from Tyre for the campaign he led against it. *19*Therefore thus says the Lord GOD:*d* I am now giving the land of Egypt to Nebuchadnezzar, king of Babylon. He shall carry off its riches, plundering and pillaging it for the wages of his soldiers, who did it for me; *20*as payment for his toil I have given him the land of Egypt, says the Lord GOD.

*21*On that day I will make a horn sprout for the house of Israel, and I will cause you to speak out in their midst; thus they shall know that I am the LORD.

See RG
325–32

CHAPTER 30

The Day of the Lord against Egypt.
*1*Thus the word of the LORD came to me: *2*Son of man, speak this prophecy: Thus says the Lord GOD: Cry, Oh, the day! *3*for near is the day, near is the day of the Lord; a day of clouds, doomsday for the nations shall it be. *4*Then a sword shall come upon Egypt, and anguish shall be in Ethiopia, when the slain fall in Egypt, when her riches are seized and her foundations are overthrown. *5*Ethiopia, Put, Lud, all Arabia, Libya, and people of the allied territory shall fall by the sword with them. *6*Those who support Egypt shall fall, and down shall come her proud strength; from Migdol to Syene they shall fall there by the sword, says the Lord GOD. *7*She shall be the most devastated of lands, and her cities shall be the most desolate of all. *8*Then they shall know that I am the LORD, when I set fire to Egypt and when all who help her are broken. *9*On that day mes-

sengers shall hasten forth at my command to terrify unsuspecting Ethiopia; they shall be in anguish on the day of Egypt, which is surely coming.

*10*Thus says the Lord GOD: I will put an end to the throngs of Egypt by the hand of Nebuchadnezzar, king of Babylon. *11*He and his people with him, the most ruthless of nations, shall be brought in to devastate the land. They shall draw their swords against Egypt, and fill the land with the slain. *12*I will turn the Niles into dry land and sell the land over to the power of the wicked. The land and everything in it I will hand over to foreigners to devastate. I, the LORD, have spoken.

*13e*Thus says the Lord GOD: I will put an end to the great ones of Memphis and the princes of the land of Egypt, that they may be no more. I will cast fear into the land of Egypt, and devastate Pathros. *14*I will set fire to Zoan, and inflict punishments on Thebes. *15*I will pour out my wrath on Pelusium, Egypt's stronghold, and cut down the crowds in Memphis. *16*I will set fire to Egypt; Syene shall writhe in anguish; Thebes shall be breached and its walls shall be demolished. *17*The young men of On and of Pibeseth shall fall by the sword, and the cities themselves shall go into captivity. *18*In Tehaphnehes the day shall be darkened when I break the scepter of Egypt. Her haughty pride shall cease from her, clouds shall cover her, and her daughters shall go into captivity. *19*Thus will I inflict punishments on Egypt, that they may know that I am the LORD.

Pharaoh's Broken Arm. *20*On the seventh day of the first month in the eleventh year,* the word of the LORD came to me: *21**Son of man, I have broken the arm of Pharaoh, the king of Egypt, and see, it has not been bound up with bandages and healing remedies that it

---

29, 17: The first day of the first month in the twenty-seventh year: April 26, 571 B.C. This is the latest date attached to any prophecy in Ezekiel.

29, 18f: The fulfillment of Ezekiel's prophecy against Tyre (chapters 26—28) was a thirteen-year siege of the city by Nebuchadnezzar (587–574 B.C.). Tyre seems to have been taken, but its resources were exhausted and the booty was small. Therefore Ezekiel now prophesies that Nebuchadnezzar will collect his wages as God's instrument in the punishment of Tyre, by plundering Egypt.

30, 20: The seventh day of the first month in the eleventh

year: April 29, 587 B.C.

30, 21-26: This oracle was uttered during the siege of Jerusalem, which had now lasted more than a year (Ez 24, 1). Pharaoh Hophra went to the aid of Jerusalem, causing the Chaldeans to lift the siege temporarily; cf Jer 34, 21; 37, 6f. In the prophet's eyes, this was interfering with the divine punishment of Judah that was to be inflicted by the Chaldeans. The Egyptians were routed by the Chaldeans, and were able to offer no more help to Jerusalem; cf chapter 31.

---

d: Jer 46, 2.   *e:* Zec 13, 2.

may be strong enough to hold the sword. [22] Therefore thus says the Lord GOD: See! I am coming at Pharaoh, the king of Egypt. I will break his strong arm, so that the sword drops from his hand. [23] I will scatter the Egyptians among the nations and strew them over foreign lands. [24] But I will strengthen the arms of the king of Babylon, and put my sword in his hand, which he will bring against Egypt so as to plunder and pillage it. [25] [I will make the arms of the king of Babylon strong, but the arms of Pharaoh shall drop.] Then they shall know that I am the LORD, when I put my sword in the hand of the king of Babylon for him to wield against the land of Egypt. [26] [I will scatter the Egyptians among the nations and strew them over foreign lands.] Thus they shall know that I am the LORD.

CHAPTER 31

See RG 325–32

Allegory of the Cypress. [1] On the first day of the third month in the eleventh year,* the word of the LORD came to me: [2] Son of man, say to Pharaoh, the king of Egypt, and to his hordes: What are you like in your greatness?

[3] Behold, a cypress [cedar] in Lebanon,
   beautiful of branch, lofty of stature,
   amid the very clouds lifted its crest.
[4] Waters made it grow, the abyss made it
      flourish,
   sending its rivers round where it was
      planted,
   turning its streams to all the trees of
      the field.
[5] Thus it grew taller than every other tree
      of the field,
   and longer of branch because of the
      abundant water.
[6] In its boughs nested all the birds of the
      air,
   under its branches all beasts of the
      field gave birth,
   in its shade dwelt numerous peoples of
      every race.
[7] It became beautiful and stately in its
      spread of foliage,
   for its roots were turned toward
      abundant water.

[8] The cedars in the garden of God were not
      its equal,
   nor could the fir trees match its
      boughs,
   Neither were the plane trees like it for
      branches;
   no tree in the garden of God matched
      its beauty.
[9] I made it beautiful, with much foliage,
   the envy of all Eden's trees in the
      garden of God.

[10] Therefore thus says the Lord GOD: Because it became lofty in stature, raising its crest among the clouds, and because it became proud in heart at its height, [11] I have handed it over to the mightiest of the nations, which has dealt with it in keeping with its wickedness. I humiliated it. [12] Foreigners, the most ruthless of the nations, cut it down and left it on the mountains. Its foliage was brought low in all the valleys, its branches lay broken in all the ravines of the land, and all the peoples of the land withdrew from its shade, abandoning it.

[13] On its fallen trunk rested all the birds of
      the air,
   and by its branches were all the beasts
      of the field.

[14] Thus no tree may grow lofty in stature or raise its crest among the clouds; no tree fed by water may stand by itself in its loftiness.

For all of them are destined for death,
   for the land below,
For the company of mortals,
   those who go down into the pit.

[15] Thus says the Lord GOD: On the day he went down to the nether world I made the abyss close up over him; I stopped its streams so that the deep waters were held back. I cast gloom over Lebanon because of him, so that all the trees in the land drooped on his account. [16] At the crash of his fall I made the nations rock, when I cast him down to the nether world with those who go down into the pit. In the land below, all Eden's trees were consoled, Lebanon's choice and best, all that were fed by water.

31, 1: The first day of the third month in the eleventh year: June 21, 587 B.C.

[17]They too have come down with him to the nether world, to those slain by the sword; those who dwelt in his shade are dispersed among the nations. [18]Which was your equal in glory or size among the trees of Eden? Yet you have been brought down with the trees of Eden to the land below. You shall lie with the uncircumcised, with those slain by the sword. Such are Pharaoh and all his hordes, says the Lord GOD.

CHAPTER 32

See RG 325-32

Dirge over Pharaoh. [1]On the first day of the twelfth month in the twelfth year,* the word of the LORD came to me: [2]Son of man, utter a lament over Pharaoh, the king of Egypt, saying to him: Lion of the nations, you are destroyed.

You were like a monster in the sea,
　spouting in your streams,
Stirring the water with your feet
　and churning its streams.
[3] Thus says the Lord GOD:
I will spread my net over you
　[with a host of many nations],
　and draw you up in my seine.[f]
[4] I will leave you on the land;
　on the open field I will cast you.
I will have all the birds of the air alight
　on you,
　and all the beasts of the earth eat their
　　fill of you.
[5] I will leave your flesh on the mountains,
　and fill the valleys with your carcass.
[6] I will water the land with what flows
　from you,
　and the river beds shall be filled with
　　your blood.
[7] When I snuff you out I will cover the
　heavens,
　and all their stars I will darken;
The sun I will cover with clouds,
　and the moon shall not give its light.[g]
[8] All the shining lights in the heavens
　I will darken on your account,
And I will spread darkness over your land,
　says the Lord GOD.

[9]I will grieve the hearts of many peoples when I lead you captive among the nations, to lands which you do not know. [10]Many peoples shall be appalled at you, and their kings shall shudder over you in horror when they see me brandish my sword, and on the day of your downfall every one of them shall continuously tremble for his own life. [11]For thus says the Lord GOD: The sword of the king of Babylon shall come upon you.

[12] I will cut down your horde with the
　blades of warriors,
　all of them the most ruthless of the
　　nations;
They shall lay waste the glory of Egypt,
　and all her hordes shall be destroyed.
[13] I will have all of her animals perish
　beside her abundant waters;
The foot of man shall stir them no longer,
　nor shall the hoof of beast disturb them.
[14] Then will I make their waters clear,
　and their streams flow like oil,
　says the Lord GOD.

[15]When I turn Egypt into a waste, the land shall be devastated of all that is in it; when I strike all who live there, they shall know that I am the LORD. [16]This is a dirge, and it shall be sung: the daughters of the nations shall chant it; over Egypt and all its hordes shall they chant it, says the Lord GOD.

Dirge over Egypt. [17]On the fifteenth day of the first month in the twelfth year, the word of the LORD came to me: [18]Son of man, lament over the throngs of Egypt, for the mighty nations have thrust them down to the bottom of the earth, with those who go down into the pit. [20]In the midst of those slain by the sword shall they fall, and place shall be made with them for all their hordes. Then from the midst of the nether world, the mighty warriors shall speak to Egypt: [19]"Whom do you excel in beauty? [21]Come down, you and your allies, lie with the uncircumcised, with those slain by the sword."

[22]There is Assyria with all her company, all of them slain, [23]whose graves have been made

---

32, 1: The first day of the twelfth month in the twelfth year: March 3, 585 B.C.

f: Ez 12, 13; 17, 20.　*g:* Is 13, 10; Jl 2, 10; 4, 15; Mt 24, 29.

in the recesses of the pit; her company is around Egypt's grave, all of them slain, fallen by the sword, who spread terror in the land of the living. ²⁴There is Elam with all her throng about Egypt's grave, all of them slain, fallen by the sword: they have gone down uncircumcised to the bottom of the earth, who spread their terror in the land of the living, and they bear their disgrace with those who go down into the pit; ²⁵in the midst of the slain they are placed. ²⁶There are Meshech and Tubal and all their throng about her grave, all of them uncircumcised, slain by the sword, for they spread their terror in the land of the living.

²⁷They do not lie with the mighty men fallen of old,* who went down to the nether world with their weapons of war, whose swords were placed under their heads and whose shields were laid over their bones, though the mighty men caused terror in the land of the living. ²⁸But in the midst of the uncircumcised shall you lie, with those slain by the sword.

²⁹There are Edom, her kings, and all her princes, who despite their might have been placed with those slain by the sword; with the uncircumcised they lie, and with those who go down into the pit. ³⁰There are all the princes of the north and all the Sidonians, who have gone down with the slain, because of the terror their might inspired; they lie uncircumcised with those slain by the sword and bear their disgrace with those who go down to the pit. ³¹When Pharaoh sees these, he shall be comforted for all his hordes slain by the sword—Pharaoh and all his army, says the Lord GOD. ³²Since he spread his terror in the land of the living, therefore is he laid to rest among the uncircumcised, with those slain by the sword—Pharaoh and all his hordes, says the Lord GOD.

IV: Salvation for Israel

CHAPTER 33

See RG
325–32

The Prophet a Watchman. ¹Thus the word of the LORD came to me: ²Son of man, speak thus to your countrymen: When I bring the sword against a country, and the people of this country select one of their number to be their watchman, ³and the watchman, seeing the sword coming against the country, blows the trumpet to warn the people, ⁴anyone hearing but not heeding the warning of the trumpet and therefore slain by the sword that comes against him, shall be responsible for his own death. ⁵He heard the trumpet blast yet refused to take warning; he is responsible for his own death, for had he taken warning he would have escaped with his life. ⁶But if the watchman sees the sword coming and fails to blow the warning trumpet, so that the sword comes and takes anyone, I will hold the watchman responsible for that person's death, even though that person is taken because of his own sin.

⁷ʰYou, son of man, I have appointed watchman for the house of Israel; when you hear me say anything, you shall warn them for me. ⁸If I tell the wicked man that he shall surely die, and you do not speak out to dissuade the wicked man from his way, he [the wicked man] shall die for his guilt, but I will hold you responsible for his death. ⁹But if you warn the wicked man, trying to turn him from his way, and he refuses to turn from his way, he shall die for his guilt, but you shall save yourself.

Individual Retribution. ¹⁰As for you, son of man, speak to the house of Israel: You people say, "Our crimes and our sins weigh us down; we are rotting away because of them. How can we survive?" ¹¹ⁱAnswer them: As I live, says the Lord GOD, I swear I take no pleasure in the death of the wicked man, but rather in the wicked man's conversion, that he may live. Turn, turn from your evil ways! Why should you die, O house of Israel?

¹²As for you, son of man, tell your countrymen: The virtue which a man has practiced will not save him on the day that he sins; neither will the wickedness that a man has done bring about his downfall on the day

---

32, 27: The mighty men fallen of old: the semilegendary heroes of the prehistoric past, who were thought to have once dominated the world; cf Is 14, 9.

---

h: Ez 3, 17.   *i:* Ez 18, 23-32.

that he turns from his wickedness [nor can the virtuous man, when he sins, remain alive]. [13]Though I say to the virtuous man that he shall surely live, if he then presumes on his virtue and does wrong, none of his virtuous deeds shall be remembered; because of the wrong he has done, he shall die. [14]And though I say to the wicked man that he shall surely die, if he turns away from his sin and does what is right and just, [15]giving back pledges, restoring stolen goods, living by the statutes that bring life, and doing no wrong, he shall surely live, he shall not die. [16]None of the sins he committed shall be held against him; he has done what is right and just, he shall surely live.

[17]Yet your countrymen say, "The way of the LORD is not fair!"; but it is their way that is not fair. [18]When a virtuous man turns away from what is right and does wrong, he shall die for it. [19]But when a wicked man turns away from wickedness and does what is right and just, because of this he shall live. [20]j And still you say, "The way of the LORD is not fair!"? I will judge every one of you according to his ways, O house of Israel.

The Fugitive from Jerusalem. [21]On the fifth day of the tenth month, in the twelfth year of our exile, the fugitive came to me from Jerusalem and said, "The city is taken!" [22]The hand of the LORD had come upon me the evening before the fugitive arrived, and he opened my mouth when the fugitive reached me in the morning. My mouth was opened, and I was dumb no longer.

The Survivors in Judah. [23]Thus the word of the Lord came to me: [24]Son of man, they who live in the ruins on the land of Israel reason thus: "Abraham, though but a single individual, received possession of the land; we, therefore, being many, have as permanent possession the land that has been given to us." [25]Give them this answer: Thus says the Lord

GOD: You eat on the mountains, you raise your eyes to your idols, you shed blood—yet you would keep possession of the land? [26]You rely on your sword, you do abominable things, each one of you defiles his neighbor's wife—yet you would keep possession of the land? [27]Tell them this: Thus says the Lord GOD: As I live, those who are in the ruins I swear shall fall by the sword; those who are in the open field I have given to the wild beasts for food; and those who are in fastnesses and in caves shall die by the plague. [28]I will make the land a desolate waste, so that its proud strength will come to an end, and the mountains of Israel shall be so desolate that no one will cross them. [29]Thus they shall know that I am the LORD, when I make the land a desolate waste because of all the abominable things they have done.

The Prophet's False Popularity. [30]As for you, son of man, your countrymen are talking about you along the walls and in the doorways of houses. They say to one another, "Come and hear the latest word that comes from the LORD."* [31]My people come to you as people always do; they sit down before you and hear your words, but they will not obey them, for lies are on their lips and their desires are fixed on dishonest gain. [32]For them you are only a ballad singer, with a pleasant voice and a clever touch. They listen to your words, but they will not obey them. [33]But when it comes—and it is surely coming!—they shall know that there was a prophet among them.

CHAPTER 34

Parable of the Shepherds. [1]Thus the word of the LORD came to me: [2]Son of man, prophesy against the shepherds of Israel,* in these words prophesy to them [to the shepherds]: Thus says the Lord GOD: Woe to the shepherds of Israel who have been pasturing

See RG
325–32

33, 21f: January 8, 585 B.C. According to Jeremiah (39, 2), Jerusalem was taken in July, 587. Some MSS read "eleventh" for twelfth year (January, 586); even so, there was ample time between the fall of Jerusalem and the arrival of the fugitive from that city to journey to Babylon. However, this is the fugitive sent to fulfill the promise of Ez 24, 25. 27, the eyewitness who would release Ezekiel from his dumbness; cf Ez, 2, 26f.

33, 23-29: News brought by the fugitive furnished the oc-

casion of this prophecy. Like Jeremiah, Ezekiel rejects the idea that the survivors in Judah have any claim to the land. The new Israel is to be formed from the exiles.

33, 30: The fulfillment of Ezekiel's prophecies about Jerusalem was responsible for this temporary enthusiasm among the unstable people.

34, 2: The shepherds of Israel: the leaders of the people.

---

j: Ez 18, 25.

themselves!k Should not shepherds, rather, pasture sheep? 3You have fed off their milk, worn their wool, and slaughtered the fatlings, but the sheep you have not pastured. 4You did not strengthen the weak nor heal the sick nor bind up the injured. You did not bring back the strayed nor seek the lost, but you lorded it over them harshly and brutally. 5So they were scattered for lack of a shepherd, and became food for all the wild beasts. My sheep were scattered 6and wandered over all the mountains and high hills; my sheep were scattered over the whole earth, with no one to look after them or to search for them.

7Therefore, shepherds, hear the word of the LORD: 8As I live, says the Lord GOD, because my sheep have been given over to pillage, and because my sheep have become food for every wild beast, for lack of a shepherd; because my shepherds did not look after my sheep, but pastured themselves and did not pasture my sheep; 9because of this, shepherds, hear the word of the LORD: 10Thus says the Lord GOD: I swear I am coming against these shepherds. I will claim my sheep from them and put a stop to their shepherding my sheep so that they may no longer pasture themselves. I will save my sheep, that they may no longer be food for their mouths.

11For thus says the Lord GOD: I myself will look after and tend my sheep. 12As a shepherd tends his flock when he finds himself among his scattered sheep, so will I tend my sheep. I will rescue them from every place where they were scattered when it was cloudy and dark. 13I will lead them out from among the peoples and gather them from the foreign lands; I will bring them back to their own country and pasture them upon the mountains of Israel [in the land's ravines and all its inhabited places]. 14In good pastures will I pasture them, and on the mountain heights of Israel shall be their grazing ground. There they shall lie down on good grazing ground, and in rich pastures shall they be pastured on the mountains of Israel.

15I myself will pasture my sheep; I myself will give them rest, says the Lord GOD. 16The lost I will seek out, the strayed I will bring back, the injured I will bind up, the sick I will heal [but the sleek and the strong I will destroy], shepherding them rightly.

Separation of the Sheep. 17As for you, my sheep, says the Lord GOD, I will judge between one sheep and another, between rams and goats. 18Was it not enough for you to graze on the best pasture, that you had to trample the rest of your pastures with your feet? Was it not enough for you to drink the clearest water, that you had to foul the remainder with your feet? 19Thus my sheep had to graze on what your feet had trampled and drink what your feet had fouled. 20Therefore thus says the Lord GOD: Now will I judge between the fat and the lean sheep. 21Because you push with side and shoulder, and butt all the weak sheep with your horns until you have driven them out, 22I will save my sheep so that they may no longer be despoiled, and I will judge between one sheep and another. 23I will appoint one shepherd over them to pasture them, my servant David;* he shall pasture them and be their shepherd. 24I, the Lord, will be their God, and my servant David shall be prince among them. I, the LORD, have spoken.

25I will make a covenant of peace with them, and rid the country of ravenous beasts, that they may dwell securely in the desert and sleep in the forests. 26I will place them about my hill, sending rain in due season, rains that shall be a blessing to them. 27The trees of the field shall bear their fruits, and the land its crops, and they shall dwell securely on their own soil. Thus they shall know that I am the LORD when I break the bonds of their yoke and free them from the power of those who enslaved them. 28They shall no longer be despoiled by the nations or devoured by beasts of the earth, but shall dwell secure, with no one to frighten them. 29I will prepare for them peaceful fields for planting; they shall no longer be carried off by famine in the land, or

34, 23: One shepherd . . . my servant David: a messianic Davidic King who will rule over the restored Israel (vv 25-31) in the name of the Lord.

k: Ez 13, 3; Jer 23, 1.   l: Is 40, 21; Hos 3, 5; Jn 10, 11. 14.

bear the reproaches of the nations. [30]Thus they shall know that I, the LORD, am their God, and they are my people, the house of Israel, says the Lord GOD. [31][You, my sheep, you are the sheep of my pasture, and I am your God, says the Lord GOD.]

See RG 325-32

CHAPTER 35

Against Edom. [1]Thus the word of the LORD came to me:[m] [2]Son of man, set your face against Mount Seir, and prophesy against it. [3]Say to it: Thus says the Lord GOD: See! I am coming at you, Mount Seir. I will stretch out my hand against you and make you a desolate waste. [4]Your cities I will turn into ruins, and you shall be a waste; thus you shall know that I am the LORD.

[5]Because you never let die your hatred for the Israelites, whom you delivered over to the power of the sword at the time of their trouble, when their crimes came to an end, [6]therefore, as I live, says the Lord GOD, you have been guilty of blood, and blood, I swear, shall pursue you. [7]I will make Mount Seir a desolate waste, and cut off from it any traveler. [8]With the slain I will fill your hills, your valleys, and all your ravines [in them the slain shall fall by the sword]: [9]desolate will I make you forever, and leave your cities without inhabitants; thus you shall know that I am the LORD.

[10]Because you said: The two nations and the two lands* have become mine; we shall possess them—although the LORD was there— [11]therefore, as I live, says the Lord GOD, I will deal with you according to your anger and your envy which you have exercised [in your hatred] against them. I will make myself known among you when I judge you, [12]and you shall know that I am the LORD. I have heard all the contemptuous things you have uttered against the mountains of Israel: "They are desolate, they have been given us to devour." [13]I have heard the insolent and wild words you have spoken against me. [14]Thus says the Lord GOD: Just as you

rejoiced over my land because it was desolate, so will I do to you. [15]In keeping with your glee over the devastation of the inheritance of the house of Israel, so will I treat you. A waste shall you be, Mount Seir, you and the whole of Edom. Thus they shall know that I am the LORD.

CHAPTER 36

See RG 325-32

Regeneration of the Land. [1]As for you, son of man, prophesy to the mountains of Israel: Mountains of Israel,[n] hear the word of the LORD! [2]Thus says the Lord GOD: Because the enemy has said of you, "Ha! the everlasting heights have become our possession" [3][therefore prophesy in these words: Thus says the Lord GOD:]; because you have been ridiculed and despised on all sides for having become a possession for the rest of the nations, and have become a byword and a popular jeer; [4]therefore, mountains of Israel, hear the word of the LORD: [Thus says the Lord GOD to the mountains and hills, the ravines and valleys, the desolate ruins and abandoned cities, which have been given over to the pillage and mockery of the remaining nations round about; [5]therefore thus says the Lord GOD:] Truly, with burning jealousy I speak against the rest of the nations [and against all of Edom] who with wholehearted joy and utter contempt have considered my land their possession to be delivered over to plunder. [6][Therefore, prophesy concerning the land of Israel, and say to the mountains and hills, the ravines and valleys: Thus says the Lord GOD:] With jealous fury I speak, because you have borne the reproach of the nations. [7]Therefore do I solemnly swear that your neighboring nations shall bear their own reproach.

[8]As for you, mountains of Israel, you shall grow branches and bear fruit for my people Israel, for they shall soon return. [9]See, I come to you, it is to you that I turn; you will be tilled and sown, [10]and I will settle crowds of men upon you, the whole house of Israel;

35, 1-15: After the fall of Jerusalem, Edom assisted the Chaldeans in devastating the land and subduing the population, and ended by occupying part of Judah's former territory. For this reason these oracles against Edom are found in the context of the city's fall.

35, 10: The two nations and the two lands: the superseded kingdoms of Israel and Judah and their territories.

---

m: 1ff: Ez 25, 12ff.   *n:* Ez 6, 3.

cities shall be repeopled, and ruins rebuilt. [11] I will settle crowds of men and beasts upon you, to multiply and be fruitful. I will repeople you as in the past, and be more generous to you than in the beginning; thus you shall know that I am the LORD.

[12] [My people Israel are the ones whom I will have walk upon you; they shall take possession of you, and you shall be their heritage. Never again shall you rob them of their children.]

[13] Thus says the Lord GOD: Because they have said of you, "You are a land that devours men,* and you rob your people of their children"; [14] therefore, never again shall you devour men or rob your people of their children, says the Lord GOD. [15] No more will I permit you to hear the reproach of nations, or bear insults from peoples, or rob your people of their children, says the Lord GOD.

Regeneration of the People. [16] Thus the word of the LORD came to me: [17] Son of man, when the house of Israel lived in their land, they defiled it by their conduct and deeds. In my sight their conduct was like the defilement of a menstruous woman. [18] Therefore I poured out my fury upon them [because of the blood which they poured out on the ground, and because they defiled it with idols]. [19] I scattered them among the nations, dispersing them over foreign lands; according to their conduct and deeds I judged them. [20o] But when they came among the nations [wherever they came], they served to profane my holy name, because it was said of them: "These are the people of the LORD, yet they had to leave their land." [21] So I have relented because of my holy name which the house of Israel profaned among the nations where they came. [22] Therefore say to the house of Israel: Thus says the Lord GOD: Not for your sakes do I act, house of Israel, but for the sake of my holy name, which you profaned among the nations to which you came. [23] I will prove the holiness of my great name, profaned among the nations, in whose midst you have profaned it. Thus the nations shall know that I am the LORD, says the Lord GOD, when in their sight I prove my holiness through you. [24] For I will take you away from among the nations, gather you from all the foreign lands, and bring you back to your own land. [25p] I will sprinkle clean water upon you to cleanse you from all your impurities, and from all your idols I will cleanse you. [26q] I will give you a new heart and place a new spirit within you, taking from your bodies your stony hearts and giving you natural hearts. [27r] I will put my spirit within you and make you live by my statutes, careful to observe my decrees. [28] You shall live in the land I gave your fathers; you shall be my people, and I will be your God. [29] I will save you from all your impurities; I will order the grain to be abundant, and I will not send famine against you. [30] I will increase the fruit on your trees and the crops in your fields; thus you shall no longer bear among the nations the reproach of famine. [31] Then you shall remember your evil conduct, and that your deeds were not good; you shall loathe yourselves for your sins and your abominations. [32] Not for your sakes do I act, says the Lord GOD—let this be known to you! Be ashamed and abashed because of your conduct, O house of Israel.

[33] Thus says the Lord GOD: When I purify you from all your crimes, I will repeople the cities, and the ruins shall be rebuilt; [34] the desolate land shall be tilled, which was formerly a wasteland exposed to the gaze of every passer-by. [35] "This desolate land has been made into a garden of Eden," they shall say. "The cities that were in ruins, laid waste, and destroyed are now repeopled and fortified." [36] Thus the neighboring nations that remain shall know that I, the LORD, have rebuilt what was destroyed and replanted what was desolate. I, the LORD, have promised, and I will do it.

[37] Thus says the Lord GOD: This also I will be persuaded to do for the house of Israel: to multiply them like sheep. [38] As with sacrificial sheep, the sheep of Jerusalem on its

---

36, 13: A land that devours men: destroys its own population, as could be seen in its disastrous political history.

o: Is 52, 5; Rom 2, 24.   *p:* Ps 51, 4; Zec 13, 1; Hb 10, 22; Jn 3, 5.   *q:* Jer 31, 33.   *r:* Ez 37, 14; 39, 29; Is 42, 1; 44, 3; 59, 21; Hg 2, 5; Jl 3, 1f.

feast days, the cities which were in ruins shall be filled with flocks of men; thus they shall know that I am the LORD.

See RG 325–32

CHAPTER 37

*Vision of the Dry Bones.** *¹*The hand of the LORD came upon me, and he led me out in the spirit of the LORD and set me in the center of the plain, which was now filled with bones. ²He made me walk among them in every direction so that I saw how many they were on the surface of the plain. How dry they were! ³He asked me: Son of man, can these bones come to life? "Lord GOD," I answered, "you alone know that." ⁴Then he said to me: Prophesy over these bones, and say to them: Dry bones, hear the word of the LORD! ⁵Thus says the Lord GOD to these bones: See! I will bring spirit into you, that you may come to life. ⁶I will put sinews upon you, make flesh grow over you, cover you with skin, and put spirit in you so that you may come to life and know that I am the LORD. ⁷I prophesied as I had been told, and even as I was prophesying I heard a noise; it was a rattling as the bones came together, bone joining bone. ⁸I saw the sinews and the flesh come upon them, and the skin cover them, but there was no spirit in them. ⁹Then he said to me: Prophesy to the spirit, prophesy, son of man, and say to the spirit: Thus says the Lord GOD: From the four winds come, O spirit, and breathe into these slain that they may come to life. ¹⁰I prophesied as he told me, and the spirit came into them; they came alive and stood upright, a vast army. ¹¹Then he said to me: Son of man, these bones are the whole house of Israel. They have been saying, "Our bones are dried up, our hope is lost, and we are cut off." ¹²Therefore, prophesy and say to them: Thus says the Lord GOD: O my people, I will open your graves and have you rise from them, and bring you back to the land of Israel. ¹³Then you shall know that I am the LORD, when I open your graves and have you rise from them, O my people! ¹⁴I will

put my spirit in you that you may live, and I will settle you upon your land; thus you shall know that I am the LORD. I have promised, and I will do it, says the LORD.

The Two Sticks. ¹⁵*Thus the word of the LORD came to me: ¹⁶Now, son of man, take a single stick, and write on it: Judah and those Israelites who are associated with him. Then take another stick and write on it: Joseph [the stick of Ephraim] and all the house of Israel associated with him. ¹⁷Then join the two sticks together, so that they form one stick in your hand. ¹⁸When your countrymen ask you, "Will you not tell us what you mean by all this?", ¹⁹answer them: Thus says the Lord GOD: [I will take the stick of Joseph, which is in the hand of Ephraim, and of the tribes of Israel associated with him, and I will join to it the stick of Judah, making them a single stick; they shall be one in my hand. ²⁰The sticks on which you write you shall hold up before them to see. ²¹Tell them: Thus speaks the Lord GOD:] I will take the Israelites from among the nations to which they have come, and gather them from all sides to bring them back to their land. ²²I will make them one nation upon the land, in the mountains of Israel, and there shall be one prince for them all. Never again shall they be two nations, and never again shall they be divided into two kingdoms.

²³No longer shall they defile themselves with their idols, their abominations, and all their transgressions. I will deliver them from all their sins of apostasy, and cleanse them so that they may be my people and I may be their God. ²⁴ˢMy servant David shall be prince over them, and there shall be one shepherd for them all; they shall live by my statutes and carefully observe my decrees. ²⁵They shall live on the land which I gave to my servant Jacob, the land where their fathers lived; they shall live on it forever, they, and their children, and their children's children, with my servant David their prince forever. ²⁶ᵗI will make with them a covenant of peace; it shall be an everlasting covenant

---

37, 1-14: This vision is a prediction of the restoration of Israel under the figure of a resurrection from the dead; it is not concerned with the doctrine of resurrection itself.

37, 15-22: The symbolic action of joining two sticks into

one signifies the future union of Israel and Judah under one messianic King.

s: Ez 34, 23; Jer 23, 5; 33, 15. *t:* Ps 110, 4.

with them, and I will multiply them, and put my sanctuary among them forever. [27]My dwelling shall be with them; I will be their God, and they shall be my people. [28]Thus the nations shall know that it is I, the LORD, who make Israel holy, when my sanctuary shall be set up among them forever.

See RG 325–32

CHAPTER 38

First Prophecy against Gog. [1]Thus the word of the LORD came to me:* [2]Son of man, turn toward Gog* [the land of Magog], [u] the chief prince of Meshech and Tubal, and prophesy against him: [3]Thus says the Lord GOD: See! I am coming at you, Gog, chief prince of Meshech and Tubal. [4]I will lead you forth with all your army, horses and riders all handsomely outfitted, a great horde with bucklers and shields, all of them carrying swords: [5]Persia, Cush, and Put with them [all with shields and helmets], [6]Gomer with all its troops, Beth-togarmah from the recesses of the north with all its troops, many peoples with you. [7]Prepare yourself, be ready, you and all your horde assembled about you, and be at my disposal. [8]After many days you will be mustered [in the last years you will come] against a nation which has survived the sword, which has been assembled from many peoples [on the mountains of Israel which were long a ruin], which has been brought forth from among the peoples and all of whom now dwell in security. [9]You shall come up like a sudden storm, advancing like a cloud to cover the earth, you and all your troops and the many peoples with you.

[10]Thus says the Lord GOD: At that time thoughts shall arise in your mind, and you shall devise an evil scheme: [11]"I will go up against a land of open villages and attack the peaceful people who are living in security,

all of them living without walls, having neither bars nor gates, [12]to plunder and pillage, turning my hand against the ruins that were repeopled and against a people gathered from the nations, a people concerned with cattle and goods, who dwell at the navel of the earth."* [13]Sheba and Dedan, the merchants of Tarshish and all her young lions shall ask you: "Is it for plunder that you have come? Is it for pillage that you have summoned your horde, to carry off silver and gold, to take away cattle and goods, to seize much plunder?"

[17]Thus says the Lord GOD: It is of you that I spoke in ancient times through my servants, the prophets of Israel, who prophesied in those days that I would bring you against them. [18]But on that day, the day when Gog invades the land of Israel, says the Lord GOD, my fury shall be aroused. In my anger [19]and in my jealousy, in my fiery wrath, I swear: On that day there shall be a great shaking upon the land of Israel. [20]Before me shall tremble the fish of the sea and the birds of the air, the beasts of the field and all the reptiles that crawl upon the ground, and all men who are on the land. Mountains shall be overturned, and cliffs shall tumble, and every wall shall fall to the ground. [21]Against him I will summon every terror, says the Lord GOD, every man's sword against his brother. I will hold judgment with him in pestilence and bloodshed; [22]flooding rain and hailstones, fire and brimstone, I will rain upon him, upon his troops, and upon the many peoples with him. [23]I will prove my greatness and holiness and make myself known in the sight of many nations; thus they shall know that I am the LORD.

Second Prophecy against Gog. [14]Therefore prophesy, son of man, and say to Gog: Thus says the Lord GOD: When my people

---

38, 1—39, 20: These three oracles against Gog may refer either to a specific foreign invasion in the future, or to the apocalyptic struggle between good and evil at the end of time. By some they are ascribed to a later author than Ezekiel, who lived after the exile and the return to Palestine.

38, 2: Gog: the name is almost certainly a symbolic one taken from that of Gyges, king of Lydia, whether or not the prophet has a specific person in mind. The gloss Magog may be an Akkadian expression, mat-Gog, "the land of Gog." Meshech and Tubal, as well as Gomer and Beth-togarmah (v 6),

were countries around the Black Sea, the northernmost countries known to the Hebrews: the north (cf also v 15) was the traditional direction from which invasion was expected; cf Jer 1, 13ff.

38, 12: Who dwell at the navel of the earth: the people of Israel (cf v 18; also Ez 5, 5). Many ancient peoples spoke of their own homelands as "the navel," that is, the center of the earth.

---

u: Rv 20, 7f.

Israel are dwelling in security, will you not bestir yourself *15* and come from your home in the recesses of the north, you and many peoples with you, all mounted on horses, a great horde and a mighty army? *16* You shall come up against my people Israel like a cloud covering the land. In the last days I will bring you against my land, that the nations may know of me, when in their sight I prove my holiness through you, O Gog.

See RG
325–32

CHAPTER 39

Third Prophecy against Gog. *1* Now, son of man, prophesy against Gog in these words: Thus says the Lord GOD: See! I am coming at you, Gog, chief prince of Meshech and Tubal. *2* I will turn you about, I will urge you on, and I will make you come up from the recesses of the north; I will lead you against the mountains of Israel. *3* Then I will strike the bow from your left hand, and make the arrows drop from your right. *4* Upon the mountains of Israel you shall fall, you and all your troops and the peoples who are with you. To birds of prey of every kind and to the wild beasts I am giving you to be eaten. *5* On the open field you shall fall, for I have decreed it, says the Lord GOD.

6 I will send fire upon Magog and upon those who live securely in the coastlands; thus they shall know that I am the LORD. *7* I will make my holy name known among my people Israel; I will no longer allow my holy name to be profaned. Thus the nations shall know that I am the LORD, the Holy One in Israel. *8* Yes, it is coming and shall be fulfilled, says the Lord GOD. This is the day I have decreed.

9 Then shall those who live in the cities of Israel go out and burn weapons: [shields and bucklers,] bows and arrows, clubs and lances; for seven years they shall make fires with them. *10* They shall not have to bring in wood from the fields or cut it down in the forests, for they shall make fires with the weapons. Thus they shall plunder those who plundered them and pillage those who pillaged them, says the Lord GOD.

11 On that day I will give Gog for his tomb a well-known place in Israel, the Valley of Abarim* east of the sea [it is blocked to travelers]. Gog shall be buried there with all his horde, and it shall be named "Valley of Hamon-gog." *12* To purify the land, the house of Israel shall need seven months to bury them. *13* All the people of the land shall bury them and gain renown for it, when I reveal my glory, says the Lord GOD. *14* Men shall be permanently employed to pass through the land burying those who lie unburied, so as to purify the land. For seven months they shall keep searching. *15* When they pass through, should they see a human bone, let them put up a marker beside it, until others have buried it in the Valley of Hamon-gog. *16* [Also the name of the city shall be Hamonah.] Thus the land shall be purified.

17 As for you, son of man, says the Lord GOD, say to birds of every kind and to all the wild beasts: Come together, from all sides gather for the slaughter I am about to provide for you, a great slaughter on the mountains of Israel: you shall have flesh to eat and blood to drink. *18* You shall eat the flesh of warriors and drink the blood of the princes of the land [rams, lambs, and goats, bullocks, fatlings of Bashan, all of them]. *19* From the slaughter which I will provide for you, you shall eat fat until you are filled and drink blood until you are drunk. *20* You shall be filled at my table with horses and riders, with warriors and soldiers of every kind, says the Lord GOD.

Israel's Return. *21* Thus I will display my glory among the nations, and all the nations shall see the judgment I have executed and the hand I have laid upon them. *22* From that day forward the house of Israel shall know that I am the LORD, their God. *23* The nations shall know that because of its sins the house of Israel went into exile; for they transgressed against me, and I hid my face from them and handed them over to their foes, so that all of them fell by the sword. *24* According to their uncleanness and their transgressions I dealt with them, hiding my face from them.

25 Therefore, thus says the Lord GOD: Now I will restore the fortunes of Jacob and

---

39, 11: The Valley of Abarim: in the Abarim mountains, east of the Jordan. Hamon-gog: means "the horde of Gog."

have pity on the whole house of Israel, and I will be jealous for my holy name. 26They shall forget their disgrace and all the times they broke faith with me, when they live in security on their land with no one to frighten them. 27When I bring them back from among the peoples, I will gather them from the lands of their enemies, and will prove my holiness through them in the sight of many nations. 28vThus they shall know that I, the LORD, am their God, since I who exiled them among the nations, will gather them back on their land, not leaving any of them behind. 29No longer will I hide my face from them, for I have poured out my spirit upon the house of Israel, says the Lord GOD.

V: The New Israel*

The New Temple

CHAPTER 40

See RG 325-32

The Man with a Measure. 1On the tenth day of the month beginning the twenty-fifth year of our exile, fourteen years after the city was taken, that very day the hand of the LORD came upon me and brought me 2in divine visions to the land of Israel, where he set me down on a very high mountain. On it there seemed to be a city being built before me. 3When he had brought me there, all at once I saw a man whose appearance was that of bronze; he was standing in the gate, holding a linen cord and a measuring rod. 4The man said to me, "Son of man, look carefully and listen intently, and pay strict attention to all that I will show you, for you have been brought here so that I might show it to you. Tell the house of Israel all that you see." 5[Then I saw an outer wall that completely surrounded the temple. The man was holding

a measuring rod six cubits long, each cubit being a cubit and a handbreadth;* he measured the width and the height of the structure, each of which was found to be one rod.]

The East Gate.* 6Then he went to the gate which faced the east, climbed its steps, and measured the gate's threshold, which was found to be a rod wide. 7The cells were a rod long and a rod wide, and the pilasters between the cells measured five cubits. The threshold of the gate adjoining the vestibule of the gate toward the inside measured one rod. 8He measured the vestibule of the gate, 9which was eight cubits, and its pilasters, which were two cubits. The vestibule of the gate was toward the inside. 10The cells of the east gate were three on either side, of equal size, and the pilasters on either side were also of equal size. 11He measured the gate's entrance, which was ten cubits wide, while the width of the gate's passage itself was thirteen cubits. 12The border before each of the cells on both sides was one cubit; the cells themselves were six cubits on either side, from opening to opening. 13He measured the gate from the back wall of one cell to the back wall of the cell on the opposite side: the width was twenty-five cubits. 14He measured the vestibule, which was twenty-five cubits. The pilasters adjoining the court on either side were six cubits. 15The length of the gate from the front entrance to the front of the vestibule on the inside was fifty cubits. 16Within the gateway on both sides there were splayed windows let into the cells [and into their pilasters]; likewise, within the vestibule on both sides there were windows. The pilasters were decorated with palms.

The Outer Court. 17Then he brought me to the outer court,* where there were cham-

---

40, 1—48, 35: This lengthy vision of the new Israel is dated (Ez 40, 1) April 28, 573 B.C. It is largely concerned with the new temple and the prescriptions to govern it, but other details of the restored commonwealth are included, forming a kind of program for the future. The literary form of the vision has been aptly termed "utopian": it is plain that the prophet did not expect a literal fulfillment of much of what he described. The passage doubtless underwent successive additions, both from the prophet and from later inspired writers.

40, 5: A cubit and a handbreadth: the ordinary cubit consisted of six handbreadths; the great cubit, of seven. In meas-

uring the temple, a rod six great cubits long was used. The ordinary cubit was about one and a half feet, or, more exactly, 17.5 inches; the large cubit, 20.4 inches.

40, 6-16: The east gate, leading into the outer court of the temple, is described more fully than the north and south gates, which, however, were of the same dimensions. On the west side of the outer court there was a large building instead of a gate (Ez 41, 12).

40, 17: The outer court: the court outside the temple area proper, which had its own inner court (vv 28-37).

v: Ez 36, 23.

bers and a pavement. The pavement was laid all around the court, and the chambers, which were on the pavement, were thirty in number. [18]The pavement lay alongside the gates, as wide as the gates were long; this was the lower pavement. [19]He measured the width of the court from the front of the lower gate to the front of the inner gate; it was one hundred cubits between them.

The North Gate. Then he proceeded north, [20]where, on the outer court, there was a gate facing north, whose length and width he measured. [21]Its cells, three on either side, its pilasters, and its vestibule had the same measurements as those of the first gate; it was fifty cubits long and twenty-five cubits wide. [22]Its windows, the windows of its vestibule, and its palm decorations were of the same proportions as those of the gate facing the east. Seven steps led up to it, and its vestibule was toward the inside. [23]The inner court had a gate opposite the north gate, just as at the east gate; he measured one hundred cubits from one gate to the other.

The South Gate. [24]Then he led me south, to where there was a southern gate, whose cells, pilasters, and vestibule he measured; they were the same size as the others. [25]The gate and its vestibule had windows on both sides, like the other windows. It was fifty cubits long and twenty-five cubits wide. [26]It was ascended by seven steps; its vestibule was toward the inside; and it was decorated with palms here and there on its pilasters. [27]The inner court also had a southern gate; from gate to gate he measured one hundred cubits.

*Gates of the Inner Court.** [28]Then he brought me to the inner court by the south gate, where he measured the south gate. Its dimensions were the same as the others; [29]its cells, its pilasters, and its vestibule were the same size as the others. The gate and its vestibule had windows on both sides; and it was fifty cubits long and twenty-five cubits wide. [31]But its vestibule was toward the outer court; palms were on its pilasters, and it had a stairway of eight steps. [32]Then he brought me to the gate facing the east, where he measured the gate, whose dimensions were found to be the same. [33]Its cells, its pilasters, and its vestibule were the same size as the others; the gate and its vestibule had windows on both sides; it was fifty cubits long and twenty-five cubits wide. [34]But its vestibule was toward the outer court; palms were on its pilasters here and there, and it had a stairway of eight steps. [35]Then he brought me to the north gate, where he measured the dimensions [36]of its cells, its pilasters, and its vestibule, and found them the same. The gate and its vestibule had windows on both sides; it was fifty cubits long and twenty-five cubits wide. [37]Its vestibule was toward the outer court; palms were on its pilasters here and there, and it had a stairway of eight steps.

Side Rooms. [38]There was a chamber opening off the vestibule of the gate, where the holocausts were rinsed. [39]In the vestibule of the gate there were two tables on either side, on which were slaughtered the sin offerings and guilt offerings. [40]Along the wall of the vestibule, but outside, near the entrance of the north gate, were two tables, and on the other side of the vestibule of the gate there were two tables. [41]There were four tables on either side of the gate [eight tables], on which the sacrifices were slaughtered. [42]There were four tables for holocausts, made of cut stone, one and a half cubits long, one and a half cubits wide, and one cubit high. [43]The ledges, a handbreadth wide, were set on the inside all around, and on them were laid the instruments with which the holocausts were slaughtered. On the tables themselves the flesh was laid. [44]He then led me to the inner court where there were two chambers, one beside the north gate, facing south, and the other beside the south gate, facing north. [45]He said to me, "This chamber which faces south is for the priests who have charge of the temple, [46]and the chamber which faces north is for the priests who have charge of the altar. These are the Zadokites,* the only Levites who may come near to minister to the LORD." [47]Then he

---

40, 28-37: The gates leading into the inner court of the temple area correspond to the gates leading into the outer court, with the exception that their vestibules are on the outer rather than the inner side. (Verse 30, a dittography of v 29, is omitted.)

40, 46: The Zadokites: descendants of the priestly line of Zadok; cf 2 Sm 15, 24-29; 1 Kgs 1, 32ff; 2, 35.

measured the court, which was a hundred cubits long and a hundred cubits wide, a perfect square. The altar stood in front of the temple.

*The Temple Building.** [48]Then he brought me into the vestibule of the temple and measured the pilasters on each side, which were five cubits. The width of the doorway was fourteen cubits, and the side walls on either side of the door measured three cubits. [49]*The vestibule was twenty cubits wide and twelve cubits deep; ten steps led up to it, and there were columns by the pilasters, one on either side.

See RG 325–32

CHAPTER 41

[1]Then he brought me to the nave and measured the pilasters, which were six cubits thick on either side. [2]The width of the entrance was ten cubits, and the walls at either side of it measured five cubits each. He measured the length of the nave, which was found to be forty cubits, while its width was twenty.

[3]Then he went in beyond and measured the pilasters flanking that entrance, which were two cubits; the width of the entrance was six cubits, and the walls at either side of it extended seven cubits each. [4]He measured the space beyond the nave, twenty cubits long and twenty cubits wide, and said to me, "This is the holy of holies."*

[5]Then he measured the wall of the temple, which was six cubits thick; the side chambers, which extended all the way around the temple, had a width of four cubits. [6]There were thirty side chambers built one above the other in three stories, and there were offsets in the outside wall of the temple that enclosed the side chambers; these served as supports, so that there were no supports in the temple wall proper. [7]There was a broad circular passageway that led upward to the side chambers, for the temple was enclosed all the way around and all the way upward; therefore the temple had a broad way running upward so that one could pass from the lowest to the middle and the highest story. [8]About the temple was a raised pavement completely enclosing it—the foundations of the side chambers—a full rod of six cubits in extent. [9]The width of the outside wall which enclosed the side chambers was five cubits. Between the side chambers of the temple [10]and the chambers of the court was an open space twenty cubits wide going all around the temple. [11]The side chambers had entrances to the open space, one entrance on the north and another on the south. The width of the wall surrounding the open space was five cubits. [12]The building* fronting the free area on the west side was seventy cubits front to back; the wall of the building was five cubits thick all around, and it measured ninety cubits from side to side. [13]He measured the temple, which was one hundred cubits long. The free area, together with the building and its walls, was a hundred cubits in length. [14]The façade of the temple, along with the free area, on the east side, was one hundred cubits wide. [15]He measured the building which lay the length of the free area and behind it, and together with its walls on both sides it was one hundred cubits.

Interior of the Temple. The inner nave and the outer vestibule [16]were paneled with precious wood all around, covered from the ground to the windows. There were splayed windows with trellises about them [facing the threshold]. [17]As high as the lintel of the door, even into the interior part of the temple as well as outside, on every wall on every side in both the inner and outer rooms were carved [18]the figures of cherubim and palmtrees: a palmtree between every two cherubim. Each cherub had two faces: [19]a man's face looking at a palmtree on one side, and a lion's face looking at a palmtree on the other; thus they were figured on every side throughout the whole temple. [20]From the ground to the lintel of the door the cherubim and palmtrees were carved on the walls. [21]The way into the nave was a square doorframe. In front of the holy place was something that looked like [22]a

40, 48—41, 15: The description of Ezekiel's visionary temple closely follows the description of the temple of Solomon (1 Kgs 6).

40, 49—41, 4: Vestibule . . . nave . . . holy of holies: the three divisions of the temple building in progressing order of sanctity. The last is called "the inner sanctuary" in 1 Kgs 6.

41, 12: The building: the function of this structure lying behind the temple is never specified.

wooden altar,* three cubits in height, two cubits long, and two cubits wide. It had corners, and its base and sides were of wood. He said to me, "This is the table which is before the LORD." 23The nave had a double door, and also the holy place had 24a double door. Each door had two movable leaves; two leaves were on one doorjamb and two on the other. 25Carved upon them [on the doors of the nave] were cherubim and palmtrees, like those carved on the walls. Before the vestibule outside was a wooden lattice. 26There were splayed windows [and palmtrees] on both side walls of the vestibule, and the side chambers of the temple. . . .

CHAPTER 42

See RG 325-32

Other Structures. ¹Then he led me north to the outer court, bringing me to some chambers on the north that lay across the free area and which were also across from the building. ²Their length was a hundred cubits on the north side, and they were fifty cubits wide. ³Across the twenty cubits of the inner court and the pavement of the outer court, there were three parallel rows of them on different levels. ⁴In front of the chambers, to the inside, was a walk ten cubits broad and a wall of one cubit; but the entrances of the chambers were on the north. ⁵The outermost chambers were the lowest, for the system of levels set them at a level lower than the closest chambers and those in between;* ⁶for they were in three rows and had no foundations to conform with the foundations of the courts, therefore they were on a lower terrace of the ground than the closest and the middle chambers. ⁷On the far side there was a wall running parallel to the chambers along the outer court; its length before these chambers was fifty cubits, ⁸for the length of the chambers belonging to the outer court was fifty cubits, but along its entire length the wall measured one hundred cubits. ⁹Below these chambers there was the way in from the east, so that one could enter from the outer court ¹⁰where the wall of the court began.

To the south along the side of the free area and the building there were also chambers, ¹¹before which was a passage. These looked like the chambers to the north, just as long and just as wide, with the same exits and plan and entrances. ¹²Below the chambers to the south there was an entrance at the beginning of the way which led to the back wall, by which one could enter from the east. ¹³He said to me, "The north and south chambers which border on the free area are the sanctuary chambers; here the priests who draw near to the LORD shall eat the most sacred meals, and here they shall keep the most sacred offerings: cereal offerings, sin offerings, and guilt offerings; for it is a holy place.* ¹⁴When the priests have once entered, they shall not leave the holy place for the outer court until they have left here the clothing in which they ministered, for it is holy. They shall put on other garments, and then approach the place destined for the people."

Measuring the Outer Court. ¹⁵When he had finished measuring the inner temple area, he brought me out by way of the gate which faces east and measured all the limits of the court. ¹⁶He measured the east side: five hundred cubits by his measuring rod. Then he turned ¹⁷and measured the north side: five hundred cubits by the measuring rod. He turned ¹⁸to the south and measured five hundred cubits by the measuring rod. ¹⁹Then he turned to the west and measured five hundred cubits by the measuring rod. ²⁰Thus he measured it in the four directions, five hundred cubits long and five hundred cubits wide. It was surrounded by a wall, to separate the sacred from the profane.

Restoration of the Temple

CHAPTER 43

See RG 325-32

The Return of the Lord. ¹Then he led me to the gate which faces the east, ²and there I saw the glory of the God of Israel coming from the east. I heard a sound like the roaring of many waters, and the earth shone with his

---

41, 22: A wooden altar: the altar of incense, standing in the nave at the entrance to the holy of holies.

42, 5f: The three rows of identical chambers, since they rested on different ground levels, necessarily had roofs on correspondingly different levels.

42, 13: The function of these chambers is explained again in Ez 46, 19f.

glory. [3w]The vision was like that which I had seen when he came to destroy the city, and like that which I had seen by the river Chebar. I fell prone [4]as the glory of the LORD entered the temple by way of the gate which faces the east, [5]but spirit lifted me up and brought me to the inner court. And I saw that the temple was filled with the glory of the LORD. [6]Then I heard someone speaking to me from the temple, while the man stood beside me. [7]The voice said to me: Son of man, this is where my throne shall be, this is where I will set the soles of my feet; here I will dwell among the Israelites forever. Never again shall they and their kings profane my holy name with their harlotries and with the corpses of their kings [their high places]. [8]When they placed their threshold against my threshold* and their doorpost next to mine, so that only a wall was between us, they profaned my holy name by their abominable deeds; therefore I consumed them in my wrath. [9]From now on they shall put far from me their harlotry and the corpses of their kings, and I will dwell in their midst forever.

The Law of the Temple. [10]As for you, son of man, describe the temple to the house of Israel [that they may be ashamed of their sins], both its measurements and its design; [11][and if they are ashamed of all that they have done,] make known to them the form and design of the temple, its exits and entrances, all its statutes and laws; write these down for them to see, that they may carefully observe all its laws and statutes. [12]This is the law of the temple: its whole surrounding area on the mountain top shall be most sacred.

The Altar. [13]These were the measurements of the altar* in cubits of one cubit plus a handbreadth. Its base was one cubit high and one cubit deep, with a rim around its edge of one span. The height of the altar itself was as follows: [14]from its base at the bottom up to the lower ledge it was two cubits high, and this ledge was one cubit deep; from the

lower to the upper ledge it was four cubits high, and this ledge also was one cubit deep; [15]the hearth of the altar was four cubits high, and extending from the top of the hearth were the four horns of the altar. [16]The hearth was a square: twelve cubits long and twelve cubits wide. [17]The upper ledge was also a square: fourteen cubits long and fourteen cubits wide. The lower ledge, likewise a square, was sixteen cubits long and sixteen cubits wide, with a half-cubit rim surrounding it. And there was a base of one cubit all around. The steps of the altar face the east.

[18]Then he said to me: Son of man, thus says the Lord GOD: These are the statutes for the altar when it is set up for the offering of holocausts upon it and for the sprinkling of blood against it. [19]Give a young bull as a sin offering to the priests, the Levites who are of the line of Zadok, who draw near me to minister to me, says the Lord GOD. [20]Take some of its blood and put it on the four horns of the altar, and on the four corners of the ledge, and on the rim all around. Thus you shall purify it and make atonement for it. [21]Then take the bull of the sin offering, which is to be burnt in a designated part of the temple, outside the sanctuary. [22]On the second day present an unblemished he-goat as a sin offering, to purify the altar as was done with the bull. [23]When you have finished the purification, bring an unblemished young bull and an unblemished ram from the flock, [24]and present them before the LORD; the priests shall strew salt on them and offer them to the LORD as holocausts. [25]Daily for seven days you shall offer a he-goat as a sin offering, and a young bull and a ram from the flock, all unblemished, shall be offered [26]for seven days. Thus atonement shall be made for the altar, and it shall be purified and dedicated. [27]And when these days are over, from the eighth day on, the priests shall offer your holocausts and peace offerings on the altar. Then I will accept you, says the Lord GOD.

43, 8: They placed their threshold against my threshold: the preexilic temple and the royal palace belonged to the same complex of buildings, and this physical proximity was reflected in the use made of the temple by kings like Ahaz and Manasseh, who treated it as their private chapel for pagan rites. In the new Israel the temple is free,

even physically, from civil jurisdiction; cf Ez 45, 7f.

43, 13: The altar: of holocausts, standing in the inner court of the temple area; cf Ez 40, 47.

w: Ez 1, 1.

CHAPTER 44

See RG 325-32

The Closed Gate. ¹Then he brought me back to the outer gate of the sanctuary, facing the east; but it was closed. ²He said to me: This gate is to remain closed; it is not to be opened for anyone to enter by it; since the LORD, the God of Israel, has entered by it, it shall remain closed. ³Only the prince may sit down in it to eat his meal in the presence of the LORD. He must enter by way of the vestibule of the gate, and leave by the same way.*

The New Law

Admission to the Temple. ⁴Then he brought me by way of the north gate to the façade of the temple, and when I looked I saw the glory of the LORD filling the LORD's temple, and I fell prone. ⁵Then he said to me: Son of man, pay strict attention, look carefully, and listen intently to all that I will tell you about the statutes and laws of the LORD's temple; be attentive in regard to those who are to be admitted to the temple and all those who are to be excluded from the sanctuary. ⁶Say to that rebellious house, the house of Israel: Thus says the Lord GOD: Enough of all these abominations of yours, O house of Israel! ⁷You have admitted foreigners, uncircumcised both in heart and flesh, to my sanctuary to profane it when you offered me food, fat, and blood;* thus you have broken my covenant by all your abominations. ⁸Instead of caring for the service of my temple, you have appointed such as these to serve me in my sanctuary in your stead. ⁹Thus says the Lord GOD: No foreigners, uncircumcised in heart and in flesh, shall ever enter my sanctuary; none of the foreigners who live among the Israelites.

*Levites.** ¹⁰But as for the Levites who departed from me when Israel strayed from me to pursue their idols, they shall bear the consequences of their sin. ¹¹They shall serve in my sanctuary as gatekeepers and temple servants; they shall slaughter the holocausts and the sacrifices for the people, and they shall stand before the people to minister for them. ¹²Because they used to minister for them before their idols, and became an occasion of sin to the house of Israel, therefore I have sworn an oath against them, says the Lord GOD: they shall bear the consequences of their sin. ¹³They shall no longer draw near me to serve as my priests, nor shall they touch any of my sacred things, or the most sacred things. Thus they shall bear their disgrace because of all their abominable deeds. ¹⁴But I will set them to the service of the temple, for all its work and for everything that is to be done in it.

Priests. ¹⁵As for the levitical priests, however, the Zadokites who cared for my sanctuary when the Israelites strayed from me, they shall draw near me to minister to me, and they shall stand before me to offer me fat and blood, says the Lord GOD. ¹⁶It is they who shall enter my sanctuary, they who shall approach my table to minister to me, and they who shall carry out my service. ¹⁷Whenever they enter the gates of the inner court, they shall wear linen garments; they shall not put on anything woolen when they minister at the gates of the inner court or within the temple. ¹⁸ˣThey shall have linen turbans on their heads and linen drawers on their loins; they shall not gird themselves with anything that causes sweat. ¹⁹ʸWhen they are to go out to the people in the outer court, they shall take off the garments in which they ministered and leave them in the chambers of the sanctuary, putting on other garments; thus they will not transmit holiness to the people* with their garments.

44, 3: The prince stands at the eastern gate of the inner court while his sacrifice is offered up (Ez 46, 2); he then goes to the vestibule of the outer court, there to partake of his sacrificial meal. The closed outer gate on the eastern side signifies that the Lord has entered the temple permanently, not to depart again.

44, 7ff: In the preexilic temple various menial services had been performed by foreigners; cf Jos 9, 22-27. In the new temple the Levites will perform these services (vv 10-14).

44, 10-14: Levites other than the Zadokite priesthood of Jerusalem had performed priestly functions at the various sanctuaries and high places in Israel and Judah, where the worship of the Lord had often been corrupted with pagan elements. The demotion of the Levites to menial service in the temple was enforced in the actual restoration after the exile, and explains why relatively few Levites were willing to return; cf Ezr 8, 15ff.

44, 19: Thus they will not transmit holiness to the people:

x: Ex 28, 40. 42; 29, 9; 38, 28; Lv 6, 3.   y: Ez 42, 13. 14.

*20z*They shall not shave their heads nor let their hair hang loose, but they shall keep their hair carefully trimmed. *21a*No priest shall drink wine when he is to enter the inner court. *22b*They shall not take for their wives either widows or divorced women, but only virgins of the race of Israel; however, they may marry women who are the widows of priests. *23*They shall teach my people to distinguish between the sacred and the profane, and make known to them the difference between the clean and the unclean. *24c*In capital cases they shall stand as judges, judging them according to my decrees. They shall observe my laws and statutes on all my festivals, and keep my sabbaths holy.

*25d*They shall not make themselves unclean by coming near any dead person, unless it be their father, mother, son, daughter, brother, or maiden sister; for these they may make themselves unclean. *26*After a priest has been cleansed, he must wait an additional seven days, *27*and on the day he enters the inner court to minister in the sanctuary, he shall present his sin offering, says the Lord GOD. *28e*They shall have no inheritance, for I am their inheritance; you shall give them no property in Israel, for I am their property. *29f*They shall eat the cereal offering, the sin offering, and the guilt offering; whatever is under the ban* in Israel shall be theirs. *30g*All the choicest first fruits of every kind, and all the best of your offerings of every kind, shall belong to the priests; likewise the best of your dough you shall give to the priests to bring a blessing down upon your house. *31h*The priests shall not eat anything, whether flesh or fowl, that has died of itself or has been killed by wild beasts.

CHAPTER 45

See RG 325-32

The Sacred Tract. *1*When you apportion the land into inheritances, you shall set apart a sacred tract of land for the LORD, twenty-five thousand cubits long and twenty thousand wide; its whole area shall be sacred. *2*Of this land a square plot, five hundred by five hundred cubits, surrounded by a free space of fifty cubits, shall be assigned to the sanctuary. *3*Also from this sector measure off a strip, twenty-five thousand cubits long and ten thousand wide, within which shall be the sanctuary, the holy of holies. *4*This shall be the sacred part of the land belonging to the priests, the ministers of the sanctuary, who draw near to minister to the LORD; it shall be a place for their homes and pasture land for their cattle. *5*Also there shall be a strip twenty-five thousand cubits long and ten thousand wide as property for the Levites, the ministers of the temple, that they may have cities to live in. *6*As property of the City you shall designate a strip five thousand cubits wide and twenty-five thousand long, parallel to the sacred tract; this shall belong to the whole house of Israel. *7*The prince shall have a section bordering on both sides of the combined sacred tract and City property, extending westward on the western side and eastward on the eastern side, corresponding in length to one of the tribal portions from the western boundary to the eastern boundary *8*of the land. This shall be his property in Israel, so that the princes of Israel will no longer oppress my people, but will leave the land to the house of Israel according to their tribes.

*Weights and Measures.** *9*Thus says the Lord GOD: Enough, you princes of Israel!

holiness was thought of as something physical, as though it were communicable, and therefore not to be brought in contact with unconsecrated persons.

44, 29: Under the ban: dedicated to the Lord, withdrawn from profane use.

45, 9-12: Besides the land monopoly fostered by royal greed and collusion with the wealthy (Mi 2, 2; Is 3, 12-15; 5, 8-10), one grave social evil of preexilic Israel was dishonesty in business; cf Hos 12, 8; Am 8, 5. Ephah: a dry measure; liquid measure: in Hebrew, a "bath," standardized according to the homer (a dry measure of about 10 bushels, or 80 gallons). In v 12 reference is made to the change in value of the mina:

before the exile it was valued at 50 shekels, but afterward, in imitation of Babylonian practice, the 60-shekel mina was adopted. The shekel was a unit of weight slightly less than half an ounce. As a monetary unit, the value obviously differed greatly, depending on whether it was a gold or a silver shekel.

z: Lv 21, 5.   *a:* Lv 10, 9.   *b:* Lv 21, 7. 14.   *c:* Dt 17, 9; 19, 17.   *d:* Lv 21, 1ff. 11.   *e:* Nm 18, 20; Dt 18, 1.   *f:* Lv 2, 3. 10; 6, 9. 22; 7, 9; 10, 12; Nm 18, 9; 18, 14.   *g:* Ex 34, 26; Dt 18, 4.   *h:* Lv 22, 8.

Put away violence and oppression, and do what is right and just! Stop evicting my people! says the Lord GOD. [10i]You shall have honest scales, an honest ephah, and an honest liquid measure. [11]The ephah and the liquid measure shall be of the same size: the liquid measure equal to a tenth of a homer, and the ephah equal to a tenth of a homer; by the homer they shall be determined. [12j]The shekel shall be twenty gerahs. Twenty shekels, twenty-five shekels, plus fifteen shekels shall be your mina.

Offerings. [13]These are the offerings you shall make: one sixth of an ephah from each homer of wheat, and one sixth of an ephah from each homer of barley. [14]The regulation for oil: for every measure of oil, a tenth of a measure, computed by the kor* of ten liquid measures [or a homer, for ten liquid measures make a homer]. [15]One sheep from the flock for every two hundred from the pasturage of Israel, for sacrifice—holocausts and peace offerings and atonement sacrifices, says the Lord GOD. [16]All the people of the land shall be bound to this offering [for the prince in Israel]. [17]It shall be the duty of the prince to provide the holocausts, cereal offerings, and libations on the feasts, new moons, and sabbaths, on all the festivals of the house of Israel. He shall offer the sin offerings, cereal offerings, holocausts, and peace offerings, to make atonement on behalf of the house of Israel.

The Passover. [18]Thus says the Lord GOD: On the first day of the first month you shall use an unblemished young bull as a sacrifice to purify the sanctuary. [19]Then the priest shall take some of the blood from the sin offering and put it on the doorposts of the temple, on the four corners of the ledge of the altar, and on the doorposts of the gates of the inner court. [20]You shall repeat this on the first day of the seventh month for those who have sinned through inadvertence or ignorance; thus you shall make atonement for the temple. [21k]On the fourteenth day of the first month you shall observe the feast of the Passover; for seven days unleavened bread is to be eaten. [22]On that day the prince shall offer on his own behalf, and on behalf of all the people of the land, a bull as a sin offering. [23]On each of the seven days of the feast he shall offer as a holocaust to the Lord seven bulls and seven rams without blemish, and as a sin offering he shall offer one male goat each day. [24]As a cereal offering he shall offer one ephah for each bull and one ephah for each ram; and he shall offer one hin* of oil for each ephah.

The Feast of Booths. [25]On the fifteenth day of the seventh month, the feast day, and for seven days, he shall perform the same rites, making the same sin offerings, the same holocausts, the same cereal offerings and offerings of oil.

CHAPTER 46

See RG 325-32

Sabbaths. [1]Thus says the Lord GOD: The gate toward the east of the inner court shall remain closed throughout the six working days, but on the sabbath and on the day of the new moon it shall be open. [2]The prince shall enter from outside by way of the vestibule of the gate and remain standing at the doorpost of the gate; then while the priests offer his holocausts and peace offerings, he shall worship at the threshold of the gate and then leave; the gate shall not be closed until evening. [3]The people of the land shall worship before the LORD at the door of this gate on the sabbaths and new moons. [4l]The holocausts which the prince presents to the LORD on the sabbath shall consist of six unblemished lambs and an unblemished ram, [5]together with a cereal offering of one ephah for the ram, whatever he pleases for the lambs, and a hin of oil for each ephah. [6m]On the day of the new moon he shall provide an unblemished young bull, also six lambs and a ram without blemish, [7]with a cereal offering of one ephah for the bull and one for the ram, for the lambs as much as he has at hand, and for each ephah a hin of oil.

45, 14: Kor: both a liquid and a dry measure, corresponding to the homer.
45, 24: Hin: a sixth part of the liquid measure called a bath.

i: Lv 19, 35; Dt 25, 13-16; Hos 12, 8; Am 8, 5; Mi 6, 10f.   j: Ex 30, 13; Lv 27, 25; Nm 3, 47; 18, 16.   k: Ex 12, 6; Lv 23, 5; Nm 28, 16.   l: Nm 28, 9f.   m: Nm 28, 11-15.

Ritual Laws. [8]The prince shall always enter and depart by the vestibule of the gate. [9n]When the people of the land enter the presence of the LORD to worship on the festivals, if they enter by the north gate they shall leave by the south gate, and if they enter by the south gate they shall leave by the north gate; no one shall return by the gate through which he has entered, but he shall leave by the opposite gate. [10]The prince shall be in their midst when they enter, and he shall also leave with them. [11]On the feasts and festivals the cereal offering shall be an ephah for a bull, an ephah for a ram, but for the lambs as much as one pleases, and a hin of oil with each ephah. [12]When the prince makes a freewill offering to the LORD, whether holocausts or peace offerings, the eastern gate shall be opened for him, and he shall offer his holocausts or his peace offerings as on the sabbath; then he shall leave, and the gate shall be closed after his departure. [13o]He shall offer as a daily holocaust to the LORD an unblemished yearling lamb; this he shall offer every morning. [14]With it every morning he shall provide as a cereal offering one sixth of an ephah, with a third of a hin of oil to moisten the fine flour. This cereal offering to the LORD is mandatory with the established holocaust. [15p]The lamb, the cereal offering, and the oil are to be offered every morning as an established holocaust.

The Prince and the Land. [16]Thus says the Lord GOD: If the prince makes a gift of part of his inheritance to any of his sons, it shall belong to his sons; that property is theirs by inheritance. [17]But if he makes a gift of part of his inheritance to one of his servants, it shall belong to the latter only until the year of release,* when it shall revert to the prince. Only the inheritance given to his sons is permanent. [18]The prince shall not seize any part of the inheritance of the people by evicting them from their property. He shall provide an inheritance for his sons from his own property, so that none of my people will be driven from their property.

The Temple Kitchens. [19]Then he brought me by the entrance which is on the side of the gate to the chambers [of the sanctuary, reserved to the priests] which face the north. There, at their west end, I saw a place, [20]concerning which he said to me, "Here the priests cook the guilt offerings and the sin offerings, and bake the cereal offerings, so that they do not have to take them into the outer court at the risk of transmitting holiness to the people." [21]Then he led me into the outer court and had me pass around the four corners of the court, and I saw that in each corner there was another court: [22]in the four corners of the court, minor courts, forty cubits long and thirty wide, all four of them the same size. [23]A wall of stones surrounded each of the four, and hearths were built beneath the stones all the way around. [24]He said to me, "These are the kitchens where the temple ministers cook the sacrifices of the people."

CHAPTER 47

See RG 325-32

*The Wonderful Stream.** [1]Then he brought me back to the entrance of the temple, and I saw water flowing out from beneath the threshold of the temple toward the east, for the façade of the temple was toward the east; the water flowed down from the southern side of the temple, south of the altar.[q] [2]He led me outside by the north gate, and around to the outer gate facing the east, where I saw water trickling from the southern side. [3]Then when he had walked off to the east with a measuring cord in his hand, he measured off a thousand cubits and had me wade through the water, which was ankle-deep. [4]He measured off another thousand and once more had me wade through the water, which was now knee-deep. Again he measured off a thousand and had me wade; the water was up to my waist. [5]Once more he measured off a thousand, but there was now a river through which I could not wade; for the water had risen so high it had

---

46, 17: The year of release: the jubilee year; cf Lv 25, 23-55.

47, 1-12: The wonderful and superabundant stream flowing from the temple, restoring to fertility traditionally arid ground, is symbolic of the return of the conditions of

primeval paradise; cf Gn 2, 10-14. Water signifies great blessings, just as dryness signifies a curse; cf Ez 26, 5. 14.

n: Ex 23, 17; 34, 23; Dt 16, 16.   *o:* Ex 29, 38-42; Nm 28, 3-8. *p:* Ex 29, 42.   *q:* Sir 24, 28f; Jl 4, 18; Zec 13, 1; Rv 22, 1f.

Tribal Territories in the Restored Israel

become a river that could not be crossed except by swimming. ⁶He asked me, "Have you seen this, son of man?" Then he brought me to the bank of the river, where he had me sit. ⁷Along the bank of the river I saw very many trees on both sides. ⁸He said to me, "This water flows into the eastern district down upon the Arabah, and empties into the sea, the salt waters, which it makes fresh. ⁹Wherever the river flows, every sort of living creature that can multiply shall live, and there shall be abundant fish, for wherever this water comes the sea shall be made fresh. ¹⁰Fishermen shall be standing along it from En-gedi to En-eglaim,* spreading their nets there. Its kinds of fish shall be like those of the Great Sea, very numerous. ¹¹Only its marshes and swamps shall not be made fresh; they shall be left for salt. ¹²Along both banks of the river, fruit trees of every kind shall grow; their leaves shall not fade, nor their fruit fail. Every month they shall bear fresh fruit, for they shall be watered by the flow from the sanctuary. Their fruit shall serve for food, and their leaves for medicine."

The New Israel

Boundaries of the Land.* ¹³Thus says the Lord GOD: These are the boundaries within which you shall apportion the land among the twelve tribes of Israel [Joseph having two portions]. ¹⁴All of you shall have a like portion in this land which I swore to give to your fathers, that it might fall to you as your inheritance. ¹⁵ʳThis is the boundary of the land on the north side: from the Great Sea in the direction of Hethlon, past Labo of Hamath,

47, 10: From En-gedi to En-eglaim: the former was about halfway down the western shore of the Dead Sea, the latter may have been at its northern extremity.

47, 13-20: These boundaries of the restored Israel correspond to those of the Davidic kingdom at its fullest extent, the so-called "ideal boundaries" of the promised land; cf Nm 34, 3-12.

r: Nm 34, 7ff.

to Zedad, [16]Berothah, and Sibraim, along the frontiers of Hamath and Damascus, to Hazar-enon which is on the border of the Hauran. [17]Thus the border shall extend from the sea to Hazar-enon, with the frontier of Hamath and Damascus to the north. This is the northern boundary. [18]The eastern boundary: between the Hauran—toward Damascus—and Gilead on the one side, and the land of Israel on the other side, the Jordan shall form the boundary down to the eastern sea as far as Tamar. This is the eastern boundary. [19]The southern boundary: from Tamar to the waters of Meribath-kadesh, thence to the Wadi of Egypt, and on to the Great Sea. This is the southern boundary. [20]The western boundary: the Great Sea forms the boundary up to a point parallel to Labo of Hamath. This is the western boundary.

The Northern Portions. [21]You shall distribute this land among yourselves according to the tribes of Israel. [22]sYou shall allot it as inheritances for yourselves and for the aliens resident in your midst who have bred children among you. The latter shall be to you like native Israelites; along with you they shall receive inheritances among the tribes of Israel. [23]In whatever tribe the alien may be resident, there you shall assign him his inheritance, says the Lord GOD.

CHAPTER 48

See RG
325–32

[1]This is the list* of the tribes.t Dan: at the northern extremity, adjoining Hamath, all along from the approaches to Hethlon through Labo of Hamath to Hazar-enon, on the northerly border with Damascus, with his possession reaching from the eastern to the western boundary. [2]Asher: on the frontier of Dan, from the eastern to the western boundary. [3]Naphtali: on the frontier of Asher, from the eastern to the western boundary. [4]Manasseh: on the frontier of Naphtali, from the eastern to the western boundary. [5]Ephraim: on the frontier of Manasseh, from the eastern to the western boundary. [6]Reuben: on the frontier of Ephraim, from the eastern to the western boundary. [7]Judah: on the frontier of Reuben, from the eastern to the western boundary.

The Sacred Tract. [8]On the frontier of Judah, from the eastern to the western boundary there shall be the tract which you shall set apart, twenty-five thousand cubits from north to south, and as wide as one of the tribal portions from the eastern to the western boundary. In the center of the tract shall be the sanctuary. [9]The tract that you set aside for the LORD shall be twenty-five thousand cubits across by twenty thousand north and south. [10]In this sacred tract the priests shall have twenty-five thousand cubits on the north, ten thousand on the west, ten thousand on the east, and twenty-five thousand on the south; and the sanctuary of the LORD shall be in its center. [11]The consecrated priests, the Zadokites, who fulfilled my service and did not stray along with the Israelites as the Levites did, [12]shall have within this tract of land their own most sacred domain, next to the territory of the Levites. [13]The Levites shall have a territory corresponding to that of the priests, twenty-five thousand cubits by ten thousand. The whole tract shall be twenty-five thousand cubits across and twenty thousand north and south. [14]They may not sell or exchange or alienate this, the best part of the land, for it is sacred to the LORD. [15]The remaining five thousand cubits along the twenty-five-thousand-cubit line are profane land, assigned to the City for dwellings and pasture; the City shall be at their center. [16]These are the dimensions of the City: the north side, forty-five hundred cubits; the south side, forty-five hundred cubits; the east side, forty-five hundred cubits; and the west side, forty-five hundred cubits. [17]The pasture lands of the City shall extend north two hundred and fifty cubits, south two hundred and fifty cubits, east two hundred and fifty cubits, and west two hundred and fifty cubits. [18]There shall remain an area along the sacred tract, ten thousand cubits to the east and ten thou-

---

48, 1-29: This distribution of the land among the tribes does not correspond to the geographical realities of Palestine. It is a description of the ideal order, like that in Ez 47, 1-12.

s: Ex 12, 48; Lv 19, 34; 24, 22; Nm 9, 14; Jos 8, 33.   t: Ez 47, 15ff.

sand to the west, whose produce shall provide food for the workers of the City. [19] The workers in the City shall be taken from all the tribes of Israel. [20] The entire tract shall be twenty-five thousand by twenty-five thousand cubits; as a perfect square you shall set apart the sacred tract together with the City property.

[21] The remainder shall belong to the prince: the land on both sides of the sacred tract and the City property, extending along the twenty-five-thousand-cubit line eastward to the eastern boundary, and westward along the twenty-five-thousand-cubit line to the western boundary, a territory parallel with the tribal portions for the prince. The sacred tract and the sanctuary of the temple shall be in the middle. [22] Thus, except for the property of the Levites and the City property, which lie in the midst of the prince's property, the territory between the portions of Judah and of Benjamin shall belong to the prince.

The Southern Portions. [23] These are the remaining tribes. Benjamin: from the eastern to the western boundary. [24] Simeon: on the frontier of Benjamin, from the eastern to the western boundary. [25] Issachar: on the frontier of Simeon, from the eastern to the western boundary. [26] Zebulun: on the frontier of Issachar, from the eastern to the western boundary. [27] Gad: on the frontier of Zebulun, from the eastern to the western boundary. [28] Along the frontier of Gad shall be the southern boundary, which shall extend from Tamar to the waters of Meribath-kadesh, and from there to the Wadi of Egypt, and on to the Great Sea. [29] Such is the land which you shall apportion as inheritances among the tribes of Israel, and these are their portions, says the Lord GOD.

The Gates of the City. [30] These are the exits of the City, the gates of which are named after the tribes of Israel. On the north side, measuring forty-five hundred cubits, [31] there shall be three gates: the gate of Reuben, the gate of Judah, and the gate of Levi. [32] On the east side, measuring forty-five hundred cubits, there shall be three gates: the gate of Joseph, the gate of Benjamin, and the gate of Dan. [33] On the south side, measuring forty-five hundred cubits, there shall be three gates: the gate of Simeon, the gate of Issachar, and the gate of Zebulun. [34] On the west side, measuring forty-five hundred cubits, there shall be three gates: the gate of Gad, the gate of Asher, and the gate of Naphtali. [35] The perimeter of the City is eighteen thousand cubits. The name of the City shall henceforth be "The LORD is here."

See RG
336–43

The Book of Daniel

This Book takes its name, not from the author, who is actually unknown, but from its hero, a young Jew taken early to Babylon, where he lived at least until 538 B.C. Strictly speaking, the book does not belong to the prophetic writings but rather to a distinctive type of literature known as "apocalyptic," of which it is an early specimen. Apocalyptic writing enjoyed its greatest popularity from 200 B.C. to 100 A.D., a time of distress and persecution for Jews, and later, for Christians. Though subsequent in time to the prophetic, apocalyptic literature has its roots in the teaching of the prophets, who often pointed ahead to the day of the Lord, the consummation of history. For both prophet and apocalyptist Yahweh was the Lord of history, and he would ultimately vindicate his people.

This work was composed during the bitter persecution carried on by Antiochus IV Epiphanes (167–164) and was written to strengthen and comfort the Jewish people in their ordeal.

The Book contains stories originating in and transmitted by popular traditions which tell of the trials and triumphs of the wise Daniel and his three companions. The moral is that men of faith can resist temptation and conquer adversity. The characters are not purely legendary but rest on older historical tradition. What is more important than the question of historicity, and closer to the intention of the author, is the fact that a persecuted Jew of the second century B.C. would quickly see the application of these stories to his own plight.

There follows a series of visions promising deliverance and glory to the Jews in the days to come. The great nations of the ancient world have risen in vain against Yahweh; his kingdom shall overthrow existing powers and last forever. Under this apocalyptic imagery are contained some of the best elements of prophetic teaching: the insistence on right conduct, the divine control over events, the certainty that the kingdom of God will ultimately triumph. The arrival of the kingdom is a central theme of the synoptic gospels, and Jesus, in calling himself the "Son of Man," reminds us that he fulfills the destiny of this mysterious figure in the seventh chapter of Daniel.

The added episodes of Susanna, Bel, and the Dragon, found only in the Greek version, are edifying short stories with a didactic purpose.

These three sections constitute the divisions of the Book of Daniel:

I: Daniel and the Kings of Babylon (1, 1—6, 29).
II: Daniel's Visions (7, 1—12, 13).
III: Appendix (13, 1—14, 42).

I: Daniel and the Kings of Babylon

CHAPTER 1

See RG
337

The Food Test. [1]In the third year of the reign of Jehoiakim, king of Judah, King Nebuchadnezzar of Babylon came and laid siege to Jerusalem.*a* [2b]The Lord handed over to him Jehoiakim, king of Judah, and some of the vessels of the temple of God, which he carried off to the land of Shinar,* and placed in the temple treasury of his god.

[3]The king told Ashpenaz, his chief chamberlain, to bring in some of the Israelites of royal blood and of the nobility, [4]young men without any defect, handsome, intelligent and wise, quick to learn, and prudent in judgment, such as could take their place in the king's palace; they were to be taught the language and literature of the Chaldeans; [5]after three years' training they were to enter the king's service. The king allotted them a daily portion of food and wine from the royal table. [6]Among these were men of Judah: Daniel, Hananiah, Mishael, and Azariah. [7]The chief chamberlain changed their names: Daniel to Belteshazzar, Hananiah to Shadrach, Mishael to Meshach, and Azariah to Abednego.*

[8]But Daniel was resolved not to defile himself with the king's food or wine; so he begged the chief chamberlain to spare him this defilement.* [9]Though God had given Daniel the favor and sympathy of the chief chamberlain, [10]he nevertheless said to Daniel, "I am afraid of my lord the king; it is he who allotted your food and drink. If he sees that you look wretched by comparison with the other young men of your age, you will endanger my life with the king." [11]Then Daniel said to the steward whom the chief chamberlain had put in charge of Daniel, Hananiah, Mishael, and Azariah, [12]"Please test your servants for ten days. Give us vegetables to eat and water to drink. [13]Then see how we look in comparison with the other young men who eat from the royal table, and treat your servants according to what you see." [14]He acceded to this request, and tested them for ten days; [15]after ten days they looked healthier and better fed than any of the young men who ate from the royal table. [16]So the steward continued to take away the food and wine they were to receive, and gave them vegetables.

[17]To these four young men God gave knowledge and proficiency in all literature and science, and to Daniel the understanding of all visions and dreams. [18]At the end of the time the king had specified for their preparation, the chief chamberlain brought them before Nebuchadnezzar. [19]When the king had spoken with all of them, none was found

---

1, 2: Shinar: ancient name for Babylonia, a deliberate archaism in this text: cf Gn 10, 10; 11, 2.

1, 7: The young men are given Babylonian names as a sign of their adoption by the king.

1, 8: This defilement: the bread, meat, and wine of the Gentiles, which were unclean (Hos 9, 3; Tb 1, 12; Jdt 10, 5;

12, 1f) because they might have been offered to idols or prepared over firewood taken from a sacred grove. Only raw vegetables and water were safe from this danger (v 12).

a: 2 Kgs 24, 1; 2 Chr 36, 6; Jer 25, 1.   *b:* Dn 5, 2; Gn 10, 10; 2 Kgs 24, 2; 2 Chr 36, 7.

equal to Daniel, Hananiah, Mishael, and Azariah; and so they entered the king's service. [20]In any question of wisdom or prudence which the king put to them, he found them ten times better than all the magicians and enchanters in his kingdom. [21c]Daniel remained there until the first year of King Cyrus.[*]

See RG 337

CHAPTER 2

The King's Dream[*] [1]In the second year of his reign, King Nebuchadnezzar had a dream which left his spirit no rest and robbed him of his sleep. [2]So he ordered that the magicians, enchanters, sorcerers, and Chaldeans[*] be summoned to interpret the dream for him. When they came and presented themselves to the king, [3]he said to them, "I had a dream which will allow my spirit no rest until I know what it means." [4]The Chaldeans answered the king [Aramaic]:[*] "O king, live forever! Tell your servants the dream and we will give its meaning." [5]The king answered the Chaldeans, "This is what I have decided: unless you tell me the dream and its meaning, you shall be cut to pieces and your houses destroyed. [6]But if you tell me the dream and its meaning, you shall receive from me gifts and presents and great honors. Now tell me the dream and its meaning."

[7]Again they answered, "Let the king tell his servants the dream and we will give its meaning." [8]But the king replied: "I know for certain that you are bargaining for time, since you know what I have decided. [9]If you do not tell me the dream, there can be but one decree for you. You have framed a false and deceitful interpretation to present me with till the crisis is past. Tell me the dream, therefore, that I may be sure that you can also give its correct interpretation."

[10]The Chaldeans answered the king: "There is not a man on earth who can do what you ask, O king; never has any king,

however great and mighty, asked such a thing of any magician, enchanter, or Chaldean. [11]What you demand, O king, is too difficult; there is no one who can tell it to the king except the gods who do not dwell among men." [12]At this the king became violently angry and ordered all the wise men of Babylon to be put to death. [13]When the decree was issued that the wise men should be slain, Daniel and his companions were also sought out.

[14]Then Daniel prudently took counsel with Arioch, the captain of the king's guard, who had set out to kill the wise men of Babylon: [15]"O officer of the king," he asked, "what is the reason for this harsh order from the king?" When Arioch told him, [16]Daniel went and asked for time from the king, that he might give him the interpretation.

[17]Daniel went home and informed his companions Hananiah, Mishael, and Azariah, [18]that they might implore the mercy of the God of heaven in regard to this mystery, so that Daniel and his companions might not perish with the rest of the wise men of Babylon. [19]During the night the mystery was revealed to Daniel in a vision, and he blessed the God of heaven:

[20] "Blessed be the name of God forever and
    ever,
  for wisdom and power are his.
[21] He causes the changes of the times and
    seasons,
  makes kings and unmakes them.
He gives wisdom to the wise
  and knowledge to those who
    understand.
[22] He reveals deep and hidden things
  and knows what is in the darkness,
  for the light dwells with him.[d]
[23] To you, O God of my fathers,
  I give thanks and praise,

1, 21: The first year of King Cyrus: the year of this Persian king's conquest of Babylon, 539/8 B.C.

2, 1-49: The chronology of v 1 is in conflict with that of Dn 1, 5. 18, and in v 25 Daniel appears to be introduced to the king for the first time. It seems that the story of this chapter was originally entirely independent of chapter 1, and later retouched slightly to fit its present setting.

2, 2: Chaldeans: here probably astrologers, who were so

associated with the Chaldeans in the Hebrew mind that in the later language they are sometimes simply called by the name of that people.

2, 4: Aramaic: from Dn 2, 4 to 7, 28 the text of Daniel is in Aramaic, not Hebrew, as indicated by this gloss.

c: Dn 6, 28. *d:* Jn 1, 9; 8, 12; 1 Cor 4, 5; 1 Jn 1, 6.

The Neo-Babylonian Empire

because you have given me wisdom and power.

Now you have shown me what we asked of you,

you have made known to us the king's dream."

²⁴So Daniel went to Arioch, whom the king had appointed to destroy the wise men of Babylon, and said to him, "Do not put the wise men of Babylon to death. Bring me before the king, and I will tell him the interpretation of the dream." Arioch quickly brought Daniel to the king and said, ²⁵"I have found a man among the Judean captives who can give the interpretation to the king." ²⁶The king asked Daniel, whose name was Belteshazzar, "Can you tell me the dream that I had, and its meaning?" ²⁷In the king's presence Daniel made this reply:

"The mystery about which the king has inquired, the wise men, enchanters, magicians, and astrologers could not explain to the king. ²⁸But there is a God in heaven who reveals mysteries, and he has shown King Nebuchadnezzar what is to happen in days to come; this was the dream you saw as you lay in bed. ²⁹To you in your bed there came thoughts about what should happen in the future, and he who reveals mysteries showed you what is to be. ³⁰To me also this mystery has been revealed; not that I am wiser than any other living person, but in order that its meaning may be made known to the king, that you may understand the thoughts in your own mind.

³¹"In your vision, O king, you saw a statue, very large and exceedingly bright, terrifying in appearance as it stood before you. ³²The head of the statue was pure gold, its chest and arms were silver, its belly and thighs bronze, ³³the legs iron, its feet partly iron and partly tile.* ³⁴While you looked at the statue, a stone which was hewn from a mountain without a hand being put to it, struck its iron and tile feet, breaking them in pieces. ³⁵The iron, tile, bronze, silver, and gold all crumbled at once, fine as the chaff on

2, 33: Partly tile: terra cotta tile was much in use among the Babylonians for decoration and for actual construction.

the threshing floor in summer, and the wind blew them away without leaving a trace. But the stone that struck the statue became a great mountain and filled the whole earth.

³⁶*"This was the dream; the interpretation we shall also give in the king's presence. ³⁷You, O king, are the king of kings; to you the God of heaven has given dominion and strength, power and glory; ³⁸men, wild beasts, and birds of the air, wherever they may dwell, he has handed over to you, making you ruler over them all; you are the head of gold. ³⁹Another kingdom shall take your place, inferior to yours, then a third kingdom, of bronze, which shall rule over the whole earth. ⁴⁰There shall be a fourth kingdom, strong as iron; it shall break in pieces and subdue all these others, just as iron breaks in pieces and crushes everything else. ⁴¹The feet and toes you saw, partly of potter's tile and partly of iron, mean that it shall be a divided kingdom, but yet have some of the hardness of iron. As you saw the iron mixed with clay tile, ⁴²and the toes partly iron and partly tile, the kingdom shall be partly strong and partly fragile. ⁴³The iron mixed with clay tile means that they shall seal their alliances by intermarriage, but they shall not stay united, any more than iron mixes with clay. ⁴⁴ᵉIn the lifetime of those kings the God of heaven will set up a kingdom that shall never be destroyed or delivered up to another people; rather, it shall break in pieces all these kingdoms and put an end to them, and it shall stand forever. ⁴⁵That is the meaning of the stone you saw hewn from the mountain without a hand being put to it, which broke in pieces the tile, iron, bronze, silver, and gold. The great God has revealed to the king what shall be in the future; this is exactly what you dreamed, and its meaning is sure."

⁴⁶Then King Nebuchadnezzar fell down and worshiped Daniel and ordered sacrifice and incense offered to him. ⁴⁷To Daniel the king said, "Truly your God is the God of gods and Lord of kings and a revealer of mysteries; that is why you were able to reveal this mystery." ⁴⁸He advanced Daniel to a high post, gave him many generous presents, made him ruler of the whole province of Babylon and chief prefect over all the wise men of Babylon. ⁴⁹At Daniel's request the king made Shadrach, Meshach, and Abednego administrators of the province of Babylon, while Daniel himself remained at the king's court.

CHAPTER 3

See RG 337

The Fiery Furnace. ¹King Nebuchadnezzar had a golden statue made, sixty cubits high and six cubits wide, which he set up in the plain of Dura* in the province of Babylon. ²He then ordered the satraps,* prefects, and governors, the counselors, treasurers, judges, magistrates and all the officials of the provinces to be summoned to the dedication of the statue which he had set up. ³The satraps, prefects, and governors, the counselors, treasurers, judges, and magistrates and all the officials of the provinces, all these came together for the dedication and stood before the statue which King Nebuchadnezzar had set up. ⁴A herald cried out: "Nations and peoples of every language, when you hear the sound of the trumpet, flute, lyre, harp, psaltery,* bagpipe, and all the other musical instruments, ⁵you are ordered to fall down and worship the golden statue which King Nebuchadnezzar has set up. ⁶Whoever does not fall down and worship shall be instantly cast into a white-hot furnace."* ⁷Therefore, as soon as they heard

2, 36-45: The four successive kingdoms in this apocalyptic perspective are the Babylonian (gold), the Median (silver), the Persian (bronze), and the Hellenistic (iron). The last, after Alexander's death, was divided among his generals (vv 41f). The two resulting kingdoms, which most affected the Jews, were the dynasty of the Ptolemies in Egypt and that of the Seleucids in Syria, who tried in vain, by war and through intermarriage, to restore the unity of Alexander's empire (v 43). The stone hewn from the mountain is the messianic kingdom awaited by the Jews (vv 44f). Our Lord made this image personal to himself; cf Lk 20, 17f.

3, 1: Dura: several places in Babylonia bore this name. Probably the present reference is to one a few miles south of Babylon. Colossi of the type mentioned here were not uncommon in antiquity; a cubit was seventeen and a half inches.

3, 2: Satraps: the Persian major governors.

3, 4: Psaltery: a harplike instrument.

3, 6: Death by fire was not unknown as a punishment in Babylonia; cf Jer 29, 22.

e: Mt 21, 44; Lk 20, 18.

the sound of the trumpet, flute, lyre, harp, psaltery, bagpipe, and all the other musical instruments, the nations and peoples of every language all fell down and worshiped the golden statue which King Nebuchadnezzar had set up.

[8]At that point, some of the Chaldeans came and accused the Jews [9]to King Nebuchadnezzar: "O king, live forever! [10]O king, you issued a decree that everyone who heard the sound of the trumpet, flute, lyre, harp, psaltery, bagpipe, and all the other musical instruments should fall down and worship the golden statue; [11]whoever did not was to be cast into a white-hot furnace. [12]There are certain Jews whom you have made administrators of the province of Babylon: Shadrach, Meshach, Abednego; these men, O king, have paid no attention to you; they will not serve your god or worship the golden statue which you set up."

[13]Nebuchadnezzar flew into a rage and sent for Shadrach, Meshach, and Abednego, who were promptly brought before the king. [14]King Nebuchadnezzar questioned them: "Is it true, Shadrach, Meshach, and Abednego, that you will not serve my god, or worship the golden statue that I set up? [15]Be ready now to fall down and worship the statue I had made, whenever you hear the sound of the trumpet, flute, lyre, harp, psaltery, bagpipe, and all the other musical instruments; otherwise, you shall be instantly cast into the white-hot furnace; and who is the God that can deliver you out of my hands?" [16]Shadrach, Meshach, and Abednego answered King Nebuchadnezzar, "There is no need for us to defend ourselves before you in this matter. [17]If our God, whom we serve, can save us* from the white-hot furnace and from your hands, O king, may he save us! [18]But even if he will not, know, O king, that we will not serve your god or worship the golden statue which you set up."

[19]Nebuchadnezzar's face became livid with utter rage against Shadrach, Meshach, and Abednego. He ordered the furnace to be heated seven times more than usual [20]and had some of the strongest men in his army bind Shadrach, Meshach, and Abednego and cast them into the white-hot furnace. [21]They were bound and cast into the white-hot furnace with their coats, hats, shoes and other garments, [22]for the king's order was urgent. So huge a fire was kindled in the furnace that the flames devoured the men who threw Shadrach, Meshach, and Abednego into it. [23]But these three fell, bound, into the midst of the white-hot furnace.

[24]*They walked about in the flames, singing to God and blessing the Lord. [25]In the fire Azariah stood up and prayed aloud:

[26] "Blessed are you, and praiseworthy,
  O Lord, the God of our fathers,
  and glorious forever is your name.
[27] For you are just in all you have done;
  all your deeds are faultless, all your
   ways right,
  and all your judgments proper.
[28] You have executed proper judgments
  in all that you have brought upon us
  and upon Jerusalem, the holy city of
   our fathers.
 By a proper judgment you have done all
   this
  because of our sins;
[29] For we have sinned and transgressed
  by departing from you,
  and we have done every kind of evil.
[30] Your commandments we have not
   heeded or observed,
  nor have we done as you ordered us
   for our good.
[31] Therefore all you have brought upon us,
  all you have done to us,
  you have done by a proper judgment.
[32] You have handed us over to our enemies,
  lawless and hateful rebels;
  to an unjust king, the worst in all the
   world.
[33] Now we cannot open our mouths;
  we, your servants, who revere you,
  have become a shame and a reproach.

3, 17: If our God . . . can save us: the youths do not question the efficacy of the divine power, but whether it will be exercised (v 18).

3, 24-90: These verses are inspired additions to the Aramaic text of Daniel, translated from the Greek form of the book. They were originally composed in Hebrew or Aramaic, which has not been preserved. The church has always regarded them as part of the canonical Scriptures.

³⁴ For your name's sake, do not deliver us
    up forever,
    or make void your covenant.
³⁵ Do not take away your mercy from us,
    for the sake of Abraham, your beloved,
    Isaac your servant, and Israel your
    holy one,
³⁶ To whom you promised to multiply their
    offspring
    like the stars of heaven,
    or the sand on the shore of the sea.
³⁷ For we are reduced, O Lord, beyond any
    other nation,
    brought low everywhere in the world
    this day
    because of our sins.
³⁸ We have in our day no prince, prophet, or
    leader,
    no holocaust, sacrifice, oblation, or
    incense,
    no place to offer first fruits, to find
    favor with you.
³⁹ But with contrite heart and humble
    spirit
    let us be received;
⁴⁰ As though it were holocausts of rams and
    bullocks,
    or thousands of fat lambs,
So let our sacrifice be in your presence
    today
    as we follow you unreservedly;
    for those who trust in you cannot be
    put to shame.
⁴¹ And now we follow you with our whole
    heart,
    we fear you and we pray to you.
⁴² Do not let us be put to shame,
    but deal with us in your kindness and
    great mercy.
⁴³ Deliver us by your wonders,
    and bring glory to your name,
    O Lord:
⁴⁴ Let all those be routed
    who inflict evils on your servants;
Let them be shamed and powerless,
    and their strength broken;
⁴⁵ Let them know that you alone are the
    Lord God,
    glorious over the whole world."

⁴⁶ Now the king's men who had thrown
them in continued to stoke the furnace with
brimstone, pitch, tow, and faggots. ⁴⁷ The
flames rose forty-nine cubits above the furnace, ⁴⁸ and spread out, burning the
Chaldeans nearby. ⁴⁹ But the angel of the
Lord went down into the furnace with Azariah and his companions, drove the fiery
flames out of the furnace, ⁵⁰ and made the inside of the furnace as though a dew-laden
breeze were blowing through it. The fire in
no way touched them or caused them pain or
harm. ⁵¹ Then these three in the furnace with
one voice sang, glorifying and blessing God:

⁵² "Blessed are you, O Lord, the God of our
    fathers,
    praiseworthy and exalted above all
    forever;
    And blessed is your holy and glorious
    name,
    praiseworthy and exalted above all for
    all ages.
⁵³ Blessed are you in the temple of your
    holy glory,
    praiseworthy and glorious above all
    forever.
⁵⁴ Blessed are you on the throne of your
    kingdom,
    praiseworthy and exalted above all
    forever.
⁵⁵ Blessed are you who look into the depths
    from your throne upon the cherubim,
    praiseworthy and exalted above all
    forever.
⁵⁶ Blessed are you in the firmament of
    heaven,
    praiseworthy and glorious forever.
⁵⁷ Bless the Lord, all you works of the
    Lord,
    praise and exalt him above all forever.
⁵⁸ Angels of the Lord, bless the Lord,
    praise and exalt him above all forever.
⁵⁹ You heavens, bless the Lord,
    praise and exalt him above all forever.ᶠ
⁶⁰ All you waters above the heavens, bless
    the Lord,
    praise and exalt him above all forever.
⁶¹ All you hosts of the Lord, bless the Lord;

f: 59f: Ps 148, 4.

praise and exalt him above all forever.
⁶² Sun and moon, bless the Lord;
  praise and exalt him above all forever.
⁶³ Stars of heaven, bless the Lord;
  praise and exalt him above all forever.
⁶⁴ Every shower and dew, bless the Lord;
  praise and exalt him above all forever.
⁶⁵ All you winds, bless the Lord;
  praise and exalt him above all forever.
⁶⁶ Fire and heat, bless the Lord;
  praise and exalt him above all forever.
⁶⁷ [Cold and chill, bless the Lord;
  praise and exalt him above all forever.
⁶⁸ Dew and rain, bless the Lord;
  praise and exalt him above all forever.]
⁶⁹ Frost and chill, bless the Lord;
  praise and exalt him above all forever.
⁷⁰ Ice and snow, bless the Lord;
  praise and exalt him above all forever.
⁷¹ Nights and days, bless the Lord;
  praise and exalt him above all forever.
⁷² Light and darkness, bless the Lord;
  praise and exalt him above all forever.
⁷³ Lightnings and clouds, bless the Lord;
  praise and exalt him above all forever.
⁷⁴ Let the earth bless the Lord,
  praise and exalt him above all forever.
⁷⁵ Mountains and hills, bless the Lord;
  praise and exalt him above all forever.
⁷⁶ Everything growing from the earth, bless
    the Lord;
  praise and exalt him above all forever.
⁷⁷ You springs, bless the Lord;
  praise and exalt him above all forever.
⁷⁸ Seas and rivers, bless the Lord;
  praise and exalt him above all forever.
⁷⁹ You dolphins and all water creatures,
    bless the Lord;
  praise and exalt him above all forever.
⁸⁰ All you birds of the air, bless the Lord;
  praise and exalt him above all forever.
⁸¹ All you beasts, wild and tame, bless the
    Lord;
  praise and exalt him above all forever.
⁸² You sons of men, bless the Lord;
  praise and exalt him above all forever.
⁸³ O Israel, bless the Lord;
  praise and exalt him above all forever.
⁸⁴ Priests of the Lord, bless the Lord;

praise and exalt him above all forever.
⁸⁵ Servants of the Lord, bless the Lord;
  praise and exalt him above all forever.
⁸⁶ Spirits and souls of the just, bless the
    Lord;
  praise and exalt him above all forever.
⁸⁷ Holy men of humble heart, bless the
    Lord;
  praise and exalt him above all forever.
⁸⁸ Hananiah, Azariah, Mishael, bless the
    Lord;
  praise and exalt him above all forever.
For he has delivered us from the nether
    world,
  and saved us from the power of death;
He has freed us from the raging flame
  and delivered us from the fire.
⁸⁹ Give thanks to the Lord, for he is good,
  for his mercy endures forever.
⁹⁰ Bless the God of gods, all you who fear
    the Lord;
  praise him and give him thanks,
  because his mercy endures forever."

Hearing them sing, and astonished at seeing them alive, ⁹¹King Nebuchadnezzar rose in haste and asked his nobles, "Did we not cast three men bound into the fire?" "Assuredly, O king," they answered. ⁹²"But," he replied, "I see four men unfettered and unhurt, walking in the fire, and the fourth looks like a son of God."* ⁹³Then Nebuchadnezzar came to the opening of the white-hot furnace and called to Shadrach, Meshach, and Abednego: "Servants of the most high God, come out." Thereupon Shadrach, Meshach, and Abednego came out of the fire. ⁹⁴When the satraps, prefects, governors, and nobles of the king came together, they saw that the fire had had no power over the bodies of these men; not a hair of their heads had been singed, nor were their garments altered; there was not even a smell of fire about them. ⁹⁵Nebuchadnezzar exclaimed, "Blessed be the God of Shadrach, Meshach, and Abednego, who sent his angel to deliver the servants that trusted in him; they disobeyed the royal command and yielded their bodies rather than serve or worship any god except their own God. ⁹⁶There-

3, 92: A son of God: an angel; cf Jb 1, 6.

fore I decree for nations and peoples of every language that whoever blasphemes the God of Shadrach, Meshach, and Abednego shall be cut to pieces and his house destroyed. For there is no other God who can rescue like this." [97]Then the king promoted Shadrach, Meshach, and Abednego in the province of Babylon.

Vision of the Great Tree.[*] [98]King Nebuchadnezzar to the nations and peoples of every language, wherever they dwell on earth: abundant peace! [99]It has seemed good to me to publish the signs and wonders which the most high God[*] has accomplished in my regard.

[100]How great are his signs, how mighty his
    wonders;
  his kingdom is an everlasting
    kingdom,
  and his dominion endures through all
    generations.[g]

See RG
337

CHAPTER 4

[1]I, Nebuchadnezzar, was at home in my palace, content and prosperous. [2]I had a terrifying dream as I lay in bed, and the images and the visions of my mind frightened me. [3]So I issued a decree that all the wise men of Babylon should be brought before me to give the interpretation of the dream. [4]When the magicians, enchanters, Chaldeans, and astrologers had come in, I related the dream before them; but none of them could tell me its meaning. [5][h]Finally there came before me Daniel, whose name is Belteshazzar after the name of my god,[*] and in whom is the spirit of the holy God. I repeated the dream to him: [6]"Belteshazzar, chief of the magicians, I know that the spirit of the holy God is in you and no mys-

tery is too difficult for you; tell me the meaning of the visions that I saw in my dream.

[7]"These were the visions I saw while in bed: I saw a tree of great height at the center of the world. [8]It was large and strong, with its top touching the heavens, and it could be seen to the ends of the earth. [9]Its leaves were beautiful and its fruit abundant, providing food for all. Under it the wild beasts found shade, in its branches the birds of the air nested; all men ate of it. [10]In the vision I saw while in bed, a holy sentinel[*] came down from heaven, [11]and cried out:

[*] 'Cut down the tree and lop off its
        branches,
    strip off its leaves and scatter its fruit;
    let the beasts flee its shade, and the
        birds its branches.
[12] But leave in the earth its stump and roots,
    fettered with iron and bronze, in the
        grass of the field.
  Let him be bathed with the dew of
        heaven;
    his lot be to eat, among beasts, the
        grass of the earth.
[13] Let his mind be changed from the
        human;
    let him be given the sense of a beast,
    till seven years pass over him.
[14] By decree of the sentinels is this decided,
    by order of the holy ones, this
        sentence;
  That all who live may know
    that the Most High rules over the
        kingdom of men:
  He can give it to whom he will,
    or set over it the lowliest of men.'[i]

[15]"This is the dream that I, King Nebuchadnezzar, had. Now, Belteshazzar, tell me

---

3, 98—4, 34: This section has the form of a letter written by Nebuchadnezzar to his subjects.

3, 99: The most high God: the Jews, especially in the diaspora, used this title to distinguish their God from those of the pagans. On the lips of a polytheist (so also in v 93) it was merely the title of another god. It was an ancient divine name used in Canaan; cf Gn 14, 18.

4, 5: After the name of my god: Belteshazzar, the Babylonian name given to Daniel at the king's orders (Dn 1, 7), is Balatsuussur, "protect his life." In the king's intention, this would be an abbreviation for Bel-balatsu-ussur. It would thus include an appeal to the god Bel, originally the name of the

city god of Nippur, and later identified with Marduk, the chief god of Babylon. Daniel's use of the name would refer the prayer rather to the true God.

4, 10: A holy sentinel: an angel. This term is found in the Bible only in this chapter of Daniel, but it is common in later Jewish literature.

4, 11ff: As the tree is Nebuchadnezzar (v 19), the description passes from metaphor to the reality.

g: Dn 4, 31; 7, 14. h: Gn 41, 38. i: 1 Sm 2, 8; 16, 11; Is 62, 6.

its meaning. Although none of the wise men in my kingdom can tell me the meaning, you can, because the spirit of the holy God is in you."

[16]Then Daniel, whose name was Belteshazzar, was appalled for a while, terrified by his thoughts. "Belteshazzar," the king said to him, "let not the dream or its meaning terrify you." [17]"My lord," Belteshazzar replied, "this dream should be for your enemies, and its meaning for your foes.[*] The large, strong tree that you saw, with its top touching the heavens, that could be seen by the whole earth, [18]which had beautiful foliage and abundant fruit, providing food for all, under which the wild beasts lived, and in whose branches the birds of the air dwelt— [19]you are that tree, O king, large and strong! Your majesty has become so great as to touch the heavens, and your rule extends over the whole earth. [20]As for the king's vision of a holy sentinel that came down from heaven and proclaimed: 'Cut down the tree and destroy it, but leave in the earth its stump and roots, fettered with iron and bronze in the grass of the field; let him be bathed with the dew of heaven, and let his lot be among wild beasts till seven years pass over him'— [21]this is its meaning, O king; this is the sentence which the Most High has passed upon my lord king: [22][j]You shall be cast out from among men and dwell with wild beasts; you shall be given grass to eat like an ox and be bathed with the dew of heaven;[*] seven years shall pass over you, until you know that the Most High rules over the kingdom of men and gives it to whom he will. [23]The command that the stump and roots of the tree are to be left means that your kingdom shall be preserved for you, once you have learned it is heaven that rules. [24][k]Therefore, O king, take my advice; atone for your sins by good deeds, and for your misdeeds by kindness to the poor; then your prosperity will be long.'"[*]

[25]All this happened to King Nebuchadnezzar. [26]Twelve months later, as he was walking on the roof of the royal palace in Babylon, [27]the king said, "Babylon the great! Was it not I, with my great strength, who built it as a royal residence for my splendor and majesty?"[*] [28]While these words were still on the king's lips, a voice spoke from heaven, "It has been decreed for you, King Nebuchadnezzar, that your kingdom is taken from you! [29]You shall be cast out from among men, and shall dwell with wild beasts; you shall be given grass to eat like an ox, and seven years shall pass over you, until you learn that the Most High rules over the kingdom of men and gives it to whom he will." [30][*]At once this was fulfilled. Nebuchadnezzar was cast out from among men, he ate grass like an ox, and his body was bathed with the dew of heaven, until his hair grew like the feathers of an eagle, and his nails like the claws of a bird.

[31][l]When this period was over, I, Nebuchadnezzar, raised my eyes to heaven; my reason was restored to me, and I blessed the Most High, I praised and glorified him who lives forever:

His dominion is an everlasting dominion,
 and his kingdom endures through all
  generations.
[32] All who live on the earth are counted as
  nothing;
 he does as he pleases with the powers
  of heaven
 as well as with those who live on the
  earth.
There is no one who can stay his hand
 or say to him, "What have you done?"

4, 17: "This dream . . . for your foes": Daniel speaks as a courtier.

4, 22: The description is of a form of insanity called lycanthropy, in which the patient acts like a wolf.

4, 24: A classic Scriptural text for the efficacy of good works.

4, 27: The words attributed to the king are similar to the boastings in the royal inscriptions by which the Mesopotamian kings testified to their mighty works.

4, 30ff: There is no certainty of any such thing happening to Nebuchadnezzar as is described here. Some scholars think that the Nebuchadnezzar of this chapter is actually Nabonidus, the father of Belshazzar, who was mysteriously absent from Babylon for a number of years. The Biblical author's chief interest was not in the historicity of this popular tale, but in the object lesson it contained for the proud "divine" kings of the Seleucid dynasty.

j: Dn 5, 21. k: Sir 3, 30; 4, 8. l: Dn 3, 100; 7, 14.

[33]At the same time my reason returned to me, and for the glory of my kingdom, my majesty and my splendor returned to me. My nobles and lords sought me out; I was restored to my kingdom, and became much greater than before. [34]Therefore, I, Nebuchadnezzar, now praise and exalt and glorify the King of heaven, because all his works are right and his ways just; and those who walk in pride he is able to humble.

CHAPTER 5

See RG 337

The Writing on the Wall. [1]King Belshazzar* gave a great banquet for a thousand of his lords, with whom he drank. [2]Under the influence of the wine, he ordered the gold and silver vessels which Nebuchadnezzar, his father,* had taken from the temple in Jerusalem, to be brought in so that the king, his lords, his wives and his entertainers might drink from them. [3]When the gold and silver vessels taken from the house of God in Jerusalem had been brought in, and while the king, his lords, his wives and his entertainers were drinking [4]wine from them, they praised their gods of gold and silver, bronze and iron, wood and stone.

[5]Suddenly, opposite the lampstand, the fingers of a human hand appeared, writing on the plaster of the wall in the king's palace. When the king saw the wrist and hand that wrote, [6]his face blanched; his thoughts terrified him, his hip joints shook, and his knees knocked. [7]The king shouted for the enchanters, Chaldeans, and astrologers to be brought in. "Whoever reads this writing and tells me what it means," he said to the wise men of Babylon, "shall be clothed in purple, wear a golden collar about his neck, and be third in the government of the kingdom." [8]But though all the king's wise men came in, none of them could either read the writing or tell the king what it meant. [9]Then King Belshazzar was greatly terrified; his face went ashen, and his lords were thrown into confusion.

[10]When the queen heard of the discussion between the king and his lords, she entered the banquet hall and said, "O king, live forever! Be not troubled in mind, nor look so pale! [11]There is a man in your kingdom in whom is the spirit of the holy God; during the lifetime of your father he was seen to have brilliant knowledge and god-like wisdom. In fact, King Nebuchadnezzar, your father, made him chief of the magicians, enchanters, Chaldeans, and astrologers, [12]because of the extraordinary mind possessed by this Daniel, whom the king named Belteshazzar. He knew and understood how to interpret dreams, explain enigmas, and solve difficulties. Now therefore, summon Daniel to tell you what this means."

[13]Then Daniel was brought into the presence of the king. The king asked him, "Are you the Daniel, the Jewish exile, whom my father, the king, brought from Judah? [14]I have heard that the spirit of God is in you, that you possess brilliant knowledge and extraordinary wisdom. [15]Now, the wise men and enchanters were brought in to me to read this writing and tell me its meaning, but they could not say what the words meant. [16]But I have heard that you can interpret dreams and solve difficulties; if you are able to read the writing and tell me what it means, you shall be clothed in purple, wear a gold collar about your neck, and be third in the government of the kingdom."

[17]Daniel answered the king: "You may keep your gifts, or give your presents to someone else; but the writing I will read for you, O king, and tell you what it means. [18]The Most High God gave your father Nebuchadnezzar a great kingdom and glorious majesty. [19]Because he made him so great, the nations and peoples of every language dreaded and feared him. Whomever he wished, he killed or let live; whomever he wished, he exalted or humbled. [20]But when his heart became proud and his spirit hardened by insolence, he was put down from his royal throne and deprived of his glory; [21][m]he

---

5, 1: King Belshazzar: Belshazzar was actually the crown prince, but he had been given royal authority in Babylon by his father Nabonidus.

5, 2: Nebuchadnezzar, his father: several kings of Babylon intervened between Nebuchadnezzar and Belshazzar. Either the term father is used here in the broad sense of "remote predecessor," or the name Nebuchadnezzar is used for "Nabonidus."

m: Dn 4, 22.

was cast out from among men and was made insensate as a beast; he lived with wild asses, and ate grass like an ox; his body was bathed with the dew of heaven, until he learned that the Most High God rules over the kingdom of men and appoints over it whom he will. [22]You, his son, Belshazzar, have not humbled your heart, though you knew all this; [23]you have rebelled against the Lord of heaven. You had the vessels of his temple brought before you, so that you and your nobles, your wives and your entertainers, might drink wine from them; and you praised the gods of silver and gold, bronze and iron, wood and stone, that neither see nor hear nor have intelligence. But the God in whose hand is your life breath and the whole course of your life, you did not glorify. [24]By him were the wrist and hand sent, and the writing set down.

[25]"This is the writing that was inscribed: MENE, TEKEL, and PERES.* These words mean: [26]*MENE, God has numbered your kingdom and put an end to it; [27]TEKEL, you have been weighed on the scales and found wanting; [28]PERES, your kingdom has been divided and given to the Medes and Persians."

[29]Then by order of Belshazzar they clothed Daniel in purple, with a gold collar about his neck, and proclaimed him third in the government of the kingdom. [30]The same night Belshazzar, the Chaldean king, was slain:

CHAPTER 6

See RG 337

[1]And Darius the Mede* succeeded to the kingdom at the age of sixty-two.

In the Lions' Den. [2]Darius decided to appoint over his entire kingdom one hundred and twenty satraps, to safeguard his inter-

ests; [3]these were accountable to three supervisors, one of whom was Daniel. [4]Daniel outshone all the supervisors and satraps because an extraordinary spirit was in him, and the king thought of giving him authority over the entire kingdom. [5]Therefore the supervisors and satraps tried to find grounds for accusation against Daniel as regards the administration. But they could accuse him of no wrongdoing; because he was trustworthy, no fault of neglect or misconduct was to be found in him. [6]Then these men said to themselves, "We shall find no grounds for accusation against this Daniel unless by way of the law of his God." [7]So these supervisors and satraps went thronging to the king and said to him, "King Darius, live forever! [8]nAll the supervisors of the kingdom, the prefects, satraps, nobles, and governors are agreed that the following prohibition ought to be put in force by royal decree: no one is to address any petition to god or man for thirty days, except to you, O king; otherwise he shall be cast into a den of lions. [9]Now, O king, issue the prohibition over your signature, immutable and irrevocable* under Mede and Persian law." [10]So King Darius signed the prohibition and made it law.

[11]Even after Daniel heard that this law had been signed, he continued his custom of going home to kneel in prayer and give thanks to his God in the upper chamber three times a day, with the windows open toward Jerusalem. [12]So these men rushed in and found Daniel praying and pleading before his God. [13]Then they went to remind the king about the prohibition: "Did you not decree, O king, that no one is to address a petition to god or man for thirty days, except to you, O

5, 25: MENE, TEKEL, and PERES: these seem to be the Aramaic names of weights and monetary values: the mina, the shekel (the sixtieth part of a mina), and the parsu (a half-mina).

5, 26ff: Daniel interprets these three terms by a play on the words: Mene, connected with the verb meaning to number; Tekel, with the verb meaning to weigh; Peres, with the verb meaning to divide. There is also a play on the last term with the word for Persians.

6, 1: Darius the Mede: unknown in profane history. The Median kingdom had already been conquered by Cyrus the Persian, and it was Cyrus who captured Babylon. Evidently the author of Daniel has deliberately adopted an apocalyptic

view of history, derived from prophecy (cf Is 13, 17ff; Jer 51, 11. 28ff), according to which the Medes formed the second of four world kingdoms preceding the messianic times; see note on Dn 2, 36-45. The character of Darius the Mede has probably been modeled on that of the Persian king Darius the Great (552–486 B.C.), the second successor of Cyrus.

6, 9: Immutable and irrevocable: the passages in Est 1, 19 and 8, 8 also refer to the immutability of Medo-Persian laws. The historian Diodorus Siculus indicates that such a concept existed in the time of Darius III (335–331 B.C.), the last of the Persian kings. Cf vv 13. 16.

n: Est 1, 19.

king; otherwise he shall be cast into a den of lions?" The king answered them, "The decree is absolute, irrevocable under the Mede and Persian law." *14*To this they replied, "Daniel, the Jewish exile, has paid no attention to you, O king, or to the decree you issued; three times a day he offers his prayer." *15*The king was deeply grieved at this news and he made up his mind to save Daniel; he worked till sunset to rescue him. *16*But these men insisted. "Keep in mind, O king," they said, "that under the Mede and Persian law every royal prohibition or decree is irrevocable." *17*So the king ordered Daniel to be brought and cast into the lions' den.* To Daniel he said, "May your God, whom you serve so constantly, save you." *18*To forestall any tampering, the king sealed with his own ring and the rings of the lords the stone that had been brought to block the opening of the den.

*19*Then the king returned to his palace for the night; he refused to eat and he dismissed the entertainers. Since sleep was impossible for him, *20*the king rose very early the next morning and hastened to the lions' den. *21*As he drew near, he cried out to Daniel sorrowfully, "O Daniel, servant of the living God, has the God whom you serve so constantly been able to save you from the lions?" *22o*Daniel answered the king: "O king, live forever! *23*My God has sent his angel and closed the lions' mouths so that they have not hurt me. For I have been found innocent before him; neither to you have I done any harm, O king!" *24*This gave the king great joy. At his order Daniel was removed from the den, unhurt because he trusted in his God. *25*The king then ordered the men who had accused Daniel, along with their chil-

dren and their wives, to be cast into the lions' den. Before they reached the bottom of the den, the lions overpowered them and crushed all their bones.

*26*Then King Darius wrote to the nations and peoples of every language, wherever they dwell on the earth: "All peace to you! *27*I decree that throughout my royal domain the God of Daniel is to be reverenced and feared:

"For he is the living God, enduring
forever;
his kingdom shall not be destroyed,
and his dominion shall be without end.
28 He is a deliverer and savior,
working signs and wonders in heaven
and on earth,
and he delivered Daniel from the
lions' power."*p*

*29*So Daniel fared well during the reign of Darius and the reign of Cyrus the Persian.

II: Daniel's Visions

CHAPTER 7

See RG 338–42

*Vision of the Four Beasts.** *1*In the first year of King Belshazzar of Babylon, Daniel had a dream as he lay in bed, and was terrified by the visions of his mind. Then he wrote down the dream; the account began: *2*In the vision I saw during the night, suddenly the four winds of heaven stirred up the great sea,* *3*from which emerged four immense beasts, each different from the others. *4*The first was like a lion, but with eagle's wings.* While I watched, the wings were plucked; it was raised from the ground to stand on two feet like a man, and given a human mind. *5*The second was like a bear;*

6, 17: The lions' den: a pit too deep to be easily scaled; its opening was blocked with a stone (v 18).

7, 1-27: The significance of this vision is the same as that of Nebuchadnezzar's dream in chapter 2; see note on Dn 2, 36-45. To the four succeeding world kingdoms, Babylonian, Median, Persian, and Greek, is opposed the messianic kingdom of the people of God. The imagery of this chapter has been used extensively in the Revelation of St. John, where it is applied to the Roman empire, the persecutor of the church.

7, 2: The great sea: the primordial ocean beneath the earth, according to primitive cosmology (Gn 7, 11; 49, 25). This was thought to contain various monsters (Is 27, 1; Jb 7, 12), and in particular mythological monsters symbolizing the

chaos which God had vanquished in ancient times (Jb 9, 13; 26, 13; etc.).

7, 4: The representation of the Babylonian empire as a winged lion, a common motif in Babylonian art, symbolizes the bestial power hostile to God. The two wings that are plucked represent Nebuchadnezzar and Belshazzar. On two feet like a man . . . a human mind: contrasts with what is said in Dn 4, 13. 30.

7, 5: A bear: represents the Median empire, its three tusks symbolizing its destructive nature; hence, the command: "Up, devour much flesh."

---

o: 1 Mc 2, 60. *p:* Dn 1, 21.

it was raised up on one side, and among the teeth in its mouth were three tusks. It was given the order, "Up, devour much flesh." ⁶After this I looked and saw another beast, like a leopard;* on its back were four wings like those of a bird, and it had four heads. To this beast dominion was given. ⁷After this, in the visions of the night I saw the fourth beast,* different from all the others, terrifying, horrible, and of extraordinary strength; it had great iron teeth with which it devoured and crushed, and what was left it trampled with its feet. ⁸I was considering the ten horns it had, when suddenly another, a little horn, sprang out of their midst, and three of the previous horns were torn away to make room for it. This horn had eyes like a man, and a mouth that spoke arrogantly. ⁹*As I watched,

Thrones were set up
and the Ancient One took his throne.
His clothing was snow bright,
and the hair on his head as white as wool;
His throne was flames of fire,
with wheels of burning fire.
¹⁰ A surging stream of fire
flowed out from where he sat;
Thousands upon thousands were ministering to him,
and myriads upon myriads attended him.�q

The court was convened, and the books were opened. ¹¹I watched, then, from the first of the arrogant words which the horn spoke, until the beast was slain and its body thrown into the fire to be burnt up. ¹²The other beasts, which also lost their dominion, were granted a prolongation of life for a time and a season. ¹³As the visions during the night continued, I saw

One like a son of man* coming,
on the clouds of heaven;
When he reached the Ancient One
and was presented before him,
¹⁴ He received dominion, glory, and kingship;
nations and peoples of every language serve him.
His dominion is an everlasting dominion
that shall not be taken away,
his kingship shall not be destroyed.ʳ

¹⁵I, Daniel, found my spirit anguished within its sheath of flesh, and I was terrified by the visions of my mind. ¹⁶I approached one of those present and asked him what all this meant in truth; in answer, he made known to me the meaning of the things: ¹⁷"These four great beasts stand for four kingdoms which shall arise on the earth. ¹⁸But the holy ones of the Most High shall receive the kingship, to possess it forever and ever."

¹⁹But I wished to make certain about the fourth beast, so very terrible and different from the others, devouring and crushing with its iron teeth and bronze claws, and trampling with its feet what was left; ²⁰about the ten horns on its head, and the other one that sprang up, before which three horns fell; about the horn with the eyes and the mouth that spoke arrogantly, which appeared greater than its fellows. ²¹For, as I watched, that horn made war against the holy ones and was victorious ²²until the Ancient One arrived; judgment was pronounced in favor of the holy ones of the Most High, and the time came when the holy ones possessed the kingdom. ²³He answered me thus:

7, 6: A leopard: used to symbolize the swiftness with which Cyrus the Persian established his kingdom. Four heads: corresponding to the four Persian kings of Dn 11, 2.

7, 7f: Alexander's empire was different from all the others in that it was Western rather than Oriental in inspiration. The ten horns represent the kings of the Seleucid dynasty, the only part of the Hellenistic empire that concerned the author. The little horn is Antiochus IV Epiphanes (175–163 B.C.), the worst of the Seleucid kings, who usurped the throne.

7, 9f: A vision of the heavenly throne of God (the Ancient One), who sits in judgment (symbolized by fire) over the nations. Some of the details of the vision, depicting the divine majesty and omnipotence, are to be found in Ez 1.

7, 13f: One like a son of man: in contrast to the worldly kingdoms opposed to God, which appear as beasts, the glorified people of God that will form his kingdom on earth is represented in human form (v 18). Just as our Lord applied the figure of the stone hewn from the mountain to himself (Dn 2, 36-45), he also made the title, "Son of Man" his most characteristic way of referring to himself, as the One in whom and through whom the salvation of God's people came to be realized.

q: Rv 5, 11.   r: Dn 3, 100; 4, 31; Mi 4, 7; Lk 1, 32.

"The fourth beast shall be a fourth
kingdom on earth,
different from all the others;
It shall devour the whole earth,
beat it down, and crush it.
24 The ten horns shall be ten kings
rising out of that kingdom;
another shall rise up after them,
Different from those before him,
who shall lay low three kings.
25 He shall speak against the Most High
and oppress the holy ones of the Most
High,
thinking to change the feast days and
the law.*
They shall be handed over to him
for a year, two years, and a half-year.
26 But when the court is convened,
and his power is taken away
by final and absolute destruction,
27 Then the kingship and dominion and
majesty
of all the kingdoms under the heavens
shall be given to the holy people of the
Most High,
Whose kingdom shall be everlasting:
all dominions shall serve and obey him."

28The report concluded: I, Daniel, was
greatly terrified by my thoughts, and my face
blanched, but I kept the matter to myself.*

See RG 338-42

CHAPTER 8

Vision of the Ram and He-goat. [1] After this first vision, I, Daniel, had another, in
the third year of the reign of King Belshazzar. 2In my vision I saw myself in the
fortress of Susa* in the province of Elam; I
was beside the river Ulai. 3I looked up and
saw standing by the river a ram with two
great horns, the one larger and newer than
the other. 4I saw the ram butting toward the
west, north, and south. No beast could withstand it or be rescued from its power; it did
what it pleased and became very powerful.

5As I was reflecting, a he-goat with a
prominent horn on its forehead suddenly
came from the west across the whole earth
without touching the ground. 6It approached
the two-horned ram I had seen standing by the
river, and rushed toward it with savage force.
7I saw it attack the ram with furious blows
when they met, and break both its horns. It
threw the ram, which had not the force to
withstand it, to the ground, and trampled upon
it; and no one could rescue it from its power.

8The he-goat became very powerful, but at
the height of its power the great horn was
shattered, and in its place came up four others,
facing the four winds of heaven. 9Out of one
of them came a little horn* which kept growing toward the south, the east, and the glorious
country. 10Its power extended to the host of
heaven,* so that it cast down to earth some of
the host and some of the stars and trampled on
them. 11It boasted even against the prince of
the host, from whom it removed the daily sacrifice, and whose sanctuary it cast down, 12as
well as the host, while sin replaced the daily
sacrifice. It cast truth to the ground, and was
succeeding in its undertaking.

13I heard a holy one speaking, and another
said to whichever one it was that spoke,
"How long shall the events of this vision last
concerning the daily sacrifice, the desolating
sin* which is placed there, the sanctuary, and

7, 25: The reference is to the persecutions of Antiochus IV
and his attempt to force the Jews to give up their customs and
to adopt Hellenistic ways (1 Mc 1, 33f). A year, two years,
and a half-year: an indefinite, evil period of time. As seven is
the Jewish "perfect" number, half of it signifies great imperfection. Actually, this corresponds fairly accurately to the duration of Antiochus' persecution.

7, 28: This verse ends the Aramaic part of the Book of
Daniel.

8, 1-27: This vision repeats the major part of the preceding one, though in a more explicit fashion. As explained in vv
20ff, the two-horned ram represents the combined kingdom
of the Medes and Persians, destroyed by Alexander's Hellenistic empire originating in the west. Once again the author
is interested only in the Seleucid dynasty, which emerged

from the dissolution of Alexander's empire after his death in
323 B.C.

8, 2: The fortress of Susa: the royal palace of the Persian
kings in the ancient territory of Elam, east of Babylonia. The
river Ulai: a canal along the northern side of Susa.

8, 9: The little horn, as in chapter 7, is Antiochus IV. The
glorious country: Palestine.

8, 10ff: The host of heaven: ordinarily meaning the stars,
here refers to the people of God; cf Dn 12, 3. The prince of
the host: God himself, with whose holy religion Antiochus in-
terfered (1 Mc 1, 45).

8, 13: The desolating sin: the Hebrew contains a wordplay
(shomem) on the name Baal Shamem ("lord of the heavens,"
the Greek Zeus Olympios), referring to the statue with which
Antiochus profaned the temple of Jerusalem (2 Mc 6, 2).

Alexander's Empire

the trampled host?" [14]He answered him, "For two thousand three hundred evenings and mornings; then the sanctuary shall be purified."

[15]While I, Daniel, sought the meaning of the vision I had seen, a manlike figure stood before me, [16]and on the Ulai I heard a human voice that cried out, "Gabriel,* explain the vision to this man." [17]When he came near where I was standing, I fell prostrate in terror. But he said to me, "Understand, son of man, that the vision refers to the end time."* [18]As he spoke to me, I fell forward in a faint; he touched me and made me stand up. [19]"I will show you," he said, "what is to happen later in the period of wrath; for at the appointed time, there will be an end.

[20]"The two-horned ram you saw represents the kings of the Medes and Persians. [21]The he-goat is the king of the Greeks, and the great horn on its forehead is the first king. [22]The four that rose in its place when it was broken are four kingdoms that will issue from his nation, but without his strength.

[23]"After their reign,
    when sinners have reached their
      measure,
There shall arise a king, impudent
    and skilled in intrigue.
[24]He shall be strong and powerful,
    bring about fearful ruin,
    and succeed in his undertaking.
He shall destroy powerful peoples;
[25]   his cunning shall be against the holy
      ones,
   his treacherous conduct shall
      succeed.
He shall be proud of heart
    and destroy many by stealth.
But when he rises against the prince of
      princes,
   he shall be broken without a hand
      being raised.

8, 16: The angel Gabriel is mentioned here for the first time in the Bible. There is wordplay in the preceding verse on ge-ber—manlike figure.

8, 17: The end time: the day of the Lord, when God sits in judgment on his enemies (v 19).

²⁶ The vision of the evenings and the
  mornings
  is true, as spoken;
Do you, however, keep this vision
  undisclosed,
  because the days are to be many."

²⁷I, Daniel, was weak and ill for some days; then I arose and took care of the king's affairs. But I was appalled at the vision, which I could not understand.

CHAPTER 9

Gabriel and the Seventy Weeks. ¹It was the first year that Darius,* son of Ahasuerus, of the race of the Medes, reigned over the kingdom of the Chaldeans; ^{2s}in the first year of his reign I, Daniel, tried to understand in the Scriptures the counting of the years of which the LORD spoke to the prophet Jeremiah: that for the ruins of Jerusalem seventy years* must be fulfilled.

³I turned to the Lord God, pleading in earnest prayer, with fasting, sackcloth, and ashes. ^{4t}I prayed to the LORD, my God, and confessed, "Ah, Lord, great and awesome God, you who keep your merciful covenant toward those who love you and observe your commandments! ^{5u}We have sinned, been wicked and done evil; we have rebelled and departed from your commandments and your laws. ⁶We have not obeyed your servants the prophets, who spoke in your name to our kings, our princes, our fathers, and all the people of the land. ⁷Justice, O Lord, is on your side; we are shamefaced even to this day: the men of Judah, the residents of Jerusalem, and all Israel, near and far, in all the countries to which you have scattered them because of their treachery toward you. ⁸O LORD, we are shamefaced, like our kings, our princes, and our fathers, for having sinned against you. ⁹But yours, O Lord, our God, are

compassion and forgiveness! Yet we rebelled against you ¹⁰and paid no heed to your command, O LORD, our God, to live by the law you gave us through your servants the prophets. ^{11v}Because all Israel transgressed your law and went astray, not heeding your voice, the sworn malediction, recorded in the law of Moses, the servant of God, was poured out over us for our sins. ¹²You carried out the threats you spoke against us and against those who governed us, by bringing upon us in Jerusalem the greatest calamity that has ever occurred under heaven. ¹³As it is written* in the law of Moses, this calamity came full upon us. As we did not appease the Lord, our God, by turning back from our wickedness and recognizing his constancy, ¹⁴so the Lord kept watch over the calamity and brought it upon us. You, O LORD, our God, are just in all that you have done, for we did not listen to your voice.

^{15w}"Now, O Lord, our God, who led your people out of the land of Egypt with a strong hand, and made a name for yourself even to this day, we have sinned, we are guilty. ¹⁶O Lord, in keeping with all your just deeds, let your anger and your wrath be turned away from your city Jerusalem, your holy mountain. On account of our sins and the crimes of our fathers, Jerusalem and your people have become the reproach of all our neighbors. ¹⁷Hear, therefore, O God, the prayer and petition of your servant; and for your own sake, O Lord, let your face shine upon your desolate sanctuary. ^{18x}Give ear, O my God, and listen; open your eyes and see our ruins and the city which bears your name. When we present our petition before you, we rely not on our just deeds, but on your great mercy. ¹⁹O Lord, hear! O Lord, pardon! O Lord, be attentive and act without delay, for your own sake, O my God, because this city and your people bear your name!"

9, 1: Darius: see the note on Dn 6, 1.

9, 2: Seventy years: the prophet Jeremiah (25, 11; 29, 10) prophesied a Babylonian captivity of seventy years, a round number signifying the complete passing away of the existing generation. Jeremiah's prophecy was fulfilled in the capture of Babylon by Cyrus and the subsequent return of the Jews to Palestine. However, the author of Daniel, living during the persecution of Antiochus, sees the conditions of the exile still existing; therefore in his mediation he extends Jeremiah's

number to seventy weeks of years (v 24, i.e., seven times seventy years, to characterize the Jewish victory over the Seleucids as the ultimate fulfillment of the prophecy.

9, 13: As it is written: the first time that this formula of Scriptural citation is used in the Bible. The reference (v 11) is to the sanctions of Lv 26, 14ff; Dt 28, 15ff.

s: 2f: Jer 25, 11; 29, 10. t: Neh 1, 5. u: Bar 1, 17. v: Dt 27, 15. w: Bar 2, 11; Ex 14, 22. x: Jer 25, 29.

[20]I was still occupied with my prayer, confessing my sin and the sin of my people Israel, presenting my petition to the LORD, my God, on behalf of his holy mountain— [21]yI was still occupied with this prayer, when Gabriel, the one whom I had seen before in vision, came to me in rapid flight at the time of the evening sacrifice.* [22]He instructed me in these words: "Daniel, I have now come to give you understanding. [23]When you began your petition, an answer was given which I have come to announce, because you are beloved. Therefore, mark the answer and understand the vision.

[24] "Seventy weeks* are decreed
for your people and for your holy city:
Then transgression will stop and sin will
end,
guilt will be expiated,
Everlasting justice will be introduced,
vision and prophecy ratified,
and a most holy will be anointed.
[25]   Know and understand this:
From the utterance of the word
that Jerusalem was to be rebuilt*
Until one who is anointed and a leader,
there shall be seven weeks.
During sixty-two weeks
it shall be rebuilt,

With streets and trenches,
in time of affliction.
[26] After the sixty-two weeks
an anointed* shall be cut down
when he does not possess the city;
And the people of a leader who will
come
shall destroy the sanctuary.
Then the end shall come like a torrent;
until the end there shall be war,
the desolation that is decreed.
[27] For one week* he shall make
a firm compact with the many;
Half the week
he shall abolish sacrifice and oblation;
On the temple wing shall be the horrible
abomination
until the ruin that is decreed
is poured out upon the horror."z

CHAPTER 10

See RG 338–42

*Vision of the Hellenistic Wars.** [1]In the third year of Cyrus, king of Persia, a revelation was given to Daniel, who had been named Belteshazzar. The revelation was certain: a great war; he understood it from the vision. [2]In those days, I, Daniel, mourned* three full weeks. [3]I ate no savory food, I took no meat or wine, and I did not anoint myself at all until the end of the three weeks.

9, 21: At the time of the evening sacrifice: between three and four in the afternoon.
9, 24: Seventy weeks: i. e., of years. Just as Jeremiah's seventy years was an approximation (see note on v 2), the four hundred and ninety years here is not to be taken literally. Similarly, the distribution of the "weeks" in the following verses indicates only relative proportions of the total figure. A most holy: an expression used almost always of an object, the altar or the temple, but once (1 Chr 23, 13) of Aaron the high priest. The author sees the definitive establishment of the kingdom of God, realized in the reconsecration of the temple after Antiochus' desecration, or personified in the holy community (like the Son of Man of chapter 7). The Fathers of the church almost unanimously understood the reference to be to Christ, the final realization of the prophecy.
9, 25: From the utterance . . . to be rebuilt: from the time of Jeremiah's prophecy. One . . . anointed and a leader: either Cyrus, who was called the anointed of the Lord to end the exile (Is 45, 1), or the high priest Joshua, who presided over the rebuilding of the altar of sacrifice after the exile (Ezr 3, 2). Seven weeks: forty-nine years, an approximation of the time of the exile. During sixty-two weeks . . . rebuilt: a period of 434 years, roughly approximating the interval between the rebuilding of Jerusalem after the exile and the beginning of the Seleucid persecution.

9, 26: An anointed: doubtless the high priest Onias III, murdered in 171 B.C., from which the author dates the beginning of the persecution. Onias was in exile when he was killed. A leader: Antiochus IV.
9, 27: One week: the final phase of the period in view, the time of Antiochus' persecution; he is Antiochus himself. The many: the faithless Jews who allied themselves with the heathen; cf 1 Mc 1, 11ff. Half the week: three and a half years; see note on Dn 7, 25. The temple was desecrated by Antiochus from 167 to 165 B.C. The temple wing: probably the main portal. The horrible abomination: see note on Dn 8, 13. Perhaps an inscription was placed on the portal of the temple dedicating it to the Olympian Zeus. Our Lord referred to this passage in his own prediction of the destruction of Jerusalem (Mt 24, 15).
10, 1—12, 13: This final vision repeats some of the material contained in the others. It is concerned with history of the worldly kingdoms from the time of Cyrus to the defeat of the tyrant Antiochus.
10, 2: Mourned: perhaps the author intends to recall the interruption in the rebuilding of the temple, which occurred during this time (Ezr 4, 1-4).

y: Dn 8, 16.   z: Mt 24, 15; 2 Mc 6, 2.

[4]On the twenty-fourth day of the first month* I was on the bank of the great river, the Tigris. [5]As I looked up, I saw a man* dressed in linen with a belt of fine gold around his waist. [6]His body was like chrysolite, his face shone like lightning, his eyes were like fiery torches, his arms and feet looked like burnished bronze, and his voice sounded like the roar of a multitude. [7]I alone, Daniel, saw the vision; but great fear seized the men who were with me; they fled and hid themselves, although they did not see the vision. [8]So I was left alone, seeing this great vision. No strength remained in me; I turned the color of death and was powerless. [9]When I heard the sound of his voice, I fell face forward in a faint.

[10]But then a hand touched me, raising me to my hands and knees. [11]"Daniel, beloved," he said to me, "understand the words which I am speaking to you; stand up, for my mission now is to you." When he said this to me, I stood up trembling. [12]"Fear not, Daniel," he continued; "from the first day you made up your mind to acquire understanding and humble yourself before God, your prayer was heard. Because of it I started out, [13]but the prince of the kingdom of Persia* stood in my way for twenty-one days, until finally Michael, one of the chief princes, came to help me. I left him there with the prince of the kings of Persia, [14]and came to make you understand what shall happen to your people in the days to come; for there is yet a vision concerning those days."

[15]While he was speaking thus to me, I fell forward and kept silent. [16]Then something like a man's hand touched my lips; I opened my mouth and said to the one facing me, "My lord, I was seized with pangs at the vision and I was powerless. [17]How can my lord's servant speak with you, my lord? For now no strength or even breath is left in me." [18]The one who looked like a man touched me again and strengthened me, saying, [19]"Fear not, beloved, you are safe; take courage and be strong." [20]When he spoke to me, I grew strong and said, "Speak, my lord, for you have strengthened me." "Do you know," he asked, "why I have come to you? Soon I must fight the prince of Persia again. When I leave, the prince of Greece will come; [21a]but I shall tell you what is written in the truthful book. No one supports me against all these except Michael, your prince, [1]standing* as a reinforcement and a bulwark for me. [2]Now I shall tell you the truth.

CHAPTER 11

See RG 338-42

"Three kings of Persia* are yet to come; and a fourth shall acquire the greatest riches of all. Strengthened by his riches, he shall rouse all the kingdom of Greece. [3]But a powerful king shall appear and rule with great might, doing as he pleases. [4]No sooner shall he appear than his kingdom shall be broken and divided in the four directions under heaven; but not among his descendants or in keeping with his mighty rule, for his kingdom shall be torn to pieces and belong to others than they.

[5]*"The king of the south shall grow strong, but one of his princes shall grow stronger still and govern a domain greater than his. [6]After some years they shall become allies: the daughter of the king of the

10, 4: The first month: the month Nisan (mid-March to mid-April).

10, 5f: The heavenly person of the vision is probably the angel Gabriel, as in Dn 9, 21. Chrysolite: or topaz, a yellowish precious stone.

10, 13: The prince of the kingdom of Persia: the guardian angel of Persia. The later Judaism ascribed protecting angels to various groups of human society, often as little more than personifications. Michael: the angel who is the protector of God's people (v 21).

11, 1f: Standing . . . truth: these are the first two verses of ch 11.

11, 2-4: The three kings of Persia who follow Cyrus are uncertain, since there were more than three Persian kings between Cyrus and the dissolution of the kingdom. The fourth is doubt-

less Xerxes I (486–465 B.C.), the great campaigner against Greece. The powerful king is Alexander the Great, who ended the Persian empire by his victory at Issus in 333 B.C.

11, 5-45: These verses describe the dynastic histories of the Ptolemies in Egypt (the king of the south) and the Seleucids in Syria (the king of the north), the two divisions of the Hellenistic empire that were of interest to the author (v 6). In vv 10-20 is described the struggle between the two kingdoms for the control of Palestine, in which the Seleucids were eventually victorious. The reference in v 20 is to Seleucus IV, who sent Heliodorus to plunder the temple treasure in Jerusalem (2 Mc 3). Finally, vv 21-45 describe the career of Antiochus IV and his persecution, in details that have been seen above.

a: Rv 12, 7.

south shall come to the king of the north in the interest of peace. But her bid for power shall fail: and her line shall not be recognized, and she shall be given up, together with those who brought her, her son and her husband. But later [7] a descendant of her line shall succeed to his rank, and shall come against the rampart and enter the stronghold of the king of the north, and conquer them. [8] Even their gods, with their molten images and their precious vessels of silver and gold, he shall carry away as booty into Egypt. For years he shall have nothing to do with the king of the north. [9] Then the latter shall invade the land of the king of the south, and return to his own country.

[10] "But his sons shall prepare and assemble a great armed host, which shall advance like a flood, then withdraw. When it returns and surges around the stronghold, [11] the king of the south, provoked, shall go out to fight against the king of the north, whose great host shall make a stand but shall be given into his hand [12] and be carried off. In the pride of his heart, he shall lay low tens of thousands, but he shall not triumph. [13] For the king of the north shall raise another army, greater than before; after some years he shall attack with this large army and great resources. [14] [b] In those times many shall resist the king of the south, and outlaws of your people shall rise up in fulfillment of vision, but they shall fail. [15] When the king of the north comes, he shall set up siegeworks and take the fortified city by storm. The power of the south shall not withstand him, and not even his picked troops shall have the strength to resist. [16] He shall attack him and do as he pleases, with no one to withstand him. He shall stop in the glorious land, dealing destruction. [17] He shall set himself to penetrate the entire strength of his kingdom. He shall conclude an agreement with him and give him a daughter in marriage in order to destroy the kingdom, but this shall not succeed in his favor. [18] He shall turn to the coastland and take many, but a leader shall

put an end to his shameful conduct, so that he cannot renew it against him. [19] He shall turn to the strongholds of his own land, but shall stumble and fall, to be found no more. [20] In his stead one shall arise who will send a tax collector through the glorious kingdom, but he shall soon be destroyed, though not in conflict or in battle.

[21] "There shall rise in his place a despicable person, to whom the royal insignia shall not be given. By stealth and fraud he shall seize the kingdom. [22] Armed might shall be completely overwhelmed by him and crushed, and even the prince of the covenant. [23] After allying with him, he shall treacherously rise to power with a small party. [24] By stealth he shall enter prosperous provinces and do that which his fathers or grandfathers never did; he shall distribute spoil, booty, and riches among them and devise plots against their strongholds; but only for a time. [25] He shall call on his strength and cleverness to meet the king of the south with a great army; the king of the south shall prepare for battle with a very large and strong army, but he shall not succeed because of the plots devised against him. [26] Even his table companions shall seek to destroy him, his army shall be overwhelmed, and many shall fall slain. [27] The two kings, resolved on evil, shall sit at table together and exchange lies, but they shall have no success, because the appointed end is not yet.

[28] "He shall turn back toward his land with great riches, his mind set against the holy covenant; he shall arrange matters and return to his land. [29] At the time appointed he shall come again to the south, but this time it shall not be as before. [30] When ships of the Kittim* confront him, he shall lose heart and retreat. Then he shall direct his rage and energy against the holy covenant; those who forsake it he shall once more single out. [31] Armed forces shall move at his command and defile the sanctuary stronghold, abolishing the daily sacrifice and setting up the horrible abomination. [32] By his deceit he shall

---

11, 30: Kittim: originally this word meant Cypriots or other island dwellers. Here it means the Romans, who forced Antiochus to withdraw from Egypt during his second campaign there.

b: Is 19, 1.

The Ptolemaic and Seleucid Kingdoms

make some who were disloyal to the covenant apostatize; but those who remain loyal to their God shall take strong action. ³³The nation's wise men shall instruct the many; though for a time they will become victims of the sword, of flames, exile, and plunder. ³⁴When they fall, few people shall help them, but many shall join them out of treachery. ³⁵Of the wise men, some shall fall, so that the rest may be tested, refined, and purified, until the end time which is still appointed to come.

³⁶*"The king shall do as he pleases, exalting himself and making himself greater than any god; he shall utter dreadful blasphemies against the God of gods. He shall prosper only till divine wrath is ready, for what is determined must take place. ³⁷He shall have no regard for the gods of his ancestors or for the one in whom women delight; for no god shall he have regard, because he shall make himself greater than all. ³⁸Instead, he shall

give glory to the god of strongholds; a god unknown to his fathers he shall glorify with gold, silver, precious stones, and other treasures. ³⁹To defend the strongholds he shall station a people of a foreign god. Whoever acknowledges him he shall provide with abundant honor; he shall make them rule over the many and distribute the land as a reward.

⁴⁰"At the appointed time the king of the south shall come to grips with him, but the king of the north shall overwhelm him with chariots and horsemen and a great fleet, passing through the countries like a flood. ⁴¹He shall enter the glorious land and many shall fall, except Edom, Moab, and the chief part of Ammon, which shall escape from his power. ⁴²He shall extend his power over the countries, and not even the land of Egypt shall escape. ⁴³He shall control the riches of gold and silver and all the treasures of Egypt; Libya and Ethiopia shall be in his

11, 36–39: Instead of venerating Apollo, one of the gods of his ancestors, Antiochus venerated, and even identified himself with, Zeus Olympios, whom the Romans equated with the god of their fortress in Rome, Jupiter Capitolinus, the god of strongholds.

train. [44]When news from the east and the north terrifies him, he shall set out with great fury to slay and to doom many. [45]He shall pitch the tents of his royal pavilion between the sea and the glorious holy mountain, but he shall come to his end with none to help him.

CHAPTER 12

See RG 338-42

[1]"At that time there shall arise
Michael, the great prince,
guardian of your people;[c]
It shall be a time unsurpassed in distress
since nations began until that time.
At that time your people shall escape,
everyone who is found written in the
book.*
[2]Many of those who sleep
in the dust of the earth shall awake;*
Some shall live forever,
others shall be an everlasting horror
and disgrace.[d]
[3]But the wise shall shine brightly
like the splendor of the firmament,
And those who lead the many to justice
shall be like the stars forever.[e]

[4]"As for you, Daniel, keep secret the message and seal the book until the end time; many shall fall away and evil shall increase."

[5]I, Daniel, looked and saw two others, one standing on either bank of the river. [6]One of them said to the man clothed in linen, who was upstream, "How long shall it be to the end of these appalling things?" [7f]The man clothed in linen, who was upstream, lifted his right and left hands to heaven; and I heard him swear by him who lives forever that it should be for a year, two years, a half-year;* and that, when the power of the destroyer of the holy people was brought to an end, all these things should end. [8]I heard, but

I did not understand; so I asked, "My lord, what follows this?" [9]"Go, Daniel," he said, "because the words are to be kept secret and sealed until the end time. [10]Many shall be refined, purified, and tested, but the wicked shall prove wicked; none of them shall have understanding, but the wise shall have it. [11]From the time that the daily sacrifice is abolished and the horrible abomination is set up, there shall be one thousand two hundred and ninety days. [12]Blessed is the man who has patience and perseveres until the one thousand three hundred and thirty-five days. [13]Go, take your rest, you shall rise for your reward at the end of days."

III: Appendix*

CHAPTER 13

See RG 342-43

Susanna's Virtue. [1]In Babylon there lived a man named Joakim, [2]who married a very beautiful and God-fearing woman, Susanna, the daughter of Hilkiah; [3]her pious parents had trained their daughter according to the law of Moses. [4]Joakim was very rich; he had a garden near his house, and the Jews had recourse to him often because he was the most respected of them all.

[5]That year, two elders of the people were appointed judges, of whom the Lord said, "Wickedness has come out of Babylon: from the elders who were to govern the people as judges." [6]These men, to whom all brought their cases, frequented the house of Joakim. [7]When the people left at noon, Susanna used to enter her husband's garden for a walk. [8]When the old men saw her enter every day for her walk, they began to lust for her. [9]They suppressed their consciences; they would not allow their eyes to look to heaven, and did not keep in mind just judgments. [10]Though both were enamored of her, they did not tell each other their trouble, [11]for

---

12, 1: Written in the book: the book of God's predestination.

12, 2: The first Israelites who have fallen (Dn 11, 33ff) shall awake, that is, rise to live forever. A resurrection of the wicked as in later, Christian teaching (Jn 5, 28f) is implied here if the others are included in the many; but cf Is 66, 24.

12, 7: A year, two years, a half-year: see note on Dn 7, 25. The author's perspective is the end of Antiochus and beyond, the final consummation of all things.

13, 1—14, 42: The short stories in these two chapters may have originally been about some other Daniel or Daniels than the hero of the main part of the book. They exist now only in Greek, but probably were first composed in Hebrew or Aramaic. They are excluded from the Jewish canon of Scripture, but the church as always included them among the inspired writings.

c: Rv 12, 7.   *d:* Mt 25, 46; Jn 5, 29.   *e:* Wis 3, 7.   *f:* Rv 10, 5f.

they were ashamed to reveal their lustful desire to have her. *12*Day by day they watched eagerly for her. *13*One day they said to each other, "Let us be off for home, it is time for lunch." So they went out and parted; *14*but both turned back, and when they met again, they asked each other the reason. They admitted their lust, and then they agreed to look for an occasion when they could meet her alone.

*15*One day, while they were waiting for the right moment, she entered the garden as usual, with two maids only. She decided to bathe, for the weather was warm. *16*Nobody else was there except the two elders, who had hidden themselves and were watching her. *17*"Bring me oil and soap," she said to the maids, "and shut the garden doors while I bathe." *18*They did as she said; they shut the garden doors and left by the side gate to fetch what she had ordered, unaware that the elders were hidden inside.

*19*As soon as the maids had left, the two old men got up and hurried to her. *20*"Look," they said, "the garden doors are shut, and no one can see us; give in to our desire, and lie with us. *21*If you refuse, we will testify against you that you dismissed your maids because a young man was here with you."

22"I am completely trapped," Susanna groaned. "If I yield, it will be my death; if I refuse, I cannot escape your power. *23*Yet it is better for me to fall into your power without guilt than to sin before the Lord." *24*Then Susanna shrieked, and the old men also shouted at her, *25*as one of them ran to open the garden doors. *26*When the people in the house heard the cries from the garden, they rushed in by the side gate to see what had happened to her. *27*At the accusations by the old men, the servants felt very much ashamed, for never had any such thing been said about Susanna.

*28*When the people came to her husband Joakim the next day, the two wicked elders also came, fully determined to put Susanna to death. Before all the people they ordered: *29*"Send for Susanna, the daughter of Hilkiah, the wife of Joakim." When she was sent for, *30*she came with her parents, children and all her relatives. *31*Susanna, very

delicate and beautiful, *32*was veiled; but those wicked men ordered her to uncover her face so as to sate themselves with her beauty. *33*All her relatives and the onlookers were weeping.

*34*In the midst of the people the two elders rose up and laid their hands on her head. *35*Through her tears she looked up to heaven, for she trusted in the Lord wholeheartedly. *36*The elders made this accusation: "As we were walking in the garden alone, this woman entered with two girls and shut the doors of the garden, dismissing the girls. *37*A young man, who was hidden there, came and lay with her. *38*When we, in a corner of the garden, saw this crime, we ran toward them. *39*We saw them lying together, but the man we could not hold, because he was stronger than we; he opened the doors and ran off. *40*Then we seized this one and asked who the young man was, *41*but she refused to tell us. We testify to this." The assembly believed them, since they were elders and judges of the people, and they condemned her to death.

*42*But Susanna cried aloud: "O eternal God, you know what is hidden and are aware of all things before they come to be: *43*you know that they have testified falsely against me. Here I am about to die, though I have done none of the things with which these wicked men have charged me."

*44*The Lord heard her prayer. *45*As she was being led to execution, God stirred up the holy spirit of a young boy named Daniel, *46*and he cried aloud: "I will have no part in the death of this woman." *47*All the people turned and asked him, "What is this you are saying?" *48*He stood in their midst and continued, "Are you such fools, O Israelites! To condemn a woman of Israel without examination and without clear evidence? *49*Return to court, for they have testified falsely against her."

*50*Then all the people returned in haste. To Daniel the elders said, "Come, sit with us and inform us, since God has given you the prestige of old age." *51*But he replied, "Separate these two far from one another that I may examine them."

*52*After they were separated one from the

other, he called one of them and said: "How you have grown evil with age! Now have your past sins come to term: ⁵³ᵍpassing unjust sentences, condemning the innocent, and freeing the guilty, although the Lord says, 'The innocent and the just you shall not put to death.' ⁵⁴Now, then, if you were a witness, tell me under what tree you saw them together." ⁵⁵"Under a mastic tree,"* he answered. "Your fine lie has cost you your head," said Daniel; "for the angel of God shall receive the sentence from him and split you in two." ⁵⁶Putting him to one side, he ordered the other one to be brought. "Offspring of Canaan, not of Judah," Daniel said to him, "beauty has seduced you, lust has subverted your conscience. ⁵⁷This is how you acted with the daughters of Israel, and in their fear they yielded to you; but a daughter of Judah did not tolerate your wickedness.* ⁵⁸Now then, tell me under what tree you surprised them together." ⁵⁹"Under an oak," he said. "Your fine lie has cost you also your head," said Daniel; "for the angel of God waits with a sword to cut you in two so as to make an end of you both."

⁶⁰The whole assembly cried aloud, blessing God who saves those that hope in him. ⁶¹ʰThey rose up against the two elders, for by their own words Daniel had convicted them of perjury. According to the law of Moses, they inflicted on them the penalty they had plotted to impose on their neighbor: ⁶²they put them to death. Thus was innocent blood spared that day.

⁶³Hilkiah and his wife praised God for their daughter Susanna, as did Joakim her husband and all her relatives, because she was found innocent of any shameful deed. ⁶⁴And from that day onward Daniel was greatly esteemed by the people.

CHAPTER 14

See RG 342–43

Bel and the Dragon. ¹After King Astyages* was laid with his fathers, Cyrus the Persian succeeded to his kingdom. ²Daniel was the king's favorite and was held in higher esteem than any of the friends of the king.* ³The Babylonians had an idol called Bel,* and every day they provided for it six barrels of fine flour, forty sheep, and six measures of wine. ⁴The king worshiped it and went every day to adore it; but Daniel adored only his God. ⁵When the king asked him, "Why do you not adore Bel?" Daniel replied, "Because I worship not idols made with hands, but only the living God who made heaven and earth and has dominion over all mankind." ⁶Then the king continued, "You do not think Bel is a living god? Do you not see how much he eats and drinks every day?" ⁷Daniel began to laugh. "Do not be deceived, O king," he said; "it is only clay inside and bronze outside; it has never taken any food or drink." ⁸Enraged, the king called his priests and said to them, "Unless you tell me who it is that consumes these provisions, you shall die. ⁹But if you can show that Bel consumes them, Daniel shall die for blaspheming Bel." Daniel said to the king, "Let it be as you say!" ¹⁰There were seventy priests of Bel, besides their wives and children.

When the king went with Daniel into the temple of Bel, ¹¹the priests of Bel said, "See, we are going to leave. Do you, O king, set out the food and prepare the wine; then shut the door and seal it with your ring. ¹²If you do not find that Bel has eaten it all when you return in the morning, we are to die; otherwise Daniel shall die for his lies against us." ¹³They were not perturbed, because under the table they had made a secret entrance

---

13, 55-59: The contrast between the mastic tree, which is small, and the majestic oak emphasizes the contradiction between the statements of the two elders. In the Greek text there is a play on words between the names of these two trees and the mortal punishment decreed by Daniel for the elders.

13, 57: Besides the evident moral intent of this story, it appears to have served the purpose of contrasting the northern and the southern kingdom, Israel and Judah, in favor of the latter.

14, 1: King Astyages: the last of the Median kings, de-

feated by Cyrus in 550 B.C. This story preserves the fiction of a successive Median and Persian rule of Babylon.

14, 2: This verse in the Septuagint Greek text reads: "There was once a priest, Daniel by name, the son of Abal, a favorite of the king of Babylon." This may represent an earlier form of the story, before it was attached to the Book of Daniel.

14, 3: Bel: see the note on Dn 4, 5.

g: Ex 23, 7.   *h:* 61f: Dt 19, 18. 19.

1169

through which they always came in to consume the food. [14]After they departed the king set the food before Bel, while Daniel ordered his servants to bring some ashes, which they scattered through the whole temple; the king alone was present. Then they went outside, sealed the closed door with the king's ring, and departed. [15]The priests entered that night as usual, with their wives and children, and they ate and drank everything.

[16]Early the next morning, the king came with Daniel. [17]"Are the seals unbroken, Daniel?" he asked. And Daniel answered, "They are unbroken, O king." [18]As soon as he had opened the door, the king looked at the table and cried aloud, "Great you are, O Bel; there is no trickery in you." [19]But Daniel laughed and kept the king from entering. "Look at the floor," he said; "whose footprints are these?" [20]"I see the footprints of men, women, and children!" said the king. [21]The angry king arrested the priests, their wives, and their children. They showed him the secret door by which they used to enter to consume what was on the table. [22]He put them to death, and handed Bel over to Daniel, who destroyed it and its temple.

[23]There was a great dragon which the Babylonians worshiped. [24]"Look!" said the king to Daniel, "you cannot deny that this is a living god, so adore it." [25]But Daniel answered, "I adore the Lord, my God, for he is the living God. [26]Give me permission, O king, and I will kill this dragon without sword or club." "I give you permission," the king said. [27]Then Daniel took some pitch, fat, and hair; these he boiled together and made into cakes. He put them into the mouth of the dragon, and when the dragon ate them, he burst asunder. "This," he said, "is what you worshiped."

[28]When the Babylonians heard this, they were angry and turned against the king. "The king has become a Jew," they said; "he has destroyed Bel, killed the dragon, and put the priests to death." [29]They went to the king and demanded: "Hand Daniel over to us, or we will kill you and your family." [30]When he saw himself threatened with violence, the king was forced to hand Daniel over to them. [31]They threw Daniel into a lions' den, where he remained six days. [32]In the den were seven lions, and two carcasses and two sheep had been given to them daily. But now they were given nothing, so that they would devour Daniel.

[33]In Judea there was a prophet, Habakkuk; he mixed some bread in a bowl with the stew he had boiled, and was going to bring it to the reapers in the field, [34]when an angel of the Lord told him, "Take the lunch you have to Daniel in the lions' den at Babylon." [35]But Habakkuk answered, "Babylon, sir, I have never seen, and I do not know the den!" [36i]The angel of the Lord seized him by the crown of his head and carried him by the hair; with the speed of the wind, he set him down in Babylon above the den. [37]"Daniel, Daniel," cried Habakkuk, "take the lunch God has sent you." [38]"You have remembered me, O God," said Daniel; "you have not forsaken those who love you." [39]While Daniel began to eat, the angel of the Lord at once brought Habakkuk back to his own place.

[40]On the seventh day the king came to mourn for Daniel. As he came to the den and looked in, there was Daniel, sitting there! [41]The king cried aloud, "You are great, O Lord, the God of Daniel, and there is no other besides you!" [42]Daniel he took out, but those who had tried to destroy him he threw into the den, and they were devoured in a moment before his eyes.

i: Ez 8, 3.

See RG
346–49

The Book of Hosea

Hosea belonged to the northern kingdom and began his prophetic career in the last years of Jeroboam II (786–746 B.C.). Some believe that he was a priest, others that he was a cult prophet; the prophecy, our only source of information concerning his life, gives us no certain answer in the matter. The collected oracles reveal a very sensitive, emotional man who could pass quickly from violent anger to the deepest tenderness. The prophecy pivots around his own unfortunate marriage to Gomer, a personal tragedy which profoundly influenced his teaching. In fact, his own prophetic vocation and message were immeasurably deepened by the painful experience he underwent in his married life.

Gomer, the adulteress, symbolized faithless Israel. And just as Hosea could not give up his wife forever even when she played the harlot, so Yahweh could not renounce Israel, who had been betrothed to him. God would chastise, but it would be the chastisement of the jealous lover, longing to bring back the beloved to the fresh and pure joy of their first love.

Israel's infidelity took the form of idolatry and ruthless oppression of the poor. No amount of mechanically offered sacrifices could atone for her serious sins. Chastisement alone remained; God would have to strip her of the rich ornaments bestowed by her false lovers and thus bring her back to the true lover. A humiliated Israel would again seek Yahweh. The eleventh chapter of Hosea is one of the summits of Old Testament theology; God's love for his people has never been expressed more tenderly. Hosea began the tradition of describing the relation between Yahweh and Israel in terms of marriage. This symbolism appears later on in the Old Testament; and, in the New, both St. John and St. Paul express in the same imagery the union between Christ and his Church.

The Book of Hosea is divided as follows:

I: The Prophet's Marriage and Its Lesson (1, 1—3, 5).

II: Israel's Guilt and Punishment (4, 1—14, 10).

I: The Prophet's Marriage and Its Lesson*

CHAPTER 1

See RG
346–47

Marriage with an Unfaithful Wife. [1]The word of the LORD that came to Hosea, the son of Beeri, in the days of Uzziah, Jotham, Ahaz, Hezekiah, kings of Judah, and in the days of Jeroboam, son of Joash, king of Israel. [2]In the beginning of the LORD's speaking to Hosea, the LORD said to Hosea:

Go, take a harlot wife* and harlot's
    children,
    for the land gives itself to harlotry,
    turning away from the LORD.

[3]So he went and took Gomer, the daughter of Diblaim; and she conceived and bore him a son. [4]Then the LORD said to him:

Give him the name Jezreel,*
    for in a little while
I will punish the house of Jehu
    for the bloodshed at Jezreel
And bring to an end the kingdom
    of the house of Israel;
[5] On that day I will break the bow of Israel
    in the valley of Jezreel.

1—3: This section is ordinarily thought to be biographical, the prophet's personal tragedy figuring as the relation of God to his people Israel. Hosea's marriage to a harlot wife represents Israel's infidelity to her Lord; hence the symbolic names of the children (Hos 1, 4-9). In Hos 2, 4-25 the Lord protests this infidelity and decrees its consequences, but promises restoration in return for amendment; his punishments are medicinal. In chapter 3 Hosea once more takes back his wife, but only conditionally, signifying God's long-suffering love for Israel and hope for her return.

1, 2: A harlot wife: this does not necessarily mean that Gomer was a harlot when Hosea married her; the verse describes the event in its final consequences.

1, 4: Jezreel: the strategic valley in northern Israel where Jehu brought the dynasty of Omri to an end through bloodshed (2 Kgs 9—10). Jeroboam II was the last king but one of the house of Jehu; the prophecy in this verse was fulfilled by the murder of his son, who reigned only six months (2 Kgs 15, 8-10).

⁶When she conceived again and bore a daughter, the LORD said to him:

Give her the name Lo-ruhama;*
I no longer feel pity for the house of Israel:
    rather, I abhor them utterly.
⁷ Yet for the house of Judah I feel pity;
    I will save them by the LORD, their
        God;
But I will not save them by war,
    by sword or bow, by horses or
        horsemen.*

⁸After she weaned Lo-ruhama, she conceived and bore a son. ⁹Then the LORD said:

Give him the name Lo-ammi,*
    for you are not my people,
    and I will not be your God.

CHAPTER 2

See RG
346–47

Israel's Punishment and Restoration

⁴ Protest against your mother, protest!*
    for she is not my wife,
    and I am not her husband.
Let her remove her harlotry from before
    her,
    her adultery from between her breasts,
⁵ Or I will strip her naked,*
    leaving her as on the day of her birth;
I will make her like the desert,
    reduce her to an arid land,
    and slay her with thirst.
⁶ I will have no pity on her children,
    for they are the children of harlotry.
⁷ Yes, their mother has played the harlot;
    she that conceived them has acted
        shamefully.

"I will go after my lovers,"* she said,
    "who give me my bread and my water,
        my wool and my flax, my oil and my
        drink."

¹⁰ Since she has not known
    that it was I who gave her
    the grain, the wine, and the oil,
And her abundance of silver,
    and of gold, which they used for Baal,
¹¹ Therefore I will take back my grain in its
        time,
    and my wine in its season;
I will snatch away my wool and my flax,
    with which she covers her nakedness.
¹² So now I will lay bare her shame
    before the eyes of her lovers,
    and no one can deliver her out of my
        hand.
¹³ I will bring an end to all her joy,
    her feasts, her new moons, her
        sabbaths,
    and all her solemnities.
¹⁴ I will lay waste her vines and fig trees,
    of which she said, "These are the hire
    my lovers have given me";
I will turn them into rank growth
    and wild beasts shall devour them.
¹⁵ I will punish her for the days of the Baals,*
    for whom she burnt incense
While she decked herself out with her
        rings and her jewels,
    and, in going after her lovers,
    forgot me, says the LORD.
⁸ Therefore, I will hedge in her way with
        thorns*
    and erect a wall against her,
    so that she cannot find her paths.

1, 6: Lo-ruhama: "she is not pitied." The "pity" that is here withheld from Israel is God's gratuitous love which inspires his beneficent acts.

1, 7: The terrible punishments announced by the prophets were so fully realized that later generations made a point of recalling the same prophets' messages of consolation also, even though it meant taking these from another context. Thus, an editor placed the words of Hos 2, 1ff after the repudiation of Israel in Hos 1, 9; here the more natural order has been restored. The present verse is another example of the same thing. In addition, it may be the work of a later hand, dating from a time when the prophecies of Hosea were circulated in the south, after the dissolution of the northern kingdom that he had prophesied. The second part of the verse emphasizes the power of the Lord, who needs no human agents to fulfill

his will. It may refer to the deliverance of Jerusalem from the siege of Sennacherib (2 Kgs 19, 35ff).

1, 9: Lo-ammi: "not my people."

2, 4: The Lord speaks of Israel, still using the example of Hosea's wife.

2, 5: I will strip her naked: contemporary documents indicate that this was a conventional punishment for adultery.

2, 7: My lovers: the local fertility deities to whom, rather than to the Lord (v 10), the unfaithful Israelites attributed the produce of the land.

2, 15: The days of the Baals: ritual observances held in various local shrines in honor of Baal.

2, 8f: The crop failures, blight, etc., sent by the Lord (vv 11-14) have as their purpose to make Israel see the folly of her ways.

⁹ If she runs after her lovers, she shall not
  overtake them;
  if she looks for them she shall not find
  them.
Then she shall say,
  "I will go back to my first husband,
  for it was better with me then than
  now."

¹⁶ So I will allure her;*
  I will lead her into the desert
  and speak to her heart.
¹⁷ From there I will give her the vineyards
  she had,
  and the valley of Achor as a door of
  hope.
She shall respond there as in the days of
  her youth,
  when she came up from the land of
  Egypt.

¹⁸   On that day, says the LORD,
She shall call me "My husband,"
  and never again "My baal."*
¹⁹ Then will I remove from her mouth the
  names of the Baals,
  so that they shall no longer be
  invoked.
²⁰ I will make a covenant for them on that
  day,
  with the beasts of the field,
With the birds of the air,
  and with the things that crawl on the
  ground.
Bow and sword and war

I will destroy from the land,
  and I will let them take their rest in
  security.

²¹ I will espouse you to me forever:*
  I will espouse you in right and in
  justice,
  in love and in mercy;
²² I will espouse you in fidelity,
  and you shall know the LORD.
²³ On that day I will respond, says the LORD;
  I will respond to the heavens,
  and they shall respond to the earth;
²⁴ The earth shall respond to the grain, and
  wine, and oil,
  and these shall respond to Jezreel.
²⁵ I will sow him for myself in the land,
  and I will have pity on Lo-ruhama.
I will say to Lo-ammi, "You are my
  people,"
  and he shall say, "My God!"ᵃ

CHAPTER 3

Triumph of Love

¹ *Again the LORD said to me:
Give your love to a woman
  beloved of a paramour, an adulteress;
Even as the LORD loves the people of
  Israel,
  though they turn to other gods
  and are fond of raisin cakes.*

²So I bought her for fifteen pieces of silver and a homer* and a lethech of barley.
³Then I said to her:

**See RG
346-47**

2, 16f: Israel's journey in the desert represents for Hosea
the time of Israel's fidelity, before it was corrupted by the
ways of Canaan; cf Jer 2, 2-7; Am 5, 25. Thus, he pictures a
restoration in terms of a new entry into the promised land.

2, 18: My baal: the word means "lord, master." It was
commonly used by women of their husbands, but it is to be
shunned as a title for the Lord because of its association with
the pagan god Baal. Probably it had been so used by many Israelites, who saw little if any difference between the worship
of the Lord and the worship of Baal.

2, 21f: The Lord will once more espouse Israel; the qualities ascribed to the renewed people are the bridal gift (cf Gn
24, 53) with which he will endow it. In right and in justice:
two terms dear to Hosea, used by him especially to condemn
the popular social injustice and corruption of the legal
processes. Here they mean right conduct in general. Love:
one of the most characteristic words of Hosea's prophecy. It
means a dutiful love, based on a social relation; here it refers

to the covenant between God and his people. It is a love fulfilled by the performance of mutual obligations. Mercy: from
the same root as the word translated pity in Hos 1, 6; cf v 25.
And you shall know the Lord: another characteristic expression of Hosea; cf Hos 4, 1; 5, 4; 6, 3. 6. It means not an abstract but a practical knowledge, i.e., acknowledgment of his
will, obedience to his law.

3, 1-5: Hosea is instructed to take Gomer back, redeeming
her from her paramours. On condition of her amendment, she
will be restored to her former position of wife. This in turn
signifies God's enduring love for his people. He will put the
people through a period of trial—the dissolution of the kingdom—in order that they may return to him wholeheartedly.

3, 1: Raisin cakes: offerings to the fertility goddess
Ashera, the female counterpart of Baal; cf Jer 7, 18; 44, 19.

3, 2: Homer: about ten bushels. Lethech: a half-homer.

---

a: Rom 9, 25; 1 Pt 2, 10.

"Many days you shall wait for me;
  you shall not play the harlot
Or belong to any man;
  I in turn will wait for you."
[4] For the people of Israel shall remain
    many days
  without king or prince,
Without sacrifice or sacred pillar,*
  without ephod or household idols.
[5] Then the people of Israel shall turn back
    and seek the LORD, their God,
    and David, their king;*
  They shall come trembling to the LORD
    and to his bounty, in the last days.[b]
[1] *The number of the Israelites
    shall be like the sand of the sea,
    which can be neither measured nor
      counted.
  Whereas they were called,
    "Lo-ammi,"
  They shall be called,
    "Children of the living God."[c]
[2] Then the people of Judah and of Israel
    shall be gathered together;
  They shall appoint for themselves one
    head
    and come up from other lands,
    for great shall be the day of Jezreel.
[3] Say to your brothers, "Ammi,"
    and to your sisters, "Ruhama."

II: Israel's Guilt and Punishment
CHAPTER 4

See RG
347–49

Crimes of Israel

[1] Hear the word of the LORD,
    O people of Israel,
    for the LORD has a grievance
    against the inhabitants of the land:
  There is no fidelity, no mercy,

no knowledge of God in the land.
[2] False swearing, lying, murder, stealing
    and adultery!
  in their lawlessness, bloodshed follows
    bloodshed.[d]
[3] Therefore the land mourns,
    and everything that dwells in it
      languishes:
  The beasts of the field,
    the birds of the air,
    and even the fish of the sea perish.

Guilt of the Priests

[4] But let no one protest, let no one
    complain;
  with you is my grievance, O priests!*
[5] You shall stumble in the day,
    and the prophets shall stumble with
      you at night;
  I will destroy your mother.
[6] My people perish for want of knowledge!
  Since you have rejected knowledge,
    I will reject you from my priesthood;
  Since you have ignored the law of your
    God,
    I will also ignore your sons.
[7] One and all they sin against me,
    exchanging their glory for shame.
[8] They feed on the sin of my people,
    and are greedy for their guilt.
[9] The priests shall fare no better than the
      people:
  I will punish them for their ways,
    and repay them for their deeds.[e]
[10] They shall eat but not be satisfied,
    they shall play the harlot but not
      increase,
  Because they have abandoned the LORD
[11] to practice harlotry.
  Old wine and new

3, 4: Sacred pillar: the stone massebah, originally perhaps a phallic symbol, representing Baal. These were also used, with another signification, in Israelite worship; see notes on Gn 28, 18; Ex 34, 13. Ephod: an instrument used in consulting the deity; cf 1 Sm 23, 6-12; 30, 7; see notes on Ex 28, 6. 15-30. Household idols: images regarded as the tutelary deities of the household; cf Gn 31, 19; Jgs 17, 5; 18, 14. 17f.

3, 5: David, their king: the messianic King of the Davidic line who will restore the kingdom of God's people; cf Jer 23, 5; Ez 34, 23f. The last days: the messianic age.

3, 1-3: These verses (The number . . . Ruhama) (transposed from ch 2) continue the conditional promise of restora-

tion made in Hos 3, 1-5, reversing the dire predictions of chapter 1; the symbolic names now become names of honor: Jezreel, "God sows"; Ammi, "my people"; Ruhama, "she is pitied."

4, 4ff: Hosea is particularly severe with the priests in the northern kingdom, who had led the way in the general apostasy from God's law. The prophets here associated with the priests (v 5) were doubtless cult prophets, who were often unworthy of their pretended calling; cf Jer 2, 8; 4, 9f; 6, 13f; 23, 9-40.

b: Ez 34, 23.   c: Rom 9, 26.   d: Ex 20, 13-17.   e: Is 24, 2.

deprive my people of understanding.
12 They consult their piece of wood,
    and their wand* makes
        pronouncements for them,
For the spirit of harlotry has led them
        astray;
    they commit harlotry, forsaking their
        God.
13 On the mountaintops they offer
        sacrifice
    and on the hills they burn incense,
Beneath oak and poplar and terebinth,
    because of their pleasant shade.
That is why your daughters play the
        harlot,
    and your daughters-in-law are
        adulteresses.
14 Am I then to punish your daughters for
        their harlotry,
    your daughters-in-law for their
        adultery?
You yourselves consort with harlots,
    and with prostitutes you offer
        sacrifice!*
So must a people without understanding
    come to ruin.
15 Though you play the harlot, O Israel,
    let not Judah become guilty!
Come not to Gilgal,*
    nor up to Beth-aven,
    to swear, "As the Lord lives!"
16 For Israel is as stubborn as a heifer;
    will the LORD now give them broad
        pastures
    as though they were lambs?
17 Ephraim* is an associate of idols,
    let him alone!
18 When their carousing is over,
    they give themselves to harlotry;
    in their arrogance they love shame.

19 The wind has bound them up in its
        pinions;*
    they shall have only shame from their
        altars.

CHAPTER 5

See RG
347–49

Guilt of the Leaders

1 Hear this, O priests,
    Pay attention, O house of Israel,
O household of the king, give ear!
    It is you who are called to judgment.f
For you have become a snare at
        Mizpah,*
    and a net spread upon Tabor.
2 In their perversity they have sunk into
        wickedness,
    and I am rejected by them all.
3 I know Ephraim,
    and Israel is not hidden from me;
Now Ephraim has played the harlot,
    Israel is defiled.
4 Their deeds do not allow them
    to return to their God;
For the spirit of harlotry is in them,
    and they do not recognize the LORD.

5 The arrogance of Israel bears witness
        against him;
    Ephraim stumbles in his guilt,
    and Judah stumbles with them.
6 With their flocks and their herds they
        shall go
    to seek the LORD, but they shall not
        find him:
    he has withdrawn himself from them.
7 They have been untrue to the LORD,
    for they have begotten illegitimate
        children;
Now shall the new moon devour them
    together with their fields.

4, 12: Wood . . . wand: an idol used in divination.

4, 14: With prostitutes you offer sacrifice: the ritual prostitution practiced at the Canaanite shrines was introduced even into sanctuaries dedicated to the Lord. In comparison, the adultery that had become common in Israel was a far less reprehensible crime.

4, 15: Gilgal: not the Gilgal of the south (Jos 4, 19f), but a sanctuary north of Bethel where there was an association of cult prophets (2 Kgs 2, 1ff; 4, 38). Beth-aven: literally, "house of iniquity," Hosea's nickname for Bethel, and a scribal substitute for Bethel, "house of god," in this context. Bethel was one of the royal shrines of Israel, where there was a schis-

matic public worship of the Lord; cf 1 Kgs 12, 26-30.

4, 17: Ephraim: the heartland of the northern kingdom. During the latter part of Hosea's prophetic career, Ephraim was all that remained of Israel after the Assyrians had overrun Transjordan and Galilee.

4, 19: The Israelites shall be carried from their country as by a whirlwind. To this their idolatry has brought them.

5, 1: Mizpah: probably the Mizpah in Transjordan is meant; cf Jos 11, 8. Tabor: the mountain that dominates the valley of Jezreel.

f: Mi 3, 1.

Political Upheavals*

8 Blow the horn in Gibeah,
   the trumpet in Ramah!
Sound the alarm in Beth-aven:
   "Look behind you, O Benjamin!"*
9 Ephraim shall become a waste
   on the day of chastisement:
Against the tribes of Israel
   I announce what is sure to be.
10 The princes of Judah have become
   like those that move a boundary line;*
Upon them I will pour out
   my wrath like water.ᵍ

11 Is Ephraim maltreated, his rights
      violated?
   No, he has willingly gone after filth!*
12 I am like a moth for Ephraim,
   like maggots* for the house of
      Judah.
13 When Ephraim saw his infirmity,
   and Judah his sore,
Ephraim went to Assyria,
   and Judah sent to the great king.*
But he cannot heal you
   nor take away your sore.
14 For I am like a lion to Ephraim,
   like a young lion to the house of
      Judah;
It is I who rend the prey and depart,
   I carry it away and no one can save it
      from me.

Insincere Conversion

15 I will go back to my place
   until they pay for their guilt
   and seek my presence.*

CHAPTER 6

See RG
347–49

*In their affliction, they shall look
      for me:
1   "Come, let us return to the LORD,
For it is he who has rent, but he will heal
      us;
   he has struck us, but he will bind our
      wounds.
2 He will revive us after two days;*
   on the third day he will raise us up,
   to live in his presence.ʰ
3 Let us know, let us strive to know the
      LORD;
   as certain as the dawn is his coming,
   and his judgment shines forth like the
      light of day!
He will come to us like the rain,
   like spring rain that waters the earth."

4 What can I do with you, Ephraim?
   What can I do with you, Judah?
Your piety* is like a morning cloud,
   like the dew that early passes away.
5 For this reason I smote them through the
      prophets,
   I slew them by the words of my
      mouth;
6 For it is love that I desire, not sacrifice,
   and knowledge of God rather than
      holocausts.ⁱ
7 But they, in their land, violated the
      covenant;
   there they were untrue to me.
8 Gilead is a city of evildoers,
   tracked with blood.
9 As brigands ambush a man,

5, 8-14: This passage refers to the Syro-Ephraimite war of 735–734 B.C., when a coalition of Arameans and Israelites attempted to dethrone the king of Judah. Judah repulsed the attempt with the aid of Assyria, and the latter devastated both Aram and Israel; cf 2 Kgs 16, 5-9. Hosea condemns both Israel and Judah for the war.

5, 8: A vision of invasion, from Gibeah and Ramah in northern Judah, into Israel.

5, 10: Like those that move a boundary line: comparison of the invaders to a classic case of social injustice; cf Dt 19, 14; 27, 17; Prv 23, 10f.

5, 11: Gone after filth: by allying himself with Aram.

5, 12: Moth . . . maggots: internal corruption will work the Lord's punishment on both Israel and Judah.

5, 13: Ephraim went . . . the great king: in 738 B.C. the Israelite king Menahem had to pay tribute to the Assyrian king

Tiglath-pileser III, whose vassal he became (2 Kgs 15, 19f). Under the threat of the Syro-Ephraimite invasion King Ahaz of Judah also submitted himself and his country to Tiglath-pileser (2 Kgs 16, 7-9). "The great king" was the title used by the Assyrian kings.

5, 15: The Lord withdraws himself from Israel, hoping for its repentance.

6, 1: In . . . me: this is the last line of ch 5.

6, 2: After two days; on the third day: after a short lapse of time.

6, 4: Piety: the word is translated "love" in Hos 2, 21 and in v 6 below.

g: Dt 19, 14; 27, 17.   h: 1 Cor 15, 4.   i: 1 Sm 15, 22; Eccl 4, 17; Mt 9, 13; 12, 7.

a band of priests slay on the way to
Shechem,
committing monstrous crime.
10 In the house of Israel I have seen a
horrible thing:
there harlotry is found in Ephraim,
Israel is defiled.
11 For you also, O Judah,
a harvest* has been appointed.

See RG
347–49

CHAPTER 7

1 When I would bring about the
restoration of my people,
when I would heal Israel,
The guilt of Ephraim stands out,
the wickedness of Samaria;
They practice falsehood,
thieves break in, bandits plunder
abroad.
2 Yet they do not remind themselves
that I remember all their wickedness.
Even now their crimes surround them,
present to my sight.

Failure of the Monarchy*
3 In their wickedness they regale the king,
the princes too, with their deceits.
4 They are all kindled to wrath
like a blazing oven,
Whose fire the baker desists from stirring
once the dough is kneaded until it has
risen.
5 On the day of our king,
the princes are overcome with the heat
of wine.
He extends his hand among dissemblers;
6 the plotters approach with hearts like
ovens.
All the night their anger sleeps;
in the morning it flares like a blazing
fire.

7 They are all heated like ovens,
and consume their rulers.
All their kings have fallen;
none of them calls upon me.

Foreign Alliances
8 Ephraim mingles with the nations,
Ephraim is a hearth cake unturned.*
9 Strangers have sapped his strength,
but he takes no notice of it;
Of gray hairs, too, there is a sprinkling,
but he takes no notice of it.
10 The arrogance of Israel bears witness
against him;
yet they do not return to the LORD,
their God,
nor seek him, for all that.
11 Ephraim is like a dove,
silly and senseless;
They call upon Egypt,
they go to Assyria.
12 Even as they go I will spread my net
around them,
like birds in the air I will bring them
down.
In an instant I will send them captive
from their land.

Perversity of Israel
13 Woe to them, they have strayed from
me!
Ruin to them, they have sinned against
me!
Though I wished to redeem them,
they spoke lies against me.
14 They have not cried to me from their
hearts
when they wailed upon their beds;
For wheat and wine they lacerated
themselves,*
while they rebelled against me.

6, 11: Harvest: when the land will reap the consequences
of its sins.

7, 3-7: This passage refers to the dynastic upheavals of Israel's declining days. Between the death of Jeroboam II and
the fall of Samaria to the Assyrians, a matter of some twenty-
five years, there were four separate dynasties on the throne
and as many murdered kings. The prophet compares the Israelite nobles who were inflamed with passion to an overheated
oven that consumes what it is supposed to bake; thus the land
consumes its kings. Regale: with wine (v 3). Like fire smoldering through the night and blazing up in the morning, the

sleeping anger of plotters soon breaks out in open rebellion;
the succession of night and morning suggests the short reigns
of the various kings of this troubled period.

7, 8: A hearth cake unturned: burnt on one side, half baked
on the other, and therefore useless. Israel's decline in power
is ascribed to its disastrous meddling in the power politics of
the neighboring nations.

7, 14: They lacerated themselves: a common oriental
practice in prayers of earnest impetration (1 Kgs 18, 28); the
practice was forbidden in Israelite religion (Lv 19, 28; Dt 14,
1).

¹⁵ Though I trained and strengthened their
arms,
yet they devised evil against me.
¹⁶ They have again become useless,
like a treacherous bow.
Their princes shall fall by the sword
because of the insolence of their
tongues;
thus they shall be mocked in the land
of Egypt.

CHAPTER 8

See RG
347–49

¹ A trumpet to your lips,
You who watch over the house of the
LORD!
Since they have violated my covenant,
and sinned against my law,
² While to me they cry out,
"O God of Israel, we know you!"
³ The men of Israel have thrown away
what is good;
the enemy shall pursue them.
⁴ *They made kings, but not by my
authority;
they established princes, but without
my approval.
With their silver and gold they made
idols for themselves, to their own
destruction.
⁵ Cast away your calf, O Samaria!
my wrath is kindled against them;
How long will they be unable to attain
innocence in Israel?
⁶ The work of an artisan,
no god at all,
Destined for the flames—
such is the calf of Samaria!

⁷ When they sow the wind,
they shall reap the whirlwind;
The stalk of grain that forms no ear
can yield no flour;
Even if it could,
strangers would swallow it.
⁸ Israel is swallowed up;
he is now among the nations
a thing of no value.
⁹ They went up to Assyria—
a wild ass off on its own—
Ephraim bargained for lovers.
¹⁰ Even though they bargain with the
nations,
I will now gather an army;
King and princes shall shortly
succumb under the burden.

¹¹ When Ephraim made many altars to
expiate sin,
his altars became occasions of sin.*
¹² Though I write for him my many
ordinances,
they are considered as a stranger's.
¹³ Though they offer sacrifice,
immolate flesh and eat it,
the LORD is not pleased with them.
He shall still remember their guilt
and punish their sins;
they shall return to Egypt.
¹⁴ Israel has forgotten his maker
and built palaces.
Judah, too, has fortified many
cities;
but I will send fire upon his cities,
to devour their castles.ʲ

CHAPTER 9

Exile without Worship

See RG
347–49

¹ Rejoice not, O Israel,
exult not like the nations!
For you have been unfaithful to your
God,
loving a harlot's hire
upon every threshing floor.*
² Threshing floor and wine press shall not
nourish them,
the new wine shall fail them.

8, 4-6: Israel's monarchy and separate sanctuary are here
associated, as in 1 Kgs 12, 20-33; both were the result of rebellion against the divinely approved Davidic dynasty and the
Jerusalem temple with the ark of the covenant. The calf image set up by Jeroboam I in the royal shrines prevented Israel
from attaining innocence (vv 5f).

8, 11: The very multiplicity of sanctuaries throughout the
land was a danger to the purity of worship. The local shrines
were speedily assimilated to the cult places used by the

Canaanites, and the Lord was identified with the god Baal
worshiped there. Thus the Deuteronomic writers, influenced
by prophetic ideas, ended by restricting sacrificial worship to
the one temple in Jerusalem.

9, 1f: Upon every threshing floor: an allusion to harvest
festivals in honor of Baal, to whom the Israelites had attributed the fertility of the land; cf Hos 2, 7.

ʲ: Am 2, 5.

3 They shall not dwell in the LORD's land;
Ephraim shall return to Egypt,
and in Assyria they shall eat unclean
food.
4 They shall not pour libations of wine to
the LORD,
or proffer their sacrifices before him.
Theirs will be like mourners' bread,*
that makes unclean all who eat of it;
Such food as they have shall be for
themselves;
it cannot enter the house of the LORD.

5 What will you do on the festival day,
the day of the LORD's feast?*
6 When they go from the ruins,
Egypt shall gather them in, Memphis
shall bury them.
Weeds shall overgrow their silver
treasures,
and thorns invade their tents.

The Prophet Ridiculed

7 They have come, the days of
punishment!
they have come, the days of
recompense!
Let Israel know it!
"The prophet is a fool,
the man of the spirit is mad!"
Because your iniquity is great,
great, too, is your hostility.
8 A prophet is Ephraim's watchman with
God,
yet a fowler's snare is on all his
ways,
hostility in the house of his God.
9 They have sunk to the depths of
corruption,
as in the days of Gibeah;*
He shall remember their iniquity
and punish their sins.

Crime of Baal-peor

10 Like grapes in the desert,
I found Israel;
Like the first fruits of the fig tree in its
prime,
I considered your fathers.
When they came to Baal-peor*
and consecrated themselves to the
Shame,
they became as abhorrent as the thing
they loved.
11 The glory of Ephraim flies away like a
bird:
no birth, no carrying in the womb, no
conception.
Were they to bear children,
I would slay the darlings of their
womb.
12 Even though they bring up their children,
I will make them childless, till not one
is left.
Woe to them
when I turn away from them!
13 Ephraim, as I saw, was like Tyre,
planted in a beauteous spot;
But Ephraim shall bring out
his children to the slayer.
14 Give them, O LORD!
give them what?
Give them an unfruitful womb,*
and dry breasts!

Crime of Gilgal

15 All their wickedness is in Gilgal;*
yes, there they incurred my hatred.
Because of their wicked deeds
I will drive them out of my house.
I will love them no longer;
all their princes are rebels.*k*
16 Ephraim is stricken,
their root is dried up;
they shall bear no fruit.

9, 4: Mourners' bread: bread eaten at funeral rites; cf Dt 26, 13f. Contact with a corpse made a person ritually unclean, together with everything he touched. Such bread could not be offered to the Lord.

9, 5: The Lord's feast: doubtless the autumn feast of Booths, the most important of the Israelite public celebrations; cf Lv 23, 34.

9, 9: The days of Gibeah: a reference to the outrage committed at Gibeah in the days of the Judges (Jgs 19, 22-30).

9, 10: At Baal-peor (Nm 25, 1-5) the Israelites conse-

crated themselves to Baal, here called the Shame.

9, 14: An unfruitful womb: this appears to be a reversal of the ancient blessing of Joseph contained in Gn 49, 25f, in which the increase, hence fruitfulness, promised to the patriarch is even signified by the name of his son Ephraim, on whose descendants the prophet now invokes the curse of extinction.

9, 15: Gilgal: see note on Hos 4, 15.

k: 1 Sm 8, 5.

[17] My God will disown them
because they have not listened to him;
they shall be wanderers among the
nations.

See RG
347–49

CHAPTER 10

Punishment of Idolatry

[1] Israel is a luxuriant vine
whose fruit matches its growth.
The more abundant his fruit,
the more altars he built;
The more productive his land,
the more sacred pillars* he set up.
[2] Their heart is false,
now they pay for their guilt;
God shall break down their altars
and destroy their sacred pillars.
[3] If they would say,
"We have no king"—
Since they do not fear the LORD,
what can the king do for them?
[4] Nothing but make promises,
swear false oaths, and make
alliances,
While justice grows wild
like wormwood* in a plowed field!
[5] The inhabitants of Samaria fear
for the calf of Beth-aven;*
The people mourn for it
and its priests wail over it,
because the glory has departed from it.
[6] It too shall be carried to Assyria,
as an offering to the great king.
Ephraim shall be taken into captivity,
Israel be shamed by his schemes.

[7] The king of Samaria shall disappear,
like foam upon the waters.
[8] The high places of Aven shall be
destroyed,
the sin of Israel;
thorns and thistles shall overgrow their
altars.

Then they shall cry out to the mountains,
"Cover us!"
and to the hills, "Fall upon us!"*[l]*

[9] Since the days of Gibeah
you have sinned, O Israel.
There they took their stand;
war was not to reach them in Gibeah.*[m]*
[10] Against the wanton people I came
and I chastised them;*[n]*
I gathered troops against them
when I chastised them for their two
crimes.*

Time To Seek the Lord

[11] Ephraim was a trained heifer,
willing to thresh;
I myself laid a yoke
upon her fair neck;
Ephraim was to be harnessed, Judah was
to plow,
Jacob was to break his furrows:
[12] "Sow for yourselves justice,
reap the fruit of piety;
Break up for yourselves a new field,
for it is time to seek the LORD,
till he come and rain down justice
upon you."*[o]*
[13] But you have cultivated wickedness,
reaped perversity,
and eaten the fruit of falsehood.

Because you have trusted in your
chariots,
and in your many warriors,
[14] Turmoil shall break out among your
tribes
and all your fortresses shall be ravaged
As Salman ravaged Beth-arbel* in time
of war,
smashing mothers and their children.*[p]*
[15] So shall it be done to you, Bethel,
because of your utter wickedness:

10, 1: Sacred pillars: see note on Hos 3, 4.

10, 4: Justice . . . like wormwood: the administration of justice, which should have been the mainstay of the people, has in corrupt hands become another instrument of oppression; cf Am 6, 13.

10, 5: The calf of Beth-aven: see notes on Hos 4, 15; 8, 4ff.

10, 10: Their two crimes: possibly the outrage described in Jgs 19 is conceived as a double crime, of adultery and murder. Or the prophet regards the proclamation of the

monarchy (cf 1 Sm 10, 23f) as a crime.

10, 14: As Salman ravaged Beth-arbel: allusion to an invasion not otherwise mentioned in the Bible. Salman may have been the Moabite king of this name mentioned in an inscription of Tiglath-pileser III. There were several Beth-arbels in Palestine; this one was probably in Transjordan.

---

l: Is 2, 19; Lk 23, 30; Rv 6, 16.   *m:* Jgs 20, 1.   *n:* Jer 4, 3.   *o:* Is 45, 8.   *p:* Jgs 8, 10ff.

At dawn the king of Israel
    shall perish utterly.

CHAPTER 11

See RG
347–49

When Israel Was a Child

[1] When Israel was a child I loved him,
    out of Egypt* I called my son.[q]
[2] The more I called them,
    the farther they went from me,
Sacrificing to the Baals
    and burning incense to idols.
[3] Yet it was I who taught Ephraim to walk,
    who took them in my arms;
[4] I drew them with human cords,
    with bands of love;*
I fostered them like one
    who raises an infant to his cheeks;
Yet, though I stooped to feed my child,
    they did not know that I was their
      healer.

[5] He shall return to the land of Egypt,
    and Assyria shall be his king;
[6] The sword shall begin with his cities
    and end by consuming his solitudes.
Because they refused to repent,
    their own counsels shall devour them.
[7] His people are in suspense about
    returning to him;
    and God, though in unison they cry out
      to him,
    shall not raise them up.

End of the Exile

[8] How could I give you up, O Ephraim,
    or deliver you up, O Israel?
How could I treat you as Admah,
    or make you like Zeboiim?*
My heart is overwhelmed,
    my pity is stirred.[r]
[9] I will not give vent to my blazing anger,

I will not destroy Ephraim again;
For I am God and not man,
    the Holy One present among you;
    I will not let the flames consume you.

[10] They shall follow the LORD,
    who roars like a lion;
When he roars,
    his sons shall come frightened from
      the west,
[11] Out of Egypt they shall come trembling,
    like sparrows,
    from the land of Assyria, like doves;
And I will resettle them in their homes,
    says the LORD.

CHAPTER 12

Infidelity of Israel

See RG
347–49

[1] Ephraim has surrounded me with lies,
    the house of Israel, with deceit;
Judah is still rebellious against God,
    against the Holy One, who is faithful.
[2] Ephraim chases the wind,
    ever pursuing the gale.
His lies and falsehoods are many:
    he comes to terms with Assyria,
    and carries oil to Egypt.*
[3] *The LORD has a grievance against Israel:
    he shall punish Jacob for his conduct,
    for his deeds he shall repay him.
[4] In the womb he supplanted his brother,
    and as a man he contended with
      God;[s]
[5] He contended with the angel and
      triumphed,
    entreating him with tears.
At Bethel he met God
    and there he spoke with him:
[6] The LORD, the God of hosts,
    the LORD is his name!
[7] You shall return by the help of your God,

11, 1: Out of Egypt: Hosea, like most of the prophets, dates the real beginning of Israel from the time of Moses and the Exodus. Mt 2, 15 applies this text to the return of the Christ Child from Egypt.

11, 4: I drew them . . . with bands of love: not forcing them like draft animals, but drawing them with kindness and affection.

11, 8: Admah . . . Zeboiim: cities destroyed with Sodom and Gomorrah (Dt 29, 22).

12, 2: He comes . . . Egypt: allusion to the commercial and military pacts with the great powers, consistently con-

demned by the prophets as derogatory of the Lord's claim on his people.

12, 3-7: Contemporary Israel and the Israel represented by its ancestor Jacob (Israel) are here alternated, a splendid example of the Hebrew concept of "corporate personality" or easy transition from the individual to the community of which he is part. Hosea recalls the history of Jacob as it now appears in Genesis, but with some differences of detail and order.

q: Mt 2, 15.   *r:* Gn 19, 24f.   *s:* Gn 25, 26; 32, 25.

if you remain loyal and do right
and always hope in your God.

8 A merchant who holds a false balance,
who loves to defraud!
9 Though Ephraim says,
"How rich I have become;
I have made a fortune!"
All his gain shall not suffice him
for the guilt of his sin.
10 I am the LORD, your God,
since the land of Egypt;
I will again have you live in tents,
as in that appointed time.
11 I granted many visions
and spoke to the prophets,
through whom I set forth examples.
12 In Gilead is falsehood, they have come to
nought,
in Gilgal they sacrifice to bullocks;
Their altars are like heaps of stones
in the furrows of the field.

13 When Jacob fled to the land of Aram,
he served for a wife;
for a wife Israel tended sheep.*t*
14 By a prophet* the LORD brought Israel
out of Egypt,
and by a prophet they were
protected.*u*
15 Ephraim has exasperated his lord;
therefore he shall cast his bloodguilt
upon him
and repay him for his outrage.

See RG
347–49

CHAPTER 13

Furrows of the Field
1 Ephraim's word caused fear,
for he was exalted in Israel;
but he sinned through Baal and died.

Punishment for Ingratitude
2 Now they continue to sin,
making for themselves molten
images,
Silver idols according to their fancy,

all of them the work of artisans.
"To these," they say, "offer sacrifice."
Men kiss calves!
3 Therefore, they shall be like a morning
cloud
or like the dew that early passes
away,
Like chaff storm-driven from the
threshing floor
or like smoke out of the window.

4 I am the LORD, your God,
since the land of Egypt;
You know no God besides me,
and there is no savior but me.*v*
5 I fed you in the desert,
in the torrid land.
6 They ate their fill;
when filled, they became proud of
heart
and forgot me.

7 Therefore, I will be like a lion to them,
like a panther by the road I will keep
watch.
8 I will attack them like a bear robbed of
its young,
and tear their hearts from their
breasts;
I will devour them on the spot like
a lion,
as though a wild beast were to rend
them.

9 Your destruction, O Israel!
who is there to help you?
10 Where now is your king,
that he may rescue you in all your
cities?
And your rulers, of whom you said,
"Give me a king and princes"?*w*
11 I give you a king in my anger,
and I take him away in my wrath.*
12 The guilt of Israel is wrapped up,
his sin is stored away.

12, 14: A prophet: Moses.

13, 11: I give you a king . . . in my wrath: the Lord punishes the people of the northern kingdom by giving them
incompetent kings who are soon deposed.

t: Gn 28, 5; 29, 20.   *u:* Ex 14, 21f.   *v:* Is 43, 11.   *w:* 1 Sm 8, 5.

¹³ The birth pangs shall come for him,
  but he shall be an unwise child;
For when it is time he shall not present
    himself
  where children break forth.*
¹⁴ Shall I deliver them from the power of
    the nether world?*
  shall I redeem them from death?ˣ
Where are your plagues, O death!
  where is your sting, O nether world!
My eyes are closed to compassion.

¹⁵ Though he be fruitful among his fellows,
  an east wind shall come, a wind from
    the LORD,
  rising from the desert,
That shall dry up his spring,
  and leave his fountain dry.
It shall loot his land
  of every precious thing.ʸ

See RG
347-49

CHAPTER 14

¹ Samaria shall expiate her guilt,
  for she has rebelled against her God.
They shall fall by the sword,
  their little ones shall be dashed to
    pieces,
  their expectant mothers shall be ripped
    open.

Sincere Conversion

² Return, O Israel, to the LORD, your God;
  you have collapsed through your guilt.
³ Take with you words,
  and return to the LORD;
Say to him, "Forgive all iniquity,
  and receive what is good, that we may
    render
  as offerings the bullocks from our
    stalls.

⁴ Assyria will not save us,
  nor shall we have horses to mount;
We shall say no more, 'Our god,'
  to the work of our hands;
  for in you the orphan finds
    compassion."

⁵ I will heal their defection,
  I will love them freely;
  for my wrath is turned away from
    them.
⁶ I will be like the dew for Israel:
  he shall blossom like the lily;
He shall strike root like the Lebanon
    cedar,
⁷ and put forth his shoots.
His splendor shall be like the olive
    tree
  and his fragrance like the Lebanon
    cedar.
⁸ Again they shall dwell in his shade
  and raise grain;
They shall blossom like the vine,
  and his fame shall be like the wine of
    Lebanon.

⁹ Ephraim! What more has he to do with
    idols?
  I have humbled him, but I will prosper
    him.
"I am like a verdant cypress tree"—
  Because of me you bear fruit!

* * *

¹⁰ Let him who is wise understand these
    things;
  let him who is prudent know them.
Straight are the paths of the LORD,
  in them the just walk,
  but sinners stumble in them.*

13, 13: Israel's sin is such as to warrant its destruction (v 12), because it refuses to do penance. It will therefore perish as surely as the unborn child which dies in its mother's body because it does not properly employ the only way to safety.

13, 14: Shall . . . nether world: a vigorous affirmation of the Lord's determination to destroy Israel. St. Paul cites these words in a different sense (1 Cor 15, 54f), that of the ultimate victory of life over death in the resurrection of the body on the last day, wrought through the merits of Christ's passion and resurrection.

14, 10: A later addition in the style of the wisdom literature.

---

x: 1 Cor 15, 54.   *y:* Ex 19, 12.

See RG
349–51

The Book of Joel

This prophecy is rich in apocalyptic imagery and strongly eschatological in tone. It was composed about 400 B.C. Its prevailing theme is the day of the Lord.

A terrible invasion of locusts ravaged Judah. So frightful was the scourge that the prophet visualized it as a symbol of the coming day of the Lord. In the face of this threatening catastrophe, the prophet summoned the people to repent, to turn to the Lord with fasting and weeping. They were ordered to convoke a solemn assembly in which the priests would pray for deliverance. The Lord answered their prayer and promised to drive away the locusts and bless the land with peace and prosperity. To these material blessings would be added an outpouring of the spirit on all flesh. St. Peter, in his first discourse before the people at Pentecost (Acts 2, 16-21), sees in the coming of the Holy Spirit the fulfillment of this promise (1, 1—3, 5).

The concluding poem pictures the nations gathered in the Valley of Jehoshaphat, where the Lord is about to pass judgment. Israel's enemies are summoned to hear the solemn indictment; their evil deeds are at last requited. The tumultuous throng assembled in the valley of decision is made up of the enemies of God and they face inevitable destruction. The oracle changes abruptly from the terrifying image of judgment to a vision of Israel restored and forever secure from her enemies. God is both the vindicator of his people and the source of their blessing (4, 1-21).

———

See RG
349

CHAPTER 1

The Land Invaded. ¹The word of the LORD which came to Joel, the son of Pethuel.

² Hear this, you elders!
Pay attention, all you who dwell in the land!
Has the like of this happened in your days,

or in the days of your fathers?
³ Tell it to your children,
and your children to their children,
and their children to the next generation.
⁴ What the cutter left,
the locust swarm has eaten;
What the locust swarm left,
the grasshopper has eaten;
And what the grasshopper left,
the devourer* has eaten.

⁵ Wake up, you drunkards, and weep;
wail, all you drinkers of wine,
Because the juice of the grape
will be withheld from your mouths.
⁶ For a people* has invaded my land,
mighty and without number;
His teeth are the teeth of a lion,
and his molars those of a lioness.
⁷ He has laid waste my vine,
and blighted my fig tree;
He has stripped it, sheared off its bark;
its branches are made white.
⁸ Lament like a virgin girt with sackcloth
for the spouse of her youth.
⁹ Abolished are offering and libation
from the house of the LORD;
In mourning are the priests,
the ministers of the LORD.
¹⁰ The field is ravaged,
the earth mourns,
Because the grain is ravaged,
the must has failed,
the oil languishes.

¹¹ Be appalled, you husbandmen!
wail, you vinedressers!
Over the wheat and the barley,
because the harvest of the field has
perished.
¹² The vine has dried up,
the fig tree is withered;
The pomegranate, the date palm also, and
the apple,

1, 4: Cutter . . . locust . . . grasshopper . . . devourer: these names refer to various species of locusts: they can only be approximate.
1, 6: A people: the locusts compared to an invading army.

all the trees of the field are dried up;
Yes, joy has withered away
 from among mankind.

Call to Penance

¹³ Gird yourselves and weep, O priests!
 wail, O ministers of the altar!
Come, spend the night in sackcloth,
 O ministers of my God!
The house of your God is deprived
 of offering and libation.
¹⁴ Proclaim a fast,
 call an assembly;
Gather the elders,
 all who dwell in the land,
Into the house of the LORD, your
   God,
 and cry to the LORD!^a

¹⁵ Alas, the day!
 for near is the day of the LORD,
 and it comes as ruin from the
   Almighty.
¹⁶ From before our very eyes
 has not the food been cut off;
And from the house of our God,
 joy and gladness?
¹⁷ The seed lies shriveled under its
   clods;
 the stores are destroyed,
The barns are broken down,
 for the grain has failed.
¹⁸ How the beasts groan!
 The herds of cattle are bewildered!
Because they have no pasturage,
 even the flocks of sheep have
   perished.

¹⁹ To you, O LORD, I cry!
 for fire has devoured the pastures of
   the plain,
 and flame has enkindled all the trees of
   the field.
²⁰ Even the beasts of the field
 cry out to you;
For the streams of water are dried
   up,
 and fire has devoured the pastures of
   the plain.

---

a: Jl 2, 15.

CHAPTER 2

The Day of the Lord

See RG
349–50

¹ Blow the trumpet in Zion,
 sound the alarm on my holy mountain!
Let all who dwell in the land tremble,
 for the day of the LORD is coming;
² Yes, it is near, a day of darkness and of
   gloom,
 a day of clouds and somberness!
Like dawn spreading over the mountains,
 a people numerous and mighty!
Their like has not been from of old,
 nor will it be after them,
 even to the years of distant generations.
³ Before them a fire devours,
 and after them a flame enkindles;
Like the garden of Eden is the land
   before them,
 and after them a desert waste;
 from them there is no escape.

⁴ Their appearance is that of horses;
 like steeds they run.
⁵ As with the rumble of chariots
 they leap on the mountaintops;
As with the crackling of a fiery flame
 devouring stubble;
Like a mighty people
 arrayed for battle.
⁶ Before them peoples are in torment,
 every face blanches.

⁷ Like warriors they run,
 like soldiers they scale the wall;
They advance, each in his own lane,
 without swerving from their paths.
⁸ No one crowds another,
 each advances in his own track;
Though they fall into the ditches,
 they are not checked.

⁹ They assault the city,
 they run upon the wall,
 they climb into the houses;
In at the windows
 they come like thieves.
¹⁰ Before them the earth trembles,
 the heavens shake;

The sun and the moon are darkened,
    and the stars withhold their
        brightness.[b]

[11] The LORD raises his voice
    at the head of his army;
For immense indeed is his camp,
    yes, mighty, and it does his bidding.
For great is the day of the LORD,
    and exceedingly terrible; who can bear
        it?[c]
[12] Yet even now, says the LORD,
    return to me with your whole heart,
    with fasting, and weeping, and
        mourning;
[13] Rend your hearts, not your garments,
    and return to the LORD, your God.
For gracious and merciful is he,
    slow to anger, rich in kindness,
    and relenting in punishment.[d]
[14] Perhaps he will again relent
    and leave behind him a blessing,
Offerings and libations
    for the LORD, your God.[e]
[15] Blow the trumpet in Zion!
    proclaim a fast,
    call an assembly;[f]
[16] Gather the people,
    notify the congregation;
Assemble the elders,
    gather the children
    and the infants at the breast;
Let the bridegroom quit his room,
    and the bride her chamber.
[17] Between the porch and the altar*
    let the priests, the ministers of the
        LORD, weep,
And say, "Spare, O LORD, your people,
    and make not your heritage a reproach,
    with the nations ruling over them!
Why should they say among the peoples,
    'Where is their God?' "

Blessings for God's People. [18]Then the
LORD was stirred to concern for his land and
took pity on his people. [19]The LORD answered and said to his people:

See, I will send you
    grain, and wine, and oil,
    and you shall be filled with them;
No more will I make you
    a reproach among the nations.
[20] No, the northerner* I will remove far
        from you,
    and drive him out into a land arid and
        waste,
With his van toward the eastern sea,
    and his rear toward the western sea;
And his foulness shall go up,
    and his stench shall go up.

[21] Fear not, O land!
    exult and rejoice!
    for the LORD has done great things.
[22] Fear not, beasts of the field!
    for the pastures of the plain are green;
The tree bears its fruit,
    the fig tree and the vine give their
        yield.
[23] And do you, O children of Zion, exult
    and rejoice in the LORD, your God!
He has given you the teacher of justice:*
    he has made the rain come down for
        you,
    the early and the late rain as before.[g]
[24] The threshing floors shall be full of grain
    and the vats shall overflow with wine
        and oil.
[25] And I will repay you for the years
    which the locust has eaten,
The grasshopper, the devourer, and the
        cutter,
    my great army which I sent among
        you.
[26] You shall eat and be filled,

2, 17: The priests stood in the open space between the outdoor altar of holocausts and the temple building, facing the latter in order thereby to look toward God present in the holy of holies.

2, 20: The northerner: the locusts, that are compared to an invading army which in Palestine came from the north; cf Jer 1, 14f; 4, 6; Ez 26, 7; 38, 6. 15.

2, 23: The teacher of justice: the rain sent by God to show his fidelity to his promises, and to teach his people to be faithful to his commandments; cf Dt 11, 14. There is also a play on

words here between the Hebrew word moreh (teacher) and the Hebrew word yoreh (the early rain). The expression like-wise has a messianic connotation; cf Is 30, 20. The founder of the Essene sect of Qumran (second century B.C.) was known as "The Teacher of Justice."

b: Jl 4, 15; Is 13, 10; Ez 32, 7f; Mt 24, 29; Mk 13, 24; Lk 21, 25f.
c: Jer 30, 7; Am 5, 18; Zep 1, 15.   d: Ps 86, 5; Jon 4, 2.   e: Jon 3, 9.   f: Jl 1, 14.   g: Hos 10, 12.

and shall praise the name of the LORD,
    your God,
Because he has dealt wondrously with
    you;
    my people shall nevermore be put to
        shame.
27 And you shall know that I am in the
        midst of Israel;
I am the LORD, your God, and there is
    no other;
    my people shall nevermore be put to
        shame.

CHAPTER 3

See RG
350

1 Then afterward I will pour out[h]
my spirit* upon all mankind.
Your sons and daughters shall prophesy,
    your old men shall dream dreams,
    your young men shall see visions;
2 Even upon the servants and the
        handmaids,
    in those days, I will pour out my spirit.

3 And I will work wonders in the heavens
        and on the earth,
    blood, fire, and columns of smoke;
4 The sun will be turned to darkness,
    and the moon to blood,
At the coming of the day of the LORD,
    the great and terrible day.[i]
5 Then everyone shall be rescued
    who calls on the name of the LORD;
For on Mount Zion there shall be a
        remnant,
    as the LORD has said,
And in Jerusalem survivors
    whom the LORD shall call.[j]

CHAPTER 4

See RG
350

Judgment upon the Nations

1 Yes, in those days, and at that time,
    when I would restore the fortunes
    of Judah and Jerusalem;

2 I will assemble all the nations
    and bring them down to the Valley of
        Jehoshaphat,*
And I will enter into judgment with them
    there
    on behalf of my people and my
        inheritance, Israel;
Because they have scattered them among
        the nations,
    and divided my land.
3 Over my people they have cast lots;
    they gave a boy for a harlot,
    and sold a girl for the wine they drank.

4 Moreover, what are you to me, Tyre and Sidon, and all the regions of Philistia? Would you take vengeance upon me by some action? But if you do take action against me, swiftly, speedily, I will return your deed upon your own head. 5 You took my silver and my gold, and brought my precious treasures into your temples! 6 You sold the people of Judah and Jerusalem to the Greeks, removing them far from their own country! 7 See, I will rouse them from the place into which you have sold them, and I will return your deed upon your own head. 8 I will sell your sons and your daughters to the people of Judah, who shall sell them to the Sabeans,* a nation far off. Indeed, the LORD has spoken.

9 Declare this among the nations:
    proclaim a war,
    rouse the warriors to arms!
Let all the soldiers
    report and march!
10 Beat your plowshares into swords,
    and your pruning hooks into spears;
    let the weak man say, "I am a
        warrior!"*

11 Hasten and come, all you neighboring
    peoples,

3, 1f: I will pour out my spirit: in the Old Testament the spirit is the gift of God bestowed on those acting as his agents. The promise of the spirit is quoted by St. Peter in Acts 2, 17-21 as fulfilled in an eminent way by the gift of the Holy Spirit, the Third Person of the Blessed Trinity, bestowed on the Apostles.

4, 2: Valley of Jehosphaphat: a symbolic name of the place of final judgment (v 14). The name Jehosha-phat signifies "Yahweh judges." This place has been pop-

ularly identified with the Kidron Valley.

4, 8: Sabeans: a south Arabian people known for their commerce.

4, 10: This imagery is used in the reverse sense in Is 2, 4; Mi 4, 3. Here the warlike weapons are made in response to God's summons to armies which he selected to expel forever the unlawful invaders from the land of his chosen people.

---

h: 1-5: Is 44, 3; Acts 2, 17-21. i: Jl 2, 10. j: Rom 10, 13.

assemble there!

[Bring down, O Lord, your warriors!*]

¹² Let the nations bestir themselves and
come up
to the Valley of Jehoshaphat;
For there will I sit in judgment
upon all the neighboring nations.

¹³ Apply the sickle,ᵏ
for the harvest is ripe;
Come and tread,
for the wine press is full;
The vats overflow,
for great is their malice.*

¹⁴ Crowd upon crowd
in the valley of decision;
For near is the day of the LORD
in the valley of decision.

¹⁵ Sun and moon are darkened,
and the stars withhold their
brightness.ˡ

¹⁶ The LORD roars from Zion,
and from Jerusalem raises his voice;
The heavens and the earth quake,
but the LORD is a refuge to his people,
a stronghold to the men of Israel.ᵐ

Salvation for God's Elect

¹⁷ Then shall you know that I, the LORD, am
your God,
dwelling on Zion, my holy mountain;
Jerusalem shall be holy,
and strangers shall pass through her no
more.

¹⁸ And then, on that day,ⁿ
the mountains shall drip new wine,
and the hills shall flow with milk;
And the channels of Judah
shall flow with water:
A fountain shall issue from the house of
the LORD,
to water the Valley of Shittim.*

¹⁹ Egypt shall be a waste,
and Edom a desert waste,
Because of violence done to the people
of Judah,
because they shed innocent blood in
their land.

²⁰ But Judah shall abide forever,
and Jerusalem for all generations.

²¹ I will avenge their blood,
and not leave it unpunished.
The LORD dwells in Zion.

4, 11: Warriors: the angels; cf Zec 14, 5.

4, 13: Because of their numerous crimes, the nations are ripe for punishment. The use of warlike weapons against them is likened to the onslaught on the fields and vines at harvest time.

4, 18: The Valley of Shittim, or "the ravine of the acacia trees": perhaps a part of the Kidron Valley southeast of

Jerusalem; the prophetic picture of a stream of water flowing from a fountain in the temple of Jerusalem is to be found in Ez 47, 1. The Shittim east of the Jordan (see note on Nm 25, 1) is hardly referred to here.

———

k: Rv 14, 15.   l: Jl 2, 10; 3, 4.   m: Jer 25, 30; Am 1, 2.   n: Am 9, 13; Ez 47, 1-12; Zec 14, 8.

See RG
351–55

The Book of Amos

Amos was a shepherd of Tekoa in Judah, who exercised his ministry during the prosperous reign of Jeroboam II (786–746 B.C.). He prophesied in Israel at the great cult center of Bethel, from which he was finally expelled by the priest in charge of this royal sanctuary. The poetry of Amos, who denounces the hollow prosperity of the northern kingdom, is filled with imagery and language taken from his own pastoral background. The book is an anthology of his oracles and was compiled either by the prophet or by some of his disciples.

The prophecy begins with a sweeping indictment of Damascus, Philistia, Tyre, and Edom; but the forthright herdsman saves his climactic de-

nunciation for Israel, whose injustice and idolatry are sins against the light granted to her. Israel could indeed expect the day of Yahweh, but it would be a day of darkness and not light. When Amos prophesied the overthrow of the sanctuary, the fall of the royal house, and the captivity of the people, it was more than Israelite officialdom could bear. The priest of Bethel drove Amos from the shrine—but not before hearing a terrible sentence pronounced upon himself.

Amos is a prophet of divine judgment, and the sovereignty of Yahweh in nature and history dominates his thought. But he was no innovator; his conservatism was in keeping with the whole prophetic tradition calling the people back to the high moral and religious demands of Yahweh's revelation. In common with the other prophets, Amos knew that divine punishment is never completely destructive; it is part of the hidden plan of God to bring salvation to men. The perversity of the human will may retard, but it cannot totally frustrate, this design of a loving God. The last oracle opens up a perspective of restoration under a Davidic king.

The Book of Amos may be divided as follows:
I: Judgment of the Nations (1, 1—2, 16).
II: Words and Woes for Israel (3, 1—6, 14).
III: Symbolic Visions: Threats and Promises (7, 1—9, 8b).
Epilogue: Messianic Perspective (9, 8c-15).

I: Judgment of the Nations

CHAPTER 1

See RG 352 ¹The words of Amos, a shepherd from Tekoa,ᵃ which he received in vision concerning Israel, in the days of Uzziah, king of Judah, and in the days of Jeroboam, son of Joash, king of Israel, two years before the earthquake:*

² The LORD will roar from Zion,
and from Jerusalem raise his voice:
The pastures of the shepherds will
languish,
and the summit of Carmel wither.ᵇ

Aram

³ Thus says the LORD:
For three crimes of Damascus, and for
four,*
I will not revoke my word;
Because they threshed Gilead
with sledges of iron,
⁴ I will send fire* upon the house of
Hazael,
to devour the castles of Ben-hadad.
⁵ I will break the bar of Damascus;*
I will root out those who live in the
Valley of Aven,
And the sceptered ruler of Beth-eden;
the people of Aram shall be exiled to
Kir,
says the LORD.

Philistia

⁶ Thus says the LORD:
For three crimes of Gaza, and for four,
I will not revoke my word;
Because they took captive whole groups
to hand over to Edom,
⁷ I will send fire upon the wall of Gaza,
to devour her castles;
⁸ I will root out those who live in Ashdod,
and the sceptered ruler of Ashkelon;
I will turn my hand against Ekron,
and the last of the Philistines shall
perish,
says the Lord God.

Tyre

⁹ Thus says the LORD:
For three crimes of Tyre, and for four,
I will not revoke my word;
Because they delivered whole groups
captive to Edom,
and did not remember the pact of
brotherhood,*
¹⁰ I will send fire upon the wall of Tyre,
to devour her castles.

1, 1: The earthquake: which according to Hebrew tradition marked the crime of Uzziah when he attempted to offer incense in the temple (2 Chr 26, 16-21). Zechariah mentions it several centuries later (Zec 14, 5).

1, 3: For three crimes . . . four: crime after crime, an indefinite number; cf Am 1, 6. The series of judgments on the foreign nations shows that the Lord demands the observance of the moral order everywhere; Israel and Judah, despite their privileged position, are no exception. I will not revoke my word: God will not withdraw his threat of punishment against each of these nations. They threshed Gilead: the people of Aram under King Hazael had devastated Gilead; cf 2 Kgs 10, 32f.

1, 4: Fire: devastation caused by the Assyrians (Am 1, 7. 10. 12. 14; 2, 2. 5); cf 1 Sm 15, 18. Hazael . . . Ben-hadad: kings of the Arameans whose capital was Damascus (v 5); they fought against Israel (2 Kgs 13, 3), and had long occupied the region of Gilead (v 3) in Transjordan.

1, 5: Bar of Damascus: the beam securing the main gate of the city against invaders, symbol of its defenses. Valley of Aven ("vale of wickedness") . . . Beth-eden ("house of pleasure"): Aramean territory from southwest to northeast.

1, 9: Pact of brotherhood: Hiram of Tyre had made a pact with Solomon and called him brother (1 Kgs 5, 12; 9, 13).

---

a: Zec 14, 5. b: Jer 25, 30; Jl 3, 16.

Edom

11 Thus says the LORD:
For three crimes of Edom, and for four,
  I will not revoke my word;
Because he pursued his brother* with the
    sword,
  choking up all pity;
Because he persisted in his anger
  and kept his wrath to the end,
12 I will send fire upon Teman,
  and it will devour the castles of
    Bozrah.*

Ammon

13 Thus says the LORD:
For three crimes of the Ammonites, and
    for four,
  I will not revoke my word;
Because they ripped open expectant
    mothers in Gilead,
  while extending their territory,
14 I will kindle a fire upon the wall of
    Rabbah,*
  and it will devour her castles
Amid clamor on the day of battle
  and stormwind in a time of tempest.
15 Their king shall go into captivity,
  he and his princes with him, says the
    LORD.

CHAPTER 2

See RG 352

Moab

1 Thus says the LORD:
For three crimes of Moab, and for four,
  I will not revoke my word;
Because he burned to ashes
  the bones of Edom's king,*
2 I will send fire upon Moab,
  to devour the castles of Kerioth;

Moab shall meet death amid uproar
  and shouts and trumpet blasts.
3 I will root out the judge from her midst,
  and her princes I will slay with him,
    says the LORD.

Judah

4 Thus says the LORD:
For three crimes of Judah, and for four,
  I will not revoke my word;
Because they spurned the law of the
    LORD,
  and did not keep his statutes;
Because the lies* which their fathers
    followed
  have led them astray,
5 I will send fire upon Judah,
  to devour the castles of Jerusalem.

Israel

6 Thus says the LORD:
For three crimes of Israel, and for four,*
  I will not revoke my word;
Because they sell the just man for silver,
  and the poor man for a pair of
    sandals.*
7 They trample the heads of the weak
  into the dust of the earth,
  and force the lowly out of the way.
Son and father go to the same prostitute,
  profaning my holy name.
8 Upon garments taken in pledge
  they recline beside any altar;*
And the wine of those who have been
    fined
  they drink in the house of their god.

9 Yet it was I who destroyed the Amorites
  before them,

1, 11: Pursued his brother: the Edomites were descended from Esau, the brother of Jacob (Gn 25—27); nevertheless they constantly nourished enmity against Jacob's descendants, the Israelites.

1, 12: Teman and Bozrah: two of the chief cities of Edom; cf Jer 49, 20.

1, 14: Rabbah: now called Amman, the modern capital of the Hashemite Kingdom of Jordan.

2, 1: Here the prophet stresses the gravity of Moab's violation of the Semitic custom of providing honorable burial for the dead.

2, 4: The lies: false gods, who exist only in the minds of their worshipers. The crimes of Judah are infidelity and idol-

atry, in contrast to the sins for which the surrounding nations are judged.

2, 6-13: The detailed crimes of Israel are placed in strong contrast with the benefits with which the Lord favored his people.

2, 6: A pair of sandals: indicating how cheaply the rich regarded the poor.

2, 8: Upon garments . . . any altar: usurers kept the garments taken as pledges from the poor; but instead of restoring them to their owners before nightfall (Ex 22, 25; Dt 24, 12), they used them in idolatrous worship. Wine . . . their god: under the guise of a religious ceremony they drink the wine obtained through unjust fines.

who were as tall as the cedars,
  and as strong as the oak trees.
I destroyed their fruit above,
  and their roots beneath.*c*

[10] It was I who brought you up from the
    land of Egypt,
  and who led you through the desert for
    forty years,
  to occupy the land of the Amorites:*d*
[11] I who raised up prophets among your sons,
  and nazirites* among your young men.
Is this not so, O men of Israel?
  says the LORD.
[12] But you gave the nazirites wine to drink,
  and commanded the prophets not to
    prophesy.

[13] Beware, I will crush you into the ground
  as a wagon crushes when laden with
    sheaves.
[14] Flight shall perish from the swift,
  and the strong man shall not retain his
    strength;
The warrior shall not save his life,
[15]   nor the bowman stand his ground;
The swift of foot shall not escape,
  nor the horseman save his life.
[16] And the most stouthearted of warriors
    shall flee naked on that day, says the
    LORD.

II: Words and Woes for Israel

CHAPTER 3

See RG
353 *First Word.* [1]Hear this word, O men
of Israel, that the LORD pronounces over
you, over the whole family that I brought up
from the land of Egypt:

[2] You alone have I favored,
  more than all the families of the earth;
Therefore I will punish you
  for all your crimes.*

[3] Do two walk together
  unless they have agreed?

[4] Does a lion roar in the forest
  when it has no prey?
Does a young lion cry out from its den
  unless it has seized something?
[5] Is a bird brought to earth by a snare
  when there is no lure for it?
Does a snare spring up from the ground
  without catching anything?
[6] If the trumpet sounds in a city,
  will the people not be frightened?
If evil befalls a city,
  has not the LORD caused it?*
[7] Indeed, the Lord GOD does nothing
  without revealing his plan
  to his servants, the prophets.

[8] The lion roars—
  who will not be afraid!
The Lord GOD speaks—
  who will not prophesy!

[9] Proclaim this in the castles of Ashdod,
  in the castles of the land of Egypt:
"Gather about the mountain of
    Samaria,
  and see the great disorders within her,
  the oppression in her midst."*
[10] For they know not how to do what is
    right,
  says the LORD,
Storing up in their castles
  what they have extorted and robbed.
[11]   Therefore, thus says the Lord GOD:
An enemy shall surround the land,
  and strip you of your strength,
  and pillage your castles.

[12]   Thus says the LORD:
As the shepherd snatches from the mouth
    of the lion
  a pair of legs or the tip of an ear of his
    sheep,
So the Israelites who dwell in Samaria
    shall escape
  with the corner of a couch or a piece of
    a cot.

2, 11: Nazirites: see note on Nm 6, 1ff.
3, 2: God's choice of Israel brought its own responsibility.
3, 6: The sufferings which sinful man experiences through
the permissive will of God are presented here, as elsewhere in
the Old Testament, simply as caused by the Lord.

3, 9: Israel's southern neighbors, beyond Judah, are invited by the prophetic orator to witness the moral disorders of
God's people.

c: Nm 21, 24; Dt 2, 24.   d: Ex 14, 21; Dt 8, 2. 14.

[13]Hear and bear witness against the house of Jacob, says the Lord GOD, the God of hosts:

[14] On the day when I punish Israel for his crimes,
I will visit also the altars of Bethel:
The horns of the altar shall be broken off
and fall to the ground.
[15] Then will I strike the winter house
and the summer house;
The ivory apartments* shall be ruined,
and their many rooms shall be no more,
says the LORD.

CHAPTER 4

See RG 353

Second Word

[1] Hear this word, women of the mountain of Samaria,
you cows of Bashan,*
You who oppress the weak
and abuse the needy;
Who say to your lords,
"Bring drink for us!"
[2] The Lord GOD has sworn by his holiness:
Truly the days are coming upon you
When they shall drag you away with hooks,
the last of you with fishhooks;
[3] You shall go out through the breached walls
each by the most direct way,
And you shall be cast into the mire,
says the LORD.

[4] Come to Bethel and sin,
to Gilgal, and sin the more;*
Each morning bring your sacrifices,
every third day, your tithes;
[5] Burn leavened food as a thanksgiving sacrifice,
proclaim publicly your freewill offerings,

For so you love to do, O men of Israel,
says the Lord GOD.

[6] Though I have made your teeth
clean of food in all your cities,
and have made bread scarce in all your dwellings,
Yet you returned not to me,
says the LORD.

[7] Though I also withheld the rain from you
when the harvest was still three months away;
I sent rain upon one city
but not upon another;
One field was watered by rain,
but another without rain dried up;
[8] Though two or three cities staggered to one city
for water that did not quench their thirst;
Yet you returned not to me,
says the LORD.

[9] I struck you with blight and searing wind;
your many gardens and vineyards,
your fig trees and olive trees the locust devoured;
Yet you returned not to me,
says the LORD.[e]

[10] I sent upon you a pestilence like that of Egypt,*
and with the sword I slew your young men;
Your horses I let be captured,
to your nostrils I brought the stench of your camps;
Yet you returned not to me,
says the LORD.

[11] I brought upon you such upheaval
as when God overthrew Sodom and Gomorrah:

3, 15: Ivory apartments: rooms containing furniture inlaid in ivory, similar to the pieces discovered in the excavations at Samaria.

4, 1: Bashan: the region east of the Sea of Galilee, famous for its rich pasture and fattened herds, to which Amos likens the indolent women of Samaria.

4, 4f: This invitation to the sanctuaries of the northern kingdom is ironical. Pilgrimages to the shrines of Bethel and

Gilgal were the more displeasing to God because they were contrary to his will and ineffective toward improvement of morals.

4, 10: Pestilence like that of Egypt: plagues were well known in Egypt; cf Dt 7, 15; 28, 27. 60. Stench of your camps: caused by the unburied bodies.

e: Hg 2, 17.

you were like a brand plucked from
the fire;
Yet you returned not to me,
says the LORD.[f]

[12] So now I will deal with you in my own
way, O Israel!
and since I will deal thus with you,
prepare to meet your God, O Israel:
[13] Him who formed the mountains, and
created the wind,
and declares to man his thoughts;
Who made the dawn and the darkness,
and strides upon the heights of the
earth:
The LORD, the God of hosts by name.

CHAPTER 5

See RG
353-54

Third Word

[1] Hear this word which I utter over you,
a lament, O house of Israel:
[2] She is fallen, to rise no more,
the virgin Israel;
She lies abandoned upon her land,
with no one to raise her up.

[3]　　　For thus says the Lord GOD:
The city that marched out with a
thousand
shall be left with a hundred,
Another that marched out with a
hundred
shall be left with ten,
of the house of Israel.

[4] For thus says the LORD
to the house of Israel:
Seek me, that you may live,
[5]　but do not seek Bethel;
Do not come to Gilgal,
and do not cross to Beer-sheba.
For Gilgal shall be led into exile,
and Bethel shall become nought.
[6] Seek the LORD, that you may live,
lest he come upon the house of
Joseph[*] like a fire

That shall consume, with none to
quench it
for the house of Israel:
[8] He who made the Pleiades and Orion,
who turns darkness into dawn,
and darkens day into night;
Who summons the waters of the sea,
and pours them out upon the surface of
the earth;[g]
[9] Who flashes destruction upon the strong,
and brings ruin upon the fortress;
whose name is LORD.

First Woe

[7] Woe to those who turn judgment to
wormwood
and cast justice to the ground!
[10] They hate him who reproves at the gate[*]
and abhor him who speaks the truth.
[11] Therefore, because you have trampled
upon the weak
and exacted of them levies of grain,
Though you have built houses of hewn
stone,
you shall not live in them!
Though you have planted choice
vineyards,
you shall not drink their wine![h]

[12] Yes, I know how many are your crimes,
how grievous your sins:
Oppressing the just, accepting bribes,
repelling the needy at the gate!
[13] Therefore the prudent man is silent at
this time,
for it is an evil time.
[14] Seek good and not evil,
that you may live;
Then truly will the LORD, the God of hosts,
be with you as you claim!
[15] Hate evil and love good,
and let justice prevail at the gate;
Then it may be that the LORD, the God of
hosts,
will have pity on the remnant of
Joseph.[i]

5, 6: House of Joseph: the kingdom of Israel or northern kingdom, the chief tribes of which were descended from Ephraim and Manasseh, the sons of Joseph; cf Am 5, 15; 6, 6.
5, 10: At the gate: see note on Ps 127, 5.

f: Gn 19, 24.　　*g:* Am 9, 6.　　*h:* Zep 1, 13.　　*i:* Ps 97, 10; Rom 12, 9.

16 Therefore, thus says the LORD,
    the God of hosts, the Lord:
In every square there shall be
    lamentation,
and in every street they shall cry, Alas!
    Alas!
They shall summon the farmers to wail
    and professional mourners to lament,
17 And in every vineyard there shall be
    lamentation
when I pass through your midst, says
    the LORD.

Second Woe

18 Woe to those who yearn for the day of
    the LORD!*
What will this day of the LORD mean
    for you?
Darkness and not light!*j*
19 As if a man were to flee from a lion,
    and a bear should meet him;
Or as if on entering his house
    he were to rest his hand against the
    wall,
    and a snake should bite him.
20 Will not the day of the LORD be darkness
    and not light,
    gloom without any brightness?

21 *I hate, I spurn your feasts,
    I take no pleasure in your solemnities;*k*
22 Your cereal offerings I will not accept,
    nor consider your stall-fed peace
    offerings.
23 Away with your noisy songs!

I will not listen to the melodies of your
    harps.
But if you would offer me holocausts,
24   then let justice surge like water,
    and goodness like an unfailing stream.
25 Did you bring me sacrifices and offerings*l*
    for forty years in the desert, O house
    of Israel?*
26 You will carry away Sakkuth, your king,
    and Kaiwan, your star god,*
    the images that you have made for
    yourselves;
27 For I will exile you beyond Damascus,
    say I, the LORD, the God of hosts by
    name.

CHAPTER 6

See RG
354

Third Woe

1 *Woe to the complacent in Zion,
    To the overconfident on the mount of
    Samaria,*
Leaders of a nation favored from the first,
    to whom the people of Israel have
    recourse!*m*
2 Pass over to Calneh and see,
    go from there to Hamath the great,
    and down to Gath of the Philistines!
Are you better than these kingdoms,
    or is your territory wider than theirs?
3 You would put off the evil day,
    yet you hasten the reign of violence!

4 Lying upon beds of ivory,
    stretched comfortably on their
    couches,

5, 18: Day of the Lord: a technical expression which in earliest times referred to God's special intervention in human affairs. Through it his power and justice triumphed in his people. The present passage is the first instance in which it means a day of punishment of sinners. During the exile it assumed the meaning of a time when God would avenge Israel against her oppressors and bring about her restoration (Jer 50, 27; Ez 30, 3ff). Still later it came to mean the day of final judgment of the world when the good will be rewarded and the wicked punished (Jl 2, 1ff; Zep 1, 14ff; Mal 3, 19ff).

5, 21-27: The Lord condemns, not ritual worship in itself, but the cult whose exterior rites and solemnity have no relation to interior morality and justice. The Israelites falsely worshiped him as neighboring nations adored Baal or Chamos, deities which were thought to protect their respective peoples against their enemies in return for ritual observances, without any relation to right conduct.

5, 25: The meaning is not certain; according to some, the

idea is that during the forty years' wandering in the desert the simple, rudimentary worship of God was accompanied by the practice of justice, in contrast to the elaborate ritual unaccompanied by works of justice in the prophet's time.

5, 26: Sakkuth . . . star god: although the text is uncertain, it seems quite probable that reference is made to the Assyrian deities, Sakkuth, god of war and light, and Kaiwan, the planet Saturn. The people will go into exile, from which these gods have been unable to save them.

6, 1-7: The luxury of the people in Samaria will be punished by exile. They failed to learn the lesson from Calneh, Hamath and Gath at the approach of the powerful and warlike Assyrians.

6, 1: The complacent in Zion . . . the overconfident . . . of Samaria: the proud and self-interested rulers of Judah and Israel.

---

j: Jer 30, 7; Jl 2, 11; Zep 1, 15.   *k:* Is 1, 11; Jer 6, 20; Mal 1, 12.   *l:* Acts 7, 42.   *m:* Lk 6, 24.

They eat lambs taken from the flock,
    and calves from the stall!
5 Improvising to the music of the harp,
    like David, they devise their own
       accompaniment.
6 They drink wine from bowls
    and anoint themselves with the best
       oils;
    yet they are not made ill by the
       collapse of Joseph!
7 Therefore, now they shall be the first to
       go into exile,
    and their wanton revelry shall be done
       away with.

8 The Lord GOD has sworn by his very
       self,
    say I, the LORD, the God of hosts:
I abhor the pride of Jacob,
    I hate his castles,
    and I give over the city with
       everything in it;[n]
9 Should there remain ten men
    in a single house, these shall die.
10 Only a few shall be left
    to carry the dead out of the houses;
If one says to a man inside a house,
    "Is anyone with you?" and he answers,
    "No one,"
Then he shall say, "Silence!"
    for no one must mention the name of
       the LORD.
11 Indeed, the LORD has given the command
    to shatter the great house to bits,
    and reduce the small house to rubble.

12 Can horses run across a cliff?
    or can one plow the sea with oxen?*
Yet you have turned judgment into gall,
    and the fruit of justice into
       wormwood.
13 You rejoice in Lodebar,
    and say, "Have we not, by our own
       strength,

seized for ourselves Karnaim?"*
14 Beware, I am raising up against you,
    O house of Israel,
    say I, the LORD, the God of hosts,
A nation* that shall oppress you
    from Labo of Hamath even to the
       Wadi Arabah.

III: Symbolic Visions: Threats and Promises

CHAPTER 7

See RG 351-52, 354

Vision of Locusts. 1This is what the Lord GOD showed me: He was forming a locust swarm when the late growth began to come up (the late growth after the king's mowing*). 2While they were eating all the grass in the land, I said:

Forgive, O Lord GOD!
    How can Jacob stand?
    He is so small!

3And the LORD repented of this. "It shall not be," said the Lord GOD.

Vision of Fire. 4Then the Lord GOD showed me this: he called for a judgment by fire.* It had devoured the great abyss, and was consuming the land, 5when I said:

Cease, O Lord GOD!
    How can Jacob stand?
    He is so small!

6The LORD repented of this. "This also shall not be," said the Lord GOD.

Vision of the Plummet. 7Then the Lord GOD showed me this: he was standing by a wall, plummet in hand.* 8The LORD asked me, "What do you see, Amos?" And when I answered, "A plummet," the LORD said:

See, I will lay the plummet
    in the midst of my people Israel;
    I will forgive them no longer.

6, 12: Can horses . . . oxen?: one cannot change the course of nature, as the Israelites attempted to do by their sins of injustice.

6, 13: Lodebar . . . Karnaim: in Transjordan; they had been captured by the Israelites. Perhaps it is in irony that reference is made to these two cities, for the root of the first suggests "nothing" and that of the second, "horns" or "strength."

6, 14: A nation: Assyria.

7, 1: The king's mowing: the first mowing, a portion of which was payable to the king as a tax.

7, 4: Fire: understood by many as a burning drought.

7, 7: Plummet in hand: signifying that God is about to withdraw his mercy from his people and that the nation is to be measured for destruction.

---

n: Jer 51, 14.

9 The high places of Isaac shall be laid
        waste,
    and the sanctuaries of Israel made
        desolate;
    I will attack the house of Jeroboam
        with the sword.

Amos and Amaziah. 10 Amaziah, the priest of Bethel, sent word to Jeroboam, king of Israel: "Amos has conspired against you here within Israel; the country cannot endure all his words. 11 For this is what Amos says:

Jeroboam shall die by the sword,
    and Israel shall surely be exiled from
        its land."

12 To Amos, Amaziah said: "Off with you, visionary, flee to the land of Judah! There earn your bread by prophesying, 13 but never again prophesy in Bethel; for it is the king's sanctuary and a royal temple." 14 Amos answered Amaziah, "I was no prophet, nor have I belonged to a company of prophets; I was a shepherd and a dresser of sycamores.* 15 The LORD took me from following the flock, and said to me, Go, prophesy to my people Israel. 16 Now hear the word of the LORD!"

You say: prophesy not against Israel,
    preach not against the house of Isaac.
17   Now thus says the LORD:
    Your wife shall be made a harlot in the
        city,
    and your sons and daughters shall fall
        by the sword;
    Your land shall be divided by measuring
        line,
    and you yourself shall die in an
        unclean land;
    Israel shall be exiled far from its land.

See RG 354

CHAPTER 8

Vision of the Fruit Basket. 1 This is what the Lord GOD showed me: a basket of ripe fruit. 2 "What do you see, Amos?" he asked. I answered, "A basket of ripe fruit." Then the LORD said to me:

The time is ripe to have done with my
        people Israel;
    I will forgive them no longer.
3 The temple songs shall become wailings
        on that day,
    says the Lord GOD.
Many shall be the corpses,
    strewn everywhere.—Silence!

Against Greed

4 Hear this, you who trample upon the
        needy
    and destroy the poor of the land!
5 "When will the new moon be over," you
        ask,
    "that we may sell our grain,
    and the sabbath, that we may display
        the wheat?
We will diminish the ephah,*
    add to the shekel,
    and fix our scales for cheating!
6 We will buy the lowly man for silver,
    and the poor man for a pair of
        sandals;
    even the refuse of the wheat we will
        sell!"
7 The LORD has sworn by the pride of
        Jacob:*
    Never will I forget a thing they have
        done!
8 Shall not the land tremble because of
        this,
    and all who dwell in it mourn,
While it rises up and tosses like the
        Nile,
    and settles back like the river of
        Egypt?*

9 On that day, says the Lord GOD,
    I will make the sun set at midday
    and cover the earth with darkness in
        broad daylight.
10 I will turn your feasts into mourning
    and all your songs into lamentations.
    I will cover the loins of all with sackcloth
    and make every head bald.

7, 14f: Amos denies that he belonged to the class of professional prophets; his vocation is due to the personal intervention of the Lord.

8, 5: Ephah: a standard of measure; a little more than a bushel.

8, 7: The pride of Jacob: the sinful pride detested by God (Am 6, 8), in contrast to God himself, who is the true Pride of Jacob.

8, 8: The figure is based on the annual flooding of the river Nile.

I will make them mourn as for an only
son,
  and bring their day to bitter end.*o*

¹¹ Yes, days are coming, says the Lord
GOD,
  when I will send famine upon the land:
Not a famine of bread, or thirst for water,
  but for hearing the word of the LORD.
¹² Then shall they wander from sea to sea
  and rove from the north to the east
In search of the word of the LORD,
  but they shall not find it.

¹³ On that day, fair virgins and young men
  shall faint from thirst;
¹⁴ Those who swear by the shameful idol of
Samaria,
  "By the life of your god, O Dan!"
"By the life of your love, O Beer-sheba!"
  those shall fall, never to rise again.*

CHAPTER 9

See RG
354-55

*Vision of the Altar.** ¹I saw the Lord
standing beside the altar, and he said:

Strike the bases, so that the doorjambs
totter
  till you break them off on the heads of
  them all!
Those who are left I will slay with the
sword;
  not one shall flee,
  no survivor shall escape.
² Though they break through to the nether
world,
  even from there my hand shall bring
  them out;
Though they climb to the heavens,
  I will bring them down;*p*
³ Though they hide on the summit of
Carmel,
  there too I will hunt them out and take
  them away;

Though they hide from my gaze
  in the bottom of the sea,
  I will command the serpent* there to
  bite them;
⁴ Though they are led into captivity by
their enemies,
  there will I command the sword to slay
  them.
I will fix my gaze upon them
  for evil, and not for good,*q*
⁵ I, the Lord GOD of hosts.
I melt the earth with my touch,
  so that all who dwell on it mourn,
While it all rises up like the Nile,
  and settles back like the river of
  Egypt;
⁶ I have built heaven, my upper chamber,
  and established my vault over the
  earth;
I summon the waters of the sea
  and pour them out upon the surface of
  the earth,
  I, the LORD by name.*r*

⁷ Are you not like the Ethiopians to me,
  O men of Israel, says the LORD?
Did I not bring the Israelites from the
  land of Egypt
As I brought the Philistines from
  Caphtor
  and the Arameans* from Kir?*s*
⁸ The eyes of the Lord GOD are on this
  sinful kingdom:
  I will destroy it from off the face of the
  earth.

Epilogue: Messianic Perspective
But I will not destroy the house of Jacob
  completely,
  says the LORD.
⁹ For see, I have given the command
  to sift the house of Israel among all the
  nations,
As one sifts with a sieve,

8, 14: Dan and Beer-sheba, the extreme northern and
southern limits of the country, where idolatrous worship was
offered.

9, 1-8: There will be no escape from God's punishment,
symbolized here by the destruction of a building, probably
the schismatic temple at Bethel.

9, 3: Serpent: the sea monster of familiar legend,
subdued by God at the time of creation and lurking still

in the ocean depths; cf Ps 89, 10f.

9, 7: The Ethiopians . . . the Philistines . . . the Arameans:
by nature Israel is not different from any other nation. It was
not because of any merit on Israel's part that God delivered
them from Egypt. Caphtor: the island of Crete.

---

o: Tb 2, 6; 1 Mc 1, 41.   *p:* Ps 139, 8.   *q:* Jer 44, 11.   *r:* Am 5,
8.   *s:* Dt 2, 23; Jer 47, 4.

letting no pebble fall to the ground.

[10] By the sword shall all sinners among my
people die,
those who say, "Evil will not reach or
overtake us."

[11] *On that day I will raise up
the fallen hut of David;
I will wall up its breaches,
raise up its ruins,
and rebuild it as in the days of old,[t]

[12] That they may conquer what is left of
Edom
and all the nations that shall bear my
name,
say I, the LORD, who will do this.

[13] Yes, days are coming,
says the LORD,

When the plowman shall overtake the
reaper,
and the vintager, him who sows the
seed;
The juice of grapes shall drip down the
mountains,
and all the hills shall run with it.[u]

[14] I will bring about the restoration of my
people Israel;
they shall rebuild and inhabit their
ruined cities,
Plant vineyards and drink the wine,
set out gardens and eat the fruits.

[15] I will plant them upon their own ground;
never again shall they be plucked
From the land I have given them,
say I, the LORD, your God.

9, 11f: In Acts 15, 15ff St. James interprets this passage in a messianic sense. Fallen hut: the kingdom. The nations that shall bear my name: the Gentile peoples who shall be converted to the Lord, that is, conquered by him, and therefore shall bear his name.

t: Acts 15, 16.   *u:* Jl 3, 18.

See RG
356

The Book of Obadiah

The twenty-one verses of this book contain the shortest and sternest prophecy in the Old Testament. Nothing is known of the author, although his oracle against Edom, a long-standing enemy of Israel, indicates a date of composition sometime in the fifth century B.C. During this period the Edomites had been forced to abandon their ancient home near the Gulf of Aqaba and had settled in southern Judah, where they appear among the adversaries of the Jews returning from exile.

The prophecy is a bitter cry for vengeance against Edom for its heinous crimes. The mountain of Esau will be occupied and ravaged by the enemy but Zion shall remain inviolate. Judah and Israel shall again form one nation; and that triumphant refrain of Israelite eschatology will be heard once more: "The Kingdom is the Lord's!" Many of the verses in this prophecy can be paralleled in Jer 49, 7-22 but it is difficult to determine the precise relationship between these similar passages.

Title and Theme

[1] The vision of Obadiah.
[Thus says the LORD God:]
Of Edom we have heard a message from
the LORD,
and a herald has been sent among the
nations:
"Up! let us go to war against him!"[a]

Edom Shall Perish

[2] See, I make you small among the
nations;[b]
you are held in dire contempt.

[3] The pride of your heart has deceived you:
you who dwell in the clefts of the rock,
whose abode is in the heights,
Who say in your heart,
"Who will bring me down to earth?"

[4] Though you go as high as the eagle,
and your nest be set among the stars,
From there will I bring you down,
says the LORD.

a: Jer 49, 14.   *b:* 2ff: Jer 49, 15f.

⁵ If thieves came to you, if robbers by
    night,ᶜ
  how could you be thus destroyed:
  would they not steal merely till they
      had enough?
  If vintagers came to you,
  would they not leave some gleanings?*
⁶ How they search Esau,
  seek out his hiding places!
⁷ To the border they drive you—
  all your allies;
  They deceive you, they overpower you—
  those at peace with you;
  Those who eat your bread
  lay snares beneath you:
  There is no understanding in him!*
⁸ Shall I not, says the LORD, on that day
  make the wise men* disappear from
      Edom,
  and understanding from the mount of
      Esau?ᵈ
⁹ Your warriors, O Teman,* shall be
      crushed,
  till all on Mount Esau are destroyed.

The Cause

¹⁰ Because of violence to your brother
    Jacob,*
  disgrace shall cover you
  and you shall be destroyed forever.ᵉ
¹¹ On the day when you stood by,
  on the day when aliens carried off his
      possessions,
  And strangers entered his gates
  and cast lots over Jerusalem,
  you too were one of them.*
¹² Gaze not upon the day of your brother,
  the day of his disaster;
  Exult not over the children of Judah

on the day of their ruin;
  Speak not haughtily
  on the day of distress!
¹³ Enter not the gate of my people
  on the day of their calamity;
  Gaze not, you at least, upon his
      misfortune
  on the day of his calamity;
  Lay not hands upon his possessions
  on the day of his calamity!
¹⁴ Stand not at the crossroads
  to slay his refugees;
  Betray not his fugitives
  on the day of distress!

Judgment upon the Nations

¹⁵ For near is the day of the LORDᶠ
  for all the nations!
  As you have done, so shall it be done to
      you,
  your deed shall come back upon your
      own head;
¹⁶ As you have drunk* upon my holy
      mountain,
  so shall all the nations drink
      continually.
  Yes, they shall drink and swallow,
  and shall become as though they had
      not been.

Judah Shall Be Restored

¹⁷ But on Mount Zion there shall be a
      portion saved;*
  the mountain shall be holy,
  And the house of Jacob shall take
      possession
  of those that dispossessed them.
¹⁸ The house of Jacob shall be a fire,
  and the house of Joseph a flame;

5: Something of value may escape the robber, and the vintager always leaves something for the gleaners, but God's devastation of Edom will be complete.

7: There is no understanding in him: Edom's faithless allies assure one another that he does not have sense enough to be able to defend himself.

8: The wise men: Edom was proverbial for its wise men; cf Jer 49, 7.

9: Teman: one of the names used for the land southeast of Palestine, here synonymous with Edom. Esau: here used as the name of the land.

10: Your brother Jacob: Esau, also called Edom, and Jacob, the father of Judah, were the sons of Isaac (Gn 25, 24ff).

11: After the devastation of Judah, Edom occupied the southern part of its territory. Edomites also joined the invading Chaldean forces (13) and assisted them in capturing the people of Judah (14).

16: As you have drunk: the Lord addresses the people of Judah. As the people of Jerusalem have drunk the cup of retribution, so shall the nations, and especially Edom (18), suffer punishment. This metaphorical use of drinking the cup of God's wrath is common in the Bible; cf Jb 21, 20; Is 19, 14; Jer 25, 15f.

17ff: The Israelites shall be restored and shall occupy the lands of those who oppressed them. The survivors of Judah shall be rejoined by the returned exiles from northern Israel.

c: Jer 49, 9.   *d:* Is 29, 14; 1 Cor 1, 19.   *e:* Gn 27, 41f.   *f:* 15f: Ps 137, 7ff.

The house of Esau shall be stubble,
 and they shall set them ablaze and
  devour them;
Then none shall survive of the house of
  Esau,
 for the LORD has spoken.
19 They shall occupy the Negeb, the mount
  of Esau,
 and the foothills of the Philistines;
And they shall occupy the lands of
  Ephraim
 and the lands of Samaria,

and Benjamin shall occupy Gilead.
20 The captives of this host of the children
  of Israel
shall occupy the Canaanite land as far
  as Zarephath,*
And the captives of Jerusalem who are in
  Sepharad
shall occupy the cities of the
  Negeb.
21 And saviors* shall ascend Mount Zion
 to rule the mount of Esau,
 and the kingship shall be the LORD's.

20: Zarephath: a town in Phoenicia, north of Tyre; cf 1 Kgs 17, 10. Ezekiel's ideal boundaries of the new Israel (Ez 47, 13ff) extend farther north. Sepharad: probably Sardis in western Asia Minor. The later rabbis thought it to be Spain.

21: Saviors: the victorious Israelites who will rule over their enemies after the fashion of the ancient Judges; cf Jgs 3, 9. 15. 31; 10, 1.

See RG
357–58

The Book of Jonah

Written in the postexilic era, probably in the fifth century B.C., this book is a didactic story with an important theological message. It concerns a disobedient prophet who attempted to run away from his divine commission, was cast overboard and swallowed by a great fish, rescued in a marvelous manner, and sent on his way to Nineveh, the traditional enemy of Israel. To the surprise of Jonah, the wicked city listened to his message of doom and repented immediately. All, from king to lowliest subject, humbled themselves in sackcloth and ashes. Seeing their repentance, God did not carry out the punishment he had planned for them. Whereupon Jonah complained to God about the unexpected success of his mission; he was bitter because Yahweh, instead of destroying, had led the people to repentance and then spared them.

From this partly humorous story, a very sublime lesson may be drawn. Jonah stands for a narrow and vindictive mentality, all too common among the Jews of that period. Because they were the chosen people, a good many of them cultivated an intolerant nationalism which limited the mercy of God to their nation. It was abhorrent to their way of thinking that nations as wicked as Assyria should escape his wrath.

The prophecy, which is both instructive and entertaining, strikes directly at this viewpoint. It is a parable of mercy, showing that God's threatened punishments are but the expression of a merciful will which moves all men to repent and seek forgiveness. The universality of the story contrasts sharply with the particularistic spirit of many in the postexilic community. The book has also prepared the way for the gospel with its message of redemption for all, both Jew and Gentile.

CHAPTER 1

See RG
357

The First Mission. *1*This is the word of the LORD that came to Jonah,*a* son of Amittai:* *2*"Set out for the great city of Nineveh, and preach against it; their wickedness has come up before me."*b* *3*But Jonah made ready to flee to Tarshish* away from the LORD. He went down to Joppa, found a ship going to Tarshish, paid the fare, and went aboard to journey with them to Tarshish, away from the LORD.

*4*The LORD, however, hurled a violent wind upon the sea, and in the furious tempest

1, 1: Jonah, son of Amittai: a prophet of this name lived at the time of Jeroboam II (786–746 B.C.).

1, 3: Tarshish: identified by many with Tartessus, an ancient Phoenician colony in southwest Spain; precise identification with any particular Phoenician center in the western

Mediterranean is uncertain. To the Hebrews it stood for the far west.

a: 2 Kgs 14, 25. *b:* Jon 3, 3; 4, 11.

that arose the ship was on the point of breaking up. ⁵Then the mariners became frightened and each one cried to his god. To lighten the ship for themselves, they threw its cargo into the sea. Meanwhile, Jonah had gone down into the hold of the ship, and lay there fast asleep. ⁶The captain came to him and said, "What are you doing asleep? Rise up, call upon your God! Perhaps God will be mindful of us so that we may not perish."

⁷Then they said to one another, "Come, let us cast lots to find out on whose account we have met with this misfortune." So they cast lots, and thus singled out Jonah. ⁸"Tell us," they said, "what is your business? Where do you come from? What is your country, and to what people do you belong?" ⁹"I am a Hebrew," Jonah answered them; "I worship the LORD, the God of heaven, who made the sea and the dry land."

¹⁰Now the men were seized with great fear and said to him, "How could you do such a thing!"—They knew that he was fleeing from the LORD, because he had told them.— ¹¹"What shall we do with you," they asked, "that the sea may quiet down for us?" For the sea was growing more and more turbulent. ¹²Jonah said to them, "Pick me up and throw me into the sea, that it may quiet down for you; since I know it is because of me that this violent storm has come upon you."

¹³Still the men rowed hard to regain the land, but they could not, for the sea grew ever more turbulent. ¹⁴Then they cried to the LORD: "We beseech you, O LORD, let us not perish for taking this man's life; do not charge us with shedding innocent blood, for you, LORD, have done as you saw fit."* ¹⁵Then they took Jonah and threw him into the sea, and the sea's raging abated. ¹⁶Struck with great fear of the LORD, the men offered sacrifice and made vows to him.

CHAPTER 2

See RG 357

¹But the LORD sent a large fish, that swallowed Jonah; and he remained in the belly of the fish three days and three nights.ᶜ ²From the belly of the fish Jonah said this prayer to the LORD, his God:

Psalm of Thanksgiving

³ Out of my distress I called to the LORD,
and he answered me;
From the midst of the nether world I
cried for help,
and you heard my voice.ᵈ
⁴ For you cast me into the deep, into the
heart of the sea,
and the flood enveloped me;
All your breakers and your billows
passed over me.ᵉ
⁵ Then I said, "I am banished from your
sight!
yet would I again look upon your holy
temple."ᶠ
⁶ The waters swirled about me, threatening
my life;
the abyss enveloped me;
seaweed clung about my head.ᵍ
⁷ Down I went to the roots of the
mountains;
the bars of the nether world
were closing behind me forever,
But you brought up my life from the pit,
O LORD, my God.ʰ
⁸ When my soul fainted within me,
I remembered the LORD;
My prayer reached you
in your holy temple.ⁱ
⁹ Those who worship vain idols
forsake their source of mercy.ʲ
¹⁰ But I, with resounding praise,
will sacrifice to you;
What I have vowed I will pay:
deliverance is from the LORD.ᵏ

¹¹Then the LORD commanded the fish to spew Jonah upon the shore.

CHAPTER 3

See RG 357–58

Conversion of Nineveh. ¹The word of the LORD came to Jonah a second time: ²"Set

---

1, 14: Since it has pleased the Lord to punish Jonah, the mariners ask that in ridding themselves of him they be not charged with the crime of murder.

c: Mt 12, 40; 16, 4; Lk 11, 30; 1 Cor 15, 4.   *d:* Pss 18, 7; 120, 1.   *e:* Ps 42, 8.   *f:* Ps 31, 23; Is 38, 11.   *g:* Pss 18, 5; 69, 2.   *h:* Pss 16, 10; 30, 4.   *i:* Pss 5, 8; 18, 7; 88, 3.   *j:* Ps 31, 7.   *k:* Ps 50, 14.

out for the great city of Nineveh, and announce to it the message that I will tell you." ³So Jonah made ready and went to Nineveh, according to the LORD's bidding. Now Nineveh was an enormously large city; it took three days to go through it. ⁴Jonah began his journey through the city, and had gone but a single day's walk announcing, "Forty days more and Nineveh shall be destroyed,"* ⁵when the people of Nineveh believed God; they proclaimed a fast and all of them, great and small, put on sackcloth.ˡ

⁶When the news reached the king of Nineveh, he rose from his throne, laid aside his robe, covered himself with sackcloth, and sat in the ashes. ⁷Then he had this proclaimed throughout Nineveh, by decree of the king and his nobles: "Neither man nor beast, neither cattle nor sheep, shall taste anything; they shall not eat, nor shall they drink water. ⁸Man and beast shall be covered with sackcloth* and call loudly to God; every man shall turn from his evil way and from the violence he has in hand. ⁹Who knows, God may relent and forgive, and withhold his blazing wrath, so that we shall not perish."ᵐ ¹⁰When God saw by their actions how they turned from their evil way, he repented of the evil that he had threatened to do to them; he did not carry it out.

CHAPTER 4

See RG 358

Jonah's Anger: God's Reproof. ¹But this was greatly displeasing to Jonah, and he became angry.* ²"I beseech you, LORD," he prayed, "is not this what I said while I was still in my own country? This is why I fled at first to Tarshish. I knew that you are a gracious and merciful God, slow to anger, rich in clemency, loathe to punish.ⁿ ³And now, LORD, please take my life from me; for it is better for me to die than to live."ᵒ ⁴But the LORD asked, "Have you reason to be angry?"

⁵Jonah then left the city for a place to the east of it, where he built himself a hut and waited under it in the shade, to see what would happen to the city. ⁶And when the LORD God provided a gourd plant,* that grew up over Jonah's head, giving shade that relieved him of any discomfort, Jonah was very happy over the plant. ⁷But the next morning at dawn God sent a worm which attacked the plant, so that it withered. ⁸And when the sun arose, God sent a burning east wind; and the sun beat upon Jonah's head till he became faint. Then he asked for death, saying, "I would be better off dead than alive."

⁹But God said to Jonah, "Have you reason to be angry over the plant?" "I have reason to be angry," Jonah answered, "angry enough to die." ¹⁰Then the LORD said, "You are concerned over the plant which cost you no labor and which you did not raise; it came up in one night and in one night it perished.* ¹¹And should I not be concerned over Nineveh, the great city, in which there are more than a hundred and twenty thousand persons who cannot distinguish their right hand from their left, not to mention the many cattle?"

3, 4: Shall be destroyed: the Hebrew expression reminds the reader of the "overthrowing" of the wicked cities, Sodom and Gomorrah, by a special act of God.

3, 8: Beast . . . sackcloth: the animals carried the signs of this repentance, as on occasions of joy they bore garlands.

4, 1: He became angry: because of his narrowly nationalistic vindictiveness, Jonah did not wish the Lord to forgive the Ninevites.

4, 6: Gourd plant: the Hebrew word, kikayon, means here a wide-leafed plant of the cucumber or castor-bean variety.

4, 10f: Jonah is selfish in bemoaning his personal loss of a shady gourd plant without any concern over the threat of loss of life to the Ninevites through the destruction of their city. If God in his kindness provided the plant for his prophet without the latter's effort or merit, how much more is he disposed to show love and mercy toward all men, Jew and Gentile, when they repent of their sins and implore his pardon! God's providence is also shown here to extend even to animals.

l: Mt 12, 41; Lk 11, 32.   m: Jl 2, 14.   n: Ps 86, 5; Jl 2, 13.   o: 1 Kgs 19, 4.

The Book of Micah

See RG
359–60

Micah was a contemporary of Isaiah. Of his personal life and call we know nothing except that he came from the obscure village of Moresheth in the foothills. His were the broad vistas of the Judean lowland and the distant sea on the western horizon. With burning eloquence he attacked the rich exploiters of the poor, fraudulent merchants, venal judges, corrupt priests and prophets. To the man of the countryside the vices of the nation seemed centered in its capitals, for both Samaria and Jerusalem are singled out for judgment. An interesting notice in Jer 26, 17f informs us that the reform of Hezekiah was influenced by the preaching of Micah.

The prophecy may be divided into three parts: I: The impending judgment of the Lord, followed by an exposition of its causes, Israel's sins. Censure of Judah's leaders for betrayal of their responsibility (1, 1—3, 12). II: The glory of the restored Zion. A prince of David's house will rule over a reunited Israel. (St. Matthew's Nativity narrative points to Christ's birth in Bethlehem as the fulfillment of this prophecy.) A remnant shall survive the chastisement of Judah and her adversaries shall be destroyed (4, 1—5, 14). III: The case against Israel, in which the Lord is portrayed as the plaintiff who has maintained fidelity to the covenant. The somber picture closes with a prayer for national restoration and a beautiful expression of trust in God's pardoning mercy (6, 1—7, 20).

It should be noted that each of these three divisions begins with reproach and the threat of punishment, and ends on a note of hope and promise.

I: Punishment of Israel's Sins

See RG
359

CHAPTER 1

Divine Judgment. [1]The word of the LORD which came to Micah of Moresheth in the days of Jotham, Ahaz, and Hezekiah, kings of Judah: that is, the vision he received concerning Samaria and Jerusalem.

[2] Hear, O peoples, all of you,
  give heed, O earth, and all that fills
    you![a]
Let the Lord GOD be witness against you,
  the Lord from his holy temple!*
[3] For see, the LORD comes forth from his
    place,[b]
  he descends and treads upon the
    heights of the earth.
[4] The mountains melt under him
  and the valleys split open,
Like wax before the fire,
  like water poured down a slope.

[5] For the crime of Jacob all this comes to
    pass,
  and for the sins of the house of Israel.
What is the crime of Jacob?
  Is it not Samaria?
And what is the sin of the house of
    Judah?
  Is it not Jerusalem?
[6] I will make Samaria a stone heap in the
    field,
  a place to plant for vineyards;
I will throw down into the valley her
    stones,
  and lay bare her foundations.
[7] All her idols shall be broken to pieces,[c]
  all her wages shall be burned in the fire,
  and all her statues I will destroy.
As the wages of a harlot they were
    gathered,
  and to the wages of a harlot shall they
    return.*
[8] For this reason I lament and wail,
  I go barefoot and naked;

1, 2: His holy temple: God's heavenly temple; the prophet pictures a theophany (3f).

1, 7: The comparison of the unfaithful people with a prostitute, first found in Hosea, is frequent with the prophets; probably ritual prostitution is meant; cf Am 2, 7f; Hos 4, 14.

a: Dt 32, 1; Is 1, 2.   *b:* 3f: Is 26, 21; Na 1, 5; Hb 3, 10.   *c:* Hos 9, 1.

I utter lamentation like the jackals,
and mourning like the ostriches.[d]
[9] There is no remedy for the blow she has
been struck;
rather, it has come even to Judah,
It reaches to the gate of my people,
even to Jerusalem.
[10] Publish it not in Gath,*
weep not at all;
In Beth-leaphrah
roll in the dust.[e]
[11] Pass by,
you who dwell in Shaphir!
The inhabitants of Zaanan
come not forth from their city.
The lamentation of Beth-ezel
finds in you its grounds.
[12] How can the inhabitants of Maroth
hope for good?
For evil has come down from the LORD
to the gate of Jerusalem.
[13] Harness steeds to the chariots,
O inhabitants of Lachish;
Lachish, the beginning of sin
for daughter Zion,
Because there were in you
the crimes of Israel.
[14] Therefore you shall give parting gifts
to Moresheth-gath;
Beth-achzib is a deception
to the kings of Israel.
[15] Yet must I bring to you the conqueror,
O inhabitants of Mareshah;
Even to Adullam shall go
the glory of Israel.

[16] Make yourself bald, pluck out your
hair,
for the children whom you cherish;
Let your baldness be as the eagle's,
because they are exiled from you.*

CHAPTER 2

Social Evils

See RG
359

[1] Woe to those who plan iniquity,
and work out evil on their couches;
In the morning light they accomplish it
when it lies within their power.
[2] They covet fields, and seize them;
houses, and they take them;
They cheat an owner of his house,
a man of his inheritance.*
[3]   Therefore thus says the LORD:
Behold, I am planning against this race
an evil
from which you shall not withdraw
your necks;
Nor shall you walk with head high,
for it will be a time of evil.

[4] On that day a satire shall be sung over
you,
and there shall be a plaintive chant:
"Our ruin is complete,
our fields are portioned out among our
captors,
The fields of my people are measured
out,
and no one can get them back!"
[5] Thus you shall have no one
to mark out boundaries by lot*
in the assembly of the LORD.

[6] "Preach not," they preach,
"let them not preach of these
things!"*
The shame will not withdraw.
[7] How can it be said, O house of Jacob,
"Is the LORD short of patience,
or are such his deeds?"
Do not my words promise good
to him who walks uprightly?

1, 10-15: The Judean cities here named were in the vicinity of Moresheth, the region with which Micah was most familiar. They were to experience divine chastisement. In the Hebrew, wordplays on the names of these cities abound. The text is partly obscure.

1, 16: Shaving the head was a sign of mourning; cf Is 3, 24; Am 8, 10.

2, 2: Land monopoly, also denounced by Isaiah, was a chronic vice in Judah. To protect the poor against it, a man's inheritance, his ancestral property, was supposed to be inviolate; cf 1 Kgs 21, 1-4; but the wealthy in their greed were enslaving men for their debts and depriving them of their land.

2, 5: To mark out boundaries by lot: an allusion to the initial distribution of the land of Palestine among the Israelites; cf Jos 13—21. The appropriate punishment of those greedy for land will be the loss of their land to their enemies (v 4), a loss that will be irrevocable.

2, 6f: The words in quotation marks are the protestations of the people against the prophet's predictions of doom.

---

d: Jb 30, 29. *e:* 2 Sm 1, 20.

8 But of late my people has risen up as an
    enemy:
you have stripped off the mantle
    covering the tunic
Of those who go their way in confidence,
    as though it were spoils of war.
9 The women of my people you drive out
    from their pleasant houses;
From their children you take away
    forever the honor I gave them.*
10 "Up! Be off,
    this is no place to rest";
For any trifle you exact
    a crippling pledge.*

11 If one, acting on impulse, should make
    the futile claim:
"I pour you wine and strong drink as
    my prophecy,"
then he would be the prophet of this
    people.
12 I will gather you, O Jacob, each and
    every one,*
I will assemble all the remnant of
    Israel;
I will group them like a flock in the fold,
    like a herd in the midst of its corral;
they shall not be thrown into panic by
    men.
13 With a leader to break the path
    they shall burst open the gate and go
    out through it;
Their king shall go through before them,
    and the LORD at their head.

CHAPTER 3

See RG 359

Downfall of Present Leaders

1   And I said:
Hear, you leaders of Jacob,
    rulers of the house of Israel!
Is it not your duty to know what is right,
2   you who hate what is good, and love
    evil?
You who tear their skin from them,

and their flesh from their bones!*f*
3 They eat the flesh of my people,
    and flay their skin from them,
    and break their bones.
They chop them in pieces like flesh in a
    kettle,
    and like meat in a caldron.
4 When they cry to the LORD,
    he shall not answer them;
Rather shall he hide his face from them
    at that time,
    because of the evil they have done.

5 Thus says the LORD regarding the
    prophets*
    who lead my people astray;
Who, when their teeth have something to
    bite,
    announce peace,
But when one fails to put something in
    their mouth,
    proclaim war against him.*g*
6 Therefore you shall have night, not
    vision,
    darkness, not divination;
The sun shall go down upon the
    prophets,
    and the day shall be dark for them.*h*
7 Then shall the seers be put to shame,
    and the diviners confounded;
They shall cover their lips, all of them,
    because there is no answer from God.
8 But as for me, I am filled with power,
    with the spirit of the LORD,
    with authority and with might;
To declare to Jacob his crimes
    and to Israel his sins.
9 Hear this, you leaders of the house of
    Jacob,
    you rulers of the house of Israel!
You who abhor what is just,
    and pervert all that is right;
10 Who build up Zion with bloodshed,
    and Jerusalem with wickedness!

2, 9: The honor I gave them: their dignity as free Israelites.

2, 10: A crippling pledge: Israelite law forbade exacting pledges for loans that would work hardship on the borrower (Ex 22, 25f; Dt 24, 6. 10-13. 17); but the law was habitually violated.

2, 12f: This messianic passage concerning the restoration after the Babylonian exile seems out of place here and is probably a later addition.

3, 5-8: Almost all the prophetic books contain oracles against the false prophets. Here Micah accuses them of prophesying for venal motives and determining the prophecy by the price that is paid them; he contrasts his own disinterested preaching of the word of God.

f: Am 2, 7.   *g:* Ez 13, 10.   *h:* Jer 15, 9; Am 8, 9; Zec 13, 3.

[11] Her leaders render judgment for a bribe,
  her priests give decisions for a salary,
  her prophets divine for money,
While they rely on the LORD, saying,
  "Is not the LORD in the midst of us?
  No evil can come upon us!"[i]
[12] Therefore, because of you,
  Zion shall be plowed like a field,
  and Jerusalem reduced to rubble,
And the mount of the temple
  to a forest ridge.[j]

II: The New Israel
CHAPTER 4

See RG 360

The People To Be Restored

[1] In days to come*
  the mount of the LORD's house
Shall be established higher than the
  mountains;
  it shall rise high above the hills,
And peoples shall stream to it:[k]
[2] Many nations shall come, and say,
"Come, let us climb the mount of the
  LORD,
  to the house of the God of Jacob,
That he may instruct us in his ways,
  that we may walk in his paths."
For from Zion shall go forth instruction,
  and the word of the LORD from
  Jerusalem.
[3] He shall judge between many peoples
  and impose terms on strong and distant
  nations;
They shall beat their swords into
  plowshares,
  and their spears into pruning hooks;
One nation shall not raise the sword
  against another,
  nor shall they train for war again.
[4] Every man shall sit under his own vine
  or under his own fig tree, undisturbed;
  for the mouth of the LORD of hosts has
  spoken.[l]
[5] For all the peoples walk
  each in the name of its god,

But we will walk in the name of the
  LORD,
  our God, forever and ever.
[6] On that day, says the LORD,
  I will gather the lame,
  And I will assemble the outcasts,
  and those whom I have afflicted.
[7] I will make of the lame a remnant,
  and of those driven far off a strong
  nation;
And the LORD shall be king over them on
  Mount Zion,
  from now on forever.[m]
[8] And you, O Magdal-eder,*
  hillock of daughter Zion!
Unto you shall it come:
  the former dominion shall be restored,
  the kingdom of daughter Jerusalem.

[9] Now why do you cry out so?
  Are you without a king?
  Or has your counselor perished,
That you are seized with pains
  like a woman in travail?
[10] Writhe in pain, grow faint,
  O daughter Zion,
  like a woman in travail;
For now shall you go forth from the city
  and dwell in the fields;
To Babylon shall you go,
  there shall you be rescued.
There shall the LORD redeem you
  from the hand of your enemies.*

[11] How many nations are gathered against
  you!
  They say, "Let her be profaned,
  let our eyes see Zion's downfall!"
[12] But they know not the thoughts of the
  LORD,
  nor understand his counsel,
When he has gathered them
  like sheaves on the threshing floor.
[13] Arise and thresh, O daughter Zion;
  your horn I will make iron
  And your hoofs bronze,

4, 1ff: See note on Is 2, 2ff.
4, 8: Magdal-eder: "tower of the flock," an ancient place name (cf Gn 35, 21), here used symbolically of Jerusalem.
4, 10: For now . . . your enemies: probably a later addition to the text, when the prediction of exile had been fulfilled in

the Babylonian captivity. The prophet sees the exile as the means whereby God will purify and restore his people.

i: Ez 22, 27; Zep 3, 3.   *j:* Jer 26, 18.   *k:* 1ff: Is 2, 2ff.   *l:* Hos 14, 8; Am 9, 14.   *m:* Is 6, 13; Dn 7, 14; Zep 3, 19; Lk 1, 32.

that you may crush many peoples;
You shall devote their spoils to the LORD,
and their riches to the Lord of the
whole earth.ⁿ

Restoration through the Messiah

14 Now fence yourself in, Bat-gader!*
"They have laid siege against us!"
With the rod they strike on the cheek
the ruler of Israel.

CHAPTER 5

See RG
360

1 But you, Bethlehem-Ephrathah,ᵒ
too small to be among the clans of
Judah,
From you shall come forth for me
one who is to be ruler in Israel;
Whose origin is from of old,
from ancient times.*
2 (Therefore the Lord will give them up,
until the time
when she who is to give birth* has
borne,
And the rest of his brethren shall return
to the children of Israel.)ᵖ
3 He shall stand firm and shepherd his
flock
by the strength of the LORD,
in the majestic name of the LORD, his
God;
And they shall remain, for now his
greatness
shall reach to the ends of the earth;
4 he shall be peace.

If Assyria invades our country*
and treads upon our land,
We shall raise against it seven shepherds,
eight men of royal rank;

5 And they shall tend the land of Assyria
with the sword,
and the land of Nimrod* with the
drawn sword;
And we shall be delivered from Assyria,
if it invades our land
and treads upon our borders.

6 The remnant of Jacob shall be
in the midst of many peoples,
Like dew coming from the LORD,
like raindrops on the grass,
Which wait for no man,
nor tarry for the sons of men.
7 And the remnant of Jacob shall be among
the nations,
in the midst of many peoples,
Like a lion among beasts of the forest,
like a young lion among flocks of
sheep;
When it passes through, it tramples
and tears, and there is none to deliver.
8 Your hand shall be lifted above your
foes,
and all your enemies shall be
destroyed.

9   On that day, says the LORD,*
I will destroy the horses from your midst
and ruin your chariots;
10 I will demolish the cities of your land
and tear down all your fortresses.
11 I will abolish the means of divination
from your use,
and there shall no longer be
soothsayers among you.
12 I will abolish your carved images
and the sacred pillars from your midst;
And you shall no longer adore

4, 14: Bat-gader: "fenced-in maiden," another symbolic
name for Jerusalem, then under siege from the Assyrians.

5, 1: In contrast to Bat-gader (Mi 4, 14), where the ruler of
Israel, the reigning king, is in peril of his life from the Assyrians, is the tiny city and clan of Bethlehem-Ephrathah, from
which comes the ancient Davidic dynasty (whose origin is
from of old, from ancient times) with its messianic King, one
who is to be ruler in Israel.

5, 2: She who is to give birth: the mother of the Messiah:
cf Is 7, 14.

5, 4f: This passage, expressing confidence in Judah's ability to deliver itself from Assyria, is in contrast with the preceding messianic oracle, which ascribes deliverance to the
Lord and his agent. Some believe that here the prophet is
quoting the words of the defiant men of Judah. The shepherds
and men of royal rank are one and the same: warriors capable
of routing Assyria. The same kind of numerical progression is
used by Amos (1, 3), and elsewhere in the Bible.

5, 5: Nimrod: the legendary ancestor of the Meso-
potamians; cf Gn 10, 10ff.

5, 9-13: Part of the messianic restoration will consist in
the removal of everything that has drawn Israel away from
the Lord; this includes not only the objects of false worship, but also the armaments in which the idolators had
trusted.

n: Is 41, 15; Hos 10, 11.   o: Ru 1, 2; 1 Sm 17, 12; Mt 2, 6; Jn 7,
42.   p: 2f: Is 7, 14; 11, 1f.

the works of your hands.^{q}

13 I will tear out the sacred poles from your
midst,
and destroy your cities.

14 I will wreak vengeance in anger and
wrath
upon the nations that have not
hearkened.

III: Admonition

CHAPTER 6

See RG
360

Accusation and Answer

1   Hear, then, what the LORD says:
Arise, present your plea before the
mountains,
and let the hills hear your voice!^{r}

2 Hear, O mountains, the plea of the
LORD,
pay attention, O foundations of the
earth!
For the LORD has a plea against his
people,
and he enters into trial with Israel.

3 O my people, what have I done to you,
or how have I wearied you? Answer
me!^{s}

4 For I brought you up from the land of
Egypt,
from the place of slavery I released
you;
And I sent before you Moses,
Aaron, and Miriam.^{t}

5 My people, remember what Moab's King
Balak planned,
and how Balaam, the son of Beor,
answered him
. . . from Shittim to Gilgal,*
that you may know the just deeds of
the LORD.^{u}

6 With what shall I come before the LORD,*
and bow before God most high?
Shall I come before him with holocausts,
with calves a year old?^{v}

7 Will the LORD be pleased with thousands
of rams,
with myriad streams of oil?
Shall I give my first-born* for my crime,
the fruit of my body for the sin of my
soul?

8 You have been told, O man, what is
good,
and what the LORD requires of you:
Only to do the right and to love
goodness,
and to walk humbly with your God.^{w}

9 Hark! the LORD cries to the city.*
[It is wisdom to fear your name!]
Hear, O tribe and city council,

12 You whose rich men are full of violence,
whose inhabitants speak falsehood
with deceitful tongues in their heads!

10 Am I to bear any longer criminal
hoarding
and the meager ephah that is accursed?

11 Shall I acquit criminal balances,
bags of false weights?

13 Rather I will begin to strike you
with devastation because of your sins.

15 You shall sow, yet not reap,
tread out the olive, yet pour no oil,
and the grapes, yet drink no wine.^{x}

14 You shall eat, without being satisfied,
food that will leave you empty;
What you acquire, you cannot save;
what you do save, I will deliver up to
the sword.^{y}

16 You have kept the decrees of Omri,
and all the works of the house of Ahab,

5, 12f: Sacred pillars . . . sacred poles: see note on Ex 34, 13.

6, 5: From Shittim to Gilgal: from the east to the west side
of the Jordan; the events described in Jos 3—5 are meant. The
text is defective; however, it is evident that this verse continues the remembrance of God's deeds of mercy to Israel, beginning with the Exodus (v 4) and extending to the conquest,
deeds which have provoked so little response from his people.

6, 6ff: The people ask how they shall worship the Lord, pro-
posing the various forms of sacrifice. The prophet replies that
sacrifice avails nothing without the true spirit of religion. This is
one of the best expressions of the prophetic teaching on religion,

the preparation for such New Testament passages as Jas 1, 27.

6, 7: Shall I give my first-born: through Canaanite influence the abominable practice of human sacrifice had been introduced under impious kings (cf 2 Kgs 16, 3; 21, 6).

6, 9: The city: Jerusalem as the embodiment of the crimes
of the entire land.

---

q: Hos 3, 4; 10, 1f. r: Is 6, 2; Ob 1. s: Jer 2, 5. t: Ex 15, 20.
u: Nm 22, 23. v: 6f: Hos 6, 6; 8, 13; Am 5, 21. w: Dt 26, 16;
Zec 7, 9; Mt 23, 23. x: Dt 28, 38; Am 5, 11; Hg 1, 6. y: Hos
4, 10.

and you have walked in their counsels;
Therefore I will deliver you up to ruin,
    and your citizens to derision;
and you shall bear the reproach of the
    nations.*

See RG 360

CHAPTER 7

Condemnation and Prayer

¹ Alas! I am as when the fruit is
    gathered,
    as when the vines have been gleaned;
There is no cluster to eat,
    no early fig that I crave.
² The faithful are gone from the earth,
    among men the upright are no more!
They all lie in wait to shed blood,
    each one ensnares the other.ᶻ
³ Their hands succeed at evil;
    the prince makes demands,
The judge is had for a price,
    the great man speaks as he pleases,ᵃ
⁴ The best of them is like a brier,
    the most upright like a thorn hedge.
The day announced by your
    watchmen!
    your punishment has come;
    now is the time of your confusion.
⁵ Put no trust in a friend,*
    have no confidence in a companion;
Against her who lies in your bosom
    guard the portals of your mouth.ᵇ
⁶ For the son dishonors his father,
    the daughter rises up against her
    mother,
The daughter-in-law against her mother-
    in-law,
    and a man's enemies are those of his
    household.ᶜ
⁷ But as for me, I will look to the LORD,
    I will put my trust in God my savior;
    my God will hear me!ᵈ

⁸ Rejoice not over me, O my enemy!*
    though I have fallen, I will arise;
    though I sit in darkness, the LORD is
    my light.
⁹ The wrath of the LORD I will endure
    because I have sinned against
    him,
Until he takes up my cause,
    and establishes my right.
He will bring me forth to the light;
    I will see his justice.
¹⁰ When my enemy sees this,
    shame shall cover her:
She who said to me,
    "Where is the LORD, thy God?"
My eyes shall see her downfall;
    now shall she be trampled
    underfoot,
    like the mire in the streets.

¹¹ It is the day for building your walls;*
    on that day the boundary shall be
    taken away.
¹² It is the day; and they shall come to
    you
    from Assyria and from Egypt,
From Tyre even to the River,
    from sea to sea, and from mountain to
    mountain;ᵉ
¹³ And the land shall be a waste
    because of its citizens,
    as a result of their deeds.

¹⁴ Shepherd your people with your staff,*
    the flock of your inheritance,
That dwells apart in a woodland,
    in the midst of Carmel.
Let them feed in Bashan and Gilead,
    as in the days of old;
¹⁵ As in the days when you came from the
    land of Egypt,

6, 16: Judah has followed the example of the northern kingdom epitomized in the semipaganism of Omri and his son Ahab (1 Kgs 16, 25-34), copying both the corrupted worship and the social injustice of their reigns.

7, 5f: Corresponding to the widespread civil corruption and apostasy from religion is the breakdown of normal human and family relations.

7, 8ff: The unnamed enemy of Judah mentioned in these verses may be Assyria or one of the neighboring countries, such as Edom, which stood by to profit at Judah's downfall.

7, 11ff: This prophecy of restoration and repopulation of

the promised land by the Jews now in exile appears to be from the period after the destruction of Jerusalem by the Chaldeans (587 B.C.).

7, 14-17: This prayer appears to be from the time after the return from exile (537 B.C.), when the people few in number, possessed only a fragment of their former land, and were surrounded by hostile nations.

---

z: Is 1, 21; Hos 4, 2.   a: Is 1, 23.   b: Jer 9, 3.   c: Mt 10, 35f.
d: Is 8, 17.   e: Zec 14, 16.

show us wonderful signs.

16 The nations shall behold and be put to
 shame,
 in spite of all their strength;
They shall put their hands over their
 mouths;
 their ears shall become deaf.
17 They shall lick the dust like the serpent,
 like reptiles on the ground;
They shall come quaking from their
 fastnesses,
 trembling in fear of you [the LORD, our
 God].

f: Jer 10, 6; Acts 10, 43. *g:* Ps 105, 6; Is 41, 8; 63, 16.

18 Who is there like you, the God who
 removes guilt
 and pardons sin for the remnant of his
 inheritance;
Who does not persist in anger forever,
 but delights rather in clemency,*f*
19 And will again have compassion on us,
 treading underfoot our guilt?
You will cast into the depths of the sea
 all our sins;
20 You will show faithfulness to Jacob,
 and grace to Abraham,
As you have sworn to our fathers
 from days of old.*g*

See RG
361

The Book of Nahum

Shortly before the fall of Nineveh in 612 B.C., Nahum uttered his prophecy against the hated city. To understand the prophet's exultant outburst of joy over the impending destruction it is necessary to recall the savage cruelty of Assyria, which had made it the scourge of the ancient Near East for almost three centuries. The royal inscriptions of Assyria afford the best commentary on the burning denunciation of "the bloody city." In the wake of their conquests, mounds of heads, impaled bodies, enslaved citizens, and avaricious looters testified to the ruthlessness of the Assyrians. Little wonder that Judah joined in the general outburst of joy over the destruction of Nineveh!

But Nahum is not a prophet of unrestrained revenge. God's moral government of the world is asserted. Yahweh is the avenger but he is also merciful, a citadel in the day of distress. Nineveh's doom was a judgment on the wicked city. Before many years passed, Jerusalem too was to learn the meaning of such a judgment.

The book is divided as follows: The Lord's Coming in Judgment (1, 2—2, 1. 3). The Fall of Nineveh (2, 2—3, 19).

CHAPTER 1
See RG
361
1 Oracle about Nineveh. The book of the vision of Nahum of Elkosh.

The Lord's Coming in Judgment
2 *A jealous and avenging God* is the
 LORD,
 an avenger is the LORD, and angry;
The LORD brings vengeance on his
 adversaries,
 and lays up wrath for his enemies;
3 The LORD is slow to anger, yet great in
 power,
 and the LORD never leaves the guilty
 unpunished.
In hurricane and tempest is his path,
 and clouds are the dust at his feet;*a*
4 He rebukes the sea and leaves it dry,
 and all the rivers he dries up.*b*
Withered are Bashan and Carmel,
 and the bloom of Lebanon fades;*
5 The mountains quake before him,
 and the hills dissolve;
The earth is laid waste before him,
 the world and all who dwell in it.

1, 2-8: A poem written in the style of the alphabetic psalms; cf Pss 9A; 25; 111; 119. Here, however, most of the verses beginning with the letters of the second half of the alphabet are not preserved.

1, 2: A jealous . . . God: see note on Ex 20, 5.

1, 4: Bashan, Carmel and Lebanon were famous for their forests.

a: Ex 19, 16ff. *b:* Is 33, 9; Hb 3, 6ff.

6 Before his wrath, who can stand firm,[c]
and who can face his blazing anger?
His fury is poured out like fire,
and the rocks are rent asunder before
him.*
7 The LORD is good,
a refuge on the day of distress;
He takes care of those who have recourse
to him,
8 when the flood rages;
He makes an end of his opponents,
and his enemies he pursues with
darkness.
9 What are you imputing to the LORD?*
It is he who will make an end!
The enemy shall not rise a second time;
10 As when a tangle of thornbushes is set
aflame,
like dry stubble, they shall be utterly
consumed.
12 For, says the LORD,
be they* ever so many and so vigorous,
still they shall be mown down and
disappear.
Though I have humbled you,
I will humble you no more.
13 Now will I break his yoke from off you,
and burst asunder your bonds.[d]
11 From you he came
who devised evil against the LORD,
the scoundrel planner.*
14 The LORD has commanded regarding
you:*
no descendant shall come to bear your
name;
From your temple I will abolish
the carved and the molten image;
I will make your grave a mockery.

See RG
361

CHAPTER 2

1 See, upon the mountains there
advances

the bearer of good news, announcing
peace!
Celebrate your feasts, O Judah,
fulfill your vows!
For nevermore shall you be invaded
by the scoundrel; he is completely
destroyed.[e]
3 The LORD will restore the vine of Jacob,
the pride of Israel,
Though ravagers have ravaged them
and ruined the tendrils.

The Fall of Nineveh

2 The hammer comes up against you;*
guard the rampart,
Keep watch on the road, gird your loins,
marshal all your strength!
4 The shields of his warriors are
crimsoned,
the soldiers colored in scarlet;
Fiery steel are the chariots
on the day of his mustering.
The horses are frenzied;
5 the chariots dash madly through the
streets
And wheel in the squares,
looking like firebrands,
flashing like lightning bolts.
6 His picked troops are called,
ranks break at their charge;
To the wall they rush,
the mantelet* is set up.
7 The river gates are opened,
the palace shudders,
8 Its mistress is led forth captive,
and her handmaids,* under guard,
Moaning like doves,
beating their breasts.
9 Nineveh is like a pool
whose waters escape;
"Stop! Stop!"
but none turns back.

1, 6f: The coming of God in judgment has two aspects: to those who oppose him it will be unbearable; to those who have recourse to him it will bring strength and consolation.

1, 9: What are you imputing to the Lord?: the people of Judah are asked what they think God has in mind.

1, 12f: They: the enemies of Judah. You: Judah. His yoke: the dominion of the Assyrian king over Judah.

1, 11: From you . . . the scoundrel planner: addressed to Nineveh, the capital city of Sennacherib, king of Assyria, who besieged Jerusalem c. 700 B.C.

1, 14: You: the king of Assyria.

2, 2: The hammer comes up against you: the enemy is about to crush Nineveh.

2, 6: Mantelet: a movable shelter protecting the besiegers.

2, 8: Mistress . . . and her handmaids: either the queen of Nineveh with the ladies of her court, or the statue of Ishtar, Nineveh's chief goddess, with her temple prostitutes.

c: Zep 1, 15; 2, 3. *d:* Is 9, 4; 10, 27. *e:* Is 52, 7; Rom 10, 15.

10 "Plunder the silver, plunder the gold!"
  There is no end to the treasure,
    to their wealth in precious things of
      every kind!

11 Emptiness, desolation, waste;
  melting hearts and trembling knees,
  Writhing in every frame,
    every face blanched!*f*
12 Where is the lions' cave,
  the young lions' den,
  Where the lion* went in and out,
    and the cub, with no one to disturb
      them?
13 The lion snatched enough for his cubs,
  and strangled for his lionesses;
  He filled his dens with prey,
    and his caves with plunder.
14 I come against you,
  says the LORD of hosts;
  I will consume in smoke your chariots,
    and the sword shall devour your young
      lions;
  Your preying on the land I will bring to
    an end,
    the cry of your lionesses shall be heard
      no more.

See RG 361

CHAPTER 3

Ruin Imminent and Inevitable

1 Woe to the bloody city, all lies,
  full of plunder, whose looting never
    stops!*g*
2 The crack of the whip, the rumbling
    sounds of wheels;
  horses a-gallop, chariots bounding,
3 Cavalry charging,
  The flame of the sword, the flash of the
    spear,
    the many slain, the heaping corpses,
    the endless bodies to stumble upon!
4 For the many debaucheries of the harlot,
  fair and charming, a mistress of
    witchcraft,
  Who enslaved nations with her harlotries,

and peoples by her witchcraft:*h*
5 I am come against you,*i*
  and I will strip your skirt from you;
  I will show your nakedness to the
    nations,
    to the kingdoms your shame!*
6 I will cast filth upon you,
  disgrace you and put you to shame;
7 Till everyone who sees you runs from
    you, saying,
  "Nineveh is destroyed; who can pity
    her?
  Where can one find any to console
    her?"

8 Are you better than No-amon*
  that was set among the streams,
  Surrounded by waters,
    with the flood for her rampart
    and water her wall?*j*
9 Ethiopia was her strength, and Egypt,
  and others without end;
  Put and the Libyans were her
    auxiliaries.
10 Yet even she went captive into exile,
  even her little ones were dashed to
    pieces
    at the corner of every street;
  For her nobles they cast lots,
    and all her great men were put into
      chains.
11 You, too, shall drink of this till you faint
    away;
  you, too, shall seek a refuge from the
    foe.*k*
12 All your fortresses are but fig trees,
  bearing early figs
  That fall, when shaken,
    into the hungry mouth.
13 See, the troops are women in your midst;
  to your foes the gates of your land are
    open wide,
    fire has consumed their bars.*l*
14 Draw water for the siege,*
  strengthen your fortresses;

2, 12: The lion: the king of Assyria.
3, 5f: The punishment of adulteresses.
3, 8: No-amon: No was the Egyptian name of the capital
of Upper Egypt, called Thebes by the Greeks; its tutelary deity was Amon. This great city was destroyed by the Assyrians
in 663 B.C.

3, 14: An ironic exhortation to prepare the city for a futile
defense. Go down . . . brick mold: make bricks for the city
walls.

f: Jl 2, 6. g: Hb 2, 12. h: Mi 1, 7; Rv 17, 1f. i: Is 47, 3; Jer
13, 26; Hos 2, 12. j: Jer 46, 25. k: Mi 2, 11. l: Jer 51, 30.

Go down into the mud and tread the
  clay,
  take hold of the brick mold!
¹⁵ There the fire shall consume you,
  the sword shall cut you down.
Multiply like the grasshoppers,
  multiply like the locusts!
¹⁶ Make your couriers more numerous than
  the stars,
¹⁷ your garrisons as many as
    grasshoppers,
And your scribes as locust swarms
  gathered on the rubble fences on a cold
    day!
Yet when the sun warms them,

the grasshoppers will spread their
  wings and fly,
  and vanish, no one knows where.
¹⁸ Alas! how your shepherds slumber, O
    king of Assyria,
  your nobles have gone to rest;
Your people are scattered upon the
    mountains,
  with none to gather them.
¹⁹ There is no healing for your hurt,
  your wound is mortal.
All who hear this news of you
  clap their hands over you;
For who has not been overwhelmed,
  steadily, by your malice?

The Book of Habakkuk

See RG
362–63

This prophecy dates from the years 605–597 B.C.,
or between the great Babylonian victory at Carchemish and Nebuchadnezzar's invasion of Judah which culminated in the capture of
Jerusalem. The situation of Judah was desperate
at this time, with political intrigue and idolatry
widespread in the small kingdom. The first two
chapters consist of a dialogue between the
prophet and the Lord. For what may be the first
time in Israelite literature, a man questions the
ways of God, as Habakkuk calls him to account
for his government of the world. To this question
God replies that he has prepared a chastising rod,
Babylon, which will be the avenging instrument
in his hand. There is added the divine assurance
that the just Israelite will not perish in the calamities about to be visited on the nation.

The third chapter is a magnificent religious
lyric, filled with reminiscences of Israel's past
and rich in literary borrowings from the poetry of
ancient Canaan, though still expressing authentic
Israelite faith. God appears in all his majestic
splendor and executes vengeance on Judah's enemies. The prophecy ends with a joyous profession of confidence in the Lord, the Savior.

CHAPTER 1

See RG
362–63

¹The oracle which Habakkuk the
prophet received in vision.

The Prophet's Complaint and Its Answer
² How long, O LORD? I cry for help*
  but you do not listen!
I cry out to you, "Violence!"
  but you do not intervene.
³ Why do you let me see ruin;
  why must I look at misery?
Destruction and violence are before me;
  there is strife, and clamorous discord.
⁴ This is why the law is benumbed,
  and judgment is never rendered:
Because the wicked circumvent the just;
  this is why judgment comes forth
    perverted.

⁵ Look over the nations and see,*
  and be utterly amazed!
For a work is being done in your days
  that you would not have believed,
    were it told.^a
⁶ For see, I am raising up Chaldea,

1, 2-4: Traditionally, these verses have been taken as the
prophet's complaint against the internal evils of Judah; the
language used is that employed by Amos, Isaiah, and Jeremiah to condemn the social abuses of their day. In vv 5ff the
Lord answers this complaint by indicating the Chaldean empire as his instrument for punishing his people for these sins.

1, 5: Look over the nations and see: after Nebuchadnezzar's defeat of Egypt in 605 B.C., there could be little doubt
that it was the Chaldean ambition to dominate the entire Near
East.

---

a: Acts 13, 41.

that bitter and unruly people,
That marches the breadth of the land
    to take dwellings not his own.
7 Terrible and dreadful is he,
    from himself derive his law and his
      majesty.
8 Swifter than leopards are his horses,
    and keener than wolves at evening.*
His horses prance,
    his horsemen come from afar:
They fly like the eagle hastening to
      devour;
9   each comes for the rapine,
Their combined onset is that of a
      stormwind
    that heaps up captives like sand.
10 He scoffs at kings,
    and princes are his laughingstock;
He laughs at any fortress,
    heaps up a ramp, and conquers it.
11 Then he veers like the wind* and is gone—
    this culprit who makes his own
      strength his god!

12 Are you not from eternity, O LORD,*
    my holy God, immortal?
O LORD, you have marked him for
      judgment,
O Rock,* you have readied him for
      punishment!
13 Too pure are your eyes to look upon evil,
    and the sight of misery you cannot
      endure.
Why, then, do you gaze on the faithless
    in silence
while the wicked man devours

one more just than himself?
14 You have made man like the fish of the
      sea,
    like creeping things without a ruler.
15 He* brings them all up with his hook,
    he hauls them away with his net,
He gathers them in his seine;
    and so he rejoices and exults.
16 Therefore he sacrifices to his net,*
    and burns incense to his seine;
For thanks to them his portion is generous,
    and his repast sumptuous.
17 Shall he, then, keep on brandishing his
      sword
    to slay peoples without mercy?

CHAPTER 2

See RG
362–63

1 I will stand at my guard post,
    and station myself upon the rampart,
And keep watch to see what he will say
    to me,
    and what answer he will give to my
      complaint.*b*

2 Then the LORD answered me and said:
    Write down the vision
Clearly upon the tablets,
    so that one can read it readily.
3 For the vision still has its time,
    presses on to fulfillment, and will not
      disappoint;
If it delays, wait for it,
    it will surely come, it will not be late.
4 The rash man has no integrity;*c*
    but the just man, because of his faith,
      shall live.*

1, 8: Wolves at evening: the wolf is apparently thought of as more rabid and vicious in the evening when setting out for prey (Jer 5, 6; Zep 3, 3).

1, 11: Veers like the wind: the conquests of the ancient Near East were mainly raiding expeditions to collect tribute. As far as administration of conquered territories was concerned, both the Assyrians and Chaldeans were usually content to install friendly rulers and then depart. This culprit: though the Chaldeans were used by God as the agents of his punishment, this did not diminish their own guilt as ruthless marauders.

1, 12—2, 1: It is generally thought that this complaint is directed against the Chaldeans and their terrible destruction. But it may well be a continuation of Hb 1, 2-4, against the wicked Judahites who have merited God's punishment.

1, 12: O Rock: an ancient title celebrating the Lord's power; cf Ps 18, 32.

1, 15: The he of this and the following verses, to whom is

attributed such extensive evil and the destruction of many peoples, may be the wicked of Judah embodied in King Jehoiakim, ally of the powerful Pharaoh Neco of Egypt; the devastation wrought by Jehoiakim and Neco together is condemned.

1, 16: He sacrifices to his net: in v 15 the wicked ruler in question is represented as catching men in a net. This verse alludes to some rite involving the sacrificial veneration of the weapons of war.

2, 4: The just man, because of his faith, shall live: the faith which here enables the virtuous man to survive the impending doom is both a confident belief in God's justice, and patience in awaiting its execution. St. Paul quotes these words (Rom 1, 17; Gal 3, 11; Heb 10, 38) to confirm his teaching that man receives justification and supernatural life through faith in Christ.

b: Ps 85, 9.   *c:* Rom 1, 17; Gal 3, 11; Heb 10, 38.

Wealth, too, is treacherous:
the proud, unstable man—
[5] He who opens wide his throat like the
nether world,
and is insatiable as death,
Who gathers to himself all the nations,
and rallies to himself all the peoples—
[6] Shall not all these take up a taunt against
him,
satire and epigrams about him, to say:

Woe to him who stores up what is not his:
how long can it last!
he loads himself down with debts.
[7] Shall not your creditors rise suddenly?
Shall not they who make you tremble
awake?
You shall become their spoil!
[8] Because you despoiled many peoples
all the rest of the nations shall despoil
you;
Because of men's blood shed,
and violence done to the land,
to the city and to all who dwell in it.

[9] Woe to him who pursues evil gain for his
household,
setting his nest on high
to escape the reach of misfortune!
[10] You have devised shame for your
household,
cutting off many peoples, forfeiting
your own life:
[11] For the stone in the wall shall cry out,*
and the beam in the woodwork shall
answer it!

[12] Woe to him who builds a city by
bloodshed,
and establishes a town by wickedness![d]

[13] Is not this from the LORD of hosts:
peoples toil for the flames,*

and nations grow weary for nought![e]
[14] But the earth shall be filled
with the knowledge of the LORD's
glory
as water covers the sea.[f]
[15] Woe to you who give your neighbors
a flood of your wrath to drink,
and make them drunk, till their
nakedness is seen!
[16] You are filled with shame instead of
glory;
drink, you too, and stagger!
On you shall revert the cup from the
LORD's right hand,
and utter shame on your glory.
[17] For the violence done to Lebanon* shall
cover you,
and the destruction of the beasts shall
terrify you;
Because of men's blood shed,
and violence done to the land,
to the city and to all who dwell in it.
[19] Woe to him who says to wood,
"Awake!"
to dumb stone, "Arise!"
Can such a thing give oracles?
See, it is overlaid with gold and silver,
but there is no life breath in it.
[18] Of what avail is the carved image,*
that its maker should carve it?
Or the molten image and lying oracle,
that its very maker should trust in it,
and make dumb idols?
[20] But the LORD is in his holy temple;
silence before him, all the earth![g]

CHAPTER 3

Canticle
[1] Prayer of Habakkuk,
the prophet. To a plaintive tune.*

See RG
362–63

[2] O LORD, I have heard your renown,
and feared, O LORD, your work.

2, 11f: The palaces, built at the expense of gross injustice
(vv 6-10), call down vengeance on their builders. This is typical prophetic language for the condemnation of social crimes
within Israel and Judah.
2, 13: Peoples toil for the flames: they build only to have
fire consume their work, when they build contrary to God's
will.
2, 17: The violence done to Lebanon: the spoliation of the
cedar forests of Lebanon, used in lavish building projects by

the great conquerors; cf Is 14, 8; 37, 24. The destruction of the
beasts: the killing-off of the wild animals through excessive
hunting by the same conquerors; cf Bar 3, 16.
2, 18-20: Idolatrous worship is here shown to be folly by
contrasting man-made idols with the majesty of the one true
God.
3, 1: A later liturgical rubric. So also the end of v 19.

---

d: Ez 24, 9; Na 3, 1.   *e:* Jer 51, 58.   *f:* Is 11, 9.   *g:* Ps 11, 4.

In the course of the years revive it,*
  in the course of the years make it
    known;
  in your wrath remember compassion!

3 *God comes from Teman,*
  the Holy One from Mount Paran.
Covered are the heavens with his glory,
  and with his praise the earth is filled.
4 His splendor spreads like the light;
  rays shine forth from beside him,
  where his power is concealed.
5 Before him goes pestilence,
  and the plague follows in his steps.
6 He pauses to survey the earth;
  his look makes the nations tremble.
The eternal mountains are shattered,
  the age-old hills bow low
  along his ancient ways.
7 I see the tents of Cushan collapse;
  trembling are the pavilions of the land
    of Midian.
8 Is your anger against the streams,
    O Lord?
Is your wrath against the streams,
  your rage against the sea,
That you drive the steeds
  of your victorious chariot?
9 Bared and ready is your bow,
  filled with arrows is your quiver.
Into streams you split the earth;
10   at sight of you the mountains tremble.
A torrent of rain descends;
  the ocean gives forth its roar.
The sun forgets to rise,
11   the moon remains in its shelter,
At the light of your flying arrows,
  at the gleam of your flashing spear.ʰ

12 In wrath you bestride the earth,
  in fury you trample the nations.
13 You come forth to save your people,
  to save your anointed one.*
You crush the heads of the wicked,
  you lay bare their bases at the neck.ⁱ
14 You pierce with your shafts the heads of
    their princes
  whose boast would be of devouring
  the wretched in their lair.
15 You tread the sea with your steeds
  amid the churning of the deep
    waters.

16 I hear, and my body trembles;
  at the sound, my lips quiver.
Decay invades my bones,
  my legs tremble beneath me.
I await the day of distress
  that will come upon the people who
    attack us.
17 For though the fig tree blossom not
  nor fruit be on the vines,
Though the yield of the olive fail
  and the terraces produce no
    nourishment,
Though the flocks disappear from the
    fold
  and there be no herd in the stalls,
18 Yet will I rejoice in the Lordʲ
  and exult in my saving God.
19 God, my Lord, is my strength;
  he makes my feet swift as those of
    hinds
  and enables me to go upon the
    heights.

For the leader; with stringed instruments.

3, 2: In the course of the years revive it: renew today your wondrous deeds of the past.

3, 3-15: Cf the theophanies in Dt 33, 2f; Jgs 5, 4f; Pss 18, 8-16; 68, 8f; 77, 17-21; 97, 1-5; Na 1, 3-6, etc. Conventional language is employed to describe the appearance of the Lord, as in Ex 19, 16-19.

3, 3: Teman: a region in Edom. Mount Paran: in the terri-tory of Edom, or the northern part of the Sinaitic peninsula. The Lord is represented as coming from Sinai, where he had appeared to Moses and given Israel the covenant and the law.

3, 13: Your anointed one: the theocratic king, the head of God's people.

---

h: Jos 10, 12.   *i:* Is 51, 9ff.   *j:* 18f: Ps 18, 32f; Mi 7, 7.

See RG
363–64

The Book of Zephaniah

The title of the prophecy informs us that the ministry of Zephaniah took place during the reign of Josiah (640–609 B.C.). The protest against the worship of false gods, and the condemnation of the pro-Assyrian court ministers who served as regents during Josiah's minority, allow us to place the work in the first decade of the reign. Accordingly, the prophecy of Zephaniah comes rightly before that of Jeremiah, who was probably influenced by it in both language and ideas.

The age of Zephaniah was a time of religious degradation, when the old idolatries reappeared and men worshiped sun, moon, and stars. Rites completely alien to the pure monotheism taught by Moses flourished in Jerusalem. To the corrupt city Zephaniah announced the impending judgment, the day of the Lord. The prophecy may be divided into three sections, corresponding to the three chapters of the book:

• The Day of the Lord: A day of doom. The last few verses of this oracle give the classic description of the Day of the Lord as an overwhelming disaster. The Christian hymn *Dies Irae* is based on this passage (1, 2-18)

• The Day of the Lord: A day of judgment of the nations, traditional enemies of God's people (2, 1-15)

• Reproach and Promise for Jerusalem: Despite Judah's infidelities, the Lord in his mercy will spare a holy remnant, which will finally enjoy peace. The prophecy closes with a hymn of joy sung by the remnant restored to Zion (3, 1-20).

———

See RG
363

CHAPTER 1

¹The word of the LORD which came to Zephaniah, the son of Cushi, the son of Gedaliah, the son of Amariah, the son of Hezekiah, in the days of Josiah, the son of Amon, king of Judah.

The Day of the Lord: A Day of Doom

² I will completely sweep away all things
   from the face of the earth, says the
   LORD.
³ I will sweep away man and beast,
   I will sweep away the birds of the sky,
   and the fishes of the sea.
I will overthrow the wicked;
   I will destroy mankind
   from the face of the earth, says the
   LORD.*a*
⁴ I will stretch out my hand against Judah,
   and against all the inhabitants of
      Jerusalem;
I will destroy from this place the last
      vestige of Baal,
   the very names of his priests,
⁵ And those who adore the host of heaven*
   on the roofs,
   with those who adore the LORD
   but swear by Milcom;*b*
⁶ And those who have fallen away from
      the LORD,
   and those who do not seek the LORD.
⁷ Silence in the presence of the Lord GOD!
   for near is the day of the LORD,
Yes, the LORD has prepared a slaughter
      feast,
   he has consecrated his guests.*
⁸   On the day of the LORD's
             slaughter feast
I will punish the princes, and the king's
             sons,
   and all that dress in foreign apparel.
⁹ I will punish, on that day,
   all who leap over the threshold,*
Who fill the house of their master
   with violence and deceit.
¹⁰   On that day, says the LORD,
A cry will be heard from the Fish Gate,

1, 5: The host of heaven: the stars, the worship of which was introduced into Judah by the Assyrians. Milcom: the god of the Ammonites; cf 1 Kgs 11, 5. 7. 33; 2 Kgs 23, 13.
1, 7: He has consecrated his guests: God has prepared those whom he has invited to share as soldiers in the booty, or as beast and bird scavengers of carrion, on the day of slaugh-

ter. Cf Jer 46, 10; Ez 39, 17.
1, 9: Leap over the threshold: the reference is to a superstitious custom of the pagans, witnessed to at least in regard to the worship of Dagon (1 Sm 5, 5).

———

a: Hos 4, 3.   *b:* Jer 8, 2; 19, 13.

a wail from the New Quarter,[*]
loud crashing from the hills.

[11] Wail, O inhabitants of the Mortar![*]
for all the merchants will be destroyed,
all who weigh out silver, done away
with.

[12] At that time I will explore Jerusalem
with lamps;
I will punish the men who thicken on
their lees,[*]
Who say in their hearts,
"Neither good nor evil can the LORD
do."

[13] Their wealth shall be given to pillage
and their houses to devastation;
They will build houses, but shall not
dwell in them,
plant vineyards, but not drink their
wine.[c]

[14] Near is the great day of the LORD,
near and very swiftly coming;
Hark, the day of the LORD!
bitter, then, the warrior's cry.

[15] A day of wrath is that day,[d]
a day of anguish and distress,
A day of destruction and desolation,
a day of darkness and gloom,
A day of thick black clouds,

[16] a day of trumpet blasts and battle alarm
Against fortified cities,
against battlements on high.[e]

[17] I will hem men in
till they walk like the blind,
because they have sinned against the
LORD;
And their blood shall be poured out like
dust,
and their brains like dung.

[18] Neither their silver nor their gold
shall be able to save them
on the day of the LORD's wrath,
When in the fire of his jealousy
all the earth shall be consumed.

For he shall make an end, yes, a sudden
end,
of all who live on the earth.[f]

CHAPTER 2

The Day of the Lord:
A Day of Judgment

See RG
363

[1] Gather, gather yourselves together,
O nation without shame![*]

[2] Before you are driven away,
like chaff that passes on;
Before there comes upon you
the blazing anger of the LORD;
Before there comes upon you
the day of the LORD's anger.

[3] Seek the LORD, all you humble of the
earth,
who have observed his law;
Seek justice, seek humility;
perhaps you may be sheltered
on the day of the LORD's anger.

[4] For Gaza shall be forsaken,
and Ashkelon shall be a waste,
Ashdod they shall drive out at midday,
and Ekron[*] shall be uprooted.[g]

[5] Woe to you who dwell by the seacoast,
to the Cretan folk![*]
The word of the LORD is against you,
I will humble you, land of the
Philistines,
and leave you to perish without an
inhabitant!

[6] The coastland of the Cretans shall
become
fields for shepherds, and folds for
flocks.

[7] The coast shall belong
to the remnant of the house of Judah;
by the sea they shall pasture.
In the houses of Ashkelon at evening
they shall couch their flocks,
For the LORD their God shall visit them,
and bring about their restoration.

1, 10f: The New Quarter . . . the Mortar: sections of Jerusalem (cf 2 Kgs 22, 14).

1, 12: The men who thicken on their lees: those who are overconfident because, like bottles of wine in which the sediment has settled to the bottom, they have remained at peace and undisturbed for a long time.

2, 1: Nation without shame: Judah.

2, 4: Gaza . . . Ashkelon . . . Ashdod . . . Ekron: four of

the five cities of the Philistine confederation. The fifth city, Gath, is not mentioned, perhaps because it was already destroyed.

2, 5: Cretan folk: the Philistines, who came from Crete; see note on Dt 2, 23.

c: Am 5, 11. d: Jer 30, 7; Jl 2, 11; Am 5, 18. e: Am 2, 2.
f: Zep 3, 8; Ez 7, 19. g: Am 1, 6ff; Zec 9, 5.

⁸ I have heard the revilings uttered by
    Moab,
  and the insults of the Ammonites,
When they reviled my people
  and made boasts against their territory.
⁹ Therefore, as I live, says the LORD of
    hosts,
  the God of Israel,
Moab shall become like Sodom,
  the land of Ammon like Gomorrah:
A field of nettles and a salt pit
  and a waste forever.
The remnant of my people shall plunder
    them,
  the survivors of my nation dispossess
    them.
¹⁰ Such shall be the requital of their pride,
  because they reviled and boasted
    against
  the people of the LORD of hosts.
¹¹ The LORD shall inspire them with fear
  when he makes all the gods of earth to
    waste away;
Then, each from its own place,
  all the coastlands of the nations shall
    adore him.

¹² You too, O Cushites,*
  shall be slain by the sword of the
    LORD.
¹³ He will stretch out his hand against the
    north,
  to destroy Assyria;
He will make Nineveh a waste,
  dry as the desert.
¹⁴ In her midst shall settle in droves
  all the wild life of the hollows;
The screech owl and the desert owl
  shall roost in her columns;
Their call shall resound from the
    window,
  the raven's croak from the doorway.^h
¹⁵ Is this the exultant city*
  that dwelt secure;
That told herself,
  "There is no other than I!"
How has she become a waste,

a lair for wild beasts?
Whoever passes by her
  hisses, and shakes his fist!

CHAPTER 3

See RG
363-64

Reproach and Promise
for Jerusalem

¹ Woe to the city, rebellious and
    polluted,
  to the tyrannical city!
² She hears no voice,
  accepts no correction;
In the LORD she has not trusted,
  to her God she has not drawn near.ⁱ
³ Her princes in her midst
  are roaring lions;
Her judges are wolves of the night
  that have had no bones to gnaw by
    morning.^j
⁴ Her prophets are insolent,
    treacherous men;
Her priests profane what is holy,
  and do violence to the law.^k
⁵ The LORD within her is just,
  who does no wrong;
Morning after morning he renders
    judgment
  unfailingly, at dawn.

⁶ I have destroyed nations,
  their battlements are laid waste;
I have made their streets deserted,
  with no one passing through;
Their cities are devastated,
  with no man dwelling in them.^l
⁷ I said, "Surely now you will fear me,
  you will accept correction";
She should not fail to see
  all I have visited upon her.
Yet all the more eagerly have they done
  all their corrupt deeds.
⁸ Therefore, wait for me, says the LORD,
  against the day when I arise as
    accuser;
For it is my decision to gather together
    the nations,
  to assemble the kingdoms,

2, 12: Cushites: the Egyptians, at this time under a Cushite or Ethiopian dynasty.
2, 15: The exultant city: Nineveh.

h: Is 34, 11.   i: Jer 2, 30; 7, 28.   j: Ez 22, 27; Mi 3, 11.   k: Jer 23, 32.   l: Jer 2, 15.

In order to pour out upon them my wrath,
  all my blazing anger;
For in the fire of my jealousy
  shall all the earth be consumed.[m]
[9] For then I will change and purify
  the lips of the peoples,
That they all may call upon the name of
  the LORD,
  to serve him with one accord;
[10] From beyond the rivers of Ethiopia
  and as far as the recesses of the North,
  they shall bring me offerings.

[11]   On that day
You need not be ashamed
  of all your deeds,
  your rebellious actions against me;
For then will I remove from your midst
  the proud braggarts,
And you shall no longer exalt yourself
  on my holy mountain.
[12] But I will leave as a remnant in your
  midst
  . a people humble and lowly,
Who shall take refuge in the name of the
  Lord:[n]
[13]   the remnant of Israel.
They shall do no wrong
  and speak no lies;
Nor shall there be found in their mouths
  a deceitful tongue;
They shall pasture and couch their
  flocks
  with none to disturb them.[o]

[14] Shout for joy, O daughter Zion!
  sing joyfully, O Israel!
Be glad and exult with all your heart,
  O daughter Jerusalem![p]
[15] The LORD has removed the judgment
  against you,
  he has turned away your enemies;
The King of Israel, the LORD, is in your
  midst,
  you have no further misfortune to fear.
[16] On that day, it shall be said to Jerusalem:
  Fear not, O Zion, be not discouraged![q]
[17] The LORD, your God, is in your midst,
  a mighty savior;
He will rejoice over you with gladness,
  and renew you in his love,
He will sing joyfully because of you,
[18]   as one sings at festivals.
I will remove disaster from among you,
  so that none may recount your
  disgrace.
[19] Yes, at that time I will deal
  with all who oppress you:
I will save the lame,
  and assemble the outcasts;
I will give them praise and renown
  in all the earth, when I bring about
  their restoration.[r]
[20] At that time I will bring you home,
  and at that time I will gather you;
For I will give you renown and praise,
  among all the peoples of the earth,
When I bring about your restoration
  before your very eyes, says the LORD.

m: Zep 1, 18.   n: Hos 14, 4.   o: Ml 4, 4.   p: Zec 9, 9.   q: Mt 14, 27.   r: Mi 4, 6.

See RG
364–65

The Book of Haggai

Postexilic prophecy begins with Haggai, who received the word of the Lord in the second year of Darius (520 B.C.). The Jews who returned from the exile in Babylonia had encountered formidable obstacles in their efforts to re-establish Jewish life in Judah. The Samaritans had succeeded in blocking the rebuilding of the temple; but after Darius acceded to the throne (522), permission was given to resume the work. At this critical moment, when defeatism and a certain lethargy had overtaken his repatriated countrymen, Haggai came forward with his exhortations to them to complete the great task. The first oracle, an appeal to the Jews, is contained in chapter 1. To this appeal Haggai added a short oracle of encouragement (chapter 2, 1-9) for the sake of those who gloomily contrasted the former magnificence of Solomon's temple with the second temple: the Lord would be present in this new abode, and its glory, enhanced by the offerings of the Gentiles, would surpass the ancient splendor.

The prophecy may be divided into five oracles: The call to rebuild the temple. The economic distress so apparent in Judah is due to the Jews' neglect of the Lord while they provide for their own needs (1, 1-15).

The future glory of the new temple, surpassing that of the old (2, 1-9).

Unworthiness of a people, who may be the Samaritans, to offer sacrifice at the newly restored altar. This oracle is cast in the literary form of a *torah*, an instruction given the people by a priest (2, 10-14).

A promise of immediate blessings, which follows upon the undertaking (chapter 1) to rebuild the temple (2, 15-19).

A pledge to Zerubbabel, descendant of David, repository of the messianic hopes (2, 20-23).

See RG 364

CHAPTER 1

Exhortation To Rebuild the Temple of the Lord. ¹On the first day of the sixth month in the second year* of King Darius, the word of the LORD came through the prophet Haggai to the governor of Judah, Zerubbabel, son of Shealtiel, and to the high priest Joshua, son of Jehozadak:*ᵃ*

²Thus says the LORD of hosts: This people says: "Not now has the time come to rebuild the house of the LORD." ³(Then this word of the LORD came through Haggai, the prophet:) ⁴Is it time for you to dwell in your own paneled houses,*ᵇ* while this house lies in ruins?*

⁵ Now thus says the LORD of hosts:
  Consider your ways!
⁶ You have sown much, but have brought
    in little;
  you have eaten, but have not been
    satisfied;
  You have drunk, but have not been
    exhilarated;
  have clothed yourselves, but not been
    warmed;

And he who earned wages
  earned them for a bag with holes in it.*ᶜ*

⁷   Thus says the LORD of hosts:
  Consider your ways!
⁸ Go up into the hill country;
  bring timber, and build the house
That I may take pleasure in it
  and receive my glory, says the LORD.
⁹ You expected much, but it came to little;
  and what you brought home, I blew
    away.
For what cause? says the LORD of hosts.
  Because my house lies in ruins,
  while each of you hurries to his own
    house.*ᵈ*
¹⁰ Therefore the heavens withheld from you
    their dew,
  and the earth her crops.*ᵉ*
¹¹ And I called for a drought
  upon the land and upon the mountains;
Upon the grain, and upon the wine, and
    upon the oil,
  and upon all that the ground brings
    forth;
Upon men and upon beasts,
  and upon all that is produced by hand.

¹²Then Zerubbabel, son of Shealtiel, and the high priest Joshua, son of Jehozadak, and all the remnant of the people* listened to the voice of the LORD, their God, and to the words of the prophet Haggai, because the LORD, their God, had sent him, and the people feared because of the LORD. ¹³And the LORD's messenger, Haggai, proclaimed to the people as the message of the LORD: I am with you, says the LORD.

¹⁴Then the LORD stirred up the spirit of the governor of Judah, Zerubbabel, son of Shealtiel, and the spirit of the high priest Joshua, son of Jehozadak, and the spirit of all the remnant of the people, so that they came and set to work on the house of the LORD of hosts, their God, ¹⁵on the twenty-fourth day of the sixth month.

1, 1: The sixth month in the second year: August/September in 520 B.C.

1, 4: The luxury of the homes of the wealthy with their paneled houses contrasts sadly with the ruined state of the Lord's house.

1, 12: The remnant of the people: a technical term in Haggai and Zechariah for the returned exiles.

---

a: Ezr 4, 24; 5, 1; 6, 14. *b:* 2 Sm 7, 2. *c:* Dt 28, 38ff; Mi 6, 15.
d: 2 Kgs 25, 9. *e:* Gn 27, 28; Am 4, 6-9.

See RG
364–65

CHAPTER 2

Future Glory of the New Temple. In the second year of King Darius, [1]on the twenty-first day of the seventh month, the word of the LORD came through the prophet Haggai: [2]Tell this to the governor of Judah, Zerubbabel, son of Shealtiel, and to the high priest Joshua, son of Jehozadak, and to the remnant of the people:

[3] Who is left among you
    that saw this house in its former
      glory?
    And how do you see it now?
      Does it not seem like nothing in your
       eyes?
[4] But now take courage, Zerubbabel, says
    the LORD,
    and take courage, Joshua, high priest,
      son of Jehozadak,
And take courage, all you people of the
    land,
    says the LORD, and work!
    For I am with you, says the LORD of
      hosts.*f*
[5] This is the pact that I made with you
    when you came out of Egypt,
And my spirit continues in your midst;
    do not fear!*g*

[6]   For thus says the LORD of hosts:*
One moment yet, a little while,
    and I will shake the heavens and the
      earth,
    the sea and the dry land.*h*
[7] I will shake all the nations,
    and the treasures of all the nations will
      come in,
And I will fill this house with glory,
    says the LORD of hosts.*i*
[8] Mine is the silver and mine the gold,
    says the LORD of hosts.

[9] Greater will be the future glory of this
    house
    than the former, says the LORD of hosts;
And in this place I will give peace,
    says the LORD of hosts!*j*

Offerings of the Unclean Rejected. [10]On the twenty-fourth day of the ninth month, in the second year of King Darius, the word of the LORD came to the prophet Haggai: [11]Thus says the LORD of hosts: Ask the priests for a decision:*k* [12]If a man carries sanctified flesh in the fold of his garment and the fold touches bread, or pottage, or wine, or oil, or any other food, do they become sanctified? "No," the priests answered.* [13]Then Haggai said: If a person unclean from contact with a corpse touches any of these, do they become unclean? The priests answered, "They become unclean."*l* [14]Then Haggai continued:

So is this people, and so is this nation
    in my sight, says the LORD:
And so are all the works of their hands;
    and what they offer there is unclean.

*Promise of Immediate Blessings.** [15]But now, consider from this day forward. Before there was a stone laid upon a stone in the temple of the LORD, [16]how did you fare?

When one went to a heap of grain for
    twenty measures,
    it would yield but ten;
When another went to the vat to draw
    fifty measures,
    there would be but twenty.*m*
[17] I struck you in all the works of your hands
    with blight, searing wind, and hail,
    yet you did not return to me, says the
      LORD.

[18][Consider from this day forward: from the twenty-fourth day of the ninth month.*

2, 6-9: From the later period of Ezekiel's preaching onward, the temple became, as here, one of the dominant messianic themes. Greater will be the future glory of this house than the former: because Christ will enter it.

2, 12ff: According to the ritual concepts of the Jews, uncleanness was more contagious than sacredness. Inasmuch as the people were unclean, their offerings became unclean (Nm 19, 22).

2, 15-19: This prophecy is intimately linked with chapter 1, and should be read with it.

2, 18: The ninth month: the ordinal ninth has been copied incorrectly from Hg 2, 10. This note clearly concerns the twenty-fourth day of the sixth month, on which the temple of the Lord was founded (Hg 1, 15).

f: Zec 8, 9.   *g:* Ex 29, 45; Lv 26, 45.   *h:* Heb 12, 26.   *i:* Gn 49, 10; Is 60, 5. 9. 11; Mal 3, 1; Rv 21, 26.   *j:* Is 2, 2ff; Zec 6, 13.   *k:* Dt 17, 8-13; Zec 7, 3.   *l:* Nm 19, 11; 13, 22.   *m:* Is 5, 10.

From the day on which the temple of the LORD was founded, consider!]

[19] Indeed, the seed has not sprouted,
nor have the vine, the fig, the
pomegranate
and the olive tree yet borne.
From this day, I will bless!

Pledge to Zerubbabel. [20]The message of the LORD came a second time to Haggai on the twenty-fourth day of the month:* [21]Tell this to Zerubbabel, the governor of Judah:

I will shake the heavens and the earth;
[22] I will overthrow the thrones of
kingdoms,

destroy the power of the kingdoms of
the nations.
I will overthrow the chariots and their
riders,
and the riders with their horses
shall go down by one another's
sword.[n]
[23] On that day, says the LORD of
hosts,[o]
I will take you, Zerubbabel,
son of Shealtiel, my servant, says the
LORD,
And I will set you as a signet ring;
for I have chosen you, says the LORD
of hosts. *

2, 20: The month: probably again the sixth month, as in Hg 1, 15 and 2, 18; see note on the latter.

2, 23: This promise to Zerubbabel, reversing the punishment of his grandfather (Jer 22, 24), is a continuation of the messianic hope; cf Zec 6, 11f.

n: Ez 38, 21; Dn 2, 44; Zec 14, 13; Lk 1, 52.   *o:* Song 8, 6; Sir 49, 11; Is 42, 1; 44, 1f.

See RG
365–68

The Book of Zechariah

Zechariah's initial prophecy is dated to 520 B.C., the same year as that in which Haggai received the prophetic call. The first eight chapters of the Book of Zechariah contain oracles which certainly belong to him while the last six (sometimes called "Deutero-Zechariah") represent the work of one or more unknown authors. In the prophecies proper to Zechariah eight symbolic visions are recorded, all meant to promote the work of rebuilding the temple and to encourage the returned exiles, especially their leaders, Joshua and Zerubbabel. In the final chapter of this first division Zechariah portrays the messianic future under the figure of a prosperous land to which the nations come in pilgrimage, eager to follow the God of Israel.

The second part of Zechariah is divided into two sections, each with its own introductory title. The first (9—11) consists of oracles whose historical background, date and authorship are extremely difficult to determine. With 9, 9 begins the messianic vision of the coming of the Prince of Peace. The verses describing the triumphant appearance of the humble king are taken up by the four Evangelists to describe the entry of Christ into Jerusalem on Palm Sunday. Chapter 12 is introduced by an oracle proclaiming the victory of God's people over the heathen. The prophecy closes by describing in apocalyptic imagery, the final assault of the enemy on Jerusalem, after which the messianic age begins.

CHAPTER 1

See RG
365

Necessity of Conversion. [1]In the second year of Darius, in the eighth month,* the word of the LORD came to the prophet Zechariah, son of Berechiah, son of Iddo:[a] [2]The LORD was indeed angry with your fathers. . . . [3]and say to them: Thus says the LORD of hosts: Return to me, says the LORD of hosts, and I will return to you, says the LORD of hosts. [4]Be not like your fathers whom the former prophets warned: Thus says the LORD of hosts: Turn from your evil ways and from your wicked deeds. But they

1, 1: The second year . . . eighth month: October/November, 520 B.C.

a: Ezr 4, 24; 5, 1; 6, 14.

would not listen or pay attention to me, says the Lord.[b] [5]Your fathers, where are they? And the prophets, can they live forever? [6]But my words and my decrees, which I entrusted to my servants the prophets, did not these overtake your fathers? Then they repented and admitted: "The Lord of hosts has treated us according to our ways and deeds, just as he had determined he would."[c]

The Four Horsemen. [7]In the second year of Darius, on the twenty-fourth day of Shebat, the eleventh month,* the word of the Lord came to the prophet Zechariah, son of Berechiah, son of Iddo, in the following way: [8]I had a vision during the night. There appeared the driver of a red horse,* standing among myrtle trees in a shady place, and behind him were red, sorrel, and white horses.[d] [9]Then I asked, "What are these, my lord?"; and the angel who spoke with me answered me, "I will show you what these are." [10]The man who was standing among the myrtle trees spoke up and said, "These are they whom the Lord has sent to patrol the earth."[e] [11]And they answered the angel of the Lord who was standing among the myrtle trees and said, "We have patrolled the earth; see, the whole earth is tranquil and at rest!"

[12f]Then the angel of the Lord spoke out and said, "O Lord of hosts, how long will you be without mercy for Jerusalem and the cities of Judah that have felt your anger these seventy years?"* [13]To the angel who spoke with me, the Lord replied with comforting words.[g]

[14]And the angel who spoke with me said to me, Proclaim: Thus says the Lord of hosts: I am deeply moved for the sake of Jerusalem and Zion,[h] [15]and I am exceedingly angry with the complacent nations;* whereas I was but a little angry, they added to the harm.[i] [16]Therefore, says the Lord: I will turn to Jerusalem in mercy; my house shall be built in it, says the Lord of hosts, and a measuring line* shall be stretched over Jerusalem.[j] [17]Proclaim further: Thus says the Lord of hosts: My cities shall again overflow with prosperity; the Lord will again comfort Zion, and again choose Jerusalem.[k]

CHAPTER 2

See RG
365

Four Horns and Four Blacksmiths. [1]I raised my eyes and looked: there were four horns.* [2]Then I asked the angel who spoke with me what these were. He answered me, "These are the horns that scattered Judah and Israel and Jerusalem."

[3]Then the Lord showed me four blacksmiths. And I asked, "What are these coming to do?" [4]And he said, "Here are the horns that scattered Judah, so that no man raised his head any more; but these have come to terrify them: to cast down the horns of the nations that raised their horns to scatter the land of Judah."

The New Jerusalem. [5]Again I raised my eyes and looked: there was a man with a measuring line in his hand.[l] [6]"Where are you going?" I asked. "To measure Jerusalem," he answered; "to see how great is its width and how great its length."[m] [7]Then the angel who spoke with me advanced, and another angel came out to meet him [8]and said to him, "Run, tell this to that young man:* People will live in Jerusalem as though in open country, because of the multitude of men and beasts in her midst.[n] [9]But I will be for her an encircling wall of fire, says the Lord, and I will be the glory in her midst."

1, 7: The second year . . . eleventh month: January/February, 519 B.C.

1, 8-11: The driver of a red horse: apparently distinct from the man, or angel of the Lord . . . standing among the myrtle trees, who spoke with the prophet. The four horsemen are sent by God to the four corners of the earth (Zec 2, 10), to see if the whole earth is at peace.

1, 12: These seventy years: see note on Jer 25, 1-14.

1, 15: The complacent nations: the neighbors of Judah, especially Edom, which enjoyed their present prosperity and security at Judah's expense.

1, 16: Measuring line: not for devastation, as in Is 34, 11, but for reconstruction.

2, 1-4: Four horns: symbolic of the hostile forces which, from the four corners of the earth, invaded and devastated the land of Judah. Four blacksmiths: the powers used by God to destroy these enemies of his people.

2, 8: That young man: the angel or man with a measuring line of v 5.

b: Jer 25, 5; 35, 15; Mal 3, 7. c: Lam 2, 17; Lv 26, 14ff; Dt 28, 15. d: Rv 6, 4. e: Zec 6, 7. f: Zec 7, 5; Jer 25, 11; Dn 9, 2. g: Jer 29, 10. h: Zec 8, 2; Jl 2, 18. i: Is 47, 6; Ob 10-14. j: Zec 8, 3; Ezr 6, 14. k: Is 51, 3. l: Rv 11, 1. m: Dt 28, 64. n: Ez 36, 11.

[10]Up, up! Flee from the land of the north,* says the LORD; for I scatter you to the four winds of heaven, says the LORD. [11]Up, escape to Zion! you who dwell in daughter Babylon. [12]For thus said the LORD of hosts (after he had already sent me) concerning the nations that have plundered you: Whoever touches you touches the apple of my eye.[o] [13]See, I wave my hand over them; they become plunder for their slaves. Thus you shall know that the LORD of hosts has sent me.

[14]Sing and rejoice, O daughter Zion! See, I am coming to dwell among you, says the LORD.[p] [15]Many nations shall join themselves to the LORD on that day, and they shall be his people, and he will dwell among you, and you shall know that the LORD of hosts has sent me to you. [16]The LORD will possess Judah as his portion in the holy land, and he will again choose Jerusalem. [17]Silence, all mankind, in the presence of the LORD! for he stirs forth from his holy dwelling.

CHAPTER 3

See RG 366

Joshua the High Priest. [1]Then he showed me Joshua the high priest standing before the angel of the LORD, while Satan stood at his right hand to accuse him.[q] [2]And the angel of the LORD said to Satan, "May the LORD rebuke you, Satan; may the LORD who has chosen Jerusalem rebuke you! Is not this man a brand snatched from the fire?"[r]

[3]Now Joshua was standing before the angel, clad in filthy garments.* [4]He spoke and said to those who were standing before him, "Take off his filthy garments, and clothe him in festal garments."[s] [5]He also said, "Put a clean miter on his head." And they put a clean miter on his head and clothed him with the garments. Then the angel of the LORD, standing, said, "See, I have taken away your guilt."

[6]The angel of the LORD then gave Joshua this assurance: [7]"Thus says the LORD of hosts: If you walk in my ways and heed my charge, you shall judge my house and keep my courts, and I will give you access among these standing here. [8]Listen, O Joshua, high priest! You and your associates who sit before you are men of good omen.* Yes, I will bring my servant the Shoot.[t] [9]Look at the stone that I have placed before Joshua, one stone with seven facets.* I will engrave its inscription, says the LORD of hosts, and I will take away the guilt of the land in one day.[u] [10]On that day, says the LORD of hosts, you will invite one another under your vines and fig trees."[v]

CHAPTER 4

See RG 366

[4]Then I said to the angel who spoke with me, "What are these things, my lord?" [5]And the angel who spoke with me replied, "Do you not know what these things are?" "No, my lord," I answered. [6]Then he said to me, "This is the LORD's message to Zerubbabel: Not by an army, nor by might, but by my spirit, says the LORD of hosts. [7]What are you, O great mountain?* Before Zerubbabel you are but a plain. He shall bring out the capstone amid exclamations of 'Hail, Hail' to it."[w]

[8]This word of the LORD then came to me: [9]The hands of Zerubbabel have laid the foundations of this house,[x] and his hands shall finish it; then you shall know that the LORD of hosts has sent me to you. [10y]For even they who were scornful on that day of small beginnings shall rejoice to see the select stone in the hands of Zerubbabel. These

---

2, 10: The land of the north: Babylonia (v 11).

3, 3: Filthy garments: symbolic of mourning for the dead, or of national catastrophe, and implying acknowledgment of guilt (v 5).

3, 8: Men of good omen: the restoration of the priesthood is a sign of the coming of the messianic times. My servant the Shoot: identified, in the earliest form of Zec 6, 11f as the prophet composed it, with Zerubbabel, direct descendant of King David and rebuilder of the temple; and, as such, a type of the Messiah; cf Jer 23, 5.

3, 9: One stone with seven facets: apparently the same as the select stone of Zec 4, 10, which seems to be a precious gem. The seven facets are explained in Zec 4, 10 as signify-

ing the Lord's vigilance over the world. I will engrave its inscription: the same Hebrew verb for engrave is used in Ex 28, 9. 11 in regard to the inscriptions on the twelve precious stones of the priestly breastpiece.

4, 7: Great mountain: figure of the obstacles confronting Zerubbabel in building the temple. A plain: figure of the ease with which he will overcome these obstacles.

o: Dt 32, 10; Ps 17, 8. *p:* Ez 37, 26. *q:* Hg 1, 1; 1 Chr 21, 1. *r:* Rom 8, 33; Jude 9. *s:* Lk 15, 22. *t:* Is 4, 2; 11, 1; Jer 23, 5; 33, 15. *u:* Zec 4, 10. *v:* 1 Kgs 4, 25. *w:* Ezr 3, 11f; Ps 118, 22. *x:* Ezr 6, 14ff. *y:* Zec 3, 9.

seven facets are the eyes of the LORD that range over the whole earth.

The Lampstand. [1]Then the angel who spoke with me returned and awakened me, like a man awakened from his sleep. [2]"What do you see?" he asked me. "I see a lampstand all of gold, with a bowl at the top," I replied; "on it are seven lamps with their tubes,[z] [3]and beside it are two olive trees, one on the right and the other on the left."[a] [11]I then asked him, "What are these two olive trees at each side of the lampstand?" [12]And again I asked, "What are the two olive tufts which freely pour out fresh oil through the two golden channels?" [13]"Do you not know what these are?" he said to me. "No, my lord," I answered him. [14]He said, "These are the two anointed* who stand by the LORD of the whole earth."

CHAPTER 5

The Flying Scroll.* [1]Then I raised my eyes again and saw a scroll flying.[b] [2]"What do you see?" he asked me. I answered, "I see a scroll flying; it is twenty cubits long and ten cubits wide." [3]Then he said to me: "This is the curse which is to go forth over the whole earth; in accordance with it shall every thief be swept away, and in accordance with it shall every perjurer be expelled from here. [4]I will send it forth, says the LORD of hosts, and it shall come into the house of the thief, or into the house of him who perjures himself with my name; it shall lodge within his house, consuming it, timber and stones."[c]

The Flying Bushel.* [5]Then the angel who spoke with me came forward and said to me, "Raise your eyes and see what this is that comes forth." [6]"What is it?" I asked. And he

answered, "This is a bushel container coming. This is their guilt in all the land." [7]Then a leaden cover was lifted, and there was a woman sitting inside the bushel. [8]"This is Wickedness," he said; and he thrust her inside the bushel, pushing the leaden cover into the opening. [9]Then I raised my eyes and saw two women coming forth with a wind ruffling their wings, for they had wings like the wings of a stork. As they lifted up the bushel into the air, [10]I said to the angel who spoke with me, "Where are they taking the bushel?" [11]He replied, "To build a temple for it in the land of Shinar; when the temple is ready, they will deposit it there in its place."[d]

CHAPTER 6

Four Chariots.* [1]Again I raised my eyes and saw four chariots coming out from between two mountains; and the mountains were of bronze. [2]The first chariot had red horses, the second chariot black horses,[e] [3]the third chariot white horses, and the fourth chariot spotted horses—all of them strong horses. [4]I asked the angel who spoke with me, "What are these, my lord?" [5]The angel said to me in reply, "These are the four winds of the heavens, which are coming forth after being reviewed by the LORD of all the earth."[f] [6]The chariot with the black horses was turning toward the land of the north, the red and the white horses went after them, and the spotted ones went toward the land of the south. [7]As these strong horses emerged, eager to set about patrolling the earth, he said, "Go, patrol the earth!" Then, as they patrolled the earth, [8]he called out to me and said, "See, they that go forth to the land of the north will make my spirit rest in the land of the north."

4, 1ff. 11-14: The two anointed: literally, "the two sons of oil," Joshua, the anointed high priest, and Zerubbabel, the anointed prince. Just as the two olive trees in this imagery supply the sacred seven-branched lampstand (Ex 25, 31-40) with oil (v 12), so these two men, in ministering to the community, stand by (serve) the Lord.

5, 1-4: The enormous scroll, thirty feet by fifteen (the dimensions in length and breadth of the portico of Solomon's temple, 1 Kgs 6, 3), contains a list of maledictions on sinners, similar to that in Dt 27, 15-26. The thief and the perjurer represent all sinners, who are expelled from the holy community.

5, 5-11: The woman sealed in the bushel container is a fig-

ure of the general corruption of the people of Judah. She is removed from the Holy Land and transported to Shinar, that is, Babylonia, where a dwelling is being prepared for her; that is a symbol of the reign of Wickedness in pagan lands, contrasted with the reign of holiness in the Lord's dwelling on Mount Zion.

6, 1-8: The four chariots represent the angelic hosts sent by the Lord to the four ends of the earth. The chariot with the black horses brings the spirit, i.e., anger of the Lord against the land of the north, Babylonia.

---

z: Rv 1, 12.   a: Rv 11, 4.   b: Ez 2, 9.   c: Lv 19, 12.   d: Gn 11, 2ff.   e: Zec 1, 8; Rv 6, 4.   f: Ps 104, 4.

The Coronation. ⁹This word of the LORD then came to me: ¹⁰Take from the returned captives Heldai, Tobijah, Jedaiah; and go the same day to the house of Josiah, son of Zephaniah (these had come from Babylon). ¹¹Silver and gold you shall take, and make a crown; place it on the head of [Joshua, son of Jehozadak, the high priest] Zerubbabel.* ¹²And say to him: Thus says the LORD of hosts: Here is a man whose name is Shoot, and where he is he shall sprout, and he shall build the temple of the LORD.ᵍ ¹³Yes, he shall build the temple of the LORD, and taking up the royal insignia, he shall sit as ruler upon his throne. The priest shall be at his right hand, and between the two of them there shall be friendly understanding.ʰ ¹⁴The crown itself shall be a memorial offering in the temple of the LORD in favor of Heldai, Tobijah, Jedaiah, and the son of Zephaniah. ¹⁵And they who are from afar shall come and build the temple of the LORD, and you shall know that the LORD of hosts has sent me to you.ⁱ And if you heed carefully the voice of the LORD your God. . . .

CHAPTER 7

See RG 366–67

True Fasting. ¹In the fourth year of Darius the king [the word of the LORD came to Zechariah], on the fourth day of Chislev, the ninth month,* ²Bethel-sarezer sent Regemmelech and his men to implore favor of the LORD ³and to ask the priests of the house of the LORD of hosts, and the prophets, "Must I mourn and abstain in the fifth month as I have been doing these many years?"ʲ ⁴Thereupon this word of the LORD of hosts came to me: ⁵Say to all the people of the land and to the priests: When you fasted and mourned in the fifth and in the seventh month these seventy years, was it really for me that you fasted?ᵏ ⁶And when you were eating and drinking, was it not for yourselves that you ate, and for yourselves that you drank? ⁷Were not these the words which

the LORD spoke through the former prophets, when Jerusalem and the surrounding cities were inhabited and at peace, when the Negeb and the foothills were inhabited?ˡ ⁸[This word of the LORD came to Zechariah: ⁹Thus says the LORD of hosts:] Render true judgment, and show kindness and compassion toward each other.ᵐ ¹⁰Do not oppress the widow or the orphan, the alien or the poor; do not plot evil against one another in your hearts.ⁿ ¹¹But they refused to listen; they stubbornly turned their backs and stopped their ears so as not to hear.ᵒ ¹²And they made their hearts diamond-hard so as not to hear the teaching and the message that the LORD of hosts had sent by his spirit through the former prophets.ᵖ ¹³Then the LORD of hosts in his great anger said that, as they had not listened when he called, so he would not listen when they called,ᑫ ¹⁴but would scatter them with a whirlwind among all the nations that they did not know. Thus the land was left desolate after them with no one traveling to and fro; they made the pleasant land into a desert.ʳ

CHAPTER 8

See RG 366–67

In the Days of the Messiah. ¹This word of the LORD of hosts came: Thus says the LORD of hosts:

² I am intensely jealous for Zion,
    stirred to jealous wrath for her.ˢ
³   Thus says the LORD:
I will return to Zion,
    and I will dwell within Jerusalem;
Jerusalem shall be called the faithful city,
    and the mountain of the LORD of hosts,
    the holy mountain.ᵗ

⁴Thus says the LORD of hosts: Old men and old women, each with staff in hand because of old age, shall again sit in the streets of Jerusalem. ⁵The city shall be filled with boys and girls playing in her streets. ⁶Thus says the

---

6, 11: Make a crown; place it on the head of [Joshua, son of Jehozadak, the high priest] Zerubbabel: according to the current Hebrew text, Joshua the high priest is to be crowned. However, since the crown is a sign of royalty, the original text must have had the name of Zerubbabel here, not that of Joshua. In Zec 3, 8 Joshua is a different man from the one called the Shoot, and in v 12 it is upon the Shoot that the crown is to be placed.

7, 1: The fourth year of Darius . . . the fourth day of Chislev, the ninth month: November, 518 B.C.

g: Zec 3, 8; Eph 2, 20; Heb 3, 3. h: Ps 110, 4; Heb 3, 1. i: Eph 2, 19f. j: Zec 8, 19. k: Is 58, 5; Rom 14, 6. l: Jer 17, 26. m: Is 58, 6. n: Ex 22, 21-24; Dt 24, 17; Is 1, 17; Jer 5, 28. o: Neh 9, 29; Hos 4, 16. p: Ez 11, 19; 36, 26; Neh 9, 29. q: Is 1, 15; Mi 3, 4. r: Dt 4, 27. s: Na 1, 2. t: Is 2, 2; Jer 31, 23.

LORD of hosts: Even if this should seem impossible in the eyes of the remnant of this people, shall it in those days be impossible in my eyes also, says the LORD of hosts? [7]Thus says the LORD of hosts: Lo, I will rescue my people from the land of the rising sun, and from the land of the setting sun.[u] [8]I will bring them back to dwell within Jerusalem. They shall be my people, and I will be their God, with faithfulness and justice.[v]

[9]Thus says the LORD of hosts: Let your hands be strong, you who in these days hear these words spoken by the prophets on the day when the foundation of the house of the LORD of hosts was laid for the building of the temple.[w] [10]For before those days there were no wages for men, or hire for beasts; those who came and went had no security from the enemy, for I set every man against his neighbor. [11]But now I will not deal with the remnant of this people as in former days, says the LORD of hosts, [12]for it is the seedtime of peace: the vine shall yield its fruit, the land shall bear its crops, and the heavens shall give their dew; all these things I will have the remnant of the people possess. [13]Just as you were a curse among the nations, O house of Judah and house of Israel, so will I save you that you may be a blessing; do not fear, but let your hands be strong.[x]

[14]Thus says the LORD of hosts: As I determined to harm you when your fathers provoked me to wrath, says the LORD of hosts, and I did not relent,[y] [15]so again in these days I have determined to favor Jerusalem and the house of Judah; do not fear! [16]These then are the things you should do: Speak the truth to one another; let there be honesty and peace in the judgments at your gates,[z] [17]and let none of you plot evil against another in his heart, nor love a false oath. For all these things I hate, says the LORD.[a]

[18]This word of the LORD of hosts came to me: [19]Thus says the LORD of hosts: The fast days of the fourth, the fifth, the seventh, and the tenth months shall become occasions of joy and gladness, cheerful festivals for the house of Judah; only love faithfulness and peace.[*] [20]Thus says the LORD of hosts: There shall yet come peoples, the inhabitants of many cities; [21]and the inhabitants of one city shall approach those of another, and say, "Come! let us go to implore the favor of the LORD"; and, "I too will go to seek the LORD."[b] [22]Many peoples and strong nations shall come to seek the LORD of hosts in Jerusalem and to implore the favor of the LORD.[c] [23]Thus says the LORD of hosts: In those days ten men of every nationality, speaking different tongues, shall take hold, yes, take hold of every Jew by the edge of his garment and say, "Let us go with you, for we have heard that God is with you."[d]

CHAPTER 9

Invasion by the Lord[*]

See RG 367

[1]   An oracle:
The word of the LORD is upon the land of Hadrach,
    and Damascus is its resting place,
For the cities of Aram are the LORD's,
    as are all the tribes of Israel,
[2] Hamath also, on its border,
    Tyre, too, and Sidon, however wise they be.[e]
[3] Tyre built herself a stronghold,
    and heaped up silver like dust,
    and gold like the mire of the streets.
[4] Lo, the LORD will strip her of her possessions,
    and smite her power on the sea,
    and she shall be devoured by fire.[f]
[5] Ashkelon shall see it and be afraid;
Gaza also: she shall be in great anguish;
Ekron, too, for her hope shall come to nought.
The king shall disappear from Gaza,

8, 19: The fast day of the fourth month recalled the fall of Jerusalem in June, 587 B.C. (2 Kgs 25, 3f); that of the fifth month, the burning of the temple by Nebuzaradan in July of the same year (2 Kgs 25, 8f); that of the seventh month, the murder of Gedaliah in September of the same year (Jer 41, 1f); that of the tenth month, the beginning of the final siege of Jerusalem in January, 588 B.C. (2 Kgs 25, 1).

9, 1-8: Divine judgment is about to fall on the surrounding hostile peoples: Aram (Syria), including the cities of Hadrach and Damascus; Phoenicia, with its cities of Tyre and Sidon; Philistia, with its cities of Ashkelon, Gaza, Ekron, and Ashdod.

---

u: Is 11, 11; Jer 30, 18.   v: Jer 4, 2.   w: Ezr 5, 1; Hg 2, 18.   x: Is 19, 24; Jer 42, 18; Hg 2, 19; Zep 3, 20.   y: Jer 31, 28.   z: Zec 7, 9.   a: Zec 7, 10.   b: Is 2, 3.   c: Is 60, 3.   d: Is 66, 23.   e: Jer 49, 23.   f: Is 23, 1-18; Ez 26, 1—28, 26.

and Ashkelon shall not be inhabited,
6 and the baseborn* shall occupy Ashdod.
I will destroy the pride of the Philistine[g]
7 and take from his mouth his bloody
   meat,
and his abominations from between
   his teeth:
He also shall become a remnant* for our
   God,
and shall be like a family in Judah,
and Ekron shall be like the Jebusites.
8 I will encamp by my house* as a guard
that none may pass to and fro;
No oppressor shall pass over them again,
for now I have regard for their
   affliction.

Restoration under the Messiah

9 Rejoice heartily, O daughter Zion,[h]
   shout for joy, O daughter Jerusalem!
See, your king shall come to you;
   a just savior is he,
Meek, and riding on an ass,
   on a colt, the foal of an ass.*
10 He shall banish the chariot from
   Ephraim,
and the horse from Jerusalem;
The warrior's bow shall be banished,
and he shall proclaim peace to the
   nations.
His dominion shall be from sea to sea,
   and from the River* to the ends of the
   earth.[i]
11 As for you, for the blood of your
   covenant with me,*
I will bring forth your prisoners from
   the dungeon.[j]
12 In the return to the fortress
of the waiting prisoners,*

This very day, I will return you
   double for your exile.[k]
13 For I will bend Judah as my bow,
   I will arm myself with Ephraim;
I will arouse your sons, O Zion,
   [against your sons, O Yavan,]
and I will use you as a warrior's sword.
14 The LORD shall appear over them,
   and his arrow shall shoot forth as
   lightning;
The LORD God shall sound the trumpet,
   and come in a storm from the south.
15 The LORD of hosts shall be a shield over
   them,
they shall overcome sling stones
   and trample them underfoot;
They shall drink blood like wine,
   till they are filled with it like libation
   bowls,
   like the corners of the altar.
16 And the LORD, their God, shall save them
   on that day,
   his people, like a flock.
For they are the jewels in a crown
   raised aloft over his land.[l]
17 For what wealth is theirs, and what
   beauty!
   grain that makes the youths flourish,
   and new wine, the maidens!

CHAPTER 10

See RG
367

The New Order of Things

1 Ask of the LORD rain in the spring
   season!
It is the LORD who makes the storm
   clouds,
And sends men the pouring rain;
   for everyone, grassy fields.[m]
2 For the teraphim* speak nonsense,

9, 6: The baseborn: people of mixed ancestry.

9, 7: Remnant: see note on Hg 1, 12. The Jebusites: the pre-Israelite inhabitants of Jerusalem, conquered by David and incorporated into Israel.

9, 8: My house: the Holy Land; cf Hos 8, 1; 9, 15; Jer 12, 7.

9, 9: The Messiah will come, not as a conquering warrior, but in lowliness and peace. Not like the last kings of Judah, who rode in chariots and on horses (Jer 17, 25; 22, 4), but like the princes of old (Gn 49, 11; Jgs 5, 10; 10, 4), the Messiah will ride on an ass. The Evangelists see a literal fulfillment of this prophecy in the Savior's triumphant entry into Jerusalem (Mt 21, 4f; Jn 12, 14f).

9, 10: The River: the Euphrates; see note on Ps 72, 8.

9, 11: The blood of your covenant with me: the covenant between the Lord and Israel sealed with sacrificial blood (Ex 24, 8).

9, 12: The waiting prisoners: the exiles awaiting the return to their country, where they will receive a double compensation for the double punishment they had suffered; cf Is 40, 2; 61, 7.

10, 2: Teraphim: household idols, used for divination; cf Gn 31, 19. 34f; Jgs 17, 5; 18, 17f. 20; Ez 21, 26; Hos 3, 4.

g: Am 1, 8.   *h:* Is 62, 11; Jer 23, 5; Mt 21, 5; Jn 12, 15.   *i:* Hos 1, 7.   *j:* Is 42, 7; Ez 24, 8.   *k:* Is 61, 7.   *l:* Is 62, 3.   *m:* Dt 11, 14; Jer 14, 22.

the diviners have false visions:
Deceitful dreams they tell,
  empty comfort they offer.
This is why they wander like sheep,
  wretched: they have no shepherd.[n]
3 My wrath is kindled against the
    shepherds,
  and I will punish the leaders;
For the LORD of hosts will visit his flock,
  the house of Judah,
  and make them his stately war horse.

4 From him shall come leader and chief,
  from him warrior's bow and every
    officer.
5 They shall all be warriors,
  trampling the mire of the streets in
    battle;
They shall wage war because the LORD is
    with them,
  and shall put the horsemen to rout.
6 I will strengthen the house of Judah,
  the house of Joseph I will save;
I will bring them back, because I have
    mercy on them,
  they shall be as though I had never
    cast them off,
  for I am the LORD, their God, and I
    will hear them.
7 Then Ephraim shall be valiant men,
  and their hearts shall be cheered as by
    wine.
Their children shall see it and be glad,
  their hearts shall rejoice in the LORD.

8 I will whistle for them to come together,
  and when I redeem them
  they will be as numerous as before.[o]
9 I sowed them among the nations,
  yet in distant lands they remember me;
  they shall rear their children and return.
10 I will bring them back from the land of
    Egypt,
  and gather them from Assyria.

I will bring them into Gilead and into
    Lebanon,
  but these shall not suffice them;[p]
11 I will cross over to Egypt
  and smite the waves of the sea
  and all the depths of the Nile shall be
    dried up.
The pride of Assyria shall be cast down,
  and the scepter of Egypt taken away.[q]
12 I will strengthen them in the LORD,
  and they shall walk in his name, says
    the LORD.[r]

CHAPTER 11

See RG 367–68

1 Open your doors, O Lebanon,
  that the fire may devour your cedars!
2 Wail, you cypress trees,
  for the cedars are fallen,
  the mighty have been despoiled.
Wail, you oaks of Bashan,
  for the impenetrable forest is cut
    down!
3 Hark! the wailing of the shepherds,
  their glory has been ruined.
Hark! the roaring of the young lions,
  the jungle of the Jordan is laid waste.

Allegory of the Shepherds.[*] 4Thus said the LORD, my God: Shepherd the flock to be slaughtered. 5For they who buy them slay them with impunity; while those who sell them say, "Blessed be the LORD, I have become rich!" Even their own shepherds do not feel for them.[s] 6(Nor shall I spare the inhabitants of the earth any more, says the LORD. Yes, I will deliver each of them into the power of his neighbor, or into the power of his king; they shall crush the earth, and I will not deliver it out of their power.)

7So I became the shepherd of the flock to be slaughtered for the sheep merchants. I took two staffs, one of which I called "Favor," and the other, "Bonds," and I fed the flock.[t] 8In a single month I did away with the

---

11, 4-17: In this allegory the prophet becomes the good shepherd of God's flock, which is being slaughtered; he is the defender of the people exploited by bad rulers. The three shepherds, rulers in general, are to destroy one another in a short time (a single month). The service of the good shepherd is contemptuously valued at thirty pieces of silver, the legal indemnity (Ex 21, 32) for a gored slave. The prophet is thus a type of Christ whose mission of salvation to his people was appraised by the Sanhedrists, the false shepherds, at the same base price (Mt 26, 14ff). In the case of the prophet as well as of Christ (Mt 27, 5), the money is thrown into the temple treasury, i.e., paid to God, showing thereby how shamefully his divine love and care are requited.

---

n: Jer 10, 8; Ez 34, 5. o: Ez 36, 37. p: Is 11, 11; 49, 20; Hos 11, 11. q: Is 11, 15; Ez 30, 13. r: Mi 4, 5. s: Jer 50, 7. t: Hos 5, 6.

three shepherds. I wearied of them, and they behaved badly toward me. [9]"I will not feed you," I said. "What is to die, let it die; what is to perish, let it perish, and let those that are left devour one another's flesh."[u]

[10]Then I took my staff "Favor" and snapped it asunder, breaking off the covenant which I had made with all peoples; [11]that day it was broken off. The sheep merchants who were watching me understood that this was the word of the LORD. [12]I said to them, "If it seems good to you, give me my wages; but if not, let it go." And they counted out my wages, thirty pieces of silver.[v] [13]But the LORD said to me, "Throw it in the treasury, the handsome price at which they valued me." So I took the thirty pieces of silver and threw them into the treasury in the house of the LORD.[w]

[14]Then I snapped asunder my other staff, "Bonds," breaking off the brotherhood between Judah and Israel. [15]The LORD said to me: This time take the gear of a foolish shepherd. [16]For I will raise up a shepherd in the land who will take no note of those that perish, nor seek the strays, nor heal the injured, nor feed what survives—he will eat the flesh of the fat ones and tear off their hoofs![x]

[17] Woe to my foolish shepherd
   who forsakes the flock!
May the sword fall upon his arm
   and upon his right eye;
Let his arm wither away entirely,
   and his right eye be blind forever![y]

See RG 368

CHAPTER 12

*Jerusalem God's Instrument.** [1]An oracle: the word of the LORD concerning Israel. Thus says the LORD, who spreads out the heavens, lays the foundations of the earth, and forms the spirit of man within him:[z] [2]See, I will make Jerusalem a bowl to stupefy all peoples round about. [Judah will be besieged, even Jerusalem.][a] [3]On that day I will make Jerusalem a weighty stone for all peoples. All who attempt to lift it shall injure themselves badly, and all the nations of the earth shall be gathered against her.[b] [4]On that day, says the LORD, I will strike every horse with fright, and its rider with madness. I will strike blind all the horses of the peoples, but upon the house of Judah I will open my eyes, [5]and the princes of Judah shall say to themselves, "The inhabitants of Jerusalem have their strength in the LORD of hosts, their God." [6]On that day I will make the princes of Judah like a brazier of fire in the woodland, and like a burning torch among sheaves, and they shall devour right and left all the surrounding peoples; but Jerusalem shall still abide on its own site.[c] [7]The LORD shall save the tents of Judah first, that the glory of the house of David and the glory of the inhabitants of Jerusalem may not be exalted over Judah. [8]On that day, the LORD will shield the inhabitants of Jerusalem, and the weakling among them shall be like David on that day, and the house of David godlike, like an angel of the LORD before them.[d] [9]On that day I will seek the destruction of all nations that come against Jerusalem.

Messianic Jerusalem. [10]I will pour out on the house of David and on the inhabitants of Jerusalem a spirit of grace and petition;[e] and they shall look on him whom they have thrust through, and they shall mourn for him as one mourns for an only son, and they shall grieve over him as one grieves over a firstborn.*

[11]*On that day the mourning in Jerusalem

12, 1-9: Under the image of the deliverance of Judah and Jerusalem from invading enemies, the prophet foretells the ultimate victory of God's people in the messianic age.

12, 10: The divine blessings (a spirit of grace and petition) will be poured out on God's people through the intervention of an unnamed sufferer (him whom they have thrust through), similar to the Servant of the Lord in Is 52, 13—53, 12. In Jn 19, 37 the Evangelist sees in this passage a prophecy fulfilled in the piercing of Christ's side.

12, 11: The mourning for the pierced victim in Jerusalem is compared to a lamentation in the plain of Megiddo apparently over a certain personage called Hadadrimmon. The ref-

erence is no longer clear. Both Hadad and Rimmon were names of the Semitic storm god, often identified with the god Baal. Some see here a reference to the annual mourning by the pagans over the death of the fertility god. According to others, Hadadrimmon is the name of a place near Megiddo, and the reference would then be to the mourning over the death of King Josiah, who was killed in battle there; cf 2 Chr 35, 22-25.

u: Jer 15, 2. *v:* Ex 21, 32; Mt 26, 15. *w:* Mt 27, 9f. *x:* Ez 34, 2ff. *y:* Jn 10, 12. *z:* Is 42, 5. *a:* Is 51, 17; Jer 51, 7. *b:* Mt 21, 44. *c:* Ob 18. *d:* Ex 32, 34. *e:* Jer 6, 26; Jn 19, 34; Rv 1, 7.

shall be as great as the mourning of Hadadrimmon in the plain of Megiddo.[f] [12] And the land shall mourn, each family apart: the family of the house of David, and their wives; the family of the house of Nathan, and their wives; [13] the family of the house of Levi, and their wives; the family of Shemei, and their wives; [14] and all the rest of the families, each family apart, and the wives apart.

CHAPTER 13

See RG 368

The End of Falsehood. [1] On that day there shall be open to the house of David and to the inhabitants of Jerusalem, a fountain to purify from sin* and uncleanness.[g] [2] On that day, says the LORD of hosts, I will destroy the names of the idols from the land, so that they shall be mentioned no more; I will also take away the prophets and the spirit of uncleanness from the land.[h] [3] If a man still prophesies, his parents, father and mother, shall say to him, "You shall not live, because you have spoken a lie in the name of the LORD." When he prophesies, his parents, father and mother, shall thrust him through.[i]

[4] On that day, every prophet shall be ashamed to prophesy his vision, neither shall he assume the hairy mantle* to mislead, [5] but he shall say, "I am no prophet, I am a tiller of the soil, for I have owned land since my youth."[j] [6] And if anyone asks him, "What are these wounds on your chest?"* he shall answer, "With these I was wounded in the house of my dear ones."

The Song of the Sword

[7] Awake, O sword, against my shepherd, against the man who is my associate,

says the LORD of hosts.
Strike the shepherd
 that the sheep may be dispersed,*
 and I will turn my hand against the
  little ones.[k]
[8] In all the land, says the LORD,
 two thirds of them shall be cut off and
  perish,
 and one third shall be left.
[9] I will bring the one third through fire,
 and I will refine them as silver is
  refined,
 and I will test them as gold is tested.[l]
 They shall call upon my name, and I
  will hear them.
I will say, "They are my people,"
 and they shall say, "The LORD is my
  God."

CHAPTER 14

See RG 368

*The Fight for Jerusalem.** [1] Lo, a day shall come for the LORD when the spoils shall be divided in your midst. [2] And I will gather all the nations against Jerusalem for battle: the city shall be taken, houses plundered, women ravished; half of the city shall go into exile, but the rest of the people shall not be removed from the city. [3] Then the LORD shall go forth and fight against those nations, fighting as on a day of battle. [4] That day his feet shall rest upon the Mount of Olives, which is opposite Jerusalem to the east. The Mount of Olives shall be cleft in two from east to west by a very deep valley, and half of the mountain shall move to the north and half of it to the south. [5] And the valley of the LORD's mountain shall be filled up when the valley of those two mountains reaches its edge; it shall be filled up as it was filled up

13, 1: A fountain to purify from sin: in contrast to the lustral water used in ritual purification; cf Nm 19, 9. 13. 20; 31, 23. The Lord himself is the fountain of living water (Jer 2, 13); cf Is 12, 2ff.

13, 4: Hairy mantle: worn by prophets as a mark of their calling; cf 2 Kgs 1, 8; Mt 3, 4.

13, 6: Wounds on your chest: literally "wounds between your hands." The false prophets, like the prophet of Baal (1 Kgs 13, 28), apparently inflicted wounds on themselves; to defend himself against the accusation of being a false prophet, a man will deny having inflicted wounds on himself and say instead that he received them at home, "in the house of my dear ones." In the liturgy this text is applied to Christ in an accommodated sense.

13, 7: When the shepherd is killed, the sheep are scattered. In Mt 26, 31 the Evangelist quotes from this verse, in somewhat different form, the words, I will smite the shepherd, and the sheep of the flock will be scattered, as said by Christ shortly before his arrest in the Garden of Olives and the flight of the Apostles.

14, 1-21: An apocalyptic description of the day of the Lord, in which Jerusalem, the figure of God's elect, after much suffering (siege: vv 1ff; riot: v 13; plague: vv 12, 15), is rescued by the Lord (vv 4f) and given great blessings (vv 6-11. 14. 16-21).

f: 2 Chr 35, 22-25. g: Heb 9, 14; 1 Pt 1, 18f; Rv 1, 5. h: Mi 5, 12; 2 Pt 2, 1. i: Dt 18, 20; Mi 3, 5ff. j: Am 7, 14. k: Mt 26, 31. l: Jer 30, 22; Ps 66, 10.

by the earthquake in the days of King Uzziah of Judah. Then the LORD, my God, shall come, and all his holy ones with him.

[6]On that day there shall no longer be cold or frost. [7]There shall be one continuous day, known to the LORD, not day and night, for in the evening time there shall be light.[m]

[8]On that day, living waters shall flow from Jerusalem, half to the eastern sea, and half to the western sea, and it shall be so in summer and in winter.[n] [9]The LORD shall become king over the whole earth; on that day the LORD shall be the only one, and his name the only one.[o]

[10]And from Geba to Rimmon in the Negeb, all the land shall turn into a plain; but Jerusalem shall remain exalted in its place. From the Gate of Benjamin to the place of the First Gate, to the Corner Gate; and from the Tower of Hananel to the king's wine presses,[p] [11]they shall occupy her. Never again shall she be doomed; Jerusalem shall abide in security.[q]

[12]And this shall be the plague with which the LORD shall strike all the nations that have fought against Jerusalem: their flesh shall rot while they stand upon their feet, and their eyes shall rot in their sockets, and their tongues shall rot in their mouths.

[13]On that day there shall be among them a great tumult from the LORD: every man shall seize the hand of his neighbor, and the hand of each shall be raised against that of his neighbor. [14]Judah also shall fight against Jerusalem. The riches of all the surrounding nations shall be gathered together, gold, silver, and garments, in great abundance.

[15]Similar to this plague shall be the plague upon the horses, mules, camels, asses, and upon all the beasts that are in those camps.

[16]All who are left of all the nations that came against Jerusalem shall come up year after year to worship the King, the LORD of hosts, and to celebrate the feast of Booths.[r] [17]If any of the families of the earth does not come up to Jerusalem to worship the King, the LORD of hosts, no rain shall fall upon them. [18]And if the family of Egypt does not come up, or enter, upon them shall fall the plague which the LORD will inflict upon all the nations that do not come up to celebrate the feast of Booths. [19]This shall be the punishment of Egypt, and the punishment of all the nations that do not come up to celebrate the feast of Booths.

[20]On that day there shall be upon the bells of the horses, "Holy to the LORD." The pots in the house of the LORD shall be as the libation bowls before the altar. [21]And every pot in Jerusalem and in Judah shall be holy to the LORD of hosts; and all who come to sacrifice shall take them and cook in them. On that day there shall no longer be any merchant in the house of the LORD of hosts.[s]

m: Rv 21, 23.   n: Zec 13, 1; Ez 47, 1-8; Jl 3, 18.   o: Dt 6, 4; Eph 4, 5f; Rv 11, 15.   p: Zec 12, 6; Neh 3, 6; 12, 38.   q: Jer 31, 40; Rv 22, 3.   r: Lv 23, 34. 43; Neh 8, 14; Is 60, 6. 9.   s: Mt 21, 12; Jn 2, 13-16.

See RG 369–70

The Book of Malachi

This work was composed by an anonymous writer shortly before Nehemiah's arrival in Jerusalem (445 B.C.). Because of the sharp reproaches he was leveling against the priests and rulers of the people, the author probably wished to conceal his identity. To do this he made a proper name out of the Hebrew expression for "My Messenger" (Malachi), which occurs in 1, 1 and 3, 1. The historical value of the prophecy is considerable in that it gives us a picture of life in the Jewish community returned from Babylon, between the period of Haggai and the reform measures of Ezra and Nehemiah. It is likely that the author's trenchant criticism of abuses and religious indifference in the community prepared the way for these necessary reforms.

The chosen people had made a sorry return for divine love. The priests, who should have been leaders, had dishonored God by their blemished sacrifices. In his first chapter, the writer foresees the time when all nations will offer a pure oblation (1, 11)—a prophecy whose fulfillment the church sees in the Sacrifice of the Mass. The author then turns from priests to people, denouncing their marriages with pagans and their callous repudiation of Israelite wives. Imbued with the rationalist and critical spirit of the times, many had wearied God with the question, "Where is the God of justice?" To this question the prophet replies that the day of the Lord is coming. But first the forerunner must come, who will prepare the soil for repentance and true worship. The Gospel writers point to John the Baptizer, as the forerunner ushering in the messianic age, the true day of the Lord. When the ground is prepared God will appear, measuring out rewards and punishments and purifying the nation in the furnace of judgment. He will create a new order in which the ultimate triumph of good is inevitable.

See RG
369

CHAPTER 1

1 An oracle. The word of the LORD to Israel through Malachi.

Israel Preferred to Edom

2 I have loved you, says the LORD;
but you say, "How have you loved
us?"*a*
3 Was not Esau Jacob's brother? says the
LORD:*
yet I loved Jacob, but hated Esau;
I made his mountains a waste,
his heritage a desert for jackals.*b*
4 If Edom says, "We have been crushed
but we will rebuild the ruins,"
Thus says the LORD of hosts:
They indeed may build, but I will tear
down,
And they shall be called the land of
guilt,*c*
the people with whom the LORD is
angry forever.
5 Your own eyes shall see it, and you will
say,

"Great is the LORD, even beyond the
land of Israel."*d*

Sins of the Priests and Levites

6 A son honors his father,
and a servant fears his master;
If then I am a father,
where is the honor due to me?
And if I am a master,
where is the reverence due to me?—
So says the LORD of hosts to you,
O priests,
who despise his name.
But you ask, "How have we despised
your name?"
7 By offering polluted food on my altar!
Then you ask, "How have we polluted
it?"
By saying the table of the LORD may
be slighted!
8 When you offer a blind animal for
sacrifice,*e*
is this not evil?
When you offer the lame or the sick,
is it not evil?
Present it to your governor; see if he will
accept it,
or welcome you, says the LORD of
hosts.*
9 So now if you implore God for mercy on
us,
when you have done the like
Will he welcome any of you?
says the LORD of hosts.

10 Oh, that one among you would shut the
temple gates*
to keep you from kindling fire on my
altar in vain!
I have no pleasure in you, says the LORD
of hosts;
neither will I accept any sacrifice from
your hands,

1, 3ff: The thought passes from the person Esau to his descendants, Edom, and from the person Jacob to his descendants, Israel. Loved: preferred; hated: rejected; cf Gn 25, 21ff. St. Paul uses this passage as an example of God's freedom of choice in calling the Gentiles to the faith (Rom 9, 13).

1, 8: The offering in sacrifice of a lame, sick or blind animal was forbidden in the law (Lv 22, 17-25; Dt 17, 1).

1, 10f: The imperfect sacrifices offered without sincerity by the people of Judah are displeasing to the Lord. He will

rather be pleased with the offerings of the Gentile nations throughout the world (from the rising of the sun, even to its setting), which anticipate the pure offering to be sacrificed in messianic times, the universal Sacrifice of the Mass, as we are told by the Council of Trent.

a: Dt 7, 6ff; Ez 16; Am 1, 11.   *b:* Gn 25, 23; Rom 9, 13.   *c:* Is 34, 5f; 63, 1-6; Jer 49, 7-22; Ob 21.   *d:* Is 60.   *e:* Lv 22, 19-25; Dt 15, 21.

11 For from the rising of the sun, even to its
setting,
my name is great among the nations;
And everywhere they bring sacrifice to
my name,
and a pure offering;
For great is my name among the nations,
says the LORD of hosts.*f*
12 But you behave profanely toward me by
thinking
the LORD's table and its offering may
be polluted,
and its food slighted.
13 You also say, "What a burden!"
and you scorn it, says the LORD of
hosts;
You bring in what you seize, or the lame,
or the sick;
yes, you bring it as a sacrifice.
Shall I accept it from your hands?
says the LORD.
14 Cursed is the deceiver, who has in his
flock a male,
but under his vow sacrifices to the
LORD a gelding;
For a great King am I, says the LORD of
hosts,
and my name will be feared among the
nations.

CHAPTER 2

See RG
369-70   *1* And now, O priests, this
commandment is for you:
If you do not listen,
2 And if you do not lay it to heart,
to give glory to my name, says the
LORD of hosts,
I will send a curse upon you
and of your blessing I will make a
curse.
Yes, I have already cursed it,
because you do not lay it to heart.*g*
3 Lo, I will deprive you of the shoulder*

and I will strew dung in your faces,
The dung of your feasts,
and you will be carried off with it.
4 Then you will know that I sent you this
commandment
because I have a covenant with Levi,
says the LORD of hosts.*h*
5 My covenant with him was one of life
and peace;
fear I put in him, and he feared me,
and stood in awe of my name.*i*
6 True doctrine was in his mouth,
and no dishonesty was found upon his
lips;
He walked with me in integrity and
uprightness,
and turned many away from evil.*j*
7 For the lips of the priest are to keep
knowledge,
and instruction is to be sought from his
mouth,
because he is the messenger of the
LORD of hosts.*k*
8 But you have turned aside from the way,
and have caused many to falter by
your instruction;
You have made void the covenant of
Levi,
says the LORD of hosts.
9 I, therefore, have made you
contemptible
and base before all the people,
Since you do not keep my ways,
but show partiality in your decisions.

Sins of the People

10 Have we not all the one Father?*
Has not the one God created us?
Why then do we break faith with each
other,
violating the covenant of our fathers?*l*
11 Judah has broken faith; an abominable
thing

2, 3: I will deprive you of the shoulder: this part of a sacrificial animal, allotted by the law (Dt 18, 3) to the priests,
will be withheld from them.
2, 10-16: Intermarriage of Israelites with foreigners was
forbidden according to Dt 7, 1-4. After the exile this law was
strictly enforced (Ezr 9—10). Foreign marriages are here portrayed as a violation of the covenant (v 10), which made the
sacrifices offered by the offenders unacceptable to God (v
13). They were all the more reprehensible when accompanied

by the divorce of Israelite wives (vv 14ff). This gradual return to the primitive ideal of the indissolubility of marriage
was fully realized in New Testament times through the teaching of Christ; cf Mt 19, 3-12.

f: Ps 113, 3; Is 59, 19.   *g:* Lv 26, 14-45; Dt 28, 15-68.   *h:* Nm
25, 12f.   *i:* Nm 25, 12; Ez 37, 26ff.   *j:* Dt 33, 8-11.   *k:* Lv 10,
10f; Dt 17, 9f; Jer 18, 18; Hg 2, 12.   *l:* Mt 23, 9; Jb 31, 15; Eph
4, 6.

has been done in Israel and in
Jerusalem.
Judah has profaned the temple which the
LORD loves,
and has married an idolatrous woman.[m]

12 May the LORD cut off from the man who
does this
both witness and advocate out of the
tents of Jacob,
and anyone to offer sacrifice to the
LORD of hosts!

13 This also you do: the altar of the LORD
you cover
with tears, weeping and groaning,
Because he no longer regards your
sacrifice
nor accepts it favorably from your
hand;
14 And you say, "Why is it?"—
Because the LORD is witness
between you and the wife of your
youth,
With whom you have broken faith
though she is your companion, your
betrothed wife.[n]
15 Did he not make one being, with flesh
and spirit:
and what does that one require but
godly offspring?
You must then safeguard life that is your
own,
and not break faith with the wife of
your youth.[o]
16 For I hate divorce,
says the LORD, the God of Israel,
And covering one's garment with
injustice,
says the LORD of hosts;
You must then safeguard life that is your
own,
and not break faith.

17 You have wearied the LORD with your
words,

yet you say, "How have we wearied
him?"
By your saying, "Every evildoer
is good in the sight of the LORD,
And he is pleased with him";
or else, "Where is the just God?"

CHAPTER 3

The Messenger of
the Covenant

See RG
370

1 Lo, I am sending my messenger
to prepare the way before me;*
And suddenly there will come to the
temple
the LORD whom you seek,
And the messenger of the covenant
whom you desire.
Yes, he is coming, says the LORD of
hosts.[p]
2 But who will endure the day of his
coming?
And who can stand when he appears?
For he is like the refiner's fire,
or like the fuller's lye.
3 He will sit refining and purifying
[silver],
and he will purify the sons of Levi,
Refining them like gold or like silver
that they may offer due sacrifice to
the LORD.[q]
4 Then the sacrifice of Judah and
Jerusalem
will please the LORD,
as in the days of old, as in years gone by.
5 I will draw near to you for judgment,
and I will be swift to bear witness
Against the sorcerers, adulterers, and
perjurers,
those who defraud the hired man of
his wages,
Against those who defraud widows and
orphans;
those who turn aside the stranger,
and those who do not fear me, says
the LORD of hosts.

3, 1: My messenger . . . before me: in v 23 this messenger is called Elijah. In Mt 11, 10 these words are quoted by Christ
as referring to John the Baptizer, who prepared the way for the coming of the Savior; cf Mt 3, 1ff. 11f; 17, 11ff; Mk 1, 2-8;
Lk 3, 2-18; Jn 1, 31-34.

m: Ezr 9, 2; Neh 13, 25.   n: Gn 31, 49f; Prv 5, 18ff.   o: Gn 2, 7. 22ff.   p: Is 40, 3; Mt 11, 10; Mk 1, 2; Lk 1, 17; 7, 27.   q: Is 1, 25;
Zec 13, 9.

THE NEW TESTAMENT

NEW AMERICAN BIBLE

PREFACE TO THE *NEW AMERICAN BIBLE*

First Edition of the New Testament

The New Testament translation has been approached with essentially the same fidelity to the thought and individual style of the biblical writers as was applied in the Old Testament. In some cases, however, the problem of marked literary peculiarities had to be met. What by any Western standard are the limited vocabularies and stylistic infelicities of the evangelists cannot be retained in the exact form in which they appear in the originals without displeasing the modern ear. A compromise is here attempted whereby some measure of the poverty of the evangelists' expression is kept and placed at the service of their message in its richness. Similarly, the syntactical shortcomings of Paul, his frequent lapses into anacoluthon, and the like, are rendered as they occur in his epistles rather than "smoothed out." Only thus, the translators suppose, will contemporary readers have some adequate idea of the kind of writing they have before them. When the prose of the original flows more smoothly, as in Luke, Acts, and Hebrews, it is reflected in the translation.

The Gospel according to John comprises a special case. Absolute fidelity to his technique of reiterated phrasing would result in an assault on the English ear, yet the softening of the vocal effect by substitution of other words and phrases would destroy the effectiveness of his poetry. Again, resort is had to compromise. This is not an easy matter when the very repetitiousness which the author deliberately employed is at the same time regarded by those who read and speak English to be a serious stylistic defect. Only those familiar with the Greek originals can know what a relentless tattoo Johannine poetry can produce. A similar observation could be made regarding other New Testament books as well. Matthew and Mark are given to identical phrasing twice and three times in the same sentence. As for the rhetorical overgrowth and mixed figures of speech in the letters of Peter, James, and Jude, the translator must resist a powerful compulsion to tidy them up if only to render these letters intelligibly.

Without seeking refuge in complaints against

the inspired authors, however, the translators of *The New American Bible* here state that what they have attempted is a translation rather than a paraphrase. To be sure, all translation can be called paraphrase by definition. Any striving for complete fidelity will shortly end in infidelity. Nonetheless, it must be pointed out that the temptation to improve overladen sentences by the consolidation or elimination of multiplied adjectives, or the simplification of clumsy hendiadys, has been resisted here. For the most part, rhetorically ineffective words and phrases are retained in this translation in some form, even when it is clear that a Western contemporary writer would never have employed them.

The spelling of proper names in *The New American Bible* follows the customary forms found in most English Bibles since the Authorized Version.

Despite the arbitrary character of the divisions into numbered verses (a scheme which in its present form is only four centuries old), the translators have made a constant effort to keep within an English verse the whole verbal content of the Greek verse. At times the effort has not seemed worth the result since it often does violence to the original author's flow of expression, which preceded it by so many centuries. If this translation had been prepared for purposes of public reading only, the editors would have foregone the effort at an early stage. But since they never departed from the threefold objective of preparing a translation suitable for liturgical use, private reading, and the purposes of students, the last-named consideration prevailed. Those familiar with Greek should be able to discover how the translators of the New Testament have rendered any given original verse of scripture, if their exegetical or theological tasks require them to know this. At the same time, the fact should be set down here that the editors did not commit themselves in the synoptic gospels to rendering repeated words or phrases identically.

This leads to a final consideration: the Greek text used for the New Testament. Here, punctuation and verse division are at least as important as variant readings. In general, Nestle-Aland's *Novum Testamentum Graece* (25th edition, 1963) was followed. Additional help was derived from *The Greek New Testament* (Aland, Black, Metzger, Wikgren), produced for the use of translators by the United Bible Societies in 1966. However, the editors did not confine themselves strictly to these texts; at times, they inclined toward readings otherwise attested. The omission of alternative translations does not mean that the translators think them without merit, but only that in every case they had to make a choice.

Poorly attested readings do not occur in this translation. Doubtful readings of some merit appear within brackets; public readers may include such words or phrases, or omit them entirely without any damage to sense. Parentheses are used, as ordinarily in English, as a punctuation device. Material they enclose is in no sense textually doubtful. It is simply thought to be parenthetical in the intention of the biblical author, even though there is no such punctuation mark in Greek. The difficulty in dealing with quotation marks is well known. Since they do not appear in any form in the original text, wherever they occur here they constitute an editorial decision.

PREFACE TO THE REVISED EDITION

The New Testament of *The New American Bible,* a fresh translation from the Greek text, was first published in complete form in 1970, together with the Old Testament translation that had been completed the previous year. Portions of the New Testament had appeared earlier, in somewhat different form, in the provisional Mass lectionary of 1964 and in the *Lectionary for Mass* of 1970.

Since 1970 many different printings of the New Testament have been issued by a number of publishers, both separately and in complete Bibles, and the text has become widely known both in the United States and in other English-speaking countries. Most American Catholics have been influenced by it because of its widespread use in the liturgy, and it has received a generally favorable reception from many other Christians as well. It has taken its place among the standard contemporary translations of the New Testament, respected for its fidelity to the original and its attempt to render this into current American English.

Although the scriptures themselves are timeless, translations and explanations of them quickly become dated in an era marked by rapid cultural change to a degree never previously experienced. The explosion of biblical studies that has taken place in our century and the changing nature of our language itself require periodic adjustment both in translations and in the accompanying explanatory materials. The experience of actual use of the New Testament of *The New American Bible*, especially in oral proclamation, has provided a basis for further improvement. Accordingly, it was decided in 1978 to proceed with a thorough revision of the New Testament to reflect advances in scholarship and to satisfy needs identified through pastoral experience.

For this purpose a steering committee was formed to plan, organize, and direct the work of revision, to engage collaborators, and to serve as an editorial board to coordinate the work of the various revisers and to determine the final form of the text and the explanatory materials. Guidelines were drawn up and collaborators selected in 1978 and early 1979, and November of 1980 was established as the deadline for manuscripts. From December 1980 through September 1986 the editorial board met a total of fifty times and carefully reviewed and revised all the material in order to ensure accuracy and consistency of approach. The editors also worked together with the bishops' ad hoc committee that was appointed by the National Conference of Catholic Bishops in 1982 to oversee the revision.

The threefold purpose of the translation that was expressed in the preface to the first edition has been maintained in the revision: to provide a version suitable for liturgical proclamation, for private reading, and for purposes of study. Special attention has been given to the first of these purposes, since oral proclamation demands special qualities in a translation, and experience had provided insights and suggestions that could lead to improvement in this area. Efforts have also been made, however, to facilitate devotional reading by providing suitable notes and introductory materials, and to assist the student by achieving greater accuracy and consistency in the translation and supplying more abundant information in the introductions and notes.

The primary aim of the revision is to produce a version as accurate and faithful to the meaning of the Greek original as is possible for a translation. The editors have consequently moved in the direction of a formal-equivalence approach to translation, matching the vocabulary, structure, and even word order of the original as closely as possible in the receptor language. Some other contemporary biblical versions have adopted, in varying degrees, a dynamic-equivalence approach, which attempts to respect the individuality of each language by expressing the meaning of the original in a linguistic structure suited to English, even though this may be very different from the corresponding Greek structure. While this approach often results in fresh and brilliant renderings, it has the disadvantages of more or less radically abandoning traditional biblical and liturgical terminology and phraseology, of expanding the text to include what more properly belongs in notes, commentaries, or preaching, and of tending toward paraphrase. A more formal approach seems better suited to the specific purposes intended for this translation.

At the same time, the editors have wished to produce a version in English that reflects contemporary American usage and is readily understandable to ordinary educated people, but one that will be recognized as dignified speech, on the level of formal rather than colloquial usage. These aims are not in fact contradictory, for there are different levels of language in current use: the language of formal situations is not that of colloquial conversation, though people understand both and may pass from one to the other without adverting to the transition. The liturgy is a formal situation that requires a level of discourse more dignified, formal, and hieratic than the world of business, sport, or informal communication. People readily understand this more formal level even though they may not often use it; our passive vocabulary is much larger than our active vocabulary. Hence this revision, while avoiding archaisms, does not shrink from traditional biblical terms that are easily understood even though not in common use in everyday speech. The level of language consciously aimed

at is one appropriate for liturgical proclamation; this may also permit the translation to serve the purposes of devotional reading and serious study.

A particular effort has been made to insure consistency of vocabulary. Always to translate a given Greek word by the same English equivalent would lead to ludicrous results and to infidelity to the meaning of the text. But in passages where a particular Greek term retains the same meaning, it has been rendered in the same way insofar as this has been feasible; this is particularly significant in the case of terms that have a specific theological meaning. The synoptic gospels have been carefully translated so as to reveal both the similarities and the differences of the Greek.

An especially sensitive problem today is the question of discrimination in language. In recent years there has been much discussion about allegations of anti-Jewish expressions in the New Testament and of language that discriminates against various minorities. Above all, however, the question of discrimination against women affects the largest number of people and arouses the greatest degree of interest and concern. At present there is little agreement about these problems or about the best way to deal with them. In all these areas the present translation attempts to display a sensitivity appropriate to the present state of the questions under discussion, which are not yet resolved and in regard to which it is impossible to please everyone, since intelligent and sincere participants in the debate hold mutually contradictory views.

The primary concern in this revision is fidelity to what the text says. When the meaning of the Greek is inclusive of both sexes, the translation seeks to reproduce such inclusivity insofar as this is possible in normal English usage, without resort to inelegant circumlocutions or neologisms that would offend against the dignity of the language. Although the generic sense of *man* is traditional in English, many today reject it; its use has therefore generally been avoided, though it is retained in cases where no fully satisfactory equivalent could be found. English does not possess a gender-inclusive third personal pronoun in the singular, and this translation continues to use the masculine resumptive pronoun after *everyone* or *anyone*, in the traditional way, where this cannot be avoided without infidelity to the meaning.

The translation of the Greek word *adelphos,* particularly in the plural form *adelphoi,* poses an especially delicate problem. While the term literally means *brothers* or other male blood relatives, even in profane Greek the plural can designate two persons, one of either sex, who were born of the same parents. It was adopted by the early Christians to designate, in a figurative sense, the members of the Christian community, who were conscious of a new familial relationship to one another by reason of their adoption as children of God. They are consequently addressed as *adelphoi.* This has traditionally been rendered into English by *brothers* or, more archaically, *brethren.* There has never been any doubt that this designation includes *all* the members of the Christian community, both male and female. Given the absence in English of a corresponding term that explicitly includes both sexes, this translation retains the usage of *brothers,* with the inclusive meaning that has been traditionally attached to it in this biblical context.

Since the New Testament is the product of a particular time and culture, the views expressed in it and the language in which they are expressed reflect a particular cultural conditioning, which sometimes makes them quite different from contemporary ideas and concerns. Discriminatory language should be eliminated insofar as possible whenever it is unfaithful to the meaning of the New Testament, but the text should not be altered in order to adjust it to contemporary concerns. This translation does not introduce any changes, expansions, additions to, or subtractions from the text of scripture. It further retains the traditional biblical ways of speaking about God and about Christ, including the use of masculine nouns and pronouns.

The Greek text followed in this translation is that of the third edition of *The Greek New Testament,* edited by Kurt Aland, Matthew Black, Carlo Martini, Bruce Metzger, and Allen Wikgren, and published by the United Bible Societies in 1975. The same text, with a different critical apparatus and variations in punctuation and typography, was published as the twenty-sixth edition of the Nestle-Aland *Novum Testamentum Graece* in 1979 by the Deutsche Bibelstiftung, Stuttgart. This edition has also been consulted.

When variant readings occur, the translation, with few exceptions, follows the reading that was placed in the text of these Greek editions, though the occurrence of the principal variants is pointed out in the notes.

The editors of the Greek text placed square brackets around words or portions of words of which the authenticity is questionable because the evidence of textual witnesses is inconclusive. The same has been done in the translation insofar as it is possible to reproduce this convention in English. It should be possible to read the text either with or without the disputed words, but in English it is not always feasible to provide this alternative, and in some passages the bracketed words must be included to make sense. As in the first edition, parentheses do not indicate textual uncertainty, but are simply a punctuation device to indicate a passage that in the editors' judgment appears parenthetical to the thought of the author.

Citations from the Old Testament are placed within quotation marks; longer citations are set off as block quotations in a separate indented paragraph. The sources of such citations, as well as those of many more or less subtle allusions to the Old Testament, are identified in the biblical cross-reference section at the bottom of each page. Insofar as possible, the translation of such Old Testament citations agrees with that of *The New American Bible* Old Testament whenever the underlying Greek agrees with the Hebrew (or, in some cases, the Aramaic or Greek) text from which the Old Testament translation was made. But citations in the New Testament frequently follow the Septuagint or some other version, or were made from memory; hence, in many cases the translation in the New Testament passage will not agree with what appears in the Old Testament. Some of these cases are explained in the notes.

It is a further aim of the revised edition to supply explanatory materials more abundantly than in the first edition. In most cases the introductions and notes have been entirely rewritten and expanded, and the cross-references checked and revised. It is intended that these materials should reflect the present state of sound biblical scholarship and should be presented in such a form that they can be assimilated by the ordinary intelligent reader without specialized biblical training. While they have been written with the ordinary educated Christian in mind, not all technical vocabulary can be entirely dispensed with in approaching the Bible, any more than in any other field. It is the hope of the editors that these materials, even if they sometimes demand an effort, will help the reader to a fuller and more intelligent understanding of the New Testament and a fruitful appropriation of its meaning for personal spiritual growth.

The New American Bible is a Roman Catholic translation. This revision, however, like the first edition, has been accomplished with the collaboration of scholars from other Christian churches, both among the revisers and on the editorial board, in response to the encouragement of Vatican Council II (*Dei Verbum,* 22). The editorial board expresses gratitude to all who have collaborated in the revision: to all the revisers, consultants, and bishops who contributed to it, to reviewers of the first edition, and to those who voluntarily submitted suggestions. May this translation fulfill its threefold purpose, "so that the word of the Lord may speed forward and be glorified" (2 Thes 3, 1).

September 30, 1986
The Feast of St. Jerome

THE GOSPELS

The collection of writings that constitutes the New Testament begins with four gospels. Next comes the Acts of the Apostles, followed by twenty-one letters that are attributed to Paul, James, Peter, John, and Jude. Finally, at the end of the early church's scriptures stands the Revelation to John. Virtually all Christians agree that these twenty-seven books constitute the "canon," a term that means "rule" and designates the list of writings that are regarded as authoritative for Christian faith and life.

It is the purpose of this Introduction to describe those features that are common to the four gospels. A similar treatment of the letters of the New Testament is provided in the two Introductions that appear before the Letter to the Romans and before the Letter of James, respectively. The Acts of the Apostles, a work that is both historical and theological, and Revelation, an apocalyptic work, have no counterparts in the New Testament; the special Introductions prefixed to these books treat of the literary characteristics proper to each of them.

While the New Testament contains four writings called "gospels," there is in reality only one gospel running through all of the Christian scriptures, the gospel of and about Jesus Christ. Our English word "gospel" translates the Greek term *euangelion*, meaning "good news." This noun was used in the plural by the Greek translators of the Old Testament to render the Hebrew term for "good news" (2 Sm 4, 10; possibly also 18, 20.25). But it is the corresponding verb *euangelizomai*, "to proclaim good news," that was especially significant in preparing for the New Testament idea of "gospel," since this term is used by Deutero-Isaiah of announcing the great victory of God that was to establish his universal kingship and inaugurate the new age (Is 40, 9; 52, 7; 61, 1).

Paul used the word *euangelion* to designate the message that he and the other apostles proclaimed, the "gospel of God" (Rom 1, 1; 15, 16; 2 Cor 11, 7; 1 Thes 2, 2.8.9). He often referred to it simply as "the gospel" (Rom 1, 16; 10, 16; 11, 28; etc.) or, because of its content and origin, as "the gospel of Christ" (Rom 15, 19; 1 Cor 9, 12; 1 Thes 3, 2; etc.). Because of its personal meaning for him and his own particular manner of telling the story about Jesus Christ and of explaining the significance of his cross and resurrection, Paul also referred to this message as "my gospel" (Rom 2, 16; cf Gal 1, 11; 2, 2) or "our gospel" (2 Cor 4, 3; 1 Thes 1, 5; 2 Thes 2, 14).

It was Mark, as far as we know, who first applied the term "gospel" to a book telling the story of Jesus; see Mk 1, 1 and the note there. This form of presenting Jesus' life, works, teachings, passion, and resurrection was developed further by the other evangelists; see the Introduction to each gospel. The first three of the canonical gospels, Matthew, Mark, and Luke, are so similar at many points when viewed together, particularly when arranged in parallel columns or lines, that they are called "synoptic" gospels, from the Greek word for such a general view. The fourth gospel, John, often differs significantly from the synoptics in outline and approach. This work never uses the word "gospel" or its corresponding verb; nevertheless, its message concerns the same Jesus, and the reader is urged to believe in him as the Messiah, "that through this belief you may have life in his name" (20, 31).

From the second century onward, the practice arose of designating each of these four books as a "gospel," understood as a title, and of adding a phrase with a name that identified the traditional author, e.g., "The Gospel according to Matthew." The arrangement of the canon that was adopted, with the four gospels grouped together at the beginning followed by Acts, provides a massive focus upon Jesus and allows Acts to serve as a framework for the letters of the New Testament. This order, however, conceals the fact that Luke's two volumes, a gospel and Acts, were intended by their author to go together. It further obscures the point that Paul's letters were written before any of our gospels, though the sayings and deeds of Jesus stand behind all the New Testament writings.

See RG 373–86

The Gospel According to Matthew

The position of the Gospel according to Matthew as the first of the four gospels in the New Testament reflects both the view that it was the first to be written, a view that goes back to the late second century A.D., and the esteem in which it was held by the church; no other was so frequently quoted in the noncanonical literature of earliest Christianity. Although the majority of scholars now reject the opinion about the time of its composition, the high estimation of this work remains. The reason for that becomes clear upon study of the way in which Matthew presents his story of Jesus, the demands of Christian discipleship, and the breaking-in of the new and final age through the ministry but particularly through the death and resurrection of Jesus.

The gospel begins with a narrative prologue (1, 1—2, 23), the first part of which is a genealogy of Jesus starting with Abraham, the father of Israel (1, 1–17). Yet at the beginning of that genealogy Jesus is designated as "the son of David, the son of Abraham" (1, 1). The kingly ancestor who lived about a thousand years after Abraham is named first, for this is the genealogy of Jesus Christ, the Messiah, the royal anointed one (1, 16). In the first of the episodes of the infancy narrative that follow the genealogy, the mystery of Jesus' person is declared. He is conceived of a virgin by the power of the Spirit of God (1, 18–25). The first of the gospel's fulfillment citations, whose purpose it is to show that he was the one to whom the prophecies of Israel were pointing, occurs here (1, 23): he shall be named Emmanuel, for in him God is with us.

The announcement of the birth of this newborn king of the Jews greatly troubles not only King Herod but all Jerusalem (2, 1–3), yet the Gentile magi are overjoyed to find him and offer him their homage and their gifts (2, 10–11). Thus his ultimate rejection by the mass of his own people and his acceptance by the Gentile nations is foreshadowed. He must be taken to Egypt to escape the murderous plan of Herod. By his sojourn there and his subsequent return after the king's death he relives the Exodus experience of Israel. The words of the Lord spoken through the prophet Hosea, "Out of Egypt I called my son," are fulfilled in him (2, 15); if Israel was God's son, Jesus is so in a way far surpassing the dignity of that nation, as his marvelous birth and the unfolding of his story show (see 3, 17; 4, 1–11; 11, 27; 14, 33; 16, 16; 27, 54). Back in the land of Israel, he must be taken to Nazareth in Galilee because of the danger to his life in Judea, where Herod's son Archelaus is now ruling (2, 22–23). The sufferings of Jesus in the infancy narrative anticipate those of his passion, and if his life is spared in spite of the dangers, it is because his destiny is finally to give it on the cross as "a ransom for many" (20, 28). Thus the word of the angel will be fulfilled, ". . . he will save his people from their sins" (1, 21; cf 26, 28).

In 4, 12 Matthew begins his account of the ministry of Jesus, introducing it by the preparatory preaching of John the Baptist (3, 1–12), the baptism of Jesus that culminates in God's proclaiming him his "beloved Son" (3, 13–17), and the temptation in which he proves his true sonship by his victory over the devil's attempt to deflect him from the way of obedience to the Father (4, 1–11). The central message of Jesus' preaching is the coming of the kingdom of heaven and the need for repentance, a complete change of heart and conduct, on the part of those who are to receive this great gift of God (4, 17). Galilee is the setting for most of his ministry; he leaves there for Judea only in 19, 1, and his ministry in Jerusalem, the goal of his journey, is limited to a few days (21, 1—25, 46).

In this extensive material there are five great discourses of Jesus, each concluding with the formula "When Jesus finished these words" or one closely similar (7, 28; 11, 1; 13, 53; 19, 1; 26, 1). These are an important structure of the gospel. In every case the discourse is preceded by a narrative section, each narrative and discourse together constituting a "book" of the gospel. The discourses are, respectively, the "Sermon on the Mount" (5, 3—7, 27), the missionary discourse (10, 5–42), the parable discourse (13, 3–52), the "church order" discourse (18, 3–35), and the eschatological discourse (24, 4—25, 46). In large measure the material of these discourses came to Matthew from his tradition, but his work in modifying and adding to what he had received is abundantly evident. No other evangelist gives the teaching of Jesus with such elegance and order as he.

In the "Sermon on the Mount" the theme of righteousness is prominent, and even at this early stage of the ministry the note of opposition is struck between Jesus and the Pharisees, who are designated as "the hypocrites" (6, 2.5.16). The righteousness of his disciples must surpass that of the scribes and Pharisees; otherwise, in spite of their alleged following of Jesus, they will not enter into the kingdom of heaven (5, 20). Righteousness means doing the will of the heavenly Father (7, 21), and his will is proclaimed in a manner that is startling to all who have identified it with the law of Moses. The antitheses of the Sermon (5, 21–48) both accept (5, 21–30.43–48) and reject (5, 31–42) elements of that law, and in the former case the understanding of the law's demands is deepened and extended. The antitheses are the best commentary on the meaning of Jesus' claim that he has come not to abolish but to fulfill the law (5, 17). What is meant by fulfillment of the law is not the demand to keep it exactly as it stood before the coming of Jesus, but rather his bringing the law to be a lasting expression of the will of God, and in that fulfillment there is much that will pass away. Should this appear contradictory to his saying that "until heaven and earth pass away" not even the smallest part of the law will pass (5, 18), that time of fulfillment is not the dissolution of the universe but the coming of the new age, which will occur with Jesus' death and resurrection. While righteousness in the new age will continue to mean conduct that is in accordance with the law, it will be conduct in accordance with the law as expounded and interpreted by Jesus (cf 28, 20, ". . . all that I have commanded you").

Though Jesus speaks harshly about the Pharisees in the Sermon, his judgment is not solely a condemnation of them. The Pharisees are portrayed as a negative example for his disciples, and his condemnation of those who claim to belong to him while disobeying his word is no less severe (7, 21–23.26–27).

In 4, 23 a summary statement of Jesus' activity speaks not only of his teaching and proclaiming the gospel but of his "curing every disease and illness among the people"; this is repeated almost verbatim in 9, 35. The narrative section that follows the Sermon on the Mount (8, 1—9, 38) is composed principally of accounts of those merciful deeds of Jesus, but it is far from being simply a collection of stories about miraculous cures. The nature of the community that Jesus will establish is shown; it will always be under the protection of him whose power can deal with all dangers (8, 23–27), but it is only for those who are prepared to follow him at whatever cost (8, 16–22), not only believing Israelites but Gentiles who have come to faith in him (8, 10–12). The disciples begin to have some insight, however imperfect, into the mystery of Jesus' person. They wonder about him whom "the winds and the sea obey" (8, 27), and they witness his bold declaration of the forgiveness of the paralytic's sins (9, 2). That episode of the narrative moves on two levels. When the crowd sees the cure that testifies to the authority of Jesus, the Son of Man, to forgive sins (9, 6), they glorify God "who had given such authority to human beings" (9, 8). The forgiveness of sins is now not the prerogative of Jesus alone but of "human beings," that is, of the disciples who constitute the community of Jesus, the church. The ecclesial character of this narrative section could hardly be more plainly indicated.

The end of the section prepares for the discourse on the church's mission (10, 5–42). Jesus is moved to pity at the sight of the crowds who are like sheep without a shepherd (9, 36), and he sends out the twelve disciples to make the proclamation with which his own ministry began, "The kingdom of heaven is at hand" (10, 7; cf 4, 17), and to drive out demons and cure the sick as he has done (10, 1). Their mission is limited to Israel (10, 5–6) as Jesus' own was (15, 24), yet in 15, 16 that perspective broadens and the discourse begins to speak of the mission that the disciples will have after the resurrection and of the severe persecution that will attend it (10, 18). Again, the discourse moves on two levels: that of the time of Jesus and that of the time of the church.

The narrative section of the third book (11, 2—12, 50) deals with the growing opposition to Jesus. Hostility toward him has already been manifested (8, 10; 9, 3.10–13.34), but here it becomes more intense. The rejection of Jesus comes, as before, from Pharisees, who take "counsel against him to put him to death" (12, 14) and repeat their earlier accusation that he drives out demons because he is in league with demonic power (12, 22–24). But they are not alone in their rejection. Jesus complains of the lack of faith of "this generation" of Israelites (11, 16–19) and reproaches the towns "where most of his mighty deeds had been done" for not heeding his call to repentance (11, 20–24). This dark picture is relieved by Jesus' praise of the Father who has enabled "the childlike" to accept him (11, 25–27), but on the whole the story is one of opposition to his word and blindness to the meaning of his deeds. The whole section ends with his declaring that not even the most intimate blood relationship with him counts for anything; his only true relatives are those who do the will of his heavenly Father (12, 48–50).

The narrative of rejection leads up to the parable discourse (13, 3–52). The reason given for Jesus' speaking to the crowds in parables is that they have hardened themselves against his clear teaching, unlike the disciples to whom knowledge of "the mysteries of the kingdom has been granted" (13, 10–16). In 13, 36 he dismisses the crowds and continues the discourse to his disciples alone, who claim, at the end, to have understood all that he has said (13, 51). But, lest the impression be given that the church of Jesus is made up only of true disciples, the explanation of the parable of the weeds among the wheat (13, 37–43), as well as the parable of the net thrown into the sea "which collects fish of every kind" (13, 47–49), shows that it is composed of both the righteous and the wicked, and that separation between the two will be made only at the time of the final judgment.

In the narrative that constitutes the first part of the fourth book of the gospel (13, 54—17, 27),

Jesus is shown preparing for the establishment of his church with its teaching authority that will supplant the blind guidance of the Pharisees (15, 13–14), whose teaching, curiously said to be that of the Sadducees also, is repudiated by Jesus as the norm for his disciples (16, 6.11–12). The church of Jesus will be built on Peter (16, 18), who will be given authority to bind and loose on earth, an authority whose exercise will be confirmed in heaven (16, 19). The metaphor of binding and loosing has a variety of meanings, among them that of giving authoritative teaching. This promise is made to Peter directly after he has confessed Jesus to be the Messiah, the Son of the living God (16, 16), a confession that he has made as the result of revelation given to him by the heavenly Father (16, 17); Matthew's ecclesiology is based on his high christology.

Directly after that confession Jesus begins to instruct his disciples about how he must go the way of suffering and death (16, 21). Peter, who has been praised for his confession, protests against this and receives from Jesus the sharpest of rebukes for attempting to deflect Jesus from his God-appointed destiny. The future rock upon whom the church will be built is still a man of "little faith" (see 14, 31). Both he and the other disciples must know not only that Jesus will have to suffer and die but that they too will have to follow him on the way of the cross if they are truly to be his disciples (16, 24–25).

The discourse following this narrative (18, 1–35) is often called the "church order" discourse, although that title is perhaps misleading since the emphasis is not on the structure of the church but on the care that the disciples must have for one another in respect to guarding each other's faith in Jesus (18, 6–7), to seeking out those who have wandered from the fold (18, 10–14), and to repeated forgiving of their fellow disciples who have offended them (18, 21–35). But there is also the obligation to correct the sinful fellow Christian and, should one refuse to be corrected, separation from the community is demanded (18, 15–18).

The narrative of the fifth book (19, 1—23, 39) begins with the departure of Jesus and his disciples from Galilee for Jerusalem. In the course of their journey Jesus for the third time predicts the passion that awaits him at Jerusalem and also his resurrection (20, 17–19). At his entrance into the city he is hailed as the Son of David by the crowds accompanying him (21, 9). He cleanses the temple (21, 12–17), and in the few days of his Jerusalem ministry he engages in a series of controversies with the Jewish religious leaders (21, 23–27; 22, 15–22.23–33.34–40.41–46), meanwhile speaking parables against them (21, 28–32.33–46), against all those Israelites who have rejected God's invitation to the messianic banquet (22, 1–10), and against all, Jew and Gentile, who have accepted but have shown themselves unworthy of it (22, 11–14). Once again, the perspective of the evangelist includes not only the time of Jesus' ministry but that of the preaching of the gospel after his resurrection. The narrative culminates in Jesus' denunciation of the scribes and Pharisees, reflecting not only his own opposition to them but that of Matthew's church (23, 1–36), and in Jesus' lament over Jerusalem (23, 37–39).

In the discourse of the fifth book (24, 1—25, 46), the last of the great structural discourses of the gospel, Jesus predicts the destruction of the temple and his own final coming. The time of the latter is unknown (24, 36.44), and the disciples are exhorted in various parables to live in readiness for it, a readiness that entails faithful attention to the duties of the interim period (24, 45—25, 30). The coming of Jesus will bring with it the great judgment by which the everlasting destiny of all will be determined (25, 31–46).

The story of Jesus' passion and resurrection (26, 1—28, 20), the climax of the gospel, throws light on all that has preceded. In Mt "righteousness" means both the faithful response to the will of God demanded of all to whom that will is announced and also the saving activity of God for his people (see 3, 15; 5, 6; 6, 33). The passion supremely exemplifies both meanings of that central Matthean word. In Jesus' absolute faithfulness to the Father's will that he drink the cup of suffering (26, 39), the incomparable model for Christian obedience is given; in his death "for the forgiveness of sins" (26, 28), the saving power of God is manifested as never before.

Matthew's portrayal of Jesus in his passion combines both the majestic serenity of the obedient Son who goes his destined way in fulfillment of the scriptures (26, 52–54), confident of his ultimate vindication by God, and the depths of fear and abandonment that he feels in face of death (26, 38–39; 27, 46). These two aspects are ex-

pressed by an Old Testament theme that occurs often in the narrative, i.e., the portrait of the suffering Righteous One who complains to God in his misery, but is certain of eventual deliverance from his terrible ordeal.

The passion-resurrection of God's Son means nothing less than the turn of the ages, a new stage of history, the coming of the Son of Man in his kingdom (28, 18; cf 16, 28). That is the sense of the apocalyptic signs that accompany Jesus' death (27, 51–53) and resurrection (28, 2). Although the old age continues, as it will until the manifestation of Jesus' triumph at his parousia, the final age has now begun. This is known only to those who have seen the Risen One and to those, both Jews and Gentiles, who have believed in their announcement of Jesus' triumph and have themselves become his disciples (cf 28, 19). To them he is constantly, though invisibly, present (28, 20), verifying the name Emmanuel, "God is with us" (cf 1, 23).

The questions of authorship, sources, and the time of composition of this gospel have received many answers, none of which can claim more than a greater or lesser degree of probability. The one now favored by the majority of scholars is the following.

The ancient tradition that the author was the disciple and apostle of Jesus named Matthew (see 10, 3) is untenable because the gospel is based, in large part, on the Gospel according to Mark (almost all the verses of that gospel have been utilized in this), and it is hardly likely that a companion of Jesus would have followed so extensively an account that came from one who admittedly never had such an association rather than rely on his own memories. The attribution of the gospel to the disciple Matthew may have been due to his having been responsible for some of the traditions found in it, but that is far from certain.

The unknown author, whom we shall continue to call Matthew for the sake of convenience, drew not only upon the Gospel according to Mark but upon a large body of material (principally, sayings of Jesus) not found in Mk that corresponds, sometimes exactly, to material found also in the Gospel according to Luke. This material, called "Q" (probably from the first letter of the German word *Quelle*, meaning "source"), represents traditions, written and oral, used by both Matthew and Luke. Mark and Q are sources common to the two other synoptic gospels; hence the name the "Two-Source Theory" given to this explanation of the relation among the synoptics.

In addition to what Matthew drew from Mk and Q, his gospel contains material that is found only there. This is often designated "M," written or oral tradition that was available to the author. Since Mk was written shortly before or shortly after A.D. 70 (see Introduction to Mk), Mt was composed certainly after that date, which marks the fall of Jerusalem to the Romans at the time of the First Jewish Revolt (A.D. 66–70), and probably at least a decade later since Matthew's use of Mk presupposes a wide diffusion of that gospel. The post-A.D. 70 date is confirmed within the text by 22, 7, which refers to the destruction of Jerusalem.

As for the place where the gospel was composed, a plausible suggestion is that it was Antioch, the capital of the Roman province of Syria. That large and important city had a mixed population of Greek-speaking Gentiles and Jews. The tensions between Jewish and Gentile Christians there in the time of Paul (see Gal 2, 1–14) in respect to Christian obligation to observe Mosaic law are partially similar to tensions that can be seen between the two groups in Matthew's gospel. The church of Matthew, originally strongly Jewish Christian, had become one in which Gentile Christians were predominant. His gospel answers the question how obedience to the will of God is to be expressed by those who live after the "turn of the ages," the death and resurrection of Jesus.

The principal divisions of the Gospel according to Matthew are the following:

I: The Infancy Narrative (1, 1—2, 23)
II: The Proclamation of the Kingdom (3, 1—7, 29)
III: Ministry and Mission in Galilee (8, 1—11, 1)
IV: Opposition from Israel (11, 2—13, 53)
V: Jesus, the Kingdom, and the Church (13, 54—18, 35)
VI: Ministry in Judea and Jerusalem (19, 1—25, 46)
VII: The Passion and Resurrection (26, 1—28, 20)

I: The Infancy Narrative

CHAPTER 1

See RG 375–76

The Genealogy of Jesus. *1a**The book of the genealogy of Jesus Christ, the son of David, the son of Abraham.

*2bc*Abraham became the father of Isaac, Isaac the father of Jacob, Jacob the father of Judah and his brothers. *3d*Judah became the father of Perez and Zerah, whose mother was Tamar. Perez became the father of Hezron, Hezron the father of Ram, *4e*Ram the father of Amminadab. Amminadab became the father of Nahshon, Nahshon the father of Salmon, *5f*Salmon the father of Boaz, whose mother was Rahab. Boaz became the father

---

1, 1—2, 23: The infancy narrative forms the prologue of the gospel. Consisting of a genealogy and five stories, it presents the coming of Jesus as the climax of Israel's history, and the events of his conception, birth, and early childhood as the fulfillment of Old Testament prophecy. The genealogy is probably traditional material that Matthew edited. In its first two sections (1, 2–11) it was drawn from Ru 4, 18–22 and 1 Chr 1–3. Except for Jechoniah, Shealtiel, and Zerubbabel, none of the names in the third section (1, 12–16) is found in any Old Testament genealogy. While the genealogy shows the continuity of God's providential plan from Abraham on, discontinuity is also present. The women Tamar (1, 3), Rahab and Ruth (1, 5), and the wife of Uriah, Bathsheba (1, 6), bore their sons through unions that were in varying degrees strange and unexpected. These "irregularities" culminate in the supreme "irregularity" of the Messiah's birth of a virgin mother; the age of fulfillment is inaugurated by a creative act of God.

Drawing upon both biblical tradition and Jewish stories, Matthew portrays Jesus as reliving the Exodus experience of Israel and the persecutions of Moses. His rejection by his own

people and his passion are foreshadowed by the troubled reaction of "all Jerusalem" to the question of the magi who are seeking the "newborn king of the Jews" (2, 2–3), and by Herod's attempt to have him killed. The magi who do him homage prefigure the Gentiles who will accept the preaching of the gospel. The infancy narrative proclaims who Jesus is, the savior of his people from their sins (1, 21), Emmanuel in whom "God is with us" (1, 23), and the Son of God (2, 15).

1, 1: The son of David, the son of Abraham: two links of the genealogical chain are singled out. Although the later, David is placed first in order to emphasize that Jesus is the royal Messiah. The mention of Abraham may be due not only to his being the father of the nation Israel but to Matthew's interest in the universal scope of Jesus' mission; cf Gn 22, 18, "... in your descendants all the nations of the earth shall find blessing."

a: Gn 5, 1 / 1 Chr 17, 11 / Gn 22, 18. *b:* Lk 3, 23-38. *c:* Gn 21, 3; 25, 26; 29, 35; 1 Chr 2, 1. *d:* Gn 38, 29-30; Ru 4, 18; 1 Chr 2, 4-9. *e:* Ru 4, 19-20; 1 Chr 2, 10-11. *f:* Ru 4, 21-22; 1 Chr 2, 11-12.

of Obed, whose mother was Ruth. Obed became the father of Jesse, ⁶ᵍJesse the father of David the king.

David became the father of Solomon, whose mother had been the wife of Uriah. ⁷ʰ*Solomon became the father of Rehoboam, Rehoboam the father of Abijah, Abijah the father of Asaph. ⁸Asaph became the father of Jehoshaphat, Jehoshaphat the father of Joram, Joram the father of Uzziah. ⁹Uzziah became the father of Jotham, Jotham the father of Ahaz, Ahaz the father of Hezekiah. ¹⁰*Hezekiah became the father of Manasseh, Manasseh the father of Amos, Amos the father of Josiah. ¹¹Josiah became the father of Jechoniah and his brothers at the time of the Babylonian exile.

¹²ⁱAfter the Babylonian exile, Jechoniah became the father of Shealtiel, Shealtiel the father of Zerubbabel, ¹³Zerubbabel the father of Abiud. Abiud became the father of Eliakim, Eliakim the father of Azor, ¹⁴Azor the father of Zadok. Zadok became the father of Achim, Achim the father of Eliud, ¹⁵Eliud the father of Eleazar. Eleazar became the father of Mat-than, Matthan the father of Jacob, ¹⁶Jacob the father of Joseph, the husband of Mary. Of her was born Jesus who is called the Messiah.

¹⁷*Thus the total number of generations from Abraham to David is fourteen generations; from David to the Babylonian exile, fourteen generations; from the Babylonian exile to the Messiah, fourteen generations.

The Birth of Jesus. ¹⁸*Now this is how the birth of Jesus Christ came about. When his mother Mary was betrothed to Joseph, but before they lived together, she was found with child through the holy Spirit. ¹⁹*Joseph her husband, since he was a righteous man, yet unwilling to expose her to shame, decided to divorce her quietly. ²⁰ʲ*Such was his intention when, behold, the angel of the Lord appeared to him in a dream and said, "Joseph, son of David, do not be afraid to take Mary your wife into your home. For it is through the holy Spirit that this child has been conceived in her. ²¹*She will bear a son and you are to name him Jesus, because he will save his people from their sins." ²²All this took place to fulfill what the Lord had said through the prophet:

1, 7: The successor of Abijah was not Asaph but Asa (see 1 Chr 3, 10). Some textual witnesses read the latter name; however, **Asaph** is better attested. Matthew may have deliberately introduced the psalmist Asaph into the genealogy (and in v 10 the prophet Amos) in order to show that Jesus is the fulfillment not only of the promises made to David (see 2 Sm 7) but of all the Old Testament.

1, 10: **Amos:** some textual witnesses read **Amon,** who was the actual successor of Manasseh (see 1 Chr 3, 14).

1, 17: Matthew is concerned with fourteen generations, probably because fourteen is the numerical value of the Hebrew letters forming the name of David. In the second section of the genealogy (6b-11), three kings of Judah, Ahaziah, Joash, and Amaziah, have been omitted (see 1 Chr 3, 11–12), so that there are fourteen generations in that section. Yet the third (12–16) apparently has only thirteen. Since Matthew here emphasizes that each section has fourteen, it is unlikely that the thirteen of the last was due to his oversight. Some scholars suggest that **Jesus who is called the Messiah** (16b) doubles the final member of the chain: **Jesus,** born within the family of David, opens up the new age as **Messiah,** so that in fact there are fourteen generations in the third section. This is perhaps too subtle, and the hypothesis of a slip not on the part of Matthew but of a later scribe seems likely. On **Messiah,** see the note on Lk 2, 11.

1, 18–25: This first story of the infancy narrative spells out what is summarily indicated in v 16. The virginal conception of Jesus is the work of the Spirit of God. Joseph's decision to divorce Mary is overcome by the heavenly command that he take her into his home and accept the child as his own. The natural genealogical line is broken but the prom-ises to David are fulfilled; through Joseph's adoption the child belongs to the family of David. Matthew sees the virginal conception as the fulfillment of Is 7, 14.

1, 18: Betrothed to Joseph: betrothal was the first part of the marriage, constituting a man and woman as husband and wife. Subsequent infidelity was considered adultery. The betrothal was followed some months later by the husband's taking his wife into his home, at which time normal married life began.

1, 19: A righteous man: as a devout observer of the Mosaic law, Joseph wished to break his union with someone whom he suspected of gross violation of the law. It is commonly said that the law required him to do so, but the texts usually given in support of that view, e.g., Dt 22, 20–21, do not clearly pertain to Joseph's situation. **Unwilling to expose her to shame:** the penalty for proved adultery was death by stoning; cf Dt 22, 21–23.

1, 20: The angel of the Lord: in the Old Testament a common designation of God in communication with a human being. **In a dream:** see 2, 13.19.22. These dreams may be meant to recall the dreams of Joseph, son of Jacob the patriarch (Gn 37, 5–11.19). A closer parallel is the dream of Amram, father of Moses, related by Josephus (**Antiquities** 2, 9, 3 §§212, 215–16).

1, 21: Jesus: in first-century Judaism the Hebrew name Joshua (Greek Iēsous) meaning "Yahweh helps" was interpreted as "Yahweh saves."

g: 2 Sm 12, 24; 1 Chr 2, 15; 3, 5. *h:* 2 Kgs 25, 1-21; 1 Chr 3, 10-15. *i:* 1 Chr 3, 16-19. *j:* 2, 13.19; Lk 1, 35.

[23] [k]*"Behold, the virgin shall be with child
        and bear a son,
     and they shall name him Emmanuel,"

which means "God is with us." [24]When Joseph awoke, he did as the angel of the Lord had commanded him and took his wife into his home. [25][l]*He had no relations with her until she bore a son, and he named him Jesus.

See RG
375–76

CHAPTER 2

The Visit of the Magi. [1]*When Jesus was born in Bethlehem of Judea, in the days of King Herod, behold, magi from the east arrived in Jerusalem, [2][m]*saying, "Where is the newborn king of the Jews? We saw his star at its rising and have come to do him homage." [3]When King Herod heard this, he was greatly troubled, and all Jerusalem with him. [4]*Assembling all the chief priests and the scribes of the people, he inquired of them where the Messiah was to be born. [5][n]They said to him, "In Bethlehem of Judea, for thus it has been written through the prophet:

[6] 'And you, Bethlehem, land of Judah,
     are by no means least among the rulers
        of Judah;
   since from you shall come a ruler,
     who is to shepherd my people
        Israel.' "

[7]Then Herod called the magi secretly and ascertained from them the time of the star's appearance. [8]He sent them to Bethlehem and said, "Go and search diligently for the child. When you have found him, bring me word, that I too may go and do him homage." [9]After their audience with the king they set out. And behold, the star that they had seen at its rising preceded them, until it came and stopped over the place where the child was. [10]They were overjoyed at seeing the star, [11][o]*and on entering the house they saw the child with Mary his mother. They prostrated themselves and did him homage. Then they opened their treasures and offered him gifts of gold, frankincense, and myrrh. [12]And having been warned in a dream not to return to Herod, they departed for their country by another way.

The Flight to Egypt. [13]*When they had departed, behold, the angel of the Lord appeared to Joseph in a dream and said, "Rise, take the child and his mother, flee to Egypt, and stay there until I tell you. Herod is going to search for the child to destroy him." [14]Joseph rose and took the child and his mother by night and departed for Egypt. [15][p]*He stayed there until the death of Herod, that what the Lord had said through the prophet might be fulfilled, "Out of Egypt I called my son."

1, 23: God is with us: God's promise of deliverance to Judah in Isaiah's time is seen by Matthew as fulfilled in the birth of Jesus, in whom God is with his people. The name Emmanuel is alluded to at the end of the gospel where the risen Jesus assures his disciples of his continued presence, ". . . I am with you always, until the end of the age" (28, 20).

1, 25: Until she bore a son: the evangelist is concerned to emphasize that Joseph was not responsible for the conception of Jesus. The Greek word translated "until" does not imply normal marital conduct after Jesus' birth, nor does it exclude it.

2, 1–12: The future rejection of Jesus by Israel and his acceptance by the Gentiles are retrojected into this scene of the narrative.

2, 1: In the days of King Herod: Herod reigned from 37 to 4 B.C. **Magi:** originally a designation of the Persian priestly caste, the word became used of those who were regarded as having more than human knowledge. Matthew's magi are astrologers.

2, 2: We saw his star: it was a common ancient belief that a new star appeared at the time of a ruler's birth. Matthew also draws upon the Old Testament story of Balaam, who had prophesied that "A star shall advance from Jacob" (Nm 24, 17), though there the star means not an astral phenomenon but the king himself.

2, 4: Herod's consultation with the chief priests and

scribes has some similarity to a Jewish legend about the child Moses in which the "sacred scribes" warn Pharaoh about the imminent birth of one who will deliver Israel from Egypt and the king makes plans to destroy him.

2, 11: Cf Ps 72, 10.15; Is 60, 6. These Old Testament texts led to the interpretation of the magi as kings.

2, 13–23: Biblical and nonbiblical traditions about Moses are here applied to the child Jesus, though the dominant Old Testament type is not Moses but Israel (see v 15).

2, 13: Flee to Egypt: Egypt was a traditional place of refuge for those fleeing from danger in Palestine (see 1 Kgs 11, 40; Jer 26, 21), but the main reason why the child is to be taken to Egypt is that he may relive the Exodus experience of Israel.

2, 15: The fulfillment citation is taken from Hos 11, 1. Israel, God's son, was called out of Egypt at the time of the Exodus; Jesus, the Son of God, will similarly be called out of that land in a new exodus. The father-son relationship between God and the nation is set in a higher key. Here the son is not a group adopted as "son of God," but the child who, as conceived by the holy Spirit, stands in unique relation to God. He is son of David and of Abraham, of Mary and of Joseph, but, above all, of God.

k: Is 7, 14 LXX. *l:* Lk 2, 7. *m:* Nm 24, 17. *n:* Mi 5, 1 / 2 Sm 5, 2. *o:* Ps 72, 10-11.15; Is 60, 6. *p:* Hos 11, 1.

The Massacre of the Infants. [16]When Herod realized that he had been deceived by the magi, he became furious. He ordered the massacre of all the boys in Bethlehem and its vicinity two years old and under, in accordance with the time he had ascertained from the magi. [17]Then was fulfilled what had been said through Jeremiah the prophet:

[18] q *"A voice was heard in Ramah,
  sobbing and loud lamentation;
Rachel weeping for her children,
  and she would not be consoled,
  since they were no more."

The Return from Egypt. [19]When Herod had died, behold, the angel of the Lord appeared in a dream to Joseph in Egypt [20]r*and said, "Rise, take the child and his mother and go to the land of Israel, for those who sought the child's life are dead." [21]He rose, took the child and his mother, and went to the land of Israel. [22]*But when he heard that Archelaus was ruling over Judea in place of his father Herod, he was afraid to go back

there. And because he had been warned in a dream, he departed for the region of Galilee. [23]s*He went and dwelt in a town called Nazareth, so that what had been spoken through the prophets might be fulfilled, "He shall be called a Nazorean."

II: The Proclamation of the Kingdom

CHAPTER 3

See RG 376

The Preaching of John the Baptist. [1]t*In those days John the Baptist appeared, preaching in the desert of Judea [2]u*[and] saying, "Repent, for the kingdom of heaven is at hand!" [3]v*It was of him that the prophet Isaiah had spoken when he said:

"A voice of one crying out in the desert,
  'Prepare the way of the Lord,
    make straight his paths.' "

[4]w*John wore clothing made of camel's hair and had a leather belt around his waist. His

---

2, 18: Jer 31, 15 portrays Rachel, wife of the patriarch Jacob, weeping for her children taken into exile at the time of the Assyrian invasion of the northern kingdom (722–21 B.C.). Bethlehem was traditionally identified with Ephrath, the place near which Rachel was buried (see Gn 35, 19; 48, 7), and the mourning of Rachel is here applied to her lost children of a later age. **Ramah:** about six miles north of Jerusalem. The lamentation of Rachel is so great as to be heard at a far distance.

2, 20: For those who sought the child's life are dead: Moses, who had fled from Egypt because the Pharaoh sought to kill him (see Ex 2, 15), was told to return there, "for all the men who sought your life are dead" (Ex 4, 19).

2, 22: With the agreement of the emperor Augustus, Archelaus received half of his father's kingdom, including Judea, after Herod's death. He had the title "ethnarch" (i.e., "ruler of a nation") and reigned from 4 B.C. to A.D. 6.

2, 23: Nazareth . . . he shall be called a Nazorean: the tradition of Jesus' residence in Nazareth was firmly established, and Matthew sees it as being in accordance with the foreannounced plan of God. The town of Nazareth is not mentioned in the Old Testament, and no such prophecy can be found there. The vague expression "through the prophets" may be due to Matthew's seeing a connection between Nazareth and certain texts in which there are words with a remote similarity to the name of that town. Some such Old Testament texts are Is 11, 1 where the Davidic king of the future is called "a bud" (nēser) that shall blossom from the roots of Jesse, and Jgs 13, 5.7 where Samson, the future deliverer of Israel from the Philistines, is called one who shall be consecrated (a nāzîr) to God.

3, 1–12: Here Matthew takes up the order of Jesus' minis-

try found in the gospel of Mark, beginning with the preparatory preaching of John the Baptist.

3, 1: Unlike Luke, Matthew says nothing of the Baptist's origins and does not make him a relative of Jesus. **The desert of Judea:** the barren region west of the Dead Sea extending up the Jordan valley.

3, 2: Repent: the Baptist calls for a change of heart and conduct, a turning of one's life from rebellion to obedience toward God. **The kingdom of heaven is at hand:** "heaven" (literally, "the heavens") is a substitute for the name "God" that was avoided by devout Jews of the time out of reverence. The expression "the kingdom of heaven" occurs only in the gospel of Matthew. It means the effective rule of God over his people. In its fullness it includes not only human obedience to God's word, but the triumph of God over physical evils, supremely over death. In the expectation found in Jewish apocalyptic, the kingdom was to be ushered in by a judgment in which sinners would be condemned and perish, an expectation shared by the Baptist. This was modified in Christian understanding where the kingdom was seen as being established in stages, culminating with the parousia of Jesus.

3, 3: See the note on Jn 1, 23.

3, 4: The clothing of John recalls the austere dress of the prophet Elijah (2 Kgs 1, 8). The expectation of the return of Elijah from heaven to prepare Israel for the final manifestation of God's kingdom was widespread, and according to Matthew this expectation was fulfilled in the Baptist's ministry (11, 14; 17, 11–13).

---

q: Jer 31, 15.   r: Ex 4, 19.   s: 13, 54; Mk 1, 9; Lk 2, 39; 4, 34; Jn 19, 19.   t: Mk 1, 2-8; Lk 3, 2-17.   u: 4, 17; 10, 7.   v: Is 40, 3.   w: 11, 7-8; 2 Kgs 1, 8; Zec 13, 4.

food was locusts and wild honey. [5]At that time Jerusalem, all Judea, and the whole region around the Jordan were going out to him [6]* and were being baptized by him in the Jordan River as they acknowledged their sins.

[7x]*When he saw many of the Pharisees and Sadducees coming to his baptism, he said to them, "You brood of vipers! Who warned you to flee from the coming wrath? [8]Produce good fruit as evidence of your repentance. [9y]And do not presume to say to yourselves, 'We have Abraham as our father.' For I tell you, God can raise up children to Abraham from these stones. [10]Even now the ax lies at the root of the trees. Therefore every tree that does not bear good fruit will be cut down and thrown into the fire. [11z]*I am baptizing you with water, for repentance, but the one who is coming after me is mightier than I. I am not worthy to carry his sandals. He will baptize you with the holy Spirit and fire. [12a]*His winnowing fan is in his hand. He will clear his threshing floor and gather his wheat into his barn, but the chaff he will burn with unquenchable fire."

The Baptism of Jesus. [13b]*Then Jesus came from Galilee to John at the Jordan to be baptized by him. [14]*John tried to prevent him, saying, "I need to be baptized by you, and yet you are coming to me?" [15]Jesus said to him in reply, "Allow it now, for thus it is fitting for us to fulfill all righteousness." Then he allowed him. [16c]*After Jesus was baptized, he came up from the water and behold, the heavens were opened [for him], and he saw the Spirit of God descending like a dove [and] coming upon him. [17d]*And a voice came from the heavens, saying, "This is my beloved Son, with whom I am well pleased."

CHAPTER 4

The Temptation of Jesus. [1e]*Then Jesus was led by the Spirit into the desert to

See RG 376-77

3, 6: Ritual washing was practiced by various groups in Palestine between 150 B.C. and A.D. 250. John's baptism may have been related to the purificatory washings of the Essenes at Qumran.

3, 7: Pharisees and Sadducees: the former were marked by devotion to the law, written and oral, and the scribes, experts in the law, belonged predominantly to this group. The Sadducees were the priestly aristocratic party, centered in Jerusalem. They accepted as scripture only the first five books of the Old Testament, followed only the letter of the law, rejected the oral legal traditions, and were opposed to teachings not found in the Pentateuch, such as the resurrection of the dead. Matthew links both of these groups together as enemies of Jesus (16, 1.6.11.12; cf Mk 8, 11–13.15). The threatening words that follow are addressed to them rather than to "the crowds" as in Lk 3, 7. **The coming wrath:** the judgment that will bring about the destruction of unrepentant sinners.

3, 11: Baptize you with the holy Spirit and fire: the water baptism of John will be followed by an "immersion" of the repentant in the cleansing power of the Spirit of God, and of the unrepentant in the destroying power of God's judgment. However, some see **the holy Spirit** and **fire** as synonymous, and the effect of this "baptism" as either purification or destruction. See the note on Lk 3, 16.

3, 12: The discrimination between the good and the bad is compared to the procedure by which a farmer separates wheat and chaff. The **winnowing fan** was a forklike shovel with which the threshed wheat was thrown into the air. The kernels fell to the ground; the light chaff, blown off by the wind, was gathered and burned up.

3, 13–17: The baptism of Jesus is the occasion on which he is equipped for his ministry by the holy Spirit and proclaimed to be the Son of God.

3, 14–15: This dialogue, peculiar to Matthew, reveals John's awareness of Jesus' superiority to him as the mightier one who is coming and who will baptize with the holy Spirit (11). His reluctance to admit Jesus among the sinners whom he is baptizing with water is overcome by Jesus' response. **To fulfill all righteousness:** in this gospel to **fulfill** usually refers to fulfillment of prophecy, and **righteousness** to moral conduct in conformity with God's will. Here, however, as in 5, 6 and 6, 33, **righteousness** seems to mean the saving activity of God. **To fulfill all righteousness** is to submit to the plan of God for the salvation of the human race. This involves Jesus' identification with sinners; hence the propriety of his accepting John's baptism.

3, 16: The Spirit . . . coming upon him: cf Is 42, 1.

3, 17: This is my beloved Son: the Marcan address to Jesus (Mk 1, 11) is changed into a proclamation. The Father's voice speaks in terms that reflect Is 42, 1, Ps 2, 7, and Gn 22, 2.

4, 1–11: Jesus, proclaimed Son of God at his baptism, is subjected to a triple temptation. Obedience to the Father is a characteristic of true sonship, and Jesus is tempted by the devil to rebel against God, overtly in the third case, more subtly in the first two. Each refusal of Jesus is expressed in language taken from the Book of Deuteronomy (Dt 8, 3; 6, 13.16). The testings of Jesus resemble those of Israel during the wandering in the desert and later in Canaan, and the victory of Jesus, the true Israel and the true Son, contrasts with the failure of the ancient and disobedient "son," the old Israel. In the temptation account Matthew is almost identical with Luke; both seem to have drawn upon the same source.

---

x: 12, 34; 23, 33; Is 59, 5.   y: Jn 8, 33.39; Rom 9, 7-8; Gal 4, 21-31.   z: Jn 1, 26-27.33; Acts 1, 5.   a: 13, 30; Is 41, 16; Jer 15, 7.   b: Mk 1, 9-11; Lk 3, 21-22; Jn 1, 31-34.   c: Is 42, 1.   d: 12, 18; 17, 5; Gn 22, 2; Ps 2, 7; Is 42, 1.   e: Mk 1, 12-13; Lk 4, 1-13.

be tempted by the devil. [2f]*He fasted for forty days and forty nights, and afterwards he was hungry. [3]The tempter approached and said to him, "If you are the Son of God, command that these stones become loaves of bread." [4g]*He said in reply, "It is written:

'One does not live by bread alone,
    but by every word that comes forth
        from the mouth of God.' "

[5]*Then the devil took him to the holy city, and made him stand on the parapet of the temple, [6h]and said to him, "If you are the Son of God, throw yourself down. For it is written:

'He will command his angels concerning
    you'
  and 'with their hands they will support
    you,
lest you dash your foot against a stone.' "

[7i]Jesus answered him, "Again it is written, 'You shall not put the Lord, your God, to the test.' " [8]Then the devil took him up to a very high mountain, and showed him all the kingdoms of the world in their magnificence, [9]*and he said to him, "All these I shall give to you, if you will prostrate yourself and worship me." [10j]At this, Jesus said to him, "Get away, Satan! It is written:

'The Lord, your God, shall you worship
  and him alone shall you serve.' "

[11]Then the devil left him and, behold, angels came and ministered to him.

The Beginning of the Galilean Ministry. [12k]*When he heard that John had been arrested, he withdrew to Galilee. [13l]He left Nazareth and went to live in Capernaum by the sea, in the region of Zebulun and Naphtali, [14]that what had been said through Isaiah the prophet might be fulfilled:

[15 m]"Land of Zebulun and land of Naphtali,
  the way to the sea, beyond the Jordan,
  Galilee of the Gentiles,
[16 n]the people who sit in darkness
  have seen a great light,
on those dwelling in a land
    overshadowed by death
  light has arisen."

[17o]*From that time on, Jesus began to preach and say, "Repent, for the kingdom of heaven is at hand."

The Call of the First Disciples. [18p]*As he was walking by the Sea of Galilee, he saw two brothers, Simon who is called Peter, and his brother Andrew, casting a net into the sea; they were fishermen. [19]He said to them, "Come after me, and I will make you fishers of men." [20]*At once they left their nets and followed him. [21]He walked along from there and saw two other brothers, James, the son of Zebedee, and his brother John. They were in a boat, with their father Zebedee, mending their nets. He called them, [22]and immedi-

4, 2: **Forty days and forty nights:** the same time as that during which Moses remained on Sinai (Ex 24, 18). The time reference, however, seems primarily intended to recall the forty years during which Israel was tempted in the desert (Dt 8, 2).

4, 4: Cf Dt 8, 3. Jesus refuses to use his power for his own benefit and accepts whatever God wills.

4, 5–7: The devil supports his proposal by an appeal to the scriptures, Ps 91, 11a.12. Unlike Israel (Dt 6, 16), Jesus refuses to "test" God by demanding from him an extraordinary show of power.

4, 9: The worship of Satan to which Jesus is tempted is probably intended to recall Israel's worship of false gods. His refusal is expressed in the words of Dt 6, 13.

4, 12–17: Isaiah's prophecy of the light rising upon Zebulun and Naphtali (Is 8, 23—9, 1) is fulfilled in Jesus' residence at Capernaum. The territory of these two tribes was the first to be devastated (733–32 B.C.) at the time of the Assyrian invasion. In order to accommodate Jesus' move to Capernaum to the prophecy, Matthew speaks of that town as being "in the region of Zebulun and Naphtali" (13), whereas it was

only in the territory of the latter, and he understands the sea of the prophecy, the Mediterranean, as the sea of Galilee.

4, 17: At the beginning of his preaching Jesus takes up the words of John the Baptist (3, 2) although with a different meaning; in his ministry the kingdom of heaven has already begun to be present (12, 28).

4, 18–22: The call of the first disciples promises them a share in Jesus' work and entails abandonment of family and former way of life. Three of the four, Simon, James, and John, are distinguished among the disciples by a closer relation with Jesus (17, 1; 26, 37).

4, 20: Here and in v 22, as in Mark (1, 16–20) and unlike the Lucan account (5, 1–11), the disciples' response is motivated only by Jesus' invitation, an element that emphasizes his mysterious power.

f: Ex 24, 18; Dt 8, 2. g: Dt 8, 3. h: Ps 91, 11-12. i: Dt 6, 16.
j: 16, 23; Dt 6, 13. k: Mk 1, 14-15; Lk 4, 14.31. l: Jn 2, 12.
m: Is 8, 23 LXX; 9, 1. n: Lk 1, 79. o: 3, 2. p: Mk 1, 16-20;
Lk 5, 1-11.

ately they left their boat and their father and followed him.

Ministering to a Great Multitude. *23q**He went around all of Galilee, teaching in their synagogues, proclaiming the gospel of the kingdom, and curing every disease and illness among the people. *24**His fame spread to all of Syria, and they brought to him all who were sick with various diseases and racked with pain, those who were possessed, lunatics, and paralytics, and he cured them. *25r**And great crowds from Galilee, the Decapolis, Jerusalem, and Judea, and from beyond the Jordan followed him.

See RG 377–78

CHAPTER 5

The Sermon on the Mount. *1**When he saw the crowds, he went up the mountain, and after he had sat down, his disciples came to him. *2*He began to teach them, saying:

The Beatitudes

3 s*"Blessed are the poor in spirit,
　　for theirs is the kingdom of heaven.
4 t*Blessed are they who mourn,
　　for they will be comforted.
5 u*Blessed are the meek,
　　for they will inherit the land.
6 *Blessed are they who hunger and thirst
　　　for righteousness,
　　for they will be satisfied.
7 v Blessed are the merciful,
　　for they will be shown mercy.
8 w*Blessed are the clean of heart,
　　for they will see God.
9 Blessed are the peacemakers,
　　for they will be called children of God.
10 x*Blessed are they who are persecuted
　　　for the sake of righteousness,
　　for theirs is the kingdom of heaven.

*11y*Blessed are you when they insult you and

4, 23–25: This summary of Jesus' ministry concludes the narrative part of the first book of Matthew's gospel (chs 3–4). The activities of his ministry are teaching, proclaiming the gospel, and healing; cf 9, 35.

4, 23: Their synagogues: Matthew usually designates the Jewish synagogues as **their synagogue(s)** (9, 35; 10, 17; 12, 9; 13, 54) or, in address to Jews, **your synagogues** (23, 34), an indication that he wrote after the break between church and synagogue.

4, 24: Syria: the Roman province to which Palestine belonged.

4, 25: The Decapolis: a federation of Greek cities in Palestine, originally ten in all, all but one east of the Jordan.

5, 1—7, 29: The first of the five discourses that are a central part of the structure of this gospel. It is the discourse section of the first book and contains sayings of Jesus derived from Q and from M. The Lucan parallel is in that gospel's "Sermon on the Plain" (Lk 6, 20–49), although some of the sayings in Matthew's "Sermon on the Mount" have their parallels in other parts of Luke. The careful topical arrangement of the sermon is probably not due only to Matthew's editing; he seems to have had a structured discourse of Jesus as one of his sources. The form of that source may have been as follows: four beatitudes (5, 3–4.6.11–12), a section on the new righteousness with illustrations (5, 17.20–24.27–28.33–48), a section on good works (6, 1–6.16–18), and three warnings (7, 1–2.15–21.24–27).

5, 1–2: Unlike Luke's sermon, this is addressed not only to the disciples but to the crowds (see 7, 28).

5, 3–12: The form **Blessed are (is)** occurs frequently in the Old Testament in the Wisdom literature and in the psalms. Although modified by Matthew, the first, second, fourth, and ninth beatitudes have Lucan parallels (5, 3 // Lk 6, 20; 5, 4 // Lk 6, 21b; 5, 6 // Lk 6, 21a; 5, 11–12 // Lk 5, 22–23). The oth-

ers were added by the evangelist and are probably his own composition. A few manuscripts, Western and Alexandrian, and many versions and patristic quotations give the second and third beatitudes in inverted order.

5, 3: The poor in spirit: in the Old Testament, the **poor** (ănāwim) are those who are without material possessions and whose confidence is in God (see Is 61, 1; Zep 2, 3; in the NAB the word is translated **lowly** and **humble**, respectively, in those texts). Matthew added **in spirit** in order either to indicate that only the devout poor were meant or to extend the beatitude to all, of whatever social rank, who recognized their complete dependence on God. The same phrase **poor in spirit** is found in the Qumran literature (1QM 14, 7).

5, 4: Cf Is 61, 2, "(The Lord has sent me) . . . to comfort all who mourn." **They will be comforted:** here the passive is a "theological passive" equivalent to the active "God will comfort them"; so also in vv 6 and 7.

5, 5: Cf Ps 37, 11, ". . . the meek shall possess the land." In the psalm "the land" means the land of Palestine; here it means the kingdom.

5, 6: For righteousness: a Matthean addition. For the meaning of **righteousness** here, see the note on 3, 14–15.

5, 8: Cf Ps 24, 4. Only one "whose heart is clean" can take part in the temple worship. To be with God in the temple is described in Ps 42, 3 as "beholding his face," but here the promise to **the clean of heart** is that they will **see God** not in the temple but in the coming kingdom.

5, 10: Righteousness here, as usually in Matthew, means conduct in conformity with God's will.

---

q: 9, 35; Mk 1, 39; Lk 4, 15.44.　*r:* Mk 3, 7-8; Lk 6, 17-19.
s: Lk 6, 20-23.　*t:* Is 61, 2-3; Rv 21, 4.　*u:* Gn 13, 15; Ps 37, 11.
v: 18, 33; Jas 2, 13.　*w:* Pss 24, 4-5; 73, 1.　*x:* 1 Pt 2, 20; 3, 14;
4, 14.　*y:* 10, 22; Acts 5, 41.

persecute you and utter every kind of evil against you [falsely] because of me. *12z**Rejoice and be glad, for your reward will be great in heaven. Thus they persecuted the prophets who were before you.

The Similes of Salt and Light. *13a**"You are the salt of the earth. But if salt loses its taste, with what can it be seasoned? It is no longer good for anything but to be thrown out and trampled underfoot. *14b*You are the light of the world. A city set on a mountain cannot be hidden. *15c*Nor do they light a lamp and then put it under a bushel basket; it is set on a lampstand, where it gives light to all in the house. *16d*Just so, your light must shine before others, that they may see your good deeds and glorify your heavenly Father.

Teaching about the Law. *17**"Do not think that I have come to abolish the law or the prophets. I have come not to abolish but to fulfill. *18e*Amen, I say to you, until heaven and earth pass away, not the smallest letter or the smallest part of a letter will pass from the law, until all things have taken place. *19**Therefore, whoever breaks one of the least of these commandments and teaches others to do so will be called least in the kingdom of heaven. But whoever obeys and teaches these commandments will be called greatest in the kingdom of heaven. *20*I tell you, unless your righteousness surpasses that of the scribes and Pharisees, you will not enter into the kingdom of heaven.

Teaching about Anger. *21f**"You have heard that it was said to your ancestors, 'You shall not kill; and whoever kills will be liable to judgment.' *22g**But I say to you, whoever is angry with his brother will be liable to judgment, and whoever says to his brother, 'Raqa,' will be answerable to the Sanhedrin, and whoever says, 'You fool,' will be liable to

5, 12: The prophets who were before you: the disciples of Jesus stand in the line of the persecuted prophets of Israel. Some would see the expression as indicating also that Matthew considered all Christian disciples as prophets.

5, 13–16: By their deeds the disciples are to influence the world for good. They can no more escape notice than **a city set on a mountain.** If they fail in good works, they are as useless as flavorless salt or as a lamp whose light is concealed.

5, 13: The unusual supposition of salt losing its flavor has led some to suppose that the saying refers to the salt of the Dead Sea that, because chemically impure, could lose its taste.

5, 17–20: This statement of Jesus' position concerning the Mosaic law is composed of traditional material from Matthew's sermon documentation (see the note on 5, 1—7, 29), other Q material (cf 18 and Lk 16, 17), and the evangelist's own editorial touches. **To fulfill** the law appears at first to mean a literal enforcement of the law in the least detail: **until heaven and earth pass away** nothing of the law **will pass** (18). Yet the "passing away" of heaven and earth is not necessarily the end of the world understood, as in much apocalyptic literature, as the dissolution of the existing universe. The "turning of the ages" comes with the apocalyptic event of Jesus' death and resurrection, and those to whom this gospel is addressed are living in the new and final age, prophesied by Isaiah as the time of "new heavens and a new earth" (Is 65, 17; 66, 22). Meanwhile, during Jesus' ministry when the kingdom is already breaking in, his mission remains within the framework of the law, though with significant anticipation of the age to come, as the following antitheses (vv 21–48) show.

5, 19: Probably **these commandments** means those of the Mosaic law. But this is an interim ethic "until heaven and earth pass away."

5, 21–48: Six examples of the conduct demanded of the Christian disciple. Each deals with a commandment of the law, introduced by **You have heard that it was said to your ancestors** or an equivalent formula, followed by Jesus' teach-

ing in respect to that commandment, **But I say to you;** thus their designation as "antitheses." Three of them accept the Mosaic law but extend or deepen it (21–22; 27–28; 43–44); three reject it as a standard of conduct for the disciples (31–32; 33–37; 38–39).

5, 21: Cf Ex 20, 13; Dt 5, 17. The second part of the verse is not an exact quotation from the Old Testament, but cf Ex 21, 12.

5, 22: Anger is the motive behind murder, as the insulting epithets are steps that may lead to it. They, as well as the deed, are all forbidden. **Raqa:** an Aramaic word **rēqā'** or **rēqâ** probably meaning "imbecile," "blockhead," a term of abuse. The ascending order of punishment, **judgment** (by a local council?), trial before **the Sanhedrin,** condemnation to **Gehenna,** points to a higher degree of seriousness in each of the offenses. **Sanhedrin:** the highest judicial body of Judaism. **Gehenna:** in Hebrew **gê-hinnōm,** "Valley of Hinnom," or **gê ben-hinnōm,** "Valley of the son of Hinnom," southwest of Jerusalem, the center of an idolatrous cult during the monarchy in which children were offered in sacrifice (see 2 Kgs 23, 10; Jer 7, 31). In Jos 18, 16 (Septuagint, Codex Vaticanus) the Hebrew is transliterated into Greek as **gaienna,** which appears in the New Testament as **geenna.** The concept of punishment of sinners by fire either after death or after the final judgment is found in Jewish apocalyptic literature (e.g., Enoch 90, 26) but the name **geenna** is first given to the place of punishment in the New Testament.

5, 22–26: Reconciliation with an offended brother is urged in the admonition of vv 23–24 and the parable of vv 25–26 (// Lk 12, 58–59). The severity of the judge in the parable is a warning of the fate of unrepentant sinners in the coming judgment by God.

z: 2 Chr 36, 16; Heb 11, 32-38; Jas 5, 10. *a:* Mk 9, 50; Lk 14, 34-35. *b:* Jn 8, 12. *c:* Mk 4, 21; Lk 8, 16; 11, 33. *d:* Jn 3, 21. *e:* Lk 16, 17. *f:* Ex 20, 13; Dt 5, 17. *g:* Jas 1, 19-20.

fiery Gehenna. [23h]Therefore, if you bring your gift to the altar, and there recall that your brother has anything against you, [24]leave your gift there at the altar, go first and be reconciled with your brother, and then come and offer your gift. [25i]Settle with your opponent quickly while on the way to court with him. Otherwise your opponent will hand you over to the judge, and the judge will hand you over to the guard, and you will be thrown into prison. [26]Amen, I say to you, you will not be released until you have paid the last penny.

Teaching about Adultery. [27j]*"You have heard that it was said, 'You shall not commit adultery.' [28]But I say to you, everyone who looks at a woman with lust has already committed adultery with her in his heart. [29k]*If your right eye causes you to sin, tear it out and throw it away. It is better for you to lose one of your members than to have your whole body thrown into Gehenna. [30]And if your right hand causes you to sin, cut it off and throw it away. It is better for you to lose one of your members than to have your whole body go into Gehenna.

Teaching about Divorce. [31l]*"It was also said, 'Whoever divorces his wife must give her a bill of divorce.' [32m]But I say to you,

whoever divorces his wife (unless the marriage is unlawful) causes her to commit adultery, and whoever marries a divorced woman commits adultery.

Teaching about Oaths. [33n]*"Again you have heard that it was said to your ancestors, 'Do not take a false oath, but make good to the Lord all that you vow.' [34o]*But I say to you, do not swear at all; not by heaven, for it is God's throne; [35]nor by the earth, for it is his footstool; nor by Jerusalem, for it is the city of the great King. [36]Do not swear by your head, for you cannot make a single hair white or black. [37]*Let your 'Yes' mean 'Yes,' and your 'No' mean 'No.' Anything more is from the evil one.

Teaching about Retaliation. [38p]*"You have heard that it was said, 'An eye for an eye and a tooth for a tooth.' [39q]But I say to you, offer no resistance to one who is evil. When someone strikes you on [your] right cheek, turn the other one to him as well. [40]If anyone wants to go to law with you over your tunic, hand him your cloak as well. [41r]*Should anyone press you into service for one mile, go with him for two miles. [42s]Give to the one who asks of you, and do not turn your back on one who wants to borrow.

5, 27: See Ex 20, 14; Dt 5, 18.

5, 29–30: No sacrifice is too great to avoid total destruction in **Gehenna**.

5, 31–32: See Dt 24, 1–5. The Old Testament commandment that a bill of divorce be given to the woman assumes the legitimacy of divorce itself. It is this that Jesus denies. (**Unless the marriage is unlawful**): this "exceptive clause," as it is often called, occurs also in 19, 9, where the Greek is slightly different. There are other sayings of Jesus about divorce that prohibit it absolutely (see Mk 10, 11–12; Lk 16, 18; cf 1 Cor 7, 10.11b), and most scholars agree that they represent the stand of Jesus. Matthew's "exceptive clauses" are understood by some as a modification of the absolute prohibition. It seems, however, that the unlawfulness that Matthew gives as a reason why a marriage must be broken refers to a situation peculiar to his community: the violation of Mosaic law forbidding marriage between persons of certain blood and/or legal relationship (Lv 18, 6–18). Marriages of that sort were regarded as incest (**porneia**), but some rabbis allowed Gentile converts to Judaism who had contracted such marriages to remain in them. Matthew's "exceptive clause" is against such permissiveness for Gentile converts to Christianity; cf the similar prohibition of **porneia** in Acts 15, 20.29. In this interpretation, the clause constitutes no exception to the absolute prohibition of divorce when the marriage is lawful.

5, 33: This is not an exact quotation of any Old Testament text, but see Ex 20, 7, Dt 5, 11, and Lv 19, 12. The purpose of

an oath was to guarantee truthfulness by one's calling on God as witness.

5, 34–36: The use of these oath formularies that avoid the divine name is in fact equivalent to swearing by it, for all the things sworn by are related to God.

5, 37: **Let your 'Yes' mean 'Yes,' and your 'No' mean 'No':** literally, "let your speech be 'Yes, yes,' 'No, no.'" Some have understood this as a milder form of oath, permitted by Jesus. In view of v 34, "Do not swear at all," that is unlikely. **From the evil one:** i.e., from the devil. Oath-taking presupposes a sinful weakness of the human race, namely, the tendency to lie. Jesus demands of his disciples a truthfulness that makes oaths unnecessary.

5, 38–42: See Lv 24, 20. The Old Testament commandment was meant to moderate vengeance; the punishment should not exceed the injury done. Jesus forbids even this proportionate retaliation. Of the five examples that follow, only the first deals directly with retaliation for evil; the others speak of liberality.

5, 41: Roman garrisons in Palestine had the right to requisition the property and services of the native population.

h: Mk 11, 25. *i:* 18, 34-35; Lk 12, 58-59. *j:* Ex 20, 14; Dt 5, 18. *k:* 18, 8-9; Mk 9, 43-47. *l:* 19, 3-9; Dt 24, 1. *m:* Lk 16, 18; 1 Cor 7, 10-11. *n:* Lv 19, 12; Nm 30, 3. *o:* Ps 48, 3; Sir 23, 9; Is 66, 1; Jas 5, 12. *p:* Ex 21, 24; Lv 24, 19-20. *q:* Lk 6, 29-30. *r:* Lam 3, 30. *s:* Dt 15, 7-8.

Love of Enemies. [43 tu]*"You have heard that it was said, 'You shall love your neighbor and hate your enemy.' [44]But I say to you, love your enemies, and pray for those who persecute you, [45]that you may be children of your heavenly Father, for he makes his sun rise on the bad and the good, and causes rain to fall on the just and the unjust. [46]*For if you love those who love you, what recompense will you have? Do not the tax collectors do the same? [47]*And if you greet your brothers only, what is unusual about that? Do not the pagans do the same? [48 v]*So be perfect, just as your heavenly Father is perfect.

See RG
377-78

CHAPTER 6

Teaching about Almsgiving. [1 w]*"[But] take care not to perform righteous deeds in order that people may see them; otherwise, you will have no recompense from your heavenly Father. [2 x]*When you give alms, do not blow a trumpet before you, as the hypocrites do in the synagogues and in the streets

to win the praise of others. Amen, I say to you, they have received their reward. [3]But when you give alms, do not let your left hand know what your right is doing, [4]so that your almsgiving may be secret. And your Father who sees in secret will repay you.

Teaching about Prayer. [5]"When you pray, do not be like the hypocrites, who love to stand and pray in the synagogues and on street corners so that others may see them. Amen, I say to you, they have received their reward. [6]But when you pray, go to your inner room, close the door, and pray to your Father in secret. And your Father who sees in secret will repay you. [7]*In praying, do not babble like the pagans, who think that they will be heard because of their many words. [8]Do not be like them. Your Father knows what you need before you ask him.

The Lord's Prayer. [9 y]*"This is how you are to pray:

Our Father in heaven,
hallowed be your name,

5, 43–48: See Lv 19, 18. There is no Old Testament commandment demanding hatred of one's enemy, but the "neighbor" of the love commandment was understood as one's fellow countryman. Both in the Old Testament (Ps 139, 19–22) and at Qumran (1QS 9, 21) hatred of evil persons is assumed to be right. Jesus extends the love commandment to the enemy and the persecutor. His disciples, as children of God, must imitate the example of their Father, who grants his gifts of sun and rain to both the good and the bad.

5, 46: Tax collectors: Jews who were engaged in the collection of indirect taxes such as tolls and customs. See the note on Mk 2, 14.

5, 47: Jesus' disciples must not be content with merely usual standards of conduct; see v 20 where the verb "surpass" (Greek **perisseuō**) is cognate with the **unusual** (**perisson**) of this verse.

5, 48: Perfect: in the gospels this word occurs only in Matthew, here and in 19, 21. The Lucan parallel (6, 36) demands that the disciples be **merciful.**

6, 1–18: The sermon continues with a warning against doing good in order to be seen and gives three examples, almsgiving (2–4), prayer (5, 15), and fasting (16–18). In each, the conduct of **the hypocrites** (2) is contrasted with that demanded of the disciples. The sayings about **reward** found here and elsewhere (5, 12.46; 10, 41–42) show that this is a genuine element of Christian moral exhortation. Possibly to underline the difference between the Christian idea of **reward** and that of **the hypocrites**, the evangelist uses two different Greek verbs to express the rewarding of the disciples and that of **the hypocrites**; in the latter case it is the verb **apechō**, a commercial term for giving a receipt for what has been paid in full (2.5.16).

6, 2: The hypocrites: the scribes and Pharisees, see 23, 13.15. 23.25.27.29. The designation reflects an attitude resulting not only from the controversies at the time of Jesus' ministry but from the opposition between Pharisaic Judaism and the church of Matthew. **They have received their reward:** they desire praise and have received what they were looking for.

6, 7–15: Matthew inserts into his basic traditional material an expansion of the material on prayer that includes the model prayer, the "Our Father." That prayer is found in Lk 11, 2–4 in a different context and in a different form.

6, 7: The example of what Christian prayer should be like contrasts it now not with the prayer of the hypocrites but with that of **the pagans.** Their babbling probably means their reciting a long list of divine names, hoping that one of them will force a response from the deity.

6, 9–13: Matthew's form of the "Our Father" follows the liturgical tradition of his church. Luke's less developed form also represents the liturgical tradition known to him, but it is probably closer than Matthew's to the original words of Jesus.

6, 9: Our Father in heaven: this invocation is found in many rabbinic prayers of the post-New Testament period. **Hallowed be your name:** though the "hallowing" of the divine name could be understood as reverence done to God by human praise and by obedience to his will, this is more probably a petition that God hallow his own name, i.e., that he manifest his glory by an act of power (cf Ez 36, 23), in this case, by the establishment of his kingdom in its fullness.

---

t: Lk 6, 27.32-36.   *u:* Lv 19, 18.   *v:* Lv 11, 44; 19, 2; Dt 18, 13; Jas 1, 4; 1 Pt 1, 16; 1 Jn 3, 3.   *w:* 23, 5.   *x:* Jn 12, 43.   *y:* Lk 11, 2-4.

10   z*your kingdom come,
      your will be done,
         on earth as in heaven.
11   a*Give us today our daily bread;
12   b*and forgive us our debts,
         as we forgive our debtors;
13   c*and do not subject us to the final
            test,
         but deliver us from the evil one.

14d*If you forgive others their transgressions, your heavenly Father will forgive you. 15eBut if you do not forgive others, neither will your Father forgive your transgressions.

Teaching about Fasting. 16*"When you fast, do not look gloomy like the hypocrites. They neglect their appearance, so that they may appear to others to be fasting. Amen, I say to you, they have received their reward. 17But when you fast, anoint your head and wash your face, 18so that you may not appear to others to be fasting, except to your Father who is hidden. And your Father who sees what is hidden will repay you.

Treasure in Heaven. 19f*"Do not store up for yourselves treasures on earth, where moth and decay destroy, and thieves break in and steal. 20gBut store up treasures in heaven, where neither moth nor decay destroy, nor thieves break in and steal. 21For where your treasure is, there also will your heart be.

The Light of the Body. 22h*"The lamp of the body is the eye. If your eye is sound, your whole body will be filled with light; 23but if your eye is bad, your whole body will be in darkness. And if the light in you is darkness, how great will the darkness be.

God and Money. 24i*"No one can serve two masters. He will either hate one and love the other, or be devoted to one and despise the other. You cannot serve God and mammon.

Dependence on God. 25j*"Therefore I tell you, do not worry about your life, what you will eat [or drink], or about your body, what you will wear. Is not life more than food and the body more than clothing? 26kLook at the birds in the sky; they do not sow or reap, they gather nothing into barns, yet your heavenly Father feeds them. Are not you more important than they? 27*Can any of you by worrying add a single moment to your life-span? 28Why are you anxious about clothes? Learn from the way the wild flowers grow. They do not work or spin. 29But I tell you that not even Solomon in all his

---

6, 10: **Your kingdom come:** this petition sets the tone of the prayer, and inclines the balance toward divine rather than human action in the petitions that immediately precede and follow it. **Your will be done, on earth as in heaven:** a petition that the divine purpose to establish the kingdom, a purpose present now **in heaven,** be executed **on earth.**

6, 11: **Give us today our daily bread:** the rare Greek word **epiousios,** here **daily,** occurs in the New Testament only here and in Lk 11, 3. A single occurrence of the word outside of these texts and of literature dependent on them has been claimed, but the claim is highly doubtful. The word may mean **daily** or "future" (other meanings have also been proposed). The latter would conform better to the eschatological tone of the whole prayer. So understood, the petition would be for a speedy coming of the kingdom (**today**), which is often portrayed in both the Old Testament and the New under the image of a feast (Is 25, 6; Mt 8, 11; 22, 1–10; Lk 13, 29; 14, 15–24).

6, 12: **Forgive us our debts:** the word **debts** is used metaphorically of sins, "debts" owed to God (see Lk 11, 4). The request is probably for forgiveness at the final judgment.

6, 13: Jewish apocalyptic writings speak of a period of severe trial before the end of the age, sometimes called the "messianic woes." This petition asks that the disciples be spared that **final test.**

6, 14–15: These verses reflect a set pattern called "Principles of Holy Law." Human action now will be met by a corresponding action of God at the final judgment.

6, 16: The only fast prescribed in the Mosaic law was that of the Day of Atonement (Lv 16, 31), but the practice of regular fasting was common in later Judaism; cf **Didache** 9, 1.

6, 19–34: The remaining material of this chapter is taken almost entirely from Q. It deals principally with worldly possessions, and the controlling thought is summed up in v 24: the disciple can serve only one master and must choose between God and wealth (**mammon**). See further the note on Lk 16, 9.

6, 22–23: In this context the parable probably points to the need for the disciple to be enlightened by Jesus' teaching on the transitory nature of earthly riches.

6, 24: **Mammon:** an Aramaic word meaning wealth or property.

6, 25–34: Jesus does not deny the reality of human needs (32), but forbids making them the object of anxious care and, in effect, becoming their slave.

6, 27: **Life-span:** the Greek word can also mean "stature." If it is taken in that sense, the word here translated **moment** (literally, "cubit") must be translated literally as a unit not of time but of spatial measure. The cubit is about eighteen inches.

z: 26, 42. a: Prv 30, 8-9. b: 18, 21-22; Sir 28, 2. c: Jn 17, 15; 2 Thes 3, 3. d: 18, 35; Sir 28, 1-5; Mk 11, 25. e: Jas 2, 13. f: Jas 5, 2-3. g: Lk 12, 33-34. h: Lk 11, 34-36. i: Lk 16, 13. j: Lk 12, 22-31. k: Pss 145, 15-16; 147, 9.

splendor was clothed like one of them. *30**If God so clothes the grass of the field, which grows today and is thrown into the oven tomorrow, will he not much more provide for you, O you of little faith? *31*So do not worry and say, 'What are we to eat?' or 'What are we to drink?' or 'What are we to wear?' *32*All these things the pagans seek. Your heavenly Father knows that you need them all. *33**But seek first the kingdom [of God] and his righteousness, and all these things will be given you besides. *34*Do not worry about tomorrow; tomorrow will take care of itself. Sufficient for a day is its own evil.

See RG
377–78

CHAPTER 7

Judging Others. *1lm**"Stop judging, that you may not be judged. *2n*For as you judge, so will you be judged, and the measure with which you measure will be measured out to you. *3*Why do you notice the splinter in your brother's eye, but do not perceive the wooden beam in your own eye? *4*How can you say to your brother, 'Let me remove that splinter from your eye,' while the wooden beam is in your eye? *5**You hypocrite, remove the wooden beam from your eye first; then you will see clearly to remove the splinter from your brother's eye.

Pearls before Swine. *6o**"Do not give what is holy to dogs, or throw your pearls before swine, lest they trample them underfoot, and turn and tear you to pieces.

The Answer to Prayers. *7pq*"Ask and it will be given to you; seek and you will find; knock and the door will be opened to you. *8r*For everyone who asks, receives; and the one who seeks, finds; and to the one who knocks, the door will be opened. *9**Which one of you would hand his son a stone when he asks for a loaf of bread, *10*or a snake when he asks for a fish? *11s*If you then, who are wicked, know how to give good gifts to your children, how much more will your heavenly Father give good things to those who ask him.

The Golden Rule. *12t**"Do to others whatever you would have them do to you. This is the law and the prophets.

The Narrow Gate. *13u**"Enter through the narrow gate; for the gate is wide and the road broad that leads to destruction, and those who enter through it are many. *14*How narrow the gate and constricted the road that leads to life. And those who find it are few.

False Prophets. *15v**"Beware of false prophets, who come to you in sheep's clothing, but underneath are ravenous wolves. *16w*By their fruits you will know them. Do

6, 30: **Of little faith:** except for the parallel in Lk 12, 28, the word translated **of little faith** is found in the New Testament only in Matthew. It is used by him of those who are disciples of Jesus but whose faith in him is not as deep as it should be (see Mt 8, 26; 14, 31; 16, 8 and the cognate noun in 17, 20).

6, 33: **Righteousness:** see the note on 3, 14–15.

7, 1–12: In v 1 Matthew returns to the basic traditional material of the sermon (Lk 6, 37–38.41–42). The governing thought is the correspondence between conduct toward one's fellows and God's conduct toward the one so acting.

7, 1: This is not a prohibition against recognizing the faults of others, which would be hardly compatible with vv 5 and 6, but against passing judgment in a spirit of arrogance, forgetful of one's own faults.

7, 5: **Hypocrite:** the designation previously given to the scribes and Pharisees is here given to the Christian disciple who is concerned with the faults of another and ignores his own more serious offenses.

7, 6: **Dogs** and **swine** were Jewish terms of contempt for Gentiles. This saying may originally have derived from a Jewish Christian community opposed to preaching the gospel (**what is holy, pearls**) to Gentiles. In the light of 28, 19 that can hardly be Matthew's meaning. He may have taken the saying as applying to a Christian dealing with an obstinately impenitent fellow Christian (18, 17).

7, 9–10: There is a resemblance between a stone and a

round loaf of bread and between a serpent and the scaleless fish called **barbut.**

7, 12: See Lk 6, 31. This saying, known since the eighteenth century as the "Golden Rule," is found in both positive and negative form in pagan and Jewish sources, both earlier and later than the gospel. **This is the law and the prophets** is an addition probably due to the evangelist.

7, 13–28: The final section of the discourse is composed of a series of antitheses, contrasting two kinds of life within the Christian community, that of those who obey the words of Jesus and that of those who do not. Most of the sayings are from Q and are found also in Luke.

7, 13–14: The metaphor of the "two ways" was common in pagan philosophy and in the Old Testament. In Christian literature it is found also in the **Didache** (1–6) and the **Epistle of Barnabas** (18–20).

7, 15–20: Christian disciples who claimed to speak in the name of God are called **prophets** (15) in 10, 41 and in 23, 34. They were presumably an important group within the church of Matthew. As in the case of the Old Testament prophets, there were both true and false ones, and for Matthew the dif-

l: Lk 6, 37-38.41-42. *m:* Rom 2, 1-2; 1 Cor 4, 5. *n:* Wis 12, 22; Mk 4, 24. *o:* Prv 23, 9. *p:* Mk 11, 24; Lk 11, 9-13. *q:* 18, 19. *r:* Lk 18, 1-8; Jn 14, 13. *s:* 1 Jn 5, 14-15. *t:* Lk 6, 31. *u:* Lk 13, 24. *v:* 2 Pt 2, 1. *w:* 12, 33; Lk 6, 43-44.

people pick grapes from thornbushes, or figs from thistles? [17]Just so, every good tree bears good fruit, and a rotten tree bears bad fruit. [18]A good tree cannot bear bad fruit, nor can a rotten tree bear good fruit. [19x]Every tree that does not bear good fruit will be cut down and thrown into the fire. [20]So by their fruits you will know them.

The True Disciple. [21y]*"Not everyone who says to me, 'Lord, Lord,' will enter the kingdom of heaven, but only the one who does the will of my Father in heaven. [22za]Many will say to me on that day, 'Lord, Lord, did we not prophesy in your name? Did we not drive out demons in your name? Did we not do mighty deeds in your name?' [23b]*Then I will declare to them solemnly, 'I never knew you. Depart from me, you evildoers.'

The Two Foundations. [24c]*"Everyone who listens to these words of mine and acts on them will be like a wise man who built his house on rock. [25d]The rain fell, the floods came, and the winds blew and buffeted the house. But it did not collapse; it had been set solidly on rock. [26]And everyone who listens to these words of mine but does not act on them will be like a fool who built his house

on sand. [27]The rain fell, the floods came, and the winds blew and buffeted the house. And it collapsed and was completely ruined."

[28]*When Jesus finished these words, the crowds were astonished at his teaching, [29e]*for he taught them as one having authority, and not as their scribes.

III: Ministry and Mission in Galilee

CHAPTER 8

See RG
378–79

The Cleansing of a Leper. [1f]*When Jesus came down from the mountain, great crowds followed him. [2]*And then a leper approached, did him homage, and said, "Lord, if you wish, you can make me clean." [3]He stretched out his hand, touched him, and said, "I will do it. Be made clean." His leprosy was cleansed immediately. [4g]*Then Jesus said to him, "See that you tell no one, but go show yourself to the priest, and offer the gift that Moses prescribed; that will be proof for them."

The Healing of a Centurion's Servant. [5h]*When he entered Capernaum, a centurion

---

ference could be recognized by the quality of their deeds, the **fruits** (16). The mention of **fruits** leads to the comparison with trees, some producing good fruit, others bad.

7, 21–23: The attack on the false prophets is continued, but is broadened to include those disciples who perform works of healing and exorcism in the name of Jesus (**Lord**) but live evil lives. Entrance into the kingdom is only for those who do the will of the Father. On the day of judgment (**on that day**) the morally corrupt prophets and miracle workers will be rejected by Jesus.

7, 23: I never knew you: cf 10, 33. **Depart from me, you evildoers:** cf Ps 6, 9.

7, 24–27: The conclusion of the discourse (cf Lk 6, 47–49). Here the relation is not between saying and doing as in vv 15–23 but between hearing and doing, and the words of Jesus are applied to every Christian (**everyone who listens**).

7, 28–29: When Jesus finished these words: this or a similar formula is used by Matthew to conclude each of the five great discourses of Jesus (cf 11, 1; 13, 53; 19, 1; 26, 1).

7, 29: Not as their scribes: scribal instruction was a faithful handing down of the traditions of earlier teachers; Jesus' teaching is based on his own authority. **Their scribes:** for the implications of **their,** see the note on 4, 23.

8, 1—9, 38: This narrative section of the second book of the gospel is composed of nine miracle stories, most of which are found in Mark, although Matthew does not follow the Marcan order and abbreviates the stories radically. The stories are arranged in three groups of three, each group followed by

a section composed principally of sayings of Jesus about discipleship. Verse 9, 35 is an almost verbatim repetition of 4, 23. Each speaks of Jesus' teaching, preaching, and healing. The teaching and preaching form the content of chs 5–7; the healing, that of chs 8–9. Some scholars speak of a portrayal of Jesus as "Messiah of the Word" in 5–7 and "Messiah of the Deed" in 8–9. That is accurate so far as it goes, but there is also a strong emphasis on discipleship in 8–9; these chapters have not only christological but ecclesiological import.

8, 2: A leper: see the note on Mk 1, 40.

8, 4: Cf Lv 14, 2–9. **That will be proof for them:** the Greek can also mean "that will be proof against them." It is not clear whether **them** refers to the priests or the people.

8, 5–13: This story comes from Q (see Lk 7, 1–10) and is also reflected in Jn 4, 46–54. The similarity between the Q story and the Johannine is due to a common oral tradition, not to a common literary source. As in the later story of the daughter of the Canaanite woman (15, 21–28) Jesus here breaks with his usual procedure of ministering only to Israelites and anticipates the mission to the Gentiles.

8, 5: A centurion: a military officer commanding a hundred men. He was probably in the service of Herod Antipas, tetrarch of Galilee; see the note on 14, 1.

x: 3, 10. *y:* Is 29, 13; Lk 6, 46. *z:* Lk 13, 26-27. *a:* 25, 11-12. *b:* Pss 5, 5; 6, 9. *c:* Lk 6, 47-49. *d:* Prv 10, 25. *e:* Mk 1, 22; Lk 4, 32. *f:* Mk 1, 40-44; Lk 5, 12-14. *g:* Lv 14, 2-32; Lk 17, 14. *h:* Lk 7, 1-10; Jn 4, 46-53.

approached him and appealed to him, [6]saying, "Lord, my servant is lying at home paralyzed, suffering dreadfully." [7]He said to him, "I will come and cure him." [8]*The centurion said in reply, "Lord, I am not worthy to have you enter under my roof; only say the word and my servant will be healed. [9]For I too am a person subject to authority, with soldiers subject to me. And I say to one, 'Go,' and he goes; and to another, 'Come here,' and he comes; and to my slave, 'Do this,' and he does it." [10]*When Jesus heard this, he was amazed and said to those following him, "Amen, I say to you, in no one in Israel have I found such faith. [11i]*I say to you, many will come from the east and the west, and will recline with Abraham, Isaac, and Jacob at the banquet in the kingdom of heaven, [12]but the children of the kingdom will be driven out into the outer darkness, where there will be wailing and grinding of teeth." [13]And Jesus said to the centurion, "You may go; as you have believed, let it be done for you." And at that very hour [his] servant was healed.

The Cure of Peter's Mother-in-Law. [14j]*Jesus entered the house of Peter, and saw his mother-in-law lying in bed with a fever. [15k]He touched her hand, the fever left her, and she rose and waited on him.

Other Healings [16]*When it was evening, they brought him many who were possessed by demons, and he drove out the spirits by a word and cured all the sick, [17l]*to fulfill what had been said by Isaiah the prophet:

"He took away our infirmities
    and bore our diseases."

The Would-be Followers of Jesus. [18m]*When Jesus saw a crowd around him, he gave orders to cross to the other side. [19n]*A scribe approached and said to him, "Teacher, I will follow you wherever you go." [20]*Jesus answered him, "Foxes have dens and birds of the sky have nests, but the Son of Man has nowhere to rest his head." [21]Another of [his] disciples said to him, "Lord, let me go first and bury my father." [22]*But Jesus answered him, "Follow me, and let the dead bury their dead."

The Calming of the Storm at Sea. [23o]*He got into a boat and his disciples followed him. [24]*Suddenly a violent storm came up on

---

8, 8–9: Acquainted by his position with the force of a command, the centurion expresses faith in the power of Jesus' mere word.

8, 10: **In no one in Israel:** there is good textual attestation (e.g., Codex Sinaiticus) for a reading identical with that of Lk 7, 9, "not even in Israel." But that seems to be due to a harmonization of Matthew with Luke.

8, 11–12: Matthew inserts into the story a Q saying (see Lk 13, 28–29) about the entrance of Gentiles into the kingdom and the exclusion of those Israelites who, though descended from the patriarchs and members of the chosen nation (**the children of the kingdom**), refused to believe in Jesus. **There will be wailing and grinding of teeth:** the first occurrence of a phrase used frequently in this gospel to describe final condemnation (13, 42.50; 22, 13; 24, 51; 25, 30). It is found elsewhere in the New Testament only in Lk 13, 28.

8, 14–15: Cf Mk 1, 29–31. Unlike Mark, Matthew has no implied request by others for the woman's cure. Jesus acts on his own initiative, and the cured woman rises and waits not on "them" (Mk 1, 31) but on **him.**

8, 16: **By a word:** a Matthean addition to Mk 1, 34; cf 8, 8.

8, 17: This fulfillment citation from Is 53, 4 follows the MT, not the LXX. The prophet speaks of the Servant of the Lord who suffers vicariously for the sins ("infirmities") of others; Matthew takes the **infirmities** as physical afflictions.

8, 18–22: This passage between the first and second series of miracles about following Jesus is taken from Q (see Lk 9, 57–62). The third of the three sayings found in the source is absent from Matthew.

8, 18: **The other side:** i.e., of the Sea of Galilee.

8, 19: **Teacher:** for Matthew, this designation of Jesus is true, for he has Jesus using it of himself (10, 24.25; 23, 8; 26, 18), yet when it is used of him by others they are either his opponents (9, 11; 12, 38; 17, 24; 22, 16.24.36) or, as here and in 19, 16, well-disposed persons who cannot see more deeply. Thus it reveals an inadequate recognition of who Jesus is.

8, 20: **Son of Man:** see the note on Mk 8, 31. This is the first occurrence in Mt of a term that appears in the New Testament only in sayings of Jesus, except for Acts 7, 56 and possibly 9, 6 (// Mk 2, 10; Lk 5, 24). In Mt it refers to Jesus in his ministry (seven times, as here), in his passion and resurrection (nine times, e.g., 17, 22), and in his glorious coming at the end of the age (thirteen times, e.g., 24, 30).

8, 22: **Let the dead bury their dead:** the demand of Jesus overrides what both the Jewish and the Hellenistic world regarded as a filial obligation of the highest importance. See the note on Lk 9, 60.

8, 23: **His disciples followed him:** the first miracle in the second group (8, 23—9, 8) is introduced by a verse that links it with the preceding sayings by the catchword "follow." In Mk the initiative in entering the boat is taken by the disciples (Mk 4, 35–41); here, Jesus enters first and the disciples follow.

8, 24: **Storm:** literally, "earthquake," a word commonly used in apocalyptic literature for the shaking of the old world

i: 13, 42.50; 22, 13; 24, 51; 25, 30; Lk 13, 28-29. *j*: Mk 1, 29-34; Lk 4, 38-41. *k*: 9, 25. *l*: Is 53, 4. *m*: Mk 4, 35. *n*: Lk 9, 57-60. *o*: Mk 4, 35-40; Lk 8, 22-25.

the sea, so that the boat was being swamped by waves; but he was asleep. *25 p**They came and woke him, saying, "Lord, save us! We are perishing!" *26**He said to them, "Why are you terrified, O you of little faith?" Then he got up, rebuked the winds and the sea, and there was great calm. *27*The men were amazed and said, "What sort of man is this, whom even the winds and the sea obey?"

The Healing of the Gadarene Demoniacs. *28q**When he came to the other side, to the territory of the Gadarenes, two demoniacs who were coming from the tombs met him. They were so savage that no one could travel by that road. *29**They cried out, "What have you to do with us, Son of God? Have you come here to torment us before the appointed time?" *30**Some distance away a herd of many swine was feeding. *31r*The demons pleaded with him, "If you drive us out, send us into the herd of swine." *32*And he said to them, "Go then!" They came out and entered the swine, and the whole herd rushed down the steep bank into the sea where they drowned. *33*The swineherds ran away, and when they came to the town they reported everything, including what had happened to the demoniacs. *34*Thereupon the whole town came out to meet Jesus, and when they saw him they begged him to leave their district.

CHAPTER 9

See RG 378–79

The Healing of a Paralytic. *1s**He entered a boat, made the crossing, and came into his own town. *2t*And there people brought to him a paralytic lying on a stretcher. When Jesus saw their faith, he said to the paralytic, "Courage, child, your sins are forgiven." *3**At that, some of the scribes said to themselves, "This man is blaspheming." *4*Jesus knew what they were thinking, and said, "Why do you harbor evil thoughts? *5*Which is easier, to say, 'Your sins are forgiven,' or to say, 'Rise and walk'? *6u**But that you may know that the Son of Man has authority on earth to forgive sins"—he then said to the paralytic, "Rise, pick up your stretcher, and go home." *7*He rose and went home. *8**When the crowds saw this they were struck with awe and glorified God who had given such authority to human beings.

The Call of Matthew. *9v**As Jesus passed

---

when God brings in his kingdom. All the synoptics use it in depicting the events preceding the parousia of the Son of Man (24, 7; Mk 13, 8; Lk 21, 11). Matthew has introduced it here and in his account of the death and resurrection of Jesus (27, 51–54; 28, 2).

8, 25: The reverent plea of the disciples contrasts sharply with their reproach of Jesus in Mk 4, 38.

8, 26: You of little faith: see the note on 6, 30. **Great calm:** Jesus' calming the sea may be meant to recall the Old Testament theme of God's control over the chaotic waters (Pss 65, 8; 89, 10; 93, 3–4; 107, 29).

8, 28: Gadarenes: this is the reading of Codex Vaticanus, supported by other important textual witnesses. The original reading of Codex Sinaiticus was Gazarines, later changed to Gergesenes, and a few versions have Gerasenes. Each of these readings points to a different territory connected, respectively, with the cities Gadara, Gergesa, and Gerasa (modern Jerash). There is the same confusion of readings in the parallel texts, Mk 5, 1 and Lk 8, 26; there the best reading seems to be "Gerasenes," whereas "Gadarenes" is probably the original reading in Mt. The town of Gadara was about five miles southeast of the Sea of Galilee, and Josephus (**Life** 9 §42) refers to it as possessing territory that lay on that sea. **Two demoniacs:** Mark (5, 1–20) has one.

8, 29: What have you to do with us?: see the note on Jn 2, 4. **Before the appointed time:** the notion that evil spirits were allowed by God to afflict human beings until the time of the final judgment is found in Enoch 16, 1 and Jubilees 10, 7–10.

8, 30: The tending of pigs, animals considered unclean by

Mosaic law (Lv 11, 6–7), indicates that the population was Gentile.

9, 1: His own town: Capernaum; see 4, 13.

9, 3: Scribes: see the note on Mk 2, 6. Matthew omits the reason given in the Marcan story for the charge of blasphemy: "Who but God alone can forgive sins?" (Mk 2, 7).

9, 6: It is not clear whether "But that you may know . . . to forgive sins" is intended to be a continuation of the words of Jesus or a parenthetical comment of the evangelist to those who would hear or read this gospel. In any case, Matthew here follows the Marcan text.

9, 8: Who had given such authority to human beings: a significant difference from Mk 2, 12 ("They . . . glorified God saying, 'We have never seen anything like this.' "). Matthew's extension to **human beings** of the authority to forgive sins points to the belief that such authority was being claimed by Matthew's church.

9, 9–17: In this section the order is the same as that of Mk 2, 13–22.

9, 9: A man named Matthew: Mark names this tax collector Levi (2, 14). No such name appears in the four lists of the twelve who were the closest companions of Jesus (10, 2–4; Mk 3, 16–19; Lk 6, 14–16; Acts 1, 13 [eleven, because of the defection of Judas Iscariot]), whereas all four list a Matthew, designated in 10, 3 as "the tax collector." The evan-

p: Ps 107, 28-29. *q:* Mk 5, 1-17; Lk 8, 26-37. *r:* Lk 4, 34.41. *s:* Mk 2, 3-12; Lk 5, 18-26. *t:* Lk 7, 48. *u:* Jn 5, 27. *v:* Mk 2, 14-17; Lk 5, 27-32.

on from there, he saw a man named Matthew sitting at the customs post. He said to him, "Follow me." And he got up and followed him. *10w**While he was at table in his house, many tax collectors and sinners came and sat with Jesus and his disciples. *11**The Pharisees saw this and said to his disciples, "Why does your teacher eat with tax collectors and sinners?" *12**He heard this and said, "Those who are well do not need a physician, but the sick do. *13x**Go and learn the meaning of the words, 'I desire mercy, not sacrifice.' I did not come to call the righteous but sinners."

The Question about Fasting. *14y*Then the disciples of John approached him and said, "Why do we and the Pharisees fast [much], but your disciples do not fast?" *15**Jesus answered them, "Can the wedding guests mourn as long as the bridegroom is with them? The days will come when the bridegroom is taken away from them, and then they will fast. *16**No one patches an old cloak with a piece of unshrunken cloth, for its fullness pulls away from the cloak and the tear gets worse. *17*People do not put new wine into old wineskins. Otherwise the skins burst, the wine spills out, and the

skins are ruined. Rather, they pour new wine into fresh wineskins, and both are preserved."

The Official's Daughter and the Woman with a Hemorrhage. *18z**While he was saying these things to them, an official came forward, knelt down before him, and said, "My daughter has just died. But come, lay your hand on her, and she will live." *19*Jesus rose and followed him, and so did his disciples. *20**A woman suffering hemorrhages for twelve years came up behind him and touched the tassel on his cloak. *21a*She said to herself, "If only I can touch his cloak, I shall be cured." *22*Jesus turned around and saw her, and said, "Courage, daughter! Your faith has saved you." And from that hour the woman was cured.

*23*When Jesus arrived at the official's house and saw the flute players and the crowd who were making a commotion, *24**he said, "Go away! The girl is not dead but sleeping." And they ridiculed him. *25*When the crowd was put out, he came and took her by the hand, and the little girl arose. *26*And news of this spread throughout all that land.

The Healing of Two Blind Men. *27bc**And

---

gelist may have changed the "Levi" of his source to **Matthew** so that this man, whose call is given special notice, like that of the first four disciples (4, 18–22), might be included among the twelve. Another reason for the change may be that the disciple Matthew was the source of traditions peculiar to the church for which the evangelist was writing.

9, 10: His house: it is not clear whether **his** refers to Jesus or Matthew. **Tax collectors:** see the note on 5, 46. Table association with such persons would cause ritual impurity.

9, 11: Teacher: see the note on 8, 19.

9, 12: See the note on Mk 2, 17.

9, 13: Go and learn . . . not sacrifice: Matthew adds the prophetic statement of Hos 6, 6 to the Marcan account (see also 12, 7). If mercy is superior to the temple sacrifices, how much more to the laws of ritual impurity.

9, 15: Fasting is a sign of mourning and would be as inappropriate at this time of joy, when Jesus is proclaiming the kingdom, as it would be at a marriage feast. Yet the saying looks forward to the time when Jesus will no longer be with the disciples visibly, the time of Matthew's church. **Then they will fast:** see **Didache** 8, 1.

9, 16–17: Each of these parables speaks of the unsuitability of attempting to combine the old and the new. Jesus' teaching is not a patching up of Judaism, nor can the gospel be contained within the limits of Mosaic law.

9, 18–34: In this third group of miracles, the first (18–26) is clearly dependent on Mark (Mk 5, 21–43). Though it tells of two miracles, the cure of the woman had already been in-

cluded within the story of the raising of the official's daughter, so that the two were probably regarded as a single unit. The other miracles seem to have been derived from Mark and Q respectively, though there Matthew's own editing is much more evident.

9, 18: Official: literally, "ruler." Mark calls him "one of the synagogue officials" (Mk 5, 22). **My daughter has just died:** Matthew heightens the Marcan "my daughter is at the point of death" (Mk 5, 23).

9, 20: Tassel: possibly "fringe." The Mosaic law prescribed that tassels be worn on the corners of one's garment as a reminder to keep the commandments (see Nm 15, 37–39; Dt 22, 12).

9, 24: Sleeping: sleep is a biblical metaphor for death (see Ps 87, 6 LXX; Dn 12, 2; 1 Thes 5, 10). Jesus' statement is not a denial of the child's real death, but an assurance that she will be roused from her sleep of death.

9, 27–31: This story was probably composed by Matthew out of Mark's story of the healing of a blind man named Bartimaeus (Mk 10, 46–52). Mark places the event late in Jesus' ministry, just before his entrance into Jerusalem, and Matthew has followed his Marcan source at that point in his gospel also (see 20, 29–34). In each of the Matthean stories the single blind man of Mark becomes two. The reason why

w: 11, 19; Lk 15, 1-2.   x: 12, 7; Hos 6, 6.   y: Mk 2, 18-22; Lk 5, 33-39.   z: Mk 5, 22-43; Lk 8, 41-56.   a: 14, 36; Nm 15, 37.
b: 20, 29-34.   c: 15, 22.

as Jesus passed on from there, two blind men followed [him], crying out, "Son of David, have pity on us!" ^{28}When he entered the house, the blind men approached him and Jesus said to them, "Do you believe that I can do this?" "Yes, Lord," they said to him. ^{29}Then he touched their eyes and said, "Let it be done for you according to your faith." ^{30}And their eyes were opened. Jesus warned them sternly, "See that no one knows about this." ^{31}But they went out and spread word of him through all that land.

The Healing of a Mute Person. ^{32d*}As they were going out, a demoniac who could not speak was brought to him, ^{33e}and when the demon was driven out the mute person spoke. The crowds were amazed and said, "Nothing like this has ever been seen in Israel." ^{34f*}But the Pharisees said, "He drives out demons by the prince of demons."

The Compassion of Jesus. ^{35g*}Jesus went around to all the towns and villages, teaching in their synagogues, proclaiming the gospel of the kingdom, and curing every disease and illness. ^{36h*}At the sight of the crowds, his heart was moved with pity for them because they were troubled and abandoned, like sheep without a shepherd. ^{37i*}Then he said to his disciples, "The harvest is abundant but the laborers are few; ^{38}so ask the master of the harvest to send out laborers for his harvest."

CHAPTER 10

See RG
379

The Mission of the Twelve. ^{1j*}Then he summoned his twelve disciples and gave them authority over unclean spirits to drive them out and to cure every disease and every illness. ^{2*}The names of the twelve apostles are these: first, Simon called Peter, and his brother Andrew; James, the son of Zebedee, and his brother John; ^{3}Philip and Bartholomew, Thomas and Matthew the tax collector; James, the son of Alphaeus, and Thaddeus; ^{4}Simon the Cananean, and Judas Iscariot who betrayed him.

The Commissioning of the Twelve. ^{5k*}Jesus sent out these twelve after instructing them

Matthew would have given a double version of the Marcan story and placed the earlier one here may be that he wished to add a story of Jesus' curing the blind at this point in order to prepare for Jesus' answer to the emissaries of the Baptist (11, 4–6) in which Jesus, recounting his works, begins with his giving sight to the blind.

9, 27: Son of David: this messianic title is connected once with the healing power of Jesus in Mark (10, 47–48) and Luke (18, 38–39) but more frequently in Matthew (see also 12, 23; 15, 22; 20, 30–31).

9, 32–34: The source of this story seems to be Q (see Lk 11, 14–15). As in the preceding healing of the blind, Matthew has two versions of this healing, the later in 12, 22–24 and earlier here.

9, 34: This spiteful accusation foreshadows the growing opposition to Jesus in chs 11 and 12.

9, 35: See the notes on 4, 23–25 and 8, 1—9, 38.

9, 36: See Mk 6, 34; Nm 27, 17; 1 Kgs 22, 17.

9, 37–38: This Q saying (see Lk 10, 2) is only imperfectly related to this context. It presupposes that only God (**the master of the harvest**) can take the initiative in sending out preachers of the gospel, whereas in Matthew's setting it leads into ch 10, where Jesus does so.

10, 1—11, 1: After an introductory narrative (10, 1–4), the second of the discourses of the gospel. It deals with the mission now to be undertaken by the disciples (5–15), but the perspective broadens and includes the missionary activity of the church between the time of the resurrection and the parousia.

10, 1: His twelve disciples: although, unlike Mark (3, 13–14) and Luke (6, 12–16), Matthew has no story of Jesus' choosing the Twelve, he assumes that the group is known to the reader. The earliest New Testament text to speak of it is

1 Cor 15, 5. The number probably is meant to recall the twelve tribes of Israel and implies Jesus' authority to call all Israel into the kingdom. While Luke (6, 13) and probably Mark (4, 10.34) distinguish between the Twelve and a larger group also termed disciples, Matthew tends to identify the disciples and the Twelve. **Authority . . . every illness:** activities the same as those of Jesus; see 4, 23; 9, 35; 10, 8. The Twelve also share in his proclamation of the kingdom (10, 7). But although he teaches (4, 23; 7, 28; 9, 35), they do not. Their commission to teach comes only after Jesus' resurrection, after they have been fully instructed by him (28, 20).

10, 2–4: Here, for the only time in Matthew, the Twelve are designated **apostles.** The word "apostle" means "one who is sent," and therefore fits the situation here described. In the Pauline letters, the place where the term occurs most frequently in the New Testament, it means primarily one who has seen the risen Lord and has been commissioned to proclaim the resurrection. With slight variants in Luke and Acts, the names of those who belong to this group are the same in the four lists given in the New Testament (see the note on 9, 9). **Cananean:** this represents an Aramaic word meaning "zealot." The meaning of that designation is unclear (see the note on Lk 6, 15).

10, 5–6: Like Jesus (15, 24), the Twelve are sent only to Israel. This saying may reflect an original Jewish Christian refusal of the mission to the Gentiles, but for Matthew it expresses rather the limitation that Jesus himself observed during his ministry.

d: 12, 22-24; Lk 11, 14-15. *e:* Mk 2, 12; 7, 37. *f:* 10, 25; Mk 3, 22. *g:* 4, 23; Lk 8, 1. *h:* Nm 27, 17; 1 Kgs 22, 17; Jer 50, 6; Ez 34, 5; Mk 6, 34. *i:* Lk 10, 2; Jn 4, 35. *j:* Mk 3, 14-19; Lk 6, 13-16; Acts 1, 13. *k:* Mk 6, 7-13; Lk 9, 1-6.

thus, "Do not go into pagan territory or enter a Samaritan town. [6l]Go rather to the lost sheep of the house of Israel. [7m]As you go, make this proclamation: 'The kingdom of heaven is at hand.' [8*]Cure the sick, raise the dead, cleanse lepers, drive out demons. Without cost you have received; without cost you are to give. [9n]Do not take gold or silver or copper for your belts; [10o]no sack for the journey, or a second tunic, or sandals, or walking stick. The laborer deserves his keep. [11p]Whatever town or village you enter, look for a worthy person in it, and stay there until you leave. [12]As you enter a house, wish it peace. [13*]If the house is worthy, let your peace come upon it; if not, let your peace return to you. [14q*]Whoever will not receive you or listen to your words—go outside that house or town and shake the dust from your feet. [15r]Amen, I say to you, it will be more tolerable for the land of Sodom and Gomorrah on the day of judgment than for that town.

Coming Persecutions. [16s]"Behold, I am sending you like sheep in the midst of wolves; so be shrewd as serpents and simple as doves. [17tu*]But beware of people, for they will hand you over to courts and scourge you in their synagogues, [18]and you will be led before governors and kings for my sake as a witness before them and the pagans. [19v]When they hand you over, do not worry about how you are to speak or what you are to say. You will be given at that moment what you are to say. [20]For it will not be you who speak but the Spirit of your Father speaking through you. [21w*]Brother will hand over brother to death, and the father his child; children will rise up against parents and have them put to death. [22*]You will be hated by all because of my name, but whoever endures to the end will be saved. [23*]When they persecute you in one town, flee to another. Amen, I say to you, you will not finish the towns of Israel before the Son of Man comes. [24x]No disciple is above his teacher, no slave above his master. [25*]It is enough for the disciple that he become like his teacher, for the slave that he become like his master. If they have called the master of the house Beelzebul, how much more those of his household!

Courage under Persecution. [26yz*]"Therefore do not be afraid of them. Nothing is concealed that will not be revealed, nor secret that will not be known. [27]What I say to you in the darkness, speak in the light; what you hear whispered, proclaim on the housetops. [28a]And do not be afraid of those who kill the body but cannot kill the soul; rather, be afraid of the one who can destroy both soul and body in Gehenna. [29]Are not two sparrows sold for a small coin? Yet not one of them falls to the ground without your Father's knowledge. [30]Even all the hairs of your head are counted. [31]So do not be afraid;

10, 8–11: The Twelve have received their own call and mission through God's gift, and the benefits they confer are likewise to be given freely. They are not to take with them money, provisions, or unnecessary clothing; their lodging and food will be provided by those who receive them.

10, 13: The greeting of peace is conceived of not merely as a salutation but as an effective word. If it finds no worthy recipient, it will return to the speaker.

10, 14: Shake the dust from your feet: this gesture indicates a complete disassociation from such unbelievers.

10, 17: The persecutions attendant upon the post-resurrection mission now begin to be spoken of. Here Matthew brings into the discourse sayings found in Mk 13, which deals with events preceding the parousia.

10, 21: See Mi 7, 6, which is cited in vv 35.36.

10, 22: To the end: the original meaning was probably "until the parousia." But it is not likely that Matthew expected no missionary disciples to suffer death before then, since he envisages the martyrdom of other Christians (21). For him, **the end** is probably that of the individual's life (see 28).

10, 23: Before the Son of Man comes: since the coming of the Son of Man at the end of the age had not taken place when this gospel was written, much less during the mission of the Twelve during Jesus' ministry, Matthew cannot have meant the coming to refer to the parousia. It is difficult to know what he understood it to be: perhaps the "proleptic parousia" of 28, 16–20, or the destruction of the temple in A.D. 70, viewed as a coming of Jesus in judgment on unbelieving Israel.

10, 25: Beelzebul: see 9, 34 for the charge linking Jesus with "the prince of demons," who is named **Beelzebul** in 12, 24. The meaning of the name is uncertain; possibly, "lord of the house."

10, 26: The **concealed** and **secret** coming of the kingdom is to be proclaimed by them, and no fear must be allowed to deter them from that proclamation.

l: 15, 24. *m:* 3, 2; 4, 17. *n:* Mk 6, 8-9; Lk 9, 3; 10, 4. *o:* Lk 10, 7; 1 Cor 9, 14; 2 Tm 5, 18. *p:* Mk 6, 10-11; Lk 9, 4-5; 10, 5-12. *q:* Acts 13, 51; 18, 6. *r:* 11, 24; Gn 19, 1-29; Jude 7. *s:* Lk 10, 3. *t:* Mk 13, 9-13; Lk 21, 12-19. *u:* Acts 5, 40. *v:* Ex 4, 11-12; Jer 1, 6-10; Lk 12, 11-12. *w:* 24, 9.13. *x:* Lk 6, 40; Jn 13, 16; 15, 20. *y:* Lk 12, 2-9. *z:* Mk 4, 22; Lk 8, 17; 1 Tm 5, 25. *a:* Jas 4, 12.

you are worth more than many sparrows. ³²*Everyone who acknowledges me before others I will acknowledge before my heavenly Father. ^{33b}But whoever denies me before others, I will deny before my heavenly Father.

Jesus: A Cause of Division. ^{34c}"Do not think that I have come to bring peace upon the earth. I have come to bring not peace but the sword. ³⁵For I have come to set

a man 'against his father,
a daughter against her mother,
and a daughter-in-law against her
mother-in-law;
³⁶   and one's enemies will be those of his
household.'

The Conditions of Discipleship. ^{37d}"Whoever loves father or mother more than me is not worthy of me, and whoever loves son or daughter more than me is not worthy of me; ³⁸*and whoever does not take up his cross and follow after me is not worthy of me. ^{39e}*Whoever finds his life will lose it, and whoever loses his life for my sake will find it.

Rewards. ^{40f}*"Whoever receives you receives me, and whoever receives me receives the one who sent me. ⁴¹*Whoever receives a prophet because he is a prophet will receive a prophet's reward, and whoever re-

ceives a righteous man because he is righteous will receive a righteous man's reward. ^{42g}And whoever gives only a cup of cold water to one of these little ones to drink because he is a disciple—amen, I say to you, he will surely not lose his reward."

CHAPTER 11

See RG 379-80

¹*When Jesus finished giving these commands to his twelve disciples, he went away from that place to teach and to preach in their towns.

IV: Opposition from Israel

The Messengers from John the Baptist. ^{2h}*When John heard in prison of the works of the Messiah, he sent his disciples to him ³*with this question, "Are you the one who is to come, or should we look for another?" ⁴Jesus said to them in reply, "Go and tell John what you hear and see: ⁵ⁱ*the blind regain their sight, the lame walk, lepers are cleansed, the deaf hear, the dead are raised, and the poor have the good news proclaimed to them. ⁶And blessed is the one who takes no offense at me."

Jesus' Testimony to John. ^{7j}*As they were going off, Jesus began to speak to the crowds

---

10, 32–33: In the Q parallel (Lk 12, 8–9), the Son of Man will acknowledge those who have acknowledged Jesus, and those who deny him will be denied (by the Son of Man) before the angels of God at the judgment. Here Jesus and the Son of Man are identified, and the acknowledgment or denial will be before his heavenly Father.

10, 38: The first mention of the cross in Matthew, explicitly that of the disciple, but implicitly that of Jesus (**and follow after me**). Crucifixion was a form of capital punishment used by the Romans for offenders who were not Roman citizens.

10, 39: One who denies Jesus in order to save one's earthly life will be condemned to everlasting destruction; loss of earthly life for Jesus' sake will be rewarded by everlasting life in the kingdom.

10, 40–42: All who receive the disciples of Jesus receive him, and God who sent him, and will be rewarded accordingly.

10, 41: **A prophet:** one who speaks in the name of God; here, the Christian prophets who proclaim the gospel. **Righteous man:** since righteousness is demanded of all the disciples, it is difficult to take the **righteous man** of this verse and **one of these little ones** (42) as indicating different groups within the followers of Jesus. Probably all three designations are used here of Christian missionaries as such.

11, 1: The closing formula of the discourse refers back to the original addressees, the Twelve.

11, 2—12, 50: The narrative section of the third book deals with the growing opposition to Jesus. It is largely devoted to disputes and attacks relating to faith and discipleship and thus contains much sayings-material, drawn in large part from Q.

11, 2: **In prison:** see 4, 12; 14, 1–12. **The works of the Messiah:** the deeds of chs 8–9.

11, 3: The question probably expresses a doubt of the Baptist that Jesus is **the one who is to come** (cf Mal 3, 1) because his mission has not been one of fiery judgment as John had expected (3, 2).

11, 5–6: Jesus' response is taken from passages of Isaiah (26, 19; 29, 18–19; 35, 5–6; 61, 1) that picture the time of salvation as marked by deeds such as those that Jesus is doing. The beatitude is a warning to the Baptist not to disbelieve because his expectations have not been met.

11, 7–19: Jesus' rebuke of John is counterbalanced by a reminder of the greatness of the Baptist's function (7–15) that is followed by a complaint about those who have heeded neither John nor Jesus (16–19).

b: Mk 8, 38; Lk 9, 26; 2 Tm 2, 12; Rv 3, 5.   *c:* Lk 12, 51-53.
d: 16, 24-25; Lk 14, 26-27.   *e:* Mk 8, 35; Lk 9, 24; Jn 12, 25.
f: Lk 10, 16; Jn 12, 44; 13, 20.   *g:* 25, 40; Mk 9, 41.   *h:* Lk 7, 18-28.   *i:* Is 26, 19; 29, 18-19; 35, 5-6; 61, 1.   *j:* 3, 3.5.

about John, "What did you go out to the desert to see? A reed swayed by the wind? [8]Then what did you go out to see? Someone dressed in fine clothing? Those who wear fine clothing are in royal palaces. [9]*Then why did you go out? To see a prophet? Yes, I tell you, and more than a prophet. [10k]This is the one about whom it is written:

'Behold, I am sending my messenger
  ahead of you;
 he will prepare your way before you.'

[11]*Amen, I say to you, among those born of women there has been none greater than John the Baptist; yet the least in the kingdom of heaven is greater than he. [12l]*From the days of John the Baptist until now, the kingdom of heaven suffers violence, and the violent are taking it by force. [13]*All the prophets and the law prophesied up to the time of John. [14m]And if you are willing to accept it, he is Elijah, the one who is to come. [15]Whoever has ears ought to hear.

[16n]*"To what shall I compare this generation? It is like children who sit in marketplaces and call to one another, [17]'We played the flute for you, but you did not dance, we sang a dirge but you did not mourn.' [18o]For John came neither eating nor drinking, and they said, 'He is possessed by a demon.'

[19p]The Son of Man came eating and drinking and they said, 'Look, he is a glutton and a drunkard, a friend of tax collectors and sinners.' But wisdom is vindicated by her works."

Reproaches to Unrepentant Towns. [20q]Then he began to reproach the towns where most of his mighty deeds had been done, since they had not repented. [21r]*"Woe to you, Chorazin! Woe to you, Bethsaida! For if the mighty deeds done in your midst had been done in Tyre and Sidon, they would long ago have repented in sackcloth and ashes. [22]But I tell you, it will be more tolerable for Tyre and Sidon on the day of judgment than for you. [23s]*And as for you, Capernaum:

'Will you be exalted to heaven?
 You will go down to the netherworld.'

For if the mighty deeds done in your midst had been done in Sodom, it would have remained until this day. [24t]But I tell you, it will be more tolerable for the land of Sodom on the day of judgment than for you."

The Praise of the Father. [25u]*At that time Jesus said in reply, "I give praise to you, Father, Lord of heaven and earth, for although you have hidden these things from the wise and the learned you have revealed them to the childlike. [26]Yes, Father, such has been

---

11, 9–10: In common Jewish belief there had been no prophecy in Israel since the last of the Old Testament prophets, Malachi. The coming of a new prophet was eagerly awaited, and Jesus agrees that John was such. Yet he was **more than a prophet,** for he was the precursor of the one who would bring in the new and final age. The Old Testament quotation is a combination of Mal 3, 1 and Ex 23, 20, with the significant change that the **before me** of Malachi becomes **before you.** The messenger now precedes not God, as in the original, but Jesus.

11, 11: John's preeminent greatness lies in his function of announcing the imminence of the kingdom (3, 1). But to be in the kingdom is so great a privilege that the least who has it is greater than the Baptist.

11, 12: The meaning of this difficult saying is probably that the opponents of Jesus are trying to prevent people from accepting the kingdom and to snatch it away from those who have received it.

11, 13: All the prophets and the law: Matthew inverts the usual order, "law and prophets," and says that both have **prophesied.** This emphasis on the prophetic character of the law points to its fulfillment in the teaching of Jesus and to the transitory nature of some of its commandments (see the note on 5, 17–20).

11, 16–19: See Lk 7, 31–35. The meaning of the parable

(16–17) and its explanation (18–19b) is much disputed. A plausible view is that the **children** of the parable are two groups, one of which proposes different entertainments to the other that will not agree with either proposal. The first represents John, Jesus, and their disciples; the second those who reject John for his asceticism and Jesus for his table association with those despised by the religiously observant. Verse 19c (**her works**) forms an inclusion with v 2 ("the works of the Messiah"). The original form of the saying is better preserved in Lk 7, 35, ". . . wisdom is vindicated by all her children." There John and Jesus are the children of Wisdom; here the works of Jesus the Messiah are those of divine Wisdom, of which he is the embodiment. Some important textual witnesses, however, have essentially the same reading as in Luke.

11, 21: Tyre and Sidon were pagan cities denounced for their wickedness in the Old Testament; cf Jl 4, 4–7.

11, 23: Capernaum's pride and punishment are described in language taken from the taunt song against the king of Babylon (Is 14, 13–15).

11, 25–27: This Q saying, identical with Lk 10, 21–22 ex-

k: Ex 23, 20; Mal 3, 1; Mk 1, 2; Lk 1, 76. l: Lk 16, 16. m: 17, 10-13; Mal 3, 23; Lk 1, 17. n: Lk 7, 31-35. o: Lk 1, 15. p: 9, 10-11. q: Lk 10, 12-15. r: Jl 4, 4-7. s: Is 14, 13-15. t: 10, 15. u: Lk 10, 21-22.

your gracious will. *27v* All things have been handed over to me by my Father. No one knows the Son except the Father, and no one knows the Father except the Son and anyone to whom the Son wishes to reveal him.

The Gentle Mastery of Christ. *28** "Come to me, all you who labor and are burdened, and I will give you rest. *29w** Take my yoke upon you and learn from me, for I am meek and humble of heart; and you will find rest for yourselves. *30* For my yoke is easy, and my burden light."

See RG 380

CHAPTER 12

Picking Grain on the Sabbath. *1xy** At that time Jesus was going through a field of grain on the sabbath. His disciples were hungry and began to pick the heads of grain and eat them. *2* When the Pharisees saw this, they said to him, "See, your disciples are doing what is unlawful to do on the sabbath." *3z** He said to them, "Have you not read what David did when he and his companions were hungry, *4a* how he went into the house of God and ate the bread of offering, which neither he nor his companions but only the priests could lawfully eat? *5b** Or have you not read in the law that on the sabbath the priests serving in the temple violate the sabbath and are innocent? *6* I say to you, something greater than the temple is here. *7c** If you knew what this meant, 'I desire mercy, not sacrifice,' you would not have condemned these innocent men. *8d** For the Son of Man is Lord of the sabbath."

The Man with a Withered Hand. *9e* Moving on from there, he went into their synagogue. *10** And behold, there was a man there who had a withered hand. They questioned him, "Is it lawful to cure on the sabbath?" so that they might accuse him. *11** He said to them, "Which one of you who has a sheep that falls into a pit on the sabbath will not take hold of it and lift it out? *12* How much more valuable a person is than a sheep. So it is lawful to do good on the sabbath." *13* Then he said to the man, "Stretch out your hand." He stretched it out, and it was restored as sound as the other. *14f** But the Pharisees went out and took counsel against him to put him to death.

cept for minor variations, introduces a joyous note into this section, so dominated by the theme of unbelief. While the **wise and the learned**, the scribes and Pharisees, have rejected Jesus' preaching and the significance of his mighty deeds, **the childlike** have accepted them. Acceptance depends upon the Father's revelation, but this is granted to those who are open to receive it and refused to the arrogant. Jesus can speak of all mysteries because he is **the Son** and there is perfect reciprocity of knowledge between him and the Father; what has been **handed over** to him is revealed only to those whom he wishes.

11, 28–29: These verses are peculiar to Matthew and are similar to Ben Sirach's invitation to learn wisdom and submit to her yoke (Sir 51, 23.26).

11, 28: Who labor and are burdened: burdened by the law as expounded by the scribes and Pharisees (23, 4).

11, 29: In place of the yoke of the law, complicated by scribal interpretation, Jesus invites the burdened to take the yoke of obedience to his word, under which they **will find rest;** cf Jer 6, 16.

12, 1–14: Matthew here returns to the Marcan order that he left in 9, 18. The two stories depend on Mk 2, 23–28 and 3, 1–6, respectively, and are the only places in either gospel that deal explicitly with Jesus' attitude toward sabbath observance.

12, 1–2: The picking of the heads of grain is here equated with reaping, which was forbidden on the sabbath (Ex 34, 21).

12, 3–4: See 1 Sm 21, 2–7. In the Marcan parallel (2, 25–26) the high priest is mistakenly called Abiathar, although in 1 Sm this action is attributed to Ahimelech. The Old Testament story is not about a violation of the sabbath rest; its pertinence to this dispute is that a violation of the law was permissible because of David's men being without food.

12, 5–6: This and the following argument (7) are peculiar to Matthew. The temple service seems to be the changing of the showbread on the sabbath (Lv 24, 8) and the doubling on the sabbath of the usual daily holocausts (Nm 28, 9–10). The argument is that the law itself requires work that breaks the sabbath rest, because of the higher duty of temple service. If temple duties outweigh the sabbath law, how much more does the presence of Jesus, with his proclamation of the kingdom (**something greater than the temple**), justify the conduct of his disciples.

12, 7: See the note on 9, 13.

12, 8: The ultimate justification for the disciples' violation of the sabbath rest is that Jesus, the Son of Man, has supreme authority over the law.

12, 10: Rabbinic tradition later than the gospels allowed relief to be given to a sufferer on the sabbath if life was in danger. This may also have been the view of Jesus' Pharisaic contemporaries. But the case here is not about one in danger of death.

12, 11: Matthew omits the question posed by Jesus in Mk 3, 4 and substitutes one about rescuing a sheep on the sabbath, similar to that in Lk 14, 5.

12, 14: See Mk 3, 6. Here the plan to bring about Jesus' death is attributed to the Pharisees only. This is probably due to the situation of Matthew's church, when the sole opponents were the Pharisees.

v: Jn 3, 35; 6, 46; 7, 28; 10, 15. *w:* Sir 51, 26; Jer 6, 16. *x:* Mk 2, 23-28; Lk 6, 1-5. *y:* Dt 23, 26. *z:* 1 Sm 21, 2-7. *a:* Lv 24, 5-9. *b:* Lv 24, 8; Nm 28, 9-10. *c:* Hos 6, 6. *d:* Jn 5, 16-17. *e:* Mk 3, 1-6; Lk 6, 6-11. *f:* Jn 5, 18.

The Chosen Servant. [15]*When Jesus realized this, he withdrew from that place. Many [people] followed him, and he cured them all, [16]but he warned them not to make him known. [17]This was to fulfill what had been spoken through Isaiah the prophet:

[18] g "Behold, my servant whom I have
    chosen,
  my beloved in whom I delight;
  I shall place my spirit upon him,
    and he will proclaim justice to the
      Gentiles.
[19] *He will not contend or cry out,
  nor will anyone hear his voice in the
    streets.
[20] A bruised reed he will not break,
  a smoldering wick he will not quench,
  until he brings justice to victory.
[21]   *And in his name the Gentiles will
    hope."

Jesus and Beelzebul. [22]h*Then they brought to him a demoniac who was blind and mute. He cured the mute person so that he could speak and see. [23]i*All the crowd was astounded, and said, "Could this perhaps be the Son of David?" [24]j*But when the Pharisees heard this, they said, "This man drives out demons only by the power of Beelzebul, the prince of demons." [25]k*But he knew what they were thinking and said to them, "Every kingdom divided against itself will be laid waste, and no town or house divided against itself will stand. [26]And if Satan drives out Satan, he is divided against himself; how, then, will his kingdom stand? [27]*And if I drive out demons by Beelzebul, by whom do your own people drive them out? Therefore they will be your judges. [28]l*But if it is by the Spirit of God that I drive out demons, then the kingdom of God has come upon you. [29]*How can anyone enter a strong man's house and steal his property, unless he first ties up the strong man? Then he can plunder his house. [30]m*Whoever is not with me is against me, and whoever does not gather with me scatters. [31]n*Therefore, I say to you, every sin and blasphemy will be forgiven people, but blasphemy against the Spirit will not be forgiven. [32]And whoever speaks a word against the Son of Man will be forgiven; but whoever speaks against the holy Spirit will not be forgiven, either in this age or in the age to come.

12, 15–21: Matthew follows Mk 3, 7–12 but summarizes his source in two verses (15.16) that pick up the withdrawal, the healings, and the command for silence. To this he adds a fulfillment citation from the first Servant Song (Is 42, 1–4) that does not correspond exactly to either the Hebrew or the LXX of that passage. It is the longest Old Testament citation in this gospel, emphasizing the meekness of Jesus, the Servant of the Lord, and foretelling the extension of his mission to the Gentiles.

12, 15: Jesus' knowledge of the Pharisees' plot and his healing **all** are peculiar to Matthew.

12, 19: The servant's not contending is seen as fulfilled in Jesus' withdrawal from the disputes narrated in 1–14.

12, 21: Except for a minor detail, Matthew here follows the LXX, although the meaning of the Hebrew ("the coastlands will wait for his teaching") is similar.

12, 22–32: For the exorcism, see the note on 9, 32–34. The long discussion combines Marcan and Q material (Mk 3, 22–30; Lk 11, 19–20.23; 12, 10). Mk 3, 20–21 is omitted, with a consequent lessening of the sharpness of 12, 48.

12, 23: See the note on 9, 27.

12, 24: See the note on 10, 25.

12, 25–26: Jesus' first response to the Pharisees' charge is that if it were true, Satan would be destroying his own kingdom.

12, 27: Besides pointing out the absurdity of the charge, Jesus asks how the work of Jewish exorcists (**your own people**) is to be interpreted. Are they, too, to be charged with collusion with Beelzebul? For an example of Jewish exorcism see Josephus, Antiquities 8, 2, 5 §§42–49.

12, 28: The Q parallel (Lk 11, 20) speaks of the "finger" rather than of the "spirit" of God. While the difference is probably due to Matthew's editing, he retains **the kingdom of God** rather than changing it to his usual "kingdom of heaven." **Has come upon you:** see 4, 17.

12, 29: A short parable illustrates what Jesus is doing. The **strong man** is Satan, whom Jesus has tied up and whose **house** he is plundering. Jewish expectation was that Satan would be chained up in the last days (Rv 20, 2); Jesus' exorcisms indicate that those days have begun.

12, 30: This saying, already attached to the preceding verses in Q (see Lk 11, 23), warns that there can be no neutrality where Jesus is concerned. Its pertinence in a context where Jesus is addressing not the neutral but the bitterly opposed is not clear. The accusation of scattering, however, does fit the situation. Jesus is the shepherd of God's people (2, 6), his mission is to the lost sheep of Israel (15, 24); the Pharisees, who oppose him, are guilty of scattering the sheep.

12, 31: **Blasphemy against the Spirit:** the sin of attributing to Satan (24) what is the work of the Spirit of God (28).

g: Is 42, 1-4. h: 9, 32-34; Lk 11, 14-15. i: 9, 27. j: 10, 25; Mk 3, 22. k: Mk 3, 23-27; Lk 11, 17-22. l: Lk 11, 20. m: Lk 11, 23. n: Mk 3, 28-30; Lk 12, 10.

A Tree and Its Fruits. ³³ᵒ*"Either declare the tree good and its fruit is good, or declare the tree rotten and its fruit is rotten, for a tree is known by its fruit. ³⁴ᵖ*You brood of vipers, how can you say good things when you are evil? For from the fullness of the heart the mouth speaks. ³⁵A good person brings forth good out of a store of goodness, but an evil person brings forth evil out of a store of evil. ³⁶�q*I tell you, on the day of judgment people will render an account for every careless word they speak. ³⁷By your words you will be acquitted, and by your words you will be condemned."

The Demand for a Sign. ³⁸ʳ*Then some of the scribes and Pharisees said to him, "Teacher, we wish to see a sign from you." ³⁹*He said to them in reply, "An evil and unfaithful generation seeks a sign, but no sign will be given it except the sign of Jonah the prophet. ⁴⁰*Just as Jonah was in the belly of the whale three days and three nights, so will the Son of Man be in the heart of the earth three days and three nights. ⁴¹*At the judgment, the men of Nineveh will arise with this generation and condemn it, because they repented at the preaching of Jonah; and there is something greater than Jonah here. ⁴²ˢAt the judgment the queen of the south will arise with this generation and condemn it, because she came from the ends of the earth to hear the wisdom of Solomon; and there is something greater than Solomon here.

The Return of the Unclean Spirit. ⁴³ᵗ*"When an unclean spirit goes out of a person it roams through arid regions searching for rest but finds none. ⁴⁴Then it says, 'I will return to my home from which I came.' But upon returning, it finds it empty, swept clean, and put in order. ⁴⁵Then it goes and brings back with itself seven other spirits more evil than itself, and they move in and dwell there; and the last condition of that person is worse than the first. Thus it will be with this evil generation."

The True Family of Jesus. ⁴⁶ᵘ*While he was still speaking to the crowds, his mother and his brothers appeared outside, wishing to speak with him. [⁴⁷*Someone told him, "Your mother and your brothers are standing outside, asking to speak with you."] ⁴⁸But he said in reply to the one who told him, "Who is my mother? Who are my brothers?" ⁴⁹And stretching out his hand toward his disciples, he said, "Here are my mother and my brothers. ⁵⁰For whoever does the will of my heavenly Father is my brother, and sister, and mother."

12, 33: Declare; literally, "make." The meaning of this verse is obscure. Possibly it is a challenge to the Pharisees either to declare Jesus and his exorcisms good or both of them bad. A tree is known by its fruit; if the fruit is good, so must the tree be. If the driving out of demons is good, so must its source be.

12, 34: The admission of Jesus' goodness cannot be made by the Pharisees, for they are evil, and the words that proceed from their evil hearts cannot be good.

12, 36–37: If on the day of judgment people will be held accountable for even their **careless** words, the vicious accusations of the Pharisees will surely lead to their condemnation.

12, 38–42: This section is mainly from Q (see Lk 11, 29–32). Mk 8, 11–12, which Matthew has followed in 16, 1–4, has a similar demand for a sign. The scribes and Pharisees refuse to accept the exorcisms of Jesus as authentication of his claims and demand a sign that will end all possibility of doubt. Jesus' response is that no such sign will be given. Because his opponents are evil and see him as an agent of Satan, nothing will convince them.

12, 38: Teacher: see the note on 8, 19. In 16, 1 the request is for a sign "from heaven" (Mk 8, 11).

12, 39: Unfaithful: literally, "adulterous." The covenant between God and Israel was portrayed as a marriage bond, and unfaithfulness to the covenant as adultery; cf Hos 2, 4–15; Jer 3, 6–10.

12, 40: See Jon 2, 1. While in Q the sign was simply Jo-

nah's preaching to the Ninevites (Lk 11, 30.32), Matthew here adds Jonah's sojourn **in the belly of the whale** for **three days and three nights,** a prefigurement of Jesus' sojourn in the abode of the dead and, implicitly, of his resurrection.

12, 41–42: The Ninevites who **repented** (see Jon 3, 1–10) **and the queen of the south** (i.e., of Sheba; see 1 Kgs 10, 1–13) were pagans who responded to lesser opportunities than have been offered to Israel in the ministry of Jesus, **something greater than Jonah** or **Solomon.** At the final judgment they will condemn the faithless **generation** that has rejected him.

12, 43–45: Another Q passage; cf 11, 24–26. Jesus' ministry has broken Satan's hold over Israel, but the refusal of **this evil generation** to accept him will lead to a worse situation than what preceded his coming.

12, 46–50: See Mk 3, 31–35. Matthew has omitted Mk 3, 20–21, which is taken up in Mk 3, 31 (see the note on 12, 22–32), yet the point of the story is the same in both gospels: natural kinship with Jesus counts for nothing; only one who **does the will** of **his heavenly Father** belongs to his true family.

12, 47: This verse is omitted in some important textual witnesses, including Codex Sinaiticus (original reading) and Codex Vaticanus.

---

o: Lk 6, 43-45. *p:* 3, 7; 23, 33; 15, 11-12; Lk 3, 7. *q:* Jas 3, 1-2. *r:* 16, 1-4; Jon 2, 1; 3, 1-10; Mk 8, 11-12; Lk 11, 29-32. *s:* 1 Kgs 10, 1-10. *t:* Lk 11, 24-26. *u:* Mk 3, 31-35; Lk 8, 19-21.

See RG
380

CHAPTER 13

The Parable of the Sower. [1v]*On that day, Jesus went out of the house and sat down by the sea. [2]Such large crowds gathered around him that he got into a boat and sat down, and the whole crowd stood along the shore. [3]*And he spoke to them at length in parables, saying: "A sower went out to sow. [4]And as he sowed, some seed fell on the path, and birds came and ate it up. [5]Some fell on rocky ground, where it had little soil. It sprang up at once because the soil was not deep, [6]and when the sun rose it was scorched, and it withered for lack of roots. [7]Some seed fell among thorns, and the thorns grew up and choked it. [8]But some seed fell on rich soil, and produced fruit, a hundred or sixty or thirtyfold. [9]Whoever has ears ought to hear."

The Purpose of Parables. [10]The disciples approached him and said, "Why do you speak to them in parables?" [11]*He said to them in reply, "Because knowledge of the mysteries of the kingdom of heaven has been granted to you, but to them it has not been granted. [12w]*To anyone who has, more will be given and he will grow rich; from anyone who has not, even what he has will be taken away. [13x]*This is why I speak to them in parables, because 'they look but do not see and hear but do not listen or understand.' [14y]Isaiah's prophecy is fulfilled in them, which says:

'You shall indeed hear but not understand,
    you shall indeed look but never see.
[15] Gross is the heart of this people,
    they will hardly hear with their ears,
    they have closed their eyes,
    lest they see with their eyes
    and hear with their ears
and understand with their heart and be
    converted,
    and I heal them.'

13, 1–53: The discourse in parables is the third great discourse of Jesus in Mt and constitutes the second part of the third book of the gospel. Matthew follows the Marcan outline (Mk 4, 1–35) but has only two of Mark's parables, the five others being from Q and M. In addition to the seven parables, the discourse gives the reason why Jesus uses this type of speech (10–15), declares the blessedness of those who understand his teaching (16–17), explains the parable of the sower (18–23) and of the weeds (36–43), and ends with a concluding statement to the disciples (51–52).

13, 3: In parables: the word "parable" (Greek **parabolē**) is used in the LXX to translate the Hebrew **māshāl**, a designation covering a wide variety of literary forms such as axioms, proverbs, similitudes, and allegories. In the New Testament the same breadth of meaning of the word is found, but there it primarily designates stories that are illustrative comparisons between Christian truths and events of everyday life. Sometimes the event has a strange element that is quite different from usual experience (e.g., in v 33, the enormous amount of dough in the parable of the yeast); this is meant to sharpen the curiosity of the hearer. If each detail of such a story is given a figurative meaning, the story is an allegory. Those who maintain a sharp distinction between parable and allegory insist that a parable has only one point of comparison, and that while parables were characteristic of Jesus' teaching, to see allegorical details in them is to introduce meanings that go beyond their original intention and even falsify it. However, to exclude any allegorical elements from a parable is an excessively rigid mode of interpretation, now abandoned by many scholars.

13, 3–8: Since in Palestine sowing often preceded plowing, much of the seed is scattered on ground that is unsuitable. Yet while much is wasted, the seed that falls on good ground bears fruit in extraordinarily large measure. The point of the parable is that, in spite of some failure because of opposition and indifference, the message of Jesus about the coming of the kingdom will have enormous success.

13, 11: Since a parable is figurative speech that demands reflection for understanding, only those who are prepared to explore its meaning can come to know it. To understand is a gift of God, granted to the disciples but not to the crowds. In Semitic fashion, both the disciples' understanding and the crowd's obtuseness are attributed to God. The question of human responsibility for the obtuseness is not dealt with, although it is asserted in v 13. **The mysteries:** as in Lk 8, 10; Mk 4, 11 has "the mystery." The word is used in Dn 2, 18.19.27 and in the Qumran literature (1QpHab 7, 8; 1QS 3, 23; 1QM 3, 9) to designate a divine plan or decree affecting the course of history that can be known only when revealed. **Knowledge of the mysteries of the kingdom of heaven** means recognition that the kingdom has become present in the ministry of Jesus.

13, 12: In the New Testament use of this axiom of practical "wisdom" (see 25, 29; Mk 4, 25; Lk 8, 18; 19, 26), the reference transcends the original level. God gives further understanding to one who accepts the revealed mystery; from the one who does not, he will take it away (note the "theological passive," **more will be given, what he has will be taken away**).

13, 13: Because 'they look . . . or understand': Matthew softens his Marcan source, which states that Jesus speaks in parables so that the crowds may not understand (Mk 4, 12), and makes such speaking a punishment given **because** they have not accepted his previous clear teaching. However, his citation of Is 6, 9–10 in v 14 supports the harsher Marcan view.

v: Mk 4, 1-12; Lk 8, 4-10.   *w:* 25, 29; Mk 4, 25; Lk 8, 18; 19, 26.
x: Jn 9, 39.   *y:* Is 6, 9-10; Jn 12, 40; Acts 28, 26-27; Rom 11, 8.

The Privilege of Discipleship. [16z]*"But blessed are your eyes, because they see, and your ears, because they hear. [17]Amen, I say to you, many prophets and righteous people longed to see what you see but did not see it, and to hear what you hear but did not hear it.

The Explanation of the Parable of the Sower. [18a]*"Hear then the parable of the sower. [19]The seed sown on the path is the one who hears the word of the kingdom without understanding it, and the evil one comes and steals away what was sown in his heart. [20]The seed sown on rocky ground is the one who hears the word and receives it at once with joy. [21]But he has no root and lasts only for a time. When some tribulation or persecution comes because of the word, he immediately falls away. [22]The seed sown among thorns is the one who hears the word, but then worldly anxiety and the lure of riches choke the word and it bears no fruit. [23]But the seed sown on rich soil is the one who hears the word and understands it, who indeed bears fruit and yields a hundred or sixty or thirtyfold."

The Parable of the Weeds among the Wheat. [24]*He proposed another parable to them. "The kingdom of heaven may be likened to a man who sowed good seed in his field. [25]*While everyone was asleep his enemy came and sowed weeds all through the wheat, and then went off. [26]When the crop grew and bore fruit, the weeds appeared as well. [27]The slaves of the householder came to him and said, 'Master, did you not sow good seed in your field? Where have the weeds come from?' [28]He answered, 'An enemy has done this.' His slaves said to him, 'Do you want us to go and pull them up?' [29]He replied, 'No, if you pull up the weeds you might uproot the wheat along with them. [30b]*Let them grow together until harvest; then at harvest time I will say to the harvesters, "First collect the weeds and tie them in bundles for burning; but gather the wheat into my barn." ' "

The Parable of the Mustard Seed. [31c]*He proposed another parable to them. "The kingdom of heaven is like a mustard seed that a person took and sowed in a field. [32d]*It is the smallest of all the seeds, yet when full-grown it is the largest of plants. It becomes a large bush, and the 'birds of the sky come and dwell in its branches.' "

The Parable of the Yeast. [33e]*He spoke to them another parable. "The kingdom of

13, 16–17: Unlike the unbelieving crowds, the disciples have seen that which the **prophets** and the **righteous** of the Old Testament **longed to see** without having their longing fulfilled.

13, 18–23: See Mk 4, 14–20; Lk 8, 11–15. In this explanation of the parable the emphasis is on the various types of soil on which the seed falls, i.e., on the dispositions with which the preaching of Jesus is received. The second and third types particularly are explained in such a way as to support the view held by many scholars that the explanation derives not from Jesus but from early Christian reflection upon apostasy from the faith that was the consequence of persecution and worldliness respectively. Others, however, hold that the explanation may come basically from Jesus even though it was developed in the light of later Christian experience. The four types of persons envisaged are (1) those who never accept **the word of the kingdom** (19); (2) those who believe for a while but fall away because of **persecution** (20–21); (3) those who believe, but in whom **the word** is choked by **worldly anxiety** and the seduction of **riches** (22); (4) those who respond to **the word** and produce **fruit** abundantly (23).

13, 24–30: This parable is peculiar to Matthew. The comparison in v 24 does not mean that **the kingdom of heaven may be likened** simply to the person in question but to the situation narrated in the whole story. The refusal of the **householder** to allow his **slaves** to separate **the wheat** from

the weeds while they are still growing is a warning to the disciples not to attempt to anticipate the final judgment of God by a definitive exclusion of sinners from the kingdom. In its present stage it is composed of the good and the bad. The judgment of God alone will eliminate the sinful. Until then there must be patience and the preaching of repentance.

13, 25: Weeds: darnel, a poisonous weed that in its first stage of growth resembles wheat.

13, 30: Harvest: a common biblical metaphor for the time of God's judgment; cf Jer 51, 33; Jl 4, 13; Hos 6, 11.

13, 31–33: See Mk 4, 30–32; Lk 13, 18–21. The parables of the mustard seed and the yeast illustrate the same point: the amazing contrast between the small beginnings of the kingdom and its marvelous expansion.

13, 32: See Dn 4, 7–9.17–19, where the birds nesting in the tree represent the people of Nebuchadnezzar's kingdom. See also Ez 17, 23 and 31, 6.

13, 33: Except in this Q parable and in 16, 12, **yeast** (or "leaven") is, in New Testament usage, a symbol of corruption (see 16, 6.11–12; Mk 8, 15; Lk 12, 1; 1 Cor 5, 6–8; Gal 5, 9). **Three measures:** an enormous amount, enough to feed a hundred people. The exaggeration of this element of the parable points to the greatness of the kingdom's effect.

z: Lk 10, 23-24; 1 Pt 1, 10-12. a: Mk 4, 13-20; Lk 8, 11-15. b: 3, 12. c: Mk 4, 30-32; Lk 13, 18-19. d: Ez 17, 23; 31, 6; Dn 4, 7-9.17-19. e: Lk 13, 20-21.

heaven is like yeast that a woman took and mixed with three measures of wheat flour until the whole batch was leavened."

The Use of Parables. *34f**All these things Jesus spoke to the crowds in parables. He spoke to them only in parables, *35g**to fulfill what had been said through the prophet:

"I will open my mouth in parables,
I will announce what has lain hidden
from the foundation [of the
world]."

The Explanation of the Parable of the Weeds. *36**Then, dismissing the crowds, he went into the house. His disciples approached him and said, "Explain to us the parable of the weeds in the field." *37**He said in reply, "He who sows good seed is the Son of Man, *38**the field is the world, the good seed the children of the kingdom. The weeds are the children of the evil one, *39**and the enemy who sows them is the devil. The harvest is the end of the age, and the harvesters are angels. *40*Just as weeds are collected and burned [up] with fire, so will it be at the end of the age. *41**The Son of Man will send his angels, and they will collect out of his king-

dom all who cause others to sin and all evildoers. *42h*They will throw them into the fiery furnace, where there will be wailing and grinding of teeth. *43i**Then the righteous will shine like the sun in the kingdom of their Father. Whoever has ears ought to hear.

More Parables. *44j**"The kingdom of heaven is like a treasure buried in a field, which a person finds and hides again, and out of joy goes and sells all that he has and buys that field. *45*Again, the kingdom of heaven is like a merchant searching for fine pearls. *46*When he finds a pearl of great price, he goes and sells all that he has and buys it. *47*Again, the kingdom of heaven is like a net thrown into the sea, which collects fish of every kind. *48*When it is full they haul it ashore and sit down to put what is good into buckets. What is bad they throw away. *49*Thus it will be at the end of the age. The angels will go out and separate the wicked from the righteous *50*and throw them into the fiery furnace, where there will be wailing and grinding of teeth.

Treasures New and Old. *51**"Do you understand all these things?" They answered, "Yes." *52**And he replied, "Then every scribe

13, 34: **Only in parables:** see vv 10–15.

13, 35: **The prophet:** some textual witnesses read "Isaiah the prophet." The quotation is actually from Ps 78, 2; the first line corresponds to the LXX text of the psalm. The psalm's title ascribes it to Asaph, the founder of one of the guilds of temple musicians. He is called "the prophet" (NAB "the seer") in 2 Chr 29, 30, but it is doubtful that Matthew averted to that; for him, any Old Testament text that could be seen as fulfilled in Jesus was prophetic.

13, 36: **Dismissing the crowds:** the return of Jesus to the house marks a break with the crowds, who represent unbelieving Israel. From now on his attention is directed more and more to his disciples and to their instruction. The rest of the discourse is addressed to them alone.

13, 37–43: In the explanation of the parable of the weeds emphasis lies on the fearful end of the wicked, whereas the parable itself concentrates on patience with them until judgment time.

13, 38: **The field is the world:** this presupposes the resurrection of Jesus and the granting to him of "all power in heaven and on earth" (28, 18).

13, 39: **The end of the age:** this phrase is found only in Mt (13, 40.49; 24, 3; 28, 20).

13, 41: **His kingdom:** the **kingdom** of the **Son of Man** is distinguished from that of the Father (43); see 1 Cor 15, 24–25. The church is the place where Jesus' kingdom is manifested, but his royal authority embraces the entire world; see the note on 13, 38.

13, 43: See Dn 12, 3.

13, 44–50: The first two of the last three parables of the discourse have the same point. The **person** who **finds** a buried **treasure** and the **merchant** who finds a **pearl of great price** sell **all** that they have to acquire these finds; similarly, the one who understands the supreme value of the kingdom gives up whatever he must to obtain it. The **joy** with which this is done is made explicit in the first parable, but it may be presumed in the second also. The concluding parable of the fishnet resembles the explanation of the parable of the weeds with its stress upon the final exclusion of evil persons from the kingdom.

13, 44: In the unsettled conditions of Palestine in Jesus' time, it was not unusual to guard valuables by burying them in the ground.

13, 51: Matthew typically speaks of the understanding of the disciples.

13, 52: Since Matthew tends to identify the disciples and the Twelve (see the note on 10, 1), this saying about the Christian **scribe** cannot be taken as applicable to all who accept the message of Jesus. While the Twelve are in many ways representative of all who believe in him, they are also distinguished from them in certain respects. The church of Matthew has leaders among whom are a group designated as "scribes" (23, 34). Like the scribes of Israel, they are teachers. It is the Twelve and these their later counterparts to whom

f: Mk 4, 33-34. *g:* Ps 78, 2. *h:* 8, 12; Rv 21, 8. *i:* Dn 12, 3. *j:* Prv 2, 4; 4, 7.

who has been instructed in the kingdom of heaven is like the head of a household who brings from his storeroom both the new and the old." [53]When Jesus finished these parables, he went away from there.

V: Jesus, the Kingdom, and the Church

The Rejection at Nazareth. [54kl*]He came to his native place and taught the people in their synagogue. They were astonished and said, "Where did this man get such wisdom and mighty deeds? [55m]Is he not the carpenter's son? Is not his mother named Mary and his brothers James, Joseph, Simon, and Judas? [56]Are not his sisters all with us? Where did this man get all this?" [57n]And they took offense at him. But Jesus said to them, "A prophet is not without honor except in his native place and in his own house." [58]And he did not work many mighty deeds there because of their lack of faith.

CHAPTER 14

See RG
380-81 **Herod's Opinion of Jesus.** [1opq*]At that time Herod the tetrarch heard of the reputation of Jesus [2]and said to his servants, "This man is John the Baptist. He has been raised from the dead; that is why mighty powers are at work in him."

The Death of John the Baptist. [3r*]Now Herod had arrested John, bound [him], and put him in prison on account of Herodias, the wife of his brother Philip, [4s]for John had said to him, "It is not lawful for you to have her." [5t]Although he wanted to kill him, he feared the people, for they regarded him as a prophet. [6]But at a birthday celebration for Herod, the daughter of Herodias performed a dance before the guests and delighted Herod [7]so much that he swore to give her whatever she might ask for. [8]Prompted by her mother, she said, "Give me here on a platter the head of John the Baptist." [9]The king was distressed, but because of his oaths and the guests who were present, he ordered that it be given, [10]and he had John beheaded in the prison. [11]His head was brought in on a platter and given to the girl, who took it to her mother. [12]His disciples came and took away the corpse and buried him; and they went and told Jesus.

The Return of the Twelve and the Feeding of the Five Thousand. [13u*]When Jesus heard

---

this verse applies. The **scribe . . . instructed in the kingdom of heaven** knows both the teaching of Jesus (**the new**) and the law and prophets (**the old**) and provides in his own teaching **both the new and the old** as interpreted and fulfilled by **the new.** On the translation **head of a household** (for the same Greek word translated **householder** in v 27), see the note on 24, 45–51.

13, 54—17, 27: This section is the narrative part of the fourth book of the gospel.

13, 54–58: After the Sermon on the Mount the crowds are in admiring astonishment at Jesus' teaching (7, 28); here the astonishment is of those who take **offense at him.** Familiarity with his background and family leads them to regard him as pretentious. Matthew modifies his Marcan source (6, 1–6). Jesus is not the carpenter but **the carpenter's son** (55), "and among his own kin" is omitted (57), **he did not work many mighty deeds** in face of such unbelief (58) rather than the Marcan ". . . he was not able to perform any mighty deed there" (6, 5), and there is no mention of his amazement at his townspeople's lack of faith.

14, 1–12: The murder of the Baptist by Herod Antipas prefigures the death of Jesus (see 17, 12). The Marcan source (6, 14–29) is much reduced and in some points changed. In Mk Herod reveres John as a holy man and the desire to kill him is attributed to Herodias (6, 19.20), whereas here that desire is Herod's from the beginning (5).

14, 1: Herod the tetrarch: Herod Antipas, son of Herod the Great. When the latter died, his territory was divided among three of his surviving sons, Archelaus who received half of it (2, 23), Herod Antipas who became ruler of Galilee and Perea, and Philip who became ruler of northern Transjordan. Since he received a quarter of his father's domain, Antipas is accurately designated **tetrarch** ("ruler of a fourth [part]", although in v 9 Matthew repeats the "king" of his Marcan source (6, 26).

14, 3: Herodias was not the wife of Herod's half-brother Philip but of another half-brother, Herod Boethus. The union was prohibited by Lv 18, 16; 20, 21. According to Josephus (**Antiquities** 18, 5, 2 §§116–19), Herod imprisoned and then executed John because he feared that the Baptist's influence over the people might enable him to lead a rebellion.

14, 13–21: The feeding of the five thousand is the only miracle of Jesus that is recounted in all four gospels. The principal reason for that may be that it was seen as anticipating the Eucharist and the final banquet in the kingdom (8, 11; 26, 29), but it looks not only forward but backward, to the feeding of Israel with manna in the desert at the time of the Exodus (Ex 16), a miracle that in some contemporary Jewish expectation would be repeated in the messianic age (2 Baruch 29, 8). It may also be meant to recall Elisha's feeding a hundred dred men with small provisions (2 Kgs 4, 42–44).

k: Mk 6, 1-6; Lk 4, 16-30. *l:* 2, 23; Jn 1, 46; 7, 15. *m:* 12, 46; 27, 56; Jn 6, 42. *n:* Jn 4, 44. *o:* Mk 6, 14-29. *p:* Lk 3, 1. *q:* Lk 9, 7-9. *r:* Lk 3, 19-20. *s:* Lv 18, 16; 20, 21. *t:* 21, 26. *u:* 15, 32-38; Mk 6, 32-44; Lk 9, 10-17; Jn 6, 1-13.

of it, he withdrew in a boat to a deserted place by himself. The crowds heard of this and followed him on foot from their towns. [14]When he disembarked and saw the vast crowd, his heart was moved with pity for them, and he cured their sick. [15]When it was evening, the disciples approached him and said, "This is a deserted place and it is already late; dismiss the crowds so that they can go to the villages and buy food for themselves." [16][Jesus] said to them, "There is no need for them to go away; give them some food yourselves." [17]But they said to him, "Five loaves and two fish are all we have here." [18]Then he said, "Bring them here to me," [19*]and he ordered the crowds to sit down on the grass. Taking the five loaves and the two fish, and looking up to heaven, he said the blessing, broke the loaves, and gave them to the disciples, who in turn gave them to the crowds. [20*]They all ate and were satisfied, and they picked up the fragments left over—twelve wicker baskets full. [21]Those who ate were about five thousand men, not counting women and children.

The Walking on the Water. [22v*]Then he made the disciples get into the boat and precede him to the other side, while he dismissed the crowds. [23w]After doing so, he went up on the mountain by himself to pray. When it was evening he was there alone. [24]Meanwhile the boat, already a few miles offshore, was being tossed about by the waves, for the wind was against it. [25*]During the fourth watch of the night, he came toward them, walking on the sea. [26]When the disciples saw him walking on the sea they were terrified. "It is a ghost," they said, and they cried out in fear. [27*]At once [Jesus] spoke to them, "Take courage, it is I; do not be afraid." [28]Peter said to him in reply, "Lord, if it is you, command me to come to you on the water." [29]He said, "Come." Peter got out of the boat and began to walk on the water toward Jesus. [30x]But when he saw how [strong] the wind was he became frightened; and, beginning to sink, he cried out, "Lord, save me!" [31*]Immediately Jesus stretched out his hand and caught him, and said to him, "O you of little faith, why did you doubt?" [32]After they got into the boat, the wind died down. [33y*]Those who were in the boat did him homage, saying, "Truly, you are the Son of God."

The Healings at Gennesaret. [34z]After making the crossing, they came to land at Gennesaret. [35]When the men of that place recognized him, they sent word to all the surrounding country. People brought to him all those who were sick [36a]and begged him that they might touch only the tassel on his cloak, and as many as touched it were healed.

CHAPTER 15

See RG 380–81

The Tradition of the Elders. [1b*]Then Pharisees and scribes came to Jesus from

---

14, 19: The **taking,** saying the blessing, breaking, and giving to the disciples correspond to the actions of Jesus over the bread at the Last Supper (26, 26). Since they were usual at any Jewish meal, that correspondence does not necessarily indicate a eucharistic reference here. Matthew's silence about Jesus' dividing the fish among the people (Mk 6, 41) is perhaps more significant in that regard.

14, 20: The **fragments left over:** as in Elisha's miracle, food was **left over** after all had been fed. The word **fragments** (Greek **klasmata**) is used, in the singular, of the broken bread of the Eucharist in **Didache** 9, 3–4.

14, 22–33: The disciples, laboring against the turbulent sea, are saved by Jesus. For his power over the waters, see the note on 8, 26. Here that power is expressed also by his **walking on the sea** (25; cf Ps 77, 20; Jb 9, 8). Matthew has inserted into the Marcan story (Mk 6, 45–52) material that belongs to his special traditions on Peter (28–31).

14, 25: The **fourth watch of the night:** between 3 a.m. and 6 a.m. The Romans divided the twelve hours between 6 p.m. and 6 a.m. into four equal parts called "watches."

14, 27: **It is I:** see the note on Mk 6, 50.

14, 31: **You of little faith:** see the note on 6, 30. **Why did you doubt?:** the verb is peculiar to Matthew and occurs elsewhere only in 28, 17.

14, 33: This confession is in striking contrast to the Marcan parallel (6, 51) where the disciples are "completely astounded."

15, 1–20: This dispute begins with the question of the Pharisees and scribes why Jesus' disciples are breaking **the tradition of the elders** about washing one's hands before eating (2). Jesus' counterquestion accuses his opponents of breaking **the commandment of God for the sake of their tradition** (3) and illustrates this by their interpretation of the commandment of the Decalogue concerning parents (4–6). Denouncing them as hypocrites, he applies to them a derogatory prophecy of Isaiah (7–8). Then with a wider audience (**the crowd,** 10) he goes beyond the violation of tradition with which the dispute has started. The parable (11) is an attack on the Mosaic law concerning clean and unclean foods, similar

---

v: Mk 6, 45-52; Jn 6, 16-21. *w:* Mk 1, 35; Lk 5, 16; 6, 12. *x:* 8, 25-26. *y:* 16, 16. *z:* Mk 6, 53-56. *a:* 9, 20-22. *b:* Mk 7, 1-23.

Jerusalem and said, ^{2c}*"Why do your disciples break the tradition of the elders? They do not wash [their] hands when they eat a meal." ³*He said to them in reply, "And why do you break the commandment of God for the sake of your tradition? ^{4d}For God said, 'Honor your father and your mother,' and 'Whoever curses father or mother shall die.' ⁵*But you say, 'Whoever says to father or mother, "Any support you might have had from me is dedicated to God," ⁶need not honor his father.' You have nullified the word of God for the sake of your tradition. ⁷Hypocrites, well did Isaiah prophesy about you when he said:

^{8 e}*'This people honors me with their lips,
        but their hearts are far from me;
^{9 f}in vain do they worship me,
    teaching as doctrines human
            precepts.' "

^{10g}He summoned the crowd and said to them, "Hear and understand. ¹¹It is not what enters one's mouth that defiles that person; but what comes out of the mouth is what defiles one." ¹²Then his disciples approached and said to him, "Do you know that the Pharisees took offense when they heard what you said?" ¹³*He said in reply, "Every plant that my heavenly Father has not planted will be uprooted. ^{14h}Let them alone; they are blind guides [of the blind]. If a blind person leads a blind person,

both will fall into a pit." ¹⁵*Then Peter said to him in reply, "Explain [this] parable to us." ¹⁶He said to them, "Are even you still without understanding? ¹⁷Do you not realize that everything that enters the mouth passes into the stomach and is expelled into the latrine? ¹⁸ⁱBut the things that come out of the mouth come from the heart, and they defile. ¹⁹*For from the heart come evil thoughts, murder, adultery, unchastity, theft, false witness, blasphemy. ²⁰These are what defile a person, but to eat with unwashed hands does not defile."

The Canaanite Woman's Faith. ^{21 j}*Then Jesus went from that place and withdrew to the region of Tyre and Sidon. ²²And behold, a Canaanite woman of that district came and called out, "Have pity on me, Lord, Son of David! My daughter is tormented by a demon." ²³But he did not say a word in answer to her. His disciples came and asked him, "Send her away, for she keeps calling out after us." ²⁴*He said in reply, "I was sent only to the lost sheep of the house of Israel." ^{25k}But the woman came and did him homage, saying, "Lord, help me." ²⁶*He said in reply, "It is not right to take the food of the children and throw it to the dogs." ²⁷She said, "Please, Lord, for even the dogs eat the scraps that fall from the table of their masters." ^{28 l}*Then Jesus said to her in reply, "O woman, great is your

---

to those antitheses that abrogate the law (5, 31–32.33–34.38–39). After a warning to his disciples not to follow the moral guidance of the Pharisees (13–14), he explains the **parable (15)** to them, saying that defilement comes not from what **enters the mouth** (17) but from the evil thoughts and deeds that rise from within, **from the heart** (18–20). The last verse returns to the starting point of the dispute (eating **with unwashed hands**). Because of Matthew's omission of Mk 7, 19b, some scholars think that Matthew has weakened the Marcan repudiation of the Mosaic food laws. But that half verse is ambiguous in the Greek, which may be the reason for its omission here.

15, 2: The tradition of the elders: see the note on Mk 7, 5. The purpose of the handwashing was to remove defilement caused by contact with what was ritually unclean.

15, 3–4: For the commandment see Ex 20, 12 (// Dt 5, 16); 21, 17. The honoring of one's parents had to do with supporting them in their needs.

15, 5: See the note on Mk 7, 11.

15, 8: The text of Is 29, 13 is quoted approximately according to the Septuagint.

15, 13–14: Jesus leads his disciples away from the teaching authority of the Pharisees.

15, 15: Matthew specifies **Peter** as the questioner, unlike Mk 7, 17. Given his tendency to present the disciples as more understanding than in his Marcan source, it is noteworthy that here he retains the Marcan rebuke, although in a slightly milder form. This may be due to his wish to correct the Jewish Christians within his church who still held to the food laws and thus separated themselves from Gentile Christians who did not observe them.

15, 19: The Marcan list of thirteen things that defile (7, 21–22) is here reduced to seven that partially cover the content of the Decalogue.

15, 21–28: See the note on 8, 5–13.

15, 24: See the note on 10, 5–6.

15, 26: The children: the people of Israel. **Dogs:** see the note on 7, 6.

15, 28: As in the case of the cure of the centurion's servant (8, 10), Matthew ascribes Jesus' granting the request to the woman's **great faith,** a point not made equally explicit in the Marcan parallel (7, 24–30).

c: Lk 11, 38. d: Ex 20, 12; 21, 17; Lv 20, 9; Dt 5, 16; Prv 20, 20. e: Is 29, 13 LXX. f: Col 2, 23. g: Mk 7, 14. h: 23, 16.19.24; Lk 6, 39; Jn 9, 40. i: 12, 34. j: Mk 7, 24-30. k: 10, 6. l: 8, 10.

faith! Let it be done for you as you wish." And her daughter was healed from that hour.

The Healing of Many People. [29]Moving on from there Jesus walked by the Sea of Galilee, went up on the mountain, and sat down there. [30m]Great crowds came to him, having with them the lame, the blind, the deformed, the mute, and many others. They placed them at his feet, and he cured them. [31]The crowds were amazed when they saw the mute speaking, the deformed made whole, the lame walking, and the blind able to see, and they glorified the God of Israel.

The Feeding of the Four Thousand. [32n]Jesus summoned his disciples and said, "My heart is moved with pity for the crowd, for they have been with me now for three days and have nothing to eat. I do not want to send them away hungry, for fear they may collapse on the way." [33]The disciples said to him, "Where could we ever get enough bread in this deserted place to satisfy such a crowd?" [34]Jesus said to them, "How many loaves do you have?" "Seven," they replied, "and a few fish." [35]He ordered the crowd to sit down on the ground. [36]Then he took the seven loaves and the fish, gave thanks, broke the loaves, and gave them to the disciples, who in turn gave them to the crowds. [37o]They all ate and were satisfied. They picked up the fragments left over—seven baskets full. [38]Those who ate were four thousand men, not counting women and children. [39]And when he had dismissed the crowds, he got into the boat and came to the district of Magadan.

CHAPTER 16

See RG 381–82

The Demand for a Sign. [1p]The Pharisees and Sadducees came and, to test him, asked him to show them a sign from heaven. [2]He said to them in reply, "[In the evening you say, 'Tomorrow will be fair, for the sky is red'; [3q]and, in the morning, 'Today will be stormy, for the sky is red and threatening.' You know how to judge the appearance of the sky, but you cannot judge the signs of the times.] [4r]An evil and unfaithful generation seeks a sign, but no sign will be given it except the sign of Jonah." Then he left them and went away.

The Leaven of the Pharisees and Sadducees. [5s]In coming to the other side of the sea, the disciples had forgotten to bring bread. [6t]Jesus said to them, "Look out, and beware of the leaven of the Pharisees and Sadducees." [7]They concluded among themselves, saying, "It is because we have brought no bread." [8]When Jesus became aware of this he said, "You of little faith, why do you conclude among yourselves that it is because you have no bread? [9u]Do you not yet understand, and do you not remember the five loaves for the five thousand, and how many wicker baskets you took up? [10v]Or the seven loaves for the four thousand, and how many baskets you took up? [11]How do you not comprehend that I was not speaking to you about bread? Beware of the

15, 32–39: Most probably this story is a doublet of that of the feeding of the five thousand (14, 13–21). It differs from it notably only in that Jesus takes the initiative, not the disciples (32), and in the numbers: the crowd has been with Jesus **three days** (32), **seven loaves** are multiplied (36), **seven baskets** of **fragments** remain after the feeding (37), and **four thousand** men are fed (38).

15, 36: **Gave thanks:** see 14, 19, "said the blessing." There is no difference in meaning. The thanksgiving was a blessing of God for his benefits.

16, 1: **A sign from heaven:** see the note on 12, 38–42.

16, 2–3: The answer of Jesus in these verses is omitted in many important textual witnesses, and it is very uncertain that it is an original part of this gospel. It resembles Lk 12, 54–56 and may have been inserted from there. It rebukes the Pharisees and Sadducees who are able to read indications of coming weather but not the indications of the coming kingdom in the signs that Jesus does offer, his mighty deeds and teaching.

16, 4: See the notes on 12, 39.40.

16, 5–12: Jesus' warning his disciples against **the teaching of the Pharisees and Sadducees** comes immediately before his promise to confer on Peter the authority to bind and to loose on earth (19), an authority that will be confirmed in heaven. Such authority most probably has to do, at least in part, with teaching. The rejection of the teaching authority of the Pharisees (see also 12, 12–14) prepares for a new one derived from Jesus.

16, 6: **Leaven:** see the note on 13, 33. **Sadducees:** Matthew's Marcan source speaks rather of "the leaven of Herod" (8, 15).

16, 7–11: The disciples, men **of little faith,** misunderstand Jesus' metaphorical use of **leaven,** forgetting that, as the feeding of the crowds shows, he is not at a loss to provide them with bread.

m: Is 35, 5-6. n: Mk 8, 1-10. o: 16, 10. p: Mk 8, 11-21. q: Lk 12, 54-56. r: 12, 39; Jon 2, 1. s: Mk 8, 14-21. t: Lk 12, 1. u: 14, 17-21; Jn 6, 9. v: 15, 34-38.

leaven of the Pharisees and Sadducees." *12**Then they understood that he was not telling them to beware of the leaven of bread, but of the teaching of the Pharisees and Sadducees.

Peter's Confession about Jesus. *13w**When Jesus went into the region of Caesarea Philippi he asked his disciples, "Who do people say that the Son of Man is?" *14x**They replied, "Some say John the Baptist, others Elijah, still others Jeremiah or one of the prophets." *15*He said to them, "But who do you say that I am?" *16y**Simon Peter said in reply, "You are the Messiah, the Son of the living God." *17**Jesus said to him in reply, "Blessed are you, Simon son of Jonah. For flesh and blood has not revealed this to you, but my heavenly Father. *18z**And so I say to you, you are Peter, and upon this rock I will build my church, and the gates of the netherworld shall not prevail against it. *19a**I will give you the keys to the kingdom of heaven.

16, 12: After his rebuke, the disciples understand that by **leaven** he meant the corrupting influence of the **teaching of the Pharisees and Sadducees.** The evangelist probably understands this **teaching** as common to both groups. Since at the time of Jesus' ministry the two differed widely on points of teaching, e.g., the resurrection of the dead, and at the time of the evangelist the Sadducee party was no longer a force in Judaism, the supposed common **teaching** fits neither period. The disciples' eventual understanding of Jesus' warning contrasts with their continuing obtuseness in the Marcan parallel (8, 14–21).

16, 13–20: The Marcan confession of Jesus as Messiah, made by Peter as spokesman for the other disciples (8, 27–29; cf also Lk 9, 18–20), is modified significantly here. The confession is of Jesus both as **Messiah** and as **Son of the living God** (16). Jesus' response, drawn principally from material peculiar to Matthew, attributes the confession to a divine revelation granted to Peter alone (17) and makes him the **rock** on which Jesus **will build** his **church** (18) and the disciple whose authority in the church **on earth** will be confirmed in **heaven**, i.e., by God (19).

16, 13: Caesarea Philippi: situated about twenty miles north of the Sea of Galilee in the territory ruled by Philip, a son of Herod the Great, tetrarch from 4 B.C. until his death in A.D. 34 (see the note on 14, 1). He rebuilt the town of Paneas, naming it **Caesarea** in honor of the emperor, and **Philippi** ("of Philip") to distinguish it from the seaport in Samaria that was also called Caesarea. **Who do people say that the Son of Man is?:** although the question differs from the Marcan parallel (8, 27: "Who . . . that I am?"), the meaning is the same, for Jesus here refers to himself as the **Son of Man** (cf 15).

16, 14: John the Baptist: see 14, 2. **Elijah:** cf Mal 3, 23–24; Sir 48, 10; and see the note on 3, 4. **Jeremiah:** an addition of Matthew to the Marcan source.

16, 16: The Son of the living God: see 2, 15; 3, 17. The addition of this exalted title to the Marcan confession eliminates whatever ambiguity was attached to the title Messiah. This, among other things, supports the view proposed by many scholars that Matthew has here combined his source's confession with a post-resurrectional confession of faith in Jesus as **Son of the living God** that belonged to the appearance of the risen Jesus to Peter; cf 1 Cor 15, 5; Lk 24, 34.

16, 17: Flesh and blood: a Semitic expression for human beings, especially in their weakness. **Has not revealed this . . . but my heavenly Father:** that Peter's faith is spoken of as coming not through human means but through a revelation from God is similar to Paul's description of his recognition of who Jesus was; see Gal 1, 15–16, ". . . when he [God] . . . was pleased to reveal his Son to me. . . ."

16, 18: You are Peter, and upon this rock I will build my church: the Aramaic word **kēpā'*** meaning **rock** and transliterated into Greek as **Kēphas** is the name by which Peter is called in the Pauline letters (1 Cor 1, 12; 3, 22; 9, 5; 15, 4; Gal 1, 18; 2, 9.11.14) except in Gal 2, 7–8 ("Peter"). It is translated as **Petros** ("Peter") in Jn 1, 42. The presumed original Aramaic of Jesus' statement would have been, in English, "You are the Rock (**Kēpā'***) and upon this rock (**kēpā'***) I will build my church." The Greek text probably means the same, for the difference in gender between the masculine noun **petros**, the disciple's new name, and the feminine noun **petra** (rock) may be due simply to the unsuitability of using a feminine noun as the proper name of a male. Although the two words were generally used with slightly different nuances, they were also used interchangeably with the same meaning, "rock." **Church:** this word (Greek **ekklēsia**) occurs in the gospels only here and in 18, 17 (twice). There are several possibilities for an Aramaic original. Jesus' **church** means the community that he **will** gather and that, like a building, will have Peter as its solid foundation. That function of Peter consists in his being witness to Jesus as **the Messiah, the Son of the living God. The gates of the netherworld shall not prevail against it;** the netherworld (Greek **Hadēs,** the abode of the dead) is conceived of as a walled city whose **gates** will not close in upon the church of Jesus, i.e., it will not be overcome by the power of death.

16, 19: The keys to the kingdom of heaven: the image of the **keys** is probably drawn from Is 22, 15–25, where Eliakim, who succeeds Shebna as master of the palace, is given "the key of the House of David," which he authoritatively "opens" and "shuts" (22, 22). **Whatever you bind . . . loosed in heaven:** there are many instances in rabbinic literature of the binding-loosing imagery. Of the several meanings given there to the metaphor, two are of special importance here: the giving of authoritative teaching, and the lifting or imposing of the ban of excommunication. It is disputed whether the image of **the keys** and that of binding and loosing are different metaphors meaning the same thing. In any case, the promise of the keys is given to Peter alone. In 18, 18 all the disciples are given the power of binding and loosing, but the context of that verse suggests that there the power of excommunication alone is intended. That **the keys** are those to **the kingdom of heaven** and that Peter's exercise of authority in the church **on earth** will be confirmed **in heaven** show an intimate connection between, but not an identification of, the church and **the kingdom of heaven.**

w: Mk 8, 27-29; Lk 9, 18-20. *x:* 14, 2. *y:* Jn 6, 69. *z:* Jn 1, 42. *a:* Is 22, 22; Rv 3, 7.

Whatever you bind on earth shall be bound in heaven; and whatever you loose on earth shall be loosed in heaven." [20b]*Then he strictly ordered his disciples to tell no one that he was the Messiah.

The First Prediction of the Passion. [21cd]*From that time on, Jesus began to show his disciples that he must go to Jerusalem and suffer greatly from the elders, the chief priests, and the scribes, and be killed and on the third day be raised. [22]*Then Peter took him aside and began to rebuke him, "God forbid, Lord! No such thing shall ever happen to you." [23e]He turned and said to Peter, "Get behind me, Satan! You are an obstacle to me. You are thinking not as God does, but as human beings do."

The Conditions of Discipleship. [24f]*Then Jesus said to his disciples, "Whoever wishes to come after me must deny himself, take up his cross, and follow me. [25g]*For whoever wishes to save his life will lose it, but whoever loses his life for my sake will find it. [26]What profit would there be for one to gain the whole world and forfeit his life? Or what can one give in exchange for his life? [27h]*For the Son of Man will come with his angels in his Father's glory, and then he will repay everyone according to his conduct. [28]*Amen, I say to you, there are some standing here who will not taste death until they see the Son of Man coming in his kingdom."

CHAPTER 17

See RG 381-82

The Transfiguration of Jesus. [1i]*After six days Jesus took Peter, James, and John

16, 20: Cf Mk 8, 30. Matthew makes explicit that the prohibition has to do with speaking of Jesus as **the Messiah;** see the note on Mk 8, 27–30.

16, 21–23: This first prediction of the passion follows Mk 8, 31–33 in the main and serves as a corrective to an understanding of Jesus' messiahship as solely one of glory and triumph. By his addition of **from that time on** (21) Matthew has emphasized that Jesus' revelation of his coming suffering and death marks a new phase of the gospel. Neither this nor the two later passion predictions (17, 22–23; 20, 17–19) can be taken as sayings that, as they stand, go back to Jesus himself. However, it is probable that he foresaw that his mission would entail suffering and perhaps death, but was confident that he would ultimately be vindicated by God (see 26, 29).

16, 21: He: the Marcan parallel (8, 31) has "the Son of Man." Since Matthew has already designated Jesus by that title (13), its omission here is not significant. The Matthean prediction is equally about the sufferings of the Son of Man. **Must:** this necessity is part of the tradition of all the synoptics; cf Mk 8, 31; Lk 9, 21. **The elders, the chief priests, and the scribes:** see the note on Mk 8, 31. **On the third day:** so also Lk 9, 22, against the Marcan "after three days" (8, 31). Matthew's formulation is, in the Greek, almost identical with the pre-Pauline fragment of the kerygma in 1 Cor 15, 4, and also with Hos 6, 2, which many take to be the Old Testament background to the confession that Jesus was raised **on the third day.** Josephus uses "after three days" and "on the third day" interchangeably (**Antiquities** 7, 11, 6 §§280–81; 8, 8, 1–2 §§214, 218) and there is probably no difference in meaning between the two phrases.

16, 22–23: Peter's refusal to accept Jesus' predicted suffering and death is seen as a satanic attempt to deflect Jesus from his God-appointed course, and the disciple is addressed in terms that recall Jesus' dismissal of the devil in the temptation account (4, 10: "Get away, Satan!"). Peter's satanic purpose is emphasized by Matthew's addition to the Marcan source of the words **You are an obstacle to me.**

16, 24–28: A readiness to follow Jesus even to giving up

one's life for him is the condition for true discipleship; this will be repaid by him at the final judgment.

16, 24: Deny himself: to deny someone is to disown him (see 10, 33; 26, 34–35) and to deny oneself is to disown oneself as the center of one's existence.

16, 25: See the notes on 10, 38.39.

16, 27: The parousia and final judgment are described in 25, 31 in terms almost identical with these.

16, 28: Coming in his kingdom: since the **kingdom** of the Son of Man has been described as "the world" and Jesus' sovereignty precedes his final coming in glory (13, 38.41), the **coming** in this verse is not the parousia as in the preceding but the manifestation of Jesus' rule after his resurrection; see the notes on 13, 38.41.

17, 1–8: The account of the transfiguration confirms that Jesus is the **Son** of God (5) and points to fulfillment of the prediction that he will come **in his Father's glory** at the end of the age (16, 27). It has been explained by some as a resurrection appearance retrojected into the time of Jesus' ministry, but that is not probable since the account lacks many of the usual elements of the resurrection-appearance narratives. It draws upon motifs from the Old Testament and noncanonical Jewish apocalyptic literature that express the presence of the heavenly and the divine, e.g., brilliant light, white garments, and the overshadowing cloud.

17, 1: These three disciples are also taken apart from the others by Jesus in Gethsemane (26, 37). **A high mountain:** this has been identified with Tabor or Hermon, but probably no specific mountain was intended by the evangelist or by his Marcan source (9, 2). Its meaning is theological rather than geographical, possibly recalling the revelation to Moses on Mount Sinai (Ex 24, 12–18) and to Elijah at the same place (1 Kgs 19, 8–18; Horeb Sinai).

b: Mk 8, 30; Lk 9, 21. c: Mk 8, 31—9, 1; Lk 9, 22-27. d: 17, 22-23; 20, 17-19. e: 4, 10. f: Lk 14, 27. g: Lk 17, 33; Jn 12, 25. h: 25, 31-33; Jb 34, 11; Ps 62, 13; Jer 17, 10; 2 Thes 1, 7-8. i: Mk 9, 2-8; Lk 9, 28-36.

his brother, and led them up a high mountain by themselves. [2j]*And he was transfigured before them; his face shone like the sun and his clothes became white as light. [3]*And behold, Moses and Elijah appeared to them, conversing with him. [4]*Then Peter said to Jesus in reply, "Lord, it is good that we are here. If you wish, I will make three tents here, one for you, one for Moses, and one for Elijah." [5k]*While he was still speaking, behold, a bright cloud cast a shadow over them, then from the cloud came a voice that said, "This is my beloved Son, with whom I am well pleased; listen to him." [6]*When the disciples heard this, they fell prostrate and were very much afraid. [7]But Jesus came and touched them, saying, "Rise, and do not be afraid." [8]And when the disciples raised their eyes, they saw no one else but Jesus alone.

The Coming of Elijah. [9l]*As they were coming down from the mountain, Jesus charged them, "Do not tell the vision to anyone until the Son of Man has been raised from the dead." [10m]*Then the disciples asked him, "Why do the scribes say that Elijah must come first?" [11n]*He said in reply, "Elijah will indeed come and restore all things; [12o]but I tell you that Elijah has already come, and they did not recognize him but did to him whatever they pleased. So also will the Son of Man suffer at their hands." [13]*Then the disciples understood that he was speaking to them of John the Baptist.

The Healing of a Boy with a Demon. [14p]*When they came to the crowd a man approached, knelt down before him, [15]*and said, "Lord, have pity on my son, for he is a lunatic and suffers severely; often he falls into fire, and often into water. [16]I brought him to your disciples, but they could not cure him." [17q]*Jesus said in reply, "O faithless and perverse generation, how long will

---

17, 2: **His face shone like the sun:** this is a Matthean addition; cf Dn 10, 6. **His clothes became white as light:** cf Dn 7, 9, where the clothing of God appears "snow bright." For the **white** garments of other heavenly beings, see Rv 4, 4; 7, 9; 19, 14.

17, 3: See the note on Mk 9, 5.

17, 4: **Three tents:** the booths in which the Israelites lived during the feast of Tabernacles (cf Jn 7, 2) were meant to recall their ancestors' dwelling in booths during the journey from Egypt to the promised land (Lv 23, 39–42). The same Greek word, **skēnē**, here translated **tents**, is used in the LXX for the booths of that feast, and some scholars have suggested that there is an allusion here to that liturgical custom.

17, 5: **Cloud cast a shadow over them:** see the note on Mk 9, 7. **This is my beloved Son . . . listen to him:** cf 3, 17. The voice repeats the baptismal proclamation about Jesus, with the addition of the command **listen to him.** The latter is a reference to Dt 18, 15 in which the Israelites are commanded to **listen** to the prophet like Moses whom God will raise up for them. The command to **listen to** Jesus is general, but in this context it probably applies particularly to the preceding predictions of his passion and resurrection (16, 21) and of his coming (16, 27.28).

17, 6–7: A Matthean addition; cf Dn 10, 9–10.18–19.

17, 9–13: In response to the disciples' question about the expected return of Elijah, Jesus interprets the mission of the Baptist as the fulfillment of that expectation. But that was not suspected by those who opposed and finally killed him, and Jesus predicts a similar fate for himself.

17, 9: **The vision:** Matthew alone uses this word to describe the transfiguration. **Until the Son of Man has been raised from the dead:** only in the light of Jesus' resurrection can the meaning of his life and mission be truly understood; until then no testimony to **the vision** will lead people to faith.

17, 10: See the notes on 3, 4; 16, 14.

17, 11–12: The preceding question and this answer may reflect later controversy with Jews who objected to the Christian claims for Jesus that Elijah had not yet come.

17, 13: See 11, 14.

17, 14–20: Matthew has greatly shortened the Marcan story (9, 14–29). Leaving aside several details of the boy's illness, he concentrates on the need for faith, not so much on the part of the boy's father (as does Mark, for Matthew omits Mk 9, 22b-24) but on that of his own disciples whose inability to drive out the demon is ascribed to their **little faith** (20).

17, 15: **A lunatic:** this description of the boy is peculiar to Matthew. The word occurs in the New Testament only here and in 4, 24 and means one affected or struck by the moon. The symptoms of the boy's illness point to epilepsy, and attacks of these were thought to be caused by phases of the moon.

17, 17: **Faithless and perverse:** so Matthew and Luke (9, 41) against Mark's **faithless** (9, 19). The Greek word here translated **perverse** is the same as that in Dt 32, 5 LXX, where Moses speaks to his people. There is a problem in knowing to whom the reproach is addressed. Since the Matthean Jesus normally chides his disciples for their **little faith** (as in 20), it would appear that the charge of lack of faith could not be made against them and that the reproach is addressed to unbelievers among the Jews. However in v 20b (**if you have faith the size of a mustard seed**), which is certainly addressed to the disciples, they appear to have not even the smallest faith; if they had, they would have been able to cure the boy. In the light of v 20b the reproach of v 17 could have applied to the disciples. There seems to be an inconsistency between the charge of **little faith** in v 20a and that of not even a little in v 20b.

j: 28, 3; Dn 7, 9; 10, 6; Rv 4, 4; 7, 9; 19, 14. *k:* 3, 17; Dt 18, 15; 2 Pt 1, 17. *l:* Mk 9, 9-13. *m:* Mal 3, 23-24. *n:* Lk 1, 17. *o:* 11, 14. *p:* Mk 9, 14-29; Lk 9, 37-43. *q:* Dt 32, 5 LXX.

I be with you? How long will I endure you? Bring him here to me." *18*Jesus rebuked him and the demon came out of him, and from that hour the boy was cured. *19*Then the disciples approached Jesus in private and said, "Why could we not drive it out?" *20r*He said to them, "Because of your little faith. Amen, I say to you, if you have faith the size of a mustard seed, you will say to this mountain, 'Move from here to there,' and it will move. Nothing will be impossible for you." [*21*]*

The Second Prediction of the Passion. *22s*As they were gathering in Galilee, Jesus said to them, "The Son of Man is to be handed over to men, *23*and they will kill him, and he will be raised on the third day." And they were overwhelmed with grief.

Payment of the Temple Tax. *24t*When they came to Capernaum, the collectors of the tem-ple tax approached Peter and said, "Doesn't your teacher pay the temple tax?" *25*"Yes," he said. When he came into the house, before he had time to speak, Jesus asked him, "What is your opinion, Simon? From whom do the kings of the earth take tolls or census tax? From their subjects or from foreigners?" *26*When he said, "From foreigners," Jesus said to him, "Then the subjects are exempt. *27*But that we may not offend them, go to the sea, drop in a hook, and take the first fish that comes up. Open its mouth and you will find a coin worth twice the temple tax. Give that to them for me and for you."

CHAPTER 18

The Greatest in the Kingdom. *1u*At

See RG 381–83

that time the disciples approached Jesus and said, "Who is the greatest in the kingdom of

---

17, 18: **The demon came out of him:** not until this verse does Matthew indicate that the boy's illness is a case of demoniacal possession.

17, 20: The entire verse is an addition of Matthew who (according to the better attested text) omits the reason given for the disciples' inability in Mk 9, 29. **Little faith:** see the note on 6, 30. **Faith the size of a mustard seed . . . and it will move:** a combination of a Q saying (cf Lk 17, 6) with a Marcan saying (cf Mk 11, 23).

17, 21: Some manuscripts add, "But this kind does not come out except by prayer and fasting"; this is a variant of the better reading of Mk 9, 29.

17, 22–23: The second passion prediction (cf 16, 21–23) is the least detailed of the three and may be the earliest. In the Marcan parallel the disciples do not understand (9, 32); here they understand and are **overwhelmed with grief** at the prospect of Jesus' death (23).

17, 24–27: Like 14, 28–31 and 16, 16b-19, this episode comes from Matthew's special material on Peter. Although the question of **the collectors** concerns Jesus' payment of **the temple tax,** it is put to **Peter.** It is he who receives instruction from Jesus about freedom from the obligation of payment and yet why it should be made. The means of doing so is provided miraculously. The pericope deals with a problem of Matthew's church, whether its members should pay the temple tax, and the answer is given through a word of Jesus conveyed to Peter. Some scholars see here an example of the teaching authority of Peter exercised in the name of Jesus (see 16, 19). The specific problem was a Jewish Christian one and may have arisen when the Matthean church was composed largely of that group.

17, 24: **The temple tax:** before the destruction of the Jerusalem temple in A.D. 70 every male Jew above nineteen years of age was obliged to make an annual contribution to its upkeep (cf Ex 30, 11–16; Neh 10, 33). After the destruction the Romans imposed upon Jews the obligation of paying that tax for the temple of Jupiter Capitolinus. There is disagreement about which period the story deals with.

17, 25: **From their subjects or from foreigners?:** the Greek word here translated **subjects** literally means "sons."

17, 26: **Then the subjects are exempt:** just as **subjects** are not bound by laws applying to **foreigners,** neither are Jesus and his disciples, who belong to the kingdom of heaven, bound by the duty of paying the temple tax imposed on those who are not of the kingdom. If the Greek is translated "sons," the freedom of Jesus, the Son of God, and of his disciples, children ("sons") of the kingdom (cf 13, 38), is even more clear.

17, 27: **That we may not offend them:** though they are **exempt** (26), Jesus and his disciples are to avoid giving offense; therefore the tax is to be paid. **A coin worth twice the temple tax:** literally, "a stater," a Greek coin worth two double drachmas. Two double drachmas were equal to the Jewish shekel and the tax was a half-shekel. **For me and for you:** not only Jesus but Peter pays the tax, and this example serves as a standard for the conduct of all the disciples.

18, 1–35: This discourse of the fourth book of the gospel is often called the "church order" discourse, but it lacks most of the considerations usually connected with church order, such as various offices in the church and the duties of each, and deals principally with the relations that must obtain among the members of the church. Beginning with the warning that greatness in **the kingdom of heaven** is measured not by rank or power but by childlikeness (1–5), it deals with the care that the disciples must take not to cause the **little ones to sin** or to neglect them if they stray from the community (6–14), the correction of members who sin (15–18), the efficacy of the prayer of the disciples because of the presence of Jesus (19–20), and the forgiveness that must be repeatedly extended to sinful members who repent (21–35).

18, 1: The initiative is taken not by Jesus as in the Marcan parallel (9, 33–34) but by the disciples. **Kingdom of heaven:** this may mean **the kingdom** in its fullness, i.e., after the parousia and the final judgment. But what follows about causes of sin, church discipline, and forgiveness, all dealing

---

r: 21, 21; Lk 17, 6; 1 Cor 13, 2.   s: 16, 21; 20, 18-19.   t: Ex 30, 11-16; Neh 10, 33.   u: Mk 9, 36-37; Lk 9, 46-48.

heaven?" [2]He called a child over, placed it in their midst, [3v*]and said, "Amen, I say to you, unless you turn and become like children, you will not enter the kingdom of heaven. [4w]Whoever humbles himself like this child is the greatest in the kingdom of heaven. [5*]And whoever receives one child such as this in my name receives me.

Temptations to Sin. [6x*]"Whoever causes one of these little ones who believe in me to sin, it would be better for him to have a great millstone hung around his neck and to be drowned in the depths of the sea. [7*]Woe to the world because of things that cause sin! Such things must come, but woe to the one through whom they come! [8y*]If your hand or foot causes you to sin, cut it off and throw it away. It is better for you to enter into life maimed or crippled than with two hands or

two feet to be thrown into eternal fire. [9]And if your eye causes you to sin, tear it out and throw it away. It is better for you to enter into life with one eye than with two eyes to be thrown into fiery Gehenna.

The Parable of the Lost Sheep. [10z*]"See that you do not despise one of these little ones, for I say to you that their angels in heaven always look upon the face of my heavenly Father.* [[11]]*a [12]What is your opinion? If a man has a hundred sheep and one of them goes astray, will he not leave the ninety-nine in the hills and go in search of the stray? [13]And if he finds it, amen, I say to you, he rejoices more over it than over the ninety-nine that did not stray. [14]In just the same way, it is not the will of your heavenly Father that one of these little ones be lost.

A Brother Who Sins. [15b*]"If your brother

---

with the present age, suggests that the question has to do with rank also in the church, where **the kingdom** is manifested here and now, although only partially and by anticipation; see the notes on 3, 2; 4, 17.

18, 3: Become like children: the child is held up as a model for the disciples not because of any supposed innocence of children but because of their complete dependence on, and trust in, their parents. So must the disciples be, in respect to God.

18, 5: Cf 10, 40.

18, 6: One of these little ones: the thought passes from the child of vv 2–4 to the disciples, **little ones** because of their becoming **like children.** It is difficult to know whether this is a designation of all who are disciples or of those who are insignificant in contrast to others, e.g., the leaders of the community. Since apart from this chapter the designation **little ones** occurs in Mt only in 10, 42 where it means disciples as such, that is its more likely meaning here. **Who believe in me:** since discipleship is impossible without at least some degree of faith, this further specification seems superfluous. However, it serves to indicate that the warning against causing a **little one** to sin is principally directed against whatever would lead such a one to a weakening or loss of faith. The Greek verb **skandalizein,** here translated **causes . . . to sin,** means literally "causes to stumble"; what the stumbling is depends on the context. It is used of falling away from faith in 13, 21. According to the better reading of Mk 9, 42, **in me** is a Matthean addition to the Marcan source. **It would be better . . . depths of the sea:** cf Mk 9, 42.

18, 7: This is a Q saying; cf Lk 17, 1. The inevitability of **things that cause sin** (literally, "scandals") does not take away the responsibility of **the one through whom they come.**

18, 8–9: These verses are a doublet of 5, 29–30. In that context they have to do with causes of sexual sin. As in the Marcan source from which they have been drawn (Mk 9, 42–48), they differ from the first warning about scandal, which deals with causing another person to sin, for they concern what **causes** oneself **to sin** and they do not seem to be re-

lated to another's loss of faith, as the first warning is. It is difficult to know how Matthew understood the logical connection between these verses and vv 6–7.

18, 10–14: The first and last verses are peculiar to Mt. The parable itself comes from Q; see Lk 15, 3–7. In Lk it serves as justification for Jesus' table-companionship with sinners; here, it is an exhortation for the disciples to seek out fellow disciples who have gone **astray.** Not only must no one cause a fellow disciple to sin, but those who have strayed must be sought out and, if possible, brought back to the community. The joy of the shepherd on finding the sheep, though not absent in Mt (13), is more emphasized in Lk. By his addition of vv 10 and 14, Matthew has drawn out explicitly the application of the parable to the care of the **little ones.**

18, 10: Their angels in heaven . . . my heavenly Father: for the Jewish belief in angels as guardians of nations and individuals, see Dn 10, 13.20–21; Tb 5, 4–7; 1QH 5, 20–22; as intercessors who present the prayers of human beings to God, see Tb 13, 12.15. The high worth of the **little ones** is indicated by their being represented before God by these heavenly beings.

18, 11: Some manuscripts add, "For the Son of Man has come to save what was lost"; cf 9, 13. This is practically identical with Lk 19, 10 and is probably a copyist's addition from that source.

18, 15–20: Passing from the duty of Christian disciples toward those who have strayed from their number, the discourse now turns to how they are to deal with one who sins and yet remains within the community. First there is to be private correction (15); if this is unsuccessful, further correction before **two or three witnesses** (16); if this fails, the matter is to be brought before the assembled community (**the church**), and if the sinner refuses to attend to the correction of **the church,** he is to be expelled (17). The church's judgment will be ratified **in heaven,** i.e., by God (18). This three-step

v: 19, 14; Mk 10, 15; Lk 18, 17. *w:* 23, 12. *x:* Mk 9, 42; Lk 17, 1-2. *y:* 5, 29-30; Mk 9, 43-47. *z:* Ez 34, 1-3.16; Lk 15, 3-7. *a:* Lk 19, 10. *b:* Lv 19, 17; Sir 19, 13; Gal 6, 1.

sins [against you], go and tell him his fault between you and him alone. If he listens to you, you have won over your brother. *16c**If he does not listen, take one or two others along with you, so that 'every fact may be established on the testimony of two or three witnesses.' *17d**If he refuses to listen to them, tell the church. If he refuses to listen even to the church, then treat him as you would a Gentile or a tax collector. *18e**Amen, I say to you, whatever you bind on earth shall be bound in heaven, and whatever you loose on earth shall be loosed in heaven. *19f**Again, [amen,] I say to you, if two of you agree on earth about anything for which they are to pray, it shall be granted to them by my heavenly Father. *20g**For where two or three are gathered together in my name, there am I in the midst of them."

The Parable of the Unforgiving Servant.

21h*Then Peter approaching asked him, "Lord, if my brother sins against me, how often must I forgive him? As many as seven times?" *22**Jesus answered, "I say to you, not seven times but seventy-seven times. *23i*That is why the kingdom of heaven may be likened to a king who decided to settle accounts with his servants. *24**When he began the accounting, a debtor was brought before him who owed him a huge amount. *25*Since he had no way of paying it back, his master ordered him to be sold, along with his wife, his children, and all his property, in payment of the debt. *26**At that, the servant fell down, did him homage, and said, 'Be patient with me, and I will pay you back in full.' *27*Moved with compassion the master of that servant let him go and forgave him the loan.

process of correction corresponds, though not exactly, to the procedure of the Qumran community; see 1QS 5, 25—6, 1; 6, 24—7, 25; CD 9, 2–8. The section ends with a saying about the favorable response of God to prayer, even to that of a very small number, for Jesus is in the midst of any gathering of his disciples, however small (19–20). Whether this prayer has anything to do with the preceding judgment is uncertain.

18, 15: Your brother: a fellow disciple; see 23, 8. The bracketed words, **against you**, are widely attested but they are not in the important codices Sinaiticus and Vaticanus or in some other textual witnesses. Their omission broadens the type of sin in question. **Won over:** literally, "gained."

18, 16: Cf Dt 19, 15.

18, 17: The church: the second of the only two instances of this word in the gospels; see the note on 16, 18. Here it refers not to the entire **church** of Jesus, as in 16, 18, but to the local congregation. **Treat him . . . a Gentile or a tax collector:** just as the observant Jew avoided the company of Gentiles and tax collectors, so must the congregation of Christian disciples separate itself from the arrogantly sinful member who refuses to repent even when convicted of his sin by the whole **church**. Such a one is to be set outside the fellowship of the community. The harsh language about **Gentile** and **tax collector** probably reflects a stage of the Matthean **church** when it was principally composed of Jewish Christians. That time had long since passed, but the principle of exclusion for such a sinner remained. Paul makes a similar demand for excommunication in 1 Cor 5, 1–13.

18, 18: Except for the plural of the verbs **bind** and **loose**, this verse is practically identical with 16, 19b, and many scholars understand it as granting to all the disciples what was previously given to Peter alone. For a different view, based on the different contexts of the two verses, see the note on 16, 19.

18, 19–20: Some take these verses as applying to prayer on the occasion of the church's gathering to deal with the sinner of v 17. Unless an **a fortiori** argument is supposed, this seems unlikely. God's answer to the prayer of **two or three** envisages a different situation from one that involves the en-

tire congregation. In addition, the object of this prayer is expressed in most general terms as **anything for which they are to pray.**

18, 20: For where two or three . . . midst of them: the presence of Jesus guarantees the efficacy of the prayer. This saying is similar to one attributed to a rabbi executed in A.D. 135 at the time of the second Jewish revolt: ". . . When two sit and there are between them the words of the Torah, the divine presence (Shekinah) rests upon them" (Pirqê 'Abôt 3, 3).

18, 21–35: The final section of the discourse deals with the forgiveness that the disciples are to give to their fellow disciples who sin against them. To the question of Peter how often forgiveness is to be granted (21), Jesus answers that it is to be given without limit (22) and illustrates this with the parable of the unmerciful servant (23–34), warning that his **heavenly Father** will give those who do not forgive the same treatment as that given to the unmerciful servant (35). Verses 21–22 correspond to Lk 17, 4; the parable and the final warning are peculiar to Mt. That the parable did not originally belong to this context is suggested by the fact that it really does not deal with repeated forgiveness, which is the point of Peter's question and Jesus' reply.

18, 22: Seventy-seven times: the Greek corresponds exactly to the LXX of Gn 4, 24. There is probably an allusion, by contrast, to the limitless vengeance of Lamech in the Gn text. In any case, what is demanded of the disciples is limitless forgiveness.

18, 24: A huge amount: literally, "ten thousand talents." The talent was a unit of coinage of high but varying value depending on its metal (gold, silver, copper) and its place of origin. It is mentioned in the New Testament only here and in 25, 14–30.

18, 26: Pay you back in full: an empty promise, given the size of the debt.

c: Dt 19, 15; Jn 8, 17; 1 Tm 5, 19.   *d:* 1 Cor 5, 1-13.   *e:* 16, 19; Jn 20, 23.   *f:* 7, 7-8; Jn 15, 7.   *g:* 1 Cor 5, 4.   *h:* 6, 12; Lk 17, 4. *i:* 25, 19.

²⁸*When that servant had left, he found one of his fellow servants who owed him a much smaller amount. He seized him and started to choke him, demanding, 'Pay back what you owe.' ²⁹Falling to his knees, his fellow servant begged him, 'Be patient with me, and I will pay you back.' ³⁰But he refused. Instead, he had him put in prison until he paid back the debt. ³¹Now when his fellow servants saw what had happened, they were deeply disturbed, and went to their master and reported the whole affair. ³²His master summoned him and said to him, 'You wicked servant! I forgave you your entire debt because you begged me to. ³³ʲShould you not have had pity on your fellow servant, as I had pity on you?' ³⁴*Then in anger his master handed him over to the torturers until he should pay back the whole debt. ³⁵ᵏ*So will my heavenly Father do to you, unless each of you forgives his brother from his heart."

VI: Ministry in Judea and Jerusalem

CHAPTER 19

See RG 382-83

Marriage and Divorce. ¹*When Jesus finished these words, he left Galilee and went to the district of Judea across the Jordan. ²Great crowds followed him, and he cured them there. ³ˡ*Some Pharisees approached him, and tested him, saying, "Is it lawful for a man to divorce his wife for any cause whatever?" ⁴ᵐ*He said in reply, "Have you not read that from the beginning the Creator 'made them male and female' ⁵ⁿand said, 'For this reason a man shall leave his father and mother and be joined to his wife, and the two shall become one flesh'? ⁶So they are no longer two, but one flesh. Therefore, what God has joined together, no human being must separate." ⁷ᵒ*They said to

18, 28: A much smaller amount: literally, "a hundred denarii." A denarius was the normal daily wage of a laborer. The difference between the two debts is enormous and brings out the absurdity of the conduct of the Christian who has received the great forgiveness of God and yet refuses to forgive the relatively minor offenses done to him.

18, 34: Since the debt is so great as to be unpayable, the punishment will be endless.

18, 35: The Father's forgiveness, already given, will be withdrawn at the final judgment for those who have not imitated his forgiveness by their own.

19, 1—23, 39: The narrative section of the fifth book of the gospel. The first part (19, 1—20, 34) has for its setting the journey of Jesus from Galilee to Jerusalem; the second (21, 1—23, 39) deals with Jesus' ministry in Jerusalem up to the final great discourse of the gospel (chs 24–25). Matthew follows the Marcan sequence of events, though adding material both special to this gospel and drawn from Q. The second part ends with the denunciation of the scribes and Pharisees (23, 1–36) followed by Jesus' lament over Jerusalem (37–39). This long and important speech raises a problem for the view that Mt is structured around five other discourses of Jesus (see Introduction) and that this one has no such function in the gospel. However, it is to be noted that this speech lacks the customary concluding formula that follows the five discourses (see the note on 7, 28), and that those discourses are all addressed either exclusively (chs 10, 18, 24–25) or primarily (chs 5–7, 13) to the disciples, whereas this is addressed primarily to the scribes and Pharisees (13–36). Consequently, it seems plausible to maintain that the evangelist did not intend to give it the structural importance of the five other discourses, and that, in spite of its being composed of sayings-material, it belongs to the narrative section of this book. In that regard, it is similar to the sayings-material of 11, 7–30. Some have proposed that Matthew wished to regard it as part of the final discourse of chs 24–25, but the intervening mate-

rial (24, 1–4) and the change in matter and style of those chapters do not support that view.

19, 1–12: In giving Jesus' teaching on divorce (3–9), Matthew here follows his Marcan source (10, 2–12) as he does Q in 5, 31–32 (cf Lk 16, 18). Verses 10–12 are peculiar to Mt.

19, 1: When Jesus finished these words: see the note on 7, 28–29. The district of Judea across the Jordan: an inexact designation of the territory. Judea did not extend across the Jordan; the territory east of the river was Perea. The route to Jerusalem by way of Perea avoided passage through Samaria.

19, 3: Tested him: the verb is used of attempts of Jesus' opponents to embarrass him by challenging him to do something they think impossible (16, 1; Mk 8, 11; Lk 11, 16) or by having him say something that they can use against him (22, 18.35; Mk 10, 2; 12, 15). For any cause whatever: this is peculiar to Mt and has been interpreted by some as meaning that Jesus was being asked to take sides in the dispute between the schools of Hillel and Shammai on the reasons for divorce, the latter holding a stricter position than the former. It is unlikely, however, that to ask Jesus' opinion about the differing views of two Jewish schools, both highly respected, could be described as "testing" him, for the reason indicated above.

19, 4–6: Matthew recasts his Marcan source, omitting Jesus' question about Moses' command (Mk 10, 3) and having him recall at once two Genesis texts that show the will and purpose of the Creator in making human beings male and female (Gn 1, 27), namely, that a man may be joined to his wife in marriage in the intimacy of one flesh (Gn 2, 24). What God has thus joined must not be separated by any human being. (The NAB translation of the Hebrew bāśār of Gn 2, 24 as "body" rather than "flesh" obscures the reference of Mt to that text.)

19, 7: See Dt 24, 1–4.

j: Sir 28, 4. k: 6, 15; Jas 2, 13. l: Mk 10, 2-12. m: Gn 1, 27. n: Gn 2, 24; 1 Cor 6, 16; Eph 5, 31. o: Dt 24, 1-4.

him, "Then why did Moses command that the man give the woman a bill of divorce and dismiss [her]?" *8*He said to them, "Because of the hardness of your hearts Moses allowed you to divorce your wives, but from the beginning it was not so. *9p**I say to you, whoever divorces his wife (unless the marriage is unlawful) and marries another commits adultery." *10*[His] disciples said to him, "If that is the case of a man with his wife, it is better not to marry." *11**He answered, "Not all can accept [this] word, but only those to whom that is granted. *12**Some are incapable of marriage because they were born so; some, because they were made so by others; some, because they have renounced marriage for the sake of the kingdom of heaven. Whoever can accept this ought to accept it."

Blessing of the Children. *13q**Then children were brought to him that he might lay his hands on them and pray. The disciples rebuked them, *14r*but Jesus said, "Let the children come to me, and do not prevent them; for the kingdom of heaven belongs to such as these." *15*After he placed his hands on them, he went away.

The Rich Young Man. *16s**Now someone approached him and said, "Teacher, what good must I do to gain eternal life?" *17**He answered him, "Why do you ask me about the good? There is only One who is good. If you wish to enter into life, keep the commandments." *18t**He asked him, "Which ones?" And Jesus replied, " 'You shall not kill; you shall not commit adultery; you shall not steal; you shall not bear false witness; *19*honor your father and your mother'; and 'you shall love your neighbor as yourself.' " *20**The young man said to him, "All of these I have observed. What do I still

19, 9: Moses' concession to human sinfulness (**the hardness of your hearts,** 8) is repudiated by Jesus, and the original will of the Creator is reaffirmed against that concession. (**Unless the marriage is unlawful**): see the note on 5, 31–32. There is some evidence suggesting that Jesus' absolute prohibition of divorce was paralleled in the Qumran community (see 11QTemple 57, 17–19; CD 4, 12b—5, 14). Matthew moves Mark's setting of this verse as spoken to the disciples alone "in the house" (Mk 10, 10) and also his extension of the divorce prohibition to the case of a woman's divorcing her husband (10, 12), probably because in Palestine, unlike the places where Roman and Greek law prevailed, the woman was not allowed to initiate the divorce.

19, 11: [**This**] **word:** probably the disciples' **it is better not to marry** (10). Jesus agrees but says that celibacy is not for all but only for those **to whom that is granted** by God.

19, 12: **Incapable of marriage:** literally, "eunuchs." Three classes are mentioned, eunuchs from birth, eunuchs by castration, and those who have voluntarily **renounced marriage** (literally, "have made themselves eunuchs") **for the sake of the kingdom,** i.e., to devote themselves entirely to its service. Some scholars take the last class to be those who have been divorced by their spouses and have refused to enter another marriage. But it is more likely that it is rather those who have chosen never to marry, since that suits better the optional nature of the decision: **whoever can . . . ought to accept it.**

19, 13–15: This account is understood by some as intended to justify the practice of infant baptism. That interpretation is based principally on the command not to **prevent** the children from coming, since that word sometimes has a baptismal connotation in the New Testament; see Acts 8, 36.

19, 16–30: Cf Mk 10, 17–31. This story does not set up a "two-tier" morality, that of those who seek (only) **eternal life** (16) and that of those who **wish to be perfect** (21). It speaks rather of the obstacle that riches constitute for the

following of Jesus and of the impossibility, humanly speaking, for one who has **many possessions** (22) **to enter the kingdom** (24). Actual renunciation of riches is not demanded of all; Matthew counts the rich Joseph of Arimathea as a disciple of Jesus (27, 57). But only the poor in spirit (5, 3) can **enter the kingdom** and, as here, such poverty may entail the sacrifice of one's **possessions.** The Twelve, who **have given up everything** (27) to follow Jesus, will have as their reward a share in Jesus' (the Son of Man's) **judging the twelve tribes of Israel** (28), and all who have similarly sacrificed family or property for his sake **will inherit eternal life** (29).

19, 16: **Gain eternal life:** this is equivalent to "entering into life" (17) and "being saved" (25); the **life** is that of the new age after the final judgment (see 25, 46). It probably is also equivalent here to "entering the kingdom of heaven" (23) or "the kingdom of God" (24), but see the notes on 3, 2; 4, 17; 18, 1 for the wider reference of **the kingdom** in Mt.

19, 17: By Matthew's reformulation of the Marcan question and reply (Mk 10, 17–18) Jesus' repudiation of the term "good" for himself has been softened. Yet the Marcan assertion that "no one is good but God alone" stands, with only unimportant verbal modification.

19, 18–19: The first five commandments cited are from the Decalogue (see Ex 20, 12–16; Dt 5, 16–20). Matthew omits Mark's "you shall not defraud" (10, 19; see Dt 24, 14) and adds Lv 19, 18. This combination of commandments of the Decalogue with Lv 19, 18 is partially the same as Paul's enumeration of the demands of Christian morality in Rom 13, 9.

19, 20: **Young man:** in Mt alone of the synoptics the questioner is said to be a **young man;** thus the Marcan "from my youth" (10, 20) is omitted.

p: 5, 32; Lk 16, 18; 1 Cor 7, 10-11.   *q:* Mk 10, 13-16; Lk 18, 15-17.   *r:* 18, 3; Acts 8, 36.   *s:* Mk 10, 17-31; Lk 18, 18-30.   *t:* Ex 20, 12-16; Dt 5, 16-20 / Lv 19, 18; Rom 13, 9.

lack?" *21u**Jesus said to him, "If you wish to be perfect, go, sell what you have and give to [the] poor, and you will have treasure in heaven. Then come, follow me." *22*When the young man heard this statement, he went away sad, for he had many possessions. *23**Then Jesus said to his disciples, "Amen, I say to you, it will be hard for one who is rich to enter the kingdom of heaven. *24v*Again I say to you, it is easier for a camel to pass through the eye of a needle than for one who is rich to enter the kingdom of God." *25**When the disciples heard this, they were greatly astonished and said, "Who then can be saved?" *26w*Jesus looked at them and said, "For human beings this is impossible, but for God all things are possible." *27x*Then Peter said to him in reply, "We have given up everything and followed you. What will there be for us?" *28y**Jesus said to them, "Amen, I say to you that you who have followed me, in the new age, when the Son of Man is seated on his throne of glory, will yourselves sit on twelve thrones, judging the twelve tribes of Israel. *29*And everyone who has given up houses or brothers or sisters or father or mother or children or lands for the sake of my name will receive a hundred times more, and will inherit eternal life. *30z**But many who are first will be last, and the last will be first.

CHAPTER 20

See RG 382–83

The Workers in the Vineyard. *1**"The kingdom of heaven is like a landowner who went out at dawn to hire laborers for his vineyard. *2*After agreeing with them for the usual daily wage, he sent them into his vineyard. *3*Going out about nine o'clock, he saw others standing idle in the marketplace, *4**and he said to them, 'You too go into my vineyard, and I will give you what is just.' *5*So they went off. [And] he went out again around noon, and around three o'clock, and did likewise. *6*Going out about five o'clock, he found others standing around, and said to them, 'Why do you stand here idle all day?' *7*They answered, 'Because no one has hired us.' He said to them, 'You too go into my vineyard.' *8a**When it was evening the owner of the vineyard said to his foreman, 'Summon the laborers and give them their pay, beginning with the last and ending with the first.' *9*When those who had started about five o'clock came, each received the usual daily wage. *10*So when the first came, they thought that they would receive more, but each of them also got the usual wage. *11*And

---

19, 21: If you wish to be perfect: to be perfect is demanded of all Christians; see 5, 48. In the case of this man, it involves selling his possessions and giving to the poor; only so can he **follow** Jesus.

19, 23–24: Riches are an obstacle to entering **the kingdom** that cannot be overcome by human power. The comparison with the impossibility of a camel's passing **through the eye of a needle** should not be mitigated by such suppositions as that **the eye of a needle** means a low or narrow gate. **The kingdom of God:** as in 12, 28; 21, 31.43, instead of Mt's usual **kingdom of heaven.**

19, 25–26: See the note on Mk 10, 23–27.

19, 28: This saying, directed to the Twelve, is from Q; see Lk 22, 29–30. **The new age:** the Greek word here translated "new age" occurs in the New Testament only here and in Ti 3, 5. Literally, it means "rebirth" or "regeneration," and is used in Ti of spiritual rebirth through baptism. Here it means the "rebirth" effected by the coming of the kingdom. Since that coming has various stages (see the notes on 3, 2; 4, 17), **the new age** could be taken as referring to the time after the resurrection when the Twelve will govern the true Israel, i.e., the church of Jesus. (For "judge" in the sense of "govern," cf Jgs 12, 8.9.11; 15, 20; 16, 31; Ps 2, 10). But since it is connected here with the time when **the Son of Man** will be **seated on his throne of glory,** language that Matthew uses in 25, 31 for the time of final judgment, it is more likely that

what the Twelve are promised is that they will be joined with Jesus then in judging the people of Israel.

19, 30: Different interpretations have been given to this saying, which comes from Mk 10, 31. In view of Matthew's associating it with the following parable (20, 1–15) and substantially repeating it (in reverse order) at the end of that parable (20, 16), it may be that his meaning is that all who respond to the call of Jesus, at whatever time (**first or last**), will be the same in respect to inheriting the benefits of the kingdom, which is the gift of God.

20, 1–16: This parable is peculiar to Mt. It is difficult to know whether the evangelist composed it or received it as part of his traditional material and, if the latter is the case, what its original reference was. In its present context its close association with 19, 30 suggests that its teaching is the equality of all the disciples in the reward of inheriting eternal life.

20, 4: What is just: although the wage is not stipulated as in the case of those first hired, it will be fair.

20, 8: Beginning with the last . . . the first: this element of the parable has no other purpose than to show how **the first** knew what **the last** were given (12).

---

u: 5, 48; 6, 20.　*v:* 7, 14.　*w:* Gn 18, 14; Jb 42, 2; Lk 1, 37.　*x:* 4, 20.22.　*y:* 25, 31; Dn 7, 9.22; Lk 22, 30; Rv 3, 21; 20, 4.　*z:* 20, 16.　*a:* Lv 19, 13; Dt 24, 15.

on receiving it they grumbled against the landowner, *12*saying, 'These last ones worked only one hour, and you have made them equal to us, who bore the day's burden and the heat.' *13**He said to one of them in reply, 'My friend, I am not cheating you. Did you not agree with me for the usual daily wage? *14**Take what is yours and go. What if I wish to give this last one the same as you? *15*[Or] am I not free to do as I wish with my own money? Are you envious because I am generous?' *16**Thus, the last will be first, and the first will be last."

The Third Prediction of the Passion. *17b**As Jesus was going up to Jerusalem, he took the twelve [disciples] aside by themselves, and said to them on the way, *18*"Behold, we are going up to Jerusalem, and the Son of Man will be handed over to the chief priests and the scribes, and they will condemn him to death, *19*and hand him over to the Gentiles to be mocked and scourged and crucified, and he will be raised on the third day."

The Request of James and John. *20c**Then the mother of the sons of Zebedee approached him with her sons and did him homage, wishing to ask him for something. *21*He said to her, "What do you wish?" She answered him, "Command that these two sons of mine sit, one at your right and the other at your left, in your kingdom." *22**Jesus said in reply, "You do not know what you are asking. Can you drink the cup that I am going to drink?" They said to him, "We can." *23*He replied, "My cup you will indeed drink, but to sit at my right and at my left [, this] is not mine to give but is for those for whom it has been prepared by my Father." *24d*When the ten heard this, they became indignant at the two brothers. *25*But Jesus summoned them and said, "You know that the rulers of the Gentiles lord it over them, and the great ones make their authority over them felt. *26*But it shall not be so among you. Rather, whoever wishes to be great among you shall be your servant; *27e*whoever wishes to be first among you shall be your slave. *28f**Just so, the Son of Man did not come to be served but to serve and to give his life as a ransom for many."

The Healing of Two Blind Men. *29g**As

20, 13: I am not cheating you: literally, "I am not treating you unjustly."

20, 14–15: The owner's conduct involves no violation of justice (4.13), and that all the workers receive the same wage is due only to his generosity to the latest arrivals; the resentment of the first comes from envy.

20, 16: See the note on 19, 30.

20, 17–19: Cf Mk 10, 32–34. This is the third and the most detailed of the passion predictions (16, 21–23; 17, 22–23). It speaks of Jesus' **being handed over to the Gentiles** (27, 2), his being **mocked** (27, 27–30), **scourged** (27, 26), and **crucified** (27, 31.35). In all but the last of these points Matthew agrees with his Marcan source, but whereas Mk speaks of Jesus' being killed (10, 34), Mt has the specific **to be . . . crucified.**

20, 20–28: Cf Mk 10, 35–45. The request of the sons of Zebedee, made through their mother, for the highest places of honor in the **kingdom,** and the indignation of **the** other **ten** disciples at this request, show that neither **the two brothers** nor the others have understood that what makes for greatness in the kingdom is not lordly power but humble service. Jesus gives the example, and his ministry of service will reach its highest point when he gives his life for the deliverance of the human race from sin.

20, 20–21: The reason for Matthew's making **the mother** the petitioner (cf Mk 10, 35) is not clear. Possibly he intends an allusion to Bathsheba's seeking the kingdom for Solomon; see 1 Kgs 1, 11–21. **Your kingdom:** see the note on 16, 28.

20, 22: You do not know what you are asking: the Greek verbs are plural and, with the rest of the verse, indicate that the answer is addressed not to the woman but to her sons. **Drink the cup:** see the note on Mk 10, 38–40. Matthew omits the Marcan "or be baptized with the baptism with which I am baptized" (10, 38).

20, 28: Ransom: this noun, which occurs in the New Testament only here and in the Marcan parallel (10, 45), does not necessarily express the idea of liberation by payment of some price. The cognate verb is used frequently in the LXX of God's liberating Israel from Egypt or from Babylonia after the Exile; see Ex 6, 6; 15, 13; Ps 77 (76 LXX), 16; Is 43, 1; 44, 22. The liberation brought by Jesus' death will be **for many;** cf Is 53, 12. **Many** does not mean that some are excluded, but is a Semitism designating the collectivity who benefit from the service of the one, and is equivalent to "all." While there are few verbal contacts between this saying and the fourth Servant Song (Is 52, 13—53, 12), the ideas of that passage are reflected here.

20, 29–34: The cure of the blind men is probably symbolic of what will happen to the disciples, now blind to the meaning of Jesus' passion and to the necessity of their sharing his suffering. As the men are given sight, so, after the resurrection, will the disciples come to see that to which they are now blind. Matthew has abbreviated his Marcan source (10, 46–52) and has made Mk's one man two. Such doubling is characteristic of this gospel; see 8, 28–34 (// Mk 5, 1–20) and the note on 9, 27–31.

b: 16, 21; 17, 22-23; Mk 10, 32-34; Lk 18, 31-33. *c:* Mk 10, 35-45. *d:* Lk 22, 25-27. *e:* Mk 9, 35. *f:* 26, 28; Is 53, 12; Rom 5, 6; 1 Tm 2, 6. *g:* Mk 10, 46-52; Lk 18, 35-43.

they left Jericho, a great crowd followed him. *30h**Two blind men were sitting by the roadside, and when they heard that Jesus was passing by, they cried out, "[Lord,] Son of David, have pity on us!" *31*The crowd warned them to be silent, but they called out all the more, "Lord, Son of David, have pity on us!" *32*Jesus stopped and called them and said, "What do you want me to do for you?" *33*They answered him, "Lord, let our eyes be opened." *34*Moved with pity, Jesus touched their eyes. Immediately they received their sight, and followed him.

See RG 383–84

CHAPTER 21

The Entry into Jerusalem. *1i**When they drew near Jerusalem and came to Bethphage on the Mount of Olives, Jesus sent two disciples, *2**saying to them, "Go into the village opposite you, and immediately you will find an ass tethered, and a colt with her. Untie them and bring them here to me. *3*And if anyone should say anything to you, reply, 'The master has need of them.' Then he will send them at once." *4**This happened so that

what had been spoken through the prophet might be fulfilled:

5 j "Say to daughter Zion,
'Behold, your king comes to you,
meek and riding on an ass,
and on a colt, the foal of a beast of burden.' "

*6*The disciples went and did as Jesus had ordered them. *7**They brought the ass and the colt and laid their cloaks over them, and he sat upon them. *8k**The very large crowd spread their cloaks on the road, while others cut branches from the trees and strewed them on the road. *9l**The crowds preceding him and those following kept crying out and saying:

"Hosanna to the Son of David;
blessed is he who comes in the name of the Lord;
hosanna in the highest."

10*And when he entered Jerusalem the whole city was shaken and asked, "Who is this?" *11**And the crowds replied, "This is

20, 30: [**Lord**]: some important textual witnesses omit this, but that may be because copyists assimilated this verse to 9, 27. **Son of David:** see the note on 9, 27.

21, 1–11: Jesus' coming to Jerusalem is in accordance with the divine will that he must go there (cf 16, 21) to suffer, die, and be raised. He prepares for his entry into the city in such a way as to make it a fulfillment of the prophecy of Zec 9, 9 (2) that emphasizes the humility of the **king** who **comes** (5). That prophecy, absent from the Marcan parallel account (11, 1–11) although found also in the Johannine account of the entry (12, 15), is the center of the Matthean story. During the procession from Bethphage to Jerusalem, Jesus is acclaimed as the Davidic messianic king by the crowds who accompany him (9). On his arrival **the whole city was shaken,** and to the inquiry of the amazed populace about Jesus' identity the crowds with him reply that he is **the prophet, from Nazareth in Galilee** (10.11).

21, 1: Bethphage: a village that can no longer be certainly identified. Mk mentions it before Bethany (11, 1), which suggests that it lay to the east of the latter. **The Mount of Olives:** the hill east of Jerusalem that is spoken of in Zec 14, 4 as the place where the Lord will come to rescue Jerusalem from the enemy nations.

21, 2: An ass tethered, and a colt with her: instead of the one animal of Mk 11, 2, Mt has two, as demanded by his understanding of Zec 9, 9.

21, 4–5: The prophet: this fulfillment citation is actually composed of two distinct Old Testament texts, Is 62, 11 (**Say to daughter Zion**) and Zec 9, 9. The **ass** and the **colt** are the same animal in the prophecy, mentioned twice in different

ways, the common Hebrew literary device of poetic parallelism. That Matthew takes them as two is one of the reasons why some scholars think that he was a Gentile rather than a Jewish Christian who would presumably not make that mistake (see Introduction).

21, 7: Upon them: upon the two animals; an awkward picture resulting from Matthew's misunderstanding of prophecy.

21, 8: Spread . . . on the road: cf 2 Kgs 9, 13. There is a similarity between the cutting and strewing of the **branches** and the festivities of Tabernacles (Lv 23, 39–40); see also 2 Mc 10, 5–8 where the celebration of the rededication of the temple is compared to that of Tabernacles.

21, 9: Hosanna: the Hebrew means "(O Lord) grant salvation"; see Ps 118, 25, but that invocation had become an acclamation of jubilation and welcome. **Blessed is he . . . in the name of the Lord:** see Ps 118, 26 and the note on Jn 12, 13. **In the highest:** probably only an intensification of the acclamation, although **Hosanna in the highest** could be taken as a prayer, "May God save (him)."

21, 10: Was shaken: in the gospels this verb is peculiar to Mt where it is used also of the earthquake at the time of the crucifixion (27, 51) and of the terror of the guards of Jesus' tomb at the appearance of the angel (28, 4). For Matthew's use of the cognate noun, see the note on 8, 24.

21, 11: The prophet: see 16, 14 ("one of the prophets") and 21, 46.

h: 9, 27. *i:* Mk 11, 1-11; Lk 19, 28-38; Jn 12, 12-15. *j:* Is 62, 11; Zec 9, 9. *k:* 2 Kgs 9, 13. *l:* Ps 118, 25-26.

Jerusalem in the Time of Jesus

Jesus the prophet, from Nazareth in Galilee."

The Cleansing of the Temple. [12mn]*Jesus entered the temple area and drove out all those engaged in selling and buying there. He overturned the tables of the money changers and the seats of those who were selling doves. [13o]*And he said to them, "It is written:

'My house shall be a house of prayer,'
    but you are making it a den of thieves.'"

21, 12–17: Matthew changes the order of Mk (11, 11.12.15) and places the cleansing of the temple on the same day as the entry into Jerusalem, immediately after it. The activities going on in **the temple area** were not secular but connected with the temple worship. Thus Jesus' attack on those so engaged and his charge that they were **making God's house of prayer a den of thieves** (12–13) constituted a claim to authority over the religious practices of Israel and were a challenge to the priestly authorities. Verses 14–17 are peculiar to Mt. Jesus' healings and his countenancing of the children's cries of praise rouse the indignation of **the chief priests and the scribes** (15). These two groups appear in the infancy narrative (2, 4) and have been mentioned in the first and third passion predictions (16, 21; 20, 18). Now, as the passion approaches, they come on the scene again, exhibiting their hostility to Jesus.

21, 12: These activities were carried on in the court of the Gentiles, the outermost court of **the temple area.** Animals for sacrifice were sold; the **doves** were for those who could not afford a more expensive offering; see Lv 5, 7. **Tables of the money changers:** only the coinage of Tyre could be used for the purchases; other money had to be exchanged for that.

21, 13: 'My house . . . prayer': cf Is 56, 7. Matthew omits

m: Mk 11, 15-19; Lk 19, 45-48; Jn 2, 14-22.   n: Lv 5, 7.   o: Is 56, 7; Jer 7, 11.

*14 p**The blind and the lame approached him in the temple area, and he cured them. *15**When the chief priests and the scribes saw the wondrous things he was doing, and the children crying out in the temple area, "Hosanna to the Son of David," they were indignant *16q**and said to him, "Do you hear what they are saying?" Jesus said to them, "Yes; and have you never read the text, 'Out of the mouths of infants and nurslings you have brought forth praise'?" *17*And leaving them, he went out of the city to Bethany, and there he spent the night.

The Cursing of the Fig Tree. *18r**When he was going back to the city in the morning, he was hungry. *19s*Seeing a fig tree by the road, he went over to it, but found nothing on it except leaves. And he said to it, "May no fruit ever come from you again." And immediately the fig tree withered. *20*When the disciples saw this, they were amazed and said, "How was it that the fig tree withered immediately?" *21t**Jesus said to them in reply, "Amen, I say to you, if you have faith and do not waver, not only will you do what has been done to the fig tree, but even if you say to this mountain, 'Be lifted up and thrown into the sea,' it will be done. *22u*Whatever you ask for in prayer with faith, you will receive."

The Authority of Jesus Questioned. *23 vw**When he had come into the temple area, the chief priests and the elders of the people approached him as he was teaching and said, "By what authority are you doing these things? And who gave you this authority?" *24**Jesus said to them in reply, "I shall ask you one question, and if you answer it for me, then I shall tell you by what authority I do these things. *25*Where was John's baptism from? Was it of heavenly or of human origin?" They discussed this among themselves and said, "If we say 'Of heavenly origin,' he will say to us, 'Then why did you not believe him?' *26x**But if we say, 'Of human origin,' we fear the crowd, for they all regard John as a prophet." *27**So they said to Jesus in reply, "We do not know." He himself said to them, "Neither shall I tell you by what authority I do these things.

The Parable of the Two Sons. *28**"What is your opinion? A man had two sons. He came

---

the final words of the quotation, "for all peoples" ("all nations"), possibly because for him the worship of the God of Israel by all nations belongs to the time after the resurrection; see 28, 19. **A den of thieves:** the phrase is taken from Jer 7, 11.

21, 14: The blind and the lame: according to 2 Sm 5, 8 (LXX) **the blind and the lame** were forbidden to enter "the house of the Lord," the temple. These are the last of Jesus' healings in Mt.

21, 15: The wondrous things: the healings.

21, 16: 'Out of the mouths . . . praise': cf Ps 8, 3 (LXX).

21, 18–22: In Mk the effect of Jesus' cursing the fig tree is not immediate; see 11, 14.20. By making it so, Matthew has heightened the miracle. Jesus' act seems arbitrary and ill-tempered, but it is a prophetic action similar to those of Old Testament prophets that vividly symbolize some part of their preaching; see, e.g., Ez 12, 1–20. It is a sign of the judgment that is to come upon the Israel that with all its apparent piety lacks the fruit of good deeds (3, 10) and will soon bear the punishment of its fruitlessness (43). Some scholars propose that this story is the development in tradition of a parable of Jesus about the destiny of a fruitless tree, such as Lk 13, 6–9. Jesus' answer to the question of the amazed disciples (20) makes the miracle an example of the power of prayer made with unwavering **faith** (21–22).

21, 21: See 17, 20.

21, 23–27: Cf Mk 11, 27–33. This is the first of five controversies between Jesus and the religious authorities of Judaism in 21, 23—22, 46, presented in the form of questions and answers.

21, 23: These things: probably his entry into the city, his cleansing of the temple, and his healings there.

21, 24: To reply by counterquestion was common in rabbinical debate.

21, 26: We fear . . . as a prophet: cf 14, 5.

21, 27: Since through embarrassment on the one hand and fear on the other the religious authorities claim ignorance of the origin of John's baptism, they show themselves incapable of speaking with authority; hence Jesus refuses to discuss with them the grounds of his authority.

21, 28–32: The series of controversies is interrupted by three parables on the judgment of Israel (21, 28—22, 14) of which this, peculiar to Mt, is the first. The second (21, 33–46) comes from Mk (12, 1–12), and the third (22, 1–14) from Q; see Lk 14, 15–24. This interruption of the controversies is similar to that in Mk, although Mk has only one parable between the first and second controversy. As regards Mt's first parable, vv 28–30 if taken by themselves could point simply to the difference between saying and doing, a theme of much importance in this gospel (cf 7, 21; 12, 50); that may have been the parable's original reference. However, it is given a more specific application by the addition of vv 31–32. The two sons represent, respectively, the religious leaders and the religious outcasts who followed John's call to repentance. By the answer they give to Jesus' question (31) the leaders con-

p: 2 Sm 5, 8 LXX. *q:* Ps 8, 2 LXX; Wis 10, 21. *r:* Mk 11, 12-14.20-24. *s:* Jer 8, 13; Lk 13, 6-9. *t:* 17, 20; Lk 17, 6. *u:* 7, 7; 1 Jn 3, 22. *v:* Mk 11, 27-33; Lk 20, 1-8. *w:* Jn 2, 18. *x:* 14, 5.

to the first and said, 'Son, go out and work in the vineyard today.' 29He said in reply, 'I will not,' but afterwards he changed his mind and went. 30The man came to the other son and gave the same order. He said in reply, 'Yes, sir,' but did not go. 31*Which of the two did his father's will?" They answered, "The first." Jesus said to them, "Amen, I say to you, tax collectors and prostitutes are entering the kingdom of God before you. 32y*When John came to you in the way of righteousness, you did not believe him; but tax collectors and prostitutes did. Yet even when you saw that, you did not later change your minds and believe him.

The Parable of the Tenants. 33za*"Hear another parable. There was a landowner who planted a vineyard, put a hedge around it, dug a wine press in it, and built a tower. Then he leased it to tenants and went on a journey. 34*When vintage time drew near, he sent his servants to the tenants to obtain his produce. 35But the tenants seized the servants and one they beat, another they killed,

and a third they stoned. 36Again he sent other servants, more numerous than the first ones, but they treated them in the same way. 37Finally, he sent his son to them, thinking, 'They will respect my son.' 38*But when the tenants saw the son, they said to one another, 'This is the heir. Come, let us kill him and acquire his inheritance.' 39b*They seized him, threw him out of the vineyard, and killed him. 40What will the owner of the vineyard do to those tenants when he comes?" 41*They answered him, "He will put those wretched men to a wretched death and lease his vineyard to other tenants who will give him the produce at the proper times." 42c*Jesus said to them, "Did you never read in the scriptures:

'The stone that the builders rejected
    has become the cornerstone;
by the Lord has this been done,
    and it is wonderful in our eyes'?

43*Therefore, I say to you, the kingdom of

---

demn themselves. There is much confusion in the textual tradition of the parable. Of the three different forms of the text given by important textual witnesses, one has the leaders answer that the son who agreed to go but did not was the one who did the father's will. Although some scholars accept that as the original reading, their arguments in favor of it seem unconvincing. The choice probably lies only between a reading that puts the son who agrees and then disobeys before the son who at first refuses and then obeys, and the reading followed in the present translation. The witnesses to the latter reading are slightly better than those that support the other.

21, 31: Entering . . . before you: this probably means "they enter; you do not."

21, 32: Cf Lk 7, 29–30. Although the thought is similar to that of the Lucan text, the formulation is so different that it is improbable that the saying comes from Q. **Came to you . . . way of righteousness:** several meanings are possible: that John himself was righteous, that he taught righteousness to others, or that he had an important place in God's plan of salvation. For the last, see the note on 3, 14–15.

21, 33–46: Cf Mk 12, 1–12. In this parable there is a close correspondence between most of the details of the story and the situation that it illustrates, the dealings of God with his people. Because of that heavy allegorizing, some scholars think that it does not in any way go back to Jesus, but represents the theology of the later church. That judgment applies to the Marcan parallel as well, although the allegorizing has gone farther in Mt. There are others who believe that while many of the allegorical elements are due to church sources, they have been added to a basic parable spoken by Jesus. This view is now supported by the Gospel of Thomas, 65, where a less allegorized and probably more primitive form of the parable is found.

21, 33: Planted a vineyard . . . a tower: cf Is 5, 1–2. The **vineyard** is defined in Is 5, 7 as "the house of Israel."

21, 34–35: His servants: Mt has two sendings of **servants** as against Mk's three sendings of a single servant (11, 2–5a) followed by a statement about the sending of "many others" (11, 2.5b). That these **servants** stand for the prophets sent by God to Israel is clearly implied but not made explicit here, but see 23, 37. **His produce:** cf Mk 12, 2, "some of the produce." The **produce** is the good works demanded by God, and his claim to them is total.

21, 38: Acquire his inheritance: if a Jewish proselyte died without heir, the tenants of his land would have final claim on it.

21, 39: Threw him out . . . and killed him: the change in the Marcan order where the son is killed and his corpse then thrown out (12, 8) was probably made because of the tradition that Jesus died outside the city of Jerusalem; see Jn 19, 17; Heb 13, 12.

21, 41: They answered: in Mk 12, 9 the question is answered by Jesus himself; here the leaders answer and so condemn themselves; cf v 31. Matthew adds that the new **tenants** to whom the vineyard will be transferred **will give** the owner **the produce at the proper times.**

21, 42: Cf Ps 118, 22–23. The psalm was used in the early church as a prophecy of Jesus' resurrection; see Acts 4, 11; 1 Pt 2, 7. If, as some think, the original parable ended at v 39, it was thought necessary to complete it by a reference to Jesus' vindication by God.

21, 43: Peculiar to Mt. **Kingdom of God:** see the note on

y: Lk 7, 29-30.   z: Mk 12, 1-12; Lk 20, 9-19.   a: Is 5, 1-2.7.
b: Heb 13, 12.   c: Ps 118, 22-23; Is 28, 16; Acts 4, 11; 1 Pt 2, 7.

God will be taken away from you and given to a people that will produce its fruit. [144] *The one who falls on this stone will be dashed to pieces; and it will crush anyone on whom it falls.]" [45]*When the chief priests and the Pharisees heard his parables, they knew that he was speaking about them. [46]And although they were attempting to arrest him, they feared the crowds, for they regarded him as a prophet.

See RG
383-84

CHAPTER 22

The Parable of the Wedding Feast.

[1d]*Jesus again in reply spoke to them in parables, saying, [2]*"The kingdom of heaven may be likened to a king who gave a wedding feast for his son. [3]*He dispatched his servants to summon the invited guests to the feast, but they refused to come. [4]A second time he sent other servants, saying, 'Tell those invited: "Behold, I have prepared my banquet, my calves and fattened cattle are killed, and everything is ready; come to the feast."' [5]Some ignored the invitation and went away, one to his farm, another to his business. [6e]The rest laid hold of his servants, mistreated them, and killed them. [7]*The king was enraged and sent his troops, destroyed those murderers, and burned their city. [8]Then he said to his servants, 'The feast is ready, but those who were invited were not worthy to come. [9]Go out, therefore, into the main roads and invite to the feast whomever you find.' [10]*The servants went out into the streets and gathered all they found, bad and good alike, and the hall was filled with guests. [11]*But when the king came in to meet the guests he saw a man there not dressed in a wedding garment. [12]He said to him, 'My friend, how is it that you came in here without a wedding garment?' But he was reduced to silence. [13f]*Then the king said to his attendants, 'Bind his hands and feet, and cast him into the darkness outside, where there will be wailing and grinding of teeth.' [14]Many are invited, but few are chosen."

Paying Taxes to the Emperor.

[15g]*Then the Pharisees went off and plotted how they might entrap him in speech. [16]*They sent their disciples to him, with the Herodians, saying,

19, 23–24. Its presence here instead of Mt's usual "kingdom of heaven" may indicate that the saying came from Matthew's own traditional material. **A people that will produce its fruit:** believing Israelites and Gentiles, the church of Jesus.

21, 44: The majority of textual witnesses omit this verse. It is probably an early addition to Mt from Lk 20, 18 with which it is practically identical.

21, 45: The Pharisees: Matthew inserts into the group of Jewish leaders (23) those who represented the Judaism of his own time.

22, 1–14: This parable is from Q; see Lk 14, 15–24. It has been given many allegorical traits by Matthew, e.g., the burning of the **city** of the guests who refused the invitation (7), which corresponds to the destruction of Jerusalem by the Romans in A.D. 70. It has similarities with the preceding parable of the tenants: the sending of two groups of **servants** (3,4), the murder of the **servants** (6), the punishment of the **murderers** (7), and the entrance of a new group into a privileged situation of which the others had proved themselves unworthy (8–10). The parable ends with a section that is peculiar to Mt (11–14), which some take as a distinct parable. Mt presents the **kingdom** in its double aspect, already present and something that can be entered here and now (1–10), and something that will be possessed only by those present members who can stand the scrutiny of the final judgment (11–14). The parable is not only a statement of God's judgment on Israel but a warning to Matthew's church.

22, 2: Wedding feast: the Old Testament's portrayal of final salvation under the image of a banquet (Is 25, 6) is taken up also in 8, 11; cf Lk 13, 15.

22, 3–4: Servants . . . other servants: probably Christian missionaries in both instances; cf 23, 34.

22, 7: See the note on vv 1–14.

22, 10: Bad and good alike: cf 13, 47.

22, 11: A wedding garment: the repentance, change of heart and mind, that is the condition for entrance into the kingdom (3, 2; 4, 17) must be continued in a life of good deeds (7, 21–23).

22, 13: Wailing and grinding of teeth: the Christian who lacks the wedding garment of good deeds will suffer the same fate as those Jews who have rejected Jesus; see the note on 8, 11–12.

22, 15–22: The series of controversies between Jesus and the representatives of Judaism (see the note on 21, 23–27) is resumed. As in the first (21, 23–27), here and in the following disputes Matthew follows his Marcan source with few modifications.

22, 15: The Pharisees: while Matthew retains the Marcan union of Pharisees and Herodians in this account, he clearly emphasizes the Pharisees' part. They alone are mentioned here, and the Herodians are joined with them only in a prepositional phrase of v 16. **Entrap him in speech:** the question that they will pose is intended to force Jesus to take either a position contrary to that held by the majority of the people or one that will bring him into conflict with the Roman authorities.

22, 16: Herodians: see the note on Mk 3, 6. They would favor payment of the tax; the Pharisees did not.

d: Lk 14, 15-24. *e:* 21, 35. *f:* 8, 12; 25, 30. *g:* Mk 12, 13-17; Lk 20, 20-26.

"Teacher, we know that you are a truthful man and that you teach the way of God in accordance with the truth. And you are not concerned with anyone's opinion, for you do not regard a person's status. *17**Tell us, then, what is your opinion: Is it lawful to pay the census tax to Caesar or not?" *18*Knowing their malice, Jesus said, "Why are you testing me, you hypocrites? *19**Show me the coin that pays the census tax." Then they handed him the Roman coin. *20*He said to them, "Whose image is this and whose inscription?" *21h**They replied, "Caesar's." At that he said to them, "Then repay to Caesar what belongs to Caesar and to God what belongs to God." *22*When they heard this they were amazed, and leaving him they went away.

The Question about the Resurrection. *23i**On that day Sadducees approached him, saying that there is no resurrection. They put this question to him, *24j**saying, "Teacher, Moses said, 'If a man dies without children,

his brother shall marry his wife and raise up descendants for his brother.' *25*Now there were seven brothers among us. The first married and died and, having no descendants, left his wife to his brother. *26*The same happened with the second and the third, through all seven. *27*Finally the woman died. *28*Now at the resurrection, of the seven, whose wife will she be? For they all had been married to her." *29**Jesus said to them in reply, "You are misled because you do not know the scriptures or the power of God. *30*At the resurrection they neither marry nor are given in marriage but are like the angels in heaven. *31**And concerning the resurrection of the dead, have you not read what was said to you by God, *32k*'I am the God of Abraham, the God of Isaac, and the God of Jacob'? He is not the God of the dead but of the living." *33*When the crowds heard this, they were astonished at his teaching.

The Greatest Commandment. *34l**When

22, 17: **Is it lawful:** the law to which they refer is the law of God.

22, 19: **They handed him the Roman coin:** their readiness in producing the money implies their use of it and their acceptance of the financial advantages of the Roman administration in Palestine.

22, 21: **Caesar's:** the emperor Tiberius (A.D. 14–37). **Repay to Caesar what belongs to Caesar:** those who willingly use the coin that is Caesar's should **repay** him in kind. The answer avoids taking sides in the question of the lawfulness of the tax. **To God what belongs to God:** Jesus raises the debate to a new level. Those who have hypocritically asked about tax in respect to its relation to the law of God should be concerned rather with repaying **God** with the good deeds that are his due; cf 21, 41.43.

22, 23–33: Here Jesus' opponents are the **Sadducees,** members of the powerful priestly party of his time; see the note on 3, 7. Denying the resurrection of the dead, a teaching of relatively late origin in Judaism (cf Dn 12, 2), they appeal to a law of the Pentateuch (Dt 25, 5–10) and present a case based on it that would make resurrection from the dead ridiculous (24–28). Jesus chides them for knowing neither **the scriptures** nor **the power of God** (29). His argument in respect to God's **power** contradicts the notion, held even by many proponents as well as by opponents of the teaching, that the life of those raised from the dead would be essentially a continuation of the type of life they had had before death (30). His argument based on the scriptures (31–32) is of a sort that was accepted as valid among Jews of the time.

22, 23: **Saying that there is no resurrection:** in the Marcan parallel (12, 18) the Sadducees are correctly defined as those "who say there is no resurrection"; see also Lk 20, 27. Matthew's rewording of Mk can mean that these particular Sadducees deny the resurrection, which would imply that he

was not aware that the denial was characteristic of the party. For some scholars this is an indication of his being a Gentile Christian; see the note on 21, 4–5.

22, 24: **'If a man dies . . . his brother':** this is known as the "law of the levirate," from the Latin **levir,** "brother-in-law." Its purpose was to continue the family line of the deceased **brother** (Dt 25, 6).

22, 29: The sexual relationships of this world will be transcended; the risen body will be the work of the creative **power of God.**

22, 31–32: Cf Ex 3, 6. In the Pentateuch, which the Sadducees accepted as normative for Jewish belief and practice, God speaks even now (**to you**) of himself as the God of the patriarchs who died centuries ago. He identifies himself in relation to them, and because of their relation to him, the living God, they too are alive. This might appear no argument for the resurrection, but simply for life after death as conceived in Wis 3, 1–3. But the general thought of early first-century Judaism was not influenced by that conception; for it human immortality was connected with the existence of the body.

22, 34–40: The Marcan parallel (12, 28–34) is an exchange between Jesus and a scribe who is impressed by the way in which Jesus has conducted himself in the previous controversy (12, 28), who compliments him for the answer he gives him (12, 32), and who is said by Jesus to be "not far from the kingdom of God" (12, 34). Matthew has sharpened that scene. The questioner, as the representative of other Pharisees, tests Jesus by his question (34–35), and both his reaction to Jesus' reply and Jesus' commendation of him are lacking.

h: Rom 13, 7.   i: Mk 12, 18-27; Lk 20, 27-40.   j: Gn 38, 8; Dt 25, 5-6.   k: Ex 3, 6.   l: Mk 12, 28-34; Lk 10, 25-28.

the Pharisees heard that he had silenced the Sadducees, they gathered together, [35*]and one of them [a scholar of the law] tested him by asking, [36*]"Teacher, which commandment in the law is the greatest?" [37m*]He said to him, "You shall love the Lord, your God, with all your heart, with all your soul, and with all your mind. [38]This is the greatest and the first commandment. [39n*]The second is like it: You shall love your neighbor as yourself. [40o*]The whole law and the prophets depend on these two commandments."

The Question about David's Son. [41p*]While the Pharisees were gathered together, Jesus questioned them, [42*]saying, "What is your opinion about the Messiah? Whose son is he?" They replied, "David's."

[43]He said to them, "How, then, does David, inspired by the Spirit, call him 'lord,' saying:

[44] [q] 'The Lord said to my lord,
"Sit at my right hand
until I place your enemies under your feet" '?

[45*]If David calls him 'lord,' how can he be his son?" [46r]No one was able to answer him a word, nor from that day on did anyone dare to ask him any more questions.

CHAPTER 23

See RG 383–84

Denunciation of the Scribes and Pharisees. [1s*]Then Jesus spoke to the crowds and to his disciples, [2*]saying, "The scribes and the Pharisees have taken their

---

22, 35: [A scholar of the law]: meaning "scribe." Although this reading is supported by the vast majority of textual witnesses, it is the only time that the Greek word so translated occurs in Mt. It is relatively frequent in Lk, and there is reason to think that it may have been added here by a copyist since it occurs in the Lucan parallel (10, 25–28). **Tested:** see the note on 19, 3.

22, 36: For the devout Jew all the commandments were to be kept with equal care, but there is evidence of preoccupation in Jewish sources with the question put to Jesus.

22, 37–38: Cf Dt 6, 5. Matthew omits the first part of Mk's fuller quotation (12, 29; Dt 6, 4–5), probably because he considered its monotheistic emphasis needless for his church. The love of God must engage the total person (**heart, soul, mind**).

22, 39: Jesus goes beyond the extent of the question put to him and joins **to the greatest and the first commandment** a **second**, that of **love** of **neighbor**, Lv 19, 18; see the note on 19, 18–19. This combination of the two commandments may already have been made in Judaism.

22, 40: The double commandment is the source from which **the whole law and the prophets** are derived.

22, 41–46: Having answered the questions of his opponents in the preceding three controversies, Jesus now puts a question to them about the sonship of the Messiah. Their easy response (43a) is countered by his quoting a verse of Ps 110 that raises a problem for their response (43b-45). They are unable to solve it and **from that day on** their questioning of him is ended.

22, 41: The Pharisees . . . questioned them: Mk is not specific about who are questioned (12, 35).

22, 42–44: David's: this view of the Pharisees was based on such Old Testament texts as Is 11, 1–9; Jer 23, 5; and Ez 34, 23; see also the extrabiblical Psalms of Solomon 17, 21. **How, then . . . saying:** Jesus cites Ps 110, 1, accepting the Davidic authorship of the psalm, a common view of his time. The psalm was probably composed for the enthronement of a Davidic king of Judah. Matthew assumes that the Pharisees interpret it as referring to the Messiah, although there is no clear evidence that it was so interpreted in the Judaism of Jesus' time. It was widely used in the early church as referring to the exaltation of the risen Jesus. **My lord:** understood as the Messiah.

22, 45: Since Matthew presents Jesus both as Messiah (16, 16) and as Son of David (1, 1; see also the note on 9, 27), the question is not meant to imply Jesus' denial of Davidic sonship. It probably means that although he is the Son of David, he is someone greater, Son of Man and Son of God, and recognized as greater by David who calls him my **'lord.'**

23, 1–39: The final section of the narrative part of the fifth book of the gospel is a denunciation by Jesus of the scribes and the Pharisees (see the note on 3, 7). It depends in part on Mk and Q (cf Mk 12, 38–39; Lk 11, 37–52; 13, 34–35), but in the main it is peculiar to Mt. (For the reasons against considering this extensive body of sayings-material either as one of the structural discourses of this gospel or as part of the one that follows in chs 24–25, see the note on 19, 1—23, 39.) While the tradition of a deep opposition between Jesus and the Pharisees is well founded, this speech reflects an opposition that goes beyond that of Jesus' ministry and must be seen as expressing the bitter conflict between Pharisaic Judaism and the church of Matthew at the time when the gospel was composed. The complaint often made that the speech ignores the positive qualities of Pharisaism and of its better representatives is true, but the complaint overlooks the circumstances that gave rise to the invective. Nor is the speech purely anti-Pharisaic. The evangelist discerns in his church many of the same faults that he finds in its opponents and warns his fellow Christians to look to their own conduct and attitudes.

23, 2–3: Have taken their seat . . . Moses: it is uncertain whether this is simply a metaphor for Mosaic teaching authority or refers to an actual chair on which the teacher sat. It has been proved that there was a seat so designated in synagogues of a later period than that of this gospel. **Do and observe . . . they tell you:** since the Matthean Jesus abrogates Mosaic law (5, 31–42), warns his disciples against the teaching of the Pharisees (14, 1–12), and, in this speech, denounces the Pharisees as blind guides in respect to their teaching on oaths (16–22), this commandment **to observe all things**

m: Dt 6, 5. *n:* Lv 19, 18; Jas 2, 8. *o:* Rom 13, 8-10; Gal 5, 14. *p:* Mk 12, 35-37; Lk 20, 41-44. *q:* Ps 110, 1; Acts 2, 35; Heb 1, 13. *r:* Lk 20, 40. *s:* Mk 12, 38-39; Lk 11, 37-52; 13, 34-35.

one swears by the temple, it means nothing, but if one swears by the gold of the temple, one is obligated.' [17]Blind fools, which is greater, the gold, or the temple that made the gold sacred? [18]And you say, 'If one swears by the altar, it means nothing, but if one swears by the gift on the altar, one is obligated.' [19]You blind ones, which is greater, the gift, or the altar that makes the gift sacred? [20a]One who swears by the altar swears by it and all that is upon it; [21]one who swears by the temple swears by it and by him who dwells in it; [22]one who swears by heaven swears by the throne of God and by him who is seated on it.

[23b]*"Woe to you, scribes and Pharisees, you hypocrites. You pay tithes of mint and dill and cummin, and have neglected the weightier things of the law: judgment and mercy and fidelity. [But] these you should have done, without neglecting the others. [24c]*Blind guides, who strain out the gnat and swallow the camel!

[25d]*"Woe to you, scribes and Pharisees, you hypocrites. You cleanse the outside of cup and dish, but inside they are full of plunder and self-indulgence. [26]Blind Pharisee, cleanse first the inside of the cup, so that the outside also may be clean.

[27]*"Woe to you, scribes and Pharisees, you hypocrites. You are like whitewashed tombs, which appear beautiful on the outside, but inside are full of dead men's bones and every kind of filth. [28e]Even so, on the outside you appear righteous, but inside you are filled with hypocrisy and evildoing.

[29]*"Woe to you, scribes and Pharisees, you hypocrites. You build the tombs of the prophets and adorn the memorials of the righteous, [30f]and you say, 'If we had lived in the days of our ancestors, we would not have joined them in shedding the prophets' blood.' [31g]Thus you bear witness against yourselves that you are the children of those who murdered the prophets; [32]now fill up what your ancestors measured out! [33h]You serpents, you brood of vipers, how can you flee from the judgment of Gehenna? [34i]*Therefore, behold, I send to you prophets

23, 23: The Mosaic law ordered tithing of the produce of the land (Lv 27, 30; Dt 14, 22–23), and the scribal tradition is said here to have extended this law to even the smallest herbs. The practice is criticized not in itself but because it shows the Pharisees' preoccupation with matters of less importance while they neglect **the weightier things of the law.**

23, 24: Cf Lv 11, 41–45 that forbids the eating of any "swarming creature." The Pharisees' scrupulosity about minor matters and neglect of greater ones (23) is further brought out by this contrast between straining liquids that might contain a tiny "swarming creature" and yet swallowing **the camel.** The latter was one of the unclean animals forbidden by the law (Lv 11, 4), but it is hardly possible that the scribes and Pharisees are being denounced as guilty of so gross a violation of the food laws. To **swallow the camel** is only a hyperbolic way of speaking of their neglect of what is important.

23, 25–26: The ritual washing of utensils for dining (cf Mk 7, 4) is turned into a metaphor illustrating a concern for appearances while inner purity is ignored. The **scribes and Pharisees** are compared to cups carefully washed on the outside but filthy within. **Self-indulgence:** the Greek word here translated means lack of self-control, whether in drinking or in sexual conduct.

23, 27–28: The sixth **woe**, like the preceding one, deals with concern for externals and neglect of what is **inside.** Since contact with dead bodies, even when one was unaware of it, caused ritual impurity (Nm 19, 11–22), tombs were whitewashed so that no one would contract such impurity inadvertently.

23, 29–36: The final **woe** is the most serious indictment of all. It portrays the **scribes and Pharisees** as standing in the same line as their **ancestors** who murdered **the prophets** and **the righteous.**

23, 29–32: In spite of honoring the slain dead by building their **tombs** and adorning their **memorials,** and claiming that they would not have joined in their ancestors' crimes if they **had lived in** their **days,** the **scribes and Pharisees** are true **children** of their ancestors and are defiantly ordered by Jesus to **fill up** what those **ancestors measured out.** This order reflects the Jewish notion that there was an allotted measure of suffering that had to be completed before God's final judgment would take place.

23, 34–36: There are important differences between the Matthean and the Lucan form of this Q material; cf Lk 11, 49–51. In Lk the one who sends the emissaries is the "wisdom of God." If, as many scholars think, that is the original wording of Q, Matthew, by making Jesus the sender, has presented him as the personified divine wisdom. In Lk, wisdom's emissaries are the Old Testament "prophets" and the Christian "apostles." Mt's **prophets and wise men and scribes** are probably Christian disciples alone; cf 10, 41 and see the note on 13, 52. **You will kill:** see 24, 9. **Scourge in your synagogues . . . town to town:** see 10, 17.23 and the note on 10, 17. **All the righteous blood shed upon the earth:** the slaying of the disciples is in continuity with all the shedding of **righteous blood** beginning with that of **Abel.** The persecution of Jesus' disciples by **this generation** involves the persecutors in the guilt of their murderous ancestors. **The blood of Zechariah:** see the note on Lk 11, 51. By identifying him as **the son of Barachiah** Matthew understands him to be Zechariah the Old Testament minor prophet; see Zec 1, 1.

a: 5, 34-35. *b:* Lv 27, 30; Dt 14, 22; Lk 11, 42. *c:* Lv 11, 41-45. *d:* Mk 7, 4; Lk 11, 39. *e:* Lk 16, 15; 18, 9. *f:* Lk 11, 47. *g:* Acts 7, 52. *h:* 3, 7; 12, 34. *i:* 5, 12; Gn 4, 8; 2 Chr 24, 20-22; Zec 1, 1; Lk 11, 49-51;Rv 18, 24.

and wise men and scribes; some of them you will kill and crucify, some of them you will scourge in your synagogues and pursue from town to town, *35* so that there may come upon you all the righteous blood shed upon earth, from the righteous blood of Abel to the blood of Zechariah, the son of Barachiah, whom you murdered between the sanctuary and the altar. *36* Amen, I say to you, all these things will come upon this generation.

The Lament over Jerusalem. *37jk**"Jerusalem, Jerusalem, you who kill the prophets and stone those sent to you, how many times I yearned to gather your children together, as a hen gathers her young under her wings, but you were unwilling! *38l* Behold, your house will be abandoned, desolate. *39m* I tell you, you will not see me again until you say, 'Blessed is he who comes in the name of the Lord.' "

23, 37–39: Cf Lk 13, 34–35. The denunciation of Pharisaic Judaism ends with this lament over **Jerusalem**, which has repeatedly rejected and murdered those whom God has **sent** to her. **How many times:** this may refer to various visits of Jesus to the city, an aspect of his ministry found in Jn but otherwise not in the synoptics. **As a hen . . . under her wings:** for imagery similar to this, see Pss 17, 8; 91, 4. **Your house . . . desolate:** probably an allusion to the destruction of the temple in A.D. 70. **You will not see me . . . in the name of the Lord:** Israel will not see Jesus again until he comes in glory for the final judgment. The acclamation has been interpreted in contrasting ways, as an indication that Israel will at last accept Jesus at that time, and as its troubled recognition of him as its dreaded judge who will pronounce its condemnation; in support of the latter view see 24, 30.

24, 1—25, 46: The discourse of the fifth book, the last of the five around which the gospel is structured. It is called the "eschatological" discourse since it deals with the coming of the new age (the **eschaton**) in its fullness, with events that will precede it, and with how the disciples are to conduct themselves while awaiting an event that is as certain as its exact time is unknown to all but the Father (24, 36). The discourse may be divided into two parts, 24, 1–44 and 24, 45—25, 46. In the first, Matthew follows his Marcan source (13, 1–37) closely. The second is drawn from Q and from the evangelist's own traditional material. Both parts show Matthew's editing of his sources by deletions, additions, and modifications. The vigilant waiting that is emphasized in the second part does not mean a cessation of ordinary activity and concentration only on what is to come, but a faithful accomplishment of duties at hand, with awareness that the end, for which the disciples must always be ready, will entail the great judgment by which the everlasting destiny of all will be determined.

24, 2: As in Mk, Jesus predicts the destruction of the temple. By omitting the Marcan story of the widow's contribution (12, 41–44) that immediately precedes the prediction in that gospel, Matthew has established a close connection between it

---

The Destruction of the Temple Foretold. *1n**Jesus left the temple area and was going away, when his disciples approached him to point out the temple buildings. *2**He said to them in reply, "You see all these things, do you not? Amen, I say to you, there will not be left here a stone upon another stone that will not be thrown down."

The Beginning of Calamities. *3**As he was sitting on the Mount of Olives, the disciples approached him privately and said, "Tell us, when will this happen, and what sign will there be of your coming, and of the end of the age?" *4**Jesus said to them in reply, "See that no one deceives you. *5* For many will come in my name, saying, 'I am the Messiah,' and they will deceive many. *6o**You will hear of wars and reports of wars;

---

and 23, 38, ". . . your house will be abandoned desolate."

24, 3: The Mount of Olives: see the note on 21, 1. **The disciples:** cf Mk 13, 3–4 where only Peter, James, John, and Andrew put the question that is answered by the discourse. In both gospels, however, the question is put **privately:** the ensuing discourse is only for those who are **disciples** of Jesus. **When will this happen . . . end of the age?:** Matthew distinguishes carefully between the destruction of the temple [**this**] and the **coming** of Jesus that will bring **the end of the age.** In Mk the two events are more closely connected, a fact that may be explained by Mark's believing that the one would immediately succeed the other. **Coming:** this translates the Greek word **parousia,** which is used in the gospels only here and in vv 27, 37, and 39. It designated the official visit of a ruler to a city or the manifestation of a saving deity, and it was used by Christians to refer to the final coming of Jesus in glory, a term first found in the New Testament with that meaning in 1 Thes 2, 19. **The end of the age:** see the note on 13, 39.

24, 4–14: This section of the discourse deals with calamities in the world (6–7) and in the church (9–12). The former **must happen** before **the end** comes (6), but they are only **the beginning of the labor pains** (8). (It may be noted that the Greek word translated **the end** in v 6 and in vv 13–14 is not the same as the phrase "the end of the age" in v 3, although the meaning is the same.) The latter are sufferings of the church, both from within and without, that will last until the **gospel is preached . . . to all nations. Then the end will come** and those who have endured the sufferings with fidelity **will be saved** (13–14).

24, 6–7: The disturbances mentioned here are a commonplace of apocalyptic language, as is the assurance that they **must happen** (see Dn 2, 28 LXX), for that is the plan of God. **Kingdom against kingdom:** see Is 19, 2.

j: Lk 13, 34-35; 19, 41-44. *k:* 21, 35. *l:* Jer 12, 7. *m:* Ps 118, 26. *n:* Mk 13, 1-37; Lk 21, 5-36. *o:* Dn 2, 28 LXX.

see that you are not alarmed, for these things must happen, but it will not yet be the end. [7p]Nation will rise against nation, and kingdom against kingdom; there will be famines and earthquakes from place to place. [8*]All these are the beginning of the labor pains. [9q*]Then they will hand you over to persecution, and they will kill you. You will be hated by all nations because of my name. [10]And then many will be led into sin; they will betray and hate one another. [11]Many false prophets will arise and deceive many; [12]and because of the increase of evildoing, the love of many will grow cold. [13r]But the one who perseveres to the end will be saved. [14s*]And this gospel of the kingdom will be preached throughout the world as a witness to all nations, and then the end will come.

The Great Tribulation. [15t*]"When you see the desolating abomination spoken of through Daniel the prophet standing in the holy place (let the reader understand), [16*]then those in Judea must flee to the mountains, [17u*]a person on the housetop must not go down to get things out of his house, [18]a person in the field must not return to get his cloak. [19]Woe to pregnant women and nursing mothers in those days. [20*]Pray that your flight not be in winter or on the sabbath, [21v*]for at that time there will be great tribulation, such as has not been since the beginning of the world until now, nor ever will be. [22]And if those days had not been

24, 8: The labor pains: the tribulations leading up to the end of the age are compared to the pains of a woman about to give birth. There is much attestation for rabbinic use of the phrase "the woes (or birth pains) of the Messiah" after the New Testament period, but in at least one instance it is attributed to a rabbi who lived in the late first century A.D. In this Jewish usage it meant the distress of the time preceding the coming of the Messiah; here, the labor pains precede the coming of the Son of Man in glory.

24, 9–12: Matthew has used Mk 13, 9–12 in his missionary discourse (10, 17–21) and omits it here. Besides the sufferings, including death, and the hatred of all nations that the disciples will have to endure, there will be worse affliction within the church itself. This is described in vv 10–12, which are peculiar to Mt. Will be led into sin: literally, "will be scandalized," probably meaning that they will become apostates; see 13, 21 where "fall away" translates the same Greek word as here. Betray: in the Greek this is the same word as the hand over of v 9. The handing over to persecution and hatred from outside will have their counterpart within the church. False prophets: these are Christians; see the note on 7, 15–20. Evildoing: see 7, 23. Because of the apocalyptic nature of much of this discourse, the literal meaning of this description of the church should not be pressed too hard. However, there is reason to think that Mt's addition of these verses reflects in some measure the condition of his community.

24, 14: Except for the last part (and then the end will come), this verse substantially repeats Mk 13, 10. The Matthean addition raises a problem since what follows in vv 15–23 refers to the horrors of the First Jewish Revolt including the destruction of the temple, and Matthew, writing after that time, knew that the parousia of Jesus was still in the future. A solution may be that the evangelist saw the events of those verses as foreshadowing the cosmic disturbances that he associates with the parousia (29) so that the period in which the former took place could be understood as belonging to the end.

24, 15–28: Cf Mk 13, 14–23; Lk 17, 23–24.37. A further stage in the tribulations that will precede the coming of the Son of Man, and an answer to the question of v 3a, "when will this (the destruction of the temple) happen?"

24, 15: The desolating abomination: in 167 B.C. the Syrian king Antiochus IV Epiphanes desecrated the temple by setting up in it a statue of Zeus Olympios (see 1 Mc 1, 54). That event is referred to in Dn 12, 11 LXX as the "desolating abomination" (NAB "horrible abomination") and the same Greek term is used here; cf also Dn 9, 27; 11, 31. Although the desecration had taken place before Dn was written, it is presented there as a future event, and Matthew sees that "prophecy" fulfilled in the desecration of the temple by the Romans. In the holy place: the temple; more precise than Mk's where he should not (13, 14). Let the reader understand: this parenthetical remark, taken from Mk 13, 14, invites the reader to realize the meaning of Dn's "prophecy."

24, 16: The tradition that the Christians of Jerusalem fled from that city to Pella, a city of Transjordan, at the time of the First Jewish Revolt is found in Eusebius (**Ecclesiastical History,** 3, 5, 3), who attributes the flight to "a certain oracle given by revelation before the war." The tradition is not improbable but the Matthean command, derived from its Marcan source, is vague in respect to the place of flight (to the mountains), although some scholars see it as applicable to the flight to Pella.

24, 17–19: Haste is essential, and the journey will be particularly difficult for women who are burdened with unborn or infant children.

24, 20: On the sabbath: this addition to in winter (cf Mk 13, 18) has been understood as an indication that Mt was addressed to a church still observing the Mosaic law of sabbath rest and the scribal limitations upon the length of journeys that might lawfully be made on that day. That interpretation conflicts with Mt's view on sabbath observance (cf 12, 1–14). The meaning of the addition may be that those undertaking on the sabbath a journey such as the one here ordered would be offending the sensibilities of law-observant Jews and would incur their hostility.

24, 21: For the unparalleled distress of that time, see Dn 12, 1.

p: Is 19, 2.   q: 10, 17.   r: 10, 22.   s: 28, 19; Rom 10, 18.   t: Dn 9, 27; 11, 31; 12, 11; Mk 13, 14.   u: Lk 17, 31.   v: Dn 12, 1.

shortened, no one would be saved; but for the sake of the elect they will be shortened. [23w]If anyone says to you then, 'Look, here is the Messiah!' or, 'There he is!' do not believe it. [24]False messiahs and false prophets will arise, and they will perform signs and wonders so great as to deceive, if that were possible, even the elect. [25]Behold, I have told it to you beforehand. [26]*So if they say to you, 'He is in the desert,' do not go out there; if they say, 'He is in the inner rooms,' do not believe it. [27x]For just as lightning comes from the east and is seen as far as the west, so will the coming of the Son of Man be. [28]Wherever the corpse is, there the vultures will gather.

The Coming of the Son of Man. [29y]*"Immediately after the tribulation of those days,

the sun will be darkened,
and the moon will not give its light,
and the stars will fall from the sky,
and the powers of the heavens will be shaken.

[30z]*And then the sign of the Son of Man will appear in heaven, and all the tribes of the earth will mourn, and they will see the Son of Man coming upon the clouds of heaven with power and great glory. [31a]*And he will send out his angels with a trumpet blast, and they will gather his elect from the four winds, from one end of the heavens to the other.

The Lesson of the Fig Tree. [32]*"Learn a lesson from the fig tree. When its branch becomes tender and sprouts leaves, you know that summer is near. [33]In the same way, when you see all these things, know that he is near, at the gates. [34]*Amen, I say to you, this generation will not pass away until all these things have taken place. [35b]Heaven and earth will pass away, but my words will not pass away.

The Unknown Day and Hour. [36c]*"But of that day and hour no one knows, neither the angels of heaven, nor the Son, but the Father alone. [37d]*For as it was in the days of Noah, so it will be at the coming of the Son of Man. [38]In [those] days before the flood, they were eating and drinking, marrying and giving in marriage, up to the day that Noah entered the ark. [39]They did not know until the flood came and carried them all away. So will it be [also] at the coming of the Son of Man. [40e]*Two men will be out in the field; one will

24, 26–28: Claims that the Messiah is to be found in some distant or secret place must be ignored. **The coming of the Son of Man** will be as clear as **lightning** is to all and as **the corpse** of an animal is to **vultures;** cf Lk 17, 24.37. Here there is clear identification of **the Son of Man** and the Messiah; cf v 23.

24, 29: The answer to the question of v 3b, "What will be the sign of your coming?" **Immediately after . . . those days:** the shortening of time between the preceding **tribulation** and the parousia has been explained as Matthew's use of a supposed device of Old Testament prophecy whereby certainty that a predicted event will occur is expressed by depicting it as imminent. While it is questionable that that is an acceptable understanding of the Old Testament predictions, it may be applicable here, for Matthew knew that the parousia had not come **immediately after** the fall of Jerusalem, and it is unlikely that he is attributing a mistaken calculation of time to Jesus. **The sun . . . be shaken:** cf Is 13, 10.13.

24, 30: **The sign of the Son of Man:** perhaps this means **the sign** that is the glorious appearance **of the Son of Man;** cf 12, 39–40 where "the sign of Jonah" is Jonah's being in the "belly of the whale." **Tribes of the earth will mourn:** peculiar to Mt; cf Zec 12, 12–14. **Coming upon the clouds . . . glory:** cf Dn 7, 13, although there the "one like a son of man" comes to God to receive kingship; here **the Son of Man** comes from heaven for judgment.

24, 31: **Send out his angels:** cf 13, 41 where they are sent out to collect the wicked for punishment. **Trumpet blast:** cf Is 27, 13; 1 Thes 4, 16.

24, 32–35: Cf Mk 13, 28–31.

24, 34: The difficulty raised by this verse cannot be satisfactorily removed by the supposition that **this generation** means the Jewish people throughout the course of their history, much less the entire human race. Perhaps for Matthew it means the **generation** to which he and his community belonged.

24, 36–44: The statement of v 34 is now counterbalanced by one that declares that the exact time of the parousia is known only to **the Father** (36), and the disciples are warned to be always ready for it. This section is drawn from Mk and Q (cf Lk 17, 26–27.34–35; 12, 39–40).

24, 36: Many textual witnesses omit **nor the Son,** which follows Mk 13, 32. Since its omission can be explained by reluctance to attribute this ignorance to **the Son,** the reading that includes it is probably original.

24, 37–39: Cf Lk 17, 26–27. **In the days of Noah:** the Old Testament account of the flood lays no emphasis upon what is central for Matthew, i.e., the unexpected coming of the flood upon those who were unprepared for it.

24, 40–41: Cf Lk 17, 34–35. **Taken . . . left:** the former probably means **taken** into the kingdom; the latter, **left** for destruction. People in the same situation will be dealt with in opposite ways. In this context, the discrimination between them will be based on their readiness for the coming of the Son of Man.

w: Lk 17, 23.   *x:* Lk 17, 24.37.   *y:* Is 13, 10.13; Ez 32, 7; Am 8, 9.   *z:* Dn 7, 13; Zec 12, 12-14; Rv 1, 7.   *a:* Is 27, 13; 1 Cor 15, 52; 1 Thes 4, 16.   *b:* Is 40, 8.   *c:* Acts 1, 7.   *d:* Gn 6, 5—7, 23; Lk 17, 26-27; 2 Pt 3, 6.   *e:* Lk 17, 34-35.

be taken, and one will be left. *41*Two women will be grinding at the mill; one will be taken, and one will be left. *42f**Therefore, stay awake! For you do not know on which day your Lord will come. *43g*Be sure of this: if the master of the house had known the hour of night when the thief was coming, he would have stayed awake and not let his house be broken into. *44*So too, you also must be prepared, for at an hour you do not expect, the Son of Man will come.

The Faithful or the Unfaithful Servant. *45h**"Who, then, is the faithful and prudent servant, whom the master has put in charge of his household to distribute to them their food at the proper time? *46*Blessed is that servant whom his master on his arrival finds doing so. *47*Amen, I say to you, he will put him in charge of all his property. *48**But if that wicked servant says to himself, 'My master is long delayed,' *49*and begins to beat his fellow servants, and eat and drink with drunkards, *50*the servant's master will come on an unexpected day and at an unknown hour *51i**and will punish him severely and assign him a place with the hypocrites, where there will be wailing and grinding of teeth.

CHAPTER 25

See RG 383–84

The Parable of the Ten Virgins. *1**"Then the kingdom of heaven will be like ten virgins who took their lamps and went out to meet the bridegroom. *2**Five of them were foolish and five were wise. *3*The foolish ones, when taking their lamps, brought no oil with them, *4*but the wise brought flasks of oil with their lamps. *5*Since the bridegroom was long delayed, they all became drowsy and fell asleep. *6*At midnight, there was a cry, 'Behold, the bridegroom! Come out to meet him!' *7*Then all those virgins got up and trimmed their lamps. *8*The foolish ones said to the wise, 'Give us some of your oil, for our lamps are going out.' *9*But the wise ones replied, 'No, for there may not be enough for us and you. Go instead to the merchants and buy some for yourselves.' *10*While they went off to buy it, the bridegroom came and those who were ready went into the wedding feast with him. Then the door was locked. *11j**Afterwards the other virgins came and said, 'Lord, Lord, open the door for us!' *12*But he said in reply, 'Amen, I say to you, I do not know you.' *13k**Therefore, stay awake, for you know neither the day nor the hour.

The Parable of the Talents. *14l**"It will be as when a man who was going on a journey called in his servants and entrusted his possessions to them. *15**To one he gave five talents; to another, two; to a third, one—to each according to his ability. Then he went away.

24, 42–44: Cf Lk 12, 39–40. The theme of vigilance and readiness is continued with the bold comparison of the Son of Man to a thief who comes to break into a house.

24, 45–51: The second part of the discourse (see the note on 24, 1—25, 46) begins with this parable of **the faithful** or unfaithful **servant;** cf Lk 12, 41–46. It is addressed to the leaders of Matthew's church; **the servant has been put in charge** of his master's **household** (45) even though that **household** is composed of those who are his **fellow servants** (49).

24, 45: To distribute . . . proper time: readiness for the master's return means a vigilance that is accompanied by faithful performance of the duty assigned.

24, 48: My master . . . delayed: the note of delay is found also in the other parables of this section; cf 25, 5.19.

24, 51: Punish him severely: the Greek verb, found in the New Testament only here and in the Lucan parallel (12, 46), means, literally, "cut in two." **With the hypocrites:** see the note on 6, 2. Matthew classes the unfaithful Christian leader with the unbelieving leaders of Judaism. **Wailing and grinding of teeth:** see the note on 8, 11–12.

25, 1–13: Peculiar to Mt.

25, 1: Then: at the time of the parousia. **Kingdom . . . will be like:** see the note on 13, 24–30.

25, 2–4: Foolish . . . wise: cf the contrasted "wise man" and "fool" of 7, 24.26, where the two are distinguished by good deeds and lack of them, and such deeds may be signified by the **oil** of this parable.

25, 11–12: Lord, Lord: cf 7, 21. **I do not know you:** cf 7, 23, where the Greek verb is different but synonymous.

25, 13: Stay awake: some scholars see this command as an addition to the original parable of Matthew's traditional material, since in v 5 all the virgins, wise and foolish, fall asleep. But the wise virgins are adequately equipped for their task, and **stay awake** may mean no more than to be prepared; cf 24, 42.44.

25, 14–30: Cf Lk 19, 12–27.

25, 14: It will be as when . . . journey: literally, "For just as a man who was going on a journey." Although the comparison is not completed, the sense is clear; the kingdom of heaven is like the situation here described. Faithful use of one's gifts will lead to participation in the fullness of the kingdom, lazy inactivity to exclusion from it.

25, 15: Talents: see the note on 18, 24.

f: 25, 13; Lk 12, 39-40. *g:* 1 Thes 5, 2. *h:* Lk 12, 41-46. *i:* 13, 42; 25, 30. *j:* 7, 21.23; Lk 13, 25.27. *k:* 24, 42; Mk 13, 33. *l:* Lk 19, 12-27.

Immediately ^{16}the one who received five talents went and traded with them, and made another five. ^{17}Likewise, the one who received two made another two. ^{18}*But the man who received one went off and dug a hole in the ground and buried his master's money. ^{19}After a long time the master of those servants came back and settled accounts with them. ^{20}*The one who had received five talents came forward bringing the additional five. He said, 'Master, you gave me five talents. See, I have made five more.' ^{21m}His master said to him, 'Well done, my good and faithful servant. Since you were faithful in small matters, I will give you great responsibilities. Come, share your master's joy.' ^{22}[Then] the one who had received two talents also came forward and said, 'Master, you gave me two talents. See, I have made two more.' ^{23}His master said to him, 'Well done, my good and faithful servant. Since you were faithful in small matters, I will give you great responsibilities. Come, share your master's joy.' ^{24}Then the one who had received the one talent came forward and said, 'Master, I knew you were a demanding person, harvesting where you did not plant and gathering where you did not scatter; ^{25}so out of fear I went off and buried your talent in the ground. Here it is back.' ^{26}*His master said to him in reply, 'You wicked, lazy servant! So

you knew that I harvest where I did not plant and gather where I did not scatter? ^{27}Should you not then have put my money in the bank so that I could have got it back with interest on my return? ^{28}Now then! Take the talent from him and give it to the one with ten. ^{29n}*For to everyone who has, more will be given and he will grow rich; but from the one who has not, even what he has will be taken away. ^{30}*And throw this useless servant into the darkness outside, where there will be wailing and grinding of teeth.'

The Judgment of the Nations. ^{31o}*"When the Son of Man comes in his glory, and all the angels with him, he will sit upon his glorious throne, ^{32p}*and all the nations will be assembled before him. And he will separate them one from another, as a shepherd separates the sheep from the goats. ^{33}He will place the sheep on his right and the goats on his left. ^{34}Then the king will say to those on his right, 'Come, you who are blessed by my Father. Inherit the kingdom prepared for you from the foundation of the world. ^{35q}For I was hungry and you gave me food, I was thirsty and you gave me drink, a stranger and you welcomed me, ^{36}naked and you clothed me, ill and you cared for me, in prison and you visited me.' ^{37}*Then the righteous will answer him and say, 'Lord, when did we see

---

25, 18: Buried his master's money: see the note on 13, 44.

25, 20–23: Although the first two servants have received and doubled large sums, their faithful trading is regarded by the master as fidelity **in small matters** only, compared with the **great responsibilities** now to be given to them. The latter are unspecified. **Share your master's joy:** probably the joy of the banquet of the kingdom; cf 8, 11.

25, 26–28: Wicked, lazy servant: this man's inactivity is not negligible but seriously culpable. As punishment, he loses the gift he had received, that is now given to the first servant, whose possessions are already great.

25, 29: See the note on 13, 12 where there is a similar application of this maxim.

25, 30: See the note on 8, 11–12.

25, 31–46: The conclusion of the discourse, which is peculiar to Mt, portrays the final judgment that will accompany the parousia. Although often called a "parable," it is not really such, for the only parabolic elements are the depiction of **the Son of Man** as a **shepherd** and of **the righteous** and the wicked as **sheep** and **goats** respectively (32–33). The criterion of judgment will be the deeds of mercy that have been done for the **least** of Jesus' **brothers** (40). A difficult and important question is the identification of these **least brothers.** Are they all people who have suffered hunger, thirst, etc. (35.36) or a

particular group of such sufferers? Scholars are divided in their response and arguments can be made for either side. But leaving aside the problem of what the traditional material that Matthew edited may have meant, it seems that a stronger case can be made for the view that in the evangelist's sense the sufferers are Christians, probably Christian missionaries whose sufferings were brought upon them by their preaching of the gospel. The criterion of judgment for **all the nations** is their treatment of those who have borne to the world the message of Jesus, and this means ultimately their acceptance or rejection of Jesus himself; cf 10, 40, "Whoever receives you, receives me."

25, 31: See the note on 16, 27.

25, 32: All the nations: before the end the gospel will have been preached throughout the world (24, 14); thus the Gentiles will be judged on their response to it. But the phrase **all the nations** includes the Jews also, for at the judgment "the Son of Man . . . will repay everyone according to his conduct" (16, 27).

25, 37–40: The righteous will be astonished that in caring for the needs of the sufferers they were ministering to the **Lord** himself. **One of these least brothers of mine:** cf 10, 42.

m: Lk 16, 10. *n:* 13, 12; Mk 4, 25; Lk 8, 18; 19, 26. *o:* 16, 27; Dt 33, 2 LXX. *p:* Ez 34, 17. *q:* Is 58, 7; Ez 18, 7.

you hungry and feed you, or thirsty and give you drink?' [38]When did we see you a stranger and welcome you, or naked and clothe you? [39]When did we see you ill or in prison, and visit you?' [40r]And the king will say to them in reply, 'Amen, I say to you, whatever you did for one of these least brothers of mine, you did for me.' [41s*]Then he will say to those on his left, 'Depart from me, you accursed, into the eternal fire prepared for the devil and his angels. [42t]For I was hungry and you gave me no food, I was thirsty and you gave me no drink, [43]a stranger and you gave me no welcome, naked and you gave me no clothing, ill and in prison, and you did not care for me.' [44*]Then they will answer and say, 'Lord, when did we see you hungry or thirsty or a stranger or naked or ill or in prison, and not minister to your needs?' [45]He will answer them, 'Amen, I say to you, what you did not do for one of these least ones, you did not do for me.' [46u]And these will go off to eternal punishment, but the righteous to eternal life."

VII: The Passion and Resurrection

CHAPTER 26

See RG 384–86

The Conspiracy against Jesus. [1*]When Jesus finished all these words, he said to his disciples, [2v]"You know that in two days' time it will be Passover, and the Son of Man will be handed over to be crucified." [3*]Then the chief priests and the elders of the people assembled in the palace of the high priest, who was called Caiaphas, [4w]and they consulted together to arrest Jesus by treachery and put him to death. [5*]But they said, "Not during the festival, that there may not be a riot among the people."

The Anointing at Bethany. [6x*]Now when Jesus was in Bethany in the house of Simon the leper, [7]a woman came up to him with an alabaster jar of costly perfumed oil, and poured it on his head while he was reclining at table. [8]When the disciples saw this, they were indignant and said, "Why this waste? [9]It could have been sold for much, and the money given to the poor." [10]Since Jesus knew this, he said to them, "Why do you make trouble for the woman? She has done a good thing for me. [11y]The poor you will always have with you; but you will not always have me. [12*]In pouring this perfumed oil upon my body, she did it to prepare me for burial. [13]Amen, I say to you, wherever this gospel is proclaimed in the whole world, what she has done will be spoken of, in memory of her."

The Betrayal by Judas. [14z*]Then one of the Twelve, who was called Judas Iscariot, went to the chief priests [15a*]and said, "What

---

25, 41: Fire prepared . . . his angels: cf 1 Enoch 10, 13 where it is said of the evil angels and Semyaza, their leader, "In those days they will lead them into the bottom of the fire—and in torment—in the prison (where) they will be locked up forever."

25, 44–45: The **accursed** (41) will be likewise astonished that their neglect of the sufferers was neglect of the **Lord** and will receive from him a similar answer.

26, 1—28, 20: The five books with alternating narrative and discourse (3, 1—25, 46) that give this gospel its distinctive structure lead up to the climactic events that are the center of Christian belief and the origin of the Christian church, the passion and resurrection of Jesus. In his passion narrative (chs 26–27) Matthew follows his Marcan source closely but with omissions (e.g., Mk 14, 51–52) and additions (e.g., 27, 3–10.19). Some of the additions indicate that he utilized traditions that he had received from elsewhere; others are due to his own theological insight (e.g., 26, 28, ". . . for the forgiveness of sins"; 27, 52). In his editing Matthew also altered Mk in some minor details. But there is no need to suppose that he knew any passion narrative other than Mark's.

26, 1–2: When Jesus finished all these words: see the note on 7, 28–29. **"You know . . . crucified":** Matthew turns

Mk's statement of the time (14, 1) into Jesus' final prediction of his passion. **Passover:** see the note on Mk 14, 1.

26, 3: Caiaphas was high priest from A.D. 18 to 36.

26, 5: Not during the festival: the plan to delay Jesus' arrest and execution until after **the festival** was not carried out, for according to the synoptics he was arrested on the night of Nisan 14 and put to death the following day. No reason is given why the plan was changed.

26, 6–13: See the notes on Mk 14, 3–9 and Jn 12, 1–8.

26, 12: To prepare me for burial: cf Mk 14, 8. In accordance with the interpretation of this act as Jesus' **burial** anointing, Matthew, more consistent than Mark, changes the purpose of the visit of the women to Jesus' tomb; they do not go to anoint him (Mk 16, 1) but "to see the tomb" (28, 1).

26, 14: Iscariot: see the note on Lk 6, 16.

26, 15: The motive of avarice is introduced by Judas's question about the price for betrayal, which is absent in the Marcan source (14, 10–11). **Hand him over:** the same Greek

---

r: 10, 40.42. s: 7, 23; Lk 13, 27. t: Jb 22, 7; Jas 2, 15-16. u: Dn 12, 2. v: Mk 14, 1-2; Lk 22, 1-2. w: Jn 11, 47-53. x: Mk 14, 3-9; Jn 12, 1-8. y: Dt 15, 11. z: Mk 14, 10-11; Lk 22, 3-6. a: Zec 11, 12.

are you willing to give me if I hand him over to you?" They paid him thirty pieces of silver, *16*and from that time on he looked for an opportunity to hand him over.

Preparations for the Passover. *17bc**On the first day of the Feast of Unleavened Bread, the disciples approached Jesus and said, "Where do you want us to prepare for you to eat the Passover?" *18**He said, "Go into the city to a certain man and tell him, 'The teacher says, "My appointed time draws near; in your house I shall celebrate the Passover with my disciples." ' " *19*The disciples then did as Jesus had ordered, and prepared the Passover.

The Betrayer. *20*When it was evening, he reclined at table with the Twelve. *21**And while they were eating, he said, "Amen, I say to you, one of you will betray me." *22*Deeply distressed at this, they began to say to him one after another, "Surely it is not I, Lord?" *23*He said in reply, "He who has dipped his hand into the dish with me is the one who will betray me. *24d**The Son of Man indeed goes, as it is written of him, but woe to that man by whom the Son of Man is betrayed. It would be better for that man if he had never been born." *25**Then Judas, his betrayer, said in reply, "Surely it is not I, Rabbi?" He answered, "You have said so."

The Lord's Supper. *26ef**While they were eating, Jesus took bread, said the blessing, broke it, and giving it to his disciples said, "Take and eat; this is my body." *27**Then he took a cup, gave thanks, and gave it to them, saying, "Drink from it, all of you, *28g*for this is my blood of the covenant, which will be shed on behalf of many for the forgiveness of sins. *29**I tell you, from now on I shall not drink this fruit of the vine until the day when I drink it with you new in the kingdom of my Father." *30**Then, after singing a hymn, they went out to the Mount of Olives.

verb is used to express the saving purpose of God by which Jesus is handed over to death (cf 17, 22; 20, 18; 26, 2) and the human malice that hands him over. **Thirty pieces of silver:** the price of the betrayal is found only in Mt. It is derived from Zec 11, 12 where it is the wages paid to the rejected shepherd, a cheap price (Zec 11, 13). That amount is also the compensation paid to one whose slave has been gored by an ox (Ex 21, 32).

26, 17: **The first day of the Feast of Unleavened Bread:** see the note on Mk 14, 1. Matthew omits Mk's "when they sacrificed the Passover lamb."

26, 18: By omitting much of Mk 14, 13–15, adding **My appointed time draws near,** and turning the question into a statement, **in your house I shall celebrate the Passover,** Matthew has given this passage a solemnity and majesty greater than that of his source.

26, 21: Given Matthew's interest in the fulfillment of the Old Testament, it is curious that he omits the Marcan designation of Jesus' betrayer as "one who is eating with me" (14, 18), since that is probably an allusion to Ps 41, 10. However, the shocking fact that the betrayer is one who shares table fellowship with Jesus is emphasized in v 23.

26, 24: **It would be better . . . born:** the enormity of the deed is such that it would be better not to exist than to do it.

26, 25: Peculiar to Mt. **You have said so:** cf 26, 64; 27, 11. This is a half-affirmative. Emphasis is laid on the pronoun and the answer implies that the statement would not have been made if the question had not been asked.

26, 26–29: See the note on Mk 14, 22–24. The Marcan-Matthean is one of the two major New Testament traditions of the words of Jesus when instituting the Eucharist. The other (and earlier) is the Pauline-Lucan (1 Cor 11, 23–25; Lk 22, 19–20). Each shows the influence of Christian liturgical usage, but the Marcan-Matthean is more developed in that regard than the Pauline-Lucan. The words over the bread and cup succeed each other without the intervening meal mentioned in 1 Cor 11, 25; Lk 22, 20; and there is parallelism between the consecratory words (**this is my body . . . this is my blood**). Matthew follows Mk closely but with some changes.

26, 26: See the note on 14, 19. **Said the blessing:** a prayer blessing God. **Take and eat:** literally, **Take, eat. Eat** is an addition to Mk's "take it" (literally, "take"; 14, 22). **This is my body:** the bread is identified with Jesus himself.

26, 27–28: **Gave thanks:** see the note on 15, 36. **Gave it to them . . . all of you:** cf Mk 14, 23–24. In the Marcan sequence the disciples drink and then Jesus says the interpretative words. Matthew has changed this into a command to **drink** followed by those words. **My blood:** see Lv 17, 11 for the concept that the **blood** is "the seat of life" and that when placed on the altar it "makes atonement." **Which will be shed:** the present participle, "being shed" or "going to be shed," is future in relation to the Last Supper. **On behalf of:** Greek **peri;** see the note on Mk 14, 24. **Many:** see the note on 20, 28. **For the forgiveness of sins:** a Matthean addition. The same phrase occurs in Mk 1, 4 in connection with John's baptism but Matthew avoids it there (3, 11). He places it here probably because he wishes to emphasize that it is the sacrificial death of Jesus that brings **forgiveness of sins.**

26, 29: Although his death will interrupt the table fellowship he has had with the disciples, Jesus confidently predicts his vindication by God and a new table fellowship with them at the banquet of the kingdom.

26, 30: See the note on Mk 14, 26.

b: Mk 14, 12-21; Lk 22, 7-23.   *c:* Ex 12, 14-20.   *d:* Is 53, 8-10.
e: Mk 14, 22-26; Lk 22, 14-23; 1 Cor 11, 23-25.   *f:* 1 Cor 10, 16.
g: Ex 24, 8; Is 53, 12.

Peter's Denial Foretold. [31hi*]Then Jesus said to them, "This night all of you will have your faith in me shaken, for it is written:

'I will strike the shepherd,
   and the sheep of the flock will be
      dispersed';

[32]but after I have been raised up, I shall go before you to Galilee." [33]Peter said to him in reply, "Though all may have their faith in you shaken, mine will never be." [34jk*]Jesus said to him, "Amen, I say to you, this very night before the cock crows, you will deny me three times." [35]Peter said to him, "Even though I should have to die with you, I will not deny you." And all the disciples spoke likewise.

The Agony in the Garden. [36lm*]Then Jesus came with them to a place called Gethsemane, and he said to his disciples, "Sit here while I go over there and pray." [37n*]He took along Peter and the two sons of Zebedee, and began to feel sorrow and distress. [38o*]Then he said to them, "My soul is sorrowful even to death. Remain here and keep watch with me." [39p*]He advanced a lit-

tle and fell prostrate in prayer, saying, "My Father, if it is possible, let this cup pass from me; yet, not as I will, but as you will." [40]When he returned to his disciples he found them asleep. He said to Peter, "So you could not keep watch with me for one hour? [41*]Watch and pray that you may not undergo the test. The spirit is willing, but the flesh is weak." [42q*]Withdrawing a second time, he prayed again, "My Father, if it is not possible that this cup pass without my drinking it, your will be done!" [43]Then he returned once more and found them asleep, for they could not keep their eyes open. [44]He left them and withdrew again and prayed a third time, saying the same thing again. [45r]Then he returned to his disciples and said to them, "Are you still sleeping and taking your rest? Behold, the hour is at hand when the Son of Man is to be handed over to sinners. [46]Get up, let us go. Look, my betrayer is at hand."

The Betrayal and Arrest of Jesus. [47s]While he was still speaking, Judas, one of the Twelve, arrived, accompanied by a large crowd, with swords and clubs, who had come from the chief priests and the eld-

---

26, 31: Will have . . . shaken: literally, "will be scandalized in me"; see the note on 24, 9–12. **I will strike . . . dispersed:** cf Zec 13, 7.

26, 34: Before the cock crows: see the note on 14, 25. The third watch of the night was called "cockcrow." **Deny me:** see the note on 16, 24.

26, 36–56: Cf Mk 14, 32–52. The account of Jesus in Gethsemane is divided between that of his agony (36–46) and that of his betrayal and arrest (47–56). Jesus' **sorrow and distress** (37) in face of death is unrelieved by the presence of his three disciples who, though urged to **watch with** him (38.41), fall asleep (40.43). He prays that **if . . . possible** his death may be avoided (39) but that his Father's will be done (39,42.44). Knowing then that his death must take place, he announces to his companions that **the hour** for his being **handed over** has come (45). Judas arrives with an armed band provided by the Sanhedrin and greets Jesus with a kiss, the prearranged sign for his identification (47–49). After his arrest, he rebukes a disciple who has attacked the **high priest's servant** with a **sword** (51–54), and chides those who have come out to seize him with **swords and clubs** as if he were a **robber** (55–56). In both rebukes Jesus declares that the treatment he is now receiving is the fulfillment of the scriptures (55.56). The subsequent flight of **all the disciples** is itself the fulfillment of his own prediction (cf 31). In this episode, Matthew follows Mk with a few alterations.

26, 36: Gethsemane: the Hebrew name means "oil press" and designates an olive orchard on the western slope of the Mount of Olives; see the note on 21, 1. The name appears

only in Mt and Mk. The place is called a "garden" in Jn 18, 1.

26, 37: Peter and the two sons of Zebedee: cf 17, 1.

26, 38: Cf Ps 42, 6.12. In the Septuagint (Ps 41, 5.12) the same Greek word for **sorrowful** is used as here. **To death:** i.e., "enough to die"; cf Jon 4, 9.

26, 39: My Father: see the note on Mk 14, 36. Matthew omits the Aramaic **'abbā'** and adds the qualifier **my. This cup:** see the note on Mk 10, 38–40.

26, 41: Undergo the test: see the note on 6, 13. In that verse "the final test" translates the same Greek word as is here translated **the test,** and these are the only instances of the use of that word in Mt. It is possible that the passion of Jesus is seen here as an anticipation of the great tribulation that will precede the parousia (see the notes on 24, 8; 24, 21) to which 6, 13 refers, and that just as Jesus prays to be delivered from death (39), so he exhorts the disciples to pray that they will not have to **undergo the** great **test** that his passion would be for them. Some scholars, however, understand **not undergo** (literally, "not enter") **the test** as meaning not that the disciples may be spared **the test** but that they may not yield to the temptation of falling away from Jesus because of his passion even though they will have to endure it.

26, 42: Your will be done: cf 6, 10.

h: Mk 14, 7-31. *i:* Zec 13, 7; Jn 16, 32. *j:* Lk 22, 33-34; Jn 13, 37-38. *k:* 26, 69-75. *l:* Mk 14, 32-42; Lk 22, 39-46. *m:* Jn 18, 1. *n:* Heb 5, 7. *o:* Ps 42, 6.12; Jon 4, 9. *p:* Jn 4, 34; 6, 38; Phil 2, 8. *q:* 6, 10; Heb 10, 9. *r:* Jn 12, 23; 13, 1; 17, 1. *s:* Mk 14, 43-50; Lk 22, 47-53; Jn 18, 3-11.

ers of the people. ⁴⁸His betrayer had arranged a sign with them, saying, "The man I shall kiss is the one; arrest him." ⁴⁹*Immediately he went over to Jesus and said, "Hail, Rabbi!" and he kissed him. ⁵⁰Jesus answered him, "Friend, do what you have come for." Then stepping forward they laid hands on Jesus and arrested him. ⁵¹And behold, one of those who accompanied Jesus put his hand to his sword, drew it, and struck the high priest's servant, cutting off his ear. ⁵²Then Jesus said to him, "Put your sword back into its sheath, for all who take the sword will perish by the sword. ⁵³Do you think that I cannot call upon my Father and he will not provide me at this moment with more than twelve legions of angels? ⁵⁴But then how would the scriptures be fulfilled which say that it must come to pass in this way?" ⁵⁵*At that hour Jesus said to the crowds, "Have you come out as against a robber, with swords and clubs to seize me? Day after day I sat teaching in the temple area, yet you did not arrest me. ⁵⁶ᵗBut all this has come to pass that the writings of the prophets may be fulfilled." Then all the disciples left him and fled.

Jesus before the Sanhedrin. ⁵⁷ᵘ*Those who had arrested Jesus led him away to Caiaphas the high priest, where the scribes and the elders were assembled. ⁵⁸Peter was following him at a distance as far as the high priest's courtyard, and going inside he sat down with the servants to see the outcome. ⁵⁹*The chief priests and the entire Sanhedrin kept trying to obtain false testimony against Jesus in order to put him to death, ⁶⁰ᵛ*but they found none, though many false witnesses came forward. Finally two came forward ⁶¹who stated, "This man said, 'I can destroy the temple of God and within three days rebuild it.' " ⁶²The high priest rose and addressed him, "Have you no answer? What are these men testifying against you?" ⁶³ʷ*But Jesus was silent. Then the high priest said to him, "I order you to tell us under oath before the living God whether you are the Messiah, the Son of God." ⁶⁴ˣ*Jesus said to him in reply, "You have said so. But I tell you:

26, 49: **Rabbi:** see the note on 23, 6–7. Jesus is so addressed twice in Mt (cf 25), both times by Judas. For the significance of the closely related address "teacher" in Mt, see the note on 8, 19.

26, 55: **Day after day . . . arrest me:** cf Mk 14, 49. This suggests that Jesus had taught for a relatively long period in Jerusalem, whereas 21, 1–11 puts his coming to the city for the first time only a few days before.

26, 57–68: Following Mk 14, 53–65, Matthew presents the nighttime appearance of Jesus before **the Sanhedrin** as a real trial. After **many false witnesses** bring charges against him that do not suffice for the death sentence (60), **two came forward** who charge him with claiming to be able to **destroy the temple . . . and within three days** to **rebuild it** (60–61). Jesus makes no answer even when challenged to do so by **the high priest,** who then orders him to declare **under oath . . . whether** he is **the Messiah, the Son of God** (62–63). Matthew changes Mk's clear affirmative response (14, 62) to the same one as that given to Judas (cf 25), but follows Mk almost verbatim in Jesus' predicting that his judges will see him (**the Son of Man**) **seated at the right hand of** God **and coming on the clouds of heaven** (64). **The high priest** then charges him with blasphemy (65), a charge with which the other members of **the Sanhedrin** agree by declaring that **he deserves to die** (66). They then attack him (67) and mockingly demand that he **prophesy** (68). This account contains elements that are contrary to the judicial procedures prescribed in the Mishnah, the Jewish code of law that dates in written form from ca. A.D. 200, e.g., trial on a feast day, a night session of the court, pronouncement of a verdict of condemnation at the same session at which testimony was re-

ceived. Consequently, some scholars regard the account entirely as a creation of the early Christians without historical value. However, it is disputable whether the norms found in the Mishnah were in force at the time of Jesus. More to the point is the question whether the Matthean-Marcan night trial derives from a combination of two separate incidents, a nighttime preliminary investigation (cf Jn 18, 13.19–24) and a formal trial on the following morning (cf Lk 22, 66–71).

26, 57: **Caiaphas:** see the note on 26, 3.

26, 59: **Sanhedrin:** see the note on Lk 22, 66.

26, 60–61: **Two:** cf Dt 19, 15. **I can destroy . . . rebuild it:** there are significant differences from the Marcan parallel (14, 58). Matthew omits "made with hands" and "not made with hands" and changes Mk's "will destroy" and "will build another" to **can destroy** and (can) **rebuild.** The charge is probably based on Jesus' prediction of the temple's destruction; see the notes on 23, 37–39; 24, 2; and Jn 2, 19. A similar prediction by Jeremiah was considered as deserving death; cf Jer 7, 1–15; 26, 1–8.

26, 63: **Silent:** possibly an allusion to Is 53, 7. **I order you . . . living God:** peculiar to Mt; cf Mk 14, 61.

26, 64: **You have said so:** see the note on 26, 25. **From now on . . . heaven:** the Son of Man who is to be crucified (cf 20, 19) will be seen in glorious majesty (cf Ps 110, 1) and **coming on the clouds of heaven** (cf Dn 7, 13). **The Power:** see the note on Mk 14, 61–62.

t: 26, 31. *u:* Mk 14, 53-65; Lk 22, 54-55.63-71; Jn 18, 12-14.19-24. *v:* Dt 19, 15; Jn 2, 19; Acts 6, 14. *w:* Is 53, 7. *x:* Ps 110, 1; Dn 7, 13.

From now on you will see 'the Son of
Man

    seated at the right hand of the Power'
and 'coming on the clouds of
heaven.' "

[65]*Then the high priest tore his robes and
said, "He has blasphemed! What further
need have we of witnesses? You have now
heard the blasphemy; [66]what is your opinion?" They said in reply, "He deserves to
die!" [67]*[y]Then they spat in his face and
struck him, while some slapped him, [68]say-
ing, "Prophesy for us, Messiah: who is it that
struck you?"

Peter's Denial of Jesus. [69]*[z]Now Peter was
sitting outside in the courtyard. One of the
maids came over to him and said, "You too
were with Jesus the Galilean." [70]*But he denied it in front of everyone, saying, "I do not
know what you are talking about!" [71]As he
went out to the gate, another girl saw him and
said to those who were there, "This man was
with Jesus the Nazorean." [72]Again he denied
it with an oath, "I do not know the man!"
[73]*A little later the bystanders came over and
said to Peter, "Surely you too are one of
them; even your speech gives you away."

[74]At that he began to curse and to swear, "I
do not know the man." And immediately a
cock crowed. [75]*[a]Then Peter remembered the
word that Jesus had spoken: "Before the cock
crows you will deny me three times." He
went out and began to weep bitterly.

CHAPTER 27

See RG 384–86

Jesus before Pilate. [1]*[b]*When it was
morning, all the chief priests and the elders of
the people took counsel against Jesus to put
him to death. [2]They bound him, led him away,
and handed him over to Pilate, the governor.

The Death of Judas. [3]*[c][d]*Then Judas, his
betrayer, seeing that Jesus had been condemned, deeply regretted what he had done.
He returned the thirty pieces of silver to the
chief priests and elders, [4]saying, "I have
sinned in betraying innocent blood." They
said, "What is that to us? Look to it yourself." [5]*Flinging the money into the temple,
he departed and went off and hanged himself.
[6]The chief priests gathered up the money, but
said, "It is not lawful to deposit this in the
temple treasury, for it is the price of blood."
[7]After consultation, they used it to buy the
potter's field as a burial place for foreigners.
[8]That is why that field even today is called

26, 65: Blasphemed: the punishment for **blasphemy** was
death by stoning (see Lv 24, 10–16). According to the Mishnah, to be guilty of **blasphemy** one had to pronounce "the
Name itself," i.e. Yahweh; cf **Sanhedrin** 7, 4.5. Those who
judge the gospel accounts of Jesus' trial by the later Mishnah
standards point out that Jesus uses the surrogate "the Power,"
and hence no Jewish court would have regarded him as guilty
of **blasphemy;** others hold that the Mishnah's narrow understanding of **blasphemy** was a later development.

26, 67–68: The physical abuse, apparently done to Jesus
by the members of the Sanhedrin themselves, recalls the sufferings of the Isaian Servant of the Lord; cf Is 50, 6. The
mocking challenge to **prophesy** is probably motivated by
Jesus' prediction of his future glory (64).

26, 70: Denied it in front of everyone: see 10, 33. Peter's
repentance (75) saves him from the fearful destiny of which
Jesus speaks there.

26, 73: Your speech . . . away: Matthew explicates Mk's
"you too are a Galilean" (14, 70).

27, 1–31: Cf Mk 15, 1–20. Matthew's account of the Roman trial before **Pilate** is introduced by a consultation of the
Sanhedrin after which Jesus is **handed over to . . . the governor** (1–2). Matthew follows his Marcan source closely but
adds some material that is peculiar to him, the death of **Judas**
(3–10), possibly the name **Jesus** as the name of **Barabbas**
also (16–17), the intervention of Pilate's **wife** (19), Pilate's
washing **his hands** in token of his disclaiming responsibility

for Jesus' death (24), and the assuming of that responsibility
by **the whole people** (25).

27, 1–2: There is scholarly disagreement about the meaning of the Sanhedrin's taking **counsel (symboulion elabon;**
cf 12, 14; 22, 15; 27, 7; 28, 12); see the note on Mk 15, 1.
Some understand it as a discussion about the strategy for putting their death sentence against **Jesus** into effect since they
lacked the right to do so themselves. Others see it as the occasion for their passing that sentence, holding that Matthew,
unlike Mark (14, 64), does not consider that it had been
passed in the night session (26, 66). Even in the latter interpretation, their handing **him over to Pilate** is best explained
on the hypothesis that they did not have competence to put
their sentence into effect, as is stated in Jn 18, 31.

27, 3: The thirty pieces of silver: see 26, 15.

27, 5–8: For another tradition about the death of Judas, cf
Acts 1, 18–19. The two traditions agree only in the purchase
of a field with **the money** paid to Judas for his betrayal of
Jesus and the name given to the **field, the Field of Blood.** In
Acts Judas himself buys the field and its name comes from
his own blood shed in his fatal accident on it. **The potter's
field:** this designation of the field is based on the fulfillment
citation in v 10.

[y]: Wis 2, 19; Is 50, 6.   [z]: Mk 14, 66-72; Lk 22, 56-62; Jn 18, 17-
18.25-27.   [a]: 26, 34.   [b]: Mk 15, 1; Lk 23, 1; Jn 18, 28.   [c]: Acts
1, 18-19.   [d]: 26, 15.

the Field of Blood. *9**Then was fulfilled what had been said through Jeremiah the prophet, "And they took the thirty pieces of silver, the value of a man with a price on his head, a price set by some of the Israelites, *10e*and they paid it out for the potter's field just as the Lord had commanded me."

Jesus Questioned by Pilate. *11f**Now Jesus stood before the governor, and he questioned him, "Are you the king of the Jews?" Jesus said, "You say so." *12g**And when he was accused by the chief priests and elders, he made no answer. *13*Then Pilate said to him, "Do you not hear how many things they are testifying against you?" *14*But he did not answer him one word, so that the governor was greatly amazed.

The Sentence of Death. *15h**Now on the occasion of the feast the governor was accustomed to release to the crowd one prisoner whom they wished. *16**And at that time they had a notorious prisoner called [Jesus] Barabbas. *17*So when they had assembled, Pilate said to them, "Which one do you want me to release to you, [Jesus] Barabbas, or Jesus called Messiah?" *18**For he knew that it was out of envy that they had handed him over. *19**While he was still seated on the bench, his wife sent him a message, "Have nothing to do with that righteous man. I suffered much in a dream today because of him." *20i*The chief priests and the elders persuaded the crowds to ask for Barabbas but to destroy Jesus. *21*The governor said to them in reply, "Which of the two do you want me to release to you?" They answered, "Barabbas!" *22**Pilate said to them, "Then what shall I do with Jesus called Messiah?" They all said, "Let him be crucified!" *23*But he said, "Why? What evil has he done?" They only shouted the louder, "Let him be crucified!" *24j**When Pilate saw that he was not

27, 9–10: Cf 26, 15. Matthew's attributing this text to Jeremiah is puzzling, for there is no such text in that book, and **the thirty pieces of silver** thrown by Judas "into the temple" (5) recall rather Zec 11, 12–13. It is usually said that the attribution of the text to Jeremiah is due to Matthew's combining the Zechariah text with texts from Jeremiah that speak of a **potter** (18, 2–3), the buying of a **field** (32, 6–9), or the breaking of a potter's flask at Topheth in the valley of Ben-Hinnom with the prediction that it will become a burial place (19, 1–13).

27, 11: King of the Jews: this title is used of Jesus only by pagans. The Matthean instances are, besides this verse, 2, 2; 27, 29.37. Matthew equates it with "Messiah"; cf 2, 2.4 and 27, 17.22 where he has changed "the king of the Jews" of his Marcan source (15, 9.12) to "(Jesus) called Messiah." The normal political connotation of both titles would be of concern to the Roman **governor. You say so:** see the note on 26, 25. An unqualified affirmative response is not made because Jesus' kingship is not what Pilate would understand it to be.

27, 12–14: Cf 26, 62–63. As in the trial before the Sanhedrin, Jesus' silence may be meant to recall Is 53, 7. **Greatly amazed:** possibly an allusion to Is 52, 14–15.

27, 15–26: The choice that Pilate offers **the crowd** between **Barabbas** and **Jesus** is said to be in accordance with a custom of releasing at the Passover feast **one prisoner** chosen **by the crowd** (15). This custom is mentioned also in Mk 15, 6 and Jn 18, 39 but not in Lk; see the note on Lk 23, 17. Outside of the gospels there is no direct attestation of it, and scholars are divided in their judgment of the historical reliability of the claim that there was such a practice.

27, 16–17: [Jesus] **Barabbas:** it is possible that the double name is the original reading; **Jesus** was a common Jewish name; see the note on 1, 21. This reading is found in only a few textual witnesses, although its absence in the majority can be explained as an omission of **Jesus** made for reverential reasons. That name is bracketed because of its uncertain textual attestation. The Aramaic name **Barabbas** means "son

of the father"; the irony of the choice offered between him and Jesus, the true son of the Father, would be evident to those addressees of Mt who knew that.

27, 18: Cf Mk 14, 10. This is an example of the tendency, found in varying degree in all the gospels, to present Pilate in a relatively favorable light and emphasize the hostility of the Jewish authorities and eventually of the people.

27, 19: Jesus' innocence is declared by a Gentile woman. **In a dream:** in Mt's infancy narrative, dreams are the means of divine communication; cf 1, 20; 2, 12.13.19.22.

27, 22: Let him be crucified: incited by the chief priests and elders (20), the crowds demand that Jesus be executed by crucifixion, a peculiarly horrible form of Roman capital punishment. The Marcan parallel, "Crucify him" (15, 3), addressed to Pilate, is changed by Matthew to the passive, probably to emphasize the responsibility of the crowds.

27, 24–25: Peculiar to Mt. **Took water . . . blood:** cf Dt 21, 1–8, the handwashing prescribed in the case of a murder when the killer is unknown. The elders of the city nearest to where the corpse is found must wash their hands, declaring, "Our hands did not shed this blood." **Look to it yourselves:** cf v 4. **The whole people:** Matthew sees in those who speak these words **the entire people** (Greek *laos*) of Israel. **His blood . . . and upon our children:** cf Jer 26, 15. The responsibility for Jesus' death is accepted by the nation that was God's special possession (Ex 19, 5), his own **people** (Hos 2, 25), and they thereby lose that high privilege; see 21, 43 and the note on that verse. The controversy between Matthew's church and Pharisaic Judaism about which was the true people of God is reflected here. As the Second Vatican Council has pointed out, guilt for Jesus' death is not attributable to all the Jews of his time or to any Jews of later times.

e: Zec 11, 12-13. *f:* Mk 15, 2-5; Lk 23, 2-3; Jn 18, 29-38. *g:* Is 53, 7. *h:* Mk 15, 6-15; Lk 23, 17-25; Jn 18, 39—19, 16. *i:* Acts 3, 14. *j:* Dt 21, 1-8.

succeeding at all, but that a riot was break-ing out instead, he took water and washed his hands in the sight of the crowd, saying, "I am innocent of this man's blood. Look to it yourselves." 25 And the whole people said in reply, "His blood be upon us and upon our children." 26*Then he released Barabbas to them, but after he had Jesus scourged, he handed him over to be crucified.

Mockery by the Soldiers. 27k*Then the soldiers of the governor took Jesus inside the praetorium and gathered the whole co-hort around him. 28*They stripped off his clothes and threw a scarlet military cloak about him. 29l*Weaving a crown out of thorns, they placed it on his head, and a reed in his right hand. And kneeling before him, they mocked him, saying, "Hail, King of the Jews!" 30m*They spat upon him and took the reed and kept striking him on the head. 31 And when they had mocked him, they stripped him of the cloak, dressed him in his own clothes, and led him off to cru-cify him.

The Way of the Cross. 32n* As they were going out, they met a Cyrenian named Si-mon; this man they pressed into service to carry his cross.

The Crucifixion. 33o And when they came to a place called Golgotha (which means Place of the Skull), 34p*they gave Jesus wine to drink mixed with gall. But when he had tasted it, he refused to drink. 35q*After they had crucified him, they divided his garments by casting lots; 36then they sat down and kept watch over him there. 37*And they placed over his head the written charge against him: This is Jesus, the King of the Jews. 38*Two revolutionaries were crucified with him, one on his right and the other on his left. 39r*Those passing by reviled him, shaking their heads 40sand saying, "You who would destroy the temple and rebuild it in three days, save yourself, if you are the Son of God, [and] come down from the cross!" 41Likewise the chief priests with the scribes and elders mocked him and said, 42*"He saved others; he cannot save himself. So he is the king of Israel! Let him come down from the cross now, and we will believe in him. 43t*He trusted in God; let him deliver him now if he wants him. For he said, 'I am

27, 26: He had Jesus scourged: the usual preliminary to crucifixion.

27, 27: The praetorium: the residence of the Roman governor. His usual place of residence was at Caesarea Mar-itima on the Mediterranean coast, but he went to Jerusalem during the great feasts, when the influx of pilgrims posed the danger of a nationalistic riot. It is disputed whether **the prae-torium** in Jerusalem was the old palace of Herod in the west of the city or the fortress of Antonia northwest of the temple area. **The whole cohort:** normally six hundred soldiers.

27, 28: Scarlet military cloak: so Mt as against the royal purple of Mk 15, 17 and Jn 19, 2.

27, 29: Crown out of thorns: probably of long **thorns** that stood upright so that it resembled the "radiant" **crown, a** diadem with spikes worn by Hellenistic kings. The soldiers' purpose was mockery, not torture. **A reed:** peculiar to Mt; a mock scepter.

27, 30: Spat upon him: cf 26, 67 where there also is a possible allusion to Is 50, 6.

27, 32: See the note on Mk 15, 21. **Cyrenian named Si-mon:** Cyrenaica was a Roman province on the north coast of Africa and Cyrene was its capital city. The city had a large population of Greek-speaking Jews. **Simon** may have been living in Palestine or have come there for the Passover as a pilgrim. **Pressed into service:** see the note on 5, 41.

27, 34: Wine . . . mixed with gall: cf Mk 15, 23 where the drink is "wine drugged with myrrh," a narcotic. Mt's text is probably an inexact allusion to Ps 69, 22. That psalm belongs to the class called the individual lament, in which a perse-cuted just man prays for deliverance in the midst of great suf-fering and also expresses confidence that his prayer will be heard. That theme of the suffering Just One is frequently ap-plied to the sufferings of Jesus in the passion narratives.

27, 35: The clothing of an executed criminal went to his executioner(s), but the description of that procedure in the case of Jesus, found in all the gospels, is plainly inspired by Ps 22, 19. However, that psalm verse is quoted only in Jn 19, 24.

27, 37: The offense of a person condemned to death by crucifixion was written on a tablet that was displayed on his cross. The **charge** against **Jesus** was that he had claimed to be the **King of the Jews** (cf 11), i.e., the Messiah (cf 17.22).

27, 38: Revolutionaries: see the note on Jn 18, 40 where the same Greek word as that found here is used for Barabbas.

27, 39–40: Reviled him . . . heads: cf Ps 22, 8. **You who would destroy . . . three days:** cf 26, 61. **If you are the Son of God:** the same words as those of the devil in the tempta-tion of Jesus; cf 4, 3.6.

27, 42: King of Israel: in their mocking of Jesus the members of the Sanhedrin call themselves and their people not "the Jews" but **Israel.**

27, 43: Peculiar to Mt. **He trusted in God . . . wants him:** cf Ps 22, 9. **He said . . . of God:** probably an allusion to Wis 2, 12–20 where the theme of the suffering just one appears.

k: Mk 15, 16-20; Jn 19, 2-3.   l: 27, 11.   m: Is 50, 6.   n: Mk 15, 21; Lk 23, 26.   o: Mk 15, 22-32; Lk 23, 32-38; Jn 19, 17-19.23-24.   p: Ps 69, 21.   q: Ps 22, 19.   r: Ps 22, 8.   s: 4, 3.6; 26, 61.   t: Ps 22, 9; Wis 2, 12-20.

the Son of God.' " [44]The revolutionaries who were crucified with him also kept abusing him in the same way.

The Death of Jesus. [45uv*]From noon onward, darkness came over the whole land until three in the afternoon. [46w*]And about three o'clock Jesus cried out in a loud voice, "*Eli, Eli, lema sabachthani?*" which means, "My God, my God, why have you forsaken me?" [47*]Some of the bystanders who heard it said, "This one is calling for Elijah." [48x]Immediately one of them ran to get a sponge; he soaked it in wine, and putting it on a reed, gave it to him to drink. [49]But the rest said, "Wait, let us see if Elijah comes to save him." [50*]But Jesus cried out again in a loud voice, and gave up his spirit. [51y*]And behold, the veil of the sanctuary was torn in two from top to bottom. The earth quaked, rocks were split, [52z]tombs were opened, and the bodies of many saints who had fallen asleep were raised. [53]And coming forth from their tombs after his resurrection, they entered the holy city and appeared to many. [54*]The centurion and the men with him who were keeping watch over Jesus feared greatly when they saw the earthquake and all that was happening, and they said, "Truly, this was the Son of God!" [55*]There were many women there, looking on from a distance, who had followed Jesus from Galilee, ministering to him. [56a]Among them were Mary Magdalene and Mary the mother of James and Joseph, and the mother of the sons of Zebedee.

The Burial of Jesus. [57bc*]When it was evening, there came a rich man from Arimathea named Joseph, who was himself a disciple of Jesus. [58]He went to Pilate and asked for the body of Jesus; then Pilate ordered it to be handed over. [59]Taking the body, Joseph wrapped it [in] clean linen [60]and laid it in his

---

27, 45: Cf Amos 8, 9 where on the day of the Lord "the sun will set at midday."

27, 46: Eli, Eli, lema sabachthani?: Jesus cries out in the words of Ps 22, 2a, a psalm of lament that is the Old Testament passage most frequently drawn upon in this narrative. In Mk the verse is cited entirely in Aramaic, which Matthew partially retains but changes the invocation of God to the Hebrew **Eli,** possibly because that is more easily related to the statement of the following verse about Jesus' calling for Elijah.

27, 47: Elijah: see the note on 3, 4. This prophet, taken up into heaven (2 Kgs 2, 11), was believed to come to the help of those in distress, but the evidences of that belief are all later than the gospels.

27, 50: Gave up his spirit: cf the Marcan parallel (15, 37), "breathed his last." Matthew's alteration expresses both Jesus' control over his destiny and his obedient giving up of his life to God.

27, 51–53: Veil of the sanctuary . . . bottom: cf Mk 15, 38; Lk 23, 45. Lk puts this event immediately before the death of Jesus. There were two veils in the Mosaic tabernacle on the model of which the temple was constructed, the outer one before the entrance of the Holy Place and the inner one before the Holy of Holies (see Ex 26, 31–36). Only the high priest could pass through the latter and that only on the Day of Atonement (see Lv 16, 1–18). Probably the **torn veil** of the gospels is the inner one. The meaning of the scene may be that now, because of Jesus' death, all people have access to the presence of God, or that the temple, its holiest part standing exposed, is now profaned and will soon be destroyed. **The earth quaked . . . appeared to many:** peculiar to Mt. The earthquake, the splitting of the **rocks,** and especially the resurrection of the dead **saints** indicate the coming of the final age. In the Old Testament the coming of God is frequently portrayed with the imagery of an earthquake (see Pss 68, 9; 77, 19), and Jesus speaks of the earthquakes that

will accompany the "labor pains" that signify the beginning of the dissolution of the old world (24, 7–8). For the expectation of the resurrection of the dead at the coming of the new and final age, see Dn 12, 1–3. Matthew knows that the end of the old age has not yet come (28, 20), but the new age has broken in with the death (and resurrection; cf the earthquake in 28, 2) of Jesus; see the note on 16, 28. **After his resurrection:** this qualification seems to be due to Matthew's wish to assert the primacy of Jesus' **resurrection** even though he has placed the resurrection of the dead **saints** immediately after Jesus' death.

27, 54: Cf Mk 15, 39. The Christian confession of faith is made by Gentiles, not only **the centurion,** as in Mk, but the other soldiers **who were keeping watch over Jesus** (cf 36).

27, 55–56: Looking on from a distance: cf Ps 38, 12. **Mary Magdalene . . . Joseph:** these two women are mentioned again in v 61 and 28, 1 and are important as witnesses of the reality of the empty tomb. A **James** and **Joseph** are referred to in 13, 55 as brothers of Jesus.

27, 57–61: Cf Mk 15, 42–47. Matthew drops Mk's designation of **Joseph** of **Arimathea** as "a distinguished member of the council" (the Sanhedrin), and makes him **a rich man** and **a disciple of Jesus.** The former may be an allusion to Is 53, 9 (the Hebrew reading of that text is disputed and the one followed in the NAB OT has nothing about the rich, but they are mentioned in the LXX version). That the tomb was the **new tomb** of **a rich man** and that it was seen by the women are indications of an apologetic intent of Matthew; there could be no question about the identity of Jesus' burial place. **The other Mary:** the mother of James and Joseph (56).

u: Mk 15, 33-41; Lk 23, 44-49; Jn 19, 28-30. *v:* Am 8, 9. *w:* Ps 22, 2. *x:* Ps 69, 21. *y:* Ex 26, 31-36; Ps 68, 9; 77, 19. *z:* Dn 12, 1-3. *a:* 13, 55. *b:* Mk 15, 42-47; Lk 23, 50-56; Jn 19, 38-42. *c:* Is 53, 9.

new tomb that he had hewn in the rock. Then he rolled a huge stone across the entrance to the tomb and departed. [61] But Mary Magdalene and the other Mary remained sitting there, facing the tomb.

The Guard at the Tomb. [62]*The next day, the one following the day of preparation, the chief priests and the Pharisees gathered before Pilate [63d] and said, "Sir, we remember that this impostor while still alive said, 'After three days I will be raised up.' [64]*Give orders, then, that the grave be secured until the third day, lest his disciples come and steal him and say to the people, 'He has been raised from the dead.' This last imposture would be worse than the first." [65]*Pilate said to them, "The guard is yours; go secure it as best you can." [66]So they went and secured

the tomb by fixing a seal to the stone and setting the guard.

CHAPTER 28

The Resurrection of Jesus. [1e]*After the sabbath, as the first day of the week was dawning, Mary Magdalene and the other Mary came to see the tomb. [2f]*And behold, there was a great earthquake; for an angel of the Lord descended from heaven, approached, rolled back the stone, and sat upon it. [3g]His appearance was like lightning and his clothing was white as snow. [4]The guards were shaken with fear of him and became like dead men. [5]Then the angel said to the women in reply, "Do not be afraid! I know that you are seeking Jesus the crucified. [6]*He is not here, for he has been raised just

27, 62–66: Peculiar to Mt. The story prepares for 28, 11–15 and the Jewish charge that the tomb was empty because the **disciples** had stolen the body of Jesus (28, 13.15).

27, 62: The next day . . . preparation: the sabbath. According to the synoptic chronology, in that year **the day of preparation** (for the sabbath) was the Passover; cf Mk 15, 42. **The Pharisees:** the principal opponents of Jesus during his ministry and, in Matthew's time, of the Christian church, join with **the chief priests** to guarantee against a possible attempt of Jesus' **disciples** to steal his body.

27, 64: This last imposture . . . the first: the claim that Jesus **has been raised from the dead** is clearly the **last imposture; the first** may be either his claim that he would **be raised up** (63) or his claim that he was the one with whose ministry the kingdom of God had come (see 12, 28).

27, 65: The guard is yours: literally, "have a guard" or "you have a guard." Either the imperative or the indicative could mean that Pilate granted the petitioners some Roman soldiers as guards, which is the sense of the present translation. However, if the verb is taken as an indicative it could also mean that Pilate told them to use their own Jewish guards.

28, 1–20: Except for vv 1–8, based on Mk 16, 1–8, the material of this final chapter is peculiar to Mt. Even where he follows Mk, Matthew has altered his source so greatly that a very different impression is given from that of the Marcan account. The two points that are common to the resurrection testimony of all the gospels are that the tomb of Jesus had been found empty and that the risen Jesus had appeared to certain persons, or, in the original form of Mk, that such an appearance was promised as soon to take place (see Mk 16, 7). On this central and all-important basis, Matthew has constructed an account that interprets the resurrection as the turning of the ages (2–4), shows the Jewish opposition to Jesus as continuing **to the present** in the claim that the resurrection is a deception perpetrated by the **disciples** who stole his body from the tomb (11–15), and marks a new stage in the mission of **the disciples** once limited to Israel (10, 5–6); now they are to **make disciples of all nations.** In this work they will be strengthened by the presence of the exalted Son of Man, who

will be with them **until** the kingdom comes in fullness at **the end of the age** (16–20).

28, 1: After the sabbath . . . dawning: since the sabbath ended at sunset, this could mean in the early evening, for **dawning** can refer to the appearance of the evening star; cf Lk 23, 54. However, it is probable that Matthew means the morning dawn of the day after the sabbath, as in the similar though slightly different text of Mk, "when the sun had risen" (16, 2). **Mary Magdalene and the other Mary:** see the notes on 27, 55–56; 57–61. **To see the tomb:** cf Mk 16, 1–2 where the purpose of the women's visit is to anoint Jesus' body.

28, 2–4: Peculiar to Mt. **A great earthquake:** see the note on 27, 51–53. **Descended from heaven:** this trait is peculiar to Mt, although his interpretation of the "young man" of his Marcan source (16, 5) as an **angel** is probably true to Mk's intention; cf Lk 24, 23 where the "two men" of 24, 4 are said to be "angels." **Rolled back the stone . . . upon it:** not to allow the risen Jesus to leave the tomb but to make evident that the tomb is empty (see 6). Unlike the apocryphal Gospel of Peter (9, 35—11, 44), the New Testament does not describe the resurrection of Jesus, nor is there anyone who sees it. **His appearance was like lightning . . . snow:** see the note on 17, 2.

28, 6–7: Cf Mk 16, 6–7. **Just as he said:** a Matthean addition referring to Jesus' predictions of his resurrection, e.g., 16, 21; 17, 23; 20, 19. **Tell his disciples:** like the angel of the Lord of the infancy narrative, the angel interprets a fact and gives a commandment about what is to be done; cf 1, 20–21. Matthew omits Mk's "and Peter" (16, 7); considering his interest in Peter, this omission is curious. Perhaps the reason is that the Marcan text may allude to a first appearance of Jesus to Peter alone (cf 1 Cor 15, 5; Lk 24, 34) which Matthew has already incorporated into his account of Peter's confession at Caesarea Philippi; see the note on 16, 16. **He is going . . . Galilee:** like Mk 16, 7, a reference to Jesus' prediction at the Last Supper (26, 32; Mk 14, 28). Matthew changes Mk's "as he told you" to a declaration of the angel.

d: 12, 40; 16, 21; 17, 23; 20, 19. *e:* Mk 16, 1-8; Lk 24, 1-12; Jn 20, 1-10. *f:* 25, 51. *g:* 17, 2.

as he said. Come and see the place where he lay. *7h*Then go quickly and tell his disciples, 'He has been raised from the dead, and he is going before you to Galilee; there you will see him.' Behold, I have told you." *8**Then they went away quickly from the tomb, fearful yet overjoyed, and ran to announce this to his disciples. *9i**And behold, Jesus met them on their way and greeted them. They approached, embraced his feet, and did him homage. *10*Then Jesus said to them, "Do not be afraid. Go tell my brothers to go to Galilee, and there they will see me."

The Report of the Guard. *11**While they were going, some of the guard went into the city and told the chief priests all that had happened. *12*They assembled with the elders and took counsel; then they gave a large sum of money to the soldiers, *13*telling them, "You are to say, 'His disciples came by night and stole him while we were asleep.' *14*And if this gets to the ears of the governor, we will satisfy [him] and keep you out of trouble." *15*The soldiers took the money and did as they were instructed. And this story has circulated among the Jews to the present [day].

The Commissioning of the Disciples. *16j**The eleven disciples went to Galilee, to the mountain to which Jesus had ordered them. *17**When they saw him, they worshiped, but they doubted. *18k**Then Jesus approached and said to them, "All power in heaven and on earth has been given to me. *19l**Go, therefore, and make disciples of all nations, baptizing them in the name of the Father, and of the Son, and of the holy Spirit, *20m**teaching them to observe all that I have commanded you. And behold, I am with you always, until the end of the age."

28, 8: Contrast Mk 16, 8 where the women in their fear "said nothing to anyone."

28, 9–10: Although these verses are peculiar to Mt, there are similarities between them and Jn's account of the appearance of Jesus to Mary Magdalene (20, 17). In both there is a touching of Jesus' body, and a command of Jesus to bear a message to his disciples, designated as his **brothers**. Matthew may have drawn upon a tradition that appears in a different form in Jn. Jesus' words to the women are mainly a repetition of those of the angel (5a; 7b).

28, 11–15: This account indicates that the dispute between Christians and Jews about the empty tomb was not whether the tomb was empty but why.

28, 16–20: This climactic scene has been called a "proleptic parousia," for it gives a foretaste of the final glorious coming of the Son of Man (26, 64). Then his triumph will be manifest to all; now it is revealed only to **the disciples,** who are commissioned to announce it to **all nations** and bring them to belief in Jesus and obedience to his commandments.

28, 16: The eleven: the number recalls the tragic defection of Judas Iscariot. **To the mountain . . . ordered them:** since the message to **the disciples** was simply that they were to go to Galilee (10), some think that **the mountain** comes from a tradition of the message known to Matthew and alluded to here. For the significance of **the mountain,** see the note on 17, 1.

28, 17: But they doubted: the Greek can also be translated, "but some doubted." The verb occurs elsewhere in the New Testament only in 14, 31 where it is associated with Peter's being of "little faith." For the meaning of that designation, see the note on 6, 30.

28, 18: All power . . . me: the Greek word here translated **power** is the same as that found in the LXX translation of Dn 7, 13–14 where one "like a son of man" is given **power** and an everlasting kingdom by God. The risen Jesus here claims universal power, i.e., **in heaven and on earth.**

28, 19: Therefore: since universal power belongs to the risen Jesus (18), he gives the eleven a mission that is universal. They are to **make disciples of all nations.** While all **nations** is understood by some scholars as referring only **to all** Gentiles, it is probable that it included the Jews as well. **Baptizing them:** baptism is the means of entrance into the community of the risen one, the Church. **In the name of the Father . . . holy Spirit:** this is perhaps the clearest expression in the New Testament of trinitarian belief. It may have been the baptismal formula of Matthew's church, but primarily it designates the effect of baptism, the union of the one baptized with the Father, Son, and holy Spirit.

28, 20: All that I have commanded you: the moral teaching found in this gospel, preeminently that of the Sermon on the Mount (chs 5–7). The commandments of Jesus are the standard of Christian conduct, not the Mosaic law as such, even though some of the Mosaic commandments have now been invested with the authority of Jesus. **Behold, I am with you always:** the promise of Jesus' real though invisible presence echoes the name Emmanuel given to him in the infancy narrative; see the note on 1, 23. End of the age: see the notes on 13, 39 and 24, 3.

h: 26, 32. *i:* Jn 20, 17. *j:* Mk 16, 14-16; Lk 24, 36-49; Jn 20, 19-23. *k:* Dn 7, 14 LXX. *l:* Acts 1, 8. *m:* 1, 23; 13, 39; 24, 3.

See RG
386-96

The Gospel According to Mark

This shortest of all New Testament gospels is likely the first to have been written, yet it often tells of Jesus' ministry in more detail than either Matthew or Luke (for example, the miracle stories at 5, 1–20 or 9, 14–29). It recounts what Jesus did in a vivid style, where one incident follows directly upon another. In this almost breathless narrative, Mark stresses Jesus' message about the kingdom of God now breaking into human life as good news (1, 14–15) and Jesus himself as the gospel of God (1, 1; 8, 35; 10, 29). Jesus is the Son whom God has sent to rescue humanity by serving and by sacrificing his life (10, 45).

The opening verse about good news in Mark (1, 1) serves as a title for the entire book. The action begins with the appearance of John the Baptist, a messenger of God attested by scripture. But John points to a mightier one, Jesus, at whose baptism God speaks from heaven, declaring Jesus his Son. The Spirit descends upon Jesus, who eventually, it is promised, will baptize "with the holy Spirit." This presentation of who Jesus really is (1, 1–13) is rounded out with a brief reference to the temptation of Jesus and how Satan's attack fails. Jesus as Son of God will be victorious, a point to be remembered as one reads of Jesus' death and the enigmatic ending to Mark's Gospel.

The key verses at 1, 14–15, which are programmatic, summarize what Jesus proclaims as gospel: fulfillment, the nearness of the kingdom, and therefore the need for repentance and for faith. After the call of the first four disciples, all fishermen (1, 16–20), we see Jesus engaged in teaching (1, 21.22.27), preaching (1, 38.39), and healing (1, 29–31.34.40–45), and exorcising demons (1, 22–27.34.39). The content of Jesus' teaching is only rarely stated, and then chiefly in parables (ch 4) about the kingdom. His cures, especially on the sabbath (3, 1–5); his claim, like God, to forgive sins (2, 3–12); his table fellowship with tax collectors and sinners (2, 14–17); and the statement that his followers need not now fast but should rejoice while Jesus is present (2, 18–22), all stir up opposition that will lead to Jesus' death (3, 6).

In Mark, Jesus is portrayed as immensely popular with the people in Galilee during his ministry (2, 2; 3, 7; 4, 1). He appoints twelve disciples to help preach and drive out demons, just as he does (3, 13–19). He continues to work many miracles; the blocks 4, 35—6, 44 and 6, 45—7, 10 are cycles of stories about healings, miracles at the Sea of Galilee, and marvelous feedings of the crowds. Jesus' teaching in ch 7 exalts the word of God over "the tradition of the elders" and sees defilement as a matter of the heart, not of unclean foods. Yet opposition mounts. Scribes charge that Jesus is possessed by Beelzebul (3, 22). His relatives think him "out of his mind" (3, 21). Jesus' kinship is with those who do the will of God, in a new eschatological family, not even with mother, brothers, or sisters by blood ties (3, 31–35; cf 6, 1–6). But all too often his own disciples do not understand Jesus (4, 13.40; 6, 52; 8, 17–21). The fate of John the Baptist (6, 17–29) hints ominously at Jesus' own passion (9, 13; cf 8, 31).

A breakthrough seemingly comes with Peter's confession that Jesus is the Christ (Messiah; 8, 27–30). But Jesus himself emphasizes his passion (8, 31; 9, 31; 10, 33–34), not glory in the kingdom (10, 35–45). Momentarily he is glimpsed in his true identity when he is transfigured before three of the disciples (9, 2–8), but by and large Jesus is depicted in Mark as moving obediently along the way to his cross in Jerusalem. Occasionally there are miracles (9, 17–27; 10, 46–52; 11, 12–14.20–21, the only such account in Jerusalem), sometimes teachings (10, 2–11.23–31), but the greatest concern is with discipleship (8, 34—9, 1; 9, 33–50). For the disciples do not grasp the mystery being revealed (9, 32; 10, 32.38). One of them will betray him, Judas (14, 10–11.43–45); one will deny him, Peter (14, 27.31.54.66–72); all eleven men will desert Jesus (14, 27.50).

The passion account, with its condemnation of Jesus by the Sanhedrin (14, 53.55–65; 15, 1a) and sentencing by Pilate (15, 1), is prefaced with the entry into Jerusalem (11, 1–11), ministry and controversies there (11, 15—12, 44), Jesus' Last Supper with the disciples (14, 1–26), and his arrest at Gethsemane (14, 32–52). A chapter of apocalyptic tone about the destruction of the temple (13, 1–2.14–23) and the coming of the Son of Man (13, 24–27), a discourse filled with promises (13, 11.31) and admonitions to be watchful (13, 2.23.37), is significant for Mark's Gospel, for it helps one see that God, in Jesus, will be victorious after the cross and at the end of history.

The Gospel of Mark ends in the most ancient manuscripts with an abrupt scene at Jesus' tomb, which the women find empty (16, 1–8). His own prophecy of 14, 28 is reiterated, that Jesus goes before the disciples into Galilee; "there you will see him." These words may imply resurrection appearances there, or Jesus' parousia there, or the start of Christian mission, or a return to the roots depicted in 1, 9.14–15 in Galilee. Other hands have attached additional endings after 16, 8; see the note on 16, 9–20.

The framework of Mark's Gospel is partly geographical: Galilee (1, 14—9, 49), through the area "across the Jordan" (10, 1) and through Jericho (10, 46–52), to Jerusalem (11, 1—16, 8). Only rarely does Jesus go into Gentile territory (5, 1–20; 7, 24–37), but those who acknowledge him there and the centurion who confesses Jesus at the cross (15, 39) presage the gospel's expansion into the world beyond Palestine.

Mark's Gospel is even more oriented to christology. Jesus is the Son of God (1, 11; 9, 7; 15, 39; cf 1, 1; 14, 61). He is the Messiah, the anointed king of Davidic descent (12, 35; 15, 32), the Greek for which, *Christos*, has, by the time Mark wrote, become in effect a proper name (1, 1; 9, 41). Jesus is also seen as Son of Man, a term used in Mark not simply as a substitute for "I" or for humanity in general (cf 2, 10.27–28; 14, 21) or with reference to a mighty figure who is to come (13, 26; 14, 62), but also in connection with Jesus' predestined, necessary path of suffering and vindication (8, 31; 10, 45).

The unfolding of Mark's story about Jesus is sometimes viewed by interpreters as centered around the term "mystery." The word is employed just once, at 4, 11, in the singular, and its content there is the kingdom, the open secret that God's reign is now breaking into human life with its reversal of human values. There is a related sense in which Jesus' real identity remained a secret during his lifetime, according to Mark, although demons and demoniacs knew it (1, 24; 3, 11; 5, 7); Jesus warned against telling of his mighty deeds and revealing his identity (1, 44;

3, 12; 5, 43; 7, 36; 8, 26.30), an injunction sometimes broken (1, 45; cf 5, 19–20). Further, Jesus teaches by parables, according to Mark, in such a way that those "outside" the kingdom do not understand, but only those to whom the mystery has been granted by God.

Mark thus shares with Paul, as well as with other parts of the New Testament, an emphasis on election (13, 20.22) and upon the gospel as Christ and his cross (cf 1 Cor 1, 23). Yet in Mark the person of Jesus is also depicted with an unaffected naturalness. He reacts to events with authentic human emotion: pity (1, 44), anger (3, 5), triumph (4, 40), sympathy (5, 36; 6, 34), surprise (6, 9), admiration (7, 29; 10, 21), sadness (14, 33–34), and indignation (14, 48–49).

Although the book is anonymous, apart from the ancient heading "According to Mark" in manuscripts, it has traditionally been assigned to John Mark, in whose mother's house (at Jerusalem) Christians assembled (Acts 12, 12). This Mark was a cousin of Barnabas (Col 4, 10) and accompanied Barnabas and Paul on a missionary journey (Acts 12, 25; 13, 3; 15, 36–39). He appears in Pauline letters (2 Tm 4, 11; Phlm 1, 24) and with Peter (1 Pt 5, 13). Papias (ca. A.D. 135) described Mark as Peter's "interpreter," a view found in other patristic writers. Petrine influence should not, however, be exaggerated. The evangelist has put together various oral and possibly written sources—miracle stories, parables, sayings, stories of controversies, and the passion—so as to speak of the crucified Messiah for Mark's own day.

Traditionally, the gospel is said to have been written shortly before A.D. 70 in Rome, at a time of impending persecution and when destruction loomed over Jerusalem. Its audience seems to have been Gentile, unfamiliar with Jewish customs (hence 7, 3–4.11). The book aimed to equip such Christians to stand faithful in the face of persecution (13, 9–13), while going on with the proclamation of the gospel begun in Galilee (13, 10; 14, 9). Modern research often proposes as the author an unknown Hellenistic Jewish Christian, possibly in Syria, and perhaps shortly after the year 70.

The principal divisions of the Gospel according to Mark are the following:

I: The Preparation for the Public Ministry of Jesus (1, 1–13)

I: The Preparation
for the Public Ministry
of Jesus

CHAPTER 1

See RG
388–90

1*The beginning of the gospel of Jesus Christ [the Son of God].

The Preaching of John the Baptist. *2ab**As it is written in Isaiah the prophet:

"Behold, I am sending my messenger
 ahead of you;
 he will prepare your way.
*3 c*A voice of one crying out in the desert:
 'Prepare the way of the Lord,
 make straight his paths.' "

*4*John [the] Baptist appeared in the desert proclaiming a baptism of repentance for the forgiveness of sins. *5*People of the whole Judean countryside and all the inhabitants of Jerusalem were going out to him and were being baptized by him in the Jordan River as they acknowledged their sins. *6**John was clothed in camel's hair, with a leather belt around his waist. He fed on locusts and wild honey. *7*And this is what he proclaimed: "One mightier than I is coming after me. I am not worthy to stoop and loosen the thongs of his sandals. *8d**I have baptized you with water; he will baptize you with the holy Spirit."

The Baptism of Jesus. *9e*It happened in those days that Jesus came from Nazareth of Galilee and was baptized in the Jordan by John. *10**On coming up out of the water he saw the heavens being torn open and the Spirit, like a dove, descending upon him. *11f*And a voice came from the heavens, "You are my beloved Son; with you I am well pleased."

The Temptation of Jesus. *12g**At once the Spirit drove him out into the desert, *13*and he remained in the desert for forty days, tempted by Satan. He was among wild beasts, and the angels ministered to him.

1, 1–13: The prologue of the Gospel according to Mark begins with the title (1) followed by three events preparatory to Jesus' preaching: (1) the appearance in the Judean wilderness of John, baptizer, preacher of repentance, and precursor of Jesus (2–8); (2) the baptism of Jesus, at which a voice from heaven acknowledges Jesus to be God's Son, and the holy Spirit descends on him (9–11); (3) the temptation of Jesus by Satan (12–13).

1, 1: The gospel of Jesus Christ [the Son of God]: the "good news" of salvation in and through Jesus, crucified and risen, acknowledged by the Christian community as Messiah (8, 29; 14, 61–62) and Son of God (11; 9, 7; 15, 39), although some important manuscripts here omit **the Son of God.**

1, 2–3: Although Mark attributes the prophecy to Isaiah, the text is a combination of Mal 3, 1; Is 40, 3; and Ex 23, 20; cf Mt 11, 10; Lk 7, 27. John's ministry is seen as God's prelude to the saving mission of his Son. **The way of the Lord:** this prophecy of Deutero-Isaiah concerning the end of the Babylonian exile is here applied to the coming of Jesus; John the Baptist is to prepare the way for him.

1, 6: Clothed in camel's hair . . . waist: the Baptist's garb recalls that of Elijah in 2 Kgs 1, 8. Jesus speaks of the Baptist as Elijah who has already come (9, 11–13; Mt 17, 10–12; cf Mal 3, 23–24; Lk 1, 17).

1, 8–9: Through the life-giving baptism with the holy Spirit (8), Jesus will create a new people of God. But first he identifies himself with the people of Israel in submitting to

John's baptism of repentance and in bearing on their behalf the burden of God's decisive judgment (9; cf 4). As in the desert of Sinai, so here in the wilderness of Judea, Israel's sonship with God is to be renewed.

1, 10–11: He saw the heavens . . . and the Spirit . . . upon him: indicating divine intervention in fulfillment of promise. Here the descent of the Spirit on Jesus is meant, anointing him for his ministry; cf Is 11, 2; 42, 1; 61, 1; 63, 9. **A voice . . . with you I am well pleased:** God's acknowledgment of Jesus as his unique Son, the object of his love. His approval of Jesus is the assurance that Jesus will fulfill his messianic mission of salvation.

1, 12–13: The same Spirit who descended on Jesus in his baptism now drives him into the desert for forty days. The result is radical confrontation and temptation by Satan who attempts to frustrate the work of God. The presence of wild beasts may indicate the horror and danger of the desert regarded as the abode of demons or may reflect the paradise motif of harmony among all creatures; cf Is 11, 6–9. The presence of ministering angels to sustain Jesus recalls the angel who guided the Israelites in the desert in the first Exodus (14, 19; 23, 20) and the angel who supplied nourishment to Elijah in the wilderness (1 Kgs 19, 5–7). The combined forces of

a: Mt 3, 1-11; Lk 3, 2-16. *b:* Mal 3, 1. *c:* Is 40, 3; Jn 1, 23. *d:* Jn 1, 27; Acts 1, 5; 11, 16. *e:* Mt 3, 13-17; Lk 3, 21-23; Jn 1, 32-33. *f:* Ps 2, 7. *g:* Mt 4, 1-11; Lk 4, 1-13.

II: The Mystery of Jesus

The Beginning of the Galilean Ministry. [14h]*After John had been arrested, Jesus came to Galilee proclaiming the gospel of God: [15i]"This is the time of fulfillment. The kingdom of God is at hand. Repent, and believe in the gospel."

The Call of the First Disciples. [16j]*As he passed by the Sea of Galilee, he saw Simon and his brother Andrew casting their nets into the sea; they were fishermen. [17]Jesus said to them, "Come after me, and I will make you fishers of men." [18]Then they abandoned their nets and followed him. [19]He walked along a little farther and saw James, the son of Zebedee, and his brother John. They too were in a boat mending their nets. [20]Then he called them. So they left their father Zebedee in the boat along with the hired men and followed him.

The Cure of a Demoniac. [21k]*Then they came to Capernaum, and on the sabbath he entered the synagogue and taught. [22l]The people were astonished at his teaching, for he taught them as one having authority and not as the scribes. [23]*In their synagogue was a man with an unclean spirit; [24]*he cried out, "What have you to do with us, Jesus of Nazareth? Have you come to destroy us? I know who you are—the Holy One of God!" [25]Jesus rebuked him and said, "Quiet! Come out of him!" [26]The unclean spirit convulsed him and with a loud cry came out of him. [27]All were amazed and asked one another, "What is this? A new teaching with authority. He commands even the unclean spirits and they obey him." [28]His fame spread everywhere throughout the whole region of Galilee.

The Cure of Simon's Mother-in-Law. [29m]On leaving the synagogue he entered the house of Simon and Andrew with James and John. [30]Simon's mother-in-law lay sick with a fever. They immediately told him about her. [31]He approached, grasped her hand, and helped her up. Then the fever left her and she waited on them.

Other Healings. [32]When it was evening, after sunset, they brought to him all who were ill or possessed by demons. [33]The whole town was gathered at the door. [34]He cured many who were sick with various diseases, and he drove out many demons, not permitting them to speak because they knew him.

Jesus Leaves Capernaum. [35n]Rising very early before dawn, he left and went off to a deserted place, where he prayed. [36]Simon and those who were with him pursued him [37]and on finding him said, "Everyone is looking for you." [38]He told them, "Let us go on to the nearby villages that I may preach there also. For this purpose have I come." [39]So he went into their synagogues, preaching and driving out demons throughout the whole of Galilee.

The Cleansing of a Leper. [40o]*A leper came to him [and kneeling down] begged

---

good and evil were present to Jesus in the desert. His sustained obedience brings forth the new Israel of God there where Israel's rebellion had brought death and alienation.

1, 14–15: After John had been arrested: in the plan of God, Jesus was not to proclaim the good news of salvation prior to the termination of the Baptist's active mission. **Galilee:** in the Marcan account, scene of the major part of Jesus' public ministry before his arrest and condemnation. **The gospel of God:** not only the good news from God but about God at work in Jesus Christ. **This is the time of fulfillment:** i.e., of God's promises. **The kingdom of God . . . Repent:** see the note on Mt 3, 2.

1, 16–20: These verses narrate the call of the first disciples. See the notes on Mt 4, 18–22 and 4, 20.

1, 21–45: The account of a single day's ministry of Jesus on a sabbath in and outside the synagogue of Capernaum (21–31) combines teaching and miracles of exorcism and healing. Mention is not made of the content of the teaching but of the effect of astonishment and alarm on the people. Jesus' teaching with authority, making an absolute claim on the hearer, was in the best tradition of the ancient prophets, not of

the scribes. The narrative continues with events that evening (32–34; see the notes on Mt 8, 14–17) and the next day (35–39). The cleansing in vv 40–45 stands as an isolated story.

1, 23: An unclean spirit: so called because of the spirit's resistance to the holiness of God. The spirit knows and fears the power of Jesus to destroy his influence; cf 32.34; 3, 11; 6, 13.

1, 24: What have you to do with us?: see the note on Jn 2, 4.

1, 24–25: The Holy One of God: not a confession but an attempt to ward off Jesus' power, reflecting the notion that use of the precise name of an opposing spirit would guarantee mastery over him. Jesus silenced the cry of the unclean spirit and drove him out of the man.

1, 40: A leper: for the various forms of skin disease, see Lv 13, 1–50 and the note on Lv 13, 2–4. There are only two instances in the Old Testament in which God is shown to have cured a leper (Nm 12, 10–15 and 2 Kgs 5, 1–14). The law of

h: Mt 4, 12-17; Lk 4, 14-15. *i:* Mt 3, 2. *j:* Mt 4, 18-22; Lk 5, 2-11. *k:* Lk 4, 31-37. *l:* Mt 7, 28-29. *m:* Mt 8, 14-16; Lk 4, 38-41. *n:* Lk 4, 42-44. *o:* Mt 8, 2-4; Lk 5, 12-14.

him and said, "If you wish, you can make me clean." *41 p*Moved with pity, he stretched out his hand, touched him, and said to him, "I do will it. Be made clean." *42 q*The leprosy left him immediately, and he was made clean. *43*Then, warning him sternly, he dismissed him at once. *44 r*Then he said to him, "See that you tell no one anything, but go, show yourself to the priest and offer for your cleansing what Moses prescribed; that will be proof for them." *45*The man went away and began to publicize the whole matter. He spread the report abroad so that it was impossible for Jesus to enter a town openly. He remained outside in deserted places, and people kept coming to him from everywhere.

CHAPTER 2

See RG 390–91

The Healing of a Paralytic. *1 s*When Jesus returned to Capernaum after some days, it became known that he was at home. *2*Many gathered together so that there was no longer room for them, not even around the door, and he preached the word to them. *3*They came bringing to him a paralytic carried by four men. *4*Unable to get near Jesus because of the crowd, they opened up the roof above him. After they had broken through, they let down the mat on which the paralytic was lying. *5*When Jesus saw their

faith, he said to the paralytic, "Child, your sins are forgiven." *6*Now some of the scribes were sitting there asking themselves, *7 t*"Why does this man speak that way? He is blaspheming. Who but God alone can forgive sins?" *8*Jesus immediately knew in his mind what they were thinking to themselves, so he said, "Why are you thinking such things in your hearts? *9*Which is easier, to say to the paralytic, 'Your sins are forgiven,' or to say, 'Rise, pick up your mat and walk'? *10*But that you may know that the Son of Man has authority to forgive sins on earth"— *11*he said to the paralytic, "I say to you, rise, pick up your mat, and go home." *12*He rose, picked up his mat at once, and went away in the sight of everyone. They were all astounded and glorified God, saying, "We have never seen anything like this."

The Call of Levi. *13 u*Once again he went out along the sea. All the crowd came to him and he taught them. *14 v*As he passed by, he saw Levi, son of Alphaeus, sitting at the customs post. He said to him, "Follow me." And he got up and followed him. *15*While he was at table in his house, many tax collectors and sinners sat with Jesus and his disciples; for there were many who followed him. *16*Some scribes who were Pharisees saw that he was eating with sinners and tax col-

---

Moses provided for the ritual purification of a leper. In curing the leper, Jesus assumes that the priests will reinstate the cured man into the religious community. See also the note on Lk 5, 14.

2, 1—3, 6: This section relates a series of conflicts between Jesus and the scribes and Pharisees in which the growing opposition of the latter leads to their plot to put Jesus to death (3, 6).

2, 1–2: He was at home: to the crowds that gathered in and outside the house Jesus **preached the word,** i.e., the gospel concerning the nearness of the kingdom and the necessity of repentance and faith (1, 14).

2, 5: It was the faith of the paralytic and those who carried him that moved Jesus to heal the sick man. Accounts of other miracles of Jesus reveal more and more his emphasis on faith as the requisite for exercising his healing powers (5, 34; 9, 23–24; 10, 52).

2, 6: Scribes: trained in oral interpretation of the written law; in Mark's gospel, adversaries of Jesus, with one exception (12, 28.34).

2, 7: He is blaspheming: an accusation made here and repeated during the trial of Jesus (14, 60–64).

2, 10: But that you may know that the Son of Man . . . on earth: although vv 8–9 are addressed to the scribes, the sudden interruption of thought and structure in v 10 seems not

addressed to them nor to the paralytic. Moreover, the early public use of the designation "Son of Man" to unbelieving scribes is most unlikely. The most probable explanation is that Mark's insertion of v 10 is a commentary addressed to Christians for whom he recalls this miracle and who already accept in faith that Jesus is Messiah and Son of God.

2, 13: He taught them: see the note on 1, 21–45.

2, 14: As he passed by: see the note on 1, 16–20. **Levi, son of Alphaeus:** see the note on Mt 9, 9. **Customs post:** such tax collectors paid a fixed sum for the right to collect customs duties within their districts. Since whatever they could collect above this amount constituted their profit, the abuse of extortion was widespread among them. Hence, Jewish customs officials were regarded as sinners (16), outcasts of society, and disgraced along with their families. **He got up and followed him:** i.e., became a disciple of Jesus.

2, 15: In his house: cf v 1; Mt 9, 10. Lk 5, 29 clearly calls it Levi's house.

2, 16–17: This and the following conflict stories reflect a similar pattern: a statement of fact, a question of protest, and a reply by Jesus.

---

p: 5, 30.   *q:* Lk 17, 14.   *r:* Lv 14, 2-32.   *s:* Mt 9, 2-8; Lk 5, 18-26.   *t:* Is 43, 25.   *u:* 4, 1.   *v:* Mt 9, 9-13; Lk 5, 27-32.

lectors and said to his disciples, "Why does he eat with tax collectors and sinners?" [17]*Jesus heard this and said to them [that], "Those who are well do not need a physician, but the sick do. I did not come to call the righteous but sinners."

The Question about Fasting. [18w]*The disciples of John and of the Pharisees were accustomed to fast. People came to him and objected, "Why do the disciples of John and the disciples of the Pharisees fast, but your disciples do not fast?" [19]*Jesus answered them, "Can the wedding guests fast while the bridegroom is with them? As long as they have the bridegroom with them they cannot fast. [20]But the days will come when the bridegroom is taken away from them, and then they will fast on that day. [21]No one sews a piece of unshrunken cloth on an old cloak. If he does, its fullness pulls away, the new from the old, and the tear gets worse. [22]Likewise, no one pours new wine into old wineskins. Otherwise, the wine will burst the skins, and both the wine and the skins are ruined. Rather, new wine is poured into fresh wineskins."

The Disciples and the Sabbath. [23x]*As he was passing through a field of grain on the sabbath, his disciples began to make a path while picking the heads of grain. [24y]At this

the Pharisees said to him, "Look, why are they doing what is unlawful on the sabbath?" [25]*He said to them, "Have you never read what David did when he was in need and he and his companions were hungry? [26z]How he went into the house of God when Abiathar was high priest and ate the bread of offering that only the priests could lawfully eat, and shared it with his companions?" [27a]*Then he said to them, "The sabbath was made for man, not man for the sabbath. [28]*That is why the Son of Man is lord even of the sabbath."

CHAPTER 3

See RG 390-91

A Man with a Withered Hand. [1b]*Again he entered the synagogue. There was a man there who had a withered hand. [2]They watched him closely to see if he would cure him on the sabbath so that they might accuse him. [3]He said to the man with the withered hand, "Come up here before us." [4]Then he said to them, "Is it lawful to do good on the sabbath rather than to do evil, to save life rather than to destroy it?" But they remained silent. [5c]Looking around at them with anger and grieved at their hardness of heart, he said to the man, "Stretch out your hand." He stretched it out and his hand was restored. [6]*The Pharisees went out and im-

2, 17: Do not need a physician: this maxim of Jesus with its implied irony was uttered to silence his adversaries who objected that he ate with **tax collectors and sinners** (16). Because the scribes and Pharisees were self-righteous, they were not capable of responding to Jesus' call to repentance and faith in the gospel.

2, 18–22: This conflict over the question of fasting has the same pattern as vv 16–17; see the notes on Mt 9, 15 and 9, 16–17.

2, 19: Can the wedding guests fast?: the bridal metaphor expresses a new relationship of love between God and his people in the person and mission of Jesus to his disciples. It is the inauguration of the new and joyful messianic time of fulfillment and the passing of the old. Any attempt at assimilating the Pharisaic practice of fasting, or of extending the preparatory discipline of John's disciples beyond the arrival of the bridegroom, would be as futile as sewing **a piece of unshrunken cloth on an old cloak** or pouring **new wine into old wineskins** with the resulting destruction of both cloth and wine (21–22). Fasting is rendered superfluous during the earthly ministry of Jesus; cf v 20.

2, 23–28: This conflict regarding the sabbath follows the same pattern as in vv 18–22.

2, 25–26: Have you never read what David did?: Jesus defends the action of his disciples on the basis of 1 Sm 21, 2–7 in which an exception is made to the regulation of Lv 24,

9 because of the extreme hunger of David and his men. According to 1 Sm, the priest who gave the bread to David was Ahimelech, father of Abiathar.

2, 27: The sabbath was made for man: a reaffirmation of the divine intent of the sabbath to benefit Israel as contrasted with the restrictive Pharisaic tradition added to the law.

2, 28: The Son of Man is lord even of the sabbath: Mark's comment on the theological meaning of the incident is to benefit his Christian readers; see the note on 2, 10.

3, 1–5: Here Jesus is again depicted in conflict with his adversaries over the question of sabbath-day observance. His opponents were already ill disposed toward him because they regarded Jesus as a violator of the sabbath. Jesus' question **Is it lawful to do good on the sabbath rather than to do evil?** places the matter in the broader theological context outside the casuistry of the scribes. The answer is obvious. Jesus heals the man with the withered hand in the sight of all and reduces his opponents to silence; cf Jn 5, 17–18.

3, 6: In reporting the plot of the Pharisees and Herodians to put Jesus to death after this series of conflicts in Galilee, Mark uses a pattern that recurs in his account of later controversies in Jerusalem (11, 17–18; 12, 13–17). The help of the Herodians,

w: Mt 9, 14-17; Lk 5, 33-39.   x: Mt 12, 1-8; Lk 6, 1-5.   y: Dt 23, 25.   z: 1 Sm 21, 2-7 / Lv 24, 5-9.   a: 2 Mc 5, 19.   b: Mt 12, 9-14; Lk 6, 6-11.   c: Lk 14, 4.

mediately took counsel with the Herodians against him to put him to death.

The Mercy of Jesus. ⁷ᵈ*Jesus withdrew toward the sea with his disciples. A large number of people [followed] from Galilee and from Judea. ⁸Hearing what he was doing, a large number of people came to him also from Jerusalem, from Idumea, from beyond the Jordan, and from the neighborhood of Tyre and Sidon. ⁹He told his disciples to have a boat ready for him because of the crowd, so that they would not crush him. ¹⁰ᵉHe had cured many and, as a result, those who had diseases were pressing upon him to touch him. ¹¹ᶠ*And whenever unclean spirits saw him they would fall down before him and shout, "You are the Son of God." ¹²He warned them sternly not to make him known.

The Mission of the Twelve. ¹³ᵍ*He went up the mountain and summoned those whom he wanted and they came to him. ¹⁴ʰ*He appointed twelve [whom he also named apostles] that they might be with him and he might send them forth to preach ¹⁵and to have authority to drive out demons: ¹⁶*[he appointed the twelve:] Simon, whom he named Peter; ¹⁷ⁱJames, son of Zebedee, and John the brother of James, whom he named Boanerges, that is, sons of thunder; ¹⁸Andrew, Philip, Bartholomew, Matthew, Thomas, James the son of Alphaeus; Thaddeus, Simon the Cananean, ¹⁹and Judas Iscariot who betrayed him.

Blasphemy of the Scribes. ²⁰ʲ*He came home. Again [the] crowd gathered, making it impossible for them even to eat. ²¹ᵏWhen his relatives heard of this they set out to seize him, for they said, "He is out of his mind." ²²ˡ*The scribes who had come from Jerusalem said, "He is possessed by Beelzebul," and "By the prince of demons he drives out demons."

Jesus and Beelzebul. ²³Summoning them, he began to speak to them in parables, "How can Satan drive out Satan? ²⁴If a kingdom is divided against itself, that kingdom cannot stand. ²⁵And if a house is divided against itself, that house will not be able to stand. ²⁶And if Satan has risen up against himself and is divided, he cannot stand; that is the end of him. ²⁷But no one can enter a strong man's house to plunder his property unless he first ties up the strong man. Then he can plunder his house. ²⁸ᵐAmen, I say to you, all sins and all blasphemies that people utter will be forgiven them. ²⁹*But whoever blasphemes against the holy Spirit will never have forgiveness, but is guilty of an everlasting sin." ³⁰For they had said, "He has an unclean spirit."

---

supporters of Herod Antipas, tetrarch of Galilee and Perea, is needed to take action against Jesus. Both series of conflicts point to their gravity and to the impending passion of Jesus.

3, 7–19: This overview of the Galilean ministry manifests the power of Jesus to draw people to himself through his teaching and deeds of power. The crowds of Jews from many regions surround Jesus (7–12). This phenomenon prepares the way for creating a new people of Israel. The choice and mission of the Twelve is the prelude (13–19).

3, 11–12: See the note on 1, 24–25.

3, 13: He went up the mountain: here and elsewhere the mountain is associated with solemn moments and acts in the mission and self-revelation of Jesus (6, 46; 9, 2–8; 13, 3). Jesus acts with authority as he **summoned those whom he wanted and they came to him.**

3, 14–15: He appointed twelve [whom he also named apostles] that they might be with him: literally "he made," i.e., instituted them as apostles to extend his messianic mission through them (6, 7–13). See the notes on Mt 10, 1 and 10, 2–4.

3, 16: Simon, whom he named Peter: Mark indicates that Simon's name was changed on this occasion. Peter is first in all lists of the apostles (Mt 10, 2; Lk 6, 14; Acts 1, 13; cf 1 Cor 15, 5–8).

3, 20–35: Within the narrative of the coming of Jesus' rel-

atives (20–21) is inserted the account of the unbelieving scribes from Jerusalem who attributed Jesus' power over demons to Beelzebul (22–30); see the note on 5, 21–43. There were those even among the relatives of Jesus who disbelieved and regarded Jesus as **out of his mind** (21). Against this background, Jesus is informed of the arrival of his mother and brothers [and sisters] (32). He responds by showing that not family ties but doing God's will (35) is decisive in the kingdom; cf the note on Mt 12, 46–50.

3, 20: He came home: cf 2, 1–2 and see the note on 2, 15.

3, 22: By Beelzebul: see the note on Mt 10, 25. Two accusations are leveled against Jesus: (1) that **he is possessed** by an unclean spirit, and (2) **by the prince of demons he drives out demons.** Jesus answers the second charge by a parable (24–27) and responds to the first charge in vv 28–29.

3, 29: Whoever blasphemes against the holy Spirit: this sin is called **an everlasting sin** because it attributes to Satan, who is the power of evil, what is actually the work of the holy Spirit, namely, victory over the demons.

d: Mt 4, 23–25; 12, 15; Lk 6, 17–19.   *e:* 5, 30.   *f:* 1, 34; Lk 4, 41.
g: Mt 10, 1–4; Lk 6, 12–16.   *h:* 6, 7.   *i:* Mt 16, 18; Jn 1, 42.   *j:* 2,
2.   *k:* Jn 10, 20.   *l:* Mt 12, 24–32; Lk 11, 15–22; 12, 10.   *m:* Lk
12, 10.

Jesus and His Family. [31n]His mother and his brothers arrived. Standing outside they sent word to him and called him. [32]*A crowd seated around him told him, "Your mother and your brothers [and your sisters] are outside asking for you." [33]But he said to them in reply, "Who are my mother and [my] brothers?" [34]And looking around at those seated in the circle he said, "Here are my mother and my brothers. [35][For] whoever does the will of God is my brother and sister and mother."

CHAPTER 4

See RG
391–92

The Parable of the Sower. [1o][p]*On another occasion he began to teach by the sea. A very large crowd gathered around him so that he got into a boat on the sea and sat down. And the whole crowd was beside the sea on land. [2]And he taught them at length in parables, and in the course of his instruction he said to them, [3]*"Hear this! A sower went out to sow. [4]And as he sowed, some seed fell on the path, and the birds came and ate it up. [5]Other seed fell on rocky ground where it had little soil. It sprang up at once because the soil was not deep. [6]And when the sun rose, it was scorched and it withered for lack of roots. [7]Some seed fell among thorns, and the thorns grew up and choked it and it produced no grain. [8]And some seed fell on rich soil and produced fruit. It came up and grew and yielded thirty, sixty, and a hundredfold." [9]He added, "Whoever has ears to hear ought to hear."

The Purpose of the Parables. [10]And when he was alone, those present along with the Twelve questioned him about the parables. [11]*He answered them, "The mystery of the kingdom of God has been granted to you. But to those outside everything comes in parables, [12q]so that

'they may look and see but not perceive,
  and hear and listen but not understand,
in order that they may not be converted
  and be forgiven.' "

[13r]*Jesus said to them, "Do you not understand this parable? Then how will you understand any of the parables? [14]The sower sows the word. [15]These are the ones on the path where the word is sown. As soon as they hear, Satan comes at once and takes away the word sown in them. [16]And these are the ones sown on rocky ground who, when they hear the word, receive it at once with joy. [17]But they have no root; they last only for a time. Then when tribulation or persecution comes because of the word, they quickly fall away. [18]Those sown among thorns are another sort. They are the people who hear the word, [19]but worldly anxiety, the lure of riches, and the craving for other things intrude and choke the word, and it bears no fruit. [20]But those sown on rich soil are the ones who hear the word and accept it and bear fruit thirty and sixty and a hundredfold."

Parable of the Lamp. [21s][t]He said to them, "Is a lamp brought in to be placed under a bushel basket or under a bed, and not to be placed on a lampstand? [22u]For there is nothing hidden except to be made visible; noth-

---

3, 32: Your brothers: see the note on 6, 3.

4, 1–34: In parables (2): see the note on Mt 13, 3. The use of parables is typical of Jesus' enigmatic method of teaching the crowds (2–9.12) as compared with the interpretation of the parables he gives to his disciples (10–25.33–34), to each group according to its capacity to understand (9–11). The key feature of the parable at hand is the sowing of the seed (3), representing the breakthrough of the kingdom of God into the world. The various types of soil refer to the diversity of response accorded the word of God (4–7). The climax of the parable is the harvest of thirty, sixty, and a hundredfold, indicating the consummation of the kingdom (8). Thus both the present and the future action of God, from the initiation to the fulfillment of the kingdom, is presented through this and other parables (26–29.30–32).

4, 1: By the sea: the shore of the Sea of Galilee or a boat near the shore (2, 13; 3, 7–8) is the place where Mark depicts Jesus teaching the crowds. By contrast the mountain is the scene of Jesus at prayer (6, 46) or in the process of forming his disciples (3, 13; 9, 2).

4, 3–8: See the note on Mt 13, 3–8.

4, 11–12: These verses are to be viewed against their background in 3, 6.22 concerning the unbelief and opposition Jesus encountered in his ministry. It is against this background that the distinction in Jesus' method becomes clear of presenting the kingdom to the disbelieving crowd in one manner and to the disciples in another. To the former it is presented in parables and the truth remains hidden; for the latter the parable is interpreted and the mystery is partially revealed because of their faith; see the notes on Mt 13, 11 and 13, 13.

4, 13–20: See the note on Mt 13, 18–23.

n: Mt 12, 46-50; Lk 8, 19-21. *o:* Mt 13, 1-13; Lk 8, 4-10. *p:* 2, 13; Lk 5, 1. *q:* Is 6, 9; Jn 12, 40; Acts 28, 26; Rom 11, 8. *r:* Mt 13, 18-23; Lk 8, 11-15. *s:* Lk 8, 16-18. *t:* Mt 5, 15; Lk 11, 33. *u:* Mt 10, 26; Lk 12, 2.

ing is secret except to come to light. [23]Anyone who has ears to hear ought to hear." [24v]He also told them, "Take care what you hear. The measure with which you measure will be measured out to you, and still more will be given to you. [25w]To the one who has, more will be given; from the one who has not, even what he has will be taken away."

Seed Grows of Itself. [26x*]He said, "This is how it is with the kingdom of God; it is as if a man were to scatter seed on the land [27]and would sleep and rise night and day and the seed would sprout and grow, he knows not how. [28]Of its own accord the land yields fruit, first the blade, then the ear, then the full grain in the ear. [29]And when the grain is ripe, he wields the sickle at once, for the harvest has come."

The Mustard Seed. [30y]He said, "To what shall we compare the kingdom of God, or what parable can we use for it? [31]It is like a mustard seed that, when it is sown in the ground, is the smallest of all the seeds on the earth. [32*]But once it is sown, it springs up and becomes the largest of plants and puts forth large branches, so that the birds of the sky can dwell in its shade." [33z]With many such parables he spoke the word to them as they were able to understand it. [34]Without parables he did not speak to them, but to his own disciples he explained everything in private.

The Calming of a Storm at Sea. [35a*]On that day, as evening drew on, he said to them, "Let us cross to the other side." [36]Leaving the crowd, they took him with them in the boat just as he was. And other boats were with him. [37]A violent squall came up and waves were breaking over the boat, so that it was already filling up. [38]Jesus was in the stern, asleep on a cushion. They woke him and said to him, "Teacher, do you not care that we are perishing?" [39*]He woke up, rebuked the wind, and said to the sea, "Quiet! Be still!" The wind ceased and there was great calm. [40]Then he asked them, "Why are you terrified? Do you not yet have faith?" [41b*]They were filled with great awe and said to one another, "Who then is this whom even wind and sea obey?"

CHAPTER 5

See RG 392-93

The Healing of the Gerasene Demoniac. [1c*]They came to the other side of the sea, to the territory of the Gerasenes. [2*]When he got out of the boat, at once a man from the tombs who had an unclean spirit met him. [3]The man had been dwelling among the tombs, and no one could restrain him any longer, even with a chain. [4]In fact, he had frequently been bound with shackles and chains, but the chains had been pulled apart by him and the shackles smashed, and no one was strong enough to subdue him. [5]Night and day among the tombs and on the hillsides he was always crying out and bruising himself with stones. [6]Catching sight of Jesus from a distance, he ran up and prostrated himself before him, [7*]crying out in a loud voice, "What have you to do with me, Jesus, Son of the Most High God? I adjure you by God, do not torment me!" [8](He had been saying to him, "Unclean spirit, come

---

4, 26–29: Only Mark records the parable of the seed's growth. Sower and harvester are the same. The emphasis is on the power of the seed to grow of itself without human intervention (27). Mysteriously it produces **blade** and **ear** and **full grain** (28). Thus the kingdom of God initiated by Jesus in proclaiming the word develops quietly yet powerfully until it is fully established by him at the final judgment (29); cf Rv 14, 15.

4, 32: The universality of the kingdom of God is indicated here; cf Ez 17, 23; 31, 6; Dn 4, 17–19.

4, 35—5, 43: After the chapter on parables, Mark narrates four miracle stories: 4, 35–41; 5, 1–20; and two joined together in 5, 21–43. See also the notes on Mt 8, 23–34 and 9, 8–26.

4, 39: Quiet! Be still!: as in the case of silencing a demon (1, 25), Jesus rebukes the wind and subdues the turbulence of the sea by a mere word; see the note on Mt 8, 26.

4, 41: Jesus is here depicted as exercising power over

wind and sea. In the Christian community this event was seen as a sign of Jesus' saving presence amid persecutions that threatened its existence.

5, 1: The territory of the Gerasenes: the reference is to pagan territory; cf Is 65, 1. Another reading is "Gadarenes"; see the note on Mt 8, 28.

5, 2–6: The man was an outcast from society, dominated by unclean spirits (8.13), living among the tombs. The prostration before Jesus (6) indicates Jesus' power over evil spirits.

5, 7: What have you to do with me?: cf 1, 24 and see the note on Jn 2, 4.

---

v: Mt 7, 2; Lk 6, 38.　w: Mt 13, 12; Lk 19, 26.　x: Jas 5, 7.
y: Mt 13, 31-32; Lk 13, 18-19.　z: Mt 13, 34.　a: Mt 8, 18.23-37; Lk 8, 22-25.　b: 1, 27.　c: Mt 8, 28-34; Lk 8, 26-39.

out of the man!") ⁹ᵈ*He asked him, "What is your name?" He replied, "Legion is my name. There are many of us." ¹⁰And he pleaded earnestly with him not to drive them away from that territory.

¹¹*Now a large herd of swine was feeding there on the hillside. ¹²And they pleaded with him, "Send us into the swine. Let us enter them." ¹³And he let them, and the unclean spirits came out and entered the swine. The herd of about two thousand rushed down a steep bank into the sea, where they were drowned. ¹⁴The swineherds ran away and reported the incident in the town and throughout the countryside. And people came out to see what had happened. ¹⁵As they approached Jesus, they caught sight of the man who had been possessed by Legion, sitting there clothed and in his right mind. And they were seized with fear. ¹⁶Those who witnessed the incident explained to them what had happened to the possessed man and to the swine. ¹⁷Then they began to beg him to leave their district. ¹⁸As he was getting into the boat, the man who had been possessed pleaded to remain with him. ¹⁹*But he would not permit him but told him instead, "Go home to your family and announce to them all that the Lord in his pity has done for you." ²⁰Then the man went off and began to proclaim in the Decapolis what Jesus had done for him; and all were amazed.

Jairus's Daughter and the Woman with a Hemorrhage. ²¹ᵉ*When Jesus had crossed again [in the boat] to the other side, a large crowd gathered around him, and he stayed close to the sea. ²²ᶠOne of the synagogue officials, named Jairus, came forward. Seeing him he fell at his feet ²³*and pleaded earnestly with him, saying, "My daughter is at the point of death. Please, come lay your hands on her that she may get well and live." ²⁴He went off with him, and a large crowd followed him and pressed upon him.

²⁵There was a woman afflicted with hemorrhages for twelve years. ²⁶She had suffered greatly at the hands of many doctors and had spent all that she had. Yet she was not helped but only grew worse. ²⁷She had heard about Jesus and came up behind him in the crowd and touched his cloak. ²⁸*She said, "If I but touch his clothes, I shall be cured." ²⁹Immediately her flow of blood dried up. She felt in her body that she was healed of her affliction. ³⁰Jesus, aware at once that power had gone out from him, turned around in the crowd and asked, "Who has touched my clothes?" ³¹But his disciples said to him, "You see how the crowd is pressing upon you, and yet you ask, 'Who touched me?'" ³²And he looked around to see who had done it. ³³The woman, realizing what had happened to her, approached in fear and trembling. She fell down before Jesus and told him the whole truth. ³⁴ᵍHe said to her, "Daughter, your faith has saved you. Go in peace and be cured of your affliction."

³⁵*While he was still speaking, people from the synagogue official's house arrived and said, "Your daughter has died; why trouble the teacher any longer?" ³⁶Disregarding the message that was reported, Jesus said to the synagogue official, "Do not be afraid; just have faith." ³⁷He did not allow anyone to accompany him inside except Peter, James, and John, the brother of James.

5, 9: Legion is my name: the demons were numerous and the condition of the possessed man was extremely serious; cf Mt 12, 45.

5, 11: Herd of swine: see the note on Mt 8, 30.

5, 19: Go home: Jesus did not accept the man's request **to remain with him** as a disciple (18), yet invited him to announce to his own people what the Lord had done for him, i.e., proclaim the gospel message to his pagan family; cf 1, 14.39; 3, 14; 13, 10.

5, 21–43: The story of the raising to life of Jairus's daughter is divided into two parts: vv 21–24 and 35–43. Between these two separated parts the account of the cure of the hemorrhage victim (25–34) is interposed. This technique of intercalating or sandwiching one story within another occurs several times in Mk: 3, 19b-21 (22–30) 31–35; 6, 6b-13 (14–29)

30; 11, 12–14 (15–19) 20–25; 14, 53 (54) 55–65 (66–73).

5, 23: Lay your hands on her: this act for the purpose of healing is frequent in Mk (6, 5; 7, 32–35; 8, 23–25; 16, 18) and is also found in Mt 9, 18; Lk 4, 40; 13, 13; Acts 9, 17; 28, 8.

5, 28: Both in the case of Jairus and his daughter (23) and in the case of the hemorrhage victim, the inner conviction that physical contact (30) accompanied by faith in Jesus' saving power could effect a cure was rewarded.

5, 35: The faith of Jairus was put to a twofold test: (1) that his daughter might be cured and, now that she had died, (2) that she might be restored to life. His faith contrasts with the lack of faith of the crowd.

d: Mt 12, 45; Lk 8, 2; 11, 26. *e:* 2, 13. *f:* Mt 9, 18-26; Lk 8, 41-56. *g:* Lk 7, 30.

*38*When they arrived at the house of the synagogue official, he caught sight of a commotion, people weeping and wailing loudly. *39h**So he went in and said to them, "Why this commotion and weeping? The child is not dead but asleep." *40*And they ridiculed him. Then he put them all out. He took along the child's father and mother and those who were with him and entered the room where the child was. *41**He took the child by the hand and said to her, "*Talitha koum*," which means, "Little girl, I say to you, arise!" *42*The girl, a child of twelve, arose immediately and walked around. [At that] they were utterly astounded. *43*He gave strict orders that no one should know this and said that she should be given something to eat.

See RG
392-93

CHAPTER 6

The Rejection at Nazareth. *1i**He departed from there and came to his native place, accompanied by his disciples. *2**When the sabbath came he began to teach in the synagogue, and many who heard him were astonished. They said, "Where did this man get all this? What kind of wisdom has been given him? What mighty deeds are wrought by his hands! *3j**Is he not the carpenter, the son of Mary, and the brother of James and Joses and Judas and Simon? And are not his sisters here with us?" And they took offense at him. *4k**Jesus said to them, "A prophet is not without honor except in his native place and among his own kin and in his own house." *5**So he was not able to perform any mighty deed there, apart from curing a few sick people by laying his hands on them. *6*He was amazed at their lack of faith.

The Mission of the Twelve. He went around to the villages in the vicinity teaching. *7l**He summoned the Twelve and began to send them out two by two and gave them authority over unclean spirits. *8**He instructed them to take nothing for the journey but a walking stick—no food, no sack, no money in their belts. *9*They were, however, to wear sandals but not a second tunic. *10**He said to them, "Wherever you enter a house,

5, 39: Not dead but asleep: the New Testament often refers to death as sleep (Mt 27, 52; Jn 11, 11; 1 Cor 15, 6; 1 Thes 4, 13–15); see the note on Mt 9, 24.

5, 41: Arise: the Greek verb **egeirein** is the verb generally used to express resurrection from death (6, 14.16; Mt 11, 5; Lk 7, 14) and Jesus' own resurrection (16, 6; Mt 28, 6; Lk 24, 6).

6, 1: His native place: the Greek word **patris** here refers to Nazareth (cf 1, 9; Lk 4, 16.23–24), though it can also mean native land.

6, 2–6: See the note on Mt 13, 54–58.

6, 3: Is he not the carpenter?: no other gospel calls Jesus a carpenter. Some witnesses have "the carpenter's son," as in Mt 13, 55. **Son of Mary:** contrary to Jewish custom, which calls a man the son of his father, this expression may reflect Mark's own faith that God is the Father of Jesus (1, 1.11; 8, 38; 13, 32; 14, 36). **The brother of James . . . Simon:** in Semitic usage, the terms 'brother,' 'sister' are applied not only to children of the same parents, but to nephews, nieces, cousins, half-brothers, and half-sisters; cf Gn 14, 16; 29, 15; Lv 10, 4. While one cannot suppose that the meaning of a Greek word should be sought in the first place from Semitic usage, the Septuagint often translates the Hebrew '**āh** by the Greek word **adelphos,** "brother," as in the cited passages, a fact that may argue for a similar breadth of meaning in some New Testament passages. For instance, there is no doubt that in v 17, "brother" is used of Philip, who was actually the half-brother of Herod Antipas. On the other hand, Mark may have understood the terms literally; see also Mt 3, 31–32; 12, 46; 13, 55–56; Lk 8, 19; Jn 7, 3.5. The question of meaning here would not have arisen but for the faith of the church in Mary's perpetual virginity.

6, 4: A prophet is not without honor except . . . in his own house: a saying that finds parallels in other literatures, espe-cially Jewish and Greek, but without reference to a prophet. Comparing himself to previous Hebrew prophets whom the people rejected, Jesus intimates his own eventual rejection by the nation especially in view of the dishonor his own relatives had shown him (3, 21) and now his townspeople as well.

6, 5: He was not able to perform any mighty deed there: according to Mark, Jesus' power could not take effect because of a person's lack of faith.

6, 7–13: The preparation for the mission of the Twelve is seen in the call (1) of the first disciples to be fishers of men (1, 16–20), (2) then of the Twelve set apart to be with Jesus and to receive authority to preach and expel demons (3, 13–19). Now they are given the specific mission to exercise that authority in word and power as representatives of Jesus during the time of their formation.

6, 8–9: In Mk the use of a **walking stick** (8) and **sandals** (9) is permitted, but not in Mt 10, 10 nor in Lk 10, 4. Mark does not mention any prohibition to visit pagan territory and to enter Samaritan towns. These differences indicate a certain adaptation to conditions in and outside of Palestine and sug-gest in Mark's account a later activity in the church. For the rest, Jesus required of his apostles a total dependence on God for food and shelter; cf vv 35–44; 8, 1–9.

6, 10–11: Remaining in the same house as a guest (10) rather than moving to another offering greater comfort avoided any impression of seeking advantage for oneself and prevented dishonor to one's host. Shaking the dust off one's feet served as testimony against those who rejected the call to repentance.

h: Acts 9, 40. *i:* Mt 13, 54-58; Lk 4, 16-30. *j:* 15, 40; Mt 12, 46; Jn 6, 42. *k:* Jn 4, 44. *l:* Mt 10, 1.9-14; Lk 9, 15; 10, 4-11.

Rulers during New Testament Times

Roman Emperors

27 B.C.–A.D. 14	Augustus
A.D. 14–37	Tiberius
A.D. 37–41	Caligula
A.D. 41–54	Claudius
A.D. 54–68	Nero
A.D. 68–69	Galba; Otho; Vitellius
A.D. 69–79	Vespasian
A.D. 79–81	Titus
A.D. 81–96	Domitian

Herodian Rulers

37–4 B.C.	Herod the Great, king of the Jews
4 B.C.–A.D. 6	Archelaus, ethnarch of Judea
4 B.C.–A.D. 39	Herod Antipas, tetrarch of Galilee and Perea
4 B.C.–A.D. 34	Philip, tetrarch of Iturea, Trachonitis, etc.
A.D. 37–44	Herod Agrippa I, from 37 to 44 king over the former tetrarchy of Philip, and from 41 to 44 over Judea, Galilee, and Perea
A.D. 53–about 100	Herod Agrippa II, king over the former tetrarchy of Philip and Lysanias, and from 56 (or 61) over parts of Galilee and Perea

Procurators of Judea after the Reign of Archelaus to the Reign of Herod Agrippa I

A.D. 6–8	Coponius
A.D. 9–12	M. Ambivius
A.D. 12–15	Annius Rufus
A.D. 15–26	Valerius Gratus
A.D. 26–36	Pontius Pilate
A.D. 37	Marullus
A.D. 37–41	Herennius Capito

Procurators of Palestine from the Reign of Herod Agrippa I to the Jewish Revolt

A.D. 44–about 46	Cuspius Fadus
A.D. about 46–48	Tiberius Alexander
A.D. 48–52	Ventidius Cumanus
A.D. 52–60	M. Antonius Felix
A.D. 60–62	Porcius Festus
A.D. 62–64	Clodius Albinus
A.D. 64–66	Gessius Florus

stay there until you leave from there. *11*Whatever place does not welcome you or listen to you, leave there and shake the dust off your feet in testimony against them." *12*So they went off and preached repentance. *13m**They drove out many demons, and they anointed with oil many who were sick and cured them.

Herod's Opinion of Jesus. *14no**King Herod heard about it, for his fame had become widespread, and people were saying, "John the Baptist has been raised from the dead; that is why mighty powers are at work in him." *15p*Others were saying, "He is Elijah"; still others, "He is a prophet like any of the prophets." *16*But when Herod learned of it, he said, "It is John whom I beheaded. He has been raised up."

The Death of John the Baptist. *17q**Herod was the one who had John arrested and bound in prison on account of Herodias, the wife of his brother Philip, whom he had married. *18r*John had said to Herod, "It is not lawful for you to have your brother's wife." *19**Herodias harbored a grudge against him and wanted to kill him but was unable to do so. *20*Herod feared John, knowing him to be a righteous and holy man, and kept him in custody. When he heard him speak he was very much perplexed, yet he liked to listen to him. *21*She had an opportunity one day when Herod, on his birthday, gave a banquet for his courtiers, his military officers, and the leading men of Galilee. *22*Herodias's own daughter came in and performed a dance that delighted Herod and his guests. The king said to the girl, "Ask of me whatever you wish and I will grant it to you." *23s*He even swore [many things] to her, "I will grant you whatever you ask of me, even to half of my kingdom." *24*She went out and said to her mother, "What shall I ask for?" She replied, "The head of John the Baptist." *25*The girl hurried back to the king's presence and made her request, "I want you to give me at once on a platter the head of John the Baptist." *26*The king was deeply distressed, but because of his oaths and the guests he did not wish to break his word to her. *27t*So he promptly dispatched an executioner with orders to bring back his head. He went off and beheaded him in the prison. *28*He brought in the head on a platter and gave it to the girl. The girl in turn gave it to her mother. *29*When his disciples heard about it, they came and took his body and laid it in a tomb.

The Return of the Twelve. *30u**The apostles gathered together with Jesus and reported all they had done and taught. *31v**He said to them, "Come away by yourselves to a deserted place and rest a while." People were coming and going in great numbers, and they had no opportunity even to eat. *32w*So they went off in the boat by themselves to a deserted place. *33*People saw them leaving and many came to know about it. They hastened there on foot from all the towns and arrived at the place before them.

6, 13: Anointed with oil . . . cured them: a common medicinal remedy, but seen here as a vehicle of divine power for healing.

6, 14–16: The various opinions about Jesus anticipate the theme of his identity that reaches its climax in 8, 27–30.

6, 14: King Herod: see the note on Mt 14, 1.

6, 17–29: Similarities are to be noted between Mark's account of the imprisonment and death of John the Baptist in this pericope, and that of the passion of Jesus (15, 1–47). Herod and Pilate, each in turn, acknowledges the holiness of life of one over whom he unjustly exercises the power of condemnation and death (26–27; 15, 9–10.14–15). The hatred of Herodias toward John parallels that of the Jewish leaders toward Jesus. After the deaths of John and of Jesus, well-disposed persons request the bodies of the victims of Herod and of Pilate in turn to give them respectful burial (29; 15, 45–46).

6, 19: Herodias: see the note on Mt 14, 3.

6, 30: Apostles: here, and in some manuscripts at 3, 14, Mark calls apostles (i.e., those sent forth) the Twelve whom Jesus sends as his emissaries, empowering them to preach, to expel demons, and to cure the sick (13). Only after Pentecost is the title used in the technical sense.

6, 31–34: The withdrawal of Jesus with his disciples to a desert place to rest attracts a great number of people to follow them. Toward this people of the new exodus Jesus is moved with pity; he satisfies their spiritual hunger by teaching them many things, thus gradually showing himself the faithful shepherd of a new Israel; cf Nm 27, 17; Ez 34, 15.

6, 35–44: See the note on Mt 14, 13–21. Compare this section with 8, 1–9. The various accounts of the multiplication of loaves and fishes, two each in Mark and in Matthew and one each in Luke and in John, indicate the wide interest of the early church in their eucharistic gatherings; see, e.g., v 41; 8, 6; 14, 22; and recall also the sign of bread in Ex 16; Dt 8, 3–16; Pss 78, 24–25; 105, 40; Wis 16, 20–21.

m: Jas 5, 14. *n:* Lk 9, 7-8. *o:* Mt 14, 1-12. *p:* Mt 16, 14. *q:* Lk 3, 19-20. *r:* Lv 18, 16. *s:* Est 5, 3. *t:* Lk 9, 9. *u:* Lk 9, 10. *v:* 3, 20; Mt 14, 13; Lk 9, 10. *w:* Mt 14, 13-21; Lk 9, 10-17; Jn 6, 1-13.

The Feeding of the Five Thousand. [34]When he disembarked and saw the vast crowd, his heart was moved with pity for them, for they were like sheep without a shepherd; and he began to teach them many things. [35]*By now it was already late and his disciples approached him and said, "This is a deserted place and it is already very late. [36]Dismiss them so that they can go to the surrounding farms and villages and buy themselves something to eat." [37]He said to them in reply, "Give them some food yourselves." But they said to him, "Are we to buy two hundred days' wages worth of food and give it to them to eat?" [38]He asked them, "How many loaves do you have? Go and see." And when they had found out they said, "Five loaves and two fish." [39]So he gave orders to have them sit down in groups on the green grass. [40]*The people took their places in rows by hundreds and by fifties. [41]*Then, taking the five loaves and the two fish and looking up to heaven, he said the blessing, broke the loaves, and gave them to [his] disciples to set before the people; he also divided the two fish among them all. [42]They all ate and were satisfied. [43]And they picked up twelve wicker baskets full of fragments and what was left of the fish. [44]Those who ate [of the loaves] were five thousand men.

The Walking on the Water. [45]x*Then he made his disciples get into the boat and precede him to the other side toward Bethsaida, while he dismissed the crowd. [46]*And when he had taken leave of them, he went off to the mountain to pray. [47]When it was evening, the boat was far out on the sea and he was alone on shore. [48]*Then he saw that they were tossed about while rowing, for the wind was against them. About the fourth watch of the night, he came towards them walking on the sea. He meant to pass by them. [49]But when they saw him walking on the sea, they thought it was a ghost and cried out. [50]*They had all seen him and were terrified. But at once he spoke with them, "Take courage, it is I, do not be afraid!" [51]He got into the boat with them and the wind died down. They were [completely] astounded. [52]y*They had not understood the incident of the loaves. On the contrary, their hearts were hardened.

The Healings at Gennesaret. [53]z After making the crossing, they came to land at Gennesaret and tied up there. [54]As they were leaving the boat, people immediately recognized him. [55]They scurried about the surrounding country and began to bring in the sick on mats to wherever they heard he was. [56a]Whatever villages or towns or countryside he entered, they laid the sick in the marketplaces and begged him that they might touch only the tassel on his cloak; and as many as touched it were healed.

CHAPTER 7

The Tradition of the Elders. [1b]*Now when the Pharisees with some scribes who

See RG 392–93

6, 40: The people . . . in rows by hundreds and by fifties: reminiscent of the groupings of Israelites encamped in the desert (Ex 18, 21–25) and of the wilderness tradition of prophets depicting the transformation of the wasteland into pastures where the true shepherd feeds his flock (Ez 34, 25–26) and makes his people beneficiaries of messianic grace.

6, 41: On the language of this verse as eucharistic (cf 14, 22), see the notes on Mt 14, 19.20. Jesus observed the Jewish table ritual of blessing God before partaking of food.

6, 45–52: See the note on Mt 14, 22–33.

6, 45: To the other side toward Bethsaida: a village at the northeastern shore of the Sea of Galilee.

6, 46: He went off to the mountain to pray: see 1, 35–38. In Jn 6, 15 Jesus withdrew to evade any involvement in the false messianic hopes of the multitude.

6, 48: Walking on the sea: see the notes on Mt 14, 22–33 and on Jn 6, 19.

6, 50: It is I, do not be afraid!: literally, "I am." This may reflect the divine revelatory formula of Ex 3, 14; Is 41, 4.10.14; 43, 1–3.10.13. Mark implies the hidden identity of Jesus as Son of God.

6, 52: They had not understood . . . the loaves: the revelatory character of this sign and that of the walking on the sea completely escaped the disciples. **Their hearts were hardened:** in 3, 5–6 hardness of heart was attributed to those who did not accept Jesus and plotted his death. Here the same disposition prevents the disciples from comprehending Jesus' self-revelation through signs; cf 8, 17.

7, 1–23: See the note on Mt 15, 1–20. Against the Pharisees' narrow, legalistic, and external practices of piety in matters of purification (2–5), external worship (6–7), and observance of commandments, Jesus sets in opposition the true moral intent of the divine law (8–13). But he goes beyond contrasting the law and Pharisaic interpretation of it. The parable of vv 14–15 in effect sets aside the law itself in respect to clean and unclean food. He thereby opens the way for unity between Jew and Gentile in the kingdom of God, intimated by Jesus' departure for pagan territory beyond Galilee. For similar contrast see 2, 1—3, 6; 3, 20–35; 6, 1–6.

x: Mt 14, 22-32; Jn 6, 15-21. y: 4, 13. z: Mt 14, 34-36. a: 5, 27-28; Acts 5, 15. b: Mt 15, 1-20.

had come from Jerusalem gathered around him, [2]they observed that some of his disciples ate their meals with unclean, that is, unwashed, hands. [3]*(For the Pharisees and, in fact, all Jews, do not eat without carefully washing their hands, keeping the tradition of the elders. [4]And on coming from the marketplace they do not eat without purifying themselves. And there are many other things that they have traditionally observed, the purification of cups and jugs and kettles [and beds].) [5]*So the Pharisees and scribes questioned him, "Why do your disciples not follow the tradition of the elders but instead eat a meal with unclean hands?" [6c]He responded, "Well did Isaiah prophesy about you hypocrites, as it is written:

'This people honors me with their lips,
    but their hearts are far from me;
[7] In vain do they worship me,
    teaching as doctrines human precepts.'

[8]You disregard God's commandment but cling to human tradition." [9]He went on to say, "How well you have set aside the commandment of God in order to uphold your tradition! [10d]For Moses said, 'Honor your father and your mother,' and 'Whoever curses father or mother shall die.' [11]*Yet you say, 'If a person says to father or mother, "Any support you might have had from me is qorban"' (meaning, dedicated to God), [12]you allow him to do nothing more for his father or mother. [13]You nullify the word of God in favor of your tradition that you have handed on. And you do many such things." [14e]He summoned the crowd again and said to them, "Hear me, all of you, and understand. [15]Nothing that enters one from outside can defile that person; but the things that come out from within are what defile." [[16]]*

[17f]*When he got home away from the crowd his disciples questioned him about the parable. [18]He said to them, "Are even you likewise without understanding? Do you not realize that everything that goes into a person from outside cannot defile, [19g]*since it enters not the heart but the stomach and passes out into the latrine?" (Thus he declared all foods clean.) [20]"But what comes out of a person, that is what defiles. [21h]From within people, from their hearts, come evil thoughts, unchastity, theft, murder, [22]adultery, greed, malice, deceit, licentiousness, envy, blasphemy, arrogance, folly. [23]All these evils come from within and they defile."

The Syrophoenician Woman's Faith. [24i]*From that place he went off to the district of Tyre. He entered a house and wanted no one to know about it, but he could not escape notice. [25]Soon a woman whose daughter had an unclean spirit heard about him. She came and fell at his feet. [26j]The woman was a Greek, a Syrophoenician by birth, and she begged him to drive the demon out of her daughter. [27]*He said to her, "Let the children be fed first. For it is not right to take the food of the children and throw it to the dogs."

7, 3: **Carefully washing their hands:** refers to ritual purification.

7, 5: **Tradition of the elders:** the body of detailed, unwritten, human laws regarded by the scribes and Pharisees to have the same binding force as that of the Mosaic law; cf Gal 1, 14.

7, 11: **Qorban:** a formula for a gift to God, dedicating the offering to the temple, so that the giver might continue to use it for himself but not give it to others, even needy parents.

7, 16: Verse 16, "Anyone who has ears to hear ought to hear," is omitted because it is lacking in some of the best Greek manuscripts and was probably transferred here by scribes from 4, (9),23.

7, 17: **Away from the crowd . . . the parable:** in this context of privacy the term **parable** refers to something hidden, about to be revealed to the disciples; cf 4, 10–11.34. Jesus sets the Mosaic food laws in the context of the kingdom of God where they are abrogated, and he declares moral defilement the only cause of uncleanness.

7, 19: **(Thus he declared all foods clean):** if this bold

declaration goes back to Jesus, its force was not realized among Jewish Christians in the early church; cf Acts 10, 1—11, 18.

7, 24–37: The withdrawal of Jesus to the district of Tyre may have been for a respite (24), but he soon moved onward to Sidon and, by way of the Sea of Galilee, to the Decapolis. These districts provided a Gentile setting for the extension of his ministry of healing because the people there acknowledged his power (29.37). The actions attributed to Jesus (33–35) were also used by healers of the time.

7, 27–28: The figure of a household in which children at table are fed first and then their leftover food is given to the dogs under the table is used effectively to acknowledge the prior claim of the Jews to the ministry of Jesus; however, Jesus accedes to the Gentile woman's plea for the cure of her afflicted daughter because of her faith.

c: Is 29, 13. d: Ex 21, 17; Lv 20, 9; Dt 5, 16; Eph 6, 2. e: Mt 15, 10-20. f: 4, 10.13. g: Acts 10, 15. h: Jer 17, 9. i: Mt 15, 21-28. j: Mt 8, 29.

28She replied and said to him, "Lord, even the dogs under the table eat the children's scraps." 29Then he said to her, "For saying this, you may go. The demon has gone out of your daughter." 30When the woman went home, she found the child lying in bed and the demon gone.

The Healing of a Deaf Man. 31kAgain he left the district of Tyre and went by way of Sidon to the Sea of Galilee, into the district of the Decapolis. 32And people brought to him a deaf man who had a speech impediment and begged him to lay his hand on him. 33He took him off by himself away from the crowd. He put his finger into the man's ears and, spitting, touched his tongue; 34then he looked up to heaven and groaned, and said to him, "*Ephphatha*!" (that is, "Be opened!") 35And [immediately] the man's ears were opened, his speech impediment was removed, and he spoke plainly. 36*He ordered them not to tell anyone. But the more he ordered them not to, the more they proclaimed it. 37lThey were exceedingly astonished and they said, "He has done all things well. He makes the deaf hear and [the] mute speak."

CHAPTER 8

See RG
392-94

The Feeding of the Four Thousand. 1m*In those days when there again was a great crowd without anything to eat, he summoned the disciples and said, 2"My heart is moved with pity for the crowd, because they have been with me now for three days and have nothing to eat. 3If I send them away hungry to their homes, they will collapse on the way, and some of them have come a great dis-

tance." 4His disciples answered him, "Where can anyone get enough bread to satisfy them here in this deserted place?" 5Still he asked them, "How many loaves do you have?" "Seven," they replied. 6*He ordered the crowd to sit down on the ground. Then, taking the seven loaves he gave thanks, broke them, and gave them to his disciples to distribute, and they distributed them to the crowd. 7They also had a few fish. He said the blessing over them and ordered them distributed also. 8They ate and were satisfied. They picked up the fragments left over—seven baskets. 9There were about four thousand people.

He dismissed them 10and got into the boat with his disciples and came to the region of Dalmanutha.

The Demand for a Sign. 11no*The Pharisees came forward and began to argue with him, seeking from him a sign from heaven to test him. 12He sighed from the depth of his spirit and said, "Why does this generation seek a sign? Amen, I say to you, no sign will be given to this generation." 13Then he left them, got into the boat again, and went off to the other shore.

The Leaven of the Pharisees. 14pThey had forgotten to bring bread, and they had only one loaf with them in the boat. 15*He enjoined them, "Watch out, guard against the leaven of the Pharisees and the leaven of Herod." 16They concluded among themselves that it was because they had no bread. 17qWhen he became aware of this he said to them, "Why do you conclude that it is because you have no bread? Do you not yet understand or comprehend? Are your hearts

---

7, 36: The more they proclaimed it: the same verb **proclaim** attributed here to the crowd in relation to the miracles of Jesus is elsewhere used in Mark for the preaching of the gospel on the part of Jesus, of his disciples, and of the Christian community (1, 14; 13, 10; 14, 9). Implied in the action of the crowd is a recognition of the salvific mission of Jesus; see the note on Mt 11, 5–6.

8, 1–10: The two accounts of the multiplication of loaves and fishes (8, 1–10 and 6, 31–44) have eucharistic significance. Their similarity of structure and themes but dissimilarity of detail are considered by many to refer to a single event that, however, developed in two distinct traditions, one Jewish Christian and the other Gentile Christian, since Jesus in Mark's presentation (7, 24–37) has extended his saving mission to the Gentiles.

8, 6: See the note on 6, 41.

8, 11–12: The objection of the Pharisees that Jesus' miracles are unsatisfactory for proving the arrival of God's kingdom is comparable to the request of the crowd for a sign in Jn 6, 30–31. Jesus' response shows that a sign originating in human demand will not be provided; cf Nm 14, 11.22.

8, 15: The leaven of the Pharisees . . . of Herod: the corruptive action of leaven (1 Cor 5, 6–8; Gal 5, 9) was an apt symbol of the evil dispositions both of the Pharisees (11–13; 7, 5–13) and of Herod (6, 14–29) toward Jesus. The disciples of Jesus are warned against sharing such rebellious attitudes toward Jesus; cf vv 17, 21.

---

k: Mt 15, 29-31. *l:* Mt 15, 31. *m:* 6, 34-44; Mt 15, 32-39. *n:* Mt 12, 38-39; 16, 1-4. *o:* Lk 11, 16. *p:* Mt 16, 5-12; Lk 12, 1. *q:* 4, 13.

Sites of Jesus' Travels in Galilee and Vicinity

1332

hardened? *18r* Do you have eyes and not see, ears and not hear? And do you not remember, *19* when I broke the five loaves for the five thousand, how many wicker baskets full of fragments you picked up?" They answered him, "Twelve." *20* "When I broke the seven loaves for the four thousand, how many full baskets of fragments did you pick up?" They answered [him], "Seven." *21* He said to them, "Do you still not understand?"

The Blind Man of Bethsaida. *22** When they arrived at Bethsaida, they brought to him a blind man and begged him to touch him. *23s* He took the blind man by the hand and led him outside the village. Putting spittle on his eyes he laid his hands on him and asked, "Do you see anything?" *24* Looking up he replied, "I see people looking like trees and walking." *25* Then he laid hands on his eyes a second time and he saw clearly; his sight was restored and he could see everything distinctly. *26* Then he sent him home and said, "Do not even go into the village."

III: The Mystery Begins to Be Revealed

Peter's Confession about Jesus. *27t** Now Jesus and his disciples set out for the villages of Caesarea Philippi. Along the way he asked his disciples, "Who do people say that I am?" *28* They said in reply, "John the Baptist, others Elijah, still others one of the prophets." *29* And he asked them, "But who do you say that I am?" Peter said to him in reply, "You are the Messiah." *30* Then he warned them not to tell anyone about him.

The First Prediction of the Passion. *31u** He began to teach them that the Son of Man must suffer greatly and be rejected by the elders, the chief priests, and the scribes, and be killed, and rise after three days. *32* He spoke this openly. Then Peter took him aside and began to rebuke him. *33* At this he turned around and, looking at his disciples, rebuked Peter and said, "Get behind me, Satan. You are thinking not as God does, but as human beings do."

The Conditions of Discipleship. *34v** He summoned the crowd with his disciples and said to them, "Whoever wishes to come after me must deny himself, take up his cross, and follow me. *35w** For whoever wishes to save his life will lose it, but whoever loses his life for my sake and that of the gospel will save it. *36* What profit is there for one to gain the whole world and forfeit his life? *37* What could one give in exchange for his

8, 22–26: Jesus' actions and the gradual cure of the blind man probably have the same purpose as in the case of the deaf man (7, 31–37). Some commentators regard the cure as an intended symbol of the gradual enlightenment of the disciples concerning Jesus' messiahship.

8, 27–30: This episode is the turning point in Mark's account of Jesus in his public ministry. Popular opinions concur in regarding him as a prophet. The disciples by contrast believe him to be the Messiah. Jesus acknowledges this identification but prohibits them from making his messianic office known to avoid confusing it with ambiguous contemporary ideas on the nature of that office. See further the notes on Mt 16, 13–20.

8, 31: Son of Man: an enigmatic title. It is used in Dn 7, 13–14 as a symbol of "the saints of the Most High," the faithful Israelites who receive the everlasting kingdom from the Ancient One (God). They are represented by a human figure that contrasts with the various beasts who represent the previous kingdoms of the earth. In the Jewish apocryphal books of 1 Enoch and 4 Ezra the "Son of Man" is not, as in Dn, a group, but a unique figure of extraordinary spiritual endowments, who will be revealed as the one through whom the everlasting kingdom decreed by God will be established. It is possible though doubtful that this individualization of the Son of Man figure had been made in Jesus' time, and therefore his use of the title in that sense is questionable. Of itself, this expression means simply a human being, or, indefinitely, someone, and there are evidences of this use in pre-Christian times. Its use in the New Testament is probably due to Jesus' speaking of himself in that way, "a human being," and the later church's taking this in the sense of the Jewish apocrypha and applying it to him with that meaning. **Rejected by the elders, the chief priests, and the scribes:** the supreme council called the Sanhedrin was made up of seventy-one members of these three groups and presided over by the high priest. It exercised authority over the Jews in religious matters. See the note on Mt 8, 20.

8, 34–35: This utterance of Jesus challenges all believers to authentic discipleship and total commitment to himself through self-renunciation and acceptance of the cross of suffering, even to the sacrifice of life itself. **Whoever wishes to save his life will lose it . . . will save it:** an expression of the ambivalence of life and its contrasting destiny. Life seen as mere self-centered earthly existence and lived in denial of Christ ends in destruction, but when lived in loyalty to Christ, despite earthly death, it arrives at fullness of life.

8, 35: For my sake and that of the gospel: Mark here, as at 10, 29, equates Jesus with the gospel.

r: Jer 5, 21; Ez 12, 2. s: 7, 33; Jn 9, 6. t: Mt 16, 13-20; Lk 9, 18-21. u: Mt 16, 21-27; Lk 9, 22-26. v: Mt 10, 38-39; 16, 24-27; Lk 14, 26-27. w: Jn 12, 25.

life? [38]xWhoever is ashamed of me and of my words in this faithless and sinful generation, the Son of Man will be ashamed of when he comes in his Father's glory with the holy angels."

See RG
393

CHAPTER 9

[1]y*He also said to them, "Amen, I say to you, there are some standing here who will not taste death until they see that the kingdom of God has come in power."

The Transfiguration of Jesus. [2]z*After six days Jesus took Peter, James, and John and led them up a high mountain apart by themselves. And he was transfigured before them, [3]and his clothes became dazzling white, such as no fuller on earth could bleach them. [4]Then Elijah appeared to them along with Moses, and they were conversing with Jesus. [5]*Then Peter said to Jesus in reply, "Rabbi, it is good that we are here! Let us make three tents: one for you, one for Moses, and one for Elijah." [6]He hardly knew what to say, they were so terrified. [7]*Then a cloud came, casting a shadow over them; then from the cloud came a voice, "This is my beloved Son. Listen to him." [8]Suddenly, looking around, they no longer saw anyone but Jesus alone with them.

The Coming of Elijah. [9a]*As they were coming down from the mountain, he charged them not to relate what they had seen to anyone, except when the Son of Man had risen from the dead. [10]So they kept the matter to themselves, questioning what rising from the dead meant. [11b]Then they asked him, "Why do the scribes say that Elijah must come first?" [12]He told them, "Elijah will indeed come first and restore all things, yet how is it written regarding the Son of Man that he must suffer greatly and be treated with contempt? [13c]But I tell you that Elijah has come and they did to him whatever they pleased, as it is written of him."

The Healing of a Boy with a Demon. [14d]*When they came to the disciples, they saw a large crowd around them and scribes arguing with them. [15]Immediately on seeing him, the whole crowd was utterly amazed. They ran up to him and greeted him. [16]He asked them, "What are you arguing about with them?" [17]Someone from the crowd answered him, "Teacher, I have brought to you my son possessed by a mute spirit. [18]Wherever it seizes him, it throws him down; he foams at the mouth, grinds his teeth, and becomes rigid. I asked your disciples to drive it out, but they were unable to do so." [19]He said to them in reply, "O faithless generation, how long will I be with you? How long will I endure you? Bring him to me." [20]They brought the boy to him. And when he saw him, the spirit immediately threw the boy into convulsions. As he fell to the ground, he began to roll

9, 1: There are some standing . . . come in power: understood by some to refer to the establishment by God's power of his kingdom on earth in and through the church; more likely, as understood by others, a reference to the imminent parousia.

9, 2–8: Mk and Mt 17, 1 place the transfiguration of Jesus six days after the first prediction of his passion and death and his instruction to the disciples on the doctrine of the cross; Lk 9, 28 has "about eight days." Thus the transfiguration counterbalances the prediction of the passion by affording certain of the disciples insight into the divine glory that Jesus possessed. His glory will overcome his death and that of his disciples; cf 2 Cor 3, 18; 2 Pt 1, 16–19. The heavenly voice (7) prepares the disciples to understand that in the divine plan Jesus must die ignominiously before his messianic glory is made manifest; cf Lk 24, 25–27. See further the note on Mt 17, 1–8.

9, 5: Moses and Elijah represent respectively law and prophecy in the Old Testament and are linked to Mt. Sinai; cf Ex 19, 16—20, 17; 1 Kgs 19, 2.8–14. They now appear with Jesus as witnesses to the fulfillment of the law and the prophets taking place in the person of Jesus as he appears in glory.

9, 7: **A cloud came, casting a shadow over them:** even

the disciples enter into the mystery of his glorification. In the Old Testament the cloud covered the meeting tent, indicating the Lord's presence in the midst of his people (Ex 40, 34–35) and came to rest upon the temple in Jerusalem at the time of its dedication (1 Kgs 8, 10).

9, 9–13: At the transfiguration of Jesus his disciples had seen Elijah. They were perplexed because, according to the rabbinical interpretation of Mal 3, 23–24, Elijah was to come first. Jesus' response shows that Elijah has come, in the person of John the Baptist, to prepare for the day of the Lord. Jesus **must suffer greatly and be treated with contempt** (12) like the Baptist (13); cf 6, 17–29.

9, 14–29: The disciples' failure to effect a cure seems to reflect unfavorably on Jesus (14–18.22). In response Jesus exposes their lack of trust in God (19) and scores their lack of prayer (29), i.e., of conscious reliance on God's power when acting in Jesus' name. For Mt, see the note on 17, 14–20. Luke 9, 37–43 centers attention on Jesus' sovereign power.

x: Mt 10, 33; Lk 12, 8.   y: Mt 16, 28; Lk 9, 27.   z: Mt 17, 1-13; Lk 9, 28-36.   a: 8, 31.   b: Is 53, 3; Mal 3, 23.   c: 1 Kgs 19, 2-10.   d: Mt 17, 14-21; Lk 9, 37-43.

around and foam at the mouth. ²¹Then he questioned his father, "How long has this been happening to him?" He replied, "Since childhood. ²²It has often thrown him into fire and into water to kill him. But if you can do anything, have compassion on us and help us." ²³Jesus said to him, " 'If you can!' Everything is possible to one who has faith." ²⁴Then the boy's father cried out, "I do believe, help my unbelief!" ²⁵Jesus, on seeing a crowd rapidly gathering, rebuked the unclean spirit and said to it, "Mute and deaf spirit, I command you: come out of him and never enter him again!" ²⁶Shouting and throwing the boy into convulsions, it came out. He became like a corpse, which caused many to say, "He is dead!" ²⁷But Jesus took him by the hand, raised him, and he stood up. ²⁸When he entered the house, his disciples asked him in private, "Why could we not drive it out?" ²⁹*He said to them, "This kind can only come out through prayer."

The Second Prediction of the Passion. ³⁰ e f They left from there and began a journey through Galilee, but he did not wish anyone to know about it. ³¹He was teaching his disciples and telling them, "The Son of Man is to be handed over to men and they will kill him, and three days after his death he will rise." ³²But they did not understand the saying, and they were afraid to question him.

IV: The Full Revelation of the Mystery

The Greatest in the Kingdom. ³³ g *They came to Capernaum and, once inside the house, he began to ask them, "What were you arguing about on the way?" ³⁴But they remained silent. They had been discussing among themselves on the way who was the greatest. ³⁵ h Then he sat down, called the Twelve, and said to them, "If anyone wishes to be first, he shall be the last of all and the servant of all." ³⁶Taking a child he placed it in their midst, and putting his arms around it he said to them, ³⁷ i "Whoever receives one child such as this in my name, receives me; and whoever receives me, receives not me but the One who sent me."

Another Exorcist. ³⁸ j *John said to him, "Teacher, we saw someone driving out demons in your name, and we tried to prevent him because he does not follow us." ³⁹Jesus replied, "Do not prevent him. There is no one who performs a mighty deed in my name who can at the same time speak ill of me. ⁴⁰ k For whoever is not against us is for us. ⁴¹ l Anyone who gives you a cup of water to drink because you belong to Christ, amen, I say to you, will surely not lose his reward.

Temptations to Sin. ⁴² m "Whoever causes one of these little ones who believe [in me] to sin, it would be better for him if a great millstone were put around his neck and he were thrown into the sea. ⁴³*If your hand causes you to sin, cut it off. It is better for you to enter into life maimed than with two hands to go into Gehenna, into the unquenchable fire. [⁴⁴]* ⁴⁵And if your foot causes you to sin, cut if off. It is better for you to enter into life crippled than with two feet to be thrown into Gehenna. [⁴⁶]* ⁴⁷And if your eye causes you to sin, pluck it out. Better for you to enter into the kingdom of God with one eye than with two eyes to be thrown into Gehenna, ⁴⁸ n where 'their worm does not die, and the fire is not quenched.'

The Simile of Salt. ⁴⁹*"Everyone will be

9, 29: This kind can only come out through prayer: a variant reading adds "and through fasting."

9, 33–37: Mark probably intends this incident and the sayings that follow as commentary on the disciples' lack of understanding (32). Their role in Jesus' work is one of service, especially to the poor and lowly. Children were the symbol Jesus used for the **anawim**, the poor in spirit, the lowly in the Christian community.

9, 38–41: Jesus warns against jealousy and intolerance toward others, such as exorcists who do **not follow us.** The saying in v 40 is a broad principle of the divine tolerance. Even the smallest courtesies shown to those who teach in Jesus' name do not go unrewarded.

9, 43.45.47: Gehenna: see the note on Mt 5, 22.

9, 44.46: These verses, lacking in some important early manuscripts, are here omitted as scribal additions. They simply repeat v 48, itself a modified citation of Is 66, 24.

9, 49: Everyone will be salted with fire: so the better manuscripts. Some add "every sacrifice will be salted with salt." The purifying and preservative use of salt in food (Lv 2, 13) and the refinement effected through fire refer here to

e: Jn 7, 1.   f: 8, 31; Mt 17, 22-23; Lk 9, 43-45.   g: Mt 18, 1-5; Lk 9, 46-48.   h: Mt 20, 27.   i: Mt 10, 40; 18, 5; Jn 13, 20.   j: Nm 11, 28; Lk 9, 49-50; 1 Cor 12, 3.   k: Mt 12, 30.   l: Mt 10, 42; 1 Cor 3, 23.   m: Mt 5, 29-30; 18, 6-9; Lk 17, 1-2.   n: Is 66, 24.

salted with fire. [50o]Salt is good, but if salt becomes insipid, with what will you restore its flavor? Keep salt in yourselves and you will have peace with one another."

See RG
393-94
CHAPTER 10

Marriage and Divorce. [1]He set out from there and went into the district of Judea [and] across the Jordan. Again crowds gathered around him and, as was his custom, he again taught them. [2p*]The Pharisees approached and asked, "Is it lawful for a husband to divorce his wife?" They were testing him. [3]He said to them in reply, "What did Moses command you?" [4q]They replied, "Moses permitted him to write a bill of divorce and dismiss her." [5]But Jesus told them, "Because of the hardness of your hearts he wrote you this commandment. [6r]But from the beginning of creation, 'God made them male and female. [7s]For this reason a man shall leave his father and mother [and be joined to his wife], [8]and the two shall become one flesh.' So they are no longer two but one flesh. [9]Therefore what God has joined together, no human being must separate." [10]In the house the disciples again questioned him about this. [11t]He said to them, "Whoever divorces his wife and marries another commits adultery against her; [12]and if she divorces her husband and marries another, she commits adultery."

Blessing of the Children. [13uv]And people were bringing children to him that he might touch them, but the disciples rebuked them. [14]When Jesus saw this he became indignant and said to them, "Let the children come to me; do not prevent them, for the kingdom of God belongs to such as these. [15w*]Amen, I say to you, whoever does not accept the kingdom of God like a child will not enter it." [16]Then he embraced them and blessed them, placing his hands on them.

The Rich Man. [17x]As he was setting out on a journey, a man ran up, knelt down before him, and asked him, "Good teacher, what must I do to inherit eternal life?" [18*]Jesus answered him, "Why do you call me good? No one is good but God alone. [19y]You know the commandments: 'You shall not kill; you shall not commit adultery; you shall not steal; you shall not bear false witness; you shall not defraud; honor your father and your mother.' " [20]He replied and said to him, "Teacher, all of these I have observed from my youth." [21]Jesus, looking at him, loved him and said to him, "You are lacking in one thing. Go, sell what you have, and give to [the] poor and you will have treasure in heaven; then come, follow me." [22]At that statement his face fell, and he went away sad, for he had many possessions.

[23z*]Jesus looked around and said to his disciples, "How hard it is for those who have wealth to enter the kingdom of God!" [24]The disciples were amazed at his words. So Jesus again said to them in reply, "Children, how hard it is to enter the kingdom of God! [25]It is easier for a camel to pass through [the] eye of [a] needle than for one who is rich to enter the kingdom of God." [26]They were exceedingly astonished and said among themselves, "Then who can be saved?" [27]Jesus looked at them and said, "For human beings it is im-

---

comparable effects in the spiritual life of the disciples of Jesus.

10, 2–9: In the dialogue between Jesus and the Pharisees on the subject of divorce, Jesus declares that the law of Moses permitted divorce (Dt 24, 1) only **because of the hardness of your hearts** (4–5). In citing Gn 1, 27 and 2, 24, Jesus proclaims permanence to be the divine intent from the beginning concerning human marriage (6–8). He reaffirms this with the declaration that **what God has joined together, no human being must separate** (9). See further the notes on Mt 5, 31–32 and 19, 3–9.

10, 15: Whoever does not accept the kingdom of God like a child: i.e., in total dependence upon and obedience to the gospel; cf Mt 18, 3–4.

10, 18: Why do you call me good?: Jesus repudiates the term "good" for himself and directs it to God, the source of all goodness who alone can grant the

gift of eternal life; cf Mt 19, 16–17.

10, 23–27: In the Old Testament wealth and material goods are considered a sign of God's favor (Jb 1, 10; Ps 128, 1–2; Is 3, 10). The words of Jesus in 23–25 provoke astonishment among the disciples because of their apparent contradiction of the Old Testament concept (24.26). Since wealth, power, and merit generate false security, Jesus rejects them utterly as a claim to enter the kingdom. Achievement of salvation is beyond human capability and depends solely on the goodness of God who offers it as a gift (27).

---

o: Lv 2, 13; Mt 5, 13; Lk 14, 34-35; Col 4, 6. p: Mt 19, 3-9. q: Dt 24, 1-4. r: Gn 1, 27. s: Gn 2, 24; 1 Cor 6, 16; Eph 5, 31. t: Mt 5, 32; Lk 16, 18; 1 Cor 7, 10-11. u: Mt 19, 13-15; Lk 18, 15-17. v: Lk 9, 47. w: Mt 18, 3. x: Mt 19, 16-30; Lk 18, 18-30. y: Ex 20, 12-16; Dt 5, 16-21. z: Prv 11, 28.

possible, but not for God. All things are possible for God." [28]Peter began to say to him, "We have given up everything and followed you." [29]Jesus said, "Amen, I say to you, there is no one who has given up house or brothers or sisters or mother or father or children or lands for my sake and for the sake of the gospel [30]who will not receive a hundred times more now in this present age: houses and brothers and sisters and mothers and children and lands, with persecutions, and eternal life in the age to come. [31a]But many that are first will be last, and [the] last will be first."

The Third Prediction of the Passion. [32b]They were on the way, going up to Jerusalem, and Jesus went ahead of them. They were amazed, and those who followed were afraid. Taking the Twelve aside again, he began to tell them what was going to happen to him. [33]"Behold, we are going up to Jerusalem, and the Son of Man will be handed over to the chief priests and the scribes, and they will condemn him to death and hand him over to the Gentiles [34]who will mock him, spit upon him, scourge him, and put him to death, but after three days he will rise."

Ambition of James and John. [35c]Then James and John, the sons of Zebedee, came to him and said to him, "Teacher, we want you to do for us whatever we ask of you." [36]He replied, "What do you wish [me] to do for you?" [37]They answered him, "Grant that in your glory we may sit one at your right and the other at your left." [38d]*Jesus said to them, "You do not know what you are asking. Can you drink the cup that I drink or be baptized with the baptism with which I am baptized?" [39]They said to him, "We can." Jesus said to them, "The cup that I drink, you will drink, and with the baptism with which

I am baptized, you will be baptized; [40]but to sit at my right or at my left is not mine to give but is for those for whom it has been prepared." [41]When the ten heard this, they became indignant at James and John. [42e]*Jesus summoned them and said to them, "You know that those who are recognized as rulers over the Gentiles lord it over them, and their great ones make their authority over them felt. [43]But it shall not be so among you. Rather, whoever wishes to be great among you will be your servant; [44]whoever wishes to be first among you will be the slave of all. [45]For the Son of Man did not come to be served but to serve and to give his life as a ransom for many."

The Blind Bartimaeus. [46f]*They came to Jericho. And as he was leaving Jericho with his disciples and a sizable crowd, Bartimaeus, a blind man, the son of Timaeus, sat by the roadside begging. [47]On hearing that it was Jesus of Nazareth, he began to cry out and say, "Jesus, son of David, have pity on me." [48]And many rebuked him, telling him to be silent. But he kept calling out all the more, "Son of David, have pity on me." [49]Jesus stopped and said, "Call him." So they called the blind man, saying to him, "Take courage; get up, he is calling you." [50]He threw aside his cloak, sprang up, and came to Jesus. [51]Jesus said to him in reply, "What do you want me to do for you?" The blind man replied to him, "Master, I want to see." [52]Jesus told him, "Go your way; your faith has saved you." Immediately he received his sight and followed him on the way.

CHAPTER 11

See RG 394

The Entry into Jerusalem. [1g]*When they drew near to Jerusalem, to Bethphage

---

10, 38–40: Can you drink the cup . . . I am baptized?: the metaphor of drinking the cup is used in the Old Testament to refer to acceptance of the destiny assigned by God; see the note on Ps 11, 6. In Jesus' case, this involves divine judgment on sin that Jesus the innocent one is to expiate on behalf of the guilty (14, 24; Is 53, 5). His baptism is to be his crucifixion and death for the salvation of the human race; cf Lk 12, 50. The request of James and John for a share in the glory (35–37) must of necessity involve a share in Jesus' sufferings, the endurance of tribulation and suffering for the gospel (39). The authority of assigning places of honor in the kingdom is reserved to God (40).

10, 42–45: Whatever authority is to be exercised by the disciples must, like that of Jesus, be rendered as service to others (45) rather than for personal aggrandizement (42–44). The service of Jesus is his passion and death for the sins of the human race (45); cf 14, 24; Is 53, 11–12; Mt 26, 28; Lk 22, 19–20.

10, 46–52: See the notes on Mt 9, 27–31 and 20, 29–34.

11, 1–11: In Mark's account Jesus takes the initiative in ordering the preparation for his entry into Jerusalem (1–6) even

a: Mt 19, 30; Lk 13, 30. b: 8, 31; Mt 20, 17-19; Lk 18, 31-33. c: Mt 20, 20-28. d: Lk 12, 50. e: Lk 22, 25-27. f: Mt 20, 29-34; Lk 18, 35-43. g: Mt 21, 1-9; Lk 19, 29-38; Jn 12, 12-15.

and Bethany at the Mount of Olives, he sent two of his disciples ²and said to them, "Go into the village opposite you, and immediately on entering it, you will find a colt tethered on which no one has ever sat. Untie it and bring it here. ³If anyone should say to you, 'Why are you doing this?' reply, 'The Master has need of it and will send it back here at once.' " ⁴So they went off and found a colt tethered at a gate outside on the street, and they untied it. ⁵Some of the bystanders said to them, "What are you doing, untying the colt?" ⁶They answered them just as Jesus had told them to, and they permitted them to do it. ⁷So they brought the colt to Jesus and put their cloaks over it. And he sat on it. ⁸Many people spread their cloaks on the road, and others spread leafy branches that they had cut from the fields. ⁹ʰThose preceding him as well as those following kept crying out:

"Hosanna!
  Blessed is he who comes in the name
        of the Lord!
¹⁰   Blessed is the kingdom of our father
        David that is to come!
  Hosanna in the highest!"

¹¹ⁱHe entered Jerusalem and went into the temple area. He looked around at everything and, since it was already late, went out to Bethany with the Twelve.

Jesus Curses a Fig Tree. ¹²ʲ*The next day as they were leaving Bethany he was hungry. ¹³Seeing from a distance a fig tree in leaf, he went over to see if he could find anything on it. When he reached it he found nothing but leaves; it was not the time for figs. ¹⁴And he said to it in reply, "May no one ever eat of your fruit again!" And his disciples heard it.

Cleansing of the Temple. ¹⁵ᵏ*They came to Jerusalem, and on entering the temple area he began to drive out those selling and buying there. He overturned the tables of the money changers and the seats of those who were selling doves. ¹⁶He did not permit anyone to carry anything through the temple area. ¹⁷ˡThen he taught them saying, "Is it not written:

'My house shall be called a house of
        prayer for all peoples'?
  But you have made it a den of
        thieves."

¹⁸The chief priests and the scribes came to hear of it and were seeking a way to put him to death, yet they feared him because the whole crowd was astonished at his teaching. ¹⁹ᵐWhen evening came, they went out of the city.

The Withered Fig Tree. ²⁰ⁿEarly in the morning, as they were walking along, they saw the fig tree withered to its roots. ²¹Peter remembered and said to him, "Rabbi, look! The fig tree that you cursed has withered." ²²Jesus said to them in reply, "Have faith in God. ²³ᵒAmen, I say to you, whoever says to this mountain, 'Be lifted up and thrown into the sea,' and does not doubt in his heart but believes that what he says will happen, it shall be done for him. ²⁴ᵖTherefore I tell you, all that you ask for in prayer, believe that you will receive it and it shall be yours. ²⁵ᑫWhen you stand to pray, forgive anyone against whom you have a grievance, so that your heavenly Father may in turn forgive you your transgressions. [²⁶]"*

The Authority of Jesus Questioned. ²⁷ʳ*They returned once more to Jerusalem. As he was walking in the temple area, the

---

as he later orders the preparation of his last Passover Supper (14, 12–16). In vv 9–10 the greeting Jesus receives stops short of proclaiming him Messiah. He is greeted rather as the prophet of the coming messianic kingdom. Contrast Mt 21, 9.

11, 12–14: Jesus' search for fruit on the fig tree recalls the prophets' earlier use of this image to designate Israel; cf Jer 8, 13; 29, 17; Jl 1, 7; Hos 9, 10.16. Cursing the fig tree is a parable in action representing Jesus' judgment (20) on barren Israel and the fate of Jerusalem for failing to receive his teaching; cf Is 34, 4; Hos 2, 14; Lk 13, 6–9.

11, 15–19: See the note on Mt 21, 12–17.

11, 26: This verse, which reads, "But if you do not forgive,

neither will your heavenly Father forgive your transgressions," is omitted in the best manuscripts. It was probably added by copyists under the influence of Mt 6, 15.

11, 27–33: The mounting hostility toward Jesus came from the chief priests, the scribes, and the elders (27); the Herodians and the Pharisees (12, 13); and the Sadducees (12,

h: 2 Sm 7, 16; Ps 118, 26.   i: Mt 21, 10.17.   j: Mt 21, 18–20; Lk 13, 6–9.   k: Mt 21, 12–13; Lk 19, 45–46; Jn 2, 14–16.   l: Is 56, 7; Jer 7, 11.   m: Lk 21, 37.   n: Mt 21, 20–22.   o: Mt 17, 20–21; Lk 17, 6.   p: Mt 7, 7; Jn 11, 22; 14, 13.   q: Mt 6, 14; 18, 35.   r: Mt 21, 23–27; Lk 20, 1–8.

chief priests, the scribes, and the elders approached him [28]and said to him, "By what authority are you doing these things? Or who gave you this authority to do them?" [29]Jesus said to them, "I shall ask you one question. Answer me, and I will tell you by what authority I do these things. [30]Was John's baptism of heavenly or of human origin? Answer me." [31]They discussed this among themselves and said, "If we say, 'Of heavenly origin,' he will say, '[Then] why did you not believe him?' [32]But shall we say, 'Of human origin'?"—they feared the crowd, for they all thought John really was a prophet. [33]So they said to Jesus in reply, "We do not know." Then Jesus said to them, "Neither shall I tell you by what authority I do these things."

CHAPTER 12

See RG 394

Parable of the Tenants. [1] [st]*He began to speak to them in parables. "A man planted a vineyard, put a hedge around it, dug a wine press, and built a tower. Then he leased it to tenant farmers and left on a journey. [2]At the proper time he sent a servant to the tenants to obtain from them some of the produce of the vineyard. [3]But they seized him, beat him, and sent him away empty-handed. [4]Again he sent them another servant. And that one they beat over the head and treated shamefully. [5]He sent yet another whom they killed. So, too, many others; some they beat, others they killed. [6]He had one other to send, a beloved son. He sent him to them last of all, thinking, 'They will respect my son.' [7]But those tenants said to one another, 'This is the heir. Come, let us kill him, and the inheritance will be ours.' [8]So they seized him and killed him, and threw him out of the vineyard. [9]What [then] will the owner of the vineyard do? He will come, put the tenants to death, and give the vineyard to others. [10u]Have you not read this scripture passage:

'The stone that the builders rejected
    has become the cornerstone;
[11] by the Lord has this been done,
    and it is wonderful in our eyes'?"

[12]They were seeking to arrest him, but they feared the crowd, for they realized that he had addressed the parable to them. So they left him and went away.

Paying Taxes to the Emperor. [13vw]*They sent some Pharisees and Herodians to him to ensnare him in his speech. [14]They came and said to him, "Teacher, we know that you are a truthful man and that you are not concerned with anyone's opinion. You do not regard a person's status but teach the way of God in accordance with the truth. Is it lawful to pay the census tax to Caesar or not? Should we pay or should we not pay?" [15]Knowing their hypocrisy he said to them, "Why are you testing me? Bring me a denarius to look at." [16]They brought one to him and he said to them, "Whose image and inscription is this?" They replied to him, "Caesar's." [17x]So Jesus said to them, "Repay to Caesar what belongs to Caesar and to God what belongs to God." They were utterly amazed at him.

The Question about the Resurrection. [18]*Some Sadducees, who say there is no resurrection, came to him and put this question to him, [19y]saying, "Teacher, Moses wrote for us, 'If someone's brother dies, leaving a wife but no child, his brother must take the wife and raise up descendants for his brother.' [20]Now there were seven brothers. The first married a woman and died, leaving no descendants. [21]So the second married her and died, leaving no descendants, and the third likewise. [22]And the seven left no descendants. Last of all the woman also died. [23]At the resurrection

---

18). By their rejection of God's messengers, John the Baptist and Jesus, they incurred the divine judgment implied in vv 27–33 and confirmed in the parable of the vineyard tenants (12, 1–12).

12, 1–12: The vineyard denotes Israel (Is 5, 1–7). The tenant farmers are the religious leaders of Israel. God is the owner of the vineyard. His servants are his messengers, the prophets. The beloved son is Jesus (1, 11; 9, 7; Mt 3, 17; 17, 5; Lk 3, 22; 9, 35). The punishment of the tenants refers to the religious leaders, and the transfer of the vineyard to others

refers to the people of the new Israel.

12, 13–34: In the ensuing conflicts (cf also 2, 1–3, 6) Jesus vanquishes his adversaries by his responses to their questions and reduces them to silence (34).

12, 13–17: See the note on Mt 22, 15–22.

12, 18–27: See the note on Mt 22, 23–33.

s: Mt 21, 33-46; Lk 20, 9-19. t: Is 5, 1-7; Jer 2, 21. u: Ps 118, 22-23; Is 28, 16. v: Mt 22, 15-33; Lk 20, 20-39. w: 3, 6. x: Rom 13, 7. y: Dt 25, 5.

[when they arise] whose wife will she be? For all seven had been married to her." [24]Jesus said to them, "Are you not misled because you do not know the scriptures or the power of God? [25]When they rise from the dead, they neither marry nor are given in marriage, but they are like the angels in heaven. [26]z As for the dead being raised, have you not read in the Book of Moses, in the passage about the bush, how God told him, 'I am the God of Abraham, [the] God of Isaac, and [the] God of Jacob'? [27]He is not God of the dead but of the living. You are greatly misled."

The Greatest Commandment. [28a]*One of the scribes, when he came forward and heard them disputing and saw how well he had answered them, asked him, "Which is the first of all the commandments?" [29]Jesus replied, "The first is this: 'Hear, O Israel! The Lord our God is Lord alone! [30]b You shall love the Lord your God with all your heart, with all your soul, with all your mind, and with all your strength.' [31]c The second is this: 'You shall love your neighbor as yourself.' There is no other commandment greater than these." [32]The scribe said to him, "Well said, teacher. You are right in saying, 'He is One and there is no other than he.' [33]d And 'to love him with all your heart, with all your understanding, with all your strength, and to love your neighbor as yourself' is worth more than all burnt offerings and sacrifices." [34]e And when Jesus saw that [he] answered with understanding, he said to him, "You are not far from the kingdom of God." And no one dared to ask him any more questions.

The Question about David's Son. [35]f*As Jesus was teaching in the temple area he said, "How do the scribes claim that the Messiah is the son of David? [36]g David himself, inspired by the holy Spirit, said:

'The Lord said to my lord,
"Sit at my right hand
until I place your enemies under your feet." '

[37]David himself calls him 'lord'; so how is he his son?" [The] great crowd heard this with delight.

Denunciation of the Scribes. [38]h*In the course of his teaching he said, "Beware of the scribes, who like to go around in long robes and accept greetings in the marketplaces, [39]seats of honor in synagogues, and places of honor at banquets. [40]They devour the houses of widows and, as a pretext, recite lengthy prayers. They will receive a very severe condemnation."

The Poor Widow's Contribution. [41]i*He sat down opposite the treasury and observed how the crowd put money into the treasury. Many rich people put in large sums. [42]A poor widow also came and put in two small coins worth a few cents. [43]Calling his disciples to himself, he said to them, "Amen, I say to you, this poor widow put in more than all the other contributors to the treasury. [44]For they have all contributed from their surplus wealth, but she, from her poverty, has contributed all she had, her whole livelihood."

CHAPTER 13

See RG 395

The Destruction of the Temple Foretold. [1]j*As he was making his way out of the temple area one of his disciples said to him, "Look, teacher, what stones and what buildings!" [2]Jesus said to him, "Do you see these great buildings? There will not be one stone left upon another that will not be thrown down."

12, 28–34: See the note on Mt 22, 34–40.

12, 35–37: Jesus questions the claim of the scribes about the Davidic descent of the Messiah, not to deny it (Mt 1, 1; Acts 2, 20.34; Rom 1, 3; 2 Tm 2, 8) but to imply that he is more than this. His superiority derives from his transcendent origin, to which David himself attested when he spoke of the Messiah with the name "Lord" (Ps 110, 1). See also the note on Mt 22, 41–46.

12, 38–40: See the notes on 7, 1–23 and Mt 23, 1–39.

12, 41–44: See the note on Lk 21, 1–4.

13, 1–2: The reconstructed temple with its precincts, be-

gun under Herod the Great ca. 20 B.C., was completed only some seven years before it was destroyed by fire in A.D. 70 at the hands of the Romans; cf Jer 26, 18; Mt 24, 1–2. For the dating of the reconstruction of the temple, see further the note on Jn 2, 20.

z: Ex 3, 6. a: Mt 22, 34-40; Lk 10, 25-28. b: Dt 6, 4-5. c: Lv 19, 18; Rom 13, 9; Gal 5, 14; Jas 2, 8. d: Dt 6, 4; Ps 40, 7-9. e: Mt 22, 46; Lk 20, 40. f: Mt 22, 41-45; Lk 20, 41-44. g: Ps 110, 1. h: Mt 23, 1-7; Lk 11, 43; 20, 45-47. i: Lk 21, 1-4. j: Mt 24, 1-2; Lk 21, 5-6.

Parables in the Synoptic Gospels

Parable	Matthew	Mark	Luke
The Weeds among the Wheat	13, 24–30		
The Hidden Treasure	13, 44		
The Fine Pearl	13, 45–46		
The Net	13, 47–48		
The Unforgiving Servant	18, 23–35		
The Workers in the Vineyard	20, 1–16		
The Two Sons	21, 28–30		
The Wedding Feast	22, 2–14		
The Talents	25, 14–30		
The Judgment of the Nations	25, 31–46		
Seed Grows of Itself		4, 26–29	
Need for Watchfulness		13, 32–37	
The Two Debtors			7, 41–42
The Good Samaritan			10, 30–35
The Persistent Friend			11, 5–8
The Rich Fool			12, 16–20
The Vigilant and Faithful Servants			12, 35–40
The Faithful and Wise Steward			12, 42–48
The Barren Fig Tree			13, 6–9
The Great Feast			14, 15–24
The Tower			14, 28–30
The King Marching into Battle			14, 31–33
The Lost Coin			15, 8–10
The Lost Son			15, 11–32
The Dishonest Steward			16, 1–8
The Rich Man and Lazarus			16, 19–31
Attitude of a Servant			17, 7–10
The Persistent Widow			18, 2–5
The Pharisee and the Tax Collector			18, 9–14
The Ten Gold Coins			19, 11–27
The Two Foundations	7, 24–29		6, 46–49
The Yeast	13, 33		13, 20–21
The Lost Sheep	18, 10–14		15, 1–7
The Lamp	5, 15	4, 21	8, 16; 11, 33
The New Cloth	9, 16	2, 21	5, 36
The New Wine in Old Wineskins	9, 17	2, 22	5, 37–38
The Sower	13, 1–9	4, 1–9	8, 4–8
The Mustard Seed	13, 31–32	4, 30–34	13, 18–19
The Tenants	21, 33–46	12, 1–12	20, 9–19
The Lesson of the Fig Tree	24, 32–35	13, 28–31	21, 29

The Signs of the End. [3][k][*]As he was sitting on the Mount of Olives opposite the temple area, Peter, James, John, and Andrew asked him privately, [4]"Tell us, when will this happen, and what sign will there be when all these things are about to come to an end?" [5][l]Jesus began to say to them, "See that no one deceives you. [6]Many will come in my name saying, 'I am he,' and they will deceive many. [7]When you hear of wars and reports of wars do not be alarmed; such things must happen, but it will not yet be the end. [8]Nation will rise against nation and kingdom against kingdom. There will be earthquakes from place to place and there will be famines. These are the beginnings of the labor pains.

The Coming Persecution. [9][m]"Watch out for yourselves. They will hand you over to the courts. You will be beaten in synagogues. You will be arraigned before governors and kings because of me, as a witness before them. [10][*]But the gospel must first be preached to all nations. [11][n]When they lead you away and hand you over, do not worry beforehand about what you are to say. But say whatever will be given to you at that hour. For it will not be you who are speaking but the holy Spirit. [12]Brother will hand over brother to death, and the father his child; children will rise up against parents and have them put to death. [13]You will be hated by all because of my name. But the one who perseveres to the end will be saved.

The Great Tribulation. [14][o][p][*]"When you see the desolating abomination standing where he should not (let the reader understand), then those in Judea must flee to the mountains, [15][q][and] a person on a housetop must not go down or enter to get anything out of his house, [16]and a person in a field must not return to get his cloak. [17]Woe to pregnant women and nursing mothers in those days. [18]Pray that this does not happen in winter. [19][r]For those times will have tribulation such as has not been since the beginning of God's creation until now, nor ever will be. [20]If the Lord had not shortened those days, no one would be saved; but for the sake of the elect whom he chose, he did shorten the days. [21]If anyone says to you then, 'Look, here is the Messiah! Look, there he is!' do not believe it. [22]False messiahs and false prophets will arise and will perform signs and wonders in order to mislead, if that were possible, the elect. [23]Be watchful! I have told it all to you beforehand.

The Coming of the Son of Man. [24][s][t]"But in those days after that tribulation

the sun will be darkened,
  and the moon will not give its light,
[25] and the stars will be falling from the sky,
  and the powers in the heavens will be shaken.

[26][u][*]And then they will see 'the Son of Man coming in the clouds' with great power and glory, [27]and then he will send out the angels and gather [his] elect from the four winds, from the end of the earth to the end of the sky.

The Lesson of the Fig Tree. [28][v]"Learn a lesson from the fig tree. When its branch becomes tender and sprouts leaves, you know that summer is near. [29]In the same way,

---

13, 3–37: Jesus' prediction of the destruction of the temple (2) provoked questions that the four named disciples put to him in private regarding the time and the sign when all **these things are about to come to an end** (3–4). The response to their questions was Jesus' eschatological discourse prior to his imminent death. It contained instruction and consolation exhorting the disciples and the church to faith and obedience through the trials that would confront them (5–13). The sign is the presence of **the desolating abomination** (14; see Dn 9, 27), i.e., of the Roman power profaning the temple. Flight from Jerusalem is urged rather than defense of the city through misguided messianic hope (14–23). Intervention will occur only after destruction (24–27), which will happen before the end of the first Christian generation (28–31). No one but the Father knows the precise time, or that of the parousia (32); hence the necessity of constant vigilance (33–37). Luke sets the parousia at a later date, after "the time of the Gen-

tiles" (Lk 21, 24). See also the notes on Mt 24, 1—25, 46.

13, 10: **The gospel . . . to all nations:** the period of the Christian mission.

13, 14: The participle **standing** is masculine, in contrast to the neuter at Mt 24, 15.

13, 26: **Son of Man . . . with great power and glory:** Jesus cites this text from Dn 7, 13 in his response to the high priest, **Are you the Messiah?** (14, 61). In Ex 34, 5; Lv 16, 2; and Nm 11, 25 the clouds indicate the presence of the divinity. Thus in his role of Son of Man, Jesus is a heavenly being who will come in power and glory.

---

k: Mt 24, 3-8; Lk 21, 7-11. l: Eph 5, 6; 2 Thes 2, 3. m: Mt 24, 9-14; Lk 21, 12-19. n: Mt 10, 19-22; Lk 12, 11-12. o: Mt 24, 15-22; Lk 21, 20-24. p: Dn 9, 27; Mt 24, 15. q: Lk 17, 31. r: Dn 12, 1. s: Mt 24, 29-31; Lk 21, 25-27. t: Is 13, 10; Ez 32, 7; Jl 2, 10. u: 14, 62; Dn 7, 13-14. v: Mt 24, 32-36; Lk 21, 29-33.

when you see these things happening, know that he is near, at the gates. [30]Amen, I say to you, this generation will not pass away until all these things have taken place. [31]Heaven and earth will pass away, but my words will not pass away.

Need for Watchfulness. [32]"But of that day or hour, no one knows, neither the angels in heaven, nor the Son, but only the Father. [33w]Be watchful! Be alert! You do not know when the time will come. [34x]It is like a man traveling abroad. He leaves home and places his servants in charge, each with his work, and orders the gatekeeper to be on the watch. [35]Watch, therefore; you do not know when the lord of the house is coming, whether in the evening, or at midnight, or at cockcrow, or in the morning. [36]May he not come suddenly and find you sleeping. [37]What I say to you, I say to all: 'Watch!' "

CHAPTER 14

See RG 395-96

The Conspiracy against Jesus. [1y*]The Passover and the Feast of Unleavened Bread were to take place in two days' time. So the chief priests and the scribes were seeking a way to arrest him by treachery and put him to death. [2]They said, "Not during the festival, for fear that there may be a riot among the people."

The Anointing at Bethany. [3z*]When he was in Bethany reclining at table in the house of Simon the leper, a woman came with an alabaster jar of perfumed oil, costly genuine spikenard. She broke the alabaster jar and poured it on his head. [4]There were some who were indignant. "Why has there been this waste of perfumed oil? [5]It could have been sold for more than three hundred days' wages and the money given to the poor." They were infuriated with her. [6]Jesus said, "Let her alone. Why do you make trouble for her? She has done a good thing for me. [7]The poor you will always have with you, and whenever you wish you can do good to them, but you will not always have me. [8]She has done what she could. She has anticipated anointing my body for burial. [9]Amen, I say to you, wherever the gospel is proclaimed to the whole world, what she has done will be told in memory of her."

The Betrayal by Judas. [10a]Then Judas Iscariot, one of the Twelve, went off to the chief priests to hand him over to them. [11]When they heard him they were pleased and promised to pay him money. Then he looked for an opportunity to hand him over.

Preparations for the Passover. [12b*]On the first day of the Feast of Unleavened Bread, when they sacrificed the Passover lamb, his disciples said to him, "Where do you want us to go and prepare for you to eat the Passover?" [13*]He sent two of his disciples and said to them, "Go into the city and a man will meet you, carrying a jar of water. Follow him. [14]Wherever he enters, say to the master of the house, 'The Teacher says, "Where is my guest room where I may eat

---

14, 1—16, 8: In the movement of Mark's gospel the cross is depicted as Jesus' way to glory in accordance with the divine will. Thus the passion narrative is seen as the climax of Jesus' ministry.

14, 1: The Passover and the Feast of Unleavened Bread: the connection between the two festivals is reflected in Ex 12, 3–20; 34, 18; Lv 23, 4–8; Nm 9, 2–14; 28, 16–17; Dt 16, 1–8. The Passover commemorated the redemption from slavery and the departure of the Israelites from Egypt by night. It began at sundown after the Passover lamb was sacrificed in the temple in the afternoon of the fourteenth day of the month of Nisan. With the Passover Supper on the same evening was associated the eating of unleavened bread. The latter was continued through Nisan 21, a reminder of the affliction of the Israelites and of the haste surrounding their departure. Praise and thanks to God for his goodness in the past were combined at this dual festival with the hope of future salvation. **The chief priests . . . to death:** the intent to put Jesus to death was plotted for a long time but delayed for fear of the crowd (3, 6; 11, 18; 12, 12).

14, 3–9: At Bethany on the Mount of Olives, a few miles from Jerusalem, **in the house of Simon the leper,** Jesus defends a woman's loving action of anointing his head with perfumed oil in view of his impending death and burial as a criminal, in which case his body would not be anointed. See further the note on Jn 12, 7. He assures the woman of the remembrance of her deed in the worldwide preaching of the good news.

14, 12: The first day of the Feast of Unleavened Bread . . . the Passover lamb: a less precise designation of the day for sacrificing the Passover lamb as evidenced by some rabbinical literature. For a more exact designation, see the note on 14, 1. It was actually Nisan 14.

14, 13: A man . . . carrying a jar of water: perhaps a prearranged signal, for only women ordinarily carried water in jars. The Greek word used here, however, implies simply a person and not necessarily a male.

w: Mt 24, 42; 25, 13-15. x: Mt 25, 14-30; Lk 19, 12-27. y: Mt 26, 2-5; Lk 22, 1-2; Jn 11, 45-53. z: Mt 26, 6-13; Jn 12, 1-8. a: Mt 26, 14-16; Lk 22, 3-6. b: Mt 26, 17-19; Lk 22, 7-13.

the Passover with my disciples?" ' *15* Then he will show you a large upper room furnished and ready. Make the preparations for us there." *16* The disciples then went off, entered the city, and found it just as he had told them; and they prepared the Passover.

The Betrayer. *17c* When it was evening, he came with the Twelve. *18** And as they reclined at table and were eating, Jesus said, "Amen, I say to you, one of you will betray me, one who is eating with me." *19* They began to be distressed and to say to him, one by one, "Surely it is not I?" *20* He said to them, "One of the Twelve, the one who dips with me into the dish. *21** For the Son of Man indeed goes, as it is written of him, but woe to that man by whom the Son of Man is betrayed. It would be better for that man if he had never been born."

The Lord's Supper. *22d** While they were eating, he took bread, said the blessing, broke it, and gave it to them, and said, "Take it; this is my body." *23* Then he took a cup, gave thanks, and gave it to them, and they all drank from it. *24** He said to them, "This is my blood of the covenant, which will be shed for many. *25* Amen, I say to you, I shall not drink again the fruit of the vine until the day when I drink it new in the kingdom of God." *26e** Then, after singing a hymn, they went out to the Mount of Olives.

Peter's Denial Foretold. *27f** Then Jesus said to them, "All of you will have your faith shaken, for it is written:

'I will strike the shepherd,
    and the sheep will be dispersed.'

28 But after I have been raised up, I shall go before you to Galilee." *29* Peter said to him, "Even though all should have their faith shaken, mine will not be." *30* Then Jesus said to him, "Amen, I say to you, this very night before the cock crows twice you will deny me three times." *31* But he vehemently replied, "Even though I should have to die with you, I will not deny you." And they all spoke similarly.

The Agony in the Garden. *32gh** Then they came to a place named Gethsemane, and he said to his disciples, "Sit here while I pray." *33* He took with him Peter, James, and John, and began to be troubled and distressed. *34* Then he said to them, "My soul is sorrowful even to death. Remain here and keep watch." *35* He advanced a little and fell to the ground and prayed that if it were possible the hour might pass by him; *36** he said, "Abba, Father, all things are possible to you. Take this cup away from me, but not what I will but what you will." *37* When he returned he found them asleep. He said to Peter, "Simon, are you asleep? Could you not keep

14, 18: One of you will betray me, one who is eating with me: contrasts the intimacy of table fellowship at the Passover meal with the treachery of the traitor; cf Ps 41, 10.

14, 21: The Son of Man indeed goes, as it is written of him: a reference to Ps 41, 10 cited by Jesus concerning Judas at the Last Supper; cf Jn 13, 18–19.

14, 22–24: The actions and words of Jesus express within the framework of the Passover meal and the transition to a new covenant the sacrifice of himself through the offering of his body and blood in anticipation of his passion and death. His **blood of the covenant** both alludes to the ancient rite of Ex 24, 4–8 and indicates the new community that the sacrifice of Jesus will bring into being (Mt 26, 26–28; Lk 22, 19–20; 1 Cor 11, 23–25).

14, 24: Which will be shed: see the note on Mt 26, 27–28. **For many:** the Greek preposition **hyper** is a different one from that at Mt 26, 28 but the same as that found at Lk 22, 19.20 and 1 Cor 11, 24. The sense of both words is vicarious, and it is difficult in Hellenistic Greek to distinguish between them. For **many** in the sense of "all," see the note on Mt 20, 28.

14, 26: After singing a hymn: Pss 114–118, thanksgiving songs concluding the Passover meal.

14, 27–31: Jesus predicted that the Twelve would waver in

their faith, even abandon him, despite their protestations to the contrary. Yet he reassured them that after his resurrection he would regather them in Galilee (16, 7; cf Mt 26, 32; 28, 7.10.16; Jn 21), where he first summoned them to be his followers as he began to preach the good news (1, 14–20).

14, 32–34: The disciples who had witnessed the raising to life of the daughter of Jairus (5, 37) and the transfiguration of their Master (9, 2) were now invited to witness his degradation and agony and to watch and pray with him.

14, 36: Abba, Father: an Aramaic term, here also translated by Mark, Jesus' special way of addressing God with filial intimacy. The word **'abbā** seems not to have been used in earlier or contemporaneous Jewish sources to address God without some qualifier. Cf Rom 8, 15; Gal 4, 6 for other occurrences of the Aramaic word in the Greek New Testament. **Not what I will but what you will:** note the complete obedient surrender of the human will of Jesus to the divine will of the Father; cf Jn 4, 34; 8, 29; Rom 5, 19; Phil 2, 8; Heb 5, 8.

c: Mt 26, 20-24; Lk 22, 21-23; Jn 13, 21-26.   *d:* Mt 26, 26-30; Lk 22, 19-20; 1 Cor 11, 23-25.   *e:* Mt 26, 30-35; Lk 22, 34.39; Jn 13, 36-38.   *f:* Zec 13, 7; Jn 16, 32.   *g:* Mt 26, 36-46; Lk 22, 40-46.   *h:* Jn 18, 1.

watch for one hour? [38i]*Watch and pray that you may not undergo the test. The spirit is willing but the flesh is weak." [39]Withdrawing again, he prayed, saying the same thing. [40]Then he returned once more and found them asleep, for they could not keep their eyes open and did not know what to answer him. [41]He returned a third time and said to them, "Are you still sleeping and taking your rest? It is enough. The hour has come. Behold, the Son of Man is to be handed over to sinners. [42]Get up, let us go. See, my betrayer is at hand."

The Betrayal and Arrest of Jesus. [43j]Then, while he was still speaking, Judas, one of the Twelve, arrived, accompanied by a crowd with swords and clubs who had come from the chief priests, the scribes, and the elders. [44]His betrayer had arranged a signal with them, saying, "The man I shall kiss is the one; arrest him and lead him away securely." [45]He came and immediately went over to him and said, "Rabbi." And he kissed him. [46]At this they laid hands on him and arrested him. [47]One of the bystanders drew his sword, struck the high priest's servant, and cut off his ear. [48]Jesus said to them in reply, "Have you come out as against a robber, with swords and clubs, to seize me? [49]Day after day I was with you teaching in the temple area, yet you did not arrest me; but that the scriptures may be fulfilled." [50]And they all left him and fled. [51]Now a young man followed him wearing nothing but a linen cloth about his body. They seized him, [52]but he left the cloth behind and ran off naked.

Jesus before the Sanhedrin. [53k]*They led Jesus away to the high priest, and all the chief priests and the elders and the scribes

came together. [54]Peter followed him at a distance into the high priest's courtyard and was seated with the guards, warming himself at the fire. [55]The chief priests and the entire Sanhedrin kept trying to obtain testimony against Jesus in order to put him to death, but they found none. [56]Many gave false witness against him, but their testimony did not agree. [57]*Some took the stand and testified falsely against him, alleging, [58l]"We heard him say, 'I will destroy this temple made with hands and within three days I will build another not made with hands.' " [59]Even so their testimony did not agree. [60]The high priest rose before the assembly and questioned Jesus, saying, "Have you no answer? What are these men testifying against you?" [61]*But he was silent and answered nothing. Again the high priest asked him and said to him, "Are you the Messiah, the son of the Blessed One?" [62m]Then Jesus answered, "I am;

and 'you will see the Son of Man
  seated at the right hand of the Power
  and coming with the clouds of
    heaven.' "

[63]At that the high priest tore his garments and said, "What further need have we of witnesses? [64]You have heard the blasphemy. What do you think?" They all condemned him as deserving to die. [65n]Some began to spit on him. They blindfolded him and struck him and said to him, "Prophesy!" And the guards greeted him with blows.

Peter's Denial of Jesus. [66o]While Peter was below in the courtyard, one of the high priest's maids came along. [67]Seeing Peter warming himself, she looked intently at him

---

14, 38: **The spirit is willing but the flesh is weak:** the spirit is drawn to what is good yet found in conflict with the flesh, inclined to sin; cf Ps 51, 7.12. Everyone is faced with this struggle, the full force of which Jesus accepted on our behalf and, through his bitter passion and death, achieved the victory.

14, 53: **They led Jesus away . . . came together:** Mark presents a formal assembly of the whole Sanhedrin (chief priests, elders, and scribes) at night, leading to the condemnation of Jesus (64), in contrast to Lk 22, 66.71, where Jesus is condemned in a daytime meeting of the council; see also Jn 18, 13.19–24.

14, 57–58: See the notes on Mt 26, 60–61 and Jn 2, 19.

14, 61–62: **The Blessed One:** a surrogate for the divine name, which Jews did not pronounce. **I am:** indicates Jesus' acknowledgment that he is the Messiah and Son of God; cf 1, 1. Contrast Mt 26, 64 and Lk 22, 67–70, in which Jesus leaves his interrogators to answer their own question. **You will see the Son of Man . . . with the clouds of heaven:** an allusion to Dn 7, 13 and Ps 110, 1, portending the enthronement of Jesus as judge in the transcendent glory of God's kingdom. **The Power:** another surrogate for the name of God.

i: Rom 7, 5. j: Mt 26, 47-56; Lk 22, 47-53; Jn 18, 3-11. k: Mt 26, 57-68; Lk 22, 54-55.63-65.67-71; Jn 18, 12-13. l: 15, 29; 2 Cor 5, 1. m: 13, 26; Ps 110, 1; Dn 7, 13; Mt 24, 30. n: Lk 22, 63-65. o: Mt 26, 69-75; Lk 22, 56-62; Jn 18, 16-18.25-27.

and said, "You too were with the Nazarene, Jesus." [68*] But he denied it saying, "I neither know nor understand what you are talking about." So he went out into the outer court. [Then the cock crowed.] [69] The maid saw him and began again to say to the bystanders, "This man is one of them." [70] Once again he denied it. A little later the bystanders said to Peter once more, "Surely you are one of them; for you too are a Galilean." [71] He began to curse and to swear, "I do not know this man about whom you are talking." [72p] And immediately a cock crowed a second time. Then Peter remembered the word that Jesus had said to him, "Before the cock crows twice you will deny me three times." He broke down and wept.

See RG 395-96

CHAPTER 15

Jesus before Pilate. [1qr*] As soon as morning came, the chief priests with the elders and the scribes, that is, the whole Sanhedrin, held a council. They bound Jesus, led him away, and handed him over to Pilate. [2*] Pilate questioned him, "Are you the king of the Jews?" He said to him in reply, "You say so." [3] The chief priests accused him of many things. [4] Again Pilate questioned him, "Have you no answer? See how many things they accuse you of." [5] Jesus gave him no further answer, so that Pilate was amazed.

The Sentence of Death. [6s*] Now on the occasion of the feast he used to release to them one prisoner whom they requested. [7*] A man called Barabbas was then in prison along with the rebels who had committed murder in a rebellion. [8] The crowd came forward and began to ask him to do for them as he was accustomed. [9] Pilate answered, "Do you want me to release to you the king of the Jews?" [10] For he knew that it was out of envy that the chief priests had handed him over. [11] But the chief priests stirred up the crowd to have him release Barabbas for them instead. [12] Pilate again said to them in reply, "Then what [do you want] me to do with [the man you call] the king of the Jews?" [13*] They shouted again, "Crucify him." [14] Pilate said to them, "Why? What evil has he done?" They only shouted the louder, "Crucify him." [15*] So Pilate, wishing to satisfy the crowd, released Barabbas to them and, after he had Jesus scourged, handed him over to be crucified.

Mockery by the Soldiers. [16t*] The soldiers led him away inside the palace, that is, the praetorium, and assembled the whole cohort. [17] They clothed him in purple and, weaving a crown of thorns, placed it on him. [18] They began to salute him with, "Hail, King of the Jews!" [19] and kept striking his head with a reed and spitting upon him. They knelt before him in homage. [20] And when they had mocked him, they stripped him of the purple cloak, dressed him in his own clothes, and led him out to crucify him.

The Way of the Cross. [21u*] They pressed into service a passer-by, Simon, a Cyrenian, who was coming in from the country, the father of Alexander and Rufus, to carry his cross.

The Crucifixion. [22v] They brought him to the place of Golgotha (which is translated

---

14, 68: [Then the cock crowed]: found in most manuscripts, perhaps in view of vv 30 and 72, but omitted in others.

15, 1: Held a council: the verb here, poieō, can mean either "convene a council" or "take counsel." This reading is preferred to a variant "reached a decision" (cf 3, 6), which 14, 64 describes as having happened at the night trial; see the note on Mt 27, 1–2. **Handed him over to Pilate:** lacking authority to execute their sentence of condemnation (14, 64), the Sanhedrin had recourse to Pilate to have Jesus tried and put to death (15); cf Jn 18, 31.

15, 2: The king of the Jews: in the accounts of the evangelists a certain irony surrounds the use of this title as an accusation against Jesus (see the note on 15, 26). While Pilate uses this term (2.9.12), he is aware of the evil motivation of the chief priests who handed Jesus over for trial and condemnation (10; Lk 23, 14–16.20; Mt 27, 18.24; Jn 18, 38; 19, 4.6.12).

15, 6–15: See the note on Mt 27, 15–26.

15, 7: Barabbas: see the note on Mt 27, 16–17.

15, 13: Crucify him: see the note on Mt 27, 22.

15, 15: See the note on Mt 27, 26.

15, 16: Praetorium: see the note on Mt 27, 27.

15, 21: They pressed into service . . . Simon, a Cyrenian: a condemned person was constrained to bear his own instrument of torture, at least the crossbeam. The precise naming of Simon and his sons is probably due to their being known among early Christian believers to whom Mark addressed his gospel. See also the notes on Mt 27, 32 and Lk 23, 26–32.

p: Jn 13, 38.   *q:* Mt 27, 1-2.11-14; Lk 23, 1-3.   *r:* Jn 18, 28.   *s:* Mt 27, 15-26; Lk 23, 17-25; Jn 18, 39-40.   *t:* Mt 27, 27-31; Jn 19, 2-3.   *u:* Mt 27, 32; Lk 23, 26.   *v:* Mt 27, 33-51; Lk 23, 32-46; Jn 19, 17-30.

Place of the Skull). ²³They gave him wine drugged with myrrh, but he did not take it. ^{24w*}Then they crucified him and divided his garments by casting lots for them to see what each should take. ^{25*}It was nine o'clock in the morning when they crucified him. ^{26*}The inscription of the charge against him read, "The King of the Jews." ^{27x}With him they crucified two revolutionaries, one on his right and one on his left. [²⁸]* ^{29y*}Those passing by reviled him, shaking their heads and saying, "Aha! You who would destroy the temple and rebuild it in three days, ³⁰save yourself by coming down from the cross." ³¹Likewise the chief priests, with the scribes, mocked him among themselves and said, "He saved others; he cannot save himself. ^{32z}Let the Messiah, the King of Israel, come down now from the cross that we may see and believe." Those who were crucified with him also kept abusing him.

The Death of Jesus. ³³At noon darkness came over the whole land until three in the afternoon. ^{34a*}And at three o'clock Jesus cried out in a loud voice, "*Eloi, Eloi, lema sabachthani?*" which is translated, "My God, my God, why have you forsaken me?" ^{35*}Some of the bystanders who heard it said, "Look, he is calling Elijah." ³⁶One of them ran, soaked a sponge with wine, put it on a reed, and gave it to him to drink, saying, "Wait, let us see if Elijah comes to take him down." ³⁷Jesus gave a loud cry and breathed his last. ^{38*}The veil of the sanctuary was torn in two from top to bottom. ^{39b*}When the centurion who stood facing him saw how he breathed his last he said, "Truly this man was the Son of God!" ^{40c*}There were also women looking on from a distance. Among them were Mary Magdalene, Mary the mother of the younger James and of Joses, and Salome. ⁴¹These women had followed him when he was in Galilee and ministered to him. There were also many other women who had come up with him to Jerusalem.

The Burial of Jesus. ^{42d}When it was already evening, since it was the day of preparation, the day before the sabbath, ^{43*}Joseph of Arimathea, a distinguished member of the council, who was himself awaiting the kingdom of God, came and courageously went to Pilate and asked for the body of Jesus. ⁴⁴Pilate was amazed that he was already dead. He summoned the centurion and asked him if Jesus had already died. ⁴⁵And when he learned of it from the centurion, he gave the body to Joseph. ⁴⁶Having bought a linen cloth, he took him down, wrapped him in the linen cloth and laid him in a tomb that had been hewn out of the rock. Then he rolled a stone against the entrance to the tomb. ⁴⁷Mary Magdalene and Mary the mother of Joses watched where he was laid.

CHAPTER 16

The Resurrection of Jesus. ^{1ef*}When the sabbath was over, Mary Magdalene, Mary, the mother of James, and Salome

See RG 396

15, 24: See the notes on Mt 27, 35 and Jn 19, 23–25a.

15, 25: It was nine o'clock in the morning: literally, "the third hour," thus between 9 a.m. and 12 noon. Cf vv 33.34.42 for Mark's chronological sequence, which may reflect liturgical or catechetical considerations rather than the precise historical sequence of events; contrast the different chronologies in the other gospels, especially Jn 19, 14.

15, 26: The inscription . . . the King of the Jews: the political reason for the death penalty falsely charged by the enemies of Jesus. See further the notes on Mt 27, 37 and Jn 19, 19.

15, 28: This verse, "And the scripture was fulfilled that says, 'And he was counted among the wicked,' " is omitted in the earliest and best manuscripts. It contains a citation from Is 53, 12, and was probably introduced from Lk 22, 37.

15, 29: See the note on Mt 27, 39–40.

15, 34: An Aramaic rendering of Ps 22, 2. See also the note on Mt 27, 46.

15, 35: Elijah: a verbal link with **Eloi** (34). See the note on 9, 9–13; cf Mal 3, 23–24. See also the note on Mt 27, 47.

15, 38: See the note on Mt 27, 51–53.

15, 39: The closing portion of Mark's gospel returns to the theme of its beginning in the Gentile centurion's climactic declaration of belief that Jesus **was the Son of God.** It indicates the fulfillment of the good news announced in the prologue (1, 1) and may be regarded as the firstfruit of the passion and death of Jesus.

15, 40–41: See the note on Mt 27, 55–56.

15, 43: Joseph of Arimathea: see the note on Mt 27, 57–61.

16, 1–8: The purpose of this narrative is to show that the tomb is empty and that Jesus **has been raised** (6) and is **going before you to Galilee** (7) in fulfillment of 14, 28. The women find the tomb empty, and an angel stationed there announces to them what has happened. They are told to proclaim the news to Peter and the disciples in order to prepare them for a reunion with him. Mark's composition of the

w: Ps 22, 18. *x:* Lk 23, 33. *y:* Jn 2, 19. *z:* Lk 23, 39. *a:* Ps 22, 2. *b:* Mt 27, 54-56; Lk 23, 47-49. *c:* 6, 3; Lk 8, 2-3. *d:* Mt 27, 57-61; Lk 23, 50-56; Jn 19, 38-42. *e:* Mt 28, 1-8; Lk 24, 1-10; Jn 20, 1-10. *f:* Mt 28, 1; Lk 23, 56.

bought spices so that they might go and anoint him. [2]Very early when the sun had risen, on the first day of the week, they came to the tomb. [3]They were saying to one another, "Who will roll back the stone for us from the entrance to the tomb?" [4]When they looked up, they saw that the stone had been rolled back; it was very large. [5g]On entering the tomb they saw a young man sitting on the right side, clothed in a white robe, and they were utterly amazed. [6]He said to them, "Do not be amazed! You seek Jesus of Nazareth, the crucified. He has been raised; he is not here. Behold, the place where they laid him. [7h]But go and tell his disciples and Peter, 'He is going before you to Galilee; there you will see him, as he told you.' " [8]Then they went out and fled from the tomb, seized with trembling and bewilderment. They said nothing to anyone, for they were afraid.

The Longer Ending

The Appearance to Mary Magdalene. [9i*]When he had risen, early on the first day of the week, he appeared first to Mary Magdalene, out of whom he had driven seven demons. [10j]She went and told his companions who were mourning and weeping. [11]When they heard that he was alive and had been seen by her, they did not believe.

The Appearance to Two Disciples. [12k]After this he appeared in another form to two of them walking along on their way to the country. [13]They returned and told the others; but they did not believe them either.

The Commissioning of the Eleven. [14l][But] later, as the eleven were at table, he appeared to them and rebuked them for their unbelief and hardness of heart because they had not believed those who saw him after he had been raised. [15m]He said to them, "Go into the whole world and proclaim the gospel to every creature. [16]Whoever believes and is baptized will be saved; whoever does not believe will be condemned. [17]These signs will accompany those who believe: in my name they will drive out demons, they will speak new languages. [18n]They will pick up serpents [with their hands], and if they drink any deadly thing, it will not harm them. They will lay hands on the sick, and they will recover."

The Ascension of Jesus. [19o]So then the Lord Jesus, after he spoke to them, was taken up into heaven and took his seat at the right hand of God. [20p]But they went forth and preached everywhere, while the Lord worked with them and confirmed the word through accompanying signs.]

The Shorter Ending

[And they reported all the instructions briefly to Peter's companions. Afterwards Jesus himself, through them, sent forth from east to west the sacred and imperishable proclamation of eternal salvation. Amen.]

---

gospel ends at v 8 with the women telling no one, because they were afraid. This abrupt termination causes some to believe that the original ending of this gospel may have been lost. See the following note.

16, 9–20: This passage, termed the Longer Ending to the Marcan gospel by comparison with a much briefer conclusion found in some less important manuscripts, has traditionally been accepted as a canonical part of the gospel and was defined as such by the Council of Trent. Early citations of it by the Fathers indicate that it was composed by the second century, although vocabulary and style indicate that it was written by someone other than Mark. It is a general resume of the material concerning the appearances of the risen Jesus, reflecting, in particular, traditions found in Luke (24) and John (20).

The Shorter Ending: Found after v 8 before the Longer Ending in four seventh-to-ninth-century Greek manuscripts as well as in one Old Latin version, where it appears alone without the Longer Ending.

The Freer Logion: Found after v 14 in a fourth-fifth century manuscript preserved in the Freer Gallery of Art, Washington, DC, this ending was known to Jerome in the fourth century. It reads: "And they excused themselves, saying, 'This age of lawlessness and unbelief is under Satan, who does not allow the truth and power of God to prevail over the unclean things dominated by the spirits [or, does not allow the unclean things dominated by the spirits to grasp the truth and power of God]. Therefore reveal your righteousness now.' They spoke to Christ. And Christ responded to them, 'The limit of the years of Satan's power is completed, but other terrible things draw near. And for those who sinned I was handed over to death, that they might return to the truth and no longer sin, in order that they might inherit the spiritual and incorruptible heavenly glory of righteousness. But . . . .' "

g: Jn 20, 12. *h:* 14, 28. *i:* Mt 28, 1-10; Jn 20, 11-18. *j:* Lk 24, 10-11; Jn 20, 18. *k:* Lk 24, 13-35. *l:* Lk 24, 36-49; 1 Cor 15, 5. *m:* 13, 10; Mt 28, 18-20; Lk 24, 47; Jn 20, 21. *n:* Mt 10, 1; Lk 10, 19; Acts 28, 3-6. *o:* Lk 24, 50-53. *p:* 1 Tm 3, 16.

See RG
397–412

The Gospel According to Luke

The Gospel according to Luke is the first part of a two-volume work that continues the biblical history of God's dealings with humanity found in the Old Testament, showing how God's promises to Israel have been fulfilled in Jesus and how the salvation promised to Israel and accomplished by Jesus has been extended to the Gentiles. The stated purpose of the two volumes is to provide Theophilus and others like him with certainty—assurance—about earlier instruction they have received (1, 4). To accomplish his purpose, Luke shows that the preaching and teaching of the representatives of the early church are grounded in the preaching and teaching of Jesus, who during his historical ministry (Acts 1, 21–22) prepared his specially chosen followers and commissioned them to be witnesses to his resurrection and to all else that he did (Acts 10, 37–42). This continuity between the historical ministry of Jesus and the ministry of the apostles is Luke's way of guaranteeing the fidelity of the church's teaching to the teaching of Jesus.

Luke's story of Jesus and the church is dominated by a historical perspective. This history is first of all salvation history. God's divine plan for human salvation was accomplished during the period of Jesus, who through the events of his life (22, 22) fulfilled the Old Testament prophecies (4, 21; 18, 31; 22, 37; 24, 26–27.44), and this salvation is now extended to all humanity in the period of the church (Acts 4, 12). This salvation history, moreover, is a part of human history. Luke relates the story of Jesus and the church to events in contemporary Palestinian (1, 5; 3, 1–2; Acts 4, 6) and Roman (2, 1–2; 3, 1; Acts 11, 28; 18, 2.12) history for, as Paul says in Acts 26, 26, "this was not done in a corner." Finally, Luke relates the story of Jesus and the church to contemporaneous church history. Luke is concerned with presenting Christianity as a legitimate form of worship in the Roman world, a religion that is capable of meeting the spiritual needs of a world empire like that of Rome. To this end, Luke depicts the Roman governor Pilate declaring Jesus innocent of any wrongdoing three times (Luke 23, 4.14.22). At the same time

Luke argues in Acts that Christianity is the logical development and proper fulfillment of Judaism and is therefore deserving of the same toleration and freedom traditionally accorded Judaism by Rome (Acts 13, 16–41; 23, 6–9; 24, 10–21; 26, 2–23).

The prominence given to the period of the church in the story has important consequences for Luke's interpretation of the teachings of Jesus. By presenting the time of the church as a distinct phase of salvation history, Luke accordingly shifts the early Christian emphasis away from the expectation of an imminent parousia to the day-to-day concerns of the Christian community in the world. He does this in the gospel by regularly emphasizing the words "each day" (9, 23; cf Mk 8, 34; 11, 3; 16, 19; 19, 47) in the sayings of Jesus. Although Luke still believes the parousia to be a reality that will come unexpectedly (12, 38.45–46), he is more concerned with presenting the words and deeds of Jesus as guides for the conduct of Christian disciples in the interim period between the ascension and the parousia and with presenting Jesus himself as the model of Christian life and piety.

Throughout the gospel, Luke calls upon the Christian disciple to identify with the master Jesus, who is caring and tender toward the poor and lowly, the outcast, the sinner, and the afflicted, toward all those who recognize their dependence on God (4, 18; 6, 20–23; 7, 36–50; 14, 12–14; 15, 1–32; 16, 19–31; 18, 9–14; 19, 1–10; 21, 1–4), but who is severe toward the proud and self-righteous, and particularly toward those who place their material wealth before the service of God and his people (6, 24–26; 12, 13–21; 16, 13–15.19–31; 18, 9–14.15–25; cf 1, 50–53). No gospel writer is more concerned than Luke with the mercy and compassion of Jesus (7, 41–43; 10, 29–37; 13, 6–9; 15, 11–32). No gospel writer is more concerned with the role of the Spirit in the life of Jesus and the Christian disciple (1, 35.41; 2, 25–27; 4, 1.14.18; 10, 21; 11, 13; 24, 49), with the importance of prayer (3, 21; 5, 16; 6, 12; 9, 28; 11, 1–13; 18, 1–8), or with Jesus' concern for women (7, 11–17.36–50; 8, 2–3; 10, 38–42). While Jesus calls all humanity to repent (5, 32; 10, 13; 11, 32; 13, 1–5; 15, 7–10; 16, 30; 17, 3–4; 24, 47), he is particularly demanding of those who would be his disciples. Of them he demands absolute and total detachment from family and material possessions (9, 57–62; 12, 32–34; 14, 25–35). To all who respond in faith and repentance to the word Jesus preaches, he brings salvation (2, 30–32; 3, 6; 7, 50; 8, 48.50; 17, 19; 19, 9) and peace (2, 14; 7, 50; 8, 48; 19, 38.42) and life (10, 25–28; 18, 26–30).

Early Christian tradition, from the late second century on, identifies the author of this gospel and of the Acts of the Apostles as Luke, a Syrian from Antioch, who is mentioned in the New Testament in Col 4, 14, Phlm 24 and 2 Tim 4, 11. The prologue of the gospel makes it clear that Luke is not part of the first generation of Christian disciples but is himself dependent upon the traditions he received from those who were eyewitnesses and ministers of the word (1, 2). His two-volume work marks him as someone who was highly literate both in the Old Testament traditions according to the Greek versions and in Hellenistic Greek writings.

Among the likely sources for the composition of this gospel (1, 3) were the Gospel of Mark, a written collection of sayings of Jesus known also to the author of the Gospel of Matthew (Q; see Introduction to Matthew), and other special traditions that were used by Luke alone among the gospel writers. Some hold that Luke used Mark only as a complementary source for rounding out the material he took from other traditions. Because of its dependence on the Gospel of Mark and because details in Luke's Gospel (13, 35a; 19, 43–44; 21, 20; 23, 28–31) imply that the author was acquainted with the destruction of the city of Jerusalem by the Romans in A.D. 70, the Gospel of Luke is dated by most scholars after that date; many propose A.D. 80–90 as the time of composition.

Luke's consistent substitution of Greek names for the Aramaic or Hebrew names occurring in his sources (e.g., 23, 33 / Mk 15, 22 / 18, 41; Mk 10, 51), his omission from the gospel of specifically Jewish Christian concerns found in his sources (e.g., Mk 7, 1–23), his interest in Gentile Christians (Mk 2, 30–32; 3, 6.38; 4, 16–30; 13, 28–30; 14, 15–24; 17, 11–19; 24, 47–48), and his incomplete knowledge of Palestinian geography, customs, and practices are among the characteristics of this gospel that suggest that Luke was a non-Palestinian writing to a non-Palestinian audience that was largely made up of Gentile Christians.

The principal divisions of the Gospel according to Luke are the following:

I: The Prologue (1, 1–4)

II: The Infancy Narrative (1, 5—2, 52)

III: The Preparation for the Public Ministry (3, 1—4, 13)

IV: The Ministry in Galilee (4, 14—9, 50)

V: The Journey to Jerusalem: Luke's Travel Narrative (9, 51—19, 27)

VI: The Teaching Ministry in Jerusalem (19, 28—21, 38)

VII: The Passion Narrative (22, 1—23, 56)

VIII: The Resurrection Narrative (24, 1–53)

I: The Prologue

CHAPTER 1

See RG 401–2

[1a]*Since many have undertaken to compile a narrative of the events that have been fulfilled among us, [2b]just as those who were eyewitnesses from the beginning and ministers of the word have handed them down to us, [3]I too have decided, after investigating everything accurately anew, to write it down in an orderly sequence for you, most excellent Theophilus, [4]so that you may realize the certainty of the teachings you have received.

1, 1–4: The Gospel according to Luke is the only one of the synoptic gospels to begin with a literary prologue. Making use of a formal, literary construction and vocabulary, the author writes the prologue in imitation of Hellenistic Greek writers and, in so doing, relates his story about Jesus to contemporary Greek and Roman literature. Luke is not only interested in the words and deeds of Jesus, but also in the larger context of the birth, ministry, death, and resurrection of Jesus as the fulfillment of the promises of God in the Old Tes-

tament. As a second- or third-generation Christian, Luke acknowledges his debt to earlier **eyewitnesses** and **ministers of the word,** but claims that his contribution to this developing tradition is a complete and accurate account, told in an orderly manner, and intended to provide **Theophilus** ("friend of God," literally) and other readers with certainty about earlier teachings they have received.

a: Acts 1, 1; 1 Cor 15, 3.　*b:* 24, 48; Jn 15, 27; Acts 1, 21-22.

II: The Infancy Narrative

Announcement of the Birth of John. ^{5c}*In the days of Herod, King of Judea, there was a priest named Zechariah of the priestly division of Abijah; his wife was from the daughters of Aaron, and her name was Elizabeth. ⁶Both were righteous in the eyes of God, observing all the commandments and ordinances of the Lord blamelessly. ^{7d}*But they had no child, because Elizabeth was barren and both were advanced in years. ⁸Once when he was serving as priest in his division's turn before God, ^{9e}according to the practice of the priestly service, he was chosen by lot to enter the sanctuary of the Lord to burn incense. ¹⁰Then, when the whole assembly of the people was praying outside at the hour of the incense offering, ¹¹the angel of the Lord appeared to him, standing at the right of the altar of incense. ¹²Zechariah was troubled by what he saw, and fear came upon him. ^{13f}*But the angel said to him, "Do not be afraid, Zechariah, because your prayer has been heard. Your wife Elizabeth will bear you a son, and you shall name him John. ¹⁴And you will have joy and gladness, and many will rejoice at his birth, ^{15g}*for he will be great in the sight of [the] Lord. He will drink neither wine nor strong drink. He will be filled with the holy Spirit even from his mother's womb, ¹⁶and he will turn many of the children of Israel to the Lord their God. ^{17h}*He will go before him in the spirit and power of Elijah to turn the hearts of fathers toward children and the disobedient to the understanding of the righteous, to prepare a people fit for the Lord." ¹⁸Then Zechariah said to the angel, "How shall I know this? For I am an old man, and my wife is advanced in years." ¹⁹ⁱ*And

1, 5—2, 52: Like the Gospel according to Matthew, this gospel opens with an infancy narrative, a collection of stories about the birth and childhood of Jesus. The narrative uses early Christian traditions about the birth of Jesus, traditions about the birth and circumcision of John the Baptist, and canticles such as the Magnificat (1, 46–55) and Benedictus (1, 67–79), composed of phrases drawn from the Greek Old Testament. It is largely, however, the composition of Luke who writes in imitation of Old Testament birth stories, combining historical and legendary details, literary ornamentation and interpretation of scripture, to answer in advance the question, "Who is Jesus Christ?" The focus of the narrative, therefore, is primarily christological. In this section Luke announces many of the themes that will become prominent in the rest of the gospel: the centrality of Jerusalem and the temple, the journey motif, the universality of salvation, joy and peace, concern for the lowly, the importance of women, the presentation of Jesus as savior, Spirit-guided revelation and prophecy, and the fulfillment of Old Testament promises. The account presents parallel scenes (diptychs) of angelic announcements of the birth of John the Baptist and of Jesus, and of the birth, circumcision, and presentation of John and Jesus. In this parallelism, the ascendency of Jesus over John is stressed: John is prophet of the Most High (1, 76); Jesus is Son of the Most High (1, 32). John is great in the sight of the Lord (1, 15); Jesus will be Great (a LXX attribute, used absolutely, of God) (1, 32). John will go before the Lord (1, 16–17); Jesus will be Lord (1, 43; 2, 11).

1, 5: In the days of Herod, King of Judea: Luke relates the story of salvation history to events in contemporary world history. Here and in 3, 1–2, he connects his narrative with events in Palestinian history; in 2, 1–2 and 3, 1, he casts the Jesus story in the light of events of Roman history. Herod the Great, the son of the Idumean Antipater, was declared "King of Judea" by the Roman Senate in 40 B.C., but became the undisputed ruler of Palestine only in 37 B.C. He continued as king until his death in 4 B.C. **Priestly division of Abijah:** a reference to the eighth

of the twenty-four divisions of priests who, for a week at a time, twice a year, served in the Jerusalem temple.

1, 7: They had no child: though childlessness was looked upon in contemporaneous Judaism as a curse or punishment for sin, it is intended here to present Elizabeth in a situation similar to that of some of the great mothers of important Old Testament figures: Sarah (Gn 15, 3; 16, 1); Rebekah (Gn 25, 21); Rachel (Gn 29, 31; 30, 1); the mother of Samson and wife of Manoah (Jgs 13, 2–3); Hannah (1 Sm 1, 2).

1, 13: Do not be afraid: a stereotyped Old Testament phrase spoken to reassure the recipient of a heavenly vision (Gn 15, 1; Jos 1, 9; Dn 10, 12.19 and elsewhere in 1, 30; 2, 10). **You shall name him John:** the name means "Yahweh has shown favor," an indication of John's role in salvation history.

1, 15: He will drink neither wine nor strong drink: like Samson (Jgs 13, 4–5) and Samuel (1 Sm 1, 11 LXX and 4QSam^a), John is to be consecrated by Nazirite vow and set apart for the Lord's service.

1, 17: He will go before him in the spirit and power of Elijah: John is to be the messenger sent before Yahweh, as described in Mal 3, 1–2. He is cast, moreover, in the role of the Old Testament fiery reformer, the prophet Elijah, who according to Mal 3, 23 (4, 5) is sent before "the great and terrible day of the Lord comes."

1, 19: I am Gabriel: "the angel of the Lord" is identified as Gabriel, the angel who in Dn 9, 20–25 announces the seventy weeks of years and the coming of an anointed one, a prince. By alluding to Old Testament themes in vv 17 and 19, such as the coming of the day of the Lord and the dawning of the messianic era, Luke is presenting his interpretation of the significance of the births of John and Jesus.

c: 1 Chr 24, 10. *d:* Gn 18, 11; Jgs 13, 2-5; 1 Sm 1, 5-6. *e:* Ex 30, 7. *f:* 1, 57.60.63; Mt 1, 20-21. *g:* 7, 33; Nm 6, 1-21; Jgs 13, 4; 1 Sm 1, 11 LXX. *h:* Sir 48, 10; Mal 3, 1; 3, 23-24; Mt 11, 14; 17, 11-13. *i:* Dn 8, 16; 9, 21.

the angel said to him in reply, "I am Gabriel, who stand before God. I was sent to speak to you and to announce to you this good news. [20]j*But now you will be speechless and unable to talk until the day these things take place, because you did not believe my words, which will be fulfilled at their proper time."

[21]Meanwhile the people were waiting for Zechariah and were amazed that he stayed so long in the sanctuary. [22]But when he came out, he was unable to speak to them, and they realized that he had seen a vision in the sanctuary. He was gesturing to them but remained mute. [23]Then, when his days of ministry were completed, he went home. [24]After this time his wife Elizabeth conceived, and she went into seclusion for five months, saying, [25]k"So has the Lord done for me at a time when he has seen fit to take away my disgrace before others."

Announcement of the Birth of Jesus. [26]*In the sixth month, the angel Gabriel was sent from God to a town of Galilee called Nazareth, [27]l to a virgin betrothed to a man named Joseph, of the house of David, and the virgin's name was Mary. [28]mAnd coming to her, he said, "Hail, favored one! The Lord is with you." [29]But she was greatly troubled at what was said and pondered what sort of greeting this might be. [30]Then the angel said to her, "Do not be afraid, Mary, for you have found favor with God. [31]nBehold, you will conceive in your womb and bear a son, and you shall name him Jesus. [32]o*He will be great and will be called Son of the Most High, and the Lord God will give him the throne of David his father, [33]pand he will rule over the house of Jacob forever, and of his kingdom there will be no end." [34]*But Mary said to the angel, "How can this be, since I have no relations with a man?" [35]qAnd the angel said to her in reply, "The holy Spirit will come upon you, and the power of the Most High will overshadow you. Therefore the child to be born will be called holy, the Son of God. [36]*And behold, Elizabeth, your relative, has also conceived a son in her old age, and this is the sixth month for her who was called barren; [37]rfor nothing will be impossible for God." [38]Mary said, "Behold, I am the handmaid of the Lord. May it be done to me according to your word." Then the angel departed from her.

Mary Visits Elizabeth. [39]During those days Mary set out and traveled to the hill country in haste to a town of Judah, [40]where she entered the house of Zechariah and greeted Elizabeth. [41]sWhen Elizabeth heard Mary's greeting, the infant leaped in her womb, and Elizabeth, filled with the holy Spirit, [42]tcried out in a loud voice and said, "Most blessed are you among women, and blessed is the fruit of your womb. [43]*And how does this happen to me, that the mother of my Lord should come to me? [44]For at the moment the sound of your greeting reached my ears, the infant in my womb leaped for joy. [45]u*Blessed are you who be-

---

1, 20: You will be speechless and unable to talk: Zechariah's becoming mute is the sign given in response to his question in v 18. When Mary asks a similar question in 1, 34, unlike Zechariah who was punished for his doubt, she, in spite of her doubt, is praised and reassured (35–37).

1, 26–38: The announcement to Mary of the birth of Jesus is parallel to the announcement to Zechariah of the birth of John. In both the angel Gabriel appears to the parent who is troubled by the vision (11–12.26–29) and then told by the angel not to fear (13.30). After the announcement is made (14–17.31–33) the parent objects (18.34) and a sign is given to confirm the announcement (20.36). The particular focus of the announcement of the birth of Jesus is on his identity as Son of David (32–33) and Son of God (32.35).

1, 32: Son of the Most High: cf 1, 76 where John is described as "prophet of the Most High." "Most High" is a title for God commonly used by Luke (35.76; 6, 35; 8, 28; Acts 7, 48; 16, 17).

1, 34: Mary's questioning response is a denial of sexual relations and is used by Luke to lead to the angel's declaration about the Spirit's role in the conception of this child (35).

According to Luke, the virginal conception of Jesus takes place through the holy Spirit, the power of God, and therefore Jesus has a unique relationship to Yahweh: he is Son of God.

1, 36–37: The sign given to Mary in confirmation of the angel's announcement to her is the pregnancy of her aged relative Elizabeth. If a woman past the childbearing age could become pregnant, why, the angel implies, should there be doubt about Mary's pregnancy, for **nothing will be impossible for God.**

1, 43: Even before his birth, Jesus is identified in Lk as the Lord.

1, 45: Blessed are you who believed: Luke portrays Mary as a believer whose faith stands in contrast to the disbelief of Zechariah (20). Mary's role as believer in the infancy narrative should be seen in connection with the explicit mention of her

j: 1, 45.   k: Gn 30, 23.   l: 2, 5; Mt 1, 16.18.   m: Jgs 6, 12; Ru 2, 4; Jdt 13, 18.   n: Gn 16, 11; Jgs 13, 3; Is 7, 14; Mt 1, 21-23.   o: 2 Sm 7, 12.13.16; Is 9, 7.   p: Dn 2, 44; 7, 14; Mi 4, 7; Mt 28, 18.   q: Mt 1, 20.   r: Gn 18, 14; Jer 32, 27; Mt 19, 26.   s: 1, 15; Gn 25, 22 LXX.   t: 11, 27-28; Jgs 5, 24; Jdt 13, 18; Dt 28, 4.   u: 1, 20.

lieved that what was spoken to you by the Lord would be fulfilled."

The Canticle of Mary. [46][v][w]*And Mary said:

"My soul proclaims the greatness of the
    Lord;
[47] [x]my spirit rejoices in God my savior.
[48] [y]For he has looked upon his handmaid's
    lowliness;
    behold, from now on will all ages call
      me blessed.
[49] [z]The Mighty One has done great things
    for me,
    and holy is his name.
[50] [a]His mercy is from age to age
    to those who fear him.
[51] [b]He has shown might with his arm,
    dispersed the arrogant of mind and
      heart.
[52] [c]He has thrown down the rulers from
    their thrones
    but lifted up the lowly.
[53] [d]The hungry he has filled with good
    things;
    the rich he has sent away empty.
[54] [e]He has helped Israel his servant,
    remembering his mercy,
[55] [f]according to his promise to our fathers,
    to Abraham and to his descendants
      forever."

[56]Mary remained with her about three months and then returned to her home.

The Birth of John. [57]*When the time arrived for Elizabeth to have her child she gave birth to a son. [58][g]Her neighbors and relatives heard that the Lord had shown his great mercy toward her, and they rejoiced with her. [59][h]*When they came on the eighth day to circumcise the child, they were going to call him Zechariah after his father, [60][i]but his mother said in reply, "No. He will be called John." [61]But they answered her, "There is no one among your relatives who has this name." [62]So they made signs, asking his father what he wished him to be called. [63]He asked for a tablet and wrote, "John is his name," and all were amazed. [64][j]Immediately his mouth was opened, his tongue freed, and he spoke blessing God. [65]Then fear came upon all their neighbors, and all these matters were discussed throughout the hill country of Judea. [66]All who heard these things took them to heart, saying, "What, then, will this child be?" For surely the hand of the Lord was with him.

The Canticle of Zechariah. [67]Then Zechariah his father, filled with the holy Spirit, prophesied, saying:

[68] [k]*"Blessed be the Lord, the God of Israel,
    for he has visited and brought
      redemption to his people.

---

presence among "those who believed" after the resurrection at the beginning of the Acts of the Apostles (14).

1, 46–55: Although Mary is praised for being the mother of the Lord and because of her belief, she reacts as the servant in a psalm of praise, the Magnificat. Because there is no specific connection of the canticle to the context of Mary's pregnancy and her visit to Elizabeth, the Magnificat (with the possible exception of v 48) may have been a Jewish Christian hymn that Luke found appropriate at this point in his story. Even if not composed by Luke, it fits in well with themes found elsewhere in Lk: joy and exultation in the Lord; the lowly being singled out for God's favor; the reversal of human fortunes; the fulfillment of Old Testament promises. The loose connection between the hymn and the context is further seen in the fact that a few Old Latin manuscripts identify the speaker of the hymn as Elizabeth, even though the overwhelming textual evidence makes Mary the speaker.

1, 57–66: The birth and circumcision of John above all emphasize John's incorporation into the people of Israel by the sign of the covenant (Gn 17, 1–12). The narrative of John's circumcision also prepares the way for the subsequent description of the circumcision of Jesus in 2, 21. At the beginning of his two-volume work Luke shows those who play crucial roles in the inauguration of Christianity to be wholly

a part of the people of Israel. At the end of the Acts of the Apostles (21, 20; 22, 3; 23, 6–9; 24, 14–16; 26, 2–8.22–23) he will argue that Christianity is the direct descendant of Pharisaic Judaism.

1, 59: The practice of Palestinian Judaism at this time was to name the child at birth; moreover, though naming a male child after the father is not completely unknown, the usual practice was to name the child after the grandfather (see 61). The naming of the child John and Zechariah's recovery from his loss of speech should be understood as fulfilling the angel's announcement to Zechariah in 1, 13 and 20.

1, 68–79: Like the canticle of Mary (46–55) the canticle of Zechariah is only loosely connected with its context. Apart from vv 76–77, the hymn in speaking of **a horn for our sal-**

---

v: 1 Sm 2, 1-10. w: Ps 35, 9; Is 61, 10; Hb 3, 18. x: Ti 3, 4; Jude 25. y: 11, 27; 1 Sm 1, 11; 2 Sm 16, 12; 2 Kgs 14, 26; Ps 113, 7. z: Dt 10, 21; Pss 71, 19; 111, 9; 126, 2-3. a: Pss 89, 2; 103, 13.17. b: Pss 89, 10; 118, 15; Jer 32, 17 (39, 17 LXX). c: 1 Sm 2, 7; 2 Sm 22, 28; Jb 5, 11; 12, 19; Ps 147, 6; Sir 10, 14; Jas 4, 6; 1 Pt 5, 5. d: 1 Sm 2, 5; Ps 107, 9. e: Ps 98, 3; Is 41, 8-9. f: Gn 13, 15; 17, 7; 18, 18; 22, 17-18; Mi 7, 20. g: 1, 14. h: 2, 21; Gn 17, 10.12; Lv 12, 3. i: 1, 13. j: 1, 20. k: 7, 16; Pss 41, 13; 72, 18; 106, 48; 111, 9.

69 *l**He has raised up a horn for our
    salvation
      within the house of David his servant,
70 even as he promised through the mouth
      of his holy prophets from of old:
71   *m*salvation from our enemies and from
    the hand of all who hate us,
72 *no*to show mercy to our fathers
    and to be mindful of his holy covenant
73 *p*and of the oath he swore to Abraham
    our father,
    and to grant us that, 74rescued from the
    hand of enemies,
      without fear we might worship him 75*q*in
    holiness and righteousness
    before him all our days.
76 *r**And you, child, will be called prophet
    of the Most High,
    for you will go before the Lord to
    prepare his ways,
77 to give his people knowledge of salvation
    through the forgiveness of their sins,
78 *st**because of the tender mercy of our God

by which the daybreak from on high
    will visit us
79 to shine on those who sit in darkness and
    death's shadow,
    to guide our feet into the path of
    peace."

80*u*The child grew and became strong in spirit, and he was in the desert until the day of his manifestation to Israel.

CHAPTER 2

See RG
401–3

The Birth of Jesus. *1**In those days a decree went out from Caesar Augustus that the whole world should be enrolled. *2*This was the first enrollment, when Quirinius was governor of Syria. *3*So all went to be enrolled, each to his own town. *4v*And Joseph too went up from Galilee from the town of Nazareth to Judea, to the city of David that is called Bethlehem, because he was of the house and family of David, *5w*to be enrolled with Mary, his betrothed, who was with child. *6*While they

vation (69) and **the daybreak from on high** (78) applies more closely to Jesus and his work than to John. Again like Mary's canticle, it is largely composed of phrases taken from the Greek Old Testament and may have been a Jewish Christian hymn of praise that Luke adapted to fit the present context by inserting vv 76–77 to give Zechariah's reply to the question asked in v 66.

1, 69: A horn for our salvation: the horn is a common Old Testament figure for strength (Pss 18, 3; 75, 5–6; 89, 18; 112, 9; 148, 14). This description is applied to God in Ps 18, 3 and is here transferred to Jesus. The connection of the phrase with **the house of David** gives the title messianic overtones and may indicate an allusion to a phrase in Hannah's song of praise (1 Sm 2, 10), "the horn of his anointed."

1, 76: You will go before the Lord: here **the Lord** is most likely a reference to Jesus (contrast 15–17 where Yahweh is meant) and John is presented as the precursor of Jesus.

1, 78: The daybreak from on high: three times in the LXX (Jer 23, 5; Zec 3, 8; 6, 12), the Greek word used here for **daybreak** translates the Hebrew word for "scion, branch," an Old Testament messianic title.

2, 1–2: Although universal registrations of Roman citizens are attested in 28 B.C., 8 B.C., and A.D. 14 and enrollments in individual provinces of those who are not Roman citizens are also attested, such a universal census of the Roman world under Caesar Augustus is unknown outside the New Testament. Moreover, there are notorious historical problems connected with Luke's dating the census **when Quirinius was governor of Syria,** and the various attempts to resolve the difficulties have proved unsuccessful. P. Sulpicius Quirinius became legate of the province of Syria in A.D. 6–7 when Judea was annexed to the province of Syria. At that time, a provincial census of Judea was taken

up. If Quirinius had been legate of Syria previously, it would have to have been before 10 B.C. because the various legates of Syria from 10 B.C. to 4 B.C. (the death of Herod) are known, and such a dating for an earlier census under Quirinius would create additional problems for dating the beginning of Jesus' ministry (3, 1.23). A previous legateship after 4 B.C. (and before A.D. 6) would not fit with the dating of Jesus' birth in the days of Herod (1, 5; Mt 2, 1). Luke may simply be combining Jesus' birth in Bethlehem with his vague recollection of a census under Quirinius (see also Acts 5, 37) to underline the significance of this birth for the whole Roman world: through this child born in Bethlehem peace and salvation come to the empire.

2, 1: Caesar Augustus: the reign of the Roman emperor Caesar Augustus is usually dated from 27 B.C. to his death in A.D. 14. According to Greek inscriptions, Augustus was regarded in the Roman Empire as "savior" and "god," and he was credited with establishing a time of peace, the **pax Augusta,** throughout the Roman world during his long reign. It is not by chance that Luke relates the birth of Jesus to the time of Caesar Augustus: the real savior (11) and peace-bearer (14; see also 19, 38) is the child born in Bethlehem. The great emperor is simply God's agent (like the Persian king Cyrus in Is 44, 28—45, 1) who provides the occasion for God's purposes to be accomplished. **The whole world:** that is, the whole Roman world: Rome, Italy, and the Roman provinces.

l: Ps 18, 3.   *m:* Ps 106, 10.   *n:* Ps 106, 45-46.   *o:* Gn 17, 7; Lv 26, 42; Ps 105, 8-9; Mi 7, 20.   *p:* Gn 22, 16-17.   *q:* Ti 2, 12. *r:* Is 40, 3; Mal 3, 1; Mt 3, 3; 11, 10.   *s:* Mal 3, 20.   *t:* Is 60, 1-2.   *u:* 2, 40; Mt 3, 1.   *v:* Mi 5, 2; Mt 2, 6.   *w:* 1, 27; Mt 1, 18.

were there, the time came for her to have her child, [7x*]and she gave birth to her firstborn son. She wrapped him in swaddling clothes and laid him in a manger, because there was no room for them in the inn.

[8*]Now there were shepherds in that region living in the fields and keeping the night watch over their flock. [9y]The angel of the Lord appeared to them and the glory of the Lord shone around them, and they were struck with great fear. [10]The angel said to them, "Do not be afraid; for behold, I proclaim to you good news of great joy that will be for all the people. [11z*]For today in the city of David a savior has been born for you who is Messiah and Lord. [12]And this will be a sign for you: you will find an infant wrapped in swaddling clothes and lying in a manger." [13]And suddenly there was a multitude of the heavenly host with the angel, praising God and saying:

[14 a*]"Glory to God in the highest
  and on earth peace to those on whom
    his favor rests."

The Visit of the Shepherds. [15]When the angels went away from them to heaven, the shepherds said to one another, "Let us go, then, to Bethlehem to see this thing that has taken place, which the Lord has made known to us." [16]So they went in haste and found Mary and Joseph, and the infant lying in the manger. [17]When they saw this, they made known the message that had been told them about this child. [18]All who heard it were amazed by what had been told them by the shepherds. [19]And Mary kept all these things, reflecting on them in her heart. [20]Then the shepherds returned, glorifying and praising God for all they had heard and seen, just as it had been told to them.

The Circumcision and Naming of Jesus. [21b*]When eight days were completed for his circumcision, he was named Jesus, the name given him by the angel before he was conceived in the womb.

The Presentation in the Temple. [22c*]When the days were completed for their purification according to the law of Moses, they took him up to Jerusalem to present him to

---

2, 7: Firstborn son: the description of Jesus as **firstborn son** does not necessarily mean that Mary had other sons. It is a legal description indicating that Jesus possessed the rights and privileges of the firstborn son (Gn 27; Ex 13, 2; Nm 3, 12–13; 18, 15–16; Dt 21, 15–17). See the notes on Mt 1, 25 and Mk 6, 3. **Wrapped him in swaddling clothes:** there may be an allusion here to the birth of another descendant of David, his son Solomon, who though a great king was wrapped in swaddling clothes like any other infant (Wis 7, 4–6). **Laid him in a manger:** a feeding trough for animals. A possible allusion to Is 1, 3 LXX.

2, 8–20: The annoucement of Jesus' birth to the shepherds is in keeping with Luke's theme that the lowly are singled out as the recipients of God's favors and blessings (see also 1, 48.52).

2, 11: The basic message of the infancy narrative is contained in the angel's announcement: this child is **savior, Messiah,** and **Lord.** Luke is the only synoptic gospel writer to use the title **savior** for Jesus (11; Acts 5, 31; 13, 23; see also 1, 69; 19, 9; Acts 4, 12). As savior, Jesus is looked upon by Luke as the one who rescues humanity from sin and delivers humanity from the condition of alienation from God. The title **christos,** "Christ," is the Greek equivalent of the Hebrew **māšiah,** "Messiah," "anointed one." Among certain groups in first-century Palestinian Judaism, the title was applied to an expected royal leader from the line of David who would restore the kingdom to Israel (see Acts 1, 6). The political overtones of the title are played down in Lk and instead the Messiah of the Lord (26) or the Lord's anointed is the one who now brings salvation to all humanity, Jew and Gentile (29–32). **Lord** is the most frequently used title for Jesus in Lk and Acts. In the New Testament it is also applied to Yahweh, as it is in the Old Testament. When used of Jesus it points to his transcendence and dominion over humanity.

2, 14: On earth peace to those on whom his favor rests: the peace that results from the Christ event is for those whom God has favored with his grace. This reading is found in the oldest representatives of the Western and Alexandrian text traditions and is the preferred one; the Byzantine text tradition, on the other hand, reads: "on earth peace, good will toward men." The peace of which Luke's gospel speaks (14; 7, 50; 8, 48; 10, 5–6; 19, 38,42; 24, 36) is more than the absence of war of the **pax Augusta;** it also includes the security and well-being characteristic of peace in the Old Testament.

2, 21: Just as John before him had been incorporated into the people of Israel through his circumcision, so too this child (see the note on 1, 57–66).

2, 22–40: The presentation of Jesus in the temple depicts the parents of Jesus as devout Jews, faithful observers of the law of the Lord (23.24.39), i.e., the law of Moses. In this respect, they are described in a fashion similar to the parents of John (1, 6) and Simeon (25) and Anna (36–37).

2, 22: Their purification: syntactically, **their** must refer to Mary and Joseph, even though the Mosaic law never mentions the purification of the husband. Recognizing the problem, some Western scribes have altered the text to read "his purification," understanding the presentation of Jesus in the temple as a form of purification; the Vulgate version has a Latin form that could be either "his" or "her." According to

---

x: Mt 1, 25.   y: 1, 11.26.   z: Mt 1, 21; 16, 16; Jn 4, 42; Acts 2, 36; 5, 31; Phil 2, 11.   a: 19, 38.   b: 1, 31; Gn 17, 12; Mt 1, 21.   c: Lv 12, 2-8.

the Lord, [23d]just as it is written in the law of the Lord, "Every male that opens the womb shall be consecrated to the Lord," [24]and to offer the sacrifice of "a pair of turtledoves or two young pigeons," in accordance with the dictate in the law of the Lord.

[25*]Now there was a man in Jerusalem whose name was Simeon. This man was righteous and devout, awaiting the consolation of Israel, and the holy Spirit was upon him. [26]It had been revealed to him by the holy Spirit that he should not see death before he had seen the Messiah of the Lord. [27]He came in the Spirit into the temple; and when the parents brought in the child Jesus to perform the custom of the law in regard to him, [28]he took him into his arms and blessed God, saying:

[29] "Now, Master, you may let your servant go
  in peace, according to your word,
[30] [e]for my eyes have seen your salvation,
[31] which you prepared in sight of all the peoples,
[32] [f]a light for revelation to the Gentiles,
  and glory for your people Israel."

[33]The child's father and mother were amazed at what was said about him; [34g]and Simeon blessed them and said to Mary his mother, "Behold, this child is destined for the fall and rise of many in Israel, and to be a sign that will be contradicted [35*](and you yourself a sword will pierce) so that the thoughts of many hearts may be revealed." [36]There was also a prophetess, Anna, the daughter of Phanuel, of the tribe of Asher. She was advanced in years, having lived seven years with her husband after her marriage, [37]and then as a widow until she was eighty-four. She never left the temple, but worshiped night and day with fasting and prayer. [38h]And coming forward at that very time, she gave thanks to God and spoke about the child to all who were awaiting the redemption of Jerusalem.

The Return to Nazareth. [39i]When they had fulfilled all the prescriptions of the law of the Lord, they returned to Galilee, to their own town of Nazareth. [40j]The child grew and became strong, filled with wisdom; and the favor of God was upon him.

The Boy Jesus in the Temple. [41k*]Each year his parents went to Jerusalem for the feast of Passover, [42]and when he was twelve years old, they went up according to festival custom. [43]After they had completed its days, as they were returning, the boy Jesus remained behind in Jerusalem, but his parents did not know it. [44]Thinking that he was in the caravan, they journeyed for a day and looked for him among their relatives and acquaintances, [45]but not finding him, they returned to Jerusalem to look for him. [46]After three days they found him in the temple, sitting in the midst of the teachers, listening to them and asking them questions, [47]and all who heard him were astounded at his understand-

---

the Mosaic law (Lv 12, 2–8), the woman who gives birth to a boy is unable for forty days to touch anything sacred or to enter the temple area by reason of her legal impurity. At the end of this period she is required to offer a year-old lamb as a burnt offering and a turtledove or young pigeon as an expiation of sin. The woman who could not afford a lamb offered instead two turtledoves or two young pigeons, as Mary does here. **They took him up to Jerusalem to present him to the Lord:** as the firstborn son (7) Jesus was consecrated to the Lord as the law required (Ex 13, 2.12), but there was no requirement that this be done at the temple. The concept of a presentation at the temple is probably derived from 1 Sm 1, 24–28, where Hannah offers the child Samuel for sanctuary services. The law further stipulated (Nm 3, 47–48) that the firstborn son should be redeemed by the parents through their payment of five shekels to a member of a priestly family. About this legal requirement Luke is silent.

2, 25: Awaiting the consolation of Israel: Simeon here and later Anna who speak about the child to all who were awaiting the redemption of Jerusalem represent the hopes and expectations of faithful and devout Jews who at this time were looking forward to the restoration of God's rule in Israel. The birth of Jesus brings these hopes to fulfillment.

2, 35: (And you yourself a sword will pierce): Mary herself will not be untouched by the various reactions to the role of Jesus (34). Her blessedness as mother of the Lord will be challenged by her son who describes true blessedness as "hearing the word of God and observing it" (11, 27–28 and 8, 20–21).

2, 41–52: This story's concern with an incident from Jesus' youth is unique in the canonical gospel tradition. It presents Jesus in the role of the faithful Jewish boy, raised in the traditions of Israel, and fulfilling all that the law requires. With this episode, the infancy narrative ends just as it began, in the setting of the Jerusalem temple.

d: Ex 13, 2.12. *e:* 3, 6; Is 40, 5 LXX; 52, 10. *f:* Is 42, 6; 46, 13; 49, 6; Acts 13, 47; 26, 23. *g:* 12, 51; Is 8, 14; Jn 9, 39; Rom 9, 33; 1 Cor 1, 23; 1 Pt 2, 7-8. *h:* Is 52, 9. *i:* Mt 2, 23. *j:* 1, 80; 2, 52. *k:* Ex 12, 24-27; 23, 15; Dt 16, 1-8.

ing and his answers. [48]When his parents saw him, they were astonished, and his mother said to him, "Son, why have you done this to us? Your father and I have been looking for you with great anxiety." [49]*And he said to them, "Why were you looking for me? Did you not know that I must be in my Father's house?" [50]But they did not understand what he said to them. [51][l]He went down with them and came to Nazareth, and was obedient to them; and his mother kept all these things in her heart. [52][m]And Jesus advanced [in] wisdom and age and favor before God and man.

III: The Preparation for the Public Ministry

CHAPTER 3

See RG
403–4

The Preaching of John the Baptist.
[1][n]*In the fifteenth year of the reign of Tiberius Caesar, when Pontius Pilate was governor

of Judea, and Herod was tetrarch of Galilee, and his brother Philip tetrarch of the region of Ituraea and Trachonitis, and Lysanias was tetrarch of Abilene, [20]*during the high priesthood of Annas and Caiaphas, the word of God came to John the son of Zechariah in the desert. [3][p]*He went throughout [the] whole region of the Jordan, proclaiming a baptism of repentance for the forgiveness of sins, [4][q][r]*as it is written in the book of the words of the prophet Isaiah:

"A voice of one crying out in the desert:
'Prepare the way of the Lord,
    make straight his paths.
[5] Every valley shall be filled
    and every mountain and hill shall be
        made low.
The winding roads shall be made straight,
    and the rough ways made smooth,
[6] [s]and all flesh shall see the salvation of
        God.' "

2, 49: I must be in my Father's house: this phrase can also be translated, "I must be about my Father's work." In either translation, Jesus refers to God as his Father. His divine sonship, and his obedience to his heavenly Father's will, take precedence over his ties to his family.

3, 1–20: Although Luke is indebted in this section to his sources, the Gospel of Mark and a collection of sayings of John the Baptist, he has clearly marked this introduction to the ministry of Jesus with his own individual style. Just as the gospel began with a long periodic sentence (1, 1–4), so too this section (1–2). He casts the call of John the Baptist in the form of an Old Testament prophetic call (2) and extends the quotation from Isaiah found in Mk 1, 3 (Is 40, 3) by the addition of Is 40, 4–5 in vv 5–6. In doing so, he presents his theme of the universality of salvation, which he has announced earlier in the words of Simeon (2, 30–32). Moreover, in describing the expectation of the people (15), Luke is characterizing the time of John's preaching in the same way as he had earlier described the situation of other devout Israelites in the infancy narrative (2, 25–26.37–38). In vv 7–18 Luke presents the preaching of John the Baptist who urges the crowds to reform in view of **the coming wrath** (7.9: eschatological preaching), and who offers the crowds certain standards for reforming social conduct (10–14: ethical preaching), and who announces to the crowds the coming of **one mightier than** he (15–18: messianic preaching).

3, 1: Tiberius Caesar: Tiberius succeeded Augustus as emperor in A.D. 14 and reigned until A.D. 37. The fifteenth year of his reign, depending on the method of calculating his first regnal year, would have fallen between A.D. 27 and 29. **Pontius Pilate:** prefect of Judea from A.D. 26 to 36. The Jewish historian Josephus describes him as a greedy and ruthless prefect who had little regard for the local Jewish population and their religious practices (see 13, 1). **Herod:** i.e., Herod Antipas, the son of Herod the Great. He ruled over Galilee

and Perea from 4 B.C. to A.D. 39. His official title **tetrarch** means literally, "ruler of a quarter," but came to designate any subordinate prince. **Philip:** also a son of Herod the Great, tetrarch of the territory to the north and east of the Sea of Galilee from 4 B.C. to A.D. 34. Only two small areas of this territory are mentioned by Luke. **Lysanias:** nothing is known about this Lysanias who is said here to have been tetrarch of Abilene, a territory northwest of Damascus.

3, 2: During the high priesthood of Annas and Caiaphas: after situating the call of John the Baptist in terms of the civil rulers of the period, Luke now mentions the religious leadership of Palestine (see the note on 1, 5). Annas had been high priest A.D. 6–15. After being deposed by the Romans in A.D. 15 he was succeeded by various members of his family and eventually by his son-in-law, Caiaphas, who was high priest A.D. 18–36. Luke refers to Annas as high priest at this time (but see Jn 18, 13.19), possibly because of the continuing influence of Annas or because the title continued to be used for the ex-high priest. **The word of God came to John:** Luke is alone among the New Testament writers in associating the preaching of John with a call from God. Luke is thereby identifying John with the prophets whose ministries began with similar calls. In 7, 26 John will be described as "more than a prophet"; he is also the precursor of Jesus (7, 27), a transitional figure inaugurating the period of the fulfillment of prophecy and promise.

3, 3: See the note on Mt 3, 2.

3, 4: The Essenes from Qumran used the same passage to explain why their community was in the desert studying and observing the law and the prophets (1QS 8, 12–15).

l: 2, 19.   *m:* 1, 80; 2, 40; 1 Sm 2, 26.   *n:* Mt 3, 1-12; Mk 1, 1-8; Jn 1, 19-28.   *o:* 1, 80.   *p:* Acts 13, 24; 19, 4.   *q:* Is 40, 3-5. *r:* Jn 1, 23.   *s:* 2, 30-31.

⁷ᵗHe said to the crowds who came out to be baptized by him, "You brood of vipers! Who warned you to flee from the coming wrath? ⁸ᵘProduce good fruits as evidence of your repentance; and do not begin to say to yourselves, 'We have Abraham as our father,' for I tell you, God can raise up children to Abraham from these stones. ⁹ᵛEven now the ax lies at the root of the trees. Therefore every tree that does not produce good fruit will be cut down and thrown into the fire."

¹⁰And the crowds asked him, "What then should we do?" ¹¹He said to them in reply, "Whoever has two cloaks should share with the person who has none. And whoever has food should do likewise." ¹²ʷEven tax collectors came to be baptized and they said to him, "Teacher, what should we do?" ¹³He answered them, "Stop collecting more than what is prescribed." ¹⁴Soldiers also asked him, "And what is it that we should do?" He told them, "Do not practice extortion, do not falsely accuse anyone, and be satisfied with your wages."

¹⁵ˣNow the people were filled with expectation, and all were asking in their hearts whether John might be the Messiah. ¹⁶ʸ*John answered them all, saying, "I am baptizing you with water, but one mightier than I is coming. I am not worthy to loosen the thongs of his sandals. He will baptize you with the holy Spirit and fire. ¹⁷ᶻ*His winnowing fan is in his hand to clear his threshing floor and to gather the wheat into his barn, but the chaff he will burn with unquenchable fire." ¹⁸Exhorting them in many other ways, he preached good news to the people. ¹⁹ᵃ*Now Herod the tetrarch, who had been censured by him because of Herodias, his brother's wife, and because of all the evil deeds Herod had committed, ²⁰added still another to these by [also] putting John in prison.

The Baptism of Jesus. ²¹ᵇ*After all the people had been baptized and Jesus also had been baptized and was praying, heaven was opened ²²ᶜ*and the holy Spirit descended upon him in bodily form like a dove. And a voice came from heaven, "You are my beloved Son; with you I am well pleased."

The Genealogy of Jesus. ²³ᵈᵉ*When Jesus began his ministry he was about thirty years of age. He was the son, as was thought, of Joseph, the son of Heli, ²⁴the son of Matthat, the son of Levi, the son of Melchi, the son of Jannai, the son of Joseph, ²⁵the son of Mattathias, the son of Amos, the son of Nahum, the son of Esli, the son of Naggai, ²⁶the son of Maath, the son of Mattathias, the son of Semein, the son of Josech, the son of Joda,

3, 16: He will baptize you with the holy Spirit and fire: in contrast to John's baptism with water, Jesus is said to baptize with the holy Spirit and with fire. From the point of view of the early Christian community, the Spirit and fire must have been understood in the light of the fire symbolism of the pouring out of the Spirit at Pentecost (Acts 2, 1–4); but as part of John's preaching, the Spirit and fire should be related to their purifying and refining characteristics (Ez 36, 25–27; Mal 3, 2–3). See the note on Mt 3, 11.

3, 17: Winnowing fan: see the note on Mt 3, 12.

3, 19–20: Luke separates the ministry of John the Baptist from that of Jesus by reporting the imprisonment of John before the baptism of Jesus (21–22). Luke uses this literary device to serve his understanding of the periods of salvation history. With John the Baptist, the time of promise, the period of Israel, comes to an end; with the baptism of Jesus and the descent of the Spirit upon him, the time of fulfillment, the period of Jesus, begins. In his second volume, the Acts of the Apostles, Luke will introduce the third epoch in salvation history, the period of the church.

3, 21–22: This episode in Luke focuses on the heavenly message identifying Jesus as **Son** and, through the allusion to Is 42, 1, as Servant of Yahweh. The relationship of Jesus to the Father has already been announced in the infancy narrative (1, 32.35; 2, 49); it occurs here at the beginning of Jesus'

Galilean ministry and will reappear in 9, 35 before another major section of Luke's gospel, the travel narrative (9, 51—19, 27). Elsewhere in Luke's writings (4, 18; Acts 10, 38), this incident will be interpreted as a type of anointing of Jesus.

3, 21: Was praying: Luke regularly presents Jesus at prayer at important points in his ministry: here at his baptism; at the choice of the Twelve (6, 12); before Peter's confession (9, 18); at the transfiguration (9, 28); when he teaches his disciples to pray (11, 1); at the Last Supper (22, 32); on the Mount of Olives (22, 41); on the cross (23, 46).

3, 22: You are my beloved Son; with you I am well pleased: this is the best attested reading in the Greek manuscripts. The Western reading, "You are my Son, this day I have begotten you," is derived from Ps 2, 7.

3, 23–38: Whereas Mt 1, 2 begins the genealogy of Jesus with Abraham to emphasize Jesus' bonds with the people of Israel, Luke's universalism leads him to trace the descent of Jesus beyond Israel to Adam and beyond that to God (38) to stress again Jesus' divine sonship.

t: Mt 12, 34. *u:* Jn 8, 39. *v:* Mt 7, 19; Jn 15, 6. *w:* 7, 29. *x:* Acts 13, 25. *y:* 7, 19-20; Jn 1, 27; Acts 1, 5; 11, 16. *z:* Mt 3, 12. *a:* Mt 14, 3-4; Mk 6, 17-18. *b:* Mt 3, 13-17; Mk 1, 9-11. *c:* 9, 35; Ps 2, 7; Is 42, 1; Mt 12, 18; 17, 5; Mk 9, 7; Jn 1, 32; 2 Pt 1, 17. *d:* Mt 1, 1-17. *e:* 4, 22; Jn 6, 42.

[27f]the son of Joanan, the son of Rhesa, the son of Zerubbabel, the son of Shealtiel, the son of Neri, [28]the son of Melchi, the son of Addi, the son of Cosam, the son of Elmadam, the son of Er, [29]the son of Joshua, the son of Eliezer, the son of Jorim, the son of Matthat, the son of Levi, [30]the son of Simeon, the son of Judah, the son of Joseph, the son of Jonam, the son of Eliakim, [31ghi*]the son of Melea, the son of Menna, the son of Mattatha, the son of Nathan, the son of David, [32]the son of Jesse, the son of Obed, the son of Boaz, the son of Sala, the son of Nahshon, [33j]the son of Amminadab, the son of Admin, the son of Arni, the son of Hezron, the son of Perez, the son of Judah, [34kl]the son of Jacob, the son of Isaac, the son of Abraham, the son of Terah, the son of Nahor, [35]the son of Serug, the son of Reu, the son of Peleg, the son of Eber, the son of Shelah, [36m]the son of Cainan, the son of Arphaxad, the son of Shem, the son of Noah, the son of Lamech, [37]the son of Methuselah, the son of Enoch, the son of Jared, the son of Mahalaleel, the son of Cainan, [38]the son of Enos, the son of Seth, the son of Adam, the son of God.

CHAPTER 4

See RG
403–4

The Temptation of Jesus. [1n*]Filled with the holy Spirit, Jesus returned from the Jordan and was led by the Spirit into the desert [2o*]for forty days, to be tempted by the devil. He ate nothing during those days, and when they were over he was hungry. [3]The devil said to him, "If you are the Son of God, command this stone to become bread." [4p]Jesus answered him, "It is written, 'One does not live by bread alone.' " [5]Then he took him up and showed him all the kingdoms of the world in a single instant. [6q]The devil said to him, "I shall give to you all this power and their glory; for it has been handed over to me, and I may give it to whomever I wish. [7]All this will be yours, if you worship me." [8r]Jesus said to him in reply, "It is written:

'You shall worship the Lord, your God,
    and him alone shall you serve.' "

[9*]Then he led him to Jerusalem, made him stand on the parapet of the temple, and said to him, "If you are the Son of God, throw yourself down from here, [10s]for it is written:

'He will command his angels concerning
        you,
    to guard you,'

[11t]and:

'With their hands they will support you,
    lest you dash your foot against a
        stone.' "

[12u]Jesus said to him in reply, "It also says, 'You shall not put the Lord, your God, to the test.' " [13v*]When the devil had finished every temptation, he departed from him for a time.

IV: The Ministry in Galilee

The Beginning of the Galilean Ministry. [14wx*]Jesus returned to Galilee in the power of the Spirit, and news of him spread throughout the whole region. [15]He taught in their synagogues and was praised by all.

3, 31: The son of Nathan, the son of David: in keeping with Jesus' prophetic role in Lk and Acts (e.g., 7, 16.39; 9, 8; 13, 33; 24, 19; Acts 3, 22–23; 7, 37) Luke traces Jesus' Davidic ancestry through the prophet Nathan (see 2 Sm 7, 2) rather than through King Solomon, as Mt 1, 6–7.

4, 1–13: See the note on Mt 4, 1–11.

4, 1: Filled with the holy Spirit: as a result of the descent of the Spirit upon him at his baptism (3, 21–22), Jesus is now equipped to overcome the devil. Just as the Spirit is prominent at this early stage of Jesus' ministry (1.14.18), so too it will be at the beginning of the period of the church in Acts (Acts 1, 4; 2, 4.17).

4, 2: For forty days: the mention of forty days recalls the forty years of the wilderness wanderings of the Israelites during the Exodus (Dt 8, 2).

4, 9: To Jerusalem: the Lucan order of the temptations

concludes on the parapet of the temple in Jerusalem, the city of destiny in Luke-Acts. It is in Jerusalem that Jesus will ultimately face his destiny (9, 51; 13, 33).

4, 13: For a time: the devil's opportune time will occur before the passion and death of Jesus (Lk 22, 3.31–32.53).

4, 14: News of him spread: a Lucan theme; see v 37; 5, 15; 7, 17.

f: 1 Chr 3, 17; Ez 3, 2.   g: 2 Sm 5, 14.   h: 1 Sm 16, 1.18.   i: Ru 4, 17-22; 1 Chr 2, 1-15.   j: Gn 29, 35; 38, 29.   k: Gn 21, 3; 25, 26; 1 Chr 1, 34; 28, 34.   l: Gn 11, 10-26; 1 Chr 1, 24-27.   m: Gn 4, 25—5, 32; 1 Chr 1, 1-4.   n: Mt 4, 1-11; Mk 1, 12-13.   o: Heb 4, 15.   p: Dt 8, 3.   q: Jer 27, 5; Mt 28, 18.   r: Dt 6, 13.   s: Ps 91, 11.   t: Ps 91, 12.   u: Dt 6, 16; 1 Cor 10, 9.   v: 22, 3; Jn 13, 2.27; Heb 4, 15.   w: Mt 4, 12-17; Mk 1, 14-15.   x: 5, 15; Mt 3, 16.

The Rejection at Nazareth. [16y]*He came to Nazareth, where he had grown up, and went according to his custom into the synagogue on the sabbath day. He stood up to read [17]and was handed a scroll of the prophet Isaiah. He unrolled the scroll and found the passage where it was written:

[18] [z]*"The Spirit of the Lord is upon me,
    because he has anointed me
      to bring glad tidings to the poor.
  He has sent me to proclaim liberty to
      captives
    and recovery of sight to the blind,
      to let the oppressed go free,
[19] and to proclaim a year acceptable to the
      Lord."

[20]Rolling up the scroll, he handed it back to the attendant and sat down, and the eyes of all in the synagogue looked intently at him. [21]*He said to them, "Today this scripture passage is fulfilled in your hearing." [22a]And all spoke highly of him and were amazed at the gracious words that came from his mouth. They also asked, "Isn't this the son of Joseph?" [23]*He said to them, "Surely you will quote me this proverb, 'Physician, cure yourself,' and say, 'Do here in your native place the things that we heard were done in Capernaum.' " [24]And he said, "Amen, I say to you, no prophet is accepted in his own native place. [25b]*Indeed, I tell you, there were many widows in Israel in the days of Elijah when the sky was closed for three and a half years and a severe famine spread over the entire land. [26c]*It was to none of these that Elijah was sent, but only to a widow in Zarephath in the land of Sidon. [27d]Again, there were many lepers in Israel during the time of Elisha the prophet; yet not one of them was cleansed, but only Naaman the Syrian." [28]When the people in the synagogue heard this, they were all filled with fury. [29]They rose up, drove him out of the town, and led him to the brow of the hill on which their town had been built, to hurl him down headlong. [30]But he passed through the midst of them and went away.

The Cure of a Demoniac. [31ef]*Jesus then went down to Capernaum, a town of Galilee. He taught them on the sabbath, [32g]and they were astonished at his teaching because he

---

4, 16–30: Luke has transposed to the beginning of Jesus' ministry an incident from his Marcan source, which situated it near the end of the Galilean ministry (Mk 6, 1–6a). In doing so, Luke turns the initial admiration (22) and subsequent rejection of Jesus (28–29) into a foreshadowing of the whole future ministry of Jesus. Moreover, the rejection of Jesus in his own hometown hints at the greater rejection of him by Israel (Acts 13, 46).

4, 16: According to his custom: Jesus' practice of regularly attending synagogue is carried on by the early Christians' practice of meeting in the temple (Acts 2, 46; 3, 1; 5, 12).

4, 18: The Spirit of the Lord is upon me, because he has anointed me: see the note on 3, 21–22. As this incident develops, Jesus is portrayed as a prophet whose ministry is compared to that of the prophets Elijah and Elisha. Prophetic anointings are known in first-century Palestinian Judaism from the Qumran literature that speaks of prophets as God's anointed ones. **To bring glad tidings to the poor:** more than any other gospel writer Luke is concerned with Jesus' attitude toward the economically and socially poor (see 6, 20.24; 12, 16–21; 14, 12–14; 16, 19–26; 19, 8). At times, the poor in Luke's gospel are associated with the downtrodden, the oppressed and afflicted, the forgotten and the neglected (18; 6, 20–22; 7, 22; 14, 12–14), and it is they who accept Jesus' message of salvation.

4, 21: Today this scripture passage is fulfilled in your hearing: this sermon inaugurates the time of fulfillment of Old Testament prophecy. Luke presents the ministry of Jesus as fulfilling Old Testament hopes and expectations (7, 22); for

Luke, even Jesus' suffering, death, and resurrection are done in fulfillment of the scriptures (24, 25–27.44–46; Acts 3, 18).

4, 23: The things that we heard were done in Capernaum: Luke's source for this incident reveals an awareness of an earlier ministry of Jesus in Capernaum that Luke has not yet made use of because of his transposition of this Nazareth episode to the beginning of Jesus' Galilean ministry. It is possible that by use of the future tense **you** will quote me. . . , Jesus is being portrayed as a prophet.

4, 25–26: The references to Elijah and Elisha serve several purposes in this episode: they emphasize Luke's portrait of Jesus as a prophet like Elijah and Elisha; they help to explain why the initial admiration of the people turns to rejection; and they provide the scriptural justification for the future Christian mission to the Gentiles.

4, 26: A widow in Zarephath in the land of Sidon: like Naaman the Syrian in v 27, a non-Israelite becomes the object of the prophet's ministry.

4, 31–44: The next several incidents in Jesus' ministry take place in Capernaum and are based on Luke's source, Mk 1, 21–39. To the previous portrait of Jesus as prophet (16–30) they now add a presentation of him as teacher (31–32), exorcist (32–37.41), healer (38–40), and proclaimer of God's kingdom (43).

y: Mt 13, 53-58; Mk 6, 1-6. *z:* Is 61, 1-2; 58, 6. *a:* 3, 23; Jn 6, 42. *b:* 1 Kgs 17, 1-7; 18, 1; Jas 5, 17. *c:* 1 Kgs 17, 9. *d:* 2 Kgs 5, 1-14. *e:* Mk 1, 21-28. *f:* Mt 4, 13; Jn 2, 12. *g:* Mt 7, 28-29.

spoke with authority. *33h*In the synagogue there was a man with the spirit of an unclean demon, and he cried out in a loud voice, *34i**"Ha! What have you to do with us, Jesus of Nazareth? Have you come to destroy us? I know who you are—the Holy One of God!" *35*Jesus rebuked him and said, "Be quiet! Come out of him!" Then the demon threw the man down in front of them and came out of him without doing him any harm. *36*They were all amazed and said to one another, "What is there about his word? For with authority and power he commands the unclean spirits, and they come out." *37*And news of him spread everywhere in the surrounding region.

The Cure of Simon's Mother-in-Law. *38j**After he left the synagogue, he entered the house of Simon. Simon's mother-in-law was afflicted with a severe fever, and they interceded with him about her. *39*He stood over her, rebuked the fever, and it left her. She got up immediately and waited on them.

Other Healings. *40k*At sunset, all who had people sick with various diseases brought them to him. He laid his hands on each of them and cured them. *41l**And demons also came out from many, shouting, "You are the Son of God." But he rebuked them and did not allow them to speak because they knew that he was the Messiah.

Jesus Leaves Capernaum. *42m**At daybreak, Jesus left and went to a deserted place. The crowds went looking for him, and when they came to him, they tried to prevent him from leaving them. *43n*But he said to them, "To the other towns also I must proclaim the good news of the kingdom of God, because for this purpose I have been sent." *44**And he was preaching in the synagogues of Judea.

CHAPTER 5

See RG
404-5

The Call of Simon the Fisherman. *1op**While the crowd was pressing in on Jesus and listening to the word of God, he was standing by the Lake of Gennesaret. *2*He saw two boats there alongside the lake; the fishermen had disembarked and were washing their nets. *3*Getting into one of the boats, the one belonging to Simon, he asked him to put out a short distance from the shore. Then he sat down and taught the crowds from the boat. *4q*After he had finished speaking, he said to Simon, "Put out into deep water and lower your nets for a catch." *5*Simon said in reply, "Master, we have worked hard all night and have caught nothing, but at your command I will lower the nets." *6*When they

---

4, 34: What have you to do with us?: see the note on Jn 2, 4. **Have you come to destroy us?:** the question reflects the current belief that before the day of the Lord control over humanity would be wrested from the evil spirits, evil destroyed, and God's authority over humanity reestablished. The synoptic gospel tradition presents Jesus carrying out this task.

4, 38: The house of Simon: because of Luke's arrangement of material, the reader has not yet been introduced to Simon (cf Mk 1, 16–18.29–31). Situated as it is before the call of Simon (5, 1–11), it helps the reader to understand Simon's eagerness to do what Jesus says (5, 5) and to follow him (5, 11).

4, 41: They knew that he was the Messiah: that is, the Christ (see the note on 2, 11).

4, 42: They tried to prevent him from leaving them: the reaction of these strangers in Capernaum is presented in contrast to the reactions of those in his hometown who rejected him (28–30).

4, 44: In the synagogues of Judea: instead of **Judea,** which is the best reading of the manuscript tradition, the Byzantine text tradition and other manuscripts read "Galilee," a reading that harmonizes Lk with Mt 4, 23 and Mk 1, 39. Up to this point Luke has spoken only of a ministry of Jesus in Galilee. Luke may be using **Judea** to refer to the land of Israel, the territory of the Jews, and not to a specific portion of it.

5, 1–11: This incident has been transposed from his source, Mk 1, 16–20, which places it immediately after Jesus makes his appearance in Galilee. By this transposition Luke uses this example of Simon's acceptance of Jesus to counter the earlier rejection of him by his hometown people, and since several incidents dealing with Jesus' power and authority have already been narrated, Luke creates a plausible context for the acceptance of Jesus by Simon and his partners. Many commentators have noted the similarity between the wondrous catch of fish reported here (4–9) and the post-resurrectional appearance of Jesus in Jn 21, 1–11. There are traces in Luke's story that the post-resurrectional context is the original one: in v 8 Simon addresses Jesus as **Lord** (a post-resurrectional title for Jesus—see 24, 34; Acts 2, 36— that has been read back into the historical ministry of Jesus) and recognizes himself as a sinner (an appropriate recognition for one who has denied knowing Jesus—22, 54–62). As used by Luke, the incident looks forward to Peter's leadership in Luke-Acts (6, 14; 9, 20; 22, 31–32; 24, 34; Acts 1, 15; 2, 14–40; 10, 11–18; 15, 7–12) and symbolizes the future success of Peter as fisherman (Acts 2, 41).

---

h: 8, 28; Mt 8, 29; Mk 1, 23-24; 5, 7. *i:* 4, 41; Jn 6, 69. *j:* Mt 8, 14-15; Mk 1, 29-31. *k:* Mt 8, 16; Mk 1, 32-34. *l:* 4, 34; Mt 8, 29; Mk 3, 11-12. *m:* Mk 1, 35-39. *n:* 8, 1; Mk 1, 14-15. *o:* Mt 4, 18-22; Mk 1, 16-20. *p:* Mt 13, 1-2; Mk 2, 13; 3, 9-10; 4, 1-2. *q:* Jn 21, 1-11.

had done this, they caught a great number of fish and their nets were tearing. *7*They signaled to their partners in the other boat to come to help them. They came and filled both boats so that they were in danger of sinking. *8*When Simon Peter saw this, he fell at the knees of Jesus and said, "Depart from me, Lord, for I am a sinful man." *9*For astonishment at the catch of fish they had made seized him and all those with him, *10r*and likewise James and John, the sons of Zebedee, who were partners of Simon. Jesus said to Simon, "Do not be afraid; from now on you will be catching men." *11s**When they brought their boats to the shore, they left everything and followed him.

The Cleansing of a Leper. *12t**Now there was a man full of leprosy in one of the towns where he was; and when he saw Jesus, he fell prostrate, pleaded with him, and said, "Lord, if you wish, you can make me clean." *13*Jesus stretched out his hand, touched him, and said, "I do will it. Be made clean." And the leprosy left him immediately. *14u**Then he ordered him not to tell anyone, but "Go, show yourself to the priest and offer for your cleansing what Moses prescribed; that will be proof for them." *15*The report about him spread all the more, and great crowds assembled to listen to him and to be cured of their ailments, *16v*but he would withdraw to deserted places to pray.

The Healing of a Paralytic. *17w**One day as Jesus was teaching, Pharisees and teachers of the law were sitting there who had come from every village of Galilee and Judea and Jerusalem, and the power of the Lord was with him for healing. *18*And some men brought on a stretcher a man who was paralyzed; they were trying to bring him in and set [him] in his presence. *19**But not finding a way to bring him in because of the crowd, they went up on the roof and lowered him on the stretcher through the tiles into the middle in front of Jesus. *20**When he saw their faith, he said, "As for you, your sins are forgiven." *21x**Then the scribes and Pharisees began to ask themselves, "Who is this who speaks blasphemies? Who but God alone can forgive sins?" *22y*Jesus knew their thoughts and said to them in reply, "What are you thinking in your hearts? *23*Which is easier, to say, 'Your sins are forgiven,' or to say, 'Rise and walk'? *24z**But that you may know that the Son of Man has authority on earth to forgive sins"—he said to the man who was paralyzed, "I say to you, rise, pick up your stretcher, and go home." *25*He stood up immediately before them, picked up what he had been lying on, and went home, glorifying God. *26*Then astonishment seized them all and they glorified God, and, struck with awe, they said, "We have seen incredible things today."

The Call of Levi. *27a*After this he went out and saw a tax collector named Levi sitting at the customs post. He said to him, "Follow me." *28**And leaving everything behind, he

---

5, 11: They left everything: in Mk 1, 16–20 and Mt 4, 18–22 the fishermen who follow Jesus leave their nets and their father; in Luke, they leave **everything** (see also 28; 12, 33; 14, 33; 18, 22), an indication of Luke's theme of complete detachment from material possessions.

5, 12: Full of leprosy: see the note on Mk 1, 40.

5, 14: Show yourself to the priest . . . what Moses prescribed: this is a reference to Lv 14, 2–9 that gives detailed instructions for the purification of one who had been a victim of leprosy and thereby excluded from contact with others (see Lv 13, 45–46.49; Nm 5, 2–3). **That will be proof for them:** see the note on Mt 8, 4.

5, 17—6, 11: From his Marcan source, Luke now introduces a series of controversies with Pharisees: controversy over Jesus' power to forgive sins (17–26); controversy over his eating and drinking with tax collectors and sinners (27–32); controversy over not fasting (33–36); and finally two episodes narrating controversies over observance of the sabbath (1–11).

5, 17: Pharisees: see the note on Mt 3, 7.

5, 19: Through the tiles: Luke has adapted the story found in Mk to his non-Palestinian audience by changing "opened up the roof" (Mk 2, 4, a reference to Palestinian straw and clay roofs) to **through the tiles,** a detail that reflects the Hellenistic Greco-Roman house with tiled roof.

5, 20: As for you, your sins are forgiven: literally, "O man, your sins are forgiven you." The connection between the forgiveness of sins and the cure of the paralytic reflects the belief of first-century Palestine (based on the Old Testament: Ex 20, 5; Dt 5, 9) that sickness and infirmity are the result of sin, one's own or that of one's ancestors (see also 13, 2; Jn 5, 14; 9, 2).

5, 21: The scribes: see the note on Mk 2, 6.

5, 24: See the notes on Mt 9, 6 and Mk 2, 10.

5, 28: Leaving everything behind: see the note on 5, 11.

r: Jer 16, 16.　s: Mt 19, 27.　t: Mt 8, 2-4; Mk 1, 40-45.　u: 8, 56; Lv 14, 2-32; Mk 7, 36.　v: Mk 1, 35.　w: Mt 9, 1-8; Mk 2, 1-12.　x: 7, 49; Is 43, 25.　y: 6, 8; 9, 47.　z: Jn 5, 8-9.27.　a: Mt 9, 9-13; Mk 2, 13-17.

got up and followed him. *29b* Then Levi gave a great banquet for him in his house, and a large crowd of tax collectors and others were at table with them. *30* The Pharisees and their scribes complained to his disciples, saying, "Why do you eat and drink with tax collectors and sinners?" *31* Jesus said to them in reply, "Those who are healthy do not need a physician, but the sick do. *32* I have not come to call the righteous to repentance but sinners."

The Question about Fasting. *33c* And they said to him, "The disciples of John fast often and offer prayers, and the disciples of the Pharisees do the same; but yours eat and drink." *34* *Jesus answered them, "Can you make the wedding guests fast while the bridegroom is with them? *35* But the days will come, and when the bridegroom is taken away from them, then they will fast in those days." *36* *And he also told them a parable. "No one tears a piece from a new cloak to patch an old one. Otherwise, he will tear the new and the piece from it will not match the old cloak. *37* Likewise, no one pours new wine into old wineskins. Otherwise, the new wine will burst the skins, and it will be spilled, and the skins will be ruined. *38* Rather, new wine must be poured into fresh wineskins. *39* *[And] no one who has been drinking old wine desires new, for he says, 'The old is good.' "

See RG 405

CHAPTER 6

Debates about the Sabbath. *1de* *While he was going through a field of grain on a sabbath, his disciples were picking the heads of grain, rubbing them in their hands, and eating them. *2* Some Pharisees said, "Why are you doing what is unlawful on the sabbath?" *3f* Jesus said to them in reply, "Have you not read what David did when he and those [who were] with him were hungry? *4g* *[How] he went into the house of God, took the bread of offering, which only the priests could lawfully eat, ate of it, and shared it with his companions." *5* Then he said to them, "The Son of Man is lord of the sabbath."

6h On another sabbath he went into the synagogue and taught, and there was a man there whose right hand was withered. *7i* The scribes and the Pharisees watched him closely to see if he would cure on the sabbath so that they might discover a reason to accuse him. *8j* But he realized their intentions and said to the man with the withered hand, "Come up and stand before us." And he rose and stood there. *9* Then Jesus said to them, "I ask you, is it lawful to do good on the sabbath rather than to do evil, to save life rather than to destroy it?" *10* Looking around at them all, he then said to him, "Stretch out your hand." He did so and his hand was restored. *11* But they became enraged and discussed together what they might do to Jesus.

The Mission of the Twelve. *12k* *In those days he departed to the mountain to pray, and he spent the night in prayer to God. *13* *When day came, he called his disciples to himself, and from them he chose Twelve,

5, 34–35: See the notes on Mt 9, 15 and Mk 2, 19.

5, 34: **Wedding guests:** literally, "sons of the bridal chamber."

5, 36–39: See the notes on Mt 9, 16–17 and Mk 2, 19.

5, 39: **The old is good:** this saying is meant to be ironic and offers an explanation for the rejection by some of the new wine that Jesus offers: satisfaction with old forms will prevent one from sampling the new.

6, 1–11: The two episodes recounted here deal with gathering grain and healing, both of which were forbidden on the sabbath. In his defense of his disciples' conduct and his own charitable deed, Jesus argues that satisfying human needs such as hunger and performing works of mercy take precedence even over the sacred sabbath rest. See also the notes on Mt 12, 1–14 and Mk 2, 25–26.

6, 4: **The bread of offering:** see the note on Mt 12, 5–6.

6, 12–16: See the notes on Mt 10, 1—11, 1 and Mk 3, 14–15.

6, 12: **Spent the night in prayer:** see the note on 3, 21.

6, 13: **He chose Twelve:** the identification of this group as the **Twelve** is a part of early Christian tradition (see 1 Cor 15, 5), and in Mt and Lk the Twelve are associated with the twelve tribes of Israel (22, 29–30; Mt 19, 28). After the fall of Judas from his position among the Twelve, the need is felt on the part of the early community to reconstitute this group before the Christian mission begins at Pentecost (Acts 1, 15–26). From Luke's perspective, they are an important group who because of their association with Jesus from the time of his baptism to his ascension (Acts 1, 21–22) provide the continuity between the historical Jesus and the church of Luke's day and who as the original eyewitnesses guarantee the fidelity of the church's beliefs and practices to the teachings of Jesus (1, 1–4). **Whom he also named apostles:** only Luke among the gospel writers attributes to Jesus the bestowal of the name **apostles** upon the Twelve. See the note on

b: 15, 1-2.   *c:* Mt 9, 14-17; Mk 2, 18-22.   *d:* Mt 12, 1-8; Mk 2, 23-28.   *e:* Dt 23, 26.   *f:* 1 Sm 21, 1-6.   *g:* Lv 24, 5-9.   *h:* Mt 12, 9-14; Mk 3, 1-6.   *i:* 14, 1.   *j:* 5, 22; 9, 47.   *k:* Mt 10, 1-4; Mk 3, 13-19.

whom he also named apostles: [141]*Simon, whom he named Peter, and his brother Andrew, James, John, Philip, Bartholomew, [15]*Matthew, Thomas, James the son of Alphaeus, Simon who was called a Zealot, [16]*and Judas the son of James, and Judas Iscariot, who became a traitor.

Ministering to a Great Multitude. [17m]*And he came down with them and stood on a stretch of level ground. A great crowd of his disciples and a large number of the people from all Judea and Jerusalem and the coastal region of Tyre and Sidon [18]came to hear him and to be healed of their diseases; and even those who were tormented by unclean spirits were cured. [19]Everyone in the crowd sought to touch him because power came forth from him and healed them all.

Sermon on the Plain. [20n]*And raising his eyes toward his disciples he said:

"Blessed are you who are poor,
    for the kingdom of God is yours.
[21] [o]Blessed are you who are now hungry,
    for you will be satisfied.

Blessed are you who are now weeping,
    for you will laugh.
[22] [p]Blessed are you when people hate you,
    and when they exclude and insult you,
    and denounce your name as evil
    on account of the Son of Man.

[23q]Rejoice and leap for joy on that day! Behold, your reward will be great in heaven. For their ancestors treated the prophets in the same way.

[24] [r]But woe to you who are rich,
    for you have received your
        consolation.
[25] [s]But woe to you who are filled now,
    for you will be hungry.
Woe to you who laugh now,
    for you will grieve and weep.
[26] [t]Woe to you when all speak well of you,
    for their ancestors treated the false
        prophets in this way.

Love of Enemies. [27uv]*"But to you who hear I say, love your enemies, do good to those who hate you, [28w]bless those who curse you, pray for those who mistreat you.

Mt 10, 2–4. "Apostle" becomes a technical term in early Christianity for a missionary sent out to preach the word of God. Although Luke seems to want to restrict the title to the Twelve (only in Acts 4, 4.14 are Paul and Barnabas termed apostles), other places in the New Testament show an awareness that the term was more widely applied (1 Cor 15, 5–7; Gal 1, 19; 1 Cor 1, 1; 9, 1; Rom 16, 7).

6, 14: Simon, whom he named Peter: see the note on Mk 3, 16.

6, 15: Simon who was called a Zealot: the Zealots were the instigators of the First Revolt of Palestinian Jews against Rome in A.D. 66–70. Because the existence of the Zealots as a distinct group during the lifetime of Jesus is the subject of debate, the meaning of the identification of Simon as a Zealot is unclear.

6, 16: Judas Iscariot: the name **Iscariot** may mean "man from Kerioth."

6, 17: The coastal region of Tyre and Sidon: not only Jews from Judea and Jerusalem, but even Gentiles from outside Palestine come to hear Jesus (see 2, 31–32; 3, 6; 4, 24–27).

6, 20–49: Luke's "Sermon on the Plain" is the counterpart to Mt's "Sermon on the Mount" (Mt 5, 1—7, 27). It is addressed to the disciples of Jesus, and, like the sermon in Mt, it begins with beatitudes (20–22) and ends with the parable of the two houses (46–49). Almost all the words of Jesus reported by Lk are found in Mt's version, but because Mt includes sayings that were related to specifically Jewish Christian problems (e.g., Mt 5, 17–20; 6, 1–8.16–18) that Luke did not find appropriate for his predominantly Gentile Christian audience, the "Sermon on the Mount" is considerably longer. Lk's sermon may be outlined as follows: an introduction consisting of blessings and woes (20–26); the love of one's enemies (27–36); the demands of loving one's neighbor (37–42); good deeds as proof of one's goodness (43–45); a parable illustrating the result of listening to and acting on the words of Jesus (46–49). At the core of the sermon is Jesus' teaching on the love of one's enemies (27–36) that has as its source of motivation God's graciousness and compassion for all humanity (35–36) and Jesus' teaching on the love of one's neighbor (37–42) that is characterized by forgiveness and generosity.

6, 20–26: The introductory portion of the sermon consists of blessings and woes that address the real economic and social conditions of humanity (the poor—the rich; the hungry—the satisfied; those grieving—those laughing; the outcast—the socially acceptable). By contrast, Matthew emphasizes the religious and spiritual values of disciples in the kingdom inaugurated by Jesus ("poor in spirit," 5, 5; "hunger and thirst for righteousness" 5, 6). In the sermon, **blessed** extols the fortunate condition of persons who are favored with the blessings of God; the woes, addressed as they are to the disciples of Jesus, threaten God's profound displeasure on those so blinded by their present fortunate situation that they do not recognize and appreciate the real values of God's kingdom. In all the blessings and woes, the present condition of the persons addressed will be reversed in the future.

6, 27–36: See the notes on Mt 5, 43–48 and 5, 48.

---

l: Acts 1, 13. *m:* Mt 4, 23-25; Mk 3, 7-10. *n:* Mt 5, 1-12. *o:* Ps 126, 5-6; Is 61, 3; Jer 31, 25; Rv 7, 16-17. *p:* Jn 15, 19; 16, 2; 1 Pt 4, 14. *q:* 11, 47-48; 2 Chr 36, 16; Mt 23, 30-31. *r:* Jas 5, 1. *s:* Is 65, 13-14. *t:* Jas 4, 4. *u:* Mt 5, 38-48. *v:* Prv 25, 21; Rom 12, 20-21. *w:* Rom 12, 14; 1 Pt 3, 9.

²⁹To the person who strikes you on one cheek, offer the other one as well, and from the person who takes your cloak, do not withhold even your tunic. ³⁰Give to everyone who asks of you, and from the one who takes what is yours do not demand it back. ³¹ˣDo to others as you would have them do to you. ³²For if you love those who love you, what credit is that to you? Even sinners love those who love them. ³³And if you do good to those who do good to you, what credit is that to you? Even sinners do the same. ³⁴ʸIf you lend money to those from whom you expect repayment, what credit [is] that to you? Even sinners lend to sinners, and get back the same amount. ³⁵ᶻBut rather, love your enemies and do good to them, and lend expecting nothing back; then your reward will be great and you will be children of the Most High, for he himself is kind to the ungrateful and the wicked. ³⁶Be merciful, just as [also] your Father is merciful.

Judging Others. ³⁷ᵃᵇ*"Stop judging and you will not be judged. Stop condemning and you will not be condemned. Forgive and you will be forgiven. ³⁸ᶜGive and gifts will be given to you; a good measure, packed together, shaken down, and overflowing, will be poured into your lap. For the measure with which you measure will in return be measured out to you." ³⁹ᵈAnd he told them a parable, "Can a blind person guide a blind person? Will not both fall into a pit? ⁴⁰ᵉNo disciple is superior to the teacher; but when fully trained, every disciple will be like his teacher. ⁴¹Why do you notice the splinter in your brother's eye, but do not perceive the wooden beam in your own? ⁴²How can you say to your brother, 'Brother, let me remove that splinter in your eye,' when you do not even notice the wooden beam in your own eye? You hypocrite! Remove the wooden beam from your eye first; then you will see clearly to remove the splinter in your brother's eye.

A Tree Known by Its Fruit. ⁴³ᶠ*"A good tree does not bear rotten fruit, nor does a rotten tree bear good fruit. ⁴⁴For every tree is known by its own fruit. For people do not pick figs from thornbushes, nor do they gather grapes from brambles. ⁴⁵A good person out of the store of goodness in his heart produces good, but an evil person out of a store of evil produces evil; for from the fullness of the heart the mouth speaks.

The Two Foundations. ⁴⁶ᵍ"Why do you call me, 'Lord, Lord,' but not do what I command? ⁴⁷ʰ*I will show you what someone is like who comes to me, listens to my words, and acts on them. ⁴⁸That one is like a person building a house, who dug deeply and laid the foundation on rock; when the flood came, the river burst against that house but could not shake it because it had been well built. ⁴⁹But the one who listens and does not act is like a person who built a house on the ground without a foundation. When the river burst against it, it collapsed at once and was completely destroyed."

CHAPTER 7

See RG 405-6

The Healing of a Centurion's Slave. ¹ⁱ*When he had finished all his words to the people, he entered Capernaum. ²*A centurion there had a slave who was ill and about to die, and he was valuable to him. ³When he heard about Jesus, he sent elders of the Jews to him, asking him to come and save the life of his slave. ⁴They approached Jesus and

6, 37–42: See the notes on Mt 7, 1–12; 7, 1; 7, 5.

6, 43–46: See the notes on Mt 7, 15–20 and 12, 33.

6, 47–49: See the note on Mt 7, 24–27.

7, 1–8, 3: The episodes in this section present a series of reactions to the Galilean ministry of Jesus and reflect some of Luke's particular interests: the faith of a Gentile (1–10); the prophet Jesus' concern for a widowed mother (11–17); the ministry of Jesus directed to the afflicted and unfortunate of Is 61, 1 (18–23); the relation between John and Jesus and their role in God's plan for salvation (24–35); a forgiven sinner's manifestation of love (36–50); the association of women with the ministry of Jesus (8, 1–3).

7, 1–10: This story about the faith of the centurion, a Gentile who cherishes the Jewish nation (5), prepares for the story

in Acts of the conversion by Peter of the Roman centurion Cornelius who is similarly described as one who is generous to the Jewish nation (Acts 10, 2). See also Acts 10, 34–35 in the speech of Peter: "God shows no partiality . . . the person who fears him and acts righteously is acceptable to him." See also the notes on Mt 8, 5–13 and Jn 4, 43–54.

7, 2: *A centurion:* see the note on Mt 8, 5.

x: Mt 7, 12. y: Dt 15, 7-8. z: Lv 25, 35-36. a: Mt 7, 1-5. b: Mt 6, 14; Jas 2, 13. c: Mk 4, 24. d: Mt 15, 14; 23, 16-17.24. e: Mt 10, 24-25; Jn 13, 16; 15, 20. f: Mt 7, 16-20; 12, 33.35. g: Mt 7, 21; Rom 2, 13; Jas 1, 22. h: Mt 7, 24-27. i: Mt 8, 5-13; Jn 4, 43-54.

strongly urged him to come, saying, "He deserves to have you do this for him, [5]for he loves our nation and he built the synagogue for us." [6*]And Jesus went with them, but when he was only a short distance from the house, the centurion sent friends to tell him, "Lord, do not trouble yourself, for I am not worthy to have you enter under my roof. [7]Therefore, I did not consider myself worthy to come to you; but say the word and let my servant be healed. [8]For I too am a person subject to authority, with soldiers subject to me. And I say to one, 'Go,' and he goes; and to another, 'Come here,' and he comes; and to my slave, 'Do this,' and he does it." [9]When Jesus heard this he was amazed at him and, turning, said to the crowd following him, "I tell you, not even in Israel have I found such faith." [10]When the messengers returned to the house, they found the slave in good health.

Raising of the Widow's Son. [11j*]Soon afterward he journeyed to a city called Nain, and his disciples and a large crowd accompanied him. [12k]As he drew near to the gate of the city, a man who had died was being carried out, the only son of his mother, and she was a widow. A large crowd from the city was with her. [13]When the Lord saw her, he was moved with pity for her and said to her, "Do not weep." [14]He stepped forward and touched the coffin; at this the bearers halted, and he said, "Young man, I tell you, arise!" [15l]The dead man sat up and began to speak, and Jesus gave him to his mother. [16m]Fear seized them all, and they glorified God, exclaiming, "A great prophet has arisen in our midst," and "God has visited his people." [17]This report about him spread through the whole of Judea and in all the surrounding region.

The Messengers from John the Baptist. [18n*]The disciples of John told him about all these things. John summoned two of his disciples [19o]and sent them to the Lord to ask, "Are you the one who is to come, or should we look for another?" [20]When the men came to him, they said, "John the Baptist has sent us to you to ask, 'Are you the one who is to come, or should we look for another?' " [21]At that time he cured many of their diseases, sufferings, and evil spirits; he also granted sight to many who were blind. [22p]And he said to them in reply, "Go and tell John what you have seen and heard: the blind regain their sight, the lame walk, lepers are cleansed, the deaf hear, the dead are raised, the poor have the good news proclaimed to them. [23*]And blessed is the one who takes no offense at me."

Jesus' Testimony to John. [24q*]When the messengers of John had left, Jesus began to speak to the crowds about John. "What did you go out to the desert to see—a reed swayed by the wind? [25]Then what did you go out to see? Someone dressed in fine garments? Those who dress luxuriously and live sumptuously are found in royal palaces. [26r]Then what did you go out to see? A prophet? Yes, I tell you, and more than a prophet. [27s]This is the one about whom scripture says:

7, 6: **I am not worthy to have you enter under my roof:** to enter the house of a Gentile was considered unclean for a Jew; cf Acts 10, 28.

7, 11–17: In the previous incident Jesus' power was displayed for a Gentile whose servant was dying; in this episode it is displayed toward a widowed mother whose only son has already died. Jesus' power over death prepares for his reply to John's disciples in v 22: "the dead are raised." This resuscitation in alluding to the prophet Elijah's resurrection of the only son of a widow of Zarephath (1 Kgs 7, 18–24) leads to the reaction of the crowd: "A great prophet has arisen in our midst" (16).

7, 18–23: In answer to John's question, **Are you the one who is to come?**—a probable reference to the return of the fiery prophet of reform, Elijah, "before the day of the Lord comes, the great and terrible day" (Mal 3, 23)—Jesus responds that his role is rather to bring the blessings spoken of in Is 61,

1 to the oppressed and neglected of society (22; cf 4, 18).

7, 23: **Blessed is the one who takes no offense at me:** this beatitude is pronounced on the person who recognizes Jesus' true identity in spite of previous expectations of what "the one who is to come" would be like.

7, 24–30: In his testimony to John, Jesus reveals his understanding of the relationship between them: John is the precursor of Jesus (27); John is the messenger spoken of in Mal 3, 1 who in Mal 3, 23 is identified as Elijah. Taken with the previous episode, it can be seen that Jesus identifies John as precisely the person John envisioned Jesus to be: the Elijah who prepares the way for the coming of the day of the Lord.

j: 4, 25-26; 1 Kgs 17, 17-24. *k:* 8, 42; 1 Kgs 17, 17. *l:* 1 Kgs 17, 23; 2 Kgs 4, 36. *m:* 1, 68; 19, 44. *n:* Mt 11, 2-6. *o:* Mal 3, 1; Rv 1, 4.8; 4, 8. *p:* 4, 18; Is 35, 5-6; 61, 1. *q:* Mt 11, 7-15. *r:* 1, 76. *s:* Mal 3, 1 / Is 40, 3.

LUKE 7, 28–50

'Behold, I am sending my messenger
ahead of you,
he will prepare your way before you.'

[28]I tell you, among those born of women, no one is greater than John; yet the least in the kingdom of God is greater than he." [29*](All the people who listened, including the tax collectors, and who were baptized with the baptism of John, acknowledged the righteousness of God; [30]but the Pharisees and scholars of the law, who were not baptized by him, rejected the plan of God for themselves.) [31u*]"Then to what shall I compare the people of this generation? What are they like? [32]They are like children who sit in the marketplace and call to one another,

'We played the flute for you, but you did
not dance.
We sang a dirge, but you did not
weep.'

[33]For John the Baptist came neither eating food nor drinking wine, and you said, 'He is possessed by a demon.' [34v]The Son of Man came eating and drinking and you said, 'Look, he is a glutton and a drunkard, a friend of tax collectors and sinners.' [35]But wisdom is vindicated by all her children."

The Pardon of the Sinful Woman. [36w*]A Pharisee invited him to dine with him, and he entered the Pharisee's house and reclined at table. [37xy]Now there was a sinful woman in the city who learned that he was at table in the house of the Pharisee. Bringing an al-abaster flask of ointment, [38]she stood behind him at his feet weeping and began to bathe his feet with her tears. Then she wiped them with her hair, kissed them, and anointed them with the ointment. [39]When the Pharisee who had invited him saw this he said to himself, "If this man were a prophet, he would know who and what sort of woman this is who is touching him, that she is a sinner." [40]Jesus said to him in reply, "Simon, I have something to say to you." "Tell me, teacher," he said. [41*]"Two people were in debt to a certain creditor; one owed five hundred days' wages and the other owed fifty. [42]Since they were unable to repay the debt, he forgave it for both. Which of them will love him more?" [43]Simon said in reply, "The one, I suppose, whose larger debt was forgiven." He said to him, "You have judged rightly." [44]Then he turned to the woman and said to Simon, "Do you see this woman? When I entered your house, you did not give me water for my feet, but she has bathed them with her tears and wiped them with her hair. [45]You did not give me a kiss, but she has not ceased kissing my feet since the time I entered. [46]You did not anoint my head with oil, but she anointed my feet with ointment. [47*]So I tell you, her many sins have been forgiven; hence, she has shown great love. But the one to whom little is forgiven, loves little." [48z]He said to her, "Your sins are forgiven." [49a]The others at table said to themselves, "Who is this who even forgives sins?" [50]But he said to the woman, "Your faith has saved you; go in peace."

7, 31–35: See the note on Mt 11, 16–19.

7, 36–50: In this story of the pardoning of the sinful woman Luke presents two different reactions to the ministry of Jesus. A Pharisee, suspecting Jesus to be a prophet, invites Jesus to a festive banquet in his house, but the Pharisee's self-righteousness leads to little forgiveness by God and consequently little love shown toward Jesus. The sinful woman, on the other hand, manifests a faith in God (50) that has led her to seek forgiveness for her sins, and because so much was forgiven, she now overwhelms Jesus with her display of love; cf the similar contrast in attitudes in 18, 9–14. The whole episode is a powerful lesson on the relation between forgiveness and love.

7, 36: Reclined at table: the normal posture of guests at a banquet. Other oriental banquet customs alluded to in this story include the reception by the host with a kiss (45), wash-ing the feet of the guests (44), and the anointing of the guests' heads (46).

7, 41: Days' wages: one denarius is the normal daily wage of a laborer.

7, 47: Her many sins have been forgiven; hence, she has shown great love: literally, "her many sins have been forgiven, seeing that she has loved much." That the woman's sins have been forgiven is attested by the great love she shows toward Jesus. Her love is the consequence of her forgiveness. This is also the meaning demanded by the parable in vv 41–43.

t: 3, 7.12; Mt 21, 32. *u:* Mt 11, 16–19. *v:* 15, 2. *w:* 11, 37; 14, 1. *x:* Mt 26, 7; Mk 14, 3. *y:* Jn 12, 3. *z:* 5, 20; Mt 9, 20; Mk 2, 5. *a:* 5, 21.

1367

CHAPTER 8

See RG
405-6

Galilean Women Follow Jesus.
[1b]*Afterward he journeyed from one town and village to another, preaching and proclaiming the good news of the kingdom of God. Accompanying him were the Twelve [2c]and some women who had been cured of evil spirits and infirmities, Mary, called Magdalene, from whom seven demons had gone out, [3]Joanna, the wife of Herod's steward Chuza, Susanna, and many others who provided for them out of their resources.

The Parable of the Sower. [4d]*When a large crowd gathered, with people from one town after another journeying to him, he spoke in a parable. [5]"A sower went out to sow his seed. And as he sowed, some seed fell on the path and was trampled, and the birds of the sky ate it up. [6]Some seed fell on rocky ground, and when it grew, it withered for lack of moisture. [7]Some seed fell among thorns, and the thorns grew with it and choked it. [8e]And some seed fell on good soil, and when it grew, it produced fruit a hundredfold." After saying this, he called out, "Whoever has ears to hear ought to hear."

The Purpose of the Parables. [9f]Then his disciples asked him what the meaning of this parable might be. [10g]He answered, "Knowledge of the mysteries of the kingdom of God has been granted to you; but to the rest, they are made known through parables so that 'they may look but not see, and hear but not understand.'

The Parable of the Sower Explained. [11hi]*"This is the meaning of the parable. The seed is the word of God. [12]Those on the path are the ones who have heard, but the devil comes and takes away the word from their hearts that they may not believe and be saved. [13]Those on rocky ground are the ones who, when they hear, receive the word with joy, but they have no root; they believe only for a time and fall away in time of trial. [14]As for the seed that fell among thorns, they are the ones who have heard, but as they go along, they are choked by the anxieties and riches and pleasures of life, and they fail to produce mature fruit. [15]But as for the seed that fell on rich soil, they are the ones who, when they have heard the word, embrace it with a generous and good heart, and bear fruit through perseverance.

The Parable of the Lamp. [16jk]*"No one who lights a lamp conceals it with a vessel or sets it under a bed; rather, he places it on a lampstand so that those who enter may see the light. [17l]For there is nothing hidden that will not become visible, and nothing secret that will not be known and come to light. [18m]Take care, then, how you hear. To anyone who has, more will be given, and from the one who has not, even what he seems to have will be taken away."

Jesus and His Family. [19n]*Then his mother and his brothers came to him but were unable to join him because of the crowd. [20o]He was told, "Your mother and your brothers are standing outside and they

8, 1–3: Luke presents Jesus as an itinerant preacher traveling in the company of the Twelve and of the Galilean women who are sustaining them out of their means. These Galilean women will later accompany Jesus on his journey to Jerusalem and become witnesses to his death (23, 49) and resurrection (24, 9–11, where Mary Magdalene and Joanna are specifically mentioned; cf also Acts 1, 14). The association of women with the ministry of Jesus is most unusual in the light of the attitude of first-century Palestinian Judaism toward women. The more common attitude is expressed in Jn 4, 27, and early rabbinic documents caution against speaking with women in public.

8, 4–21: The focus in this section is on how one should hear the word of God and act on it. It includes the parable of the sower and its explanation (4–15), a collection of sayings on how one should act on the word that is heard (16–18), and the identification of the mother and brothers of Jesus as the ones who hear the word and act on it (19–

21). See also the notes on Mt 13, 1–53 and Mk 4, 1–34.

8, 4–8: See the note on Mt 13, 3–8.

8, 11–15: On the interpretation of the parable of the sower, see the note on Mt 13, 18–23.

8, 16–18: These sayings continue the theme of responding to the word of God. Those who hear the word must become a light to others (16); even the mysteries of the kingdom that have been made known to the disciples (9–10) must come to light (17); a generous and persevering response to the word of God leads to a still more perfect response to the word.

8, 19: His brothers: see the note on Mk 6, 3.

b: 4, 43. *c:* 23, 49; 24, 10; Mt 27, 55-56; Mk 15, 40-41; Jn 19, 5. *d:* Mt 13, 1-9; Mk 4, 1-9. *e:* 14, 35; Mt 11, 15; 13, 43; Mk 4, 23. *f:* Mt 13, 10-13; Mk 4, 10-12. *g:* Is 6, 9. *h:* Mt 13, 18-23; Mk 4, 13-20. *i:* 1 Pt 1, 23. *j:* Mk 4, 21-25. *k:* 11, 33; Mt 5, 15. *l:* 12, 2; Mt 10, 26. *m:* 19, 26; Mt 13, 12; 25, 29. *n:* Mt 12, 46-50; Mk 3, 31-35. *o:* 11, 27-28.

wish to see you." [21]*He said to them in reply, "My mother and my brothers are those who hear the word of God and act on it."

The Calming of a Storm at Sea. [22]p*One day he got into a boat with his disciples and said to them, "Let us cross to the other side of the lake." So they set sail, [23]and while they were sailing he fell asleep. A squall blew over the lake, and they were taking in water and were in danger. [24]They came and woke him saying, "Master, master, we are perishing!" He awakened, rebuked the wind and the waves, and they subsided and there was a calm. [25]Then he asked them, "Where is your faith?" But they were filled with awe and amazed and said to one another, "Who then is this, who commands even the winds and the sea, and they obey him?"

The Healing of the Gerasene Demoniac. [26]q*Then they sailed to the territory of the Gerasenes, which is opposite Galilee. [27]When he came ashore a man from the town who was possessed by demons met him. For a long time he had not worn clothes; he did not live in a house, but lived among the tombs. [28]r When he saw Jesus, he cried out and fell down before him; in a loud voice he shouted, "What have you to do with me, Jesus, son of the Most High God? I beg you, do not torment me!" [29]For he had ordered the unclean spirit to come out of the man. (It had taken hold of him many times, and he used to be bound with chains and shackles as a restraint, but he would break his bonds and be driven by the demon into deserted places.) [30]*Then Jesus asked him, "What is your name?" He replied, "Legion," because many demons had entered him. [31]*And they pleaded with him not to order them to depart to the abyss.

[32]A herd of many swine was feeding there on the hillside, and they pleaded with him to allow them to enter those swine; and he let them. [33]The demons came out of the man and entered the swine, and the herd rushed down the steep bank into the lake and was drowned. [34]When the swineherds saw what had happened, they ran away and reported the incident in the town and throughout the countryside. [35]*People came out to see what had happened and, when they approached Jesus, they discovered the man from whom the demons had come out sitting at his feet. He was clothed and in his right mind, and they were seized with fear. [36]Those who witnessed it told them how the possessed man had been saved. [37]The entire population of the region of the Gerasenes asked Jesus to leave them because they were seized with great fear. So he got into a boat and returned. [38]The man from whom the demons had come out begged to remain with him, but he sent him away, saying, [39]"Return home and recount what God has done for you." The man went off and proclaimed throughout the whole town what Jesus had done for him.

Jairus's Daughter and the Woman with a Hemorrhage. [40]s*When Jesus returned, the

---

8, 21: The family of Jesus is not constituted by physical relationship with him but by obedience to the word of God. In this, Luke agrees with the Marcan parallel (3, 31–35), although by omitting Mk 3, 33 and especially Mk 3, 20–21 Luke has softened the Marcan picture of Jesus' natural family. Probably he did this because Mary has already been presented in 1, 38 as the obedient handmaid of the Lord who fulfills the requirement for belonging to the eschatological family of Jesus; cf also 11, 27–28.

8, 22–56: This section records four miracles of Jesus that manifest his power and authority: (1) the calming of a storm on the lake (22–25); (2) the exorcism of a demoniac (26–39); (3) the cure of a hemorrhaging woman (40–48); (4) the raising of Jairus's daughter to life (49–56). They parallel the same sequence of stories at Mk 4, 35—5, 43.

8, 26: Gerasenes: other manuscripts read Gadarenes or Gergesenes. See also the note on Mt 8, 28. **Opposite Galilee:** probably Gentile territory (note the presence in the area of pigs—unclean animals to Jews) and an indication that the person who receives salvation (36) is a Gentile.

8, 30: What is your name?: the question reflects the popular belief that knowledge of the spirit's name brought control over the spirit. **Legion:** to Jesus' question the demon replies with a Latin word transliterated into Greek. The Roman legion at this period consisted of 5,000 to 6,000 foot soldiers; hence the name implies a very large number of demons.

8, 31: Abyss: the place of the dead (Rom 10, 7) or the prison of Satan (Rv 20, 3) or the subterranean "watery deep" that symbolizes the chaos before the order imposed by creation (Gn 1, 2).

8, 35: Sitting at his feet: the former demoniac takes the position of a disciple before the master (10, 39; Acts 22, 3).

8, 40–56: Two interwoven miracle stories, one a healing and the other a resuscitation, present Jesus as master over sickness and death. In the Lucan account, faith in Jesus is responsible for the cure (48) and for the raising to life (50).

p: Mt 8, 18.23-27; Mk 4, 35-41.   q: Mt 8, 28-34; Mk 5, 1-20.
r: 4, 33-35; Mt 8, 29; Mk 1, 23-24.   s: Mt 9, 18-26; Mk 5, 21-43.

crowd welcomed him, for they were all waiting for him. *41* And a man named Jairus, an official of the synagogue, came forward. He fell at the feet of Jesus and begged him to come to his house, *42** because he had an only daughter, about twelve years old, and she was dying. As he went, the crowds almost crushed him. *43** And a woman afflicted with hemorrhages for twelve years, who [had spent her whole livelihood on doctors and] was unable to be cured by anyone, *44* came up behind him and touched the tassel on his cloak. Immediately her bleeding stopped. *45* Jesus then asked, "Who touched me?" While all were denying it, Peter said, "Master, the crowds are pushing and pressing in upon you." *46t* But Jesus said, "Someone has touched me; for I know that power has gone out from me." *47* When the woman realized that she had not escaped notice, she came forward trembling. Falling down before him, she explained in the presence of all the people why she had touched him and how she had been healed immediately. *48u* He said to her, "Daughter, your faith has saved you; go in peace."

49 While he was still speaking, someone from the synagogue official's house arrived and said, "Your daughter is dead; do not trouble the teacher any longer." *50* On hearing this, Jesus answered him, "Do not be afraid; just have faith and she will be saved." *51* When he arrived at the house he allowed no one to enter with him except Peter and John and James, and the child's father and mother. *52v** All

were weeping and mourning for her, when he said, "Do not weep any longer, for she is not dead, but sleeping." *53* And they ridiculed him, because they knew that she was dead. *54* But he took her by the hand and called to her, "Child, arise!" *55* Her breath returned and she immediately arose. He then directed that she should be given something to eat. *56* Her parents were astounded, and he instructed them to tell no one what had happened.

CHAPTER 9

See RG 405-7

The Mission of the Twelve. *1w** He summoned the Twelve and gave them power and authority over all demons and to cure diseases, *2* and he sent them to proclaim the kingdom of God and to heal [the sick]. *3** He said to them, "Take nothing for the journey, neither walking stick, nor sack, nor food, nor money, and let no one take a second tunic. *4x* Whatever house you enter, stay there and leave from there. *5y** And as for those who do not welcome you, when you leave that town, shake the dust from your feet in testimony against them." *6* Then they set out and went from village to village proclaiming the good news and curing diseases everywhere.

Herod's Opinion of Jesus. *7za** Herod the tetrarch heard about all that was happening, and he was greatly perplexed because some were saying, "John has been raised from the dead"; *8* others were saying, "Elijah has appeared"; still others, "One of the ancient prophets has arisen." *9b** But Herod said,

---

8, 42: An only daughter: cf the son of the widow of Nain whom Luke describes as an "only" son (7, 12; see also 9, 38).

8, 43: Afflicted with hemorrhages for twelve years: according to the Mosaic law (Lv 15, 25–30) this condition would render the woman unclean and unfit for contact with other people.

8, 52: Sleeping: her death is a temporary condition; cf Jn 11, 11–14.

9, 1–6: Armed with the power and authority that Jesus himself has been displaying in the previous episodes, the Twelve are now sent out to continue the work that Jesus has been performing throughout his Galilean ministry: (1) proclaiming the kingdom (4, 43; 8, 1); (2) exorcising demons (4, 33–37.41; 8, 26–39) and (3) healing the sick (4, 38–40; 5, 12–16.17–26; 6, 6–10; 7, 1–10.17.22; 8, 40–56).

9, 3: Take nothing for the journey: the absolute detachment required of the disciple (14, 33) leads to complete reliance on God (12, 22–31).

9, 5: Shake the dust from your feet: see the note on Mt 10, 14.

9, 7–56: This section in which Luke gathers together incidents that focus on the identity of Jesus is introduced by a question that Herod is made to ask in this gospel: "Who then is this about whom I hear such things?" (9). In subsequent episodes, Luke reveals to the reader various answers to Herod's question: Jesus is one in whom God's power is present and who provides for the needs of God's people (10–17); Peter declares Jesus to be "the Messiah of God" (18–21); Jesus says he is the suffering Son of Man (22.43–45); Jesus is the Master to be followed, even to death (23–27); Jesus is God's Son, his Chosen One (28–36).

9, 7: Herod the tetrarch: see the note on 3, 1.

9, 9: And he kept trying to see him: this indication of Herod's interest in Jesus prepares for 13, 31–33 and for 23, 8–12 where Herod's curiosity about Jesus' power to perform miracles remains unsatisfied.

t: 6, 19. *u:* 7, 50; 17, 19; 18, 42. *v:* 7, 13. *w:* Mt 10, 1.5-15; Mk 6, 7-13. *x:* 10, 5-7. *y:* 10, 10-11; Acts 13, 51. *z:* Mt 14, 1-12; Mk 6, 14-29. *a:* 9, 19; Mt 16, 14; Mk 8, 28. *b:* 23, 8.

"John I beheaded. Who then is this about whom I hear such things?" And he kept trying to see him.

The Return of the Twelve and the Feeding of the Five Thousand. *10c* When the apostles returned, they explained to him what they had done. He took them and withdrew in private to a town called Bethsaida. *11* The crowds, meanwhile, learned of this and followed him. He received them and spoke to them about the kingdom of God, and he healed those who needed to be cured. *12* As the day was drawing to a close, the Twelve approached him and said, "Dismiss the crowd so that they can go to the surrounding villages and farms and find lodging and provisions; for we are in a deserted place here." *13d* He said to them, "Give them some food yourselves." They replied, "Five loaves and two fish are all we have, unless we ourselves go and buy food for all these people." *14* Now the men there numbered about five thousand. Then he said to his disciples, "Have them sit down in groups of [about] fifty." *15* They did so and made them all sit down. *16e** Then taking the five loaves and the two fish, and looking up to heaven, he said the blessing over them, broke them, and gave them to the disciples to set before the crowd. *17* They all ate and were satisfied. And when the leftover fragments were picked up, they filled twelve wicker baskets.

Peter's Confession about Jesus. *18f** Once when Jesus was praying in solitude, and the disciples were with him, he asked them, "Who do the crowds say that I am?" *19g* They said in reply, "John the Baptist; others, Elijah; still others, 'One of the ancient prophets has arisen.'" *20** Then he said to them, "But who do you say that I am?" Peter said in reply, "The Messiah of God." *21* He rebuked them and directed them not to tell this to anyone.

The First Prediction of the Passion. *22h* He said, "The Son of Man must suffer greatly and be rejected by the elders, the chief priests, and the scribes, and be killed and on the third day be raised."

The Conditions of Discipleship. *23i j** Then he said to all, "If anyone wishes to come after me, he must deny himself and take up his cross daily and follow me. *24k* For whoever wishes to save his life will lose it, but whoever loses his life for my sake will save it. *25* What profit is there for one to gain the whole world yet lose or forfeit himself? *26l* Whoever is ashamed of me and of my words, the Son of Man will be ashamed of when he comes in his glory and in the glory of the Father and of the holy angels. *27* Truly I say to you, there are some standing here who will not taste death until they see the kingdom of God."

The Transfiguration of Jesus. *28m** About eight days after he said this, he took Peter, John, and James and went up the mountain to pray. *29* While he was praying his face changed in appearance and his clothing became dazzling white. *30** And behold, two men were conversing with him, Moses and

9, 16: **Then taking . . . :** the actions of Jesus recall the institution of the Eucharist in 22, 19; see also the note on Mt 14, 19.

9, 18–22: This incident is based on Mk 8, 27–33, but Luke has eliminated Peter's refusal to accept Jesus as suffering Son of Man (Mk 8, 32) and the rebuke of Peter by Jesus (Mk 8, 33). Elsewhere in the gospel, Luke softens the harsh portrait of Peter and the other apostles found in his Marcan source (cf 22, 39–46, which similarly lacks a rebuke of Peter that occurs in the source, Mk 14, 37–38).

9, 18: **When Jesus was praying in solitude:** see the note on 3, 21.

9, 20: **The Messiah of God:** on the meaning of this title in first-century Palestinian Judaism, see the notes on 2, 11 and on Mt 16, 13–20 and Mk 8, 27–30.

9, 23: **Daily:** this is a Lucan addition to a saying of Jesus, removing the saying from a context that envisioned the imminent suffering and death of the disciple of Jesus (as does the saying in Mk 8, 34–35) to one that focuses on the demands of daily Christian existence.

9, 28–36: Situated shortly after the first announcement of the passion, death, and resurrection, this scene of Jesus' transfiguration provides the heavenly confirmation to Jesus' declaration that his suffering will end in glory (32); see also the notes on Mt 17, 1–8 and Mk 9, 2–8.

9, 28: **Up the mountain to pray:** the "mountain" is the regular place of prayer (see 6, 12; 22, 39–41).

9, 30: **Moses and Elijah:** the two figures represent the Old Testament law and the prophets. At the end of this episode, the heavenly voice will identify Jesus as the one to be listened to now (35). See also the note on Mk 9, 5.

c: Mt 14, 13-21; Mk 6, 30-44; Jn 6, 1-14. d: 2 Kgs 4, 42-44. e: 22, 19; 24, 30-31; Acts 2, 42; 20, 11; 27, 35. f: Mt 16, 13-20; Mk 8, 27-30. g: 9, 7-8. h: 24, 7.26; Mt 16, 21; 20, 18-19; Mk 8, 31; 10, 33-34. i: Mt 16, 24-28; Mk 8, 34—9, 1. j: 14, 27; Mt 10, 38. k: 17, 33; Mt 10, 39; Jn 12, 25. l: 12, 9; Mt 10, 33; 2 Tm 2, 12. m: Mt 17, 1-8; Mk 9, 2-8.

Elijah, [31n*]who appeared in glory and spoke of his exodus that he was going to accomplish in Jerusalem. [32o*]Peter and his companions had been overcome by sleep, but becoming fully awake, they saw his glory and the two men standing with him. [33*]As they were about to part from him, Peter said to Jesus, "Master, it is good that we are here; let us make three tents, one for you, one for Moses, and one for Elijah." But he did not know what he was saying. [34*]While he was still speaking, a cloud came and cast a shadow over them, and they became frightened when they entered the cloud. [35p*]Then from the cloud came a voice that said, "This is my chosen Son; listen to him." [36*]After the voice had spoken, Jesus was found alone. They fell silent and did not at that time tell anyone what they had seen.

The Healing of a Boy with a Demon. [37q*]On the next day, when they came down from the mountain, a large crowd met him. [38]There was a man in the crowd who cried out, "Teacher, I beg you, look at my son; he is my only child. [39]For a spirit seizes him and he suddenly screams and it convulses him until he foams at the mouth; it releases him only with difficulty, wearing him out. [40]I begged your disciples to cast it out but they could not." [41]Jesus said in reply, "O faithless and perverse generation, how long will I be with you and endure you? Bring your son here." [42]As he was coming forward, the demon threw him to the ground in a convulsion; but Jesus rebuked the unclean spirit, healed the boy, and returned him to his father. [43r]And all were astonished by the majesty of God.

The Second Prediction of the Passion. While they were all amazed at his every deed, he said to his disciples, [44]"Pay attention to what I am telling you. The Son of Man is to be handed over to men." [45]But they did not understand this saying; its meaning was hidden from them so that they should not understand it, and they were afraid to ask him about this saying.

The Greatest in the Kingdom. [46s1*]An argument arose among the disciples about which of them was the greatest. [47]Jesus realized the intention of their hearts and took a child and placed it by his side [48u]and said to them, "Whoever receives this child in my name receives me, and whoever receives me receives the one who sent me. For the one who is least among all of you is the one who is the greatest."

Another Exorcist. [49v]Then John said in reply, "Master, we saw someone casting out demons in your name and we tried to prevent him because he does not follow in our company." [50]Jesus said to him, "Do not prevent him, for whoever is not against you is for you."

V: The Journey to Jerusalem: Luke's Travel Narrative

Departure for Jerusalem; Samaritan Inhospitality. [51w*]When the days for his being taken

---

9, 31: His exodus that he was going to accomplish in Jerusalem: Luke identifies the subject of the conversation as the **exodus** of Jesus, a reference to the death, resurrection, and ascension of Jesus that will take place in Jerusalem, the city of destiny (see 9, 51). The mention of exodus, however, also calls to mind the Israelite Exodus from Egypt to the promised land.

9, 32: They saw his glory: the **glory** that is proper to God is here attributed to Jesus (see 24, 26).

9, 33: Let us make three tents: in a possible allusion to the feast of Tabernacles, Peter may be likening his joy on the occasion of the transfiguration to the joyful celebration of this harvest festival.

9, 34: Over them: it is not clear whether **them** refers to Jesus, Moses, and Elijah, or to the disciples. For the cloud casting its shadow, see the note on Mk 9, 7.

9, 35: Like the heavenly voice that identified Jesus at his baptism prior to his undertaking the Galilean ministry (3, 22), so too here before the journey to the city of destiny is begun

(51) the heavenly voice again identifies Jesus as Son. **Listen to him:** the two representatives of Israel of old depart (33) and Jesus is left alone (36) as the teacher whose words must be heeded (see also Acts 3, 22).

9, 36: At that time: i.e., before the resurrection.

9, 37–43a: See the note on Mk 9, 14–29.

9, 46–50: These two incidents focus on attitudes that are opposed to Christian discipleship: rivalry and intolerance of outsiders.

9, 51—18, 14: The Galilean ministry of Jesus finishes with the previous episode and a new section of Luke's gospel

n: 9, 22; 13, 33. o: Jn 1, 14; 2 Pt 1, 16. p: 3, 22; Dt 18, 15; Ps 2, 7; Is 42, 1; Mt 3, 17; 12, 18; Mk 1, 11; 2 Pt 1, 17-18. q: Mt 17, 14-18; Mk 9, 14-27. r: 18, 32-34; Mt 17, 22-23; Mk 9, 30-32. s: Mt 18, 1-5; Mk 9, 33-37. t: 22, 24. u: 10, 16; Mt 10, 40; Jn 13, 20. v: Mk 9, 38-40. w: 9, 53; 13, 22.33; 17, 11; 18, 31; 19, 28; 24, 51; Acts 1, 2.9-11.22.

up were fulfilled, he resolutely determined to journey to Jerusalem, [52x*]and he sent messengers ahead of him. On the way they entered a Samaritan village to prepare for his reception there, [53]but they would not welcome him because the destination of his journey was Jerusalem. [54y]When the disciples James and John saw this they asked, "Lord, do you want us to call down fire from heaven to consume them?" [55]Jesus turned and rebuked them, [56]and they journeyed to another village.

The Would-be Followers of Jesus. [57z*]As they were proceeding on their journey someone said to him, "I will follow you wherever you go." [58]Jesus answered him, "Foxes have dens and birds of the sky have nests, but the Son of Man has nowhere to rest his head." [59]And to another he said, "Follow me." But he replied, "[Lord,] let me go first and bury my father." [60*]But he answered him, "Let the dead bury their dead. But you, go and proclaim the kingdom of God." [61a]And another said, "I will follow you, Lord, but first let me say farewell to my family at home." [62][To him] Jesus said, "No one who sets a hand to the plow and looks to what was left behind is fit for the kingdom of God."

CHAPTER 10

The Mission of the Seventy-two. See RG 406-7 [1b*]After this the Lord appointed seventy [-two] others whom he sent ahead of him in pairs to every town and place he intended to visit. [2c]He said to them, "The harvest is abundant but the laborers are few; so ask the master of the harvest to send out laborers for his harvest. [3d]Go on your way; behold, I am sending you like lambs among wolves. [4ef*]Carry no money bag, no sack, no sandals; and greet no one along the way. [5*]Into whatever house you enter, first say, 'Peace to this household.' [6*]If a peaceful person lives

---

begins, the journey to Jerusalem. This journey is based on Mk 10, 1–52, but Luke uses his Marcan source only in 18, 15—19, 27. Before that point he has inserted into his gospel a distinctive collection of sayings of Jesus and stories about him that he has drawn from Q, a collection of sayings of Jesus used also by Matthew, and from his own special traditions. All of the material collected in this section is loosely organized within the framework of a journey of Jesus to Jerusalem, the city of destiny, where his exodus (suffering, death, resurrection, ascension) is to take place (9, 31), where salvation is accomplished, and from where the proclamation of God's saving word is to go forth (24, 47; Acts 1, 8). Much of the material in the Lucan travel narrative is teaching for the disciples. During the course of this journey Jesus is preparing his chosen Galilean witnesses for the role they will play after his exodus (9, 31): they are to be his witnesses to the people (Acts 10, 39; 13, 31) and thereby provide certainty to the readers of Luke's gospel that the teachings they have received are rooted in the teachings of Jesus (1, 1–4).

9, 51–55: Just as the Galilean ministry began with a rejection of Jesus in his hometown, so too the travel narrative begins with the rejection of him by Samaritans. In this episode Jesus disassociates himself from the attitude expressed by his disciples that those who reject him are to be punished severely. The story alludes to 2 Kgs 1, 10.12, where the prophet Elijah takes the course of action Jesus rejects, and Jesus thereby rejects the identification of himself with Elijah.

9, 51: Days for his being taken up: like the reference to his exodus in v 31, this is probably a reference to all the events (suffering, death, resurrection, ascension) of his last days in Jerusalem, He resolutely determined: literally, "he set his face."

9, 52: Samaritan: Samaria was the territory between Judea and Galilee west of the Jordan river. For ethnic and religious reasons, the Samaritans and the Jews were bitterly opposed to one another (see Jn 4, 9).

9, 57–62: In these sayings Jesus speaks of the severity and

the unconditional nature of Christian discipleship. Even family ties and filial obligations, such as burying one's parents, cannot distract one no matter how briefly from proclaiming the kingdom of God. The first two sayings are paralleled in Mt 8, 19–22; see also the notes there.

9, 60: Let the dead bury their dead: i.e., let the spiritually dead (those who do not follow) bury their physically dead. See also the note on Mt 8, 22.

10, 1–12: Only the Gospel of Luke contains two episodes in which Jesus sends out his followers on a mission: the first (9, 1–6) is based on the mission in Mk 6, 6b-13 and recounts the sending out of the Twelve; here in vv 1–12 a similar report based on Q becomes the sending out of seventy-two in this gospel. The episode continues the theme of Jesus preparing witnesses to himself and his ministry. These witnesses include not only the Twelve but also the seventy-two who may represent the Christian mission in Luke's own day. Note that the instructions given to the Twelve and to the seventy-two are similar and that what is said to the seventy-two in v 4 is directed to the Twelve in 22, 35.

10, 1: Seventy[-two]: important representatives of the Alexandrian and Caesarean text types read "seventy," while other important Alexandrian texts and Western readings have "seventy-two."

10, 4: Carry no money bag . . . greet no one along the way: because of the urgency of the mission and the single-mindedness required of missionaries, attachment to material possessions should be avoided and even customary greetings should not distract from the fulfillment of the task.

10, 5: First say, 'Peace to this household': see the notes on 2, 14 and Mt 10, 13.

10, 6: A peaceful person: literally, "a son of peace."

---

x: Mal 3, 1.   y: 2 Kgs 1, 10.12.   z: Mt 8, 19-22.   a: 1 Kgs 19, 20.   b: Mk 6, 7.   c: Mt 9, 37-38; Jn 4, 35.   d: Mt 10, 16.   e: 9, 3; 2 Kgs 4, 29.   f: Mt 10, 7-14.

there, your peace will rest on him; but if not, it will return to you. [7g]Stay in the same house and eat and drink what is offered to you, for the laborer deserves his payment. Do not move about from one house to another. [8h]Whatever town you enter and they welcome you, eat what is set before you, [9i]cure the sick in it and say to them, 'The kingdom of God is at hand for you.' [10j]Whatever town you enter and they do not receive you, go out into the streets and say, [11k]'The dust of your town that clings to our feet, even that we shake off against you.' Yet know this: the kingdom of God is at hand. [12l]I tell you, it will be more tolerable for Sodom on that day than for that town.

Reproaches to Unrepentant Towns. [13mn]*"Woe to you, Chorazin! Woe to you, Bethsaida! For if the mighty deeds done in your midst had been done in Tyre and Sidon, they would long ago have repented, sitting in sackcloth and ashes. [14]But it will be more tolerable for Tyre and Sidon at the judgment than for you. [15o]*And as for you, Capernaum, 'Will you be exalted to heaven? You will go down to the netherworld.' " [16p]Whoever listens to you listens to me. Whoever rejects you rejects me. And whoever rejects me rejects the one who sent me."

Return of the Seventy-two. [17]The seventy [-two] returned rejoicing, and said, "Lord, even the demons are subject to us because of your name." [18q]*Jesus said, "I have observed Satan fall like lightning from the sky. [19r]Be-

hold, I have given you the power 'to tread upon serpents' and scorpions and upon the full force of the enemy and nothing will harm you. [20s]Nevertheless, do not rejoice because the spirits are subject to you, but rejoice because your names are written in heaven."

Praise of the Father. [21tu]*At that very moment he rejoiced [in] the holy Spirit and said, "I give you praise, Father, Lord of heaven and earth, for although you have hidden these things from the wise and the learned you have revealed them to the childlike. Yes, Father, such has been your gracious will. [22v]All things have been handed over to me by my Father. No one knows who the Son is except the Father, and who the Father is except the Son and anyone to whom the Son wishes to reveal him."

The Privileges of Discipleship. [23w]Turning to the disciples in private he said, "Blessed are the eyes that see what you see. [24]For I say to you, many prophets and kings desired to see what you see, but did not see it, and to hear what you hear, but did not hear it."

The Greatest Commandment. [25xy]*There was a scholar of the law who stood up to test him and said, "Teacher, what must I do to inherit eternal life?" [26]Jesus said to him, "What is written in the law? How do you read it?" [27z]He said in reply, "You shall love the Lord, your God, with all your heart, with all your being, with all your strength, and with all your mind, and your neighbor as yourself." [28a]He replied to him, "You have

10, 13–16: The call to repentance that is a part of the proclamation of the kingdom brings with it a severe judgment for those who hear it and reject it.

10, 15: The netherworld: the underworld, the place of the dead (Acts 2, 27.31), here contrasted with heaven; see also the note on Mt 11, 23.

10, 18: I have observed Satan fall like lightning: the effect of the mission of the seventy-two is characterized by the Lucan Jesus as a symbolic fall of Satan. As the kingdom of God is gradually being established, evil in all its forms is being defeated; the dominion of Satan over humanity is at an end.

10, 21: Revealed them to the childlike: a restatement of the theme announced in 8, 10: the mysteries of the kingdom are revealed to the disciples. See also the note on Mt 11, 25–27.

10, 25–37: In response to a question from a Jewish legal expert about inheriting eternal life, Jesus illustrates the superiority of love over legalism through the story of the good Samaritan. The law of love proclaimed in the "Sermon on the Plain" (6, 27–36) is exemplified by one whom the legal ex-

pert would have considered ritually impure (see Jn 4, 9). Moreover, the identity of the "neighbor" requested by the legal expert (29) turns out to be a Samaritan, the enemy of the Jew (see the note on 9, 52).

10, 25: Scholar of the law: an expert in the Mosaic law, and probably a member of the group elsewhere identified as the scribes (5, 21).

g: 9, 4; Mt 10, 10; 1 Cor 9, 6-14; 1 Tm 5, 18.   h: 1 Cor 10, 27.   i: Mt 3, 2; 4, 17; Mk 1, 15.   j: 9, 5.   k: Acts 13, 51; 18, 6.   l: Mt 10, 15; 11, 24.   m: Mt 11, 20-24.   n: Is 23; Ez 26-28; Jl 3, 4-8; Am 1, 1-10; Zec 9, 2-4.   o: Is 14, 13-15.   p: Mt 10, 40; Jn 5, 23; 13, 20; 15, 23.   q: Is 14, 12; Jn 12, 31; Rv 12, 7-12.   r: Ps 19, 13; Mk 16, 18.   s: Ex 32, 32; Dn 12, 1; Mt 7, 22; Phil 4, 3; Heb 12, 23; Rv 3, 5; 21, 27.   t: Mt 11, 25-27.   u: 1 Cor 1, 26-28.   v: Jn 3, 35; 10, 15.   w: Mt 13, 16-17.   x: Mt 22, 34-40; Mk 12, 28-34.   y: 18, 18; Mt 19, 16; Mk 10, 17.   z: Lv 19, 18; Dt 6, 5; 10, 12; Jos 22, 5; Mt 19, 19; 22, 37-39; Rom 13, 9; Gal 5, 14; Jas 2, 8.   a: Lv 18, 5; Prv 19, 16; Rom 10, 5; Gal 3, 12.

answered correctly; do this and you will live."

The Parable of the Good Samaritan. [29]But because he wished to justify himself, he said to Jesus, "And who is my neighbor?" [30]Jesus replied, "A man fell victim to robbers as he went down from Jerusalem to Jericho. They stripped and beat him and went off leaving him half-dead. [31]*A priest happened to be going down that road, but when he saw him, he passed by on the opposite side. [32]Likewise a Levite came to the place, and when he saw him, he passed by on the opposite side. [33]But a Samaritan traveler who came upon him was moved with compassion at the sight. [34]He approached the victim, poured oil and wine over his wounds and bandaged them. Then he lifted him up on his own animal, took him to an inn and cared for him. [35]The next day he took out two silver coins and gave them to the innkeeper with the instruction, 'Take care of him. If you spend more than what I have given you, I shall repay you on my way back.' [36]Which of these three, in your opinion, was neighbor to the robbers' victim?" [37]He answered, "The one who treated him with mercy." Jesus said to him, "Go and do likewise."

Martha and Mary. [38b]*As they continued their journey he entered a village where a woman whose name was Martha welcomed him. [39]*She had a sister named Mary [who] sat beside the Lord at his feet listening to him speak. [40]Martha, burdened with much serving, came to him and said, "Lord, do you not care that my sister has left me by myself to do the serving? Tell her to help me." [41]The Lord said to her in reply, "Martha, Martha, you are anxious and worried about many things. [42]*There is need of only one thing. Mary has chosen the better part and it will not be taken from her."

CHAPTER 11

See RG 406-8

The Lord's Prayer. [1c]*He was praying in a certain place, and when he had finished, one of his disciples said to him, "Lord, teach us to pray just as John taught his disciples." [2]*He said to them, "When you pray, say:

> Father, hallowed be your name,
>   your kingdom come.
> [3]   *Give us each day our daily bread
> [4]   and forgive us our sins
>   for we ourselves forgive everyone in debt to us,
> and do not subject us to the final test."

Further Teachings on Prayer. [5d]And he said to them, "Suppose one of you has a friend to whom he goes at midnight and says, 'Friend, lend me three loaves of bread, [6]for a friend of mine has arrived at my house from a journey and I have nothing to offer him,' [7]and he says in reply from within, 'Do not bother me; the door has already been locked and my children and I are already in bed. I cannot get up to give you anything.' [8]I tell you, if he does not get up to give him the loaves because of their friendship, he will get up to give him whatever he needs because of his persistence.

10, 31–32: Priest . . . Levite: those religious representatives of Judaism who would have been expected to be models of "neighbor" to the victim pass him by.

10, 38–42: The story of Martha and Mary further illustrates the importance of hearing the words of the teacher and the concern with women in Lk.

10, 39: Sat beside the Lord at his feet: it is remarkable for first-century Palestinian Judaism that a woman would assume the posture of a disciple at the master's feet (see also 8, 35; Acts 22, 3), and it reveals a characteristic attitude of Jesus toward women in this gospel (see 8, 2–3).

10, 42: There is need of only one thing: some ancient versions read, "there is need of few things"; another important, although probably inferior, reading found in some manuscripts is, "there is need of few things, or of one."

11, 1–13: Luke presents three episodes concerned with prayer. The first (1–4) recounts Jesus teaching his disciples the Christian communal prayer, the "Our Father"; the second (5–8), the importance of persistence in prayer; the third

(9–13), the effectiveness of prayer.

11, 1–4: The Matthean form of the "Our Father" occurs in the "Sermon on the Mount" (Mt 6, 9–15); the shorter Lucan version is presented while Jesus is at prayer (see the note on 3, 21) and his disciples ask him to teach them to pray just as John taught his disciples to pray. In answer to their question, Jesus presents them with an example of a Christian communal prayer that stresses the fatherhood of God and acknowledges him as the one to whom the Christian disciple owes daily sustenance (3), forgiveness (4), and deliverance from the final trial (4). See also the notes on Mt 6, 9–13.

11, 2: Your kingdom come: in place of this petition, some early church Fathers record: "May your holy Spirit come upon us and cleanse us," a petition that may reflect the use of the "Our Father" in a baptismal liturgy.

11, 3–4: Daily bread: see the note on Mt 6, 11. **The final test:** see the note on Mt 6, 13.

b: Jn 11, 1; 12, 2-3.   *c:* Mt 6, 9-15.   *d:* 18, 1-5.

The Answer to Prayer. [9ef]"And I tell you, ask and you will receive; seek and you will find; knock and the door will be opened to you. [10]For everyone who asks, receives; and the one who seeks, finds; and to the one who knocks, the door will be opened. [11]What father among you would hand his son a snake when he asks for a fish? [12]Or hand him a scorpion when he asks for an egg? [13*]If you then, who are wicked, know how to give good gifts to your children, how much more will the Father in heaven give the holy Spirit to those who ask him?"

Jesus and Beelzebul. [14g]He was driving out a demon [that was] mute, and when the demon had gone out, the mute person spoke and the crowds were amazed. [15h]Some of them said, "By the power of Beelzebul, the prince of demons, he drives out demons." [16i]Others, to test him, asked him for a sign from heaven. [17]But he knew their thoughts and said to them, "Every kingdom divided against itself will be laid waste and house will fall against house. [18]And if Satan is divided against himself, how will his kingdom stand? For you say that it is by Beelzebul that I drive out demons. [19*]If I, then, drive out demons by Beelzebul, by whom do your own people drive them out? Therefore they will be your judges. [20j]But if it is by the finger of God that [I] drive out demons, then the kingdom of God has come upon you. [21]When a strong man fully armed guards his palace, his possessions are safe. [22*]But when one stronger than he attacks and overcomes him, he takes away the armor on which he relied and distributes the spoils. [23k]Whoever is not with me is against me, and whoever does not gather with me scatters.

The Return of the Unclean Spirit. [24l]"When an unclean spirit goes out of someone, it roams through arid regions searching for rest but, finding none, it says, 'I shall return to my home from which I came.' [25]But upon returning, it finds it swept clean and put in order. [26m]Then it goes and brings back seven other spirits more wicked than itself who move in and dwell there, and the last condition of that person is worse than the first."

True Blessedness. [27n*]While he was speaking, a woman from the crowd called out and said to him, "Blessed is the womb that carried you and the breasts at which you nursed." [28]He replied, "Rather, blessed are those who hear the word of God and observe it."

The Demand for a Sign. [29o p*]While still more people gathered in the crowd, he said to them, "This generation is an evil generation; it seeks a sign, but no sign will be given it, except the sign of Jonah. [30]Just as Jonah became a sign to the Ninevites, so will the Son of Man be to this generation. [31q]At the judgment the queen of the south will rise with the men of this generation and she will condemn them, because she came from the ends of the earth to hear the wisdom of Solomon, and there is something greater than Solomon here. [32r]At the judgment the men of Nineveh will arise with this generation and condemn it, because at the preaching of Jonah they repented, and there is something greater than Jonah here.

The Simile of Light. [33s]"No one who lights a lamp hides it away or places it [under a bushel basket], but on a lampstand so that those who enter might see the light. [34t]The lamp of the body is your eye. When your eye is sound, then your whole body is filled with

---

11, 13: The holy Spirit: this is a Lucan editorial alteration of a traditional saying of Jesus (see Mt 7, 11). Luke presents the gift of the holy Spirit as the response of the Father to the prayer of the Christian disciple.

11, 19: Your own people: the Greek reads "your sons." Other Jewish exorcists (see Acts 19, 13–20), who recognize that the power of God is active in the exorcism, would themselves convict the accusers of Jesus. See also the note on Mt 12, 27.

11, 22: One stronger: i.e., Jesus. Cf 3, 16 where John the Baptist identifies Jesus as "more powerful than I."

11, 27–28: The beatitude in v 28 should not be interpreted as a rebuke of the mother of Jesus; see the note on 8, 21. Rather, it emphasizes (like 2, 35) that attentiveness to God's

word is more important than biological relationship to Jesus.

11, 29–32: The "sign of Jonah" in Lk is the preaching of the need for repentance by a prophet who comes from afar. Cf Mt 12, 38–42 (and see the notes there) where the "sign of Jonah" is interpreted by Jesus as his death and resurrection.

e: Mt 7, 7-11. *f:* Mt 21, 22; Mk 11, 24; Jn 14, 13; 15, 7; 1 Jn 5, 14-15. *g:* Mt 12, 22-30; Mk 3, 20-27. *h:* Mt 9, 34. *i:* Mt 12, 38; 16, 1; Mk 8, 11; 1 Cor 1, 22. *j:* Ex 8, 19. *k:* 9, 50; Mk 9, 40. *l:* Mt 12, 43-45. *m:* Jn 5, 14. *n:* 1, 28.42.48. *o:* Mt 12, 38-42; Mk 8, 12. *p:* Mt 16, 1.4; Jn 6, 30; 1 Cor 1, 22. *q:* 1 Kgs 10, 1-10; 2 Chr 9, 1-12. *r:* Jon 3, 8.10. *s:* 8, 16; Mt 5, 15; Mk 4, 21. *t:* Mt 6, 22-23.

light, but when it is bad, then your body is in darkness. [35]Take care, then, that the light in you not become darkness. [36]If your whole body is full of light, and no part of it is in darkness, then it will be as full of light as a lamp illuminating you with its brightness."

Denunciation of the Pharisees and Scholars of the Law. [37uv]*After he had spoken, a Pharisee invited him to dine at his home. He entered and reclined at table to eat. [38w]The Pharisee was amazed to see that he did not observe the prescribed washing before the meal. [39x]The Lord said to him, "Oh you Pharisees! Although you cleanse the outside of the cup and the dish, inside you are filled with plunder and evil. [40]You fools! Did not the maker of the outside also make the inside? [41]But as to what is within, give alms, and behold, everything will be clean for you. [42y]Woe to you Pharisees! You pay tithes of mint and of rue and of every garden herb, but you pay no attention to judgment and to love for God. These you should have done, without overlooking the others. [43z]Woe to you Pharisees! You love the seat of honor in synagogues and greetings in marketplaces. [44a]*Woe to you! You are like unseen graves over which people unknowingly walk."

[45b]*Then one of the scholars of the law said to him in reply, "Teacher, by saying this you are insulting us too." [46]And he said, "Woe also to you scholars of the law! You impose on people burdens hard to carry, but you yourselves do not lift one finger to touch them. [47c]Woe to you! You build the memorials of the prophets whom your ancestors killed. [48]Consequently, you bear witness and give consent to the deeds of your ancestors, for they killed them and you do the building. [49d]*Therefore, the wisdom of God said, 'I will send to them prophets and apostles; some of them they will kill and persecute' [50]in order that this generation might be charged with the blood of all the prophets shed since the foundation of the world, [51e]*from the blood of Abel to the blood of Zechariah who died between the altar and the temple building. Yes, I tell you, this generation will be charged with their blood! [52f]Woe to you, scholars of the law! You have taken away the key of knowledge. You yourselves did not enter and you stopped those trying to enter." [53g]When he left, the scribes and Pharisees began to act with hostility toward him and to interrogate him about many things, [54h]for they were plotting to catch him at something he might say.

CHAPTER 12

See RG 406-8

The Leaven of the Pharisees. [1i]*Meanwhile, so many people were crowding together that they were trampling one another underfoot. He began to speak, first to his disciples, "Beware of the leaven—that is, the hypocrisy—of the Pharisees.

Courage under Persecution. [2jk]*"There is nothing concealed that will not be revealed, nor secret that will not be known. [3]Therefore whatever you have said in the darkness will be heard in the light, and what you have whispered behind closed doors will be proclaimed on the housetops. [4]I tell you, my friends, do

---

11, 37–54: This denunciation of the Pharisees (39–44) and the scholars of the law (45–52) is set by Luke in the context of Jesus' dining at the home of a Pharisee. Controversies with or reprimands of Pharisees are regularly set by Luke within the context of Jesus' eating with Pharisees (see 5, 29–39; 7, 36–50; 14, 1–24). A different compilation of similar sayings is found in Mt 23 (see also the notes there).

11, 44: Unseen graves: contact with the dead or with human bones or graves (see Nm 19, 16) brought ritual impurity. Jesus presents the Pharisees as those who insidiously lead others astray through their seeming attention to the law.

11, 45: Scholars of the law: see the note on 10, 25.

11, 49: I will send to them prophets and apostles: Jesus connects the mission of the church (apostles) with the mission of the Old Testament prophets who often suffered the rebuke of their contemporaries.

11, 51: From the blood of Abel to the blood of Zechariah: the murder of Abel is the first murder recounted in the Old Testament (Gn 4, 8). The Zechariah mentioned here may be the Zechariah whose murder is recounted in 2 Chr 24, 20–22, the last murder presented in the Hebrew canon of the Old Testament.

12, 1: See the notes on Mk 8, 15 and Mt 16, 5–12.

12, 2–9: Luke presents a collection of sayings of Jesus exhorting his followers to acknowledge him and his mission fearlessly and assuring them of God's protection even in times of persecution. They are paralleled in Mt 10, 26–33.

u: 20, 45-47; Mt 23, 1-36; Mk 12, 38-40. *v:* 7, 36; 14, 1. *w:* Mt 15, 2; Mk 7, 2-5. *x:* Mt 23, 25-26. *y:* Lv 27, 30; Mt 23, 23. *z:* 20, 46; Mt 23, 6; Mk 12, 38-39. *a:* Mt 23, 27. *b:* Mt 23, 4. *c:* Mt 23, 29-32. *d:* Mt 23, 34-36. *e:* Gn 4, 8; 2 Chr 24, 20-22. *f:* Mt 23, 13. *g:* 6, 11; Mt 22, 15-22. *h:* 20, 20. *i:* Mt 16, 6; Mk 8, 15. *j:* Mt 10, 26-33. *k:* 8, 17; Mk 4, 22.

not be afraid of those who kill the body but after that can do no more. 5*I shall show you whom to fear. Be afraid of the one who after killing has the power to cast into Gehenna; yes, I tell you, be afraid of that one. 6*Are not five sparrows sold for two small coins? Yet not one of them has escaped the notice of God. 7l Even the hairs of your head have all been counted. Do not be afraid. You are worth more than many sparrows. 8I tell you, everyone who acknowledges me before others the Son of Man will acknowledge before the angels of God. 9m But whoever denies me before others will be denied before the angels of God.

Sayings about the holy Spirit. 10n*"Everyone who speaks a word against the Son of Man will be forgiven, but the one who blasphemes against the holy Spirit will not be forgiven. 11o When they take you before synagogues and before rulers and authorities, do not worry about how or what your defense will be or about what you are to say. 12For the holy Spirit will teach you at that moment what you should say."

Saying against Greed. 13*Someone in the crowd said to him, "Teacher, tell my brother to share the inheritance with me." 14p He replied to him, "Friend, who appointed me as your judge and arbitrator?" 15q Then he said to the crowd, "Take care to guard against all greed, for though one may be rich, one's life does not consist of possessions."

Parable of the Rich Fool. 16Then he told them a parable. "There was a rich man whose land produced a bountiful harvest. 17He asked himself, 'What shall I do, for I do not have space to store my harvest?' 18And he said, 'This is what I shall do: I shall tear down my barns and build larger ones. There

I shall store all my grain and other goods 19rs and I shall say to myself, "Now as for you, you have so many good things stored up for many years, rest, eat, drink, be merry!" ' 20But God said to him, 'You fool, this night your life will be demanded of you; and the things you have prepared, to whom will they belong?' 21*Thus will it be for the one who stores up treasure for himself but is not rich in what matters to God."

Dependence on God. 22t He said to [his] disciples, "Therefore I tell you, do not worry about your life and what you will eat, or about your body and what you will wear. 23For life is more than food and the body more than clothing. 24u Notice the ravens: they do not sow or reap; they have neither storehouse nor barn, yet God feeds them. How much more important are you than birds! 25Can any of you by worrying add a moment to your life-span? 26If even the smallest things are beyond your control, why are you anxious about the rest? 27v Notice how the flowers grow. They do not toil or spin. But I tell you, not even Solomon in all his splendor was dressed like one of them. 28If God so clothes the grass in the field that grows today and is thrown into the oven tomorrow, will he not much more provide for you, O you of little faith? 29As for you, do not seek what you are to eat and what you are to drink, and do not worry anymore. 30All the nations of the world seek for these things, and your Father knows that you need them. 31Instead, seek his kingdom, and these other things will be given you besides. 32w Do not be afraid any longer, little flock, for your Father is pleased to give you the kingdom. 33x Sell your belongings and give

---

12, 5: **Gehenna:** see the note on Mt 5, 22.

12, 6: **Two small coins:** the Roman copper coin, the assarion (Latin *as*), was worth about one-sixteenth of a denarius (see the note on 7, 41).

12, 10–12: The sayings about the holy Spirit are set in the context of fearlessness in the face of persecution (2–9; cf Mt 12, 31–32). The holy Spirit will be presented in Luke's second volume, the Acts of the Apostles, as the power responsible for the guidance of the Christian mission and the source of courage in the face of persecution.

12, 13–34: Luke has joined together sayings contrasting those whose focus and trust in life is on material possessions, symbolized here by the rich fool of the parable (16–21), with

those who recognize their complete dependence on God (21), those whose radical detachment from material possessions symbolizes their heavenly treasure (33–34).

12, 21: **Rich in what matters to God:** literally, "rich for God."

---

l: 12, 24; 21, 18; Acts 27, 34.   *m*: 9, 26; Mk 8, 38; 2 Tm 2, 12.   *n*: Mt 12, 31-32; Mk 3, 28-29.   *o*: 21, 12-15; Mt 10, 17-20; Mk 13, 11.   *p*: Ex 2, 14; Acts 7, 27.   *q*: 1 Tm 6, 9-10.   *r*: Mt 6, 19-21; 1 Tm 6, 17.   *s*: Sir 11, 19.   *t*: Mt 6, 25-34.   *u*: 12, 7.   *v*: 1 Kgs 10, 4-7; 2 Chr 9, 3-6.   *w*: 22, 29; Rv 1, 6.   *x*: 18, 22; Mt 6, 20-21; Mk 10, 21.

alms. Provide money bags for yourselves that do not wear out, an inexhaustible treasure in heaven that no thief can reach nor moth destroy. [34]For where your treasure is, there also will your heart be.

Vigilant and Faithful Servants. [35y]*"Gird your loins and light your lamps [36z]and be like servants who await their master's return from a wedding, ready to open immediately when he comes and knocks. [37]Blessed are those servants whom the master finds vigilant on his arrival. Amen, I say to you, he will gird himself, have them recline at table, and proceed to wait on them. [38]And should he come in the second or third watch and find them prepared in this way, blessed are those servants. [39a]Be sure of this: if the master of the house had known the hour when the thief was coming, he would not have let his house be broken into. [40]You also must be prepared, for at an hour you do not expect, the Son of Man will come."

[41]Then Peter said, "Lord, is this parable meant for us or for everyone?" [42]And the Lord replied, "Who, then, is the faithful and prudent steward whom the master will put in charge of his servants to distribute [the] food allowance at the proper time? [43]Blessed is that servant whom his master on arrival finds doing so. [44]Truly, I say to you, he will put him in charge of all his property. [45]*But if that servant says to himself, 'My master is delayed in coming,' and begins to beat the menservants and the maidservants, to eat and drink and get drunk, [46]then that servant's master will come on an unexpected day and at an unknown hour and will punish him severely and assign him a place with the unfaithful. [47b]That servant who knew his master's will but did not make preparations nor act in accord with his will shall be beaten se-verely; [48]and the servant who was ignorant of his master's will but acted in a way deserving of a severe beating shall be beaten only lightly. Much will be required of the person entrusted with much, and still more will be demanded of the person entrusted with more.

Jesus: A Cause of Division. [49]*"I have come to set the earth on fire, and how I wish it were already blazing! [50c]*There is a baptism with which I must be baptized, and how great is my anguish until it is accomplished! [51de]Do you think that I have come to establish peace on the earth? No, I tell you, but rather division. [52]From now on a household of five will be divided, three against two and two against three; [53f]a father will be divided against his son and a son against his father, a mother against her daughter and a daughter against her mother, a mother-in-law against her daughter-in-law and a daughter-in-law against her mother-in-law."

Signs of the Times. [54g]He also said to the crowds, "When you see [a] cloud rising in the west you say immediately that it is going to rain—and so it does; [55]and when you notice that the wind is blowing from the south you say that it is going to be hot—and so it is. [56]You hypocrites! You know how to interpret the appearance of the earth and the sky; why do you not know how to interpret the present time?

Settlement with an Opponent. [57h]"Why do you not judge for yourselves what is right? [58]If you are to go with your opponent before a magistrate, make an effort to settle the matter on the way; otherwise your opponent will turn you over to the judge, and the judge hand you over to the constable, and the constable throw you into prison. [59]*I say to you, you will not be released until you have paid the last penny."

12, 35–48: This collection of sayings relates to Luke's understanding of the end time and the return of Jesus. Luke emphasizes for his readers the importance of being faithful to the instructions of Jesus in the period before the parousia.

12, 45: My master is delayed in coming: this statement indicates that early Christian expectations for the imminent return of Jesus had undergone some modification. Luke cautions his readers against counting on such a delay and acting irresponsibly. Cf the similar warning in Mt 24, 48.

12, 49–53: Jesus' proclamation of the kingdom is a refining and purifying fire. His message that meets with accept-ance or rejection will be a source of conflict and dissension even within families.

12, 50: Baptism: i.e., his death.

12, 59: The last penny: Greek, **lepton,** a very small amount. Mt 5, 26 has for "the last penny" the Greek word **ko-drantēs** (Latin **quadrans,** "farthing").

y: Mt 24, 45-51. z: Mt 25, 1-13; Mk 13, 35-37. a: Mt 24, 43-44; 1 Thes 5, 2. b: Jas 4, 17. c: Mk 10, 38-39. d: Mt 10, 34-35. e: 2, 14. f: Mi 7, 6. g: Mt 16, 2-3. h: Mt 5, 25-26.

See RG
407–8

CHAPTER 13

A Call to Repentance. [1]*At that time some people who were present there told him about the Galileans whose blood Pilate had mingled with the blood of their sacrifices. [2i]He said to them in reply, "Do you think that because these Galileans suffered in this way they were greater sinners than all other Galileans? [3j]By no means! But I tell you, if you do not repent, you will all perish as they did! [4]*Or those eighteen people who were killed when the tower at Siloam fell on them—do you think they were more guilty than everyone else who lived in Jerusalem? [5]By no means! But I tell you, if you do not repent, you will all perish as they did!"

The Parable of the Barren Fig Tree. [6k]*And he told them this parable: "There once was a person who had a fig tree planted in his orchard, and when he came in search of fruit on it but found none, [7]he said to the gardener, 'For three years now I have come in search of fruit on this fig tree but have found none. [So] cut it down. Why should it exhaust the soil?' [8]He said to him in reply, 'Sir, leave it for this year also, and I shall cultivate the ground around it and fertilize it; [9]it may bear fruit in the future. If not you can cut it down.' "

Cure of a Crippled Woman on the Sabbath. [10]*He was teaching in a synagogue on the sabbath. [11]And a woman was there who for eighteen years had been crippled by a spirit; she was bent over, completely incapable of standing erect. [12]When Jesus saw her, he called to her and said, "Woman, you are set free of your infirmity." [13]He laid his hands on her, and she at once stood up straight and glorified God. [14l]But the leader of the synagogue, indignant that Jesus had cured on the sabbath, said to the crowd in reply, "There are six days when work should be done. Come on those days to be cured, not on the sabbath day." [15m]*The Lord said to him in reply, "Hypocrites! Does not each one of you on the sabbath untie his ox or his ass from the manger and lead it out for watering? [16n]*This daughter of Abraham, whom Satan has bound for eighteen years now, ought she not to have been set free on the sabbath day from this bondage?" [17]When he said this, all his adversaries were humiliated; and the whole crowd rejoiced at all the splendid deeds done by him.

The Parable of the Mustard Seed. [18o]*Then he said, "What is the kingdom of God like? To what can I compare it? [19p]It is like a mustard seed that a person took and

---

13, 1–5: The death of the Galileans at the hands of Pilate (1) and the accidental death of those on whom the tower fell (4) are presented by the Lucan Jesus as timely reminders of the need for all to repent, for the victims of these tragedies should not be considered outstanding sinners who were singled out for punishment.

13, 1: The slaughter of the Galileans by Pilate is unknown outside Lk; but from what is known about Pilate from the Jewish historian Josephus, such a slaughter would be in keeping with the character of Pilate. Josephus reports that Pilate had disrupted a religious gathering of the Samaritans on Mt. Gerizim with a slaughter of the participants (**Antiquities** 18, 4, 1 §§86–87), and that on another occasion Pilate had killed many Jews who had opposed him when he appropriated money from the temple treasury to build an aqueduct in Jerusalem (**Jewish War** 2, 9, 4 §§175–77; **Antiquities** 18, 3, 2 §§60–62).

13, 4: Like the incident mentioned in v 1, nothing of this accident in Jerusalem is known outside Lk and the New Testament.

13, 6–9: Following on the call to repentance in vv 1–5, the parable of the barren fig tree presents a story about the continuing patience of God with those who have not yet given evidence of their repentance (see 3, 8). The parable may also be alluding to the delay of the end time, when punishment will be meted out, and the importance of preparing for the end of the age because the delay will not be permanent (8–9).

13, 10–17: The cure of the crippled woman on the sabbath and the controversy that results furnishes a parallel to an incident that will be reported by Lk in 14, 1–6, the cure of the man with dropsy on the sabbath. A characteristic of Luke's style is the juxtaposition of an incident that reveals Jesus' concern for a man with an incident that reveals his concern for a woman; cf, e.g., 7, 11–17 and 8, 49–56.

13, 15–16: If the law as interpreted by Jewish tradition allowed for the untying of bound animals on the sabbath, how much more should this woman who has been bound by Satan's power be freed on the sabbath from her affliction.

13, 16: Whom Satan has bound: affliction and infirmity are taken as evidence of Satan's hold on humanity. The healing ministry of Jesus reveals the gradual wresting from Satan of control over humanity and the establishment of God's kingdom.

13, 18–21: Two parables are used to illustrate the future proportions of the kingdom of God that will result from its deceptively small beginning in the preaching and healing ministry of Jesus. They are paralleled in Mt 13, 31–33 and Mk 4, 30–32.

---

i: Jn 9, 2. *j:* Jn 8, 24. *k:* Jer 8, 13; Hb 3, 17; Mt 21, 19; Mk 11, 13. *l:* 6, 7; 14, 3; Ex 20, 8-11; Dt 5, 12-15; Mt 12, 10; Mk 3, 2-4; Jn 5, 16; 7, 23; 9, 14.16. *m:* 14, 5; Dt 22, 4; Mt 12, 11. *n:* 19, 9. *o:* Mt 13, 31-32; Mk 4, 30-32. *p:* Ez 17, 23-24; 31, 6.

planted in the garden. When it was fully grown, it became a large bush and 'the birds of the sky dwelt in its branches.' "

The Parable of the Yeast. *20q*Again he said, "To what shall I compare the kingdom of God? *21*It is like yeast that a woman took and mixed [in] with three measures of wheat flour until the whole batch of dough was leavened."

The Narrow Door; Salvation and Rejection. *22**He passed through towns and villages, teaching as he went and making his way to Jerusalem. *23*Someone asked him, "Lord, will only a few people be saved?" He answered them, *24rs*"Strive to enter through the narrow gate, for many, I tell you, will attempt to enter but will not be strong enough. *25t*After the master of the house has arisen and locked the door, then will you stand outside knocking and saying, 'Lord, open the door for us.' He will say to you in reply, 'I do not know where you are from.' *26*And you will say, 'We ate and drank in your company and you taught in our streets.' *27u*Then he will say to you, 'I do not know where [you] are from. Depart from me, all you evildoers!' *28v*And there will be wailing and grinding of teeth when you see Abraham, Isaac, and Jacob and all the prophets in the kingdom of God and you yourselves cast out. *29w*And people will come from the east and the west and from the north and the south and will recline at table in the kingdom of God. *30x*For behold, some are last who will be first, and some are first who will be last."

Herod's Desire to Kill Jesus. *31*At that

time some Pharisees came to him and said, "Go away, leave this area because Herod wants to kill you." *32**He replied, "Go and tell that fox, 'Behold, I cast out demons and I perform healings today and tomorrow, and on the third day I accomplish my purpose. *33y**Yet I must continue on my way today, tomorrow, and the following day, for it is impossible that a prophet should die outside of Jerusalem.'

The Lament over Jerusalem. *34z*"Jerusalem, Jerusalem, you who kill the prophets and stone those sent to you, how many times I yearned to gather your children together as a hen gathers her brood under her wings, but you were unwilling! *35a*Behold, your house will be abandoned. [But] I tell you, you will not see me until [the time comes when] you say, 'Blessed is he who comes in the name of the Lord.' "

CHAPTER 14 See RG 406-8

Healing of the Man with Dropsy on the Sabbath. *1bc**On a sabbath he went to dine at the home of one of the leading Pharisees, and the people there were observing him carefully. *2**In front of him there was a man suffering from dropsy. *3d*Jesus spoke to the scholars of the law and Pharisees in reply, asking, "Is it lawful to cure on the sabbath or not?" *4*But they kept silent; so he took the man and, after he had healed him, dismissed him. *5e**Then he said to them, "Who among you, if your son or ox falls into a cistern, would not immediately pull him out on the sabbath day?" *6f*But they were unable to answer his question.

13, 22–30: These sayings of Jesus follow in Lk upon the parables of the kingdom (18–21) and stress that great effort is required for entrance into the kingdom (24) and that there is an urgency to accept the present opportunity to enter because the narrow door will not remain open indefinitely (25). Lying behind the sayings is the rejection of Jesus and his message by his Jewish contemporaries (26) whose places at table in the kingdom will be taken by Gentiles from the four corners of the world (29). Those called last (the Gentiles) will precede those to whom the invitation to enter was first extended (the Jews). See also 14, 15–24.

13, 32: Nothing, not even Herod's desire to kill Jesus, stands in the way of Jesus' role in fulfilling God's will and in establishing the kingdom through his exorcisms and healings.

13, 33: It is impossible that a prophet should die outside of Jerusalem: Jerusalem is the city of destiny and the

goal of the journey of the prophet Jesus. Only when he reaches the holy city will his work be accomplished.

14, 1–6: See the note on 13, 10–17.

14, 2: Dropsy: an abnormal swelling of the body because of the retention and accumulation of fluid.

14, 5: Your son or ox: this is the reading of many of the oldest and most important New Testament manuscripts. Because of the strange collocation of **son** and **ox**, some copyists have altered it to "your ass or ox," on the model of the saying in 13, 15.

q: Mt 13, 33.　r: Mt 7, 13-14.21-23.　s: Mk 10, 25.　t: Mt 25, 10-12.　u: Ps 6, 9; Mt 7, 23; 25, 41.　v: Mt 8, 11-12.　w: Ps 107, 2-3.　x: Mt 19, 20; 20, 16; Mk 10, 31.　y: 2, 38; Jn 6, 30; 8, 20.　z: 19, 41-44; Mt 23, 37-39.　a: 19, 38; 1 Kgs 9, 7-8; Ps 118, 26; Jer 7, 4-7.13-15; 12, 7; 22, 5.　b: 6, 6-11; 13, 10-17.　c: 11, 37.　d: 6, 9; Mk 3, 4.　e: 13, 15; Dt 22, 4; Mt 12, 11.　f: Mt 22, 46.

Conduct of Invited Guests and Hosts.
[7g]*He told a parable to those who had been invited, noticing how they were choosing the places of honor at the table. [8h]"When you are invited by someone to a wedding banquet, do not recline at table in the place of honor. A more distinguished guest than you may have been invited by him, [9]and the host who invited both of you may approach you and say, 'Give your place to this man,' and then you would proceed with embarrassment to take the lowest place. [10]Rather, when you are invited, go and take the lowest place so that when the host comes to you he may say, 'My friend, move up to a higher position.' Then you will enjoy the esteem of your companions at the table. [11i]For everyone who exalts himself will be humbled, but the one who humbles himself will be exalted." [12j]Then he said to the host who invited him, "When you hold a lunch or a dinner, do not invite your friends or your brothers or your relatives or your wealthy neighbors, in case they may invite you back and you have repayment. [13]Rather, when you hold a banquet, invite the poor, the crippled, the lame, the blind; [14k]blessed indeed will you be because of their inability to repay you. For you will be repaid at the resurrection of the righteous."

The Parable of the Great Feast. [15]*One of his fellow guests on hearing this said to him, "Blessed is the one who will dine in the kingdom of God." [16l]He replied to him, "A man gave a great dinner to which he invited many. [17]When the time for the dinner came, he dispatched his servant to say to those invited, 'Come, everything is now ready.' [18]But one by one, they all began to excuse themselves.

The first said to him, 'I have purchased a field and must go to examine it; I ask you, consider me excused.' [19]And another said, 'I have purchased five yoke of oxen and am on my way to evaluate them; I ask you, consider me excused.' [20]And another said, 'I have just married a woman, and therefore I cannot come.' [21]The servant went and reported this to his master. Then the master of the house in a rage commanded his servant, 'Go out quickly into the streets and alleys of the town and bring in here the poor and the crippled, the blind and the lame.' [22]The servant reported, 'Sir, your orders have been carried out and still there is room.' [23]The master then ordered the servant, 'Go out to the highways and hedgerows and make people come in that my home may be filled. [24]For, I tell you, none of those men who were invited will taste my dinner.' "

Sayings on Discipleship. [25]*Great crowds were traveling with him, and he turned and addressed them, [26mn]*"If anyone comes to me without hating his father and mother, wife and children, brothers and sisters, and even his own life, he cannot be my disciple. [27o]Whoever does not carry his own cross and come after me cannot be my disciple. [28]Which of you wishing to construct a tower does not first sit down and calculate the cost to see if there is enough for its completion? [29]Otherwise, after laying the foundation and finding himself unable to finish the work the onlookers should laugh at him [30]and say, 'This one began to build but did not have the resources to finish.' [31]Or what king marching into battle would not first sit down and decide whether with ten thousand troops he can successfully oppose another king ad-

14, 7–14: The banquet scene found only in Luke provides the opportunity for these teachings of Jesus on humility and presents a setting to display Luke's interest in Jesus' attitude toward the rich and the poor (see the notes on 4, 18; 6, 20–26; 12, 13–34).

14, 15–24: The parable of the great dinner is a further illustration of the rejection by Israel, God's chosen people, of Jesus' invitation to share in the banquet in the kingdom and the extension of the invitation to other Jews whose identification as the poor, crippled, blind, and lame (21) classifies them among those who recognize their need for salvation, and to Gentiles (23). A similar parable is found in Mt 22, 1–10.

14, 25–33: This collection of sayings, most of which are peculiar to Lk, focuses on the total dedication necessary for

the disciple of Jesus. No attachment to family (26) or possessions (33) can stand in the way of the total commitment demanded of the disciple. Also, acceptance of the call to be a disciple demands readiness to accept persecution and suffering (27) and a realistic assessment of the hardships and costs (28–32).

14, 26: Hating his father . . . : cf the similar saying in Mt 10, 37. The disciple's family must take second place to the absolute dedication involved in following Jesus (see also 9, 59–62).

g: 11, 43; Mt 23, 6; Mk 12, 38-39. h: Prv 25, 6-7. i: 18, 14. j: 6, 32-35. k: Jn 5, 29. l: Mt 22, 2-10. m: Mt 10, 37-38. n: 9, 57-62; 18, 29; Jn 12, 25. o: 9, 23; Mt 16, 24; Mk 8, 34.

vancing upon him with twenty thousand troops? *32* But if not, while he is still far away, he will send a delegation to ask for peace terms. *33 p* In the same way, everyone of you who does not renounce all his possessions cannot be my disciple.

The Simile of Salt. *34q* *"Salt is good, but if salt itself loses its taste, with what can its flavor be restored? *35r* It is fit neither for the soil nor for the manure pile; it is thrown out. Whoever has ears to hear ought to hear."

See RG 406–8

CHAPTER 15

The Parable of the Lost Sheep. *1s* *The tax collectors and sinners were all drawing near to listen to him, *2t* but the Pharisees and scribes began to complain, saying, "This man welcomes sinners and eats with them." *3* So to them he addressed this parable. *4uvw* "What man among you having a hundred sheep and losing one of them would not leave the ninety-nine in the desert and go after the lost one until he finds it? *5* And when he does find it, he sets it on his shoulders with great joy *6* and, upon his arrival home, he calls together his friends and neighbors and says to them, 'Rejoice with me because I have found my lost sheep.' *7x* I tell you, in just the same way there will be more joy in heaven over one sinner who repents than over ninety-nine righteous people who have no need of repentance.

The Parable of the Lost Coin. *8* *"Or what woman having ten coins and losing one would not light a lamp and sweep the house, searching carefully until she finds it? *9* And when she does find it, she calls together her friends and neighbors and says to them, 'Rejoice with me because I have found the coin that I lost.' *10* In just the same way, I tell you, there will be rejoicing among the angels of God over one sinner who repents."

The Parable of the Lost Son. *11* Then he said, "A man had two sons, *12* and the younger son said to his father, 'Father, give me the share of your estate that should come to me.' So the father divided the property between them. *13y* After a few days, the younger son collected all his belongings and set off to a distant country where he squandered his inheritance on a life of dissipation. *14* When he had freely spent everything, a severe famine struck that country, and he found himself in dire need. *15* So he hired himself out to one of the local citizens who sent him to his farm to tend the swine. *16* And he longed to eat his fill of the pods on which the swine fed, but nobody gave him any. *17* Coming to his senses he thought, 'How many of my father's hired workers have more than enough food to eat, but here am I, dying from hunger. *18* I shall get up and go to my father and I shall say to him, "Father, I have sinned against heaven and against you. *19* I no longer deserve to be called your son; treat me as you would treat one of your hired workers." ' *20* So he got up and went back to his father. While he was still a long way off, his father caught sight of him, and was filled with compassion. He ran to his son, embraced him and kissed him. *21* His son said to him, 'Father, I have sinned against heaven and against you; I no longer deserve to be called your son.' *22* But his father ordered his servants, 'Quickly bring the finest robe and put it on him; put a ring on his finger and sandals on his feet. *23* Take the fattened calf and slaughter it. Then let us celebrate with a feast, *24* because this son of mine was dead, and has come to life again; he was lost, and has been found.' Then the celebration began. *25* Now the older son had been out in the field and, on his way back, as he neared the house, he heard the sound of music and dancing. *26* He called one of the servants and asked what this might mean. *27* The servant said to him, 'Your brother has returned and

---

14, 34–35: The simile of salt follows the sayings of Jesus that demanded of the disciple total dedication and detachment from family and possessions and illustrates the condition of one who does not display this total commitment. The half-hearted disciple is like salt that cannot serve its intended purpose. See the simile of salt in Mt 5, 13 and the note there.

15, 1–32: To the parable of the lost sheep (1–7) that Luke shares with Matthew (Mt 18, 12–14), Luke adds two parables (the lost coin, 8–10; the prodigal son, 11–32) from his own

special tradition to illustrate Jesus' particular concern for the lost and God's love for the repentant sinner.

15, 8: Ten coins: literally, "ten drachmas." A drachma was a Greek silver coin.

---

p: 5, 11.   *q:* Mt 5, 13; Mk 9, 50.   *r:* 8, 8; Mt 11, 15; 13, 9; Mk 4, 9.23.   *s:* Mt 9, 10-13.   *t:* 5, 30; 19, 7.   *u:* Mt 18, 12-14.   *v:* 19, 10.   *w:* Ez 34, 11-12.16.   *x:* Ez 18, 23.   *y:* Prv 29, 3.

your father has slaughtered the fattened calf because he has him back safe and sound.' [28]He became angry, and when he refused to enter the house, his father came out and pleaded with him. [29]He said to his father in reply, 'Look, all these years I served you and not once did I disobey your orders; yet you never gave me even a young goat to feast on with my friends. [30]But when your son returns who swallowed up your property with prostitutes, for him you slaughter the fattened calf.' [31]He said to him, 'My son, you are here with me always; everything I have is yours. [32]But now we must celebrate and rejoice, because your brother was dead and has come to life again; he was lost and has been found.' "

See RG 406–8

CHAPTER 16

The Parable of the Dishonest Steward.

[1]*Then he also said to his disciples, "A rich man had a steward who was reported to him for squandering his property. [2]He summoned him and said, 'What is this I hear about you? Prepare a full account of your stewardship, because you can no longer be my steward.' [3]The steward said to himself, 'What shall I do, now that my master is taking the position of steward away from me? I am not strong enough to dig and I am ashamed to beg. [4]I know what I shall do so that, when I am removed from the stewardship, they may welcome me into their homes.' [5]He called in his master's debtors one by one. To the first he said, 'How much do you owe my master?' [6]*He replied, 'One hundred measures of olive oil.' He said to him, 'Here is your promissory note. Sit down and quickly write one for fifty.' [7]*Then to another he said, 'And you, how much do you owe?' He replied, 'One hundred kors of wheat.' He said to him, 'Here is your promissory note; write one for eighty.' [8z]*And the master commended that dishonest steward for acting prudently.

Application of the Parable. "For the children of this world are more prudent in dealing with their own generation than are the children of light. [9a]*I tell you, make friends for yourselves with dishonest wealth, so that when it fails, you will be welcomed into eternal dwellings. [10b]*The person who is trustworthy in very small matters is also trustworthy in great ones; and the person who is dishonest in very small matters is also dishonest in great ones. [11]If, therefore, you are not trustworthy with dishonest wealth, who will trust you with true wealth? [12]If you are not trustworthy with what belongs to another, who will give you what is yours? [13c]*No servant can serve two masters. He will either hate one and love the other, or be devoted to one and despise the other. You cannot serve God and mammon.' "

16, 1–8a: The parable of the dishonest steward has to be understood in the light of the Palestinian custom of agents acting on behalf of their masters and the usurious practices common to such agents. The dishonesty of the steward consisted in the squandering of his master's property (1) and not in any subsequent graft. The master commends the dishonest steward who has forgone his own usurious commission on the business transaction by having the debtors write new notes that reflected only the real amount owed the master (i.e., minus the steward's profit). The dishonest steward acts in this way in order to ingratiate himself with the debtors because he knows he is being dismissed from his position (3). The parable, then, teaches the prudent use of one's material goods in light of an imminent crisis.

16, 6: One hundred measures: literally, "one hundred baths." A bath is a Hebrew unit of liquid measurement equivalent to eight or nine gallons.

16, 7: One hundred kors: a kor is a Hebrew unit of dry measure for grain or wheat equivalent to ten or twelve bushels.

16, 8b-13: Several originally independent sayings of Jesus are gathered here by Luke to form the concluding application of the parable by the dishonest steward.

16, 8b-9: The first conclusion recommends the prudent use of one's wealth (in the light of the coming of the end of the age) after the manner of the children of this world, represented in the parable by the dishonest steward.

16, 9: Dishonest wealth: literally, "mammon of iniquity." Mammon is the Greek transliteration of a Hebrew or Aramaic word that is usually explained as meaning "that in which one trusts." The characterization of this wealth as **dishonest** expresses a tendency of wealth to lead one to dishonesty. **Eternal dwellings:** or, "eternal tents," i.e., heaven.

16, 10–12: The second conclusion recommends constant fidelity to those in positions of responsibility.

16, 13: The third conclusion is a general statement about the incompatibility of serving God and being a slave to riches. To be dependent upon wealth is opposed to the teachings of Jesus who counseled complete dependence on the Father as one of the characteristics of the Christian disciple (12, 22–39). **God and mammon:** see the note on 16, 9. Mammon is used here as if it were itself a god.

---

z: Eph 5, 8; 1 Thes 5, 5.   a: 12, 33.   b: 19, 17; Mt 25, 20-23.   c: Mt 6, 24.

A Saying against the Pharisees. [14]*The Pharisees, who loved money, heard all these things and sneered at him. [15d]And he said to them, "You justify yourselves in the sight of others, but God knows your hearts; for what is of human esteem is an abomination in the sight of God.

Sayings about the Law. [16e]*"The law and the prophets lasted until John; but from then on the kingdom of God is proclaimed, and everyone who enters does so with violence. [17f]It is easier for heaven and earth to pass away than for the smallest part of a letter of the law to become invalid.

Sayings about Divorce. [18g]"Everyone who divorces his wife and marries another commits adultery, and the one who marries a woman divorced from her husband commits adultery.

The Parable of the Rich Man and Lazarus. [19]*"There was a rich man who dressed in purple garments and fine linen and dined sumptuously each day. [20]And lying at his door was a poor man named Lazarus, covered with sores, [21h]who would gladly have eaten his fill of the scraps that fell from the rich man's table. Dogs even used to come and lick his sores. [22]When the poor man died, he was carried away by angels to the bosom of Abraham. The rich man also died and was buried, [23]*and from the netherworld, where he was in torment, he raised his eyes and saw Abraham far off and Lazarus at his side. [24]And he cried out, 'Father Abraham, have pity on me. Send Lazarus to dip the tip of his finger in water and cool my tongue, for I am suffering torment in these flames.' [25i]Abraham replied, 'My child, remember that you received what was good during your lifetime while Lazarus likewise received what was bad; but now he is comforted here, whereas you are tormented. [26]Moreover, between us and you a great chasm is established to prevent anyone from crossing who might wish to go from our side to yours or from your side to ours.' [27]He said, 'Then I beg you, father, send him to my father's house, [28]for I have five brothers, so that he may warn them, lest they too come to this place of torment.' [29]But Abraham replied, 'They have Moses and the prophets. Let them listen to them.' [30]*He said, 'Oh no, father Abraham, but if someone from the dead goes to them, they will repent.' [31j]Then Abraham said, 'If they will not listen to Moses and the prophets, neither will they be persuaded if someone should rise from the dead.' "

CHAPTER 17

See RG 406–8

Temptations to Sin. [1k]He said to his disciples, "Things that cause sin will inevitably occur, but woe to the person through whom they occur. [2]It would be better for him if a millstone were put around his neck and he be thrown into the sea than for him to cause one of these little ones to sin. [3l]*Be on your guard! If your brother sins, rebuke him; and if he repents, forgive him. [4m]And if he wrongs you seven times in one day and returns to you seven times saying, 'I am sorry,' you should forgive him."

Saying of Faith. [5]And the apostles said to

16, 14–18: The two parables about the use of riches in ch 16 are separated by several isolated sayings of Jesus on the hypocrisy of the Pharisees (14–15), on the law (16–17), and on divorce (18).

16, 14–15: The Pharisees are here presented as examples of those who are slaves to wealth (see 16, 13) and, consequently, they are unable to serve God.

16, 16: John the Baptist is presented in Luke's gospel as a transitional figure between the period of Israel, the time of promise, and the period of Jesus, the time of fulfillment. With John, the fulfillment of the Old Testament promises has begun.

16, 19–31: The parable of the rich man and Lazarus again illustrates Luke's concern with Jesus' attitude toward the rich and the poor. The reversal of the fates of the rich man and Lazarus (22–23) illustrates the teachings of Jesus in Luke's "Sermon on the Plain" (6, 20–21.24–25).

16, 19: The oldest Greek manuscript of Lk dating from ca. A.D. 175–225 records the name of the rich man as an abbreviated form of "Nineveh," but there is very little textual support in other manuscripts for this reading. "Dives" of popular tradition is the Latin Vulgate's translation for "rich man."

16, 23: The netherworld: see the note on 10, 15.

16, 30–31: A foreshadowing in Luke's gospel of the rejection of the call to repentance even after Jesus' resurrection.

17, 3a: Be on your guard: the translation takes v 3a as the conclusion to the saying on scandal in vv 1–2. It is not impossible that it should be taken as the beginning of the saying on forgiveness in vv 3b–4.

d: 18, 9-14. e: Mt 11, 12-13. f: Mt 5, 18. g: Mt 5, 32; 19, 9; Mk 10, 11-12; 1 Cor 7, 10-11. h: Mt 15, 27; Mk 7, 28. i: 6, 24-25. j: Jn 5, 46-47; 11, 44-48. k: Mt 18, 6-7. l: Mt 18, 15. m: Mt 6, 14; 18, 21-22.35; Mk 11, 25.

Sites of Jesus' Journey to Jerusalem and within It

the Lord, "Increase our faith." [6n]The Lord replied, "If you have faith the size of a mustard seed, you would say to [this] mulberry tree, 'Be uprooted and planted in the sea,' and it would obey you.

Attitude of a Servant. [7*]"Who among you would say to your servant who has just come in from plowing or tending sheep in the field, 'Come here immediately and take your place at table'? [8]Would he not rather say to him, 'Prepare something for me to eat. Put on your apron and wait on me while I eat and drink. You may eat and drink when I am finished'? [9]Is he grateful to that servant because he did what was commanded? [10]So should it be with you. When you have done all you have been commanded, say, 'We are unprofitable servants; we have done what we were obliged to do.'"

The Cleansing of Ten Lepers. [11o*]As he continued his journey to Jerusalem, he traveled through Samaria and Galilee. [12]As he was entering a village, ten lepers met [him]. They stood at a distance from him [13p]and raised their voice, saying, "Jesus, Master! Have pity on us!" [14q*]And when he saw them, he said, "Go show yourselves to the priests." As they were going they were cleansed. [15]And one of them, realizing he had been healed, returned, glorifying God in a loud voice; [16]and he fell at the feet of Jesus and thanked him. He was a Samaritan. [17]Jesus said in reply, "Ten were cleansed, were they not? Where are the other nine? [18]Has none but this foreigner returned to give thanks to God?" [19r]Then he said to him, "Stand up and go; your faith has saved you."

The Coming of the Kingdom of God. [20s*]Asked by the Pharisees when the kingdom of God would come, he said in reply, "The coming of the kingdom of God cannot be observed, [21t*]and no one will announce, 'Look, here it is,' or, 'There it is.' For behold, the kingdom of God is among you."

The Day of the Son of Man. [22]Then he said to his disciples, "The days will come when you will long to see one of the days of the Son of Man, but you will not see it. [23u]There will be those who will say to you, 'Look, there he is,' [or] 'Look, here he is.' Do not go off, do not run in pursuit. [24v]For just as lightning flashes and lights up the sky from one side to the other, so will the Son of Man be [in his day]. [25w]But first he must suffer greatly and be rejected by this generation. [26x]As it was in the days of Noah, so it will be in the days of the Son of Man; [27]they were eating and drinking, marrying and giving in marriage up to the day that Noah entered the ark, and the flood came and destroyed them all. [28y]Similarly, as it was in the days of Lot: they were eating, drinking, buying, selling, planting, building; [29]on the day when Lot left Sodom, fire and brimstone rained from the sky to destroy them all. [30]So it will be on the day the Son of Man is revealed. [31za]On that day, a person who is on the housetop and whose belongings are in the house must not go down to get them, and likewise a person in the field must not return to what was left

17, 7–10: These sayings of Jesus, peculiar to Luke, which continue his response to the apostles' request to increase their faith (5–6), remind them that Christian disciples can make no claim on God's graciousness; in fulfilling the exacting demands of discipleship, they are only doing their duty.

17, 11–19: This incident recounting the thankfulness of the cleansed Samaritan leper is narrated only in Luke's gospel and provides an instance of Jesus holding up a non-Jew (18) as an example to his Jewish contemporaries (cf 10, 33 where a similar purpose is achieved in the story of the good Samaritan). Moreover, it is the faith in Jesus manifested by the foreigner that has brought him salvation (19; cf the similar relationship between faith and salvation in 7, 50; 8, 48.50).

17, 11: Through Samaria and Galilee: or, "between Samaria and Galilee."

17, 14: See the note on 5, 14.

17, 20–37: To the question of the Pharisees about the time of the coming of God's kingdom, Jesus replies that the kingdom is **among you** (20–21). The emphasis has thus been shifted from an imminent observable coming of the kingdom to something that is already present in Jesus' preaching and healing ministry. Luke has also appended further traditional sayings of Jesus about the unpredictable suddenness of the day of the Son of Man, and assures his readers that in spite of the delay of that day (12, 45), it will bring judgment unexpectedly on those who do not continue to be vigilant.

17, 21: Among you: the Greek preposition translated as **among** can also be translated as "within." In the light of other statements in Luke's gospel about the presence of the kingdom (see 10, 9.11; 11, 20) "among" is to be preferred.

n: Mt 17, 20; 21, 21; Mk 11, 23.   o: 9, 51-53; 13, 22.33; 18, 31; 19, 28; Jn 4, 4.   p: 18, 38; Mt 9, 27; 15, 22.   q: 5, 14; Lv 14, 2-32; Mt 8, 4; Mk 1, 44.   r: 7, 50; 18, 42.   s: Jn 3, 3.   t: 17, 23; Mt 24, 23; Mk 13, 21.   u: 17, 21; Mt 24, 23.26; Mk 13, 21.   v: Mt 24, 27.   w: 9, 22; 18, 32-33; Mt 16, 21; 17, 22-23; 20, 18-19; Mk 8, 31; 9, 31; 10, 33-34.   x: Gn 6-8; Mt 24, 37-39.   y: Gn 18, 20-21; 19, 1-29.   z: Mt 24, 17-18; Mk 13, 15-16.   a: Gn 19, 17.26.

behind. ³²Remember the wife of Lot. ^{33b}Whoever seeks to preserve his life will lose it, but whoever loses it will save it. ³⁴I tell you, on that night there will be two people in one bed; one will be taken, the other left. ^{35c}And there will be two women grinding meal together; one will be taken, the other left." [³⁶]* ^{37d}They said to him in reply, "Where, Lord?" He said to them, "Where the body is, there also the vultures will gather."

See RG
406-8

CHAPTER 18

The Parable of the Persistent Widow.

^{1e}*Then he told them a parable about the necessity for them to pray always without becoming weary. He said, ²"There was a judge in a certain town who neither feared God nor respected any human being. ³And a widow in that town used to come to him and say, 'Render a just decision for me against my adversary.' ⁴For a long time the judge was unwilling, but eventually he thought, 'While it is true that I neither fear God nor respect any human being, ^{5f}*because this widow keeps bothering me I shall deliver a just decision for her lest she finally come and strike me.'" ⁶The Lord said, "Pay attention to what the dishonest judge says. ⁷Will not God then secure the rights of his chosen ones who call out to him day and night? Will he be slow to answer them? ⁸I tell you, he will see to it that justice is done for them speedily. But when the Son of Man comes, will he find faith on earth?"

The Parable of the Pharisee and the Tax Collector

^{9g}He then addressed this parable to those who were convinced of their own righteousness and despised everyone else. ¹⁰"Two people went up to the temple area to pray; one was a Pharisee and the other was a tax collector. ¹¹The Pharisee took up his position and spoke this prayer to himself, 'O God, I thank you that I am not like the rest of humanity—greedy, dishonest, adulterous—or even like this tax collector. ^{12h}I fast twice a week, and I pay tithes on my whole income.' ¹³ⁱBut the tax collector stood off at a distance and would not even raise his eyes to heaven but beat his breast and prayed, 'O God, be merciful to me a sinner.' ^{14j}I tell you, the latter went home justified, not the former; for everyone who exalts himself will be humbled, and the one who humbles himself will be exalted."

Saying on Children and the Kingdom.

^{15k}*People were bringing even infants to him that he might touch them, and when the disciples saw this, they rebuked them. ¹⁶Jesus, however, called the children to himself and said, "Let the children come to me and do not prevent them; for the kingdom of God belongs to such as these. ^{17l}Amen, I say to you, whoever does not accept the kingdom of God like a child will not enter it."

The Rich Official.

^{18mn}An official asked him this question, "Good teacher, what must I do to inherit eternal life?" ¹⁹Jesus answered him, "Why do you call me good? No one is good but God alone. ^{20o}You know the com-

---

17, 36: The inclusion of v 36, "There will be two men in the field; one will be taken, the other left," in some Western manuscripts appears to be a scribal assimilation to Mt 24, 40.

18, 1–14: The particularly Lucan material in the travel narrative concludes with two parables on prayer. The first (1–8) teaches the disciples the need of persistent prayer so that they not fall victims to apostasy (8). The second (9–14) condemns the self-righteous, critical attitude of the Pharisee and teaches that the fundamental attitude of the Christian disciple must be the recognition of sinfulness and complete dependence on God's graciousness. The second parable recalls the story of the pardoning of the sinful woman (7, 36–50) where a similar contrast is presented between the critical attitude of the Pharisee Simon and the love shown by the pardoned sinner.

18, 5: Strike me: the Greek verb translated as strike means "to strike under the eye" and suggests the extreme situation to which the persistence of the widow might lead. It may, however, be used here in the much weaker sense of "to wear one out."

18, 15—19, 27: Luke here includes much of the material about the journey to Jerusalem found in his Marcan source (10, 1–52) and adds to it the story of Zacchaeus (19, 1–10) from his own particular tradition and the parable of the gold coins (minas) (19, 11–27) from Q, the source common to Lk and Mt.

18, 15–17: The sayings on children furnish a contrast to the attitude of the Pharisee in the preceding episode (9–14) and that of the wealthy official in the following one (18–23) who think that they can lay claim to God's favor by their own merit. The attitude of the disciple should be marked by the receptivity and trustful dependence characteristic of the child.

---

b: 9, 24; Mt 10, 39; 16, 25; Mk 8, 35; Jn 12, 25. *c:* Mt 24, 40-41. *d:* Jb 39, 30; Mt 24, 28. *e:* Rom 12, 12; Col 4, 2; 1 Thes 5, 17. *f:* 11, 8. *g:* 16, 5; Mt 23, 25-28. *h:* Mt 23, 23. *i:* Ps 51, 3. *j:* 14, 11; Mt 23, 12. *k:* Mt 19, 13-15; Mk 10, 13-16. *l:* Mt 18, 3. *m:* Mt 19, 16-30; Mk 10, 17-31. *n:* 10, 25. *o:* Ex 20, 12-16; Dt 5, 16-20.

mandments, 'You shall not commit adultery; you shall not kill; you shall not steal; you shall not bear false witness; honor your father and your mother.'" 21And he replied, "All of these I have observed from my youth." 22p*When Jesus heard this he said to him, "There is still one thing left for you: sell all that you have and distribute it to the poor, and you will have a treasure in heaven. Then come, follow me." 23But when he heard this he became quite sad, for he was very rich.

On Riches and Renunciation. 24Jesus looked at him [now sad] and said, "How hard it is for those who have wealth to enter the kingdom of God! 25For it is easier for a camel to pass through the eye of a needle than for a rich person to enter the kingdom of God." 26Those who heard this said, "Then who can be saved?" 27qAnd he said, "What is impossible for human beings is possible for God." 28Then Peter said, "We have given up our possessions and followed you." 29rHe said to them, "Amen, I say to you, there is no one who has given up house or wife or brothers or parents or children for the sake of the kingdom of God 30who will not receive [back] an overabundant return in this present age and eternal life in the age to come."

The Third Prediction of the Passion. 31s*Then he took the Twelve aside and said to them, "Behold, we are going up to Jerusalem and everything written by the prophets about the Son of Man will be fulfilled. 32tHe will be handed over to the Gentiles and he will be mocked and insulted and

spat upon; 33and after they have scourged him they will kill him, but on the third day he will rise." 34uBut they understood nothing of this; the word remained hidden from them and they failed to comprehend what he said.

The Healing of the Blind Beggar. 35vNow as he approached Jericho a blind man was sitting by the roadside begging, 36and hearing a crowd going by, he inquired what was happening. 37They told him, "Jesus of Nazareth is passing by." 38w*He shouted, "Jesus, Son of David, have pity on me!" 39The people walking in front rebuked him, telling him to be silent, but he kept calling out all the more, "Son of David, have pity on me!" 40Then Jesus stopped and ordered that he be brought to him; and when he came near, Jesus asked him, 41x"What do you want me to do for you?" He replied, "Lord, please let me see." 42yJesus told him, "Have sight; your faith has saved you." 43He immediately received his sight and followed him, giving glory to God. When they saw this, all the people gave praise to God.

CHAPTER 19

See RG
408

Zacchaeus the Tax Collector. 1*He came to Jericho and intended to pass through the town. 2Now a man there named Zacchaeus, who was a chief tax collector and also a wealthy man, 3was seeking to see who Jesus was; but he could not see him because of the crowd, for he was short in stature. 4So he ran ahead and climbed a sycamore tree in order to see Jesus, who was about to pass that way.

18, 22: Detachment from material possessions results in the total dependence on God demanded of one who would inherit eternal life. **Sell all that you have:** the original saying (cf Mk 10, 21) has characteristically been made more demanding by Luke's addition of "all."

18, 31–33: The details included in this third announcement of Jesus' suffering and death suggest that the literary formulation of the announcement has been directed by the knowledge of the historical passion and death of Jesus.

18, 31: **Everything written by the prophets . . . will be fulfilled:** this is a Lucan addition to the words of Jesus found in the Marcan source (Mk 10, 32–34). Luke understands the events of Jesus' last days in Jerusalem to be the fulfillment of Old Testament prophecy, but, as is usually the case in Luke-Acts, the author does not specify which Old Testament prophets he has in mind; cf 24, 25.27.44; Acts 3, 8; 13, 27; 26, 22–23.

18, 38: **Son of David:** the blind beggar identifies Jesus

with a title that is related to Jesus' role as Messiah (see the note on 2, 11). Through this Son of David, salvation comes to the blind man. Note the connection between salvation and house of David mentioned earlier in Zechariah's canticle (1, 69). See also the note on Mt 9, 27.

19, 1–10: The story of the tax collector Zacchaeus is unique to this gospel. While a rich man (2), Zacchaeus provides a contrast to the rich man of 18, 18–23 who cannot detach himself from his material possessions to become a follower of Jesus. Zacchaeus, according to Luke, exemplifies the proper attitude toward wealth: he promises to give half of his possessions to the poor (8) and consequently is the recipient of salvation (9–10).

p: 12, 33; Sir 29, 11; Mt 6, 20.   q: Mk 14, 36.   r: 14, 26.   s: 24, 25-27.44; Mt 20, 17-19; Mk 10, 32-34; Acts 3, 18.   t: 9, 22.44.   u: Mk 9, 32.   v: Mt 20, 29-34; Mk 10, 46-52.   w: 17, 13; Mt 9, 27; 15, 22.   x: Mk 10, 36.   y: 7, 50; 17, 19.

[5]When he reached the place, Jesus looked up and said to him, "Zacchaeus, come down quickly, for today I must stay at your house." [6]And he came down quickly and received him with joy. [7z]When they all saw this, they began to grumble, saying, "He has gone to stay at the house of a sinner." [8a]But Zacchaeus stood there and said to the Lord, "Behold, half of my possessions, Lord, I shall give to the poor, and if I have extorted anything from anyone I shall repay it four times over." [9b*]And Jesus said to him, "Today salvation has come to this house because this man too is a descendant of Abraham. [10c*]For the Son of Man has come to seek and to save what was lost."

The Parable of the Ten Gold Coins. [11d*]While they were listening to him speak, he proceeded to tell a parable because he was near Jerusalem and they thought that the kingdom of God would appear there immediately. [12e]So he said, "A nobleman went off to a distant country to obtain the kingship for himself and then to return. [13*]He called ten of his servants and gave them ten gold coins and told them, 'Engage in trade with these until I return.' [14]His fellow citizens, however, despised him and sent a delegation after him to announce, 'We do not want this man to be our king.' [15]But when he returned after obtaining the kingship, he had the servants called, to whom he had given the money, to learn what they had gained by trading. [16]The first came forward and said, 'Sir, your gold coin has earned ten additional ones.' [17f]He replied, 'Well done, good servant! You have been faithful in this very small matter; take charge of ten cities.' [18]Then the second came and reported, 'Your gold coin, sir, has earned five more.' [19]And to this servant too he said, 'You, take charge of five cities.' [20]Then the other servant came and said, 'Sir, here is your gold coin; I kept it stored away in a handkerchief, [21]for I was afraid of you, because you are a demanding person; you take up what you did not lay down and you harvest what you did not plant.' [22]He said to him, 'With your own words I shall condemn you, you wicked servant. You knew I was a demanding person, taking up what I did not lay down and harvesting what I did not plant; [23]why did you not put my money in a bank? Then on my return I would have collected it with interest.' [24]And to those standing by he said, 'Take the gold coin from him and give it to the servant who has ten.' [25]But they said to him, 'Sir, he has ten gold coins.' [26g]'I tell you, to everyone who has, more will be given, but from the one who has not, even what he has will be taken away. [27]Now as for those enemies of mine who did not want me as their king, bring them here and slay them before me.' "

VI: The Teaching Ministry in Jerusalem

The Entry into Jerusalem. [28h*]After he had said this, he proceeded on his journey up to

---

19, 9: A descendant of Abraham: literally, "a son of Abraham." The tax collector Zacchaeus, whose repentance is attested by his determination to amend his former ways, shows himself to be a true descendant of Abraham, the true heir to the promises of God in the Old Testament. Underlying Luke's depiction of Zacchaeus as a descendant of Abraham, the father of the Jews (1, 73; 16, 22–31), is his recognition of the central place occupied by Israel in the plan of salvation.

19, 10: This verse sums up for Luke his depiction of the role of Jesus as savior in this gospel.

19, 11–27: In this parable Luke has combined two originally distinct parables: (1) a parable about the conduct of faithful and productive servants (13.15b–26) and (2) a parable about a rejected king (12.14–15a.27). The story about the conduct of servants occurs in another form in Mt 25, 14–20. The story about the rejected king may have originated with a contemporary historical event. After the death of Herod the Great, his son Archelaus traveled to Rome to receive the title of king. A delegation of Jews appeared in Rome before Caesar Augustus to oppose the request of Archelaus. Although

not given the title of king, Archelaus was made ruler over Judea and Samaria. As the story is used by Luke, however, it furnishes a correction to the expectation of the imminent end of the age and of the establishment of the kingdom in Jerusalem (11). Jesus is not on his way to Jerusalem to receive the kingly power; for that, he must go away and only after returning from the distant country (a reference to the parousia) will reward and judgment take place.

19, 13: Ten gold coins: literally, "ten minas." A mina was a monetary unit that in ancient Greece was the equivalent of one hundred drachmas.

19, 28—21, 38: With the royal entry of Jesus into Jerusalem, a new section of Luke's gospel begins, the ministry of Jesus in Jerusalem before his death and resurrection. Luke suggests that this was a lengthy ministry in Jerusalem

z: 5, 30; 15, 2. a: Ex 21, 37; Nm 5, 6-7; 2 Sm 12, 6. b: 13, 16; Mt 21, 31. c: 15, 4-10; Ez 34, 16. d: Mt 25, 14-30. e: Mk 13, 34. f: 16, 10. g: 8, 18; Mt 13, 12; Mk 4, 25. h: Mt 21, 1-11; Mk 11, 1-11; Jn 12, 12-19.

Jerusalem. [29i]As he drew near to Bethphage and Bethany at the place called the Mount of Olives, he sent two of his disciples. [30j]He said, "Go into the village opposite you, and as you enter it you will find a colt tethered on which no one has ever sat. Untie it and bring it here. [31]And if anyone should ask you, 'Why are you untying it?' you will answer, 'The Master has need of it.' " [32k]So those who had been sent went off and found everything just as he had told them. [33]And as they were untying the colt, its owners said to them, "Why are you untying this colt?" [34]They answered, "The Master has need of it." [35l]So they brought it to Jesus, threw their cloaks over the colt, and helped Jesus to mount. [36]As he rode along, the people were spreading their cloaks on the road; [37]and now as he was approaching the slope of the Mount of Olives, the whole multitude of his disciples began to praise God aloud with joy for all the mighty deeds they had seen. [38m*]They proclaimed:

"Blessed is the king who comes
    in the name of the Lord.
Peace in heaven
    and glory in the highest."

[39*]Some of the Pharisees in the crowd said to him, "Teacher, rebuke your disciples." [40]He said in reply, "I tell you, if they keep silent, the stones will cry out!"

The Lament for Jerusalem. [41no*]As he drew near, he saw the city and wept over it, [42p]saying, "If this day you only knew what makes for peace—but now it is hidden from your eyes. [43q*]For the days are coming upon you when your enemies will raise a palisade against you; they will encircle you and hem you in on all sides. [44r]They will smash you to the ground and your children within you, and they will not leave one stone upon another within you because you did not recognize the time of your visitation."

The Cleansing of the Temple. [45st*]Then Jesus entered the temple area and proceeded to drive out those who were selling things, [46u]saying to them, "It is written, 'My house shall be a house of prayer, but you have made it a den of thieves.' " [47vw]And every day he was teaching in the temple area. The chief priests, the scribes, and the leaders of the people, meanwhile, were seeking to put him to death, [48]but they could find no way to accomplish their purpose because all the people were hanging on his words.

CHAPTER 20

See RG
408-9

The Authority of Jesus Questioned. [1x*]One day as he was teaching the people in the temple area and proclaiming the good news, the chief priests and scribes, together with the elders, approached him [2y]and said

---

(19, 47; 20, 1; 21, 37–38; 22, 53) and it is characterized by Jesus' daily teaching in the temple (21, 37–38). For the story of the entry of Jesus into Jerusalem, see Mt 21, 1–11; Mk 11, 1–10; Jn 12, 12–19 and the notes there.

19, 38: Blessed is the king who comes in the name of the Lord: only in Lk is Jesus explicitly given the title **king** when he enters Jerusalem in triumph. Luke has inserted this title into the words of Ps 118, 26 that heralded the arrival of the pilgrims coming to the holy city and to the temple. Jesus is thereby acclaimed as **king** (see 1, 32) and as the one **who comes** (see Mal 3, 1; Lk 7, 19). **Peace in heaven . . . :** the acclamation of the disciples of Jesus in Lk echoes the announcement of the angels at the birth of Jesus (2, 14). The peace Jesus brings is associated with the salvation to be accomplished here in Jerusalem.

19, 39: Rebuke your disciples: this command, found only in Lk, was given so that the Roman authorities would not interpret the acclamation of Jesus as king as an uprising against them; cf 23, 2–3.

19, 41–44: The lament for Jerusalem is found only in Lk. By not accepting Jesus (the one who mediates peace), Jerusalem will not find peace but will become the victim of devastation.

19, 43–44: Luke may be describing the actual disaster that

befell Jerusalem in A.D. 70 when it was destroyed by the Romans during the First Revolt.

19, 45–46: Immediately upon entering the holy city, Jesus in a display of his authority enters the temple (see Mal 3, 1–3) and lays claim to it after cleansing it that it might become a proper place for his teaching ministry in Jerusalem (19, 47; 20, 1; 21, 37; 22, 53). See Mt 21, 12–17; Mk 11, 15–19; Jn 2, 13–17 and the notes there.

20, 1–47: The Jerusalem religious leaders or their representatives, in an attempt to incriminate Jesus with the Romans and to discredit him with the people, pose a number of questions to him (about his authority, 2; about payment of taxes, 22; about the resurrection, 28–33).

i: Zec 14, 4. j: Nm 19, 2; Dt 21, 3, 1 Sm 6, 7; Zec 9, 9. k: 22, 13. l: 2 Kgs 9, 13. m: 2, 14; Ps 118, 26. n: 13, 34-35. o: 2 Kgs 8, 11-12; Jer 14, 17; 15, 5. p: 8, 10; Is 6, 9-10; Mt 13, 14; Mk 4, 12; Acts 28, 26-27; Rom 11, 8.10. q: Is 29, 3. r: 1, 68; 21, 6; Ps 137, 9; Mt 24, 2; Mk 13, 2. s: Mt 21, 12-13; Mk 11, 15-17; Jn 2, 13-17. t: 3, 1 / Hos 9, 15. u: Is 56, 7; Jer 7, 11. v: 20, 19; 22, 2; Mt 21, 46; Mk 11, 18; 12, 12; 14, 1-2; Jn 5, 18; 7, 30. w: 21, 37; 22, 53; Jn 18, 20. x: Mt 21, 23-27; Mk 11, 27-33. y: Acts 4, 7.

to him, "Tell us, by what authority are you doing these things? Or who is the one who gave you this authority?" ³He said to them in reply, "I shall ask you a question. Tell me, ⁴ᶻwas John's baptism of heavenly or of human origin?" ⁵ᵃThey discussed this among themselves, and said, "If we say, 'Of heavenly origin,' he will say, 'Why did you not believe him?' ⁶But if we say, 'Of human origin,' then all the people will stone us, for they are convinced that John was a prophet." ⁷So they answered that they did not know from where it came. ⁸Then Jesus said to them, "Neither shall I tell you by what authority I do these things."

The Parable of the Tenant Farmers. ⁹ᵇᶜ*Then he proceeded to tell the people this parable. "[A] man planted a vineyard, leased it to tenant farmers, and then went on a journey for a long time. ¹⁰ᵈAt harvest time he sent a servant to the tenant farmers to receive some of the produce of the vineyard. But they beat the servant and sent him away empty-handed. ¹¹So he proceeded to send another servant, but him also they beat and insulted and sent away empty-handed. ¹²Then he proceeded to send a third, but this one too they wounded and threw out. ¹³ᵉThe owner of the vineyard said, 'What shall I do? I shall send my beloved son; maybe they will respect him.' ¹⁴But when the tenant farmers saw him they said to one another, 'This is the heir. Let us kill him that the inheritance may become ours.' ¹⁵*So they threw him out of the vineyard and killed him. What will the owner of the vineyard do to them? ¹⁶He will come and put those ten-

ant farmers to death and turn over the vineyard to others." When the people heard this, they exclaimed, "Let it not be so!" ¹⁷ᶠBut he looked at them and asked, "What then does this scripture passage mean:

'The stone which the builders rejected
    has become the cornerstone'?

¹⁸Everyone who falls on that stone will be dashed to pieces; and it will crush anyone on whom it falls." ¹⁹ᵍThe scribes and chief priests sought to lay their hands on him at that very hour, but they feared the people, for they knew that he had addressed this parable to them.

Paying Taxes to the Emperor. ²⁰ʰⁱ*They watched him closely and sent agents pretending to be righteous who were to trap him in speech, in order to hand him over to the authority and power of the governor. ²¹ʲThey posed this question to him, "Teacher, we know that what you say and teach is correct, and you show no partiality, but teach the way of God in accordance with the truth. ²²*Is it lawful for us to pay tribute to Caesar or not?" ²³Recognizing their craftiness he said to them, ²⁴*"Show me a denarius; whose image and name does it bear?" They replied, "Caesar's." ²⁵ᵏSo he said to them, "Then repay to Caesar what belongs to Caesar and to God what belongs to God." ²⁶They were unable to trap him by something he might say before the people, and so amazed were they at his reply that they fell silent.

The Question about the Resurrection. ²⁷ˡᵐ*Some Sadducees, those who deny that there is a resurrection, came forward and put

---

20, 9–19: This parable about an absentee landlord and a tenant farmers' revolt reflects the social and economic conditions of rural Palestine in the first century. The synoptic gospel writers use the parable to describe how the rejection of the landlord's son becomes the occasion for the vineyard to be taken away from those to whom it was entrusted (the religious leadership of Judaism that rejects the teaching and preaching of Jesus; 19).

20, 15: They threw him out of the vineyard and killed him: cf Mk 12, 8. Luke has altered his Marcan source and reports that the murder of the son takes place outside the vineyard to reflect the tradition of Jesus' death outside the walls of the city of Jerusalem (see Heb 13, 12).

20, 20: The governor: i.e., Pontius Pilate, the Roman administrator responsible for the collection of taxes and maintenance of order in Palestine.

20, 22: Through their question the agents of the Jerusalem religious leadership hope to force Jesus to take sides on one of the sensitive political issues of first-century Palestine. The issue of nonpayment of taxes to Rome becomes one of the focal points of the First Jewish Revolt (A.D. 66–70) that resulted in the Roman destruction of Jerusalem and the temple. See also the note on Mt 22, 15–22.

20, 24: Denarius: a Roman silver coin (see the note on 7, 41).

20, 27: Sadducees: see the note on Mt 3, 7.

z: 3, 3.16. a: Mt 21, 32. b: Mt 21, 33-46; Mk 12, 1-12. c: Is 5, 1-7. d: 2 Chr 36, 15-16. e: 3, 22. f: Ps 118, 22; Is 28, 16. g: 19, 47-48; 22, 2; Mt 21, 46; Mk 11, 18; 12, 12; 14, 1-2; Jn 5, 18; 7, 30. h: Mt 22, 15-22; Mk 12, 13-17. i: 11, 54. j: Jn 3, 2. k: Rom 13, 6-7. l: Mt 22, 23-33; Mk 12, 18-27. m: Acts 23, 8.

this question to him, [28n*]saying, "Teacher, Moses wrote for us, 'If someone's brother dies leaving a wife but no child, his brother must take the wife and raise up descendants for his brother.' [29]Now there were seven brothers; the first married a woman but died childless. [30]Then the second [31]and the third married her, and likewise all the seven died childless. [32]Finally the woman also died. [33]Now at the resurrection whose wife will that woman be? For all seven had been married to her." [34]Jesus said to them, "The children of this age marry and remarry; [35]but those who are deemed worthy to attain to the coming age and to the resurrection of the dead neither marry nor are given in marriage. [36*]They can no longer die, for they are like angels; and they are the children of God because they are the ones who will rise. [37o]That the dead will rise even Moses made known in the passage about the bush, when he called 'Lord' the God of Abraham, the God of Isaac, and the God of Jacob; [38p]and he is not God of the dead, but of the living, for to him all are alive." [39]Some of the scribes said in reply, "Teacher, you have answered well." [40q]And they no longer dared to ask him anything.

The Question about David's Son. [41r*]Then he said to them, "How do they claim that the Messiah is the Son of David? [42s]For David himself in the Book of Psalms says:

'The Lord said to my lord,
"Sit at my right hand
[43] till I make your enemies your footstool." '

[44]Now if David calls him 'lord,' how can he be his son?"

Denunciation of the Scribes. [45t]Then, within the hearing of all the people, he said to [his] disciples, [46u]"Be on guard against the scribes, who like to go around in long robes and love greetings in marketplaces, seats of honor in synagogues, and places of honor at banquets. [47]They devour the houses of widows and, as a pretext, recite lengthy prayers. They will receive a very severe condemnation."

CHAPTER 21

The Poor Widow's Contribution. **See RG 408-9**
[1v*]When he looked up he saw some wealthy people putting their offerings into the treasury [2]and he noticed a poor widow putting in two small coins. [3]He said, "I tell you truly, this poor widow put in more than all the rest; [4]for those others have all made offerings from their surplus wealth, but she, from her poverty, has offered her whole livelihood."

The Destruction of the Temple Foretold. [5w*]While some people were speaking about how the temple was adorned with costly stones and votive offerings, he said, [6x]"All

20, 28–33: The Sadducees' question, based on the law of levirate marriage recorded in Dt 25, 5–10, ridicules the idea of the resurrection. Jesus rejects their naive understanding of the resurrection (35–36) and then argues on behalf of the resurrection of the dead on the basis of the written law (37–38) that the Sadducees accept. See also the notes on Mt 22, 23–33.

20, 36: Because they are the ones who will rise: literally, "being sons of the resurrection."

20, 41–44: After successfully answering the three questions of his opponents, Jesus now asks them a question. Their inability to respond implies that they have forfeited their position and authority as the religious leaders of the people because they do not understand the scriptures. This series of controversies between the religious leadership of Jerusalem and Jesus reveals Jesus as the authoritative teacher whose words are to be listened to (see 9, 35). See also the notes on Mt 22, 41–46.

21, 1–4: The widow is another example of the poor ones in this gospel whose detachment from material possessions and dependence on God leads to their blessedness (6, 20). Her simple offering provides a striking contrast to the pride and pretentiousness of the scribes denounced in the preceding section (20, 45–47). The story is taken from Mk 12, 41–44.

21, 5–36: Jesus' eschatological discourse in Lk is inspired by Mk 13, but Luke has made some significant alterations to the words of Jesus found there. Luke maintains, though in a modified form, the belief in the early expectation of the end of the age (see 27.28. 31.32.36), but, by focusing attention throughout the gospel on the importance of the day-to-day following of Jesus and by reinterpreting the meaning of some of the signs of the end from Mk 13, he has come to terms with what seemed to the early Christian community to be a delay of the parousia. Mark, for example, described the desecration of the Jerusalem temple by the Romans (Mk 13, 14) as the apocalyptic symbol (see Dn 9, 27; 12, 11) accompanying the end of the age and the coming of the Son of Man. Luke (21, 20–24), however, removes the apocalyptic setting and separates the historical destruction of Jerusalem from the signs of the coming of the Son of Man by a period that he refers to as "the times of the Gentiles" (21, 24). See also the notes on Mt 24, 1–36 and Mk 13, 1–37.

n: Gn 38, 8; Dt 25, 5. o: Ex 3, 2.6.15-16. p: Rom 14, 8-9. q: Mt 22, 46; Mk 12, 34. r: Mt 22, 41-45; Mk 12, 35-37. s: Ps 110, 1. t: 11, 37-54; Mt 23, 1-36; Mk 12, 38-40. u: 14, 7-11. v: Mk 12, 41-44. w: Mt 24, 1-2; Mk 13, 1-2. x: 19, 44.

that you see here—the days will come when there will not be left a stone upon another stone that will not be thrown down."

The Signs of the End. [7y]Then they asked him, "Teacher, when will this happen? And what sign will there be when all these things are about to happen?" [8z*]He answered, "See that you not be deceived, for many will come in my name, saying, 'I am he,' and 'The time has come.' Do not follow them! [9]When you hear of wars and insurrections, do not be terrified; for such things must happen first, but it will not immediately be the end." [10a]Then he said to them, "Nation will rise against nation, and kingdom against kingdom. [11]There will be powerful earthquakes, famines, and plagues from place to place; and awesome sights and mighty signs will come from the sky.

The Coming Persecution. [12bc*]"Before all this happens, however, they will seize and persecute you, they will hand you over to the synagogues and to prisons, and they will have you led before kings and governors because of my name. [13]It will lead to your giving testimony. [14]Remember, you are not to prepare your defense beforehand, [15d*]for I myself shall give you a wisdom in speaking that all your adversaries will be powerless to resist or refute. [16ef]You will even be handed over by parents, brothers, relatives, and friends, and they will put some of you to death. [17]You will be hated by all because of my name, [18g]but not a hair on your head will be destroyed. [19h]By your perseverance you will secure your lives.

The Great Tribulation. [20ij*]"When you see Jerusalem surrounded by armies, know that its desolation is at hand. [21k]Then those in Judea must flee to the mountains. Let those within the city escape from it, and let those in the countryside not enter the city, [22]for these days are the time of punishment when all the scriptures are fulfilled. [23l]Woe to pregnant women and nursing mothers in those days, for a terrible calamity will come upon the earth and a wrathful judgment upon this people. [24m*]They will fall by the edge of the sword and be taken as captives to all the Gentiles; and Jerusalem will be trampled underfoot by the Gentiles until the times of the Gentiles are fulfilled.

The Coming of the Son of Man. [25no]"There will be signs in the sun, the moon, and the stars, and on earth nations will be in dismay, perplexed by the roaring of the sea and the waves. [26p*]People will die of fright in anticipation of what is coming upon the world, for the powers of the heavens will be shaken. [27q]And then they will see the Son of Man coming in a cloud with power and great glory. [28r]But when these signs begin to happen, stand erect and raise your heads because your redemption is at hand."

The Lesson of the Fig Tree. [29s]He taught them a lesson. "Consider the fig tree and all the other trees. [30]When their buds burst open, you see for yourselves and know that summer is now near; [31]in the same way, when you see these things happening, know that the kingdom of God is near. [32t]Amen, I say to you, this generation will not pass away until all these things have taken place. [33u]Heaven and earth will pass away, but my words will not pass away.

21, 8: **The time has come:** in Lk, the proclamation of the imminent end of the age has itself become a false teaching.

21, 12: **Before all this happens . . . :** to Luke and his community, some of the signs of the end just described (10–11) still lie in the future. Now in dealing with the persecution of the disciples (12–19) and the destruction of Jerusalem (20–24) Luke is pointing to eschatological signs that have already been fulfilled.

21, 15: **A wisdom in speaking:** literally, "a mouth and wisdom."

21, 20–24: The actual destruction of Jerusalem by Rome in A.D. 70 upon which Luke and his community look back provides the assurance that, just as Jesus' prediction of Jerusalem's destruction was fulfilled, so too will be his announcement of their final redemption (27–28).

21, 24: **The times of the Gentiles:** a period of indeterminate length separating the destruction of Jerusalem from the cosmic signs accompanying the coming of the Son of Man.

21, 26: **The powers of the heavens:** the heavenly bodies mentioned in v 25 and thought of as cosmic armies.

---

y: Mt 24, 3-14; Mk 13, 3-13.   z: 17, 23; Mk 13, 5.6.21; 1 Jn 2, 18. a: 2 Chr 15, 6; Is 19, 2.   b: 12, 11-12; Mt 10, 17-20; Mk 13, 9-11.   c: Jn 16, 2; Acts 25, 24.   d: Acts 6, 10.   e: Mt 10, 21-22. f: 12, 52-53.   g: 12, 7; 1 Sm 14, 45; Mt 10, 30; Acts 27, 34. h: 8, 15.   i: Mt 24, 15-21; Mk 13, 14-19.   j: 19, 41-44.   k: 17, 31.   l: 1 Cor 7, 26.   m: Tb 14, 5; Ps 79, 1; Is 63, 18; Jer 21, 7; Rom 11, 25; Rv 11, 2.   n: Mt 24, 29-31; Mk 13, 24-27.   o: Wis 5, 22; Is 13, 10; Ez 32, 7; Jl 2, 10; 3, 3-4; 4, 15; Rv 6, 12-14. p: Hg 2, 6.21.   q: Dn 7, 13-14; Mt 26, 64; Rv 1, 7.   r: 2, 38. s: Mt 24, 32-35; Mk 13, 28-31.   t: 9, 27; Mt 16, 28.   u: 16, 17.

Exhortation to be Vigilant. [34v]"Beware that your hearts do not become drowsy from carousing and drunkenness and the anxieties of daily life, and that day catch you by surprise [35]like a trap. For that day will assault everyone who lives on the face of the earth. [36w]Be vigilant at all times and pray that you have the strength to escape the tribulations that are imminent and to stand before the Son of Man."

Ministry in Jerusalem. [37x]During the day, Jesus was teaching in the temple area, but at night he would leave and stay at the place called the Mount of Olives. [38]And all the people would get up early each morning to listen to him in the temple area.

VII: The Passion Narrative

CHAPTER 22

See RG
409–10

The Conspiracy against Jesus. [1y]*Now the feast of Unleavened Bread, called the Passover, was drawing near, [2z]and the chief priests and the scribes were seeking a way to put him to death, for they were afraid of the people. [3ab]*Then Satan entered into Judas, the one surnamed Iscariot, who was counted among the Twelve, [4]and he went to the chief priests and temple guards to discuss a plan for handing him over to them. [5]They were pleased and agreed to pay him money. [6]He accepted

their offer and sought a favorable opportunity to hand him over to them in the absence of a crowd.

Preparations for the Passover. [7cd]When the day of the feast of Unleavened Bread arrived, the day for sacrificing the Passover lamb, [8]he sent out Peter and John, instructing them, "Go and make preparations for us to eat the Passover." [9]They asked him, "Where do you want us to make the preparations?" [10]*And he answered them, "When you go into the city, a man will meet you carrying a jar of water. Follow him into the house that he enters [11]and say to the master of the house, 'The teacher says to you, "Where is the guest room where I may eat the Passover with my disciples?" ' [12]He will show you a large upper room that is furnished. Make the preparations there." [13e]Then they went off and found everything exactly as he had told them, and there they prepared the Passover.

The Last Supper. [14f]When the hour came, he took his place at table with the apostles. [15]*He said to them, "I have eagerly desired to eat this Passover with you before I suffer, [16g]for, I tell you, I shall not eat it [again] until there is fulfillment in the kingdom of God." [17]*Then he took a cup, gave thanks, and said, "Take this and share it among yourselves; [18]for I tell you [that] from this time on I shall not drink of the fruit of the vine until the kingdom of God comes."

22, 1–23, 56a: The passion narrative. Luke is still dependent upon Mk for the composition of the passion narrative but has incorporated much of his own special tradition into the narrative. Among the distinctive sections in Lk are: (1) the tradition of the institution of the Eucharist (22, 15–20); (2) Jesus' farewell discourse (22, 21–38); (3) the mistreatment and interrogation of Jesus (22, 63–71); (4) Jesus before Herod and his second appearance before Pilate (23, 6–16); (5) words addressed to the women followers on the way to the crucifixion (23, 27–32); (6) words to the penitent thief (23, 39–41); (7) the death of Jesus (23, 46.47b-49). Luke stresses the innocence of Jesus (23, 4.14–15.22) who is the victim of the powers of evil (22, 3.31.53) and who goes to his death in fulfillment of his Father's will (22, 42.46). Throughout the narrative Luke emphasizes the mercy, compassion, and healing power of Jesus (22, 51; 23, 43) who does not go to death lonely and deserted, but is accompanied by others who follow him on the way of the cross (23, 26–31.49).

22, 1: Feast of Unleavened Bread, called the Passover: see the note on Mk 14, 1.

22, 3: Satan entered into Judas: see the note on 4, 13.

22, 10: A man will meet you carrying a jar of water: see the note on Mk 14, 13.

22, 15: This Passover: Luke clearly identifies this last supper of Jesus with the apostles as a Passover meal that commemorated the deliverance of the Israelites from slavery in Egypt. Jesus reinterprets the significance of the Passover by setting it in the context of the kingdom of God (16). The "deliverance" associated with the Passover finds its new meaning in the blood that will be shed (20).

22, 17: Because of a textual problem in vv 19 and 20, some commentators interpret this cup as the eucharistic cup.

v: 12, 45-46; Mt 24, 48-50; 1 Thes 5, 3.6-7. *w:* Mk 13, 33. *x:* 19, 47; 22, 39. *y:* Mt 26, 1-5; Mk 14, 1-2; Jn 11, 47-53. *z:* 19, 47-48; 20, 19; Mt 21, 46; Mk 12, 12; Jn 5, 18; 7, 30. *a:* Mt 26, 14-16; Mk 14, 10-11; Jn 13, 2.27. *b:* Acts 1, 17. *c:* Mt 26, 17-19; Mk 14, 12-16. *d:* Ex 12, 6.14-20. *e:* 19, 32. *f:* Mt 26, 20.26-30; Mk 14, 17.22-26; 1 Cor 11, 23-25. *g:* 13, 29.

[19h]*Then he took the bread, said the blessing, broke it, and gave it to them, saying, "This is my body, which will be given for you; do this in memory of me." [20i]And likewise the cup after they had eaten, saying, "This cup is the new covenant in my blood, which will be shed for you.

The Betrayal Foretold. [21j]"And yet behold, the hand of the one who is to betray me is with me on the table; [22]for the Son of Man indeed goes as it has been determined; but woe to that man by whom he is betrayed." [23]And they began to debate among themselves who among them would do such a deed.

The Role of the Disciples. [24k]*Then an argument broke out among them about which of them should be regarded as the greatest. [25l]*He said to them, "The kings of the Gentiles lord it over them and those in authority over them are addressed as 'Benefactors'; [26m]but among you it shall not be so. Rather, let the greatest among you be as the youngest, and the leader as the servant. [27]For who is greater: the one seated at table or the one who serves? Is it not the one seated at table? I am among you as the one who serves. [28]It is you who have stood by me in my trials; [29n]and I confer a kingdom on you, just as my Father has conferred one on me, [30o]that you may eat and drink at my table in my kingdom; and you will sit on thrones judging the twelve tribes of Israel.

Peter's Denial Foretold. [31pq]*"Simon, Si-mon, behold Satan has demanded to sift all of you like wheat, [32]but I have prayed that your own faith may not fail; and once you have turned back, you must strengthen your brothers." [33r]He said to him, "Lord, I am prepared to go to prison and to die with you." [34s]But he replied, "I tell you, Peter, before the cock crows this day, you will deny three times that you know me."

Instructions for the Time of Crisis. [35t]He said to them, "When I sent you forth without a money bag or a sack or sandals, were you in need of anything?" "No, nothing," they replied. [36u]*He said to them, "But now one who has a money bag should take it, and likewise a sack, and one who does not have a sword should sell his cloak and buy one. [37v]For I tell you that this scripture must be fulfilled in me, namely, 'He was counted among the wicked'; and indeed what is written about me is coming to fulfillment." [38]*Then they said, "Lord, look, there are two swords here." But he replied, "It is enough!"

The Agony in the Garden. [39w]Then going out he went, as was his custom, to the Mount of Olives, and the disciples followed him. [40x]When he arrived at the place he said to them, "Pray that you may not undergo the test." [41y]After withdrawing about a stone's throw from them and kneeling, he prayed, [42z]saying, "Father, if you are willing, take this cup away from me; still, not my will but yours be done." [[43]*And to strengthen him

22, 19c-20: Which will be given . . . do this in memory of me: these words are omitted in some important Western text manuscripts and a few Syriac manuscripts. Other ancient text types, including the oldest papyrus manuscript of Lk dating from the late second or early third century, contain the longer reading presented here. The Lucan account of the words of institution of the Eucharist bears a close resemblance to the words of institution in the Pauline tradition (see 1 Cor 11, 23–26). See also the notes on Mt 26, 26–29; 26, 27–28; and Mk 14, 22–24.

22, 24–38: The Gospel of Luke presents a brief farewell discourse of Jesus; compare the lengthy farewell discourses and prayer in Jn, chs 13–17.

22, 25: 'Benefactors': this word occurs as a title of rulers in the Hellenistic world.

22, 31: All of you: literally, "you." The translation reflects the meaning of the Greek text that uses a second person plural pronoun here.

22, 31–32: Jesus' prayer for Simon's faith and the commission to strengthen his brothers anticipates the post-resurrectional prominence of Peter in the first half of Acts, where

he appears as the spokesman for the Christian community and the one who begins the mission to the Gentiles (Acts 10–11).

22, 36: In contrast to the ministry of the Twelve and of the seventy-two during the period of Jesus (9, 3; 10, 4), in the future period of the church the missionaries must be prepared for the opposition they will face in a world hostile to their preaching.

22, 38: It is enough!: the farewell discourse ends abruptly with these words of Jesus spoken to the disciples when they take literally what was intended as figurative language about being prepared to face the world's hostility.

22, 43–44: These verses, though very ancient, were probably not part of the original text of Lk. They are absent from

h: 24, 30; Acts 27, 35. i: Ex 24, 8; Jer 31, 31; 32, 40; Zec 9, 11. j: Ps 41, 10; Mt 26, 21-25; Mk 14, 18-21; Jn 13, 21-30. k: 9, 46; Mt 18, 1; Mk 9, 34. l: Mt 20, 25-27; Mk 10, 42-44; Jn 13, 3-16. m: Mt 23, 11; Mk 9, 35. n: 12, 32. o: Mt 19, 28. p: Mt 26, 33-35; Mk 14, 29-31; Jn 13, 37-38. q: Jb 1, 6-12; Am 9, 9. r: 22, 54. s: 22, 54-62. t: 9, 3; 10, 4; Mt 10, 9-10; Mk 6, 7-9. u: 22, 49. v: Is 53, 12. w: Mt 26, 30.36-46; Mk 14, 26.32-42; Jn 18, 1-2. x: 22, 46. y: Heb 5, 7-8. z: Mt 6, 10.

an angel from heaven appeared to him. [44]He was in such agony and he prayed so fervently that his sweat became like drops of blood falling on the ground.] [45]When he rose from prayer and returned to his disciples, he found them sleeping from grief. [46a]He said to them, "Why are you sleeping? Get up and pray that you may not undergo the test."

The Betrayal and Arrest of Jesus. [47b]While he was still speaking, a crowd approached and in front was one of the Twelve, a man named Judas. He went up to Jesus to kiss him. [48]Jesus said to him, "Judas, are you betraying the Son of Man with a kiss?" [49c]His disciples realized what was about to happen, and they asked, "Lord, shall we strike with a sword?" [50d]And one of them struck the high priest's servant and cut off his right ear. [51*]But Jesus said in reply, "Stop, no more of this!" Then he touched the servant's ear and healed him. [52e]And Jesus said to the chief priests and temple guards and elders who had come for him, "Have you come out as against a robber, with swords and clubs? [53f]Day after day I was with you in the temple area, and you did not seize me; but this is your hour, the time for the power of darkness."

Peter's Denial of Jesus. [54gh]After arresting him they led him away and took him into the house of the high priest; Peter was following at a distance. [55]They lit a fire in the middle of the courtyard and sat around it, and Peter sat down with them. [56]When a maid saw him seated in the light, she looked intently at him and said, "This man too was with him." [57]But he denied it saying,

"Woman, I do not know him." [58]A short while later someone else saw him and said, "You too are one of them"; but Peter answered, "My friend, I am not." [59]About an hour later, still another insisted, "Assuredly, this man too was with him, for he also is a Galilean." [60]But Peter said, "My friend, I do not know what you are talking about." Just as he was saying this, the cock crowed, [61i*]and the Lord turned and looked at Peter; and Peter remembered the word of the Lord, how he had said to him, "Before the cock crows today, you will deny me three times." [62]He went out and began to weep bitterly. [63j]The men who held Jesus in custody were ridiculing and beating him. [64]They blindfolded him and questioned him, saying, "Prophesy! Who is it that struck you?" [65]And they reviled him in saying many other things against him.

Jesus before the Sanhedrin. [66kl*]When day came the council of elders of the people met, both chief priests and scribes, and they brought him before their Sanhedrin. [67m]They said, "If you are the Messiah, tell us," but he replied to them, "If I tell you, you will not believe, [68]and if I question, you will not respond. [69n]But from this time on the Son of Man will be seated at the right hand of the power of God." [70]They all asked, "Are you then the Son of God?" He replied to them, "You say that I am." [71]Then they said, "What further need have we for testimony? We have heard it from his own mouth."

CHAPTER 23

See RG 410-11

Jesus before Pilate. [1o*]Then the whole assembly of them arose and brought

---

the oldest papyrus manuscripts of Lk and from manuscripts of wide geographical distribution.

22, 51: And healed him: only Luke recounts this healing of the injured servant.

22, 61: Only Luke recounts that the **Lord turned and looked at Peter.** This look of Jesus leads to Peter's weeping bitterly over his denial (62).

22, 66–71: Luke recounts one daytime trial of Jesus (66–71) and hints at some type of preliminary nighttime investigation (54–65). Mark (and Matthew who follows Mk) has transferred incidents of this day into the nighttime interrogation with the result that there appear to be two Sanhedrin trials of Jesus in Mk (and Mt); see the note on Mk 14, 53.

22, 66: Sanhedrin: the word is a Hebraized form of a Greek word meaning a "council," and refers to the elders, chief priests, and scribes who met under the high priest's

leadership to decide religious and legal questions that did not pertain to Rome's interests. Jewish sources are not clear on the competence of the Sanhedrin to sentence and to execute during this period.

23, 1–5.13–25: Twice Jesus is brought before Pilate in Luke's account, and each time Pilate explicitly declares Jesus innocent of any wrongdoing (4.14.22). This stress on the innocence of Jesus before the Roman authorities is also charac-

---

a: 22, 40.   *b*: Mt 26, 47-56; Mk 14, 43-50; Jn 18, 3-4.   *c*: 22, 36. *d*: Jn 18, 26.   *e*: 22, 37.   *f*: 19, 47; 21, 37; Jn 7, 30; 8, 20; Col 1, 13.   *g*: Mt 26, 57-58.69-75; Mk 14, 53-54.66-72; Jn 18, 12-18.25-27.   *h*: 22, 33.   *i*: 22, 34.   *j*: Mt 26, 67-68; Mk 14, 65. *k*: Mt 26, 59-66; Mk 14, 55-64.   *l*: Mt 27, 1; Mk 15, 1.   *m*: Jn 3, 12; 8, 45; 10, 24.   *n*: Ps 110, 1; Dn 7, 13-14; Acts 7, 56.   *o*: Mt 27, 1-2.11-14; Mk 15, 1-5; Jn 18, 28-38.

him before Pilate. [2p]They brought charges against him, saying, "We found this man misleading our people; he opposes the payment of taxes to Caesar and maintains that he is the Messiah, a king." [3q]Pilate asked him, "Are you the king of the Jews?" He said to him in reply, "You say so." [4r]Pilate then addressed the chief priests and the crowds, "I find this man not guilty." [5]But they were adamant and said, "He is inciting the people with his teaching throughout all Judea, from Galilee where he began even to here."

Jesus before Herod. [6*]On hearing this Pilate asked if the man was a Galilean; [7s]and upon learning that he was under Herod's jurisdiction, he sent him to Herod who was in Jerusalem at that time. [8t]Herod was very glad to see Jesus; he had been wanting to see him for a long time, for he had heard about him and had been hoping to see him perform some sign. [9u]He questioned him at length, but he gave him no answer. [10v]The chief priests and scribes, meanwhile, stood by accusing him harshly. [11w][Even] Herod and his soldiers treated him contemptuously and mocked him, and after clothing him in resplendent garb, he sent him back to Pilate. [12]Herod and Pilate became friends that very day, even though they had been enemies formerly. [13]Pilate then summoned the chief priests, the rulers, and the people [14x]and said to them, "You brought this man to me and accused him of inciting the people to revolt. I have conducted my investigation in your presence and have not found this man guilty of the charges you have brought against him, [15]nor did Herod, for he sent him back to us. So no capital crime has been committed by

him. [16y]Therefore I shall have him flogged and then release him." [[17]]*

The Sentence of Death. [18z]But all together they shouted out, "Away with this man! Release Barabbas to us." [19](Now Barabbas had been imprisoned for a rebellion that had taken place in the city and for murder.) [20]Again Pilate addressed them, still wishing to release Jesus, [21]but they continued their shouting, "Crucify him! Crucify him!" [22]Pilate addressed them a third time, "What evil has this man done? I found him guilty of no capital crime. Therefore I shall have him flogged and then release him." [23]With loud shouts, however, they persisted in calling for his crucifixion, and their voices prevailed. [24]The verdict of Pilate was that their demand should be granted. [25]So he released the man who had been imprisoned for rebellion and murder, for whom they asked, and he handed Jesus over to them to deal with as they wished.

The Way of the Cross. [26a*]As they led him away they took hold of a certain Simon, a Cyrenian, who was coming in from the country; and after laying the cross on him, they made him carry it behind Jesus. [27]A large crowd of people followed Jesus, including many women who mourned and lamented him. [28b]Jesus turned to them and said, "Daughters of Jerusalem, do not weep for me; weep instead for yourselves and for your children, [29]for indeed, the days are coming when people will say, 'Blessed are the barren, the wombs that never bore and the breasts that never nursed.' [30c]At that time people will say to the mountains, 'Fall upon us!' and to the hills, 'Cover us!' [31]for if these things are done when the wood is green what

teristic of John's gospel (Jn 18, 38; 19, 4.6). Luke presents the Jerusalem Jewish leaders as the ones who force the hand of the Roman authorities (1–2.5.10.13.18.21.23–25).

23, 6–12: The appearance of Jesus before Herod is found only in this gospel. Herod has been an important figure in Lk (9, 7–9; 13, 31–33) and has been presented as someone who has been curious about Jesus for a long time. His curiosity goes unrewarded. It is faith in Jesus, not curiosity, that is rewarded (7, 50; 8, 48.50; 17, 19).

23, 17: This verse, "He was obliged to release one prisoner for them at the festival," is not part of the original text of Lk. It is an explanatory gloss from Mk 15, 6 (also Mt 27, 15) and is not found in many early and important Greek manuscripts. On its historical background, see the notes on Mt 27, 15–26.

23, 26–32: An important Lucan theme throughout the

gospel has been the need for the Christian disciple to follow in the footsteps of Jesus. Here this theme comes to the fore with the story of Simon of Cyrene who takes up the cross and follows Jesus (see 9, 23; 14, 27) and with the large crowd who likewise follow Jesus on the way of the cross. See also the note on Mk 15, 21.

p: 20, 22-25; Acts 17, 7; 24, 5. q: 22, 70; 1 Tm 6, 13. r: 23, 14.22.41; Mt 27, 24; Jn 19, 4.6; Acts 13, 28. s: 3, 1; 9, 7. t: 9, 9; Acts 4, 27-28. u: Mk 15, 5. v: Mt 27, 12; Mk 15, 3. w: Mt 27, 28-30; Mk 15, 17-19; Jn 19, 2-3. x: 23, 4.22.41. y: 23, 22; Jn 19, 12-14. z: Mt 27, 20-26; Mk 15, 6-7.11-15; Jn 18, 38b-40; 19, 14-16; Acts 3, 13-14. a: Mt 27, 32.38; Mk 15, 21.27; Jn 19, 17. b: 19, 41-44; 21, 23-24. c: Hos 10, 8; Rv 6, 16.

will happen when it is dry?" *32*Now two others, both criminals, were led away with him to be executed.

The Crucifixion. *33de*When they came to the place called the Skull, they crucified him and the criminals there, one on his right, the other on his left. *34f*[Then Jesus said, "Father, forgive them, they know not what they do."] They divided his garments by casting lots. *35gh*The people stood by and watched; the rulers, meanwhile, sneered at him and said, "He saved others, let him save himself if he is the chosen one, the Messiah of God." *36i*Even the soldiers jeered at him. As they approached to offer him wine *37*they called out, "If you are King of the Jews, save yourself." *38*Above him there was an inscription that read, "This is the King of the Jews."

39*Now one of the criminals hanging there reviled Jesus, saying, "Are you not the Messiah? Save yourself and us." *40*The other, however, rebuking him, said in reply, "Have you no fear of God, for you are subject to the same condemnation? *41j*And indeed, we have been condemned justly, for the sentence we received corresponds to our crimes, but this man has done nothing criminal." *42k*Then he said, "Jesus, remember me when you come into your kingdom." *43l*He replied to him, "Amen, I say to you, today you will be with me in Paradise."

The Death of Jesus. *44mn**It was now about noon and darkness came over the whole land until three in the afternoon *45o*because of an eclipse of the sun. Then the veil of the temple was torn down the middle. *46p*Jesus cried out in a loud voice, "Father,

into your hands I commend my spirit"; and when he had said this he breathed his last. *47**The centurion who witnessed what had happened glorified God and said, "This man was innocent beyond doubt." *48q*When all the people who had gathered for this spectacle saw what had happened, they returned home beating their breasts; *49r*but all his acquaintances stood at a distance, including the women who had followed him from Galilee and saw these events.

The Burial of Jesus. *50s*Now there was a virtuous and righteous man named Joseph who, though he was a member of the council, *51t*had not consented to their plan of action. He came from the Jewish town of Arimathea and was awaiting the kingdom of God. *52*He went to Pilate and asked for the body of Jesus. *53u*After he had taken the body down, he wrapped it in a linen cloth and laid him in a rock-hewn tomb in which no one had yet been buried. *54*It was the day of preparation, and the sabbath was about to begin. *55v*The women who had come from Galilee with him followed behind, and when they had seen the tomb and the way in which his body was laid in it, *56w*they returned and prepared spices and perfumed oils. Then they rested on the sabbath according to the commandment.

VIII: The Resurrection Narrative

CHAPTER 24

The Resurrection of Jesus. *1x**But at daybreak on the first day of the week they

---

23, 34a: [Then Jesus said, "Father, forgive them, they know not what they do."]: this portion of v 34 does not occur in the oldest papyrus manuscript of Lk and in other early Greek manuscripts and ancient versions of wide geographical distribution.

23, 39–43: This episode is recounted only in this gospel. The penitent sinner receives salvation through the crucified Jesus. Jesus' words to the penitent thief reveal Luke's understanding that the destiny of the Christian is "to be with Jesus."

23, 44: Noon . . . three in the afternoon: literally, the sixth and ninth hours. See the note on Mk 15, 25.

23, 47: This man was innocent: or, "This man was righteous."

24, 1–53: The resurrection narrative in Lk consists of five sections: (1) the women at the empty tomb (23, 56b—24, 12); (2) the appearance to the two disciples on the way to Emmaus

(24, 13–35); (3) the appearance to the disciples in Jerusalem (24, 36–43); (4) Jesus' final instructions (24, 44–49); (5) the ascension (24, 50–53). In Lk, all the resurrection appearances take place in and around Jerusalem; moreover, they are all recounted as having taken place on Easter Sunday. A consistent

d: Mt 27, 33-44; Mk 15, 22-32; Jn 19, 17-24. *e:* 22, 37; Is 53, 12. *f:* Nm 15, 27-31; Ps 22, 19; Mt 5, 44; Acts 7, 60. *g:* Ps 22, 8-9. *h:* 4, 23. *i:* Ps 69, 22; Mt 27, 48; Mk 15, 36. *j:* 23, 4.14.22. *k:* 9, 27; 23, 2.3.38. *l:* 2 Cor 12, 3; Rv 2, 7. *m:* Mt 27, 45-56; Mk 15, 33-41; Jn 19, 25-30. *n:* Am 8, 9. *o:* Ex 26, 31-33; 36, 35. *p:* Ps 31, 6; Acts 7, 59. *q:* 18, 13; Zec 12, 10. *r:* 8, 1-3; 23, 55-56; 24, 10; Ps 38, 12. *s:* Mt 27, 57-61; Mk 15, 42-47; Jn 19, 38-42; Acts 13, 29. *t:* 2, 25.38. *u:* 19, 30; Acts 13, 29. *v:* 8, 2; 23, 49; 24, 10. *w:* Ex 12, 16; 20, 10; Dt 5, 14. *x:* Mt 28, 1-8; Mk 16, 1-8; Jn 20, 1-17.

took the spices they had prepared and went to the tomb. ²They found the stone rolled away from the tomb; ³but when they entered, they did not find the body of the Lord Jesus. ⁴ʸWhile they were puzzling over this, behold, two men in dazzling garments appeared to them. ⁵ᶻThey were terrified and bowed their faces to the ground. They said to them, "Why do you seek the living one among the dead? ⁶*He is not here, but he has been raised. Remember what he said to you while he was still in Galilee, ⁷ᵃthat the Son of Man must be handed over to sinners and be crucified, and rise on the third day." ⁸ᵇAnd they remembered his words. ⁹ᶜ*Then they returned from the tomb and announced all these things to the eleven and to all the others. ¹⁰ᵈThe women were Mary Magdalene, Joanna, and Mary the mother of James; the others who accompanied them also told this to the apostles, ¹¹but their story seemed like nonsense and they did not believe them. ¹²ᵉ*But Peter got up and ran to the tomb, bent down, and saw the burial cloths alone; then he went home amazed at what had happened.

The Appearance on the Road to Emmaus. ¹³ᶠ*Now that very day two of them were going to a village seven miles from Jerusalem called Emmaus, ¹⁴and they were conversing about all the things that had occurred. ¹⁵And

it happened that while they were conversing and debating, Jesus himself drew near and walked with them, ¹⁶ᵍ*but their eyes were prevented from recognizing him. ¹⁷He asked them, "What are you discussing as you walk along?" They stopped, looking downcast. ¹⁸One of them, named Cleopas, said to him in reply, "Are you the only visitor to Jerusalem who does not know of the things that have taken place there in these days?" ¹⁹ʰAnd he replied to them, "What sort of things?" They said to him, "The things that happened to Jesus the Nazarene, who was a prophet mighty in deed and word before God and all the people, ²⁰how our chief priests and rulers both handed him over to a sentence of death and crucified him. ²¹ⁱBut we were hoping that he would be the one to redeem Israel; and besides all this, it is now the third day since this took place. ²²ʲSome women from our group, however, have astounded us: they were at the tomb early in the morning ²³and did not find his body; they came back and reported that they had indeed seen a vision of angels who announced that he was alive. ²⁴ᵏThen some of those with us went to the tomb and found things just as the women had described, but him they did not see." ²⁵ˡAnd he said to them, "Oh, how foolish you are! How slow of heart to believe all that the prophets spoke! ²⁶*Was it not neces-

---

theme throughout the narrative is that the suffering, death, and resurrection of Jesus were accomplished in fulfillment of Old Testament promises and of Jewish hopes (19a.21.26–27.44.46). In his second volume, Acts, Luke will argue that Christianity is the fulfillment of the hopes of Pharisaic Judaism and its logical development (see Acts 24, 10–21).

24, 6a: He is not here, but he has been raised: this part of the verse is omitted in important representatives of the Western text tradition, but its presence in other text types and the slight difference in wording from Mt 28, 6 and Mk 16, 6 argue for its retention.

24, 9: The women in this gospel do not flee from the tomb and tell no one, as in Mk 16, 8, but return and tell the disciples about their experience. The initial reaction to the testimony of the women is disbelief (11).

24, 12: This verse is missing from the Western textual tradition but is found in the best and oldest manuscripts of other text types.

24, 13–35: This episode focuses on the interpretation of scripture by the risen Jesus and the recognition of him in the breaking of the bread. The references to the quotations of scripture and explanation of it (25–27), the kerygmatic proclamation (34), and the liturgical gesture (30) suggest that

the episode is primarily catechetical and liturgical rather than apologetic.

24, 13: Seven miles: literally, "sixty stades." A stade was 607 feet. Some manuscripts read "160 stades" or more than eighteen miles. The exact location of Emmaus is disputed.

24, 16: A consistent feature of the resurrection stories is that the risen Jesus was different and initially unrecognizable (37; Mk 16, 12; Jn 20, 14; 21, 4).

24, 26: That the Messiah should suffer . . . : Luke is the only New Testament writer to speak explicitly of a suffering Messiah (26.46; Acts 3, 18; 17, 3; 26, 23). The idea of a suffering Messiah is not found in the Old Testament or in other Jewish literature prior to the New Testament period, although the idea is hinted at in Mk 8, 31–33. See the notes on Mt 26, 63 and 26, 67–68.

y: 2 Mc 3, 26; Acts 1, 10.　z: Acts 2, 9.　a: 9, 22.44; 17, 25; 18, 32-33; Mt 16, 21; 17, 22-23; Mk 9, 31; Acts 17, 3.　b: Jn 2, 22.　c: Mk 16, 10-11; Jn 20, 18.　d: 8, 2-3; Mk 16, 9.　e: Jn 20, 3-7.　f: Mk 16, 12-13.　g: Jn 20, 14; 21, 4.　h: Mt 2, 23; 21, 11; Acts 2, 22.　i: 1, 54.68; 2, 38.　j: 24, 1-11; Mt 28, 1-8; Mk 16, 1-8.　k: Jn 20, 3-10.　l: 9, 22; 18, 31; 24, 44; Acts 3, 24; 17, 3.

sary that the Messiah should suffer these things and enter into his glory?" [27m]Then beginning with Moses and all the prophets, he interpreted to them what referred to him in all the scriptures. [28]As they approached the village to which they were going, he gave the impression that he was going on farther. [29]But they urged him, "Stay with us, for it is nearly evening and the day is almost over." So he went in to stay with them. [30]And it happened that, while he was with them at table, he took bread, said the blessing, broke it, and gave it to them. [31]With that their eyes were opened and they recognized him, but he vanished from their sight. [32]Then they said to each other, "Were not our hearts burning [within us] while he spoke to us on the way and opened the scriptures to us?" [33]So they set out at once and returned to Jerusalem where they found gathered together the eleven and those with them [34n]who were saying, "The Lord has truly been raised and has appeared to Simon!" [35]Then the two recounted what had taken place on the way and how he was made known to them in the breaking of the bread.

The Appearance to the Disciples in Jerusalem. [36o p*]While they were still speaking about this, he stood in their midst and said to them, "Peace be with you." [37q]But they were startled and terrified and thought that they were seeing a ghost. [38]Then he said to them, "Why are you troubled? And why do questions arise in your hearts? [39*]Look at my hands and my feet, that it is I myself. Touch me and see, because a ghost does not have flesh and bones as you can see I have." [40r]And as he said this, he showed them his hands and his feet. [41]While they were still incredulous for joy and were amazed, he asked them, "Have you anything here to eat?" [42s]They gave him a piece of baked fish; [43]he took it and ate it in front of them.

[44t]He said to them, "These are my words that I spoke to you while I was still with you, that everything written about me in the law of Moses and in the prophets and psalms must be fulfilled." [45u]Then he opened their minds to understand the scriptures. [46v*]And he said to them, "Thus it is written that the Messiah would suffer and rise from the dead on the third day [47w]and that repentance, for the forgiveness of sins, would be preached in his name to all the nations, beginning from Jerusalem. [48x]You are witnesses of these things. [49y*]And [behold] I am sending the promise of my Father upon you; but stay in the city until you are clothed with power from on high."

The Ascension. [50z*]Then he led them [out] as far as Bethany, raised his hands, and blessed them. [51]As he blessed them he parted from them and was taken up to heaven. [52a]They did him homage and then returned to Jerusalem with great joy, [53*]and they were continually in the temple praising God.

24, 36–43.44–49: The Gospel of Luke, like each of the other gospels (Mt 28, 16–20; Mk 16, 14–15; Jn 20, 19–23), focuses on an important appearance of Jesus to the Twelve in which they are commissioned for their future ministry. As in vv 6 and 12, so in vv 36 and 40 there are omissions in the Western text.

24, 39–42: The apologetic purpose of this story is evident in the concern with the physical details and the report that Jesus ate food.

24, 46: See the note on 24, 26.

24, 49: The promise of my Father: i.e., the gift of the holy Spirit.

24, 50–53: Luke brings his story about the time of Jesus to a close with the report of the ascension. He will also begin the story of the time of the church with a recounting of the ascension. In the gospel, Luke recounts the ascension of Jesus on Easter Sunday night, thereby closely associating it with the resurrection. In Acts (1, 3.9–11; 13, 31) he historicizes the ascension by speaking of a forty-day period between the resurrection and the ascension. The Western text omits some phrases in vv 51 and 52, perhaps to avoid any chronological conflict with Acts 1 about the time of the ascension.

24, 53: The Gospel of Luke ends as it began (1, 9), in the Jerusalem temple.

m: 24, 44; Dt 18, 25; Ps 22, 1-18; Is 53; 1 Pt 1, 10-11.   n: 1 Cor 15, 4-5.   o: Mk 16, 14-19; Jn 20, 19-20.   p: 1 Cor 15, 5.   q: Mt 14, 26.   r: Jn 21, 5.9-10.13.   s: Acts 10, 41.   t: 18, 31; 24, 27; Mt 16, 21; Jn 5, 39.46.   u: Jn 20, 9.   v: 9, 22; Is 53; Hos 6, 2.   w: Mt 3, 2; 28, 19-20; Mk 16, 15-16; Acts 10, 41.   x: Acts 1, 8.   y: Jn 14, 26; Acts 1, 4; 2, 3-4.   z: Mk 16, 19; Acts 1, 9-11.   a: Acts 1, 12.

See RG
412–23

The Gospel According to John

The Gospel according to John is quite different in character from the three synoptic gospels. It is highly literary and symbolic. It does not follow the same order or reproduce the same stories as the synoptic gospels. To a much greater degree, it is the product of a developed theological reflection and grows out of a different circle and tradition. It was probably written in the 90s of the first century.

The Gospel of John begins with a magnificent prologue, which states many of the major themes and motifs of the gospel, much as an overture does for a musical work. The prologue proclaims Jesus as the preexistent and incarnate Word of God who has revealed the Father to us. The rest of the first chapter forms the introduction to the gospel proper and consists of the Baptist's testimony about Jesus (there is no baptism of Jesus in this gospel—John simply points him out as the Lamb of God), followed by stories of the call of the first disciples, in which various titles predicated of Jesus in the early church are presented.

The gospel narrative contains a series of "signs"—the gospel's word for the wondrous deeds of Jesus. The author is primarily interested in the significance of these deeds, and so interprets them for the reader by various reflections, narratives, and discourses. The first sign is the transformation of water into wine at Cana (2, 1–11); this represents the replacement of the Jewish ceremonial washings and symbolizes the entire creative and transforming work of Jesus. The second sign, the cure of the royal official's son (4, 46–54) simply by the word of Jesus at a distance, signifies the power of Jesus' life-giving word. The same theme is further developed by other signs, probably for a total of seven. The third sign, the cure of the paralytic at the pool with five porticoes in ch 5, continues the theme of water offering newness of life. In the preceding chapter, to the woman at the well in Samaria Jesus had offered living water springing up to eternal life, a symbol of the revelation that Jesus brings; here Jesus' life-giving word replaces the water of the pool that failed to bring life. Chapter 6 contains two signs, the multiplication of loaves and the walking on the waters of the Sea of Galilee. These signs are connected much as the manna and the crossing of the Red Sea are in the Passover narrative and symbolize a new exodus. The multiplication of the loaves is interpreted for the reader by the discourse that follows, where the bread of life is used first as a figure for the revelation of God in Jesus and then for the Eucharist. After a series of dialogues reflecting Jesus' debates with the Jewish authorities at the Feast of Tabernacles in chapters 7 and 8, the sixth sign is presented in ch 9, the sign of the young man born blind. This is a narrative illustration of the theme of conflict in the preceding two chapters; it proclaims the triumph of light over darkness, as Jesus is presented as the Light of the world. This is interpreted by a narrative of controversy between the Pharisees and the young man who had been given his sight by Jesus, ending with a discussion of spiritual blindness and spelling out the symbolic meaning of the cure. And finally, the seventh sign, the raising of Lazarus in ch 11, is the climax of signs. Lazarus is presented as a token of the real life that Jesus, the Resurrection and the Life, who will now ironically be put to death because of his gift of life to Lazarus, will give to all who believe in him once he has been raised from the dead.

After the account of the seven signs, the "hour" of Jesus arrives, and the author passes from sign to reality, as he moves into the discourses in the upper room that interpret the meaning of the passion, death, and resurrection narratives that follow. The whole gospel of John is a progressive revelation of the glory of God's only Son, who comes to reveal the Father and then returns in glory to the Father. The author's purpose is clearly expressed in what must have been the original ending of the gospel at the end of ch 20: "Now Jesus did many other signs in the presence of [his] disciples that are not written in this book. But these are written that you may [come to] believe that Jesus is the Messiah, the Son of God, and that through this belief you may have life in his name."

Critical analysis makes it difficult to accept the idea that the gospel as it now stands was written by one person. Chapter 21 seems to have been added after the gospel was completed; it exhibits a Greek style somewhat different from that of the rest of the work. The prologue (1, 1–18) apparently contains an independent hymn, subsequently adapted to serve as a preface to the gospel. Within the gospel itself there are also some inconsistencies, e.g., there are two endings of Jesus' discourse in the upper room (14, 31; 18, 1). To solve these problems, scholars have proposed various rearrangements that would produce a smoother order. However, most have come to the conclusion that the inconsistencies were probably produced by subsequent editing in which homogeneous materials were added to a shorter original.

Other difficulties for any theory of eyewitness authorship of the gospel in its present form are presented by its highly developed theology and by certain elements of its literary style. For instance, some of the wondrous deeds of Jesus have been worked into highly effective dramatic scenes (ch 9); there has been a careful attempt to have these followed by discourses that explain them (chs 5 and 6); and the sayings of Jesus have been woven into long discourses of a quasi-poetic form resembling the speeches of personified Wisdom in the Old Testament.

The polemic between synagogue and church produced bitter and harsh invective, especially regarding the hostility toward Jesus of the authorities—Pharisees and Sadducees—who are combined and referred to frequently as "the Jews" (see the note on 1, 19). These opponents are even described in 8, 44 as springing from their father the devil, whose conduct they imitate in opposing God by rejecting Jesus, whom God has sent. On the other hand, the author of this gospel seems to take pains to show that women are not inferior to men in the Christian community: the woman at the well in Samaria (4) is presented as a prototype of a missionary (4, 4–42), and the first witness of the resurrection is a woman (20, 11–18).

The final editing of the gospel and arrangement in its present form probably dates from between A.D. 90 and 100. Traditionally, Ephesus has been favored as the place of composition, though many support a location in Syria, perhaps the city of Antioch, while some have suggested other places, including Alexandria.

The principal divisions of the Gospel according to John are the following:

  I: Prologue (1, 1–18)
  II: The Book of Signs (1, 19—12, 50)
  III: The Book of Glory (13, 1—20, 31)
  IV: Epilogue: The Resurrection Appearance in
     Galilee (21, 1–25)

I: Prologue

CHAPTER 1

See RG
415–16

[1] *a**In the beginning was the Word,
    and the Word was with God,
    and the Word was God.
[2] He was in the beginning with God.
[3] *b**All things came to be through him,
    and without him nothing came to be.
What came to be [4]*c*through him was life,
    and this life was the light of the human
     race;
[5] *d**the light shines in the darkness,
    and the darkness has not overcome it.

1, 1–18: The prologue states the main themes of the gospel: life, light, truth, the world, testimony, and the preexistence of Jesus Christ, the incarnate **Logos,** who reveals God the Father. In origin, it was probably an early Christian hymn. Its closest parallel is in other christological hymns, Col 1, 15–20 and Phil 2, 6–11. Its core (1–5.10–11.14) is poetic in structure, with short phrases linked by "staircase parallelism," in which the last word of one phrase becomes the first word of the next. Prose inserts (at least 6–8 and 15) deal with John the Baptist.

  1, 1: In the beginning: also the first words of the Old Testament (Gn 1, 1). **Was:** this verb is used three times with different meanings in this verse: existence, relationship, and predication. **The Word** (Greek **logos**): this term combines God's dynamic, creative word (Genesis), personified preexistent Wisdom as the instrument of God's creative activity (Proverbs), and the ultimate intelligibility of reality (Hellenistic philosophy). **With God:** the Greek preposition here connotes communication with another. **Was God:** lack of a definite article with "God" in Greek signifies predication rather than identification.

  1, 3: What came to be: while the oldest manuscripts have no punctuation here, the corrector of Bodmer Papyrus P[75], some manuscripts, and the Ante-Nicene Fathers take this phrase with what follows, as staircase parallelism. Connection with v 3 reflects fourth-century anti-Arianism.

  1, 5: The ethical dualism of light and darkness is paralleled in intertestamental literature and in the Dead Sea Scrolls. **Overcome:** "comprehend" is another possible translation, but cf 12, 35; Wis 7, 29–30.

a: 10, 30; Gn 1, 1-5; Jb 28, 12-27; Prv 8, 22-25; Wis 9, 1-2; 1 Jn 1, 1-2; Col 1, 1.15; Rv 3, 14; 19, 13. *b:* Ps 33, 9; Wis 9, 1; Sir 42, 15; 1 Cor 8, 6; Col 1, 16; Heb 1, 2; Rv 3, 14. *c:* 5, 26; 8, 12; 1 Jn 1, 2. *d:* 3, 19; 8, 12; 9, 5; 12, 35.46; Wis 7, 29-30; 1 Thes 5, 4; 1 Jn 2, 8.

6e*A man named John was sent from God. 7f*He came for testimony, to testify to the light, so that all might believe through him. 8gHe was not the light, but came to testify to the light. 9hThe true light, which enlightens everyone, was coming into the world.

10 He was in the world,
    and the world came to be through him,
    but the world did not know him.
11 *He came to what was his own,
    but his own people did not accept him.

12iBut to those who did accept him he gave power to become children of God, to those who believe in his name, 13j*who were born not by natural generation nor by human choice nor by a man's decision but of God.

14 k*And the Word became flesh
    and made his dwelling among us,

and we saw his glory,
    the glory as of the Father's only Son,
    full of grace and truth.

15l*John testified to him and cried out, saying, "This was he of whom I said, 'The one who is coming after me ranks ahead of me because he existed before me.' " 16*From his fullness we have all received, grace in place of grace, 17mbecause while the law was given through Moses, grace and truth came through Jesus Christ. 18n*No one has ever seen God. The only Son, God, who is at the Father's side, has revealed him.

II: The Book of Signs

John the Baptist's Testimony to Himself. 19*And this is the testimony of John. When the Jews from Jerusalem sent priests and Levites [to him] to ask him, "Who are

---

1, 6: John was **sent** just as Jesus was "sent" (4, 34) in divine mission. Other references to John the Baptist in this gospel emphasize the differences between them and John's subordinate role.

1, 7: Testimony: the testimony theme of Jn is introduced, which portrays Jesus as if on trial throughout his ministry. All testify to Jesus: John the Baptist, the Samaritan woman, scripture, his works, the crowds, the Spirit, and his disciples.

1, 11: What was his own . . . his own people: first a neuter, literally, "his own property/possession" (probably = Israel), then a masculine, "his own people" (the Israelites).

1, 13: Believers in Jesus become children of God not through any of the three natural causes mentioned but through God who is the immediate cause of the new spiritual life. **Were born:** the Greek verb can mean "begotten" (by a male) or "born" (from a female or of parents). The variant "he who was begotten," asserting Jesus' virginal conception, is weakly attested in Old Latin and Syriac versions.

1, 14: Flesh: the whole person, used probably against docetic tendencies (cf 1 Jn 4, 2; 2 Jn 7). **Made his dwelling:** literally, "pitched his tent/tabernacle." Cf the tabernacle or tent of meeting that was the place of God's presence among his people (Ex 25, 8–9). The incarnate Word is the new mode of God's presence among his people. The Greek verb has the same consonants as the Aramaic word for God's presence (Shekinah). **Glory:** God's visible manifestation of majesty in power, which once filled the tabernacle (Ex 40, 34) and the temple (1 Kgs 8, 10–11.27), is now centered in Jesus. **Only Son:** Greek, **monogenēs**, but see the note on 1, 18. **Grace and truth:** these words may represent two Old Testament terms describing Yahweh in covenant relationship with Israel (cf Ex 34, 6), thus God's "love" and "fidelity." The Word shares Yahweh's covenant qualities.

1, 15: This verse, interrupting vv 14 and 16, seems drawn from v 30.

1, 16: Grace in place of grace: replacement of the Old Covenant with the New (cf 17). Other possible translations are "grace upon grace" (accumulation) and "grace for grace" (correspondence).

1, 18: The only Son, God: while the vast majority of later textual witnesses have another reading, "the Son, the only one" or "the only Son," the translation above follows the best and earliest manuscripts, **monogenēs theos**, but takes the first term to mean not just "Only One" but to include a filial relationship with the Father, as at Lk 9, 38 ("only child") or Heb 11, 17 ("only son") and as translated at Jn 1, 14. The Logos is thus "only Son" and God but not Father/God.

1, 19–51: The testimony of John the Baptist about the Messiah and Jesus' self-revelation to the first disciples. This section constitutes the introduction to the gospel proper and is connected with the prose inserts in the prologue. It develops the major theme of testimony in four scenes: John's negative testimony about himself; his positive testimony about Jesus; the revelation of Jesus to Andrew and Peter; the revelation of Jesus to Philip and Nathanael.

1, 19: The Jews: throughout most of the gospel, the "Jews" does not refer to the Jewish people as such but to the hostile authorities, both Pharisees and Sadducees, particularly in Jerusalem, who refuse to believe in Jesus. The usage reflects the atmosphere, at the end of the first century, of polemics between church and synagogue, or possibly it refers to Jews as representative of a hostile world (10–11).

e: Mt 3, 1; Mk 1, 4; Lk 3, 2-3. *f:* 1, 19-34; 5, 33. *g:* 5, 35. *h:* 3, 19; 8, 12; 9, 39; 12, 46. *i:* 3, 11-12; 5, 43-44; 12, 46-50; Gal 3, 26; 4, 6-7; Eph 1, 5; 1 Jn 3, 2. *j:* 3, 5-6. *k:* Ex 16, 10; 24, 17; 25, 8-9; 33, 22; 34, 6; Sir 24, 4.8; Is 60,1; Ez 43, 7; Jl 4, 17; Hb 2, 14; 1 Jn 1, 2; 4, 2; 2 Jn 7. *l:* 1, 30; 3, 27-30. *m:* 7, 19; Ex 31, 18; 34, 28. *n:* 5, 37; 6, 46; Ex 33, 20; Jgs 13, 21-22; 1 Tm 6, 16; 1 Jn 4, 12.

you?" [20o]*he admitted and did not deny it, but admitted, "I am not the Messiah." [21p]*So they asked him, "What are you then? Are you Elijah?" And he said, "I am not." "Are you the Prophet?" He answered, "No." [22]So they said to him, "Who are you, so we can give an answer to those who sent us? What do you have to say for yourself?" [23q]*He said:

"I am 'the voice of one crying out in the desert,
"Make straight the way of the Lord," '

as Isaiah the prophet said." [24]*Some Pharisees were also sent. [25r]They asked him, "Why then do you baptize if you are not the Messiah or Elijah or the Prophet?" [26s]*John answered them, "I baptize with water; but there is one among you whom you do not recognize, [27]the one who is coming after me, whose sandal strap I am not worthy to untie." [28]*This happened in Bethany across the Jordan, where John was baptizing.

John the Baptist's Testimony to Jesus. [29t]*The next day he saw Jesus coming toward him and said, "Behold, the Lamb of God, who takes away the sin of the world. [30u]*He is the one of whom I said, 'A man is coming after me who ranks ahead of me because he existed before me.' [31]*I did not know him, but the reason why I came baptizing with water was that he might be made known to Israel." [32v]*John testified further, saying, "I saw the Spirit come down like a dove from the sky and remain upon him. [33w]I did not know him, but the one who sent me to baptize with water told me, 'On whomever you see the Spirit come down and remain, he is the one who will baptize with the holy Spirit.' [34x]*Now I have seen and testified that he is the Son of God."

The First Disciples. [35y]The next day John was there again with two of his disciples, [36]*and as he watched Jesus walk by, he said, "Behold, the Lamb of God." [37]*The two disciples heard what he said and followed Jesus. [38]Jesus turned and saw them following him and said to them, "What are you looking for?" They said to him, "Rabbi" (which translated means Teacher), "where

1, 20: Messiah: the anointed agent of Yahweh, usually considered to be of Davidic descent. See further the note on 1, 41.

1, 21: Elijah: the Baptist did not claim to be Elijah returned to earth (cf Mal 3, 23; Mt 11, 14). **The Prophet:** probably the prophet like Moses (Dt 18, 15; cf Acts 3, 22).

1, 23: This is a repunctuation and reinterpretation (as in the synoptic gospels and Septuagint) of the Hebrew text of Is 40, 3, which reads, "A voice cries out: In the desert prepare the way of the LORD."

1, 24: Some Pharisees: other translations, such as "Now they had been sent from the Pharisees," misunderstand the grammatical construction. This is a different group from that in v 19; the priests and Levites would have been Sadducees, not Pharisees.

1, 26: I baptize with water: the synoptics add "but he will baptize you with the holy Spirit" (Mk 1, 8) or ". . . holy Spirit and fire" (Mt 3, 11; Lk 3, 16). John's emphasis is on purification and preparation for a better baptism.

1, 28: Bethany across the Jordan: site unknown. Another reading is "Bethabara."

1, 29: The Lamb of God: the background for this title may be the victorious apocalyptic lamb who would destroy evil in the world (Rv 5–7; 17, 14); the paschal lamb, whose blood saved Israel (Ex 12); and/or the suffering servant led like a lamb to the slaughter as a sin-offering (Is 53, 7.10).

1, 30: He existed before me: possibly as Elijah (to come, 27); for the evangelist and his audience, Jesus' preexistence would be implied (see the note on 1, 1).

1, 31: I did not know him: this gospel shows no knowledge of the tradition (Lk 1) about the kinship of Jesus and

John the Baptist. **The reason why I came baptizing with water:** in this gospel, John's baptism is not connected with forgiveness of sins; its purpose is revelatory, that Jesus may be made known to Israel.

1, 32: Like a dove: a symbol of the new creation (Gn 8, 8) or the community of Israel (Hos 11, 11). **Remain:** the first use of a favorite verb in Jn, emphasizing the permanency of the relationship between Father and Son (as here) and between the Son and the Christian. Jesus is the permanent bearer of the Spirit.

1, 34: The Son of God: this reading is supported by good Greek manuscripts, including the Chester Beatty and Bodmer Papyri and the Vatican Codex, but is suspect because it harmonizes this passage with the synoptic version: "This is my beloved Son" (Mt 3, 17; Mk 1, 11; Lk 3, 22). The poorly attested alternate reading, "God's chosen One," is probably a reference to the Servant of Yahweh (Is 42, 1).

1, 36: John the Baptist's testimony makes his disciples' following of Jesus plausible.

1, 37: The two disciples: Andrew (40) and, traditionally, John, son of Zebedee (see the note on 13, 23).

o: 3, 28; Lk 3, 15; Acts 13, 25. p: Dt 18, 15.18; 2 Kgs 2, 11; Sir 48, 10; Mal 3, 1.23; Mt 11, 14; 17, 11-13; Mk 9, 13; Acts 3, 22. q: Is 40, 3; Mt 3, 3; Mk 1, 2; Lk 3, 4. r: Ez 36, 25; Zec 13, 1; Mt 16, 14. s: Mt 3, 11; Mk 1, 7-8; Lk 3, 16; Acts 13, 25. t: 1, 36; Ex 12; Is 53, 7; Rv 5-7; 17, 14. u: 1, 15; Mt 3, 11; Mk 1, 7; Lk 3, 16. v: Sg 5, 2; Is 11, 2; Hos 11, 11; Mt 3, 16; Mk 1, 10; Lk 3, 21-22. w: Is 42, 1; Mt 3, 11; Mk 1, 8; Lk 3, 16. x: Is 42, 1; Mt 3, 17; Mk 1, 11; Lk 9, 35. y: Mt 4, 18-22; Mk 1, 16-20; Lk 5, 1-11.

are you staying?" *39**He said to them, "Come, and you will see." So they went and saw where he was staying, and they stayed with him that day. It was about four in the afternoon. *40*Andrew, the brother of Simon Peter, was one of the two who heard John and followed Jesus. *41z**He first found his own brother Simon and told him, "We have found the Messiah" (which is translated Anointed). *42a**Then he brought him to Jesus. Jesus looked at him and said, "You are Simon the son of John; you will be called Cephas" (which is translated Peter).

*43**The next day he decided to go to Galilee, and he found Philip. And Jesus said to him, "Follow me." *44*Now Philip was from Bethsaida, the town of Andrew and Peter. *45b*Philip found Nathanael and told him, "We have found the one about whom Moses wrote in the law, and also the prophets, Jesus son of Joseph, from Nazareth." *46*But Nathanael said to him, "Can anything good come from Nazareth?" Philip said to him, "Come and see." *47**Jesus saw Nathanael

coming toward him and said of him, "Here is a true Israelite. There is no duplicity in him." *48c**Nathanael said to him, "How do you know me?" Jesus answered and said to him, "Before Philip called you, I saw you under the fig tree." *49d**Nathanael answered him, "Rabbi, you are the Son of God; you are the King of Israel." *50**Jesus answered and said to him, "Do you believe because I told you that I saw you under the fig tree? You will see greater things than this." *51e**And he said to him, "Amen, amen, I say to you, you will see the sky opened and the angels of God ascending and descending on the Son of Man."

CHAPTER 2

See RG
416–17

The Wedding at Cana. *1f**On the third day there was a wedding in Cana in Galilee, and the mother of Jesus was there. *2*Jesus and his disciples were also invited to the wedding. *3*When the wine ran short, the mother of Jesus said to him, "They have no wine." *4g**[And] Jesus said to her, "Woman, how does your concern affect me? My hour

---

1, 39: Four in the afternoon: literally, the tenth hour, from sunrise, in the Roman calculation of time. Some suggest that the next day, beginning at sunset, was the sabbath; they would have stayed with Jesus to avoid travel on it.

1, 41: Messiah: the Hebrew word **māšiah,** "anointed one" (see the note on Lk 2, 11), appears in Greek as the transliterated **messias** only here and in 4, 25. Elsewhere the Greek translation **christos** is used.

1, 42: Simon the son of John: in Mt 16, 17, Simon is called **Bariōna,** "son of Jonah," a different tradition for the name of Simon's father. **Cephas:** in Aramaic = the Rock; cf Mt 16, 18. Neither the Greek equivalent **Petros** nor, with one isolated exception, **Cephas** is attested as a personal name before Christian times.

1, 43: He: grammatically, could be Peter, but logically is probably Jesus.

1, 47: A true Israelite. There is no duplicity in him: Jacob was the first to bear the name "Israel" (Gn 32, 29), but Jacob was a man of duplicity (Gn 27, 35–36).

1, 48: Under the fig tree: a symbol of messianic peace (cf Mi 4, 4; Zec 3, 10).

1, 49: Son of God: this title is used in the Old Testament, among other ways, as a title of adoption for the Davidic king (2 Sm 7, 14; Pss 2, 7; 89, 27), and thus here, with **King of Israel,** in a messianic sense. For the evangelist, Son of God also points to Jesus' divinity (cf 20, 28).

1, 50: Possibly a statement: "You [singular] believe because I saw you under the fig tree."

1, 51: The double "Amen" is characteristic of John. **You** is plural in Greek. The allusion is to Jacob's ladder (Gn 28, 12).

2, 1—6, 71: Signs revealing Jesus as the Messiah to all Israel. "Sign" (sēmeion) is John's symbolic term for Jesus'

wondrous deeds (see Introduction). The Old Testament background lies in the Exodus story (cf Dt 11, 3; 29, 2). John is interested primarily in what the **sēmeia** signify: God's intervention in human history in a new way through Jesus.

2, 1–11: The first sign. This story of replacement of Jewish ceremonial washings (6) presents the initial revelation about Jesus at the outset of his ministry. He manifests his glory; the disciples believe. There is no synoptic parallel.

2, 1: The mother of Jesus: she is never named in John. **Cana:** unknown from the Old Testament.

2, 4: This verse may seek to show that Jesus did not work miracles to help his family and friends, as in the apocryphal gospels. **Woman:** a normal, polite form of address, but unattested in reference to one's mother. Cf also 19, 26. **How does your concern affect me?:** literally, "What is this to me and to you?"—a Hebrew expression of either hostility (Jgs 11, 12; 2 Chr 35, 21; 1 Kgs 17, 18) or denial of common interest (Hos 14, 9; 2 Kgs 3, 13). Cf Mk 1, 24; 5, 7, used by demons to Jesus. **My hour has not yet come:** the translation as a question ("Has not my hour now come?"), while preferable grammatically and supported by Greek Fathers, seems unlikely from a comparison with 7, 6.30. The "hour" is that of Jesus' passion, death, resurrection, and ascension (13, 1).

---

z: 4, 25.   a: Mt 16, 18; Mk 3, 16.   b: 21, 2.   c: Mi 4, 4; Zec 3, 10.   d: 12, 13; Ex 4, 22; Dt 14, 1; 2 Sm 7, 14; Jb 1, 6; 2, 1; 38, 7; Pss 2, 7; 29, 1; 89, 27; Wis 2, 18; Sir 4, 10; Dn 3, 25; Hos 11, 1; Mt 14, 33; 16, 16; Mk 13, 32.   e: Gn 28, 10-17; Dn 7, 13.   f: 4, 46; Jgs 14, 12; Tb 11, 8.   g: 7, 30; 8, 20; 12, 23; 13, 1; Jgs 11, 12; 1 Kgs 17, 18; 2 Kgs 3, 13; 2 Chr 35, 21; Hos 14, 9; Mk 1, 24; 5, 7; 7, 30; 8, 20; 12, 23; 13, 1.

Geography of the Gospel of John

has not yet come." [5h]His mother said to the servers, "Do whatever he tells you." [6i]*Now there were six stone water jars there for Jewish ceremonial washings, each holding twenty to thirty gallons. [7]Jesus told them, "Fill the jars with water." So they filled them to the brim. [8]*Then he told them, "Draw some out now and take it to the headwaiter." So they took it. [9]And when the headwaiter tasted the water that had become wine, without knowing where it came from (although the servers who had drawn the water knew), the headwaiter called the bridegroom [10]and said to him, "Everyone serves good wine first, and then when people have drunk freely, an inferior one; but you have kept the good wine until now." [11j]*Jesus did this as the beginning of his signs in Cana in Galilee and so revealed his glory, and his disciples began to believe in him.

[12]*After this, he and his mother, [his] brothers, and his disciples went down to Capernaum and stayed there only a few days.

Cleansing of the Temple. [13k]*Since the Passover of the Jews was near, Jesus went up to Jerusalem. [14l]*He found in the temple area those who sold oxen, sheep, and doves, as well as the money-changers seated there. [15]He made a whip out of cords and drove them all out of the temple area, with the sheep and oxen, and spilled the coins of the money-changers and overturned their tables, [16m]and to those who sold doves he said, "Take these out of here, and stop making my Father's house a marketplace." [17n]*His disciples recalled the words of scripture, "Zeal for your house will consume me." [18o]At this the Jews answered and said to him, "What sign can you show us for doing this?" [19p]*Jesus answered and said to them, "Destroy this temple and in three days I will raise it up." [20]*The Jews said, "This temple has been under construction for forty-six years, and you will raise it up in three days?" [21]But he was speaking about the temple of his body. [22q]Therefore, when he was raised from the dead, his disciples remembered that he had said this, and they came to believe the scripture and the word Jesus had spoken.

[23r]While he was in Jerusalem for the feast of Passover, many began to believe in his name when they saw the signs he was doing. [24]But Jesus would not trust himself to them because he knew them all, [25s]and did not need anyone to testify about human nature. He himself understood it well.

2, 6: Twenty to thirty gallons: literally, "two or three measures"; the Attic liquid measure contained 39.39 liters. The vast quantity recalls prophecies of abundance in the last days; cf Am 9, 13–14; Hos 14, 7; Jer 31, 12.

2, 8: Headwaiter: used of the official who managed a banquet, but there is no evidence of such a functionary in Palestine. Perhaps here a friend of the family acted as master of ceremonies; cf Sir 32, 1.

2, 11: The beginning of his signs: the first of seven (see Introduction).

2, 12—3, 21: The next three episodes take place in Jerusalem. Only the first is paralleled in the synoptic gospels.

2, 12: This transitional verse may be a harmonization with the synoptic tradition in Lk 4, 31 and Mt 4, 13. There are many textual variants. John depicts no extended ministry in Capernaum as do the synoptics.

2, 13–22: This episode indicates the post-resurrectional replacement of the temple by the person of Jesus.

2, 13: Passover: this is the first Passover mentioned in John; a second is mentioned in 6, 4, a third in 13, 1. Taken literally, they point to a ministry of at least two years.

2, 14–22: The other gospels place the cleansing of the temple in the last days of Jesus' life (Mt, on the day Jesus entered Jerusalem; Mk, on the next day). The order of events in the gospel narratives is often determined by theological motives rather than by chronological data.

2, 14: Oxen, sheep, and doves: intended for sacrifice.

The doves were the offerings of the poor (Lv 5, 7). **Money-changers:** for a temple tax paid by every male Jew more than nineteen years of age, with a half-shekel coin (Ex 30, 11–16), in Tyrian currency. See the note on Mt 17, 24.

2, 17: Ps 69, 10, changed to future tense to apply to Jesus.

2, 19: This saying about the destruction of the temple occurs in various forms (Mt 24, 2; 27, 40; Mk 13, 2; 15, 29; Lk 21, 6; cf Acts 6, 14). Mt 26, 61 has: "I **can** destroy the temple of God . . ."; see the note there. In Mk 14, 58, there is a metaphorical contrast with a new temple: "I will destroy this temple **made with hands** and within three days I will build another **not made with hands.**" Here it is symbolic of Jesus' resurrection and the resulting community (see 21 and Rv 21, 2). **In three days:** an Old Testament expression for a short, indefinite period of time; cf Hos 6, 2.

2, 20: Forty-six years: based on references in Josephus (**Jewish Wars** 1, 21, 1 §§401; **Antiquities** 15, 11, 1 §380), possibly the spring of A.D. 28. Cf the note on Lk 3, 1.

---

h: Gn 41, 55. *i:* 3, 25; Lv 11, 33; Am 9, 13-14; Mt 15, 2; 23, 25-26; Mk 7, 2-4; Lk 11, 38. *j:* 4, 54. *k:* Mt 21, 12-13; Mk 11, 15-17; Lk 19, 45-46. *l:* Ex 30, 11-16; Lv 5, 7. *m:* Zec 14, 21. *n:* Ps 69, 9. *o:* 6, 30. *p:* Mt 24, 2; 26, 61; 27, 40; Mk 13, 2; 14, 58; 15, 29; Lk 21, 6; Acts 6, 14. *q:* 5, 39; 12, 16; 14, 26; 20, 9; Mt 12, 6; Lk 24, 6-8; Rv 21, 22. *r:* 4, 45. *s:* 1 Kgs 8, 39; Pss 33, 15; 94, 11; Sir 42, 18; Jer 17, 10; 20, 12.

CHAPTER 3

See RG
417–18

Nicodemus. *1t**Now there was a Pharisee named Nicodemus, a ruler of the Jews. *2u*He came to Jesus at night and said to him, "Rabbi, we know that you are a teacher who has come from God, for no one can do these signs that you are doing unless God is with him." *3**Jesus answered and said to him, "Amen, amen, I say to you, no one can see the kingdom of God without being born from above." *4v*Nicodemus said to him, "How can a person once grown old be born again? Surely he cannot reenter his mother's womb and be born again, can he?" *5w*Jesus answered, "Amen, amen, I say to you, no one can enter the kingdom of God without being born of water and Spirit. *6x*What is born of flesh is flesh and what is born of spirit is spirit. *7*Do not be amazed that I told you, 'You must be born from above.' *8y**The wind blows where it wills, and you can hear the sound it makes, but you do not know where it comes from or where it goes; so it is with everyone who is born of the Spirit." *9*Nicodemus answered and said to him, "How can this happen?" *10*Jesus answered and said to him, "You are the teacher of Israel and you do not understand this? *11z*Amen, amen, I say to you, we speak of what we know and we testify to what

we have seen, but you people do not accept our testimony. *12a*If I tell you about earthly things and you do not believe, how will you believe if I tell you about heavenly things? *13b*No one has gone up to heaven except the one who has come down from heaven, the Son of Man. *14c**And just as Moses lifted up the serpent in the desert, so must the Son of Man be lifted up, *15**so that everyone who believes in him may have eternal life."

16d*For God so loved the world that he gave his only Son, so that everyone who believes in him might not perish but might have eternal life. *17e**For God did not send his Son into the world to condemn the world, but that the world might be saved through him. *18f*Whoever believes in him will not be condemned, but whoever does not believe has already been condemned, because he has not believed in the name of the only Son of God. *19g**And this is the verdict, that the light came into the world, but people preferred darkness to light, because their works were evil. *20h*For everyone who does wicked things hates the light and does not come toward the light, so that his works might not be exposed. *21i*But whoever lives the truth comes to the light, so that his works may be clearly seen as done in God.

Final Witness of the Baptist. *22j**After this, Jesus and his disciples went into the region of

---

3, 1–21: Jesus instructs Nicodemus on the necessity of a new birth from above. This scene in Jerusalem at Passover exemplifies the faith engendered by signs (2, 23). It continues the self-manifestation of Jesus in Jerusalem begun in ch 2. This is the first of the Johannine discourses, shifting from dialogue to monologue (11–15) to reflection of the evangelist (16–21). The shift from singular through v 10 to plural in v 11 may reflect the early church's controversy with the Jews.

3, 1: A ruler of the Jews: most likely a member of the Jewish council, the Sanhedrin; see the note on Mk 8, 31.

3, 3: Born: see the note on 1, 13. **From above:** the Greek adverb **anōthen** means both "from above" and "again." Jesus means "from above" (see 31), but Nicodemus misunderstands it as "again." This misunderstanding serves as a springboard for further instruction.

3, 8: Wind: the Greek word **pneuma** (as well as the Hebrew **rûah**) means both "wind" and "spirit." In the play on the double meaning, "wind" is primary.

3, 14: Lifted up: in Nm 21, 9, Moses simply "mounted" a serpent upon a pole. John here substitutes a verb implying glorification. Jesus, exalted to glory at his cross and resurrection, represents healing for all.

3, 15: Eternal life: used here for the first time in John, this term stresses quality of life rather than duration.

3, 16: Gave: as a gift in the incarnation, and also "over to death" in the crucifixion; cf Rom 8, 32.

3, 17–19: Condemn: the Greek root means both judgment and condemnation. Jesus' purpose is to save, but his coming provokes judgment; some condemn themselves by turning from the light.

3, 19: Judgment is not only future but is partially realized here and now.

3, 22–26: Jesus' ministry in Judea is only loosely connected with 2, 13—3, 21; cf 1, 19–36. Perhaps John the Baptist's further testimony was transposed here to give meaning to "water" in v 5. Jesus is depicted as baptizing (22); contrast 4, 2.

---

t: 7, 50-51; 19, 39. *u:* 9, 4.16.33; 10, 21; 11, 10; 13, 30; Mt 22, 16; Mk 12, 14; Lk 20, 21. *v:* 1, 13. *w:* 1, 32; 7, 39; 19, 30.34-35; Is 32, 15; 44, 3; Ez 36, 25-27; Jl 3, 1-2. *x:* 6, 63; 1 Cor 15, 44-50. *y:* Eccl 11, 4-5; Acts 2, 2-4. *z:* 3, 32.34; 8, 14; Mt 11, 27. *a:* 6, 62-65; Wis 9, 16-17; 1 Cor 15, 40; 2 Cor 5, 1; Phil 2, 10; 3, 19-20. *b:* 1, 18; 6, 62; Dn 7, 13; Rom 10, 6; Eph 4, 9. *c:* 8, 28; 12, 32.34; Nm 21, 4-9; Wis 16, 5-7. *d:* 1 Jn 4, 9. *e:* 5, 22.30; 8, 15-18; 12, 47. *f:* 5, 24; Mk 16, 16. *g:* 1, 5.9-11; 8, 12; 9, 5. *h:* Jb 24, 13-17. *i:* Gn 47, 29 LXX; Jos 2, 14 LXX; 2 Sm 2, 6 LXX; 15, 20 LXX; Tb 4, 6 LXX; 13, 6; Is 26, 10 LXX; Mt 5, 14-16. *j:* 4, 1-2.

Judea, where he spent some time with them baptizing. [23]*John was also baptizing in Aenon near Salim, because there was an abundance of water there, and people came to be baptized, [24]k*for John had not yet been imprisoned. [25]*Now a dispute arose between the disciples of John and a Jew about ceremonial washings. [26]lSo they came to John and said to him, "Rabbi, the one who was with you across the Jordan, to whom you testified, here he is baptizing and everyone is coming to him." [27]mJohn answered and said, "No one can receive anything except what has been given him from heaven. [28]nYou yourselves can testify that I said [that] I am not the Messiah, but that I was sent before him. [29]o*The one who has the bride is the bridegroom; the best man, who stands and listens to him, rejoices greatly at the bridegroom's voice. So this joy of mine has been made complete. [30]pHe must increase; I must decrease."

The One from Heaven. [31]q*The one who comes from above is above all. The one who is of the earth is earthly and speaks of earthly things. But the one who comes from heaven [is above all]. [32]rHe testifies to what he has seen and heard, but no one accepts his testimony. [33]sWhoever does accept his testimony certifies that God is trustworthy. [34]*For the one whom God sent speaks the words of God. He does not ration his gift of the Spirit.

[35]tThe Father loves the Son and has given everything over to him. [36]uWhoever believes in the Son has eternal life, but whoever disobeys the Son will not see life, but the wrath of God remains upon him.

CHAPTER 4

See RG 417-18

[1]*Now when Jesus learned that the Pharisees had heard that Jesus was making and baptizing more disciples than John [2]*(although Jesus himself was not baptizing, just his disciples), [3]he left Judea and returned to Galilee.

The Samaritan Woman. [4]*He had to pass through Samaria. [5]v*So he came to a town of Samaria called Sychar, near the plot of land that Jacob had given to his son Joseph. [6]Jacob's well was there. Jesus, tired from his journey, sat down there at the well. It was about noon.

[7]A woman of Samaria came to draw water. Jesus said to her, "Give me a drink." [8]His disciples had gone into the town to buy food. [9]w*The Samaritan woman said to him, "How can you, a Jew, ask me, a Samaritan woman, for a drink?" (For Jews use nothing in common with Samaritans.) [10]x*Jesus answered and said to her, "If you knew the gift of God and who is saying to you, 'Give me a drink,' you would have asked him and he would have given you living water." [11]*[The

---

3, 23: Aenon near Salim: site uncertain, either in the upper Jordan valley or in Samaria.

3, 24: A remark probably intended to avoid objections based on a chronology like that of the synoptics (Mt 4, 12; Mk 1, 14).

3, 25: A Jew: some think Jesus is meant. Many manuscripts read "Jews."

3, 29: The best man: literally, "the friend of the groom," the **shoshben** of Jewish tradition, who arranged the wedding. Competition between him and the groom would be unthinkable.

3, 31–36: It is uncertain whether these are words by the Baptist, Jesus, or the evangelist. They are reflections on the two preceding scenes.

3, 34: His gift: of God or to Jesus, perhaps both. This verse echoes vv 5 and 8.

4, 1–42: Jesus in Samaria. The self-revelation of Jesus continues with his second discourse, on his mission to "half-Jews." It continues the theme of replacement, here with regard to cult (21). Water (7–15) serves as a symbol (as at Cana and in the Nicodemus episode).

4, 2: An editorial refinement of 3, 22, perhaps directed against followers of John the Baptist who claimed that Jesus imitated him.

4, 4: He had to: a theological necessity; geographically, Jews often bypassed Samaria by taking a route across the Jordan.

4, 5: Sychar: Jerome identifies this with Shechem, a reading found in Syriac manuscripts.

4, 9: Samaritan women were regarded by Jews as ritually impure, and therefore Jews were forbidden to drink from any vessel they had handled.

4, 10: Living water: the water of life, i.e., the revelation that Jesus brings; the woman thinks of "flowing water," so much more desirable than stagnant cistern water. On John's device of such misunderstanding, cf the note on 3, 3.

4, 11: Sir: the Greek **kyrios** means "master" or "lord," as a respectful mode of address for a human being or a deity; cf 4, 19. It is also the word used in the Septuagint for the Hebrew **'ădônai,** substituted for the tetragrammaton YHWH.

k: Mt 4, 12; 14, 3; Mk 1, 14; 6, 17; Lk 3, 20. l: 1, 26.32-34.36. m: 19, 11; 1 Cor 4, 7; 2 Cor 3, 5; Heb 5, 4. n: 1, 20-23; Lk 3, 15. o: 15, 11; 17, 13; Mt 9, 15. p: 2 Sm 3, 1. q: 8, 23. r: 3, 11. s: 8, 26; 12, 44-50; 1 Jn 5, 10. t: 13, 3; Mt 11, 27; 28, 18; Lk 10, 22. u: 3, 16; 1 Jn 5, 13. v: Gn 33, 18-19; 48, 22; Jos 24, 32. w: Sir 50, 25-26; Mt 10, 5. x: Sir 24, 20-21; Is 55, 1; Jer 2, 13.

woman] said to him, "Sir, you do not even have a bucket and the cistern is deep; where then can you get this living water? *12y*Are you greater than our father Jacob, who gave us this cistern and drank from it himself with his children and his flocks?" *13*Jesus answered and said to her, "Everyone who drinks this water will be thirsty again; *14z*but whoever drinks the water I shall give will never thirst; the water I shall give will become in him a spring of water welling up to eternal life." *15*The woman said to him, "Sir, give me this water, so that I may not be thirsty or have to keep coming here to draw water."

*16*Jesus said to her, "Go call your husband and come back." *17*The woman answered and said to him, "I do not have a husband." Jesus answered her, "You are right in saying, 'I do not have a husband.' *18a*For you have had five husbands, and the one you have now is not your husband. What you have said is true." *19b*The woman said to him, "Sir, I can see that you are a prophet. *20c**Our ancestors worshiped on this mountain; but you people say that the place to worship is in Jerusalem." *21*Jesus said to her, "Believe me, woman, the hour is coming when you will worship the Father neither on this mountain nor in Jerusalem. *22d*You people worship what you do not understand; we worship what we understand, because salvation is from the Jews. *23**But the hour is coming, and is now here, when true worshipers will worship the Father in Spirit and truth; and indeed the Father seeks such people to worship him. *24e*God is Spirit, and those who worship him must worship in Spirit and truth." *25f**The woman said to him, "I know

that the Messiah is coming, the one called the Anointed; when he comes, he will tell us everything." *26g**Jesus said to her, "I am he, the one who is speaking with you."

27*At that moment his disciples returned, and were amazed that he was talking with a woman, but still no one said, "What are you looking for?" or "Why are you talking with her?" *28*The woman left her water jar and went into the town and said to the people, *29*"Come see a man who told me everything I have done. Could he possibly be the Messiah?" *30*They went out of the town and came to him. *31*Meanwhile, the disciples urged him, "Rabbi, eat." *32*But he said to them, "I have food to eat of which you do not know." *33*So the disciples said to one another, "Could someone have brought him something to eat?" *34h*Jesus said to them, "My food is to do the will of the one who sent me and to finish his work. *35i**Do you not say, 'In four months the harvest will be here'? I tell you, look up and see the fields ripe for the harvest. *36j**The reaper is already receiving his payment and gathering crops for eternal life, so that the sower and reaper can rejoice together. *37k*For here the saying is verified that 'One sows and another reaps.' *38*I sent you to reap what you have not worked for; others have done the work, and you are sharing the fruits of their work."

39*Many of the Samaritans of that town began to believe in him because of the word of the woman who testified, "He told me everything I have done." *40*When the Samaritans came to him, they invited him to stay with them; and he stayed there two days. *41*Many more began to believe in him be-

---

4, 20: This mountain: Gerizim, on which a temple was erected in the fourth century B.C. by Samaritans to rival Mt. Zion in Jerusalem; cf Dt 27, 4 (Mt. Ebal = the Jews' term for Gerizim).

4, 23: In Spirit and truth: not a reference to an interior worship within one's own spirit. The Spirit is the spirit given by God that reveals truth and enables one to worship God appropriately (14, 16–17). Cf "born of water and Spirit" (3, 5).

4, 25: The expectations of the Samaritans are expressed here in Jewish terminology. They did not expect a messianic king of the house of David but a prophet like Moses (Dt 18, 15).

4, 26: I am he: it could also be translated "I am," an Old Testament self-designation of Yahweh (Is 43, 3, etc.); cf 6, 20; 8, 24.28.58; 13, 19; 18, 5.6.8. See the note on Mk 6, 50.

4, 27: Talking with a woman: a religious and social re-

striction that Jesus is pictured treating as unimportant.

4, 35: 'In four months . . .': probably a proverb; cf Mt 9, 37–38.

4, 36: Already: this word may go with the preceding verse rather than with 36.

4, 39: The woman is presented as a missionary, described in virtually the same words as the disciples are in Jesus' prayer (17, 20).

y: 8, 53; Mt 12, 41.   *z:* 6, 35.58; 7, 37-39; Is 44, 3; 49, 10; Jl 4, 18; Rv 7, 16; 21, 6.   *a:* 2 Kgs 17, 24-34.   *b:* 9, 17; Hos 1, 3.   *c:* Dt 11, 29; 27, 4; Jos 8, 33; Ps 122, 1-5.   *d:* 2 Kgs 17, 27; Ps 76, 2-3.   *e:* 2 Cor 3, 17.   *f:* 1, 41.   *g:* 9, 37.   *h:* 5, 30.36; 6, 38; 9, 4; 17, 4.   *i:* Mt 9, 37-38; Lk 10, 2; Rv 14, 15.   *j:* Ps 126, 5-6; Am 9, 13-14.   *k:* Dt 20, 6; 28, 30; Jb 31, 8; Mi 6, 15.

cause of his word, [421]and they said to the woman, "We no longer believe because of your word; for we have heard for ourselves, and we know that this is truly the savior of the world."

Return to Galilee. [43]*After the two days, he left there for Galilee. [44m]*For Jesus himself testified that a prophet has no honor in his native place. [45]When he came into Galilee, the Galileans welcomed him, since they had seen all he had done in Jerusalem at the feast; for they themselves had gone to the feast.

Second Sign at Cana. [46n]*Then he returned to Cana in Galilee, where he had made the water wine. Now there was a royal official whose son was ill in Capernaum. [47]When he heard that Jesus had arrived in Galilee from Judea, he went to him and asked him to come down and heal his son, who was near death. [48o]Jesus said to him, "Unless you people see signs and wonders, you will not believe." [49]The royal official said to him, "Sir, come down before my child dies." [50p]Jesus said to him, "You may go; your son will live." The man believed what Jesus said to him and left. [51]While he was on his way back, his slaves met him and told him that his boy would live. [52]He asked them when he began to recover. They told him, "The fever left him yesterday, about

one in the afternoon." [53]The father realized that just at that time Jesus had said to him, "Your son will live," and he and his whole household came to believe. [54q][Now] this was the second sign Jesus did when he came to Galilee from Judea.

CHAPTER 5

See RG 418

Cure on a Sabbath. [1r]*After this, there was a feast of the Jews, and Jesus went up to Jerusalem. [2s]*Now there is in Jerusalem at the Sheep [Gate] a pool called in Hebrew Bethesda, with five porticoes. [3]*In these lay a large number of ill, blind, lame, and crippled. [[4]]* [5]One man was there who had been ill for thirty-eight years. [6]When Jesus saw him lying there and knew that he had been ill for a long time, he said to him, "Do you want to be well?" [7]The sick man answered him, "Sir, I have no one to put me into the pool when the water is stirred up; while I am on my way, someone else gets down there before me." [8t]Jesus said to him, "Rise, take up your mat, and walk." [9u]Immediately the man became well, took up his mat, and walked.

Now that day was a sabbath. [10v]So the Jews said to the man who was cured, "It is the sabbath, and it is not lawful for you to carry your mat." [11]He answered them, "The man who made me well told me, 'Take up

4, 43–54: Jesus' arrival in Cana in Galilee; the second sign. This section introduces another theme, that of the life-giving word of Jesus. It is explicitly linked to the first sign (2, 11). The royal official believes (50). The natural life given his son is a sign of eternal life.

4, 44: Probably a reminiscence of a tradition as in Mk 6, 4. Cf Gospel of Thomas 31: "No prophet is acceptable in his village, no physician heals those who know him."

4, 46–54: The story of the cure of the royal official's son may be a third version of the cure of the centurion's son (Mt 8, 5–13) or servant (Lk 7, 1–10). Cf also Mt 15, 21–28 // Mk 7, 24–30.

5, 1–47: The self-revelation of Jesus continues in Jerusalem at a feast. The third sign (cf 2, 11; 4, 54) is performed, the cure of a paralytic by Jesus' life-giving word. The water of the pool fails to bring life; Jesus' word does.

5, 1: The reference in vv 45–46 to Moses suggests that the feast was Pentecost. The connection of that feast with the giving of the law to Moses on Sinai, attested in later Judaism, may already have been made in the first century. The feast could also be Passover (cf 6, 4). John stresses that the day was a sabbath (9).

5, 2: There is no noun with **Sheep**. "Gate" is supplied on the grounds that there must have been a gate in the NE wall of the temple area where animals for sacrifice were brought

in; cf Neh 3, 1.32; 12, 39. **Hebrew:** more precisely, Aramaic. **Bethesda:** preferred to variants "Be(th)zatha" and "Bethsaida"; bêt-'ešdatayīn is given as the name of a double pool northeast of the temple area in the Qumran Copper Roll. **Five porticoes:** a pool excavated in Jerusalem actually has five porticoes.

5, 3: The Caesarean and Western recensions, followed by the Vulgate, add "waiting for the movement of the water." Apparently an intermittent spring in the pool bubbled up occasionally (see 7). This turbulence was believed to cure.

5, 4: Toward the end of the second century in the West and among the fourth-century Greek Fathers, an additional verse was known: "For [from time to time] an angel of the Lord used to come down into the pool; and the water was stirred up, so the first one to get in [after the stirring of the water] was healed of whatever disease afflicted him." The angel was a popular explanation of the turbulence and the healing powers attributed to it. This verse is missing from all early Greek

l: 1 Jn 4, 14.   m: Mt 13, 57; Mk 6, 4; Lk 4, 24.   n: 2, 1-11; Mt 8, 5-13; 15, 21-28; Mk 7, 24-30; Lk 7, 1-10.   o: 2, 18.23; Wis 8, 8; Mt 12, 38; 1 Cor 1, 22.   p: 1 Kgs 17, 23.   q: 2, 11.   r: 6, 4. s: Neh 3, 1.32; 12, 39.   t: Mt 9, 6; Mk 2, 11; Lk 5, 24; Acts 3, 6. u: Mk 2, 12; Lk 5, 25 / 9, 14.   v: Ex 20, 8; Jer 17, 21-27; Mk 3, 2; Lk 13, 10; 14, 1.

your mat and walk.' " [12]They asked him, "Who is the man who told you, 'Take it up and walk'?" [13w]The man who was healed did not know who it was, for Jesus had slipped away, since there was a crowd there. [14x]*After this Jesus found him in the temple area and said to him, "Look, you are well; do not sin any more, so that nothing worse may happen to you." [15]The man went and told the Jews that Jesus was the one who had made him well. [16y]Therefore, the Jews began to persecute Jesus because he did this on a sabbath. [17z]*But Jesus answered them, "My Father is at work until now, so I am at work." [18a]For this reason the Jews tried all the more to kill him, because he not only broke the sabbath but he also called God his own father, making himself equal to God.

The Work of the Son. [19b]*Jesus answered and said to them, "Amen, amen, I say to you, a son cannot do anything on his own, but only what he sees his father doing; for what he does, his son will do also. [20c]For the Father loves his Son and shows him everything that he himself does, and he will show him greater works than these, so that you may be amazed. [21d]*For just as the Father raises the dead and gives life, so also does the Son give life to whomever he wishes. [22e]*Nor does the Father judge anyone, but he has given all judgment to his Son, [23]so that all may honor the Son just as they honor the Father. Whoever does not honor the Son does not honor the Father who sent him. [24f]Amen, amen, I say to you, whoever hears my word and believes in the one who sent me has eternal life and will not come to condemnation, but has passed from death to life. [25g]Amen, amen, I say to you, the hour is coming and is now here when the dead will hear the voice of the Son of God, and those who hear will live. [26h]For just as the Father has life in himself, so also he gave to his Son the possession of life in himself. [27i]And he gave him power to exercise judgment, because he is the Son of Man. [28j]*Do not be amazed at this, because the hour is coming in which all who are in the tombs will hear his voice [29k]and will come out, those who have done good deeds to the resurrection of life, but those who have done wicked deeds to the resurrection of condemnation.

[30l]"I cannot do anything on my own; I judge as I hear, and my judgment is just, because I do not seek my own will but the will of the one who sent me.

Witnesses to Jesus. [31m]"If I testify on my own behalf, my testimony cannot be verified. [32]*But there is another who testifies on my behalf, and I know that the testimony he gives on my behalf is true. [33n]You sent emissaries to John, and he testified to the truth. [34o]I do not accept testimony from a human being, but I say this so that you may

manuscripts and the earliest versions, including the original Vulgate. Its vocabulary is markedly non-Johannine.

5, 14: While the cure of the paralytic in Mk 2, 1–12 is associated with the forgiveness of sins, Jesus never drew a one-to-one connection between sin and suffering (cf 9, 3; Lk 12, 1–5), as did Ez 18, 20.

5, 17: Sabbath observance (10) was based on God's resting on the seventh day (cf Gn 2, 2–3; Ex 20, 11). Philo and some rabbis insisted that God's providence remains active on the sabbath, keeping all things in existence, giving life in birth and taking it away in death. Other rabbis taught that God rested from creating, but not from judging (= ruling, governing). Jesus here claims the same authority to work as the Father, and, in the discourse that follows, the same divine prerogatives: power over life and death (21.24–26) and judgment (22.27).

5, 19: This proverb or parable is taken from apprenticeship in a trade: the activity of a son is modeled on that of his father. Jesus' dependence on the Father is justification for doing what the Father does.

5, 21: Gives life: in the Old Testament, a divine prerogative (Dt 32, 39; 1 Sm 2, 6; 2 Kgs 5, 7; Tob 13, 2; Is 26, 19; Dan 12, 2).

5, 22: Judgment: another divine prerogative, often expressed as acquittal or condemnation (Dt 32, 36; Ps 43, 1).

5, 28–29: While vv 19–27 present realized eschatology, vv 28–29 are future eschatology; cf Dn 12, 2.

5, 32: Another: likely the Father, who in four different ways gives testimony to Jesus, as indicated in the verse groupings 33–34, 36, 37–38, 39–40.

w: Mt 8, 18; 13, 36; Mk 4, 36; 7, 17.   x: 8, 11; 9, 2; Ez 18, 20.   y: 7, 23; Mt 12, 8.   z: Ex 20, 11.   a: 7, 1.25; 8, 37.40; 10, 33.36; 14, 28; Gn 3, 5-6; Wis 2, 16; Mt 26, 4; 2 Thes 2, 4.   b: 3, 34; 8, 26; 12, 49; 9, 4; 10, 30.   c: 3, 35.   d: 11, 25; Dt 32, 39; 1 Sm 2, 6; 2 Kgs 5, 7; Tb 13, 2; Wis 16, 13; Is 26, 19; Dn 7, 10.13; 12, 2; Rom 4, 17; 2 Cor 1, 9.   e: Acts 10, 42; 17, 31.   f: 3, 18; 8, 51; 1 Jn 3, 14.   g: 5, 28; 8, 51; 11, 25-26; Eph 2, 1; 5, 14; Rv 3, 1.   h: 1, 4; 1 Jn 5, 11.   i: 5, 22; Dn 7, 13.22; Mt 25, 31; Lk 21, 36.   j: 11, 43.   k: Dn 12, 2; Mt 16, 27; 25, 46; Acts 24, 15; 2 Cor 5, 10.   l: 6, 38.   m: 8, 13-14.18.   n: 1, 19-27; Mt 11, 10-11.   o: 1 Jn 5, 9.

be saved. [35 p*]He was a burning and shining lamp, and for a while you were content to rejoice in his light. [36q]But I have testimony greater than John's. The works that the Father gave me to accomplish, these works that I perform testify on my behalf that the Father has sent me. [37r]Moreover, the Father who sent me has testified on my behalf. But you have never heard his voice nor seen his form, [38s]and you do not have his word remaining in you, because you do not believe in the one whom he has sent. [39t*]You search the scriptures, because you think you have eternal life through them; even they testify on my behalf. [40]But you do not want to come to me to have life.

Unbelief of Jesus' Hearers. [41*]"I do not accept human praise; [42u]moreover, I know that you do not have the love of God in you. [43v]I came in the name of my Father, but you do not accept me; yet if another comes in his own name, you will accept him. [44w]How can you believe, when you accept praise from one another and do not seek the praise that comes from the only God? [45x]Do not think that I will accuse you before the Father: the one who will accuse you is Moses, in whom you have placed your hope. [46y]For if you had believed Moses, you would have believed me, because he wrote about me. [47]But if you do not believe his writings, how will you believe my words?"

CHAPTER 6

See RG 418-19

Multiplication of the Loaves. [1z*]After this, Jesus went across the Sea of Galilee [of Tiberias]. [2]A large crowd followed him, because they saw the signs he was performing on the sick. [3]Jesus went up on the mountain, and there he sat down with his disciples. [4a]The Jewish feast of Passover was near. [5b*]When Jesus raised his eyes and saw that a large crowd was coming to him, he said to Philip, "Where can we buy enough food for them to eat?" [6*]He said this to test him, because he himself knew what he was going to do. [7c*]Philip answered him, "Two hundred days' wages worth of food would not be enough for each of them to have a little [bit]." [8]One of his disciples, Andrew, the brother of Simon Peter, said to him, [9d*]"There is a boy here who has five barley loaves and two fish; but what good are these for so many?" [10e*]Jesus said, "Have the people recline." Now there was a great deal of grass in that place. So the men reclined, about five thousand in number. [11f]Then Jesus took the loaves, gave thanks, and distributed them to those who were reclining, and also as much of the fish as they wanted. [12]When they had had their fill, he said to his disciples, "Gather the fragments left over, so that nothing will be wasted." [13*]So they collected them, and filled twelve wicker baskets with fragments from the five barley

---

5, 35: **Lamp:** cf Ps 132, 17: "I will place a lamp for my Anointed (= David)," and possibly the description of Elijah in Sir 48, 1. But only **for a while,** indicating the temporary and subordinate nature of John's mission.

5, 39: **You search:** this may be an imperative: "Search the scriptures, because you think that you have eternal life through them."

5, 41: **Praise:** the same Greek word means "praise" or "honor" (from others) and "glory" (from God). There is a play on this in v 44.

6, 1–15: This story of the multiplication of the loaves is the fourth sign (cf the note on 5, 1–47). It is the only miracle story found in all four gospels (occurring twice in Mk and Mt). See the notes on Mt 14, 13–21 and 15, 32–39. John differs on the roles of Philip and Andrew, the proximity of Passover (4), and the allusion to Elisha (see 9). The story here symbolizes the food that is really available through Jesus. It connotes a new exodus and has eucharistic overtones.

6, 1: **[Of Tiberias]:** the awkward apposition represents a later name of the Sea of Galilee. It was probably originally a marginal gloss.

6, 5: Jesus takes the initiative (in the synoptics, the disciples do), possibly pictured as (cf 14) the new Moses (cf Nm 11, 13).

6, 6: Probably the evangelist's comment; in this gospel Jesus is never portrayed as ignorant of anything.

6, 7: **Days' wages:** literally, "denarii"; a Roman denarius is a day's wage in Mt 20, 2.

6, 9: **Barley loaves:** the food of the poor. There seems an allusion to the story of Elisha multiplying the barley bread in 2 Kgs 4, 42–44.

6, 10: **Grass:** implies springtime, and therefore Passover. **Five thousand:** so Mk 6, 39.44 and parallels.

6, 13: **Baskets:** the word describes the typically Palestinian wicker basket, as in Mk 6, 43 and parallels.

p: 1, 8; Ps 132, 17; Sir 48, 1.   *q:* 10, 25.   *r:* 8, 18; Dt 4, 12.15; 1 Jn 5, 9.   *s:* 1 Jn 2, 14.   *t:* 12, 16; 19, 28; 20, 9; Lk 24, 27.44; 1 Pt 1, 10.   *u:* 1 Jn 2, 15.   *v:* Mt 24, 5.24.   *w:* 12, 43.   *x:* Dt 31, 26.   *y:* 5, 39; Dt 18, 15; Lk 16, 31; 24, 44.   *z:* Mt 14, 13-21; Mk 6, 32-44; Lk 9, 10-17.   *a:* 2, 13; 11, 55.   *b:* Nm 11, 13.   *c:* Mt 20, 2.   *d:* 2 Kgs 4, 42-44.   *e:* Mt 14, 21; Mk 6, 44.   *f:* 21, 13.

loaves that had been more than they could eat. [14g]*When the people saw the sign he had done, they said, "This is truly the Prophet, the one who is to come into the world." [15h]Since Jesus knew that they were going to come and carry him off to make him king, he withdrew again to the mountain alone.

Walking on the Water. [16i]*When it was evening, his disciples went down to the sea, [17]embarked in a boat, and went across the sea to Capernaum. It had already grown dark, and Jesus had not yet come to them. [18]The sea was stirred up because a strong wind was blowing. [19j]*When they had rowed about three or four miles, they saw Jesus walking on the sea and coming near the boat, and they began to be afraid. [20]*But he said to them, "It is I. Do not be afraid." [21]They wanted to take him into the boat, but the boat immediately arrived at the shore to which they were heading.

The Bread of Life Discourse. [22]*The next day, the crowd that remained across the sea saw that there had been only one boat there, and that Jesus had not gone along with his disciples in the boat, but only his disciples had left. [23]*Other boats came from Tiberias near the place where they had eaten the bread when the Lord gave thanks. [24]When the crowd saw that neither Jesus nor his disciples were there, they themselves got into boats and came to Capernaum looking for Jesus. [25]And when they found him across the sea they said to him, "Rabbi, when did you get here?" [26]Jesus answered them and said,

"Amen, amen, I say to you, you are looking for me not because you saw signs but because you ate the loaves and were filled. [27k]*Do not work for food that perishes but for the food that endures for eternal life, which the Son of Man will give you. For on him the Father, God, has set his seal." [28]So they said to him, "What can we do to accomplish the works of God?" [29]Jesus answered and said to them, "This is the work of God, that you believe in the one he sent." [30l]So they said to him, "What sign can you do, that we may see and believe in you? What can you do? [31m]*Our ancestors ate manna in the desert, as it is written:

'He gave them bread from heaven to eat.' "

[32n]So Jesus said to them, "Amen, amen, I say to you, it was not Moses who gave the bread from heaven; my Father gives you the true bread from heaven. [33]For the bread of God is that which comes down from heaven and gives life to the world."

[34o]So they said to him, "Sir, give us this bread always." [35p]*Jesus said to them, "I am the bread of life; whoever comes to me will never hunger, and whoever believes in me will never thirst. [36q]But I told you that although you have seen [me], you do not believe. [37]Everything that the Father gives me will come to me, and I will not reject anyone who comes to me, [38r]because I came down from heaven not to do my own will but the will of the one who sent me. [39s]And this is the will of the one who sent me, that I should not

6, 14: **The Prophet:** probably the prophet like Moses (see the note on 1, 21). **The one who is to come into the world:** probably Elijah; cf Mal 3, 1.23.

6, 16–21: The fifth sign is a nature miracle, portraying Jesus sharing Yahweh's power. Cf the parallel stories following the multiplication of the loaves in Mk 6, 45–52 and Mt 14, 22–33.

6, 19: **Walking on the sea:** although the Greek (cf 16) could mean "on the seashore" or "by the sea" (cf 21, 1), the parallels, especially Mt 14, 25, make clear that Jesus walked upon the water. John may allude to Job 9, 8: God "treads upon the crests of the sea."

6, 20: **It is I:** literally, "I am." See also the notes on 4, 26 and Mk 6, 50.

6, 22–71: Discourse on the bread of life; replacement of the manna. Verses 22–34 serve as an introduction, vv 35–59 constitute the discourse proper, vv 60–71 portray the reaction of the disciples and Peter's confession.

6, 23: Possibly a later interpolation, to explain how the crowd got to Capernaum.

6, 27: **The food that endures for eternal life:** cf 4, 14, on water "springing up to eternal life."

6, 31: **Bread from heaven:** cf Ex 16, 4.15.32–34 and the notes there; Ps 78, 24. The manna, thought to have been hidden by Jeremiah (2 Mc 2, 5–8), was expected to reappear miraculously at Passover, in the last days.

6, 35–59: Up to v 50, "bread of life" is a figure for God's revelation in Jesus; in vv 51–58, the eucharistic theme comes to the fore. There may thus be a break between vv 50 and 51.

g: Dt 18, 15.18; Mal 3, 1.23; Acts 3, 22. h: 18, 36. i: Mt 14, 22-27; Mk 6, 45-52. j: Jb 9, 8; Pss 29, 3-4; 77, 20; Is 43, 16. k: 6, 50.51.54.58. l: Mt 16, 1-4; Lk 11, 29-30. m: Ex 16, 4-5; Nm 11, 7-9; Ps 78, 24. n: Mt 6, 11. o: 4, 15. p: Is 55, 1-3; Am 8, 11-13. q: 20, 29. r: 4, 34; Mt 26, 39; Heb 10, 9. s: 10, 28-29; 17, 12; 18, 9.

lose anything of what he gave me, but that I should raise it [on] the last day. [40t]For this is the will of my Father, that everyone who sees the Son and believes in him may have eternal life, and I shall raise him [on] the last day."

[41]The Jews murmured about him because he said, "I am the bread that came down from heaven," [42u]and they said, "Is this not Jesus, the son of Joseph? Do we not know his father and mother? Then how can he say, 'I have come down from heaven'?" [43v*]Jesus answered and said to them, "Stop murmuring among yourselves. [44]No one can come to me unless the Father who sent me draw him, and I will raise him on the last day. [45w]It is written in the prophets:

'They shall all be taught by God.'

Everyone who listens to my Father and learns from him comes to me. [46x]Not that anyone has seen the Father except the one who is from God; he has seen the Father. [47]Amen, amen, I say to you, whoever believes has eternal life. [48]I am the bread of life. [49y]Your ancestors ate the manna in the desert, but they died; [50]this is the bread that comes down from heaven so that one may eat it and not die. [51z]I am the living bread that came down from heaven; whoever eats this bread will live forever; and the bread that I will give is my flesh for the life of the world."

[52]The Jews quarreled among themselves, saying, "How can this man give us [his] flesh to eat?" [53]Jesus said to them, "Amen, amen, I say to you, unless you eat the flesh of the Son of Man and drink his blood, you do not have life within you. [54*]Whoever eats my flesh and drinks my blood has eternal life, and I will raise him on the last day. [55]For my flesh is true food, and my blood is true drink. [56]Whoever eats my flesh and drinks my blood remains in me and I in him. [57a]Just as the living Father sent me and I have life because of the Father, so also the one who feeds on me will have life because of me. [58]This is the bread that came down from heaven. Unlike your ancestors who ate and still died, whoever eats this bread will live forever." [59]These things he said while teaching in the synagogue in Capernaum.

The Words of Eternal Life. [60*]Then many of his disciples who were listening said, "This saying is hard; who can accept it?" [61]Since Jesus knew that his disciples were murmuring about this, he said to them, "Does this shock you? [62*]What if you were to see the Son of Man ascending to where he was before? [63*]It is the spirit that gives life, while the flesh is of no avail. The words I have spoken to you are spirit and life. [64b]But there are some of you who do not believe." Jesus knew from the beginning the ones who would not believe and the one who would betray him. [65]And he said, "For this reason I have told you that no one can come to me unless it is granted him by my Father."

[66]As a result of this, many [of] his disciples returned to their former way of life and no longer accompanied him. [67]Jesus then said to the Twelve, "Do you also want to leave?" [68]Simon Peter answered him, "Master, to whom shall we go? You have the words of eternal life. [69c]We have come to believe and are convinced that you are the Holy One of God." [70]Jesus answered them, "Did I not choose you twelve? Yet is not one of you a devil?" [71d]He was referring to Judas, son of Simon the Iscariot; it was he who would betray him, one of the Twelve.

6, 43: Murmuring: the word may reflect the Greek of Ex 16, 2.7.8.

6, 54–58: Eats: the verb used in these verses is not the classical Greek verb used of human eating, but that of animal eating: "munch," "gnaw." This may be part of John's emphasis on the reality of the flesh and blood of Jesus (cf 55), but the same verb eventually became the ordinary verb in Greek meaning "eat."

6, 60–71: These verses refer more to themes of vv 35–50 than to those of 51–58 and seem to be addressed to members of the Johannine community who found it difficult to accept the high christology reflected in the bread of life discourse.

6, 62: This unfinished conditional sentence is obscure.

Probably there is a reference to vv 49–51. Jesus claims to be the bread that comes down from heaven (50); this claim provokes incredulity (60); and so Jesus is pictured as asking what his disciples will say when he goes up to heaven.

6, 63: Spirit . . . flesh: probably not a reference to the eucharistic body of Jesus but to the supernatural and the natural, as in 3, 6. **Spirit and life:** all Jesus said about the bread of life is the revelation of the Spirit.

t: 1 Jn 2, 25. *u:* Mt 13, 54-57; Mk 6, 1-4; Lk 4, 22. *v:* Ex 16, 2.7.8; Lk 4, 22. *w:* Is 54, 13; Jer 31, 33-34. *x:* 1, 18; 7, 29; Ex 33, 20. *y:* 1 Cor 10, 3.5. *z:* Mt 26, 26-27; Lk 22, 19. *a:* 5, 26. *b:* 13, 11. *c:* 11, 27; Mt 16, 16; Mk 1, 24; Lk 4, 34. *d:* 12, 4; 13, 2.27.

CHAPTER 7*

The Feast of Tabernacles. *1eAfter this, Jesus moved about within Galilee; but he did not wish to travel in Judea, because the Jews were trying to kill him. *2fBut the Jewish feast of Tabernacles was near. *3*So his brothers said to him, "Leave here and go to Judea, so that your disciples also may see the works you are doing. *4gNo one works in secret if he wants to be known publicly. If you do these things, manifest yourself to the world." *5For his brothers did not believe in him. *6*So Jesus said to them, "My time is not yet here, but the time is always right for you. *7hThe world cannot hate you, but it hates me, because I testify to it that its works are evil. *8*You go up to the feast. I am not going up to this feast, because my time has not yet been fulfilled." *9After he had said this, he stayed on in Galilee.

*10But when his brothers had gone up to the feast, he himself also went up, not openly but [as it were] in secret. *11The Jews were looking for him at the feast and saying, "Where is he?" *12And there was considerable murmuring about him in the crowds. Some said, "He is a good man," [while] others said, "No; on the contrary, he misleads the crowd." *13iStill, no one spoke openly about him because they were afraid of the Jews.

The First Dialogue. *14*When the feast was already half over, Jesus went up into the temple area and began to teach. *15j*The Jews were amazed and said, "How does he know scripture without having studied?" *16Jesus answered them and said, "My teaching is not my own but is from the one who sent me. *17k*Whoever chooses to do his will shall know whether my teaching is from God or whether I speak on my own. *18Whoever speaks on his own seeks his own glory, but whoever seeks the glory of the one who sent him is truthful, and there is no wrong in him. *19lDid not Moses give you the law? Yet none of you keeps the law. Why are you trying to kill me?" *20m*The crowd answered, "You are possessed! Who is trying to kill you?" *21n*Jesus answered and said to them, "I performed one work and all of you are amazed *22obecause of it. Moses gave you circumcision—not that it came from Moses but rather from the patriarchs—and you circumcise a man on the sabbath. *23pIf a man can receive circumcision on a sabbath so that the law of Moses may not be broken, are you angry with me because I made a whole person well on a sabbath? *24qStop judging by appearances, but judge justly."

*25So some of the inhabitants of Jerusalem said, "Is he not the one they are trying to

---

7—8: These chapters contain events about the feast of Tabernacles (Sukkoth, Ingathering: Ex 23, 16; Tents, Booths: Dt 16, 13–16), with its symbols of booths (originally built to shelter harvesters), rain (water from Siloam poured on the temple altar), and lights (illumination of the four torches in the Court of the Women). They continue the theme of the replacement of feasts (Passover, 2, 13; 6, 4; Hanukkah, 10, 22; Pentecost, 5, 1), here accomplished by Jesus as the Living Water. These chapters comprise seven miscellaneous controversies and dialogues. There is a literary inclusion with Jesus in hiding in 7, 4.10 and 8, 59. There are frequent references to attempts on his life: 7, 1.13.19.25.30.32.44; 8, 37.40.59.

7, 3: Brothers: these relatives (cf 2, 12 and see the note on Mk 6, 3) are never portrayed as disciples until after the resurrection (Acts 1, 14). Mt 13, 55 and Mk 6, 3 give the names of four of them. Jesus has already performed works/signs in Judea; cf 2, 23; 3, 2; 4, 45; 5, 8.

7, 6: Time: the Greek word means "opportune time," here a synonym for Jesus' "hour" (see the note on 2, 4), his death and resurrection. In the wordplay, any time is suitable for Jesus' brothers, because they are not dependent on God's will.

7, 8: I am not going up: an early attested reading "not yet" seems a correction, since Jesus in the story does go up to

the feast. "Go up," in a play on words, refers not only to going up to Jerusalem but also to exaltation at the cross, resurrection, and ascension; cf 3, 14; 6, 62; 20, 17.

7, 14–31: Jesus teaches in the temple; debate with the Jews.

7, 15: Without having studied: literally, "How does he know letters without having learned?" Children were taught to read and write by means of the scriptures. But here more than Jesus' literacy is being discussed; the people are wondering how he can teach like a rabbi. Rabbis were trained by other rabbis and traditionally quoted their teachers.

7, 17: To do his will: presumably a reference back to the "work" of 6, 29: belief in the one whom God has sent.

7, 20: You are possessed: literally, "You have a demon." The insane were thought to be possessed by a demoniacal spirit.

7, 21: One work: the cure of the paralytic (5, 1–9) because of the reference to the sabbath (22; 5, 9–10).

---

e: 5, 18; 8, 37.40. *f:* Ex 23, 16; Lv 23, 34; Nm 29, 12; Dt 16, 13-16; Zec 14, 16-19. *g:* 14, 22. *h:* 15, 18. *i:* 9, 22; 19, 38; 20, 19. *j:* Lk 2, 47. *k:* 6, 29. *l:* Acts 7, 53. *m:* 8, 48-49; 10, 20. *n:* 5, 1-9. *o:* Gn 17, 10; Lv 12, 3. *p:* 5, 2-9.16; Mt 12, 11-12; Lk 14, 5. *q:* 8, 15; Lv 19, 15; Is 11, 3-4.

kill? [26*]And look, he is speaking openly and they say nothing to him. Could the authorities have realized that he is the Messiah? [27r]But we know where he is from. When the Messiah comes, no one will know where he is from." [28s]So Jesus cried out in the temple area as he was teaching and said, "You know me and also know where I am from. Yet I did not come on my own, but the one who sent me, whom you do not know, is true. [29t]I know him, because I am from him, and he sent me." [30u]So they tried to arrest him, but no one laid a hand upon him, because his hour had not yet come. [31v]But many of the crowd began to believe in him, and said, "When the Messiah comes, will he perform more signs than this man has done?"

Officers Sent to Arrest Jesus. [32*]The Pharisees heard the crowd murmuring about him to this effect, and the chief priests and the Pharisees sent guards to arrest him. [33w]So Jesus said, "I will be with you only a little while longer, and then I will go to the one who sent me. [34x]You will look for me but not find [me], and where I am you cannot come." [35*]So the Jews said to one another, "Where is he going that we will not find him? Surely he is not going to the dispersion among the Greeks to teach the Greeks, is he? [36]What is the meaning of his saying, 'You will look for me and not find [me], and where I am you cannot come'?"

Rivers of Living Water. [37y*]On the last and greatest day of the feast, Jesus stood up and exclaimed, "Let anyone who thirsts come to me and drink. [38z*]Whoever believes in me, as scripture says:

'Rivers of living water will flow from
within him.' "

[39a*]He said this in reference to the Spirit that those who came to believe in him were to receive. There was, of course, no Spirit yet, because Jesus had not yet been glorified.

Discussion about the Origins of the Messiah. [40b*]Some in the crowd who heard these words said, "This is truly the Prophet." [41]Others said, "This is the Messiah." But others said, "The Messiah will not come from Galilee, will he? [42c]Does not scripture say that the Messiah will be of David's family and come from Bethlehem, the village where David lived?" [43]So a division occurred in the crowd because of him. [44]Some of them even wanted to arrest him, but no one laid hands on him.

[45]So the guards went to the chief priests and Pharisees, who asked them, "Why did you not bring him?" [46]The guards answered, "Never before has anyone spoken like this one." [47]So the Pharisees answered them, "Have you also been deceived? [48d]Have any of the authorities or the Pharisees believed in him? [49]But this crowd, which does not know the law, is accursed." [50e]Nicodemus, one of their members who had come to him earlier, said to them, [51f]"Does our law condemn a person before it first hears him and finds out

7, 26: **The authorities:** the members of the Sanhedrin (same term as 3, 1).

7, 32–36: Jesus announces his approaching departure (cf also 8, 21; 12, 36; 13, 33) and complete control over his destiny.

7, 35: **Dispersion:** or "diaspora": Jews living outside Palestine. **Greeks:** probably refers to the Gentiles in the Mediterranean area; cf 12, 20.

7, 37–39: Promise of living water through the Spirit.

7, 38: **Living water:** not an exact quotation from any Old Testament passage; in the gospel context the gift of the Spirit is meant; cf 3, 5. **From within him:** either Jesus or the believer; if Jesus, it continues the Jesus-Moses motif (water from the rock, Ex 17, 6; Nm 20, 11) as well as Jesus as the new temple (cf Ez 47, 1). Grammatically, it goes better with the believer.

7, 39: **No Spirit yet:** Codex Vaticanus and early Latin, Syriac, and Coptic versions add "given." In this gospel, the sending of the Spirit cannot take place until Jesus' glorification through his death, resurrection, and ascension; cf 20, 22.

7, 40–53: Discussion of the Davidic lineage of the Messiah.

7, 53—8, 11: The story of the woman caught in adultery is a later insertion here, missing from all early Greek manuscripts. A Western text-type insertion, attested mainly in Old Latin translations, it is found in different places in different manuscripts: here, or after 7, 36, or at the end of this gospel, or after Lk 21, 38, or at the end of that gospel. There are many non-Johannine features in the language, and there are also many doubtful readings within the passage. The style and motifs are similar to those of Luke, and it fits better with the general situation at the end of Lk 21, but it was probably inserted here because of the allusion to Jer 17, 13 (cf the note on 8, 6) and the statement, "I do not judge anyone," in 8, 15. The Catholic Church accepts this passage as canonical scripture.

r: Heb 7, 3. s: 8, 19. t: 6, 46; 8, 55. u: 7, 44; 8, 20; Lk 4, 29-30. v: 2, 11; 10, 42; 11, 45. w: 13, 33; 16, 16. x: 8, 21; 12, 36; 13, 33.36; 16, 5; Dt 4, 29; Prv 1, 28; Is 55, 6; Hos 5, 6. y: Rv 21, 6. z: 4, 10.14; 19, 34; Is 12, 3; Ez 47, 1. a: 16, 7. b: Dt 18, 15.18. c: 2 Sm 7, 12-14; Pss 89, 3-4; 132, 11; Mi 5, 1; Mt 2, 5-6. d: 12, 42. e: 3, 1; 19, 39. f: Dt 1, 16-17.

what he is doing?" [52]They answered and said to him, "You are not from Galilee also, are you? Look and see that no prophet arises from Galilee."

CHAPTER 8

A Woman Caught in Adultery. [[53]*Then each went to his own house, [1g]*while Jesus went to the Mount of Olives. [2]But early in the morning he arrived again in the temple area, and all the people started coming to him, and he sat down and taught them. [3]Then the scribes and the Pharisees brought a woman who had been caught in adultery and made her stand in the middle. [4]They said to him, "Teacher, this woman was caught in the very act of committing adultery. [5h]*Now in the law, Moses commanded us to stone such women. So what do you say?" [6]*They said this to test him, so that they could have some charge to bring against him. Jesus bent down and began to write on the ground with his finger. [7i]*But when they continued asking him, he straightened up and said to them, "Let the one among you who is without sin be the first to throw a stone at her." [8]Again he bent down and wrote on the ground. [9]And in response, they went away one by one, beginning with the elders. So he was left alone with the woman before him. [10j]Then Jesus straightened up and said to her, "Woman, where are they? Has no one condemned you?" [11k]She replied, "No one, sir." Then Jesus said, "Neither do I condemn you. Go, [and] from now on do not sin any more."]

The Light of the World. [12l]*Jesus spoke to them again, saying, "I am the light of the world. Whoever follows me will not walk in darkness, but will have the light of life." [13]So the Pharisees said to him, "You testify on your own behalf, so your testimony cannot be verified." [14m]*Jesus answered and said to them, "Even if I do testify on my own behalf, my testimony can be verified, because I know where I came from and where I am going. But you do not know where I come from or where I am going. [15n]*You judge by appearances, but I do not judge anyone. [16o]And even if I should judge, my judgment is valid, because I am not alone, but it is I and the Father who sent me. [17p]*Even in your law it is written that the testimony of two men can be verified. [18q]I testify on my behalf and so does the Father who sent me." [19r]So they said to him, "Where is your father?" Jesus answered, "You know neither me nor my Father. If you knew me, you would know my Father also." [20s]He spoke these words while teaching in the treasury in the temple area. But no one arrested him, because his hour had not yet come.

Jesus, the Father's Ambassador. [21t]*He said to them again, "I am going away and you will look for me, but you will die in your sin. Where I am going you cannot come." [22]*So the Jews said, "He is not going to kill himself, is he, because he said, 'Where I am going you cannot come'?" [23u]He said to them, "You belong to what is below, I belong to what is above. You belong to this world,

---

8, 1: Mount of Olives: not mentioned elsewhere in the gospel tradition outside of passion week.

8, 5: Lv 20, 10 and Dt 22, 22 mention only death, but Dt 22, 23–24 prescribes stoning for a betrothed virgin.

8, 6: Cf Jer 17, 13 (RSV): "Those who turn away from thee shall be written in the earth, for they have forsaken the LORD, the fountain of living water"; cf 7, 38.

8, 7: The first stones were to be thrown by the witnesses (Dt 17, 7).

8, 12–20: Jesus the light of the world. Jesus replaces the four torches of the illumination of the temple as the light of joy.

8, 14: My testimony can be verified: this seems to contradict 5, 31, but the emphasis here is on Jesus' origin from the Father and his divine destiny. **Where I am going:** indicates Jesus' passion and glorification.

8, 15: By appearances: literally, "according to the flesh." **I do not judge anyone:** superficial contradiction of 5,

22.27.30; here the emphasis is that the judgment is not by material standards.

8, 17: Your law: a reflection of later controversy between church and synagogue.

8, 21–30: He whose ambassador I am is with me. Jesus' origin is from God; he can reveal God.

8, 21: You will die in your sin: i.e., of disbelief; cf v 24. **Where I am going you cannot come:** except through faith in Jesus' passion-resurrection.

8, 22: The Jews suspect that he is referring to his death. Johannine irony is apparent here; Jesus' death will not be self-inflicted but destined by God.

g: Lk 21, 37-38.   h: Lv 20, 10; Dt 22, 22-29.   i: Dt 17, 7.   j: Ez 33, 11.   k: 5, 14.   l: 1, 4-5.9; 12, 46; Ex 13, 22; Is 42, 6; Zec 14, 8.   m: 5, 31.   n: 12, 47; 1 Sm 16, 7.   o: 5, 30.   p: Dt 17, 6; 19, 15; Nm 35, 30.   q: 5, 23.37.   r: 7, 28; 14, 7; 15, 21.   s: 7, 30.   t: 7, 34; 13, 33.   u: 3, 31; 17, 14; 18, 36.

but I do not belong to this world. [24v]*That is why I told you that you will die in your sins. For if you do not believe that I AM, you will die in your sins." [25w]*So they said to him, "Who are you?" Jesus said to them, "What I told you from the beginning. [26x]I have much to say about you in condemnation. But the one who sent me is true, and what I heard from him I tell the world." [27]They did not realize that he was speaking to them of the Father. [28y]So Jesus said [to them], "When you lift up the Son of Man, then you will realize that I AM, and that I do nothing on my own, but I say only what the Father taught me. [29]The one who sent me is with me. He has not left me alone, because I always do what is pleasing to him." [30]Because he spoke this way, many came to believe in him.

Jesus and Abraham. [31]*Jesus then said to those Jews who believed in him, "If you remain in my word, you will truly be my disciples, [32z]and you will know the truth, and the truth will set you free." [33a]*They answered him, "We are descendants of Abraham and have never been enslaved to anyone. How can you say, 'You will become free'?" [34b]Jesus answered them, "Amen, amen, I say to you, everyone who commits sin is a slave of sin. [35c]*A slave does not remain in a household forever, but a son always remains. [36]So if a son frees you, then you will truly be free. [37]I know that you are descendants of Abraham. But you are trying to kill me, because my word has no room among you. [38]*I tell you what I have seen in the Father's presence; then do what you have heard from the Father."

[39d]*They answered and said to him, "Our father is Abraham." Jesus said to them, "If you were Abraham's children, you would be doing the works of Abraham. [40]But now you are trying to kill me, a man who has told you the truth that I heard from God; Abraham did not do this. [41e]You are doing the works of your father!" [So] they said to him, "We are not illegitimate. We have one Father, God." [42f]Jesus said to them, "If God were your Father, you would love me, for I came from God and am here; I did not come on my own, but he sent me. [43]Why do you not understand what I am saying? Because you cannot bear to hear my word. [44g]You belong to your father the devil and you willingly carry out your father's desires. He was a murderer from the beginning and does not stand in truth, because there is no truth in him. When he tells a lie, he speaks in character, because he is a liar and the father of lies. [45]But because I speak the truth, you do not believe me. [46h]Can any of you charge me with sin? If I am telling the truth, why do you not believe me? [47i]Whoever belongs to God hears the words of God; for this reason you do not listen, because you do not belong to God."

[48]*The Jews answered and said to him, "Are we not right in saying that you are a Samaritan and are possessed?" [49]Jesus answered, "I am not possessed; I honor my Father, but you dishonor me. [50j]I do not seek my own glory; there is one who seeks it and

---

8, 24.28: I AM: an expression that late Jewish tradition understood as Yahweh's own self-designation (Is 43, 10); see the note on 4, 26. Jesus is here placed on a par with Yahweh.

8, 25: What I told you from the beginning: this verse seems textually corrupt, with several other possible translations: "(I am) what I say to you"; "Why do I speak to you at all?" The earliest attested reading (Bodmer Papyrus P66) has (in a second hand), "I told you at the beginning what I am also telling you (now)." The answer here (cf Prv 8, 22) seems to hinge on a misunderstanding of v 24 "**that I AM**" as "**what I am.**"

8, 31–59: Jesus' origin ("before Abraham") and destiny are developed; the truth will free them from sin (34) and death (51).

8, 31: Those Jews who believed in him: a rough editorial suture, since in v 37 they are described as trying to kill Jesus.

8, 33: Have never been enslaved to anyone: since, historically, the Jews were enslaved almost continuously, this verse is probably Johannine irony, about slavery to sin.

8, 35: A slave . . . a son: an allusion to Ishmael and Isaac (Gn 16 and 21), or to the release of a slave after six years (Ex 21, 2; Dt 15, 12).

8, 38: The Father: i.e., God. It is also possible, however, to understand the second part of the verse as a sarcastic reference to descent of the Jews from the devil (44), "You do what you have heard from [your] father."

8, 39: The works of Abraham: Abraham believed; cf Rom 4, 11–17; Jas 2, 21–23.

8, 48: Samaritan: therefore interested in magical powers; cf Acts 7, 14–24.

---

v: Ex 3, 14; Dt 32, 39; Is 43, 10. w: 10, 24. x: 12, 44-50. y: 3, 14; 12, 32.34. z: Is 42, 7; Gal 4, 31. a: Mt 3, 9. b: Rom 6, 16-17. c: Gn 21, 10; Gal 4, 30; Heb 3, 5-6. d: Gn 26, 5; Rom 4, 11-17; Jas 2, 21-23. e: Mal 2, 10. f: 1 Jn 5, 1. g: Gn 3, 4; Wis 1, 13; 2, 24; Acts 13, 10; 1 Jn 3, 8-15. h: Heb 4, 15; 1 Pt 2, 22; 1 Jn 3, 5. i: 10, 26; 1 Jn 4, 6. j: 7, 18.

he is the one who judges. ⁵¹ᵏAmen, amen, I say to you, whoever keeps my word will never see death." ⁵²[So] the Jews said to him, "Now we are sure that you are possessed. Abraham died, as did the prophets, yet you say, 'Whoever keeps my word will never taste death.' ⁵³ˡ*Are you greater than our father Abraham, who died? Or the prophets, who died? Who do you make yourself out to be?" ⁵⁴Jesus answered, "If I glorify myself, my glory is worth nothing; but it is my Father who glorifies me, of whom you say, 'He is our God.' ⁵⁵ᵐYou do not know him, but I know him. And if I should say that I do not know him, I would be like you a liar. But I do know him and I keep his word. ⁵⁶ⁿ*Abraham your father rejoiced to see my day; he saw it and was glad. ⁵⁷*So the Jews said to him, "You are not yet fifty years old and you have seen Abraham?" ⁵⁸ᵒ*Jesus said to them, "Amen, amen, I say to you, before Abraham came to be, I AM." ⁵⁹ᵖSo they picked up stones to throw at him; but Jesus hid and went out of the temple area.

CHAPTER 9

See RG
420

The Man Born Blind. ¹�q*As he passed by he saw a man blind from birth. ²ʳ*His disciples asked him, "Rabbi, who sinned, this man or his parents, that he was born blind?" ³ˢJesus answered, "Neither he nor his parents sinned; it is so that the works of God might be made visible through him. ⁴ᵗWe have to do the works of the one who sent me while it is day. Night is coming when no one can work. ⁵ᵘWhile I am in the world, I am the light of the world." ⁶ᵛWhen he had said this, he spat on the ground and made clay with the saliva, and smeared the clay on his eyes, ⁷ʷ*and said to him, "Go wash in the Pool of Siloam" (which means Sent). So he went and washed, and came back able to see.

⁸His neighbors and those who had seen him earlier as a beggar said, "Isn't this the one who used to sit and beg?" ⁹Some said, "It is," but others said, "No, he just looks like him." He said, "I am." ¹⁰So they said to him, "[So] how were your eyes opened?" ¹¹He replied, "The man called Jesus made clay and anointed my eyes and told me, 'Go to Siloam and wash.' So I went there and washed and was able to see." ¹²And they said to him, "Where is he?" He said, "I don't know."

¹³They brought the one who was once blind to the Pharisees. ¹⁴ˣ*Now Jesus had made clay and opened his eyes on a sabbath. ¹⁵So then the Pharisees also asked him how he was able to see. He said to them, "He put clay on my eyes, and I washed, and now I can see." ¹⁶ʸSo some of the Pharisees said, "This man is not from God, because he does not keep the sabbath." [But] others said, "How can a sinful man do such signs?" And there was a division among them. ¹⁷ᶻSo they said to the blind man again, "What do you have to say about him, since he opened your eyes?" He said, "He is a prophet."

¹⁸Now the Jews did not believe that he had been blind and gained his sight until they summoned the parents of the one who had gained his sight. ¹⁹They asked them, "Is this your son, who you say was born blind? How does he

---

8, 53: Are you greater than our father Abraham?: cf 4, 12.

8, 56: He saw it: this seems a reference to the birth of Isaac (Gn 17, 7; 21, 6), the beginning of the fulfillment of promises about Abraham's seed.

8, 57: The evidence of the third-century Bodmer Papyrus P⁷⁵ and the first hand of Codex Sinaiticus indicates that the text originally read: "How can Abraham have seen you?"

8, 58: Came to be, I AM: the Greek word used for "came to be" is the one used of all creation in the prologue, while the word used for "am" is the one reserved for the Logos.

9, 1—10, 21: Sabbath healing of the man born blind. This sixth sign is introduced to illustrate the saying, "I am the light of the world" (8, 12; 9, 5). The narrative of conflict about Jesus contrasts Jesus (light) with the Jews (blindness, 39–41). The theme of water is reintroduced in the reference to the pool of Siloam. Ironically, Jesus is being judged by the Jews, yet the Jews are judged by the Light of the world; cf 3, 19–21.

9, 2: See the note on 5, 14, and Ex 20, 5, that parents' sins were visited upon their children. Jesus denies such a cause and emphasizes the purpose: the infirmity was providential.

9, 7: Go wash: perhaps a test of faith; cf 2 Kgs 5, 10–14. The water tunnel Siloam (= Sent) is used as a symbol of Jesus, sent by his Father.

9, 14: In using spittle, kneading clay, and healing, Jesus had broken the sabbath rules laid down by Jewish tradition.

k: 5, 24-29; 6, 40.47; 11, 25-26. *l:* 4, 12. *m:* 7, 28-29. *n:* Gn 17, 17; Mt 13, 17; Lk 17, 22. *o:* 1, 30; 17, 5. *p:* 10, 31.39; 11, 8; Lk 4, 29-30. *q:* Is 42, 7. *r:* Ex 20, 5; Ez 18, 20; Lk 13, 2. *s:* 5, 14; 11, 4. *t:* 11, 9-10; 12, 35-36. *u:* 8, 12. *v:* 5, 11; Mk 7, 33; 8, 23. *w:* 2 Kgs 5, 10-14. *x:* 5, 9. *y:* 3, 2; Mt 12, 10-11; Lk 13, 10-11; 14, 1-4. *z:* 4, 19.

now see?" [20]His parents answered and said, "We know that this is our son and that he was born blind. [21]We do not know how he sees now, nor do we know who opened his eyes. Ask him, he is of age; he can speak for himself." [22a*]His parents said this because they were afraid of the Jews, for the Jews had already agreed that if anyone acknowledged him as the Messiah, he would be expelled from the synagogue. [23b]For this reason his parents said, "He is of age; question him."

[24c*]So a second time they called the man who had been blind and said to him, "Give God the praise! We know that this man is a sinner." [25]He replied, "If he is a sinner, I do not know. One thing I do know is that I was blind and now I see." [26]So they said to him, "What did he do to you? How did he open your eyes?" [27]He answered them, "I told you already and you did not listen. Why do you want to hear it again? Do you want to become his disciples, too?" [28]They ridiculed him and said, "You are that man's disciple; we are disciples of Moses! [29d]We know that God spoke to Moses, but we do not know where this one is from." [30]The man answered and said to them, "This is what is so amazing, that you do not know where he is from, yet he opened my eyes. [31e]We know that God does not listen to sinners, but if one is devout and does his will, he listens to him. [32*]It is unheard of that anyone ever opened the eyes of a person born blind. [33f]If this man were not from God, he would not be able to do anything." [34]They answered and said to him, "You were born totally in sin, and are you trying to teach us?" Then they threw him out.

[35]When Jesus heard that they had thrown him out, he found him and said, "Do you believe in the Son of Man?" [36]He answered and said, "Who is he, sir, that I may believe in him?" [37g]Jesus said to him, "You have seen him and the one speaking with you is he." [38]He said, "I do believe, Lord," and he worshiped him. [39h*]Then Jesus said, "I came into this world for judgment, so that those who do not see might see, and those who do see might become blind."

[40i]Some of the Pharisees who were with him heard this and said to him, "Surely we are not also blind, are we?" [41j]Jesus said to them, "If you were blind, you would have no sin; but now you are saying, 'We see,' so your sin remains.

CHAPTER 10

See RG 420

The Good Shepherd. [1k*]"Amen, amen, I say to you, whoever does not enter a sheepfold through the gate but climbs over elsewhere is a thief and a robber. [2]But whoever enters through the gate is the shepherd of the sheep. [3]The gatekeeper opens it for him, and the sheep hear his voice, as he calls his own sheep by name and leads them out. [4l*]When he has driven out all his own, he walks ahead of them, and the sheep follow him, because they recognize his voice. [5]But they will not follow a stranger; they will run away from him, because they do not recognize the voice of strangers." [6*]Although Jesus used this figure of speech, they did not realize what he was trying to tell them.

9, 22: This comment of the evangelist (in terms used again in 12, 42 and 16, 2) envisages a situation after Jesus' ministry. Rejection/excommunication from the synagogue of Jews who confessed Jesus as Messiah seems to have begun ca. A.D. 85, when the curse against the **minim** or heretics was introduced into the "Eighteen Benedictions."

9, 24: Give God the praise!: an Old Testament formula of adjuration to tell the truth; cf Jos 7, 19; 1 Sm 6, 5 LXX. Cf 5, 41.

9, 32: A person born blind: the only Old Testament cure from blindness is found in Tobit (cf Tb 7, 7; 11, 7–13; 14, 1–2), but Tobit was not born blind.

9, 39–41: These verses spell out the symbolic meaning of the cure; the Pharisees are not the innocent blind, willing to accept the testimony of others.

10, 1–21: The good shepherd discourse continues the theme of attack on the Pharisees that ends ch 9. The figure is allegorical: the hired hands are the Pharisees who excommunicated the cured blind man. It serves as a commentary on ch 9. For the shepherd motif, used of Yahweh in the Old Testament, cf Ex 34; Gn 48, 15; 49, 24; Mi 7, 14; Pss 23, 1–4; 80, 1.

10, 1: Sheepfold: a low stone wall open to the sky.

10, 4: Recognize his voice: the Pharisees do not recognize Jesus, but the people of God, symbolized by the blind man, do.

10, 6: Figure of speech: John uses a different word for illustrative speech than the "parable" of the synoptics, but the idea is similar.

a: 7, 13; 12, 42; 16, 2; 19, 38. *b:* 12, 42. *c:* Jos 7, 19; 1 Sm 6, 5 LXX. *d:* Ex 33, 11. *e:* 10, 21; Pss 34, 16; 66, 18; Prv 15, 29; Is 1, 15. *f:* 3, 2. *g:* 4, 26; Dn 7, 13. *h:* Mt 13, 33-35. *i:* Mt 15, 14; 23, 26; Rom 2, 19. *j:* 15, 22. *k:* Gn 48, 15; 49, 24; Pss 23, 1-4; 80, 2; Jer 23, 1-4; Ez 34, 1-31; Mi 7, 14. *l:* Mi 2, 12-13.

[7]*So Jesus said again, "Amen, amen, I say to you, I am the gate for the sheep. [8]*All who came [before me] are thieves and robbers, but the sheep did not listen to them. [9]I am the gate. Whoever enters through me will be saved, and will come in and go out and find pasture. [10]A thief comes only to steal and slaughter and destroy; I came so that they might have life and have it more abundantly. [11m]I am the good shepherd. A good shepherd lays down his life for the sheep. [12n]A hired man, who is not a shepherd and whose sheep are not his own, sees a wolf coming and leaves the sheep and runs away, and the wolf catches and scatters them. [13]This is because he works for pay and has no concern for the sheep. [14]I am the good shepherd, and I know mine and mine know me, [15o]just as the Father knows me and I know the Father; and I will lay down my life for the sheep. [16p]*I have other sheep that do not belong to this fold. These also I must lead, and they will hear my voice, and there will be one flock, one shepherd. [17q]This is why the Father loves me, because I lay down my life in order to take it up again. [18r]*No one takes it from me, but I lay it down on my own. I have power to lay it down, and power to take it up again. This command I have received from my Father."

[19s]Again there was a division among the Jews because of these words. [20t]Many of them said, "He is possessed and out of his mind; why listen to him?" [21u]Others said, "These are not the words of one possessed; surely a demon cannot open the eyes of the blind, can he?"

Feast of the Dedication. [22v]*The feast of the Dedication was then taking place in Jerusalem. It was winter. [23]*And Jesus walked about in the temple area on the Portico of Solomon. [24w]*So the Jews gathered around him and said to him, "How long are you going to keep us in suspense? If you are the Messiah, tell us plainly." [25x]*Jesus answered them, "I told you and you do not believe. The works I do in my Father's name testify to me. [26y]But you do not believe, because you are not among my sheep. [27]My sheep hear my voice; I know them, and they follow me. [28z]I give them eternal life, and they shall never perish. No one can take them out of my hand. [29a]*My Father, who has given them to me, is greater than all, and no one can take them out of the Father's hand. [30b]*The Father and I are one."

[31c]The Jews again picked up rocks to stone him. [32]Jesus answered them, "I have shown you many good works from my Father. For which of these are you trying to stone me?" [33d]The Jews answered him, "We are not stoning you for a good work but for blasphemy. You, a man, are making yourself God." [34e]*Jesus answered them, "Is it not written in

---

10, 7–10: In vv 7–8, the figure is of a gate for the shepherd to come to the sheep; in vv 9–10, the figure is of a gate for the sheep to **come in and go out.**

10, 8: [**Before me**]: these words are omitted in many good early manuscripts and versions.

10, 16: Other sheep: the Gentiles, possibly a reference to "God's dispersed children" of 11, 52 destined to be gathered into one, or "apostolic Christians" at odds with the community of the beloved disciple.

10, 18: Power to take it up again: contrast the role of the Father as the efficient cause of the resurrection in Acts 2, 24; 4, 10; etc.; Rom 1, 4; 4, 24. Yet even here is added: **This command I have received from my Father.**

10, 22: Feast of the Dedication: an eight-day festival of lights (Hebrew, Hanukkah) held in December, three months after the feast of Tabernacles (7, 2), to celebrate the Maccabees' rededication of the altar and reconsecration of the temple in 164 B.C., after their desecration by Antiochus IV Epiphanes (Dn 8, 13; 9, 27; cf 1 Mc 4, 36–59; 2 Mc 1, 18—2, 19; 10, 1–8).

10, 23: Portico of Solomon: on the east side of the temple area, offering protection against the cold winds from the desert.

10, 24: Keep us in suspense: literally, "How long will

you take away our life?" Cf 11, 48–50. **If you are the Messiah, tell us plainly:** cf Lk 22, 67. This is the climax of Jesus' encounters with the Jewish authorities. There has never yet been an open confession before them.

10, 25: I told you: probably at 8, 25, which was an evasive answer.

10, 29: The textual evidence for the first clause is very divided; it may also be translated: "As for the Father, what he has given me is greater than all," or "My Father is greater than all, in what he has given me."

10, 30: This is justification for v 29; it asserts unity of power and reveals that the words and deeds of Jesus are the words and deeds of God.

10, 34: This is a reference to the judges of Israel who, since they exercised the divine prerogative to judge (Dt 1,

m: Ps 23, 1-4; Is 40, 11; 49, 9-10; Heb 13, 20; Rv 7, 17. *n:* Zec 11, 17. *o:* 15, 13; 1 Jn 3, 16. *p:* 11, 52; Is 56, 8; Jer 23, 3; Ez 34, 23; 37, 24; Mi 2, 12. *q:* Heb 10, 10. *r:* 19, 11. *s:* 7, 43; 9, 16. *t:* 7, 20; 8, 48. *u:* 3, 2. *v:* 1 Mc 4, 54.59. *w:* Lk 22, 67. *x:* 8, 25 / 5, 36; 10, 38. *y:* 8, 45.47. *z:* Dt 32, 39. *a:* Wis 3, 1; Is 43, 13. *b:* 1, 1; 12, 45; 14, 9; 17, 21. *c:* 8, 59. *d:* 5, 18; 19, 7; Lv 24, 16. *e:* Ps 82, 6.

your law, 'I said, "You are gods" '? [35]If it calls them gods to whom the word of God came, and scripture cannot be set aside, [36]f*can you say that the one whom the Father has consecrated and sent into the world blasphemes because I said, 'I am the Son of God'? [37]If I do not perform my Father's works, do not believe me; [38]gbut if I perform them, even if you do not believe me, believe the works, so that you may realize [and understand] that the Father is in me and I am in the Father." [39][Then] they tried again to arrest him; but he escaped from their power.

[40]hHe went back across the Jordan to the place where John first baptized, and there he remained. [41]*Many came to him and said, "John performed no sign, but everything John said about this man was true." [42]iAnd many there began to believe in him.

See RG 420

CHAPTER 11

The Raising of Lazarus. [1]j*Now a man was ill, Lazarus from Bethany, the village of Mary and her sister Martha. [2]Mary was the one who had anointed the Lord with perfumed oil and dried his feet with her hair; it was her brother Lazarus who was ill. [3]So the sisters sent word to him, saying, "Master, the one you love is ill." [4]k*When Jesus heard this he said, "This illness is not to end in death, but is for the glory of God, that the Son of God may be glorified through it." [5]Now Jesus loved Martha and her sister and Lazarus. [6]So when he heard that he was ill,

he remained for two days in the place where he was. [7]Then after this he said to his disciples, "Let us go back to Judea." [8]lThe disciples said to him, "Rabbi, the Jews were just trying to stone you, and you want to go back there?" [9]mnJesus answered, "Are there not twelve hours in a day? If one walks during the day, he does not stumble, because he sees the light of this world. [10]*But if one walks at night, he stumbles, because the light is not in him." [11]He said this, and then told them, "Our friend Lazarus is asleep, but I am going to awaken him." [12]So the disciples said to him, "Master, if he is asleep, he will be saved." [13]oBut Jesus was talking about his death, while they thought that he meant ordinary sleep. [14]So then Jesus said to them clearly, "Lazarus has died. [15]And I am glad for you that I was not there, that you may believe. Let us go to him." [16]p*So Thomas, called Didymus, said to his fellow disciples, "Let us also go to die with him."

[17]When Jesus arrived, he found that Lazarus had already been in the tomb for four days. [18]*Now Bethany was near Jerusalem, only about two miles away. [19]qAnd many of the Jews had come to Martha and Mary to comfort them about their brother. [20]When Martha heard that Jesus was coming, she went to meet him; but Mary sat at home. [21]rMartha said to Jesus, "Lord, if you had been here, my brother would not have died. [22][But] even now I know that whatever you ask of God, God will give you." [23]Jesus said

---

17), were called "gods"; cf Ex 21, 6, besides Ps 82, 6, from which the quotation comes.

10, 36: Consecrated: this may be a reference to the rededicated altar at the Hanukkah feast; see the note on 10, 22.

10, 41: Performed no sign: this is to stress the inferior role of John the Baptist. The Transjordan topography recalls the great witness of John the Baptist to Jesus, as opposed to the hostility of the authorities in Jerusalem.

11, 1–44: The raising of Lazarus, the longest continuous narrative in John outside of the Passion account, is the climax of the signs. It leads directly to the decision of the Sanhedrin to kill Jesus. The theme of life predominates. Lazarus is a token of the real life that Jesus dead and raised will give to all who believe in him. Johannine irony is found in the fact that Jesus' gift of life leads to his own death. The story is not found in the synoptics, but cf Mk 5, 21 and parallels; Lk 7, 11–17. There are also parallels between this story and Luke's parable of the rich man and poor Lazarus (Lk 16, 19–31). In both a man named Lazarus dies; in Luke, there is a request that he return to convince his contemporaries of the need for

faith and repentance, while in John, Lazarus does return and some believe but others do not.

11, 4: Not to end in death: this is misunderstood by the disciples as referring to physical death, but it is meant as spiritual death.

11, 10: The light is not in him: the ancients apparently did not grasp clearly the entry of light **through** the eye; they seem to have thought of it as being **in** the eye; cf Lk 11, 34; Mt 6, 23.

11, 16: Called Didymus: Didymus is the Greek word for twin. Thomas is derived from the Aramaic word for twin; in an ancient Syriac version and in the Gospel of Thomas (80, 11–12) his given name, Judas, is supplied.

11, 18: About two miles: literally, "about fifteen stades"; a stade was 607 feet.

f: 5, 18.   *g:* 14, 10-11.20.   *h:* 1, 28.   *i:* 2, 23; 7, 31; 8, 30. *j:* 12, 1-8; Lk 10, 38-42; 16, 19-31.   *k:* 9, 3.24.   *l:* 8, 59; 10, 31. *m:* 8, 12; 9, 4.   *n:* 12, 35; 1 Jn 2, 10.   *o:* Mt 9, 24.   *p:* 14, 5.22. *q:* 12, 9.17-18.   *r:* 11, 32.

to her, "Your brother will rise." ^{24s}Martha said to him, "I know he will rise, in the resurrection on the last day." ^{25t}Jesus told her, "I am the resurrection and the life; whoever believes in me, even if he dies, will live, ²⁶and everyone who lives and believes in me will never die. Do you believe this?" ^{27u}*She said to him, "Yes, Lord. I have come to believe that you are the Messiah, the Son of God, the one who is coming into the world."

²⁸When she had said this, she went and called her sister Mary secretly, saying, "The teacher is here and is asking for you." ²⁹As soon as she heard this, she rose quickly and went to him. ³⁰For Jesus had not yet come into the village, but was still where Martha had met him. ³¹So when the Jews who were with her in the house comforting her saw Mary get up quickly and go out, they followed her, presuming that she was going to the tomb to weep there. ³²When Mary came to where Jesus was and saw him, she fell at his feet and said to him, "Lord, if you had been here, my brother would not have died." ³³*When Jesus saw her weeping and the Jews who had come with her weeping, he became perturbed and deeply troubled, ³⁴and said, "Where have you laid him?" They said to him, "Sir, come and see." ^{35v}And Jesus wept. ³⁶So the Jews said, "See how he loved him." ³⁷But some of them said, "Could not the one who opened the eyes of the blind man have done something so that this man would not have died?"

³⁸So Jesus, perturbed again, came to the tomb. It was a cave, and a stone lay across it. ³⁹Jesus said, "Take away the stone." Martha, the dead man's sister, said to him, "Lord, by now there will be a stench; he has been dead for four days." ⁴⁰Jesus said to her, "Did I not tell you that if you believe you will see the glory of God?" ⁴¹*So they took away the stone. And Jesus raised his eyes and said, "Father, I thank you for hearing me. ^{42w}I know that you always hear me; but because of the crowd here I have said this, that they may believe that you sent me." ⁴³*And when he had said this, he cried out in a loud voice, "Lazarus, come out!" ⁴⁴The dead man came out, tied hand and foot with burial bands, and his face was wrapped in a cloth. So Jesus said to them, "Untie him and let him go."

Session of the Sanhedrin. ^{45x}Now many of the Jews who had come to Mary and seen what he had done began to believe in him. ⁴⁶But some of them went to the Pharisees and told them what Jesus had done. ^{47y}So the chief priests and the Pharisees convened the Sanhedrin and said, "What are we going to do? This man is performing many signs. ⁴⁸*If we leave him alone, all will believe in him, and the Romans will come and take away both our land and our nation." ^{49z}*But one of them, Caiaphas, who was high priest that year, said to them, "You know nothing, ⁵⁰nor do you consider that it is better for you that one man should die instead of the people, so that the whole nation may not perish." ⁵¹He did not say this on his own, but since he was high priest for that year, he prophesied that Jesus was going to die for the nation, ⁵²*and not only for the nation, but also to gather into one the dispersed children of God. ^{53a}So from that day on they planned to kill him.

⁵⁴*So Jesus no longer walked about in public among the Jews, but he left for the region near the desert, to a town called Ephraim, and there he remained with his disciples.

11, 27: The titles here are a summary of titles given to Jesus earlier in the gospel.

11, 33: Became perturbed: a startling phrase in Greek, literally, "He snorted in spirit," perhaps in anger at the presence of evil (death).

11, 41: Father: in Aramaic, 'abbā'. See the note on Mk 14, 36.

11, 43: Cried out in a loud voice: a dramatization of 5, 28: "the hour is coming when all who are in the tombs will hear his voice."

11, 48: The Romans will come: Johannine irony; this is precisely what happened after Jesus' death.

11, 49: That year: emphasizes the conjunction of the office and the year. Actually, Caiaphas was high priest A.D. 18–36. The Jews attributed a gift of prophecy, sometimes unconscious, to the high priest.

11, 52: Dispersed children of God: perhaps the "other sheep" of 10, 16.

11, 54: Ephraim is usually located about twelve miles northeast of Jerusalem, where the mountains descend into the Jordan valley.

s: 5, 29; 6, 39-40.44.54; 12, 48; Is 2, 2; Mi 4, 1; Acts 23, 8;24, 15. t: 5, 24; 8, 51; 14, 6; Dn 12, 2. u: 1, 9; 6, 69. v: Lk 19, 41. w: 12, 30. x: Lk 16, 31. y: 12, 19; Mt 26, 3-5; Lk 22, 2; Acts 4, 16. z: 18, 13-14. a: 5, 18; 7, 1; Mt 12, 14.

The Last Passover. *55b**Now the Passover of the Jews was near, and many went up from the country to Jerusalem before Passover to purify themselves. *56*They looked for Jesus and said to one another as they were in the temple area, "What do you think? That he will not come to the feast?" *57*For the chief priests and the Pharisees had given orders that if anyone knew where he was, he should inform them, so that they might arrest him.

See RG 420

CHAPTER 12

The Anointing at Bethany. *1cd**Six days before Passover Jesus came to Bethany, where Lazarus was, whom Jesus had raised from the dead. *2e*They gave a dinner for him there, and Martha served, while Lazarus was one of those reclining at table with him. *3f**Mary took a liter of costly perfumed oil made from genuine aromatic nard and anointed the feet of Jesus and dried them with her hair; the house was filled with the fragrance of the oil. *4*Then Judas the Iscariot, one [of] his disciples, and the one who would betray him, said, *5**"Why was this oil not sold for three hundred days' wages and given to the poor?" *6g*He said this not because he cared about the poor but because he was a thief and held the money bag and used to steal the contributions. *7**So Jesus said, "Leave her alone. Let her keep this for the day of my burial. *8h*You always have the poor with you, but you do not always have me."

9i[The] large crowd of the Jews found out that he was there and came, not only because of Jesus, but also to see Lazarus, whom he had raised from the dead. *10*And the chief priests plotted to kill Lazarus too, *11j*because many of the Jews were turning away and believing in Jesus because of him.

The Entry into Jerusalem. *12k**On the next day, when the great crowd that had come to the feast heard that Jesus was coming to Jerusalem, *13l**they took palm branches and went out to meet him, and cried out:

"Hosanna!
Blessed is he who comes in the name of
    the Lord,
    [even] the king of Israel."

*14*Jesus found an ass and sat upon it, as is written:

15 m*"Fear no more, O daughter Zion;
see, your king comes, seated upon an
    ass's colt."

16n*His disciples did not understand this at first, but when Jesus had been glorified they remembered that these things were written about him and that they had done this for him. *17**So the crowd that was with him when he called Lazarus from the tomb and raised him from death continued to testify. *18*This

---

11, 55: Purify: prescriptions for purity were based on Ex 19, 10–11.15; Nm 9, 6–14; 2 Chr 30, 1–3.15–18.

12, 1–8: This is probably the same scene of anointing found in Mk 14, 3–9 (see the note there) and Mt 26, 6–13. The anointing by a penitent woman in Lk 7, 36–38 is different. Details from these various episodes have become interchanged.

12, 3: The feet of Jesus: so Mk 14, 3; but in Mt 26, 6, Mary anoints Jesus' head as a sign of regal, messianic anointing.

12, 5: Days' wages: literally, "denarii." A denarius is a day's wage in Mt 20, 2; see the note on 6, 7.

12, 7: Jesus' response reflects the rabbinical discussion of what was the greatest act of mercy, almsgiving or burying the dead. Those who favored proper burial of the dead thought it an essential condition for sharing in the resurrection.

12, 12–19: In Jn, the entry into Jerusalem follows the anointing whereas in the synoptics it precedes. In John, the crowd, not the disciples, are responsible for the triumphal procession.

12, 13: Palm branches: used to welcome great conquerors; cf 1 Mc 13, 51; 2 Mc 10, 7. They may be related to the lûlāb, the twig bundles used at the feast of Tabernacles.

Hosanna: see Ps 118, 25–26. The Hebrew word means: "(O Lord), grant salvation." **He who comes in the name of the Lord:** referred in Ps 118, 26 to a pilgrim entering the temple gates, but here a title for Jesus (see the notes on Mt 11, 3 and Jn 6, 14; 11, 27). **The king of Israel:** perhaps from Zep 3, 14–15, in connection with the next quotation from Zec 9, 9.

12, 15: Daughter Zion: Jerusalem. Ass's colt: symbol of peace, as opposed to the war-horse.

12, 16: They had done this: the antecedent of **they** is ambiguous.

12, 17–18: There seem to be two different crowds in these verses. There are some good witnesses to the text that have another reading for v 17: "Then the crowd that was with him began to testify that he had called Lazarus out of the tomb and raised him from the dead."

---

b: 2, 13; 5, 1; 6, 4; 18, 28; Ex 19, 10-11.15; Nm 9, 6-14; 19, 12; Dt 16, 6; 2 Chr 30, 1-3.15-18. *c*: Mt 26, 6-13; Mk 14, 3-9. *d*: 11, 1. *e*: Lk 10, 38-42. *f*: 11, 2. *g*: 13, 29. *h*: Dt 15, 11. *i*: 11, 19. *j*: 11, 45. *k*: Mt 21, 1-16; Mk 11, 1-10; Lk 19, 28-40. *l*: 1, 49; Lv 23, 40; 1 Mc 13, 51; 2 Mc 10, 7; Rv 7, 9. *m*: Is 40, 9; Zec 9, 9. *n*: 2, 22.

was [also] why the crowd went to meet him, because they heard that he had done this sign. ¹⁹ᵒ*So the Pharisees said to one another, "You see that you are gaining nothing. Look, the whole world has gone after him."

The Coming of Jesus' Hour. ²⁰ᵖ*Now there were some Greeks among those who had come up to worship at the feast. ²¹�q*They came to Philip, who was from Bethsaida in Galilee, and asked him, "Sir, we would like to see Jesus." ²²ʳPhilip went and told Andrew; then Andrew and Philip went and told Jesus. ²³ˢ*Jesus answered them, "The hour has come for the Son of Man to be glorified. ²⁴ᵗ*Amen, amen, I say to you, unless a grain of wheat falls to the ground and dies, it remains just a grain of wheat; but if it dies, it produces much fruit. ²⁵ᵘ*Whoever loves his life loses it, and whoever hates his life in this world will preserve it for eternal life. ²⁶ᵛWhoever serves me must follow me, and where I am, there also will my servant be. The Father will honor whoever serves me.

²⁷ʷ*"I am troubled now. Yet what should I say? 'Father, save me from this hour'? But it was for this purpose that I came to this hour. ²⁸ˣFather, glorify your name." Then a voice came from heaven, "I have glorified it and will glorify it again." ²⁹ʸThe crowd there

heard it and said it was thunder; but others said, "An angel has spoken to him." ³⁰ᶻJesus answered and said, "This voice did not come for my sake but for yours. ³¹ᵃ*Now is the time of judgment on this world; now the ruler of this world will be driven out. ³²ᵇAnd when I am lifted up from the earth, I will draw everyone to myself." ³³He said this indicating the kind of death he would die. ³⁴ᶜ*So the crowd answered him, "We have heard from the law that the Messiah remains forever. Then how can you say that the Son of Man must be lifted up? Who is this Son of Man?" ³⁵ᵈJesus said to them, "The light will be among you only a little while. Walk while you have the light, so that darkness may not overcome you. Whoever walks in the dark does not know where he is going. ³⁶ᵉWhile you have the light, believe in the light, so that you may become children of the light."

Unbelief and Belief among the Jews. After he had said this, Jesus left and hid from them. ³⁷ᶠ*Although he had performed so many signs in their presence they did not believe in him, ³⁸ᵍ*in order that the word which Isaiah the prophet spoke might be fulfilled:

"Lord, who has believed our preaching,
 to whom has the might of the Lord
 been revealed?"

12, 19: The whole world: the sense is that everyone is following Jesus, but John has an ironic play on **world;** he alludes to the universality of salvation (3, 17; 4, 42).

12, 20–36: This announcement of glorification by death is an illustration of "the whole world" (19) going after him.

12, 20: Greeks: not used here in a nationalistic sense. These are probably Gentile proselytes to Judaism; cf 7, 35.

12, 21–22: Philip . . . Andrew: the approach is made through disciples who have distinctly Greek names, suggesting that access to Jesus was mediated to the Greek world through his disciples. Philip and Andrew were from Bethsaida (1, 44); Galileans were mostly bilingual. **See:** here seems to mean "have an interview with."

12, 23: Jesus' response suggests that only after the crucifixion could the gospel encompass both Jew and Gentile.

12, 24: This verse implies that through his death Jesus will be accessible to all. **It remains just a grain of wheat:** this saying is found in the synoptic triple and double traditions (Mk 8, 35 // Mt 16, 25 // Lk 9, 24; Mt 10, 39 // Lk 17, 33). John adds the phrases (25) **in this world** and **for eternal life.**

12, 25: His life: the Greek word **psychē** refers to a person's natural life. It does not mean "soul," for Hebrew anthropology did not postulate body/soul dualism in the way that is familiar to us.

12, 27: I am troubled: perhaps an allusion to the Geth-

semane agony scene of the synoptics.

12, 31: Ruler of this world: Satan.

12, 34: There is no passage in the Old Testament that states precisely that **the Messiah remains forever.** Perhaps the closest is Ps 89, 37.

12, 37–50: These verses, on unbelief of the Jews, provide an epilogue to the Book of Signs.

12, 38–41: John gives a historical explanation of the disbelief of the Jewish people, not a psychological one. The Old Testament had to be fulfilled; the disbelief that met Isaiah's message was a foreshadowing of the disbelief that Jesus encountered. In v 42 and also in 3, 20, we see that there is no negation of freedom.

o: 11, 47-48. *p:* Acts 10, 2. *q:* 1, 44. *r:* 1, 40. *s:* 2, 4. *t:* Is 53, 10-12; 1 Cor 15, 36. *u:* Mt 10, 39; 16, 25; Mk 8, 35; Lk 9, 24; 17, 33. *v:* 14, 3; 17, 24; Mt 16, 24; Mk 8, 34; Lk 9, 23. *w:* 6, 38; 18, 11; Mt 26, 38-39; Mk 14, 34-36; Lk 22, 42; Heb 5, 7-8. *x:* 2, 11; 17, 5; Dn 4, 31.34. *y:* Ex 9, 28; 2 Sm 22, 14; Jb 37, 4; Ps 29, 3; Lk 22, 43; Acts 23, 9. *z:* 11, 42. *a:* 16, 11; Lk 10, 18; Rv 12, 9. *b:* 3, 14; 8, 28; Is 52, 13. *c:* Pss 89, 5; 110, 4; Is 9, 7; Dn 7, 13-14; Rv 20, 1-6. *d:* 9, 4; 11, 10; Jb 5, 14. *e:* Eph 5, 8. *f:* Dt 29, 2-4; Mk 4, 11-12; Rom 9-11. *g:* Is 53, 1; Rom 10, 16.

39For this reason they could not believe, because again Isaiah said:

40 h"He blinded their eyes
and hardened their heart,
so that they might not see with their eyes
and understand with their heart and be
converted,
and I would heal them."

41i*Isaiah said this because he saw his glory and spoke about him. 42jNevertheless, many, even among the authorities, believed in him, but because of the Pharisees they did not acknowledge it openly in order not to be expelled from the synagogue. 43kFor they preferred human praise to the glory of God.

Recapitulation. 44lJesus cried out and said, "Whoever believes in me believes not only in me but also in the one who sent me, 45mand whoever sees me sees the one who sent me. 46nI came into the world as light, so that everyone who believes in me might not remain in darkness. 47oAnd if anyone hears my words and does not observe them, I do not condemn him, for I did not come to condemn the world but to save the world. 48pWhoever rejects me and does not accept my words has something to judge him: the word that I spoke, it will condemn him on the last day, 49qbecause I did not speak on my own, but the Father who sent me commanded me what to say and speak. 50And I know that his commandment is eternal life. So what I say, I say as the Father told me."

III: The Book Of Glory*

CHAPTER 13

See RG 420–21

The Washing of the Disciples' Feet.

1r*Before the feast of Passover, Jesus knew that his hour had come to pass from this world to the Father. He loved his own in the world and he loved them to the end. 2s*The devil had already induced Judas, son of Simon the Iscariot, to hand him over. So, during supper, 3tfully aware that the Father had put everything into his power and that he had come from God and was returning to God, 4he rose from supper and took off his outer garments. He took a towel and tied it around his waist. 5u*Then he poured water into a basin and began to wash the disciples' feet and dry them with the towel around his waist. 6He came to Simon Peter, who said to him, "Master, are you going to wash my feet?" 7Jesus answered and said to him, "What I am doing, you do not understand now, but you will understand later." 8vPeter said to him, "You will never wash my feet." Jesus answered him, "Unless I wash you, you will have no inheritance with me." 9Simon Peter said to him, "Master, then not only my feet, but my hands and head as well." 10w*Jesus said to him, "Whoever has bathed has no need except to have his feet washed, for he is clean all over; so you are clean, but not all." 11xFor he knew who would betray him; for this reason, he said, "Not all of you are clean."

12, 41: **His glory:** Isaiah saw the glory of Yahweh enthroned in the heavenly temple, but in John the antecedent of **his** is Jesus.

13, 1—19, 42: The Book of Glory. There is a major break here; the word "sign" is used again only in 20, 30. In this phase of Jesus' return to the Father, the discourses (chs 13–17) precede the traditional narrative of the passion (chs 18–20) to interpret them for the Christian reader. This is the only extended example of esoteric teaching of disciples in John.

13, 1–20: Washing of the disciples' feet. This episode occurs in John at the place of the narration of the institution of the Eucharist in the synoptics. It may be a dramatization of Lk 22, 27: "I am your servant." It is presented as a "model" ("pattern") of the crucifixion. It symbolizes cleansing from sin by sacrificial death.

13, 1: **Before the feast of Passover:** this would be Thursday evening, before the day of preparation; in the synoptics, the Last Supper is a Passover meal taking place, in John's

chronology, on Friday evening. **To the end:** or, "completely."

13, 2: **Induced:** literally, "The devil put into the heart that Judas should hand him over."

13, 5: The act of washing another's feet was one that could not be required of the lowliest Jewish slave. It is an allusion to the humiliating death of the crucifixion.

13, 10: **Bathed:** many have suggested that this passage is a symbolic reference to baptism. The Greek root involved is used in baptismal contexts in 1 Cor 6, 11; Eph 5, 26; Ti 3, 5; Heb 10, 22.

---

h: Is 6, 9-10; Mt 13, 13-15; Mk 4, 12. i: 5, 39; Is 6, 1.4. j: 9, 22. k: 5, 44. l: 13, 20; 14, 1. m: 14, 7-9. n: 1, 9; 8, 12. o: 3, 17. p: Lk 10, 16; Heb 4, 12. q: 14, 10.31; Dt 18, 18-19. r: 2, 4; 7, 30; 8, 20; Mt 26, 17.45; Mk 14, 12.41; Lk 22, 7. s: 6, 71; 17, 12; Mt 26, 20-21; Mk 14, 17-18; Lk 22, 3. t: 3, 35. u: 1 Sm 25, 41. v: 2 Sm 20, 1. w: 15, 3. x: 6, 70.

[12]So when he had washed their feet [and] put his garments back on and reclined at table again, he said to them, "Do you realize what I have done for you? [13y]You call me 'teacher' and 'master,' and rightly so, for indeed I am. [14]If I, therefore, the master and teacher, have washed your feet, you ought to wash one another's feet. [15z]I have given you a model to follow, so that as I have done for you, you should also do. [16a*]Amen, amen, I say to you, no slave is greater than his master nor any messenger greater than the one who sent him. [17]If you understand this, blessed are you if you do it. [18b]I am not speaking of all of you. I know those whom I have chosen. But so that the scripture might be fulfilled, 'The one who ate my food has raised his heel against me.' [19]From now on I am telling you before it happens, so that when it happens you may believe that I AM. [20c]Amen, amen, I say to you, whoever receives the one I send receives me, and whoever receives me receives the one who sent me."

Announcement of Judas's Betrayal. [21d]When he had said this, Jesus was deeply troubled and testified, "Amen, amen, I say to you, one of you will betray me." [22]The disciples looked at one another, at a loss as to whom he meant. [23e*]One of his disciples, the one whom Jesus loved, was reclining at Jesus' side. [24]So Simon Peter nodded to him to find out whom he meant. [25f]He leaned back against Jesus' chest and said to him, "Master, who is it?" [26*]Jesus answered, "It is the one to whom I hand the morsel after I

have dipped it." So he dipped the morsel and [took it and] handed it to Judas, son of Simon the Iscariot. [27g]After he took the morsel, Satan entered him. So Jesus said to him, "What you are going to do, do quickly." [28][Now] none of those reclining at table realized why he said this to him. [29h]Some thought that since Judas kept the money bag, Jesus had told him, "Buy what we need for the feast," or to give something to the poor. [30]So he took the morsel and left at once. And it was night.

The New Commandment. [31*]When he had left, Jesus said, "Now is the Son of Man glorified, and God is glorified in him. [32i][If God is glorified in him,] God will also glorify him in himself, and he will glorify him at once. [33j]My children, I will be with you only a little while longer. You will look for me, and as I told the Jews, 'Where I go you cannot come,' so now I say it to you. [34k*]I give you a new commandment: love one another. As I have loved you, so you also should love one another. [35]This is how all will know that you are my disciples, if you have love for one another."

Peter's Denial Predicted. [36l]Simon Peter said to him, "Master, where are you going?" Jesus answered [him], "Where I am going, you cannot follow me now, though you will follow later." [37]Peter said to him, "Master, why can't I follow you now? I will lay down my life for you." [38m]Jesus answered, "Will you lay down your life for me? Amen, amen, I say to you, the cock will not crow before you deny me three times."

13, 16: Messenger: the Greek has **apostolos,** the only occurrence of the term in John. It is not used in the technical sense here.

13, 23: The one whom Jesus loved: also mentioned in 19, 26; 20, 2; 21, 7. A disciple, called "another disciple" or "the other disciple," is mentioned in 18, 15 and 20, 2; in the latter reference he is identified with the disciple whom Jesus loved. There is also an unnamed disciple in 1, 35–40; see the note on 1, 37.

13, 26: Morsel: probably the bitter herb dipped in salt water.

13, 31—17, 26: Two farewell discourses and a prayer. These seem to be Johannine compositions, including sayings of Jesus at the Last Supper and on other occasions, modeled on similar farewell discourses in Greek literature and the Old Testament (of Moses, Joshua, David).

13, 31–38: Introduction: departure and return. Terms of

coming and going predominate. These verses form an introduction to the last discourse of Jesus, which extends through chs 14 to 17. In it John has collected Jesus' words to **his own** (13, 1). There are indications that several speeches have been fused together, e.g., in 14, 31 and 17, 1.

13, 34: I give you a new commandment: this puts Jesus on a par with Yahweh. The commandment itself is not new; cf Lv 19, 18 and the note there.

y: Mt 23, 8.10. z: Lk 22, 27; 1 Pt 2, 21. a: 15, 20; Mt 10, 24; Lk 6, 40. b: Ps 41, 10. c: Mt 10, 40; Mk 9, 37; Lk 9, 48. d: Mt 26, 21-25; Mk 14, 18-21; Lk 22, 21-23. e: 19, 26; 20, 2; 21, 7.20; Mt 10, 37. f: 21, 20. g: 13, 2; Lk 22, 3. h: 12, 5-6. i: 17, 1-5. j: 7, 33; 8, 21. k: 15, 12-13.17; Lv 19, 18; 1 Thes 4, 9; 1 Jn 2, 7-10; 3, 23; 2 Jn 5. l: Mk 14, 27; Lk 22, 33. m: 18, 27; Mt 26, 33-35; Mk 14, 29-31; Lk 22, 33-34.

CHAPTER 14

Last Supper Discourses. [1]*"Do not let your hearts be troubled. You have faith in God; have faith also in me. [2]In my Father's house there are many dwelling places. If there were not, would I have told you that I am going to prepare a place for you? [3n]*And if I go and prepare a place for you, I will come back again and take you to myself, so that where I am you also may be. [4]*Where [I] am going you know the way." [5]Thomas said to him, "Master, we do not know where you are going; how can we know the way?" [6q]*Jesus said to him, "I am the way and the truth and the life. No one comes to the Father except through me. [7p]*If you know me, then you will also know my Father. From now on you do know him and have seen him." [8q]*Philip said to him, "Master, show us the Father, and that will be enough for us." [9r]Jesus said to him, "Have I been with you for so long a time and you still do not know me, Philip? Whoever has seen me has seen the Father. How can you say, 'Show us the Father'? [10s]Do you not believe that I am in the Father and the Father is in me? The words that I speak to you I do not speak on my own. The Father who dwells in me is doing his works. [11t]Believe me that I am in the Father and the Father is in me, or else, believe because of the works themselves. [12u]Amen, amen, I say to you, whoever believes in me will do the works that I do, and will do greater ones than these, because I am going to the Father. [13v]And whatever you ask in my name, I will do, so that the Father may be glorified in the Son. [14]If you ask anything of me in my name, I will do it.

The Advocate. [15w]"If you love me, you will keep my commandments. [16x]*And I will ask the Father, and he will give you another Advocate to be with you always, [17y]*the Spirit of truth, which the world cannot accept, because it neither sees nor knows it. But you know it, because it remains with you, and will be in you. [18]*I will not leave you orphans; I will come to you. [19z]In a little while the world will no longer see me, but you will see me, because I live and you will live. [20a]On that day you will realize that I am in my Father and you are in me and I in you. [21b]Whoever has my commandments and observes them is the one who loves me. And whoever loves me will be loved by my Father, and I will love him and reveal myself to him." [22c]*Judas, not the Iscariot, said to him, "Master, [then] what happened that you will reveal yourself to us and not to the world?" [23d]Jesus answered and said to him, "Whoever loves me will keep my

14, 1–31: Jesus' departure and return. This section is a dialogue marked off by a literary inclusion in vv 1 and 27: "Do not let your hearts be troubled."

14, 1: You have faith: could also be imperative: "Have faith."

14, 3: Come back again: a rare Johannine reference to the parousia; cf 1 Jn 2, 28.

14, 4: The way: here, of Jesus himself; also a designation of Christianity in Acts 9, 2; 19, 9.23; 22, 4; 24, 14.22.

14, 6: The truth: in John, the divinely revealed reality of the Father manifested in the person and works of Jesus. The possession of truth confers knowledge and liberation from sin (8, 32).

14, 7: An alternative reading, "If you knew me, then you would have known my Father also," would be a rebuke, as in 8, 19.

14, 8: Show us the Father: Philip is pictured asking for a theophany like Ex 24, 9–10; 33, 18.

14, 16: Another Advocate: Jesus is the first advocate (paraclete); see 1 Jn 2, 1, where Jesus is an advocate in the sense of intercessor in heaven. The Greek term derives from legal terminology for an advocate or defense attorney, and can mean spokesman, mediator, intercessor, comforter, consoler, although no one of these terms encompasses the meaning in John. The Paraclete in John is a teacher, a witness to

Jesus, and a prosecutor of the world, who represents the continued presence on earth of the Jesus who has returned to the Father.

14, 17: The Spirit of truth: this term is also used at Qumran, where it is a moral force put into a person by God, as opposed to the spirit of perversity. It is more personal in John; it will teach the realities of the new order (26), and testify to the truth (6). While it has been customary to use masculine personal pronouns in English for the Advocate, the Greek word for "spirit" is neuter, and the Greek text and manuscript variants fluctuate between masculine and neuter pronouns.

14, 18: I will come to you: indwelling, not parousia.

14, 22: Judas, not the Iscariot: probably not the brother of Jesus in Mk 6, 3 // Mt 13, 55 or the apostle named Jude in Lk 6, 16, but Thomas (see the note on 11, 16), although other readings have "Judas the Cananean."

n: 12, 26; 17, 24; 1 Jn 2, 28. *o:* 8, 31-47. *p:* 8, 19; 12, 45. *q:* Ex 24, 9-10; 33, 18. *r:* 1, 18; 10, 30; 12, 45; 2 Cor 4, 4; Col 1, 15; Heb 1, 3. *s:* 1, 1; 10, 37-38; 12, 49. *t:* 10, 38. *u:* 1, 50; 5, 20. *v:* 15, 7.16; 16, 23-24; Mt 7, 7-11. *w:* 15, 10; Dt 6, 4-9; Ps 119; Wis 6, 18; 1 Jn 5, 3; 2 Jn 6. *x:* 15, 26; Lk 24, 49; 1 Jn 2, 1. *y:* 16, 13; Mt 28, 20; 2 Jn 1-2. *z:* 16, 16. *a:* 10, 38; 17, 21; Is 2, 17; 4, 2-3. *b:* 16, 27; 1 Jn 2, 5; 3, 24. *c:* 7, 4; Acts 10, 40-41. *d:* Rv 3, 20.

word, and my Father will love him, and we will come to him and make our dwelling with him. [24]Whoever does not love me does not keep my words; yet the word you hear is not mine but that of the Father who sent me.

[25]"I have told you this while I am with you. [26e]The Advocate, the holy Spirit that the Father will send in my name—he will teach you everything and remind you of all that [I] told you. [27f*]Peace I leave with you; my peace I give to you. Not as the world gives do I give it to you. Do not let your hearts be troubled or afraid. [28g*]You heard me tell you, 'I am going away and I will come back to you.' If you loved me, you would rejoice that I am going to the Father; for the Father is greater than I. [29h]And now I have told you this before it happens, so that when it happens you may believe. [30*]I will no longer speak much with you, for the ruler of the world is coming. He has no power over me, [31i]but the world must know that I love the Father and that I do just as the Father has commanded me. Get up, let us go.

See RG 420–21

CHAPTER 15

The Vine and the Branches. [1j*]"I am the true vine, and my Father is the vine grower. [2*]He takes away every branch in me that does not bear fruit, and every one that does he prunes so that it bears more fruit. [3k]You are already pruned because of the word that I spoke to you. [4]Remain in me, as I remain in you. Just as a branch cannot bear fruit on its own unless it remains on the vine, so neither can you unless you remain in me. [5]I am the vine, you are the branches. Whoever remains in me and I in him will bear much fruit, because without me you can do nothing. [6l*]Anyone who does not remain in me will be thrown out like a branch and wither; people will gather them and throw them into a fire and they will be burned. [7m]If you remain in me and my words remain in you, ask for whatever you want and it will be done for you. [8n]By this is my Father glorified, that you bear much fruit and become my disciples. [9o]As the Father loves me, so I also love you. Remain in my love. [10p]If you keep my commandments, you will remain in my love, just as I have kept my Father's commandments and remain in his love.

[11q]"I have told you this so that my joy may be in you and your joy may be complete. [12r]This is my commandment: love one another as I love you. [13s*]No one has greater love than this, to lay down one's life for one's friends. [14]You are my friends if you do what I command you. [15t*]I no longer call you slaves, because a slave does not know what his master is doing. I have called you friends, because I have told you everything I have heard from my Father. [16u]It was not you who chose me, but I who chose you and appointed you to go and bear fruit that will remain, so that whatever you ask the Father in my name he may give you. [17v]This I command you: love one another.

14, 27: Peace: the traditional Hebrew salutation šālôm; but Jesus' "Shalom" is a gift of salvation, connoting the bounty of messianic blessing.

14, 28: The Father is greater than I: because he **sent, gave,** etc., and Jesus is "a man who has told you the truth that I heard from God" (8, 40).

14, 30: The ruler of the world: Satan; cf 12, 31; 16, 11.

15, 1—16, 4: Discourse on the union of Jesus with his disciples. His words become a monologue and go beyond the immediate crisis of the departure of Jesus.

15, 1–17: Like 10, 1–5, this passage resembles a parable. Israel is spoken of as a vineyard at Is 5, 1–7; Mt 21, 33–46 and as a vine at Ps 80, 9–17; Jer 2, 21; Ez 15, 2; 17, 5–10; 19, 10; Hos 10, 1. The identification of the vine as the Son of Man in Ps 80, 16, and Wisdom's description of herself as a vine in Sir 24, 17, are further background for portrayal of Jesus by this figure. There may be secondary eucharistic symbolism here; cf Mk 14, 25, "the fruit of the vine."

15, 2: Takes away . . . prunes: in Greek there is a play on two related verbs.

15, 6: Branches were cut off and dried on the wall of the vineyard for later use as fuel.

15, 13: For one's friends: or: "those whom one loves." In 9–13a, the words for love are related to the Greek agapaō. In 13b-15, the words for love are related to the Greek phileō. For John, the two roots seem synonymous and mean "to love"; cf also 21, 15–17. The word **philos** is used here.

15, 15: Slaves . . . friends: in the Old Testament, Moses (Dt 34, 5), Joshua (Jos 24, 29), and David (Ps 89, 21) were called "servants" or "slaves of Yahweh"; only Abraham (Is 41, 8; 2 Chr 20, 7; cf Jas 2, 23) was called a "friend of God."

e: 15, 26; 16, 7.13-14; Ps 51, 13; Is 63, 10. *f:* 16, 33; Eph 2, 14-18. *g:* 8, 40. *h:* 13, 19; 16, 4. *i:* 6, 38. *j:* Ps 80, 9-17; Is 5, 1-7; Jer 2, 21; Ez 15, 2; 17, 5-10; 19, 10. *k:* 13, 10. *l:* Ez 15, 6-7; 19, 10-14. *m:* 14, 13; Mt 7, 7; Mk 11, 24; 1 Jn 5, 14. *n:* Mt 5, 16. *o:* 17, 23. *p:* 8, 29; 14, 15. *q:* 16, 22; 17, 13. *r:* 13, 34. *s:* Rom 5, 6-8; 1 Jn 3, 16. *t:* Dt 34, 5; Jos 24, 29; 2 Chr 20, 7; Ps 89, 21; Is 41, 8; Rom 8, 15; Gal 4, 7; Jas 2, 23. *u:* 14, 13; Dt 7, 6. *v:* 13, 34; 1 Jn 3, 23; 4, 21.

The World's Hatred. [18w]*"If the world hates you, realize that it hated me first. [19x]If you belonged to the world, the world would love its own; but because you do not belong to the world, and I have chosen you out of the world, the world hates you. [20y]*Remember the word I spoke to you, 'No slave is greater than his master.' If they persecuted me, they will also persecute you. If they kept my word, they will also keep yours. [21z]*And they will do all these things to you on account of my name, because they do not know the one who sent me. [22a]*If I had not come and spoken to them, they would have no sin; but as it is they have no excuse for their sin. [23b]Whoever hates me also hates my Father. [24c]If I had not done works among them that no one else ever did, they would not have sin; but as it is, they have seen and hated both me and my Father. [25d]*But in order that the word written in their law might be fulfilled, 'They hated me without cause.'

[26e]*"When the Advocate comes whom I will send you from the Father, the Spirit of truth that proceeds from the Father, he will testify to me. [27f]And you also testify, because you have been with me from the beginning.

See RG 420-21

CHAPTER 16

[1]"I have told you this so that you may not fall away. [2g]*They will expel you from the synagogues; in fact, the hour is coming when everyone who kills you will think he is offering worship to God. [3h]They will do this because they have not known either the Father or me. [4i]*I have told you this so that when their hour comes you may remember that I told you.

Jesus' Departure; Coming of the Advocate. "I did not tell you this from the beginning, because I was with you. [5j]*But now I am going to the one who sent me, and not one of you asks me, 'Where are you going?' [6]But because I told you this, grief has filled your hearts. [7k]But I tell you the truth, it is better for you that I go. For if I do not go, the Advocate will not come to you. But if I go, I will send him to you. [8]*And when he comes he will convict the world in regard to sin and righteousness and condemnation: [9]sin, because they do not believe in me; [10]righteousness, because I am going to the Father and you will no longer see me; [11m]condemnation, because the ruler of this world has been condemned.

[12]"I have much more to tell you, but you cannot bear it now. [13n]*But when he comes, the Spirit of truth, he will guide you to all truth. He will not speak on his own, but he will speak what he hears, and will declare to you the things that are coming. [14]He will glorify me, because he will take from what is

---

15, 18—16, 4: The hostile reaction of the world. There are synoptic parallels, predicting persecution, especially at Mt 10, 17–25; 24, 9–10.

15, 20: The word I spoke to you: a reference to 13, 16.

15, 21: On account of my name: the idea of persecution for Jesus' name is frequent in the New Testament (Mt 10, 22; 24, 9; Acts 9, 14). For John, association with Jesus' name implies union with Jesus.

15, 22.24: Jesus' words (**spoken**) and deeds (**works**) are the great motives of credibility. **They have seen and hated:** probably means that they have seen his works and still have hated; but the Greek can be read: "have seen both me and my Father and still have hated both me and my Father." **Works . . . that no one else ever did:** so Yahweh in Dt 4, 32–33.

15, 25: In their law: law is here used as a larger concept than the Pentateuch, for the reference is to Ps 35, 19 or 69, 5. See the notes on 10, 34; 12, 34. **Their law** reflects the argument of the church with the synagogue.

15, 26: Whom I will send: in 14, 16.26, the Paraclete is to be sent by the Father, at the request of Jesus. Here the Spirit comes from both Jesus and the Father in mission; there is no reference here to the eternal procession of the Spirit.

16, 2: Hour: of persecution, not Jesus' "hour" (see the note on 2, 4).

16, 4b–33: A duplicate of 14, 1–31 on departure and return.

16, 5: Not one of you asks me: the difficulty of reconciling this with Simon Peter's question in 13, 36 and Thomas' words in 14, 5 strengthens the supposition that the last discourse has been made up of several collections of Johannine material.

16, 8–11: These verses illustrate the forensic character of the Paraclete's role: in the forum of the disciples' conscience he prosecutes the world. He leads believers to see (a) that the basic sin was and is refusal to believe in Jesus; (b) that, although Jesus was found guilty and apparently died in disgrace, in reality righteousness has triumphed, for Jesus has returned to his Father; (c) finally, that it is **the ruler of this world,** Satan, who has been condemned through Jesus' death (12, 32).

16, 13: Declare to you the things that are coming: not a reference to new predictions about the future, but interpretation of what has already occurred or been said.

---

w: 7, 7; 14, 17; Mt 10, 22; 24, 9; Mk 13, 13; Lk 6, 22; 1 Jn 3, 13. x: 17, 14-16; 1 Jn 4, 5. y: 13, 16; Mt 10, 24. z: 8, 19; 16, 3. a: 8, 21.24; 9, 41. b: 5, 23; Lk 10, 16; 1 Jn 2, 23. c: 3, 2; 9, 32; Dt 4, 32-33. d: Ps 35, 19; 69, 4. e: 14, 16.26; Mt 10, 19-20. f: Lk 1, 2; Acts 1, 8. g: 9, 22; 12, 42; Mt 10, 17; Lk 21, 12; Acts 26, 11. h: 15, 21. i: 13, 19; 14, 29. j: 7, 33; 13, 36; 14, 5. k: 7, 39; 14, 16-17.26; 15, 26. l: 8, 21-24; 15, 22. m: 12, 31. n: 14, 17.26; 15, 26; Pss 25, 5; 143, 10; 1 Jn 2, 27; Rv 7, 17.

mine and declare it to you. [15]Everything that the Father has is mine; for this reason I told you that he will take from what is mine and declare it to you.

[16o]"A little while and you will no longer see me, and again a little while later and you will see me." [17]So some of his disciples said to one another, "What does this mean that he is saying to us, 'A little while and you will not see me, and again a little while and you will see me,' and 'Because I am going to the Father'?" [18]So they said, "What is this 'little while' [of which he speaks]? We do not know what he means." [19]Jesus knew that they wanted to ask him, so he said to them, "Are you discussing with one another what I said, 'A little while and you will not see me, and again a little while and you will see me'? [20p]Amen, amen, I say to you, you will weep and mourn, while the world rejoices; you will grieve, but your grief will become joy. [21q]When a woman is in labor, she is in anguish because her hour has arrived; but when she has given birth to a child, she no longer remembers the pain because of her joy that a child has been born into the world. [22r]So you also are now in anguish. But I will see you again, and your hearts will rejoice, and no one will take your joy away from you. [23s]On that day you will not question me about anything. Amen, amen, I say to you, whatever you ask the Father in my name he will give you. [24]Until now you have not asked anything in my name; ask and you will receive, so that your joy may be complete.

[25*]"I have told you this in figures of speech. The hour is coming when I will no longer speak to you in figures but I will tell you clearly about the Father. [26u]On that day you will ask in my name, and I do not tell you that I will ask the Father for you. [27]For the Father himself loves you, because you have loved me and have come to believe that I came from God. [28v]I came from the Father and have come into the world. Now I am leaving the world and going back to the Father." [29]His disciples said, "Now you are talking plainly, and not in any figure of speech. [30*]Now we realize that you know everything and that you do not need to have anyone question you. Because of this we believe that you came from God." [31]Jesus answered them, "Do you believe now? [32w*]Behold, the hour is coming and has arrived when each of you will be scattered to his own home and you will leave me alone. But I am not alone, because the Father is with me. [33x]I have told you this so that you might have peace in me. In the world you will have trouble, but take courage, I have conquered the world."

CHAPTER 17

The Prayer of Jesus. [1y*]When Jesus had said this, he raised his eyes to heaven and said, "Father, the hour has come. Give glory to your son, so that your son may glorify you, [2z*]just as you gave him authority over all people, so that he may give eternal life to all you gave him. [3a*]Now this is eternal life, that they should know you, the only true God,

See RG 420–21

16, 25: See the note on 10, 6. Here, possibly a reference to 15, 1–16 or 16, 21.

16, 30: The reference is seemingly to the fact that Jesus could anticipate their question in v 19. The disciples naively think they have the full understanding that is the climax of "the hour" of Jesus' death, resurrection, and ascension (25), but the only part of the hour that is at hand for them is their share in the passion (32).

16, 32: You will be scattered: cf Mk 14, 27 and Mt 26, 31, where both cite Zec 13, 7 about the sheep being dispersed.

17, 1–26: Climax of the last discourse(s). Since the sixteenth century, this chapter has been called the "high priestly prayer" of Jesus. He speaks as intercessor, with words addressed directly to the Father and not to the disciples, who supposedly only overhear. Yet the prayer is one of petition, for immediate (6–19) and future (20–21) disciples. Many phrases reminiscent of the Lord's Prayer occur. Although still in the world (13), Jesus looks on his earthly ministry as a

thing of the past (4.12). Whereas Jesus has up to this time stated that the disciples could follow him (13, 33.36), now he wishes them to be with him in union with the Father (12–14).

17, 1: The action of looking up to heaven and the address **Father** are typical of Jesus at prayer; cf 11, 41 and Lk 11, 2.

17, 2: Another possible interpretation is to treat the first line of the verse as parenthetical and the second as an appositive to the clause that ends v 1: **so that your son may glorify you (just as . . . all people), so that he may give eternal life. . . .**

17, 3: This verse was clearly added in the editing of the gospel as a reflection on the preceding verse; Jesus nowhere else refers to himself as Jesus Christ.

o: 7, 33; 14, 19.   p: Ps 126, 6.   q: Is 26, 17-18; Jer 31, 13; Mic 4, 9.   r: 14, 19; 15, 11; 20, 20.   s: 14, 13.   t: Mt 13, 34-35.   u: 14, 13.   v: 1, 1.   w: 8, 29; Zec 13, 7; Mt 26, 31; Mk 14, 27.   x: 14, 27.   y: 13, 31.   z: 3, 35; Mt 28, 18.   a: 1, 17; Wis 14, 7; 15, 3; 1 Jn 5, 20.

and the one whom you sent, Jesus Christ. *4*I glorified you on earth by accomplishing the work that you gave me to do. *5b*Now glorify me, Father, with you, with the glory that I had with you before the world began.

6**"I revealed your name to those whom you gave me out of the world. They belonged to you, and you gave them to me, and they have kept your word. *7*Now they know that everything you gave me is from you, *8*because the words you gave to me I have given to them, and they accepted them and truly understood that I came from you, and they have believed that you sent me. *9c*I pray for them. I do not pray for the world but for the ones you have given me, because they are yours, *10d*and everything of mine is yours and everything of yours is mine, and I have been glorified in them. *11*And now I will no longer be in the world, but they are in the world, while I am coming to you. Holy Father, keep them in your name that you have given me, so that they may be one just as we are. *12e*When I was with them I protected them in your name that you gave me, and I guarded them, and none of them was lost except the son of destruction, in order that the scripture might be fulfilled. *13f*But now I am coming to you. I speak this in the world so that they may share my joy completely. *14g*I gave them your word, and the world hated them, because they do not belong to the world any more than I belong to the world. *15h**I do not ask that you take them out of the world but that you keep them from the evil one. *16*They do not belong to the world any more than I belong to the world. *17i*Consecrate them in the truth. Your word is truth. *18j*As you sent me into the world, so I sent them into the world. *19*And I consecrate myself for them, so that they also may be consecrated in truth.

20"I pray not only for them, but also for those who will believe in me through their word, *21k*so that they may all be one, as you, Father, are in me and I in you, that they also may be in us, that the world may believe that you sent me. *22*And I have given them the glory you gave me, so that they may be one, as we are one, *23*I in them and you in me, that they may be brought to perfection as one, that the world may know that you sent me, and that you loved them even as you loved me. *24l**Father, they are your gift to me. I wish that where I am they also may be with me, that they may see my glory that you gave me, because you loved me before the foundation of the world. *25m*Righteous Father, the world also does not know you, but I know you, and they know that you sent me. *26**I made known to them your name and I will make it known, that the love with which you loved me may be in them and I in them."

CHAPTER 18

See RG 421-22

Jesus Arrested. *1n**When he had said this, Jesus went out with his disciples across the Kidron valley to where there was a garden, into which he and his disciples entered. *2*Judas his betrayer also knew the place, because Jesus had often met there with his disciples. *3o**So Judas got a band of soldiers and guards from the chief priests and the Pharisees and went there with lanterns, torches, and weapons. *4*Jesus, knowing everything that was going to happen to him, went out and said to them, "Whom are you looking for?"

17, 6: I revealed your name: perhaps the name **I AM**; cf 8, 24. 28.58; 13, 19.

17, 15: Note the resemblance to the petition of the Lord's Prayer, "deliver us from the evil one." Both probably refer to the devil rather than to abstract evil.

17, 24: Where I am: Jesus prays for the believers ultimately to join him in heaven. Then they will not see his glory as in a mirror but clearly (2 Cor 3, 18; 1 Jn 3, 2).

17, 26: I will make it known: through the Advocate.

18, 1–14: John does not mention the agony in the garden and the kiss of Judas, nor does he identify the place as Gethsemane or the Mount of Olives.

18, 1: Jesus went out: see 14, 31, where it seems he is leaving the supper room. **Kidron valley:** literally, "the winter-flowing Kidron"; this wadi has water only during the winter rains.

18, 3: Band of soldiers: seems to refer to Roman troops, either the full cohort of 600 men (1/10 of a legion), or more likely the maniple of 200 under their tribune (12). In this case, John is hinting at Roman collusion in the action against Jesus before he was brought to Pilate. The lanterns and torches may be symbolic of the hour of darkness.

b: 1, 1.2; 12, 28; Phil 2, 6.9-11. *c:* 17, 20. *d:* 16, 15; 2 Thes 1, 10.12. *e:* 13, 18; 18, 9; Ps 41, 10; Mt 26, 24; Acts 1, 16. *f:* 15, 11. *g:* 15, 19. *h:* Mt 6, 13; 2 Thes 3, 3; 1 Jn 5, 18. *i:* 1 Pt 1, 22 *j:* 20, 21-22. *k:* 10, 30; 14, 10-11.20. *l:* 14, 3; 1 Thes 4, 17. *m:* 1, 10. *n:* 2 Sm 15, 23; Mt 26, 30.36; Mk 14, 26.32; Lk 22, 39. *o:* Mt 26, 47-51; Mk 14, 43-44; Lk 22, 47.

5*They answered him, "Jesus the Nazorean." He said to them, "I AM." Judas his betrayer was also with them. 6When he said to them, "I AM," they turned away and fell to the ground. 7So he again asked them, "Whom are you looking for?" They said, "Jesus the Nazorean." 8Jesus answered, "I told you that I AM. So if you are looking for me, let these men go." 9p*This was to fulfill what he had said, "I have not lost any of those you gave me." 10*Then Simon Peter, who had a sword, drew it, struck the high priest's slave, and cut off his right ear. The slave's name was Malchus. 11q*Jesus said to Peter, "Put your sword into its scabbard. Shall I not drink the cup that the Father gave me?"

12rSo the band of soldiers, the tribune, and the Jewish guards seized Jesus, bound him, 13s*and brought him to Annas first. He was the father-in-law of Caiaphas, who was high priest that year. 14tIt was Caiaphas who had counseled the Jews that it was better that one man should die rather than the people.

Peter's First Denial. 15u*Simon Peter and another disciple followed Jesus. Now the other disciple was known to the high priest, and he entered the courtyard of the high priest with Jesus. 16But Peter stood at the gate outside. So the other disciple, the acquaintance of the high priest, went out and spoke to the gatekeeper and brought Peter in. 17Then the maid who was the gatekeeper said to Peter, "You are not one of this man's disciples, are you?" He said, "I am not."

18Now the slaves and the guards were standing around a charcoal fire that they had made, because it was cold, and were warming themselves. Peter was also standing there keeping warm.

The Inquiry before Annas. 19vThe high priest questioned Jesus about his disciples and about his doctrine. 20w*Jesus answered him, "I have spoken publicly to the world. I have always taught in a synagogue or in the temple area where all the Jews gather, and in secret I have said nothing. 21Why ask me? Ask those who heard me what I said to them. They know what I said." 22xWhen he had said this, one of the temple guards standing there struck Jesus and said, "Is this the way you answer the high priest?" 23Jesus answered him, "If I have spoken wrongly, testify to the wrong; but if I have spoken rightly, why do you strike me?" 24y*Then Annas sent him bound to Caiaphas the high priest.

Peter Denies Jesus Again. 25zNow Simon Peter was standing there keeping warm. And they said to him, "You are not one of his disciples, are you?" He denied it and said, "I am not." 26One of the slaves of the high priest, a relative of the one whose ear Peter had cut off, said, "Didn't I see you in the garden with him?" 27*Again Peter denied it. And immediately the cock crowed.

The Trial before Pilate. 28a*Then they brought Jesus from Caiaphas to the praetorium. It was morning. And they themselves did not enter the praetorium, in order not to

18, 5: Nazorean: the form found in Mt 26, 71 (see the note on Mt 2, 23) is here used, not **Nazarene** of Mark. **I AM:** or "I am he," but probably intended by the evangelist as an expression of divinity (cf their appropriate response in 6); see the note on 8, 24. John sets the confusion of the arresting party against the background of Jesus' divine majesty.

18, 9: The citation may refer to 6, 39; 10, 28; or 17, 12.

18, 10: Only John gives the names of the two antagonists; both John and Luke mention the right ear.

18, 11: The theme of the cup is found in the synoptic account of the agony (Mk 14, 36 and parallels).

18, 13: Annas: only John mentions an inquiry before Annas; cf 16.19–24; see the note on Lk 3, 2. It is unlikely that this nighttime interrogation before Annas is the same as the trial before Caiaphas placed by Matthew and Mark at night and by Luke in the morning.

18, 15–16: Another disciple . . . the other disciple: see the note on 13, 23.

18, 20: I have always taught . . . in the temple area: cf Mk 14, 49 for a similar statement.

18, 24: Caiaphas: see Mt 26, 3.57; Lk 3, 2; and the notes there. John may leave room here for the trial before Caiaphas described in the synoptic gospels.

18, 27: Cockcrow was the third Roman division of the night, lasting from midnight to 3 a.m.

18, 28: Praetorium: see the note on Mt 27, 27. **Morning:** literally, "the early hour," or fourth Roman division of the night, 3 to 6 a.m. **The Passover:** the synoptic gospels give the impression that the Thursday night supper was the Passover meal (Mk 14, 12); for John that meal is still to be eaten Friday night.

p: 6, 39; 10, 28; 17, 12.   q: Mt 20, 22; 26, 39; Mk 10, 38; Lk 22, 42.   r: Mt 26, 57-58; Mk 14, 53-54; Lk 22, 54-55.   s: Lk 3, 2. t: 11, 49-50.   u: Mt 26, 58.69-70; Mk 14, 54.66-68; Lk 22, 54-57.   v: Mt 26, 59-66; Mk 14, 55-64; Lk 22, 66-71.   w: 6, 59; 7, 14.26; Is 48, 16; Mt 26, 55; Mk 14, 23; Lk 19, 47; 22, 53.   x: Acts 23, 2.   y: Mt 26, 57.   z: Mt 26, 71-75; Mk 14, 69-72; Lk 22, 58-62.   a: Mt 27, 1-2.11-25; Mk 15, 1-5; Lk 23, 1-5.

be defiled so that they could eat the Passover. [29] So Pilate came out to them and said, "What charge do you bring [against] this man?" [30] They answered and said to him, "If he were not a criminal, we would not have handed him over to you." [31]* At this, Pilate said to them, "Take him yourselves, and judge him according to your law." The Jews answered him, "We do not have the right to execute anyone," [32b]* in order that the word of Jesus might be fulfilled that he said indicating the kind of death he would die. [33] So Pilate went back into the praetorium and summoned Jesus and said to him, "Are you the King of the Jews?" [34] Jesus answered, "Do you say this on your own or have others told you about me?" [35c] Pilate answered, "I am not a Jew, am I? Your own nation and the chief priests handed you over to me. What have you done?" [36d] Jesus answered, "My kingdom does not belong to this world. If my kingdom did belong to this world, my attendants [would] be fighting to keep me from being handed over to the Jews. But as it is, my kingdom is not here." [37e]* So Pilate said to him, "Then you are a king?" Jesus answered, "You say I am a king. For this I was born and for this I came into the world, to testify to the truth. Everyone who belongs to the truth listens to my voice." [38f] Pilate said to him, "What is truth?"

When he had said this, he again went out to the Jews and said to them, "I find no guilt in him. [39]* But you have a custom that I release one prisoner to you at Passover. Do you want me to release to you the King of the Jews?" [40]* They cried out again, "Not this one but Barabbas!" Now Barabbas was a revolutionary.

CHAPTER 19

See RG 421-22

[1]* Then Pilate took Jesus and had him scourged. [2] And the soldiers wove a crown out of thorns and placed it on his head, and clothed him in a purple cloak, [3] and they came to him and said, "Hail, King of the Jews!" And they struck him repeatedly. [4h] Once more Pilate went out and said to them, "Look, I am bringing him out to you, so that you may know that I find no guilt in him." [5i] So Jesus came out, wearing the crown of thorns and the purple cloak. And he said to them, "Behold, the man!" [6j] When the chief priests and the guards saw him they cried out, "Crucify him, crucify him!" Pilate said to them, "Take him yourselves and crucify him. I find no guilt in him." [7k]* The Jews answered, "We have a law, and according to that law he ought to die, because he made himself the Son of God." [8] Now when Pilate heard this statement, he became even more afraid, [9l] and went back into the praetorium and said to Jesus, "Where are you from?" Jesus did not answer him. [10] So Pilate said to him, "Do you not speak to me? Do you not know that I have power to release you and I have power to crucify you?" [11m] Jesus answered [him], "You would have no power over me if it had not been given to you from above. For this reason the one who handed me over to you has the greater sin." [12n]* Consequently, Pilate tried to release him; but the

---

18, 31: We do not have the right to execute anyone: only John gives this reason for their bringing Jesus to Pilate. Jewish sources are not clear on the competence of the Sanhedrin at this period to sentence and to execute for political crimes.

18, 32: The Jewish punishment for blasphemy was stoning (Lv 24, 16). In coming to the Romans to ensure that Jesus would be crucified, the Jewish authorities fulfilled his prophecy that he would be **exalted** (3, 14; 12, 32–33). There is some historical evidence, however, for Jews crucifying Jews.

18, 37: You say I am a king: see Mt 26, 64 for a similar response to the high priest. It is at best a reluctant affirmative.

18, 39: See the note on Mt 27, 15.

18, 40: Barabbas: see the note on Mt 27, 16–17. **Revolutionary:** a guerrilla warrior fighting for nationalistic aims, though the term can also denote a robber. See the note on Mt 27, 38.

19, 1: Luke places the mockery of Jesus at the midpoint in the trial when Jesus was sent to Herod. Mark and Matthew place the scourging and mockery at the end of the trial after the sentence of death. Scourging was an integral part of the crucifixion penalty.

19, 7: Made himself the Son of God: this question was not raised in John's account of the Jewish interrogations of Jesus as it was in the synoptic account. Nevertheless, see 5, 18; 8, 53; 10, 36.

19, 12: Friend of Caesar: a Roman honorific title bestowed upon high-ranking officials for merit.

b: 3, 14; 8, 28; 12, 32-33.   *c:* 1, 11.   *d:* 1, 10; 8, 23.   *e:* 8, 47; 1 Tm 6, 13.   *f:* Mt 27, 15-26; Mk 15, 6-15; Lk 23, 18-25; Acts 3, 14.   *g:* Mt 27, 27-31; Mk 15, 16-20; Lk 23, 13-25.   *h:* 18, 38. *i:* Is 52, 14.   *j:* 18, 31; 19, 15.   *k:* 10, 33-36; Lv 24, 16.   *l:* 7, 28. *m:* 3, 27; 10, 18; Rom 13, 1.   *n:* Acts 17, 7.

Jews cried out, "If you release him, you are not a Friend of Caesar. Everyone who makes himself a king opposes Caesar."

13*When Pilate heard these words he brought Jesus out and seated him on the judge's bench in the place called Stone Pavement, in Hebrew, Gabbatha. *14**It was preparation day for Passover, and it was about noon. And he said to the Jews, "Behold, your king!" *15*They cried out, "Take him away, take him away! Crucify him!" Pilate said to them, "Shall I crucify your king?" The chief priests answered, "We have no king but Caesar." *16**Then he handed him over to them to be crucified.

The Crucifixion of Jesus. So they took Jesus, *17o**and carrying the cross himself he went out to what is called the Place of the Skull, in Hebrew, Golgotha. *18*There they crucified him, and with him two others, one on either side, with Jesus in the middle. *19**Pilate also had an inscription written and put on the cross. It read, "Jesus the Nazorean, the King of the Jews." *20*Now many of the Jews read this inscription, because the place where Jesus was crucified was near the city; and it was written in Hebrew, Latin, and Greek. *21p*So the chief priests of the Jews said to Pilate, "Do not write 'The King of the Jews,' but that he said, 'I am the King of the Jews.' " *22*Pilate answered, "What I have written, I have written."

23qr*When the soldiers had crucified Jesus, they took his clothes and divided them into four shares, a share for each soldier. They also took his tunic, but the tunic was seamless, woven in one piece from the top down. *24*So they said to one another, "Let's not tear it, but cast lots for it to see whose it will be," in order that the passage of scripture might be fulfilled [that says]:

"They divided my garments among them,
and for my vesture they cast lots."

This is what the soldiers did. *25s**Standing by the cross of Jesus were his mother and his mother's sister, Mary the wife of Clopas, and Mary of Magdala. *26t**When Jesus saw his mother and the disciple there whom he loved, he said to his mother, "Woman,

---

19, 13: Seated him: others translate "(Pilate) sat down." In John's thought, Jesus is the real judge of the world, and John may here be portraying him seated on the judgment bench. **Stone Pavement:** in Greek **lithostrotos;** under the fortress Antonia, one of the conjectured locations of the praetorium, a massive stone pavement has been excavated. **Gabbatha** (Aramaic rather than Hebrew) probably means "ridge, elevation."

19, 14: Noon: Mk 15, 25 has Jesus crucified "at the third hour," which means either 9 a.m. or the period from 9 to 12. Noon, the time when, according to John, Jesus was sentenced to death, was the hour at which the priests began to slaughter Passover lambs in the temple; see Jn 1, 29.

19, 16: He handed him over to them to be crucified: in context this would seem to mean "handed him over to the chief priests." Lk 23, 25 has a similar ambiguity. There is a polemic tendency in the gospels to place the guilt of the crucifixion on the Jewish authorities and to exonerate the Romans from blame. But John later mentions the Roman soldiers (23), and it was to these soldiers that Pilate handed Jesus over.

19, 17: Carrying the cross himself: a different picture from that of the synoptics, especially Lk 23, 26, where Simon of Cyrene is made to carry the cross, walking behind Jesus. In John's theology, Jesus remained in complete control and master of his destiny (cf 10, 18). **Place of the Skull:** the Latin word for skull is **Calvaria;** hence "Calvary." **Golgotha** is actually an Aramaic rather than a Hebrew word.

19, 19: The inscription differs with slightly different words in each of the four gospels. John's form is fullest and gives the equivalent of the Latin **INRI = Iesus Nazarenus Rex Iudaeorum.** Only John mentions its polyglot character (20) and Pilate's role in keeping the title unchanged (21–22).

19, 23–25a: While all four gospels describe the soldiers casting lots to divide Jesus' garments (see the note on Mt 27, 35), only John quotes the underlying passage from Ps 22, 19, and only John sees each line of the poetic parallelism literally carried out in two separate actions (23a; 23b-24).

19, 25: It is not clear whether four women were meant, or three (i.e., **Mary the wife of Cl[e]opas** [cf Lk 24, 18] is in apposition with **his mother's sister**) or two (his mother and his mother's sister, i.e., Mary of Cl[e]opas and Mary of Magdala). Only John mentions the mother of Jesus here. The synoptics have a group of women looking on from a distance at the cross (Mk 15, 40).

19, 26–27: This scene has been interpreted literally, of Jesus' concern for his mother; and symbolically, e.g., in the light of the Cana story in ch 2 (the presence of the mother of Jesus, the address **woman,** and the mention of the **hour**) and of the upper room in ch 13 (the presence of the beloved disciple; the **hour**). Now that the hour has come (28), Mary (a symbol of the church?) is given a role as the mother of Christians (personified by the beloved disciple); or, as a representative of those seeking salvation, she is supported by the disciple who interprets Jesus' revelation; or Jewish and Gentile Christianity (or Israel and the Christian community) are reconciled.

---

o: Mt 27, 32-37; Mk 15, 21-26; Lk 23, 26-35. *p:* 18, 33; Lk 19, 14. *q:* Mt 27, 38-44; Mk 15, 27-32; Lk 23, 36-43. *r:* Ps 22, 19; Mt 27, 35; Mk 15, 24; Lk 23, 34. *s:* Mt 27, 55; Mk 15, 40-41; Lk 8, 2; 23, 49. *t:* 13, 23.

behold, your son." *27*Then he said to the disciple, "Behold, your mother." And from that hour the disciple took her into his home.

*28uv**After this, aware that everything was now finished, in order that the scripture might be fulfilled, Jesus said, "I thirst." *29**There was a vessel filled with common wine. So they put a sponge soaked in wine on a sprig of hyssop and put it up to his mouth. *30w**When Jesus had taken the wine, he said, "It is finished." And bowing his head, he handed over the spirit.

The Blood and Water. *31x*Now since it was preparation day, in order that the bodies might not remain on the cross on the sabbath, for the sabbath day of that week was a solemn one, the Jews asked Pilate that their legs be broken and they be taken down. *32*So the soldiers came and broke the legs of the first and then of the other one who was crucified with Jesus. *33*But when they came to Jesus and saw that he was already dead, they did not break his legs, *34y**but one soldier thrust his lance into his side, and immediately blood and water flowed out. *35z**An eyewitness has testified, and his testimony is true; he knows that he is speaking the truth, so that you also may [come to] believe. *36a*For this happened so that the scripture passage might be fulfilled:

"Not a bone of it will be broken."

*37b*And again another passage says:

"They will look upon him whom they have pierced."

The Burial of Jesus. *38c**After this, Joseph of Arimathea, secretly a disciple of Jesus for fear of the Jews, asked Pilate if he could remove the body of Jesus. And Pilate permitted it. So he came and took his body. *39d*Nicodemus, the one who had first come to him at night, also came bringing a mixture of myrrh and aloes weighing about one hundred pounds. *40*They took the body of Jesus and bound it with burial cloths along with the spices, according to the Jewish burial custom. *41*Now in the place where he had been crucified there was a garden, and in the garden a new tomb, in which no one had yet been buried. *42*So they laid Jesus there because of the Jewish preparation day; for the tomb was close by.

CHAPTER 20

See RG 421–22

The Empty Tomb. *1ef**On the first day of the week, Mary of Magdala came to the tomb early in the morning, while it was still dark, and saw the stone removed from the tomb. *2**So she ran and went to Simon Peter and to the other disciple whom Jesus loved, and told them, "They have taken the Lord

19, 28: The scripture . . . fulfilled: either in the scene of vv 25–27, or in the **I thirst** of v 28. If the latter, Pss 22, 16 and 69, 22 deserve consideration.

19, 29: Wine: John does not mention the drugged wine, a narcotic that Jesus refused as the crucifixion began (Mk 15, 23), but only this final gesture of kindness at the end (Mk 15, 36). **Hyssop,** a small plant, is scarcely suitable for carrying a sponge (Mark mentions a reed) and may be a symbolic reference to the hyssop used to daub the blood of the paschal lamb on the doorpost of the Hebrews (Ex 12, 22).

19, 30: Handed over the spirit: there is a double nuance of dying (giving up the last breath or spirit) and that of passing on the holy Spirit; see 7, 39, which connects the giving of the Spirit with Jesus' glorious return to the Father, and 20, 22, where the author portrays the conferral of the Spirit.

19, 34–35: John probably emphasizes these verses to show the reality of Jesus' death, against the docetic heretics. In the blood and water there may also be a symbolic reference to the Eucharist and baptism.

19, 35: He knows: it is not certain from the Greek that this **he** is the **eyewitness** of the first part of the sentence. **May [come to] believe:** see the note on 20, 31.

19, 38–42: In the first three gospels there is no anointing on Friday. In Mt and Lk, the women come to the tomb on Sunday morning precisely to anoint Jesus.

20, 1–31: The risen Jesus reveals his glory and confers the Spirit. This story fulfills the basic need for testimony to the resurrection. What we have here is not a record but a series of single stories.

20, 1–10: The story of the empty tomb is found in both the Matthean and the Lucan traditions; John's version seems to be a fusion of the two.

20, 1: Still dark: according to Mark the sun had risen, Matthew describes it as "dawning," and Luke refers to early dawn. Mary sees the stone removed, not the empty tomb.

20, 2: Mary runs away, not directed by an angel/young man as in the synoptic accounts. The plural "we" in the second part of her statement might reflect a tradition of more women going to the tomb.

u: Mt 27, 45-56; Mk 15, 33-41; Lk 23, 44-49. *v:* Pss 22, 16; 69, 22. *w:* 4, 34; 10, 18; 17, 4; Lk 23, 46. *x:* Ex 12, 16; Dt 21, 23. *y:* Nm 20, 11; 1 Jn 5, 6. *z:* 7, 37-39; 21, 24. *a:* Ex 12, 46; Nm 9, 12; Ps 34, 21. *b:* Nm 21, 9; Zec 12, 10; Rv 1, 7. *c:* Mt 27, 57-60; Mk 15, 42-46; Lk 34, 50-54. *d:* 3, 1-2; 7, 50; Ps 45, 9. *e:* Mt 28, 1-10; Mk 16, 1-11; Lk 24, 1-12. *f:* 19, 25.

from the tomb, and we don't know where they put him." *3*So Peter and the other disciple went out and came to the tomb. *4*They both ran, but the other disciple ran faster than Peter and arrived at the tomb first; *5*he bent down and saw the burial cloths there, but did not go in. *6g*When Simon Peter arrived after him, he went into the tomb and saw the burial cloths there, *7h*and the cloth that had covered his head, not with the burial cloths but rolled up in a separate place. *8*Then the other disciple also went in, the one who had arrived at the tomb first, and he saw and believed. *9i*For they did not yet understand the scripture that he had to rise from the dead. *10*Then the disciples returned home.

The Appearance to Mary of Magdala. *11j*But Mary stayed outside the tomb weeping. And as she wept, she bent over into the tomb *12*and saw two angels in white sitting there, one at the head and one at the feet where the body of Jesus had been. *13*And they said to her, "Woman, why are you weeping?" She said to them, "They have taken my Lord, and I don't know where they

laid him." *14k*When she had said this, she turned around and saw Jesus there, but did not know it was Jesus. *15l*Jesus said to her, "Woman, why are you weeping? Whom are you looking for?" She thought it was the gardener and said to him, "Sir, if you carried him away, tell me where you laid him, and I will take him." *16*Jesus said to her, "Mary!" She turned and said to him in Hebrew, "Rabbouni," which means Teacher. *17m*Jesus said to her, "Stop holding on to me, for I have not yet ascended to the Father. But go to my brothers and tell them, 'I am going to my Father and your Father, to my God and your God.' " *18*Mary of Magdala went and announced to the disciples, "I have seen the Lord," and what he told her.

Appearance to the Disciples. *19n*On the evening of that first day of the week, when the doors were locked, where the disciples were, for fear of the Jews, Jesus came and stood in their midst and said to them, "Peace be with you." *20o*When he had said this, he showed them his hands and his side. The disciples rejoiced when they saw the Lord. *21p*[Jesus] said to them again, "Peace be

20, 3–10: The basic narrative is told of Peter alone in Lk 24, 12, a verse missing in important manuscripts and which may be borrowed from tradition similar to John. Cf also Lk 24, 24.

20, 6–8: Some special feature about the state of the burial cloths caused the beloved disciple to believe. Perhaps the details emphasized that the grave had not been robbed.

20, 9: Probably a general reference to the scriptures is intended, as in Lk 24, 26 and 1 Cor 15, 4. Some individual Old Testament passages suggested are Ps 16, 10; Hos 6, 2; Jon 2, 1.2.11.

20, 11–18: This appearance to Mary is found only in Jn, but cf Mt 28, 8–10 and Mk 16, 9–11.

20, 16: Rabbouni: Hebrew or Aramaic for "my master."

20, 17: Stop holding on to me: see Mt 28, 9, where the women take hold of his feet. **I have not yet ascended:** for John and many of the New Testament writers, the ascension in the theological sense of going to the Father to be glorified took place with the resurrection as one action. This scene in John dramatizes such an understanding, for by Easter night Jesus is glorified and can give the Spirit. Therefore his ascension takes place immediately after he has talked to Mary. In such a view, the ascension after forty days described in Acts 1, 1–11 would be simply a termination of earthly appearances or, perhaps better, an introduction to the conferral of the Spirit upon the early church, modeled on Elisha's being able to have a (double) share in the spirit of Elijah if he saw him being taken up (same verb as ascending) into heaven (2 Kgs 2, 9–12). **To my Father and your Father, to my God**

and your God: this echoes Ru 1, 16: "Your people shall be my people, and your God my God." The Father of Jesus will now become the Father of the disciples because, once ascended, Jesus can give them the Spirit that comes from the Father and they can be reborn as God's children (3, 5). That is why he calls them **my brothers.**

20, 19–29: The appearances to the disciples, without or with Thomas (cf 11, 16; 14, 5), have rough parallels in the other gospels only for vv 19–23; cf Lk 24, 36–39; Mk 16, 14–18.

20, 19: The disciples: by implication from v 24, this means ten of the Twelve, presumably in Jerusalem. **Peace be with you:** although this could be an ordinary greeting, John intends here to echo 14, 27. The theme of rejoicing in v 20 echoes 16, 22.

20, 20: Hands and . . . side: Lk 24, 39–40 mentions "hands and feet," based on Ps 22, 17.

20, 21: By means of this sending, the Eleven were made apostles, that is, "those sent" (cf 17, 18), though John does not use the noun in reference to them (see the note on 13, 16). A solemn mission or "sending" is also the subject of the post-resurrection appearances to the Eleven in Mt 28, 19; Lk 24, 47; Mk 16, 15.

g: Lk 24, 12. h: 11, 44; 19, 40. i: Acts 2, 26-27; 1 Cor 15, 4. j: Mk 16, 9-11. k: 21, 4; Mk 16, 12; Lk 24, 16; 1 Cor 15, 43-44. l: Mt 28, 9-10. m: Acts 1, 9. n: Mt 28, 16-20; Mk 16, 14-18; Lk 24, 36-44. o: 14, 27. p: 17, 18; Mt 28, 19; Mk 16, 15; Lk 24, 47-48.

with you. As the Father has sent me, so I send you." [22q]*And when he had said this, he breathed on them and said to them, "Receive the holy Spirit. [23r]*Whose sins you forgive are forgiven them, and whose sins you retain are retained."

Thomas. [24]Thomas, called Didymus, one of the Twelve, was not with them when Jesus came. [25s]So the other disciples said to him, "We have seen the Lord." But he said to them, "Unless I see the mark of the nails in his hands and put my finger into the nailmarks and put my hand into his side, I will not believe." [26t]Now a week later his disciples were again inside and Thomas was with them. Jesus came, although the doors were locked, and stood in their midst and said, "Peace be with you." [27]Then he said to Thomas, "Put your finger here and see my hands, and bring your hand and put it into my side, and do not be unbelieving, but believe." [28u]*Thomas answered and said to him, "My Lord and my God!" [29v]*Jesus said to him, "Have you come to believe because you have seen me? Blessed are those who have not seen and have believed."

Conclusion. [30w]*Now Jesus did many other signs in the presence of [his] disciples that are not written in this book. [31x]But these are written that you may [come to] believe that Jesus is the Messiah, the Son of God, and that through this belief you may have life in his name.

IV: Epilogue:
The Resurrection Appearance in Galilee

CHAPTER 21

See RG 422

The Appearance to the Seven Disciples. [1y]*After this, Jesus revealed himself again to his disciples at the Sea of Tiberias. He revealed himself in this way. [2]*Together were Simon Peter, Thomas called Didymus, Nathanael from Cana in Galilee, Zebedee's sons, and two others of his disciples. [3z]*Simon Peter said to them, "I am going fishing." They said to him, "We also will come with you." So they went out and got into the boat, but that night they caught nothing. [4a]When it was already dawn, Jesus was standing on the shore; but the disciples did not realize that it was Jesus. [5b]Jesus said to them, "Children, have you caught anything to eat?" They answered him, "No." [6]So he said to them, "Cast the net over the right side of the boat and you will find something." So they cast it, and were not able to pull it in because of the number of fish. [7]So the disciple whom Jesus loved said to Peter, "It is the Lord." When Simon Peter heard that it was the Lord, he tucked in his garment, for he was lightly clad, and jumped into the sea. [8]The other disciples came in the boat, for they were not far from shore, only about a hundred yards, dragging

20, 22: This action recalls Gn 2, 7, where God breathed on the first man and gave him life; just as Adam's life came from God, so now the disciples' new spiritual life comes from Jesus. Cf also the revivification of the dry bones in Ez 37. This is the author's version of Pentecost. Cf also the note on 19, 30.

20, 23: The Council of Trent defined that this power to forgive sins is exercised in the sacrament of penance. See Mt 16, 19 and 18, 18.

20, 28: My Lord and my God: this forms a literary inclusion with the first verse of the gospel: "and the Word was God."

20, 29: This verse is a beatitude on future generations; faith, not sight, matters.

20, 30–31: These verses are clearly a conclusion to the gospel and express its purpose. While many manuscripts read **come to believe,** possibly implying a missionary purpose for John's gospel, a small number of quite early ones read "continue to believe," suggesting that the audience consists of Christians whose faith is to be deepened by the book; cf 19, 35.

21, 1–23: There are many non-Johannine peculiarities in this chapter, some suggesting Lucan Greek style; yet this passage is closer to John than 7, 53—8, 11. There are many Jo-

hannine features as well. Its closest parallels in the synoptic gospels are found in Lk 5, 1–11 and Mt 14, 28–31. Perhaps the tradition was ultimately derived from John but preserved by some disciple other than the writer of the rest of the gospel. The appearances narrated seem to be independent of those in ch 20. Even if a later addition, the chapter was added before publication of the gospel, for it appears in all manuscripts.

21, 2: Zebedee's sons: the only reference to James and John in this gospel (but see the note on 1, 37). Perhaps the phrase was originally a gloss to identify, among the five, the **two others of his disciples.** The anonymity of the latter phrase is more Johannine (1, 35). The total of seven may suggest the community of the disciples in its fullness.

21, 3–6: This may be a variant of Luke's account of the catch of fish; see the note on Lk 5, 1–11.

q: Gn 2, 7; Ez 37, 9; 1 Cor 15, 45.   *r:* Mt 16, 19; 18, 18.   *s:* 1 Jn 1, 1.   *t:* 21, 14.   *u:* 1, 1.   *v:* 4, 48; Lk 1, 45; 1 Pt 1, 8.   *w:* 21, 25.   *x:* 3, 14.15; 1 Jn 5, 13.   *y:* Mt 26, 32; 28, 7.   *z:* Mt 4, 18; Lk 5, 4-10.   *a:* 20, 14; Mt 28, 17; Lk 24, 16.   *b:* Lk 24, 41.

the net with the fish. [9c]*When they climbed out on shore, they saw a charcoal fire with fish on it and bread. [10]Jesus said to them, "Bring some of the fish you just caught." [11d]*So Simon Peter went over and dragged the net ashore full of one hundred fifty-three large fish. Even though there were so many, the net was not torn. [12]*Jesus said to them, "Come, have breakfast." And none of the disciples dared to ask him, "Who are you?" because they realized it was the Lord. [13e]Jesus came over and took the bread and gave it to them, and in like manner the fish. [14f]*This was now the third time Jesus was revealed to his disciples after being raised from the dead.

Jesus and Peter. [15]*When they had finished breakfast, Jesus said to Simon Peter, "Simon, son of John, do you love me more than these?" He said to him, "Yes, Lord, you know that I love you." He said to him, "Feed my lambs." [16]He then said to him a second time, "Simon, son of John, do you love me?" He said to him, "Yes, Lord, you know that I love you." He said to him, "Tend my sheep." [17g]He said to him the third time, "Simon, son of John, do you love me?" Peter was distressed that he had said to him a third time, "Do you love me?" and he said to him, "Lord, you know everything; you know that I love you." [Jesus] said to him, "Feed my sheep. [18h]*Amen, amen, I say to you, when you were younger, you used to dress yourself and go where you wanted; but when you grow old, you will stretch out your hands, and someone else will dress you and lead you where you do not want to go." [19i]He said this signifying by what kind of death he would glorify God. And when he had said this, he said to him, "Follow me."

The Beloved Disciple. [20j]Peter turned and saw the disciple following whom Jesus loved, the one who had also reclined upon his chest during the supper and had said, "Master, who is the one who will betray you?" [21]When Peter saw him, he said to Jesus, "Lord, what about him?" [22k]*Jesus said to him, "What if I want him to remain until I come? What concern is it of yours? You follow me." [23]*So the word spread among the brothers that that disciple would not die. But Jesus had not told him that he would not die, just "What if I want him to remain until I come? [What concern is it of yours?]"

Conclusion. [24l]*It is this disciple who testifies to these things and has written them, and we know that his testimony is true. [25m]There are also many other things that Jesus did, but if these were to be described individually, I do not think the whole world would contain the books that would be written.

21, 9.12–13: It is strange that Jesus already has fish since none have yet been brought ashore. This meal may have had eucharistic significance for early Christians since v 13 recalls Jn 6, 11, which uses the vocabulary of Jesus' action at the Last Supper; but see also the note on Mt 14, 19.

21, 11: The exact number 153 is probably meant to have a symbolic meaning in relation to the apostles' universal mission; Jerome claims that Greek zoologists catalogued 153 species of fish. Or 153 is the sum of the numbers from 1 to 17. Others invoke Ez 47, 10.

21, 12: None . . . dared to ask him: is Jesus' appearance strange to them? Cf Lk 24, 16; Mk 16, 12; Jn 20, 14. The disciples do, however, recognize Jesus **before** the breaking of the bread (opposed to Lk 24, 35).

21, 14: This verse connects chs 20 and 21; cf 20, 19.26.

21, 15–23: This section constitutes Peter's rehabilitation and emphasizes his role in the church.

21, 15–17: In these three verses there is a remarkable variety of synonyms: two different Greek verbs for **love** (see the note on 15, 13); two verbs for **feed/tend;** two nouns for **sheep;** two verbs for **know.** But apparently there is no difference of meaning. The threefold confession of Peter is meant to counteract his earlier threefold denial (18, 17.25.27). The First Vatican Council cited these verses in defining that Jesus

after his resurrection gave Peter the jurisdiction of supreme shepherd and ruler over the whole flock.

21, 15: More than these: probably "more than these disciples do" rather than "more than you love them" or "more than you love these things [fishing, etc.]."

21, 18: Originally probably a proverb about old age, now used as a figurative reference to the crucifixion of Peter.

21, 22: Until I come: a reference to the parousia.

21, 23: This whole scene takes on more significance if the disciple is already dead. The death of the apostolic generation caused problems in the church because of a belief that Jesus was to have returned first. Loss of faith sometimes resulted; cf 2 Pt 3, 4.

21, 24: Who . . . has written them: this does not necessarily mean he wrote them with his own hand. The same expression is used in 19, 22 of Pilate, who certainly would not have written the inscription himself. **We know:** i.e., the Christian community; cf 1, 14.16.

---

c: Lk 24, 41-43. d: 2 Chr 2, 16. e: Lk 24, 42. f: 20, 19.26. g: 13, 37-38; 18, 15-18.25-27; Mt 26, 69-75; Mk 14, 66-72; Lk 22, 55-62. h: Acts 21, 11.14; 2 Pt 1, 14. i: 13, 36. j: 13, 25. k: Mt 16, 28. l: 19, 35. m: 20, 30.

See RG
423–38

The Acts of the Apostles

The Acts of the Apostles, the second volume of Luke's two-volume work, continues Luke's presentation of biblical history, describing how the salvation promised to Israel in the Old Testament and accomplished by Jesus has now under the guidance of the holy Spirit been extended to the Gentiles. This was accomplished through the divinely chosen representatives (10, 41) whom Jesus prepared during his historical ministry (1, 21–22) and commissioned after his resurrection as witnesses to all that he taught (1, 8; 10, 37–43; Lk 24, 48). Luke's preoccupation with the Christian community as the Spirit-guided bearer of the word of salvation rules out of his book detailed histories of the activity of most of the preachers. Only the main lines of the roles of Peter and Paul serve Luke's interest.

Peter was the leading member of the Twelve (1, 13.15), a miracle worker like Jesus in the gospel (3, 1–10; 5, 1–11.15; 9, 32–35.36–42), the object of divine care (5, 17–21; 12, 6–11), and the spokesman for the Christian community (2, 14–36; 3, 12–26; 4, 8–12; 5, 29–32; 10, 34–43; 15, 7–11), who, according to Luke, was largely responsible for the growth of the community in the early days (2, 4; 4, 4). Paul eventually joined the community at Antioch (11, 25–26), which subsequently commissioned him and Barnabas to undertake the spread of the gospel to Asia Minor. This missionary venture generally failed to win the Jews of the diaspora to the gospel but enjoyed success among the Gentiles (13, 14—14, 27).

Paul's refusal to impose the Mosaic law upon his Gentile converts provoked very strong objection among the Jewish Christians of Jerusalem (15, 1), but both Peter and James supported his position (15, 6–21). Paul's second and third missionary journeys (16, 36—21, 16) resulted in the same pattern of failure among the Jews generally but of some success among the Gentiles. Paul, like Peter, is presented as a miracle worker (14, 8–18; 19, 12; 20, 7–12; 28, 7–10) and the object of divine care (16, 25–31).

In Acts, Luke has provided a broad survey of the church's development from the resurrection of Jesus to Paul's first Roman imprisonment, the point at which the book ends. In telling this story, Luke describes the emergence of Christianity from its origins in Judaism to its position as a religion of worldwide status and appeal. Originally a Jewish Christian community in Jerusalem, the church was placed in circumstances impelling it to include within its membership people of other cultures: the Samaritans (8, 4–25), at first an occasional Gentile (8, 26–30; 10, 1–48), and finally the Gentiles on principle (11, 20–21). Fear on the part of the Jewish people that Christianity, particularly as preached to the Gentiles, threatened their own cultural heritage caused them to be suspicious of Paul's gospel (13, 42–45; 15, 1–5; 28, 17–24). The inability of Christian missionaries to allay this apprehension inevitably created a situation in which the gospel was preached more and more to the Gentiles. Toward the end of Paul's career, the Christian communities, with the exception of those in Palestine itself (9, 31), were mainly of Gentile membership. In tracing the emergence of Christianity from Judaism, Luke is insistent upon the prominence of Israel in the divine plan of salvation (see the note on 1, 26; see also 2, 5–6; 3, 13–15; 10, 36; 13, 16–41; 24, 14–15) and that the extension of salvation to the Gentiles has been a part of the divine plan from the beginning (see 15, 13–18; 26, 22–23).

In the development of the church from a Jewish Christian origin in Jerusalem, with its roots in Jewish religious tradition, to a series of Christian communities among the Gentiles of the Roman empire, Luke perceives the action of God in history laying open the heart of all humanity to the divine message of salvation. His approach to the history of the church is motivated by his theological interests. His history of the apostolic church is the story of a Spirit-guided community and a Spirit-guided spread of the Word of God (1, 8). The travels of Peter and Paul are in reality the travels of the Word of God as it spreads from Jerusalem, the city of destiny for Jesus, to Rome, the capital of the civilized world of Luke's day. Nonetheless, the historical data he utilizes are of value for the understanding of the church's early life and development and as general background to the Pauline epistles. In the interpretation of Acts, care must be exercised to determine Luke's theological aims and interests and to evaluate his historical data without either exaggerating their literal accuracy or underestimating their factual worth.

Finally, an apologetic concern is evident throughout Acts. By stressing the continuity between Judaism and Christianity (13, 16–41; 23, 6–9; 24, 10–21; 26, 2–23), Luke argues that Christianity is deserving of the same toleration accorded Judaism by Rome. Part of Paul's defense before Roman authorities is to show that Christianity is not a disturber of the peace of the Roman Empire (24, 5.12–13; 25, 7–8). Moreover, when he stands before Roman authorities, he is declared innocent of any crime against the empire (18, 13–15; 23, 29; 25, 25–27; 26, 31–32). Luke tells his story with the hope that Christianity will be treated as fairly.

Concerning the date of Acts, see the Introduction to the Gospel according to Luke.

The principal divisions of the Acts of the Apostles are the following:

I: The Preparation for the Christian Mission (1, 1—2, 13)

II: The Mission in Jerusalem (2, 14—8, 3)

III: The Mission in Judea and Samaria (8, 4—9, 43)

IV: The Inauguration of the Gentile Mission (10, 1—15, 35)

V: The Mission of Paul to the Ends of the Earth (15, 36—28, 31)

I: The Preparation For The Christian Mission

CHAPTER 1

See RG 426

The Promise of the Spirit. ¹ᵃ*In the first book, Theophilus, I dealt with all that Jesus did and taught ²ᵇuntil the day he was taken up, after giving instructions through the holy Spirit to the apostles whom he had chosen. ³ᶜ*He presented himself alive to them by many proofs after he had suffered, appearing to them during forty days and speaking about the kingdom of God. ⁴ᵈ*While meeting with them, he enjoined them not to depart from Jerusalem, but to wait for "the promise of the Father about which you have heard me speak; ⁵ᵉfor John baptized with water, but in a few days you will be baptized with the holy Spirit."

The Ascension of Jesus. ⁶*When they had gathered together they asked him, "Lord, are you at this time going to restore the kingdom to Israel?" ⁷ᶠ*He answered them, "It is not for you to know the times or seasons that the Father has established by his own authority. ⁸ᵍ*But you will receive power when the holy Spirit comes upon you, and you will be my witnesses in Jerusalem, throughout Judea and Samaria, and to the ends of the earth."

1, 1–26: This introductory material (1–2) connects Acts with the Gospel of Luke, shows that the apostles were instructed by the risen Jesus (3–5), points out that the parousia or second coming in glory of Jesus will occur as certainly as his ascension occurred (6–11), and lists the members of the Twelve, stressing their role as a body of divinely mandated witnesses to his life, teaching, and resurrection (12–26).

1, 3: Appearing to them during forty days: Luke considered especially sacred the interval in which the appearances and instructions of the risen Jesus occurred and expressed it therefore in terms of the sacred number forty (cf Dt 8, 2). In his gospel, however, Luke connects the ascension of Jesus with the resurrection by describing the ascension on Easter Sunday evening (Lk 24, 50–53). What should probably be understood as one event (resurrection, glorification, ascension, sending of the Spirit—the paschal mystery) has been historicized by Luke when he writes of a visible ascension of Jesus after forty days and the descent of the Spirit at Pentecost. For Luke, the ascension marks the end of the appearances of Jesus except for the extraordinary appearance to Paul. With regard to Luke's understanding of salvation history, the ascension also marks the end of the time of Jesus (Lk 24, 50–53) and signals the beginning of the time of the church.

1, 4: The promise of the Father: the holy Spirit, as is clear from the next verse. This gift of the Spirit was first promised in Jesus' final instructions to his chosen witnesses in Luke's gospel (Lk 24, 49) and formed part of the continuing instructions of the risen Jesus on the kingdom of God, of which Luke speaks in v 3.

1, 6: The question of the disciples implies that in believing Jesus to be the Christ (see the note on Lk 2, 11) they had expected him to be a political leader who would restore self-rule to Israel during his historical ministry. When this had not taken place, they ask if it is to take place at this time, the period of the church.

1, 7: This verse echoes the tradition that the precise time of the parousia is not revealed to human beings; cf Mk 13, 32; 1 Thes 5, 1–3.

1, 8: Just as Jerusalem was the city of destiny in the Gospel of Luke (the place where salvation was accomplished), so here at the beginning of Acts, Jerusalem occupies a central position. It is the starting point for the mission of the Christian disciples to "the ends of the earth," the place where the apostles were situated and the doctrinal focal point in the early days of the community (15, 2.6). **The ends of the earth:** for Luke, this means Rome.

a: Lk 1, 1-4. *b:* Mt 28, 19-20; Lk 24, 44-49; Jn 20, 22; 1 Tm 3, 16. *c:* 10, 41; 13, 31. *d:* Jn 14, 16.17.26. *e:* 11, 16; Mt 3, 11; Mk 1, 8; Lk 3, 16; Jn 1, 26; Eph 1, 13. *f:* Mt 24, 36; 1 Thes 5, 1-2. *g:* 2, 1-13; 10, 39; Is 43, 10; Mt 28, 19; Lk 24, 47-48.

9h When he had said this, as they were looking on, he was lifted up, and a cloud took him from their sight. 10i While they were looking intently at the sky as he was going, suddenly two men dressed in white garments stood beside them. 11j They said, "Men of Galilee, why are you standing there looking at the sky? This Jesus who has been taken up from you into heaven will return in the same way as you have seen him going into heaven." 12k Then they returned to Jerusalem from the mount called Olivet, which is near Jerusalem, a sabbath day's journey away.

The First Community in Jerusalem. 13 When they entered the city they went to the upper room where they were staying, Peter and John and James and Andrew, Philip and Thomas, Bartholomew and Matthew, James son of Alphaeus, Simon the Zealot, and Judas son of James. 14l All these devoted themselves with one accord to prayer, together with some women, and Mary the mother of Jesus, and his brothers.

The Choice of Judas's Successor. 15 During those days Peter stood up in the midst of the brothers (there was a group of about one hundred and twenty persons in the one place). He said, 16m "My brothers, the scripture had to be fulfilled which the holy Spirit spoke beforehand through the mouth of David, concerning Judas, who was the guide for those who arrested Jesus. 17 He was numbered among us and was allotted a share in this ministry. 18n* He bought a parcel of land with the wages of his iniquity, and falling headlong, he burst open in the middle, and all his insides spilled out. 19 This became known to everyone who lived in Jerusalem, so that the parcel of land was called in their language 'Akeldama,' that is, Field of Blood. 20o For it is written in the Book of Psalms:

'Let his encampment become desolate,
    and may no one dwell in it.'

And:

'May another take his office.'

21 Therefore, it is necessary that one of the men who accompanied us the whole time the Lord Jesus came and went among us, 22p beginning from the baptism of John until the day on which he was taken up from us, become with us a witness to his resurrection." 23 So they proposed two, Joseph called Barsabbas, who was also known as Justus, and Matthias. 24 Then they prayed, "You, Lord, who know the hearts of all, show which one of these two you have chosen 25 to take the place in this apostolic ministry from which Judas turned away to go to his own place." 26q* Then they gave lots to them, and the lot fell upon Matthias, and he was counted with the eleven apostles.

CHAPTER 2

See RG 426-27

The Coming of the Spirit. 1r* When the time for Pentecost was fulfilled, they were all in one place together. 2s* And suddenly there came from the sky a noise like a strong driving wind, and it filled the entire house in which they were. 3t* Then there appeared to them tongues as of fire, which parted and

---

1, 18: Luke records a popular tradition about the death of Judas that differs from the one in Mt 27, 5, according to which Judas hanged himself. Here, although the text is not certain, Judas is depicted as purchasing a piece of property with the betrayal money and being killed on it in a fall.

1, 26: The need to replace Judas was probably dictated by the symbolism of the number twelve, recalling the twelve tribes of Israel. This symbolism also indicates that for Luke (see Lk 22, 30) the Christian church is a reconstituted Israel.

2, 1–41: Luke's pentecostal narrative consists of an introduction (1–13), a speech ascribed to Peter declaring the resurrection of Jesus and its messianic significance (14–36), and a favorable response from the audience (37–41). It is likely that the narrative telescopes events that took place over a period of time and on a less dramatic scale. The Twelve were not originally in a position to proclaim publicly the messianic office of Jesus without incurring immediate reprisal from those religious authorities in Jerusalem who had brought about Jesus' death precisely to stem the rising tide in his favor.

2, 2: There came from the sky a noise like a strong driving wind: wind and spirit are associated in Jn 3, 8. The sound of a great rush of wind would herald a new action of God in the history of salvation.

2, 3: Tongues as of fire: see Ex 19, 18 where fire symbolizes the presence of God to initiate the covenant on Sinai. Here the holy Spirit acts upon the apostles, preparing them to proclaim the new covenant with its unique gift of the Spirit (38).

h: 2 Kgs 2, 11; Mk 16, 19; Lk 24, 51. i: Jn 20, 17. j: Lk 24, 51; Eph 4, 8-10; 1 Pt 3, 22; Rv 1, 7. k: Lk 6, 14-16. l: Lk 23, 49. m: Pss 41, 10; Lk 22, 47. n: Mt 27, 3-10. o: Pss 69, 26; 109, 8; Jn 17, 12. p: 1, 8-9; 10, 39. q: Prv 16, 33. r: Lv 23, 15-21; Dt 16, 9-11. s: Jn 3, 8. t: Lk 3, 16.

The Native Lands of Pentecost Pilgrims

came to rest on each one of them. [4u]*And they were all filled with the holy Spirit and began to speak in different tongues, as the Spirit enabled them to proclaim.

[5]Now there were devout Jews from every nation under heaven staying in Jerusalem. [6]At this sound, they gathered in a large crowd, but they were confused because each one heard them speaking in his own language. [7v]They were astounded, and in amazement they asked, "Are not all these people who are speaking Galileans? [8]Then how does each of us hear them in his own native language? [9]We are Parthians, Medes, and Elamites, inhabitants of Mesopotamia, Judea and Cappadocia, Pontus and Asia, [10]Phrygia and Pamphylia, Egypt and the districts of Libya near Cyrene, as well as travelers from Rome, [11w]both Jews and converts to Judaism, Cretans and Arabs, yet we hear them speaking in our own tongues of the mighty acts of God." [12]They were all astounded and bewildered, and said to one another, "What does this mean?" [13x]But others said, scoffing, "They have had too much new wine."

II: The Mission in Jerusalem

Peter's Speech at Pentecost. [14]*Then Peter stood up with the Eleven, raised his voice, and proclaimed to them, "You who are Jews, indeed all of you staying in Jerusalem. Let this be known to you, and listen to my words. [15]These people are not drunk, as you suppose, for it is only nine o'clock in the morning. [16]No, this is what was spoken through the prophet Joel:

[17y]'It will come to pass in the last days,'
    God says,
  'that I will pour out a portion of my spirit
    upon all flesh.
  Your sons and your daughters shall
    prophesy,

your young men shall see visions,
    your old men shall dream dreams.
[18] Indeed, upon my servants and my
    handmaids
  I will pour out a portion of my spirit in
    those days,
    and they shall prophesy.
[19] And I will work wonders in the heavens
    above
  and signs on the earth below:
    blood, fire, and a cloud of smoke.
[20] The sun shall be turned to darkness,
    and the moon to blood,
    before the coming of the great and
    splendid day of the Lord,
[21 z]and it shall be that everyone shall be
    saved who calls on the name of
    the Lord.'

[22a]You who are Israelites, hear these words. Jesus the Nazorean was a man commended to you by God with mighty deeds, wonders, and signs, which God worked through him in your midst, as you yourselves know. [23b]This man, delivered up by the set plan and foreknowledge of God, you killed, using lawless men to crucify him. [24c]But God raised him up, releasing him from the throes of death, because it was impossible for him to be held by it. [25d]For David says of him:

'I saw the Lord ever before me,
    with him at my right hand I shall not
    be disturbed.
[26] Therefore my heart has been glad and my
    tongue has exulted;
    my flesh, too, will dwell in hope,
[27 e]because you will not abandon my soul
    to the nether world,
    nor will you suffer your holy one to
    see corruption.
[28] You have made known to me the paths of
    life;
  you will fill me with joy in your
    presence.'

2, 4: **To speak in different tongues:** ecstatic prayer in praise of God, interpreted in vv 6 and 11 as speaking in foreign languages, symbolizing the worldwide mission of the church.

2, 14–36: The first of six discourses in Acts (along with 3, 12–26; 4, 8–12; 5, 29–32; 10, 34–43; 13, 16–41) dealing with the resurrection of Jesus and its messianic import. Five of these are attributed to Peter, the final one to Paul. Modern

scholars term these discourses in Acts the "kerygma," the Greek word for proclamation (cf 1 Cor 15, 11).

---

u: 1, 5; 4, 31; 8, 15.17; 10, 44; 11, 15-16; 15, 8; 19, 6; Ps 104, 30; Jn 20, 33. v: 1, 11. w: 10, 46. x: 1 Cor 14, 23. y: Is 2, 2; 44, 3; Jl 3, 1-5. z: Rom 10, 13. a: 10, 38; Lk 24, 19. b: 1 Thes 2, 15. c: 13, 34. d: Ps 16, 8-11. e: 13, 35.

²⁹My brothers, one can confidently say to you about the patriarch David that he died and was buried, and his tomb is in our midst to this day. ³⁰ᶠBut since he was a prophet and knew that God had sworn an oath to him that he would set one of his descendants upon his throne, ³¹ᵍhe foresaw and spoke of the resurrection of the Messiah, that neither was he abandoned to the netherworld nor did his flesh see corruption. ³²God raised this Jesus; of this we are all witnesses. ³³ʰ*Exalted at the right hand of God, he received the promise of the holy Spirit from the Father and poured it forth, as you [both] see and hear. ³⁴ⁱFor David did not go up into heaven, but he himself said:

'The Lord said to my Lord,
"Sit at my right hand
³⁵   until I make your enemies your
        footstool." '

³⁶ʲTherefore let the whole house of Israel know for certain that God has made him both Lord and Messiah, this Jesus whom you crucified."

³⁷ᵏNow when they heard this, they were cut to the heart, and they asked Peter and the other apostles, "What are we to do, my brothers?" ³⁸*Peter [said] to them, "Repent and be baptized, every one of you, in the name of Jesus Christ for the forgiveness of your sins;

and you will receive the gift of the holy Spirit. ³⁹ᵐFor the promise is made to you and to your children and to all those far off, whomever the Lord our God will call." ⁴⁰ⁿHe testified with many other arguments, and was exhorting them, "Save yourselves from this corrupt generation." ⁴¹ᵒThose who accepted his message were baptized, and about three thousand persons were added that day.

Communal Life. ⁴²ᵖ۹*They devoted themselves to the teaching of the apostles and to the communal life, to the breaking of the bread and to the prayers. ⁴³ʳAwe came upon everyone, and many wonders and signs were done through the apostles. ⁴⁴ˢAll who believed were together and had all things in common; ⁴⁵they would sell their property and possessions and divide them among all according to each one's need. ⁴⁶Every day they devoted themselves to meeting together in the temple area and to breaking bread in their homes. They ate their meals with exultation and sincerity of heart, ⁴⁷praising God and enjoying favor with all the people. And every day the Lord added to their number those who were being saved.

CHAPTER 3

See RG 427

Cure of a Crippled Beggar. ¹*Now Peter and John were going up to the temple

---

2, 33: **At the right hand of God:** or "by the right hand of God."

2, 38: **Repent and be baptized:** repentance is a positive concept, a change of mind and heart toward God reflected in the actual goodness of one's life. It is in accord with the apostolic teaching derived from Jesus (42) and ultimately recorded in the four gospels. Luke presents baptism in Acts as the expected response to the apostolic preaching about Jesus and associates it with the conferring of the Spirit (1, 5; 10, 44–48; 11, 16).

2, 42–47: The first of three summary passages (along with 4, 32–37 and 5, 12–16) that outline, somewhat idyllically, the chief characteristics of the Jerusalem community: adherence to the teachings of the Twelve and the centering of its religious life in the eucharistic liturgy (42); a system of distribution of goods that led wealthier Christians to sell their possessions when the needs of the community's poor required it (44 and the note on 4, 32–37); and continued attendance at the temple, since in this initial stage there was little or no thought of any dividing line between Christianity and Judaism (46).

3, 1—4, 31: This section presents a series of related events: the dramatic cure of a lame beggar (3, 1–10) produces a large audience for the kerygmatic discourse of Peter (3, 11–26). The Sadducees, taking exception to the doctrine of

resurrection, have Peter, John, and apparently the beggar as well, arrested (4, 1–4) and brought to trial before the Sanhedrin. The issue concerns the authority by which Peter and John publicly teach religious doctrine in the temple (4, 5–7). Peter replies with a brief summary of the kerygma, implying that his authority is prophetic (4, 8–12). The court warns the apostles to abandon their practice of invoking prophetic authority in the name of Jesus (4, 13–18). When Peter and John reply that the prophetic role cannot be abandoned to satisfy human objections, the court nevertheless releases them, afraid to do otherwise since the beggar, lame from birth and over forty years old, is a well-known figure in Jerusalem and the facts of his cure are common property (4, 19–22). The narrative concludes with a prayer of the Christian community imploring divine aid against threats of persecution (4, 23–31).

3, 1: **For the three o'clock hour of prayer:** literally, "at the ninth hour of prayer." With the day beginning at 6 a.m., the ninth hour would be 3 p.m.

f: 2 Sm 7, 12; Ps 132, 11.   g: 13, 35; Ps 16, 10.   h: 1, 4-5.   i: Ps 110, 1.   j: 9, 22; Rom 10, 9; Phil 2, 11.   k: Lk 3, 10.   l: 3, 19; 16, 31; Lk 3, 3.   m: Is 57, 19; Jl 3, 5; Eph 2, 17.   n: Dt 32, 5; Ps 78, 8; Lk 9, 41; Phil 2, 15.   o: 2, 47; 4, 4; 5, 14; 6, 7; 11, 21.24; 21, 20.   p: 4, 32-35.   q: 1, 14; 6, 4.   r: 5, 12-16.   s: 4, 32.34-35.

area for the three o'clock hour of prayer. [2t]And a man crippled from birth was carried and placed at the gate of the temple called "the Beautiful Gate" every day to beg for alms from the people who entered the temple. [3]When he saw Peter and John about to go into the temple, he asked for alms. [4]But Peter looked intently at him, as did John, and said, "Look at us." [5]He paid attention to them, expecting to receive something from them. [6u]*Peter said, "I have neither silver nor gold, but what I do have I give you: in the name of Jesus Christ the Nazorean, [rise and] walk." [7]Then Peter took him by the right hand and raised him up, and immediately his feet and ankles grew strong. [8v]He leaped up, stood, and walked around, and went into the temple with them, walking and jumping and praising God. [9]When all the people saw him walking and praising God, [10]they recognized him as the one who used to sit begging at the Beautiful Gate of the temple, and they were filled with amazement and astonishment at what had happened to him.

Peter's Speech. [11w]As he clung to Peter and John, all the people hurried in amazement toward them in the portico called "Solomon's Portico." [12x]When Peter saw

this, he addressed the people, "You Israelites, why are you amazed at this, and why do you look so intently at us as if we had made him walk by our own power or piety? [13y]*The God of Abraham, [the God] of Isaac, and [the God] of Jacob, the God of our ancestors, has glorified his servant Jesus whom you handed over and denied in Pilate's presence, when he had decided to release him. [14z]*You denied the Holy and Righteous One and asked that a murderer be released to you. [15a]*The author of life you put to death, but God raised him from the dead; of this we are witnesses. [16]And by faith in his name, this man, whom you see and know, his name has made strong, and the faith that comes through it has given him this perfect health, in the presence of all of you. [17b]*Now I know, brothers, that you acted out of ignorance, just as your leaders did; [18c]*but God has thus brought to fulfillment what he had announced beforehand through the mouth of all the prophets, that his Messiah would suffer. [19d]Repent, therefore, and be converted, that your sins may be wiped away, [20]*and that the Lord may grant you times of refreshment and send you the Messiah already appointed for you, Jesus, [21]*whom heaven must receive until the times of universal

---

3, 6–10: The miracle has a dramatic cast; it symbolizes the saving power of Christ and leads the beggar to enter the temple, where he hears Peter's proclamation of salvation through Jesus.

3, 13: Has glorified: through the resurrection and ascension of Jesus, God reversed the judgment against him on the occasion of his trial. **Servant:** the Greek word can also be rendered as "son" or even "child" here and also in 3, 26; 4, 25 (applied to David); 4, 27; and 4, 30. Scholars are of the opinion, however, that the original concept reflected in the words identified Jesus with the suffering Servant of the Lord of Is 52, 13—53, 12.

3, 14: The Holy and Righteous One: so designating Jesus emphasizes his special relationship to the Father (see Lk 1, 35; 4, 34) and emphasizes his sinlessness and religious dignity that are placed in sharp contrast with the guilt of those who rejected him in favor of Barabbas.

3, 15: The author of life: other possible translations of the Greek title are "leader of life" or "pioneer of life." The title clearly points to Jesus as the source and originator of salvation.

3, 17: Ignorance: a Lucan motif, explaining away the actions not only of the people but also of their leaders in crucifying Jesus. On this basis the presbyters in Acts could continue to appeal to the Jews in Jerusalem to believe in Jesus, even while affirming their involvement in his death because they were unaware of his messianic dignity. See also 13, 27 and Lk 23, 34.

3, 18: Through the mouth of all the prophets: Christian

prophetic insight into the Old Testament saw the crucifixion and death of Jesus as the main import of messianic prophecy. The Jews themselves did not anticipate a suffering Messiah; they usually understood the Servant Song in Is 52, 13—53, 12 to signify their own suffering as a people. In his typical fashion (cf Lk 18, 31; 24, 25.27.44), Luke does not specify the particular Old Testament prophecies that were fulfilled by Jesus. See also the note on Lk 24, 26.

3, 20: The Lord . . . and send you the Messiah already appointed for you, Jesus: an allusion to the parousia or second coming of Christ, judged to be imminent in the apostolic age. This reference to its nearness is the only explicit one in Acts. Some scholars believe that this verse preserves a very early christology, in which the title "Messiah" (Greek "Christ") is applied to him as of his parousia, his second coming (contrast 2, 36). This view of a future messiahship of Jesus is not found elsewhere in the New Testament.

3, 21: The times of universal restoration: like "the times of refreshment" (20), an apocalyptic designation of the messianic age, fitting in with the christology of v 20 that associates the messiahship of Jesus with his future coming.

t: 14, 8-10. *u:* 4, 10. *v:* Is 35, 6; Lk 7, 22. *w:* 5, 12; Jn 10, 23. *x:* 14, 15. *y:* Ex 3, 6.15; Is 52, 13; Lk 23, 14-25. *z:* Mt 27, 20-21; Mk 15, 11; Lk 23, 18; Jn 18, 40. *a:* 4, 10; 5, 31 / 1, 8; 2, 32. *b:* 13, 27; Lk 23, 34; 1 Cor 2, 8; 1 Tm 1, 13. *c:* Lk 18, 31. *d:* 2, 38.

restoration of which God spoke through the mouth of his holy prophets from of old. [22e]*For Moses said:

'A prophet like me will the Lord, your God, raise up for you
from among your own kinsmen;
to him you shall listen in all that he may say to you.
[23f]Everyone who does not listen to that prophet
will be cut off from the people.'

[24]Moreover, all the prophets who spoke, from Samuel and those afterwards, also announced these days. [25g]You are the children of the prophets and of the covenant that God made with your ancestors when he said to Abraham, 'In your offspring all the families of the earth shall be blessed.' [26h]For you first, God raised up his servant and sent him to bless you by turning each of you from your evil ways."

See RG 427–28

CHAPTER 4

[1]*While they were still speaking to the people, the priests, the captain of the temple guard, and the Sadducees confronted them, [2i]disturbed that they were teaching the people and proclaiming in Jesus the resurrection of the dead. [3]They laid hands on them and put them in custody until the next day, since it was already evening. [4]But many of those who heard the word came to believe and [the] number of men grew to [about] five thousand.

Before the Sanhedrin. [5]On the next day, their leaders, elders, and scribes were assembled in Jerusalem, [6]with Annas the high priest, Caiaphas, John, Alexander, and all who were of the high-priestly class. [7]They

brought them into their presence and questioned them, "By what power or by what name have you done this?" [8j]Then Peter, filled with the holy Spirit, answered them, "Leaders of the people and elders: [9]If we are being examined today about a good deed done to a cripple, namely, by what means he was saved, [10]then all of you and all the people of Israel should know that it was in the name of Jesus Christ the Nazorean whom you crucified, whom God raised from the dead; in his name this man stands before you healed. [11k]*He is 'the stone rejected by you, the builders, which has become the cornerstone.' [12l]*There is no salvation through anyone else, nor is there any other name under heaven given to the human race by which we are to be saved."

[13]Observing the boldness of Peter and John and perceiving them to be uneducated, ordinary men, they were amazed, and they recognized them as the companions of Jesus. [14]Then when they saw the man who had been cured standing there with them, they could say nothing in reply. [15]So they ordered them to leave the Sanhedrin, and conferred with one another, saying, [16]"What are we to do with these men? Everyone living in Jerusalem knows that a remarkable sign was done through them, and we cannot deny it. [17m]But so that it may not be spread any further among the people, let us give them a stern warning never again to speak to anyone in this name."

[18]So they called them back and ordered them not to speak or teach at all in the name of Jesus. [19n]Peter and John, however, said to them in reply, "Whether it is right in the sight of God for us to obey you rather than

---

3, 22: A loose citation of Dt 18, 15, which teaches that the Israelites are to learn the will of Yahweh from no one but their prophets. At the time of Jesus, some Jews expected a unique prophet to come in fulfillment of this text. Early Christianity applied this tradition and text to Jesus and used them especially in defense of the divergence of Christian teaching from traditional Judaism.
4, 1: **The priests, the captain of the temple guard, and the Sadducees:** the priests performed the temple liturgy; the temple guard was composed of Levites, whose captain ranked next after the high priest. The Sadducees, a party within Judaism at this time, rejected those doctrines, including bodily resurrection, which they believed alien to the ancient Mosaic religion. The Sadducees were drawn from

priestly families and from the lay aristocracy.
4, 11: Early Christianity applied this citation from Ps 118, 22 to Jesus; cf Mk 12, 10; 1 Pt 2, 7.
4, 12: In the Roman world of Luke's day, salvation was often attributed to the emperor who was hailed as "savior" and "god." Luke, in the words of Peter, denies that deliverance comes through anyone other than Jesus.

e: 7, 37; Dt 18, 15.18. *f:* Lv 23, 29; Dt 18, 19. *g:* Gn 12, 3; 18, 18; 22, 18; Sir 44, 19-21; Gal 3, 8-9. *h:* 13, 46; Rom 1, 16. *i:* 23, 6-8; 24, 21. *j:* Mt 10, 20. *k:* Ps 118, 22; Is 28, 16; Mt 21, 42; Mk 12, 10; Lk 20, 17; Rom 9, 33; 1 Pt 2, 7. *l:* Mt 1, 21; 1 Cor 3, 11. *m:* 5, 28. *n:* 5, 29-32.

God, you be the judges. *20*It is impossible for us not to speak about what we have seen and heard." *21*After threatening them further, they released them, finding no way to punish them, on account of the people who were all praising God for what had happened. *22*For the man on whom this sign of healing had been done was over forty years old.

Prayer of the Community. *23*After their release they went back to their own people and reported what the chief priests and elders had told them. *24*And when they heard it, they raised their voices to God with one accord and said, "Sovereign Lord, maker of heaven and earth and the sea and all that is in them, *25o*you said by the holy Spirit through the mouth of our father David, your servant:

'Why did the Gentiles rage
   and the peoples entertain folly?
26 The kings of the earth took their stand
   and the princes gathered together
      against the Lord and against his
      anointed.'

27p*Indeed they gathered in this city against your holy servant Jesus whom you anointed, Herod and Pontius Pilate, together with the Gentiles and the peoples of Israel, *28*to do what your hand and [your] will had long ago planned to take place. *29*And now, Lord, take note of their threats, and enable your servants to speak your word with all boldness, *30*as you stretch forth [your] hand to heal, and signs and wonders are done through the name of your holy servant Jesus." *31q**As they prayed, the place where they were gathered shook, and they were all filled with the holy Spirit and continued to speak the word of God with boldness.

Life in the Christian Community. *32**The community of believers was of one heart and mind, and no one claimed that any of his possessions was his own, but they had everything in common. *33*With great power the apostles bore witness to the resurrection of the Lord Jesus, and great favor was accorded them all. *34r*There was no needy person among them, for those who owned property or houses would sell them, bring the proceeds of the sale, *35*and put them at the feet of the apostles, and they were distributed to each according to need.

*36s*Thus Joseph, also named by the apostles Barnabas (which is translated "son of encouragement"), a Levite, a Cypriot by birth, *37*sold a piece of property that he owned, then brought the money and put it at the feet of the apostles.

CHAPTER 5

See RG 427–28

Ananias and Sapphira. *1**A man named Ananias, however, with his wife Sapphira, sold a piece of property. *2*He retained for himself, with his wife's knowledge, some of the purchase price, took the remainder, and put it at the feet of the apostles. *3t*But Peter said, "Ananias, why has Satan filled your heart so that you lied to the holy Spirit and retained part of the price of the land? *4*While it remained unsold, did it not remain yours? And when it was sold, was it not still under your control? Why did you contrive this deed? You have lied not to human beings, but to God." *5*When Ananias heard these words, he fell down and breathed his last,

---

4, 27: Herod: Herod Antipas, ruler of Galilee and Perea from 4 B.C. to A.D. 39, who executed John the Baptist and before whom Jesus was arraigned; cf Lk 23, 6–12.

4, 31: The place . . . shook: the earthquake is used as a sign of the divine presence in Ex 19, 18; Is 6, 4. Here the shaking of the building symbolizes God's favorable response to the prayer. Luke may have had as an additional reason for using the symbol in this sense the fact that it was familiar in the Hellenistic world. Ovid and Virgil also employ it.

4, 32–37: This is the second summary characterizing the Jerusalem community (see the note on 2, 42–47). It emphasizes the system of the distribution of goods and introduces Barnabas, who appears later in Acts as the friend and companion of Paul, and who, as noted here (37), endeared himself

to the community by a donation of money through the sale of property. This sharing of material possessions continues a practice that Luke describes during the historical ministry of Jesus (Lk 8, 3) and is in accord with the sayings of Jesus in Luke's gospel (Lk 12, 33; 16, 9.11.13).

5, 1–11: The sin of Ananias and Sapphira did not consist in the withholding of part of the money but in their deception of the community. Their deaths are ascribed to a lie to the holy Spirit (3.9), i.e., they accepted the honor accorded them by the community for their generosity, but in reality they were not deserving of it.

o: Ps 2, 1-2. *p:* Lk 23, 12-13. *q:* 2, 4. *r:* 2, 44-45. *s:* 9, 27; 11, 22.30; 12, 25; 13, 15; 1 Cor 9, 6; Gal 2, 1.9.13; Col 4, 10. *t:* Lk 22, 3; Jn 13, 2.

and great fear came upon all who heard of it. [6]The young men came and wrapped him up, then carried him out and buried him.

[7]After an interval of about three hours, his wife came in, unaware of what had happened. [8]Peter said to her, "Tell me, did you sell the land for this amount?" She answered, "Yes, for that amount." [9]Then Peter said to her, "Why did you agree to test the Spirit of the Lord? Listen, the footsteps of those who have buried your husband are at the door, and they will carry you out." [10]At once, she fell down at his feet and breathed her last. When the young men entered they found her dead, so they carried her out and buried her beside her husband. [11u]And great fear came upon the whole church and upon all who heard of these things.

Signs and Wonders of the Apostles. [12v*]Many signs and wonders were done among the people at the hands of the apostles. They were all together in Solomon's portico. [13]None of the others dared to join them, but the people esteemed them. [14]Yet more than ever, believers in the Lord, great numbers of men and women, were added to them. [15w]Thus they even carried the sick out into the streets and laid them on cots and mats so that when Peter came by, at least his shadow might fall on one or another of them. [16]A large number of people from the towns in the vicinity of Jerusalem also gathered, bringing the sick and those disturbed by unclean spirits, and they were all cured.

Trial before the Sanhedrin. [17x*]Then the high priest rose up and all his companions, that is, the party of the Sadducees, and, filled with jealousy, [18]laid hands upon the apostles and put them in the public jail. [19y]But during the night, the angel of the Lord opened the doors of the prison, led them out, and said, [20]"Go and take your place in the temple area, and tell the people everything about this life." [21]When they heard this, they went to the temple early in the morning and taught. When the high priest and his companions arrived, they convened the Sanhedrin, the full senate of the Israelites, and sent to the jail to have them brought in. [22]But the court officers who went did not find them in the prison, so they came back and reported, [23]"We found the jail securely locked and the guards stationed outside the doors, but when we opened them, we found no one inside." [24]When they heard this report, the captain of the temple guard and the chief priests were at a loss about them, as to what this would come to. [25]Then someone came in and reported to them, "The men whom you put in prison are in the temple area and are teaching the people." [26z]Then the captain and the court officers went and brought them in, but without force, because they were afraid of being stoned by the people.

[27]When they had brought them in and made them stand before the Sanhedrin, the high priest questioned them, [28a]"We gave you strict orders [did we not?] to stop teaching in that name. Yet you have filled Jerusalem with your teaching and want to bring this man's blood upon us." [29b]But Peter and the apostles said in reply, "We must obey God rather than men. [30c*]The God of our ancestors raised Jesus, though you had him killed by hanging him on a tree. [31d*]God exalted him at his right hand as leader and savior to grant Israel repentance and for-

5, 12–16: This, the third summary portraying the Jerusalem community, underscores the Twelve as its bulwark, especially because of their charismatic power to heal the sick; cf 2, 42–47; 4, 32–37.

5, 17–42: A second action against the community is taken by the Sanhedrin in the arrest and trial of the Twelve; cf 4, 1–3. The motive is the jealousy of the religious authorities over the popularity of the apostles (17) who are now charged with the defiance of the Sanhedrin's previous order to them to abandon their prophetic role (28; cf 4, 18). In this crisis the apostles are favored by a miraculous release from prison (18–24). (For similar incidents involving Peter and Paul, see 12, 6–11; 16, 25–29.) The real significance of such an event, however, would be manifest only to people of faith, not to unbelievers; since the Sanhedrin already judged the Twelve to be inauthentic prophets, it could disregard reports of their miracles. When the Twelve immediately resumed public teaching, the Sanhedrin determined to invoke upon them the penalty of death (33) prescribed in Dt 13, 6–10. Gamaliel's advice against this course finally prevailed, but it did not save the Twelve from the punishment of scourging (40) in a last endeavor to shake their conviction of their prophetic mission.

5, 30: Hanging him on a tree: that is, crucifying him (cf also Gal 3, 13).

5, 31: At his right hand: see the note on 2, 33.

u: 2, 43; 5, 5; 19, 17.   v: 2, 43; 6, 8; 14, 3; 15, 12.   w: 19, 11-12; Mk 6, 56.   x: 4, 1-3.6.   y: 12, 7-10; 16, 25-26.   z: Lk 20, 19.   a: Mt 27, 25.   b: 4, 19.   c: 2, 23-24.   d: 2, 38.

giveness of sins. *32e*We are witnesses of these things, as is the holy Spirit that God has given to those who obey him."

*33*When they heard this, they became infuriated and wanted to put them to death. *34f*But a Pharisee in the Sanhedrin named Gamaliel, a teacher of the law, respected by all the people, stood up, ordered the men to be put outside for a short time, *35*and said to them, "Fellow Israelites, be careful what you are about to do to these men. *36**Some time ago, Theudas appeared, claiming to be someone important, and about four hundred men joined him, but he was killed, and all those who were loyal to him were disbanded and came to nothing. *37*After him came Judas the Galilean at the time of the census. He also drew people after him, but he too perished and all who were loyal to him were scattered. *38*So now I tell you, have nothing to do with these men, and let them go. For if this endeavor or this activity is of human origin, it will destroy itself. *39*But if it comes from God, you will not be able to destroy them; you may even find yourselves fighting against God." They were persuaded by him. *40g*After recalling the apostles, they had them flogged, ordered them to stop speaking in the name of Jesus, and dismissed them. *41h*So they left the presence of the Sanhedrin, rejoicing that they had been found worthy to suffer dishonor for the sake of the name. *42i*And all day long, both at the temple and in their homes, they did not stop teaching and proclaiming the Messiah, Jesus.

CHAPTER 6

See RG 428

The Need for Assistants. 1j*At that time, as the number of disciples continued to grow, the Hellenists complained against the Hebrews because their widows were being neglected in the daily distribution. *2**So the Twelve called together the community of the disciples and said, "It is not right for us to neglect the word of God to serve at table. *3*Brothers, select from among you seven reputable men, filled with the Spirit and wisdom, whom we shall appoint to this task, *4*whereas we shall devote ourselves to prayer and to the ministry of the word." *5*The proposal was acceptable to the whole community, so they chose Stephen, a man filled with faith and the holy Spirit, also Philip, Prochorus, Nicanor, Timon, Parmenas, and Nicholas of Antioch, a convert to Judaism. *6k**They presented these men to the apostles who prayed and laid hands on them. *7l*The word of God continued to spread, and the number of the disciples in Jerusalem increased greatly; even a large group of priests were becoming obedient to the faith.

Accusation against Stephen. 8*Now Ste-

5, 34: Gamaliel: in 22, 3, Paul identifies himself as a disciple of this Rabbi Gamaliel I who flourished in Jerusalem between A.D. 25 and 50.

5, 36–37: Gamaliel offers examples of unsuccessful contemporary movements to argue that if God is not the origin of this movement preached by the apostles it will perish by itself. The movement initiated by Theudas actually occurred when C. Cuspius Fadus was governor, A.D. 44–46. Luke's placing of Judas the Galilean after Theudas and at the time of the census (see the note on Lk 2, 1–2) is an indication of the vagueness of his knowledge of these events.

6, 1–7: The Hellenists . . . the Hebrews: the Hellenists were not necessarily Jews from the diaspora, but were more probably Palestinian Jews who spoke only Greek. The Hebrews were Palestinian Jews who spoke Hebrew or Aramaic and who may also have spoken Greek. Both groups belong to the Jerusalem Jewish Christian community. The conflict between them leads to a restructuring of the community that will better serve the community's needs. The real purpose of the whole episode, however, is to introduce Stephen as a prominent figure in the community whose long speech and martyrdom will be recounted in ch 7.

6, 2–4: The essential function of the Twelve is the "service

of the word," including development of the kerygma by formulation of the teachings of Jesus.

6, 2: To serve at table: some commentators think that it is not the serving of food that is described here but rather the keeping of the accounts that recorded the distribution of food to the needy members of the community. In any case, after Stephen and the others are chosen, they are never presented carrying out the task for which they were appointed (2–3). Rather, two of their number, Stephen and Philip, are presented as preachers of the Christian message. They, the Hellenist counterpart of the Twelve, are active in the ministry of the word.

6, 6: They . . . laid hands on them: the customary Jewish way of designating persons for a task and invoking upon them the divine blessing and power to perform it.

6, 8—8, 1: The summary (6, 7) on the progress of the Jerusalem community, illustrated by the conversion of the priests, is followed by a lengthy narrative regarding Stephen. Stephen's defense is not a response to the charges made

---

e: Lk 24, 48; Jn 15, 26. *f:* 22, 3. *g:* Mt 10, 17; Acts 4, 17-18. *h:* Mt 5, 10-11; 1 Pt 4, 13. *i:* 2, 46; 5, 20-21.25; 8, 35; 17, 3; 18, 5.28; 19, 4-5. *j:* 2, 45; 4, 34-35. *k:* 1, 24; 13, 3; 14, 23. *l:* 9, 31; 12, 24; 16, 5; 19, 20; 28, 30-31.

phen, filled with grace and power, was working great wonders and signs among the people. [9]Certain members of the so-called Synagogue of Freedmen, Cyrenians, and Alexandrians, and people from Cilicia and Asia, came forward and debated with Stephen, [10m]but they could not withstand the wisdom and the spirit with which he spoke. [11n]Then they instigated some men to say, "We have heard him speaking blasphemous words against Moses and God." [12]They stirred up the people, the elders, and the scribes, accosted him, seized him, and brought him before the Sanhedrin. [13*]They presented false witnesses who testified, "This man never stops saying things against [this] holy place and the law. [14o]For we have heard him claim that this Jesus the Nazorean will destroy this place and change the customs that Moses handed down to us." [15]All those who sat in the Sanhedrin looked intently at him and saw that his face was like the face of an angel.

CHAPTER 7

See RG
428–29

Stephen's Discourses. [1]Then the high priest asked, "Is this so?" [2p*]And he replied, "My brothers and fathers, listen. The God of glory appeared to our father Abraham while he was in Mesopotamia, before he had settled in Haran, [3q]and said to him, 'Go forth from your land and [from] your kinsfolk to the land that I will show you.' [4r]So he went forth from the land of the Chaldeans and set-

tled in Haran. And from there, after his father died, he made him migrate to this land where you now dwell. [5s]Yet he gave him no inheritance in it, not even a foot's length, but he did promise to give it to him and his descendants as a possession, even though he was childless. [6t]And God spoke thus, 'His descendants shall be aliens in a land not their own, where they shall be enslaved and oppressed for four hundred years; [7u]but I will bring judgment on the nation they serve,' God said, 'and after that they will come out and worship me in this place.' [8v]Then he gave him the covenant of circumcision, and so he became the father of Isaac, and circumcised him on the eighth day, as Isaac did Jacob, and Jacob the twelve patriarchs.

[9w]"And the patriarchs, jealous of Joseph, sold him into slavery in Egypt; but God was with him [10x]and rescued him from all his afflictions. He granted him favor and wisdom before Pharaoh, the king of Egypt, who put him in charge of Egypt and [of] his entire household. [11y]Then a famine and great affliction struck all Egypt and Canaan, and our ancestors could find no food; [12z]but when Jacob heard that there was grain in Egypt, he sent our ancestors there a first time. [13a]The second time, Joseph made himself known to his brothers, and Joseph's family became known to Pharaoh. [14b]Then Joseph sent for his father Jacob, inviting him and his whole clan, seventy-five persons; [15c]and Jacob

against him but takes the form of a discourse that reviews the fortunes of God's word to Israel and leads to a prophetic declaration: a plea for the hearing of that word as announced by Christ and now possessed by the Christian community.

The charges that Stephen depreciated the importance of the temple and the Mosaic law and elevated Jesus to a stature above Moses (6, 13–14) were in fact true. Before the Sanhedrin, no defense against them was possible. With Stephen, who thus perceived the fuller implications of the teachings of Jesus, the differences between Judaism and Christianity began to appear. Luke's account of Stephen's martyrdom and its aftermath shows how the major impetus behind the Christian movement passed from Jerusalem, where the temple and law prevailed, to Antioch in Syria, where these influences were less pressing.

6, 13: False witnesses: here, and in his account of Stephen's execution (7, 54–60), Luke parallels the martyrdom of Stephen with the death of Jesus.

7, 2–53: Stephen's speech represents Luke's description of Christianity's break from its Jewish matrix. Two motifs become prominent in the speech: (1) Israel's reaction to God's chosen

leaders in the past reveals that the people have consistently rejected them; and (2) Israel has misunderstood God's choice of the Jerusalem temple as the place where he is to be worshiped.

7, 2: God . . . appeared to our father Abraham . . . in Mesopotamia: the first of a number of minor discrepancies between the data of the Old Testament and the data of Stephen's discourse. According to Gn 12, 1, God first spoke to Abraham in Haran. The main discrepancies are these: in v 16 it is said that Jacob was buried in Shechem, whereas Gn 50, 13 says he was buried at Hebron; in the same verse it is said that the tomb was purchased by Abraham, but in Gn 33, 19 and Jos 24, 32 the purchase is attributed to Jacob himself.

m: Lk 21, 15.   n: Mt 26, 59-61; Mk 14, 55-58; Acts 21, 21.   o: Mt 26, 59-61; 27, 40; Jn 2, 19.   p: Gn 11, 31; 12, 1; Ps 29, 3.   q: Gn 12, 1.   r: Gn 12, 5; 15, 7.   s: Gn 12, 7; 13, 15; 15, 2; 16, 1; Dt 2, 5.   t: Gn 15, 13-14.   u: Ex 3, 12.   v: Gn 17, 10-14; 21, 2-4.   w: Gn 37, 11.28; 39, 2.3.21.23.   x: Gn 41, 37-43; Ps 105, 21; Wis 10, 13-14.   y: Gn 41, 54-57; 42, 5.   z: Gn 42, 1-2.   a: Gn 45, 3-4.16.   b: Gn 45, 9-11.18-19; 46, 27; Ex 1, 5 LXX; Dt 10, 22.   c: Gn 46, 5-6; 49, 33.

went down to Egypt. And he and our ancestors died [16d]and were brought back to Shechem and placed in the tomb that Abraham had purchased for a sum of money from the sons of Hamor at Shechem.

[17e]"When the time drew near for the fulfillment of the promise that God pledged to Abraham, the people had increased and become very numerous in Egypt, [18f]until another king who knew nothing of Joseph came to power [in Egypt]. [19]He dealt shrewdly with our people and oppressed [our] ancestors by forcing them to expose their infants, that they might not survive. [20g]At this time Moses was born, and he was extremely beautiful. For three months he was nursed in his father's house; [21h]but when he was exposed, Pharaoh's daughter adopted him and brought him up as her own son. [22]Moses was educated [in] all the wisdom of the Egyptians and was powerful in his words and deeds.

[23i]"When he was forty years old, he decided to visit his kinsfolk, the Israelites. [24]When he saw one of them treated unjustly, he defended and avenged the oppressed man by striking down the Egyptian. [25]He assumed [his] kinsfolk would understand that God was offering them deliverance through him, but they did not understand. [26j]The next day he appeared to them as they were fighting and tried to reconcile them peacefully, saying, 'Men, you are brothers. Why are you harming one another?' [27]Then the one who was harming his neighbor pushed him aside, saying, 'Who appointed you ruler and judge over us? [28]Are you thinking of killing me as you killed the Egyptian yesterday?' [29k]Moses fled when he heard this and settled as an alien in the land of Midian, where he became the father of two sons.

[30l]"Forty years later, an angel appeared to him in the desert near Mount Sinai in the flame of a burning bush. [31]When Moses saw it, he was amazed at the sight, and as he drew near to look at it, the voice of the Lord came, [32]'I am the God of your fathers, the God of Abraham, of Isaac, and of Jacob.' Then Moses, trembling, did not dare to look at it. [33]But the Lord said to him, 'Remove the sandals from your feet, for the place where you stand is holy ground. [34]I have witnessed the affliction of my people in Egypt and have heard their groaning, and I have come down to rescue them. Come now, I will send you to Egypt.' [35m]This Moses, whom they had rejected with the words, 'Who appointed you ruler and judge?' God sent as [both] ruler and deliverer, through the angel who appeared to him in the bush. [36n]This man led them out, performing wonders and signs in the land of Egypt, at the Red Sea, and in the desert for forty years. [37o]It was this Moses who said to the Israelites, 'God will raise up for you, from among your own kinsfolk, a prophet like me.' [38p]It was he who, in the assembly in the desert, was with the angel who spoke to him on Mount Sinai and with our ancestors, and he received living utterances to hand on to us.

[39q]"Our ancestors were unwilling to obey him; instead, they pushed him aside and in their hearts turned back to Egypt, [40r]saying to Aaron, 'Make us gods who will be our leaders. As for that Moses who led us out of the land of Egypt, we do not know what has happened to him.' [41s]So they made a calf in those days, offered sacrifice to the idol, and reveled in the works of their hands. [42tu]Then God turned and handed them over to worship the host of heaven, as it is written in the book of the prophets:

'Did you bring me sacrifices and
  offerings
    for forty years in the desert, O house
      of Israel?
[43] No, you took up the tent of Moloch
  and the star of [your] god Rephan,
    the images that you made to
      worship.
So I shall take you into exile beyond
  Babylon.'

[44v]Our ancestors had the tent of testimony in the desert just as the One who spoke to Moses directed him to make it according to the

d: Gn 23, 3-20; 33, 19; 49, 29-30; 50, 13; Jos 24, 32.   e: Ex 1, 7.   f: Ex 1, 8.   g: Ex 2, 2; Heb 11, 23.   h: Ex 2, 3-10.   i: Ex 2, 11-12.   j: Ex 2, 13-14.   k: Ex 2, 15.21-22; 18, 3-4.   l: Ex 3, 2-3.   m: Ex 2, 14.   n: Ex 7, 3.10; 14, 21; Nm 14, 33.   o: Dt 18, 15; Acts 3, 22.   p: Ex 19, 3; 20, 1-17; Dt 5, 4-22; 6, 4-25.   q: Nm 14, 3.   r: Ex 32, 1.23.   s: Ex 32, 4-6.   t: Am 5, 25-27.   u: Jer 7, 18; 8, 2; 19, 13.   v: Ex 25, 9.40.

pattern he had seen. [45w]Our ancestors who inherited it brought it with Joshua when they dispossessed the nations that God drove out from before our ancestors, up to the time of David, [46x]who found favor in the sight of God and asked that he might find a dwelling place for the house of Jacob. [47y]But Solomon built a house for him. [48z]Yet the Most High does not dwell in houses made by human hands. As the prophet says:

[49] [a]'The heavens are my throne,
the earth is my footstool.
What kind of house can you build for me? says the Lord,
or what is to be my resting place?
[50] Did not my hand make all these things?'

Conclusion. [51]"You stiff-necked people, uncircumcised in heart and ears, you always oppose the holy Spirit; you are just like your ancestors. [52b]Which of the prophets did your ancestors not persecute? They put to death those who foretold the coming of the righteous one, whose betrayers and murderers you have now become. [53c]You received the law as transmitted by angels, but you did not observe it."

Stephen's Martyrdom. [54]When they heard this, they were infuriated, and they ground their teeth at him. [55d*]But he, filled with the holy Spirit, looked up intently to heaven and saw the glory of God and Jesus standing at the right hand of God, [56]and he said, "Behold, I see the heavens opened and the Son of Man standing at the right hand of God." [57*]But they cried out in a loud voice, covered their ears, and rushed upon him together. [58e]They threw him out of the city, and began to stone him. The witnesses laid down their cloaks at the feet of a young man named Saul. [59f*]As they were stoning Stephen, he called out, "Lord Jesus, receive my spirit." [60g]Then he fell to his knees and cried out in a loud voice, "Lord, do not hold this sin against them"; and when he said this, he fell asleep.

CHAPTER 8

See RG 428–30

[1h*]Now Saul was consenting to his execution.

Persecution of the Church. On that day, there broke out a severe persecution of the church in Jerusalem, and all were scattered throughout the countryside of Judea and Samaria, except the apostles. [2]Devout men buried Stephen and made a loud lament over him. [3i*]Saul, meanwhile, was trying to destroy the church; entering house after house and dragging out men and women, he handed them over for imprisonment.

III: The Mission in Judea and Samaria

Philip in Samaria. [4j]Now those who had been scattered went about preaching the word. [5k]Thus Philip went down to [the] city

---

7, 55: He . . . saw . . . Jesus standing at the right hand of God: Stephen affirms to the Sanhedrin that the prophecy Jesus made before them has been fulfilled (Mk 14, 62).

7, 57: Covered their ears: Stephen's declaration, like that of Jesus, is a scandal to the court, which regards it as blasphemy.

7, 59: Compare Lk 23, [34].46.

8, 1–40: Some idea of the severity of the persecution that now breaks out against the Jerusalem community can be gathered from 22, 4 and 26, 9–11. Luke, however, concentrates on the fortunes of the word of God among people, indicating how the dispersal of the Jewish community resulted in the conversion of the Samaritans (4–17.25). His narrative is further expanded to include the account of Philip's acceptance of an Ethiopian (26–39).

8, 1: All were scattered . . . except the apostles: this observation leads some modern scholars to conclude that the persecution was limited to the Hellenist Christians and that the Hebrew Christians were not molested, perhaps because their attitude toward the law and temple was still more in line with that of their fellow Jews (see the charge leveled against the Hellenist Stephen in 6, 13–14). Whatever the facts, it appears that the Twelve took no public stand regarding Stephen's position, choosing, instead, to await the development of events.

8, 3: Saul . . . was trying to destroy the church: like Stephen, Saul was able to perceive that the Christian movement contained the seeds of doctrinal divergence from Judaism. A pupil of Gamaliel, according to 22, 3, and totally dedicated to the law as the way of salvation (Gal 1, 13–14), Saul accepted the task of crushing the Christian movement, at least insofar as it detracted from the importance of the temple and the law. His vehement opposition to Christianity reveals how difficult it was for a Jew of his time to accept a messianism that differed so greatly from the general expectation.

---

w: Jos 3, 14-17; 18, 1; 2 Sm 7, 5-7. x: 2 Sm 7, 1-2; 1 Kgs 8, 17; Ps 132, 1-5. y: 1 Kgs 6, 1; 1 Chr 17, 12. z: 17, 24. a: Is 66, 1-2. b: 2 Chr 36, 16; Mt 23, 31.34. c: Gal 3, 19; Heb 2, 2. d: Mt 26, 64; Mk 14, 62; Lk 22, 69; Acts 2, 34. e: 22, 20. f: Ps 31, 6; Lk 23, 46. g: Mt 27, 46.50; Mk 15, 34; Lk 23, 46. h: 22, 20. i: 9, 1.13; 22, 4; 26, 9-11; 1 Cor 5, 9; Gal 1, 13. j: 11, 19. k: 6, 5; 21, 8-9.

Sites of Early Christian Missionary Activities

of Samaria and proclaimed the Messiah to them. 6With one accord, the crowds paid attention to what was said by Philip when they heard it and saw the signs he was doing. 7lFor unclean spirits, crying out in a loud voice, came out of many possessed people, and many paralyzed and crippled people were cured. 8There was great joy in that city.

Simon the Magician. 9*A man named Simon used to practice magic in the city and astounded the people of Samaria, claiming to be someone great. 10All of them, from the least to the greatest, paid attention to him, saying, "This man is the 'Power of God' that is called 'Great.' " 11They paid attention to him because he had astounded them by his magic for a long time, 12mbut once they began to believe Philip as he preached the good news about the kingdom of God and the name of Jesus Christ, men and women alike were baptized. 13Even Simon himself believed and, after being baptized, became devoted to Philip; and when he saw the signs and mighty deeds that were occurring, he was astounded.

14Now when the apostles in Jerusalem heard that Samaria had accepted the word of God, they sent them Peter and John, 15who went down and prayed for them, that they might receive the holy Spirit, 16*for it had not yet fallen upon any of them; they had only been baptized in the name of the Lord Jesus. 17nThen they laid hands on them and they received the holy Spirit.

18*When Simon saw that the Spirit was conferred by the laying on of the apostles' hands, he offered them money 19and said, "Give me this power too, so that anyone upon whom I lay my hands may receive the holy Spirit." 20But Peter said to him, "May your money perish with you, because you thought that you could buy the gift of God with money. 21You have no share or lot in this matter, for your heart is not upright before God. 22Repent of this wickedness of yours and pray to the Lord that, if possible, your intention may be forgiven. 23For I see that you are filled with bitter gall and are in the bonds of iniquity." 24Simon said in reply, "Pray for me to the Lord, that nothing of what you have said may come upon me." 25So when they had testified and proclaimed the word of the Lord, they returned to Jerusalem and preached the good news to many Samaritan villages.

Philip and the Ethiopian. 26*Then the angel of the Lord spoke to Philip, "Get up and head south on the road that goes down from Jerusalem to Gaza, the desert route." 27o*So he got up and set out. Now there was an Ethiopian eunuch, a court official of the Candace, that is, the queen of the Ethiopians, in charge of her entire treasury, who had come to Jerusalem to worship, 28and was returning home. Seated in his chariot, he was reading the prophet Isaiah. 29The Spirit said to Philip, "Go and join up with that chariot." 30*Philip ran up and heard him reading Isaiah the prophet and said, "Do you understand what you are reading?" 31pHe replied, "How can I, unless someone instructs me?" So he invited

8, 9–13.18–24: Sorcerers were well known in the ancient world. Probably the incident involving Simon and his altercation with Peter is introduced to show that the miraculous charisms possessed by members of the Christian community (6–7) were not to be confused with the magic of sorcerers.

8, 16: Here and in 10, 44–48 and 19, 1–6, Luke distinguishes between baptism in the name of the Lord Jesus and the reception of the Spirit. In each case, the Spirit is conferred through members of the Twelve (Peter and John) or their representative (Paul). This may be Luke's way of describing the role of the church in the bestowal of the Spirit. Elsewhere in Acts, baptism and the Spirit are more closely related (1, 5; 11, 16).

8, 18–20: Simon attempts to buy the gift of God (20) with money. Peter's cursing of Simon's attempt so to use his money expresses a typically Lucan attitude toward material wealth (cf Lk 6, 24; 12, 16–21; 16, 13).

8, 26–40: In the account of the conversion of the Ethiopian eunuch, Luke adduces additional evidence to show that the spread of Christianity outside the confines of Judaism it-

self was in accord with the plan of God. He does not make clear whether the Ethiopian was originally a convert to Judaism or, as is more probable, a "God-fearer" (10, 1), i.e., one who accepted Jewish monotheism and ethic and attended the synagogue but did not consider himself bound by other regulations such as circumcision and observance of the dietary laws. The story of his conversion to Christianity is given a strong supernatural cast by the introduction of an angel (26), instruction from the holy Spirit (29), and the strange removal of Philip from the scene (39).

8, 27: The Candace: Candace is not a proper name here but the title of a Nubian queen.

8, 30–34: Philip is brought alongside the carriage at the very moment when the Ethiopian is pondering the meaning of Is 53, 7–8, a passage that Christianity, from its earliest origins, has applied to Jesus; cf the note on 3, 13.

l: Mk 16, 17. m: 1, 3; 19, 8; 28, 23.31. n: 2, 4; 4, 31; 10, 44-47; 15, 8-9; 19, 2.6. o: Is 56, 3-5. p: Jn 16, 13.

Philip to get in and sit with him. ³²𝑞This was the scripture passage he was reading:

"Like a sheep he was led to the slaughter,
and as a lamb before its shearer is
    silent,
so he opened not his mouth.
³³ In [his] humiliation justice was denied
    him.
Who will tell of his posterity?
For his life is taken from the earth."

³⁴Then the eunuch said to Philip in reply, "I beg you, about whom is the prophet saying this? About himself, or about someone else?" ³⁵Then Philip opened his mouth and, beginning with this scripture passage, he proclaimed Jesus to him. ³⁶𝑟As they traveled along the road they came to some water, and the eunuch said, "Look, there is water. What is to prevent my being baptized?" [³⁷]* ³⁸Then he ordered the chariot to stop, and Philip and the eunuch both went down into the water, and he baptized him. ³⁹𝑠When they came out of the water, the Spirit of the Lord snatched Philip away, and the eunuch saw him no more, but continued on his way rejoicing. ⁴⁰𝑡Philip came to Azotus, and went about proclaiming the good news to all the towns until he reached Caesarea.

CHAPTER 9

See RG
430–31 **Saul's Conversion.** ¹𝑢𝑣*Now Saul, still breathing murderous threats against the disciples of the Lord, went to the high priest ²*and asked him for letters to the syna-gogues in Damascus, that, if he should find any men or women who belonged to the Way, he might bring them back to Jerusalem in chains. ³𝑤On his journey, as he was nearing Damascus, a light from the sky suddenly flashed around him. ⁴𝑥He fell to the ground and heard a voice saying to him, "Saul, Saul, why are you persecuting me?" ⁵𝑦He said, "Who are you, sir?" The reply came, "I am Jesus, whom you are persecuting. ⁶𝑧Now get up and go into the city and you will be told what you must do." ⁷𝑎The men who were traveling with him stood speechless, for they heard the voice but could see no one. ⁸𝑏*Saul got up from the ground, but when he opened his eyes he could see nothing; so they led him by the hand and brought him to Damascus. ⁹For three days he was unable to see, and he neither ate nor drank.

Saul's Baptism. ¹⁰𝑐There was a disciple in Damascus named Ananias, and the Lord said to him in a vision, "Ananias." He answered, "Here I am, Lord." ¹¹𝑑The Lord said to him, "Get up and go to the street called Straight and ask at the house of Judas for a man from Tarsus named Saul. He is there praying, ¹²and [in a vision] he has seen a man named Ananias come in and lay [his] hands on him, that he may regain his sight." ¹³𝑒*But Ananias replied, "Lord, I have heard from many sources about this man, what evil things he has done to your holy ones in Jerusalem. ¹⁴𝑓And here he has authority from the chief priests to imprison all who call upon your name." ¹⁵𝑔But the Lord said to him, "Go, for

8, 37: The oldest and best manuscripts of Acts omit this verse, which is a Western text reading: "And Philip said, 'If you believe with all your heart, you may.' And he said in reply, 'I believe that Jesus Christ is the Son of God.' "

9, 1–19: This is the first of three accounts of Paul's conversion (with 22, 3–16 and 26, 2–18) with some differences of detail owing to Luke's use of different sources. Paul's experience was not visionary but was precipitated by the appearance of Jesus, as he insists in 1 Cor 15, 8. The words of Jesus, "Saul, Saul, why are you persecuting me?" related by Luke with no variation in all three accounts, exerted a profound and lasting influence on the thought of Paul. Under the influence of this experience he gradually developed his understanding of justification by faith (see the letters to the Galatians and Romans) and of the identification of the Christian community with Jesus Christ (see 1 Cor 12, 27). That Luke would narrate this conversion three times is testimony to the importance he attaches to it. This first account occurs when the word is first

spread to the Gentiles. At this point, the conversion of the hero of the Gentile mission is recounted. The emphasis in the account is on Paul as a divinely chosen instrument (15).

9, 2: The Way: a name used by the early Christian community for itself (18, 26; 19, 9.23; 22, 4; 24, 14.22). The Essene community at Qumran used the same designation to describe its mode of life.

9, 8: He could see nothing: a temporary blindness (18) symbolizing the religious blindness of Saul as persecutor (cf 26, 18).

9, 13: Your holy ones: literally, "your saints."

𝑞: Is 53, 7-8 LXX. 𝑟: 10, 47. 𝑠: 1 Kgs 18, 12. 𝑡: 21, 8. 𝑢: 8, 3; 9, 13; 22, 4; 1 Cor 15, 9; Gal 1, 13-14. 𝑣: 9, 14; 26, 10. 𝑤: 1 Cor 9, 1; 15, 8; Gal 1, 16. 𝑥: 22, 6; 26, 14. 𝑦: 22, 8; 26, 15; Mt 25, 40. 𝑧: 22, 10; 26, 16. 𝑎: 22, 9; 26, 13-14. 𝑏: 22, 11. 𝑐: 22, 12-16. 𝑑: 21, 39. 𝑒: 8, 3; 9, 1. 𝑓: 9, 1-2; 26, 10; 1 Cor 1, 2; 2 Tm 2, 22. 𝑔: 22, 15; 26, 1; 27, 24.

this man is a chosen instrument of mine to carry my name before Gentiles, kings, and Israelites, [16]and I will show him what he will have to suffer for my name." [17]So Ananias went and entered the house; laying his hands on him, he said, "Saul, my brother, the Lord has sent me, Jesus who appeared to you on the way by which you came, that you may regain your sight and be filled with the holy Spirit." [18]Immediately things like scales fell from his eyes and he regained his sight. He got up and was baptized, [19]*and when he had eaten, he recovered his strength.

Saul Preaches in Damascus. He stayed some days with the disciples in Damascus, [20]*and he began at once to proclaim Jesus in the synagogues, that he is the Son of God. [21]All who heard him were astounded and said, "Is not this the man who in Jerusalem ravaged those who call upon this name, and came here expressly to take them back in chains to the chief priests?" [22]But Saul grew all the stronger and confounded [the] Jews who lived in Damascus, proving that this is the Messiah.

Saul Visits Jerusalem. [23]After a long time had passed, the Jews conspired to kill him, [24]hbut their plot became known to Saul. Now they were keeping watch on the gates day and night so as to kill him, [25]but his disciples took him one night and let him down through an opening in the wall, lowering him in a basket.

[26]i*When he arrived in Jerusalem he tried to join the disciples, but they were all afraid of him, not believing that he was a disciple. [27]Then Barnabas took charge of him and brought him to the apostles, and he reported to them how on the way he had seen the Lord and that he had spoken to him, and how in Damascus he had spoken out boldly in the name of Jesus. [28]He moved about freely with them in Jerusalem, and spoke out boldly in the name of the Lord. [29]*He also spoke and debated with the Hellenists, but they tried to kill him. [30]jAnd when the brothers learned of this, they took him down to Caesarea and sent him on his way to Tarsus.

The Church at Peace. [31]*The church throughout all Judea, Galilee, and Samaria was at peace. It was being built up and walked in the fear of the Lord, and with the consolation of the holy Spirit it grew in numbers.

Peter Heals Aeneas at Lydda. [32]As Peter was passing through every region, he went down to the holy ones living in Lydda. [33]There he found a man named Aeneas, who had been confined to bed for eight years, for he was paralyzed. [34]Peter said to him, "Aeneas, Jesus Christ heals you. Get up and make your bed." He got up at once. [35]And all the inhabitants of Lydda and Sharon saw him, and they turned to the Lord.

Peter Restores Tabitha to Life. [36]*Now in Joppa there was a disciple named Tabitha (which translated means Dorcas). She was completely occupied with good deeds and almsgiving. [37]Now during those days she fell sick and died, so after washing her, they laid [her] out in a room upstairs. [38]Since Lydda was near Joppa, the disciples, hearing that Peter was there, sent two men to him with the request, "Please come to us without delay." [39]So Peter got up and went with them. When he arrived, they took him to the room upstairs where all the widows came to him weeping and showing him the tunics and cloaks that Dorcas had made while she

9, 19–30: This is a brief resume of Paul's initial experience as an apostolic preacher. At first he found himself in the position of being regarded as an apostate by the Jews and suspect by the Christian community of Jerusalem. His acceptance by the latter was finally brought about through his friendship with Barnabas (27).

9, 20: Son of God: the title "Son of God" occurs in Acts only here, but cf the citation of Ps 2, 7 in Paul's speech at Antioch in Pisidia (13, 33).

9, 26: This visit of Paul to Jerusalem is mentioned by Paul in Gal 1, 18.

9, 29: Hellenists: see the note on 6, 1–7.

9, 31–43: In the context of the period of peace enjoyed by the community through the cessation of Paul's activities against it, Luke introduces two traditions concerning the miraculous power exercised by Peter as he was making a tour of places where the Christian message had already been preached. The towns of Lydda, Sharon, and Joppa were populated by both Jews and Gentiles and their Christian communities may well have been mixed.

9, 36: Tabitha (Dorcas), respectively the Aramaic and Greek words for "gazelle," exemplifies the right attitude toward material possessions expressed by Jesus in the Lucan Gospel (Lk 6, 30; 11, 41; 12, 33; 18, 22; 19, 8).

h: 2 Cor 11, 32-33.   *i:* Gal 1, 18.   *j:* 11, 25.

was with them. [40k]Peter sent them all out and knelt down and prayed. Then he turned to her body and said, "Tabitha, rise up." She opened her eyes, saw Peter, and sat up. [41]He gave her his hand and raised her up, and when he had called the holy ones and the widows, he presented her alive. [42]This became known all over Joppa, and many came to believe in the Lord. [43l*]And he stayed a long time in Joppa with Simon, a tanner.

IV: The Inauguration of the Gentile Mission

CHAPTER 10

See RG 431

The Vision of Cornelius. [1m*]Now in Caesarea there was a man named Cornelius, a centurion of the Cohort called the Italica, [2*]devout and God-fearing along with his whole household, who used to give alms generously to the Jewish people and pray to God constantly. [3*]One afternoon about three o'clock, he saw plainly in a vision an angel of God come in to him and say to him, "Cornelius." [4]He looked intently at him and, seized with fear, said, "What is it, sir?" He said to him, "Your prayers and almsgiving have ascended as a memorial offering before God. [5]Now send some men to Joppa and summon one Simon who is called Peter. [6n]He is staying with another Simon, a tanner, who has a house by the sea." [7*]When the an-

gel who spoke to him had left, he called two of his servants and a devout soldier from his staff, [8]explained everything to them, and sent them to Joppa.

The Vision of Peter. [9*]The next day, while they were on their way and nearing the city, Peter went up to the roof terrace to pray at about noontime. [10]He was hungry and wished to eat, and while they were making preparations he fell into a trance. [11o]He saw heaven opened and something resembling a large sheet coming down, lowered to the ground by its four corners. [12]In it were all the earth's four-legged animals and reptiles and the birds of the sky. [13]A voice said to him, "Get up, Peter. Slaughter and eat." [14p]But Peter said, "Certainly not, sir. For never have I eaten anything profane and unclean." [15q]The voice spoke to him again, a second time, "What God has made clean, you are not to call profane." [16]This happened three times, and then the object was taken up into the sky.

[17*]While Peter was in doubt about the meaning of the vision he had seen, the men sent by Cornelius asked for Simon's house and arrived at the entrance. [18]They called out inquiring whether Simon, who is called Peter, was staying there. [19r]As Peter was pondering the vision, the Spirit said [to him], "There are three men here looking for you. [20]So get up, go downstairs, and accompany them without hesitation, because I have sent them." [21]Then Peter went down to the men

---

9, 43: The fact that Peter lodged with a tanner would have been significant to both the Gentile and Jewish Christians, for Judaism considered the tanning occupation unclean.

10, 1–48: The narrative centers on the conversion of Cornelius, a Gentile and a "God-fearer" (see the note on 8, 26–40). Luke considers the event of great importance, as is evident from his long treatment of it. The incident is again related in 11, 1-18 where Peter is forced to justify his actions before the Jerusalem community and alluded to in 15, 7–11 where at the Jerusalem "Council" Peter supports Paul's missionary activity among the Gentiles. The narrative divides itself into a series of distinct episodes, concluding with Peter's presentation of the Christian kerygma (34–43) and a pentecostal experience undergone by Cornelius' household preceding their reception of baptism (44–48).

10, 1: The Cohort called the Italica: this battalion was an auxiliary unit of archers formed originally in Italy but transferred to Syria shortly before A.D. 69.

10, 2: Used to give alms generously: like Tabitha (9, 36), Cornelius exemplifies the proper attitude toward wealth (see the note on 9, 36).

10, 3: About three o'clock: literally, "about the ninth hour." See the note on 3, 1.

10, 7: A devout soldier: by using this adjective, Luke probably intends to classify him as a "God-fearer" (see the note on 8, 26–40).

10, 9–16: The vision is intended to prepare Peter to share the food of Cornelius' household without qualms of conscience (48). The necessity of such instructions to Peter reveals that at first not even the apostles fully grasped the implications of Jesus' teaching on the law. In Acts, the initial insight belongs to Stephen.

10, 9: At about noontime: literally, "about the sixth hour."

10, 17–23: The arrival of the Gentile emissaries with their account of the angelic apparition illuminates Peter's vision: he is to be prepared to admit Gentiles, who were considered unclean like the animals of his vision, into the Christian community.

k: Mk 5, 40-41. l: 10, 6. m: 10, 30-33. n: 9, 43. o: 11, 5-12.
p: Lv 11, 1-47; Ez 4, 14. q: Mk 7, 15-19; Gal 2, 12. r: 13, 2.

and said, "I am the one you are looking for. What is the reason for your being here?" [22s]They answered, "Cornelius, a centurion, an upright and God-fearing man, respected by the whole Jewish nation, was directed by a holy angel to summon you to his house and to hear what you have to say." [23]So he invited them in and showed them hospitality.

The next day he got up and went with them, and some of the brothers from Joppa went with him. [24*]On the following day he entered Caesarea. Cornelius was expecting them and had called together his relatives and close friends. [25t]When Peter entered, Cornelius met him and, falling at his feet, paid him homage. [26]Peter, however, raised him up, saying, "Get up. I myself am also a human being." [27]While he conversed with him, he went in and found many people gathered together [28u*]and said to them, "You know that it is unlawful for a Jewish man to associate with, or visit, a Gentile, but God has shown me that I should not call any person profane or unclean. [29]And that is why I came without objection when sent for. May I ask, then, why you summoned me?"

[30*]Cornelius replied, "Four days ago at this hour, three o'clock in the afternoon, I was at prayer in my house when suddenly a man in dazzling robes stood before me and said,

[31]'Cornelius, your prayer has been heard and your almsgiving remembered before God. [32]Send therefore to Joppa and summon Simon, who is called Peter. He is a guest in the house of Simon, a tanner, by the sea.' [33]So I sent for you immediately, and you were kind enough to come. Now therefore we are all here in the presence of God to listen to all that you have been commanded by the Lord."

Peter's Speech. [34v*]Then Peter proceeded to speak and said, "In truth, I see that God shows no partiality. [35]Rather, in every nation whoever fears him and acts uprightly is acceptable to him. [36w*]You know the word [that] he sent to the Israelites as he proclaimed peace through Jesus Christ, who is Lord of all, [37x]what has happened all over Judea, beginning in Galilee after the baptism that John preached, [38y*]how God anointed Jesus of Nazareth with the holy Spirit and power. He went about doing good and healing all those oppressed by the devil, for God was with him. [39*]We are witnesses of all that he did both in the country of the Jews and [in] Jerusalem. They put him to death by hanging him on a tree. [40]This man God raised [on] the third day and granted that he be visible, [41z]not to all the people, but to us, the witnesses chosen by God in advance, who ate and drank with him after he rose from the

---

10, 24–27: So impressed is Cornelius with the apparition that he invites close personal friends to join him in his meeting with Peter. But his understanding of the person he is about to meet is not devoid of superstition, suggested by his falling down before him. For a similar experience of Paul and Barnabas, see 14, 11–18.

10, 28: Peter now fully understands the meaning of his vision; see the note on 10, 17–23.

10, 30: Four days ago: literally, "from the fourth day up to this hour."

10, 34–43: Peter's speech to the household of Cornelius typifies early Christian preaching to Gentiles.

10, 34–35: The revelation of God's choice of Israel to be the people of God did not mean he withheld the divine favor from other people.

10, 36–43: These words are more directed to Luke's Christian readers than to the household of Cornelius, as indicated by the opening words, "You know." They trace the continuity between the preaching and teaching of Jesus of Nazareth and the proclamation of Jesus by the early community. The emphasis on this divinely ordained continuity (41) is meant to assure Luke's readers of the fidelity of Christian tradition to the words and deeds of Jesus.

10, 36: To the Israelites: Luke, in the words of Peter,

speaks of the prominent position occupied by Israel in the history of salvation.

10, 38: Jesus of Nazareth: God's revelation of his plan for the destiny of humanity through Israel culminated in Jesus of Nazareth. Consequently, the ministry of Jesus is an integral part of God's revelation. This viewpoint explains why the early Christian communities were interested in conserving the historical substance of the ministry of Jesus, a tradition leading to the production of the four gospels.

10, 39: We are witnesses: the apostolic testimony was not restricted to the resurrection of Jesus but also included his historical ministry. This witness, however, was theological in character; the Twelve, divinely mandated as prophets, were empowered to interpret his sayings and deeds in the light of his redemptive death and resurrection. The meaning of these words and deeds was to be made clear to the developing Christian community as the bearer of the word of salvation (cf 1, 21–26). **Hanging him on a tree:** see the note on 5, 30.

s: Lk 7, 4-5. t: 14, 13-15; Rv 19, 10. u: Gal 2, 11-16. v: Dt 17, 2; 2 Chr 19, 7; Jb 34, 19; Wis 6, 7; Rom 2, 11; Gal 2, 6; Eph 6, 9; 1 Pt 1, 17. w: Is 52, 7; Na 2, 1. x: Mt 4, 12; Mk 1, 14; Lk 4, 14. y: Is 61, 1; Lk 4, 18. z: Lk 24, 41-43.

dead. *42a**He commissioned us to preach to the people and testify that he is the one appointed by God as judge of the living and the dead. *43*To him all the prophets bear witness, that everyone who believes in him will receive forgiveness of sins through his name."

The Baptism of Cornelius. *44b**While Peter was still speaking these things, the holy Spirit fell upon all who were listening to the word. *45*The circumcised believers who had accompanied Peter were astounded that the gift of the holy Spirit should have been poured out on the Gentiles also, *46*for they could hear them speaking in tongues and glorifying God. Then Peter responded, *47c*"Can anyone withhold the water for baptizing these people, who have received the holy Spirit even as we have?" *48*He ordered them to be baptized in the name of Jesus Christ. *49*Then they invited him to stay for a few days.

CHAPTER 11

See RG 430–31

The Baptism of the Gentiles Explained. *1**Now the apostles and the brothers who were in Judea heard that the Gentiles too had accepted the word of God. *2*So when Peter went up to Jerusalem the circumcised believers confronted him, *3**saying, "You entered the house of uncircumcised people and ate with them." *4*Peter began and explained it to them step by step, saying, *5d*"I was at prayer in the city of Joppa when in a trance I had a vision, something resembling a large sheet coming down, lowered from the sky by its four corners, and it came to me. *6*Looking intently into it, I observed and saw the four-legged animals of the earth, the wild beasts,

the reptiles, and the birds of the sky. *7*I also heard a voice say to me, 'Get up, Peter. Slaughter and eat.' *8*But I said, 'Certainly not, sir, because nothing profane or unclean has ever entered my mouth.' *9*But a second time a voice from heaven answered, 'What God has made clean, you are not to call profane.' *10*This happened three times, and then everything was drawn up again into the sky. *11*Just then three men appeared at the house where we were, who had been sent to me from Caesarea. *12**The Spirit told me to accompany them without discriminating. These six brothers also went with me, and we entered the man's house. *13e*He related to us how he had seen [the] angel standing in his house, saying, 'Send someone to Joppa and summon Simon, who is called Peter, *14*who will speak words to you by which you and all your household will be saved.' *15f*As I began to speak, the holy Spirit fell upon them as it had upon us at the beginning, *16g*and I remembered the word of the Lord, how he had said, 'John baptized with water but you will be baptized with the holy Spirit.' *17h*If then God gave them the same gift he gave to us when we came to believe in the Lord Jesus Christ, who was I to be able to hinder God?" *18*When they heard this, they stopped objecting and glorified God, saying, "God has then granted life-giving repentance to the Gentiles too."

The Church at Antioch. *19i**Now those who had been scattered by the persecution that arose because of Stephen went as far as Phoenicia, Cyprus, and Antioch, preaching the word to no one but Jews. *20*There were

---

10, 42: As judge of the living and the dead: the apostolic preaching to the Jews appealed to their messianic hope, while the preaching to Gentiles stressed the coming divine judgment; cf 1 Thes 1, 10.

10, 44: Just as the Jewish Christians received the gift of the Spirit, so too do the Gentiles.

11, 1–18: The Jewish Christians of Jerusalem were scandalized to learn of Peter's sojourn in the house of the Gentile Cornelius. Nonetheless, they had to accept the divine directions given to both Peter and Cornelius. They concluded that the setting aside of the legal barriers between Jew and Gentile was an exceptional ordinance of God to indicate that the apostolic kerygma was also to be directed to the Gentiles. Only in ch 15 at the "Council" in Jerusalem does the evangelization of the Gentiles become the official position of the church leadership in Jerusalem.

11, 3: You entered . . . : alternatively, this could be punctuated as a question.

11, 12: These six brothers: companions from the Christian community of Joppa (see 10, 23).

11, 19–26: The Jewish Christian antipathy to the mixed community was reflected by the early missionaries generally. The few among them who entertained a different view succeeded in introducing Gentiles into the community at Antioch (in Syria). When the disconcerted Jerusalem community sent Barnabas to investigate, he was so favorably impressed by what he observed that he persuaded his friend Saul to participate in the Antioch mission.

a: 1, 8; 3, 15; 17, 31; Lk 24, 48; Rom 14, 9; 2 Tm 4, 1. *b*: 11, 15; 15, 8. *c*: 8, 36. *d*: 10, 11-20. *e*: 10, 3-5.22.30-32. *f*: 10, 44. *g*: 1, 5; 19, 4; Lk 3, 16. *h*: 15, 8-9. *i*: 8, 1-4.

some Cypriots and Cyrenians among them, however, who came to Antioch and began to speak to the Greeks as well, proclaiming the Lord Jesus. *21*The hand of the Lord was with them and a great number who believed turned to the Lord. *22*The news about them reached the ears of the church in Jerusalem, and they sent Barnabas [to go] to Antioch. *23*When he arrived and saw the grace of God, he rejoiced and encouraged them all to remain faithful to the Lord in firmness of heart, *24*for he was a good man, filled with the holy Spirit and faith. And a large number of people was added to the Lord. *25*Then he went to Tarsus to look for Saul, *26**and when he had found him he brought him to Antioch. For a whole year they met with the church and taught a large number of people, and it was in Antioch that the disciples were first called Christians.

The Prediction of Agabus. *27**At that time some prophets came down from Jerusalem to Antioch, *28j*and one of them named Agabus stood up and predicted by the Spirit that there would be a severe famine all over the world, and it happened under Claudius. *29k*So the disciples determined that, according to ability, each should send relief to the brothers who lived in Judea. *30**This they did, sending it to the presbyters in care of Barnabas and Saul.

See RG 431

CHAPTER 12

Herod's Persecution of the Christians. *1**About that time King Herod laid hands upon some members of the church to harm them. *2**He had James, the brother of John, killed by the sword, *3**and when he saw that this was pleasing to the Jews he proceeded to arrest Peter also. (It was [the] feast of Un-leavened Bread.) *4*He had him taken into custody and put in prison under the guard of four squads of four soldiers each. He intended to bring him before the people after Passover. *51*Peter thus was being kept in prison, but prayer by the church was fervently being made to God on his behalf.

*6*On the very night before Herod was to bring him to trial, Peter, secured by double chains, was sleeping between two soldiers, while outside the door guards kept watch on the prison. *7*Suddenly the angel of the Lord stood by him and a light shone in the cell. He tapped Peter on the side and awakened him, saying, "Get up quickly." The chains fell from his wrists. *8*The angel said to him, "Put on your belt and your sandals." He did so. Then he said to him, "Put on your cloak and follow me." *9*So he followed him out, not realizing that what was happening through the angel was real; he thought he was seeing a vision. *10*They passed the first guard, then the second, and came to the iron gate leading out to the city, which opened for them by itself. They emerged and made their way down an alley, and suddenly the angel left him. *11*Then Peter recovered his senses and said, "Now I know for certain that [the] Lord sent his angel and rescued me from the hand of Herod and from all that the Jewish people had been expecting." *12m*When he realized this, he went to the house of Mary, the mother of John who is called Mark, where there were many people gathered in prayer. *13*When he knocked on the gateway door, a maid named Rhoda came to answer it. *14*She was so overjoyed when she recognized Peter's voice that, in-

---

11, 26: Christians: "Christians" is first applied to the members of the community at Antioch because the Gentile members of the community enable it to stand out clearly from Judaism.

11, 27–30: It is not clear whether the prophets from Jerusalem came to Antioch to request help in view of the coming famine or whether they received this insight during their visit there. The former supposition seems more likely. Suetonius and Tacitus speak of famines during the reign of Claudius (A.D. 41–54), while the Jewish historian Josephus mentions a famine in Judea in A.D. 46–48. Luke is interested, rather, in showing the charity of the Antiochene community toward the Jewish Christians of Jerusalem despite their differences on mixed communities.

11, 30: Presbyters: this is the same Greek word that else-where is translated "elders," primarily in reference to the Jewish community.

12, 1–19: Herod Agrippa ruled Judea A.D. 41–44. While Luke does not assign a motive for his execution of James and his intended execution of Peter, the broad background lies in Herod's support of Pharisaic Judaism. The Jewish Christians had lost the popularity they had had in Jerusalem (2, 47), perhaps because of suspicions against them traceable to the teaching of Stephen.

12, 2: James, the brother of John: this James, the son of Zebedee, was beheaded by Herod Agrippa ca. A.D. 44.

12, 3.4: Feast of Unleavened Bread . . . Passover: see the note on Lk 22, 1.

j: 21, 10. *k:* 12, 25. *l:* Jas 5, 16. *m:* 12, 25; 15, 37.

stead of opening the gate, she ran in and announced that Peter was standing at the gate.
*15*They told her, "You are out of your mind,"
but she insisted that it was so. But they kept
saying, "It is his angel." *16*But Peter continued to knock, and when they opened it, they
saw him and were astounded. *17**He motioned to them with his hand to be quiet and
explained [to them] how the Lord had led
him out of the prison, and said, "Report this
to James and the brothers." Then he left and
went to another place. *18n*At daybreak there
was no small commotion among the soldiers over what had become of Peter.
*19*Herod, after instituting a search but not
finding him, ordered the guards tried and
executed. Then he left Judea to spend some
time in Caesarea.

Herod's Death. *20**He had long been
very angry with the people of Tyre and Sidon, who now came to him in a body. After
winning over Blastus, the king's chamberlain, they sued for peace because their
country was supplied with food from the
king's territory. *21*On an appointed day,
Herod, attired in royal robes, [and] seated
on the rostrum, addressed them publicly.
*22*The assembled crowd cried out, "This is
the voice of a god, not of a man." *23*At once
the angel of the Lord struck him down because he did not ascribe the honor to God,
and he was eaten by worms and breathed

his last. *24o*But the word of God continued
to spread and grow.

Mission of Barnabas and Saul. *25p**After
Barnabas and Saul completed their relief
mission, they returned to Jerusalem, taking
with them John, who is called Mark.

CHAPTER 13

See RG 431

*1**Now there were in the church at
Antioch prophets and teachers: Barnabas,
Symeon who was called Niger, Lucius of Cyrene, Manaen who was a close friend of Herod
the tetrarch, and Saul. *2*While they were worshiping the Lord and fasting, the holy Spirit
said, "Set apart for me Barnabas and Saul for
the work to which I have called them." *3*Then,
completing their fasting and prayer, they laid
hands on them and sent them off.

First Mission Begins in Cyprus. *4**So
they, sent forth by the holy Spirit, went down
to Seleucia and from there sailed to Cyprus.
*5**When they arrived in Salamis, they proclaimed the word of God in the Jewish synagogues. They had John also as their assistant. *6**When they had traveled through the
whole island as far as Paphos, they met a
magician named Bar-Jesus who was a Jewish false prophet. *7*He was with the proconsul Sergius Paulus, a man of intelligence,
who had summoned Barnabas and Saul and
wanted to hear the word of God. *8*But Elymas the magician (for that is what his name

12, 17: To James: this James is not the son of Zebedee
mentioned in v 2, but is James, the "brother of the Lord" (Gal
1, 19), who in chs 15 and 21 is presented as leader of the
Jerusalem Christian community. **He left and went to another place:** the conjecture that Peter left for Rome at this
time has nothing to recommend it. His chief responsibility
was still the leadership of the Jewish Christian community in
Palestine (see Gal 2, 7). The concept of the great missionary
effort of the church was yet to come (see 13, 1–3).

12, 20–23: Josephus gives a similar account of Herod's
death that occurred in A.D. 44. Early Christian tradition considered the manner of it to be a divine punishment upon his
evil life. See 2 Kgs 19, 35 for the figure of the angel of the
Lord in such a context.

12, 25: They returned to Jerusalem: many manuscripts
read "from Jerusalem," since 11, 30 implies that Paul and
Barnabas are already in Jerusalem. This present verse could
refer to a return visit or subsequent relief mission.

13, 1–3: The impulse for the first missionary effort in Asia
Minor is ascribed to the prophets of the Antiochene commu-
nity, under the inspiration of the holy Spirit. Just as the
Jerusalem community had earlier been the center of mission-

ary activity, so too Antioch becomes the center from which
the missionaries Barnabas and Saul are sent out.

13, 4—14, 27: The key event in Luke's account of the first
missionary journey is the experience of Paul and Barnabas at
Pisidian Antioch (13, 14–52). The Christian kerygma proclaimed by Paul in the synagogue was favorably received.
Some Jews and "God-fearers" (see the note on 8, 26–40) became interested and invited the missionaries to speak again
on the following sabbath (13, 42). By that time, however, the
appearance of a large number of Gentiles from the city had so
disconcerted the Jews that they became hostile toward the
apostles (13, 44–50). This hostility of theirs appears in all
three accounts of Paul's missionary journeys in Acts, the Jews
of Iconium (14, 1–2) and Beroea (17, 11) being notable exceptions.

13, 5: John: that is, John Mark (see 12, 12.25).

**13, 6: A magician named Bar-Jesus who was a Jewish
false prophet:** that is, he posed as a prophet. Again Luke
takes the opportunity to dissociate Christianity from the magical acts of the time (7–11); see also 8, 18–24.

n: 5, 22-24.   *o:* 6, 7.   *p:* 11, 29-30.

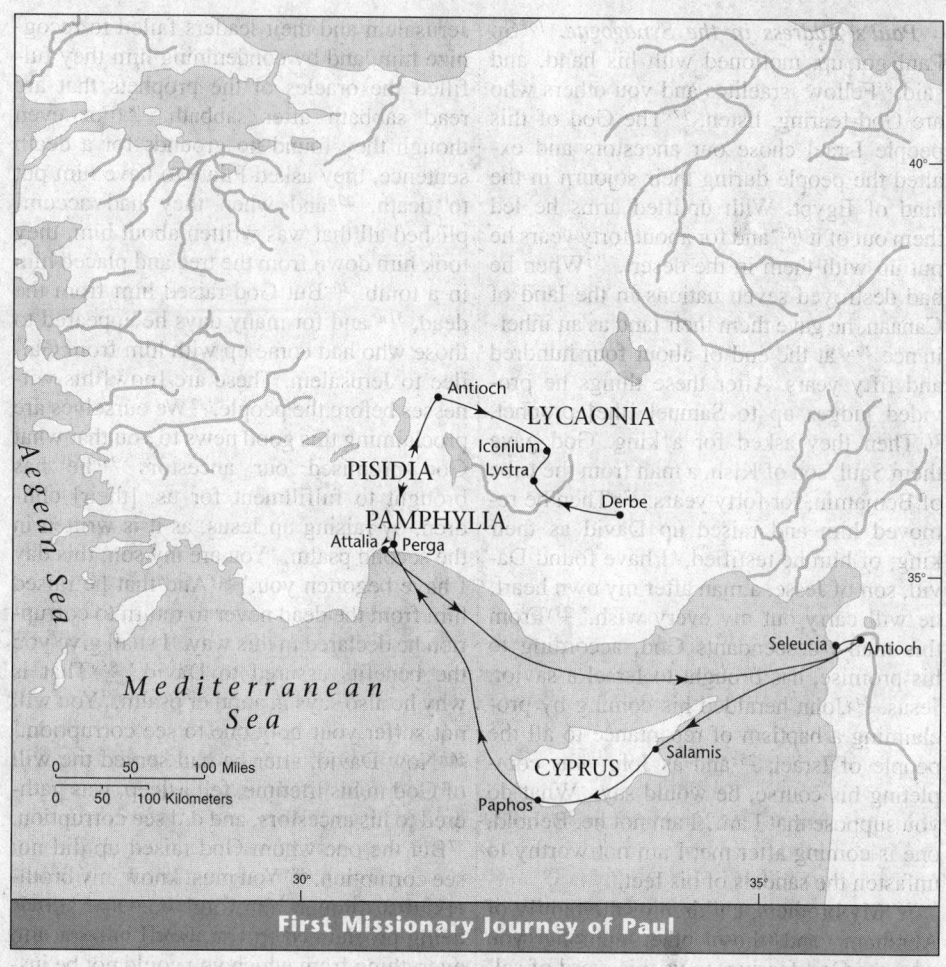

First Missionary Journey of Paul

means) opposed them in an attempt to turn the proconsul away from the faith. [9]*But Saul, also known as Paul, filled with the holy Spirit, looked intently at him [10]and said, "You son of the devil, you enemy of all that is right, full of every sort of deceit and fraud. Will you not stop twisting the straight paths of [the] Lord? [11]Even now the hand of the Lord is upon you. You will be blind, and unable to see the sun for a time." Immediately a dark mist fell upon him, and he went about seeking people to lead him by the hand. [12]When the proconsul saw what had happened, he came to believe, for he was astonished by the teaching about the Lord.

Paul's Arrival at Antioch in Pisidia. [13q]From Paphos, Paul and his companions set sail and arrived at Perga in Pamphylia. But John left them and returned to Jerusalem. [14]They continued on from Perga and reached Antioch in Pisidia. On the sabbath they entered [into] the synagogue and took their seats. [15]After the reading of the law and the prophets, the synagogue officials sent word to them, "My brothers, if one of you has a word of exhortation for the people, please speak."

13, 9: **Saul, also known as Paul:** there is no reason to believe that his name was changed from Saul to Paul upon his conversion. The use of a double name, one Semitic (Saul), the other Greco-Roman (Paul), is well attested (cf 1, 23, Joseph Justus; 12, 12.25, John Mark).

q: 15, 38.

Paul's Address in the Synagogue. ^16*^So Paul got up, motioned with his hand, and said, "Fellow Israelites and you others who are God-fearing, listen. ^17r^The God of this people Israel chose our ancestors and exalted the people during their sojourn in the land of Egypt. With uplifted arms he led them out of it ^18s*^and for about forty years he put up with them in the desert. ^19t^When he had destroyed seven nations in the land of Canaan, he gave them their land as an inheritance ^20u*^at the end of about four hundred and fifty years. After these things he provided judges up to Samuel [the] prophet. ^21v^Then they asked for a king. God gave them Saul, son of Kish, a man from the tribe of Benjamin, for forty years. ^22w^Then he removed him and raised up David as their king; of him he testified, 'I have found David, son of Jesse, a man after my own heart; he will carry out my every wish.' ^23x^From this man's descendants God, according to his promise, has brought to Israel a savior, Jesus. ^24y^John heralded his coming by proclaiming a baptism of repentance to all the people of Israel; ^25z^and as John was completing his course, he would say, 'What do you suppose that I am? I am not he. Behold, one is coming after me; I am not worthy to unfasten the sandals of his feet.'

^26^"My brothers, children of the family of Abraham, and those others among you who are God-fearing, to us this word of salvation has been sent. ^27^The inhabitants of Jerusalem and their leaders failed to recognize him, and by condemning him they fulfilled the oracles of the prophets that are read sabbath after sabbath. ^28a^For even though they found no grounds for a death sentence, they asked Pilate to have him put to death, ^29b^and when they had accomplished all that was written about him, they took him down from the tree and placed him in a tomb. ^30c^But God raised him from the dead, ^31d*^and for many days he appeared to those who had come up with him from Galilee to Jerusalem. These are [now] his witnesses before the people. ^32^We ourselves are proclaiming this good news to you that what God promised our ancestors ^33e^he has brought to fulfillment for us, [their] children, by raising up Jesus, as it is written in the second psalm, 'You are my son; this day I have begotten you.' ^34f^And that he raised him from the dead never to return to corruption he declared in this way, 'I shall give you the benefits assured to David.' ^35g^That is why he also says in another psalm, 'You will not suffer your holy one to see corruption.' ^36h^Now David, after he had served the will of God in his lifetime, fell asleep, was gathered to his ancestors, and did see corruption. ^37^But the one whom God raised up did not see corruption. ^38*^You must know, my brothers, that through him forgiveness of sins is being proclaimed to you, [and] in regard to everything from which you could not be justified under the law of Moses, ^39i^in him

---

13, 16–41: This is the first of several speeches of Paul to Jews proclaiming that the Christian church is the logical development of Pharisaic Judaism (see also 24, 10–21; 26, 2–23).

13, 16: Who are God-fearing: see the note on 8, 26–40.

13, 18: Put up with: some manuscripts read "sustained."

13, 20: At the end of about four hundred and fifty years: the manuscript tradition makes it uncertain whether the mention of four hundred and fifty years refers to the sojourn in Egypt before the Exodus, the wilderness period and the time of the conquest (see Ex 12, 40–41), as the translation here suggests, or to the time between the conquest and the time of Samuel, the period of the judges, if the text is read, "After these things, for about four hundred and fifty years, he provided judges."

13, 31: The theme of the Galilean witnesses is a major one in the Gospel of Luke and in Acts and is used to signify the continuity between the teachings of Jesus and the teachings of the church and to guarantee the fidelity of the church's teachings to the words of Jesus.

13, 38–39: Justified: the verb is the same as that used in Paul's letters to speak of the experience of justification and, as in Paul, is here connected with the term "to have faith" ("every believer"). But this seems the only passage about Paul in Acts where justification is mentioned. In Lucan fashion it is paralleled with "forgiveness of sins" (a theme at 2, 38; 3, 19; 5, 31; 10, 43) based on Jesus' resurrection (37) rather than his cross, and is put negatively (38). Therefore, some would translate, "in regard to everything from which you could not be acquitted . . . every believer is acquitted."

r: Ex 6, 1.6; 12, 51. s: Ex 16, 1.35; Nm 14, 34. t: Dt 7, 1; Jos 14, 1-2. u: Jgs 2, 16; 1 Sm 3, 20. v: 1 Sm 8, 5.19; 9, 16; 10, 1.20-21.24; 11, 15. w: 1 Sm 13, 14; 16, 12-13; Ps 89, 20-21. x: Is 11, 1. y: Mt 3, 1-2; Mk 1, 4-5; Lk 3, 2-3. z: Mt 3, 11; Mk 1, 7; Lk 3, 16; Jn 1, 20.27. a: Mt 27, 20.22-23; Mk 15, 13-14; Lk 23, 4.14-15.21-23; Jn 19, 4-6.15. b: Mt 27, 59-60; Mk 15, 46; Lk 23, 53; Jn 19, 38.41-42. c: 2, 24.32; 3, 15; 4, 10; 17, 31. d: 1, 3.8; 10, 39.41; Mt 28, 8-10.16-20; Mk 16, 9.12-20; Lk 24, 13-53; Jn 20, 11-29; 21, 1-23. e: Ps 2, 7. f: Is 55, 3. g: Ps 16, 10. h: 2, 29; 1 Kgs 2, 10. i: Rom 3, 20.

every believer is justified. ⁴⁰Be careful, then, that what was said in the prophets not come about:

⁴¹ *j*'Look on, you scoffers,
be amazed and disappear.
For I am doing a work in your days,
a work that you will never believe
even if someone tells you.' "

⁴²As they were leaving, they invited them to speak on these subjects the following sabbath. ⁴³After the congregation had dispersed, many Jews and worshipers who were converts to Judaism followed Paul and Barnabas, who spoke to them and urged them to remain faithful to the grace of God.

Address to the Gentiles. ⁴⁴On the following sabbath almost the whole city gathered to hear the word of the Lord. ⁴⁵When the Jews saw the crowds, they were filled with jealousy and with violent abuse contradicted what Paul said. ^{46k*}Both Paul and Barnabas spoke out boldly and said, "It was necessary that the word of God be spoken to you first, but since you reject it and condemn yourselves as unworthy of eternal life, we now turn to the Gentiles. ^{47l}For so the Lord has commanded us, 'I have made you a light to the Gentiles, that you may be an instrument of salvation to the ends of the earth.' "

⁴⁸The Gentiles were delighted when they heard this and glorified the word of the Lord. All who were destined for eternal life came to believe, ⁴⁹and the word of the Lord continued to spread through the whole region. ⁵⁰The Jews, however, incited the women of prominence who were worshipers and the leading men of the city, stirred up a persecution against Paul and Barnabas, and expelled them from their territory. ^{51m*}So they shook the dust from their feet in protest against them and went to Iconium. ⁵²The disciples were filled with joy and the holy Spirit.

CHAPTER 14

See RG
432

Paul and Barnabas at Iconium. ¹In Iconium they entered the Jewish synagogue together and spoke in such a way that a great number of both Jews and Greeks came to believe, ²although the disbelieving Jews stirred up and poisoned the minds of the Gentiles against the brothers. ³ⁿSo they stayed for a considerable period, speaking out boldly for the Lord, who confirmed the word about his grace by granting signs and wonders to occur through their hands. ⁴The people of the city were divided: some were with the Jews; others, with the apostles. ^{5o}When there was an attempt by both the Gentiles and the Jews, together with their leaders, to attack and stone them, ⁶they realized it and fled to the Lycaonian cities of Lystra and Derbe and to the surrounding countryside, ⁷where they continued to proclaim the good news.

Paul and Barnabas at Lystra. ^{8*}At Lystra there was a crippled man, lame from birth, who had never walked. ⁹He listened to Paul speaking, who looked intently at him, saw that he had the faith to be healed, ¹⁰and called out in a loud voice, "Stand up straight on your feet." He jumped up and began to walk about. ^{11p}When the crowds saw what Paul had done, they cried out in Lycaonian, "The gods have come down to us in human form." ^{12*}They called Barnabas "Zeus" and Paul "Hermes," because he was the chief speaker. ¹³And the priest of Zeus, whose temple was at the entrance to the city, brought oxen and garlands to the gates, for he together with the people intended to offer sacrifice.

^{14*}The apostles Barnabas and Paul tore their garments when they heard this and

---

13, 46: The refusal to believe frustrates God's plan for his chosen people; however, no adverse judgment is made here concerning their ultimate destiny. Again, Luke, in the words of Paul, speaks of the priority of Israel in the plan for salvation (see 10, 36).

13, 51: See the note on Lk 9, 5.

14, 8–18: In an effort to convince his hearers that the divine power works through his word, Paul cures the cripple. However, the pagan tradition of the occasional appearance of gods among human beings leads the people astray in interpreting the miracle. The incident reveals the cultural difficul-

ties with which the church had to cope. Note the similarity of the miracle worked here by Paul to the one performed by Peter in 3, 2–10.

14, 12: Zeus . . . Hermes: in Greek religion, Zeus was the chief of the Olympian gods, the "father of gods and men"; Hermes was a son of Zeus and was usually identified as the herald and messenger of the gods.

14, 14: Tore their garments: a gesture of protest.

j: Hb 1, 5. *k*: 3, 26; Rom 1, 16. *l*: Is 49, 6. *m*: Mt 10, 14; Mk 6, 11; Lk 9, 5; 10, 11. *n*: Mk 16, 17-20. *o*: 2 Tm 3, 11. *p*: 28, 6.

rushed out into the crowd, shouting, [15q]*"Men, why are you doing this? We are of the same nature as you, human beings. We proclaim to you good news that you should turn from these idols to the living God, 'who made heaven and earth and sea and all that is in them.' [16r]In past generations he allowed all Gentiles to go their own ways; [17s]yet, in bestowing his goodness, he did not leave himself without witness, for he gave you rains from heaven and fruitful seasons, and filled you with nourishment and gladness for your hearts." [18]Even with these words, they scarcely restrained the crowds from offering sacrifice to them.

[19t]However, some Jews from Antioch and Iconium arrived and won over the crowds. They stoned Paul and dragged him out of the city, supposing that he was dead. [20]But when the disciples gathered around him, he got up and entered the city. On the following day he left with Barnabas for Derbe.

End of the First Mission. [21]After they had proclaimed the good news to that city and made a considerable number of disciples, they returned to Lystra and to Iconium and to Antioch. [22u]They strengthened the spirits of the disciples and exhorted them to persevere in the faith, saying, "It is necessary for us to undergo many hardships to enter the kingdom of God." [23]*They appointed presbyters for them in each church and, with prayer and fasting, commended them to the Lord in whom they had put their faith. [24]Then they traveled through Pisidia and reached Pam-

phylia. [25]After proclaiming the word at Perga they went down to Attalia. [26v]From there they sailed to Antioch, where they had been commended to the grace of God for the work they had now accomplished. [27]And when they arrived, they called the church together and reported what God had done with them and how he had opened the door of faith to the Gentiles. [28]Then they spent no little time with the disciples.

CHAPTER 15

See RG 432

Council of Jerusalem. [1wx]*Some who had come down from Judea were instructing the brothers, "Unless you are circumcised according to the Mosaic practice, you cannot be saved." [2]Because there arose no little dissension and debate by Paul and Barnabas with them, it was decided that Paul, Barnabas, and some of the others should go up to Jerusalem to the apostles and presbyters about this question. [3]They were sent on their journey by the church, and passed through Phoenicia and Samaria telling of the conversion of the Gentiles, and brought great joy to all the brothers. [4]When they arrived in Jerusalem, they were welcomed by the church, as well as by the apostles and the presbyters, and they reported what God had done with them. [5]But some from the party of the Pharisees who had become believers stood up and said, "It is necessary to circumcise them and direct them to observe the Mosaic law."

[6]*The apostles and the presbyters met together to see about this matter. [7y]*After

---

14, 15–17: This is the first speech of Paul to Gentiles recorded by Luke in Acts (cf 17, 22–31). Rather than showing how Christianity is the logical outgrowth of Judaism, as he does in speeches before Jews, Luke says that God excuses past Gentile ignorance and then presents a natural theology arguing for the recognition of God's existence and presence through his activity in natural phenomena.

14, 23: **They appointed presbyters:** the communities are given their own religious leaders by the traveling missionaries. The structure in these churches is patterned on the model of the Jerusalem community (11, 30; 15, 2.5.22; 21, 18).

15, 1–35: The Jerusalem "Council" marks the official rejection of the rigid view that Gentile converts were obliged to observe the Mosaic law completely. From here to the end of Acts, Paul and the Gentile mission become the focus of Luke's writing.

15, 1–5: When some of the converted Pharisees of Jerusalem discover the results of the first missionary journey

of Paul, they urge that the Gentiles be taught to follow the Mosaic law. Recognizing the authority of the Jerusalem church, Paul and Barnabas go there to settle the question of whether Gentiles can embrace a form of Christianity that does not include this obligation.

15, 6–12: The gathering is possibly the same as that recalled by Paul in Gal 2, 1–10. Note that in v 2 it is only the apostles and presbyters, a small group, with whom Paul and Barnabas are to meet. Here Luke gives the meeting a public character because he wishes to emphasize its doctrinal significance (see 22).

15, 7–11: Paul's refusal to impose the Mosaic law on the Gentile Christians is supported by Peter on the ground that within his own experience God bestowed the holy Spirit upon

---

q: 3, 12; 10, 26; Ex 20, 11; Ps 146, 6. *r:* 17, 30. *s:* Wis 13, 1. *t:* 2 Cor 11, 25; 2 Tm 3, 11. *u:* 1 Thes 3, 3. *v:* 13, 1-3. *w:* Gal 2, 1-9. *x:* Lv 12, 3; Gal 5, 2. *y:* 10, 27-43.

much debate had taken place, Peter got up and said to them, "My brothers, you are well aware that from early days God made his choice among you that through my mouth the Gentiles would hear the word of the gospel and believe. [8z]And God, who knows the heart, bore witness by granting them the holy Spirit just as he did us. [9a]He made no distinction between us and them, for by faith he purified their hearts. [10b]Why, then, are you now putting God to the test by placing on the shoulders of the disciples a yoke that neither our ancestors nor we have been able to bear? [11c]*On the contrary, we believe that we are saved through the grace of the Lord Jesus, in the same way as they." [12]The whole assembly fell silent, and they listened while Paul and Barnabas described the signs and wonders God had worked among the Gentiles through them.

James on Dietary Law. [13]*After they had fallen silent, James responded, "My brothers, listen to me. [14]*Symeon has described how God first concerned himself with acquiring from among the Gentiles a people for his name. [15]The words of the prophets agree with this, as is written:

[16] [d]'After this I shall return
  and rebuild the fallen hut of
    David;
  from its ruins I shall rebuild it
    and raise it up again,
[17] so that the rest of humanity may seek out
    the Lord,
  even all the Gentiles on whom my
    name is invoked.

Thus says the Lord who accomplishes
    these things,
[18] known from of old.'

[19e]It is my judgment, therefore, that we ought to stop troubling the Gentiles who turn to God, [20f]but tell them by letter to avoid pollution from idols, unlawful marriage, the meat of strangled animals, and blood. [21]For Moses, for generations now, has had those who proclaim him in every town, as he has been read in the synagogues every sabbath."

Letter of the Apostles. [22]Then the apostles and presbyters, in agreement with the whole church, decided to choose representatives and to send them to Antioch with Paul and Barnabas. The ones chosen were Judas, who was called Barsabbas, and Silas, leaders among the brothers. [23]This is the letter delivered by them: "The apostles and the presbyters, your brothers, to the brothers in Antioch, Syria, and Cilicia of Gentile origin: greetings. [24]Since we have heard that some of our number [who went out] without any mandate from us have upset you with their teachings and disturbed your peace of mind, [25]we have with one accord decided to choose representatives and to send them to you along with our beloved Barnabas and Paul, [26]who have dedicated their lives to the name of our Lord Jesus Christ. [27]So we are sending Judas and Silas who will also convey this same message by word of mouth: [28g]'It is the decision of the holy Spirit and of us not to place on you any burden beyond these necessities, [29h]namely, to abstain from meat sacrificed to idols, from blood, from

Cornelius and his household without preconditions concerning the adoption of the Mosaic law (see 10, 44–47).

15, 11: In support of Paul, Peter formulates the fundamental meaning of the gospel: that all are invited to be saved through faith in the power of Christ.

15, 13–35: Some scholars think that this apostolic decree suggested by James, the immediate leader of the Jerusalem community, derives from another historical occasion than the meeting in question. This seems to be the case if the meeting is the same as the one related in Gal 2, 1–10. According to that account, nothing was imposed upon Gentile Christians in respect to Mosaic law; whereas the decree instructs Gentile Christians of mixed communities to abstain from meats sacrificed to idols and from blood-meats, and to avoid marriage within forbidden degrees of consanguinity and affinity (Lv 18), all of which practices were especially abhorrent to Jews. Luke seems to have telescoped two originally independent in-

cidents here: the first a Jerusalem "Council" that dealt with the question of circumcision, and the second a Jerusalem decree dealing mainly with Gentile observance of dietary laws (see 21, 25 where Paul seems to be learning of the decree for the first time).

15, 14: **Symeon:** elsewhere in Acts he is called either Peter or Simon. The presence of the name Symeon here suggests that, in the source Luke is using for this part of the Jerusalem "Council" incident, the name may have originally referred to someone other than Peter (see 13, 1 where the Antiochene Symeon Niger is mentioned). As the text now stands, however, it is undoubtedly a reference to Simon Peter (7).

z: 10, 44-48. a: 10, 34-35. b: Mt 23, 4; Gal 5, 1. c: Gal 2, 16; 3, 11; Eph 2, 5-8. d: Am 9, 11-12. e: 15, 28-29; 21, 25. f: Gn 9, 4; Lv 3, 17; 17, 10-14. g: 15, 19-20. h: Gn 9, 4; Lv 3, 17; 17, 10-14.

Second Missionary Journey of Paul

meats of strangled animals, and from unlawful marriage. If you keep free of these, you will be doing what is right. Farewell.' "

Delegates at Antioch. *30* And so they were sent on their journey. Upon their arrival in Antioch they called the assembly together and delivered the letter. *31* When the people read it, they were delighted with the exhortation. *32* Judas and Silas, who were themselves prophets, exhorted and strengthened the brothers with many words. *33* After they had spent some time there, they were sent off with greetings of peace from the brothers to those who had commissioned them. [*34*]* *35* But Paul and Barnabas remained in Antioch, teaching and proclaiming with many others the word of the Lord.

V: The Mission of Paul to the Ends of the Earth

Paul and Barnabas Separate. *36* *After some time, Paul said to Barnabas, "Come, let us make a return visit to see how the brothers are getting on in all the cities where we proclaimed the word of the Lord." *37* Barnabas wanted to take with them also John, who was called Mark, *38i* but Paul insisted that they should not take with them someone who had deserted them at Pamphylia and who had not continued with them in their work. *39* So sharp was their disagreement that they separated. Barnabas took Mark and sailed to Cyprus. *40* But Paul chose Silas and departed after being commended by the

brothers to the grace of the Lord. *41* He traveled through Syria and Cilicia bringing strength to the churches.

CHAPTER 16

See RG 432-33

Paul in Lycaonia: Timothy. *1j* He reached [also] Derbe and Lystra where there was a disciple named Timothy, the son of a Jewish woman who was a believer, but his father was a Greek. *2k* The brothers in Lystra and Iconium spoke highly of him, *3* *and Paul wanted him to come along with him. On account of the Jews of that region, Paul had him circumcised, for they all knew that his father was a Greek. *4* As they traveled from city to city, they handed on to the people for observance the decisions reached by the apostles and presbyters in Jerusalem. *5* Day after day the churches grew stronger in faith and increased in number.

Through Asia Minor. *6* They traveled through the Phrygian and Galatian territory because they had been prevented by the holy Spirit from preaching the message in the province of Asia. *7* *When they came to Mysia, they tried to go on into Bithynia, but the Spirit of Jesus did not allow them, *8* so they crossed through Mysia and came down to Troas. *9* During [the] night Paul had a vision. A Macedonian stood before him and implored him with these words, "Come over to Macedonia and help us." *10* *When he had seen the vision, we sought passage to Macedonia at once, concluding that God had called us to proclaim the good news to them.

15, 34: Some manuscripts add, in various wordings, "But Silas decided to remain there."

15, 36—18, 22: This continuous narrative recounts Paul's second missionary journey. On the internal evidence of the Lucan account, it lasted about three years. Paul first visited the communities he had established on his first journey (16, 1–5), then pushed on into Macedonia, where he established communities at Philippi, Thessalonica, and Beroea (16, 7—17, 5). To escape the hostility of the Jews of Thessalonica, he left for Greece and while resident in Athens attempted, without success, to establish an effective Christian community there. From Athens he proceeded to Corinth and, after a stay of a year and a half, returned to Antioch by way of Ephesus and Jerusalem (17, 16—18, 22). Luke does not concern himself with the structure or statistics of the communities but aims to show the general progress of the gospel in the Gentile world as well as its continued failure to take root in the Jewish community.

16, 3: Paul had him circumcised: he did this in order that

Timothy might be able to associate with the Jews and so perform a ministry among them. Paul did not object to the Jewish Christians' adherence to the law. But he insisted that the law could not be imposed on the Gentiles. Paul himself lived in accordance with the law, or as exempt from the law, according to particular circumstances (see 1 Cor 9, 19–23).

16, 7: The Spirit of Jesus: this is an unusual formulation in Luke's writings. The parallelism with v 6 indicates its meaning, the holy Spirit.

16, 10–17: This is the first of the so-called "we-sections" in Acts, where Luke writes as one of Paul's companions. The other passages are 20, 5–15; 21, 1–18; 27, 1—28, 16. Scholars debate whether Luke may not have used the first person plural simply as a literary device to lend color to the narrative. The realism of the narrative, however, lends weight to the argument that the "we" includes Luke or another companion of Paul whose data Luke used as a source.

i: 13, 13.   *j:* 1 Tm 1, 2; 2 Tm 1, 5.   *k:* Phil 2, 20.

Into Europe. [11]*We set sail from Troas, making a straight run for Samothrace, and on the next day to Neapolis, [12]and from there to Philippi, a leading city in that district of Macedonia and a Roman colony. We spent some time in that city. [13]On the sabbath we went outside the city gate along the river where we thought there would be a place of prayer. We sat and spoke with the women who had gathered there. [14]*One of them, a woman named Lydia, a dealer in purple cloth, from the city of Thyatira, a worshiper of God, listened, and the Lord opened her heart to pay attention to what Paul was saying. [15]After she and her household had been baptized, she offered us an invitation, "If you consider me a believer in the Lord, come and stay at my home," and she prevailed on us.

Imprisonment at Philippi. [16]*As we were going to the place of prayer, we met a slave girl with an oracular spirit, who used to bring a large profit to her owners through her fortune-telling. [17]She began to follow Paul and us, shouting, "These people are slaves of the Most High God, who proclaim to you a way of salvation." [18]She did this for many days. Paul became annoyed, turned, and said to the spirit, "I command you in the name of Jesus Christ to come out of her." Then it came out at that moment.

[19]When her owners saw that their hope of profit was gone, they seized Paul and Silas and dragged them to the public square before the local authorities. [20]*They brought them before the magistrates and said, "These people are Jews and are disturbing our city [21]and are advocating customs that are not lawful for us Romans to adopt or practice." [22]The crowd joined in the attack on them, and the magistrates had them stripped and ordered them to be beaten with rods. [23]After inflicting many blows on them, they threw them into prison and instructed the jailer to guard them securely. [24]When he received these instructions, he put them in the innermost cell and secured their feet to a stake.

Deliverance from Prison. [25]About midnight, while Paul and Silas were praying and singing hymns to God as the prisoners listened, [26]there was suddenly such a severe earthquake that the foundations of the jail shook; all the doors flew open, and the chains of all were pulled loose. [27]When the jailer woke up and saw the prison doors wide open, he drew [his] sword and was about to kill himself, thinking that the prisoners had escaped. [28]But Paul shouted out in a loud voice, "Do no harm to yourself; we are all here." [29]He asked for a light and rushed in and, trembling with fear, he fell down before Paul and Silas. [30]Then he brought them out and said, "Sirs, what must I do to be saved?" [31]And they said, "Believe in the Lord Jesus and you and your household will be saved." [32]So they spoke the word of the Lord to him and to everyone in his house. [33]He took them in at that hour of the night and bathed their wounds; then he and all his family were baptized at once. [34]He brought them up into his house and provided a meal and with his household rejoiced at having come to faith in God.

[35]*But when it was day, the magistrates sent the lictors with the order, "Release those men." [36]The jailer reported the[se] words to Paul, "The magistrates have sent orders that you be released. Now, then, come out and go in peace." [37m]*But Paul said to them, "They have beaten us publicly, even though we are Roman citizens and have not been tried, and have thrown us into prison. And now, are they going to release us se-

---

16, 11–40: The church at Philippi became a flourishing community to which Paul addressed one of his letters (see Introduction to the Letter to the Philippians).

16, 14: A worshiper of God: a "God-fearer." See the note on 8, 26–40.

16, 16: With an oracular spirit: literally, "with a Python spirit." The Python was the serpent or dragon that guarded the Delphic oracle. It later came to designate a "spirit that pronounced oracles" and also a ventriloquist who, it was thought, had such a spirit in the belly.

16, 20: Magistrates: in Greek, **stratēgoi,** the popular designation of the **duoviri,** the highest officials of the Roman colony of Philippi.

16, 35: The lictors: the equivalent of police officers, among whose duties were the apprehension and punishment of criminals.

16, 37: Paul's Roman citizenship granted him special privileges in regard to criminal process. Roman law forbade under severe penalty the beating of Roman citizens (see also 22, 25).

l: 2 Cor 11, 25; Phil 1, 30; 1 Thes 2, 2. *m:* 22, 25.

cretly? By no means. Let them come themselves and lead us out." [38n]The lictors reported these words to the magistrates, and they became alarmed when they heard that they were Roman citizens. [39]So they came and placated them, and led them out and asked that they leave the city. [40]When they had come out of the prison, they went to Lydia's house where they saw and encouraged the brothers, and then they left.

CHAPTER 17

Paul in Thessalonica. [1o]When they took the road through Amphipolis and Apollonia, they reached Thessalonica, where there was a synagogue of the Jews. [2]Following his usual custom, Paul joined them, and for three sabbaths he entered into discussions with them from the scriptures, [3p]expounding and demonstrating that the Messiah had to suffer and rise from the dead, and that "This is the Messiah, Jesus, whom I proclaim to you." [4]Some of them were convinced and joined Paul and Silas; so, too, a great number of Greeks who were worshipers, and not a few of the prominent women. [5q]But the Jews became jealous and recruited some worthless men loitering in the public square, formed a mob, and set the city in turmoil. They marched on the house of Jason, intending to bring them before the people's assembly. [6*]When they could not find them, they dragged Jason and some of the brothers before the city magistrates, shouting, "These people who have been creating a disturbance all over the world have now come here,

[7r*]and Jason has welcomed them. They all act in opposition to the decrees of Caesar and claim instead that there is another king, Jesus." [8]They stirred up the crowd and the city magistrates who, upon hearing these charges, [9]took a surety payment from Jason and the others before releasing them.

Paul in Beroea. [10]The brothers immediately sent Paul and Silas to Beroea during the night. Upon arrival they went to the synagogue of the Jews. [11s]These Jews were more fair-minded than those in Thessalonica, for they received the word with all willingness and examined the scriptures daily to determine whether these things were so. [12]Many of them became believers, as did not a few of the influential Greek women and men. [13]But when the Jews of Thessalonica learned that the word of God had now been proclaimed by Paul in Beroea also, they came there too to cause a commotion and stir up the crowds. [14t]So the brothers at once sent Paul on his way to the seacoast, while Silas and Timothy remained behind. [15]After Paul's escorts had taken him to Athens, they came away with instructions for Silas and Timothy to join him as soon as possible.

Paul in Athens. [16*]While Paul was waiting for them in Athens, he grew exasperated at the sight of the city full of idols. [17]So he debated in the synagogue with the Jews and with the worshipers, and daily in the public square with whoever happened to be there. [18*]Even some of the Epicurean and Stoic philosophers engaged him in discussion. Some asked, "What is this scavenger trying

17, 6–7: The accusations against Paul and his companions echo the charges brought against Jesus in Lk 23, 2.

17, 7: There is another king, Jesus: a distortion into a political sense of the apostolic proclamation of Jesus and the kingdom of God (see 8, 12).

17, 16–21: Paul's presence in Athens sets the stage for the great discourse before a Gentile audience in vv 22–31. Although Athens was a politically insignificant city at this period, it still lived on the glories of its past and represented the center of Greek culture. The setting describes the conflict between Christian preaching and Hellenistic philosophy.

17, 18: Epicurean and Stoic philosophers: for the followers of Epicurus (342–271 B.C.), the goal of life was happiness attained through sober reasoning and the searching out of motives for all choice and avoidance. The Stoics were followers of Zeno, a younger contemporary of Alexander the Great. Zeno and his followers believed in a type of pan-

theism that held that the spark of divinity was present in all reality and that, in order to be free, each person must live "according to nature." **This scavenger:** literally, "seed-picker," as of a bird that picks up grain. The word is later used of scrap collectors and of people who take other people's ideas and propagate them as if they were their own. **Promoter of foreign deities:** according to Xenophon, Socrates was accused of promoting new deities. The accusation against Paul echoes the charge against Socrates. **'Jesus' and 'Resurrection':** the Athenians are presented as misunderstanding Paul from the outset; they think he is preaching about Jesus and a goddess named **Anastasis,** i.e., Resurrection.

n: 22, 29. *o:* 1 Thes 2, 1-2. *p:* 3, 18; Lk 24, 25-26.46. *q:* Rom 16, 21. *r:* Lk 23, 2; Jn 19, 12-15. *s:* Jn 5, 39. *t:* 1 Thes 3, 1-2.

to say?" Others said, "He sounds like a promoter of foreign deities," because he was preaching about 'Jesus' and 'Resurrection.' [19u]*They took him and led him to the Areopagus and said, "May we learn what this new teaching is that you speak of? [20]For you bring some strange notions to our ears; we should like to know what these things mean." [21]Now all the Athenians as well as the foreigners residing there used their time for nothing else but telling or hearing something new.

Paul's Speech at the Areopagus. [22]*Then Paul stood up at the Areopagus and said:

"You Athenians, I see that in every respect you are very religious. [23]*For as I walked around looking carefully at your shrines, I even discovered an altar inscribed, 'To an Unknown God.' What therefore you unknowingly worship, I proclaim to you. [24v]The God who made the world and all that is in it, the Lord of heaven and earth, does not dwell in sanctuaries made by human hands, [25]nor is he served by human hands because he needs anything. Rather it is he who gives to everyone life and breath and everything. [26]*He made from one the whole human race to dwell on the entire surface of the earth, and he fixed the ordered seasons and the boundaries of their regions, [27w]so that people might seek God, even perhaps grope for him and find him, though indeed he is not far from any one of us. [28]*For 'In him we live and move and have our being,' as even some of your poets have said, 'For we too are his offspring.' [29x]Since therefore we are the offspring of God, we ought not to think that the divinity is like an image fashioned from gold, silver, or stone by human art and imagination. [30]God has overlooked the times of ignorance, but now he demands that all people everywhere repent [31y]because he has established a day on which he will 'judge the world with justice' through a man he has appointed, and he has provided confirmation for all by raising him from the dead."

[32]When they heard about resurrection of the dead, some began to scoff, but others said, "We should like to hear you on this some other time." [33]And so Paul left them. [34]But some did join him, and became believers. Among them were Dionysius, a member of the Court of the Areopagus, a woman named Damaris, and others with them.

CHAPTER 18

See RG 434

Paul in Corinth. [1]After this he left Athens and went to Corinth. [2z]*There he met a Jew named Aquila, a native of Pontus, who had recently come from Italy with his wife Priscilla because Claudius had ordered all the Jews to leave Rome. He went to visit them [3]and, because he practiced the same trade, stayed with them and worked, for they were tentmakers by trade. [4]Every sabbath, he

---

17, 19: **To the Areopagus:** the "Areopagus" refers either to the Hill of Ares west of the Acropolis or to the Council of Athens, which at one time met on the hill but which at this time assembled in the Royal Colonnade (**Stoa Basileios**).

17, 22–31: In Paul's appearance at the Areopagus he preaches his climactic speech to Gentiles in the cultural center of the ancient world. The speech is more theological than christological. Paul's discourse appeals to the Greek world's belief in divinity as responsible for the origin and existence of the universe. It contests the common belief in a multiplicity of gods supposedly exerting their powers through their images. It acknowledges that the attempt to find God is a constant human endeavor. It declares, further, that God is the judge of the human race, that the time of the judgment has been determined, and that it will be executed through a man whom God raised from the dead. The speech reflects sympathy with pagan religiosity, handles the subject of idol worship gently, and appeals for a new examination of divinity, not from the standpoint of creation but from the standpoint of judgment.

17, 23: **'To an Unknown God':** ancient authors such as Pausanias, Philostratus, and Tertullian speak of Athenian altars with no specific dedication as altars of "unknown gods" or "nameless altars."

17, 26: **From one:** many manuscripts read "from one blood." **Fixed . . . seasons:** or "fixed limits to the epochs."

17, 28: **'In him we live and move and have our being':** some scholars understand this saying to be based on an earlier saying of Epimenides of Knossos (6th century B.C.). **'For we too are his offspring':** here Paul is quoting Aratus of Soli, a third-century B.C. poet from Cilicia.

18, 2: **Aquila . . . Priscilla:** both may already have been Christians at the time of their arrival in Corinth (see 26). According to 1 Cor 16, 19, their home became a meeting place for Christians. **Claudius:** the Emperor Claudius expelled the Jews from Rome ca. A.D. 49. The Roman historian Suetonius gives as reason for the expulsion disturbances among the Jews "at the instigation of Chrestos," probably meaning disputes about the messiahship of Jesus.

---

u: 1 Cor 1, 22. v: 7, 48-50; Gn 1, 1; 1 Kgs 8, 27; Is 42, 5. w: Jer 23, 23; Wis 13, 6; Rom 1, 19. x: 19, 26; Is 40, 18-20; 44, 10-17; Rom 1, 22-23. y: 10, 42. z: Rom 16, 3.

entered into discussions in the synagogue, attempting to convince both Jews and Greeks.

[5]When Silas and Timothy came down from Macedonia, Paul began to occupy himself totally with preaching the word, testifying to the Jews that the Messiah was Jesus. [6a*]When they opposed him and reviled him, he shook out his garments and said to them, "Your blood be on your heads! I am clear of responsibility. From now on I will go to the Gentiles." [7b*]So he left there and went to a house belonging to a man named Titus Justus, a worshiper of God; his house was next to a synagogue. [8c*]Crispus, the synagogue official, came to believe in the Lord along with his entire household, and many of the Corinthians who heard believed and were baptized. [9d]One night in a vision the Lord said to Paul, "Do not be afraid. Go on speaking, and do not be silent, [10]for I am with you. No one will attack and harm you, for I have many people in this city." [11]He settled there for a year and a half and taught the word of God among them.

Accusations before Gallio. [12*]But when Gallio was proconsul of Achaia, the Jews rose up together against Paul and brought him to the tribunal, [13*]saying, "This man is inducing people to worship God contrary to the law." [14]When Paul was about to reply, Gallio spoke to the Jews, "If it were a matter of some crime or malicious fraud, I should with reason hear the complaint of you Jews; [15]but since it is a question of arguments over doctrine and titles and your own law, see to it yourselves. I do not wish to be a judge of such matters." [16]And he drove them away

from the tribunal. [17]They all seized Sosthenes, the synagogue official, and beat him in full view of the tribunal. But none of this was of concern to Gallio.

Return to Syrian Antioch. [18e*]Paul remained for quite some time, and after saying farewell to the brothers he sailed for Syria, together with Priscilla and Aquila. At Cenchreae he had his hair cut because he had taken a vow. [19]When they reached Ephesus, he left them there, while he entered the synagogue and held discussions with the Jews. [20]Although they asked him to stay for a longer time, he did not consent, [21]but as he said farewell he promised, "I shall come back to you again, God willing." Then he set sail from Ephesus. [22*]Upon landing at Caesarea, he went up and greeted the church and then went down to Antioch. [23*]After staying there some time, he left and traveled in orderly sequence through the Galatian country and Phrygia, bringing strength to all the disciples.

Apollos. [24f*]A Jew named Apollos, a native of Alexandria, an eloquent speaker, arrived in Ephesus. He was an authority on the scriptures. [25]He had been instructed in the Way of the Lord and, with ardent spirit, spoke and taught accurately about Jesus, although he knew only the baptism of John. [26*]He began to speak boldly in the synagogue; but when Priscilla and Aquila heard him, they took him aside and explained to him the Way [of God] more accurately. [27]And when he wanted to cross to Achaia, the brothers encouraged him and wrote to the disciples there to welcome him. After his arrival he gave great assistance

---

18, 6: Shook out his garments: a gesture indicating Paul's repudiation of his mission to the Jews there; cf 28, 17–31.

18, 7: A worshiper of God: see the note on 8, 26–40.

18, 8: Crispus: in 1 Cor 1, 14, Paul mentions that Crispus was one of the few he himself baptized at Corinth.

18, 12: When Gallio was proconsul of Achaia: Gallio's proconsulship in Achaia is dated to A.D. 51–52 from an inscription discovered at Delphi. This has become an important date in establishing a chronology of the life and missionary work of Paul.

18, 13: Contrary to the law: Gallio (15) understands this to be a problem of Jewish, not Roman, law.

18, 18: He had his hair cut because he had taken a vow: a reference to a Nazirite vow (see Nm 6, 1–21, especially 6, 18) taken by Paul (see also 21, 23–27).

18, 22: He went up and greeted the church: "going up"

suggests a visit to the church in Jerusalem.

18, 23—21, 16: Luke's account of Paul's third missionary journey devotes itself mainly to his work at Ephesus (19, 1—20, 1). There is a certain restiveness on Paul's part and a growing conviction that the Spirit bids him return to Jerusalem and prepare to go to Rome (19, 21).

18, 24–25: Apollos appears as a preacher who knows the teaching of Jesus in the context of John's baptism of repentance. Aquila and Priscilla instruct him more fully. He is referred to in 1 Cor 1, 12; 3, 5–6.22.

18, 26: The Way [of God]: for the Way, see the note on 9, 2. Other manuscripts here read "the Way of the Lord," "the word of the Lord," or simply "the Way."

a: 13, 51; Mt 10, 14; 27, 24-25; Mk 6, 11; Lk 9, 5; 10, 10-11. *b:* 13, 46-47; 28, 28. *c:* 1 Cor 1, 14. *d:* Jer 1, 8. *e:* 21, 24; Nm 6, 18. *f:* 1 Cor 1, 12.

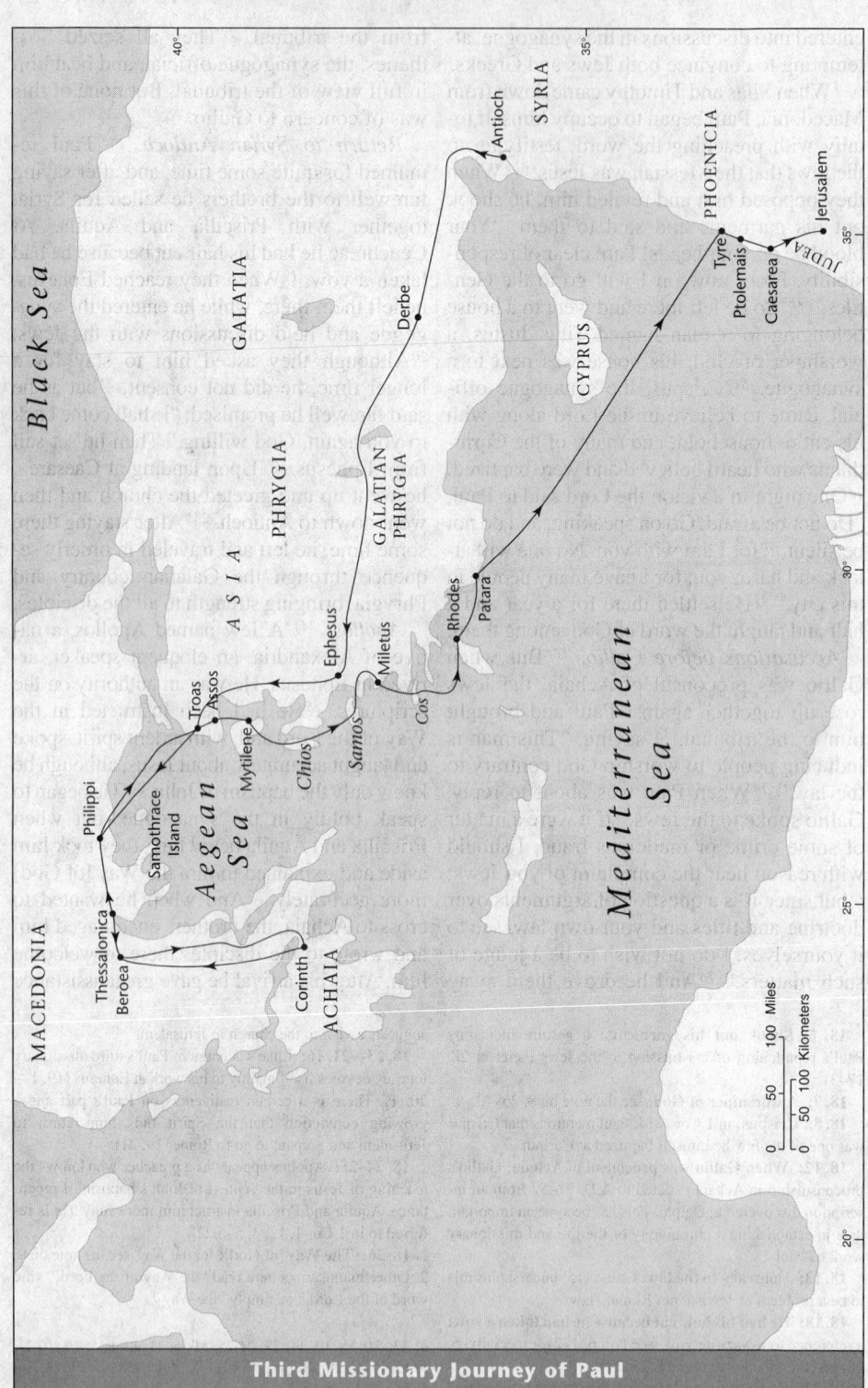

Third Missionary Journey of Paul

to those who had come to believe through grace. [28]He vigorously refuted the Jews in public, establishing from the scriptures that the Messiah is Jesus.

CHAPTER 19

See RG 434-35

Paul in Ephesus. [1]*While Apollos was in Corinth, Paul traveled through the interior of the country and came [down] to Ephesus where he found some disciples. [2]He said to them, "Did you receive the holy Spirit when you became believers?" They answered him, "We have never even heard that there is a holy Spirit." [3]He said, "How were you baptized?" They replied, "With the baptism of John." [4]gPaul then said, "John baptized with a baptism of repentance, telling the people to believe in the one who was to come after him, that is, in Jesus." [5]When they heard this, they were baptized in the name of the Lord Jesus. [6]hAnd when Paul laid [his] hands on them, the holy Spirit came upon them, and they spoke in tongues and prophesied. [7]Altogether there were about twelve men.

[8]He entered the synagogue, and for three months debated boldly with persuasive arguments about the kingdom of God. [9]But when some in their obstinacy and disbelief disparaged the Way before the assembly, he withdrew and took his disciples with him and began to hold daily discussions in the lecture hall of Tyrannus. [10]This continued for two years with the result that all the inhabitants of the province of Asia heard the word of the Lord, Jews and Greeks alike. [11]So extraordinary were the mighty deeds God accomplished at the hands of Paul [12]ithat when face cloths or aprons that touched his skin were applied to the sick, their diseases left them and the evil spirits came out of them.

The Jewish Exorcists. [13]Then some itinerant Jewish exorcists tried to invoke the name of the Lord Jesus over those with evil spirits, saying, "I adjure you by the Jesus whom Paul preaches." [14]When the seven sons of Sceva, a Jewish high priest, tried to do this, [15]the evil spirit said to them in reply, "Jesus I recognize, Paul I know, but who are you?" [16]The person with the evil spirit then sprang at them and subdued them all. He so overpowered them that they fled naked and wounded from that house. [17]When this became known to all the Jews and Greeks who lived in Ephesus, fear fell upon them all, and the name of the Lord Jesus was held in great esteem. [18]Many of those who had become believers came forward and openly acknowledged their former practices. [19]Moreover, a large number of those who had practiced magic collected their books and burned them in public. They calculated their value and found it to be fifty thousand silver pieces. [20]Thus did the word of the Lord continue to spread with influence and power.

Paul's Plans. [21]jWhen this was concluded, Paul made up his mind to travel through Macedonia and Achaia, and then to go on to Jerusalem, saying, "After I have been there, I must visit Rome also." [22]Then he sent to Macedonia two of his assistants, Timothy and Erastus, while he himself stayed for a while in the province of Asia.

The Riot of the Silversmiths. [23]About that time a serious disturbance broke out concerning the Way. [24]*There was a silversmith named Demetrius who made miniature silver shrines of Artemis and provided no little work for the craftsmen. [25]He called a meeting of these and other workers in related crafts and said, "Men, you know well that our prosperity derives from this work. [26]kAs you can now see and hear, not only in Ephesus but throughout most of the province of Asia this Paul has persuaded and misled a great number of people by saying that gods made by hands are not gods at all. [27]The dan-

---

19, 1–6: Upon his arrival in Ephesus, Paul discovers other people at the same religious stage as Apollos, though they seem to have considered themselves followers of Christ, not of the Baptist. On the relation between baptism and the reception of the Spirit, see the note on 8, 16.

19, 24: Miniature silver shrines of Artemis: the temple of Artemis at Ephesus was one of the seven wonders of the ancient world. Artemis, originally the Olympian virgin hunter, moon goddess, and goddess of wild nature, was worshiped at Ephesus as an Asian mother goddess and goddess of fertility. She was one of the most widely worshiped female deities in the Hellenistic world (see 18, 27).

g: 1, 5; 11, 16; 13, 24-25; Mt 3, 11; Mk 1, 8; Lk 3, 16. h: 8, 15-17; 10, 44.46. i: 5, 15-16; Lk 8, 44-47. j: 23, 11; Rom 1, 13; 15, 22-32. k: 17, 29.

ger grows, not only that our business will be discredited, but also that the temple of the great goddess Artemis will be of no account, and that she whom the whole province of Asia and all the world worship will be stripped of her magnificence."

[28]When they heard this, they were filled with fury and began to shout, "Great is Artemis of the Ephesians!" [29]lThe city was filled with confusion, and the people rushed with one accord into the theater, seizing Gaius and Aristarchus, the Macedonians, Paul's traveling companions. [30]Paul wanted to go before the crowd, but the disciples would not let him, [31]*and even some of the Asiarchs who were friends of his sent word to him advising him not to venture into the theater. [32]Meanwhile, some were shouting one thing, others something else; the assembly was in chaos, and most of the people had no idea why they had come together. [33]Some of the crowd prompted Alexander, as the Jews pushed him forward, and Alexander signaled with his hand that he wished to explain something to the gathering. [34]But when they recognized that he was a Jew, they all shouted in unison, for about two hours, "Great is Artemis of the Ephesians!" [35]*Finally the town clerk restrained the crowd and said, "You Ephesians, what person is there who does not know that the city of the Ephesians is the guardian of the temple of the great Artemis and of her image that fell from the sky? [36]Since these things are undeniable, you must calm yourselves and not do anything rash. [37]The men you brought here are not temple robbers, nor have they insulted our goddess. [38]If Demetrius and his fellow craftsmen have a complaint against

anyone, courts are in session, and there are proconsuls. Let them bring charges against one another. [39]If you have anything further to investigate, let the matter be settled in the lawful assembly, [40]*for, as it is, we are in danger of being charged with rioting because of today's conduct. There is no cause for it. We shall [not] be able to give a reason for this demonstration." With these words he dismissed the assembly.

CHAPTER 20

See RG 434-35

Journey to Macedonia and Greece. [1]mWhen the disturbance was over, Paul had the disciples summoned and, after encouraging them, he bade them farewell and set out on his journey to Macedonia. [2]As he traveled throughout those regions, he provided many words of encouragement for them. Then he arrived in Greece, [3]where he stayed for three months. But when a plot was made against him by the Jews as he was about to set sail for Syria, he decided to return by way of Macedonia.

Return to Troas. [4]nSopater, the son of Pyrrhus, from Beroea, accompanied him, as did Aristarchus and Secundus from Thessalonica, Gaius from Derbe, Timothy, and Tychicus and Trophimus from Asia [5]o*who went on ahead and waited for us at Troas. [6]*We sailed from Philippi after the feast of Unleavened Bread, and rejoined them five days later in Troas, where we spent a week.

Eutychus Restored to Life. [7]*On the first day of the week when we gathered to break bread, Paul spoke to them because he was going to leave on the next day, and he kept on speaking until midnight. [8]There were many lamps in the upstairs room where we

---

19, 31: **Asiarchs:** the precise status and role of the Asiarchs is disputed. They appear to have been people of wealth and influence who promoted the Roman imperial cult and who may also have been political representatives in a league of cities in the Roman province of Asia.

19, 35: **Guardian of the temple:** this title was accorded by Rome to cities that provided a temple for the imperial cult. Inscriptional evidence indicates that Ephesus was acknowledged as the temple keeper of Artemis and of the imperial cult. **That fell from the sky:** many scholars think that this refers to a meteorite that was worshiped as an image of the goddess.

19, 40: Some manuscripts omit the negative in [**not**] be

able, making the meaning, "There is no cause for which we shall be able to give a reason for this demonstration."

20, 5: The second "we-section" of Acts begins here. See the note on 16, 10–17.

20, 6: **Feast of Unleavened Bread:** see the note on Lk 22, 1.

20, 7: **The first day of the week:** the day after the sabbath and the first day of the Jewish week, apparently chosen originally by the Jerusalem community for the celebration of the liturgy of the Eucharist in order to relate it to the resurrection of Christ.

l: Col 4, 10. *m:* 1 Cor 16, 1. *n:* Rom 16, 21. *o:* 21, 29; 2 Tm 4, 20.

were gathered, [9]and a young man named Eutychus who was sitting on the window sill was sinking into a deep sleep as Paul talked on and on. Once overcome by sleep, he fell down from the third story and when he was picked up, he was dead. [10p]*Paul went down, threw himself upon him, and said as he embraced him, "Don't be alarmed; there is life in him." [11]Then he returned upstairs, broke the bread, and ate; after a long conversation that lasted until daybreak, he departed. [12]And they took the boy away alive and were immeasurably comforted.

Journey to Miletus. [13]We went ahead to the ship and set sail for Assos where we were to take Paul on board, as he had arranged, since he was going overland. [14]When he met us in Assos, we took him aboard and went on to Mitylene. [15]We sailed away from there on the next day and reached a point off Chios, and a day later we reached Samos, and on the following day we arrived at Miletus. [16]*Paul had decided to sail past Ephesus in order not to lose time in the province of Asia, for he was hurrying to be in Jerusalem, if at all possible, for the day of Pentecost.

Paul's Farewell Speech at Miletus. [17]From Miletus he had the presbyters of the church at Ephesus summoned. [18]When they came to him, he addressed them, "You know how I lived among you the whole time from the day I first came to the province of Asia. [19]I served the Lord with all humility and with the tears and trials that came to me because of the plots of the Jews, [20]and I did not at all shrink from telling you what was for your benefit, or from teaching you in public or in your homes. [21]I earnestly bore witness for both Jews and Greeks to repentance before God and to faith in our Lord Jesus. [22]But now, compelled by the Spirit, I am going to Jerusalem. What will happen to me there I do not know, [23q]except that in one city after another the holy Spirit has been warning me that imprisonment and hardships await me. [24r]Yet I consider life of no importance to me, if only I may finish my course and the ministry that I received from the Lord Jesus, to bear witness to the gospel of God's grace.

[25]"But now I know that none of you to whom I preached the kingdom during my travels will ever see my face again. [26]And so I solemnly declare to you this day that I am not responsible for the blood of any of you, [27]for I did not shrink from proclaiming to you the entire plan of God. [28s]*Keep watch over yourselves and over the whole flock of which the holy Spirit has appointed you overseers, in which you tend the church of God that he acquired with his own blood. [29]I know that after my departure savage wolves will come among you, and they will not spare the flock. [30u]And from your own group, men will come forward perverting the truth to draw the disciples away after them. [31v]So be vigilant and remember that for three years, night and day, I unceasingly admonished each of you with tears. [32]And now I commend you to God and to that gracious word of his that can build you up and give you the inheritance among all who are consecrated. [33]I have never wanted anyone's silver or gold or clothing. [34w]You know well that these very hands have served my needs and my companions. [35x]In every way I have shown you that by hard work of that sort we must help the weak, and keep in mind the words of the Lord Jesus who himself said, 'It is more blessed to give than to receive.' "

20, 10: The action of Paul in throwing himself upon the dead boy recalls that of Elijah in 1 Kgs 17, 21 where the son of the widow of Zarephath is revived and that of Elisha in 2 Kgs 4, 34 where the Shunamite woman's son is restored to life.

20, 16–35: Apparently aware of difficulties at Ephesus and neighboring areas, Paul calls the presbyters together at Miletus, about thirty miles from Ephesus. He reminds them of his dedication to the gospel (18–21), speaks of what he is about to suffer for the gospel (22–27), and admonishes them to guard the community against false prophets, sure to arise upon his departure (28–31). He concludes by citing a saying of Jesus (35) not recorded in the gospel tradition. Luke pre-

sents this farewell to the Ephesian presbyters as Paul's last will and testament.

20, 28: Overseers: see the note on Phil 1, 1. **The church of God:** because the clause "that he acquired with his own blood" following "the church of God" suggests that "his own blood" refers to God's blood, some early copyists changed "the church of God" to "the church of the Lord." Some prefer the translation "acquired with the blood of his own," i.e., Christ.

p: 1 Kgs 17, 17-24; 2 Kgs 4, 30-37; Mt 9, 24; Mk 5, 39; Lk 8, 52. *q:* 9, 16. *r:* 2 Tm 4, 7. *s:* Jn 21, 15-17; 1 Pt 5, 2. *t:* Jn 10, 12. *u:* Mt 7, 15; 2 Pt 2, 1-3; 1 Jn 2, 18-19. *v:* 1 Thes 2, 11. *w:* 1 Cor 4, 12; 1 Thes 2, 9; 2 Thes 3, 8. *x:* Sir 4, 31.

[36] When he had finished speaking he knelt down and prayed with them all. [37] They were all weeping loudly as they threw their arms around Paul and kissed him, [38] for they were deeply distressed that he had said that they would never see his face again. Then they escorted him to the ship.

CHAPTER 21

See RG 435-36

Arrival at Tyre. [1*] When we had taken leave of them we set sail, made a straight run for Cos, and on the next day for Rhodes, and from there to Patara. [2] Finding a ship crossing to Phoenicia, we went on board and put out to sea. [3] We caught sight of Cyprus but passed by it on our left and sailed on toward Syria and put in at Tyre where the ship was to unload cargo. [4] There we sought out the disciples and stayed for a week. They kept telling Paul through the Spirit not to embark for Jerusalem. [5] At the end of our stay we left and resumed our journey. All of them, women and children included, escorted us out of the city, and after kneeling on the beach to pray, [6] we bade farewell to one another. Then we boarded the ship, and they returned home.

Arrival at Ptolemais and Caesarea. [7] We continued the voyage and came from Tyre to Ptolemais, where we greeted the brothers and stayed a day with them. [8y*] On the next day we resumed the trip and came to Caesarea, where we went to the house of Philip the evangelist, who was one of the Seven, and stayed with him. [9] He had four virgin daughters gifted with prophecy. [10*] We had been there several days when a prophet named Agabus came down from Judea. [11z*] He came up to us, took Paul's belt, bound his own feet and hands with it, and said, "Thus says the holy Spirit: This is the way the Jews will bind the owner of this belt in Jerusalem, and they will hand him over to the Gentiles." [12] When we heard this, we and the local residents begged him not to go up to Jerusalem. [13a] Then Paul replied, "What are you doing, weeping and breaking my heart? I am prepared not only to be bound but even to die in Jerusalem for the name of the Lord Jesus." [14b*] Since he would not be dissuaded we let the matter rest, saying, "The Lord's will be done."

Paul and James in Jerusalem. [15] After these days we made preparations for our journey, then went up to Jerusalem. [16] Some of the disciples from Caesarea came along to lead us to the house of Mnason, a Cypriot, a disciple of long standing, with whom we were to stay. [17*] When we reached Jerusalem the brothers welcomed us warmly. [18] The next day, Paul accompanied us on a visit to James, and all the presbyters were present. [19] He greeted them, then proceeded to tell them in detail what God had accomplished among the Gentiles through his ministry. [20] They praised God when they heard it but said to him, "Brother, you see how many thousands of believers there are from among the Jews, and they are all zealous observers of the law. [21] They have been informed that you are teaching all the Jews who live among the Gentiles to abandon Moses and that you are telling them not to circumcise their children or to observe their customary practices. [22] What is to be done? They will surely hear that you have arrived. [23c*] So do what we tell you. We have four men who have taken a vow. [24*] Take these men and purify yourself

---

21, 1–18: The third "we-section" of Acts (see the note on 16, 10–17).

21, 8: One of the Seven: see the note on 6, 2–4.

21, 10: Agabus: mentioned in 11, 28 as the prophet who predicted the famine that occurred when Claudius was emperor.

21, 11: The symbolic act of Agabus recalls those of Old Testament prophets. Compare Is 20, 2; Ez 4, 1; Jer 13, 1.

21, 14: The Christian disciples' attitude reflects that of Jesus (see Lk 22, 42).

21, 17–26: The leaders of the Jewish Christians of Jerusalem inform Paul that the Jews there believe he has encouraged the Jews of the diaspora to abandon the Mosaic law. According to Acts, Paul had no objection to the retention of the law by the Jewish Christians of Jerusalem and left the Jews of the diaspora who accepted Christianity free to follow the same practice.

21, 23–26: The leaders of the community suggest that Paul, on behalf of four members of the Jerusalem community, make the customary payment for the sacrifices offered at the termination of the Nazirite vow (see Nm 6, 1–24) in order to impress favorably the Jewish Christians in Jerusalem with his high regard for the Mosaic law. Since Paul himself had once made this vow (18, 18), his respect for the law would be on public record.

21, 24: Pay their expenses: according to Nm 6, 14–15 the Nazirite had to present a yearling lamb for a holocaust, a yearling ewe lamb for a sin offering, and a ram for a peace offering, along with food and drink offerings, upon completion of the period of the vow.

---

y: 6, 5; 8, 5-6.   z: 11, 28; 20, 23.   a: 19, 15-16.   b: Mt 6, 10; 26, 39; Mk 14, 36; Lk 22, 42.   c: 18, 18; Nm 6, 1-21.

with them, and pay their expenses that they may have their heads shaved. In this way everyone will know that there is nothing to the reports they have been given about you but that you yourself live in observance of the law. *25d**As for the Gentiles who have come to believe, we sent them our decision that they abstain from meat sacrificed to idols, from blood, from the meat of strangled animals, and from unlawful marriage." *26e*So Paul took the men, and on the next day after purifying himself together with them entered the temple to give notice of the day when the purification would be completed and the offering made for each of them.

Paul's Arrest. *27*When the seven days were nearly completed, the Jews from the province of Asia noticed him in the temple, stirred up the whole crowd, and laid hands on him, *28f**shouting, "Fellow Israelites, help us. This is the man who is teaching everyone everywhere against the people and the law and this place, and what is more, he has even brought Greeks into the temple and defiled this sacred place." *29*For they had previously seen Trophimus the Ephesian in the city with him and supposed that Paul had brought him into the temple. *30*The whole city was in turmoil with people rushing together. They seized Paul and dragged him out of the temple, and immediately the gates were closed. *31**While they were trying to kill him, a report reached the cohort commander that all Jerusalem was rioting. *32*He immediately took soldiers and centurions and charged down on them. When

they saw the commander and the soldiers they stopped beating Paul. *33*The cohort commander came forward, arrested him, and ordered him to be secured with two chains; he tried to find out who he might be and what he had done. *34*Some in the mob shouted one thing, others something else; so, since he was unable to ascertain the truth because of the uproar, he ordered Paul to be brought into the compound. *35*When he reached the steps, he was carried by the soldiers because of the violence of the mob, *36g**for a crowd of people followed and shouted, "Away with him!" *37*Just as Paul was about to be taken into the compound, he said to the cohort commander, "May I say something to you?" He replied, "Do you speak Greek? *38h**So then you are not the Egyptian who started a revolt some time ago and led the four thousand assassins into the desert?" *39*Paul answered, "I am a Jew, of Tarsus in Cilicia, a citizen of no mean city; I request you to permit me to speak to the people." *40**When he had given his permission, Paul stood on the steps and motioned with his hand to the people; and when all was quiet he addressed them in Hebrew.

CHAPTER 22

See RG 436

Paul's Defense before the Jerusalem Jews. *1**"My brothers and fathers, listen to what I am about to say to you in my defense." *2*When they heard him addressing them in Hebrew they became all the more quiet. And he continued, *3i*"I am a Jew, born in Tarsus in Cilicia, but brought up in this

21, 25: Paul is informed about the apostolic decree, seemingly for the first time (see the note on 15, 13–35). The allusion to the decree was probably introduced here by Luke to remind his readers that the Gentile Christians themselves were asked to respect certain Jewish practices deriving from the law.

21, 28: The charges against Paul by the diaspora Jews are identical to the charges brought against Stephen by diaspora Jews in 6, 13. **Brought Greeks into the temple:** non-Jews were forbidden, under penalty of death, to go beyond the Court of the Gentiles. Inscriptions in Greek and Latin on a stone ballustrade marked off the prohibited area.

21, 31: Cohort commander: literally, "the leader of a thousand in a cohort." At this period the Roman cohort commander usually led six hundred soldiers, a tenth of a legion; but the number in a cohort varied.

21, 36: Away with him: at the trial of Jesus before Pilate in Lk 23, 18, the people similarly shout, "Away with this man."

21, 38: The Egyptian: according to the Jewish historian

Josephus, an Egyptian gathered a large crowd on the Mount of Olives to witness the destruction of the walls of Jerusalem that would fall at the Egyptian "prophet's" word. The commotion was put down by the Roman authorities and the Egyptian escaped, but only after thousands had been killed. **Four thousand assassins:** literally, **sicarii.** According to Josephus, these were political nationalists who removed their opponents by assassination with a short dagger, called in Latin a sica.

21, 40: In Hebrew: meaning, perhaps, in Aramaic, which at this time was the Semitic tongue in common use.

22, 1–21: Paul's first defense speech is presented to the Jerusalem crowds. Luke here presents Paul as a devout Jew (3) and zealous persecutor of the Christian community (4–5), and then recounts the conversion of Paul for the second time in Acts (see the note on 9, 1–19).

d: 15, 19-20.28-29.   *e:* 1 Cor 9, 20.   *f:* Rom 15, 31.   *g:* 22, 22; Lk 23, 18; Jn 19, 15.   *h:* 5, 36-37.   *i:* 5, 34; 26, 4-5; 2 Cor 11, 22; Gal 1, 13-14; Phil 3, 5-6.

city. At the feet of Gamaliel I was educated strictly in our ancestral law and was zealous for God, just as all of you are today. [4] [j] I persecuted this Way to death, binding both men and women and delivering them to prison. [5] Even the high priest and the whole council of elders can testify on my behalf. For from them I even received letters to the brothers and set out for Damascus to bring back to Jerusalem in chains for punishment those there as well.

[6] [k] "On that journey as I drew near to Damascus, about noon a great light from the sky suddenly shone around me. [7] [l] I fell to the ground and heard a voice saying to me, 'Saul, Saul, why are you persecuting me?' [8] [m] I replied, 'Who are you, sir?' And he said to me, 'I am Jesus the Nazorean whom you are persecuting.' [9] [n] My companions saw the light but did not hear the voice of the one who spoke to me. [10] [o] I asked, 'What shall I do, sir?' The Lord answered me, 'Get up and go into Damascus, and there you will be told about everything appointed for you to do.' [11] [p] Since I could see nothing because of the brightness of that light, I was led by hand by my companions and entered Damascus.

[12] [q] "A certain Ananias, a devout observer of the law, and highly spoken of by all the Jews who lived there, [13] came to me and stood there and said, 'Saul, my brother, regain your sight.' And at that very moment I regained my sight and saw him. [14] Then he said, 'The God of our ancestors designated you to know his will, to see the Righteous One, and to hear the sound of his voice; [15] [*] for you will be his witness before all to what you have seen and heard. [16] Now, why delay? Get up and have yourself baptized and your sins washed away, calling upon his name.'

[17] "After I had returned to Jerusalem and while I was praying in the temple, I fell into a trance [18] and saw the Lord saying to me, 'Hurry, leave Jerusalem at once, because they will not accept your testimony about me.' [19] [r] But I replied, 'Lord, they themselves know that from synagogue to synagogue I used to imprison and beat those who believed in you. [20] [s] And when the blood of your witness Stephen was being shed, I myself stood by giving my approval and keeping guard over the cloaks of his murderers.' [21] [t] [*] Then he said to me, 'Go, I shall send you far away to the Gentiles.'"

Paul Imprisoned. [22] [u] [*] They listened to him until he said this, but then they raised their voices and shouted, "Take such a one as this away from the earth. It is not right that he should live." [23] And as they were yelling and throwing off their cloaks and flinging dust into the air, [24] the cohort commander ordered him to be brought into the compound and gave instruction that he be interrogated under the lash to determine the reason why they were making such an outcry against him. [25] [v] [*] But when they had stretched him out for the whips, Paul said to the centurion on duty, "Is it lawful for you to scourge a man who is a Roman citizen and has not been tried?" [26] When the centurion heard this, he went to the cohort commander and reported it, saying, "What are you going to do? This man is a Roman citizen." [27] Then the commander came and said to him, "Tell me, are you a Roman citizen?" "Yes," he answered. [28] The commander replied, "I acquired this citizenship for a large sum of money," Paul said, "But I was born one." [29] At once those who were going to interrogate him backed away from him, and the commander became alarmed when he realized that he was a Roman citizen and that he had had him bound.

22, 15: His witness: like the Galilean followers during the historical ministry of Jesus, Paul too, through his experience of the risen Christ, is to be a witness to the resurrection (compare 1, 8; 10, 39–41; Lk 24, 48).

22, 21: Paul endeavors to explain that his position on the law has not been identical with that of his audience because it has been his prophetic mission to preach to the Gentiles to whom the law was not addressed and who had no faith in it as a way of salvation.

22, 22: Paul's suggestion that his prophetic mission to the Gentiles did not involve his imposing the law on them pro-

vokes the same opposition as occurred in Pisidian Antioch (13, 45).

22, 25: Is it lawful for you to scourge a man who is a Roman citizen and has not been tried?: see the note on 16, 37.

j: 8, 3; 9, 1-2; 22, 19; 26, 9-11; Phil 3, 6. *k:* 9, 3; 26, 13; 1 Cor 15, 8. *l:* 9, 4; 26, 14. *m:* 9, 5; 26, 15; Mt 25, 40. *n:* 9, 7; 26, 13-14. *o:* 9, 6; 26, 16. *p:* 9, 8. *q:* 9, 10-19. *r:* 8, 3; 9, 1-2; 22, 4-5; 26, 9-11. *s:* 7, 58; 8, 1. *t:* 9, 15; Gal 2, 7-9. *u:* 21, 36; Lk 23, 18; Jn 19, 15. *v:* 16, 37.

Paul before the Sanhedrin. *30*The next day, wishing to determine the truth about why he was being accused by the Jews, he freed him and ordered the chief priests and the whole Sanhedrin to convene. Then he brought Paul down and made him stand before them.

See RG 436

CHAPTER 23

*1w*Paul looked intently at the Sanhedrin and said, "My brothers, I have conducted myself with a perfectly clear conscience before God to this day." *2**The high priest Ananias ordered his attendants to strike his mouth. *3x**Then Paul said to him, "God will strike you, you whitewashed wall. Do you indeed sit in judgment upon me according to the law and yet in violation of the law order me to be struck?" *4*The attendants said, "Would you revile God's high priest?" *5y**Paul answered, "Brothers, I did not realize he was the high priest. For it is written, 'You shall not curse a ruler of your people.' "

*6z*Paul was aware that some were Sadducees and some Pharisees, so he called out before the Sanhedrin, "My brothers, I am a Pharisee, the son of Pharisees; [I] am on trial for hope in the resurrection of the dead." *7*When he said this, a dispute broke out between the Pharisees and Sadducees, and the group became divided. *8a*For the Sadducees say that there is no resurrection or angels or spirits, while the Pharisees acknowledge all three. *9*A great uproar occurred, and some scribes belonging to the Pharisee party stood up and sharply argued, "We find nothing wrong with this man. Suppose a spirit or an angel has spoken to him?" *10*The dispute was so serious that the commander, afraid that Paul would be torn to pieces by them, ordered his troops to go down and rescue him from their midst and take him into the compound.

*11b**The following night the Lord stood by him and said, "Take courage. For just as you have borne witness to my cause in Jerusalem, so you must also bear witness in Rome."

Transfer to Caesarea. *12*When day came, the Jews made a plot and bound themselves by oath not to eat or drink until they had killed Paul. *13*There were more than forty who formed this conspiracy. *14*They went to the chief priests and elders and said, "We have bound ourselves by a solemn oath to taste nothing until we have killed Paul. *15*You, together with the Sanhedrin, must now make an official request to the commander to have him bring him down to you, as though you meant to investigate his case more thoroughly. We on our part are prepared to kill him before he arrives." *16*The son of Paul's sister, however, heard about the ambush; so he went and entered the compound and reported it to Paul. *17**Paul then called one of the centurions and requested, "Take this young man to the commander; he has something to report to him." *18*So he took him and brought him to the commander and explained, "The prisoner Paul called me and asked that I bring this young man to you; he has something to say to you." *19*The commander took him by the hand, drew him aside, and asked him privately, "What is it you have to report to me?" *20*He replied, "The Jews have conspired to ask you to bring Paul down to the Sanhedrin tomorrow, as though they meant to inquire about him more thoroughly, *21*but do not believe them. More than forty of them are lying in wait for him; they have bound themselves by oath not to eat or drink until they have killed him. They are now ready and only wait for your consent." *22*As the commander dismissed the young man he directed him, "Tell no one that you gave me this information."

23, 2: The high priest Ananias: Ananias, son of Nedebaeus, was high priest from A.D. 47 to 59.

23, 3: God will strike you: Josephus reports that Ananias was later assassinated in A.D. 66 at the beginning of the First Revolt.

23, 5: Luke portrays Paul as a model of one who is obedient to the Mosaic law. Paul, because of his reverence for the law (Ex 22, 27), withdraws his accusation of hypocrisy, "whitewashed wall" (cf Mt 23, 27), when he is told Ananias is the high priest.

23, 11: The occurrence of the vision of Christ consoling Paul and assuring him that he will be his witness in Rome prepares the reader for the final section of Acts: the journey of Paul and the word he preaches to Rome under the protection of the Romans.

23, 17: Centurions: a centurion was a military officer in charge of one hundred soldiers.

w: 24, 16.   *x:* Ez 13, 10-15; Mt 23, 27.   *y:* Ex 22, 27.   *z:* 24, 15.21; 26, 5; Phil 3, 5.   *a:* Mt 22, 23; Lk 20, 27.   *b:* 19, 21.

23*Then he summoned two of the centurions and said, "Get two hundred soldiers ready to go to Caesarea by nine o'clock tonight, along with seventy horsemen and two hundred auxiliaries. 24Provide mounts for Paul to ride and give him safe conduct to Felix the governor." 25Then he wrote a letter with this content: 26*"Claudius Lysias to his excellency the governor Felix, greetings. 27cThis man, seized by the Jews and about to be murdered by them, I rescued after intervening with my troops when I learned that he was a Roman citizen. 28I wanted to learn the reason for their accusations against him so I brought him down to their Sanhedrin. 29dI discovered that he was accused in matters of controversial questions of their law and not of any charge deserving death or imprisonment. 30Since it was brought to my attention that there will be a plot against the man, I am sending him to you at once, and have also notified his accusers to state [their case] against him before you."

31So the soldiers, according to their orders, took Paul and escorted him by night to Antipatris. 32The next day they returned to the compound, leaving the horsemen to complete the journey with him. 33When they arrived in Caesarea they delivered the letter to the governor and presented Paul to him. 34When he had read it and asked to what province he belonged, and learned that he was from Cilicia, 35he said, "I shall hear your case when your accusers arrive." Then he ordered that he be held in custody in Herod's praetorium.

CHAPTER 24

See RG
436

Trial before Felix. 1Five days later the high priest Ananias came down with some elders and an advocate, a certain Tertullus, and they presented formal charges against Paul to the governor. 2When he was called, Tertullus began to accuse him, saying, "Since we have attained much peace through you, and reforms have been accomplished in this nation through your provident care, 3we acknowledge this in every way and everywhere, most excellent Felix, with all gratitude. 4But in order not to detain you further, I ask you to give us a brief hearing with your customary graciousness. 5e*We found this man to be a pest; he creates dissension among Jews all over the world and is a ringleader of the sect of the Nazoreans. 6fHe even tried to desecrate our temple, but we arrested him. [7]* 8If you examine him you will be able to learn from him for yourself about everything of which we are accusing him." 9The Jews also joined in the attack and asserted that these things were so.

10*Then the governor motioned to him to speak and Paul replied, "I know that you have been a judge over this nation for many years and so I am pleased to make my defense before you. 11As you can verify, not more than twelve days have passed since I went up to Jerusalem to worship. 12Neither in the temple, nor in the synagogues, nor anywhere in the city did they find me arguing with anyone or instigating a riot among the people. 13Nor can they prove to you the accusations they are now making against me. 14gBut this I do admit to you, that according to the Way, which they call a sect, I worship the God of our ancestors and I believe everything that is in accordance with the law and written in the prophets. 15hI have

---

23, 23: **By nine o'clock tonight:** literally, "by the third hour of the night." The night hours began at 6 p.m. **Two hundred auxiliaries:** the meaning of the Greek is not certain. It seems to refer to spearmen from the local police force and not from the cohort of soldiers, which would have numbered only 500–1000 men.

23, 26–30: The letter emphasizes the fact that Paul is a Roman citizen and asserts the lack of evidence that he is guilty of a crime against the empire. The tone of the letter implies that the commander became initially involved in Paul's case because of his Roman citizenship, but this is not an exact description of what really happened (see 21, 31–33; 22, 25–29).

23, 26: M. Antonius Felix was procurator of Judea from A.D. 52 to 60. His procuratorship was marked by cruelty toward and oppression of his Jewish subjects.

24, 5: **Nazoreans:** that is, followers of Jesus of Nazareth.

24, 7: The Western text has added here a verse (really 6b-8a) that is not found in the best Greek manuscripts. It reads, "and would have judged him according to our own law, but the cohort commander Lysias came and violently took him out of our hands and ordered his accusers to come before you."

24, 10–21: Whereas the advocate Tertullus referred to Paul's activities on his missionary journeys, the apostle narrowed the charges down to the riot connected with the incident in the temple (see 21, 27–30; 24, 17–20). In his defense, Paul stresses the continuity between Christianity and Judaism.

c: 21, 30-34; 22, 27.   d: 18, 14-15; 25, 18-19.   e: 24, 14; Lk 23, 2.   f: 21, 28.   g: 24, 5.   h: Dn 12, 2; Jn 5, 28-29.

the same hope in God as they themselves have that there will be a resurrection of the righteous and the unrighteous. ¹⁶ⁱBecause of this, I always strive to keep my conscience clear before God and man. ^{17j}After many years, I came to bring alms for my nation and offerings. ^{18k}While I was so engaged, they found me, after my purification, in the temple without a crowd or disturbance. ¹⁹But some Jews from the province of Asia, who should be here before you to make whatever accusation they might have against me— ²⁰or let these men themselves state what crime they discovered when I stood before the Sanhedrin, ^{21l}unless it was my one outcry as I stood among them, that 'I am on trial before you today for the resurrection of the dead.'"

²²Then Felix, who was accurately informed about the Way, postponed the trial, saying, "When Lysias the commander comes down, I shall decide your case." ²³He gave orders to the centurion that he should be kept in custody but have some liberty, and that he should not prevent any of his friends from caring for his needs.

Captivity in Caesarea. ^{24*}Several days later Felix came with his wife Drusilla, who was Jewish. He had Paul summoned and listened to him speak about faith in Christ Jesus. ²⁵But as he spoke about righteousness and self-restraint and the coming judgment, Felix became frightened and said, "You may go for now; when I find an opportunity I shall summon you again." ²⁶At the same time he hoped that a bribe would be offered him by Paul, and so he sent for him very often and conversed with him.

^{27*}Two years passed and Felix was succeeded by Porcius Festus. Wishing to ingratiate himself with the Jews, Felix left Paul in prison.

CHAPTER 25

See RG 436

Appeal to Caesar. ¹Three days after his arrival in the province, Festus went up from Caesarea to Jerusalem ^{2*}where the chief priests and Jewish leaders presented him their formal charges against Paul. They asked him ³as a favor to have him sent to Jerusalem, for they were plotting to kill him along the way. ⁴Festus replied that Paul was being held in custody in Caesarea and that he himself would be returning there shortly. ⁵He said, "Let your authorities come down with me, and if this man has done something improper, let them accuse him."

⁶After spending no more than eight or ten days with them, he went down to Caesarea, and on the following day took his seat on the tribunal and ordered that Paul be brought in. ⁷When he appeared, the Jews who had come down from Jerusalem surrounded him and brought many serious charges against him, which they were unable to prove. ⁸In defending himself Paul said, "I have committed no crime either against the Jewish law or against the temple or against Caesar." ^{9*}Then Festus, wishing to ingratiate himself with the Jews, said to Paul in reply, "Are you willing to go up to Jerusalem and there stand trial before me on these charges?" ¹⁰Paul answered, "I am standing before the tribunal of Caesar; this is where I should be tried. I have committed no crime against the Jews, as you very well know. ¹¹If I have committed a crime or done anything deserving death, I do not seek to escape the death penalty; but if there is no substance to the charges they are bringing against me, then no one has the right to hand me over to them. I appeal to Caesar." ¹²Then Festus, after conferring with his council, replied, "You have appealed to Caesar. To Caesar you will go."

24, 24–25: The way of Christian discipleship greatly disquiets Felix, who has entered into an adulterous marriage with Drusilla, daughter of Herod Agrippa I. This marriage provides the background for the topics Paul speaks about and about which Felix does not want to hear.

24, 27: Very little is known of Porcius Festus who was a procurator of Judea from A.D. 60 to 62.

25, 2: Even after two years the animosity toward Paul in Jerusalem had not subsided (see 24, 27).

25, 9–12: Paul refuses to acknowledge that the Sanhedrin in Jerusalem has any jurisdiction over him now (11). Paul uses his right as a Roman citizen to appeal his case to the jurisdiction of the Emperor (Nero, ca. A.D. 60) (12). This move broke the deadlock between Roman protective custody of Paul and the plan of his enemies to kill him (3).

i: 23, 1. *j:* Rom 15, 25-26; Gal 2, 10. *k:* 21, 26-30. *l:* 23, 6; 24, 15.

Paul before King Agrippa. [13]*When a few days had passed, King Agrippa and Bernice arrived in Caesarea on a visit to Festus. [14m]Since they spent several days there, Festus referred Paul's case to the king, saying, "There is a man here left in custody by Felix. [15]When I was in Jerusalem the chief priests and the elders of the Jews brought charges against him and demanded his condemnation. [16]I answered them that it was not Roman practice to hand over an accused person before he has faced his accusers and had the opportunity to defend himself against their charge. [17]So when [they] came together here, I made no delay; the next day I took my seat on the tribunal and ordered the man to be brought in. [18n]His accusers stood around him, but did not charge him with any of the crimes I suspected. [19]Instead they had some issues with him about their own religion and about a certain Jesus who had died but who Paul claimed was alive. [20]Since I was at a loss how to investigate this controversy, I asked if he were willing to go to Jerusalem and there stand trial on these charges. [21]And when Paul appealed that he be held in custody for the Emperor's decision, I ordered him held until I could send him to Caesar." [22]Agrippa said to Festus, "I too should like to hear this man." He replied, "Tomorrow you will hear him."

[23]The next day Agrippa and Bernice came with great ceremony and entered the audience hall in the company of cohort commanders and the prominent men of the city and, by command of Festus, Paul was brought in. [24]And Festus said, "King Agrippa and all you here present with us, look at this man about whom the whole Jewish populace petitioned me here and in Jerusalem, clamoring that he should live no longer. [25]I found, however, that he had done nothing deserving death, and so when he appealed to the Emperor, I decided to send him. [26]But I have nothing definite to write about him to our

sovereign; therefore I have brought him before all of you, and particularly before you, King Agrippa, so that I may have something to write as a result of this investigation. [27]For it seems senseless to me to send up a prisoner without indicating the charges against him."

CHAPTER 26

See RG 436

King Agrippa Hears Paul. [1]Then Agrippa said to Paul, "You may now speak on your own behalf." So Paul stretched out his hand and began his defense. [2]*"I count myself fortunate, King Agrippa, that I am to defend myself before you today against all the charges made against me by the Jews, [3]especially since you are an expert in all the Jewish customs and controversies. And therefore I beg you to listen patiently. [4]*My manner of living from my youth, a life spent from the beginning among my people and in Jerusalem, all [the] Jews know. [5o]They have known about me from the start, if they are willing to testify, that I have lived my life as a Pharisee, the strictest party of our religion. [6p]But now I am standing trial because of my hope in the promise made by God to our ancestors. [7]Our twelve tribes hope to attain to that promise as they fervently worship God day and night; and on account of this hope I am accused by Jews, O king. [8]Why is it thought unbelievable among you that God raises the dead? [9q]I myself once thought that I had to do many things against the name of Jesus the Nazorean, [10r]and I did so in Jerusalem. I imprisoned many of the holy ones with the authorization I received from the chief priests, and when they were to be put to death I cast my vote against them. [11]Many times, in synagogue after synagogue, I punished them in an attempt to force them to blaspheme; I was so enraged against them that I pursued them even to foreign cities.

[12]"On one such occasion I was traveling to Damascus with the authorization and com-

---

25, 13: **King Agrippa and Bernice:** brother and sister, children of Herod Agrippa I whose activities against the Jerusalem community are mentioned in 12, 1–19. Agrippa II was a petty ruler over small areas in northern Palestine and some villages in Perea. His influence on the Jewish population of Palestine was insignificant.

26, 2–23: Paul's final defense speech in Acts is now made before a king (see 9, 15). In the speech Paul presents himself as

a zealous Pharisee and Christianity as the logical development of Pharisaic Judaism. The story of his conversion is recounted for the third time in Acts in this speech (see the note on 9, 1–19).

26, 4: **Among my people:** that is, among the Jews.

m: 24, 27.   n: 18, 14-15; 23, 29.   o: Phil 3, 5-6; Gal 1, 13-14; 2 Cor 11, 22.   p: 23, 6; 24, 15.21; 28, 20.   q: 8, 3; 9, 1-2; 22, 19; Phil 3, 6.   r: 9, 14.

mission of the chief priests. *13st*At midday, along the way, O king, I saw a light from the sky, brighter than the sun, shining around me and my traveling companions. *14u**We all fell to the ground and I heard a voice saying to me in Hebrew, 'Saul, Saul, why are you persecuting me? It is hard for you to kick against the goad.' *15v*And I said, 'Who are you, sir?' And the Lord replied, 'I am Jesus whom you are persecuting. *16w**Get up now, and stand on your feet. I have appeared to you for this purpose, to appoint you as a servant and witness of what you have seen [of me] and what you will be shown. *17x*I shall deliver you from this people and from the Gentiles to whom I send you, *18y**to open their eyes that they may turn from darkness to light and from the power of Satan to God, so that they may obtain forgiveness of sins and an inheritance among those who have been consecrated by faith in me.'

19"And so, King Agrippa, I was not disobedient to the heavenly vision. *20*On the contrary, first to those in Damascus and in Jerusalem and throughout the whole country of Judea, and then to the Gentiles, I preached the need to repent and turn to God, and to do works giving evidence of repentance. *21z*That is why the Jews seized me [when I was] in the temple and tried to kill me. *22a**But I have enjoyed God's help to this very day, and so I stand here testifying to small and great alike, saying nothing different from what the prophets and Moses fore-

told, *23b**that the Messiah must suffer and that, as the first to rise from the dead, he would proclaim light both to our people and to the Gentiles."

Reactions to Paul's Speech. *24*While Paul was so speaking in his defense, Festus said in a loud voice, "You are mad, Paul; much learning is driving you mad." *25*But Paul replied, "I am not mad, most excellent Festus; I am speaking words of truth and reason. *26**The king knows about these matters and to him I speak boldly, for I cannot believe that [any] of this has escaped his notice; this was not done in a corner. *27**King Agrippa, do you believe the prophets? I know you believe." *28*Then Agrippa said to Paul, "You will soon persuade me to play the Christian." *29*Paul replied, "I would pray to God that sooner or later not only you but all who listen to me today might become as I am except for these chains."

*30*Then the king rose, and with him the governor and Bernice and the others who sat with them. *31**And after they had withdrawn they said to one another, "This man is doing nothing [at all] that deserves death or imprisonment." *32c*And Agrippa said to Festus, "This man could have been set free if he had not appealed to Caesar."

CHAPTER 27

See RG 436–37

Departure for Rome. *1**When it was decided that we should sail to Italy, they handed Paul and some other prisoners over

---

26, 14: In Hebrew: see the note on 21, 40. **It is hard for you to kick against the goad:** this proverb is commonly found in Greek literature and in this context signifies the senselessness and ineffectiveness of any opposition to the divine influence in his life.

26, 16: The words of Jesus directed to Paul here reflect the dialogues between Christ and Ananias (9, 15) and between Ananias and Paul (22, 14–15) in the two previous accounts of Paul's conversion.

26, 18: To open their eyes: though no mention is made of Paul's blindness in this account (cf 9, 8–9.12.18; 22, 11–13), the task he is commissioned to perform is the removal of other people's spiritual blindness.

26, 22: Saying nothing different from what the prophets and Moses foretold: see the note on Lk 18, 31.

26, 23: That the Messiah must suffer: see the note on Lk 24, 26.

26, 26: Not done in a corner: for Luke, this Greek proverb expresses his belief that he is presenting a story about Jesus and the church that is already well known. As such, the

entire history of Christianity is public knowledge and incontestable. Luke presents his story in this way to provide "certainty" to his readers about the instructions they have received (Lk 1, 4).

26, 27–28: If the Christian missionaries proclaim nothing different from what the Old Testament prophets had proclaimed (22–23), then the logical outcome for the believing Jew, according to Luke, is to become a Christian.

26, 31–32: In recording the episode of Paul's appearance before Agrippa, Luke wishes to show that, when Paul's case was judged impartially, no grounds for legal action against him were found (see 23, 29; 25, 25).

27, 1—28, 16: Here Luke has written a stirring account of adventure on the high seas, incidental to his main purpose of showing how well Paul got along with his captors and how

s: 9, 7. *t:* 9, 3; 22, 6. *u:* 9, 4; 22, 7. *v:* 9, 5; 22, 8; Mt 25, 40. *w:* 9, 6; 22, 10; Ez 2, 1. *x:* Jer 1, 7. *y:* Is 42, 7.16; 61, 1 LXX; Col 1, 13. *z:* 21, 31. *a:* 3, 18; Lk 24, 26-27.44-47. *b:* Is 42, 6; 49, 6; Lk 2, 32; 1 Cor 15, 20-23. *c:* 25, 11-12.

to a centurion named Julius of the Cohort Augusta. [2d]We went on board a ship from Adramyttium bound for ports in the province of Asia and set sail. Aristarchus, a Macedonian from Thessalonica, was with us. [3]On the following day we put in at Sidon where Julius was kind enough to allow Paul to visit his friends who took care of him. [4]From there we put out to sea and sailed around the sheltered side of Cyprus because of the headwinds, [5]and crossing the open sea off the coast of Cilicia and Pamphylia we came to Myra in Lycia.

Storm and Shipwreck. [6]There the centurion found an Alexandrian ship that was sailing to Italy and put us on board. [7]For many days we made little headway, arriving at Cnidus only with difficulty, and because the wind would not permit us to continue our course we sailed for the sheltered side of Crete off Salmone. [8]We sailed past it with difficulty and reached a place called Fair Havens, near which was the city of Lasea.

[9e*]Much time had now passed and sailing had become hazardous because the time of the fast had already gone by, so Paul warned them, [10]"Men, I can see that this voyage will result in severe damage and heavy loss not only to the cargo and the ship, but also to our lives." [11]The centurion, however, paid more attention to the pilot and to the owner of the ship than to what Paul said. [12]Since the harbor was unfavorably situated for spending the winter, the majority planned to put out to sea from there in the hope of reaching Phoenix, a port in Crete facing west-northwest, there to spend the winter.

[13]A south wind blew gently, and thinking they had attained their objective, they weighed anchor and sailed along close to the coast of Crete. [14]Before long an offshore wind of hurricane force called a "Northeaster" struck. [15]Since the ship was caught up in it and could not head into the wind we

gave way and let ourselves be driven. [16]We passed along the sheltered side of an island named Cauda and managed only with difficulty to get the dinghy under control. [17]They hoisted it aboard, then used cables to undergird the ship. Because of their fear that they would run aground on the shoal of Syrtis, they lowered the drift anchor and were carried along in this way. [18]We were being pounded by the storm so violently that the next day they jettisoned some cargo, [19]and on the third day with their own hands they threw even the ship's tackle overboard. [20]Neither the sun nor the stars were visible for many days, and no small storm raged. Finally, all hope of our surviving was taken away.

[21]When many would no longer eat, Paul stood among them and said, "Men, you should have taken my advice and not have set sail from Crete and you would have avoided this disastrous loss. [22]I urge you now to keep up your courage; not one of you will be lost, only the ship. [23]For last night an angel of the God to whom [I] belong and whom I serve stood by me [24f]and said, 'Do not be afraid, Paul. You are destined to stand before Caesar; and behold, for your sake, God has granted safety to all who are sailing with you.' [25]Therefore, keep up your courage, men; I trust in God that it will turn out as I have been told. [26]We are destined to run aground on some island."

[27]On the fourteenth night, as we were still being driven about on the Adriatic Sea, toward midnight the sailors began to suspect that they were nearing land. [28]They took soundings and found twenty fathoms; a little farther on, they again took soundings and found fifteen fathoms. [29]Fearing that we would run aground on a rocky coast, they dropped four anchors from the stern and prayed for day to come. [30]The sailors then tried to abandon ship; they lowered the dinghy to the sea on the pretext of going to lay out anchors from the bow. [31]But

his prophetic influence saved the lives of all on board. The recital also establishes the existence of Christian communities in Puteoli and Rome. This account of the voyage and shipwreck also constitutes the final "we-section" in Acts (see the note on 16, 10–17).

27, 1: **Cohort Augusta:** the presence of a Cohort Augusta in Syria during the first century A.D. is attested in inscriptions. Whatever the historical background to this information

given by Luke may be, the name Augusta serves to increase the prominence and prestige of the prisoner Paul whose custodians bear so important a Roman name.

27, 9: **The time of the fast:** the fast kept on the occasion of the Day of Atonement (Lv 16, 29–31), which occurred in late September or early October.

d: 19, 29; 20, 4.   e: Lv 16, 29-31.   f: 23, 11.

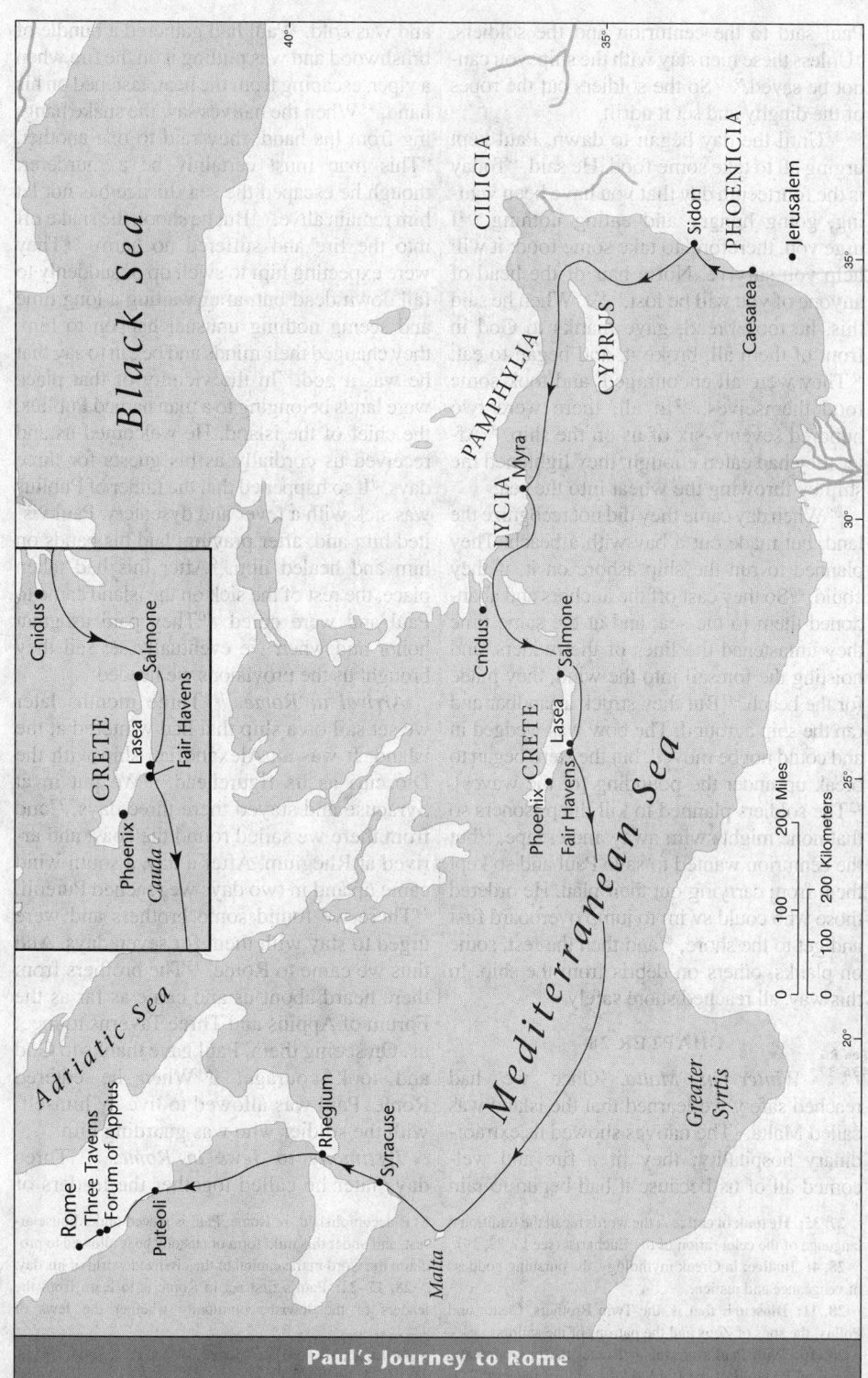

Black Sea

Adriatic Sea

Mediterranean Sea

CILICIA

PHOENICIA

Sidon

Jerusalem

Caesarea

CYPRUS

PAMPHYLIA

LYCIA

Myra

Cnidus

Salmone

CRETE

Phoenix

Lasea

Fair Havens

Cauda

Greater
Syrtis

Rome

Three Taverns

Forum of Appius

Puteoli

Rhegium

Syracuse

Malta

Cnidus

Salmone

Lasea

CRETE

Fair Havens

Phoenix

Cauda

200 Miles

100

200 Kilometers

100

0

0

Paul's Journey to Rome

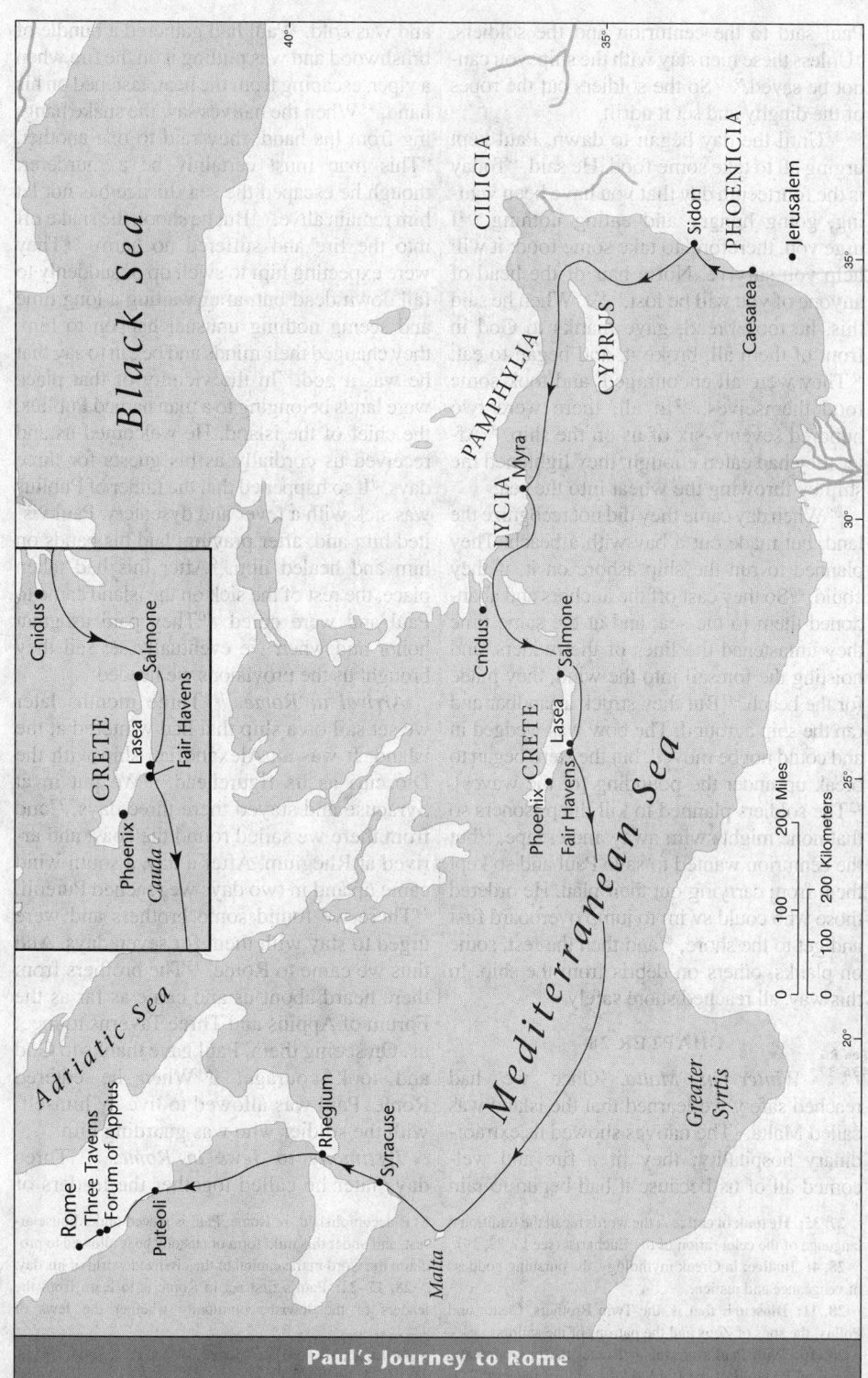

Paul said to the centurion and the soldiers, "Unless these men stay with the ship, you cannot be saved." [32]So the soldiers cut the ropes of the dinghy and set it adrift.

[33]Until the day began to dawn, Paul kept urging all to take some food. He said, "Today is the fourteenth day that you have been waiting, going hungry and eating nothing. [34]I urge you, therefore, to take some food; it will help you survive. Not a hair of the head of anyone of you will be lost." [35]g*When he said this, he took bread, gave thanks to God in front of them all, broke it, and began to eat. [36]They were all encouraged, and took some food themselves. [37]In all, there were two hundred seventy-six of us on the ship. [38]After they had eaten enough, they lightened the ship by throwing the wheat into the sea.

[39]When day came they did not recognize the land, but made out a bay with a beach. They planned to run the ship ashore on it, if they could. [40]So they cast off the anchors and abandoned them to the sea, and at the same time they unfastened the lines of the rudders, and hoisting the foresail into the wind, they made for the beach. [41]But they struck a sandbar and ran the ship aground. The bow was wedged in and could not be moved, but the stern began to break up under the pounding [of the waves]. [42]The soldiers planned to kill the prisoners so that none might swim away and escape, [43]but the centurion wanted to save Paul and so kept them from carrying out their plan. He ordered those who could swim to jump overboard first and get to the shore, [44]and then the rest, some on planks, others on debris from the ship. In this way, all reached shore safely.

CHAPTER 28

See RG
436–37 *Winter in Malta.* [1]Once we had reached safety we learned that the island was called Malta. [2]The natives showed us extraordinary hospitality; they lit a fire and welcomed all of us because it had begun to rain

and was cold. [3]Paul had gathered a bundle of brushwood and was putting it on the fire when a viper, escaping from the heat, fastened on his hand. [4]*When the natives saw the snake hanging from his hand, they said to one another, "This man must certainly be a murderer; though he escaped the sea, Justice has not let him remain alive." [5]But he shook the snake off into the fire and suffered no harm. [6]hThey were expecting him to swell up or suddenly to fall down dead but, after waiting a long time and seeing nothing unusual happen to him, they changed their minds and began to say that he was a god. [7]In the vicinity of that place were lands belonging to a man named Publius, the chief of the island. He welcomed us and received us cordially as his guests for three days. [8]It so happened that the father of Publius was sick with a fever and dysentery. Paul visited him and, after praying, laid his hands on him and healed him. [9]After this had taken place, the rest of the sick on the island came to Paul and were cured. [10]They paid us great honor and when we eventually set sail they brought us the provisions we needed.

Arrival in Rome. [11]*Three months later we set sail on a ship that had wintered at the island. It was an Alexandrian ship with the Dioscuri as its figurehead. [12]We put in at Syracuse and stayed there three days, [13]and from there we sailed round the coast and arrived at Rhegium. After a day, a south wind came up and in two days we reached Puteoli. [14]There we found some brothers and were urged to stay with them for seven days. And thus we came to Rome. [15]The brothers from there heard about us and came as far as the Forum of Appius and Three Taverns to meet us. On seeing them, Paul gave thanks to God and took courage. [16]*When he entered Rome, Paul was allowed to live by himself, with the soldier who was guarding him.

Testimony to Jews in Rome. [17]i*Three days later he called together the leaders of

---

27, 35: **He took bread . . . :** the words recall the traditional language of the celebration of the Eucharist (see Lk 22, 19).

28, 4: **Justice:** in Greek mythology, the pursuing goddess of vengeance and justice.

28, 11: **Dioscuri:** that is, the Twin Brothers, Castor and Pollux, the sons of Zeus and the patrons of the sailors.

28, 16: With Paul's arrival in Rome, the programmatic spread of the word of the Lord to "the ends of the earth" (1,

8) is accomplished. In Rome, Paul is placed under house arrest, and under this mild form of custody he is allowed to proclaim the word in the capital of the civilized world of his day.

28, 17–22: Paul's first act in Rome is to learn from the leaders of the Jewish community whether the Jews of

g: Mt 15, 36; Mk 6, 41; 8, 6; Lk 22, 19; 1 Cor 11, 23-24.   h: 14, 11.   i: 24, 12-13; 25, 8.

the Jews. When they had gathered he said to them, "My brothers, although I had done nothing against our people or our ancestral customs, I was handed over to the Romans as a prisoner from Jerusalem. *18j*After trying my case the Romans wanted to release me, because they found nothing against me deserving the death penalty. *19k*But when the Jews objected, I was obliged to appeal to Caesar, even though I had no accusation to make against my own nation. *20l**This is the reason, then, I have requested to see you and to speak with you, for it is on account of the hope of Israel that I wear these chains." *21*They answered him, "We have received no letters from Judea about you, nor has any of the brothers arrived with a damaging report or rumor about you. *22m*But we should like to hear you present your views, for we know that this sect is denounced everywhere."

*23*So they arranged a day with him and came to his lodgings in great numbers. From early morning until evening, he expounded his position to them, bearing witness to the kingdom of God and trying to convince them about Jesus from the law of Moses and the prophets. *24*Some were convinced by what he had said, while others did not believe. *25**Without reaching any agreement among themselves they began to leave; then Paul made one final statement. "Well did the holy Spirit speak to your ancestors through the prophet Isaiah, saying:

26 n'Go to this people and say:
You shall indeed hear but not understand.
You shall indeed look but never see.
27 Gross is the heart of this people;
they will not hear with their ears;
they have closed their eyes,
so they may not see with their eyes
and hear with their ears
and understand with their heart and be converted,
and I heal them.'

*28o*Let it be known to you that this salvation of God has been sent to the Gentiles; they will listen." [*29*]*

30*He remained for two full years in his lodgings. He received all who came to him, *31*and with complete assurance and without hindrance he proclaimed the kingdom of God and taught about the Lord Jesus Christ.

Jerusalem plan to pursue their case against him before the Roman jurisdiction. He is informed that no such plan is afoot, but that the Jews of Rome have heard the Christian teaching denounced. Paul's offer to explain it to them is readily accepted.

28, 20: The hope of Israel: in the words of Paul (23, 6), Luke has identified this hope as hope in the resurrection of the dead.

28, 25–28: Paul's final words in Acts reflect a major concern of Luke's writings: how the salvation promised in the Old Testament, accomplished by Jesus, and offered first to Israel (13, 26), has now been offered to and accepted by the Gentiles. Quoting Is 6, 9–10, Paul presents the scriptural support for his indictment of his fellow Jews who refuse to accept the message he proclaims. Their rejection leads to its proclamation among the Gentiles.

28, 29: The Western text has added here a verse that is not found in the best Greek manuscripts: "And when he had said this, the Jews left, seriously arguing among themselves."

28, 30–31: Although the ending of Acts may seem to be abrupt, Luke has now completed his story with the establishment of Paul and the proclamation of Christianity in Rome. Paul's confident and unhindered proclamation of the gospel in Rome forms the climax to the story whose outline was provided in 1, 8: "You will be my witnesses in Jerusalem . . . and to the ends of the earth."

j: 23, 29; 25, 25; 26, 31-32. *k:* 25, 11. *l:* 23, 6; 24, 15.21; 26, 6-8. *m:* 24, 5.14. *n:* Is 6, 9-10; Mt 13, 14-15; Mk 4, 12; Lk 8, 10; Jn 12, 40; Rom 11, 8. *o:* 13, 46; 18, 6; Ps 67, 2; Is 40, 5 LXX; Lk 3, 6.

NEW TESTAMENT LETTERS

In the New Testament canon, between the Acts of the Apostles and Revelation, there are twenty-one documents that take the form of letters or epistles. Most of these are actual letters, but some are more like treatises in the guise of letters. In a few cases even some of the more obvious elements of the letter form are absent; see the Introductions to Hebrews and to 1 John.

The virtually standard form found in these documents, though with some variation, is dependent upon the conventions of letter writing common in the ancient world, but these were modified to suit the purposes of Christian writers. The New Testament letters usually begin with a greeting including an identification of the sender or senders and of the recipients. Next comes a prayer, usually in the form of a thanksgiving. The body of the letter provides an exposition of Christian teaching, usually provoked by concrete circumstances, and generally also draws conclusions regarding ethical behavior. There often follows a discussion of practical matters, such as the writer's travel plans, and the letter concludes with further advice and a formula of farewell.

Fourteen of the twenty-one letters have been traditionally attributed to Paul. One of these, the Letter to the Hebrews, does not itself claim to be the work of Paul; when it was accepted into the canon after much discussion, it was attached at the very end of the Pauline corpus. The other thirteen identify Paul as their author, but most scholars believe that some of them were actually written by his disciples; see the Introductions to

Ephesians, Colossians, 2 Thessalonians, and 1 Timothy.

Four of the letters in the Pauline corpus (Ephesians, Philippians, Colossians, and Philemon) are called the "Captivity Epistles" because in each of them the author speaks of being in prison at the time of writing. Three others (1–2 Timothy and Titus) are known as the "Pastoral Epistles" because, addressed to individuals rather than communities, they give advice to disciples about caring for the flock. The letters of the Pauline corpus are arranged in roughly descending order of length from Romans to Philemon, with Hebrews added at the end.

The other seven letters of the New Testament that follow the Pauline corpus are collectively referred to as the "Catholic Epistles." This term, which means "universal," refers to the fact that most of them are directed not to a single Christian community, as are most of the Pauline letters, but to a wider audience; see the Introduction to the catholic letters. Three of them (1–2–3 John) are closely related to the fourth gospel and thus belong to the Johannine corpus. The catholic letters, like those of the Pauline corpus, are also arranged in roughly descending order of length, but the three Johannine letters are kept together and Jude is placed at the end.

The genuine letters of Paul are earlier in date than any of our written gospels. The dates of the other New Testament letters are more difficult to determine, but for the most part they belong to the second and third Christian generations rather than to the first.

See RG
441-50

The Letter to the Romans

Of all the letters of Paul, that to the Christians at Rome has long held pride of place. It is the longest and most systematic unfolding of the apostle's thought, expounding the gospel of God's righteousness that saves all who believe (1, 16–17); it reflects a universal outlook, with special implications for Israel's relation to the church (chs 9—11). Yet, like all Paul's letters, Romans too arose out of a specific situation, when the apostle wrote from Greece, likely Corinth, between A.D. 56 and 58 (cf Acts 20, 2–3).

Paul at that time was about to leave for Jerusalem with a collection of funds for the impoverished Jewish Christian believers there, taken up from his predominantly Gentile congregations (15, 25–27). He planned then to travel on to Rome and to enlist support there for a mission to Spain (15, 24.28). Such a journey had long been on his mind (1, 9–13; 15, 23). Now, with much missionary preaching successfully accomplished in the East (15, 19), he sought new opportunities in the West (15, 20–21), in order to complete the divine plan of evangelization in the Roman world. Yet he recognized that the visit to Jerusalem would be hazardous (15, 30–32), and we know from Acts that Paul was arrested there and came to Rome only in chains, as a prisoner (Acts 21–28, especially 21, 30–33 and 28, 14.30–31).

The existence of a Christian community in Rome antedates Paul's letter there. When it arose, likely within the sizable Jewish population at Rome, and how, we do not know. The Roman historian Suetonius mentions an edict of the Emperor Claudius about A.D. 49 ordering the expulsion of Jews from Rome in connection with a certain "Chrestus," probably involving a dispute in the Jewish community over Jesus as the Messiah ("Christus"). According to Acts 18, 2, Aquila and Priscilla (or Prisca, as in 16, 3) were among those driven out; from them, in Corinth, Paul may have learned about conditions in the church at Rome.

Opinions vary as to whether Jewish or Gentile Christians predominated in the house churches (cf 16, 5) in the capital city of the empire at the time Paul wrote. Perhaps already by then Gentile Christians were in the majority. Paul speaks in Romans of both Jews and Gentiles (3, 9.29; see the note on 1, 14). The letter also refers to those "weak in faith" (14, 1) and those "who are strong" (15, 1); this terminology may reflect not so much differences between believers of Jewish and of Gentile background, respectively, as an ascetic tendency in some converts (14, 2) combined with Jewish laws about clean and unclean foods (14, 14.20). The issues were similar to problems that Paul had faced in Corinth (1 Cor 8). If Romans 16 is part of the Letter to Rome (see the note on 16, 1–23), then Paul had considerable information about conditions in Rome through all these people there whom he knew, and our letter does not just reflect a generalized picture of an earlier situation in Corinth.

In any case, Paul writes to introduce himself and his message to the Christians at Rome, seeking to enlist their support for the proposed mission to Spain. He therefore employs formulations likely familiar to the Christians at Rome; see the note on the confessional material at 1, 3–4 and compare 3, 25–26; and 4, 25. He cites the Old Testament frequently (1, 17; 3, 10–18; ch 4; 9, 7.12–13.15.17.25–29.33; 10, 5–13.15–21; 15, 9–12). The gospel Paul presents is meant to be a familiar one to those in Rome, even though they heard it first from other preachers.

As the outline below shows, this gospel of Paul (see 16, 25) finds its center in salvation and justification through faith in Christ (1, 16–17). While God's wrath is revealed against all sin and wickedness of Gentile and Jew alike (1, 18—3, 20), God's power to save by divine righteous or justifying action in Christ is also revealed (1, 16–17; 3, 21—5, 21). The consequences and implications for those who believe are set forth (6, 1—8, 39), as are results for those in Israel (ch 9—11) who, to Paul's great sorrow (9, 1–5), disbelieve. The apostle's hope is that, just as rejection of the gospel by some in Israel has led to a ministry of salvation for non-Jews, so one day, in God's mercy, "all Israel" will be saved (11, 11–15.25–29.30–32). The fuller ethical response of believers is also drawn out, both with reference to life in Christ's body (12) and with regard to the world (ch 13, 1–7), on the basis of the eschatological situation (13, 11–14) and conditions in the community (14, 1—15, 13).

Others have viewed Romans more in the light of Paul's earlier, quite polemical Letter to the Galatians and so see the theme as the relationship between Judaism and Christianity, a topic judged to be much in the minds of the Roman Christians. Each of these religious faiths claimed to be the way of salvation based upon a covenant between God and a people chosen and made the beneficiary of divine gifts. But Christianity regarded itself as the prophetic development and fulfillment of the faith of the Old Testament, declaring that the preparatory Mosaic covenant must now give way to the new and more perfect covenant in Jesus Christ. Paul himself had been the implacable advocate of freedom of Gentiles from the laws of the Mosaic covenant and, especially in Galatia, had refused to allow attempts to impose them on Gentile converts to the gospel. He had witnessed the personal hostilities that developed between the adherents of the two faiths and had written his strongly worded Letter to the Galatians against those Jewish Christians who were seeking to persuade Gentile Christians to adopt the religious practices of Judaism. For him, the purity of the religious understanding of Jesus as the source of salvation would be seriously impaired if Gentile Christians were obligated to amalgamate the two religious faiths.

Still others find the theme of Israel and the church as expressed in Romans 9—11 to be the heart of Romans. Then the implication of Paul's exposition of justification by faith rather than by means of law is that the divine plan of salvation works itself out on a broad theological plane to include the whole of humanity, despite the differences in the content of the given religious system to which a human culture is heir. Romans presents a plan of salvation stretching from Adam through Abraham and Moses to Christ (chs 4 and 5) and on to the future revelation at Christ's parousia (8, 18–25). Its outlook is universal.

Paul's Letter to the Romans is a powerful exposition of the doctrine of the supremacy of Christ and of faith in Christ as the source of salvation. It is an implicit plea to the Christians at Rome, and to all Christians, to hold fast to that faith. They are to resist any pressure put on them to accept a doctrine of salvation through works of the law (see the note on 10, 4). At the same time they are not to exaggerate Christian freedom as an abdication of responsibility for others (12, 1–2) or as a repudiation of God's law and will (see the notes on 3, 9–26; 3, 31; 7, 7–12.13–25).

The principal divisions of the Letter to the Romans are the following:

I: Address (1, 1–15)

II: Humanity Lost without the Gospel (1, 16—3, 20)

III: Justification through Faith in Christ (3, 21—5, 21)

IV: Justification and the Christian Life (6, 1—8, 39)

V: Jews and Gentiles in God's Plan (9, 1—11, 36)

VI: The Duties of Christians (12, 1—15, 13)

VII: Conclusion (15, 14—16, 27)

I: Address

CHAPTER 1

See RG 442–45

Greeting. 1a*Paul, a slave of Christ Jesus, called to be an apostle and set apart for the gospel of God, 2bwhich he promised previously through his prophets in the holy

---

1, 1–7: In Paul's letters the greeting or **praescriptio** follows a standard form, though with variations. It is based upon the common Greco-Roman epistolary practice, but with the addition of Semitic and specifically Christian elements. The three basic components are: name of sender; name of addressee; greeting. In identifying himself, Paul often adds phrases to describe his apostolic mission; this element is more developed in Rom than in any other letter. Elsewhere he associates co-workers with himself in the greeting: Sosthenes (1 Cor), Timothy (2 Cor; Phil; Phlm), Silvanus (1–2 Thes). The standard secular greeting was the infinitive **chairein,** "greetings." Paul uses instead the similar-sounding **charis,** "grace," together with the Semitic greeting **šālôm** (Greek **eirēnē**), "peace." These gifts, foreshadowed in God's deal-

ings with Israel (see Nm 6, 24–26), have been poured out abundantly in Christ, and Paul wishes them to his readers. In Rom the Pauline **praescriptio** is expanded and expressed in a formal tone; it emphasizes Paul's office as apostle to the Gentiles. Verses 3–4 stress the gospel or kerygma, v 2 the fulfillment of God's promise, and vv 1 and 5 Paul's office. On his call, see Gal 1, 15–16; 1 Cor 9, 1; 15, 8–10; Acts 9, 1–22; 22, 3–16; 26, 4–18.

1, 1: Slave of Christ Jesus: Paul applies the term slave to himself in order to express his undivided allegiance to the Lord of the church, the Master of all, including slaves and

a: Gal 1, 10; Phil 1, 1; Jas 1, 1 / Acts 9, 15; 13, 2; 1 Cor 1, 1; Gal 1, 15; Ti 1, 1. b: 16, 25-26; Ti 1, 2.

scriptures, ^{3c}*the gospel about his Son, descended from David according to the flesh, ^{4d}but established as Son of God in power according to the spirit of holiness through resurrection from the dead, Jesus Christ our Lord. ^{5e}*Through him we have received the grace of apostleship, to bring about the obedience of faith, for the sake of his name, among all the Gentiles, ^{6f}among whom are you also, who are called to belong to Jesus Christ; ^{7g}*to all the beloved of God in Rome, called to be holy. Grace to you and peace from God our Father and the Lord Jesus Christ.

Thanksgiving. ^{8h}*First, I give thanks to my God through Jesus Christ for all of you, because your faith is heralded throughout the world. ⁹ⁱGod is my witness, whom I serve with my spirit in proclaiming the gospel of his Son, that I remember you constantly, ^{10j}*always asking in my prayers that some-

how by God's will I may at last find my way clear to come to you. ^{11k}For I long to see you, that I may share with you some spiritual gift so that you may be strengthened, ¹²that is, that you and I may be mutually encouraged by one another's faith, yours and mine. ^{13l}*I do not want you to be unaware, brothers, that I often planned to come to you, though I was prevented until now, that I might harvest some fruit among you, too, as among the rest of the Gentiles. ¹⁴*To Greeks and non-Greeks alike, to the wise and the ignorant, I am under obligation; ^{15m}that is why I am eager to preach the gospel also to you in Rome.

II: Humanity Lost without the Gospel

God's Power for Salvation. ¹⁶ⁿ*For I am not ashamed of the gospel. It is the power of God for the salvation of everyone who be-

---

masters. "No one can serve (i.e., be a slave to) two masters," said Jesus (Mt 6, 24). It is this aspect of the slave-master relationship rather than its degrading implications that Paul emphasizes when he discusses Christian commitment.

1, 3–4: Paul here cites an early confession that proclaims Jesus' sonship as messianic descendant of David (cf Mt 22, 42; 2 Tm 2, 8; Rv 22, 16) and as Son of God by the resurrection. As "life-giving spirit" (1 Cor 15, 45), Jesus Christ is able to communicate the Spirit to those who believe in him.

1, 5: Paul recalls his apostolic office, implying that the Romans know something of his history. **The obedience of faith:** as Paul will show at length in chs 6–8 and 12–15, faith in God's justifying action in Jesus Christ relates one to God's gift of the new life that is made possible through the death and resurrection of Jesus Christ and the activity of the holy Spirit (see especially 8, 1–11).

1, 7: Called to be holy: Paul often refers to Christians as "the holy ones" or "the saints." The Israelite community was called a "holy assembly" because they had been separated for the worship and service of the Lord (see Lv 11, 44; 23, 1–44). The Christian community regarded its members as sanctified by baptism (6, 22; 15, 16; 1 Cor 6, 11; Eph 5, 26–27). Christians are called to holiness (1 Cor 1, 2; 1 Thes 4, 7), that is, they are called to make their lives conform to the gift they have already received.

1, 8: In Greco-Roman letters, the greeting was customarily followed by a prayer. The Pauline letters usually include this element (except Gal and Ti), expressed in Christian thanksgiving formulas and usually stating the principal theme of the letter. In 2 Cor the thanksgiving becomes a blessing, and in Eph it is preceded by a lengthy blessing. Sometimes the thanksgiving is blended into the body of the letter, especially in 1 Thes. In Rom it is stated briefly.

1, 10–12: Paul lays the groundwork for his more detailed statement in 15, 22–24 about his projected visit to Rome.

1, 13: Brothers is idiomatic for all Paul's "kin in Christ," all those who believe in the gospel; it includes women as well as men (cf 4, 3).

1, 14: Greeks and non-Greeks: literally, "Greeks and barbarians." As a result of Alexander's conquests, Greek became the standard international language of the Mediterranean world. **Greeks** in Paul's statement therefore means people who know Greek or who have been influenced by Greek culture. **Non-Greeks** were people whose cultures remained substantially unaffected by Greek influences. Greeks called such people "barbarians" (cf Acts 28, 2), meaning people whose speech was foreign. Roman citizens would scarcely classify themselves as such, and Nero, who was reigning when Paul wrote this letter, prided himself on his admiration for Greek culture. **Under obligation:** Paul will expand on the theme of obligation in 13, 8; 15, 1.27.

1, 16–17: The principal theme of the letter is salvation through faith. **I am not ashamed of the gospel:** Paul is not ashamed to proclaim the gospel, despite the criticism that Jews and Gentiles leveled against the proclamation of the crucified savior; cf 1 Cor 1, 23–24. Paul affirms, however, that it is precisely through the crucifixion and resurrection of Jesus that God's saving will and power become manifest. **Jew first** (cf 2, 9–10) means that Jews especially, in view of the example of Abraham (ch 4), ought to be the leaders in the response of faith.

---

c: 9, 5; 2 Sm 7, 12; Mt 1, 1; Mk 12, 35; Jn 7, 42; Acts 13, 22-23; 2 Tm 2, 8; Rv 22, 16. *d:* 10, 9; Acts 13, 33; Phil 3, 10. *e:* 15, 15; Gal 2, 7.9 / 15, 18; Acts 9, 15; 26, 16-18; Gal 1, 16; 2, 7.9. *f:* 1 Cor 1, 9. *g:* Nm 6, 25-26; 1 Cor 1, 2-3; 2 Cor 1, 1-2. *h:* 16, 19; 1 Thes 1, 8. *i:* 2 Cor 1, 23; Eph 1, 16; Phil 1, 8; 1 Thes 1, 2; 2, 5.10; 2 Tm 1, 3. *j:* 15, 23.32; Acts 18, 21; 1 Cor 4, 19; 1 Thes 2, 17. *k:* 1 Thes 2, 17; 3, 10. *l:* 15, 22; Jn 15, 16; Acts 19, 21. *m:* Acts 28, 30-31. *n:* Ps 119, 46; 1 Cor 1, 18.24 / 2, 9; Acts 3, 26; 13, 46.

lieves: for Jew first, and then Greek. [17o]*For in it is revealed the righteousness of God from faith to faith; as it is written, "The one who is righteous by faith will live."

Punishment of Idolators. [18p]*The wrath of God is indeed being revealed from heaven against every impiety and wickedness of those who suppress the truth by their wickedness. [19q]For what can be known about God is evident to them, because God made it evident to them. [20r]Ever since the creation of the world, his invisible attributes of eternal power and divinity have been able to be understood and perceived in what he has made. As a result, they have no excuse; [21s]for although they knew God they did not accord him glory as God or give him thanks. Instead, they became vain in their reasoning, and their senseless minds were darkened. [22t]While claiming to be wise, they became fools [23u]and exchanged the glory of the immortal God for the likeness of an image of mortal man or of birds or of four-legged animals or of snakes. [24v]*Therefore, God handed them over to impurity through the lusts of their hearts for the mutual degradation of their bodies.

[25w]They exchanged the truth of God for a lie and revered and worshiped the creature rather than the creator, who is blessed forever. Amen. [26]Therefore, God handed them over to degrading passions. Their females exchanged natural relations for unnatural, [27x]and the males likewise gave up natural relations with females and burned with lust for one another. Males did shameful things with males and thus received in their own persons the due penalty for their perversity. [28]And since they did not see fit to acknowledge God, God handed them over to their undiscerning mind to do what is improper. [29y]They are filled with every form of wickedness, evil, greed, and malice; full of envy, murder, rivalry, treachery, and spite. They are gossips [30]and scandalmongers and they hate God. They are insolent, haughty, boastful, ingenious in their wickedness, and rebellious toward their parents. [31]They are senseless, faithless, heartless, ruthless. [32z]Although they know the just decree of God that all who practice such things deserve death, they not only do them but give approval to those who practice them.

1, 17: In it is revealed the righteousness of God from faith to faith: the gospel centers in Jesus Christ, in whom God's saving presence and righteousness in history have been made known. Faith is affirmation of the basic purpose and meaning of the Old Testament as proclamation of divine promise (2; 4, 13) and exposure of the inability of humanity to effect its salvation even through covenant law. Faith is the gift of the holy Spirit and denotes acceptance of salvation as God's righteousness, that is, God's gift of a renewed relationship in forgiveness and power for a new life. Faith is response to God's total claim on people and their destiny. The one who is righteous by faith will live: see the note on Hb 2, 4.

1, 18—3, 20: Paul aims to show that all humanity is in a desperate plight and requires God's special intervention if it is to be saved.

1, 18–32: In this passage Paul uses themes and rhetoric common in Jewish-Hellenistic mission proclamation (cf Wis 13, 1—14, 31) to indict especially the non-Jewish world. The close association of idolatry and immorality is basic, but the generalization needs in all fairness to be balanced against the fact that non-Jewish Christian society on many levels displayed moral attitudes and performance whose quality would challenge much of contemporary Christian culture. Romans themselves expressed abhorrence over devotion accorded to animals in Egypt. Paul's main point is that the wrath of God does not await the end of the world but goes into action at each present moment in humanity's history when misdirected piety serves as a facade for self-interest.

1, 18: The wrath of God: God's reaction to human sinfulness, an Old Testament phrase that expresses the irreconcilable opposition between God and evil (see Is 9, 11.16.18.20; 10, 4; 30, 27). It is not contrary to God's universal love for his creatures, but condemns Israel's turning aside from the covenant obligations. Hosea depicts Yahweh as suffering intensely at the thought of having to punish Israel (Hos 11, 8–9). God's wrath was to be poured forth especially on the "Day of Yahweh" and thus took on an eschatological connotation (see Zep 1, 15).

1, 24: In order to expose the depth of humanity's rebellion against the Creator, God handed them over to impurity through the lusts of their hearts. Instead of curbing people's evil interests, God abandoned them to self-indulgence, thereby removing the facade of apparent conformity to the divine will. Subsequently Paul will show that the Mosaic law produces the same effect; cf 5, 20; 7, 13–24. The divine judgment expressed here is related to the theme of hardness of heart described in 9, 17–18.

o: 3, 21-22; Hb 2, 4; Gal 3, 11; Heb 10, 38.   p: 2, 5.8-9; Is 66, 15; Eph 5, 6; Col 3, 6.   q: Wis 13-19; Acts 14, 15-17; 17, 23-29.   r: Jb 12, 7-9; Pss 8, 4; 19, 2; Sir 17, 7-9; Is 40, 26; Acts 14, 17;17, 25-28.   s: Eph 4, 17-18.   t: Wis 13, 1-9; Is 5, 21; Jer 10, 14; Acts 17, 29-30;1 Cor 1, 19-21.   u: Dt 4, 15-19; Ps 106, 20; Wis 11, 15; 12, 24; 13, 10-19;Jer 2, 11.   v: Wis 12, 25; 14, 22-31; Acts 7, 41-42; Eph 4, 19.   w: 9, 5; Jer 13, 25-27.   x: Lv 18, 22; 20, 13; Wis 14, 26; 1 Cor 6, 9; 1 Tm 1, 10.   y: 13, 13; Mt 15, 19; Mk 7, 21-22; Gal 5, 19-21; 2 Tm 3, 2-4.   z: Acts 8, 1; 2 Thes 2, 12.

See RG
444-45

CHAPTER 2

God's Just Judgment. ¹ᵃ*Therefore, you are without excuse, every one of you who passes judgment. For by the standard by which you judge another you condemn yourself, since you, the judge, do the very same things. ²We know that the judgment of God on those who do such things is true. ³ᵇDo you suppose, then, you who judge those who engage in such things and yet do them yourself, that you will escape the judgment of God? ⁴ᶜOr do you hold his priceless kindness, forbearance, and patience in low esteem, unaware that the kindness of God would lead you to repentance? ⁵ᵈBy your stubbornness and impenitent heart, you are storing up wrath for yourself for the day of wrath and revelation of the just judgment of God, ⁶ᵉ*who will repay everyone according to his works: ⁷eternal life to those who seek glory, honor, and immortality through perseverance in good works, ⁸ᶠbut wrath and fury to those who selfishly disobey the truth and obey wickedness. ⁹Yes, affliction and distress will come upon every human being who does evil, Jew first and then Greek. ¹⁰ᵍBut there will be glory, honor, and peace for everyone who does good, Jew first and then Greek. ¹¹ʰ*There is no partiality with God.

Judgment by the Interior Law. ¹²ⁱ*All who sin outside the law will also perish without reference to it, and all who sin under the law will be judged in accordance with it. ¹³ʲFor it is not those who hear the law who are just in the sight of God; rather, those who observe the law will be justified. ¹⁴ᵏFor when the Gentiles who do not have the law by nature observe the prescriptions of the law, they are a law for themselves even though they do not have the law. ¹⁵*They show that the demands of the law are written in their hearts, while their conscience also bears witness and their conflicting thoughts accuse or even defend them ¹⁶ˡon the day when, according to my gospel, God will judge people's hidden works through Christ Jesus.

Judgment by the Mosaic Law. ¹⁷ᵐ*Now if you call yourself a Jew and rely on the law and boast of God ¹⁸ⁿand know his will and are able to discern what is important since you are instructed from the law, ¹⁹ᵒand if you are confident that you are a guide for the blind and a light for those in darkness, ²⁰ᵖthat you are a trainer of the foolish and teacher of the simple, because in the law you have the formulation of knowledge and truth— ²¹�q then you who teach another, are you failing to teach yourself? You who preach against stealing, do you steal? ²²You who forbid adultery, do you commit adultery? You who detest idols, do you rob temples? ²³You who boast of the law, do you dis-

---

2, 1—3, 20: After his general indictment of the Gentile, Paul shows that in spite of special revelation Jews enjoy no advantage in moral status before God (3, 1–8). With the entire human race now declared guilty before God (3, 9–20), Paul will then be able to display the solution for the total problem: salvation through God's redemptive work that is revealed in Christ Jesus for all who believe (3, 21–31).

2, 1–11: As a first step in his demonstration that Jews enjoy no real moral supremacy over Gentiles, Paul explains that the final judgment will be a review of performance, not of privilege. From this perspective Gentiles stand on an equal footing with Jews, and Jews cannot condemn the sins of Gentiles without condemning themselves.

2, 6: Will repay everyone according to his works: Paul reproduces the Septuagint text of Ps 62, 12 and Prv 24, 12.

2, 11: No partiality with God: this sentence is not at variance with the statements in vv 9–10. Since Jews are the first to go under indictment, it is only fair that they be given first consideration in the distribution of blessings. Basic, of course, is the understanding that God accepts no bribes (Dt 10, 17).

2, 12–16: Jews cannot reasonably demand from Gentiles the standard of conduct inculcated in the Old Testament since

God did not address its revelation to them. Rather, God made it possible for Gentiles to know instinctively the difference between right and wrong. But, as Paul explained in 1, 18–32, humanity misread the evidence of God's existence, power, and divinity, and "while claiming to be wise, they became fools" (1, 22).

2, 15: Paul expands on the thought of Jer 31, 33; Wis 17, 11.

2, 17–29: Mere possession of laws is no evidence of virtue. By eliminating circumcision as an elitist moral sign, Paul clears away the last obstacle to his presentation of justification through faith without claims based on the receipt of circumcision and its attendant legal obligations.

a: Mt 7, 1-2. *b:* Wis 16, 15-16. *c:* 3, 25-26; 9, 22; Wis 11, 23; 15, 1; 2 Pt 3, 9.15. *d:* Ex 33, 3; Acts 7, 51; Rv 6, 17; 11, 18.
e: Ps 62, 12; Prv 24, 12; Sir 16, 14; Mt 16, 27; Jn 5, 29;2 Cor 5, 10. *f:* 2 Thes 1, 8. *g:* 1, 16; 3, 9. *h:* Dt 10, 17; 2 Chr 19, 7; Sir 35, 12-13; Acts 10, 34; Gal 2, 6;Eph 6, 9; Col 3, 25; 1 Pt 1, 17. *i:* 3, 19. *j:* Mt 7, 21; Lk 6, 46-49; 8, 21; Jas 1, 22-25; 1 Jn 3, 7. *k:* Acts 10, 35. *l:* Acts 10, 42; 17, 31. *m:* Is 48, 1-2; Mi 3, 11; Phil 3, 4-6. *n:* Phil 1, 10. *o:* Mt 15, 14; Lk 6, 39. *p:* 2 Tm 3, 15. *q:* Ps 50, 16-21; Mt 23, 3-4.

honor God by breaking the law? [24r*]For, as it is written, "Because of you the name of God is reviled among the Gentiles."

[25st]Circumcision, to be sure, has value if you observe the law; but if you break the law, your circumcision has become uncircumcision. [26u]Again, if an uncircumcised man keeps the precepts of the law, will he not be considered circumcised? [27]Indeed, those who are physically uncircumcised but carry out the law will pass judgment on you, with your written law and circumcision, who break the law. [28v]One is not a Jew outwardly. True circumcision is not outward, in the flesh. [29w]Rather, one is a Jew inwardly, and circumcision is of the heart, in the spirit, not the letter; his praise is not from human beings but from God.

CHAPTER 3

See RG 444-45 *Answers to Objections.* [1*]What advantage is there then in being a Jew? Or what is the value of circumcision? [2x]Much, in every respect. [For] in the first place, they were entrusted with the utterances of God. [3y]What if some were unfaithful? Will their infidelity nullify the fidelity of God? [4z*]Of course not! God must be true, though every human being is a liar, as it is written:

"That you may be justified in your
        words,
    and conquer when you are judged."

[5a]But if our wickedness provides proof of God's righteousness, what can we say? Is God unjust, humanly speaking, to inflict his wrath? [6]Of course not! For how else is God to judge the world? [7]But if God's truth redounds to his glory through my falsehood, why am I still being condemned as a sinner? [8b]And why not say—as we are accused and as some claim we say—that we should do evil that good may come of it? Their penalty is what they deserve.

Universal Bondage to Sin. [9c*]Well, then, are we better off? Not entirely, for we have already brought the charge against Jews and Greeks alike that they are all under the domination of sin, [10d]as it is written:

"There is no one just, not one,
[11]   there is no one who understands,
        there is no one who seeks God.
[12] All have gone astray; all alike are
            worthless;
    there is not one who does good,
        [there is not] even one.
[13] [e]Their throats are open graves;
        they deceive with their tongues;
    the venom of asps is on their lips;
[14]   [f]their mouths are full of bitter cursing.
[15] [g]Their feet are quick to shed blood;
[16]   ruin and misery are in their ways,
[17]   and the way of peace they know not.
[18]   [h]There is no fear of God before their
            eyes."

[19i*]Now we know that what the law says is addressed to those under the law, so that every mouth may be silenced and the whole world stand accountable to God, [20j*]since no

2, 24: According to Is 52, 5 the suffering of Israel prompts her enemies to revile God. Paul uses the passage in support of his point that the present immorality of Israelites is the cause of such defamation.

3, 1–4: In keeping with the popular style of diatribe, Paul responds to the objection that his teaching on the sinfulness of all humanity detracts from the religious prerogatives of Israel. He stresses that Jews have remained the vehicle of God's revelation despite their sins, though this depends on the fidelity of God.

3, 4: Though every human being is a liar: these words reproduce the Greek text of Ps 116, 11. The rest of the verse is from Ps 51, 6.

3, 9–20: Well, then, are we better off?: this phrase can also be translated "Are we at a disadvantage?" but the latter version does not substantially change the overall meaning of the passage. Having explained that Israel's privileged status is guaranteed by God's fidelity, Paul now demonstrates the infidelity of the Jews by a catena of citations from scripture, possibly derived from an existing collection of **testimonia.**

These texts show that all human beings share the common burden of sin. They are linked together by mention of organs of the body: throat, tongue, lips, mouth, feet, eyes.

3, 19: The law: Paul here uses the term in its broadest sense to mean all of the scriptures; none of the preceding texts is from the Torah or Pentateuch.

3, 20: No human being will be justified in his sight: these words are freely cited from Ps 143, 2. In place of the psalmist's "no living person," Paul substitutes "no human being" (literally "no flesh," a Hebraism), and he adds "by observing the law."

r: Is 52, 5; Ez 36, 20; 2 Pt 2, 2.   s: Jer 4, 4; 9, 24-25.   t: 1 Cor 7, 19; Gal 5, 3.   u: Gal 5, 6.   v: Jn 7, 24; 8, 15.39.   w: Dt 30, 6; Jer 4, 4; 9, 25; Col 2, 11 / 1 Cor 4, 5; 2 Cor 10, 18.   x: 9, 4; Dt 4, 7-8; Pss 103, 7; 147, 19-20.   y: 9, 6; 11, 1.29; Ps 89, 30-37; 2 Tm 2, 13.   z: Ps 116, 11 / Ps 51, 6.   a: 9, 14; Jb 34, 12-17.   b: 6, 1.   c: 1, 18—2, 25; 3, 23; Sir 8, 5.   d: Pss 14, 1-3; 53, 2-4; Eccl 7, 20.   e: Pss 5, 10; 140, 4.   f: Ps 10, 7.   g: Prv 1, 16; Is 59, 7-8.   h: Ps 36, 2.   i: 7, 7.   j: Ps 143, 2; Gal 2, 16 / 7, 7.

human being will be justified in his sight by observing the law; for through the law comes consciousness of sin.

III: Justification through Faith in Christ

Justification apart from the Law. [21k]*But now the righteousness of God has been manifested apart from the law, though testified to by the law and the prophets, [22l]the righteousness of God through faith in Jesus Christ for all who believe. For there is no distinction; [23m]all have sinned and are deprived of the glory of God. [24n]They are justified freely by his grace through the redemption in Christ Jesus, [25o]*whom God set forth as an expiation, through faith, by his blood, to prove his righteousness because of the forgiveness of sins previously committed, [26]through the forbearance of God—to prove his righteousness in the pres-

ent time, that he might be righteous and justify the one who has faith in Jesus.

[27p]*What occasion is there then for boasting? It is ruled out. On what principle, that of works? No, rather on the principle of faith. [28q]For we consider that a person is justified by faith apart from works of the law. [29r]Does God belong to Jews alone? Does he not belong to Gentiles, too? Yes, also to Gentiles, [30s]for God is one and will justify the circumcised on the basis of faith and the uncircumcised through faith. [31t]*Are we then annulling the law by this faith? Of course not! On the contrary, we are supporting the law.

CHAPTER 4

See RG 445

Abraham Justified by Faith. [1u]*What then can we say that Abraham found, our ancestor according to the flesh? [2]*Indeed, if Abraham was justified on the basis of his works, he has reason to boast; but this was not so in the sight of God. [3v]*For what does

---

3, 21–31: These verses provide a clear statement of Paul's "gospel," i.e., the principle of justification by faith in Christ. God has found a means of rescuing humanity from its desperate plight: Paul's general term for this divine initiative is the righteousness of God (21). Divine mercy declares the guilty innocent and makes them so. God does this not as a result of the law but apart from it (21), and not because of any merit in human beings but through forgiveness of their sins (24), in virtue of the redemption wrought in Christ Jesus for all who believe (22.24–25). God has manifested his righteousness in the coming of Jesus Christ, whose saving activity inaugurates a new era in human history.

3, 21: But now: Paul adopts a common phrase used by Greek authors to describe movement from disaster to prosperity. The expressions indicate that vv 21–26 are the consolatory answer to vv 9–20.

3, 25: Expiation: this rendering is preferable to "propitiation," which suggests hostility on the part of God toward sinners. As Paul will be at pains to point out (5, 8–10), it is humanity that is hostile to God.

3, 27–31: People cannot boast of their own holiness, since it is God's free gift (27), both to the Jew who practices circumcision out of faith and to the Gentile who accepts faith without the Old Testament religious culture symbolized by circumcision (29–30).

3, 27: Principle of faith: literally, "law of faith." Paul is fond of wordplay involving the term "law"; cf 7, 21.23; 8, 2. Since "law" in Greek may also connote "custom" or "principle," his readers and hearers would have sensed no contradiction in the use of the term after the negative statement concerning law in v 20.

3, 31: We are supporting the law: giving priority to God's intentions. God is the ultimate source of law, and the essence of law is fairness. On the basis of the Mosaic cov-

enant, God's justice is in question if those who sinned against the law are permitted to go free (see 23–26). In order to rescue all humanity rather than condemn it, God thinks of an alternative: the law or "principle" of faith (27). What can be more fair than to admit everyone into the divine presence on the basis of forgiveness grasped by faith? Indeed, this principle of faith antedates the Mosaic law, as Paul will demonstrate in ch 4, and does not therefore mark a change in divine policy.

4, 1–25: This is an expanded treatment of the significance of Abraham's faith, which Paul discusses in Gal 3, 6–18; see the notes there.

4, 2–5: Verse 2 corresponds to v 4, and v 3 to v 5. The Greek term here rendered **credited** means "made an entry." The context determines whether it is credit or debit. Verse 8 speaks of "recording sin" as a debit. Paul's repeated use of accountants' terminology in this and other passages can be traced both to the Old Testament texts he quotes and to his business activity as a tentmaker. The commercial term in Gn 15, 6, "credited it to him," reminds Paul in vv 7–8 of Ps 32, 2, in which the same term is used and applied to forgiveness of sins. Thus Paul is able to argue that Abraham's faith involved receipt of forgiveness of sins and that all believers benefit as he did through faith.

4, 3: Jas 2, 24 appears to conflict with Paul's statement. However, James combats the error of extremists who used the doctrine of justification through faith as a screen for moral self-determination. Paul discusses the subject of holiness in greater detail than does James and beginning with ch 6 shows

k: Is 51, 6-8; Acts 10, 43. l: 1, 17; Gal 2, 16; Phil 3, 9. m: 3, 9; 5, 12. n: Eph 2, 8; Ti 3, 7 / 5, 1-2; Eph 1, 7. o: Lv 16, 12-15; Acts 17, 31; 1 Jn 4, 10. p: 8, 2; 1 Cor 1, 29-31. q: 5, 1; Gal 2, 16. r: 10, 12. s: Dt 6, 4; Gal 3, 20; Jas 2, 19 / 4, 11-12. t: 8, 4; Mt 5, 17. u: Gal 3, 6-9. v: Gn 15, 6; Gal 3, 6; Jas 2, 14.20-24.

the scripture say? "Abraham believed God, and it was credited to him as righteousness." [4w]A worker's wage is credited not as a gift, but as something due. [5]But when one does not work, yet believes in the one who justifies the ungodly, his faith is credited as righteousness. [6]So also David declares the blessedness of the person to whom God credits righteousness apart from works:

[7x]"Blessed are they whose iniquities are forgiven
    and whose sins are covered.
[8] Blessed is the man whose sin the Lord does not record."

[9y]*Does this blessedness apply only to the circumcised, or to the uncircumcised as well? Now we assert that "faith was credited to Abraham as righteousness." [10]Under what circumstances was it credited? Was he circumcised or not? He was not circumcised, but uncircumcised. [11z]And he received the sign of circumcision as a seal on the righteousness received through faith while he was uncircumcised. Thus he was to be the father of all the uncircumcised who believe, so that to them [also] righteousness might be credited, [12]as well as the father of the circumcised who not only are circumcised but also follow the path of faith that our father Abraham walked while still uncircumcised.

Inheritance through Faith. [13a]It was not through the law that the promise was made to Abraham and his descendants that he would inherit the world, but through the righteousness that comes from faith. [14b]For if those who adhere to the law are the heirs, faith is null and the promise is void. [15c]*For the law produces wrath; but where there is no law, neither is there violation. [16d]For this reason, it depends on faith, so that it may be a gift, and the promise may be guaranteed to all his descendants, not to those who only adhere to the law but to those who follow the faith of Abraham, who is the father of all of us, [17e]as it is written, "I have made you father of many nations." He is our father in the sight of God, in whom he believed, who gives life to the dead and calls into being what does not exist. [18f]He believed, hoping against hope, that he would become "the father of many nations," according to what was said, "Thus shall your descendants be." [19g]He did not weaken in faith when he considered his own body as [already] dead (for he was almost a hundred years old) and the dead womb of Sarah. [20]*He did not doubt God's promise in unbelief; rather, he was empowered by faith and gave glory to God [21h]and was fully convinced that what he had promised he was also able to do. [22i]That is why "it was credited to him as righteousness." [23]But it was not for him alone that it was written that "it was credited to him"; [24j]it was also for us, to whom it will be credited, who believe in the one who raised Jesus our Lord from the dead, [25k]who was handed over for our transgressions and was raised for our justification.

how justification through faith introduces one to the gift of a new life in Christ through the power of the holy Spirit.

4, 9: Blessedness: evidence of divine favor.

4, 15: Law has the negative function of bringing the deep-seated rebellion against God to the surface in specific sins; see the note on 1, 18–32.

4, 20: He did not doubt God's promise in unbelief: any doubts Abraham might have had were resolved in commitment to God's promise. Heb 11, 8–12 emphasizes the faith of Abraham and Sarah.

5, 1–11: Popular piety frequently construed reverses and troubles as punishment for sin; cf Jn 9, 2. Paul therefore assures believers that God's justifying action in Jesus Christ is a declaration of peace. The crucifixion of Jesus Christ displays God's initiative in certifying humanity for unimpeded access into the divine presence. Reconciliation is God's gift of pardon to the entire human race. Through faith one benefits personally from this pardon or, in Paul's term, is justified. The ultimate aim of God is to liberate believers from the pre-Christian self as described in chs 1–3. Since this libera-tion will first find completion in the believer's resurrection, salvation is described as future in 5, 10. Because this fullness of salvation belongs to the future it is called the Christian hope. Paul's Greek term for hope does not, however, suggest a note of uncertainty, to the effect: "I wonder whether God really means it." Rather, God's promise in the gospel fills believers with expectation and anticipation for the climactic gift of unalloyed commitment in the holy Spirit to the performance of the will of God. The persecutions that attend Christian commitment are to teach believers patience and to strengthen this hope, which will not disappoint them because the holy Spirit dwells in their hearts and imbues them with God's love (5).

w: 11, 6.   x: Ps 32, 1-2.   y: 4, 3.   z: Gn 17, 10-11; Gal 3, 6-8.   a: Gn 12, 7; 18, 18; 22, 17-18; Sir 44, 21; Gal 3, 16-18.29.   b: Gal 3, 18.   c: 3, 20; 5, 13; 7, 8; Gal 3, 19.   d: Sir 44, 19; Gal 3, 7-9.   e: Gn 17, 5; Heb 11, 19 / Is 48, 13.   f: Gn 15, 5.   g: Gn 17, 17; Heb 11, 11.   h: Gn 18, 14; Lk 1, 37.   i: Gn 15, 6.   j: 10, 9; 1 Pt 1, 21.   k: Is 53, 4-5.12; 1 Cor 15, 17; 1 Pt 1, 3 / 8, 11.

CHAPTER 5

See RG
445–46

Faith, Hope, and Love. [1]*Therefore, since we have been justified by faith, we have peace with God through our Lord Jesus Christ, [2]m through whom we have gained access [by faith] to this grace in which we stand, and we boast in hope of the glory of God. [3]Not only that, but we even boast of our afflictions, knowing that affliction produces endurance, [4]n and endurance, proven character, and proven character, hope, [5]o and hope does not disappoint, because the love of God has been poured out into our hearts through the holy Spirit that has been given to us. [6]For Christ, while we were still helpless, yet died at the appointed time for the ungodly. [7]*Indeed, only with difficulty does one die for a just person, though perhaps for a good person one might even find courage to die. [8]p But God proves his love for us in that while we were still sinners Christ died for us. [9]q How much more then, since we are now justified by his blood, will we be saved through him from the wrath. [10]r Indeed, if, while we were enemies, we were reconciled to God through the death of his Son, how much more, once reconciled, will we be saved by his life. [11]Not only that, but we also boast of God through our Lord Jesus Christ, through whom we have now received reconciliation.

Humanity's Sin through Adam. [12]s*Therefore, just as through one person sin entered the world, and through sin, death, and thus death came to all, inasmuch as all sinned—

[13]t for up to the time of the law, sin was in the world, though sin is not accounted when there is no law. [14]u But death reigned from Adam to Moses, even over those who did not sin after the pattern of the trespass of Adam, who is the type of the one who was to come.

Grace and Life through Christ. [15]But the gift is not like the transgression. For if by that one person's transgression the many died, how much more did the grace of God and the gracious gift of the one person Jesus Christ overflow for the many. [16]And the gift is not like the result of the one person's sinning. For after one sin there was the judgment that brought condemnation; but the gift, after many transgressions, brought acquittal. [17]For if, by the transgression of one person, death came to reign through that one, how much more will those who receive the abundance of grace and of the gift of justification come to reign in life through the one person Jesus Christ. [18]v In conclusion, just as through one transgression condemnation came upon all, so through one righteous act acquittal and life came to all. [19]w For just as through the disobedience of one person the many were made sinners, so through the obedience of one the many will be made righteous. [20]x*The law entered in so that transgression might increase but, where sin increased, grace overflowed all the more, [21]y so that, as sin reigned in death, grace also might reign through justification for eternal life through Jesus Christ our Lord.

5, 1: **We have peace:** a number of manuscripts, versions, and church Fathers read "Let us have peace"; cf 14, 19.

5, 7: In the world of Paul's time the **good person** is especially one who is magnanimous to others.

5, 12–21: Paul reflects on the sin of Adam (Gn 3, 1–13) in the light of the redemptive mystery of Christ. Sin, as used in the singular by Paul, refers to the dreadful power that has gripped humanity, which is now in revolt against the Creator and engaged in the exaltation of its own desires and interests. But no one has a right to say, "Adam made me do it," for all are culpable (12): Gentiles under the demands of the law written in their hearts (2, 14–15), and Jews under the Mosaic covenant. Through the Old Testament law, the sinfulness of humanity that was operative from the beginning (13) found further stimulation, with the result that sins were generated in even greater abundance. According to vv 15–21, God's act in Christ is in total contrast to the disastrous effects of the virus

of sin that invaded humanity through Adam's crime.

5, 12: **Inasmuch as all sinned:** others translate "because all sinned," and understand v 13 as a parenthetical remark. Unlike Wis 2, 24, Paul does not ascribe the entry of death to the devil.

5, 20: **The law entered in:** sin had made its entrance (12); now the law comes in alongside sin. See the notes on 1, 18–32; 5, 12–21. **Where sin increased, grace overflowed all the more:** Paul declares that grace outmatches the productivity of sin.

l: 3, 24-28; Gal 2, 16. *m:* Eph 2, 18; 3, 12. *n:* 2 Cor 12, 9-10; Jas 1, 2-4; 1 Pt 1, 5-7; 4, 12-14. *o:* 8, 14-16; Pss 22, 5-6; 25, 20. *p:* Jn 3, 16; 1 Jn 4, 10.19. *q:* 1, 18; 1 Thes 1, 10. *r:* 8, 7-8; 2 Cor 5, 18; Col 1, 21-22. *s:* Gn 2, 17; 3, 1-19; Wis 2, 24 / 3, 19.23. *t:* 4, 15. *u:* 1 Cor 15, 21. *v:* 1 Cor 15, 21-22. *w:* Is 53, 11; Phil 2, 8-9. *x:* 4, 15; 7, 7-8; Gal 3, 19. *y:* 6, 23.

IV: Justification and the Christian Life

CHAPTER 6

See RG
446

Freedom from Sin; Life in God.
¹ᶻ*What then shall we say? Shall we persist in sin that grace may abound? Of course not! ²ᵃHow can we who died to sin yet live in it? ³ᵇOr are you unaware that we who were baptized into Christ Jesus were baptized into his death? ⁴ᶜWe were indeed buried with him through baptism into death, so that, just as Christ was raised from the dead by the glory of the Father, we too might live in newness of life.

⁵ᵈFor if we have grown into union with him through a death like his, we shall also be united with him in the resurrection. ⁶ᵉWe know that our old self was crucified with him, so that our sinful body might be done away with, that we might no longer be in slavery to sin. ⁷For a dead person has been absolved from sin. ⁸ᶠIf, then, we have died with Christ, we believe that we shall also live with him. ⁹ᵍWe know that Christ, raised from the dead, dies no more; death no longer has power over him. ¹⁰ʰAs to his death, he died to sin once and for all; as to his life, he lives for God. ¹¹ⁱConsequently, you too must think of yourselves as [being] dead to sin and living for God in Christ Jesus.

¹²ʲ*Therefore, sin must not reign over your mortal bodies so that you obey their desires. ¹³ᵏAnd do not present the parts of your bodies to sin as weapons for wickedness, but present yourselves to God as raised from the dead to life and the parts of your bodies to God as weapons for righteousness. ¹⁴ˡFor sin is not to have any power over you, since you are not under the law but under grace.

¹⁵ᵐWhat then? Shall we sin because we are not under the law but under grace? Of course not! ¹⁶ⁿᵒDo you not know that if you present yourselves to someone as obedient slaves, you are slaves of the one you obey, either of sin, which leads to death, or of obedience, which leads to righteousness? ¹⁷*But thanks be to God that, although you were once slaves of sin, you have become obedient from the heart to the pattern of teaching to which you were entrusted. ¹⁸Freed from sin, you have become slaves of righteousness. ¹⁹I am speaking in human terms because of the weakness of your nature. For just as you presented the parts of your bodies as slaves to impurity and to lawlessness for lawlessness, so now present them as slaves to righteousness for sanctification. ²⁰ᵖ*For when you were slaves of sin, you were free from righteousness. ²¹qBut what profit did you get then from the things of which you are now ashamed? For the end of those things is death. ²²ʳ*But now that you have been freed from sin and have become slaves of God, the benefit that you have leads to sanctification,

6, 1–11: To defend the gospel against the charge that it promotes moral laxity (cf 3, 5–8), Paul expresses himself in the typical style of spirited diatribe. God's display of generosity or grace is not evoked by sin but, as stated in 5, 8, is the expression of God's love, and this love pledges eternal life to all believers (5, 21). Paul views the present conduct of the believers from the perspective of God's completed salvation when the body is resurrected and directed totally by the holy Spirit. Through baptism believers share the death of Christ and thereby escape from the grip of sin. Through the resurrection of Christ the power to live anew becomes reality for them, but the fullness of participation in Christ's resurrection still lies in the future. But life that is lived in dedication to God now is part and parcel of that future. Hence anyone who sincerely claims to be interested in that future will scarcely be able to say, "Let us sin so that grace may prosper" (cf 1).

6, 12–19: Christians have been released from the grip of sin, but sin endeavors to reclaim its victims. The antidote is constant remembrance that divine grace has claimed them and identifies them as people who are alive only for God's interests.

6, 17: In contrast to humanity, which was handed over to self-indulgence (1, 24–32), believers are **entrusted** ("handed over") to God's **pattern of teaching,** that is, the new life God aims to develop in Christians through the productivity of the holy Spirit. Throughout this passage Paul uses the slave-master model in order to emphasize the fact that one cannot give allegiance to both God and sin.

6, 20: You were free from righteousness: expressed ironically, for such freedom is really tyranny. The commercial metaphors in vv 21–23 add up only one way: sin is a bad bargain.

6, 22: Sanctification: or holiness.

z: 3, 5-8. a: 1 Pt 4, 1. b: Gal 3, 27. c: Col 2, 12; 1 Pt 3, 21-22. d: Phil 3, 10-11; 2 Tm 2, 11. e: Gal 5, 24; 6, 14; Eph 4, 22-23. f: 1 Thes 4, 17. g: Acts 13, 34; 1 Cor 15, 26; 2 Tm 1, 10; Rv 1, 18. h: Heb 9, 26-28; 1 Pt 3, 18. i: 2 Cor 5, 15; 1 Pt 2, 24. j: Gn 4, 7. k: 12, 1; Eph 2, 5; 5, 14 / Col 3, 5. l: Gal 5, 18; 1 Jn 3, 6. m: 5, 17.21. n: Jn 8, 31-34; 2 Pt 2, 19. o: Jn 8, 32-36. p: Jn 8, 34. q: 8, 6.13; Prv 12, 28; Ez 16, 61.63. r: 1 Pt 1, 9.

and its end is eternal life. [23s]For the wages of sin is death, but the gift of God is eternal life in Christ Jesus our Lord.

See RG 446

CHAPTER 7

Freedom from the Law. [1*]Are you unaware, brothers (for I am speaking to people who know the law), that the law has jurisdiction over one as long as one lives? [2t]Thus a married woman is bound by law to her living husband; but if her husband dies, she is released from the law in respect to her husband. [3]Consequently, while her husband is alive she will be called an adulteress if she consorts with another man. But if her husband dies she is free from that law, and she is not an adulteress if she consorts with another man.

[4]In the same way, my brothers, you also were put to death to the law through the body of Christ, so that you might belong to another, to the one who was raised from the dead in order that we might bear fruit for God. [5u]For when we were in the flesh, our sinful passions, awakened by the law, worked in our members to bear fruit for death. [6v]But now we are released from the law, dead to what held us captive, so that we may serve in the newness of the spirit and not under the obsolete letter.

Acquaintance with Sin through the Law. [7w*]What then can we say? That the law is sin? Of course not! Yet I did not know sin except through the law, and I did not know what it is to covet except that the law said, "You shall not covet." [8x]But sin, finding an opportunity in the commandment, produced in me every kind of covetousness. Apart from the law sin is dead. [9]I once lived outside the law, but when the commandment came, sin became alive; [10y]then I died, and the commandment that was for life turned out to be death for me. [11z]For sin, seizing an opportunity in the commandment, deceived me and through it put me to death. [12a]So then the law is holy, and the commandment is holy and righteous and good.

Sin and Death. [13b*]Did the good, then, become death for me? Of course not! Sin, in order that it might be shown to be sin, worked death in me through the good, so that sin might become sinful beyond measure through the commandment. [14c]We know that the law is spiritual; but I am carnal, sold into slavery to sin. [15]What I do, I do not understand. For I do not do what I want, but I do what I hate. [16]Now if I do what I do not want, I concur that the law is good. [17]So now it is no longer I who do it, but sin that dwells in me. [18d]For I know that good does not dwell in me, that is, in my flesh. The willing is ready at hand, but doing the good is not. [19]For I do not do the good I want, but I do the evil I do not want. [20]Now if [I] do what I do not want, it is no longer I who do it, but sin that dwells in me. [21]So, then, I discover the principle that when I want to do right, evil is at hand. [22]For I take delight in the law of God, in my inner self, [23e*]but I see in my members another principle at war with the law of my mind, taking me captive to the

---

7, 1–6: Paul reflects on the fact that Christians have a different understanding of the law because of their faith in Christ. Law binds the living, not the dead, as exemplified in marriage, which binds in life but is dissolved through death. Similarly, Christians who through baptism have died with Christ to sin (cf 6, 2–4) are freed from the law that occasioned transgressions, which in turn were productive of death. Now that Christians are joined to Christ, the power of Christ's resurrection makes it possible for them to bear the fruit of newness of life for God.

7, 7–25: In this passage Paul uses the first person singular in the style of diatribe for the sake of argument. He aims to depict the disastrous consequences when a Christian reintroduces the law as a means to attain the objective of holiness pronounced in 6, 22.

7, 7–12: The apostle defends himself against the charge of identifying the law with sin. Sin does not exist in law but in human beings, whose sinful inclinations are not overcome by the proclamation of law.

7, 13–25: Far from improving the sinner, law encourages sin to expose itself in transgressions or violations of specific commandments (see 1, 24; 5, 20). Thus persons who do not experience the justifying grace of God, and Christians who revert to dependence on law as the criterion for their relationship with God, will recognize a rift between their reasoned desire for the goodness of the law and their actual performance that is contrary to the law. Unable to free themselves from the slavery of sin and the power of death, they can only be rescued from defeat in the conflict by the power of God's grace working through Jesus Christ.

7, 23: As in 3, 27, Paul plays on the term **law**, which in Greek can connote custom, system, or **principle**.

s: Gn 2, 17; Gal 6, 7-9; Jas 1, 15. t: 1 Cor 7, 39. u: 6, 21; 8, 6.13. v: 8, 2; 2 Cor 3, 6. w: 3, 20; Ex 20, 17; Dt 5, 21. x: 5, 13.20; 1 Cor 15, 56/4, 15. y: Lv 18, 5. z: Gn 3, 13; Heb 3, 13. a: 1 Tm 1, 8. b: 4, 15; 5, 20. c: 8, 7-8; Ps 51, 7. d: Gn 6, 5; 8, 21; Phil 2, 13. e: Gal 5, 17; 1 Pt 2, 11.

law of sin that dwells in my members. [24]Miserable one that I am! Who will deliver me from this mortal body? [25]*f*Thanks be to God through Jesus Christ our Lord. Therefore, I myself, with my mind, serve the law of God but, with my flesh, the law of sin.

See RG 446–47

CHAPTER 8

The Flesh and the Spirit. [1]*Hence, now there is no condemnation for those who are in Christ Jesus. [2]*g*For the law of the spirit of life in Christ Jesus has freed you from the law of sin and death. [3]*h*For what the law, weakened by the flesh, was powerless to do, this God has done: by sending his own Son in the likeness of sinful flesh and for the sake of sin, he condemned sin in the flesh, [4]*i*so that the righteous decree of the law might be fulfilled in us, who live not according to the flesh but according to the spirit. [5]For those who live according to the flesh are concerned with the things of the flesh, but those who live according to the spirit with the things of the spirit. [6]*j*The concern of the flesh is death, but the concern of the spirit is life and peace. [7]*k*For the concern of the flesh is hostility toward God; it does not submit to the law of God, nor can it; [8]*l*and those who are in the flesh cannot please God. [9]*m*But you are not in the flesh; on the contrary, you are in the spirit, if only the Spirit of God dwells in you. Whoever does not have the

Spirit of Christ does not belong to him. [10]*n*But if Christ is in you, although the body is dead because of sin, the spirit is alive because of righteousness. [11]If the Spirit of the one who raised Jesus from the dead dwells in you, the one who raised Christ from the dead will give life to your mortal bodies also, through his Spirit that dwells in you. [12]Consequently, brothers, we are not debtors to the flesh, to live according to the flesh. [13]*o*For if you live according to the flesh, you will die, but if by the spirit you put to death the deeds of the body, you will live.

Children of God through Adoption. [14]*p*For those who are led by the Spirit of God are children of God. [15]*q*For you did not receive a spirit of slavery to fall back into fear, but you received a spirit of adoption, through which we cry, "*Abba,* Father!" [16]*r*The Spirit itself bears witness with our spirit that we are children of God, [17]*s*and if children, then heirs, heirs of God and joint heirs with Christ, if only we suffer with him so that we may also be glorified with him.

Destiny of Glory. [18]*t*I consider that the sufferings of this present time are as nothing compared with the glory to be revealed for us. [19]For creation awaits with eager expectation the revelation of the children of God; [20]*u*for creation was made subject to futility, not of its own accord but because of the one who subjected it, in hope [21]*v*that creation it-

---

8, 1–13: After his warning in ch 7 against the wrong route to fulfillment of the objective of holiness expressed in 6, 22, Paul points his addressees to the correct way. Through the redemptive work of Christ, Christians have been liberated from the terrible forces of sin and death. Holiness was impossible so long as the **flesh** (or our "old self"), that is, self-interested hostility toward God (7), frustrated the divine objectives expressed in the law. What is worse, sin used the law to break forth into all manner of lawlessness (8). All this is now changed. At the cross God broke the power of sin and pronounced sentence on it (3). Christians still retain the flesh, but it is alien to their new being, which is life in the spirit, namely the new self, governed by the holy Spirit. Under the direction of the holy Spirit Christians are able to fulfill the divine will that formerly found expression in the law (4). The same Spirit who enlivens Christians for holiness will also resurrect their bodies at the last day (11). Christian life is therefore the experience of a constant challenge to put to death the evil deeds of the body through life of the spirit (13).

8, 14–17: Christians, by reason of the Spirit's presence within them, enjoy not only new life but also a new relationship to God, that of adopted children and heirs

through Christ, whose sufferings and glory they share.

8, 15: Abba: see the note on Mk 14, 36.

8, 18–27: The glory that believers are destined to share with Christ far exceeds the sufferings of the present life. Paul considers the destiny of the created world to be linked with the future that belongs to the believers. As it shares in the penalty of corruption brought about by sin, so also will it share in the benefits of redemption and future glory that comprise the ultimate liberation of God's people (19–22). After patient endurance in steadfast expectation, the full harvest of the Spirit's presence will be realized. On earth believers enjoy the first-fruits, i.e., the Spirit, as a guarantee of the total liberation of their bodies from the influence of the rebellious old self (23).

f: 1 Cor 15, 57.   *g:* 7, 23-24; 2 Cor 3, 17.   *h:* Acts 13, 38; 15, 10 / Jn 3, 16-17; 2 Cor 5, 21; Gal 3, 13; 4, 4;Phil 2, 7; Col 1, 22; Heb 2, 17; 4, 15; 1 Jn 4, 9.   *i:* Gal 5, 16-25.   *j:* 6, 21; 7, 5; 8, 13; Gal 6, 8.   *k:* 5, 10; Jas 4, 4.   *l:* 1 Jn 2, 16.   *m:* 1 Cor 3, 16.   *n:* Gal 2, 20; 1 Pt 4, 6.   *o:* Gal 5, 24; 6, 8; Eph 4, 22-24.   *p:* Gal 5, 18. *q:* Mk 14, 36; Gal 4, 5-6; 2 Tm 1, 7.   *r:* Jn 1, 12; Gal 3, 26-29. *s:* Gal 4, 7; 1 Pt 4, 13; 5, 1.   *t:* 2 Cor 4, 17.   *u:* Gn 3, 17-19. *v:* 2 Pt 3, 12-13; Rv 21, 1.

self would be set free from slavery to corruption and share in the glorious freedom of the children of God. [22w]We know that all creation is groaning in labor pains even until now; [23x]and not only that, but we ourselves, who have the firstfruits of the Spirit, we also groan within ourselves as we wait for adoption, the redemption of our bodies. [24y]For in hope we were saved. Now hope that sees for itself is not hope. For who hopes for what one sees? [25]But if we hope for what we do not see, we wait with endurance.

[26]In the same way, the Spirit too comes to the aid of our weakness; for we do not know how to pray as we ought, but the Spirit itself intercedes with inexpressible groanings. [27z]And the one who searches hearts knows what is the intention of the Spirit, because it intercedes for the holy ones according to God's will.

God's Indomitable Love in Christ. [28a*]We know that all things work for good for those who love God, who are called according to his purpose. [29b*]For those he foreknew he also predestined to be conformed to the image of his Son, so that he might be the firstborn among many brothers. [30c]And those he predestined he also called; and those he called he also justified; and those he justified he also glorified.

[31d*]What then shall we say to this? If God is for us, who can be against us? [32e]He who did not spare his own Son but handed him

over for us all, how will he not also give us everything else along with him? [33f]Who will bring a charge against God's chosen ones? It is God who acquits us. [34g]Who will condemn? It is Christ [Jesus] who died, rather, was raised, who also is at the right hand of God, who indeed intercedes for us. [35]What will separate us from the love of Christ? Will anguish, or distress, or persecution, or famine, or nakedness, or peril, or the sword? [36h]As it is written:

> "For your sake we are being slain all the day;
> we are looked upon as sheep to be slaughtered."

[37i]No, in all these things we conquer overwhelmingly through him who loved us. [38j*]For I am convinced that neither death, nor life, nor angels, nor principalities, nor present things, nor future things, nor powers, [39*]nor height, nor depth, nor any other creature will be able to separate us from the love of God in Christ Jesus our Lord.

V: Jews And Gentiles in God's Plan

CHAPTER 9

See RG 447–48

Paul's Love for Israel. [1k*]I speak the truth in Christ, I do not lie; my conscience joins with the holy Spirit in bearing me wit-

---

8, 28–30: These verses outline the Christian vocation as it was designed by God: **to be conformed to the image of his Son,** who is to be **the firstborn among many brothers** (29). God's redemptive action on behalf of the believers has been in process before the beginning of the world. Those whom God chooses are **those he foreknew** (29) or elected. Those who are **called** (30) are **predestined** or predetermined. These expressions do not mean that God is arbitrary. Rather, Paul uses them to emphasize the thought and care that God has taken for the Christian's salvation.

8, 28: **We know that all things work for good for those who love God:** a few ancient authorities have God as the subject of the verb, and some translators render: "We know that God makes everything work for good for those who love God . . . ."

8, 29: **Image:** while man and woman were originally created in God's image (Gn 1, 26–27), it is through baptism into Christ, the image of God (2 Cor 4, 4; Col 1, 15), that we are renewed according to the image of the Creator (Col 3, 10).

8, 31–39: The all-conquering power of God's love has overcome every obstacle to Christians' salvation and every

threat to separate them from God. That power manifested itself fully when God's own Son was delivered up to death for their salvation. Through him Christians can overcome all their afflictions and trials.

8, 38: **Present things** and **future things** may refer to astrological data. Paul appears to be saying that the gospel liberates believers from dependence on astrologers.

8, 39: **Height, depth** may refer to positions in the zodiac, positions of heavenly bodies relative to the horizon. In astrological documents the term for "height" means "exaltation" or the position of greatest influence exerted by a planet. Since hostile spirits were associated with the planets and stars, Paul includes **powers** (38) in his list of malevolent forces.

9, 1—11, 36: Israel's unbelief and its rejection of Jesus as

w: 2 Cor 5, 2-5.   *x:* 2 Cor 1, 22; Gal 5, 5.   *y:* 2 Cor 5, 7; Heb 11, 1.   *z:* Ps 139, 1; 1 Cor 4, 5.   *a:* Eph 1, 4-14; 3, 11.   *b:* Eph 1, 5; 1 Pt 1, 2.   *c:* Is 45, 25; 2 Thes 2, 13-14.   *d:* Ps 118, 6; Heb 13, 6.   *e:* Jn 3, 16.   *f:* Is 50, 8.   *g:* Ps 110, 1; Heb 7, 25; 1 Jn 2, 1.   *h:* Ps 44, 23; 1 Cor 4, 9; 15, 30; 2 Cor 4, 11; 2 Tm 3, 12.   *i:* 1 Jn 5, 4.   *j:* 1 Cor 3, 22; Eph 1, 21; 1 Pt 3, 22.   *k:* 2 Cor 11, 31; 1 Tm 2, 7.

ness [2]that I have great sorrow and constant anguish in my heart. [3t]For I could wish that I myself were accursed and separated from Christ for the sake of my brothers, my kin according to the flesh. [4m]They are Israelites; theirs the adoption, the glory, the covenants, the giving of the law, the worship, and the promises; [5n*]theirs the patriarchs, and from them, according to the flesh, is the Messiah. God who is over all be blessed forever. Amen.

God's Free Choice. [6o]But it is not that the word of God has failed. For not all who are of Israel are Israel, [7p]nor are they all children of Abraham because they are his descendants; but "It is through Isaac that descendants shall bear your name." [8q]This means that it is not the children of the flesh who are the children of God, but the children of the promise are counted as descendants. [9r]For this is the wording of the promise, "About this time I shall return and Sarah will have a son." [10s*]And not only that, but also when Rebecca had conceived children by one husband, our father Isaac— [11]before they had yet been born or had done anything,

good or bad, in order that God's elective plan might continue, [12t]not by works but by his call—she was told, "The older shall serve the younger." [13u*]As it is written:

"I loved Jacob
but hated Esau."

[14v*]What then are we to say? Is there injustice on the part of God? Of course not! [15w]For he says to Moses:

"I will show mercy to whom I will,
I will take pity on whom I will."

[16x]So it depends not upon a person's will or exertion, but upon God, who shows mercy. [17y]For the scripture says to Pharaoh, "This is why I have raised you up, to show my power through you that my name may be proclaimed throughout the earth." [18z*]Consequently, he has mercy upon whom he wills, and he hardens whom he wills.

[19a*]You will say to me then, "Why [then] does he still find fault? For who can oppose his will?" [20b]But who indeed are you, a human being, to talk back to God? Will what

---

savior astonished and puzzled Christians. It constituted a serious problem for them in view of God's specific preparation of Israel for the advent of the Messiah. Paul addresses himself here to the essential question of how the divine plan could be frustrated by Israel's unbelief. At the same time, he discourages both complacency and anxiety on the part of Gentiles. To those who might boast of their superior advantage over Jews, he warns that their enjoyment of the blessings assigned to Israel can be terminated. To those who might anxiously ask, "How can we be sure that Israel's fate will not be ours?" he replies that only unbelief can deprive one of salvation.

9, 1–5: The apostle speaks in strong terms of the depth of his grief over the unbelief of his own people. He would willingly undergo a curse himself for the sake of their coming to the knowledge of Christ (3; cf Lv 27, 28–29). His love for them derives from God's continuing choice of them and from the spiritual benefits that God bestows on them and through them on all of humanity (4–5).

9, 5: Some editors punctuate this verse differently and prefer the translation, "Of whom is Christ according to the flesh, who is God over all." However, Paul's point is that **God who is over all** aimed to use Israel, which had been entrusted with every privilege, in outreach to the entire world through the Messiah.

9, 10: Children by one husband, our father Isaac: Abraham had two children, Ishmael and Isaac, by two wives, Hagar and Sarah, respectively. In that instance Isaac, although born later than Ishmael, became the bearer of the messianic promise. In the case of twins born to Rebecca, God's elective procedure is seen even more dramatically, and again the younger, contrary to Semitic custom, is given the preference.

9, 13: The literal rendering, **"Jacob I loved, but Esau I hated,"** suggests an attitude of divine hostility that is not implied in Paul's statement. In Semitic usage "hate" means to love less; cf Lk 14, 26 with Mt 10, 37. Israel's unbelief reflects the mystery of the divine election that is always operative within it. Mere natural descent from Abraham does not ensure the full possession of the divine gifts; it is God's sovereign prerogative to bestow this fullness upon, or to withhold it from, whomsoever he wishes; cf Mt 3, 9; Jn 8, 39. The choice of Jacob over Esau is a case in point.

9, 14–18: The principle of divine election does not invite Christians to theoretical inquiry concerning the nonelected, nor does this principle mean that God is unfair in his dealings with humanity. The instruction concerning divine election is a part of the gospel and reveals that the gift of faith is the enactment of God's mercy (16). God raised up Moses to display that mercy, and Pharaoh to display divine severity in punishing those who obstinately oppose their Creator.

9, 18: The basic biblical principle is: those who will not see or hear **shall** not see or hear. On the other hand, the same God who thus makes stubborn or hardens the heart can reconstruct it through the work of the holy Spirit.

9, 19–29: The apostle responds to the objection that if God rules over faith through the principle of divine election, God

l: Ex 32, 32. m: 3, 2; Ex 4, 22; Dt 7, 6; 14, 1-2. n: Mt 1, 1-16; Lk 3, 23-38 / 1, 25; Ps 41, 14. o: Nm 23, 19 / Mt 3, 9. p: Gn 21, 12; Gal 3, 29. q: Gal 4, 23.28. r: Gn 18, 10.14. s: Gn 25, 21. t: 11, 5-6 / Gn 25, 23-24. u: Mal 1, 3. v: Dt 32, 4. w: Ex 33, 19. x: Eph 2, 8; Ti 3, 5. y: Ex 9, 16. z: 11, 30-32; Ex 4, 21; 7, 3. a: 3, 7; Wis 12, 12. b: Wis 15, 7; Is 29, 16; 45, 9; Jer 18, 6.

is made say to its maker, "Why have you created me so?" *21* Or does not the potter have a right over the clay, to make out of the same lump one vessel for a noble purpose and another for an ignoble one? *22c* What if God, wishing to show his wrath and make known his power, has endured with much patience the vessels of wrath made for destruction? *23* This was to make known the riches of his glory to the vessels of mercy, which he has prepared previously for glory, *24* namely, us whom he has called, not only from the Jews but also from the Gentiles.

Witness of the Prophets. *25d** As indeed he says in Hosea:

"Those who were not my people I will
        call 'my people,'
    and her who was not beloved I will
        call 'beloved.'
26 e And in the very place where it was said
        to them, 'You are not my people,'
    there they shall be called children of
        the living God."

27f And Isaiah cries out concerning Israel, "Though the number of the Israelites were like the sand of the sea, only a remnant will be saved; *28* for decisively and quickly will the Lord execute sentence upon the earth." *29g* And as Isaiah predicted:

"Unless the Lord of hosts had left us
        descendants,
    we would have become like Sodom
    and have been made like Gomorrah."

Righteousness Based on Faith. *30h** What then shall we say? That Gentiles, who did not pursue righteousness, have achieved it, that is, righteousness that comes from faith; *31i* but that Israel, who pursued the law of righteousness, did not attain to that law? *32 j** Why not? Because they did it not by faith, but as if it could be done by works. They stumbled over the stone that causes stumbling, *33k* as it is written:

"Behold, I am laying a stone in Zion
        that will make people stumble
    and a rock that will make them fall,
    and whoever believes in him shall not be
        put to shame."

CHAPTER 10

See RG 447-48

*11** Brothers, my heart's desire and prayer to God on their behalf is for salvation. *2m* I testify with regard to them that they have zeal for God, but it is not discerning. *3n* For, in their unawareness of the righteousness that comes from God and their attempt to establish their own [righteousness], they did not submit to the righteousness of God. *4o** For Christ is the end of the law for the justification of everyone who has faith.

---

cannot then accuse unbelievers of sin (19). For Paul, this objection is in the last analysis a manifestation of human insolence, and his "answer" is less an explanation of God's ways than the rejection of an argument that places humanity on a level with God. At the same time, Paul shows that God is far less arbitrary than appearances suggest, for God endures **with much patience** (22) a person like the Pharaoh of the Exodus.

9, 25: Beloved: in Semitic discourse means "preferred" or "favorite" (cf 13). See Hos 2, 1, which is transposed after Hos 3, 5 in the NAB.

9, 30–33: In the conversion of the Gentiles and, by contrast, of relatively few Jews, the Old Testament prophecies are seen to be fulfilled; cf 25–29. Israel feared that the doctrine of justification through faith would jeopardize the validity of the Mosaic law, and so they never reached their goal of righteousness that they had sought to attain through meticulous observance of the law (31). Since Gentiles, including especially Greeks and Romans, had a great regard for righteousness, Paul's statement concerning Gentiles in v 30 is to be understood from a Jewish perspective: quite evidently they had not been interested in "God's" righteousness, for it had not been revealed to them; but now in response to the proclamation of the gospel they respond in faith.

9, 32: Paul discusses Israel as a whole from the perspective of contemporary Jewish rejection of Jesus as Messiah. The Old Testament and much of Jewish noncanonical literature in fact reflect a fervent faith in divine mercy.

10, 1–13: Despite Israel's lack of faith in God's act in Christ, Paul does not abandon hope for her salvation (1). However, Israel must recognize that the Messiah's arrival in the person of Jesus Christ means the termination of the Mosaic law as the criterion for understanding oneself in a valid relationship to God. Faith in God's saving action in Jesus Christ takes precedence over any such legal claim (6).

10, 4: The Mosaic legislation has been superseded by God's action in Jesus Christ. Others understand **end** here in the sense that Christ is the goal of the law, i.e., the true meaning of the Mosaic law, which cannot be correctly understood apart from him. Still others believe that both meanings are intended.

---

c: 2, 4; Wis 12, 20-21; Jer 50, 25. *d:* Hos 2, 25. *e:* Hos 2, 1. *f:* Is 10, 22-23; Hos 2, 1 / 11, 5 / Is 28, 22. *g:* Is 1, 9; Mt 10, 15. *h:* 10, 4.20. *i:* 10, 3. *j:* Is 8, 14. *k:* Is 28, 16; 1 Pt 2, 6-8. *l:* 9, 1.3. *m:* Acts 22, 3. *n:* 9, 31-32; Phil 3, 9. *o:* Acts 13, 38-39; 2 Cor 3, 14; Heb 8, 13.

[5p]*Moses writes about the righteousness that comes from [the] law, "The one who does these things will live by them." [6q]But the righteousness that comes from faith says, "Do not say in your heart, 'Who will go up into heaven?' (that is, to bring Christ down) [7r]*or 'Who will go down into the abyss?' (that is, to bring Christ up from the dead)." [8s]But what does it say?

"The word is near you,
in your mouth and in your heart"

(that is, the word of faith that we preach), [9t]*for, if you confess with your mouth that Jesus is Lord and believe in your heart that God raised him from the dead, you will be saved. [10]For one believes with the heart and so is justified, and one confesses with the mouth and so is saved. [11u]For the scripture says, "No one who believes in him will be put to shame." [12v]For there is no distinction between Jew and Greek; the same Lord is Lord of all, enriching all who call upon him. [13w]For "everyone who calls on the name of the Lord will be saved."

[14x]*But how can they call on him in whom they have not believed? And how can they believe in him of whom they have not heard? And how can they hear without someone to preach? [15y]*And how can people preach unless they are sent? As it is written, "How beautiful are the feet of those who bring [the] good news!" [16z]But not everyone has heeded the good news; for Isaiah says, "Lord, who has believed what was heard from us?" [17a]Thus faith comes from what is heard, and what is heard comes through the word of Christ. [18b]But I ask, did they not hear? Certainly they did; for

"Their voice has gone forth to all the
earth,
and their words to the ends of the
world."

[19c]But I ask, did not Israel understand? First Moses says:

"I will make you jealous of those who
are not a nation;
with a senseless nation I will make
you angry."

[20d]Then Isaiah speaks boldly and says:

"I was found [by] those who were not
seeking me;
I revealed myself to those who were
not asking for me."

[21]But regarding Israel he says, "All day long I stretched out my hands to a disobedient and contentious people."

CHAPTER 11

See RG
447–48

The Remnant of Israel. [1ef]*I ask, then, has God rejected his people? Of course not! For I too am an Israelite, a descendant of Abraham, of the tribe of Benjamin. [2]God has not rejected his people whom he foreknew. Do you not know what the scripture says about Elijah, how he pleads with God against Israel? [3g]"Lord, they have

---

10, 5–6: The subject of the verb **says** (6) is **righteousness** personified. Both of the statements in vv 5 and 6 derive from Moses, but Paul wishes to contrast the language of law and the language of faith.

10, 7: Here Paul blends Dt 30, 13 and Ps 107, 26.

10, 9–11: To confess Jesus as Lord was frequently quite hazardous in the first century (cf Mt 10, 18; 1 Thes 2, 2; 1 Pt 2, 18–21; 3, 14). For a Jew it could mean disruption of normal familial and other social relationships, including great economic sacrifice. In the face of penalties imposed by the secular world, Christians are assured that **no one who believes in** Jesus **will be put to shame** (11).

10, 14–21: The gospel has been sufficiently proclaimed to Israel, and Israel has adequately understood God's plan for the messianic age, which would see the gospel brought to the uttermost parts of the earth. As often in the past, Israel has not accepted the prophetic message; cf Acts 7, 51–53.

10, 15: How beautiful are the feet of those who bring

[the] good news: in Semitic fashion, the parts of the body that bring the messenger with welcome news are praised; cf Lk 11, 27.

11, 1–10: Although Israel has been unfaithful to the prophetic message of the gospel (10, 14–21), God remains faithful to Israel. Proof of the divine fidelity lies in the existence of Jewish Christians like Paul himself. The unbelieving Jews, says Paul, have been blinded by the Christian teaching concerning the Messiah.

p: Lv 18, 5; Gal 3, 12.   *q:* Dt 9, 4; 30, 12.   *r:* Dt 30, 13; 1 Pt 3, 19.   *s:* Dt 30, 14.   *t:* 1 Cor 12, 3.   *u:* 9, 33; Is 28, 16.   *v:* 1, 16; 3, 22.29; Acts 10, 34; 15, 9.11; Gal 3, 28; Eph 2, 14.   *w:* Jl 3, 5; Acts 2, 21.   *x:* Acts 8, 31.   *y:* Is 52, 7; Na 2, 1; Eph 6, 15.   *z:* Is 53, 1; Jn 12, 38.   *a:* Jn 17, 20.   *b:* Ps 19, 5; Mt 24, 14.   *c:* 11, 11.14; Dt 32, 21.   *d:* 9, 30; Is 65, 1-2.   *e:* 2 Cor 11, 22; Phil 3, 5.   *f:* 1 Sm 12, 22; Ps 94, 14.   *g:* 1 Kgs 19, 10.14.

killed your prophets, they have torn down your altars, and I alone am left, and they are seeking my life." [4h]But what is God's response to him? "I have left for myself seven thousand men who have not knelt to Baal." [5i]So also at the present time there is a remnant, chosen by grace. [6j]But if by grace, it is no longer because of works; otherwise grace would no longer be grace. [7k]What then? What Israel was seeking it did not attain, but the elect attained it; the rest were hardened, [8l]as it is written:

"God gave them a spirit of deep sleep,
    eyes that should not see
    and ears that should not hear,
down to this very day."

[9m]And David says:

"Let their table become a snare and a
    trap,
    a stumbling block and a retribution for
    them;
[10] let their eyes grow dim so that they may
    not see,
    and keep their backs bent forever."

The Gentiles' Salvation. [11n*]Hence I ask, did they stumble so as to fall? Of course not! But through their transgression salvation has come to the Gentiles, so as to make them jealous. [12]Now if their transgression is enrichment for the world, and if their diminished number is enrichment for the Gentiles, how much more their full number.

[13o]Now I am speaking to you Gentiles. Inasmuch then as I am the apostle to the Gentiles, I glory in my ministry [14]in order to make my race jealous and thus save some of them. [15]For if their rejection is the reconciliation of the world, what will their acceptance be but life from the dead? [16p*]If the firstfruits are holy, so is the whole batch of dough; and if the root is holy, so are the branches.

[17q]But if some of the branches were broken off, and you, a wild olive shoot, were grafted in their place and have come to share in the rich root of the olive tree, [18r]do not boast against the branches. If you do boast, consider that you do not support the root; the root supports you. [19]Indeed you will say, "Branches were broken off so that I might be grafted in." [20s]That is so. They were broken off because of unbelief, but you are there because of faith. So do not become haughty, but stand in awe. [21t]For if God did not spare the natural branches, [perhaps] he will not spare you either. [22u]See, then, the kindness and severity of God: severity toward those who fell, but God's kindness to you, provided you remain in his kindness; otherwise you too will be cut off. [23v]And they also, if they do not remain in unbelief, will be grafted in, for God is able to graft them in again. [24]For if you were cut from what is by nature a wild olive tree, and grafted, contrary to nature, into a cultivated one, how much more will they who belong to it by nature be grafted back into their own olive tree.

God's Irrevocable Call. [25w*]I do not want you to be unaware of this mystery, brothers, so that you will not become wise [in] your own estimation: a hardening has come upon Israel in part, until the full number of the Gentiles comes in, [26xy]and thus all Israel will be saved, as it is written:

11, 11–15: The unbelief of the Jews has paved the way for the preaching of the gospel to the Gentiles and for their easier acceptance of it outside the context of Jewish culture. Through his mission to the Gentiles Paul also hopes to fill his fellow Jews with jealousy. Hence he hastens to fill the entire Mediterranean world with the gospel. Once all the Gentile nations have heard the gospel, Israel as a whole is expected to embrace it. This will be tantamount to resurrection of the dead, that is, the reappearance of Jesus Christ with all the believers at the end of time.

11, 16–24: Israel remains holy in the eyes of God and stands as a witness to the faith described in the Old Testament because of **the firstfruits** (or the first piece baked) (16), that is, the converted remnant, and **the root** that **is holy**, that is, the patriarchs (16). The Jews' failure to believe in Christ is a warning to Gentile Christians to be on guard against any semblance of anti-Jewish arrogance, that is, failure to recognize their total dependence on divine grace.

11, 25–29: In God's design, Israel's unbelief is being used to grant the light of faith to the Gentiles. Meanwhile, Israel remains dear to God (cf 9, 13), still the object of special providence, the mystery of which will one day be revealed.

h: 1 Kgs 19, 18. *i:* 9, 27. *j:* 4, 4; Gal 3, 18. *k:* 9, 31. *l:* Dt 29, 3; Is 29, 10; Mt 13, 13-15; Acts 28, 26-27. *m:* Pss 69, 23-24; 35, 8. *n:* Acts 13, 46; 18, 6; 28, 28 / 10, 19; Dt 32, 21. *o:* 1, 5. *p:* Nm 15, 17-21; Ez 44, 30; Neh 10, 36-38. *q:* Eph 2, 11-19. *r:* 1 Cor 1, 31. *s:* 12, 16. *t:* 1 Cor 10, 12. *u:* Jn 15, 2.4; Heb 3, 14. *v:* 2 Cor 3, 16. *w:* Prv 3, 7 / 12, 16; Mk 13, 10; Lk 21, 24; Jn 10, 16. *x:* Mt 23, 39. *y:* Ps 14, 7; Is 59, 20-21.

"The deliverer will come out of Zion,
he will turn away godlessness from
Jacob;
27 ᶻand this is my covenant with them
when I take away their sins."

28ᵃIn respect to the gospel, they are enemies
on your account; but in respect to election,
they are beloved because of the patriarchs.
29ᵇFor the gifts and the call of God are irrevocable.

Triumph of God's Mercy. 30*Just as you
once disobeyed God but have now received
mercy because of their disobedience, 31so
they have now disobeyed in order that, by
virtue of the mercy shown to you, they too
may [now] receive mercy. 32ᶜFor God delivered all to disobedience, that he might have
mercy upon all.

33ᵈ*Oh, the depth of the riches and wisdom and knowledge of God! How inscrutable are his judgments and how un-
searchable his ways!

34 ᵉ*"For who has known the mind of the
Lord
or who has been his counselor?"
35 ᶠ*"Or who has given him anything
that he may be repaid?"

36ᵍFor from him and through him and for
him are all things. To him be glory forever.
Amen.

VI: The Duties of Christians

CHAPTER 12

See RG
448

Sacrifice of Body and Mind. 1ʰ*I urge
you therefore, brothers, by the mercies of
God, to offer your bodies as a living sacrifice, holy and pleasing to God, your spiritual
worship. 2ⁱDo not conform yourselves to this
age but be transformed by the renewal of
your mind, that you may discern what is the
will of God, what is good and pleasing and
perfect.

Many Parts in One Body. 3ʲFor by the
grace given to me I tell everyone among
you not to think of himself more highly
than one ought to think, but to think
soberly, each according to the measure of
faith that God has apportioned. 4ᵏFor as in
one body we have many parts, and all the
parts do not have the same function, 5*so
we, though many, are one body in Christ
and individually parts of one another.
6ˡ*Since we have gifts that differ according
to the grace given to us, let us exercise

11, 30–32: Israel, together with the Gentiles who have
been handed over to all manner of vices (ch 1), has been **delivered . . . to disobedience.** The conclusion of v 32 repeats
the thought of 5, 20, "Where sin increased, grace overflowed
all the more."

11, 33–36: This final reflection celebrates the wisdom of
God's plan of salvation. As Paul has indicated throughout
these chapters, both Jew and Gentile, despite the religious re-
calcitrance of each, have received the gift of faith. The methods used by God in making this outreach to the world stagger
human comprehension but are at the same time a dazzling invitation to abiding faith.

11, 34: The citation is from the Greek text of Is 40, 13. Paul
does not explicitly mention Isaiah in this verse, nor Job in v 35.

11, 35: Paul quotes from an old Greek version of Jb 41, 3a,
which differs from the Hebrew text (Jb 41, 11a).

12, 1—13, 14: Since Christ marks the termination of the
Mosaic law as the primary source of guidance for God's people (10, 4), the apostle explains how Christians can function,
in the light of the gift of justification through faith, in their relation to one another and the state.

12, 1–8: The Mosaic code included elaborate directions on
sacrifices and other cultic observances. The gospel, however,
invites believers to present their **bodies as a living sacrifice**
(1). Instead of being limited by specific legal maxims, Christians are liberated for the exercise of good judgment as they
are confronted with the many and varied decisions required in

the course of daily life. To assist them, God distributes a variety of gifts to the fellowship of believers, including those of
prophecy, teaching, and exhortation (6–8). Prophets assist the
community to understand the will of God as it applies to the
present situation (6). Teachers help people to understand
themselves and their responsibilities in relation to others (7).
One who **exhorts** offers encouragement to the community to
exercise their faith in the performance of all that is pleasing to
God (8). Indeed, this very section, beginning with v 1, is a
specimen of Paul's own style of exhortation.

12, 5: **One body in Christ:** on the church as the body of
Christ, see 1 Cor 12, 12–27.

12, 6: Everyone has some gift that can be used for the benefit of the community. When the instruction on justification
through faith is correctly grasped, the possesser of a gift will
understand that it is not an instrument of self-aggrandizement. Possession of a gift is not an index to quality of faith.
Rather, the gift is a challenge to faithful use.

z: Is 27, 9; Jer 31, 33-34. *a:* 15, 8; 1 Thes 2, 15-16. *b:* 9, 6; Nm
23, 19; Is 54, 10. *c:* Gal 3, 22; 1 Tm 2, 4. *d:* Jb 11, 7-8; Ps 139,
6.17-18; Wis 17, 1; Is 55, 8-9. *e:* Jb 15, 8; Wis 9, 13; Is 40, 13;
Jer 23, 18; 1 Cor 2, 11-16. *f:* Jb 41, 3; Is 40, 14. *g:* 1 Cor 8, 6;
Col 1, 16-17. *h:* 2 Cor 1, 3 / 6, 13; 1 Pt 2, 5. *i:* Eph 4, 17.22-
23; 1 Pt 1, 14 / Eph 5, 10.17; Phil 1, 10. *j:* 15, 15 / Phil 2, 3 /
1 Cor 12, 11; Eph 4, 7. *k:* 1 Cor 12, 12.27; Eph 4, 25. *l:* 1 Cor
12, 4-11.28-31; Eph 4, 7-12; 1 Pt 4, 10-11 / 2 Cor 9, 7.

them: if prophecy, in proportion to the faith; [7]if ministry, in ministering; if one is a teacher, in teaching; [8*]if one exhorts, in exhortation; if one contributes, in generosity; if one is over others, with diligence; if one does acts of mercy, with cheerfulness.

Mutual Love. [9m]Let love be sincere; hate what is evil, hold on to what is good; [10n]love one another with mutual affection; anticipate one another in showing honor. [11o]Do not grow slack in zeal, be fervent in spirit, serve the Lord. [12p]Rejoice in hope, endure in affliction, persevere in prayer. [13q]Contribute to the needs of the holy ones, exercise hospitality. [14rs*]Bless those who persecute [you], bless and do not curse them. [15t]Rejoice with those who rejoice, weep with those who weep. [16u]Have the same regard for one another; do not be haughty but associate with the lowly; do not be wise in your own estimation. [17v]Do not repay anyone evil for evil; be concerned for what is noble in the sight of all. [18w]If possible, on your part, live at peace with all. [19x]Beloved, do not look for revenge but leave room for the wrath; for it is written, "Vengeance is mine, I will repay, says the Lord." [20y]Rather, "if your enemy is hungry, feed him; if he is thirsty, give him something to drink; for by so doing you will heap burning coals upon his head." [21]Do not be conquered by evil but conquer evil with good.

CHAPTER 13

See RG 448

Obedience to Authority. [1z*]Let every person be subordinate to the higher authorities, for there is no authority except from God, and those that exist have been established by God. [2]Therefore, whoever resists authority opposes what God has appointed, and those who oppose it will bring judgment upon themselves. [3a]For rulers are not a cause of fear to good conduct, but to evil. Do you wish to have no fear of authority? Then do what is good and you will receive approval from it, [4b]for it is a servant of God for your good. But if you do evil, be afraid, for it does not bear the sword without purpose; it is the servant of God to inflict wrath on the evildoer. [5c]Therefore, it is necessary to be subject not only because of the wrath but also because of conscience. [6]This is why you also pay taxes, for the authorities are ministers of God, devoting themselves to this very thing. [7d]Pay to all their dues, taxes to whom taxes are due, toll to whom toll is due, respect to whom respect is due, honor to whom honor is due.

Love Fulfills the Law. [8e*]Owe nothing to anyone, except to love one another; for the

---

12, 8: **Over others:** usually taken to mean "rule over" but possibly "serve as a patron." Wealthier members in Greco-Roman communities were frequently asked to assist in public service projects. In view of the references to contributing **in generosity** and to **acts of mercy,** Paul may have in mind people like Phoebe (16, 1–2), who is called a **benefactor** (or "patron") because of the services she rendered to many Christians, including Paul.

12, 14–21: Since God has justified the believers, it is not necessary for them to take justice into their own hands by taking vengeance. God will ultimately deal justly with all, including those who inflict injury on the believers. This question of personal rights as a matter of justice prepares the way for more detailed consideration of the state as adjudicator.

13, 1–7: Paul must come to grips with the problem raised by a message that declares people free from the law. How are they to relate to Roman authority? The problem was exacerbated by the fact that imperial protocol was interwoven with devotion to various deities. Paul builds on the traditional instruction exhibited in Wis 6, 1–3, according to which kings and magistrates rule by consent of God. From this perspective, then, believers who render obedience to the governing authorities are obeying the one who is highest in command. At the same time, it is recognized that Caesar has the responsibility to make just ordinances and to commend uprightness;

cf Wis 6, 4–21. That Caesar is not entitled to obedience when such obedience would nullify God's prior claim to the believers' moral decision becomes clear in the light of the following verses.

13, 8–10: When love directs the Christian's moral decisions, the interest of law in basic concerns, such as familial relationships, sanctity of life, and security of property, is safeguarded (9). Indeed, says Paul, the same applies to any **other commandment** (9), whether one in the Mosaic code or one drawn up by local magistrates under imperial authority. Love anticipates the purpose of public legislation, namely, to secure the best interests of the citizenry. Since Caesar's obligation is to punish the wrongdoer (4), the Christian who acts in love is free from all legitimate indictment.

m: 2 Cor 6, 6; 1 Tm 1, 5; 1 Pt 1, 22 / Am 5, 15.   n: Jn 13, 34; 1 Thes 4, 9; 1 Pt 2, 17; 2 Pt 1, 7 / Phil 2, 3.   o: Acts 18, 25.   p: 5, 2-3; Col 4, 2; 1 Thes 5, 17.   q: Heb 13, 2; 1 Pt 4, 9.   r: Mt 5, 38-48; 1 Cor 4, 12; 1 Pt 3, 9.   s: Lk 6, 27-28.   t: Ps 35, 13; Sir 7, 34; 1 Cor 12, 26.   u: 15, 5; Phil 2, 2-3 / 11, 20; Prv 3, 7; Is 5, 21.   v: Prv 3, 4; 1 Thes 5, 15; 1 Pt 3, 9.   w: Heb 12, 14.   x: Lv 19, 18; Dt 32, 35.41; Mt 5, 39; 1 Cor 6, 6-7; Heb 10, 30.   y: Prv 25, 21-22; Mt 5, 44.   z: Prv 8, 15-16; Wis 6, 3; Jn 19, 11; 1 Pt 2, 13-17; Ti 3, 1.   a: 1 Pt 2, 13-14; 3, 13.   b: 12, 19.   c: 1 Pt 2, 19.   d: Mt 22, 21; Mk 12, 17; Lk 20, 25.   e: Jn 13, 34; Gal 5, 14.

one who loves another has fulfilled the law. [9f]The commandments, "You shall not commit adultery; you shall not kill; you shall not steal; you shall not covet," and whatever other commandment there may be, are summed up in this saying, [namely] "You shall love your neighbor as yourself." [10g]Love does no evil to the neighbor; hence, love is the fulfillment of the law.

Awareness of the End of Time. [11h*]And do this because you know the time; it is the hour now for you to awake from sleep. For our salvation is nearer now than when we first believed; [12i]the night is advanced, the day is at hand. Let us then throw off the works of darkness [and] put on the armor of light; [13j*]let us conduct ourselves properly as in the day, not in orgies and drunkenness, not in promiscuity and licentiousness, not in rivalry and jealousy. [14k]But put on the Lord Jesus Christ, and make no provision for the desires of the flesh.

CHAPTER 14

See RG 448

To Live and Die for Christ. [11m*]Welcome anyone who is weak in faith, but not for disputes over opinions. [2n]One person believes that one may eat anything, while the weak person eats only vegetables. [3o]The one who eats must not despise the one who abstains, and the one who abstains must not pass judgment on the one who eats; for God has welcomed him. [4p]Who are you to pass judgment on someone else's servant? Before his own master he stands or falls. And he will be upheld, for the Lord is able to make him stand. [5q*][For] one person considers one day more important than another, while another person considers all days alike. Let everyone be fully persuaded in his own mind. [6]Whoever observes the day, observes it for the Lord. Also whoever eats, eats for the Lord, since he gives thanks to God; while whoever abstains, abstains for the Lord and gives thanks to God. [7]None of us lives for oneself, and no one dies for oneself. [8r*]For if we live, we live for the Lord, and if we die, we die for the Lord; so then, whether we live or die, we are the Lord's. [9s]For this is why Christ died and came to life, that he might be Lord of both the dead and the living. [10t]Why then do you judge your brother? Or you, why do you look down on your brother? For we shall all stand before the judgment seat of God; [11u]for it is written:

"As I live, says the Lord, every knee
shall bend before me,
and every tongue shall give praise to
God."

[12v]So [then] each of us shall give an account of himself [to God].

Consideration for the Weak Conscience. [13w]Then let us no longer judge one another, but rather resolve never to put a stumbling block or hindrance in the way of a brother. [14x]I know and am convinced in the Lord

---

13, 11–14: These verses provide the motivation for the love that is encouraged in vv 8–10.

13, 13: Let us conduct ourselves properly as in the day: the behavior described in 1, 29–30 is now to be reversed. Secular moralists were fond of making references to people who could not wait for nightfall to do their carousing. Paul says that Christians claim to be people of the new day that will dawn with the return of Christ. Instead of planning for nighttime behavior they should be concentrating on conduct that is consonant with avowed interest in the Lord's return.

14, 1–15, 6: Since Christ spells termination of the law, which included observance of specific days and festivals as well as dietary instruction, the jettisoning of long-practiced customs was traumatic for many Christians brought up under the Mosaic code. Although Paul acknowledges that in principle no food is a source of moral contamination (14), he recommends that the consciences of Christians who are scrupulous in this regard be respected by other Christians (21). On the other hand, those who have scruples are not to sit in judgment on those who know that the gospel has liberated them from such ordinances (10). See 1 Cor 8 and 10.

14, 5: Since the problem to be overcome was humanity's perverted mind or judgment (1, 28), Paul indicates that the **mind** of the Christian is now able to function with appropriate discrimination (cf 12, 2).

14, 8: The Lord: Jesus, our Master. The same Greek word, **kyrios,** was applied to both rulers and holders of slaves. Throughout the Letter to the Romans Paul emphasizes God's total claim on the believer; see the note on 1, 1.

---

f: Ex 20, 13-17 / Lv 19, 18; Dt 5, 17-21; Mt 5, 43-44; 19, 18-19;22, 39; Mk 12, 31; Lk 10, 27; Gal 5, 14; Jas 2, 8.   *g:* Mt 22, 40; 1 Cor 13, 4-7.   *h:* Eph 5, 8-16; 1 Thes 5, 5-7.   *i:* Jn 8, 12; 1 Thes 5, 4-8; 1 Jn 2, 8 / 2 Cor 6, 7; 10, 4;Eph 5, 11; 6, 13-17.   *j:* Lk 21, 34; Eph 5, 18.   *k:* Gal 3, 27; 5, 16; Eph 4, 24; 6, 11.   *l:* 1 Cor 8, 1-13.   *m:* 15, 1.7; 1 Cor 9, 22.   *n:* Gn 1, 29; 9, 3; 1 Cor 8, 1-13; 10, 14-33.   *o:* Col 2, 16.   *p:* 2, 1; Mt 7, 11; Jas 4, 11-12.   *q:* Gal 4, 10.   *r:* Lk 20, 38; 2 Cor 5, 15; Gal 2, 20; 1 Thes 5, 10.   *s:* Acts 10, 42.   *t:* Acts 17, 31; 2 Cor 5, 10.   *u:* Is 49, 18 / Is 45, 23; Phil 2, 10-11.   *v:* Gal 6, 5.   *w:* 1 Cor 8, 9.13.   *x:* Mk 7, 5.20; Acts 10, 15; 1 Cor 10, 25-27; 1 Tm 4, 4.

Jesus that nothing is unclean in itself; still, it is unclean for someone who thinks it unclean. *15y*If your brother is being hurt by what you eat, your conduct is no longer in accord with love. Do not because of your food destroy him for whom Christ died. *16z*So do not let your good be reviled. *17a*For the kingdom of God is not a matter of food and drink, but of righteousness, peace, and joy in the holy Spirit; *18*whoever serves Christ in this way is pleasing to God and approved by others. *19b**Let us then pursue what leads to peace and to building up one another. *20c*For the sake of food, do not destroy the work of God. Everything is indeed clean, but it is wrong for anyone to become a stumbling block by eating; *21*it is good not to eat meat or drink wine or do anything that causes your brother to stumble. *22*Keep the faith [that] you have to yourself in the presence of God; blessed is the one who does not condemn himself for what he approves. *23d**But whoever has doubts is condemned if he eats, because this is not from faith; for whatever is not from faith is sin.

CHAPTER 15

See RG 448–49

Patience and Self-Denial. *1e*We who are strong ought to put up with the failings of the weak and not to please ourselves; *2f*let each of us please our neighbor for the good, for building up. *3g**For Christ did not please himself; but, as it is written, "The insults of those who insult you fall upon me." *4h*For whatever was written previously was written for our instruction, that by endurance and by the encouragement of the scriptures we

might have hope. *5i**May the God of endurance and encouragement grant you to think in harmony with one another, in keeping with Christ Jesus, *6*that with one accord you may with one voice glorify the God and Father of our Lord Jesus Christ.

God's Fidelity and Mercy. *7j**Welcome one another, then, as Christ welcomed you, for the glory of God. *8k*For I say that Christ became a minister of the circumcised to show God's truthfulness, to confirm the promises to the patriarchs, *9l*but so that the Gentiles might glorify God for his mercy. As it is written:

"Therefore, I will praise you among the
  Gentiles
  and sing praises to your name."

*10m**And again it says:

"Rejoice, O Gentiles, with his people."

*11n*And again:

"Praise the Lord, all you Gentiles,
  and let all the peoples praise him."

*12o*And again Isaiah says:

"The root of Jesse shall come,
  raised up to rule the Gentiles;
in him shall the Gentiles hope."

*13p*May the God of hope fill you with all joy and peace in believing, so that you may abound in hope by the power of the holy Spirit.

VII: Conclusion

Apostle to the Gentiles. *14**I myself am convinced about you, my brothers, that you your-

---

14, 19: Some manuscripts, versions, and church Fathers read, "We then pursue . . ."; cf 5, 1.

14, 23: Whatever is not from faith is sin: Paul does not mean that all the actions of unbelievers are sinful. He addresses himself to the question of intracommunity living. **Sin** in the singular is the dreadful power described in 5, 12–14.

15, 3: Liberation from the law of Moses does not make the scriptures of the old covenant irrelevant. Much consolation and motivation for Christian living can be derived from the Old Testament, as in the citation from Ps 69, 10. Because this psalm is quoted several times in the New Testament, it has been called indirectly messianic.

15, 5: Think in harmony: a Greco-Roman ideal. Not rigid uniformity of thought and expression but thoughtful consideration of other people's views finds expression here.

15, 7–13: True oneness of mind is found in pondering the

ultimate mission of the church: to bring it about that God's name be glorified throughout the world and that Jesus Christ be universally recognized as God's gift to all humanity. Paul here prepares his addressees for the climactic appeal he is about to make.

15, 10: Paul's citation of Dt 32, 43 follows the Greek version.

15, 14–33: Paul sees himself as apostle and benefactor in

y: 1 Cor 8, 11-13. *z:* 2, 24; Ti 2, 5. *a:* 1 Cor 8, 8. *b:* 12, 18 / 15, 2. *c:* 1 Cor 8, 11-13; 10, 28-29; Ti 1, 15. *d:* Ti 1, 15; Jas 4, 17. *e:* 14, 1-2. *f:* 14, 1.19; 1 Cor 9, 19; 10, 24.33. *g:* Ps 69, 10. *h:* 4, 23-24; 1 Mc 12, 9; 1 Cor 10, 11; 2 Tm 3, 16. *i:* 12, 16; Phil 2, 2, 5. *j:* 14, 1. *k:* Mt 15, 24 / Mi 7, 20; Acts 3, 25. *l:* 11, 30 / 2 Sm 22, 50; Ps 18, 50. *m:* Dt 32, 43. *n:* Ps 117, 1. *o:* Is 11, 10; Rv 5, 5; 22, 16. *p:* 5, 1-2.

selves are full of goodness, filled with all knowledge, and able to admonish one another. [15q]But I have written to you rather boldly in some respects to remind you, because of the grace given me by God [16r]to be a minister of Christ Jesus to the Gentiles in performing the priestly service of the gospel of God, so that the offering up of the Gentiles may be acceptable, sanctified by the holy Spirit. [17]In Christ Jesus, then, I have reason to boast in what pertains to God. [18s]For I will not dare to speak of anything except what Christ has accomplished through me to lead the Gentiles to obedience by word and deed, [19*]by the power of signs and wonders, by the power of the Spirit [of God], so that from Jerusalem all the way around to Illyricum I have finished preaching the gospel of Christ. [20t*]Thus I aspire to proclaim the gospel not where Christ has already been named, so that I do not build on another's foundation, [21u*]but as it is written:

"Those who have never been told of him
        shall see,
and those who have never heard of
        him shall understand."

Paul's Plans; Need for Prayers. [22]That is why I have so often been prevented from coming to you. [23v]But now, since I no longer have any opportunity in these regions and since I have desired to come to you for many years, [24w]I hope to see you in passing as I go to Spain and to be sent on my way there by you, after I have enjoyed being with you for a time. [25x*]Now, however, I am going to Jerusalem to minister to the holy ones. [26y*]For Macedonia and Achaia have decided to make some contribution for the poor among the holy ones in Jerusalem; [27z]they decided to do it, and in fact they are indebted to them, for if the Gentiles have come to share in their spiritual blessings, they ought also to serve them in material blessings. [28]So when I have completed this and safely handed over this contribution to them, I shall set out by way of you to Spain; [29]and I know that in coming to you I shall come in the fullness of Christ's blessing.

[30a]I urge you, [brothers,] by our Lord Jesus Christ and by the love of the Spirit, to join me in the struggle by your prayers to God on my behalf, [31]that I may be delivered from the disobedient in Judea, and that my ministry for Jerusalem may be acceptable to the holy ones, [32]so that I may come to you with joy by the will of God and be refreshed together with you. [33b]The God of peace be with all of you. Amen.

CHAPTER 16

See RG 449

Phoebe Commended. [1c*]I commend to you Phoebe our sister, who is [also] a minister of the church at Cenchreae, [2]that you may receive her in the Lord in a manner wor-

---

the priestly service of the gospel and so sketches plans for a mission in Spain, supported by those in Rome.

15, 14: Full of goodness: the opposite of what humanity was filled with according to 1, 29–30.

15, 19: Illyricum: Roman province northwest of Greece on the eastern shore of the Adriatic.

15, 20: I aspire: Paul uses terminology customarily applied to philanthropists. Unlike some philanthropists of his time, Paul does not engage in cheap competition for public acclaim. This explanation of his missionary policy is to assure the Christians in Rome that he is also not planning to remain in that city and build on other people's foundations (cf 2 Cor 10, 12–18). However, he does solicit their help in sending him on his way to Spain, which was considered the limit of the western world. Thus Paul's addressees realize that evangelization may be understood in the broader sense of mission or, as in Rom 1, 15, of instruction within the Christian community that derives from the gospel.

15, 21: The citation from Is 52, 15 concerns the Servant of the Lord. According to Isaiah, the Servant is first of all Israel, which was to bring the knowledge of Yahweh to the nations. In chs 9–11 Paul showed how Israel failed in this mission. Therefore, he himself undertakes almost singlehandedly Is-

rael's responsibility as the Servant and moves as quickly as possible with the gospel through the Roman empire.

15, 25–27: Paul may have viewed the contribution he was gathering from Gentile Christians for the poor in Jerusalem (cf 2 Cor 8 and 9) as a fulfillment of the vision of Is 60, 5–6. In confidence that the messianic fulfillment was taking place, Paul stresses in chs 14–16 the importance of harmonious relationships between Jews and Gentiles.

15, 26: Achaia: the Roman province of southern Greece.

16, 1–23: Some authorities regard these verses as a later addition to the letter, but in general the evidence favors the view that they were included in the original. Paul endeavors through the long list of greetings (3–16; 21–23) to establish strong personal contact with congregations that he has not personally encountered before. The combination of Jewish and Gentile names dramatically attests the unity in the gospel

q: 1, 5; 12, 3. *r:* 11, 13; Phil 2, 17. *s:* Acts 15, 12; 2 Cor 12, 12. *t:* 2 Cor 10, 13-18. *u:* Is 52, 15. *v:* 1, 10-13; Acts 19, 21-22. *w:* 1 Cor 16, 6. *x:* Acts 19, 21; 20, 22. *y:* 1 Cor 16, 1; 2 Cor 8, 1-4; 9, 2.12. *z:* 9, 4 / 1 Cor 9, 11. *a:* 2 Cor 1, 11; Phil 1, 27; Col 4, 3; 2 Thes 3, 1. *b:* 16, 20; 2 Cor 13, 11; Phil 4, 9; 1 Thes 5, 23; 2 Thes 3, 16; Heb 13, 20. *c:* Acts 18, 18.

thy of the holy ones, and help her in whatever she may need from you, for she has been a benefactor to many and to me as well.

Paul's Greetings. [3d*]Greet Prisca and Aquila, my co-workers in Christ Jesus, [4]who risked their necks for my life, to whom not only I am grateful but also all the churches of the Gentiles; [5e*]greet also the church at their house. Greet my beloved Epaenetus, who was the firstfruits in Asia for Christ. [6]Greet Mary, who has worked hard for you. [7*]Greet Andronicus and Junia, my relatives and my fellow prisoners; they are prominent among the apostles and they were in Christ before me. [8]Greet Ampliatus, my beloved in the Lord. [9]Greet Urbanus, our co-worker in Christ, and my beloved Stachys. [10]Greet Apelles, who is approved in Christ. Greet those who belong to the family of Aristobulus. [11]Greet my relative Herodion. Greet those in the Lord who belong to the family of Narcissus. [12]Greet those workers in the Lord, Tryphaena and Tryphosa. Greet the beloved Persis, who has worked hard in the Lord. [13f*]Greet Rufus, chosen in the Lord, and his mother and mine. [14]Greet Asyncritus, Phlegon, Hermes, Patrobas, Hermas, and the brothers who are with them. [15]Greet Philologus, Julia, Nereus and his sister, and Olympas, and all the holy ones who are with them. [16g]Greet one another with a holy kiss. All the churches of Christ greet you.

Against Factions. [17h*]I urge you, brothers, to watch out for those who create dissensions and obstacles, in opposition to the teaching that you learned; avoid them. [18i]For such people do not serve our Lord Christ but their own appetites, and by fair and flattering speech they deceive the hearts of the innocent. [19j]For while your obedience is known to all, so that I rejoice over you, I want you to be wise as to what is good, and simple as to what is evil; [20k*]then the God of peace will quickly crush Satan under your feet. The grace of our Lord Jesus be with you.

Greetings from Corinth. [21l]Timothy, my co-worker, greets you; so do Lucius and Jason and Sosipater, my relatives. [22]I, Tertius, the writer of this letter, greet you in the Lord. [23m*]Gaius, who is host to me and to the whole church, greets you. Erastus, the city treasurer, and our brother Quartus greet you. [24]*

Doxology. [25 n*]Now to him who can strengthen you, according to my gospel and the proclamation of Jesus Christ, according to the revelation of the mystery kept secret for long ages [26o]but now manifested through the prophetic writings and, according to the command of the eternal God, made known to all nations to bring about the obedience of faith, [27p]to the only wise God, through Jesus Christ be glory forever and ever. Amen.]

---

that transcends previous barriers of nationality, religious ceremony, or racial status.

16, 1: Minister: in Greek, **diakonos;** see the note on Phil 1, 1.

16, 3: Prisca and Aquila: presumably the couple mentioned at Acts 18, 2; 1 Cor 16, 19; 2 Tm 4, 19.

16, 5: The church at their house: i.e., that meets there. Such local assemblies (cf 1 Cor 16, 19; Col 4, 15; Phlm 2) might consist of only one or two dozen Christians each. It is understandable, therefore, that such smaller groups might experience difficulty in relating to one another on certain issues. **Firstfruits:** cf 8, 23; 11, 16; 1 Cor 16, 15.

16, 7: The name Junia is a woman's name. One ancient Greek manuscript and a number of ancient versions read the name "Julia." Most editors have interpreted it as a man's name, Junias.

16, 13: This Rufus cannot be identified to any degree of certainty with the Rufus of Mk 15, 21.

16, 17–18: Paul displays genuine concern for the congregations in Rome by warning them against self-seeking teachers. It would be a great loss, he intimates, if their obedience, which is known to all (cf 1, 8), would be diluted.

16, 20: This verse contains the only mention of Satan in Romans.

16, 23: This Erastus is not necessarily to be identified with the Erastus of Acts 19, 22 or of 2 Tm 4, 20.

16, 24: Some manuscripts add, similarly to v 20, "The grace of our Lord Jesus Christ be with you all. Amen."

16, 25–27: This doxology is assigned variously to the end of chs 14, 15, and 16 in the manuscript tradition. Some manuscripts omit it entirely. Whether written by Paul or not, it forms an admirable conclusion to the letter at this point.

16, 25: Paul's gospel reveals **the mystery kept secret for long ages:** justification and salvation through faith, with all the implications for Jews and Gentiles that Paul has developed in the letter.

---

d: Acts 18, 2.18-26; 1 Cor 16, 19; 2 Tm 4, 19.   *e:* 1 Cor 16, 19; Col 4, 15; Phlm 2 / 1 Cor 16, 15.   *f:* Mk 15, 21.   *g:* 1 Cor 16, 20; 2 Cor 13, 12; 1 Thes 5, 26; 1 Pt 5, 14.   *h:* Mt 7, 15; Ti 3, 10.   *i:* Phil 3, 18-19 / Col 2, 4; 2 Pt 2, 3.   *j:* 1, 8; Mt 10, 16; 1 Cor 14, 20.   *k:* 15, 33; Gn 3, 15; Lk 10, 19 / 1 Cor 16, 23; 1 Thes 5, 28;2 Thes 3, 18. *l:* Acts 16, 1-2; 19, 22; 20, 4; 1 Cor 4, 17; 16, 10; Phil 2, 19-22;Heb 13, 23.   *m:* Acts 19, 29; 1 Cor 1, 14 / 2 Tm 4, 20.   *n;* 1 Cor 2, 7; Eph 1, 9; 3, 3-9; Col 1, 26.   *o:* 2 Tm 1, 10 / 1, 5; Eph 3, 4-5.9; 1 Pt 1, 20.   *p:* 11, 36; Gal 1, 5; Eph 3, 20-21; Phil 4, 20; 1 Tm 1, 17; 2 Tm 4, 18; Heb 13, 21; 1 Pt 4, 11; 2 Pt 3, 18; Jude 25, Rev 1, 6.

See RG
450–58

The First Letter to the Corinthians

Paul's first letter to the church of Corinth provides us with a fuller insight into the life of an early Christian community of the first generation than any other book of the New Testament. Through it we can glimpse both the strengths and the weaknesses of this small group in a great city of the ancient world, men and women who had accepted the good news of Christ and were now trying to realize in their lives the implications of their baptism. Paul, who had founded the community and continued to look after it as a father, responds both to questions addressed to him and to situations of which he had been informed. In doing so, he reveals much about himself, his teaching, and the way in which he conducted his work of apostleship. Some things are puzzling because we have the correspondence only in one direction. For the person studying this letter, it seems to raise as many questions as it answers, but without it our knowledge of church life in the middle of the first century would be much poorer.

Paul established a Christian community in Corinth about the year 51, on his second missionary journey. The city, a commercial crossroads, was a melting pot full of devotees of various pagan cults and marked by a measure of moral depravity not unusual in a great seaport. The Acts of the Apostles suggests that moderate success attended Paul's efforts among the Jews in Corinth at first, but that they soon turned against him (Acts 18, 1–8). More fruitful was his year and a half spent among the Gentiles (Acts 18, 11), which won to the faith many of the city's poor and underprivileged (1, 26). After his departure the eloquent Apollos, an Alexandrian Jewish Christian, rendered great service to the community, expounding "from the scriptures that the Messiah is Jesus" (Acts 18, 24–28).

While Paul was in Ephesus on his third journey (16, 8; Acts 19, 1–20), he received disquieting news about Corinth. The community there was displaying open factionalism, as certain members were identifying themselves exclusively with individual Christian leaders and interpreting Christian teaching as a superior wisdom for the initiated few (1, 10—4, 21). The community lacked the decisiveness to take appropriate action

against one of its members who was living publicly in an incestuous union (5, 1–13). Other members engaged in legal conflicts in pagan courts of law (6, 1–11); still others may have participated in religious prostitution (6, 12–20) or temple sacrifices (10, 14–22).

The community's ills were reflected in its liturgy. In the celebration of the Eucharist certain members discriminated against others, drank too freely at the agape, or fellowship meal, and denied Christian social courtesies to the poor among the membership (11, 17–22). Charisms such as ecstatic prayer, attributed freely to the impulse of the holy Spirit, were more highly prized than works of charity (13, 1–2.8), and were used at times in a disorderly way (14, 1–40). Women appeared at the assembly without the customary head-covering (11, 3–16), and perhaps were quarreling over their right to address the assembly (14, 34–35).

Still other problems with which Paul had to deal concerned matters of conscience discussed among the faithful members of the community: the eating of meat that had been sacrificed to idols (8, 1–13), the use of sex in marriage (7, 1–7), and the attitude to be taken by the unmarried toward marriage in view of the possible proximity of Christ's second coming (7, 25–40). There was also a doctrinal matter that called for Paul's attention, for some members of the community, despite their belief in the resurrection of Christ, were denying the possibility of general bodily resurrection.

To treat this wide spectrum of questions, Paul wrote this letter from Ephesus about the year 56. The majority of the Corinthian Christians may well have been quite faithful. Paul writes on their behalf to guard against the threats posed to the community by the views and conduct of various minorities. He writes with confidence in the authority of his apostolic mission, and he presumes that the Corinthians, despite their deficiencies, will recognize and accept it. On the other hand, he does not hesitate to exercise his authority as his judgment dictates in each situation, even going so far as to promise a direct confrontation with recalcitrants, should the abuses he scores remain uncorrected (4, 18–21).

The letter illustrates well the mind and character of Paul. Although he is impelled to insist on his office as founder of the community, he recognizes that he is only one servant of God among many and generously acknowledges the labors of Apollos (3, 5–8). He provides us in this letter with many valuable examples of his method of theological reflection and exposition. He always treats the questions at issue on the level of the purity of Christian teaching and conduct. Certain passages of the letter are of the greatest importance for the understanding of early Christian teaching on the Eucharist (10, 14–22; 11, 17–34) and on the resurrection of the body (15, 1–58).

Paul's authorship of 1 Corinthians, apart from a few verses that some regard as later interpolations, has never been seriously questioned. Some scholars have proposed, however, that the letter as we have it contains portions of more than one original Pauline letter. We know that Paul wrote at least two other letters to Corinth (see 5, 9; 2 Cor 2, 3–4) in addition to the two that we now have; this theory holds that the additional letters are actually contained within the two canonical ones. Most commentators, however, find 1 Corinthians quite understandable as a single coherent work.

The principal divisions of the First Letter to the Corinthians are the following:

I: Address

CHAPTER 1

See RG 452–53

Greeting. *1a**Paul, called to be an apostle of Christ Jesus by the will of God, and Sosthenes our brother, *2b*to the church of God that is in Corinth, to you who have been sanctified in Christ Jesus, called to be holy, with all those everywhere who call upon the name of our Lord Jesus Christ, their Lord and ours. *3*Grace to you and peace from God our Father and the Lord Jesus Christ.

Thanksgiving. *4*I give thanks to my God always on your account for the grace of God bestowed on you in Christ Jesus, *5*that in him you were enriched in every way, with all discourse and all knowledge, *6**as the testimony to Christ was confirmed among you, *7c*so that you are not lacking in any spiritual gift as you wait for the revelation of our Lord Jesus Christ. *8d*He will keep you firm to the end, irreproachable on the day of our Lord Jesus [Christ]. *9e*God is faithful, and by him you were called to fellowship with his Son, Jesus Christ our Lord.

II: Disorders in the Corinthian Community

A. Divisions in the Church

Groups and Slogans. *10f**I urge you, brothers, in the name of our Lord Jesus Christ,

---

1, 1–9: Paul follows the conventional form for the opening of a Hellenistic letter (cf Rom 1, 1–7), but expands the opening with details carefully chosen to remind the readers of their situation and to suggest some of the issues the letter will discuss.

1, 1: Called ... by the will of God: Paul's mission and the church's existence are grounded in God's initiative. God's call, grace, and fidelity are central ideas in this introduction, emphasized by repetition and wordplays in the Greek.

1, 6: The testimony: this defines the purpose of Paul's mission (see also 15, 15 and the note on 2, 1). The forms of his testimony include oral preaching and instruction, his letters, and the life he leads as an apostle.

1, 10—4, 21: The first problem Paul addresses is that of divisions within the community. Although we are unable to

a: Rom 1, 1. *b:* Acts 18, 1-11. *c:* Ti 2, 13. *d:* Phil 1, 6. *e:* 1 Jn 1, 3. *f:* Phil 2, 2.

that all of you agree in what you say, and that there be no divisions among you, but that you be united in the same mind and in the same purpose. [11]For it has been reported to me about you, my brothers, by Chloe's people, that there are rivalries among you. [12g*]I mean that each of you is saying, "I belong to Paul," or "I belong to Apollos," or "I belong to Cephas," or "I belong to Christ." [13*]Is Christ divided? Was Paul crucified for you? Or were you baptized in the name of Paul? [14h]I give thanks [to God] that I baptized none of you except Crispus and Gaius, [15]so that no one can say you were baptized in my name. [16i](I baptized the household of Stephanas also; beyond that I do not know whether I baptized anyone else.) [17j*]For Christ did not send me to baptize but to preach the gospel, and not with the wisdom of human eloquence, so that the cross of Christ might not be emptied of its meaning.

Paradox of the Cross. [18k]The message of the cross is foolishness to those who are perishing, but to us who are being saved it is the power of God. [19l]For it is written:

"I will destroy the wisdom of the wise,
  and the learning of the learned I will
    set aside."

[20m]Where is the wise one? Where is the scribe? Where is the debater of this age? Has not God made the wisdom of the world foolish? [21*]For since in the wisdom of God the world did not come to know God through wisdom, it was the will of God through the foolishness of the proclamation to save those who have faith. [22n]For Jews demand signs and Greeks look for wisdom, [23o]but we proclaim Christ crucified, a stumbling block to Jews and foolishness to Gentiles, [24]but to those who are called, Jews and Greeks alike, Christ the power of God and the wisdom of God. [25]For the foolishness of God is wiser than human wisdom, and the weakness of God is stronger than human strength.

The Corinthians and Paul. [26*]Consider your own calling, brothers. Not many of you were wise by human standards, not many were powerful, not many were of noble birth. [27p]Rather, God chose the foolish of the world to shame the wise, and God chose the weak

reconstruct the situation in Corinth completely, Paul clearly traces the divisions back to a false self-image on the part of the Corinthians, coupled with a false understanding of the apostles who preached to them (cf 4, 6.9; 9, 1–5) and of the Christian message itself. In these chapters he attempts to deal with those underlying factors and to bring the Corinthians back to a more correct perspective.

1, 12: I belong to: the activities of Paul and Apollos in Corinth are described in Acts 18. Cephas (i.e., "the Rock," a name by which Paul designates Peter also in 3, 22; 9, 5; 15, 5 and in Gal 1, 18; 2, 9.11.14) may well have passed through Corinth; he could have baptized some members of the community either there or elsewhere. The reference to Christ may be intended ironically here.

1, 13–17: The reference to baptism and the contrast with preaching the gospel in v 17a suggest that some Corinthians were paying special allegiance to the individuals who initiated them into the community.

1, 17b-18: The basic theme of chs 1–4 is announced. Adherence to individual leaders has something to do with differences in rhetorical ability and also with certain presuppositions regarding wisdom, eloquence, and effectiveness (power), which Paul judges to be in conflict with the gospel and the cross.

1, 17b: Not with the wisdom of human eloquence: both of the nouns employed here involve several levels of meaning, on which Paul deliberately plays as his thought unfolds. Wisdom (sophia) may be philosophical and speculative, but in biblical usage the term primarily denotes practical knowl-

edge such as is demonstrated in the choice and effective application of means to achieve an end. The same term can designate the arts of building (cf 3, 10) or of persuasive speaking (cf 2, 4) or effectiveness in achieving salvation. Eloquence (logos): this translation emphasizes one possible meaning of the term logos (cf the references to rhetorical style and persuasiveness in 2, 1.4). But the term itself may denote an internal reasoning process, plan, or intention, as well as an external word, speech, or message. So by his expression ouk en sophia logou in the context of gospel preaching, Paul may intend to exclude both human ways of reasoning or thinking about things and human rhetorical technique. Human: this adjective does not stand in the Greek text but is supplied from the context. Paul will begin immediately to distinguish between sophia and logos from their divine counterparts and play them off against each other.

1, 21–25: True wisdom and power are to be found paradoxically where one would least expect them, in the place of their apparent negation. To human eyes the crucified Christ symbolizes impotence and absurdity.

1, 26—2, 5: The pattern of God's wisdom and power is exemplified in their own experience, if they interpret it rightly (1, 26–31), and can also be read in their experience of Paul as he first appeared among them preaching the gospel (2, 1–5).

g: 3, 4.22; 16, 12; Acts 18, 24-28. h: Acts 18, 8 / Rom 16, 23. i: 16, 15-17. j: 2, 1.4. k: 2, 14 / Rom 1, 16. l: Is 29, 14. m: Is 19, 12. n: Mt 12, 38; 16, 1 / Acts 17, 18-21. o: 2, 2; Gal 3, 1 / Gal 5, 11. p: Jas 2, 5.

of the world to shame the strong, [28]and God chose the lowly and despised of the world, those who count for nothing, to reduce to nothing those who are something, [29q]*so that no human being might boast before God. [30r]It is due to him that you are in Christ Jesus, who became for us wisdom from God, as well as righteousness, sanctification, and redemption, [31s]so that, as it is written, "Whoever boasts, should boast in the Lord."

See RG
452–53

CHAPTER 2

[1t]*When I came to you, brothers, proclaiming the mystery of God, I did not come with sublimity of words or of wisdom. [2u]For I resolved to know nothing while I was with you except Jesus Christ, and him crucified. [3]*I came to you in weakness and fear and much trembling, [4v]*and my message and my proclamation were not with persuasive [words of] wisdom, but with a demonstration of spirit and power, [5w]so that your faith might rest not on human wisdom but on the power of God.

The True Wisdom. [6]*Yet we do speak a wisdom to those who are mature, but not a wisdom of this age, nor of the rulers of this age who are passing away. [7]*Rather, we speak God's wisdom, mysterious, hidden, which God predetermined before the ages for our glory, [8]*and which none of the rulers of this age knew; for, if they had known it, they would not have crucified the Lord of glory. [9x]But as it is written:

> "What eye has not seen, and ear has not heard,
> and what has not entered the human heart,
> what God has prepared for those who love him,"

[10y]this God has revealed to us through the Spirit.

For the Spirit scrutinizes everything, even the depths of God. [11]Among human beings, who knows what pertains to a person except the spirit of the person that is within? Similarly, no one knows what pertains to God except the Spirit of God. [12]We have not received the spirit of the world but the Spirit that is from God, so that we may understand the things freely given us by God. [13]*And we speak about them not with words taught by

---

1, 29–31: "Boasting (about oneself)" is a Pauline expression for the radical sin, the claim to autonomy on the part of a creature, the illusion that we live and are saved by our own resources. "Boasting in the Lord" (31), on the other hand, is the acknowledgment that we live only from God and for God.

2, 1: The mystery of God: God's secret, known only to himself, is his plan for the salvation of his people; it is clear from 1, 18–25; 2, 2.8–10 that this secret involves Jesus and the cross. In place of **mystery,** other good manuscripts read "testimony" (cf 1, 6).

2, 3: The **weakness** of the crucified Jesus is reflected in Paul's own bearing (cf 2 Cor 10–13). **Fear and much trembling:** reverential fear based on a sense of God's transcendence permeates Paul's existence and preaching. Compare his advice to the Philippians to work out their salvation with "fear and trembling" (Phil 2, 12), because God is at work in them just as his exalting power was paradoxically at work in the emptying, humiliation, and obedience of Jesus to death on the cross (Phil 2, 6–11).

2, 4: Among many manuscript readings here the best is either "not with the persuasion of wisdom" or "not with persuasive words of wisdom," which differ only by a nuance. Whichever reading is accepted, the inefficacy of human wisdom for salvation is contrasted with the power of the cross.

2, 6–3, 4: Paul now asserts paradoxically what he has previously been denying. To the Greeks who "are looking for wisdom" (1, 22), he does indeed bring a wisdom, but of a higher order and an entirely different quality, the only wisdom really worthy of the name. The Corinthians would be

able to grasp Paul's preaching as wisdom and enter into a wisdom-conversation with him if they were more open to the Spirit and receptive to the new insight and language that the Spirit teaches.

2, 7–10a: God's wisdom: his plan for our salvation. This was his own eternal secret that no one else could fathom, but in this new age of salvation he has graciously revealed it to us. For the pattern of God's secret, hidden to others and now revealed to the Church, cf also Rom 11, 25–36; 16, 25–27; Eph 1, 3–10; 3, 3–11; Col 1, 25–28.

2, 8: The rulers of this age: this suggests not only the political leaders of the Jews and Romans under whom Jesus was crucified (cf Acts 4, 25–28) but also the cosmic powers behind them (cf Eph 1, 20–23; 3, 10). **They would not have crucified the Lord of glory:** they became the unwitting executors of God's plan, which will paradoxically bring about their own conquest and submission (15, 24–28).

2, 13: In spiritual terms: the Spirit teaches spiritual people a new mode of perception (12) and an appropriate language by which they can share their self-understanding, their knowledge about what God has done in them. The final phrase in v 13 can also be translated "describing spiritual realities to spiritual people," in which case it prepares for vv 14–16.

---

q: Eph 2, 9. *r:* Rom 4, 17 / 6, 11; Rom 3, 24-26; 2 Cor 5, 21 / Eph 1, 7;Col 1, 14; 1 Thes 5, 23. *s:* Jer 9, 23; 2 Cor 10, 17. *t:* 1, 17. *u:* 1, 23; Gal 6, 14. *v:* 4, 20; Rom 15, 19; 1 Thes 1, 5. *w:* 2 Cor 4, 7. *x:* Is 64, 3. *y:* Mt 11, 25; 13, 11; 16, 17.

human wisdom, but with words taught by the Spirit, describing spiritual realities in spiritual terms.

14*Now the natural person does not accept what pertains to the Spirit of God, for to him it is foolishness, and he cannot understand it, because it is judged spiritually. *15**The spiritual person, however, can judge everything but is not subject to judgment by anyone.

*16z*For "who has known the mind of the Lord, so as to counsel him?" But we have the mind of Christ.

CHAPTER 3

See RG 452-53

1*Brothers, I could not talk to you as spiritual people, but as fleshly people, as infants in Christ. *2a*I fed you milk, not solid food, because you were unable to take it. Indeed, you are still not able, even now, *3b**for you are still of the flesh. While there is jealousy and rivalry among you, are you not of the flesh and behaving in an ordinary human way? *4c*Whenever someone says, "I belong to Paul," and another, "I belong to Apollos," are you not merely human?

The Role of God's Ministers. *5**What is Apollos, after all, and what is Paul? Ministers through whom you became believers, just as the Lord assigned each one. *6d*I planted, Apollos watered, but God caused the growth. *7*Therefore, neither the one who plants nor the one who waters is anything, but only God, who causes the growth. *8*The one who plants and the one who waters are equal, and each will receive wages in proportion to his labor. *9e*For we are God's co-workers; you are God's field, God's building.

10*According to the grace of God given to me, like a wise master builder I laid a foundation, and another is building upon it. But each one must be careful how he builds upon it, *11*for no one can lay a foundation other than the one that is there, namely, Jesus Christ. *12*If anyone builds on this foundation with gold, silver, precious stones, wood, hay, or straw, *13f**the work of each will come to light, for the Day will disclose it. It will be revealed with fire, and the fire [itself] will test the quality of each one's work. *14*If the work stands that someone built upon the foundation, that person will receive a wage. *15**But if someone's work is burned up, that

2, 14: **The natural person:** see the note on 3, 1.

2, 15: **The spiritual person . . . is not subject to judgment:** since spiritual persons have been given knowledge of what pertains to God (11–12), they share in God's own capacity to judge. One to whom the mind of the Lord (and of Christ) is revealed (16) can be said to share in some sense in God's exemption from counseling and criticism.

3, 1–4: The Corinthians desire a sort of wisdom dialogue or colloquy with Paul; they are looking for solid, adult food, and he appears to disappoint their expectations. Paul counters: if such a dialogue has not yet taken place, the reason is that they are still at an immature stage of development (cf 2, 6).

3, 1: **Spiritual people . . . fleshly people:** Paul employs two clusters of concepts and terms to distinguish what later theology will call the "natural" and the "supernatural." (1) The natural person (2, 14) is one whose existence, perceptions, and behavior are determined by purely natural principles, the **psyche** (2, 14) and the **sarx** (flesh, a biblical term that connotes creatureliness, 1.3). Such persons are only infants (1); they remain on a purely human level (**anthrōpoi,** 4). (2) On the other hand, they are called to be animated by a higher principle, the **pneuma,** God's spirit. They are to become spiritual (**pneumatikoi,** 1) and mature (2, 6) in their perceptions and behavior (cf Gal 5, 16–26). The culmination of existence in the Spirit is described in 15, 44–49.

3, 3–4: Jealousy, rivalry, and divisions in the community are symptoms of their arrested development; they reveal the immaturity both of their self-understanding (4) and of their judgments about their apostles (21).

3, 5—4, 5: The Corinthians tend to evaluate their leaders by the criteria of human wisdom and to exaggerate their importance. Paul views the role of the apostles in the light of his theology of spiritual gifts (cf chs 12–14, where the charism of the apostle heads the lists). The essential aspects of all spiritual gifts (12, 4–6 presents them as gifts of grace, as services, and as modes of activity) are exemplified by the apostolate, which is a gift of grace (3, 10) through which God works (3, 9) and a form of service (3, 5) for the common good (elsewhere expressed by the verb "build up," suggested here by the image of the building, 3, 9). The apostles serve the church, but their accountability is to God and to Christ (4, 1–5).

3, 5: **Ministers:** for other expressions of Paul's understanding of himself as minister or steward to the church, cf 4, 1; 9, 17.19–27; 2 Cor 3, 6–9; 4, 1; 5, 18; 6, 3–4; and 11, 23 (the climax of Paul's defense).

3, 10–11: There are diverse functions in the service of the community, but each individual's task is serious, and each will stand accountable for the quality of his contribution.

3, 13: **The Day:** the great day of Yahweh, the day of judgment, which can be a time of either gloom or joy. **Fire** both destroys and purifies.

3, 15: **Will be saved:** although Paul can envision very harsh divine punishment (cf 17), he appears optimistic about the success of divine corrective means both here and elsewhere (cf 5, 5; 11, 32 [discipline]). The text of v 15 has sometimes been used to support the notion of purgatory, though it does not envisage this.

z: Wis 9, 13; Is 40, 13; Rom 11, 34. a: Heb 5, 12-14. b: Jas 3, 13-16. c: 1, 12. d: Acts 18, 1-11.24-28. e: Eph 2, 20-22; 1 Pt 2, 5. f: Mt 3, 11-12; 2 Thes 1, 7-10.

one will suffer loss; the person will be saved, but only as through fire. [16g]Do you not know that you are the temple of God, and that the Spirit of God dwells in you? [17]*If anyone destroys God's temple, God will destroy that person; for the temple of God, which you are, is holy.

[18h]Let no one deceive himself. If anyone among you considers himself wise in this age, let him become a fool so as to become wise. [19i]For the wisdom of this world is foolishness in the eyes of God, for it is written:

"He catches the wise in their own ruses,"

[20j]and again:

"The Lord knows the thoughts of the
        wise, that they are vain."

[21k]*So let no one boast about human beings, for everything belongs to you, [22]Paul or Apollos or Cephas, or the world or life or death, or the present or the future: all belong to you, [23]and you to Christ, and Christ to God.

CHAPTER 4

See RG
452–53

[11]Thus should one regard us: as servants of Christ and stewards of the mysteries of God. [2]Now it is of course required of stewards that they be found trustworthy. [3]It does not concern me in the least that I be judged by you or any human tribunal; I do not even pass judgment on myself; [4m]I am not conscious of anything against me, but I do not thereby stand acquitted; the one who judges me is the Lord. [5]Therefore, do not make any judgment before the appointed time, until the Lord comes, for he will bring to light what is hidden in darkness and will manifest the motives of our hearts, and then everyone will receive praise from God.

Paul's Life as Pattern. [6]*I have applied these things to myself and Apollos for your benefit, brothers, so that you may learn from us not to go beyond what is written, so that none of you will be inflated with pride in favor of one person over against another. [7]Who confers distinction upon you? What do you possess that you have not received? But if you have received it, why are you boasting as if you did not receive it? [8]*You are already satisfied; you have already grown rich; you have become kings without us! Indeed, I wish that you had become kings, so that we also might become kings with you.

[9n]*For as I see it, God has exhibited us apostles as the last of all, like people sen-

---

3, 17: Holy: i.e., "belonging to God." The cultic sanctity of the community is a fundamental theological reality to which Paul frequently alludes (cf 1, 2.30; 6, 11; 7, 14).

3, 21–23: These verses pick up the line of thought of 1, 10–13. If the Corinthians were genuinely wise (18–20), their perceptions would be reversed, and they would see everything in the world and all those with whom they exist in the church in their true relations with one another. Paul assigns all the persons involved in the theological universe a position on a scale: God, Christ, church members, church leaders. Read from top to bottom, the scale expresses ownership; read from bottom to top, the obligation to serve. This picture should be complemented by similar statements such as those in 8, 6 and 15, 20–28.

4, 6–21: This is an emotionally charged peroration to the discussion about divisions. It contains several exhortations and statements of Paul's purpose in writing (cf 6.14–17.21) that counterbalance the initial exhortation at 1, 10.

4, 6: That you may learn from us not to go beyond what is written: the words "to go" are not in the Greek, but have here been added as the minimum necessary to elicit sense from this difficult passage. It probably means that the Corinthians should avoid the false wisdom of vain speculation, contenting themselves with Paul's proclamation of the cross, which is the fulfillment of God's promises in the Old Testament (what is written). **Inflated with pride:** literally, "puffed up," i.e., arrogant, filled with a sense of self-impor-

tance. The term is particularly Pauline, found in the New Testament only in 1 Cor 4, 6.18–19; 5, 2; 8, 1; 13, 4; Col 2, 18 (cf the related noun at 2 Cor 12, 20). It sometimes occurs in conjunction with the theme of "boasting," as in vv 6–7 here.

4, 8: Satisfied . . . rich . . . kings: these three statements could also be punctuated as questions continuing the series begun in v 7. In any case these expressions reflect a tendency at Corinth toward an overrealized eschatology, a form of self-deception that draws Paul's irony. The underlying attitude has implications for the Corinthians' thinking about other issues, notably morality and the resurrection, that Paul will address later in the letter.

4, 9–13: A rhetorically effective catalogue of the circumstances of apostolic existence, in the course of which Paul ironically contrasts his own sufferings with the Corinthians' illusion that they have passed beyond the folly of the passion and have already reached the condition of glory. His language echoes that of the beatitudes and woes, which assert a future reversal of present conditions. Their present sufferings ("to this very hour," 11) place the apostles in the class of those to whom the beatitudes promise future relief (Mt 5, 3–11; Lk 6, 20–23); whereas the Corinthians' image of themselves as "al-

g: 6, 19; 2 Cor 6, 16; Eph 2, 20-22.   *h:* 8, 2; Is 5, 21; Gal 6, 3.
i: 1, 20 / Jb 5, 13.   *j:* Ps 94, 11.   *k:* 4, 6 / Rom 8, 32.   *l:* Ti 1, 7;
1 Pt 4, 10.   *m:* 2 Cor 1, 12 / Rom 2, 16; 2 Cor 5, 10.   *n:* 15, 31;
Rom 8, 36; 2 Cor 4, 8-12; 11, 23 / Heb 10, 33.

tenced to death, since we have become a spectacle to the world, to angels and human beings alike. [10o]We are fools on Christ's account, but you are wise in Christ; we are weak, but you are strong; you are held in honor, but we in disrepute. [11p]To this very hour we go hungry and thirsty, we are poorly clad and roughly treated, we wander about homeless [12q]and we toil, working with our own hands. When ridiculed, we bless; when persecuted, we endure; [13]when slandered, we respond gently. We have become like the world's rubbish, the scum of all, to this very moment.

[14*]I am writing you this not to shame you, but to admonish you as my beloved children. [15r]Even if you should have countless guides to Christ, yet you do not have many fathers, for I became your father in Christ Jesus through the gospel. [16s]Therefore, I urge you, be imitators of me. [17t]For this reason I am sending you Timothy, who is my beloved and faithful son in the Lord; he will remind you of my ways in Christ [Jesus], just as I teach them everywhere in every church.

[18*]Some have become inflated with pride, as if I were not coming to you. [19]But I will come to you soon, if the Lord is willing, and I shall ascertain not the talk of these inflated people but their power. [20u]For the kingdom of God is not a matter of talk but of power. [21v]Which do you prefer? Shall I come to you with a rod, or with love and a gentle spirit?

B. Moral Disorders

CHAPTER 5

See RG 453

A Case of Incest. [1w*]It is widely reported that there is immorality among you, and immorality of a kind not found even among pagans—a man living with his father's wife. [2*]And you are inflated with pride. Should you not rather have been sorrowful? The one who did this deed should be expelled from your midst. [3x]I, for my part, although absent in body but present in spirit, have already, as if present, pronounced judgment on the one who has committed this deed, [4]in the name of [our] Lord Jesus: when you have gathered together and I am with you in spirit with the power of the Lord Jesus, [5y*]you are to deliver this man to Satan for the destruction of his flesh, so that his spirit may be saved on the day of the Lord.

[6z*]Your boasting is not appropriate. Do you not know that a little yeast leavens all

---

ready" filled, rich, ruling (8), as wise, strong, and honored (10) places them paradoxically in the position of those whom the woes threaten with future undoing (Lk 6, 24–26). They have lost sight of the fact that the reversal is predicted for the future.

4, 14–17: My beloved children: the close of the argument is dominated by the tender metaphor of the father who not only gives his children life but also educates them. Once he has begotten them through his preaching, Paul continues to present the gospel to them existentially, by his life as well as by his word, and they are to learn, as children do, by imitating their parents (16). The reference to the **rod** in v 21 belongs to the same image-complex. So does the image of the **ways** in v 17: the ways that Paul teaches everywhere, "his ways in Christ Jesus," mean a behavior pattern quite different from the human ways along which the Corinthians are walking (3, 3).

4, 18–21: Verse 20 picks up the contrast between a certain kind of talk (**logos**) and true power (**dynamis**) from 1, 17–18 and 2, 4–5. The kingdom, which many of them imagine to be fully present in their lives (8), will be rather unexpectedly disclosed in the strength of Paul's encounter with them, if they make a powerful intervention on his part necessary. Compare the similar ending to an argument in 2 Cor 13, 1–4.10.

5, 1—6, 20: Paul now takes up a number of other matters that require regulation. These have come to his attention by hearsay (5, 1), probably in reports brought by "Chloe's people" (1, 11).

5, 1–13: Paul first deals with the incestuous union of a man with his stepmother (1–8) and then attempts to clarify general admonitions he has given about associating with fellow Christians guilty of immorality (9–13). Each of these three brief paragraphs expresses the same idea: the need for separation between the holy and the unholy.

5, 2: Inflated with pride: this remark and the reference to **boasting** in v 6 suggest that they are proud of themselves despite the infection in their midst, tolerating and possibly even approving the situation. The attitude expressed in 6, 2.13 may be influencing their thinking in this case.

5, 5: Deliver this man to Satan: once the sinner is expelled from the church, the sphere of Jesus' lordship and victory over sin, he will be in the region outside over which Satan is still master. **For the destruction of his flesh:** the purpose of the penalty is medicinal: through affliction, sin's grip over him may be destroyed and the path to repentance and reunion laid open. With Paul's instructions for an excommunication ceremony here, contrast his recommendations for the reconciliation of a sinner in 2 Cor 2, 5–11.

5, 6: A little yeast: yeast, which induces fermentation, is

o: 1, 18; 3, 18; 2 Cor 11, 19 / 2, 3; 2 Cor 13, 9. *p:* Rom 8, 35; 2 Cor 11, 23-27. *q:* Acts 9, 6-14; 18, 3; 20, 34; 1 Thes 2, 9 / 1 Pt 3, 9. *r:* Gal 4, 19; Phlm 10. *s:* 11, 1; Phil 3, 17; 4, 9; 1 Thes 1, 6; 2 Thes 3, 7.9. *t:* 16, 10; Acts 19, 22. *u:* 2, 4; 1 Thes 1, 5. *v:* 2 Cor 1, 23; 10, 2. *w:* Lv 18, 7-8; 20, 11; Dt 27, 20. *x:* Col 2, 5. *y:* 1 Tm 1, 20. *z:* Gal 5, 9.

the dough? [7a]*Clear out the old yeast, so that you may become a fresh batch of dough, inasmuch as you are unleavened. For our paschal lamb, Christ, has been sacrificed. [8b]Therefore, let us celebrate the feast, not with the old yeast, the yeast of malice and wickedness, but with the unleavened bread of sincerity and truth.

[9]*I wrote you in my letter not to associate with immoral people, [10c]not at all referring to the immoral of this world or the greedy and robbers or idolaters; for you would then have to leave the world. [11d]But I now write to you not to associate with anyone named a brother, if he is immoral, greedy, an idolater, a slanderer, a drunkard, or a robber, not even to eat with such a person. [12]For why should I be judging outsiders? Is it not your business to judge those within? [13e]God will judge those outside. "Purge the evil person from your midst."

See RG
453

CHAPTER 6

Lawsuits before Unbelievers. [1]*How can any one of you with a case against another dare to bring it to the unjust for judgment instead of to the holy ones? [2f]*Do you not know that the holy ones will judge the world? If the world is to be judged by you, are you unqualified for the lowest law courts? [3]Do you not know that we will judge angels? Then why not everyday matters? [4]If, therefore, you have courts for everyday matters, do you seat as judges people of no standing in the church? [5]I say this to shame you. Can it be that there is not one among you wise enough to be able to settle a case between brothers? [6]But rather brother goes to court against brother, and that before unbelievers?

[7g]Now indeed [then] it is, in any case, a failure on your part that you have lawsuits against one another. Why not rather put up with injustice? Why not rather let yourselves be cheated? [8]Instead, you inflict injustice and cheat, and this to brothers. [9h]*Do you not know that the unjust will not inherit the kingdom of God? Do not be deceived; neither fornicators nor idolaters nor adulterers nor boy prostitutes nor sodomites [10]nor thieves nor the greedy nor drunkards nor slanderers nor robbers will inherit the kingdom of God. [11i]That is what some of you used to be; but now you have had yourselves washed, you were sanctified, you were justified in the name of the Lord Jesus Christ and in the Spirit of our God.

Sexual Immorality. [12j]*"Everything is

a natural symbol for a source of corruption that becomes all-pervasive. The expression is proverbial.

5, 7–8: In the Jewish calendar, Passover was followed immediately by the festival of Unleavened Bread. In preparation for this feast all traces of old bread were removed from the house, and during the festival only unleavened bread was eaten. The sequence of these two feasts provides Paul with an image of Christian existence: Christ's death (the true Passover celebration) is followed by the life of the Christian community, marked by newness, purity, and integrity (a perpetual feast of unleavened bread). Paul may have been writing around Passover time (cf 16, 5); this is a little Easter homily, the earliest in Christian literature.

5, 9–13: Paul here corrects a misunderstanding of his earlier directives against associating with immoral fellow Christians. He concedes the impossibility of avoiding contact with sinners in society at large but urges the Corinthians to maintain the inner purity of their own community.

6, 1–11: Christians at Corinth are suing one another before pagan judges in Roman courts. A barrage of rhetorical questions (1–9) betrays Paul's indignation over this practice, which he sees as an infringement upon the holiness of the Christian community.

6, 2–3: The principle to which Paul appeals is an eschatological prerogative promised to Christians: they are to share with Christ the judgment of the world (cf Dn 7, 22.27). Hence they ought to be able to settle minor disputes within the community.

6, 9–10: A catalogue of typical vices that exclude from the kingdom of God and that should be excluded from God's church. Such lists (cf 5, 10) reflect the common moral sensibility of the New Testament period.

6, 9: The Greek word translated as **boy prostitutes** may refer to catamites, i.e., boys or young men who were kept for purposes of prostitution, a practice not uncommon in the Greco-Roman world. In Greek mythology this was the function of Ganymede, the "cupbearer of the gods," whose Latin name was Catamitus. The term translated **sodomites** would then refer to adult males who indulged in homosexual practices with such boys. See similar condemnations of such practices in Rom 1, 26–27; 1 Tm 1, 10.

6, 12–20: Paul now turns to the opinion of some Corinthians that sexuality is a morally indifferent area (12–13). This leads him to explain the mutual relation between the Lord Jesus and our bodies (13b) in a densely packed paragraph that contains elements of a profound theology of sexuality (15–20).

6, 12–13: Everything is lawful for me: the Corinthians may have derived this slogan from Paul's preaching about Christian freedom, but they mean something different by it:

a: Ex 12, 1-13; Dt 16, 1-2; 1 Pt 1, 19.   *b:* Ex 12, 15-20; 13, 7; Dt 16, 3.   *c:* 10, 27; Jn 17, 15.   *d:* Mt 18, 17; 2 Thes 3, 6.14; 2 Jn 10.   *e:* Dt 13, 6; 17, 7; 22, 24.   *f:* Wis 3, 8; Mt 19, 28; Rv 20, 4.   *g:* Mt 5, 38-42; Rom 12, 17-21; 1 Thes 5, 15.   *h:* 15, 50; Gal 5, 19-21; Eph 5, 5.   *i:* Ti 3, 3-7.   *j:* 10, 23.

lawful for me," but not everything is beneficial. "Everything is lawful for me," but I will
not let myself be dominated by anything.
13"Food for the stomach and the stomach for
food," but God will do away with both the
one and the other. The body, however, is not
for immorality, but for the Lord, and the
Lord is for the body; *14k*God raised the Lord
and will also raise us by his power.

*15l*Do you not know that your bodies are
members of Christ? Shall I then take Christ's
members and make them the members of a
prostitute? Of course not! *16m*[Or] do you not
know that anyone who joins himself to a prostitute becomes one body with her? For "the
two," it says, "will become one flesh." *17n*But
whoever is joined to the Lord becomes one
spirit with him. *18*Avoid immorality. Every
other sin a person commits is outside the body,
but the immoral person sins against his own
body. *19o*Do you not know that your body is a
temple of the holy Spirit within you, whom
you have from God, and that you are not your
own? *20p*For you have been purchased at a
price. Therefore glorify God in your body.

they consider sexual satisfaction a matter as indifferent as food,
and they attribute no lasting significance to bodily functions
(13a). Paul begins to deal with the slogan by two qualifications,
which suggest principles for judging sexual activity. **Not everything is beneficial:** cf 10, 23, and the whole argument of chs
8–10 on the finality of freedom and moral activity. **Not let myself be dominated:** certain apparently free actions may involve
in fact a secret servitude in conflict with the lordship of Jesus.

6, 15b-16: A prostitute: the reference may be specifically
to religious prostitution, an accepted part of pagan culture at
Corinth and elsewhere; but the prostitute also serves as a symbol for any sexual relationship that conflicts with Christ's claim
over us individually. **The two . . . will become one flesh:** the
text of Gn 2, 24 is applied positively to human marriage in Mt
and Mk, and in Eph 5, 29–32: love of husband and wife reflect
the love of Christ for his church. The application of the text to
union with a prostitute is jarring, for such a union is a parody,
an antitype of marriage, which does conflict with Christ's
claim over us. This explains the horror expressed in 15b.

6, 18: Against his own body: expresses the intimacy and
depth of sexual disorder, which violates the very orientation
of our bodies.

6, 19–20: Paul's vision becomes trinitarian. **A temple:**
sacred by reason of God's gift, his indwelling Spirit. **Not
your own:** but "for the Lord," who acquires ownership by
the act of redemption. **Glorify God in your body:** the argument concludes with a positive imperative to supplement
the negative "avoid immorality" of v 18. Far from
being a terrain that is morally indifferent, the area of
sexuality is one in which our relationship with God (and
his Christ and his Spirit) is very intimately expressed:

III: Answers to the Corinthians' Questions

A. Marriage and Virginity

CHAPTER 7

See RG 453–54

Advice to the Married. *1*Now in regard to the matters about which you wrote:
"It is a good thing for a man not to touch a
woman," *2*but because of cases of immorality every man should have his own wife, and
every woman her own husband. *3*The husband should fulfill his duty toward his wife,
and likewise the wife toward her husband.
*4*A wife does not have authority over her own
body, but rather her husband, and similarly a
husband does not have authority over his
own body, but rather his wife. *5*Do not deprive each other, except perhaps by mutual
consent for a time, to be free for prayer, but
then return to one another, so that Satan may
not tempt you through your lack of self-control. *6*This I say by way of concession, however, not as a command. *7q*Indeed, I wish
everyone to be as I am, but each has a partic-

he is either highly glorified or deeply offended.

7, 1–40: Paul now begins to answer questions addressed
to him by the Corinthians (7, 1—11, 1). The first of these concerns marriage. This chapter contains advice both to the married (1–16) and to the unmarried (25–38) or widowed
(39–40); these two parts are separated by vv 17–24, which
enunciate a principle applicable to both.

7, 1–16: It seems that some Christians in Corinth were advocating asceticism in sexual matters. The pattern **it is a good
thing . . . , but** occurs twice (1–2.8–9; cf 26), suggesting that
in this matter as in others the Corinthians have seized upon a
genuine value but are exaggerating or distorting it in some
way. Once again Paul calls them to a more correct perspective
and a better sense of their own limitations. The phrase **it is a
good thing** (1) may have been the slogan of the ascetic party
at Corinth.

7, 1–7: References to Paul's own behavior (7–8) suggest
that his celibate way of life and his preaching to the unmarried
(cf 25–35) have given some the impression that asceticism
within marriage, i.e., suspension of normal sexual relations,
would be a laudable ideal. Paul points to their experience of
widespread immorality to caution them against overestimating
their own strength (2); as individuals they may not have the
particular gift that makes such asceticism feasible (7) and
hence are to abide by the principle to be explained in vv 17–24.

7, 6: By way of concession: this refers most likely to the

k: Rom 8, 11; 2 Cor 4, 14.   *l:* 12, 27; Rom 6, 12-13; 12, 5; Eph 5,
30.   *m:* Gn 2, 24; Mt 19, 5; Mk 10, 8; Eph 5, 31.   *n:* Rom 8, 9-
10; 2 Cor 3, 17.   *o:* 3, 16-17; Rom 5, 5.   *p:* 3, 23; 7, 23; Acts 20,
28 / Rom 12, 1; Phil 1, 20.   *q:* Mt 19, 11-12.

ular gift from God, one of one kind and one of another.

8r*Now to the unmarried and to widows I say: It is a good thing for them to remain as they are, as I do, *9*but if they cannot exercise self-control they should marry, for it is better to marry than to be on fire. *10s**To the married, however, I give this instruction (not I, but the Lord): A wife should not separate from her husband *11*—and if she does separate she must either remain single or become reconciled to her husband—and a husband should not divorce his wife.

12*To the rest I say (not the Lord): If any brother has a wife who is an unbeliever, and she is willing to go on living with him, he should not divorce her; *13*and if any woman has a husband who is an unbeliever, and he is willing to go on living with her, she should not divorce her husband. *14t*For the unbelieving husband is made holy through his wife, and the unbelieving wife is made holy through the brother. Otherwise your children would be unclean, whereas in fact they are holy.

15*If the unbeliever separates, however, let him separate. The brother or sister is not bound in such cases; God has called you to peace. *16*For how do you know, wife, whether you will save your husband; or how do you know, husband, whether you will save your wife?

The Life That the Lord Has Assigned. *17**Only, everyone should live as the Lord has assigned, just as God called each one. I give this order in all the churches. *18u*Was someone called after he had been circumcised? He should not try to undo his circumcision. Was an uncircumcised person called? He should not be circumcised. *19v*Circumcision means nothing, and uncircumcision means nothing; what matters is keeping God's commandments. *20*Everyone should remain in the state in which he was called.

*21*Were you a slave when you were called? Do not be concerned but, even if you can gain your freedom, make the most of it. *22w*For the slave called in the Lord is a freed person in the Lord, just as the free person who has been called is a slave of Christ. *23x*You have been purchased at a price. Do not become slaves to human beings. *24*Brothers, everyone should continue before God in the state in which he was called.

Advice to Virgins and Widows. *25**Now in regard to virgins I have no commandment from the Lord, but I give my opinion as one who by the Lord's mercy is trustworthy. *26y*So this is what I think best because of the present distress: that it is a good thing for a person to remain as he is. *27*Are you bound to a wife? Do not seek a separation. Are you free of a wife? Then do not look for a wife. *28*If you marry, however, you do not sin, nor does an unmarried woman sin if she marries; but such people will experience affliction in their earthly life, and I would like to spare you that.

29z*I tell you, brothers, the time is running out. From now on, let those having wives act

concession mentioned in v 5a: temporary interruption of relations for a legitimate purpose.

7, 7: A particular gift from God: use of the term **charisma** suggests that marriage and celibacy may be viewed in the light of Paul's theology of spiritual gifts (chs 12–14).

7, 8: Paul was obviously unmarried when he wrote this verse. Some interpreters believe that he had previously been married and widowed; there is no clear evidence either for or against this view, which was expressed already at the end of the second century by Clement of Alexandria.

7, 10–11: (Not I, but the Lord): Paul reminds the married of Jesus' principle of nonseparation (Mk 10, 9). This is one of his rare specific references to the teaching of Jesus.

7, 12–14: To the rest: marriages in which only one partner is a baptized Christian. Jesus' prohibition against divorce is not addressed to them, but Paul extends the principle of nonseparation to such unions, provided they are marked by peacefulness and shared sanctification.

7, 15–16: If the unbeliever separates: the basis of the "Pauline privilege" in Catholic marriage legislation.

7, 17–24: On the ground that distinct human conditions are less significant than the whole new existence opened up by God's call, Paul urges them to be less concerned with changing their states of life than with answering God's call where it finds them. The principle applies both to the married state (1–16) and to the unmarried (25–38).

7, 25–28: Paul is careful to explain that the principle of v 17 does not bind under sin but that present earthly conditions make it advantageous for the unmarried to remain as they are (28). These remarks must be complemented by the statement about "particular gifts" from v 7.

7, 29–31: The world . . . is passing away: Paul advises Christians to go about the ordinary activities of life in a manner different from those who are totally immersed in them and unaware of their transitoriness.

r: 1 Tm 5, 11-16 / 9, 5; *s:* Mt 5, 32; 19, 9. *t:* Rom 11, 16. *u:* 1 Mc 1, 15 / Acts 15, 1-2. *v:* Rom 2, 25.29; Gal 5, 6; 6, 15. *w:* Eph 6, 5-9; Col 3, 11; Phlm 16. *x:* 6, 20. *y:* 8. *z:* Rom 13, 11.

as not having them, ³⁰those weeping as not weeping, those rejoicing as not rejoicing, those buying as not owning, ³¹those using the world as not using it fully. For the world in its present form is passing away.

³²I should like you to be free of anxieties. An unmarried man is anxious about the things of the Lord, how he may please the Lord. ³³ᵃBut a married man is anxious about the things of the world, how he may please his wife, ³⁴ᵇand he is divided. An unmarried woman or a virgin is anxious about the things of the Lord, so that she may be holy in both body and spirit. A married woman, on the other hand, is anxious about the things of the world, how she may please her husband. ³⁵ᶜI am telling you this for your own benefit, not to impose a restraint upon you, but for the sake of propriety and adherence to the Lord without distraction.

³⁶*If anyone thinks he is behaving improperly toward his virgin, and if a critical moment has come and so it has to be, let him do as he wishes. He is committing no sin; let them get married. ³⁷The one who stands firm in his resolve, however, who is not under compulsion but has power over his own will, and has made up his mind to keep his virgin,

will be doing well. ³⁸So then, the one who marries his virgin does well; the one who does not marry her will do better.

³⁹ᵈ*A wife is bound to her husband as long as he lives. But if her husband dies, she is free to be married to whomever she wishes, provided that it be in the Lord. ⁴⁰ᵉShe is more blessed, though, in my opinion, if she remains as she is, and I think that I too have the Spirit of God.

B. Offerings to Idols

CHAPTER 8

See RG 454-55

Knowledge Insufficient. ¹ᶠ*Now in regard to meat sacrificed to idols: we realize that "all of us have knowledge"; knowledge inflates with pride, but love builds up. ²If anyone supposes he knows something, he does not yet know as he ought to know. ³ᵍBut if one loves God, one is known by him.

⁴ʰSo about the eating of meat sacrificed to idols: we know that "there is no idol in the world," and that "there is no God but one." ⁵Indeed, even though there are so-called gods in heaven and on earth (there are, to be sure, many "gods" and many "lords"), ⁶ⁱ*yet for us there is

---

7, 36–38: The passage is difficult to interpret, because it is unclear whether Paul is thinking of a father and his unmarried daughter (or slave), or of a couple engaged in a betrothal or spiritual marriage. The general principles already enunciated apply: there is no question of sin, even if they should marry, but staying as they are is "better" (for the reasons mentioned in 28–35). Once again the **charisma** of v 7, which applies also to the unmarried (8–9), is to be presupposed.

7, 36: **A critical moment has come:** either because the woman will soon be beyond marriageable age, or because their passions are becoming uncontrollable (cf 9).

7, 39–40: Application of the principles to the case of widows. If they do choose to remarry, they ought to prefer Christian husbands.

8, 1–11, 1: The Corinthians' second question concerns meat that has been sacrificed to idols; in this area they were exhibiting a disordered sense of liberation that Paul here tries to rectify. These chapters contain a sustained and unified argument that illustrates Paul's method of theological reflection on a moral dilemma. Although the problem with which he is dealing is dated, the guidelines for moral decisions that he offers are of lasting validity.

Essentially Paul urges them to take a communitarian rather than an individualistic view of their Christian freedom. Many decisions that they consider pertinent only to their private relationship with God have, in fact, social consequences. Nor can moral decisions be determined by merely theoretical consider-

ations; they must be based on concrete circumstances, specifically on the value and needs of other individuals and on mutual responsibility within the community. Paul here introduces the theme of "building up" (**oikodomē**), i.e., of contributing by individual action to the welfare and growth of the community. This theme will be further developed in ch 14; see the note on 14, 3b-5. Several years later Paul would again deal with the problem of meat sacrificed to idols in Rom 14, 1—15, 6.

8, 1a: **Meat sacrificed to idols:** much of the food consumed in the city could have passed through pagan religious ceremonies before finding its way into markets and homes. **"All of us have knowledge":** a slogan, similar to 6, 12, which reveals the self-image of the Corinthians. Verse 4 will specify the content of this knowledge.

8, 6: This verse rephrases the monotheistic confession of v 4 in such a way as to contrast it with polytheism (5) and to express our relationship with the one God in concrete, i.e., in personal and Christian terms. **And for whom we exist:** since the Greek contains no verb here and the action intended must be inferred from the preposition **eis,** another translation is equally possible: "toward whom we return." **Through whom all things:** the earliest reference in the New Testament to Jesus' role in creation.

a: Lk 14, 20. *b:* 1 Tm 5, 5. *c:* Lk 10, 39-42. *d:* Rom 7, 2. *e:* 25. *f:* Rom 15, 14 / 13, 1-13; Rom 14, 15.19. *g:* Rom 8, 29; Gal 4, 9; *h:* 10, 19; Dt 6, 4. *i:* Mal 2, 10 / Rom 11, 36; Eph 4, 5-6 / 1, 2-3 / Jn 1, 3; Col 1, 16.

one God, the Father,
   from whom all things are and for
     whom we exist,
and one Lord, Jesus Christ,
   through whom all things are and
     through whom we exist.

Practical Rules. *7j*But not all have this knowledge. There are some who have been so used to idolatry up until now that, when they eat meat sacrificed to idols, their conscience, which is weak, is defiled. *8k**Now food will not bring us closer to God. We are no worse off if we do not eat, nor are we better off if we do. *9l*But make sure that this liberty of yours in no way becomes a stumbling block to the weak. *10*If someone sees you, with your knowledge, reclining at table in the temple of an idol, may not his conscience too, weak as it is, be "built up" to eat the meat sacrificed to idols? *11m*Thus through your knowledge, the weak person is brought to destruction, the brother for whom Christ died. *12*When you sin in this way against your brothers and wound their consciences, weak as they are, you are sinning against Christ. *13n**Therefore if food causes my brother to sin, I will never eat meat again, so that I may not cause my brother to sin.

CHAPTER 9

See RG 455

Paul's Rights as an Apostle. *1o**Am I not free? Am I not an apostle? Have I not seen Jesus our Lord? Are you not my work in the Lord? *2*Although I may not be an apostle for others, certainly I am for you, for you are the seal of my apostleship in the Lord.

3*My defense against those who would pass judgment on me is this. *4**Do we not have the right to eat and drink? *5*Do we not have the right to take along a Christian wife, as do the rest of the apostles, and the brothers of the Lord, and Cephas? *6p*Or is it only myself and Barnabas who do not have the right not to work? *7q*Who ever serves as a soldier at his own expense? Who plants a vineyard without eating its produce? Or who shepherds a flock without using some of the milk from the flock? *8*Am I saying this on human authority, or does not the law also speak of these things? *9r*It is written in the law of Moses, "You shall not muzzle an ox while it is treading out the grain." Is God concerned about oxen, *10s*or is he not really speaking for our sake? It was written for our sake, because the plowman should plow in hope, and the thresher in hope of receiving a share. *11t*If we have sown spiritual seed for you, is it a great thing that we reap a material harvest from you? *12u**If

---

8, 8–9: Although the food in itself is morally neutral, extrinsic circumstances may make the eating of it harmful. A **stumbling block:** the image is that of tripping or causing someone to fall (cf 13; 9, 12; 10, 12.32; 2 Cor 6, 3; Rom 14, 13.20–21). This is a basic moral imperative for Paul, a counterpart to the positive imperative to "build one another up"; compare the expression "giving offense" as opposed to "pleasing" in 10, 32–33.

8, 13: His own course is clear: he will avoid any action that might harm another Christian. This statement prepares for the paradigmatic development in ch 9.

9, 1–27: This chapter is an emotionally charged expansion of Paul's appeal to his own example in 8, 13; its purpose is to reinforce the exhortation of 8, 9. The two opening questions introduce the themes of Paul's freedom and his apostleship (1), themes that the chapter will develop in reverse order, vv 1–18 treating the question of his apostleship and the rights that flow from it, and vv 19–27 exploring dialectically the nature of Paul's freedom. The language is highly rhetorical, abounding in questions, wordplays, paradoxes, images, and appeals to authority and experience. The argument is unified by repetitions; its articulations are highlighted by inclusions and transitional verses.

9, 3: **My defense against those who would pass judgment on me:** the reference to a defense (**apologia**) is surprising, and suggests that Paul is incorporating some material here that he has previously used in another context. The defense will touch on two points: the fact of Paul's rights as an apostle (4–12a and 13–14) and his nonuse of those rights (12b and 15–18).

9, 4–12a: Apparently some believe that Paul is not equal to the other apostles and therefore does not enjoy equal privileges. His defense on this point (here and in 13–14) reinforces the assertion of his apostolic character in v 2. It consists of a series of analogies from natural equity (7) and religious custom (13) designed to establish his equal right to support from the churches (4–6.11–12a); these analogies are confirmed by the authority of the law (8–10) and of Jesus himself (14).

9, 12b: It appears, too, that suspicion or misunderstanding has been created by Paul's practice of not living from his

j: 10, 28; Rom 14, 23 / Rom 14, 1; 15, 1. *k:* Rom 14, 17. *l:* Rom 14, 13.20-21. *m:* Rom 14, 15.20. *n:* Mt 18, 6; Rom 14, 20-21. *o:* 19 / 2 Cor 12, 12 / 15, 8-9; Acts 9, 17; 26, 16. *p:* Acts 4, 36-37; 13, 1-2; Gal 2, 1.9.13; Col 4, 10. *q:* 2 Tm 2, 3-4. *r:* Dt 25, 4; 1 Tm 5, 18. *s:* 2 Tm 2, 6. *t:* Rom 15, 27. *u:* 2 Cor 11, 7-12; 12, 13-18; 2 Thes 3, 6-12.

others share this rightful claim on you, do not we still more?

Reason for Not Using His Rights. Yet we have not used this right. On the contrary, we endure everything so as not to place an obstacle to the gospel of Christ. *13v**Do you not know that those who perform the temple services eat [what] belongs to the temple, and those who minister at the altar share in the sacrificial offerings? *14w*In the same way, the Lord ordered that those who preach the gospel should live by the gospel.

15x*I have not used any of these rights, however, nor do I write this that it be done so in my case. I would rather die. Certainly no one is going to nullify my boast. *16y*If I preach the gospel, this is no reason for me to boast, for an obligation has been imposed on me, and woe to me if I do not preach it! *17z*If I do so willingly, I have a recompense, but if unwillingly, then I have been entrusted with a stewardship. *18a*What then is my recompense? That, when I preach, I offer the gospel free of charge so as not to make full use of my right in the gospel.

All Things to All. *19b**Although I am free in regard to all, I have made myself a slave to all so as to win over as many as possible. *20*To the Jews I became like a Jew to win over Jews; to those under the law I became like one under the law—though I myself am not under the law—to win over those under the law. *21*To those outside the law I became like one outside the law—though I am not outside God's law but within the law of Christ—to win over those outside the law. *22c*To the weak I became weak, to win over the weak. I have become all things to all, to save at least some. *23*All this I do for the sake of the gospel, so that I too may have a share in it.

24d*Do you not know that the runners in the stadium all run in the race, but only one wins the prize? Run so as to win. *25e*Every athlete exercises discipline in every way. They do it to win a perishable crown, but we an imperishable one. *26*Thus I do not run aimlessly; I do not fight as if I were shadowboxing. *27**No, I drive my body and train it, for fear that, after having preached to others, I myself should be disqualified.

CHAPTER 10

See RG 454-55

Warning against Overconfidence. *1f**I do not want you to be unaware, brothers, that our ancestors were all under the cloud and all passed through the sea, *2g*and all of them were baptized into Moses in the cloud and in the sea. *3*All ate the same spiritual food,

preaching. The first reason he asserts in defense of this practice is an entirely apostolic one; it anticipates the developments to follow in vv 19–22. He will give a second reason in vv 15–18.

9, 13–14: The position of these verses produces an interlocking of the two points of Paul's defense. These arguments by analogy (13) and from authority (14) belong with those of vv 7–10 and ground the first point. But Paul defers them until he has had a chance to mention "the gospel of Christ" (12b), after which it is more appropriate to mention Jesus' injunction to his preachers and to argue by analogy from the sacred temple service to his own liturgical service, the preaching of the gospel (cf Rom 1, 9; 15, 16).

9, 15–18: Paul now assigns a more personal motive to his nonuse of his right to support. His preaching is not a service spontaneously undertaken on his part but a stewardship imposed by a sort of divine compulsion. Yet to merit any reward he must bring some spontaneous quality to his service, and this he does by freely renouncing his right to support. The material here is quite similar to that contained in Paul's "defense" at 2 Cor 11, 5–12; 12, 11–18.

9, 19–23: In a rhetorically balanced series of statements Paul expands and generalizes the picture of his behavior and explores the paradox of apostolic freedom. It is not essentially freedom **from** restraint but freedom **for** service—a possibility of constructive activity.

9, 24–27: A series of miniparables from sports, appealing to readers familiar with Greek gymnasia and the nearby Isthmian games.

9, 27: For fear that . . . I myself should be disqualified: a final paradoxical turn to the argument: what appears at first a free, spontaneous renunciation of rights (12–18) seems subsequently to be required for fulfillment of Paul's stewardship (to preach effectively he must reach his hearers wherever they are, 19–22), and finally is seen to be necessary for his own salvation (23–27). Mention of the possibility of disqualification provides a transition to ch 10.

10, 1–5: Paul embarks unexpectedly upon a panoramic survey of the events of the Exodus period. The privileges of Israel in the wilderness are described in terms that apply strictly only to the realities of the new covenant ("baptism," "spiritual food and drink"); interpreted in this way they point forward to the Christian experience (1–4). But those privileges did not guarantee God's permanent pleasure (5).

v: Nm 18, 8.31; Dt 18, 1-5. *w:* Mt 10, 10; Lk 10, 7-8. *x:* 2 Cor 11, 9-10. *y:* Acts 26, 14-18. *z:* 4, 1; Gal 2, 7. *a:* 2 Cor 11, 7-12. *b:* Mt 20, 26-27. *c:* 10, 33; Rom 15, 1; 2 Cor 11, 29. *d:* Heb 12, 1. *e:* 2 Tm 2, 5 / 2 Tm 4, 7-8; Jas 1, 12; 1 Pt 5, 4. *f:* Ex 13, 21-22; 14, 19-20 / Ex 14, 21-22.26-30. *g:* Rom 6, 3; Gal 3, 27 / Ex 16, 4-35.

4h*and all drank the same spiritual drink, for they drank from a spiritual rock that followed them, and the rock was the Christ. *5i*Yet God was not pleased with most of them, for they were struck down in the desert.

6j*These things happened as examples for us, so that we might not desire evil things, as they did. *7k*And do not become idolaters, as some of them did, as it is written, "The people sat down to eat and drink, and rose up to revel." *8l*Let us not indulge in immorality as some of them did, and twenty-three thousand fell within a single day. *9m**Let us not test Christ as some of them did, and suffered death by serpents. *10n*Do not grumble as some of them did, and suffered death by the destroyer. *11**These things happened to them as an example, and they have been written down as a warning to us, upon whom the end of the ages has come. *12**Therefore whoever thinks he is standing secure should take care not to fall. *13o*No trial has come to you but what is human. God is faithful and will not let you be tried beyond your strength; but with the trial he will also provide a way out, so that you may be able to bear it.

Warning against Idolatry. *14p**Therefore, my beloved, avoid idolatry. *15*I am speaking as to sensible people; judge for yourselves what I am saying. *16q*The cup of blessing that we bless, is it not a participation in the blood of Christ? The bread that we break, is it not a participation in the body of Christ? *17r*Because the loaf of bread is one, we, though many, are one body, for we all partake of the one loaf.

*18s*Look at Israel according to the flesh; are not those who eat the sacrifices participants in the altar? *19*So what am I saying? That meat sacrificed to idols is anything? Or that an idol is anything? *20t**No, I mean that what they sacrifice, [they sacrifice] to demons, not to God, and I do not want you to become participants with demons. *21u*You cannot drink the cup of the Lord and also the cup of demons. You cannot partake of the table of the Lord and of the table of demons. *22v*Or are we provoking the Lord to jealous anger? Are we stronger than he?

Seek the Good of Others. *23w**"Everything is lawful," but not everything is beneficial. "Everything is lawful," but not everything builds up. *24x*No one should seek his own advantage, but that of his neighbor. *25**Eat any-

---

10, 4: A spiritual rock that followed them: the Torah speaks only about a rock from which water issued, but rabbinic legend amplified this into a spring that followed the Israelites throughout their migration. Paul uses this legend as a literary type: he makes the rock itself accompany the Israelites, and he gives it a spiritual sense. **The rock was the Christ:** in the Old Testament, Yahweh is the Rock of his people (cf Dt 32, Moses' song to Yahweh the Rock). Paul now applies this image to the Christ, the source of the living water, the true Rock that accompanied Israel, guiding their experiences in the desert.

10, 6–13: This section explicitates the typological value of these Old Testament events: the desert experiences of the Israelites are examples, meant as warnings, to deter us from similar sins (idolatry, immorality, etc.) and from a similar fate.

10, 9: Christ: to avoid Paul's concept of Christ present in the wilderness events, some manuscripts read "the Lord."

10, 11: Upon whom the end of the ages has come: it is our period in time toward which past ages have been moving and in which they arrive at their goal.

10, 12–13: Take care not to fall: the point of the whole comparison with Israel is to caution against overconfidence, a sense of complete security (12). This warning is immediately balanced by a reassurance, based, however, on God (13).

10, 14–22: The warning against idolatry from v 7 is now repeated (14) and explained in terms of the effect of sacrifices: all sacrifices, Christian (16–17), Jewish (18), or pagan (20), establish communion. But communion with Christ is exclusive, incompatible with any other such communion (21). Compare the line of reasoning at 6, 15.

10, 20: To demons: although Jews denied divinity to pagan gods, they often believed that there was some nondivine reality behind the idols, such as the dead, or angels, or demons. The explanation Paul offers in v 20 is drawn from Dt 32, 7: the power behind the idols, with which the pagans commune, consists of demonic powers hostile to God.

10, 23—11, 1: By way of peroration Paul returns to the opening situation (ch 8) and draws conclusions based on the intervening considerations (chs 9–10).

10, 23–24: He repeats in the context of this new problem the slogans of liberty from 6, 12, with similar qualifications. Liberty is not merely an individual perfection, nor an end in itself, but is to be used for the common good. The language of v 24 recalls the descriptions of Jesus' self-emptying in Phil 2.

10, 25–30: A summary of specific situations in which the eating of meat sacrificed to idols could present problems of conscience. Three cases are considered. In the first (the marketplace, 25–26) and the second (at table, 27), there is no need to be concerned with whether food has passed through a pagan

h: Ex 17, 1-7; Nm 20, 7-11; Dt 8, 15. *i:* Nm 14, 28-38; Jude 5. *j:* Nm 11, 4.34. *k:* Ex 32, 6. *l:* Nm 25, 1-9. *m:* Nm 21, 5-9. *n:* Nm 14, 2-37; 16, 1-35. *o:* Mt 6, 13; Jas 1, 13-14 / 1, 9. *p:* 1 Jn 5, 21. *q:* Mt 26, 26-29; Acts 2, 42. *r:* Rom 12, 5; Eph 4, 4. *s:* Lv 7, 6. *t:* Dt 32, 17. *u:* 2 Cor 6, 14-18. *v:* Dt 32, 21 / Eccl 6, 10. *w:* 6, 12. *x:* Rom 15, 2; Phil 2, 4.21.

thing sold in the market, without raising questions on grounds of conscience, [26]yfor "the earth and its fullness are the Lord's." [27]If an unbeliever invites you and you want to go, eat whatever is placed before you, without raising questions on grounds of conscience. [28]But if someone says to you, "This was offered in sacrifice," do not eat it on account of the one who called attention to it and on account of conscience; [29]I mean not your own conscience, but the other's. For why should my freedom be determined by someone else's conscience? [30]zIf I partake thankfully, why am I reviled for that over which I give thanks?

[31]So whether you eat or drink, or whatever you do, do everything for the glory of God. [32]*Avoid giving offense, whether to Jews or Greeks or the church of God, [33]ajust as I try to please everyone in every way, not seeking my own benefit but that of the many, that they may be saved.

See RG
454–56

CHAPTER 11

[1]bBe imitators of me, as I am of Christ.

IV: Problems In Liturgical Assemblies

[2]c*I praise you because you remember me in everything and hold fast to the traditions, just as I handed them on to you.

A. Women's Headdresses

Man and Woman. [3]d*But I want you to know that Christ is the head of every man, and a husband the head of his wife, and God the head of Christ. [4]*Any man who prays or prophesies with his head covered brings shame upon his head. [5]But any woman who prays or prophesies with her head unveiled brings shame upon her head, for it is one and the same thing as if she had had her head shaved. [6]For if a woman does not have her head veiled, she may as well have her hair cut off. But if it is shameful for a woman to have her hair cut off or her head shaved, then she should wear a veil.

[7]e*A man, on the other hand, should not cover his head, because he is the image and glory of God, but woman is the glory of

sacrifice or not, for the principle of 8, 4–6 still stands, and the whole creation belongs to the one God. But in the third case (28), the situation changes if someone present explicitly raises the question of the sacrificial origin of the food; eating in such circumstances may be subject to various interpretations, some of which could be harmful to individuals. Paul is at pains to insist that the enlightened Christian conscience need not change its judgment about the neutrality, even the goodness, of the food in itself (29–30); yet the total situation is altered to the extent that others are potentially endangered, and this calls for a different response, for the sake of others.

10, 32—11, 1: In summary, the general rule of mutually responsible use of their Christian freedom is enjoined first negatively (32), then positively, as exemplified in Paul (33), and finally grounded in Christ, the pattern for Paul's behavior and theirs (11, 1; cf Rom 15, 1–3).

11, 2—14, 40: This section of the letter is devoted to regulation of conduct at the liturgy. The problems Paul handles have to do with the dress of women in the assembly (11, 3–16), improprieties in the celebration of community meals (11, 17–34), and the use of charisms or spiritual gifts (12, 1–14, 40). The statement in 11, 2 introduces all of these discussions, but applies more appropriately to the second (cf the mention of praise in 11, 17 and of tradition in 11, 23).

11, 3–16: Women have been participating in worship at Corinth without the head-covering normal in Greek society of the period. Paul's stated goal is to bring them back into conformity with contemporary practice and propriety. In his desire to convince, he reaches for arguments from a variety of sources, though he has space to develop them only sketchily and is perhaps aware that they differ greatly in persuasiveness.

11, 3: A husband the head of his wife: the specific problem suggests to Paul the model of the head as a device for clarifying relations within a hierarchical structure. The model is similar to that developed later in greater detail and nuance in Eph 5, 21–33. It is a hybrid model, for it grafts onto a strictly theological scale of existence (cf 3, 21–23) the hierarchy of sociosexual relations prevalent in the ancient world: men, dominant, reflect the active function of Christ in relation to his church; women, submissive, reflect the passive role of the church with respect to its savior. This gives us the functional scale: God, Christ, man, woman.

11, 4–6: From man's direct relation to Christ, Paul infers that his head should not be covered. But woman, related not directly to Christ on the scale but to her husband, requires a covering as a sign of that relationship. **Shameful . . . to have her hair cut off:** certain less honored classes in society, such as lesbians and prostitutes, are thought to have worn their hair close-cropped.

11, 7–9: The hierarchy of v 3 is now expressed in other metaphors: the image (**eikōn**) and the reflected glory (**doxa**). Paul is alluding basically to the text of Gn 1, 27, in which mankind as a whole, the male-female couple, is created in God's image and given the command to multiply and together dominate the lower creation. But Gn 1, 24 is interpreted here in the light of the second creation narrative in Gn 2, in which each of the sexes is created separately (first the man and then the woman **from** man and **for** him, to be his helpmate, Gn 2,

y: Pss 24, 1; 50, 12.   z: Rom 14, 6; 1 Tm 4, 3-4.   a: 9, 22; Rom 15, 2.   b: 4, 16; Phil 3, 17.   c: 15, 3; 2 Thes 2, 15.   d: Eph 5, 23.   e: Gn 1, 26-27; 5, 1.

man. [8][f]For man did not come from woman, but woman from man; [9][g]nor was man created for woman, but woman for man; [10][*]for this reason a woman should have a sign of authority on her head, because of the angels. [11][h][*]Woman is not independent of man or man of woman in the Lord. [12][i]For just as woman came from man, so man is born of woman; but all things are from God.

[13][*]Judge for yourselves: is it proper for a woman to pray to God with her head unveiled? [14]Does not nature itself teach you that if a man wears his hair long it is a disgrace to him, [15]whereas if a woman has long hair it is her glory, because long hair has been given [her] for a covering? [16]But if anyone is inclined to be argumentative, we do not have such a custom, nor do the churches of God.

B. The Lord's Supper

An Abuse at Corinth. [17][*]In giving this instruction, I do not praise the fact that your meetings are doing more harm than good. [18][j]First of all, I hear that when you meet as a church there are divisions among you, and to a degree I believe it; [19][*]there have to be factions among you in order that [also]

those who are approved among you may become known. [20]When you meet in one place, then, it is not to eat the Lord's supper, [21]for in eating, each one goes ahead with his own supper, and one goes hungry while another gets drunk. [22][k]Do you not have houses in which you can eat and drink? Or do you show contempt for the church of God and make those who have nothing feel ashamed? What can I say to you? Shall I praise you? In this matter I do not praise you.

Tradition of the Institution. [23][l][*]For I received from the Lord what I also handed on to you, that the Lord Jesus, on the night he was handed over, took bread, [24]and, after he had given thanks, broke it and said, "This is my body that is for you. Do this in remembrance of me." [25][m]In the same way also the cup, after supper, saying, "This cup is the new covenant in my blood. Do this, as often as you drink it, in remembrance of me." [26]For as often as you eat this bread and drink the cup, you proclaim the death of the Lord until he comes.

[27][*]Therefore whoever eats the bread or drinks the cup of the Lord unworthily will have to answer for the body and blood of the

---

20–23), and under the influence of the story of the fall, as a result of which the husband rules over the woman (Gn 3, 16). This interpretation splits the single image of God into two, at different degrees of closeness.

11, 10: A sign of authority: "authority" (**exousia**) may possibly be due to mistranslation of an Aramaic word for "veil"; in any case, the connection with v 9 indicates that the covering is a sign of woman's subordination. **Because of the angels:** a surprising additional reason, which the context does not clarify. Presumably the reference is to cosmic powers who might inflict harm on women or whose function is to watch over women or the cult.

11, 11–12: These parenthetical remarks relativize the argument from Gn 2–3. **In the Lord:** in the Christian economy the relation between the sexes is characterized by a mutual dependence, which is not further specified. And even in the natural order conditions have changed: the mode of origin described in Gn 2 has been reversed (12a). But the ultimately significant fact is the origin that all things have in common (12b).

11, 13–16: The argument for conformity to common church practice is summed up and pressed home. Verses 14–15 contain a final appeal to the sense of propriety that contemporary Greek society would consider "natural" (cf 5–6).

11, 17–34: Paul turns to another abuse connected with the liturgy, and a more serious one, for it involves neglect of basic Christian tradition concerning the meaning of the Lord's Supper. Paul recalls that tradition for them and reminds them of its implications.

11, 19: That . . . those who are approved among you may become known: Paul situates their divisions within the context of the eschatological separation of the authentic from the inauthentic and the final revelation of the difference. The notion of authenticity-testing recurs in the injunction to self-examination in view of present and future judgment (28–32).

11, 23–25: This is the earliest written account of the institution of the Lord's Supper in the New Testament. The narrative emphasizes Jesus' action of self-giving (expressed in the words over the bread and the cup) and his double command to repeat his own action.

11, 27: It follows that the only proper way to celebrate the Eucharist is one that corresponds to Jesus' intention, which fits with the meaning of his command to reproduce his action in the proper spirit. If the Corinthians eat and drink unworthily, i.e., without having grasped and internalized the meaning of his death for them, **they will have to answer for the body and blood,** i.e., will be guilty of a sin against the Lord himself (cf 8, 12).

---

f: Gn 2, 21-23.   *g:* Gn 2, 18.   *h:* Gal 3, 27-28.   *i:* 8, 6; Rom 11, 36.   *j:* 1, 10-12; Gal 5, 20.   *k:* Jas 2, 1-7.   *l:* 2; 15, 3 / 10, 16-17; Mt 26, 26-29; Mk 14, 22-25; Lk 22, 14-20.   *m:* Ex 24, 8; 2 Cor 3, 6; Heb 8, 6-13.

Lord. [28*]A person should examine himself, and so eat the bread and drink the cup. [29*]For anyone who eats and drinks without discerning the body, eats and drinks judgment on himself. [30]That is why many among you are ill and infirm, and a considerable number are dying. [31]If we discerned ourselves, we would not be under judgment; [32n]but since we are judged by [the] Lord, we are being disciplined so that we may not be condemned along with the world.

[33]Therefore, my brothers, when you come together to eat, wait for one another. [34]If anyone is hungry, he should eat at home, so that your meetings may not result in judgment. The other matters I shall set in order when I come.

C. Spiritual Gifts

CHAPTER 12

Unity and Variety. [1*]Now in regard to spiritual gifts, brothers, I do not want you to be unaware. [2o*]You know how, when you were pagans, you were constantly attracted and led away to mute idols. [3p]Therefore, I tell you that nobody speaking by the spirit of God says, "Jesus be accursed." And no one can say, "Jesus is Lord," except by the holy Spirit.

[4q*]There are different kinds of spiritual gifts but the same Spirit; [5]there are different forms of service but the same Lord; [6]there are different workings but the same God who produces all of them in everyone. [7]To each individual the manifestation of the Spirit is given for some benefit. [8r]To one is given through the Spirit the expression of wisdom; to another the expression of knowledge according to the same Spirit; [9]to another faith by the same Spirit; to another gifts of healing by the one Spirit; [10s]to another mighty deeds; to another prophecy; to another discernment of spirits; to another varieties of tongues; to another interpretation of tongues. [11t]But one and the same Spirit produces all of these, distributing them individually to each person as he wishes.

One Body, Many Parts. [12u*]As a body is one though it has many parts, and all the parts of the body, though many, are one body, so also Christ. [13v]For in one Spirit we were all baptized into one body, whether Jews or Greeks, slaves or free persons, and we were all given to drink of one Spirit.

[14]Now the body is not a single part, but many. [15]If a foot should say, "Because I am not a hand I do not belong to the body," it does not for this reason belong any less to

11, 28: Examine himself: the Greek word is similar to that for "approved" in v 19, which means "having been tested and found true." The self-testing required for proper eating involves *discerning the body* (29), which, from the context, must mean understanding the sense of Jesus' death (26), perceiving the imperative to unity that follows from the fact that Jesus gives himself to all and requires us to repeat his sacrifice in the same spirit (18–25).

11, 29–32: Judgment: there is a series of wordplays in these verses that would be awkward to translate literally into English; it includes all the references to judgment (**krima,** 29.34; **krinō,** 31.32), discernment (**diakrinō,** 29.31), and condemnation (**katakrinō,** 32). The judgment is concretely described as the illness, infirmity, and death that have visited the community. These are signs that the power of Jesus' death is not yet completely recognized and experienced. Yet even the judgment incurred is an expression of God's concern; it is a medicinal measure meant to rescue us from condemnation with God's enemies.

12, 1—14, 40: Ecstatic and charismatic activity were common in early Christian experience, as they were in other ancient religions. But the Corinthians seem to have developed a disproportionate esteem for certain phenomena, especially tongues, to the detriment of order in the liturgy. Paul's response to this development provides us with the fullest exposition we have of his theology of the charisms.

12, 2–3: There is an experience of the Spirit and an understanding of ecstatic phenomena that are specifically Christian and that differ, despite apparent similarities, from those of the pagans. It is necessary to discern which spirit is leading one; ecstatic phenomena must be judged by their effect (2). Verse 3 illustrates this by an example: power to confess Jesus as Lord can come only from the Spirit, and it is inconceivable that the Spirit would move anyone to curse the Lord.

12, 4–6: There are some features common to all charisms, despite their diversity: all are **gifts** (**charismata**), grace from outside ourselves; all are **forms of service** (**diakoniai**), an expression of their purpose and effect; and all are **workings** (**energēmata**), in which God is at work. Paul associates each of these aspects with what later theology will call one of the persons of the Trinity, an early example of "appropriation."

12, 12–26: The image of **a body** is introduced to explain Christ's relationship with believers (12). Verse 13 applies this model to the church: by baptism all, despite diversity of ethnic or social origins, are integrated into one organism. Verses 14–26 then develop the need for diversity of function among the parts of a body without threat to its unity.

n: Dt 8, 5; Heb 12, 5-11. *o:* Eph 2, 11-18. *p:* Rom 10, 9; 1 Jn 4, 2-3. *q:* Rom 12, 6; Eph 4, 7.11. *r:* 2, 6-13. *s:* 14, 5.26.39; Acts 2, 4. *t:* 7, 7; Eph 4, 7. *u:* 10, 17; Rom 12, 4-5; Eph 2, 16; Col 3, 15. *v:* Gal 3, 28; Eph 2, 13-18; Col 3, 11 / Jn 7, 37-39.

the body. *16*Or if an ear should say, "Because I am not an eye I do not belong to the body," it does not for this reason belong any less to the body. *17*If the whole body were an eye, where would the hearing be? If the whole body were hearing, where would the sense of smell be? *18*But as it is, God placed the parts, each one of them, in the body as he intended. *19*If they were all one part, where would the body be? *20*But as it is, there are many parts, yet one body. *21*The eye cannot say to the hand, "I do not need you," nor again the head to the feet, "I do not need you." *22*Indeed, the parts of the body that seem to be weaker are all the more necessary, *23*and those parts of the body that we consider less honorable we surround with greater honor, and our less presentable parts are treated with greater propriety, *24*whereas our more presentable parts do not need this. But God has so constructed the body as to give greater honor to a part that is without it, *25*so that there may be no division in the body, but that the parts may have the same concern for one another. *26*If [one] part suffers, all the parts suffer with it; if one part is honored, all the parts share its joy.

Application to Christ. *27w**Now you are Christ's body, and individually parts of it. *28x**Some people God has designated in the church to be, first, apostles; second, prophets; third, teachers; then, mighty deeds; then gifts of healing, assistance, administration,

and varieties of tongues. *29*Are all apostles? Are all prophets? Are all teachers? Do all work mighty deeds? *30*Do all have gifts of healing? Do all speak in tongues? Do all interpret? *31*Strive eagerly for the greatest spiritual gifts.

The Way of Love. But I shall show you a still more excellent way.

CHAPTER 13

See RG 456–57

1y*If I speak in human and angelic tongues, but do not have love, I am a resounding gong or a clashing cymbal. *2z*And if I have the gift of prophecy and comprehend all mysteries and all knowledge; if I have all faith so as to move mountains, but do not have love, I am nothing. *3a*If I give away everything I own, and if I hand my body over so that I may boast but do not have love, I gain nothing.

4b*Love is patient, love is kind. It is not jealous, [love] is not pompous, it is not inflated, *5c*it is not rude, it does not seek its own interests, it is not quick-tempered, it does not brood over injury, *6*it does not rejoice over wrongdoing but rejoices with the truth. *7d*It bears all things, believes all things, hopes all things, endures all things.

8*Love never fails. If there are prophecies, they will be brought to nothing; if tongues, they will cease; if knowledge, it will be brought to nothing. *9*For we know partially and we prophesy partially, *10*but when the

12, 27–30: Paul now applies the image again to the church as a whole and its members (27). The lists in vv 28–30 spell out the parallelism by specifying the diversity of functions found in the church (cf Rom 12, 6–8; Eph 4, 11).

12, 28: First, apostles: apostleship was not mentioned in vv 8–10, nor is it at issue in these chapters, but Paul gives it pride of place in his listing. It is not just one gift among others but a prior and fuller gift that includes the others. They are all demonstrated in Paul's apostolate, but he may have developed his theology of charisms by reflecting first of all on his own grace of apostleship (cf 3, 5—4, 14; 9, 1–27; 2 Cor 2, 14—6, 13; 10, 1—13, 30, esp. 11, 23 and 12, 12).

13, 1–13: This chapter involves a shift of perspective and a new point. All or part of the material may once have been an independent piece in the style of Hellenistic eulogies of virtues, but it is now integrated, by editing, into the context of chs 12–14 (cf the reference to tongues and prophecy) and into the letter as a whole (cf the references to knowledge and to behavior). The function of ch 13 within the discussion of spiritual gifts is to relativize all the charisms by contrasting them with the more basic, pervasive, and enduring value that gives

them their purpose and their effectiveness. The rhetoric of this chapter is striking.

13, 1–3: An inventory of gifts, arranged in careful gradation: neither tongues (on the lowest rung), nor prophecy, knowledge, or faith, nor even self-sacrifice has value unless informed by love.

13, 4–7: This paragraph is developed by personification and enumeration, defining love by what it does or does not do. The Greek contains fifteen verbs; it is natural to translate many of them by adjectives in English.

13, 8–13: The final paragraph announces its topic, Love never fails (8), then develops the permanence of love in contrast to the charisms (9–12), and finally asserts love's superiority even over the other "theological virtues" (13).

w: Rom 12, 5-8; Eph 1, 23; 4, 12; 5, 30; Col 1, 18.24. *x:* Eph 2, 20; 3, 5; 4, 11. *y:* 8, 1; 16, 14; Rom 12, 9-10; 13, 8-10. *z:* 4, 1; 14, 2 / 1, 5; 8, 1-3; 12, 8 / Mt 17, 20; 21, 21; Col 2, 3. *a:* Mt 6, 2. *b:* Eph 4, 2 / 4, 6.18; 5, 2; 8, 1. *c:* 10, 24.33; Phil 2, 4.21; 1 Thes 5, 15. *d:* Prv 10, 12; 1 Pt 4, 8.

perfect comes, the partial will pass away. [11]When I was a child, I used to talk as a child, think as a child, reason as a child; when I became a man, I put aside childish things. [12e]At present we see indistinctly, as in a mirror, but then face to face. At present I know partially; then I shall know fully, as I am fully known. [13f*]So faith, hope, love remain, these three; but the greatest of these is love.

See RG
456-57

CHAPTER 14

Prophecy Greater than Tongues. [1g*]Pursue love, but strive eagerly for the spiritual gifts, above all that you may prophesy. [2*]For one who speaks in a tongue does not speak to human beings but to God, for no one listens; he utters mysteries in spirit. [3h*]On the other hand, one who prophesies does speak to human beings, for their building up, encouragement, and solace. [4]Whoever speaks in a tongue builds himself up, but whoever prophesies builds up the church. [5]Now I should like all of you to speak in tongues, but even more to prophesy. One who prophesies is greater than one who speaks in tongues, unless he interprets, so that the church may be built up.

[6*]Now, brothers, if I should come to you speaking in tongues, what good will I do you if I do not speak to you by way of revelation, or knowledge, or prophecy, or instruction? [7]Likewise, if inanimate things that produce sound, such as flute or harp, do not give out the tones distinctly, how will what is being played on flute or harp be recognized? [8]And if the bugle gives an indistinct sound, who will get ready for battle? [9]Similarly, if you, because of speaking in tongues, do not utter intelligible speech, how will anyone know what is being said? For you will be talking to the air. [10]It happens that there are many different languages in the world, and none is meaningless; [11]but if I do not know the meaning of a language, I shall be a foreigner to one who speaks it, and one who speaks it a foreigner to me. [12]So with yourselves: since you strive eagerly for spirits, seek to have an abundance of them for building up the church.

Need for Interpretation. [13*]Therefore, one who speaks in a tongue should pray to be able to interpret. [14*][For] if I pray in a tongue, my spirit is at prayer but my mind is unproductive. [15i]So what is to be done? I will pray with the spirit, but I will also pray with the mind. I will sing praise with the

13, 13: In speaking of love, Paul is led by spontaneous association to mention faith and hope as well. They are already a well-known triad (cf 1 Thes 1, 3), three interrelated (cf 7) features of Christian life, more fundamental than any particular charism. **The greatest . . . is love:** love is operative even within the other members of the triad (7), so that it has a certain primacy among them. Or, if the perspective is temporal, love will remain (cf "never fails," 8) even when faith has yielded to sight and hope to possession.

14, 1–5: Verse 1b returns to the thought of 12, 31a and reveals Paul's primary concern. The series of contrasts in vv 2–5 discloses the problem at Corinth: a disproportionate interest in tongues, with a corresponding failure to appreciate the worth of prophecy. Paul attempts to clarify the relative values of those gifts by indicating the kind of communication achieved in each and the kind of effect each produces.

14, 2–3a: They involve two kinds of communication: tongues, private speech toward God in inarticulate terms that need interpretation to be intelligible to others (see 27–28); prophecy, communication with others in the community.

14, 3b-5: They produce two kinds of effect. One who speaks in tongues **builds himself up;** it is a matter of individual experience and personal perfection, which inevitably recalls Paul's previous remarks about being inflated, seeking one's own good, pleasing oneself. But a prophet **builds up the church:** the theme of "building up" or "edifying" others, the main theme of the letter, comes to clearest expression in

this chapter (3.4.5.12.17). It has been anticipated at 8, 1 and 10, 23, and by the related concept of "the beneficial" in 6, 12; 10, 23; 12, 7; etc.

14, 6–12: Sound, in order to be useful, must be intelligible. This principle is illustrated by a series of analogies from music (7–8) and from ordinary human speech (10–11); it is applied to the case at hand in v 9 and v 12.

14, 13–19: The charism of interpretation lifts tongues to the level of intelligibility, enabling them to produce the same effect as prophecy (cf 5.26–28).

14, 14–15: **My spirit:** Paul emphasizes the exclusively ecstatic, nonrational quality of tongues. The tongues at Pentecost are also described as an ecstatic experience (Acts 2, 4.12–13), though Luke superimposes further interpretations of his own. **My mind:** the ecstatic element, dominant in earliest Old Testament prophecy as depicted in 1 Sam 10, 5–13; 19, 20–24, seems entirely absent from Paul's notion of prophecy and completely relegated to tongues. He emphasizes the role of reason when he specifies instruction as a function of prophecy (6.19.31). But he does not exclude intuition and emotion; cf references to encouragement and consolation (3.31) and the scene describing the ideal exercise of prophecy (24–25).

e: 2 Cor 5, 7; Heb 11, 1 / 2 Tm 2, 19; 1 Jn 3, 2. *f:* Col 1, 4; 1 Thes 1, 3; 5, 8. *g:* 5.12.39. *h:* 4-5.12.17.26; 3, 9; 8, 1.10; 10, 23. *i:* Eph 5, 19; Col 3, 16.

spirit, but I will also sing praise with the mind. [16]Otherwise, if you pronounce a blessing [with] the spirit, how shall one who holds the place of the uninstructed say the "Amen" to your thanksgiving, since he does not know what you are saying? [17]For you may be giving thanks very well, but the other is not built up. [18]I give thanks to God that I speak in tongues more than any of you, [19]but in the church I would rather speak five words with my mind, so as to instruct others also, than ten thousand words in a tongue.

Functions of These Gifts. [20][j]*Brothers, stop being childish in your thinking. In respect to evil be like infants, but in your thinking be mature. [21][k]It is written in the law:

"By people speaking strange tongues
  and by the lips of foreigners
I will speak to this people,
  and even so they will not listen to me,

says the Lord." [22]Thus, tongues are a sign not for those who believe but for unbelievers, whereas prophecy is not for unbelievers but for those who believe.

[23][l]*So if the whole church meets in one place and everyone speaks in tongues, and then uninstructed people or unbelievers should come in, will they not say that you are out of your minds? [24]But if everyone is prophesying, and an unbeliever or uninstructed person should come in, he will be convinced by everyone and judged by everyone, [25][m]and the secrets of his heart will be disclosed, and so he will fall down and worship God, declaring, "God is really in your midst."

Rules of Order. [26][n]*So what is to be done, brothers? When you assemble, one has a psalm, another an instruction, a revelation, a tongue, or an interpretation. Everything should be done for building up. [27]If anyone speaks in a tongue, let it be two or at most three, and each in turn, and one should interpret. [28]But if there is no interpreter, the person should keep silent in the church and speak to himself and to God.

[29]Two or three prophets should speak, and the others discern. [30]But if a revelation is given to another person sitting there, the first one should be silent. [31]For you can all prophesy one by one, so that all may learn and all be encouraged. [32]Indeed, the spirits of prophets are under the prophets' control, [33]*since he is not the God of disorder but of peace.

As in all the churches of the holy ones, [34][o]women should keep silent in the churches, for they are not allowed to speak, but should be subordinate, as even the law says. [35]But if they want to learn anything,

14, 20–22: The Corinthians pride themselves on tongues as a sign of God's favor, a means of direct communication with him (2.28). To challenge them to a more mature appraisal, Paul draws from scripture a less flattering explanation of what speaking in tongues may signify. Isaiah threatened the people that if they failed to listen to their prophets, the Lord would speak to them (in punishment) through the lips of Assyrian conquerors (Is 28, 11–12). Paul compresses Isaiah's text and makes God address his people directly. Equating tongues with foreign languages (cf 10–11), Paul concludes from Isaiah that **tongues are a sign not for those who believe,** i.e., not a mark of God's pleasure for those who listen to him but a mark of his displeasure with those in the community who are faithless, who have not heeded the message that he has sent through the prophets.

14, 23–25: Paul projects the possible missionary effect of two hypothetical liturgical experiences, one consisting wholly of tongues, the other entirely of prophecy. **Uninstructed (idiōtai):** the term may simply mean people who do not speak or understand tongues, as in v 16, where it seems to designate Christians. But coupled with the term "unbelievers" it may be another way of designating those who have not been initiated into the community of faith; some believe it denotes a special class of non-Christians who are close to the

community, such as catechumens. **Unbelievers (apistoi):** he has shifted from the inner-community perspective of v 22; the term here designates non-Christians (cf 6, 6; 7, 15; 10, 27).

14, 26–33a: Paul concludes with specific directives regarding exercise of the gifts in their assemblies. Verse 26 enunciates the basic criterion in the use of any gift: it must contribute to "building up."

14, 33b–36: Verse 33b may belong with what precedes, so that the new paragraph would begin only with v 34. Verses 34–35 change the subject. These two verses have the theme of submission in common with ch 11, despite differences in vocabulary, and a concern with what is or is not becoming; but it is difficult to harmonize the injunction to silence here with ch 11, which appears to take it for granted that women do pray and prophesy aloud in the assembly (cf 11, 5.13). Hence the verses are often considered an interpolation, reflecting the discipline of later churches; such an interpolation would have to have antedated our manuscripts, all of which contain them, though some transpose them to the very end of the chapter.

j: Mt 10, 16; Rom 16, 19; Eph 4, 14. *k:* Is 28, 11-12; Dt 28, 49. *l:* Acts 2, 6.13. *m:* 4, 5 / Is 45, 14; Zec 8, 23. *n:* Eph 4, 12. *o:* 1 Tm 2, 11-15; 1 Pt 3, 1.

they should ask their husbands at home. For it is improper for a woman to speak in the church. *36*Did the word of God go forth from you? Or has it come to you alone?

*37*If anyone thinks that he is a prophet or a spiritual person, he should recognize that what I am writing to you is a commandment of the Lord. *38*If anyone does not acknowledge this, he is not acknowledged. *39*So, [my] brothers, strive eagerly to prophesy, and do not forbid speaking in tongues, *40*but everything must be done properly and in order.

V: The Resurrection
A. The Resurrection of Christ

CHAPTER 15

See RG
457

The Gospel Teaching. *1**Now I am reminding you, brothers, of the gospel I preached to you, which you indeed received and in which you also stand. *2*Through it you are also being saved, if you hold fast to the word I preached to you, unless you believed in vain. *3 p**For I handed on to you as of first importance what I also received: that Christ died for our sins in accordance with the scriptures; *4q*that he was buried; that he was raised on the third day in accordance with

the scriptures; *5r*that he appeared to Cephas, then to the Twelve. *6*After that, he appeared to more than five hundred brothers at once, most of whom are still living, though some have fallen asleep. *7*After that he appeared to James, then to all the apostles. *8s*Last of all, as to one born abnormally, he appeared to me. *9t**For I am the least of the apostles, not fit to be called an apostle, because I persecuted the church of God. *10*But by the grace of God I am what I am, and his grace to me has not been ineffective. Indeed, I have toiled harder than all of them; not I, however, but the grace of God [that is] with me. *11*Therefore, whether it be I or they, so we preach and so you believed.

B. The Resurrection of the Dead

Results of Denial. *12**But if Christ is preached as raised from the dead, how can some among you say there is no resurrection of the dead? *13u*If there is no resurrection of the dead, then neither has Christ been raised. *14*And if Christ has not been raised, then empty [too] is our preaching; empty, too, your faith. *15v*Then we are also false witnesses to God, because we testified against God that he raised Christ, whom he did not raise if in fact the dead are not raised. *16*For if the dead are not raised, nei-

15, 1–58: Some consider this chapter an earlier Pauline composition inserted into the present letter. The problem that Paul treats is clear to a degree: some of the Corinthians are denying the resurrection of the dead (12), apparently because of their inability to imagine how any kind of bodily existence could be possible after death (35). It is plausibly supposed that their attitude stems from Greek anthropology, which looks with contempt upon matter and would be content with the survival of the soul, and perhaps also from an overrealized eschatology of gnostic coloration, such as that reflected in 2 Tm 2, 18, which considers the resurrection a purely spiritual experience already achieved in baptism and in the forgiveness of sins. Paul, on the other hand, will affirm both the essential corporeity of the resurrection and its futurity.

His response moves through three steps: a recall of the basic kerygma about Jesus' resurrection (1–11), an assertion of the logical inconsistencies involved in denial of the resurrection (12–34), and an attempt to perceive theologically what the properties of the resurrected body must be (35–58).

15, 1–11: Paul recalls the tradition (3–7), which he can presuppose as common ground and which provides a starting point for his argument. This is the fundamental content of all Christian preaching and belief (1–2.11).

15, 3–7: The language by which Paul expresses the essence of the "gospel" (1) is not his own but is drawn from older credal formulas. This credo highlights Jesus' death for

our sins (confirmed by his burial) and Jesus' resurrection (confirmed by his appearances) and presents both of them as fulfillment of prophecy. **In accordance with the scriptures:** conformity of Jesus' passion with the scriptures is asserted in Mt 16, 1; Lk 24, 25–27.32.44–46. Application of some Old Testament texts (Pss 2, 7; 16, 8–11) to his resurrection is illustrated by Acts 2, 27–31; 13, 29–39; and Is 52, 13—53, 12 and Hos 6, 2 may also have been envisaged.

15, 9–11: A persecutor may have appeared disqualified (**ouk . . . hikanos**) from apostleship, but in fact God's grace has qualified him. Cf the remarks in 2 Cor about his qualifications (2, 16; 3, 5) and his greater labors (11, 23). These verses are parenthetical, but a nerve has been touched (the references to his abnormal birth and his activity as a persecutor may echo taunts from Paul's opponents), and he is instinctively moved to self-defense.

15, 12–19: Denial of the resurrection (12) involves logical inconsistencies. The basic one, stated twice (13.16), is that if there is no such thing as (bodily) resurrection, then it has not taken place even in Christ's case.

p: 11, 23 / 1 Pt 2, 24; 3, 18 / Is 53, 4-12.   *q:* Acts 2, 23-24 / Ps 16, 8-11; Hos 6, 1-2; Jon 2, 1.   *r:* Mk 16, 14; Mt 28, 16-17; Lk 24, 36; Jn 20, 19.   *s:* 9, 1; Acts 9, 3-6; Gal 1, 16.   *t:* Acts 8, 3; 9, 1-2; Gal 1, 23; Eph 3, 8; 1 Tm 1, 15.   *u:* 1 Thes 4, 14. *v:* Acts 5, 32.

ther has Christ been raised, *17**and if Christ has not been raised, your faith is vain; you are still in your sins. *18*Then those who have fallen asleep in Christ have perished. *19*If for this life only we have hoped in Christ, we are the most pitiable people of all.

Christ the Firstfruits. *20w**But now Christ has been raised from the dead, the firstfruits of those who have fallen asleep. *21**For since death came through a human being, the resurrection of the dead came also through a human being. *22x*For just as in Adam all die, so too in Christ shall all be brought to life, *23y*but each one in proper order: Christ the firstfruits; then, at his coming, those who belong to Christ; *24z**then comes the end, when he hands over the kingdom to his God and Father, when he has destroyed every sovereignty and every authority and power. *25a*For he must reign until he has put all his enemies under his feet. *26b**The last enemy to be destroyed is death, *27c**for "he subjected everything under his feet." But when it says that

everything has been subjected, it is clear that it excludes the one who subjected everything to him. *28d*When everything is subjected to him, then the Son himself will [also] be subjected to the one who subjected everything to him, so that God may be all in all.

Practical Arguments. *29**Otherwise, what will people accomplish by having themselves baptized for the dead? If the dead are not raised at all, then why are they having themselves baptized for them?

*30e**Moreover, why are we endangering ourselves all the time? *31f*Every day I face death; I swear it by the pride in you [brothers] that I have in Christ Jesus our Lord. *32g*If at Ephesus I fought with beasts, so to speak, what benefit was it to me? If the dead are not raised:

"Let us eat and drink,
    for tomorrow we die."

*33*Do not be led astray:

"Bad company corrupts good morals."

15, 17–18: The consequences for the Corinthians are grave: both forgiveness of sins and salvation are an illusion, despite their strong convictions about both. Unless Christ is risen, their faith does not save.

15, 20–28: After a triumphant assertion of the reality of Christ's resurrection (20a), Paul explains its positive implications and consequences. As a soteriological event of both human (20–23) and cosmic (24–28) dimensions, Jesus' resurrection logically and necessarily involves ours as well.

15, 20: The firstfruits: the portion of the harvest offered in thanksgiving to God implies the consecration of the entire harvest to come. Christ's resurrection is not an end in itself; its finality lies in the whole harvest, ourselves.

15, 21–22: Our human existence, both natural and supernatural, is corporate, involves solidarity. **In Adam . . . in Christ:** the Hebrew word **'ādām** in Genesis is both a common noun for mankind and a proper noun for the first man. Paul here presents Adam as at least a literary type of Christ; the parallelism and contrast between them will be developed further in vv 45–49 and in Rom 5, 12–21.

15, 24–28: Paul's perspective expands to cosmic dimensions, as he describes the climax of history, **the end.** His viewpoint is still christological, as in vv 20–23. Verses 24 and 28 describe Christ's final relations to his enemies and his Father in language that is both royal and military; vv 25–28 insert a proof from scripture (Pss 110, 1; 8, 7) into this description. But the viewpoint is also theological, for God is the ultimate agent and end, and likewise soteriological, for we are the beneficiaries of all the action.

15, 26: The last enemy . . . is death: a parenthesis that specifies the final fulfillment of the two Old Testament texts just referred to, Ps 110, 1 and Ps 8, 7. Death is not just one cosmic power among many, but the ultimate effect of sin in

the universe (cf 56; Rom 5, 12). Christ defeats death where it prevails, in our bodies. The destruction of the last enemy is concretely the "coming to life" (22) of "those who belong to Christ" (23).

15, 27b-28: The one who subjected everything to him: the Father is the ultimate agent in the drama, and the final end of the process, to whom the Son and everything else is ordered (24.28). **That God may be all in all:** his reign is a dynamic exercise of creative power, an outpouring of life and energy through the universe, with no further resistance. This is the supremely positive meaning of "subjection": that God may fully be God.

15, 29–34: Paul concludes his treatment of logical inconsistencies with a listing of miscellaneous Christian practices that would be meaningless if the resurrection were not a fact.

15, 29: Baptized for the dead: this practice is not further explained here, nor is it necessarily mentioned with approval, but Paul cites it as something in their experience that attests in one more way to belief in the resurrection.

15, 30–34: A life of sacrifice, such as Paul describes in 4, 9–13 and 2 Cor, would be pointless without the prospect of resurrection; a life of pleasure, such as that expressed in the Epicurean slogan of v 32, would be far more consistent. **I fought with beasts:** since Paul does not elsewhere mention a combat with beasts at Ephesus, he may be speaking figuratively about struggles with adversaries.

w: Rom 8, 11; Col 1, 18; 1 Thes 4, 14. *x:* Gn 3, 17-19; Rom 5, 12-19. *y:* 1 Thes 4, 15-17. *z:* Eph 1, 22. *a:* Ps 110, 1. *b:* Rom 6, 9; 2 Tm 1, 10; Rv 20, 14; 21, 4. *c:* Ps 8, 7; Eph 1, 22; Phil 3, 21. *d:* Eph 4, 6; Col 3, 11. *e:* 2 Cor 4, 8-12; 11, 23-27. *f:* Ps 44, 23; Rom 8, 36. *g:* 4, 9; 2 Cor 4, 10-11 / Wis 2, 5-7; Is 22, 13.

34h Become sober as you ought and stop sinning. For some have no knowledge of God; I say this to your shame.

C. The Manner of the Resurrection

35* But someone may say, "How are the dead raised? With what kind of body will they come back?"

The Resurrection Body. 36i* You fool! What you sow is not brought to life unless it dies. 37 And what you sow is not the body that is to be but a bare kernel of wheat, perhaps, or of some other kind; 38j but God gives it a body as he chooses, and to each of the seeds its own body. 39* Not all flesh is the same, but there is one kind for human beings, another kind of flesh for animals, another kind of flesh for birds, and another for fish. 40 There are both heavenly bodies and earthly bodies, but the brightness of the heavenly is one kind and that of the earthly another. 41 The brightness of the sun is one kind, the brightness of the moon another,

and the brightness of the stars another. For star differs from star in brightness.

42* So also is the resurrection of the dead. It is sown corruptible; it is raised incorruptible. 43k It is sown dishonorable; it is raised glorious. It is sown weak; it is raised powerful. 44 It is sown a natural body; it is raised a spiritual body. If there is a natural body, there is also a spiritual one.

45l* So, too, it is written, "The first man, Adam, became a living being," the last Adam a life-giving spirit. 46 But the spiritual was not first; rather the natural and then the spiritual. 47 The first man was from the earth, earthly; the second man, from heaven. 48 As was the earthly one, so also are the earthly, and as is the heavenly one, so also are the heavenly. 49m* Just as we have borne the image of the earthly one, we shall also bear the image of the heavenly one.

The Resurrection Event. 50n* This I declare, brothers: flesh and blood cannot inherit the kingdom of God, nor does corruption inherit incorruption. 51o* Behold, I tell you a mystery. We shall not all fall asleep,

15, 35–58: Paul imagines two objections that the Corinthians could raise: one concerning the manner of the resurrection (**how?**), the other pertaining to the qualities of the risen body (**what kind?**). These questions probably lie behind their denial of the resurrection (12), and seem to reflect the presumption that no kind of body other than the one we now possess would be possible. Paul deals with these objections in inverse order, in vv 36–49 and vv 50–58. His argument is fundamentally theological and its appeal is to the understanding.

15, 35–49: Paul approaches the question of the nature of the risen body (**what kind of body?**) by means of two analogies: the seed (36–44) and the first man, Adam (45–49).

15, 36–38: The analogy of the seed: there is a change of attributes from seed to plant; the old life-form must be lost for the new to emerge. By speaking about the seed as a **body** that dies and comes to life, Paul keeps the point of the analogy before the reader's mind.

15, 39–41: The expression "its own body" (38) leads to a development on the marvelous diversity evident in bodily life.

15, 42–44: The principles of qualitative difference before and after death (36–38) and of diversity on different levels of creation (39–41) are now applied to the human body. Before: a body animated by a lower, natural life-principle (**psychē**) and endowed with the properties of natural existence (corruptibility, lack of glory, weakness). After: a body animated by a higher life-principle (**pneuma**; cf 45) and endowed with other qualities (incorruptibility, glory, power, spirituality), which are properties of God himself.

15, 45: The analogy of **the first man, Adam,** is introduced by a citation from Gn 2, 7. Paul alters the text slightly, adding the adjective **first,** and translating the Hebrew 'ādām

twice, so as to give it its value both as a common noun (**man**) and as a proper name (**Adam**). Verse 45b then specifies similarities and differences between the two Adams. **The last Adam,** Christ (cf 21–22) has become **a . . . spirit (pneuma)**, a life-principle transcendent with respect to the natural soul (**psychē**) of the first Adam (on the terminology here, cf the note on 3, 1). Further, he is not just alive, but **life-giving,** a source of life for others.

15, 49: We shall also bear the image: although it has less manuscript support, this reading better fits the context's emphasis on futurity and the transforming action of God; on future transformation as conformity to the image of the Son, cf Rom 8, 29; Phil 3, 21. The majority reading, "let us bear the image," suggests that the image of the heavenly man is already present and exhorts us to conform to it.

15, 50–57: These verses, an answer to the first question of v 35, explain theologically how the change of properties from one image to another will take place: God has the power to transform, and he will exercise it.

15, 50–53: Flesh and blood . . . corruption: living persons and the corpses of the dead, respectively. In both cases, the gulf between creatures and God is too wide to be bridged unless God himself transforms us.

15, 51–52: A mystery: the last moment in God's plan is disclosed; cf the notes on 2, 1.7–10a. The final trumpet and the awakening of the dead are stock details of the apocalyptic scenario. **We shall not all fall asleep:** Paul expected that some of

h: Mt 22, 29; Mk 12, 24.   i: Jn 12, 24.   j: Gn 1, 11.   k: Phil 3, 20-21; Col 3, 4.   l: Gn 2, 7 / Jn 5, 21-29; 2 Cor 3, 6.17.   m: Gn 5, 3 / Rom 8, 29; Phil 3, 21.   n: Jn 3, 3-6.   o: 1 Thes 4, 14-17.

but we will all be changed, [52p]in an instant, in the blink of an eye, at the last trumpet. For the trumpet will sound, the dead will be raised incorruptible, and we shall be changed. [53q]For that which is corruptible must clothe itself with incorruptibility, and that which is mortal must clothe itself with immortality. [54r*]And when this which is corruptible clothes itself with incorruptibility and this which is mortal clothes itself with immortality, then the word that is written shall come about:

"Death is swallowed up in victory.
[55s]Where, O death, is your victory?
Where, O death, is your sting?"

[56t*]The sting of death is sin, and the power of sin is the law. [57u]But thanks be to God who gives us the victory through our Lord Jesus Christ.

[58]Therefore, my beloved brothers, be firm, steadfast, always fully devoted to the work of the Lord, knowing that in the Lord your labor is not in vain.

VI: Conclusion

CHAPTER 16

See RG 457–58

The Collection. [1v*]Now in regard to the collection for the holy ones, you also should do as I ordered the churches of Galatia. [2]On the first day of the week each of you should set aside and save whatever he can afford, so that collections will not be going on when I come. [3]And when I arrive, I shall send those whom you have approved with letters of recommendation to take your gracious gift to Jerusalem. [4*]If it seems fitting that I should go also, they will go with me.

Paul's Travel Plans. [5w*]I shall come to you after I pass through Macedonia (for I am going to pass through Macedonia), [6]and perhaps I shall stay or even spend the winter with you, so that you may send me on my way wherever I may go. [7x]For I do not wish to see you now just in passing, but I hope to spend some time with you, if the Lord permits. [8y]I shall stay in Ephesus until Pentecost, [9z]because a door has opened for me wide and productive for work, but there are many opponents.

[10a]If Timothy comes, see that he is without fear in your company, for he is doing the work of the Lord just as I am. [11]Therefore, no one should disdain him. Rather, send him on his way in peace that he may come to me, for I am expecting him with the brothers. [12b]Now in regard to our brother Apollos, I urged him strongly to go to you with the brothers, but it was not at all his will that he go now. He will go when he has an opportunity.

Exhortation and Greetings. [13]Be on your guard, stand firm in the faith, be courageous, be strong. [14]Your every act should be done with love.

[15c]I urge you, brothers—you know that the household of Stephanas is the firstfruits of Achaia and that they have devoted them-

---

his contemporaries might still be alive at Christ's return; after the death of Paul and his whole generation, copyists altered this statement in various ways. **We will all be changed:** the statement extends to all Christians, for Paul is not directly speaking about anyone else. Whether they have died before the end or happen still to be alive, all must be transformed.

15, 54–55: Death is swallowed up in victory: scripture itself predicts death's overthrow. **O death:** in his prophetic vision Paul may be making Hosea's words his own, or imagining this cry of triumph on the lips of the risen church.

15, 56: The sting of death is sin: an explanation of Hosea's metaphor. Death, scorpion-like, is equipped with a sting, sin, by which it injects its poison. Christ defeats sin, the cause of death (Gn 3, 19; Rom 5, 12).

16, 1–4: This paragraph contains our earliest evidence for a project that became a major undertaking of Paul's ministry. The collection for the church at Jerusalem was a symbol in his mind for the unity of Jewish and Gentile Christianity. Cf Gal 2, 10; Rom 15, 25–29; 2 Cor 8–9 and the notes to this last passage.

16, 1: In regard to the collection: it has already begun in Galatia and Macedonia (cf 2 Cor 8), and presumably he has already instructed the Corinthians about its purpose.

16, 4: That I should go also: presumably Paul delivered the collection on his final visit to Jerusalem; cf Rom 15, 25–32; Acts 24, 14.

16, 5–12: The travel plans outlined here may not have materialized precisely as Paul intended; cf 2 Cor 1, 8—2, 13; 7, 4–16.

16, 8: In Ephesus until Pentecost: this tells us the place from which he wrote the letter and suggests he may have composed it about Easter time (cf 5, 7–8).

p: Jl 2, 1; Zec 9, 14; Mt 24, 31; Rv 11, 15-18.   *q:* 2 Cor 5, 2-4. *r:* Is 25, 8; 2 Cor 5, 4; 2 Tm 1, 10; Heb 2, 14-15.   *s:* Hos 13, 14. *t:* Rom 4, 15; 7, 7.13.   *u:* Jn 16, 33; 1 Jn 5, 4.   *v:* Acts 24, 17; Rom 15, 25-32; 2 Cor 8-9; Gal 2, 10.   *w:* Acts 19, 21; Rom 15, 26; 2 Cor 1, 15-16.   *x:* Acts 18, 21.   *y:* 15, 32; Acts 18, 19; 19, 1-10.   *z:* Acts 14, 27; 2 Cor 2, 12.   *a:* 4, 17; Acts 16, 1; 19, 22; Phil 2, 19-23.   *b:* 1, 12; 3, 4-6.22; Acts 18, 24-28.   *c:* 1, 16.

selves to the service of the holy ones— [16]be subordinate to such people and to everyone who works and toils with them. [17]I rejoice in the arrival of Stephanas, Fortunatus, and Achaicus, because they made up for your absence, [18d]for they refreshed my spirit as well as yours. So give recognition to such people. [19e*]The churches of Asia send you greet-ings. Aquila and Prisca together with the church at their house send you many greet-ings in the Lord. [20f]All the brothers greet you. Greet one another with a holy kiss.

[21g]I, Paul, write you this greeting in my own hand. [22h*]If anyone does not love the Lord, let him be accursed. *Marana tha*. [23i]The grace of the Lord Jesus be with you. [24]My love to all of you in Christ Jesus.

16, 19–24: These paragraphs conform to the normal epis-tolary conclusion, but their language is overlaid with liturgi-cal coloration as well. The **greetings** of the Asian churches are probably to be read, along with the letter, in the liturgy at Corinth, and the union of the church is to be expressed by **a holy kiss** (19–20). Paul adds to this his own greeting (21) and blessings (23–24).

16, 22: Accursed: literally, "anathema." This expression (cf 12, 3) is a formula for exclusion from the community; it may imply here a call to self-examination before celebration of the Eucharist, in preparation for the Lord's coming and judgment (cf 11, 17–34). **Marana tha:** an Aramaic expres-sion, probably used in the early Christian liturgy. As under-stood here ("O Lord, come!"), it is a prayer for the early re-turn of Christ. If the Aramaic words are divided differently (**Maran atha,** "Our Lord has come"), it becomes a credal declaration. The former interpretation is supported by what appears to be a Greek equivalent of this acclamation in Rv 22, 20: "Amen. Come, Lord Jesus!"

d: 1 Thes 5, 12-13.   *e:* Acts 18, 2.18.26; Rom 16, 3-5.   *f:* Rom 16, 16; 2 Cor 13, 12; 1 Thes 5, 26; 1 Pt 5, 14.   *g:* Gal 6, 11; Col 4, 18; 2 Thes 3, 17.   *h:* 12, 3; Rom 9, 3; Gal 1, 8-9; Rv 22, 20.   *i:* Rom 16, 20.

See RG
458–64

The Second Letter to the Corinthians

The Second Letter to the Corinthians is the most personal of all of Paul's extant writings, and it re-veals much about his character. In it he deals with one or more crises that have arisen in the Corinthian church. The confrontation with these problems caused him to reflect deeply on his re-lationship with the community and to speak about it frankly. One moment he is venting his feelings of frustration and uncertainty, the next he is pour-ing out his relief and affection. The importance of the issues at stake between them calls forth from him an enormous effort of personal persuasion, as well as doctrinal considerations that are of great value for us. Paul's ability to produce profound theological foundations for what may at first sight appear to be rather commonplace circum-stances is perhaps nowhere better exemplified than in Second Corinthians. The emotional tone of the letter, its lack of order, and our ignorance of some of its background do not make it easy to follow, but it amply repays the effort required of the reader.

Second Corinthians is rich and varied in con-tent. The interpretation of Exodus in chapter 3, for instance, offers a striking example of early apologetic use of the Old Testament. Paul's dis-cussion of the collection in chs 8–9 contains a theology of sharing of possessions, of community of goods among Christian churches, which is both balanced and sensitive. Furthermore, the closing chapters provide an illustration of early Christian invective and polemic, because the con-flict with intruders forces Paul to assert his au-thority. But in those same chapters Paul articu-lates the vision and sense of values that animate his own apostolate, revealing his faith that Jesus' passion and resurrection are the pattern for all Christian life and expressing a spirituality of min-istry unsurpassed in the New Testament.

The letter is remarkable for its rhetoric. Paul falls naturally into the style and argumentation of contemporary philosophic preachers, employing with ease the stock devices of the "diatribe." By a barrage of questions, by challenges both serious and ironic, by paradox heaped upon paradox, even by insults hurled at his opponents, he strives to awaken in his hearers a true sense of values and an appropriate response. All his argument centers on the destiny of Jesus, in which a paradoxical re-versal of values is revealed. But Paul appeals to his own personal experience as well. In passages of great rhetorical power (4, 7–15; 6, 3–10; 11, 21–29; 12, 5–10; 13, 3–4) he enumerates the circumstances of his ministry and the tribulations he has had to endure for Jesus and the gospel, in the hope of illustrating the pattern of Jesus' existence in his own and of drawing the Corinthians into a reappraisal of the values they cherish. Similar passages in the same style in his other letters (cf especially Rom 8, 31–39; 1 Cor 1, 26–31; 4, 6–21; 9, 1–27; 13, 1–13; Phil 4, 10–19) confirm Paul's familiarity with contemporary rhetoric and demonstrate how effectively it served to express his vision of Christian life and ministry.

Second Corinthians was occasioned by events and problems that developed after Paul's first letter reached Corinth. We have no information about these circumstances except what is contained in the letter itself, which of course supposes that they are known to the readers. Consequently the reconstruction of the letter's background is an uncertain enterprise about which there is not complete agreement.

The letter deals principally with these three topics: (1) a crisis between Paul and the Corinthians, occasioned at least partially by changes in his travel plans (1, 12—2, 13), and the successful resolution of that crisis (7, 5–16); (2) further directives and encouragement in regard to the collection for the church in Jerusalem (8, 1—9, 15); (3) the definition and defense of Paul's ministry as an apostle. Paul's reflections on this matter are occasioned by visitors from other churches who passed through Corinth, missionaries who differed from Paul in a variety of ways, both in theory and in practice. Those differences led to comparisons. Either the visitors themselves or some of the local church members appear to have sown confusion among the Corinthians with regard to Paul's authority or his style, or both. Paul deals at length with aspects of this situation in 2, 14—7, 4 and again in 10, 1—13, 10, though the manner of treatment and the thrust of the argument differ in each of these sections.

Scholars have noticed a lack of continuity in this document. For example, the long section of 2, 14—7, 4 seems abruptly spliced into the narrative of a crisis and its resolution. Identical or similar topics, moreover, seem to be treated several times during the letter (compare 2, 14—7, 4 with 10, 1—13, 10, and 8, 1–24 with 9, 1–15). Many judge, therefore, that this letter as it stands incorporates several briefer letters sent to Corinth over a certain span of time. If this is so, then Paul himself or, more likely, some other editor clearly took care to gather those letters together and impose some literary unity upon the collection, thus producing the document that has come down to us as the Second Letter to the Corinthians. Others continue to regard it as a single letter, attributing its inconsistencies to changes of perspective in Paul that may have been occasioned by the arrival of fresh news from Corinth during its composition. The letter, or at least some sections of it, appears to have been composed in Macedonia(2, 12–13; 7, 5–6; 8, 1–4; 9, 2–4). It is generally dated about the autumn of A.D. 57; if it is a compilation, of course, the various parts may have been separated by intervals of at least some months.

The principal divisions of the Second Letter to the Corinthians are the following:

I: Address (1, 1–11)
II: The Crisis between Paul and the Corinthians (1, 12—7, 16)
  A: Past Relationships (1, 12—2, 13)
  B: Paul's Ministry (2, 14—7, 4)
  C: Resolution of the Crisis (7, 5–16)
III: The Collection for Jerusalem (8, 1—9, 15)
IV: Paul's Defense of His Ministry (10, 1—13, 10)
V: Conclusion (13, 11–13)

I: Address

CHAPTER 1

See RG 459–60

Greeting. [1a]*Paul, an apostle of Christ Jesus by the will of God, and Timothy our brother, to the church of God that is in Corinth, with all the holy ones throughout Achaia: [2]grace to you and peace from God our Father and the Lord Jesus Christ.

1, 1–11: The opening follows the usual Pauline form, except that the thanksgiving takes the form of a doxology or glorification of God (3). This introduces a meditation on the experience of suffering and encouragement shared by Paul and the Corinthians (4–7), drawn, at least in part, from Paul's reflections on a recent affliction (8–10). The section ends with a modified and delayed allusion to thanksgiving (11).

a: Eph 1, 1; Col 1, 1 / 1, 19; Acts 16 / Rom 1, 7; 1 Cor 1, 2.

Thanksgiving. *3b**Blessed be the God and Father of our Lord Jesus Christ, the Father of compassion and God of all encouragement, *4c*who encourages us in our every affliction, so that we may be able to encourage those who are in any affliction with the encouragement with which we ourselves are encouraged by God. *5**For as Christ's sufferings overflow to us, so through Christ does our encouragement also overflow. *6*If we are afflicted, it is for your encouragement and salvation; if we are encouraged, it is for your encouragement, which enables you to endure the same sufferings that we suffer. *7**Our hope for you is firm, for we know that as you share in the sufferings, you also share in the encouragement.

8d*We do not want you to be unaware, brothers, of the affliction that came to us in the province of Asia; we were utterly weighed down beyond our strength, so that we despaired even of life. *9e**Indeed, we had accepted within ourselves the sentence of death, that we might trust not in ourselves but in God who raises the dead. *10f*He rescued us from such great danger of death, and he will continue to rescue us; in him we have put our hope [that] he will also rescue us again, *11g*as you help us with prayer, so that thanks may be given by many on our behalf for the gift granted us through the prayers of many.

II: The Crisis Between Paul and the Corinthians
A. Past Relationships

Paul's Sincerity and Constancy. *12**For our boast is this, the testimony of our conscience that we have conducted ourselves in the world, and especially toward you, with the simplicity and sincerity of God, [and] not by human wisdom but by the grace of God. *13*For we write you nothing but what you can read and understand, and I hope that you will understand completely, *14h*as you have come to understand us partially, that we are your boast as you also are ours, on the day of [our] Lord Jesus.

15*With this confidence I formerly intended to come to you so that you might receive a double favor, *16i*namely, to go by way of you to Macedonia, and then to come to you again on my return from Macedonia, and have you send me on my way to Judea. *17j**So when I intended this, did I act lightly?

1, 3: God of all encouragement: Paul expands a standard Jewish blessing so as to state the theme of the paragraph. The theme of "encouragement" or "consolation" (**paraklēsis**) occurs ten times in this opening, against a background formed by multiple references to "affliction" and "suffering."

1, 5: Through Christ: the Father of compassion is the Father of our Lord Jesus (3); Paul's sufferings and encouragement (or "consolation") are experienced in union with Christ. Cf Lk 2, 25: the "consolation of Israel" is Jesus himself.

1, 7: You also share in the encouragement: the eschatological reversal of affliction and encouragement that Christians expect (cf Mt 5, 4; Lk 6, 24) permits some present experience of reversal in the Corinthians' case, as in Paul's.

1, 8: Asia: a Roman province in western Asia Minor, the capital of which was Ephesus.

1, 9–10: The sentence of death: it is unclear whether Paul is alluding to a physical illness or to an external threat to life. The result of the situation was to produce an attitude of faith in God alone. **God who raises the dead:** rescue is the constant pattern of God's activity; his final act of encouragement is the resurrection.

1, 12—2, 13: The autobiographical remarks about the crisis in Asia Minor lead into consideration of a crisis that has arisen between Paul and the Corinthians. Paul will return to this question, after a long digression, in 7, 5–16. Both of these sections deal with travel plans Paul had made, changes in the plans, alternative measures adopted, a breach that opened between him and the community, and finally a reconciliation between them.

1, 12–14: Since Paul's own conduct will be under discussion here, he prefaces the section with a statement about his habitual behavior and attitude toward the community. He protests his openness, single-mindedness, and conformity to God's grace; he hopes that his relationship with them will be marked by mutual understanding and pride, which will constantly increase until it reaches its climax at the judgment. Two references to boasting frame this paragraph (12.14), the first appearances of a theme that will be important in the letter, especially in chs 10–13; the term is used in a positive sense here (cf the note on 1 Cor 1, 29–31).

1, 15: I formerly intended to come: this plan reads like a revision of the one mentioned in 1 Cor 16, 5. Not until 1, 23—2, 1 will Paul tell us something his original readers already knew, that he has canceled one or the other of these projected visits.

1, 17: Did I act lightly?: the subsequent change of plans casts suspicion on the original intention, creating the impression that Paul is vacillating and inconsistent or that **human**

b: 1 Cor 15, 24; Eph 1, 3; 1 Pt 1, 3 / Rom 15, 5. *c:* 7, 6-7.13; 1 Thes 3, 6-8; 2 Thes 2, 16. *d:* Acts 20, 18-19; 1 Cor 15, 32. *e:* 4, 7-11; Rom 4, 17. *f:* 2 Tm 4, 18. *g:* 4, 15; 9, 12. *h:* Phil 2, 16; 1 Thes 2, 19-20. *i:* 1 Cor 16, 5-9; Acts 19, 21. *j:* Mt 5, 37; Jas 5, 12.

Or do I make my plans according to human considerations, so that with me it is "yes, yes" and "no, no"? [18]*As God is faithful, our word to you is not "yes" and "no." [19k]For the Son of God, Jesus Christ, who was proclaimed to you by us, Silvanus and Timothy and me, was not "yes" and "no," but "yes" has been in him. [20l]For however many are the promises of God, their Yes is in him; therefore, the Amen from us also goes through him to God for glory. [21m]*But the one who gives us security with you in Christ and who anointed us is God; [22n]he has also put his seal upon us and given the Spirit in our hearts as a first installment.

Paul's Change of Plan. [23o]*But I call upon God as witness, on my life, that it is to spare you that I have not yet gone to Corinth. [24]Not that we lord it over your faith; rather, we work together for your joy, for you stand firm in the faith.

See RG
460–61

CHAPTER 2

[1]For I decided not to come to you again in painful circumstances. [2]For if I inflict pain upon you, then who is there to cheer me except the one pained by me? [3]*And I wrote as I did so that when I came I might not be pained by those in whom I should have rejoiced, confident about all of you that my joy is that of all of you. [4]For out of much affliction and anguish of heart I wrote to you with many tears, not that you might be pained but that you might know the abundant love I have for you.

The Offender. [5]*If anyone has caused pain, he has caused it not to me, but in some measure (not to exaggerate) to all of you. [6]This punishment by the majority is enough for such a person, [7p]so that on the contrary you should forgive and encourage him instead, or else the person may be overwhelmed by excessive pain. [8]Therefore, I urge you to reaffirm your love for him. [9q]For this is why I wrote, to know your proven character, whether you were obedient in everything. [10]Whomever you forgive anything, so do I. For indeed what I have forgiven, if I have forgiven anything, has been for you in the presence of Christ, [11r]so that

considerations keep dictating shifts in his goals and projects (cf the counterclaim of 12). **"Yes, yes" and "no, no":** stating something and denying it in the same or the next breath; being of two minds at once, or from one moment to the next.
1, 18–22: As God is faithful: unable to deny the change in plans, Paul nonetheless asserts the firmness of the original plan and claims a profound constancy in his life and work. He grounds his defense in God himself, who is firm and reliable; this quality can also be predicated in various ways of those who are associated with him. Christ, Paul, and the Corinthians all participate in analogous ways in the constancy of God. A number of the terms here, which appear related only conceptually in Greek or English, would be variations of the same root, 'mn, in a Semitic language, and thus naturally associated in a Semitic mind, such as Paul's. These include the words **yes** (17–20), **faithful** (18), **Amen** (20), **gives us security** (21), **faith, stand firm** (24).
1, 21–22: The commercial terms **gives us security, seal, first installment** are here used analogously to refer to the process of initiation into the Christian life, perhaps specifically to baptism. The passage is clearly trinitarian. The Spirit is the **first installment** or "down payment" of the full messianic benefits that God guarantees to Christians. Cf Eph 1, 13–14.
1, 23–24: I have not yet gone to Corinth: some suppose that Paul received word of some affair in Corinth, which he decided to regulate by letter even before the first of his projected visits (cf 16). Others conjecture that he did pay the first visit, was offended there (cf 2, 5), returned to Ephesus, and sent a letter (2, 3–9) in place of the second visit. The expressions **to spare you** (23) and **work together for your joy** (24)

introduce the major themes of the next two paragraphs, which are remarkable for insistent repetition of key words and ideas. These form two clusters of terms in the English translation: (1) cheer, rejoice, encourage, joy; (2) pain, affliction, anguish. These clusters reappear when Paul resumes treatment of this subject in 7, 5–16.
2, 3–4: I wrote as I did: we learn for the first time about the sending of a letter in place of the proposed visit. Paul mentions the letter in passing, but emphasizes his motivation in sending it: to avoid being saddened by them (cf 1), and to help them realize the depth of his love. Another motive will be added in 7, 12: to bring to light their own concern for him. **With many tears:** it has been suggested that we may have all or part of this "tearful letter" somewhere in the Corinthian correspondence, either in 1 Cor 5 (the case of the incestuous man), or in 1 Cor as a whole, or in 2 Cor 10–13. None of these hypotheses is entirely convincing. See the note on 13, 1.
2, 5–11: The nature of the **pain** (5) is unclear, though some believe an individual at Corinth rejected Paul's authority, thereby scandalizing many in the community. In any case, action has been taken, and Paul judges the measures adequate to right the situation (6). The follow-up directives he now gives are entirely positive: forgive, encourage, love. **Overwhelmed** (7): a vivid metaphor (literally "swallowed") that Paul employs positively at 5, 4 and in 1 Cor 15, 54 (7). It is often used to describe satanic activity (cf 1 Pt 5, 8); note the reference to Satan here in v 11.

k: Acts 16, 1-3; 1 Thes 1, 1; 2 Thes 1, 1. *l:* 1 Cor 14, 16; Rv 3, 14. *m:* 1 Jn 2, 20.27. *n:* Eph 1, 13-14; 4, 30 / 5, 5; Rom 5, 5; 8, 16.23. *o:* 13, 2. *p:* Col 3, 13. *q:* 7, 15. *r:* Eph 4, 27.

we might not be taken advantage of by Satan, for we are not unaware of his purposes.

Paul's Anxiety. [12s*]When I went to Troas for the gospel of Christ, although a door was opened for me in the Lord, [13t*]I had no relief in my spirit because I did not find my brother Titus. So I took leave of them and went on to Macedonia.

B. Paul's Ministry

Ministers of a New Covenant. [14*]But thanks be to God, who always leads us in triumph in Christ and manifests through us the odor of the knowledge of him in every place. [15u]For we are the aroma of Christ for God among those who are being saved and among those who are perishing, [16*]to the latter an odor of death that leads to death, to the former an odor of life that leads to life. Who is qualified for this? [17v]For we are not like the many who trade on the word of God; but as out of sincerity, indeed as from God and in the presence of God, we speak in Christ.

[1w*]Are we beginning to commend ourselves again? Or do we need, as some do, letters of recommendation to you or from you? [2*]You are our letter, written on our hearts, known and read by all, [3x*]shown to

---

2, 12–13: I had no relief: Paul does not explain the reason for his anxiety until he resumes the thread of his narrative at 7, 5: he was waiting to hear how the Corinthians would respond to his letter. Since 7, 5–16 describes their response in entirely positive terms, we never learn in detail why he found it necessary to defend and justify his change of plans, as in 1, 15–24. Was this portion of the letter written before the arrival of Titus with his good news (7, 6–7)?

2, 13: Macedonia: a Roman province in northern Greece.

2, 14—7, 4: This section constitutes a digression within the narrative of the crisis and its resolution (1, 12—2, 13 and 7, 5–16). The main component (2, 14—6, 10) treats the nature of Paul's ministry and his qualifications for it; this material bears some similarity to the defense of his ministry in chs 10–13, but it may well come from a period close to the crisis. This is followed by a supplementary block of material quite different in character and tone (6, 14—7, 1). These materials may have been brought together into their present position during final editing of the letter; appeals to the Corinthians link them to one another (6, 11–13) and lead back to the interrupted narrative (7, 2–4).

2, 14—6, 10: The question of Paul's adequacy (16; cf 3, 5) and his credentials (3, 1–2) has been raised. Paul responds by an extended treatment of the nature of his ministry. It is a ministry of glory (3, 7—4, 6), of life (4, 7—5, 10), of reconciliation (5, 11—6, 10).

2, 14–16a: The initial statement plunges us abruptly into another train of thought. Paul describes his personal existence and his function as a preacher in two powerful images (14) that constitute a prelude to the development to follow.

2, 14a: Leads us in triumph in Christ: this metaphor of a festive parade in honor of a conquering military hero can suggest either a positive sharing in Christ's triumph or an experience of defeat, being led in captivity and submission (cf 4, 8–11; 1 Cor 4, 9). Paul is probably aware of the ambiguity, as he is in the case of the next metaphor.

2, 14b-16a: The odor of the knowledge of him: incense was commonly used in triumphal processions. The metaphor suggests the gradual diffusion of the knowledge of God through the apostolic preaching. **The aroma of Christ:** the image shifts from the fragrance Paul diffuses to the aroma that he is. Paul is probably thinking of the "sweet odor" of the sacrifices in the Old Testament (e.g., Gn 8, 21; Ex 29, 18) and per-

haps of the metaphor of wisdom as a sweet odor (Sir 24, 15). **Death . . . life:** the aroma of Christ that comes to them through Paul is perceived differently by various classes of people. To some his preaching and his life (cf 1 Cor 1, 17—2, 6) are perceived as **death,** and the effect is death for them; others perceive him, despite appearances, as **life,** and the effect is life for them. This fragrance thus produces a separation and a judgment (cf the function of the "light" in John's gospel).

2, 16b-17: Qualified: Paul may be echoing either the self-satisfied claims of other preachers or their charges about Paul's deficiencies. No one is really qualified, but the apostle contrasts himself with those who dilute or falsify the preaching for personal advantage and insists on his totally good conscience: his ministry is from God, and he has exercised it with fidelity and integrity (cf 3, 5–6).

3, 1: Paul seems to allude to certain preachers who pride themselves on their written credentials. Presumably they reproach him for not possessing similar credentials and compel him to spell out his own qualifications (4, 2; 5, 12; 6, 4). The Corinthians themselves should have performed this function for Paul (5, 12; cf 12, 11). Since he is forced to find something that can recommend him, he points to them: their very existence constitutes his **letter** of recommendation (1–2). Others who engage in self-commendation will also be mentioned in 10, 12–18.

3, 2–3: Mention of "letters of recommendation" generates a series of metaphors in which Paul plays on the word "letter": (1) the community is Paul's letter of recommendation (2a); (2) they are a letter engraved on his affections for all to see and read (2b); (3) they are a letter from Christ that Paul merely delivers (3a); (4) they are a letter written by the Spirit on the tablets of human hearts (3b). One image dissolves into another.

3, 3b: This verse contrasts Paul's letter with those **written . . . in ink** (like the credentials of other preachers) and those **written . . . on tablets of stone** (like the law of Moses). These contrasts suggest that the other preachers may have claimed special relationship with Moses. If they were Judaizers zealous for the Mosaic law, that would explain the detailed contrast between the old and the new covenants (6; 4, 7—6, 10). If they were charismatics who claimed Moses as their model,

---

s: Acts 16, 8.   *t:* 7, 6; 1 Tm 1, 3.   *u:* 4, 3; 1 Cor 1, 18.   *v:* 4, 2; 1 Cor 5, 8.   *w:* Acts 18, 27; Rom 16, 1; 1 Cor 16, 3.   *x:* Ex 24, 12; 31, 18; 32, 15-19 / Jer 31, 33; Ez 11, 19; 36, 26-27.

be a letter of Christ administered by us, written not in ink but by the Spirit of the living God, not on tablets of stone but on tablets that are hearts of flesh.

*4**Such confidence we have through Christ toward God. *5y*Not that of ourselves we are qualified to take credit for anything as coming from us; rather, our qualification comes from God, *6z**who has indeed qualified us as ministers of a new covenant, not of letter but of spirit; for the letter brings death, but the Spirit gives life.

Contrast with the Old Covenant. *7a**Now if the ministry of death, carved in letters on stone, was so glorious that the Israelites could not look intently at the face of Moses because of its glory that was going to fade, *8**how much more will the ministry of the Spirit be glorious? *9*For if the ministry of condemnation was glorious, the ministry of righteousness will abound much more in glory. *10*Indeed, what was endowed with glory has come to have no glory in this respect because of the glory that surpasses it. *11*For if what was going to fade was glorious, how much more will what endures be glorious.

*12**Therefore, since we have such hope, we act very boldly *13**and not like Moses, who put a veil over his face so that the Israelites could not look intently at the cessation of what was fading. *14**Rather, their thoughts were rendered dull, for to this present day the same veil remains unlifted when they read the old covenant, because through Christ it is taken away. *15b*To this day, in fact, whenever Moses is read, a veil lies over their hearts, *16c*but whenever a person turns to the Lord the veil is removed. *17**Now the Lord is the Spirit, and where the Spirit of the Lord is, there is

that would explain the extended treatment of Moses himself and his glory (3, 7—4, 6). **Hearts of flesh:** cf Ezekiel's contrast between the heart of flesh that the Spirit gives and the heart of stone that it replaces (Ez 36, 26); the context is covenant renewal and purification that makes observance of the law possible.

3, 4–6: These verses resume 2, 1—3, 3. Paul's confidence (4) is grounded in his sense of God-given mission (2, 17), the specifics of which are described in vv 1–3. Verses 5–6 return to the question of his qualifications (2, 16), attributing them entirely to God. Verse 6 further spells out the situation described in v 3b and "names" it: Paul is living within **a new covenant,** characterized by the Spirit, which **gives life.** The usage of a **new covenant** is derived from Jer 31, 31–33, a passage that also speaks of writing on the heart; cf 2.

3, 6b: This verse serves as a topic sentence for 3, 7—6, 10. For the contrast between **letter** and **spirit,** cf Rom 2, 29; 7, 5–6.

3, 7—4, 6: Paul now develops the contrast enunciated in 3, 6b in terms of the relative glory of the two covenants, insisting on the greater glory of the new. His polemic seems directed against individuals who appeal to the glorious Moses and fail to perceive any comparable glory either in Paul's life as an apostle or in the gospel he preaches. He asserts in response that Christians have a glory of their own that far surpasses that of Moses.

3, 7: The **ministry of death:** from his very first words, Paul describes the Mosaic covenant and ministry from the viewpoint of their limitations. They lead to **death** rather than life (6–7; cf 4, 7—5, 10), to **condemnation** rather than reconciliation (9; cf 5, 11—6, 10). **Was so glorious:** the basic text to which Paul alludes is Ex 34, 29–35, to which his opponents have undoubtedly laid claim. **Going to fade:** Paul concedes the glory of Moses' covenant and ministry, but grants them only temporary significance.

3, 8–11: **How much more:** the argument "from the less to the greater" is repeated three times (8.9.11). Verse 10 expresses another point of view: the difference in glory is so

great that only the new covenant and ministry can properly be called "glorious" at all.

3, 12: **Such hope:** the glory is not yet an object of experience, but that does not lessen Paul's confidence. **Boldly:** the term *parrēsia* expresses outspoken declaration of Christian conviction (cf 4, 1–2). Paul has nothing to hide and no reason for timidity.

3, 13–14a: **Not like Moses:** in Exodus Moses veiled his face to protect the Israelites from God's reflected glory. Without impugning Moses' sincerity, Paul attributes another effect to the veil. Since it lies between God's glory and the Israelites, it explains how they could fail to notice the glory disappearing. **Their thoughts were rendered dull:** the problem lay with their understanding. This will be expressed in vv 14b-16 by a shift in the place of the veil: it is no longer over Moses' face but over their perception.

3, 14b-16: The parallelism in these verses makes it necessary to interpret corresponding parts in relation to one another. **To this present day:** this signals the shift of Paul's attention to his contemporaries; his argument is typological, as in 1 Cor 10. The Israelites of Moses' time typify the Jews of Paul's time, and perhaps also Christians of Jewish origin or mentality who may not recognize the temporary character of Moses' glory. **When they read the old covenant:** the lasting dullness prevents proper appraisal of Moses' person and covenant. When his writings are read in the synagogue, a veil still impedes their understanding. **Through Christ:** i.e., in the new covenant. **Whenever a person turns to the Lord:** Moses in Exodus appeared before God without the veil and gazed on his face unprotected. Paul applies that passage to converts to Christianity: when they turn to the Lord fully and authentically, the impediment to their understanding is removed.

3, 17: **The Lord is the Spirit:** the "Lord" to whom the Christian turns (16) is the Spirit of whom Paul has been

y: Jn 3, 27. *z:* Eph 3, 7 / Jer 31, 31-34. *a:* Ex 34, 29-35. *b:* Rom 11, 7-10. *c:* Ex 34, 34.

freedom. *18d**All of us, gazing with unveiled face on the glory of the Lord, are being transformed into the same image from glory to glory, as from the Lord who is the Spirit.

See RG 461-62

CHAPTER 4

Integrity in the Ministry. *1**Therefore, since we have this ministry through the mercy shown us, we are not discouraged. *2e*Rather, we have renounced shameful, hidden things; not acting deceitfully or falsifying the word of God, but by the open declaration of the truth we commend ourselves to everyone's conscience in the sight of God. *3f**And even though our gospel is veiled, it is veiled for those who are perishing, *4g*in whose case the god of this age has blinded the minds of the unbelievers, so that they may not see the light of the gospel of the glory of Christ, who is the image of God. *5**For we do not preach our-

selves but Jesus Christ as Lord, and ourselves as your slaves for the sake of Jesus. *6h**For God who said, "Let light shine out of darkness," has shone in our hearts to bring to light the knowledge of the glory of God on the face of [Jesus] Christ.

The Paradox of the Ministry. *7**But we hold this treasure in earthen vessels, that the surpassing power may be of God and not from us. *8i**We are afflicted in every way, but not constrained; perplexed, but not driven to despair; *9*persecuted, but not abandoned; struck down, but not destroyed; *10j**always carrying about in the body the dying of Jesus, so that the life of Jesus may also be manifested in our body. *11k*For we who live are constantly being given up to death for the sake of Jesus, so that the life of Jesus may be manifested in our mortal flesh. *12**So death is at work in us, but life in

speaking, the life-giving Spirit of the living God (6.8), the inaugurator of the new covenant and ministry, who is also the Spirit of Christ. **The Spirit of the Lord:** the Lord here is the living God (3), but there may also be an allusion to Christ as Lord (14.16). **Freedom:** i.e., from the ministry of death (7) and the covenant that condemned (9).

3, 18: Another application of the veil image. **All of us . . . with unveiled face:** Christians (Israelites from whom the veil has been removed) are like Moses, standing in God's presence, beholding and reflecting his glory. **Gazing:** the verb may also be translated "contemplating as in a mirror"; 4, 6 would suggest that the mirror is Christ himself. **Are being transformed:** elsewhere Paul speaks of transformation, conformity to Jesus, God's image, as a reality of the end time, and even v 12 speaks of the glory as an object of hope. But the life-giving Spirit, the distinctive gift of the new covenant, is already present in the community (cf 1, 22, the "first installment"), and the process of transformation has already begun. **Into the same image:** into the image of God, which is Christ (4, 4).

4, 1–2: A ministry of this sort generates confidence and forthrightness; cf 1, 12–14; 2, 17.

4, 3–4: **Though our gospel is veiled:** the final application of the image. Paul has been reproached either for obscurity in his preaching or for his manner of presenting the gospel. But he confidently asserts that there is no veil over his gospel. If some fail to perceive its light, that is because of unbelief. The veil lies over their eyes (3, 14), a blindness induced by Satan, and a sign that they are headed for destruction (cf 2, 15).

4, 5: **We do not preach ourselves:** the light seen in his gospel is the glory of Christ (4). Far from preaching himself, the preacher should be a transparent medium through whom Jesus is perceived (cf 10–11). **Your slaves:** Paul draws attention away from individuals as such and toward their role in relation to God, Christ, and the community; cf 1 Cor 3, 5; 4, 1.

4, 6: Autobiographical allusion to the episode at Damascus clarifies the origin and nature of Paul's service; cf Acts 9, 1–19;

22, 3–16; 26, 2–18. **"Let light shine out of darkness":** Paul seems to be thinking of Gn 1, 3 and presenting his apostolic ministry as a new creation. There may also be an allusion to Is 9, 1, suggesting his prophetic calling as servant of the Lord and light to the nations; cf Is 42, 6.16; 49, 6; 60, 1–2, and the use of light imagery in Acts 26, 13–23. **To bring to light the knowledge:** Paul's role in the process of revelation, expressed at the beginning under the image of the odor and aroma (2, 14–15), is restated now, at the end of this first moment of the development, in the imagery of light and glory (3–6).

4, 7—5, 10: Paul now confronts the difficulty that his present existence does not appear glorious at all; it is marked instead by suffering and death. He deals with this by developing the topic already announced in 3, 3.6, asserting his faith in the presence and ultimate triumph of life, in his own and every Christian existence, despite the experience of death.

4, 7: **This treasure:** the glory that he preaches and into which they are being transformed. **In earthen vessels:** the instruments God uses are human and fragile; some imagine small terracotta lamps in which light is carried.

4, 8–9: A catalogue of his apostolic trials and afflictions. Yet in these the negative never completely prevails; there is always some experience of rescue, of salvation.

4, 10–11: Both the negative and the positive sides of the experience are grounded christologically. The logic is similar to that of 1, 3–11. His sufferings are connected with Christ's, and his deliverance is a sign that he is to share in Jesus' resurrection.

4, 12–15: His experience does not terminate in himself, but in others (12.15; cf 1, 4–5). Ultimately, everything is ordered even beyond the community, toward God (15; cf 1, 11).

d: Rom 8, 29-30; 12, 2; Gal 4, 19; Phil 3, 10.20-21 / 4, 4-6;1 Cor 15, 49; Col 1, 15; 3, 9-11; 1 Jn 3, 2. *e:* 2, 17; 1 Thes 2, 4-7. *f:* 2, 15-16; 2 Thes 2, 10. *g:* Jn 12, 31-36 / 1 Tm 1, 11. *h:* Gn 1, 3; Is 9, 1; Acts 26, 13-23; Gal 1, 15-16 / Jn 8, 12;Heb 1, 3. *i:* 6, 4-10; 1 Cor 4, 9-13. *j:* Col 1, 24. *k:* Rom 8, 36; 1 Cor 15, 31.

"In an acceptable time I heard you,
　　and on the day of salvation I helped
　　　　you."

Behold, now is a very acceptable time; behold, now is the day of salvation. ^{3h*}We cause no one to stumble in anything, in order that no fault may be found with our ministry; ^{4i*}on the contrary, in everything we commend ourselves as ministers of God, through much endurance, in afflictions, hardships, constraints, ^{5j}beatings, imprisonments, riots, labors, vigils, fasts; ^{6k*}by purity, knowledge, patience, kindness, in a holy spirit, in unfeigned love, ^{7l}in truthful speech, in the power of God; with weapons of righteousness at the right and at the left; ^{8*}through glory and dishonor, insult and praise. We are treated as deceivers and yet are truthful; ^{9m}as unrecognized and yet acknowledged; as dy-ing and behold we live; as chastised and yet not put to death; ^{10n}as sorrowful yet always rejoicing; as poor yet enriching many; as having nothing and yet possessing all things.

^{11*}We have spoken frankly to you, Corinthians; our heart is open wide. ^{12o}You are not constrained by us; you are constrained by your own affections. ^{13p}As recompense in kind (I speak as to my children), be open yourselves.

Call to Holiness. ^{14*}Do not be yoked with those who are different, with unbelievers. For what partnership do righteousness and lawlessness have? Or what fellowship does light have with darkness? ^{15}What accord has Christ with Beliar? Or what has a believer in common with an unbeliever? ^{16q*}What agreement has the temple of God with idols? For we are the temple of the living God; as God said:

ministry of reconciliation (cf 5, 20) and describes how his ministry is exercised: the "message of reconciliation" (5, 19) is lived existentially in his apostolic experience.

6, 1: Not to receive . . . in vain: i.e., conform to the gift of justification and new creation. The context indicates how this can be done concretely: become God's righteousness (5, 21), not live for oneself (5, 15), be reconciled with Paul (6, 11–13; 7, 2–3).

6, 2: In an acceptable time: Paul cites the Septuagint text of Is 49, 8; the Hebrew reads "in a time of favor"; it is parallel to "on the day of salvation." **Now:** God is bestowing favor and salvation at this very moment, as Paul is addressing his letter to them.

6, 3: Cause no one to stumble: the language echoes that of 1 Cor 8–10, as does the expression "no longer live for themselves" in 5, 15. **That no fault may be found:** i.e., at the eschatological judgment (cf 1 Cor 4, 2–5).

6, 4a: This is the central assertion, the topic statement for the catalogue that follows. **We commend ourselves:** Paul's self-commendation is ironical (with an eye on the charges mentioned in 3, 1–3) and paradoxical (pointing mostly to experiences that would not normally be considered points of pride but are perceived as such by faith). Cf also the self-commendation in 11, 23–29. **As ministers of God:** the same Greek word, **diakonos,** means "minister" and "servant"; cf 11, 23, the central assertion in a similar context, and 1 Cor 3, 5.

6, 4b-5: Through much endurance: this phrase functions as a subtitle; it is followed by an enumeration of nine specific types of trials endured.

6, 6–7a: A list of virtuous qualities in two groups of four, the second fuller than the first.

6, 8b-10: A series of seven rhetorically effective antitheses, contrasting negative external impressions with positive inner reality. Paul perceives his existence as a reflection of Jesus' own and affirms an inner reversal that escapes outward observation. The final two members illustrate two distinct kinds of paradox or apparent contradiction that are characteristic of apostolic experience.

6, 11–13: Paul's tone becomes quieter, but his appeal for acceptance and affection is emotionally charged. References to the heart and their mutual relations bring the development begun in 2, 14—3, 3 to an effective conclusion.

6, 14—7, 1: Language and thought shift noticeably here. Suddenly we are in a different atmosphere, dealing with a quite different problem. Both the vocabulary and the thought, with their contrast between good and evil, are more characteristic of Qumran documents or the Book of Revelation than they are of Paul. Hence, critics suspect that this section was inserted by another hand.

6, 14–16a: The opening injunction to separate from unbelievers is reinforced by five rhetorical questions to make the point that Christianity is not compatible with paganism. Their opposition is emphasized also by the accumulation of five distinct designations for each group. These verses are a powerful statement of God's holiness and the exclusiveness of his claims.

6, 16c-18: This is a chain of scriptural citations carefully woven together. God's covenant relation to his people and his presence among them (16) is seen as conditioned on cultic separation from the profane and cultically impure (17); that relation is translated into the personal language of the parent-child relationship, an extension to the community of the language of 2 Sm 7, 14 (18). Some remarkable parallels to this chain found in the final chapters of Revelation. God's presence among his people (21, 22) is expressed there, too, by applying 2 Sm 7, 14 to the community (21, 7). There is a call to separation (18, 4) and exclusion of the unclean from the community and its liturgy (21, 27). The title "Lord Almighty" (**Pantokratōr**) occurs in the New Testament only here in 18 and nine times in Rv.

h: 1 Cor 9, 12; 10, 32 / 8, 20-21.　i: 4, 8-11; 11, 23-27; 1 Cor 4, 9-13.　j: Acts 16, 23.　k: Gal 5, 22-23.　l: 10, 4; Rom 13, 12; Eph 6, 11-17.　m: 4, 10-11; Rom 8, 36.　n: Rom 8, 32; 1 Cor 3, 21.　o: 7, 3.　p: Gal 4, 19.　q: 1 Cor 10, 20-21 / 1 Cor 3, 16-17; 6, 19 / Ex 25, 8; 29, 45;Lv 26, 12; Jer 31, 1; 32, 38; Ez 37, 27.

"I will live with them and move among them,
  and I will be their God
  and they shall be my people.
[17] [r]Therefore, come forth from them
  and be separate," says the Lord,
  "and touch nothing unclean;
  then I will receive you
[18] [s]and I will be a father to you,
  and you shall be sons and daughters to me,
  says the Lord Almighty."

See RG 462

CHAPTER 7

[1]Since we have these promises, beloved, let us cleanse ourselves from every defilement of flesh and spirit, making holiness perfect in the fear of God. [2]*Make room for us; we have not wronged anyone, or ruined anyone, or taken advantage of anyone. [3t]I do not say this in condemnation, for I have already said that you are in our hearts, that we may die together and live together. [4]I have great confidence in you, I have great pride in you; I am filled with encouragement, I am overflowing with joy all the more because of all our affliction.

C. Resolution of the Crisis

Paul's Joy in Macedonia. [5u]*For even when we came into Macedonia, our flesh had no rest, but we were afflicted in every way— external conflicts, internal fears. [6v]But God, who encourages the downcast, encouraged us by the arrival of Titus, [7]and not only by his arrival but also by the encouragement with which he was encouraged in regard to you, as he told us of your yearning, your lament, your zeal for me, so that I rejoiced even more. [8w]*For even if I saddened you by my letter, I do not regret it; and if I did regret it ([for] I see that that letter saddened you, if only for a while), [9]I rejoice now, not because you were saddened, but because you were saddened into repentance; for you were saddened in a godly way, so that you did not suffer loss in anything because of us. [10]For godly sorrow produces a salutary repentance without regret, but worldly sorrow produces death. [11]For behold what earnestness this godly sorrow has produced for you, as well as readiness for a defense, and indignation, and fear, and yearning, and zeal, and punishment. In every way you have shown yourselves to be innocent in the matter. [12x]So then even though I wrote to you, it was not on account of the one who did the wrong, or on account of the one who suffered the wrong, but in order that your concern for us might be made plain to you in the sight of God. [13]*For this reason we are encouraged.

And besides our encouragement, we rejoice even more because of the joy of Titus, since his spirit has been refreshed by all of you. [14]For if I have boasted to him about you, I was not put to shame. No, just as everything we said to you was true, so our boasting before Titus proved to be the truth. [15y]And his heart goes out to you all the more,

7, 2–4: These verses continue the thought of 6, 11–13, before the interruption of 6, 14—7, 1. Verse 4 serves as a transition to the next section: the four themes it introduces (confidence; pride or "boasting"; encouragement; joy in affliction) are developed in vv 5–16. All have appeared previously in the letter.

7, 5–16: This section functions as a peroration or formal summing up of the whole first part of the letter, chs 1–7. It deals with the restoration of right relations between Paul and the Corinthians, and it is marked by fullness and intensity of emotion.

7, 5–7: Paul picks up the thread of the narrative interrupted at 2, 13 (5) and describes the resolution of the tense situation there depicted (6–7). Finally Titus arrives and his coming puts an end to Paul's restlessness (2, 13; 7, 5), casts out his fears, and reverses his mood. The theme of encouragement and affliction is reintroduced (cf 1, 3–11); here, too, encouragement is traced back to God and is described as contagious (6). The language of joy and sorrow also reappears in v 11.

7 (cf 1, 23—2, 1 and the note on 1, 23–24).

7, 5: Macedonia: see the note on 2, 13.

7, 8–12: Paul looks back on the episode from the viewpoint of its ending. The goal of their common activity, promotion of their joy (1, 24), has been achieved, despite and because of the sorrow they felt. That sorrow was God-given. Its salutary effects are enumerated fully and impressively in vv 10–11; not the least important of these is that it has revealed to them the attachment they have to Paul.

7, 13–16: Paul summarizes the effect of the experience on Titus: encouragement, joy, love, relief. Finally, he describes its effects on himself: encouragement, joy, confidence, pride or "boasting" (i.e., the satisfaction resulting from a boast that proves well-founded; cf 4; 1, 12.14).

r: Is 52, 11; Ez 20, 34.41; Rv 18, 4; 21, 27. s: 2 Sm 7, 14; Ps 2, 7; Is 43, 6; Jer 31, 9; Rv 21, 7 / Rv 4, 8;11, 17; 15, 3; 21, 22. t: 6, 11-13. u: 2, 13. v: 7, 13-14; 1 Thes 3, 6-8. w: 2, 2-4; Heb 12, 11. x: 2, 3.9; 7, 8. y: 2, 9.

as he remembers the obedience of all of you, when you received him with fear and trembling. [16]I rejoice, because I have confidence in you in every respect.

III: The Collection for Jerusalem

CHAPTER 8

See RG 462-63

Generosity in Giving. [1z*]We want you to know, brothers, of the grace of God that has been given to the churches of Macedonia, [2*]for in a severe test of affliction, the abundance of their joy and their profound poverty overflowed in a wealth of generosity on their part. [3*]For according to their means, I can testify, and beyond their means,

spontaneously, [4a]they begged us insistently for the favor of taking part in the service to the holy ones, [5*]and this, not as we expected, but they gave themselves first to the Lord and to us through the will of God, [6b*]so that we urged Titus that, as he had already begun, he should also complete for you this gracious act also. [7c*]Now as you excel in every respect, in faith, discourse, knowledge, all earnestness, and in the love we have for you, may you excel in this gracious act also.

[8]I say this not by way of command, but to test the genuineness of your love by your concern for others. [9d*]For you know the gracious act of our Lord Jesus Christ, that for your sake he became poor although he was

---

8, 1—9, 15: Paul turns to a new topic, the collection for the church in Jerusalem. There is an early precedent for this project in the agreement mentioned in Gal 2, 6–10. According to Acts, the church at Antioch had sent Saul and Barnabas to Jerusalem with relief (Acts 11, 27–30). Subsequently Paul organized a project of relief for Jerusalem among his own churches. Our earliest evidence for it comes in 1 Cor 16, 1–4, after it had already begun (see the notes there); by the time Paul wrote Rom 15, 25–28 the collection was completed and ready for delivery. Chapters 8 and 9 contain what appear to be two letters on the subject. In them Paul gives us his fullest exposition of the meaning he sees in the enterprise, presenting it as an act of Christian charity and as an expression of the unity of the church, both present and eschatological. These chapters are especially rich in the recurrence of key words, on which Paul plays; it is usually impossible to do justice to these wordplays in the translation.

8, 1–24: This is a letter of recommendation for Titus and two unnamed companions, written from Macedonia probably at least a year later than 1 Cor 16. The recommendation proper is prefaced by remarks about the ideals of sharing and equality within the Christian community (1–15). Phil 4, 10–20 shows that Paul has reflected on his personal experience of need and relief in his relations with the community at Philippi; he now develops his reflections on the larger scale of relations between his Gentile churches and the mother church in Jerusalem.

8, 1–5: The example of the Macedonians, a model of what ought to be happening at Corinth, provides Paul with the occasion for expounding his theology of "giving."

8, 1: The grace of God: the fundamental theme is expressed by the Greek noun **charis,** which will be variously translated throughout these chapters as "grace" (8, 1; 9, 8.14), "favor" (8, 4), "gracious act" (8, 6.7.9) or "gracious work" (8, 19), to be compared to "gracious gift" (1 Cor 16, 3). The related term, **eucharistia,** "thanksgiving," also occurs at 9, 11.12. The wordplay is not superficial; various mutations of the same root signal inner connection between aspects of a single reality, and Paul consciously exploits the similarities in vocabulary to highlight that connection.

8, 2: Three more terms are now introduced. **Test**

(**dokimē**): the same root is translated as "to test" (8) and "evidence" (9, 13); it means to be tried and found genuine. **Abundance:** variations on the same root lie behind "overflow" (8, 2; 9, 12), "excel" (8, 7), "surplus" (8, 14), "superfluous" (9, 1), "make abundant" and "have an abundance" (9, 8). These expressions of fullness contrast with references to need (8, 14; 9, 12). **Generosity:** the word **haplotēs** has nuances of both simplicity and sincerity; here and in 9, 11.13 it designates the singleness of purpose that manifests itself in generous giving.

8, 3–4: Paul emphasizes the spontaneity of the Macedonians and the nature of their action. **They begged us insistently:** the same root is translated as "urge," "appeal," "encourage" (8, 6.17; 9, 5). **Taking part:** the same word is translated "contribution" in 9, 13 and a related term as "partner" in 8, 23. **Service (diakonia):** this word occurs also in 9, 1.13 as "service"; in 9, 12 it is translated "administration," and in 8, 19.20 the corresponding verb is rendered "administer."

8, 5: They gave themselves ... to the Lord and to us: on its deepest level their attitude is one of self-giving.

8, 6: Titus: 1 Cor 16 seemed to leave the organization up to the Corinthians, but apparently Paul has sent Titus to initiate the collection as well; 8, 16–17 will describe Titus' attitude as one of shared concern and cooperation.

8, 7: The charitable service Paul is promoting is seen briefly and in passing within the perspective of Paul's theology of the charisms. **Earnestness (spoudē):** this or related terms occur also in v 22 ("earnest") and 8, 8.16.17 ("concern").

8, 9: The dialectic of Jesus' experience, expressed earlier in terms of life and death (5, 15), sin and righteousness (5, 21), is now rephrased in terms of poverty and wealth. Many scholars think this is a reference to Jesus' preexistence with God (his "wealth") and to his incarnation and death (his "poverty"), and they point to the similarity between this verse and Phil 2, 6–8. Others interpret the wealth and poverty as succeeding phases of Jesus' earthly existence, e.g., his sense of intimacy with God and then the desolation and the feeling of abandonment by God in his death (cf Mk 15, 34).

---

z: 11, 9; Rom 15, 26. a: Acts 24, 17; Rom 15, 31. b: 2, 13; 7, 6-7.13-14; 8, 16.23; 12, 18. c: 1 Cor 1, 5. d: 6, 10; Phil 2, 6-8.

rich, so that by his poverty you might become rich. [10e]And I am giving counsel in this matter, for it is appropriate for you who began not only to act but to act willingly last year: [11*]complete it now, so that your eager willingness may be matched by your completion of it out of what you have. [12*]For if the eagerness is there, it is acceptable according to what one has, not according to what one does not have; [13]not that others should have relief while you are burdened, but that as a matter of equality [14]your surplus at the present time should supply their needs, so that their surplus may also supply your needs, that there may be equality. [15f]As it is written:

"Whoever had much did not have more,
and whoever had little did not have
less."

Titus and His Collaborators. [16*]But thanks be to God who put the same concern for you into the heart of Titus, [17]for he not only welcomed our appeal but, since he is very concerned, he has gone to you of his own accord. [18g*]With him we have sent the brother who is praised in all the churches for his preaching of the gospel. [19h]And not only that, but he has also been appointed our traveling companion by the churches in this gracious work administered by us for the glory of the Lord [himself] and for the expression

of our eagerness. [20*]This we desire to avoid, that anyone blame us about this lavish gift administered by us, [21i]for we are concerned for what is honorable not only in the sight of the Lord but also in the sight of others. [22]And with them we have sent our brother whom we often tested in many ways and found earnest, but who is now much more earnest because of his great confidence in you. [23]As for Titus, he is my partner and co-worker for you; as for our brothers, they are apostles of the churches, the glory of Christ. [24*]So give proof before the churches of your love and of our boasting about you to them.

CHAPTER 9

See RG 462–63

God's Indescribable Gift. [1*]Now about the service to the holy ones, it is superfluous for me to write to you, [2j*]for I know your eagerness, about which I boast of you to the Macedonians, that Achaia has been ready since last year; and your zeal has stirred up most of them. [3*]Nonetheless, I sent the brothers so that our boast about you might not prove empty in this case, so that you might be ready, as I said, [4]for fear that if any Macedonians come with me and find you not ready we might be put to shame (to say nothing of you) in this conviction. [5]So I thought it necessary to encourage the brothers to go on ahead of you and arrange in advance for your promised gift, so that in this

8, 11: Eager: the word **prothymia** also occurs in 8, 12.19; 9, 2.

8, 12–15: Paul introduces the principle of **equality** into the discussion. The goal is not impoverishment but sharing of resources; balance is achieved at least over the course of time. In v 15 Paul grounds his argument unexpectedly in the experience of Israel gathering manna in the desert: equality was achieved, independently of personal exertion, by God, who gave with an even hand according to need. Paul touches briefly here on the theme of "living from God."

8, 16–24: In recommending Titus and his companions, Paul stresses their personal and apostolic qualities, their good dispositions toward the Corinthians, and their authority as messengers of the churches and representatives of Christ.

8, 18: The brother: we do not know the identity of this co-worker of Paul, nor of the third companion mentioned below in v 22.

8, 20–22: That anyone blame us: 12, 16–18 suggests that misunderstandings may indeed have arisen concerning Paul's management of the collection through the messengers mentioned here, but those same verses seem to imply that the Corinthians by and large would recognize the honesty of Paul's

conduct in this area as in others (cf 6, 3).

8, 24: As Paul began by holding up the Macedonians as examples to be imitated, he closes by exhorting the Corinthians to show their love (by accepting the envoys and by cooperating as the Macedonians do), thus justifying the pride Paul demonstrates because of them before other churches.

9, 1–15: Quite possibly this was originally an independent letter, though it deals with the same subject and continues many of the same themes. In that case, it may have been written a few weeks later than ch 8, while the delegation there mentioned was still on its way.

9, 2: Achaia: see the note on Rom 15, 26.

9, 3: I sent the brothers: the Greek aorist tense here could be epistolary, referring to the present; in that case Paul would be sending them now, and ch 9 would merely conclude the letter of recommendation begun in ch 8. But the aorist may also refer to a sending that is past as Paul writes; then ch 9, with its apparently fresh beginning, is a follow-up message entrusted to another carrier.

e: 9, 2; 1 Cor 16, 1-4. *f:* Ex 16, 18. *g:* 12, 18. *h:* 1 Cor 16, 3-4. *i:* Rom 12, 17. *j:* 8, 10; Rom 15, 26.

way it might be ready as a bountiful gift and not as an exaction.

⁶ᵏConsider this: whoever sows sparingly will also reap sparingly, and whoever sows bountifully will also reap bountifully. ⁷ˡEach must do as already determined, without sadness or compulsion, for God loves a cheerful giver. ⁸*Moreover, God is able to make every grace abundant for you, so that in all things, always having all you need, you may have an abundance for every good work. ⁹ᵐAs it is written:

"He scatters abroad, he gives to the poor;
his righteousness endures forever."

¹⁰ⁿThe one who supplies seed to the sower and bread for food will supply and multiply your seed and increase the harvest of your righteousness. ¹¹*You are being enriched in every way for all generosity, which through us produces thanksgiving to God, ¹²for the administration of this public service is not only supplying the needs of the holy ones but is also overflowing in many acts of thanksgiving to God. ¹³ᵒThrough the evidence of this service, you are glorifying God for your obedient confession of the gospel of Christ and the generosity of your contribution to them and to all others, ¹⁴while in prayer on your behalf they long for you, because of the surpassing grace of God upon you. ¹⁵ᵖThanks be to God for his indescribable gift!

IV: Paul's Defense of His Ministry

CHAPTER 10

See RG
463–64

Accusation of Weakness. ¹*Now I myself, Paul, urge you through the gentleness and clemency of Christ, I who am humble when face to face with you, but brave toward you when absent, ²�q*I beg you that, when present, I may not have to be brave with that confidence with which I intend to act boldly

---

9, 8–10: The behavior to which he exhorts them is grounded in God's own pattern of behavior. God is capable of overwhelming generosity, as scripture itself attests (9), so that they need not fear being short. He will provide in abundance, both supplying their natural needs and increasing their righteousness. Paul challenges them to godlike generosity and reminds them of the fundamental motive for encouragement: God himself cannot be outdone.

9, 11–15: Paul's vision broadens to take in all the interested parties in one dynamic picture. His language becomes liturgically colored and conveys a sense of fullness. With a final play on the words **charis** and **eucharistia** (see the note on 8, 1), he describes a circle that closes on itself: the movement of grace overflowing from God to them and handed on from them through Paul to others is completed by the prayer of praise and thanksgiving raised on their behalf to God.

10, 1—13, 10: These final chapters have their own unity of structure and theme and could well have formed the body of a separate letter. They constitute an **apologia** on Paul's part, i.e., a legal defense of his behavior and his ministry; the writing is emotionally charged and highly rhetorical. In the central section (11, 16—12, 10), the **apologia** takes the form of a boast. This section is prepared for by a prologue (11, 1–15) and followed by an epilogue (12, 11–18), which are similar in content and structure. These sections, in turn, are framed by an introduction (10, 1–18) and a conclusion (12, 19—13, 10), both of which assert Paul's apostolic authority and confidence and define the purpose of the letter. The structure that results from this disposition of the material is chiastic, i.e., the first element corresponds to the last, the second to the second last, etc., following the pattern **a b c b¹ a¹**.

10, 1–18: Paul asserts his apostolic authority and ex-

presses the confidence this generates in him. He writes in response to certain opinions that have arisen in the community and certain charges raised against him and in preparation for a forthcoming visit in which he intends to set things in order. This section gives us an initial glimpse of the situation in Corinth that Paul must address; much of its thematic material will be taken up again in the finale (12, 19—13, 10).

10, 1–2: A strong opening plunges us straight into the conflict. Contrasts dominate here: presence versus absence, gentleness-clemency-humility versus boldness-confidence-bravery. **Through the gentleness and clemency of Christ:** the figure of the gentle Christ, presented in a significant position before any specifics of the situation are suggested, forms a striking contrast to the picture of the bold and militant Paul (2–6); this tension is finally resolved in 13, 3–4. **Absent . . . present:** this same contrast, with a restatement of the purpose of the letter, recurs in 13, 10, which forms an inclusion with 10, 1–2.

10, 2b–4a: Flesh: the Greek word **sarx** can express both the physical life of the body without any pejorative overtones (as in "we are in the flesh," 3) and also our natural life insofar as it is marked by limitation and weakness (as in the other expressions) in contrast to the higher life and power conferred by the Spirit; cf the note on 1 Cor 3, 1. The wordplay is intended to express the paradoxical situation of a life already taken over by the Spirit but not yet seen as such except by faith. Lack of empirical evidence of the Spirit permits misunderstanding and misjudgment, but Paul resolutely denies that his behavior and effectiveness are as limited as some suppose.

k: Prv 11, 24-25. *l:* Prv 22, 8 LXX. *m:* Ps 112, 9. *n:* Is 55, 10. *o:* 8, 4; Rom 15, 31. *p:* Rom 5, 15-16. *q:* 13, 2.10; 1 Cor 4, 21.

against some who consider us as acting according to the flesh. *3**For, although we are in the flesh, we do not battle according to the flesh, *4r*for the weapons of our battle are not of flesh but are enormously powerful, capable of destroying fortresses. We destroy arguments *5*and every pretension raising itself against the knowledge of God, and take every thought captive in obedience to Christ, *6s*and we are ready to punish every disobedience, once your obedience is complete.

7t*Look at what confronts you. Whoever is confident of belonging to Christ should consider that as he belongs to Christ, so do we. *8u*And even if I should boast a little too much of our authority, which the Lord gave for building you up and not for tearing you down, I shall not be put to shame. *9**May I not seem as one frightening you through letters. *10v*For someone will say, "His letters are severe and forceful, but his bodily presence is weak, and his speech contemptible." *11w*Such a person must understand that what we are in word through letters when absent, that we also are in action when present.

12x*Not that we dare to class or compare ourselves with some of those who recommend themselves. But when they measure themselves by one another and compare themselves with one another, they are without understanding. *13**But we will not boast beyond measure but will keep to the limits God has apportioned us, namely, to reach even to you. *14*For we are not overreaching ourselves, as though we did not reach you; we indeed first came to you with the gospel of Christ. *15*We are not boasting beyond measure, in other people's labors; yet our hope is that, as your faith increases, our influence among you may be greatly enlarged, within our proper limits, *16y*so that we may preach the gospel even beyond you, not boasting of work already done in another's sphere. *17z**"Whoever boasts, should boast in the Lord." *18a**For it is not the one who recommends himself who is approved, but the one whom the Lord recommends.

CHAPTER 11

See RG 463–64

Preaching without Charge. *1b**If only you would put up with a little foolishness

10, 3b-6: Paul is involved in combat. The strong military language and imagery are both an assertion of his confidence in the divine power at his disposal and a declaration of war against those who underestimate his resources. The threat is echoed in 13, 2–3.

10, 7–8: Belonging to Christ . . . so do we: these phrases already announce the pattern of Paul's boast in 11, 21b-29, especially 11, 22–23. For building you up and not for tearing you down: Paul draws on the language by which Jeremiah described the purpose of the prophetic power the Lord gave to him (Jer 1, 9–10; 12, 16–17; 24, 6). Though Paul's power may have destructive effects on others (2–6), its intended effect on the community is entirely constructive (cf 13, 10). I shall not be put to shame: his assertions will not be refuted; they will be revealed as true at the judgment.

10, 9–10: Paul cites the complaints of some who find him lacking in personal forcefulness and holds out the threat of a personal parousia (both "return" and "presence") that will be forceful, indeed will be a demonstration of Christ's own power (cf 13, 2–4).

10, 12–18: Paul now qualifies his claim to boldness, indicating its limits. He distinguishes his own behavior from that of others, revealing those "others" as they appear to him: as self-recommending, immoderately boastful, encroaching on territory not assigned to them, and claiming credit not due to them.

10, 13: Will keep to the limits: the notion of proper limits is expressed here by two terms with overlapping meanings, metron and kanōn, which are played off against several expressions denoting overreaching or expansion beyond a legitimate sphere.

10, 17: Boast in the Lord: there is a legitimate boasting, in contrast to the immoderate boasting to which vv 13 and 15 allude. God's work through Paul in the community is the object of his boast (13–16; 1, 12–14) and constitutes his recommendation (3, 1–3). Cf the notes on 1, 12–14 and 1 Cor 1, 29–31.

10, 18: Approved: to be approved is to come successfully through the process of testing for authenticity (cf 13, 3–7 and the note on 8, 2). Whom the Lord recommends: self-commendation is a premature and unwarranted anticipation of the final judgment, which the Lord alone will pass (cf 1 Cor 4, 3–5). Paul alludes to this judgment throughout chs 10–13, frequently in final or transitional positions; cf 11, 15; 12, 19a; 13, 3–7.

11, 1–15: Although these verses continue to reveal information about Paul's opponents and the differences he perceives between them and himself, 11, 1 signals a turn in Paul's thought. This section constitutes a prologue to the boasting that he will undertake in 11, 16—12, 10, and it bears remarkable similarities to the section that follows the central boast, 12, 11–18.

11, 1: Put up with a little foolishness from me: this verse indicates more clearly than the general statement of intent in 10, 13 the nature of the project Paul is about to undertake. He alludes ironically to the Corinthians' toleration for others. Foolishness: Paul qualifies his project as folly from beginning to end; see the note on 11, 16—12, 10.

r: 6, 7; 13, 2-3; 1 Cor 1, 25; Eph 6, 10-14. s: 2, 9. t: 1 Cor 1, 12. u: 13, 10. v: 1 Cor 2, 3. w: 13, 1-2. x: 3, 1-2; 4, 2; 5, 12; 6, 4; 10, 18; 12, 11. y: Rom 15, 20-21. z: Jer 9, 22-23; 1 Cor 1, 31. a: 13, 3-9. b: 11, 21; 12, 11.

from me! Please put up with me. [2c]*For I am jealous of you with the jealousy of God, since I betrothed you to one husband to present you as a chaste virgin to Christ. [3d]*But I am afraid that, as the serpent deceived Eve by his cunning, your thoughts may be corrupted from a sincere [and pure] commitment to Christ. [4e]*For if someone comes and preaches another Jesus than the one we preached, or if you receive a different spirit from the one you received or a different gospel from the one you accepted, you put up with it well enough. [5f]*For I think that I am not in any way inferior to these "superapostles." [6g]*Even if I am untrained in speaking, I am not so in knowledge; in every way we have made this plain to you in all things.

[7h]*Did I make a mistake when I humbled myself so that you might be exalted, because I preached the gospel of God to you without charge? [8]I plundered other churches by accepting from them in order to minister to you. [9i]And when I was with you and in need, I did not burden anyone, for the brothers who came from Macedonia supplied my needs. So I refrained and will refrain from burdening you in any way. [10j]By the truth of Christ in me, this boast of mine shall not be silenced in the regions of Achaia. [11k]*And why? Because I do not love you? God knows I do!

[12]And what I do I will continue to do, in order to end this pretext of those who seek a pretext for being regarded as we are in the mission of which they boast. [13]*For such people are false apostles, deceitful workers, who masquerade as apostles of Christ. [14]And no wonder, for even Satan masquerades as an angel of light. [15]So it is not strange that his ministers also masquerade as ministers of righteousness. Their end will correspond to their deeds.

11, 2: Paul gives us a sudden glimpse of the theological values that are at stake. **The jealousy of God:** the perspective is that of the covenant, described in imagery of love and marriage, as in the prophets; cf 1 Cor 10, 22. **I betrothed you:** Paul, like a father (cf 12, 14), betroths the community to Christ as his bride (cf Eph 5, 21–33) and will present her to him at his second coming. Cf Mt 25, 1–13 and the nuptial imagery in Rv 21.

11, 3: **As the serpent deceived Eve:** before Christ can return for the community Paul fears a repetition of the primal drama of seduction. Corruption of minds is satanic activity (see 2, 11; 4, 4). Satanic imagery recurs in 11, 13–15.20; 12, 7b.16–17; see the notes on these passages.

11, 4: **Preaches another Jesus:** the danger is specified, and Paul's opponents are identified with the cunning serpent. The battle for minds has to do with the understanding of Jesus, the Spirit, the gospel; the Corinthians have flirted with another understanding than the one that Paul handed on to them as traditional and normative.

11, 5: **These "superapostles":** this term, employed again in 12, 11b, designates the opponents of whom Paul has spoken in ch 10 and again in 11, 4. They appear to be intruders at Corinth. Their preaching is marked at least by a different emphasis and style, and they do not hesitate to accept support from the community. Perhaps these itinerants appeal to the authority of church leaders in Jerusalem and even carry letters of recommendation from them. But it is not those distant leaders whom Paul is attacking here. The intruders are "superapostles" not in the sense of the "pillars" at Jerusalem (Gal 2), but in their own estimation. They consider themselves superior to Paul as apostles and ministers of Christ, and they are obviously enjoying some success among the Corinthians. Paul rejects their claim to be apostles in any superlative sense (**hyperlian**), judging them bluntly as "false apostles," ministers of Satan masquerading as apostles of Christ (13–15). On the contrary, he himself will claim to be a superminister of Christ (**hyper egō**, 23).

11, 6: Apparently found deficient in both rhetorical ability (cf 10, 10) and knowledge (cf 10, 5), Paul concedes the former charge but not the latter. **In every way:** in all their contacts with him revelation has been taking place. Paul, through whom God reveals the knowledge of himself (2, 14), and in whom the death and life of Jesus are revealed (4, 10–11; cf 6, 4), also demonstrates his own role as the bearer of true knowledge. Cf 1 Cor 1, 18—2, 16.

11, 7–10: Abruptly Paul passes to another reason for complaints: his practice of preaching without remuneration (cf 1 Cor 9, 3–18). He deftly defends his practice by situating it from the start within the pattern of Christ's own self-humiliation (cf 10, 1) and reduces objections to absurdity by rhetorical questions (cf 12, 13).

11, 11–12: Paul rejects lack of affection as his motive (possibly imputed to him by his opponents) and states his real motive, a desire to emphasize the disparity between himself and the others (cf 19–21). The topic of his gratuitous service will be taken up once more in 12, 13–18. 1 Cor 9, 15–18 gives a different but complementary explanation of his motivation.

11, 13–15: Paul picks up again the imagery of v 3 and applies it to the opponents: they are false apostles of Christ, really serving another master. **Deceitful . . . masquerade:** deception and simulation, like cunning (3), are marks of the satanic. **Angel of light:** recalls the contrast between light and darkness, Christ and Beliar at 6, 14–15. **Ministers of righteousness:** recalls the earlier contrast between the ministry of condemnation and that of righteousness (3, 9). **Their end:** the section closes with another allusion to the judgment, when all participants in the final conflict will be revealed or unmasked and dealt with as they deserve.

c: Hos 2, 21-22; Eph 5, 26-27. d: Gn 3, 1-6. e: Gal 1, 6-9. f: 12, 11. g: 1 Cor 1, 5.17; 2, 1-5. h: 12, 13-18; Acts 18, 3; 1 Cor 9, 6-18. i: Phil 4, 15.18. j: 1 Cor 9, 15. k: 12, 15.

Paul's Boast: His Labors. ¹⁶*I repeat, no one should consider me foolish; but if you do, accept me as a fool, so that I too may boast a little. ¹⁷What I am saying I am not saying according to the Lord but as in foolishness, in this boastful state. ¹⁸Since many boast according to the flesh, I too will boast. ¹⁹For you gladly put up with fools, since you are wise yourselves. ²⁰*For you put up with it if someone enslaves you, or devours you, or gets the better of you, or puts on airs, or slaps you in the face. ²¹*To my shame I say that we were too weak!

But what anyone dares to boast of (I am speaking in foolishness) I also dare. ²²*Are they Hebrews? So am I. Are they Israelites? So am I. Are they descendants of Abraham? So am I. ^{23m}*Are they ministers of Christ? (I am talking like an insane person.) I am still more, with far greater labors, far more imprisonments, far worse beatings, and numerous brushes with death. ²⁴ⁿFive times at the hands of the Jews I received forty lashes minus one. ^{25o}Three times I was beaten with rods, once I was stoned, three times I was shipwrecked, I passed a night and a day on the deep; ²⁶on frequent journeys, in dangers from rivers, dangers from robbers, dangers from my own race, dangers from Gentiles, dangers in the city, dangers in the wilderness, dangers at sea, dangers among false brothers; ^{27p}in toil and hardship, through many sleepless nights, through hunger and thirst, through frequent fastings, through cold and exposure. ²⁸And apart from these things, there is the daily pressure upon me of my anxiety for all the churches. ^{29q}Who is weak, and I am not weak? Who is led to sin, and I am not indignant?

Paul's Boast: His Weakness. ³⁰*If I must boast, I will boast of the things that show my weakness. ³¹*The God and Father of the Lord Jesus knows, he who is blessed forever, that I do not lie. ³²At Damascus, the governor under King Aretas guarded the city of Damascus, in order to seize me, ^{33r}but I was lowered in a basket through a window in the wall and escaped his hands.

CHAPTER 12

See RG
463-64

¹*I must boast; not that it is profitable, but I will go on to visions and revelations of

---

11, 16—12, 10: Paul now accepts the challenge of his opponents and indulges in boasting similar to theirs, but with differences that he has already signaled in 10, 12–18 and that become clearer as he proceeds. He defines the nature of his project and unmistakably labels it as folly at the beginning and the end (11, 16–23; 12, 11). Yet his boast does not spring from ignorance (11, 21; 12, 6) nor is it concerned merely with human distinctions (11, 18). Paul boasts "in moderation" (10, 13.15) and "in the Lord" (10, 17).

11, 16–29: The first part of Paul's boast focuses on labors and afflictions, in which authentic service of Christ consists.

11, 16–21: These verses recapitulate remarks already made about the foolishness of boasting and the excessive toleration of the Corinthians. They form a prelude to the boast proper.

11, 20: Paul describes the activities of the "others" in terms that fill out the picture drawn in vv 3–4.13–15. Much of the vocabulary suggests fleshly or even satanic activity. **Enslaves:** cf Gal 2, 4. **Devours:** cf 1 Pt 5, 8. **Gets the better:** the verb **lambanō** means "to take," but is used in a variety of senses; here it may imply financial advantage, as in the English colloquialism "to take someone." It is similarly used at 12, 16 and is there connected with cunning and deceit. **Puts on airs:** the same verb is rendered "raise oneself" (10, 5) and "be too elated" (12, 7).

11, 21: Paul ironically concedes the charge of personal weakness from 10, 1–18 but will refute the other charge there mentioned, that of lack of boldness, accepting the challenge to demonstrate it by his boast.

11, 22: The opponents apparently pride themselves on their "Jewishness." Paul, too, can claim to be a Jew by race, religion, and promise. **Descendants of Abraham:** elsewhere Paul distinguishes authentic from inauthentic heirs of Abraham and the promise (Rom 4, 13–18; 9, 7–13; 11, 1; Gal 3, 9.27–29; cf Jn 8, 33–47). Here he grants his opponents this title in order to concentrate on the principal claim that follows.

11, 23a: Ministers of Christ . . . I am still more: the central point of the boast (cf the note on 11, 5). **Like an insane person:** the climax of his folly.

11, 23b–29: Service of the humiliated and crucified Christ is demonstrated by trials endured for him. This rhetorically impressive catalogue enumerates many of the labors and perils Paul encountered on his missionary journeys.

11, 30—12, 10: The second part of Paul's boast, marked by a change of style and a shift in focus. After recalling the project in which he is engaged, he states a new topic: his weaknesses as matter for boasting. Everything in this section, even the discussion of privileges and distinctions, will be integrated into this perspective.

11, 31–32: The episode at Damascus is symbolic. It aptly illustrates Paul's weakness but ends in deliverance (cf 4, 7–11).

12, 1–4: In the body or out of the body: he seemed no longer confined to bodily conditions, but he does not claim to understand the mechanics of the experience. **Caught up:** i.e., in ecstasy. **The third heaven . . . Paradise:** ancient cosmolo-

l: Acts 22, 3 / Rom 11, 1; Phil 3, 5-6.   *m:* 6, 5; Acts 16, 22-24; 1 Cor 15, 31-32.   *n:* Dt 25, 2-3.   *o:* Acts 14, 19; 27, 43-44. *p:* 1 Cor 4, 11.   *q:* 1 Cor 9, 22.   *r:* Acts 9, 23-25.

the Lord. [2]I know someone in Christ who, fourteen years ago (whether in the body or out of the body I do not know, God knows), was caught up to the third heaven. [3]And I know that this person (whether in the body or out of the body I do not know, God knows) [4s]was caught up into Paradise and heard ineffable things, which no one may utter. [5*]About this person I will boast, but about myself I will not boast, except about my weaknesses. [6]Although if I should wish to boast, I would not be foolish, for I would be telling the truth. But I refrain, so that no one may think more of me than what he sees in me or hears from me [7t*]because of the abundance of the revelations. Therefore, that I might not become too elated, a thorn in the flesh was given to me, an angel of Satan, to beat me, to keep me from being too elated. [8u*]Three times I begged the Lord about this, that it might leave me, [9v*]but he said to me, "My grace is sufficient for you, for power is made perfect in weakness." I will rather boast most gladly of my weaknesses, in order that the power of Christ may dwell with me. [10w*]Therefore, I am content with weaknesses, insults, hardships, persecutions, and constraints, for the sake of Christ; for when I am weak, then I am strong.

Selfless Concern for the Church. [11x*]I have been foolish. You compelled me, for I ought to have been commended by you. For I am in no way inferior to these "superapostles," even though I am nothing. [12y*]The

---

gies depicted a multitiered universe. Jewish intertestamental literature contains much speculation about the number of heavens. Seven is the number usually mentioned, but the Testament of Levi (2, 7–10; 3, 1–4) speaks of three; God himself dwelt in the third of these. Without giving us any clear picture of the cosmos, Paul indicates a mental journey to a nonearthly space, set apart by God, in which secrets were revealed to him. **Ineffable things:** i.e., privileged knowledge, which it was not possible or permitted to divulge.

12, 5–7: This person: the indirect way of referring to himself has the effect of emphasizing the distance between that experience and his everyday life, just as the indirect **someone in Christ** (2) and all the passive verbs emphasize his passivity and receptivity in the experience. The revelations were not a personal achievement, nor were they meant to draw attention to any quality of his own.

12, 7b: That I might not become too elated: God assures that there is a negative component to his experience, so that he cannot lose proper perspective; cf 1, 9; 4, 7–11. **A thorn in the flesh:** variously interpreted as a sickness or physical disability, a temptation, or a handicap connected with his apostolic activity. But since Hebrew "thorn in the flesh," like English "thorn in my side," refers to persons (cf Nm 33, 55; Ez 28, 24), Paul may be referring to some especially persistent and obnoxious opponent. The language of vv 7–8 permits this interpretation. If this is correct, the frequent appearance of singular pronouns in depicting the opposition may not be merely a stylistic variation; the singular may be provoked and accompanied by the image of one individual in whom criticism of Paul's preaching, way of life, and apostolic consciousness is concentrated, and who embodies all the qualities Paul attributes to the group. **An angel of Satan:** a personal messenger from Satan; cf the satanic language already applied to the opponents in 11, 3.13–15.20.

12, 8: Three times: his prayer was insistent, like that of Jesus in Gethsemane, a sign of how intolerable he felt the thorn to be.

12, 9: But he said to me: Paul's petition is denied; release and healing are withheld for a higher purpose. The Greek perfect tense indicates that Jesus' earlier response still holds at the time of writing. **My grace is sufficient for you:** this is not a statement about the sufficiency of grace in general. Jesus speaks directly to Paul's situation. **Is made perfect:** i.e., is given most fully and manifests itself fully.

12, 9b-10a: Paul draws the conclusion from the autobiographical anecdote and integrates it into the subject of this part of the boast. **Weaknesses:** the apostolic hardships he must endure, including active personal hostility, as specified in a final catalogue (10a). **That the power of Christ may dwell with me:** Paul pinpoints the ground for the paradoxical strategy he has adopted in his self-defense.

12, 10b: When I am weak, then I am strong: Paul recognizes a twofold pattern in the resolution of the weakness-power (and death-life) dialectic, each of which looks to Jesus as the model and is experienced in him. The first is personal, involving a reversal in oneself (Jesus, 13, 4a; Paul, 1, 9–10; 4, 10–11; 6, 9). The second is apostolic, involving an effect on others (Jesus, 5, 14–15; Paul, 1, 6; 4, 12; 13, 9). The specific kind of "effectiveness in ministry" that Paul promises to demonstrate on his arrival (13, 4b; cf 10, 1–11) involves elements of both; this, too, will be modeled on Jesus' experience and a participation in that experience (9; 13, 3b).

12, 11–18: This brief section forms an epilogue or concluding observation to Paul's boast, corresponding to the prologue in 11, 1–15. A four-step sequence of ideas is common to these two sections: Paul qualifies his boast as folly (11, 1; 12, 11a), asserts his noninferiority to the "superapostles" (11, 5; 12, 11b), exemplifies this by allusion to charismatic endowments (11, 6; 12, 12), and finally denies that he has been a financial burden to the community (11, 7–12; 12, 13–18).

12, 12: Despite weakness and affliction (suggested by the mention of endurance), his ministry has been accompanied by demonstrations of power (cf 1 Cor 2, 3–4). **Signs of an apostle:** visible proof of belonging to Christ and of mediating Christ's power, which the opponents require as touchstones of apostleship (11; cf 13, 3).

s: Lk 23, 43; Rv 2, 7. *t:* Nm 33, 55; Jos 23, 13; Ez 28, 24. *u:* Mt 26, 39-44. *v:* 4, 7. *w:* 6, 4-5; Rom 5, 3 / Phil 4, 13. *x:* 11, 5. *y:* Rom 15, 19; 1 Thes 1, 5.

signs of an apostle were performed among you with all endurance, signs and wonders, and mighty deeds. [13z]*In what way were you less privileged than the rest of the churches, except that on my part I did not burden you? Forgive me this wrong!

[14]Now I am ready to come to you this third time. And I will not be a burden, for I want not what is yours, but you. Children ought not to save for their parents, but parents for their children. [15]I will most gladly spend and be utterly spent for your sakes. If I love you more, am I to be loved less? [16a]But granted that I myself did not burden you, yet I was crafty and got the better of you by deceit. [17]Did I take advantage of you through any of those I sent to you? [18b]I urged Titus to go and sent the brother with him. Did Titus take advantage of you? Did we not walk in the same spirit? And in the same steps?

Final Warnings and Appeals. [19]*Have you been thinking all along that we are defending ourselves before you? In the sight of God we are speaking in Christ, and all for building you up, beloved. [20c]*For I fear that when I come I may find you not such as I wish, and that you may find me not as you wish; that there may be rivalry, jealousy, fury, selfishness, slander, gossip, conceit, and disorder. [21]*I fear that when I come again my God may humiliate me before you, and I may have to mourn over many of those who sinned earlier and have not repented of the impurity, immorality, and licentiousness they practiced.

CHAPTER 13

See RG 463-64

[1d]*This third time I am coming to you. "On the testimony of two or three witnesses a fact shall be established." [2]*I warned those who sinned earlier and all the others, and I warn them now while absent, as I did when present on my second visit, that if I come again I will not be lenient, [3]*since you are looking for proof of Christ speaking in me. He is not weak toward you but powerful in you. [4]For indeed he was crucified out of

---

12, 13–18: Paul insists on his intention to continue refusing support from the community (cf 11, 8–12). In defending his practice and his motivation, he once more protests his love (cf 11, 11) and rejects the suggestion of secret self-enrichment. He has recourse here again to language applied to his opponents earlier: "cunning" (11, 3), "deceit" (11, 13), "got the better of you" (see the note on 11, 20), "take advantage" (2, 11).

12, 19—13, 10: This concludes the development begun in ch 10. In the chiastic arrangement of the material (see the note on 10, 1—13, 10), this final part corresponds to the opening; there are important similarities of content between the two sections as well.

12, 19: This verse looks back at the previous chapters and calls them by their proper name, a defense, an **apologia** (cf 1 Cor 9, 3). Paul insists on an important distinction: he has indeed been speaking for their benefit, but the ultimate judgment to which he submits is God's (cf 1 Cor 4, 3–5). This verse also leads into the final section, announcing two of its themes: judgment and building up.

12, 20: I fear that . . . : earlier Paul expressed fear that the Corinthians were being victimized, exploited, seduced from right thinking by his opponents (11, 3–4.19–21). Here he alludes unexpectedly to moral disorders among the Corinthians themselves. The catalogue suggests the effects of factions that have grown up around rival apostles.

12, 21: Again: one can also translate, "I fear that when I come my God may again humiliate me." Paul's allusion to the humiliation and mourning that may await him recall the mood he described in 2, 1–4, but there is no reference here to any individual such as there is in 2, 5–11. The crisis of ch 2 has happily been resolved by integration of the offender and repentance (7, 4–16), whereas 12, 21 is preoccupied with still

unrepentant sinners. The sexual sins recall 1 Cor 5–7.

13, 1: This third time I am coming: designation of the forthcoming visit as the "third" (cf 12, 14) may indicate that, in addition to his founding sojourn in Corinth, Paul had already made the first of two visits mentioned as planned in 1, 15, and the next visit will be the long-postponed second of these. If so, the materials in 1, 12—2, 13 plus 7, 4–16 and chs 10–13 may date from the same period of time, presumably of some duration, between Paul's second and third visit, though it is not clear that they are addressing the same crisis. The chronology is too unsure and the relations between sections of 2 Cor too unclear to yield any certainty. The hypothesis that chs 10–13 are themselves the "tearful letter" mentioned at 2, 3–4 creates more problems than it solves.

13, 2: I warned those who sinned earlier: mention of unrepentant sinners (12, 21 and here) and of an oral admonition given them on an earlier visit complicates the picture at the very end of Paul's development. It provides, in fact, a second explanation for the show of power that has been threatened from the beginning (10, 1–6), but a different reason for it, quite unsuspected until now. It is not clear whether Paul is merely alluding to a dimension of the situation that he has not previously had occasion to mention, or whether some other community crisis, not directly connected with that behind chs 10–13, has influenced the final editing. **I will not be lenient:** contrast Paul's hesitation and reluctance to inflict pain in 1, 23 and 2, 1–4. The next visit will bring the showdown.

13, 3–4: Paul now gives another motive for severity when he comes, the charge of weakness leveled against him as an apostle. The motive echoes more closely the opening section

z: 11, 9-12. a: 11, 3.13. b: 2, 13; 8, 16.23. c: 1 Cor 1, 11; 3, 3. d: Dt 19, 15; Mt 18, 16; Jn 8, 17; Heb 10, 28.

weakness, but he lives by the power of God. So also we are weak in him, but toward you we shall live with him by the power of God.

⁵*Examine yourselves to see whether you are living in faith. Test yourselves. Do you not realize that Jesus Christ is in you?—unless, of course, you fail the test. ⁶I hope you will discover that we have not failed. ⁷But we pray to God that you may not do evil, not that we may appear to have passed the test but that you may do what is right, even though we may seem to have failed. ⁸For we cannot do anything against the truth, but only for the truth. ⁹For we rejoice when we are weak but you are strong. What we pray for is your improvement.

¹⁰ᵉ*I am writing this while I am away, so that when I come I may not have to be severe in virtue of the authority that the Lord has given me to build up and not to tear down.

V: Conclusion

¹¹*Finally, brothers, rejoice. Mend your ways, encourage one another, agree with one another, live in peace, and the God of love and peace will be with you. ¹²ᶠGreet one another with a holy kiss. All the holy ones greet you.

¹³ᵍThe grace of the Lord Jesus Christ and the love of God and the fellowship of the holy Spirit be with all of you.

(10, 1–18) and the intervening development (especially 11, 30—12, 10). **Proof of Christ speaking in me:** the threat of 10, 1–2 is reworded to recall Paul's conformity with the pattern of Christ, his insertion into the interplay of death and life, weakness and power (cf the note on 12, 10b).

13, 5–9: Paul turns the challenge mentioned in v 3 on them: they are to put themselves to the test to demonstrate whether Christ is in them. These verses involve a complicated series of plays on the theme of **dokimē** (testing, proof, passing and failing a test). Behind this stands the familiar distinction between present human judgment and final divine judgment. This is the final appearance of the theme (cf 10, 18; 11, 15; 12, 19).

13, 10: Authority . . . to build up and not to tear down: Paul restates the purpose of his letter in language that echoes 10, 2.8, emphasizing the positive purpose of his authority in

their regard. This verse forms an inclusion with the topic sentence of the section (12, 19), as well as with the opening of this entire portion of the letter (10, 1–2).

13, 11–13: These verses may have originally concluded chs 10–13, but they have nothing specifically to do with the material of that section. It is also possible to consider them a conclusion to the whole of 2 Cor in its present edited form. The exhortations are general, including a final appeal for peace in the community. The letter ends calmly, after its many storms, with the prospect of ecclesial unity and divine blessing. The final verse is one of the clearest trinitarian passages in the New Testament.

e: 10, 8. *f:* Rom 16, 16; 1 Cor 16, 20 / Phil 4, 22; 1 Thes 5, 26; 1 Pt 5, 14. *g:* Rom 16, 20; 1 Cor 16, 23.

See RG 464–71

The Letter to the Galatians

The Galatians to whom the letter is addressed were Paul's converts, most likely among the descendants of Celts who had invaded western and central Asia Minor in the third century B.C. and had settled in the territory around Ancyra (modern Ankara, Turkey). Paul had passed through this area on his second missionary journey (Acts 16, 6) and again on his third (Acts 18, 23). It is less likely that the recipients of this letter were Paul's churches in the southern regions of Pisidia, Lycaonia, and Pamphylia where he had preached earlier in the Hellenized cities of Perge, Iconium, Pisidian Antioch, Lystra, and Derbe (Acts 13, 13—14, 27); this area was part of the Roman province of Galatia, and some scholars think that South Galatia was the destination of this letter.

If it is addressed to the Galatians in the north, the letter was probably written around A.D. 54 or 55, most likely from Ephesus after Paul's arrival there for a stay of several years on his third missionary journey (Acts 19; 20, 31). On the South Galatian theory, the date would be earlier, perhaps A.D. 48–50. Involved is the question of how one relates the events of 2, 1–10 to the "Council of Jerusalem" described in Acts 15 (see the notes on each passage).

In any case, the new Christians whom Paul is addressing were converts from paganism (4, 8–9) who were now being enticed by other missionaries to add the observances of the Jewish law, including the rite of circumcision, to the cross of Christ as a means of salvation. For, since Paul's visit, some other interpretation of Christianity had been brought to these neophytes, probably by converts from Judaism (the name "Judaizers" is sometimes applied to them); it has specifically been suggested that they were Jewish Christians who had come from the austere Essene sect.

These interlopers insisted on the necessity of following certain precepts of the Mosaic law along with faith in Christ. They were undermining Paul's authority also, asserting that he had not been trained by Jesus himself, that his gospel did not agree with that of the original and true apostles in Jerusalem, that he had kept from his converts in Galatia the necessity of accepting circumcision and other key obligations of the Jewish law, in order more easily to win them to Christ, and that his gospel was thus not the full and authentic one held by "those of repute" in Jerusalem (2, 2). Some scholars also see in chapters 5 and 6 another set of opponents against whom Paul writes, people who in their emphasis on the Spirit set aside all norms for conduct and became libertines in practice.

When Paul learned of the situation, he wrote this defense of his apostolic authority and of the correct understanding of the faith. He set forth the unique importance of Christ and his redemptive sacrifice on the cross, the freedom that Christians enjoy from the old burdens of the law, the total sufficiency of Christ and of faith in Christ as the way to God and to eternal life, and the beauty of the new life of the Spirit. Galatians is thus a summary of basic Pauline theology. Its themes were more fully and less polemically developed in the Letter to the Romans.

Autobiographically, the letter gives us Paul's own accounts of how he came to faith (1, 15–24), the agreement in "the truth of the gospel" (2, 5.14) that he shared with the Jewish Christian leaders in Jerusalem, James, Cephas, and John (2, 1–10), and the rebuke he had to deliver to Cephas in Antioch for inconsistency, contrary to the gospel, on the issue of table fellowship in the racially mixed church of Jewish and Gentile

Christians in Antioch (2, 11–14; cf 2, 15–21). At the conclusion of the letter (6, 11–18), Paul wrote in his own hand (cf 2 Thes 3, 17–18) a vivid summary of the message to the Galatians.

In his vigorous emphasis on the absolute pre-eminence of Christ and his cross as God's way to salvation and holiness, Paul stresses Christian freedom and the ineffectiveness of the Mosaic law for gaining divine favor and blessings (3, 19–29). The pious Jew saw in the law a way established by God to win divine approval by a life of meticulous observance of ritual, social, and moral regulations. But Paul's profound insight into the higher designs of God in Christ led him to understand and welcome the priority of promise and faith (shown in the experience of Abraham, 3, 6–18) and the supernatural gifts of the Spirit (3, 2–5; 5, 16—6, 10). His enthusiasm for this new vision of the life of grace in Christ and of the uniquely salvific role of Christ's redemptive death on the cross shines through this whole letter.

The principal divisions of the Letter to the Galatians are the following:

  I: Address (1, 1–5)
  II: Loyalty to the Gospel (1, 6–10)
  III: Paul's Defense of His Gospel and His Authority (1, 11—2, 21)
  IV: Faith and Liberty (3, 1—4, 31)
  V: Exhortation to Christian Living (5, 1—6, 10)
  VI: Conclusion (6, 11–18)

I: Address

CHAPTER 1

See RG 466-67

Greeting. [1ab*]Paul, an apostle not from human beings nor through a human being but through Jesus Christ and God the Father who raised him from the dead, [2*]and all the brothers who are with me, to the churches of Galatia: [3]grace to you and peace from God our Father and the Lord Jesus Christ, [4c*]who

---

1, 1–5: See the note on Rom 1, 1–7, concerning the greeting.

1, 1: Apostle: because of attacks on his authority in Galatia, Paul defends his apostleship. He is not an apostle commissioned by a congregation (Phil 2, 25; 2 Cor 8, 23) or even by prophets (1 Tm 1, 18 and 4, 14) but through Jesus Christ and God the Father.

1, 2: All the brothers: fellow believers in Christ, male and female; cf 3, 27–28. Paul usually mentions the co-

sender(s) at the start of a letter, but the use of all is unique, adding weight to the letter. Galatia: central Turkey more likely than the Roman province of Galatia; see Introduction.

1, 4: The greeting in v 3 is expanded by a christological

a: Rom 1, 1-7; 1 Cor 1, 1-3. b: 1, 11-12. c: 2, 20; Eph 5, 2; 1 Tm 2, 6 / 1 Jn 5, 19 / Rom 12, 2; Eph 5, 16; Heb 10, 10.

Paul's Journeys to Asia Minor

gave himself for our sins that he might rescue us from the present evil age in accord with the will of our God and Father, *5d*to whom be glory forever and ever. Amen.

II: Loyalty To The Gospel

6e*I am amazed that you are so quickly for-saking the one who called you by [the] grace [of Christ] for a different gospel *7*(not that there is another). But there are some who are disturbing you and wish to pervert the gospel of Christ. *8f**But even if we or an angel from heaven should preach [to you] a gospel other than the one that we preached

formula that stresses deliverance through the Lord Jesus from a world dominated by Satan; cf 2 Cor 4, 4; Eph 2, 2; 6, 12.

1, 6–10: In place of the usual thanksgiving (see the note on Rom 1, 8), Paul, with little to be thankful for in the Galatian situation, expresses amazement at the way his converts are deserting the gospel of Christ for a perverted message. He reasserts the one gospel he has preached (7–9) and begins to defend himself (10).

1, 6: The one who called you: God or Christ, though in actuality Paul was the divine instrument to call the Galatians.

1, 8: Accursed: in Greek, **anathema;** cf Rom 9, 3; 1 Cor 12, 3; 16, 22.

d: Rom 16, 27; 2 Tm 4, 18. *e:* 5, 8.10; Acts 15, 1.24; 2 Cor 11, 4. *f:* 1 Cor 16, 22 / 5, 3.21; 2 Cor 13, 2.

to you, let that one be accursed! ⁹As we have said before, and now I say again, if anyone preaches to you a gospel other than the one that you received, let that one be accursed!

¹⁰ᵍ*Am I now currying favor with human beings or God? Or am I seeking to please people? If I were still trying to please people, I would not be a slave of Christ.

III: Paul's Defense of His Gospel and His Authority

His Call by Christ. ¹¹ʰ*Now I want you to know, brothers, that the gospel preached by me is not of human origin. ¹²*For I did not receive it from a human being, nor was I taught it, but it came through a revelation of Jesus Christ.

¹³ⁱ*For you heard of my former way of life in Judaism, how I persecuted the church of God beyond measure and tried to destroy it, ¹⁴ʲand progressed in Judaism beyond many of my contemporaries among my race, since

I was even more a zealot for my ancestral traditions. ¹⁵ᵏBut when [God], who from my mother's womb had set me apart and called me through his grace, was pleased ¹⁶ᶫ*to reveal his Son to me, so that I might proclaim him to the Gentiles, I did not immediately consult flesh and blood, ¹⁷*nor did I go up to Jerusalem to those who were apostles before me; rather, I went into Arabia and then returned to Damascus.

¹⁸ᵐ*Then after three years I went up to Jerusalem to confer with Cephas and remained with him for fifteen days. ¹⁹ⁿ*But I did not see any other of the apostles, only James the brother of the Lord. ²⁰ᵒ(As to what I am writing to you, behold, before God, I am not lying.) ²¹ᵖThen I went into the regions of Syria and Cilicia. ²²And I was unknown personally to the churches of Judea that are in Christ; ²³ᑫthey only kept hearing that "the one who once was persecuting us is now preaching the faith he once tried to destroy." ²⁴So they glorified God because of me.

1, 10: This charge by Paul's opponents, that he sought to conciliate people with flattery and to curry favor with God, might refer to his mission practices (cf 1 Cor 9, 19–23) but the word **still** suggests it refers to his pre-Christian days (cf 14; Phil 3, 6). The self-description **slave of Christ** is one Paul often uses in a greeting (Rom 1, 1).

1, 11—2, 21: Paul's presentation on behalf of his message and of his apostleship reflects rhetorical forms of his day: he first narrates the facts about certain past events (1, 12—2, 14) and then states his contention regarding justification by faith as the gospel message (2, 15–21). Further arguments follow from both experience and scripture in chs 3 and 4, before he draws out the ethical consequences (5, 1—6, 10). The specific facts that he takes up here to show that his gospel is not a human invention (1, 11) but **came through a revelation of Jesus Christ** (1, 12) deal with his own calling as a Christian missionary (1, 13–17), his initial relations with the apostles in Jerusalem (1, 18–24), a later journey to Jerusalem (2, 1–10), and an incident in Antioch involving Cephas and persons from James (2, 11–14). The content of Paul's revealed gospel is then set forth in the heart of the letter (2, 15–21).

1, 12: Although Paul received his gospel **through a revelation** from Christ, this did not exclude his use of early Christian confessional formulations. See the note on 1, 4.

1, 13–17: Along with Phil 3, 4–11, which also moves from autobiography to its climax in a discussion on justification by faith (cf Gal 2, 15–21), this passage is Paul's chief account of the change from his **former way of life** (13) to service as a Christian missionary (16); cf Acts 9, 1–22; 22, 4–16; 26, 9–18. Paul himself does not use the term "conversion" but stresses revelation (12.16). In v 15 his language echoes the

Old Testament prophetic call of Jeremiah. Unlike the account in Acts (cf 22, 4–16), the calling of Paul here includes the mission to proclaim Christ **to the Gentiles** (16).

1, 16: Flesh and blood: human authorities (cf Mt 16, 17; 1 Cor 15, 50). Paul's apostleship comes from God (1).

1, 17: Arabia: probably the region of the Nabataean Arabs, east and south of Damascus.

1, 18–24: Paul's first journey to Jerusalem as a Christian, according to Galatians (cf Acts 9, 23–31 and the note on Acts 12, 25). He is quite explicit about contacts there, testifying under oath (20). On returning to **Syria** (perhaps specifically Damascus, cf v 17) **and Cilicia** (including his home town Tarsus, cf Acts 9, 30; 22, 3), Paul most likely engaged in missionary work. He underscores the fact that Christians in Judea knew of him only by reputation.

1, 18: After three years: two years and more, since Paul's call. To **confer with** Cephas may mean simply "pay a visit" or more specifically "get information from" him about Jesus, over a two-week period. **Cephas:** Aramaic name of Simon (Peter); cf Mt 16, 16–18 and the notes there.

1, 19: James the brother of the Lord: not one of the Twelve, but a brother of Jesus (see the note on Mk 6, 3). He played an important role in the Jerusalem church (see the note on Gal 2, 9), the leadership of which he took over from Peter (Acts 12, 17). Paul may have regarded James as an apostle.

g: 2 Cor 5, 11 / 1 Thes 2, 4. h: 1 Cor 15, 1 / 1, 11; Eph 3, 3. i: Acts 8, 1-3; 9, 1-2; 1 Cor 15, 9. j: Acts 26, 4-5. k: Is 49, 1; Jer 1, 4. l: 1, 11-12; Rom 1, 5; 1 Cor 15, 10; Acts 9, 3-9 / 2, 2.7 /Mt 16, 17. m: Acts 9, 26-30 / Jn 1, 42. n: 2, 9; Mt 13, 55; Acts 12, 17. o: Rom 9, 1; 2 Cor 11, 31. p: Acts 9, 30. q: 1, 13.

See RG
467–68

CHAPTER 2

The Council of Jerusalem. ^{1r*}Then after fourteen years I again went up to Jerusalem with Barnabas, taking Titus along also. ^{2s*}I went up in accord with a revelation, and I presented to them the gospel that I preach to the Gentiles—but privately to those of repute—so that I might not be running, or have run, in vain. ^{3t*}Moreover, not even Titus, who was with me, although he was a Greek, was compelled to be circumcised, ^{4u*}but because of the false brothers secretly brought in, who slipped in to spy on our freedom that we have in Christ Jesus, that they might enslave us— ^{5v*}to them we did not submit even for a moment, so that the truth of the gospel might remain intact for you. ^{6w}But from those who were reputed to be important (what they once were makes no difference to me; God shows no partiality)—those of repute made me add nothing. ^{7x*}On the contrary, when they saw that I had been entrusted with the gospel to the uncircumcised, just as Peter to the circumcised, ⁸for the one who worked in Peter for an apostolate to the circumcised worked also in me for the Gentiles, ^{9y*}and when they recognized the grace bestowed upon me, James and Cephas and John, who were reputed to be pillars, gave me and Barnabas their right hands in partnership, that we should go to the Gentiles and they to the circumcised. ^{10z*}Only, we were to be mindful of the poor, which is the very thing I was eager to do.

Peter's Inconsistency at Antioch. ^{11a*}And when Cephas came to Antioch, I opposed him to his face because he clearly was wrong.

2, 1–10: Paul's second journey to Jerusalem, according to Galatians, involved a private meeting with **those of repute** (2). At issue was a Gentile, Titus, and the question of circumcision, which **false brothers** (4) evidently demanded for him. Paul insists that the gospel he preaches (2; cf 1, 9.11) remained intact with no addition by those of repute (6); that **Titus** was not **compelled** to accept circumcision (3); and that he and the reputed **pillars** in Jerusalem agreed on how each would advance the missionary task (7–10). Usually, 1–10 is equated with the "Council of Jerusalem," as it is called, described in Acts 15. See the notes on Acts 15, 6–12 and 15, 13–35, the latter concerning the "decree" that Paul does not mention.

2, 1: **After fourteen years:** thirteen or more years, probably reckoned from the return to Syria and Cilicia (1, 21), though possibly from Paul's calling as a Christian (1, 15). **Barnabas:** cf 9.13; 1 Cor 9, 6. A Jewish Christian missionary, with whom Paul worked (Acts 4, 36–37; 11, 22.25.30; 12, 25; 13, 1–3; 15, 2). **Titus:** a missionary companion of Paul (2 Cor 2, 13; 7, 6.13–15; 8, 6.16.23; 12, 18), non-Jewish (Gal 2, 3), never mentioned in Acts.

2, 2: **A revelation:** cf 1, 1.12. Paul emphasizes it was God's will, not Jerusalem authority, that led to the journey. Acts 15, 2 states that the church in Antioch appointed Paul and Barnabas for the task. **Those of repute:** leaders of the Jerusalem church; the term, while positive, may be slightly ironic (cf 6.9). **Run, in vain:** while Paul presents a positive picture in what follows, his missionary work in Galatia would have been to no purpose if his opponents were correct that circumcision is needed for complete faith in Christ.

2, 3: **Not even** a Gentile Christian like Titus was compelled to receive the rite of circumcision. The Greek text could be interpreted that he voluntarily accepted circumcision, but this is unlikely in the overall argument.

2, 4: **False brothers:** Jewish Christians who took the position that Gentile Christians must first become Jews through circumcision and observance of the Mosaic law in order to become Christians; cf Acts 15, 1.

2, 5: **The truth of the gospel:** the true gospel, in contrast to the false one of the opponents (1, 6–9); the gospel of grace, used as a norm (14).

2, 7–9: Some think that actual "minutes" of the meeting are here quoted. Paul's apostleship to the Gentiles (1, 16) is recognized alongside that of Peter to the Jews. Moreover, the right to proclaim the gospel without requiring circumcision and the Jewish law is sealed by a handshake. That Paul and colleagues **should go to the Gentiles** did not exclude his preaching to Jews as well (Rom 1, 13–16) or Cephas to Gentile areas.

2, 9: **James and Cephas and John:** see the notes on 1, 18 and 19; on Peter and John as leaders in the Jerusalem church, cf Acts 3, 1 and 8, 14. The order here, with James first, may reflect his prominence in Jerusalem after Peter (Cephas) departed (Acts 12, 17).

2, 10: **The poor:** Jerusalem Christians or a group within the church there (cf Rom 15, 26). The collection for them was extremely important in Paul's thought and labor (cf Rom 15, 25–28; 1 Cor 16, 1–4; 2 Cor 8 and 9).

2, 11–14: The decision reached in Jerusalem (3–7) recognized the freedom of Gentile Christians from the Jewish law. But the problem of table fellowship between Jewish Christians, who possibly still kept kosher food regulations, and Gentile believers was not yet settled. When Cephas first came to the racially mixed community of Jewish and Gentile Christians in Antioch (12), he ate with non-Jews. Pressure from persons arriving later from Jerusalem caused him and Barnabas to draw back. Paul therefore publicly rebuked Peter's inconsistency toward the gospel (14). Some think that what Paul said on that occasion extends through v 16 or v 21.

2, 11: **Clearly was wrong:** literally, "stood condemned," by himself and also by Paul. His action in breaking table fel-

---

r: Acts 15, 2. *s:* 1, 11-12.16 / 1, 16 / Phil 2, 16. *t:* 2 Cor 2, 13; 7, 6-7; 8, 16-17; 12, 18; Ti 1, 4 / 2, 14; 6, 12. *u:* 5, 1; Acts 15, 1.24. *v:* 2, 14; 4, 16. *w:* Dt 10, 17; Rom 2, 11. *x:* 1, 15-16; Acts 9, 15; 15, 12; 22, 21; Rom 1, 5. *y:* Rom 15, 15 / 1, 18-19; Jn 1, 42; Acts 12, 17 / 2, 1. *z:* Acts 11, 29-30; Rom 15, 25-28; 1 Cor 16, 1-4; 2 Cor 8, 9. *a:* 1, 18 / Acts 11, 19-30; 15, 1-2.

12b*For, until some people came from James, he used to eat with the Gentiles; but when they came, he began to draw back and separated himself, because he was afraid of the circumcised. *13c**And the rest of the Jews [also] acted hypocritically along with him, with the result that even Barnabas was carried away by their hypocrisy. *14d**But when I saw that they were not on the right road in line with the truth of the gospel, I said to Cephas in front of all, "If you, though a Jew, are living like a Gentile and not like a Jew, how can you compel the Gentiles to live like Jews?"

Faith and Works. *15**We, who are Jews by nature and not sinners from among the Gentiles, *16e**[yet] who know that a person is not justified by works of the law but through faith in Jesus Christ, even we have believed in Christ Jesus that we may be justified by faith in Christ and not by works of the law, because by works of the law no one will be justified. *17**But if, in seeking to be justified in Christ, we ourselves are found to be sinners, is Christ then a minister of sin? Of course not! *18**But if I am building up again those things that I tore down, then I show myself to be a transgressor. *19f**For through the law I died to the law, that I might live for God. I have been crucified with Christ; *20g*yet I live, no longer I, but Christ lives in me; insofar as I now live in the flesh, I live by faith in the Son of God who has loved me and given himself up for me. *21h*I do not nullify the grace of God; for if justification comes through the law, then Christ died for nothing.

IV: Faith and Liberty

CHAPTER 3

See RG 468-70

Justification by Faith. *1i**O stupid Galatians! Who has bewitched you, before whose eyes Jesus Christ was publicly portrayed as crucified? *2j**I want to learn only this from you: did you receive the Spirit from works of the law, or from faith in what you heard? *3k**Are you so stupid? After beginning with the Spirit, are you now ending with the flesh? *4**Did you experience so many things

lowship was especially grievous if the eating involved the meal at the Lord's supper (cf 1 Cor 11, 17–25).

2, 12: Some people came from James: strict Jewish Christians (cf Acts 15, 1.5; 21, 20–21), either sent by James (1, 19; 2, 9) or claiming to be from the leader of the Jerusalem church. **The circumcised:** presumably Jewish Christians, not Jews.

2, 13: The Jews: Jewish Christians, like Barnabas. **Hypocrisy:** literally, "pretense," "play-acting"; moral insincerity.

2, 14: Compel the Gentiles to live like Jews: that is, conform to Jewish practices, such as circumcision (3–5) or regulations about food (12).

2, 15–21: Following on the series of incidents cited above, Paul's argument, whether spoken to Cephas at Antioch or only now articulated, is pertinent to the Galatian situation, where believers were having themselves circumcised (6, 12–13) and obeying other aspects of Jewish law (4, 9–10; 5, 1–4). He insists that salvation is by faith in Christ, not by works of the law. His teaching on the gospel concerns justification by faith (16) in relation to sin (17), law (19), life in Christ (19–20), and grace (21).

2, 16: No one will be justified: Ps 143, 2 is reflected.

2, 17: A minister of sin: literally, "a servant of sin" (cf Rom 15, 8), an agent of sin, one who promotes it. This is possibly a claim by opponents that justification on the basis of faith in Christ makes Christ an abettor of sin when Christians are found to be sinners. Paul denies the conclusion (cf Rom 6, 1–4).

2, 18: To return to observance of the law as the means to salvation would entangle one not only in inevitable transgressions of it but also in the admission that it was wrong to have abandoned the law in the first place.

2, 19: Through the law I died to the law: this is vari-

ously explained: the law revealed sin (Rom 7, 7–9) and led to death and then to belief in Christ; or, the law itself brought the insight that law cannot justify (16; Ps 143, 2); or, the "law of Christ" (6, 2) led to abandoning the Mosaic law; or, the law put Christ to death (cf 3, 13) and so provided a way to our salvation, through baptism into Christ, through which we die (**crucified with Christ;** see Rom 6, 6). Cf also 3, 19–25 on the role of the law in reference to salvation.

3, 1–14: Paul's contention that justification comes not through the law or the works of the law but by faith in Christ and in his death (2, 16.21) is supported by appeals to Christian experience (1–5) and to scripture (6–14). The gift of God's Spirit to the Galatians came from the gospel received in faith, not from doing what the law enjoins. The story of Abraham shows that faith in God brings **righteousness** (6; Gn 15, 6). The promise to Abraham (8; Gn 12, 3) extends to the Gentiles (14).

3, 1: Stupid: not just senseless, for they were in danger of deserting their salvation.

3, 2: Faith in what you heard: Paul's message received with faith. The Greek can also mean "the proclamation of the faith" or "a hearing that comes from faith."

3, 3: On the contrast of **Spirit** and **flesh,** cf Rom 8, 1–11. Having received the Spirit, they need not be circumcised now.

3, 4: Experience so many things: probably the **mighty deeds** of v 5 but possibly the experience of sufferings.

---

b: Acts 10, 15.28; 11, 3.   *c*: 2, 1.9.   *d*: 2, 5 / 1, 18; 2, 9 / 2, 3.   *e*: 3, 2.11; Ps 143, 1-2; Rom 3, 20.28; 4, 5; 11, 6; Eph 2, 8-9; Phil 3, 9.   *f*: 6, 14; Rom 6, 6.8.10; 7, 6.   *g*: 1, 4; Rom 8, 10-11; Col 3, 3-4.   *h*: 5, 2.   *i*: 5, 7; 1 Cor 1, 23.   *j*: 2, 16 / 3, 14; Rom 10, 17.   *k*: 5, 16-18.

in vain?—if indeed it was in vain. [51]Does, then, the one who supplies the Spirit to you and works mighty deeds among you do so from works of the law or from faith in what you heard? [6m*]Thus Abraham "believed God, and it was credited to him as righteousness."

[7n*]Realize then that it is those who have faith who are children of Abraham. [8o]Scripture, which saw in advance that God would justify the Gentiles by faith, foretold the good news to Abraham, saying, "Through you shall all the nations be blessed." [9p]Consequently, those who have faith are blessed along with Abraham who had faith. [10q*]For all who depend on works of the law are under a curse; for it is written, "Cursed be everyone who does not persevere in doing all the things written in the book of the law." [11r]And that no one is justified before God by the law is clear, for "the one who is righteous by faith will live." [12s]But the law does not depend on faith; rather, "the one who does these things will live by them." [13t]Christ

ransomed us from the curse of the law by becoming a curse for us, for it is written, "Cursed be everyone who hangs on a tree," [14u]that the blessing of Abraham might be extended to the Gentiles through Christ Jesus, so that we might receive the promise of the Spirit through faith.

The Law Did Not Nullify the Promise. [15v*]Brothers, in human terms I say that no one can annul or amend even a human will once ratified. [16w*]Now the promises were made to Abraham and to his descendant. It does not say, "And to descendants," as referring to many, but as referring to one, "And to your descendant," who is Christ. [17x*]This is what I mean: the law, which came four hundred and thirty years afterward, does not annul a covenant previously ratified by God, so as to cancel the promise. [18y*]For if the inheritance comes from the law, it is no longer from a promise; but God bestowed it on Abraham through a promise.

[19z*]Why, then, the law? It was added for

3, 6: Abraham . . . righteousness: see Gn 15, 6; Rom 4, 3. The Galatians like Abraham heard with faith and experienced justification. This first argument forms the basis for the further scriptural evidence that follows.

3, 7–9: Faith is what matters, for **Abraham** and the **children of Abraham,** in contrast to the claims of the opponents that circumcision and observance of the law are needed to bring the promised blessing of Gn 12, 3; cf Gn 18, 18; Sir 44, 21; Acts 3, 25.

3, 10–14: Those **who depend** not on promise and faith but **on works of the law are under a curse** because they do **not persevere in doing all the things written in the book of the law** (10; Dt 27, 26) in order to gain life (12; Lv 18, 5; cf Rom 10, 5). But scripture teaches that **no one is justified before God by the law** (11; Hb 2, 4, adapted from the Greek version of Habakkuk; cf Rom 1, 17; Heb 10, 38). Salvation, then, depends on faith in Christ who died on the cross (13), taking upon himself a curse found in Dt 21, 23 (about executed criminals hanged in public view), to free us from **the curse of the law** (13). That the Gentile Galatians have received the promised Spirit (14) by faith and in no other way returns the argument to the experience cited in vv 1–5.

3, 15–18: A third argument to support Paul's position that salvation is not through the law but by promise (1–14) comes from legal practice and scriptural history. A legal agreement or **human will,** duly **ratified,** is unalterable (15). God's **covenant** with **Abraham** and its repeated promises (Gn 12, 2–3.7; 13, 15; 17, 7–8; 22, 16–18; 24, 7) is not superseded by **the law,** which came much later, in the time of Moses. **The inheritance** (of the Spirit and the blessings) is by promise, not by law (18). Paul's argument hinges on the fact that the same Greek word, **diathēkē,** can be rendered as **will** or testament (15) and as **covenant** (17).

3, 16: Descendant: literally, "and to his seed." The Hebrew, as in Gn 12, 7; 15, 18; 22, 17–18, is a collective singular, traditionally rendered as a plural, **descendants,** but taken by Paul in its literal number to refer to **Christ** as descendant of Abraham.

3, 17: Four hundred and thirty years afterward: follows Ex 12, 40 in the Greek (Septuagint) version, in contrast to Gn 15, 13 and Acts 7, 6, for chronology.

3, 18: This refutes the opponents' contention that the promises of God are fulfilled only as a reward for human observance of the law.

3, 19–22: A digression: if the Mosaic law, then, does not save or **bring life,** why was it given? Elsewhere, Paul says the law served to show what sin is (Rom 3, 20; 7, 7–8). Here the further implication is that the law in effect served to produce transgressions. Moreover, it was received at second hand **by angels,** through a **mediator,** not directly from God (19). The law does not, however, oppose God's purposes, for it carries out its function (22), so that **righteousness** comes by **faith** and **promise,** not by human works of the law.

3, 19: The descendant: Christ (16). **By angels:** Dt 33, 2–4 stressed their presence as enhancing the importance of the law; Paul uses their role to diminish its significance (cf Acts 7, 38.53). **A mediator:** Moses. But in a covenant of

l: 2, 16. *m:* Gn 15, 6; Rom 4, 3; Jas 2, 23. *n:* 3, 29; Rom 4, 11-12 / Sir 44, 19-21. *o:* Gn 12, 3; 18, 17-19; Acts 3, 25. *p:* Rom 4, 16. *q:* Dt 27, 26; Jas 2, 10. *r:* 2, 16; Hb 2, 4; Rom 1, 17. *s:* Lv 18, 5; Rom 10, 5. *t:* Dt 21, 23; Rom 8, 3; 2 Cor 5, 21. *u:* 3, 2-3.5; Is 44, 3; Jl 3, 1-2; Acts 2, 33. *v:* Rom 3, 5 / Heb 9, 16-17. *w:* Gn 12, 7; 13, 15; 17, 8; 22, 17; 24, 7; Mt 1, 1. *x:* Ex 12, 40. *y:* Rom 4, 16; 11, 6. *z:* Rom 4, 15; 5, 20; 7, 7.13 / Acts 7, 38.53.

transgressions, until the descendant came to whom the promise had been made; it was promulgated by angels at the hand of a mediator. [20a]Now there is no mediator when only one party is involved, and God is one. [21b]Is the law then opposed to the promises [of God]? Of course not! For if a law had been given that could bring life, then righteousness would in reality come from the law. [22c]But scripture confined all things under the power of sin, that through faith in Jesus Christ the promise might be given to those who believe.

What Faith Has Brought Us. [23d*]Before faith came, we were held in custody under law, confined for the faith that was to be revealed. [24e*]Consequently, the law was our disciplinarian for Christ, that we might be justified by faith. [25f]But now that faith has come, we are no longer under a disciplinarian. [26g*]For through faith you are all children of God in Christ Jesus. [27h*]For all of you who were baptized into Christ have clothed yourselves with Christ. [28i]There is neither Jew nor Greek, there is neither slave nor free person, there is not male and female; for you are all one in Christ Jesus. [29j]And if you belong to Christ, then you are Abraham's descendant, heirs according to the promise.

CHAPTER 4

See RG 469–70

God's Free Children in Christ. [1*]I mean that as long as the heir is not of age, he is no different from a slave, although he is the owner of everything, [2]but he is under the supervision of guardians and administrators until the date set by his father. [3k*]In the same way we also, when we were not of age, were enslaved to the elemental powers of the world. [4l]But when the fullness of time had come, God sent his Son, born of a woman, born under the law, [5m]to ransom those under the law, so that we might receive adoption. [6n*]As proof that you are children, God sent the spirit of his Son into our hearts, crying out, "Abba, Father!" [7o]So you are no longer a slave but a child, and if a child then also an heir, through God.

Do Not Throw This Freedom Away. [8p*]At a time when you did not know God, you became slaves to things that by nature are not

promise, where all depends on the one God, no mediator is needed (20).

3, 23–29: Paul adds a further argument in support of righteousness or justification by faith and through God's promise rather than by works of the law (2, 16; 3, 22): as **children of God, baptized into Christ,** the Galatians are all **Abraham's descendant** and **heirs** of the promise to Abraham (8.14.16–18.29). The teaching in 23–25, that since **faith** (Christianity) **has come, we are no longer under** the law, could be taken with the previous paragraph on the role of the Mosaic law, but it also fits here as a contrast between the situation **before faith** (23) and the results after faith has come (25–29).

3, 24–25: **Disciplinarian:** the Greek **paidagōgos** referred to a slave who escorted a child to school but did not teach or tutor; hence, a guardian or monitor. Applying this to the law fits the role of the law described in vv 19–25.

3, 26: **Children of God:** literally "sons," in contrast to the young child under the disciplinarian in vv 24–25. The term includes males and females (28).

3, 27–28: Likely a formula used at baptism that expresses racial, social-economic, and sexual equality in Christ (cf Col 3, 11).

3, 27: **Clothed yourselves with Christ:** literally, "have put on Christ"; cf Rom 13, 14; Eph 4, 24; Col 3, 10. Baptismal imagery, traceable to the Old Testament (Jb 29, 14; Is 59, 17) but also found in pagan mystery cults.

4, 1–7: What Paul has argued in 3, 26–29 is now elaborated in terms of the Christian as **the heir** (1.7; cf 3, 18.29) freed from control by others. Again, as in 3, 2–5, the proof

that Christians are children of God is the gift of the Spirit of Christ relating them intimately to God.

4, 1.3: **Not of age:** an infant or minor.

4, 3: **The elemental powers of the world:** while the term can refer to the "elements" like earth, air, fire, and water or to elementary forms of religion, the sense here is more likely that of celestial beings that were thought in pagan circles to control the world; cf 8; Col 2, 8.20.

4, 6: **Children:** see the note on 3, 26; here in contrast to the infant or young person **not of age** (1.3). **Abba:** cf Mk 14, 36 and the note; Rom 8, 15.

4, 8–11: On the basis of the arguments advanced from 3, 1 through 4, 7, Paul now launches his appeal to the Galatians with the question, **how can you turn back** to the slavery of the law (9)? The question is posed with reference to bondage to the **elemental powers** (see the note on 4, 3) because the Galatians had originally been converted to Christianity from paganism, not Judaism (8). The use of the direct question is like 3, 3–5.

4, 8: **Things that by nature are not gods:** or "gods that by nature do not exist."

---

a: Dt 6, 4.   *b:* Rom 7, 7.10; 8, 2-4.   *c:* Rom 3, 9-20.23; 11, 32.
d: 4, 3-5; 5, 18.   *e:* 2, 16.   *f:* Rom 10, 4.   *g:* 4, 5-7; Jn 1, 12;
Rom 8, 14-17.   *h:* Rom 6, 3; 13, 14; Eph 4, 24.   *i:* Rom 10, 12;
1 Cor 12, 13; Col 3, 11.   *j:* 3, 7.14.16.18; Rom 4, 16-17; 9, 7 / 4,
1.7; Rom 4, 13-14; 8, 17;Heb 6, 12; Jas 2, 5.   *k:* 3, 23 / 4, 9; Col
2, 20.   *l:* Mk 1, 15.   *m:* 3, 13.26.   *n:* 3, 26; Rom 8, 15.   *o:* 3,
29; Rom 8, 16-17.   *p:* 1 Cor 12, 2.

gods; [9q]but now that you have come to know God, or rather to be known by God, how can you turn back again to the weak and destitute elemental powers? Do you want to be slaves to them all over again? [10r*]You are observing days, months, seasons, and years. [11*]I am afraid on your account that perhaps I have labored for you in vain.

Appeal to Former Loyalty. [12s*]I implore you, brothers, be as I am, because I have also become as you are. You did me no wrong; [13*]you know that it was because of a physical illness that I originally preached the gospel to you, [14]and you did not show disdain or contempt because of the trial caused you by my physical condition, but rather you received me as an angel of God, as Christ Jesus. [15*]Where now is that blessedness of yours? Indeed, I can testify to you that, if it had been possible, you would have torn out your eyes and given them to me. [16]So now have I become your enemy by telling you the truth? [17t*]They show interest in you, but not in a good way; they want to isolate you, so that you may show interest in them. [18]Now it is good to be shown interest for good reason at all times, and not only when I am with you. [19u]My children, for whom I am again in labor until Christ be formed in you! [20]I would like to be with you now and to change my tone, for I am perplexed because of you.

An Allegory on Christian Freedom. [21*]Tell me, you who want to be under the law, do you not listen to the law? [22v]For it is written that Abraham had two sons, one by the slave woman and the other by the freeborn woman. [23w]The son of the slave woman was born naturally, the son of the freeborn through a promise. [24x]Now this is an allegory. These women represent two covenants. One was from Mount Sinai, bearing children for slavery; this is Hagar. [25*]Hagar represents Sinai, a mountain in Arabia; it corresponds to the present Jerusalem, for she is in slavery along with her children. [26y]But the Jerusalem above is freeborn, and she is our mother. [27z*]For it is written:

"Rejoice, you barren one who bore no children;
break forth and shout, you who were not in labor;
for more numerous are the children of the deserted one
than of her who has a husband."

4, 10: This is likely a reference to ritual observances from the Old Testament, promoted by opponents: sabbaths or Yom Kippur, new moon, Passover or Pentecost, sabbatical years.

4, 11: Cf 2, 2. If the Galatians become **slaves . . . all over again** to the law (9), Paul will have worked in vain among them.

4, 12–20: A strongly personal section. Paul appeals to past ties between the Galatians and himself. He speaks sharply of the opponents (17–18) and pastorally to the Galatians (19–20).

4, 12: Because I have also become as you are: a terse phrase in Greek, meaning "Be as I, Paul, am," i.e., living by faith, independent of the law, for, in spite of my background in Judaism (1, 13), I have become as you Galatians are now, a brother in Christ.

4, 13: Physical illness: because its nature is not described, some assume an eye disease (15); others, epilepsy; some relate it to 2 Cor 12, 7–9. **Originally:** this may also be translated "formerly" or "on the first (of two) visit(s)"; cf Acts 16, 6; 18, 23.

4, 15: That blessedness of yours: possibly a reference to the Galatians' initial happy reception of Paul (14) and of his gospel (1, 6; 3, 1–4) and their felicitation at such blessedness, but the phrase could also refer ironically to earlier praise by Paul of the Galatians, no longer possible when they turn from the gospel to the claims of the opponents (17–18; 1, 7). If the word is a more literal reference to a beatitude, Gal 3, 26–28 may be in view.

4, 17: Isolate you: that is, from the blessings of the gospel and/or from Paul.

4, 21–31: Paul supports his appeal for the gospel (9; 1, 6–9; 2, 16; 3, 2) by a further argument from scripture (cf 3, 6–18). It involves the relationship of **Abraham** (3, 6–16) to his wife, Sarah, the **freeborn woman,** and to Hagar, **the slave woman,** and the contrast between the sons born to each, **Isaac,** child of promise, and Ishmael, son of Hagar (Gn 16 and 21). Only through Isaac is the promise of God preserved. This **allegory** (24), with its equation of the Sinai covenant and Mosaic law with slavery and of the promise of God with freedom, Paul uses only in light of previous arguments. His quotation of Gn 21, 10 at v 30 suggests on a scriptural basis that the Galatians should expel those who are troubling them (1, 7).

4, 25: Hagar represents Sinai . . . : some manuscripts have what seems a geographical note, "For Sinai is a mountain in Arabia."

4, 27: Is 54, 1 in the Septuagint translation is applied to Sarah as the **barren one** (in Gn 15) who ultimately becomes the mother not only of Isaac but now of numerous children, i.e., of all those who believe, the **children of the promise** (28).

q: 4, 3; Col 2, 20. r: Col 2, 16-20. s: 1 Cor 11, 1. t: 1, 7; 6, 12; Acts 20, 30. u: 1 Cor 4, 14-15; 2 Cor 6, 13; 1 Thes 2, 7-8. v: Gn 16, 15; 21, 2-3. w: Gn 17, 16; Rom 4, 19-20; 9, 7-9. x: 3, 17 / Ex 19, 20 / Gn 16, 1. y: Heb 12, 22; Rv 21, 2. z: Is 54, 1.

28a Now you, brothers, like Isaac, are children of the promise. 29But just as then the child of the flesh persecuted the child of the spirit, it is the same now. 30b But what does the scripture say?

"Drive out the slave woman and her son!
For the son of the slave woman shall
not share the inheritance with the
son"

of the freeborn. 31c Therefore, brothers, we are children not of the slave woman but of the freeborn woman.

V: Exhortation to Christian Living

CHAPTER 5

See RG
470

The Importance of Faith. 1d*For freedom Christ set us free; so stand firm and do not submit again to the yoke of slavery.

2e It is I, Paul, who am telling you that if you have yourselves circumcised, Christ will be of no benefit to you. 3f*Once again I declare to every man who has himself circumcised that he is bound to observe the entire law. 4You are separated from Christ, you who are trying to be justified by law; you have fallen from grace. 5g For through the

Spirit, by faith, we await the hope of righteousness. 6h*For in Christ Jesus, neither circumcision nor uncircumcision counts for anything, but only faith working through love.

Be Not Misled. 7*You were running well; who hindered you from following [the] truth? 8i*That enticement does not come from the one who called you. 9j A little yeast leavens the whole batch of dough. 10k I am confident of you in the Lord that you will not take a different view, and that the one who is troubling you will bear the condemnation, whoever he may be. 11l*As for me, brothers, if I am still preaching circumcision, why am I still being persecuted? In that case, the stumbling block of the cross has been abolished. 12*Would that those who are upsetting you might also castrate themselves!

Freedom for Service. 13m*For you were called for freedom, brothers. But do not use this freedom as an opportunity for the flesh; rather, serve one another through love. 14n*For the whole law is fulfilled in one statement, namely, "You shall love your neighbor as yourself." 15But if you go on biting and devouring one another, beware that you are not consumed by one another.

16o*I say, then: live by the Spirit and you will certainly not gratify the desire of the

---

5, 1–6: Paul begins the exhortations, continuing through 6, 10, with an appeal to the Galatians to side with freedom instead of slavery (1). He reiterates his message of justification or righteousness by faith instead of law and circumcision (2–5); cf 2, 16; 3, 3. Faith, not circumcision, is what counts (6).

5, 1: Freedom: Paul stresses as the conclusion from the allegory in 4, 21–31 this result of Christ's work for us. It is a principle previously mentioned (2, 4), the responsible use of which v 13 will emphasize.

5, 3: Cf 3, 10–12. Just as those who seek to live by the law must carry out all its contents, so those who have faith and live by promise must stand firm in their freedom (1.13).

5, 6: Cf Rom 2, 25–26; 1 Cor 7, 19; Gal 6, 15. The Greek for **faith working through love** or "faith expressing itself through love" can also be rendered as "faith energized by (God's) love."

5, 7–12: Paul addresses the Galatians directly: with questions (7.11), a proverb (9), a statement (8), and biting sarcasm (12), seeking to persuade the Galatians to break with those trying to add law and circumcision to Christ as a basis for salvation.

5, 7: Running well: as in an athletic contest; cf 2, 2; 1 Cor 9, 24–26; Phil 2, 16; 3, 14.

5, 8: The one who called you: see the note on 1, 6.

5, 11: Preaching circumcision: this could refer to Paul's

pre-Christian period (possibly as a missionary for Judaism); more probably it arose as a charge from opponents, based perhaps on the story in Acts 16, 1–3 that Paul had circumcised Timothy "on account of the Jews." Unlike the Gentile Titus in Gal 2, 3, Timothy was the son of a Jewish mother. **The stumbling block of the cross:** cf 1 Cor 1, 23.

5, 12: A sarcastic half-wish that their knife would go beyond mere circumcision; cf Phil 3, 2 and the note there.

5, 13–26: In light of another reminder of the freedom of the gospel (13; cf 1), Paul elaborates on what believers are called to do and be: they fulfill the law by love of neighbor (14–15), walking in the Spirit (16–26), as is illustrated by concrete **fruit of the Spirit** in their lives.

5, 13: Serve . . . through love: cf v 6.

5, 14: Lv 19, 18, emphasized by Jesus (Mt 22, 39; Lk 10, 27); cf Rom 13, 8–10.

5, 16–25: Spirit . . . flesh: cf 3, 3 and the note on Rom 8, 1–13.

a: Rom 9, 8. b: Gn 21, 10. c: 3, 29; Jn 8, 35. d: 2, 4; 4, 5.9; Jn 8, 32.36. e: 2, 21; Acts 15, 1-29. f: 3, 10; Rom 2, 25; Jas 2, 10. g: Rom 8, 23.25. h: 3, 28; 6, 15; 1 Cor 7, 19. i: 1, 6. j: 1 Cor 5, 6. k: 1, 7. l: 6, 12.14; 1 Cor 1, 23. m: 5, 1 / Rom 6, 18; 1 Cor 8, 9; 1 Pt 2, 16. n: Lv 19, 18; Mt 22, 39; Rom 13, 8-10. o: 5, 24-25; Rom 8, 5.

flesh. [17p]For the flesh has desires against the Spirit, and the Spirit against the flesh; these are opposed to each other, so that you may not do what you want. [18q]But if you are guided by the Spirit, you are not under the law. [19r*]Now the works of the flesh are obvious: immorality, impurity, licentiousness, [20s]idolatry, sorcery, hatreds, rivalry, jealousy, outbursts of fury, acts of selfishness, dissensions, factions, [21*]occasions of envy, drinking bouts, orgies, and the like. I warn you, as I warned you before, that those who do such things will not inherit the kingdom of God. [22t]In contrast, the fruit of the Spirit is love, joy, peace, patience, kindness, generosity, faithfulness, [23u]gentleness, self-control. Against such there is no law. [24v]Now those who belong to Christ [Jesus] have crucified their flesh with its passions and desires. [25w]If we live in the Spirit, let us also follow the Spirit. [26x]Let us not be conceited, provoking one another, envious of one another.

See RG
470–71

CHAPTER 6

Life in the Community of Christ. [1y*]Brothers, even if a person is caught in some transgression, you who are spiritual should correct that one in a gentle spirit,

looking to yourself, so that you also may not be tempted. [2z*]Bear one another's burdens, and so you will fulfill the law of Christ. [3a]For if anyone thinks he is something when he is nothing, he is deluding himself. [4*]Each one must examine his own work, and then he will have reason to boast with regard to himself alone, and not with regard to someone else; [5b]for each will bear his own load.

[6c*]One who is being instructed in the word should share all good things with his instructor. [7]Make no mistake: God is not mocked, for a person will reap only what he sows, [8d]because the one who sows for his flesh will reap corruption from the flesh, but the one who sows for the spirit will reap eternal life from the spirit. [9e]Let us not grow tired of doing good, for in due time we shall reap our harvest, if we do not give up. [10f*]So then, while we have the opportunity, let us do good to all, but especially to those who belong to the family of the faith.

VI: Conclusion

Final Appeal. [11g*]See with what large letters I am writing to you in my own hand! [12h*]It is those who want to make a good appearance in the flesh who are trying to compel you to

5, 19–23: Such lists of vices and virtues (cf Rom 1, 29–31; 1 Cor 6, 9–10) were common in the ancient world. Paul contrasts **works of the flesh** (19) with **fruit** (not "works") **of the Spirit** (22). Not law, but the Spirit, leads to such traits.

5, 21: Occasions of envy: after the Greek word **phthonoi,** "envies," some manuscripts add a similar sounding one, **phonoi,** "murders."

6, 1–10: The ethical exhortations begun at 5, 1 continue with a variety of admonitions to the community (**brothers:** see the note on 1, 2). Nearly every sentence contains a separate item of practical advice; the faith and freedom of the gospel underlie each maxim. Tensions and temptation within communal life have previously been addressed in 5, 15,26, and v 1 continues with a case in which **a person is caught in some transgression** such as those in 5, 19–21; cf 2, 17.

6, 2: The law of Christ: cf Rom 8, 2; 1 Cor 9, 21; Gal 5, 14. The principle of love for others is meant. To **bear one another's burdens** is to "serve one another through love" (5, 13).

6, 4–5: Self-examination is the cure for self-deception. Compare what you are with what you were before, and give the glory to God; cf Rom 6, 19–22. **Load:** used elsewhere of a soldier's pack. Correcting one's own conduct avoids burdening others with it.

6, 6: Implies oral instruction in the faith by catechists; these are to be remunerated for their service; cf Rom 15, 27.

6, 10: The family of the faith: the Christian household or church. Doing good has a universal object (**to all**), but the lo-

cal community makes specific the reality of those to be served.

6, 11–18: A postscript in Paul's own hand, as was his practice (see 1 Cor 16, 21; 2 Thes 3, 17). Paul summarizes his appeal against his opponents (12–13), then returns to his message of glorying in the cross, not in circumcision, as the means of salvation (14–15; cf 5, 11). A benediction follows at v 16. In the polemical spirit that the attack on his apostleship called forth (1, 11—2, 21), Paul reasserts his missionary credentials (17) before giving a final benediction (18).

6, 11: Large letters: in contrast to the finer hand of the scribe who wrote the letter up to this point. The larger Greek letters make Paul's message even more emphatic. Some find a hint of poor eyesight on Paul's part. See the note on 4, 13.

6, 12–15: The Jewish Christian opponents wished **not to be persecuted,** possibly by Jews. But since Judaism seems to have had a privileged status as a religion in the Roman empire, circumcised Christians might, if taken as Jews, thereby

p: Rom 7, 15.23; 8, 6. *q:* Rom 6, 14; 8, 14. *r:* Rom 1, 29-31; 1 Cor 6, 9-10; Col 3, 5-6.8. *s:* Rv 22, 15. *t:* Eph 5, 9 / 1 Cor 13, 4-7; 2 Cor 6, 6; 1 Tm 4, 12; 2 Pt 1, 6. *u:* 1 Tm 1, 9. *v:* 2, 19; Rom 6, 6; 8, 13. *w:* 5, 16. *x:* Phil 2, 3. *y:* Mt 18, 15; Jas 5, 19 / 1 Cor 10, 12-13. *z:* Col 3, 13 / 1 Cor 9, 21. *a:* 1 Cor 3, 18; 8, 2; 2 Cor 12, 11. *b:* Rom 14, 12. *c:* 1 Cor 9, 14. *d:* Prv 11, 18; Rom 8, 6.13. *e:* 2 Thes 3, 13; Heb 12, 1-3. *f:* 1 Thes 5, 15. *g:* 1 Cor 16, 21. *h:* 5, 2.11.

have yourselves circumcised, only that they may not be persecuted for the cross of Christ. *13**Not even those having themselves circumcised observe the law themselves; they only want you to be circumcised so that they may boast of your flesh. *14i**But may I never boast except in the cross of our Lord Jesus Christ, through which the world has been crucified to me, and I to the world. *15 j**For neither does

avoid persecution from the Romans. In any case, Paul instead stresses conformity with **the cross of our Lord Jesus Christ;** cf 2, 19–21; 5, 11.

6, 13: Those having themselves circumcised: other manuscripts read, "those who have had themselves circumcised."

6, 14: Through which: or "through whom."

6, 15: New creation: or "new creature"; cf 2 Cor 5, 17.

6, 16: This rule: the principle in vv 14 and 15. **The Israel of God:** while the church may be meant (the phrase can be translated "to all who follow this rule, even the Israel of God"; cf 10; 1 Cor 10, 18), the reference may also be to God's ancient people, Israel; cf Pss 125, 5; 128, 6.

circumcision mean anything, nor does uncircumcision, but only a new creation. *16k**Peace and mercy be to all who follow this rule and to the Israel of God.

17 l*From now on, let no one make troubles for me; for I bear the marks of Jesus on my body.

*18m*The grace of our Lord Jesus Christ be with your spirit, brothers. Amen.

6, 17: The marks of Jesus: slaves were often branded by marks (**stigmata**) burned into their flesh to show to whom they belonged; so also were devotees of pagan gods. Paul implies that instead of outdated circumcision, his body bears the scars of his apostolic labors (2 Cor 11, 22–31), such as floggings (Acts 16, 22; 2 Cor 11, 25) and stonings (Acts 14, 19), that mark him as belonging to the Christ who suffered (cf Rom 6, 3; 2 Cor 4, 10; Col 1, 24) and will protect his own.

i: 2, 20; 1 Cor 2, 2.   *j:* 5, 6; 1 Cor 7, 19 / 2 Cor 5, 17.   *k:* Pss 125, 5; 128, 6.   *l:* 2 Cor 4, 10.   *m:* Phil 4, 23; 2 Tm 4, 22; Phlm 25.

See RG
471–75

The Letter to the Ephesians

Ephesians is the great Pauline letter about the church. It deals, however, not so much with a congregation in the city of Ephesus in Asia Minor as with the worldwide church, the head of which is Christ (4, 15), the purpose of which is to be the instrument for making God's plan of salvation known throughout the universe (3, 9–10). Yet this ecclesiology is anchored in God's saving love, shown in Jesus Christ (2, 4–10), and the whole of redemption is rooted in the plan and accomplishment of the triune God (1, 3–14). The language is often that of doxology (1, 3–14) and prayer (cf 1, 15–23; 3, 14–19), indeed of liturgy and hymns (3, 20–21; 5, 14).

The majestic chapters of Ephesians emphasize the unity in the church of Christ that has come about for both Jews and Gentiles within God's household (1, 15—2, 22, especially 2, 11–22) and indeed the "seven unities" of church, Spirit, hope; one Lord, faith, and baptism; and the one God (4, 4–6). Yet the concern is not with the church for its own sake but rather as the means for mission in the world (3, 1—4, 24). The gifts Christ gives its members are to lead to growth and renewal (4, 7–24). Ethical admonition is not lacking either; all aspects of human life and relationships are illumined by the light of Christ (4, 25—6, 20).

The letter is seemingly addressed by Paul to Christians in Ephesus (1, 1), a place where the apostle labored for well over two years (Acts 19, 10). Yet there is a curiously impersonal tone to the writing for a community with which Paul was so intimately acquainted (cf 3, 2 and 4, 21). There are no personal greetings (cf 6, 23). More significantly, important early manuscripts omit the words "in Ephesus" (see the note on 1, 1). Many therefore regard the letter as an encyclical or "circular letter" sent to a number of churches in Asia Minor, the addressees to be designated in each place by its bearer, Tychicus (6, 21–22). Others think that Ephesians is the letter referred to in Colossians 4, 16 as "to the Laodiceans."

Paul, who is designated as the sole author at 1, 1, is described in almost unparalleled terms with regard to the significant role he has in God's plan for bringing the Gentiles to faith in Christ (3, 1–12). Yet at the time of writing he is clearly in prison (3, 1; 4, 1; 6, 20), suffering afflictions (3, 13). Traditionally this "Captivity Epistle" has, along with Colossians, Philippians, and Philemon, been dated to an imprisonment in Rome, likely in A.D. 61–63. Others appeal to an earlier imprisonment, perhaps in Caesarea (Acts 23, 27—27, 2). Since the early nineteenth century, however, much of critical scholarship has considered the letter's style and use of words (especially when compared with Colossians), its concept of the church, and other points of doctrine put forward by the writer as grounds for serious doubt about authorship by Paul. The letter may then be the work of a secretary writing at the apostle's direction or of a later disciple who sought to develop Paul's ideas for a new situation around A.D. 80–100.

The principal divisions of the Letter to the Ephesians are the following:

I: Address (1, 1–14)

II: Unity of the Church in Christ (1, 15— 2, 22)

III: World Mission of the Church (3, 1—4, 24)

IV: Daily Conduct, an Expression of Unity (4, 25—6, 20)

V: Conclusion (6, 21–24).

I: Address

CHAPTER 1

See RG
472-73
Greeting. *1a**Paul, an apostle of Christ Jesus by the will of God, to the holy ones who are [in Ephesus] faithful in Christ

Jesus: *2b*grace to you and peace from God our Father and the Lord Jesus Christ.

The Father's Plan of Salvation. *3c**Blessed be the God and Father of our Lord Jesus Christ, who has blessed us in Christ with every spiritual blessing in the heavens, *4d*as he chose us in him, before the foundation of the world, to be holy and without blemish before him. In love *5e*he destined us for adoption to himself through Jesus Christ, in accord with the favor of his will, *6f*for the praise of the glory of his grace that he granted us in the beloved.

Fulfillment through Christ. *7g*In him we have redemption by his blood, the forgiveness of transgressions, in accord with the riches of his grace *8h*that he lavished upon us. In all wisdom and insight, *9i**he has made known to us the mystery of his will in accord with his favor that he set forth in him *10j*as a plan for the fullness of times, to sum up all things in Christ, in heaven and on earth.

Inheritance through the Spirit. *11k*In him we were also chosen, destined in accord with the purpose of the One who accomplishes all things according to the intention of his will, *12**so that we might exist for the

----

1, 1–2: For the epistolary form used at the beginning of letters, see the note on Rom 1, 1–7. Twenty-two of the thirty Greek words in vv 1–2 also occur in Col 1, 1–2.

1, 1: [In Ephesus]: the phrase is lacking in important early witnesses such as P46 (3rd cent.), and Sinaiticus and Vaticanus (4th cent.), appearing in the latter two as a fifth-century addition. Basil and Origen mention its absence from manuscripts. See Introduction. Without the phrase, the Greek can be rendered, as in Col 1, 2, "to the holy ones and faithful brothers in Christ."

1, 3–14: While a Pauline letter usually continues after the greeting with a prayer of thanksgiving, as in 15–23 below, Ephesians first inserts a blessing of God for the blessings Christians have experienced, as in 2 Cor 1, 3–4 and 1 Pt 1, 3–12. The blessing here, akin to a Jewish **berakah,** is rich in images almost certainly drawn from hymns and liturgy. Many ideas here are also found in Col 1, 3–23. Certain phrases are frequently repeated, such as **in Christ** (3.10.12) or **in him** (4.7.9.11.13) or **in the beloved** (6) and **(for) the praise of (his) glory** (6.12.14). Some terms like **chose** (4) and **destined** (5) reflect Old Testament theology (Dt 7, 7; 9, 4–6; 23, 5) or Pauline themes (**redemption,** 7.14; **grace,** 6.7) or specific emphases in Col (**forgiveness,** Col 1, 14).

A triadic structure is discernible in vv 3–14: **God the Father** (3–6.8.11), **Christ** (3.5.7–10.12), and the **Spirit** (13–14). The spiritual blessings Christians have received through Christ (3) are gratefully enumerated: the call to holi-

ness (4; cf Col 1, 22); the gift of divine **adoption** establishing a unique spiritual relationship with God the Father through Christ (5; cf Gal 4, 5); liberation from sin through Christ's sacrificial death (7); revelation of God's plan of salvation in Christ (9; cf 3, 3–4; Rom 16, 25); the gift of election and faith in Christ bestowed upon Jewish Christians (see the note on 12, **we who first hoped in Christ**); and finally, the same gift granted to Gentiles (13, **you also**). In the Christ-centered faith and existence of the Christian communities the apostle sees the predetermined **plan** of God to bring all creation under the final rule of Christ (4–5.9–10) being **made known** (9) and carried through, to God's glory (6.12.14).

1, 3: In the heavens: literally, "in the heavenlies" or "in the heavenly places," a term in Eph for the divine realm.

1, 9: Mystery: as in Rom 16, 25; Col 1, 26.27 and elsewhere, a secret of God now revealed in the **plan** to save and **sum up all things in Christ** (10); cf 3, 3–6.

1, 12: We who first hoped: probably Jewish Christians (contrast 13, **you,** the Gentiles); possibly the people of Israel, "we who already enjoyed the hope of Christ," or perhaps present hope in contrast to future redemption (cf 14).

----

a: Rom 1, 7; 1 Cor 1, 1-2; Col 1, 1. *b:* Col 1, 2. *c:* 2, 6; 2 Cor 1, 3. *d:* 5, 27; Jn 15, 16; 17, 24; Rom 8, 29; 2 Thes 2, 13. *e:* Jn 1, 12; 1 Jn 3, 1. *f:* Mt 3, 17; Col 1, 13. *g:* 2, 7-13; Rom 3, 24; Col 1, 14.20. *h:* Col 1, 9. *i:* 3, 3.9; Rom 16, 25. *j:* Gal 4, 4; Col 1, 16.20. *k:* Is 46, 10; Rom 8, 28; Col 1, 12; Rv 4, 11.

praise of his glory, we who first hoped in Christ. [13] [1]*In him you also, who have heard the word of truth, the gospel of your salvation, and have believed in him, were sealed with the promised holy Spirit, [14m]*which is the first installment of our inheritance toward redemption as God's possession, to the praise of his glory.

II: Unity of the Church in Christ

The Church as Christ's Body. [15n]*Therefore, I, too, hearing of your faith in the Lord Jesus and of your love for all the holy ones, [16o]do not cease giving thanks for you, remembering you in my prayers, [17p]that the God of our Lord Jesus Christ, the Father of glory, may give you a spirit of wisdom and revelation resulting in knowledge of him. [18q]May the eyes of [your] hearts be enlightened, that you may know what is the hope that belongs to his call, what are the riches of glory in his inheritance among the holy ones, [19r]and what is the surpassing greatness of his power for us who believe, in accord with the exercise of his great might, [20s]which he worked in Christ, raising him from the dead and seating him at his right hand in the heavens, [21t]far above every principality, authority, power, and dominion, and every name that is named not only in this age but also in the one to come. [22u]And he put all things beneath his feet and gave him as head over all things to the church, [23v]*which is his body, the fullness of the one who fills all things in every way.

CHAPTER 2

See RG 472–73

Generosity of God's Plan. [1w]*You were dead in your transgressions and sins [2x]*in which you once lived following the

---

1, 13: Sealed: by God, in baptism; cf 4, 30; 2 Cor 1, 22.

1, 14: First installment: down payment by God on full salvation, as at 2 Cor 1, 22.

1, 15–23: See the note on Rom 1, 8 for the thanksgiving form in a letter. Much of the content parallels thoughts in Col 1, 3–20. The prayer moves from God and Christ (17.20–21) to the Ephesians (17–19) and the church (22–23). Paul asks that the blessing imparted by God the Father (3) to the Ephesians will be strengthened in them through the message of the gospel (13.17–19). Those blessings are seen in the context of God's **might** in establishing the sovereignty of Christ over all other creatures (19–21) and in appointing him **head** of the church (22–23). For the allusion to angelic spirits in v 21, see Rom 8, 38 and Col 1, 16. Here, as in 1 Cor 15, 24–25 and Col 2, 15, every such **principality** and **power** is made subject to Christ.

1, 15: Your faith . . . your love: some manuscripts omit the latter phrase, but cf Col 1, 4.

1, 23: His body: the church (22); cf the note on Col 1, 18. Only in Eph and Col is Christ the **head** of the **body,** in contrast to the view in 1 Cor 12 and Rom 12, 4–8 where Christ is equated with the entire body or community. **Fullness:** see the note on Col 1, 19. Some take **the one who fills** as God, others as Christ (cf 4, 10). If in Christ "dwells the fullness of the deity bodily" (Col 2, 9), then, as God "fills" Christ, Christ in turn fills the church and the believer (3, 19; 5, 18). But the difficult phrases here may also allow the church to be viewed as the "complement" of Christ who is "being filled" as God's plan for the universe is carried out through the church (cf 3, 9–10).

2, 1–22: The gospel of **salvation** (1, 13) that God **worked in Christ** (1, 20) is reiterated in terms of what God's **great love** (4), expressed in Christ, means for us. The passage sometimes addresses **you,** Gentiles (1–2.8.11–13.19.22), but other times speaks of **all of us** who believe (3–7.10.14.18). In urging people to **remember** their grim past when they were **dead** in sins (1–3.11–12) and what they are **now in Christ** (4–10.13), the author sees both Jew and Gentile reconciled

with God, now **one new person,** a new humanity, **one body, the household of God, a temple** and **dwelling place** of God's Spirit (15–16.19–22). The presentation falls into two parts, the second stressing more the meaning for the church.

2, 1–10: The recipients of Paul's letter have experienced, in their redemption from **transgressions and sins,** the effect of Christ's supremacy over the power of the devil (1–2; cf 6, 11–12), who rules not from the netherworld but from the **air** between God in heaven and human beings on earth. Both Jew and Gentile have experienced, through Christ, God's free gift of salvation that already marks them for a future heavenly destiny (3–7). The language **dead, raised us up,** and **seated us . . . in the heavens** closely parallels Jesus' own passion and Easter experience. The terms in vv 8–9 describe salvation in the way Paul elsewhere speaks of justification: **by grace, through faith, the gift of God, not from works;** cf Gal 2, 16–21; Rom 3, 24–28. Christians are a newly created people in Christ, fashioned by God for a life of goodness (10).

2, 1–7: These verses comprise one long sentence in Greek, the main verb coming in v 5, God **brought us to life,** the object you/us **dead in . . . transgressions** being repeated in 1 and 5; cf Col 2, 13.

2, 2: Age of this world: or "aeon," a term found in gnostic thought, possibly synonymous with the **rulers of this world,** but also reflecting the Jewish idea of "two ages," this present evil age and "the age to come"; cf 1 Cor 3, 19; 5, 10; 7, 31; Gal 1, 4; Ti 2, 12. **The disobedient:** literally, "the sons of disobedience," a Semitism as at Is 30, 9.

l: 4, 30; Acts 2, 33; Col 1, 5-6. *m:* 2 Cor 1, 22; 5, 5. *n:* Col 1, 3-4; Phlm 4-5. *o:* Col 1, 3.9. *p:* 3, 14.16; Col 1, 9-10; 1 Jn 5, 20. *q:* 4, 4; Col 1, 12.27. *r:* 2 Cor 13, 4; Col 1, 11; 2, 12. *s:* Ps 110, 1; Heb 1, 3. *t:* Phil 2, 9; Col 1, 16; 1 Pt 3, 22. *u:* 4, 15; Ps 8, 7; Mt 28, 18; Col 1, 18. *v:* 4, 10.12; Rom 12, 5; 1 Cor 12, 27; Col 1, 19. *w:* Col 1, 21; 2, 13. *x:* 6, 12; Jn 12, 31; Col 1, 13.

age of this world, following the ruler of the power of the air, the spirit that is now at work in the disobedient. [3y]All of us once lived among them in the desires of our flesh, following the wishes of the flesh and the impulses, and we were by nature children of wrath, like the rest. [4]But God, who is rich in mercy, because of the great love he had for us, [5z*]even when we were dead in our transgressions, brought us to life with Christ (by grace you have been saved), [6a]raised us up with him, and seated us with him in the heavens in Christ Jesus, [7b]that in the ages to come he might show the immeasurable riches of his grace in his kindness to us in Christ Jesus. [8c]For by grace you have been saved through faith, and this is not from you; it is the gift of God; [9d]it is not from works, so no one may boast. [10e]For we are his handiwork, created in Christ Jesus for the good works that God has prepared in advance, that we should live in them.

One in Christ. [11*]Therefore, remember that at one time you, Gentiles in the flesh, called the uncircumcision by those called the circumcision, which is done in the flesh by human hands, [12f*]were at that time without Christ, alienated from the community of Israel and strangers to the covenants of promise, without hope and without God in the world. [13g]But now in Christ Jesus you

who once were far off have become near by the blood of Christ. [14h*]For he is our peace, he who made both one and broke down the dividing wall of enmity, through his flesh, [15i*]abolishing the law with its commandments and legal claims, that he might create in himself one new person in place of the two, thus establishing peace, [16j]and might reconcile both with God, in one body, through the cross, putting that enmity to death by it. [17k]He came and preached peace to you who were far off and peace to those who were near, [18l]for through him we both have access in one Spirit to the Father.

[19m]So then you are no longer strangers and sojourners, but you are fellow citizens with the holy ones and members of the household of God, [20n*]built upon the foundation of the apostles and prophets, with Christ Jesus himself as the capstone. [21o]Through him the whole structure is held together and grows into a temple sacred in the Lord; [22p]in him you also are being built together into a dwelling place of God in the Spirit.

III: World Mission of the Church

CHAPTER 3

Commission to Preach God's Plan. See RG 473 [1q*]Because of this, I, Paul, a prisoner of

---

2, 5: Our relation through baptism **with Christ**, the risen Lord, is depicted in terms of realized eschatology, as already exaltation, though v 7 brings in the future aspect too.

2, 11–22: The Gentiles lacked Israel's messianic expectation, lacked the various **covenants** God made with **Israel**, lacked **hope** of salvation and knowledge of the true **God** (11–12); but through Christ all these religious barriers between Jew and Gentile have been transcended (13–14) by the abolition of the Mosaic covenant-law (15) for the sake of uniting Jew and Gentile into a single religious community (15–16), imbued with the same holy **Spirit** and worshiping the same **Father** (18). The Gentiles are now included in God's **household** (19) as it arises upon the **foundation** of apostles assisted by those endowed with the prophetic gift (3, 5), the preachers of Christ (20; cf 1 Cor 12, 28). With Christ as the **capstone** (20; cf Is 28, 16; Mt 21, 42), they are being built into the holy **temple** of God's people where the divine presence dwells (21–22).

2, 12: The community of Israel: or "commonwealth"; cf 4, 18. The covenants: cf Rom 9, 4: with Abraham, with Moses, with David.

2, 14–16: The elaborate imagery here combines pictures

of Christ as **our peace** (Is 9, 5), his crucifixion, the ending of the Mosaic law (cf Col 2, 14), reconciliation (2 Cor 5, 18–21), and the destruction of **the dividing wall** such as kept people from God in the temple or a barrier in the heavens.

2, 15: One new person: a corporate body, the Christian community, made up of Jews and Gentiles, replacing ancient divisions; cf Rom 1, 16.

2, 20: Capstone: the Greek can also mean cornerstone or keystone.

3, 1–13: Paul reflects on his mission to the Gentiles. He alludes to his call and appointment to the apostolic office (2–3) and how his **insight** through revelation, as well as that of the other apostles and charismatic prophets in the church (4–5),

y: Col 3, 6-7. z: Rom 5, 8; 6, 13; Col 2, 13. a: Rom 8, 10-11; Phil 3, 20; Col 2, 12. b: 1, 7. c: Rom 3, 24; Gal 2, 16. d: 1 Cor 1, 29. e: 4, 24; Ti 2, 14. f: Rom 9, 4; Col 1, 21.27. g: 2, 17; Is 57, 19; Col 1, 20. h: Gal 3, 28. i: 2 Cor 5, 17; Col 2, 14. j: Col 1, 20.22. k: Is 57, 19; Zec 9, 10. l: 3, 12. m: Heb 12, 22-23. n: Is 28, 16; Rv 21, 14. o: 1 Cor 3, 16; Col 2, 19. p: 1 Pt 2, 5. q: Phil 1, 7.13; Col 1, 24-29; 4, 18; Phlm 1, 9; 2 Tm 2, 9.

Christ [Jesus] for you Gentiles— [2r*]if, as I suppose, you have heard of the stewardship of God's grace that was given to me for your benefit, [3s*][namely, that] the mystery was made known to me by revelation, as I have written briefly earlier. [4]When you read this you can understand my insight into the mystery of Christ, [5t]which was not made known to human beings in other generations as it has now been revealed to his holy apostles and prophets by the Spirit, [6u]that the Gentiles are coheirs, members of the same body, and copartners in the promise in Christ Jesus through the gospel.

[7v]Of this I became a minister by the gift of God's grace that was granted me in accord with the exercise of his power. [8w]To me, the very least of all the holy ones, this grace was given, to preach to the Gentiles the inscrutable riches of Christ, [9x*]and to bring to light [for all] what is the plan of the mystery hidden from ages past in God who created all things, [10y*]so that the manifold wisdom of God might now be made known through the church to the principalities and authorities in the heavens. [11]This was according to the eternal purpose that he accomplished in Christ Jesus our Lord, [12z]in whom we have boldness of speech and confidence of access through faith in him. [13a]So I ask you not to lose heart over my afflictions for you; this is your glory.

Prayer for the Readers. [14*]For this reason I kneel before the Father, [15]from whom every family in heaven and on earth is named, [16b]that he may grant you in accord with the riches of his glory to be strengthened with power through his Spirit in the inner self, [17c]and that Christ may dwell in your hearts through faith; that you, rooted and grounded in love, [18d]may have strength to comprehend with all the holy ones what is the breadth and length and height and depth, [19e]and to know the love of Christ that surpasses knowledge, so that you may be filled with all the fullness of God.

[20f]Now to him who is able to accomplish far more than all we ask or imagine, by the power at work within us, [21]to him be glory in the church and in Christ Jesus to all generations, forever and ever. Amen.

CHAPTER 4

Unity in the Body. [1g*]I, then, a prisoner for the Lord, urge you to live in a manner worthy of the call you have received, [2h]with all humility and gentleness, with pa-

---

has deepened understanding of God's plan of salvation in Christ. Paul is the special herald (7) of a new **promise** to the **Gentiles** (6): that the divine plan includes them in the spiritual benefits promised to Israel. Not only is this unique apostolic role his; Paul also has been given the task of explaining to all the divine **plan** of salvation (8–9), once **hidden.** Through **the church,** God's plan to save through Christ is becoming manifest to angelic beings (10; cf 1, 21), in accord with God's **purpose** (11). The fulfillment of the plan in Christ gives the whole church more **confidence** through **faith** in God (12). The readers of this letter are also thereby encouraged to greater confidence despite Paul's imprisonment (13).

3, 1: A **prisoner of Christ:** see Introduction. Paul abruptly departs from his train of thought at the end of v 1, leaving an incomplete sentence.

3, 2: Stewardship: the Greek is the same term employed at 1, 10 for the **plan** that God administers (Col 1, 25) and in which Paul plays a key role.

3, 3–4: The mystery: God's resolve to deliver Gentiles along with Israel through Christ; cf the notes on 1, 10; 3, 9.

3, 9: [For all]: while some think this phrase was added so as to yield the sense "to enlighten all about the plan . . . ," it is more likely that some manuscripts and Fathers omitted it accidentally or to avoid the idea that **all** conflicted with Paul's assignment to preach to **the Gentiles** (8) specifically.

3, 10: Principalities and authorities: see the note on 1, 15–23 regarding v 21.

3, 14–21: The apostle prays that those he is addressing may, like the rest of the church, deepen their understanding of God's plan of salvation in Christ. It is a plan that affects the whole universe (15) with **the breadth and length and height and depth** of God's love in Christ (18) or possibly the universe in all its dimensions. The apostle prays that they may perceive the redemptive love of Christ for them and be completely immersed in the fullness of God (19). The prayer concludes with a doxology to God (20–21).

3, 14–15: Every family: in the Greek there is wordplay on the word for **the Father (patria, patēr).** The phrase could also mean "God's whole family" (cf 2, 21).

4, 1–16: A general plea for unity in the church. Christians have been fashioned through the **Spirit** into a single harmonious religious community (one **body,** 4.12; cf 16), belonging to a single **Lord** (in contrast to the many gods of the pagan world), and by one way of salvation through **faith,** brought out especially by the significance of **baptism** (1–6; cf Rom 6, 1–11). But Christian unity is more than adherence to a com-

---

r: Col 1, 25. *s:* 1, 9-10; Col 1, 26. *t:* Col 1, 26. *u:* 2, 13.18-19. *v:* Rom 15, 15; Col 1, 25.29. *w:* 1 Cor 15, 8-10; Gal 1, 16; 2, 7-9. *x:* Rom 16, 25; Col 1, 26-27. *y:* 1 Pt 1, 12. *z:* Rom 5, 1-2; Heb 4, 16. *a:* Col 1, 22.24; 2 Tm 2, 10. *b:* 6, 10; Rom 7, 22; 2 Cor 4, 16; Col 1, 11. *c:* Jn 14, 23; Col 1, 23; 2, 7. *d:* Col 2, 2. *e:* Col 2, 3.9. *f:* Rom 16, 25-27; Col 1, 29. *g:* 3, 1; Col 1, 10. *h:* Col 3, 12-13.

tience, bearing with one another through love, [3i]striving to preserve the unity of the spirit through the bond of peace: [4j*]one body and one Spirit, as you were also called to the one hope of your call; [5k]one Lord, one faith, one baptism; [6l]one God and Father of all, who is over all and through all and in all. *Diversity of Gifts.* [7m]But grace was given to each of us according to the measure of Christ's gift. [8n*]Therefore, it says:

"He ascended on high and took prisoners captive;

he gave gifts to men."

[9]What does "he ascended" mean except that he also descended into the lower [regions] of the earth? [10]The one who descended is also the one who ascended far above all the heavens, that he might fill all things.

[11o*]And he gave some as apostles, others as prophets, others as evangelists, others as pastors and teachers, [12*]to equip the holy ones for the work of ministry, for building up the body of Christ, [13p*]until we all attain to the unity of faith and knowledge of the Son of God, to mature manhood, to the extent of the full stature of Christ, [14q]so that we may no longer be infants, tossed by waves and swept along by every wind of teaching arising from human trickery, from their cunning in the interests of deceitful scheming. [15r*]Rather, living the truth in love, we should grow in every way into him who is the head, Christ, [16s]from whom the whole body, joined and held together by every supporting ligament, with the proper functioning of each part, brings about the body's growth and builds itself up in love.

Renewal in Christ. [17t*]So I declare and testify in the Lord that you must no longer live as the Gentiles do, in the futility of their minds; [18u]darkened in understanding, alienated from the life of God because of their ignorance, because of their hardness of heart, [19v]they have become callous and have handed themselves over to licentiousness for the practice of every kind of impurity to excess. [20]That is not how you learned Christ, [21]assuming that you have heard of him and were taught in him, as truth is in Jesus, [22w]that you should put away the old self of your former way of life, corrupted through deceitful desires, [23x]and be renewed in the spirit of your minds, [24y*]and put on the new self, created in God's way in righteousness and holiness of truth.

---

mon belief. It is manifested in the exalted Christ's gifts to individuals to serve so as to make the community more Christlike (11–16). This teaching on Christ as the source of the gifts is introduced in v 8 by a citation of Ps 68, 18, which depicts Yahweh triumphantly leading Israel to salvation in Jerusalem. It is here understood of Christ, ascending **above all the heavens**, the **head** of the church; through his redemptive death, resurrection, and ascension he has become the source of the church's spiritual gifts. The "descent" of Christ (9–10) refers more probably to the incarnation (cf Phil 2, 6–8) than to Christ's presence after his death in the world of the dead (cf 1 Pt 3, 19).

4, 4–6: The "seven unities" (church, **Spirit, hope; Lord, faith** in Christ [1, 13], **baptism; one God**) reflect the triune structure of later creeds in reverse.

4, 8–10: While the emphasis is on an ascension and giftgiving by Christ, there is also a reference in taking **prisoners captive** to the aeons and powers mentioned at 1, 21; 2, 2; 3, 10; and 6, 12.

4, 11: Concerning this list of ministers, cf 1 Cor 12, 28 and Rom 12, 6–8. **Evangelists:** missionary preachers (cf Acts 21, 8 and 2 Tm 4, 5), not those who wrote gospels. **Pastors and teachers:** a single group in the Greek, shepherding congregations.

4, 12: The ministerial leaders in v 11 are to equip the whole people of God for their **work of ministry.**

4, 13: Mature manhood: literally, "a perfect man" (cf Col 1, 28), possibly the "one new person" of 2, 15, though there **anthrōpos** suggests humanity, while here **anēr** is the term for male. This personage becomes visible in the church's growing to its fullness in the unity of those who believe in Christ.

4, 15–16: The head, Christ: cf Col 1, 18 and contrast 1 Cor 12, 12–27 and Rom 12, 4–5 where Christ is identified with the whole body, including the head. The imagery may derive from ancient views in medicine, the **head** coordinating and caring for the body, each **ligament** (perhaps the ministers of v 11) supporting the whole. But as at 2, 19–22, where the temple is depicted as a growing organism, there may also be the idea here of growing toward the capstone, Christ.

4, 17–24: Paul begins to indicate how the new life in Christ contrasts with the Gentiles' old way of existence. Literally, **the old self** (22) and **the new self** (24) are "the old man" and "the new man" (**anthrōpos**, person), as at 2, 15; cf the note on 4, 13.

4, 24: Put on: in baptism. See the note on Gal 3, 27.

---

i: Col 3, 14-15. *j:* Rom 12, 5; 1 Cor 10, 17; 12, 12-13. *k:* 1 Cor 8, 6. *l:* 1 Cor 12, 6. *m:* Rom 12, 3.6; 1 Cor 12, 28. *n:* Ps 68, 19; Col 2, 15. *o:* 1 Cor 12, 28. *p:* Col 1, 28. *q:* 1 Cor 14, 20; Col 2, 4.8; Heb 13, 9; Jas 1, 6. *r:* 1 Cor 11, 3; Col 1, 18; 2, 19. *s:* Col 2, 19. *t:* Rom 1, 21. *u:* Col 1, 21; 1 Pt 1, 14. *v:* Col 3, 5. *w:* Rom 8, 13; Gal 6, 8; Col 3, 9. *x:* Rom 12, 2. *y:* Gn 1, 26-27; Col 3, 10.

IV: Daily Conduct, an Expression of Unity

Rules for the New Life. [25z]*Therefore, putting away falsehood, speak the truth, each one to his neighbor, for we are members one of another. [26a]*Be angry but do not sin; do not let the sun set on your anger, [27b]and do not leave room for the devil. [28c]*The thief must no longer steal, but rather labor, doing honest work with his [own] hands, so that he may have something to share with one in need. [29d]No foul language should come out of your mouths, but only such as is good for needed edification, that it may impart grace to those who hear. [30]*And do not grieve the holy Spirit of God, with which you were sealed for the day of redemption. [31e]All bitterness, fury, anger, shouting, and reviling must be removed from you, along with all malice. [32f][And] be kind to one another, compassionate, forgiving one another as God has forgiven you in Christ.

CHAPTER 5

See RG 473–74 [1g]*So be imitators of God, as beloved children, [2h]and live in love, as Christ loved us and handed himself over for us as a sacrificial offering to God for a fragrant aroma. [3i]Immorality or any impurity or greed must not even be mentioned among you, as is fitting among holy ones, [4j]no obscenity or silly or suggestive talk, which is out of place, but instead, thanksgiving. [5k]Be sure of this, that no immoral or impure or greedy person, that is, an idolater, has any inheritance in the kingdom of Christ and of God.

Duty to Live in the Light. [6l]*Let no one deceive you with empty arguments, for because of these things the wrath of God is coming upon the disobedient. [7]So do not be associated with them. [8m]For you were once darkness, but now you are light in the Lord. Live as children of light, [9n]for light produces every kind of goodness and righteousness and truth. [10o]Try to learn what is pleasing to the Lord. [11p]Take no part in the fruitless works of darkness; rather expose them, [12]for it is shameful even to mention the things done by them in secret; [13q]but everything exposed by the light becomes visible, [14r]for everything that becomes visible is light. Therefore, it says:

"Awake, O sleeper,
  and arise from the dead,
and Christ will give you light."

[15s]*Watch carefully then how you live, not as foolish persons but as wise, [16]making the most of the opportunity, because the days are evil. [17]Therefore, do not continue in ignorance, but try to understand what is the will of the Lord. [18t]And do not get drunk on wine, in which lies debauchery, but be filled with the Spirit, [19u]addressing one another [in] psalms and hymns and spiritual songs, singing and playing to the Lord in your hearts, [20v]giving thanks always and for everything in the name of our Lord Jesus Christ to God the Father.

Wives and Husbands. [21w]*Be subordinate

4, 25—6, 20: For similar exhortations to a morally good life in response to God's gift of faith, see the notes on Rom 12, 1—13, 14 and Gal 5, 13–26.

4, 26: If angry, seek reconciliation that day, not giving the devil (6, 11) opportunity to lead into sin.

4, 28: **Honest work:** literally, "the good." **His [own] hands:** some manuscripts have the full phrase as in 1 Cor 4, 12.

4, 30: See the note on 1, 13.

5, 1: **Imitators of God:** in forgiving (4, 32) and in loving (as exhibited in how **Christ loved us**).

5, 6: See the note on 2, 2.

5, 14: An early Christian hymn, possibly from a baptismal liturgy. For the content compare 2, 5–6; 3, 9 and Is 60, 1.

5, 15—16.19–20: The wording is similar to Col 4, 5 and 3, 16–17.

5, 21—6, 9: Cf the notes on Col 3, 18—4, 1 and 1 Pt 2, 18—3, 7 for a similar listing of household duties where the inferior is admonished first (**wives,** 5, 22; **children,** 6, 1; **slaves,** 6, 5),

then the superior (**husbands,** 5, 25; **fathers,** 6, 4; **masters,** 6, 9). Paul varies this pattern by an emphasis on mutuality (see 5, 20); use of Old Testament material about **father and mother** in 6, 2; the judgment to come for slave-owners (**you have a Master in heaven,** 6, 9); and above all the initial principle of subordination **to one another** under **Christ,** thus effectively undermining exclusive claims to domination by one party. Into the section on **wives** and **husbands** an elaborate teaching on

z: Zec 8, 16. a: Ps 4, 5 LXX; Mt 5, 22. b: 2 Cor 2, 11.
c: 1 Thes 4, 11. d: 5, 4; Col 3, 16; 4, 6. e: Col 3, 8. f: Mt 6, 14;
Col 3, 12-13. g: Mt 5, 45.48. h: Ex 29, 18; Ps 40, 7; Gal 2, 20;
1 Jn 3, 16. i: Gal 5, 19; Col 3, 5. j: 4, 29; Col 3, 8. k: 1 Cor 6,
9-10; Gal 5, 21; Col 3, 5. l: Rom 1, 18; Col 2, 4.8. m: 2, 11-13;
Jn 12, 36; Col 1, 12-13. n: Gal 5, 22. o: Rom 12, 2. p: Rom
13, 12. q: Jn 3, 20-21. r: Is 26, 19; 60, 1. s: Col 4, 5. t: Prv
23, 31 LXX; Lk 21, 34. u: Ps 33, 2-3; Col 3, 16. v: Col 3, 17.
w: 1 Pt 5, 5.

to one another out of reverence for Christ. [22x]Wives should be subordinate to their husbands as to the Lord. [23y]For the husband is head of his wife just as Christ is head of the church, he himself the savior of the body. [24]As the church is subordinate to Christ, so wives should be subordinate to their husbands in everything. [25z]Husbands, love your wives, even as Christ loved the church and handed himself over for her [26a]to sanctify her, cleansing her by the bath of water with the word, [27b]that he might present to himself the church in splendor, without spot or wrinkle or any such thing, that she might be holy and without blemish. [28]So [also] husbands should love their wives as their own bodies. He who loves his wife loves himself. [29]For no one hates his own flesh but rather nourishes and cherishes it, even as Christ does the church, [30c]because we are members of his body.

[31] [d]"For this reason a man shall leave [his]
father and [his] mother
and be joined to his wife,
and the two shall become one flesh."

[32e]This is a great mystery, but I speak in reference to Christ and the church. [33]In any case, each one of you should love his wife as himself, and the wife should respect her husband.

See RG
473–74

CHAPTER 6

Children and Parents. [1f]Children, obey your parents [in the Lord], for this is right. [2g]"Honor your father and mother." This is the first commandment with a promise, [3]"that it may go well with you and that

you may have a long life on earth." [4h]Fathers, do not provoke your children to anger, but bring them up with the training and instruction of the Lord.

Slaves and Masters. [5i]Slaves, be obedient to your human masters with fear and trembling, in sincerity of heart, as to Christ, [6j]not only when being watched, as currying favor, but as slaves of Christ, doing the will of God from the heart, [7]willingly serving the Lord and not human beings, [8]knowing that each will be requited from the Lord for whatever good he does, whether he is slave or free. [9k]Masters, act in the same way toward them, and stop bullying, knowing that both they and you have a Master in heaven and that with him there is no partiality.

Battle against Evil. [10*]Finally, draw your strength from the Lord and from his mighty power. [11l]Put on the armor of God so that you may be able to stand firm against the tactics of the devil. [12m]For our struggle is not with flesh and blood but with the principalities, with the powers, with the world rulers of this present darkness, with the evil spirits in the heavens. [13n]Therefore, put on the armor of God, that you may be able to resist on the evil day and, having done everything, to hold your ground. [14o]So stand fast with your loins girded in truth, clothed with righteousness as a breastplate, [15p]and your feet shod in readiness for the gospel of peace. [16q]In all circumstances, hold faith as a shield, to quench all [the] flaming arrows of the evil one. [17r]And take the helmet of salvation and the sword of the Spirit, which is the word of God.

Constant Prayer. [18s]With all prayer and supplication, pray at every opportunity in

---

Christ and the church has been woven (5, 22–33).

5, 21–33: The apostle exhorts married Christians to a strong mutual love. Holding with Gn 2, 24 that marriage is a divine institution (31), Paul sees Christian marriage as taking on a new meaning symbolic of the intimate relationship of love between Christ and the church. The wife should serve her husband in the same spirit as that of the church's service to Christ (22.24), and the husband should care for his wife with the devotion of Christ to the church (25–30). Paul gives to the Genesis passage its highest meaning in the light of the union of Christ and the church, of which Christlike loyalty and devotion in Christian marriage are a clear reflection (31–33).

6, 10–20: A general exhortation to courage and prayer. Drawing upon the imagery and ideas of Is 11, 5; 59, 16–17; and Wis 5, 17–23, Paul describes the Christian in terms of the

dress and equipment of Roman soldiers. He observes, however, that the Christian's readiness for combat is not directed against human beings but against the spiritual powers of evil (10–17; cf 1, 21; 2, 2; 3, 10). Unique importance is placed upon prayer (18–20).

x: Col 3, 18—4, 1; 1 Pt 3, 1-7.   y: 1 Cor 11, 3; Col 1, 18.   z: Col 3, 19; 1 Tm 2, 6.   a: Rom 6, 4; Ti 3, 5-7.   b: 2 Cor 11, 2; Col 1, 22.   c: Rom 12, 5; 1 Cor 6, 15.   d: Gn 2, 24; Mt 19, 5; Mk 10, 7-8.   e: Rv 19, 7.   f: Prv 6, 20; Sir 3, 1-6; Col 3, 20.   g: Ex 20, 12; Dt 5, 16.   h: Col 3, 21-22.   i: Col 3, 22-25; 1 Tm 6, 1-2; Ti 2, 9-10.   j: 1 Pt 2, 18.   k: Col 4, 1.   l: Rom 13, 12; 2 Cor 6, 7; 10, 4; Jas 4, 7.   m: 1, 21; 2, 2; Col 1, 13.   n: Rom 13, 12.   o: Wis 5, 17-20; Is 11, 5; Lk 12, 35; 1 Thes 5, 8.   p: Is 52, 7.   q: 1 Pt 5, 9.   r: Is 59, 17; 1 Thes 5, 8.   s: Mt 26, 41; Col 4, 2-3.

the Spirit. To that end, be watchful with all perseverance and supplication for all the holy ones ^{19t}and also for me, that speech may be given me to open my mouth, to make known with boldness the mystery of the gospel ^{20u}for which I am an ambassador in chains, so that I may have the courage to speak as I must.

V: Conclusion

A Final Message. ^{21v}*So that you also may

have news of me and of what I am doing, Tychicus, my beloved brother and trustworthy minister in the Lord, will tell you everything. ^{22w}I am sending him to you for this very purpose, so that you may know about us and that he may encourage your hearts.

²³Peace be to the brothers, and love with faith, from God the Father and the Lord Jesus Christ. ^{24x}Grace be with all who love our Lord Jesus Christ in immortality.

6, 21–24: Tychicus: the bearer of the letter; see the note on Col 4, 7. Verses 21–22 parallel Col 4, 7–8, often word for word. If Ephesians is addressed to several Christian communities (see Introduction), it is understandable that no greetings to individual members of these communities should have been included in it.

t: Acts 4, 29; Col 4, 3; 2 Thes 3, 1.   *u:* 2 Cor 5, 20; Col 4, 4.   *v:* Acts 20, 4; Col 4, 7; 2 Tm 4, 12.   *w:* Col 4, 8.   *x:* 1 Pt 1, 8.

See RG
475–78

The Letter to the Philippians

Philippi, in northeastern Greece, was a city of some importance in the Roman province of Macedonia. Lying on the great road from the Adriatic coast to Byzantium, the Via Egnatia, and in the midst of rich agricultural plains near the gold deposits of Mt. Pangaeus, it was in Paul's day a Roman town (Acts 16, 21), with a Greek-Macedonian population and a small group of Jews (see Acts 16, 13). Originally founded in the sixth century B.C. as Krenides by the Thracians, the town was taken over after 360 B.C. by Philip II of Macedon, the father of Alexander the Great, and was renamed for himself, "Philip's City." The area became Roman in the second century B.C. On the plains near Philippi in October 42 B.C., Antony and Octavian decisively defeated the forces of Brutus and Cassius, the slayers of Julius Caesar. Octavian (Augustus) later made Philippi a Roman colony and settled many veterans of the Roman armies there.

Paul, according to Acts (16, 9–40), established at Philippi the first Christian community in Europe. He came to Philippi, via its harbor town of Neapolis (modern Kavalla), on his second missionary journey, probably in A.D. 49 or 50, accompanied by Silas and Timothy (Acts 15, 40; 16, 3; cf Phil 1, 1) and Luke, if he is to be included in the "we" references of Acts 16, 10–17. The Acts account tells of the conversion of a business woman, Lydia; the exorcism of a slave girl;

and, after an earthquake, while Paul and Silas were imprisoned in Philippi, the faith and baptism of a jailer and his family. None of these persons, however, is directly mentioned in Philippians (cf the notes on 4, 2 and 4, 3). Acts 16 concludes its account by describing how Paul (and Silas), asked by the magistrates to leave Philippi, went on to Thessalonica (Acts 17, 1–10), where several times his loyal Philippians continued to support him with financial aid (Phil 4, 16). Later, Paul may have passed through Philippi on his way from Ephesus to Greece (Acts 20, 1–2), and he definitely stopped there on his fateful trip to Jerusalem (Acts 20, 6).

Paul's letter to the Christians at Philippi was written while he was in a prison somewhere (1, 7.13.14.17), indeed in danger of death (1, 20–23). Although under guard for preaching Christ, Paul rejoices at the continuing progress of the gospel (1, 12–26) and expresses gratitude for the Philippians' renewed concern and help in an expression of thanks most clearly found at 4, 10–20. Much of the letter is devoted to instruction about unity and humility within the Christian community at Philippi (1, 27—2, 18) and exhortations to growth, joy, and peace in their life together (4, 1–9). The letter seems to be drawing to a close at the end of what we number as ch 2, as Paul reports the plans of his helper Timothy and of Epaphroditus (whom the Philippians had sent to aid Paul) to come to Philippi (2, 19—3, 1), and even Paul's own expectation that he will go free-and come to Philippi (1, 25–26; 2, 24). Yet quite abruptly at 3, 2, Paul erupts into warnings against false teachers who threaten to impose on the Philippians the burdens of the Mosaic law, including circumcision. The section that follows, 3, 2–21, is a vigorous attack on these Judaizers (cf Gal 2, 11—3, 29) or Jewish Christian teachers (cf 2 Cor 11, 12–23), giving us insights into Paul's own life story (3, 4–6) and into the doctrine of justification, the Christian life, and ultimate hope (3, 7–21).

The location of Paul's imprisonment when he wrote to the Philippians, and thus the date of the letter, are uncertain. The traditional view has been that it stems from Paul's confinement in Rome, between A.D. 59 and 63 (cf Acts 28, 14–31). One modern view suggests the period when he was imprisoned at Caesarea, on the coast of Palestine, A.D. 57 or 58 (Acts 23, 23—26, 32); another suggests Corinth (cf 2 Cor 11, 9). Much recent scholarship favors Ephesus, around A.D. 55, a situation referred to in 2 Cor 1, 8 concerning "the affliction that came to us" in Asia Minor (cf also 1 Cor 15, 32). The reference at 1, 13 to the "praetorium" (cf also 4, 22) can be understood to mean the imperial guard or government house at Ephesus (or Caesarea), or the praetorian camp in Rome. Involved in a decision are the several journeys back and forth between Philippi and wherever Paul is imprisoned, mentioned in the letter (2, 25–28; 4, 14); this factor causes many to prefer Ephesus because of its proximity to Philippi. The Ephesian hypothesis dates the composition of Philippians to the mid-50s when most of Paul's major letters were written.

There is also a likelihood, according to some scholars, that the letter as we have it is a composite from parts of three letters by Paul to the Philippians. Seemingly 4, 10–20 is a brief note of appreciation for help sent through Epaphroditus. The long section from 1, 3 to 3, 1 is then another letter, with news of Paul's imprisonment and reports on Timothy and Epaphroditus (who has fallen ill while with Paul), along with exhortations to the Philippians about Christian conduct; and 3, 2–21 a third communication warning about threats to Philippian Christianity. The other verses in ch 4 and 1, 1–2, are vari-

ously assigned by critics to these three underlying letters, which an editor presumably put together to produce a picture of Paul writing earnestly from prison (1–2), facing opponents of the faith (ch 3), and with serene joy advising and thanking his Philippians (ch 4). If all four chapters were originally a unity, then one must assume that a break occurred between the writing of 3, 1 and 3, 2, possibly involving the receipt of bad news from Philippi, and that Paul had some reasons for delaying his words of thanks for the aid brought by Epaphroditus till the end of his letter.

This beautiful letter is rich in insights into Paul's theology and his apostolic love and concern for the gospel and his converts. In Philippians, Paul reveals his human sensitivity and tenderness, his enthusiasm for Christ as the key to life and death (1, 21), and his deep feeling for those in Christ who dwell in Philippi. With them he shares his hopes and convictions, his anxieties and fears, revealing the total confidence in Christ that constitutes faith (3, 8–10). The letter incorporates a hymn about the salvation that God has brought about through Christ (2, 6–11), applied by Paul to the relations of Christians with one another (2, 1–5). Philippians has been termed "the letter of joy" (4, 4.10). It is the rejoicing of faith, based on true understanding of Christ's unique role in the salvation of all who profess his lordship (2, 11; 3, 8–12.14; 20–21).

The principal divisions of the Letter to the Philippians are the following:

I: Address (1, 1–11)

II: Progress of the Gospel (1, 12–26)

III: Instructions for the Community (1, 27—2, 18)

IV: Travel Plans of Paul and His Assistants (2, 19—3, 1)

V: Polemic: Righteousness and the Goal in Christ (3, 2–21)

VI: Instructions for the Community (4, 1–9)

VII: Gratitude for the Philippians' Generosity (4, 10–20)

VIII: Farewell (4, 21–23)

I: Address

CHAPTER 1

See RG
476

Greeting. *1a**Paul and Timothy, slaves of Christ Jesus, to all the holy ones in Christ Jesus who are in Philippi, with the overseers and ministers: *2b**grace to you and peace from God our Father and the Lord Jesus Christ.

Thanksgiving. *3c**I give thanks to my God at every remembrance of you, *4*praying always with joy in my every prayer for all of you, *5*because of your partnership for the gospel from the first day until now. *6d**I am confident of this, that the one who began a good work in you will continue to complete it until the day of Christ Jesus. *7*It is right that I should think this way about all of you, because I hold you in my heart, you who are all partners with me in grace, both in my imprisonment and in the defense and confirmation of the gospel. *8e*For God is my witness, how I long for all of you with the affection of Christ Jesus. *9f*And this is my prayer: that your love may increase ever more and more in knowledge and every kind of perception, *10g*to discern what is of value, so that you may be pure and blameless for the day of Christ, *11h*filled with the fruit of righteousness that comes through Jesus Christ for the glory and praise of God.

II: Progress of the Gospel

12i*I want you to know, brothers, that my situation has turned out rather to advance the gospel, *13j**so that my imprisonment has become well known in Christ throughout the whole praetorium and to all the rest, *14**and so that the majority of the brothers, having taken encouragement in the Lord from my

---

1, 1–2: See the note on Rom 1, 1–7, concerning the greeting.

1, 1: Slaves: Paul usually refers to himself at the start of a letter as an apostle. Here he substitutes a term suggesting the unconditional obligation of himself and Timothy to the service of Christ, probably because, in view of the good relationship with the Philippians, he wishes to stress his status as a co-servant rather than emphasize his apostolic authority. Reference to Timothy is a courtesy: Paul alone writes the letter, as the singular verb throughout shows (3–26), and the reference (2, 19–24) to Timothy in the third person. **Overseers:** the Greek term **episkopos** literally means "one who oversees" or "one who supervises," but since the second century it has come to designate the "bishop," the official who heads a local church. In New Testament times this office had not yet developed into the form that it later assumed, though it seems to be well on the way to such development in the Pastorals; see 1 Tm 3, 2 and Ti 1, 7, where it is translated **bishop.** At Philippi, however (and at Ephesus, according to Acts 20, 28), there was more than one **episkopos,** and the precise function of these officials is uncertain. In order to distinguish this office from the later stages into which it developed, the term is here translated as **overseers. Ministers:** the Greek term **diakonoi** is used frequently in the New Testament to designate "servants," "attendants," or "ministers." Paul refers to himself and to other apostles as "ministers of God" (2 Cor 6, 4) or "ministers of Christ" (2 Cor 11, 23). In the Pastorals (1 Tm 3, 8.12) the **diakonos** has become an established official in the local church; hence the term is there translated as **deacon.** The **diakonoi** at Philippi seem to represent an earlier stage of development of the office; we are uncertain about their precise functions. Hence the term is here translated as **ministers.** See Rom 16, 1, where Phoebe is described as a **diakonos** (**minister**) of the church of Cenchreae.

1, 2: The gifts come **from** Christ the Lord, not simply through him from the Father; compare the christology in 2, 6–11.

1, 3–11: As in Rom 1, 8–15 and all the Pauline letters except Galatians, a thanksgiving follows, including a direct prayer for the Philippians (9–11); see the note on Rom 1, 8. On their **partnership for the gospel** (5), cf 29–30; 4, 10–20. Their devotion to the faith and to Paul made them his pride and joy (4, 1). The characteristics thus manifested are evidence of the community's continuing preparation for the Lord's parousia (6.10). Paul's especially warm relationship with the Philippians is suggested here (7.8) as elsewhere in the letter. The eschatology serves to underscore a concern for ethical growth (9–11), which appears throughout the letter.

1, 6: The day of Christ Jesus: the parousia or triumphant return of Christ, when those loyal to him will be with him and share in his eternal glory; cf 10; 2, 16; 3, 20–21; 1 Thes 4, 17; 5, 10; 2 Thes 1, 10; 1 Cor 1, 8.

1, 12–26: The body of the letter begins with an account of Paul's present **situation,** i.e., his **imprisonment** (12–13; see Introduction), and then goes on with advice for the Philippians (1, 27—2, 18). The **advance** of **the gospel** (12) and the **progress** of the Philippians **in the faith** (25) frame what is said.

1, 13: Praetorium: either the praetorian guard in the city where Paul was imprisoned or the governor's official residence in a Roman province (cf Mk 15, 16; Acts 23, 35). See Introduction on possible sites.

1, 14–18: Although Paul is imprisoned, Christians there nonetheless go on preaching Christ. But they do so with varied motives, **some** with personal hostility toward Paul, others out of personal ambition.

---

a: Rom 1, 1; 2 Cor 1, 1; 1 Thes 1, 1; Phlm 1 / 1 Tm 3, 1-13. *b:* Rom 1, 7; Gal 1, 3; Phlm 3. *c:* Rom 1, 8; 1 Cor 1, 4; 1 Thes 1, 2. *d:* 2, 13 / 1, 10; 2, 16; 1 Cor 1, 8. *e:* Rom 1, 9; 2 Cor 1, 23; 1 Thes 2, 5. *f:* Eph 3, 14-19; Col 1, 9-10; Phlm 6. *g:* Rom 2, 18; 12, 2 / 1, 6. *h:* Jn 15, 8. *i:* Eph 3, 1; 6, 20; 2 Tm 2, 9; Phlm 9. *j:* 4, 22.

imprisonment, dare more than ever to proclaim the word fearlessly.

[15]Of course, some preach Christ from envy and rivalry, others from good will. [16]The latter act out of love, aware that I am here for the defense of the gospel; [17]the former proclaim Christ out of selfish ambition, not from pure motives, thinking that they will cause me trouble in my imprisonment. [18k]*What difference does it make, as long as in every way, whether in pretense or in truth, Christ is being proclaimed? And in that I rejoice.

Indeed I shall continue to rejoice, [19l]*for I know that this will result in deliverance for me through your prayers and support from the Spirit of Jesus Christ. [20m]My eager expectation and hope is that I shall not be put to shame in any way, but that with all boldness, now as always, Christ will be magnified in my body, whether by life or by death. [21n]For to me life is Christ, and death is gain. [22o]If I go on living in the flesh, that means fruitful labor for me. And I do not know which I shall choose. [23p]I am caught between the two. I long to depart this life and be with Christ, [for] that is far better. [24]Yet that I remain [in] the flesh is more necessary for your benefit. [25]And this I know with confidence, that I shall remain and continue in the service of all of you for your progress and joy in the faith, [26]so that your boasting in Christ Jesus may abound on account of me when I come to you again.

III: Instructions for the Communtiy

Steadfastness in Faith. [27q]*Only, conduct yourselves in a way worthy of the gospel of Christ, so that, whether I come and see you or am absent, I may hear news of you, that you are standing firm in one spirit, with one mind struggling together for the faith of the gospel, [28]not intimidated in any way by your opponents. This is proof to them of destruction, but of your salvation. And this is God's doing. [29r]For to you has been granted, for the sake of Christ, not only to believe in him but also to suffer for him. [30s]*Yours is the same struggle as you saw in me and now hear about me.

CHAPTER 2

See RG
476–77

Plea for Unity and Humility. [1]*If there is any encouragement in Christ, any solace in love, any participation in the Spirit, any compassion and mercy, [2t]complete my joy by being of the same mind, with the same love, united in heart, thinking one thing. [3u]Do nothing out of selfishness or out of vainglory; rather, humbly regard others as more important than yourselves, [4v]each looking out not for his own interests, but [also] everyone for those of others.

[5]*Have among yourselves the same attitude that is also yours in Christ Jesus,

1, 18: Rejoice: a major theme in the letter; see Introduction.

1, 19–25: Paul earnestly debates his prospects of martyrdom or continued missionary labor. While he may **long to depart this life** and thus **be with Christ** (23), his overall and final expectation is that he will be delivered from this imprisonment and **continue in the service** of the Philippians and of others (19.25; 2, 24). In either case, Christ is central (20.21); if to live means Christ for Paul, death means to be united with Christ in a deeper sense.

1, 19: Result in deliverance for me: an echo of Jb 13, 16, hoping that God will turn suffering to ultimate good and deliverance from evil.

1, 27–30: Ethical admonition begins at this early point in the letter, emphasizing steadfastness and congregational unity in the face of possible suffering. The **opponents** (28) are those in Philippi, probably pagans, who oppose the gospel cause. **This is proof . . .** (28) may refer to the whole outlook and conduct of the Philippians, turning out for their salvation but to the judgment of the opponents (cf 2 Cor 2, 15–16), or possibly the sentence refers to the opinion of the opponents,

who hold that the obstinacy of the Christians points to the destruction of such people as defy Roman authority (though in reality, Paul holds, such faithfulness leads to salvation).

1, 30: A reference to Paul's earlier imprisonment in Philippi (Acts 16, 19–24; 1 Thes 2, 2) and to his present confinement.

2, 1–11: The admonition to likemindedness and unity (2–5) is based on the believers' threefold experience with Christ, God's love, and the Spirit. The appeal to humility (3) and to obedience (12) is rooted in christology, specifically in a statement about Christ Jesus (6–11) and his humbling of self and obedience to the point of death (8).

2, 5: Have . . . the same attitude that is also yours in Christ Jesus: or, "that also Christ Jesus had." While it is often held that Christ here functions as a model for moral imi-

k: 4, 10. l: Jb 13, 16 / 2 Cor 1, 11. m: 1 Cor 6, 20; 1 Pt 4, 16. n: Gal 2, 20. o: Rom 1, 13. p: 2 Cor 5, 8. q: Eph 4, 1; Col 1, 10; 1 Thes 2, 12 / 4, 3. r: Mt 5, 10; 10, 38; Mk 8, 34; Acts 5, 41. s: 1, 13; Acts 16, 22-24. t: Rom 15, 5; 1 Cor 1, 10. u: Rom 12, 3.10; Gal 5, 26. v: 1 Cor 10, 24.33; 13, 5.

6 *w**Who, though he was in the form of God,
  did not regard equality with God
      something to be grasped.
7   *x**Rather, he emptied himself,
  taking the form of a slave,
  coming in human likeness;
  and found human in appearance,
8   *y**he humbled himself,
  becoming obedient to death,
      even death on a cross.
9 *z**Because of this, God greatly exalted him
  and bestowed on him the name
  that is above every name,
10   *a**that at the name of Jesus
  every knee should bend,
  of those in heaven and on earth and
      under the earth,
11   *b**and every tongue confess that
  Jesus Christ is Lord,
  to the glory of God the Father.

Obedience and Service in the World. *12c**So
then, my beloved, obedient as you have always been, not only when I am present but
all the more now when I am absent, work out
your salvation with fear and trembling.
*13d*For God is the one who, for his good purpose, works in you both to desire and to
work. *14e*Do everything without grumbling
or questioning, *15f**that you may be blameless and innocent, children of God without
blemish in the midst of a crooked and perverse generation, among whom you shine
like lights in the world, *16g*as you hold on to
the word of life, so that my boast for the day
of Christ may be that I did not run in vain or
labor in vain. *17h**But, even if I am poured out
as a libation upon the sacrificial service of
your faith, I rejoice and share my joy with all
of you. *18i*In the same way you also should
rejoice and share your joy with me.

IV: Travel Plans of Paul and His Assistants

Timothy and Paul. *19j**I hope, in the Lord
Jesus, to send Timothy to you soon, so that I
too may be heartened by hearing news of

tation, it is not the historical Jesus but the entire Christ event
that vv 6–11 depict. Therefore, the appeal is to have in relations among yourselves that same relationship you have in
Jesus Christ, i.e., serving one another as you serve Christ (4).
  2, 6–11: Perhaps an early Christian hymn quoted here by
Paul. The short rhythmic lines fall into two parts, vv 6–8
where the subject of every verb is Christ, and vv 9–11 where
the subject is God. The general pattern is thus of Christ's humiliation and then exaltation. More precise analyses propose
a division into six three-line stanzas (6; 7abc; 7d-8; 9; 10; 11)
or into three stanzas (6–7ab; 7cd-8; 9–11). Phrases such as
even death on a cross (8c) are considered by some to be additions (by Paul) to the hymn, as are vv 10c and 11c.
  2, 6: Either a reference to Christ's preexistence and those
aspects of divinity that he was willing to give up in order to
serve in human form, or to what the man Jesus refused to
grasp at to attain divinity. Many see an allusion to the Genesis story: unlike Adam, Jesus, **though . . . in the form of God**
(Gn 1, 26–27), did not reach out for **equality with God,** in
contrast with the first Adam in Gn 3, 5–6.
  **2, 7: Taking the form of a slave, coming in human like-
ness:** or ". . . taking the form of a slave. // Coming in human
likeness, and found human in appearance." While it is common to take vv 6 and 7 as dealing with Christ's preexistence
and v 8 with his incarnate life, so that lines 7b and c are parallel, it is also possible to interpret so as to exclude any reference
to preexistence (see the note on 2, 6) and to take vv 6–8 as presenting two parallel stanzas about Jesus' human state (6–7b;
7cd-8); in the latter alternative, **coming in human likeness**
begins the second stanza and parallels 6a to some extent.
  2, 8: There may be reflected here language about the servant of the Lord, Is 52, 13—53, 12, especially 53, 12.
  2, 9: The name: "Lord" (11), revealing the true nature of

the one who is named.
  **2, 10–11: Every knee should bend . . . every tongue con-
fess:** into this language of Is 45, 23 there has been inserted a
reference to the three levels in the universe, according to ancient thought, **heaven, earth, under the earth.**
  2, 11: Jesus Christ is Lord: a common early Christian acclamation; cf 1 Cor 12, 3; Rom 10, 9. But doxology to God
the Father is not overlooked here (11c) in the final version of
the hymn.
  2, 12–18: Paul goes on to draw out further ethical implications for daily life (14–18) from the salvation God works in
Christ.
  2, 12: Fear and trembling: a common Old Testament expression indicating awe and seriousness in the service of God
(cf Ex 15, 16; Jdt 2, 28; Ps 2, 11; Is 19, 16).
  2, 15–16: Generation . . . as you hold on to . . . : or ". . .
generation. Among them shine like lights in the world because you hold the word of life . . . ."
  2, 17: Libation: in ancient religious ritual, the pouring out
on the ground of a liquid offering as a sacrifice. Paul means
that he may be facing death.
  2, 19—3, 1: The plans of Paul and his assistants for future

w: Jn 1, 1-2; 17, 5; Col 2, 9; Heb 1, 3. *x:* Is 53, 3.11; Jn 1, 14;
Rom 8, 3; 2 Cor 8, 9; Gal 4, 4; Heb 2, 14.17. *y:* Mt 26, 39; Jn 10,
17; Heb 5, 8; 12, 2. *z:* Acts 2, 33; Mt 23, 12; Eph 1, 20-21; Heb
1, 3-4. *a:* Is 45, 23; Jn 5, 23; Rom 14, 11; Rv 5, 13. *b:* Acts 2,
36; Rom 10, 9; 1 Cor 12, 3. *c:* Ps 2, 11; 1 Cor 2, 3; 2 Cor 7, 15.
d: 1, 6; 1 Cor 12, 6; 15, 10; 2 Cor 3, 5. *e:* 1 Cor 10, 10; 1 Pt 4, 9.
f: 1 Thes 3, 13 / Dt 32, 5; Mt 10, 16; Acts 2, 40 / Dn 12, 3;Mt 5,
14.16; Eph 5, 8. *g:* 1 Thes 2, 19 / Is 49, 4; 65, 23; Gal 2, 2.
h: Rom 15, 16; 2 Tm 4, 6. *i:* 3, 1; 4, 4. *j:* Acts 16, 1-3; 17, 14-
15; 1 Cor 4, 17; 16, 10.

you. [20]For I have no one comparable to him for genuine interest in whatever concerns you. [21k]For they all seek their own interests, not those of Jesus Christ. [22]But you know his worth, how as a child with a father he served along with me in the cause of the gospel. [23]He it is, then, whom I hope to send as soon as I see how things go with me, [24*]but I am confident in the Lord that I myself will also come soon.

Epaphroditus. [25l]*With regard to Epaphroditus, my brother and co-worker and fellow soldier, your messenger and minister in my need, I consider it necessary to send him to you. [26]For he has been longing for all of you and was distressed because you heard that he was ill. [27]He was indeed ill, close to death; but God had mercy on him, not just on him but also on me, so that I might not have sorrow upon sorrow. [28]I send him therefore with the greater eagerness, so that, on seeing him, you may rejoice again, and I may have less anxiety. [29m]Welcome him then in the Lord with all joy and hold such people in esteem, [30]because for the sake of the work of Christ he came close to death,

risking his life to make up for those services to me that you could not perform.

See RG 477

CHAPTER 3

Concluding Admonitions. [1n]*Finally, my brothers, rejoice in the Lord. Writing the same things to you is no burden for me but is a safeguard for you.

V: Polemic: Righteousness and the Goal in Christ

Against Legalistic Teachers. [2o]*Beware of the dogs! Beware of the evil-workers! Beware of the mutilation! [3p]*For we are the circumcision, we who worship through the Spirit of God, who boast in Christ Jesus and do not put our confidence in flesh, [4q]although I myself have grounds for confidence even in the flesh.

Paul's Autobiography. If anyone else thinks he can be confident in flesh, all the more can I. [5r]*Circumcised on the eighth day, of the race of Israel, of the tribe of Benjamin, a Hebrew of Hebrew parentage, in observance of the law a Pharisee, [6s]in zeal I

travel are regularly a part of a Pauline letter near its conclusion; cf Rom 15, 22–29; 1 Cor 16, 5–12.

2, 19: Timothy: already known to the Philippians (Acts 16, 1–15; cf 1 Cor 4, 17; 16, 10).

2, 24: I myself will also come soon: cf 1, 19–25 for the significance of this statement.

2, 25: Epaphroditus: sent by the Philippians as their messenger (literally, "apostle") to aid Paul in his imprisonment, he had fallen seriously ill; Paul commends him as he sends him back to Philippi.

3, 1: Finally . . . rejoice: the adverb often signals the close of a letter; cf 4, 8; 2 Cor 13, 11. While the verb could also be translated "good-bye" or "farewell," although it is never so used in Greek epistolography, the theme of joy has been frequent in the letter (1, 18; 2, 2.18); note also 4, 4 and the addition of "always" there as evidence for the meaning "rejoice." To write the same things may refer to what Paul has previously taught in Philippi or to what he has just written or to what follows.

3, 2–21: An abrupt change in content and tone, either because Paul at this point responds to disturbing news he has just heard about a threat to the faith of the Philippians in the form of false teachers, or because part of another Pauline letter was inserted here; see Introduction. The chapter describes these teachers in strong terms as dogs. The persons meant are evidently different from the rival preachers of 1, 14–18 and the opponents of 1, 28. Since vv 2–4 emphasize Jewish terms like circumcision (2–3.5), some relate them to the "Judaizers" of the Letter to the Galatians. Other phrases make them

appear more like the false teachers of 2 Cor 11, 12–15, the evil-workers. The latter part of the chapter depicts the many who are enemies of Christ's cross in terms that may sound more Gentile or even "gnostic" than Jewish (18–19). Accordingly, some see two groups of false teachers in ch 3, others one group characterized by a claim of having attained "perfect maturity" (12–15).

3, 2–11: Paul sets forth the Christian claim, especially using personal, autobiographical terms that are appropriate to the situation. He presents his own experience in coming to know Christ Jesus in terms of righteousness or justification (cf Rom 1, 16–17; 3, 21—5, 11; Gal 2, 5–11), contrasting the righteousness from God through faith and that of one's own based on the law as two exclusive ways of pleasing God.

3, 2: Beware of the mutilation: literally, "incision," an ironic wordplay on "circumcision"; cf Gal 5, 12. There may be an association with the self-inflicted mutilations of the prophets of Baal (1 Kgs 18, 28) and of devotees of Cybele who slashed themselves in religious frenzy.

3, 3: We are the circumcision: the true people of God, seed and offspring of Abraham (Gal 3, 7.29; 6, 15). Spirit of God: some manuscripts read "worship God by the Spirit."

3, 5: Circumcised on the eighth day: as the law required (Gn 17, 12; Lv 12, 3).

k: 1 Cor 13, 5; 2 Tm 4, 10. l: 4, 10-11.15-16.18. m: 1 Cor 16, 18. n: 2, 18; 4, 4. o: Ps 22, 17.21; Rv 22, 15 / 2 Cor 11, 13 / Gal 5, 6.12. p: Rom 2, 28-29; Col 2, 11. q: 2 Cor 11, 18.21-23. r: Lk 1, 59; 2, 21 / Acts 22, 3; 23, 6; 26, 5. s: Acts 8, 3; 22, 4; 26, 9-11.

persecuted the church, in righteousness based on the law I was blameless.

Righteousness from God. [7t]*[But] whatever gains I had, these I have come to consider a loss because of Christ. [8]More than that, I even consider everything as a loss because of the supreme good of knowing Christ Jesus my Lord. For his sake I have accepted the loss of all things and I consider them so much rubbish, that I may gain Christ [9u]and be found in him, not having any righteousness of my own based on the law but that which comes through faith in Christ, the righteousness from God, depending on faith [10v]to know him and the power of his resurrection and [the] sharing of his sufferings by being conformed to his death, [11w]if somehow I may attain the resurrection from the dead.

Forward in Christ. [12x]*It is not that I have already taken hold of it or have already attained perfect maturity, but I continue my pursuit in hope that I may possess it, since I have indeed been taken possession of by Christ [Jesus]. [13]Brothers, I for my part do not consider myself to have taken possession. Just one thing: forgetting what lies behind but straining forward to what lies ahead, [14y]I continue my pursuit toward the goal, the prize of God's upward calling, in Christ Jesus. [15]Let us, then, who are "perfectly mature", adopt this attitude. And if you have a different attitude, this too God will reveal to you. [16]*Only, with regard to what we have attained, continue on the same course.

Wrong Conduct and Our Goal. [17z]*Join with others in being imitators of me, brothers, and observe those who thus conduct themselves according to the model you have in us. [18a]For many, as I have often told you and now tell you even in tears, conduct themselves as enemies of the cross of Christ. [19b]Their end is destruction. Their God is their stomach; their glory is in their "shame." Their minds are occupied with earthly things. [20c]*But our citizenship is in heaven, and from it we also await a savior, the Lord Jesus Christ. [21d]He will change our lowly body to conform with his glorified body by the power that enables him also to bring all things into subjection to himself.

VI: Instructions for the Community

CHAPTER 4

See RG 477-78

Live in Concord. [1e]*Therefore, my brothers, whom I love and long for, my joy and crown, in this way stand firm in the Lord, beloved.

[2]*I urge Euodia and I urge Syntyche to come to a mutual understanding in the Lord. [3f]*Yes, and I ask you also, my true yoke-

3, 7: **Loss:** his knowledge of Christ led Paul to reassess the ways of truly pleasing and serving God. His reevaluation indicates the profound and lasting effect of his experience of the meaning of Christ on the way to Damascus some twenty years before (Gal 1, 15–16; Acts 9, 1–22).

3, 12–16: To be **taken possession of by Christ** does not mean that one has already arrived at perfect spiritual maturity. Paul and the Philippians instead press on, trusting in God.

3, 12: **Attained perfect maturity:** possibly an echo of the concept in the mystery religions of being an initiate, admitted to divine secrets.

3, 16: Some manuscripts add, probably to explain Paul's cryptic phrase, "thinking alike."

3, 17–21: Paul and those who live a life centered in Christ, envisaging both his suffering and resurrection, provide a model that is the opposite of opponents who reject Christ's cross (cf 1 Cor 1, 23).

3, 17: **Being imitators of me:** not arrogance, but humble simplicity, since all his converts know that Paul is wholly dedicated to imitating Christ (1 Cor 11, 1; cf also Phil 4, 9; 1 Thes 1, 6; 2 Thes 3, 7.9; 1 Cor 4, 6).

3, 20: **Citizenship:** Christians constitute a colony of

heaven, as Philippi was a **colonia** of Rome (Acts 16, 12). The hope Paul expresses involves the final coming of Christ, not a status already attained, such as the opponents claim.

4, 1–9: This series of ethical admonitions rests especially on the view of Christ and his coming (cf 5) in 3, 20–21. Paul's instructions touch on unity within the congregation, joy, prayer, and the Christian outlook on life.

4, 2: **Euodia ... Syntyche:** two otherwise unknown women in the Philippian congregation; on the advice to them, cf 2, 2–4.

4, 3: **Yokemate:** or "comrade," although the Greek **syzygos** could also be a proper name. **Clement:** otherwise unknown, although later writers sought to identify him with Clement, bishop of Rome (Eusebius, **Ecclesiastical History** 3.15.1).

t: Mt 13, 44.46; Lk 14, 33. u: Rom 3, 21-22. v: Rom 6, 3-5; 8, 17; Gal 6, 17. w: Jn 11, 23-26; Acts 4, 2; Rv 20, 5-6. x: 1 Tm 6, 12.19. y: 1 Cor 9, 24-25; 2 Tm 4, 7. z: 1 Cor 4, 16; 11, 1; 1 Thes 1, 7; 1 Pt 5, 3. a: 1 Cor 1, 17.23; Gal 6, 12. b: Rom 8, 5-6; 16, 18. c: Eph 2, 6.19; Col 3, 1-3; Heb 12, 22. d: Rom 8, 23.29; 1 Cor 15, 42-57; 2 Cor 3, 18; 5, 1-5 /1 Cor 15, 27-28. e: 1 Thes 2, 19-20. f: Ex 32, 32-33; Ps 69, 29; Dn 12, 1; Lk 10, 20; Rv 3, 5; 13, 8;17, 8; 20, 12.15; 21, 27.

mate, to help them, for they have struggled at my side in promoting the gospel, along with Clement and my other co-workers, whose names are in the book of life.

Joy and Peace. [4g]*Rejoice in the Lord always. I shall say it again: rejoice! [5h]*Your kindness should be known to all. The Lord is near. [6i]Have no anxiety at all, but in everything, by prayer and petition, with thanksgiving, make your requests known to God. [7j]Then the peace of God that surpasses all understanding will guard your hearts and minds in Christ Jesus.

[8k]*Finally, brothers, whatever is true, whatever is honorable, whatever is just, whatever is pure, whatever is lovely, whatever is gracious, if there is any excellence and if there is anything worthy of praise, think about these things. [9l]*Keep on doing what you have learned and received and heard and seen in me. Then the God of peace will be with you.

VII: Gratitude for the Philippians' Generosity

[10m]*I rejoice greatly in the Lord that now at last you revived your concern for me. You were, of course, concerned about me but lacked an opportunity. [11n]Not that I say this because of need, for I have learned, in whatever situation I find myself, to be self-sufficient. [12]I know indeed how to live in humble circumstances; I know also how to live with abundance. In every circumstance and in all things I have learned the secret of being well fed and of going hungry, of living in abundance and of being in need. [13o]I have the strength for everything through him who empowers me. [14]Still, it was kind of you to share in my distress.

[15]*You Philippians indeed know that at the beginning of the gospel, when I left Macedonia, not a single church shared with me in an account of giving and receiving, except you alone. [16]For even when I was at Thessalonica you sent me something for my needs, not only once but more than once. [17]It is not that I am eager for the gift; rather, I am eager for the profit that accrues to your account. [18p]*I have received full payment and I abound. I am very well supplied because of what I received from you through Epaphroditus, "a fragrant aroma," an acceptable sacrifice, pleasing to God. [19q]My God will fully supply whatever you need, in accord with his glorious riches in Christ Jesus. [20r]To our God and Father, glory forever and ever. Amen.

VIII: Farewell

[21]*Give my greetings to every holy one in Christ Jesus. The brothers who are with me send you their greetings; [22s]*all the holy ones send you their greetings, especially those of Caesar's household. [23]The grace of the Lord Jesus Christ be with your spirit.

4, 4: Rejoice: see the note on 3, 1.

4, 5: Kindness: considerateness, forbearance, fairness. **The Lord is near:** most likely a reference to Christ's parousia (1, 6.10; 3, 20–21; 1 Cor 16, 22), although some sense an echo of Ps 119, 151 and the perpetual presence of the Lord.

4, 8: The language employs terms from Roman Stoic thought.

4, 9: Cf the note on 3, 17.

4, 10–20: Paul, more directly than anywhere else in the letter (cf 1, 3–5), here thanks the Philippians for their gift of money sent through Epaphroditus (2, 25). Paul's own policy was **to be self-sufficient** as a missionary, supporting himself by his own labor (1 Thes 2, 5–9; 1 Cor 9, 15–18; cf Acts 18, 2–3). In spite of this reliance on self and on God to provide (11–13), Paul accepted gifts from the Philippians **not only once but more than once** (16) when he was in Thessalonica (Acts 17, 1–9), as he does now, in prison (**my distress,** 14). While commercial terms appear in the passage, like **an account of giving and receiving** (15) and **received full payment** (18), Paul is most concerned about the spiritual growth of the Philippians (10.17.19); he emphasizes that God will care for their needs, through Christ.

4, 15: The beginning of the gospel: it was at Philippi that Paul first preached Christ in Europe, going on from there to Thessalonica and Beroea (Acts 16, 9—17, 14).

4, 18: Aroma . . . sacrifice: Old Testament cultic language (cf Gn 8, 21; Ex 29, 18.25.41; Lv 1, 9.13; Ez 20, 41) applied to the Philippians' gift; cf Eph 5, 2; 2 Cor 2, 14–16.

4, 21–23: On the usual greetings at the conclusion of a letter, see the note on 1 Cor 16, 19–24. Inclusion of greetings from **all the holy ones** in the place from which Paul writes would involve even the Christians of 1, 14–18 who had their differences with Paul.

4, 22: Those of Caesar's household: minor officials or even slaves and freedmen, found in Ephesus or Rome, among other places.

g: 2, 18; 3, 1. *h:* Ti 3, 2 / Ps 145, 18; Heb 10, 37; Jas 5, 8-9. *i:* Mt 6, 25-34; 1 Pt 5, 7 / Col 4, 2. *j:* Jn 14, 27; Col 3, 15. *k:* Rom 12, 17. *l:* 1 Thes 4, 1 / Rom 15, 33; 16, 20; 1 Cor 14, 33; 1 Thes 5, 23. *m:* 1, 18; 2, 25; 1 Cor 9, 11; 2 Cor 11, 9. *n:* 1 Cor 4, 11; 2 Cor 6, 10; 11, 27 / 2 Cor 12, 9-10. *o:* Col 1, 29; 2 Tm 4, 17. *p:* Gn 8, 21; Ex 29, 18; Eph 5, 2; Heb 13, 16. *q:* 1 Thes 3, 11.13. *r:* Rom 16, 27; Eph 5, 20. *s:* 1, 13.

See RG
478–80

The Letter to the Colossians

This letter is addressed to a congregation at Colossae in the Lycus Valley in Asia Minor, east of Ephesus. At the time of writing, Paul had not visited there, the letter says (1, 4; 2, 1). The community had apparently been established by Epaphras of Colossae (1, 7; 4, 12; Phlm 23). Problems, however, had arisen, brought on by teachers who emphasized Christ's relation to the universe (cosmos). Their teachings stressed angels (2, 18; "principalities and powers," 2, 15), which were connected with astral powers and cultic practices (see the note on 2, 16) and rules about food and drink and ascetical disciplines (2, 16.18). These teachings, Paul insists, detract from the person and work of Christ for salvation as set forth magnificently in a hymnic passage at Col 1, 15–20 and reiterated throughout the letter. Such teachings are but "shadows"; Christ is "reality" (2, 17).

For help in dealing with these problems that the new teachers posed at Colossae, Epaphras sought out Paul, who was then imprisoned (4, 10.18) at a place that the letter does not mention. Paul, without entering into debate over the existence of angelic spirits or their function, simply affirms that Christ possesses the sum total of redemptive power (1, 19) and that the spiritual renewal of the human person occurs through contact in baptism with the person of Christ, who died and rose again (2, 9–14). It is unnecessary for the Christian to be concerned about placating spirits (2, 15) or avoiding imagined defilement through ascetical practices in regard to food and drink (2, 20–23). True Christian asceticism consists in the conquering of personal sins (3, 5–10) and the practice of love of neighbor in accordance with the standard set by Christ (3, 12–16).

Paul commends the community as a whole (1, 3–8); this seems to indicate that, though the Colossians have been under pressure to adopt the false doctrines, they have not yet succumbed. The apostle expresses his prayerful concern for them (1, 9–14). His preaching has cost him persecution, suffering, and imprisonment, but he regards these as reflective of the sufferings of Christ, a required discipline for the sake of the gospel (see the note on 1, 24; cf 1, 29; 2, 1). His instructions to the Christian family and to slaves and masters

require a new spirit of reflection and action. Love, obedience, and service are to be rendered "in the Lord" (3, 18—4, 1).

Colossians follows the outline of a typical Pauline letter. It is distinguished by the poetic lines in 1, 15–20 concerning who Christ is and what Christ means in creation and redemption. This hymn may be compared with similar passages in Philippians 2, 6–11; 1 Timothy 3, 16; and Jn 1, 1–18. It was apparently familiar liturgical material to the author, the audience, and the false teachers. In 1, 21—2, 7, however, Paul interprets the relation between the body of Christ, which he insists is the church (1, 18), and the world or cosmos to be one not simply of Christ's preexistence and rule but one of missionary advance into the world by the spreading of the word (1, 25.28). In this labor of the missionary body of Christ, Paul as a minister plays a prime part in bringing Christ and the gospel as hope to the Gentiles (1, 23.25.27). To "every creature under heaven" the word is to be proclaimed, so that everyone receives Christ, is established in faith, and walks in Christ (1, 28; 2, 6.7).

Paul wrote the Letter to the Colossians while in prison, but his several imprisonments leave the specific place and date of composition uncertain. On this point the same problem exists as with Ephesians and Philippians (see the Introductions to these letters). Traditionally the house arrest at Rome, in which Paul enjoyed a certain restricted freedom in preaching (see Acts 28, 16–28), or a second Roman imprisonment has been claimed as the setting. Others suggest a still earlier imprisonment at Caesarea (see Acts 23, 12—27, 1) or in Ephesus (see Acts 19). Still others regard the letter as the work of some pupil or follower of Paul, writing in his name. In any case, the contents are often closely paralleled by thoughts in Ephesians.

The principal divisions of the Letter to the Colossians are the following:

I: Address (1, 1–14)

II: The Preeminence of Christ (1, 15—2, 3)

III: Warnings against False Teachers (2, 4–23)

IV: The Ideal Christian Life in the World (3, 1—4, 6)

V: Conclusion (4, 7–18)

I: Address

See RG
479

CHAPTER 1

Greeting. *1a**Paul, an apostle of Christ Jesus by the will of God, and Timothy our brother, *2*to the holy ones and faithful brothers in Christ in Colossae: grace to you and peace from God our Father.

Thanksgiving. *3b**We always give thanks to God, the Father of our Lord Jesus Christ, when we pray for you, *4*for we have heard of your faith in Christ Jesus and the love that you have for all the holy ones *5c*because of the hope reserved for you in heaven. Of this you have already heard through the word of truth, the gospel, *6*that has come to you. Just as in the whole world it is bearing fruit and growing, so also among you, from the day you heard it and came to know the grace of God in truth, *7d**as you learned it from Epaphras our beloved fellow slave, who is a trustworthy minister of Christ on your behalf *8*and who also told us of your love in the Spirit.

Prayer for Continued Progress. *9e**There-fore, from the day we heard this, we do not cease praying for you and asking that you may be filled with the knowledge of his will through all spiritual wisdom and under-standing *10*to live in a manner worthy of the Lord, so as to be fully pleasing, in every good work bearing fruit and growing in the knowledge of God, *11*strengthened with every power, in accord with his glorious might, for all endurance and patience, with joy *12f**giving thanks to the Father, who has made you fit to share in the inheritance of the holy ones in light. *13*He delivered us from the power of darkness and transferred us to the kingdom of his beloved Son, *14g*in whom we have redemption, the forgiveness of sins.

II: The Preeminence of Christ— His Person and Work

15 h*He is the image of the invisible God,
    the firstborn of all creation.
16 i*For in him were created all things in
    heaven and on earth,
    the visible and the invisible,

1, 1–2: For the epistolary form used by Paul at the beginning of his letters, see the note on Rom 1, 1–7. On **holy ones** or "God's people," see the note on Rom 1, 7. Awareness of their calling helps this group to be **faithful brothers** and sisters in **Christ,** i.e., dedicated to the tasks implied in their calling.

1, 3–8: On thanksgiving at the start of a letter, see the note on Rom 1, 8. The apostle, recalling his own prayers for them and the good report about them he has received (3–4), congratulates the Colossians upon their acceptance of Christ and their faithful efforts to live the gospel (3, 6–8). To encourage them he mentions the success of the gospel elsewhere (6) and assures them that his knowledge of their community is accurate, since he has been in personal contact with Epaphras (7–8), who likely had evangelized Colossae and other cities in the Lycus Valley of Asia Minor (cf 4, 12.13; Phlm 23). On **faith, love,** and **hope** (4.5.8), see the note on 1 Cor 13, 13; cf 1 Thes 1, 3; 5, 8.

1, 7: Epaphras: now with Paul but a Colossian, founder of the church there.

1, 9–14: Moved by Epaphras' account, the apostle has prayed and continues to pray fervently for the Colossians that, in their response to the gospel, they **may be filled with the knowledge of** God's will (9; cf 3, 10). Paul expects a mutual interaction between their life according to the gospel and this knowledge (10), yielding results (**fruit;** 10; cf 6) **in every good work:** growth, strength, **endurance, patience, with joy** (11), and the further giving of thanks (12).

1, 12–14: A summary about **redemption** by **the Father** precedes the statement in vv 15–20 about the **beloved Son** who is God's love in person (13). Christians share **the inher-**itance . . . in light with the holy ones, here probably the angels (12). The imagery reflects the Exodus (**delivered . . . transferred**) and Jesus' theme of the **kingdom. Redemption** is explained as **forgiveness of sins** (cf Acts 2, 38; Rom 3, 24–25; Eph 1, 7).

1, 15–20: As the poetic arrangement indicates, these lines are probably an early Christian hymn, known to the Colossians and taken up into the letter from liturgical use (cf Phil 2, 6–11; 1 Tm 3, 16). They present Christ as the mediator of creation (15–18a) and of redemption (18b-20). There is a parallelism between **firstborn of all creation** (15) and firstborn from the dead (18). While many of the phrases were at home in Greek philosophical use and even in gnosticism, the basic ideas also reflect Old Testament themes about Wisdom found in Prv 8, 22–31; Wis 7, 22—8, 1; and Sir 1, 4. See also the notes on what is possibly a hymn in Jn 1, 1–18.

1, 15: Image: cf Gn 1, 27. Whereas the man and the woman were originally created in the image and likeness of God (see also Gn 1, 26), Christ as image (2 Cor 4, 4) of **the invisible God** (Jn 1, 18) now shares this new nature in baptism with those redeemed (cf 3, 10–11).

1, 16–17: Christ (though not mentioned by name) is preeminent and supreme as God's agent in the creation of **all things** (cf Jn 1, 3), as prior to **all things** (17; cf Heb 1, 3).

---

a: Eph 1, 1.   *b:* Eph 1, 15-16; Phlm 4-5.   *c:* Eph 1, 13.18; 1 Pt 1, 4.   *d:* Phlm 23.   *e:* Eph 1, 15-17; 5, 17; Phil 1, 9.   *f:* 3, 17; Jn 8, 12; Acts 26, 18; 1 Tm 6, 16; 1 Pt 2, 9.   *g:* Eph 1, 7.   *h:* Ps 89, 28; Jn 1, 3.18; 2 Cor 4, 4.   *i:* 1 Cor 8, 6; Eph 1, 10.21.

whether thrones or dominions or
    principalities or powers;
  all things were created through him
    and for him.
[17] He is before all things,
  and in him all things hold together.
[18] *j** He is the head of the body, the
    church.
He is the beginning, the firstborn from
    the dead,
  that in all things he himself might be
    preeminent.
[19] *For in him all the fullness was pleased
    to dwell,
[20]   *k** and through him to reconcile all
    things for him,
  making peace by the blood of his cross
  [through him], whether those on earth
    or those in heaven.

[21] *l** And you who once were alienated and
hostile in mind because of evil deeds [22] he
has now reconciled in his fleshly body
through his death, to present you holy, without blemish, and irreproachable before him,
[23] provided that you persevere in the faith,
firmly grounded, stable, and not shifting
from the hope of the gospel that you heard,
which has been preached to every creature
under heaven, of which I, Paul, am a minister.

Christ in Us. [24]*Now I rejoice in my sufferings for your sake, and in my flesh I am
filling up what is lacking in the afflictions of
Christ on behalf of his body, which is the
church, [25]of which I am a minister in accordance with God's stewardship given to me to
bring to completion for you the word of
God, [26]*m*the mystery hidden from ages and
from generations past. But now it has been
manifested to his holy ones, [27]*n*to whom God
chose to make known the riches of the glory
of this mystery among the Gentiles; it is
Christ in you, the hope for glory. [28]*o*It is he
whom we proclaim, admonishing everyone
and teaching everyone with all wisdom, that
we may present everyone perfect in Christ.
[29]*p*For this I labor and struggle, in accord
with the exercise of his power working
within me.

1, 18: Church: such a reference seemingly belongs under
"redemption" in the following lines, not under the "creation"
section of the hymn. Stoic thought sometimes referred to the
world as "the body of Zeus." Pauline usage is to speak of the
church as the body of Christ (1 Cor 12, 12–27; Rom 12, 4–5).
Some think that the author of Colossians has inserted the reference to the church here so as to define "head of the body"
in Paul's customary use. See v 24. **Preeminent:** when Christ
was raised by God as **firstborn from the dead** (cf Acts 26,
23; Rv 1, 5), he was placed over the community, the church,
that he had brought into being, but he is also indicated as
crown of the whole new creation, over **all things**. His further
role is to **reconcile all things** (20) for God or possibly "to
himself."
1, 19: Fullness: in gnostic usage this term referred to a
spiritual world of beings above, between God and the world;
many later interpreters take it to refer to **the fullness of the
deity** (2, 9); the reference could also be to the fullness of
grace (cf Jn 1, 16).
1, 20: The blood of his cross: the most specific reference
in the hymn to redemption through Christ's death, a central
theme in Paul; cf 2, 14–15; 1 Cor 1, 17.18.23. **[Through
him]:** the phrase, lacking in some manuscripts, seems superfluous but parallels the reference to reconciliation through
Christ earlier in the verse.
1, 21–23: Paul, in applying this hymn to the Colossians,
reminds them that they have experienced the reconciling effect of Christ's death. He sees the effects of the cross in the
redemption of human beings, not of cosmic powers such as
those referred to in vv 16 and 20 (**all things**). Paul also urges
adherence to Christ in faith and begins to point to his own
role as minister (23), sufferer (24), and proclaimer (27–28)
of this gospel.
1, 24—2, 3: As the community at Colossae was not personally known to Paul (see Introduction), he here invests
his teaching with greater authority by presenting a brief
sketch of his apostolic ministry and sufferings as they reflect those of Christ on behalf of the church (24). The
preaching of God's word (25) carries out the divine plan
(**the mystery,** 26) to make Christ known to the Gentiles
(27). It teaches the God-given wisdom about Christ (28),
whose power works mightily in the apostle (29). Even in
those communities that do not know him personally (2, 1),
he can increase the perception of God in Christ, unite the
faithful more firmly in love, and so bring encouragement to
them (2). He hopes that his apostolic authority will make
the Colossians perceive more readily the defects in the
teaching of others who have sought to delude them, the
next concern in the letter.
1, 24: What is lacking: although variously interpreted,
this phrase does not imply that Christ's atoning death on the
cross was defective. It may refer to the apocalyptic concept
of a quota of "messianic woes" to be endured before the end
comes; cf Mk 13, 8.19–20.24 and the note on Mt 23, 29–32.
Others suggest that Paul's mystical unity with Christ allowed him to call his own **sufferings the afflictions of
Christ.**

j: 1 Cor 11, 3; 12, 12.27; 15, 20; Eph 1, 22-23; Rv 1, 5. *k:* 2 Cor
5, 18-19; Eph 1, 10. *l:* Eph 2, 14-16. *m:* Rom 16, 25-26; 1 Cor
2, 7; Eph 3, 3.9. *n:* 3, 4; Rom 8, 10. *o:* Eph 4, 13. *p:* 2, 1; 4,
12; Phil 4, 13.

CHAPTER 2

See RG 479–80

*1**For I want you to know how great a struggle I am having for you and for those in Laodicea and all who have not seen me face to face, *2q*that their hearts may be encouraged as they are brought together in love, to have all the richness of fully assured understanding, for the knowledge of the mystery of God, Christ, *3r*in whom are hidden all the treasures of wisdom and knowledge.

III: Warnings against False Teachers

A General Admonition. *4s**I say this so that no one may deceive you by specious arguments. *5t*For even if I am absent in the flesh, yet I am with you in spirit, rejoicing as I observe your good order and the firmness of your faith in Christ. *6*So, as you received Christ Jesus the Lord, walk in him, *7u*rooted in him and built upon him and established in the faith as you were taught, abounding in thanksgiving. *8v**See to it that no one captivate you with an empty, seductive philosophy according to human tradition, according to the elemental powers of the world and not according to Christ.

Sovereign Role of Christ. *9w**For in him dwells the whole fullness of the deity bodily, *10*and you share in this fullness in him, who is the head of every principality and power. *11x**In him you were also circumcised with a circumcision not administered by hand, by stripping off the carnal body, with the circumcision of Christ. *12y*You were buried with him in baptism, in which you were also raised with him through faith in the power of God, who raised him from the dead. *13z*And even when you were dead [in] transgressions and the uncircumcision of your flesh, he brought you to life along with him, having forgiven us all our transgressions; *14a**obliterating the bond against us, with its legal claims, which was opposed to us, he also removed it from our midst, nailing it to the cross; *15b**despoiling the principalities and the powers, he made a public spectacle of them, leading them away in triumph by it.

Practices Contrary to Faith. *16c**Let no one, then, pass judgment on you in matters of food and drink or with regard to a festival or new moon or sabbath. *17d*These are shad-

---

2, 1: Laodicea: chief city in Phrygia, northwest of Colossae; cf 4, 13.16; Rv 3, 14–22.

2, 4–23: In face of the threat posed by false teachers (4), the Colossians are admonished to adhere to the gospel as it was first preached to them (6), steeping themselves in it with grateful hearts (7). They must reject religious teachings originating in any source except the gospel (8) because in Christ alone will they have access to God, **the deity** (9), So fully has Christ enlightened them that they need no other source of religious knowledge or virtue (10). They do not require **circumcision** (11), for **in baptism** their whole being has been affected by Christ (12) through forgiveness of sin and resurrection to a new life (13; cf 3, 1 and Rom 6, 1–11).

On the cross Christ canceled the record of the debt that stood against us with all its claims (14), i.e., he eliminated the law (cf Eph 2, 15) that human beings could not observe—and that could not save them. He forgave sins against the law (14) and exposed as false and misleading (15) all other powers (cf 1, 16) that purport to offer salvation. Therefore, the Colossians are not to accept judgments from such teachers on **food and drink** or to keep certain religious festivals or engage in certain cultic practices (16), for the Colossians would thereby risk severing themselves from Christ (19). If, when they accepted the gospel, they believed in Christ as their savior, they must be convinced that their salvation cannot be achieved by appeasing ruling spirits through dietary practices or through a wisdom gained simply by means of harsh asceticism (20–23).

2, 8: Elemental powers of the world: see the note on Gal 4, 3.

2, 9: Fullness of the deity: the divine nature, not just attributes; see the note on 1, 19.

2, 11: A description of baptism (12) in symbolic terms of the Old Testament rite for entry into the community. The false teachers may have demanded physical circumcision of the Colossians.

2, 14: The elaborate metaphor here about how God canceled the legal claims against us through Christ's cross depicts not Christ being nailed to the cross by men but **the bond . . . with its legal claims** being nailed to the cross by God.

2, 15: The picture derives from the **public spectacle** and **triumph** of a Roman emperor's victory parade, where captives marched in subjection. **The principalities and the powers** are here conquered, not reconciled (cf 1, 16.20). An alternate rendering for **by it** (the cross) is "by him" (Christ).

2, 16: Festival or new moon or sabbath: yearly, monthly, and weekly observances determined by religious powers associated with a calendar set by the heavenly bodies, sun, moon, and stars (cf 8).

q: 1, 26-27; Eph 3, 18-19. *r:* Prv 2, 4-5; Is 45, 3; Rom 11, 33; 1 Cor 1, 30. *s:* Eph 4, 14. *t:* 1 Cor 5, 3; Phil 1, 27. *u:* Eph 2, 20-22; 3, 17. *v:* Gal 4, 3; Eph 5, 6. *w:* 1, 19; Eph 3, 19. *x:* 1, 22; Jer 4, 4; Rom 2, 25-29; Phil 3, 3. *y:* Rom 6, 3-4. *z:* Eph 2, 1.5. *a:* Eph 2, 14-15. *b:* 1, 16.20; 2 Cor 2, 14; Eph 1, 21. *c:* Rom 14, 3-4; 1 Tm 4, 3. *d:* Heb 8, 5; 10, 1.

ows of things to come; the reality belongs to Christ. [18e]*Let no one disqualify you, delighting in self-abasement and worship of angels, taking his stand on visions, inflated without reason by his fleshly mind, [19f] and not holding closely to the head, from whom the whole body, supported and held together by its ligaments and bonds, achieves the growth that comes from God.

[20] If you died with Christ to the elemental powers of the world, why do you submit to regulations as if you were still living in the world? [21] "Do not handle! Do not taste! Do not touch!" [22g] These are all things destined to perish with use; they accord with human precepts and teachings. [23] While they have a semblance of wisdom in rigor of devotion and self-abasement [and] severity to the body, they are of no value against gratification of the flesh.

IV: The Ideal Christian Life in the World

CHAPTER 3

See RG 480

Mystical Death and Resurrection. [1h]*If then you were raised with Christ, seek what is above, where Christ is seated at the right hand of God. [2] Think of what is above, not of what is on earth. [3i] For you have died, and your life is hidden with Christ in God. [4] When Christ your life appears, then you too will appear with him in glory.

Renunciation of Vice. [5j]*Put to death,

then, the parts of you that are earthly: immorality, impurity, passion, evil desire, and the greed that is idolatry. [6k]*Because of these the wrath of God is coming [upon the disobedient]. [7] By these you too once conducted yourselves, when you lived in that way. [8l]*But now you must put them all away: anger, fury, malice, slander, and obscene language out of your mouths. [9m] Stop lying to one another, since you have taken off the old self with its practices [10n]*and have put on the new self, which is being renewed, for knowledge, in the image of its creator. [11o]*Here there is not Greek and Jew, circumcision and uncircumcision, barbarian, Scythian, slave, free; but Christ is all and in all.

[12p] Put on then, as God's chosen ones, holy and beloved, heartfelt compassion, kindness, humility, gentleness, and patience, [13q] bearing with one another and forgiving one another, if one has a grievance against another; as the Lord has forgiven you, so must you also do. [14r] And over all these put on love, that is, the bond of perfection. [15s] And let the peace of Christ control your hearts, the peace into which you were also called in one body. And be thankful. [16t] Let the word of Christ dwell in you richly, as in all wisdom you teach and admonish one another, singing psalms, hymns, and spiritual songs with gratitude in your hearts to God. [17u] And whatever you do, in word or in deed, do everything in the name of the Lord Jesus, giving thanks to God the Father through him.

The Christian Family. [18v]*Wives, be sub-

2, 18: Ascetic practices encouraged by the false teachers included subjection of self humbly to their rules, worship of angels, and cultivation of visions, though exact details are unclear.

3, 1–4: By retaining the message of the gospel that the risen, living Christ is the source of their salvation, the Colossians will be free from false religious evaluations of the things of the world (1–2). They have died to these; but one day **when Christ . . . appears,** they will live with Christ in the presence of God (3–4).

3, 5–17: In lieu of false asceticism and superstitious festivals, the apostle reminds the Colossians of the moral life that is to characterize their response to God through Christ. He urges their participation in the liturgical hymns and prayers that center upon God's plan of salvation in Christ (16).

3, 5.8: The two lists of five vices each are similar to enumerations at Rom 1, 29–31 and Gal 5, 19–21.

3, 6: **The wrath of God:** see the note on Rom 1, 18. Many manuscripts add, as at Eph 5, 6, "upon the disobedient."

3, 8–10: Put . . . away; have taken off; have put on: the

terms may reflect baptismal practice, taking off garments and putting on new ones after being united with Christ, here translated into ethical terms.

3, 10: Image: see the note on 1, 15.

3, 11: **Scythian:** a barbarous people from north of the Black Sea.

3, 18—4, 6: After general recommendations that connect family life and the social condition of slavery with the service of Christ (3, 18—4, 1), Paul requests prayers for himself, especially in view of his imprisonment (2–3), and recommends

e: 2, 23; Mt 24, 4. f: Eph 2, 21-22; 4, 16. g: Is 29, 13. h: 2, 12; Ps 110, 1; Phil 3, 20; Eph 2, 6. i: Rom 6, 2-5. j: Mt 15, 19; Rom 1, 29-30; Gal 5, 19-21; Eph 5, 3.5. k: Rom 1, 18. l: Eph 4, 22.25.31. m: Rom 6, 4.6; Eph 4, 22-25; Heb 12, 1; 1 Pt 2, 1; 4, 2. n: Gn 1, 26-27. o: 1 Cor 12, 13; Gal 3, 27-28. p: Eph 4, 1-2.32; 1 Thes 5, 15. q: Mt 6, 14; 18, 21-35; Eph 4, 32. r: Rom 13, 8-10. s: Rom 12, 5; 1 Cor 12, 12; Eph 2, 16; 4, 3-4; Phil 4, 7. t: Eph 5, 19-20. u: 1 Cor 10, 31. v: Eph 5, 22; Ti 2, 5; 1 Pt 3, 1.

ordinate to your husbands, as is proper in the Lord. ¹⁹Husbands, love your wives, and avoid any bitterness toward them. ²⁰ʷChildren, obey your parents in everything, for this is pleasing to the Lord. ²¹ˣFathers, do not provoke your children, so they may not become discouraged.

Slaves and Masters. ²²ʸ*Slaves, obey your human masters in everything, not only when being watched, as currying favor, but in simplicity of heart, fearing the Lord. ²³Whatever you do, do from the heart, as for the Lord and not for others, ²⁴knowing that you will receive from the Lord the due payment of the inheritance; be slaves of the Lord Christ. ²⁵ᶻFor the wrongdoer will receive recompense for the wrong he committed, and there is no partiality.

CHAPTER 4

See RG 480

¹Masters, treat your slaves justly and fairly, realizing that you too have a Master in heaven.

Prayer and Apostolic Spirit. ²ᵃPersevere in prayer, being watchful in it with thanksgiving; ³ᵇat the same time, pray for us, too, that God may open a door to us for the word, to speak of the mystery of Christ, for which I am in prison, ⁴that I may make it clear, as I must speak. ⁵ᶜConduct yourselves wisely toward outsiders, making the most of the opportunity. ⁶Let your speech always be gracious, seasoned with salt, so that you know how you should respond to each one.

V: Conclusion

Tychicus and Onesimus. ⁷ᵈ*Tychicus, my beloved brother, trustworthy minister, and fellow slave in the Lord, will tell you all the news of me. ⁸I am sending him to you for this very purpose, so that you may know about us and that he may encourage your hearts, ⁹ᵉtogether with Onesimus, a trustworthy and beloved brother, who is one of you. They will tell you about everything here.

From Paul's Co-Workers. ¹⁰ᶠ*Aristarchus, my fellow prisoner, sends you greetings, as does Mark the cousin of Barnabas (concerning whom you have received instructions; if he comes to you, receive him), ¹¹*and Jesus, who is called Justus, who are of the circumcision; these alone are my co-workers for the kingdom of God, and they have been a comfort to me. ¹²ᵍ*Epaphras sends you greetings; he is one of you, a slave of Christ [Jesus], always striving for you in his prayers so that you may be perfect and fully assured in all the will of God. ¹³*For I can testify that he works very hard for you and for those in Laodicea and those in Hierapolis. ¹⁴ʰ*Luke the beloved physician sends greetings, as does Demas.

A Message for the Laodiceans. ¹⁵*Give greetings to the brothers in Laodicea and to Nympha and to the church in her house. ¹⁶*And when this letter is read before you, have it read also in the church of the Laodiceans, and you yourselves read the one from

friendly relations and meaningful discussions of Christian teaching with **outsiders,** i.e., non-Christians (5–6). See the note on Eph 5, 21—6, 9.

3, 22–25: Slaves: within this table of duties in family and societal relations, involving wives and husbands, children and parents (18–21), such as also appears in Eph 5, 22—6, 9, slaves here receive special attention because of the case of Onesimus the slave returning to his master (4, 9; Phlm 10–12).

4, 7–18: Paul concludes with greetings and information concerning various Christians known to the Colossians.

4, 7: Tychicus: Acts 20, 4 mentions his role in the collection for Jerusalem; Eph 6, 21 repeats what is said here; see also 2 Tm 4, 12; Ti 3, 12.

4, 10: Aristarchus: a Thessalonian who was with Paul at Ephesus and Caesarea and on the voyage to Rome (Acts 19, 29; 20, 4; 27, 2). **Mark:** also referred to at Phlm 24 and 2 Tm 4, 11 and, as "John Mark," in Acts (12, 12.25; 13, 13; 15, 37–40). See also 1 Pt 5, 13 and the note there. Traditionally the author of the second gospel.

4, 11: Jesus: a then common Jewish name, the Greek form of Joshua.

4, 12: Epaphras: see the notes on 1, 3–8 and 1, 7.

4, 13: Laodicea: see the note on 2, 1. **Hierapolis:** a city northeast of Laodicea and northwest of Colossae.

4, 14: Luke: only here described as a medical doctor; cf Phlm 24 and 2 Tm 4, 11. Traditionally the author of the third gospel. **Demas:** cf Phlm 24; he later deserted Paul (2 Tm 4, 10).

4, 15: Nympha and . . . her house: some manuscripts read a masculine for the house-church leader, "Nymphas and . . . his house."

4, 16: The one from Laodicea: either a letter by Paul that

w: Eph 6, 1. x: Eph 6, 4. y: Eph 6, 5; 1 Tm 6, 1; Ti 2, 9-10; 1 Pt 2, 18. z: Rom 2, 11. a: Lk 18, 1; Rom 12, 12; Eph 6, 18-20; 1 Thes 5, 17. b: Rom 15, 30; 1 Cor 16, 9; Eph 6, 19; 2 Thes 3, 1. c: Eph 5, 15-16. d: Acts 20, 4; Eph 6, 21-22; Phil 1, 12. e: Phlm 10-11. f: Acts 19, 29; 20, 4; 27, 2 / Acts 12, 12.25; 13, 13; 15, 37.40; 2 Tm 4, 11; Phlm 24; 1 Pt 5, 13. g: 1, 7; Rom 15, 30. h: Phlm 24; 2 Tm 4, 10-11.

Laodicea. *17i**And tell Archippus, "See that you fulfill the ministry that you received in the Lord."

has been lost or the Letter to the Ephesians (cf the note on Eph 1, 1, **in Ephesus**).

4, 17: Fulfill the ministry: usually taken to mean that **Archippus,** the son of Philemon and Apphia (Phlm 1–2), is "pastor" at Colossae. An alternate interpretation is that Archippus, not Philemon, is the owner of the slave Onesimus and that Paul is asking Archippus to complete the service he

18j*The greeting is in my own hand, Paul's. Remember my chains. Grace be with you.

has received in the Lord by sending Onesimus back to minister to Paul in his captivity (cf Phlm 20).

4, 18: My own hand: a postscript in Paul's own hand was his custom; cf Gal 6, 11–18 and 2 Thes 3, 17–18.

i: Phlm 2.   *j:* 1 Cor 16, 21; Gal 6, 11; Eph 3, 1; 2 Thes 3, 17.

See RG 481–84

The First Letter to the Thessalonians

When Paul parted from Barnabas (Acts 15, 36–41) at the beginning of what is called his second missionary journey, he chose Silvanus (Silas) as his traveling companion. Soon afterwards he took Timothy along with him (Acts 16, 1–3). Paul was now clearly at the head of his own missionary band. About A.D. 50, he arrived in Greece for the first time. In making converts in Philippi and, soon afterwards, in Thessalonica, he was beset by persecution from Jews and Gentiles alike. Moving on to Beroea, he was again harassed by enemies from Thessalonica and hurriedly left for Athens (Acts 16, 11—17, 15). Silvanus and Timothy remained behind for a while. Paul soon sent Timothy back to Thessalonica to strengthen that community in its trials (3, 1–5). Timothy and Silvanus finally returned to Paul when he reached Corinth (Acts 18, 1–18), probably in the early summer of A.D. 51. Timothy's return with a report on conditions at Thessalonica served as the occasion for Paul's first letter (3, 6–8).

The letter begins with a brief address (1, 1) and concludes with a greeting (5, 26–28). The body of the letter consists of two major parts. The first (1, 2—3, 13) is a set of three sections of thanksgiving connected by two *apologiae* (defenses) dealing, respectively, with the missionaries' previous conduct and their current concerns. Paul's thankful optimism regarding the Thessalonians' spiritual welfare is tempered by his insistence on their recognition of the selfless love shown by the missionaries. In an age of itinerant peddlers of new religions, Paul found it necessary to emphasize not only the content of his gospel but also his

manner of presenting it, for both attested to God's grace as freely bestowed and powerfully effected.

The second part of the letter (4, 1—5, 25) is specifically hortatory or parenetic. The superabundant love for which Paul has just prayed (3, 12–13) is to be shown practically by living out the norms of conduct that he has communicated to them. Specific "imperatives" of Christian life, principles for acting morally, stem from the "indicative" of one's relationship to God through Christ by the sending of the holy Spirit. Thus, moral conduct is the practical, personal expression of one's Christian faith, love, and hope.

The principal divisions of the First Letter to the Thessalonians are the following:

I: Address (1, 1–10)

II: Previous Relations with the Thessalonians (2, 1—3, 13)

III: Specific Exhortations (4, 1—5, 25)

IV: Final Greeting (5, 26–28)

I: Address

CHAPTER 1

See RG 482

Greeting. *1a**Paul, Silvanus, and Timothy to the church of the Thessalonians in God the Father and the Lord Jesus Christ: grace to you and peace.

Thanksgiving for Their Faith. *2b*We give thanks to God always for all of you, remembering you in our prayers, unceasingly *3**calling to mind your work of faith and labor of

1, 1: On the address, see the note on Rom 1, 1–7.

1, 3: Faith . . . love . . . hope: this, along with 5, 8, is the earliest mention in Christian literature of the three "theological virtues" (see 1 Cor 13, 13). The order here stresses escha-

tological hope, in line with the letter's emphasis on the Lord's second, triumphant coming, or parousia (10; 2, 12.19; 3, 13; 4,

a: Acts 15, 40; 16, 1-3.19; 17, 14-15; 2 Thes 1, 1-2.   *b:* 2 Thes 1, 3.

love and endurance in hope of our Lord Jesus Christ, before our God and Father, [4c]knowing, brothers loved by God, how you were chosen. [5d]For our gospel did not come to you in word alone, but also in power and in the holy Spirit and [with] much conviction. You know what sort of people we were [among] you for your sake. [6*]And you became imitators of us and of the Lord, receiving the word in great affliction, with joy from the holy Spirit, [7e]so that you became a model for all the believers in Macedonia and in Achaia. [8f]For from you the word of the Lord has sounded forth not only in Macedonia and [in] Achaia, but in every place your faith in God has gone forth, so that we have no need to say anything. [9g]For they themselves openly declare about us what sort of reception we had among you, and how you turned to God from idols to serve the living and true God [10h]and to await his Son from heaven, whom he raised from [the] dead, Jesus, who delivers us from the coming wrath.

II: Previous Relations with the Thessalonians

CHAPTER 2

See RG 482–83

Paul's Ministry Among Them. [1]For you yourselves know, brothers, that our reception among you was not without effect. [2i]Rather, after we had suffered and been insolently treated, as you know, in Philippi, we drew courage through our God to speak to you the gospel of God with much struggle. [3]Our exhortation was not from delusion or impure motives, nor did it work through deception. [4j*]But as we were judged worthy by God to be entrusted with the gospel, that is how we speak, not as trying to please human beings, but rather God, who judges our hearts. [5]Nor, indeed, did we ever appear with flattering speech, as you know, or with a pretext for greed—God is witness— [6k]nor did we seek praise from human beings, either from you or from others, [7*]although we were able to impose our weight as apostles of Christ. Rather, we were gentle among you, as a nursing mother cares for her children. [8]With such affection for you, we were determined to share with you not only the gospel of God, but our very selves as well, so dearly beloved had you become to us. [9l]You recall, brothers, our toil and drudgery. Working night and day in order not to burden any of you, we proclaimed to you the gospel of God. [10]You are witnesses, and so is God, how devoutly and justly and blamelessly we behaved toward you believers. [11m]As you know, we treated each one of you as a father treats his children, [12n]exhorting and encouraging you and insisting that you conduct yourselves as worthy of the God who calls you into his kingdom and glory.

Further Thanksgiving. [13]And for this reason we too give thanks to God unceasingly, that, in receiving the word of God from hearing us, you received not a human word but, as it truly is, the word of God, which is now at work in you who believe. [14*]For you, brothers, have become imitators of the churches of God that are in Judea in Christ Jesus. For you suffer the same things from your compatriots as they did from the Jews, [15o*]who killed both the Lord Jesus and the

---

13—5, 11; 5, 23).

1, 6: Imitators: the Pauline theme of "imitation" (see 2, 14; 1 Cor 4, 16; 11, 1; 2 Thes 3, 9) is rooted in Paul's view of solidarity in Christ through sharing in Jesus' cross and in the Spirit of the risen Lord.

2, 4: Judged worthy: Paul regards "worthiness" not as grounded in one's own talent or moral self-righteousness but in God's discernment of genuinely selfless attitudes and actions (see 2 Cor 10, 17–18).

2, 7: Gentle: many excellent manuscripts read "infants" (nēpioi), but "gentle" (ēpioi) better suits the context here.

2, 14: Luke's picture of the persecutions at Philippi (by Gentiles) and in Thessalonica and Beroea (by Jews) seems to be considerably schematized (Acts 16, 11–40; 17, 1–15). Paul pictures the Thessalonian community as composed of con-

verts from paganism (1, 9) and speaks here of persecution by their (pagan) compatriots rather than by Jews.

2, 15–16: Paul is speaking of historical opposition on the part of Palestinian Jews in particular and does so only some twenty years after Jesus' crucifixion. Even so, he quickly proceeds to depict the persecutors typologically, in apocalyptic terms. His remarks give no grounds for anti-Semitism to those willing to understand him, especially in view of

c: 2 Thes 2, 13. d: Acts 13, 52; 17, 1-9. e: 2 Thes 1, 4; 1 Cor 4, 16; 11, 1 / 2, 14; Phil 3, 17. f: Rom 1, 8. g: Acts 14, 15; Gal 4, 8 / 4, 5. h: Rom 2, 1-16; 5, 9; 13, 4 / 5, 9. i: Acts 16, 19—17, 10. j: Gal 1, 10. k: Jn 5, 41.44; 1 Cor 10, 31; 2 Cor 4, 17. l: Acts 20, 34; 1 Cor 4, 12; 9, 3-18; 2 Thes 3, 7-9. m: Acts 20, 31. n: 1 Pt 5, 10 / 4, 7; 2 Thes 2, 14. o: Acts 2, 23; 7, 52.

prophets and persecuted us; they do not please God, and are opposed to everyone, [16p]trying to prevent us from speaking to the Gentiles that they may be saved, thus constantly filling up the measure of their sins. But the wrath of God has finally begun to come upon them.

Paul's Recent Travel Plans. [17q]Brothers, when we were bereft of you for a short time, in person, not in heart, we were all the more eager in our great desire to see you in person. [18r]We decided to go to you—I, Paul, not only once but more than once—yet Satan thwarted us. [19s]For what is our hope or joy or crown to boast of in the presence of our Lord Jesus at his coming if not you yourselves? [20]For you are our glory and joy.

See RG 482-83

CHAPTER 3

[1t]That is why, when we could bear it no longer, we decided to remain alone in Athens [2u]and sent Timothy, our brother and co-worker for God in the gospel of Christ, to strengthen and encourage you in your faith, [3*]so that no one be disturbed in these afflictions. For you yourselves know that we are destined for this. [4v]For even when we were among you, we used to warn you in advance that we would undergo affliction, just as has happened, as you know. [5]For this reason, when I too could bear it no longer, I sent to learn about your faith, for fear that somehow the tempter had put you to the test and our toil might come to nothing.

[6]But just now Timothy has returned to us from you, bringing us the good news of your faith and love, and that you always think kindly of us and long to see us as we long to see you. [7]Because of this, we have been reassured about you, brothers, in our every distress and affliction, through your faith. [8]For we now live, if you stand firm in the Lord.

Concluding Thanksgiving and Prayer. [9*]What thanksgiving, then, can we render to God for you, for all the joy we feel on your account before our God? [10]Night and day we pray beyond measure to see you in person and to remedy the deficiencies of your faith. [11]Now may God himself, our Father, and our Lord Jesus direct our way to you, [12w]and may the Lord make you increase and abound in love for one another and for all, just as we have for you, [13x]so as to strengthen your hearts, to be blameless in holiness before our God and Father at the coming of our Lord Jesus with all his holy ones. [Amen.]

III: Specific Exhortations

CHAPTER 4

See RG 483-84

General Exhortations. [1]Finally, brothers, we earnestly ask and exhort you in the Lord Jesus that, as you received from us how you should conduct yourselves to please God—and as you are conducting yourselves—you do so even more. [2*]For you know what instructions we gave you through the Lord Jesus.

Holiness in Sexual Conduct. [3*]This is the

Paul's pride in his own ethnic and religious background (Rom 9, 1–5; 10, 1; 11, 1–3; Phil 3, 4–6). Sinful conduct (16) is itself an anticipation of the ultimate wrath or judgment of God (Rom 1, 18—2, 5), whether or not it is perceived as such.

3, 3: We are destined: the Greek phraseology and the context suggest Paul's concern to alert his readers to difficulties he knew they would necessarily face and to enable them to see their present experience in the light of what he warned them would happen in the future. This line of thought is followed in 2 Thes 2, 1–15.

3, 9–10: The tension between Paul's optimism concerning the Thessalonians' faith and his worries about their perseverance remains unresolved. Perhaps this is accounted for not only by the continuing harassment but also by the shortness of his own stay in Thessalonica (even if that were over twice as long as the conventional three weeks that Luke assigns to it, Acts 17, 2).

4, 2: Instructions: these include specific guidelines on the basis of the Lord's authority, not necessarily sayings Jesus

actually uttered. More profoundly, as v 8 implies, the instructions are practical principles that Paul worked out in accordance with his understanding of the role of the Spirit.

4, 3–8: Many think that this passage deals with a variety of moral regulations (fornication, adultery, sharp business practices). It can be more specifically interpreted as bringing general norms to bear on a specific problem, namely, marriage within degrees of consanguinity (as between uncle and niece) forbidden in Jewish law but allowed according to a Greek heiress law, which would insure retention of an inheritance within the family and perhaps thereby occasion divorce. In that case, "immorality" (3) should be rendered as "unlawful marriage" and "this matter" (6) as "a lawsuit." The phrase in v 4, "acquire a wife for himself," has often been interpreted to mean "control one's body."

---

p: Gn 15, 16; 2 Mc 6, 14 / Rom 1, 18; 2, 5-6. q: 3, 10; Rom 1, 10-11. r: Rom 15, 22. s: 2 Cor 1, 14; Phil 2, 16; 4, 1. t: Acts 17, 14. u: Acts 16, 1-2; 1 Cor 3, 5-9. v: Acts 14, 22; 2 Thes 2, 5-7; 2 Tm 3, 12. w: 4, 9-10; 2 Thes 1, 3. x: 5, 23; 1 Cor 1, 8.

will of God, your holiness: that you refrain from immorality, [4]that each of you know how to acquire a wife for himself in holiness and honor, [5y]not in lustful passion as do the Gentiles who do not know God; [6]not to take advantage of or exploit a brother in this matter, for the Lord is an avenger in all these things, as we told you before and solemnly affirmed. [7]For God did not call us to impurity but to holiness. [8z]Therefore, whoever disregards this, disregards not a human being but God, who [also] gives his holy Spirit to you.

Mutual Charity. [9a]On the subject of mutual charity you have no need for anyone to write you, for you yourselves have been taught by God to love one another. [10b]Indeed, you do this for all the brothers throughout Macedonia. Nevertheless we urge you, brothers, to progress even more, [11]and to aspire to live a tranquil life, to mind your own affairs, and to work with your [own] hands, as we instructed you, [12]that you may conduct yourselves properly toward outsiders and not depend on anyone.

Hope for the Christian Dead. [13]We do not want you to be unaware, brothers, about those who have fallen asleep, so that you may not grieve like the rest, who have no hope. [14c]For if we believe that Jesus died and rose, so too will God, through Jesus, bring with him those who have fallen asleep. [15d*]Indeed, we tell you this, on the word of the Lord, that we who are alive, who are left until the coming of the Lord, will surely not precede those who have fallen asleep. [16e]For the Lord himself, with a word of command, with the voice of an archangel and with the trumpet of God, will come down from heaven, and the dead in Christ will rise first. [17*]Then we who are alive, who are left, will be caught up together with them in the clouds to meet the Lord in the air. Thus we shall always be with the Lord. [18]Therefore, console one another with these words.

CHAPTER 5

See RG
483-84

Vigilance. [1f]Concerning times and seasons, brothers, you have no need for anything to be written to you. [2g]For you yourselves know very well that the day of the Lord will come like a thief at night. [3]When people are saying, "Peace and security," then sudden disaster comes upon them, like labor pains upon a pregnant woman, and they will not escape.

[4h]But you, brothers, are not in darkness, for that day to overtake you like a thief. [5*]For all of you are children of the light and children of the day. We are not of the night or of darkness. [6i]Therefore, let us not sleep as the rest do, but let us stay alert and sober. [7]Those who sleep go to sleep at night, and those who are drunk get drunk at night. [8j]But since we are of the day, let us be sober, putting on the breastplate of faith and love and the helmet that is hope for salvation. [9]For God did not destine us for wrath, but to gain salvation through our Lord Jesus Christ, [10*]who died for us, so that whether we are awake or asleep we may live together with him. [11k]Therefore, encourage one another and build one another up, as indeed you do.

Church Order. [12]We ask you, brothers, to respect those who are laboring among you and who are over you in the Lord and who

---

4, 15: Coming of the Lord: Paul here assumes that the second coming, or parousia, will occur within his own lifetime but insists that the time or season is unknown (5, 1–2). Nevertheless, the most important aspect of the parousia for him was the fulfillment of union with Christ. His pastoral exhortation focuses first on hope for the departed faithful, then (5, 1–3) on the need of preparedness for those who have to achieve their goal.

4, 17: Will be caught up together: literally, snatched up, carried off; cf 2 Cor 12, 2; Rv 12, 5. From the Latin verb here used, **rapiemur,** has come the idea of "the rapture," when believers will be transported away from the woes of the world; this construction combines this verse with Mt 24, 40–41 (see the note there) // Lk 17, 34–35 and passages from Rv in a scheme of millennial dispensationalism.

5, 5: Children of the light: that is, belonging to the daylight

of God's personal revelation and expected to achieve it (an analogous development of imagery that appears in Jn 12, 36).

5, 10: Characteristically, Paul plays on words suggesting ultimate and anticipated death and life. Union with the crucified and risen Lord at his parousia is anticipated in some measure in contrasted states of our temporal life. The essential element he urges is our indestructible personal union in Christ's own life (see Rom 5, 1–10).

y: Ps 79, 6; Jer 10, 25; 2 Thes 1, 8; 1 Pt 3, 7. z: Lk 10, 16. a: Jn 6, 45; 13, 34; 1 Jn 2, 20-21.27; 4, 7. b: 2 Thes 3, 6-12. c: 1 Cor 15, 3-4.12.20. d: 1 Cor 15, 51; Rv 14, 13; 20, 4-6. e: Mt 24, 31; 1 Cor 15, 23.52. f: Mt 24, 36-45. g: 2 Pt 3, 10. h: Eph 5, 8-9. i: Mt 24, 42; Rom 13, 12-13; 1 Pt 5, 8. j: Is 59, 17; Rom 13, 11-14; Eph 6, 11.14-17. k: Rom 15, 2; 1 Cor 8, 1; 14, 12.26; Eph 4, 29.

admonish you, [13] and to show esteem for them with special love on account of their work. Be at peace among yourselves.

[14] We urge you, brothers, admonish the idle, cheer the fainthearted, support the weak, be patient with all. [15] *l* See that no one returns evil for evil; rather, always seek what is good [both] for each other and for all. [16] Rejoice always. [17] Pray without ceasing. [18] *m* In all circumstances give thanks, for this is the will of God for you in Christ Jesus. [19] *Do not quench the Spirit. [20] Do not despise prophetic utterances. [21] Test everything; retain what is good. [22] Refrain from every kind of evil.

Concluding Prayer. [23] *n* *May the God of peace himself make you perfectly holy and may you entirely, spirit, soul, and body, be preserved blameless for the coming of our Lord Jesus Christ. [24] The one who calls you is faithful, and he will also accomplish it. [25] Brothers, pray for us [too].

IV: Final Greeting

[26] *Greet all the brothers with a holy kiss. [27] I adjure you by the Lord that this letter be read to all the brothers. [28] The grace of our Lord Jesus Christ be with you.

5, 19–21: Paul's buoyant encouragement of charismatic freedom sometimes occasioned excesses that he or others had to remedy (see 1 Cor 14; 2 Thes 2, 1–15; 2 Pt 3, 1–16).

5, 23: Another possible translation is, "May the God of peace himself make you perfectly holy and sanctify your spirit fully, and may both soul and body be preserved blameless for the coming of our Lord Jesus Christ." In either case, Paul is not offering an anthropological or philosophical analysis of human nature. Rather, he looks to the wholeness

of what may be called the supernatural and natural aspects of a person's service of God.

5, 26: Kiss: the holy embrace (see Rom 16, 16; 1 Cor 16, 20; 2 Cor 13, 12; 1 Pt 5, 14) was a greeting of respect and affection, perhaps given during a liturgy at which Paul's letter would have been read.

l: Prv 20, 22; Mt 5, 38-42; Rom 12, 17. *m:* Eph 5, 20. *n:* 2 Thes 3, 16.

See RG
484–86
The Second Letter to the Thessalonians

This letter is addressed to the same church as the letter that precedes it in the canon and contains many expressions parallel to those in the First Letter to the Thessalonians, indeed verbatim with them. Yet other aspects of the contents of the Second Letter to the Thessalonians suggest a more impersonal tone and changed circumstances in the situation at Thessalonica.

The letter begins with an address (1, 1–2) that expands only slightly on that of 1 Thes 1, 1. It ends with a greeting insisting on its Pauline authority in the face of false claims made in Paul's name (see the note on 2, 2). The body of the letter falls into three short parts, of which the second is notoriously difficult (ch 2).

The opening thanksgiving and prayer (1, 3–12) speak of the Thessalonians' increasing faith and love in the face of outside persecution. God's eventual judgment against persecutors and his salvation for the faithful are already evidenced by the very fact of persecution. The second part (2, 1–17), the heart of the letter, deals with a problem threatening the faith of the community. A message involving a prophetic oracle and appar-

ently a forged letter, possibly presented at a liturgical gathering (cf 2, 2 and 1Cor 14, 26–33), to the effect that the day of the Lord and all that it means have already come, has upset the life of the Thessalonian church.

The writer counters their preoccupation with the date of the parousia (or coming again of the Lord Jesus from heaven, 2, 1) by recalling Paul's teaching concerning what must happen first and by going on to describe what will happen at the Lord's coming (2, 8); he indicates the twofold process by which the "activity of Satan" and God's actions (2, 9–11) are working out, namely, a growing division between believers and those who succumb to false prophecy and "the lie." He concludes by insisting on Pauline traditions and by praying for divine strength (2, 13–17). The closing part of the letter (3, 1–16) deals in particular with the apostle's directives and model style of life and with correction of disorderly elements within the community.

Traditional opinion holds that this letter was written shortly after 1 Thessalonians. Occasionally it has been argued that 2 Thessalonians was written first or that the two letters are addressed to different segments within the church at Thessalonica(2 Thessalonians being directed to the Jewish Christians there) or even that 2 Thessalonians was originally written to some other nearby place where Paul carried out mission work, such as Philippi or Beroea. Increasingly in recent times, however, the opinion has been advanced that 2 Thessalonians is a pseudepigraph, that is, a letter written authoritatively in Paul's name, to maintain apostolic traditions in a later period, perhaps during the last two decades of the first century.

In any case, the presumed audience of Second Thessalonians and certain features of its style and content require that it be read and studied in a Pauline context, particularly that provided by 1 Thessalonians. At the same time, and especially if the letter is regarded as not by Paul himself, its apocalyptic presentation of preconditions for the parousia (2, 1–12) may profit from and require recourse to a wider biblical basis for interpretation, namely Old Testament books such as Daniel and Isaiah and especially, in the New Testament, the synoptic apocalyptic discourse (Mk 13; Mt 24–25; Lk 21, 5–36) and the Book of Revelation.

The principal divisions of the Second Letter to the Thessalonians are the following:

I: Address (1, 1–12)
II: Warning against Deception Concerning the Parousia (2, 1–17)
III: Concluding Exhortations (3, 1–16)
IV: Final Greetings (3, 17–18)

I: Address

CHAPTER 1

Greeting. *1a**Paul, Silvanus, and Timothy to the church of the Thessalonians in God our Father and the Lord Jesus Christ: *2*grace to you and peace from God [our] Father and the Lord Jesus Christ.

Thanksgiving. *3b**We ought to thank God always for you, brothers, as is fitting, because your faith flourishes ever more, and the love of every one of you for one another grows ever greater. *4*Accordingly, we ourselves boast of you in the churches of God regarding your endurance and faith in all your persecutions and the afflictions you endure.

*5c*This is evidence of the just judgment of God, so that you may be considered worthy of the kingdom of God for which you are suffering. *6*For it is surely just on God's part to repay with afflictions those who are afflicting you, *7*and to grant rest along with us to you who are undergoing afflictions, at the revelation of the Lord Jesus from heaven with his mighty angels, *8d*in blazing fire, inflicting punishment on those who do not acknowledge God and on those who do not obey the gospel of our Lord Jesus. *9e*These will pay the penalty of eternal ruin, separated from the presence of the Lord and from the glory of his power, *10f**when he comes to be glorified among his holy ones and to be marveled at on that day among all who have believed, for our testimony to you was believed.

Prayer. *11g*To this end, we always pray for you, that our God may make you worthy of his calling and powerfully bring to fulfillment every good purpose and every effort of faith, *12h**that the name of our Lord Jesus may be glorified in you, and you in him, in accord with the grace of our God and Lord Jesus Christ.

1, 1–2: On the address, see the note on Rom 1, 1–7 and cf 1 Thes 1, 1.

1, 3–12: On the thanksgiving, see the note on Rom 1, 8 and cf 1 Thes 1, 2–10. Paul's gratitude to God for the faith and love of the Thessalonians (3) and his Christian pride in their faithful endurance (4–5) contrast with the condemnation announced for those who afflict them, a judgment to be carried out at the parousia (6–10), which is described in vivid language drawn from Old Testament apocalyptic. A prayer for the fulfillment of God's purpose in the Thessalonians (11–12) completes the section, as is customary in a Pauline letter (cf 1 Thes 1, 2–3).

1, 10: Among his holy ones: in the Old Testament, this term can refer to an angelic throng (cf also Jude 14), but here, in parallel with **among all who have believed,** it can refer to the triumphant people of God.

1, 12: The grace of our God and Lord Jesus Christ: the Greek can also be translated, "the grace of our God and of the Lord Jesus Christ."

---

a: 1 Thes 1, 1. *b:* 1 Cor 1, 4; 1 Thes 1, 2; 3, 12. *c:* Phil 1, 28; 1 Thes 2, 12. *d:* Ps 79, 5-6; Is 66, 15; Jer 10, 25. *e:* Is 2, 10.19.21. *f:* Ps 89, 8; Dn 7, 18-22.27; 1 Thes 3, 13. *g:* 1 Thes 1, 2-3. *h:* Is 66, 5.

II: Warning against Deception Concerning the Parousia

CHAPTER 2

See RG 485–86

Christ and the Lawless One. [1][i]*We ask you, brothers, with regard to the coming of our Lord Jesus Christ and our assembling with him, [2][j]*not to be shaken out of your minds suddenly, or to be alarmed either by a "spirit," or by an oral statement, or by a let- ter allegedly from us to the effect that the day of the Lord is at hand. [3]*Let no one de- ceive you in any way. For unless the apos- tasy comes first and the lawless one is re- vealed, the one doomed to perdition, [4][k]*who opposes and exalts himself above every so- called god and object of worship, so as to seat himself in the temple of God, claiming that he is a god— [5]do you not recall that while I was still with you I told you these things? [6]*And now you know what is re- straining, that he may be revealed in his time. [7][l]*For the mystery of lawlessness is

---

2, 1–17: The Thessalonians have been **shaken** by a mes- sage purporting to come from Paul himself that **the day of the Lord** is already present. He warns against this deception in eschatology by citing a scenario of events that must first occur (3–12) before the end will come. The overall point Paul makes is the need to reject such lies as Satan sends; he also reaffirms the Thessalonians in their calling (13–14). They are to uphold what Paul himself has taught (15). There is a con- cluding prayer for their strengthening (16–17). As in 1, 8–10, the Old Testament provides a good deal of coloring; cf espe- cially Is 14, 13–14; 66, 15.18–21; Ez 28, 2–9; Dn 11, 36–37. The contents of 2, 3b-8 may come from a previously existing apocalypse. The details have been variously interpreted.

An alternative to the possibilities noted below understands that an oracular utterance, supposedly coming from a prophetic spirit (2–3a), has so disrupted the community's thinking that its effects may be compared to those of the ma- nia connected with the worship of the Greek god Dionysus. On this view, the writer seems to allude in vv 6–8 to Dionysiac "seizure," although, of course, ironically, some- what as Paul alludes to witchcraft ("an evil eye") in Gal 3, 1 in speaking of the threat to faith posed by those disturbing the Galatians (Gal 1, 6–7; 5, 10b). On this view of 2 Thes 2, the Greek participles **katechon** (rendered above as **what is re- straining**) and **katechōn** (**the one who restrains**) are to be translated "the seizing power" in v 6 and "the seizer" in v 7. They then allude to a pseudocharismatic force or spirit of Dionysiac character that has suddenly taken hold of the Thes- salonian community (see 2). The addressees **know** (6) this force or spirit because of the problem it is causing. This pseudocharismatic force or spirit is a kind of anticipation and advance proof of the ultimate, climactic figure (**the lawless one** or the rebel, 3), of which the community has been warned (see the note on 1 Thes 3, 3). It is, however, only the begin- ning of the end that the latter's manifestation entails; the end is not yet. For in the course of **the mystery of lawlessness** (7), false prophetism, after it ceases in the Thessalonian com- munity, will be manifested in the world at large (8–12), where it will also be eliminated in turn by the Lord Jesus.

2, 2: "**Spirit**": a Spirit-inspired utterance or ecstatic revela- tion. **An oral statement:** literally, a "word" or pronouncement, not necessarily of ecstatic origin. **A letter allegedly from us:** possibly a forged letter, so that Paul calls attention in 3, 17 to his practice of concluding a genuine letter with a summary note or greeting in his own hand, as at Gal 6, 11–18 and elsewhere.

2, 3b-5: This incomplete sentence (anacoluthon, 4) recalls what the Thessalonians had already been taught, an apoca- lyptic scenario depicting, in terms borrowed especially from Dn 11, 36–37 and related verses, human self-assertiveness against God in **the temple of God** itself. **The lawless one** represents the climax of such activity in this account.

2, 4: **Seat himself in the temple of God:** a reflection of the language in Dn 7, 23–25; 8, 9–12; 9, 27; 11, 36–37; and 12, 11 about the attempt of Antiochus IV Epiphanes to set up a statue of Zeus in the Jerusalem temple and possibly of the Roman emperor Caligula to do a similar thing (Mk 13, 14). Here the imagery suggests an attempt to install someone in the place of God, **claiming that he is a god** (cf Ez 28, 2). Usually, it is the Jerusalem temple that is assumed to be meant; on the alternative view sketched above (see the note on 2, 1–17), **the temple** refers to the Christian community.

2, 6–7: **What is restraining . . . the one who restrains:** neuter and masculine, respectively, of a force and person holding back the lawless one. The Thessalonians know what is meant (6), but the terms, seemingly found only in this pas- sage and in writings dependent on it, have been variously in- terpreted. Traditionally, v 6 has been applied to the Roman empire and v 7 to the Roman emperor (in Paul's day, Nero) as bulwarks holding back chaos (cf Rom 13, 1–7). A second in- terpretation suggests that cosmic or angelic powers are bind- ing Satan (9) and so restraining him; some relate this to an anti-Christ figure (1 Jn 2, 18) or to Michael the archangel (Rv 12, 7–9; 20, 1–3). A more recent view suggests that it is the preaching of the Christian gospel that restrains the end, for in God's plan the end cannot come until the gospel is preached to all nations (Mk 13, 10); in that case, Paul as missionary preacher par excellence is "the one who restrains," whose re- moval (death) will bring the end (7). On the alternative view (see the note on 2, 1–17), the phrases should be referred to that which and to him who seizes (a prophet) in ecstasy so as to have him speak pseudo-oracles.

2, 7–12: **The lawless one** and **the one who restrains** are involved in an activity or process, **the mystery of lawless- ness,** behind which **Satan** stands (9). The action of the **Lord** [**Jesus**] in overcoming the lawless one is described in Old Testament language (**with the breath of his mouth;** cf Is 11,

---

i: 1 Thes 4, 13-17. *j*: Mt 24, 6; 1 Cor 14, 26.32-33; 1 Thes 5, l- 2. *k*: Dn 11, 36-37; Ez 28, 2. *l*: Mt 13, 36-43; Acts 20, 29; Gal 5, 10; 2 Pt 2, 1; Rv 22, 11.

already at work. But the one who restrains is to do so only for the present, until he is removed from the scene. ^{8m}And then the lawless one will be revealed, whom the Lord [Jesus] will kill with the breath of his mouth and render powerless by the manifestation of his coming, ^{9n}the one whose coming springs from the power of Satan in every mighty deed and in signs and wonders that lie, ^{10}and in every wicked deceit for those who are perishing because they have not accepted the love of truth so that they may be saved. ^{11}Therefore, God is sending them a deceiving power so that they may believe the lie, ^{12}that all who have not believed the truth but have approved wrongdoing may be condemned.

^{13o*}But we ought to give thanks to God for you always, brothers loved by the Lord, because God chose you as the firstfruits for salvation through sanctification by the Spirit and belief in truth. ^{14p}To this end he has [also] called you through our gospel to possess the glory of our Lord Jesus Christ. ^{15*}Therefore, brothers, stand firm and hold fast to the traditions that you were taught, either by an oral statement or by a letter of ours.

^{16}May our Lord Jesus Christ himself and God our Father, who has loved us and given us everlasting encouragement and good hope through his grace, ^{17}encourage your hearts and strengthen them in every good deed and word.

III: Concluding Exhortations

CHAPTER 3

See RG 486

Request for Prayers. ^{1q*}Finally, brothers, pray for us, so that the word of the Lord may speed forward and be glorified, as it did among you, ^{2}and that we may be delivered from perverse and wicked people, for not all have faith. ^{3r}But the Lord is faithful; he will strengthen you and guard you from the evil one. ^{4s}We are confident of you in the Lord that what we instruct you, you [both] are doing and will continue to do. ^{5}May the Lord direct your hearts to the love of God and to the endurance of Christ.

Neglect of Work. ^{6*}We instruct you, brothers, in the name of [our] Lord Jesus Christ, to shun any brother who conducts himself in a disorderly way and not according to the tradition they received from us. ^{7}For you know how one must imitate us. For we did not act in a disorderly way among you, ^{8t}nor did we eat food received free from anyone. On the contrary, in toil and drudgery, night and day we worked, so as not to burden any of you. ^{9u}Not that we do not have the right. Rather, we wanted to present ourselves as a model for you, so that you might imitate us. ^{10v}In fact, when we were with you, we instructed you that if anyone was unwilling to work, neither should that one eat. ^{11w}We hear that some are conducting themselves among you in a

---

4; Jb 4, 9; Rv 19, 15). His **coming** is literally the Lord's "parousia." The biblical concept of the "holy war," eschatologically conceived, may underlie the imagery.

2, 13: As the **firstfruits:** there is also strong manuscript evidence for the reading, "God chose you from the beginning," thus providing a focus on God's activity from beginning to end; **firstfruits** is a Pauline term, however; cf Rom 8, 23; 11, 16; 16, 5, among other references.

2, 15: Reference to **an oral statement** and **a letter** (2) and the content here, including a formula of conclusion (cf 1 Cor 16, 13; Gal 5, 1), suggest that vv 1–15 or even 1–17 are to be taken as a literary unit, notwithstanding the incidental thanksgiving formula in v 13.

3, 1–18: The final chapter urges the Thessalonians to pray for Paul and his colleagues (1–2) and reiterates confidence in the Thessalonians (3–5), while admonishing them about a specific problem in their community that has grown out of the intense eschatological speculation, namely, not to work but to become instead disorderly busybodies (6–15). A benediction

(16) and postscript in Paul's own hand round out the letter. On vv 17–18, cf the note on 2, 2.

3, 6: Some members of the community, probably because they regarded the parousia as imminent or the new age of the Lord to be already here (2, 2), had apparently ceased to work for a living. The disciplinary problem they posed could be rooted in distorted thinking about Paul's own teaching (cf 1 Thes 2, 16; 3, 3–4; 5, 4–5) or, more likely, in a forged letter (2, 2) and the type of teaching dealt with in 2, 1–15. The apostle's own moral teaching, reflected in his selfless labors for others, was rooted in a deep doctrinal concern for the gospel message (cf 1 Thes 2, 3–10).

m: Is 11, 4; Rv 19, 15. *n:* Mt 24, 24; Rv 13, 13. *o:* 1 Thes 2, 13; 5, 9. *p:* Rom 5, 1-10; 8, 29-30; 1 Thes 4, 7; 5, 9. *q:* Eph 6, 19; Col 4, 3. *r:* 1 Thes 5, 24 / 1 Cor 16, 13 / Mt 6, 13. *s:* 2 Cor 7, 16; 1 Thes 4, 1-2. *t:* 1 Thes 2, 9. *u:* Mt 10, 10; Phil 3, 17. *v:* 1 Thes 4, 11. *w:* 1 Thes 5, 14.

disorderly way, by not keeping busy but minding the business of others. *12*Such people we instruct and urge in the Lord Jesus Christ to work quietly and to eat their own food. *13*But you, brothers, do not be remiss in doing good. *14*If anyone does not obey our word as expressed in this letter, take note of this person not to associate with him, that he may be put to shame. *15x*Do not regard him as an enemy but ad-

monish him as a brother. *16y*May the Lord of peace himself give you peace at all times and in every way. The Lord be with all of you.

IV: Final Greetings

*17z*This greeting is in my own hand, Paul's. This is the sign in every letter; this is how I write. *18*The grace of our Lord Jesus Christ be with all of you.

x; 2 Cor 2, 7; Gal 6, 1.   *y:* Jn 14, 27; Rom 15, 33.   *z:* 1 Cor 16, 21; Gal 6, 11.

See RG
487–89

The First Letter to Timothy

The three letters, First and Second Timothy and Titus, form a distinct group within the Pauline corpus. In the collection of letters by the Apostle to the Gentiles, they differ from the others in form and contents. All three suggest they were written late in Paul's career. The opponents are not "Judaizers" as in Galatians but false teachers stressing "knowledge" (*gnosis;* see the note on 1 Tm 6, 20–21). Attention is given especially to correct doctrine and church organization. Jesus' second coming recedes into the background compared to references in Paul's earlier letters (though not Colossians and Ephesians). The three letters are addressed not to congregations but to those who shepherd congregations (Latin, *pastores*). These letters were first named "Pastoral Epistles" in the eighteenth century because they all are concerned with the work of a pastor in caring for the community or communities under his charge.

The first of the Pastorals, 1 Timothy, is presented as having been written from Macedonia. Timothy, whom Paul converted, was of mixed Jewish and Gentile parentage (Acts 16, 1–3). He was the apostle's companion on both the second and the third missionary journeys (Acts 16, 3; 19, 22) and was often sent by him on special missions (Acts 19, 22; 1 Cor 4, 17; 1 Thes 3, 2). In 1 Timothy (1, 3), he is described as the administrator of the entire Ephesian community.

The letter instructs Timothy on his duty to restrain false and useless teaching (1, 3–11; 4, 1–5; 6, 3–16) and proposes principles pertaining to his relationship with the older members of the community (5, 1–2) and with the presbyters (5, 17–22). It gives rules for aid to widows

(5, 3–8) and their selection for charitable ministrations (5, 9–16) and also deals with liturgical celebrations (2, 1–15), selections for the offices of bishop and deacon (3, 1–13), relation of slaves with their masters (6, 1–2), and obligations of the wealthier members of the community (6, 17–19). This letter also reminds Timothy of the prophetic character of his office (1, 12–20) and encourages him in his exercise of it (4, 6–16). The central passage of the letter (3, 14–16) expresses the principal motive that should guide the conduct of Timothy—preservation of the purity of the church's doctrine against false teaching. On this same note the letter concludes (6, 20–21).

From the late second century to the nineteenth, Pauline authorship of the three Pastoral Epistles went unchallenged. Since then, the attribution of these letters to Paul has been questioned. Most scholars are convinced that Paul could not have been responsible for the vocabulary and style, the concept of church organization, or the theological expressions found in these letters. A second group believes, on the basis of statistical evidence, that the vocabulary and style are Pauline, even if at first sight the contrary seems to be the case. They state that the concept of church organization in the letters is not as advanced as the questioners of Pauline authorship hold since the notion of hierarchical order in a religious community existed in Israel before the time of Christ, as evidenced in the Dead Sea Scrolls. Finally, this group sees affinities between the theological thought of the Pastorals and that of the unquestionably genuine letters of Paul. Other scholars, while conceding a degree of validity to the positions mentioned above, suggest that the apostle made use of a secretary who was responsible for the composition of the letters. A fourth group of scholars believes that these letters are the work of a compiler, that they are based on traditions about Paul in his later years, and that they include, in varying amounts, actual fragments of genuine Pauline correspondence.

If Paul is considered the more immediate author, the Pastorals are to be dated between the end of his first Roman imprisonment (Acts 28, 16) and his execution under Nero (A.D. 63–67); if they are regarded as only more remotely Pauline, their date may be as late as the early second century. In spite of these problems of authorship and dating, the Pastorals are illustrative of early Christian life and remain an important element of canonical scripture.

The principal divisions of the First Letter to Timothy are the following:

   I: Address (1, 1–2)
   II: Sound Teaching (1, 3–20)
   III: Problems of Discipline (2, 1—4, 16)
   IV: Duties toward Others (5, 1—6, 2a)
   V: False Teaching and True Wealth (6, 2)
   VI: Final Recommendation and Warning
      (6, 20–21)

I: Address

CHAPTER 1

See RG
487–88 *Greeting.* ^{1a*}Paul, an apostle of Christ Jesus by command of God our savior and of

Christ Jesus our hope, ^{2b}to Timothy, my true child in faith: grace, mercy, and peace from God the Father and Christ Jesus our Lord.

II: Sound Teaching

Warning against False Doctrine. ^{3c*}I repeat the request I made of you when I was on my way to Macedonia, that you stay in Ephesus to instruct certain people not to teach false doctrines ^{4d*}or to concern themselves with myths and endless genealogies, which promote speculations rather than the plan of God that is to be received by faith. ^{5e}The aim of this instruction is love from a pure heart, a good conscience, and a sincere faith. ^{6f}Some people have deviated from these and turned to meaningless talk, ^{7}wanting to be teachers of the law, but without understanding either what they are saying or what they assert with such assurance.

^{8g*}We know that the law is good, provided that one uses it as law, ^{9}with the understanding that law is meant not for a righteous person but for the lawless and unruly, the godless and sinful, the unholy and profane, those who kill their fathers or mothers, murderers, ^{10h*}the unchaste, sodomites, kidnappers, liars, perjurers, and whatever else is opposed to sound teaching, ^{11i}according to the glorious gospel of the blessed God, with which I have been entrusted.

Gratitude for God's Mercy. ^{12j*}I am grateful to him who has strengthened me, Christ Jesus our Lord, because he considered me trustworthy in appointing me to the ministry.

1, 1–2: For the Pauline use of the conventional epistolary form, see the note on Rom 1, 1–7.

1, 3–7: Here Timothy's initial task **in Ephesus** (cf Acts 20, 17–35) is outlined: to suppress the idle religious speculations, probably about Old Testament figures (3–4, but see the note on 6, 20–21), which do not contribute to the development of love within the community (5) but rather encourage similar useless conjectures (6–7).

1, 4: The **plan of God that is to be received by faith:** the Greek may also possibly mean "God's trustworthy plan" or "the training in faith that God requires."

1, 8–11: Those responsible for the speculations that are to be suppressed by Timothy do not present the Old Testament from the Christian viewpoint. The Christian values the Old Testament not as a system of law but as the first stage in God's revelation of his saving plan, which is brought to fulfillment in the good news of salvation through faith in Jesus Christ.

1, 10: Sodomites: see 1 Cor 6, 9 and the note there.

1, 12–17: Present gratitude for the Christian apostleship leads Paul to recall an earlier time when he had been a fierce persecutor of the Christian communities (cf Acts 26, 9–11) until his conversion by intervention of divine mercy through the appearance of Jesus. This and his subsequent apostolic experience testify to the saving purpose of Jesus' incarnation. The fact of his former ignorance of the truth has not kept the apostle from regarding himself as having been the worst of sinners (15). Yet he was chosen to be an apostle, that God might manifest his firm will to save sinful humanity through Jesus Christ (16). The recounting of so great a mystery leads to a spontaneous outpouring of adoration (17).

---

a: 2, 3; Lk 1, 47; Ti 1, 3; 2, 10 / Col 1, 27.   *b:* 2 Tm 1, 2; Ti 1, 4.   *c:* Acts 20, 1.   *d:* 4, 7; Ti 1, 14; 3, 9; 2 Pt 1, 16.   *e:* Rom 13, 10. *f:* 6, 4.20; Ti 1, 10.   *g:* Rom 7, 12.16.   *h:* 4; 6; 6, 3; 2 Tm 4, 3; Ti 1, 9; 2, 1.   *i:* Ti 1, 3.   *j:* Phil 4, 13 / Acts 9, 15; Gal 1, 15-16.

[13k]I was once a blasphemer and a persecutor and an arrogant man, but I have been mercifully treated because I acted out of ignorance in my unbelief. [14l]Indeed, the grace of our Lord has been abundant, along with the faith and love that are in Christ Jesus. [15m]*This saying is trustworthy and deserves full acceptance: Christ Jesus came into the world to save sinners. Of these I am the foremost. [16]But for that reason I was mercifully treated, so that in me, as the foremost, Christ Jesus might display all his patience as an example for those who would come to believe in him for everlasting life. [17n]*To the king of ages, incorruptible, invisible, the only God, honor and glory forever and ever. Amen.

Responsibility of Timothy. [18o]*I entrust this charge to you, Timothy, my child, in accordance with the prophetic words once spoken about you. Through them may you fight a good fight [19p]by having faith and a good conscience. Some, by rejecting conscience, have made a shipwreck of their faith, [20q]*among them Hymenaeus and Alexander, whom I have handed over to Satan to be taught not to blaspheme.

III: Problems of Discipline

CHAPTER 2

Prayer and Conduct. [1r]*First of all, then, I ask that supplications, prayers, petitions, and thanksgivings be offered for everyone, [2]for kings and for all in authority, that we may lead a quiet and tranquil life in all devotion and dignity. [3s]This is good and pleasing to God our savior, [4t]who wills everyone to be saved and to come to knowledge of the truth.

[5] [u]For there is one God.
There is also one mediator between God
    and the human race,
Christ Jesus, himself human,
[6] [v]*who gave himself as ransom for all.

This was the testimony at the proper time. [7w]For this I was appointed preacher and apostle (I am speaking the truth, I am not lying), teacher of the Gentiles in faith and truth.

[8]*It is my wish, then, that in every place the men should pray, lifting up holy hands,

See RG
488

1, 15: This saying is trustworthy: this phrase regularly introduces in the Pastorals a basic truth of early Christian faith; cf 3, 1; 4, 9; 2 Tm 2, 11; Ti 3, 8.

1, 17: King of ages: through Semitic influence, the Greek expression could mean "everlasting king"; it could also mean "king of the universe."

1, 18–20: Timothy is to be mindful of his calling, which is here compared to the way Barnabas and Saul were designated by Christ as prophets for missionary service; cf Acts 13, 1–3. Such is probably the sense of the allusion to the prophetic words (18). His task is not to yield, whether in doctrine or in conduct, to erroneous opinions, taking warning from what has already happened at Ephesus in the case of Hymenaeus and Alexander (19–20).

1, 18: The prophetic words once spoken about you: the Greek may also be translated, "the prophecies that led (me) to you." It probably refers to testimonies given by charismatic figures in the Christian communities. **Fight a good fight:** this translation preserves the play on words in Greek. The Greek terms imply a lengthy engagement in battle and might well be translated "wage a good campaign."

1, 20: Hymenaeus: mentioned in 2 Tm 2, 17 as saying that the resurrection has already taken place (in baptism). **Alexander:** probably the Alexander mentioned in 2 Tm 4, 14 as the coppersmith who "did me a great deal of harm." **Whom I have handed over to Satan:** the same terms are used in the condemnation of the incestuous man in 1 Cor 5, 5.

2, 1–7: This marked insistence that the liturgical prayer of the community concern itself with the needs of all, whether

Christian or not, and especially of those in authority, may imply that a disposition existed at Ephesus to refuse prayer for pagans. In actuality, such prayer aids the community to achieve peaceful relationships with non-Christians (2) and contributes to salvation, since it derives its value from the presence within the community of Christ, who is the one and only savior of all (3–6). The vital apostolic mission to the Gentiles (7) reflects Christ's purpose of universal salvation.

Verse 5 contains what may well have been a very primitive creed. Some interpreters have called it a Christian version of the Jewish **shema:** "Hear, O Israel, the LORD is our God, the LORD alone . . ." (Dt 6, 4–5). The assertion in v 7, "I am speaking the truth, I am not lying," reminds one of similar affirmations in Rom 9, 1; 2 Cor 11, 31; and Gal 1, 20.

2, 6: The testimony: to make sense of this overly concise phrase, many manuscripts supply "to which" (or "to whom"); two others add "was given." The translation has supplied "this was."

2, 8–15: The prayer of the community should be unmarred by internal dissension (8); cf Mt 5, 21–26; 6, 14; Mk 11, 25. At the liturgical assembly the dress of women should be ap-

k: Acts 8, 3; 9, 1-2; 1 Cor 15, 9; Gal 1, 13. *l:* Rom 5, 20; 2 Tm 1, 13. *m:* Lk 15, 2; 19, 10. *n:* Rom 16, 27. *o:* 4, 14 / 6, 12; 2 Tm 4, 7; Jude 3. *p:* 3, 9. *q:* 2 Tm 2, 17; 4, 14 / 1 Cor 5, 5. *r:* Eph 6, 18; Phil 4, 6. *s:* 1, 1; 4, 10. *t:* 2 Tm 3, 7; 2 Pt 3, 9. *u:* 1 Cor 8, 6; Heb 8, 6; 9, 15; 12, 24 / Rom 5, 15. *v:* Mk 10, 45; Gal 1, 4; 2, 20; Eph 5, 25; Ti 2, 14. *w:* Acts 9, 15; 1 Cor 9, 1; Gal 2, 7-8.

without anger or argument. [9x]Similarly, [too,] women should adorn themselves with proper conduct, with modesty and self-control, not with braided hairstyles and gold ornaments, or pearls, or expensive clothes, [10y]but rather, as befits women who profess reverence for God, with good deeds. [11z]A woman must receive instruction silently and under complete control. [12*]I do not permit a woman to teach or to have authority over a man. She must be quiet. [13a]For Adam was formed first, then Eve. [14b]Further, Adam was not deceived, but the woman was deceived and transgressed. [15c]But she will be saved through motherhood, provided women persevere in faith and love and holiness, with self-control.

See RG 488

CHAPTER 3

Qualifications of Various Ministers. [1d*]This saying is trustworthy: whoever aspires to the office of bishop desires a noble task. [2]Therefore, a bishop must be irreproachable, married only once, temperate, self-controlled, decent, hospitable, able to teach, [3e]not a drunkard, not aggressive, but gentle, not contentious, not a lover of money.

[4]He must manage his own household well, keeping his children under control with perfect dignity; [5]for if a man does not know how to manage his own household, how can he take care of the church of God? [6*]He should not be a recent convert, so that he may not become conceited and thus incur the devil's punishment. [7f]He must also have a good reputation among outsiders, so that he may not fall into disgrace, the devil's trap.

[8*]Similarly, deacons must be dignified, not deceitful, not addicted to drink, not greedy for sordid gain, [9]holding fast to the mystery of the faith with a clear conscience. [10]Moreover, they should be tested first; then, if there is nothing against them, let them serve as deacons. [11g*]Women, similarly, should be dignified, not slanderers, but temperate and faithful in everything. [12]Deacons may be married only once and must manage their children and their households well. [13]Thus those who serve well as deacons gain good standing and much confidence in their faith in Christ Jesus.

The Mystery of Our Religion. [14*]I am writing you about these matters, although I hope to visit you soon. [15h]But if I should be delayed, you should know how to behave in the house-

---

propriate to the occasion (9); their chief adornment is to be reputation for good works (10). Women are not to take part in the charismatic activity of the assembly (11–12; cf 1 Cor 14, 34) or exercise authority; their conduct there should reflect the role of man's helpmate (13; cf Gn 2, 18) and not the later relationship of Eve to Adam (14; cf Gn 3; 6–7). As long as women perform their role as wives and mothers in faith and love, their salvation is assured (15).

2, 12: A man: this could also mean "her husband."

3, 1–7: The passage begins by commending those who aspire to the office of bishop (**episkopos;** see the note on Phil 1, 1) within the community, but this first sentence (1) may also imply a warning about the great responsibilities involved. The writer proceeds to list the qualifications required: personal stability and graciousness; talent for teaching (2); moderation in habits and temperament (3); managerial ability (4); and experience in Christian living (5–6). Moreover, the candidate's previous life should provide no grounds for the charge that he did not previously practice what he now preaches. No list of qualifications for presbyters appears in 1 Tm. The presbyter-bishops here and in Ti (see the note on Ti 1, 5–9) lack certain functions reserved here for Paul and Timothy.

3, 1: This saying is trustworthy: the saying introduced is so unlike others after this phrase that some later Western manuscripts read, "This saying is popular." It is understood by some interpreters as concluding the preceding section (2, 8–15). **Bishop:** literally, "overseer"; see the note on Phil 1, 1.

3, 6: The devil's punishment: this phrase could mean the

punishment once incurred by the devil (objective genitive) or a punishment brought about by the devil (subjective genitive).

3, 8–13: Deacons, besides possessing the virtue of moderation (8), are to be outstanding for their faith (9) and well respected within the community (10). Women in the same role, although some interpreters take them to mean wives of deacons, must be dignified, temperate, dedicated, and not given to malicious talebearing (11). Deacons must have shown stability in marriage and have a good record with their families (12), for such experience prepares them well for the exercise of their ministry on behalf of the community (13). See further the note on Phil 1, 1.

3, 11: Women: this seems to refer to women deacons but may possibly mean wives of deacons. The former is preferred because the word is used absolutely; if deacons' wives were meant, a possessive "their" would be expected. Moreover, they are also introduced by the word "similarly," as in v 8; this parallel suggests that they too exercised ecclesiastical functions.

3, 14–16: In case there is some delay in the visit to Timothy at Ephesus planned for the near future, the present letter is being sent on ahead to arm and enlighten him in his task of preserving sound Christian conduct in the Ephesian church. The care he must exercise over this community is required by

x: 1 Pt 3, 3-5. *y:* 5, 10; 1 Pt 3, 1. *z:* 1 Cor 14, 34-35. *a:* Gn 1, 27; 2, 7.22; 1 Cor 11, 8-9. *b:* Gn 3, 6.13; 2 Cor 11, 3. *c:* 5, 14. *d:* Ti 1, 6-9. *e:* Heb 13, 5. *f:* 2 Cor 8, 21; 2 Tm 2, 26. *g:* Ti 2, 3. *h:* Eph 2, 19-22.

hold of God, which is the church of the living God, the pillar and foundation of truth. ¹⁶ⁱ*Undeniably great is the mystery of devotion,

> Who was manifested in the flesh,
> vindicated in the spirit,
> seen by angels,
> proclaimed to the Gentiles,
> believed in throughout the world,
> taken up in glory.

See RG 488

CHAPTER 4

False Asceticism. ¹ʲ*Now the Spirit explicitly says that in the last times some will turn away from the faith by paying attention to deceitful spirits and demonic instructions ²through the hypocrisy of liars with branded consciences. ³ᵏThey forbid marriage and require abstinence from foods that God created to be received with thanksgiving by those who believe and know the truth. ⁴ˡFor everything created by God is good, and nothing is to be rejected when received with thanksgiving, ⁵*for it is made holy by the invocation of God in prayer.

Counsel to Timothy. ⁶*If you will give these instructions to the brothers, you will be a good minister of Christ Jesus, nourished on the words of the faith and of the sound teaching you have followed. ⁷ᵐAvoid profane and silly myths. Train yourself for devotion, ⁸ⁿfor, while physical training is of limited value, devotion is valuable in every respect, since it holds a promise of life both for the present and for the future. ⁹ᵒThis saying is trustworthy and deserves full acceptance. ¹⁰ᵖ*For this we toil and struggle, because we have set our hope on the living God, who is the savior of all, especially of those who believe.

¹¹*Command and teach these things. ¹²�q*Let no one have contempt for your youth, but set an example for those who believe, in speech, conduct, love, faith, and purity. ¹³*Until I arrive, attend to the reading, exhortation, and teaching. ¹⁴ʳ*Do not neglect the gift you have, which was conferred on you through the prophetic word with the imposition of hands of the presbyterate. ¹⁵Be diligent in these matters, be absorbed in them, so that your progress may be evident

the profound nature of Christianity. It centers in Christ, appearing in human flesh, vindicated by the holy Spirit; the mystery of his person was revealed to the angels, announced to the Gentiles, and accepted by them in faith. He himself was taken up (through his resurrection and ascension) to the divine glory (16). This passage apparently includes part of a liturgical hymn used among the Christian communities in and around Ephesus. It consists of three couplets in typical Hebrew balance: flesh-spirit (contrast), seen-proclaimed (complementary), world-glory (contrast).

3, 16: Who: the reference is to Christ, who is himself "the mystery of our devotion." Some predominantly Western manuscripts read "which," harmonizing the gender of the pronoun with that of the Greek word for mystery; many later (eighth/ninth century on), predominantly Byzantine manuscripts read "God," possibly for theological reasons.

4, 1–5: Doctrinal deviations from the true Christian message within the church have been prophesied, though the origin of the prophecy is not specified (1–2); cf Acts 20, 29–30. The letter warns against a false asceticism that prohibits marriage and regards certain foods as forbidden, though they are part of God's good creation (3).

4, 5: The invocation of God in prayer: literally, "the word of God and petition." The use of "word of God" without an article in Greek suggests that it refers to the name of God being invoked in blessing rather than to the "word of God" proclaimed to the community.

4, 6–10: Timothy is urged to be faithful, both in his teaching and in his own life, as he looks only to God for salvation.

4, 10: Struggle: other manuscripts and patristic witnesses read "suffer reproach."

4, 11–16: Timothy is urged to preach and teach with confidence, relying on the gifts and the mission that God has bestowed on him.

4, 12: Youth: some commentators find this reference a sign of pseudepigraphy. Timothy had joined Paul as a missionary already in A.D. 49, some fifteen years before the earliest supposed date of composition.

4, 13: Reading: the Greek word refers to private or public reading. Here, it probably designates the public reading of scripture in the Christian assembly.

4, 14: Prophetic word: this may mean the utterance of a Christian prophet designating the candidate or a prayer of blessing accompanying the rite. **Imposition of hands:** this gesture was used in the Old Testament to signify the transmission of authority from Moses to Joshua (Nm 27, 18–23; Dt 34, 9). The early Christian community used it as a symbol of installation into an office: the Seven (Acts 6, 6) and Paul and Barnabas (Acts 13, 3). **Of the presbyterate:** this would mean that each member of the college of presbyters imposed hands and appears to contradict 2 Tm 1, 6, in which Paul says that he imposed hands on Timothy. This latter text, however, does not exclude participation by others in the rite. Some prefer to translate "for the presbyterate," and thus understand it to designate the office into which Timothy was installed rather than the agents who installed him.

i: Jn 1, 14; Rom 1, 3-4. *j:* 2 Tm 3, 1; 4, 3; 2 Pt 3, 3; Jude 18. *k:* Gn 9, 3; Rom 14, 6; 1 Cor 10, 30-31. *l:* Gn 1, 31; Acts 10, 15. *m:* 1, 4; 2 Tm 2, 16; Ti 1, 14. *n:* 6, 6. *o:* 1, 15; 2 Tm 2, 11; Ti 3, 8. *p:* 2, 4; Ti 2, 11. *q:* 1 Cor 16, 11; Ti 2, 15 / Phil 3, 17. *r:* 5, 22; Acts 6, 6; 8, 17; 2 Tm 1, 6.

to everyone. [16]Attend to yourself and to your teaching; persevere in both tasks, for by doing so you will save both yourself and those who listen to you.

IV: Duties toward Others

CHAPTER 5

See RG
488–89 [1s]*Do not rebuke an older man, but appeal to him as a father. Treat younger men as brothers, [2]older women as mothers, and younger women as sisters with complete purity.

Rules for Widows. [3]Honor widows who are truly widows. [4]But if a widow has children or grandchildren, let these first learn to perform their religious duty to their own family and to make recompense to their parents, for this is pleasing to God. [5t]The real widow, who is all alone, has set her hope on God and continues in supplications and prayers night and day. [6]But the one who is self-indulgent is dead while she lives. [7]Command this, so that they may be irreproachable. [8]And whoever does not provide for relatives and especially family members has denied the faith and is worse than an unbeliever.

[9]Let a widow be enrolled if she is not less than sixty years old, married only once, [10u]with a reputation for good works, namely, that she has raised children, practiced hospitality, washed the feet of the holy ones,

helped those in distress, involved herself in every good work. [11]But exclude younger widows, for when their sensuality estranges them from Christ, they want to marry [12]and will incur condemnation for breaking their first pledge. [13v]And furthermore, they learn to be idlers, going about from house to house, and not only idlers but gossips and busybodies as well, talking about things that ought not to be mentioned. [14w]So I would like younger widows to marry, have children, and manage a home, so as to give the adversary no pretext for maligning us. [15]For some have already turned away to follow Satan. [16]*If any woman believer has widowed relatives, she must assist them; the church is not to be burdened, so that it will be able to help those who are truly widows.

Rules for Presbyters. [17x]*Presbyters who preside well deserve double honor, especially those who toil in preaching and teaching. [18y]For the scripture says, "You shall not muzzle an ox when it is threshing," and, "A worker deserves his pay." [19z]Do not accept an accusation against a presbyter unless it is supported by two or three witnesses. [20a]Reprimand publicly those who do sin, so that the rest also will be afraid. [21]I charge you before God and Christ Jesus and the elect angels to keep these rules without prejudice, doing nothing out of favoritism. [22b]Do not lay hands too readily on anyone, and do not share in another's sins.

5, 1–16: After a few words of general advice based on common sense (1–2), the letter takes up, in its several aspects, the subject of widows. The first responsibility for their care belongs to the family circle, not to the Christian community as such (3–4.16). The widow left without the aid of relatives may benefit the community by her prayer, and the community should consider her material sustenance its responsibility (5–8). Widows who wish to work directly for the Christian community should not be accepted unless they are well beyond the probability of marriage, i.e., sixty years of age, married only once, and with a reputation for good works (9–10). Younger widows are apt to be troublesome and should be encouraged to remarry (11–15).

5, 16: Woman believer: some early Latin manuscripts and Fathers have a masculine here, while most later manuscripts and patristic quotations conflate the two readings, perhaps to avoid unfair restriction to women.

5, 17–25: The function of presbyters is not exactly the same as that of the **episkopos,** "bishop" (3, 1); in fact, the relation of the two at the time of this letter is obscure (but cf the note on Ti 1, 5–9). The Pastorals seem to reflect a transitional stage that developed in many regions of the church into the

monarchical episcopate of the second and third centuries. The presbyters possess the responsibility of preaching and teaching, for which functions they are supported by the community (17–18). The realization that their position subjects them to adverse criticism is implied in the direction to Timothy (19–20) to make sure of the truth of any accusation against them before public reproof is given. He must be as objective as possible in weighing charges against presbyters (21), learning from his experience to take care in selecting them (22). Some scholars take v 22 as a reference not to ordination of presbyters but to reconciliation of public sinners. The letter now sounds an informal note of personal concern in its advice to Timothy not to be so ascetic that he even avoids wine (23). Judgment concerning the fitness of candidates to serve as presbyters is easy with persons of open conduct, more difficult and prolonged with those of greater reserve (24–25).

s: Lv 19, 32; Ti 2, 2. *t:* Jer 49, 11; Lk 2, 37; 18, 7. *u:* Jn 13, 14; Heb 13, 2. *v:* 2 Thes 3, 11. *w:* 1 Cor 7, 9. *x:* 1 Cor 16, 18; Phil 2, 29. *y:* Dt 25, 4; 1 Cor 9, 8 / Mt 10, 10; Lk 10, 7. *z:* Dt 17, 6; 19, 15; Mt 18, 16; 2 Cor 13, 1. *a:* Gal 2, 14; Eph 5, 11; 2 Tm 4, 2; Ti 1, 9.13. *b:* 4, 14; 2 Tm 1, 6.

Keep yourself pure. [23]Stop drinking only water, but have a little wine for the sake of your stomach and your frequent illnesses.

[24]Some people's sins are public, preceding them to judgment; but other people are followed by their sins. [25]Similarly, good works are also public; and even those that are not cannot remain hidden.

See RG 489

CHAPTER 6

Rules for Slaves. [1c]*Those who are under the yoke of slavery must regard their masters as worthy of full respect, so that the name of God and our teaching may not suffer abuse. [2d]*Those whose masters are believers must not take advantage of them because they are brothers but must give better service because those who will profit from their work are believers and are beloved.

V: False Teaching and True Wealth

Teach and urge these things. [3e]Whoever teaches something different and does not agree with the sound words of our Lord Jesus Christ and the religious teaching [4]is conceited, understanding nothing, and has a morbid disposition for arguments and verbal disputes. From these come envy, rivalry, insults, evil suspicions, [5f]and mutual friction among people with corrupted minds, who are deprived of the truth, supposing religion to be a means of gain. [6g]*Indeed, religion with contentment is a great gain. [7h]For we brought nothing into the world, just as we shall not be able to take anything out of it.

[8i]If we have food and clothing, we shall be content with that. [9j]Those who want to be rich are falling into temptation and into a trap and into many foolish and harmful desires, which plunge them into ruin and destruction. [10]For the love of money is the root of all evils, and some people in their desire for it have strayed from the faith and have pierced themselves with many pains.

Exhortations to Timothy. [11k]*But you, man of God, avoid all this. Instead, pursue righteousness, devotion, faith, love, patience, and gentleness. [12l]Compete well for the faith. Lay hold of eternal life, to which you were called when you made the noble confession in the presence of many witnesses. [13m]I charge [you] before God, who gives life to all things, and before Christ Jesus, who gave testimony under Pontius Pilate for the noble confession, [14]to keep the commandment without stain or reproach until the appearance of our Lord Jesus Christ [15n]that the blessed and only ruler will make manifest at the proper time, the King of kings and Lord of lords, [16o]who alone has immortality, who dwells in unapproachable light, and whom no human being has seen or can see. To him be honor and eternal power. Amen.

Right Use of Wealth. [17p]*Tell the rich in the present age not to be proud and not to rely on so uncertain a thing as wealth but rather on God, who richly provides us with all things for our enjoyment. [18]Tell them to do good, to be rich in good works, to be generous, ready to share, [19q]thus accumulating as treasure a good foundation for the future, so as to win the life that is true life.

6, 1–2: Compare the tables for household duties, such as that of Col 3, 18—4, 1. Domestic relationships derive new meaning from the Christian faith.

6, 1: Our teaching: this refers to the teaching of the Christian community.

6, 2b-10: Timothy is exhorted to maintain steadfastly the position outlined in this letter, not allowing himself to be pressured into any other course. He must realize that false teachers can be discerned by their pride, envy, quarrelsomeness, and greed for material gain. Verse 6 is rather obscure and is interpreted, and therefore translated, variously. The suggestion seems to be that the important gain that religion brings is spiritual, but that there is material gain, too, up to the point of what is needed for physical sustenance (cf 17–19).

6, 6: Contentment: the word **autarkeia** is a technical Greek philosophical term for the virtue of independence from material goods (Aristotle, Cynics, Stoics).

6, 11–16: Timothy's position demands total dedication to God and faultless witness to Christ (11–14) operating from an awareness, through faith, of the coming revelation in Jesus of the invisible God (15–16).

6, 11: Man of God: a title applied to Moses and the prophets (Dt 33, 1; 1 Sm 2, 27; 1 Kgs 12, 22; 13, 1; etc.).

6, 17–19: Timothy is directed to instruct the rich, advising them to make good use of their wealth by aiding the poor.

c: Eph 6, 5; Ti 2, 9-10. *d:* Phlm 16. *e:* Gal 1, 6-9; 2 Tm 1, 13; Ti 1, 1. *f:* 2 Tm 3, 8; 4, 4; Ti 1, 14. *g:* 4, 8; Phil 4, 11-12; Heb 13, 5. *h:* Jb 1, 21; Eccl 5, 14. *i:* Prv 30, 8. *j:* Prv 23, 4; 28, 22. *k:* 2 Tm 2, 22. *l:* 1 Cor 9, 26; 2 Tm 4, 7. *m:* Jn 18, 36-37; 19, 11. *n:* 2 Mc 13, 4; Rv 17, 14. *o:* Ex 33, 20; Ps 104, 2. *p:* Ps 62, 11; Lk 12, 20. *q:* Mt 6, 20.

VI: Final Recommendation and Warning

²⁰r*O Timothy, guard what has been entrusted to you. Avoid profane babbling and the absurdities of so-called knowledge. ²¹sBy professing it, some people have deviated from the faith.

Grace be with all of you.

6, 20–21: A final solemn warning against the heretical teachers, with what seems to be a specific reference to gnosticism, the great rival and enemy of the church for two centuries and more (the Greek word for "knowledge" is **gnōsis**). If gnosticism is being referred to here, it is probable that the warnings against "speculations" and "myths and genealogies" (cf especially 1, 4; Ti 3, 9) involve allusions to that same kind of heresy. Characteristic of the various gnostic systems of speculation was an elaborate mythology of innumerable superhuman intermediaries, on a descending scale ("genealogies"), between God and the world. Thus would be explained the emphasis upon Christ's being the one mediator (as in 2, 5). Although fully developed gnosticism belonged to the second and later centuries, there are signs that incipient forms of it belonged to Paul's own period.

r: 2 Tm 1, 14 / 4, 7.   s: 1, 6; 2 Tm 2, 18.

The Second Letter to Timothy

**See RG
489–91**

The authorship and date of this letter, as one of the Pastoral Epistles, are discussed in the Introduction to the First Letter to Timothy.

The tone here is more personal than in First Timothy, for this letter addresses Timothy in vivid terms (1, 6–14; 2, 1–13) and depicts Paul's courage and hope in the face of discouragements late in the course of his apostolic ministry (1, 15–18; 3, 10–17; 4, 9–18). Indeed, the letter takes on the character of a final exhortation and testament from Paul to the younger Timothy (4, 1–8). Paul is portrayed as a prisoner (1, 8,16; 2, 9) in Rome (1, 17), and there is a hint that Timothy may be in Ephesus (2, 17). The letter reveals that, with rare exceptions, Christians have not rallied to Paul's support (1, 15–18) and takes a pessimistic view of the outcome of his case (4, 6). It describes Paul as fully aware of what impends, looking to God, not to human beings, for his deliverance (4, 3—8,18). It recalls his mission days with Timothy (1, 3–5; cf Acts 16, 1–4). It points to his preaching of the gospel as the reason for his imprisonment and offers Timothy, as a motive for steadfastness, his own example of firmness in faith despite adverse circumstances (1, 6–14). The letter suggests that Timothy should prepare others to replace himself as Paul has prepared Timothy to replace him (2, 1–2). Paul urges him not to desist out of fear from preserving and spreading the Christian message (2, 3–7). It presents the resurrection of Jesus and his messianic role as the heart of the gospel for which Paul has been ready to lay down his life (2, 8–9) and thus not only to express his own conviction fully but to support the conviction of others (2, 10–13).

This letter, like the preceding one, urges Timothy to protect the community from the inevitable impact of false teaching (2, 14—3, 9), without fear of the personal attacks that may result (3, 10–13). It recommends that he rely on the power of the scriptures, on proclamation of the word, and on sound doctrine (3, 14—4, 2), without being troubled by those who do not accept him (4, 3–5). The letter poignantly observes in passing that Paul has need of his reading materials and his cloak (4, 13) and, what will be best of all, a visit from Timothy.

On the theory of authorship by Paul himself, Second Timothy appears to be the last of the three Pastoral Epistles. The many scholars who argue that the Pastorals are products of the Pauline school often incline toward Second Timothy as the earliest of the three and the one most likely to have actual fragments of material from Paul himself.

The principal divisions of the Second Letter to Timothy are the following:

I: Address (1, 1–5)

II: Exhortations to Timothy (1, 6—2, 13)

III: Instructions Concerning False Teaching (2, 14—4, 8)

IV: Personal Requests and Final Greetings (4, 9–22)

I: Address

CHAPTER 1

See RG 490

Greeting. [1a]*Paul, an apostle of Christ Jesus by the will of God for the promise of life in Christ Jesus, [2]to Timothy, my dear child: grace, mercy, and peace from God the Father and Christ Jesus our Lord.

Thanksgiving. [3b]*I am grateful to God, whom I worship with a clear conscience as my ancestors did, as I remember you constantly in my prayers, night and day. [4]*I yearn to see you again, recalling your tears, so that I may be filled with joy, [5c]as I recall your sincere faith that first lived in your grandmother Lois and in your mother Eunice and that I am confident lives also in you.

II: Exhortations to Timothy

The Gifts Timothy Has Received. [6d]*For this reason, I remind you to stir into flame the gift of God that you have through the imposition of my hands. [7e]For God did not give us a spirit of cowardice but rather of power and love and self-control. [8f]*So do not be ashamed of your testimony to our Lord, nor of me, a prisoner for his sake; but bear your share of hardship for the gospel with the strength that comes from God.

[9g]*He saved us and called us to a holy life, not according to our works but according to his own design and the grace bestowed on us in Christ Jesus before time began, [10h]but now made manifest through the appearance of our savior Christ Jesus, who destroyed death and brought life and immortality to light through the gospel, [11i]*for which I was appointed preacher and apostle and teacher. [12j]*On this account I am suffering these things; but I am not ashamed, for I know him in whom I have believed and am confident that he is able to guard what has been entrusted to me until that day. [13k]Take as your norm the sound words that you heard from me, in the faith and love that are in Christ Jesus. [14l]Guard this rich trust with the help of the holy Spirit that dwells within us.

Paul's Suffering. [15m]*You know that everyone in Asia deserted me, including Phygelus and Hermogenes. [16n]*May the Lord grant mercy to the family of Onesiphorus because he often gave me new heart and was not ashamed of my chains. [17]But when he came to Rome, he promptly searched for me and found me. [18o]*May the

---

1, 1–2: For the formula of address and greeting, see the note on Rom 1, 1–7.

1, 1: The promise of life in Christ Jesus: that God grants through union with Christ in faith and love; cf Col 3, 4; 1 Tm 4, 8.

1, 3: As my ancestors did: this emphasizes the continuity of Judaism and Christianity; for a similar view, see Rom 9, 3–5; Phil 3, 4–6.

1, 4–5: Purportedly written from prison in Rome (8.17; 4, 6–8) shortly before the writer's death, the letter recalls the earlier sorrowful parting from Timothy, commending him for his faith and expressing the longing to see him again.

1, 6: The gift of God: the grace resulting from the conferral of an ecclesiastical office. **The imposition of my hands:** see the note on 1 Tm 4, 14.

1, 8: Do not be ashamed of your testimony to our Lord: i.e., of preaching and suffering for the sake of the gospel.

1, 9–10: Redemption from sin and the call to holiness of life are not won by personal deeds but are freely and graciously bestowed according to God's eternal plan; cf Eph 1, 4.

1, 11: Teacher: the overwhelming majority of manuscripts and Fathers read "teacher of the nations," undoubtedly a harmonization with 1 Tm 2, 7.

1, 12: He is able to guard . . . until that day: the intervening words can also be translated "what I have entrusted to him" (i.e., the fruit of his ministry) as well as "what has been

entrusted to me" (i.e., the faith). The same difficult term occurs in v 14, where it is modified by the adjective "rich" and used without a possessive.

1, 15: Keen disappointment is expressed, here and later (4, 16), that the Christians of the province of Asia, especially Phygelus and Hermogenes, should have abandoned the writer and done nothing to defend his case in court.

1, 16–18: The family of Onesiphorus because he . . . of my chains: Onesiphorus seems to have died before this letter was written. His family is mentioned twice (here and in 4, 19), though it was Onesiphorus himself who was helpful to Paul in prison and rendered much service to the community of Ephesus. Because the apostle complains of abandonment by all in Asia during his second imprisonment and trial, the assistance of Onesiphorus seems to have been given to Paul during his first Roman imprisonment (A.D. 61–63).

1, 18: Lord . . . Lord: the first "Lord" here seems to refer to Christ, the second "Lord" to the Father.

a: 1 Tm 4, 8.   *b:* 1 Tm 3, 9 / Phil 3, 5.   *c:* 1 Tm 1, 5 / Acts 16, 1.   *d:* 1 Tm 4, 14; 5, 22 / Acts 6, 6; 8, 17.   *e:* Rom 5, 5; 8, 15; 1 Cor 2, 4.   *f:* 2, 3.15; Rom 1, 16.   *g:* Eph 2, 8-9; Ti 3, 5 / Eph 1, 4; Ti 1, 2.   *h:* Rom 16, 26; 1 Pt 1, 20 / 1 Tm 6, 14 / Phil 3, 20; Ti 1, 4; 2, 13; 2 Pt 1, 11 / 1 Cor 15, 54-55; Heb 2, 14 / 1 Cor 15, 53-54.   *i:* 1 Tm 2, 7.   *j:* 1 Pt 4, 16 / 1 Tm 1, 10-11.   *k:* 1 Tm 1, 14.   *l:* 1 Tm 6, 20 / Rom 8, 11.   *m:* 4, 16.   *n:* 4, 19.   *o:* Jude 21.

Lord grant him to find mercy from the Lord on that day. And you know very well the services he rendered in Ephesus.

See RG
490

CHAPTER 2

Timothy's Conduct. ¹*So you, my child, be strong in the grace that is in Christ Jesus. ²And what you heard from me through many witnesses entrust to faithful people who will have the ability to teach others as well. ³ᵖBear your share of hardship along with me like a good soldier of Christ Jesus. ⁴ᵍTo satisfy the one who recruited him, a soldier does not become entangled in the business affairs of life. ⁵ʳSimilarly, an athlete cannot receive the winner's crown except by competing according to the rules. ⁶ˢThe hardworking farmer ought to have the first share of the crop. ⁷ᵗReflect on what I am saying, for the Lord will give you understanding in everything.

⁸ᵘ*Remember Jesus Christ, raised from the dead, a descendant of David: such is my gospel, ⁹ᵛfor which I am suffering, even to the point of chains, like a criminal. But the word of God is not chained. ¹⁰ʷTherefore, I bear with everything for the sake of those who are chosen, so that they too may obtain the salvation that is in Christ Jesus, together with eternal glory. ¹¹ˣThis saying is trustworthy:

If we have died with him
  we shall also live with him;

¹² ʸif we persevere
  we shall also reign with him.
But if we deny him
  he will deny us.
¹³ ᶻIf we are unfaithful
  he remains faithful,
  for he cannot deny himself.

III: Instructions Concerning False Teaching

Warning against Useless Disputes. ¹⁴ᵃ*Remind people of these things and charge them before God to stop disputing about words. This serves no useful purpose since it harms those who listen. ¹⁵ᵇBe eager to present yourself as acceptable to God, a workman who causes no disgrace, imparting the word of truth without deviation. ¹⁶ᶜAvoid profane, idle talk, for such people will become more and more godless, ¹⁷ᵈand their teaching will spread like gangrene. Among them are Hymenaeus and Philetus, ¹⁸ᵉwho have deviated from the truth by saying that [the] resurrection has already taken place and are upsetting the faith of some. ¹⁹ᶠNevertheless, God's solid foundation stands, bearing this inscription, "The Lord knows those who are his"; and, "Let everyone who calls upon the name of the Lord avoid evil."

²⁰In a large household there are vessels not only of gold and silver but also of wood

---

2, 1–7: This passage manifests a characteristic deep concern for safeguarding the faith and faithfully transmitting it through trustworthy people (1–2; cf 1, 14; 1 Tm 6, 20; Ti 1, 9). Comparisons to the soldier's detachment, the athlete's sportsmanship, and the farmer's arduous work as the price of recompense (4–6) emphasize the need of singleness of purpose in preaching the word, even at the cost of hardship, for the sake of Christ (3).

2, 8–13: The section begins with a sloganlike summary of Paul's gospel about Christ (8) and concludes with what may be part of an early Christian hymn (11b-12a; most exegetes include the rest of v 12 and all of v 13 as part of the quotation). The poetic lines suggest that through baptism Christians die spiritually with Christ and hope to live with him and reign with him forever, but the Christian life includes endurance, witness, and even suffering, as the final judgment will show and as Paul's own case makes clear; while he is imprisoned for preaching the gospel (9), his sufferings are helpful to the elect for obtaining the salvation and glory available in Christ (10), who will be true to those who are faithful and will disown those who deny him (12–13).

2, 14–19: For those who dispute about mere words (cf 23–24) and indulge in irreligious talk to the detriment of their listeners (16–19), see the notes on 1 Tm 1, 3–7; 6, 20–21. Hymenaeus and Philetus (17), while accepting the Christian's mystical death and resurrection in Christ through baptism, claimed that baptized Christians are already risen with Christ in this life and thus that there is no future bodily resurrection or eternal glory to come. The first quotation in v 19 is from Nm 16, 5; the other quotation is from some unidentified Jewish or Christian writing.

2, 14: Before God: many ancient manuscripts read "before the Lord."

p: 1, 8; 4, 5; Phlm 2.   *q:* 1 Cor 9, 6.   *r:* 1 Cor 9, 25.   *s:* 1 Cor 9, 7-10.   *t:* Prv 2, 6.   *u:* Rom 1, 3; 1 Cor 15, 4.20 / Rom 2, 16; Gal 1, 11; 2, 2.   *v:* Phil 1, 12-14.   *w:* Col 1, 24; 1 Tm 1, 15.   *x:* Rom 6, 8.   *y:* Mt 10, 22.33; Lk 12, 9.   *z:* Nm 23, 19; Rom 3, 3-4; 1 Cor 10, 13; Ti 1, 2.   *a:* 1 Tm 6, 4.   *b:* 1, 8; 2 Cor 6, 7; Eph 1, 13; Col 1, 5.   *c:* 1 Tm 4, 7.   *d:* 1 Tm 1, 20.   *e:* 2 Thes 2, 2. *f:* Is 28, 16; 1 Cor 3, 10-15 / Nm 16, 5; Jn 10, 14.

and clay, some for lofty and others for humble use. [21g]If anyone cleanses himself of these things, he will be a vessel for lofty use, dedicated, beneficial to the master of the house, ready for every good work. [22h*]So turn from youthful desires and pursue righteousness, faith, love, and peace, along with those who call on the Lord with purity of heart. [23i]Avoid foolish and ignorant debates, for you know that they breed quarrels. [24j]A slave of the Lord should not quarrel, but should be gentle with everyone, able to teach, tolerant, [25k]correcting opponents with kindness. It may be that God will grant them repentance that leads to knowledge of the truth, [26l*]and that they may return to their senses out of the devil's snare, where they are entrapped by him, for his will.

CHAPTER 3

The Dangers of the Last Days. [1m*]But understand this: there will be terrifying times in the last days. [2n]People will be self-centered and lovers of money, proud, haughty, abusive, disobedient to their parents, ungrateful, irreligious, [3]callous, implacable, slanderous, licentious, brutal, hating what is good, [4]traitors, reckless, conceited, lovers of pleasure rather than lovers of God, [5o]as they make a pretense of religion but deny its power. Reject them. [6p]For some of these slip into homes and make captives of women weighed down by sins, led by various desires, [7q]always trying to

learn but never able to reach a knowledge of the truth. [8r]Just as Jannes and Jambres opposed Moses, so they also oppose the truth—people of depraved mind, unqualified in the faith. [9]But they will not make further progress, for their foolishness will be plain to all, as it was with those two.

Paul's Example and Teaching. [10*]You have followed my teaching, way of life, purpose, faith, patience, love, endurance, [11s]persecutions, and sufferings, such as happened to me in Antioch, Iconium, and Lystra, persecutions that I endured. Yet from all these things the Lord delivered me. [12t]In fact, all who want to live religiously in Christ Jesus will be persecuted. [13]But wicked people and charlatans will go from bad to worse, deceivers and deceived. [14u]But you, remain faithful to what you have learned and believed, because you know from whom you learned it, [15v]and that from infancy you have known [the] sacred scriptures, which are capable of giving you wisdom for salvation through faith in Christ Jesus. [16w*]All scripture is inspired by God and is useful for teaching, for refutation, for correction, and for training in righteousness, [17x]so that one who belongs to God may be competent, equipped for every good work.

CHAPTER 4

Solemn Charge. [1y*]I charge you in the presence of God and of Christ Jesus, who will

---

2, 22: Those who call on the Lord: those who believe in Christ and worship him as Lord, i.e., Christians (Acts 9, 14–16.20–21; Rom 10, 12–13; cf 19, literally, "Everyone who names the name of the Lord").

2, 26: Some interpreters would render this passage, "Thus they may come to their senses and, forced to do his (i.e., God's) will, may escape the devil's trap." This interpretation of the Greek is possible, but the one accepted in the text seems more likely.

3, 1–9: The moral depravity and false teaching that will be rampant in the last days are already at work (1–5). The frivolous and superficial, too, devoid of the true spirit of religion, will be easy victims of those who pervert them by falsifying the truth (6–8), just as Jannes and Jambres, Pharaoh's magicians of Egypt (Ex 7, 11–12.22), discredited the truth in Moses' time. Exodus does not name the magicians, but the two names are widely found in much later Jewish, Christian, and even pagan writings. Their origins are legendary.

3, 10–17: Paul's example for Timothy includes persecution, a frequent emphasis in the Pastorals. Timothy is to be steadfast to what he has been taught and to scripture. The scriptures are the source of wisdom, i.e., of belief in and lov-

ing fulfillment of God's word revealed in Christ, through whom salvation is given.

3, 16: All scripture is inspired by God: this could possibly also be translated, "All scripture inspired by God is useful for . . . ." In this classic reference to inspiration, God is its principal author, with the writer as the human collaborator. Thus the scriptures are the word of God in human language. See also 2 Pt 1, 20–21.

3, 16–17: Useful for teaching . . . every good work: because as God's word the scriptures share his divine authority. It is exercised through those who are ministers of the word.

4, 1–5: The gravity of the obligation incumbent on Timo-

g: 3, 17. *h:* Gal 5, 22; 1 Tm 6, 11 / Rom 10, 13; 1 Cor 1, 2. *i:* 1 Tm 1, 4; 4, 7; 6, 4; Ti 3, 9. *j:* 1 Tm 3, 2-3. *k:* 3, 7; 1 Tm 2, 4. *l:* 1 Tm 3, 7. *m:* 1 Tm 4, 1; 2 Pt 3, 3; Jude 18. *n:* Rom 1, 29-31. *o:* Rom 2, 20-22; Ti 1, 16. *p:* Ti 1, 11. *q:* 2, 25. *r:* Ex 7, 11.22; 1 Tm 6, 5. *s:* Acts 13, 50; 14, 5.19 / Ps 34, 20. *t:* Jn 15, 20; Acts 14, 22. *u:* 2, 2. *v:* Jn 5, 39. *w:* Rom 15, 4; 2 Pt 1, 19-21. *x:* 2, 21. *y:* 1 Tm 5, 21; 6, 14 / Acts 10, 42; Rom 14, 9-10; 1 Pt 4, 5.

judge the living and the dead, and by his appearing and his kingly power: ²ᶻproclaim the word; be persistent whether it is convenient or inconvenient; convince, reprimand, encourage through all patience and teaching. ³ᵃ*For the time will come when people will not tolerate sound doctrine but, following their own desires and insatiable curiosity, will accumulate teachers ⁴ᵇand will stop listening to the truth and will be diverted to myths. ⁵But you, be self-possessed in all circumstances; put up with hardship; perform the work of an evangelist; fulfill your ministry.

Reward for Fidelity. ⁶ᶜ*For I am already being poured out like a libation, and the time of my departure is at hand. ⁷ᵈ*I have competed well; I have finished the race; I have kept the faith. ⁸ᵉ*From now on the crown of righteousness awaits me, which the Lord, the just judge, will award to me on that day, and not only to me, but to all who have longed for his appearance.

IV: Personal Requests and Final Greetings

Paul's Loneliness. ⁹*Try to join me soon, ¹⁰ᶠ*for Demas, enamored of the present world, deserted me and went to Thessalonica, Crescens to Galatia, and Titus to Dalmatia. ¹¹ᵍLuke is the only one with me. Get Mark and bring him with you, for he is helpful to me in the ministry. ¹²ʰI have sent Tychicus to Ephesus. ¹³ⁱWhen you come, bring the cloak I left with Carpus in Troas, the papyrus rolls, and especially the parchments.

¹⁴ʲ*Alexander the coppersmith did me a great deal of harm; the Lord will repay him according to his deeds. ¹⁵You too be on guard against him, for he has strongly resisted our preaching.

¹⁶ᵏAt my first defense no one appeared on my behalf, but everyone deserted me. May it not be held against them! ¹⁷ˡBut the Lord stood by me and gave me strength, so that through me the proclamation might be completed and all the Gentiles might hear it. And I was rescued from the lion's mouth. ¹⁸ᵐThe Lord will rescue me from every evil threat and will bring me safe to his heavenly kingdom. To him be glory forever and ever. Amen.

Final Greeting. ¹⁹ⁿ*Greet Prisca and Aq-

---

thy to preach the word can be gauged from the solemn adjuration: in the presence of God, and of Christ coming as universal judge, and by his appearance and his kingly power (1). Patience, courage, constancy, and endurance are required despite the opposition, hostility, indifference, and defection of many to whom the truth has been preached (2–5).

4, 3: Insatiable curiosity: literally, "with itching ears."

4, 6: The apostle recognizes his death through martyrdom to be imminent. He regards it as an act of worship in which his blood will be poured out in sacrifice; cf Ex 29, 38–40; Phil 2, 17.

4, 7: At the close of his life Paul could testify to the accomplishment of what Christ himself foretold concerning him at the time of his conversion, "I will show him what he will have to suffer for my name" (Acts 9, 16).

4, 8: When the world is judged at the parousia, all who have eagerly looked for the Lord's appearing and have sought to live according to his teachings will be rewarded. The crown is a reference to the laurel wreath placed on the heads of victorious athletes and conquerors in war; cf 2, 5; 1 Cor 9, 25.

4, 9–13: Demas either abandoned the work of the ministry for worldly affairs or, perhaps, gave up the faith itself (10). Luke (11) may have accompanied Paul on parts of his second and third missionary journeys (Acts 16, 10–12; 20, 5–7). Notice the presence of the first personal pronoun "we" in these Acts passages, suggesting to some that Luke (or at least some

traveling companion of Paul's) was the author of Acts. Mark, once rejected by Paul (Acts 13, 13; 15, 39), is now to render him a great service (11); cf Col 4, 10; Phlm 24. For Tychicus, see Eph 6, 21; cf also Acts 20, 4; Col 4, 7.

4, 10: Galatia: some manuscripts read "Gaul" or "Gallia."

4, 14–18: Alexander: an opponent of Paul's preaching (14–15), perhaps the one who is mentioned in 1 Tm 1, 20. Despite Paul's abandonment by his friends in the province of Asia (cf 1, 15–16), the divine assistance brought this first trial to a successful issue, even to the point of making the gospel message known to those who participated in or witnessed the trial (16–17).

4, 19: Prisca and Aquila: they assisted Paul in his ministry in Corinth (Acts 18, 2–3) and Ephesus (Acts 18, 19.26; 1 Cor 16, 19). They risked death to save his life, and all the Gentile communities are indebted to them (Rom 16, 3–5).

z: Acts 20, 20.31; 1 Tm 5, 20.   a: 1 Tm 4, 1.   b: 1 Tm 1, 4; 4, 7; Ti 1, 14.   c: Phil 2, 17.   d: 1 Tm 1, 18; 6, 12; Jude 3 / Acts 20, 24; 1 Cor 9, 24; Heb 12, 1.   e: 2, 5; Wis 5, 16; 1 Cor 9, 25; Phil 3, 14; Jas 1, 12; 1 Pt 5, 4; Rv 2, 10.   f: Col 4, 14; Phlm 24 / 2 Cor 2, 13; 7, 6-7; 8, 23; Gal 2, 3;Ti 1, 4.   g: Col 4, 14; Phlm 24 / Col 4, 10; Phlm 24.   h: Acts 20, 4; Eph 6, 21; Col 4, 7.   i: Acts 16, 8; 20, 6.   j: 1 Tm 1, 20 / 2 Sm 3, 39; Pss 28, 4; 62, 12; Prv 24, 12; Rom 2, 6.   k: 1, 15.   l: Acts 23, 11; 27, 23; Phil 4, 13 / 1 Mc 2, 60; Ps 22, 22; Dn 6, 23.   m: 2 Cor 1, 10 / Rom 16, 27.   n: Acts 18, 2; Rom 16, 3; 1 Cor 16, 19 / 1, 16.

uila and the family of Onesiphorus. ²⁰*Erastus remained in Corinth, while I left Trophimus sick at Miletus. ²¹*Try to get here before winter. Eubulus, Pudens, Linus,

Claudia, and all the brothers send greetings.

²² ᵖThe Lord be with your spirit. Grace be with all of you.

4, 20: Erastus: he was the treasurer of the city of Corinth (Rom 16, 24); cf also Acts 19, 22. **Trophimus:** from the province of Asia, he accompanied Paul from Greece to Troas (Acts 20, 4–5).

4, 21: Linus: Western tradition sometimes identified this Linus with the supposed successor of Peter as bishop of Rome, and Claudia as the mother of Linus (**Apostolic Constitutions,** fourth century).

---

o: Acts 19, 22; Rom 16, 24 / Acts 20, 4; 21, 29.   *p:* Gal 6, 18; Phil 4, 23; Col 4, 18; 1 Tm 6, 21; Ti 3, 15.

See RG
491–93

The Letter to Titus

The third of the Pastoral Epistles in the New Testament is addressed to a different co-worker of Paul than are First and Second Timothy. The situation is different, too, for Titus is addressed as the person in charge of developing the church on the large Mediterranean island of Crete (1, 5), a place Paul had never, according to the New Testament, visited. The tone is closer to that of First Timothy as three topics of church life and structure are discussed: presbyter-bishops (see the note on 1, 5–9), groups with which one must work in the church (2, 1–10), and admonitions for conduct based on the grace and love of God that appeared in Jesus Christ (2, 11—3, 10). The warmer personal tone of Second Timothy is replaced by emphasis on church office and on living in the society of the day, in which deceivers and heretics abound (1, 10–16; 3, 9–10).

The Pauline assistant who is addressed, Titus, was a Gentile Christian, but we are nowhere informed of his place of birth or residence. He went from Antioch with Paul and Barnabas to Jerusalem (Gal 2, 1; cf Acts 15, 2). According to 2 Corinthians (2, 13; 7, 6.13–14), he was with Paul on his third missionary journey; his name, however, does not appear in Acts. Besides being the bearer of Paul's severe letter to the Corinthians (2 Cor 7, 6–8), he had the responsibility of taking up the collection in Corinth for the Christian community of Jerusalem (2 Cor 8, 6.16–19.23). In the present letter (1, 5), he is mentioned as the administrator of the Christian community in Crete, charged with the task of organizing it through the appointment of presbyters and bish-

ops (1, 5–9; here the two terms refer to the same personages).

The letter instructs Titus about the character of the assistants he is to choose in view of the pastoral difficulties peculiar to Crete (1, 5–16). It suggests the special individual and social virtues that the various age groups and classes in the Christian community should be encouraged to acquire (2, 1–10). The motivation for transformation of their lives comes from christology, especially the redemptive sacrifice of Christ and his future coming, as applied through baptism and justification (2, 11–14; 3, 4–8). The community is to serve as a leaven for Christianizing the social world about it (3, 1–3). Good works are to be the evidence of their faith in God (3, 8); those who engage in religious controversy are, after suitable warning, to be ignored (3, 9–11).

The authorship and date of the Letter to Titus are discussed in the Introduction to 1 Timothy. Those who assume authorship by Paul himself usually place Titus after 1 Timothy and before 2 Timothy. Others see it as closely related to 1 Timothy, in a growing emphasis on church structure and opposition to heresy, later than the letters of Paul himself and 2 Timothy. It has also been suggested that, if the three Pastorals once circulated as a literary unit, Titus was meant to be read ahead of 1 and 2 Timothy.

The principal divisions of the Letter to Titus are the following:

I: Address (1, 1–4)

II: Pastoral Charge (1, 5–16)

III: Teaching the Christian Life (2, 1—3, 15)

I: Address

CHAPTER 1

See RG
491-92

Greeting. *1a**Paul, a slave of God and apostle of Jesus Christ for the sake of the faith of God's chosen ones and the recognition of religious truth, *2b*in the hope of eternal life that God, who does not lie, promised before time began, *3c*who indeed at the proper time revealed his word in the proclamation with which I was entrusted by the command of God our savior, *4d*to Titus, my true child in our common faith: grace and peace from God the Father and Christ Jesus our savior.

II: Pastoral Charge

Titus in Crete. *5**For this reason I left you in Crete so that you might set right what remains to be done and appoint presbyters in every town, as I directed you, *6e*on condition that a man be blameless, married only once, with believing children who are not accused of licentiousness or rebellious. *7*For a bishop as God's steward must be blameless, not arrogant, not irritable, not a drunkard, not aggressive, not greedy for sordid gain, *8*but hospitable, a lover of goodness, temperate, just, holy, and self-controlled, *9f*holding fast to the true message as taught so that he will be able both to exhort with sound doctrine and to refute opponents. *10**For there are also many rebels, idle talkers and deceivers, especially the Jewish Christians. *11*It is imperative to silence them, as they are upsetting whole families by teaching for sordid gain what they should not. *12**One of them, a prophet of their own, once said, "Cretans have always been liars, vicious beasts, and lazy gluttons." *13g*That testimony is true. Therefore, admonish them sharply, so that they may be sound in the faith, *14h*instead of paying attention to Jewish myths and regulations of people who have repudiated the truth. *15i*To the clean all things are clean, but to those who are defiled and unbelieving nothing is clean; in fact, both their minds and their consciences are tainted. *16*They claim to know God, but by their deeds they deny him. They are vile and disobedient and unqualified for any good deed.

III: Teaching the Christian Life

CHAPTER 2

See RG
492

Christian Behavior. *1j**As for yourself, you must say what is consistent with sound doctrine, namely, *2*that older men should be temperate, dignified, self-controlled, sound in faith, love, and endurance. *3*Similarly, older women should be reverent in their behavior, not slanderers, not addicted to drink, teaching what is good, *4*so that they may train younger women to love their husbands and children, *5k*to be self-controlled, chaste, good homemakers, under the control of their husbands, so that the word of God may not be discredited.

1, 1–4: On the epistolary form, see the note on Rom 1, 1–7. The apostolate is the divinely appointed mission to lead others to the true faith and through it to eternal salvation (1–3).

1, 5–9: This instruction on the selection and appointment of presbyters, substantially identical with that in 1 Tm 3, 1–7 on a bishop (see the note there), was aimed at strengthening the authority of Titus by apostolic mandate; cf 2, 15. In vv 5.7 and Acts 20, 17.28, the terms **episkopos** and **presbyteros** ("bishop" and "presbyter") refer to the same persons. Deacons are not mentioned in Titus. See also the note on Phil 1, 1.

1, 10–16: This adverse criticism of the defects within the community is directed especially against certain Jewish Christians, who busy themselves with useless speculations over persons mentioned in the Old Testament, insist on the observance of Jewish ritual purity regulations, and thus upset whole families by teaching things they have no right to teach; cf 3, 9; 1 Tm 1, 3–10.

1, 10: Jewish Christians: literally, "those of the circumcision."

1, 12: Cretans . . . gluttons: quoted from Epimenides, a Cretan poet of the sixth century B.C.

2, 1–10: One of Titus' main tasks in Crete is to become acquainted with the character of the Cretans and thereby learn to cope with its deficiencies (see 1, 12). The counsel is not only for Titus himself but for various classes of people with whom he must deal: older men and women (2–4), younger women and men (4–7), and slaves (9–10); cf Eph 6, 1–9; Col 3, 18—4, 1.

---

a: 1 Tm 2, 4; 4, 3; 2 Tm 2, 25; 3, 7; Heb 10, 26. *b:* 3, 7; 2 Tm 1, 1; 1 Jn 2, 25. *c:* 2, 10; 3, 4; Ps 24, 5; 1 Tm 1, 1; 2, 3; 4, 10; Jude 25. *d:* 2, 13; 3, 6; Phil 3, 20; 2 Tm 1, 10; 2 Pt 1, 1.11; 2, 20; 3, 2.18. *e:* 1 Tm 3, 2-7; 2 Tm 2, 24-26. *f:* 1, 13; 2, 1-2.8; 1 Tm 1, 10; 6, 3; 2 Tm 1, 13; 4, 3. *g:* 1, 9. *h:* 3, 9; 1 Tm 1, 4; 4, 7; 2 Tm 4, 4; 2 Pt 1, 16. *i:* Mk 7, 18-23; Acts 10, 15; Rom 14, 14-23. *j:* 1, 9.13; 2, 8; 1 Tm 1, 10; 6, 3; 2 Tm 1, 13; 4, 3. *k:* 1 Cor 11, 3; 14, 34; Eph 5, 22-24; Col 3, 18; 1 Tm 2, 11-15; 1 Pt 3, 1-6.

⁶Urge the younger men, similarly, to control themselves, ⁷showing yourself as a model of good deeds in every respect, with integrity in your teaching, dignity, ⁸and sound speech that cannot be criticized, so that the opponent will be put to shame without anything bad to say about us.

⁹ˡSlaves are to be under the control of their masters in all respects, giving them satisfaction, not talking back to them ¹⁰ᵐor stealing from them, but exhibiting complete good faith, so as to adorn the doctrine of God our savior in every way.

Transformation of Life. ¹¹ⁿ*For the grace of God has appeared, saving all ¹²and training us to reject godless ways and worldly desires and to live temperately, justly, and devoutly in this age, ¹³ᵒ*as we await the blessed hope, the appearance of the glory of the great God and of our savior Jesus Christ, ¹⁴ᵖwho gave himself for us to deliver us from all lawlessness and to cleanse for himself a people as his own, eager to do what is good.

¹⁵ᵠSay these things. Exhort and correct with all authority. Let no one look down on you.

See RG
492-93

CHAPTER 3

¹ʳ*Remind them to be under the control of magistrates and authorities, to be obedient, to be open to every good enterprise. ²They are to slander no one, to be peaceable, considerate, exercising all graciousness toward everyone. ³ˢFor we ourselves were once foolish, disobedient, deluded, slaves to various desires and pleasures, living in malice and envy, hateful ourselves and hating one another.

⁴ ᵗBut when the kindness and generous
   love
   of God our savior appeared,
⁵ ᵘnot because of any righteous deeds we
   had done
   but because of his mercy,
he saved us through the bath of rebirth
   and renewal by the holy Spirit,
⁶ ᵛwhom he richly poured out on us
   through Jesus Christ our savior,
⁷ ʷso that we might be justified by his
   grace
   and become heirs in hope of eternal
   life.

⁸ˣ*This saying is trustworthy.

Advice to Titus. I want you to insist on these points, that those who have believed in God be careful to devote themselves to good works; these are excellent and beneficial to others. ⁹ʸ*Avoid foolish arguments, genealogies, rivalries, and quarrels about the law, for they are useless and futile. ¹⁰ᶻAfter a first and second warning, break off contact with a heretic, ¹¹realizing that such a person is perverted and sinful and stands self-condemned.

Directives, Greetings, and Blessing. ¹²ᵃ*When I send Artemas to you, or Tychicus,

2, 11–15: Underlying the admonitions for moral improvement in 1–10 as the moving force is the constant appeal to God's revelation of salvation in Christ, with its demand for transformation of life.

2, 13: **The blessed hope, the appearance:** literally, "the blessed hope and appearance," but the use of a single article in Greek strongly suggests an epexegetical, i.e., explanatory sense. **Of the great God and of our savior Jesus Christ:** another possible translation is "of our great God and savior Jesus Christ."

3, 1–8: The list of Christian duties continues from 2, 9–10, undergirded again as in 2, 11–13 by appeal to what God in Christ has done (4–7; cf 2, 11–14). The spiritual renewal of the Cretans, signified in God's merciful gift of baptism (4–7), should be reflected in their improved attitude toward civil authority and in their Christian relationship with all (1–3).

3, 1: **Magistrates and authorities:** some interpreters understand these terms as referring to the principalities and powers of the heavenly hierarchy. **To be open to every good enterprise:** this implies being good citizens. It could also be

translated "ready to do every sort of good work" (as Christians); cf 14.

3, 8–11: In matters of good conduct and religious doctrine, Titus is to stand firm.

3, 9: See the note on 1 Tm 6, 20–21.

3, 12–15: **Artemas** or **Tychicus** (2 Tm 4, 12) is to replace

l: 1 Cor 7, 21-22; Eph 6, 5-8; Col 3, 22-25; 1 Tm 6, 1-2; 1 Pt 2, 18. *m:* 1, 3; 3, 4; Ps 24, 5; 1 Tm 1, 1; 2, 3; 4, 10; Jude 25. *n:* 1 Tm 2, 4; 4, 10. *o:* 1 Cor 1, 7; Phil 3, 20; 1 Thes 1, 10 / 2 Tm 1, 10 / 1, 4; 3, 6; 2 Pt 1, 1.11; 2, 20; 3, 2.18. *p:* Gal 1, 4; 2, 20; Eph 5, 2.25; 1 Tm 2, 6; 1 Pt 1, 18-19 /Ps 130, 8. *q:* 1 Tm 4, 12. *r:* Rom 13, 1-7; 1 Tm 2, 1-2; 1 Pt 2, 13-14. *s:* 1 Cor 6, 9-11; Eph 2, 1-3; 5, 8; Col 3, 5-7; 1 Pt 4, 3. *t:* 1, 3; 2, 10; Ps 24, 5; 1 Tm 1, 1; 2, 3; 4, 10; Jude 25. *u:* Dt 9, 5; Eph 2, 4-5.8-9; 2 Tm 1, 9. *v:* 1, 4; 2, 13; Phil 3, 20; 2 Tm 1, 10; 2 Pt 1, 1.11; 2, 20; 3, 2.18. *w:* 1, 2; 2 Tm 1, 1; 1 Jn 2, 25. *x:* 1 Tm 1, 15; 3, 1; 4, 9; 2 Tm 2, 11. *y:* 1 Tm 1, 4; 4, 7; 2 Tm 2, 23. *z:* Mt 18, 15-18; Rom 16, 17; 1 Cor 5, 11; 2 Thes 3, 6.14-15. *a:* Acts 20, 4; Eph 6, 21; Col 4, 7; 2 Tm 4, 12.

try to join me at Nicopolis, where I have decided to spend the winter. ^{13b}Send Zenas the lawyer and Apollos on their journey soon, and see to it that they have everything they need. ^{14c}But let our people, too, learn to devote

themselves to good works to supply urgent needs, so that they may not be unproductive. ^{15d}All who are with me send you greetings. Greet those who love us in the faith. Grace be with all of you.

Titus, who will join Paul in his winter sojourn at Nicopolis in Epirus, on the western coast of Greece.

b: Acts 18, 24-26; 1 Cor 1, 12; 3, 4-6.22; 4, 6; 16, 12.   c: 2, 14; 3, 8; Heb 10, 24; 1 Pt 3, 13.   d: Heb 13, 25.

See RG 493–95

The Letter to Philemon

This short letter addressed to three specific individuals was written by Paul during an imprisonment, perhaps in Rome between A.D. 61 and 63 (see the Introduction to Colossians for other possible sites). It concerns Onesimus, a slave from Colossae (Col 4, 9), who had run away from his master, perhaps guilty of theft in the process (18). Onesimus was converted to Christ by Paul (10). Paul sends him back to his master (12) with this letter asking that he be welcomed willingly by his old master (8–10.14.17) not just as a slave but as a brother in Christ (16). Paul uses very strong arguments (especially 19) in his touching appeal on behalf of Onesimus. It is unlikely that Paul is subtly hinting that he would like to retain Onesimus as his own slave, lent to Paul by his master. Rather, he suggests he would like to have Onesimus work with him for the gospel (13.20–21). There is, however, little evidence connecting this Onesimus with a bishop of Ephesus of the same name mentioned by Ignatius of Antioch (ca. A.D. 110).

Paul's letter deals with an accepted institution of antiquity, human slavery. But Paul breathes into this letter the spirit of Christ and of equality within the Christian community. He does not at-

tack slavery directly, for this is something the Christian communities of the first century were in no position to do, and the expectation that Christ would soon come again militated against social reforms. Yet Paul, by presenting Onesimus as "brother, beloved . . . to me, but even more so to you" (16), voiced an idea revolutionary in that day and destined to break down worldly barriers of division "in the Lord."

See RG 494

Address and Greeting. ^{1a*}Paul, a prisoner for Christ Jesus, and Timothy our brother, to Philemon, our beloved and our co-worker, ^{2b*}to Apphia our sister, to Archippus our fellow soldier, and to the church at your house. ^{3c*}Grace to you and peace from God our Father and the Lord Jesus Christ.

Thanksgiving. ^{4d*}I give thanks to my God always, remembering you in my prayers, ^{5*}as I hear of the love and the faith you have in the Lord Jesus and for all the holy ones, ^{6e*}so that your partnership in the faith may become effective in recognizing every good there is in us that leads to Christ.

Plea for Onesimus. ^{7f*}For I have experi-

1: **Prisoner:** as often elsewhere (cf Rom, 1 Cor, Gal especially), the second word in Greek enunciates the theme and sets the tone of the letter. Here it is the prisoner appealing rather than the apostle commanding.

2: **Apphia our sister:** sister is here used (like brother) to indicate a fellow Christian. **The church at your house: your** here is singular. It more likely refers to Philemon than to the last one named, Archippus; Philemon is then the owner of the slave Onesimus (10). An alternate view is that the actual master of the slave is Archippus and that the one to whom the letter is addressed, Philemon, is the most prominent Christian there; see the note on Col 4, 17.

3: **Grace . . . and peace:** for this greeting, which may be a combination of Greek and Aramaic epistolary formulae, see the note on Rom 1, 1–7.

4: **In my prayers:** literally, "at the time of my prayers."

5: **Holy ones:** a common term for members of the Christian community (so also 7).

6: **In us:** some good ancient manuscripts have in you (plural). **That leads to Christ: leads to** translates the Greek preposition **eis,** indicating direction or purpose.

7: **Encouragement:** the Greek word **paraklēsis** is cognate with the verb translated "urge" in vv 9.10, and serves as an introduction to Paul's plea. **Hearts:** literally, "bowels," expressing in Semitic fashion the seat of the emotions, one's "inmost self." The same Greek word is used in v 12 and again

a: 9; Eph 3, 1; 4, 1; Phil 1, 7.13.   b: Col 4, 17.   c: Rom 1, 7; Gal 1, 3; Phil 1, 2.   d: Rom 1, 8-9; Eph 1, 15-16.   e: Phil 1, 9; Col 1, 9.   f: 2 Cor 7, 4.

enced much joy and encouragement from your love, because the hearts of the holy ones have been refreshed by you, brother. [8]*Therefore, although I have the full right in Christ to order you to do what is proper, [9]g*I rather urge you out of love, being as I am, Paul, an old man, and now also a prisoner for Christ Jesus. [10]hI urge you on behalf of my child Onesimus, whose father I have become in my imprisonment, [11]*who was once useless to you but is now useful to [both] you and me. [12]I am sending him, that is, my own heart, back to you. [13]i*I should have liked to retain him for myself, so that he might serve me on your behalf in my imprisonment for the gospel, [14]jbut I did not want to do anything without your consent, so that the good you do might not be forced but voluntary. [15]*Perhaps this is why he was away from you for a while, that you might have him back forever, [16]k*no longer as a

slave but more than a slave, a brother, beloved especially to me, but even more so to you, as a man and in the Lord. [17]So if you regard me as a partner, welcome him as you would me. [18]*And if he has done you any injustice or owes you anything, charge it to me. [19]lI, Paul, write this in my own hand: I will pay. May I not tell you that you owe me your very self. [20]Yes, brother, may I profit from you in the Lord. Refresh my heart in Christ.

[21]With trust in your compliance I write to you, knowing that you will do even more than I say. [22]mAt the same time prepare a guest room for me, for I hope to be granted to you through your prayers.

Final Greetings. [23]n*Epaphras, my fellow prisoner in Christ Jesus, greets you, [24]oas well as Mark, Aristarchus, Demas, and Luke, my co-workers. [25]The grace of the Lord Jesus Christ be with your spirit.

in v 20, where it forms a literary inclusion marking off the body of the letter.

8: Full right: often translated "boldness," the Greek word **parrēsia** connotes the full franchise of speech, as the right of a citizen to speak before the body politic, claimed by the Athenians as their privilege (Euripides).

9: Old man: some editors conjecture that Paul here used a similar Greek word meaning "ambassador" (cf Eph 6, 20). This conjecture heightens the contrast with "prisoner" but is totally without manuscript support.

11: Useless . . . useful: here Paul plays on the name Onesimus, which means "useful" or "beneficial." The verb translated "profit" in v 20 is cognate.

13: Serve: the Greek **diakoneō** could connote a ministry.

15: Was away from: literally, "was separated from," but the same verb means simply "left" in Acts 18, 1. It is a euphemism for his running away.

16: As a man: literally, "in the flesh." With this and the following phrase, Paul describes the natural and spiritual orders.

18–19: Charge it to me . . . I will pay: technical legal and commercial terms in account keeping and acknowledgment of indebtedness.

23–24: Epaphras: a Colossian who founded the church there (Col 1, 7) and perhaps also in Laodicea and Hierapolis (Col 2, 1; 4, 12–13). **Aristarchus:** a native of Thessalonica and fellow worker of Paul (Acts 19, 29; 20, 4; 27, 2). For Mark, Demas, and Luke, see 2 Tm 4, 9–13 and the note there.

g: 1; Eph 3, 1; 4, 1; Phil 1, 7.13.   *h:* 1 Cor 4, 14-15; Gal 4, 19; Col 4, 9.   *i:* Phil 2, 30.   *j:* 2 Cor 9, 7; 1 Pt 5, 2.   *k:* 1 Tm 6, 2. *l:* Gal 6, 11; 2 Thes 3, 17.   *m:* Heb 13, 19.   *n:* Col 1, 7; 4, 12-13. *o:* Acts 12, 12.15; 13, 13; 15, 37-39; 19, 29; 20, 4; 27, 2; Col 4, 10.14; 2 Tm 4, 10-13.

See RG
496–501

The Letter to the Hebrews

As early as the second century, this treatise, which is of great rhetorical power and force in its admonition to faithful pilgrimage under Christ's leadership, bore the title "To the Hebrews." It was assumed to be directed to Jewish Christians. Usually Hebrews was attached in Greek manuscripts to the collection of letters by Paul. Although no author is mentioned (for there is no address), a reference to Timothy (13, 23) suggested connections to the circle of Paul and his assistants. Yet the exact audience, the author, and

even whether Hebrews is a letter have long been disputed.

The author saw the addressees in danger of apostasy from their Christian faith. This danger was due not to any persecution from outsiders but to a weariness with the demands of Christian life and a growing indifference to their calling (2, 1; 4, 14; 6, 1–12; 10, 23–32). The author's main theme, the priesthood and sacrifice of Jesus (ch 3–10), is not developed for its own sake but as a means of restoring their lost fervor and strengthening them in their faith. Another important theme of the letter is that of the pilgrimage of the people of God to the heavenly Jerusalem (11, 10; 12, 1–3. 18–29; 13, 14). This theme is intimately connected with that of Jesus' ministry in the heavenly sanctuary (9, 11—10, 22).

The author calls this work a "message of encouragement" (13, 22), a designation that is given to a synagogue sermon in Acts 13, 15. Hebrews is probably therefore a written homily, to which the author gave an epistolary ending (13, 22–25).

The author begins with a reminder of the pre-existence, incarnation, and exaltation of Jesus (1, 3) that proclaimed him the climax of God's word to humanity (1, 1–3). He dwells upon the dignity of the person of Christ, superior to the angels (1, 4—2, 2). Christ is God's final word of salvation communicated (in association with accredited witnesses to his teaching: cf 2, 3–4) not merely by word but through his suffering in the humanity common to him and to all others (2, 5–16). This enactment of salvation went beyond the pattern known to Moses, faithful prophet of God's word though he was, for Jesus as high priest expiated sin and was faithful to God with the faithfulness of God's own Son (2, 17—3, 6).

Just as the infidelity of the people thwarted Moses' efforts to save them, so the infidelity of any Christian may thwart God's plan in Christ (3, 6—4, 13). Christians are to reflect that it is their humanity that Jesus took upon himself, with all its defects save sinfulness, and that he bore the burden of it until death out of obedience to God. God declared this work of his Son to be the cause of salvation for all (4, 14—5, 10). Although Christians recognize this fundamental teaching, they may grow weary of it and of its implications, and therefore require other reflections to stimulate their faith (5, 11—6, 20).

Therefore, the author presents to the readers for their reflection the everlasting priesthood of Christ (7, 1–28), a priesthood that fulfills the promise of the Old Testament (8, 1–13). It also provides the meaning God ultimately intended in the sacrifices of the Old Testament (9, 1–28): these pointed to the unique sacrifice of Christ, which alone obtains forgiveness of sins (10, 1–18). The trial of faith experienced by the readers should resolve itself through their consideration of Christ's ministry in the heavenly sanctuary and his perpetual intercession there on their behalf (7, 25; 8, 1–13). They should also be strengthened by the assurance of his foreordained parousia, and by the fruits of faith that they have already enjoyed (10, 19–39).

It is in the nature of faith to recognize the reality of what is not yet seen and is the object of hope, and the saints of the Old Testament give striking example of that faith (11, 1–40). The perseverance to which the author exhorts the readers is shown forth in the early life of Jesus. Despite the afflictions of his ministry and the supreme trial of his suffering and death, he remained confident of the triumph that God would bring him (12, 1–3). The difficulties of human life have meaning when they are accepted as God's discipline (12, 4–13), and if Christians persevere in fidelity to the word in which they have believed, they are assured of possessing forever the unshakable kingdom of God (12, 14–29).

The letter concludes with specific moral commandments (13, 1–17), in the course of which the author recalls again his central theme of the sacrifice of Jesus and the courage needed to associate oneself with it in faith (13, 9–16).

As early as the end of the second century, the church of Alexandria in Egypt accepted Hebrews as a letter of Paul, and that became the view commonly held in the East. Pauline authorship was contested in the West into the fourth century, but then accepted. In the sixteenth century, doubts about that position were again raised, and the modern consensus is that the letter was not written by Paul. There is, however, no widespread agreement on any of the other suggested authors, e.g., Barnabas, Apollos, or Prisc(ill)a and Aquila. The document itself has no statement about its author.

Among the reasons why Pauline authorship has been abandoned are the great difference of vocabulary and style between Hebrews and Paul's letters, the alternation of doctrinal teaching with moral exhortation, the different manner of citing the Old Testament, and the resemblance between the thought of Hebrews and that of Alexandrian Judaism. The Greek of the letter is in many ways the best in the New Testament.

Since the letter of Clement of Rome to the Corinthians, written about A.D. 96, most probably cites Hebrews, the upper limit for the date of composition is reasonably certain. While the letter's references in the present tense to the Old

Testament sacrificial worship do not necessarily show that temple worship was still going on, many older commentators and a growing number of recent ones favor the view that it was and that the author wrote before the destruction of the temple of Jerusalem in A.D. 70. In that case, the argument of the letter is more easily explained as directed toward Jewish Christians rather than those of Gentile origin, and the persecutions they have suffered in the past (cf 10, 32–34) may have been connected with the disturbances that preceded the expulsion of the Jews from Rome in A.D. 49 under the emperor Claudius. These were probably caused by disputes between Jews who accepted Jesus as the Messiah and those who did not.

The principal divisions of the Letter to the Hebrews are the following:

    I: Introduction (1, 1–4)

    II: The Son Higher than the Angels (1, 5—2, 18)

    III: Jesus, Faithful and Compassionate High Priest (3, 1—5, 10)

    IV: Jesus' Eternal Priesthood and Eternal Sacrifice (5, 11—10, 39)

    V: Examples, Discipline, Disobedience (11, 1—12, 29)

    VI: Final Exhortation, Blessing, Greetings (13, 1–25)

I: Introduction

CHAPTER 1

See RG
497–98

[1]*In times past, God spoke in partial and various ways to our ancestors through the prophets; [2a]in these last days, he spoke to us through a son, whom he made heir of all things and through whom he created the universe,

[3] [b]who is the refulgence of his glory,
    the very imprint of his being,
and who sustains all things by his mighty word.
When he had accomplished purification from sins,
he took his seat at the right hand of the Majesty on high,
[4] [c]as far superior to the angels
as the name he has inherited is more excellent than theirs.

II: The Son Higher than the Angels

Messianic Enthronement. [5d]*For to which of the angels did God ever say:

"You are my son; this day I have begotten you"?

Or again:

"I will be a father to him, and he shall be a son to me"?

1, 1–4: The letter opens with an introduction consisting of a reflection on the climax of God's revelation to the human race in his Son. The divine communication was initiated and maintained during Old Testament times in fragmentary and varied ways through **the prophets** (1), including Abraham, Moses, and all through whom God spoke. But now **in these last days** (2), the final age, God's revelation of his saving purpose is achieved **through a son**, i.e., one who is Son, whose role is redeemer and mediator of creation. He was made **heir of all things** through his death and exaltation to glory, yet he existed before he appeared as man; through him God **created the universe.** Verses 3–4, which may be based upon a liturgical hymn, assimilate the Son to the personified Wisdom of the Old Testament as **refulgence of** God's **glory** and **imprint of his being** (3; cf Wis 7, 26). These same terms are used of the Logos in Philo. The author now turns from the cosmological role of the preexistent Son to the redemptive work of Jesus: he brought about purification from sins and has been exalted to the right hand of God (see Ps 110, 1). The once-humiliated and crucified Jesus has been declared God's Son, and this name shows his superiority to the angels. The reason for the author's insistence on that superiority is,

among other things, that in some Jewish traditions angels were mediators of the old covenant (see Acts 7, 53; Gal 3, 19). Finally, Jesus' superiority to the angels emphasizes the superiority of the new covenant to the old because of the heavenly priesthood of Jesus.

1, 5–14: Jesus' superiority to the angels is now demonstrated by a series of seven Old Testament texts. Some scholars see in the stages of Jesus' exaltation an order corresponding to that of enthronement ceremonies in the ancient Near East, especially in Egypt, namely, elevation to divine status (5–6); presentation to the angels and proclamation of everlasting lordship (7–12); enthronement and conferral of royal power (13). The citations from the Psalms in vv 5 and 13 were traditionally used of Jesus' messianic sonship (cf Acts 13, 33) through his resurrection and exaltation (cf Acts 2, 33–35); those in vv 8 and 10–12 are concerned with his divine king-

a: Is 2, 2; Jer 23, 20; Ez 38, 16; Dn 10, 14 / Jn 3, 17; Rom 8, 3; Gal 4, 4 / Prv 8, 30; Wis 7, 22; Jn 1, 3; 1 Cor 8, 6; Col 1, 16. *b:* Wis 7, 26; 2 Cor 4, 4; Col 1, 15 / 8, 1; 10, 12; 12, 2; Mk 16, 19; Acts 2, 33; 7, 55-56; Rom 8, 34; Eph 1, 20; Col 3, 1; 1 Pt 3, 22. *c:* Eph 1, 21; Phil 2, 9-11. *d:* Ps 2, 7 / 2 Sm 7, 14.

6e*And again, when he leads the first-born into the world, he says:

"Let all the angels of God worship him."

7fOf the angels he says:

"He makes his angels winds
and his ministers a fiery flame";

8g*but of the Son:

"Your throne, O God, stands forever and
ever;
and a righteous scepter is the scepter
of your kingdom.
9 You loved justice and hated wickedness;
therefore God, your God, anointed you
with the oil of gladness above your
companions";

10hand:

"At the beginning, O Lord, you
established the earth,
and the heavens are the works of your
hands.
11 They will perish, but you remain;
and they will all grow old like a
garment.
12 You will roll them up like a cloak,
and like a garment they will be changed.
But you are the same, and your years will
have no end."

13iBut to which of the angels has he ever said:

"Sit at my right hand
until I make your enemies your
footstool"?

14jAre they not all ministering spirits sent to serve, for the sake of those who are to inherit salvation?

CHAPTER 2

See RG
497–98

Exhortation to Faithfulness. 1*Therefore, we must attend all the more to what we have heard, so that we may not be carried away. 2kFor if the word announced through angels proved firm, and every transgression and disobedience received its just recompense, 3lhow shall we escape if we ignore so great a salvation? Announced originally through the Lord, it was confirmed for us by those who had heard. 4mGod added his testimony by signs, wonders, various acts of power, and distribution of the gifts of the holy Spirit according to his will.

Exaltation through Abasement. 5*For it was not to angels that he subjected the world to come, of which we are speaking. 6nInstead, someone has testified somewhere:

"What is man that you are mindful of
him,

---

ship and his creative function. The central quotation in v 7 serves to contrast the angels with the Son. The author quotes it according to the Septuagint translation, which is quite different in meaning from that of the Hebrew ("You make the winds your messengers, and flaming fire your ministers"). The angels are only **sent to serve . . . those who are to inherit salvation** (14).

1, 6: And again, when he leads: the Greek could also be translated "And when he again leads" in reference to the parousia.

1, 8–12: O God: the application of the name "God" to the Son derives from the preexistence mentioned in vv 2–3; the psalmist had already used it of the Hebrew king in the court style of the original. See the note on Ps 45, 7. It is also important for the author's christology that in vv 10–12 an Old Testament passage addressed to God is redirected to Jesus.

2, 1–4: The author now makes a transition into exhortation, using an a fortiori argument (as at 7, 21–22; 9, 13–14; 10, 28–29; 12, 25). The **word announced through angels** (2), the Mosaic law, is contrasted with the more powerful word that Christians have received (3–4). Christ's supremacy strengthens Christians against being **carried away** from their faith.

2, 5–18: The humanity and the suffering of Jesus do not constitute a valid reason for relinquishing the Christian faith.

Ps 8 (6–7) is also applied to Jesus in 1 Cor 15, 27; Eph 1, 22; and probably 1 Pt 3, 22. This christological interpretation, therefore, probably reflects a common early Christian tradition, which may have originated in the expression **the son of man** (6). The psalm contrasts God's greatness with man's relative insignificance but also stresses the superiority of man to the rest of creation, of which he is lord. Heb applies this christologically: Jesus lived a truly human existence, **lower than the angels,** in the days of his earthly life, particularly in his suffering and death; now, **crowned with glory and honor,** he is raised above all creation. The author considers all things as already **subject to him** because of his exaltation (8–9), though **we do not see** this yet. The reference to Jesus as **leader** (10) sounds the first note of an important leitmotif in Heb: the journey of the people of God to the sabbath rest (4, 9), the heavenly sanctuary, following Jesus, their "forerunner" (6, 20). It was fitting that God should make him **perfect through suffering,** consecrated by obedient suffering. Because he is perfected as high priest, Jesus is then able to consecrate his peo-

e: Dt 32, 43 LXX; Ps 97, 7.   *f:* Ps 104, 4 LXX.   *g:* Ps 45, 7-8.
h: Ps 102, 26-28.   *i:* Ps 110, 1.   *j:* Ps 91, 11; Dn 7, 10.   *k:* Acts 7, 38.53; Gal 3, 19.   *l:* 10, 29; 12, 25.   *m:* Mk 16, 20; Acts 14, 3; 19, 11.   *n:* Ps 8, 5-7.

or the son of man that you care for
    him?

[7] You made him for a little while lower
    than the angels;

you crowned him with glory and honor,

[8] *o*subjecting all things under his feet."

In "subjecting" all things [to him], he left
nothing not "subject to him." Yet at present
we do not see "all things subject to him,"
[9] *p*but we do see Jesus "crowned with glory
and honor" because he suffered death, he
who "for a little while" was made "lower
than the angels," that by the grace of God he
might taste death for everyone.

[10] *q*For it was fitting that he, for whom and
through whom all things exist, in bringing
many children to glory, should make the
leader to their salvation perfect through suffering. [11] He who consecrates and those who
are being consecrated all have one origin.
Therefore, he is not ashamed to call them
"brothers," [12] *r*saying:

"I will proclaim your name to my
    brothers,
in the midst of the assembly I will
    praise you";

[13] *s*and again:

"I will put my trust in him";

and again:

"Behold, I and the children God has
    given me."

[14] *t*Now since the children share in blood and
flesh, he likewise shared in them, that
through death he might destroy the one who
has the power of death, that is, the devil,
[15] and free those who through fear of death
had been subject to slavery all their life.
[16] Surely he did not help angels but rather the
descendants of Abraham; [17] *u*therefore, he
had to become like his brothers in every
way, that he might be a merciful and faithful
high priest before God to expiate the sins of
the people. [18] Because he himself was tested
through what he suffered, he is able to help
those who are being tested.

III: Jesus, Faithful and Compassionate High Priest

CHAPTER 3

See RG
498–99

Jesus, Superior to Moses. [1]*Therefore, holy "brothers," sharing in a heavenly
calling, reflect on Jesus, the apostle and high
priest of our confession, [2] *v*who was faithful
to the one who appointed him, just as Moses
was "faithful in [all] his house." [3] *w*But he is
worthy of more "glory" than Moses, as the

ple (11); access to God is made possible by each of these two
consecrations. If Jesus is able to help human beings, it is because he has become one of us; we are his "brothers." The author then cites three Old Testament texts as proofs of this unity
between ourselves and the Son. Psalm 22, 23 is interpreted so
as to make Jesus the singer of this lament, which ends with
joyful praise of the Lord in the assembly of "brothers." The
other two texts are from Is 8, 17.18. The first of these seems
intended to display in Jesus an example of the trust in God that
his followers should emulate. The second curiously calls these
followers "children"; probably this is to be understood to
mean children of Adam, but the point is our solidarity with
Jesus. By sharing human nature, including the ban of death,
Jesus broke the power of the devil over death (14); the author
shares the view of Hellenistic Judaism that death was not intended by God and that it had been introduced into the world
by the devil. The **fear of death** (15) is a religious fear based
on the false conception that death marks the end of a person's
relations with God (cf Ps 115, 17–18; Is 38, 18). Jesus deliberately allied himself with the **descendants of Abraham** (16)
in order to be a **merciful and faithful high priest.** This is the
first appearance of the central theme of Heb, Jesus the great
high priest expiating the **sins of the people** (17), as one who
experienced the same tests as they (18).

3, 1–6: The author now takes up the two qualities of Jesus
mentioned in 2, 17, but in inverse order: faithfulness (3, 1—4,
13) and mercy (4, 14—5, 10). Christians are called **holy
"brothers"** because of their common relation to him (2, 11),
the **apostle,** a designation for Jesus used only here in the New
Testament (cf Jn 13, 16; 17, 3), meaning one sent as God's final word to us (1, 2). He is compared with Moses probably because he is seen as mediator of the new covenant (9, 15) just
as Moses was of the old (9, 19–22, including his sacrifice). But
when the author of Heb speaks of Jesus' sacrifice, he does not
consider Moses as the Old Testament antitype, but rather the
high priest on the Day of Atonement (9, 6–15). Moses' faithfulness **"in [all] his house"** refers back to Nm 12, 7, on which
this section is a midrashic commentary. In vv 3–6, the author
does not indicate that he thinks of either Moses or Christ as the
founder of the household. **His house** (2.5.6) means God's
house, not that of Moses or Christ; in the case of Christ, compare v 6 with 10, 21. The **house** of v 6 is the Christian com-

o: Mt 28, 18; 1 Cor 15, 25-28; Eph 1, 20-23; Phil 3, 21; 1 Pt 3, 22.
p: Phil 2, 6-11. *q:* 12, 2; Is 53, 4 / Rom 11, 36; 1 Cor 8, 6. *r:* Ps
22, 23. *s:* Is 8, 17.18. *t:* Is 25, 8; Hos 13, 14; Jn 12, 31; Rom 6,
9; 1 Cor 15, 54-55; 2 Tm 1, 10; Rv 12, 10. *u:* 4, 15; 5, 1-3.
v: Nm 12, 7. *w:* 2 Cor 3, 7-8.

founder of a house has more "honor" than the house itself. [4]Every house is founded by someone, but the founder of all is God. [5]Moses was "faithful in all his house" as a "servant" to testify to what would be spoken, [6x*]but Christ was faithful as a son placed over his house. We are his house, if [only] we hold fast to our confidence and pride in our hope.

Israel's Infidelity a Warning. [7y*]Therefore, as the holy Spirit says:

"Oh, that today you would hear his
       voice,
[8]   'Harden not your hearts as at the
         rebellion
       in the day of testing in the desert,
[9]   [z]where your ancestors tested and tried
         me
       and saw my works [10]for forty
         years.
       Because of this I was provoked with
         that generation
       and I said, "They have always been
         of erring heart,
       and they do not know my ways."
[11]   As I swore in my wrath,
       "They shall not enter into my
         rest." ' "

[12]Take care, brothers, that none of you may have an evil and unfaithful heart, so as to forsake the living God. [13]Encourage yourselves daily while it is still "today," so that none of you may grow hardened by the deceit of sin. [14a]We have become partners of Christ if only we hold the beginning of the reality firm until the end, [15b]for it is said:

"Oh, that today you would hear his
       voice:
   'Harden not your hearts as at the
       rebellion.' "

[16c]Who were those who rebelled when they heard? Was it not all those who came out of Egypt under Moses? [17d]With whom was he "provoked for forty years"? Was it not those who had sinned, whose corpses fell in the desert? [18e]And to whom did he "swear that they should not enter into his rest," if not to those who were disobedient? [19]And we see that they could not enter for lack of faith.

CHAPTER 4

See RG
498–99

The Sabbath Rest. [1]Therefore, let us be on our guard while the promise of entering into his rest remains, that none of you seem to have failed. [2]For in fact we have received the good news just as they did. But the word that they heard did not profit them, for they were not united in faith with those who listened. [3f]For we who believed enter into [that] rest, just as he has said:

"As I swore in my wrath,
   'They shall not enter into my rest,' "

---

munity; the author suggests its continuity with Israel by speaking not of two houses but of only one. Verse 6 brings out the reason why Jesus is superior to Moses: the latter was the faithful **servant** laboring **in** the house founded by God, but Jesus is God's **son,** placed **over** the house.

3, 6: The majority of manuscripts add "firm to the end," but these words are not found in the three earliest and best witnesses and are probably an interpolation derived from v 14.

3, 7—4, 13: The author appeals for steadfastness of faith in Jesus, basing his warning on the experience of Israel during the Exodus. In the Old Testament the Exodus had been invoked as a symbol of the return of Israel from the Babylonian exile (Is 42, 9; 43, 16–21; 51, 9–11). In the New Testament the redemption was similarly understood as a new exodus, both in the experience of Jesus himself (Lk 9, 31) and in that of his followers (1 Cor 10, 1–4). The author cites Ps 95, 7–11, a salutary example of hardness of heart, as a warning against the danger of growing weary and giving up the journey. To call God **living** (12) means that he reveals himself in his works (cf Jos 3, 10; Jer 10, 10). The **rest** (11) into which Israel was to enter was only a foreshadowing of that rest to which Christians are called. They are to remember the example of Israel's revolt in the desert that cost a whole generation the loss of the promised land (15–19; cf Nm 14, 20–29). In 4, 1–11, the symbol of **rest** is seen in deeper dimension: because the promise to the ancient Hebrews foreshadowed that given to Christians, it is **good news;** and because the promised land was the place of rest that God provided for his people, it was a share in his own rest, which he enjoyed after he had finished his creative work (3–4; cf Gn 2, 2). The author attempts to read this meaning of God's rest into Ps 95, 7–11 (6–9). The Greek form of the name of Joshua, who led Israel into the promised land, is Jesus (8). The author plays upon the name but stresses the superiority of Jesus, who leads his followers into heavenly rest. Verses 12 and 13 are meant as a continuation of the warning, for the word of God brings judgment as well as salvation. Some would capitalize **the word of God** and see it as a personal title of Jesus, comparable to that of Jn 1, 1–18.

x: 10, 21; Eph 2, 19; 1 Tm 3, 15; 1 Pt 4, 17.   y: Ps 95, 7-11.   z: Ex 17, 7; Nm 20, 2-5.   a: Rom 8, 17.   b: Ps 95, 7-8.   c: Nm 14, 1-38; Dt 1, 19-40.   d: Nm 14, 29.   e: Nm 14, 22-23; Dt 1, 35.   f: 3, 11; Ps 95, 11.

and yet his works were accomplished at the foundation of the world. *4g*For he has spoken somewhere about the seventh day in this manner, "And God rested on the seventh day from all his works"; *5h*and again, in the previously mentioned place, "They shall not enter into my rest." *6*Therefore, since it remains that some will enter into it, and those who formerly received the good news did not enter because of disobedience, *7i*he once more set a day, "today," when long afterwards he spoke through David, as already quoted:

"Oh, that today you would hear his voice:
   'Harden not your hearts.' "

*8j*Now if Joshua had given them rest, he would not have spoken afterwards of another day. *9*Therefore, a sabbath rest still remains for the people of God. *10*And whoever enters into God's rest, rests from his own works as God did from his. *11*Therefore, let us strive to enter into that rest, so that no one may fall after the same example of disobedience.

*12k*Indeed, the word of God is living and effective, sharper than any two-edged sword, penetrating even between soul and spirit, joints and marrow, and able to discern reflections and thoughts of the heart. *13 l*No creature is concealed from him, but everything is naked and exposed to the eyes of him to whom we must render an account.

Jesus, Compassionate High Priest.

14m*Therefore, since we have a great high priest who has passed through the heavens, Jesus, the Son of God, let us hold fast to our confession. *15n*For we do not have a high priest who is unable to sympathize with our weaknesses, but one who has similarly been tested in every way, yet without sin. *16o*So let us confidently approach the throne of grace to receive mercy and to find grace for timely help.

CHAPTER 5

See RG
498-99

1*Every high priest is taken from among men and made their representative before God, to offer gifts and sacrifices for sins. *2**He is able to deal patiently with the ignorant and erring, for he himself is beset by weakness *3p*and so, for this reason, must make sin offerings for himself as well as for the people. *4q*No one takes this honor upon himself but only when called by God, just as Aaron was. *5r*In the same way, it was not Christ who glorified himself in becoming high priest, but rather the one who said to him:

"You are my son;
   this day I have begotten you";

6s*just as he says in another place:

"You are a priest forever
   according to the order of Melchizedek."

4, 14–16: These verses, which return to the theme first sounded in 2, 16—3, 1, serve as an introduction to the section that follows. The author here alone calls Jesus **a great high priest** (14), a designation used by Philo for the Logos; perhaps he does so in order to emphasize Jesus' superiority over the Jewish high priest. He has **been tested in every way, yet without sin** (15); this indicates an acquaintance with the tradition of Jesus' temptations, not only at the beginning (as in Mk 1, 13) but throughout his public life (cf Lk 22, 28). Although the reign of the exalted Jesus is a theme that occurs elsewhere in Heb, and Jesus' throne is mentioned in 1, 8, **the throne of grace** (16) refers to the throne of God. The similarity of v 16 to 10, 19–22 indicates that the author is thinking of our confident access to God, made possible by the priestly work of Jesus.

5, 1–10: The true humanity of Jesus (see the note on 2, 5–18) makes him a more rather than a less effective high priest to the Christian community. In Old Testament tradition, the high priest was identified with the people, guilty of personal sin just as they were (1–3). Even so, the office was of divine appointment (4), as was also the case with the sinless Christ (5). For v 6, see the note on Ps 110, 4. Although Jesus was Son of God, he was destined as a human being to learn obedience by accepting the suffering he had to endure (8).

Because of his perfection through this experience of human suffering, he is the cause of salvation for all (9), a **high priest according to the order of Melchizedek** (10; cf 6 and 7, 3).

5, 1: To offer gifts and sacrifices for sins: the author is thinking principally of the Day of Atonement rite, as is clear from 9, 7. This ritual was celebrated to atone for "all the sins of the Israelites" (Lv 16, 34).

5, 2: Deal patiently: the Greek word **metriopathein** occurs only here in the Bible; this term was used by the Stoics to designate the golden mean between excess and defect of passion. Here it means rather the ability to sympathize.

5, 6–8: The author of Heb is the only New Testament writer to cite v 4 of Ps 110, here and in 7, 17.21, to show that Jesus has been called by God to his role as priest. Verses 7–8 deal with his ability to sympathize with sinners, because of his own experience of the trials and weakness of human nature, especially fear of death. In his present exalted state,

g: Gn 2, 2. *h:* Ps 95, 11. *i:* 3, 7-8.15; Ps 95, 7-8. *j:* Dt 31, 7; Jos 22, 4. *k:* Wis 18, 15-16; Is 49, 2; Eph 6, 17; Rv 1, 16; 2, 12. *l:* Jb 34, 21-22; Pss 90, 8; 139, 2-4. *m:* 9, 11.24. *n:* 2, 17-18; 5, 2. *o:* 8, 1; 10, 19.22.35; 12, 2; Eph 3, 12. *p:* Lv 9, 7; 16, 15-17.30.34. *q:* Ex 28, 1. *r:* Ps 2, 7. *s:* Ps 110, 4.

[7t]*In the days when he was in the flesh, he offered prayers and supplications with loud cries and tears to the one who was able to save him from death, and he was heard because of his reverence. [8u]*Son though he was, he learned obedience from what he suffered; [9v]and when he was made perfect, he became the source of eternal salvation for all who obey him, [10w]declared by God high priest according to the order of Melchizedek.

IV: Jesus' Eternal Priesthood and Eternal Sacrifice

Exhortation to Spiritual Renewal. [11]*About this we have much to say, and it is difficult to explain, for you have become sluggish in hearing. [12x]Although you should be teachers by this time, you need to have someone teach you again the basic elements of the utterances of God. You need milk, [and] not solid food. [13]Everyone who lives on milk lacks experience of the word of righteousness, for he is a child. [14]But solid food is for the mature, for those whose faculties are trained by practice to discern good and evil.

CHAPTER 6

See RG 499

[1y]Therefore, let us leave behind the basic teaching about Christ and advance to maturity, without laying the foundation all over again: repentance from dead works and faith in God, [2z]*instruction about baptisms and laying on of hands, resurrection of the dead and eternal judgment. [3]And we shall do this, if only God permits. [4a]*For it is impossible in the case of those who have once been enlightened and tasted the heavenly gift and shared in the holy Spirit [5]*and tasted the good word of God and the powers of the age to come, [6b]*and then have fallen away, to bring them to repentance again, since they are recrucifying the Son of God for themselves and holding him up to contempt. [7c]Ground that has absorbed the rain falling upon it repeatedly and brings forth crops useful to those for whom it is cultivated receives a blessing from God. [8d]But if it produces thorns and thistles, it is rejected; it will soon be cursed and finally burned.

weakness is foreign to him, but he understands what we suffer because of his previous earthly experience.

5, 7: He offered prayers . . . to the one who was able to save him from death: at Gethsemane (cf Mk 14, 35), though some see a broader reference (see the note on Jn 12, 27).

5, 8: Son though he was: two different though not incompatible views of Jesus' sonship coexist in Heb, one associating it with his exaltation, the other with his preexistence. The former view is the older one (cf Rom 1, 4).

5, 11—6, 20: The central section of Heb (5, 11—10, 39) opens with a reprimand and an appeal. Those to whom the author directs his teaching about Jesus' priesthood, which is **difficult to explain,** have become **sluggish in hearing** and forgetful of even **the basic elements** (5, 12). But rather than treating of basic teachings, the author apparently believes that the challenge of more advanced ones may shake them out of their inertia (**therefore,** 6, 1). The six examples of **basic teaching** in 6, 1–3 are probably derived from a traditional catechetical list. No effort is made to address apostates, for their very hostility to the Christian message cuts them off completely from Christ (6, 4–8). This harsh statement seems to rule out repentance after apostasy, but perhaps the author deliberately uses hyperbole in order to stress the seriousness of abandoning Christ. With 6, 9 a milder tone is introduced, and the criticism of the community (6, 1–3.9) is now balanced by an expression of confidence that its members are living truly Christian lives, and that God will justly reward their efforts (10). The author is concerned especially about their persevering (11–12), citing in this regard the achievement of Abraham, who relied on God's

promise and on God's oath (13–18; cf Gn 22, 16), and proposes to them as a firm anchor of Christian hope the high priesthood of Christ, who is now living with God (19–20).

6, 2: Instruction about baptisms: not simply about Christian baptism but about the difference between it and similar Jewish rites, such as proselyte baptism, John's baptism, and the washings of the Qumran sectaries. **Laying on of hands:** in Acts 8, 17; 19, 6 this rite effects the infusion of the holy Spirit; in Acts 6, 6; 13, 3; 1 Tm 4, 14; 5, 22; 2 Tm 1, 6 it is a means of conferring some ministry or mission in the early Christian community.

6, 4: Enlightened and tasted the heavenly gift: this may refer to baptism and the Eucharist, respectively, but more probably means the neophytes' enlightenment by faith and their experience of salvation.

6, 5: Tasted the good word of God and the powers of the age to come: the proclamation of the **word of God** was accompanied by signs of the Spirit's power (1 Thes 1, 5; 1 Cor 2, 4).

6, 6: They are recrucifying the Son of God for themselves: a colorful description of the malice of apostasy, which is portrayed as again crucifying and deriding the Son of God.

t: Mt 26, 38-44; Mk 14, 34-40; Lk 22, 41-46; Jn 12, 27. *u:* Rom 5, 19; Phil 2, 8. *v:* 7, 24-25.28. *w:* 6, 20; Ps 110, 4. *x:* 1 Cor 3, 1-3. *y:* 9, 14. *z:* 9, 10; Mk 7, 4 / Acts 6, 6; 8, 17; 13, 3; 19, 6; 1 Tm 4, 14; 5, 22; 2 Tm 1, 6. *a:* 10, 26.32; Ps 34, 6; 2 Cor 4, 6. *b:* 2 Pt 2, 21. *c:* Gn 1, 11-12; Dt 11, 11. *d:* Gn 3, 17-18; Mt 7, 16; 13, 7; Mk 4, 7; Lk 8, 7.

⁹But we are sure in your regard, beloved, of better things related to salvation, even though we speak in this way. ¹⁰For God is not unjust so as to overlook your work and the love you have demonstrated for his name by having served and continuing to serve the holy ones. ¹¹ᵉWe earnestly desire each of you to demonstrate the same eagerness for the fulfillment of hope until the end, ¹²ᶠ*so that you may not become sluggish, but imitators of those who, through faith and patience, are inheriting the promises.

God's Promise Immutable. ¹³ᵍ*When God made the promise to Abraham, since he had no one greater by whom to swear, "he swore by himself," ¹⁴ʰand said, "I will indeed bless you and multiply" you. ¹⁵ⁱ*And so, after patient waiting, he obtained the promise. ¹⁶Human beings swear by someone greater than themselves; for them an oath serves as a guarantee and puts an end to all argument. ¹⁷ʲSo when God wanted to give the heirs of his promise an even clearer demonstration of the immutability of his purpose, he intervened with an oath, ¹⁸ᵏ*so that by two immutable things, in which it was impossible for God to lie, we who have taken refuge might be strongly encouraged to hold fast to the hope that lies before us. ¹⁹ˡ*This we have as an anchor of the soul, sure and firm, which reaches into the interior behind the veil, ²⁰ᵐwhere Jesus has entered on our behalf as forerunner, becoming high priest forever according to the order of Melchizedek.

CHAPTER 7

See RG 498-99

Melchizedek, a Type of Christ. ¹ⁿ*This "Melchizedek, king of Salem and priest of God Most High," "met Abraham as he returned from his defeat of the kings" and "blessed him." ²*And Abraham apportioned to him "a tenth of everything." His name first means righteous king, and he was also "king of Salem," that is, king of peace. ³ᵒ*Without father, mother, or ancestry, without beginning of days or end of life, thus made to resemble the Son of God, he remains a priest forever.

⁴ᵖ*See how great he is to whom the patriarch "Abraham [indeed] gave a tenth" of his spoils. ⁵�q The descendants of Levi who receive the office of priesthood have a com-

6, 12: Imitators of those . . . inheriting the promises: the author urges the addressees to imitate the faith of the holy people of the Old Testament, who now possess the promised goods of which they lived in hope. This theme will be treated fully in ch 11.

6, 13: He swore by himself: God's promise to Abraham, which he confirmed by an oath ("I swear by myself," Gen 22, 16) was the basis for the hope of all Abraham's descendants.

6, 15: He obtained the promise: this probably refers not to Abraham's temporary possession of the land but to the eschatological blessings that Abraham and the other patriarchs have now come to possess.

6, 18: Two immutable things: the promise and the oath, both made by God.

6, 19: Anchor . . . into the interior behind the veil: a mixed metaphor. The Holy of Holies, beyond the veil that separates it from the Holy Place (Ex 26, 31–33), is seen as the earthly counterpart of the heavenly abode of God. This theme will be developed in ch 9.

7, 1–3: Recalling the meeting between Melchizedek and Abraham described in Gn 14, 17–20, the author enhances the significance of this priest by providing the popular etymological meaning of his name and that of the city over which he ruled (2). Since Genesis gives no information on the parentage or the death of Melchizedek, he is seen here as a type of Christ, representing a priesthood that is unique and eternal (3).

7, 1: The author here assumes that Melchizedek was a priest of the God of Israel (cf Gn 14, 22 and the note there).

7, 2: In Gn 14, the Hebrew text does not state explicitly who gave tithes to whom. The author of Heb supplies Abra-

ham as the subject, according to a contemporary interpretation of the passage. This supports the argument of the midrash and makes it possible to see in Melchizedek a type of Jesus. The messianic blessings of righteousness and peace are foreshadowed in the names "Melchizedek" and "Salem."

7, 3: Without father, mother, or ancestry, without beginning of days or end of life: this is perhaps a quotation from a hymn about Melchizedek. The rabbis maintained that anything not mentioned in the Torah does not exist. Consequently, since the Old Testament nowhere mentions Melchizedek's ancestry, birth, or death, the conclusion can be drawn that he **remains . . . forever.**

7, 4–10: The tithe that Abraham gave to Melchizedek (4), a practice later followed by the levitical priesthood (5), was a gift (6) acknowledging a certain superiority in Melchizedek, the foreign priest (7). This is further indicated by the fact that the institution of the levitical priesthood was sustained by hereditary succession in the tribe of Levi, whereas the absence of any mention of Melchizedek's death in Gn implies that his personal priesthood is permanent (8). The levitical priesthood itself, through Abraham, its ancestor, paid tithes to Melchizedek, thus acknowledging the superiority of his priesthood over its own (9–10).

e: 3, 14. *f:* 5, 11; Gal 3, 14; Eph 1, 13-14. *g:* Gn 22, 16. *h:* Gn 22, 17. *i:* 12; Rom 4, 20. *j:* 12. *k:* Nm 23, 19; 1 Sm 15, 29; Jn 8, 17; 2 Tm 2, 13. *l:* 10, 20; Ex 26, 31-33; Lv 16, 2. *m:* 5, 10; Ps 110, 4. *n:* Gn 14, 17-20. *o:* 4, 14; 6, 6; 10, 29. *p:* Gn 14, 20. *q:* Nm 18, 21 / Gn 35, 11.

mandment according to the law to exact tithes from the people, that is, from their brothers, although they also have come from the loins of Abraham. ⁶But he who was not of their ancestry received tithes from Abraham and blessed him who had received the promises. ⁷*Unquestionably, a lesser person is blessed by a greater. ⁸In the one case, mortal men receive tithes; in the other, a man of whom it is testified that he lives on. ⁹*One might even say that Levi himself, who receives tithes, was tithed through Abraham, ¹⁰for he was still in his father's loins when Melchizedek met him.

¹¹ʳ*If, then, perfection came through the levitical priesthood, on the basis of which the people received the law, what need would there still have been for another priest to arise according to the order of Melchizedek, and not reckoned according to the order of Aaron? ¹²When there is a change of priesthood, there is necessarily a change of law as well. ¹³*Now he of whom these things are said belonged to a different tribe, of which no member ever officiated at the altar. ¹⁴ˢ*It is clear that our Lord arose from Judah,

and in regard to that tribe Moses said nothing about priests. ¹⁵*It is even more obvious if another priest is raised up after the likeness of Melchizedek, ¹⁶*who has become so, not by a law expressed in a commandment concerning physical descent but by the power of a life that cannot be destroyed. ¹⁷ᵗFor it is testified:

"You are a priest forever
according to the order of
Melchizedek."

¹⁸ᵘOn the one hand, a former commandment is annulled because of its weakness and uselessness, ¹⁹*for the law brought nothing to perfection; on the other hand, a better hope is introduced, through which we draw near to God. ²⁰*And to the degree that this happened not without the taking of an oath—for others became priests without an oath, ²¹ᵛbut he with an oath, through the one who said to him:

"The Lord has sworn, and he will not repent:
'You are a priest forever' "—

7, 7: **A lesser person is blessed by a greater:** though this sounds like a principle, there are some examples in the Old Testament that do not support it (cf 2 Sm 14, 22; Jb 31, 20). The author may intend it as a statement of a liturgical rule.

7, 9: **Levi:** for the author this name designates not only the son of Jacob mentioned in Genesis but the priestly tribe that was thought to be descended from him.

7, 11–14: The levitical priesthood was not typified by the priesthood of Melchizedek, for Ps 110, 4 speaks of a priesthood of a new order, the order of Melchizedek, to arise in messianic times (11). Since the levitical priesthood served the Mosaic law, a new priesthood (12) would not come into being without a change in the law itself. Thus Jesus was not associated with the Old Testament priesthood, for he was a descendant of the tribe of Judah, which had never exercised the priesthood (13–14).

7, 13: **He of whom these things are said:** Jesus, the priest "according to the order of Melchizedek." According to the author's interpretation, Ps 110 spoke prophetically of Jesus.

7, 14: **Judah:** the author accepts the early Christian tradition that Jesus was descended from the family of David (cf Mt 1, 1–2.16.20; Lk 1, 27; 2, 4; Rom 1, 3). The Qumran community expected two Messiahs, one descended from Aaron and one from David; Heb shows no awareness of this view or at least does not accept it. Our author's view is not attested in contemporaneous Judaism.

7, 15–19: Jesus does not exercise a priesthood through family lineage but through his immortal existence (15–16),

fulfilling Ps 110, 4 (17; cf 3). Thus he abolishes forever both the levitical priesthood and the law it serves, because neither could effectively sanctify people (18) by leading them into direct communication with God (19).

7, 16: **A life that cannot be destroyed:** the life to which Jesus has attained by virtue of his resurrection; it is his exaltation rather than his divine nature that makes him priest. The Old Testament speaks of the Aaronic priesthood as eternal (see Ex 40, 15); our author does not explicitly consider this possible objection to his argument but implicitly refutes it in vv 23–24.

7, 19: **A better hope:** this hope depends upon the sacrifice of the Son of God; through it we "approach the throne of grace" (4, 16); cf 6, 19.20.

7, 20–25: As was the case with the promise to Abraham (6, 13), though not with the levitical priesthood, the eternal priesthood of the order of Melchizedek was confirmed by God's oath (20–21); cf Ps 110, 4. Thus Jesus becomes the guarantee of a permanent covenant (22) that does not require a succession of priests as did the levitical priesthood (23) because his high priesthood is eternal and unchangeable (24). Consequently, Jesus is able to save all who draw near to God through him since he is their ever-living intercessor (25).

7, 20: **An oath:** God's oath in Ps 110, 4.

---

r: 5, 6; Ps 110, 4.　s: Gn 49, 10; Is 11, 1; Mt 1, 1-2.16.20; 2, 6; Lk 1, 27; 2, 4; Rom 1, 3; Rv 5, 5.　t: 5, 6; Ps 110, 4.　u: 10, 1.　v: Ps 110, 4.

²²ʷ*to that same degree has Jesus [also] become the guarantee of an [even] better covenant. ²³Those priests were many because they were prevented by death from remaining in office, ²⁴ˣbut he, because he remains forever, has a priesthood that does not pass away. ²⁵ʸ*Therefore, he is always able to save those who approach God through him, since he lives forever to make intercession for them.

²⁶ᶻ*It was fitting that we should have such a high priest: holy, innocent, undefiled, separated from sinners, higher than the heavens. ²⁷ᵃ*He has no need, as did the high priests, to offer sacrifice day after day, first for his own sins and then for those of the people; he did that once for all when he offered himself. ²⁸ᵇFor the law appoints men subject to weakness to be high priests, but the word of the oath, which was taken after the law, appoints a son, who has been made perfect forever.

CHAPTER 8

See RG
499

Heavenly Priesthood of Jesus. ¹ᶜ*The main point of what has been said is this: we have such a high priest, who has taken his seat at the right hand of the throne of the Majesty in heaven, ²ᵈ*a minister of the sanctuary and of the true tabernacle that the Lord, not man, set up. ³ᵉNow every high priest is appointed to offer gifts and sacrifices; thus the necessity for this one also to have something to offer. ⁴ᶠIf then he were on earth, he would not be a priest, since there are those who offer gifts according to the law. ⁵ᵍThey worship in a copy and shadow of the heavenly sanctuary, as Moses was warned when he was about to erect the tabernacle. For he says, "See that you make everything according to the pattern shown you on the mountain." ⁶ʰNow he has obtained so much more excellent a ministry as he is mediator of a better covenant, enacted on better promises.

Old and New Covenants. ⁷*For if that first covenant had been faultless, no place would have been sought for a second one. ⁸ⁱ*But he finds fault with them and says:

7, 22: **An [even] better covenant:** better than the Mosaic covenant because it will be eternal, like the priesthood of Jesus upon which it is based. Verse 12 argued that a change of priesthood involves a change of law; since "law" and "covenant" are used correlatively, a new covenant is likewise instituted.

7, 25: **To make intercession:** the intercession of the exalted Jesus, not the sequel to his completed sacrifice but its eternal presence in heaven; cf Rom 8, 34.

7, 26–28: Jesus is precisely the high priest whom the human race requires, holy and sinless, installed far above humanity (26); one having no need to offer sacrifice daily for sins but making a single offering of himself (27) once for all. The law could only appoint high priests with human limitations, but the fulfillment of God's oath regarding the priesthood of Melchizedek (Ps 110, 4) makes the Son of God the perfect priest forever (28).

7, 26: This verse with its list of attributes is reminiscent of v 3 and is perhaps a hymnic counterpart to it, contrasting the exalted Jesus with Melchizedek.

7, 27: Such daily sacrifice is nowhere mentioned in the Mosaic law; only on the Day of Atonement is it prescribed that the high priest must **offer sacrifice . . . for his own sins and then for those of the people** (Lv 16, 11–19). **Once for all:** this translates the Greek words **ephapax/hapax** that occur eleven times in Heb.

8, 1–6: The Christian community has in Jesus the kind of high priest described in 7, 26–28. In virtue of his ascension Jesus has taken his place at God's right hand in accordance with Ps 110, 1 (1), where he presides over the heavenly sanctuary established by God himself (2). Like every high priest, he has his offering to make (3; cf 9, 12.14), but it differs from

that of the levitical priesthood in which he had no share (4) and which was in any case but a shadowy reflection of the true offering in the heavenly sanctuary (5). But Jesus' ministry in the heavenly sanctuary is that of mediator of a superior covenant that accomplishes what it signifies (6).

8, 2: **The sanctuary:** the Greek term could also mean "holy things" but bears the meaning "sanctuary" elsewhere in Heb (9, 8.12.24.25; 10, 19; 13, 11). **The true tabernacle:** the heavenly tabernacle **that the Lord . . . set up** is contrasted with the earthly tabernacle that Moses set up in the desert. **True** means "real" in contradistinction to a mere "copy and shadow" (5); compare the Johannine usage (e.g., Jn 1, 9; 6, 32; 15, 1). The idea that the earthly sanctuary is a reflection of a heavenly model may be based upon Ex 25, 9, but probably also derives from the Platonic concept of a real world of which our observable world is merely a shadow.

8, 7–13: Since the first covenant was deficient in accomplishing what it signified, it had to be replaced (7), as Jeremiah (31, 31–34) had prophesied (8–12). Even in the time of Jeremiah, the first covenant was antiquated (13). In 7, 22–24, the superiority of the new covenant was seen in the permanence of its priesthood; here the superiority is based on better promises, made explicit in the citation of Jer 31 (LXX: 38), 31–34, namely, in the immediacy of the people's knowledge of God (11) and in the forgiveness of sin (12).

w: 8, 6-10; 9, 15-20; 10, 29; 12, 24; 13, 20.   *x:* 5, 6; 13, 8.
y: Rom 8, 34; 1 Jn 2, 1; Rv 1, 18.   *z:* 4, 14.15.   *a:* 5, 3; 9, 12.25-28; 10, 11-14; Ex 29, 38-39; Lv 16, 6.11.15-17; Nm 28, 3-4; Is 53, 10; Rom 6, 10.   *b:* 5, 1.2.9.   *c:* 1, 3; 4, 14; 7, 26-28.   *d:* 9, 11; Ex 33, 7; Nm 24, 6 LXX.   *e:* 5, 1.   *f:* 7, 13.   *g:* 9, 23; Ex 25, 40; Acts 7, 44; Col 2, 17.   *h:* 7, 22; 9, 15.   *i:* Jer 31, 31-34.

"Behold, the days are coming, says the Lord,

when I will conclude a new covenant with the house of Israel and the house of Judah.

9 It will not be like the covenant I made with their fathers

the day I took them by the hand to lead them forth from the land of Egypt;

for they did not stand by my covenant and I ignored them, says the Lord.

10 jBut this is the covenant I will establish with the house of Israel

after those days, says the Lord:

I will put my laws in their minds and I will write them upon their hearts.

I will be their God,

and they shall be my people.

11 And they shall not teach, each one his fellow citizen

and kinsman, saying, 'Know the Lord,'

for all shall know me,

from least to greatest.

12 For I will forgive their evildoing and remember their sins no more."

13k*When he speaks of a "new" covenant, he declares the first one obsolete. And what has become obsolete and has grown old is close to disappearing.

CHAPTER 9

The Worship of the First Covenant.

See RG 500

1*Now [even] the first covenant had regulations for worship and an earthly sanctuary. 2l*For a tabernacle was constructed, the outer one, in which were the lampstand, the table, and the bread of offering; this is called the Holy Place. 3m*Behind the second veil was the tabernacle called the Holy of Holies, 4n*in which were the gold altar of incense and the ark of the covenant entirely covered with gold. In it were the gold jar containing the manna, the staff of Aaron that had sprouted, and the tablets of the covenant. 5o*Above it were the cherubim of glory overshadowing the place of expiation. Now is not the time to speak of these in detail.

6p*With these arrangements for worship, the priests, in performing their service, go into the outer tabernacle repeatedly, 7q*but the high priest alone goes into the inner one once a year, not without blood that he offers

8, 8–12: In citing Jer the author follows the Septuagint; some apparent departures from it may be the result of a different Septuagintal text rather than changes deliberately introduced.

8, 13: Close to disappearing: from the prophet's perspective, not that of the author of Heb.

9, 1–10: The regulations for worship under the old covenant permitted all the priests to enter the Holy Place (2, 6), but only the high priest to enter the Holy of Holies and then only once a year (3–5.7). The description of the sanctuary and its furnishings is taken essentially from Ex 25–26. This exclusion of the people from the Holy of Holies signified that they were not allowed to stand in God's presence (8) because their offerings and sacrifices, which were merely symbols of their need of spiritual renewal (10), could not obtain forgiveness of sins (9).

9, 2: The outer one: the author speaks of the outer tabernacle (6) and the inner one (7) rather than of one Mosaic tabernacle divided into two parts or sections.

9, 3: The second veil: what is meant is the veil that divided the Holy Place from the Holy of Holies. It is here called the second, because there was another veil at the entrance to the Holy Place, or "outer tabernacle" (Ex 26, 36).

9, 4: The gold altar of incense: Ex 30, 6 locates this altar in the Holy Place, i.e., the first tabernacle, rather than in the Holy of Holies. Neither is there any Old Testament support for the assertion that the jar of manna and the staff of Aaron were in the ark of the covenant. For the tablets of the

covenant, see Ex 25, 16.

9, 5: The place of expiation: the gold "mercy seat" (Greek hilastērion, as in Rom 3, 25), where the blood of the sacrificial animals was sprinkled on the Day of Atonement (Lv 16, 14–15). This rite achieved "expiation" or atonement for the sins of the preceding year.

9, 6: In performing their service: the priestly services that had to be performed regularly in the Holy Place or outer tabernacle included burning incense on the incense altar twice each day (Ex 30, 7), replacing the loaves on the table of the bread of offering once each week (Lv 24, 8), and constantly caring for the lamps on the lampstand (Ex 27, 21).

9, 7: Not without blood: blood was essential to Old Testament sacrifice because it was believed that life was located in the blood. Hence blood was especially sacred, and its outpouring functioned as a meaningful symbol of cleansing from sin and reconciliation with God. Unlike Heb, the Old Testament never says that the blood is "offered." The author is perhaps retrojecting into his description of Mosaic ritual a concept that belongs to the New Testament antitype, as Paul does when he speaks of the Israelites' passage through the sea as a "baptism" (1 Cor 10, 2).

j: 10, 16-17.   k: Rom 10, 4.   l: Ex 25, 23-30.   m: Ex 26, 31-34.   n: Ex 16, 32-34; 25, 10.16.21; 30, 1-10; Lv 16, 12-13; Nm 17, 2-7.16-26.   o: Ex 25, 16-22; 26, 34; Lv 16, 14-15.   p: Ex 27, 21; 30, 7; Lv 24, 8.   q: Ex 30, 10; Lv 16, 1-14.

for himself and for the sins of the people. [8]In this way the holy Spirit shows that the way into the sanctuary had not yet been revealed while the outer tabernacle still had its place. [9]*This is a symbol of the present time, in which gifts and sacrifices are offered that cannot perfect the worshiper in conscience [10r]but only in matters of food and drink and various ritual washings: regulations concerning the flesh, imposed until the time of the new order.

Sacrifice of Jesus. [11s]*But when Christ came as high priest of the good things that have come to be, passing through the greater and more perfect tabernacle not made by hands, that is, not belonging to this creation, [12t]he entered once for all into the sanctuary, not with the blood of goats and calves but with his own blood, thus obtaining eternal redemption. [13u]*For if the blood of goats and bulls and the sprinkling of a heifer's ashes can sanctify those who are defiled so that their flesh is cleansed, [14v]*how much more

will the blood of Christ, who through the eternal spirit offered himself unblemished to God, cleanse our consciences from dead works to worship the living God.

[15w]*For this reason he is mediator of a new covenant: since a death has taken place for deliverance from transgressions under the first covenant, those who are called may receive the promised eternal inheritance. [16]*Now where there is a will, the death of the testator must be established. [17]For a will takes effect only at death; it has no force while the testator is alive. [18]Thus not even the first covenant was inaugurated without blood. [19x]*When every commandment had been proclaimed by Moses to all the people according to the law, he took the blood of calves [and goats], together with water and crimson wool and hyssop, and sprinkled both the book itself and all the people, [20y]saying, "This is 'the blood of the covenant which God has enjoined upon you.' " [21z]*In the same way, he sprinkled also the taberna-

9, 9: **The present time:** this expression is equivalent to the "present age," used in contradistinction to the "age to come."

9, 11–14: Christ, the high priest of the spiritual blessings foreshadowed in the Old Testament sanctuary, has actually entered the true sanctuary of heaven that is not of human making (11). His place there is permanent, and his offering is his own blood that won eternal redemption (12). If the sacrifice of animals could bestow legal purification (13), how much more effective is the blood of the sinless, divine Christ who spontaneously offered himself to purge the human race of sin and render it fit for the service of God (14).

9, 11: **The good things that have come to be:** the majority of later manuscripts here read "the good things to come"; cf 10, 1.

9, 13: **A heifer's ashes:** ashes from a red heifer that had been burned were mixed with water and used for the cleansing of those who had become ritually defiled by touching a corpse; see Nm 19, 9.14–21.

9, 14: **Through the eternal spirit:** this expression does not refer either to the holy Spirit or to the divine nature of Jesus but to the life of the risen Christ, "a life that cannot be destroyed" (7, 16).

9, 15–22: Jesus' role as **mediator of a new covenant** is based upon his sacrificial **death** (cf 8, 6). His death has effected **deliverance from transgressions,** i.e., deliverance from sins committed under the old covenant, which the Mosaic sacrifices were incapable of effacing. Until this happened, the **eternal inheritance** promised by God could not be obtained (15). This effect of his work follows the human pattern by which a last will and testament becomes effective only with the death of the testator (16–17). The Mosaic covenant was also associated with death, for Moses made use of

blood to seal the pact between God and the people (18–21). In Old Testament tradition, guilt could normally not be remitted without the use of blood (22; cf Lv 17, 11).

9, 16–17: **A will . . . death of the testator:** the same Greek word **diathēkē,** meaning "covenant" in vv 15 and 18, is used here with the meaning **will.** The new covenant, unlike the old, is at the same time a will that requires the **death of the testator.** Jesus as eternal Son is the one who established the new covenant together with his Father, author of both covenants; at the same time he is the testator whose death puts his **will** into effect.

9, 19–20: A number of details here are different from the description of this covenant rite in Ex 24, 5–8. Exodus mentions only calves ("young bulls," NAB), not goats (but this addition in Heb is of doubtful authenticity), says nothing of the use of **water and crimson wool and hyssop** (these features probably came from a different rite; cf Lv 14, 3–7; Nm 19, 6–18), and describes Moses as splashing blood on the altar, whereas Heb says he sprinkled it on the book (but both book and altar are meant to symbolize the agreement of God). The words of Moses are also slightly different from those in Exodus and are closer to the words of Jesus at the Last Supper in Mk 14, 24 // Mt 26, 28.

9, 21: According to Ex, the tabernacle did not yet exist at the time of the covenant rite. Moreover, nothing is said of sprinkling it with blood at its subsequent dedication (Ex 40, 9–11).

r: 13, 9; Lv 11; 14, 8; Nm 19, 11-21; Col 2, 16. s: 4, 14; 10, 1.20. t: 7, 27; Mt 26, 28. u: 10, 4; Lv 16, 6-16; Nm, 19, 9.14-21. v: 10, 10; Rom 5, 9; 1 Tm 3, 9; Ti 2, 14; 1 Pt 1, 18-19; 1 Jn 1, 7; Rv 1, 5. w: 1 Tm 2, 5. x: 12-13. y: Ex 24, 3-8; Mt 26, 28; Mk 14, 24. z: Ex 40, 9; Lv 8, 15.19.

cle and all the vessels of worship with blood. ²²ᵃ*According to the law almost everything is purified by blood, and without the shedding of blood there is no forgiveness.

²³ᵇ*Therefore, it was necessary for the copies of the heavenly things to be purified by these rites, but the heavenly things themselves by better sacrifices than these. ²⁴ᶜFor Christ did not enter into a sanctuary made by hands, a copy of the true one, but heaven itself, that he might now appear before God on our behalf. ²⁵Not that he might offer himself repeatedly, as the high priest enters each year into the sanctuary with blood that is not his own; ²⁶ᵈ*if that were so, he would have had to suffer repeatedly from the foundation of the world. But now once for all he has appeared at the end of the ages to take away sin by his sacrifice. ²⁷ᵉJust as it is appointed that human beings die once, and after this the judgment, ²⁸ᶠ*so also Christ, offered once to take away the sins of many, will appear a second time, not to take away sin but to bring salvation to those who eagerly await him.

CHAPTER 10

One Sacrifice instead of Many.

See RG 500

¹ᵍ*Since the law has only a shadow of the good things to come, and not the very image of them, it can never make perfect those who come to worship by the same sacrifices that they offer continually each year. ²Otherwise, would not the sacrifices have ceased to be offered, since the worshipers, once cleansed, would no longer have had any consciousness of sins? ³ʰBut in those sacrifices there is only a yearly remembrance of sins, ⁴ⁱfor it is impossible that the blood of bulls and goats take away sins. ⁵ʲ*For this reason, when he came into the world, he said:

"Sacrifice and offering you did not desire,
 but a body you prepared for me;

9, 22: Without the shedding of blood there is no forgiveness: in fact, ancient Israel did envisage other means of obtaining forgiveness; the Old Testament mentions contrition of heart (Ps 51, 19), fasting (Jl 2, 12), and almsgiving (Sir 3, 29). The author is limiting his horizon to the sacrificial cult, which did always involve the shedding of blood for its expiatory and unitive value.

9, 23–28: Since the blood of animals became a cleansing symbol among Old Testament prefigurements, it was necessary that the realities foreshadowed be brought into being by a shedding of blood that was infinitely more effective by reason of its worth (23). Christ did not simply prefigure the heavenly realities (24) by performing an annual sacrifice with a blood not his own (25); he offered the single sacrifice of himself as the final annulment of sin (26). Just as death is the unrepeatable act that ends a person's life, so Christ's offering of himself for all is the unrepeatable sacrifice that has once for all achieved redemption (27–28).

9, 26: At the end of the ages: the use of expressions such as this shows that the author of Heb, despite his interest in the Platonic concept of an eternal world above superior to temporal reality here below, nevertheless still clings to the Jewish Christian eschatology with its sequence of "the present age" and "the age to come."

9, 28: To take away the sins of many: the reference is to Is 53, 12. Since the Greek verb **anapherō** can mean both "to take away" and "to bear," the author no doubt intended to play upon both senses: Jesus took away sin by bearing it himself. See the similar wordplay in Jn 1, 29. **Many** is used in the Semitic meaning of "all" in the inclusive sense, as in Mk 14, 24. **To those who eagerly await him:** Jesus will appear a second time at the parousia, as the high priest reappeared on the Day of Atonement, emerging from the Holy of Holies, which

he had entered **to take away sin.** This dramatic scene is described in Sir 50, 5–11.

10, 1–10: Christian faith now realizes that the Old Testament sacrifices did not effect the spiritual benefits to come but only prefigured them (1). For if the sacrifices had actually effected the forgiveness of sin, there would have been no reason for their constant repetition (2). They were rather a continual reminder of the people's sins (3). It is not reasonable to suppose that human sins could be removed by the blood of animal sacrifices (4). Christ, therefore, is here shown to understand his mission in terms of Ps 40, 6–8, cited according to the Septuagint (5–7). Jesus acknowledged that the Old Testament sacrifices did not remit the sins of the people and so, perceiving the will of God, offered his own body for this purpose (8–10).

10, 1: A shadow of the good things to come: the term **shadow** was used in 8, 5 to signify the earthly counterpart of the Platonic heavenly reality. But here it means a prefiguration of what is to come in Christ, as it is used in the Pauline literature; cf Col 2, 17.

10, 5–7: A passage from Ps 40, 7–9a is placed in the mouth of the Son at his incarnation. As usual, the author follows the Septuagint text. There is a notable difference in v 5 (Ps 40, 7b), where the Masoretic text reads "ears you have dug for me" ("ears open to obedience you gave me," NAB), but most Septuagint manuscripts have "a body you prepared for me," a reading obviously more suited to the interpretation of Heb.

---

a: Lv 17, 11. *b*: Jb 15, 15. *c*: 7, 25; Rom 8, 34; 1 Jn 2, 1-2. *d*: 7, 27; Jn 1, 29; Gal 4, 4. *e*: Gn 3, 19. *f*: 10, 10; Is 53, 12. *g*: 8, 5; Col 2, 17. *h*: Lv 16, 21; Nm 5, 15 LXX. *i*: Is 1, 11; Mi 6, 6-8. *j*: Ps 40, 7-9.

⁶ holocausts and sin offerings you took no
delight in.
⁷ Then I said, 'As is written of me in the
scroll,
Behold, I come to do your will,
O God.' "

⁸ᵏ*First he says, "Sacrifices and offerings,
holocausts and sin offerings, you neither desired nor delighted in." These are offered according to the law. ⁹ˡThen he says, "Behold, I
come to do your will." He takes away the first
to establish the second. ¹⁰ᵐBy this "will," we
have been consecrated through the offering of
the body of Jesus Christ once for all.

¹¹ⁿ*Every priest stands daily at his ministry, offering frequently those same sacrifices
that can never take away sins. ¹²ᵒBut this one
offered one sacrifice for sins, and took his
seat forever at the right hand of God; ¹³*now
he waits until his enemies are made his footstool. ¹⁴ᵖFor by one offering he has made
perfect forever those who are being consecrated. ¹⁵*The holy Spirit also testifies to us,
for after saying:

¹⁶ �q"This is the covenant I will establish
with them after those days, says
the Lord:
'I will put my laws in their hearts,
and I will write them upon their
minds,' "

¹⁷ʳ*he also says:

"Their sins and their evildoing
I will remember no more."

¹⁸Where there is forgiveness of these, there
is no longer offering for sin.

Recalling the Past. ¹⁹ˢ*Therefore, brothers, since through the blood of Jesus we
have confidence of entrance into the sanctuary ²⁰ᵗ*by the new and living way he
opened for us through the veil, that is, his

**10, 8: Sacrifices and offerings, holocausts and sin of-
ferings:** these four terms taken from the preceding passage of
Ps 40 (with the first two changed to plural forms) are probably intended as equivalents to the four principal types of Old
Testament sacrifices: peace offerings (Lv 3, here called **sacrifices**); cereal offerings (Lv 2, here called **offerings**); holo-
causts (Lv 1); and **sin offerings** (Lv 4–5). This last category
includes the guilt offerings of Lv 5, 14–26.

10, 11–18: Whereas the levitical priesthood offered daily
sacrifices that were ineffectual in remitting sin (11), Jesus offered a single sacrifice that won him a permanent place at
God's right hand. There he has only to await the final outcome of his work (12–13; cf Ps 110, 1). Thus he has brought
into being in his own person the new covenant prophesied by
Jeremiah (31, 33–34) that has rendered meaningless all other
offerings for sin (14–18).

10, 13: Until his enemies are made his footstool: Ps 110,
1 is again used; the reference here is to the period of time between the enthronement of Jesus and his second coming. The
identity of the **enemies** is not specified; cf 1 Cor 15, 25–27.

10, 15–17: The testimony of the scriptures is now invoked
to support what has just preceded. The passage cited is a portion of the new covenant prophecy of Jer 31, 31–34, which
the author previously used in 8, 8–12.

10, 17: He also says: these words are not in the Greek
text, which has only **kai**, "also," but the expression **after saying** in v 15 seems to require such a phrase to divide the Jeremiah text into two sayings. Others understand "the Lord
says" of v 16 (here rendered **says the Lord**) as outside the
quotation and consider v 16b as part of the second saying.
Two ancient versions and a number of minuscules introduce
the words "then he said" or a similar expression at the beginning of v 17.

10, 19–39: Practical consequences from these reflections
on the priesthood and the sacrifice of Christ should make it
clear that Christians may now have direct and confident access
to God through the person of Jesus (19–20), who rules God's
house as high priest (21). They should approach God with sincerity and faith, in the knowledge that through baptism their
sins have been remitted (22), reminding themselves of the hope
they expressed in Christ at that event (23). They are to encourage one another to Christian love and activity (24), not refusing, no matter what the reason, to participate in the community's assembly, especially in view of the parousia (25; cf
1 Thes 4, 13–18). If refusal to participate in the assembly indicates rejection of Christ, no sacrifice exists to obtain forgiveness for so great a sin (26); only the dreadful judgment of God
remains (27). For if violation of the Mosaic law could be punished by death, how much worse will be the punishment of
those who have turned their backs on Christ by despising his
sacrifice and disregarding the gifts of the holy Spirit (28–29).
Judgment belongs to the Lord, and he enacts it by his living
presence (30–31). There was a time when the spirit of their
community caused them to welcome and share their sufferings
(32–34). To revitalize that spirit is to share in the courage of the
Old Testament prophets (cf Is 26, 20; Hb 2, 3–4), the kind of
courage that must distinguish the faith of the Christian (35–39).

10, 20: Through the veil, that is, his flesh: the term **flesh**
is used pejoratively. As the temple veil kept people from entering the Holy of Holies (it was rent at Christ's death, Mk 15,
38), so the flesh of Jesus constituted an obstacle to approaching God.

10, 21: The house of God: this refers back to 3, 6, "we are
his house."

k: 5-6; Ps 40, 7. l: 7; Ps 40, 8; Mt 26, 39; Mk 14, 36; Lk 22, 42;
Jn 6, 38. m: 9, 12.14. n: 7, 27; Dt 10, 8; 18, 7. o: Ps 110, 1.
p: 9, 28. q: 8, 10; Jer 31, 33. r: 8, 12; Jer 31, 34. s: 3, 6; 4,
16; 6, 19-20; Eph 1, 7; 3, 12. t: Jn 14, 6 / 6, 19-20; 9, 8.11-12;
Mt 27, 51; Mk 15, 38; Lk 23, 45.

flesh, 21u*and since we have "a great priest over the house of God," 22v*let us approach with a sincere heart and in absolute trust, with our hearts sprinkled clean from an evil conscience and our bodies washed in pure water. 23wLet us hold unwaveringly to our confession that gives us hope, for he who made the promise is trustworthy. 24We must consider how to rouse one another to love and good works. 25x*We should not stay away from our assembly, as is the custom of some, but encourage one another, and this all the more as you see the day drawing near.

26y*If we sin deliberately after receiving knowledge of the truth, there no longer remains sacrifice for sins 27zbut a fearful prospect of judgment and a flaming fire that is going to consume the adversaries. 28a*Anyone who rejects the law of Moses is put to death without pity on the testimony of two or three witnesses. 29bDo you not think that a much worse punishment is due the one who has contempt for the Son of God, considers unclean the covenant-blood by which he was consecrated, and insults the spirit of grace? 30cWe know the one who said:

"Vengeance is mine; I will repay,"

and again:

"The Lord will judge his people."

31dIt is a fearful thing to fall into the hands of the living God.

32e*Remember the days past when, after you had been enlightened, you endured a great contest of suffering. 33fAt times you were publicly exposed to abuse and affliction; at other times you associated yourselves with those so treated. 34gYou even joined in the sufferings of those in prison and joyfully accepted the confiscation of your property, knowing that you had a better and lasting possession. 35hTherefore, do not throw away your confidence; it will have great recompense. 36iYou need endurance to do the will of God and receive what he has promised.

37 j*"For, after just a brief moment,
he who is to come shall come;
he shall not delay.
38 kBut my just one shall live by faith,
and if he draws back I take no pleasure
in him."

39We are not among those who draw back and perish, but among those who have faith and will possess life.

V: Examples, Discipline, Disobedience

CHAPTER 11

See RG
500

Faith of the Ancients. 1 1*Faith is the realization of what is hoped for and evidence

---

10, 22: With our hearts sprinkled clean from an evil conscience: as in 9, 13 (see the note there), the sprinkling motif refers to the Mosaic rite of cleansing from ritual impurity. This could produce only an external purification, whereas sprinkling with the blood of Christ (9, 14) cleanses the **conscience. Washed in pure water:** baptism is elsewhere referred to as a washing; cf 1 Cor 6, 11; Eph 5, 26.

10, 25: Our assembly: the liturgical **assembly** of the Christian community, probably for the celebration of the Eucharist. **The day:** this designation for the parousia also occurs in the Pauline letters, e.g., Rom 2, 16; 1 Cor 3, 13; 1 Thes 5, 2.

10, 26: If we sin deliberately: verse 29 indicates that the author is here thinking of apostasy; cf 3, 12; 6, 4–8.

10, 28: Rejects the law of Moses: evidently not any sin against the law, but idolatry. Dt 17, 2–7 prescribed capital punishment for idolaters who were convicted on the testimony of two or three witnesses.

10, 32: After you had been enlightened: "enlightenment" is an ancient metaphor for baptism (cf Eph 5, 14; Jn 9, 11), but see 6, 4 and the note there.

10, 37–38: In support of his argument, the author uses Hb

2, 3–4 in a wording almost identical with the text of the Codex Alexandrinus of the Septuagint but with the first and second lines of v 4 inverted. He introduces it with a few words from Is 26, 20: **after just a brief moment.** Note the Pauline usage of Hb 2, 4 in Rom 1, 17; Gal 3, 11.

11, 1–40: This chapter draws upon the people and events of the Old Testament to paint an inspiring portrait of religious faith, firm and unyielding in the face of any obstacles that confront it. These pages rank among the most eloquent and lofty to be found in the Bible. They expand the theme announced in 6, 12, to which the author now returns (10, 39). The material of this chapter is developed chronologically. Verses 3–7 draw upon the first nine chapters of Gn; vv 8–22,

---

u: 3, 6. v: 9, 13-14; Ez 36, 25; 1 Cor 6, 11; Ti 3, 5; 1 Pt 3, 21. w: 3, 1.6; 4, 14; 1 Cor 10, 13. x: Rom 13, 12; 1 Cor 3, 13. y: 3, 12; 6, 4-8. z: 31; 9, 27; Is 26, 11 LXX; Zep 1, 18. a: Dt 17, 6. b: 6, 6. c: Dt 32, 35.36; Rom 12, 19. d: 27; Mt 10, 28; Lk 12, 4-5. e: 6, 4. f: 1 Cor 4, 9. g: 13, 3; Mt 6, 19-20; Lk 12, 33-34. h: 4, 16. i: Lk 21, 19. j: Is 26, 20; Hb 2, 3. k: Hb 2, 4; Rom 1, 17; Gal 3, 11. l: 1, 3; 3, 14; Rom 8, 24; 2 Cor 4, 18.

of things not seen. ²Because of it the ancients were well attested. ³ᵐ*By faith we understand that the universe was ordered by the word of God, so that what is visible came into being through the invisible. ⁴ⁿ*By faith Abel offered to God a sacrifice greater than Cain's. Through this he was attested to be righteous, God bearing witness to his gifts, and through this, though dead, he still speaks. ⁵ᵒBy faith Enoch was taken up so that he should not see death, and "he was found no more because God had taken him." Before he was taken up, he was attested to have pleased God. ⁶ᵖ*But without faith it is impossible to please him, for anyone who approaches God must believe that he exists and that he rewards those who seek him. ⁷qBy faith Noah, warned about what was not yet seen, with reverence built an ark for the salvation of his household. Through this he condemned the world and inherited the righteousness that comes through faith.

⁸ʳBy faith Abraham obeyed when he was called to go out to a place that he was to receive as an inheritance; he went out, not knowing where he was to go. ⁹ˢBy faith he sojourned in the promised land as in a foreign country, dwelling in tents with Isaac and Jacob, heirs of the same promise; ¹⁰ᵗfor

he was looking forward to the city with foundations, whose architect and maker is God. ¹¹ᵘBy faith he received power to generate, even though he was past the normal age—and Sarah herself was sterile—for he thought that the one who had made the promise was trustworthy. ¹²ᵛSo it was that there came forth from one man, himself as good as dead, descendants as numerous as the stars in the sky and as countless as the sands on the seashore.

¹³ʷAll these died in faith. They did not receive what had been promised but saw it and greeted it from afar and acknowledged themselves to be strangers and aliens on earth, ¹⁴for those who speak thus show that they are seeking a homeland. ¹⁵If they had been thinking of the land from which they had come, they would have had opportunity to return. ¹⁶ˣBut now they desire a better homeland, a heavenly one. Therefore, God is not ashamed to be called their God, for he has prepared a city for them.

¹⁷ʸBy faith Abraham, when put to the test, offered up Isaac, and he who had received the promises was ready to offer his only son, ¹⁸ᶻof whom it was said, "Through Isaac descendants shall bear your name." ¹⁹ᵃ*He reasoned that God was able to raise even from

upon the period of the patriarchs; vv 23–31, upon the time of Moses; vv 32–38, upon the history of the judges, the prophets, and the Maccabean martyrs. The author gives the most extensive description of faith provided in the New Testament, though his interest does not lie in a technical, theological definition. In view of the needs of his audience he describes what authentic faith does, not what it is in itself. Through faith God guarantees the blessings to be hoped for from him, providing evidence in the gift of faith that what he promises will eventually come to pass (1). Because they accepted in faith God's guarantee of the future, the biblical personages discussed in vv 3–38 were themselves commended by God (2). Christians have even greater reason to remain firm in faith since they, unlike the Old Testament men and women of faith, have perceived the beginning of God's fulfillment of his messianic promises (39–40).

11, 1: Faith is the realization . . . evidence: the author is not attempting a precise definition. There is dispute about the meaning of the Greek words **hypostasis** and **elenchos,** here translated **realization** and **evidence,** respectively. **Hypostasis** usually means "substance," "being" (as translated in 1, 3), or "reality" (as translated in 3, 14); here it connotes something more subjective, and so **realization** has been chosen rather than "assurance" (RSV). **Elenchos,** usually "proof," is used here in an objective sense and so translated **evidence** rather than the transferred sense of "(inner) conviction" (RSV).

11, 3: By faith . . . God: this verse does not speak of the faith of the Old Testament men and women but is in the first person plural. Hence it seems out of place in the sequence of thought.

11, 4: The "Praise of the Ancestors" in Sir 44, 1—50, 21 gives a similar list of heroes. The Cain and Abel narrative in Gn 4, 1–16 does not mention Abel's faith. It says, however, that God "looked with favor on Abel and his offering" (Gn 4, 4); in view of v 6 the author probably understood God's favor to have been activated by Abel's faith. **Though dead, he still speaks:** possibly because his blood "cries out to me from the soil" (Gn 4, 10), but more probably a way of saying that the repeated story of Abel provides ongoing witness to faith.

11, 6: One must believe not only that God exists but that he is concerned about human conduct; the Old Testament defines folly as the denial of this truth; cf Ps 52, 2.

11, 19: As a symbol: Isaac's "return from death" is seen

m: Gn 1, 3; Ps 33, 6; Wis 9, 1; Jn 1, 3.   n: 12, 24; Gn 4, 4.10.   o: Gn 5, 24; Sir 44, 16.   p: Wis 4, 10.   q: Gn 6, 8-22; Sir 44, 17-18; Mt 24, 37-39; Lk 17, 26-27;1 Pt 3, 20; 2, Pt 2, 5.   r: Gn 12, 1-4; 15, 7-21; Sir 44, 19-22; Acts 7, 2-8; Rom 4, 16-22.   s: Gn 12, 8; 13, 12; 23, 4; 26, 3; 35, 27.   t: 12, 22; 13, 14; Rv 21, 10-22.   u: Gn 17, 19; 21, 2; Rom 4, 19-21 / 1 Cor 10, 13.   v: Gn 15, 5; 22, 17; 32, 13; Ex 32, 13; Dt 10, 22; Dn 3, 36 LXX.   w: Gn 23, 4; Ps 39, 13.   x: 13, 14; Ex 3, 6.   y: Gn 22, 1-10; Sir 44, 20; 1 Mc 2, 52; Jas 2, 21.   z: Gn 21, 12 LXX; Rom 9, 7.   a: Rom 4, 16-22.

the dead, and he received Isaac back as a symbol. [20b]*By faith regarding things still to come Isaac blessed Jacob and Esau. [21c]By faith Jacob, when dying, blessed each of the sons of Joseph and "bowed in worship, leaning on the top of his staff." [22d]By faith Joseph, near the end of his life, spoke of the Exodus of the Israelites and gave instructions about his bones.

[23e]By faith Moses was hidden by his parents for three months after his birth, because they saw that he was a beautiful child, and they were not afraid of the king's edict. [24f]*By faith Moses, when he had grown up, refused to be known as the son of Pharaoh's daughter; [25]he chose to be ill-treated along with the people of God rather than enjoy the fleeting pleasure of sin. [26]He considered the reproach of the Anointed greater wealth than the treasures of Egypt, for he was looking to the recompense. [27g]By faith he left Egypt, not fearing the king's fury, for he persevered as if seeing the one who is invisible. [28h]By faith he kept the Passover and sprinkled the blood, that the Destroyer of the firstborn might not touch them. [29i]By faith they crossed the Red Sea as if it were dry land, but when the Egyptians attempted it they were drowned. [30j]By faith the walls of Jericho fell after being encircled for seven days. [31k]By faith Rahab the harlot did not perish with the disobedient, for she had received the spies in peace.

[32l]What more shall I say? I have not time to tell of Gideon, Barak, Samson, Jephthah, of David and Samuel and the prophets, [33m]who by faith conquered kingdoms, did what was righteous, obtained the promises; they closed the mouths of lions, [34n]put out raging fires, escaped the devouring sword; out of weakness they were made powerful, became strong in battle, and turned back foreign invaders. [35o]Women received back their dead through resurrection. Some were tortured and would not accept deliverance, in order to obtain a better resurrection. [36p]Others endured mockery, scourging, even chains and imprisonment. [37q]They were stoned, sawed in two, put to death at sword's point; they went about in skins of sheep or goats, needy, afflicted, tormented. [38r]The world was not worthy of them. They wandered about in deserts and on mountains, in caves and in crevices in the earth.

[39]Yet all these, though approved because of their faith, did not receive what had been promised. [40]*God had foreseen something better for us, so that without us they should not be made perfect.

CHAPTER 12

God our Father. [1]*Therefore, since we are surrounded by so great a cloud of witnesses, let us rid ourselves of every burden and sin that clings to us and persevere in running the race that lies before us [2s]while keeping our eyes fixed on Jesus, the leader and perfecter of faith. For the sake of the joy

See RG 500–501

---

as a **symbol** of Christ's resurrection. Others understand the words **en parabolē** to mean "in figure," i.e., the word **dead** is used figuratively of Isaac, since he did not really die. But in the one other place that **parabolē** occurs in Heb, it means symbol (9, 9).

11, 20–22: Each of these three patriarchs, Isaac, Jacob, and Joseph, had faith in the future fulfillment of God's promise and renewed this faith when near death.

11, 24–27: The reason given for Moses' departure from Egypt differs from the account in Ex 2, 11–15. The author also gives a christological interpretation of his decision to share the trials of his people.

11, 40: So that without us they should not be made perfect: the heroes of the Old Testament obtained their recompense only after the saving work of Christ had been accomplished. Thus they already enjoy what Christians who are still struggling do not yet possess in its fullness.

12, 1–13: Christian life is to be inspired not only by the Old Testament men and women of faith (1) but above all by Jesus. As the architect of Christian faith, he had himself to endure the cross before receiving the glory of his triumph (2). Reflection on his sufferings should give his followers courage to continue the struggle, if necessary even to the shedding of blood (3–4). Christians should regard their own sufferings as the affectionate correction of the Lord, who loves them as a father loves his children.

12, 1: That clings to us: the meaning is uncertain, since the Greek word **euperistatos,** translated **cling,** occurs only here. The papyrus P[46] and one minuscule read **euperispastos,** "easily distracting," which also makes good sense.

---

b: Gn 27, 27-40.   c: Gn 27, 38-40; 47, 31 LXX; 48, 15-16.   d: Gn 50, 24-25.   e: Ex 2, 2; Acts 7, 20.   f: Ex 2, 10-15; Acts 7, 23-29.   g: Ex 2, 15; Acts 7, 29.   h: Ex 12, 21-23; Wis 18, 25; 1 Cor 10, 10.   i: Ex 14, 22-28.   j: Jos 6, 12-21.   k: Jos 2, 1-21; 6, 22-25; Jas 2, 25.   l: Jgs 4, 6-22; 6, 11—8, 32; 11, 1-12, 7.   m: Dn 6, 23.   n: Dn 3, 22-25.49-50.   o: 1 Kgs 17, 17-24; 2 Kgs 4, 18-37; 2 Mc 6, 18—7, 42.   p: 2 Chr 36, 16; Jer 20, 2; 37, 15.   q: 2 Chr 24, 21.   r: 1 Mc 2, 28-30.   s: 2, 10; Ps 110, 1; Phil 2, 6-8.

that lay before him he endured the cross, despising its shame, and has taken his seat at the right of the throne of God. *3*Consider how he endured such opposition from sinners, in order that you may not grow weary and lose heart. *4*In your struggle against sin you have not yet resisted to the point of shedding blood. *5t*You have also forgotten the exhortation addressed to you as sons:

"My son, do not disdain the discipline of the Lord
    or lose heart when reproved by him;
6 for whom the Lord loves, he disciplines;
    he scourges every son he
        acknowledges."

*7u*Endure your trials as "discipline"; God treats you as sons. For what "son" is there whom his father does not discipline? *8*If you are without discipline, in which all have shared, you are not sons but bastards. *9v*Besides this, we have had our earthly fathers to discipline us, and we respected them. Should we not [then] submit all the more to the Father of spirits and live? *10*They disciplined us for a short time as seemed right to them, but he does so for our benefit, in order that we may share his holiness. *11w*At the time, all discipline seems a cause not for joy but for pain, yet later it brings the peaceful fruit of righteousness to those who are trained by it. *12x*So strengthen your drooping hands and your weak knees. *13y*Make straight paths for your feet, that what is lame may not be dislocated but healed.

Penalties of Disobedience. *14z*Strive for peace with everyone, and for that holiness without which no one will see the Lord. *15a**See to it that no one be deprived of the grace of God, that no bitter root spring up and cause trouble, through which many may become defiled, *16b*that no one be an immoral or profane person like Esau, who sold his birthright for a single meal. *17c*For you know that later, when he wanted to inherit his father's blessing, he was rejected because he found no opportunity to change his mind, even though he sought the blessing with tears.

*18d**You have not approached that which could be touched and a blazing fire and gloomy darkness and storm *19e*and a trumpet blast and a voice speaking words such that those who heard begged that no message be further addressed to them, *20f*for they could not bear to hear the command: "If even an animal touches the mountain, it shall be stoned." *21g*Indeed, so fearful was the spectacle that Moses said, "I am terrified and trembling." *22h*No, you have approached Mount Zion and the city of the living God, the heavenly Jerusalem, and countless angels in festal gathering, *23i**and the assembly of the firstborn enrolled in heaven, and God the judge of all, and the spirits of the just made perfect, *24j**and Jesus, the mediator of

---

12, 15–17: Esau serves as an example in two ways: his **profane** attitude illustrates the danger of apostasy, and his inability to secure a blessing afterward illustrates the impossibility of repenting after falling away (see 6, 4–6).

12, 18–29: As a final appeal for adherence to Christian teaching, the two covenants, of Moses and of Christ, are compared. The Mosaic covenant, the author argues, is shown to have originated in fear of God and threats of divine punishment (18–21). The covenant in Christ gives us direct access to God (22), makes us members of the Christian community, God's children, a sanctified people (23), who have Jesus as mediator to speak for us (24). Not to heed the voice of the risen Christ is a graver sin than the rejection of the word of Moses (25–26). Though Christians fall away, God's kingdom in Christ will remain and his justice will punish those guilty of deserting it (28–29).

12, 18–24: This remarkably beautiful passage contrasts two great assemblies of people: that of the Israelites gathered at Mount Sinai for the sealing of the old covenant and the promulgation of the Mosaic law, and that of the followers of Jesus gathered at **Mount Zion, the heavenly Jerusalem,** the

assembly of the **new covenant.** This latter scene, marked by the presence of **countless angels** and of **Jesus** with his redeeming **blood,** is reminiscent of the celestial liturgies of the Book of Revelation.

12, 23: The assembly of the firstborn enrolled in heaven: this expression may refer to the angels of v 22, or to the heroes of the Old Testament (see ch 11), or to the entire assembly of the new covenant.

12, 24: Speaks more eloquently: the blood of Abel, the first human blood to be shed, is contrasted with that of Jesus. Abel's blood cried out from the earth for vengeance, but the blood of Jesus has opened the way for everyone, providing cleansing and access to God (10, 19).

t: Prv 3, 11-12 / Dt 8, 5; 1 Cor 11, 32. *u:* Prv 13, 24; Sir 30, 1. *v:* Nm 16, 22; 27, 16 LXX. *w:* 2 Cor 4, 17; Phil 1, 11; Jas 3, 18. *x:* Is 35, 3; Sir 25, 23; Jb 4, 3-4. *y:* Prv 4, 26 LXX. *z:* Rom 12, 18; 14, 19. *a:* Dt 29, 18 (17 LXX). *b:* Gn 25, 33. *c:* Gn 27, 34-38. *d:* Ex 19, 12-14; Dt 4, 11; 5, 22-23. *e:* Ex 19, 16.19; 20, 18-19. *f:* Ex 19, 12-13. *g:* Dt 9, 19. *h:* Gal 4, 26; Rv 21, 2. *i:* Lk 10, 20; Rv 5, 11. *j:* 7, 22; 8, 6; 9, 15 / 11, 4; Gn 4, 10.

a new covenant, and the sprinkled blood that speaks more eloquently than that of Abel.

[25k]See that you do not reject the one who speaks. For if they did not escape when they refused the one who warned them on earth, how much more in our case if we turn away from the one who warns from heaven. [26l]His voice shook the earth at that time, but now he has promised, "I will once more shake not only earth but heaven." [27m]That phrase, "once more," points to [the] removal of shaken, created things, so that what is unshaken may remain. [28n]Therefore, we who are receiving the unshakable kingdom should have gratitude, with which we should offer worship pleasing to God in reverence and awe. [29o]For our God is a consuming fire.

VI: Final Exhortation, Blessing, Greetings

CHAPTER 13

See RG 501

[1*]Let mutual love continue. [2p]Do not neglect hospitality, for through it some have unknowingly entertained angels. [3q]Be mindful of prisoners as if sharing their imprisonment, and of the ill-treated as of yourselves, for you also are in the body. [4r]Let marriage be honored among all and the marriage bed be kept undefiled, for God will judge the immoral and adulterers. [5s]Let your life be free from love of money but be content with what you have, for he has said, "I will never forsake you or abandon you." [6t]Thus we may say with confidence:

"The Lord is my helper,
[and] I will not be afraid.
What can anyone do to me?"

[7]Remember your leaders who spoke the word of God to you. Consider the outcome of their way of life and imitate their faith. [8u]Jesus Christ is the same yesterday, today, and forever. [9v*]Do not be carried away by all kinds of strange teaching. It is good to have our hearts strengthened by grace and not by foods, which do not benefit those who live by them. [10*]We have an altar from which those who serve the tabernacle have no right to eat. [11w]The bodies of the animals whose blood the high priest brings into the sanctuary as a sin offering are burned outside the camp. [12x]Therefore, Jesus also suffered outside the gate, to consecrate the people by his own blood. [13]Let us then go to him outside the camp, bearing the reproach that he bore. [14y]For here we have no lasting city, but we seek the one that is to come. [15z]Through him [then] let us continually offer God a sacrifice of praise, that is, the fruit of lips that confess his name. [16a]Do not neglect to do good and to share what you have; God is pleased by sacrifices of that kind.

[17*]Obey your leaders and defer to them, for they keep watch over you and will have to give an account, that they may fulfill their task with joy and not with sorrow, for that would be of no advantage to you.

[18]Pray for us, for we are confident that we have a clear conscience, wishing to act rightly in every respect. [19]I especially ask for

---

13, 1–16: After recommendations on social and moral matters (1–6), the letter turns to doctrinal issues. The fact that the original leaders are dead should not cause the recipients of this letter to lose their faith (7), for Christ still lives and he remains always the same (8). They must not rely for their personal sanctification on regulations concerning foods (9), nor should they entertain the notion that Judaism and Christianity can be intermingled (10; cf the notes on Gal 2, 11–14 and 2, 15–21). As Jesus died separated from his own people, so must the Christian community remain apart from the religious doctrines of Judaism (11–14). Christ must be the heart and center of the community (15–16).

13, 9: Strange teaching: this doctrine about **foods** probably refers to the Jewish food laws; in view of v 10, however, the author may be thinking of the Mosaic sacrificial banquets.

13, 10: We have an altar: this does not refer to the Eu-

charist, which is never clearly mentioned in Heb, but to the sacrifice of Christ.

13, 17–25: Recommending obedience to the leaders of the community, the author asks for prayers (17–19). The letter concludes with a blessing (20–21), a final request for the acceptance of its message (22), information regarding Timothy (23), and general greetings (24–25).

k: Ex 20, 19. *l:* Ex 19, 18; Jgs 5, 4-5; Ps 68, 9; Hg 2, 6. *m:* Is 66, 22; Mt 24, 35; Mk 13, 31; Lk 21, 33. *n:* Dn 7, 14.18 / Rom 1, 9. *o:* Dt 4, 24; Is 33, 14. *p:* Gn 18, 3; 19, 2-3; Jgs 6, 11-22; Tb 5, 4. *q:* Mt 25, 36. *r:* 1 Cor 5, 13; Eph 5, 5. *s:* Dt 31, 6.8; Jos 1, 5. *t:* Pss 27, 1-3; 118, 6. *u:* 1, 12; 7, 24; Rv 1, 17. *v:* Rom 14, 17; 1 Cor 8, 8; Eph 4, 14; Col 2, 16. *w:* Ex 29, 14; Lv 16, 27. *x:* Mt 21, 39; Mk 12, 8; Lk 20, 15; Jn 19, 17. *y:* 11, 10.14. *z:* Hos 14, 3. *a:* Phil 4, 18.

your prayers that I may be restored to you very soon.

20b*May the God of peace, who brought up from the dead the great shepherd of the sheep by the blood of the eternal covenant, Jesus our Lord, 21furnish you with all that is good, that you may do his will. May he carry out in you what is pleasing to him through Jesus Christ, to whom be glory forever [and ever]. Amen.

22Brothers, I ask you to bear with this message of encouragement, for I have written to you rather briefly. 23cI must let you know that our brother Timothy has been set free. If he comes soon, I shall see you together with him. 24Greetings to all your leaders and to all the holy ones. Those from Italy send you greetings. 25dGrace be with all of you.

13, 20–21: These verses constitute one of the most beautiful blessings in the New Testament. The resurrection of Jesus is presupposed throughout Heb, since it is included in the author's frequently expressed idea of his exaltation, but this is the only place where it is explicitly mentioned.

b: Is 63, 11; Zec 9, 11; Jn 10, 11; Acts 2, 24; Rom 15, 33. *c:* Acts 16, 1. *d:* Ti 3, 15.

THE CATHOLIC LETTERS

See RG
501-20

In addition to the thirteen letters attributed to Paul and the Letter to the Hebrews, the New Testament contains seven other letters. Three of these are attributed to John, two to Peter, and one each to James and Jude, all personages of the apostolic age. The term "catholic letter" first appears, with reference only to 1 John, in the writings of Apollonius of Ephesus, a second-century apologist, known only from a citation in Eusebius's *Ecclesiastical History*. Eusebius himself (A.D. 260–340) used the term to refer to all seven letters.

The reason for the term "catholic," which means "universal," was the perception that these letters, unlike those of Paul, which were directed to a particular local church, were apparently addressed more generally to the universal church. This designation is not entirely accurate, however. On the one hand, Hebrews has no specifically identified addressees, and originally this was probably true of Ephesians as well. On the other hand, 3 John is addressed to a named individual, 2 John to a specific, though unnamed, community, and 1 Peter to a number of churches that are specified as being located in Asia Minor.

While all seven of these writings begin with an epistolary formula, several of them do not appear to be real letters in the modern sense of the term. In the ancient world it was not unusual to cast an exhortation in the form of a letter for literary effect, a phenomenon comparable to the "open letter" that is sometimes used today.

With the exception of 1 Peter and 1 John, the ancient church showed reluctance to include the catholic letters in the New Testament canon. The reason for this was widespread doubt whether they had actually been written by the apostolic figures to whom they are attributed. The early Christians saw the New Testament as the depository of apostolic faith; therefore, they wished to include only the testimony of apostles. Today we distinguish more clearly between the authorship of a work and its canonicity: even though written by other, later witnesses than those whose names they bear, these writings nevertheless testify to the apostolic faith and constitute canonical scripture. By the late fourth or early fifth centuries, most objections had been overcome in both the Greek and Latin churches (though not in the Syriac), and all seven of the catholic letters have since been acknowledged as canonical.

The Letter of James

See RG
501-6

The person to whom this letter is ascribed can scarcely be one of the two members of the Twelve who bore the name James (see Mt 10, 2–3; Mk 3, 17–18; Lk 6, 14–15), for he is not identified as an apostle but only as "slave of God and of the Lord Jesus Christ" (1, 1). This designation most probably refers to the third New Testament personage named James, a relative of Jesus who is usually called "brother of the Lord" (see Mt 13, 55; Mk 6, 3). He was the leader of the Jewish Christian community in Jerusalem whom Paul acknowledged as one of the "pillars" (Gal 2, 9). In Acts he appears as the authorized spokesman for the Jewish Christian position in the early Church (Acts 12, 17; 15, 13–21). According to the Jewish historian Josephus (Antiquities 20, 9, 1 § 200–203), he was stoned to death by the Jews under the high priest Ananus II in A.D. 62.

The letter is addressed to "the twelve tribes in the dispersion." In Old Testament terminology the term "twelve tribes" designates the people of Israel; the "dispersion" or "diaspora" refers to the non-Palestinian Jews who had settled throughout the Greco-Roman world (see Jn 7, 35). Since in Christian thought the church is the new Israel, the address probably designates the Jewish Christian churches located in Palestine, Syria, and elsewhere. Or perhaps the letter is meant more generally for all Christian communities, and the "dispersion" has the symbolic meaning of exile from our true home, as it has in the address of 1 Peter (1, 1). The letter is so markedly Jewish in character that some scholars have regarded it as a Jewish document subsequently "baptized" by a few Christian insertions, but such an origin is scarcely tenable in view of the numerous contacts discernible between the Letter of James and other New Testament literature.

From the viewpoint of its literary form, James is a letter only in the most conventional sense; it has none of the characteristic features of a real letter except the address. It belongs rather to the genre of *parenesis* or exhortation and is concerned almost exclusively with ethical conduct. It therefore falls within the tradition of Jewish wisdom literature, such as can be found in the Old Testament (Proverbs, Sirach) and in the extracanonical Jewish literature (*Testaments of the Twelve Patriarchs, the Books of Enoch, the Manual of Discipline* found at Qumran). More specifically, it consists of sequences of didactic proverbs, comparable to Tob 4, 5–19, to many passages in Sirach, and to sequences of sayings in the synoptic gospels. Numerous passages in James treat of subjects that also appear in the synoptic sayings of Jesus, especially in Matthew's Sermon on the Mount, but the correspondences are too general to establish any literary dependence. James represents a type of early Christianity that emphasized sound teaching and responsible moral behavior. Ethical norms are derived not primarily from christology, as in Paul, but from a concept of salvation that involves conversion, baptism, forgiveness of sin, and expectation of judgment (1, 17; 4, 12).

Paradoxically, this very Jewish work is written in an excellent Greek style, which ranks among the best in the New Testament and appears to be the work of a trained Hellenistic writer. Those who continue to regard James of Jerusalem as its author are therefore obliged to suppose that a secretary must have put the letter into its present literary form. This assumption is not implausible in the light of ancient practice. Some regard the letter as one of the earliest writings in the New Testament and feel that its content accurately reflects what we would expect of the leader of Jewish Christianity. Moreover, they argue that the type of Jewish Christianity reflected in the letter cannot be situated historically after the fall of Jerusalem in A.D. 70.

Others, however, believe it more likely that James is a pseudonymous work of a later period. In addition to its Greek style, they observe further that (a) the prestige that the writer is assumed to enjoy points to the later legendary reputation of James; (b) the discussion of the importance of good works seems to presuppose a debate subsequent to that in Paul's own day; (c) the author does not rely upon prescriptions of the Mosaic law, as we would expect from the historical James; (d) the letter contains no allusions to James's own history and to his relationship with Jesus or to the early Christian community of Jerusalem. For these reasons, many recent interpreters assign James to the period A.D. 90–100.

The principal divisions of the Letter of James are the following:

I: Address (1, 1)

II: The Value of Trials and Temptation (1, 2–18)

III: Exhortations and Warnings (1, 19—5, 12)

IV: The Power of Prayer (5, 13–20)

I: Address

See RG
502

CHAPTER 1

1a*James, a slave of God and of the Lord Jesus Christ, to the twelve tribes in the dispersion, greetings.

II: The Value of Trials and Temptation

Perseverance in Trial. *2b**Consider it all joy, my brothers, when you encounter various trials, *3**for you know that the testing of your faith produces perseverance. *4*And let perseverance be perfect, so that you may be perfect and complete, lacking in nothing. *5c**But if any of you lacks wisdom, he should ask God who gives to all generously and ungrudgingly, and he will be given it. *6d*But he should ask in faith, not doubting, for the one who doubts is like a wave of the sea that is driven and tossed about by the wind. *7*For that person must not suppose that he will receive anything from the Lord, *8*since he is a man of two minds, unstable in all his ways.

9e*The brother in lowly circumstances should take pride in his high standing, *10f*and the rich one in his lowliness, for he will pass away "like the flower of the field." *11*For the sun comes up with its scorching heat and dries up the grass, its flower droops, and the beauty of its appearance vanishes. So will the rich person fade away in the midst of his pursuits.

Temptation. *12g**Blessed is the man who perseveres in temptation, for when he has been proved he will receive the crown of life that he promised to those who love him. *13h**No one experiencing temptation should say, "I am being tempted by God"; for God is not subject to temptation to evil, and he himself tempts no one. *14*Rather, each person is tempted when he is lured and enticed by his own desire. *15*Then desire conceives and brings forth sin, and when sin reaches maturity it gives birth to death.

16*Do not be deceived, my beloved brothers: *17**all good giving and every perfect gift is from above, coming down from the Father of lights, with whom there is no alteration or shadow caused by change. *18i**He willed to give us birth by the word of truth that we may be a kind of firstfruits of his creatures.

1, 1: James, a slave of God and of the Lord Jesus Christ: a declaration of the writer's authority for instructing the Christian communities; cf Rom 1, 1. Regarding the identity of the author, see Introduction. **Dispersion:** see Introduction.

1, 2: Consider it all joy . . . various trials: a frequent teaching of the New Testament derived from the words and sufferings of Jesus (Mt 5, 10–12; Jn 10, 11; Acts 5, 41).

1, 3–8: The sequence of testing, perseverance, and being perfect and complete indicates the manner of attaining spiritual maturity and full preparedness for the coming of Christ (5, 7–12; cf 1 Pt 1, 6–7; Rom 5, 3–5). These steps require wisdom (5).

1, 5: Wisdom: a gift that God readily grants to all who ask in faith and that sustains the Christian in times of trial. It is a kind of knowledge or understanding not accessible to the unbeliever or those who doubt, which gives the recipient an understanding of the real importance of events. In this way a Christian can deal with adversity with great calm and hope (cf 1 Cor 2, 6–12).

1, 9–11: Throughout his letter (see 2, 5; 4, 10.13–16; 5, 1–6), the author reaffirms the teaching of Jesus that worldly prosperity is not necessarily a sign of God's favor but can even be a hindrance to proper humility before God (cf Lk 6, 20–25; 12, 16–21; 16, 19–31).

1, 12: Temptation: the Greek word used here is the same one used for "trials" in v 2. The crown of life: in ancient Palestine, crowns or wreaths of flowers were worn at festive occasions as signs of joy and honor. In the Hellenistic world,

wreaths were given as a reward to great statesmen, soldiers, athletes. **Life:** here means eternal life. **He promised:** some manuscripts read "God" or "the Lord," while the best witnesses do not specify the subject of "promised."

1, 13–15: It is contrary to what we know of God for God to be the author of human temptation (13). In the commission of a sinful act, one is first beguiled by passion (14), then consent is given, which in turn causes the sinful act. When sin permeates the entire person, it incurs the ultimate penalty of death (15).

1, 16–18: The author here stresses that God is the source of all good and of good alone, and the evil of temptation does not come from him.

1, 17: All good giving and every perfect gift may be a proverb written in hexameter. **Father of lights:** God is here called the Father of the heavenly luminaries, i.e., the stars, sun, and moon that he created (Gn 1, 14–18). Unlike orbs moving from nadir to zenith, he never changes or diminishes in brightness.

1, 18: Acceptance of the gospel message, **the word of truth,** constitutes new birth (Jn 3, 5–6) and makes the recipient the **firstfruits** (i.e., the cultic offering of the earliest grains, symbolizing the beginning of an abundant harvest) of a new creation; cf 1 Cor 15, 20; Rom 8, 23.

a: Jn 7, 35; 1 Pt 1, 1. *b:* Rom 5, 3-5; 1 Pt 1, 6; 4, 13-16. *c:* Prv 2, 2-6; Wis 9, 4.9-12. *d:* Mt 7, 7; Mk 11, 24. *e:* 2, 5. *f:* Is 40, 6-7. *g:* 1 Cor 9, 25; 2 Tm 4, 8; 1 Pt 5, 4; Rv 2, 10. *h:* Sir 15, 11-20; 1 Cor 10, 13. *i:* Jn 1, 12-13; 1 Pt 1, 23.

III: Exhortations and Warnings

Doers of the Word. [19] [j]*Know this, my dear brothers: everyone should be quick to hear, slow to speak, slow to wrath, [20] [k]for the wrath of a man does not accomplish the righteousness of God. [21] [l]Therefore, put away all filth and evil excess and humbly welcome the word that has been planted in you and is able to save your souls.

[22] [m]Be doers of the word and not hearers only, deluding yourselves. [23]For if anyone is a hearer of the word and not a doer, he is like a man who looks at his own face in a mirror. [24]He sees himself, then goes off and promptly forgets what he looked like. [25] [n]*But the one who peers into the perfect law of freedom and perseveres, and is not a hearer who forgets but a doer who acts, such a one shall be blessed in what he does.

[26] [o]*If anyone thinks he is religious and does not bridle his tongue but deceives his heart, his religion is vain. [27] [p]*Religion that is pure and undefiled before God and the Father is this: to care for orphans and widows in their affliction and to keep oneself unstained by the world.

CHAPTER 2

See RG
502-3

Sin of Partiality. [1]*My brothers, show no partiality as you adhere to the faith in our glorious Lord Jesus Christ. [2]For if a man with gold rings on his fingers and in fine clothes comes into your assembly, and a poor person in shabby clothes also comes in, [3]and you pay attention to the one wearing the fine clothes and say, "Sit here, please," while you say to the poor one, "Stand there," or "Sit at my feet," [4]*have you not made distinctions among yourselves and become judges with evil designs?

[5] [q]*Listen, my beloved brothers. Did not God choose those who are poor in the world to be rich in faith and heirs of the kingdom that he promised to those who love him? [6]But you dishonored the poor person. Are not the rich oppressing you? And do they themselves not haul you off to court? [7] [r]Is it not they who blaspheme the noble name that was invoked over you? [8] [s]*However, if you fulfill the royal law according to the scripture, "You shall love your neighbor as yourself," you are doing well. [9] [t]But if you show partiality, you commit sin, and are convicted by the law as transgressors. [10] [u]For whoever keeps the whole law, but falls short in one particular, has become guilty in respect to all of it. [11] [v]For he who said, "You shall not commit adultery," also said, "You shall not kill." Even if you do not commit adultery but kill, you have become a transgressor of the law. [12] [w]*So speak and so act as people who will be judged by the

---

1, 19–25: To **be quick to hear** the gospel is to accept it readily and to act in conformity with it, removing from one's soul whatever is opposed to it, so that it may take root and effect salvation (19–21). To listen to the gospel message but not practice it is failure to improve oneself (22–24). Only conformity of life to the perfect law of true freedom brings happiness (25).

1, 25: Peers into the perfect law: the image of a person doing this is paralleled to that of hearing God's word. The **perfect law** applies the Old Testament description of the Mosaic law to the gospel of Jesus Christ that brings freedom.

1, 26–27: A practical application of v 22 is now made.

1, 26: For control of the tongue, see the note on 3, 1–12.

1, 27: In the Old Testament, orphans and widows are classical examples of the defenseless and oppressed.

2, 1–13: In the Christian community there must be no discrimination or favoritism based on status or wealth (2–4; cf Mt 5, 3; 11, 5; 23, 6; 1 Cor 1, 27–29). Divine favor rather consists in God's election and promises (5). The rich who oppress the poor blaspheme the name of Christ (6–7). By violating one law of love of neighbor, they offend against the whole law (8–11). On the other hand, conscious awareness of the final judgment helps the faithful to fulfill the whole law (12).

2, 4: When Christians show favoritism to the rich they are guilty of the worst kind of prejudice and discrimination. The author says that such Christians set themselves up as judges who judge not by divine law but by the basest, self-serving motives.

2, 5: The poor, "God's poor" of the Old Testament, were seen by Jesus as particularly open to God for belief in and reliance on him alone (Lk 6, 20). God's law cannot tolerate their oppression in any way (9).

2, 8: Royal: literally, "kingly"; because the Mosaic law came from God, the universal king. There may be an allusion to Jesus' uses of this commandment in his preaching of the kingdom of God (Mt 22, 39; Mk 12, 31; Lk 10, 27).

2, 12–13: The law upon which the last judgment will be based is the law of freedom. As Jesus taught, mercy (which participates in God's own loving mercy) includes forgiveness of those who wrong us (see Mt 6, 12.14–15).

j: Prv 14, 17; Sir 5, 11. *k:* Eph 4, 26. *l:* Col 3, 8. *m:* Mt 7, 26; Rom 2, 13. *n:* 2, 12; Ps 19, 8; Rom 8, 2. *o:* 3, 2; Ps 34, 14. *p:* Ex 22, 21. *q:* 1 Cor 1, 26-28; Rv 2, 9. *r:* 1 Pt 4, 4. *s:* Lv 19, 18; Mt 22, 39; Rom 13, 9. *t:* Dt 1, 17. *u:* Gal 3, 10. *v:* Ex 20, 13-14; Dt 5, 17-18. *w:* 1, 25; Rom 8, 2.

law of freedom. [13x]For the judgment is merciless to one who has not shown mercy; mercy triumphs over judgment.

Faith and Works. [14y]*What good is it, my brothers, if someone says he has faith but does not have works? Can that faith save him? [15]If a brother or sister has nothing to wear and has no food for the day, [16z]and one of you says to them, "Go in peace, keep warm, and eat well," but you do not give them the necessities of the body, what good is it? [17]So also faith of itself, if it does not have works, is dead.

[18]Indeed someone may say, "You have faith and I have works." Demonstrate your faith to me without works, and I will demonstrate my faith to you from my works. [19]You believe that God is one. You do well. Even the demons believe that and tremble. [20]Do you want proof, you ignoramus, that faith without works is useless? [21a]Was not Abraham our father justified by works when he offered his son Isaac upon the altar? [22]You see that faith was active along with his works, and faith was completed by the works. [23b]Thus the scripture was fulfilled that says, "Abraham believed God, and it was credited to him as righteousness," and he was called "the friend of God." [24]See how a person is justified by works and not by faith alone. [25c]And in the same way, was not Rahab the harlot also justified by works when she welcomed the messengers and sent them out by a different route? [26]For just as a body without a spirit is dead, so also faith without works is dead.

CHAPTER 3

See RG 503–4

Power of the Tongue. [1]*Not many of you should become teachers, my brothers, for you realize that we will be judged more strictly, [2d]for we all fall short in many respects. If anyone does not fall short in speech, he is a perfect man, able to bridle his whole body also. [3]If we put bits into the mouths of horses to make them obey us, we also guide their whole bodies. [4]It is the same with ships: even though they are so large and driven by fierce winds, they are steered by a very small rudder wherever the pilot's inclination wishes. [5]In the same way the tongue is a small member and yet has great pretensions.

Consider how small a fire can set a huge forest ablaze. [6]The tongue is also a fire. It exists among our members as a world of malice, defiling the whole body and setting the entire course of our lives on fire, itself set on fire by Gehenna. [7]For every kind of beast and bird, of reptile and sea creature, can be tamed and has been tamed by the human species, [8e]but no human being can tame the tongue. It is a restless evil, full of deadly poison. [9]With it we bless the Lord and Father, and with it we curse human beings who are made in the likeness of God. [10]From the same mouth come blessing and cursing. This need not be so, my brothers. [11]Does a spring gush forth from the same opening both pure and brackish water? [12f]Can a fig tree, my brothers, produce olives, or a grapevine figs? Neither can salt water yield fresh.

True Wisdom. [13g]*Who among you is wise and understanding? Let him show his works by a good life in the humility that comes from wisdom. [14]But if you have bitter jealousy and selfish ambition in your hearts, do not boast and be false to the truth. [15]Wisdom of this kind does not come down from above but is earthly, unspiritual, demonic. [16]For where

---

2, 14–26: The theme of these verses is the relationship of faith and works (deeds). It has been argued that the teaching here contradicts that of Paul (see especially Rom 4, 5–6). The problem can only be understood if the different viewpoints of the two authors are seen. Paul argues against those who claim to participate in God's salvation because of their good deeds as well as because they have committed themselves to trust in God through Jesus Christ (Paul's concept of faith). Paul certainly understands, however, the implications of true faith for a life of love and generosity (see Gal 5, 6.13–15). The author of James is well aware that proper conduct can only come about with an authentic commitment to God in faith (18.26). Many think he was seeking to correct a misunderstanding of Paul's view.

3, 1–12: The use and abuse of the important role of teaching in the church (1) are here related to the good and bad use of the tongue (9–12), the instrument through which teaching was chiefly conveyed (see Sir 5, 11—6, 1; 28, 12–26).

3, 13–18: This discussion of true wisdom is related to the previous reflection on the role of the teacher as one who is in control of his speech. The qualities of the wise man endowed from above are detailed (17–18; cf Gal 5, 22–23), in contrast to the qualities of earthbound wisdom (14–16; cf 2 Cor 12, 20).

x: Mt 5, 7; 6, 14-15; 18, 32-33. y: Mt 25, 31-46; Gal 5, 6. z: 1 Jn 3, 17. a: Gn 22, 9-12; Heb 11, 17. b: Gn 15, 6; Rom 4, 3; Gal 3, 6 / 2 Chr 20, 7; Is 41, 8. c: Jos 2, 1-21. d: 1, 26; Prv 13, 3; Sir 28, 12-26. e: Ps 140, 4. f: Mt 7, 16-17. g: Eph 4, 1-2.

jealousy and selfish ambition exist, there is disorder and every foul practice. [17h]But the wisdom from above is first of all pure, then peaceable, gentle, compliant, full of mercy and good fruits, without inconstancy or insincerity. [18i]And the fruit of righteousness is sown in peace for those who cultivate peace.

CHAPTER 4

See RG 504–5 *Causes of Division.* [1j]*Where do the wars and where do the conflicts among you come from? Is it not from your passions that make war within your members? [2]You covet but do not possess. You kill and envy but you cannot obtain; you fight and wage war. You do not possess because you do not ask. [3]You ask but do not receive, because you ask wrongly, to spend it on your passions. [4k]*Adulterers! Do you not know that to be a lover of the world means enmity with God? Therefore, whoever wants to be a lover of the world makes himself an enemy of God. [5]*Or do you suppose that the scripture speaks without meaning when it says, "The spirit that he has made to dwell in us tends toward jealousy"? [6l]*But he bestows a greater grace; therefore, it says:

"God resists the proud,
but gives grace to the humble."

[7m]So submit yourselves to God. Resist the devil, and he will flee from you. [8n]Draw near to God, and he will draw near to you. Cleanse your hands, you sinners, and purify your hearts, you of two minds. [9]Begin to lament, to mourn, to weep. Let your laughter be turned into mourning and your joy into dejection. [10o]Humble yourselves before the Lord and he will exalt you.

[11]*Do not speak evil of one another, brothers. Whoever speaks evil of a brother or judges his brother speaks evil of the law and judges the law. If you judge the law, you are not a doer of the law but a judge. [12p]There is one lawgiver and judge who is able to save or to destroy. Who then are you to judge your neighbor?

Warning against Presumption. [13]*Come now, you who say, "Today or tomorrow we shall go into such and such a town, spend a year there doing business, and make a profit"— [14q]*you have no idea what your life will be like tomorrow. You are a puff of smoke that appears briefly and then disappears. [15]*Instead you should say, "If the Lord wills it, we shall live to do this or that." [16]But

---

4, 1–12: The concern here is with the origin of conflicts in the Christian community. These are occasioned by love **of the world,** which **means enmity with God** (4). Further, the conflicts are bound up with failure to pray properly (cf Mt 7, 7–11; Jn 14, 13; 15, 7; 16, 23), that is, not asking God at all or using God's kindness only for one's pleasure (2–3). In contrast, the proper dispositions are submission to God, repentance, humility, and resistance to evil (7–10).

4, 1: Passions: the Greek word here (literally, "pleasures") does not indicate that pleasure is evil. Rather, as the text points out (2–3), it is the manner in which one deals with needs and desires that determines good or bad. The motivation for any action can be wrong, especially if one does not pray properly but seeks only selfish enjoyment (3).

4, 4: Adulterers: a common biblical image for the covenant between God and his people is the marriage bond. In this image, breaking the covenant with God is likened to the unfaithfulness of adultery.

4, 5: The meaning of this saying is difficult because the author of Jas cites, probably from memory, a passage that is not in any extant manuscript of the Bible. Other translations of the text with a completely different meaning are possible: "The Spirit that he (God) made to dwell in us yearns (for us) jealously," or, "He (God) yearns jealously for the spirit that he has made to dwell in us." If this last translation is correct, the author perhaps had in mind an apocryphal religious text that

echoes the idea that God is zealous for his creatures; cf Ex 20, 5; Dt 4, 24; Zec 8, 2.

4, 6: The point of this whole argument is that God wants the happiness of all, but that selfishness and pride can make that impossible. We must work with him in humility (10).

4, 11: Slander of a fellow Christian does not break just one commandment but makes mockery of the authority of law in general and therefore of God.

4, 13–17: The uncertainty of life (14), its complete dependence on God, and the necessity of submitting to God's will (15) all help one know and do what is right (17). To disregard this is to live in pride and arrogance (16); failure to do what is right is a sin (17).

4, 14: Some important Greek manuscripts here have, "You who have no idea what tomorrow will bring. Why, what is your life?"

4, 15: If the Lord wills it: often in piety referred to as the **"conditio Jacobaea,"** the condition James says we should employ to qualify all our plans.

---

h: 1, 17; Wis 7, 22-23. *i:* Mt 5, 9. *j:* Rom 7, 23; 1 Pt 2, 11. *k:* Mt 6, 24; Lk 16, 13; Rom 8, 7; 1 Jn 2, 15-16. *l:* Jb 22, 29; Prv 3, 34; Mt 23, 12; 1 Pt 5, 5. *m:* 1 Pt 5, 8-9. *n:* Zec 1, 3; Mal 3, 7. *o:* Jb 5, 11; Mt 23, 12; Lk 14, 11; 18, 14; 1 Pt 5, 6. *p:* Mt 7, 1; Rom 2, 1; 14, 4. *q:* Prv 27, 1 / Ps 39, 6-7.

now you are boasting in your arrogance. All such boasting is evil. [17r*]So for one who knows the right thing to do and does not do it, it is a sin.

See RG 505–6

CHAPTER 5

Warning to the Rich. [1s*]Come now, you rich, weep and wail over your impending miseries. [2t]Your wealth has rotted away, your clothes have become moth-eaten, [3u]your gold and silver have corroded, and that corrosion will be a testimony against you; it will devour your flesh like a fire. You have stored up treasure for the last days. [4v]Behold, the wages you withheld from the workers who harvested your fields are crying aloud, and the cries of the harvesters have reached the ears of the Lord of hosts. [5w]You have lived on earth in luxury and pleasure; you have fattened your hearts for the day of slaughter. [6x*]You have condemned; you have murdered the righteous one; he offers you no resistance.

Patience and Oaths. [7*]Be patient, therefore, brothers, until the coming of the Lord. See how the farmer waits for the precious fruit of the earth, being patient with it until it receives the early and the late rains. [8y]You too must be patient. Make your hearts firm, because the coming of the Lord is at hand. [9]Do not complain, brothers, about one another, that you may not be judged. Behold, the Judge is standing before the gates. [10]Take as an example of hardship and patience, brothers, the prophets who spoke in the name of the Lord. [11]Indeed we call blessed those who have persevered. You have heard of the perseverance of Job, and you have seen the purpose of the Lord, because "the Lord is compassionate and merciful."

[12a*]But above all, my brothers, do not swear, either by heaven or by earth or with any other oath, but let your "Yes" mean "Yes" and your "No" mean "No," that you may not incur condemnation.

IV: The Power of Prayer

Anointing of the Sick. [13]Is anyone among you suffering? He should pray. Is anyone in good spirits? He should sing praise. [14b*]Is anyone among you sick? He should summon the presbyters of the church, and they should pray over him and anoint [him] with oil in the name of the Lord, [15*]and the prayer of faith will save the sick person, and the Lord will raise him up. If he has committed any sins, he will be forgiven.

Confession and Intercession. [16]Therefore, confess your sins to one another and pray for one another, that you may be healed. The fervent prayer of a righteous person is very

---

4, 17: It is a sin: those who live arrogantly, forgetting the contingency of life and our dependence on God (13–16), are guilty of sin.

5, 1–6: Continuing with the theme of the transitory character of life on earth, the author points out the impending ruin of the godless. He denounces the unjust rich, whose victims cry to heaven for judgment on their exploiters (4–6). The decay and corrosion of the costly garments and metals, which symbolize wealth, prove them worthless and portend the destruction of their possessors (2–3).

5, 6: The author does not have in mind any specific crime in his readers' communities but rather echoes the Old Testament theme of the harsh oppression of the righteous poor (see Prv 1, 11; Wis 2, 10.12.20).

5, 7–11: Those oppressed by the unjust rich are reminded of the need for patience, both in bearing the sufferings of human life (9) and in their expectation of the coming of the Lord. It is then that they will receive their reward (7–8.10–11; cf Heb 10, 25; 1 Jn 2, 18).

5, 7: The early and the late rains: an expression related to the agricultural season in ancient Palestine (see Dt 11, 14; Jer 5, 24; Jl 2, 23).

5, 12: This is the threat of condemnation for the abuse of

swearing oaths (cf Mt 5, 33–37). **By heaven or by earth:** these words were substitutes for the original form of an oath, to circumvent its binding force and to avoid pronouncing the holy name of God (see Ex 22, 10).

5, 14: In case of sickness a Christian should ask for the presbyters of the church, i.e., those who have authority in the church (cf Acts 15, 2.22–23; 1 Tm 5, 17; Ti 1, 5). They are to pray over the person and anoint with oil; oil was used for medicinal purposes in the ancient world (see Is 1, 6; Lk 10, 34). In Mk 6, 13, the Twelve anoint the sick with oil on their missionary journey. **In the name of the Lord:** by the power of Jesus Christ.

5, 15: The results of the prayer and anointing are physical health and forgiveness of sins. The Roman Catholic Church (Council of Trent, Session 14) declared that this anointing of the sick is a sacrament "instituted by Christ and promulgated by blessed James the apostle."

r: Lk 12, 47.   *s:* Lk 6, 24.   *t:* Mt 6, 19.   *u:* Ps 21, 10; Prv 11, 4; Jdt 16, 17.   *v:* Lv 19, 13; Dt 24, 14-15; Mal 3, 5.   *w:* Jer 12, 3; Lk 16, 19-25.   *x:* Wis 2, 10-20.   *y:* Lk 21, 19; Heb 10, 36 / Heb 10, 25; 1 Pt 4, 7.   *z:* Ex 34, 6; Ps 103, 8.   *a:* Mt 5, 34-37.   *b:* Mk 6, 13.

powerful. [17c]Elijah was a human being like us; yet he prayed earnestly that it might not rain, and for three years and six months it did not rain upon the land. [18d]Then he prayed again, and the sky gave rain and the earth produced its fruit.

Conversion of Sinners. [19e]My brothers, if anyone among you should stray from the truth and someone bring him back, [20f]*he should know that whoever brings back a sinner from the error of his way will save his soul from death and will cover a multitude of sins.

5, 20: When a Christian is instrumental in the conversion of a sinner, the result is forgiveness of sins and a reinstatement of the sinner to the life of grace.

---

c: 1 Kgs 17, 1; Lk 4, 25.   *d:* 1 Kgs 18, 45.   *e:* Mt 18, 15; Gal 6, 1.   *f:* Prv 10, 12; 1 Pt 4, 8.

See RG
506–10

The First Letter of Peter

This letter begins with an address by Peter to Christian communities located in five provinces of Asia Minor (1, 1), including areas evangelized by Paul (Acts 16, 6–7; 18, 23). Christians there are encouraged to remain faithful to their standards of belief and conduct in spite of threats of persecution. Numerous allusions in the letter suggest that the churches addressed were largely of Gentile composition (1, 14.18; 2, 9–10; 4, 3–4), though considerable use is made of the Old Testament (1, 24; 2, 6–7, 9–10.22; 3, 10–12).

The contents following the address both inspire and admonish these "chosen sojourners" (1, 1) who, in seeking to live as God's people, feel an alienation from their previous religious roots and the society around them. Appeal is made to Christ's resurrection and the future hope it provides (1, 3–5) and to the experience of baptism as new birth (1, 3.23–25; 3, 21). The suffering and death of Christ serve as both source of salvation and example (1, 19; 2, 21–25; 3, 18). What Christians are in Christ, as a people who have received mercy and are to proclaim and live according to God's call (2, 9–10), is repeatedly spelled out for all sorts of situations in society (2, 11–17), work (even as slaves, 2, 18–20), the home (3, 1–7), and general conduct (3, 8–12; 4, 1–11). But over all hangs the possibility of suffering as a Christian (3, 13–17). In 4, 12–19 persecution is described as already occurring, so that some have supposed the letter was addressed both to places where such a "trial by fire" was already present and to places where it might break out.

The letter constantly mingles moral exhortation (*paraklēsis*) with its catechetical summaries of mercies in Christ. Encouragement to fidelity in spite of suffering is based upon a vision of the meaning of Christian existence. The emphasis on baptism and allusions to various features of the baptismal liturgy suggest that the author has incorporated into his exposition numerous homiletic, credal, hymnic, and sacramental elements of the baptismal rite that had become traditional at an early date.

From Irenaeus in the late second century until modern times, Christian tradition regarded Peter the apostle as author of this document. Since he was martyred at Rome during the persecution of Nero between A.D. 64 and 67, it was supposed that the letter was written from Rome shortly before his death. This is supported by its reference to "Babylon" (5, 13), a code name for Rome in the early church.

Some modern scholars, however, on the basis of a number of features that they consider incompatible with Petrine authenticity, regard the letter as the work of a later Christian writer. Such features include the cultivated Greek in which it is written, difficult to attribute to a Galilean fisherman, together with its use of the Greek Septuagint translation when citing the Old Testament; the similarity in both thought and expression to the Pauline literature; and the allusions to widespread persecution of Christians, which did not occur until at least the reign of Domitian (A.D. 81–96). In this view the letter would date from the end of the first century or even the beginning of the second, when there is evidence for persecution of Christians in Asia Minor (the letter of Pliny the Younger to Trajan, A.D. 111–12).

Other scholars believe, however, that these objections can be met by appeal to use of a secretary, Silvanus, mentioned in 5, 12. Such secretaries often gave literary expression to the author's thoughts in their own style and language. The persecutions may refer to local harassment rather than to systematic repression by the state. Hence there is nothing in the document incompatible with Petrine authorship in the 60s.

Still other scholars take a middle position. The many literary contacts with the Pauline literature, James, and 1 John suggest a common fund of traditional formulations rather than direct dependence upon Paul. Such liturgical and catechetical traditions must have been very ancient and in some cases of Palestinian origin.

Yet it is unlikely that Peter addressed a letter to the Gentile churches of Asia Minor while Paul was still alive. This suggests a period after the death of the two apostles, perhaps A.D. 70–90. The author would be a disciple of Peter in Rome, representing a Petrine group that served as a bridge between the Palestinian origins of Christianity and its flowering in the Gentile world. The problem addressed would not be official persecution but the difficulty of living the Christian life in a hostile, secular environment that espoused different values and subjected the Christian minority to ridicule and oppression.

The principal divisions of the First Letter of Peter are the following:

I: Address (1, 1–2)
II: The Gift and Call of God in Baptism (1, 3—2, 10)
III: The Christian in a Hostile World (2, 11—4, 11)
IV: Advice to the Persecuted (4, 12—5, 11)
V: Conclusion (5, 12–14)

I: Address

CHAPTER 1

See RG 507–8

Greeting. *1a**Peter, an apostle of Jesus Christ, to the chosen sojourners of the dispersion in Pontus, Galatia, Cappadocia, Asia, and Bithynia, *2b*in the foreknowledge of God the Father, through sanctification by the Spirit, for obedience and sprinkling with the blood of Jesus Christ: may grace and peace be yours in abundance.

II: The Gift and Call of God in Baptism

Blessing. *3c**Blessed be the God and Father of our Lord Jesus Christ, who in his great mercy gave us a new birth to a living hope through the resurrection of Jesus Christ from the dead, *4d*to an inheritance that is imperishable, undefiled, and unfading, kept in heaven for you *5*who by the power of God are safeguarded through faith, to a salvation that is ready to be revealed in the final time. *6e**In this you rejoice, although now for a little while you may have to suffer through various trials, *7f*so that the genuineness of your faith, more precious than gold that is perishable even though tested by fire, may prove to be for praise, glory, and honor at the revelation of Jesus Christ. *8g*Although you have not seen him you love him; even though you do not see him now yet believe in him, you rejoice with an indescribable and glorious joy, *9*as you attain the goal of [your] faith, the salvation of your souls.

10*Concerning this salvation, prophets

1, 1–2: The introductory formula names **Peter** as the writer (but see Introduction). In his comments to the presbyters (5, 1), the author calls himself a "fellow presbyter." He addresses himself to the Gentile converts of Asia Minor. Their privileged status as a **chosen** and sanctified people makes them worthy of God's **grace** and **peace**. In contrast is their actual existence as aliens and **sojourners,** scattered among pagans, far from their true country.

1, 1: Dispersion: literally, diaspora; see Jas 1, 1 and Introduction to that letter. **Pontus . . . Bithynia:** five provinces in Asia Minor, listed in clockwise order from the north, perhaps in the sequence in which a messenger might deliver the letter.

1, 3–5: A prayer of praise and thanksgiving to God who bestows the gift of new life and hope in baptism (**new birth,** 3) **through the resurrection of Jesus Christ from the dead.** The new birth is a sign of an **imperishable inheritance** (4),

of **salvation** that is still in the future (**to be revealed in the final time,** 5).

1, 6–9: As the glory of Christ's resurrection was preceded by his sufferings and death, the new life of faith that it bestows is to be subjected to many **trials** (6) while achieving its goal: the glory of the fullness of **salvation** (9) at the coming of Christ (7).

1, 10–12: The **Spirit of Christ** (11) is here shown to have been present in the prophets, moving them to search, investigate, and prophesy about the **grace** of **salvation** that was to come (10), and in the apostles impelling them to preach the fulfillment of salvation in the message of Christ's sufferings and glory (12).

---

a: Jas 1, 1. *b:* Rom 8, 29. *c:* Ti 3, 5. *d:* Mt 6, 19-20. *e:* Jas 1, 2-3. *f:* 1 Cor 3, 13. *g:* 2 Cor 5, 6-7.

who prophesied about the grace that was to be yours searched and investigated it, [11h]investigating the time and circumstances that the Spirit of Christ within them indicated when it testified in advance to the sufferings destined for Christ and the glories to follow them. [12]It was revealed to them that they were serving not themselves but you with regard to the things that have now been announced to you by those who preached the good news to you [through] the holy Spirit sent from heaven, things into which angels longed to look.

Obedience. [13*]Therefore, gird up the loins of your mind, live soberly, and set your hopes completely on the grace to be brought to you at the revelation of Jesus Christ. [14*]Like obedient children, do not act in compliance with the desires of your former ignorance [15i]but, as he who called you is holy, be holy yourselves in every aspect of your conduct, [16j]for it is written, "Be holy because I [am] holy."

Reverence. [17k]Now if you invoke as Father him who judges impartially according to each one's works, conduct yourselves with reverence during the time of your sojourning, [18l]realizing that you were ransomed from your futile conduct, handed on by your ancestors, not with perishable things like silver or gold [19m*]but with the precious blood of Christ as of a spotless unblemished lamb. [20]He was known before the foundation of the world but revealed in the final time for you, [21]who through him believe in God who raised him from the dead and gave him glory, so that your faith and hope are in God.

Mutual Love. [22n*]Since you have purified yourselves by obedience to the truth for sincere mutual love, love one another intensely from a [pure] heart. [23o*]You have been born anew, not from perishable but from imperishable seed, through the living and abiding word of God, [24p]for:

"All flesh is like grass,
  and all its glory like the flower of the field;
the grass withers,
  and the flower wilts;
[25] but the word of the Lord remains forever."

This is the word that has been proclaimed to you.

CHAPTER 2

See RG 508-9

God's House and People. [1q*]Rid yourselves of all malice and all deceit, insincerity, envy, and all slander; [2]like newborn infants, long for pure spiritual milk so that through it you may grow into salvation, [3r*]for you have tasted that the Lord is good. [4s*]Come to him, a living stone, rejected by human beings but chosen and precious in the sight of God, [5t*]and, like living stones, let yourselves be built into a spiritual house to be a holy priesthood to offer spiritual sacri-

1, 13–25: These verses are concerned with the call of God's people to holiness and to mutual love by reason of their redemption through the blood of Christ (18–21).

1, 13: Gird up the loins of your mind: a figure reminiscent of the rite of Passover when the Israelites were in flight from their oppressors (Ex 12, 11), and also suggesting the vigilance of the Christian people in expectation of the parousia of Christ (Lk 12, 35).

1, 14–16: The ignorance here referred to (14) was their former lack of knowledge of God, leading inevitably to godless conduct. Holiness (15–16), on the contrary, is the result of their call to the knowledge and love of God.

1, 19: Christians have received the redemption prophesied by Isaiah (52, 3), through the blood (Jewish symbol of life) of the spotless lamb (Is 53, 7.10; Jn 1, 29; Rom 3, 24–25; cf 1 Cor 6, 20).

1, 22–25: The new birth of Christians (23) derives from Christ, the imperishable seed or sowing that produces a new and lasting existence in those who accept the gospel (24–25), with the consequent duty of loving one another (22).

1, 23: The living and abiding word of God: or, "the word of the living and abiding God."

2, 1–3: Growth toward salvation is seen here as two steps: first, stripping away all that is contrary to the new life in Christ; second, the nourishment (pure spiritual milk) that the newly baptized have received.

2, 3: Tasted that the Lord is good: cf Ps 34, 9.

2, 4–8: Christ is the cornerstone (cf Is 28, 16) that is the foundation of the spiritual edifice of the Christian community (5). To unbelievers, Christ is an obstacle and a stumbling block on which they are destined to fall (8); cf Rom 11, 11.

2, 5: Let yourselves be built: the form of the Greek word could also be indicative passive, "you are being built" (cf 9).

h: Is 52, 13—53, 12; Dn 9, 24. i: Mt 5, 48; 1 Jn 3, 3. j: Lv 11, 44; 19, 2. k: 2, 11. l: Is 52, 3; 1 Cor 6, 20. m: Ex 12, 5; Jn 1, 29; Heb 9, 14. n: Rom 12, 10. o: 1 Jn 3, 9. p: Is 40, 6-8. q: Jas 1, 21. r: Ps 34, 9. s: Ps 118, 22; Mt 21, 42; Acts 4, 11. t: Eph 2, 21-22.

fices acceptable to God through Jesus Christ. [6u]For it says in scripture:

"Behold, I am laying a stone in Zion,
a cornerstone, chosen and precious,
and whoever believes in it shall not be
put to shame."

[7v]Therefore, its value is for you who have faith, but for those without faith:

"The stone which the builders rejected
has become the cornerstone,"

[8w]and

"A stone that will make people
stumble,
and a rock that will make them fall."

They stumble by disobeying the word, as is their destiny. [9x*]But you are "a chosen race, a royal priesthood, a holy nation, a people of his own, so that you may announce the praises" of him who called you out of darkness into his wonderful light.

[10 y]Once you were "no people"
but now you are God's people;
you "had not received mercy"
but now you have received mercy.

III: The Christian in a Hostile World

Christian Examples. [11z*]Beloved, I urge you as aliens and sojourners to keep away from worldly desires that wage war against the soul. [12]Maintain good conduct among the Gentiles, so that if they speak of you as evildoers, they may observe your good works and glorify God on the day of visitation.

Christian Citizens. [13a*]Be subject to every human institution for the Lord's sake, whether it be to the king as supreme [14]or to governors as sent by him for the punishment of evildoers and the approval of those who do good. [15]For it is the will of God that by doing good you may silence the ignorance of foolish people. [16b]Be free, yet without using freedom as a pretext for evil, but as slaves of God. [17c]Give honor to all, love the community, fear God, honor the king.

Christian Slaves. [18d*]Slaves, be subject to your masters with all reverence, not only to those who are good and equitable but also to those who are perverse. [19]For whenever anyone bears the pain of unjust suffering because of consciousness of God, that is a grace. [20]But

2, 9–10: The prerogatives of ancient Israel mentioned here are now more fully and fittingly applied to the Christian people: "a chosen race" (cf Is 43, 20–21) indicates their divine election (Eph 1, 4–6); "a royal priesthood" (cf Ex 19, 6) to serve and worship God in Christ, thus continuing the priestly functions of his life, passion, and resurrection; "a holy nation" (Ex 19, 6) reserved for God, a people he claims for his own (cf Mal 3, 17) in virtue of their baptism into his death and resurrection. This transcends all natural and national divisions and unites the people into one community to glorify the one who led them from the darkness of paganism to the light of faith in Christ. From being "no people" deprived of all mercy, they have become the very people of God, the chosen recipients of his mercy (cf Hos 1, 9; 2, 25).

2, 11–3, 12: After explaining the doctrinal basis for the Christian community, the author makes practical applications in terms of the virtues that should prevail in all the social relationships of the members of the community: good example to Gentile neighbors (2, 11–12); respect for human authority (2, 13–17); obedience, patience, and endurance of hardship in domestic relations (2, 18–25); Christian behavior of husbands and wives (3, 1–7); mutual charity (3, 8–12).

2, 11: Aliens and sojourners: no longer signifying absence from one's native land (Gn 23, 4), this image denotes

rather their estrangement from the world during their earthly pilgrimage (see also 1, 1.17).

2, 13–17: True Christian freedom is the result of being servants of God (16; see the note on 2, 18–23). It includes reverence for God, esteem for every individual, and committed love for fellow Christians (17). Although persecution may threaten, subjection to human government is urged (13.17) and concern for the impact of Christians' conduct on those who are not Christians (12.15).

2, 18–21: Most of the labor in the commercial cities of first-century Asia Minor was performed by a working class of slaves. The sense of freedom contained in the gospel undoubtedly caused great tension among Christian slaves: witness the special advice given concerning them here and in 1 Cor 7, 21–24; Eph 6, 5–8; Col 3, 22–25; Phlm. The point made here does not have so much to do with the institution of slavery, which the author does not challenge, but with the nonviolent reaction (20) of slaves to unjust treatment. Their patient suffering is compared to that of Jesus (21), which won righteousness for all humanity.

u: Is 28, 16. v: Ps 118, 22; Mt 21, 42; Lk 20, 17; Acts 4, 11. w: Is 8, 14; Rom 9, 33. x: Ex 19, 6; Is 61, 6; Rv 1, 6; 20, 6. y: Hos 1, 9; 2, 25 / Hos 1, 6. z: Gal 5, 24. a: Rom 13, 1-7. b: Gal 5, 13. c: Prv 24, 21; Mt 22, 21. d: Eph 6, 5.

what credit is there if you are patient when beaten for doing wrong? But if you are patient when you suffer for doing what is good, this is a grace before God. [21e]*For to this you have been called, because Christ also suffered for you, leaving you an example that you should follow in his footsteps.

[22] [f]*"He committed no sin,
    and no deceit was found in his mouth."

[23g]When he was insulted, he returned no insult; when he suffered, he did not threaten; instead, he handed himself over to the one who judges justly. [24h]He himself bore our sins in his body upon the cross, so that, free from sin, we might live for righteousness. By his wounds you have been healed. [25i]*For you had gone astray like sheep, but you have now returned to the shepherd and guardian of your souls.

CHAPTER 3

See RG 508-9

Christian Spouses. [1]*Likewise, you wives should be subordinate to your husbands so that, even if some disobey the word, they may be won over without a word by their wives' conduct [2j]when they observe your reverent and chaste behavior. [3k]Your adornment should not be an external one: braiding the hair, wearing gold jewelry, or dressing in fine clothes, [4]but rather the hidden character of the heart, expressed in the imperishable beauty of a gentle and calm

disposition, which is precious in the sight of God. [5]For this is also how the holy women who hoped in God once used to adorn themselves and were subordinate to their husbands; [6]thus Sarah obeyed Abraham, calling him "lord." You are her children when you do what is good and fear no intimidation.

[7l]*Likewise, you husbands should live with your wives in understanding, showing honor to the weaker female sex, since we are joint heirs of the gift of life, so that your prayers may not be hindered.

Christian Conduct. [8]*Finally, all of you, be of one mind, sympathetic, loving toward one another, compassionate, humble. [9m]Do not return evil for evil, or insult for insult; but, on the contrary, a blessing, because to this you were called, that you might inherit a blessing. [10n]For:

"Whoever would love life
    and see good days
must keep the tongue from evil
    and the lips from speaking deceit,
[11] must turn from evil and do good,
    seek peace and follow after it.
[12] For the eyes of the Lord are on the
    righteous
    and his ears turned to their prayer,
but the face of the Lord is against
    evildoers."

Christian Suffering. [13]*Now who is going to harm you if you are enthusiastic for what

---

2, 21: Suffered: some ancient manuscripts and versions read "died" (cf 3, 18).

2, 22–25: After the quotation of Is 53, 9b, the passage describes Jesus' passion with phrases concerning the Suffering Servant from Is 53, 4–12, perhaps as employed in an early Christian confession of faith; cf 1, 18–21 and 3, 18–22.

2, 25: The shepherd and guardian of your souls: the familiar shepherd and flock figures express the care, vigilance, and love of God for his people in the Old Testament (Ps 23; Is 40, 11; Jer 23, 4–5; Ez 34, 11–16) and of Jesus for all humanity in the New Testament (Mt 18, 10–14; Lk 15, 4–7; Jn 10, 1–16; Heb 13, 20).

3, 1–6: The typical marital virtues of women of the ancient world, obedience, reverence, and chastity (1–2), are outlined here by the author, who gives them an entirely new motivation: Christian wives are to be virtuous so that they may be instrumental in the conversion of their husbands. In imitation of **holy women** in the past (5) they are to cultivate the interior life (4) instead of excessive concern with their appearance (3).

3, 7: Husbands who do not respect their wives will have as little success in prayer as those who, according to Paul, have

no love: their prayers will be "a resounding gong or a clashing cymbal" (1 Cor 13, 1). Consideration for others is shown as a prerequisite for effective prayer also in Mt 5, 23–24; 1 Cor 11, 20–22; Jas 4, 3. After all, whatever the social position of women in the world and in the family, they are equal recipients of the gift of God's salvation. Paul is very clear on this point, too (see 1 Cor 11, 11–12; Gal 3, 28).

3, 8–12: For the proper ordering of Christian life in its various aspects as described in 2, 11—3, 9, there is promised the blessing expressed in Ps 34, 13–17. In the Old Testament this refers to longevity and prosperity; here, it also refers to eternal life.

3, 13–22: This exposition, centering on v 17, runs as follows: by his suffering and death Christ the righteous one saved the unrighteous (18); by his resurrection he received new life in the spirit, which he communicates to believers

e: Mt 16, 24. *f:* Is 53, 9. *g:* Mt 5, 39. *h:* Is 53, 4.12 / Is 53, 5. *i:* Is 53, 6. *j:* 1 Cor 7, 12-16; Eph 5, 22-24; Col 3, 18; 1 Tm 2, 9-15. *k:* 1 Tm 2, 9-10. *l:* Eph 5, 25-33; Col 3, 19. *m:* Mt 5, 44; Lk 6, 28; Rom 12, 14. *n:* Ps 34, 13-17.

is good? *14*But even if you should suffer because of righteousness, blessed are you. Do not be afraid or terrified with fear of them, *15o*but sanctify Christ as Lord in your hearts. Always be ready to give an explanation to anyone who asks you for a reason for your hope, *16*but do it with gentleness and reverence, keeping your conscience clear, so that, when you are maligned, those who defame your good conduct in Christ may themselves be put to shame. *17*For it is better to suffer for doing good, if that be the will of God, than for doing evil.

*18 p*For Christ also suffered for sins once, the righteous for the sake of the unrighteous, that he might lead you to God. Put to death in the flesh, he was brought to life in the spirit. *19*In it he also went to preach to the spirits in prison, *20q*who had once been disobedient while God patiently waited in the days of Noah during the building of the ark, in which a few persons, eight in all, were saved through water. *21r*This prefigured baptism, which saves you now. It is not a removal of dirt from the body but an appeal to God for a clear conscience, through the resurrection of Jesus Christ, *22s*who has gone into heaven and is at the right hand of God, with angels, authorities, and powers subject to him.

CHAPTER 4

See RG 509-10

Christian Restraint. *1*Therefore, since Christ suffered in the flesh, arm yourselves also with the same attitude (for whoever suffers in the flesh has broken with sin), *2*so as not to spend what remains of one's life in the flesh on human desires, but on the will of God. *3t*For the time that has passed is sufficient for doing what the Gentiles like to do: living in debauchery, evil desires, drunkenness, orgies, carousing, and wanton idolatry. *4*They are surprised that you do not plunge into the same swamp of profligacy, and they vilify you; *5u*but they will give an account to him who stands ready to judge the living and the dead. *6*For this is why the gospel was preached even to the dead that, though condemned in the flesh in human estimation, they might live in the spirit in the estimation of God.

Christian Charity. *7*The end of all things is at hand. Therefore, be serious and sober for prayers. *8v*Above all, let your love for one another be intense, because love covers a multitude of sins. *9w*Be hospitable to one another without complaining. *10x*As each one has received a gift, use it to serve one another as good stewards of God's varied grace. *11y*Whoever preaches, let it be with the words of God; whoever serves, let it be

through the baptismal bath that cleanses their consciences from sin. As Noah's family was saved **through water,** so Christians are saved through the waters of baptism (19–22). Hence they need not share the fear of sinners; they should rather rejoice in suffering because of their hope in Christ. Thus their innocence disappoints their accusers (13–16; cf Mt 10, 28; Rom 8, 35–39).

3, 18: Suffered: very many ancient manuscripts and versions read "died." **Put to death in the flesh:** affirms that Jesus truly died as a human being. **Brought to life in the spirit:** that is, in the new and transformed existence freed from the limitations and weaknesses of natural human life (cf 1 Cor 15, 45).

3, 19: The spirits in prison: it is not clear just who these spirits are. They may be the spirits of the sinners who died in the flood, or angelic powers, hostile to God, who have been overcome by Christ (cf 22; Gn 6, 4; Enoch 6–36, especially 21, 6; 2 Enoch 7, 1–5).

3, 21: Appeal to God: this could also be translated "pledge," that is, a promise on the part of Christians to live with a good conscience before God, or a pledge from God of forgiveness and therefore a good conscience for us.

4, 1–6: Willingness to suffer with Christ equips the Christian with the power to conquer sin (1). Christ is here por-

trayed as the judge to whom those guilty of pagan vices must render an account (5; cf Jn 5, 22–27; Acts 10, 42; 2 Tm 4, 1).

4, 6: The dead: these may be the sinners of the flood generation who are possibly referred to in 3, 19. But many scholars think that there is no connection between these two verses, and that **the dead** here are Christians who have died since hearing the preaching of the gospel.

4, 7–11: The inner life of the eschatological community is outlined as **the end** (the parousia of Christ) and the judgment draws near in terms of seriousness, sobriety, prayer, and love expressed through hospitality and the use of one's gifts for the glory of God and of Christ.

4, 8: Love covers a multitude of sins: a maxim based on Prv 10, 12; see also Ps 32, 1; Jas 5, 20.

4, 11: Some scholars feel that this doxology concludes the part of the homily addressed specifically to the newly baptized, begun in 1, 3; others that it concludes a baptismal liturgy. Such doxologies do occur within a New Testament letter, e.g., Rom 9, 5. Some propose that v 11 was an alternate

o: Is 8, 12. p: 1 Cor 15, 45. q: Gn 7, 7.17; 2 Pt 2, 5. r: Eph 5, 26; Heb 10, 22. s: Eph 1, 20-21. t: Eph 2, 2-3; 4, 17-19; Col 3, 7; Ti 3, 3. u: Acts 10, 42; 2 Tm 4, 1. v: Prv 10, 12; Jas 5, 20. w: Heb 13, 2. x: Rom 12, 6-8; 1 Cor 12, 4-11. y: 1 Cor 10, 31.

with the strength that God supplies, so that in all things God may be glorified through Jesus Christ, to whom belong glory and dominion forever and ever. Amen.

IV: Advice to the Persecuted

Trial of Persecution. ^{12z}*Beloved, do not be surprised that a trial by fire is occurring among you, as if something strange were happening to you. ^{13a}But rejoice to the extent that you share in the sufferings of Christ, so that when his glory is revealed you may also rejoice exultantly. ^{14b}If you are insulted for the name of Christ, blessed are you, for the Spirit of glory and of God rests upon you. ¹⁵But let no one among you be made to suffer as a murderer, a thief, an evildoer, or as an intriguer. ¹⁶But whoever is made to suffer as a Christian should not be ashamed but glorify God because of the name. ^{17c}For it is time for the judgment to begin with the household of God; if it begins with us, how will it end for those who fail to obey the gospel of God?

^{18 d}"And if the righteous one is barely saved,
    where will the godless and the sinner appear?"

¹⁹As a result, those who suffer in accord with God's will hand their souls over to a faithful creator as they do good.

See RG
509–10

CHAPTER 5

Advice to Presbyters. ¹*So I exhort the presbyters among you, as a fellow presbyter and witness to the sufferings of Christ and one who has a share in the glory to be revealed. ^{2e}Tend the flock of God in your midst, [overseeing] not by constraint but willingly, as God would have it, not for shameful profit but eagerly. ³Do not lord it over those assigned to you, but be examples to the flock. ^{4f}*And when the chief Shepherd is revealed, you will receive the unfading crown of glory.

Advice to the Community. ^{5g}*Likewise, you younger members, be subject to the presbyters. And all of you, clothe yourselves with humility in your dealings with one another, for:

"God opposes the proud
    but bestows favor on the humble."

^{6h}So humble yourselves under the mighty hand of God, that he may exalt you in due time. ⁷ⁱCast all your worries upon him because he cares for you.

^{8j}Be sober and vigilant. Your opponent the devil is prowling around like a roaring lion looking for [someone] to devour. ⁹Resist him, steadfast in faith, knowing that your fellow believers throughout the world undergo the same sufferings. ^{10k}The God of all grace who called you to his eternal glory through Christ [Jesus] will himself restore, confirm, strengthen, and establish you after you have suffered a little. ¹¹To him be dominion forever. Amen.

---

ending, with 4, 12—5, 14 being read in places where persecution was more pressing. But such doxologies usually do not occur at the end of letters (the only examples are 2 Pt 3, 18, Jude 25, and Rom 16, 27, the last probably a liturgical insertion).

4, 12–19: The suffering to which the author has already frequently referred is presented in more severe terms. This has led some scholars to see these verses as referring to an actual persecution. Others see the heightening of the language as only a rhetorical device used at the end of the letter to emphasize the suffering motif.

5, 1–4: In imitation of Christ, the chief shepherd, those entrusted with a pastoral office are to tend the flock by their care and example.

5, 1: Presbyters: the officially appointed leaders and teachers of the Christian community (cf 1 Tm 5, 17–18; Ti 1, 5–8; Jas 5, 14).

5, 4: See the note on 2, 25.

5, 5–11: The community is to be subject to the presbyters and to show humility toward one another and trust in God's love and care (5–7). With sobriety, alertness, and steadfast faith they must resist the evil one; their sufferings are shared with Christians everywhere (8–9). They will be strengthened and called to eternal glory (10–11).

5, 5: Younger members: this may be a designation for office-holders of lesser rank.

---

z: 1, 6-7; 3, 14.17.   *a:* Rom 5, 3-5; 8, 17; 2 Tm 2, 12.   *b:* Acts 5, 41 / Is 11, 2.   *c:* Lk 23, 31; 2 Thes 1, 8.   *d:* Prv 11, 31 LXX. *e:* Acts 20, 28; Ti 1, 7.   *f:* Wis 5, 15-16; 1 Cor 9, 25; 2 Tm 4, 8; Jas 1, 12.   *g:* Prv 3, 34.   *h:* Jb 22, 29; Jas 4, 10.   *i:* Ps 55, 23; Mt 6, 25-33; Lk 12, 22-31; Phil 4, 6.   *j:* 1 Thes 5, 6.   *k:* Rom 8, 18; 2 Cor 4, 17.

V: Conclusion

^{12*}I write you this briefly through Silvanus, whom I consider a faithful brother, exhorting you and testifying that this is the true grace of God. Remain firm in it. ^{13*}The chosen one at Babylon sends you greeting, as does Mark, my son. ^{14l}Greet one another with a loving kiss. Peace to all of you who are in Christ.

5, 12: Silvanus: the companion of Paul (see 2 Cor 1, 19; 1 Thes 1, 1; 2 Thes 1, 1). Jews and Jewish Christians, like Paul, often had a Hebrew name (Saoul, Silas) and a Greek or Latin name (Paul, Silvanus). On Silvanus's possible role as amanuensis, see Introduction.
5, 13: The chosen one: feminine, referring to the Christian community (**ekklēsia**) at **Babylon,** the code name for Rome in Rv 14, 8; 17, 5; 18, 2. **Mark, my son:** traditionally

a prominent disciple of Peter and co-worker at the church in Rome, perhaps the John Mark referred to in Acts 12, 12.25; 13, 5.13; and in 15, 37–39, a companion of Barnabas. Perhaps this is the same Mark mentioned as Barnabas's cousin in Col 4, 10, a co-worker with Paul in Phlm 24 (see also 2 Tm 4, 11).

l: Rom 16, 16; 1 Cor 16, 20; 2 Cor 13, 12.

See RG 510–13

The Second Letter of Peter

This letter can be appreciated both for its positive teachings and for its earnest warnings. It seeks to strengthen readers in faith (1, 1), hope for the future (3, 1–10), knowledge (1, 2.6.8), love (1, 7), and other virtues (1, 5–6). This aim is carried out especially by warning against false teachers, the condemnation of whom occupies the long central section of the letter (2, 1–22). A particular crisis is the claim by "scoffers" that there will be no second coming of Jesus, a doctrine that the author vigorously affirms (3, 1–10). The concept of God's "promises" is particularly precious in the theology of 2 Peter (1, 4; 3, 4.9.13). Closing comments at 3, 17–18 well sum up the twin concerns: that you not "be led into" error and "fall" but instead "grow in grace" and "knowledge" of Jesus Christ.

Second Peter is clearly structured in its presentation of these points. It reminds its readers of the divine authenticity of Christ's teaching (1, 3–4), continues with reflections on Christian conduct (1, 5–15), then returns to the exalted dignity of Jesus by incorporating into the text the apostolic witness to his transfiguration (1, 16–18). It takes up the question of the interpretation of scripture by pointing out that it is possible to misunderstand the sacred writings (1, 19–21) and that divine punishment will overtake false teachers (2, 1–22). It proclaims that the parousia is the teaching of the Lord and of the apostles and is therefore an eventual certainty (3, 1–13). At the same time, it warns that the meaning of Paul's writings on this question should not be distorted (3, 14–18).

In both content and style this letter is very different from 1 Peter, which immediately precedes it in the canon. The opening verse attributes it to "Symeon Peter, a slave and apostle of Jesus Christ." Moreover, the author in 3, 1 calls his work a "second letter," referring probably to 1 Peter as his first, and in 1, 18 counts himself among those present at the transfiguration of Jesus.

Nevertheless, acceptance of 2 Peter into the New Testament canon met with great resistance in the early church. The oldest certain reference to it comes from Origen in the early third century. While he himself accepted both Petrine letters as canonical, he testifies that others rejected 2 Peter. As late as the fifth century some local churches still excluded it from the canon, but eventually it was universally adopted. The principal reason for the long delay was the persistent doubt that the letter stemmed from the apostle Peter.

Among modern scholars there is wide agreement that 2 Peter is a pseudonymous work, i.e., one written by a later author who attributed it to Peter according to a literary convention popular at the time. It gives the impression of being more remote in time from the apostolic period than 1 Peter; indeed, many think it is the latest work in the New Testament and assign it to the first or even the second quarter of the second century.

The principal reasons for this view are the following. The author refers to the apostles and "our ancestors" as belonging to a previous generation, now dead (3, 2–4). A collection of Paul's letters exists and appears to be well known, but disputes have arisen about the interpretation of them (3, 14–16). The passage about false teachers

(2, 1–18) contains a number of literary contacts with Jude 4–16, and it is generally agreed that 2 Peter depends upon Jude, not vice versa. Finally, the principal problem exercising the author is the false teaching of "scoffers" who have concluded from the delay of the parousia that the Lord is not going to return. This could scarcely have been an issue during the lifetime of Simon Peter.

The Christians to whom the letter is addressed are not identified, though it may be the intent of 3, 1 to identify them with the churches of Asia Minor to which 1 Peter was sent. Except for the epistolary greeting in 1, 1–2, 2 Peter does not have the features of a genuine letter at all, but is rather a general exhortation cast in the form of a letter. The author must have been a Jewish Christian of the dispersion for, while his Jewish heritage is evident in various features of his thought and style, he writes in the rather stilted literary Greek of the Hellenistic period. He appeals to tradition against the twin threat of doctrinal error and moral laxity, which appear to reflect an early stage of what later developed into full-blown gnosticism. Thus he forms a link between the apostolic period and the church of subsequent ages.

The principal divisions of the Second Letter of Peter are the following:

I: Address (1, 1–2)
II: Exhortation to Christian Virtue (1, 3–21)
III: Condemnation of the False Teachers (2, 1–22)
IV: The Delay of the Second Coming (3, 1–16)
V: Final Exhortation and Doxology (3, 17–18)

I: Address

CHAPTER 1

See RG 000–00

Greeting. [1]*Symeon Peter, a slave and apostle of Jesus Christ, to those who have received a faith of equal value to ours through the righteousness of our God and savior Jesus Christ: [2]*may grace and peace be yours in abundance through knowledge of God and of Jesus our Lord.

II: Exhortation to Christian Virtue

The Power of God's Promise. [3a]*His divine power has bestowed on us everything that makes for life and devotion, through the knowledge of him who called us by his own glory and power. [4b]Through these, he has bestowed on us the precious and very great promises, so that through them you may come to share in the divine nature, after escaping from the corruption that is in the world because of evil desire. [5c]*For this very reason, make every effort to supplement your faith with virtue, virtue with knowledge, [6]knowledge with self-control, self-control with endurance, endurance with devotion, [7]devotion with mutual affection, mutual affection with love. [8]If these are yours and increase in abundance, they will keep you from being idle or unfruitful in the knowledge of our Lord Jesus Christ. [9d]Anyone who lacks them is blind and shortsighted, forgetful of the cleansing of his past sins. [10]*Therefore, brothers, be all the

---

1, 1: Symeon Peter: on the authorship of 2 Peter, see Introduction; on the spelling here of the Hebrew name **Šim'ôn,** cf Acts 15, 14. The greeting is especially similar to those in 1 Peter and Jude. The words translated **our God and savior Jesus Christ** could also be rendered "our God and the savior Jesus Christ"; cf 11; 2, 20; 3, 2.18.

1, 2: Knowledge: a key term in the letter (3.8; 2, 20; 3, 18), perhaps used as a Christian emphasis against gnostic claims.

1, 3–4: Christian life in its fullness is a gift of divine power effecting a knowledge of Christ and the bestowal of divine promises (3, 4.9). **To share in the divine nature,** escaping from a corrupt world, is a thought found elsewhere in the Bible but expressed only here in such Hellenistic terms, since it is said to be accomplished through knowledge (3); cf 2; 2, 20; but see also Jn 15, 4; 17, 22–23; Rom 8, 14–17; Heb 3, 14; 1 Jn 1, 3; 3, 2.

1, 3: By his own glory and power: the most ancient papyrus and the best codex read "through glory and power."

1, 5–9: Note the climactic gradation of qualities (5–7), beginning with faith and leading to the fullness of Christian life, which is love; cf Rom 5, 3–4; Gal 5, 6.22 for a similar series of "virtues," though the program and sense here are different than in Paul. The fruit of these is knowledge of Christ (8) referred to in v 3; their absence is spiritual blindness (9).

1, 10–11: Perseverance in the Christian vocation is the best preventative against losing it and the safest provision for attaining its goal, the kingdom. **Kingdom of . . . Christ,** instead of "God," is unusual; cf Col 1, 13 and Mt 13, 41, as well as the **righteousness of . . . Christ** (1).

a: 2 Cor 4, 6; 1 Pt 2, 9. *b:* 2 Cor 7, 1; 1 Jn 2, 15. *c:* Gal 5, 22-23. *d:* 1 Jn 2, 9.11.

more eager to make your call and election firm, for, in doing so, you will never stumble. ¹¹For, in this way, entry into the eternal kingdom of our Lord and savior Jesus Christ will be richly provided for you.

Apostolic Witness. ¹²*Therefore, I will always remind you of these things, even though you already know them and are established in the truth you have. ¹³*I think it right, as long as I am in this "tent," to stir you up by a reminder, ^{14e}since I know that I will soon have to put it aside, as indeed our Lord Jesus Christ has shown me. ¹⁵I shall also make every effort to enable you always to remember these things after my departure.

^{16f}*We did not follow cleverly devised myths when we made known to you the power and coming of our Lord Jesus Christ, but we had been eyewitnesses of his majesty. ^{17g}*For he received honor and glory from God the Father when that unique declaration came to him from the majestic glory, "This is my Son, my beloved, with whom I am well pleased." ¹⁸*We ourselves heard this voice come from heaven while we were with him on the holy mountain. ^{19h}Moreover, we possess the prophetic message that is altogether reliable. You will do well to be attentive to it, as to a lamp shining in a dark place, until day dawns and the morning star rises in your hearts. ²⁰*Know this first of all, that there is no prophecy of scripture that is a matter of personal interpretation, ²¹for no prophecy ever came through human will; but rather human beings moved by the holy Spirit spoke under the influence of God.

III: Condemnation of the False Teachers

CHAPTER 2

See RG
511-12

False Teachers. ¹ⁱ*There were also false prophets among the people, just as there will be false teachers among you, who will introduce destructive heresies and even deny the Master who ransomed them, bringing swift destruction on themselves. ^{2j}Many will follow their licentious ways, and because of them the way of truth will be reviled. ^{3k}In their greed they will exploit you with fabrications, but from of old their condemnation has not been idle and their destruction does not sleep.

Lessons from the Past. ^{4l}*For if God did

1, 12–19: The purpose in writing is to call to mind the apostle's witness to the truth, even as he faces the end of his life (12–15), his eyewitness testimony to Christ (16–18), and the true prophetic message (19) through the Spirit in scripture (20–21), in contrast to what false teachers are setting forth (ch 2).

1, 13: **Tent:** a biblical image for transitory human life (Is 38, 12), here combined with a verb that suggests not folding or packing up a tent but its being discarded in death (cf 2 Cor 5, 1–4).

1, 16: **Coming:** in Greek **parousia,** used at 3, 4.12 of the second coming of Christ. The word was used in the extrabiblical writings for the visitation of someone in authority; in Greek cult and Hellenistic Judaism it was used for the manifestation of the divine presence. What the apostles **made known** has been interpreted to refer to Jesus' transfiguration (17) or to his entire first coming or to his future coming in power (ch 3).

1, 17: The author assures the readers of the reliability of the apostolic message (including Jesus' power, glory, and coming; cf the note on 1, 16) by appeal to the transfiguration of Jesus in glory (cf Mt 17, 1–8 and parallels) and by appeal to the prophetic message (19; perhaps Nm 24, 17). Here, as elsewhere, the New Testament insists on continued reminders as necessary to preserve the historical facts about Jesus and the truths of the faith; cf 3, 1–2; 1 Cor 11, 2; 15, 1–3. **My Son, my beloved:** or, "my beloved Son."

1, 18: **We:** at Jesus' transfiguration, referring to Peter, James, and John (Mt 17, 1).

1, 20–21: Often cited, along with 2 Tm 3, 16, on the "inspiration" of scripture or against private interpretation, these verses in context are directed against the false teachers of ch 2 and clever tales (16). The prophetic word in scripture comes admittedly through **human beings** (21), but **moved by the holy Spirit,** not from their own interpretation, and is a matter of what the author and Spirit intended, not the **personal interpretation** of false teachers. Instead of **under the influence of God,** some manuscripts read "holy ones of God."

2, 1–3: The pattern of **false prophets** among the Old Testament people of God will recur through **false teachers** in the church. Such destructive opinions of heretical sects bring loss of faith in Christ, contempt for the way of salvation (cf 21), and immorality.

2, 4–6: The false teachers will be punished just as surely and as severely as were the fallen **angels** (4; cf Jude 6; Gn 6, 1–4), the sinners of Noah's day (5; Gn 7, 21–23), and the inhabitants of the cities of the Plain (6; Jude 7; Gn 19, 25). Whereas there are three examples in Jude 5–7 (Exodus and wilderness; rebellious angels; Sodom and Gomorrah), 2 Peter omitted the first of these, has inserted a new illustration about Noah (5) between Jude's second and third examples, and listed the resulting three examples in their Old Testament order (Gn 6; 7; 19).

2, 4: **Chains of Tartarus:** cf Jude 6; other manuscripts in

e: Is 38, 12; Jn 21, 18-19. *f:* Lk 9, 28-36; Jn 1, 14. *g:* Ps 2, 7; Mt 17, 4-6. *h:* Lk 1, 78-79; Rv 2, 28. *i:* Mt 24, 11.24; 1 Tm 4, 1; Jude 4. *j:* Is 52, 5. *k:* Rom 16, 18. *l:* Jude 6.

not spare the angels when they sinned, but condemned them to the chains of Tartarus and handed them over to be kept for judgment; [5m*]and if he did not spare the ancient world, even though he preserved Noah, a herald of righteousness, together with seven others, when he brought a flood upon the godless world; [6n]and if he condemned the cities of Sodom and Gomorrah [to destruction], reducing them to ashes, making them an example for the godless [people] of what is coming; [7]and if he rescued Lot, a righteous man oppressed by the licentious conduct of unprincipled people [8](for day after day that righteous man living among them was tormented in his righteous soul at the lawless deeds that he saw and heard), [9o]then the Lord knows how to rescue the devout from trial and to keep the unrighteous under punishment for the day of judgment, [10p*]and especially those who follow the flesh with its depraved desire and show contempt for lordship.

False Teachers Denounced. Bold and arrogant, they are not afraid to revile glorious beings, [11q*]whereas angels, despite their superior strength and power, do not bring a reviling judgment against them from the Lord. [12r]But these people, like irrational animals born by nature for capture and destruction, revile things that they do not understand, and in their destruction they will also be destroyed, [13s*]suffering wrong as payment for wrongdoing. Thinking daytime revelry a delight, they are stains and defilements as they revel in their deceits while carousing with you. [14]Their eyes are full of adultery and insatiable for sin. They seduce unstable people, and their hearts are trained in greed. Accursed children! [15t*]Abandoning the straight road, they have gone astray, following the road of Balaam, the son of Bosor, who loved payment for wrongdoing, [16u]but he received a rebuke for his own crime: a mute beast spoke with a human voice and restrained the prophet's madness.

[17v]These people are waterless springs and mists driven by a gale; for them the gloom of darkness has been reserved. [18w*]For, talking empty bombast, they seduce with licentious desires of the flesh those who have barely escaped from people who live in error. [19x]They promise them freedom, though they themselves are slaves of corruption, for a person is a slave of whatever overcomes him. [20y]For if they, having escaped the defilements of the world through the knowledge of [our] Lord and savior Jesus Christ, again become entangled and overcome by them, their last condition is worse than their first. [21z*]For it would have been better for them not to have known the way of righteousness than after knowing it to turn back from the holy commandment handed down to them. [22a*]What

2 Peter read "pits of Tartarus." **Tartarus:** a term borrowed from Greek mythology to indicate the infernal regions.

2, 5–10a: Although God did not spare the sinful, he kept and saved the righteous, such as **Noah** (5) and **Lot** (7), and he **knows how to rescue the devout** (9), who are contrasted with the false teachers of the author's day. On Noah, cf Gn 5, 32—9, 29, especially 7, 1. On Lot, cf Gn 13 and 19.

2, 10b–22: Some take 10b and 11 with the preceding paragraph. Others begin the new paragraph with 10a, supplying from v 9 **The Lord knows how . . . to keep . . . under punishment,** with reference to God and probably specifically Christ (1). The conduct of the false teachers is described and condemned in language similar to that of Jude 8–16. This arrogance knows no bounds; animal-like, they are due to be caught and destroyed. They seduce even those who have knowledge of Christ (20).

2, 10b: Glorious beings: literally, "glories"; cf Jude 8. While some think that illustrious personages are meant or even political officials behind whom (fallen) angels stand, it is more likely that the reference is to glorious angelic beings (cf Jude 9).

2, 11: From the Lord: some manuscripts read "before the Lord"; cf Jude 9.

2, 13: Suffering wrong: some manuscripts read "receiving a reward." **In their deceits:** some manuscripts read "in their love feasts" (Jude 12).

2, 15: Balaam, the son of Bosor: in Nm 22, 5, Balaam is said to be the son of Beor, and it is this name that turns up in a few ancient Greek manuscripts by way of "correction" of the text. Balaam is not portrayed in such a bad light in Nm 22. His evil reputation and his **madness** (16), and possibly his surname Bosor, may have come from a Jewish tradition about him in the first/second century, of which we no longer have any knowledge.

2, 18: Barely escaped: some manuscripts read "really escaped."

2, 21: Commandment handed down: cf 3, 2 and Jude 3.

2, 22: The second proverb is of unknown origin, while the first appears in Prv 26, 11.

m: Gn 8, 15-19; Heb 11, 7. *n:* Gn 19, 24-25; Jude 7. *o:* 1 Cor 10, 13; Rv 3, 10. *p:* Jude 8. *q:* Jude 9. *r:* Ps 49, 13-15; Jude 10. *s:* Jude 12. *t:* Nm 31, 16; Jude 11. *u:* Nm 22, 28-33. *v:* Jude 12-13. *w:* Jude 16. *x:* Jn 8, 34; Rom 6, 16-17. *y:* Mt 12, 45. *z:* Ez 3, 20. *a:* Prv 26, 11.

is expressed in the true proverb has happened to them, "The dog returns to its own vomit," and "A bathed sow returns to wallowing in the mire."

IV: The Delay of the Second Coming

CHAPTER 3

See RG
512

Denial of the Parousia. *¹*This* is now, beloved, the second letter I am writing to you; through them by way of reminder I am trying to stir up your sincere disposition, *²ᵇ*to recall the words previously spoken by the holy prophets and the commandment of the Lord and savior through your apostles. *³ᶜ*Know* this first of all, that in the last days scoffers will come [to] scoff, living according to their own desires *⁴ᵈ*and* saying, "Where is the promise of his coming? From the time when our ancestors fell asleep, everything has remained as it was from the beginning of creation." *⁵ᵉ*They* deliberately ignore the fact that the heavens existed of old and earth was formed out of water and

through water by the word of God; *⁶ᶠ*through* these the world that then existed was destroyed, deluged with water. *⁷ᵍ*The present heavens and earth have been reserved by the same word for fire, kept for the day of judgment and of destruction of the godless.

⁸ʰ*But do not ignore this one fact, beloved, that with the Lord one day is like a thousand years and a thousand years like one day. *⁹ⁱ*The Lord does not delay his promise, as some regard "delay," but he is patient with you, not wishing that any should perish but that all should come to repentance. *¹⁰ʲ*But* the day of the Lord will come like a thief, and then the heavens will pass away with a mighty roar and the elements will be dissolved by fire, and the earth and everything done on it will be found out.

Exhortation to Preparedness. *¹¹ᵏ*Since* everything is to be dissolved in this way, what sort of persons ought [you] to be, conducting yourselves in holiness and devotion, *¹² ˡ*waiting* for and hastening the coming of the day of God, because of which the heavens will be dissolved in

---

3, 1–4: The false teachers not only flout Christian morality (cf Jude 8–19); they also deny the second coming of Christ and the judgment (4; cf 7). They seek to justify their licentiousness by arguing that the promised return of Christ has not been realized and the world is the same, no better than it was before (3–4). The author wishes to strengthen the faithful against such errors by reminding them in this **second letter** of the instruction in 1 Pt and of the teaching of the **prophets** and of Christ, conveyed through the **apostles** (1–2; cf Jude 17); cf 1 Pt 1, 10–12.16–21, especially 16–21; Eph 2, 20.

3, 3: Scoffers: cf Jude 18, where, however, only the passions of the scoffers are mentioned, not a denial on their part of Jesus' parousia.

3, 4–7: The false teachers tried to justify their immorality by pointing out that the promised **coming (parousia)** of the Lord has not yet occurred, even though early Christians expected it in their day. They thus insinuate that God is not guiding the world's history anymore, since nothing has changed and the first generation of Christians, **our ancestors** (4) has all died by this time. The author replies that, just as God destroyed the earth with water in the flood (5–6, cf 2, 5), so he will destroy it along with the false teachers on judgment day (7). **The word of God,** which called the world into being (Gn 1; Ps 33, 6) and **destroyed** it by the waters of a flood, will destroy it again by fire on **the day of judgment** (5–7).

3, 5: Formed out of water and through water: Gn 1, 2.6–8 is reflected as well as Greek views that water was the basic element from which all is derived.

3, 6: Destroyed, deluged with water: cf 2, 5; Gn 7, 11—8, 2.

3, 8–10: The scoffers' objection (4) is refuted also by showing that **delay** of the Lord's second coming is not a failure to fulfill his word but rather a sign of his patience: God is giving time for repentance before the final judgment (cf Wis 11, 23–26; Ez 18, 23; 33, 11).

3, 8: Cf Ps 90, 4.

3, 10: Like a thief: Mt 24, 43; 1 Thes 5, 2; Rv 3, 3. **Will be found out:** cf 1 Cor 3, 13–15. Some few versions read, as the sense may demand, "will not be found out"; many manuscripts read "will be burned up"; there are further variants in other manuscripts, versions, and Fathers. Total destruction is assumed (11).

3, 11–16: The second coming of Christ and the judgment of the world are the doctrinal bases for the moral exhortation to readiness through vigilance and a virtuous life; cf Mt 24, 42.50–51; Lk 12, 40; 1 Thes 5, 1–11; Jude 20–21.

3, 12: Flames . . . fire: although this is the only New Testament passage about a final conflagration, the idea was common in apocalyptic and Greco-Roman thought. **Hastening:** eschatology is here used to motivate ethics (11), as elsewhere in the New Testament. Jewish sources and Acts 3, 19–20 assume that proper ethical conduct can help bring the promised day of the Lord; cf 9. Some render the phrase, however, "desiring it earnestly."

---

b: Jude 17. *c:* 1 Tm 4, 1; 2 Tm 3, 1; Jude 18. *d:* Is 5, 19. *e:* Gn 1, 2.6.8; Ps 24, 2. *f:* Gn 7, 21. *g:* Is 51, 6; Mt 3, 12. *h:* Ps 90, 4. *i:* Ez 18, 23; 1 Tm 2, 4. *j:* Is 66, 15-16; Mt 24, 29. *k:* Acts 3, 19-21. *l:* Is 34, 4; Heb 10, 27.

flames and the elements melted by fire. [13m]*But according to his promise we await new heavens and a new earth in which righteousness dwells.

[14]Therefore, beloved, since you await these things, be eager to be found without spot or blemish before him, at peace. [15n]And consider the patience of our Lord as salvation, as our beloved brother Paul, according to the wisdom given to him, also wrote to you, [16]*speaking of these things as he does in all his letters. In them there are some things hard to understand that the ignorant and un-stable distort to their own destruction, just as they do the other scriptures.

V: Final Exhortation and Doxology

[17o]*Therefore, beloved, since you are forewarned, be on your guard not to be led into the error of the unprincipled and to fall from your own stability. [18p]But grow in grace and in the knowledge of our Lord and savior Jesus Christ. To him be glory now and to the day of eternity. [Amen.]

3, 13: New heavens and a new earth: cf Is 65, 17; 66, 22. The divine promises will be fulfilled after the day of judgment will have passed. The universe will be transformed by the reign of God's **righteousness** or justice; cf Is 65, 17–18; Acts 3, 21; Rom 8, 18–25; Rv 21, 1.

3, 16: These things: the teachings of this letter find parallels in Paul, e.g., God's will to save (Rom 2, 4; 9, 22–23; 1 Cor 1, 7–8), the coming of Christ (1 Thes 4, 16–17; 1 Cor 15, 23–52), and preparedness for the judgment (Col 1, 22–23; Eph 1, 4–14; 4, 30; 5, 5–14). **Other scriptures:** used to guide the faith and life of the Christian community. The letters of

Paul are thus here placed on the same level as books of the Old Testament. Possibly other New Testament writings could also be included.

3, 17–18: To avoid the dangers **of error** and loss of **stability,** Christians are **forewarned** to be **on guard** and to **grow in grace and knowledge** (1, 2) of Christ. The doxology (18) recalls 1 Pt 4, 11. Some manuscripts add **Amen.**

m: Is 65, 17; 66, 22; Rom 8, 21; Rv 21, 1.27.   *n:* Rom 8, 19; Jude 24.   *o:* Mk 13, 5; Heb 2, 1.   *p:* Rom 16, 27.

See RG 513–16

The First Letter of John

Early Christian tradition identified this work as a letter of John the apostle. Because of its resemblance to the fourth gospel in style, vocabulary, and ideas, it is generally agreed that both works are the product of the same school of Johannine Christianity. The terminology and the presence or absence of certain theological ideas in 1 John suggest that it was written after the gospel; it may have been composed as a short treatise on ideas that were developed more fully in the fourth gospel. To others, the evidence suggests that 1 John was written after the fourth gospel as part of a debate on the proper interpretation of that gospel. Whatever its relation to the gospel, 1 John may be dated toward the end of the first century. Unlike 2 and 3 John, it lacks in form the salutation and epistolary conclusion of a letter. These features, its prologue, and its emphasis on doctrinal teaching make it more akin to a theological treatise than to most other New Testament letters.

The purpose of the letter is to combat certain false ideas, especially about Jesus, and to deepen the spiritual and social awareness of the Christian community (3, 17). Some former members (2, 19) of the community refused to acknowledge Jesus as the Christ (2, 22) and denied that he was a true man (4, 2). The specific heresy described in this letter cannot be identified exactly, but it is a form of docetism or gnosticism; the former doctrine denied the humanity of Christ to insure that his divinity was untainted, and the latter viewed the appearance of Christ as a mere stepping-stone to higher knowledge of God. These theological errors are rejected by an appeal to the reality and continuity of the apostolic witness to Jesus. The author affirms that authentic Christian love, ethics, and faith take place only within the historical revelation and sacrifice of Jesus Christ. The fullness of Christian life as fellowship with the Father must be based on true belief and result in charitable living; knowledge of God and love for one another are inseparable, and error in one area inevitably affects the other. Although the author recognizes that Christian doctrine presents intangible mysteries of faith about Christ, he insists that the concrete Christian life brings to light the deeper realities of the gospel.

The structure and language of the letter are straightforward yet repetitive. The author sets forth the striking contrasts between light and darkness, Christians and the world, and truth and error to illustrate the threats and responsibilities of Christian life. The result is not one of theological argument but one of intense religious conviction expressed in simple truths. The letter is of particular value for its declaration of the humanity and divinity of Christ as an apostolic teaching and for its development of the intrinsic connection between Christian moral conduct and Christian doctrine.

The principal divisions of the First Letter of John are the following:

I: Prologue (1, 1–4)

II: God as Light (1, 5—3, 10)

III: Love for One Another (3, 11—5, 12)

IV: Epilogue (5, 13–21)

I: Prologue

CHAPTER 1

See RG
514

The Word of Life

1a*What was from the beginning,
what we have heard,
what we have seen with our eyes,
what we looked upon
and touched with our hands
concerns the Word of life—
*2 b*for the life was made visible;
we have seen it and testify to it
and proclaim to you the eternal life
that was with the Father and was made
visible to us—

*3 c*what we have seen and heard
we proclaim now to you,
so that you too may have fellowship with
us;
for our fellowship is with the Father
and with his Son, Jesus Christ.
*4 d*We are writing this so that our joy may
be complete.

II: God as Light

God is Light. *5**Now this is the message that we have heard from him and proclaim to you: God is light, and in him there is no darkness at all. *6e*If we say, "We have fellowship with him," while we continue to walk in darkness, we lie and do not act in truth. *7f*But if we walk in the light as he is in the light, then we have fellowship with one another, and the blood of his Son Jesus cleanses us from all sin. *8**If we say, "We are without sin," we deceive ourselves, and the truth is not in us. *9h*If we acknowledge our sins, he is faithful and just and will forgive our sins and cleanse us from every wrongdoing. *10i*If we say, "We have not sinned," we make him a liar, and his word is not in us.

CHAPTER 2

See RG
514–15

Christ and His Commandments. *1j**My children, I am writing this to you so that you may not commit sin. But if anyone does sin, we have an Advocate with the Father, Jesus Christ the righteous one. *2k*He is expiation for our sins, and not for our sins only but for those of the whole world.

1, 1–4: There is a striking parallel to the prologue of the gospel of John (Jn 1, 1–18), but the emphasis here is not on the preexistent Word but rather on the apostles' witness to the incarnation of life by their experience of the historical Jesus. He is **the Word of life** (1; cf Jn 1, 4), **the eternal life that was with the Father and was made visible** (2; cf Jn 1, 14), and was **heard, seen, looked upon,** and **touched** by the apostles. The purpose of their teaching is to share that life, called **fellowship . . . with the Father and with his Son, Jesus Christ,** with those who receive their witness (3; Jn 1, 14.16).

1, 5–7: **Light** is to be understood here as truth and goodness; **darkness** here is error and depravity (cf Jn 3, 19–21; 17, 17; Eph 5, 8). To **walk** in light or darkness is to live according to truth or error, not merely intellectual but moral as well. Fellowship with God and with one another consists in a life according to the truth as found in God and in Christ.

1, 8–10: Denial of the condition of sin is self-deception and even contradictory of divine revelation; there is also the continual possibility of sin's recurrence. Forgiveness and deliverance from sin through Christ are assured through acknowledgment of them and repentance.

2, 1: Children: like the term "beloved," this is an expression of pastoral love (cf Jn 13, 33; 21, 5; 1 Cor 4, 14). **Advocate:** for the use of the term, see Jn 14, 16. Forgiveness of sin is assured through Christ's intercession and expiation or "offering"; the death of Christ effected the removal of sin.

a: 2, 13; Jn 1, 1.14; 20, 20.25.27. *b:* Jn 15, 27; 17, 5. *c:* Jn 17, 21; Acts 4, 20. *d:* Jn 15, 11; 2 Jn 12. *e:* Jn 12, 35. *f:* Mt 26, 28; Rom 3, 24-25; Heb 9, 14; 1 Pt 1, 19; Rv 1, 5. *g:* 2 Chr 6, 36; Prv 20, 9. *h:* Prv 28, 13; Jas 5, 16. *i:* 5, 10. *j:* Jn 14, 16; Heb 7, 25. *k:* 4, 10.

31*The way we may be sure that we know him is to keep his commandments. *4m*Whoever says, "I know him," but does not keep his commandments is a liar, and the truth is not in him. *5n*But whoever keeps his word, the love of God is truly perfected in him. This is the way we may know that we are in union with him: *6*whoever claims to abide in him ought to live [just] as he lived.

The New Commandment. *7o**Beloved, I am writing no new commandment to you but an old commandment that you had from the beginning. The old commandment is the word that you have heard. *8p**And yet I do write a new commandment to you, which holds true in him and among you, for the darkness is passing away, and the true light is already shining. *9q*Whoever says he is in the light, yet hates his brother, is still in the darkness. *10r*Whoever loves his brother remains in the light, and there is nothing in him to cause a fall. *11*Whoever hates his brother is in darkness; he walks in darkness and does not know where he is going because the darkness has blinded his eyes.

Members of the Community. *12s**I am writing to you, children, because your sins have been forgiven for his name's sake.

*13t*I am writing to you, fathers, because you know him who is from the beginning.

I am writing to you, young men, because you have conquered the evil one.

*14*I write to you, children, because you know the Father.

I write to you, fathers, because you know him who is from the beginning.

I write to you, young men, because you are strong and the word of God remains in you, and you have conquered the evil one.

15u*Do not love the world or the things of the world. If anyone loves the world, the love of the Father is not in him. *16**For all that is in the world, sensual lust, enticement for the eyes, and a pretentious life, is not from the Father but is from the world. *17v*Yet the world and its enticement are passing away. But whoever does the will of God remains forever.

Antichrists. *18w**Children, it is the last hour; and just as you heard that the antichrist was coming, so now many antichrists have appeared. Thus we know this is the last hour. *19**They went out from us, but they were not really of our number; if they had been, they would have remained with us. Their desertion shows that none of them was of our number. *20x**But you have the anointing that comes

---

2, 3–6: The way we may be sure: to those who claim, "I have known Christ and therefore I know him," our author insists on not mere intellectual knowledge but obedience to God's commandments in a life conformed to the example of Christ; this confirms our knowledge of him and is **the love of God . . . perfected.** Disparity between moral life and the commandments proves improper belief.

2, 7–11: The author expresses the continuity and freshness of mutual charity in Christian experience. Through Christ the commandment of love has become the **light** defeating the **darkness** of evil in a new age. All hatred as darkness is incompatible with the light and Christian life. Note also the characteristic Johannine polemic in which a positive assertion is emphasized by the negative statement of its opposite.

2, 8: Which holds true in him and among you: literally, "a thing that holds true in him and in you."

2, 12–17: The Christian community that has experienced the grace of God through forgiveness of sin and knowledge of Christ is armed against the evil one.

2, 12: For his name's sake: because of Christ our sins are forgiven.

2, 15: The world: all that is hostile toward God and alienated from him. Love of the **world** and love of God are thus mutually exclusive; cf Jas 4, 4.

2, 16: Sensual lust: literally, "the lust of the flesh," inordinate desire for physical gratification. **Enticement for the**

eyes: literally, "the lust of the eyes," avarice or covetousness; the eyes are regarded as the windows of the soul. **Pretentious life:** literally, "pride of life," arrogance or ostentation in one's earthly style of life that reflects a willful independence from God and others.

2, 18: It is the last hour: literally, "a last hour," the period between the death and resurrection of Christ and his second coming. **The antichrist:** opponent or adversary of Christ; the term appears only in 1–2 John, but "pseudochrists" (translated "false messiahs") in Mt 24, 24 and Mk 13, 22, and Paul's "lawless one" in 2 Thes 2, 3, are similar figures. **Many antichrists:** Mt, Mk, and Rv seem to indicate a collectivity of persons, here related to the false teachers.

2, 19: Not really of our number: the apostate teachers only proved their lack of faith by leaving the community.

2, 20: The anointing that comes from the holy one: this anointing is in the Old Testament sense of receiving the Spirit of God. The **holy one** probably refers to Christ. True knowledge is the gift of the Spirit (cf Is 11, 2), and the function of the Spirit is to lead Christians to the truth (Jn 14, 17.26; 16, 13).

l: Jn 14, 15; 15, 10. *m:* 4, 20. *n:* Jn 14, 23. *o:* 3, 11; Dt 6, 5; Mt 22, 37-40. *p:* Jn 13, 34 / Jn 1, 5; Rom 13, 12. *q:* Jn 8, 12. *r:* Eccl 2, 14; Jn 11, 10. *s:* 1 Cor 6, 11. *t:* 1, 1; Jn 1, 1. *u:* Rom 8, 7-8; Jas 4, 4; 2 Pt 1, 4. *v:* Is 40, 8; Mt 7, 21; 1 Cor 7, 31; 1 Pt 4, 2. *w:* 1 Tim 4, 1. *x:* Jn 14, 26.

from the holy one, and you all have knowledge. *21y*I write to you not because you do not know the truth but because you do, and because every lie is alien to the truth. *22z**Who is the liar? Whoever denies that Jesus is the Christ. Whoever denies the Father and the Son, this is the antichrist. *23a*No one who denies the Son has the Father, but whoever confesses the Son has the Father as well.

Life from God's Anointing. *24b**Let what you heard from the beginning remain in you. If what you heard from the beginning remains in you, then you will remain in the Son and in the Father. *25c*And this is the promise that he made us: eternal life. *26*I write you these things about those who would deceive you. *27*As for you, the anointing that you received from him remains in you, so that you do not need anyone to teach you. But his anointing teaches you about everything and is true and not false; just as it taught you, remain in him.

Children of God. *28**And now, children, remain in him, so that when he appears we may have confidence and not be put to shame by him at his coming. *29*If you consider that he is righteous, you also know that everyone who acts in righteousness is begotten by him.

See RG 514–15

CHAPTER 3

*1d**See what love the Father has bestowed on us that we may be called the children of God. Yet so we are. The reason the world does not know us is that it did not know him. *2e**Beloved, we are God's children now; what we shall be has not yet been revealed. We do know that when it is revealed we shall be like him, for we shall see him as he is. *3f*Everyone who has this hope based on him makes himself pure, as he is pure.

Avoiding Sin. *4**Everyone who commits sin commits lawlessness, for sin is lawlessness. *5g*You know that he was revealed to take away sins, and in him there is no sin. *6*No one who remains in him sins; no one who sins has seen him or known him. *7*Children, let no one deceive you. The person who acts in righteousness is righteous, just as he is righteous. *8h*Whoever sins belongs to the devil, because the devil has sinned from the beginning. Indeed, the Son of God was revealed to destroy the works of the devil. *9**No one who is begotten by God commits sin, because God's seed remains in him; he cannot sin because he is begotten by God. *10*In this way, the children of God and the children of the devil are made plain; no one who fails to act in righteousness belongs to God, nor anyone who does not love his brother.

III: Love for One Another

*11i**For this is the message you have heard from the beginning: we should love one another, *12j*unlike Cain who belonged to the evil one and slaughtered his brother. Why

---

2, 22–23: Certain gnostics denied that the earthly Jesus was the Christ; to deny knowledge of the Son is to deny the Father, since only through the Son has God been fully revealed (Jn 1, 18; 14, 8–9).

2, 24: Continuity with the apostolic witness as proclaimed in the prologue is the safeguard of right belief.

2, 28–29: Our confidence at his judgment is based on the daily assurance of salvation. Our actions reflect our true relation to him.

3, 1–3: The greatest sign of God's love is the gift of his Son (Jn 3, 16) that has made Christians true children of God. This relationship is a present reality and also part of the life to come; true knowledge of God will ultimately be gained, and Christians prepare themselves now by virtuous lives in imitation of the Son.

3, 2: When it is revealed: or "when he is revealed" (the subject of the verb could be Christ).

3, 4: Lawlessness: a reference to the activity of the antichrist, so it is expressed as hostility toward God and a rejection of Christ. The author goes on to contrast the states of sin and righteousness. Christians do not escape sin but realize

that when they sin they cease to have fellowship with God. Virtue and sin distinguish the children of God from the children of the devil.

3, 9: A habitual sinner is a child of the devil, while a child of God, who by definition is in fellowship with God, cannot sin. **Seed:** Christ or the Spirit who shares the nature of God with the Christian.

3, 11–18: Love, even to the point of self-sacrifice, is the point of the commandment. The story of Cain and Abel (12–15; Gn 4, 1–16) presents the rivalry of two brothers, in a contrast of evil and righteousness, where envy led to murder. For Christians, proof of deliverance is love toward others, after the example of Christ. This includes concrete acts of charity, out of our material abundance.

y: 3, 19; 2 Pt 1, 12. *z:* 2 Thes 2, 4. *a:* Jn 14, 7-9. *b:* Jn 14, 23. *c:* Jn 5, 24; 10, 28; 17, 2. *d:* Jn 1, 12; Eph 1, 5 / Jn 15, 21; 17, 25. *e:* Phil 3, 21. *f:* 2, 6. *g:* Is 53, 9; Jn 1, 29; 8, 46; 1 Pt 2, 22. *h:* Jn 8, 44; 12, 31-32. *i:* 2, 7; Jn 13, 34; 15, 12.17. *j:* Gn 4, 8; Jude 11.

did he slaughter him? Because his own works were evil, and those of his brother righteous. [13k]Do not be amazed, [then,] brothers, if the world hates you. [14l]We know that we have passed from death to life because we love our brothers. Whoever does not love remains in death. [15m]Everyone who hates his brother is a murderer, and you know that no murderer has eternal life remaining in him. [16n]The way we came to know love was that he laid down his life for us; so we ought to lay down our lives for our brothers. [17o]If someone who has worldly means sees a brother in need and refuses him compassion, how can the love of God remain in him? [18p]Children, let us love not in word or speech but in deed and truth.

Confidence before God. [19*][Now] this is how we shall know that we belong to the truth and reassure our hearts before him [20]in whatever our hearts condemn, for God is greater than our hearts and knows everything. [21]Beloved, if [our] hearts do not condemn us, we have confidence in God [22q]and receive from him whatever we ask, because we keep his commandments and do what pleases him. [23r]And his commandment is this: we should believe in the name of his Son, Jesus Christ, and love one another just as he commanded us. [24s]Those who keep his commandments remain in him, and he in them, and the way we know that he remains in us is from the Spirit that he gave us.

CHAPTER 4

See RG 515-16

Testing the Spirits. [1t*]Beloved, do not trust every spirit but test the spirits to see whether they belong to God, because many false prophets have gone out into the world. [2u]This is how you can know the Spirit of God: every spirit that acknowledges Jesus Christ come in the flesh belongs to God, [3v*]and every spirit that does not acknowledge Jesus does not belong to God. This is the spirit of the antichrist that, as you heard, is to come, but in fact is already in the world. [4]You belong to God, children, and you have conquered them, for the one who is in you is greater than the one who is in the world. [5w]They belong to the world; accordingly, their teaching belongs to the world, and the world listens to them. [6x]We belong to God, and anyone who knows God listens to us, while anyone who does not belong to God refuses to hear us. This is how we know the spirit of truth and the spirit of deceit.

God's Love and Christian Life. [7*]Beloved, let us love one another, because love is of God; everyone who loves is begotten by God and knows God. [8]Whoever is without love does not know God, for God is love. [9y]In this way the love of God was revealed to us: God sent his only Son into the world so that we might have life through him. [10z]In this is love: not that we have loved God, but that he loved us and sent his Son as expiation for our sins. [11]Beloved, if God so loved us, we also must love one another. [12a]No one has ever

---

3, 19–24: Living a life of faith in Jesus and of Christian love assures us of abiding in God no matter what our feelings may at times tell us. Our obedience gives us confidence in prayer and trust in God's judgment. This obedience includes our belief in Christ and love for one another.

3, 19b-20: This difficult passage may also be translated "we shall be at peace before him in whatever our hearts condemn, for . . ." or "and before God we shall convince our hearts, if our hearts condemn us, that God is greater than our hearts."

4, 1–6: Deception is possible in spiritual phenomena and may be tested by its relation to Christian doctrine (cf 1 Cor 12, 3): those who fail to acknowledge Jesus Christ in the flesh are false prophets and belong to the antichrist. Even though these false prophets are well received in the world, the Christian who belongs to God has a greater power in the truth.

4, 3: Does not acknowledge Jesus: some ancient manuscripts add "Christ" and/or "to have come in the flesh" (cf 2),

and others read "every spirit that annuls (or severs) Jesus."

4, 7–12: Love as we share in it testifies to the nature of God and to his presence in our lives. One who loves shows that one is a child of God and knows God, for God's very being is love; one without love is without God. The revelation of the nature of God's love is found in the free gift of his Son to us, so that we may share life with God and be delivered from our sins. The love we have for one another must be of the same sort: authentic, merciful; this unique Christian love is our proof that we know God and can "see" the invisible God.

---

k: Mt 24, 9; Jn 15, 18; 17, 14. l: Lv 19, 17; Jn 5, 24. m: Jn 8, 44. n: Mt 20, 28; Jn 10, 11; 15, 13. o: Dt 15, 7.11; Jas 2, 15-16. p: Jas 1, 22. q: 5, 15; Mt 7, 7-11; 21, 22; Jn 14, 13-14. r: Jn 13, 34; 15, 17. s: 4, 13; Jn 14, 21-23. t: 2, 18; Mt 24, 24. u: 1 Cor 12, 3; 1 Thes 5, 21. v: 1, 22. w: Jn 15, 19. x: Jn 8, 47; 10, 16. y: Jn 3, 16. z: Rom 5, 8. a: Jn 1, 18; 1 Tm 6, 16.

seen God. Yet, if we love one another, God remains in us, and his love is brought to perfection in us.

[13]*This is how we know that we remain in him and he in us, that he has given us of his Spirit. [14]Moreover, we have seen and testify that the Father sent his Son as savior of the world. [15]Whoever acknowledges that Jesus is the Son of God, God remains in him and he in God. [16]We have come to know and to believe in the love God has for us.

God is love, and whoever remains in love remains in God and God in him. [17b]In this is love brought to perfection among us, that we have confidence on the day of judgment because as he is, so are we in this world. [18]There is no fear in love, but perfect love drives out fear because fear has to do with punishment, and so one who fears is not yet perfect in love. [19]We love because he first loved us. [20c]*If anyone says, "I love God," but hates his brother, he is a liar; for whoever does not love a brother whom he has seen cannot love God whom he has not seen. [21d]This is the commandment we have from him: whoever loves God must also love his brother.

See RG 515–16

CHAPTER 5

Faith is Victory over the World. [1e]*Everyone who believes that Jesus is the Christ is begotten by God, and everyone who loves the father loves [also] the one begotten by him. [2]In this way we know that we love the children of God when we love God and obey his commandments. [3f]For the love of God is this, that we keep his commandments. And his commandments are not burdensome, [4g]for whoever is begotten by God conquers the world. And the victory that conquers the world is our faith. [5h]Who [indeed] is the victor over the world but the one who believes that Jesus is the Son of God?

[6i]*This is the one who came through water and blood, Jesus Christ, not by water alone, but by water and blood. The Spirit is the one that testifies, and the Spirit is truth. [7]So there are three that testify, [8j]the Spirit, the water, and the blood, and the three are of one accord. [9k]If we accept human testimony, the testimony of God is surely greater. Now the testimony of God is this, that he has testified on behalf of his Son. [10l]Whoever believes in the Son of God has this testimony within himself. Whoever does not believe God has made him a liar by not believing the testimony God has given about his Son. [11m]And this is the testimony: God gave us eternal life, and this life is in his Son. [12]Whoever possesses the Son has life; whoever does not possess the Son of God does not have life.

IV: Epilogue

Prayer for Sinners. [13n]*I write these things to you so that you may know that you have

---

4, 13–21: The testimony of the Spirit and that of faith join the testimony of love to confirm our knowledge of God. Our love is grounded in the confession of Jesus as the Son of God and the example of God's love for us. Christian life is founded on the knowledge of God as love and on his continuing presence that relieves us from fear of judgment (16–18). What Christ gives us confidence, even as we live and love in this world. Yet Christian love is not abstract but lived in the concrete manner of love for one another.

4, 20: Cannot love God: some ancient manuscripts read "how can he love . . . ?"

5, 1–5: Children of God are identified not only by their love for others (4, 7–9) and for God (5, 1–2) but by their belief in the divine sonship of Jesus Christ. Faith, the acceptance of Jesus in his true character and the obedience in love to God's commands (3), is the source of the Christian's power in the world and conquers the world of evil (4–5), even as Christ overcame the world (Jn 16, 33).

5, 6–12: Water and blood (6) refers to Christ's baptism (Mt 3, 16–17) and to the shedding of his blood on the cross (Jn 19, 34). **The Spirit** was present at the baptism (Mt 3, 16; Mk 1, 10; Lk 3, 22; Jn 1, 32.34). **The testimony** to Christ as

the Son of God is confirmed by divine witness (7–9), greater by far than the two legally required human witnesses (Dt 17, 6). To deny this is to deny God's truth; cf Jn 8, 17–18. The gist of the divine witness or **testimony** is that **eternal life** (11–12) is given in Christ and nowhere else. To **possess the Son** is not acceptance of a doctrine but of a person who lives now and provides life.

5, 13–21: As children of God we have confidence in prayer because of our intimate relationship with him (14–15). In love, we pray (16–17) for those who are in **sin**, but not in **deadly sin** (literally, "sin unto death"), probably referring to apostasy or activities brought on under the antichrist; cf Mk 3, 29; Heb 6, 4–6; 10, 26–31. Even in the latter case, however, prayer, while not enjoined, is not forbidden. The letter concludes with a summary of the themes of the letter (18–20). There is a sharp antithesis between the children of God and those belonging to the world and to the evil one. The Son re-

b: 2, 28. *c:* 2, 4. *d:* Jn 13, 34; 14, 15.21; 15, 17. *e:* Jn 8, 42; 1 Pt 1, 23. *f:* Jn 14, 15. *g:* Jn 16, 33. *h:* 1 Cor 15, 57. *i:* Jn 15, 26; 19, 34. *j:* Jn 5, 32.36; 15, 26. *k:* Jn 5, 32.37. *l:* 3, 33. *m:* 1, 2; Jn 1, 4; 5, 21.26; 17, 3. *n:* Jn 1, 12; 20, 31.

eternal life, you who believe in the name of the Son of God. [14o]And we have this confidence in him, that if we ask anything according to his will, he hears us. [15]And if we know that he hears us in regard to whatever we ask, we know that what we have asked him for is ours. [16p]If anyone sees his brother sinning, if the sin is not deadly, he should pray to God and he will give him life. This is only for those whose sin is not deadly. There is such a thing as deadly sin, about which I do not say that you should pray. [17]All

wrongdoing is sin, but there is sin that is not deadly.

[18]We know that no one begotten by God sins; but the one begotten by God he protects, and the evil one cannot touch him. [19]We know that we belong to God, and the whole world is under the power of the evil one. [20q]We also know that the Son of God has come and has given us discernment to know the one who is true. And we are in the one who is true, in his Son Jesus Christ. He is the true God and eternal life. [21]Children, be on your guard against idols.

veals the God of truth; Christians dwell in the true God, **in his Son,** and have eternal life. The final verse (21) voices a perennial warning about **idols,** any type of rival to God.

o: 3, 21-22; Mt 7, 7; Jn 14, 13-14.   *p:* Mt 12, 31.   *q:* Jer 24, 7; Jn 17, 3; Eph 1, 17.

The Second Letter of John

See RG
516–17

Written in response to similar problems, the Second and Third Letters of John are of the same length, perhaps determined by the practical consideration of the writing space on one piece of papyrus. In each letter the writer calls himself "the Presbyter," and their common authorship is further evidenced by internal similarities in style and wording, especially in the introductions and conclusions. The literary considerations that link 2 John and 3 John also link them with the First Letter and the Gospel of John. The concern with "truth," christology, mutual love, the new commandment, antichrist, and the integrity of witness to the earthly Jesus mark these works as products of the Johannine school. The identity of the Presbyter is problematic. The use of the title implies more than age, and refers to his position of leadership in the early church. The absence of a proper name indicates that he was well known and acknowledged in authority by the communities to which he writes. Although traditionally attributed to John the apostle, these letters were probably written by a disciple or scribe of an apostle. The traditional place and date of composition, Ephesus at the end of the first century, are plausible for both letters.

The Second Letter is addressed to "the chosen Lady" and "to her children." This literary image of a particular Christian community reflects the specific destination and purpose of the letter. Unlike 1 John, this brief letter is not a theological treatise but a reply to problems within the church. The Johannine themes of love and truth are used to support practical advice on Christian living. The Presbyter encourages community members to show their Christianity by adhering to the great commandment of mutual love and to the historical truth about Jesus. The false teaching present among them is a spiritualizing christology that may tempt some members to discount teachings about the incarnation and death of Jesus the Christ; cf 1 Jn 4, 2. For their protection the Presbyter forbids hospitality toward unknown or "progressive" Christians to prevent their infiltration of the community. The Second Letter preserves the Johannine concerns of doctrinal purity and active love in the form of pastoral advice to a threatened community.

———

See RG
516–17

[1a]*The Presbyter to the chosen Lady and to her children whom I love in

1: The chosen Lady: literally "elected"; this could also be translated "Kyria (a woman's name) chosen (by God)" or "the lady Electa" or "Electa Kyria." The adjective "chosen" is applied to all Christians at the beginning of other New Testament letters (1 Pt 1, 1; Ti 1, 1). The description is of a spe-

cific community with "children" who are its members. **The truth:** the affirmation of Jesus in the flesh and in contrast to false teaching (7).

———

a: Jn 8, 32; 3 Jn 1.

truth—and not only I but also all who know the truth— [2]because of the truth that dwells in us and will be with us forever. [3]*Grace, mercy, and peace will be with us from God the Father and from Jesus Christ the Father's Son in truth and love.

[4b]*I rejoiced greatly to find some of your children walking in the truth just as we were commanded by the Father. [5c]But now, Lady, I ask you, not as though I were writing a new commandment but the one we have had from the beginning: let us love one another. [6d]*For this is love, that we walk according to his commandments; this is the commandment, as you heard from the beginning, in which you should walk.

[7e]*Many deceivers have gone out into the world, those who do not acknowledge Jesus Christ as coming in the flesh; such is the deceitful one and the antichrist. [8]*Look to yourselves that you do not lose what we worked for but may receive a full recompense. [9f]*Anyone who is so "progressive" as not to remain in the teaching of the Christ does not have God; whoever remains in the teaching has the Father and the Son. [10g]*If anyone comes to you and does not bring this doctrine, do not receive him in your house or even greet him; [11]for whoever greets him shares in his evil works.

[12h]*Although I have much to write to you, I do not intend to use paper and ink. Instead, I hope to visit you and to speak face to face so that our joy may be complete. [13]*The children of your chosen sister send you greetings.

3: Grace, mercy, and peace: like 1 and 2 Tm this letter adds **mercy** to the terms used frequently in a salutation to describe Christian blessing; it appears only here in the Johannine writings. The author also puts the blessing in relation to **truth** and **love,** the watchwords of the Johannine teaching. **The Father's Son:** the title that affirms the close relationship of Christ to God; similar variations of this title occur elsewhere (Jn 1, 14; 3, 35), but the precise wording is not found elsewhere in the New Testament.

4: Some of your children: this refers to those whom the Presbyter has recently encountered, but it may also indicate the presence of false doctrine in the community: the Presbyter encourages those who have remained faithful. **Walking in the truth:** an expression used in the Johannine writings to describe a way of living in which the Christian faith is visibly expressed; cf 1 Jn 1, 6–7; 2, 6.11, 3 Jn 3.

6: His commandments: cf 1 Jn 2, 7–8; 3, 23; 4, 21; obedience to the commandment of faith and love includes all others.

7: The antichrist: see 1 Jn 2, 18–19.22; 4, 3.

8: You (plural): it is not certain whether this means the Christians addressed or includes the Presbyter, since some of the ancient Greek manuscripts and Greek Fathers have "we."

9: Anyone who is so "progressive": literally, "Anyone who goes ahead." Some gnostic groups held the doctrine of the Christ come in the flesh to be a first step in belief, which the more advanced and spiritual believer surpassed and abandoned in his knowledge of the spiritual Christ. The author affirms that fellowship with God may be gained only by holding to the complete doctrine of Jesus Christ (1 Jn 2, 22–23; 4, 2; 5, 5–6).

10–11: At this time false teachers were considered so dangerous and divisive as to be shunned completely. From this description they seem to be wandering preachers. We see here a natural suspicion of early Christians concerning such itinerants and can envisage the problems faced by missionaries such as those mentioned in 3 Jn 10.

12: Our joy: a number of other Greek manuscripts read "your joy."

13: Chosen sister: the community of which the Presbyter is now a part greets you (singular), the community of the Lady

b: 3 Jn 3.   c: Jn 13, 34; 15, 12; 1 Jn 4, 7.   d: Jn 13, 34; 14, 15; 1 Jn 5, 3.   e: 1 Jn 2, 22; 4, 2.   f: Jn 8, 31; 1 Jn 2, 23; 4, 15.   g: Rom 16, 17; 2 Thes 3, 6.   h: Jn 15, 11; 1 Jn 1, 4; 3 Jn 13.

See RG
517–18

The Third Letter of John

The Third Letter of John preserves a brief glimpse into the problems of missionary activity and local autonomy in the early church. In contrast to the other two letters of John, this work was addressed to a specific individual, Gaius. This letter is less theological in content and purpose. The author's goal was to secure hospitality and material support for his missionaries, and the Presbyter is writing to another member of the church who has welcomed missionaries in the past. The Presbyter commends Gaius for his hospitality and encourages his future help. He indicates he may come to challenge the policy of Diotrephes that is based on evil gossip.

The problems of the Presbyter in this short letter provide us with valuable evidence of the flexible and personal nature of authority in the early church. The Presbyter writes to Gaius, whom perhaps he had converted or instructed, on the basis of their personal links. The brothers have also confirmed him as a loyal Christian in action and belief. Gaius accepted the missionaries from the Presbyter and presumably will accept Demetrius on the Presbyter's recommendation. In contrast, Diotrephes refuses to receive either letters or friends of the Presbyter. Although he is portrayed as ambitious and hostile, he perhaps exemplifies the cautious and sectarian nature of early Christianity; for its own protection the local community mistrusted missionaries as false teachers. Most interestingly, Diotrephes seems comfortable in ignoring the requests of the Presbyter. The Presbyter seems to acknowledge that only a personal confrontation with Diotrephes will remedy the situation (10). The division, however, may also rest on doctrinal disagreement in which Gaius and the other "friends" accept the teaching of the Presbyter, and Diotrephes does not; the missionaries are not received for suspicion of theological error. Diotrephes has thus been viewed by some as an overly ambitious local upstart trying to thwart the advance of orthodox Christianity, by others as an orthodox church official suspicious of the teachings of the Presbyter and those in the Johannine school who think as he does, or by still others as a local leader anxious to keep the debates in the Johannine community out of his own congregation.

This brief letter and the situation that it mirrors show us how little we know about some details of early development in the church: schools of opinion existed around which questions of faith and life were discussed, and personal ties as well as doctrine and authority played a role in what happened amid divisions and unity.

^{1a*}The Presbyter to the beloved Gaius whom I love in truth. **See RG 517–18** ^{2}Beloved, I hope you are prospering in every respect and are in good health, just as your soul is prospering. ^{3b*}I rejoiced greatly when some of the brothers came and testified to how truly you walk in the truth. ^{4c}Nothing gives me greater joy than to hear that my children are walking in the truth.

^{5d*}Beloved, you are faithful in all you do for the brothers, especially for strangers; ^{6e*}they have testified to your love before the church. Please help them in a way worthy of God to continue their journey. ^{7*}For they have set out for the sake of the Name and are accepting nothing from the pagans. ^{8}Therefore, we ought to support such persons, so that we may be co-workers in the truth.

^{9*}I wrote to the church, but Diotrephes, who loves to dominate, does not acknowledge us. ^{10*}Therefore, if I come, I will draw attention to what he is doing, spreading evil nonsense about us. And not content with that, he will not receive the brothers, hindering those who wish to do so and expelling them from the church.

^{11f*}Beloved, do not imitate evil but imitate good. Whoever does what is good is of God; whoever does what is evil has never seen God. ^{12g*}Demetrius receives a good report from all, even from the truth itself. We give our testimonial as well, and you know our testimony is true.

1: Beloved Gaius: a frequent form of address for fellow Christians in New Testament epistolary literature.

3: The brothers: in this letter, the term may refer to Christians who have been missionaries and received hospitality from Gaius (5–6). **Walk in the truth:** the common Johannine term to describe Christian living; this description presents Gaius as following the teachings of the Presbyter in contrast to Diotrephes.

5: You are faithful in all you do: Gaius's aid to the missionaries is a manifestation of his true Christian faith.

6: Help them . . . to continue their journey: the Presbyter asks Gaius not only to continue to welcome the missionaries to his community but also to equip them for further travels.

7: The Name: of Jesus Christ (cf Acts 5, 41; 1 Jn 2, 12; 3, 23; 5, 13). **Accepting nothing:** not expecting support from the pagans to whom they preach the gospel, so that they will not be considered as beggars; they required support from

other Christians; cf Paul's complaints to the Corinthians (1 Cor 9, 3–12).

9: Who loves to dominate: the Presbyter does not deny Diotrephes' place as leader but indicates that his ambition may have caused him to disregard his letter and his influence.

10: If I come: the Presbyter may visit the community to challenge the actions of Diotrephes toward himself and the missionaries. **Will not receive the brothers:** Diotrephes may have been critical of the teachings of the Presbyter and sought to maintain doctrinal purity; cf 1 Jn 2, 19 and 2 Jn 10–11.

11: Do not imitate evil: Gaius should not be influenced by the behavior of Diotrephes.

12: Demetrius: because of the fear of false teachers,

a: 2 Jn 1. *b:* 5; Gal 6, 10; 2 Jn 4. *c:* 1 Thes 2, 11-12; 1 Tm 1, 2; 2 Tm 1, 2; 1 Jn 2, 1; 2 Jn 4. *d:* Rom 12, 13; Gal 6, 10; Heb 13, 2. *e:* Acts 15, 3; Col 1, 10; 1 Thes 2, 12. *f:* 1 Jn 2, 29; 3, 6.10. *g:* Jn 19, 35; 21, 24; 1 Tm 3, 7.

*13h*I have much to write to you, but I do not wish to write with pen and ink. *14*Instead, I hope to see you soon, when we can talk face to face. *15i**Peace be with you. The friends greet you; greet the friends there each by name.

Demetrius, perhaps the bearer of the letter, is provided with a recommendation from the Presbyter; cf 2 Cor 3, 1; Rom 16, 1. **Even from the truth itself:** this refers probably to the manner of Demetrius's life that testifies to his true belief; cf Gaius above (v 3).

15: Friends: although a Johannine term for Christians (Jn 15, 15), the word here may refer to those in the community loyal to the Presbyter and to Gaius.

h: 2 Jn 12.   *i:* Jn 20, 19.21.26; Eph 6, 23; 1 Pt 5, 14.

See RG 519–20

The Letter of Jude

This letter is by its address attributed to "Jude, a slave of Jesus Christ and brother of James" (1). Since he is not identified as an apostle, this designation can hardly be meant to refer to the Jude or Judas who is listed as one of the Twelve (Lk 6, 16; Acts 1, 13; cf Jn 14, 22). The person intended is almost certainly the other Jude, named in the gospels among the relatives of Jesus (Mt 13, 55; Mk 6, 3), and the James who is listed there as his brother is the one to whom the Letter of James is attributed (see the Introduction to James). Nothing else is known of this Jude, and the apparent need to identify him by reference to his better-known brother indicates that he was a rather obscure personage in the early church.

The letter is addressed in the most general terms to "those who are called, beloved in God the Father and kept safe for Jesus Christ" (1), hence apparently to all Christians. But since its purpose is to warn the addressees against false teachers, the author must have had in mind one or more specific Christian communities located in the unidentified region where the errors in question constituted a danger. While the letter contains some Semitic features, there is nothing to identify the addressees specifically as Jewish Christians; indeed, the errors envisaged seem to reflect an early form of gnosticism, opposed to law, that points rather to the cultural context of the Gentile world. Like James and 2 Peter, the Letter of Jude manifests none of the typical features of the letter form except the address.

There is so much similarity between Jude and 2 Peter, especially Jude 4–16 and 2 Peter 2, 1–18, that there must be a literary relationship between them. Since there is no evidence for the view that both authors borrowed from the same source, it is usually supposed that one of them borrowed from the other. Most scholars believe that Jude is the earlier of the two, principally because he quotes two apocryphal Jewish works, the Assumption of Moses (9) and the Book of Enoch (14–15) as part of his structured argument, whereas 2 Peter omits both references. Since there was controversy in the early church about the propriety of citing noncanonical literature that included legendary material, it is more probable that a later writer would omit such references than that he would add them.

Many interpreters today consider Jude a pseudonymous work dating from the end of the first century or even later. In support of this view they adduce the following arguments: (a) the apostles are referred to as belonging to an age that has receded into the past (17–18); (b) faith is understood as a body of doctrine handed down by a process of tradition (3); (c) the author's competent Greek style shows that he must have had a Hellenistic cultural formation; (d) the gnostic character of the errors envisaged fits better into the early second century than into a period several decades earlier. While impressive, these arguments are not entirely compelling and do not completely rule out the possibility of composition around the year A.D. 80, when the historical Jude may still have been alive.

This little letter is an urgent note by an author who intended to write more fully about salvation to an unknown group of readers, but who was forced by dangers from false teachers worming their way into the community (3–4) to dash off a warning against them (5–16) and to deliver some pressing Christian admonitions (17–23). The letter is justly famous for its majestic closing doxology (24–25).

See RG
519–20 *Address and Greeting.* ^{1a}*Jude, a slave of Jesus Christ and brother of James, to those who are called, beloved in God the Father and kept safe for Jesus Christ: ^{2b}may mercy, peace, and love be yours in abundance.

Occasion for Writing. ^{3c}*Beloved, although I was making every effort to write to you about our common salvation, I now feel a need to write to encourage you to contend for the faith that was once for all handed down to the holy ones. ^{4d}For there have been some intruders, who long ago were designated for this condemnation, godless persons, who pervert the grace of our God into licentiousness and who deny our only Master and Lord, Jesus Christ.

The False Teachers. ^{5e}*I wish to remind you, although you know all things, that [the] Lord who once saved a people from the land of Egypt later destroyed those who did not believe. ^{6f}*The angels too, who did not keep to their own domain but deserted their proper dwelling, he has kept in eternal chains, in gloom, for the judgment of the great day. ^{7g}*Likewise, Sodom, Gomorrah, and the surrounding towns, which, in the same manner as they, indulged in sexual promiscuity and practiced unnatural vice, serve as an example by undergoing a punishment of eternal fire.

⁸*Similarly, these dreamers nevertheless also defile the flesh, scorn lordship, and revile glorious beings. ^{9h}*Yet the archangel Michael, when he argued with the devil in a dispute over the body of Moses, did not venture to pronounce a reviling judgment upon him but said, "May the Lord rebuke you!" ¹⁰ⁱBut these people revile what they do not understand and are destroyed by what they know by nature like irrational animals. ^{11j}*Woe to them! They followed the way of Cain, abandoned themselves to Balaam's error for the sake of gain, and perished in the rebellion of Korah. ^{12k}*These are blemishes on your love feasts, as they carouse fearlessly and look after themselves. They are

1: Jude . . . brother of James: for the identity of the author of this letter, see Introduction. **To those who are called:** the vocation to the Christian faith is God's free gift to those whom he loves and whom he safely protects in Christ until the Lord's second coming.

3–4: Our common salvation: the teachings of the Christian faith derived from the apostolic preaching and to be kept by the Christian community.

5: For this first example of divine punishment on those who had been saved but did not then keep faith, see Nm 14, 28–29 and the note there. Some manuscripts have the word "once" (**hapax** as at 3) after "you know"; some commentators have suggested that it means "knowing one thing" or "you know all things once for all." Instead of "[the] Lord" manuscripts vary, having "Jesus," "God," or no subject stated.

6: This second example draws on Gn 6, 1–4 as elaborated in the apocryphal Book of Enoch (cf 14): heavenly beings came to earth and had sexual intercourse with women. God punished them by casting them out of heaven into darkness and bondage.

7: Practiced unnatural vice: literally, "went after alien flesh." This example derives from Gn 19, 1–25, especially 4–11, when the townsmen of Sodom violated both hospitality and morality by demanding that Lot's two visitors (really messengers of Yahweh) be handed over to them so that they could abuse them sexually. **Unnatural vice:** this refers to the desire for intimacies by human beings with angels (the reverse of the example in 6). Sodom (whence "sodomy") and Gomorrah became proverbial as object lessons for God's punishment on sin (Is 1, 9; Jer 50, 40; Am 4, 11; Mt 10, 15; 2 Pt 2, 6).

8: Dreamers: the writer returns to the false teachers of v

4, applying charges from the three examples in vv 5, 6, 7. This may apply to claims they make for revelations they have received by night (to the author, hallucinations). **Defile the flesh:** this may mean bodily pollutions from the erotic dreams of sexual license (7). **Lordship . . . glorious beings:** these may reflect the Lord (5; Jesus, 4) whom they spurn and the angels (6; cf the note on 2 Pt 2, 10, here, as there, literally, "glories").

9: The archangel Michael . . . judgment: a reference to an incident in the apocryphal Assumption of Moses. Dt 34, 6 had said of Moses, literally in Greek, "they buried him" or "he (God?) buried him" (taken to mean "he was buried"). The later account tells how Michael, who was sent to bury him, was challenged by the devil's interest in the body. Our author draws out the point that if an archangel refrained from reviling even the devil, how wrong it is for mere human beings to revile glorious beings (angels).

11: Cain . . . Balaam . . . Korah: examples of rebellious men and of the punishment their conduct incurred; cf Gn 4, 8–16; Nm 16, 1–35; 31, 16. See the note on 2 Pt 2, 15.

12: Blemishes on your love feasts: or "hidden rocks" or "submerged reefs" (cf 13). The opponents engaged in scandalous conduct in connection with community gatherings called **love feasts** (agape meals), which were associated with eucharistic celebrations at certain stages of early Christian practice; cf 1 Cor 11, 18–34 and the note on 2 Pt 2, 13.

a: Mt 13, 55; Mk 6, 3; Acts 12, 17; Rom 1, 7.   *b:* Gal 6, 16; 1 Tm 1, 2; 2 Pt 1, 2.   *c:* 17.20; 1 Tm 6, 12.   *d:* Gal 2, 4; 2 Tm 3, 6; 2 Pt 2, 1.   *e:* Nm 14, 35; 1 Cor 10, 5; Heb 3, 16.17.   *f:* 2 Pt 2, 4.9. *g:* Dt 29, 22-24; Mt 25, 41; 2 Thes 1, 8-9; 2 Pt 2, 6; 3, 7.   *h:* Dn 10, 21; 12, 1.   *i:* 2 Pt 2, 12.   *j:* Gn 4, 8-16; 1 Jn 3, 12 / Nm 31, 15-16; 2 Pt 2, 15; Rv 2, 14 / Nm 16, 19-35.   *k:* 2 Pt 2, 13.17.

waterless clouds blown about by winds, fruitless trees in late autumn, twice dead and uprooted. [13]They are like wild waves of the sea, foaming up their shameless deeds, wandering stars for whom the gloom of darkness has been reserved forever.

[14]*Enoch, of the seventh generation from Adam, prophesied also about them when he said, "Behold, the Lord has come with his countless holy ones [15]to execute judgment on all and to convict everyone for all the godless deeds that they committed and for all the harsh words godless sinners have uttered against him." [16]mThese people are complainers, disgruntled ones who live by their desires; their mouths utter bombast as they fawn over people to gain advantage.

Exhortations. [17]nBut you, beloved, remember the words spoken beforehand by the apostles of our Lord Jesus Christ, [18]o*for they told you, "In [the] last time there will be scoffers who will live according to their own godless desires." [19]pThese are the ones who cause divisions; they live on the natural plane, devoid of the Spirit. [20]qBut you, beloved, build yourselves up in your most holy faith; pray in the holy Spirit. [21]rKeep yourselves in the love of God and wait for the mercy of our Lord Jesus Christ that leads to eternal life. [22]*On those who waver, have mercy; [23]*save others by snatching them out of the fire; on others have mercy with fear, abhorring even the outer garment stained by the flesh.

Doxology. [24]s*To the one who is able to keep you from stumbling and to present you unblemished and exultant, in the presence of his glory, [25]tto the only God, our savior, through Jesus Christ our Lord be glory, majesty, power, and authority from ages past, now, and for ages to come. Amen.

14–15: Cited from the apocryphal Book of Enoch 1, 9.

18: This is the substance of much early Christian preaching rather than a direct quotation of any of the various New Testament passages on this theme (see Mk 13, 22; Acts 20, 30; 1 Tm 4, 1–3; 2 Pt 3, 3).

22: Have mercy: some manuscripts read "convince," "confute," or reprove." Others have "even though you waver" or "doubt" instead of **who waver.**

23: With fear: some manuscripts connect the phrase "with fear" with the imperative "save" or with the participle "snatching." Other manuscripts omit the phrase "on others have mercy," so that only two groups are envisioned. Rescue of those led astray and caution in the endeavor are both enjoined. **Outer garment stained by the flesh:** the imagery may come from Zec 3, 3–5, just as that of **snatching . . . out of the fire** comes from Zec 3, 2; the very garments of the godless are to be abhorred because of their contagion.

24–25: With this liturgical statement about the power of God to keep the faithful from stumbling, and praise to him through Jesus Christ, the letter reaches its conclusion by returning to the themes with which it began (1–2).

l: Mt 16, 27; Heb 12, 22-23. *m:* 18; 1 Cor 10, 10; 2 Pt 2, 10.18. *n:* Heb 2, 3; 2 Pt 3, 2. *o:* 1 Tm 4, 1; 2 Tm 3, 1-5; 2 Pt 3, 3. *p:* 1 Cor 2, 14; Jas 3, 15. *q:* Eph 6, 18; Col 2, 7. *r:* Ti 2, 13. *s:* 2 Cor 4, 14; 1 Pt 4, 13. *t:* Rom 11, 36; 1 Tm 1, 17.

See RG 520–25

The Revelation to John

The Apocalypse, or Revelation to John, the last book of the Bible, is one of the most difficult to understand because it abounds in unfamiliar and extravagant symbolism, which at best appears unusual to the modern reader. Symbolic language, however, is one of the chief characteristics of apocalyptic literature, of which this book is an outstanding example. Such literature enjoyed wide popularity in both Jewish and Christian circles from ca. 200 B.C. to A.D. 200.

This book contains an account of visions in symbolic and allegorical language borrowed extensively from the Old Testament, especially Ezekiel, Zechariah, and Daniel. Whether or not these visions were real experiences of the author or simply literary conventions employed by him is an open question.

This much, however, is certain: symbolic descriptions are not to be taken as literal descriptions, nor is the symbolism meant to be pictured realistically. One would find it difficult and repulsive to visualize a lamb with seven horns and seven eyes; yet Jesus Christ is described in precisely such words (5, 6). The author used these images to suggest Christ's universal (seven) power (horns) and knowledge (eyes). A significant feature of apocalyptic writing is the use of symbolic colors, metals, garments (1, 13–16; 3, 18; 4, 4; 6, 1–8; 17, 4; 19, 8), and numbers (*four* signifies the world, *six* imperfection, *seven* totality or perfection, *twelve* Israel's tribes or the apostles, *one thousand* immensity). Finally the vindictive language in the book (6, 9–10; 18, 1—19, 4) is also to be understood symbolically and not literally. The cries for vengeance on the lips of Christian martyrs that sound so harsh are in fact literary devices the author employed to evoke in the reader and hearer a feeling of horror for apostasy and rebellion that will be severely punished by God.

The lurid descriptions of the punishment of Jezebel (2, 22) and of the destruction of the great harlot, Babylon (16, 9—19, 2), are likewise literary devices. The metaphor of Babylon as harlot would be wrongly construed if interpreted literally. On the other hand, the stylized figure of the woman clothed with the sun (12, 1–6), depicting the New Israel, may seem to be a negative stereotype. It is necessary to look beyond the literal meaning to see that these images mean to convey a sense of God's wrath at sin in the former case and trust in God's providential care over the church in the latter.

The Book of Revelation cannot be adequately understood except against the historical background that occasioned its writing. Like Daniel and other apocalypses, it was composed as resistance literature to meet a crisis. The book itself suggests that the crisis was ruthless persecution of the early church by the Roman authorities; the harlot Babylon symbolizes pagan Rome, the city on seven hills (17, 9). The book is, then, an exhortation and admonition to Christians of the first century to stand firm in the faith and to avoid compromise with paganism, despite the threat of adversity and martyrdom; they are to await patiently the fulfillment of God's mighty promises. The triumph of God in the world of men and women remains a mystery, to be accepted in faith and longed for in hope. It is a triumph that unfolded in the history of Jesus of Nazareth and continues to unfold in the history of the individual Christian who follows the way of the cross, even, if necessary, to a martyr's death.

Though the perspective is eschatological—ultimate salvation and victory are said to take place at the end of the present age when Christ will come in glory at the parousia—the book presents the decisive struggle of Christ and his followers against Satan and his cohorts as already over. Christ's overwhelming defeat of the kingdom of Satan ushered in the everlasting reign of God (11, 15; 12, 10). Even the forces of evil unwittingly carry out the divine plan (17, 17), for God is the sovereign Lord of history.

The Book of Revelation had its origin in a time of crisis, but it remains valid and meaningful for Christians of all time. In the face of apparently insuperable evil, either from within or from without, all Christians are called to trust in Jesus' promise, "Behold, I am with you always, until the end of the age" (Mt 28, 20). Those who remain steadfast in their faith and confidence in the risen Lord need have no fear. Suffering, persecution, even death by martyrdom, though remaining impenetrable mysteries of evil, do not comprise an absurd dead end. No matter what adversity or sacrifice Christians may endure, they will in the end triumph over Satan and his forces because of their fidelity to Christ the victor. This is the enduring message of the book; it is a message of hope and consolation and challenge for all who dare to believe.

The author of the book calls himself John (1, 1.4.9; 22, 8), who because of his Christian faith has been exiled to the rocky island of Patmos, a Roman penal colony. Although he never claims to be John the apostle, whose name is attached to the fourth gospel, he was so identified by several of the early church Fathers, including Justin, Irenaeus, Clement of Alexandria, Tertullian, Cyprian, and Hippolytus. This identification, however, was denied by other Fathers, including Denis of Alexandria, Eusebius of Caesarea, Cyril of Jerusalem, Gregory Nazianzen, and John Chrysostom. Indeed, vocabulary, grammar, and style make it doubtful that the book could have been put into its present form by the same person(s) responsible for the fourth gospel. Nevertheless, there are definite linguistic and theological affinities between the two books. The tone of the letters to the seven churches (1, 4—3, 22) is indicative of the great authority the author enjoyed over the Christian communities in Asia. It is possible, therefore, that he was a disciple of John the apostle, who is traditionally associated with that part of the world. The date of the book in its present form is probably near the end of the reign of Domitian (A.D. 81–96), a fierce persecutor of the Christians.

The principal divisions of the Book of Revelation are the following:

I: Prologue (1, 1–3)

I: Prologue

CHAPTER 1

See RG 521–22

1a*The revelation of Jesus Christ, which God gave to him, to show his servants what must happen soon. He made it known by sending his angel to his servant John, *2*who gives witness to the word of God and to the testimony of Jesus Christ by reporting what he saw. *3b**Blessed is the one who reads aloud and blessed are those who listen to this prophetic message and heed what is written in it, for the appointed time is near.

II: Letters to the Churches of Asia

Greeting. *4c**John, to the seven churches in Asia: grace to you and peace from him who is and who was and who is to come, and from the seven spirits before his throne, *5d**and from Jesus Christ, the faithful witness, the firstborn of the dead and ruler of the kings of the earth. To him who loves us and has freed us from our sins by his blood, *6e*who has made us into a kingdom, priests for his God and Father, to him be glory and power forever [and ever]. Amen.

> *7* *f*Behold, he is coming amid the clouds,
>> and every eye will see him,
>> even those who pierced him.
> All the peoples of the earth will lament
>> him.
> Yes. Amen.

8g*"I am the Alpha and the Omega," says the Lord God, "the one who is and who was and who is to come, the almighty."

The First Vision. *9**I, John, your brother, who share with you the distress, the kingdom, and the endurance we have in Jesus, found myself on the island called Patmos because I proclaimed God's word and gave testimony to Jesus. *10**I was caught up in spirit on the Lord's day and heard behind me a voice as loud as a trumpet, *11**which said, "Write on a scroll what you see and send it to the seven churches: to Ephesus, Smyrna, Pergamum, Thyatira, Sardis, Philadelphia,

---

1, 1–3: This prologue describes the source, contents, and audience of the book and forms an inclusion with the epilogue (22, 6–21), with its similar themes and expressions.

1, 3: Blessed is the one: this is the first of seven beatitudes in this book; the others are in 14, 13; 16, 15; 19, 9; 20, 6; 22, 7.14. **This prophetic message:** literally, "the words of the prophecy"; so 22, 7.10.18.19 by inclusion. **The appointed time:** when Jesus will return in glory; cf 1, 7; 3, 11; 22, 7.10.12.20.

1, 4–8: Although Revelation begins and ends (22, 21) with Christian epistolary formulae, there is nothing between chs 4 and 22 resembling a letter. The author here employs the standard word order for greetings in Greek letter writing: "N. to N., greetings . . .."; see the note on Rom 1, 1.

1, 4: Seven churches in Asia: Asia refers to the Roman province of that name in western Asia Minor (modern Turkey); these representative churches are mentioned by name in v 11, and each is the recipient of a message (2, 1—3, 22). **Seven** is the biblical number suggesting fullness and completeness; thus the seer is writing for the whole church.

1, 5: Freed us: the majority of Greek manuscripts and several early versions read "washed us"; but "freed us" is supported by the best manuscripts and fits well with Old Testament imagery, e.g., Is 40, 2.

1, 8: The Alpha and the Omega: the first and last letters of the Greek alphabet. In 22, 13 the same words occur together with the expressions "the First and the Last, the Beginning and the End"; cf 17; 2, 8; 21, 6; Is 41, 4; 44, 6.

1, 9–20: In this first vision, the seer is commanded to write what he sees to the seven churches (9–11). He sees Christ in glory, whom he depicts in stock apocalyptic imagery (12–16), and hears him describe himself in terms meant to encourage Christians by emphasizing his victory over death (17–20).

1, 9: Island called Patmos: one of the Sporades islands in the Aegean Sea, some fifty miles south of Ephesus, used by the Romans as a penal colony. **Because I proclaimed God's word:** literally, "on account of God's word."

1, 10: The Lord's day: Sunday. **As loud as a trumpet:** the imagery is derived from the theophany at Sinai (Ex 19, 16.19; cf Heb 12, 19 and the trumpet in other eschatological settings in Is 27, 13; Jl 2, 1; Mt 24, 31; 1 Cor 15, 52; 1 Thes 4, 16).

1, 11: Scroll: a papyrus roll.

---

a: 22, 6-8.20; Dn 2, 28 / 19, 10. *b:* 22, 7 / Lk 11, 28. *c:* 8; 4, 8; 11, 17; 16, 5; Ex 3, 14. *d:* 3, 14; 1 Cor 15, 20; Col 1, 18 / Heb 9, 14; 1 Pt 1, 19; 1 Jn 1, 7. *e:* Ex 19, 6; 1 Pt 2, 9. *f:* Dn 7, 13 / Zec 12, 10; Mt 24, 30; Jn 19, 37. *g:* 17; 21, 6; 22, 13; Is 41, 4; 44, 6; 48, 12.

and Laodicea." *12**Then I turned to see whose voice it was that spoke to me, and when I turned, I saw seven gold lampstands *13h**and in the midst of the lampstands one like a son of man, wearing an ankle-length robe, with a gold sash around his chest. *14**The hair of his head was as white as white wool or as snow, and his eyes were like a fiery flame. *15**His feet were like polished brass refined in a furnace, and his voice was like the sound of rushing water. *16i**In his right hand he held seven stars. A sharp two-edged sword came out of his mouth, and his face shone like the sun at its brightest.

17j*When I caught sight of him, I fell down at his feet as though dead. He touched me with his right hand and said, "Do not be afraid. I am the first and the last, *18**the one who lives. Once I was dead, but now I am alive forever and ever. I hold the keys to death and the netherworld. *19**Write down, therefore, what you have seen, and what is happening, and what will happen after-

wards. *20**This is the secret meaning of the seven stars you saw in my right hand, and of the seven gold lampstands: the seven stars are the angels of the seven churches, and the seven lampstands are the seven churches.

CHAPTER 2

See RG 522

To Ephesus. *1**"To the angel of the church in Ephesus, write this:

" 'The one who holds the seven stars in his right hand and walks in the midst of the seven gold lampstands says this: *2**"I know your works, your labor, and your endurance, and that you cannot tolerate the wicked; you have tested those who call themselves apostles but are not, and discovered that they are impostors. *3*Moreover, you have endurance and have suffered for my name, and you have not grown weary. *4*Yet I hold this against you: you have lost the love you had at first. *5*Realize how far you have fallen. Repent, and do the works you did at first. Otherwise, I will come to you and remove

1, 12–16: A symbolic description of Christ in glory. The metaphorical language is not to be understood literally; cf Introduction.

1, 13: Son of man: see the note on Mk 8, 31. **Ankle-length robe:** Christ is priest; cf Ex 28, 4; 29, 5; Wis 18, 24; Zec 3, 4. **Gold sash:** Christ is king; cf Ex 28, 4; 1 Mc 10, 89; 11, 58; Dn 10, 5.

1, 14: Hair . . . as white as white wool or as snow: Christ is eternal, clothed with the dignity that belonged to the "Ancient of Days"; cf 18; Dn 7, 9. **His eyes were like a fiery flame:** Christ is portrayed as all-knowing; cf 2, 23; Ps 7, 10; Jer 17, 10; and similar expressions in 2, 18; 19, 12; cf Dn 10, 6.

1, 15: His feet . . . furnace: Christ is depicted as unchangeable; cf Ez 1, 27; Dn 10, 6. The Greek word translated "refined" is unconnected grammatically with any other word in the sentence. **His voice . . . water:** Christ speaks with divine authority; cf Ez 1, 24.

1, 16: Seven stars: in the pagan world, Mithras and the Caesars were represented with seven stars in their right hand, symbolizing their universal dominion. **A sharp two-edged sword:** this refers to the word of God (cf Eph 6, 17; Heb 4, 12) that will destroy unrepentant sinners; cf 2, 16; 19, 15; Wis 18, 15; Is 11, 4; 49, 2. **His face . . . brightest:** this symbolizes the divine majesty of Christ; cf 10, 1; 21, 23; Jgs 5, 31; Is 60, 19; Mt 17, 2.

1, 17: It was an Old Testament belief that for sinful human beings to see God was to die; cf Ex 19, 21; 33, 20; Jgs 6, 22–23; Is 6, 5.

1, 18: Netherworld: Greek Hades, Hebrew Sheol, the abode of the dead; cf 20, 13–14; Nm 16, 33.

1, 19: What you have seen, and what is happening, and what will happen afterwards: the three parts of the Book of Revelation, the vision (10–20), the situation in the seven

churches (chs 2–3), and the events of chs 6–22.

1, 20: Secret meaning: literally, "mystery." **Angels:** these are the presiding spirits of the seven churches. Angels were thought to be in charge of the physical world (cf 7, 1; 14, 18; 16, 5) and of nations (Dn 10, 13; 12, 1), communities (the seven churches), and individuals (Mt 18, 10; Acts 12, 15). Some have seen in the "angel" of each of the seven churches its pastor or a personification of the spirit of the congregation.

2, 1–3, 22: Each of the seven letters follows the same pattern: address; description of the exalted Christ; blame and/or praise for the church addressed; threat and/or admonition; final exhortation and promise to all Christians.

2, 1–7: The letter to Ephesus praises the members of the church there for their works and virtues, including discerning false teachers (2–3), but admonishes them to repent and return to their former devotion (4–5). It concludes with a reference to the Nicolaitans (see the note on 6) and a promise that the victor will have access to eternal life (7).

2, 1: Ephesus: this great ancient city had a population of ca. 250,000; it was the capital of the Roman province of Asia and the commercial, cultural, and religious center of Asia. The other six churches were located in the same province, situated roughly in a circle; they were selected for geographical reasons rather than for the size of their Christian communities. **Walks in the midst of the seven gold lampstands:** this signifies that Christ is always present in the church; see the note on 1, 4.

2, 2: Who call themselves . . . impostors: this refers to unauthorized and perverse missionaries; cf Acts 20, 29–30.

h: Dn 7, 13; 10, 5.   *i:* Heb 4, 12.   *j:* Dn 8, 18 / 1, 8.

your lampstand from its place, unless you repent. *6**But you have this in your favor: you hate the works of the Nicolaitans, which I also hate.

7k*' "Whoever has ears ought to hear what the Spirit says to the churches. To the victor I will give the right to eat from the tree of life that is in the garden of God." '

To Smyrna. *8**"To the angel of the church in Smyrna, write this:

" 'The first and the last, who once died but came to life, says this: *9l**"I know your tribulation and poverty, but you are rich. I know the slander of those who claim to be Jews and are not, but rather are members of the assembly of Satan. *10*Do not be afraid of anything that you are going to suffer. Indeed, the devil will throw some of you into prison, that you may be tested, and you will face an ordeal for ten days. Remain faithful until death, and I will give you the crown of life. *11m**' "Whoever has ears ought to hear what the Spirit says to the churches. The victor shall not be harmed by the second death." '

To Pergamum. *12**"To the angel of the church in Pergamum, write this:

" 'The one with the sharp two-edged sword says this: *13**"I know that you live where Satan's throne is, and yet you hold fast to my name and have not denied your faith in me, not even in the days of Antipas, my faithful witness, who was martyred among you, where Satan lives. *14n*Yet I have a few things against you. You have some people there who hold to the teaching of Balaam, who instructed Balak to put a stumbling block before the Israelites: to eat food sacrificed to idols and to play the harlot. *15*Likewise, you also have some people who hold to the teaching of [the] Nicolaitans. *16*Therefore, repent. Otherwise, I will come to you quickly and wage war against them with the sword of my mouth.

17o*' "Whoever has ears ought to hear what the Spirit says to the churches. To the victor I shall give some of the hidden manna; I shall also give a white amulet upon which is inscribed a new name, which no one knows except the one who receives it." '

2, 6: Nicolaitans: these are perhaps the impostors of v 2; see the note on vv 14–15. There is little evidence for connecting this group with Nicolaus, the proselyte from Antioch, mentioned in Acts 6, 5.

2, 7: Victor: referring to any Christian individual who holds fast to the faith and does God's will in the face of persecution. **The tree of life that is in the garden of God:** this is a reference to the tree in the primeval paradise (Gn 2, 9); cf 22, 2.14.19. The decree excluding humanity from the tree of life has been revoked by Christ.

2, 8–11: The letter to Smyrna encourages the Christians in this important commercial center by telling them that although they are impoverished, they are nevertheless rich, and calls those Jews who are slandering them members of the assembly of Satan (9). There is no admonition; rather, the Christians are told that they will suffer much, even death, but the time of tribulation will be short compared to their eternal reward (10), and they will thus escape final damnation (11).

2, 8: Smyrna: modern Izmir, ca. thirty miles north of Ephesus, and the chief city of Lydia, with a temple to the goddess Roma. It was renowned for its loyalty to Rome, and it also had a large Jewish community very hostile toward Christians.

2, 9–10: The church in Smyrna was materially poor but spiritually rich. Accusations made by Jewish brethren there occasioned the persecution of Christians; cf Acts 14, 2.19; 17, 5.13.

2, 11: The second death: this refers to the eternal death, when sinners will receive their final punishment; cf 20, 6.14–15; 21, 8.

2, 12–17: The letter to Pergamum praises the members of

the church for persevering in their faith in Christ even in the midst of a pagan setting and in face of persecution and martyrdom (13). But it admonishes them about members who advocate an unprincipled morality (14; cf 2 Pt 2, 15; Jude 11) and others who follow the teaching of the Nicolaitans (15; see the note there). It urges them to repent (16) and promises them the hidden manna and Christ's amulet (17).

2, 12: Pergamum: modern Bergama, ca. forty-five miles northeast of Smyrna, a center for various kinds of pagan worship. It also had an outstanding library (the word **parchment** is derived from its name).

2, 13: Satan's throne: the reference is to emperor worship and other pagan practices that flourished in Pergamum, perhaps specifically to the white marble altar erected and dedicated to Zeus by Eumenes II (197–160 B.C.).

2, 14–15: Like Balaam, the biblical prototype of the religious compromiser (cf Nm 25, 1–3; 31, 16; 2 Pt 2, 15; Jude 11), the Nicolaitans in Pergamum and Ephesus (6) accommodated their Christian faith to paganism. They abused the principle of liberty enunciated by Paul (1 Cor 9, 19–23).

2, 17: The hidden manna: this is the food of life; cf Ps 78, 24–25. **White amulet:** literally, "white stone," on which was written a magical name, whose power could be tapped by one who knew the secret name. It is used here as a symbol of victory and joy; cf 3, 4–5. **New name:** this is a reference to the Christian's rebirth in Christ; cf 3, 12; 19, 12; Is 62, 2; 65, 15.

---

k: 11.17.29; 3, 6.13.22; 13, 9; Mt 11, 15. *l:* Jas 2, 5. *m:* 20, 6.14; 21, 8. *n:* Nm 22-24; 25, 1-3; 31, 16; 2 Pt 2, 15; Jude 11. *o:* Is 62, 2; 65, 15.

Pergamum

Thyatira

A S I A

Sardis

Philadelphia

Smyrna

Ephesus

Laodicea

Patmos

Aegean Sea

0   50   100 Miles

0   50   100 Kilometers

Mediterranean Sea

The Seven Churches

To Thyatira. ¹⁸*"To the angel of the church in Thyatira, write this:

" 'The Son of God, whose eyes are like a fiery flame and whose feet are like polished brass, says this: ¹⁹"I know your works, your love, faith, service, and endurance, and that your last works are greater than the first. ²⁰*Yet I hold this against you, that you tolerate the woman Jezebel, who calls herself a prophetess, who teaches and misleads my servants to play the harlot and to eat food sacrificed to idols. ²¹I have given her time to repent, but she refuses to repent of her harlotry. ²²So I will cast her on a sickbed and plunge those who commit adultery with her into intense suffering unless they repent of her works. ²³ᵖ*I will also put her children to death. Thus shall all the churches come to know that I am the searcher of hearts and minds and that I will give each of you what your works deserve. ²⁴*But I say to the rest of you in Thyatira, who do not uphold this teaching and know nothing of the so-called deep secrets of Satan: on you I will place no further burden, ²⁵except that you must hold fast to what you have until I come.

²⁶ �q*" ' "To the victor, who keeps to my ways until the end,

2, 18–29: The letter to Thyatira praises the progress in virtue of this small Christian community (19) but admonishes them for tolerating a false prophet who leads them astray (20). Her fate is sealed, but there is hope of repentance for her followers (21–22). Otherwise, they too shall die (23). They are warned against Satanic power or knowledge (24–25). Those who remain faithful will share in the messianic reign, having authority over nations (26–27), and will in fact possess Christ himself (28).

2, 18: Thyatira: modern Akhisar, ca. forty miles southeast of Pergamum, a frontier town famous for its workers' guilds (cf Acts 16, 14), membership in which may have involved festal meals in pagan temples.

2, 20: The scheming and treacherous Jezebel of old (cf 1 Kgs 19, 1–2; 21, 1–14; 2 Kgs 9, 22.30–34) introduced pagan customs into the religion of Israel; this new Jezebel was doing the same to Christianity.

2, 23: Children: spiritual descendants.

2, 24: The so-called deep secrets of Satan: literally, "the deep things of Satan," a scathing reference to the perverse teaching of the Nicolaitans (15).

2, 26–28: The Christian who perseveres in faith will share

p: 1 Sm 16, 7; Jer 11, 20; 17, 10.   q: 12, 5; Ps 2, 8-9.

I will give authority over the nations. [27] He will rule them with an iron rod.

Like clay vessels will they be
smashed,

[28] just as I received authority from my Father. And to him I will give the morning star. [29]" ' "Whoever has ears ought to hear what the Spirit says to the churches." '

See RG
522

CHAPTER 3

To Sardis. [1]*"To the angel of the church in Sardis, write this:

" 'The one who has the seven spirits of God and the seven stars says this: "I know your works, that you have the reputation of being alive, but you are dead. [2] Be watchful and strengthen what is left, which is going to die, for I have not found your works complete in the sight of my God. [3r] Remember then how you accepted and heard; keep it, and repent. If you are not watchful, I will come like a thief, and you will never know at what hour I will come upon you. [4s] However, you have a few people in Sardis who have not soiled their garments; they will walk with me dressed in white, because they are worthy.

[5t]*" ' "The victor will thus be dressed in white, and I will never erase his name from the

book of life but will acknowledge his name in the presence of my Father and of his angels.

[6]" ' "Whoever has ears ought to hear what the Spirit says to the churches." '

To Philadelphia. [7u]*"To the angel of the church in Philadelphia, write this:

" 'The holy one, the true,
who holds the key of David,
who opens and no one shall close,
who closes and no one shall open,

says this:

[8]*" ' "I know your works (behold, I have left an open door before you, which no one can close). You have limited strength, and yet you have kept my word and have not denied my name. [9v] Behold, I will make those of the assembly of Satan who claim to be Jews and are not, but are lying, behold I will make them come and fall prostrate at your feet, and they will realize that I love you. [10]*Because you have kept my message of endurance, I will keep you safe in the time of trial that is going to come to the whole world to test the inhabitants of the earth. [11w] I am coming quickly. Hold fast to what you have, so that no one may take your crown.

[12x]*" ' "The victor I will make into a pillar in the temple of my God, and he will never

in Christ's messianic authority (cf Ps 2, 8–9) and resurrection victory over death, symbolized by the morning star; cf 22, 16.

2, 26: Who keeps to my ways: literally, "who keeps my works."

3, 1–6: The letter to Sardis does not praise the community but admonishes its members to watchfulness, mutual support, and repentance (2–3). The few who have remained pure and faithful will share Christ's victory and will be inscribed in the book of life (4–5).

3, 1: Sardis: this city, located ca. thirty miles southeast of Thyatira, was once the capital of Lydia, known for its wealth at the time of Croesus (6th century B.C.). Its citadel, reputed to be unassailable, was captured by surprise, first by Cyrus and later by Antiochus. The church is therefore warned to be on guard.

3, 5: In white: white is a sign of victory and joy as well as resurrection; see the note on 2, 17. **The book of life:** the roll in which the names of the redeemed are kept; cf 13, 8; 17, 8; 20, 12.15; 21, 27; Phil 4, 3; Dn 12, 1. They will be acknowledged by Christ in heaven; cf Mt 10, 32.

3, 7–13: The letter to Philadelphia praises the Christians there for remaining faithful even with their limited strength (8). Members of the assembly of Satan are again singled out (9; see 2, 9 above). There is no admonition; rather, the letter promises that they will be kept safe at the great trial (10–11) and that the victors will become pillars of the heavenly temple, upon which three names will be

inscribed: God, Jerusalem, and Christ (12).

3, 7: Philadelphia: modern Alasehir, ca. thirty miles southeast of Sardis, founded by Attalus II Philadelphus of Pergamum to be an "open door" (8) for Greek culture; it was destroyed by an earthquake in A.D. 17. Rebuilt by money from the Emperor Tiberius, the city was renamed Neo-Caesarea; this may explain the allusions to "name" in v 12. **Key of David:** to the heavenly city of David (cf Is 22, 22), "the new Jerusalem" (12), over which Christ has supreme authority.

3, 8: An open door: opportunities for sharing and proclaiming the faith; cf Acts 14, 27; 1 Cor 16, 9; 2 Cor 2, 12.

3, 10: My message of endurance: this does not refer to a saying of Jesus about patience but to the example of Christ's patient endurance. **The inhabitants of the earth:** literally, "those who live on the earth." This expression, which also occurs in 6, 10; 8, 13; 11, 10; 13, 8.12.14; 17, 2.8, always refers to the pagan world.

3, 12: Pillar: this may be an allusion to the rebuilding of the city; see the note on v 7. **New Jerusalem:** it is described in 21, 10—22, 5.

r: Mt 24, 42-44; Mk 13, 33; 1 Thes 5, 2; 2 Pt 3, 10. s: 7, 13-14. t: Ps 69, 29; Dn 12, 1 / Mt 10, 32. u: Is 22, 22; Mt 16, 19. v: 2, 9 / Is 45, 14; 60, 14. w: 2, 25; 22, 7.20. x: 21, 2-3; Ez 48, 35 / 19, 13.

leave it again. On him I will inscribe the name of my God and the name of the city of my God, the new Jerusalem, which comes down out of heaven from my God, as well as my new name.

13" ' "Whoever has ears ought to hear what the Spirit says to the churches." '

To Laodicea. *14y**"To the angel of the church in Laodicea, write this:

" 'The Amen, the faithful and true witness, the source of God's creation, says this: *15**"I know your works; I know that you are neither cold nor hot. I wish you were either cold or hot. *16**So, because you are lukewarm, neither hot nor cold, I will spit you out of my mouth. *17z**For you say, 'I am rich and affluent and have no need of anything,' and yet do not realize that you are wretched, pitiable, poor, blind, and naked. *18**I advise you to buy from me gold refined by fire so that you may be rich, and white garments to put on so that your shameful nakedness may not be exposed, and buy ointment to smear on your eyes so that you may see. *19a*Those whom I love, I reprove and chastise. Be earnest, therefore, and repent. *20**" ' "Behold, I stand at the door and knock. If anyone hears my voice and opens

the door, [then] I will enter his house and dine with him, and he with me. *21b*I will give the victor the right to sit with me on my throne, as I myself first won the victory and sit with my Father on his throne.

22" ' "Whoever has ears ought to hear what the Spirit says to the churches." ' "

III: God and the Lamb in Heaven

CHAPTER 4

See RG 522-23

Vision of Heavenly Worship. *1**After this I had a vision of an open door to heaven, and I heard the trumpetlike voice that had spoken to me before, saying, "Come up here and I will show you what must happen afterwards." *2c**At once I was caught up in spirit. A throne was there in heaven, and on the throne sat *3*one whose appearance sparkled like jasper and carnelian. Around the throne was a halo as brilliant as an emerald. *4d**Surrounding the throne I saw twenty-four other thrones on which twenty-four elders sat, dressed in white garments and with gold crowns on their heads. *5**From the throne came flashes of lightning,

---

3, 14–22: The letter to Laodicea reprimands the community for being lukewarm (15–16), but no particular faults are singled out. Their material prosperity is contrasted with their spiritual poverty, the violet tunics that were the source of their wealth with the white robe of baptism, and their famous eye ointment with true spiritual perception (17–18). But Christ's chastisement is inspired by love and a desire to be allowed to share the messianic banquet with his followers in the heavenly kingdom (19–21).

3, 14: Laodicea: ca. forty miles southeast of Philadelphia and ca. eighty miles east of Ephesus, a wealthy industrial and commercial center, with a renowned medical school. It exported fine woolen garments and was famous for its eye salves. It was so wealthy that it was proudly rebuilt without outside aid after the devastating earthquake of A.D. 60/61. **The Amen:** this is a divine title (cf Hebrew text of Is 65, 16) applied to Christ; cf 2 Cor 1, 20. **Source of God's creation:** literally, "the beginning of God's creation," a concept found also in Jn 1, 3; Col 1, 16–17; Heb 1, 2; cf Prv 8, 22–31; Wis 9, 1–2.

3, 15–16: Halfhearted commitment to the faith is nauseating to Christ; cf Rom 12, 11.

3, 16: Spit: literally, "vomit." The image is that of a beverage that should be either hot or cold. Perhaps there is an allusion to the hot springs of Hierapolis across the Lycus river from Laodicea, which would have been lukewarm by the time they reached Laodicea.

3, 17: Economic prosperity occasioned spiritual bankruptcy. **3, 18: Gold . . . fire:** God's grace. **White garments:** sym-

bol of an upright life; the city was noted for its violet/purple cloth. **Ointment . . . eyes:** to remove spiritual blindness; one of the city's exports was eye ointment (see the note on 3, 14).

3, 20: Christ invites all to the messianic banquet in heaven; cf Is 25, 6; Lk 14, 15; 22, 30.

4, 1–11: The seer now describes a vision of the heavenly court in worship of God enthroned. He reverently avoids naming or describing God but pictures twenty-four elders in priestly and regal attire (4) and God's throne and its surroundings made of precious gems and other symbols that traditionally express the majesty of God (5–6). Universal creation is represented by the four living creatures (6–7). Along with the twenty-four elders, they praise God unceasingly in humble adoration (8–11).

4, 1: The ancients viewed heaven as a solid vault, entered by way of actual doors.

4, 2–8: Much of the imagery here is taken from Ez 1 and 10.

4, 4: Twenty-four elders: these represent the twelve tribes of Israel and the twelve apostles; cf 21, 12–14.

4, 5: Flashes of lightning, rumblings, and peals of thunder: as in other descriptions of God's appearance or activity; cf 8, 5; 11, 19; 16, 18; Ex 19, 16; Ez 1, 4.13. **The seven spirits of God:** the seven "angels of the presence" as in 8, 2 and Tb 12, 15.

---

y: 1, 5. *z:* Prv 13, 7; Lk 12, 21. *a:* Prv 3, 11-12; 1 Cor 11, 32; Heb 12, 5-11. *b:* Lk 22, 28-30; Mt 19, 28. *c:* Is 6, 1 / Ez 1, 26-28. *d:* Is 24, 23.

rumblings, and peals of thunder. Seven flaming torches burned in front of the throne, which are the seven spirits of God. *6e**In front of the throne was something that resembled a sea of glass like crystal.

In the center and around the throne, there were four living creatures covered with eyes in front and in back. *7**The first creature resembled a lion, the second was like a calf, the third had a face like that of a human being, and the fourth looked like an eagle in flight. *8f**The four living creatures, each of them with six wings, were covered with eyes inside and out. Day and night they do not stop exclaiming:

> "Holy, holy, holy is the Lord God
>   almighty,
>   who was, and who is, and who is to
>   come."

*9*Whenever the living creatures give glory and honor and thanks to the one who sits on the throne, who lives forever and ever, *10*the twenty-four elders fall down before the one who sits on the throne and worship him, who lives forever and ever. They throw down their crowns before the throne, exclaiming:

11 g"Worthy are you, Lord our God,
>   to receive glory and honor and power,
>   for you created all things;
>   because of your will they came to be
>   and were created."

CHAPTER 5

The Scroll and the Lamb. *1h**I saw a scroll in the right hand of the one who sat on the throne. It had writing on both sides and was sealed with seven seals. *2*Then I saw a mighty angel who proclaimed in a loud voice, "Who is worthy to open the scroll and break its seals?" *3*But no one in heaven or on earth or under the earth was able to open the scroll or to examine it. *4*I shed many tears because no one was found worthy to open the scroll or to examine it. *5i**One of the elders said to me, "Do not weep. The lion of the tribe of Judah, the root of David, has triumphed, enabling him to open the scroll with its seven seals."

6j*Then I saw standing in the midst of the throne and the four living creatures and the elders a Lamb that seemed to have been slain. He had seven horns and seven eyes; these are the [seven] spirits of God sent out into the whole world. *7*He came and received the scroll from the right hand of the one who sat on the throne. *8*When he took it, the four living creatures and the twenty-four elders fell down before the Lamb. Each of the elders held a harp and gold bowls filled with incense, which are the prayers of the holy ones. *9*They sang a new hymn:

> "Worthy are you to receive the scroll
>   and to break open its seals,

4, 6: **A sea of glass like crystal:** an image adapted from Ez 1, 22–26. **Four living creatures:** these are symbols taken from Ez 1, 5–21; they are identified as cherubim in Ez 10, 20. **Covered with eyes:** these suggest God's knowledge and concern.

4, 7: **Lion . . . calf . . . human being . . . eagle:** these symbolize, respectively, what is noblest, strongest, wisest, and swiftest in creation. **Calf:** traditionally translated "ox," the Greek word refers to a heifer or young bull. Since the second century, these four creatures have been used as symbols of the evangelists Mark, Luke, Matthew, and John, respectively.

4, 8: **Six wings:** like the seraphim of Is 6, 2.

5, 1–14: The seer now describes a papyrus roll in God's right hand (1) with seven seals indicating the importance of the message. A mighty angel asks who is worthy to open the scroll, i.e., who can accomplish God's salvific plan (2). There is despair at first when no one in creation can do it (3–4). But the seer is comforted by an elder who tells him that Christ, called the lion of the tribe of Judah, has won the right to open it (5). Christ then appears as a Lamb, coming to receive the scroll from God (6–7), for which he is acclaimed as at a coronation (8–10). This is followed by a doxology of the angels

(11–12) and then finally by the heavenly church united with all of creation (13–14).

5, 1: **A scroll:** a papyrus roll possibly containing a list of afflictions for sinners (cf Ez 2, 9–10) or God's plan for the world. **Sealed with seven seals:** it is totally hidden from all but God. Only the Lamb (7–9) has the right to carry out the divine plan.

5, 5: **The lion of the tribe of Judah, the root of David:** these are the messianic titles applied to Christ to symbolize his victory; cf 22, 16; Gn 49, 9; Is 11, 1.10; Mt 1, 1.

5, 6: Christ is the Paschal Lamb without blemish, whose blood saved the new Israel from sin and death; cf Ex 12; Is 53, 7; Jn 1, 29.36; Acts 8, 32; 1 Pt 1, 18–19. This is the main title for Christ in Rv, used twenty-eight times. **Seven horns and seven eyes:** Christ has the fullness (see the note on 1, 4) of power (horns) and knowledge (eyes); cf Zec 4, 10. **[Seven] spirits:** as in 1, 4; 3, 1; and 4, 5.

e: Ex 24, 10. *f:* Is 6, 2-3 / 1, 4.8; 11, 17; 16, 5. *g:* Rom 4, 17; 16, 27. *h:* Is 29, 11. *i:* Is 11, 1.10; Rom 15, 12. *j:* Jn 1, 29.

for you were slain and with your blood
       you purchased for God
those from every tribe and tongue,
       people and nation.
[10] *k* You made them a kingdom and priests
       for our God,
and they will reign on earth."

[11] *I looked again and heard the voices of many angels who surrounded the throne and the living creatures and the elders. They were countless in number, [12] and they cried out in a loud voice:

"Worthy is the Lamb that was slain
       to receive power and riches, wisdom
              and strength,
       honor and glory and blessing."

[13] Then I heard every creature in heaven and on earth and under the earth and in the sea, everything in the universe, cry out:

"To the one who sits on the throne and to
              the Lamb
       be blessing and honor, glory and
              might,
       forever and ever."

[14] The four living creatures answered, "Amen," and the elders fell down and worshiped.

IV: The Seven Seals, Trumpets, and Plagues, with Interludes

CHAPTER 6

See RG 523

The First Six Seals. [1] *Then I watched while the Lamb broke open the first of the seven seals, and I heard one of the four living creatures cry out in a voice like thunder, "Come forward." [2] *m* *I looked, and there was a white horse, and its rider had a bow. He was given a crown, and he rode forth victorious to further his victories.

[3] When he broke open the second seal, I heard the second living creature cry out, "Come forward." [4] *n* *Another horse came out, a red one. Its rider was given power to take peace away from the earth, so that people would slaughter one another. And he was given a huge sword.

[5] *When he broke open the third seal, I heard the third living creature cry out, "Come forward." I looked, and there was a black horse, and its rider held a scale in his hand. [6] *o* *I heard what seemed to be a voice in the midst of the four living creatures. It said, "A ration of wheat costs a day's pay, and three rations of barley cost a day's pay. But do not damage the olive oil or the wine."
[7] When he broke open the fourth seal, I

5, 11: Countless: literally, "100,000,000 plus 1,000,000," used by the author to express infinity.

6, 1—16, 21: A series of seven disasters now begins as each seal is broken (6, 1—8, 1), followed by a similar series as seven trumpets sound (8, 2—11, 19) and as seven angels pour bowls on the earth causing plagues (15, 1—16, 21). These gloomy sequences are interrupted by longer or shorter scenes suggesting the triumph of God and his witnesses (e.g., chs 7, 10, 11, 12, 13, 14).

6, 1—17: This chapter provides a symbolic description of the contents of the sealed scroll. The breaking of the first four seals reveals four riders. The first rider (of a white horse) is a conquering power (1–2), the second (red horse) a symbol of bloody war (3–4), the third (black horse) a symbol of famine (5–6), the fourth (pale green horse) a symbol of Death himself, accompanied by Hades (the netherworld) as his page (7–8). Verse 8b summarizes the role of all four riders. The breaking of the fifth seal reveals Christian martyrs in an attitude of sacrifice as blood poured out at the foot of an altar begging God for vindication, which will come only when their quota is filled; but they are given a white robe symbolic of victory (9–11). The breaking of the sixth seal reveals typical apocalyptic signs in the sky and the sheer terror of all people at the imminent divine judgment (12–17).

6, 1–8: The imagery is adapted from Zec 1, 8–10; 6, 1–8.
6, 2: White horse . . . bow: this may perhaps allude specifically to the Parthians on the eastern border of the Roman empire. Expert in the use of the bow, they constantly harassed the Romans and won a major victory in A.D. 62; see the note on 9, 13–21. But the Old Testament imagery typifies the history of oppression of God's people at all times.
6, 4: Huge sword: this is a symbol of war and violence; cf Ez 21, 14–17.
6, 5: Black horse: this is a symbol of famine, the usual accompaniment of war in antiquity; cf Lv 26, 26; Ez 4, 16–17. The scale is a symbol of shortage of food with a corresponding rise in price.
6, 6: A day's pay: literally, "a denarius," a Roman silver coin that constitutes a day's wage in Mt 20, 2. Because of the famine, food was rationed and sold at an exorbitant price. A liter of flour was considered a day's ration in the Greek historians Herodotus and Diogenes Laertius. **Barley:** food of the poor (Jn 6, 9.13; cf 2 Kgs 7, 1.16.18); it was also used to feed animals; cf 1 Kgs 5, 8. **Do not damage:** the olive and the vine are to be used more sparingly in time of famine.

---

k: 1, 6; Ex 19, 6; Is 61, 6.   *l:* Dn 7, 10; Jude 14-15.   *m:* Zec 1, 8-10; 6, 1-3.   *n:* Ez 21, 14-16.   *o:* Lv 26, 26; Ez 4, 16-17.

heard the voice of the fourth living creature cry out, "Come forward." *8 p**I looked, and there was a pale green horse. Its rider was named Death, and Hades accompanied him. They were given authority over a quarter of the earth, to kill with sword, famine, and plague, and by means of the beasts of the earth.

9*When he broke open the fifth seal, I saw underneath the altar the souls of those who had been slaughtered because of the witness they bore to the word of God. *10**They cried out in a loud voice, "How long will it be, holy and true master, before you sit in judgment and avenge our blood on the inhabitants of the earth?" *11*Each of them was given a white robe, and they were told to be patient a little while longer until the number was filled of their fellow servants and brothers who were going to be killed as they had been.

12 q*Then I watched while he broke open the sixth seal, and there was a great earthquake; the sun turned as black as dark sackcloth and the whole moon became like blood. *13**The stars in the sky fell to the earth like unripe figs shaken loose from the tree in a strong wind. *14 r**Then the sky was divided like a torn scroll curling up, and every mountain and is-

land was moved from its place. *15**The kings of the earth, the nobles, the military officers, the rich, the powerful, and every slave and free person hid themselves in caves and among mountain crags. *16 s*They cried out to the mountains and the rocks, "Fall on us and hide us from the face of the one who sits on the throne and from the wrath of the Lamb, *17**because the great day of their wrath has come and who can withstand it?"

CHAPTER 7

See RG 523

The 144,000 Sealed. *1 t**After this I saw four angels standing at the four corners of the earth, holding back the four winds of the earth so that no wind could blow on land or sea or against any tree. *2**Then I saw another angel come up from the East, holding the seal of the living God. He cried out in a loud voice to the four angels who were given power to damage the land and the sea, *3 u*"Do not damage the land or the sea or the trees until we put the seal on the foreheads of the servants of our God." *4 v**I heard the number of those who had been marked with the seal, one hundred and forty-four thousand marked from every tribe of the Israelites: *5**twelve thousand were marked from the

---

6, 8: Pale green: symbol of death and decay; cf Ez 14, 21.

6, 9: The altar: this altar corresponds to the altar of holocausts in the temple in Jerusalem; see also 11, 1. **Because of the witness ... word of God:** literally, "because of the word of God and the witness they had borne."

6, 10: Holy and true master: Old Testament usage as well as the context indicates that this is addressed to God rather than to Christ.

6, 12–14: Symbolic rather than literal description of the cosmic upheavals attending the day of the Lord when the martyrs' prayer for vindication (10) would be answered; cf Am 8, 8–9; Is 34, 4; 50, 3; Jl 2, 10; 3, 3–4; Mt 24, 4–36; Mk 13, 5–37; Lk 21, 8–36.

6, 12: Dark sackcloth: for mourning, sackcloth was made from the skin of a black goat.

6, 13: Unripe figs: literally, "summer (or winter) fruit."

6, 14: Was divided: literally, "was split," like a broken papyrus roll torn in two, each half then curling up to form a roll on either side.

6, 15: Nobles: literally, "courtiers," "grandees." **Military officers:** literally, "commanders of 1,000 men," used in Josephus and other Greek authors as the equivalent of the Roman *tribunus militum.* The listing of various ranks of society represents the universality of terror at the impending doom.

6, 17: Their: this reading is attested in the best manuscripts, but the vast majority read "his" in reference to the wrath of the Lamb in the preceding verse.

7, 1–17: An interlude of two visions precedes the breaking of the seventh seal, just as two more will separate the sixth and seventh trumpets (ch 10). In the first vision (1–8), the elect receive the seal of the living God as protection against the coming cataclysm; cf 14, 1; Ez 9, 4–6; 2 Cor 1, 22; Eph 1, 13; 4, 30. The second vision (9–17) portrays the faithful Christians before God's throne to encourage those on earth to persevere to the end, even to death.

7, 1: The four corners of the earth: the earth is seen as a table or rectangular surface.

7, 2: East: literally, "rising of the sun." The east was considered the source of light and the place of paradise (Gn 2, 8). **Seal:** whatever was marked by the impression of one's signet ring belonged to that person and was under his protection.

7, 4–9: One hundred and forty-four thousand: the square of twelve (the number of Israel's tribes) multiplied by a thousand, symbolic of the new Israel (cf 14, 1–5; Gal 6, 16; Jas 1, 1) that embraces people **from every nation, race, people, and tongue** (9).

7, 5–8: Judah is placed first because of Christ; cf "the Lion of the tribe of Judah" (5, 5). Dan is omitted because of a later tradition that the antichrist would arise from it.

---

p: Ez 14, 21. *q:* Jl 3, 4; Mt 24, 29. *r:* Is 34, 4 / 16, 20. *s:* Is 2, 19; Hos 10, 8; Lk 23, 30. *t:* Jer 49, 36; Zec 6, 5. *u:* Ex 12, 7-14; Ez 9, 4; 2 Cor 1, 22; Eph 1, 13; 4, 30. *v:* 14, 1.

tribe of Judah, twelve thousand from the tribe of Reuben, twelve thousand from the tribe of Gad, [6]twelve thousand from the tribe of Asher, twelve thousand from the tribe of Naphtali, twelve thousand from the tribe of Manasseh, [7]twelve thousand from the tribe of Simeon, twelve thousand from the tribe of Levi, twelve thousand from the tribe of Issachar, [8]twelve thousand from the tribe of Zebulun, twelve thousand from the tribe of Joseph, and twelve thousand were marked from the tribe of Benjamin.

Triumph of the Elect. [9]*After this I had a vision of a great multitude, which no one could count, from every nation, race, people, and tongue. They stood before the throne and before the Lamb, wearing white robes and holding palm branches in their hands. [10]*They cried out in a loud voice:

"Salvation comes from our God, who is
    seated on the throne,
  and from the Lamb."

[11]All the angels stood around the throne and around the elders and the four living creatures. They prostrated themselves before the throne, worshiped God, [12]and exclaimed:

"Amen. Blessing and glory, wisdom and
    thanksgiving,
  honor, power, and might
  be to our God forever and ever.
    Amen."

[13]Then one of the elders spoke up and said to me, "Who are these wearing white robes, and where did they come from?" [14w]*I said to him, "My lord, you are the one who knows." He said to me, "These are the ones who have survived the time of great distress; they have washed their robes and made them white in the blood of the Lamb.

[15] "For this reason they stand before God's
    throne
  and worship him day and night in his
    temple.
  The one who sits on the throne will
    shelter them.
[16] [x]They will not hunger or thirst anymore,
  nor will the sun or any heat strike them.
[17] [y]*For the Lamb who is in the center of
    the throne will shepherd them
  and lead them to springs of life-giving
    water,
  and God will wipe away every tear
    from their eyes."

CHAPTER 8

See RG 523

The Seven Trumpets. [1z]*When he broke open the seventh seal, there was silence in heaven for about half an hour. [2a]And I saw that the seven angels who stood before God were given seven trumpets.

The Gold Censer. [3b]*Another angel came and stood at the altar, holding a gold censer. He was given a great quantity of incense to offer, along with the prayers of all the holy ones, on the gold altar that was before the throne. [4]The smoke of the incense along with the prayers of the holy ones went up before God from the hand of the angel. [5c]Then the angel took the censer, filled it with burning coals from the altar, and hurled it down to the earth. There were peals of thunder, rumblings, flashes of lightning, and an earthquake.

The First Four Trumpets. [6d]The seven an-

7, 9: **White robes ... palm branches:** symbols of joy and victory; see the note on 3, 5.

7, 10: **Salvation comes from:** literally, "(let) salvation (be ascribed) to." A similar hymn of praise is found at the fall of the dragon (12, 10) and of Babylon (19, 1).

7, 14: **Time of great distress:** fierce persecution by the Romans; cf Introduction.

7, 17: **Life-giving water:** literally, "the water of life," God's grace, which flows from Christ; cf 21, 6; 22, 1.17; Jn 4, 10.14.

8, 1–13: The breaking of the seventh seal produces at first silence and then seven symbolic disasters, each announced by a trumpet blast, of which the first four form a unit as did the first four seals. A minor liturgy (3–5) is enclosed by a vision of seven angels (2.6). Then follow the first four trumpet blasts, each heralding catastrophes modeled on the plagues of Egypt affecting the traditional prophetic third (cf Ez 5, 12) of the earth, sea, fresh water, and stars (7–12). Finally, there is a vision of an eagle warning of the last three trumpet blasts (13).

8, 1: **Silence in heaven:** as in Zep 1, 7, a prelude to the eschatological woes that are to follow; cf Introduction.

8, 3: **Altar:** there seems to be only one altar in the heavenly temple, corresponding to the altar of holocausts in 6, 9, and here to the altar of incense in Jerusalem; cf also 9, 13; 11, 1; 14, 18; 16, 7.

---

w: Mt 24, 21.   x: Is 49, 10.   y: 21, 4; Is 25, 8.   z: Hb 2, 20; Zep 1, 7; Zec 2, 17.   a: 4, 5; Tb 12, 15.   b: Ps 141, 2; Tb 12, 12. c: Ez 10, 2; Ps 11, 6 / 4, 5; 11, 19; 16, 18.   d: 16, 1-21.

gels who were holding the seven trumpets prepared to blow them.

⁷*When the first one blew his trumpet, there came hail and fire mixed with blood, which was hurled down to the earth. A third of the land was burned up, along with a third of the trees and all green grass.

⁸ᵉ*When the second angel blew his trumpet, something like a large burning mountain was hurled into the sea. A third of the sea turned to blood, ⁹*a third of the creatures living in the sea died, and a third of the ships were wrecked.

¹⁰ᶠWhen the third angel blew his trumpet, a large star burning like a torch fell from the sky. It fell on a third of the rivers and on the springs of water. ¹¹ᵍ*The star was called "Wormwood," and a third of all the water turned to wormwood. Many people died from this water, because it was made bitter.

¹²ʰWhen the fourth angel blew his trumpet, a third of the sun, a third of the moon, and a third of the stars were struck, so that a third of them became dark. The day lost its light for a third of the time, as did the night.

¹³*Then I looked again and heard an eagle flying high overhead cry out in a loud voice, "Woe! Woe! Woe to the inhabitants of the earth from the rest of the trumpet blasts that the three angels are about to blow!"

CHAPTER 9

See RG
523

The Fifth Trumpet. ¹ⁱ*Then the fifth angel blew his trumpet, and I saw a star that had fallen from the sky to the earth. It was

given the key for the passage to the abyss. ²ʲIt opened the passage to the abyss, and smoke came up out of the passage like smoke from a huge furnace. The sun and the air were darkened by the smoke from the passage. ³ᵏ*Locusts came out of the smoke onto the land, and they were given the same power as scorpions of the earth. ⁴They were told not to harm the grass of the earth or any plant or any tree, but only those people who did not have the seal of God on their foreheads. ⁵*They were not allowed to kill them but only to torment them for five months; the torment they inflicted was like that of a scorpion when it stings a person. ⁶ⁱDuring that time these people will seek death but will not find it, and they will long to die but death will escape them.

⁷ᵐ*The appearance of the locusts was like that of horses ready for battle. On their heads they wore what looked like crowns of gold; their faces were like human faces, ⁸ⁿand they had hair like women's hair. Their teeth were like lions' teeth, ⁹and they had chests like iron breastplates. The sound of their wings was like the sound of many horse-drawn chariots racing into battle. ¹⁰They had tails like scorpions, with stingers; with their tails they had power to harm people for five months. ¹¹*They had as their king the angel of the abyss, whose name in Hebrew is Abaddon and in Greek Apollyon.

¹²The first woe has passed, but there are two more to come.

8, 7: This woe resembles the seventh plague of Egypt (Ex 9, 23–24); cf Jl 3, 3.

8, 8–11: The background of these two woes is the first plague of Egypt (Ex 7, 20–21).

8, 9: Creatures living in the sea: literally, "creatures in the sea that had souls."

8, 11: Wormwood: an extremely bitter and malignant plant symbolizing the punishment God inflicts on the ungodly; cf Jer 9, 12–14; 23, 15.

8, 13: Woe! Woe! Woe: each of the three woes pronounced by the angel represents a separate disaster; cf 9, 12; 11, 14. The final woe, released by the seventh trumpet blast, includes the plagues of ch 16.

9, 1–12: The fifth trumpet heralds a woe containing elements from the eighth and ninth plagues of Egypt (Ex 10, 12–15.21–23) but specifically reminiscent of the invasion of locusts in Jl 1, 4—2, 10.

9, 1: A star: late Judaism represented fallen powers as stars (Is 14, 12–15; Lk 10, 18; Jude 13), but a comparison

with 1, 20 and 20, 1 suggests that here it means an angel. **The passage to the abyss:** referring to Sheol, the netherworld, where Satan and the fallen angels are kept for a thousand years, to be cast afterwards into the pool of fire; cf 20, 7–10. The abyss was conceived of as a vast subterranean cavern full of fire. Its only link with the earth was a kind of passage or mine shaft, which was kept locked.

9, 3: Scorpions: their poisonous sting was proverbial; Ez 2, 6; Lk 11, 12.

9, 5: For five months: more or less corresponding to the life-span of locusts.

9, 7–10: Eight characteristics are listed to show the eschatological and diabolical nature of these locusts.

9, 11: Abaddon: Hebrew (more precisely, Aramaic) for destruction or ruin. **Apollyon:** Greek for the "Destroyer."

e: Ex 7, 20. *f:* Is 14, 12. *g:* Jer 9, 14. *h:* Ex 10, 21-23. *i:* 20, 1. *j:* Gn 19, 28. *k:* Ex 10, 12-15; Wis 16, 9. *l:* Jb 3, 21. *m:* Jl 2, 4. *n:* Jl 1, 6.

The Sixth Trumpet. ¹³ᵒ*Then the sixth angel blew his trumpet, and I heard a voice coming from the [four] horns of the gold altar before God, ¹⁴*telling the sixth angel who held the trumpet, "Release the four angels who are bound at the banks of the great river Euphrates." ¹⁵So the four angels were released, who were prepared for this hour, day, month, and year to kill a third of the human race. ¹⁶The number of cavalry troops was two hundred million; I heard their number. ¹⁷ᵖ*Now in my vision this is how I saw the horses and their riders. They wore red, blue, and yellow breastplates, and the horses' heads were like heads of lions, and out of their mouths came fire, smoke, and sulfur. ¹⁸By these three plagues of fire, smoke, and sulfur that came out of their mouths a third of the human race was killed. ¹⁹For the power of the horses is in their mouths and in their tails; for their tails are like snakes, with heads that inflict harm.

²⁰�q*The rest of the human race, who were not killed by these plagues, did not repent of the works of their hands, to give up the worship of demons and idols made from gold, silver, bronze, stone, and wood, which cannot see or hear or walk. ²¹Nor did they repent of their murders, their magic potions, their unchastity, or their robberies.

See RG
523

CHAPTER 10

The Angel with the Small Scroll.

¹*Then I saw another mighty angel come down from heaven wrapped in a cloud, with a halo around his head; his face was like the sun and his feet were like pillars of fire. ²*In his hand he held a small scroll that had been opened. He placed his right foot on the sea and his left foot on the land, ³ʳand then he cried out in a loud voice as a lion roars. When he cried out, the seven thunders raised their voices, too. ⁴When the seven thunders had spoken, I was about to write it down; but I heard a voice from heaven say, "Seal up what the seven thunders have spoken, but do not write it down." ⁵Then the angel I saw standing on the sea and on the land raised his right hand to heaven ⁶ˢ*and swore by the one who lives forever and ever, who created heaven and earth and sea and all that is in them, "There shall be no more delay. ⁷ᵗ*At the time when you hear the seventh angel blow his trumpet, the mysterious plan of God shall be fulfilled, as he promised to his servants the prophets."

⁸Then the voice that I had heard from heaven spoke to me again and said, "Go, take the scroll that lies open in the hand of the angel who is standing on the sea and on the land." ⁹*So I went up to the angel and told him to give me the small scroll. He said to me, "Take and swallow it. It will turn your stomach sour, but in your mouth it will taste as sweet as honey." ¹⁰ᵘI took the small scroll

---

9, 13–21: The sixth trumpet heralds a woe representing another diabolical attack symbolized by an invasion by the Parthians living east of the Euphrates; see the note on 6, 2. At the appointed time (15), the frightful horses act as God's agents of judgment. The imaginative details are not to be taken literally; see Introduction and the note on 6, 12–14.

9, 13: [Four]: many Greek manuscripts and versions omit the word. The horns were situated at the four corners of the altar (Ex 27, 2; 30, 2–3); see the note on 8, 3.

9, 14–15: The four angels: they are symbolic of the destructive activity that will be extended throughout the universe.

9, 17: Blue: literally, "hyacinth-colored." Yellow: literally, "sulfurous."

9, 20: The works of their hands: i.e., the gods their hands had made.

10, 1—11, 14: An interlude in two scenes (10, 1–11 and 11, 1–14) precedes the sounding of the seventh trumpet; cf 7, 1–17. The first vision describes an angel astride sea and land like a colossus, with a small scroll open, the contents of which indicate that the end is imminent (ch 10). The second vision is of the measuring of the temple and of two witnesses,

whose martyrdom means that the kingdom of God is about to be inaugurated.

10, 1–4: The seven thunders: God's voice announcing judgment and doom; cf Ps 29, 3–9, where thunder, as the voice of Yahweh, is praised seven times.

10, 2: He placed . . . on the land: this symbolizes the universality of the angel's message, as does the figure of the small scroll open to be read.

10, 6: Heaven and earth and sea: the three parts of the universe. No more delay: cf Dn 12, 7; Hb 2, 3.

10, 7: The mysterious plan of God: literally, "the mystery of God," the end of the present age when the forces of evil will be put down (17, 1—19, 4.11–21; 20, 7–10; cf 2 Thes 2, 6–12; Rom 16, 25–26), and the establishment of the reign of God when all creation will be made new (21, 1—22, 5).

10, 9–10: The small scroll was sweet because it predicted the final victory of God's people; it was sour because it also announced their sufferings. Cf Ez 3, 1–3.

o: Ex 30, 1-3.   p: Jb 41, 10-13.   q: Ps 135, 15-17; Is 17, 8; Dn 5, 4.   r: Ps 29, 3-9; Jer 25, 30; Am 3, 8.   s: Dt 32, 40; Dn 12, 7 / Ez 12, 28.   t: Am 3, 7.   u: Ez 3, 1-3.

from the angel's hand and swallowed it. In my mouth it was like sweet honey, but when I had eaten it, my stomach turned sour. *11**Then someone said to me, "You must prophesy again about many peoples, nations, tongues, and kings."

See RG
523

CHAPTER 11

The Two Witnesses. *1v**Then I was given a measuring rod like a staff and I was told, "Come and measure the temple of God and the altar, and count those who are worshiping in it. *2**But exclude the outer court of the temple; do not measure it, for it has been handed over to the Gentiles, who will trample the holy city for forty-two months. *3**I will commission my two witnesses to prophesy for those twelve hundred and sixty days, wearing sackcloth." *4w**These are the two olive trees and the two lampstands that stand before the Lord of the earth. *5**If anyone wants to harm them, fire comes out of their mouths and devours their enemies. In this way, anyone wanting to harm them is sure to be slain. *6x*They have the power to close up the sky so that no rain can fall during the time of their prophesying. They also have power to turn water into blood and to afflict the earth with any plague as often as they wish.

7y*When they have finished their testimony, the beast that comes up from the abyss will wage war against them and conquer them and kill them. *8**Their corpses will lie in the main street of the great city, which has the symbolic names "Sodom" and "Egypt," where indeed their Lord was crucified. *9**Those from every people, tribe, tongue, and nation will gaze on their corpses for three and a half days, and they will not allow their corpses to be buried. *10*The inhabitants of the earth will gloat over them and be glad and exchange gifts because these two prophets tormented the inhabitants of the earth. *11z*But after the three and a half days, a breath of life from God entered them. When they stood on their feet, great fear fell on those who saw them. *12a*Then they heard a loud voice from heaven say to them, "Come up here." So they went up to heaven in a cloud as their enemies looked on. *13**At that moment there was a great earthquake, and a tenth of the city fell in ruins. Seven thousand people were killed during the earthquake; the rest were terrified and gave glory to the God of heaven.

*14*The second woe has passed, but the third is coming soon.

The Seventh Trumpet. *15**Then the sev-

10, 11: This further prophecy is contained in chs 12–22.

11, 1: The temple and altar symbolize the new Israel; see the note on 7, 4–9. The worshipers represent Christians. The measuring of the temple (cf Ez 40, 3—42, 20; 47, 1–12; Zec 2, 5–6) suggests that God will preserve the faithful remnant (cf Is 4, 2–3) who remain true to Christ (14, 1–5).

11, 2: The outer court: the Court of the Gentiles. **Trample . . . forty-two months:** the duration of the vicious persecution of the Jews by Antiochus IV Epiphanes (Dn 7, 25; 12, 7); this persecution of three and a half years (half of seven, counted as 1260 days in 3; 12, 6) became the prototype of periods of trial for God's people; cf Lk 4, 25; Jas 5, 17. The reference here is to the persecution by the Romans; cf Introduction.

11, 3: The two witnesses, wearing sackcloth symbolizing lamentation and repentance, cannot readily be identified. Do they represent Moses and Elijah, or the Law and the Prophets, or Peter and Paul? Most probably they refer to the universal church, especially the Christian martyrs, fulfilling the office of witness (two because of Dt 19, 15; cf Mk 6, 7; Jn 8, 17).

11, 4: The two olive trees and the two lampstands: the martyrs who stand in the presence of the Lord; the imagery is taken from Zec 4, 1–3.11–14, where the olive trees refer to Zerubbabel and Joshua.

11, 5–6: These details are derived from stories of Moses, who turned **water into blood** (Ex 7, 17–20), and of Elijah, who called down fire from heaven (1 Kgs 18, 36–40; 2 Kgs 1, 10)

and closed up the sky for three years (1 Kgs 17, 1; cf 18, 1).

11, 7: The beast . . . from the abyss: the Roman emperor Nero, who symbolizes the forces of evil, or the antichrist (13, 1.8; 17, 8); cf Dn 7, 2–8.11–12.19–22 and Introduction.

11, 8: The great city: this expression is used constantly in Rv for Babylon, i.e., Rome; cf 14, 8; 16, 19; 17, 18; 18, 2.10.21. **"Sodom" and "Egypt":** symbols of immorality (cf Is 1, 10) and oppression of God's people (cf Ex 1, 11–14). **Where indeed their Lord was crucified:** not the geographical but the symbolic Jerusalem that rejects God and his witnesses, i.e., Rome, called Babylon in chs 16–18; see the note on 17, 9 and Introduction.

11, 9–12: Over the martyrdom (7) of the two witnesses, now called prophets, the ungodly rejoice **for three and a half days,** a symbolic period of time; see the note on v 2. Afterwards they go in triumph to heaven, as did Elijah (2 Kgs 2, 11).

11, 13: Seven thousand people: a symbolic sum to represent all social classes (seven) and large numbers (thousands); cf Introduction.

11, 15–19: The seventh trumpet proclaims the coming of God's reign after the victory over diabolical powers; see the note on 10, 7.

---

v: Ez 40, 3-5 / Zec 2, 5-9. *w:* Zec 4, 3.14. *x:* Ex 7, 17. *y:* Dn 7, 21. *z:* Ez 37, 5.10. *a:* 2 Kgs 2, 11.

enth angel blew his trumpet. There were loud voices in heaven, saying, "The kingdom of the world now belongs to our Lord and to his Anointed, and he will reign forever and ever." [16]The twenty-four elders who sat on their thrones before God prostrated themselves and worshiped God [17]and said:

"We give thanks to you, Lord God
almighty,
who are and who were.
For you have assumed your great power
and have established your reign.
[18] [b]The nations raged,
but your wrath has come,
and the time for the dead to be judged,
and to recompense your servants, the
prophets,
and the holy ones and those who fear
your name,
the small and the great alike,
and to destroy those who destroy the
earth."

[19]Then God's temple in heaven was opened, and the ark of his covenant could be seen in the temple. There were flashes of lightning, rumblings, and peals of thunder, an earthquake, and a violent hailstorm.

CHAPTER 12

The Woman and the Dragon. [1][c]*A great sign appeared in the sky, a woman clothed with the sun, with the moon under her feet, and on her head a crown of twelve stars. [2]*She was with child and wailed aloud in pain as she labored to give birth. [3][d]*Then another sign appeared in the sky; it was a huge red dragon, with seven heads and ten horns, and on its heads were seven diadems. [4][e]Its tail swept away a third of the stars in the sky and hurled them down to the earth. Then the dragon stood before the woman about to give birth, to devour her child when she gave birth. [5][f]*She gave birth to a son, a male child, destined to rule all the nations with an iron rod. Her child was caught up to God and his throne. [6]*The woman herself fled into the desert where she had a place prepared by God, that there she might be taken care of for twelve hundred and sixty days.

[7]*Then war broke out in heaven; Michael and his angels battled against the dragon. The dragon and its angels fought back, [8]but they did not prevail and there was no longer any place for them in heaven. [9][g]*The huge dragon, the ancient serpent, who is called the Devil and Satan, who deceived the whole

---

12, 1—14, 20: This central section of Rv portrays the power of evil, represented by a dragon, in opposition to God and his people. First, the dragon pursues the woman about to give birth, but her son is saved and "caught up to God and his throne" (12, 5). Then Michael and his angels cast the dragon and his angels out of heaven (12, 7–9). After this, the dragon tries to attack the boy indirectly by attacking members of his church (12, 13–18). A beast, symbolizing the Roman empire, then becomes the dragon's agent, mortally wounded but restored to life and worshiped by all the world (13, 1–10). A second beast arises from the land, symbolizing the antichrist, which leads people astray by its prodigies to idolize the first beast (13, 11–18). This is followed by a vision of the Lamb and his faithful ones, and the proclamation of imminent judgment upon the world in terms of the wine of God's wrath (14, 1–20).

12, 1–6: The woman adorned with the sun, the moon, and the stars (images taken from Gn 37, 9–10) symbolizes God's people in the Old and the New Testament. The Israel of old gave birth to the Messiah (5) and then became the new Israel, the church, which suffers persecution by the dragon (6.13–17); cf Is 50, 1; 66, 7; Jer 50, 12. This corresponds to a widespread myth throughout the ancient world that a goddess pregnant with a savior was pursued by a horrible monster; by miraculous intervention, she bore a son who then killed the monster.

12, 2: Because of Eve's sin, the woman gives birth in distress and pain (Gn 3, 16; cf Is 66, 7–14).

12, 3: Huge red dragon: the Devil or Satan (cf 9; 20, 2), symbol of the forces of evil, a mythical monster known also as Leviathan (Ps 74, 13–14) or Rahab (Jb 26, 12–13; Ps 89, 11). **Seven diadems:** these are symbolic of the fullness of the dragon's sovereignty over the kingdoms of this world; cf Christ with many diadems (19, 12).

12, 5: Rule . . . iron rod: fulfilled in 19, 15; cf Ps 2, 9. **Was caught up to God:** reference to Christ's ascension.

12, 6: God protects the persecuted church in the desert, the traditional Old Testament place of refuge for the afflicted, according to the typology of the Exodus; see the note on 11, 2.

12, 7–12: Michael, mentioned only here in Rv, wins a victory over the dragon. A hymn of praise follows.

12, 7: Michael; the archangel, guardian and champion of Israel; cf Dn 10, 13.21; 12, 1; Jude 9. In Hebrew, the name Michael means "Who can compare with God?"; cf 13, 4.

12, 9: The ancient serpent: who seduced Eve (Gn 3, 1–6), mother of the human race; cf 20, 2; Eph 6, 11–12. **Was thrown down:** allusion to the expulsion of Satan from heaven; cf Lk 10, 18.

---

b: Ps 2, 1.5 / Am 3, 7.   *c:* Gn 37, 9.   *d:* Dn 7, 7.   *e:* Dn 8, 10.
f: Is 66, 7 / Ps 2, 9.   *g:* Gn 3, 1-4 / Lk 10, 18.

world, was thrown down to earth, and its angels were thrown down with it.

*10**Then I heard a loud voice in heaven say:

"Now have salvation and power come,
  and the kingdom of our God
  and the authority of his Anointed.
For the accuser of our brothers is cast out,
  who accuses them before our God day
    and night.
11 They conquered him by the blood of the
    Lamb
  and by the word of their testimony;
  love for life did not deter them from
    death.
12 Therefore, rejoice, you heavens,
  and you who dwell in them.
But woe to you, earth and sea,
  for the Devil has come down to you in
    great fury,
  for he knows he has but a short time."

*13h*When the dragon saw that it had been thrown down to the earth, it pursued the woman who had given birth to the male child. *14i**But the woman was given the two wings of the great eagle, so that she could fly to her place in the desert, where, far from the serpent, she was taken care of for a year, two years, and a half-year. *15**The serpent, however, spewed a torrent of water out of his mouth after the woman to sweep her away with the current. *16*But the earth helped the woman and opened its mouth and swallowed the flood that the dragon spewed out

of its mouth. *17j**Then the dragon became angry with the woman and went off to wage war against the rest of her offspring, those who keep God's commandments and bear witness to Jesus. *18**It took its position on the sand of the sea.

CHAPTER 13

See RG 523

The First Beast. *1k**Then I saw a beast come out of the sea with ten horns and seven heads; on its horns were ten diadems, and on its heads blasphemous name[s]. *2 l**The beast I saw was like a leopard, but it had feet like a bear's, and its mouth was like the mouth of a lion. To it the dragon gave its own power and throne, along with great authority. *3**I saw that one of its heads seemed to have been mortally wounded, but this mortal wound was healed. Fascinated, the whole world followed after the beast. *4**They worshiped the dragon because it gave its authority to the beast; they also worshiped the beast and said, "Who can compare with the beast or who can fight against it?"

*5m**The beast was given a mouth uttering proud boasts and blasphemies, and it was given authority to act for forty-two months. *6*It opened its mouth to utter blasphemies against God, blaspheming his name and his dwelling and those who dwell in heaven. *7n*It was also allowed to wage war against the holy ones and conquer them, and it was granted authority over every tribe, people, tongue, and nation. *8o*All the inhabitants of

---

12, 10: The accuser: the meaning of the Hebrew word "Satan," found in v 9; Jb 1—2; Zec 3, 1; 1 Chr 21, 1; he continues to accuse Christ's disciples.

12, 14: Great eagle: symbol of the power and swiftness of divine help; cf Ex 19, 4; Dt 32, 11; Is 40, 31.

12, 15: The serpent is depicted as the sea monster; cf 13, 1; Is 27, 1; Ez 32, 2; Ps 74, 13–14.

12, 17: Although the church is protected by God's special providence (16), the individual Christian is to expect persecution and suffering.

12, 18: It took its position: many later manuscripts and versions read "I took my position," thus connecting the sentence to the following paragraph.

13, 1–10: This wild beast, combining features of the four beasts in Dn 7, 2–28, symbolizes the Roman empire; the seven heads represent the emperors; see the notes on 17, 10 and 17, 12–14. The blasphemous names are the divine titles assumed by the emperors.

13, 2: Satan (12, 9), the prince of this world (Jn 12, 31), commissioned the beast to persecute the church (5–7).

13, 3: This may be a reference to the popular legend that Nero would come back to life and rule again after his death (which occurred in A.D. 68 from a self-inflicted stab wound in the throat); cf v 14; 17, 8. Domitian (A.D. 81–96) embodied all the cruelty and impiety of Nero. Cf Introduction.

13, 4: Worshiped the beast: allusion to emperor worship, which Domitian insisted upon and ruthlessly enforced. **Who can compare with the beast:** perhaps a deliberate parody of the name Michael; see the note on 12, 7.

13, 5–6: Domitian, like Antiochus IV Epiphanes (Dn 7, 8.11.25), demanded that he be called by divine titles such as "our lord and god" and "Jupiter." See the note on 11, 2.

13, 5: Forty-two months: this is the same duration as the profanation of the holy city (11, 2), the prophetic mission of the two witnesses (11, 3), and the retreat of the woman into the desert (12, 6.14).

---

h: Gn 3, 15. *i:* Ex 19, 4; Dn 7, 25; 12, 7. *j:* Gn 3, 15. *k:* 2 Thes 2, 3-12. *l:* Dn 7, 3-6. *m:* Dn 7, 8.11.25; 8, 14; 9, 27; 11, 36; 12, 7. *n:* Dn 7, 21. *o:* 3, 5; 17, 8; 20, 12.

the earth will worship it, all whose names were not written from the foundation of the world in the book of life, which belongs to the Lamb who was slain.

9 ᵖWhoever has ears ought to hear these words.

10 �q Anyone destined for captivity goes into captivity.
Anyone destined to be slain by the sword shall be slain by the sword.
Such is the faithful endurance of the holy ones.

The Second Beast. 11*Then I saw another beast come up out of the earth; it had two horns like a lamb's but spoke like a dragon. 12It wielded all the authority of the first beast in its sight and made the earth and its inhabitants worship the first beast, whose mortal wound had been healed. 13ʳIt performed great signs, even making fire come down from heaven to earth in the sight of everyone. 14It deceived the inhabitants of the earth with the signs it was allowed to perform in the sight of the first beast, telling them to make an image for the beast who had been wounded by the sword and revived. 15sIt was then permitted to breathe life into the beast's image, so that the beast's image could speak and [could] have anyone who did not worship it put to death. 16tIt forced all the people, small and great, rich and poor, free and

slave, to be given a stamped image on their right hands or their foreheads, 17so that no one could buy or sell except one who had the stamped image of the beast's name or the number that stood for its name.

18u*Wisdom is needed here; one who understands can calculate the number of the beast, for it is a number that stands for a person. His number is six hundred and sixty-six.

CHAPTER 14

See RG 523

The Lamb's Companions. 1v*Then I looked and there was the Lamb standing on Mount Zion, and with him a hundred and forty-four thousand who had his name and his Father's name written on their foreheads. 2I heard a sound from heaven like the sound of rushing water or a loud peal of thunder. The sound I heard was like that of harpists playing their harps. 3w*They were singing [what seemed to be] a new hymn before the throne, before the four living creatures and the elders. No one could learn this hymn except the hundred and forty-four thousand who had been ransomed from the earth. 4x*These are they who were not defiled with women; they are virgins and these are the ones who follow the Lamb wherever he goes. They have been ransomed as the firstfruits of the human race for God and the Lamb. 5y*On their lips no deceit has been found; they are unblemished.

The Three Angels. 6*Then I saw another

13, 11–18: The second beast is described in terms of the false prophets (cf 16, 13; 19, 20; 20, 10) who accompany the false messiahs (the first beast); cf Mt 24, 24; Mk 13, 22; 2 Thes 2, 9; cf also Dt 13, 2–4. Christians had either to worship the emperor and his image or to suffer martyrdom.
13, 18: Each of the letters of the alphabet in Hebrew as well as in Greek has a numerical value. Many possible combinations of letters will add up to 666, and many candidates have been nominated for this infamous number. The most likely is the emperor Caesar Nero (see the note on 13, 3), the Greek form of whose name in Hebrew letters gives the required sum. (The Latin form of this name equals 616, which is the reading of a few manuscripts.) Nero personifies the emperors who viciously persecuted the church. It has also been observed that "6" represents imperfection, falling short of the perfect number "7," and is represented here in a triple or superlative form.
14, 1–5: Now follows a tender and consoling vision of the Lamb and his companions.
14, 1: Mount Zion: in Jerusalem, the traditional place where the true remnant, the Israel of faith, is to be gathered in the messianic reign; cf 2 Kgs 19, 30–31; Jl 3, 5; Ob 17; Mi 4,

6–8; Zep 3, 12–20. **A hundred and forty-four thousand:** see the note on 7, 4–9. **His Father's name . . . foreheads:** in contrast to the pagans who were marked with the name or number of the beast (13, 16–17).
14, 4: Virgins: metaphorically, because they never indulged in any idolatrous practices, which are considered in the Old Testament to be adultery and fornication (2, 14–15.20–22; 17, 1–6; cf Ez 16, 1–58; 23, 1–49). The parallel passages (7, 3; 22, 4) indicate that the 144,000 whose foreheads are sealed represent all Christian people.
14, 5: No deceit: because they did not deny Christ or do homage to the beast. Lying is characteristic of the opponents of Christ (Jn 8, 44), but the Suffering Servant spoke no falsehood (Is 53, 9; 1 Pt 2, 22). **Unblemished:** a cultic term taken from the vocabulary of sacrificial ritual.
14, 6–13: Three angels proclaim imminent judgment on the pagan world, calling all peoples to worship God the cre-

p: Mt 13, 9.   q: Jer 15, 2.   r: Dt 13, 2-4; Mt 24, 24; 2 Thes 2, 9-10.   s: Dn 3, 5-7.15.   t: 14, 9; 16, 2; 19, 20; 20, 4.   u: 17, 9.   v: Jl 3, 5; Ob 17; Acts 2, 21.   w: Pss 33, 3; 96, 1; 98, 1; Is 42, 10.   x: Jer 2, 2; Jas 1, 18.   y: Zep 3, 13.

angel flying high overhead, with everlasting good news to announce to those who dwell on earth, to every nation, tribe, tongue, and people. *7z*He said in a loud voice, "Fear God and give him glory, for his time has come to sit in judgment. Worship him who made heaven and earth and sea and springs of water."

8a*A second angel followed, saying:

"Fallen, fallen is Babylon the great,
  that made all the nations drink
  the wine of her licentious passion."

*9*A third angel followed them and said in a loud voice, "Anyone who worships the beast or its image, or accepts its mark on forehead or hand, *10**will also drink the wine of God's fury, poured full strength into the cup of his wrath, and will be tormented in burning sulfur before the holy angels and before the Lamb. *11b*The smoke of the fire that torments them will rise forever and ever, and there will be no relief day or night for those who worship the beast or its image or accept the mark of its name." *12c**Here is what sustains the holy ones who keep God's commandments and their faith in Jesus.

13d*I heard a voice from heaven say, "Write this: Blessed are the dead who die in the Lord from now on." "Yes," said the Spirit, "let them find rest from their labors, for their works accompany them."

The Harvest of the Earth. *14e**Then I looked and there was a white cloud, and sitting on the cloud one who looked like a son of man, with a gold crown on his head and a sharp sickle in his hand. *15f*Another angel came out of the temple, crying out in a loud voice to the one sitting on the cloud, "Use your sickle and reap the harvest, for the time to reap has come, because the earth's harvest is fully ripe." *16*So the one who was sitting on the cloud swung his sickle over the earth, and the earth was harvested.

*17*Then another angel came out of the temple in heaven who also had a sharp sickle. *18**Then another angel [came] from the altar, [who] was in charge of the fire, and cried out in a loud voice to the one who had the sharp sickle, "Use your sharp sickle and cut the clusters from the earth's vines, for its grapes are ripe." *19g*So the angel swung his sickle over the earth and cut the earth's vintage. He threw it into the great wine press of God's fury. *20**The wine press was trodden outside the city and blood poured out of the wine press to the height of a horse's bridle for two hundred miles.

CHAPTER 15

The Seven Last Plagues. *1**Then I saw in heaven another sign, great and awe-inspiring: seven angels with the seven last plagues, for through them God's fury is accomplished.

2h*Then I saw something like a sea of glass mingled with fire. On the sea of glass

See RG 523

---

ator. Babylon (Rome) will fall, and its supporters will be tormented forever.

14, 6: Everlasting good news: that God's eternal reign is about to begin; see the note on 10, 7.

14, 8: This verse anticipates the lengthy dirge over Babylon (Rome) in 18, 1—19, 4. The oracle of Is 21, 9 to Babylon is applied here.

14, 10–11: The wine of God's fury: image taken from Is 51, 17; Jer 25, 15–16; 49, 12; 51, 7; Ez 23, 31–34. Eternal punishment in the fiery pool of burning sulfur (or "fire and brimstone"; cf Gn 19, 24) is also reserved for the Devil, the beast, and the false prophet (19, 20; 20, 10; 21, 8).

14, 12: In addition to **faith in Jesus,** the seer insists upon the necessity and value of works, as in 2, 23; 20, 12–13; 22, 12; cf Mt 16, 27; Rom 2, 6.

14, 13: See the note on 1, 3. According to Jewish thought, people's actions followed them as witnesses before the court of God.

14, 14–20: The reaping of the harvest symbolizes the gathering of the elect in the final judgment, while the reaping and treading of the grapes symbolizes the doom of the un-

godly (cf Jl 4, 12–13; Is 63, 1–6) that will come in 19, 11–21.

14, 18: Altar: there was only one altar in the heavenly temple; see the notes above on 6, 9; 8, 3; 11, 1.

14, 20: Two hundred miles: literally sixteen hundred stades. The **stadion,** a Greek unit of measurement, was about 607 feet in length, approximately the length of a furlong.

15, 1—16, 21: The seven bowls, the third and last group of seven after the seven seals and the seven trumpets, foreshadow the final cataclysm. Again, the series is introduced by a heavenly prelude, in which the victors over the beast sing the canticle of Moses (15, 2–4).

15, 1–4: A vision of the victorious martyrs precedes the vision of woe in 15, 5—16, 21; cf 7, 9–12.

15, 2: Mingled with fire: fire symbolizes the sanctity involved in facing God, reflected in the trials that have prepared the victorious Christians or in God's wrath.

z: 2, 10; Mt 10, 28. *a:* 18, 2-3; Is 21, 9; Jer 51, 8 / Is 51, 17; Jer 25, 15-17. *b:* 19, 3. *c:* 12, 17. *d:* Mt 11, 28-29; 2 Thes 1, 7; Heb 4, 10. *e:* 1, 7; Dn 7, 13. *f:* Jl 4, 13; Mt 13, 36-43. *g:* 19, 15; Is 63, 1-6. *h:* 7, 9.14; 13, 15-18.

were standing those who had won the victory over the beast and its image and the number that signified its name. They were holding God's harps, ³ⁱ*and they sang the song of Moses, the servant of God, and the song of the Lamb:

"Great and wonderful are your works,
Lord God almighty.
Just and true are your ways,
O king of the nations.
⁴ ʲWho will not fear you, Lord,
or glorify your name?
For you alone are holy.
All the nations will come
and worship before you,
for your righteous acts have been
revealed."

⁵*After this I had another vision. The temple that is the heavenly tent of testimony opened, ⁶ᵏand the seven angels with the seven plagues came out of the temple. They were dressed in clean white linen, with a gold sash around their chests. ⁷One of the four living creatures gave the seven angels seven gold bowls filled with the fury of God, who lives forever and ever. ⁸ˡThen the temple became so filled with the smoke from God's glory and might that no one could enter it until the seven plagues of the seven angels had been accomplished.

See RG 523

CHAPTER 16

The Seven Bowls. ¹*I heard a loud voice speaking from the temple to the seven angels, "Go and pour out the seven bowls of God's fury upon the earth."

²*The first angel went and poured out his bowl on the earth. Festering and ugly sores broke out on those who had the mark of the beast or worshiped its image.

³*The second angel poured out his bowl on the sea. The sea turned to blood like that from a corpse; every creature living in the sea died.

⁴ᵐThe third angel poured out his bowl on the rivers and springs of water. These also turned to blood. ⁵ⁿThen I heard the angel in charge of the waters say:

"You are just, O Holy One,
who are and who were,
in passing this sentence.
⁶ ᵒFor they have shed the blood of the holy
ones and the prophets,
and you [have] given them blood to
drink;
it is what they deserve."

⁷ᵖThen I heard the altar cry out,

"Yes, Lord God almighty,
your judgments are true and just."

⁸The fourth angel poured out his bowl on the sun. It was given the power to burn people with fire. ⁹�vPeople were burned by the scorching heat and blasphemed the name of God who had power over these plagues, but they did not repent or give him glory.

¹⁰ʳ*The fifth angel poured out his bowl on the throne of the beast. Its kingdom was plunged into darkness, and people bit their tongues in pain ¹¹ˢand blasphemed the God of heaven because of their pains and sores. But they did not repent of their works.

¹²*The sixth angel emptied his bowl on the great river Euphrates. Its water was dried up to prepare the way for the kings of the East. ¹³ᵗ*I saw three unclean spirits like frogs come from the mouth of the dragon, from

---

15, 3: The song of Moses: the song that Moses and the Israelites sang after their escape from the oppression of Egypt (Ex 15, 1–18). The martyrs have escaped from the oppression of the Devil. **Nations:** many other Greek manuscripts and versions read "ages."

15, 5–8: Seven angels receive the bowls of God's wrath.

15, 5: Tent of testimony: the name of the meeting tent in the Greek text of Ex 40. Cf 2 Mc 2, 4–7.

16, 1–21: These seven bowls, like the seven seals (6, 1–17; 8, 1) and the seven trumpets (8, 2—9, 21; 11, 15–19), bring on a succession of disasters modeled in part on the plagues of Egypt (Ex 7—12). See the note on 6, 12–14.

16, 2: Like the sixth Egyptian plague (Ex 9, 8–11).

16, 3–4: Like the first Egyptian plague (Ex 7, 20–21). The same woe followed the blowing of the second trumpet (8, 8–9).

16, 10: The throne of the beast: symbol of the forces of evil. **Darkness:** like the ninth Egyptian plague (Ex 10, 21–23); cf 9, 2.

16, 12: The kings of the East: Parthians; see the notes on 6, 2 and 17, 12–13. **East:** literally, "rising of the sun," as in 7, 2.

16, 13: Frogs: possibly an allusion to the second Egyptian

i: Pss 92, 6; 98, 1 / Dt 32, 4; Ps 145, 17.   *j:* Ps 86, 9-10; Jer 10, 7.
k: 19, 8.   *l:* 1 Kgs 8, 10; Is 6, 4.   *m:* Ex 7, 14-24.   *n:* 1, 4.
o: Ez 35, 6; Mt 23, 34-35.   *p:* Dn 3, 27; Tb 3, 2.   *q:* Am 4, 6.
r: Ex 10, 21-23.   *s:* Ex 9, 8-11 / Jer 5, 3.   *t:* Ex 8, 2-3.

the mouth of the beast, and from the mouth of the false prophet. *14u*These were demonic spirits who performed signs. They went out to the kings of the whole world to assemble them for the battle on the great day of God the almighty. *15v**("Behold, I am coming like a thief." Blessed is the one who watches and keeps his clothes ready, so that he may not go naked and people see him exposed.) *16**They then assembled the kings in the place that is named Armageddon in Hebrew.

*17w*The seventh angel poured out his bowl into the air. A loud voice came out of the temple from the throne, saying, "It is done." *18x*Then there were lightning flashes, rumblings, and peals of thunder, and a great earthquake. It was such a violent earthquake that there has never been one like it since the human race began on earth. *19**The great city was split into three parts, and the gentile cities fell. But God remembered great Babylon, giving it the cup filled with the wine of his fury and wrath. *20**Every island fled, and mountains disappeared. *21y*Large hailstones like huge weights came down from the sky on people, and they blasphemed God for the plague of hail because this plague was so severe.

V: The Punishment of Babylon and the Destruction of Pagan Nations

CHAPTER 17

See RG
523–24

Babylon the Great. *1z**Then one of the seven angels who were holding the seven bowls came and said to me, "Come here. I will show you the judgment on the great harlot who lives near the many waters. *2a**The kings of the earth have had intercourse with her, and the inhabitants of the earth became drunk on the wine of her harlotry." *3b**Then he carried me away in spirit to a deserted place where I saw a woman seated on a scarlet beast that was covered with blasphemous names, with seven heads and ten horns. *4c**The woman was wearing purple and scarlet and adorned with gold, precious stones, and pearls. She held in her hand a gold cup that was filled with the abominable and sordid deeds of her harlotry. *5*On her forehead was written a name, which is a mystery, "Babylon the great, the mother of harlots and of the abominations of the earth." *6**I saw that the woman was drunk on the blood of the holy ones and on the blood of the witnesses to Jesus.

Meaning of the Beast and Harlot When I saw her I was greatly amazed. *7*The angel said to me, "Why are you amazed? I will explain to you the mystery of the woman and of the beast that carries her, the beast with the seven heads and the ten horns. *8d**The beast that you saw existed once but now exists no longer. It will come up from the abyss and is headed for destruction. The inhabitants of the earth whose names have not been written in the book of life from the foundation of the world shall be amazed when they see the beast, because it existed once but exists no longer, and yet it will

---

plague (Ex 7, 26—8, 11). **The false prophet:** identified with the two-horned second beast (13, 11–18 and the note there).

16, 15: Like a thief: as in 3, 3 (cf Mt 24, 42–44; 1 Thes 5, 2). **Blessed:** see the note on 1, 3.

16, 16: Armageddon: in Hebrew, this means "Mountain of Megiddo." Since Megiddo was the scene of many decisive battles in antiquity (Jgs 5, 19–20; 2 Kgs 9, 27; 2 Chr 35, 20–24), the town became the symbol of the final disastrous rout of the forces of evil.

16, 19: The great city: Rome and the empire.

16, 20–21: See the note on 6, 12–14. **Hailstones:** as in the seventh Egyptian plague (Ex 9, 23–24); cf 8, 7. **Like huge weights:** literally, "weighing a talent," about one hundred pounds.

17, 1—19, 10: The punishment of Babylon is now described as a past event and, metaphorically, under the image of the great harlot who leads people astray into idolatry.

17, 1–6: Babylon, the symbolic name (5) of Rome, is graphically described as "the great harlot."

17, 2: Intercourse . . . harlotry: see the note on 14, 4. The pagan kings subject to Rome adopted the cult of the emperor.

17, 3: Scarlet beast: see the note on 13, 1–10. **Blasphemous names:** divine titles assumed by the Roman emperors; see the note on 13, 5–6.

17, 4: Reference to the great wealth and idolatrous cults of Rome.

17, 6b-18: An interpretation of the vision is here given.

17, 8: Allusion to the belief that the dead Nero would return to power (11); see the note on 13, 3.

---

u: 1 Cor 1, 8. *v:* Mt 24, 42-44 / 3, 17. *w:* Is 66, 6. *x:* Mk 13, 19. *y:* Ex 9, 22-26. *z:* Jer 50, 38; 51, 13. *a:* Jer 51, 7. *b:* 13, 1. *c:* 18, 16. *d:* 13, 3-4 / 3, 5; 13, 8; 20, 12.

come again. 9e*Here is a clue for one who has wisdom. The seven heads represent seven hills upon which the woman sits. They also represent seven kings: 10*five have already fallen, one still lives, and the last has not yet come, and when he comes he must remain only a short while. 11*The beast that existed once but exists no longer is an eighth king, but really belongs to the seven and is headed for destruction. 12f*The ten horns that you saw represent ten kings who have not yet been crowned; they will receive royal authority along with the beast for one hour. 13They are of one mind and will give their power and authority to the beast. 14gThey will fight with the Lamb, but the Lamb will conquer them, for he is Lord of lords and king of kings, and those with him are called, chosen, and faithful."

15Then he said to me, "The waters that you saw where the harlot lives represent large numbers of peoples, nations, and tongues. 16h*The ten horns that you saw and the beast will hate the harlot; they will leave her desolate and naked; they will eat her flesh and consume her with fire. 17For God has put it into their minds to carry out his purpose and to make them come to an agreement to give their kingdom to the beast until the words of God are accomplished. 18The woman whom you saw represents the great city that has sovereignty over the kings of the earth."

CHAPTER 18

See RG 524

The Fall of Babylon. 1i*After this I saw another angel coming down from heaven, having great authority, and the earth became illumined by his splendor. 2j*He cried out in a mighty voice:

"Fallen, fallen is Babylon the great.
  She has become a haunt for demons.
She is a cage for every unclean spirit,
  a cage for every unclean bird,
  [a cage for every unclean] and
    disgusting [beast].
3 k*For all the nations have drunk
  the wine of her licentious passion.
The kings of the earth had intercourse
    with her,
  and the merchants of the earth grew
    rich from her drive for luxury."

4l*Then I heard another voice from heaven say:

"Depart from her, my people,
  so as not to take part in her sins
  and receive a share in her plagues,
5 mfor her sins are piled up to the sky,
  and God remembers her crimes.
6 nPay her back as she has paid others.
  Pay her back double for her deeds.
  Into her cup pour double what she
    poured.
7 oTo the measure of her boasting and
    wantonness

17, 9: Here is a clue: literally, "Here a mind that has wisdom." **Seven hills:** of Rome.

17, 10: There is little agreement as to the identity of the Roman emperors alluded to here. The number seven (9) suggests that all the emperors are meant; see the note on 1, 4.

17, 11: The beast: Nero; see the note on v 8.

17, 12–13: Ten kings who have not yet been crowned: perhaps Parthian satraps who are to accompany the revived Nero (the beast) in his march on Rome to regain power; see the note on 13, 3. In 19, 11–21, the Lamb and his companions will conquer them.

17, 16–18: The ten horns: the ten pagan kings (12) who unwittingly fulfill God's will against harlot Rome, the great city; cf Ez 16, 37.

18, 1—19, 4: A stirring dirge over the fall of Babylon-Rome. The perspective is prophetic, as if the fall of Rome had already taken place. The imagery here, as elsewhere in this book, is not to be taken literally. The vindictiveness of some of the language, borrowed from the scathing Old Tes-

tament prophecies against Babylon, Tyre, and Nineveh (Is 23; 24; 27; Jer 50–51; Ez 26–27), is meant to portray symbolically the inexorable demands of God's holiness and justice; cf Introduction. The section concludes with a joyous canticle on the future glory of heaven.

18, 2: Many Greek manuscripts and versions omit a cage for every unclean . . . beast.

18, 3–24: Rome is condemned for her immorality, symbol of idolatry (see the note on 14, 4), and for persecuting the church; cf 19, 2.

18, 4: Depart from her: not evacuation of the city but separation from sinners, as always in apocalyptic literature.

e: 13, 18. f: Dn 7, 24. g: 19, 11-21; 2 Mc 13, 4; 1 Tm 6, 15 / Rom 1, 6; 1 Pt 2, 9; Jude 1. h: Ez 16, 37-41; 23, 25-29. i: Ez 43, 2. j: 14, 8; Is 21, 9; Jer 50, 2-3; 51, 8. k: 17, 2; Jer 51, 7. l: Is 48, 20; Jer 50, 8. m: Jer 51, 9. n: Jer 50, 15 / Jer 16, 18. o: Is 47, 8-9.

repay her in torment and grief;
for she said to herself,
  'I sit enthroned as queen;
  I am no widow,
  and I will never know grief.'
[8] Therefore, her plagues will come in one
    day,
  pestilence, grief, and famine;
  she will be consumed by fire.
For mighty is the Lord God who judges
    her."

[9]The kings of the earth who had intercourse with her in their wantonness will weep and mourn over her when they see the smoke of her pyre. [10]They will keep their distance for fear of the torment inflicted on her, and they will say:

"Alas, alas, great city,
  Babylon, mighty city.
In one hour your judgment has
    come."

[11]*The merchants of the earth will weep and mourn for her, because there will be no more markets for their cargo: [12]their cargo of gold, silver, precious stones, and pearls; fine linen, purple silk, and scarlet cloth; fragrant wood of every kind, all articles of ivory and all articles of the most expensive wood, bronze, iron, and marble; [13]*cinnamon, spice, incense, myrrh, and frankincense; wine, olive oil, fine flour, and wheat; cattle and sheep, horses and chariots, and slaves, that is, human beings.

[14] p"The fruit you craved
  has left you.
All your luxury and splendor are gone,
  never again will one find them."

[15]The merchants who deal in these goods, who grew rich from her, will keep their distance for fear of the torment inflicted on her. Weeping and mourning, [16]qthey cry out:

"Alas, alas, great city,
  wearing fine linen, purple and scarlet,
adorned [in] gold, precious stones, and
    pearls.
[17] In one hour this great wealth has been
    ruined."

Every captain of a ship, every traveler at sea, sailors, and seafaring merchants stood at a distance [18]and cried out when they saw the smoke of her pyre, "What city could compare with the great city?" [19]rThey threw dust on their heads and cried out, weeping and mourning:

"Alas, alas, great city,
  in which all who had ships at sea
  grew rich from her wealth.
In one hour she has been ruined.
[20] sRejoice over her, heaven,
  you holy ones, apostles, and prophets.
For God has judged your case against
    her."

[21]tA mighty angel picked up a stone like a huge millstone and threw it into the sea and said:

"With such force will Babylon the great
    city be thrown down,
  and will never be found again.
[22] uNo melodies of harpists and musicians,
    flutists and trumpeters,
  will ever be heard in you again.
No craftsmen in any trade
  will ever be found in you again.
No sound of the millstone
  will ever be heard in you again.
[23] vNo light from a lamp
  will ever be seen in you again.
No voices of bride and groom
  will ever be heard in you again.
Because your merchants were the great
    ones of the world,
  all nations were led astray by your
    magic potion.
[24] wIn her was found the blood of prophets
    and holy ones
  and all who have been slain on the
    earth."

18, 11: Ironically, the merchants weep not so much for Babylon-Rome, but for their lost markets; cf Ez 27, 36.

18, 13: Spice: an unidentified spice plant called in Greek amōmon.

p: Hos 10, 5 / Am 6, 7.   *q:* 17, 4.   *r:* Ez 27, 27-32.   *s:* 19, 1-2; Dt 32, 43.   *t:* Jer 51, 63-64; Ez 26, 21.   *u:* Is 24, 8; Ez 26, 13.   *v:* Jer 7, 34; 16, 9; 25, 10.   *w:* 16, 6.

See RG
524

CHAPTER 19

1*After this I heard what sounded like the loud voice of a great multitude in heaven, saying:

"Alleluia!
Salvation, glory, and might belong to our God,
2   *x*for true and just are his judgments.
He has condemned the great harlot
    who corrupted the earth with her harlotry.
He has avenged on her the blood of his servants."

*3y*They said a second time:

"Alleluia! Smoke will rise from her forever and ever."

*4*The twenty-four elders and the four living creatures fell down and worshiped God who sat on the throne, saying, "Amen. Alleluia."

The Victory Song. *5z**A voice coming from the throne said:

"Praise our God, all you his servants,
    [and] you who revere him, small and great."

*6*Then I heard something like the sound of a great multitude or the sound of rushing water or mighty peals of thunder, as they said:

"Alleluia!
The Lord has established his reign,
    [our] God, the almighty.

7 a*Let us rejoice and be glad
    and give him glory.
For the wedding day of the Lamb has come,
    his bride has made herself ready.
8 b*She was allowed to wear
    a bright, clean linen garment."

(The linen represents the righteous deeds of the holy ones.)

9c*Then the angel said to me, "Write this: Blessed are those who have been called to the wedding feast of the Lamb." And he said to me, "These words are true; they come from God." *10d**I fell at his feet to worship him. But he said to me, "Don't! I am a fellow servant of yours and of your brothers who bear witness to Jesus. Worship God. Witness to Jesus is the spirit of prophecy."

The King of Kings. *11e**Then I saw the heavens opened, and there was a white horse; its rider was [called] "Faithful and True." He judges and wages war in righteousness. *12f**His eyes were [like] a fiery flame, and on his head were many diadems. He had a name inscribed that no one knows except himself. *13g**He wore a cloak that had been dipped in blood, and his name was called the Word of God. *14h*The armies of heaven followed him, mounted on white horses and wearing clean white linen. *15i**Out of his mouth came a sharp sword to strike the nations. He will rule them with an iron rod, and he himself will tread out in the wine press the wine of the fury and wrath of

19, 1.3.4.6: Alleluia: found only here in the New Testament, this frequent exclamation of praise in the Hebrew psalms was important in Jewish liturgy.

19, 5–10: A victory song follows, sung by the entire church, celebrating the marriage of the Lamb, the union of the Messiah with the community of the elect.

19, 7: The wedding day of the Lamb: symbol of God's reign about to begin (21, 1—22, 5); see the note on 10, 7. **His bride:** the church; cf 2 Cor 11, 2; Eph 5, 22–27. Marriage is one of the biblical metaphors used to describe the covenant relationship between God and his people; cf Hos 2, 16–22; Is 54, 5–6; 62, 5; Ez 16, 6–14. Hence, idolatry and apostasy are viewed as adultery and harlotry (Hos 2, 4–15; Ez 16, 15–63); see the note on 14, 4.

19, 8: See the note on 14, 12.

19, 9: Blessed: see the note on 1, 3.

19, 10: The spirit of prophecy: as the prophets were inspired to proclaim God's word, so the Christian is called to give witness to the Word of God (13) made flesh; cf 1, 2; 6, 9; 12, 17.

19, 11–16: Symbolic description of the exalted Christ (cf 1, 13–16) who together with the armies of heaven overcomes the beast and its followers; cf 17, 14.

19, 12: A name: in Semitic thought, the name conveyed the reality of the person; cf Mt 11, 27; Lk 10, 22.

19, 13: Had been dipped in: other Greek manuscripts and versions read "had been sprinkled with"; cf v 15. **The Word of God:** Christ is the revelation of the Father; cf Jn 1, 1.14; 1 Jn 2, 14.

19, 15: The treading of the wine press is a prophetic symbol used to describe the destruction of God's enemies; cf Is 63, 1–6; Jl 4, 13.

x: Dn 3, 27 / Jer 51, 48-49.   *y:* 14, 11; Is 34, 10.   *z:* 11, 18; Ps 115, 13.   *a:* Mt 22, 9; Eph 5, 27.   *b:* 15, 6; Is 61, 10; Mt 22, 11-12.   *c:* Mt 8, 11; Lk 14, 15.   *d:* 22, 8-9.   *e:* Is 11, 4.   *f:* 1, 14-16; 2, 18 / Lk 10, 22.   *g:* Is 63, 1 / Jn 1, 1.   *h:* 15, 6; 19, 8.   *i:* 14, 20; Is 63, 3.

God the almighty. [16j]He has a name written on his cloak and on his thigh, "King of kings and Lord of lords."

[17*]Then I saw an angel standing on the sun. He cried out [in] a loud voice to all the birds flying high overhead, "Come here. Gather for God's great feast, [18k]to eat the flesh of kings, the flesh of military officers, and the flesh of warriors, the flesh of horses and of their riders, and the flesh of all, free and slave, small and great." [19]Then I saw the beast and the kings of the earth and their armies gathered to fight against the one riding the horse and against his army. [20l*]The beast was caught and with it the false prophet who had performed in its sight the signs by which he led astray those who had accepted the mark of the beast and those who had worshiped its image. The two were thrown alive into the fiery pool burning with sulfur. [21]The rest were killed by the sword that came out of the mouth of the one riding the horse, and all the birds gorged themselves on their flesh.

See RG
524

CHAPTER 20

The Thousand-year Reign. [1m*]Then I saw an angel come down from heaven, holding in his hand the key to the abyss and a heavy chain. [2n*]He seized the dragon, the ancient serpent, which is the Devil or Satan, and tied it up for a thousand years [3]and threw it into the abyss, which he locked over it and sealed, so that it could no longer lead the nations astray until the thousand years

are completed. After this, it is to be released for a short time.

[4o*]Then I saw thrones; those who sat on them were entrusted with judgment. I also saw the souls of those who had been beheaded for their witness to Jesus and for the word of God, and who had not worshiped the beast or its image nor had accepted its mark on their foreheads or hands. They came to life and they reigned with Christ for a thousand years. [5]The rest of the dead did not come to life until the thousand years were over. This is the first resurrection. [6*]Blessed and holy is the one who shares in the first resurrection. The second death has no power over these; they will be priests of God and of Christ, and they will reign with him for [the] thousand years.

[7*]When the thousand years are completed, Satan will be released from his prison. [8p*]He will go out to deceive the nations at the four corners of the earth, Gog and Magog, to gather them for battle; their number is like the sand of the sea. [9q*]They invaded the breadth of the earth and surrounded the camp of the holy ones and the beloved city. But fire came down from heaven and consumed them. [10]The Devil who had led them astray was thrown into the pool of fire and sulfur, where the beast and the false prophet were. There they will be tormented day and night forever and ever.

The Large White Throne. [11r*]Next I saw a large white throne and the one who was sitting on it. The earth and the sky fled from his

---

19, 17–21: The certainty of Christ's victory is proclaimed by an angel, followed by a reference to the mustering of enemy forces and a fearsome description of their annihilation. The gruesome imagery is borrowed from Ez 39, 4.17–20.

19, 20: Beast . . . false prophet: see the notes on ch 13. The fiery pool . . . sulfur: symbol of God's punishment (14, 10; 20, 10.14–15), different from the abyss; see the note on 9, 1.

20, 1–6: Like the other numerical values in this book, the thousand years are not to be taken literally; they symbolize the long period of time between the chaining up of Satan (a symbol for Christ's resurrection-victory over death and the forces of evil) and the end of the world. During this time God's people share in the glorious reign of God that is present to them by virtue of their baptismal victory over death and sin; cf Rom 6, 1–8; Jn 5, 24–25; 16, 33; 1 Jn 3, 14; Eph 2, 1.

20, 1: Abyss: see the note on 9, 1.

20, 2: Dragon . . . serpent . . . Satan: see the notes on 12, 3.9.10.15.

20, 4: Beast . . . mark: see ch 13 and its notes.

20, 6: Blessed: see the note on 1, 3. Second death: see the note on 2, 11. Priests: as in 1, 6; 5, 10; cf 1 Pt 2, 9.

20, 7–10: A description of the symbolic battle to take place when Satan is released at the end of time, when the thousand years are over; see the note on vv 1–6.

20, 8: Gog and Magog: symbols of all pagan nations; the names are taken from Ez 38, 1—39, 20.

20, 9: The breadth of the earth: Palestine. The beloved city: Jerusalem; see the note on 14, 1.

20, 11–15: A description of the final judgment. After the intermediate reign of Christ, all the dead are raised and judged, thus inaugurating the new age.

j: 17, 14; 2 Mc 13, 4.   k: Ez 39, 17-20.   l: 14, 10.   m: 9, 1.   n: Gn 3, 1.   o: Mt 19, 28.   p: Ez 38, 2.9.16.   q: Ez 38, 22.   r: 2 Pt 3, 7.10.12.

presence and there was no place for them. *12s*I saw the dead, the great and the lowly, standing before the throne, and scrolls were opened. Then another scroll was opened, the book of life. The dead were judged according to their deeds, by what was written in the scrolls. *13*The sea gave up its dead; then Death and Hades gave up their dead. All the dead were judged according to their deeds. *14t*Then Death and Hades were thrown into the pool of fire. (This pool of fire is the second death.) *15*Anyone whose name was not found written in the book of life was thrown into the pool of fire.

VI: The New Creation

CHAPTER 21

See RG
524

The New Heaven and the New Earth.

*1u*Then I saw a new heaven and a new earth. The former heaven and the former earth had passed away, and the sea was no more. *2v*I also saw the holy city, a new Jerusalem, coming down out of heaven from God, prepared as a bride adorned for her husband. *3w*I heard a loud voice from the throne saying, "Behold, God's dwelling is with the human race. He will dwell with them and they will be his people and God himself will always be with them [as their God]. *4x*He will wipe every tear from their eyes, and there shall be no more death or mourning, wailing or pain, [for] the old order has passed away."

*5y*The one who sat on the throne said, "Behold, I make all things new." Then he said, "Write these words down, for they are trustworthy and true." *6z*He said to me, "They are accomplished. I [am] the Alpha and the Omega, the beginning and the end. To the thirsty I will give a gift from the spring of life-giving water. *7a*The victor will inherit these gifts, and I shall be his God, and he will be my son. *8b*But as for cowards, the unfaithful, the depraved, murderers, the unchaste, sorcerers, idol-worshipers, and deceivers of every sort, their lot is in the burning pool of fire and sulfur, which is the second death."

The New Jerusalem. *9*One of the seven angels who held the seven bowls filled with the seven last plagues came and said to me, "Come here. I will show you the bride, the wife of the Lamb." *10c*He took me in spirit to a great, high mountain and showed me the holy city Jerusalem coming down out of heaven from God. *11d*It gleamed with the splendor of God. Its radiance was like that of a precious stone, like jasper, clear as crystal. *12*It had a massive, high wall, with twelve gates where twelve angels were stationed and on which names were inscribed, [the names] of the twelve tribes of the Israelites. *13e*There were three gates facing east, three north, three south, and three west. *14f*The wall of the city had twelve courses of stones as its foundation, on which were inscribed the twelve names of the twelve apostles of the Lamb.

20, 12: The book of life: see the note on 3, 5. **Judged . . . scrolls:** see the note on 14, 12.

20, 13: Hades: the netherworld; see the note on 1, 18.

20, 14: Second death: see the note on 2, 11.

21, 1—22, 5: A description of God's eternal kingdom in heaven under the symbols of a new heaven and a new earth; cf Is 65, 17–25; 66, 22; Mt 19, 28.

21, 1: Sea . . . no more: because as home of the dragon it was doomed to disappear; cf Jb 7, 12.

21, 2: New Jerusalem . . . bride: symbol of the church (Gal 4, 26); see the note on 19, 7.

21, 3: People: other ancient manuscripts read a plural, "peoples."

21, 3–4: Language taken from Ez 37, 27; Is 25, 8; 35, 10; cf 7, 17.

21, 5: The one . . . on the throne: God himself; cf 4, 1–11.

21, 6: They are accomplished: God's reign has already begun; see the note on 20, 1–6. **Alpha . . . Omega:** see the note on 1, 8. **Life-giving water:** see the note on 7, 17.

21, 7: The victor: over the forces of evil; see the conclu-

sions of the seven letters (2, 7.11.17.26; 3, 5.12.21). **He will be my son:** the victorious Christian enjoys divine affiliation by adoption (Gal 4, 4–7; Rom 8, 14–17); see the note on 2, 26–28.

21, 8: Cowards: their conviction is so weak that they deny Christ in time of trial and become traitors. **Second death:** see the note on 2, 11.

21, 9—22, 5: Symbolic descriptions of the new Jerusalem, the church. Most of the images are borrowed from Ez 40—48.

21, 9: The bride, the wife of the Lamb: the church (2), the new Jerusalem (10); cf 2 Cor 11, 2.

21, 14: Courses of stones . . . apostles: literally, "twelve foundations"; cf Eph 2, 19–20.

s: Rom 2, 6. *t:* 1 Cor 15, 26.54-55. *u:* Is 65, 17; 66, 22; Rom 8, 19-23; 2 Pt 3, 13. *v:* 19, 7-9. *w:* Ez 37, 27. *x:* 7, 17; Is 25, 8; 35, 10. *y:* Is 43, 19; 2 Cor 5, 17. *z:* 22, 17; Ps 36, 8-9; Is 55, 1. *a:* 2 Sm 7, 14. *b:* 22, 15; Rom 1, 29-32. *c:* Ez 40, 2. *d:* Heb 11, 10. *e:* Ez 48, 31-35. *f:* Eph 2, 20.

15*The one who spoke to me held a gold measuring rod to measure the city, its gates, and its wall. *16**The city was square, its length the same as [also] its width. He measured the city with the rod and found it fifteen hundred miles in length and width and height. *17**He also measured its wall: one hundred and forty-four cubits according to the standard unit of measurement the angel used. *18**The wall was constructed of jasper, while the city was pure gold, clear as glass. *19g*The foundations of the city wall were decorated with every precious stone; the first course of stones was jasper, the second sapphire, the third chalcedony, the fourth emerald, *20*the fifth sardonyx, the sixth carnelian, the seventh chrysolite, the eighth beryl, the ninth topaz, the tenth chrysoprase, the eleventh hyacinth, and the twelfth amethyst. *21*The twelve gates were twelve pearls, each of the gates made from a single pearl; and the street of the city was of pure gold, transparent as glass.

22h*I saw no temple in the city, for its temple is the Lord God almighty and the Lamb. *23i**The city had no need of sun or moon to shine on it, for the glory of God gave it light, and its lamp was the Lamb. *24j**The nations will walk by its light, and to it the kings of the earth will bring their treasure. *25*During the day its gates will never be shut, and there will be no night there. *26*The treasure and wealth of the nations will be brought there, *27k*but nothing unclean will enter it, nor any[one] who does abominable things or tells lies. Only those will enter whose names are written in the Lamb's book of life.

CHAPTER 22

See RG 524

1*Then the angel showed me the river of life-giving water, sparkling like crystal, flowing from the throne of God and of the Lamb *2**down the middle of its street. On either side of the river grew the tree of life that produces fruit twelve times a year, once each month; the leaves of the trees serve as medicine for the nations. *3*Nothing accursed will be found there anymore. The throne of God and of the Lamb will be in it, and his servants will worship him. *4**They will look upon his face, and his name will be on their foreheads. *5m*Night will be no more, nor will they need light from lamp or sun, for the Lord God shall give them light, and they shall reign forever and ever.

VII: Epilogue

6n*And he said to me, "These words are trustworthy and true, and the Lord, the God of prophetic spirits, sent his angel to show his servants what must happen soon." *7o**"Behold, I am coming soon." Blessed is the one who keeps the prophetic message of this book.

*8*It is I, John, who heard and saw these things, and when I heard and saw them I fell down to worship at the feet of the angel who showed them to me. *9p*But he said to me,

---

21, 15–17: The city is shaped like a gigantic cube, a symbol of perfection (cf 1 Kgs 6, 19–20). The measurements of the city and its wall are multiples of the symbolic number twelve; see the note on 7, 4–9.

21, 16: Fifteen hundred miles: literally, twelve thousand stades, about 12,000 furlongs (see the note on 14, 20); the number is symbolic: twelve (the apostles as leaders of the new Israel) multiplied by 1,000 (the immensity of Christians); cf Introduction. **In length and width and height:** literally, "its length and width and height are the same."

21, 17: One hundred and forty-four cubits: the cubit was about eighteen inches in length. **Standard unit of measurement the angel used:** literally, "by a human measure, i.e., an angel's."

21, 18–21: The gold and precious gems symbolize the beauty and excellence of the church; cf Ex 28, 15–21; Tb 13, 16–17; Is 54, 11–12.

21, 22: Christ is present throughout the church; hence, no temple is needed as an earthly dwelling for God; cf Mt 18, 20; 28, 20; Jn 4, 21.

21, 23: Lamp ... Lamb: cf Jn 8, 12.

21, 24–27: All men and women of good will are welcome in the church; cf Is 60, 1.3.5.11. **The ... book of life:** see the note on 3, 5.

22, 1.17: Life-giving water: see the note on 7, 17.

22, 2: The tree of life: cf v 14; see the note on 2, 7. **Fruit ... medicine:** cf Ez 47, 12.

22, 4: Look upon his face: cf Mt 5, 8; 1 Cor 13, 12; 1 Jn 3, 2.

22, 6–21: The book ends with an epilogue consisting of a series of warnings and exhortations and forming an inclusion with the prologue by resuming its themes and expressions; see the note on 1, 1–3.

22, 7.12.20: I am coming soon: Christ is the speaker; see the note on 1, 3.

22, 7.14: Blessed: see the note on 1, 3.

---

g: Is 54, 11-12.   *h:* Jn 2, 19-20.   *i:* Is 60, 1-2.19-20.   *j:* Is 60, 11.   *k:* Is 35, 8; 52, 1; Zec 13, 2 / Rv 3, 5; 20, 12.   *l:* Ez 47, 1-12.   *m:* Is 60, 20.   *n:* 1, 1.   *o:* 12.20 / 1, 3.   *p:* 19, 10.

"Don't! I am a fellow servant of yours and of your brothers the prophets and of those who keep the message of this book. Worship God."

10*Then he said to me, "Do not seal up the prophetic words of this book, for the appointed time is near. *11*Let the wicked still act wickedly, and the filthy still be filthy. The righteous must still do right, and the holy still be holy."

12q"Behold, I am coming soon. I bring with me the recompense I will give to each according to his deeds. *13r**I am the Alpha and the Omega, the first and the last, the beginning and the end."

14s*Blessed are they who wash their robes so as to have the right to the tree of life and enter the city through its gates. *15t*Outside are the dogs, the sorcerers, the unchaste, the murderers, the idol-worshipers, and all who love and practice deceit.

16u*"I, Jesus, sent my angel to give you this testimony for the churches. I am the root and offspring of David, the bright morning star."

17v*The Spirit and the bride say, "Come." Let the hearer say, "Come." Let the one who thirsts come forward, and the one who wants it receive the gift of life-giving water.

*18*I warn everyone who hears the prophetic words in this book: if anyone adds to them, God will add to him the plagues described in this book, *19w*and if anyone takes away from the words in this prophetic book, God will take away his share in the tree of life and in the holy city described in this book.

20x*The one who gives this testimony says, "Yes, I am coming soon." Amen! Come, Lord Jesus!

*21*The grace of the Lord Jesus be with all.

22, 10: The appointed time: see the note on 1, 3.

22, 13: Christ applies to himself words used by God in 1, 8.

22, 14: The city: heavenly Jerusalem; see the note on 21, 2.

22, 16: The root ... of David: see the note on 5, 5. **Morning star:** see the note on 2, 26–28.

22, 17: Bride: the church; see the note on 21, 2.

22, 20: Come, Lord Jesus: a liturgical refrain, similar to

the Aramaic expression **Marana tha**—"Our Lord, come!"—in 1 Cor 16, 22; cf the note there. It was a prayer for the coming of Christ in glory at the parousia; see the note on 1, 3.

---

q: 7.20 / Ps 62, 12; 2 Tm 4, 14.   *r:* 1, 8; 21, 6; Is 41, 4; 44, 6.   *s:* 7, 14-15; 22, 2.   *t:* 21, 8; Rom 1, 29-32.   *u:* 1, 1.11-12; 22, 6 / 2, 28.   *v:* 21, 6; Is 55, 1.   *w:* Dt 4, 2.   *x:* 7.12 / Acts 3, 20-21; 1 Cor 15, 23; 16, 22.

**GLOSSARY
MEASURES AND WEIGHTS
LECTIONARY**

GLOSSARY

acrostic a poetic form in which the first letter of each new line or series of lines within a larger group follows the order of letters in the Hebrew alphabet. The supreme example in the Bible is Psalm 119 and, outside the psalter, the Book of Lamentations.

allegory an extended comparison in which persons or objects stand for abstract ideas, moral qualities, or spiritual realities. Some people read the Song of Songs, which uses the language of a passionate love affair, as an allegory of God's love for the people of God, or of Christ's love for the church. Allegorical: characterized by allegory; symbolic.

alleluia a Greek and Latin form of a Hebrew verb, meaning "praise the Lord." *See* hallelujah.

anawim the Hebrew word for "the poor," "the afflicted," "the meek or humble." Often used in the Psalms for the group to which the Psalmist belongs.

aphorism a short memorable saying. Many of the Proverbs are aphorisms, and so are many of Jesus' statements. Aphorisms are easy to remember.

apocalypse the Greek word for "revelation." It is also used as the name for a type of literature that contains mysterious revelations, usually veiled in symbolic language and interpreted by an angel. The subject matter of an apocalypse deals with the heavenly world and with the future, especially the final judgment. Biblical examples are found in Daniel 7–12 and in the Book of Revelation.

apocrypha a Greek word meaning "hidden." Pious literature, related to the Scriptures but not included in the canon. Protestants regard several books of the Catholic Old Testament as apocryphal because they are not found in the Hebrew Bible (Sirach, Wisdom, Baruch, 1 and 2 Maccabees, Tobit, Judith). *See* canon; deuterocanonical.

apologia Greek, "explanation." A defense of one's actions or beliefs, usually given in a formal speech or written document.

apostasy the act of abandoning a set of beliefs, or the position of having abandoned them.

B

Base Community a translation of a Spanish term, *comunidad de base:* "basic or foundational society," for certain popular church groups in Central and South America that are empowering cultural, educational, and political organizations among the oppressed—particularly peasants.

basilica a church built according to an ancient Roman plan, with a rectangular nave and a semicircular apse at one end; also, a Catholic church with certain ceremonial or liturgical privileges.

Booths, Feast of the final harvest festival of grapes and olives, falling within our month of October. It was called "Booths" because the harvesters lived in the field in makeshift tents or booths. *See* Tabernacles; *Sukkoth.*

C

Canaan the land infiltrated by the Israelites after the Exodus. It was more extensive than biblical Israel. Canaanite: an inhabitant of that land.

canon a Greek word meaning "measuring rod," and later the rule by which something was judged. Christian tradition uses the word for the official list of the individual books that make up the Scriptures. The canon of the Catholic Church is more extensive than that of the Protestant churches, but less extensive than that of the Orthodox churches. *See* apocrypha; pseudepigraphy. Canonical: conforming to the canon.

canonical criticism a way of reading the text of the Bible that tries to understand its final form, rather than working only with the parts that make it up or trying to reconstruct earlier versions of it. *See* form criticism; historical-critical method; literary criticism; redaction criticism.

casemate two parallel walls that are joined by short cross walls. They form small rooms that are used for storage or are filled with earth to strengthen fortifications.

ceramic typology a way of dating different levels of an archaeological site by classifying the pieces of pottery found in them according to the approximate eras in which they were made.

chaos complete lack of order. In the mythology of the ancient Near East, chaos was sometimes personified as divine beings who had to be conquered by other gods in order to establish an orderly and habitable universe.

charisma a gift of spiritual grace, particularly a gift of one of the manifestations of the Holy Spirit in the New Testament church, such as speaking in tongues. Charismatic: gifted with charisma.

Christ the Greek word for the Hebrew *masiah* (*see* messiah). Both words mean anointed, that is, blessed by having oil poured over the head. By applying this title to Jesus, the early Christians expressed their belief that he was the messiah of Israel.

Christology the theological doctrines covering the nature of Jesus as the Christ. High christology emphasizes the divinity of Jesus; low christology stresses his humanity.

chronicler scholarly name for the author, or group of authors, of the books of 1 and 2 Chronicles, Ezra, and Nehemiah.

circumcision the ritual removal of the foreskin of the penis in male infants. It symbolized, for Jews, the membership of the infant in the people of God (Genesis 17,9–14). It came to have spiritual significance, an image of repentance (Jeremiah 4,4). In Paul's writings (see in particular Galatians 5,2–6), it means the reliance upon one's own good deeds, rather than on God's mercy, for salvation.

Cisjordan Latin for "this side of Jordan," that is, the western bank of the river Jordan ("this side" as viewed from Jerusalem). *See* Transjordan.

codex a manuscript made up of separate leaves of writing that are bound into a unit along one edge. Our modern books are a development of the codex form. *See* scroll.

cosmos Greek for "order, regularity." The cosmos is the created world of order, stability, and relative permanence, as opposed to the impermanence and disorder of chaos.

Council of Trent the twenty-ninth ecumenical council of the Catholic Church, held 1545–1563, after the Protestant Reformation had begun. Among other things, it defined the books that are part of the Catholic canon of Scripture.

covenant an agreement between two parties. There are several important covenants in the Old Testament. After the Flood, God made a covenant with Noah not to destroy the earth again. The covenants with Abraham and David have the character of unconditional promises by God. The most central covenant is that made with Moses on Mt. Sinai, and described in the Books of Exodus and Deuteronomy. That covenant has specific requirements (the commandments) and resembles the international treaties of the ancient Near East.

cult the rituals and religious practices at a temple or other place of worship. For instance, the cult of the Jerusalem Temple means the religious practices observed there, with no judgment about their value implied in the term.

D

Dead Sea Scrolls a group of manuscripts that were found in 1947 in caves near the Dead Sea, at a place called *wadi Qumran* (Qumran gulch). The scrolls appear to have been the library of an Essene settlement, which flourished at the site from the late second century B.C. until it was destroyed by the Romans in 68 A.D. The importance of the scrolls for biblical studies is twofold. They include Hebrew manuscripts of biblical books that are several centuries older than those previously known, and they shed new light on Jewish beliefs and practices around the time of Jesus. *See* Essenes.

decalogue Greek, "ten words." The traditional name for the list of commandments given in Exodus 20,1–17 and Deuteronomy 5,6–21.

demon a spiritual or nonphysical being, generally hostile to human beings, but in most Old Testament passages still under God's control (*see* Job 1 and 2). A common Hebrew name was *satan,* meaning "adversary." By the time of the New Testament demons were generally regarded as hostile to God as well, and therefore evil, or the cause of bad influences—disease, mental distress—on human beings. Demonic: marked by spiritual evil, like a demon.

deuterocanonical Greek, "second canon." The name for those books in the Catholic Old Testament that are not in the Hebrew canon, but were added in the Greek translation, the Septuagint, and taken over into the Latin versions. The deuterocanonical books (and additions) are: Sirach, Wisdom, Baruch, 1 and 2 Maccabees, Tobit, Judith, and additions to Esther and Daniel. *See* canon.

Deuteronomic History the books of Joshua, Judges, 1 and 2 Samuel, and 1 and 2 Kings, giving a history of Israel from the conquest of the land to the exile. The Book of Deuteronomy serves as a sort of preface to this work.

deuteronomic reform the religious reform and revival that took place under King Josiah beginning in 621 B.C. Scholars generally assume that the book from which the religious instructions were read to the people was the newly rediscovered Book of Deuteronomy (see 2 Kings 22,8—23,25). During this reform the Temple worship was purged of many pagan influences that had crept in under the political overlordship of the Assyrian Empire.

deuteronomist the scholarly name for the author or authors of the books of Joshua, Judges, 1 and 2 Samuel, and 1 and 2 Kings, which form a continuous history of Israel from the conquest of the land to the exile in Babylon. *See* Deuteronomic History.

discernment the ability to distinguish between what is valuable and what is not, especially in the spiritual or moral realms.

disciple a follower. The disciples of Jesus were those who followed, or tried to follow, his teachings.

E

ecclesiology the theology of the meaning of the church or the study of the church's forms, structures, importance, etc.

ecumenism from the Greek *oikoumene*, "the whole inhabited world." Any attempts to deal with the relations between different Christian groups, or to think about ways in which divisions might be overcome. Since the Second Vatican Council (1963–65) ecumenical activity has become a major goal of the Catholic Church. Ecumenical: aimed at fostering ecumenism, or characterized by ecumenical aims; having the character of ecumenism.

Elohist the scholarly name for the author of one of the source documents for the Pentateuch. The Elohist's writing is marked by the use of Hebrew *'elohim* (God) rather than the proper name *yahweh* (Lord) in the period before Moses. *See* Yahwist.

Ephraim the most important tribe of the Northern Kingdom. *See* Northern Kingdom.

Epicurean a follower of the Greek philosopher Epicurus, who taught (among other things) that more permanent pleasures should be preferred to passing ones, and that one should remain unaffected as far as possible by the changes and passions of everyday life.

epigraph an inscription, usually carved or etched in stone. Epigraphs, which can be recovered from archae-ological sites, provide information about the language and customs of the time when they were written.

epistle a letter, generally intended for public reading and written according to a set literary style. Epistolary: having the form of a letter.

eschatology teaching about "the end." In the Hebrew prophets, the end in question is that of Israel or Judah as independent nations. In later apocalyptic writings it came to mean the end of the world.

Essenes a Jewish sect around the time of Jesus. They are described by the first-century Jewish authors. Philo and Josephus, and by the Roman Pliny. The Dead Sea Scrolls are believed to be the documents of an Essene community. *See* Dead Sea Scrolls.

ethnology the study of races or ethnic groups.

etiology an account or story that gives the cause of something. Many stories in the Bible may have originated in this way; for instance, the story of Lot's wife (Genesis 19,26) may have been told to explain the existence of a pillar of salt.

exegesis the explanation of a text.

exile removal from one's own country. In the context of the Old Testament, "the Exile" refers to the period between 586 and 539 B.C. when the upper classes of Judah were exiles in Babylon. A previous exile, from the northern kingdom of Israel, had been enforced in 722–721 B.C. Exilic: taking place during the Exile, or dealing with it.

F

festival a religious celebration.

form criticism an approach to a text that focuses on the smaller literary forms contained in a larger work (for instance, parables or miracle stories in the Gospels) and tries to discover the historical settings in which they might have originated, before they were incorporated in the larger work.

Former Prophets the name in the Hebrew Scriptures for the first part of the larger section called the Prophets. The Former Prophets consist of Joshua, Judges, 1 and 2 Samuel, and 1 and 2 Kings. *See* Latter Prophets; Prophets; Writings.

fundamentalist in its narrow meaning, a fundamentalist is a conservative Protestant who believes in the five fundamentals: the sole authority of Scripture; the Virgin Birth of Jesus Christ; the doctrine of the substitutionary atonement of the death of Christ; the physical, bodily resurrection of Christ; and the literal Second Coming of Christ to judge the world. In its larger meaning, fundamentalist has come to mean any rigidly conservative adherent to a belief system, who regards all those outside the belief system as without hope of salvation, and who treats the sacred text of the tradition as an infallible guide to belief and action.

G

Gemara *see* Talmud.

genre a literary form or type. Biblical genres include oracles, laments, hymns, parables, letters, gospels, and apocalypses.

Gentile a non-Jew.

gnosticism from the Greek word *gnosis,* "knowledge." A kind of religion that claims secret knowledge about the real nature of the universe. Gnosticism flourished in the second to fourth centuries A.D., but tendencies to it can also be found in New Testament times. Gnostic philosophies differ greatly in their actual beliefs, but all claim to have and impart secret knowledge to those who join their group. Some New Testament writings, such as the letters of Paul and John, may be combatting forms of gnosticism in some of their passages. Gnosticism was denounced as heretical by the early theologians of the church. A major library of gnostic documents was discovered at Nag Hammadi in Egypt in 1946. Gnostic: an adherent of gnosticism, or a person or writing with characteristics of gnosticism.

H

haggadah Jewish tales, anecdotes, and other materials in the Talmud that are distinguished from the legal traditions that also became part of the Talmud. *See* Talmud.

halakah Jewish laws and regulations, other than those found in the Bible, that make up the legal part of the Talmud. *See* Talmud.

hallelujah a Hebrew word meaning "praise the Lord." The Greek and Latin spelling of it, alleluia, is more familiar in the liturgy.

Hasmonean the name given to the dynasty descended from the Maccabee brothers. It ruled Israel from 135 to 36 B.C.; the last Hasmonean was overthrown by Herod the Great.

hellenic conforming to, or characterized by, the ideals of Greek culture. The Greek conquest of the countries of the eastern Mediterranean by Alexander the Great, during the years 333–323 B.C., was followed by the adoption of the Greek language and educational practices in the areas under Greek political influence. Hellenistic: having this Greek cultural character or idealizing it. Hellenization: the process of adopting Greek culture and practices.

herem the practice of sacrificing all the spoils of war to God.

Herodian followers and members of the court of the dynasty of Herod the Great and his sons (about 40 B.C. to A.D. 40).

historical-critical method any method of reading a text that tries to understand it in its historical context, that is, its original setting and what it meant to its original hearers or readers. For example, a historical-critical reading of Isaiah 7:14 ("the virgin shall be with child") asks what this prophecy meant to the people of Jerusalem in the eighth century B.C., not what it later came to mean for the Christian faith. The method uses the tools of historical research to understand the conditions of the past, and critical tools to understand the traditions and development that lie behind the surface of the text. Historical criticism is an umbrella term that includes such methods as form criticism and redaction criticism.

holocaust a sacrifice entirely consumed by fire, a whole burnt offering. This sacrifice was one of adoration of God.

Holocaust, the the European persecution of the Jews, 1938–1945, that culminated in the death-camp slaughter of up to six million European Jews.

holocausts, altar of in the Temple, the altar on which the whole burnt offerings were made.

humanist one who upholds the value and dignity of the human person and human culture. Some humanists believe in God; others do not, but believe that human endeavors and accomplishments are the highest ones we know of. Some scholars have thought that humanism marks some of the passages in Ecclesiastes and other wisdom materials.

hymn a religious poem set to music and sung as part of worship.

hypostasization (or hypostatization) speaking of an abstract quality as if it were a living being, for instance, Wisdom in Proverbs 8 or Sirach 24.

Hyksos Egyptian dynasty (1850–1500 B.C.) that may have been of Semitic origin, and therefore have provided the historical basis for the stories of the Israelite patriarchs in Egypt (Genesis 37–50).

I

inerrancy the doctrine that the biblical materials are without error. In its strict form, as held, for instance, by Protestant fundamentalists, inerrancy includes the assertion that in the original manuscripts of the biblical books there are no errors of fact, whether theological, historical, or scientific. A more restrained version of the doctrine would claim that the Bible is an inerrant guide in matters of faith, but that it may contain historical errors or assertions that cannot be reconciled with present-day science. Vatican II expressed it this way: "Therefore, since everything asserted by the inspired authors or sacred writers must be held to be asserted by the Holy Spirit, it follows that the books of Scripture must be acknowledged as teaching firmly, faithfully, and without error that truth which God wanted put into the sacred writings for the sake of our salvation" (Document on Revelation, *Dei Verbum,* n. 11). The final phrase, "for the sake of our salvation"—that is, not for the sake of giving us historical or scientific information—establishes the limits of inerrancy.

inspiration the belief that words uttered by a human being are really the words of a divinity. In the ancient world, prophets and oracles were thought to be inspired. In Christian tradition, the notion of inspiration was eventually applied to the whole Bible. Inspiration in a more expanded sense speaks of an inspired tradition, in which numerous authors, anonymous contributors, editors, and others all worked together more or less consciously to create the biblical materials; in this view, God used all these people and their human traditions to express the Bible's teachings. The Second Vatican Council affirms the inspiration of Scripture, but warns that God speaks "through men in human fashion" so that careful attention must be given "to what the sacred writers really intended" (*Dogmatic Constitution on Divine Revelation*, III.12).

Israel the name for both the kingdom of twelve tribal groups, of which David and Solomon were kings, and for the northern section of this kingdom, which split off after the death of Solomon and began a separate political existence under Jeroboam I (1 Kings 12). *See* Northern Kingdom, Southern Kingdom.

J

Jahvist the author of one of the source documents of the Pentateuch (German spelling). *See* Yahwist.

Josephus a Roman Jewish historian of the first century A.D., whose works of Jewish history were written partly to make the Jewish religion and people more acceptable to the Roman government. His two major works are the *Jewish Wars* and the *Jewish Antiquities,* which provide valuable information about the background of the later Old Testament writings and the New Testament.

Judah the major tribal group of the Southern Kingdom. *See* Southern Kingdom.

K

kosher according to specific regulations; fit or proper. Food that is *kosher* does not fall into any of the forbidden food groups and has been prepared according to the cleanliness regulations.

L

lament a Hebrew verse form that is used for poetic elegies, psalms of suffering or anguish, and other treatments of painful parts of the human condition. The Book of Lamentations and many psalms are in the form of laments. See *qinah.*

Latter Prophets the name given in Jewish tradition to the second part of the section of the Hebrew Scriptures called the Prophets. The Latter Prophets are Isaiah, Jeremiah, Ezekiel, and the Book of Twelve (Hosea, Joel, Amos, Obadiah, Jonah, Micah, Nahum, Habakkuk, Zephaniah, Haggai, Zechariah, Malachi). *See* Prophets.

Law the usual English translation of the Hebrew word *Torah,* which means "guidance" or "teaching." The Torah in the narrower sense of the Pentateuch (Genesis, Exodus, Leviticus, Numbers, and Deuteronomy) is the first of the three divisions of the Hebrew Scriptures (followed by the Prophets and the Writings). It is often called the "Law of Moses" although it contains much else besides legal material. Despite Paul's attacks on attempts to win salvation through the Law, the dominant biblical attitude to law sees it as a gift of God and source of joy. It is the opportunity to show faithfulness to God in one's daily activities. *See* Pentateuch; Prophets; Torah; Writings.

Levite a member of the tribe charged with responsibility for Israel's worship. The Levites owned no land of their own, but rather lived on the offerings of the Temple sacrifices.

levirate marriage from Latin *levir,* "husband's brother." A practice in the earlier stages of Judaism in which a man had to take his dead brother's wife as his own if his brother had died before fathering any children who could carry on his name. The children that would result from the union of the widow and her brother-in-law would be treated as if they were the dead man's offspring, inheriting his property and carrying on his name. It is generally agreed that the practice died out well before the time of Jesus (along with the practice of polygamy), but it forms the basis of the question that the Sadducees present to Jesus (Matthew 22, 23–33; Mark 12, 18–27; Luke 20, 27–40): in the next life, which of seven brothers will be the husband of a woman whom they all successively married under the levirate law.

libation from the Latin for "pour." Pouring out a liquid (such as wine or oil) onto the ground as a sacrifice to a deity.

literal meaning the plain sense of a text, whether historical, instructional, or otherwise. The literal meaning was traditionally treated in opposition to the allegorical meaning. *See* allegory.

literary criticism in older usage literary criticism meant what is now called "source criticism," that is, the search for the underlying documents in a biblical text. The isolation of the Yahwistic, Elohistic, and other basic documents in the first four books of the Bible is an example of this. More recently, a form of literary criticism has arisen which accepts the text in its final form and does not try to reconstruct earlier stages of it. This more recent type of criticism is concerned with the meaning of the text for the modern reader rather than with its historical context. *See* canonical criticism; historical-critical method; source criticism.

liturgy originally a term for a public good work, paid for by a wealthy citizen but intended to benefit everyone. Liturgy now means the official public worship of the church. "The Liturgy" is increasingly used, following Orthodox writers, to mean the celebration of the Eucharist.

love feasts early Christian celebrations, perhaps held together with the Eucharist or as part of it, that included a full meal for the whole church community. Paul criticizes some of the church members in Corinth for the fact that in their assemblies they do not share food and drink, but rather the wealthy bring their own and consume it, while the poor have nothing extra to eat (1 Corinthians 11, 17–22). Perhaps because of such abuses, the institution of the love feast seems to have disappeared at a relatively early date.

M

matriarch Greek "mother-ruler," a female leader, elder, or ruler. *See* patriarch.

Megillah, (plural Megilloth) Hebrew, "scroll," a long strip of parchment or papyrus on which the text of a book was written. The festal *megilloth* are the books of Ruth, Song of Songs, Ecclesiastes, Esther, and Lamentations, each of which is read in the synagogue at a specific special feast.

messiah Hebrew for "anointed." It could be applied to various officials, including priests, but came to refer especially to the king who was descended from David. (As part of the ritual when a king was enthroned, his head was anointed with oil.) In the period after the Exile, when there was no longer a king in Judah, the "messiah" came to mean an ideal figure who would restore the kingdom of Israel in the future. *See also* Christ (the Greek translation of Messiah).

metaphor a direct comparison, one that does not use the words "like" or "as," between two things. Jesus used a metaphor when he said, "I am the gate for the sheep" (John 10,7). *See* simile.

midrash Hebrew, "explanation." A method of interpretation, developed among Jewish teachers before the time of Christ, in which a biblical passage is quoted up to the point of contemporary application. At that point the passage is discontinued and the explanation or application is given. A New Testament example is found in Matthew 2,16–23. Matthew alludes to Jeremiah 31, 15–17, but quotes only Jeremiah 31,15 (the tears of Rachel). Whereas Jeremiah goes on to announce the reward of those tears and the return of the Israelites from Exile, Matthew writes of the return of Jesus, Mary, and Joseph from Egypt.

millennium a thousand years. In Revelation 20,1–5, the thousand-year reign of Christ is predicted, and this reign has been called "the Millennium" because it is supposed to bring in an era of peace and well-being. A millennarian is one who takes this passage as predicting a literal, physical reign of Christ on Earth (as opposed to treating it as a metaphor for heaven, for example) and who tries to identify the events that will occur in order to bring the Millennium about.

Mishnah *see* Talmud.

motif a characteristic image or theme in a work.

mystery a spiritual reality that can never be fully understood. A mystery is not opaque to reason, but rather has a character that human reason cannot fully comprehend. The love of God for us is a mystery, not because we cannot understand what love is, but because we cannot comprehend the fullness of God's love, no matter how hard we try.

myth a story that expresses a spiritual truth or basic conviction of a culture through narrative. In particular, myths give explanations of origins, often through the struggles of divine beings or superhuman creatures. Because the Bible firmly believes in only one God, in biblical myths the presence of multiple deities has faded out, but the titanic struggle between good and evil is still maintained, as in the story of Paradise in Genesis 2—3, or the Tower of Babel story in Genesis 11,1–9. (For an alternate form of the Paradise myth, see Ezekiel 28,11–19.) Such stories, for example, express the impossibility of human efforts to attain the level of God.

N

Nazirite one who takes a religious vow of strict observance to dedicate himself or herself to the Lord, as explained in Numbers 6,1–21. The vow involves keeping purity laws very strictly, abstaining from alcoholic drink, and refraining from cutting one's hair. Samson, whose story is told in Judges 13–16, was a Nazirite, though his observance was marked by a number of relapses. Paul took the Nazirite vow (Acts 18,18; 21,23–24).

Northern Kingdom the political assembly of tribal groups that split off from the kingdom of Israel after Solomon's death (1 Kings 12). This newly-formed kingdom was itself called Israel, and in some of the prophets (for instance, Hosea 8,11), Ephraim, after its most important tribe.

O

oracle a message from God to a priest or prophet, and by the prophet to others, often in response to an inquiry. The content and style vary, from a call to prophesy to a message of salvation or a statement of threat and condemnation. Prophetic books are often made up of a series of oracles, usually in poetical form, which were collected and written down later, not necessarily in the order in which the prophet originally spoke them.

ostraca pieces of pottery with writing scratched on them. Ostraca are recovered from archaeological digs and provide evidence about the language at the time they were written; their existence reflects the fact that paper was a relatively rare and valuable substance, and was not used for casual writing, such as messages intended to be read once and thrown away, lists, and the like. Instead, people scratched a few words on a piece of broken pottery—useless for anything else—and thousands of these casual messages have been discovered.

P

palaeography the study of ancient forms of writing. Palaeography can be used to date manuscripts, since writing styles changed over the years and different manuscripts of the same book can be arranged in the likely order in which they were written. Palaeography can also classify the writing in inscriptions (epigraphs) and scratched on broken pieces of pottery (ostraca).

paraenesis moral exhortation, urging the reader or hearer to better behavior or a better mode of living, usually accompanied with or in the form of proverbial wisdom. The letter of James contains much of this sort of moral exhortation.

parousia Greek, "presence," by extension "appearance." The second coming of Christ.

Passover the Jewish feast commemorating the Exodus from Egypt.

patriarch Greek, "father-ruler," a male leader, elder, or ruler. *See* matriarch.

patristic (from the Greek word for "father"). Having to do with, or in the period of, the early theologians of the Christian church, usually referred to as "the fathers." The patristic period begins with the close of the New Testament writings, sometime after 100 A.D., and continues for several centuries. During this time creeds

and many classic Christian doctrines, such as the Incarnation, were worked out and put in final form.

Pentateuch a Greek word meaning "five scrolls" that is used to designate the first five books of the Bible (Genesis, Exodus, Leviticus, Numbers, Deuteronomy). Modern scholars now hold that the first four of these books are a later compilation (perhaps assembled during or after the Exile) of earlier independent sources, which are distinguished by various literary characteristics. The oldest of these, the "J" source (from the German name for it, Jahvist), uses the Hebrew word *Yahweh* as the name of God from the beginning, and may be connected to the court of King David. Another source, "E," uses *'elohim* instead of Yahweh before the time of Moses, and reflects traditions (about sites of worship, for instance) that probably derive from the northern tribes of the kingdom of Israel rather than from the southern sources of the kingdom of Judah that are contained in "J." A third source, "P," is a compilation of laws and Temple practices that the priests developed. The fourth source, "D," is found almost exclusively in the book of Deuteronomy. *See* Law; source criticism; Torah.

personification a literary device that takes an abstract quality or spiritual reality and speaks of it in human terms. The Book of Proverbs, 3,16 says of Wisdom, "Long life is in her right hand,/ in her left are riches and honor." Speaking of wisdom as if it were a human being is personification.

Pharisaism a reform movement in Judaism that probably began in the century before the birth of Jesus and, after the destruction of Jerusalem in 70 A.D., became an increasingly important influence in the religious life of Judaism. Essentially a lay movement, Pharisaism sought to invigorate Jewish life by emphasizing fidelity to Jewish law. Its base was the local synagogue with its study of the Jewish Scriptures and traditions and its strong sense of piety. Although Jesus may have shared many of the goals of Pharisaism, the gospels report him in conflict with it over interpretation of the religious law. *See* Pharisee.

Pharisee Hebrew, "separatist." One of a group of observant Jews, beginning before the time of Jesus and continuing with important leadership roles afterwards. They helped to develop an elaborate system of oral laws to apply the written law of Moses to Jewish life after the destruction of the Temple and the Roman conquest of their homeland. They were influential in the evolution of the synagogue and staunchly defended new doctrinal developments, such as belief in angels, bodily resurrection, and life after death. Some of the negative image of Pharisees in the Gospels may reflect later clashes between these Jewish leaders and the early church. *See* Pharisaism; Torah.

Platonism a philosophical system, derived in part from Plato but going beyond what he taught, that (among other things) saw a distinct separation between the worlds of the spirit and of material things, and that regarded the material world as inferior. There has certainly been Platonic influence on Christianity, though how much is difficult to say; but the Christian doctrine of the goodness of creation has helped to moderate the harshness of the Platonic judgment about the evil of material existence in and of itself.

pogrom the organized killing of a group, especially of Jews.

polemic a denunciation or condemnation of an opponent.

potsherd a broken piece (sherd or shard) of pottery. By studying decoration, shape, materials, etc., archaeologists can tell the level of pottery-making in a given era by examining the broken pieces from archaeological sites. *See* ceramic typology; ostraca; stratigraphy.

pre-exilic before the Exile of the Jewish people, that is, either before 721 B.C., when the Northern Kingdom (Israel) went into exile, or before 587–86 B.C., when the Southern Kingdom (Judah) was exiled by the Babylonians.

Priestly source the source that scholars assume was put together by the remains of the Israelite priesthood in Exile, containing the rules and regulations for worship in the Temple and other genealogical and legal information. This source, usually abbreviated "P," is one of the documents assumed to make up the Pentateuch *(see)*.

primeval history the term for the first ten chapters and part of the eleventh chapter of Genesis, dealing with events before the time of Abraham, who was regarded as the direct ancestor of the Israelites. "Primeval" designates the long stretch of time before literary documents enable us to reconstruct historical data.

prophet Greek, "one who speaks out." A prophet, called by God to speak the truth no matter what the cost, was one of the main participants in classical Israelite religion. The prophet was charged with the role of delivering God's message to the rulers, whether religious or political, and, as a result, many prophets were unpopular with the kings and priests. Prophets did not specialize in predicting the future, but rather in analyzing the present and announcing the consequences of current behavior. Most prophets spoke in a very memorable poetic form, delivering their statements orally in the streets or sanctuaries; only later were these written down, and still later put in some sort of order.

Prophets the second of the three divisions of the classical Hebrew Scriptures (the other two divisions are the Law and the Writings). The Prophets, in turn, are divided into the Former Prophets—Joshua, Judges, 1 and 2 Samuel, and 1 and 2 Kings—and the Latter Prophets—Isaiah, Jeremiah, Ezekiel, and the Twelve Minor Prophets. *See* canon; Former Prophets; Latter Prophets; Law; Writings.

proverb a statement of traditional wisdom, supported by long experience and expressed in memorable form. Generally the second line repeats or develops, sometimes by contrast, the thought of the first line. This feature is called parallelism, and is common in Hebrew poetry. Proverbs are quoted in many books of the Bible, but the major collection is in Proverbs. There are also proverbs in Wisdom and, in a longer "essay" form, in Sirach. *See* wisdom.

psalm from the Greek, a song accompanied by musical instruments. In the Bible these songs cover a wide variety of style and content; psalms appear in many places, but the principal collection of them is found in the Book of Psalms. The Hebrew name for this book is *Tehillim,* meaning "praises," even though the majority of the psalms are not hymns of praise but spread over many other categories such as laments, prayers of thanksgiving and confidence, wisdom, and psalms of royalty.

pseudepigraphy Greek, "false writing," meaning a false claim to authorship. The term is used for those ancient writings, Jewish and Christian, which went under the name of an important or fascinating biblical person, like Solomon or Enoch, or the apostles Thomas or James. Such works purported to be of equal status with works whose authority was already accepted. Some found their way into the Bible, at least in the Catholic and Orthodox canon: for instance, the Wisdom of Solomon. *See* apocrypha; canon; deuterocanonical.

pseudonymous under a false name. A pseudonymous writing is one that is published under the name of a well-known figure (usually long dead) in order to establish its authority or to continue the traditions of a revered but now dead leader. In the ancient world this was an accepted literary device. *See* pseudepigraphy.

Q

Q the abbreviation of the German word *quelle,* "source." It designates one of the original sources of Matthew and Luke, containing sayings of Jesus that they added to material they took from Mark's gospel. *See* synoptic gospels.

qinah a Hebrew poetical form (the lament) usually characterized by a two-line structure in which the first line has three stresses and the second line has two stresses. Normally in Hebrew poetry, each line of a strophe has the same number of stresses.

Qoheleth the Hebrew name, meaning "one who leads the assembly," of Ecclesiastes.

R

rabbi a teacher of the Jewish laws and traditions. Some of the followers of Jesus called him "rabbi"; in the time after Jesus, and after the Romans had destroyed the Temple in 70 A.D., the rabbis reconstituted the Jewish religion as one of study and meditation on the Scripture.

reader-response criticism a method for analyzing a literary text that focuses on the relationship between the text and its reader, paying attention to the literary clues in the text that guide the reader in drawing meaning from it.

redaction criticism the analysis of how a text was put together by an editor (or redactor) from already existing sources. The editor sometimes adds bridging sentences, uses characteristic language, adds or subtracts material, or uses the sources in a particular way, that reveal the concerns of the author and the audience at a point later in time than the original sources. Chapter 5 of Vatican II's document on Revelation speaks of the Gospels as the product of redactors: "The sacred authors wrote the four Gospels, selecting some things from the many which had been handed on by word of mouth or in writing, reducing some of them to a synthesis, explicating some things in view of the situation of their churches, and preserving the form of proclamation, but always in such fashion that they told us the honest truth about Jesus" (*Dei Verbum*, n. 19).

revelation Latin, "taking away the veil" (a translation of Greek, *apokalypsis*). The Book of Revelation in the Bible is an example of the apocalyptic genre (*see* apocalypse), which explains current happenings by means of a heavenly interpreter so that the reader understands the real importance of what is going on. The idea of revelation in theology is that what is revealed either could not have been discovered by unaided human reason or would take the reason too long to discover.

rhetorical criticism analysis of a text that shows how it uses literary devices to achieve its aims and effects.

Rosh Hashanah Hebrew, "head of the year." The Jewish New Year.

S

sacrifice the practice of giving something of value to God, in order to show one's devotion or commitment. In Israelite religion, sacrifice, usually of an animal or bird (though grain was also offered), was carried out by the ritual destruction of part or all of it by fire on an altar. This symbolized the bonding of oneself with God or the reunion with God after a sinful or unclean person received forgiveness and purification. Christianity took over this idea of sacrifice and applied it to the death of Jesus Christ, teaching that Christ's sacrifice was in atonement for human sin. In modern-day Christianity, sacrifice usually entails doing without things of value (money, material possessions, or time) by giving them away, to the church to promote its work of worship and service, to any organization engaged in the service of others, or directly to those in need.

Sadducee a member of the priestly family descended from Zadok, one of the two high priestly families under King David (2 Samuel 8, 17). They were granted supreme control over the Temple by King Solomon (1 Kings 2,35) and were further secured in their position by Ezekiel (Ezekiel 44,10–31). The Sadducees formed one of the ruling parties of Judaism from the time of the Hasmonean Dynasty (around 146 B.C.) to the destruction of the Temple in 70 A.D. They believed in the religious authority only of the Torah, or first five books of the Bible, and opposed the new interpretations advanced by the Pharisees, especially belief in the resurrection, life after death, and the existence of angels (*see* Acts 23,6–11). The Sadducees, despite their religious conservatism, were strongly influenced by the secular aspects of Greek culture and may have been willing to sacrifice strict Jewish ideals to maintain their power and wealth. *See* Pharisees.

saga a popular account of the prehistory or early heroic period of a people. Sagas are usually tales about the ancestors of a particular group, or the founders of a country. Many of the stories in the early chapters of Genesis are sagas.

Samaritan a member of a group resident in Israel at the time of the New Testament, and descended from the survivors in the land at the time of the Exile, who had intermarried with non-Israelites brought into the land by the Assyrians (2 Kings 17,24). After the restoration of the nation of Israel under Ezra and Nehemiah, they had not been reassimilated into the Hebrew nation. The Jews of Jesus' time looked down on Samaritans as not being true adherents of the Jewish religion, though the Samaritans themselves thought otherwise. Jesus, characteristically, treated the Samaritans with respect (John 4,4–42), and told one of his best-known parables using a Samaritan to illustrate true neighborliness, against two presumably religious characters who do not stop to help someone in need (Luke 10,30–37).

scroll a long strip of parchment or papyrus on which a manuscript was written. A scroll was difficult to handle and refer to, since in order to be read it had to be unrolled and it could be thirty or more feet long. It was replaced, some time after the first century A.D., by the bound book, or codex (*see*), but synagogues even today have scrolls of the Hebrew Scriptures for religious use.

Second Temple the reconstruction of Solomon's Temple, after the return from Exile, under the encouragement of the prophets Haggai and Zechariah and the direction of Ezra and Nehemiah. The Second Temple period began at the end of the sixth century B.C. and lasted through the extensive reconstruction of the Temple under Herod the Great's initiative until the fiery destruction by the Romans in 70 A.D.

Septuagint from the Latin for "seventy," therefore abbreviated LXX, the Latin numeral for seventy. It is the name of the main ancient Greek translation of the Hebrew Bible (with additions originally in Greek), undertaken by the Jewish community in Greek-speaking Egypt beginning about 250 B.C. This version included a larger number of books than was eventually accepted by the Jews for their collection of the Scriptures. It became very popular among Christians and was in fact their premier edition of the Bible. (The name "seventy" derives from a legend that Ptolemy II (285–247 B.C.) commissioned seventy (or seventy-two) learned elders to prepare this translation, a task they accomplished in seventy-two days.) Because the Septuagint is not a literal translation, but rather introduces modifications and explanatory remarks, it witnesses to Jewish interpretation of the Bible in the one or two centuries before Christ.

simile a comparison between two things, using "like" or "as." Malachi speaks of the Lord as "like the refiner's fire" (3,2) and the Psalms say the soul longs for God "as the hind longs for the running waters" (42,1). *See* metaphor.

soteriology from the Greek word for "savior." The study of the theology of salvation, or the explanation of different understandings of salvation.

source criticism the isolation and study of the different sources that go to make up a text. The most famous hypotheses of source criticism include the theory that the Books of Genesis through Numbers are made up of three sources ("J," or Yahwist, "E," or Elohist, "P," or Priestly) that were combined by later editors or redactors. Another source hypothesis is that Matthew and Luke used the gospel of Mark and another source (called "Q") when they wrote their gospels. *See* redaction criticism.

Southern Kingdom the remaining part of the undivided kingdom of Israel, after the northern tribes withdrew from Israel at Solomon's death (1 Kings 12). It is also called Judah. *See* Northern Kingdom.

stoa a covered walkway or portico.

stratigraphy the analysis of the sequence of layers, or strata, of a tell, or mound, at an archaeological site formed by successive periods of human occupation.

strophe (Greek, "turning"). Two or more lines of poetry that are treated as a unit; a stanza.

structural analysis a critical method that studies a text by looking for recurring patterns of meaning or imagery common to all languages and cultures. It wrestles with the text itself and is not concerned with the meaning intended by the original author nor with the historical context of the first composition.

Sukkoth Hebrew, "booths" or "tents," temporary structures built in the fields for the laborers to live in while the crops were being harvested. The Feast of *Sukkoth* is the major harvest festival. *See* Booths; Tabernacles.

synoptic gospels Matthew, Mark, and Luke. They are called "synoptic" because they can be "viewed together" or compared in parallel fashion. Similarities in the order of events, material, and even language, suggest that the Synoptics have a literary interrelationship. Scholars have theorized that Matthew and Luke are based on Mark and on another source, a list of Jesus' sayings, that is called "Q" (from the German word *Quelle,* "source"). This common basis would account for their similar character.

T

Tabernacles, Feast of the Hebrew harvest festival. *See* Booths; *Sukkoth.*

Talmud from the Hebrew, "learning" or "instruction." A collection of laws, regulations, and other material that, after the Hebrew Scriptures, is the authoritative religious document of Judaism. It consists primarily of the Mishnah, a collection of legal and procedural interpretations and practices from the Pharisees and other respected teachers. These materials themselves were further explained and expanded in the Gemara, which is a commentary on the Mishnah. All these materials were handed down orally until they were given a written form in what is called the Palestinian or Jerusalem Talmud (fourth century A.D.). A century later, the scholars of Judaism living outside the land of Israel put together the longer and more authoritative version called the Babylonian Talmud (which contains over two and a half million words, more than twice as many words as are in the entire Bible, and about four times as many words as are in the Hebrew Scriptures). See *haggadah, halakah.*

Temple a place of worship. The Temple in Hebrew religion was a permanent structure in Jerusalem, built by Solomon as a substitute for the tent of worship that the Israelites had used in the wilderness and continued to use through David's reign. This Temple was destroyed by the Babylonians in 587–86 B.C. A Second Temple was constructed under Ezra and Nehemiah in the fifth century, after the return from Exile. *See* Second Temple.

testament a documentary witness or testifier to something; in the Bible, specifically, the two Testaments are witnesses, respectively, to the relations between God and Israel, and to the work of God in Jesus Christ and in the beginnings of the Christian church.

text any unit of writing that is the subject of critical reading. It can be as small as one word (in the case of determining misprints, copying errors, etc.) or as large as an entire section or book. In biblical studies the term strictly applies only to editions of the Bible in the original language; very early renditions into another language are called versions; modern language versions are called translations. *See* Septuagint; Vulgate.

textual criticism the examination of the written text (usually in a number of different manuscripts) in order to determine what its accurate form is. Textual criticism compares one manuscript with another, to choose the variant form that is preferable in cases where the manuscripts disagree about a particular word. In translations, textual variations are sometimes explained in footnotes. *The New American Bible* says that it is "Translated from the Original Languages with Critical Use of All the Ancient Sources" (*see* the title page).

theodicy the theological effort to "justify God," that is, to explain the existence of evil while maintaining the goodness and power of God. The Book of Job is a long argument in theodicy.

theophany a Greek word meaning "appearance of God," that is, the manifestation of the divine to human perception in some way.

toledoth Hebrew, "generations, descendants, offspring"; a list of descendants; a genealogical account. There is a list of generations in Genesis 5,1–32 or in the first nine chapters of 1 Chronicles. Biblical genealogies generally, like the ones for Jesus in Matthew 1,1–7 and Luke 3,23–38, communicate a religious message within the list of names.

Torah a Hebrew word meaning "guide" or "teaching." The Torah consists of the first five books of the Bible (Genesis, Exodus, Leviticus, Numbers, Deuteronomy) and is the most important part of the Hebrew Scriptures for the Jewish religion. *See* Law; Pentateuch.

tradition the means by which beliefs, customs, stories, laws, religious practices, and other cultural phenomena are handed down from one generation to the next. The Bible is in part a record of traditions, first among the Hebrew people and then among the Christians. The Bible itself was first represented in tradition: in traditional stories and beliefs, in religious practices, and so on; only later was it written down and handed on in that form. The study of tradition—of how things are handed on, and how they change or stay the same during the process—is of great importance for understanding the

Bible and the beliefs that are based upon it. *See* redaction criticism.

transcendence the quality of going beyond ordinary experience. In theology, transcendence teaches that God is not contained in creation, or identical with it, but surpasses it in an absolute sense.

Transjordan Latin for "the other side of the (river) Jordan" as seen from Jerusalem. *See* Cisjordan.

transmission history the account of how a text came down to us from its originator. The transmission can begin in spoken form: a story told to others, a proverbial saying. It may then result in a written document, which is copied and combined with other documents or oral traditions, until it is in the form in which we have it. Scholars studying the text of the books of the Bible have assumed that, because of such things as two different accounts of the same event, or different names for God, the text as we have it is the result of a complicated process. Their efforts to understand this process are transmission history.

Trent, Council of see Council of Trent.

typology from the Greek word *typos,* the raised design on a seal for imprinting in wax, then a pattern or model; a theological way of understanding persons, events, or explanations, especially in the New Testament, by referring back to Old Testament "types." A type can be an event, like the Exodus from Egypt (1 Corinthians 10,1–6); a real person, like Solomon (Luke 11,31); or a story or parable like that of Jonah (Luke 11,29–30).

typology, ceramic see ceramic typology.

V

Vatican II the council of the Church held in the Vatican from 1962–65. The Second Vatican Council made many far-reaching decisions about the life of the Church, such as putting the liturgy into the language of the people. The Council also promoted the study and reading of the Scriptures and encouraged new Catholic translations and commentaries to help the understanding of nonexperts.

Vulgate the Latin translation of the Bible by St. Jerome, made in the fifth century A.D. Jerome went back to the original languages, Greek and Hebrew, in making his translation; it is called the Vulgate (from the Latin meaning "of the common people") because Latin was the language that most people spoke at that time.

W

wisdom the tradition of human learning, handed down from teacher to pupil and from parent to child. Wisdom relied on seeing recurring patterns in human behavior and in moral consequences of action, and in presenting these in a memorable form, usually a proverb. Wisdom

Literature: the collection of wisdom writings in the Bible, consisting of the books of Proverbs, Ecclesiastes, Wisdom, and Sirach, and including parts of Job and Psalms as well.

Writings the third part of the Hebrew Scriptures, after the Law (Torah) and Prophets. The Writings consisted of Psalms, Proverbs, Job, The Song of Songs, Ruth, Lamentations, Ecclesiastes, Esther, Daniel, Ezra, Nehemiah, and 1 and 2 Chronicles.

Y

Yahweh the Hebrew name for God. It is usually explained as based on the Hebrew verb for "to be or become," but it is not easy to translate. "The one who is" or "who causes to be" are possibilities. *The New American Bible,* following a tradition of English-language translations, uses the word Lord (or occasionally God) to indicate when the word Yahweh appears in the text. Yahweh is given as God's name to Moses in Exodus 3,14.

Yahwist the name for the author of one of the source documents of the Pentateuch. The Yahwist, from the beginning of his work (Genesis 2,4), habitually uses the name Yahweh for God (as opposed to the author of another of the documents, the Elohist, who uses the Hebrew word *'elohim*, or God). It is generally agreed among scholars that the Yahwist's account is the oldest of the documents. *See* Elohist; Pentateuch; Priestly.

Yom Kippur Hebrew, "Day of Atonement." The Jewish holy day of fasting and repentance.

Z

Zealot a Jew who was committed to the violent overthrow of the Roman rulers of Israel. Zealots were not a unified party or group but formed a number of sometimes conflicting factions, united only by their aversion to Roman oppression. They practiced assassination and other terror tactics, as well as engaging in political agitation. Although Zealots may have been active during Jesus' lifetime, there is little evidence of their emergence as a significant movement and force in Judaism until the time of the Jewish revolt that began about thirty years after the death of Jesus. Zealots captured by the Romans were usually crucified as a deterrent to their followers. The Zealot-inspired revolt in 66–70 A.D. was crushed by the Romans and the Temple in Jerusalem was pulled down.

Zion original meaning uncertain. It is sometimes spelled according to its Greek form, Sion. The name refers to the fortification within ancient Jerusalem conquered by David or to the entire city (2 Samuel 5,6–10). Still later Zion designated the area immediately north of this original city where Solomon built the Temple (Psalms 2,6; 48,2), and in some prophetical writings it stood for the heavenly Jerusalem (Isaiah 60,14; see Hebrews 12,22). From the fourth century A.D. the name has been attached to the southwest part of Jerusalem, where the tomb of David was relocated and the upper room of the Last Supper is pointed out. At the present time it is outside the medieval walls of Jerusalem.

MEASURES AND WEIGHTS

The modern equivalents for biblical measures and weights are presented in the following tables.

Hebrew Measures of Capacity: Liquid Measures

HEBREW	NAB	EQUIVALENCE	U.S. MEASURES	METRIC UNITS
kor	kor	10 baths	60.738 gallons	230 liters
bat	bath	6 hins	6.073 gallons	23 liters
hin	hin	3 kabs	1.012 gallons	3.829 liters
qab	kab	4 logs	1.4349 quarts	1.276 liters
log	log		.674 pint	.32 liter

Hebrew Measures of Capacity: Dry Measures

HEBREW	NAB	EQUIVALENCE	U.S. MEASURES	METRIC UNITS
homer	homer	2 lethechs	6.524 bushels	229.7 liters
kor	measure, cor	2 lethechs	6.524 bushels	229.7 liters
letek	lethech, measure	5 ephahs	3.262 bushels	114.8 liters
'epah	ephah, measure	3 seahs	20.878 quarts	22.9 liters
tse'ah	measure	3.33 omers	6.959 quarts	7.7 liters
'omer	omer	1.8 kabs	2.087 quarts	2.3 liters
'issaron	tenth part (of ephah)			
qab	kab		1.159 quarts	1.3 liters

Measures of Capacity in the New Testament

GREEK	NAB	EQUIVALENCE	U.S. MEASURES	METRIC UNITS
batos	measure	(Hebrew) bat	6.073 gallons	23 liters
koros	kor	(Hebrew) kor	60.738 gallons or 6.524 bushels	230 liters
saton	measure	(Hebrew) tse'ah	6.959 dry quarts	7.71 liters
metretes	measure		10.3 gallons	39 liters
choinix	ration		.98 dry quart	1.079 liters
modios	bushel	(Latin) modius	7.68 dry quarts	8.458 liters

Hebrew Measures of Length

HEBREW	NAB	EQUIVALENCE	U.S. MEASURES	METRIC UNITS
'ammaḥ	cubit	2 spans	17.49 inches	.443 meter
zeret	span	3 handbreadths	8.745 inches	.221 meter
topaḥ, tepaḥ	handbreadth	4 fingers	2.915 inches	.074 meter
'etsbaʿ	finger		.728 inch	.019 meter

The cubit described in Ezekiel 40, 5; 43, 13 is equal to seven (not six) handbreadths, namely 20.405 inches.

Measures of Length in the New Testament

GREEK	NAB	U.S. MEASURES	METRIC UNITS
pechus	cubit	about 1.5 feet	.456 meter
orguia	fathom	about 72.44 inches	1.839 meters
stadion	stade	about 606 feet	184.7 meters
milion	mile	about 4,854 feet	1.482 kilometers

Hebrew Weights

HEBREW	NAB	EQUIVALENCE	U.S. AVOIRDUPOIS	METRIC UNITS
kikkar	talent	60 minas	75.558 pounds	34.3 kilograms
maneh	mina	50 shekels	20.148 ounces	571.2 grams
sheqel	shekel	2 bekas	176.29 grains	11.42 grams
beqaʿ	bekah, half a shekel	10 gerahs	88.14 grains	5.71 grams
gerah	gerah		8.81 grains	.57 gram

The practice of weighing unmarked ingots of metal used in commercial transactions prior to the invention of money explains that the names of the units of weight were used later as indications of value, and as names for monetary standards. There is, however, no direct relation between the shekel-weight and the weight of a shekel piece.

Weights in the New Testament

GREEK	NAB	EQUIVALENCE	U.S. AVOIRDUPOIS	METRIC UNITS
talenton	talent	(Hebrew) talent	75.558 pounds	34.3 kilograms
mna	gold coin	(Hebrew) mina	20.148 ounces	571.2 grams
litra	pound	(Latin) libra	.719 pound	326.4 grams

LECTIONARY

THE NEW 3-YEAR CYCLE OF READINGS
FOR SUNDAY MASS

See pp. 1716–17 for Readings of Feasts that displace the Sunday Readings.
Guide: 1 refers to Reading I; 2 refers to Reading II; 3 refers to Gospel reading.

YEAR A
2005 2008 2011 2014
2017 2020 2023

Advent Season

1st Sunday of Advent
1 Is 2, 1–5
2 Rom 13, 11–14
3 Mt 24, 37–44

2nd Sunday of Advent
1 Is 11, 1–10
2 Rom 15, 4–9
3 Mt 3, 1–12

3rd Sunday of Advent
1 Is 35, 1–6a. 10
2 Jas 5, 7–10
3 Mt 11, 2–11

4th Sunday of Advent
1 Is 7, 10–14
2 Rom 1, 1–7
3 Mt 1, 18–24

Christmas Season

Christmas Vigil
1 Is 62, 1–5
2 Acts 13, 16–17.
   22–25
3 Mt 1, 1–25

Christmas
(At Midnight)
1 Is 9, 1–6

2 Ti 2, 11–14
3 Lk 2, 1–14

Christmas (At Dawn)
1 Is 62, 11–12
2 Ti 3, 4–7
3 Lk 2, 15–20

Christmas
(During the Day)
1 Is 52, 7–10
2 Heb 1, 1–6
3 Jn 1, 1–18

Sunday After
Christmas
(Holy Family)
1 Sir 3, 3–7. 14–
   17a
2 Col 3, 12–21
3 Mt 2, 13–15. 19–
   23

January 1
(Solemnity of Mary,
Mother of God)
1 Nm 6, 22–27
2 Gal 4, 4–7
3 Lk 2, 16–21

2nd Sunday After
Christmas
1 Sir 24, 1–4. 12–16
2 Eph 1, 3–6. 15–18
3 Jn 1, 1–18

Epiphany
1 Is 60, 1–6
2 Eph 3, 2–3a. 5–6
3 Mt 2, 1–12

Sunday After Epiphany
(Baptism of the Lord)
1 Is 42, 1–4. 6–7
2 Acts 10, 34–38
3 Mt 3, 13–17

Lenten Season

Ash Wednesday
1 Jl 2, 12–18
2 2 Cor 5, 20—6, 2
3 Mt 6, 1–6. 16–18

1st Sunday of Lent
1 Gn 2, 7–9; 3, 1–7
2 Rom 5, 12–19
3 Mt 4, 1–11

2nd Sunday of Lent
1 Gn 12, 1–4a
2 2 Tm 1, 8b–10
3 Mt 17, 1–9

3rd Sunday of Lent
1 Ex 17, 3–7
2 Rom 5, 1–2. 5–8
3 Jn 4, 5–42

4th Sunday of Lent
1 1 Sm 16, 1b. 6–7.
   10–13a
2 Eph 5, 8–14
3 Jn 9, 1–41

5th Sunday of Lent
1 Ez 37, 12–14
2 Rom 8, 8–11
3 Jn 11, 1–45

Passion Sunday
(Palm Sunday)
Procession: Mt 21, 1–11
1 Is 50, 4–7
2 Phil 2, 6–11
3 Mt 26, 14—27, 66

Easter Triduum and
Easter Season

Mass of Lord's Supper
1 Ex 12, 1–8. 11–14
2 1 Cor 11, 23–26
3 Jn 13, 1–15

Good Friday
1 Is 52, 13—53, 12
2 Heb 4, 14–16; 5,
   7–9
3 Jn 18, 1—19, 42

Easter Vigil
1 Gn 1, 1—2, 2
   Gn 22, 1–18
   Ex 14, 15—15, 1

Is 54, 5–14
Is 55, 1–11
Bar 3, 9–15. 32—
4, 4
Ez 36, 16–17a.
18–28
2 Rom 6, 3–11
3 Mt 28, 1–10

Easter Sunday
1 Acts 10, 34a. 37–
43
2 Col 3, 1–4
or 1 Cor 5, 6b–8
3 Jn 20, 1–9
or Mt 28, 1–10
Evening: 3 Lk 24,
13–35

2nd Sunday of Easter
1 Acts 2, 42–47
2 1 Pt 1, 3–9
3 Jn 20, 19–31

3rd Sunday of Easter
1 Acts 2, 14. 22–33
2 1 Pt 1, 17–21
3 Lk 24, 13–35

4th Sunday of Easter
1 Acts 2, 14a. 36–41
2 1 Pt 2, 20b–25
3 Jn 10, 1–10

5th Sunday of Easter
1 Acts 6, 1–7
2 1 Pt 2, 4–9
3 Jn 14, 1–12

6th Sunday of Easter
1 Acts 8, 5–8. 14–17
2 1 Pt 3, 15–18
3 Jn 14, 15–21

Ascension of Our Lord
1 Acts 1, 1–11
2 Eph 1, 17–23
3 Mt 28, 16–20

7th Sunday of Easter
1 Acts 1, 12–14
2 1 Pt 4, 13–16
3 Jn 17, 1–11a

Pentecost Vigil
1 Gn 11, 1–9
or Ex 19, 3–8a.
16–20b
or Ez 37, 1–14
or Jl 3, 1–5

2 Rom 8, 22–27
3 Jn 7, 37–39

Mass of the Day
1 Acts 2, 1–11
2 1 Cor 12, 3b–7.
12–13
3 Jn 20, 19–23

**Solemnities of the Lord
During Ordinary Time**

**Trinity Sunday
(Sunday after
Pentecost)**
1 Ex 34, 4b–6. 8–9
2 2 Cor 13, 11–13
3 Jn 3, 16–18

Corpus Christi
1 Dt 8, 2–3. 14b–16a
2 1 Cor 10, 16–17
3 Jn 6, 51–58

Sacred Heart of Jesus
1 Dt 7, 6–11
2 1 Jn 4, 7–16
3 Mt 11, 25–30

Ordinary Time

1st Sunday
*(See Baptism of the Lord,
above)*

2nd Sunday
1 Is 49, 3. 5–6
2 1 Cor 1, 1–3
3 Jn 1, 29–34

3rd Sunday
1 Is 8, 23b—9, 3
2 1 Cor 1, 10–13. 17
3 Mt 4, 12–23

4th Sunday
1 Zep 2, 3; 3, 12–13
2 1 Cor 1, 26–31
3 Mt 5, 1–12a

5th Sunday
1 Is 58, 7–10
2 1 Cor 2, 1–5
3 Mt 5, 13–16

6th Sunday
1 Sir 15, 16–21
2 1 Cor 2, 6–10
3 Mt 5, 17–37

7th Sunday
1 Lv 19, 1–2. 17–18

2 1 Cor 3, 16–23
3 Mt 5, 38–48

8th Sunday
1 Is 49, 14–15
2 1 Cor 4, 1–5
3 Mt 6, 24–34

9th Sunday
1 Dt 11, 18. 26–28.
32
2 Rom 3, 21–25a.
28
3 Mt 7, 21–27

10th Sunday
1 Hos 6, 3–6
2 Rom 4, 18–25
3 Mt 9, 9–13

11th Sunday
1 Ex 19, 2–6a
2 Rom 5, 6–11
3 Mt 9, 36—10, 8

12th Sunday
1 Jer 20, 10–13
2 Rom 5, 12–15
3 Mt 10, 26–33

13th Sunday
1 2 Kgs 4, 8–11.
14–16a
2 Rom 6, 3–4. 8–11
3 Mt 10, 37–42

14th Sunday
1 Zec 9, 9–10
2 Rom 8, 9. 11–13
3 Mt 11, 25–30

15th Sunday
1 Is 55, 10–11
2 Rom 8, 18–23
3 Mt 13, 1–23

16th Sunday
1 Wis 12, 13. 16–
19
2 Rom 8, 26–27
3 Mt 13, 24–43

17th Sunday
1 1 Kgs 3, 5. 7–12
2 Rom 8, 28–30
3 Mt 13, 44–52

18th Sunday
1 Is 55, 1–3
2 Rom 8, 35. 37–39
3 Mt 14, 13–21

19th Sunday
1 1 Kgs 19, 9a.
11–13a
2 Rom 9, 1–5
3 Mt 14, 22–33

20th Sunday
1 Is 56, 1. 6–7
2 Rom 11, 13–15.
29–32
3 Mt 15, 21–28

21st Sunday
1 Is 22, 19–23
2 Rom 11, 33–36
3 Mt 16, 13–20

22nd Sunday
1 Jer 20, 7–9
2 Rom 12, 1–2
3 Mt 16, 21–27

23rd Sunday
1 Ez 33, 7–9
2 Rom 13, 8–10
3 Mt 18, 15–20

24th Sunday
1 Sir 27, 30—28, 7
2 Rom 14, 7–9
3 Mt 18, 21–35

25th Sunday
1 Is 55, 6–9
2 Phil 1, 20c–24. 27a
3 Mt 20, 1–16a

26th Sunday
1 Ez 18, 25–28
2 Phil 2, 1–11
3 Mt 21, 28–32

27th Sunday
1 Is 5, 1–7
2 Phil 4, 6–9
3 Mt 21, 33–43

28th Sunday
1 Is 25, 6–10a
2 Phil 4, 12–14,
19–20
3 Mt 22, 1–14

29th Sunday
1 Is 45, 1. 4–6
2 1 Thes 1, 1–5b
3 Mt 22, 15–21

30th Sunday
1 Ex 22, 20–26
2 1 Thes 1, 5c–10
3 Mt 22, 34–40

31st Sunday
1   Mal 1, 14b—2, 2b.
     8–10
2   1 Thes 2, 7b–9,
     13
3   Mt 23, 1–12

32nd Sunday
1   Wis 6, 12–16
2   1 Thes 4, 13–18
3   Mt 25, 1–13

33rd Sunday
1   Prv 31, 10–13.
     19–20. 30–31
2   1 Thes 5, 1–6
3   Mt 25, 14–30

**34th Sunday
(Christ the King)**
1   Ez 34, 11–12.
     15–17
2   1 Cor 15, 20–26.
     28
3   Mt 25, 31–46

**YEAR B
2006 2009 2012 2015
2018 2021 2024**

Advent Season

1st Sunday of Advent
1   Is 63, 16b–17. 19b;
     64, 2b–7
2   1 Cor 1, 3–9
3   Mk 13, 33–37

2nd Sunday of Advent
1   Is 40, 1–5. 9–11
2   2 Pt 3, 8–14
3   Mk 1, 1–8

3rd Sunday of Advent
1   Is 61, 1–2a. 10–11
2   1 Thes 5, 16–24
3   Jn 1, 6–8. 19–28

4th Sunday of Advent
1   2 Sm 7, 1–5. 8b–12.
     14a. 16
2   Rom 16, 25–27
3   Lk 1, 26–38

Christmas Season

Christmas Vigil
1   Is 62, 1–5
2   Acts 13, 16–17.
     22–25
3   Mt 1, 1–25

Christmas (At Midnight)
1   Is 9, 1–6
2   Ti 2, 11–14
3   Lk 2, 1–14

Christmas (At Dawn)
1   Is 62, 11–12
2   Ti 3, 4–7
3   Lk 2, 15–20

Christmas (During the Day)
1   Is 52, 7–10
2   Heb 1, 1–6
3   Jn 1, 1–18

Sunday After Christmas (Holy Family)
1   Gn 15, 1–6; 21, 1–3
2   Heb 11, 8. 11–12.
     17–19
3   Lk 2, 22–40 or 22.
     39–40

January 1 (Solemnity of Mary, Mother of God)
1   Nm 6, 22–27
2   Gal 4, 4–7
3   Lk 2, 16–21

2nd Sunday After Christmas
1   Sir 24, 1–2. 8–12
2   Eph 1, 3–6. 15–18
3   Jn 1, 1–18

Epiphany
1   Is 60, 1–6
2   Eph 3, 2–3a. 5–6
3   Mt 2, 1–12

Sunday After Epiphany (Baptism of the Lord)
1   Is 55, 1–11
2   1 Jn 5, 1–9
3   Mk 1, 7–11

Lenten Season

Ash Wednesday
1   Jl 2, 12–18
2   2 Cor 5, 20—6, 2
3   Mt 6, 1–6. 16–18

1st Sunday of Lent
1   Gn 9, 8–15
2   1 Pt 3, 18–22
3   Mk 1, 12–15

2nd Sunday of Lent
1   Gn 22, 1–2. 9a.
     10–13. 15–18
2   Rom 8, 31b–34
3   Mk 9, 2–10

3rd Sunday of Lent
1   Ex 20, 1–17
2   1 Cor 1, 22–25
3   Jn 2, 13–25

4th Sunday of Lent
1   2 Chr 36, 14–16.
     19–23
2   Eph 2, 4–10
3   Jn 3, 14–21

5th Sunday of Lent
1   Jer 31, 31–34
2   Heb 5, 7–9
3   Jn 12, 20–33

Passion Sunday (Palm Sunday)
Procession: Mk 11,
     1–10 or Jn 12,
     12–16
1   Is 50, 4–7
2   Phil 2, 6–11
3   Mk 14, 1—15,47

Easter Triduum and Easter Season

Mass of Lord's Supper
1   Ex 12, 1–8. 11–14
2   1 Cor 11, 23–26
3   Jn 13, 1–15

Good Friday
1   Is 52, 13–53, 12
2   Heb 4, 14—16. 5,
     7–9
3   Jn 18, 1—19, 42

Easter Vigil
1   Gn 1, 1—2, 2
     Gn 22, 1–18
     Ex 14, 15—15, 1
     Is 54, 5–14
     Is 55, 1–11
     Bar 3, 9–15. 32—
     4, 4
     Ez 36, 16–28
2   Rom 6, 3–11
3   Mk 16, 1–7

Easter Sunday
1   Acts 10, 34a. 37–43
2   Col 3, 1–4
     or 1 Cor 5, 6b–8

3   Jn 20, 1–9
     or Mk 16, 1–8
Evening: 3 Lk 24,
     13–35

2nd Sunday of Easter
1   Acts 4, 32–35
2   1 Jn 5, 1–6
3   Jn 20, 19–31

3rd Sunday of Easter
1   Acts 3, 13–15.
     17–19
2   1 Jn 2, 1–5a
3   Lk 24, 35–48

4th Sunday of Easter
1   Acts 4, 8–12
2   1 Jn 3, 1–2
3   Jn 10, 11–18

5th Sunday of Easter
1   Acts 9, 26–31
2   1 Jn 3, 18–24
3   Jn 15, 1–8

6th Sunday of Easter
1   Acts 10, 25–26.
     34–35. 44–48
2   1 Jn 4, 7–10
3   Jn 15, 9–17

Ascension of Our Lord
1   Acts 1, 1–11
2   Eph 1, 17–23 or 4,
     1–13
3   Mk 16, 15–20

7th Sunday of Easter
1   Acts 1, 15–17. 20a.
     20c–26
2   1 Jn 4, 11–16
3   Jn 17, 11b–19

Pentecost Vigil
1   Gn 11, 1–9
     or Ex 19, 3–8a.
     16–20b
     or Ez 37, 1–14
     or Jl 3, 1–5
2   Rom 8, 22–27
3   Jn 7, 37–39

Mass of the Day
1   Acts 2, 1–11
2   1 Cor 12, 3b–7.
     12–13
3   Jn 20, 19–23
Pentecost-Optional
2   Gal 5, 16–25

3   Jn 15, 26–27; 16, 12–15

Solemnities of the Lord During Ordinary Time

Trinity Sunday (Sunday after Pentecost)
1   Dt 4, 32–34. 39–40
2   Rom 8, 14–17
3   Mt 28, 16–20

Corpus Christi
1   Ex 24, 3–8
2   Heb 9, 11–15
3   Mk 14, 12–16. 22–26

Sacred Heart of Jesus
1   Hos 11, 1. 3–4. 8c–9
2   Eph 3, 8–12. 14–19
3   Jn 19, 31–37

Ordinary Time

1st Sunday
(See Baptism of the Lord, above)

2nd Sunday
1   1 Sm 3, 3b–10. 19
2   1 Cor 6, 13c–15a. 17–20
3   Jn 1, 35–42

3rd Sunday
1   Jon 3, 1–5. 10
2   1 Cor 7, 29–31
3   Mk 1, 14–20

4th Sunday
1   Dt 18, 15–20
2   1 Cor 7, 32–35
3   Mk 1, 21–28

5th Sunday
1   Jb 7, 1–4. 6–7
2   1 Cor 9, 16–19. 22–23
3   Mk 1, 29–39

6th Sunday
1   Lv 13, 1–2. 45–46
2   1 Cor 10, 31—11, 1
3   Mk 1, 40–45

7th Sunday
1   Is 43, 18–19. 21–22. 24b–25
2   2 Cor 1, 18–22
3   Mk 2, 1–12

8th Sunday
1   Hos 2, 16b. 17b. 21–22
2   2 Cor 3, 1b–6
3   Mk 2, 18–22

9th Sunday
1   Dt 5, 12–15
2   2 Cor 4, 6–11
3   Mk 2, 23—3, 6

10th Sunday
1   Gn 3, 9–15
2   2 Cor 4, 13—5, 1
3   Mk 3, 20–35

11th Sunday
1   Ez 17, 22–24
2   2 Cor 5, 6–10
3   Mk 4, 26–34

12th Sunday
1   Jb 38, 1. 8–11
2   2 Cor 5, 14–17
3   Mk 4, 35–41

13th Sunday
1   Wis 1, 13–15; 2, 23–24
2   2 Cor 8, 7. 9. 13–15
3   Mk 5, 21–43

14th Sunday
1   Ez 2, 2–5
2   2 Cor 12, 7–10
3   Mk 6, 1–6

15th Sunday
1   Am 7, 12–15
2   Eph 1, 3–14
3   Mk 6, 7–13

16th Sunday
1   Jer 23, 1–6
2   Eph 2, 13–18
3   Mk 6, 30–34

17th Sunday
1   2 Kgs 4, 42–44
2   Eph 4, 1–6
3   Jn 6, 1–15

18th Sunday
1   Ex 16, 2–4. 12–15
2   Eph 4, 17. 20–24
3   Jn 6, 24–35

19th Sunday
1   1 Kgs 19, 4–8
2   Eph 4, 30—5, 2
3   Jn 6, 41–51

20th Sunday
1   Prv 9, 1–6
2   Eph 5, 15–20
3   Jn 6, 51–58

21st Sunday
1   Jos 24, 1–2a. 15–17. 18b
2   Eph 5, 21–32
3   Jn 6, 60–69

22nd Sunday
1   Dt 4, 1–2. 6–8
2   Jas 1, 17–18. 21b–22. 27
3   Mk 7, 1–8. 14–15. 21–23

23rd Sunday
1   Is 35, 4–7a
2   Jas 2, 1–5
3   Mk 7, 31–37

24th Sunday
1   Is 50, 5–9a
2   Jas 2, 14–18
3   Mk 8, 27–35

25th Sunday
1   Wis 2, 12. 17–20
2   Jas 3, 16—4, 3
3   Mk 9, 30–37

26th Sunday
1   Nm 11, 25–29
2   Jas 5, 1–6
3   Mk 9, 38–43. 45. 47–48

27th Sunday
1   Gn 2, 18–24
2   Heb 2, 9–11
3   Mk 10, 2–16

28th Sunday
1   Wis 7, 7–11
2   Heb 4, 12–13
3   Mk 10, 17–30

29th Sunday
1   Is 53, 10–11
2   Heb 4, 14–16
3   Mk 10, 35–45

30th Sunday
1   Jer 31, 7–9
2   Heb 5, 1–6
3   Mk 10, 46–52

31st Sunday
1   Dt 6, 2–6

2   Heb 7, 23–28
3   Mk 12, 28b–34

32nd Sunday
1   1 Kgs 17, 10–16
2   Heb 9, 24–28
3   Mk 12, 38–44

33rd Sunday
1   Dn 12, 1–3
2   Heb 10, 11–14. 18
3   Mk 13, 24–32

34th Sunday (Christ the King)
1   Dn 7, 13–14
2   Rv 1, 5–8
3   Jn 18, 33b–37

YEAR C
**2007 2010 2013 2016
2019 2022 2025**

Advent Season

1st Sunday of Advent
1   Jer 33, 14–16
2   1 Thes 3, 12—4, 2
3   Lk 21, 25–28. 34–36

2nd Sunday of Advent
1   Bar 5, 1–9
2   Phil 1, 4–6. 8–11
3   Lk 3, 1–6

3rd Sunday of Advent
1   Zep 3, 14–18a
2   Phil 4, 4–7
3   Lk 3, 10–18

4th Sunday of Advent
1   Mi 5, 1–4a
2   Heb 10, 5–10
3   Lk 1, 39–45

Christmas Season

Christmas Vigil
1   Is 62, 1–6
2   Acts 13, 16–17. 22–25
3   Mt 1, 1–25

Christmas (At Midnight)
1   Is 9, 1–6
2   Ti 2, 11–14
3   Lk 2, 1–14

Christmas (At Dawn)
1   Is 62, 11–12

2   Ti 3, 4–7
3   Lk 2, 15–20

**Christmas
(During the Day)**
1   Is 57, 7–10
2   Heb 1, 1–6
3   Jn 1, 1–18

**Sunday After
Christmas
(Holy Family)**
1   1 Sm 1, 20–22.
     24–28
2   1 Jn 3, 1–2. 21–24
3   Lk 2, 41–52

**January 1
(Solemnity of Mary,
Mother of God)**
1   Nm 6, 22–27
2   Gal 4, 4–7
3   Lk 2, 16–21

**2nd Sunday After
Christmas**
1   Sir 24, 1–2. 8–12
2   Eph 1, 3–6. 15–18
3   Jn 1, 1–18

Epiphany
1   Is 60, 1–6
2   Eph 3, 2–3a. 5–6
3   Mt 2, 1–12

**Sunday After Epiphany
(Baptism of the Lord)**
1   Is 40, 1–5. 9–11
2   Ti 2, 11–14; 3, 4–7
3   Lk 3, 15–16. 21–
     22

Lenten Season

Ash Wednesday
1   Jl 2, 12–18
2   2 Cor 5, 20—6, 2
3   Mt 6, 1–6. 16–18

1st Sunday of Lent
1   Dt 26, 4–10
2   Rom 10, 8–13
3   Lk 4, 1–13

2nd Sunday of Lent
1   Gn 15, 5–12. 17–18
2   Phil 3, 17–4, 1
3   Lk 9, 28b–36

3rd Sunday of Lent
1   Ex 3, 1–8a. 13–15

2   1 Cor 10, 1–6.
     10–12
3   Lk 13, 1–9

4th Sunday of Lent
1   Jos 5, 9a. 10–12
2   2 Cor 5, 17–21
3   Lk 15, 1–3. 11–32

5th Sunday of Lent
1   Is 43, 16–21
2   Phil 3, 8–14
3   Jn 8, 1–11

**Passion Sunday
(Palm Sunday)**
Procession: Lk 19,
     28–40
1   Is 50, 4–7
2   Phil 2, 6–11
3   Lk 22, 14—23, 56

**Easter Triduum and
Easter Season**

Mass of Lord's Supper
1   Ex 12, 1–8. 11–14
2   1 Cor 11, 23–26
3   Jn 13, 1–15

Good Friday
1   Is 52, 13–53, 12
2   Heb 4, 14–16; 5,
     7–9
3   Jn 18, 1—19, 42

Easter Vigil
1   Gn 1, 1–2, 2
     Gn 22, 1–18
     Ex 14, 15—15, 1
     Is 54, 5–14
     Is 55, 1–11
     Bar 3, 9–15. 32—
     4, 4
     Ez 36, 16–28
2   Rom 6, 3–11
3   Lk 24, 1–12

Easter Sunday
1   Acts 10, 34a. 37–
     43
2   Col 3, 1–4
     or 1 Cor 5, 6b–8
3   Jn 20, 1–9
     or Lk 24, 1–12
Evening: 3 Lk 24,
     13–35

2nd Sunday of Easter
1   Acts 5, 12–16

2   Rv 1, 9–11a. 12–13.
     17–19
3   Jn 20, 19–31

3rd Sunday of Easter
1   Acts 5, 27b–32.
     40b–41
2   Rv 5, 11–14
3   Jn 21, 1–19 or
     1–14

4th Sunday of Easter
1   Acts 13, 14.
     43–52
2   Rv 7, 9. 14b–17
3   Jn 10, 27–30

5th Sunday of Easter
1   Acts 14, 21b–27
2   Rv 21, 1–5a
3   Jn 13, 31–33a.
     34–35

6th Sunday of Easter
1   Acts 15, 1–2.
     22–29
2   Rv 21, 10–14.
     22–23
3   Jn 14, 23–29

Ascension of the Lord
1   Acts 1, 1–11
2   Eph 1, 17–23 or
     Heb 9, 24–28;
     10, 19–23
3   Lk 24, 46–53

7th Sunday of Easter
1   Acts 7, 55–60
2   Rv 22, 12–14.
     16–17. 20
3   Jn 17, 20–26

Pentecost Vigil
1   Gn 11, 1–9
     or Ex 19, 3–8a.
     16–20b
     or Ez 37, 1–14
     or Jl 3, 1–5
2   Rom 8, 22–27
3   Jn 7, 37–39

Mass of the Day
1   Acts 2, 1–11
2   1 Cor 12, 3b–7.
     12–13
     or Rom 8, 8–27
3   Jn 20, 19–23
     or Jn 14, 15–16.
     23b–26

**Solemnities of the Lord
During Ordinary Time**

**Trinity Sunday
(Sunday After
Pentecost)**
1   Prv 8, 22–31
2   Rom 5, 1–5
3   Jn 16, 12–15

Corpus Christi
1   Gn 14, 18–20
2   1 Cor 11, 23–26
3   Lk 9, 11b–17

Sacred Heart of Jesus
1   Ez 34, 11–16
2   Rom 5, 5b–11
3   Lk 15, 3–7

Ordinary Time

1st Sunday
*(See Baptism of the Lord,
above)*

2nd Sunday
1   Is 62, 1–5
2   1 Cor 12, 4–11
3   Jn 2, 1–12

3rd Sunday
1   Neh 8, 2–4a. 5–6.
     8–10
2   1 Cor 12, 12–30
3   Lk 1, 1–4; 4, 14–21

4th Sunday
1   Jer 1, 4–5. 17–19
2   1 Cor 12. 31—13,
     13
3   Lk 4, 21–30

5th Sunday
1   Is 6, 1–2a. 3–8
2   1 Cor 15, 1–11
3   Lk 5, 1–11

6th Sunday
1   Jer 17, 5–8
2   1 Cor 15, 12. 16–20
3   Lk 6, 17. 20–26

7th Sunday
1   1 Sm 26, 2. 7–9.
     12–13. 22–23
2   1 Cor 15, 45–49
3   Lk 6, 27–38

8th Sunday
1   Sir 27, 5–8
2   1 Cor 15, 54–58
3   Lk 6, 39–45

9th Sunday
1   1 Kgs 8, 41–43
2   Gal 1, 1–2. 6–10
3   Lk 7, 1–10

10th Sunday
1   1 Kgs 17, 17–24
2   Gal 1, 11–19
3   Lk 7, 11–17

11th Sunday
1   2 Sm 12, 7–10. 13
2   Gal 2, 16. 19–21
3   Lk 7, 36—8, 3

12th Sunday
1   Zec 12, 10–11
2   Gal 3, 26–29
3   Lk 9, 18–24

13th Sunday
1   1 Kgs 19, 16b. 19–21
2   Gal 5, 1. 13–18
3   Lk 9, 51–62

14th Sunday
1   Is 66, 10–14c
2   Gal 6, 14–18
3   Lk 10, 1–12. 17–20

15th Sunday
1   Dt 30, 10–14

2   Col 1, 15–20
3   Lk 10, 25–37

16th Sunday
1   Gn 18, 1–10a
2   Col 1, 24–28
3   Lk 10, 38–42

17th Sunday
1   Gn 18, 20–32
2   Col 2, 12–14
3   Lk 11, 1–13

18th Sunday
1   Eccl 1, 2; 2, 21–23
2   Col 3, 1–5. 9–11
3   Lk 12, 13–31

19th Sunday
1   Wis 18, 6–9
2   Heb 11, 1–2. 8–19
3   Lk 12, 32–48

20th Sunday
1   Jer 38, 4–6. 8–10
2   Heb 12, 1–4
3   Lk 12, 49–53

21st Sunday
1   Is 66, 18–21
2   Heb 12, 5–7. 11–13
3   Lk 13, 22–30

22nd Sunday
1   Sir 3, 19–21. 30–31

2   Heb 12, 18–19. 22–24a
3   Lk 14, 1. 7–14

23rd Sunday
1   Wis 9, 13–19
2   Phlm 9b–10. 12–17
3   Lk 14, 25–33

24th Sunday
1   Ex 32, 7–11. 13–14
2   1 Tm 1, 12–17
3   Lk 15, 1–32

25th Sunday
1   Am 8, 4–7
2   1 Tm 2, 1–8
3   Lk 16, 1–13

26th Sunday
1   Am 6, 1a. 4–7
2   1 Tm 6, 11–16
3   Lk 16, 19–31

27th Sunday
1   Hb 1, 2–3; 2, 2–4
2   2 Tm 1, 6–8. 13–14
3   Lk 17, 5–10

28th Sunday
1   2 Kgs 5, 14–17

2   2 Tm 2, 8–13
3   Lk 17, 11–19

29th Sunday
1   Ex 17, 8–13
2   2 Tm 3, 14—4, 2
3   Lk 18, 1–8

30th Sunday
1   Sir 35, 15b–17. 20–22a
2   2 Tm 4, 6–8. 16–18
3   Lk 18, 9–14

31st Sunday
1   Wis 11, 23—12, 2
2   2 Thes 1, 11—2, 2
3   Lk 19, 1–10

32nd Sunday
1   2 Mc 7, 1–2. 9–14
2   2 Thes 2, 16—3, 5
3   Lk 20, 27–38

33rd Sunday
1   Mal 3, 19–20a
2   2 Thes 3, 7–12
3   Lk 21, 5–19

34th Sunday
(Christ the King)
1   2 Sm 5, 1–3
2   Col 1, 12–20
3   Lk 23, 35–43

READINGS FOR THE MAJOR FEASTS OF THE YEAR

Feb. 2: Presentation of the Lord
1   Mal 3, 1–4
2   Heb 2, 14–18
3   Lk 2, 22–40

Mar. 19: Joseph, Husband of Mary
1   2 Sm 7, 4–5a. 12–14a. 16
2   Rom 4, 13. 16–18. 22
3   Mt 1, 16. 18–21. 24a
    or Lk 2, 41–51a

Mar. 25: Annunciation
1   Is 7, 10–14
2   Heb 10, 4–10
3   Lk 1, 26–28

June 24: John the Baptist Vigil
1   Jer 1, 4–10
2   1 Pt 1, 8–12
3   Lk 1, 5–17

Mass of the Day
1   Is 49, 1–6
2   Acts 13, 22–26
3   Lk 1, 57–66. 80

June 29: Peter and Paul Vigil
1   Acts 3, 1–10
2   Gal 1, 11–20
3   Jn 21, 15–19

Mass of the Day
1   Acts 12, 1–11
2   2 Tm 4, 6–8. 17–18
3   Mt 16, 13–19

Aug. 6: Transfiguration
1   Dn 7, 9–10. 13–14
2   2 Pt 1, 16–19
3   (A) Mt 7, 1–9
    (B) Mk 9, 2–10
    (C) Lk 9, 28b–36

Aug. 15: Assumption Vigil
1   1 Chr 15, 3–4. 15; 16, 1–2
2   1 Cor 15, 54–57
3   Lk 11, 27–28

Mass of the Day
1   Rv 11, 19a; 12, 1–6a. 10ab
2   1 Cor 15, 20–26
3   Lk 1, 39–56

Sept. 14: Triumph of the Cross
1   Nm 21, 4–9
2   Phil 2, 6–11
3   Jn 3, 13–17

Nov. 1: All Saints
1   Rv 7, 2–4. 9–14
2   1 Jn 3, 1–3
3   Mt 5, 1–12a

Nov. 2: All Souls
First Mass
1   Jb 19, 1. 23–27
2   1 Cor 15, 51–57
3   Jn 6, 37–40

Second Mass
1   Wis 3, 1–9
2   Phil 3, 20–21
3   Jn 11, 17–27

Third Mass
1   2 Mc 12, 43–46
2   Rv 14, 13
3   Jn 14, 1–6
(Other Readings may be chosen)

Nov. 9: Dedication of St. John Lateran
1   2 Chr 5, 6–10.
    13—6, 2

2   1 Cor 3, 9–13.
    16–17
3   Lk 19, 1–10
(Other Readings may be chosen)

Dec. 8: Immaculate Conception
1   Gn 3, 9–15. 20
2   Eph 1, 3–6. 11–12
3   Lk 1, 26–38

WEEKDAY READINGS

Advent Season

First Week of Advent

Monday: Is 2, 1–5 (Year A Is 4, 2–6); Mt 8, 5–11

Tuesday: Is 11, 1–10; Lk 10, 21–24

Wednesday: Is 25, 6–10a; Mt 15, 29–37

Thursday: Is 26, 1–6; Mt 7, 21. 24–27

Friday: Is 29, 17–24; Mt 9, 27–31

Saturday: Is 30, 19–21. 23–26; Mt 9, 35—10, 1. 6–8

Second Week of Advent

Monday: Is 35, 1–10; Lk 5, 17–26

Tuesday: Is 40, 1–11; Mt 18, 12–14

Wednesday: Is 40, 25–31; Mt 11, 28–30

Thursday: Is 41, 13–20; Mt 11, 11–15

Friday: Is 48, 17–19; Mt 11, 16–19

Saturday: Sir 48, 1–4. 9–11; Mt 17, 10–13

Third Week of Advent

Monday: Num 24, 2–7. 15–17a; Mt 21, 23–27

Tuesday: Zep 3, 1–2. 9–13; Mt 21, 28–32

Wednesday: Is 45, 6b–8. 18. 21b–25; Lk 7, 18b–23

Thursday: Is 54, 1–10; Lk 7, 24–30

Friday: Is 56, 1–3a. 6–8; Jn 5, 33–36

Dec. 17: Gn 49, 2. 8–10; Mt 1, 1–17

Dec. 18: Jer 23, 5–8; Mt 1, 18–24

Dec. 19: Jgs 13, 2–7. 24–25a; Lk 1, 5–25

Dec. 20: Is 7, 10–14; Lk 1, 26–38

Dec. 21: Sg 2, 8–14 or Zep 3, 14–18a; Lk 1, 39–45

Dec. 22: 1 Sm 1, 24–28; Lk 1, 46–56

Dec. 23: Mal 3, 1–4. 23–24; Lk 1, 57–66

Dec. 24: 2 Sm 7, 1–5. 8b–11. 16; Lk 1, 67–79

Christmas Season

Octave of Christmas

Second day (St. Stephen): Acts 6, 8–10; 7, 54–59; Mt 10, 17–22

Third day (St. John): 1 Jn 1, 1–4; Jn 20, 2–8

Fourth day (Holy Innocents): 1 Jn 1, 5—2, 2; Mt 2, 13–18

Fifth day: 1 Jn 2, 3–11; Lk 2:22–35

Sixth day: 1 Jn 2, 12–17; Lk 2, 36–40

Seventh day: 1 Jn 2, 18–21; Jn 1, 1–18

January 2: 1 Jn 2, 22–28; Jn 1, 19–28

January 3: 1 Jn 2, 29–3, 6; Jn 1, 29–34

January 4: 1 Jn 3, 7–10; Jn 1, 35–42

January 5: 1 Jn 3, 11–21; Jn 1, 43–51

January 6 (if Epiphany not celebrated): 1 Jn 5, 5–13; Mk 1, 6b–11

Readings may vary slightly depending on when Epiphany is celebrated

Week After Epiphany

Monday after Epiphany: 1 Jn 3, 22—4, 6; Mt 4, 12–17. 23–25

Tuesday after Epiphany: 1 Jn 4, 7–10; Mk 6, 34–44

Wednesday after Epiphany: 1 Jn 4, 11–18; Mk 6, 45–52

Thursday after Epiphany: 1 Jn 4, 19—5, 4; Lk 4, 14–22a

Friday after Epiphany: 1 Jn 5, 5–13; Lk 5, 12–16

Saturday after Epiphany: 1 Jn 5, 14–21; Jn 3, 22–30

Lenten Season

Ash Wednesday: Jl 2, 12–18; 2 Cor 5, 20—6, 2; Mt 6, 1–6. 16–18

Thursday after Ash Wednesday: Dt 30, 15–20; Lk 9, 22–25

Friday after Ash Wednesday: Is 58, 1–9a; Mt 9, 14–15

Saturday after Ash Wednesday: Is 58, 9b–14; Lk 5, 27–32

First Week of Lent

Monday: Lv 19, 1–2. 11–18; Mt 25, 31–46

Tuesday: Is 55. 10–11; Mt 6, 7–15

Wednesday: Jon 3, 1–10; Lk 11, 29–32

Thursday: Est C, 12. 14–16. 23–25; Mt 7, 7–12

Friday: Ez 18, 21–28; Mt 5, 20–26

Saturday: Dt 26, 16–19; Mt 5, 43–48

Second Week of Lent

Monday: Dn 9, 4b–10; Lk 6, 36–38

Tuesday: Is 1, 10. 16–20; Mt 23, 1–12

Wednesday: Jer 18, 18–20; Mt 20, 17–28

Thursday: Jer 17, 5–10; Lk 16, 19–31

Friday: Gn 37, 3–4. 12–13a. 17b–28; Mt 21, 33–43. 45–46

Saturday: Mi 7, 14–15. 18–20; Lk 15, 1–3. 11–32

Third Week of Lent

Monday: 2 Kgs 5, 1–15a; Lk 4, 24–30

Tuesday: Dn 3, 25. 34–43; Mt 18, 21–35

Wednesday: Dt 4, 1. 5–9; Mt 5, 17–19

Thursday: Jer 7, 23–28; Lk 11, 14–23

Friday: Hos 14, 2–10; Mk 12, 28b–34

Saturday: Hos 6, 1–6; Lk 18, 19–24

Fourth Week of Lent

Monday: Is 65, 17–21; Jn 4, 43–54

Tuesday: Ez 47, 1–9. 12; Jn 5, 1–3a. 5–16

Wednesday: Is 49, 8–15; Jn 5, 17–30

Thursday: Ex 32, 7–14; Jn 5, 31–47

Friday: Wis 2, 1a. 12–22; Jn 7, 1–2. 10. 25–30

Saturday: Jer 11, 18–20; Jn 7, 40–53

Fifth Week of Lent

Monday: Dn 13, 1–9. 15–17. 19–30. 33–62; Jn 8, 1–11 (Year C: Jn 8, 12–20)

Tuesday: Nm 21, 4–9; Jn 8, 21–30

Wednesday: Dn 3, 14–20. 91–92. 95; Jn 8, 31–42

Thursday: Gn 17, 3–9; Jn 8, 51–59

Friday: Jer 20, 10–13; Jn 10, 31–42

Saturday: Ez 37, 21–28; Jn 11, 45–56

Holy Week

Monday: Is 42, 1–7; Jn 12, 1–11

Tuesday: Is 49, 1–6; Jn 13, 21–33. 36–38

Wednesday: Is 50, 4–9a; Mt 26, 14–25

Thursday Chrism Mass: Is 61, 1–3a. 6a. 8b–9; Rv 1, 5–8; Lk 4, 16–21

Easter Season

Octave of Easter

Monday: Acts 2, 14. 22–32; Mt 28, 8–15

Tuesday: Acts 2, 36–41; Jn 20, 11–18

Wednesday: Acts 3, 1–10; Lk 24, 13–35

Thursday: Acts 3, 11–26; Lk 24, 35–48

Friday: Acts 4, 1–12; Jn 21, 1–14

Saturday: Acts 4, 13–21; Mk 16, 9–15

Second Week of Easter

Monday: Acts 4, 23–31; Jn 3, 1–8

Tuesday: Acts 4, 32–37; Jn 3, 7–15

Wednesday: Acts 5, 17–26; Jn 3, 16–21

Thursday: Acts 5, 27–33; Jn 3, 31–36

Friday: Acts 5, 34–42; Jn 6; 1–15

Saturday: Acts 6, 1–7; Jn 6, 16–21

Third Week of Easter

Monday: Acts 6, 8–15; Jn 6, 22–29

Tuesday: Acts 7, 51—8, 1a; Jn 6, 30–35

Wednesday: Acts 8, 1–8; Jn 6, 35–40

Thursday: Acts 8, 26–40; Jn 6, 44–51

Friday: Acts 9, 1–20; Jn 6, 52–59

Saturday: Acts 9, 31–42; Jn 6, 60–69

Fourth Week of Easter

Monday: Acts 11, 1–18; Jn 10, 1–10 (Year A: Jn 10, 11–18)

Tuesday: Acts 11, 19–26; Jn 10, 22–30

Wednesday: Acts 12, 24—13, 5a; Jn 12, 44–50

Thursday: Acts 13, 13–25; Jn 13, 16–20

Friday: Acts 13, 26–33; Jn 14, 1–6

Saturday: Acts 13, 44–52; Jn 14, 7–14

Fifth Week of Easter

Monday: Acts 14, 5–18; Jn 14, 21–26

Tuesday: Acts 14, 19–28; Jn 14, 27–31a

Wednesday: Acts 15, 1–6; Jn 15, 1–8

Thursday: Acts 15, 7–21; Jn 15, 9–11

Friday: Acts 15, 22–31; Jn 15, 12–17

Saturday: Acts 16, 1–10; Jn 15, 18–21

Sixth Week of Easter

Monday: Acts 16, 11–15; John 15, 26—16, 4a

Tuesday: Acts 16, 22–34; Jn 16, 5–11

Wednesday: Acts 17, 15. 22—18, 1; Jn 16, 12–15

Thursday: Acts 18, 1–8; Jn 16, 16–20

Friday: Acts 18, 9–18; Jn 16, 20–23a

Saturday: Acts 18, 23–28; Jn 16, 23b–28

Seventh Week of Easter

Monday: Acts 19, 1–8; Jn 16, 29–33

Tuesday: Acts 20, 17–27; Jn 17, 1–11a

Wednesday: Acts 20, 28–38; Jn 17, 11b–19

Thursday: Acts 22, 30; 23, 6–11; Jn 17, 20–26

Friday: Acts 25, 13–21; Jn 21, 15–19

Saturday: Acts 28, 16–20. 30–31; Jn 21, 20–25

SEASON OF THE YEAR

(I is the reading for Year 1; II is the reading for Year II; the Gospel is the same each year)

Week One

Monday: I – Heb 1, 1–6; II – 1 Sm 1, 1–8; Mk 1, 14–20

Tuesday: I – Heb 2, 5–12; II – 1 Sm 1, 9–20; Mk 1, 21–28

Wednesday: I – Heb 2, 14–18; II – 1 Sm 3, 1–10. 19–20; Mk 1, 29–39

Thursday: I – Heb 3, 7–14; II – 1 Sm 4, 1–11; Mk 1, 40–45

Friday: I – Heb 4, 1–5. 11; II – 1 Sm 8, 4–7. 10–22a; Mk 2, 1–12

Saturday: I – Heb 4, 12–16; II – 1 Sm 9, 1–14. 17–19; 10, 1a; Mk 2, 13–17

Week Two

Monday: I – Heb 5, 1–10; II – 1 Sm 15, 16–23; Mk 2, 18–22

Tuesday: I – Heb 6, 10–20; II – 1 Sm 16, 1–13; Mk 2, 23–28

Wednesday: I – Heb 7, 1–3. 15–17; II – 1 Sm 17, 32–33. 37. 40–51; Mk 3, 1–6

Thursday: I – Heb 7, 25—8, 6; II – 1 Sm 18, 6–9; 19, 1–7; Mk 3, 7–12

Friday: I – Heb 8, 6–13; II – 1 Sm 24, 3–21; Mk 3, 13–19

Saturday: I – Heb 9, 2–3. 11–14; II – 2 Sm 1, 1–4. 11–12. 19. 23–27; Mk 3, 20–21

Week Three

Monday: I – Heb 9, 15. 24–28; II – 2 Sm 5, 1–7. 10; Mk 3, 22–30

Tuesday: I – Heb 10, 1–10; II – 2 Sm 6, 12b–15. 17–19; Mk 3, 31–35

Wednesday: I – Heb 10, 11–18; II – 2 Sm 7, 4–17; Mk 4, 1–20

Thursday: I – Heb 10, 19–25; II – 2 Sm 7, 18–19. 24–29; Mk 4, 21–25

Friday: I – Heb 10, 32–39; II – 2 Sm 11, 1–4a. 5–10a. 13–17; Mk 4, 26–34

Saturday: I – Heb 11, 1–2. 8–9; II – 2 Sm 12, 1–7a. 10–17; Mk 4, 35–41

Week Four

Monday: I – Heb 11, 32–40; II – 2 Sm 15, 13–14. 30; 16, 5–13a; Mk 5, 1–20

Tuesday: I – Heb 12, 1–4; II – 2 Sm 18, 9–10. 14b. 24–25a. 30—19, 3; Mk 5, 21–43

Wednesday: I – Heb 12, 4–7. 11–15; II – 2 Sm 24, 2. 9–17; Mk 6, 1–6

Thursday: I – Heb 12, 18–19. 21–24; II – 1 Kgs 2, 1–4. 10–12; Mk 6, 7–13

Friday: I – Heb 13, 1–8; II – Sir 47, 2–11; Mk 6, 14–29

Saturday: 1 – Heb 13, 15–17. 20–21; II – 1 Kgs 3, 4–13; Mk 6, 30–34

Week Five

Monday: I – Gn 1, 1–19; II – 1 Kgs 8, 1–7. 9–13; Mk 6, 53–56

Tuesday: I – Gn 1, 20—2, 4a; II – 1 Kgs 8, 22–23. 27–30; Mk 7, 1–13

Wednesday: I – Gn 2, 4b–9. 15–17; II – 1 Kgs 10, 1–10; Mk 7, 14–23

Thursday: I – Gn 2, 18–25; II – 1 Kgs 11, 4–13; Mk 7, 24–30

Friday: I – Gn 3, 1–8; II – 1 Kgs 11, 29–32; 12, 19; Mk 7, 31–37

Saturday: I – Gn 3, 9–24; II – 1 Kgs 12, 26–32; 13, 33–34; Mk 8, 1–10

Week Six

Monday: I – Gn 4, 1–15. 25; II – Jas 1, 1–11; Mk 8, 11–13

Tuesday: I – Gn 6, 5–8; 7, 1–5. 10; II – Jas 1, 12–18; Mk 8, 14–21

Wednesday: I – Gn 8, 6–13. 20–22; II – Jas 1, 19–27; Mk 8, 22–26

Thursday: I – Gn 9, 1–13; II – Jas 2, 1–9; Mk 8, 27–33

Friday: I – Gn 11, 1–9; II – Jas 2, 14–24. 26; Mk 8, 34—9, 1

Saturday: I – Heb 11, 1–7; II – Jas 3, 1–10; Mk 9, 2–13

Week Seven

Monday: I – Sir 1, 1–10; II – Jas 3, 13–18; Mk 9, 14–29

Tuesday: I – Sir 2, 1–11; II – Jas 4, 1–10; Mk 9, 30–37

Wednesday: I – Sir 4, 11–19; II – Jas 4, 13–17; Mk 9, 38–40

Thursday: I – Sir 5, 1–8; II – Jas 5, 1–6; Mk 9, 41–50

Friday: I – Sir 6, 5–17; II – Jas 5, 9–12; Mk 10, 1–12

Saturday: I – Sir 17, 1–15; II – Jas 5, 13–20; Mk 10, 13–16

Week Eight

Monday: I – Sir 17, 19–27; II – 1 Pt 1, 3–9; Mk 10, 17–27

Tuesday: I – Sir 35, 1–12; II – 1 Pt 1, 10–16; Mk 10, 28–31

Wednesday: I – Sir 36, 1. 5–6. 10–17; II – 1 Pt 1, 18–25; Mk 10, 32–45

Thursday: I – Sir 42, 15–25; II – 1 Pt 2, 2–5. 9–12; Mk 10, 46–52

Friday: I – Sir 44, 1. 9–13; II – 1 Pt 4, 7–13; Mk 11, 11–26

Saturday: I – Sir 51, 12b–20; II – Jude 17, 20b–25; Mk 11, 27–33

Week Nine

Monday: I – Tb 1, 1a–2; 2, 1–9; II – 2 Pt 1, 2–7; Mk 12, 1–12

Tuesday: I – Tb 2, 9–14; II – 2 Pt 3, 12–15a. 17–18; Mk 12, 13–17

Wednesday: I – Tb 3, 1–11. 16; II – 2 Tm 1, 1–3. 6–12; Mk 12, 18–27

Thursday: I – Tb 6, 10–11; 7, 1. 9–17; 8, 4–7; II – 2 Tm 2, 8–15; Mk 12, 28b–34

Friday: I – Tb 11, 5–17; II – 2 Tm 3, 10–17; Mk 12, 35–37

Saturday: I – Tb 12, 1. 5–15. 20; II – 2 Tm 4, 1–8; Mk 12, 38–44

Week Ten

Monday: I – 2 Cor 1, 1–7; II – 1 Kgs 17, 1–6; Mt 5, 1–12

Tuesday: I – 2 Cor 1, 18–22; II – 1 Kgs 17, 7–16; Mt 5, 13–16

Wednesday: I – 2 Cor 3, 4–11; II – 1 Kgs 18, 20–39; Mt 5, 17–19

Thursday: I – 2 Cor 3, 15—4, 1. 3–6; II – 1 Kgs 18, 41–46; Mt 5, 20–26

Friday: I – 2 Cor 4, 7–15; II – 1 Kgs 19, 9a. 11–16; Mt 5, 27–32

Saturday: I – 2 Cor 5, 14–21; II – 1 Kgs 19, 19–21; Mt 5, 33–37

Week Eleven

Monday: I – 2 Cor 6, 1–10; II – 1 Kgs 21, 1–16; Mt 5, 38–42

Tuesday: I – 2 Cor 8, 1–9; II – 1 Kgs 21, 17–29; Mt 5, 43–48

Wednesday: I – 2 Cor 9, 6–11; II – 1 Kgs 2, 1. 6–14; Mt 6, 1–6. 16–18

Thursday: I – 2 Cor 11, 1–11; II – Sir 48, 1–15; Mt 6, 7–15

Friday: I – 2 Cor 11, 18. 21b–30; II – 2 Kgs 11, 1–4. 9–18. 20; Mt 6, 19–23

Saturday: I – 2 Cor 12, 1–10; II – 2 Chr 24, 17–25; Mt 6, 24–34

Week Twelve

Monday: I – Gn 12, 1–9; II – 2 Kgs 17, 5–8. 13–15a. 18; Mt 7, 1–5

Tuesday: I – Gn 13, 2. 5–8; II – 2 Kgs 19, 9b–11. 14–21. 31–35a. 36; Mt 7, 6. 12–14

Wednesday: I – Gn 15, 1–12. 17–18; II – 2 Kgs 22, 8–13; 23, 1–3; Mt 7, 15–20

Thursday: I – Gn 16, 1–12. 15–16; II – 2 Kgs 24, 8–17; Mt 7, 21–29

Friday: I – Gn 17, 1. 9–10. 15–22;
 II – 2 Kgs 25, 1–12; Mt 8,
 1–4
Saturday: I – Gn 18, 1–15; II –
 Lam 2, 2. 10–14. 18–19; Mt
 8, 5–17

Week Thirteen
Monday: I – Gn 18, 16–33; II –
 Am 2, 6–10. 13–16; Mt 8,
 18–22
Tuesday: I – Gn 19, 15–29; II –
 Am 3, 1–8; 4, 11–12; Mt 8,
 23–27
Wednesday: I – Gn 21, 5. 8–20;
 II – Am 5, 14–15. 21–24; Mt
 8, 28–34
Thursday: I – Gn 22, 1–19; II –
 Am 7, 10–17; Mt 9, 1–8
Friday: I – Gn 23, 1–4. 19; 24,
 1–8. 62–67; II – Am 8, 4–6.
 9–12; Mt 9, 9–13
Saturday: I – Gn 27, 1–5. 15–29;
 II – Am 9, 11–15; Mt 9,
 14–17

Week Fourteen
Monday: I – Gn 28, 10–22a; II –
 Hos 2, 16. 17b–18. 21–22; Mt
 9, 18–26
Tuesday: I – Gn 32, 22–33; II –
 Hos 8, 4–7. 11–13; Mt 9,
 32–38
Wednesday: I – Gn 41, 51–57; 42,
 5–7a. 17–24a; II – Hos 10,
 1–3. 7–8. 12; Mt 10, 1–7
Thursday: I – Gn 44, 18–21.
 23b–29; 45, 1–5; II – Hos 11,
 1. 3–4. 8c–9; Mt 10, 7–15
Friday: I – Gn 46, 1–7. 28–30; II –
 Hos 14, 2–10; Mt 10, 16–23
Saturday: I – Gn 49, 29–33; 50,
 15–24; II – Is 6, 1–8; Mt 10,
 24–33

Week Fifteen
Monday: I – Ex 1, 8–14. 22; II –
 Is 1, 10–17; Mt 10, 34—
 11, 1
Tuesday: I – Ex 2, 1–15a; II – Is 7,
 1–9; Mt 11, 20–24
Wednesday: I – Ex 3, 1–6. 9–12;
 II – Is 10, 5–7. 13–16; Mt 11,
 25–27
Thursday: I – Ex 3, 13–20; II – Is
 26, 7–9. 12. 16–19; Mt 11,
 28–30

Friday: I – Ex 11, 10–12. 14;
 II – Is 38, 1–6. 21–22. 7–8;
 Mt 12, 1–8
Saturday: I – Ex 12, 37–42; II –
 Mi 2, 1–5; Mt 12, 14–21

Week Sixteen
Monday: I – Ex 14, 5–18; II –
 Mi 6, 1–4. 6–8; Mt 12,
 38–42
Tuesday: I – Ex 14, 21—15, 1;
 II – Mi 7, 14–15. 18–20; Mt
 12, 46–50
Wednesday: I – Ex 16, 1–5. 9–15;
 II – Jer 1, 1. 4–10; Mt 13, 1–9
Thursday: I – Ex 19, 1–2. 9–11.
 16–20b; II – Jer 2, 1–3. 7–8.
 12–13; Mt 13, 10–17
Friday: I – Ex 20, 1–17; II – Jer 3,
 14–17; Mt 13, 18–23
Saturday: I – Ex 24, 3–8; II – Jer
 7, 1–11; Mt 13, 24–30

Week Seventeen
Monday: I – Ex 32, 15–24. 30–34;
 II – Jer 13, 1–11; Mt 13,
 31–35
Tuesday: I – Ex 33, 7–11; 34,
 5b–9. 28; II – Jer 14, 17–22;
 Mt 13, 36–43
Wednesday: I – Ex 34, 29–34; II –
 Jer 15, 10. 16–21; Mt 13,
 44–46
Thursday: I – Ex 40, 16–21.
 34–38; II – Jer 18, 1–6; Mt
 13, 47–53
Friday: I – Lv 23, 1. 4–11. 15–16.
 27. 34b–37; II – Jer 26, 1–9;
 Mt 13, 54–58
Saturday: I – Lv 25, 1. 8–17; II –
 Jer 26, 11–16. 24; Mt 14,
 1–12

Week Eighteen
Monday: I – Nm 11, 4b–15; II –
 Jer 28, 1–17; Mt 14, 13–21 or
 Mt 14, 22–36
Tuesday: I – Nm 12, 1–13; II – Jer
 30, 1–2. 12–15. 18–22; Mt
 14, 22–36 or Mt 15, 1–2.
 10–14
Wednesday: I – Nm 13, 1–2a.
 25—14, 1. 26–29. 34–35;
 II – Jer 31, 1–7; Mt 15, 21–28
Thursday: I – Nm 20, 1–13; II –
 Jer 31, 31–34; Mt 16,
 13–23

Friday: I – Dt 4, 32–40; II – Na 2,
 1. 3; 3, 1–3. 6–7; Mt 16,
 24–28
Saturday: I – Dt 6, 4–13; II – Hb 1,
 12—2, 4; Mt 17, 14–20

Week Nineteen
Monday: I – Dt 10, 12–22; II –
 Ez 1, 2–5. 24–28c; Mt 17,
 22–27
Tuesday: I – Dt 31, 1–8; II – Ez 2,
 8—3, 4; Mt 18, 1–5. 10.
 12–14
Wednesday: I – Dt 34, 1–12; II –
 Ez 9, 1–7; 10, 18–22; Mt 18,
 15–20
Thursday: I – Jos 3, 7–10a. 11.
 13–17; II – Ez 12, 1–12; Mt
 18, 21—19, 1
Friday: I – Jos 24, 1–13; II – Ez
 16, 1–15. 60. 63; Mt 19, 3–12
Saturday: I – Jos 24, 14–29; II –
 Ez 18, 1–10. 13b. 30–32; Mt
 19, 13–15

Week Twenty
Monday: I – Jgs 2, 11–19; II –
 Ez 24, 15–24; Mt 19, 16–22
Tuesday: I – Jgs 6, 11–24a; II –
 Ez 28, 1–10; Mt 19, 23–30
Wednesday: I – Jgs 9, 6–15; II –
 Ez 34, 1–11; Mt 20, 1–16a
Thursday: I – Jgs 11, 29–39a; II –
 Ez 36, 23–28; Mt 22, 1–14
Friday: I – Ru 1, 1. 3–6. 14b–16.
 22; II – Ez 37, 1–14; Mt 22,
 34–40
Saturday: I – Ru 2, 1–3. 8–11; 4,
 13–17; II – Ez 43, 1–7a; Mt
 23, 1–12

Week Twenty-one
Monday: I – Thes 1, 2b–5. 8b–10;
 II – 2 Thes 1, 1–5. 11b–12;
 Mt 23, 13–22
Tuesday: I – 1 Thes 2, 1–18; II –
 2 Thes 2, 1–3a. 13–17; Mt 23,
 23–26
Wednesday: I – 1 Thes 2, 9–13;
 II – 2 Thes 3, 6–10. 16–18;
 Mt 23, 27–32
Thursday: I – 1 Thes 3, 7–13; II –
 1 Cor 1, 1–9; Mt 24, 42–51
Friday: I – 1 Thes 4, 1–8; II –
 1 Cor 1, 17–25; Mt 25, 1–13
Saturday: I – 1 Thes 4, 9–12; II –
 1 Cor 1, 26–31; Mt 25, 14–30

Week Twenty-two

Monday: I – 1 Thes 4, 13–18; II –
1 Cor 2, 1–5; Lk 4, 16–30

Tuesday: I – 1 Thes 5, 1–6. 9–11;
II – 1 Cor 2, 10b–16; Lk 4,
31–37

Wednesday: I – Col 1, 1–8; II –
1 Cor 3, 1–9; Lk 4, 38–44

Thursday: I – Col 1, 9–14; II –
1 Cor 3, 18–23; Lk 5, 1–11

Friday: I – Col 1, 15–20; II – 1 Cor
4, 1–5; Lk 5, 33–39

Saturday: I – Col 1, 21–23; II –
1 Cor 4, 9–15; Lk 6, 1–5

Week Twenty-three

Monday: I – Col 1, 24—2, 3; II –
1 Cor 5, 1–8; Lk 6, 6–11

Tuesday: I – Col 2, 6–15; II –
1 Cor 6, 1–11; Lk 6, 12–19

Wednesday: I – Col 3, 1–11; II –
1 Cor 7, 25–31; Lk 6, 20–26

Thursday: I – Col 3, 12–17; II –
1 Cor 8, 1b–7. 11–13; Lk 6,
27–38

Friday: I – 1 Tm 1, 1–2. 12–14;
II – 1 Cor 9, 16–19. 22b–27;
Lk 6, 39–42

Saturday: I – 1 Tm 1, 15–17; II –
1 Cor 10, 14–22a; Lk 6,
43–49

Week Twenty-four

Monday: I – 1 Tm 2, 1–8; II –
1 Cor 11, 17–26. 33; Lk 7,
1–10

Tuesday: I – 1 Tm 3, 1–13; II –
1 Cor 12, 12–14. 27–31a; Lk
7, 11–17

Wednesday: I – 1 Tm 3, 14–16; II
– 1 Cor 12, 31—13, 13; Lk 7,
31–35

Thursday: I – 1 Tm 4, 12–16;
II – 1 Cor 15, 1–11; Lk 7,
36–50

Friday: I – 1 Tm 6, 2c–12; II –
1 Cor 15, 12–20; Lk 8, 1–3

Saturday: I – 1 Tm 6, 13–16; II –
1 Cor 15, 36–37. 42–49; Lk
8, 4–15

Week Twenty-five

Monday: I – Ezr 1, 1–6; II – Prv 3,
27–34; Lk 8, 16–18

Tuesday: I – Ezr 6, 7–8. 12b.
14–20; II – Prv 21, 1–6.
10–13; Lk 8, 19–21

Wednesday: I – Ezr 9, 5–9; II –
Prv 30, 5–9; Lk 9, 1–6

Thursday: I – Hg 1, 1–8; II – Eccl
1, 2–11; Lk 9, 7–9

Friday: I – Hg 1, 15b—2, 9; II –
Eccl 3, 1–11; Lk 9, 18–22

Saturday: I – Zec 2, 5–9a. 14–15a;
II – Eccl 11, 9—12, 8; Lk 9,
43b–45

Week Twenty-six

Monday: I – Zec 8, 1–8; II – Jb 1,
6–22; Lk 9, 46–50

Tuesday: I – Zec 8, 20–23; II – Jb
3, 1–3. 11–17. 20–23; Lk 9,
51–56

Wednesday: I – Neh 2, 1–8; II –
Jb 9, 1–12. 14–16; Lk 9,
57–62

Thursday: I – Neh 8, 1–4a. 5–6.
7b–12; II – Jb 19, 12–27; Lk
10, 1–12

Friday: I – Bar 1, 15–22; II – Jb
38, 1. 12–21; 40, 3–5; Lk 10,
13–16

Saturday: I – Bar 4, 5–12. 27–29;
II – Jb 42, 1–3. 5–6. 12–17;
Lk 10, 17–24

Week Twenty-seven

Monday: I – Jon 1, 1—2, 1. 11;
II – Gal 1, 6–12; Lk 10,
25–37

Tuesday: I – Jon 3, 1–10; II – Gal
1, 13–24; Lk 10, 38–42

Wednesday: I – Jon 4, 1–11; II –
Gal 2, 1–2. 7–14; Lk 11, 1–4

Thursday: I – Mal 3, 13–20a;
II – Gal 3, 1–5; Lk 11, 5–13

Friday: I – Jl 1, 13–15; 2, 1–2;
II – Gal 3, 7–14; Lk 11,
15–26

Saturday: I – Jl 4, 12–21; II – Gal
3, 22–29; Lk 11, 27–28

Week Twenty-eight

Monday: I – Rom 1, 1–7; II – Gal
4, 22–24. 26–27; Lk 11,
29–32

Tuesday: I – Rom 1, 16–25; II –
Gal 5, 1–6; Lk 11, 37–41

Wednesday: I – Rom 2, 1–11; II –
Gal 5, 18–25; Lk 11, 42–46

Thursday: I – Rom 3, 21–29; II –
Eph 1, 3–10; Lk 11, 47–54

Friday: I – Rom 4, 1–8; II – Eph 1,
11–14; Lk 12, 1–7

Saturday: I – Rom 4, 13. 16–18;
II – Eph 1, 15–23; Lk 12,
8–12

Week Twenty-nine

Monday: I – Rom 4, 20–25; II –
Eph 2, 1–10; Lk 12, 13–21

Tuesday: I – Rom 5, 12. 15b.
17–19. 20b–21; II – Eph 2,
12–22; Lk 12, 35; 38

Wednesday: I – Rom 6, 12–18;
II – Eph 3, 2–12; Lk 12,
39–48

Thursday: I – Rom 6, 19–23; II –
Eph 3, 14–21; Lk 12, 49–53

Friday: I – Rom 7, 18–25a; II –
Eph 4, 1–6; Lk 12, 54–59

Saturday: I – Rom 8, 1–11; II –
Eph 4, 7–16; Lk 13, 1–9

Week Thirty

Monday: I – Rom 8, 12–17; II –
Eph 4, 32—5, 8; Lk 13,
10–17

Tuesday: I – Rom 8, 18–25; II –
Eph 5, 21–33; Lk 13, 18–21

Wednesday: I – Rom 8, 26–30; II –
Eph 6, 1–9; Lk 13, 22–30

Thursday: I – Rom 3, 31b–39; II –
Eph 6, 10–20; Lk 13, 31–35

Friday: I – Rom 9, 1–5; II – Phil 1,
1–11; Lk 14, 1–6

Saturday: I – Rom 11, 1–2a.
11–12. 25–29; II – Phil 1,
18b–26; Lk 14, 1. 7–11

Week Thirty-one

Monday: I – Rom 11, 29–36; II –
Phil 2, 1–4; Lk 14, 12–14

Tuesday: I – Rom 12, 5–16a; II –
Phil 2, 5–11; Lk 14, 15–24

Wednesday: I – Rom 13, 8–10; II –
Phil 2, 12–18; Lk 14, 25–33

Thursday: I – Rom 14, 7–12; II –
Phil 3, 3–8a; Lk 15, 1–10

Friday: I – Rom 15, 14–21; II –
Phil 3, 17—4, 1; Lk 16, 1–8

Saturday: I – Rom 16, 3–9. 16.
22–27; II – Phil 4, 10–19; Lk
16, 9–15

Week Thirty-two

Monday: I – Wis 1, 1–7; II – Ti 1,
1–9; Lk 17, 1–6

Tuesday: I – Wis 2, 23—3, 9; II –
Ti 2, 1–8. 11–14; Lk 17, 7–10

Wednesday: I – Wis 6, 1–11; II –
Ti 3, 1–7; Lk 17, 11–19

Thursday: I – Wis 7, 22—8, 1; II –
Phlm 7–20; Lk 17, 20–25

Friday: I – Wis 13, 1–9; II – 2 Jn
4–9; Lk 17, 26–37

Saturday: I – Wis 18, 14–16; 19,
6–9; II – 3 Jn 5–8; Lk 18, 1–8

Week Thirty-three
Monday: I – 1 Mc 1, 10–15.
41–43. 54. 57. 62. 64; II – Rv
1, 1–4; 2, 1–5a; Lk 18, 35–43

Tuesday: I – 2 Mc 6, 18–31; II –
Rv 3, 1–6. 14–22; Lk 19,
1–10

Wednesday: I – 2 Mc 7, 1. 20–31;
II – Rv 4, 1–11; Lk 19,
11–28

Thursday: I – 1 Mc 2, 15–29; II –
Rv 5, 1–10; Lk 19, 41–44

Friday: I – 1 Mc 4, 36–37. 52–59;
II – Rv 10, 8–11; Lk 19,
45–48

Saturday: I – 1 Mc 6, 1–13; II –
Rv 11, 4–12; Lk 20, 27–40

Week Thirty-four
Monday: I – Dn 1, 1–6. 8–20; II –
Rv 14, 1–3. 4b–5; Lk 21, 1–4

Tuesday: I – Dn 2, 31–45; II –
Rv 14, 14–19; Lk 21,
5–11

Wednesday: I – Dn 5, 1–6. 13–14.
16–17. 23–28; II – Rv 15,
1–4; Lk 21, 12–19

Thursday: I – Dn 6, 11–28; II – Rv
18, 1–2. 21–23; 19, 1–3. 9a;
Lk 21, 20–28

Friday: I – Dn 7, 2–14; II – Rv 20,
1–4; 20, 11—21, 2; Lk 21,
29–33

Saturday: I – Dn 7, 15–27; II Rv
22, 1–7; Lk 21, 34–36

INDEX TO READING GUIDE

COLLABORATORS
on the Old Testament of the *New American Bible*

BISHOPS' COMMITTEE OF THE CONFRATERNITY OF CHRISTIAN DOCTRINE

Most Rev. Charles P. Greco, D.D., *Chairman*   Most Rev. Joseph T. McGucken, S.T.D.   Most Rev. Vincent S. Waters, D.D.
Most Rev. Romeo Blanchette, D.D.   Most Rev. Christopher J. Weldon, D.D.

EDITORS IN CHIEF

Rev. Louis F. Hartman, C.SS.R., S.S.L., LING. OR. L., *Chairman*   Rev. Msgr. Patrick W. Skehan, S.T.D., LL.D., *Vice-Chairman*
Rev. Stephen J. Hartdegen, O.F.M., S.S.L., *Secretary*

ASSOCIATE EDITORS AND TRANSLATORS

Rev. Edward P. Arbez, S.S., S.T.D.   Rev. Msgr. Edward J. Byrne, PH.D., S.T.D.   Rev. Edward A. Cerny, S.S., S.T.D.
Rev. James E. Coleran, S.J., S.T.L., S.S.L.   Rev. John J. Collins, S.J., M.A., S.S.L.
Sr. M. Emmanuel Collins, O.S.F., PH.D.   Prof. Frank M. Cross, Jr., PH.D.   Rev. Patrick Cummins, O.S.B., S.T.D.
Rev. Antonine A. DeGuglielmo, O.F.M., S.T.D., S.S.L., S.S. LECT. GEN.   Rev. Alexander A. DiLella, O.F.M., S.T.L., S.S.L., PH.D.
Most Rev. John J. Dougherty, S.T.L., S.S.D.   William A. Dowd, S.J., S.T.D., S.S.L.   Prof. David Noel Freedman, PH.D.
Rev. Michael J. Gruenthaner, S.J., S.T.D., S.S.D.   Rev. Msgr. Maurice A. Hofer, S.S.L.   Rev. Justin Krellner, O.S.B., S.T.D.
Rev. Joseph L. Lilly, C.M., S.T.D., S.S.L.   Rev. Roderick F. MacKenzie, S.J., M.A., S.S.D.
Rev. Edward A. Mangan, C.SS.R., S.S.L.   Rev. Daniel W. Martin, C.M., S.T.L., S.S.L.   Rev. William H. McClellan, S.J.
Rev. James McGlinchey, C.M., S.T.D.   Rev. Frederick Moriarty, S.J., S.S.L., S.T.D.   Rev. Richard T. Murphy, O.P., S.T.D., S.S.D.
Rev. Roland E. Murphy, O. CARM., M.A., S.T.D., S.S.L.   Rev. Msgr. William R. Newton, M.S., S.S.D.
Rev. Eberhard Olinger, O.S.B.   Rev. Charles H. Pickar, O.S.A., S.T.L., S.S.L.
Rev. Christopher Rehwinkel, O.F.M., S.T.D., S.S. LECT. GEN.   Rev. Msgr. John R. Rowan, S.T.D., S.S.L.
Prof. J. A. Sanders, PH.D.   Rev. Edward F. Siegman, C.PP.S., S.T.D., S.S.L.   Rev. Msgr. Matthew P. Stapleton, S.T.D., S.S.L.
Rev. Msgr. John E. Steinmueller, S.T.D., S.S.L.   Rev. John Ujlaki, O.S.B., LITT.D.
Rev. Bruce Vawter, C.M., S.T.L., S.S.D.   Rev. John B. Weisengoff, S.T.D., S.S.L.

COLLABORATORS
on the Revised New Testament of the *New American Bible*

BISHOPS' AD HOC COMMITTEE

Most Rev. Theodore E. McCarrick, D.D.   Most Rev. Richard J. Sklba, D.D.   Most Rev. J. Francis Stafford, D.D.
Most Rev. John F. Whealon, D.D., *Chairman*

BOARD OF EDITORS

Rev. Msgr. Myles M. Bourke   Rev. Francis T. Gignac, S.J., *Chairman*   Rev. Stephen J. Hartdegen, O.F.M., *Secretary*
Rev. Claude J. Peifer, O.S.B.   Rev. John H. Reumann

REVISERS

Rev. Msgr. Myles M. Bourke   Rev. Frederick W. Danker   Rev. Alexander A. Di Lella, O.F.M.   Rev. Charles H. Giblin, S.J.
Rev. Francis T. Gignac, S.J.   Rev. Stephen J. Hartdegen, O.F.M.   Dr. Maurya P. Horgan   Rev. John R. Keating, S.J.
Rev. John Knox   Dr. Paul J. Kobelski   Dr. J. Rebecca Lyman   Bro. Elliott C. Maloney, O.S.B.   Dr. Janet A. Timbie

CONSULTANTS

Rev. Joseph Jensen, O.S.D.   Rev. Aidan Kavanagh, O.S.D.   Dr. Marianne Sawicki

BUSINESS MANAGER

Charles A. Buggé

WORD PROCESSOR

Suzanna Jordan

1752

COLLABORATORS
on the Revised Psalms of the *New American Bible*

BISHOPS' AD HOC COMMITTEE

Most Rev. Enrique San Pedro, S.J.   Most Rev. Richard Sklba, D.D.   Most Rev. Donald W. Trautman, S.T.D., S.S.L.

Most Rev. Emil A. Wcela   Most Rev. John F. Whealon, S.S.L., *Chairman*

BOARD OF EDITORS

Rev. Richard Clifford, S.J.   Bro. Aloysius Fitzgerald, F.S.C.   Rev. Joseph Jensen, O.S.B.   Rev. Roland Murphy, O. CARM.

Sr. Irene Nowell, O.S.B.   Dr. Judith Sanderson

REVISERS

Prof. Gary Anderson   Rev. Michael L. Barré   Rev. Christopher T. Begg   Dr. Joseph Blenkinsopp

Rev. Anthony R. Ceresko, O.S.F.S.   Rev. Richard J. Clifford, S.J.   Rev. Aelred Cody, O.S.B.   Prof. Michael D. Coogan

Rev. Alexander A. Di Leila, O.F.M.   Dr. Robert A. Di Vito   Bro. Aloysius Fitzgerald, F.S.C.   Rev. Michael D. Guinan, O.F.M.

Rev. William L. Holladay   Rev. William Irwin, C.S.B.   Rev. Joseph Jensen, O.S.B.   Rev. John S. Kselman

Dr. Conrad E. L'Heureux   Rev. Leo Laberge, O.M.I.   Dr. Paul G. Mosca   Rev. Dr. Roland E. Murphy, O. CARM.

Dr. Michael Patrick O'Connor   Rev. Brian J. Peckham, S.J.   Prof. Jimmy J. Roberts   Sr. Eileen M. Schuller, O.S.U.

Dr. Byron E. Shafer   Prof. Mark S. Smith

ENGLISH CONSULTANTS

Dr. Catherine Dunn   Bro. Daniel Burke, F.S.C.

BUSINESS MANAGER

Charles A. Buggé

1753

A CONCORDANCE
TO THE *NEW AMERICAN BIBLE*

SPECIAL SYMBOLS

* *GOD, *LORD and *LORD'S index the proper name of God *(Yahweh)* typeset in small capital letters (GOD, LORD, LORD's) in the NAB.

→ An arrow following an entry heading points to related words for additional study

= An equals sign marks an alternate proper name for additional study (e.g., ISRAEL = JACOB)

John R. Kohlenberger III

TABLE OF ABBREVIATIONS

Ac . . . . Acts	Jer . . . . Jeremiah	2Pe . . . . 2 Peter
Am . . . . Amos	Jn . . . . John	Phm . . . . Philemon
Bar . . . . Baruch	1Jn . . . . 1 John	Php . . . . Philippians
1Ch . . . . 1 Chronicles	2Jn . . . . 2 John	Pr . . . . Proverbs
2Ch . . . . 2 Chronicles	3Jn . . . . 3 John	Ps . . . . Psalms
1Co . . . . 1 Corinthians	Jnh . . . . Jonah	Rev . . . . Revelation
2Co . . . . 2 Corinthians	Job . . . . Job	Ro . . . . Romans
Col . . . . Colossians	Joel . . . . Joel	Ru . . . . Ruth
Da . . . . Daniel	Jos . . . . Joshua	1Sa . . . . 1 Samuel
Dt . . . . Deuteronomy	Jude . . . . Jude	2Sa . . . . 2 Samuel
Ecc . . . . Ecclesiastes	1Ki . . . . 1 Kings	Sir . . . . Sirach
Eph . . . . Ephesians	2Ki . . . . 2 Kings	SS . . . . Song of Songs
Est . . . . Esther	La . . . . Lamentations	1Th . . . . 1 Thessalonians
Ex . . . . Exodus	Lev . . . . Leviticus	2Th . . . . 2 Thessalonians
Eze . . . . Ezekiel	Lk . . . . Luke	1Ti . . . . 1 Timothy
Ezr . . . . Ezra	Mal . . . . Malachi	2Ti . . . . 2 Timothy
Gal . . . . Galatians	1Mc . . . . 1 Maccabees	Tit . . . . Titus
Ge . . . . Genesis	2Mc . . . . 2 Maccabees	Tob . . . . Tobit
Hab . . . . Habakkuk	Mic . . . . Micah	Wis . . . . Wisdom
Hag . . . . Haggai	Mk . . . . Mark	Zec . . . . Zechariah
Heb . . . . Hebrews	Mt . . . . Matthew	Zep . . . . Zephaniah
Hos . . . . Hosea	Na . . . . Nahum	
Isa . . . . Isaiah	Ne . . . . Nehemiah	
Jas . . . . James	Nu . . . . Numbers	**OTHER**
Jdg . . . . Judges	Ob . . . . Obadiah	S . . . . Shorter Ending of Mark
Jdt . . . . Judith	1Pe . . . . 1 Peter	Pr: . . . . Sirach Prologue

A

AARON

Genealogy (Ex 6:16-20; Jos 21:4, 10; 1Ch 6:3-15). Priesthood of (Ex 28:1; Nu 17; Heb 5:1-4; 7), vestments of (Ex 28; 39), consecration of (Ex 29), ordination of (Lev 8).

Spokesman for Moses (Ex 4:14-16, 27-31; 7:1-2). Supported Moses' hands in battle (Ex 17:8-13). Built golden calf (Ex 32; Dt 9:20). Spoke against Moses (Nu 12). Priesthood opposed (Nu 16); staff budded (Nu 17). Forbidden to enter the promised land (Nu 20:1-12). Death of (Nu 20:22-29; 33:38-39). Praise of (Sir 45:6-22).

ABANDON → ABANDONED

Dt   4:31 God, he will not a and destroy you,

2Ch 15: 2 you; but if you a him, he will a you.

Ac   2:27 because you will not a my soul

ABANDONED → ABANDON

Jdg   2:13 Because they had thus a him

2Ch 12: 5 'You have a me, and therefore I have

     12: 5 therefore I have a you to the power

Sir   49: 4 They a the law of the Most High,

Isa   54: 7 For a brief moment I a you,

ABBA

Mk 14:36 he said, "A, Father, all things are

Ro   8:15 through which we cry, "A, Father!"

Gal   4: 6 our hearts, crying out, "A, Father!"

ABEDNEGO → = AZARIAH

Deported to Babylon with Daniel (Da 1:1-6). Name changed from Azariah (Da 1:7). Refused defilement by food (Da 1:8-20). Refused idol worship (Da 3:1-12); saved from furnace (Da 3:13-30).

ABEL

Second son of Adam (Ge 4:2). Offered acceptable sacrifice (Ge 4:4; Heb 11:4; 12:24). Murdered by Cain (Ge 4:8; Mt 23:35; Lk 11:51; 1Jn 3:12).

ABIATHAR

High priest in days of Saul and David (1Sa 22; 2Sa 15; 1Ki 1-2; Mk 2:26). Escaped Saul's slaughter of priests (1Sa 22:18-23). Supported David in Absalom's revolt (2Sa 15:24-29). Supported Adonijah (1Ki 1:7-42); deposed by Solomon (1Ki 2:22-35; cf. 1Sa 2:31-35).

ABIDE

Ps   15: 1 LORD, who may a in your tent?

     91: 1 High, who a in the shadow

Wis   3: 9 the faithful shall a with him in love:

ABIGAIL

1. Sister of David (1Ch 2:16-17).

2. Wife of Nabal (1Sa 25:30); pled for his life with David (1Sa 25:14-35). Became David's wife after Nabal's death (1Sa 25:36-42).

ABIHU

Son of Aaron (Ex 6:23; 24:1, 9); killed for offering illicit fire (Lev 10; Nu 3:2-4; 1Ch 24:1-2).

ABIJAH

1. Second son of Samuel (1Ch 6:28); a corrupt judge (1Sa 8:1-5).

2. An Aaronic priest (1Ch 24:10; Lk 1:5).

3. Son of Jeroboam I; died as prophesied by Ahijah (1Ki 14:1-18).

4. Son of Rehoboam, also called Abijam; king of Judah who fought Jeroboam I attempting to reunite Israel (1Ki 14:31-15:8; 2Ch 12:16-14:1).

ABILITY → ABLE

Mt   25:15 third, one—to each according to his a.

ABIMELECH

1. King of Gerar who took Abraham's wife Sarah, believing her to be his sister (Ge 20). Covenanted with Abraham (Ge 21:22-33).

2. King of Gerar who took Isaac's wife Rebekah, believing her to be his sister (Ge 26:1-11). Covenanted with Isaac (Ge 26:26-31).

3. Son of Gideon (Jdg 8:31). Attempted to become king (Jdg 9).

ABIRAM

Sided with Dathan in rebellion against Moses and Aaron (Nu 16; 26:9; Dt 11:6; Sir 45:18).

ABISHAI

Son of Zeruiah, David's sister (1Sa 26:6; 1Ch 2:16). One of David's chief warriors (1Ch 11:15-21): against Edom (1Ch 18:12-13), Ammon (2Sa 10), Absalom (2Sa 18), Sheba (2Sa 20). Wanted to kill Saul (1Sa 26), killed Abner (2Sa 2:18-27; 3:22-39).

ABLE → ABILITY

Ex   18:25 He picked out a men from all Israel

Jdt   11:18 of them will be a to withstand you.

Ro   14: 4 for the Lord is a to make him stand.

2Co   9: 8 God is a to make every grace

Eph   6:11 you may be a to stand firm against

2Ti   1:12 that he is a to guard what has been

Heb   2:18 he is a to help those who are being

     5: 2 He is a to deal patiently

     7:25 he is always a to save those who

Rev   5: 3 or under the earth was a to open

ABNER

Cousin of Saul and commander of his army (1Sa 14:50; 17:55-57; 26). Made Ish-Bosheth king after Saul (2Sa 2:8-10), but later defected to David (2Sa 3:6-21). Killed Asahel (2Sa 2:18-32), for which he was killed by Joab and Abishai (2Sa 3:22-39).

ABOLISH → ABOLISHING

Mt   5:17 think that I have come to a the law

Mt   5:17 I have come not to a but to fulfill.

ABOLISHING → ABOLISH

Da   11:31 a the daily sacrifice and setting

ABOMINABLE → ABOMINATION

2Ch 28: 3 by fire according to the a practice

Eze   7:20 of them their a images [their idols].

ABOMINATION → ABOMINABLE, ABOMINATIONS

1Ma   6: 7 they had pulled down the A

Pr   6:16 hates, yes, seven are an a to him;

Da   9:27 temple wing shall be the horrible a

ABOMINATIONS → ABOMINATION

Eze   44: 7 broken my covenant by all your a.

Rev   17: 5 of harlots and of the a of the earth."

ABOUND

Ro   6: 1 we persist in sin that grace may a?

ABOVE

Dt   4:39 the LORD is God in the heavens a

Jn   3: 7 told you, 'You must be born from a.'

Php   2: 9 him the name that is a every name,

Col   3: 2 Think of what is a, not of what is

ABRAHAM

Abram, son of Terah (Ge 11:26-27), husband of Sarah (Ge 11:29).

Covenant relation with the LORD (Ge 12:1-3; 13:14-17; 15; 17; 22:15-18; Ex 2:24; Ne 9:8; Ps 105; Mic 7:20; Lk 1:68-75; Ro 4; Heb 6:13-15).

Called from Ur, via Haran, to Canaan (Ge 12:1; Ac 7:2-4; Heb 11:8-10). Moved to Egypt, nearly lost Sarah to Pharoah (Ge 12:10-20). Divided the land with Lot; settled in Hebron (Ge 13). Saved Lot from four kings (Ge 14:1-16); blessed by Melchizedek (Ge 14:17-20; Heb 7:1-10). Declared righteous by faith (Ge 15:6; Ro 4:3; Gal 3:6-9; 1Ma 2:52). Fathered Ishmael by Hagar (Ge 16).

Name changed from Abram (Ge 17:5; Ne 9:7). Circumcised (Ge 17; Ro 4:9-12). Entertained three visitors (Ge 18); promised a son by Sarah (Ge 18:9-15; 17:16). Questioned destruction of Sodom and Gomorrah (Ge 18:16-33). Moved to Gerar; nearly lost Sarah to Abimelech (Ge 20). Fathered Isaac by Sarah (Ge 21:1-7; Ac 7:8; Heb 11:11-12); sent away Hagar and Ishmael (Ge 21:8-21; Gal 4:22-30). Covenant with Abimelech (Ge 21:22-32). Tested by offering Isaac (Ge 22; Heb 11:17-19; Jas 2:21-24). Sarah died; bought field of Ephron for burial (Ge 23). Secured wife for Isaac (Ge 24). Fathered children by Keturah (Ge 25:1-6; 1Ch 1:32-33). Death (Ge 25:7-11).

Called servant of God (Ge 26:24), friend of God (2Ch 20:7; Isa 41:8; Jas 2:23), prophet (Ge 20:7), father of Israel (Ex 3:15; Isa 51:2; Mt 3:9; Jn 8:39-58). Praised (Sir 44:19-45:1).

ABSALOM
Son of David by Maacah (2Sa 3:3; 1Ch 3:2). Killed Amnon for rape of his sister Tamar; banished by David (2Sa 13). Returned to Jerusalem; received by David (2Sa 14). Rebelled against David (2Sa 15-17). Killed (2Sa 18).

ABSENT
1Co 5: 3 although **a** in body but present
Col   2: 5 For even if I am **a** in the flesh, yet I

ABUNDANCE → ABUNDANTLY
2Co 9: 8 you may have an **a** for every good

ABUNDANTLY → ABUNDANCE
Jn 10:10 might have life and have it more **a**.

ABYSS
Lk   8:31 not to order them to depart to the **a**.
Ro 10: 7 or "Who will go down into the **a**?"

ACCEPT → ACCEPTED
Mt 19:11 "Not all can **a** [this] word, but only
Jn   1:11 but his own people did not **a** him.

ACCEPTED → ACCEPT
Lk   4:24 no prophet is **a** in his own native

ACCESS
Ro   5: 2 through whom we have gained **a**
Eph 2:18 through him we both have **a** in one

ACCORDING
Sir 16:12 he judges men, each **a** to his deeds.
Mt   9:29 it be done for you **a** to your faith."
Ro   8: 4 who live not **a** to the flesh but **a**
Heb 2: 4 gifts of the holy Spirit **a** to his will.
1Jn 5:14 that if we ask anything **a** to his will,
Rev 20:12 life. The dead were judged **a** to their

ACCOUNT
Mt 12:36 of judgment people will render an **a**
Heb 4:13 him to whom we must render an **a**.

ACCURSED → CURSE
Ro   9: 3 I could wish that I myself were **a**
Rev 22: 3 Nothing **a** will be found there

ACCUSE → ACCUSER
Zec 3: 1 stood at his right hand to **a** him.
Mt 12:10 sabbath?" so that they might **a** him.

ACCUSER → ACCUSE
Rev 12:10 For the **a** of our brothers is cast out,

ACHAN
Sinned at Jericho; stoned (Jos 7; 22:20; 1Ch 2:7).

ACHISH
King of Gath before whom David feigned insanity (1Sa 21:10-15). Later "ally" of David (2Sa 27-29).

ACKNOWLEDGE
Mt 10:32 others I will **a** before my heavenly
Ro   1:28 since they did not see fit to **a** God,

ACT → ACTED, ACTIVE, ACTS
Ps 37: 5 to the LORD; trust that God will **a**

ACTED → ACT
Eze 20: 9 but I **a** for my name's sake, that it
Ac   3:17 that you **a** out of ignorance, just as
1Ti 1:13 been mercifully treated because I **a**

ACTIVE → ACT
Jas 2:22 faith was **a** along with his works,

ACTS → ACT
Ex   6: 6 arm and with mighty **a** of judgment.
Ps 71:15 day after day your **a** of deliverance,
Mt   7:24 **a** on them will be like a wise man
Jas 1:25 who forgets but a doer who **a**,

ADAM
First man (Tob 8:6; Ge 1:26-2:25; Ro 5:14; 1Ti 2:13). Sin of (Ge 3; Hos 6:7 [note]; Ro 5:12-21). Children of (Ge 4:1-5:5). Death of (Ge 5:5; Ro 5:12-21; 1Co 15:22).

ADD
Dt   4: 2 you shall not **a** to what I command
Pr 30: 6 **A** nothing to his words, lest he
Lk 12:25 of you by worrying **a** a moment

ADMONISH → ADMONITION
Col 3:16 you teach and **a** one another,

ADMONITION → ADMONISH
Pr 15: 5 The fool spurns his father's **a**,

ADONIJAH
1. Son of David by Haggith (2Sa 3:4; 1Ch 3:2). Attempted to be king after David; killed at Solomon's order (1Ki 1-2).
2. Levite; teacher of the Law (2Ch 17:8).

ADOPTION
Ro   8:15 fear, but you received a spirit of **a**,
    8:23 within ourselves as we wait for **a**,
Gal 4: 5 the law, so that we might receive **a**.

ADORNED → ADORNMENT
Lk 21: 5 how the temple was **a** with costly
Rev 17: 4 purple and scarlet and **a** with gold,
    21: 2 God, prepared as a bride **a** for her

ADORNMENT → ADORNED
Pr   3:22 to your soul, and an **a** for your neck.

ADULTERERS → ADULTERY
Jer 23:10 With **a** the land is filled; on their
1Co 6: 9 nor idolaters nor **a** nor boy

ADULTERESS → ADULTERY
Lev 20:10 and the **a** shall be put to death.
Pr   2:16 from the **a** with her smooth words,

ADULTERY → ADULTERERS, ADULTERESS
Ex 20:14 "You shall not commit **a**.
Jer 3: 9 committing **a** with stone and wood.
Mt   5:28 lust has already committed **a**
Lk 16:18 and marries another commits **a**,
    16:18 from her husband commits **a**.
Jn   8: 3 a woman who had been caught in **a**

ADVANTAGE
Ecc 7:12 the **a** of knowledge is that wisdom
Ro   3: 1 What **a** is there then in being a Jew?
1Co 10:24 No one should seek his own **a**,

ADVERSARIES → ADVERSARY
2Sa 22:49 Above my **a** you exalt me

ADVERSARY
1Ti 5:14 so as to give the **a** no pretext

ADVICE
2Ch 10:13 Ignoring the **a** the elders had given
Tob 4:18 lightly of any **a** that can be useful.
Pr   8:14 Mine are counsel and **a**; Mine is
Sir 37:11 pay no attention to any **a** they give.

ADVOCATE
Jn 14:26 The **A**, the holy Spirit
    15:26 the **A** comes whom I will send you
1Jn 2: 1 sin, we have an **A** with the Father,

AFFLICT → AFFLICTED, AFFLICTION
2Sa 7:10 continue to **a** them as they did

AFFLICTED → AFFLICT
2Co 4: 8 We are **a** in every way, but not

AFFLICTION → AFFLICT
Dt 16: 3 bread, the bread of **a**, that you may
Ps 25:18 Put an end to my **a** and suffering;
2Co 4:17 this momentary light **a** is producing

AFRAID → FEAR
Ge   3:10 but I was **a**, because I was naked,
Ex   3: 6 face, for he was **a** to look at God.
Dt 20: 3 Be not weakhearted or **a**; be neither
Mt 10:31 So do not be **a**; you are worth more
      28:10 Jesus said to them, "Do not be **a**.
Lk 12:32 Do not be **a** any longer, little flock,
Heb 13: 6 [and] I will not be **a**. What can

AGABUS
A Christian prophet (Ac 11:28; 21:10).

AGAG
King of Amalekites; not killed by Saul (1Sa 15).

AGAIN
Job 14:14 a man has died, were he to live **a**,
Jn 14: 3 I will come back **a** and take you
Heb 6: 6 to bring them to repentance **a**,

AGE → AGES
Ge 21: 2 bore Abraham a son in his old **a**,
Mt 28:20 you always, until the end of the **a**."
Gal 1: 4 us from the present evil **a** in accord

AGES → AGE
1Co 2: 7 God predetermined before the **a**
Col 1:26 the mystery hidden from **a**
1Ti 1:17 To the king of **a**, incorruptible,

AGREE
Mt 18:19 you, if two of you **a** on earth
Mk 14:56 him, but their testimony did not **a**.

AGRIPPA
Descendant of Herod; king before whom Paul argued his case in Caesarea (Ac 25:13-26:32).

AHAB
1. Son of Omri; king of Israel (1Ki 16:28-22:40), husband of Jezebel (1Ki 16:31). Promoted Baal worship (1Ki 16:31-33); opposed by Elijah (1Ki 17:1; 18; 21), a prophet (1Ki 20:35-43), Micaiah (1Ki 22:1-28). Defeated Ben-Hadad (1Ki 20). Killed for failing to kill Ben-Hadad and for murder of Naboth (1Ki 20:35-21:40).
2. A false prophet (Jer 29:21-22).

AHASUERUS → = ARTAXERXES
King of Persia (Ezr 4:6), husband of Esther (called Artaxerxes in Est 11:1; 12:2; 13:1; 16:1). Deposed Vashti; replaced her with Esther (Est 1-2). Sealed Haman's edict to annihilate the Jews (Est 3). Received Esther without having called her (Est 5:1-8). Honored Mordecai (Est 6). Hanged Haman (Est 7). Issued edict allowing Jews to defend themselves (Est 8). Promoted Mordecai (Est 8:1-2, 15; 9:4; 10).

AHAZ
Son of Jotham; king of Judah, (2Ki 16; 2Ch 28; Mt 1:9). Idolatry of (2Ki 16:3-4, 10-18; 2Ch 28:1-4, 22-25). Defeated by Aram and Israel (2Ki 16:5-6; 2Ch 28:5-15). Sought help from Assyria rather than the LORD (2Ki 16:7-9; 2Ch 28:16-21; Isa 7).

AHAZIAH → = JEHOAHAZ
1. Son of Ahab; king of Israel (1Ki 22:51-2Ki 1:18; 2Ch 20:35-37). Made an unsuccessful alliance with Jehoshaphat (2Ch 20:35-37). Died for seeking Baal rather than the LORD (2Ki 1).
2. Son of Jehoram; king of Judah (2Ki 8:25-29; 9:14-29), also called Jehoahaz (2Ch 21:17-22:9; 25:23). Killed by Jehu while visiting Joram (2Ki 9:14-29; 2Ch 22:1-9).

AHEAD
Mt 11:10 I am sending my messenger **a**
Php 3:13 but straining forward to what lies **a**,

AHIJAH
1. Priest during Saul's reign (1Sa 14:3,18).
2. Prophet of Shiloh (1Ki 11:29-39; 14:1-18).

AHIKAM
Father of Gedaliah (2Ki 25:22), protector of Jeremiah (Jer 26:24).

AHIMAAZ
1. Father-in-law of Saul (1Sa 14:50).
2. Son of Zadok, the high priest, loyal to David (2Sa 15:27,36; 17:17-20; 18:19-33).

AHIMELECH
1. Priest who helped David in his flight from Saul (1Sa 21-22).
2. One of David's warriors (1Sa 26:6).

AHITHOPHEL
One of David's counselors who sided with Absalom (2Sa 15:12, 31-37; 1Ch 27:33-34); committed suicide when his advice was ignored (2Sa 16:15-17:23).

AI
Jos 7: 4 they were defeated by those at **A**,

AIR
Eph 2: 2 the ruler of the power of the **a**,
1Th 4:17 the clouds to meet the Lord in the **a**.
Rev 16:17 poured out his bowl into the **a**.

ALARMED
Mk 13: 7 and reports of wars do not be **a**;
2Th 2: 2 or to be **a** either by a "spirit,"

ALEXANDER
1Ma 1: 1 After **A** the Macedonian,

ALIEN → ALIENS
Lev 19:34 You shall treat the **a** who resides
Dt 24:17 shall not violate the rights of the **a**

ALIENS → ALIEN
Ge 15:13 that your descendants shall be **a**
1Pe 2:11 I urge you as **a** and sojourners

ALIVE → LIVE
Ge 6:19 that you may keep them **a** with you.
Ac 1: 3 He presented himself **a** to them
1Th 4:17 Then we who are **a**, who are left,
Rev 1:18 but now I am **a** forever and ever.
      19:20 The two were thrown **a**

ALL
Ge 6:13 to put an end to **a** mortals on earth;
      6:13 destroy them and **a** life on earth.
Dt 6: 5 with **a** your heart, and with **a** your
      6: 5 your soul, and with **a** your strength.
Sir 7:29 With **a** your soul, fear God,
Jer 29:13 you seek me with **a** your heart,
Lk 10:27 God, with **a** your heart, with **a** your
     10:27 with **a** your strength, and with **a**
Ro 3:23 **a** have sinned and are deprived
     6:10 death, he died to sin once and for **a**;
1Co 15:51 We shall not **a** fall asleep, but we will **a** be changed,
2Co 5:15 He indeed died for **a**, so that those
Eph 1:23 the one who fills **a** things in every
Col 3:11 slave, free; but Christ is **a** and in **a**.
2Ti 3:16 **A** scripture is inspired by God and is
2Pe 3: 9 that **a** should come to repentance.
Rev 21: 5 said, "Behold, I make **a** things new."

ALMIGHTY → MIGHT
Ge 17: 1 to him and said: "I am God the **A**.
Ex 6: 3 As God the **A** I appeared
Ps 91: 1 who abide in the shadow of the **A**,
Bar 3: 1 "LORD **A**, God of Israel,
Rev 1: 8 who was and who is to come, the **a**."
     21:22 for its temple is the Lord God **a**

ALMS
Tob 12: 8 It is better to give **a** than to store
Sir 7:10 and neglect not the giving of **a**.
Mt 6: 2 When you give **a**, do not blow

ALONE → LONELY
Ge 2:18 "It is not good for the man to be **a**.
Dt 6: 4 The LORD is our God, the LORD **a**!
Isa 2:11 and the LORD **a** will be exalted,
Mk 2: 7 Who but God **a** can forgive sins?"
     10:18 good? No one is good but God **a**.
Jas 2:24 by works and not by faith **a**.

ALPHA

Rev 1: 8 "I am the **A** and the Omega,"
22:13 I am the **A** and the Omega, the first

ALTAR → ALTARS

Ge 22: 9 him, Abraham built an **a** there
22: 9 put him on top of the wood on the **a**.
Ex 27: 1 "You shall make an **a** of acacia
30: 1 burning incense you shall make an **a**
Ezr 3: 2 about rebuilding the **a** of the God
Jdt 4:12 The **a**, too, they draped in sackcloth;
1Ma 1:54 upon the **a** of holocausts,
4:47 built a new **a** like the former one.
Mt 5:24 leave your gift there at the **a**,
Heb 13:10 We have an **a** from which those
Jas 2:21 he offered his son Isaac upon the **a**?
Rev 6: 9 I saw underneath the **a** the souls

ALTARS → ALTAR

Ex 34:13 Tear down their **a**; smash their
Nu 3:31 the **a**, the utensils
1Ma 2:45 about and tore down the pagan **a**;

ALWAYS

Mt 28:20 I am with you **a**, until the end
Lk 18: 1 to pray **a** without becoming weary.
Php 4: 4 Rejoice in the Lord **a**. I shall say it

AMALEK

Ex 17: 8 **A** came and waged war against
1Sa 15: 3 attack **A**, and deal with him and all

AMASA

Nephew of David (1Ch 2:17). Commander of Absalom's forces (2Sa 17:24-27). Returned to David (2Sa 19:13). Killed by Joab (2Sa 20:4-13).

AMAZED

Mt 8:27 The men were **a** and said, "What sort
Mk 6: 6 He was **a** at their lack of faith.

AMAZIAH

1. Son of Joash; king of Judah (2Ki 14; 2Ch 25). Defeated Edom (2Ki 14:7; 2Ch 25:5-13); defeated by Israel for worshiping Edom's gods (2Ki 14:8-14; 2Ch 25:14-24).
2. Idolatrous priest; opposed Amos (Am 7:10-17).

AMBASSADOR → AMBASSADORS

Eph 6:20 for which I am an **a** in chains,

AMBASSADORS → AMBASSADOR

2Co 5:20 So we are **a** for Christ, as if God

AMBITION

Jas 3:14 and selfish **a** in your hearts, do not

AMEN

Dt 27:15 And all the people shall answer, 'A'!'

2Co 1:20 the **A** from us also goes through him
Rev 3:14 " 'The **A**, the faithful and true witness,

AMMONITES

Ge 19:38 He is the ancestor of the **A** of today.
Jer 49: 6 the lot of the **A**, says the LORD.

AMNON

Firstborn of David (2Sa 3:2; 1Ch 3:1). Killed by Absalom for raping his sister Tamar (2Sa 13).

AMON

1. Son of Manasseh; king of Judah (2Ki 21:18-26; 1Ch 3:14; 2Ch 33:21-25).
2. Ruler of Samaria (1Ki 22:26; 2Ch 18:25).

AMORITES

Ge 15:16 the **A** will not have reached its full
Nu 21:31 had settled in the land of the **A**,

AMOS

Prophet from Tekoa (Am 1:1; 7:10-17; Tob 2:6).

ANANIAS

1. Early disciple; died for lying to God (Ac 5:1-11).
2. Disciple who baptized Saul (Ac 9:10-19).
3. High priest at Paul's arrest (Ac 22:30-24:1).

ANCESTORS

Ac 5:30 The God of our **a** raised Jesus,
Heb 1: 1 ways to our **a** through the prophets;

ANCHOR

Heb 6:19 This we have as an **a** of the soul,

ANCIENT

Ps 24: 7 rise up, you **a** portals, that the king
Da 7: 9 and the **A** One took his throne.
Rev 20: 2 He seized the dragon, the **a** serpent,

ANDREW

Apostle; brother of Simon Peter (Mt 4:18; 10:2; Mk 1:16-18, 29; 3:18; 13:3; Lk 6:14; Jn 1:35-44; 6:8-9; 12:22; Ac 1:13).

ANGEL → ANGELS, ARCHANGEL

Ex 3: 2 There an **a** of the LORD appeared
23:20 I am sending an **a** before you,
Nu 22:22 the **a** of the LORD stationed himself
1Ch 21:15 also sent an **a** to destroy Jerusalem;
21:15 and said to the destroying **a**,
21:15 The **a** of the LORD was then standing
Tob 5: 4 he found the **a** Raphael standing
5: 4 not know that this was an **a** of God.
1Ma 7:41 your **a** went out and killed
Ps 34: 8 The **a** of the LORD, who encamps

Isa 37:36 The **a** of the LORD went forth
Da 3:49 the **a** of the Lord went down
3:95 who sent his **a** to deliver
13:59 "for the **a** of God waits with a sword
14:34 when an **a** of the Lord told him,
Mt 1:20 the **a** of the Lord appeared to him
Lk 1:26 the **a** Gabriel was sent from God
Ac 5:19 the **a** of the Lord opened the doors
2Co 11:14 even Satan masquerades as an **a**
Gal 1: 8 an **a** from heaven should preach

ANGELS → ANGEL

Ge 19: 1 The two **a** reached Sodom
Tob 11:14 and blessed be all his holy **a**.
Ps 103:20 Bless the LORD, all you **a**,
Mk 12:25 but they are like the **a** in heaven.
Lk 4:10 will command his **a** concerning you,
Jn 1:51 opened and the **a** of God ascending
Ac 23: 8 say that there is no resurrection or **a**
Ro 8:38 nor life, nor **a**, nor principalities,
1Co 6: 3 you not know that we will judge **a**?
Col 2:18 in self-abasement and worship of **a**,
Heb 2: 7 for a little while lower than the **a**;
1Pe 1:12 things into which **a** longed to look.
2Pe 2: 4 if God did not spare the **a** when they
Rev 1:20 the seven stars are the **a** of the seven
7: 1 this I saw four **a** standing at the four
21:12 gates where twelve **a** were stationed

ANGER → ANGRY

Ex 34: 6 slow to **a** and rich in kindness
1Ki 16:13 the god of Israel, to **a** by their idols.
Ps 30: 6 For divine **a** lasts but a moment;
Pr 12:16 The fool immediately shows his **a**,
Isa 48: 9 sake of my name I restrain my **a**,
Joel 2:13 is he, slow to **a**, rich in kindness,
Jnh 4: 2 God, slow to **a**, rich in clemency,
Mk 3: 5 Looking around at them with **a**
Eph 4:26 sin; do not let the sun set on your **a**,

ANGRY → ANGER

Jer 3:12 LORD, I will not remain **a** with you;
Mt 5:22 whoever is **a** with his brother will

ANGUISH
Zep　1:15　is that day, a day of **a** and dis-
　　　　　tress,

ANIMAL → ANIMALS
Ps　50:10　For every **a** of the forest is
　　　　　mine,

ANIMALS → ANIMAL
Ge　2:19　out of the ground various wild
　　　　　a
　　3:14　from all the **a** and from all the
　　　　　wild
　　9: 2　come upon all the **a** of the
　　　　　earth

ANNA
　　1. Prophetess; spoke of the child Jesus (Lk
2:36-38).
　　2. Wife of Tobit (Tob 1:20; 2:1, 11).

ANNAS
　　High priest A.D. 6-15 (Lk 3:2; Jn 18:13,
24; Ac 4:6).

ANOINT → ANOINTED, ANOINTING
Ex　30:30　and his sons you shall also **a**
1Sa　15: 1　to **a** you king over his people
　　　　　Israel.
Ps　23: 5　watch; You **a** my head with oil;

ANOINTED → ANOINT
1Sa　2:10　his king and exalt the horn of
　　　　　his **a**!"
　　26: 9　who can lay hands on the
　　　　　LORD's **a**
1Ch　16:22　"Touch not my **a**, and to my
　　　　　prophets
Ps　2: 2　together against the LORD and
　　　　　his **a**:
Isa　61: 1　because the LORD has **a** me; He
　　　　　has
Da　9:24　ratified, and a most holy will
　　　　　be **a**.
　　9:26　weeks an **a** shall be cut down
Zec　4:14　"These are the two **a** who stand
Lk　4:18　because he has **a** me to bring
　　　　　glad
Jn　1:41　the Messiah" (which is trans-
　　　　　lated **A**).
　　12: 3　nard and **a** the feet of Jesus

ANOINTING → ANOINT
Ex　30:25　and blend them into sacred **a**
　　　　　oil,
1Jn　2:27　the **a** that you received from
　　　　　him
　　2:27　his **a** teaches you about every-
　　　　　thing

ANOTHER
Pr　27: 2　Let **a** praise you—not your
　　　　　own
Isa　48:11　My glory I will not give to **a**.
Jn　14:16　he will give you **a** Advocate
　　　　　to be
Gal　1: 7　(not that there is **a**). But there
　　　　　are

ANSWER → ANSWERED
1Ki　18:37　**A** me, LORD! **A** me, that this
　　　　　people
Job　30:20　I cry to you, but you do not
　　　　　a me;
Pr　15: 1　A mild **a** calms wrath, but a
　　　　　harsh

Isa　65:24　Before they call, I will **a**; while
　　　　　they
Lk　23: 9　him at length, but he gave him
　　　　　no **a**.

ANSWERED → ANSWER
1Ch　21:26　he **a** him by sending down fire
Ps　118:21　I thank you for you **a** me; you
　　　　　have

ANT
Pr　6: 6　Go to the **a**, O sluggard, study
　　　　　her

ANTICHRIST
1Jn　2:18　as you heard that the **a** was
　　　　　coming,
　　2:22　the Father and the Son, this is
　　　　　the **a**.
　　4: 3　This is the spirit of the **a** that,
　　　　　as you
2Jn　1: 7　such is the deceitful one and
　　　　　the **a**.

ANTIOCH
Ac　11:26　had found him he brought him
　　　　　to **A**.
　　11:26　it was in **A** that the disciples
　　　　　were
　　13: 1　were in the church at **A**
　　　　　prophets
Gal　2:11　And when Kephas came to **A**,

ANTIOCHUS
　　Antiochus IV Epiphanes, king of the
Syrian Greeks B.C. 175-164 (1Ma 1:10-19).
Plundered the temple in Jerusalem (1Ma
1:20-28). Attempted to force the Hellenization of the Jewish people (1Ma 1:41-53), including defiling the altar and holy place
(1Ma 1:54-64). His policies sparked the
Maccabean revolt.

ANXIETIES
1Co　7:32　I should like you to be free
　　　　　of **a**.

ANYTHING
Ge　18:14　Is **a** too marvelous for the
　　　　　LORD
Jer　32:27　all mankind! Is **a** impossible to
　　　　　me?
Mt　18:19　of you agree on earth about **a**
Jn　16:23　you will not question me
　　　　　about **a**.

APART
Ro　3:21　God has been manifested **a**

APOLLOS
　　Christian from Alexandria, learned in the
Scriptures; instructed by Aquila and Priscilla
(Ac 18:24-28). At Corinth (Ac 19:1; 1Co
1:12; 3; Tit 3:13).

APOSTASY
1Ma　2:15　of enforcing the **a** came to the
　　　　　city

APOSTLE → APOSTLES
Ro　11:13　then as I am the **a** to the Gen-
　　　　　tiles,
1Co　9: 1　Am I not an **a**? Have I not seen
2Co　12:12　of an **a** were performed among
　　　　　you
Heb　3: 1　Jesus, the **a** and high priest
　　　　　of our

APOSTLES → APOSTLE
　　See also Andrew, Bartholomew, Barnabas,
James, John, Judas, Matthew, Matthias, Nathanael, Paul, Peter, Philip, Simon, Thaddaeus, Thomas.
Mt　10: 2　names of the twelve **a** are
　　　　　these:
Lk　6:13　Twelve, whom he also
　　　　　named **a**:
Ac　2:43　and signs were done through
　　　　　the **a**.
1Co　12:28　in the church to be, first, **a**;
　　　　　second,
Eph　2:20　built upon the foundation of
　　　　　the **a**
　　4:11　And he gave some as **a**,
　　　　　others as
Rev　21:14　names of the twelve **a** of the
　　　　　Lamb.

APPEAL
Ac　25:11　hand me over to them. I **a** to
　　　　　Caesar."
1Pe　3:21　an **a** to God for a clear con-
　　　　　science,

APPEAR → APPEARANCE, APPEAR-
　　　　　ANCES, APPEARED, APPEARING
Mt　24:30　of the Son of Man will **a** in
　　　　　heaven,
2Co　5:10　we must all **a** before the judg-
　　　　　ment
Heb　9:28　sins of many, will **a** a second
　　　　　time,

APPEARANCE → APPEAR
1Sa　16: 7　"Do not judge from his **a** or
　　　　　from his
　　16: 7　because man sees the **a** but the
　　　　　LORD
2Co　5:12　who boast of external **a** rather
　　　　　than

APPEARANCES → APPEAR
Jn　7:24　Stop judging by **a**, but judge
　　　　　justly."

APPEARED → APPEAR
1Co　15: 5　that he **a** to Kephas,
Heb　9:26　now once for all he has **a** at the
　　　　　end

APPEARING → APPEAR
Ac　1: 3　**a** to them during forty days

APPETITES
Ro　16:18　our Lord Christ but their
　　　　　own **a**,

APPLE
Dt　32:10　guarding them as the **a** of his
　　　　　eye.

APPOINT → APPOINTED
1Sa　8: 5　your example, **a** a king over us,
Isa　60:17　iron; I will **a** peace your gov-
　　　　　ernor,

APPOINTED → APPOINT
Mk　3:16　[he **a** the twelve:] Simon,
　　　　　whom he
Ac　3:20　send you the Messiah already **a**
Heb　9:27　Just as it is **a** that human be-
　　　　　ings die

APPROACH
Heb　4:16　So let us confidently **a** the
　　　　　throne

AQUILA

Husband of Priscilla; co-worker with Paul, instructor of Apollos (Ac 18; Ro 16:3; 1Co 16:19; 2Ti 4:19).

ARABS

1Ma 5:39 they have also hired A to help them,

ARAM → ARAMAIC, ARAMEAN

Jdg 10: 6 the gods of A, the gods of Sidon,

2Ch 16: 7 "Because you relied on the king of A

16: 7 king of A has escaped your hand,

ARAMAIC → ARAM

2Ki 18:26 "Please speak to your servants in A;

Ezr   4: 7 The document was written in A

4: 7 accompanied by a translation. [A:]

Da   2: 4 Chaldeans answered the king [A]:

ARAMEAN → ARAM

Dt   26: 5 was a wandering A who went down

ARARAT

Ge   8: 4 came to rest on the mountains of A.

ARAUNAH → = ORNAN

2Sa 24:16 the threshing floor of A the Jebusite.

ARCHANGEL → ANGEL

Jude 1: 9 Yet the a Michael, when he argued

ARCHITECT

Heb 11:10 whose a and maker is God.

AREOPAGUS

Ac   17:22 Paul stood up at the A and said:

ARGUMENT → ARGUMENTS

Lk   9:46 An a arose among the disciples

1Ti   2: 8 up holy hands, without anger or a.

ARGUMENTS → ARGUMENT

2Co 10: 4 destroying fortresses. We destroy a

Col   4: 4 one may deceive you by specious a.

ARIMATHEA

Jn   19:38 Joseph of A, secretly a disciple

ARISE → ARISES, RISE

SS   2:10 "A, my beloved, my beautiful one,

Mt   24:11 Many false prophets will a

ARISES → ARISE, RISE

1Ma 14:41 high priest until a true prophet a.

ARK

Ge   6:14 "Make yourself an a of gopherwood,

Ex   25:10 "You shall make an a of acacia

1Sa   4:11 The a of God was captured, and Eli's

1Ki   8: 9 There was nothing in the a

2Ma   2: 4 and the a should accompany him

1Pe   3:20 Noah during the building of the a,

Rev 11:19 the a of his covenant could be seen

ARM → ARMIES, ARMOR, ARMS, ARMY

Ex   6: 6 rescue you by my outstretched a

Dt   7:19 outstretched a with which the LORD,

2Ch 32: 8 For he has only an a of flesh, but we

Job 40: 9 Have you an a like that of God,

Isa 53: 1 To whom has the a of the LORD been

ARMIES → ARM

1Sa 17:36 because he has insulted the a

Lk   21:20 you see Jerusalem surrounded by a,

Rev 19:14 The a of heaven followed him,

ARMOR → ARM

Wis   5:17 He shall take his zeal for a and he

Ro   13:12 darkness [and] put on the a of light;

Eph   6:11 Put on the a of God so that you may

ARMS → ARM

Pr   31:17 with strength, and sturdy are her a.

Hos 11: 3 to walk, who took them in my a;

ARMY → ARM

Ex   15: 4 and a he hurled into the sea;

Ps   27: 3 Though an a encamp against me,

33:16 A king is not saved by a mighty a,

Rev 19:19 riding the horse and against his a.

AROMA

2Co   2:15 For we are the a of Christ for God

ARRESTED

Mt   14: 3 Now Herod had a John,

26:50 they laid hands on Jesus and a him.

ARROGANCE → ARROGANT

1Ma   1:24 after he had spoken with great a

Pr   8:13 to hate evil;] Pride, a, the evil way,

Sir 10: 7 Odious to the LORD and to men is a,

ARROGANT → ARROGANCE

Ps   73: 3 Because I was envious of the a

Da   7:11 the first of the a words

ARROW → ARROWS

Isa 49: 2 He made me a polished a, in his

ARROWS → ARROW

1Sa 20:20 day of the month I will shoot a,

Ps   64: 8 But God will shoot a at them

Eph   6:16 to quench all [the] flaming a

ARTAXERXES → = AHASUERUS

1. King of Persia; allowed rebuilding of temple under Ezra (Ezr 4; 7), and of walls of Jerusalem under his cupbearer Nehemiah (Ne 2; 5:14; 13:6).

2. See Ahasuerus.

ARTEMIS

Ac   19:27 of the great goddess A will be of no

ASA

King of Judah (1Ki 15:8-24; 1Ch 3:10; 2Ch 14-16). Godly reformer (2Ch 15); in later years defeated Israel with help of Aram, not the LORD (1Ki 15:16-22; 2Ch 16).

ASAHEL

Nephew of David, one of his warriors (2Sa 23:24; 1Ch 2:16; 11:26; 27:7). Killed by Abner (2Sa 2); avenged by Joab (2Sa 3:22-39).

ASAPH

1. Recorder to Hezekiah (2Ki 18:18, 37; Isa 36:3, 22).

2. Levitical musician (1Ch 6:39; 15:17-19; 16:4-7, 37), seer (2Ch 29:30). Sons of (1Ch 25; 2Ch 5:12; 20:14; 29:13; 35:15; Ezr 2:41; 3:10; Ne 7:44; 11:17; 12:27-47). Psalms of (2Ch 29:30; Ps 50; 73-83).

ASCEND → ASCENDING, ASCENTS

Ps 139: 8 If I a to the heavens, you are there;

ASCENDING → ASCEND

Jn   1:51 the angels of God a and descending

ASCENTS → ASCEND

Songs of ascents (Ps 120-134).

ASHAMED → SHAME

Isa 29:22 Jacob shall have nothing to be a of,

Mk   8:38 Whoever is a of me and of my

8:38 the Son of Man will be a

Ro   1:16 For I am not a of the gospel. It is

Heb   2:11 he is not a to call them "brothers,"

11:16 God is not a to be called their God,

ASHER

Son of Jacob by Zilpah (Ge 30:13; 35:26; 46:17; Ex 1:4; 1Ch 2:2). Tribe of blessed (Ge 49:20; Dt 33:24-25), numbered (Nu 1:40-41; 26:44-47), allotted land (Jos 10:24-31; Eze 48:2), failed to fully possess (Jdg 1:31-32), failed to support Deborah (Jdg 5:17), supported Gideon (Jdg 6:35; 7:23) and David (1Ch 12:36), 12,000 from (Rev 7:6).

ASHERAH → ASHERAHS, ASTARTE

1Ki 18:19 four hundred prophets of A who eat

2Ch 15:16 made an outrageous object for A;

ASHERAHS → ASHERAH

Jdg   3: 7 and serving the Baals and the A,

ASHES

Ge   18:27 Lord, though I am but dust and a!

ASHES (*cont.*)
Jdt 4:11 with a strewn on their heads,
Est 4: 1 put on sackcloth and **a**, and walked
Job 42: 6 have said, and repent in dust and **a**.
Jnh 3: 6 with sackcloth, and sat in the **a**.
Mt 11:21 have repented in sackcloth and **a**.

ASIA
Ac 16: 6 the message in the province of **A**.
Rev 1: 4 John, to the seven churches in **A**:

ASIDE → SIDE
Ex 32: 8 They have soon turned **a**
Dt 28:14 not turning **a** to the right

ASK
Ps 2: 8 Only **a** it of me, and I will make
Mt 6: 8 what you need before you **a** him.
   7: 7 "A and it will be given to you;
Jn 16:24 **a** and you will receive, so that your
Jas 4: 3 You **a** but do not receive,
   4: 3 because you **a** wrongly, to spend it
1Jn 5:14 if we **a** anything according to his

ASLEEP → SLEEP
Jnh 1: 5 hold of the ship, and lay there fast **a**.
Mt 8:24 swamped by waves; but he was **a**.

ASSEMBLE → ASSEMBLY
Zep 3: 8 to **a** the kingdoms, In order to pour
Rev 16:14 of the whole world to **a** them

ASSEMBLY → ASSEMBLE
Ne 8: 2 priest brought the law before the **a**,
Ps 149: 1 song, a hymn in the **a** of the faithful.
Heb 12:23 and the **a** of the firstborn enrolled

ASSIGNED
1Co 3: 5 just as the Lord **a** each one.
   7:17 should live as the Lord has **a**, just as

ASSYRIA
2Ki 18:11 The king of **A** then deported
   18:11 then deported the Israelites to **A**
Jer 50:18 as once I punished the king of **A**;

ASTARTE → ASHERAH
1Ki 11: 5 By adoring **A**, the goddess

ASTONISHED
Lk 2:48 they were **a**, and his mother said

ASTRAY → STRAY
Dt 30:17 but are led **a** and adore and serve
Isa 53: 6 We had all gone **a** like sheep,
Mt 18:12 sheep and one of them goes **a**,
1Pe 2:25 For you had gone **a** like sheep,

ATE → EAT
Ge 3: 6 she took some of its fruit and **a** it;
   3: 6 who was with her, and he **a** it.
Ex 16:35 The Israelites **a** this manna for forty
   16:35 they **a** manna until they reached
Ps 78:25 All **a** a meal fit for heroes; food he
Eze 3: 3 I **a** it, and it was as sweet as honey
Mt 14:20 They all **a** and were satisfied,
   15:37 They all **a** and were satisfied.

ATHALIAH
Granddaughter of Omri; wife of Jehoram and mother of Ahaziah; encouraged their evil ways (2Ki 8:18, 27; 2Ch 22:2). At death of Ahaziah she made herself queen, killing all his sons but Joash (2Ki 11:1-3; 2Ch 22:10-12); killed six years later when Joash revealed (2Ki 11:4-16; 2Ch 23:1-15).

ATHLETE
2Ti 2: 5 an **a** cannot receive the winner's

ATONEMENT → ATONES
Ex 29:36 day as a sin offering, to make **a**.
   29:36 purge the altar in making **a** for it;
   30:10 a year Aaron shall perform the **a** rite
   30:10 your generations this **a** is to be
   32:30 may be able to make **a** for your sin."
Lev 23:28 because it is the Day of **A**, when **a** is

ATONES → ATONEMENT
Sir 3: 3 He who honors his father **a** for sins;

ATTAIN → ATTAINED
Pr 8:12 and judicious knowledge I **a**.
Php 3:11 if somehow I may **a** the resurrection

ATTAINED → ATTAIN
Php 3:16 with regard to what we have **a**,

AUTHOR
Ac 3:15 The **a** of life you put to death,

AUTHORITIES → AUTHORITY
Ro 13: 1 be subordinate to the higher **a**,

AUTHORITY → AUTHORITIES
Mk 1:27 is this? A new teaching with **a**.
Lk 5:24 the Son of Man has **a** on earth
Ro 13: 1 for there is no **a** except from God,
1Co 11:10 a woman should have a sign of **a**
1Ti 2:12 to teach or to have **a** over a man.
Rev 12:10 and the **a** of his Anointed.

AVENGE → VENGEANCE
1Ma 2:67 and you shall **a** the wrongs of your
Rev 6:10 **a** our blood on the inhabitants

AVENGER → VENGEANCE
Nu 35:12 of asylum from the **a** of blood,
Ps 8: 3 your foes, to silence enemy and **a**.
1Th 4: 6 the Lord is an **a** in all these things,

AVENGES → VENGEANCE
Dt 32:43 For he **a** the blood of his servants

AVENGING → VENGEANCE
Na 1: 2 A jealous and **a** God is the LORD,

AVOID → AVOIDS
2Ti 2:16 A profane, idle talk, for such people
Tit 3: 9 A foolish arguments, genealogies,

AVOIDS → AVOID
Pr 16: 6 by the fear of the LORD man **a** evil.

AWAKE
Ps 44:24 A! Why do you sleep, O Lord?
   57: 9 A, my soul; **a**, lyre and harp! I will
Isa 51: 9 A, **a**, put on strength, O arm
   51: 9 of the LORD! A as in the days of old,
Da 12: 2 sleep in the dust of the earth shall **a**;
Eph 5:14 Therefore, it says: "A, O sleeper,

AWE → AWESOME
Isa 29:23 and be in **a** of the God of Israel.
Mt 9: 8 saw this they were struck with **a**
Ac 2:43 A came upon everyone, and many
Ro 11:20 not become haughty, but stand in **a**.

AWESOME → AWE
Dt 10:17 mighty and **a**, who has no favorites,
Ne 1: 5 great and **a** God, you who preserve
Ps 65: 6 You answer us with **a** deeds
   68:36 A is God in his holy place, the God
Da 9: 4 great and **a** God, you who keep your

AX
Mt 3:10 Even now the **a** lies at the root

AZARIAH → = ABEDNEGO, = UZZIAH
1. King of Judah; see Uzziah (2Ki 15:1-7).
2. Prophet (2Ch 15:1-8).
3. Opponent of Jeremiah (Jer 43:2).
4. Jewish exile; see Abednego (Da 1:6-19).

AZAZEL
Lev 16: 8 one is for the LORD and which for **A**.

B

BAAL → BAALS
Nu 25: 3 submitted to the rites of **B** of Peor,

Jdg   2:13   him and served **B** and the Ashtaroth,

1Ki   18:25   Elijah then said to the prophets of **B**,

     19:18   those who have not knelt to **B**

Jer   2: 8   The prophets prophesied by **B**,

Ro   11: 4   men who have not knelt to **B**."

BAALS → BAAL

Jdg   3: 7   and serving the **B** and the Asherahs,

1Sa   7: 4   So the Israelites put away their **B**

BAASHA

   King of Israel (1Ki 15:16-16:7; 2Ch 16:1-6).

BABEL → BABYLON

Ge   11: 9   That is why it was called **B**,

BABES

Ps   8: 3   Out of the mouths of **b** and infants

BABYLON → BABEL

2Ki   24:15   He deported Jehoiachin to **B**,

     24:15   Jerusalem to **B** the king's mother

Ps   137: 1   By the rivers of **B** we sat mourning

Isa   14: 4   taunt-song against the king of **B**:

     21: 9   says, 'Fallen, fallen is **B**, And all

Jer   25:11   shall be enslaved to the king of **B**:

Da   14:36   he set him down in **B** above the den.

1Pe   5:13   chosen one at **B** sends you greeting,

Rev   14: 8   "Fallen, fallen is **B** the great,

BACK

Ge   19:26   But Lot's wife looked **b**, and she was

BAD

Pr   20:14   "**B**, **b**!" says the buyer; but once he

Mt   7:17   fruit, and a rotten tree bears **b** fruit.

1Co   15:33   "**B** company corrupts good morals."

BALAAM

   Prophet who attempted to curse Israel (Nu 22-24; Dt 23:4-5; 2Pe 2:15; Jude 11; Rev 2:14). Killed in Israel's vengeance on Midianites (Nu 31:8; Jos 13:22).

BALAK

   Moabite king who hired Balaam to curse Israel (Nu 22-24; Jos 24:9; Mic 6:5).

BALANCE

Isa   40:12   in scales and the hills in a **b**?

BALM

Jer   8:22   Is there no **b** in Gilead, no physician

BAPTISM → BAPTIZE

Mk   1: 4   in the desert proclaiming a **b**

     10:38   be baptized with the **b** with which I

Lk   20: 4   was John's **b** of heavenly

Ac   18:25   although he knew only the **b**

Ac   19: 3   They replied, "With the **b** of John."

Ro   6: 4   with him through **b** into death,

Eph   4: 5   one Lord, one faith, one **b**;

Col   2:12   You were buried with him in **b**,

1Pe   3:21   This prefigured **b**, which saves you

BAPTISMS → BAPTIZE

Heb   6: 2   instruction about **b** and laying

BAPTIST → BAPTIZE

Mt   3: 1   In those days John the **B** appeared,

     11:11   been none greater than John the **B**;

     14: 8   on a platter the head of John the **B**."

     16:14   "Some say John the **B**, others Elijah,

BAPTIZE → BAPTISM, BAPTISMS, BAPTIST, BAPTIZED, BAPTIZING

Mt   3:11   He will **b** you with the holy Spirit

Lk   3:16   He will **b** you with the holy Spirit

1Co   1:17   For Christ did not send me to **b**

BAPTIZED → BAPTIZE

Mt   3:13   to John at the Jordan to be **b** by him.

Ac   1: 5   for John **b** with water, but in a few

     1: 5   in a few days you will be **b**

     2:38   "Repent and be **b**, every one of you,

Ro   6: 3   we who were **b** into Christ Jesus

     6: 3   Christ Jesus were **b** into his death?

1Co   10: 2   all of them were **b** into Moses

     12:13   in one Spirit we were all **b** into one

BAPTIZING → BAPTIZE

Mt   28:19   **b** them in the name of the Father,

Jn   4: 1   and **b** more disciples than John

BARABBAS

   Prisoner released by Pilate instead of Jesus (Mt 27:16-26; Mk 15:7-15; Lk 23:18-19; Jn 18:40).

BARAK

   Judge who fought with Deborah against Canaanites (Jdg 4-5; 1Sa 12:11; Heb 11:32).

BARBARIAN

Col   3:11   circumcision and uncircumcision, **b**,

BARBS

Nu   33:55   to remain will become as **b** in your

BARE → BARED

Ps   18:16   the world's foundations lay **b**,

BARED → BARE

Isa   52:10   The LORD has **b** his holy arm

BARN → BARNS

Lk   12:24   they have neither storehouse nor **b**,

BARNABAS → = JOSEPH

   Disciple, originally Joseph (Ac 4:36), prophet (Ac 13:1), apostle (Ac 14:14). Brought Paul to apostles (Ac 9:27), Antioch (Ac 11:22-29; Gal 2:1-13), on the first missionary journey (Ac 13-14). Together at Jerusalem Council, they separated over John Mark (Ac 15). Later co-workers (1Co 9:6; Col 4:10).

BARNS → BARN

Dt   28: 8   upon you, on your **b** and on all your

Ps   144:13   May our **b** be full with every kind

Lk   12:18   do: I shall tear down my **b** and build

BARREN

Ge   11:30   Sarai was **b**; she had no child.

Ex   23:26   no woman in your land will be **b**

1Sa   2: 5   spoil. The **b** wife bears seven sons,

Isa   54: 1   cry, you **b** one who did not bear,

Lk   1: 7   because Elizabeth was **b** and both

BARTHOLOMEW → = NATHANAEL?

   Apostle (Mt 10:3; Mk 3:18; Lk 6:14; Ac 1:13). Possibly also called Nathanael (Jn 1:45-49; 21:2).

BARUCH

   Jeremiah's secretary (Jer 32:12-16; 36; 43:1-6; 45:1-2). Deuterocanonical book ascribed to (Bar 1:1, 3, 8).

BARZILLAI

   1. Gileadite who aided David during Absalom's revolt (2Sa 17:27; 19:31-39).

   2. Son-in-law of 1. (Ezr 2:61; Ne 7:63).

BASHAN

Nu   21:33   and went up along the road to **B**.

     21:33   king of **B**, advanced against them

Ps   22:13   me; fierce bulls of **B** encircle me.

Mic   7:14   Let them feed in **B** and Gilead,

BASIN

Jn   13: 5   he poured water into a **b** and began

BASKET

Ex   2: 3   she took a papyrus **b**, daubed it

Mt   5:15   and then put it under a bushel **b**; it is

Ac   9:25   in the wall, lowering him in a **b**.

BATHING

2Sa   11: 2   From the roof he saw a woman **b**,

BATHSHEBA

   Wife of Uriah; committed adultery with and married David (2Sa 11; Ps 51), mother of Solomon (2Sa 12:24; 1Ki 1-2; 1Ch 3:5).

BATTLE

1Sa   17:47   For the **b** is the LORD'S, and he shall

2Ch   20:15   for the **b** is not yours but God's.

BATTLE (*cont.*)
Ps 24: 8 warrior, the LORD, mighty in **b**.
Ecc 9:11 the swift, nor the **b** by the valiant,
Rev 16:14 them for the **b** on the great day
    20: 8 and Magog, to gather them for **b**;

BEAR → BEARS, BIRTH, BIRTHRIGHT, BORE, BORN, CHILDBEARING, FIRSTBORN
Ge 4:13 "My punishment is too great t o **b**.
    17:19 your wife Sarah is to **b** you a son,
Isa 7:14 and **b** a son, and shall name him
Mt 1:23 shall be with child and **b** a son,
    7:18 A good tree cannot **b** bad fruit,
    7:18 nor can a rotten tree **b** good fruit.
Jn 15: 2 branch in me that does not **b** fruit,
Gal 6: 2 **B** one another's burdens, and so you

BEARS → BEAR
1Co 13: 7 It **b** all things, believes all things,

BEAST → BEASTS
Rev 11: 7 the **b** that comes up from the abyss
    13:18 can calculate the number of the **b**,
    16: 2 on those who had the mark of the **b**
    19:20 The **b** was caught and with it
    19:20 who had accepted the mark of the **b**

BEASTS → BEAST
Da 7: 3 which emerged four immense **b**,
Mk 1:13 He was among wild **b**,

BEAT → BEATEN, BEATING
Isa 2: 4 They shall **b** their swords

BEATEN → BEAT
2Co 11:25 Three times I was **b** with rods,
1Pe 2:20 if you are patient when **b** for doing

BEATING → BEAT
Lk 22:63 custody were ridiculing and **b** him.

BEAUTIFUL → BEAUTY
Ge 12:11 "I know well how **b** a woman you
Tob 6:12 is sensible, courageous, and very **b**;
Job 42:15 women were as **b** as the daughters
Isa 52: 7 How **b** upon the mountains
Da 13: 2 who married a very **b**
Ac 3: 2 temple called "the **B** Gate" every day
Ro 10:15 "How **b** are the feet of those who

BEAUTY → BEAUTIFUL
2Sa 14:25 so be praised for his **b** as Absalom,
Jdt 16: 9 and her **b** captivated his mind.

1Ma 2:12 We see our sanctuary and our **b**
Ps 27: 4 To gaze on the LORD's **b**, to visit his
Pr 6:25 Lust not in your heart after her **b**,
    31:30 Charm is deceptive and **b** fleeting;
Wis 13: 3 in their **b** they thought them gods,
    13: 3 original source of **b** fashioned them.
Sir 9: 8 gaze not upon the **b** of another's wife—
    9: 8 Through woman's **b** many perish,
Da 13:56 said to him, "**b** has seduced you,
1Pe 3: 4 in the imperishable **b** of a gentle

BED → BEDS
Ge 47:31 Israel bowed at the head of the **b**.
Heb 13: 4 the marriage **b** be kept undefiled,

BEDS → BED
Ps 36: 5 In their **b** they hatch plots; they set

BEE → BEES
Sir 11: 3 Least is the **b** among winged things,
Isa 7:18 and for the **b** in the land of Assyria.

BEER-SHEBA
Ge 21:31 This is why the place is called **B**;
1Sa 3:20 Israel from Dan to **B** came to know

BEES → BEE
Jdg 14: 8 found a swarm of **b** and honey

BEFORE
Ex 33: 2 Jebusites, I will send an angel **b** you
Isa 43:10 that it is I. **B** me no god was formed,
    65:24 **B** they call, I will answer;
Mal 3: 1 to prepare the way **b** me;
Mt 6: 8 what you need **b** you ask him.
Lk 22:61 said to him, "**B** the cock crows today,
Heb 12: 2 that lay **b** him he endured the cross,

BEGGAR
Jn 9: 8 had seen him earlier as a **b** said,

BEGINNING
Ge 1: 1 In the **b**, when God created
Ps 111:10 fear of the LORD is the **b** of wisdom;
Pr 1: 7 of the LORD is the **b** of knowledge;
Ecc 7: 8 is the end of speech than its **b**;
Isa 40:21 Was it not foretold you from the **b**?
Mt 24: 8 All these are the **b** of the labor
Jn 1: 1 In the **b** was the Word,
1Jn 1: 1 What was from the **b**, what we have
2Jn 1: 6 as you heard from the **b**,

Rev 21: 6 and the Omega, the **b** and the end.

BEGOTTEN
Ac 13:33 are my son; this day I have **b** you.'
Heb 1: 5 are my son; this day I have **b** you"?

BEHEADED → HEAD
Lk 9: 9 But Herod said, "John I **b**.
Rev 20: 4 of those who had been **b** for their

BEHEMOTH
Job 40:15 See, besides you I made **B**,

BEHIND
Isa 38:17 When you cast **b** your back all my
Mt 16:23 turned and said to Peter, "Get **b** me,
Php 3:13 forgetting what lies **b** but straining

BEING
Ge 2: 7 life, and so man became a living **b**.
1Co 15:45 became a living **b**," the last Adam
Heb 1: 3 the very imprint of his **b**, and who

BEL
  Babylonian deity (Isa 46:1; Jer 50:2; 51:44; Bar 6:40; Da 14:3-28).

BELIEF → BELIEVE
2Th 2:13 by the Spirit and **b** in truth.

BELIEVE → BELIEF, BELIEVED, BELIEVER, BELIEVES
Ex 4: 5 will take place so that they may **b**,"
Nu 14:11 How long will they refuse to **b**
Jer 12: 6 you. Do not **b** them, even if they are
Mt 18: 6 one of these little ones who **b** in me
    24:23 Messiah!' or, 'There he is!' do not **b** it.
Mk 1:15 at hand. Repent, and **b** in the gospel."
    9:24 cried out, "I do **b**, help my unbelief!"
Lk 24:25 of heart to **b** all that the prophets
Jn 1: 7 so that all might **b** through him.
    3:18 but whoever does not **b** has already
    6:29 God, that you **b** in the one he sent."
    10:38 them, even if you do not **b** me,
    17:20 those who will **b** in me through their
    20:29 to **b** because you have seen me?
Ac 16:31 "**B** in the Lord Jesus and you
    28:24 he had said, while others did not **b**.
Ro 3:22 faith in Jesus Christ for all who **b**.
    10: 9 **b** in your heart that God raised him

1Th 4:14 For if we **b** that Jesus died and rose,

Heb 11: 6 anyone who approaches God must **b**

Jas 2:19 You **b** that God is one. You do well.

2:19 do well. Even the demons **b**

1Pe 1: 8 you do not see him now yet **b**

Jude 1: 5 later destroyed those who did not **b**.

BELIEVED → BELIEVE

Ex 14:31 they feared the LORD and **b** in him

Jdt 14:10 of Israel had done, **b** firmly in him.

Jn 12:38 "Lord, who has **b** our preaching,

20: 8 at the tomb first, and he saw and **b**.

Ac 2:44 All who **b** were together and had all

Ro 4: 3 "Abraham **b** God, and it was credited

10:16 who has **b** what was heard from us?"

2Co 4:13 is written, "I **b**, therefore I spoke,"

Gal 3: 6 Thus Abraham "**b** God, and it was

1Ti 3:16 Gentiles, **b** in throughout the world,

Heb 4: 3 For we who **b** enter into [that] rest,

Jas 2:23 fulfilled that says, "Abraham **b** God,

BELIEVER → BELIEVE

2Co 6:15 Or what has a **b** in common

BELIEVES → BELIEVE

Pr 14:15 The simpleton **b** everything,

Jn 3:15 everyone who **b** in him may have

11:26 lives and **b** in me will never die.

Ro 9:33 whoever **b** in him shall not be put

10:10 For one **b** with the heart and so is

1Co 13: 7 It bears all things, **b** all things,

BELLY

Ge 3:14 On your **b** shall you crawl, and dirt

Lev 11:42 Whether it crawls on its **b**,

Mt 12:40 was in the **b** of the whale three days

BELONG → BELONGS

Jn 10:16 sheep that do not **b** to this fold.

15:19 because you do not **b** to the world,

1Co 12:15 "Because I am not a hand I do not **b**

12:15 it does not for this reason **b** any less

BELONGS → BELONG

Ps 22:29 For kingship **b** to the LORD, the ruler

62:12 I have heard: Power **b** to God;

BELOVED → LOVE

Mt 3:17 "This is my **b** Son, with whom I am

Mt 12:18 chosen, my **b** in whom I delight;

17: 5 "This is my **b** Son, with whom I am

Col 3:12 holy and **b**, heartfelt compassion,

Rev 20: 9 of the holy ones and the **b** city.

BELSHAZZAR
King of Babylon (Da 5; Bar 1:11-12).

BELT

1Sa 18: 4 and his sword, his bow and his **b**.

Isa 11: 5 and faithfulness a **b** upon his hips.

Mk 1: 6 with a leather **b** around his waist.

BELTESHAZZAR → See DANIEL

BEN-HADAD
1. King of Syria in time of Asa (1Ki 15:18-20; 2Ch 16:2-4).
2. King of Syria in time of Ahab (1Ki 20; 2Ki 6:24; 8:7-15).
3. King of Syria in time of Jehoahaz (2Ki 13:3, 24-25; Jer 49:27; Am 1:4).

BENAIAH
A commander of David's army (2Sa 8:18; 20:23; 23:20-30); loyal to Solomon (1Ki 1:8-2:46; 4:4).

BEND → BENT

Php 2:10 every knee should **b**, of those

BENEFICIAL → BENEFIT

1Co 6:12 for me," but not everything is **b**.

10:23 is lawful," but not everything is **b**.

BENEFIT

Gal 5: 2 Christ will be of no **b** to you.

BENJAMIN → BENJAMINITE
Twelfth son of Jacob by Rachel (Ge 35:16-24; 46:19-21; 1Ch 2:2). Jacob refused to send him to Egypt, but relented (Ge 42-45). Tribe of blessed (Ge 49:27; Dt 33:12), numbered (Nu 1:37; 26:41), allotted land (Jos 18:11-28; Eze 48:23), failed to fully possess (Jdg 1:21), nearly obliterated (Jdg 20-21), sided with Ish-Bosheth (2Sa 2), but turned to David (1Ch 12:2, 29). 12,000 from (Rev 7:8).

BENJAMINITE → BENJAMIN

Jdg 3:15 up for them a savior, the **B** Ehud,

1Sa 9:21 "Am I not a **B**, of one of the smallest

BENT → BEND

Jn 8: 6 Jesus **b** down and began to write

20: 5 he **b** down and saw the burial cloths

BEREAVES

La 1:20 In the streets the sword **b**, at home

BESIDES

Wis 12:13 is there any god **b** you who have

Isa 45:21 **b** whom there is no other God?

Da 14:41 Daniel, and there is no other **b** you!"

BEST → GOOD

Dt 33:21 He saw that the **b** should be his

BETHANY

Mt 26: 6 when Jesus was in **B** in the house

Jn 11: 1 Lazarus from **B**, the village of Mary

BETHEL

Ge 12: 8 on to the hill country east of **B**,

12: 8 pitching his tent with **B** to the west

28:19 He called that site **B**,

1Sa 7:16 passing through **B**,

BETHLEHEM

Ru 4:11 in Ephrathah and win fame in **B**.

1Sa 17:12 Jesse, who was from **B** in Judah.

Mt 2: 1 When Jesus was born in **B** of Judea,

Lk 2:15 to **B** to see this thing that has taken

BETRAY

Jn 13:11 For he knew who would **b** him;

BETTER → GOOD

1Sa 15:22 LORD? Obedience is **b** than sacrifice,

Tob 12: 8 but **b** than either is almsgiving

12: 8 righteousness is **b** than abundance.

12: 8 It is **b** to give alms than to store

Ps 63: 4 For your love is **b** than life; my lips

Pr 15:16 **B** a little with fear of the LORD

27: 5 **B** is an open rebuke than a love

Ecc 2:24 There is nothing **b** for man than

9: 4 a live dog is **b** off than a dead lion.

Sir 40:26 but **b** than either, fear of God.

Da 1:20 found them ten times **b** than all

Mt 5:29 It is **b** for you to lose one of your

Mk 14:21 would be **b** for that man if he had

Jn 11:50 do you consider that it is **b** for you

Php 1:23 be with Christ, [for] that is far **b**.

Heb 7:22 guarantee of an [even] **b** covenant.

9:23 by **b** sacrifices than these.

1Pe 3:17 For it is **b** to suffer for doing good,

BETWEEN

Ge 3:15 I will put enmity **b** you

3:15 and **b** your offspring and hers;

9:13 serve as a sign of the covenant **b** me

16: 5 May the LORD decide **b** you and me!"

Isa 2: 4 He shall judge **b** the nations,

Eze 34:17 GOD, I will judge **b** one sheep

34:17 and another, **b** rams and goats.

Ro 10:12 For there is no distinction **b** Jew

BETWEEN (*cont.*)
1Ti   2: 5 one mediator **b** God and the human

BEWARE
Ecc 12:12 As to more than these, my son, **b**.
Php   3: 2 **B** of the dogs!
        3: 2 evil-workers! **B** of the mutilation!

BEYOND
Ps 147: 5 in power, with wisdom **b** measure.
2Co 4:17 weight of glory **b** all comparison,

BEZALEL
Judahite craftsman in charge of building the tabernacle (Ex 31:1-11; 35:30-39:31).

BILDAD
One of Job's friends (Job 2:11; 8; 18; 25; 42:9).

BILHAH
Servant of Rachel, mother of Jacob's sons Da and Naphtali (Ge 30:1-7; 35:25; 46:23-25).

BIND → BINDS
Dt   6: 8 **B** them at your wrist as a sign
Mt 16:19 Whatever you **b** on earth shall be

BINDS → BIND
Job 5:18 For he wounds, but he **b** up;

BIRD → BIRDS
Lev 20:25 the uncleanness of any beast or **b**

BIRDS → BIRD
Ge 1:21 teems, and all kinds of winged **b**.
      1:22 and let the **b** multiply on the earth."
      7: 3 and of all the unclean **b**, one pair,
Jer 7:33 will be food for the **b** of the sky
Mt 6:26 Look at the **b** in the sky; they do not
Rev 19:21 all the **b** gorged themselves on their

BIRTH → BEAR
Dt 32:18 forgot the God who gave you **b**.
Ps 22:11 the womb; since **b** you are my God.
Jas 1:18 He willed to give us **b** by the word
1Pe 1: 3 his great mercy gave us a new **b**

BIRTHRIGHT → BEAR, RIGHT
Ge 25:34 his way. Esau cared little for his **b**.
Heb 12:16 who sold his **b** for a single meal.

BISHOP
1Ti   3: 1 the office of **b** desires a noble task.
Tit   1: 7 For a **b** as God's steward must be

BIT → BITE, BITS
Ps 32: 9 with **b** and bridle their temper is

BITE → BIT
Sir 21: 2 that will **b** you if you go near it;

BITS → BIT
Jas   3: 3 If we put **b** into the mouths

BITTER → BITTERNESS
Ex 1:14 making life **b** for them with hard
   12: 8 with unleavened bread and **b** herbs.
  15:23 the water, because it was too **b**.
Ru 1:13 my lot is too **b** for you,
Rev 8:11 this water, because it was made **b**.

BITTERNESS → BITTER
Pr 14:10 The heart knows its own **b**,
Eph 4:31 All **b**, fury, anger, shouting,

BLACK
Zec 6: 2 horses, the second chariot **b** horses,
Mt 5:36 make a single hair white or **b**.
Rev 6: 5 and there was a **b** horse, and its

BLAMELESS
Ge 17: 1 Walk in my presence and be **b**.
1Ma 4:42 He chose **b** priests,
Job 1: 1 In the land of Uz there was a **b**
Ps 37:18 LORD watches over the days of the **b**;
Php 2:15 that you may be **b** and innocent,
1Th 5:23 be preserved **b** for the coming
Tit   1: 7 a bishop as God's steward must be **b**,

BLASPHEME → BLASPHEMED, BLASPHEMER, BLASPHEMES, BLASPHEMIES, BLASPHEMOUS
Ac 26:11 in an attempt to force them to **b**;
1Ti 1:20 over to Satan to be taught not to **b**.

BLASPHEMED → BLASPHEME
Eze 20:27 In this way also your fathers **b** me,
Mt 26:65 tore his robes and said, "He has **b**!

BLASPHEMER → BLASPHEME
Sir   3:16 A **b** is he who despises his father;
1Ti 1:13 I was once a **b** and a persecutor

BLASPHEMES → BLASPHEME
Lev 24:16 whoever **b** the name of the LORD
Lk 12:10 but the one who **b** against the holy

BLASPHEMIES → BLASPHEME
Mk   3:28 and all **b** that people utter will be
Rev 13: 6 its mouth to utter **b** against God,

BLASPHEMOUS → BLASPHEME
Ac   6:11 heard him speaking **b** words against
Rev 13: 1 and on its heads **b** name[s].

BLAZING
Heb 12:18 which could be touched and a **b** fire

BLEMISH
Ex 12: 5 be a year-old male and without **b**.
Eph 5:27 she might be holy and without **b**.

BLESS → BLESSED, BLESSING, BLESSINGS
Ge 12: 2 and I will **b** you; I will make your
  17:16 I will **b** her, and I will give you
  17:16 Him also will I **b**; he shall give rise
  22:17 I will **b** you abundantly and make
  26: 3 and I will be with you and **b** you;
Ex 20:24 name I will come to you and **b** you.
Nu 6:24 The LORD **b** you and keep you!
Dt 7:13 He will love and **b** and multiply
   7:13 he will **b** the fruit of your womb
  30:16 God, will **b** you in the land you are
1Ch 29:20 "Now **b** the LORD your God!"
Tob 4:19 At all times **b** the Lord God, and ask
Ps 5:13 For you, LORD, **b** the just;
  29:11 may the LORD **b** his people
  34: 2 I will **b** the LORD at all times;
  103: 1 Of David. **B** the LORD, my soul;
  103: 1 soul; all my being, **b** his holy name!
  109:28 Though they curse, may you **b**;
Hag 2:19 yet borne. From this day, I will **b**!
Lk   6:28 **b** those who curse you,
Ro 12:14 **B** those who persecute [you],
1Co 4:12 hands. When ridiculed, we **b**;
Jas   3: 9 With it we **b** the Lord and Father,

BLESSED → BLESS
Ge 1:22 and God **b** them, saying, "Be fertile,
   2: 3 So God **b** the seventh day and made
  14:19 "**B** be Abram by God Most High,
Nu 24: 9 him? **B** is he who blesses you,
Tob 3:11 be you, O Lord, merciful God!
   3:11 Forever **b** and honored is your holy
Jdt 13:17 saying with one accord, "**B** are you,
Job 1:21 away; **b** be the name of the LORD!"
  42:12 Thus the LORD **b** the latter days
Ps 118:26 **B** is he who comes in the name
Isa 30:18 justice: **b** are all who wait for him!
Jer 17: 7 **B** is the man who trusts in the LORD,
Da 3:26 "**B** are you, and praiseworthy,
Mt 5: 3 "**B** are the poor in spirit, for theirs is

Mt 16:17 said to him in reply, "**B** are you,

Mk 10:16 Then he embraced them and **b** them,

Lk   1:42 said, "Most **b** are you among women,

       1:42 and **b** is the fruit of your womb.

       6:20 he said: "**B** are you who are poor,

Jn 12:13 **B** is he who comes in the name

    20:29 **B** are those who have not seen

Ac 20:35 'It is more **b** to give than to receive.' "

Gal   3: 8 you shall all the nations be **b**."

Eph   1: 3 **B** be the God and Father of our Lord

       1: 3 who has **b** us in Christ with every

1Pe   3:14 because of righteousness, **b** are you.

Rev   1: 3 **B** is the one who reads aloud and **b**

    22: 7 soon." **B** is the one who keeps

BLESSING → BLESS

Ge 12: 2 name great, so that you will be a **b**.

    22:18 all the nations of the earth shall find **b**—

    27:36 and now he has taken away my **b**."

    27:36 "Haven't you saved a **b** for me?"

Nu 23:20 It is a **b** I have been given

    23:20 a **b** which I cannot restrain.

Dt 11:26 you here, this day, a **b** and a curse:

Ne 13: 2 our God turned the curse into a **b**."

Tob   8:15 O God, with every holy and pure **b**!

Eze 34:26 rains that shall be a **b** to them.

Mal   3:10 to pour down **b** upon you without

Mk 14:22 he took bread, said the **b**, broke it,

1Co 10:16 The cup of **b** that we bless, is it not

Gal   3:14 that the **b** of Abraham might be

Eph   1: 3 every spiritual **b** in the heavens,

Rev   5:12 and strength, honor and glory and **b**."

     7:12 "Amen. **B** and glory,

BLESSINGS → BLESS

Dt 28: 2 all these **b** will come upon you

Jos   8:34 of the law, the **b** and the curses,

Ps 21: 7 make him the pattern of **b** forever,

Pr 10: 6 **B** are for the head of the just,

Ro 15:27 come to share in their spiritual **b**,

    15:27 also to serve them in material **b**.

BLIND → BLINDED, BLINDNESS

Ex   4:11 sight to one and makes another **b**?

Dt 27:18 'Cursed be he who misleads a **b** man

Ps 146: 8 the Lᴏʀᴅ gives sight to the **b**.

Isa 35: 5 will the eyes of the **b** be opened,

    42:19 Who is **b** but my servant, or deaf

Mt 11: 5 the **b** regain their sight, the lame

Lk   6:39 "Can a **b** person guide a **b** person?

Jn   9:25 One thing I do know is that I was **b**

Ro   2:19 that you are a guide for the **b**

2Pe   1: 9 Anyone who lacks them is **b**

BLINDED → BLIND

Jn 12:40 "He **b** their eyes and hardened their

2Co   4: 4 of this age has **b** the minds

BLINDNESS → BLIND

Dt 28:28 you with madness, **b** and panic,

BLOCK

Sir 31: 7 It is a stumbling **b** to those who are

Isa 44:19 of the rest, or worship a **b** of wood?"

Ro 11: 9 a stumbling **b** and a retribution

1Co   1:23 crucified, a stumbling **b** to Jews

BLOOD → BLOODSHED

Ge   4:10 Your brother's **b** cries out to me

     9: 6 If anyone sheds the **b** of man,

     9: 6 by man shall his **b** be shed;

Ex   7:17 hold, and it shall be changed into **b**.

    12:13 the **b** will mark the houses where

    12:13 Seeing the **b**, I will pass over you;

    24: 8 he took the **b** and sprinkled it

    24: 8 "This is the **b** of the covenant

Lev   1: 5 shall offer up its **b** by splashing it

     3:17 shall not partake of any fat or any **b**."

    17:11 the life of a living body is in its **b**,

    17:11 because it is the **b**, as the seat

Nu 35:33 have no atonement for the **b** shed

    35:33 it except through the **b** of him who

Ps 72:14 for precious is their **b** in his sight.

Isa   1:11 In the **b** of calves, lambs and goats

Mt 27: 8 even today is called the Field of **B**.

Mk 14:24 them, "This is my **b** of the covenant,

Lk 22:44 sweat became like drops of **b** falling

Jn   6:53 of the Son of Man and drink his **b**,

    19:34 immediately **b** and water flowed

Ac   2:20 and the moon to **b**,

Ro   5: 9 since we are now justified by his **b**,

1Co 11:25 cup is the new covenant in my **b**.

Eph   1: 7 him we have redemption by his **b**,

     6:12 our struggle is not with flesh and **b**

Heb   9:12 not with the **b** of goats and calves

     9:12 goats and calves but with his own **b**,

     9:22 almost everything is purified by **b**,

     9:22 of **b** there is no forgiveness.

1Jn   5: 6 one who came through water and **b**,

     5: 6 by water alone, but by water and **b**.

Rev   1: 5 has freed us from our sins by his **b**,

     5: 9 with your **b** you purchased for God

     6:12 and the whole moon became like **b**.

    12:11 conquered him by the **b** of the Lamb

BLOODSHED → BLOOD, SHED

Isa   5: 7 He looked for judgment, but see, **b**!

BLOSSOMS

Ex 25:33 shaped like almond **b**, each with its

    25:33 shaped like almond **b**, each with its

BLOT

Ps 51: 3 your abundant compassion **b** out my

BLOW → BLOWING

Joel   2: 1 **B** the trumpet in Zion,

Rev   8: 6 seven trumpets prepared to **b** them.

BOAST → BOASTING

Pr 27: 1 **B** not of tomorrow, for you know

Ro   2:23 You who **b** of the law, do you

1Co   1:31 boasts, should **b** in the Lord."

2Co 11:30 If I must **b**, I will **b** of the things

Gal   6:14 may I never **b** except in the cross

Eph   2: 9 is not from works, so no one may **b**.

BOASTING → BOAST

1Co   5: 6 Your **b** is not appropriate. Do you

BOAZ

    Bethlehemite who showed favor to Ruth (Ru 2), married her (Ru 4). Ancestor of David (Ru 4:18-22; 1Ch 2:12-15), Jesus (Mt 1:5-16; Lk 3:23-32).

BODIES → BODY

Ro 12: 1 to offer your **b** as a living sacrifice,

1Co   6:15 not know that your **b** are members

Heb 10:22 and our **b** washed in pure water.

BODILY → BODY

Lk   3:22 upon him in **b** form like a dove.

BODILY → BODY (*cont.*)
Col 2: 9 the whole fullness of the deity **b**,

BODY → BODIES, BODILY
Mic 6: 7 the fruit of my **b** for the sin of my
Mt 6:22 "The lamp of the **b** is the eye. If your
     6:22 your whole **b** will be filled
Mk 14:22 them, and said, "Take it; this is my **b**."
Lk 12: 4 not be afraid of those who kill the **b**
Jn 2:21 speaking about the temple of his **b**.
Ro 7:24 will deliver me from this mortal **b**?
1Co 6:13 the other. The **b**, however, is not
     6:13 the Lord, and the Lord is for the **b**;
     10:17 are one **b**, for we all partake
     15:44 It is sown a natural **b**; it is raised
     15:44 a natural **b**; it is raised a spiritual **b**.
     15:44 If there is a natural **b**, there is
2Co 5: 8 we would rather leave the **b** and go
Eph 4: 4 one **b** and one Spirit, as you were
Col 2:19 from whom the whole **b**,

BOLDNESS
Eph 3:12 in whom we have **b** of speech

BONE → BONES
Ge 2:23 "This one, at last, is **b** of my bones
Eze 37: 7 bones came together, **b** joining **b**.

BONES → BONE
Ex 12:46 You shall not break any of its **b**.
Ps 34:21 God watches over all their **b**;

BOOK → BOOKS
Jos 1: 8 Keep this **b** of the law on your lips.
Ps 69:29 Strike them from the **b** of the living;
Rev 21:27 are written in the Lamb's **b** of life.

BOOKS → BOOK
Ecc 12:12 making of many **b** there is no end,
Da 7:10 convened, and the **b** were opened.
Jn 21:25 whole world would contain the **b**

BOOTHS
Lev 23:34 month is the LORD's feast of **B**,
Ezr 3: 4 kept the feast of **B** in the manner
Zec 14:16 and to celebrate the feast of **B**.

BORE → BEAR
Mt 8:17 our infirmities and **b** our diseases."
1Pe 2:24 He himself **b** our sins in his body

BORN → BEAR
Ecc 3: 2 A time to be **b**, and a time to die;
Isa 66: 8 or a nation be **b** in a single moment?
Lk 2:11 of David a savior has been **b** for you
Jn 3: 7 you, 'You must be **b** from above.'
1Co 15: 8 as to one **b** abnormally, he appeared
1Pe 1:23 You have been **b** anew,

BORROW → BORROWER
Dt 28:12 to many nations and **b** from none.
Ps 37:21 The wicked **b** but do not repay;
Mt 5:42 your back on one who wants to **b**.

BORROWER → BORROW
Pr 22: 7 and the **b** is the slave of the lender.

BOW → BOWED
Ge 9:13 I set my **b** in the clouds to serve as
Ex 20: 5 you shall not **b** down before them
Ps 95: 6 Enter, let us **b** down in worship;

BOWED → BOW
Ps 146: 8 raises up those who are **b** down;

BOWLS
Rev 16: 1 pour out the seven **b** of God's fury

BOY → BOYS
Lk 2:43 the **b** Jesus remained behind

BOYS → BOY
Ex 1:18 acted thus, allowing the **b** to live?"

BRANCH → BRANCHES
Isa 4: 2 The **b** of the LORD will be luster
Jn 15: 2 He takes away every **b** in me

BRANCHES → BRANCH
Jn 15: 5 I am the vine, you are the **b**.
Ro 11:21 if God did not spare the natural **b**,

BREAD
Ge 3:19 of your face shall you get **b** to eat,
Ex 12: 8 its roasted flesh with unleavened **b**
Dt 8: 3 that not by **b** alone does man live,
Ecc 11: 1 Cast your **b** upon the waters;
Wis 16:20 and furnished them **b** from heaven,
Sir 15: 3 him with the **b** of understanding,
Mt 6:11 Give us today our daily **b**;
Lk 4: 4 'One does not live by **b** alone.'"
Jn 6:35 said to them, "I am the **b** of life;
Ac 2:42 to the breaking of the **b**
1Co 10:17 Because the loaf of **b** is one, we,
     11:26 For as often as you eat this **b**

BREAK → BREAKING, BROKEN, BROKENHEARTED
Mt 6:19 destroys, and thieves **b** in and steal.
Jn 19:33 dead, they did not **b** his legs,

BREASTPIECE → BREASTPLATE
Ex 28:15 "The **b** of decision you shall

BREASTPLATE → BREASTPIECE
Wis 5:18 He shall don justice for a **b** and shall
Isa 59:17 He put on justice as his **b**, salvation,
Eph 6:14 clothed with righteousness as a **b**,

BREATH
Ge 2: 7 blew into his nostrils the **b** of life,
     6:17 in which there is the **b** of life;
Ecc 12: 7 the life **b** returns to God who gave
2Th 2: 8 will kill with the **b** of his mouth

BRIBE
Dt 16:19 You shall not take a **b**; for a **b** blinds

BRIDE → BRIDEGROOM
Isa 62: 5 as a bridegroom rejoices in his **b**
Rev 19: 7 come, his **b** has made herself ready.
     21: 9 I will show you the **b**, the wife

BRIDEGROOM → BRIDE
Mt 9:15 guests mourn as long as the **b** is
     9:15 will come when the **b** is taken away
Jn 3:29 The one who has the bride is the **b**;

BRIDLE
Ps 32: 9 bit and **b** their temper is curbed,
Jas 3: 2 man, able to **b** his whole body also.

BRIGHT → BRIGHTNESS
Mt 17: 5 a **b** cloud cast a shadow over them,
Rev 22:16 of David, the **b** morning star."

BRIGHTNESS → BRIGHT
Am 5:20 and not light, gloom without any **b**?

BRING → BRINGS, BROUGHT
Ge 6:19 living creatures you shall **b** two
Ecc 12:14 Because God will **b** to judgment
Jer 24: 6 and **b** them back to this land,
Mt 10:34 I have come to **b** peace
     10:34 I have come to **b** not peace
Ro 10:15 of those who **b** [the] good news!"

BRINGS → BRING
Jas 5:20 know that whoever **b** back a sinner

BROKE → BREAK
Ex 32:19 **b** them on the base of the mountain.

Jer 31:32 for they **b** my covenant and I
            had
Mt   14:19 he said the blessing, **b** the
            loaves,
1Co 11:24 he had given thanks, **b** it and
            said,

BROKEN → BREAK
Ps   51:19 My sacrifice, God, is a **b** spirit;
     51:19 do not spurn a **b**, humbled
            heart.
Ro   11:20 is so. They were **b** off because

BROKENHEARTED → BREAK,
HEART
Ps 147: 3 Heals the **b**, binds up their
            wounds,
Isa 61: 1 to heal the **b**, To proclaim
            liberty

BRONZE
Nu   21: 9 Moses accordingly made a **b**
            serpent
     21: 9 by a serpent looked at the **b**
            serpent,
Dt   28:23 sky over your heads will be
            like **b**
Da   10: 6 and feet looked like bur-
            nished **b**,

BROOD
Mt   3: 7 he said to them, "You **b** of
            vipers!
Lk   13:34 a hen gathers her **b** under her
            wings,

BROTHER → BROTHER'S, BROTHER-
IN-LAW, BROTHERS
Ge   4: 8 Cain said to his **b** Abel, "Let
            us go
      4: 8 Cain attacked his **b** Abel and
            killed
Mt   5:24 first and be reconciled with
            your **b**,
     10:21 **B** will hand over **b** to death,

BROTHER'S → BROTHER
Dt   25: 7 does not care to marry his **b**
            wife,
Dt   25: 7 to perpetuate his **b** name in Is-
            rael.'
Mk   6:18 lawful for you to have your **b**
            wife."

BROTHER-IN-LAW → BROTHER
Ge   38: 8 in fulfillment of your duty
            as **b**,

BROTHERS → BROTHER
Ge   9:25 lowest of slaves shall he be to
            his **b**."
     37:11 So his **b** were wrought up
            against
Mk   3:33 "Who are my mother and
            [my] **b**?"
Lk   22:32 back, you must strengthen
            your **b**."
Heb   2:11 he is not ashamed to call
            them "**b**,"

BROUGHT → BRING
Ge   15: 7 "I am the LORD who **b** you
            from Ur
Jdg   2: 1 "It was I who **b** you up from
            Egypt
2Ch 36:18 princes, all these he **b** to Bab-
            ylon.

Ezr   6: 5 **b** to Babylon are to be sent
            back:
1Ti   6: 7 For we **b** nothing into the
            world,

BUILD → BUILDERS, BUILDING,
BUILDS, BUILT, REBUILD
Ge   11: 4 let us **b** ourselves a city and a
            tower
Dt   6:10 fine, large cities that you did
            not **b**,
Ps 127: 1 Unless the LORD **b** the house,
     127: 1 they labor in vain who **b**.
Isa 57:14 **B** up, **b** up, prepare the way,
Mt   16:18 upon this rock I will **b** my
            church,

BUILDERS → BUILD
Ps 118:22 The stone the **b** rejected has
            become
Mk   12:10 'The stone that the **b** rejected
1Pe   2: 7 "The stone which the **b** re-
            jected

BUILDING → BUILD
1Co   3: 9 you are God's field, God's **b**.
2Co   5: 1 destroyed, we have a **b** from
            God,
Eph   4:12 for **b** up the body of Christ,

BUILDS → BUILD
Pr   14: 1 Wisdom **b** her house, but Folly
            tears
1Co   3:10 each one must be careful how
            he **b**
      8: 1 inflates with pride, but love
            b up.
     10:23 is lawful," but not everything
            b up.

BUILT → BUILD
Tob 13:16 Jerusalem shall be **b** with sap-
            phire
     13:16 of Jerusalem shall be **b** with
            gold,
1Ma   4:47 **b** a new altar like the former
            one.
Pr   9: 1 Wisdom has **b** her house, she
            has set
Eph   2:20 **b** upon the foundation

BULLS
1Ch 29:21 a thousand **b**, a thousand
            rams,
Ps   22:13 Many **b** surround me; fierce **b**
Heb 10: 4 it is impossible that the blood
            of **b**

BURDEN → BURDENS,
BURDENSOME
Mt   11:30 For my yoke is easy, and my **b**
            light."

BURDENS → BURDEN
Lk   11:46 You impose on people **b** hard
Gal   6: 2 Bear one another's **b**, and so
            you will

BURDENSOME → BURDEN
1Jn   5: 3 And his commandments are
            not **b**,

BURIED → BURY
Ro   6: 4 We were indeed **b** with him
            through
1Co 15: 4 that he was **b**; that he was
            raised

BURN → BURNED, BURNING, BURNT
Ex   21:25 **b** for **b**, wound for wound,
Lk   3:17 his barn, but the chaff he will **b**

BURNED → BURN
Ex   3: 3 sight, and see why the bush is
            not **b**."
Jn   15: 6 them into a fire and they will
            be **b**.
1Co   3:15 But if someone's work is **b** up,

BURNING → BURN
Ps   79: 5 Will your rage keep **b** like fire?
Lk   24:32 not our hearts **b** [within us]
            while he

BURNT → BURN
Ps   51:18 a **b** offering you would not ac-
            cept,
Mk   12:33 is worth more than all **b** offer-
            ings

BURY → BURIED
Lk   9:60 him, "Let the dead **b** their
            dead.

BUSH
Ex   3: 2 to him in fire flaming out
            of a **b**.
      3: 2 he was surprised to see that
            the **b**,

BUY → BUYS
Rev   3:18 I advise you to **b** from me gold
      3:18 **b** ointment to smear on your
            eyes so

BUYS → BUY
Mt   13:44 sells all that he has and **b** that
            field,

BYWORD → WORD
Job 17: 6 and I am made a **b** of the
            people;
Ps   44:15 You make us a **b** among the
            nations;

C

CAESAREA
Mt   16:13 of C Philippi he asked his dis-
            ciples,
Ac   10: 1 Now in **C** there was a man
            named
     25: 4 Paul was being held in custody
            in **C**

CAIAPHAS
High priest at trial of Jesus (Mt 26:3, 57;
Lk 3:2; Jn 11:49; 18:13-28); at trial of disci-
ples (Ac 4:6).

CAIN
Firstborn of Adam (Ge 4:1), murdered
brother Abel (Ge 4:1-25; Heb 11:4; 1Jn 3:12;
Jude 11).

CALAMITIES → CALAMITY
1Sa 10:19 you from all your evils and **c**,

CALAMITY → CALAMITIES
Da   9:13 of Moses, this **c** came full
            upon us.

CALEB
Judahite who spied out Canaan (Nu 13:6);
allowed to enter land (Nu 13:30-14:38; Dt
1:36; Sir 46:7-9; 1Ma 2:56). Given Hebron
(Jos 14:6-15:19).

CALF → CALVES

Ex　32: 4　a graving tool, made a molten **c**.

Lk　15:23　Take the fattened **c** and slaughter it.

CALL → CALLED, CALLING

Dt　 4:26　I **c** heaven and earth this day

1Sa　 3: 5　called me." "I did not **c** you," Eli said.

1Ki　18:24　You shall **c** on your gods, and I will

　　　18:24　your gods, and I will **c** on the LORD.

Ps　61: 3　From the brink of Sheol I **c**;

Pr　 8: 1　Does not Wisdom **c**,

Isa　65:24　Before they **c**, I will answer;

Mt　 9:13　I did not come to **c** the righteous

Lk　 6:46　"Why do you **c** me, 'Lord, Lord,'

Jn　15:15　I no longer **c** you slaves,

Ro　10:12　of all, enriching all who **c** upon him.

　　　11:29　the gifts and the **c** of God are irrevocable.

CALLED → CALL

2Sa　22: 7　In my distress I **c** upon the LORD

Isa　43: 1　I have **c** you by name: you are mine.

Mt　23: 8　As for you, do not be **c** 'Rabbi.'

1Co　 7:15　such cases; God has **c** you to peace.

1Jn　 3: 1　we may be **c** the children of God.

CALLING → CALL

Php　 3:14　goal, the prize of God's upward **c**,

CALVES → CALF

1Ki　12:28　the king made two **c** of gold

CAMEL

Mt　23:24　out the gnat and swallow the **c**!

Mk　10:25　for a **c** to pass through [the] eye

CANA

Jn　 2: 1　third day there was a wedding in **C**

CANAAN → CANAANITE, CANAANITES

Ge　 9:25　"Cursed be **C**! The lowest of slaves

Nu　13: 2　men to reconnoiter the land of **C**,

1Ch　16:18　"To you will I give the land of **C**

CANAANITE → CANAAN

Ge　28: 1　"You shall not marry a **C** woman!

Mt　15:22　a **C** woman of that district came

CANAANITES → CANAAN

Ex　33: 2　Driving out the **C**, Amorites,

Jdg　 3: 5　Israelites were living among the **C**,

CAPERNAUM

Mt　 4:13　and went to live in **C** by the sea,

Jn　 6:59　teaching in the synagogue in **C**.

CAPTIVE → CAPTIVITY

2Ki　24:16　led **c** to Babylon all seven thousand

Ro　 7:23　taking me **c** to the law of sin

Eph　 4: 8　on high and took prisoners **c**;

CAPTIVITY → CAPTIVE

Dt　28:41　remain with you, but will go into **c**.

Ezr　 8:35　those who had returned from the **c**,

CARE → CARELESS, CARES, CARING

Ps　 8: 5　mere mortals that you **c** for them?

Heb　 2: 6　the son of man that you **c** for him?

Jas　 1:27　to **c** for orphans and widows in their

CARELESS → CARE

Mt　12:36　for every **c** word they speak.

CARES → CARE

1Pe　 5: 7　upon him because he **c** for you.

CARMEL

1Ki　18:20　the prophets assemble on Mount **C**.

CARPENTER'S

Mt　13:55　Is he not the **c** son? Is not his

CARRY

Lk　14:27　Whoever does not **c** his own cross

CASE

Isa　41:21　Present your **c**, says the LORD;

CAST

Est　 9:24　to destroy them and had **c** the pur,

Ps　22:19　them; for my clothing they **c** lots.

　　　55:23　**C** your care upon the LORD, who will

Pr　16:33　When the lot is **c** into the lap,

Jn　19:24　**c** lots for it to see whose it will be,"

　　　19:24　and for my vesture they **c** lots."

1Pe　 5: 7　**C** all your worries upon him

CATTLE

Ge　 1:25　all kinds of **c**, and all kinds

CAUGHT

2Co　12: 2　was **c** up to the third heaven.

1Th　 4:17　will be **c** up together with them

CAUSE

Ps　 9: 5　You upheld my right and my **c**,

Jn　15:25　fulfilled, 'They hated me without **c**.'

CAVE

Ge　23: 9　to sell me the **c** of Machpelah

1Sa　22: 1　and escaped to the **c** of Adullam.

CEASE

Ge　 8:22　and day and night shall not **c**."

Jer　31:36　Then shall the race of Israel **c**

1Co　13: 8　to nothing; if tongues, they will **c**;

CEDAR

2Sa　 7: 2　"Here I am living in a house of **c**,

Ps　92:13　tree, shall grow like a **c** of Lebanon.

CELEBRATE

1Co　 5: 8　Therefore let us **c** the feast,

CENSER → CENSERS

Eze　 8:11　each of them with his **c** in his hand,

Rev　 8: 3　stood at the altar, holding a gold **c**.

CENSERS → CENSER

Lev　10: 1　Nadab and Abihu took their **c** and,

CENSUS

Nu　 1: 2　"Take a **c** of the whole community

CENTURION

Mt　 8: 5　a **c** approached him and appealed

Lk　23:47　The **c** who witnessed what had

Ac　10: 1　a **c** of the Cohort called the Italica,

CEPHAS → = PETER
　Name given to the apostle Peter (Jn 1:42; 1Co 1:12; 3:22; 9:5; 15:5; Gal 1:18; 2:9, 11, 14).

CHAFF

Ps　 1: 4　They are like **c** driven by the wind.

Lk　 3:17　his barn, but the **c** he will burn

CHAINED → CHAINS

2Ti　 2: 9　But the word of God is not **c**.

CHAINS → CHAINED

Eph　 6:20　for which I am an ambassador in **c**,

Heb　11:36　even **c** and imprisonment.

2Pe　 2: 4　them to the **c** of Tartarus

CHALDEANS

Ge　15: 7　of the **C** to give you this land as

Da　 1: 4　the language and literature of the **C**;

CHANGE → CHANGED, CHANGERS

Nu　23:19　human, that he should **c** his mind.

Jas　 1:17　no alteration or shadow caused by **c**.

CHANGED → CHANGE

1Co　15:51　all fall asleep, but we will all be **c**,

Heb　 1:12　and like a garment they will be **c**.

CHANGERS → CHANGE

Mk　11:15　overturned the tables of the money **c**

Jn　 2:15　and spilled the coins of the **m**

CHARACTER

Ro　 5: 4　endurance, proven **c**, and proven **c**,

CHARGE
Mk 15:26 of the **c** against him read, "The King
Ro 8:33 will bring a **c** against God's chosen
1Co 9:18 I offer the gospel free of **c** so as not

CHARIOT → CHARIOTS
2Ki 2:11 a flaming **c** and flaming horses
Ps 104: 3 You make the clouds your **c**;

CHARIOTS → CHARIOT
Ex 14:28 it covered the **c** and the charioteers
Zec 6: 1 and saw four **c** coming

CHARM
Pr 31:30 **C** is deceptive and beauty fleeting;

CHEEK
Mt 5:39 strikes you on [your] right **c**,

CHEERFUL
2Co 9: 7 compulsion, for God loves a **c** giver.

CHEMOSH
1Ki 11: 7 then built a high place to **C**, the idol
Jer 48: 7 be captured. **C** shall go into exile,

CHERUB → CHERUBIM
Ps 18:11 Mounted on a **c** he flew,
Eze 28:14 With the **C** I placed you; you were

CHERUBIM → CHERUB
Ge 3:24 and he stationed the **c** and the fiery
Ex 25:18 Make two **c** of beaten gold
2Ch 3:11 wings of the **c** spanned twenty cubits:
Ps 80: 2 throne upon the **c** reveal yourself
Heb 9: 5 Above it were the **c** of glory

CHIEF
Mk 15: 3 The **c** priests accused him of many
1Pe 5: 4 when the **c** Shepherd is revealed,

CHILD → CHILDBEARING, CHILDISH, CHILDREN
Ge 17:17 "Can a **c** be born to a man who is
Isa 11: 6 with a little **c** to guide them.
49:15 tenderness for the **c** of her womb?
Hos 11: 1 When Israel was a **c** I loved him,
Mt 1:18 with **c** through the holy Spirit.
Mk 10:15 of God like a **c** will not enter it."
1Co 13:11 When I was a **c**, I used to talk as a **c**,
13:11 as a **c**, think as a **c**, reason as a **c**;
Gal 4: 7 So you are no longer a slave but a **c**,
4: 7 but a **c**, and if a **c** then also an heir,
Rev 12: 4 to devour her **c** when she gave birth.

CHILDBEARING → CHILD, BEAR
Ge 3:16 "I will intensify the pangs of your **c**;

CHILDISH → CHILD
1Co 13:11 I became a man, I put aside **c** things.

CHILDREN → CHILD
Ex 12:26 When your **c** ask you, 'What does
Dt 6: 7 Drill them into your **c**.
11:19 Teach them to your **c**,
Mt 3: 9 you, God can raise up **c** to Abraham
Lk 18:16 called the **c** to himself and said,
18:16 "Let the **c** come to me and do not
Jn 1:12 he gave power to become **c** of God,
Ro 8:14 by the Spirit of God are **c** of God.
Eph 6: 4 do not provoke your **c** to anger,
1Jn 3:10 the **c** of God and the **c** of the devil

CHOOSE → CHOOSES, CHOSE, CHOSEN
Dt 30:19 curse. **C** life, then, that you and your

CHOOSES → CHOOSE
Dt 12:14 the Lord **c** from among your tribes;

CHOSE → CHOOSE
Dt 4:37 your fathers he **c** their descendants
Ne 9: 7 are the God who **c** Abram,
Mk 13:20 for the sake of the elect whom he **c**,
1Co 1:27 God **c** the foolish of the world
1:27 and God **c** the weak of the world

CHOSEN → CHOOSE
Isa 42: 1 my **c** one with whom I am pleased,
Mt 22:14 Many are invited, but few are **c**."
Ro 11: 5 time there is a remnant, **c** by grace.
1Pe 2: 6 a cornerstone, **c** and precious,
2: 9 But you are "a **c** race, a royal

CHRIST → CHRISTIAN, CHRISTIANS, MESSIAH
Ro 5: 6 For **C**, while we were still helpless,
8:35 will separate us from the love of **C**?
10: 4 For **C** is the end of the law
1Co 1:23 but we proclaim **C** crucified,
3:11 one that is there, namely, Jesus **C**.
11: 1 Be imitators of me, as I am of **C**.
15: 3 received: that **C** died for our sins
Gal 5: 1 For freedom **C** set us free; so stand
Eph 4:15 way into him who is the head, **C**,
Php 1:21 For to me life is **C**, and death too

Php 2:11 tongue confess that Jesus **C** is Lord,
Col 1:27 it is **C** in you, the hope for glory.
Rev 20: 4 they reigned with **C** for a thousand

CHRISTIAN → CHRIST
Ac 26:28 will soon persuade me to play the **C**."
1Pe 4:16 suffer as a **C** should not be ashamed

CHRISTIANS → CHRIST
Ac 11:26 that the disciples were first called **C**.

CHURCH
Mt 16:18 and upon this rock I will build my **c**,
Ac 8: 1 persecution of the **c** in Jerusalem,
1Co 12:28 God has designated in the **c** to be,
14: 4 whoever prophesies builds up the **c**.
Col 1:18 He is the head of the body, the **c**.

CIRCUMCISE → CIRCUMCISED, CIRCUMCISION
Ge 17:11 **C** the flesh of your foreskin,
Dt 10:16 **C** your hearts, therefore, and be no
Lk 1:59 on the eighth day to **c** the child,
Jn 7:22 you **c** a man on the sabbath.

CIRCUMCISED → CIRCUMCISE
Ge 17:10 every male among you shall be **c**.
1Ma 1:60 had had their children **c** were put
Ac 15: 1 "Unless you are **c** according
Gal 6:13 having themselves **c** observe
6:13 they only want you to be **c** so
Col 2:11 were also **c** with a circumcision not

CIRCUMCISION → CIRCUMCISE
Ro 2:29 and **c** is of the heart, in the spirit,
Gal 5: 6 neither **c** nor uncircumcision counts

CISTERN
Pr 5:15 Drink water from your own **c**,
Jer 38: 6 him into the **c** of Prince Malchiah,
38: 6 There was no water in the **c**,

CITIES → CITY
Ge 19:25 He overthrew those **c** and the whole
19:25 with the inhabitants of the **c**
Jos 20: 2 the Israelites to designate the **c**
Rev 16:19 three parts, and the gentile **c** fell.

CITIZENSHIP
Php 3:20 But our **c** is in heaven, and from it

CITY → CITIES
1Ch 11: 7 thenceforth was called the **C**
Ps 127: 1 Unless the Lord guard the **c**, in vain

CITY → CITIES (*cont.*)

Pr   31:31   her works praise her at the **c** gates.

La   1: 1   the once crowded **c**! Widowed is

Da   9:24   for your people and for your holy **c**;

Mt   5:14   A **c** set on a mountain cannot be

Heb 12:22   Zion and the **c** of the living God,

Rev 21: 2   I also saw the holy **c**, a new

CLAP

Ps   47: 2   All you peoples, **c** your hands,

Isa 55:12   the countryside shall **c** their hands.

CLAY

Isa 45: 9   Dare the **c** say to its modeler,

Jer 18: 6   like **c** in the hand of the potter,

Ro   9:21   the potter have a right over the **c**,

2Ti   2:20   and silver but also of wood and **c**,

CLEAN → CLEANSE, CLEANSING

Ge   7: 2   Of every **c** animal, take with you

Lev 10:10   between what is **c** and what is

Mk   7:19   (Thus he declared all foods **c**.)

Jn 13:10   his feet washed, for he is **c** all over;

      13:10   **c** all over; so you are **c**, but not all."

Ac 10:15   "What God has made **c**, you are not

Heb 10:22   our hearts sprinkled **c** from an evil

CLEANSE → CLEAN

Ps   51: 4   all my guilt; from my sin **c** me.

Sir 38:10   be just, **c** your heart of every sin;

1Jn   1: 9   and **c** us from every wrongdoing.

CLEANSING → CLEAN

Eph   5:26   **c** her by the bath of water

2Pe   1: 9   forgetful of the **c** of his past sins.

CLEAR

Ps   19: 9   The command of the LORD is **c**,

1Ti   3: 9   of the faith with a **c** conscience.

Rev 21:18   the city was pure gold, **c** as glass.

CLINGS

Ge   2:24   father and mother and **c** to his wife,

Heb 12: 1   of every burden and sin that **c** to us

CLOAK

Ex 22:26   this **c** of his is the only covering he

Heb   1:12   You will roll them up like a **c**,

CLOTHE → CLOTHED, CLOTHING

1Pe   5: 5   **c** yourselves with humility in your

CLOTHED → CLOTHE

2Co   5: 2   to be further **c** with our heavenly

Gal   3:27   into Christ have **c** yourselves

Rev 12: 1   in the sky, a woman **c** with the sun,

CLOTHING → CLOTHE

Ps   22:19   among them; for my **c** they cast lots.

CLOUD → CLOUDS

Ex 13:21   of a column of **c** to show them

1Ki   8:10   the **c** filled the temple of the LORD

     18:44   "There is a **c** as small as a man's hand

Eze 10: 4   the temple was filled with the **c**,

Mk   9: 7   Then a **c** came, casting a shadow

      9: 7   then from the **c** came a voice,

Lk 21:27   of Man coming in a **c** with power

Heb 12: 1   by so great a **c** of witnesses, let us

Rev 14:14   I looked and there was a white **c**,

Rev 14:14   on the **c** one who looked like a son

CLOUDS → CLOUD

Ge   9:13   my bow in the **c** to serve as a sign

Da   7:13   on the **c** of heaven; When he

Mt 24:30   Man coming upon the **c** of heaven

1Th   4:17   them in the **c** to meet the Lord

Rev   1: 7   Behold, he is coming amid the **c**,

CLUSTER

Nu 13:23   a branch with a single **c** of grapes

COALS

Ps   11: 6   the wicked fiery **c** and brimstone,

Pr   25:22   For live **c** you will heap on his head,

Ro 12:20   by so doing you will heap burning **c**

COIN

Mt 17:27   you will find a **c** worth twice

     22:19   Show me the **c** that pays the census

     22:19   Then they handed him the Roman **c**.

Lk 15: 9   me because I have found the **c** that I

COLD

Zec 14: 6   that day there shall no longer be **c**

Mt 24:12   the love of many will grow **c**.

Rev   3:16   neither hot nor **c**, I will spit you

COLLECTOR → COLLECTORS

Mt 10: 3   Thomas and Matthew the tax **c**;

Lk 18:10   a Pharisee and the other was a tax **c**.

    19: 2   who was a chief tax **c**

COLLECTORS → COLLECTOR

Mt   5:46   have? Do not the tax **c** do the same?

    11:19   a friend of tax **c** and sinners.'

COLT

Zec   9: 9   on an ass, on a **c**, the foal of an ass.

Jn 12:15   king comes, seated upon an ass's **c**."

COME → COMES, COMING

Ps 144: 5   LORD, incline your heavens and **c**,

Isa 59:20   He shall **c** to Zion a redeemer

Zec 14: 5   shall **c**, and all his holy ones

Mt   6:10   your kingdom **c**, your will be done,

Lk   7:20   ask, 'Are you the one who is to **c**,

Jn   6:37   the Father gives me will **c**

Rev   1: 4   is and who was and who is to **c**,

    22:20   coming soon." Amen! C, Lord Jesus!

COMES → COME

Ps 118:26   is he who **c** in the name of the LORD.

Lk 19:38   "Blessed is the king who **c**

Jn 14: 6   life. No one **c** to the Father except

COMFORT → COMFORTED, COMFORTERS, COMFORTS

Isa 40: 1   C, give **c** to my people, says your

COMFORTED → COMFORT

Mt   5: 4   they who mourn, for they will be **c**.

COMFORTERS → COMFORT

Job 16: 2   times. Wearisome **c** are you all!

Ps   69:21   was none, for **c**, but found none.

COMFORTS → COMFORT

Isa 66:13   As a mother **c** her son, so will I

COMING → COME

Mal   3: 2   who will endure the day of his **c**?

2Pe   3: 4   "Where is the promise of his **c**?

Rev 22:20   testimony says, "Yes, I am **c** soon."

COMMAND → COMMANDED, COMMANDMENT, COMMANDMENTS

Dt   1:26   and after defying the **c** of the LORD,

COMMANDED → COMMAND

Ge   7: 5   Noah did just as the LORD had **c** him.

Ex 40:32   the altar, as the LORD **c** Moses.

Jos   1:16   "We will do all you have **c** us,"

Mt 28:20   to observe all that I have **c** you.

Jn 14:31   that I do just as the Father has **c** me.

COMMANDMENT → COMMAND

Mt 22:38   This is the greatest and the first **c**.

Ro   7:12   and the **c** is holy and righteous

1Jn   3:23   And his **c** is this: we should believe

COMMANDMENTS → COMMAND

Ex   20: 6   those who love me and keep my **c**.

Dt   4:13   the ten **c**, which he wrote on two

     6: 1   "These then are the **c**, the statutes

Ecc   12:13   Fear God and keep his **c**, for this is

Mt   19:17   wish to enter into life, keep the **c**."

     22:40   the prophets depend on these two **c**."

Jn   14:15   "If you love me, you will keep my **c**.

1Co   7:19   what matters is keeping God's **c**.

1Jn   5: 3   of God is this, that we keep his **c**.

     5: 3   his **c**. And his **c** are not burdensome,

Rev   14:12   the holy ones who keep God's **c**

COMMIT → COMMITS

Dt   5:18   'You shall not **c** adultery.

2Ki   17:21   LORD, causing them to **c** a great sin.

Mt   5:27   it was said, 'You shall not **c** adultery.'

COMMITS → COMMIT

Jn   8:34   everyone who **c** sin is a slave of sin.

COMMON

Ac   2:44   together and had all things in **c**;

COMPANY

1Co   15:33   astray: "Bad **c** corrupts good morals."

COMPARE

Pr   8:11   no choice possession can **c** with her.

Lk   7:31   to what shall I **c** the people of this

COMPASSION → COMPASSIONATE

Ps   103:13   As a father has **c** on his children,

     103:13   so the LORD has **c** on the faithful.

Col   3:12   and beloved, heartfelt **c**, kindness,

COMPASSIONATE → COMPASSION

Sir   2:11   **C** and merciful is the LORD;

Jas   5:11   because "the Lord is **c** and merciful."

COMPETING

2Ti   2: 5   crown except by **c** according

COMPLAINING → COMPLAINT

1Pe   4: 9   hospitable to one another without **c**.

COMPLAINT → COMPLAINING

Job   10: 1   life. I will give myself up to **c**; I will

Ps   142: 3   Before God I pour out my **c**,

Hab   2: 1   what answer he will give to my **c**.

CONCEITED

Gal   5:26   Let us not be **c**, provoking one

1Ti   6: 4   is **c**, understanding nothing, and has

1Ti   3: 6   so that he may not become **c**

CONCEIVE

Lk   1:31   you will **c** in your womb and bear

CONDEMN → CONDEMNATION, CONDEMNED

Lk   11:31   this generation and she will **c** them,

Jn   3:17   Son into the world to **c** the world,

Ro   8:34   Who will **c**? It is Christ [Jesus] who

1Jn   3:21   if [our] hearts do not **c** us, we have

CONDEMNATION → CONDEMN

Mk   12:40   They will receive a very severe **c**."

Ro   5:18   as through one transgression **c** came

Jas   5:12   mean "No," that you may not incur **c**.

CONDEMNED → CONDEMN

Mt   12:37   and by your words you will be **c**."

Jn   3:18   believes in him will not be **c**,

     3:18   does not believe has already been **c**,

     16:11   the ruler of this world has been **c**.

1Co   11:32   that we may not be **c** along

CONDUCT

Tob   4:14   and discipline yourself in all your **c**.

Sir   37:17   The root of all **c** is the mind;

Eze   22:31   I have brought down their **c**

Ro   13: 3   are not a cause of fear to good **c**,

1Pe   1:15   in every aspect of your **c**,

CONFESS → CONFESSES, CONFESSION

Lev   5: 5   of these cases shall **c** the sin he has

     16:21   he shall **c** over it all the sinful faults

Php   2:11   and every tongue **c** that Jesus Christ

CONFESSES → CONFESS

Ro   10:10   and one **c** with the mouth and so is

1Jn   2:23   whoever **c** the Son has the Father as

CONFESSION → CONFESS

1Ti   6:12   when you made the noble **c**

Heb   4:14   Son of God, let us hold fast to our **c**.

CONFIDENCE

Php   3: 3   Jesus and do not put our **c** in flesh,

Heb   10:19   of Jesus we have **c** of entrance

CONFIRM

2Sa   7:25   **c** for all time the prophecy you have

Ro   15: 8   to **c** the promises to the patriarchs,

CONFORMED

Ro   8:29   predestined to be **c** to the image

CONFUSE

Ge   11: 7   go down and there **c** their language,

CONQUER → CONQUERED, CONQUERS

Rev   17:14   but the Lamb will **c** them, for he is

CONQUERED → CONQUER

Jn   16:33   but take courage, I have **c** the world."

Heb   11:33   who by faith **c** kingdoms, did what

1Jn   2:13   because you have **c** the evil one.

CONQUERS → CONQUER

1Jn   5: 4   is begotten by God **c** the world,

     5: 4   victory that **c** the world is our faith.

CONSCIENCE

Ro   2:15   while their **c** also bears witness

1Co   8: 7   to idols, their **c**, which is weak,

1Ti   1: 5   heart, a good **c**, and a sincere faith.

1Pe   3:21   but an appeal to God for a clear **c**,

CONSECRATE → CONSECRATED

Ex   13: 2   "**C** to me every first-born that opens

CONSECRATED → CONSECRATE

2Ch   7:16   this house that my name may be **c**

CONSIDER → CONSIDERED

Jas   1: 2   **C** it all joy, my brothers, when you

CONSIDERED → CONSIDER

Pr   17:28   a fool, if he keeps silent, is **c** wise;

CONSOLATION

Lk   2:25   and devout, awaiting the **c** of Israel,

CONSULT → CONSULTED

Isa   40:14   Whom did he **c** to gain knowledge?

CONSULTED → CONSULT

Eze   20: 3   not allow myself to be **c** by you,

CONSUME → CONSUMED, CONSUMING

Nu   16:21   this band, that I may **c** them at once."

Jn   2:17   "Zeal for your house will **c** me."

CONSUMED → CONSUME

Ex   3: 2   the bush, though on fire, was not **c**.

Ps   90: 7   Truly we are **c** by your anger,

Zep   3: 8   my jealousy shall all the earth be **c**.

Gal   5:15   that you are not **c** by one another.

CONSUMING → CONSUME
Heb 12:29 For our God is a **c** fire.

CONTAIN
Jn 21:25 the whole world would **c** the books

CONTEMPT
Mk 9:12 suffer greatly and be treated with **c**?
Heb 6: 6 themselves and holding him up to **c**.

CONTEND
Jude 1: 3 to encourage you to **c** for the faith

CONTENT → CONTENTMENT
Sir 29:23 or much, be **c** with what you have,
2Co 12:10 Therefore, I am **c** with weaknesses,
Heb 13: 5 money but be **c** with what you have,

CONTENTMENT → CONTENT
1Ti 6: 6 religion with **c** is a great gain.

CONTRIBUTE
Ro 12:13 **C** to the needs of the holy ones,

CONVERT
Mt 23:15 traverse sea and land to make one **c**,
1Ti 3: 6 He should not be a recent **c**,

CONVICT
Jude 1:15 and to **c** everyone for all the godless

CONVINCE → CONVINCED, CONVINCING
Ac 28:23 trying to **c** them about Jesus
2Ti 4: 2 **c**, reprimand, encourage through all

CONVINCED → CONVINCE
Ro 8:38 For I am **c** that neither death,

COPY
Dt 17:18 he shall have a **c** of this law made
Heb 9:24 made by hands, a **c** of the true one,

CORDS
2Sa 22: 6 The **c** of the nether world enmeshed
Hos 11: 4 I drew them with human **c**,

CORNELIUS
First Gentile Christian (Ac 10).

CORNERSTONE → STONE
Ps 118:22 builders rejected has become the **c**.
Isa 28:16 A precious **c** as a sure foundation;
Lk 20:17 builders rejected has become the **c**"?
1Pe 2: 6 in Zion, a **c**, chosen and precious,

CORRECTING → CORRECTION
2Ti 2:25 **c** opponents with kindness. It may

CORRECTION → CORRECTING
Jer 5: 3 laid them low, but they refused **c**;
2Ti 3:16 refutation, for **c**, and for training

CORRUPT → CORRUPTION
Ge 6:11 In the eyes of God the earth was **c**
Ac 2:40 yourselves from this **c** generation."

CORRUPTION → CORRUPT
Ac 2:31 netherworld nor did his flesh see **c**.
2Pe 1: 4 escaping from the **c** that is

COST
1Ch 21:24 up holocausts that **c** me nothing."
Lk 14:28 and calculate the **c** to see if there is

COUNCIL
Jer 23:18 who has stood in the **c** of the LORD,

COUNSEL → COUNSELOR, COUNSELORS
Isa 28:29 wonderful is his **c** and great his

COUNSELOR → COUNSEL
Ro 11:34 of the Lord or who has been his **c**?"

COUNSELORS → COUNSEL
Pr 11:14 people falls; security lies in many **c**.
24: 6 the victory is due to a wealth of **c**.

COUNT → COUNTED, COUNTS
Ps 90:12 Teach us to **c** our days aright,

COUNTED → COUNT
Ge 13:16 your descendants too might be **c**.
Mt 10:30 all the hairs of your head are **c**.

COURAGE → COURAGEOUS
Jn 16:33 but take **c**, I have conquered

COURAGEOUS → COURAGE
1Ma 2:64 be **c** and strong in keeping the law,
1Co 16:13 firm in the faith, be **c**, be strong.

COURT → COURTS
Ex 27: 9 also make a **c** for the Dwelling.
27: 9 south side the **c** shall have hangings
Da 7:10 The **c** was convened, and the books
Mt 5:25 while on the way to **c** with him.
1Co 6: 6 brother goes to **c** against brother,

COURTS → COURT
Ps 84:11 Better one day in your **c**
96: 8 name! Bring gifts and enter his **c**;

COVENANT → COVENANTS
Ge 6:18 But with you I will establish my **c**;

CORRECTION → CORRECTING
Ge 9: 9 I am now establishing my **c**
15:18 that the LORD made a **c** with Abram,
Ex 2:24 was mindful of his **c** with Abraham,
19: 5 hearken to my voice and keep my **c**,
24: 7 Taking the book of the **c**, he read it
Lev 26:42 I will remember my **c** with Jacob,
26:42 my **c** with Jacob, my **c** with Isaac,
26:42 with Isaac, and my **c** with Abraham;
Jdg 2: 1 I would never break my **c** with you,
1Ki 8:23 you keep your **c** of kindness
Ezr 10: 3 enter into a **c** before our God
Jdt 9:13 planned dire things against your **c**,
1Ma 1:15 and abandoned the holy **c**;
Ps 105: 8 He remembers forever his **c**,
Sir 28: 7 of the Most High's **c**, and overlook
Isa 61: 8 a lasting **c** I will make with them.
Jer 31:31 I will make a new **c** with the house
Eze 16:60 Yet I will remember the **c** I made
16:60 set up an everlasting **c** with you.
Mal 3: 1 of the **c** whom you desire. Yes, he is
Lk 22:20 "This cup is the new **c** in my blood,
1Co 11:25 "This cup is the new **c** in my blood.
2Co 3: 6 qualified us as ministers of a new **c**,
Heb 7:22 the guarantee of an [even] better **c**.
12:24 the mediator of a new **c**,
Rev 11:19 the ark of his **c** could be seen

COVENANTS → COVENANT
Ro 9: 4 glory, the **c**, the giving of the law,
Gal 4:24 These women represent two **c**.

COVER
Ex 33:22 will **c** you with my hand until I have
Jas 5:20 death and will **c** a multitude of sins.

COVET
Ex 20:17 "You shall not **c** your neighbor's
20:17 You shall not **c** your neighbor's
Ro 7: 7 I did not know what it is to **c** except
7: 7 that the law said, "You shall not **c**."
Jas 4: 2 You **c** but do not possess. You kill

CRAFTY
2Co 12:16 yet I was **c** and got the better of you

CREATE → CREATED, CREATION, CREATOR
Ps   51:12   A clean heart **c** for me, God;
Isa   65:17   Lo, I am about to **c** new heavens
Eph   2:15   that he might **c** in himself one new

CREATED → CREATE
Ge   1: 1   when God **c** the heavens
    1:27   God **c** man in his image;
    1:27   in the divine image he **c** him;
    1:27   **c** him; male and female he **c** them.
Dt   32: 6   Is he not your father who **c** you?
Sir   1: 4   all things else wisdom was **c**;
Mal   2:10   Has not the one God **c** us?
1Co   11: 9   nor was man **c** for woman,
Eph   2:10   **c** in Christ Jesus for the good works
Col   1:16   in him were **c** all things in heaven
    1:16   all things were **c** through him
1Ti   4: 4   For everything **c** by God is good,
Rev   4:11   for you **c** all things; because of your
    4:11   will they came to be and were **c**."

CREATION → CREATE
Ge   2: 3   from all the work he had done in **c**.
Mk   10: 6   But from the beginning of **c**,
Ro   8:19   For **c** awaits with eager expectation
2Co   5:17   So whoever is in Christ is a new **c**:
Gal   6:15   uncircumcision, but only a new **c**.
Col   1:15   invisible God, the firstborn of all **c**.
2Pe   3: 4   as it was from the beginning of **c**."

CREATOR → CREATE
Ecc   12: 1   Remember your **C** in the days
Ro   1:25   the creature rather than the **c**, who is
Col   3:10   for knowledge, in the image of its **c**.
1Pe   4:19   over to a faithful **c** as they do good.

CREATURE → CREATURES
Ro   1:25   and worshiped the **c** rather than

CREATURES → CREATURE
Ps   104:24   them all; the earth is full of your **c**.
Eze   1: 5   figures resembling four living **c**
Rev   4: 6   there were four living **c** covered
    19: 4   and the four living **c** fell down

CREDIT
Lk   6:33   good to you, what **c** is that to you?
1Pe   2:20   But what **c** is there if you are patient

CREEPING
Ge   1:24   cattle, **c** things, and wild animals

CRIED → CRY
Ex   2:23   and **c** out because of their slavery.
Nu   20:16   when we **c** to the LORD, he heard our
Jdg   3: 9   But when the Israelites **c**
Ps   22: 6   To you they **c** out and they escaped;
Mt   27:46   about three o'clock Jesus **c**

CRIMINAL → CRIMINALS
Jn   18:30   "If he were not a **c**, we would not
2Ti   2: 9   even to the point of chains, like a **c**.

CRIMINALS → CRIMINAL
Lk   23:32   both **c**, were led away with him

CROOKED
Dt   32: 5   children, a perverse and **c** race!
Ecc   1:15   What is **c** cannot be made straight,
Php   2:15   without blemish in the midst of a **c**

CROSS → CROSSROADS
Dt   31: 3   your God, who will **c** before you;
    31: 3   [It is Joshua who will **c** before you,
Mk   15:30   by coming down from the **c**.
Lk   14:27   Whoever does not carry his own **c**
1Co   1:18   The message of the **c** is foolishness
Gal   6:14   in the **c** of our Lord Jesus Christ,
Php   2: 8   obedient to death, even death on a **c**.
Col   1:20   making peace by the blood of his **c**
Heb   12: 2   lay before him he endured the **c**,

CROSSROADS → CROSS, ROAD
Pr   8: 2   road, at the **c** she takes her stand;

CROWD → CROWDS
Mk   8: 2   heart is moved with pity for the **c**,
    14:43   accompanied by a **c** with swords

CROWDS → CROWD
Mt   7:28   words, the **c** were astonished at his

CROWN → CROWNED, CROWNS
Pr   4: 9   a glorious **c** will she bestow on you."
Jn   19: 2   the soldiers wove a **c** out of thorns
Php   4: 1   my joy and **c**, in this way stand firm
2Ti   4: 8   on the **c** of righteousness awaits me,
1Pe   5: 4   you will receive the unfading **c**
Rev   6: 2   He was given a **c**, and he rode forth
    14:14   man, with a gold **c** on his head

CROWNED → CROWN
Ps   8: 6   a god, **c** them with glory and honor.

Heb   2: 9   but we do see Jesus "**c** with glory

CROWNS → CROWN
Rev   4:10   They throw down their **c** before

CRUCIFIED → CRUCIFY
Mt   27:22   They all said, "Let him be **c**!"
Lk   24: 7   be handed over to sinners and be **c**,
Ac   4:10   Christ the Nazorean whom you **c**,
Ro   6: 6   that our old self was **c** with him,
1Co   1:23   but we proclaim Christ **c**,
Gal   2:19   for God. I have been **c** with Christ;

CRUCIFY → CRUCIFIED
Lk   23:21   continued their shouting, "C him!
Jn   19:15   him away, take him away! C him!"
    19:15   said to them, "Shall I **c** your king?"

CRUSH → CRUSHED
Job   6: 9   that God would decide to **c** me,
Isa   53:10   was pleased to **c** him in infirmity.]
Ro   16:20   of peace will quickly **c** Satan under

CRUSHED → CRUSH
Ps   34:19   saves those whose spirit is **c**.

CRY → CRIED, CRYING
Ex   2:23   As their **c** for release went
Ps   5: 3   Hear my **c** for help, my king,
Hab   1: 2   How long, O LORD? I **c** for help
    1: 2   not listen! I **c** out to you, "Violence!"
Mk   15:37   Jesus gave a loud **c** and breathed his

CRYING → CRY
Mk   1: 3   A voice of one **c** out in the desert:

CRYSTAL
Eze   1:22   seeming like glittering **c**,
Rev   22: 1   sparkling like **c**,

CUP
Ps   23: 5   my head with oil; my **c** overflows.
Jer   25:15   Take this **c** of foaming wine
Mt   10:42   And whoever gives only a **c** of cold
    26:39   is possible, let this **c** pass from me;
Mk   10:38   Can you drink the **c** that I drink
Lk   22:17   Then he took a **c**, gave thanks,
1Co   11:25   In the same way also the **c**,
    11:25   "This **c** is the new covenant in my
Rev   14:10   full strength into the **c** of his wrath,

CURED
Mt   8:16   spirits by a word and **c** all the sick,
Ac   5:16   unclean spirits, and they were all **c**.

CURSE → ACCURSED, CURSED, CURSES

Ge 12: 3 you and **c** those who **c** you.
Nu 22:12 with them and do not **c** this people,
Dt 21:23 since God's **c** rests on him who
23: 5 Pethor in Aram Naharaim, to **c** you;
Job 2: 9 to your innocence? **C** God and die."
Ps 109:28 Though they **c**, may you bless;
Sir 4: 5 eyes, give no man reason to **c** you;
Mk 14:71 He began to **c** and to swear, "I do not
Lk 6:28 bless those who **c** you,
Ro 12:14 [you], bless and do not **c** them.
Gal 3:13 ransomed us from the **c** of the law
3:13 **c** of the law by becoming a **c** for us,

CURSED → CURSE

Ge 3:17 "**C** be the ground because of you!
9:25 he said: "**C** be Canaan! The lowest
27:29 to you. **C** be those who curse you,
Nu 23: 8 can I curse whom God has not **c**?
Job 3: 1 Job opened his mouth and **c** his day.
Mk 11:21 The fig tree that you **c** has withered."
Gal 3:10 "**C** be everyone who does not
Heb 6: 8 it will soon be **c** and finally burned.

CURSES → CURSE

Lev 24:15 Anyone who **c** his God shall bear
2Ch 34:24 all the **c** written in the book that has

CUSTOM → CUSTOMS

Jn 18:39 But you have a **c** that I release one

CUSTOMS → CUSTOM

1Ma 1:42 each abandoning his particular **c**.
Ac 16:21 are advocating **c** that are not lawful

CUT

Ps 37: 9 Those who do evil will be **c** off,
Isa 53: 8 When he was **c** off from the land
Mt 3:10 not bear good fruit will be **c** down
Mk 9:43 your hand causes you to sin, **c** it off.
Ro 11:22 otherwise you too will be **c** off.

CYMBAL → CYMBALS

1Co 13: 1 a resounding gong or a clashing **c**.

CYMBALS → CYMBAL

2Sa 6: 5 harps, tambourines, sistrums and **c**.
Ne 12:27 hymns and the music of **c**, harps,

Ps 150: 5 Give praise with crashing **c**,
150: 5 **c**, praise him with sounding **c**.

CYRUS
Persian king who allowed exiles to return (2Ch 36:22-Ezr 1:8), to rebuild temple (Ezr 5:13-6:14), as appointed by the LORD (Isa 44:28-45:13).

D

DAGON

Jdg 16:23 offer a great sacrifice to their god **D**
1Sa 5: 2 and brought it into the temple of **D**,
5: 2 the temple of **D**, placing it beside **D**.

DAILY → DAY

Mt 6:11 Give us today our **d** bread;
Lk 9:23 take up his cross **d** and follow me.

DAMASCUS

Ac 9: 3 as he was nearing **D**, a light

DAN
1. Son of Jacob by Bilhah (Ge 30:4-6; 35:25; 46:23). Tribe of blessed (Ge 49:16-17; Dt 33:22), numbered (Nu 1:39; 26:43), allotted land (Jos 19:40-48; Eze 48:1), failed to fully possess (Jdg 1:34-35), failed to support Deborah (Jdg 5:17), possessed Dan (Jdg 18).
2. Northernmost city in Israel (Ge 14:14; Jdg 18; 20:1).

DANCE

Ps 150: 4 Give praise with tambourines and **d**,
Ecc 3: 4 a time to mourn, and a time to **d**.
Lk 7:32 the flute for you, but you did not **d**.

DANIEL → = BELTESHAZZAR
1. Hebrew exile to Babylon, name changed to Belteshazzar (Da 1:6-7). Refused to eat unclean food (Da 1:8-21). Interpreted Nebuchadnezzar's dreams (Da 2; 4), writing on the wall (Da 5). Thrown into lion's den (Da 6; 14:31-42). Visions of (Da 7-12). Saves Susanna (Da 13). Destroys Bel and its priests (Da 14).
2. Son of David (1Ch 3:1).

DARE

Mt 22:46 did anyone **d** to ask him any more

DARIUS
1. King of Persia (Ezr 4:5), allowed rebuilding of temple (Ezr 5-6).
2. Mede who conquered Babylon (Da 5:31).

DARK → DARKNESS

Ps 139:12 Darkness is not **d** for you, and night
2Pe 1:19 it, as to a lamp shining in a **d** place,

DARKNESS → DARK

Ge 1: 2 and **d** covered the abyss,
Ex 10:22 there was dense **d** throughout
Dt 5:23 the voice from the midst of the **d**,

Zep 1:15 desolation, a day of **d** and gloom,
Mt 4:16 the people who sit in **d** have seen
6:23 bad, your whole body will be in **d**.
6:23 **d**. And if the light in you is **d**,
6:23 in you is **d**, how great will the **d** be.
Jn 1: 5 the light shines in the **d**, and the **d**
Eph 5: 8 For you were once **d**, but now you
Col 1:13 He delivered us from the power of **d**
1Jn 1: 5 light, and in him there is no **d** at all.

DATHAN
Involved in Korah's rebellion against Moses and Aaron (Nu 16:1-27; 26:9; Dt 11:6; Ps 106:17; Sir 45:18).

DAUGHTER → DAUGHTERS

Ex 2: 5 Pharaoh's **d** came down to the river
Jdt 10:12 "I am a **d** of the Hebrews, and I am
Est 2: 7 had taken her as his own **d**.
Ps 9:15 salvation in the gates of **d** Zion.
La 2: 1 has detested **d** Zion! He has cast
Mic 7: 6 the **d** rises up against her mother,
Zec 9: 9 Rejoice heartily, O **d** Zion,
9: 9 shout for joy, O **d** Jerusalem! See,
Mt 14: 6 the **d** of Herodias performed a dance
Lk 12:53 a mother against her **d** and a **d**

DAUGHTERS → DAUGHTER

Ge 6: 4 had intercourse with the **d** of man,
19:36 both of Lot's **d** became pregnant
Nu 27: 1 son of Joseph, had **d** named Mahlah,
Dt 12:31 their sons and **d** to their gods.
Job 42:15 women were as beautiful as the **d**
Ac 2:17 sons and your **d** shall prophesy,
2Co 6:18 and you shall be sons and **d** to me,

DAVID
Son of Jesse (Ru 4:17-22; 1Ch 2:13-15), ancestor of Jesus (Mt 1:1-17; Lk 3:31). Wives and children (1Sa 18; 25:39-44; 2Sa 3:2-5; 5:13-16; 11:27; 1Ch 3:1-9).
Anointed king by Samuel (1Sa 16:1-13). Musician to Saul (1Sa 16:14-23; 18:10). Killed Goliath (1Sa 17). Relation with Jonathan (1Sa 18:1-4; 19-20; 23:16-18; 2Sa 1). Disfavor of Saul (1Sa 18:6-23:29). Spared Saul's life (1Sa 24; 26). Among Philistines (1Sa 21:10-14; 27-30). Lament for Saul and Jonathan (2Sa 1).
Anointed king of Judah (2Sa 2:1-11). Conflict with house of Saul (2Sa 2-4). Anointed king of Israel (2Sa 5:1-4; 1Ch 11:1-3). Conquered Jerusalem (2Sa 5:6-10; 1Ch 11;4-9). Brought ark to Jerusalem (2Sa

6; 1Ch 13; 15-16). The LORD promised eternal dynasty (2Sa 7; 1Ch 17; Ps 132). Showed kindness to Mephibosheth (2Sa 9). Adultery with Bathsheba, murder of Uriah (2Sa 11-12). Son Amnon raped daughter Tamar; killed by Absalom (2Sa 13). Absalom's revolt (2Sa 14-17); death (2Sa 18). Sheba's revolt (2Sa 20). Victories: Philistines (2Sa 5:17-25; 21:15-22; 1Ch 14:8-17; 20:4-8), Ammonites (2Sa 10; 1Ch 19), various (2Sa 8; 1Ch 18). Mighty men (2Sa 23:8-39; 1Ch 11-12). Punished for numbering army (2Sa 24; 1Ch 21). Appointed Solomon king (1Ki 1:28-2:9). Prepared for building of temple (1Ch 22-29). Last words (2Sa 23:1-7). Death (1Ki 2:10-12; 1Ch 29:28).

Psalmist (Mt 22:43-45), musician (Am 6:5), prophet (2Sa 23:2-7; Ac 1:16; 2:30).

Psalms of: 2 (Ac 4:25), 3-32, 34-41, 51-65, 68-70, 86, 95 (Heb 4:7), 101, 103, 108-110, 122, 124, 131, 133, 138-145.

DAWN → DAWNS
Isa 14:12 O morning star, son of the **d**!
Hos   6: 3 as certain as the **d** is his coming,

DAWNS → DAWN
Ps 97:11 Light **d** for the just; gladness,
2Pe 1:19 until day **d** and the morning star

DAY → DAILY, DAYS
Ge   1: 5 God called the light "**d**,"
     1: 5 and morning followed—the first **d**.
     8:22 Summer and winter, and **d** and night
Ex 13:21 Thus they could travel both **d**
    20: 8 to keep holy the sabbath **d**.
Jos   1: 8 Recite it by **d** and by night, that you
Ps   1: 2 God's law they study **d** and night.
   118:24 This is the **d** the LORD has made;
Isa 66: 8 a country be brought forth in one **d**,
Joel 1:15 Alas, the **d**! for near is the **d**
Zec 14: 1 a **d** shall come for the LORD
Mal   3: 2 But who will endure the **d** of his
Mt   25:13 you know neither the **d** nor the hour.
Lk   11: 3 Give us each **d** our daily bread
     24:46 and rise from the dead on the third **d**
Jn   6:40 and I shall raise him [on] the last **d**."
Ro   14: 5 considers one **d** more important
2Co   6: 2 on the **d** of salvation I helped you."
      6: 2 behold, now is the **d** of salvation.
1Th   5: 2 the **d** of the Lord will come like
2Pe   3: 8 the Lord one **d** is like a thousand
      3: 8 and a thousand years like one **d**.
      3:10 the **d** of the Lord will come like

DAYS → DAY
Ge   1:14 the fixed times, the **d** and the years,
      7: 4 Seven **d** from now I will bring rain
      7: 4 rain down on the earth for forty **d**
Ex   24:18 there he stayed for forty **d** and forty
1Ki 19: 8 he walked forty **d** and forty nights
1Ma   4:56 For eight **d** they celebrated
Mk   1:13 remained in the desert for forty **d**,
Eph   5:16 opportunity, because the **d** are evil.
2Ti   3: 1 will be terrifying times in the last **d**.
Heb   1: 2 in these last **d**, he spoke to us

DEACONS
1Ti   3: 8 Similarly, **d** must be dignified,

DEAD → DEATH, DIE, DIED, DYING
Dt   18:11 spirits or seeks oracles from the **d**.
Ps 115:17 The **d** do not praise the LORD,
Ecc   9: 4 a live dog is better off than a **d** lion.
Mt   8:22 me, and let the **d** bury their **d**."
Mk   12:27 He is not God of the **d**
Lk   24: 5 seek the living one among the **d**?
Ro   6:11 of yourselves as [being] **d** to sin
Eph   2: 1 You were **d** in your transgressions
Col   1:18 beginning, the firstborn from the **d**,
1Pe   4: 5 ready to judge the living and the **d**.
Rev   1: 5 the firstborn of the **d** and ruler
     20:12 I saw the **d**, the great and the lowly,
     20:12 life. The **d** were judged according

DEAF
Ex   4:11 and makes another **d** and dumb?
Isa 29:18 On that day the **d** shall hear
Lk   7:22 lepers are cleansed, the **d** hear,

DEATH → DEAD
Dt   30:19 I have set before you life and **d**,
Ru   1:17 aught but **d** separates me from you!"
Ps   22:16 palate; you lay me in the dust of **d**.
Pr   18:21 **D** and life are in the power
SS   8: 6 For stern as **d** is love, relentless as
Sir 15:17 Before man are life and **d**,
Hos 13:14 shall I redeem them from **d**?
     13:14 Where are your plagues, O **d**!
Mt   16:28 who will not taste **d** until they see

1Jn   4:17 the **d** of judgment because as he is,
Rev   1:10 caught up in spirit on the Lord's **d**
     16:14 on the great **d** of God the almighty.

Jn   5:24 but has passed from **d** to life.
Ro   6:23 For the wages of sin is **d**,
1Co 15:55 Where, O **d**, is your victory? Where,
     15:55 victory? Where, O **d**, is your sting?"
2Co   2:16 to the latter an odor of **d** that leads
      2:16 latter an odor of **d** that leads to **d**,
Heb   2:14 through **d** he might destroy the one
      2:14 the one who has the power of **d**,
1Jn   3:14 that we have passed from **d** to life
      3:14 does not love remains in **d**.
Rev   1:18 ever. I hold the keys to **d**
     20:14 Then **D** and Hades were thrown
     20:14 (This pool of fire is the second **d**.)
     21: 4 and there shall be no more **d**

DEBAUCHERY
Eph   5:18 in which lies **d**, but be filled

DEBORAH
    Prophetess; led victory over Canaanites (Jdg 4-5).

DEBTS
Dt   15: 1 you shall have a relaxation of **d**,
Mt   6:12 and forgive us our **d**, as we forgive

DECEIT → DECEITFUL, DECEIVE, DECEIVED, DECEIVERS
Dt   32: 4 A faithful God, without **d**, how just
1Pe   2:22 and no **d** was found in his mouth."

DECEITFUL → DECEIT
Ps   35:20 in the land they fashion **d** speech.
Zep   3:13 be found in their mouths a **d** tongue;
1Ti   4: 1 faith by paying attention to **d** spirits

DECEIVE → DECEIT
Eph   5: 6 Let no one **d** you with empty
1Jn   1: 8 "We are without sin," we **d** ourselves,
Rev 20: 8 to **d** the nations at the four corners

DECEIVED → DECEIT
1Ti   2:14 Adam was not **d**, but the woman
      2:14 the woman was **d** and transgressed.

DECEIVERS → DECEIT
Tit   1:10 idle talkers and **d**,
2Jn   1: 7 Many **d** have gone

DECISION
Pr   16:33 its **d** depends entirely on the LORD.

DECLARED
Mk   7:19 latrine?" (Thus he **d** all foods clean.)

DECREASE
Jn 3:30 He must increase; I must **d**."

DECREE → DECREED, DECREES
Ps 2: 7 I will proclaim the **d** of the LORD,
Lk 2: 1 In those days a **d** went

DECREED → DECREE
Da 9:24 "Seventy weeks are **d** for your people

DECREES → DECREE
Ps 119: 2 Happy those who observe God's **d**,

DEDICATED → DEDICATION
1Ki 8:63 all the Israelites **d** the temple

DEDICATION → DEDICATED
2Ch 7: 9 they had celebrated the **d** of the altar
Ezr 6:16 other returned exiles— celebrated the **d**
1Ma 4:56 eight days they celebrated the **d**

DEED → DEEDS
Jer 32:10 I had written and sealed the **d**,
Col 3:17 in word or in **d**, do everything

DEEDS → DEED
Dt 3:24 on earth can perform **d** as mighty as
Ps 9: 2 I will declare all your wondrous **d**.
Jer 50:29 Repay her for her **d**; as she has
Rev 19: 8 linen represents the righteous **d**

DEFEND
Ps 72: 4 he may **d** the oppressed among
Pr 31: 9 is just, **d** the needy and the poor!

DEFILE → DEFILED
Nu 35:34 Do not **d** the land in which you live
Mk 7:15 one from outside can **d** that person;
  7:15 come out from within are what **d**."

DEFILED → DEFILE
1Ma 1:37 the sanctuary; they **d** the sanctuary.
Ps 79: 1 they have **d** your holy temple,

DEFRAUD
Lev 19:13 "You shall not **d** or rob your
Mk 10:19 you shall not **d**; honor your father

DEITY
Col 2: 9 the whole fullness of the **d** bodily,

DELAY
Ps 70: 6 help and deliverer. LORD, do not **d**!
Heb 10:37 to come shall come; he shall not **d**.

DELIGHT → DELIGHTS
1Sa 15:22 "Does the LORD so **d** in holocausts
Ps 40: 9 To do your will is my **d**; my God,
Pr 8:30 and I was his **d** day by day,
Ro 7:22 For I take **d** in the law of God,

DELIGHTS → DELIGHT
Ps 5: 5 You are not a god who **d** in evil;

DELILAH
  Philistine who betrayed Samson (Jdg 16:4-22).

DELIVER → DELIVERANCE, DELIVERER, DELIVERS
Mt 27:43 let him **d** him now if he wants him.

DELIVERANCE → DELIVER
Est 4:14 and **d** will come to the Jews
Php 1:19 this will result in **d** for me through

DELIVERER → DELIVER
Ro 11:26 "The **d** will come out of Zion, he will

DEMON → DEMONIACS, DEMONIC, DEMONS
Tob 3: 8 the wicked **d** Asmodeus killed them
  6: 8 a woman who is afflicted by a **d**
Mt 11:18 they said, 'He is possessed by a **d**.'
  17:18 him and the **d** came out of him,
Jn 10:21 surely a **d** cannot open the eyes

DEMONIACS → DEMON
Mt 8:28 two **d** who were coming

DEMONIC → DEMON
Rev 16:14 These were **d** spirits who performed

DEMONS → DEMON
Dt 32:17 They offered sacrifice to **d**,
Bar 4: 7 with sacrifices to **d**, to no-gods;
Lk 11:18 it is by Beelzebul that I drive out **d**.
1Co 10:20 [they sacrifice] to **d**, not to God,
  10:20 you to become participants with **d**.
Jas 2:19 Even the **d** believe that and tremble.
Rev 9:20 to give up the worship of **d**

DEN
Jer 7:11 become in your eyes a **d** of thieves?
Mk 11:17 But you have made it a **d** of thieves."

DENARIUS
Mk 12:15 testing me? Bring me a **d** to look at."

DENIED → DENY
Mt 26:70 But he **d** it in front of everyone,
1Ti 5: 8 family members has **d** the faith
Rev 3: 8 my word and have not **d** my name.

DENIES → DENY
Lk 12: 9 whoever **d** me before others will be
1Jn 2:22 Whoever **d** that Jesus is the Christ.
  2:22 Whoever **d** the Father and the Son,

DENY → DENIED, DENIES
Mt 16:24 to come after me must **d** himself,
2Ti 2:12 him. But if we **d** him he will **d** us.
2Pe 2: 1 even **d** the Master who ransomed

DEPART
Ge 49:10 The scepter shall never **d**
Php 1:23 two. I long to **d** this life and be

DEPRAVED
2Pe 2:10 follow the flesh with its **d** desire

DEPRIVE
1Co 7: 5 Do not **d** each other, except perhaps

DEPTH → DEPTHS
Ro 11:33 the **d** of the riches and wisdom
Eph 3:18 breadth and length and height and **d**,

DEPTHS → DEPTH
Ps 130: 1 Out of the **d** I call to you, LORD;
1Co 2:10 everything, even the **d** of God.

DESCENDANTS
Ge 15:18 "To your **d** I give this land,
Dt 4:37 love of your fathers he chose their **d**
Isa 44: 3 and my blessing upon your **d**.
Ro 9: 7 of Abraham because they are his **d**;
  9: 7 Isaac that **d** shall bear your name."

DESCENDED → DESCENDING
Eph 4: 9 also **d** into the lower [regions]

DESCENDING → DESCENDED
Mk 1:10 the Spirit, like a dove, **d** upon him.
Jn 1:51 ascending and **d** on the Son of Man."

DESERT → DESERTED
Ps 106:14 In the **d** they gave way to their
Isa 40: 3 out: In the **d** prepare the way

DESERTED → DESERT
Mk 8: 4 to satisfy them here in this **d** place?"

DESERVE
Rev 2:23 give each of you what your works **d**.

DESIRE → DESIRED, DESIRES
Hos 6: 6 For it is love that I **d**, not sacrifice,
Mt 9:13 meaning of the words, 'I **d** mercy,
Jas 1:14 is lured and enticed by his own **d**.

DESIRED → DESIRE
Lk 22:15 "I have eagerly **d** to eat this Passover

DESIRES → DESIRE
Sir 18:30 your lusts, but keep your **d** in check.
2Ti 4: 3 following their own **d** and insatiable

DESOLATE → DESOLATING
Ex 23:29 else the land will become so **d**
1Ma 1:39 sanctuary was as **d** as a wilderness;
Mt 23:38 your house will be abandoned, **d**.

DESOLATING → DESOLATE
Mk 13:14 you see the **d** abomination standing

DESPAIR → DESPAIRED
2Co 4: 8 perplexed, but not driven to **d**;

DESPAIRED → DESPAIR
2Co 1: 8 strength, so that we **d** even of life.

DESPISE → DESPISED
Pr 1: 7 wisdom and instruction fools **d**.
Lk 16:13 be devoted to one and **d** the other.

DESPISED → DESPISE
1Co 1:28 chose the lowly and **d** of the world,

DESTINED
Eph 1: 5 he **d** us for adoption to himself
1Pe 1:11 to the sufferings **d** for Christ

DESTROY → DESTROYED, DESTROYER, DESTRUCTION
Ge 6:13 So I will **d** them and all life
Est 3: 6 he sought to **d** all the Jews,
Mt 10:28 of the one who can **d** both soul
Jn 10:10 only to steal and slaughter and **d**;
Jas 4:12 judge who is able to save or to **d**.
1Jn 3: 8 God was revealed to **d** the works

DESTROYED → DESTROY
1Co 15:26 The last enemy to be **d** is death,
2Co 5: 1 should be **d**, we have a building

DESTROYER → DESTROY
Ex 12:23 not let the **d** come into your houses
1Co 10:10 did, and suffered death by the **d**.

DESTRUCTION → DESTROY
Mt 7:13 and the road broad that leads to **d**,
Ro 9:22 the vessels of wrath made for **d**?
2Pe 3:16 and unstable distort to their own **d**,

DEVIL
Mt 4: 1 the desert to be tempted by the **d**.
Lk 8:12 but the **d** comes and takes away
Jn 8:44 You belong to your father the **d**
Eph 4:27 and do not leave room for the **d**.
6:11 firm against the tactics of the **d**.
Heb 2:14 the power of death, that is, the **d**,
Jas 4: 7 Resist the **d**, and he will flee

1Pe 5: 8 Your opponent the **d** is prowling

1Jn 3: 8 Whoever sins belongs to the **d**,
3: 8 **d**, because the **d** has sinned
3: 8 to destroy the works of the **d**.
Jude 1: 9 with the **d** in a dispute over the body
Rev 12: 9 who is called the **D** and Satan,
20: 2 serpent, which is the **D** or Satan,

DEVOTED → DEVOTION
Mt 6:24 or be **d** to one and despise the other.

DEVOTION → DEVOTED
Wis 10:12 that **d** to God is mightier than all else.
1Ti 4: 7 Train yourself for **d**,
2Pe 1: 3 everything that makes for life and **d**,

DEVOUR → DEVOURING
1Pe 5: 8 lion looking for [someone] to **d**.
Rev 12: 4 to **d** her child when she gave birth.

DEVOURING → DEVOUR
Gal 5:15 you go on biting and **d** one another,

DEW
Jdg 6:37 If **d** comes on the fleece alone,

DICTATED
Jer 36:18 "Jeremiah **d** all these words to me,"

DIE → DEAD
Ge 2:17 from it you are surely doomed to **d**."
3: 4 woman: "You certainly will not **d**!
Ex 11: 5 Every first-born in this land shall **d**,
Ru 1:17 Wherever you **d** I will **d**, and there
Job 2: 9 your innocence? Curse God and **d**."
Pr 10:21 many, but fools **d** for want of sense.
Ecc 3: 2 A time to be born, and a time to **d**;
Isa 22:13 "Eat and drink, for tomorrow we **d**!"
Jer 31:30 his own fault only shall anyone **d**:
Mt 26:35 "Even though I should have to **d**
Jn 11:26 and believes in me will never **d**.
Ro 14: 8 and if we **d**, we **d** for the Lord;
14: 8 whether we live or **d**, we are
1Co 15:32 eat and drink, for tomorrow we **d**."
Heb 9:27 that human beings **d** once,

DIED → DEAD
Ro 5: 6 yet **d** at the appointed time
1Co 15: 3 that Christ **d** for our sins
Gal 2:19 For through the law I **d** to the law,

DIFFERENT
2Co 11: 4 if you receive a **d** spirit from the one
11: 4 or a **d** gospel from the one you
Gal 1: 6 [the] grace [of Christ] for a **d** gospel

DILIGENCE
Ro 12: 8 if one is over others, with **d**; if one

DINAH
Only daughter of Jacob, by Leah (Ge 30:21; 46:15). Raped by Shechem; avenged by Simeon and Levi (Ge 34).

DIRECT → DIRECTS
2Th 3: 5 May the Lord **d** your hearts

DIRECTS → DIRECT
Pr 16: 9 his course, but the LORD **d** his steps.

DISAPPOINT
Ro 5: 5 and hope does not **d**,

DISASTER
Eze 7: 5 Thus says the Lord GOD: **D** upon **d**!

DISCERNMENT
1Co 12:10 to another **d** of spirits; to another

DISCIPLE → DISCIPLES
Mt 10:24 No **d** is above his teacher, no slave
Lk 14:26 his own life, he cannot be my **d**.

DISCIPLES → DISCIPLE
Isa 8:16 sealed instruction kept among my **d**.
Mt 26:56 Then all the **d** left him and fled.
28:19 and make **d** of all nations,
Lk 6:13 day came, he called his **d** to himself,
Jn 8:31 in my word, you will truly be my **d**,
Ac 11:26 the **d** were first called Christians.

DISCIPLINE → DISCIPLINED
Pr 5:23 He will die from lack of **d**,
Heb 12: 5 son, do not disdain the **d** of the Lord

DISCIPLINED → DISCIPLINE
1Co 11:32 we are being **d** so that we may not

DISEASE → DISEASES
Mt 4:23 curing every **d** and illness among
9:35 and curing every **d** and illness.

DISEASES → DISEASE
Ex 15:26 any of the **d** with which I afflicted
Mt 8:17 away our infirmities and bore our **d**."

DISGRACE
1Ma 4:58 the **d** of the Gentiles was removed.
Pr 11: 2 When pride comes, **d** comes;

DISHONEST
Lk 16:10 the person who is **d** in very small
16:10 small matters is also **d** in great ones.

DISHONOR
Jn 8:49 I honor my Father, but you **d** me.
Ac 5:41 worthy to suffer **d** for the sake

DISMAYED
Jos 1: 9 Do not fear nor be **d**, for the LORD,

DISOBEDIENT → DISOBEYING
Ro 10:21 long I stretched out my hands to a **d**
Tit 3: 3 we ourselves were once foolish, **d**,

DISOBEYING → DISOBEDIENT
Lev 26:27 you still persist in **d** and defying me,
1Pe 2: 8 They stumble by **d** the word, as is

DISPERSION
Jn 7:35 not going to the **d** among the Greeks

DISQUALIFIED → DISQUALIFY
1Co 9:27 to others, I myself should be **d**.

DISQUALIFY → DISQUALIFIED
Col 2:18 Let no one **d** you,

DISSENSIONS
Gal 5:20 fury, acts of selfishness, **d**, factions,

DISTINCTION → DISTINCTIONS
Ro 3:22 all who believe. For there is no **d**;

DISTINCTIONS → DISTINCTION
Jas 2: 4 you not made **d** among yourselves

DISTRESS
Dt 4:30 In your **d**, when all these things
Jdg 2:15 would do, till they were in great **d**.
2Sa 22: 7 In my **d** I called upon the LORD
Ps 81: 8 In **d** you called and I rescued you;
Jer 30: 7 it! At time of **d** for Jacob, though he
Ro 8:35 Will anguish, or **d**, or persecution,

DISTRIBUTED
Ac 4:35 they were **d** to each according

DIVIDE → DIVIDED
Ps 22:19 they **d** my garments among them;

DIVIDED → DIVIDE
Lk 11:18 And if Satan is **d** against himself,

DIVINATION → DIVINE
1Sa 15:23 For a sin like **d** is rebellion,
2Ki 17:17 practiced fortune-telling and **d**,

DIVINE → DIVINATION
2Pe 1: 4 may come to share in the **d** nature,

DIVORCE → DIVORCED
Dt 24: 1 therefore he writes out a bill of **d**
Isa 50: 1 Where is the bill of **d** with which I
Jer 3: 8 her away and gave her a bill of **d**,
Mal 2:16 For I hate **d**, says the LORD, the God
Mt 5:31 his wife must give her a bill of **d**.'
19: 3 a man to **d** his wife for any cause
1Co 7:11 a husband should not **d** his wife.

DIVORCED → DIVORCE
Lev 21: 7 nor a woman who has been **d** by her
Mt 5:32 marries a **d** woman commits

DOCTRINE → DOCTRINES
2Ti 4: 3 people will not tolerate sound **d** but,
Tit 1: 9 be able both to exhort with sound **d**

DOCTRINES → DOCTRINE
Mk 7: 7 me, teaching as **d** human precepts.'
1Ti 1: 3 certain people not to teach false **d**

DOEG
Edomite; Saul's chief shepherd; murdered 85 priests at Nob (1Sa 21:7; 22:6-23; Ps 52).

DOERS → DOES, DONE
Jas 1:22 Be **d** of the word and not hearers

DOES → DOERS
Ps 135: 6 wishes he **d** in heaven and on earth,
Ecc 3:14 whatever God **d** will endure forever;
Mk 3:35 [For] whoever **d** the will of God is

DOG → DOGS
Jdg 7: 5 up the water as a **d** does with its
Pr 26:11 As the **d** returns to his vomit,
2Pe 2:22 "The **d** returns to its own vomit,"

DOGS → DOG
Mt 7: 6 "Do not give what is holy to **d**,
15:26 of the children and throw it to the **d**."
Php 3: 2 Beware of the **d**!
Rev 22:15 Outside are the **d**, the sorcerers,

DOMINION
Ge 1:26 Let them have **d** over the fish
Da 7:14 He received **d**, glory, and kingship;
7:14 serve him. His **d** is an everlasting **d**

DONE → DOERS
Mt 6:10 come, your will be **d**, on earth as
26:42 my drinking it, your will be **d**!"

Rev 16:17 from the throne, saying, "It is **d**."

DOOM → DOOMED
Dt 32:35 and their **d** is rushing upon them!
Ps 81:16 tremble, their **d** sealed forever.

DOOMED → DOOM
Ps 102:21 prisoners, to release those **d** to die."

DOOR → DOORPOSTS
Mt 7: 7 and the **d** will be opened to you,
Rev 3:20 " ' 'Behold, I stand at the **d** and knock.
3:20 hears my voice and opens the **d**.

DOORPOSTS → DOOR
Ex 12: 7 apply it to the two **d** and the lintel

DORCAS
Disciple; raised from the dead (Ac 9:36-43).

DOUBLE
Dt 21:17 giving him a **d** share of whatever he
1Sa 1: 5 a **d** portion to Hannah because he
2Ki 2: 9 "May I receive a **d** portion of your
Rev 18: 6 others. Pay her back **d** for her deeds.
Rev 18: 6 her cup pour **d** what she poured.

DOUBT → DOUBTED, DOUBTING
Mt 14:31 "O you of little faith, why did you **d**?"

DOUBTED → DOUBT
Mt 28:17 him, they worshiped, but they **d**.

DOUBTING → DOUBT
Jas 1: 6 not **d**, for the one who doubts is like

DOUGH
Ex 12:39 Since the **d** they had brought
Gal 5: 9 yeast leavens the whole batch of **d**.

DOVE
Ge 8: 8 Then he sent out a **d**, to see
Mk 1:10 like a **d**, descending upon him.

DRAGON
Isa 27: 1 he will slay the **d** that is in the sea.
Da 14:23 There was a great **d**
Rev 12: 3 sky; it was a huge red **d**, with seven
20: 2 He seized the **d**, the ancient serpent,

DRANK → DRINK
Mk 14:23 it to them, and they all **d** from it,
1Co 10: 4 and all **d** the same spiritual drink,
10: 4 for they **d** from a spiritual rock

DRAW
Jn 12:32 earth, I will **d** everyone to my-self."
Jas 4: 8 **D** near to God, and he will **d** near

DREAM → DREAMER, DREAMS
1Ki 3: 5 appeared to Solomon in a **d** at night.
Da 7: 1 Daniel had a **d** as he lay in bed,
    7: 1 Then he wrote down the **d**;
Mt 1:20 of the Lord appeared to him in a **d**
Ac 2:17 your old men shall **d** dreams.

DREAMER → DREAM
Ge 37:19 another: "Here comes that master **d**!

DREAMS → DREAM
Nu 12: 6 to him, in **d** I will speak to him;
1Sa 28: 6 whether in **d** or by the Urim
Sir 34: 7 For **d** have led many astray,

DRIED → DRY
Jos 5: 1 that the LORD had **d** up the wa-ters
Isa 51:10 Was it not you who **d** up the sea,

DRINK → DRANK, DRUNK, DRUNKARD, DRUNKENNESS
Ex 32: 6 Then they sat down to eat and **d**,
Ecc 9: 7 and **d** your wine with a merry heart,
Isa 22:13 You eat meat and **d** wine: "Eat and **d**,
Mt 20:22 Can you **d** the cup that I am going
    20:22 you **d** the cup that I am going to **d**?"
Jn 18:11 Shall I not **d** the cup that the Father
Ro 14:17 of God is not a matter of food and **d**,
1Co 12:13 we were all given to **d** of one Spirit.
Rev 14:10 will also **d** the wine of God's fury,

DRIVE → DROVE
Ex 23:30 I will **d** them out little by little
Nu 33:52 **d** out all the inhabitants of the land
Mk 11:15 the temple area he began to **d**

DROSS
Ps 119:119 Like **d** you regard all the wicked
Isa 1:25 and refine your **d** in the fur-nace,
Eze 22:18 of Israel has become **d** for me.
    22:18 **d** from silver have they be-come.

DROVE → DRIVE
Jos 24:18 our approach the LORD **d** out [all
Mk 1:12 At once the Spirit **d** him

DRUNK → DRINK
Ge 9:21 he became **d** and lay naked inside
1Sa 1:13 not be heard. Eli, thinking her **d**,

Jn 2:10 and then when people have **d** freely,
Ac 2:15 These people are not **d**, as you
Eph 5:18 And do not get **d** on wine,

DRUNKARD → DRINK
Pr 23:21 For the **d** and the glutton come
Mt 11:19 he is a glutton and a **d**, a friend
1Co 5:11 a slanderer, a **d**, or a robber,
1Ti 3: 3 not a **d**, not aggressive, but gentle,

DRUNKENNESS → DRINK
Tob 4:15 nor let **d** accompany you on your

DRY → DRIED
Ge 1: 9 basin, so that the **d** land may appear."
    1: 9 its basin, and the **d** land ap-peared.
Ex 14:16 may pass through it on **d** land.
Jos 3:17 all Israel crossed over on **d** ground,
    3:17 remained motionless on **d** ground
Jdg 6:37 while all the ground is **d**, I shall
Eze 37: 4 **D** bones, hear the word of the LORD!

DUE
1Ch 16:29 to the LORD the glory **d** his name!
Mal 1: 6 father, where is the honor **d** to me?
    1: 6 where is the reverence **d** to me?—
Ro 13: 7 taxes to whom taxes are **d**,
    13: 7 **d**, toll to whom toll is **d**,
    13: 7 respect to whom respect is **d**,
    13: 7 is **d**, honor to whom honor is **d**.

DULL
Isa 6:10 to **d** their ears and close their eyes;
    59: 1 to save, nor his ear too **d** to hear.

DUST
Ge 13:16 make your descendants like the **d**
1Sa 2: 8 He raises the needy from the **d**;
Ps 103:14 formed, remembers that we are **d**.
Ecc 3:20 both were made from the **d**,
    3:20 the **d**, and to the **d** they both return.
Na 1: 3 and clouds are the **d** at his feet;
Mt 10:14 and shake the **d** from your feet.

DWELL → DWELLING, DWELLS
Ex 25: 8 for me, that I may **d** in their midst.
Ps 23: 6 life; I will **d** in the house of the LORD
Eph 3:17 Christ may **d** in your hearts through
Col 1:19 all the fullness was pleased to **d**,
Rev 21: 3 He will **d** with them and they will

DWELLING → DWELL
Lev 26:11 I will set my **D** among you, and will
Dt 12:11 chooses as the **d** place for his name
Jn 14: 2 house there are many **d** places.
Eph 2:22 being built together into a **d** place

DWELLS → DWELL
1Ki 8:27 it indeed be that God **d** among men
Jn 14:10 The Father who **d** in me is doing his
Ro 7:17 I who do it, but sin that **d** in me.
1Co 3:16 and that the Spirit of God **d** in you?
Col 2: 9 in him **d** the whole fullness

DYING → DEAD
2Co 6: 9 as **d** and behold we live;

E

EAGLE → EAGLES
Eze 1:10 finally each had the face of an **e**.
    17: 3 The great **e**, with great wings,
Rev 4: 7 the fourth looked like an **e** in flight.

EAGLES → EAGLE
Isa 40:31 they will soar as with **e'** wings;

EAR → EARS
Lk 22:51 he touched the servant's **e** and healed
1Co 2: 9 has not seen, and **e** has not heard,

EARLY
Dt 11:14 land, the **e** rain and the late rain,
Lk 24:22 were at the tomb **e** in the morning
Jas 5: 7 patient with it until it receives the **e**

EARS → EAR
Isa 35: 5 opened, the **e** of the deaf be cleared;
Mt 11:15 Whoever has **e** ought to hear.
Rev 2: 7 " ' "Whoever has **e** ought to hear what

EARTH → EARTHLY, EARTHQUAKE, EARTHQUAKES
Ge 1: 1 God created the heavens and the **e**,
    6:11 In the eyes of God the **e** was corrupt
Ex 19: 5 people, though all the **e** is mine.
Ps 47: 3 awe, the great king over all the **e**,
Sir 40:11 All that is of **e** returns to **e**, and
Isa 6: 3 "All the **e** is filled with his glory!"
    65:17 and a new **e**; The things of the past
Jer 23:24 both heaven and **e**? says the LORD.
Mt 24:35 Heaven and **e** will pass away,
Lk 5:24 of Man has authority on **e** to forgive

EARTH → EARTHLY, EARTHQUAKE, EARTHQUAKES (*cont.*)
2Pe 3:13 and a new **e** in which righteousness
Rev 21: 1 I saw a new heaven and a new **e**.
    21: 1 and the former **e** had passed away,

EARTHLY → EARTH
Jn 3:12 If I tell you about **e** things and you
2Co 5: 1 For we know that if our **e** dwelling,

EARTHQUAKE → EARTH, QUAKE
1Ki 19:11 the LORD was not in the **e**.
Mt 28: 2 And behold, there was a great **e**;
Ac 16:26 there was suddenly such a severe **e**
Rev 6:12 sixth seal, and there was a great **e**;

EARTHQUAKES → EARTH, QUAKE
Mt 24: 7 famines and **e** from place to place.

EASIER → EASY
Mt 9: 5 Which is **e**, to say, 'Your sins are
Lk 16:17 It is **e** for heaven and earth to pass
    18:25 For it is **e** for a camel to pass

EAST
Ge 2: 8 in the **e**, and he placed there
Ps 103:12 As far as the **e** is from the west,
Mt 2: 1 behold, magi from the **e** arrived

EASY → EASIER
Mt 11:30 For my yoke is **e**, and my burden

EAT → ATE, EATING, EATS
Ge 2:16 "You are free to **e** from any
Ex 2:11 "This is how you are to **e** it:
    12:11 you shall **e** like those who are
Lev 11: 4 you shall not **e** any of the following
Ecc 2:24 is nothing better for man than to **e**
Mt 26:26 it to his disciples said, "Take and **e**;
Ac 10:13 him, "Get up, Peter. Slaughter and **e**."
1Co 10:31 So whether you **e** or drink,

EATING → EAT
Lk 7:34 The Son of Man came **e**
1Co 8: 4 So about the **e** of meat sacrificed

EATS → EAT
Jn 6:51 whoever **e** this bread will live
1Co 11:27 Therefore whoever **e** the bread

EDEN
Ge 2: 8 the LORD God planted a garden in **E**,
Isa 51: 3 Her deserts he shall make like **E**,
Eze 28:13 In **E**, the garden of God, you were,

EDOM → = ESAU
Ge 25:30 (That is why he was called **E**.)
Nu 20:18 But **E** answered him, "You shall not
Ob 1: 1 Of **E** we have heard a message
Mal 1: 4 If **E** says, "We have been crushed

EFFORT
2Pe 1: 5 make every **e** to supplement your

EGYPT
Ge 12:10 land; so Abram went down to **E**
    37:28 out of the cistern and took him to **E**.
    47:27 as Israel settled in the land of **E**,
Ex 1: 8 of Joseph, came to power in **E**.
    12:40 had stayed in **E** was four hundred
Jos 15:47 as far as the Wadi of **E** and the coast
Ne 9:18 God who brought you up out of **E**,'
Ps 78:51 He struck all the firstborn of **E**,
Hos 11: 1 loved him, out of **E** I called my son.
Mt 2:15 fulfilled, "Out of **E** I called my son."
Rev 11: 8 the symbolic names "Sodom" and "**E**,"

EHUD
Judge of Israel (Jdg 3:12-30).

ELAH
1. Son of Baasha; king of Israel (1Ki 16:6-14).
2. Valley in which David fought Goliath (1Sa 17:2, 19; 21:9).

ELDERS
Ex 24: 1 and seventy of the **e** of Israel.
Jdg 2: 7 of those **e** who outlived Joshua
Isa 3:14 with his people's **e** and princes: It is
Da 13:61 They rose up against the two **e**,
Mt 27:12 accused by the chief priests and **e**,
Mk 7: 3 hands, keeping the tradition of the **e**.
Rev 4: 4 thrones on which twenty-four **e** sat,

ELEAZAR
1. Third son of Aaron (Ex 6:23-25). Succeeded Aaron as high priest (Nu 20:26; Dt 10:6). Allotted land to tribes (Jos 14:1). Death (Jos 24:33).
2. Brother of Judas Maccabeus (1Ma 2:5; 6:43-46).

ELECT → ELECTION
Mt 24:22 sake of the **e** they will be shortened.
Mk 13:22 mislead, if that were possible, the **e**.

ELECTION → ELECT
Ro 11:28 but in respect to **e**, they are beloved
2Pe 1:10 eager to make your call and **e** firm,

ELEMENTS
Heb 5:12 someone teach you again the basic **e**
2Pe 3:10 and the **e** will be dissolved by fire,

ELEVEN
Mt 28:16 The **e** disciples went to Galilee,
Ac 1:26 he was counted with the **e** apostles.

ELI
1. High priest in youth of Samuel (1Sa 1-4). Blessed Hannah (1Sa 1:12-18); raised Samuel (1Sa 2:11-26). Prophesied against because of wicked sons (1Sa 2:27-36). Death of Eli and sons (1Sa 4:11-22).
2. "Eli, Eli, lema sabachthani?" (Mt 27:46).

ELIAKIM → = JEHOIAKIM
1. Original name of Jehoiakim (2Ki 23:34; 2Ch 36:4).
2. Hezekiah's palace administrator (2Ki 18:17-37; 19:2; Isa 36:1-22; 37:2).

ELIEZER
1. Servant of Abraham (Ge 15:2).
2. Son of Moses (Ex 18:4; 1Ch 23:15-17).

ELIHU
A friend of Job (Job 32-37).

ELIJAH
Prophet; predicted famine in Israel (1Ki 17:1; Jas 5:17). Fed by ravens (1Ki 17:2-6). Raised Sidonian widow's son (1Ki 17:7-24). Defeated prophets of Baal at Carmel (1Ki 18:16-46). Ran from Jezebel (1Ki 19:1-9). Prophesied death of Azariah (2Ki 1). Succeeded by Elisha (1Ki 19:19-21; 2Ki 2:1-18). Taken to heaven in whirlwind (2Ki 2:11-12; Sir 48:1-12; 1Ma 2:58).
Return prophesied (Mal 4:5-6); equated with John the Baptist (Mt 17:9-13; Mk 9:9-13; Lk 1:17). Appeared with Moses in transfiguration of Jesus (Mt 17:1-8; Mk 9:1-8).

ELIMELECH
Ru 1: 3 **E**, the husband of Naomi, died,

ELIPHAZ
A friend of Job (Job 4-5; 15; 22; 42:7, 9).

ELISHA
Prophet; successor of Elijah (1Ki 19:16-21; Sir 48:12-14); inherited his mantle (2Ki 2:1-18). Purified bad water (2Ki 2:19-22). Cursed young men (2Ki 2:23-25). Aided Israel's defeat of Moab (2Ki 3). Provided widow with oil (2Ki 4:1-7). Raised Shunammite woman's son (2Ki 4:8-37). Purified food (2Ki 4:38-41). Fed 100 men (2Ki 4:42-44). Healed Naaman's leprosy (2Ki 5). Made axhead float (2Ki 6:1-7). Captured Arameans (2Ki 6:8-23). Political adviser to Israel (2Ki 6:24-8:6; 9:1-3; 13:14-19), Aram (2Ki 8:7-15). Death (2Ki 13:20).

ELIZABETH
Mother of John the Baptist (Lk 1:5-58).

ELKANAH
Husband of Hannah, father of Samuel (1Sa 1-2).

EMMANUEL → = IMMANUEL
Mt 1:23 and they shall name him **E**,"

EMMAUS
Lk 24:13 miles from Jerusalem called **E**,

EMPTIED → EMPTY
1Co 1:17 cross of Christ might not be **e** of its
Php 2: 7 Rather, he **e** himself,

EMPTY → EMPTIED, EMPTY-HANDED
Eph 5: 6 one deceive you with **e** arguments,

EMPTY-HANDED → EMPTY, HAND
Ex 23:15 No one shall appear before me **e**.
Ru 3:17 come back to my mother-in-law **e**!"

ENCOURAGEMENT
Ac 4:36 (which is translated "son of **e**"),
Ro 15: 5 and **e** grant you to think in harmony
Php 2: 1 If there is any **e** in Christ,

END → ENDS
Ge 6:13 decided to put an **e** to all mortals
Pr 14:12 a man, but the **e** of it leads to death!
Ecc 12:12 making of many books there is no **e**,
Mt 24:13 perseveres to the **e** will be saved.
  28:20 you always, until the **e** of the age."
Jn 13: 1 world and he loved them to the **e**.
Ro 10: 4 For Christ is the **e** of the law
Rev 22:13 the last, the beginning and the **e**."

ENDOR
1Sa 28: 7 is a woman in **E** who is a medium."

ENDS → END
Ps 2: 8 your possession the **e** of the earth.
Isa 40:28 creator of the **e** of the earth. He does
Ro 10:18 their words to the **e** of the world."

ENDURANCE → ENDURE
Ro 5: 3 knowing that affliction produces **e**,
Heb 10:36 You need **e** to do the will of God
2Pe 1: 6 self-control with **e**, **e** with devotion,
Rev 1: 9 and the **e** we have in Jesus,

ENDURE → ENDURANCE, ENDURED, ENDURES
Mal 3: 2 who will **e** the day of his coming?

ENDURED → ENDURE
Heb 12: 2 that lay before him he **e** the cross,

ENDURES → ENDURE
1Ch 16:41 "because his kindness **e** forever,"
Sir 40:17 off, and justice **e** forever.
Bar 4: 1 the law that **e** forever; All who cling

Mt 10:22 whoever **e** to the end will be saved.
Jn 6:27 for the food that **e** for eternal life,
1Co 13: 7 things, hopes all things, **e** all things.

ENEMIES → ENEMY
Ex 23:22 I will be an enemy to your **e**
Jdt 8:35 you to take vengeance upon our **e**!"
Est 9: 5 The Jews struck down all their **e**
  9: 5 they did to their **e** as they pleased.
1Ma 4:36 "Now that our **e** have been crushed,
Ps 110: 1 while I make your **e** your footstool."
Mt 5:44 love your **e**, and pray for those who
Lk 20:43 till I make your **e** your footstool." '
Ro 5:10 if, while we were **e**, we were

ENEMY → ENEMIES, ENMITY
Mt 13:39 the **e** who sows them is the devil.
1Co 15:26 The last **e** to be destroyed is death,
Jas 4: 4 of the world makes himself an **e**

ENJOY → ENJOYMENT
Ecc 9: 9 **E** life with the wife whom you love,

ENJOYMENT → ENJOY
1Ti 6:17 provides us with all things for our **e**.

ENLIGHTENED → LIGHT
Eph 1:18 May the eyes of [your] hearts be **e**,
Heb 6: 4 case of those who have once been **e**

ENLIGHTENS → LIGHT
Jn 1: 9 which **e** everyone, was coming

ENMITY → ENEMY
Ge 3:15 I will put **e** between you
Jas 4: 4 of the world means **e** with God?

ENOCH
Walked with God and taken by him (Ge 5:18-24; Heb 11:5; Sir 44:16). Prophet (Jude 14).

ENSLAVE → SLAVE
Gal 2: 4 in Christ Jesus, that they might **e** us—

ENTER → ENTRY
Ex 40:35 Moses could not **e** the meeting tent,
Nu 20:24 he shall not **e** the land I am giving
Ps 95:11 anger: "They shall never **e** my rest."
Mt 5:20 you will not **e** into the kingdom
  7:13 "**E** through the narrow gate;
  7:13 those who **e** through it are many.
Mk 10:15 of God like a child will not **e** it."

Jn 3: 5 no one can **e** the kingdom of God
Heb 3:11 "They shall not **e** into my rest." ' "
Rev 21:27 but nothing unclean will **e** it,
  21:27 Only those will **e** whose names are

ENTHRONED → THRONE
1Ch 13: 6 the name "LORD **e** upon the cherubim."

ENTRUSTED → TRUST
Lk 12:48 required of the person **e** with much,
  12:48 of the person **e** with more.
2Ti 1:12 to guard what has been **e** to me until

ENVY
Mk 7:22 deceit, licentiousness, **e**, blasphemy,
Ro 1:29 full of **e**, murder, rivalry, treachery,

EPHOD
Ex 28: 6 "The **e** they shall make of gold
Jdg 8:27 Gideon made an **e** out of the gold

EPHRAIM
1. Second son of Joseph (Ge 41:52; 46:20). Blessed as firstborn by Jacob (Ge 48). Tribe of numbered (Nu 1:33; 26:37), blessed (Dt 33:17), allotted land (Jos 16:4-9; Eze 48:5), failed to fully possess (Jos 16:10; Jdg 1:29).
2. Term for the Northern Kingdom (Isa 7:17; Hos 5).

EQUAL → EQUALITY
Isa 40:25 To whom can you liken me as an **e**?
  46: 5 you compare me with, as an **e**,
Jn 5:18 father, making himself **e** to God.

EQUALITY → EQUAL
Php 2: 6 of God, did not regard **e** with God

EQUIPPED
2Ti 3:17 competent, **e** for every good work.

ESAU → = EDOM
Firstborn of Isaac, twin of Jacob (Ge 25:21-26). Also called Edom (Ge 25:30). Sold Jacob his birthright (Ge 25:29-34); lost blessing (Ge 27). Married Hittites (Ge 26:34), Ishmaelites (Ge 28:6-9). Reconciled to Jacob (Ge 33). Genealogy (Ge 36). The LORD chose Jacob over Esau (Mal 1:2-3), but gave Esau land (Dt 2:2-12). Descendants eventually obliterated (Ob 1-21; Jer 49:7-22).

ESCAPE
Ps 68:21 **e** from death is in the LORD God's
Ro 2: 3 that you will **e** the judgment
1Th 5: 3 woman, and they will not **e**.
Heb 12:25 they did not **e** when they refused

ESTABLISH → ESTABLISHED
Ge 6:18 But with you I will **e** my covenant;

1785

ESTABLISH → ESTABLISHED (*cont.*)

Dt 28: 9 he will **e** you as a people sacred

Ps 89: 5 and **e** your throne through all ages."

Ro 10: 3 to **e** their own [righteousness],

ESTABLISHED → ESTABLISH

Ps 89: 3 For you said, "My love is **e** forever;

103:19 The LORD's throne is **e** in heaven;

Jer 10:12 power, **e** the world by his wisdom,

2Pe 1:12 and are **e** in the truth you have.

ESTHER

Jewess, originally named Hadassah, who lived in Persia; cousin of Mordecai (Est 2:7). Chosen queen of Xerxes (Est 2:8-18). Persuaded by Mordecai to foil Haman's plan to exterminate the Jews (Est 3-4). Revealed Haman's plans to Xerxes, resulting in Haman's death (Est 7), the Jews' preservation (Est 8-9), Mordecai's exaltation (Est 8:15; 9:4; 10). Decreed celebration of Purim (Est 9:18-32).

ETERNAL → ETERNITY

Mt 25:46 these will go off to **e** punishment,

25:46 but the righteous to **e** life."

Mk 10:17 what must I do to inherit **e** life?"

Jn 3:16 not perish but might have **e** life.

4:14 spring of water welling up to **e** life."

10:28 I give them **e** life, and they shall

Ro 5:21 **e** life through Jesus Christ our Lord.

2Co 4:17 us an **e** weight of glory beyond all

Heb 5: 9 he became the source of **e** salvation

1Jn 5:13 you may know that you have **e** life,

ETERNITY → ETERNAL

Sir 42:21 he is from all **e** one and the same,

2Pe 3:18 be glory now and to the day of **e**.

EUNUCH → EUNUCHS

Ac 8:27 Now there was an Ethiopian **e**,

EUNUCHS → EUNUCH

Isa 56: 4 To the **e** who observe my sabbaths

EUPHRATES

Ge 2:14 of Asshur. The fourth river is the **E**.

15:18 of Egypt to the Great River [the **E**],

Rev 16:12 his bowl on the great river **E**.

EUTYCHUS

Ac 20: 9 and a young man named **E** who was

EVANGELIST → EVANGELISTS

Ac 21: 8 we went to the house of Philip the **e**,

2Ti 4: 5 perform the work of an **e**;

EVANGELISTS → EVANGELIST

Eph 4:11 others as **e**, others as pastors

EVE

Ge 3:20 The man called his wife **E**,

4: 1 man had relations with his wife **E**,

Tob 8: 6 Adam and you gave him his wife **E**

2Co 11: 3 as the serpent deceived **E** by his

1Ti 2:13 For Adam was formed first, then **E**.

EVENING

Ge 1: 5 "night." Thus **e** came, and morning

Ecc 11: 6 and at **e** let not your hand be idle;

Zec 14: 7 for in the **e** time there shall be light.

EVERLASTING → LAST

Ge 9:16 and recall the **e** covenant that I have

EVERY → EVERYTHING

Ge 7:23 The LORD wiped out **e** living thing

Ex 11: 5 **E** first-born in this land shall die,

Dt 8: 3 by **e** word that comes forth

Ecc 12:14 God will bring to judgment **e** work,

Isa 45:23 To me **e** knee shall bend; by me **e**

Mt 12:25 "**E** kingdom divided against itself

Ro 14:11 Lord, **e** knee shall bend before me,

14:11 **e** tongue shall give praise to God."

Php 2:10 name of Jesus **e** knee should bend,

2Ti 3:17 equipped for **e** good work.

1Jn 4: 1 do not trust **e** spirit but test

Rev 21: 4 He will wipe **e** tear from their eyes,

EVERYTHING → EVERY

Ge 1:31 God looked at **e** he had made,

Ex 19: 8 together, "**E** the LORD has said,

Ecc 3: 1 There is an appointed time for **e**,

1Co 10:31 you do, do **e** for the glory of God.

1Ti 4: 4 For **e** created by God is good,

2Pe 1: 3 has bestowed on us **e** that makes

EVIL → EVILDOERS, EVILS

Ge 6: 5 conceived was ever anything but **e**,

Ex 32:22 how prone the people are to **e**.

Tob 12: 7 and **e** will not find its way to you.

Pr 8:13 [The fear of the LORD is to hate **e**;]

8:13 Pride, arrogance, the **e** way,

Sir 7: 1 Do no **e**, and **e** will not overtake

Isa 5:20 Woe to those who call **e** good,

5:20 those who call **e** good, and good **e**,

Mt 6:13 test, but deliver us from the **e** one.

12:35 an **e** person brings forth **e**

12:35 brings forth **e** out of a store of **e**.

Jn 17:15 that you keep them from the **e** one.

Ro 12:17 Do not repay anyone **e** for **e**;

Eph 5:16 opportunity, because the days are **e**.

1Pe 2:16 using freedom as a pretext for **e**,

1Jn 5:18 and the **e** one cannot touch him.

2Jn 1:11 greets him shares in his **e** works.

3Jn 1:11 do not imitate **e** but imitate good.

1:11 does what is **e** has never seen God.

EVILDOERS → EVIL

Ps 34:17 The LORD's face is against **e** to wipe

Lk 13:27 are from. Depart from me, all you **e**!'

1Pe 2:12 so that if they speak of you as **e**,

EVILS → EVIL

1Ti 6:10 love of money is the root of all **e**,

EXALT → EXALTED, EXALTS

Pr 4: 8 Extol her, and she will **e** you;

Jas 4:10 before the Lord and he will **e** you.

EXALTED → EXALT

Ps 97: 9 all the earth, **e** far above all gods.

Isa 2:11 and the LORD alone will be **e**,

Php 2: 9 Because of this, God greatly **e** him

EXALTS → EXALT

Pr 14:34 Virtue **e** a nation, but sin is

Sir 7:11 man; be mindful of him who **e**

Lk 14:11 For everyone who **e** himself will be

EXAMINE

1Co 11:28 A person should **e** himself, and so

2Co 13: 5 **E** yourselves to see whether you are

EXAMPLES

1Co 10: 6 These things happened as **e** for us,

1Pe 5: 3 to you, but be **e** to the flock.

EXCELLENCE → EXCELLENT

Php 4: 8 if there is any **e** and if there is

EXCELLENT → EXCELLENCE

1Co 12:31 I shall show you a still more **e** way.

Heb 1: 4 has inherited is more **e** than theirs.

EXCEPT

2Sa 22:32 "For who is God **e** the LORD? Who is

Mt 11:27 No one knows the Son **e** the Father,

Mt 11:27 no one knows the Father **e** the Son

Lk 11:29 will be given it, **e** the sign of Jonah.

Jn 14: 6 comes to the Father **e** through me.

EXCHANGED

Ps 106:20 They **e** their glorious God

Ro 1:23 **e** the glory of the immortal God

EXCUSE

Jn 15:22 as it is they have no **e** for their sin.

Ro 1:20 made. As a result, they have no **e**;

EXHORT

Tit 2:15 **E** and correct with all authority.

EXILE

2Ki 25:11 led into **e** the last of the people

Ezr 6:21 had returned from the **e** partook of it

EXIST → EXISTED, EXISTS

1Co 8: 6 all things are and for whom we **e**,

      8: 6 things are and through whom we **e**.

Heb 2:10 and through whom all things **e**,

EXISTED → EXIST

2Pe 3: 5 the fact that the heavens **e** of old

EXISTS → EXIST

Heb 11: 6 God must believe that he **e**

EXPECTING

Lk 6:35 to them, and lend **e** nothing back;

EXPLAIN → EXPLAINED

2Ch 9: 2 Solomon that he could not **e** to her.

Da 5:12 how to interpret dreams, **e** enigmas,

EXPLAINED → EXPLAIN

Mk 4:34 his own disciples he **e** everything

EXPOSE → EXPOSED

Mt 1:19 yet unwilling to **e** her to shame,

Eph 5:11 works of darkness; rather **e** them,

EXPOSED → EXPOSE

Jn 3:20 so that his works might not be **e**.

Eph 5:13 everything **e** by the light becomes

Heb 10:33 times you were publicly **e** to abuse

EYE → EYES, EYEWITNESSES

Ex 21:24 **e** for **e**, tooth for tooth,

Ps 17: 8 Keep me as the apple of your **e**;

Mt 5:29 If your right **e** causes you to sin,

      5:38 'An **e** for an **e** and a tooth for a tooth.'

      7: 3 the splinter in your brother's **e**,

Mt 7: 3 the wooden beam in your own **e**?

Mk 10:25 to pass through [the] **e** of [a] needle

1Co 15:52 in the blink of an **e**, at the last

Rev 1: 7 and every **e** will see him, even those

EYES → EYE

Ge 3: 7 the **e** of both of them were opened,

2Ch 16: 9 The **e** of the LORD roam over

Ps 121: 1 I raise my **e** toward the mountains.

Pr 3: 7 Be not wise in your own **e**,

     22:12 The **e** of the LORD safeguard

Eze 1:18 their rims were full of **e** all around.

Da 10: 6 his **e** were like fiery torches,

Zec 4:10 These seven facets are the **e**

Mt 9:30 And their **e** were opened.

     13:15 they have closed their **e**, lest they

     13:15 **e**, lest they see with their **e** and hear

Lk 24:31 With that their **e** were opened

Eph 1:18 May the **e** of [your] hearts be

1Pe 3:12 For the **e** of the Lord are

1Jn 2:16 lust, enticement for the **e**,

Rev 1:14 and his **e** were like a fiery flame.

     4: 6 four living creatures covered with **e**

     21: 4 He will wipe every tear from their **e**,

EYEWITNESSES → EYE, WITNESS

Lk 1: 2 just as those who were **e**

2Pe 1:16 but we had been **e** of his majesty.

EZEKIEL

Priest called to be prophet to the exiles (Eze 1-3; Sir 49:8). Symbolically acted out destruction of Jerusalem (Eze 4-5; 12; 24).

EZRA

Priest and teacher of the Law who led a return of exiles to Israel to reestablish temple and worship (Ezr 7-8). Corrected intermarriage of priests (Ezr 9-10). Read Law at celebration of Feast of Tabernacles (Ne 8). Participated in dedication of Jerusalem's walls (Ne 12).

F

FACE → FACES

Ex 3: 6 Moses hid his **f**, for he was afraid

     34:30 radiant the skin of his **f** had become,

Nu 6:25 The LORD let his **f** shine upon you,

     12: 8 **f** to **f** I speak to him, plainly and not

Ps 4: 7 LORD, show us the light of your **f**!"

Isa 54: 8 for a moment I hid my **f** from you;

Eze 39:29 No longer will I hide my **f**

Lk 9:29 While he was praying his **f** changed

2Co 3: 7 intently at the **f** of Moses because

Rev 1:16 and his **f** shone like the sun at its

FACES → FACE

Eze 1: 6 but each had four **f** and four wings,

Rev 9: 7 of gold; their **f** were like human **f**,

FACTIONS

1Co 11:19 there have to be **f** among you

Gal 5:20 acts of selfishness, dissensions, **f**,

FAIL → FAILED

Dt 31: 6 he will never **f** you or forsake you."

Eze 47:12 shall not fade, nor their fruit **f**.

FAILED → FAIL

Ro 9: 6 it is not that the word of God has **f**.

FAINT

Ps 142: 4 My spirit is **f** within me, but you

Isa 40:31 grow weary, walk and not grow **f**.

FAITH → FAITHFUL, FAITHFULNESS, FAITHLESS

Ps 146: 6 that is in them, Who keeps **f** forever,

Isa 7: 9 a nation. Unless your **f** is firm

Hab 2: 4 just man, because of his **f**, shall live.

Mt 17:20 to them, "Because of your little **f**.

     17:20 if you have **f** the size of a mustard

Mk 2: 5 When Jesus saw their **f**, he said

Lk 7:50 the woman, "Your **f** has saved you;

     18: 8 Man comes, will he find **f** on earth?"

Ac 3:16 And by **f** in his name, this man,

     3:16 the **f** that comes through it has given

Ro 1:17 the righteousness of God from **f** to **f**;

     1:17 one who is righteous by **f** will live."

     3:28 a person is justified by **f** apart

1Co 13:13 So **f**, hope, love remain, these three;

Gal 3:11 one who is righteous by **f** will live."

     5: 6 but only **f** working through love.

Eph 4: 5 one Lord, one **f**, one baptism;

Php 3: 9 which comes through **f** in Christ,

     3: 9 from God, depending on **f**

1Ti 6:11 righteousness, devotion, **f**, love,

2Ti 4: 7 finished the race; I have kept the **f**.

Heb 11: 1 **F** is the realization of what is hoped

     12: 2 Jesus, the leader and perfecter of **f**.

Jas 2:17 So also **f** of itself, if it does not have

     2:24 by works and not by **f** alone.

FAITH → FAITHFUL, FAITHFULNESS,
    FAITHLESS (*cont.*)
2Pe 1: 1 those who have received a **f** of
        equal
1Jn 5: 4 that conquers the world is
        our **f**.
Jude 1: 3 contend for the **f** that was once
Rev 2:13 and have not denied your **f** in
        me,

FAITHFUL → FAITH
Dt 32: 4 his ways! A **f** God, without
        deceit,
Ps   4: 4 the LORD works wonders for
        the **f**;
  116:15 eyes of the LORD is the death
        of his **f**.
Wis 3: 9 the **f** shall abide with him in
        love:
Mic 7: 2 The **f** are gone from the earth,
Zec 8: 3 Jerusalem shall be called the **f**
        city,
Mt 24:45 then, is the **f** and prudent ser-
        vant,
1Co 10:13 God is **f** and will not let you be
        tried
1Th 5:24 The one who calls you is **f**,
        and he
1Pe 4:19 over to a **f** creator as they do
        good.
1Jn 1: 9 he is **f** and just and will forgive
        our
Rev 1: 5 and from Jesus Christ, the **f**
        witness,
  19:11 its rider was [called] "**F** and
        True."

FAITHFULNESS → FAITH
Ps 26: 3 my eyes; I walk guided by
        your **f**.
Isa 11: 5 his waist, and **f** a belt upon his
        hips.
La 3:23 each morning, so great is his **f**.
Gal 5:22 patience, kindness, generos-
        ity, **f**,

FAITHLESS → FAITH
Mt 17:17 reply, "O **f** and perverse gener-
        ation,

FALL → FALLEN, FALLING, FELL
Ps 91: 7 Though a thousand **f** at your
        side,
Pr 16:18 and a haughty spirit before a **f**.
Sir 28:23 who forsake the LORD will **f**
        victims
Lk 10:18 have observed Satan **f** like
        lightning
Ro 9:33 and a rock that will make
        them **f**,
1Co 10:12 secure should take care not
        to **f**.
Heb 10:31 It is a fearful thing to **f**

FALLEN → FALL
2Sa 1:19 how can the warriors have **f**!
Isa 14:12 How have you **f** from the heav-
        ens,
  21: 9 calls out and says, '**F**, **f** is Bab-
        ylon,
Rev 9: 1 I saw a star that had **f** from the
        sky
  18: 2 voice: "**F**, **f** is Babylon the
        great.

FALLING → FALL
Lk 22:44 like drops of blood **f** on the
        ground.]

FALSE
Mt 7:15 "Beware of **f** prophets, who
        come
Mk 13:22 **F** messiahs and **f** prophets will
        arise
2Pe 2: 1 also **f** prophets among the
        people,
   2: 1 there will be **f** teachers among
        you,
Rev 16:13 and from the mouth of the **f**
        prophet.
  20:10 the beast and the **f** prophet
        were.

FAMILIES → FAMILY
Ac 3:25 your offspring all the **f** of the
        earth
Tit 1:11 as they are upsetting whole **f**

FAMILY → FAMILIES
Gal 6:10 who belong to the **f** of the
        faith.
Eph 3:15 from whom every **f** in heaven

FAMINE
Ge 12:10 There was **f** in the land; so
        Abram
  12:10 since the **f** in the land was
        severe.
  41:27 ears; they are seven years of **f**.
Ru 1: 1 the judges there was a **f** in the
        land;
Ps 37:19 in days of **f** they will have
        plenty.
Am 8:11 when I will send **f** upon the
        land:
   8:11 Not a **f** of bread, or thirst for
        water,
Ac 11:28 would be a severe **f** all over
Ro 8:35 or persecution, or **f**, or naked-
        ness,

FAR
Isa 57:19 Peace, peace to the **f** and the
        near,
Jer 23:23 says the LORD, and not a God **f**
        off?
Mk 7: 6 lips, but their hearts are **f**
        from me;
  12:34 "You are not **f** from the
        kingdom

FAST → FASTED, FASTING
Isa 58: 5 ashes? Do you call this a **f**, a
        day
Mt 6:16 "When you **f**, do not look
        gloomy
Lk 18:12 I **f** twice a week, and I pay
        tithes

FASTED → FAST
Mt 4: 2 He **f** for forty days and forty
        nights,

FASTING → FAST
Mt 6:16 they may appear to others to
        be **f**.

FATHER → FATHER'S
Ge 2:24 That is why a man leaves his **f**
Ex 20:12 "Honor your **f** and your
        mother,

Ex 21:15 Whoever strikes his **f** or
        mother
2Sa 7:14 I will be a **f** to him, and he
        shall be
Ps 89:27 He shall cry to me, 'You are
        my **f**,
Pr 28:24 He who defrauds **f** or mother
Wis 2:16 the just and boasts that God is
        his **F**.
Sir 3: 3 He who honors his **f** atones for
        sins;
Isa 8: 4 the child knows how to call
        his **f**
Jer 3:19 would call me, "My **F**," I
        thought,
Mal 1: 6 A son honors his **f**, and a ser-
        vant
   1: 6 If then I am a **f**, where is the
        honor
Mt 6: 9 you are to pray: Our **F** in
        heaven,
  28:19 baptizing them in the name of
        the **F**,
Lk 18:20 honor your **f** and your
        mother.' "
Jn 5:18 but he also called God his
        own **f**,
  8:44 You belong to your **f** the devil
  8:44 because he is a liar and the **f** of
        lies.
  14: 6 comes to the **F** except through
        me.
Ro 8:15 through which we cry,
        "*Abba*, **F**!"
Gal 4: 6 into our hearts, crying out,
        "*Abba*, **F**!"
Eph 6: 2 "Honor your **f** and mother."
        This is
Heb 1: 5 "I will be a **f** to him, and he
        shall be
  12: 9 all the more to the **F** of spirits
Jas 1:17 coming down from the **F** of
        lights,
Rev 3: 5 his name in the presence of
        my **F**

FATHER'S → FATHER
Lk 2:49 know that I must be in my **F**
        house?"
Jn 1:14 the glory as of the **F** only Son,
  2:16 here, and stop making my **F**
        house
  10:29 can take them out of the **F**
        hand.
  14: 2 In my **F** house there are many

FAULT
Sir 11: 7 Before investigating, find no **f**;
Ro 9:19 "Why [then] does he still
        find **f**?

FAVOR → FAVORED
Ge 6: 8 But Noah found **f** with the
        LORD.
Ex 33:12 and also, 'You have found **f**
        with me.'
Ps 30: 5 a moment; divine **f** lasts a life-
        time.
Isa 49: 8 In a time of **f** I answer you,
Zec 11: 7 one of which I called "**F**,"

FAVORED → FAVOR
Lk 1:28 coming to her, he said, "Hail,
        one!

FEAR → AFRAID, FEARED, FEARS
Dt   6:13 The Lord, your God, shall
            you f;
Ps   19:10 The f of the Lord is pure,
     23: 4 I f no harm for you are at my
            side;
     27: 1 whom do I f? The Lord is my
            life's
Pr   1: 7 The f of the Lord is the begin-
            ning
Ecc 12:13 all is heard: F God and keep
            his
Php   2:12 work out your salvation with f
1Pe   3:14 be afraid or terrified with f of
            them,
1Jn   4:18 There is no f in love, but per-
            fect
      4:18 love drives out f because f has
            to do
Rev 14: 7 voice, "F God and give him
            glory,

FEARED → FEAR
Ex   14:31 they f the Lord and believed in
            him
Job   1: 1 Job, who f God and avoided
            evil.
Hag   1:12 the people f because of the
            Lord.

FEARS → FEAR
Jdt 16:16 one who f the Lord is forever
            great.
Ps   34: 5 me, delivered me from all my
            f.
Pr   31:30 the woman who f the Lord is
            to be
Sir   1:11 He who f the Lord will have
     15: 1 He who f the Lord will do
            this;

FED → FEED
Dt   8:16 and f you in the desert with
            manna.
Ps   80: 6 You have f them the bread of
            tears,

FEED → FED, FEEDS
Jn   21:15 He said to him, "F my lambs."
Ro   12:20 "if your enemy is hungry, f
            him; if he

FEEDS → FED
Isa 40:11 Like a shepherd he f his flock;
            in his

FEET → FOOT
Ps   8: 7 your hands, put all things at
            their f:
    119:105 Your word is a lamp for my f,
Da   2:33 iron, its f partly iron and partly
            tile.
Mt   22:44 I place your enemies under
            your f" '?
Lk   24:39 Look at my hands and my f,
            that it
Jn   12: 3 nard and anointed the f of Je-
            sus
     13: 5 began to wash the disciples' f
Ro   16:20 quickly crush Satan under your
            f.
1Co 15:25 has put all his enemies under
            his f.
Rev   1:15 His f were like polished brass

FELLOWSHIP
2Co   6:14 Or what f does light have
1Jn   1: 3 so that you too may have f
            with us;
      1: 3 f with us; for our f is with the
            Father

FEMALE
Ge   1:27 him; male and f he created
            them.
Mk   10: 6 'God made them male and f.
Gal   3:28 free person, there is not male
            and f;

FESTIVALS
Lev 23: 2 The following are the f of the
            Lord,

FEVER
Dt   28:22 will strike you with wasting
            and f,
Mk   1:30 mother-in-law lay sick with a f.

FEW
Ps 105:12 When they were f in number,
Mt   22:14 Many are invited, but f are
            chosen."
Lk   13:23 "Lord, will only a f people be
            saved?"

FIELD → FIELDS
Pr   31:16 She picks out a f to purchase;
Mt   13:44 is like a treasure buried in a f,
     13:44 sells all that he has and buys
            that f.
     24:40 Two men will be out in the f;
1Co   3: 9 you are God's f, God's
            building.

FIELDS → FIELD
Lk   2: 8 in that region living in the f
Jn   4:35 up and see the f ripe for the
            harvest.

FIG → FIGS
Ge   3: 7 so they sewed f leaves together
Hab   3:17 For though the f tree blossom
            not
Mt   24:32 "Learn a lesson from the f tree.
Lk   13: 6 a person who had a f tree
            planted

FIGHT → FOUGHT
Ex   14:14 The Lord himself will f for
            you;
1Ti   1:18 Through them may you f a
            good f

FIGS → FIG
Jer 24: 1 of f placed before the temple
Lk   6:44 fruit. For people do not pick f

FILL → FILLED, FULL, FULLNESS
Ge   1:28 multiply; f the earth and sub-
            due it.
      9: 1 fertile and multiply and f the
            earth.
Jer 23:24 Do I not f both heaven and
            earth?
Eph   4:10 heavens, that he might f all
            things.

FILLED → FILL
Ex   1: 7 strong that the land was f with
            them.
     40:34 the glory of the Lord f the
            Dwelling.

1Ki   8:11 the Lord's glory had f the
            temple
Ps   72:19 may all the earth be f with the
            Lord's
Eze 43: 5 that the temple was f with the
            glory
Lk   1:15 He will be f with the holy
            Spirit
Ac   2: 4 they were all f with the holy
            Spirit
Eph   5:18 debauchery, but be f with the
            Spirit,

FILTHY
Zec   3: 3 before the angel, clad in f
            garments.
Rev 22:11 still act wickedly, and the f still
            be f.

FIND → FINDS, FOUND
Dt   4:29 you shall indeed f him when
Jer 29:13 you look for me, you will f me.
            Yes,
Mt   11:29 and you will f rest for your-
            selves.
     16:25 loses his life for my sake will
            f it.
Lk   11: 9 seek and you will f;

FINDS → FIND
Pr   8:35 For he who f me f life, and
            wins
     18:22 He who f a wife f happiness;
            it is

FINGER
Dt   9:10 by God's own f, with a copy of
            all
Mt   23: 4 they will not lift a f to move
            them.
Lk   11:20 if it is by the f of God that [I]
            drive

FINISHED
Ge   2: 2 the seventh day God was f
Ex   40:33 court. Thus Moses f all the
            work.
Jn   19:30 had taken the wine, he said, "It
            is f."

FIRE → FIERY
Ex   3: 2 appeared to him in f flaming
      3: 2 though on f, was not con-
            sumed.
     13:21 of a column of f to give them
            light.
Lev   9:24 f came forth from the Lord's
Nu   11: 1 that the f of the Lord burned
            among
Dt   4:24 is a consuming f, a jealous
            God.
1Ki 19:12 fire—but the Lord was not in
            the f.
1Ki 19:12 the f there was a tiny whis-
            pering
2Ch   7: 1 f came down from heaven
Isa 66:24 not die, nor their f be extin-
            guished;
Da   3:92 walking in the f, and the fourth
Mal   3: 2 For he is like the refiner's f, or
            like
Mt   3:11 you with the holy Spirit and f
Mk   9:43 Gehenna, into the unquench-
            able f.

FIRE → FIERY (*cont.*)

Ac	2: 3	appeared to them tongues as of f.
1Co	3:13	It will be revealed with f, and the f
Heb	12:29	For our God is a consuming f.
Jas	3: 6	The tongue is also a f. It exists
	3: 6	the entire course of our lives on f,
	3: 6	lives on f, itself set on f by Gehenna.
2Pe	3:10	the elements will be dissolved by f,
Rev	20:14	were thrown into the pool of f.
	20:14	(This pool of f is the second death.)

FIRM

Isa	7: 9	Unless your faith is f you shall not
	7: 9	your faith is f you shall not be f!
2Co	1:24	your joy, for you stand f in the faith.

FIRST → FIRSTBORN

Ge	1: 5	and morning followed—the f day.
Isa	41: 4	I, the LORD, am the f,
Mt	6:33	But seek f the kingdom [of God]
Mk	10:31	But many that are f will be last,
	10:31	f will be last, and [the] last will be f."
	16: 2	had risen, on the f day of the week,
Ac	11:26	disciples were f called Christians.
Ro	1:16	believes: for Jew f, and then Greek.
1Co	15:45	too, it is written, "The f man, Adam,
1Th	4:16	and the dead in Christ will rise f.
1Jn	4:19	We love because he f loved us.
Rev	1:17	not be afraid. I am the f and the last,
	20: 5	were over. This is the f resurrection.

FIRSTBORN, FIRST-BORN → BEAR, FIRST

Ex	4:22	Israel is my son, my f.
	12:29	At midnight the LORD slew every f
	13: 2	"Consecrate to me every f that opens
Ps	78:51	He struck all the f of Egypt,
Zec	12:10	over him as one grieves over a f.
Lk	2: 7	and she gave birth to her f son.
Col	1:15	invisible God, the f of all creation.
Rev	1: 5	the f of the dead and ruler

FISH

Ge	1:26	Let them have dominion over the f
Jnh	2: 1	But the LORD sent a large f,
	2: 1	in the belly of the f three days
Mt	7:10	or a snake when he asks for a f?
Jn	6: 9	has five barley loaves and two f;

FIVE

1Sa	17:40	David selected f smooth stones
Mt	14:19	Taking the f loaves and the two fish,
1Co	14:19	church I would rather speak f words

FLAME → FLAMES

Isa	10:17	Israel's Holy One a f, That burns
Rev	19:12	His eyes were [like] a fiery f,

FLAMES → FLAME

Da	3:49	drove the fiery f out of the furnace,

FLED → FLEE

Ex	2:15	But Moses f from him and stayed
Mk	14:50	And they all left him and f.
Rev	12: 6	The woman herself f into the desert
	20:11	and the sky f from his presence

FLEE → FLED

Ps	11: 1	me, "F like a bird to the mountains!
	139: 7	From your presence, where can I f?
Isa	30:17	one; if five threaten you, you shall f,
Jas	4: 7	the devil, and he will f from you.

FLESH

Ge	2:23	and f of my f; This one shall be
Job	19:26	And from my f I shall see God;
Mt	16:17	For f and blood has not revealed this
	26:41	spirit is willing, but the f is weak."
Jn	1:14	And the Word became f and made
	3: 6	What is born of f is f and what is
Ro	8: 4	who live not according to the f
	8:13	For if you live according to the f,
2Co	12: 7	a thorn in the f was given to me,
Gal	5:19	Now the works of the f are obvious:
Eph	6:12	For our struggle is not with f
1Pe	1:24	for: "All f is like grass, and all its
1Jn	4: 2	Jesus Christ come in the f belongs

FLOCK

Isa	40:11	Like a shepherd he feeds his f; in his
Mt	26:31	the sheep of the f will be dispersed';
Lk	12:32	little f, for your Father is pleased
Jn	10:16	voice, and there will be one f,
1Pe	5: 3	to you, but be examples to the f.

FLOGGED

Ac	5:40	they had them f, ordered them

FLOOD

Ge	7: 7	ark because of the waters of the f.

Ge	9:15	waters shall never again become a f
Ps	29:10	The LORD sits enthroned above the f!
2Pe	2: 5	he brought a f upon the godless

FLOW → FLOWING, FLOWS

Zec	14: 8	living waters shall f from Jerusalem,
Jn	7:38	living water will f from within him.' "

FLOWER

Isa	40: 7	The grass withers, the f wilts,
1Pe	1:24	all its glory like the f of the field;
	1:24	the grass withers, and the f wilts;

FLOWING → FLOW

Ex	3: 8	land, a land f with milk and honey,
Jos	5: 6	he would not let them see the land f
Eze	47: 1	I saw water f out from beneath
Rev	22: 1	f from the throne of God

FOE

Ex	23:22	to your enemies and a f to your foes.
Ps	60:13	Give us aid against the f;

FOLLOW → FOLLOWED

Ex	16: 4	see whether they f my instructions
Dt	6:14	You shall not f other gods, such as
1Ki	18:21	If the LORD is God, f him; if Baal,
Lk	9:23	and take up his cross daily and f me.
Jn	10:27	voice; I know them, and they f me.
Rev	14: 4	the ones who f the Lamb wherever

FOLLOWED → FOLLOW

Jdg	2:12	they f the other gods of the various
Mk	1:18	Then they left their nets and f him.
Rev	13: 3	the whole world f after the beast.

FOLLY → FOOL

Pr	13:16	prudence, but the fool peddles f.
	26: 4	not the fool according to his f,
Ecc	2:13	has the advantage over f as much as
Mk	7:22	envy, blasphemy, arrogance, f.

FOOD → FOODS

Ge	1:30	I give all the green plants for f."
1Ma	1:63	than to be defiled with unclean f
Ps	136:25	And gives f to all flesh, God's love
Mt	6:25	Is not life more than f and the body
Jn	6:55	For my flesh is true f, and my blood
1Co	8: 8	Now f will not bring us closer

FOODS → FOOD
Mk 7:19 (Thus he declared all **f** clean.)
1Ti 4: 3 require abstinence from **f** that God

FOOL → FOLLY, FOOLISH, FOOLISHNESS, FOOLS
Pr 15: 5 The **f** spurns his father's admonition,
20: 3 strife, while every **f** starts a quarrel.
Mt 5:22 says, 'You **f**,' will be liable to fiery

FOOLISH → FOOL
Pr 17:25 A **f** son is vexation to his father,
Jer 5:21 to this, **f** and senseless people
Mt 25: 2 Five of them were **f** and five were
1Co 1:20 made the wisdom of the world **f**?
Tit 3: 3 For we ourselves were once **f**,

FOOLISHNESS → FOOL
1Co 1:18 of the cross is **f** to those who are
3:19 wisdom of this world is **f** in the eyes

FOOLS → FOOL
Ps 14: 1 Of David. F say in their hearts,
Pr 1: 7 wisdom and instruction **f** despise.
10:21 many, but **f** die for want of sense.
Ro 1:22 claiming to be wise, they became **f**
1Co 4:10 We are **f** on Christ's account, but you

FOOT → FEET, FOOTSTOOL
Ps 91:12 lest you strike your **f** against a stone.
Mt 18: 8 If your hand or **f** causes you to sin,
Lk 4:11 lest you dash your **f** against a stone.' "

FOOTSTOOL → FOOT
Ps 110: 1 while I make your enemies your **f**."
Isa 66: 1 the earth is my **f**. What kind
Heb 10:13 until his enemies are made his **f**.

FOREHEAD → FOREHEADS
Ex 13: 9 hand and as a reminder on your **f**;
1Sa 17:49 and struck the Philistine on the **f**.

FOREHEADS → FOREHEAD
Eze 9: 4 an X on the **f** of those who moan
Rev 7: 3 put the seal on the **f** of the servants
13:16 image on their right hands or their **f**,
20: 4 nor had accepted its mark on their **f**

FOREIGN → FOREIGNER, FOREIGNERS
Ps 81:10 There must be no **f** god among you;

FOREIGNER → FOREIGN
Ex 12:43 the Passover. No **f** may partake of it.
1Co 14:11 I shall be a **f** to one who speaks it,
14:11 it, and one who speaks it a **f** to me.

FOREIGNERS → FOREIGN
1Co 14:21 and by the lips of **f** I will speak

FOREKNEW → KNOW
Ro 8:29 For those he **f** he also predestined
11: 2 not rejected his people whom he **f**.

FORERUNNER → RUN
Heb 6:20 Jesus has entered on our behalf as **f**,

FORESKIN
Ge 17:14 flesh of his **f** has not been cut away,

FORETOLD → TELL
Isa 43: 9 this, or **f** to us the earlier things?

FOREVER
Ge 3:22 life also, and thus eat of it and live **f**."
6: 3 "My spirit shall not remain in man **f**,
Ex 3:15 "This is my name **f**; this is my title
2Sa 7:13 I will make his royal throne firm **f**.
1Ch 16:15 He remembers **f** his covenant
Ps 19:10 enduring **f**. The statutes of the LORD
110: 4 "Like Melchizedek you are a priest **f**."
117: 2 the LORD is faithful **f**. Hallelujah!
Ecc 3:14 whatever God does will endure **f**;
Wis 5:15 But the just live **f**, and in the LORD is
Isa 40: 8 wilts, the word of our God stands **f**."
51: 6 My salvation shall remain **f** and my
Jn 6:51 whoever eats this bread will live **f**;
Heb 5: 6 "You are a priest **f**
13: 8 is the same yesterday, today, and **f**.
1Pe 1:25 but the word of the Lord remains **f**."
Rev 1:18 dead, but now I am alive **f** and ever.
11:15 and he will reign **f** and ever."
22: 5 and they shall reign **f** and ever.

FORFEIT
Mk 8:36 gain the whole world and **f** his life?

FORGAVE → FORGIVE
Ps 85: 3 You **f** the guilt of your people,

FORGET → FORGOT, FORGOTTEN
Dt 6:12 take care not to **f** the LORD,
Ps 137: 5 If I **f** you, Jerusalem, may my right
Pr 4: 5 Do not **f** or turn aside

Isa 49:15 Can a mother **f** her infant,
49:15 Even should she **f**, I will never **f**

FORGIVE → FORGAVE, FORGIVEN, FORGIVENESS, FORGIVING
Ex 32:32 If you would only **f** their sin! If you
Sir 5: 6 his mercy; my many sins he will **f**."
Mt 6:12 and **f** us our debts, as we **f** our
Lk 5:24 earth to **f** sins"—he said to the man who
1Jn 1: 9 just and will **f** our sins and cleanse

FORGIVEN → FORGIVE
Lev 4:20 for them, and they will be **f**.
Ps 32: 1 fault is removed, whose sin is **f**.
Mt 12:31 sin and blasphemy will be **f** people,
12:31 against the Spirit will not be **f**.
Mk 2: 9 paralytic, 'Your sins are **f**,' or to say,
Ro 4: 7 are they whose iniquities are **f**
Eph 4:32 one another as God has **f** you

FORGIVENESS → FORGIVE
Mk 1: 4 of repentance for the **f** of sins.
3:29 the holy Spirit will never have **f**,
Col 1:14 we have redemption, the **f** of sins.
Heb 9:22 the shedding of blood there is no **f**.

FORGIVING → FORGIVE
Ex 34: 7 and **f** wickedness and crime and sin;
Ps 86: 5 Lord, you are kind and **f**,
Eph 4:32 **f** one another as God has forgiven

FORGOT → FORGET
Dt 32:18 You **f** the God who gave you birth.
Jer 23:27 just as their fathers **f** my name

FORGOTTEN → FORGET
Ps 77:10 Has God **f** mercy, in anger withheld
Isa 49:14 has forsaken me; my Lord has **f** me."
Heb 12: 5 **f** the exhortation addressed to you as

FORM → FORMED, FORMLESS
Lk 3:22 upon him in bodily **f** like a dove.

FORMED → FORM
Ge 2: 7 the LORD God **f** man out of the clay
Ps 139:13 You **f** my inmost being; you knit me
Gal 4:19 in labor until Christ be **f** in you!

FORMLESS → FORM
Ge 1: 2 the earth was a **f** wasteland,
Wis 11:17 the universe from **f** matter, to send

FORSAKE → FORSAKEN
Dt 31: 6 you; he will never fail you or **f** you."

FORSAKE → FORSAKEN (*cont.*)
Jos 1: 5 I will not leave you nor f you.
Jer 17:13 all who f you shall be in disgrace;
Heb 13: 5 "I will never f you or abandon you."

FORSAKEN → FORSAKE
Mt 27:46 God, my God, why have you f me?"

FORTRESS
2Sa 22: 2 LORD, my rock, my f, my deliverer,
Ps 71: 3 for you are my rock and f.

FORTY
Ge 7: 4 rain down on the earth for f days
    7: 4 on the earth for f days and f nights,
Nu 14:34 F days you spent in scouting
    14:34 f years shall you suffer for your
1Ki 19: 8 he walked f days and f nights
Jnh 3: 4 "F days more and Nineveh shall be
Mt 4: 2 He fasted for f days and f nights,
Heb 3:17 whom was he "provoked for f years"?

FOUGHT → FIGHT
Jos 10:42 LORD, the God of Israel, f for Israel.
Rev 12: 7 The dragon and its angels f back,

FOUND → FIND
Isa 55: 6 Seek the LORD while he may be f,
    65: 1 to be f by those who sought me not.
Lk 15:24 again; he was lost, and has been f.'
Ro 10:20 "I was f [by] those who were not
Rev 20:15 whose name was not f written

FOUNDATION → FOUNDATIONS
Ezr 3: 6 though the f of the temple
Isa 28:16 A precious cornerstone as a sure f;
1Co 3:11 no one can lay a f other than the one
Eph 2:20 built upon the f of the apostles
2Ti 2:19 God's solid f stands, bearing this

FOUNDATIONS → FOUNDATION
1Ki 6:37 The f of the LORD's temple were laid
Heb 11:10 looking forward to the city with f,

FOUNTAIN
Ps 36:10 For with you is the f of life,
Pr 16:22 Good sense is a f of life to its
Zec 13: 1 Jerusalem, a f to purify from sin

FOUR
Eze 1: 5 figures resembling f living creatures
    10:14 Each had f faces: the first face was

Rev 4: 6 there were f living creatures covered

FOXES
Jdg 15: 4 left and caught three hundred f.
Lk 9:58 "F have dens and birds of the sky

FRAGRANT
Ex 25: 6 anointing oil and for the f incense;
Eph 5: 2 offering to God for a f aroma.

FRANKINCENSE → INCENSE
Isa 60: 6 bearing gold and f, and proclaiming
Mt 2:11 and offered him gifts of gold, f,

FREE → FREED, FREEDOM
Ps 146: 7 hungry. The LORD sets prisoners f;
Sir 15:14 him subject to his own f choice.
Jn 8:32 the truth, and the truth will set you f."
Gal 3:28 there is neither slave nor f person,
Eph 6: 8 he does, whether he is slave or f.

FREED → FREE
Rev 1: 5 has f us from our sins by his blood,

FREEDOM → FREE
2Co 3:17 the Spirit of the Lord is, there is f.
Gal 5: 1 For f Christ set us free; so stand
1Pe 2:16 yet without using f as a pretext

FRIEND → FRIENDS
Pr 17:17 He who is a f is always a f,
    18:24 a true f is more loyal than a brother.
Sir 7:18 Barter not a f for money, nor a dear
Mt 11:19 a f of tax collectors and sinners.'
Jas 2:23 and he was called "the f of God."

FRIENDS → FRIEND
Job 2:11 when three of Job's f heard of all
Jn 15:13 this, to lay down one's life for one's f.
    15:15 I have called you f, because I have

FRUIT → FRUITFUL, FRUITLESS, FRUITS
Ge 3: 6 So she took some of its f and ate it;
Dt 28: 4 "Blessed be the f of your womb.
Ps 1: 3 that yields its f in season; Its leaves
Pr 8:19 My f is better than gold, yes,
Eze 47:12 f trees of every kind shall grow;
    47:12 leaves shall not fade, nor their f fail.
    47:12 Every month they shall bear fresh f,
    47:12 Their f shall serve for food,

Mt 3: 8 Produce good f as evidence of your
Lk 1:42 and blessed is the f of your womb.
    6:44 every tree is known by its own f.
Jn 15: 2 branch in me that does not bear f,
    15: 2 he prunes so that it bears more f.
Gal 5:22 contrast, the f of the Spirit is love,
Col 1:10 in every good work bearing f
Heb 13:15 the f of lips that confess his name.
Rev 22: 2 that produces f twelve times a year,

FRUITFUL → FRUIT
Ex 1: 7 the Israelites were f and prolific.

FRUITS → FRUIT
Pr 3: 9 with first f of all your produce;
Mt 7:16 By their f you will know them.

FULFILL → FULFILLED
Ecc 5: 4 a vow than make it and not f it.
Mt 5:17 I have come not to abolish but to f.
Gal 6: 2 and so you will f the law of Christ.
Jas 2: 8 if you f the royal law according

FULFILLED → FULFILL
Lk 24:44 the prophets and psalms must be f."
Ro 8: 4 decree of the law might be f in us,

FULL → FILL
Eze 10:12 of the four wheels were f of eyes all
Jn 1:14 only Son, f of grace and truth.

FULLNESS → FILL
Jn 1:16 From his f we have all received,
1Co 10:26 for "the earth and its f are the Lord's.'
Gal 4: 4 But when the f of time had come,
Eph 1:10 as a plan for the f of times, to sum
    3:19 may be filled with all the f of God.
Col 1:19 him all the f was pleased to dwell,
    2: 9 him dwells the whole f of the deity

FURNACE
Isa 48:10 tested you in the f of affliction.
Da 3: 6 be instantly cast into a whitehot f."
    3:49 went down into the f with Azariah
    3:49 drove the fiery flames out of the f,
Mt 13:42 will throw them into the fiery f,

FURY
Ro 2: 8 f to those who selfishly disobey

Rev 16:19 the cup filled with the wine of his **f**

FUTURE
Pr   24:20 For the evil man has no **f**, the lamp
Jer 31:17 There is hope for your **f**,
1Co   3:22 life or death, or the present or the **f**:
1Ti   6:19 treasure a good foundation for the **f**,

G

GABRIEL
   Angel who interpreted Daniel's visions (Da 8:16-26; 9:20-27); announced births of John (Lk 1:11-20), Jesus (Lk 1:26-38).

GAD
   1. Son of Jacob by Zilpah (Ge 30:9-11; 35:26; 1Ch 2:2). Tribe of blessed (Ge 49:19; Dt 33:20-21), numbered (Nu 1:25; 26:18), allotted land east of the Jordan (Nu 32; 34:14; Jos 18:7; 22), west (Eze 48:27-28), 12,000 from (Rev 7:5).
   2. Prophet; seer of David (1Sa 22:5; 2Sa 24:11-19; 1Ch 29:29).

GAIN
Lk   9:25 one to **g** the whole world yet lose
Php   1:21 to me life is Christ, and death is **g**.
      3: 8 so much rubbish, that I may **g** Christ
1Ti   6: 5 religion to be a means of **g**.

GALILEAN → GALILEE
Mt   26:69 "You too were with Jesus the **G**."

GALILEANS → GALILEE
Ac   2: 7 these people who are speaking **G**?

GALILEE → GALILEAN, GALILEANS
Mt   4:15 the Jordan, **G** of the Gentiles,
Jn   7:41 "The Messiah will not come from **G**,

GAMALIEL
   Pharisee (Ac 5:34-39), teacher of Paul (Ac 22:5).

GARDEN
Ge   2: 8 the Lᴏʀᴅ God planted a **g** in Eden,
Eze 28:13 In Eden, the **g** of God, you were,
Jn   19:41 he had been crucified there was a **g**,
     19:41 **g**, and in the **g** a new tomb,

GARMENT → GARMENTS
Ps 102:27 they all wear out like a **g**;

GARMENTS → GARMENT
Ge   3:21 wife the Lᴏʀᴅ God made leather **g**,

GATE → GATES
Mt   7:13 "Enter through the narrow **g**;
      7:13 for the **g** is wide and the road broad
Jn   10: 7 say to you, I am the **g** for the sheep.
Heb 13:12 Jesus also suffered outside the **g**,

GATES → GATE
Ge   24:60 possession of the **g** of their enemies!"
Dt   6: 9 of your houses and on your **g**.
Ps 100: 4 Enter the temple **g** with praise,
Mt   16:18 the **g** of the netherworld shall not
Rev 21:21 The twelve **g** were twelve pearls,
     21:21 each of the **g** made from a single

GATH
1Sa 17: 4 champion named Goliath of **G** came
2Sa   1:20 "Tell it not in **G**, herald it not

GATHER → GATHERED
Ex   16: 4 to go out and **g** their daily portion;
Ru   2: 7 She asked leave to **g** the gleanings
Isa 11:12 and **g** the outcasts of Israel;
Mt   12:30 and whoever does not **g** with me
Lk   13:34 to **g** your children together as a hen

GATHERED → GATHER
Mt   18:20 or three are **g** together in my name,

GAVE → GIVE
Ge   28: 4 your descendants the blessing he **g**
Ex   31:18 he **g** him the two tablets
Ne   9:15 heaven you **g** them in their hunger,
Ecc 12: 7 life breath returns to God who **g** it.
Mt   25:35 I was hungry and you **g** me food,
     25:35 I was thirsty and you **g** me drink,
Jn   1:12 who did accept him he **g** power
      3:16 the world that he **g** his only Son,
Eph   4:11 And he **g** some as apostles, others as
1Ti   2: 6 who **g** himself as ransom for all.

GEDALIAH
   Governor of Judah (2Ki 25:22-26; Jer 39-41).

GEHAZI
   Servant of Elisha (2Ki 4:12-5:27; 8:4-5).

GENEALOGY
Mt   1: 1 The book of the **g** of Jesus Christ,

GENERATION → GENERATIONS
Ex   20: 6 mercy down to the thousandth **g**,
     34: 7 third and fourth **g** for their fathers'
Mt   12:39 evil and unfaithful **g** seeks a sign,
Lk   21:32 this **g** will not pass away until all

GENERATIONS → GENERATION
Isa 51: 8 forever and my salvation, for all **g**.

GENEROSITY
Ro   12: 8 if one contributes, in **g**; if one is
Gal   5:22 patience, kindness, **g**, faithfulness,

GENTILE → GENTILES
1Ma   1:14 according to the **G** custom.
Mt   18:17 treat him as you would a **G** or a tax
Gal   2:14 are living like a **G** and not like

GENTILES → GENTILE
1Ma   1:11 an alliance with the **G** all around us;
Lk   21:24 be taken as captives to all the **G**;
     21:24 underfoot by the **G** until the times
     21:24 until the times of the **G** are fulfilled.
Ac   15:19 to stop troubling the **G** who turn
Ro   3:29 Does he not belong to **G**, too? Yes,
      3:29 belong to **G**, too? Yes, also to **G**,
Gal   3: 8 God would justify the **G** by faith,
Eph   4:17 you must no longer live as the **G** do,

GENTLE → GENTLENESS
1Pe   3: 4 in the imperishable beauty of a **g**

GENTLENESS → GENTLE
Gal   5:23 **g**, self-control. Against such there is
1Ti   6:11 faith, love, patience, and **g**.

GETHSEMANE
Mk   14:32 Then they came to a place named **G**,

GHOST
Mt   14:26 "It is a **g**," they said, and they cried
Lk   24:39 because a **g** does not have flesh

GIANT
Sir 47: 4 As a youth he slew the **g** and wiped

GIBEON
Jos 10:12 Stand still, O sun, at **G**, O moon,
1Ki   3: 5 In **G** the Lᴏʀᴅ appeared to Solomon

GIDEON → = JERUBBAAL
   Judge, also called Jerubbaal; freed Israel from Midianites (Jdg 6-8; Heb 11:32). The fleece (Jdg 8:36-40).

GIFT → GIFTS
Nu   18: 7 I give you the priesthood as a **g**.
Mt   5:23 if you bring your **g** to the altar,
Jn   4:10 "If you knew the **g** of God and who
Ac   2:38 you will receive the **g** of the holy
Ro   6:23 the **g** of God is eternal life in Christ
1Co   7: 7 each has a particular **g** from God,

GIFT → GIFTS (*cont.*)

Jas   1:17   and every perfect **g** is from above,

Rev   21: 6   the thirsty I will give a **g**

GIFTS → GIFT

Mt   2:11   treasures and offered him **g** of gold,

Lk   11:13   how to give good **g** to your children,

Ro   11:29   For the **g** and the call of God are

1Co   12: 1   Now in regard to spiritual **g**,

     14: 1   but strive eagerly for the spiritual **g**,

Eph   4: 8   prisoners captive; he gave **g** to men."

GILGAL

Jos   5: 9   Therefore the place is called **G**

1Sa   7:16   **G** and Mizpah and judging Israel

GIRL

Ex   1:16   him; but if it is a **g**, she may live."

Mk   5:41   which means, "Little **g**, I say to you,

GIVE → GAVE, GIVEN, GIVER, GIVES

Ge   9: 3   I **g** them all to you as I did the green

     12: 7   your descendants I will **g** this land."

1Ki   3: 5   of me and I will **g** it to you."

Tob   12: 9   Those who regularly **g** alms shall

Pr   25:21   enemy be hungry, **g** him food to eat,

     25:21   eat, if he be thirsty, **g** him to drink;

     30:15   two daughters of the leech are, "**G**,

     30:15   daughters of the leech are, "**G, G**."

Eze   36:26   I will **g** you a new heart and place

Mt   6:11   **G** us today our daily bread;

     7: 6   "Do not **g** what is holy to dogs,

Mk   10:45   to **g** his life as a ransom for many."

Jn   10:28   I **g** them eternal life, and they shall

Ac   20:35   said, 'It is more blessed to **g** than

GIVEN → GIVE

Mt   7: 7   "Ask and it will be **g** to you;

Mk   4:25   To the one who has, more will be **g**;

Lk   22:19   is my body, which will be **g** for you;

Ro   5: 5   the holy Spirit that has been **g** to us.

GIVER → GIVE

2Co   9: 7   for God loves a cheerful **g**.

GIVES → GIVE

2Co   3: 6   brings death, but the Spirit **g** life.

Jas   4: 6   proud, but **g** grace to the humble."

GLAD → GLADNESS

Ps   16: 9   Therefore my heart is **g**, my soul

     90:15   Make us **g** as many days as you

Pr   10: 1   A wise son makes his father **g**,

Mt   5:12   Rejoice and be **g**, for your reward

Ac   2:26   Therefore my heart has been **g**

GLADNESS → GLAD

Ps   100: 2   worship the LORD with cries of **g**;

Isa   16:10   joy and **g**, In the vineyards there is

Zep   3:17   He will rejoice over you with **g**,

Heb   1: 9   the oil of **g** above your companions";

GLASS

Rev   4: 6   resembled a sea of **g** like crystal.

     21:18   the city was pure gold, clear as **g**.

GLEAN

Ru   2: 2   **g** ears of grain in the field of anyone

GLOOM

Isa   9: 1   those who dwelt in the land of **g**

Joel   2: 2   is near, a day of darkness and of **g**,

GLORIFIED → GLORY

Jn   13:31   "Now is the Son of Man **g**, and God

     13:31   Son of Man **g**, and God is **g** in him.

     17: 4   I **g** you on earth by accomplishing

Ac   3:13   has **g** his servant Jesus whom you

Ro   8:30   and those he justified he also **g**.

GLORIFY → GLORY

Ps   86:12   **g** your name forever, Lord my God.

Jn   17: 1   son, so that your son may **g** you,

1Co   6:20   Therefore **g** God in your body.

Rev   15: 4   or **g** your name? For you alone are

GLORIOUS → GLORY

Jdt   16:13   God. O LORD, great are you and **g**,

Da   3:26   fathers, and **g** forever is your name.

Jas   2: 1   the faith in our **g** Lord Jesus Christ.

GLORY → GLORIFIED, GLORIFY, GLORIOUS

Ex   24:16   The **g** of the LORD settled

     33:18   Moses said, "Do let me see your **g**!"

     40:34   tent, and the **g** of the LORD filled

1Sa   4:21   saying, "Gone is the **g** from Israel,"

1Ki   8:11   since the LORD's **g** had filled

1Ma   1:40   was as great as her **g** had been,

Ps   8: 6   crowned them with **g** and honor.

     19: 2   The heavens declare the **g** of God;

     24: 7   portals, that the king of **g** may enter.

Isa   6: 3   "All the earth is filled with his **g**!"

     40: 5   the **g** of the LORD shall be revealed,

Bar   5: 4   of justice, the **g** of God's worship.

Eze   44: 4   I looked I saw the **g** of the LORD

Hos   4: 7   me, exchanging their **g** for shame.

Mt   25:31   the Son of Man comes in his **g**,

Lk   2:14   "**G** to God in the highest and on earth

Jn   1:14   us, and we saw his **g**, the **g** as

     12:41   Isaiah said this because he saw his **g**

Ro   3:23   and are deprived of the **g** of God.

     8:18   compared with the **g** to be revealed

     9: 4   the adoption, the **g**, the covenants,

1Co   10:31   do, do everything for the **g** of God.

2Co   4:17   weight of **g** beyond all comparison,

Heb   1: 3   who is the refulgence of his **g**,

2Pe   1:17   **g** from God the Father

     1:17   came to him from the majestic **g**,

Rev   4:11   to receive **g** and honor and power,

     21:23   for the **g** of God gave it light, and its

GLUTTON

Pr   23:21   drunkard and the **g** come to poverty,

Mt   11:19   'Look, he is a **g** and a drunkard,

GNAT

Mt   23:24   who strain out the **g** and swallow

GO

Ex   5: 1   Let my people **g**, that they may

Jos   1: 9   God, is with you wherever you **g**."

Ru   1:16   you! for wherever you **g** I will **g**,

Mt   28:19   **G**, therefore, and make disciples

Jn   14: 3   if I **g** and prepare a place for you,

GOAT → GOATS

Lev   16: 9   The **g** that is determined by lot

Da   8:21   The **h** is the king of the Greeks,

GOATS → GOAT

Ps   50:13   of bulls or drink the blood of **g**?

Mt   25:32   separates the sheep from the **g**.

Heb   10: 4   blood of bulls and **g** take away sins.

GOD → GOD'S, GODDESS, GODLESS, GODLY, GODS

Ge 1: 1 when **G** created the heavens
    1:27 **G** created man in his image;
    3: 5 **G** knows well that the moment you
   17: 1 him and said: "I am **G** the Almighty.
Ex 3: 4 **G** called out to him from the bush,
   15: 2 my savior. He is my **G**, I praise him;
   15: 2 him; the **G** of my father, I extol him.
   20: 5 I, the LORD, your **G**, am a jealous **G**,
   34: 6 a merciful and gracious **G**,
Nu 23:19 **G** is not man that he should speak
Dt 4: 7 our **G**, is to us whenever we call
   6: 5 LORD, your **G**, with all your heart,
Jos 22:34 among them that the LORD is **G**.
1Sa 2: 2 LORD; there is no Rock like our **G**.
1Ki 8:27 indeed be that **G** dwells among men
   18:24 The **G** who answers with fire is **G**."
2Ki 17: 7 their **G**, who had brought them
Ezr 6:16 of this house of **G** with joy.
Ne 8:18 book of the law of **G** day after day,
Tob 4:19 At all times bless the Lord **G**,
Ps 19: 2 The heavens declare the glory of **G**;
   22: 2 My **G**, my **G**, why have you
   46: 2 **G** is our refuge and our strength,
   46:11 "Be still and confess that I am **G**!
   47: 8 **G** is king over all the earth;
   53: 2 "There is no **G**." Their deeds are
   68:21 Our **G** is a **G** who saves;
   90: 2 from eternity to eternity you are **G**.
   136: 2 Praise the **G** of gods; God's love
   145: 1 I will extol you, my **G** and king;
Ecc 12:13 all is heard: Fear **G** and keep his
Sir 32:14 He who would find **G** must accept
Isa 12: 2 **G** indeed is my savior; I am
   40:28 The LORD is the eternal **G**,
   44: 6 I am the last; there is no **G** but me.
Jer 10:10 The LORD is true **G**, he is the living
   10:10 he is the living **G**, the eternal King,
Bar 4: 8 the Eternal **G** who nourished you,
Eze 28: 2 of Tyre: Thus says the Lord **G**:
   28: 2 you say, "A **g** am I! I occupy a godly
   28: 2 And yet you are a man, and not a **g**,

Eze 28: 2 you may think yourself like a **g**.
Da 14: 4 it; but Daniel adored only his **G**.
Hos 12: 6 The LORD, the **G** of hosts, the LORD
Am 4:12 prepare to meet your **G**, O Israel:
Mic 6: 8 and to walk humbly with your **G**.
Hab 3:18 the LORD and exult in my saving **G**.
Mal 2:10 Has not the one **G** created us?
Mt 1:23 which means "**G** is with us."
   4: 4 comes forth from the mouth of **G**.' "
   4: 7 put the Lord, your **G**, to the test.' "
   4:10 Lord, your **G**, shall you worship
   6:24 You cannot serve **G** and mammon.
   27:40 if you are the Son of **G**, [and] come
Mk 1: 1 of Jesus Christ [the Son of **G**].
   2: 7 Who but **G** alone can forgive sins?"
   10: 9 Therefore what **G** has joined
   12:30 You shall love the Lord your **G**
Lk 2:14 "Glory to **G** in the highest
   18:19 good? No one is good but **G** alone.
   22:70 asked, "Are you then the Son of **G**?"
Jn 1: 1 and the Word was with **G**,
   1: 1 was with **G**, and the Word was **G**.
   1:18 No one has ever seen **G**. The only
   1:18 **G**. The only Son, **G**, who is
   3:16 For **G** so loved the world that he
   5:18 but he also called **G** his own father,
   5:18 father, making himself equal to **G**.
   20:28 said to him, "My Lord and my **G**!"
Ac 5:29 "We must obey **G** rather than men.
Ro 4: 3 "Abraham believed **G**, and it was
   6:23 the gift of **G** is eternal life in Christ
   8:31 If **G** is for us, who can be against
1Co 10:31 do, do everything for the glory of **G**.
2Co 4: 4 in whose case the **g** of this age has
   4: 4 of Christ, who is the image of **G**.
   6:16 agreement has the temple of **G**
   6:16 we are the temple of the living **G**;
   6:16 temple of the living **G**; as **G** said:
   6:16 and I will be their **G** and they shall
Eph 4: 6 one **G** and Father of all, who is over

Php 2: 6 though he was in the form of **G**,
   2: 6 regard equality with **G** something
Tit 2:13 of the glory of the great **G**
Heb 4:12 Indeed, the word of **G** is living
   10:31 to fall into the hands of the living **G**.
   12:29 For our **G** is a consuming fire.
Jas 2:23 "Abraham believed **G**, and it was
   2:23 and he was called "the friend of **G**."
   4: 8 Draw near to **G**, and he will draw
1Jn 1: 5 **G** is light, and in him there is no
   4:16 to believe in the love **G** has for us.
   4:16 **G** is love, and whoever remains
   4:16 remains in love remains in **G** and **G**
   5: 2 we love the children of **G** when we
   5: 2 the children of **G** when we love **G**
Jude 1:21 Keep yourselves in the love of **G**
Rev 4: 8 holy, holy is the Lord **G** almighty,
   19:13 his name was called the Word of **G**.
   22: 5 for the Lord **G** shall give them light,

*GOD → *LORD
Ge 15: 2 "O Lord **G**, what good will your gifts
2Sa 7:18 I, Lord **G**, and who are the members
Isa 25: 8 forever. The Lord **G** will wipe away
   61: 1 The spirit of the Lord **G** is upon me,

GOD'S → GOD
1Co 3: 9 For we are **G** co-workers; you are **G**
   3: 9 you are **G** field, **G** building.
1Jn 3: 2 Beloved, we are **G** children now;

GODDESS → GOD
1Ki 11: 5 Astarte, the **g** of the Sidonians,
Ac 19:27 of the great **g** Artemis will be of no

GODLESS → GOD
Job 8:13 shall the hope of the **g** man perish.
1Ti 1: 9 lawless and unruly, the **g** and sinful,
2Pe 3: 7 and of destruction of the **g**.

GODLY → GOD
Mal 2:15 that one require but **g** offspring?
2Co 7:10 For **g** sorrow produces a salutary

GODS → GOD
Ex 12:12 judgment on all the **g** of Egypt—I,

GODS → GOD (*cont.*)

Ex 20: 3 shall not have other **g** besides me.

Jdg 2:17 to the worship of other **g**. They were

2Ki 17: 7 and because they venerated other **g**.

Jn 10:34 in your law, 'I said, "You are **g**" "?

1Co 8: 5 even though there are so-called **g**

8: 5 to be sure, many "**g**" and many "lords"),

GOG

Eze 38:18 the day when **G** invades the land

Rev 20: 8 corners of the earth, **G** and Magog,

GOLD

Ex 20:23 silver nor gods of **g** shall you make

25:17 then make a propitiatory of pure **g**,

25:31 lampstand of pure beaten **g** — its shaft

28: 6 ephod they shall make of **g** thread

32:31 making a god of **g** for themselves!

1Ki 6:21 interior of the temple with pure **g**.

6:21 overlaid it with **g**, and looped it

Tob 12: 8 to give alms than to store up **g**;

Job 28:15 Solid **g** cannot purchase it, nor can

Sir 31: 5 The lover of **g** will not be free

Isa 60:17 In place of bronze I will bring **g**,

Ac 3: 6 "I have neither silver nor **g**, but what

1Pe 1: 7 faith, more precious than **g** that is

Rev 21:21 the street of the city was of pure **g**,

GOLGOTHA

Mt 27:33 to a place called **G** (which means

GOLIATH

Giant killed by David (1Sa 17; 21:9; Sir 47:4).

GOMORRAH

Ge 19:24 **G** [from the Lord out of heaven].

Isa 1: 9 as Sodom, we should be like **G**.

Jude 1: 7 Sodom, **G**, and the surrounding

GOOD → BEST, BETTER, GOODNESS

Ge 1:31 he had made, and he found it very **g**.

2: 9 delightful to look at and **g** for food,

2: 9 the tree of the knowledge of **g**

3:22 knowing what is **g** and what is bad!

50:20 God meant it for **g**, to achieve his

Dt 6:18 right and **g** in the sight of the Lord,

Dt 6:18 possess the **g** land which the Lord

2Ch 7: 3 "for he is **g**, for his mercy endures

Ps 34: 9 Learn to savor how **g** the Lord is;

84:12 The Lord withholds no **g** thing

Ecc 12:14 hidden qualities, whether **g** or bad.

Isa 52: 7 Announcing peace, bearing **g** news,

Da 3:89 Give thanks to the Lord, for he is **g**.

Mt 5:45 his sun rise on the bad and the **g**,

25:21 done, my **g** and faithful servant.

Mk 10:18 him, "Why do you call me **g**? No one

10:18 me **g**? No one is **g** but God alone.

Lk 2:10 I proclaim to you **g** news of great

Lk 6:43 "A **g** tree does not bear rotten fruit,

6:43 nor does a rotten tree bear **g** fruit.

Jn 10:11 I am the **g** shepherd. A **g** shepherd

Ro 7:16 not want, I concur that the law is **g**.

12: 2 what is **g** and pleasing and perfect.

12:21 by evil but conquer evil with **g**.

Eph 2:10 in Christ Jesus for the **g** works

1Ti 4: 4 For everything created by God is **g**,

Heb 10: 1 has only a shadow of the **g** things

1Pe 3:17 For it is better to suffer for doing **g**,

GOODNESS → GOOD

Ps 23: 6 Only **g** and love will pursue me

GOSHEN

Ge 45:10 You will settle in the region of **G**,

GOSPEL

Mk 8:35 sake and that of the **g** will save it.

Ro 1:16 For I am not ashamed of the **g**. It is

1Co 9:16 If I preach the **g**, this is no reason

2Co 4: 3 And even though our **g** is veiled,

Gal 1: 6 grace [of Christ] for a different **g**

Php 1:27 in a way worthy of the **g** of Christ,

1:27 together for the faith of the **g**,

GOSSIP

2Co 12:20 selfishness, slander, **g**, conceit,

GRACE → GRACIOUS

Wis 3: 9 Because **g** and mercy are with his

Jn 1:14 Father's only Son, full of **g** and truth.

1:16 have all received, **g** in place of **g**,

Ac 15:11 we are saved through the **g**

Ro 3:24 by his **g** through the redemption

6: 1 we persist in sin that **g** may abound?

6:14 are not under the law but under **g**.

11: 6 But if by **g**, it is no longer because

11: 6 otherwise **g** would no longer be **g**.

1Co 15:10 But by the **g** of God I am what I am,

15:10 his **g** to me has not been ineffective.

15:10 but the **g** of God [that is] with me.

2Co 12: 9 to me, "My **g** is sufficient for you,

Gal 5: 4 by law; you have fallen from **g**.

Eph 2: 5 Christ (by **g** you have been saved),

2Th 2:16 and good hope through his **g**,

Tit 2:11 For the **g** of God has appeared,

Heb 4:16 confidently approach the throne of **g**

4:16 mercy and to find **g** for timely help.

Jas 4: 6 But he bestows a greater **g**;

4: 6 proud, but gives **g** to the humble."

1Pe 5:10 The God of all **g** who called you

Jude 1: 4 who pervert the **g** of our God

Rev 22:21 The **g** of the Lord Jesus be with all.

GRACIOUS → GRACE

Ex 34: 6 a merciful and **g** God, slow to anger

Nu 6:25 shine upon you, and be **g** to you!

Ps 116: 5 **G** is the Lord and just; yes, our God

Col 4: 6 Let your speech always be **g**,

GRAFTED

Ro 11:17 were **g** in their place and have come

GRAIN

Dt 25: 4 an ox when it is treading out **g**.

Mk 2:23 he was passing through a field of **g**

2:23 a path while picking the heads of **g**.

GRAPES

Nu 13:23 with a single cluster of **g** on it,

Isa 5: 2 Then he looked for the crop of **g**,

5: 2 of **g**, but what it yielded was wild **g**.

Jer 31:29 "The fathers ate unripe **g**,

Mt 7:16 Do people pick **g** from thornbushes,

Rev 14:18 the earth's vines, for its **g** are ripe."

GRASS

Isa 40: 6 "All mankind is **g**, and all their glory

Mt 6:30 If God so clothes the **g** of the field,

1Pe 1:24 "All flesh is like **g**, and all its glory

1Pe 1:24 flower of the field; the **g** withers,

GRATIFY

Gal 5:16 you will certainly not **g** the desire

GRAVE → GRAVES

Ps 49:15 Straight to the **g** they descend,

Isa 53: 9 A **g** was assigned him among

GRAVES → GRAVE

Eze 37:12 I will open your **g** and have you rise

Lk 11:44 You are like unseen **g** over

GRAY

Pr 16:31 **G** hair is a crown of glory; it is

GREAT → GREATER, GREATEST

Ge 1:16 God made the two **g** lights,

12: 2 "I will make of you a **g** nation, and I

12: 2 I will make your name **g**,

Ex 32:11 the land of Egypt with such **g** power

Dt 10:17 the LORD of lords, the **g** God,

Ne 8: 6 Ezra blessed the LORD, the **g** God,

Jdt 16:13 O LORD, **g** are you and glorious,

Ps 95: 3 For the LORD is the **g** God, the **g**

Jer 10: 6 one is like you, O LORD, **g** are you,

La 3:23 morning, so is his faithfulness.

Da 9: 4 Lord, **g** and awesome God, you who

Joel 2:11 For **g** is the day of the LORD,

Mt 4:16 have seen a **g** light, on those

13:46 When he finds a pearl of **g** price,

20:26 to be **g** among you shall be your

Eph 2: 4 because of the **g** love he had for us,

Tit 2:13 of the glory of the **g** God and of our

Heb 2: 3 if we ignore so **g** a salvation?

12: 1 we are surrounded by so **g** a cloud

13:20 the dead the **g** shepherd of the sheep

Rev 14: 8 "Fallen, fallen is Babylon the **g**,

GREATER → GREAT

Mt 12: 6 something **g** than the temple is here.

Mk 12:31 other commandment **g** than these."

Jn 14:12 I do, and will do **g** ones than these,

15:13 No one has **g** love than this, to lay

1Jn 4: 4 is in you is **g** than the one who is

GREATEST → GREAT

Mt 22:38 This is the **g** and the first

Lk 9:48 all of you is the one who is the **g**."

1Co 13:13 three; but the **g** of these is love.

GREECE → GREEK, GREEKS

1Ma 1: 1 in his place, having first ruled in **G**.

GREED → GREEDY

Lk 12:15 "Take care to guard against all **g**,

Col 3: 5 evil desire, and the **g** that is idolatry.

GREEDY → GREED

Pr 28:25 The **g** man stirs up disputes, but he

1Co 6:10 thieves nor the **g** nor drunkards nor

Tit 1: 7 aggressive, not **g** for sordid gain,

GREEK → GREECE

Jn 19:20 written in Hebrew, Latin, and **G**.

Ro 1:16 believes: for Jew first, and then **G**.

Gal 3:28 There is neither Jew nor **G**, there is

GREEKS → GREECE

1Co 1:22 signs and **G** look for wisdom,

GREEN

Ge 1:30 I give all the **g** plants for food."

Ps 23: 2 In **g** pastures you let me graze;

GREW → GROW

1Sa 2:21 while young Samuel **g**

Isa 53: 2 He **g** up like a sapling before him,

Lk 1:80 The child **g** and became strong,

2:40 The child **g** and became strong,

GRIEVE → GRIEVED

Eph 4:30 And do not **g** the holy Spirit of God,

1Th 4:13 so that you may not **g** like the rest,

GRIEVED → GRIEVE

Isa 63:10 But they rebelled, and **g** his holy

GRINDING

Lk 17:35 will be two women **g** meal together;

GROAN → GROANING

Ro 8:23 **g** within ourselves as we wait

2Co 5: 2 For in this tent we **g**, longing to be

GROANING → GROAN

Ex 2:24 he heard their **g** and was mindful

GROUND

Ge 2: 7 formed man out of the clay of the **g**

3:17 eat, "Cursed be the **g** because of you!

Ex 3: 5 the place where you stand is holy **g**.

Mt 13: 5 Some fell on rocky **g**, where it had

GROW → GREW, GROWTH

Eze 47:12 fruit trees of every kind shall **g**;

2Pe 3:18 But **g** in grace and in the knowledge

GROWTH → GROW

1Co 3: 7 but only God, who causes the **g**.

Col 2:19 achieves the **g** that comes

GUARANTEE → GUARANTEED

Heb 7:22 become the **g** of an [even] better

GUARANTEED → GUARANTEE

Ro 4:16 and the promise may be **g** to all his

GUARD → GUARDIAN, GUARDS

Pr 2:11 over you, understanding will **g** you;

2Th 3: 3 you and **g** you from the evil one.

2Ti 1:12 is able to **g** what has been entrusted

GUARDIAN → GUARD

1Pe 2:25 to the shepherd and **g** of your souls.

GUARDS → GUARD

Mt 28: 4 The **g** were shaken with fear of him

GUIDANCE → GUIDE

Pr 11:14 For lack of **g** a people falls;

GUIDE → GUIDANCE

Isa 58:11 Then the LORD will **g** you always

Lk 6:39 a blind person **g** a blind person?

Jn 16:13 of truth, he will **g** you to all truth.

GUILT → GUILTY

Lev 5:15 to the LORD as his **g** offering

Ps 32: 5 my sin to you; my **g** I did not hide.

32: 5 and you took away the **g** of my sin.

Hos 14: 2 you have collapsed through your **g**.

Zec 3: 9 I will take away the **g** of the land

GUILTY → GUILT

Ex 23: 7 to death, nor shall you acquit the **g**.

Nu 14:18 yet not declaring the guiltless **g**,

Da 13:53 and freeing the **g**, although the Lord

Mk 3:29 but is **g** of an everlasting sin."

H

HABAKKUK

Prophet to Judah (Hab 1:1; 3:1; Da 14:33-39).

HADASSAH → See ESTHER

HADES

Rev 20:14 **H** were thrown into the pool of fire.

HAGAR

Servant of Sarah, wife of Abraham, mother of Ishmael (Ge 16:1-6; 25:12). Driven away by Sarah while pregnant (Ge 16:5-16); after birth of Isaac (Ge 21:9-21; Gal 4:21-31).

HAGGAI

Post-exilic prophet who encouraged rebuilding of the temple (Ezr 5:1; 6:14; Hag 1-2).

HAIL → HAILSTONES

Ex   9:19   shelter shall die when the **h** comes

Rev   8: 7   there came **h** and fire mixed

HAILSTONES → HAIL

Jos 10:11   from these **h** than the Israelites slew

Rev 16:21   Large **h** like huge weights came

HAIR → HAIRS

Jdg 16:22   the **h** of his head began to grow as

Lk   7:44   her tears and wiped them with her **h**.

Jn   12: 3   of Jesus and dried them with her **h**;

1Co 11: 6   she may as well have her **h** cut off.

     11: 6   for a woman to have her **h** cut off

HAIRS → HAIR

Ps   40:13   see. They are more than the **h** of my

Mt 10:30   Even all the **h** of your head are

HALF

Est   5: 3   Even if it is **h** of my kingdom,

Mk   6:23   of me, even to **h** of my kingdom.”

Lk   19: 8   “Behold, **h** of my possessions, Lord,

HALLOWED

Mt   6: 9   Father in heaven, **h** be your name,

HAM

Son of Noah (Ge 5:32; 1Ch 1:4), father of Canaan (Ge 9:18; 10:6-20; 1Ch 1:8-16). Saw Noah's nakedness (Ge 9:20-27).

HAMAN

Agagite nobleman honored by Xerxes (Est 3:1-2). Plotted to exterminate the Jews because of Mordecai (Est 3:3-15). Forced to honor Mordecai (Est 5-6). Plot exposed by Esther (Est 5:1-8; 7:1-8). Hanged (Est 7:9-10).

HANANIAH → = SHADRACH

1. False prophet; adversary of Jeremiah (Jer 28).

2. Original name of Shadrach (Da 1:6-19; 2:17).

HAND → EMPTY-HANDED, HANDED, HANDS

Ex   15: 6   Your right **h**, O Lord,

     15: 6   your right **h**, O Lord, has shattered

Dt   19:21   tooth for tooth, **h** for **h**, and foot

1Ki 18:44   a cloud as small as a man's **h** rising

Jdt   9:10   their pride by the **h** of a woman.

Ps 110: 1   “Take your throne at my right **h**,

Pr   3:16   Long life is in her right **h**, in her left

Isa   5:25   he raises his **h** to strike them;

     5:25   back, and his **h** is still outstretched.

Da   5: 5   the fingers of a human **h** appeared,

     5: 5   king saw the wrist and **h** that wrote,

Hab 2:16   the cup from the Lord's right **h**.

Mt   3:12   His winnowing fan is in his **h**.

Mk   9:43   If your **h** causes you to sin, cut it

Lk   20:42   said to my lord, “Sit at my right **h**

Jn   10:28   No one can take them out of my **h**.

Ro   8:34   who also is at the right **h** of God,

1Co 12:15   I am not a **h** I do not belong

Heb 10:12   seat forever at the right **h** of God;

Rev   1:16   In his right **h** he held seven stars.

     5: 1   in the right **h** of the one who sat

HANDED → HAND

Mt 27:26   he **h** him over to be crucified.

Ro   4:25   who was **h** over for our

HANDS → HAND

Ps 115: 7   They have **h** but do not feel,

Isa 49:16   of my **h** I have written your name;

Lk   23:46   into your **h** I commend my spirit”;

     24:40   he showed them his **h** and his feet.

Ac   8:18   by the laying on of the apostles' **h**,

Ro   10:21   I stretched out my **h** to a disobedient

Heb   6: 2   about baptisms and laying on of **h**,

     10:31   to fall into the **h** of the living God.

HANNAH

Wife of Elkanah, mother of Samuel (1Sa 1). Prayer at dedication of Samuel (1Sa 2:1-10). Blessed (1Sa 2:18-21).

HAPPY

Tob 13:14   **H** are those who love you, and **h**

     13:14   **H** are all the men who shall grieve

Ps   1: 1   **H** those who do not follow

     33:12   **H** the nation whose God is the Lord,

     84:13   hosts, **h** are those who trust in you!

Pr   3:13   **H** the man who finds wisdom,

HARD → HARDEN, HARDENED, HARDENING, HARDSHIPS

Ex   1:14   for them with **h** work in mortar

Mt   19:23   it will be **h** for one who is rich

HARDEN → HARD

Ps   95: 8   Do not **h** your hearts as at Meribah,

Heb   3: 8   '**H** not your hearts as at the rebellion

HARDENED → HARD

Mk   8:17   or comprehend? Are your hearts **h**?

Ro   11: 7   the elect attained it; the rest were **h**,

HARDENING → HARD

Ro   11:25   a **h** has come upon Israel in part,

HARDSHIPS → HARD

2Co 12:10   weaknesses, insults, **h**, persecutions,

HARM

Ge   50:20   Even though you meant **h** to me,

Ne   6: 2   They were planning to do me **h**.

Pr   12:21   No **h** befalls the just, but the wicked

1Pe   3:13   Now who is going to **h** you if you

HARP → HARPS

Ps 150: 3   the horn, praise him with **h** and lyre.

Rev   5: 8   Each of the elders held a **h** and gold

HARPS → HARP

1Ch 15:16   to play on musical instruments, **h**,

Ne   12:27   hymns and the music of cymbals, **h**,

Ps 137: 2   of that land we hung up our **h**.

HARVEST

Ge   8:22   lasts, seedtime and **h**, cold and heat,

Ex   23:16   the feast of the grain **h** with the first

     23:16   the feast at the fruit **h** at the end

Mt   13:39   The **h** is the end of the age,

Mk   4:29   sickle at once, for the **h** has come.”

Lk   10: 2   “The **h** is abundant but the laborers

     10: 2   so ask the master of the **h** to send

     10: 2   the **h** to send out laborers for his **h**.

Rev 14:15   “Use your sickle and reap the **h**,

     14:15   because the earth's **h** is fully ripe.”

HASTENING

2Pe   3:12   and **h** the coming of the day of God,

HATE → HATED, HATING

Ps   45: 8   You love justice and **h** wrongdoing;

     97:10   The Lord loves those who **h** evil,

Ecc   3: 8   A time to love, and a time to **h**;

Am   5:15   **H** evil and love good, and let justice

Mal   2:16   For I **h** divorce, says the Lord,

Mt   5:43   your neighbor and **h** your enemy.'

Lk   6:27 do good to those who **h** you,
Jn   7: 7 The world cannot **h** you, but it
             hates
Ro   7:15 do what I want, but I do what
             I **h**.

HATED → HATE
Jn   15:18 hates you, realize that it **h** me
             first.
Ro   9:13 is written: "I loved Jacob but **h**
             Esau."

HATES → HATE
Pr   6:16 There are six things the LORD
             h, yes,
Sir   15:13 Abominable wickedness the
             LORD **h**,
Jn   15:23 Whoever **h** me also **h** my
             Father.

HAUGHTY
Pr   6:17 **H** eyes, a lying tongue, and
             hands
      16:18 disaster, and a **h** spirit before a
             fall.

HAY
1Co   3:12 precious stones, wood, **h**, or
             straw,

HEAD → BEHEADED, HEADS
Isa   59:17 salvation, as the helmet on
             his **h**;
Mt   8:20 of Man has nowhere to rest
             his **h**."
Mk   6:28 He brought in the **h** on a
             platter
1Co   11: 3 that Christ is the **h** of every
             man,
      11: 3 and a husband the **h** of his
             wife,
      11: 3 of his wife, and God the **h** of
             Christ.
Eph   1:22 gave him as **h** over all things

HEADS → HEAD
Eze   11:21 down their conduct upon
             their **h**,
Rev   12: 3 dragon, with seven **h** and ten
             horns,
      12: 3 and on its **h** were seven
             diadems.

**HEAL → HEALED, HEALING, HEALS,
HEALTH**
Dt   32:39 I who inflict wounds and **h**
             them,
Ecc   3: 3 A time to kill, and a time to **h**;
Isa   57:19 says the LORD; and I will **h**
             them.
Jn   12:40 be converted, and I would **h**
             them."

HEALED → HEAL
Isa   6:10 and they will turn and be **h**.
      53: 5 us whole, by his stripes we
             were **h**.
Jas   5:16 for one another, that you may
             be **h**.
1Pe   2:24 By his wounds you have
             been **h**.

HEALING → HEAL
Pr   12:18 but the tongue of the wise is **h**.
1Co   12: 9 another gifts of **h** by the one
             Spirit;

HEALS → HEAL
Ps   103: 3 pardons all your sins, **h** all
             your ills,

HEALTH → HEAL
Sir   30:15 More precious than gold is **h**
3Jn   1: 2 in every respect and are in
             good **h**,

**HEAR → HEARD, HEARERS,
HEARING, HEARS**
Dt   6: 4 "**H**, O Israel! The LORD is our
             God,
      31:13 know it yet, must **h** it and
             learn it,
Isa   59: 1 to save, nor his ear too dull
             to **h**.
Jer   5:21 see not, who have ears and **h**
             not.
Eze   37: 4 Dry bones, **h** the word of the
             LORD!
Mt   13:17 and to **h** what you **h** but did not
             h it.
Mk   12:29 replied, "The first is this: '**H**,
             O Israel!
Lk   7:22 the deaf **h**, the dead are raised,
Heb   3: 7 that today you would **h** his
             voice,

HEARD → HEAR
Isa   40:21 Have you not **h**? Was it not
             foretold
Ro   10:17 Thus faith comes from what
             is **h**,
      10:17 what is **h** comes through the
             word
1Co   2: 9 eye has not seen, and ear has
             not **h**,
1Jn   1: 3 what we have seen and **h**
Rev   22: 8 I, John, who **h** and saw these
             things,
      22: 8 when I **h** and saw them I fell
             down

HEARERS → HEAR
Jas   1:22 doers of the word and not **h**
             only,

HEARING → HEAR
Am   8:11 but for **h** the word of the LORD.
1Co   12:17 were an eye, where would the
             h be?
      12:17 be? If the whole body were **h**,

HEARS → HEAR
Ps   69:34 For the LORD **h** the poor, does
             not
Pr   15:29 but the prayer of the just he **h**.
Jn   5:24 whoever **h** my word and be-
             lieves
1Jn   5:14 according to his will, he **h** us.
Rev   22:18 warn everyone who **h** the
             prophetic

**HEART → BROKENHEARTED,
HEART'S, HEARTLESS, HEARTS**
Ge   6: 6 on the earth, and his **h** was
             grieved.
Dt   6: 5 with all your **h**, and with all
             your
Jos   22: 5 serve him with your whole **h**
1Sa   16: 7 but the LORD looks into the **h**."
Ps   19:15 the thoughts of my **h** before
             you,
      51:12 A clean **h** create for me, God;

Pr   3: 5 Trust in the LORD with all
             your **h**,
      7: 3 write them on the tablet of
             your **h**.
Eze   36:26 I will give you a new **h** and
             place
Da   3:39 with contrite **h** and humble
             spirit
Mt   5: 8 Blessed are the clean of **h**, for
             they
      5:28 adultery with her in his **h**.
Mk   12:30 the Lord your God with all
             your **h**,
Lk   12:34 treasure is, there also will your
             h be.
Ro   2:29 and circumcision is of the **h**,
      10: 9 in your **h** that God raised him
Heb   10:22 let us approach with a sin-
             cere **h**

HEART'S → HEART
Ro   10: 1 my **h** desire and prayer to God

HEARTLESS → HEART
Ro   1:31 are senseless, faithless, **h**, ruth-
             less.

HEARTS → HEART
Dt   30:14 in your mouths and in your **h**;
Ps   95: 8 Do not harden your **h** as at
             Meribah,
Jer   31:33 them, and write it upon their **h**;
Mk   7: 6 lips, but their **h** are far
             from me;
Jn   14: 1 "Do not let your **h** be troubled.
Ro   2:15 of the law are written in
             their **h**,
      5: 5 into our **h** through the holy
             Spirit
Eph   3:17 may dwell in your **h** through
             faith;
Col   3:15 the peace of Christ control
             your **h**,
Heb   3: 8 'Harden not your **h** as
      10:16 "I will put my laws in their **h**,
             and I
2Pe   1:19 and the morning star rises in
             your **h**.
1Jn   3:20 in whatever our **h** condemn,
             for God
      3:20 for God is greater than our **h**
Rev   2:23 to know that I am the searcher
             of **h**

HEAVEN → HEAVENLY, HEAVENS
Ge   14:19 High, the creator of **h** and
             earth;
Ex   16: 4 "I will now rain down bread
             from **h**
Dt   31:28 so may call **h** and earth to wit-
             ness
Job   16:19 now, behold, my witness is
             in **h**,
Jer   23:24 Do I not fill both **h** and earth?
Mt   3: 2 for the kingdom of **h** is at
             hand!"
      6: 9 Our Father in **h**, hallowed be
             your
      24:35 **H** and earth will pass away,
             but my
      26:64 and 'coming on the clouds
             of **h**.'"
Mk   10:21 and you will have treasure
             in **h**;

HEAVEN → HEAVENLY, HEAVENS
  (*cont.*)
Lk 19:38 Peace in **h** and glory in the highest."
    24:51 from them and was taken up to **h**.
Jn   3:13 to **h** except the one who has come
    3:13 the one who has come down from **h**,
Ac   1:11 you into **h** will return in the same
    1:11 as you have seen him going into **h**."
Ro 10: 6 your heart, 'Who will go up into **h**?"
2Co 12: 2 was caught up to the third **h**.
Php 3:20 But our citizenship is in **h**,
1Th 1:10 and to await his Son from **h**,
Heb 9:24 one, but **h** itself, that he might now
2Pe 1:18 voice come from **h** while we were
Rev 4: 1 I had a vision of an open door to **h**,
    21: 1 Then I saw a new **h** and a new earth.
    21: 1 The former **h** and the former earth

HEAVENLY → HEAVEN
Mt   5:48 just as your **h** Father is perfect.
2Co 5: 2 further clothed with our **h** habitation
Heb 3: 1 sharing in a **h** calling,

HEAVENS → HEAVEN
Ge   1: 1 when God created the **h**
    28:12 with its top reaching to the **h**;
1Ki 8:27 If the **h** and the highest **h** cannot
Dt 10:14 The **h**, even the highest **h**,
Ps 57: 6 Show yourself over the **h**, God;
  115:16 The **h** belong to the LORD,
Ecc 3: 1 a time for every affair under the **h**.
Isa 14:12 How have you fallen from the **h**,
   65:17 Lo, I am about to create new **h**
Jer 10:11 the earth, and from beneath these **h**!
Eph 4:10 who ascended far above all the **h**,
Heb 4:14 priest who has passed through the **h**,
2Pe 3:10 the **h** will pass away with a mighty

HEAVY
Mt 23: 4 They tie up **h** burdens [hard

HEBREW → HEBREWS
Jnh 1: 9 "I am a **H**," Jonah answered them;
Jn 19:20 and it was written in **H**, Latin,
Php 3: 5 of Benjamin, a **H** of **H** parentage,

HEBREWS → HEBREW
Ex 3:18 the God of the **H**, has sent us word.
Jdt 10:12 "I am a daughter of the **H**, and I am
2Co 11:22 Are they **H**? So am I. Are they

HEBRON
Ge 13:18 terebinth of Mamre, which is at **H**.
2Sa 2:11 and six months in **H** as king

HEEL
Ge 3:15 your head, while you strike at his **h**."
    25:26 came out next, gripping Esau's **h**;
Jn 13:18 my food has raised his **h** against me.'

HEIGHT → HIGH
Ro 8:39 nor **h**, nor depth, nor any other
Eph 3:18 breadth and length and **h** and depth,

HEIGHTS → HIGH
Ps 148: 1 the heavens; give praise in the **h**.
Hab 3:19 and enables me to go upon the **h**.

HEIR → HEIRS
Ge 15: 4 "No, that one shall not be your **h**;
    15: 4 **h**; your own issue shall be your **h**."
Gal 4: 7 a child, and if a child then also an **h**,
Heb 1: 2 whom he made **h** of all things

HEIRS → HEIR
Ro 8:17 then **h**, **h** of God and joint **h**
Tit 3: 7 become **h** in hope of eternal life.
1Pe 3: 7 since we are joint **h** of the gift

HELMET
Isa 59:17 salvation, as the **h** on his head;
Eph 6:17 And take the **h** of salvation

HELP → HELPED, HELPER, HELPS
Jdt 6:21 called upon the God of Israel for **h**.
Ps 33:20 the LORD, who is our **h** and shield.
    46: 2 an ever-present **h** in distress.
Sir 2: 6 Trust God and he will **h** you;
Mk 9:24 out, "I do believe, **h** my unbelief!"
Heb 2:18 able to **h** those who are being tested.
    4:16 and to find grace for timely **h**.

HELPED → HELP
1Sa 7:12 "To this point has the LORD **h** us."

HELPER → HELP
Ps 30:11 have mercy on me; LORD, be my **h**."
Heb 13: 6 "The Lord is my **h**, [and] I will not

HELPS → HELP
Ps 37:40 The LORD **h** and rescues them,

HERBS
Ex 12: 8 with unleavened bread and bitter **h**.

HERMON
Dt 3: 8 from the Wadi Arnon to Mount **H**
Ps 133: 3 Like dew of **H** coming down

HEROD → HERODIANS
  1. King of Judea; tried to kill Jesus (Mt 2; Lk 1:5).
  2. Son of 1. Tetrarch of Galilee who arrested and beheaded John the Baptist (Mt 14:1-12; Mk 6:14-29; Lk 3:1, 19-20; 9:7-9); tried Jesus (Lk 23:6-15).
  3. Grandson of 1. King of Judea who killed James (Ac 12:2); arrested Peter (Ac 12:3-19). Death (Ac 12:19-23).

HERODIANS → HEROD
Mk 3: 6 took counsel with the **H** against him
    12:13 and **H** to him to ensnare him in his

HERODIAS
  Wife of Herod the Tetrarch who persuaded her daughter to ask for John the Baptist's head (Mt 14:1-12; Mk 6:14-29; Lk 3:19).

HEWN
Mk 15:46 in a tomb that had been **h**

HEZEKIAH
  King of Judah (Sir 48:17-25). Restored the temple and worship (2Ch 29-31). Sought the LORD for help against Assyria (2Ki 18-19; 2Ch 32:1-23; Isa 36-37). Illness healed (2Ki 20:1-11; 2Ch 32:24-26; Isa 38). Judged for showing Babylonians his treasures (2Ki 20:12-21; 2Ch 32:31; Isa 39).

HID → HIDE
Ge 3: 8 his wife **h** themselves from the LORD
Ex 2: 2 child, she **h** him for three months.
    3: 6 Moses **h** his face, for he was afraid
Jos 6:17 because she **h** the messengers we
1Ki 18:13 of the LORD—that I **h** a hundred
Isa 49: 2 arrow, in his quiver he **h** me.
    54: 8 for a moment I **h** my face from you;

HIDDEN → HIDE
Pr 2: 4 and like **h** treasures search her out:
Isa 40:27 Israel, "My way is **h** from the LORD,
Mk 4:22 there is nothing **h** except to be made
Col 3: 3 your life is **h** with Christ in God.
Rev 2:17 I shall give some of the **h** manna;

HIDE → HID, HIDDEN
Dt 31:17 them and **h** my face from them,
Ps 13: 2 How long will you **h** your face
    17: 8 **h** me in the shadow of your wings

HIGH → HEIGHT, HEIGHTS, HIGHEST, HIGHLY
Ge 14:18 and being a priest of God Most **H**,
1Ki 3: 2 were sacrificing on the **h** places,
Ps 91: 1 dwell in the shelter of the Most **H**,

Mt   4: 8 took him up to a very **h** moun-
            tain,
    17: 1 and led them up a **h** mountain
Mk   5: 7 me, Jesus, Son of the Most **H**
            God?
Eph 4: 8 it says: "He ascended on **h** and
            took
Heb 2:17 and faithful **h** priest before
            God
     7:26 that we should have such a **h**
            priest:

HIGHEST → HIGH
1Ki 8:27 the **h** heavens cannot contain
            you,
Mt 21: 9 name of the Lord; hosanna in
            the **h**."
Lk   2:14 "Glory to God in the **h** and on
            earth

HIGHLY → HIGH
Ro 12: 3 of himself more **h** than one
            ought

HILL
Isa 40: 4 mountain and **h** shall be made
            low;
Lk   3: 5 mountain and **h** shall be made
            low.

HINDERED
1Pe 3: 7 so that your prayers may not
            be **h**.

HIRAM
    King of Tyre; helped David build his
palace (2Sa 5:11-12; 1Ch 14:1); helped
Solomon build the temple (1Ki 5; 2Ch 2) and
his navy (1Ki 9:10-27; 2Ch 8).

HITTITE → HITTITES
Ge 23:10 Hittites. So Ephron the **H**
            replied
2Sa 11: 3 [Joab's armor-bearer] Uriah
            the **H**."

HITTITES → HITTITE
Dt 20:17 You must doom them all—t
            he **H**,
Ezr 9: 1 their abominations [Canaan-
            ites, **H**,

HOLD → HOLDS
Ps 73:23 you; you take **h** of my right
            hand.
Col 1:17 and in him all things **h** to-
            gether.

HOLDS → HOLD
Ps 37:24 never fall, for the Lord **h** their
            hand.
Rev 2: 1 " 'The one who **h** the seven
            stars

HOLES
Hag 1: 6 earned them for a bag with **h**
            in it.

HOLINESS → HOLY
Ex 15:11 is like to you, magnificent in
            h?
Ps 89:36 By my **h** I swore once for all: I
            will
Ro   1: 4 the spirit of **h** through resurrec-
            tion
1Ti 2:15 persevere in faith and love
            and **h**,

Heb 12:14 that **h** without which no one
            will see

HOLOCAUST → HOLOCAUSTS
Lev 1: 3 "If his **h** offering is from the
            herd,

HOLOCAUSTS → HOLOCAUST
Ex 40: 6 Put the altar of **h** in front of the
            entrance
1Sa 15:22 "Does the Lord so delight in **h**
1Ma 1:45 to prohibit **h**, sacrifices, and li-
            bations
     4:56 and joyfully offered **h** and sac-
            rifices
Hos 6: 6 and knowledge of God rather
            than **h**.
Mic 6: 6 Shall I come before him
            with **h**,

HOLOFERNES
    Assyrian general (Jdt 2:4). Beguiled and
beheaded by Judith (Jdt 10-13).

HOLY → HOLINESS
Ex   3: 5 place where you stand is **h**
            ground.
    20: 8 to keep the **h** the sabbath day.
    26:33 which divides the **h** place from
            the **h**
Lev 11:44 shall make and keep your-
            selves **h**,
    11:44 keep yourselves **h**, because I
            am **h**.
Jos 5:15 on which you are standing
            is **h**."
1Sa 2: 2 There is no **H** One like the
            Lord;
1Ma 1:15 and abandoned the **h** covenant;
Ps   2: 6 my king on Zion, my **h** moun-
            tain."
    11: 4 The Lord is in his **h** temple;
Isa 6: 3 "**H, h, h** is the Lord of hosts!"
    40:25 me as an equal? says the **H**
            One.
Da   9:24 for your people and for your **h**
            city:
     9:24 and a most **h** will be anointed.
Mt   1:18 with child through the **h** Spirit.
     3:11 He will baptize you with the **h**
            Spirit
    24:15 in the **h** place (let the reader
Mk   1:24 I know who you are—the **H**
            One
     3:29 blasphemes against the **h** Spirit
            will
Lk   3:22 the **h** Spirit descended upon
            him
    11:13 in heaven give the **h** Spirit to
            those
Jn 14:26 the **h** Spirit that the Father will
            send
Ac   2: 4 they were all filled with the **h**
            Spirit
     2:27 nor will you suffer your **h** one
            to see
     5: 3 heart so that you lied to the **h**
            Spirit
Ro 12: 1 sacrifice, **h** and pleasing to
            God,
Eph 1: 4 to be **h** and without blemish
            before
     4:30 do not grieve the **h** Spirit of
            God,

Heb 6: 4 gift and shared in the **h** Spirit
1Pe 1:16 it is written, "Be **h** because I
            [am] **h**."
1Jn 2:20 that comes from the **h** one, and
            you
Jude 1:14 has come with his countless **h**
            ones
Rev 4: 8 "**H, h, h** is the Lord God
            almighty,
    21: 2 I also saw the **h** city, a new
    22:11 still do right, and the **h** still
            be **h**."

HOME → HOMELESS
Dt   6: 7 Speak of them at **h** and abroad,
Ps 68: 7 Who gives a **h** to the forsaken,
2Co 5: 8 leave the body and go **h** to the
            Lord.

HOMELESS → HOME
Isa 58: 7 sheltering the oppressed and
            the **h**;
1Co 4:11 roughly treated, we wander
            about **h**

HONEST
Lev 19:36 weights, an **h** ephah and an **h**
            hin. I,

HONEY
Ex   3: 8 a land flowing with milk
            and **h**,
Jdg 14: 8 of bees and **h** in the lion's
            carcass.
Ps 19:11 Sweeter also than **h** or drip-
            pings
Mt   3: 4 His food was locusts and
            wild **h**.

HONOR → HONORABLE, HONORED,
        HONORS
Dt   5:16 '**H** your father and your
            mother,
1Ch 29:12 "Riches and **h** are from you,
            and you
Tob 4: 3 **H** your mother, and do not
            abandon
Ps   8: 6 crowned them with glory
            and **h**.
Mal 1: 6 a father, where is the **h** due
            to me?
Mt 13:57 "A prophet is not without **h**
            except
    15: 4 said, '**H** your father and your
            mother,'
Jn 12:26 The Father will **h** whoever
            serves
Ro 13: 7 respect is due, **h** to whom **h** is
            due.
Eph 6: 2 "**H** your father and mother."
            This is
1Ti 5:17 who preside well deserve
            double **h**,
Heb 2: 7 you crowned him with glory
            and **h**,
Rev 4:11 to receive glory and **h** and
            power,

HONORABLE → HONOR
Php 4: 8 true, whatever is **h**, whatever is
            just,

HONORED → HONOR
1Co 12:26 if one part is **h**, all the parts
            share its

1801

HONORS → HONOR
Mal 1: 6 A son **h** his father, and a servant
Mt 15: 8 'This people **h** me with their lips,

HOOFS
Lev 11: 3 any animal that has **h** you may eat,

HOOK → HOOKS
Mt 17:27 drop in a **h**, and take the first fish

HOOKS → HOOK
Isa 2: 4 and their spears into pruning **h**;

HOPE → HOPED, HOPES
Job 17:15 Where then is my **h**, and my
Ps 62: 6 alone, from whom comes my **h**.
      146: 5 whose **h** is in the LORD, their God,
Pr 23:18 and your **h** will not be cut off.
Jer 14: 8 O **H** of Israel, O LORD, our savior
Da 13:60 blessing God who saves those that **h**
La 3:21 to mind, as my reason to have **h**:
Mt 12:21 And in his name the Gentiles will **h**."
Ro 5: 5 and **h** does not disappoint,
      12:12 Rejoice in **h**, endure in affliction,
1Co 13:13 So faith, **h**, love remain, these three;
Col 1:27 it is Christ in you, the **h** for glory.
1Th 5: 8 the helmet that is **h** for salvation.
Heb 7:19 other hand, a better **h** is introduced,
1Pe 1: 3 a living **h** through the resurrection
1Jn 3: 3 Everyone who has this **h** based

HOPED → HOPE
Heb 11: 1 is the realization of what is **h**
1Pe 3: 5 how the holy women who **h** in God

HOPES → HOPE
1Co 13: 7 believes all things, **h** all things,

HOREB → = SINAI
Ex 3: 1 he came to **H**, the mountain of God.
Dt 5: 2 God, made a covenant with us at **H**;
1Ki 19: 8 nights to the mountain of God, **H**.

HORN → HORNS
Ps 18: 3 shield, my saving **h**, my stronghold!
Da 7: 8 a little **h**, sprang out of their midst,
      7: 8 it. This **h** had eyes like a man,
      8: 5 with a prominent **h** on its forehead

HORNS → HORN
Ge 22:13 a ram caught by its **h** in the thicket.
Ex 27: 2 At the four corners there are to be **h**,

Da 8: 3 by the river a ram with two great **h**,
Rev 5: 6 He had seven **h** and seven eyes;
      9:13 the [four] **h** of the gold altar before
      17: 3 names, with seven heads and ten **h**.

HORSE → HORSES
Ex 15: 1 **h** and chariot he has cast
Ps 33:17 Useless is the **h** for safety; its great
Zec 1: 8 There appeared the driver of a red **h**,
Rev 6: 2 and there was a white **h**, and its
      19:11 opened, and there was a white **h**;

HORSES → HORSE
2Ki 2:11 and flaming **h** came between them,
Ps 20: 8 Some rely on chariots, others on **h**,
Joel 2: 4 Their appearance is that of **h**;
Rev 9: 7 was like that of **h** ready for battle.
      19:14 mounted on white **h** and wearing

HOSANNA
Mk 11:10 that is to come! **H** in the highest!"
Jn 12:13 out to meet him, and cried out: "**H**!

HOSEA
  Prophet whose wife and family pictured the unfaithfulness of Israel (Hos 1-3).

HOSHEA → = JOSHUA
  1. Original name of Joshua (Nu 13:8, 16).
  2. Last king of Israel (2Ki 15:30; 17:1-6).

HOSPITABLE → HOSPITALITY
1Ti 3: 2 decent, **h**, able to teach,
Tit 1: 8 but **h**, a lover of goodness,
1Pe 4: 9 Be **h** to one another without

HOSPITALITY → HOSPITABLE
Ro 12:13 needs of the holy ones, exercise **h**.
1Ti 5:10 practiced **h**, washed the feet
Heb 13: 2 Do not neglect **h**, for through it

HOST → HOSTS
2Ki 17:16 and worshiped all the **h** of heaven,
Lk 2:13 of the heavenly **h** with the angel,

HOSTILE
Col 1:21 and **h** in mind because of evil deeds

HOSTS → HOST
Dt 4:19 or any star among the heavenly **h**,
1Sa 1: 3 his city to worship the LORD of **h**
Ps 46: 8 The LORD of **h** is with us;
Isa 48: 2 Israel, whose name is the LORD of **h**.

HOT
Rev 3:15 that you are neither cold nor **h**.
      3:15 **h**. I wish you were either cold or **h**.

HOUR
Mt 24:36 "But of that day and **h** no one knows,
Jn 2: 4 affect me? My **h** has not yet come."
      17: 1 and said, "Father, the **h** has come.

HOUSE → HOUSEHOLD, HOUSES, HOUSETOP, HOUSETOPS, STOREHOUSE
Ex 20:17 shall not covet your neighbor's **h**.
2Sa 7:11 that he will establish a **h** for you.
Ezr 1: 5 to go up to build the **h** of the LORD
Ps 69:10 zeal for your **h** consumes me, I am
      127: 1 Unless the LORD build the **h**,
Pr 9: 1 Wisdom has built her **h**, she has set
Isa 56: 7 and make joyful in my **h** of prayer;
      56: 7 altar, For my **h** shall be called a **h**
Mt 7:24 be like a wise man who built his **h**
      21:13 written: 'My **h** shall be a **h** of prayer,'
Mk 3:25 And if a **h** is divided against itself,
      3:25 that **h** will not be able to stand.
Jn 2:17 "Zeal for your **h** will consume me."
      14: 2 In my Father's **h** there are many
1Pe 2: 5 a spiritual **h** to be a holy priesthood

HOUSEHOLD → HOUSE
Jos 24:15 As for me and my **h**, we will serve
Mic 7: 6 a man's enemies are those of his **h**.
Mt 10:36 one's enemies will be those of his **h**.'
Eph 2:19 ones and members of the **h** of God,
1Ti 3: 4 He must manage his own **h** well,
      3:15 how to behave in the **h** of God,
1Pe 4:17 to begin with the **h** of God; if it

HOUSES → HOUSE
Ex 12:27 LORD, who passed over the **h**
      12:27 the Egyptians, he spared our **h**."
Mt 19:29 everyone who has given up **h**

HOUSETOP → HOUSE
Mt 24:17 a person on the **h** must not go down

HOUSETOPS → HOUSE
Mt 10:27 hear whispered, proclaim on the **h**.

HULDAH
  Prophetess inquired by Hilkiah for Josiah (2Ki 22; 2Ch 34:14-28).

HUMAN → HUMANKIND, HUMANS
Jdt 8:16 nor he, that he may be given
Da 5: 5 the fingers of a **h** hand appeared,

Hos 11: 4 I drew them with **h** cords,
Mt 15: 9 teaching as doctrines **h** precepts.' "
1Co 2:13 not with words taught by **h** wisdom,
Php 2: 7 coming in **h** likeness; and found **h**
1Ti 2: 5 There is also one mediator between God and the **h** race, Christ Jesus, himself **h**,
Rev 4: 7 had a face like that of a **h** being,

HUMANS → HUMAN
Ps 8: 5 What are **h** that you are mindful

HUMBLE → HUMBLED, HUMBLY, HUMILITY
Ps 25: 9 Guides the **h** rightly, and teaches
 25: 9 **h** rightly, and teaches the **h** the way.
Zep 2: 3 the LORD, all you **h** of the earth,
Mt 11:29 me, for I am meek and **h** of heart;
Jas 4:10 **H** yourselves before the Lord and he
1Pe 5: 5 proud but bestows favor on the **h**."

HUMBLED → HUMBLE
Lk 14:11 who exalts himself will be **h**,
Php 2: 8 he **h** himself, becoming obedient

HUMBLY → HUMBLE
Mic 6: 8 and to walk **h** with your God.

HUMILITY → HUMBLE
Pr 15:33 wisdom, and **h** goes before honors.
Zep 2: 3 Seek justice, seek **h**; perhaps you
Col 3:12 kindness, **h**, gentleness,
1Pe 5: 5 clothe yourselves with **h** in your

HUNDRED
Ge 17:17 born to a man who is a **h** years old?
Isa 65:20 youth who reaches but a **h** years,
 65:20 of a **h** shall be thought accursed.
Ro 4:19 (for he was almost a **h** years old)

HUNG
Ps 137: 2 of that land we **h** up our harps.

HUNGER → HUNGRY
Dt 8: 3 therefore let you be afflicted with **h**,
Mt 5: 6 Blessed are they who **h** and thirst
Rev 7:16 They will not **h** or thirst anymore,

HUNGRY → HUNGER
Ps 50:12 Were I **h**, I would not tell you,
 146: 7 gives food to the **h**. The LORD sets
Pr 25:21 If your enemy be **h**, give him food

Mt 12: 1 His disciples were **h** and began
Ro 12:20 "if your enemy is **h**, feed him; if he is

HUSBAND → HUSBANDS
Ge 3: 6 it; and she also gave some to her **h**,
 3:16 Yet your urge shall be for your **h**,
Pr 31:28 praise her; her **h**, too, extols her:
Sir 26: 1 Happy the **h** of a good wife,
Isa 54: 5 has become your **h** is your Maker;
1Co 7:10 wife should not separate from her **h**
Eph 5:23 For the **h** is head of his wife just as
Rev 21: 2 as a bride adorned for her **h**.

HUSBANDS → HUSBAND
Jn 4:18 For you have had five **h**,
Eph 5:25 **H**, love your wives, even as Christ
Col 3:18 be subordinate to your **h**, as is
Tit 2: 4 train younger women to love their **h**
1Pe 3: 7 you **h** should live with your wives

HUSHAI
Wise man of David; foiled Absalom's revolt (2Sa 15:32-37; 16:15-17:16).

HYMN → HYMNS
Mt 26:30 after singing a **h**, they went

HYMNS → HYMN
Eph 5:19 one another [in] psalms and **h**
Col 3:16 singing psalms, **h**, and spiritual

HYPOCRISY → HYPOCRITE, HYPOCRITES
Mt 23:28 but inside you are filled with **h**
Mk 12:15 Knowing their **h** he said to them,

HYPOCRITE → HYPOCRISY
Lk 6:42 You **h**! Remove the wooden beam

HYPOCRITES → HYPOCRISY
Mt 6: 5 do not be like the **h**, who love
 23:13 to you, scribes and Pharisees, you **h**,
Mk 7: 6 did Isaiah prophesy about you **h**,

HYSSOP
Ex 12:22 Then take a bunch of **h**, and dipping
Nu 19: 6 **h** and scarlet yarn and throw them
Ps 51: 9 Cleanse me with **h**, that I may be
Jn 19:29 soaked in wine on a sprig of **h**

I

IDLE
Ecc 11: 6 at evening let not your hand be **i**:

IDOL → IDOLS
Isa 40:19 An **i**, cast by a craftsman,
1Co 10:19 anything? Or that an **i** is anything?

IDOLS → IDOL
Ex 20: 4 You shall not carve **i** for yourselves
1Ma 1:43 they sacrificed to **i** and profaned
Ps 115: 4 Their **i** are silver and gold, the work
1Co 8: 1 in regard to meat sacrificed to **i**:

IGNORANCE → IGNORANT
Ac 17:30 God has overlooked the times of **i**,
1Pe 2:15 doing good you may silence the **i**

IGNORANT → IGNORANCE
Heb 5: 2 is able to deal patiently with the **i**
2Pe 3:16 things hard to understand that the **i**

ILL
1Co 11:30 That is why many among you are **i**

ILLEGITIMATE
Jn 8:41 [So] they said to him, "We are not **i**.

IMAGE → IMAGES
Ge 1:26 "Let us make man in our **i**, after our
1Co 15:49 Just as we have borne the **i**
 15:49 also bear the **i** of the heavenly one.
Col 1:15 He is the **i** of the invisible God,
Rev 20: 4 or its **i** nor had accepted its mark

IMAGES → IMAGE
Nu 33:52 all their stone figures and molten **i**,

IMITATE → IMITATORS
Heb 13: 7 of their way of life and **i** their faith.
3Jn 1:11 Beloved, do not **i** evil but **i** good.

IMITATORS → IMITATE
1Co 11: 1 Be **i** of me, as I am of Christ.
Eph 5: 1 So be **i** of God, as beloved children,

IMMANUEL → = EMMANUEL
Isa 7:14 bear a son, and shall name him **I**.
 8: 8 wings the full width of your land, **I**!

IMMORAL → IMMORALITY
1Co 5: 9 letter not to associate with **i** people,
Heb 12:16 that no one be an **i** or profane

IMMORALITY → IMMORAL
2Co 12:21 have not repented of the impurity, **i**,

IMMORTAL → IMMORTALITY
Ro 1:23 exchanged the glory of the **i** God

IMMORTALITY → IMMORTAL
1Co 15:53 is mortal must clothe itself with **i**.
1Ti 6:16 who alone has **i**, who dwells

IMPERISHABLE
1Co 9:25 a perishable crown, but we an **i** one.
1Pe 1: 4 to an inheritance that is **i**, undefiled,

IMPORTANCE
1Co 15: 3 handed on to you as of first **i** what I

IMPOSSIBLE
Zec 8: 6 if this should seem **i** in the eyes
8: 6 it in those days be **i** in my eyes also,
Mt 17:20 move. Nothing will be **i** for you."
Mk 10:27 "For human beings it is **i**, but not
Heb 11: 6 without faith it is **i** to please him,

IMPURE → IMPURITY
Eph 5: 5 this, that no immoral or **i** or greedy
1Th 2: 3 was not from delusion or **i** motives,

IMPURITY → IMPURE
Gal 5:19 immorality, **i**, licentiousness,
1Th 4: 7 For God did not call us to **i**

INCENSE → FRANKINCENSE
Ex 25: 6 anointing oil and for the fragrant **i**;

INCREASE → INCREASED
Lk 17: 5 apostles said to the Lord, "I our faith."
Jn 3:30 He must **i**; I must decrease."

INCREASED → INCREASE
Ro 5:20 where sin **i**, grace overflowed all

INDEPENDENT
1Co 11:11 Woman is not **i** of man or man

INFANTS
Ps 8: 3 Out of the mouths of babes and **i**
Mt 21:16 'Out of the mouths of **i** and nurslings
1Co 14:20 In respect to evil be like **i**,

INFIRMITIES
Isa 53: 4 Yet it was our **i** that he bore,
Mt 8:17 "He took away our **i** and bore our

INHERIT → INHERITANCE
Lk 10:25 what must I do to **i** eternal life?'
1Co 6: 9 the unjust will not **i** the kingdom
Heb 1:14 sake of those who are to **i** salvation?

INHERITANCE → INHERIT
Col 1:12 to share in the **i** of the holy ones
Heb 9:15 may receive the promised eternal **i**.

INIQUITIES
Lev 16:22 is to carry off their **i** to an isolated
Ro 4: 7 are they whose **i** are forgiven

INJURY
Lev 24:20 The same **i** that a man gives another

INJUSTICE
Ro 9:14 to say? Is there **i** on the part of God?

INN
Lk 2: 7 there was no room for them in the **i**.
10:34 took him to an **i** and cared for him.

INNER → INWARDLY
Mt 24:26 'He is in the **i** rooms,' do not believe
2Co 4:16 our **i** self is being renewed day

INNOCENCE → INNOCENT
Ps 26: 6 I will wash my hands in **i** and walk
Hos 8: 5 they be unable to attain **i** in Israel?

INNOCENT → INNOCENCE
Pr 6:17 tongue, and hands that shed **i** blood;
Mt 27:24 saying, "I am **i** of this man's blood.

INQUIRE
Dt 12:30 Do not **i** regarding their gods,

INSCRIBED → INSCRIPTION
Rev 19:12 He had a name **i** that no one knows

INSCRIPTION → INSCRIBED
Mk 15:26 The **i** of the charge against him
2Ti 2:19 bearing this **i**, "The Lord knows

INSIGHT
Eph 1: 8 upon us. In all wisdom and **i**,

INSPIRED
2Ti 3:16 All scripture is **i** by God and is

INSTITUTION
1Pe 2:13 to every human **i** for the Lord's sake,

INSTRUCT → INSTRUCTED, INSTRUCTION
1Co 14:19 mind, so as to **i** others also, than ten

INSTRUCTED → INSTRUCT
Isa 40:13 LORD, or has **i** him as his counselor?

INSTRUCTION → INSTRUCT
Pr 8:10 Receive my **i** in preference to silver,
Mic 4: 2 For from Zion shall go forth **i**,
Ro 15: 4 previously was written for our **i**,
1Ti 1: 5 The aim of this **i** is love from a pure

INSULTS
2Co 12:10 I am content with weaknesses, **i**,

INTEGRITY
Tit 2: 7 respect, with **i** in your teaching,

INTELLIGENT
Pr 11:12 no sense, but the **i** man keeps silent.

INTERCEDES → INTERCESSION
Ro 8:26 the Spirit itself **i** with inexpressible

INTERCESSION → INTERCEDES
Heb 7:25 he lives forever to make **i** for them.

INTERMARRY → MARRIAGE
Dt 7: 3 You shall not **i** with them,

INTERPRET → INTERPRETATION, INTERPRETATIONS
Ge 41:15 certain dreams that no one can **i**.
41:15 you are told a dream you can **i** it."
1Co 12:30 Do all speak in tongues? Do all **i**?

INTERPRETATION → INTERPRET
1Co 12:10 of tongues; to another **i** of tongues.
2Pe 1:20 that is a matter of personal **i**,

INTERPRETATIONS → INTERPRET
Ge 40: 8 to them, "Surely, **i** come from God.

INVISIBLE
Col 1:15 He is the image of the **i** God,
1Ti 1:17 ages, incorruptible, **i**, the only God,

INVITE → INVITES
Lk 14:13 you hold a banquet, **i** the poor,

INVITES → INVITE
1Co 10:27 If an unbeliever **i** you and you want

INVOKE
1Pe 1:17 if you **i** as Father him who judges

INWARDLY → INNER
Ro 2:29 one is a Jew, and circumcision is

IRON
Ps 2: 9 an **i** rod you shall shepherd them,
Pr 27:17 As **i** sharpens **i**, so man sharpens his
Da 2:33 the legs **i**, its feet partly **i** and partly
Rev 19:15 He will rule them with an **i** rod,

IRREVOCABLE
Ro 11:29 the gifts and the call of God are **i**.

ISAAC
Son of Abraham by Sarah (Ge 17:19; 21:1-7; 1Ch 1:28). Abrahamic covenant perpetuated with (Ge 17:21; 26:2-5). Offered up by Abraham (Ge 22; Heb 11:17-19). Rebekah taken as wife (Ge 24). Inherited Abraham's estate (Ge 25:5). Father of Esau and Jacob (Ge 25:19-26; 1Ch 1:34). Nearly lost Rebekah to Abimelech (Ge 26:1-11). Covenant with Abimelech (Ge 26:12-31). Tricked into blessing Jacob (Ge 27). Death (Ge 35:27-29). Father of Israel (Ex 3:6; Dt 29:13; Ro 9:10).

ISAIAH

Prophet to Judah (Isa 1:1). Called by the LORD (Isa 6). Announced judgment to Ahaz (Isa 7), deliverance from Assyria to Hezekiah (2Ki 19; Isa 36-37), deliverance from death to Hezekiah (2Ki 20:1-11; Isa 38). Chronicler of Judah's history (2Ch 26:22; 32:32).

ISCARIOT

Mt 10: 4 and Judas **I** who betrayed him.

Lk 22: 3 Judas, the one surnamed **I**, who was

ISHBAAL

Son of Saul; would-be king (2Sa 2:8-4:12).

ISHMAEL

Son of Abraham by Hagar (Ge 16; 1Ch 1:28). Blessed, but not son of covenant (Ge 17:18-21; Gal 4:21-31). Sent away by Sarah (Ge 21:8-21). Children (Ge 25:12-18; 1Ch 1:29-31). Death (Ge 25:17).

ISRAEL → ISRAELITE, ISRAELITES, = JACOB

1. Name given to Jacob (Ge 32:28; 35:10).
2. Corporate name of Jacob's descendants; often specifically Northern Kingdom.

Ge 49:28 All these are the twelve tribes of **I**,

Ex 28:11 with the names of the sons of **I**

Nu 24:17 and a staff shall rise from **I**,

Dt 6: 4 "Hear, O **I**! The LORD is our God,

Ps 125: 5 with the wicked. Peace upon **I**!

Jer 31:31 a new covenant with the house of **I**

Hos 11: 1 When **I** was a child I loved him,

Mt 2: 6 who is to shepherd my people **I**.' "

Mk 12:29 replied, "The first is this: 'Hear, O **I**!

Lk 22:30 judging the twelve tribes of **I**.

Ac 1: 6 going to restore the kingdom to **I**?"

Ro 9: 6 failed. For not all who are of **I** are **I**,

Heb 8: 8 house of **I** and the house of Judah.

ISRAELITE → ISRAEL

Jn 1:47 and said of him, "Here is a true **I**.

Ro 11: 1 For I too am an **I**, a descendant

ISRAELITES → ISRAEL

Ex 2:23 Still the **I** groaned and cried

29:45 I will dwell in the midst of the **I**

ISSACHAR

Son of Jacob by Leah (Ge 30:18; 35:23; 1Ch 2:1). Tribe of blessed (Ge 49:14-15; Dt 33:18-19), numbered (Nu 1:29; 26:25), allotted land (Jos 19:17-23; Eze 48:25), assisted Deborah (Jdg 5:15), 12,000 from (Rev 7:7).

ITCHING

J

JACOB → = ISRAEL

1. Son of Isaac, younger twin of Esau (Ge 26:21-26; 1Ch 1:34). Bought Esau's birthright (Ge 26:29-34); tricked Isaac into blessing him (Ge 27:1-37). Fled to Haran (Ge 28:1-5). Abrahamic covenant perpetuated through (Ge 28:13-15; Mal 1:2). Vision at Bethel (Ge 28:10-22). Served Laban for Rachel and Leah (Ge 29:1-30). Children (Ge 29:31-30:24; 35:16-26; 1Ch 2-9). Flocks increased (Ge 30:25-43). Returned to Canaan (Ge 31). Wrestled with God; name changed to Israel (Ge 32:22-32). Reconciled to Esau (Ge 33). Returned to Bethel (Ge 35:1-15). Favored Joseph (Ge 37:3). Sent sons to Egypt during famine (Ge 42-43). Settled in Egypt (Ge 46). Blessed Ephraim and Manasseh (Ge 48). Blessed sons (Ge 49:1-28; Heb 11:21). Death (Ge 49:29-33). Burial (Ge 50:1-14).

2. Corporate name of Jacob's descendants; often specifically Northern Kingdom.

1Ma 1:28 all the house of **J** was covered

Ps 135: 4 For the LORD has chosen **J**, Israel as

Mic 7:20 You will show faithfulness to **J**,

Ro 9:13 is written: "I loved **J** but hated Esau."

JAEL

Woman who killed the Canaanite general, Sisera (Jdg 4:17-22; 5:6, 24-27).

JAIRUS

Synagogue ruler whose daughter Jesus raised (Mk 5:22-43; Lk 8:41-56).

JAMES

1. Apostle; brother of John (Mt 4:21-22; 10:2; Mk 3:17; Lk 5:1-10). At transfiguration (Mt 17:1-13; Mk 9:1-13; Lk 9:28-36). Killed by Herod (Ac 12:2).

2. Apostle (Mt 10:3; Mk 3:18; Lk 6:15).

3. Brother of Jesus (Mt 13:55; Mk 6:3; Lk 24:10; Gal 1:19) and Judas (Jude 1). With believers before Pentecost (Ac 1:13). Leader of church at Jerusalem (Ac 12:17; 15; 21:18; Gal 2:9, 12). Author of epistle (Jas 1:1).

JAPHETH

Son of Noah (Ge 5:32; 1Ch 1:4-5). Blessed (Ge 9:18-28). Sons of (Ge 10:2-5).

JAR → JARS

1Ki 17:14 'The **j** of flour shall not go empty,

Mk 14: 3 with an alabaster **j** of perfumed oil,

14: 3 She broke the alabaster **j** and poured

Lk 22:10 a man will meet you carrying a **j**

JARS → JAR

Jn 2: 6 there were six stone water **j** there

JEALOUS

Ex 34:14 other god, for the LORD is 'the **J** One';

34:14 the LORD is 'the **J** One'; a **j** God is he.

Dt 4:24 God, is a consuming fire, a **j** God.

Eze 39:25 and I will be **j** for my holy name.

Ro 10:19 "I will make you **j** of those who are

JEBUSITES

Ex 3: 8 Amorites, Perizzites, Hivites and **J**.

Jos 15:63 the **J** who lived in Jerusalem

15:63 so the **J** dwell in Jerusalem beside

JECONIAH → See JEHOIACHIN

JEHOAHAZ

1. Son of Jehu; king of Israel (2Ki 13:1-9).

2. Son of Josiah; king of Judah (2Ki 23:31-34; 2Ch 36:1-4).

JEHOASH → = JOASH

1. Son of Ahaziah, king of Judah (2Ki 12). See Joash, 1.

2. Son of Jehoahaz; king of Israel. Defeat of Aram prophesied by Elisha (2Ki 13:10-25). Defeated Amaziah in Jerusalem (2Ki 14:1-16). See Joash, 2.

JEHOIACHIN → = CONIAH, = JECONIAH

Son of Jehoiakim; king of Judah exiled by Nebuchadnezzar (2Ki 24:8-17; 2Ch 36:8-10; Eze 1:2). Status improved (2Ki 25:27-30; Jer 52:31-34).

JEHOIADA

Priest who sheltered Joash from Athaliah (2Ki 11-12; 2Ch 22:11-24:16).

JEHOIAKIM → = ELIAKIM

Son of Josiah; made king of Judah by Nebuchadnezzar (2Ki 23:34-24:6; 2Ch 36:4-8; Jer 22:18-23). Burned scroll of Jeremiah's prophecies (Jer 36).

JEHORAM → = JORAM

1. Son of Jehoshaphat; king of Judah. Prophesied against by Elijah; killed by the LORD (2Ch 21). See Joram, 1.

2. Son of Ahab; king of Israel (2Ch 22:5). Joined Jehoshaphat against Moab (2Ki 3). See Joram, 2.

JEHOSHAPHAT

1. Son of Asa; king of Judah. Strengthened his kingdom (2Ch 17). Joined with Ahab against Aram (2Ki 22; 2Ch 18). Established judges (2Ch 19). Joined Joram against Moab (2Ki 3; 2Ch 20).

2. Valley of judgment (Joel 3:2, 12).

JEHU

1. Prophet against Baasha (2Ki 16:1-7).

2. King of Israel. Anointed by Elijah to obliterate house of Ahab (1Ki 19:16-17); anointed by servant of Elisha (2Ki 9:1-13). Killed Joram and Ahaziah (2Ki 9:14-29; 2Ch 22:7-9), Jezebel (2Ki 9:30-37), relatives of Ahab (2Ki 10:1-17; Hos 1:4), ministers of Baal (2Ki 10:18-29). Death (2Ki 10:30-36).

JEPHTHAH

Judge from Gilead who delivered Israel from Ammon (Jdg 10:6-12:7). Made rash vow concerning his daughter (Jdg 11:30-40).

JEREMIAH

Prophet to Judah (Jer 1:1-3). Called by the LORD (Jer 1). Put in stocks (Jer 20:1-3). Threatened for prophesying (Jer 11:18-23; 26). Opposed by Hananiah (Jer 28). Scroll burned (Jer 36). Imprisoned (Jer 37). Thrown into cistern (Jer 38). Forced to Egypt with those fleeing Babylonians (Jer 43).

JERICHO

Jos 6: 2 "I have delivered **J** and its king

1Ki 16:34 his reign, Hiel from Bethel rebuilt **J**,

Lk 18:35 as he approached **J** a blind man was

JEROBOAM

1. Official of Solomon; rebelled to become first king of Israel (1Ki 11:26-40; 12:1-20; 2Ch 10). Idolatry (1Ki 12:25-33; Tob 1:5; Sir 47:23); judgment for (1Ki 13-14; 2Ch 13).

2. Son of Jehoash; king of Israel (1Ki 14:23-29).

JERUSALEM

2Sa 5: 5 thirty-three years in **J** over all Israel

     15:29 took the ark of God back to **J**

2Ki 25:10 down the walls that surrounded **J**.

Ezr 2: 1 and who came back to **J** and Judah,

Ne 2:17 how **J** lies in ruins and its gates

      2:17 let us rebuild the wall of **J**,

1Ma 1:29 he came to **J** with a strong force.

Isa 40: 2 Speak tenderly to **J**, and proclaim

La   1: 8 of which she is guilty, **J** is defiled;

Da 9:25 of the word that **J** was to be rebuilt

Mic 4: 2 and the word of the LORD from **J**.

Zec 1:14 I am deeply moved for the sake of **J**

Zec 14: 8 living waters shall flow from **J**,

Mt 23:37 "**J**, **J**, you who kill the prophets

Lk 4: 9 Then he led him to **J**, made him

Gal 4:25 it corresponds to the present **J**,

Heb 12:22 the heavenly **J**, and countless angels

Rev 21: 2 city, a new **J**, coming down

JESSE

Father of David (Ru 4:17-22; 1Sa 16; 1Ch 2:12-17).

JESUS

1. Jesus the Messiah.

LIFE: Genealogy (Mt 1:1-17; Lk 3:21-37). Birth announced (Mt 1:18-25; Lk 1:26-45). Birth (Mt 2:1-12; Lk 2:1-40). Escape to Egypt (Mt 2:13-23). As a boy in the temple (Lk 2:41-52). Baptism (Mt 3:13-17; Mk 1:9-11; Lk 3:21-22; Jn 1:32-34). Temptation (Mt 4:1-11; Mk 1:12-13; Lk 4:1-13). Ministry in Galilee (Mt 4:12-18:35; Mk 1:14-9:50; Lk 4:14-13:9; Jn 1:35-2:11; 4; 6), Transfiguration (Mt 17:1-8; Mk 9:2-8; Lk 9:28-36), on the way to Jerusalem (Mt 19-20; Mk 10; Lk 13:10-19:27), in Jerusalem (Mt 21; Mk 11-13; Lk 19:28-21:38; Jn 2:12-3:36; 5; 7-12). Last supper (Mt 26:17-35; Mk 14:12-31; Lk 22:1-38; Jn 13-17). Arrest and trial (Mt 26:36-27:31; Mk 14:43-15:20; Lk 22:39-23:25; Jn 18:1-19:16). Crucifixion (Mt 27:32-66; Mk 15:21-47; Lk 23:26-55; Jn 19:28-42). Resurrection and appearances (Mt 28; Mk 16; Lk 24; Jn 20-21; Ac 1:1-11; 7:56; 9:3-6; 1Co 15:1-8; Rev 1:1-20).

MIRACLES. *Healings:* official's son (Jn 4:43-54), demoniac in Capernaum (Mk 1:23-26; Lk 4:33-35), Peter's mother-in-law (Mt 8:14-17; Mk 1:29-31; Lk 4:38-39), leper (Mt 8:2-4; Mk 1:40-45; Lk 5:12-16), paralytic (Mt 9:1-8; Mk 2:1-12; Lk 5:17-26), cripple (Jn 5:1-9), shriveled hand (Mt 12:10-13; Mk 3:1-5; Lk 6:6-11), centurion's servant (Mt 8:5-13; Lk 7:1-10), widow's son raised (Lk 7:11-17), demoniac (Mt 12:22-23; Lk 11:14), Gadarene demoniacs (Mt 8:28-34; Mk 5:1-20; Lk 8:26-39), woman's bleeding and Jairus' daughter (Mt 9:18-26; Mk 5:21-43; Lk 8:40-56), blind man (Mt 9:27-31), mute man (Mt 9:32-33), Canaanite woman's daughter (Mt 15:21-28; Mk 7:24-30), deaf man (Mt 7:31-37), blind man (Mk 8:22-26), demoniac boy (Mt 17:14-18; Mk 9:14-29; Lk 9:37-43), ten lepers (Lk 17:11-19), man born blind (Jn 9:1-7), Lazarus raised (Jn 11), crippled woman (Lk 13:11-17), man with dropsy (Lk 14:1-6), two blind men (Mt 20:29-34; Mk 10:46-52; Lk 18:35-43), Malchus' ear (Lk 22:50-51). *Other Miracles:* water to wine (Jn 2:1-11), catch of fish (Lk 5:1-11), storm stilled (Mt 8:23-27; Mk 4:37-41; Lk 8:22-25), 5,000 fed (Mt 14:15-21; Mk 6:35-44; Lk 9:10-17; Jn 6:1-14), walking on water (Mt 14:25-33; Mk 6:48-52; Jn 6:15-21), 4,000 fed (Mt 15:32-39; Mk 8:1-9), money from fish (Mt 17:24-27), fig tree cursed (Mt 21:18-22; Mk 11:12-14), catch of fish (Jn 21:1-14).

MAJOR TEACHING: Sermon on the Mount (Mt 5-7; Lk 6:17-49), to Nicodemus (Jn 3), to Samaritan woman (Jn 4), Bread of Life (Jn 6:22-59), at Feast of Tabernacles (Jn 7-8), woes to Pharisees (Mt 23; Lk 11:37-54), Good Shepherd (Jn 10:1-18), Olivet Discourse (Mt 24-25; Mk 13; Lk 21:5-36), Upper Room Discourse (Jn 13-16).

PARABLES: Sower (Mt 13:3-23; Mk 4:3-25; Lk 8:5-18), seed's growth (Mk 4:26-29), wheat and weeds (Mt 13:24-30, 36-43), mustard seed (Mt 13:31-32; Mk 4:30-32), yeast (Mt 13:33; Lk 13:20-21), hidden treasure (Mt 13:44), valuable pearl (Mt 13:45-46), net (Mt 13:47-51), house owner (Mt 13:52), good Samaritan (Lk 10:25-37), unmerciful servant (Mt 18:15-35), lost sheep (Mt 18:10-14; Lk 15:4-7), lost coin (Lk 15:8-10), prodigal son (Lk 15:11-32), dishonest manager (Lk 16:1-13), rich man and Lazarus (Lk 16:19-31), persistent widow (Lk 18:1-8), Pharisee and tax collector (Lk 18:9-14), payment of workers (Mt 20:1-16), tenants and the vineyard (Mt 21:28-46; Mt 12:1-12; Lk 20:9-19), wedding banquet (Mt 22:1-14), faithful servant (Mt 24:45-51), ten virgins (Mt 25:1-13), talents (Mt 25:1-30; Lk 19:12-27).

DISCIPLES see APOSTLES. Call (Jn 1:35-51; Mt 4:18-22; 9:9; Mk 1:16-20; 2:13-14; Lk 5:1-11, 27-28). Named Apostles (Mt 3:13-19; Lk 6:12-16). Twelve sent out (Mt 10; Mk 6:7-11; Lk 9:1-5). Seventy sent out (Lk 10:1-24). Defection of (Jn 6:60-71; Mt 26:56; Mk 14:50-52). Final commission (Mt 28:16-20; Jn 21:15-23; Ac 1:3-8).

Ac 9: 5 "I am **J**, whom you are persecuting.

1Co 8: 6 and one Lord, **J** Christ,

Php 2:10 that at the name of **J** every knee

2Th 2: 1 to the coming of our Lord **J** Christ

1Ti 1:15 Christ **J** came into the world to save

Heb 12: 2 while keeping our eyes fixed on **J**,

     13: 8 **J** Christ is the same yesterday,

1Jn 1: 7 the blood of his Son **J** cleanses us

Rev 1: 1 The revelation of **J** Christ,

     22:20 coming soon." Amen! Come, Lord **J**!

2. Disciple, also called Justus (Col 4:11).
3. Writer of Sirach (Sir Pr:1; 50:27; 51:1).

JETHRO

Father-in-law and adviser of Moses (Ex 3:1; 4:18; 18). Also known as Reuel (Ex 2:18).

JEW → JEWS, JUDAISM

Est 10: 3 The **J** Mordecai was next in rank

Zec 8:23 take hold of every **J** by the edge

Ro 1:16 believes: for **J** first, and then Greek.

     2:29 Rather, one is a **J** inwardly,

1Co 9:20 To the Jews I became like a **J** to win

Col 3:11 Here there is not Greek and **J**,

JEWS → JEW

Est 3:13 that all the **J**, young and old,

Mt 2: 2 "Where is the newborn king of the **J**?

     27:11 him, "Are you the king of the **J**?"

Jn 4:22 because salvation is from the **J**.

Ro 3:29 Does God belong to **J** alone?

JEZEBEL

Sidonian wife of Ahab (1Ki 16:31). Promoted Baal worship (1Ki 16:32-33). Killed prophets of the LORD (1Ki 18:4, 13). Opposed Elijah (1Ki 19:1-2). Had Naboth killed (1Ki 21). Death (1Ki 21:17-24; 2Ki 9:30-37). Metaphor of immorality (Rev 2:20).

JEZREEL

2Ki 10: 7 baskets, and sent them to Jehu in **J**.

Hos 1: 4 Give him the name **J**, for in a little

      1: 4 for the bloodshed at **J** And bring

JOAB

Nephew of David (1Ch 2:16). Commander of his army (2Sa 8:16). Victorious over Ammon (2Sa 10; 1Ch 19), Rabbah (2Sa 11; 1Ch 20), Jerusalem (1Ch 11:6), Absalom (2Sa 18), Sheba (2Sa 20). Killed Abner (2Sa 3:22-39), Amasa (2Sa 20:1-13). Numbered David's army (2Sa 24; 1Ch 21). Sided with Adonijah (1Ki 1:17, 19). Killed by Benaiah (1Ki 2:5-6, 28-35).

JOASH → = JEHOASH
1. Son of Ahaziah; king of Judah. Sheltered from Athaliah by Jehoiada (2Ki 11; 2Ch 22:10-23:21). Repaired temple (2Ch 24). See Jehoash, 1.
2. Son of Jehoahaz, king of Israel (2Ki 13; 2Ch 25:17-25). See Jehoash, 2.

JOB
Wealthy man from Uz; feared God (Job 1:1-5). Integrity tested by disaster (Job 1:6-22), personal affliction (Job 2). Maintained innocence in debate with three friends (Job 3-31), Elihu (Job 32-37). Rebuked by the LORD (Job 38-41). Vindicated and restored to greater stature by the LORD (Job 42). Example of righteousness (Eze 14:14, 20; Sir 49:9).

JOEL
1. Son of Samuel (1Sa 8:2; 1Ch 6:28).
2. Prophet (Joel 1:1; Ac 2:16).

JOHANAN
1. First high priest in the temple (1Ch 6:9-10).
2. Jewish leader who tried to save Gedaliah from assassination (Jer 40:13-14); took Jews, including Jeremiah, to Egypt (Jer 40-43).

JOHN
1. Son of Zechariah and Elizabeth (Lk 1). Called the Baptist (Mt 3:1-12; Mk 1:2-8). Witness to Jesus (Mt 3:11-12; Mk 1:7-8; Lk 3:15-18; Jn 1:6-35; 3:27-30; 5:33-36). Doubts about Jesus (Mt 11:2-6; Lk 7:18-23). Arrest (Mt 4:12; Mk 1:14). Execution (Mt 14:1-12; Mk 6:14-29; Lk 9:7-9). Ministry compared to Elijah (Mt 11:7-19; Mk 9:11-13; Lk 7:24-35).
2. Apostle; brother of James (Mt 4:21-22; 10:2; Mk 3:17; Lk 5:1-10). At transfiguration (Mt 17:1-13; Mk 9:1-13; Lk 9:28-36). Desire to be greatest (Mk 10:35-45). Leader of church at Jerusalem (Ac 4:1-3; Gal 2:9). Elder who wrote epistles (2Jn 1; 3Jn 1). Prophet who wrote Revelation (Rev 1:1; 22:8).
3. Cousin of Barnabas, co-worker with Paul, (Ac 12:12-13:13; 15:37; see Mark).
4. Son of Simon Maccabeus (1Ma 13:53; 16).

JOIN → JOINED
Eze 37:17 Then **j** the two sticks together,

JOINED → JOIN
Mt 19: 6 what God has **j** together, no human

JOINT → JOINTS
Ro 8:17 heirs of God and **j** heirs with Christ,

JOINTS → JOINT
Heb 4:12 soul and spirit, **j** and marrow,

JONAH
Prophet in days of Jeroboam II (2Ki 14:25). Called to Nineveh; fled to Tarshish (Jnh 1:1-3). Cause of storm; thrown into sea (Jnh 1:4-16). Swallowed by fish (Jnh 1:17). Prayer (Jnh 2). Preached to Nineveh (Jnh 3). Attitude reproved by the LORD (Jnh 4). Sign of (Mt 12:39-41; Lk 11:29-32).

JONATHAN
1. Son of Saul (1Sa 13:16; 1Ch 8:33). Valiant warrior (1Sa 13-14). Relation to David (1Sa 18:1-4; 19-20; 23:16-18). Killed at Gilboa (1Sa 31). Mourned by David (2Sa 1).
2. Brother and successor of Judas Maccabeus (1Ma 2:5; 9:28-31).

JOPPA
Jnh 1: 3 He went down to **J**, found a ship
Ac 9:43 And he stayed a long time in **J**

JORAM → = JEHORAM
1. Son of Jehoshaphat; king of Judah (2Ki 8:16-24). See Jehoram, 1.
2. Son of Ahab; king of Israel. Killed with Ahaziah by Jehu (2Ki 8:25-29; 9:14-26; 2Ch 22:5-9). See Jehoram, 2.

JORDAN
Ge 13:10 watered the whole **J** Plain was as far
Nu 34:12 boundary shall continue along the **J**
Jos 3:17 of the **J** until the whole nation had
Mt 3: 6 in the **J** River as they acknowledged

JOSEPH → = BARNABAS, = BARSABBAS
1. Son of Jacob by Rachel (Ge 30:24; 1Ch 2:2). Favored by Jacob, hated by brothers (Ge 37:3-4). Dreams (Ge 37:5-11). Sold by brothers (Ge 37:12-36). Served Potiphar; imprisoned by false accusation (Ge 39). Interpreted dreams of Pharaoh's servants (Ge 40), of Pharaoh (Ge 41:4-40). Made greatest in Egypt (Ge 41:41-57). Sold grain to brothers (Ge 42-45). Brought Jacob and sons to Egypt (Ge 46-47). Sons Ephraim and Manasseh blessed (Ge 48). Blessed (Ge 49:22-26; Dt 33:13-17). Death (Ge 50:22-26; Ex 13:19; Heb 11:22). 12,000 from (Rev 7:8).
2. Husband of Mary mother of Jesus (Mt 1:16-24; 2:13-19; Lk 1:27; 2; Jn 1:45).
3. Disciple from Arimathea; buried Jesus in his tomb (Mt 27:57-61; Mk 15:43-47; Lk 24:50-52).
4. Original name of Barnabas (Ac 4:36).

JOSHUA → = HOSHEA, = JESHUA
1. Son of Nun; name changed from Hoshea (Nu 13:8, 16; 1Ch 7:27). Fought Amalekites under Moses (Ex 17:9-14). Servant of Moses on Sinai (Ex 24:13; 32:17). Spied Canaan (Nu 13). With Caleb, allowed to enter land (Nu 14:6, 30). Succeeded Moses (Dt 1:38; 31:1-8; 34:9). Charged Israel to conquer Canaan (Jos 1). Crossed Jordan (Jos 3-4). Circumcised sons of wilderness wanderings (Jos 5). Conquered Jericho (Jos 6), Ai (Jos 7-8), five kings at Gibeon (Jos 10:1-28), southern Canaan (Jos 10:29-43), northern Canaan (Jos 11-12). Defeated at Ai (Jos 7). Deceived by Gibeonites (Jos 9). Renewed covenant (Jos 8:30-35; 24:1-27). Divided land among tribes (Jos 13-22). Last words (Jos 23). Death (Jos 24:28-31).
2. High priest during rebuilding of temple (Hag 1-2; Zec 3:1-9; 6:11). See Jeshua.

JOSIAH
Son of Amon; king of Judah (2Ki 21:26; 1Ch 3:14). Prophesied (1Ki 13:2). Book of the Law discovered during his reign (2Ki 22; 2Ch 34:14-31). Reforms (2Ki 23:1-25; 2Ch 34:1-13; 35:1-19; Sir 49:1-4). Killed in battle (2Ki 23:29-30; 2Ch 35:20-27).

JOTHAM
1. Son of Gideon (Jdg 9).
2. Son of Azariah (Uzziah); king of Judah (2Ki 15:32-38; 2Ch 26:21-27:9).

JOY
Job 20: 5 and the **j** of the impious
Ps 51:14 Restore my **j** in your salvation;
Pr 21:15 To practice justice is a **j** for the just,
Isa 12: 3 With **j** you will draw water
35:10 crowned with everlasting **j**;
35:10 They will meet with **j** and gladness,
La 2:15 city, the **j** of the whole earth?"
Bar 5: 9 For God is leading Israel in **j**
Mk 4:16 the word, receive it at once with **j**.
Lk 1:44 the infant in my womb leaped for **j**.
2:10 good news of great **j** that will be
Jn 16:22 no one will take your **j** away
Ro 14:17 peace, and **j** in the holy Spirit;
Gal 5:22 the fruit of the Spirit is love, **j**,
Php 4: 1 I love and long for, my **j** and crown,
Heb 12: 2 the **j** that lay before him he endured
Jas 1: 2 Consider it all **j**, my brothers,

JUBILEE
Lev 25:10 It shall be a **j** for you, when every
Nu 36: 4 the Israelites celebrate the **j** year,

JUDAH → JUDEA
1. Son of Jacob by Leah (Ge 29:35; 35:23; 1Ch 2:1). Did not want to kill Joseph (Ge 37:26-27). Among Canaanites, fathered Perez by Tamar (Ge 38). Tribe of blessed as ruling tribe (Ge 49:8-12; Dt 33:7), numbered (Nu 1:27; 26:22), allotted land (Jos 15; Eze 48:7), failed to fully possess (Jos 15:63; Jdg 1:1-20).
2. Name used for Southern Kingdom.
2Sa 2: 4 Then the men of **J** came there
La 1: 3 **J** has fled into exile from oppression
Mt 2: 6 'And you, Bethlehem, land of **J**,
2: 6 means least among the rulers of **J**;
Heb 7:14 is clear that our Lord arose from **J**,
Rev 5: 5 The lion of the tribe of **J**, the root

JUDAISM → JEW
Ac 13:43 were converts to **J** followed Paul
Gal 1:13 heard of my former way of life in **J**,

JUDAS → = BARSABBAS, = JUDE, = THADDAEUS, MACCABEUS

1. Apostle; son of James (Lk 6:16; Jn 14:22; Ac 1:13). Probably also called Thaddaeus (Mt 10:3; Mk 3:18).

2. Brother of James and Jesus (Mt 13:55; Mk 6:3), also called Jude (Jude 1).

3. Christian prophet (Ac 15:22-32).

4. Apostle, also called Iscariot, who betrayed Jesus (Mt 10:4; 26:14-56; Mk 3:19; 14:10-50; Lk 6:16; 22:3-53; Jn 6:71; 12:4; 13:2-30; 18:2-11). Suicide of (Mt 27:3-5; Ac 1:16-25).

5. Leader of the Maccabean revolt (1Ma 2:4, 66). Recaptured Jerusalem and rededicated the temple and altar (1Ma 4:36-61). Death of (1Ma 9).

JUDE → See JUDAS, 2

JUDEA → JUDAH
Mt	2: 1	Jesus was born in Bethlehem of **J**,
Lk	3: 1	Pontius Pilate was governor of **J**,
Ac	1: 8	throughout **J** and Samaria,

JUDGE → JUDGED, JUDGES, JUDGMENT, JUDGMENTS
Ex	2:14	appointed you ruler and **j** over us?
Isa	11: 3	Not by appearance shall he **j**,
Eze	34:17	GOD, I will **j** between one sheep
Jn	7:24	judging by appearances, but **j** justly."
	18:31	and **j** him according to your law."
Ro	3: 6	For how else is God to **j** the world?
1Co	6: 2	that the holy ones will **j** the world?
2Ti	4: 1	who will **j** the living and the dead,
Heb	12:23	and God the **j** of all, and the spirits
Jas	5: 9	the **J** is standing before the gates.

JUDGED → JUDGE
Mt	7: 1	"Stop judging, that you may not be **j**.
Jas	3: 1	that we will be **j** more strictly,
Rev	20:12	The dead were **j** according to their

JUDGES → JUDGE
Jdg	2:16	the LORD raised up **j** to deliver them
1Sa	2:10	The LORD **j** the ends of the earth.
Sir	16:12	he **j** men, each according to his
Lk	11:19	out? Therefore they will be your **j**.
Ac	4:19	you rather than God, you be the **j**.
Jas	4:11	**j** his brother speaks evil of the law
	4:11	speaks evil of the law and **j** the law.
Rev	19:11	and True." He **j** and wages war

JUDGMENT → JUDGE
Ex	6: 6	arm and with mighty acts of **j**.
Ps	1: 5	the wicked will not survive **j**,

Ecc	12:14	God will bring to **j** every work,
Jer	25:31	he is to pass **j** upon all mankind:
Da	7:22	**j** was pronounced in favor
Mal	3: 5	I will draw near to you for **j**, and I
Mt	11:24	Sodom on the day of **j** than for you."
Ro	14:10	we shall all stand before the **j** seat
2Co	5:10	we must all appear before the **j** seat
Heb	9:27	beings die once, and after this the **j**,
	10:27	a fearful prospect of **j** and a flaming
Jas	2:13	For the **j** is merciless to one who has
	2:13	mercy; mercy triumphs over **j**.
1Pe	4:17	it is time for the **j** to begin
1Jn	4:17	on the day of **j** because as he is,
Rev	18:10	city. In one hour your **j** has come."

JUDGMENTS → JUDGE
Ro	11:33	How inscrutable are his **j** and how
Rev	19: 2	for true and just are his **j**. He has

JUDITH

Virtuous widow and heroine of the deuterocanonical book of Judith (Jdt 8-16).

JUST → JUSTICE, JUSTIFICATION, JUSTIFIED, JUSTIFY
Dt	32: 4	deceit, how **j** and upright he is!
Tob	3: 2	and all your deeds are **j**; All your
1Jn	1: 9	he is faithful and **j** and will forgive
Rev	15: 3	almighty. **J** and true are your ways,

JUSTICE → JUST
Job	37:23	his great **j** owes no one
Ps	33: 5	The LORD loves **j** and right and fills
Pr	21:15	To practice **j** is a joy for the just,
Isa	30:18	For the LORD is a God of **j**:
	42: 4	Until he establishes **j** on the earth;
Am	5:24	then let **j** surge like water,

JUSTIFICATION → JUST
Ro	4:25	and was raised for our **j**.
Gal	2:21	for if **j** comes through the law,

JUSTIFIED → JUST
Ro	3:24	They are **j** freely by his grace
	5: 1	since we have been **j** by faith,
	10:10	believes with the heart and so is **j**,
1Co	6:11	you were **j** in the name of the Lord
Gal	2:16	know that a person is not **j** by works
	2:16	Jesus that we may be **j** by faith
	2:16	works of the law no one will be **j**.
Jas	2:24	See how a person is **j** by works

JUSTIFY → JUST
Ro	3:30	will **j** the circumcised on the basis
Gal	3: 8	that God would **j** the Gentiles

K

KADESH → KADESH-BARNEA
Nu	20: 1	month, and the people settled at **K**.
Dt	1:46	had to stay as long as you did at **K**.

KADESH-BARNEA → KADESH
Nu	32: 8	I sent them from **K** to reconnoiter

KEEP → KEEPER, KEEPS, KEPT
Ge	17: 9	you must **k** my covenant throughout
Ex	19: 5	to my voice and **k** my covenant,
Nu	6:24	The LORD bless you and **k** you!
Dt	5:10	love me and **k** my commandments.
Ne	1: 5	you and **k** your commandments,
Pr	7: 2	**K** my commands and live,
Ecc	3: 6	a time to **k**, and a time to cast away.
	12:13	Fear God and **k** his commandments,
Sir	1:26	before men; over your lips **k** watch.
Jude	1:24	the one who is able to **k** you.
Rev	22: 9	of those who **k** the message of this

KEEPER → KEEP
Ge	4: 9	"I do not know. Am I my brother's **k**?"

KEEPS → KEEP
Jas	2:10	For whoever **k** the whole law,

KEPT → KEEP
Jn	17: 6	to me, and they have **k** your word.
2Ti	4: 7	finished the race; I have **k** the faith.

KEY → KEYS
Isa	22:22	I will place the **k** of the House
Lk	11:52	law! You have taken away the **k**
Rev	3: 7	the true, who holds the **k** of David,

KEYS → KEY
Mt	16:19	I will give you the **k** to the kingdom
Rev	1:18	ever. I hold the **k** to death

KIDRON
2Sa	15:23	the king crossed the **K** Valley
Jn	18: 1	his disciples across the **K** valley

KILL
Ex	4:23	I warn you, I will **k** your son,
Ecc	3: 3	A time to **k**, and a time to heal;
Mt	10:28	be afraid of those who **k** the body
	10:28	**k** the body but cannot **k** the soul;

KIND → KINDNESS, KINDS
1Co 13: 4 Love is patient, love is **k**. It is not
Eph 4:32 [And] be **k** to one another,

KINDNESS → KIND
Ro 2: 4 Or do you hold his priceless **k**,
 2: 4 that the **k** of God would lead you
Gal 5:22 joy, peace, patience, **k**, generosity,

KINDS → KIND
Ge 6:20 Of all **k** of birds, of all **k** of beasts,
 6:20 and of all **k** of creeping things,
Lev 19:19 yours with two different **k** of seed;
 19:19 with two different **k** of thread.

KING → KINGDOM, KINGS
Ex 1: 8 Then a new **k**, who knew nothing
Dt 17:14 to have a **k** over you like all
1Sa 8: 7 they are rejecting me as their **k**.
2Sa 2: 4 anointed David **k** of the Judahites.
Jdt 9:12 waters, **K** of all you have created,
Ps 2: 6 "I myself have installed my **k**
 10:16 The LORD is **k** forever; the nations
Isa 6: 5 yet my eyes have seen the **K**,
Jer 10:10 he is the living God, the eternal **K**,
Mt 2: 2 "Where is the newborn **k**
 27:37 This is Jesus, the **K** of the Jews.
Lk 19:38 "Blessed is the **k** who comes
Jn 1:49 Son of God; you are the **K** of Israel."
1Ti 1:17 To the **k** of ages, incorruptible,
Rev 19:16 thigh, "**K** of kings and Lord of lords."

KINGDOM → KING
Ex 19: 6 You shall be to me a **k** of priests,
2Sa 7:12 loins, and I will make his **k** firm.
1Ki 11:31 says: 'I will tear away the **k**
Wis 10:10 ways, Showed him the **k** of God
Mt 4:17 for the **k** of heaven is at hand."
 5: 3 spirit, for theirs is the **k** of heaven.
 6:10 your **k** come, your will be done,
 13:24 "The **k** of heaven may be likened
Mk 1:15 fulfillment. The **k** of God is at hand.
 6:23 you ask of me, even to half of my **k**."
 10:24 how hard it is to enter the **k** of God!
 12:34 "You are not far from the **k** of God."
 13: 8 rise against nation and **k** against **k**.
Lk 17:21 behold, the **k** of God is among you.'

Lk 22:16 there is fulfillment in the **k** of God."
Jn 3: 5 you, no one can enter the **k** of God
 18:36 "My **k** does not belong to this world.
 18:36 If my **k** did belong to this world,
 18:36 Jews. But as it is, my **k** is not here."
Ac 1: 6 time going to restore the **k** to Israel?"
Ro 14:17 For the **k** of God is not a matter
1Co 6: 9 the unjust will not inherit the **k**
Eph 5: 5 any inheritance in the **k** of Christ
Col 1:13 us to the **k** of his beloved Son,
1Th 2:12 of the God who calls you into his **k**
Heb 12:28 the unshakable **k** should have
2Pe 1:11 entry into the eternal **k** of our Lord
Rev 11:15 "The **k** of the world now belongs

KINGS → KING
Ge 17: 6 of you; **k** shall stem from you.
Ps 2: 2 **K** on earth rise up and princes plot
 138: 4 All the **k** of earth will praise you,
Pr 8:15 By me **k** reign, and lawgivers
Isa 52:15 of him **k** shall stand speechless;
Da 7:24 The ten horns shall be ten **k**
 7:24 him, who shall lay low three **k**.
Ac 4:26 The **k** of the earth took their stand
1Ti 6:15 the King of **k** and Lord of lords,
Rev 19:16 thigh, "King of **k** and Lord of lords."

KISS
SS 1: 2 B Let him **k** me with kisses of his
Mt 26:48 saying, "The man I shall **k** is the one;
2Co 13:12 Greet one another with a holy **k**.

KNEE
Isa 45:23 To me every **k** shall bend; by me
Ro 14:11 Lord, every **k** shall bend before me,
Php 2:10 name of Jesus every **k** should bend,

KNEEL → KNELT
Ps 95: 6 let us **k** before the LORD who made

KNELT → KNEEL
2Ch 6:13 it, Solomon **k** in the presence

KNEW → KNOW
Dt 34:10 whom the LORD **k** face to face.
Jer 1: 5 I formed you in the womb I **k** you,
Mt 7:23 to them solemnly, 'I never **k** you.
Ro 1:21 for although they **k** God they did not

KNOCK
Lk 11: 9 **k** and the door will be opened

KNOW → FOREKNEW, KNEW, KNOWING, KNOWLEDGE, KNOWN, KNOWS
Ge 22:12 I **k** now how devoted you are
Ex 6: 7 You will **k** that I, the LORD, am your
1Ki 8:39 You who alone **k** the hearts of all
Job 19:25 for me, I **k** that my Vindicator lives,
Ecc 8:16 I applied my heart to **k** wisdom
Isa 1: 3 But Israel does not **k**, my people has
Jer 31:34 and kinsmen how to **k** the LORD. All,
 31:34 from least to greatest, shall **k** me.
Mt 6: 3 let your left hand **k** what your right
 24:42 For you do not **k** on which day your
Lk 11:13 **k** how to give good gifts to your
 22:34 will deny three times that you **k** me."
Jn 10:14 and I **k** mine and mine **k** me,
 13:35 This is how all will **k** that you are
 21:24 and we **k** that his testimony is true.
Ac 1: 7 "It is not for you to **k** the times
Ro 8:28 We **k** that all things work for good
1Co 8: 2 he does not yet **k** as he ought to **k**.
 13:12 At present I **k** partially; then I shall
 13:12 I shall **k** fully as I am fully known.
Eph 3:19 to **k** the love of Christ that surpasses
Php 3:10 to **k** him and the power of his
Tit 1:16 They claim to **k** God, but by their
Heb 8:11 and kinsman, saying, "**K** the Lord,"
 8:11 for all shall **k** me, from least
1Jn 2: 4 Whoever says, "I **k** him," but does not
 3:16 The way we came to **k** love was
Rev 3: 3 you will never **k** at what hour I will

KNOWING → KNOW
Ge 3:22 us, **k** what is good and what is bad!
Jn 18: 4 everything that was going
Php 3: 8 good of **k** Christ Jesus my Lord.

KNOWLEDGE → KNOW
Ge 2: 9 the tree of the **k** of good and bad.
Ps 94:10 who teaches humans not have **k**?
Pr 1: 7 of the LORD is the beginning of **k**;
 8:10 silver, and **k** rather than choice gold.

KNOWLEDGE → KNOW (cont.)

Ecc	1:18	he who stores up **k** stores up grief.
Isa	11: 2	a spirit of **k** and of fear of the LORD,
Hos	4: 6	My people perish for want of **k**!
	4: 6	**k**! Since you have rejected **k**, I will
Lk	11:52	You have taken away the key of **k**.
Ro	11:33	riches and wisdom and **k** of God!
1Co	8: 1	we realize that "all of us have **k**";
Eph	3:19	the love of Christ that surpasses **k**,
Col	2: 3	all the treasures of wisdom and **k**.
1Ti	6:20	and the absurdities of so-called **k**.
2Pe	1: 5	your faith with virtue, virtue with **k**,
1Jn	2:20	the holy one, and you all have **k**.

KNOWN → KNOW

Lk	6:44	For every tree is **k** by its own fruit.
1Co	2:16	For "who has **k** the mind of the Lord,
Eph	1: 9	he has made **k** to us the mystery

KNOWS → KNOW

Ps	103:14	For he **k** how we are formed,
Mt	6: 8	Your Father **k** what you need before
	24:36	"But of that day and hour no one **k**,
Ro	8:27	who searches hearts **k** what is
2Ti	2:19	"The Lord **k** those who are his"; and,
1Jn	4: 7	loves is begotten by God and **k** God.

KORAH → KORAHITES

Levite; led rebels against Moses (Nu 16; Jude 11).

KORAHITES → KORAH

Psalms of: Pss 42; 44-49; 84; 85; 87; 88.

L

LABAN

Brother of Rebekah (Ge 24:29), father of Rachel and Leah (Ge 29:16). Received Abraham's servant (Ge 24:29-51). Provided daughters as wives for Jacob in exchange for Jacob's service (Ge 29:1-30). Provided flocks for Jacob's service (Ge 30:25-43). Pursued and covenanted with Jacob (Ge 31).

LABOR → LABORER

Ex	1:11	to oppress them with forced **l**.
	20: 9	Six days you may **l** and do all your
1Co	15:58	that in the Lord your **l** is not in vain.

LABORER → LABOR

Lev	19:13	overnight the wages of your day **l**.
Lk	10: 7	you, for the **l** deserves his payment.

LACKING

Col	1:24	filling up what is **l** in the afflictions

LAID → LAY

Isa	53: 6	But the LORD **l** upon him the guilt
Mk	16: 6	Behold, the place where they **l** him.
1Jn	3:16	love was that he **l** down his life

LAMB → LAMBS

Isa	53: 7	mouth; Like a **l** led to the slaughter
Mk	14:12	when they sacrificed the Passover **l**,
Jn	1:29	"Behold, the **L** of God, who takes
1Co	5: 7	For our paschal **l**, Christ, has been
1Pe	1:19	as of a spotless unblemished **l**.
Rev	5:12	"Worthy is the **L** that was slain
	19: 7	the wedding day of the **L** has come,
	21:23	gave it light, and its lamp was the **L**.

LAMBS → LAMB

Ex	12:21	"Go and procure **l** for your families,
Isa	40:11	flock; in his arms he gathers the **l**,
Jn	21:15	love you." He said to him, "Feed my **l**."

LAME

Isa	35: 6	Then will the **l** leap like a stag,
Zep	3:19	I will save the **l**, and assemble
Mt	11: 5	blind regain their sight, the **l** walk,

LAMP → LAMPS, LAMPSTAND, LAMPSTANDS

1Ki	11:36	may always have a **l** before me
Ps	18:29	You, LORD, give light to my **l**;
	119:105	Your word is a **l** for my feet, a light
Mt	5:15	Nor do they light a **l** and then put it
	6:22	"The **l** of the body is the eye. If your
Rev	22: 5	nor will they need light from **l**

LAMPS → LAMP

Ex	25:37	You shall then make seven **l** for it
	25:37	set up the **l** that they shed their light
Mt	25: 1	be like ten virgins who took their **l**

LAMPSTAND → LAMP

Ex	25:31	"You shall make a **l** of pure beaten
1Ma	4:50	altar and lighted the lamps on the **l**,
Zec	4: 2	"I see a **l** all of gold, with a bowl

LAMPSTANDS → LAMP

Rev	1:20	right hand, and of the seven gold **l**:
Rev	1:20	the seven **l** are the seven churches.
	11: 4	the two **l** that stand before the Lord

LAND

Ge	1:10	God called the dry **l** "the earth,"
	12: 7	your descendants I will give this **l**."
Ex	3: 8	lead them out of that **l** into a good
	3: 8	of that **l** into a good and spacious **l**,
	3: 8	**l**, a **l** flowing with milk and honey,
	20: 2	brought you out of the **l** of Egypt,
Nu	13: 2	men to reconnoiter the **l** of Canaan,
Jos	11:23	the tribes. And the **l** enjoyed peace.
2Ki	17: 5	occupied the whole **l** and attacked
	25:21	death in Riblah, in the **l** of Hamath.
	25:21	Thus was Judah exiled from her **l**.
2Ch	7:14	pardon their sins and revive their **l**.
Ps	37:11	But the poor will possess the **l**,
Jer	22:29	O **l**, **l**, **l**, hear the word of the LORD—
Da	11:41	He shall enter the glorious **l**

LANGUAGE

Ac	2: 6	heard them speaking in his own **l**.

LAP

Pr	16:33	When the lot is cast into the **l**,

LASHES

2Co	11:24	Jews I received forty **l** minus one.

LAST → EVERLASTING

2Sa	23: 1	These are the **l** words of David:
Isa	44: 6	I am the first and I am the **l**; there is
Mt	19:30	But many who are first will be **l**,
	19:30	first will be **l**, and the **l** will be first.
Mk	9:35	first, he shall be the **l** of all
1Co	15:26	The **l** enemy to be destroyed is
	15:52	the blink of an eye, at the **l** trumpet.
2Ti	3: 1	will be terrifying times in the **l** days.
Heb	1: 2	in these **l** days, he spoke to us
1Jn	2:18	Children, it is the **l** hour; and just as
	2:18	Thus we know this is the **l** hour.
Rev	1:17	be afraid. I am the first and the **l**,

LAUGH → LAUGHINGSTOCK, LAUGHTER

Ge	18:13	"Why did Sarah **l** and say, 'Shall I
Ecc	3: 4	A time to weep, and a time to **l**;
Lk	6:21	are now weeping, for you will **l**.

LAUGHINGSTOCK → LAUGH

La	3:14	I have become a **l** for all nations,

LAUGHTER → LAUGH
Ps 126: 2 Our mouths were filled with l;
Jas   4: 9 Let your l be turned into
              mourning

LAW → LAWFUL, LAWLESSNESS
Dt   1: 5 began to explain the l in the
              land
      31: 9 Moses had written down this l,
Jos   1: 8 Keep this book of the l on your
              lips.
1Ma   2:48 They saved the l from the
              hands
Ps   1: 2 Rather, the l of the LORD is
              their joy;
       1: 2 God's l they study day and
              night.
Jer   31:33 I will place my l within them,
Mt   5:17 that I have come to abolish
              the l
      23:23 the weightier things of the l:
Lk   24:44 written about me in the l of
              Moses
Jn   1:17 because while the l was given
Ro   2:15 the demands of the l are
              written
       6:14 since you are not under the l
      10: 4 the end of the l for the justifi-
              cation
Gal   2:19 For through the l I died to the l,
Heb   10: 1 Since the l has only a shadow
Jas   2:10 For whoever keeps the whole l,

LAWFUL → LAW
Mt   12:12 So it is l to do good on the sab-
              bath."
1Co   6:12 "Everything is l for me," but
              not
       6:12 "Everything is l for me," but I
              will not
      10:23 "Everything is l," but not
              everything
      10:23 "Everything is l," but not
              everything

LAWLESSNESS → LAW
2Th   2: 7 the mystery of l is already at
              work.
1Jn   3: 4 who commits sin commits l,
              for sin
       3: 4 commits sin commits l, for sin
              is l.

LAY → LAID
Mt   28: 6 Come and see the place where
              he l.
Jn   10:15 I will l down my life for the
              sheep.
1Co   3:11 no one can l a foundation other
              than

LAZARUS
   1. Poor man in Jesus' parable (Lk 16:19-
31).
   2. Brother of Mary and Martha whom Jesus raised from the dead (Jn 11:1-12:19).

LAZY
Ex   5:17 "It is just because you are l that
              you

LEAD → LEADER, LEADERS, LEADS,
       LED
Ex   32:34 l the people whither I have told
              you.

Ro   2: 4 of God would l you to repen-
              tance?

LEADER → LEAD
1Ch   28: 4 For he chose Judah as l, then
              one

LEADERS → LEAD
Isa   3:12 O my people, your l mislead,
Lk   19:47 and the l of the people, mean-
              while,
Heb   13: 7 Remember your l who spoke

LEADS → LEAD
Ro   6:16 either of sin, which l to
              death,
       6:16 which l to righteousness?

LEAH
   Wife of Jacob (Ge 29:16-30); bore six
sons and one daughter (Ge 29:31-30:21;
34:1; 35:23; Ru 4:11).

LEAPED → LEAPING
Lk   1:41 greeting, the infant l in her
              womb,

LEAPING → LEAPED
1Ch   15:29 and when she saw King
              David l

LEARN → LEARNED, LEARNING
Dt   4:10 that they may l to fear me as
              long as
Isa   1:17 l to do good. Make justice your
              aim:

LEARNED → LEARN
Php   4:11 for I have l, in whatever situa-
              tion I

LEARNING → LEARN
Ac   26:24 Paul; much l is driving you
              mad."

LEAST → LESS
Mt   2: 6 are by no means l among the
              rulers
       5:19 one of the l of these command-
              ments
       5:19 do so will be called l in the
              kingdom
Lk   9:48 the one who is l among all of
              you is

LEAVE → LEFT
Nu   11:20 wailed, 'Why did we ever l
              Egypt?' "
Mk   10: 7 this reason a man shall l his
              father
Jn   14:18 I will not l you orphans; I will
              come

LEAVEN → LEAVENS
Ex   12:15 shall have your houses clear of
              all l.

LEAVENS → LEAVEN
Gal   5: 9 A little yeast l the whole
              batch

LEAVES
Ge   3: 7 so they sewed fig l together
Eze   47:12 their l shall not fade, nor their
              fruit
      47:12 for food, and their l for medi-
              cine."
Rev   22: 2 the l of the trees serve as medi-
              cine

LEBANON
Dt   11:24 from the desert and from L,
Isa   40:16 L would not suffice for fuel,
              nor its

LED → LEAD
Isa   53: 7 Like a lamb l to the slaughter
Mt   4: 1 Jesus was l by the Spirit
      27:31 and l him off to crucify him.
Ro   8:14 For those who are l by the
              Spirit

LEFT → LEAVE
Dt   28:14 the right or to the l from any
Mt   6: 3 do not let your l hand know
              what
      25:33 on his right and the goats on
              his l.
Lk   17:34 bed; one will be taken, the
              other l.

LEGION
Lk   8:30 name?" He replied, "L," be-
              cause many

LEGS
Jn   19:33 dead, they did not break his l,

LENDER
Pr   22: 7 the borrower is the slave of
              the l.

LEPER → LEPROUS
Mt   8: 2 And then a l approached, did
              him
      26: 6 Bethany in the house of Simon
              the l,

LEPERS → LEPROUS
Lk   7:22 the lame walk, l are cleansed,

LEPROUS → LEPER, LEPERS
Ex   4: 6 it, to his surprise his hand
              was l,

LESS → LEAST
Ex   30:15 nor shall the poor give l,
Ezr   9:13 have made l of our sinfulness
              than it

LETTER
Mt   5:18 not the smallest l or the
              smallest
       5:18 l or the smallest part of a l will
              pass
2Co   3: 6 new covenant, not of l but of
              spirit;
       3: 6 for the l brings death, but the
              Spirit

LEVI → LEVITES, LEVITICAL,
       = MATTHEW
   1. Son of Jacob by Leah (Ge 29:34; 46:11;
1Ch 2:1). With Simeon avenged rape of Dinah (Ge 34). Tribe of blessed (Ge 49:5-7; Dt
33:8-11), chosen as priests (Nu 3-4), numbered (Nu 3:39; 26:62), given cities, but not
land (Nu 18; 35; Dt 10:9; Jos 13:14; 21), land
(Eze 48:8-22), 12,000 from (Rev 7:7).
   2. See Matthew.

LEVIATHAN
Ps   74:14 You crushed the heads of L,

LEVITES → LEVI
Nu   1:53 the L shall camp around
       1:53 The L, then, shall have charge
Jos   14: 4 The L themselves received no
              share

CONCORDANCE

LEVITES → LEVI (*cont.*)
Ne 8: 9 [and the **L** who were instructing

LEVITICAL → LEVI
Heb 7:11 came through the **l** priesthood,

LIAR → LIE
Pr 19:22 rather be a poor man than a **l**.
Jn 8:44 because he is a **l** and the father
Ro 3: 4 though every human being is a **l**,
1Jn 2:22 Who is the **l**? Whoever denies

LIARS → LIE
1Ti 1:10 kidnapers, **l**, perjurers, and whatever

LIBERTY
Lev 25:10 sacred by proclaiming **l** in the land
Isa 61: 1 To proclaim **l** to the captives
1Co 8: 9 make sure that this **l** of yours in no

LICENTIOUSNESS
Mk 7:22 malice, deceit, **l**, envy, blasphemy,
Gal 5:19 are obvious: immorality, impurity, **l**,
Jude 1: 4 pervert the grace of our God into **l**

LIE → LIAR, LIARS, LIES, LYING
Isa 11: 6 the leopard shall **l** down
1Jn 2:21 because every **l** is alien to the truth.

LIES → LIE
Php 3:13 thing: forgetting what **l** behind
3:13 straining forward to what **l** ahead,

LIFE → LIVE
Ge 2: 7 blew into his nostrils the breath of **l**,
2: 9 with the tree of **l** in the middle
9: 5 demand an accounting for human **l**.
Ex 21:23 injury ensues, you shall give **l** for **l**,
Dt 12:23 for blood is **l**, and you shall not
12:23 you shall not consume this seat of **l**
30:19 I have set before you **l** and death,
30:19 Choose **l**, then, that you and your
Ps 34:13 Who among you loves **l**,
Pr 18:21 and **l** are in the power of the tongue;
Ecc 7:12 wisdom preserves the **l** of its owner.
Sir 4:12 He who loves her loves **l**; those who
Isa 53:10 If he gives his **l** as an offering
53:10 shall see his descendants in a long **l**,
Mt 7:14 constricted the road that leads to **l**.
10:39 Whoever finds his **l** will lose it,
10:39 whoever loses his **l** for my sake will
20:28 to give his **l** as a ransom for many."

Mk 10:30 and eternal **l** in the age to come.
Jn 1: 4 through him was **l**, and this **l** was
3:15 believes in him may have eternal **l**."
6:35 said to them, "I am the bread of **l**;
11:25 her, "I am the resurrection and the **l**;
14: 6 "I am the way and the truth and the **l**.
Ac 3:15 The author of **l** you put to death,
Ro 5:21 eternal **l** through Jesus Christ our
8:11 the dead will give **l** to your mortal
8:38 that neither death, nor **l**, nor angels,
2Co 3: 6 brings death, but the Spirit gives **l**.
Php 4: 3 whose names are in the book of **l**.
1Jn 3:14 to **l** because we love our brothers.
5:20 He is the true God and eternal **l**.
Rev 2: 8 who once died but came to **l**,
20: 4 They came to **l** and they reigned
20:12 scroll was opened, the book of **l**
22: 2 of the river grew the tree of **l**

LIFTED
Jn 3:14 just as Moses **l** up the serpent
3:14 so must the Son of Man be **l** up,

LIGHT → ENLIGHTENED, ENLIGHTENS, LIGHTS
Ge 1: 3 said, "Let there be **l**," and there was **l**.
Ex 13:21 of a column of fire to give them **l**.
Ps 27: 1 The LORD is my **l** and my salvation;
Pr 4:18 the path of the just is like shining **l**,
Ecc 2:13 folly as much as **l** has the advantage
Isa 42: 6 of the people, a **l** for the nations,
Isa 60: 1 up in splendor! Your **l** has come,
Mt 4:16 have seen a great **l**, on those
4:16 overshadowed by death **l** has arisen."
5:14 You are the **l** of the world. A city
11:30 my yoke is easy, and my burden **l**."
Jn 1: 9 The true **l**, which enlightens
8:12 saying, "I am the **l** of the world.
8:12 darkness, but will have the **l** of life."
Ro 13:12 [and] put on the armor of **l**;
2Co 11:14 Satan masquerades as an angel of **l**.
1Pe 2: 9 out of darkness into his wonderful **l**.

1Jn 1: 7 if we walk in the **l** as he is in the **l**,
Rev 22: 5 nor will they need **l** from lamp
22: 5 for the Lord God shall give them **l**,

LIGHTNING
Ex 19:16 there were peals of thunder and **l**,
Da 10: 6 his face shone like **l**, his eyes were
Lk 10:18 "I have observed Satan fall like **l**
Rev 4: 5 From the throne came flashes of **l**,

LIGHTS → LIGHT
Ge 1:16 God made the two great **l**,
Jas 1:17 coming down from the Father of **l**,

LIKE → LIKENESS
Ge 3: 5 you will be **l** gods who know what
Ex 15:11 Who is **l** to you among the gods,
15:11 Who is **l** to you,
2Sa 7:22 There is none **l** you and there is no
Ps 113: 5 Who is **l** the LORD, our God
Isa 46: 9 other; I am God, there is none **l** me.
Jer 10: 6 No one is **l** you, O LORD, great are
Lk 13:18 said, "What is the kingdom of God **l**?
Rev 1:13 the lampstands one **l** a son of man,
10: 1 his face was **l** the sun and his feet
10: 1 and his feet were **l** pillars of fire.
16:15 ("Behold, I am coming **l** a thief."

LIKENESS → LIKE
Ge 1:26 make man in our image, after our **l**.
Ro 8: 3 his own Son in the **l** of sinful flesh
Php 2: 7 coming in human **l**; and found

LINEN
Ex 26: 1 out of sheets woven of fine **l** twined
Da 10: 5 I saw a man dressed in **l** with a belt
Rev 19: 8 a bright, clean **l** garment." (The **l**

LION → LION'S, LIONS
1Sa 17:34 whenever a **l** or bear came to carry
Ecc 9: 4 a live dog is better off than a dead **l**.
Isa 11: 7 rest; the **l** shall eat hay like the ox.
Da 7: 4 The first was like a **l**,
Rev 4: 7 The first creature resembled a **l**,
5: 5 The **l** of the tribe of Judah, the root

LION'S → LION
2Ti 4:17 I was rescued from the **l** mouth.

1812

LIONS → LION
Da 6:20 morning and hastened to the l' den.

LIPS
Isa 6: 5 For I am a man of unclean l,
6: 5 living among a people of unclean l;
Mt 15: 8 'This people honors me with their l,
Heb 13:15 the fruit of l that confess his name.

LISTEN → LISTENS
2Ki 17:40 They did not l, however,
Mk 9: 7 "This is my beloved Son. L to him."
Lk 16:31 'If they will not l to Moses
Ac 3:22 to him you shall l in all that he may

LISTENS → LISTEN
Jn 18:37 belongs to the truth l to my voice."
1Jn 4: 6 and anyone who knows God l to us,

LITTLE
Ex 16:18 a small amount did not have too l.
Ps 8: 6 you have made them l less than
Pr 15:16 Better a l with fear of the LORD
Sir 29:23 Be it l or much, be content
Mt 8:26 are you terrified, O you of l faith?"
2Co 8:15 and whoever had l did not have less."
Gal 5: 9 A l yeast leavens the whole batch

LIVE → ALIVE, LIFE, LIVES, LIVING
Ge 3:22 also, and thus eat of it and l forever."
Ex 1:16 kill him; but if it is a girl, she may l."
Dt 8: 3 that not by bread alone does man l,
Wis 5:15 But the just l forever,
Hab 2: 4 man, because of his faith, shall l.
Mt 4: 4 'One does not l by bread alone,
Jn 11:25 in me, even if he dies, will l,
Ro 1:17 one who is righteous by faith will l."
14: 8 For if we l, we l for the Lord,
14: 8 so then, whether we l or die, we are
2Co 5:15 that those who l might no longer l
Gal 3:12 "the one who does these things will l

LIVES → LIVE
Ex 33:20 for no man sees me and still l.
Tob 13: 1 Blessed be God who l forever,
Job 19:25 for me, I know that my Vindicator l,
Ps 18:47 The LORD l! Blessed be my rock!
Jn 11:26 everyone who l and believes in me
Ro 6:10 for all; as to his life, he l for God.
1Jn 3:16 to lay down our l for our brothers.

Rev 15: 7 fury of God, who l forever and ever.

LIVING → LIVE
Ge 2: 7 life, and so man became a l being.
3:20 she became the mother of all the l.
6:19 all other l creatures you shall bring
Dt 5:26 the voice of the l God speaking
Jer 2:13 forsaken me, the source of l waters;
Zec 14: 8 l waters shall flow from Jerusalem,
Mt 16:16 the Messiah, the Son of the l God."
Jn 4:10 he would have given you l water."
6:51 I am the l bread that came down
Ro 12: 1 to offer your bodies as a l sacrifice,
2Co 6:16 For we are the temple of the l God;
Heb 4:12 the word of God is l and effective,
1Pe 2: 4 Come to him, a l stone,

LOAVES
Mk 6:41 taking the five l and the two fish
6:41 broke the l, and gave them to [his]
8: 6 taking the seven l he gave thanks,

LOCK
Mt 23:13 You l the kingdom of heaven before

LOCUST → LOCUSTS
Joel 2:25 the years which the l has eaten,

LOCUSTS → LOCUST
Ex 10: 4 tomorrow I will bring l into your
2Ch 6:28 or mildew, or l, or caterpillars;
Mt 3: 4 His food was l and wild honey.
Rev 9: 3 L came out of the smoke onto

LONELY → ALONE
La 1: 1 How l she is now, the once crowded

LONG → LONGING
Ex 20:12 you may have a l life in the land
Ps 13: 2 How l, LORD? Will you utterly
13: 2 How l will you hide your face
Pr 3:16 L life is in her right hand, in her left
1Co 11:14 man wears his hair l it is a disgrace
1Pe 2: 2 l for pure spiritual milk so
Rev 6:10 out in a loud voice, "How l will it be,

LONGING → LONG
2Co 5: 2 l to be further clothed with our

LOOK → LOOKED, LOOKS
Ex 3: 6 face, for he was afraid to l at God.
Ps 80:15 hosts; l down from heaven and see;

Lk 24:39 L at my hands and my feet, that it is

LOOKED → LOOK
Ge 19:26 But Lot's wife l back, and she was

LOOKS → LOOK
1Sa 16: 7 but the LORD l into the heart."
Ps 14: 2 The LORD l down from heaven
Mt 5:28 everyone who l at a woman

LORD → LORD'S, LORDS
Ge 18:27 I am presuming to speak to my L,
Ex 4:10 said to the L, "If you please, L,
Dt 10:17 For the L, your God, is the God
10:17 is the God of gods, the L of lords,
Jdt 6:19 "L, God of heaven, behold their
Ps 16: 2 I say to the L, you are my L,
you are
110: 1 of David. The L says to you, my l:
Wis 8: 3 God; even the L of all loved her.
Sir 1: 1 All wisdom comes from the L
Isa 6: 1 I saw the L seated on a high
Da 2:47 is the God of gods and L of kings
3:57 Bless the L, all you works of the L,
Mic 1: 2 Let the L GOD be witness against
1: 2 you, the L from his holy temple!
Mt 7:22 Many will say to me on that day, 'L,
7:22 'L, L, did we not prophesy in your
12: 8 the Son of Man is L of the sabbath."
Mk 1: 3 'Prepare the way of the L,
12:29 O Israel! The L our God is L alone!
Lk 2:11 born for you who is Messiah and L.
10:27 "You shall love the L, your God,
19:38 in the name of the L.
Jn 20:28 and said to him, "My L and my God!"
Ac 2:34 he himself said: 'The L said to my L,
Ro 4:24 the one who raised Jesus our L
10:12 the same L is L of all, enriching all
1Co 2:16 "who has known the mind of the L,
8: 6 we exist, and one L, Jesus Christ,
12: 3 "Jesus is L," except by the holy Spirit.
2Co 3:17 Now the L is the Spirit, and where
3:17 and where the Spirit of the L is,
Eph 4: 5 one L, one faith, one baptism;
Php 2:11 that Jesus Christ is L, to the glory
4: 5 be known to all. The L is near.

LORD → LORD'S, LORDS (*cont.*)

Col 3:13 as the **L** has forgiven you, so must

1Th 4:15 on the word of the **L**, that we who

4:15 are left until the coming of the **L**,

1Ti 6:15 the King of kings and **L** of lords,

Heb 12:14 without which no one will see the **L**.

Jas 4:10 Humble yourselves before the **L**

1Pe 3:15 sanctify Christ as **L** in your hearts.

2Pe 3:9 The **L** does not delay his promise,

Jude 1:4 who deny our only Master and **L**,

Rev 4:8 holy, holy is the **L** God almighty,

Rev 19:16 thigh, "King of kings and **L** of lords."

22:20 soon." Amen! Come, **L** Jesus!

*LORD → *GOD, *LORD'S

Ge 2:7 the **L** God formed man

13:4 and there he invoked the **L** by name.

18:14 too marvelous for the **L** to do?

22:14 say, "On the mountain the **L** will see."

Ex 3:15 The **L**, the God of your fathers,

5:2 "Who is the **L**, that I should heed his

5:2 I do not know the **L**; even if I did,

6:7 the **L**, am your God when I free you

15:3 The **L** is a warrior, **L** is his name!

34:6 Thus the **L** passed before him

34:6 him and cried out, "The **L**, the **L**,

Lev 19:2 for I, the **L**, your God, am holy.

Nu 6:24 The **L** bless you and keep you!

14:18 'The **L** is slow to anger and rich

Dt 6:4 The **L** is our God, the **L** alone!

Jos 24:15 does not please you to serve the **L**,

24:15 my household, we will serve the **L**."

1Sa 2:2 There is no Holy One like the **L**;

1Ki 8:11 glory had filled the temple of the **L**.

18:21 If the **L** is God, follow him; if Baal,

1Ch 16:11 Look to the **L** in his strength;

Ezr 7:10 practice of the law of the **L**

Ne 8:10 prepared; for today is holy to our **L**.

8:10 in the **L** must be your strength!"

Job 1:21 The **L** gave and the **L** has taken

1:21 away; blessed be the name of the **L**!"

42:12 Thus the **L** blessed the latter days

Ps 1:2 Rather, the law of the **L** is their joy;

10:16 The **L** is king forever; the nations

18:2 He said: I love you, **L**, my strength,

23:1 of David. The **L** is my shepherd;

33:12 the nation whose God is the **L**,

84:12 For a sun and shield is the **L** God,

84:12 The **L** withholds no good thing

110:1 David. The **L** says to you, my lord:

113:5 Who is like the **L**, our God

125:2 the **L** surrounds his people both now

128:1 Happy are all who fear the **L**,

145:18 You, **L**, are near to all who call

150:6 give praise to the **L**! Hallelujah!

Pr 1:7 The fear of the **L** is the beginning

3:5 Trust in the **L** with all your heart,

19:23 The fear of the **L** is an aid to life;

21:2 but it is the **L** who proves hearts.

Isa 2:11 and the **L** alone will be exalted,

6:3 "Holy, holy is the **L** of hosts!"

33:22 Indeed the **L** will be there with us,

33:22 yes, the **L** our judge, the **L** our

33:22 the **L** our king, he it is who will

53:6 But the **L** laid upon him the guilt

64:8 Be not so very angry, **L**, keep not

Jer 4:4 For the sake of the **L**,

31:34 and kinsmen how to know the **L**.

31:34 says the **L**, for I will forgive their

32:27 I am the **L**, the God of all mankind!

La 3:25 Good is the **L** to one who waits

Eze 3:23 I saw that the glory of the **L** was

10:18 the glory of the **L** left the threshold

37:4 Dry bones, hear the word of the **L**!

44:4 of the **L** filling the LORD's temple,

48:35 shall henceforth be "The **L** is here."

Joel 1:15 for near is the day of the **L**, and it

Am 5:6 Seek the **L**, that you may live,

Ob 1:15 For near is the day of the **L** for all

Na 1:3 The **L** is slow to anger, yet great

1:3 and the **L** never leaves the guilty

Zep 1:14 Near is the great day of the **L**,

1:14 Hark, the day of the **L**! bitter, then,

Zec 14:9 The **L** shall become king over

14:9 that day the **L** shall be the only one,

Mal 3:6 Surely I, the **L**, do not change,

LORD'S → LORD

Ro 14:8 whether we live or die, we are the **L**.

1Co 10:26 "the earth and its fullness are the **L**."

*LORD'S → *LORD

Nu 11:23 Moses, "Is this beyond the **L** reach?

Dt 32:9 While the **L** own portion was Jacob,

Ps 24:1 The earth is the **L** and all it holds,

Ob 1:21 and the kingship shall be the **L**.

LORDS → LORD

Dt 10:17 gods, the LORD of l, the great God,

Ps 136:3 Praise the Lord of l; God's love

1Co 8:5 to be sure, many "gods" and many "l"),

Rev 19:16 thigh, "King of kings and Lord of l."

LOSE → LOSS, LOST

Mk 8:35 wishes to save his life will l it,

Heb 12:3 may not grow weary and l heart.

2Jn 1:8 that you do not l what we worked

LOSS → LOSE

1Co 3:15 is burned up, that one will suffer l,

Php 3:8 consider everything as a l because

3:8 his sake I have accepted the l of all

LOST → LOSE

Ps 119:176 I have wandered like a l sheep;

Jer 50:6 L sheep were my people,

Eze 34:16 The l I will seek out, the strayed l

Mt 10:6 Go rather to the l sheep of the house

Lk 15:6 because I have found my l sheep.'

19:10 to seek and to save what was l."

LOT → LOT'S, LOTS

1. Nephew of Abraham (Ge 11:27; 12:5). Chose to live in Sodom (Ge 13). Rescued from four kings (Ge 14). Rescued from Sodom (Ge 19:1-29; 2Pe 2:7). Fathered Moab and Ammon (Ge 19:30-38).

2. Object cast to make decisions.

Nu 33:54 the land among yourselves by l,

33:54 Wherever anyone's l falls, there shall

Est 3:7 or l, was cast in Haman's presence,

3:7 the l fell on the thirteenth day

Pr 16:33 When the l is cast into the lap,

Ac 1:26 and the l fell upon Matthias, and he

LOT'S → LOT, 1

Ge 19:26 But **L** wife looked back, and she

LOTS → LOT, 2

Ps 22:19 them; for my clothing they cast **l**.

Jnh 1: 7 let us cast **l** to find out on whose

1: 7 So they cast **l**, and thus singled

Mt 27:35 divided his garments by casting **l**;

LOVE → BELOVED, LOVED, LOVER, LOVERS, LOVES

Ex 20: 6 on the children of those who **l** me

Lev 19:18 You shall **l** your neighbor as

Dt 6: 5 Therefore, you shall **l** the LORD,

Ne 1: 5 of mercy toward those who **l** you

1Ma 4:33 by the sword of those who **l** you,

Ps 18: 2 He said: I **l** you, LORD, my strength,

Ps 116: 1 I **l** the LORD, who listened to my

119:97 How I **l** your teaching, LORD! I study

136: 1 is so good; God's **l** endures forever;

Pr 5:19 Her **l** will invigorate you always,

5:19 through her **l** you will flourish

8:17 "Those who **l** me I also **l**, and those

Ecc 3: 8 A time to **l**, and a time to hate;

SS 1: 2 More delightful is your **l** than wine!

8: 6 For stern as death is **l**, relentless as

Sir 2:15 those who **l** him keep his ways.

7:30 all your strength, **l** your Creator,

Isa 54: 8 with enduring **l** I take pity on you,

Da 9: 4 covenant toward those who **l** you

14:38 have not forsaken those who **l** you."

Hos 11: 4 with bands of **l**; I fostered them like

Mt 5:44 But I say to you, **l** your enemies,

6:24 will either hate one and **l** the other,

Mk 12:31 is this: 'You shall **l** your neighbor as

Lk 6:32 For if you **l** those who **l** you,

6:32 Even sinners **l** those who **l** them.

10:27 said in reply, "You shall **l** the Lord,

Jn 13:34 a new commandment: **l** one another.

13:34 so you also should **l** one another.

14:15 "If you **l** me, you will keep my

15:13 No one has greater **l** than this, to lay

Jn 21:16 "Simon, son of John, do you **l** me?"

21:16 "Yes, Lord, you know that I **l** you."

Ro 5: 5 because the **l** of God has been

5: 8 God proves his **l** for us in that while

12: 9 Let **l** be sincere; hate what is evil,

13: 8 to anyone, except to **l** one another;

1Co 8: 1 inflates with pride, but **l** builds up.

13: 4 **L** is patient, **l** is kind. It is not

13: 4 It is not jealous, [**l**] is not pompous,

13:13 So faith, hope, **l** remain, these three;

13:13 three; but the greatest of these is **l**.

Gal 5: 6 but only faith working through **l**.

5:22 the fruit of the Spirit is **l**, joy, peace,

Eph 2: 4 because of the great **l** he had for us,

3:19 and to know the **l** of Christ

5:25 Husbands, **l** your wives, even as

Col 3:14 And over all these put on **l**, that is,

1Th 5: 8 on the breastplate of faith and **l**

1Ti 6:10 For the **l** of money is the root of all

Tit 2: 2 sound in faith, **l**, and endurance.

Heb 10:24 how to rouse one another to **l**

13: 5 Let your life be free from **l**

Jas 2: 8 "You shall **l** your neighbor as

1Pe 1: 8 you have not seen him you **l** him;

2Pe 1: 7 affection, mutual affection with **l**.

1Jn 2:15 Do not **l** the world or the things

2:15 the **l** of the Father is not in him.

3: 1 See what **l** the Father has bestowed

3:16 The way we came to know **l** was

4: 7 Beloved, let us **l** one another,

4: 7 **l** one another, because **l** is of God;

4: 8 Whoever is without **l** does not know

4: 8 **l** does not know God, for God is **l**.

5: 3 For the **l** of God is this, that we keep

2Jn 1: 6 For this is **l**, that we walk according

Jude 1:21 Keep yourselves in the **l** of God

Rev 2: 4 you have lost the **l** you had at first.

LOVED → LOVE

Jer 31: 3 With age-old love I have **l** you; so I

Hos 11: 1 When Israel was a child I **l** him,

Mal 1: 2 I have **l** you, says the LORD; but you

1: 2 but you say, "How have you **l** us?"

Jn 3:16 For God so **l** the world that he gave

13: 1 He **l** his own in the world and he **l**

Gal 2:20 in the Son of God who has **l** me

Eph 5: 2 as Christ **l** us and handed himself

1Jn 4:19 We love because he first **l** us.

LOVER → LOVE

Ps 99: 4 O mighty king, **l** of justice,

1Ti 3: 3 not contentious, not a **l** of money.

LOVERS → LOVE

Jer 3: 1 But you have sinned with many **l**,

2Ti 3: 2 be self-centered and **l** of money,

LOVES → LOVE

Ps 33: 5 The LORD **l** justice and right and fills

Pr 3:12 For whom the LORD **l** he reproves,

Sir 4:12 He who **l** her **l** life; those who seek

Mt 10:37 "Whoever **l** father or mother more

10:37 and whoever **l** son or daughter more

Lk 7:47 to whom little is forgiven, **l** little."

Ro 13: 8 the one who **l** another has fulfilled

Eph 5:28 bodies. He who **l** his wife **l** himself.

Heb 12: 6 for whom the Lord **l**, he disciplines;

1Jn 4: 7 everyone who **l** is begotten by God

Rev 1: 5 To him who **l** us and has freed us

LOW → LOWER, LOWLY

Isa 40: 4 mountain and hill shall be made **l**;

Lk 3: 5 mountain and hill shall be made **l**.

LOWER → LOW

Heb 2: 7 for a little while **l** than the angels;

LOWLY → LOW

Jdt 9:11 but you are the God of the **l**,

Lk 1:52 from their thrones but lifted up the **l**.

Ro 12:16 be haughty but associate with the **l**;

LOYAL

Da 11:32 but those who remain **l** to their God

LUKE

Associate of Paul (Col 4:14; 2Ti 4:11; Phm 24).

LUKEWARM

Rev 3:16 because you are **l**, neither hot nor

LUST → LUSTS
Mt 5:28 **l** has already committed adultery

LUSTS → LUST
Ro 1:24 impurity through the **l** of their hearts

LYDIA
Ac 16:14 them, a woman named **L**, a dealer

LYING → LIE
1Ki 22:23 the LORD has put a **l** spirit
Pr 6:17 Haughty eyes, a **l** tongue, and hands
Wis 1:11 and a **l** mouth slays the soul.
Hos 4: 2 False swearing, **l**, murder,

LYRE
Ps 33: 2 on the ten-stringed **l** offer praise.

M

MACCABEUS → JUDAS
1Ma 2:66 And Judas **M**, a warrior from his

MACEDONIA
Ac 16: 9 words, "Come over to **M** and help us."

MADE → MAKE
Ge 1:31 God looked at everything he had **m**,
  3:21 the LORD God **m** leather garments,
Ge 6: 6 that he had **m** man on the earth,
  15:18 occasion that the LORD **m** a covenant
Ex 20:11 In six days the LORD **m** the heavens
  20:11 the sabbath day and **m** it holy.
  36: 8 **m** the Dwelling with its ten sheets
Ps 8: 6 Yet you have **m** them little less than
  118:24 This is the day the LORD has **m**;
  139:14 you, so wonderfully you **m** me;
Jer 27: 5 It was I who **m** the earth, and man
Mk 2:27 them, "The sabbath was **m** for man,
Ac 2:36 that God has **m** him both Lord
Rev 14: 7 Worship him who **m** heaven

MADNESS
Dt 28:28 the LORD will strike you with **m**,
Ecc 9: 3 and **m** is in their hearts during life;

MAGDALENE
Mt 27:56 Among them were Mary **M**

MAGICIANS
Ex 7:11 and they also, the **m** of Egypt,
Da 2: 2 So he ordered that the **m**,

MAGNIFY
Ps 34: 4 **M** the LORD with me; let us exalt his

MAJESTIC → MAJESTY
2Pe 1:17 came to him from the **m** glory,

MAJESTY → MAJESTIC
1Ch 29:11 and power, **m**, splendor, and glory.
Ps 93: 1 The LORD is king, robed with **m**;
Heb 1: 3 at the right hand of the **M** on high,
2Pe 1:16 we had been eyewitnesses of his **m**.

MAKE → MADE, MAKER
Ge 1:26 "Let us **m** man in our image,
  2:18 I will **m** a suitable partner for him."
  12: 2 "I will **m** of you a great nation, and I
  12: 2 bless you; I will **m** your name great,
Ex 32: 1 **m** us a god who will be our leader;
Isa 61: 8 a lasting covenant I will **m**
  66:22 which I will **m** Shall endure before
Jer 31:31 when I will **m** a new covenant
Mt 28:19 and **m** disciples of all nations,
Mk 1:17 me, and I will **m** you fishers of men."

MAKER → MAKE
Job 4:17 mortal be blameless against his **M**?
Isa 54: 5 become your husband is your **M**;

MALACHI
Post-exilic prophet (Mal 1:1).

MALE
Ge 1:27 him; **m** and female he created them.
  17:10 keep: every **m** among you shall be
Lev 20:13 If a man lies with a **m** as
Mt 19: 4 beginning the Creator 'made them **m**
Rev 12: 5 She gave birth to a son, a **m** child,

MALICE
Ro 1:29 of wickedness, evil, greed, and **m**;
1Co 5: 8 the yeast of **m** and wickedness,

MAN → MEN
Ge 2: 7 the LORD God formed **m**
  2: 7 and so **m** became a living being.
  2:18 "It is not good for the **m** to be alone.
1Sa 13:14 sought out a **m** after his own heart
Mt 9: 6 the Son of **M** has authority on earth
Lk 6: 5 "The Son of **M** is lord of the sabbath."
Jn 9:35 "Do you believe in the Son of **M**?"
1Co 11: 3 that Christ is the head of every **m**,
Rev 1:13 the lampstands one like a son of **m**,
  14:14 one who looked like a son of **m**,

MANAGE
1Ti 3: 4 He must **m** his own household well,
  5:14 and **m** a home, so as to give

MANASSEH
1. Firstborn of Joseph (Ge 41:51; 46:20). Blessed by Jacob but not as firstborn (Ge 48). Tribe of blessed (Dt 33:17), numbered (Nu 1:35; 26:34), half allotted land east of Jordan (Nu 32; Jos 13:8-33), half west (Jos 16; Eze 48:4), failed to fully possess (Jos 17:12-13; Jdg 1:27), 12,000 from (Rev 7:6).
2. Son of Hezekiah; king of Judah (2Ki 21:1-18; 2Ch 33:1-20). Judah exiled for his detestable sins (2Ki 21:10-15). Repented (2Ch 33:12-19).

MANGER
Lk 2:12 swaddling clothes and lying in a **m**."

MANNA
Ex 16:31 The Israelites called this food **m**.
Jos 5:12 produce of the land, the **m** ceased.
  5:12 No longer was there **m**
Jn 6:49 Your ancestors ate the **m**
Rev 2:17 I shall give some of the hidden **m**;

MANTLE
2Ki 2: 8 Elijah took his **m**, rolled it

MANY
Isa 53:12 he shall take away the sins of **m**,
Mt 22:14 **M** are invited, but few are chosen."
Mk 10:45 to give his life as a ransom for **m**."
Jn 20:30 Now Jesus did **m** other signs
Ro 12: 5 though **m**, are one body in Christ

MARAH
Ex 15:23 they arrived at **M**, where they could
  15:23 Hence this place was called **M**.

MARK → MARKED, MARKS
1. Cousin of Barnabas (Ac 12:12; 15:37-39; Col 4:10; 2Ti 4:11; Phm 24; 1Pe 5:13), see John.
2. Brand or symbol:
Ge 4:15 So the LORD put a **m** on Cain,
Rev 14: 9 or accepts its **m** on forehead
  19:20 astray those who had accepted the **m**

MARKED → MARK
Eze 9: 6 But do not touch any **m** with the X;
Hab 1:12 LORD, you have **m** him for judgment,

MARKET → MARKETPLACE
1Co 10:25 Eat anything sold in the **m**,

MARKETPLACE → MARKET
Jn 2:16 stop making my Father's house a **m**."

MARKS → MARK
Gal 6:17 me; for I bear the **m** of Jesus on my

MARRIAGE → INTERMARRY, MARRIED, MARRIES

Mt 22:30 neither marry nor are given in **m**

Heb 13: 4 Let **m** be honored among all

13: 4 all and the **m** bed be kept undefiled,

MARRIED → MARRIAGE

Mal 2:11 and has **m** an idolatrous woman.

Mk 12:23 be? For all seven had been **m** to her."

1Ti 3: 2 be irreproachable, **m** only once,

Tit 1: 6 a man be blameless, **m** only once,

MARRIES → MARRIAGE

Mk 10:11 **m** another commits adultery against

1Co 7:28 an unmarried woman sin if she **m**;

MARTHA

Sister of Mary and Lazarus (Lk 10:38-42; Jn 11; 12:2).

MARVELOUS

Ps 98: 1 who has done **m** deeds, have won

MARY

1. Mother of Jesus (Mt 1:16-25; Lk 1:27-56; 2:1-40). With Jesus at temple (Lk 2:41-52), at the wedding in Cana (Jn 2:1-5), questioning his sanity (Mk 3:21), at the cross (Jn 19:25-27). Among disciples (Ac 1:14).

2. Magdalene; former demoniac (Lk 8:2). Helped support Jesus' ministry (Lk 8:1-3). At the cross (Mt 27:56; Mk 15:40; Jn 19:25), burial (Mt 27:61; Mk 15:47). Saw angel after resurrection (Mt 28:1-10; Mk 16:1-9; Lk 24:1-12); also Jesus (Jn 20:1-18).

3. Sister of Martha and Lazarus (Jn 11). Washed Jesus' feet (Jn 12:1-8).

4. Mother of James and Joses; witnessed crucifixion (Mt 27:56; Mk 15:40) and empty tomb (Mk 16:1; Lk 24:10).

MASTER → MASTERS, TASKMASTERS

Ge 4: 7 is toward you, yet you can be his **m**."

Mal 1: 6 and a servant fears his **m**; If then I

1: 6 to me? And if I am a **m**, where is

Mt 25:21 His **m** said to him, 'Well done,

Jn 15:20 you, 'No slave is greater than his **m**.'

2Pe 2: 1 and even deny the **M** who ransomed

MASTERS → MASTER

Mt 6:24 "No one can serve two **m**. He will

MATTANIAH → See ZEDEKIAH

MATTATHIAS

Priest who started the Maccabean revolt (1Ma 2).

MATTHEW → = LEVI

Apostle; former tax collector (Mt 9:9-13; 10:3; Mk 3:18; Lk 6:15; Ac 1:13). Also called Levi (Mk 2:14-17; Lk 5:27-32).

MATTHIAS

Disciple chosen to replace Judas (Ac 1:23-26).

MATURE

1Co 2: 6 speak a wisdom to those who are **m**,

Php 3:15 then, who are "perfectly **m**" adopt this

Heb 5:14 But solid food is for the **m**, for those

MEAN → MEANING

Ex 12:26 you, 'What does this rite of yours **m**?'

Jos 4: 6 ask you what these stones **m** to you,

MEANING → MEAN

Ge 40: 5 night, each dream with its own **m**.

MEASURE

Dt 25:15 and a true and just **m**, that you may

Mk 4:24 The **m** with which you **m** will be

Lk 6:38 a good **m**, packed together,

6:38 For the **m** with which you **m** will

MEAT

Ro 14:21 it is good not to eat **m** or drink wine

MEDIATOR

Gal 3:19 by angels at the hand of a **m**.

1Ti 2: 5 There is also one **m** between God

Heb 8: 6 more excellent a ministry as he is **m**

MEDIUM

Lev 20:27 man or a woman who acts as a **m**

MEEK

Mt 5: 5 Blessed are the **m**, for they will

MEET → MEETING

Ex 30:36 the meeting tent where I will **m** you.

Am 4:12 prepare to **m** your God, O Israel;

1Th 4:17 the clouds to **m** the Lord in the air.

MEETING → MEET

Ex 27:21 them before the Lord in the **m** tent,

40:34 Then the cloud covered the **m** tent,

MELCHIZEDEK

Ge 14:18 **M**, king of Salem, brought out bread

Ps 110: 4 "Like **M** you are a priest forever."

Heb 7: 1 This "**M**, king of Salem and priest

MELT

Ps 97: 5 The mountains **m** like wax before

MEMBERS

Ro 7:23 I see in my **m** another principle

7:23 the law of sin that dwells in my **m**.

1Co 6:15 that your bodies are **m** of Christ?

6:15 take Christ's **m** and make them the **m**

MEMORIAL

Jos 4: 7 are to serve as a perpetual **m**

MEN → MAN

Ge 18: 2 up, he saw three **m** standing nearby.

Sir 44: 1 Now will I praise those godly **m**,

Da 3:92 "I see four **m** unfettered and unhurt,

Lk 9:30 two **m** were conversing with him,

MENAHEM

King of Israel (2Ki 15:14-23).

MENE

Da 5:25 was inscribed: **M**, Tekel, and Peres.

MEPHIBOSHETH

Son of Jonathan shown kindness by David (2Sa 4:4; 9; 21:7). Accused of siding with Absalom (2Sa 16:1-4; 19:24-30).

MERCIES → MERCY

La 3:22 not exhausted, his **m** are not spent;

MERCIFUL → MERCY

Dt 4:31 is a **m** God, he will not abandon

Ps 111: 4 deeds; gracious and **m** is the Lord.

Sir 2:11 Compassionate and **m** is the Lord;

Jer 3:12 with you; For I am **m**, says the Lord,

Mt 5: 7 Blessed are the **m**, for they will be

Lk 6:36 Be **m**, just as [also] your Father is

6:36 **m**, just as [also] your Father is **m**.

Heb 2:17 that he might be a **m** and faithful

MERCY → MERCIES, MERCIFUL

1Ch 21:13 of the Lord, whose **m** is very great,

Zec 1:12 how long will you be without **m**

Mt 9:13 the words, 'I desire **m**, not sacrifice.'

23:23 law: judgment and **m** and fidelity.

Ro 9:15 "I will show **m** to whom I will, I will

Eph 2: 4 who is rich in **m**,

Tit 3: 5 but because of his **m**, he saved us

Heb 4:16 the throne of grace to receive **m**

Jas 2:13 to one who has not shown **m**;

MERIBAH

Ex 17: 7 place was called Massah and **M**,

Ps 95: 8 Do not harden your hearts as at **M**,

1817

MESHACH → = MISHAEL
Hebrew exiled to Babylon; name changed from Mishael (Da 1:6-7). Refused defilement by food (Da 1:8-20). Refused to worship idol (Da 3:1-18); saved from furnace (Da 3:19-30).

MESSAGE → MESSENGER
1Co 1:18 The **m** of the cross is foolishness
2Co 5:19 to us the **m** of reconciliation.

MESSENGER → MESSAGE
Isa 42:19 servant, or deaf like the **m** I send?
Mt 11:10 I am sending my **m** ahead of you;

MESSIAH → CHRIST, MESSIAHS
Mt 16:16 "You are the **M**, the Son of the living
Lk 2:11 has been born for you who is **M**
Ac 2:36 has made him both Lord and **M**,
Ro 9: 5 according to the flesh, is t he **M**.

MESSIAHS → MESSIAH
Mk 13:22 False **m** and false prophets will arise

MICAH
1. Idolater from Ephraim (Jdg 17-18).
2. Prophet from Moresheth (Jer 26:18-19; Mic 1:1).

MICAIAH
Prophet of the LORD who spoke against Ahab (1Ki 22:1-28; 2Ch 18:1-27).

MICHAEL
Archangel (Jude 9); warrior in angelic realm, protector of Israel (Da 10:13, 21; 12:1; Rev 12:7).

MICHAL
Daughter of Saul, wife of David (1Sa 14:49; 18:20-28). Warned David of Saul's plot (1Sa 19). Saul gave her to Paltiel (1Sa 25:44); David retrieved her (2Sa 3:13-16). Criticized David for dancing before the ark (2Sa 6:16-23; 1Ch 15:29).

MIDDLE
Ge 3: 3 the tree in the **m** of the garden
Rev 22: 2 down the **m** of its street. On either

MIDIAN → MIDIANITES
Ex 18: 1 the priest of **M**, heard of all

MIDIANITES → MIDIAN
Ge 37:36 The **M**, meanwhile, sold Joseph
Nu 31: 2 "Avenge the Israelites on the **M**,

MIDWIVES
Ex 1:17 The **m**, however, feared God;

MIGHT → ALMIGHTY, MIGHTY
2Ch 20: 6 In your hand is power and **m**,
Zec 4: 6 an army, nor by **m**, but by my spirit,

MIGHTY → MIGHT
Ge 49:24 the power of the **M** One of Jacob,

MILE
Mt 5:41 press you into service for one **m**,

MILK
Ex 3: 8 a land flowing with **m** and honey,
Heb 5:12 You need **m**, [and] not solid food.
1Pe 2: 2 pure spiritual **m** so that through it

MILLSTONE → STONE
Lk 17: 2 him if a **m** were put around his neck

MIND → MINDFUL, MINDS
Nu 23:19 human, that he should change his **m**.
Sir 37:17 The root of all conduct is t he **m**;
Mt 22:37 all your soul, and with all your **m**.
Ro 1:28 their undiscerning **m** to do what is
1Co 2:16 "who has known the **m** of the Lord,
2:16 him?" But we have the **m** of Christ.

MINDFUL → MIND
Ps 8: 5 are humans that you are **m** of them,
111: 5 you, **m** of your covenant forever.
Heb 2: 6 "What is man that you are **m** of him,

MINDS → MIND
2Co 4: 4 of this age has blinded the **m**
Eph 4:23 be renewed in the spirit of your **m**,
Php 4: 7 your hearts and **m** in Christ Jesus.

MINISTER → MINISTERS, MINISTRY
Ex 28:43 tent or approach the altar to **m**

MINISTERS → MINISTER
2Co 3: 6 who has indeed qualified us as **m**
11:15 So it is not strange that his **m**
11:15 masquerade as **m** of righteousness.

MINISTRY → MINISTER
2Co 5:18 and given us the **m** of reconciliation,
Eph 4:12 the holy ones for the work of **m**,
Heb 8: 6 so much more excellent a **m** as he is

MIRACLES → See also JESUS: MIRACLES

MIRIAM
Sister of Moses and Aaron (Nu 26:59). Led dancing at Red Sea (Ex 15:20-21).

Ex 6: 1 Forced by my **m** hand, he will send
Ps 99: 4 O **m** king, lover of justice,
Lk 1:49 The **M** One has done great things
Rev 18: 8 **m** is the Lord God who judges her."

Struck with leprosy for criticizing Moses (Nu 12). Death (Nu 20:1).

MIRROR
1Co 13:12 as in a **m**, but then face to face.
Jas 1:23 who looks at his own face in a **m**.

MISHAEL → See MESHACH

MOAB
Ge 19:37 birth to a son whom she named **M**,
Ru 1: 1 sons to reside on the plateau of **M**.
Isa 15: 1 Oracle on **M**: Laid waste in a night,
15: 1 Ar of **M** is destroyed; Laid waste
15: 1 in a night, Kir of **M** is destroyed.

MOCK → MOCKED
Ps 22: 8 All who see me **m** me; they curl
Mk 10:34 who will **m** him, spit upon him,

MOCKED → MOCK
Gal 6: 7 God is not **m**, for a person will reap

MOLECH
Lev 18:21 offspring to be immolated to **M**,

MOMENT → MOMENTARY
Ex 33: 5 up in your company even f or a **m**,
Ps 30: 6 For divine anger lasts but a **m**;
Isa 54: 7 For a brief **m** I abandoned you,
66: 8 or a nation be born in a single **m**?

MOMENTARY → MOMENT
2Co 4:17 this **m** light affliction is producing

MONEY
Ecc 10:19 glad, but **m** answers for everything.
Mk 11:15 the tables of the **m** changers
1Ti 3: 3 not contentious, not a lover of **m**.
1Ti 6:10 the love of **m** is the root of all evils,
Heb 13: 5 Let your life be free from love of **m**

MONTH
Ex 12: 2 "This **m** shall stand at the head
12: 2 you shall reckon it the first **m**
Eze 47:12 Every **m** they shall bear fresh fruit,
Rev 22: 2 twelve times a year, once each **m**;

MOON → MOONS
Ge 37: 9 the **m** and eleven stars were bowing
Dt 17: 3 the **m** or any of the host of the sky,
Jos 10:13 and the **m** stayed, while the nation
Ac 2:20 and the **m** to blood,
Rev 6:12 and the whole **m** became like blood.

Rev 21:23 no need of sun or **m** to shine on it,

MOONS → MOON

2Ch 8:13 at the new **m**, and on the fixed

MORALS

1Co 15:33 "Bad company corrupts good **m**."

MORDECAI

Benjamite exile who raised Esther (Est 2:5-15). Mordecai's dream (Est 11; 10:4-13). Exposed plot to kill Xerxes (Est 2:19-23; 12:1-6). Refused to honor Haman (Est 3:1-6; 5:9-14). Mordecai's prayer (Est 13). Charged Esther to foil Haman's plot against the Jews (Est 4). Xerxes forced Haman to honor Mordecai (Est 6). Mordecai exalted (Est 8-10). Established Purim (Est 9:18-32).

MORE → MOST

Ps 19:11 **M** desirable than gold, than a hoard
69:32 will please the LORD **m** than oxen,
Mk 4:25 the one who has, **m** will be given;
Lk 12:23 For life is **m** than food and the body
12:23 food and the body than clothing.
1Co 12:31 show you a still **m** excellent way.
Rev 21: 4 and there shall be no **m** death

MORIAH

Ge 22: 2 you love, and go to the land of **M**.
2Ch 3: 1 the LORD in Jerusalem on Mount **M**,

MORNING

Ge 1: 5 came, and **m** followed—the first day.
La 3:23 They are renewed each **m**, so great
Lk 24:22 they were at the tomb early in the **m**
2Pe 1:19 and the **m** star rises in your hearts.
Rev 22:16 of David, the bright **m** star."

MORTAL

1Co 15:53 this which is **m** must clothe itself
2Co 5: 4 so that what is **m** may be swallowed

MOSES

Levite; brother of Aaron (Ex 6:20; 1Ch 6:3). Put in basket into Nile; discovered and raised by Pharaoh's daughter (Ex 2:1-10). Fled to Midian after killing Egyptian (Ex 2:11-15). Married to Zipporah, fathered Gershom (Ex 2:16-22).
Called by the LORD to deliver Israel (Ex 3-4). Pharaoh's resistance (Ex 5). Ten plagues (Ex 7-11). Passover and Exodus (Ex 12-13). Led Israel through Red Sea (Ex 14). Song of deliverance (Ex 15:1-21). Brought water from rock (Ex 17:1-7). Raised hands to defeat Amalekites (Ex 17:8-16). Delegated judges (Ex 18; Dt 1:9-18).
Received Law at Sinai (Ex 19-23; 25-31; Jn 1:17). Announced Law to Israel (Ex 19:7-

8; 24; 35). Broke tablets because of golden calf (Ex 32; Dt 9). Saw glory of the LORD (Ex 33-34). Supervised building of tabernacle (Ex 36-40). Set apart Aaron and priests (Lev 8-9). Numbered tribes (Nu 1-4; 26). Opposed by Aaron and Miriam (Nu 12). Sent spies into Canaan (Nu 13). Announced forty years of wandering for failure to enter land (Nu 14). Opposed by Korah (Nu 16). Forbidden to enter land for striking rock (Nu 20:1-13; Dt 1:37). Lifted bronze snake for healing (Nu 21:4-9; Jn 3:14). Final address to Israel (Dt 1-33). Succeeded by Joshua (Nu 27:12-23; Dt 34). Death and burial by God (Dt 34:5-12). Praise of (Sir 45).
Law of (1Ki 2:3; Ezr 3:2; Mk 12:26; Lk 24:44). Book of (2Ch 25:12; Ne 13:1). Song of (Ex 15:1-21; Rev 15:3). Prayer of (Ps 90).

MOST → MORE

Ge 14:18 and being a priest of God **M** High,
Ps 91: 1 dwell in the shelter of the **M** High,
Mk 5: 7 me, Jesus, Son of the **M** High God?
Col 4: 5 making the **m** of the opportunity.
Jude 1:20 yourselves up in your **m** holy faith;

MOTH

Mt 6:19 earth, where **m** and decay destroys,

MOTHER → MOTHER'S, MOTHERS

Ge 2:24 why a man leaves his father and **m**
3:20 because she became the **m** of all
Ex 20:12 "Honor your father and your **m**,
Jdg 5: 7 rose, when I rose, a **m** in Israel,
Tob 4: 3 Honor your **m**, and do not abandon
Pr 31: 1 The advice which his **m** gave him:
Sir 3: 6 LORD who brings comfort to his **m**.
Isa 66:13 As a **m** comforts her son, so will I
Mt 10:37 or **m** more than me is not worthy
Lk 14:26 me without hating his father and **m**,
Jn 2: 3 ran short, the **m** of Jesus said to him,
19:27 said to the disciple, "Behold, your **m**."
Gal 4:26 above is freeborn, and she is our **m**.
Eph 5:31 shall leave [his] father and [his] **m**
Rev 17: 5 the great, the **m** of harlots

MOTHER'S → MOTHER

Job 1:21 I came forth from my **m** womb,
Pr 1: 8 and reject not your **m** teaching;
Jn 3: 4 he cannot reenter his **m** womb

MOTHERS → MOTHER

Mk 10:30 and sisters and **m** and children

MOUNT → MOUNTAIN, MOUNTAINS

Ex 19:20 came down to the top of **M** Sinai,
Dt 11:29 the blessing on **M** Gerizim,
11:29 on **M** Gerizim, the curse on **M** Ebal.
Ps 78:68 of Judah, **M** Zion which he favored.
Mic 4: 7 shall be king over them on **M** Zion,
Zec 14: 4 feet shall rest upon the **M** of Olives,
14: 4 The **M** of Olives shall be cleft
Mk 13: 3 the **M** of Olives opposite the temple
Heb 12:22 you have approached **M** Zion
Rev 14: 1 was the Lamb standing on **M** Zion,

MOUNTAIN → MOUNT

Ex 3: 1 he came to Horeb, the **m** of God.
24:18 of the cloud as he went up on the **m**;
Isa 2: 2 to come, The **m** of the LORD's house
2: 2 shall be established as the highest **m**
Da 2:45 from the **m** without a hand being put
Mt 4: 8 devil took him up to a very high **m**,
17:20 you will say to this **m**,
2Pe 1:18 we were with him on the holy **m**.

MOUNTAINS → MOUNT

Ge 7:20 cubits higher than the submerged **m**.
Ps 125: 2 As **m** surround Jerusalem, the LORD
Isa 52: 7 How beautiful upon the **m**
1Co 13: 2 if I have all faith so as to move **m**,
Rev 16:20 island fled, and **m** disappeared.

MOURN → MOURNFUL, MOURNING

Ecc 3: 4 a time to **m**, and a time to dance.
Sir 7:34 who weep, but **m** with those who **m**;
Zec 12:10 they shall **m** for him as one mourns
Mt 5: 4 Blessed are they who **m**, for they

MOURNING → MOURN

Ps 30:12 You changed my **m** into dancing;
Isa 61: 3 them oil of gladness in place of **m**,
Rev 21: 4 there shall be no more death or **m**,

MOUTH → MOUTHS

Dt 8: 3 comes forth from the **m** of the LORD.
Ps 19:15 Let the words of my **m** meet
Mt 4: 4 comes forth from the **m** of God.' "
15:11 It is not what enters one's **m**
15:11 out of the **m** is what defiles one."
Jas 3:10 From the same **m** come blessing

MOUTH → MOUTHS (*cont.*)
Rev 19:15 Out of his **m** came a sharp sword

MOUTHS → MOUTH
Ps 115: 5 They have **m** but do not speak,

MUCH
Ecc 12:12 in **m** study there is weariness
Lk 12:48 **M** will be required of the person
　 12:48 of the person entrusted with **m**,
Jn 12:24 but if it dies, it produces **m** fruit.

MULTIPLY
Ge 1:28 "Be fertile and **m**; fill the earth
　 9: 7 Be fertile, then, and **m**;

MULTITUDE
Jas 5:20 death and will cover a **m** of sins.
1Pe 4: 8 because love covers a **m** of sins.

MURDER → MURDERER, MURDERERS
Hos 4: 2 lying, **m**, stealing and adultery!

MURDERER → MURDER
Nu 35:16 he is a **m** and shall be put to death.
Jn 8:44 He was a **m** from the beginning

MURDERERS → MURDER
Rev 21: 8 the depraved, **m**, the unchaste,

MUSTARD
Mt 17:20 you have faith the size of a **m** seed,
Mk 4:31 It is like a **m** seed that, when it is

MUTUAL
Ro 12:10 love one another with **m** affection;
Heb 13: 1 Let **m** love continue.

MYRRH
Mt 2:11 gifts of gold, frankincense, and **m**.
Mk 15:23 gave him wine drugged with **m**,

MYSTERY
Da 2:19 During the night the **m** was revealed
Ro 11:25 want you to be unaware of this **m**,
1Co 15:51 Behold, I tell you a **m**. We shall not
Eph 3: 4 my insight into the **m** of Christ,
1Ti 3: 9 holding fast to the **m** of the faith
Rev 17: 5 which is a **m**, "Babylon the great,

MYTHS
2Pe 1:16 did not follow cleverly devised **m**

N

NAAMAN
　 Aramean general whose leprosy was cleansed by Elisha (2Ki 5; Lk 4:27).

NABAL
　 Wealthy Carmelite the LORD killed for refusing to help David (1Sa 25). David married Abigail, his widow (1Sa 25:39-42).

NABOTH
　 Jezreelite killed for his vineyard (1Ki 21). Ahab's family punished (1Ki 21:17-24; 2Ki 9:21-37).

NADAB
　 1. Firstborn of Aaron (Ex 6:23); killed with Abihu for offering unauthorized fire (Lev 10; Nu 3:4).
　 2. Son of Jeroboam I; king of Israel (1Ki 15:25-32).

NAHUM
　 Prophet against Nineveh (Na 1:1; Tob 14:4).

NAILING → NAILS
Col 2:14 it from our midst, **n** it to the cross;

NAILS → NAILING
Jn 20:25 I see the mark of the **n** in his hands

NAKED → NAKEDNESS
Ge 2:25 The man and his wife were both **n**,
Job 1:21 "**N** I came forth from my mother's
　 1:21 and **n** shall I go back again.
2Co 5: 3 taken it off, we shall not be found **n**.

NAKEDNESS → NAKED
Ro 8:35 or famine, or **n**, or peril,

NAME → NAMES
Ge 2:19 called each of them would be its **n**.
　 4:26 men began to invoke the LORD by **n**.
　 12: 2 I will make your **n** great, so that you
Ex 3:15 "This is my **n** forever; this is my title
　 20: 7 "You shall not take the **n** of the LORD,
　 20: 7 unpunished him who takes his **n**
　 34: 5 him there and proclaimed his **n**,
Dt 12:11 for his **n** you shall bring all
Ps 9:11 Those who honor your **n** trust
Pr 18:10 The **n** of the LORD is a strong tower;
Isa 42: 8 I am the LORD, this is my **n**;
Zec 14: 9 the only one, and his **n** the only one.
Mt 1:21 a son and you are to **n** him Jesus,
　 6: 9 in heaven, hallowed be your **n**,
　 28:19 them in the **n** of the Father,
Jn 1:12 God, to those who believe in his **n**,
　 20:31 belief you may have life in his **n**.
Ac 4:12 is there any other **n** under heaven
Php 2: 9 and bestowed on him the **n** that is

Php 2: 9 on him the **n** that is above every **n**,
Rev 13:17 the stamped image of the beast's **n**
　 13:17 **n** or the number that stood for its **n**.
　 19:13 his **n** was called the Word of God.
　 22: 4 and his **n** will be on their foreheads.

NAMES → NAME
Ge 2:20 The man gave **n** to all the cattle,
Ex 28: 9 engrave on them the **n** of the sons
Mt 10: 2 The **n** of the twelve apostles are
Rev 21:14 were inscribed the twelve **n**

NAOMI
　 Wife of Elimelech, mother-in-law of Ruth (Ru 1:2, 4). Left Bethlehem for Moab during famine (Ru 1:1). Returned a widow, with Ruth (Ru 1:6-22). Advised Ruth to seek marriage with Boaz (Ru 2:17-3:4). Cared for Ruth's son Obed (Ru 4:13-17).

NAPHTALI
　 Son of Jacob by Bilhah (Ge 30:8; 35:25; 1Ch 2:2). Tribe of blessed (Ge 49:21; Dt 33:23), numbered (Nu 1:43; 26:50), allotted land (Jos 19:32-39; Eze 48:3), failed to fully possess (Jdg 1:33), supported Deborah (Jdg 4:10; 5:18), David (1Ch 12:34), 12,000 from (Rev 7:6).

NARROW
Lk 13:24 "Strive to enter through the **n** gate,

NATHAN
　 Prophet and chronicler of Israel's history (1Ch 29:29; 2Ch 9:29). Announced the Davidic covenant (2Sa 7; 1Ch 17). Denounced David's sin with Bathsheba (2Sa 12). Supported Solomon (1Ki 1).

NATHANAEL → = BARTHOLOMEW?
　 Apostle (Jn 1:45-49; 21:2). Probably also called Bartholomew (Mt 10:3).

NATION → NATIONS
Ge 12: 2 "I will make of you a great **n**, and I
Ex 32:10 Then I will make of you a great **n**."
Ps 33:12 Happy the **n** whose God is the LORD,
Pr 14:34 Virtue exalts a **n**, but sin is
Isa 2: 4 One **n** shall not raise the sword
　 66: 8 or a **n** be born in a single moment?
Mt 24: 7 **N** will rise against **n**, and kingdom
1Pe 2: 9 a holy **n**, a people of his own,

NATIONS → NATION
Ge 18:18 and all the **n** of the earth are to find
2Ki 17:15 the surrounding **n** whom the LORD
Ps 47: 9 God rules over the **n**; God sits
Isa 2: 2 hills. All **n** shall stream toward it;

Isa 42: 1 he shall bring forth justice to the **n**,
Am 9:12 all the **n** that shall bear my name,
Mt 28:19 and make disciples of all **n**,
Ro 4:18 would become "the father of many **n**,"
Rev 22: 2 the trees serve as medicine for the **n**.

NATURAL → NATURE
Ro 11:21 if God did not spare the **n** branches,

NATURE → NATURAL
2Pe 1: 4 may come to share in the divine **n**,

NAZARETH
Mt 2:23 went and dwelt in a town called **N**,
Jn 1:46 "Can anything good come from **N**?"

NAZIRITE
Nu 6: 2 a woman) solemnly takes the **n** vow

NEAR
Dt 30:14 No, it is something very **n** to you,
Isa 55: 6 be found, call him while he is **n**.
Zep 1:14 **N** is the great day of the LORD,
Jas 4: 8 Draw **n** to God, and he will draw **n**
Rev 22:10 book, for the appointed time is **n**.

NEBUCHADNEZZAR
Babylonian king, also spelled Nebuchadrezzar. Subdued and exiled Judah (2Ki 24-25; 2Ch 36; Jer 39). Dreams interpreted by Daniel (Da 2; 4). Worshiped God (Da 3:28-29; 4:34-37).

NECK → STIFF-NECKED
Pr 3:22 soul, and an adornment for your **n**.
Mt 18: 6 a great millstone hung around his **n**

NECO
Pharaoh who killed Josiah (2Ki 23:29-30; 2Ch 35:20-22), deposed Jehoahaz (2Ki 23:33-35; 2Ch 36:3-4).

NEED → NEEDY
Mt 6: 8 knows what you **n** before you ask
1Co 12:21 "I do not **n** you," nor again the head
12:21 the head to the feet, "I do not **n** you."
1Jn 2:27 you do not **n** anyone to teach you.

NEEDLE
Lk 18:25 pass through the eye of a **n** than

NEEDY → NEED
1Sa 2: 8 He raises the **n** from the dust;
Job 29:16 I was a father to the **n**; the rights
Ps 113: 7 The LORD raises the **n** from the dust,

NEGLECT
1Ti 4:14 Do not **n** the gift you have,

NEHEMIAH
Cupbearer of Artaxerxes (Ne 2:1); governor of Israel (Ne 8:9). Returned to Jerusalem to rebuild walls (Ne 2-6). With Ezra, reestablished worship (Ne 8). Prayer confessing nation's sin (Ne 9). Dedicated wall (Ne 12). Story of the miraculous fire (2Ma 1).

NEIGHBOR
Lev 19:18 You shall love your **n** as yourself.
Dt 5:20 dishonest witness against your **n**.
Mt 19:19 'you shall love your **n** as yourself.' "
Jas 2: 8 "You shall love your **n** as yourself,"

NESTS
Mt 8:20 dens and birds of the sky have **n**,

NEVER
Ps 15: 5 acts like this shall **n** be shaken.
Da 2:44 a kingdom that shall **n** be destroyed
Mt 7:23 to them solemnly, 'I **n** knew you.
Jn 10:28 eternal life, and they shall **n** perish.
1Co 13: 8 Love **n** fails. If there are prophecies,
Heb 13: 5 "I will **n** forsake you or abandon you."

NEW
Ex 1: 8 Then a **n** king, who knew nothing
Ps 33: 3 Sing to God a **n** song; skillfully play
Ecc 1: 9 be done. Nothing is **n** under the sun.
Isa 43:19 See, I am doing something **n**!
65:17 Lo, I am about to create **n** heavens
65:17 and a **n** earth; The things of the past
Jer 31:31 I will make a **n** covenant
Eze 36:26 I will give you a **n** heart and place
36:26 heart and place a **n** spirit within you,
Mt 9:17 People do not put **n** wine into old
9:17 Rather, they pour **n** wine into fresh
Mk 1:27 is this? A **n** teaching with authority.
Lk 22:20 "This cup is the **n** covenant in my
Jn 13:34 I give you a **n** commandment:
2Co 3: 6 us as ministers of a **n** covenant,
Col 3:10 and have put on the **n** self, which is
Heb 8: 8 I will conclude a **n** covenant
1Pe 1: 3 his great mercy gave us a **n** birth
2Pe 3:13 to his promise we await **n** heavens
3:13 and a **n** earth in which righteousness

1Jn 2: 7 I am writing no **n** commandment
Rev 21: 1 Then I saw a **n** heaven and a **n** earth.
21: 2 saw the holy city, a **n** Jerusalem,
21: 5 said, "Behold, I make all things **n**."

NEWS
Isa 52: 7 Announcing peace, bearing good **n**,
Mt 11: 5 poor have the good **n** proclaimed

NICODEMUS
Pharisee who visted Jesus at night (Jn 3). Argued for fair treatment of Jesus (Jn 7:50-52). With Joseph, prepared Jesus for burial (Jn 19:38-42).

NIGHT → NIGHTS
Ge 1: 5 "day," and the darkness he called "**n**."
Ex 13:21 at **n** by means of a column of fire
13:21 they could travel both day and **n**.
Jos 1: 8 Recite it by day and by **n**, that you
Mt 24:43 the house had known the hour of **n**
1Th 5: 2 the Lord will come like a thief at **n**.
Rev 22: 5 **N** will be no more, nor will they

NIGHTS → NIGHT
Ge 7:12 forty **n** heavy rain poured down
Ex 24:18 he stayed for forty days and forty **n**.
1Ki 19: 8 and forty **n** to the mountain of God,
Mt 4: 2 He fasted for forty days and forty **n**,
12:40 of the whale three days and three **n**,
12:40 of the earth three days and three **n**.

NINEVEH
Jnh 1: 2 "Set out for the great city of **N**,
Na 1: 1 Oracle about **N**. The book
Mt 12:41 the men of **N** will arise with this

NOAH
Righteous man (Eze 14:14, 20) called to build ark (Ge 6-8; Heb 11:7; 1Pe 3:20; 2Pe 2:5). God's covenant with (Ge 9:1-17). Drunkenness of (Ge 9:18-23). Blessed sons, cursed Canaan (Ge 9:24-27). Praised (Sir 44:17-18).

NOISE
Ex 32:17 Joshua heard the **n** of the people

NOON
Mk 15:33 At **n** darkness came over the whole

NORTH
Jer 4: 6 Evil I bring from the **n**, and great

NORTH (*cont.*)
Da   11: 6   to the king of the **n** in the interest

NOTHING
Ecc   1: 9   be done. **N** is new under the sun.
Sir   39:20   ages; to him there is **n** unexpected.
Jer   32:17   arm; **n** is impossible to you.
Mt   17:20   move. **N** will be impossible for you."
Jn   15: 5   because without me you can do **n**.
1Co   13: 2   but do not have love, I am **n**.

NULLIFY
Ro   3: 3   Will their infidelity **n** the fidelity
Gal   2:21   I do not **n** the grace of God;

NUMBER → NUMBERED, NUMEROUS
Nu   1:45   The total **n** of the Israelites
Ro   11:25   part, until the full **n** of the Gentiles
Rev   13:18   who understands can calculate the **n**
      13:18   for it is a **n** that stands for a person.
      13:18   His **n** is six hundred and sixty-six.

NUMBERED → NUMBER
2Sa   24:10   David regretted having **n** the people,

NUMEROUS → NUMBER
Ex   1: 9   "Look how **n** and powerful
Zec   10: 8   them they will be as **n** as before.

O

OATH
Dt   7: 8   his fidelity to the **o** he had sworn
Ps   132:11   The LORD swore an **o** to David,
Heb   7:20   others became priests without an **o**,

OBADIAH
   1. Believer who sheltered 100 prophets from Jezebel (1Ki 18:1-16).
   2. Prophet against Edom (Ob 1).

OBEDIENCE → OBEY
Ro   5:19   so through the **o** of one the many
Heb   5: 8   he learned **o** from what he suffered;

OBEDIENT → OBEY
Php   2: 8   himself, becoming **o** to death,

OBEY → OBEDIENCE, OBEDIENT, OBEYED
Jos   24:24   the LORD, our God, and **o** his voice."
Ac   5:29   "We must **o** God rather than men.
Eph   6: 1   **o** your parents [in the Lord], for this

OBEYED → OBEY
Heb   11: 8   faith Abraham **o** when he was called

OBSERVE
Lev   20: 8   therefore, to **o** what I, the LORD,

OBSTACLE
1Co   9:12   so as not to place an **o** to the gospel

OBTAIN → OBTAINED
2Ti   2:10   they too may **o** the salvation that is

OBTAINED → OBTAIN
Heb   8: 6   Now he has **o** so much more

ODOR
Ge   8:21   When the LORD smelled the sweet **o**,

OFFENSE
Mk   6: 3   with us?" And they took **o** at him.

OFFER → OFFERING, OFFERINGS
Ps   4: 6   **O** fitting sacrifice and trust
Heb   9:25   that he might **o** himself repeatedly,

OFFERING → OFFER
Ge   4: 4   with favor on Abel and his **o**,
Ps   40: 7   Sacrifice and **o** you do not want;
Eph   5: 2   over for us as a sacrificial **o** to God
Heb   10:14   one **o** he has made perfect forever

OFFERINGS → OFFER
Mk   12:33   is worth more than all burnt **o**

OFFSPRING
Ge   3:15   and between your **o** and hers;

OHOLIAB
   Craftsman who worked on the tabernacle (Ex 31:6; 35:34; 36:1-2; 38:23).

OIL
Ex   25: 6   **o** for the light;
      25: 6   spices for the anointing **o**
Dt   14:23   wine and **o**, as well as the firstlings
Ps   23: 5   You anoint my head with **o**; my cup
Heb   1: 9   with the **o** of gladness above your
Jas   5:14   anoint [him] with **o** in the name

OLD
Ge   21: 7   I have borne him a son in his **o** age."
Ps   74:12   you, God, are my king from of **o**,
Mk   2:22   pours new wine into **o** wineskins.
Ro   4:19   he was almost a hundred years **o**)
Eph   4:22   you should put away the **o** self

OLIVE → OLIVES
Zec   4: 3   and beside it are two **o** trees,
Ro   11:17   a wild **o** shoot, were grafted in their
      11:17   to share in the rich root of the **o** tree,
Rev   11: 4   These are the two **o** trees

OLIVES → OLIVE
Zec   14: 4   feet shall rest upon the Mount of **O**,
      14: 4   The Mount of **O** shall be cleft
Mt   24: 3   he was sitting on the Mount of **O**,

OMEGA
Rev   1: 8   "I am the Alpha and the **O**,"

OMRI
   King of Israel (1Ki 16:21-26).

ONCE → ONE
Ex   30:10   **O** a year Aaron shall perform
      30:10   atonement is to be made **o** a year
Ro   6:10   death, he died to sin **o** and for all;
Heb   7:27   he did that **o** for all when he offered
      9:27   appointed that human beings die **o**,

ONE → FIRST, ONCE
Ge   2:24   and the two of them become **o** body.
Zec   14: 9   day the LORD shall be the only **o**,
      14: 9   the only **o**, and his name the only **o**.
Jn   10:30   The Father and I are **o**."
1Co   12:13   in **o** Spirit we were all baptized
      12:13   we were all baptized into **o** body,
      12:13   were all given to drink of **o** Spirit.
Gal   3:28   for you are all **o** in Christ Jesus.
Eph   4: 5   **o** Lord, **o** faith, **o** baptism;

ONLY
Ge   22: 2   "Take your son Isaac, your **o** one,
1Ki   18:22   "I am the **o** surviving prophet
Jn   1:14   the glory as of the Father's **o** Son,
      3:16   the world that he gave his **o** Son,
1Ti   1:17   invisible, the **o** God,
1Jn   4: 9   God sent his **o** Son into the world so

OPEN → OPENED, OPENS
Rev   5: 2   "Who is worthy to **o** the scroll

OPENED → OPEN
Ge   3: 7   the eyes of both of them were **o**,
Isa   53: 7   and **o** not his mouth; Like a lamb
      53: 7   he was silent and **o** not his mouth.
Da   7:10   convened, and the books were **o**.
Lk   11: 9   knock and the door will be **o** to you
Heb   10:20   living way he **o** for us through
Rev   20:12   the throne, and scrolls were **o**.
      20:12   Then another scroll was **o**, the book

OPENS → OPEN
Rev   3: 7   who **o** and no one shall close,

OPPORTUNITY
Mt 26:16 he looked for an **o** to hand him over.
Gal 5:13 do not use this freedom as an **o**

OPPRESSED → OPPRESSION
Ge 15:13 and **o** for four hundred years.
Ex 1:12 Yet the more they were **o**, the more
Jdt 9:11 the helper of the **o**, the supporter
Ps 146: 7 secures justice for the **o**, gives food

OPPRESSION → OPPRESSED
Eze 45: 9 Put away violence and **o**, and do

ORDAIN
Ex 29: 9 thus shall you **o** Aaron and his sons.

ORDER
Heb 5:10 according to the **o** of Melchizedek.

ORIGIN
Mt 21:26 say, "Of human **o**," we fear the crowd,
Ac 5:38 or this activity is of human **o**, it will

ORNAMENTS
Ex 33: 6 the Israelites laid aside their **o**.

ORPHANS
Jas 1:27 to care for **o** and widows in their

OTHER → OTHERS
Ex 20: 3 shall not have **o** gods besides me.
Jdg 2:19 following **o** gods in service
2Ki 17: 7 and because they venerated **o** gods.
Isa 45: 5 I am the LORD and there is no **o**,
Mt 6:24 will either hate one and love the **o**,
     6:24 be devoted to one and despise the **o**.

OTHERS → OTHER
Lk 6:31 Do to **o** as you would have them do
Php 2: 3 humbly regard **o** as more important

OTHNIEL
Nephew of Caleb (Jos 15:15-19; Jdg 1:12-15). Judge who freed Israel from Aram (Jdg 3:7-11).

OUTSIDE
Lk 11:39 Although you cleanse the **o**
Heb 13:12 Jesus also suffered **o** the gate,
Rev 22:15 **O** are the dogs, the sorcerers,

OUTSTRETCHED → STRETCH
Ex 6: 6 I will rescue you by my **o** arm
Ps 136:12 With mighty hand and **o** arm,
Jer 27: 5 by my great power, with my **o** arm;

OVERCOME
Jn 1: 5 and the darkness has not **o** it.

OVERSEERS
Ac 20:28 the holy Spirit has appointed you **o**,

OVERSHADOW
Lk 1:35 power of the Most High will **o** you.

OWE → OWES
Mt 18:28 demanding, 'Pay back what you **o**.'
Ro 13: 8 **O** nothing to anyone, except to love

OWN
Isa 53: 6 each following his **o** way;
Jer 31:30 but through his **o** fault only shall
Jn 1:11 He came to what was his **o**, but his
     1:11 but his **o** people did not accept him.
     10:18 from me, but I lay it down on my **o**.
1Co 6:19 God, and that you are not your **o**?

OX → OXEN
Dt 25: 4 "You shall not muzzle an **o** when it is
Isa 65:25 and the lion shall eat hay like the **o**
Eze 1:10 and on the left side the face of an **o**,
1Ti 5:18 "You shall not muzzle an **o** when it is

P

PAGANS
1Co 12: 2 how, when you were **p**, you were

PAIN → PAINS
Ge 3:16 in **p** shall you bring forth children.
1Pe 2:19 For whenever anyone bears the **p**
Rev 21: 4 wailing or **p**, [for] the old order has

PAINS → PAIN
Ro 8:22 groaning in labor **p** even until now;
1Th 5: 3 them, like labor **p** upon a pregnant

PALM → PALMS
Jn 12:13 they took **p** branches and went
Rev 7: 9 holding **p** branches in their hands.

PALMS → PALM
Isa 49:16 the **p** of my hands I have written

PANGS
Ge 3:16 he said: "I will intensify the **p** of your

PARABLE → PARABLES
Mt 13:18 "Hear then the **p** of the sower.

PARABLES → PARABLE; See also JESUS: PARABLES
Mt 13:35 "I will open my mouth in **p**, I will

PARADISE
Lk 23:43 you, today you will be with me in **P**."
2Co 12: 4 was caught up into **P** and heard

PARALYTIC → PARALYZED
Mt 9: 2 to him a **p** lying on a stretcher.
     9: 2 their faith, he said to the **p**, "Courage,

PARALYZED → PARALYTIC
Ac 8: 7 many **p** and crippled people were

PARCHMENTS
2Ti 4:13 papyrus rolls, and especially the **p**.

PARDON
Ex 34: 9 yet **p** our wickedness and sins,

PARENTS
Eph 6: 1 Children, obey your **p** [in the Lord],

PARTAKE
1Co 10:17 body, for we all **p** of the one loaf.

PARTIALITY
Pr 24:23 To show **p** in judgment is not good.
Ro 2:11 There is no **p** with God.

PARTNERSHIP
2Co 6:14 For what **p** do righteousness

PASHHUR
Priest; opponent of Jeremiah (Jer 20:1-6).

PASS → PASSED, PASSING
Ex 12:13 Seeing the blood, I will **p** over you;
     33:19 make all my beauty **p** before you,
Am 5:17 when I **p** through your midst,
Mt 24:35 Heaven and earth will **p** away,
     24:35 but my words will not **p** away.
2Pe 3:10 then the heavens will **p** away

PASSED → PASS
Ge 15:17 which **p** between those pieces.
Ex 12:27 LORD, who **p** over the houses
     33:22 you with my hand until I have **p** by.
2Co 5:17 the old things have **p** away; behold,
1Jn 3:14 We know that we have **p** from death
Rev 21: 4 pain, [for] the old order has **p** away."

PASSING → PASS
1Co 7:31 world in its present form is **p** away.
1Jn 2:17 and its enticement are **p** away.

PASSIONS
Gal 5:24 have crucified their flesh with its **p**

PASSOVER
Ex 12:11 are in flight. It is the **P** of the LORD.
Dt 16: 1 Abib by keeping the **P** of the LORD,
Mk 14:12 when they sacrificed the **P** lamb,

PASSOVER (*cont.*)
Mk 14:12 go and prepare for you to eat the **P**?"

PASTORS
Eph 4:11 others as **p** and teachers,

PASTURES
Ps 23: 2 In green **p** you let me graze; to safe

PATH → PATHS
Ps 16:11 You will show me the **p** to life,
      119:105 a lamp for my feet, a light for my **p**.
Mt 13: 4 some seed fell on the **p**, and birds

PATHS → PATH
Pr 3: 6 and he will make straight your **p**.
Mt 3: 3 of the Lord, make straight his **p**.'"
Heb 12:13 Make straight **p** for your feet,

PATIENCE → PATIENT
Mic 2: 7 "Is the LORD short of **p**, or are such
Ro 2: 4 and **p** in low esteem,
Gal 5:22 joy, peace, **p**, kindness, generosity,
2Pe 3:15 And consider the **p** of our Lord as

PATIENT → PATIENCE
1Co 13: 4 Love is **p**, love is kind. It is not
2Pe 3: 9 but he is **p** with you, not wishing

PATTERN
Ex 25:40 them according to the **p** shown you
Heb 8: 5 according to the **p** shown you

PAUL → = SAUL
Also called Saul (Ac 13:9). Pharisee from Tarsus (Ac 9:11; Php 3:5). Apostle (Gal 1). At stoning of Stephen (Ac 8:1). Persecuted Church (Ac 9:1-2; Gal 1:13). Vision of Jesus on road to Damascus (Ac 9:4-9; 26:12-18). In Arabia (Gal 1:17). Preached in Damascus; escaped death through the wall in a basket (Ac 9:19-25). In Jerusalem; back to Tarsus (Ac 9:26-30).
Brought to Antioch by Barnabas (Ac 11:22-26). First missionary journey to Cyprus and Galatia (Ac 13-14). Stoned at Lystra (Ac 14:19-20). At Jerusalem council (Ac 15). Split with Barnabas over Mark (Ac 15:36-41).
Second missionary journey with Silas (Ac 16-20). Called to Macedonia (Ac 16:6-10). Freed from prison in Philippi (Ac 16:16-40). In Thessalonica (Ac 17:1-9). Speech in Athens (Ac 17:16-33). In Corinth (Ac 18). In Ephesus (Ac 19). Return to Jerusalem (Ac 20). Farewell to Ephesian elders (Ac 20:13-38). Arrival in Jerusalem (Ac 21:1-26). Arrested (Ac 21:27-36). Addressed crowds (Ac 22), Sanhedrin (Ac 23:1-11). Sent to Caesarea (Ac 23:12-35). Trial before Felix (Ac 24), Festus (Ac 25:1-12). Before Agrippa (Ac 25:13-26:32). Voyage to Rome; shipwreck (Ac 27). Arrival in Rome (Ac 28).

PAVEMENT
Jn 19:13 bench in the place called Stone **P**,

PAY → REPAY
Dt 24:15 You shall **p** him each day's wages
Mt 22:17 Is it lawful to **p** the census tax
Ro 13: 7 **P** to all their dues, taxes to whom

PEACE → PEACEMAKERS
Lev 26: 6 I will establish **p** in the land,
Ps 122: 6 For the **p** of Jerusalem pray:
Isa 26: 3 of firm purpose you keep in **p**; in **p**,
      57:19 life. **P**, **p** to the far and the near,
Isa 57:21 No **p** for the wicked! says my God.
Jer 6:14 the injury to my people: "**P**, **p**!"
      6:14 "**P**, **p**!" they say, though there is no **p**.
Lk 2:14 and on earth **p** to those on whom his
Jn 14:27 **P** I leave with you; my **p** I give
Ro 16:20 of **p** will quickly crush Satan under
1Co 14:33 is not the God of disorder but of **p**.
Gal 5:22 of the Spirit is love, joy, **p**, patience,
Eph 4: 3 of the spirit through the bond of **p**:
Php 4: 7 Then the **p** of God that surpasses all
2Ti 2:22 and **p**, along with those who call

PEACEMAKERS → PEACE
Mt 5: 9 Blessed are the **p**, for they will be

PEARL → PEARLS
Mt 13:46 When he finds a **p** of great price,
Rev 21:21 of the gates made from a single **p**;

PEARLS → PEARL
Mt 7: 6 or throw your **p** before swine,

PEKAH
King of Israel (2Ki 15:25-31; 2Ch 28:6; Isa 7:1).

PEKAHIAH
Son of Menahem; king of Israel (2Ki 15:22-26).

PENALTY
Ro 1:27 their own persons the due **p** for their

PENTECOST
Ac 2: 1 When the time for **P** was fulfilled,

PEOPLE → PEOPLES
Ex 5: 1 Israel: Let my **p** go, that they may
      33:13 this nation is, after all, your own **p**."
Dt 4:20 that you might be his very own **p**,

Ru 1:16 I will lodge, your **p** shall be my **p**,
2Sa 5: 2 'You shall shepherd my **p** Israel
Ps 29:11 May the LORD give might to his **p**;
      29:11 his **p**; may the LORD bless his **p**
      125: 2 the LORD surrounds his **p** both now
Isa 40: 1 Comfort, give comfort to my **p**,
      42: 6 as a covenant of the **p**, a light
      53: 8 and smitten for the sin of his **p**,
Jer 50: 6 Lost sheep were my **p**,
Da 9:24 for your **p** and for your holy city:
Zec 13: 9 I will say, "They are my **p**," and they
Mt 1:21 because he will save his **p**
Jn 11:50 one man should die instead of the **p**,
      18:14 man should die rather than the **p**.
Ro 9:25 who were not my **p** I will call 'my **p**,"
Heb 8:10 their God, and they shall be my **p**.
1Pe 2: 9 a holy nation, a **p** of his own,

PEOPLES → PEOPLE
Ge 17:16 and rulers of **p** shall issue from him."
Ps 117: 1 you nations! Give glory, all you **p**!

PERFECT → PERFECTER
Ps 19: 8 The law of the LORD is **p**,
Mt 5:48 So be **p**, just as your heavenly
      5:48 **p**, just as your heavenly Father is **p**.
Ro 12: 2 what is good and pleasing and **p**.
2Co 12: 9 for power is made **p** in weakness."
Heb 5: 9 and when he was made **p**,
1Jn 4:18 **p** love drives out fear because fear
      4:18 and so one who fears is not yet **p**

PERFECTER → PERFECT
Heb 12: 2 on Jesus, the leader and **p** of faith.

PERISH → PERISHABLE
Jos 23:13 until you **p** from this good land
Est 4:16 king, contrary to the law. If I **p**, I **p**!"
Jn 3:16 who believes in him might not **p**
2Pe 3: 9 not wishing that any should **p**

PERISHABLE → PERISH
1Co 9:25 They do it to win a **p** crown, but we
1Pe 1:23 not from **p** but from imperishable

PERSECUTE → PERSECUTED, PERSECUTION
Mt 5:44 and pray for those who **p** you,
Ro 12:14 Bless those who **p** [you],

PERSECUTED → PERSECUTE

Jn 15:20 master.' If they **p** me, they will

2Co 4: 9 **p**, but not abandoned; struck down,

2Ti 3:12 religiously in Christ Jesus will be **p**.

PERSECUTION → PERSECUTE

Mt 13:21 or **p** comes because of the word,

Ro 8:35 or distress, or **p**, or famine,

PERSEVERE

Ro 12:12 endure in affliction, **p** in prayer.

PERSIA

Ezr 1: 1 king of **P**, in order to fulfill

1: 1 the LORD inspired King Cyrus of **P**

PESTILENCE

Dt 32:24 and bitter **p**, And the teeth of wild

Ps 91: 6 Nor the **p** that roams in darkness,

PETER → = CEPHAS, = SIMON

Apostle, brother of Andrew, also called Simon (Mt 10:2; Mk 3:16; Lk 6:14; Ac 1:13), and Cephas (Jn 1:42). Confession of Christ (Mt 16:13-20; Mk 8:27-30; Lk 9:18-27). At transfiguration (Mt 17:1-8; Mk 9:2-8; Lk 9:28-36; 2Pe 1:16-18). Caught fish with coin (Mt 17:24-27). Denial of Jesus predicted (Mt 26:31-35; Mk 14:27-31; Lk 22:31-34; Jn 13:31-38). Denied Jesus (Mt 26:69-75; Mk 14:66-72; Lk 22:54-62; Jn 18:15-27). Commissioned by Jesus to shepherd his flock (Jn 21:15-23).

Speech at Pentecost (Ac 2). Healed beggar (Ac 3:1-10). Speech at temple (Ac 3:11-26), before Sanhedrin (Ac 4:1-22). In Samaria (Ac 8:14-25). Sent by vision to Cornelius (Ac 10). Announced salvation of Gentiles in Jerusalem (Ac 11; 15). Freed from prison (Ac 12). Inconsistency at Antioch (Gal 2:11-21). At Jerusalem Council (Ac 15).

PHARAOH → PHARAOH'S

Ge 41:14 **P** therefore had Joseph summoned,

Ex 3:11 "Who am I that I should go to **P**

14:17 I will receive glory through **P**

Ro 9:17 For the scripture says to **P**, "This is

PHARAOH'S → PHARAOH

Heb 11:24 be known as the son of **P** daughter;

PHARISEE → PHARISEES

Lk 11:37 a **P** invited him to dine at his home.

Jn 3: 1 there was a **P** named Nicodemus,

Ac 5:34 But a **P** in the Sanhedrin named

Php 3: 5 in observance of the law a **P**,

PHARISEES → PHARISEE

Mt 5:20 surpasses that of the scribes and **P**,

16: 6 beware of the leaven of the **P**

23:13 you, scribes and **P**, you hypocrites.

PHILEMON

Phm 1: 1 brother, to **P**, our beloved and our

PHILIP

1. Apostle (Mt 10:3; Mk 3:18; Lk 6:14; Jn 1:43-48; 14:8; Ac 1:13).

2. Deacon (Ac 6:1-7); evangelist in Samaria (Ac 8:4-25), to Ethiopian (Ac 8:26-40).

PHILISTINE → PHILISTINES

1Sa 17:37 me safe from the clutches of this **P**."

PHILISTINES → PHILISTINE

Ge 26: 1 Abimelech, king of the **P** in Gerar.

1Sa 5: 1 The **P**, having captured the ark

17: 1 The **P** rallied their forces for battle

2Sa 8: 1 After this David attacked the **P**

8: 1 them, wresting . . . from the **P**.

Am 1: 8 and the last of the **P** shall perish,

PHILOSOPHERS → PHILOSOPHY

Ac 17:18 Stoic **p** engaged him in discussion.

PHILOSOPHY → PHILOSOPHERS

Col 2: 8 seductive **p** according to human

PHINEHAS

1. Grandson of Aaron (Ex 6:25; Jos 22:30-32). Zeal for the LORD (Nu 25:7-13; Ps 106:30).

2. A wicked priest (1Sa 1:3; 2:12-17; 4:1-19).

PHOEBE

Ro 16: 1 I commend to you **P** our sister,

PHYSICAL

1Ti 4: 8 while **p** training is of limited value,

PHYSICIAN

Mt 9:12 "Those who are well do not need a **p**,

Col 4:14 Luke the beloved **p** sends greetings,

PIECES

Ge 15:17 which passed between those **p**.

Lk 20:18 on that stone will be dashed to **p**;

PIERCED

Jn 19:37 look upon him whom they have **p**."

Rev 1: 7 him, even those who **p** him.

PIG

Dt 14: 8 and the **p**, which indeed has hoofs

PILATE

Governor of Judea. Questioned Jesus (Mt 27:1-26; Mk 15:15; Lk 22:66-23:25; Jn 18:28-19:16); sent him to Herod (Lk 23:6-12); consented to his crucifixion when crowds chose Barabbas (Mt 27:15-26; Mk 15:6-15; Lk 23:13-25; Jn 19:1-10).

PILLAR

Ge 19:26 and she was turned into a **p** of salt.

PIT

Ps 103: 4 Delivers your life from the **p**,

PITY

Dt 7:16 You are not to look on them with **p**,

Hos 1: 6 I no longer feel **p** for the house

PLACE → PLACES

Ex 26:33 divides the holy **p** from the holy

Ps 24: 3 LORD? Who can stand in his holy **p**?

Jn 14: 3 And if I go and prepare a **p** for you,

PLACES → PLACE

Lev 26:30 I will demolish your high **p**,

Ps 78:58 They enraged him with their high **p**;

PLAGUE → PLAGUES

Zec 14:12 this shall be the **p**

Rev 11: 6 with any **p** as often as they wish.

PLAGUES → PLAGUE

Hos 13:14 death? Where are your **p**, O death!

Rev 15: 1 seven angels with the seven last **p**,

22:18 to him the **p** described in this book,

PLAIN

Ge 13:12 settled among the cities of the **P**,

Isa 40: 4 The rugged land shall be made a **p**,

PLANNED

Isa 46:11 it; I have **p** it, and I will do it.

PLANT → PLANTED

Ge 1:29 you every seed-bearing **p** all over

Ecc 3: 2 a time to **p**, and a time to uproot

3: 2 time to **p**, and a time to uproot the **p**.

PLANTED → PLANT

Ge 2: 8 the LORD God **p** a garden in Eden,

Ps 1: 3 like a tree **p** near streams of water,

1Co 3: 6 I **p**, Apollos watered, but God

PLEASE → PLEASED, PLEASES, PLEASING, PLEASURE

Ps 69:32 My song will **p** the LORD more than

Sir 2:16 who fear the LORD seek to **p** him,

Ro 8: 8 who are in the flesh cannot **p** God.

15: 3 For Christ did not **p** himself; but,

1Co 10:33 just as I try to **p** everyone in every

1Th 4: 1 you should conduct yourselves to **p**

Heb 11: 6 faith it is impossible to **p** him,

PLEASED → PLEASE

Mic 6: 7 Will the LORD be **p** with thousands

Mt 3:17 Son, with whom I am well **p**."

PLEASED → PLEASE (*cont.*)
Col 1:19 him all the fullness was **p** to dwell,
2Pe 1:17 beloved, with whom I am well **p**."

PLEASES → PLEASE
1Jn 3:22 commandments and do what **p** him.

PLEASING → PLEASE
Ps 104:34 May my theme be **p** to God; I will
Eph 5:10 Try to learn what is **p** to the Lord.
Php 4:18 an acceptable sacrifice, **p** to God.

PLEASURE → PLEASE
Pr 21:17 He who loves **p** will suffer want;
Eze 18:32 For I have no **p** in the death
2Ti 3: 4 lovers of **p** rather than lovers

PLOWSHARES
Isa 2: 4 They shall beat their swords into **p**

PLUNDER
Eze 39:10 Thus they shall **p** those who

POISON
Jas 3: 8 It is a restless evil, full of deadly **p**.

POLE → POLES
Nu 21: 8 "Make a saraph and mount it on a **p**,
Dt 16:21 "You shall not plant a sacred **p**

POLES → POLE
2Ki 17:10 sacred **p** for themselves on every

POOR → POVERTY
1Sa 2: 8 from the ash heap he lifts up the **p**,
Ps 113: 7 dust, lifts the **p** from the ash heap,
Pr 19:22 shame; rather be a **p** man than a liar.
Mt 5: 3 "Blessed are the **p** in spirit, for theirs
Mk 10:21 give to [the] **p** and you will have
12:42 A **p** widow also came and put
Jn 12: 8 You always have the **p** with you,
2Co 6:10 rejoicing; as **p** yet enriching many;
2Co 8: 9 sake he became **p** although he was
Jas 2: 5 Did not God choose those who are **p**

PORTION
Dt 32: 9 While the LORD's own **p** was Jacob,
Ps 142: 6 my **p** in the land of the living.
La 3:24 My **p** is the LORD, says my soul;

POSSESS → POSSESSED, POSSESSION, POSSESSIONS
Isa 60:21 they shall always **p** the land, They,

POSSESSED → POSSESS
Mt 8:16 they brought him many who were **p**

POSSESSION → POSSESS
Ex 19: 5 you shall be my special **p**,
Jos 1:11 take **p** of the land which the LORD.
Ps 2: 8 nations, your **p** the ends of the earth.

POSSESSIONS → POSSESS
Lk 12:15 rich, one's life does not consist of **p**."

POSSIBLE
Mt 19:26 but for God all things are **p**."
26:39 if it is **p**, let this cup pass from me;

POTIPHAR
Egyptian who bought Joseph (Ge 37:36; 39:1-6), sent him to prison (Ge 39:7-30).

POTTER → POTTER'S
Sir 33:13 Like clay in the hands of a **p**, to be
Ro 9:21 does not the **p** have a right over

POTTER'S → POTTER
Jer 18: 2 Rise up, be off to the **p** house;
Mt 27: 7 it to buy the **p** field as a burial place

POUR → POURED
Dt 12:16 but must **p** it out on the ground like
Isa 44: 3 I will **p** out water upon the thirsty
44: 3 I will **p** out my spirit upon your
Ac 2:17 'that I will **p** out a portion of my
Rev 16: 1 **p** out the seven bowls of God's fury

POURED → POUR
Eze 39:29 for I have **p** out my spirit
Ac 2:33 Spirit from the Father and **p** it forth,
Ro 5: 5 the love of God has been **p**
Tit 3: 6 whom he richly **p** out on us

POVERTY → POOR
Pr 30: 8 me, give me neither **p** nor riches;
Sir 11:14 **p** and riches, are from the LORD.
Mk 12:44 from her **p**, has contributed all she
2Co 8: 9 by his **p** you might become rich.

POWER → POWERFUL, POWERS
Ex 9:16 to show you my **p** and to make my
15: 6 hand, O LORD, magnificent in **p**,
1Ch 29:11 "Yours, O LORD, are grandeur and **p**,
Jdt 9:14 clearly that you are the God of all **p**
Ps 68:35 Confess the **p** of God,
68:35 Israel, whose **p** is in the sky.
Pr 18:21 and life are in the **p** of the tongue;

Mt 22:29 know the scriptures or the **p** of God.
Mk 13:26 coming in the clouds' with great **p**
Ro 1:20 his invisible attributes of eternal **p**
1Co 15:24 and every authority and **p**.
Eph 1:19 of his **p** for us who believe,
Php 3:10 him and the **p** of his resurrection
2Ti 3: 5 a pretense of religion but deny its **p**.
2Pe 1: 3 His divine **p** has bestowed on us
1: 3 called us by his own glory and **p**.
Rev 20: 6 second death has no **p** over these;

POWERFUL → POWER
1Co 1:26 not many were **p**, not many were

POWERS → POWER
Ro 8:38 things, nor future things, nor **p**,
Eph 6:12 with the **p**, with the world rulers

PRACTICE → PRACTICES
Sir 50:29 If he puts them into **p**, he can cope
Mt 23: 3 For they preach but they do not **p**.

PRACTICES → PRACTICE
Col 3: 9 have taken off the old self with its **p**

PRAISE → PRAISED, PRAISES
Ex 15: 2 He is my God, I **p** him; the God
Tob 12: 6 God! Give him the **p** and the glory.
Ps 56: 5 God, I **p** your promise; in you I
150: 6 that has breath give **p** to the LORD!
Pr 27: 2 Let another **p** you—not your own
31:31 let her works **p** her at the city gates.
Mt 21:16 nurslings you have brought forth **p**'?"
1Co 14:15 I will sing **p** with the spirit, but I
14:15 but I will also sing **p** with the mind.
Rev 19: 5 "**P** our God, all you his servants,

PRAISED → PRAISE
Ps 48: 2 Great is the LORD and highly **p**

PRAISES → PRAISE
Sir 24: 1 Wisdom sings her own **p**, before her

PRAY → PRAYED, PRAYER, PRAYERS, PRAYING, PRAYS
1Sa 12:23 the LORD by ceasing to **p** for you
2Ch 7:14 humble themselves and **p**, and seek
Ps 5: 3 king, my God! To you I **p**, O LORD;
122: 6 For the peace of Jerusalem **p**:
Sir 37:15 Most important of all, **p** to God

Mt   5:44 and **p** for those who persecute you,

       6: 5 "When you **p**, do not be like

       6: 5 to stand and **p** in the synagogues

Lk 11: 1 to **p** just as John taught his disciples."

Ro 8:26 do not know how to **p** as we ought,

1Co 14:15 I will **p** with the spirit, but I will

    14:15 but I will also **p** with the mind.

1Th 5:17 **P** without ceasing.

Jas 5:16 one another and **p** for one another,

PRAYED → PRAY

Mk 1:35 off to a deserted place, where he **p**.

    14:35 **p** that if it were possible the hour

PRAYER → PRAY

Ps 6:10 The Lᴏʀᴅ has heard my **p**; the Lᴏʀᴅ

Pr 15:29 but the **p** of the just he hears.

Isa 56: 7 and make joyful in my house of **p**;

    56: 7 called a house of **p** for all peoples.

Mt 21:13 'My house shall be a house of **p**,'

Mk 11:24 all that you ask for in **p**,

Ro 12:12 endure in affliction, persevere in **p**.

Jas 5:16 The fervent **p** of a righteous person

PRAYERS → PRAY

Mk 12:40 and, as a pretext, recite lengthy **p**.

Heb 5: 7 he offered **p** and supplications

Rev 5: 8 which are the **p** of the holy ones.

PRAYING → PRAY

2Ma 15:12 was **p** with outstretched arms

PRAYS → PRAY

2Ma 15:14 and fervently **p** for his people

PREACHING

1Ti 5:17 especially those who toil in **p**

PRECEPTS

Ps 19: 9 The **p** of the Lᴏʀᴅ are right,

  119:15 I will ponder your **p** and consider

Mt 15: 9 me, teaching as doctrines human **p**.' "

PRECIOUS

Ps 72:14 for **p** is their blood in his sight.

Pr 3:15 She is more **p** than corals, and none

Isa 28:16 tested, A **p** cornerstone as a sure

1Pe 1:19 with the **p** blood of Christ as

    2: 6 a cornerstone, chosen and **p**,

PREDESTINED

Ro 8:30 And those he **p** he also called;

PREPARE → PREPARED

Mal 3: 1 to **p** the way before me;

Mt 3: 3 in the desert, '**P** the way of the Lord,

Jn 14: 2 that I am going to **p** a place for you?

PREPARED → PREPARE

1Co 2: 9 what God has **p** for those who love

PRESENCE → PRESENT

Ps 51:13 Do not drive me from your **p**,

  139: 7 From your **p**, where can I flee?

PRESENT → PRESENCE

Ro 6:13 do not **p** the parts of your bodies

    6:13 **p** yourselves to God as raised

1Co 3:22 life or death, or the **p** or the future:

Eph 5:27 he might **p** to himself the church

2Ti 2:15 Be eager to **p** yourself as acceptable

PREVAIL

1Sa 2: 9 For not by strength does man **p**;

PRICE

Mt 27: 9 value of a man with a **p** on his head,

    27: 9 a **p** set by some of the Israelites,

1Co 6:20 For you have been purchased at a **p**.

PRIDE → PROUD

Pr 16:18 **P** goes before disaster,

Sir 10:13 For **p** is the reservoir of sin,

PRIEST → PRIESTHOOD, PRIESTS

Ge 14:18 and being a **p** of God Most High,

Ex 2:16 daughters of a **p** of Midian came

Ps 110: 4 Melchizedek you are a **p** forever."

Mk 14:63 At that the high **p** tore his garments

Heb 3: 1 and high **p** of our confession,

    5:10 God high **p** according to the order

    7: 3 Son of God, he remains a **p** forever.

  10:21 we have "a great **p** over the house

PRIESTHOOD → PRIEST

Ex 29: 9 them. Thus shall the **p** be theirs

Heb 7:24 has a **p** that does not pass away.

1Pe 2: 5 to be a holy **p** to offer spiritual

PRIESTS → PRIEST

Ex 28: 1 to you, that they may be my **p**.

Dt 31: 9 it to the livitical **p** who carry the ark

Mic 3:11 her **p** give decisions for a salary,

Mk 15: 3 The chief **p** accused him of many

Heb 7:27 as did the high **p**, to offer sacrifice

Rev 20: 6 they will be **p** of God and of Christ,

PRINCE → PRINCES

Eze 37:25 my servant David their **p** forever.

Da 10:21 all these except Michael, your **p**,

PRINCES → PRINCE

Da 8:25 he rises against the prince of **p**,

PRISCILLA

Wife of Aquila, also called Prisca; co-worker with Paul (Ac 18; Ro 16:3; 1Co 16:19; 2Ti 4:19); instructor of Apollos (Ac 18:24-28).

PRISON → PRISONER, PRISONERS

Ge 39:20 But even while he was in **p**,

Mt 14:10 and he had John beheaded in the **p**.

Ac 12: 5 Peter thus was being kept in **p**,

PRISONER → PRISON

Mk 15: 6 to them one **p** whom they requested.

Eph 3: 1 I, Paul, a **p** of Christ [Jesus] for you

PRISONERS → PRISON

Ps 146: 7 the hungry. The Lᴏʀᴅ sets **p** free;

Isa 61: 1 to the captives and release to the **p**,

PRIZE

1Co 9:24 in the race, but only one wins the **p**?

Php 3:14 goal, the **p** of God's upward calling,

PROCLAIM

Ps 97: 6 The heavens **p** God's justice;

Mt 10:27 hear whispered, **p** on the housetops.

Mk 16:15 and **p** the gospel to every creature.

Lk 4:19 to **p** a year acceptable to the Lord."

PRODUCE → PRODUCES

Jos 5:11 they ate of the **p** of the land

Pr 3: 9 wealth, with first fruits of all your **p**;

PRODUCES → PRODUCE

2Co 7:10 For godly sorrow **p** a salutary

    7:10 regret, but worldly sorrow **p** death.

Jas 1: 3 testing of your faith **p** perseverance.

PROFANE

Lev 22:32 and do not **p** my holy name;

1Ma 1:45 to **p** the sabbaths and feast days,

PROFIT

Sir 29:11 that will **p** you more than the gold.

Mt 16:26 What **p** would there be for one

PROMISE → PROMISED, PROMISES

Ac 2:39 For the **p** is made to you and to your

Eph 2:12 and strangers to the covenants of **p**,

1Ti 4: 8 since it holds a **p** of life both

2Pe 3: 9 The Lord does not delay his **p**,

PROMISED → PROMISE

Dt 1:11 times over, and bless you as he **p**!

PROMISED → PROMISE (*cont.*)
Eph　1:13　were sealed with the **p** holy Spirit,

PROMISES → PROMISE
Ps　12: 7　The **p** of the LORD are sure,
2Co　1:20　For however many are the **p** of God,
Heb　8: 6　better covenant, enacted on better **p**.

PROOFS
Ac　1: 3　by many **p** after he had suffered,

PROPHECIES → PROPHESY
1Co 13: 8　If there are **p**, they will be brought

PROPHECY → PROPHESY
Ac　21: 9　four virgin daughters gifted with **p**.
1Co 12:10　to another **p**; to another discernment
2Pe　1:20　that there is no **p** of scripture that is

PROPHESY → PROPHECIES, PROPHECY, PROPHET, PROPHETS
Mt　7:22　Lord, did we not **p** in your name?
1Co 13: 9　know partially and we **p** partially,
Rev 11: 3　commission my two witnesses to **p**

PROPHET → PROPHESY
Ex　7: 1　your brother shall act as your **p**.
Dt　18:18　for them a **p** like you from among
1Ma　4:46　until a **p** should come and decide
Lk　4:24　no **p** is accepted in his own native
　　　20: 6　are convinced that John was a **p**.”
Rev 16:13　and from the mouth of the false **p**.
　　　20:10　the beast and the false **p** were.

PROPHETS → PROPHESY
Nu　11:29　all the people of the LORD were **p**!
1Ki 18:40　said to them, “Seize the **p** of Baal.
1Ma　9:27　in Israel since the time **p** ceased
Ps　105:15　my anointed, to my **p** do no harm.”
Mt　5:17　come to abolish the law or the **p**.
　　　22:40　law and the **p** depend on these two
Lk　24:44　and in the **p** and psalms must be
1Co 12:28　apostles; second, **p**; third, teachers;
Eph　2:20　the foundation of the apostles and **p**,
　　　4:11　others as **p**, others as evangelists,
Rev 11:10　because these two **p** tormented
　　　18:20　you holy ones, apostles, and **p**.

PROSPERITY → PROSPERS
Dt　30:15　have today set before you life and **p**,
Ps　73: 3　when I saw the **p** of the wicked.
Isa　48:18　your **p** would be like a river,

PROSPERS → PROSPERITY
Ps　1: 3　never wither; whatever they do **p**.

PROSTITUTE → PROSTITUTES
1Co　6:15　and make them the members of a **p**?

PROSTITUTES → PROSTITUTE
Mt　21:31　**p** are entering the kingdom of God
1Co　6: 9　adulterers nor boy **p** nor practicing

PROTECTS
Jdt　9:14　there is no other who **p** the people
Ps　116: 6　The LORD **p** the simple; I was

PROUD → PRIDE
Ps　94: 2　earth; give the **p** what they deserve.
Pr　21: 4　Haughty eyes and a **p** heart—
Sir　10: 9　Why are dust and ashes **p**?
Jas　4: 6　“God resists the **p**, but gives grace

PROVERBS
Pr　1: 1　The **p** of Solomon, the son
Ecc 12: 9　scrutinized and arranged many **p**.

PROVIDE → PROVIDES
Ge　22: 8　“God himself will **p** the sheep
1Co 10:13　the trial he will also **p** a way out,

PROVIDES → PROVIDE
1Ti　6:17　who richly **p** us with all things

PROVOKE → PROVOKED
Dt　32:21　I will **p** them with a ‘no-people’;
Jer　25: 6　lest you **p** me with your handiwork,

PROVOKED → PROVOKE
Ps　78:41　God, **p** the Holy One of Israel.

PRUNES
Jn　15: 2　does he **p** so that it bears more fruit.

PSALMS
Lk　24:44　the prophets and **p** must be fulfilled.”
Eph　5:19　addressing one another [in] **p**

PUBLIC
Col　2:15　he made a **p** spectacle of them,

PUNISH → PUNISHMENT
Ex　32:34　When it is time for me to **p**, I will **p**
Jer　21:14　I will **p** you, says the LORD, as your

PUNISHMENT → PUNISH
Ge　4:13　the LORD: “My **p** is too great to bear.
Mt　25:46　And these will go off to eternal **p**,

1Jn　4:18　fear because fear has to do with **p**,

PURE → PURIFICATION, PURIFIED, PURITY
Ps　19:10　The fear of the LORD is **p**,
Hab　1:13　Too **p** are your eyes to look
Php　4: 8　whatever is **p**, whatever is lovely,
1Jn　3; 3　hope based on him makes himself **p**,
　　　3: 3　on him makes himself **p**, as he is **p**.

PURIFICATION → PURE
Heb　1: 3　he had accomplished **p** from sins,

PURIFIED → PURE
Da　12:10　Many shall be refined, **p**, and tested,
1Pe　1:22　Since you have **p** yourselves

PURIM
Est　9:26　so these days have been named **P**

PURITY → PURE
2Co　6: 6　by **p**, knowledge, patience,

PURPLE
Ex　25: 4　violet, **p** and scarlet yarn; fine linen
Mk　15:17　They clothed him in **p** and,

PURPOSE
Isa　46:10　stand, I accomplish my every **p**.
Ro　8:28　who are called according to his **p**.
Eph　3:11　the eternal **p** that he accomplished

PURSUE → PURSUED, PURSUES
Ps　34:15　and do good; seek peace and **p** it.
Ro　14:19　Let us then **p** what leads to peace
1Ti　6:11　Instead, **p** righteousness, devotion,

PURSUED → PURSUE
Ps　18:38　I **p** my enemies and overtook them;

PURSUES → PURSUE
Pr　21:21　He who **p** justice and kindness
Sir　31: 5　for he who **p** wealth is led astray

PUT
Isa　42: 1　Upon whom I have **p** my spirit;
Eze　36:27　I will **p** my spirit within you
Eph　6:11　**P** on the armor of God so that you

Q

QUARRELED
Ex　17: 7　because the Israelites **q** there

QUEEN
1Ki 10: 1　The **q** of Sheba, having heard
Est　2:17　and made her **q** in place of Vashti.
Mt　12:42　the judgment the **q** of the south will
Rev 18: 7　‘I sit enthroned as **q**; I am no widow,

QUESTIONS
2Ch 9: 1 Jerusalem to test him with subtle **q**,
Mt 22:46 anyone dare to ask him any more **q**.

QUICK → QUICKLY
Jas 1:19 everyone should be **q** to hear,

QUICKLY → QUICK
Jn 13:27 "What you are going to do, do **q**."
Ro 9:28 **q** will the Lord execute sentence
Gal 1: 6 you are so **q** forsaking the one who

QUIET
1Ti 2: 2 that we may lead a **q** and tranquil

QUIVER
Isa 49: 2 a polished arrow, in his **q** he hid me.

R

RABBI
Mt 23: 8 As for you, do not be called '**R**.'
Jn 1:38 to him, "**R**" (which translated means

RACE
Ecc 9:11 under the sun that the **r** is not won
1Co 9:24 in the stadium all run in the **r**,
Heb 12: 1 in running the **r** that lies before us
1Pe 2: 9 But you are "a chosen **r**, a royal

RACHEL
Daughter of Laban (Ge 29:16); wife of Jacob (Ge 29:28); bore two sons (Ge 30:22-24; 35:16-24; 46:19). Stole Laban's gods (Ge 31:19, 32-35). Death (Ge 35:19-20).

RAHAB
Prostitute who hid Israelite spies (Jos 2; 6:22-25; Heb 11:31; Jas 2:25). Mother of Boaz (Mt 1:5).

RAIN → RAINED, RAINS
Ge 7: 4 now I will bring **r** down on the earth
1Ki 17: 1 be no dew or **r** except at my word."
Isa 45: 8 like gentle **r** let the skies drop it
Mt 5:45 and causes **r** to fall on the just
Rev 11: 6 so that no **r** can fall during the time

RAINED → RAIN
Ge 19:24 time the LORD **r** down sulphurous
Ex 9:23 the LORD **r** down hail upon the land

RAINS → RAIN
Jas 5: 7 it receives the early and the late **r**.

RAISE → RISE
Dt 18:15 **r** up for you from among your own
2Ma 7: 9 the King of the world will **r** us

Jn 2:19 and in three days I will **r** it up."
2Co 4:14 who raised the Lord Jesus will **r** us

RAISED → RISE
Mt 17:23 and he will be **r** on the third day."
Ac 2:24 But God **r** him up, releasing him
Ro 4:25 and was **r** for our justification.
1Co 15: 4 that he was **r** on the third day

RAM → RAMS
Ge 22:13 he spied a **r** caught by its horns
22:13 and took the **r** and offered it up as
Ex 29:22 from this **r** you shall take its fat:
29:22 thigh, since this is the ordination **r**;
Da 8: 3 the river a **r** with two great horns,

RAMS → RAM
1Sa 15:22 and submission than the fat of **r**.

RANSOM → RANSOMED
Mt 20:28 and to give his life as a **r** for many."
1Ti 2: 6 who gave himself as **r** for all.

RANSOMED → RANSOM
Isa 35:10 whom the LORD has **r** will return

RAVENS
1Ki 17: 6 **R** brought him bread and meat
Lk 12:24 Notice the **r**: they do not sow

READ → READING
Ex 24: 7 he **r** it aloud to the people,
Jos 8:34 were **r** aloud all the words
Ne 8: 8 Ezra **r** plainly from the book
8: 8 all could understand what was **r**.
Lk 4:16 on the sabbath day. He stood up to **r**
2Co 3:15 whenever Moses is **r**, a veil lies

READING → READ
Ac 8:30 and heard him **r** Isaiah the prophet
8:30 "Do you understand what you are **r**?"

READY
Rev 19: 7 come, his bride has made herself **r**.

REAP
Gal 6: 7 a person will **r** only what he sows,
Rev 14:15 "Use your sickle and **r** the harvest,
14:15 for the time to **r** has come,

REBEKAH
Sister of Laban, secured as bride for Isaac (Ge 24). Mother of Esau and Jacob (Ge 25:19-26). Taken by Abimelech as sister of Isaac; returned (Ge 26:1-11). Encouraged Jacob to trick Isaac out of blessing (Ge 27:1-17).

REBEL → REBELLED, REBELLION
Ex 23:21 Do not **r** against him, for he will not
1Sa 12:14 him and do not **r** against the LORD's

REBELLED → REBEL
Nu 20:24 because you both **r** against my

REBELLION → REBEL
1Sa 15:23 For a sin like divination is **r**,

REBUILD → BUILD
Ne 2:17 let us **r** the wall of Jerusalem,
Ac 15:16 and **r** the fallen hut of David;
15:16 from its ruins I shall **r** it and raise it

REBUKE
Pr 27: 5 Better is an open **r** than a love
Zec 3: 2 Satan, "May the LORD **r** you, Satan;
3: 2 who has chosen Jerusalem **r** you!
Mk 8:32 took him aside and began to **r** him.

RECEIVE → RECEIVED
Jn 3:27 "No one can **r** anything except what
16:24 ask and you will **r**, so that your joy
20:22 and said to them, "**R** the holy Spirit.
Ac 2:38 you will **r** the gift of the holy Spirit.
20:35 'It is more blessed to give than to **r**.' "
1Co 4: 7 you boasting as if you did not **r** it?
Rev 4:11 to **r** glory and honor and power,

RECEIVED → RECEIVE
Mt 6: 2 say to you, they have **r** their reward.
1Co 11:23 For I **r** from the Lord what I

RECONCILE → RECONCILED, RECONCILIATION
Ac 7:26 and tried to **r** them peacefully,
Col 1:20 through him to **r** all things for him,

RECONCILED → RECONCILE
Mt 5:24 go first and be **r** with your brother,
1Co 7:11 remain single or become **r** to her

RECONCILIATION → RECONCILE
Ro 5:11 whom we have now received **r**.
2Co 5:18 and given us the ministry of **r**,

RED
Ex 15: 4 were submerged in the **R** Sea.
Mt 16: 3 for the sky is **r** and threatening.'
Rev 12: 3 it was a huge **r** dragon, with seven

REDEEMED → REDEMPTION
2Sa 7:23 which you **r** for yourself
Ps 107: 2 Let that be the prayer of the LORD's **r**,
107: 2 **r**, those **r** from the hand of the foe,

REDEEMER → REDEMPTION

Ps   19:15   you, Lord, my rock and my **r**.
Isa   48:17   Thus says the Lord, your **r**, the Holy

REDEMPTION → REDEEMED, REDEEMER

Lk   21:28   raise your heads because your **r** is
Ro   3:24   by his grace through the **r** in Christ
Eph   1: 7   In him we have **r** by his blood,
Heb   9:12   own blood, thus obtaining eternal **r**.

REFINE → REFINED

Zec   13: 9   and I will **r** them as silver is refined,

REFINED → REFINE

Da   12:10   Many shall be **r**, purified,

REFUGE

Nu   35:11   unintentionally may take **r**.
Pr   30: 5   a shield to those who take **r** in him.
Jer   16:19   fortress, my **r** in the day of distress!

REGARD

Php   2: 6   of God, did not **r** equality with God

REGULATIONS

Col   2:20   why do you submit to **r** as if you
Heb   9:10   **r** concerning the flesh,

REHOBOAM

Son of Solomon (1Ki 11:43; 1Ch 3:10). Harsh treatment of subjects caused divided kingdom (1Ki 12:1-24; 14:21-31; 2Ch 10-12).

REIGN

Ex   15:18   The Lord shall **r** forever and ever.
Ps   146:10   The Lord shall **r** forever, your God,
1Co   15:25   For he must **r** until he has put all his
2Ti   2:12   we shall also **r** with him. But if we
Rev   11:15   and he will **r** forever and ever."
       22: 5   and they shall **r** forever and ever.

REJECT → REJECTED

Isa   30:12   of Israel: Because you **r** this word,

REJECTED → REJECT

Ps   60: 3   O God, you **r** us, broke our
      118:22   The stone the builders **r** has become
Mt   21:42   'The stone that the builders **r**
1Pe   2: 4   by human beings but chosen

REJOICE → REJOICING

Ps   118:24   has made; let us **r** in it and be glad.
Isa   62: 5   his bride so shall your God **r** in you.
Zep   3:17   He will **r** over you with gladness,
Lk   6:23   **R** and leap for joy on that day!
Php   4: 4   **R** in the Lord always. I shall say it

Php   4: 4   Lord always. I shall say it again: **r**!

REJOICING → REJOICE

2Co   6:10   as sorrowful yet always **r**; as poor

RELEASE

Isa   61: 1   the captives and **r** to the prisoners,
Mt   27:15   the governor was accustomed to **r**

RELENT

Joel   2:14   Perhaps he will again **r** and leave
Jnh   3: 9   knows, God may **r** and forgive,

RELIGION

Jas   1:27   **R** that is pure and undefiled before

RELY

Pr   3: 5   on your own intelligence **r** not;
Sir   5: 1   **R** not on your wealth; say not:

REMAIN → REMAINS

1Co   7:20   Everyone should **r** in the state
Heb   1:11   They will perish, but you **r**;

REMAINS → REMAIN

Heb   7: 3   Son of God, he **r** a priest forever.
      10:26   there no longer **r** sacrifice for sins

REMEMBER → REMEMBERED

Ex   20: 8   "**R** to keep holy the sabbath day.
Dt   8:18   **R** then, it is the Lord, your God,
Job   10: 9   **r** that you fashioned me from clay!
Ecc   12: 1   **R** your Creator in the days of your
Jer   31:34   evildoing and **r** their sin no more.
2Ti   2: 8   **R** Jesus Christ, raised from the dead,
Heb   8:12   evildoing and **r** their sins no more."

REMEMBERED → REMEMBER

Ps   78:35   They **r** that God was their rock,
      106:45   For their sake he **r** his covenant
Rev   16:19   But God **r** great Babylon, giving it

REMNANT

Ge   45: 7   of you to ensure for you a **r** on earth
Isa   10:21   A **r** will return, the **r** of Jacob,
Jer   50:20   for I will forgive the **r** I preserve.
Ro   9:27   of the sea, only a **r** will be saved;

RENEW → RENEWED

Isa   40:31   in the Lord will **r** their strength,

RENEWED → RENEW

2Co   4:16   our inner self is being **r** day by day.
Eph   4:23   and be **r** in the spirit of your minds,

REPAY → PAY

Ps   28: 4   **R** them for their deeds, for the evil
      28: 4   For the work of their hands **r** them;
Ro   12:17   Do not **r** anyone evil for evil;

REPENT → REPENTANCE

1Ki   8:47   may they **r** in the land of their
Job   42: 6   I have said, and **r** in dust and ashes.
Mt   3: 2   [and] saying, "**R**, for the kingdom
Ac   2:38   [said] to them, "**R** and be baptized,
Rev   16: 9   but they did not **r** or give him glory.

REPENTANCE → REPENT

Mk   1: 4   desert proclaiming a baptism of **r**
Lk   3: 8   good fruits as evidence of your **r**;
Ro   2: 4   of God would lead you to **r**?
2Co   7:10   produces a salutary **r** without regret,
2Pe   3: 9   perish but that all should come to **r**.

REPROVE

Rev   3:19   Those whom I love, I **r** and chastise.

RESCUE → RESCUES

Ps   22: 9   you; if he loves you, let him **r** you."
2Pe   2: 9   the Lord knows how to **r** the devout

RESCUES → RESCUE

Ps   37:40   The Lord helps and **r** them,

RESIST

Jas   4: 7   **R** the devil, and he will flee

RESPECT

Ro   13: 7   toll is due, **r** to whom **r** is due,

REST → RESTED

Ex   31:15   day is the sabbath of complete **r**,
2Sa   7:11   I will give you **r** from all your
Ps   95:11   anger: "They shall never enter my **r**."
Mt   11:28   are burdened, and I will give you **r**.
Heb   4:10   And whoever enters into God's **r**,

RESTED → REST

Ge   2: 2   he **r** on the seventh day from all
Ex   20:11   them; but on the seventh day he **r**.

RESTORE

Ps   51:14   **R** my joy in your salvation;
Mt   17:11   will indeed come and **r** all things;

RESURRECTION

Mt   22:30   At the **r** they neither marry nor are
Mk   12:18   who say there is no **r**, came to him
Jn   11:25   told her, "I am the **r** and the life;

1Co 15:12 some among you say there is no **r**

Php 3:10 the power of his **r** and [the] sharing

Rev 20: 5 years were over. This is the first **r**.

RETAIN

Jn 20:23 and whose sins you **r** are retained."

RETURN

Ge 3:19 to eat, Until you **r** to the ground,

3:19 you are dirt, and to dirt you shall **r**.

Dt 30: 2 you and your children **r** to the Lord,

Mal 3: 7 them. **R** to me, and I will **r** to you,

3: 7 hosts. Yet you say, "How must we **r**?"

REUBEN

Firstborn of Jacob by Leah (Ge 29:32; 46:8; 1Ch 2:1). Attempted to rescue Joseph (Ge 37:21-30). Lost birthright for sleeping with Bilhah (Ge 35:22; 49:4). Tribe of blessed (Ge 49:3-4; Dt 33:6), numbered (Nu 1:21; 26:7), allotted land east of Jordan (Nu 32; 34:14; Jos 13:15), west (Eze 48:6), failed to help Deborah (Jdg 5:15-16), supported David (1Ch 12:37), 12,000 from (Rev 7:5).

REVEAL → REVEALED, REVELATION, REVELATIONS

Mt 11:27 to whom the Son wishes to **r** him.

REVEALED → REVEAL

Isa 40: 5 the glory of the Lord shall be **r**,

Mt 16:17 and blood has not **r** this to you,

Lk 17:30 be on the day the Son of Man is **r**.

Ro 1:17 in it is **r** the righteousness of God

1Jn 3: 2 what we shall be has not yet been **r**.

3: 2 when it is **r** we shall be like him,

REVELATION → REVEAL

1Co 14: 6 if I do not speak to you by way of **r**,

Eph 3: 3 was made known to me by **r**, as I

Rev 1: 1 The **r** of Jesus Christ, which God

REVELATIONS → REVEAL

2Co 12: 1 go on to visions and **r** of the Lord.

REVERENCE

Eph 5:21 to one another out of **r** for Christ.

REWARD → REWARDED, REWARDS

Ps 19:12 obeying them brings much **r**.

Isa 40:10 strong arm; Here is his **r** with him,

Mt 6: 5 to you, they have received their **r**.

Lk 6:23 day! Behold, your **r** will be great

REWARDED → REWARD

2Sa 22:21 "The Lord **r** me according to my

REWARDS → REWARD

Heb 11: 6 and that he **r** those who seek him.

RIB

Ge 2:22 into a woman the **r** that he had taken

RICH → RICHES

Mt 19:23 one who is **r** to enter the kingdom

Lk 12:21 but is not **r** in what matters to God."

2Co 8: 9 he became poor although he was **r**,

8: 9 by his poverty you might become **r**.

Eph 2: 4 But God, who is **r** in mercy,

1Ti 6:18 good, to be **r** in good works, to be

Jas 1:10 and the **r** one in his lowliness, for he

RICHES → RICH

Pr 30: 8 me, give me neither poverty nor **r**;

Lk 8:14 are choked by the anxieties and **r**

Ro 11:33 the depth of the **r** and wisdom

RID

1Pe 2: 1 **R** yourselves of all malice and all

RIDER → RIDES, RIDING

Rev 19:11 its **r** was [called] "Faithful and True."

RIDES → RIDER

Dt 33:26 who **r** the heavens in his power,

33:26 and **r** the skies in his majesty;

RIDING → RIDER

Zec 9: 9 Meek, and **r** on an ass, on a colt,

RIGHT → BIRTHRIGHT

Ex 15: 6 Your **r** hand, O Lord,

15: 6 your **r** hand, O Lord, has shattered

Dt 6:18 Do what is **r** and good in the sight

Ps 110: 1 lord: "Take your throne at my **r** hand,

Pr 14:12 Sometimes a way seems **r** to a man,

Mt 25:33 He will place the sheep on his **r**

Ac 2:34 said to my Lord, "Sit at my **r** hand

Heb 1:13 "Sit at my **r** hand until I make your

RIGHTEOUS → RIGHTEOUSNESS

Job 4:17 "Can a man be **r** as against God?

Jer 23: 5 I will raise up a **r** shoot to David;

Mk 2:17 do. I did not come to call the **r**

Ro 1:17 "The one who is **r** by faith will live."

Ro 5:19 of one the many will be made **r**.

1Jn 2: 1 the Father, Jesus Christ the **r** one.

Rev 19: 8 (The linen represents the **r** deeds

RIGHTEOUSNESS → RIGHTEOUS

Ge 15: 6 who credited it to him as an act of **r**.

Mt 5: 6 are they who hunger and thirst for **r**,

Jn 16: 8 the world in regard to sin and **r**

Ro 3:22 the **r** of God through faith in Jesus

Gal 3: 6 God, and it was credited to him as **r**."

Eph 6:14 truth, clothed with **r** as a breastplate,

1Pe 2:24 free from sin, we might live for **r**.

2Pe 3:13 and a new earth in which **r** dwells.

Rev 19:11 True." He judges and wages war in **r**.

RIPE

Jn 4:35 and see the fields **r** for the harvest.

Rev 14:15 because the earth's harvest is fully **r**."

RISE → ARISE, RAISE, RAISED, ROSE

Nu 24:17 and a staff shall **r** from Israel,

2Ma 12:44 not expecting the fallen to **r** again,

Ps 94: 2 **R** up, judge of the earth;

Da 12:13 you shall **r** for your reward

1Th 4:16 and the dead in Christ will **r** first.

RIVER → RIVERS

Ps 46: 5 Streams of the **r** gladden the city

Isa 48:18 your prosperity would be like a **r**,

Eze 47:12 Along both banks of the **r**,

Mt 3: 6 the Jordan **R** as they acknowledged

Rev 22: 1 Then the angel showed me the **r**

RIVERS → RIVER

Ps 137: 1 By the **r** of Babylon we sat

Rev 8:10 It fell on a third of the **r**

ROAD → CROSSROADS

Mt 7:13 the **r** broad that leads to destruction,

ROARING → ROARS

1Pe 5: 8 around like a **r** lion looking

ROARS → ROARING

Hos 11:10 follow the Lord, who **r** like a lion;

11:10 lion; When he **r**, his sons shall come

Jer 25:30 The Lord **r** from on high,

25:30 Mightily he **r** over the range,

ROB → ROBBER

Mal 3: 8 Dare a man **r** God? Yet you are

3: 8 And you say, "How do we **r** you?"

ROBBER → ROB
1Co 5:11 or a **r**, not even to eat with such

ROBE → ROBED, ROBES
Ex 28: 4 an ephod, a **r**, a brocaded tunic,
Lk 15:22 'Quickly bring the finest **r** and put it
Rev 6:11 Each of them was given a white **r**,

ROBED → ROBE
Ps 93: 1 The LORD is king, **r** with majesty;
    93: 1 the LORD is **r**, girded with might.

ROBES → ROBE
Mk 12:38 who like to go around in long **r**
Rev 22:14 are they who wash their **r** so as

ROCK
Ex 17: 6 in front of you on the **r** in Horeb.
    17: 6 Strike the **r**, and the water will flow
Nu 20: 8 their presence order the **r** to yield its
    20: 8 the **r** you shall bring forth water
1Sa 2: 2 the LORD; there is no **R** like our God.
Ps 19:15 you, LORD, my **r** and my redeemer.
Isa 44: 8 Is there a God or any **R** besides me?
Mt 16:18 upon this **r** I will build my church.
Mk 15:46 that had been hewn out of the **r**.
1Pe 2: 8 and a **r** that will make them fall."

ROD
2Sa 7:14 I will correct him with the **r** of men
Ps 2: 9 an iron **r** you shall shepherd them,
    23: 4 your **r** and staff give me courage.
Pr 13:24 He who spares his **r** hates his son,
Rev 2:27 He will rule them with an iron **r**.

ROLL
Mk 16: 3 "Who will **r** back the stone for us

ROOF
Jos 2: 6 Now, she had led them to the **r**,
2Sa 11: 2 strolled about on the **r** of the palace.
    11: 2 the **r** he saw a woman bathing,
Mk 2: 4 they opened up the **r** above him.

ROOM
Mk 14:15 show you a large upper **r** furnished
Ro 12:19 revenge but leave **r** for the wrath;
Eph 4:27 and do not leave **r** for the devil.

ROOT → ROOTED
Isa 11:10 On that day, The **r** of Jesse,
Ro 11:16 and if the **r** is holy, so are
    15:12 says: "The **r** of Jesse shall come,
1Ti 6:10 love of money is the **r** of all evils,
Rev 5: 5 of the tribe of Judah, the **r** of David,

ROOTED → ROOT
Eph 3:17 that you, **r** and grounded in love,

ROSE → RISE
1Th 4:14 if we believe that Jesus died and **r**,

ROUGH
Isa 40: 4 plain, the **r** country, a broad valley.
Lk 3: 5 and the **r** ways made smooth,

ROYAL
Jas 2: 8 you fulfill the **r** law according
1Pe 2: 9 are "a chosen race, a **r** priesthood,

RUBBISH
1Co 4:13 We have become like the world's **r**,
Php 3: 8 and I consider them so much **r**,

RUINS
Ezr 9: 9 house of our God and restore its **r**,
Ne 2:17 how Jerusalem lies in **r** and its gates
Ac 15:16 from its **r** I shall rebuild it and raise

RULE → RULER, RULERS, RULES
Ps 110: 2 LORD says: "**R** over your enemies!
Rev 19:15 He will **r** them with an iron rod,

RULER → RULE
Ex 2:14 "Who has appointed you **r** and judge
Mt 2: 6 since from you shall come a **r**,
Rev 1: 5 dead and **r** of the kings of the earth.

RULERS → RULE
Isa 40:23 makes the **r** of the earth as nothing.
Eph 6:12 the world **r** of this present darkness,

RULES → RULE
Ps 66: 7 who **r** by might forever,
Isa 40:10 Lord GOD, who **r** by his strong arm;
2Ti 2: 5 by competing according to the **r**.

RUN → FORERUNNER, RUNNERS
Isa 40:31 They will **r** and not grow weary,
Gal 2: 2 not be running, or have **r**, in vain.

RUNNERS → RUN
1Co 9:24 that the **r** in the stadium all run

RUTH
 Moabitess; widow who went to Bethlehem with mother-in-law Naomi (Ru 1).

Gleaned in field of Boaz; shown favor (Ru 2). Proposed marriage to Boaz (Ru 3). Married (Ru 4:1-12); bore Obed, ancestor of David (Ru 4:13-22), Jesus (Mt 1:5).

S

SABBATH
Ex 20: 8 "Remember to keep holy the **s** day.
1Ma 1:43 to idols and profaned the **s**.
Mt 12: 1 through a field of grain on the **s**.
Mk 2:28 the Son of Man is lord even of the **s**."

SACKCLOTH
Da 9: 3 prayer, with fasting, **s**, and ashes.
Mt 11:21 would long ago have repented in **s**

SACRED
Ex 28: 2 you shall have **s** vestments made.
    34:13 smash their **s** pillars, and cut down
Ex 34:13 **s** pillars, and cut down their **s** poles.

SACRIFICE → SACRIFICED, SACRIFICES
Ex 12:27 'This is the Passover **s** of the LORD.
1Sa 15:22 Obedience is better than **s**,
Ps 40: 7 **S** and offering you do not want;
Pr 15: 8 The **s** of the wicked is
Da 9:27 he shall abolish **s** and oblation;
Hos 6: 6 For it is love that I desire, not **s**,
Mt 9:13 of the words, 'I desire mercy, not **s**.'
Php 4:18 an acceptable **s**, pleasing to God.
Heb 13:15 let us continually offer God a **s**

SACRIFICED → SACRIFICE
1Co 5: 7 paschal lamb, Christ, has been **s**.
    8: 1 Now in regard to meat **s** to idols:

SACRIFICES → SACRIFICE
Mk 12:33 more than all burnt offerings and **s**."

SADDUCEES
Mt 16: 6 of the leaven of the Pharisees and **S**."
Mk 12:18 Some **S**, who say there is no

SAFE
Pr 18:10 the just man runs to it and is **s**.

SALT
Ge 19:26 and she was turned into a pillar of **s**.
Mt 5:13 "You are the **s** of the earth. But if

SALVATION → SAVE
Ps 27: 1 The LORD is my light and my **s**;
    51:14 Restore my joy in your **s**;
Isa 12: 3 will draw water at the fountain of **s**,

Isa 52: 7 announcing **s**, and saying to Zion,

Lk 3: 6 and all flesh shall see the **s** of God.' "

Ac 4:12 There is no **s** through anyone else,

2Co 6: 2 and on the day of **s** I helped you."

6: 2 time; behold, now is the day of **s**.

Php 2:12 work out your **s** with fear

Heb 2: 3 we escape if we ignore so great a **s**?

2Pe 3:15 the patience of our Lord as **s**, as our

Rev 19: 1 **S**, glory, and might belong to our

SAMARIA → SAMARITAN

1Ki 16:24 bought the hill of **S** from Shemer

16:24 hill, naming the city he built **S**

2Ki 17: 6 the king of Assyria took **S**,

Jn 4: 4 He had to pass through **S**.

Ac 1: 8 throughout Judea and **S**,

SAMARITAN → SAMARIA

Lk 10:33 But a **S** traveler who came upon him

SAME

Ro 10:12 the **s** Lord is Lord of all,

1Co 12: 4 of spiritual gifts but the **s** Spirit;

Heb 13: 8 Jesus Christ is the **s** yesterday,

SAMSON

Danite judge. Birth promised (Jdg 13). Married a Philistine, but his wife given away (Jdg 14). Vengeance on the Philistines (Jdg 15). Betrayed by Delilah (Jdg 16:1-22). Death (Jdg 16:23-31). Feats of strength: killed lion (Jdg 14:6), 30 Philistines (Jdg 14:19), 1,000 Philistines with jawbone (Jdg 15:13-17), carried off gates of Gaza (Jdg 16:3), pushed down temple of Dagon (Jdg 16:25-30; Heb 11:32).

SAMUEL

Ephraimite judge and prophet (Heb 11:32). Birth prayed for (1Sa 1:10-18). Dedicated to temple by Hannah (1Sa 1:21-28). Raised by Eli (1Sa 2:11, 18-26). Called as prophet (1Sa 3). Led Israel to victory over Philistines (1Sa 7). Asked by Israel for a king (1Sa 8). Anointed Saul as king (1Sa 9-10). Farewell speech (1Sa 12). Rebuked Saul for sacrifice (1Sa 13). Announced rejection of Saul (1Sa 15). Anointed David as king (1Sa 16). Protected David from Saul (1Sa 19:18-24). Death (1Sa 25:1). Returned from dead to condemn Saul (1Sa 28).

SANCTIFICATION → SANCTIFIED

Ro 6:19 as slaves to righteousness for **s**.

SANCTIFIED → SANCTIFICATION

1Co 6:11 you were **s**, you were justified

SANCTUARY

Ex 25: 8 "They shall make a **s** for me, that I

1Ch 22:19 to build the **s** of the LORD God,

1Ma 1:21 He insolently invaded the **s** and took

4:36 let us go up to purify the **s**

Eze 37:26 and put my **s** among them forever.

Da 9:26 shall destroy the **s**. Then the end

Heb 9:24 Christ did not enter into a **s** made

SAND

Mt 7:26 like a fool who built his house on **s**.

SANDALS

Ex 3: 5 Remove the **s** from your feet,

Mt 3:11 I. I am not worthy to carry his **s**.

SARAH

1. Wife of Abraham, originally named Sarai; barren (Ge 11:29-31; 1Pe 3:6). Taken by Pharaoh as Abraham's sister; returned (Ge 12:10-20). Gave Hagar to Abraham; sent her away in pregnancy (Ge 16). Name changed; Isaac promised (Ge 17:15-21; 18:10-15; Heb 11:11). Taken by Abimelech as Abraham's sister; returned (Ge 20). Isaac born; Hagar and Ishmael sent away (Ge 21:1-21; Gal 4:21-31). Death (Ge 23).

2. Daughter of Raguel, wife of Tobias (Tob 3; 6-8; 10-12).

SATAN

1Ch 21: 1 A **s** rose up against Israel, and he

Job 1: 6 the LORD, **S** also came among them.

Zec 3: 2 And the angel of the LORD said to **S**,

3: 2 to **S**, "May the LORD rebuke you, **S**;

Mt 4:10 this, Jesus said to him, "Get away, **S**!

12:26 And if **S** drives out **S**, he is divided

16:23 and said to Peter, "Get behind me, **S**!

2Co 11:14 for even **S** masquerades as an angel

Rev 12: 9 who is called the Devil and **S**,

20: 7 **S** will be released from his prison.

SATISFY

Isa 55: 2 your wages for what fails to **s**?

SAUL → = PAUL

1. Benjamite; anointed by Samuel as first king of Israel (1Sa 9-10). Defeated Ammonites (1Sa 11). Rebuked for offering sacrifice (1Sa 13:1-15). Defeated Philistines (1Sa 14). Rejected as king for failing to annihilate Amalekites (1Sa 15). Soothed from evil spirit by David (1Sa 16:14-23). Sent David against Goliath (1Sa 17). Jealousy and attempted murder of David (1Sa 18:1-11). Gave David Michal as wife (1Sa 18:12-30). Second attempt to kill David (1Sa 19). Anger at Jonathan (1Sa 20:26-34). Pursued David: killed priests at Nob (1Sa 22), went to Keilah and Ziph (1Sa 23), life spared by David at En Gedi (1Sa 24) and in his tent (1Sa 26). Rebuked by Samuel's spirit for consulting witch at Endor (1Sa 28). Wounded by Philistines; took his own life (1Sa 31; 1Ch 10). Lamented by David (2Sa 1:17-27). Children (1Sa 14:49-51; 1Ch 8).

2. See Paul.

SAVE → SALVATION, SAVED, SAVIOR

Ps 54: 3 O God, by your name **s** me. By your

Isa 59: 1 of the LORD is not too short to **s**,

Mt 1:21 because he will **s** his people

16:25 wishes to **s** his life will lose it,

Lk 19:10 come to seek and to **s** what was lost."

Heb 7:25 **s** those who approach God through

SAVED → SAVE

Mt 10:22 endures to the end will be **s**.

Mk 15:31 themselves and said, "He **s** others;

Lk 13:23 "Lord, will only a few people be **s**?"

Ac 2:21 everyone shall be **s** who calls on

16:30 said, "Sirs, what must I do to be **s**?"

Ro 10:13 on the name of the Lord will be **s**."

Eph 2: 8 grace you have been **s** through faith,

SAVIOR → SAVE

Isa 49:26 that I, the LORD, am your **s**,

Hos 13: 4 me, and there is no **s** but me.

Lk 2:11 the city of David a **s** has been born

Ac 13:23 has brought to Israel a **s**, Jesus.

1Ti 4:10 the living God, who is the **s** of all,

Tit 2:13 great God and of our **s** Jesus Christ,

2Pe 3:18 of our Lord and **s** Jesus Christ.

SCARLET

Isa 1:18 Though your sins be like **s**,

Mt 27:28 threw a **s** military cloak about him.

SCATTER → SCATTERED

Dt 4:27 The LORD will **s** you among

SCATTERED → SCATTER

Dt 30: 3 all the nations wherein he has **s** you.

Jer 31:10 He who **s** Israel, now gathers them

SCEPTER

Ge 49:10 The **s** shall never depart from Judah,

Heb 1: 8 and a righteous **s** is the **s** of your

SCOFFERS

Ps 1: 1 sinners, nor sit in company with **s**.

2Pe 3: 3 the last days **s** will come [to] scoff,

SCRIBES

Mt 7:29 having authority, and not as their **s**.

23:13 "Woe to you, **s** and Pharisees,

SCRIPTURE → SCRIPTURES

Lk 4:21 "Today this **s** passage is fulfilled

Jn 10:35 came, and **s** cannot be set aside,

2Ti 3:16 All **s** is inspired by God and is

SCRIPTURES → SCRIPTURE
Mt 22:29 because you do not know the **s**
Lk 24:45 their minds to understand the **s**.
Jn   5:39 You search the **s**, because you think
1Co 15: 3 our sins in accordance with the **s**;

SCROLL
Lk   4:17 and was handed a **s** of the prophet
     4:17 He unrolled the **s** and found
Rev 5: 2 "Who is worthy to open the **s**

SEA
Ge   1:26 dominion over the fish of the **s**,
Ex 15: 1 and chariot he has cast into the **s**.
Dt 30:13 Nor is it across the **s**, that you
Dt 30:13 'Who will cross the **s** to get it for us
Ps 95: 5 The **s** and dry land belong to God,
Mic 7:19 into the depths of the **s** all our sins;
Rev 4: 6 resembled a **s** of glass like crystal.
    13: 1 come out of the **s** with ten horns
    21: 1 away, and the **s** was no more.

SEAL → SEALS
2Co 1:22 he has also put his **s** upon us
Rev 7: 3 or the trees until we put the **s**
    22:10 "Do not **s** up the prophetic words

SEALS → SEAL
Rev 5: 2 to open the scroll and break its **s**?"

SEARCH → SEARCHES
Dt   4:29 find him when you **s** after him

SEARCHES → SEARCH
Ro   8:27 the one who **s** hearts knows what is

SEASON → SEASONS
Ps   1: 3 that yields its fruit in **s**; Its leaves

SEASONS → SEASON
Gal 4:10 days, months, **s**, and years.
1Th 5: 1 Concerning times and **s**, brothers,

SEAT → SEATED
Ro 14:10 shall all stand before the judgment **s**
2Co 5:10 all appear before the judgment **s**

SEATED → SEAT
Lk 22:69 of Man will be **s** at the right hand

SECOND → TWO
Mt 22:39 The **s** is like it: You shall love your
Rev 20:14 (This pool of fire is the **s** death.)

SECURITY → SECURE
1Th 5: 3 "Peace and **s**," then sudden disaster

SEE → SEEN, SEES, SIGHT
Ex 33:20 But my face you cannot **s**, for no
Ps 115: 5 but do not speak, eyes but do not **s**.
Jn   9:25 is that I was blind and now I **s**."
1Co 13:12 At present we **s** indistinctly,
1Jn 3: 2 like him, for we shall **s** him as he is.
Rev 1: 7 and every eye will **s** him, even those

SEED → SEEDS, SEEDTIME
Mt 17:20 have faith the size of a mustard **s**,
1Pe 1:23 perishable but from imperishable **s**,

SEEDS → SEED
Mk   4:31 the smallest of all the **s** on the earth.

SEEK
1Ch 28: 9 If you **s** him, he will let himself be
Ps 34:11 those who **s** the LORD lack no good
   119:10 With all my heart I **s** you; do not let
Isa 55: 6 **S** the LORD while he may be found,
Sir 2:16 Those who fear the LORD **s** to please
Lk 19:10 For the Son of Man has come to **s**
Heb 11: 6 that he rewards those who **s** him.

SEEMS
Pr 16:25 Sometimes a way **s** right to a man,
Heb 12:11 all discipline **s** a cause not for joy

SEEN → SEE
Jn   1:18 No one has ever **s** God. The only
    14: 9 Whoever has **s** me has **s** the Father.
    20:29 to believe because you have **s** me?
    20:29 Blessed are those who have not **s**
1Pe 1: 8 you have not **s** him you love him;

SELF-CONTROL → SELF-CONTROLLED
1Co 7: 5 tempt you through your lack of **s**.
2Pe 1: 6 knowledge with **s**, with **s** endurance,

SELF-CONTROLLED → SELF-CONTROL
Tit 1: 8 temperate, just, holy, and **s**,
     2: 5 to be **s**, chaste, good homemakers,

SELFISH → SELFISHNESS
Php 1:17 proclaim Christ out of **s** ambition,
Jas 3:14 and **s** ambition in your hearts,

SELFISHNESS → SELFISH
2Co 12:20 jealousy, fury, **s**, slander, gossip,

SELL
Pr 23:23 Get the truth, and **s** it not—wisdom,
Mk 10:21 go, **s** what you have, and give

SEND → SENT
Ex 33: 2 I will **s** an angel before you
Isa 6: 8 of the Lord saying, "Whom shall I **s**?
     6: 8 go for us?" "Here I am;" I said; "**s** me!"
Jn   3:17 God did not **s** his Son into the world
    14:26 the Father will **s** in my name—he will

SENNACHERIB
Assyrian king; siege of Jerusalem was overthrown by the LORD following prayer of Hezekiah and Isaiah (2Ki 18:13-19:37; 2Ch 32:1-21; Isa 36-37).

SENT → SEND
Ex   3:14 tell the Israelites: I AM **s** me to you."
Lk 10:16 rejects me rejects the one who **s** me."
Jn 17:18 As you **s** me into the world, so I **s**
    20:21 As the Father has **s** me, so I send
1Jn 4:10 **s** his Son as expiation for our sins.

SEPARATE → SEPARATED
Mt 19: 6 together, no human being must **s**."
Ro   8:35 What will **s** us from the love
1Co 7:10 Lord): A wife should not **s** from her

SEPARATED → SEPARATE
Heb 7:26 undefiled, **s** from sinners,

SERPENT → SERPENTS
Ge   3: 1 Now the **s** was the most cunning
     3: 1 The **s** asked the woman, "Did God
Nu 21: 9 Moses accordingly made a bronze **s**
    21: 9 who had been bitten by a **s** looked
    21: 9 bitten by a **s** looked at the bronze **s**,
2Co 11: 3 that, as the **s** deceived Eve by his
Rev 20: 2 the ancient **s**, which is the Devil

SERPENTS → SERPENT
Mt 10:16 so be shrewd as **s** and simple as

SERVANT → SERVANTS
Ps 19:12 By them your **s** is instructed;
Isa 42: 1 Here is my **s** whom I uphold,
    53:11 suffering, my **s** shall justify many,
Zec 3: 8 Yes, I will bring my **s** the Shoot.
Ac   3:13 has glorified his **s** Jesus whom you

Heb 3: 5 in all his house" as a "s" to testify

SERVANTS → SERVANT

2Ki 17:23 as he had foretold through all his s,

Rev 7: 3 the foreheads of the s of our God."

SERVE

Jos 24:15 it does not please you to s the LORD,

24:15 decide today whom you will s,

24:15 my household, we will s the LORD."

Mt 6:24 "No one can s two masters. He will

6:24 You cannot s God and mammon.

Mk 10:45 to s and to give his life as a ransom

1Pe 4:10 it to s one another as good stewards

SETH

Ge 4:25 birth to a son whom she called S.

SETTLE

Nu 33:53 possession of the land and s in it,

SEVEN → SEVENTH

Ge 7: 2 take with you s pairs, a male and its

Ex 25:37 You shall then make s lamps for it

Jos 6: 4 s priests carrying ram's horns ahead

6: 4 day march around the city s times,

Da 9:25 there shall be s weeks.

Mt 18:22 "I say to you, not s times but s times.

Rev 1:12 I turned, I saw s gold lamp-stands

5: 1 sides and was sealed with s seals.

8: 2 the s angels who stood before God

8: 2 before God were given s trumpets.

12: 3 dragon, with s heads and ten horns,

12: 3 and on its heads were s diadems.

15: 1 s angels with the s last plagues,

SEVENTH → SEVEN

Ge 2: 2 Since on the s day God was finished

2: 2 he rested on the s day from all

Ex 20:10 the s day is the sabbath of the LORD,

23:11 the s year you shall let the land lie

Heb 4: 4 spoken somewhere about the s day

4: 4 God rested on the s day from all his

SEVENTY → SEVENTY-SEVEN

Ge 46:27 Egypt amounted to s persons in all.

2Ch 36:21 have rest while s years are ful-filled."

Jer 25:12 but when the s years have elapsed,

Da 9:24 "S weeks are decreed for your people

SEVENTY-SEVEN → SEVENTY

Mt 18:22 to you, not seven times but s times.

SHADOW

2Ki 20:11 who made the s retreat the ten steps

Ps 17: 8 eye; hide me in the s of your wings

91: 1 who abide in the s of the Almighty,

SHADRACH → = HANANIAH

Hebrew exiled to Babylon; name changed from Hananiah (Da 1:6-7). Refused defile-ment by food (Da 1:8-20). Refused to wor-ship idol (Da 3:1-18); saved from furnace (Da 3:19-30).

SHALLUM

King of Israel (2Ki 15:10-16).

SHALMANESER

King of Assyria; conquered and deported Israel (2Ki 17:3-4; 18:9; Tob 1:2).

SHAME → ASHAMED, SHAMEFUL

1Co 1:27 foolish of the world to s the wise,

1:27 weak of the world to s the strong,

Heb 12: 2 despising its s, and has taken his

1Jn 2:28 not be put to s by him at his coming.

SHAMEFUL → SHAME

2Co 4: 2 we have renounced s, hidden things;

Eph 5:12 for it is s even to mention the things

SHAMGAR

Judge; killed 600 Philistines (Jdg 3:31; 5:6).

SHARE

Lk 3:11 "Whoever has two cloaks should s

Ro 15:27 the Gentiles have come to s in their

Col 1:12 who has made you fit to s

Heb 12:10 in order that we may s his holiness.

SHARP → SHARPENS, SHARPER

Pr 5: 4 as s as a two-edged sword.

Rev 19:15 his mouth came a s sword to strike

SHARPENS → SHARP

Pr 27:17 As iron s iron, so man s his fellow

SHARPER → SHARP

Heb 4:12 s than any two-edged sword,

SHEBA

1. Benjamite; rebelled against David (2Sa 20).

2. Queen of Sheba (1Ki 10; 2Ch 9; Mt 12:42; Lk 11:31).

SHECHEM

1. Raped Jacob's daughter Dinah; killed (Ge 34).

2. City where Joshua renewed the cov-enant (Jos 24). Abimelech as king (Jdg 9).

SHED → BLOODSHED, SHEDDING

Ge 9: 6 by man shall his blood be s;

Pr 6:17 and hands that s innocent blood;

Mt 23:35 you all the righteous blood s

Rev 16: 6 For they have s the blood

SHEDDING → SHED

Heb 9:22 without the s of blood there is no

12: 4 yet resisted to the point of s blood.

SHEEP → SHEEPFOLD

1Ki 22:17 like s without a shepherd,

Isa 53: 6 We had all gone astray like s,

Eze 34:15 I myself will pasture my s; I myself

Zec 13: 7 that the s may be dispersed, and I

Mt 9:36 like s without a shepherd.

Lk 15: 4 man among you having a hun-dred s

Jn 10: 7 I say to you, I am the gate for the s.

10:15 I will lay down my life for the s.

Heb 13:20 great shepherd of the s by the blood

1Pe 2:25 For you had gone astray like s,

SHEEPFOLD → SHEEP

Jn 10: 1 does not enter a s through the gate

SHELTER

Ps 91: 1 dwell in the s of the Most High,

Rev 7:15 who sits on the throne will s them.

SHEM

Son of Noah (Ge 5:32; 6:10). Blessed (Ge 9:26). Descendants (Ge 10:21-31; 11:10-32; Lk 3:36).

SHEOL

Ps 139: 8 if I lie down in S, you are there too.

SHEPHERD → SHEPHERDS

Ps 23: 1 The LORD is my s; there is nothing I

Isa 40:11 Like a s he feeds his flock; in his

Mt 2: 6 ruler, who is to s my people Israel.' "

26:31 'I will strike the s, and the sheep

Jn 10:11 I am the good s. A good s lays down

Heb 13:20 the dead the great s of the sheep

1Pe 5: 4 And when the chief S is re-vealed,

SHEPHERDS → SHEPHERD

Eze 34: 2 prophesy against the s of Is-rael,

34: 2 words prophesy to them [to the s]:

SHEPHERDS → SHEPHERD (*cont.*)

Eze 34: 2 to the **s** of Israel who have
been

34: 2 Should not **s**, rather, pasture
sheep?

Lk 2: 8 Now there were **s** in that
region

SHIELD

Ge 15: 1 I am your **s**; I will make your

Ps 7:11 A **s** before me is God who
saves

Eph 6:16 hold faith as a **s**, to quench all

SHILOH

1Sa 1:24 him at the temple of the LORD
in S.

SHIMEI

Cursed David (2Sa 16:5-14); spared (2Sa
19:16-23). Killed by Solomon (1Ki 2:8-9,
36-46).

SHINE → SHINES, SHINING

Nu 6:25 The LORD let his face **s** upon
you,

Da 12: 3 But the wise shall **s** brightly

Mt 5:16 your light must **s** before others,

SHINES → SHINE

Jn 1: 5 the light **s** in the darkness,

Isa 60: 1 the glory of the Lord **s** upon
you.

SHINING → SHINE

2Pe 1:19 as to a lamp **s** in a dark place,

1Jn 2: 8 away, and the true light is already **s**.

SHORT

Isa 59: 1 hand of the LORD is not too **s** to
save,

SHOUT

Ps 47: 2 hands; **s** to God with joyful
cries.

Zec 9: 9 **s** for joy, O daughter Jerusalem!

SHOW → SHOWED

Ge 12: 1 house to a land that I will **s**
you.

Ps 85: 8 S us, LORD, your love; grant us
your

Jn 14: 8 "Master, **s** us the Father, and
that will

1Co 12:31 I shall **s** you a still more
excellent

Rev 4: 1 and I will **s** you what must
happen

SHOWED → SHOW

Dt 34: 1 the LORD **s** him all the land—
Gilead,

Jn 20:20 he **s** them his hands and his
side.

SHUT

Isa 22:22 when he opens, no one
shall **s**,

SICK → SICKNESS

Mt 8:16 spirits by a word and cured all
the **s**,

9:12 not need a physician, but the
s do.

Jas 5:14 Is anyone among you **s**? He
should

SICKLE

Rev 14:14 his head and a sharp **s** in his
hand.

SICKNESS → SICK

Ex 23:25 I will remove all **s** from your
midst;

SIDE → ASIDE

Ps 91: 7 Though a thousand fall at
your **s**,

Jn 19:34 soldier thrust his lance into
his **s**,

SIFT

Lk 22:31 behold Satan has demanded to
s all

SIGHT → SEE

Ps 72:14 for precious is their blood in
his **s**.

Mt 11: 5 the blind regain their **s**, the
lame

2Co 5: 7 for we walk by faith, not by **s**.

1Pe 3: 4 which is precious in the **s** of
God.

SIGN → SIGNS

Ge 9:12 "This is the **s** that I am giving
for all

Isa 7:14 Lord himself will give you
this **s**:

Mt 24: 3 what **s** will there be of your
coming,

Mk 8:12 "Why does this generation
seek a **s**?

8:12 no **s** will be given to this
generation."

SIGNS → SIGN

Ex 7: 3 despite the many **s** and
wonders

Mt 16: 3 you cannot judge the **s** of the
times.]

Jn 20:30 Now Jesus did many other **s**

1Co 1:22 For Jews demand **s** and Greeks
look

Rev 16:14 demonic spirits who performed **s**.

SILAS

Prophet (Ac 15:22-32); co-worker with
Paul on second missionary journey (Ac 16-
18; 2Co 1:19). Co-writer with Paul (1Th 1:1;
2Th 1:1); Peter (1Pe 5:12).

SILENT

Isa 53: 7 he was **s** and opened not his
mouth.

Mk 14:61 But he was **s** and answered
nothing.

1Co 14:34 women should keep **s**

SILVER

Ps 66:10 us, O God, tried us as **s** tried by
fire.

Pr 8:10 my instruction in preference
to **s**,

Isa 48:10 See, I have refined you like **s**,

Zec 13: 9 I will refine them as **s** is refined,

Mt 26:15 They paid him thirty pieces
of **s**,

Ac 3: 6 "I have neither **s** nor gold, but
what I

1Co 3:12 on this foundation with gold, **s**,

SIMEON → = SIMON

1. Son of Jacob by Leah (Ge 29:33; 35:23;
1Ch 2:1). With Levi killed Shechem for rape
of Dinah (Ge 34:25-29). Held hostage by
Joseph in Egypt (Ge 42:24-43:23). Tribe of
blessed (Ge 49:5-7), numbered (Nu 1:23;
26:14), allotted land (Jos 19:1-9; Eze 48:24),
12,000 from (Rev 7:7).

2. Godly Jew who blessed the infant Jesus
(2:25-35).

3. See Peter (Ac 15:14; 2Pe 1:1).

SIMON → = PETER, = SIMEON

1. See Peter.

2. Apostle; the Zealot (Mt 10:4; Mk 3:18;
Lk 6:15; Ac 1:13).

3. Samaritan sorcerer (Ac 8:9-24).

SIMPLE

Ps 19: 8 trustworthy, giving wisdom to
the **s**.

Pr 1:22 "How long, you **s** ones, will
you love

SIN → SINFUL, SINNED, SINNER,
SINNERS, SINS

Ge 4: 7 **s** is a demon lurking at the
door;

Ex 32:32 If you would only forgive
their **s**!

Nu 32:23 do this, you will **s** against the
LORD,

32:23 escape the consequences of
your **s**.

1Ki 8:46 "When they **s** against you (for
there

8:46 there is no man who does
not **s**),

Tob 12:10 of **s** are their own worst
enemies.

Ps 119:11 that I may not **s** against you.

Wis 10:13 was sold, but delivered him
from **s**.

Da 9:20 confessing my **s** and the **s**
of my

Mt 5:29 If your right eye causes you
to **s**,

Jn 1:29 who takes away the **s** of the
world.

Ro 5:12 as through one person **s**
entered

5:12 the world, and through **s**,
death,

6:23 For the wages of **s** is death,

2Co 5:21 him to be **s** who did not
know **s**,

Heb 4:15 tested in every way, yet without **s**.

1Jn 1: 7 his Son Jesus cleanses us from
all **s**.

SINAI → = HOREB

Ex 19:20 came down to the top of
Mount S,

Ps 68:18 S the Lord entered the holy
place.

Gal 4:25 Hagar represents S, a mountain

SINFUL → SIN

1Ma 1:10 sprang from these a **s** offshoot,

Lk 5: 8 from me, Lord, for I am a **s**
man."

Ro 8: 3 own Son in the likeness of **s**
flesh

SING → SINGERS, SONG, SONGS, SUNG
Ex 15: 1 LORD: I will s to the LORD, for he is
Jdt 16:13 "A new hymn I will s to my God.
Ps 47: 7 S praise to God, s praise; s praise
47: 7 praise; s praise to our king, s praise.
Isa 5: 1 Let me now s of my friend,
1Co 14:15 I will s praise with the spirit, but I
14:15 I will also s praise with the mind.

SINGERS → SING
Ezr 2:70 but the s, the gatekeepers,

SINGLE
Mt 6:27 by worrying add a s moment to your
Rev 21:21 of the gates made from a s pearl;

SINNED → SIN
Ps 51: 6 Against you alone have I s; I have
La 5: 7 Our fathers, who s, are no more;
Da 9: 5 We have s, been wicked and done
Ro 3:23 all have s and are deprived
1Jn 1:10 "We have not s," we make him a liar,

SINNER → SIN
Lk 15: 7 heaven over one s who repents than
Jas 5:20 whoever brings back a s

SINNERS → SIN
Ps 1: 1 Nor go the way of s, nor sit
Pr 23:17 Let not your heart emulate s, but be
Lk 6:33 is that to you? Even s do the same.
Ro 5: 8 while we were still s Christ died
1Ti 1:15 Jesus came into the world to save s.

SINS → SIN
1Sa 2:25 If a man s against another man,
2:25 but if a man s against the LORD,
2Ch 7:14 pardon their s and revive their land.
Ps 103:10 Has not dealt with us as our s merit,
Sir 2:11 he forgives s, he saves in time
Isa 1:18 LORD: Though your s be like scarlet,
53:12 he shall take away the s of many,
Eze 18: 4 mine; only the one who s shall die.
Mic 7:19 into the depths of the sea all our s;
Mt 9: 6 has authority on earth to forgive s
Mk 1: 5 River as they acknowledged their s.
Lk 11: 4 and forgive us our s for we
Ac 3:19 that your s may be wiped away,

1Co 15: 3 Christ died for our s in accordance
Heb 9:28 once to take away the s of many,
1Jn 1: 9 If we acknowledge our s, he is
1: 9 will forgive our s and cleanse us
Rev 1: 5 freed us from our s by his blood,

SISTER
Ge 12:13 that you are my s, so that it may go
20: 2 said of his wife Sarah, "She is my s."
Pr 7: 4 Say to Wisdom, "You are my s!"
Mk 3:35 the will of God is my brother and s

SIT → SITS
Ps 1: 1 nor s in company with scoffers.
Mt 20:23 but to s at my right and at my left [,
Heb 1:13 has he ever said: "S at my right hand

SITS → SIT
Isa 28: 6 to him who s in judgment,

SIX
Ex 20: 9 S days you may labor and do all
Pr 6:16 There are s things the LORD hates,
Isa 6: 2 each of them had s wings: with two
Rev 4: 8 each of them with s wings,

SKILL
Ex 28: 3 whom I have endowed with s,
1Ki 7:14 from Tyre. He was endowed with s,

SKIN
Job 2: 4 answered the LORD and said, "S for s!
Jer 13:23 Can the Ethiopian change his s?

SKULL
2Ki 9:35 they found nothing of her but the s,
Mt 27:33 (which means Place of the S),

SKY
Dt 28:23 The s over your heads will be like
Mt 16: 3 for the s is red and threatening.'
16: 3 to judge the appearance of the s,
Rev 6:14 the s was divided like a torn scroll

SLANDER → SLANDERED
Ps 15: 3 Who does not s a neighbor, does no
1Pe 2: 1 deceit, insincerity, envy, and all s;

SLANDERED → SLANDER
1Co 4:13 when s, we respond gently.

SLAUGHTER → SLAUGHTERED
Pr 7:22 like an ox that is led to s;
Isa 53: 7 Like a lamb led to the s or a sheep

Ac 8:32 "Like a sheep he was led to the s,

SLAUGHTERED → SLAUGHTER
Zec 11: 4 my God: Shepherd the flock to be s.
Rev 6: 9 those who had been s because

SLAVE → ENSLAVE, SLAVERY, SLAVES
Ge 21:10 "Drive out that s and her son! No son
21:10 son of that s is going to share
Mk 10:44 be first among you will be the s
Jn 8:34 everyone who commits sin is a s
Gal 3:28 there is neither s nor free person,
Php 2: 7 taking the form of a s,
Phm 1:16 no longer as a s but more than a s,

SLAVERY → SLAVE
Ex 20: 2 of the land of Egypt, that place of s.
Ro 7:14 but I am carnal, sold into s to sin.
8:15 you did not receive a spirit of s
Gal 5: 1 do not submit again to the yoke of s.

SLAVES → SLAVE
Ro 6:16 to someone as obedient s, you are s
6:20 For when you were s of sin,
2Pe 2:19 though they themselves are s

SLEEP → ASLEEP, SLEEPER, SLEEPING, SLEEPS
Ge 2:21 So the LORD God cast a deep s
Da 12: 2 Many of those who s in the dust

SLEEPER → SLEEP
Eph 5:14 "Awake, O s, and arise

SLEEPING → SLEEP
Mt 9:24 The girl is not dead but s." And they

SLEEPS → SLEEP
Ps 121: 4 of Israel never slumbers nor s.

SLING
1Sa 17:50 overcame the Philistine with s

SLOW
Ex 34: 6 s to anger and rich in kindness
Nu 14:18 'The LORD is s to anger and rich
Ps 145: 8 s to anger and abounding in love.
Na 1: 3 The LORD is s to anger, yet great
Lk 24:25 How s of heart to believe all

SMALL → SMALLEST
Jas 3: 5 same way the tongue is a s member
3: 5 Consider how s a fire can set a huge

SMALLEST → SMALL
Mk 4:31 is the s of all the seeds on the earth.

SMOKE → SMOKING
Ex 19:18 Mount Sinai was all wrapped in s,
       19:18 The s rose from it as though
Isa   6: 4 and the house was filled with s.
Rev 15: 8 so filled with the s from God's glory

SMOKING → SMOKE
Ge 15:17 there appeared a s brazier
Ex 20:18 trumpet blast and the mountain s,

SNAKE
Lk 11:11 among you would hand his son a s

SNARE
Jdg 2: 3 their gods shall become a s for you."

SNOW
Ps 51: 9 wash me, make me whiter than s.
Isa   1:18 they may become white as s;
Da   7: 9 His clothing was s bright,
Rev 1:14 was as white as white wool or as s,

SOBER
1Th 5: 6 rest do, but let us stay alert and s.

SODOM
Ge 19:24 rained down sulphurous fire upon S
Isa   1: 9 We had become as S, we should be
Lk 10:12 it will be more tolerable for S
Rev 11: 8 which has the symbolic names "S"

SOLDIERS
Mt 28:12 gave a large sum of money to the s,
Jn 19:23 When the s had crucified Jesus,

SOLID
1Co 3: 2 I fed you milk, not s food,
Heb 5:14 But s food is for the mature,

SOLOMON
    Son of David by Bathsheba; king of Judah (2Sa 12:24; 1Ch 3:5, 10). Appointed king by David (1Ki 1); adversaries Adonijah, Joab, Shimei killed by Benaiah (1Ki 2). Asked for wisdom (1Ki 3; 2Ch 1). Judged between two prostitutes (1Ki 3:16-28). Built temple (1Ki 5-7; 2Ch 2-5); prayer of dedication (1Ki 8; 2Ch 6). Visited by Queen of Sheba (1Ki 10; 2Ch 9). Wives turned his heart from God (1Ki 11:1-13). Jeroboam rebelled against (1Ki 11:26-40). Death (1Ki 11:41-43; 2Ch 9:29-31).
    Proverbs of (1Ki 4:32; Pr 1:1; 10:1; 25:1); psalms of (Ps 72; 127); song of (SS 1:1).

SON → SONS
Ge 21: 2 bore Abraham a s in his old age,
Ex   4:23 Let my s go, that he may serve me.
      4:23 I will kill your s, your first-born."
2Sa 7:14 to him, and he shall be a s to me."
Ps   2: 7 who said to me, "You are my s;

Sir   4:10 Thus will you be like a s
Isa   7:14 and bear a s, and shall name him
Mt   1:23 shall be with child and bear a s,
      2:15 fulfilled, "Out of Egypt I called my s."
      3:17 "This is my beloved S, with whom I
Mt 12: 8 For the S of Man is Lord
    16:16 Messiah, the S of the living God."
Mk 10:45 For the S of Man did not come to be
Lk   1:35 will be called holy, the S of God.
    20:44 calls him 'lord,' how can he be his s?"
Jn   1:34 and testified that he is the S of God."
      3:16 the world that he gave his only S,
Ro 8:29 be conformed to the image of his S,
1Th 1:10 and to await his S from heaven,
Heb 1: 2 he spoke to us through a s, whom he
    1: 5 say: "You are my s; this day I have
    1: 5 to him, and he shall be a s to me"?
2Pe 1:17 glory, "This is my S, my beloved,
1Jn 4: 9 God sent his only S into the world
Rev 12: 5 She gave birth to a s, a male child,
    14:14 the cloud one who looked like a s

SONG → SING
Ex 15: 1 the Israelites sang this s to the Lᴏʀᴅ:
Dt 31:21 this s, which their descendants will
Ps 40: 4 And put a new s in my mouth,
Rev 15: 3 and they sang the s of Moses,
    15: 3 of God, and the s of the Lamb:

SONGS → SING
Col 3:16 and spiritual s with gratitude in your

SONS → SON
Ge   6: 2 the s of heaven saw how beautiful
    35:22 The s of Jacob were now twelve.
Dt   7: 3 to their s nor taking their daughters
      7: 3 taking their daughters for your s.
Ac   2:17 Your s and your daughters shall
2Co 6:18 you shall be s and daughters to me,

SOON
Rev 22:20 testimony says, "Yes, I am coming s."

SORCERERS → SORCERY
Rev 22:15 are the dogs, the s, the unchaste,

SORCERY → SORCERERS
Gal 5:20 idolatry, s, hatreds, rivalry,

SORROW → SORROWFUL
Est 9:22 was turned for them from s into joy,
Ecc 1:18 in much wisdom there is much s,
Isa 35:10 gladness, s and mourning will flee.

SORROWFUL → SORROW
2Co 6:10 as s yet always rejoicing; as poor

SOUL → SOULS
Dt   6: 5 and with all your s, and with all
Jos 22: 5 him with your whole heart and s."
Ps 16: 9 my heart is glad, my s rejoices;
    25: 1 I wait for you, O Lᴏʀᴅ; I lift up my s
    42: 2 so my s longs for you, O God.
Sir 7:29 With all your s, fear God, revere his
Mic 6: 7 fruit of my body for the sin of my s?
Mt 10:28 kill the body but cannot kill the s;
    10:28 of the one who can destroy both s
Heb 4:12 penetrating even between s
Jas 5:20 his way will save his s from death
3Jn 1: 2 health, just as your s is prospering.

SOULS → SOUL
Jer 6:16 it; thus you will find rest for your s.
1Pe 2:25 the shepherd and guardian of your s.

SOUND
Eze 1:24 Then I heard the s of their wings,
    1:24 the s of the tumult was like the din
1Co 15:52 For the trumpet will s, the dead will
2Ti 4: 3 will not tolerate s doctrine but,
Tit 1: 9 able both to exhort with s doctrine
Rev 1:15 his voice was like the s of rushing

SOW → SOWED, SOWER, SOWS
Ex 23:10 "For six years you may s your land
Ecc 11: 6 In the morning s your seed,
Hos 10:12 "S for yourselves justice,
Mt 13: 3 saying: "A sower went out to s.
1Co 15:36 What you s is not brought to life

SOWED → SOW
Mt 13:24 a man who s good seed in his field.

SOWER → SOW
Mk 4:14 The s sows the word.

SOWS → SOW
Jn   4:37 the saying is verified that 'One s

2Co 9: 6 whoever s sparingly will also reap

9: 6 and whoever s bountifully will

SPAN

Isa 40:12 marked off the heavens with a s?

Mt 6:27 add a single moment to your l?

SPARE

Ro 11:21 God did not s the natural branches,

11:21 [perhaps] he will not s you either.

2Pe 2: 4 God did not s the angels when they

SPARROWS

Lk 12: 7 You are worth more than many s.

SPEAK → SPEAKING, SPEECH, SPOKE

Ge 18:27 "See how I am presuming to s to my

Nu 12: 8 face to face I s to him,

12: 8 fear to s against my servant Moses?"

Dt 18:20 a prophet presumes to s in my name

18:20 that I have not commanded him to s,

Job 13: 3 But I would s with the Almighty;

Ecc 3: 7 a time to be silent, and a time to s.

Mt 13:13 This is why I s to them in parables,

Ac 2: 4 and began to s in different tongues,

1Co 12:30 of healing? Do all s in tongues?

Jas 1:19 to hear, slow to s, slow to wrath,

SPEAKING → SPEAK

1Co 14:39 and do not forbid s in tongues,

SPEAR → SPEARS

1Sa 19:10 to nail David to the wall with the s,

19:10 so that the s struck only the wall,

SPEARS → SPEAR

Mic 4: 3 and their s into pruning hooks;

SPECTACLE

1Co 4: 9 since we have become a s

SPEECH → SPEAK

Ex 4:10 but I am slow of s and tongue."

Sir 4:29 Be not surly in your s, nor lazy

1Ti 4:12 for those who believe, in s, conduct,

1Jn 3:18 let us love not in word or s

SPICES

Ex 25: 6 s for the anointing oil

Jn 19:40 with burial cloths along with the s,

SPIES

Jos 2: 1 secretly sent out two s from Shittim,

SPIRIT → SPIRITS, SPIRITUAL

Ge 6: 3 said: "My s shall not remain in man

Nu 11:25 Taking some of the s that was

11:25 and as the s came to rest on them,

2Ki 2: 9 I receive a double portion of your s."

Ne 9:20 "Your good s you bestowed on them,

Job 33: 4 For the s of God has made me,

Ps 31: 6 Into your hands I commend my s;

51:19 My sacrifice, God, is a broken s;

Pr 16:18 and a haughty s before a fall.

Isa 42: 1 Upon whom I have put my s;

Eze 36:26 heart and place a new s within you,

Mt 1:18 found with child through the holy S.

5: 3 "Blessed are the poor in s, for theirs

12:31 blasphemy against the S will not be

26:41 test. The s is willing, but the flesh is

Mk 1: 8 he will baptize you with the holy S."

Jn 3: 5 without being born of water and S.

4:24 God is S, and those who worship

4:24 who worship him must worship in S

6:63 It is the s that gives life,

6:63 words I have spoken to you are s

14:26 the holy S that the Father will send

Ac 2: 4 they were all filled with the holy S

2: 4 as the S enabled them to proclaim.

2:38 will receive the gift of the holy S.

Ro 8: 9 you are in the s, if only the S of God

8: 9 Whoever does not have the S

8:26 the S too comes to the aid of our

8:26 but the S itself intercedes

1Co 6:19 is a temple of the holy S within you,

12: 4 of spiritual gifts but the same S;

2Co 3: 6 new covenant, not of letter but of s;

3: 6 brings death, but the S gives life.

Gal 4: 6 God sent the s of his Son into our

5:22 the fruit of the S is love, joy, peace,

Eph 1:13 sealed with the promised holy S,

2:18 have access in one S to the Father.

4:30 do not grieve the holy S of God,

5:18 debauchery, but be filled with the S,

1Th 5:19 Do not quench the S.

Heb 4:12 even between soul and s,

1Jn 4: 1 do not trust every s but test

Rev 1:10 was caught up in s on the Lord's day

SPIRITS → SPIRIT

Nu 16:22 God of the s of all mankind,

Dt 18:11 nor one who consults ghosts and s

Lk 4:36 power he commands the unclean s,

1Co 12:10 to another discernment of s;

Rev 1: 4 from the seven s before his throne,

SPIRITUAL → SPIRIT

Ro 7:14 We know that the law is s; but I am

1Co 2:13 describing s realities in s terms.

12: 1 Now in regard to s gifts, brothers,

14: 1 but strive eagerly for the s gifts,

15:46 But the s was not first;

15:46 rather the natural and then the s.

Eph 1: 3 Christ with every s blessing

Col 1: 9 of his will through all s wisdom

1Pe 2: 2 long for pure s milk so that through

2: 5 let yourselves be built into a s house

2: 5 to offer s sacrifices acceptable

SPIT

Mk 14:65 Some began to s on him.

Rev 3:16 cold, I will s you out of my mouth.

SPLENDOR

Eph 5:27 present to himself the church in s,

SPOKE → SPEAK

Mk 4:33 many such parables he s the word

Heb 1: 1 God s in partial and various ways

2Pe 1:21 the holy Spirit s under the influence

SPOT

Eph 5:27 without s or wrinkle or any such

2Pe 3:14 be eager to be found without s

SPRING

Isa 45: 8 let justice also s up! I, the LORD,

Jn 4:14 become in him a s of water welling

Rev 21: 6 gift from the s of life-giving water.

SPRINKLE → SPRINKLED

Nu 8: 7 S them with the water of remission;

Eze 36:25 I will s clean water upon you

SPRINKLED → SPRINKLE

Lev 8:11 he s some of this oil seven times

Heb 10:22 with our hearts s clean from an evil

STAFF

Ex 4: 4 of it, and it became a s in his hand.

STAFF *(cont.)*

Ps 23: 4 your rod and s give me courage.

Zec 11:10 I took my s "Favor" and snapped it

STAND → STANDING

Ex 14:13 S your ground, and you will see

Job 19:25 he will at last s forth upon the dust;

Mt 12:25 house divided against itself will s.

Ro 14: 4 for the Lord is able to make him s.

14:10 we shall all s before the judgment

Eph 6:11 be able to s firm against the tactics

STANDARDS

1Co 1:26 many of you were wise by human s,

STANDING → STAND

1Co 10:12 thinks he is s secure should take

Jas 5: 9 the Judge is s before the gates.

STAR → STARS

Nu 24:17 near: A s shall advance from Jacob,

Isa 14:12 O morning s, son of the dawn!

Mt 2: 2 We saw his s at its rising and have

2Pe 1:19 the morning s rises in your hearts.

Rev 9: 1 I saw a s that had fallen

22:16 of David, the bright morning s."

STARS → STAR

Ge 1:16 govern the night; and he made the s.

Job 38: 7 While the morning s sang in chorus

Ps 148: 3 and moon; give praise, all shining s.

Da 12: 3 to justice shall be like the s forever.

Rev 1:16 In his right hand he held seven s.

12: 4 away a third of the s in the sky

STATUE

Da 2:31 O king, you saw a s, very large

STATUTES

Dt 4: 1 hear the s and decrees which I am

Ne 9:13 laws, good s, and commandments;

STEADFAST

Ps 57: 8 My heart is s, God, my heart is s.

1Pe 5: 9 Resist him, s in faith,

STEAL

Ex 20:15 "You shall not s.

Mt 6:19 destroys, and thieves break in and s.

Jn 10:10 A thief comes only to s

STEPHEN

Early church leader (Ac 6:5). Arrested (Ac 6:8-15). Speech to Sanhedrin (Ac 7). Stoned (Ac 7:54-60; 8:2; 11:19; 22:20).

STEPS

Pr 16: 9 course, but the LORD directs his s.

STIFF-NECKED → NECK

Ex 32: 9 I see how s this people is,"

Ac 7:51 "You s people,

STILL

Ex 14:14 for you; you have only to keep s."

Jos 10:13 And the sun stood s, and the moon

Ps 46:11 "Be s and confess that I am God!

Mk 4:39 Be s!" The wind ceased and there

Ro 5: 8 while we were s sinners Christ died

Heb 11: 4 this, though dead, he s speaks.

STING

1Co 15:55 victory? Where, O death, is your s?"

STONE → CORNERSTONE, MILLSTONE, STONED, STONES

Ge 28:18 the next morning Jacob took the s

28:18 head, set it up as a memorial s,

Ex 28:10 six of their names on one s,

28:10 s, and the other six on the other s,

31:18 the s tablets inscribed by God's own

1Sa 17:50 the Philistine with sling and s;

Ps 118:22 The s the builders rejected

Isa 28:16 See, I am laying a s in Zion, a s

Mt 4: 6 lest you dash your foot against a s.' "

Mk 12:10 'The s that the builders rejected

16: 3 "Who will roll back the s for us

Ro 9:32 They stumbled over the s

2Co 3: 3 not on tablets of s but on tablets

1Pe 2: 4 a living s, rejected by human beings

STONED → STONE

2Ch 24:21 the king's order they s him to death

Ac 14:19 They s Paul and dragged him

Heb 11:37 They were s, sawed in two,

STONES → STONE

Jos 4: 3 to take up twelve s from this spot

1Sa 17:40 David selected five smooth s

Mt 3: 9 children to Abraham from these s.

Lk 19:40 they keep silent, the s will cry out!"

1Co 3:12 gold, silver, precious s, wood, hay,

1Pe 2: 5 like living s, let yourselves be built

STORE → SHOREHOUSE, STORING

Mt 6:19 "Do not s up for yourselves treasures

STOREHOUSE → HOUSE, STORE

Mal 3:10 into the s, That there may be food

STORING → STORE

Ro 2: 5 you are s up wrath for yourself

STRAIGHT

Pr 3: 6 him, and he will make s your paths.

Sir 2: 6 make s your ways and hope in him.

Isa 40: 3 Make s in the wasteland a highway

Mt 3: 3 way of the Lord, make s his paths.' "

Ac 9:11 go to the street called S and ask

STRANGE → STRANGER, STRANGERS

Dt 32:16 They provoked him with s gods

1Co 14:21 "By people speaking s tongues

STRANGER → STRANGE

Mt 25:35 drink, a s and you welcomed me,

STRANGERS → STRANGE

Eph 2:12 and s to the covenants of promise,

Heb 11:13 acknowledged themselves to be s

STRAW

Ex 5:10 I will not provide you with s.

1Co 3:12 precious stones, wood, hay, or s,

STRAY → ASTRAY

Ps 119:10 seek you; do not let me s from your

STREAM → STREAMS

Isa 2: 2 hills. All nations shall s toward it;

Am 5:24 and goodness like an unfailing s.

STREAMS → STREAM

Ps 1: 3 like a tree planted near s of water,

42: 2 As the deer longs for s of water,

STREET

Pr 1:20 Wisdom cries aloud in the s,

Mt 6: 5 on s corners so that others may see

Rev 21:21 the s of the city was of pure gold,

STRENGTH → STRONG

Ex 15: 2 My s and my courage is the LORD,

1Ch 16:11 Look to the LORD in his s;

Ne 8:10 in the LORD must be your s!"

Jdt 9:11 "Your s is not in numbers, nor does

1Ma 3:19 but on s that comes from Heaven.

Ps 46: 2 God is our refuge and our s,

Pr 31:25 She is clothed with s and dignity,

Isa 40:31 hope in the LORD will renew their s,

Mk 12:30 all your mind, and with all your s.'

1Co 1:25 of God is stronger than human s.

1840

STRENGTHEN → STRONG

Jdg 16:28 **S** me, O God, this last time

Ps 119:28 in accord with your word to **s** me.

Lk 22:32 back, you must **s** your brothers."

Heb 12:12 So **s** your drooping hands and your

STRETCH → OUTSTRETCHED, STRETCHED

Mk 3: 5 he said to the man, "**S** out your hand."

STRETCHED → STRETCH

2Sa 24:16 the angel **s** forth his hand toward

STRIFE → STRIVE

Pr 23:29 Who have **s**? Who have anxiety?

STRIKE

Ge 3:15 and hers; He will **s** at your head,

3:15 at your head, while you **s** at his heel."

Ex 17: 6 **S** the rock, and the water will flow

Zec 13: 7 the LORD of hosts. **S** the shepherd

Mk 14:27 it is written: 'I will **s** the shepherd,

Rev 19:15 came a sharp sword to **s** the nations.

STRIVE → STRIFE

1Co 12:31 **S** eagerly for the greatest spiritual

STRONG → STRENGTH, STRENGTHEN, STRONGHOLD

Ps 140: 8 My revered LORD, my **s** helper,

Pr 18:10 The name of the LORD is a **s** tower;

Ro 15: 1 We who are **s** ought to put

1Co 1:27 weak of the world to shame the **s**,

2Co 12:10 for when I am weak, then I am **s**.

STRONGHOLD → STRONG

Ps 9:10 The LORD is a **s** for the oppressed,

9:10 oppressed, a **s** in times of trouble.

STRUGGLE

Eph 6:12 For our **s** is not with flesh and blood

Heb 12: 4 your **s** against sin you have not yet

STUBBORN

Hos 4:16 For Israel is as **s** as a heifer;

STUDY

Ezr 7:10 Ezra had set his heart on the **s**

Ecc 12:12 in much **s** there is weariness

STUMBLE → STUMBLING

Ps 37:24 May **s**, but they will never fall,

Pr 4:12 and should you run, you will not **s**.

Ro 9:33 that will make people **s** and a rock

1Pe 2: 8 "A stone that will make people **s**,

2: 8 They **s** by disobeying the word, as is

STUMBLING → STUMBLE

Ro 11: 9 a **s** block and a retribution for them;

1Co 8: 9 in no way becomes a **s** block

STUMP

Isa 11: 1 shall sprout from the **s** of Jesse,

SUBDUE

Ge 1:28 and multiply; fill the earth and **s** it.

1Ch 17:10 Israel. And I will **s** all your enemies.

SUBJECTED

Ro 8:20 but because of the one who **s** it,

1Co 15:28 When everything is **s** to him,

15:28 be **s** to the One who **s** everything

SUBMIT

Gal 5: 1 and do not **s** again to the yoke

SUCCEED

Pr 15:22 they **s** when counselors are many.

SUDDENLY

Mal 3: 1 And **s** there will come to the temple

Mk 13:36 May he not come **s** and find you

SUFFER → SUFFERED, SUFFERING, SUFFERINGS, SUFFERS

Lk 22:15 this Passover with you before I **s**,

24:46 is written that the Messiah would **s**

Ro 8:17 if only we **s** with him so that we

Heb 9:26 he would have had to **s** repeatedly

1Pe 3:17 For it is better to **s** for doing good,

SUFFERED → SUFFER

1Pe 2:21 because Christ also **s** for you,

SUFFERING → SUFFER

Job 2:13 for they saw how great was his **s**.

Isa 53: 3 a man of **s**, accustomed to infirmity,

SUFFERINGS → SUFFER

Ro 8:18 that the **s** of this present time are as

1Pe 4:13 that you share in the **s** of Christ,

SUFFERS → SUFFER

1Co 12:26 If [one] part **s**, all the parts suffer

SUFFICIENT

2Co 12: 9 he said to me, "My grace is **s** for you,

SULFUR

Rev 21: 8 is in the burning pool of fire and **s**,

SUMMED

Ro 13: 9 there may be, are **s** up in this saying,

SUN

Jos 10:13 And the **s** stood still, and the moon

10:13 The **s** halted in the middle

Ps 84:12 For a **s** and shield is the LORD God,

Ecc 1: 9 done. Nothing is new under the **s**.

Mt 5:45 for he makes his **s** rise on the bad

Ac 2:20 The **s** shall be turned to darkness,

Rev 1:16 and his face shone like the **s** at its

19:17 I saw an angel standing on the **s**,

Rev 22: 5 will they need light from lamp or **s**,

SUPERIOR

Heb 1: 4 as far **s** to the angels as the name he

SUPPLICATION → SUPPLICATIONS

Eph 6:18 With all prayer and **s**, pray at every

6:18 and **s** for all the holy ones

SUPPLICATIONS → SUPPLICATION

1Ti 2: 1 then, I ask that **s**, prayers, petitions,

Heb 5: 7 offered prayers and **s** with loud cries

SUPPORT

Ps 18:19 distress, but the LORD came to my **s**.

Ro 11:18 consider that you do not **s** the root;

SURE

Nu 32:23 and you can be **s** that you will not

Isa 28:16 cornerstone as a **s** foundation;

Heb 6:19 as an anchor of the soul, **s** and firm,

SURPASSES → SURPASSING

Sir 25:11 Fear of the LORD **s** all else,

Eph 3:19 the love of Christ that **s** knowledge,

Php 4: 7 **s** all understanding will guard your

SURPASSING → SURPASSES

2Co 9:14 because of the **s** grace of God

SURPRISED

1Pe 4:12 do not be **s** that a trial by fire is

SURROUNDED → SURROUNDS

Lk 21:20 you see Jerusalem **s** by armies,

Heb 12: 1 since we are **s** by so great a cloud

Rev 20: 9 and **s** the camp of the holy ones

SURROUNDS → SURROUNDED

Ps 125: 2 Jerusalem, the LORD **s** his people

SURVIVORS

Eze 14:22 still some **s** shall be left in it who

SUSA
Ne 1: 1 year, I was in the citadel of **S**
Est 1: 2 royal throne in the stronghold of **S**,

SUSANNA
Righteous woman wrongly accused of immorality (Da 13:1-44); vindicated by Daniel (Da 13:45-64).

SUSTAINS
Heb 1: 3 who s all things by his mighty word.

SWALLOW → SWALLOWED
Mt 23:24 strain out the gnat and s the camel!

SWALLOWED → SWALLOW
Ge 41: 7 the seven thin ears s up the seven
Nu 16:32 earth opened its mouth and s them
1Co 15:54 about: "Death is s up in victory.

SWEAR → SWORE, SWORN
Dt 10:20 hold fast to him and s by his name.
Mt 5:34 But I say to you, do not s at all;

SWEAT
Ge 3:19 By the s of your face shall you get
Lk 22:44 that his s became like drops

SWEET → SWEETER
Ps 119:103 How s to my tongue is your mouth.
Eze 3: 3 it was as s as honey in my mouth.
Rev 10:10 it. In my mouth it was like s honey,

SWEETER → SWEET
Jdg 14:18 said to him, "What is s than honey,
Ps 19:11 of purest gold; S also than honey

SWIFT
Ecc 9:11 sun that the race is not won by the s,
2Pe 2: 1 them, bringing s destruction

SWINE
1Ma 1:47 to sacrifice s and unclean animals,
Mt 7: 6 or throw your pearls before s,
Mk 5:12 with him, "Send us into the s. Let us

SWORD → SWORDS
Ge 3:24 cherubim and the fiery revolving s,
1Sa 17:47 shall learn that it is not by s or spear
1Ch 21:30 he was fearful of the s of the angel
Sir 21: 3 Every offense is a two-edged s;
Isa 2: 4 shall not raise the s against another,
49: 2 He made of me a sharp-edged s
Mt 10:34 come to bring not peace but the s.
Lk 2:35 you yourself a s will pierce) so
Eph 6:17 of salvation and the s of the Spirit,

Heb 4:12 sharper than any two-edged s,
Rev 1:16 A sharp two-edged s came
19:15 his mouth came a sharp s to strike

SWORDS → SWORD
Isa 2: 4 peoples. They shall beat their s

SWORE → SWEAR
Ex 6: 8 into the land which I s to give
32:13 and how you s to them by your own
Ps 132:11 The LORD s an oath to David,
Heb 6:13 by whom to swear, "he s by himself,"

SWORN → SWEAR
Ps 110: 4 The LORD has s and will not waver:
Heb 7:21 him: "The Lord has s, and he will not

SYMPATHIZE
Heb 4:15 have a high priest who is unable to s

SYNAGOGUE → SYNAGOGUES
Lk 4:16 into the s on the sabbath day.
8:41 an official of the s, came forward.
Ac 18:26 He began to speak boldly in the s;

SYNAGOGUES → SYNAGOGUE
Mt 4:23 teaching in their s,

T

TABITHA → See DORCAS

TABLE → TABLES
Ex 25:23 shall also make a t of acacia wood,
Ps 23: 5 You set a t before me as my

TABLES → TABLE
Mk 11:15 He overturned the t of the money

TABLETS
Ex 31:18 Sinai, he gave him the two t
31:18 the stone t inscribed by God's own
2Co 3: 3 not on t of stone but on t that are

TAKE → TAKEN, TAKES
Mt 11:29 T my yoke upon you and learn
Mk 8:34 must deny himself, t up his cross,

TAKEN → TAKE
Sir 44:16 walked with the LORD and was t up,
Heb 11: 5 By faith Enoch was t up so that he
11: 5 no more because God had t him."
11: 5 Before he was t up, he was attested

TAKES → TAKE
Jn 1:29 who t away the sin of the world.
10:18 No one t it from me, but I lay it
Rev 22:19 if anyone t away from the words

TALENT
Mt 25:25 off and buried your t in the ground.

TAMAR
1. Wife of Judah's sons Er and Onan (Ge 38:1-10). Children by Judah (Ge 38:11-30; Mt 1:3).
2. Daughter of David, raped by Amnon (2Sa 13).

TASTE → TASTED
Mt 16:28 here who will not t death until they
Col 2:21 not handle! Do not t! Do not touch!"

TASTED → TASTE
Heb 6: 4 enlightened and t the heavenly gift
1Pe 2: 3 for you have t that the Lord is good.

TAUGHT → TEACH
Isa 40:14 Who t him the path of judgment,
Jn 6:45 prophets: 'They shall all be t by God.'

TAX → TAXES
Mt 11:19 a friend of t collectors and sinners.'
Lk 18:10 and the other was a t collector.

TAXES → TAX
Ro 13: 7 all their dues, t to whom t are due,

TEACH → TAUGHT, TEACHER, TEACHERS, TEACHING
Ps 90:12 T us to count our days aright,
Jer 31:34 will they have need to t their friends
Jn 14:26 in my name—he will t you everything
Col 3:16 richly, as in all wisdom you t
1Ti 2:12 I do not permit a woman to t
1Jn 2:27 you do not need anyone to t you.

TEACHER → TEACH
Mt 10:24 No disciple is above his t, no slave
Jn 1:38 "Rabbi" (which translated means T),

TEACHERS → TEACH
Ps 119:99 more understanding than all my t,
1Co 12:28 third, t; then, mighty deeds;
Eph 4:11 evangelists, others as pastors and t,
Jas 3: 1 Not many of you should become t,

TEACHING → TEACH
Mk 1:27 is this? A new t with authority.
Tit 1:11 are upsetting whole families by t
2Jn 1: 9 in the t of the Christ does not have
1: 9 remains in the t has the Father

TEAR → TORN
Mk 2:21 from the old, and the t gets worse.
Rev 7:17 God will wipe away every t

TEETH → TOOTH
Mt 8:12 will be wailing and grinding of t."

TEKEL
Da 5:27 T, you have been weighed

TELL → FORETOLD
Ps 50:12 Were I hungry, I would not t you,
1Co 15:51 Behold, I t you a mystery. We shall

TEMPERATE
1Ti 3: 2 irreproachable, married only once, t,
Tit 2: 2 that older men should be t,

TEMPLE
1Sa 3: 3 in the t of the LORD where the ark
1Ma 4:48 the interior of the t and purified
Ps 11: 4 The LORD is in his holy t; the LORD's
Mt 4: 5 him stand on the parapet of the t,
Mt 12: 6 something greater than the t is here.
Jn 2:21 speaking about the t of his body.
1Co 3:16 not know that you are the t of God,
Eph 2:21 grows into a t sacred in the Lord;
Rev 21:22 I saw no t in the city, for its t is

TEMPTATION → TEMPTED, TEMPTER
1Ti 6: 9 who want to be rich are falling into t
Jas 1:12 is the man who perseveres in t,

TEMPTED → TEMPTATION
Mk 1:13 the desert for forty days, t by Satan.
Gal 6: 1 so that you also may not be t.

TEMPTER → TEMPTATION
Mt 4: 3 The t approached and said to him,
1Th 3: 5 fear that somehow the t had put you

TEN → TENTH
Ex 34:28 the covenant, the t commandments.
Da 7:24 The t horns shall be t kings
Mt 25: 1 will be like t virgins who took their
Rev 17:12 The t horns that you saw represent t

TENDER
Lk 1:78 because of the t mercy of our God

TENT
Ex 27:21 before the LORD in the meeting t,
2Sa 7: 2 while the ark of God dwells in a t!"
2Co 5: 1 dwelling, a t, should be destroyed,

TENTH → TEN
Ge 14:20 Abram gave him a t of everything.
Isa 6:13 If there be still a t part in it,

TERROR
Ps 91: 5 You shall not fear the t of the night

TEST → TESTED, TESTING
Dt 6:16 God, to the t, as you did at Massah.
Lk 4:12 not put the Lord, your God, to the t.' "
   10:25 of the law who stood up to t him
2Co 13: 5 you are living in faith. T yourselves.
   13: 5 you?—unless, of course, you fail the t.
1Jn 4: 1 but t the spirits to see whether they

TESTED → TEST
Ps 78:41 Again and again they t God,
Heb 4:15 but one who has similarly been t

TESTIFIED → TESTIFY
Jn 1:15 John t to him and cried out, saying,
1Pe 1:11 them indicated when it t in advance

TESTIFIES → TESTIFY
1Jn 5: 6 The Spirit is the one that t,

TESTIFY → TESTIFIED, TESTIFIES, TESTIMONY
Jn 15:26 from the Father, he will t to me.
1Jn 5: 7 So there are three that t,

TESTIMONY → TESTIFY
Mk 14:59 Even so their t did not agree.
Rev 1: 9 God's word and gave t to Jesus.

TESTING → TEST
Jas 1: 3 that the t of your faith produces

THADDAEUS → = JUDAS
Apostle (Mt 10:3; Mk 3:18); probably also known as Judas son of James (Lk 6:16; Ac 1:13).

THANK → THANKS, THANKSGIVING
2Ch 29:31 t offerings for the house of the LORD."
   29:31 the sacrifices and t offerings and all

THANKS → THANK
1Ch 16: 8 Give t to the LORD, invoke his name;
Ps 107: 1 "Give t to the LORD who is good,
Ro 1:21 him glory as God or give him t.
1Co 11:24 and after he had given t, broke it
2Co 9:15 T be to God for his indescribable
Rev 4: 9 t to the one who sits on the throne,

THANKSGIVING → THANK
Lev 7:12 anyone makes a peace offering in t,
   7:12 with his t sacrifice he shall offer
Php 4: 6 with t, make your requests known
Rev 7:12 Blessing and glory, wisdom and t,

THEFT → THIEF
Mt 15:19 adultery, unchastity, t, false witness,

THIEF → THEFT, THIEVES
Ex 22: 1 "[If a t is caught in the act
Jn 10:10 A t comes only to steal
1Th 5: 2 the Lord will come like a t at night.
Rev 16:15 ("Behold, I am coming like a t."

THIEVES → THIEF
Mt 6:19 destroys, and t break in and steal.

THINK → THINKING, THOUGHT, THOUGHTS
Ro 12: 3 I tell everyone among you not to t
   12: 3 more highly than one ought to t,
   12: 3 t, but to t soberly, each according

THINKING → THINK
1Co 14:20 stop being childish in your t.
   14:20 like infants, but in your t be mature.

THIRD → THREE
Hos 6: 2 on the t day he will raise us up,
Mt 26:44 withdrew again and prayed a t time,
Lk 18:33 him, but on the t day he will rise."
2Co 12: 2 was caught up to the t heaven.

THIRST → THIRSTY
Mt 5: 6 who hunger and t for righteousness,
Rev 7:16 They will not hunger or t anymore,

THIRSTY → THIRST
Mt 25:35 I was t and you gave me drink,

THOMAS
Apostle (Mt 10:3; Mk 3:18; Lk 6:15; Jn 11:16; 14:5; 21:2; Ac 1:13). Doubted resurrection (Jn 20:24-28).

THORN → THORNS
2Co 12: 7 a t in the flesh was given to me,

THORNS → THORN
Ge 3:18 T and thistles shall it bring forth
Mt 13: 7 Some seed fell among t, and the t
Jn 19: 2 the soldiers wove a crown out of t

THOUGHT → THINK
2Co 10: 5 take every t captive in obedience

THOUGHTS → THINK
Isa 55: 8 For my t are not your t, nor are your
1Co 3:20 "The Lord knows the t of the wise,
Heb 4:12 reflections and t of the heart.

THOUSAND → THOUSANDS
Ps 90: 4 A t years in your eyes are merely
2Pe 3: 8 the Lord one day is like a t years
3: 8 a t years and a t years like one day.
Rev 20: 4 reigned with Christ for a t years.

THOUSANDS → THOUSAND
1Sa 18: 7 "Saul has slain his t, and David his
1Sa 18: 7 has slain his t, and David his ten t."
Da 7:10 T upon t were ministering to him,

THREE → THIRD
Ge 18: 2 up, he saw t men standing nearby.
Ex 23:14 "T times a year you shall celebrate
Mt 18:20 t are gathered together in my name,
26:34 crows, you will deny me t times."
Mk 8:31 and be killed, and rise after t days.
2Co 12: 8 T times I begged the Lord
1Jn 5: 7 So there are t that testify,

THRONE → THRONES
2Sa 7:13 I will make his royal t firm forever.
Ps 45: 7 Your t, O god, stands forever;
Isa 6: 1 Lord seated on a high and lofty t,
Jer 33:21 not have a son to be king upon his t,
Mt 19:28 of Man is seated on his t of glory,
Heb 4:16 So let us confidently approach the t
12: 2 his seat at the right of the t of God.
Rev 4:10 before the one who sits on the t
4:10 down their crowns before the t,
20:11 Next I saw a large white t

THRONES → THRONE
Da 7: 9 As I watched, T were set up
Rev 4: 4 the throne I saw twenty-four other t

THROW → THROWN
Ex 1:22 "T into the river every boy that is
Mt 7: 6 or t your pearls before swine,

THROWN → THROW
Rev 20:10 Devil who had led them astray was t

THUMMIM
Ex 28:30 you shall put the Urim and T,

THUNDER → THUNDERS
Ex 9:23 LORD sent forth hail and peals of t.

Rev 4: 5 lightning, rumblings, and peals of t.

THUNDERS → THUNDER
Rev 10: 3 out, the seven t raised their voices,

TIBNI
King of Israel (1Ki 16:21-22).

TIE
Mt 23: 4 They t up heavy burdens [hard

TIME → TIMES
Est 4:14 that it was for a t like this that you
Ecc 3: 1 There is an appointed t
3: 1 and a t for every affair under
Ro 5: 6 at the appointed t for the ungodly.
2Co 6: 2 "In an acceptable t I heard you,
6: 2 Behold, now is a very acceptable t;
Gal 4: 4 when the fullness of t had come,
Rev 22:10 book, for the appointed t is near.

TIMES → TIME
Jos 6: 4 day march around the city seven t.
Mt 16: 3 you cannot judge the signs of the t.]
18:22 you, not seven t but seventy-seven t.
Mk 14:30 twice you will deny me three t."

TIMOTHY
Believer from Lystra (Ac 16:1). Joined Paul on second missionary journey (Ac 16-20). Sent to settle problems at Corinth (1Co 4:17; 16:10). Led church at Ephesus (1Ti 1:3). Co-writer with Paul (1Th 1:1; 2Th 1:1; Phm 1).

TITHE
Dt 12:17 partake of your t of grain or wine
Mal 3:10 Bring the whole t

TITUS
Gentile co-worker of Paul (Gal 2:1-3; 2Ti 4:10); sent to Corinth (2Co 2:13; 7-8; 12:18), Crete (Tit 1:4-5).

TOBIAH
Enemy of Nehemiah (Ne 2:10-19; 4; 6; 13:4-9).

TOBIT
Tob 1: 1 This book tells the story of T,

TODAY
Dt 30:15 then, I have t set before you life
Ps 2: 7 "You are my son; t I am your father.
Lk 23:43 t you will be with me in Paradise."
Heb 13: 8 Jesus Christ is the same yesterday, t,

TOGETHER
Mt 19: 6 what God has joined t, no human

TOLA
A judge of Israel (Jdg 10:1-2).

TOMB
Mk 15:46 laid him in a t that had been hewn
15:46 a stone against the entrance to the t.
Lk 24: 2 the stone rolled away from the t;

TOMORROW
Isa 22:13 wine: "Eat and drink, for t we die!"
Mt 6:34 Do not worry about t; t will take
Jas 4:14 no idea what your life will be like t.

TONGUE → TONGUES
Ex 4:10 but I am slow of speech and t."
Ps 139: 4 Even before a word is on my t,
Pr 18:21 and life are in the power of the t;
Isa 45:23 bend; by me every t shall swear,
1Co 14:19 also, than ten thousand words in a t.
Php 2:11 and every t confess that Jesus Christ
Jas 3: 8 but no human being can tame the t.

TONGUES → TONGUE
Ac 2: 3 there appeared to them t as of fire,
1Co 12:10 to another varieties of t; to another
12:10 of t; to another interpretation of t.
14: 5 I should like all of you to speak in t,
14: 5 is greater than one who speaks in t,

TOOTH → TEETH
Ex 21:24 eye for eye, t for t, hand for hand,
Mt 5:38 'An eye for an eye and a t for a t.'

TORCHES
Da 10: 6 his eyes were like fiery t, his arms
Rev 4: 5 Seven flaming t burned in front

TORMENTED
Rev 20:10 There they will be t day and night

TORN → TEAR
1Sa 28:17 me: he has t the kingdom from your
Lk 23:45 the temple was t down the middle.

TORTURED
Heb 11:35 Some were t and would not accept

TOUCH
Ge 3: 3 'You shall not eat it or even t it,
Mt 9:21 "If only I can t his cloak, I shall be
Lk 24:39 T me and see, because a ghost does
Col 2:21 not handle! Do not taste! Do not t!"

TOWER
Ge   11: 4   a city and a t with its top in the sky,
Pr   18:10   The name of the LORD is a strong t;

TRADITION
Mt   15: 2   "Why do your disciples break the t
Col   2: 8   philosophy according to human t,

TRAIN → TRAINING
Pr   22: 6   T a boy in the way he should go;
1Ti   4: 7   silly myths. T yourself for devotion,

TRAINING → TRAIN
1Ti   4: 8   while physical t is of limited value,
2Ti   3:16   and for t in righteousness,

TRAITOR
Lk   6:16   and Judas Iscariot, who became a t.

TRANSFIGURED
Mt   17: 2   And he was t before them; his face

TRANSFORMED
Ro   12: 2   be t by the renewal of your mind,
2Co   3:18   are being t into the same image

TRANSGRESSION
Da   9:24   Then t will stop and sin will end,
Gal   6: 1   even if a person is caught in some t,

TRAP
Lk   20:20   to be righteous who were to t him
Ro   11: 9   their table become a snare and a t,

TREAD → TREADING
Rev   19:15   and he himself will t out in the wine

TREADING → TREAD
Dt   25: 4   muzzle an ox when it is t out grain.
Mic   7:19   on us, t underfoot our guilt?
1Co   9: 9   shall not muzzle an ox while it is t

TREASURE → TREASURES
Ps   119:11   In my heart I t your promise, that I
Mt   6:21   For where your t is, there also will
2Co   4: 7   we hold this t in earthen vessels,

TREASURES → TREASURE
Col   2: 3   in whom are hidden all the t

TREE → TREES
Ge   3:24   to guard the way to the t of life.
Dt   21:23   shall not remain on the t overnight.
      21:23   curse rests on him who hangs on a t,
Mt   12:33   "Either declare the t good and its

Mt   12:33   or declare the t rotten and its fruit is
      12:33   rotten, for a t is known by its fruit.
Ac   5:30   him killed by hanging him on a t.
Ro   11:24   what is by nature a wild olive t,
      11:24   grafted back into their own olive t
Rev   22: 2   side of the river grew the t of life

TREES → TREE
Ps   96:12   Then let all the t of the forest rejoice
Zec   4:11   "What are these two olive t at each
Rev   11: 4   These are the two olive t

TREMBLE → TREMBLED, TREMBLING
Ps   114: 7   T, earth, before the Lord,
Hab   3: 6   his look makes the nations t.

TREMBLED → TREMBLE
Ex   20:18   smoking, they all feared and t.

TREMBLING → TREMBLE
Ps   2:11   fear; with t bow down in homage,
Php   2:12   out your salvation with fear and t.

TRESPASSES
2Co   5:19   not counting their t against them

TRIAL → TRIALS
2Pe   2: 9   how to rescue the devout from t
Rev   3:10   safe in the time of t that is going

TRIALS → TRIAL
Jas   1: 2   when you encounter various t,
1Pe   1: 6   have to suffer through various t,

TRIBE → TRIBES
Nu   1: 4   there shall be a man from each t,
Ps   78:68   God chose the t of Judah,
Rev   5: 5   The lion of the t of Judah, the root

TRIBES → TRIBE
Ge   49:28   All these are the twelve t of Israel,
Ex   24: 4   pillars for the twelve t of Israel.
Mt   19:28   judging the twelve t of Israel.
Rev   21:12   of the twelve t of the Israelites.

TRIUMPHS
Jas   2:13   mercy; mercy t over judgment.

TROUBLE → TROUBLED
Job   14: 1   woman is short-lived and full of t,
Ps   9:10   a stronghold in times of t.
Pr   11: 8   The just man escapes t,
Sir   51:10   Do not abandon me in time of t,
Isa   33: 2   morning, our salvation in time of t!

TROUBLED → TROUBLE
Jn   14: 1   "Do not let your hearts be t.

TRUE → TRUTH
Jn   1: 9   The t light, which enlightens
      21:24   and we know that his testimony is t.
Ro   3: 4   God must be t, though every human
1Jn   5:20   to know the one who is t. And we
      5:20   t. And we are in the one who is t,
      5:20   He is the t God and eternal life.
Rev   3:14   the faithful and t witness, the source
      19:11   its rider was [called] "Faithful and T."
      22: 6   "These words are trustworthy and t,

TRUMPET → TRUMPETS
Ex   19:16   and a very loud t blast, so that all
Joel   2:15   Blow the t Zion! proclaim a fast,
1Co   15:52   in the blink of an eye, at the last t.
      15:52   t. For the t will sound, the dead will
1Th   4:16   an archangel and with the t of God,

TRUMPETS → TRUMPET
Nu   10: 2   "Make two t of beaten silver,
Rev   8: 2   before God were given seven t.

TRUST → ENTRUSTED, TRUSTED, TRUSTEES, TRUSTS, TRUSTWORTHY
Ps   9:11   Those who honor your name t
      37: 3   In the LORD and do good that you
      119:42   with a word, for I t in your word.
Pr   3: 5   T in the LORD with all your heart,
Sir   2: 6   T God and he will help you;
Heb   2:13   and again: "I will put my t in him";

TRUSTED → TRUST
Ps   22: 5   In you our ancestors t; they t
Da   3:95   to deliver the servants that t in him;
      13:35   she t in the Lord wholeheartedly.

TRUSTS → TRUST
Ps   86: 2   save your servant who t in you.
Jer   17: 7   Blessed is the man who t

TRUSTWORTHY → TRUST
1Co   7:25   as one who by the Lord's mercy is t.
Rev   22: 6   to me, "These words are t and true,

TRUTH → TRUE
Tob   3: 2   All your ways are mercy and t;
Ps   25: 5   Guide me in your t and teach me,
Pr   23:23   Get the t, and sell it not— wisdom,
Jn   1:17   and t came through Jesus Christ.

TRUTH → TRUE (*cont.*)
Jn 4:23 worship the Father in Spirit and t;
8:32 and you will know the t, and the t
14: 6 "I am the way and the t and the life.
14:17 the Spirit of t, which the world
16:13 the Spirit of t, he will guide you
16:13 Spirit of t, he will guide you to all t.
Eph 4:15 Rather, living the t in love,
1Ti 3:15 God, the pillar and foundation of t.
2Ti 2:15 the word of t without deviation.

TUNIC
Lk 9: 3 and let no one take a second t.
Jn 19:23 They also took his t, but the t was

TURN
Isa 6:10 and they will t and be healed.
45:22 T to me and be safe, all you ends
Lk 1:17 of Elijah to t the hearts of fathers

TWELVE
Ge 49:28 All these are the t tribes of Israel.
Ex 24: 4 and t pillars for the t tribes of Israel.
Jos 4: 3 to take up t stones from this spot
Mt 10: 1 he summoned his t disciples
Lk 9:17 up, they filled t wicker baskets.
Rev 21:12 with t gates where t angels were
21:12 [the names] of the t tribes
22: 2 that produces fruit t times a year,

TWO → TWICE, TWO-EDGED
Ge 1:16 God made the t great lights,
6:19 living creatures you shall bring t
Ex 31:18 he gave him the t tablets
Dt 17: 6 The testimony of t or three
Mt 6:24 "No one can serve t masters. He will
19: 5 and the t shall become one flesh'?

TWO-EDGED → TWO
Heb 4:12 effective, sharper than any t sword,
Rev 1:16 A sharp t sword came out of his

TYRE
Eze 28:12 utter a lament over the king of T,
Mt 11:22 it will be more tolerable for T

U

UNBELIEF → UNBELIEVER, UNBELIEVERS
Mk 9:24 cried out, "I do believe, help my u!"
Ro 11:20 They were broken off because of u,

1Ti 1:13 I acted out of ignorance in my u.

UNBELIEVER → UNBELIEF
1Co 10:27 If an u invites you and you want
2Co 6:15 a believer in common with an u?

UNBELIEVERS → UNBELIEF
2Co 6:14 with those who are different, with u.

UNCIRCUMCISED → UNCIRCUMCISION
Ex 12:48 no man who is u may partake of it.
1Ma 1:48 to leave their sons u, and to let
Ac 7:51 people, u in heart and ears,
Ro 4:11 through faith while he was u.
4:11 the father of all the u who believe,

UNCIRCUMCISION → UNCIRCUMCISED
1Co 7:19 nothing, and u means nothing;
Gal 5: 6 neither circumcision nor u counts

UNCLEAN → UNCLEANNESS
Lev 5: 2 touches any u thing, as the carcass
5: 2 as the carcass of an u wild animal,
5: 2 or that of an u domestic animal,
5: 2 or that of an u swarming creature,
5: 2 and thus becomes u and guilty;
Isa 52:11 touch nothing u! Out from there!
Mk 3:11 whenever u spirits saw him they
Rev 21:27 but nothing u will enter it,

UNDER
Ac 4:12 any other name u heaven given
Ro 6:14 since you are not u the law but u

UNDERSTAND → UNDERSTANDING
Job 42: 3 with great things that I do not u;
Pr 2: 5 will you u the fear of the LORD;
Mt 13:15 ears and u with their heart and be
Lk 24:45 their minds to u the scriptures.
Ac 8:30 "Do you u what you are reading?"
Eph 5:17 try to u what is the will of the Lord.

UNDERSTANDING → UNDERSTAND
Ex 36: 1 u in knowing how to execute all
Pr 2: 6 his mouth come knowledge and u;
Isa 40:14 or showed him the way of u?
Lk 2:47 heard him were astounded at his u
Php 4: 7 that surpasses all u will guard your
2Ti 2: 7 for the Lord will give you u

UNFAITHFUL
Ro 3: 3 What if some were u? Will their

UNGODLY
Ro 5: 6 died at the appointed time for the u.

UNITY
Eph 4: 3 preserve the u of the spirit through

UNJUST
Ro 3: 5 say? Is God u, humanly speaking,
Heb 6:10 God is not u so as to overlook your

UNLEAVENED
Ex 12:17 then, this custom of the u bread.
Mt 26:17 first day of the Feast of U Bread,

UNPRODUCTIVE
1Co 14:14 spirit is at prayer but my mind is u.
Tit 3:14 needs, so that they may not be u.

UNRIGHTEOUS
2Pe 2: 9 to keep the u under punishment

UPHOLD
Isa 42: 1 Here is my servant whom I u,

UPRIGHT
Job 1: 1 a blameless and u man named Job,

UR
Ge 15: 7 the LORD who brought you from U

URIAH
    Hittite husband of Bathsheba, killed (2Sa 11).

URIM
Ex 28:30 of decision you shall put the U

USE → USEFUL
Gal 5:13 But do not u this freedom as
2Ti 2:20 for lofty and others for humble u.

USEFUL → USE
2Ti 3:16 by God and is u for teaching,

UZZIAH → = AZARIAH
    Son of Amaziah; king of Judah also known as Azariah (2Ki 15:1-7; 1Ch 6:24; 2Ch 26). Struck with leprosy because of pride (2Ch 26:16-23).

V

VAIN → VANITY
Lev 26:16 You will sow your seed in v,
Ps 2: 1 and the peoples grumble in v?
Mt 15: 9 in v do they worship me, teaching as
Php 2:16 Christ may be that I did not run in v
2:16 that I did not run in v or labor in v,

VALLEY
Ps 23: 4 Even when I walk through a dark v,

Isa 40: 4 Every **v** shall be filled in,
    40: 4 plain, the rough country, a broad **v**.
Lk 3: 5 Every **v** shall be filled and every

VALUE
Ro 3: 1 Or what is the **v** of circumcision?
1Ti 4: 8 physical training is of limited **v**,

VANITY → VAIN
Ecc 1: 2 **V** of vanities, says Qoheleth,
    1: 2 **v** of vanities! All things are **v**!
    12: 8 **V** of vanities, says Qoheleth,
    12: 8 says Qoheleth, all things are **v**!

VASHTI
    Persian queen replaced by Esther (Est 1-2).

VEIL
Ex 34:33 with them, he put a **v** over his face.
2Co 3:15 is read, a **v** lies over their hearts,

VENGEANCE → AVENGE, AVENGER, AVENGES, AVENGING
Isa 34: 8 For the LORD has a day of **v**, a year
Na 1: 2 and angry; The LORD brings **v** on his

VICTORY
Pr 21:31 the day of battle, but **v** is the LORD's.
1Co 15:54 about: "Death is swallowed up in **v**.
1Jn 5: 4 the **v** that conquers the world is our

VINDICATED
Mt 11:19 But wisdom is **v** by her works."
1Ti 3:16 in the flesh, **v** in the spirit,

VINE → VINEYARD
Ps 80: 9 You brought a **v** out of Egypt;
Jer 2:21 I had planted you, a choice **v**
    2:21 out obnoxious to me, a spurious **v**?
Jn 15: 1 "I am the true **v**, and my Father is
    15: 1 **v**, and my Father is the **v** grower.

VINEYARD → VINE
1Ki 21: 1 as Naboth the Jezreelite had a **v**
Isa 5: 1 my friend's song concerning his **v**.
    5: 1 his **v**. My friend had a **v** on a fertile
Mt 21:33 was a landowner who planted a **v**,

VIOLENCE
Hab 2:17 For the **v** done to Lebanon shall
    2:17 and **v** done to the land, to the city

VIPERS
Mt 23:33 you brood of **v**, how can you flee

VIRGIN
Jer 31:21 Turn back, O **v** Israel, turn back
Mt 1:23 the **v** shall be with child and bear
2Co 11: 2 present you as a chaste **v** to Christ.

VISION → VISIONS
Isa 22: 1 Oracle of the Valley of **V**: What is
Da 8:26 The **v** of the evenings
    8:26 however, keep this **v** undisclosed,
Ac 26:19 not disobedient to the heavenly **v**.

VISIONS → VISION
Nu 12: 6 you, in **v** will I reveal myself to him,
Eze 1: 1 heavens opened, and I saw divine **v**.
Da 1:17 to Daniel the understanding of all **v**
Ac 2:17 your young men shall see **v**,

VOICE
Isa 40: 3 A **v** cries out: In the desert prepare
Jn 1:23 "I am 'the **v** of one crying
    10: 3 and the sheep hear his **v**, as he calls
Heb 3: 7 "Oh, that today you would hear his **v**,
Rev 3:20 If anyone hears my **v** and opens

VOW → VOWS
Ecc 5: 4 had better not make a **v** than make it
Sir 18:23 Before making a **v** have the means

VOWS → VOW
Ps 22:26 my **v** I will fulfill before those who

W

WAGES
Ro 6:23 For the **w** of sin is death, but the gift

WAIT
Ps 27:14 **W** for the LORD, take courage;
    27:14 be stouthearted, **w** for the LORD!
Sir 2: 7 who fear the LORD, **w** for his mercy.
Hab 2: 3 If it delays, **w** for it, it will surely
Ro 8:23 groan within ourselves as we **w**

WALK → WALKED, WALKING
Ge 17: 1 **W** in my presence and be blameless.
Ps 23: 4 when I **w** through a dark valley,
Isa 2: 5 let us **w** in the light of the LORD!
    40:31 grow weary, **w** and not grow faint.
Jer 6:16 Which is the way to good, and **w** it;
    6:16 But they said, "We will not **w** it."

Jn 8:12 Whoever follows me will not **w**
2Co 5: 7 for we **w** by faith, not by sight.
Rev 21:24 The nations will **w** by its light,

WALKED → WALK
Ge 5:24 Then Enoch **w** with God, and he

WALKING → WALK
Mt 14:26 the disciples saw him **w** on the sea

WALL
Jos 6:20 The **w** collapsed, and the people
Ne 2:17 let us rebuild the **w** of Jerusalem,
Eph 2:14 and broke down the dividing **w**

WAR → WARRIOR, WARS
Ecc 3: 8 a time of **w**, and a time of peace.
Da 9:26 until the end there shall be **w**,
Ro 7:23 my members another principle at **w**
Rev 19:11 and wages **w** in righteousness.

WARRIOR → WAR
Ex 15: 3 The LORD is a **w**, LORD is his name!

WARS → WAR
Mt 24: 6 You will hear of **w** and reports of **w**;

WASH → WASHED
Ps 51: 9 **w** me, make me whiter than snow.
Jn 13: 5 began to **w** the disciples' feet and dry
Rev 22:14 are they who **w** their robes so as

WASHED → WASH
1Co 6:11 but now you have had yourselves **w**,

WATCH → WATCHES
Lk 2: 8 keeping the night **w** over their flock.
Heb 13:17 for they keep **w** over you and will

WATCHES → WATCH
Ps 1: 6 The LORD **w** over the way of the just,

WATER → WATERS
Ex 17: 1 Here there was no **w** for the people
Nu 20: 2 As the community had no **w**,
Jer 2:13 broken cisterns, that hold no **w**.
Eze 36:25 I will sprinkle clean **w** upon you
Mk 1: 8 I have baptized you with **w**; will
Jn 2: 9 the headwaiter tasted the **w** that had
    2: 9 who had drawn the **w** knew),
    3: 5 of God without being born of **w**
    4:10 he would have given you living **w**."
1Jn 5: 6 This is the one who came through **w**

WATER → WATERS (*cont.*)
1Jn 5: 6 not by **w** alone, but by **w** and blood.
Rev 22: 1 me the river of life-giving **w**,

WATERS → WATER
Ge 7: 7 ark because of the **w** of the flood.
Ecc 11: 1 Cast your bread upon the **w**;

WAY → WAYS
Ps 1: 6 The LORD watches over the **w**
1: 6 the **w** of the wicked leads to ruin.
86:11 Teach me, LORD, your **w** that I may
Pr 12:15 The **w** of the fool seems right in his
22: 6 Train a boy in the **w** he should go;
Isa 40: 3 the desert prepare the **w** of the LORD!
Mal 3: 1 to prepare the **w** before me;
Mt 3: 3 desert, 'Prepare the **w** of the Lord,
Jn 14: 6 "I am the **w** and the truth and the life.
Ac 9: 2 or women who belonged to the **W**,
1Co 12:31 show you a still more excellent **w**.
Heb 10:20 living **w** he opened for us through

WAYS → WAY
Dt 10:12 your and follow his **w** exactly,
Sir 2:15 those who love him keep his **w**.
Rev 15: 3 Just and true are your **w**, O king

WEAK → WEAKNESS, WEAKNESSES
Mt 26:41 spirit is willing, but the flesh is **w**."
Ro 14: 1 Welcome anyone who is **w** in faith,
1Co 1:27 and God chose the **w** of the world
2Co 12:10 for when I am **w**, then I am strong.

WEAKNESS → WEAK
Ro 8:26 Spirit too comes to the aid of our **w**;

WEAKNESSES → WEAK
2Co 12:10 I am content with **w**, insults,
Heb 4:15 is unable to sympathize with our **w**,

WEALTH
Ps 49: 7 Those who trust in their **w** and boast
Pr 19: 4 **W** adds many friends, but the friend
Sir 5: 1 Rely not on your **w**; say not: "I have

WEAPONS
2Co 6: 7 with **w** of righteousness at the right

WEAR
Mt 6:31 we to drink?' or 'What are we to **w**?'

WEARY
Isa 40:31 They will run and not grow **w**,
Heb 12: 3 in order that you may not grow **w**

WEDDING
Jn 2: 1 the third day there was a **w** in Cana

WEEKS
Ex 34:22 "You shall keep the feast of **W**
Lev 23:15 sheaf, you shall count seven full **w**,
Da 9:24 "Seventy **w** are decreed for your

WEEP → WEEPING
Ecc 3: 4 A time to **w**, and a time to laugh;
Ro 12:15 who rejoice, **w** with those who **w**.

WEEPING → WEEP
Ps 30: 6 At dusk **w** comes for the night;
Mt 2:18 Rachel **w** for her children, and she

WEIGHED
Da 5:27 you have been **w** on the scales

WELL
Mt 3:17 Son, with whom I am **w** pleased."
17: 5 Son, with whom I am **w** pleased;
2Pe 1:17 with whom I am **w** pleased,"

WEST
Ps 103:12 As far as the east is from the **w**,
Isa 43: 5 from the **w** I will gather you.

WHEAT
Mt 13:25 and sowed weeds all through the **w**,
Lk 22:31 demanded to sift all of you like **w**,
Jn 12:24 you, unless a grain of **w** falls
12:24 dies, it remains just a grain of **w**;

WHIRLWIND → WIND
2Ki 2:11 and Elijah went up to heaven in a **w**.

WHITE → WHITER
Da 7: 9 the hair on his head as **w** as wool;
Mt 5:36 for you cannot make a single hair **w**
Rev 1:14 hair of his head was as **w** as wool
20:11 Next I saw a large **w** throne

WHITER → WHITE
Ps 51: 9 wash me, make me **w** than snow.

WICKED → WICKEDNESS
Ge 13:13 Sodom were very **w** in the sins they
Ps 1: 5 Therefore the **w** will not survive
73: 3 when I saw the prosperity of the **w**.
Isa 48:22 [There is no peace for the **w**,
Eze 18:23 pleasure from the death of the **w**?

Da 12:10 and tested, but the **w** shall prove **w**;

WICKEDNESS → WICKED
Ge 6: 5 the LORD saw how great was man's **w**

WIDE
Mt 7:13 for the gate is **w** and the road broad

WIDOW → WIDOWS
Ps 146: 9 sustains the orphan and the **w**,
1Ti 5: 4 if a **w** has children or grandchildren,
Rev 18: 7 have no **w**, and I will never know

WIDOWS → WIDOW
1Ti 5: 3 Honor **w** who are truly **w**.
Jas 1:27 for orphans and **w** in their affliction

WIFE → WIVES
Ge 2:24 and mother and clings to his **w**,
Ex 20:17 shall not covet your neighbor's **w**,
Tob 8: 6 Adam and you gave him his **w** Eve
Pr 18:22 He who finds a **w** finds happiness;
Sir 26: 3 A good **w** is a generous gift
Mt 5:32 whoever divorces his **w** (unless
19: 3 a man to divorce his **w** for any cause
Eph 5:28 He who loves his **w** loves himself.
Rev 21: 9 you the bride, the **w** of the Lamb."

WILD
Ex 32:25 Aaron had let the people run **w**,
Mk 1:13 He was among **w** beasts,
Ro 11:17 off, and you, a **w** olive shoot,

WILL → WILLING
Ps 40: 9 To do your **w** is my delight;
143:10 Teach me to do your **w**, for you are
Isa 53:10 life, and the **w** of the LORD shall be
Mt 6:10 kingdom come, your **w** be done,
Lk 22:42 still, not my **w** but yours be done."
Jn 4:34 to do the **w** of the one who sent me
Ro 9:19 You **w** say to me then,
9:19 fault? For who can oppose his **w**?"
Eph 6: 6 doing the **w** of God from the heart,
1Jn 5:14 we ask anything according to his **w**,

WILLING → WILL
Mt 26:41 test. The spirit is **w**, but the flesh is
Lk 22:42 if you are **w**, take this cup away

WIND → WHIRLWIND
1Ki 19:11 heavy **w** was rending the mountains
19:11 LORD—but the LORD was not in the **w**.

1Ki 19:11 in the **w**. After the **w** there was
Ps 1: 4 They are like chaff driven by the **w**.
Ecc 1:14 all is vanity and a chase after **w**.
Jn 3: 8 The **w** blows where it wills, and you
Ac 2: 2 sky a noise like a strong driving **w**,

WINE
Dt 7:13 your soil, your grain and **w** and oil,
Ps 104:15 and **w** to gladden our hearts,
Pr 20: 1 **W** is arrogant, strong drink is
SS 1: 2 More delightful is your love than **w**!
Sir 40:20 **W** and music delight the soul,
Mt 9:17 People do not put new **w** into old
9:17 the skins burst, the **w** spills out,
9:17 Rather, they pour new **w** into fresh
Jn 2: 9 tasted the water that had become **w**,
Eph 5:18 And do not get drunk on **w**,
Rev 18: 3 the **w** of her licentious passion.

WINGS
Ex 19: 4 how I bore you up on eagle **w**
Ps 17: 8 hide me in the shadow of your **w**
Lk 13:34 a hen gathers her brood under her **w**,

WIPE → WIPED
Isa 25: 8 The Lord GOD will **w** away the tears
Rev 21: 4 He will **w** every tear from their

WIPED → WIPE
Ac 3:19 that your sins may be **w** away,

WISDOM → WISE
Dt 4: 6 will you give evidence of your **w**
Job 11: 6 And tell you that the secrets of **w**
Pr 1:20 **W** cries aloud in the street,
9:10 The beginning of **w** is the fear
Ecc 1:13 investigate in **w** all things that are
Wis 6:12 Resplendent and unfading is **W**,
Sir 1: 1 All **w** comes from the LORD
24: 1 **W** sings her own praises, before her
Mt 13:54 "Where did this man get such **w**
Lk 2:52 And Jesus advanced [in] **w** and age
Ro 11:33 the depth of the riches and **w**
1Co 1:19 "I will destroy the **w** of the wise,
Col 2: 3 are hidden all the treasures of **w**
Jas 3:17 the **w** from above is first of all pure,
Rev 5:12 power and riches, **w** and strength,

WISE → WISDOM
Dt 4: 6 'This great nation is truly a **w**
Pr 3: 7 Be not **w** in your own eyes,

Pr 13:20 Walk with **w** men and you will
13:20 with **w** men and you will become **w**,
Ecc 12:11 The sayings of the **w** are like goads;
Da 12: 3 But the **w** shall shine brightly
Mt 25: 2 them were foolish and five were **w**.
1Co 1:26 of you were **w** by human standards,
Eph 5:15 live, not as foolish persons but as **w**,

WITHER → WITHERED, WITHERS
Ps 1: 3 Its leaves never **w**; whatever they do

WITHERED → WITHER
Mt 13: 6 scorched, and it **w** for lack of roots.
21:19 And immediately the fig tree **w**.

WITHERS → WITHER
1Pe 1:24 the grass **w**, and the flower wilts;

WITHOUT
2Ch 18:16 mountains, like sheep **w** a shepherd,
Pr 19: 2 **W** knowledge even zeal is not good;
Mt 9:36 abandoned, like sheep **w** a shepherd.
Eph 2:12 were at that time **w** Christ,
2:12 **w** hope and **w** God in the world.
Heb 4:15 been tested in every way, yet **w** sin.

WITNESS → EYEWITNESSES, WITNESSES
Dt 19:15 "One **w** alone shall not take the stand
Job 16:19 now, behold, my **w** is in heaven,
Ro 2:15 also bears **w** and their conflicting
Rev 1: 5 the faithful **w**, the firstborn

WITNESSES → WITNESS
Mt 26:60 though many false **w** came forward.
Heb 12: 1 surrounded by so great a cloud of **w**,
Rev 11: 3 I will commission my two **w**

WIVES → WIFE
1Ki 11: 3 He had seven hundred **w** of princely
11: 3 and his **w** turned his heart.
Eph 5:22 **W** should be subordinate to their
1Pe 3: 1 you **w** should be subordinate to your
3: 1 without a word by their **w'** conduct

WOE
Mt 23:13 "**W** to you, scribes and Pharisees.
Rev 8:13 overhead cry out in a loud voice, "**W**!
8:13 cry out in a loud voice, "**W**! **W**!

WOLF → WOLVES
Isa 11: 6 the **w** shall be a guest of the lamb,
Jn 10:12 sees a **w** coming and leaves
10:12 and the **w** catches and scatters them.

WOLVES → WOLF
Mt 7:15 but underneath are ravenous **w**.

WOMAN → WOMEN
Ge 2:22 up into a **w** the rib that he had taken
3:15 put enmity between you and the **w**,
Pr 11:16 A gracious **w** wins esteem, but she
31:30 the **w** who fears the LORD is to be
Da 13: 2 a very beautiful and God-fearing **w**,
Jn 19:26 he said to his mother, "**W**, behold,
Gal 4: 4 born of a **w**, born under the law,
Rev 12: 1 in the sky, a **w** clothed with the sun,

WOMB
Job 1:21 I came forth from my mother's **w**,
Ps 139:13 you knit me in my mother's **w**.
Jer 1: 5 I formed you in the **w** I knew you,
Lk 1:42 and blessed is the fruit of your **w**.
1:44 the infant in my **w** leaped for joy.

WOMEN → WOMAN
Ezr 10: 2 by taking as wives foreign **w**
Mt 24:41 Two **w** will be grinding at the mill;
Lk 1:42 "Most blessed are you among **w**,
23:55 The **w** who had come from Galilee
1Pe 3: 5 how the holy **w** who hoped in God

WONDERS
Ps 136: 4 Who alone has done great **w**,
Jn 4:48 "Unless you people see signs and **w**,
2Th 2: 9 deed and in signs and **w** that lie,

WOOD
Dt 28:64 you will serve strange gods of **w**
1Co 3:12 silver, precious stones, **w**, hay,

WORD → BYWORD, WORDS
1Ki 8:56 Not a single **w** has gone unfulfilled
Ps 119:105 Your **w** is a lamp for my feet, a light
Pr 30: 5 Every **w** of God is tested; he is
Isa 40: 8 the **w** of our God stands forever."
55:11 So shall my **w** be that goes forth
Mk 4:14 The sower sows the **w**.
Lk 1:38 be done to me according to your **w**."

WORD → BYWORD, WORDS (*cont.*)

Jn	1: 1	In the beginning was the **W**,
	1: 1	and the **W** was with God, and the **W**
	1:14	And the **W** became flesh and made
	14:23	"Whoever loves me will keep my **w**,
	17:17	them in the truth. Your **w** is truth.
Ro	9: 6	it is not that the **w** of God has failed.
2Ti	2:15	imparting the **w** of truth without
Jas	1:22	Be doers of the **w** and not hearers
1Jn	2: 5	But whoever keeps his **w**, the love
Rev	19:13	his name was called the **W** of God.

WORDS → WORD

Dt	11:18	take these **w** of mine into your heart
Ps	5: 2	Hear my **w**, O LORD; listen to my
Pr	30: 6	Add nothing to his **w**, lest he
Hos	6: 5	I slew them by the **w** of my mouth;
Mt	24:35	away, but my **w** will not pass away.
Lk	6:47	listens to my **w**, and acts on them.
1Co	2:13	them not with **w** taught by human
	2:13	but with **w** taught by the Spirit,
Rev	22:19	from the **w** in this prophetic book,

WORK → WORKS

Ge	2: 2	with the **w** he had been doing,
	2: 2	from all the **w** he had undertaken.
Ex	20:10	No **w** may be done then either
Ps	8: 4	your heavens, the **w** of your fingers,
Jn	6:27	Do not **w** for food that perishes
Php	1: 6	the one who began a good **w** in you
	2:12	**w** out your salvation with fear
2Ti	3:17	equipped for every good **w**.
Heb	6:10	not unjust so as to overlook your **w**

WORKS → WORK

Ps	8: 7	have given them rule over the **w**
	92: 6	How great are your **w**, LORD!
Gal	2:16	a person is not justified by **w**
	2:16	in Christ and not by **w** of the law,
	2:16	because by **w** of the law no one will
	5:19	Now the **w** of the flesh are obvious:
Eph	2: 9	it is not from **w**, so no one may
1Ti	6:18	to be rich in good **w**, to be generous,
Jas	2:17	itself, if it does not have **w**, is dead.

WORLD

Ps	9: 9	It is God who governs the **w**
Mt	5:14	You are the light of the **w**. A city set
	16:26	there be for one to gain the whole **w**
Jn	1:10	He was in the **w**, and the **w** came
	1:10	him, but the **w** did not know him.
	3:16	God so loved the **w** that he gave his
	8:12	saying, "I am the light of the **w**.
	16:33	In the **w** you will have trouble,
	16:33	courage, I have conquered the **w**."
1Ti	6: 7	For we brought nothing into the **w**,
Jas	4: 4	to be a lover of the **w** means enmity
	4: 4	of the **w** makes himself an enemy
1Jn	2: 2	only but for those of the whole **w**.
	2:15	Do not love the **w** or the things
	2:15	not love the **w** or the things of the **w**.
	2:15	**w**. If anyone loves the **w**, the love
Rev	11:15	"The kingdom of the **w** now belongs

WORM

Ps	22: 7	But I am a **w**, hardly human,
Mk	9:48	where 'their **w** does not die,

WORRY

Mt	6:25	I tell you, do not **w** about your life,
	10:19	over, do not **w** about how you are

WORSHIP → WORSHIPED

Ex	20: 5	bow down before them or **w** them.
Ps	100: 2	**w** the LORD with cries of gladness;
Mt	4: 9	will prostrate yourself and **w** me."
Jn	4:24	those who **w** him must win Spirit
Ro	12: 1	pleasing to God, your spiritual **w**.
Rev	22: 3	be in it, and his servants will **w** him.

WORSHIPED → WORSHIP

Rev	5:14	and the elders fell down and **w**.

WORTHY

Mt	10:38	and follow after me is not **w** of me.
Eph	4: 1	in a manner **w** of the call you have
Heb	3: 3	he is **w** of more "glory" than Moses,
Rev	4:11	"**W** are you, Lord our God, to receive
	5:12	voice: "**W** is the Lamb that was slain

WOUND → WOUNDS

Ex	21:25	burn for burn, **w** for **w**,
Rev	13: 3	but this mortal **w** was healed.

WOUNDS → WOUND

Ps	147: 3	the brokenhearted, binds up their **w**,
1Pe	2:24	By his **w** you have been healed.

WRAPPED

Mk	15:46	**w** him in the linen cloth and laid
Lk	2: 7	She **w** him in swaddling clothes

WRATH

Ps	2: 5	to them in anger, terrifies them in **w**:
	6: 2	LORD, nor punish me in your **w**.
Pr	15: 1	A mild answer calms **w**, but a harsh
Sir	16:11	though on the wicked alights his **w**.
La	4:11	poured out his blazing **w**; He has
Zep	1:15	A day of **w** is that day, a day
Mt	3: 7	you to flee from the coming **w**?
Ro	1:18	The **w** of God is indeed being
Eph	2: 3	we were by nature children of **w**,
1Th	1:10	who delivers us from the coming **w**.
Rev	6:17	the great day of their **w** has come

WRITE → WRITING, WRITTEN, WROTE

Ex	34:27	said to Moses, "**W** down these words,
Dt	6: 9	**W** them on the doorposts of your
Pr	7: 3	**w** them on the tablet of your heart.
Jer	31:33	them, and **w** it upon their hearts;
Heb	8:10	and I will **w** them upon their hearts.
Rev	21: 5	Then he said, "**W** these words down,

WRITING → WRITE

Da	5: 7	"Whoever reads this **w** and tells me

WRITTEN → WRITE

Jos	23: 6	all that is **w** in the book of the law
Da	12: 1	everyone who is found **w**
Lk	24:44	that everything **w** about me
Jn	21:25	contain the books that would be **w**.
Rev	21:27	those will enter whose names are **w**

WRONG → WRONGDOING

Nu	5: 7	he shall confess the **w** he has done,
Ac	23: 9	"We find nothing **w** with this man.

WRONGDOING → DO, WRONG

1Jn	5:17	All **w** is sin, but there is sin that is

WROTE → WRITE

Ex	24: 4	**w** down all the words of the LORD
	34:28	he **w** on the tablets the words
Jn	5:46	me, because he **w** about me.

Y

YEAR → YEARS
Ex 23:14 "Three times a **y** you shall celebrate
Heb 10: 1 that they offer continually each **y**.

YEARS → YEAR
Ge   1:14 the fixed times, the days and the **y**,
Ex 12:40 was four hundred and thirty **y**.
Nu 14:34 forty **y** shall you suffer for your
2Ch 36:21 rest while seventy **y** are fulfilled."
Ps 90: 4 A thousand **y** in your eyes
Jer 25:12 when the seventy **y** have elapsed,
Da   9: 2 Scriptures the counting of the **y**
     9: 2 of Jerusalem seventy **y** must be
Gal 4:10 days, months, seasons, and **y**.
2Pe 3: 8 Lord one day is like a thousand **y**
     3: 8 **y** and a thousand **y** like one day.
Rev 20: 2 and tied it up for a thousand **y**

YEAST
Gal 5: 9 A little **y** leavens the whole batch

YESTERDAY
Heb 13: 8 Jesus Christ is the same **y**, today,

YOKE
Mt 11:30 For my **y** is easy, and my burden
Gal 5: 1 not submit again to the **y** of slavery.

YOUNG → YOUTH
Ps 119: 9 How can the **y** walk without fault?
Ac   2:17 your **y** men shall see visions,

YOUTH → YOUNG
Ps 71: 5 Lord; my trust, GOD, from my **y**.
Ecc 12: 1 your Creator in the days of your **y**,

Z

ZACCHAEUS
Lk 19: 2 Now a man there named **Z**, who was

ZEAL → ZEALOUS
1Ma 2:26 Thus he showed his **z** for the law,
Ps 69:10 Because **z** for your house consumes
Isa 37:32 The **z** of the LORD of hosts shall do
Jn   2:17 "**Z** for your house will consume me."
Ro 10: 2 to them that they have **z** for God,
Php 3: 6 in **z** I persecuted the church,

ZEALOUS → ZEAL
Nu 25:13 because he was **z** on behalf of his
1Ki 19:10 "I have been most **z** for the LORD,

ZEBULUN
Son of Jacob by Leah (Ge 30:20; 35:23; 1Ch 2:1). Tribe of blessed (Ge 49:13; Dt 33:18-19), numbered (Nu 1:31; 26:27), allotted land (Jos 19:10-16; Eze 48:26), failed to fully possess (Jdg 1:30), supported Deborah (Jdg 4:6-10; 5:14, 18), David (1Ch 12:33), 12,000 from (Rev 7:8).

ZECHARIAH
1. Son of Jeroboam II; king of Israel (2Ki 15:8-12).
2. Post-exilic prophet who encouraged rebuilding of temple (Ezr 5:1; 6:14; Zec 1:1).

ZEDEKIAH → = MATTANIAH
1. False prophet (1Ki 22:11-24; 2Ch 18:10-23).

2. Mattaniah, son of Josiah (1Ch 3:15), made king of Judah by Nebuchadnezzar (2Ki 24:17-25:7; 2Ch 36:10-14; Jer 37-39; 52:1-11).

ZEPHANIAH
Prophet; descendant of Hezekiah (Zep 1:1).

ZERUBBABEL
Descendant of David (1Ch 3:19; Mt 1:3). Led return from exile (Ezr 2:2; Ne 7:7). Governor of Israel; helped rebuild temple (Ezr 3; Hag 1-2; Zec 4).

ZIMRI
King of Israel (1Ki 16:9-20).

ZION
2Sa 5: 7 David did take the stronghold of **Z**,
Ps   2: 6 my king on **Z**, my holy mountain."
     48: 3 Mount **Z**, the heights of Zaphon,
     78:68 Judah, Mount **Z** which he favored.
Isa 28:16 GOD: See, I am laying a stone in **Z**,
Mic 4: 2 from **Z** shall go forth instruction,
Zec 9: 9 Rejoice heartily, O daughter **Z**,
Mt 21: 5 "Say to daughter **Z**, 'Behold,
Ro 11:26 "The deliverer will come out of **Z**,
1Pe 2: 6 "Behold, I am laying a stone in **Z**,
Rev 14: 1 was the Lamb standing on Mount **Z**,

ZIPPORAH
Daughter of Reuel; wife of Moses (Ex 2:21-22; 4:20-26; 18:1-6).

ZOPHAR
One of Job's friends (Job 2:11; 11; 20; 42:9).

MAP 1

Jerusalem in New Testament times

Medieval and Turkish Jerusalem

Approximate lines of City Walls:
of original Zion
under Herod the Great
added by Agrippa I
Wall of Aelia
Modern roads

Original Rock Contours are shown.

B = Bridge
C. of I. = Court of Israel
C. of P. = Court of Priests
C. of W. = Court of Women
G = Gate
G⁺ = Gate of Coponius = Barclay's Gate
G⁺ = Double (Huldah) Gate

© Oxford University Press

Mount of Olives

Kidron Valley

Gethsemane

Tombs
Monument of Bene Hezir

Fullers Tower
Pool

Siloam Gate
Solomon's Portico
Portico
Pinnacle of Temple

TEMPLE
Court of Gentiles
C. of W.
C. of I.
C. of P.

Ophel
Gihon Spring

Bezetha

BEZETHA
CAVERNS
ROYAL

ANTONIA TOWER
Arch
Warren's Gate
Gate (by Wilson's Arch)
Western Wall
Gate (by Robinson's Arch)
Beautiful Gate
Triple Gate
Huldah Gate

Tyropoeon Valley

Herodian Street

Tomb of Helena Princess of Adiabene

OUTWORK OF UNCERTAIN ORIGIN

Solomon's Pool
Pool of Siloam
Conduit

Takoa Gate G

300 Metres
300 Yards

Damascus Gate
Jewish Tombs
Golgotha?
Gennath Gate
Calvary?
Pool

? Hippicus
ROYAL PALACE
PRAE-TORIUM
? Phasephinus

Aqueduct

TURKISH

Essene Gate G

Hinnom Valley

Pool

Family Tomb of Herod

Bethlehem

Jerusalem in Old Testament times

Medieval and Turkish Jerusalem

Approximate lines of City Walls:
of original Zion (2 Sam 5:7)
extended under the Kings
extended after the Exile (by Maccabees, 2nd Cent.B.C.?)
Eastern wall of Nehemiah's city
Modern roads

Original Rock Contours are shown.

Mount of Olives

Kidron Valley

Post-exilic Jewish tombs
Monument of Bene Hezir

Pre-exilic Judean tombs

300 Metres
300 Yards

Tower of Hananel
Baris

TEMPLE ALTAR

? PALACE

Manasseh's Wall
Gihon Spring
Upper Pool
Old Conduit
Conduit

Wall
Solomon's Wall

? MISHNA (SECOND QUARTER)

Central (Cheesemakers) Valley

Tombs

UPPER CITY

Wall of Hezekiah (Manasseh)

The lines of the southern walls of the city after the Exile are uncertain

CITY OF DAVID (LOWER CITY)
OPHEL
SILOAM
Wall of Zion

Lower Pool
Old Pool
Gate

En-rogel Spring

Hinnom Valley (? Topheth)

?

© Oxford University Press

OUTER BORDER SHOWS 200 YARD SUBDIVISIONS

Prepared by Oxford Cartographers
and based on the Oxford Bible Atlas

MAP 2

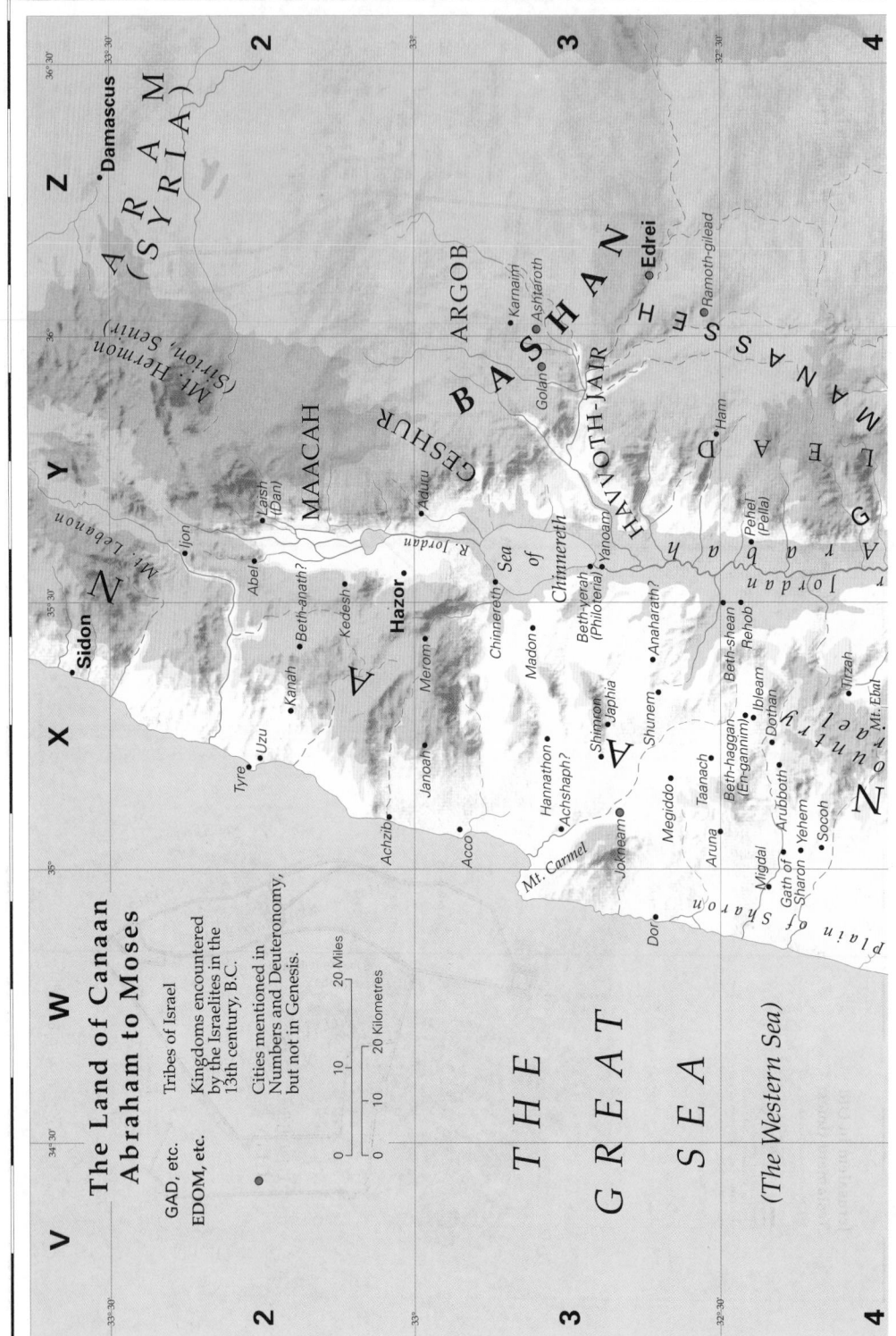

The Land of Canaan
Abraham to Moses

GAD, etc.   Tribes of Israel

EDOM, etc.   Kingdoms encountered by the Israelites in the 13th century, B.C.

● Cities mentioned in Numbers and Deuteronomy, but not in Genesis.

0   10   20 Miles

0   10   20 Kilometres

THE

GREAT

SEA

(The Western Sea)

A R A M
(S Y R I A)
● Damascus

Mt. Hermon
(Sirion, Senir)

Mt. Lebanon

● Sidon

● Tyre

Uzu

Achzib

Acco

Mt. Carmel

Dor

Plain of Sharon

Ijon

Abel
Laish
(Dan)

Kanah ● Beth-anath?

Kedesh ●

Hazor ●

Janoah ●

Hannathon ●
Achshaph?

Jokneam ●

Megiddo ●

Taanach ●

Aruna

Migdal

Gath of
Sharon

Yehem

Socoh

Merom ●

Madon ●

Chinnereth ●

Sea
of
Chinnereth

MAACAH

GESHUR

BASHAN

ARGOB

Karnaim ●
● Ashtaroth

Golan ●

Edrei ●

Ramoth-gilead ●

HAVVOTH-JAIR

M A N A S S E H

Beth-yerah
(Philoteria)

Yanoam ●

Anaharath? ●

Beth-shean ●

Rehob ●

● Ham

Pehel
(Pella) ●

● Tirzah

● Mt. Ebal

hill country of Israel

Shimron ●

Japhia ●

Shunem ●

Beth-haggan
(En-gannim) ●

Ibleam ●

Dothan ●

Arubboth ●

Adamah ●

R. Jordan

Jordan

A r a b a h

G i l e a d

G A D

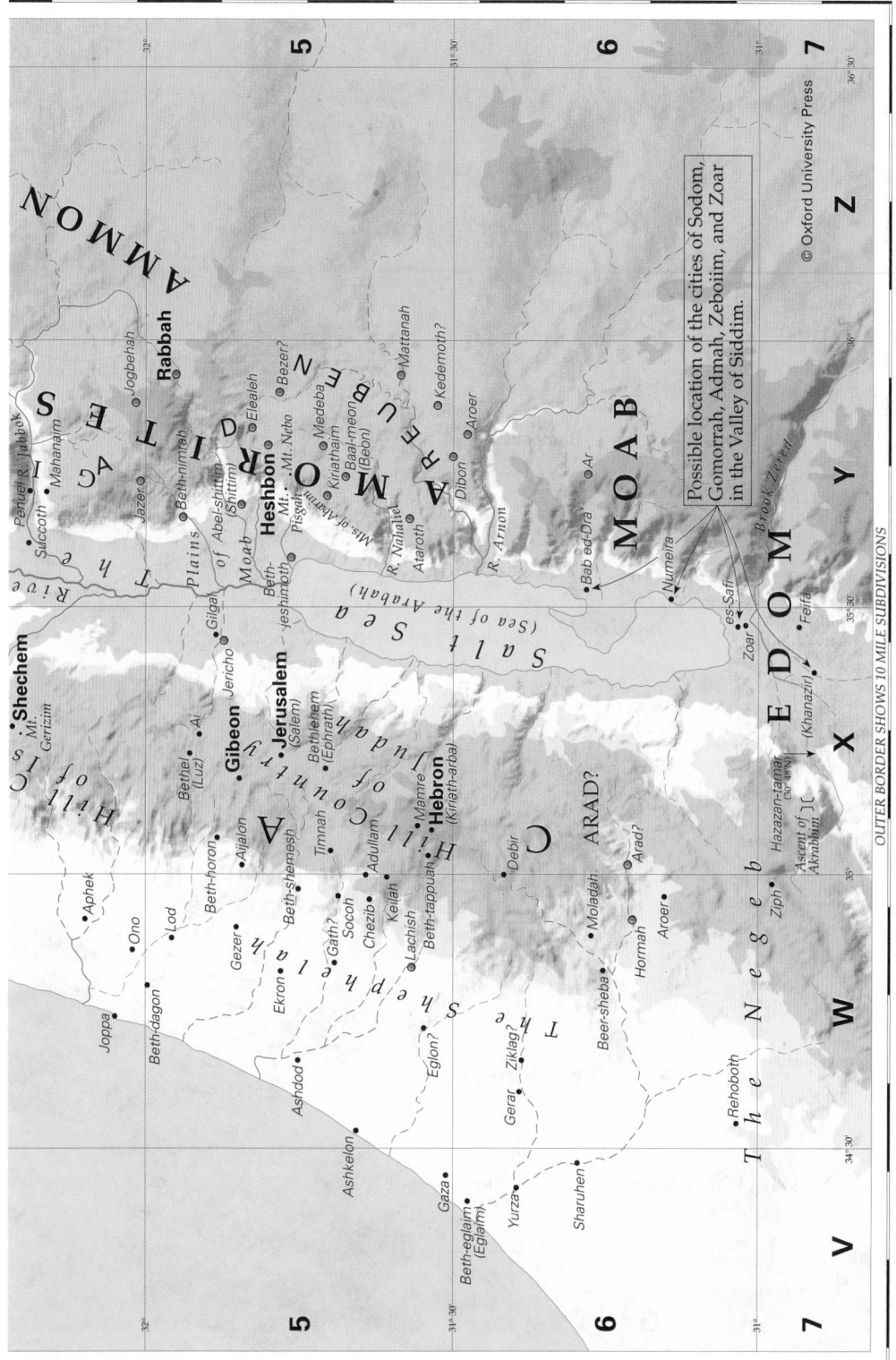

MAP 2

5

6

7

Z

Y

X

W

V

5

6

7

A M M O N

S   I   T   E   S

A M O R I T E S

R E U B E N

G A D

M O A B

E D O M

I S R A E L

Hill   Country

Hill   Country   of   Judah

Sea of the Arabah)

Salt Sea

The   Shephelah

The   Negeb

The   River

The   Plains   of   Moab

Rabbah

Jogbehah

Peniel R. Jabbok

Succoth

Mahanaim

Jazer

Beth-nimrah

Abel-shittim (Shittim)

Heshbon

Pisgah

Mt. Nebo

Mts. of Abarim

Beth-jeshimoth

Gilgal

Elealeh

Bezer?

Medeba

Kiriathaim

Baal-meon (Beon)

R. Nahaliel

Ataroth

R. Arnon

Mattanah

Kedemoth?

Dibon

Aroer

Ar

Bab ed-Dra

Numeira

es-Safi

Zoar

Feifa

Brook Zered

(Khanazir)

Hazazan-tamar (30° 48'N)

Ascent of Akrabbim

Ziph

Moladah

Arad?

ARAD?

Aroer

Hormah

Beer-sheba

Rehoboth

Sharuhen

Gaza

Beth-eglaim (Eglaim)

Yurza

Gerar

Ziklag?

Ashkelon

Ashdod

Eglon?

Beth-dagon

Joppa

Aphek

Ono

Lod

Gezer

Ekron

Beth-horon

Aijalon

Beth-shemesh

Timnah

Gath?

Socoh

Chezib

Keilah

Beth-tappuah

Adullam

Lachish

Debir

Shechem

Mt. Gerizim

Bethel (Luz)

Ai

Jericho

Gibeon

Jerusalem (Salem)

Bethlehem (Ephrath)

Mamre

Hebron (Kiriath-arba)

Possible location of the cities of Sodom, Gomorrah, Admah, Zeboiim, and Zoar in the Valley of Siddim.

© Oxford University Press

32°

31° 30'

31°

36° 30'

36°

35° 30'

35°

34° 30'

MAP 3

P   Q   R

1

THE   GREAT

T

P

Y

G

E

Lake
Menzaleh

Mons Casius
Lake *Sirbonis*

Pelusium
(Sin)

The Way to the Land of the

Zoan (Tanis)

•Busiris

Baal-zephon•

Zilu
(Tjaru)

Rameses
(Qantir)

G O S H E N

Lake
Timsah

W i l d e r n e s s

2

•Pi-beseth
(Bubastis)

Pithom• Succoth

•Athribis

(Tell el-Yahudiyeh)

Great
Bitter
Lake

Possible Northern Exodus

Little Bitter
Lake

R. Nile

•Heliopolis
(On)

Baal-zephon

Saqqarah•

Memphis
(Noph)

Traditional Exodus route

3

31°

32°

33°

31°

29°

Heracleopolis•

The Exodus

—————— Probable route of the Exodus

- - - - - - Alternative routes

·-·-·-·-· Line of border fortresses

G u l f   o f   S u e z

0   20   40 Miles

0   20   40 Kilometres

4

Q   R

33°

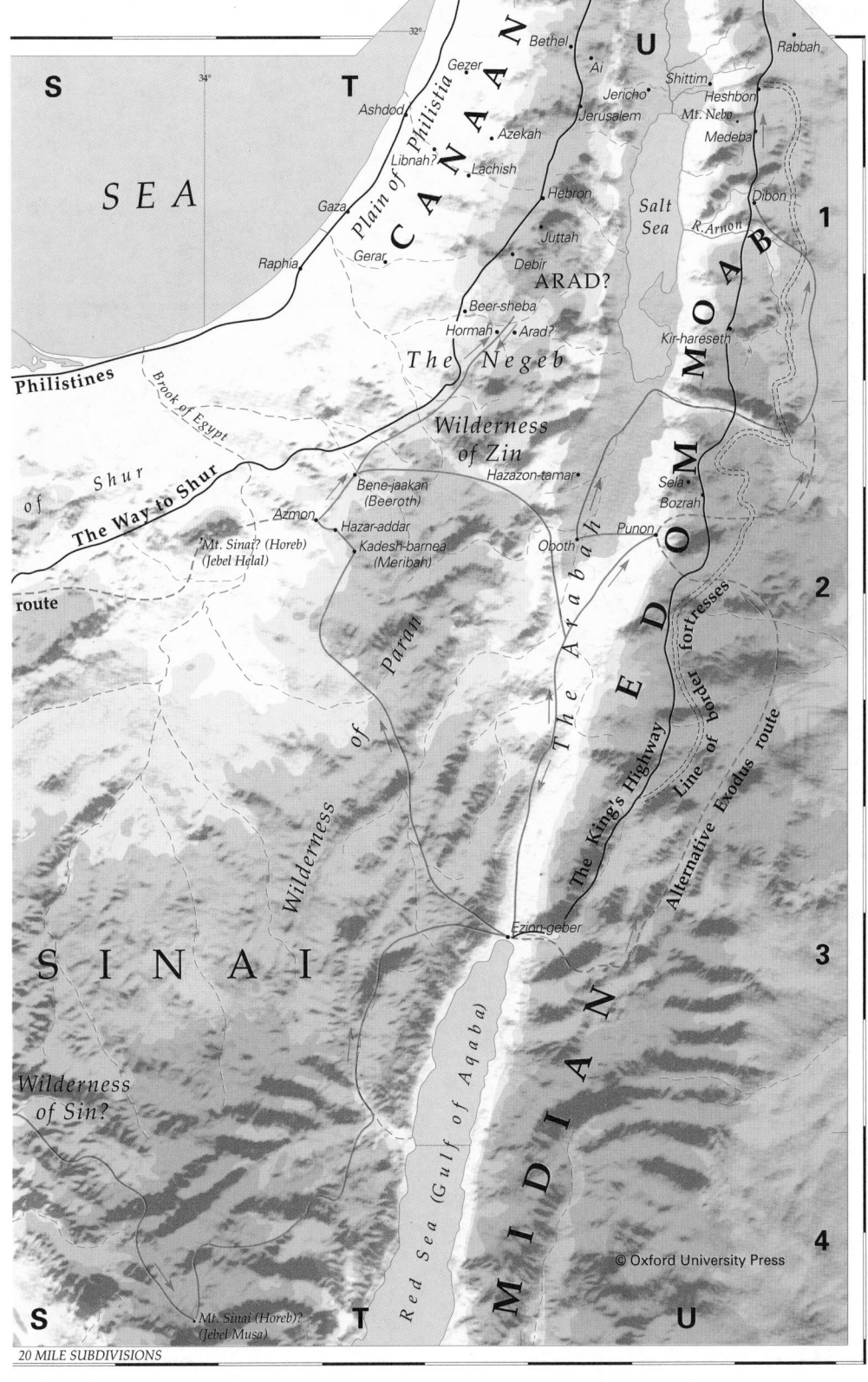

S T U

S
SEA

32°
34°

Bethel
Ai
Jericho
Jerusalem
Shittim
Heshbon
Mt. Nebo
Medeba
Rabbah
Gezer
Ashdod
Plain of Philistia
Azekah
Libnah?
Lachish
Gaza
Gerar
Hebron
Salt Sea
Dibon
R. Arnon
CANAAN
Raphia
Juttah
Debir
ARAD?
Beer-sheba
Hormah
Arad?
Kir-hareseth
The Negeb
Philistines
Brook of Egypt
Wilderness of Zin
Hazazon-tamar
Sela
Bozrah
Shur
The Way to Shur
of
Bene-jaakan (Beeroth)
Azmon
Hazar-addar
Kadesh-barnea (Meribah)
Oboth
Punon
M O A B
1
'Mt. Sinai? (Horeb) (Jebel Helal)
Parah
The Arabah
E D O M
route
2
Line of border fortresses
of
Wilderness
The King's Highway
Alternative Exodus route
SINAI
Ezion-geber
3
Wilderness of Sin?
Red Sea (Gulf of Aqaba)
M I D I A N
© Oxford University Press
4

S T U

20 MILE SUBDIVISIONS

Mt. Sinai (Horeb)? (Jebel Musa)

MAP 4

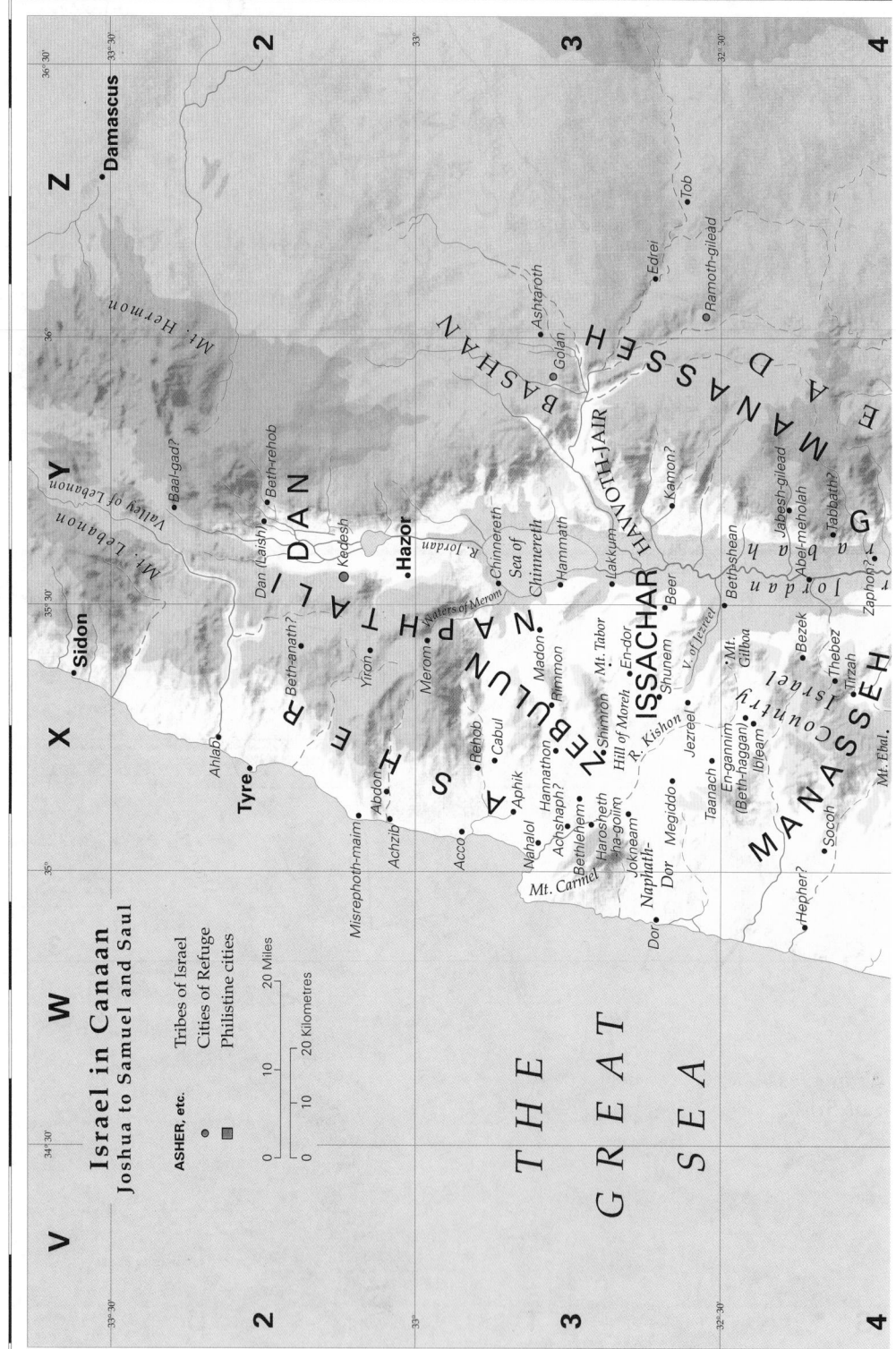

Israel in Canaan
Joshua to Samuel and Saul

ASHER, etc.   Tribes of Israel
● Cities of Refuge
■ Philistine cities

0   10   20 Miles

0   10   20 Kilometres

V   W   X   Y   Z

Damascus

Mt. Hermon

Sidon

Valley of Lebanon

Mt. Lebanon

Baal-gad?

Beth-rehob

DAN

Dan (Laish

Kedesh

Hazor

Ahlab?

Tyre

Misrephoth-maim

Beth-anath?

Yiron

Merom

Waters of Merom

R. Jordan

Chinnereth

Sea of Chinnereth

BASHAN

Ashtaroth

Golan

Edrei

Tob

Ramoth-gilead

MANASSEH

GAD

Hammath

HAVVOTH-JAIR

Jakkum?

Kamon?

Beer

Jabesh-gilead

Tabbath?

Abel-meholah

Bethshean

Jordan

Zaphon?

Abdon

Achzib

Acco

Nahalol

Bethlehem

Cabul

Hannathon

Aphik

Rehob

Achshaph?

ASHER

ZEBULUN

Shimron

Madon

Rimmon

Mt. Tabor

En-dor

ISSACHAR

Hill of Moreh

Shunem

R. Kishon

V. of Jezreel

Jezreel

Harosheth ha-goiim

Joknéam

Naphath-Dor

Mt. Carmel

Taanach

Megiddo

En-gannim (Beth-haggan)

Ibleam

Bezek

Thebez

Tirzah

Mt. Ebal

Socoh

Hepher?

MANASSEH

Hill Country of Israel

Mt. Gilboa

Dor

THE

GREAT

SEA

NAPHTALI

SHER

36° 30'   36°   35° 30'   35°   34° 30'   33° 30'

33° 30'   33°   32° 30'

2   3   4

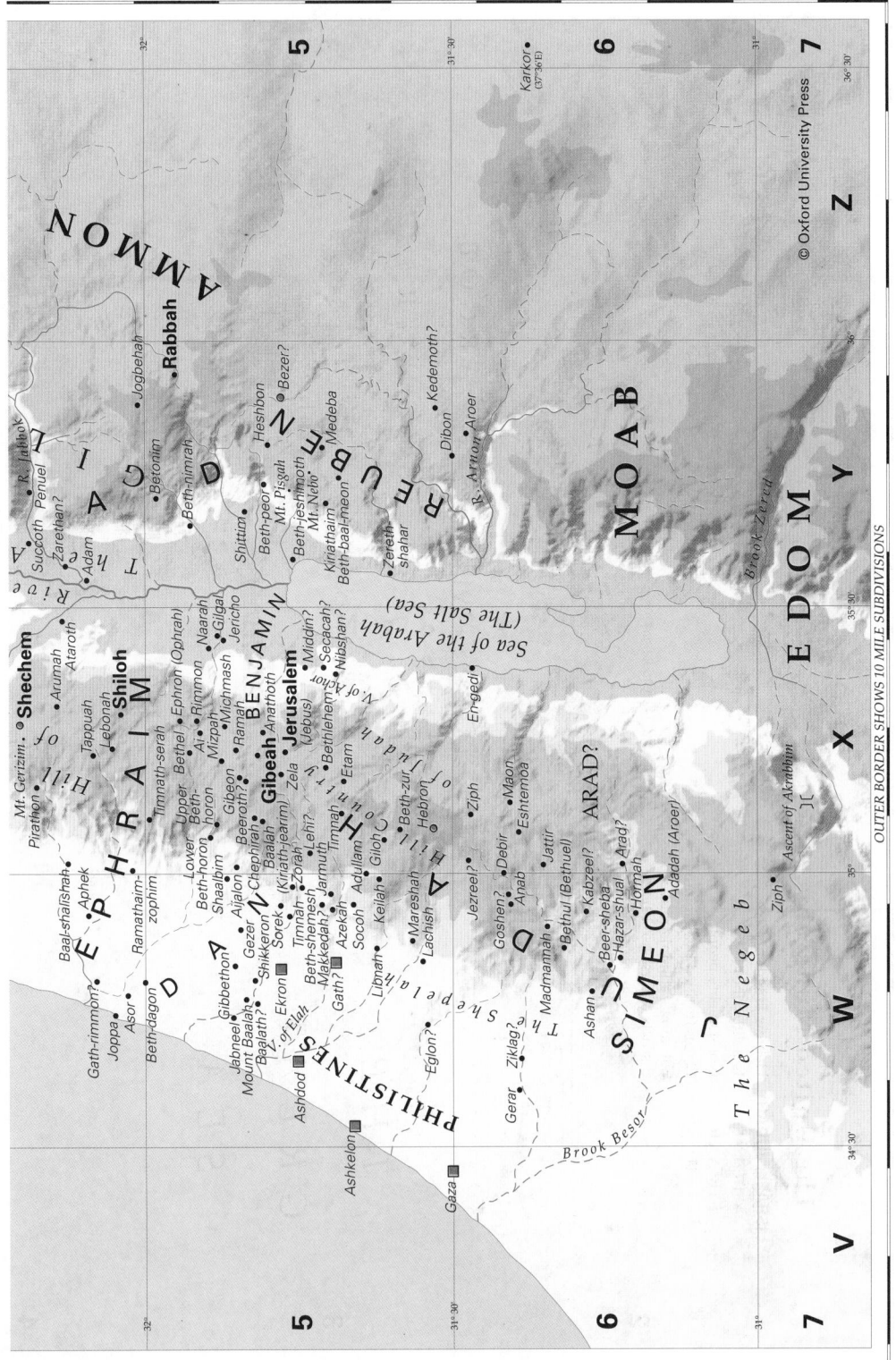

MAP 4

Shechem ●

Mt. Gerizim ●

Arumah ●
Ataroth ●

Pirathon ●

Baal-shalishah ●

Aphek ●

Tappuah ●

Lebonah ●

Shiloh

E P H R A I M

H I L L

Timnath-serah ●

Ephron (Ophrah) ●

Naarah ●

Bethel ●

Ai ●

Upper
Beth-
horon ●

Mizpah ●

Michmash ●

Ramah ●

B E N J A M I N

Anathoth ●

Gibeah

Jerusalem

(Jebus)

Gilgal ●

Jericho ●

Rimmon ●

Gibeon ●

Beeroth ●

Chephirah ●

Baalah ●

Zela ●

Bethlehem ●

Etam ●

Midddin? ●

Secacah? ●

Nibshan? ●

V. of Achor

D A N

Gath-rimmon? ●

Joppa ●

Beth-dagon ●

Asor ●

Gibbethon ●

Ramathaim-
zophim ●

Lower
Beth-horon ●

Shaalbim ●

Aijalon ●

Gezer ●

Jabneel ●

Mount Baalah ●

Baalath? ●

Shikkeron ●

Ekron ●

Timnah ●

Sorek (Kiriath-jearim) ●

Beth-shemesh ●

Makkedah? ●

Zorah? ●

Jarmuth ●

Beth-zur? ●

Giloh? ●

Lehi? ●

Adullam ●

Socoh ●

Azekah ●

Keilah ●

Libnah ●

Mareshah ●

Gath? ●

V. of Elah

Ashdod ■

Ashkelon ●

Gaza ■

P H I L I S T I N E S

Eglon? ●

Lachish ●

H I L L C o u n t r y o f J u d a h

J U D A H

Hebron ●

Jezreel? ●

Ziph ●

Maon ●

Debir ●

Anab ●

Eshtemoa ●

Jattir ●

Goshen? ●

Bethul (Bethuel) ●

Kabzeel? ●

Arad? ●

Hormah ●

Beer-sheba ●

Hazar-shual ●

Ashan ●

Madmannah ●

Adadah (Aroer) ●

A R A D?

S I M E O N

The Negeb

Ziph ●

Ascent of Akrabbim

Gerar ●

Ziklag? ●

Brook Besor

The Shephelah

R. Jabbok

Succoth ●

Penuel ●

Zarethan? ●

Adam ●

The Jordan River

G I L E A D

Jogbehah ●

Rabbah ●

A M M O N

Betonim ●

Beth-nimrah ●

Shittim ●

Beth-peor? ●

Heshbon ●

Bezer? ●

Beth-jeshimoth ●

Mt. Pisgah ●

Mt. Nebo ●

Kiriathaim ●

Medeba ●

Beth-baal-meon ●

Zereth-
shahar ●

Dibon ●

R E U B E N

R. Arnon Aroer ●

Kedemoth? ●

Karkor ●
(37° 36' E)

Sea of the Arabah
(The Salt Sea)

M O A B

Brook Zered

E D O M

© Oxford University Press

MAP 5

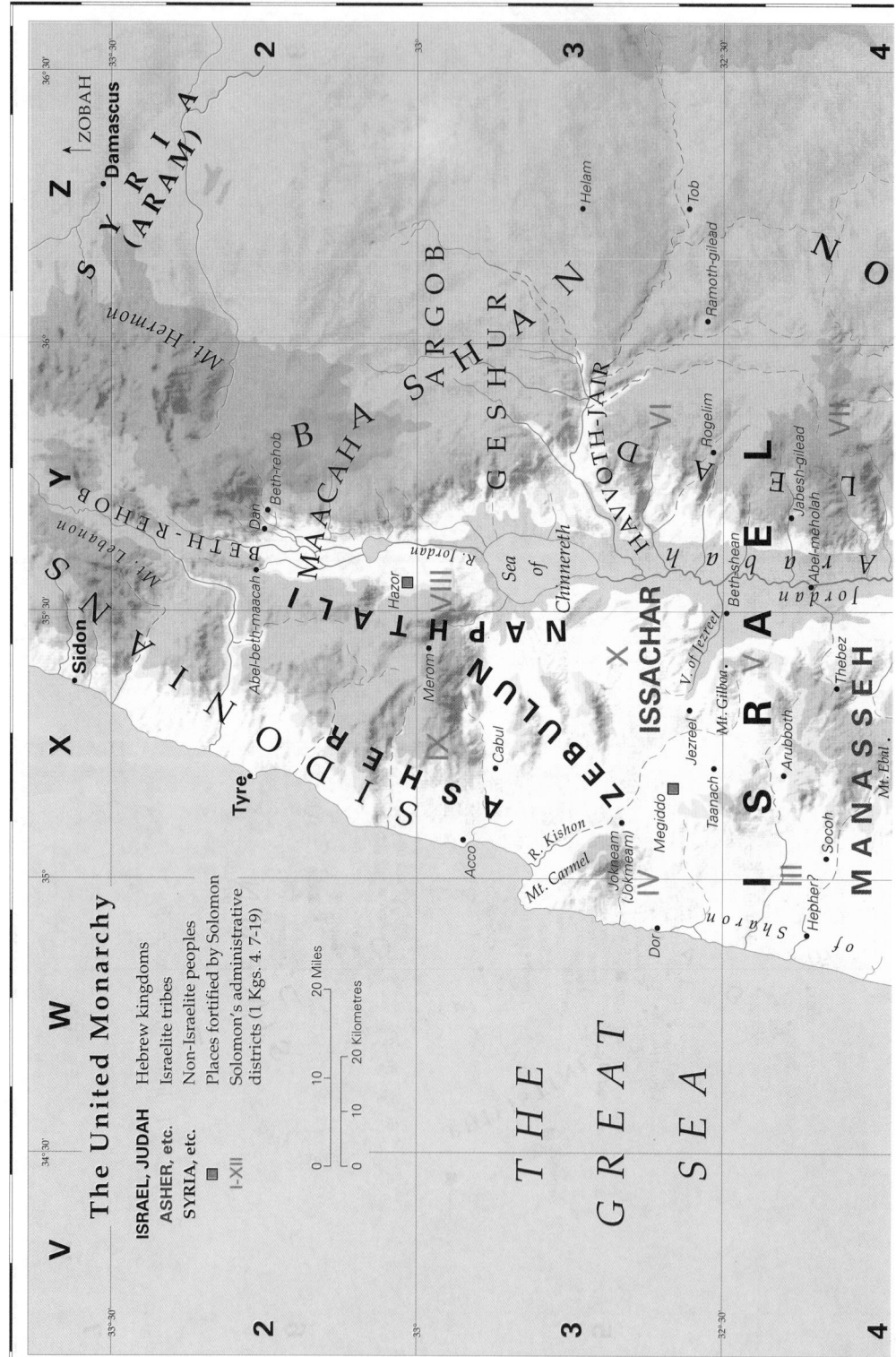

The United Monarchy

ISRAEL, JUDAH Hebrew kingdoms
ASHER, etc. Israelite tribes
SYRIA, etc. Non-Israelite peoples
■ Places fortified by Solomon
I–XII Solomon's administrative districts (1 Kgs. 4. 7-19)

0   10   20 Miles
0   10   20 Kilometres

THE GREAT SEA

S Y R I A (ARAM)
ZOBAH
• Damascus
Mt. Hermon

S I D O N I A N S
Mt. Lebanon
• Sidon
BETH-REHOB
Tyre •
Acco •

• Helam
• Tob
• Ramoth-gilead

B E T H - R E H O B
MAACAH
• Beth-rehob
• Dan
• Abel-beth-maacah

SARGOB
SAHUR
GESHUN
HAVVOTH-JAIR
• Rogelim
• Jabesh-gilead
• Abel-meholah

N A P H T A L I
■ Hazor
VIII
Sea of Chinnereth
R. Jordan

A S H E R
• Abel-beth-maacah
Merom •
• Cabul
IX

Z E B U L U N
Mt. Carmel
R. Kishon

I S S A C H A R
×
V. of Jezreel
Jezreel •
• Mt. Gilboa
Bethshean •

I S R A E L
Jordan
Gilead

Dor •
Jokneam (Jokmeam) •
■ Megiddo
IV
Taanach •
III
• Hepher?
• Socoh
• Arubboth
• Thebez
Mt. Ebal •

M A N A S S E H
of Sharon

V   W   X
2   3   4

MAP 5

© Oxford University Press

OUTER BORDER SHOWS 10 MILE SUBDIVISIONS

5

6

7

Z

Rabbah
(Rabbath-ammon)

A M M O N

To-debar?
R. Jabbok
Mahanaim
Succoth
Zarethan?
Jazer

The River

X I

C

I

• Heshbon

• Medeba

R. Nahaliel

Dibon •
Aroer •

R. Arnon

M O A B

Kir-hareseth •

Brook Zered

E D O M

Y

X

The River

Salt Sea
(Sea of the Arabah)

Wilderness of Judah

Mt. Gerizim • • Shechem

Pirathon •

Shiloh

• Baal-hazor
• Ephraim
Gilgal •
• Jericho

Zeredah •

Bethel •
Upper Beth-horon •
Beeroth? •
Elon • • Gibeon
Kiriath- • Gibeah
jearim
• Anathoth

X I
BENJAMIN

Jerusalem ■

EPHRAIM

Beth-hanan
Lower Beth-horon
Gezer ■

Shaalbim •

Makaz ■
Sorek •

Baalath? ■

• Bethlehem
Netophah •
• Tekoa

H

J U D A H

S

Ekron •
Beth-shemesh •
• Gath?
Libnah? •

Gath-rimmon •

Plain

Joppa •

P H I L I S T I N E S

Ashdod •

Ashkelon •

Gaza •

Adullam •
Giloh •

• Hebron

Carmel •
• Debir
Kabzeel? •
Valley of Salt

• Arad

The Shephelah (Lowland)

The Negeb

Gerar • Ziklag?
Beer-sheba •

A M A L E K

Brook Besor

Tamar
(En-gedi) ■

V

W

32°

31° 30'

31°

32°

31° 30'

31°

36° 30'

36°

35° 30'

35°

34° 30'

5

6

7

MAP 6

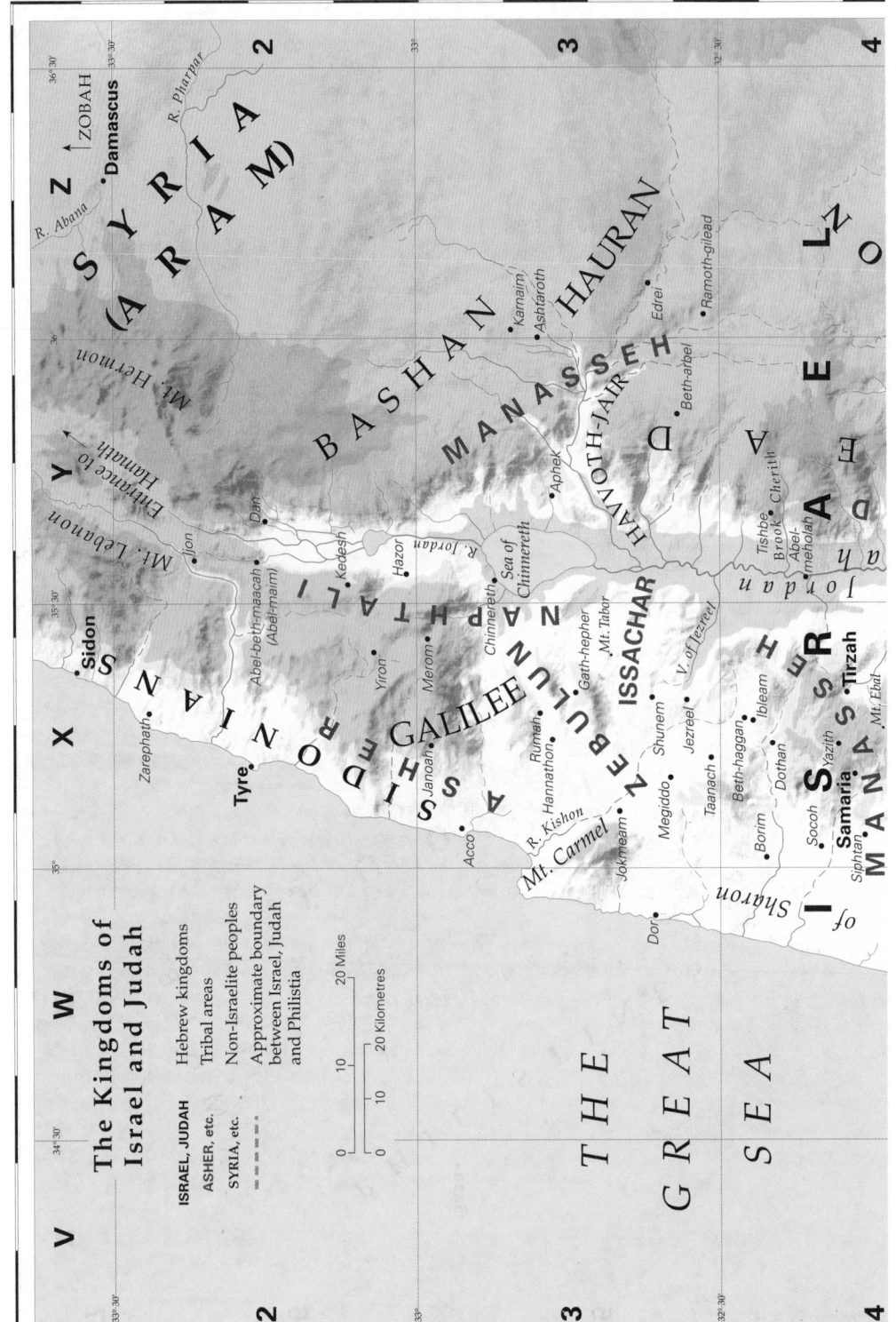

The Kingdoms of
Israel and Judah

ISRAEL, JUDAH   Hebrew kingdoms
ASHER, etc.   Tribal areas
SYRIA, etc.   Non-Israelite peoples
‒ ‒ ‒ ‒   Approximate boundary
between Israel, Judah
and Philistia

0   10   20 Miles

0   10   20 Kilometres

THE
GREAT
SEA

ZOBAH
Damascus
R. Pharpar
R. Abana
SYRIA
(ARAM)
Mt. Hermon
Entrance to
Hamath
Mt. Lebanon
Ijon
Sidon
Zarephath
SIDONIANS
Tyre
Acco
Dan
Kedesh
Hazor
Abel-beth-maacah
(Abel-maim)
Yiron
NAPHTALI
Merom
Janoah
ASHER
GALILEE
Rumah
Hannathon
R. Kishon
Jokmeam
Mt. Carmel
Dor
of Sharon
ZEBULUN
Chinnereth
Sea of
Chinnereth
R. Jordan
Gath-hepher
Mt. Tabor
ISSACHAR
Shunem
V. of Jezreel
Jezreel
Megiddo
Taanach
Beth-haggan
Dothan
Ibleam
Borim
Socoh
Siphtan
Samaria
Yazith
MANASSEH
Mt. Ebal
Tirzah
BASHAN
Karnaim
Ashtaroth
HAURAN
MANASSEH
Edrei
HAVVOTH-JAIR
Aphek
Beth-arbel
Ramoth-gilead
GAD
Tishbe
Brook Cherith
Abel-meholah
Jordan
of
ISRAEL

V   W   X   Y   Z   2   3   4

MAP 6

© Oxford University Press

OUTER BORDER SHOWS 10 MILE SUBDIVISIONS

MAP 7

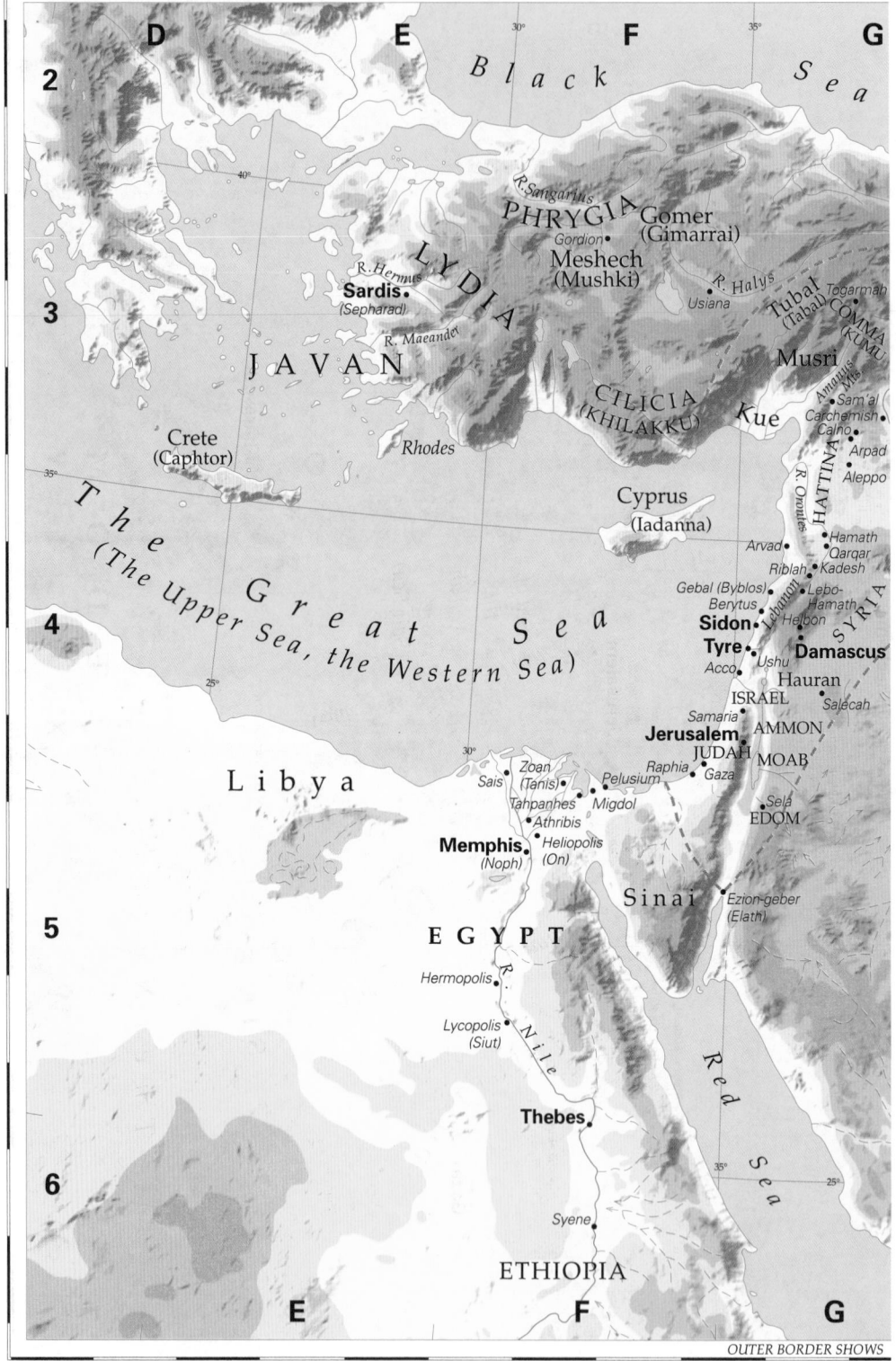

B l a c k   S e a

D   E   F   G

2

R. Sangarius

PHRYGIA   Gomer
Gordion •   (Gimarrai)

Meshech
(Mushki)   R. Halys

LYDIA   Usiana •   Tubal   Togarmah
Sardis •   (Tabal)   COMMA
(Sepharad)   KLMU

3   R. Hermus   Musri

R. Maeander   JAVAN   Amanus
                    Mts
            CILICIA   Sam'al
            (KHILAKKU)   Carchemish •
                    Calno •
            Kue   HATTINA   Arpad •
                        Aleppo •

Crete   Rhodes
(Caphtor)   R. Orontes
                    Hamath
            Cyprus   Arvad •   Qarqar
            (Iadanna)   Riblah • Kadesh
                    Gebal (Byblos) • Lebo-
T h e   G r e a t   S e a   Berytus •   Hamath
                    Helbon •   SYRIA
(The Upper Sea, the Western Sea)   Sidon •   Lebanon
                    Tyre •   Damascus
                    Acco • Ushu
4   Hauran
                    ISRAEL   Salecah •
                    Samaria •
            L i b y a   AMMON
                    Jerusalem   MOAB
                    JUDAH
                Zoan   Raphia • Gaza •
                (Tanis)   Pelusium
                Sais •   Sela •
                Tahpanhes •   Migdol   EDOM
                Athribis •
            Memphis •   Heliopolis
            (Noph)   (On)   Sinai
                        Ezion-geber
                        (Elath)
5   E G Y P T

        Hermopolis •   R.
                Nile
        Lycopolis •
        (Siut)   Red

                    Sea
            Thebes •

6   Syene •

            ETHIOPIA

        E   F   G

OUTER BORDER SHOWS

MAP 7

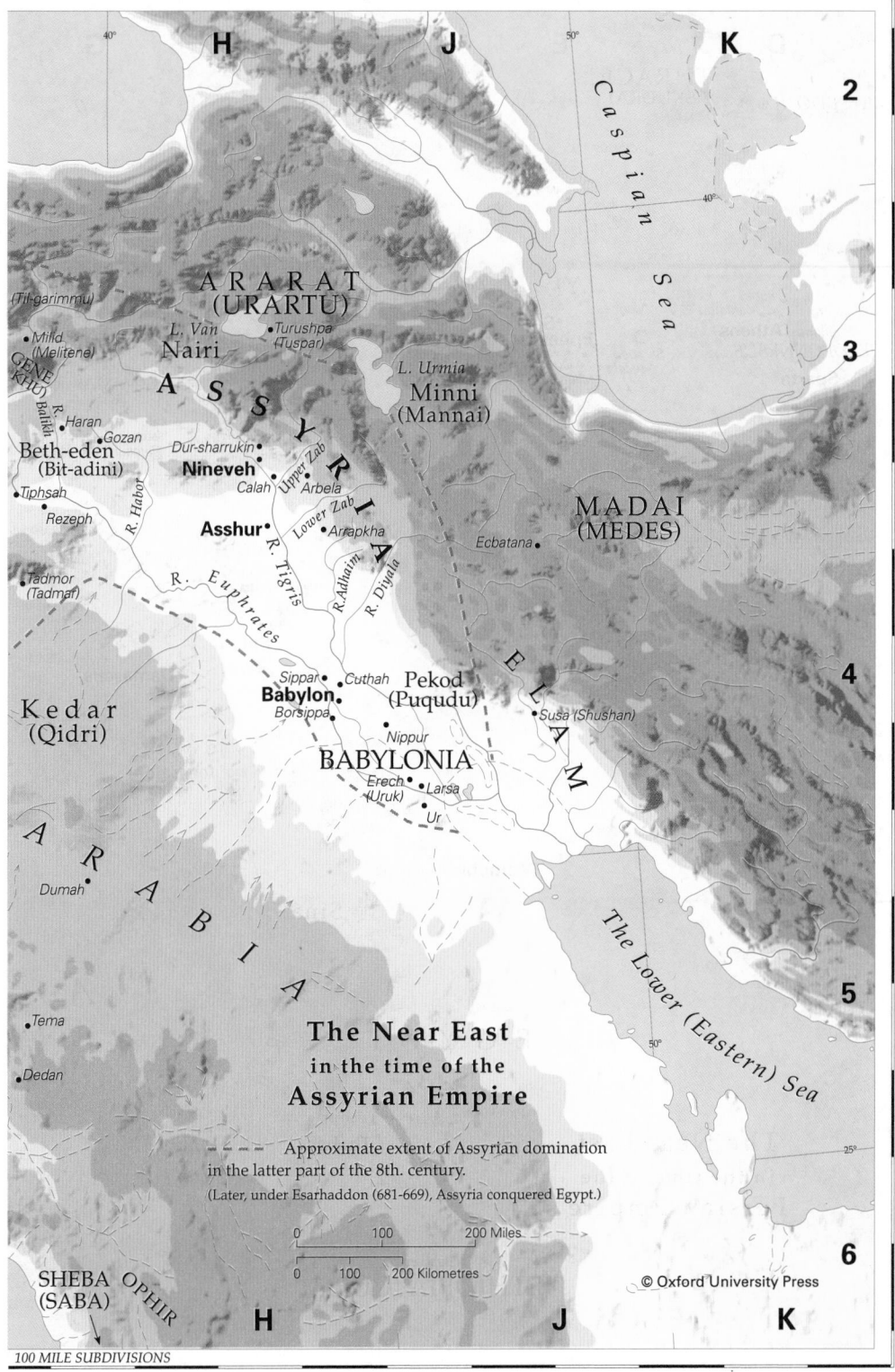

The Near East
in the time of the
Assyrian Empire

- - - Approximate extent of Assyrian domination
in the latter part of the 8th. century.
(Later, under Esarhaddon (681-669), Assyria conquered Egypt.)

0   100   200 Miles
0   100   200 Kilometres

100 MILE SUBDIVISIONS

Caspian Sea

ARARAT
(URARTU)

(Til-garimmu)

*Milid.
(Melitene)* L. Van *Turushpa
(Tuspar)* Nairi

L. Urmia
Minni
(Mannai)

A S S Y R I A

R. Habor
R. Balikh
Haran *Gozan* Dur-sharrukin
Nineveh Calah Upper Zab *Arbela*

Beth-eden
(Bit-adini)

Tiphsah
Rezeph

Asshur Lower Zab *Arrapkha*

MADAI
(MEDES)

Ecbatana

R. Tigris
R. Adhaim
R. Diyala

*Tadmor
(Tadmaf)*

R. Euphrates

Kedar
(Qidri)

Sippar *Cuthah* Pekod
Babylon (Puqudu)
Borsippa

E L A M

Susa (Shushan)

Nippur

BABYLONIA

Erech *Larsa*
(Uruk)
Ur

A R A B I A

Dumah

The Lower (Eastern) Sea

Tema

Dedan

SHEBA
(SABA) OPHIR

MAP 8

D   **E**   **F**   **G**

MACEDONIA

THRACE
(SKUDRA)

B l a c k   *S e a*

Doriscus

• *Sinope*

Byzantium

PAPHLAGONIANS

THESSALY

Aegean

30°

R. Sangarius

35°

MOSCHI

Thermopylae

Sea

Hellespont

40°

R. *Granicus*

Mt. Ida

D A S C Y L I U M

CAPPADOCIA

Delphi

Lesbos

Mytilene

Gordion •

CIMMERIANS

• *Pteria?*

Thebes *Marathon*

Corinth

LYDIA

PHRYGIA

Melitene •

3

Salamis **Athens**

Magnesia

Sardis

R. *Halys*

PELOPONNESUS

Samos

Ephesus

COMMAGENE

Sparta

C. *Mycale*

Magnesia on Maeander

Miletus

Cilician

Issus

CARIA

Tarsus

Gates

Carchemish

Haran

LYCIA

PAMPHYLIA

CILICIA

Aleppo

Arpad

Rhodes

Xanthus

Thapsacus

35°

Crete

Kyrenia

Hamath

Tadmor

Gortyna

Soli

Salamis

Arvad

U
p
p
e
r

Cyprus

Citium

Amathus

Gebal

S e a

Sidon

25°

• *Cyrene*

(Mediterranean Sea)

Tyre

Damascus

4

K E D

Samaria

B E Y O N D   T H E   R I V E R

30°

AMMON

(Alexandria)

Ashdod

Jerusalem

Sais

Zoan

Tahpanhes

Gaza JUDAH

Busiris

Pelusium

MOAB

EDOMITES

Memphis • *Heliopolis*

Sela

• *Dumah*

Sinai

L I B Y A

5

Hermopolis

R. *Nile*

A

E G Y P T

• *Tema*

Abydos

Coptos

Red

Thebes

• *Dedan*

Edfu

S e a

35°

The Near East
in the time of the
Persian Empire

25°

Yeb
(Elephantine)

Syene

ETHIOPIA (CUSH)

E   **F**   **G**

OUTER BORDER SHOWS

MAP 8

COLCHI

Caucasus Mountains

Trapezus
(MESHECH)

R. Cyrus

R. Araxes

Hyrcanian

Sea

(Caspian Sea)

L. Van

ARMENIA
(URARTU)

L. Urmia

H Y R C A N I A

A S S Y R I A

Nineveh • *Arbela*

Asshur • *Arrapkha*

R. Tigris

R. Euphrates

M E D I A

Astrabad
(Gorgan) • *Zadrakarta*
(Turang Tepe)
• (Damghan)

PARTHIA

Rages
(Rhagae)

Ecbatana
(Achmetha)

Behistun
(Bisutun)

SAGARTIA

B A B Y L O N I A

Eshnunna

• *Der*

Sippar

Babylon

Borsippa

Nippur

Gabae
• (Isfahan)

E L A M
(SUSIANA)

Susa
(Shushan)

A R

Erech (Uruk)
Larsa • *Ur*

Anshan
(Tall-i Malyan) •

Parsagarda
• (Pasargadae)

Persepolis

R A B I A

P E R S I S
(P E R S I A)

Lower Sea (Persian Gulf)

0		100		200 Miles
0	100		200 Kilometres	

© Oxford University Press

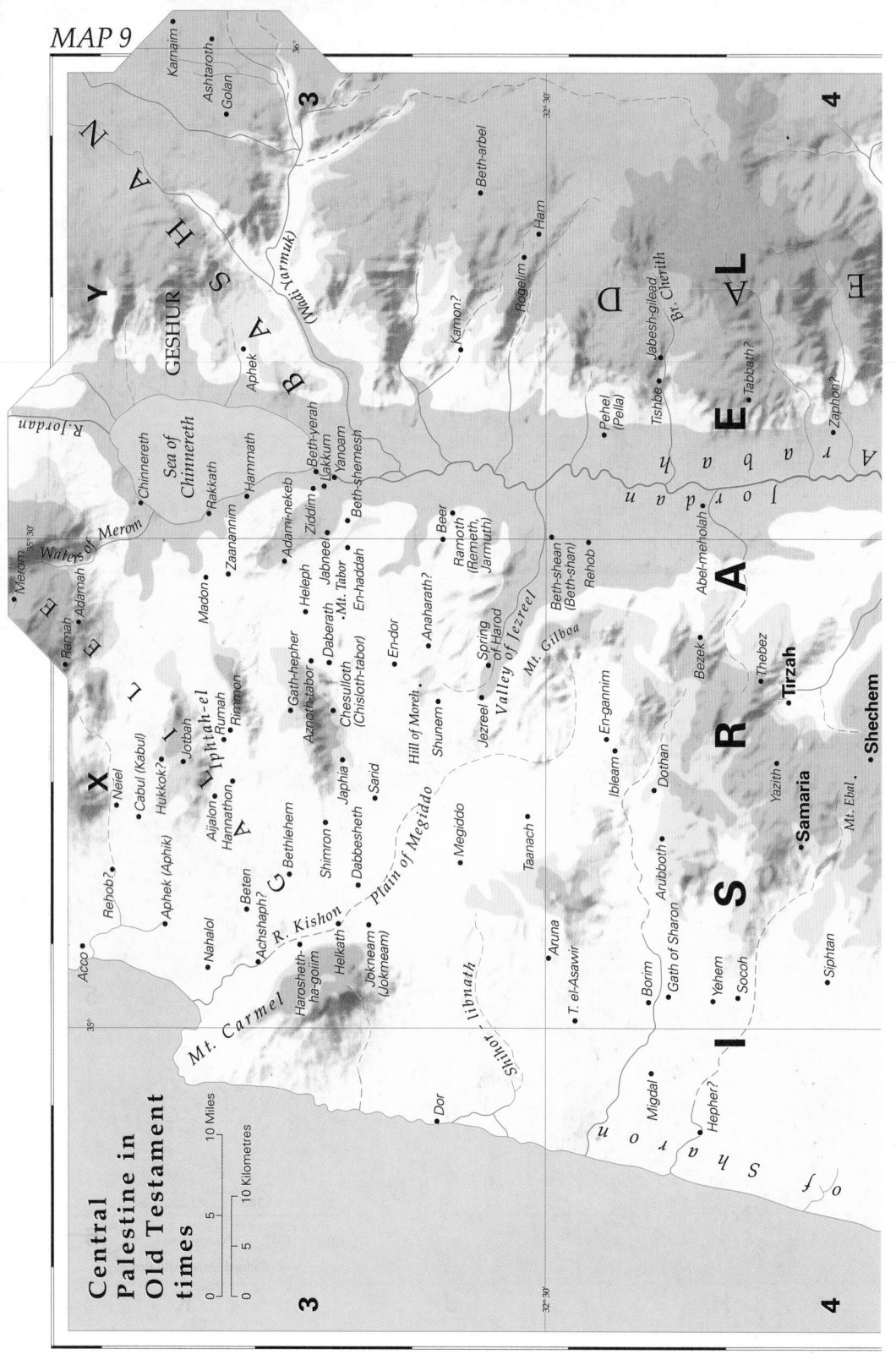

MAP 9

Central Palestine in Old Testament times

10 Miles

10 Kilometres

Acco

Rehob?

Aphek (Aphik)

Nahalol

Achshaph?

Beten

Bethlehem

Shimron

Dabbesheth

Helkath

Haroshethha-goiim

Mt. Carmel

R. Kishon

Dor

Shihor-libnath

Aphek (Aphik)

Neiel

Cabul (Kabul)

Hukkok?

Jotbah

Ijon

Iphtah-el

Hannathon

Ajalon

Rimmon

Rumah

Japhia

Sarid

Jokneam (Jokneam)

Plain of Megiddo

Megiddo

Taanach

Aruna

T. el-Asawir

Borim

Gath of Sharon

Migdal

Hepher?

of Sharon

Yehem

Socoh

Siphtan

Yazith

Mt. Ebal

Samaria

Shechem

Tirzah

ISRAEL

Ibleam

Dothan

En-gannim

Bezek

Thebez

Abel-meholah

Rehob

Beth-shean (Beth-shan)

Mt. Gilboa

Spring of Harod

Valley of Jezreel

Jezreel

Shunem

Hill of Moreh

En-dor

Anaharath?

Beer

Ramoth (Remeth, Jarmuth)

En-haddah

Mt. Tabor

Chesulloth (Chisloth-tabor)

Daberath

Anoth-tabor

Gath-hepher

Heleph

Jabneel

Ziddim

Adami-nekeb

Zaanannim

Madon

Rakkath

Hammath

Chinnereth

Sea of Chinnereth

Beth-shemesh

Yanoam

Lakkum

Beth-yerah

Waters of Merom

Merom

Adamah?

Ramah

ASHER

GESHUR

Aphek

R. Jordan

Jordan

Arabah

Pehel (Pella)

Tishbe

Jabesh-gilead

Br. Cherith

Tabbath?

Zaphon?

Rogelim

Ham

Kamon?

Beth-arbel

Karnaim

Ashtaroth

Golan

BASHAN

GILEAD

Jordan

MAP 9

MAP 10

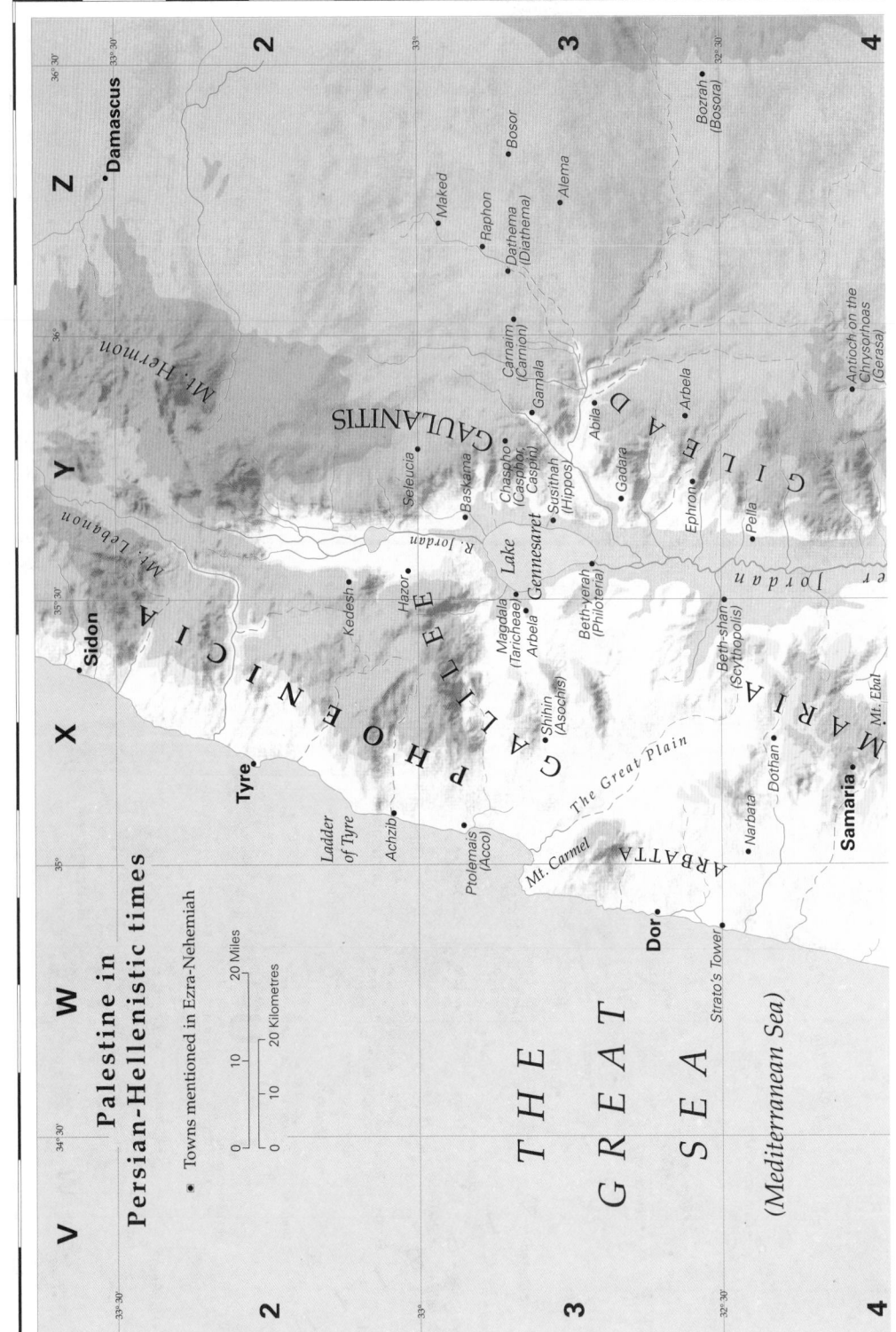

Palestine in
Persian-Hellenistic times

• Towns mentioned in Ezra-Nehemiah

20 Miles

20 Kilometres

0   10

0   10

THE

GREAT

SEA

(Mediterranean Sea)

Strato's Tower

Dor

Samaria

Mt. Ebal

Narbata

Dothan

ARBATTA

Mt. Carmel

The Great Plain

SAMARIA

Beth-shan
(Scythopolis)

Shihin
(Asochis)

GALILEE

Ptolemais
(Acco)

Achzib

Ladder
of Tyre

Tyre

PHOENICIA

Sidon

Kedesh

Hazor

Magdala
(Tarichea)   Arbela

Beth-yerah
(Philoteria)

Lake
Gennesaret

Abila

Gadara

Pella

Ephron

GILEAD

Arbela

Antioch on the
Chrysorhoas
(Gerasa)

Jordan

R. Jordan

GAULANITIS

Seleucia

Baskama

Chaspho
(Caspho,
Casphi)

Susithah
(Hippos)

Gamala

Carnaim
(Carnion)

Alema

Dathema
(Diathema)

Raphon

Bosor

Maked

Mt. Hermon

Mt. Lebanon

Damascus

Bozrah
(Bosora)

V   W   X   Y   Z

2

3

4

33° 30'   34° 30'   35°   35° 30'   36°   36° 30'

33°

32° 30'

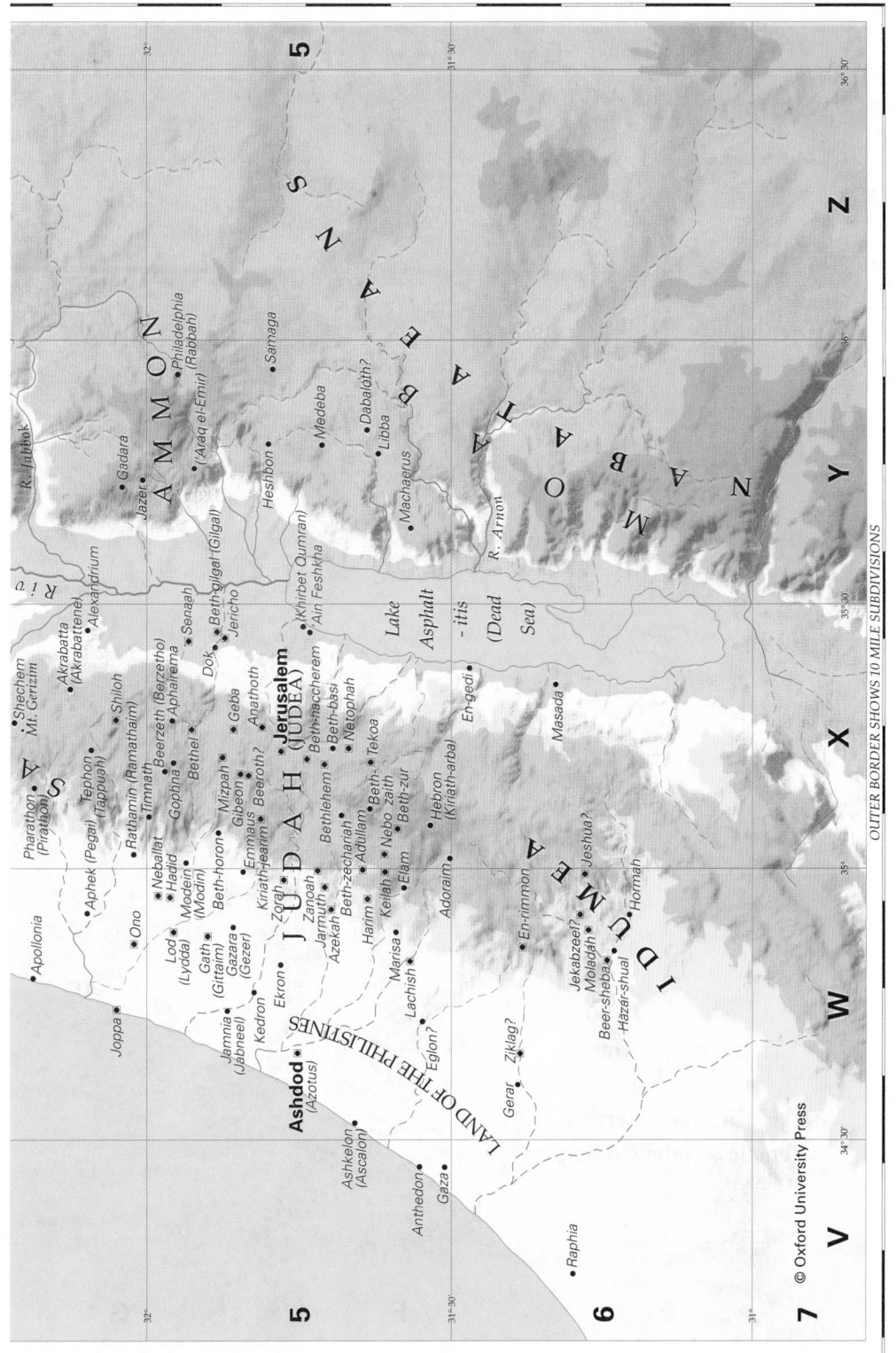

MAP 10

OUTER BORDER SHOWS 10 MILE SUBDIVISIONS

© Oxford University Press

MAP 11

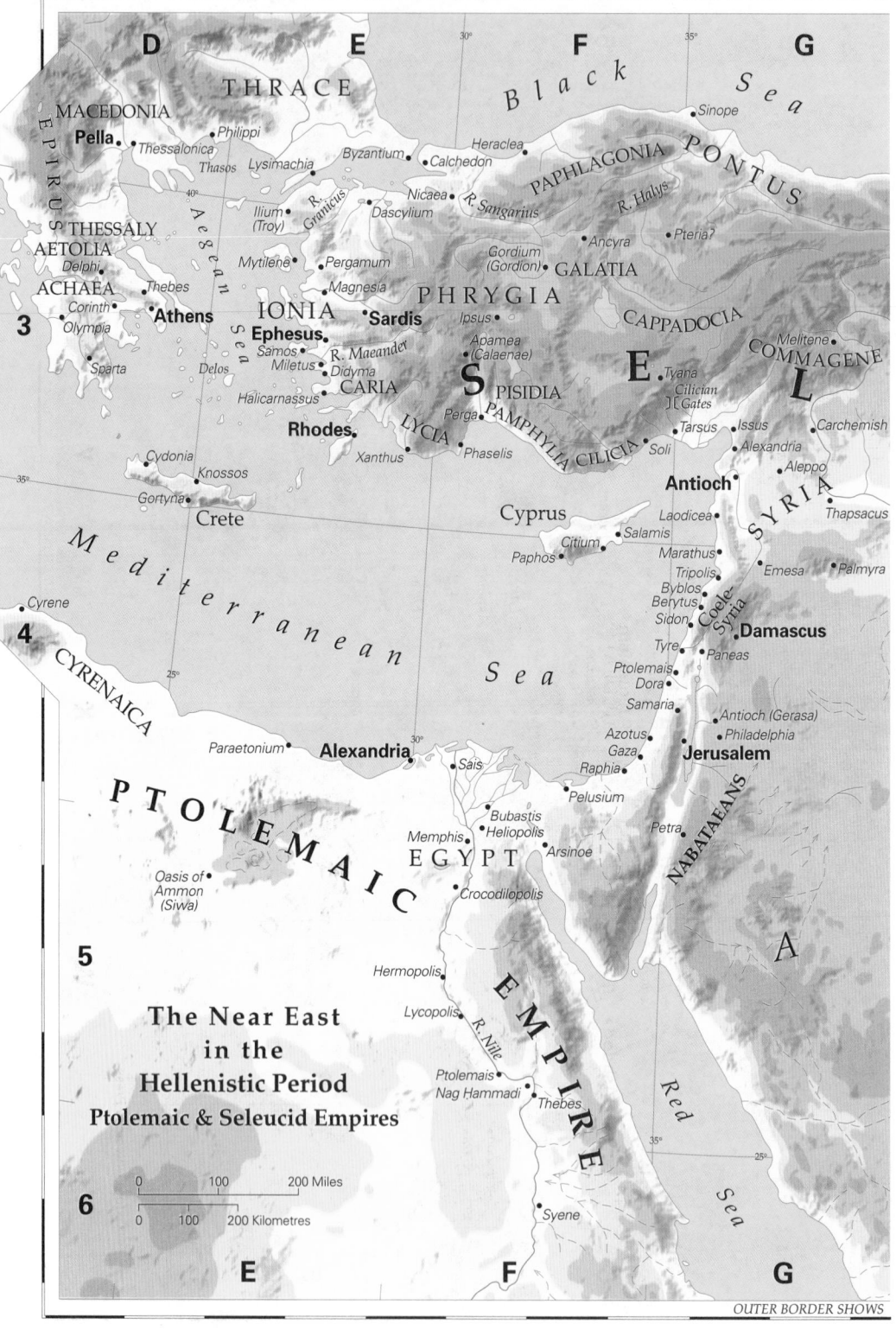

**The Near East
in the
Hellenistic Period**
Ptolemaic & Seleucid Empires

0   100   200 Miles

0   100   200 Kilometres

MAP 11

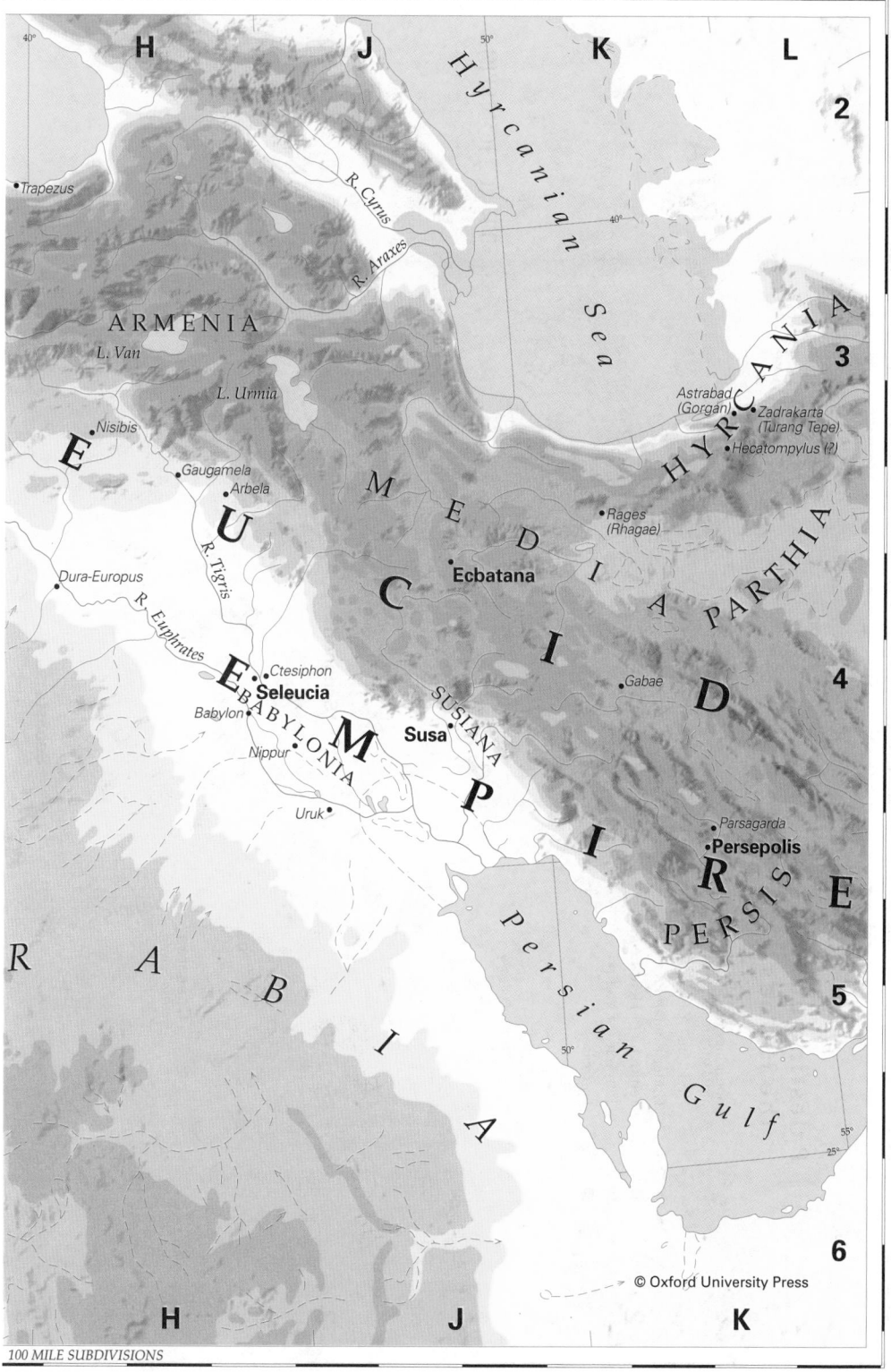

H   J   K   L

2

•*Trapezus*

ARMENIA

L. Van

3

L. Urmia

H
y
r
c
a
n
i
a
n

Sea

Astrabad
(Gorgan)•   •Zadrakarta
(Turang Tepe)

H
Y
R
C
A
N
I
A

•*Nisibis*

•*Gaugamela*
•*Arbela*

M

E

D

•Hecatompylus (?)

E

U

R. Tigris

Rages
(Rhagae)

Ecbatana

I

A

PARTHIA

•*Dura-Europus*

R. Euphrates

•*Ctesiphon*
Seleucia

Babylon•

•*Nippur*

B
A
B
Y
L
O
N
I
A

C

SUSIANA

Susa

•*Gabae*

D

4

E

M

P

•*Uruk*

•*Parsagarda*

Persepolis

I

R

PERSIS

E

R

A

B

I

A

P
e
r
s
i
a
n

Gulf

5

6

H   J   K

MAP 12

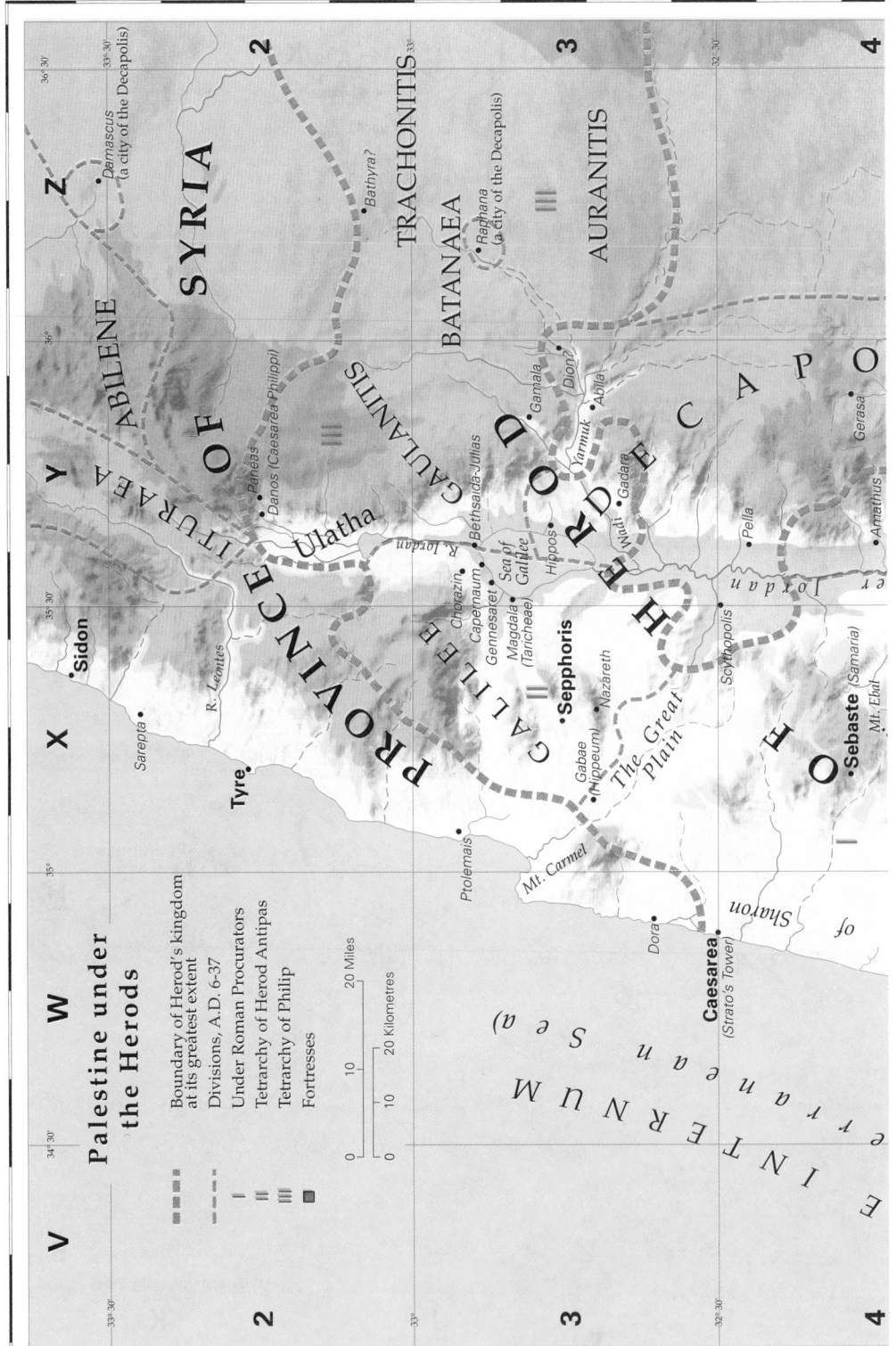

Palestine under
the Herods

Boundary of Herod's kingdom
at its greatest extent
Divisions, A.D. 6-37
Under Roman Procurators
Tetrarchy of Herod Antipas
Tetrarchy of Philip
Fortresses

20 Miles

20 Kilometres

SYRIA

Damascus
(a city of the Decapolis)

Bathyra?

ABILENE

ITURAEA

TRACHONITIS

BATANAEA

Raphana
(a city of the Decapolis)

AURANITIS

PROVINCE

OF

Paneas

Danos (Caesarea Philippi)

GAULANITIS

Ulatha

Gamala

Dion

Abila

DECAPO

HEROD

R. Jordan

Bethsaida-Julias

Sea of
Galilee

Hippos

Wadi

Yarmuk

Gadara

Sidon

Sarepta

R. Leontes

Chorazin

Capernaum

Gennesaret

*Magdala
(Taricheae)*

Sepphoris

Nazareth

GALILEE

Pella

Gerasa

Amathus

Tyre

*Gabae
(Hippeum)*

The Great
Plain

Scythopolis

Jordan

OF

Ptolemais

Mt. Carmel

Sebaste (Samaria)

Mt. Ebal

of
Sharon

Dora

Caesarea
(Strato's Tower)

*M
INTERNUM*

Mediterranean Sea

MAP 12

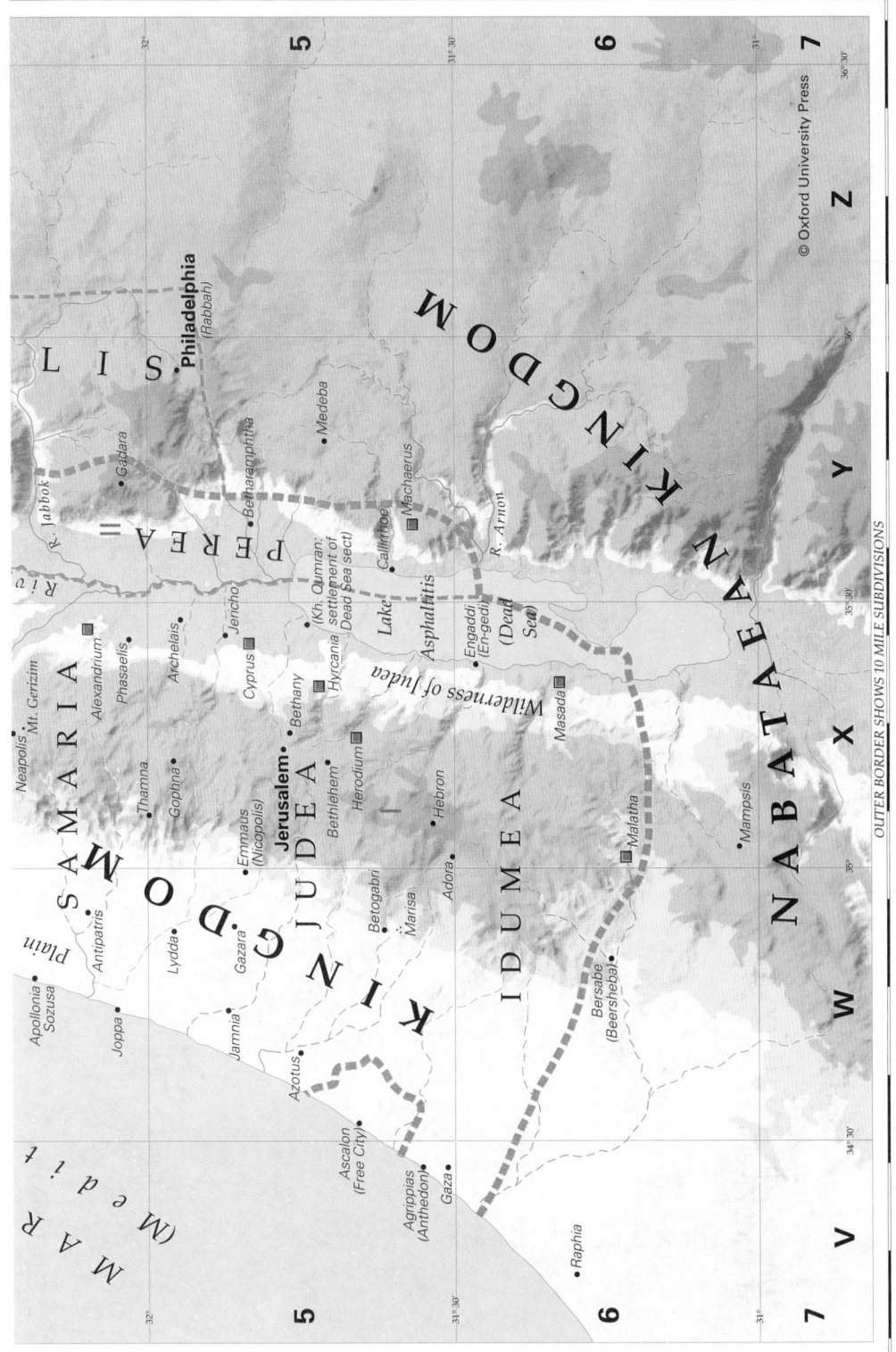

© Oxford University Press

OUTER BORDER SHOWS 10 MILE SUBDIVISIONS

Philadelphia
(Rabbah)

L I S

Gadara

R. Jabbok

Bethramphtha

Medeba

Machaerus

Callirrhoe

R. Arnon

P E R E A =

River

Jericho

Archelais

Phasaelis

Cyprus

(Kh. Qumran:
settlement of
Dead Sea sect)

Hyrcania

Lake
Asphaltitis

Engaddi
(En-gedi)

(Dead
Sea)

Bethany

Wilderness of Judea

Alexandrium

Neapolis. Mt. Gerizim

S A M A R I A

Thamna

Gophna

Emmaus
(Nicopolis)

Jerusalem

J U D E A

Bethlehem

Herodium

Masada

Hebron

N A B A T A E A N   K I N G D O M

Y

Z

X

Apollonia
Sozusa

Plain

Antipatris

Lydda

Gazara

Betogabri

Marisa

Adora

I D U M E A

Mampsis

K I N G D O M

Joppa

Jamnia

Azotus

Bersabe
(Beersheba)

Malatha

W

Ascalon
(Free City)

Agrippias
(Anthedon)

Gaza

Raphia

M A R
(M e d i t

V

5

6

7

5

6

7

MAP 13

North and Central Palestine at the time of the Ministry of Christ c.A.D. 30

- – – – – Political boundaries
- JUDEA, etc. Political units
- ◦ Places mentioned in the New Testament
- ▲ Cities of the Decapolis
- ▲ Cities of the Decapolis mentioned in the New Testament
- ▪ Fortresses

10 Miles
5
0

10 Kilometres
5
0

TETRARCHY OF PHILIP

Caesarea Philippi (Paneas)

Daphne

Ulatha

Lake Semechonitis (Lake Hûleh)

Thella

Seleucia

Sogane

GAULANITIS

Bethsaida-Julias

Gamala

Gergesa?

Hippos (Susithah)

R. Jordan

Sea of Galilee

Capernaum

Ginnesar (Gennesaret)

Chorazin

Cadasa

Capar Ganaeol

Gischala

Jamneith

Acchabare

Sepph

Bersabe

Meroth

Selame

Baca

Sogane

Cana

Magdala (Taricheae)

Arbela

Tiberias

Bethmaus

Ammathus

Bethyerah (Philoteria)

Sennabris

Agrippina

Scythopolis

GALILEE (Tetrarchy

Rumah

Garis

Sigoph

Dabaritta (Dabira)

Itabyrium (Tabor)

Exaloth

Nain

Sepphoris

Nazareth

Japha

Simonias

Besara

Asochis

Jotapata

Chabulon

Saab

Mt. of Jezreel

The Great Plain (Esdraelon)

R. Kishon

Gabae (Hippeum)

PROVINCE OF SYRIA

Tyre (33.16N)

PHOENICIA

Ladder of Tyre

Ecdippa (Achzib)

Ptolemais

Mt. Carmel

Sycaminum

Bucolon Polis

Gabata

Dora (Dor)

Crocodilon Polis

Caesarea

DECAPOLIS

Dion?

Abila

Capitolias

Arbela

Wadi Yarmuk

Emmatha

Gadara

X

Y

3

MAP 13

© Oxford University Press

4

5

Gerasa

Philadelphia
(*Rabbah*)

A P O L I S

A N D   P E R E A

Herod

(Antipas)

Zia

Gadara

Brook Cherith

R. Jabbok

Amathus

Pella

A

of

Salim?
Aenon?

Betharamphtha
(*Livias, Julias*)

Esbus

River Jordan

35° 30′

32°

Gilboa

Alexandrium

Coreae

Phasaelis

Archelais

Jericho

Cyprus

Taurus

(*Kh. Qumran:
settlement of
Dead Sea sect*)

Ginae

S A M A R I A

(*Wadi Farah*)

Bernesilis

Sebaste
(*Samaria*)

Neapolis
Mt. Gerizim

Mt. Ebal

Sychar

Tirathana

Pharaton

Mahnayim

Acrabbein

Selo (Shiloh)

Anathu Borcaeus

Taphon

Ephraim
(*Aphairema*)

Gophna

Michmash

Capharsalama?

Anathoth

Berzetho

Aialon?

Gabath Saul

Bethel

Mt. Scopus

Jerusalem

Bethphage
Bethany

X

E

A

(under Roman administration)

Arus

Thamna (Timnath)

Ilon

Lower Beth-horon

Upper Beth-horon

Adasa

Gabaon

Berea?

*Colonia Amasa
(Emmaus?)*

J U D E A

Narbata

Gitta

Yishub

Capparetaea

Tower of Aphek

Modein

Sappho

*Emmaus
(Nicopolis)*

D

Plain of Sharon

Brook of Kanah

Capharsaba

Antipatris
(*Pegai*)

*Rathamin
(Arimathea?)*

Adida

U

Gazara

W

Lydda

R. Belus (Kedron)

Cariathiareim

*Apollonia
Sozusa*

Joppa

Jamnia

Kedron

Kedron

4

5

OUTER BORDER SHOWS 10 MILE SUBDIVISIONS

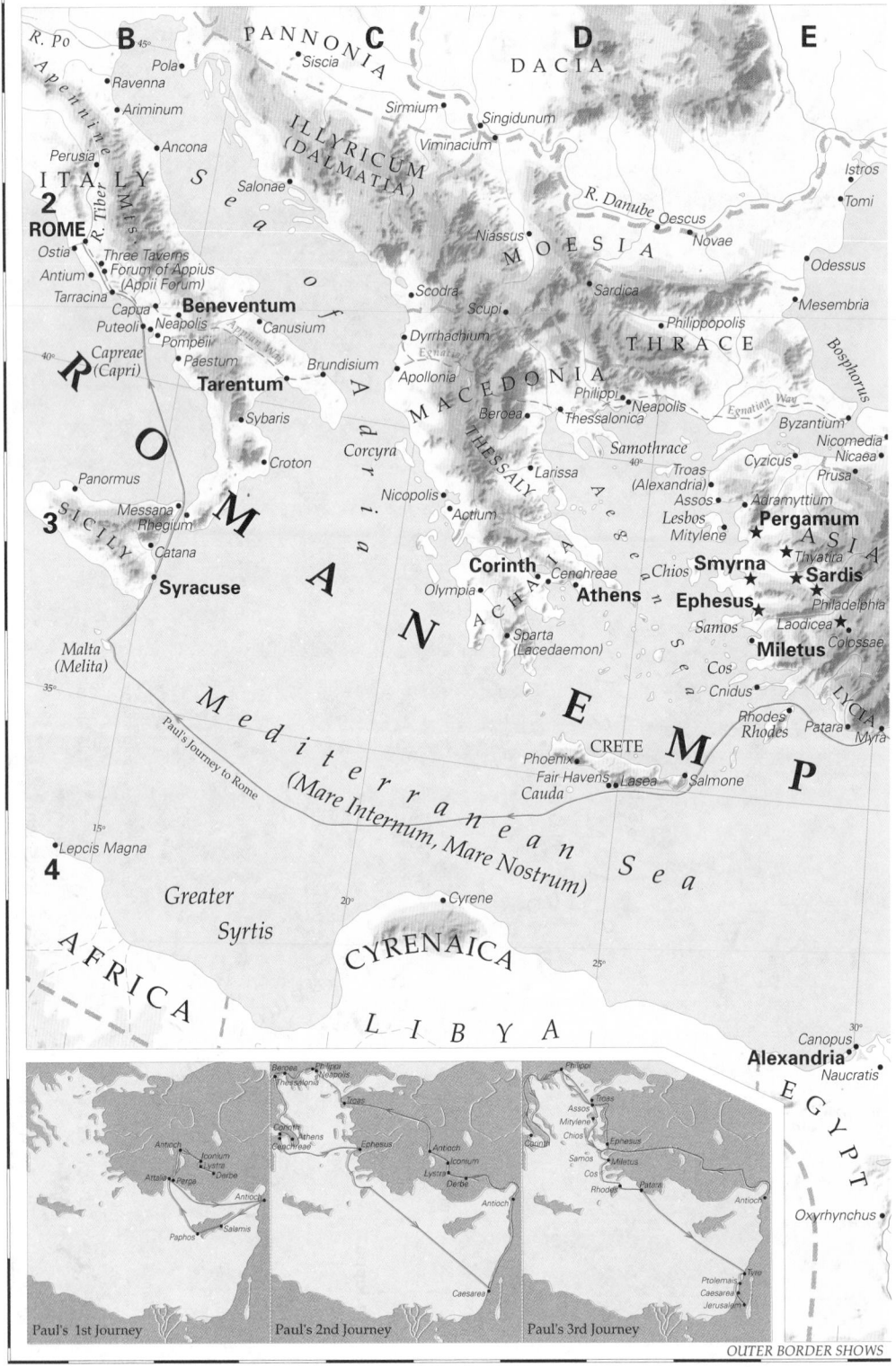

MAP 14

B 45° PANNONIA **C** **D** DACIA **E**

R. Po
Pola•
•Ravenna
•Ariminum
•Ancona
SISCIA•
SIRMIUM•
•SINGIDUNUM
VIMINACIUM•
ILLYRICUM
(DALMATIA)
Salonae•

Perusia•
2
ROME
Ostia•
Antium•
Tarracina•
R. Tiber
Apennine Mts.
Sea of
Three Taverns
Forum of Appius
(Appii Forum)
Scodra•
NIASSUS•
R. Danube Oescus•
•Novae
MOESIA
Sardica•
•Philippopolis
THRACE
•Istros
•Tomi
•Odessus
•Mesembria

40°
Capua•
Puteoli•
Neapolis•
Pompeii•
Beneventum
Canusium•
Paestum•
Appian Way
Dyrrhachium•
Apollonia•
Beroea•
MACEDONIA
Philippi• Neapolis•
Thessalonica•
Egnatian Way
Byzantium•
Nicomedia•
Nicaea•
Prusa•
Bosphorus

**Capreae
(Capri)**
R O M A N
SICILY
Sybaris•
Croton•
Corcyra
THESSALY
Larissa•
40°
Samothrace
Troas
(Alexandria)
Assos•
Lesbos
Mitylene
Cyzicus•
Adramyttium•
Pergamum ★
ASIA
★Thyatira
★**Sardis**

Panormus•
Messana•
Rhegium•
Catana•
Syracuse
Nicopolis•
Actium•
ACHAIA
Corinth
Cenchreae
Olympia•
Athens
Sparta
(Lacedaemon)
Chios
Smyrna ★
Ephesus ★
Samos•
Cos•
Cnidus•
Rhodes
Rhodes
Miletus
Colossae
Laodicea ★
★Philadelphia
Aegean Sea
LYCIA
Patara•
•Myra

35°
**Malta
(Melita)**
Paul's Journey to Rome
M e d i t e r r a n e a n   S e a
(Mare Internum, Mare Nostrum)
Phoenix•
CRETE
Fair Havens•
Cauda
Lasea•
Salmone•
E M P

4
•Lepcis Magna
15°
**Greater
Syrtis**
20°
•Cyrene
25°
Canopus•
Alexandria•
Naucratis•
30°

A F R I C A
C Y R E N A I C A
L I B Y A
EGYPT
•Oxyrhynchus

Antioch•
Iconium•
Lystra•
Derbe•
Attalia• Perga•
Antioch•
Paphos• Salamis•

Paul's 1st Journey

Beroea• Philippi• Neapolis•
Thessalonica•
Troas•
Corinth• Athens•
Cenchreae
Ephesus•
Antioch•
Iconium•
Lystra• Derbe•
Antioch•
Caesarea•

Paul's 2nd Journey

Philippi•
Assos•
Troas•
Mitylene•
Chios•
Cauda
Samos•
Cos•
Rhodes•
Ephesus•
Miletus•
Patara•
Antioch•
Ptolemais• Tyre•
Caesarea•
Jerusalem•

Paul's 3rd Journey

MAP 14

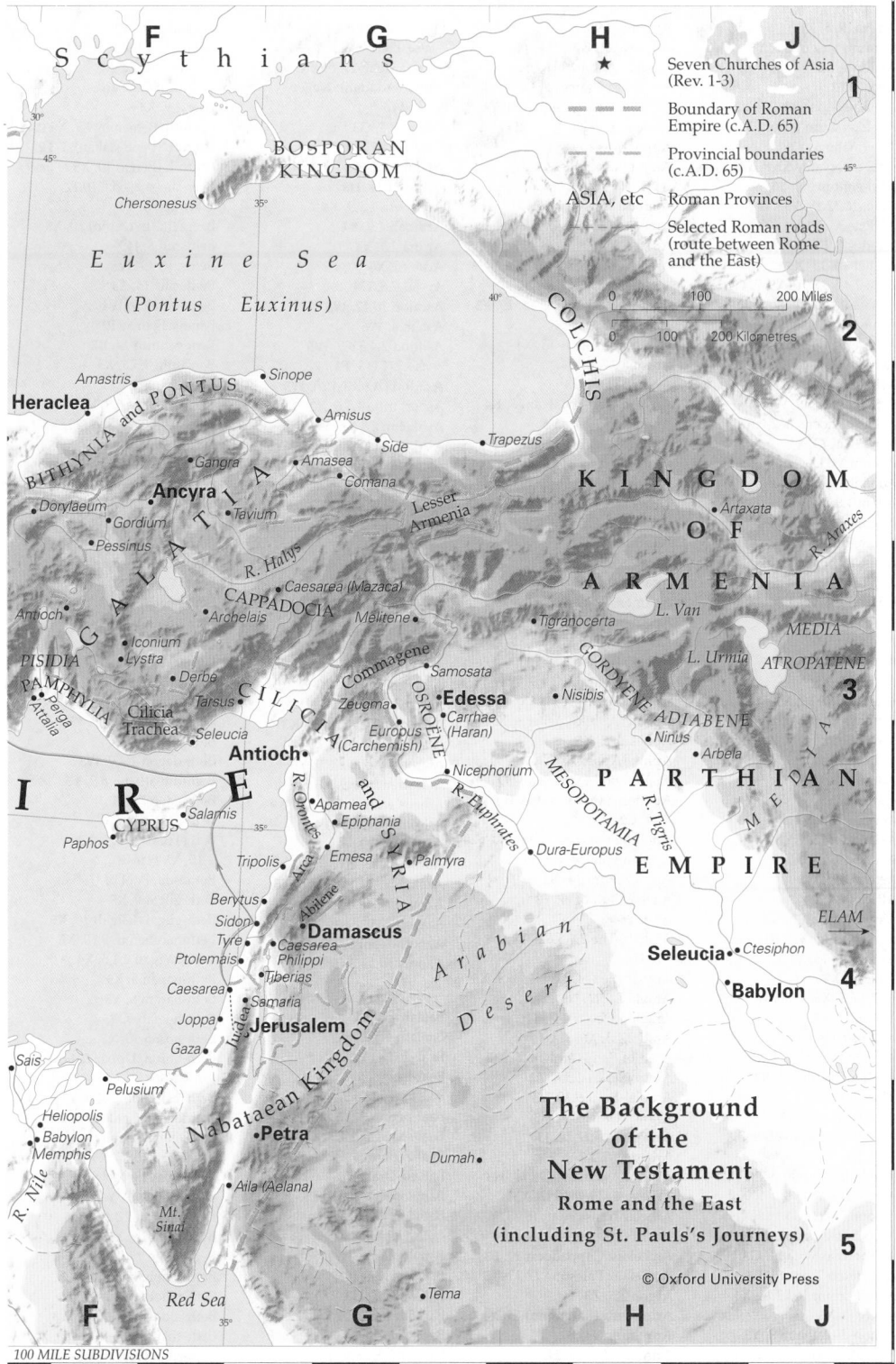

S c y t h i a n s   ★

★   Seven Churches of Asia
(Rev. 1-3)

– – –   Boundary of Roman
Empire (c.A.D. 65)

– – –   Provincial boundaries
(c.A.D. 65)

ASIA, etc   Roman Provinces

Selected Roman roads
(route between Rome
and the East)

1

BOSPORAN
KINGDOM

Chersonesus

E u x i n e   S e a

(Pontus   Euxinus)

COLCHIS

0   100   200 Miles

0   100   200 Kilometres

2

Amastris   *Sinope*

Heraclea   BITHYNIA and PONTUS

Amisus

Side   *Trapezus*

Gangra   *Amasea*

Dorylaeum   **Ancyra**   *Comana*

Gordium   *Tavium*

Pessinus   GALATIA   Lesser Armenia

R. Halys

K I N G D O M

O F

A R M E N I A

Artaxata

R. Araxes

Antioch   CAPPADOCIA   *Caesarea (Mazaca)*

Iconium   *Archelais*   *Melitene*

PISIDIA   *Lystra*

Tigranocerta   *L. Van*

MEDIA

L. Urmia   ATROPATENE

PAMPHYLIA   *Derbe*   Commagene   *Samosata*

Perga   *Tarsus*   CILICIA   *Zeugma*   OSROENE   **Edessa**   *Nisibis*

Attalia   Cilicia Trachea   *Europus (Carchemish)*   *Carrhae (Haran)*

3

Seleucia   *Nicephorium*

GORDYENE   ADIABENE

Ninus

Arbela

I R E   **Antioch**   and   MESOPOTAMIA

R. Orontes   *Apamea*   SYRIA   *R. Euphrates*

P A R T H I A N

R. Tigris   MEDIA

CYPRUS   *Salamis*   *Epiphania*

Paphos   *Emesa*   *Palmyra*   *Dura-Europus*

E M P I R E

Tripolis

ELAM →

Berytus

Sidon   *Abilene*

Tyre   **Damascus**

Ptolemais   *Caesarea Philippi*

Caesarea   *Tiberias*

Samaria

Seleucia   *Ctesiphon*

Babylon

4

Joppa   Judaea   **Jerusalem**

Gaza

Sais

Pelusium

A r a b i a n

Nabataean Kingdom

D e s e r t

Heliopolis

Babylon

Memphis

Petra

Dumah

**The Background
of the
New Testament**

Rome and the East

(including St. Pauls's Journeys)

R. Nile

Aila (Aelana)

Mt. Sinai

© Oxford University Press

5

Red Sea   *Tema*

INDEX TO MAPS